TABLE OF CONTENTS—Continued

SATURN

MOTOR
AUTO REPAIR MANUAL

GENERAL MOTORS CORPORATION

57th Edition, Volume 1

First Printing

John R. Lypen, SAE
Editor

Marian A. Maasshoff, SAE
Managing Editor

Warren Schildknecht, SAE
Senior Editor

Christopher P. Jakubowski, SAE
Senior Editor

Richard F. Cahoon
Assistant Editor

Richard G. Glover
Assistant Editor

Mark C. Ferrand
Technical Assistance Editor

Donald R. Cobb
Assistant Editor

Charles R. Burstall
Assistant Editor

Lynda Slater
Production Assistant

Timothey L. Martin
Assistant Editor

Bruce W. Clippert
Assistant Editor

Kirk D. Lashbrook
Assistant Editor

Timothy J. Hoch
Assistant Editor

Brad A. Harris
Assistant Editor

Debra L. Bibb
Assistant Editor

Daniel Reynolds
Assistant Editor

Published by
MOTOR

A Division of Hearst Business Publishing, Inc.

5600 Crooks Road, Troy, MI 48098

Printed in the U.S.A.
Copyright © 1993 Hearst Business Publishing, Inc.
All rights reserved
ISBN 0-87851-817-7

Frank A. Bennack, Jr.
President

Gilbert C. Maurer
Executive Vice-President

Richard P. Malloch
*General Manager
Hearst Books/Business
Publishing Group*

Nelson J. Maione
*Vice-President &
Resident Controller*

Michael J. Kromida, SAE
Product Manager

Randolph A. Hearst
Chairman

Gordon L. Jones
*Vice-President
Hearst Books/Business
Publishing Group*

Thomas H. King
Managing Director

Kevin F. Carr
*Vice-President/Publisher
Motor Books*

Philip C. Cunningham, SAE
Editorial Director

VEHICLE IDENTIFICATION

1991–92 BUICK
V.I.N. DEFINED

1st POSITION
COUNTRY
1 = United States
2 = Canada

2nd POSITION
MANUFACTURER
G = General Motors

3rd POSITION
DIVISION
4 = Buick
7 = GM of Canada

4th POSITION
CARLINE CODE
A = Century
B = LeSabre, Electra (RWD)
B = Estate Wagon (RWD)
B = Coachbuilder Wagon
B = Roadmaster
C = Electra/Park Ave (FWD)
D = Electra (RWD)
E = Riviera/Reatta
G = Regal
H = LeSabre (FWD)
J = Skyhawk
N = Somerset Regal/Skylark
W = Regal
X = Skylark

5th POSITION, 1985-88
CARLINE SERIES
B = Skylark Custom
C = Skylark Limited
D = Skylark Sport
E = Skylark T-Type
F = Electra T-Type
G = Century Sport
H = Century Custom
J = Regal/Somerset
K = Regal/Somerset
L = Century Limited
M = Regal/Somerset Limited
N = LeSabre Custom
P = Lesabre Limited
R = Electra Limited
S = Skyhawk Custom
T = Skyhawk Limited
U = Park Avenue (RWD)
V = Electra Estate
W = Park Avenue (FWD)
X = Electra Limited (FWD)
Y = Riviera T-TYPE
Z = Riviera Luxury

5th POSITION, 1989-92
CARLINE SERIES
B = Regal Custom
B = Coachbuilder Wagon
C = Reatta
C = Skylark Custom 4 Door
D = Regal/Skylark Limited
E = Skyhawk Sport
F = Electra T-Type
H = Century Custom/Wagon
J = Skylark Custom 2 Door
K = Regal/Somerset

5th POSITION, 89-92 (CONT'D)
L = Century Limited/Wagon
L = Estate Wagon
M = Skylark Limited
M = Skylark Grand Sport
N = Roadmaster
P = Lesabre Custom
R = LeSabre Limited
R = LeSabre Estate Wagon
R = Roadmaster Est Wagon
S = Skyhawk Custom
T = Roadmaster ITT Ltd.
U = Elect Park Ave (Ultra)
V = Electra Estate (RWD)
V = Skylark
W = Electra Park Avenue
X = Electra Limited (FWD)
Z = Riviera Luxury

6th & 7th POSITION, 1985-86
BODY TYPE
19 = 4 Door Sedan
27 = 2 Door Coupe
35 = 4 Door Wagon
37 = 2 Door Coupe
47 = 2 Door Coupe
57 = 2 Door Coupe
67 = 2 Door Convertable
69 = 4 Door Sedan
77 = 2 Door Hatchback
87 = 2 Door Coupe

6th POSITION, 1987-92
BODY TYPE
1 = 2 Door Coupe
2 = 2 Door Hatchback
3 = 2 Door Convertable
5 = 4 Door Sedan
6 = 4 Door Sedan
8 = 4 Door Wagon

7th POSITION, 1987-92
RESTRAINT SYSTEM
1 = Manual Belts
2 = Manual Belts (Built In Safety)
2 = Manual Belts (Dual Air Bags)
3 = Manual Belts (Driver Air Bag)
4 = Automatic Belts
5 = Automatic Belts (Driver Air Bag)

8th POSITION, 1985-88
ENGINE CODE
A = 3.8-V6, 2 Barrel
B = 3.8-V6, 2 Barrel
D = 2.3-L4, Fuel Injected
E = 3.0-V6, 2 Barrel
H = 5.0-V8, 4 Barrel
J = 1.8-L4, MFI
M = 3.0-V6, Fuel Injected
N = 5.7-V8, Diesel
P = 2.0-L4, EFI
R = 2.5-L4, TBI
T = 4.3-V6, Diesel
U = 2.5-L4, TBI
V = 4.3-V6, Diesel
W = 2.8-V6, MFI
X = 2.8-V6, 2 Barrel
Y = 5.0-V8, 4 Barrel
Z = 4.3-V6, TBI

8th POSITION, 85-88 (CONT'D)
0 = 1.8-L4, TBI
1 = 2.0-L4, EFI
3 = 3.8-V6, MFI
7 = 3.8-V6, SFI
9 = 3.8-V6, SFI

8th POSITION, 1989-92
ENGINE CODE
C = 3.8-V6, MFI
D = 2.3-L4, MFI
E = 5.0-V8, TBI
G = 2.2-L4, TBI
L = 3.8-V6, MFI
N = 3.3-V6, MFI
R = 2.5-L4, TBI
T = 3.1-V6, MFI
U = 2.5-L4, TBI
W = 2.8-V6, Fuel Injected
Y = 5.0-V8, 4 Barrel
Z = 4.3-V6, MFI
1 = 2.0-L4, Fuel Injected
1 = 3.8-V6, MFI
3 = 2.3-L4, MFI
4 = 2.2-L4, MFI
7 = 5.7-V8, TBI

9th POSITION
CHECK DIGIT

10th POSITION
MODEL YEAR
F = 1985
G = 1986
H = 1987
J = 1988
K = 1989
L = 1990
M = 1991
N = 1992

11th POSITION
ASSEMBLY PLANT
A = Lakewood, GA
B = Lansing, MI
C = Lansing, MI
D = Doraville, GA
H = Flint, MI
K = Leeds, MO
M = Lansing, MI
P = Pontiac, MI
R = Arlington, TX
S = Ramos Arizpe, Mexico
T = Tarrytown, NY
U = Hamtramck, MI
X = Fairfax, KS
Z = Fremont, Ca
1 = Oshawa #2, Canada
1 = Wentzville, MO
2 = Ste. Therese, Canada
4 = Orion, MI
6 = Oklahoma City, OK
7 = Lordstown, OH
9 = Oshawa #1, Canada

12th Thru 17th POSITION
PRODUCTION SEQUENCE NUMBER

1993–94 BUICK
V.I.N. DEFINED

1st POSITION
COUNTRY
1 = United States
2 = Canada

2nd POSITION
MANUFACTURER
G = General Motors

3rd POSITION
DIVISION
4 = Buick
7 = GM of Canada

4th POSITION
CARLINE CODE
A = Century
B = Estate Wagon (RWD)
B = Coachbuilder Wagon
B = Roadmaster
C = Park Avenue (FWD)
E = Riviera
H = LeSabre (FWD)
N = Somerset/Skylark
W = Regal

5th POSITION
CARLINE SERIES
B = Regal Custom
B = Coachbuilder Wagon
D = Regal Limited
F = Regal Gran Sport
G = Century/Spl Wagon
H = Century Custom/Wagon
J = Skylark
L = Century Limited Wagon
M = Skylark Gran Sport
P = LeSabre Custom
R = LeSabre Limited
R = Roadmaster Est Wgn
T = Roadmaster Limited
U = Park Avenue - Ultra
V = Somerset
V = Skylark Custom
W = Park Avenue
Z = Riviera

6th POSITION
BODY TYPE
1 = 2 Door Coupe
3 = 2 Door Convertible
5 = 4 Door Sedan
8 = 4 Door Wagon

7th POSITION
RESTRAINT SYSTEM
1 = Manual Belts
2 = Manual Belts (Dual Air Bags)
3 = Manual Belts (Driver Air Bag)
4 = Automatic Belts
5 = Automatic Belts (Driver Air Bag)
6 = Automatic Belts (Dual Air Bags)

8th POSITION
ENGINE CODE
L = 3.8-V6, MFI
N = 3.3-V6, MFI
R = 2.5-L4, TBI
T = 3.1-V6, MFI
1 = 3.8-V6, MFI
3 = 2.3-L4, MFI
4 = 2.2-L4, MFI
7 = 5.7-V8, TBI

9th POSITION
CHECK DIGIT

10th POSITION
MODEL YEAR
P = 1993
R = 1994

11th POSITION
ASSEMBLY PLANT
B = Lansing, MI
C = Lansing, MI
H = Flint, MI
R = Arlington, TX
S = Ramos Arizpe, ME
U = Hamtramck, MI
W = Willow Run, MI
1 = Wentzville, MO
6 = Oklahoma City, OK

12th Thru 17th POSITION
PRODUCTION SEQUENCE NUMBER

CADILLAC
V.I.N. DEFINED

1st POSITION
COUNTRY
1 = United States
2 = Canada

2nd POSITION
MANUFACTURER
G = General Motors

3rd POSITION
DIVISION
6 = Cadillac
7 = GM of Canada

4th POSITION
CARLINE CODE
C = Fleetwood/DeVille (FWD)
C = Commercial Chassis
C = Sixty Special
C = DeVille/DeVille Touring
D = Fleetwood/DeVille (RWD)
D = Brougham
D = Commercial Chassis (RWD)
E = Eldorado
J = Cimarron
K = Concours
K = DeVille
K = Seville
K = Seville Touring
V = Allante'

5th POSITION
CARLINE SERIES
B = Fleetwood (FWD)
B = Sixty Special
D = DeVille (FWD)
F = Concours
F = Fleetwood Limo
G = Cimarron
G = Fleetwood 60 Special
H = Fleetwood Limo
H = Commercial Chassis (RWD)
L = Eldorado
M = DeVille (RWD)
R = Allante' Conv. & HT
S = Seville
S = Allante' Convertible
S = Fleetwood 60 Special
T = Eldorado Touring
W = Fleetwood Brougham
Y = Seville Touring Sedan
Z = Commercial Chassis

6th POSITION, 1987-94
BODY TYPE
1 = 2 Door Coupe
3 = 2 Door Convertible
5 = 4 Door Sedan

6th & 7th POSITION, 1985-86
BODY TYPE
19 = 4 Door Sedan
27 = 2 Door Coupe
35 = 4 Door Wagon
37 = 2 Door Coupe
47 = 2 Door Coupe
57 = 2 Door Coupe
67 = 2 Door Convertible
69 = 4 Door Sedan
77 = 2 Door Hatchback
87 = 2 Door Coupe

7th POSITION, 1987-94
RESTRAINT SYSTEM
1 = Manual Belts
2 = Manual Belts (Built In Safety)
2 = Manual Belts (Dual Air Bags)
3 = Manual Belts (Driver Air Bag)
4 = Automatic Belts
5 = Automatic Belts (Driver Air Bag)
6 = Automatic Belts (Dual Air Bags)

8th POSITION
ENGINE CODE
B = 4.9-V8, MFI
E = 5.0-V8, TBI
N = 5.7-V8, Diesel
P = 2.0-L4, EFI
W = 2.8-V6, MFI
Y = 5.0-V8, 4 Barrel
Y = 4.6-V8, MFI
3 = 4.5-V8, MFI
5 = 4.5-V8, Fuel Injected
6 = 4.5-V8, Fuel Injected
7 = 4.1-V8, Fuel Injected
7 = 5.7-V8, TBI
8 = 4.5-V8, MFI
9 = 5.0-V8, 4 Barrel
9 = 4.6-V8, MFI

9th POSITION
CHECK DIGIT

10th POSITION
MODEL YEAR
F = 1985
G = 1986
H = 1987
J = 1988
K = 1989
L = 1990
M = 1991
N = 1992
P = 1993
R = 1994

11th POSITION
ASSEMBLY PLANT
J = GMAD Janesville, WI
R = Arlington, TX
U = Hamtramck, MI
4 = Lake Orion, MI
9 = Detroit, MI

12th Thru 17th POSITION
PRODUCTION SEQUENCE NUMBER

GEO
V.I.N. DEFINED

1st POSITION
COUNTRY
1 = United States
2 = Canada
J = Japan

2nd POSITION
MANUFACTURER
G = Canada
G = General Motors
G = Suzuki
Y = N.U.M.M.I.
8 = General Motors

3rd POSITION
DIVISION
1 = Chevrolet
1 = GEO
7 = GM of Canada
7 = GEO

4th POSITION
CARLINE CODE
M = Metro
R = Spectrum
R = Storm
S = Prizm

5th POSITION
CARLINE SERIES
F = Spectrum Level I
F = Storm Level I
G = Spectrum Level II
G = Storm Level II
K = Prizm
L = Prizm GSI
R = Metro GEO, Base
R = Metro LSI
R = Metro FXI
S = Metro
S = Metro FXI
T = Storm GSI Level II

6th POSITION
BODY TYPE
2 = 2 Door Coupe Sedan
2 = 2 Door Hatchback
2 = 3 Door 2+2 Coupe
2 = 3 Door Convertible
4 = 3 Door Hatchback Cpe/Wagon
5 = 4 Door Sedan
6 = 4 Door Notchback
6 = 4 Door Hatchback
7 = 4 Door Liftback
8 = 4 Door Wagon

7th POSITION
RESTRAINT SYSTEM
1 = Manual Belts
2 = Manual Belts (Built in Safety)
3 = Manual Belts (Driver Air Bag)
4 = Automatic Belts (Passive)

8th POSITION
ENGINE CODE
K = 1.5-L4, 2 Barrel
L = 1.0-L3, Turbo
5 = 1.6-L4, EFI
6 = 1.0-L3, TBI
6 = 1.6-L4, EFI
7 = 1.5-L4, 2 Barrel
8 = 1.8-L4, EFI
9 = 1.5-L4, Turbo
9 = 1.3-L4, TBI

9th POSITION
CHECK DIGIT

10th POSITION
MODEL YEAR
K = 1989
L = 1990
M = 1991
N = 1992
P = 1993
R = 1994

11th POSITION
ASSEMBLY PLANT
K = Kosia, Japan
Z = Fremont, Ca
6 = Ingersoll, Ont. (CAMI)
7 = Fujisawa, Japan
8 = Fujisawa, Japan

12th Thru 17th POSITION
PRODUCTION SEQUENCE NUMBER

CHEVROLET
V.I.N. DEFINED

1st POSITION
COUNTRY
1 = United States
2 = Canada

2nd POSITION
MANUFACTURER
G = General Motors
Y = N.U.M.M.I.
8 = General Motors

3rd POSITION
DIVISION
1 = Chevrolet
7 = GM of Canada

4th POSITION
CARLINE CODE
A = Celebrity
B = Impala
B = Caprice/Hearse/Limo
F = Camaro & Convertible
G = El Camino, Monte Carlo
J = Cavalier/Conv./Wagon
L = Corsica, Beretta
M = Sprint
R = Spectrum
S = Nova, TVS, Venture
T = Chevette
W = Lumina
X = Citation
Y = Corvette & Convertible

5th POSITION
CARLINE SERIES
B = Chevette
C = Hearse/Limo Chassis
C = Cavalier Cadet
C = Cavalier Conv. & Wag (1992-94)
D = Cavalier CS
D = Corsica
E = Cavalier Hatchback, Type 10
F = Cavalier Convertible (1989-94)
F = Cavalier Z24 (1989-94)
F = Spectrum Level I
G = Spectrum Level II
H = Citation
J = Chevette Scooter
K = Nova, TVX
L = Impala
L = Caprice/Caprice Wagon
L = Lumina
L = Nova Twin Cam
M = Lumina Coupe
N = Caprice Classic LS
N = Lumina Eurosport/LS
P = Lumina Z34
R = Sprint
S = Camaro Berlinetta
S = Sprint E/R
T = Corsica
T = Corsica LT
T = Sprint
U = Caprice Classic Brougham & LS
V = Celebrity
W = Beretta & Convertible
W = Beretta GT/Z26

5th POSITION (CONTINUED)
X = Citation
Z = Corvette & Convertible
Z = Beretta GTZ
Z = Corsica LTZ
Z = Corvette ZR1
Z = Monte Carlo

6th & 7th POSITION, 1985-86
BODY TYPE
08 = 2 Door Hatchback
19 = 4 Door Sedan
27 = 2 Door Coupe
35 = 4 Door Wagon
37 = 2 Door Coupe
47 = 2 Door Coupe
57 = 2 Door Coupe
67 = 2 Door Convertible
68 = 4 Door Hatchback
69 = 4 Door Sedan
77 = 2 Door Hatchback
87 = 2 Door Coupe

6th POSITION, 1987-94
BODY TYPE
1 = 2 Door Coupe
2 = 2 Door Coupe
2 = 2 Door Hatchback
2 = 2 Door Convertible
3 = 2 Door Convertible
5 = 4 Door Sedan
6 = 4 Door Hatchback
6 = 4 Door Sedan
8 = 4 Door Wagon
8 = Commercial Chassis

7th POSITION, 1987-94
RESTRAINT SYSTEM
1 = Manual Belts
2 = Manual Belts (Built In Safety)
2 = Manual Belts (Dual Air Bags)
3 = Manual Belts (Driver Air Bag)
4 = Automatic Belts
5 = Automatic Belts (Driver Air Bag)
6 = Automatic Belts (Dual Air Bags)

8th POSITION, 1985-88
ENGINE CODE
A = 3.8-V6, 2 Barrel
B = 3.8-V6, 2 Barrel
C = 1.6-L4, 2 Barrel
D = 1.8-L4, Diesel
E = 5.0-V8, Fuel Injected
F = 5.0-V8, Fuel Injected
G = 5.0-V8, 4 Barrel
H = 5.0-V8, 4 Barrel
K = 2.0-L4, EFI
M = 1.3-L3, 2 Barrel
N = 2.0-L4, MFI
N = 5.7-V8, Diesel
P = 2.0-L4, EFI
R = 2.5-L4, TBI
S = 2.8-V6, MFI
T = 4.3-V6, Diesel
V = 2.8-V6, MFI
W = 2.8-V6, MFI
X = 2.8-V6, 2 Barrel
1 = 2.0-L4, EFI

8th POSITION, 85-88(CONT'D)
2 = 1.0-L3, EFI
2 = 1.0-L3, Turbo
2 = 2.5-L4, TFI
4 = 1.6-L4, 2 Barrel
5 = 1.0-L3, 2 Barrel
5 = 1.5-L4, Diesel
6 = 1.6-L4, EFI
6 = 1.0-L3, TBI
6 = 5.7-V8, 4 Barrel
7 = 1.5-L4, 2 Barrel
8 = 5.7-V8, MFI
9 = 1.5-L4, Fuel Injected
9 = 1.5-L4, Turbocharged

8th POSITION, 1989-94
ENGINE CODE
A = 2.3-L4, MFI
E = 5.0-V8, TBI
F = 5.0-V8, MFI
G = 2.2-L4, TBI
P = 5.7-V8, MFI
R = 2.5-L4, TBI
S = 2.8-V6, Fuel Injected
S = 3.4-V6, MFI
T = 3.1-V6, MFI
W = 2.8-V6, Fuel Injected
W = 3.1-V6, MFI
W = 4.3-V6, MFI
X = 3.4-V6, MFI
Y = 5.0-V8, 4 Barrel
Y = 4.3-V6, MFI
1 = 2.0-L4, Fuel Injected
2 = 1.0-L3, MFI
2 = 2.2-L4, MFI
5 = 1.6-L4, MFI
6 = 1.0-L3, TBI
6 = 1.6-L4, MFI
7 = 5.7-V8, TBI
8 = 5.7 V8, MFI

9th POSITION
CHECK DIGIT

10th POSITION
MODEL YEAR
F = 1985
G = 1986
H = 1987
J = 1988
K = 1989
L = 1990
M = 1991
N = 1992
P = 1993
R = 1994

11th POSITION
ASSEMBLY PLANT

12th Thru 17th POSITION
PRODUCTION SEQUENCE NUMBER

1991-92 OLDSMOBILE V.I.N. DEFINED

1st POSITION COUNTRY
1 = United States
2 = Canada

2nd POSITION MANUFACTURER
G = General Motors

3rd POSITION DIVISION
3 = Oldsmobile
7 = GM of Canada

4th POSITION CARLINE CODE
A = Cutlass Ciera/Cruiser
B = 88 Custom Cruiser (RWD)
C = 98 Regency/Brougham (FWD)
C = 98 Regency Elite
D = 98 Regency (RWD)
E = Toronado
E = Toronado Trofe'o
G = Cutlass
G = Cutlass Supreme
H = Delta 88 (FWD)
H = 88 Royale/LS (FWD)
J = Firenza
N = Calais
N = Achieva
W = Cutlass Supreme & S
W = Cutlass International
W = Cutlass Convertible

5th POSITION, 1985-88 CARLINE SERIES
C = Firenza
D = Firenza
F = Calais
F = Calais S
H = Cutlass Supreme
J = Cutlass Ciera/Wagon
K = Cutlass International
L = Cutlass Calais
L = Cutlass Ciera
L = Cutlass Ciera S
L = Achieva S
M = Cutlass Ciera SL
M = Cutlass Cruiser SL Wagon
M = Delta 88

5th POSITION, 1989-92 CARLINE SERIES
F = Achieva SL
F = Calais
F = Calais S
H = Cutlass Supreme
J = Cutlass Ciera/Wagon
K = Cutlass International
L = Cutlass Calais
L = Cutlass Ciera
L = Cutlass Ciera S
L = Achieva S
M = Cutlass Ciera SL
M = Cutlass Cruiser SL Wagon
M = Delta 88

5th POSITION, 89-92 (CONT'D)
N = 88 Royale
P = Custom Cruiser
R = Cutlass Supreme Int'l
S = Cutlass Ciera Int'l
T = Calais SL
T = Cutlass Convertible
V = Toronado Trofe'o
V = 98 Touring Sedan
W = 98 Regency Brougham
W = 98 Regency Elite
X = 98 Regency (FWD)
Y = Delta 88 Brougham
Y = 88 Royale LS
Z = Toronado

6th & 7th POSITION, 1985-86 BODY TYPE
19 = 4 Door Sedan
27 = 2 Door Coupe
35 = 4 Door Wagon
37 = 2 Door Coupe
47 = 2 Door Coupe
57 = 2 Door Coupe
67 = 2 Door Convertible
69 = 4 Door Sedan
77 = 2 Door Hatchback
87 = 2 Door Coupe

6th POSITION, 1987-92 BODY TYPE
1 = 2 Door Coupe
1 = 2 Door Sedan
2 = 2 Door Sedan
3 = 2 Door Convertible
5 = 4 Door Sedan
6 = 4 Door Sedan
8 = 4 Door Wagon

7th POSITION, 1987-92 RESTRAINT SYSTEM
1 = Manual Belts
2 = Manual Belts (Built In Safety)
2 = Manual Belts (Dual Air Bags)
3 = Manual Belts (Driver Air Bag)
4 = Automatic Belts
5 = Automatic Belts (Driver Air Bag)

8th POSITION, 1985-88 ENGINE CODE
A = 3.8-V6, 2 barrel
B = 3.8-V6, 2 barrel
D = 2.3-L4, Fuel Injected
E = 3.0-V6, 2 barrel
L = 5.0-V8, 4 barrel
L = 3.0-V6, MFI
M = 3.0-V6, MFI
P = 2.0-L4, EFI
R = 2.5-L4, TBI
T = 4.3-V6, Diesel
U = 2.5-L4, TBI
W = 4.3-V6, Diesel
X = 2.8-V6, 2 barrel
Y = 5.0-V8, 4 barrel

8th POSITION, 89-92 (CONT'D)
0 = 1.8-L4, TBI
1 = 2.0-L4, EFI
3 = 3.8-V6, MBI
7 = 4.3-V8, Diesel
9 = 5.0-V8, 4 barrel

8th POSITION, 1989-92 ENGINE CODE
A = 2.3-L4, MFI
C = 2.3-L4, MFI
D = 2.3-L4, MFI
E = 5.0-V8, TBI
L = 3.8-V6, MFI
N = 3.3-V6, MFI
R = 2.5-L4, TBI
T = 3.1-V6, MFI
U = 2.5-L4, TBI
W = 2.8-V6, MFI
X = 3.4-V6, MFI
1 = 3.8-V6, MFI
3 = 2.3-L4, MFI
7 = 3.8-V6, MFI
7 = 5.7-V8, TBI

9th POSITION CHECK DIGIT

10th POSITION MODEL YEAR
F = 1985
G = 1986
H = 1987
J = 1988
K = 1989
L = 1990
M = 1991
N = 1992

11th POSITION ASSEMBLY PLANT
B = Lansing, MI
C = Lansing, MI
D = Doraville, GA
E = Linden, NJ
F = Flint, MI
G = Framingham, MA
K = Leeds, MO
M = Lansing, MI
R = Arlington, TX
U = Hamtramck, MI
W = Willow Run, MI
X = Fairfax, KS
Y = Wilmington, DE
Z = Fremont, Ca
1 = Wentzville, MO
1 = Oshawa #2, Canada
2 = Ste. Therese, Canada
4 = Orion, MI
7 = Lordstown, OH
9 = Oshawa #1, Canada

12th Thru 17th POSITION PRODUCTION SEQUENCE NUMBER

1993-94 OLDSMOBILE V.I.N. DEFINED

1st POSITION COUNTRY
1 = United States
2 = Canada

2nd POSITION MANUFACTURER
G = General Motors

3rd POSITION DIVISION
3 = Oldsmobile
7 = GM of Canada

4th POSITION CARLINE CODE
A = Cutlass Ciera/Cruiser
B = 88 Custom Cruiser (RWD)
C = 98 Touring Sedan
C = 98 Regency/Elite
E = Toronado
E = Toronado Trofe'o
H = 88 Royale/LS (FWD)
N = Achieva
W = Cutlass Supreme S
T = Cutlass Supreme Int'l
W = Cutlass International
W = Cutlass Convertible

5th POSITION CARLINE SERIES
F = Achieva SL
G = Cutlass Ciera S
H = Cutlass Supreme S
J = Cutlass S/Wagon
L = Cutlass Ciera S
L = Achieva S
M = Cutlass Ciera SL
M = Cutlass Cruiser SL Wagon
N = 88 Royale
P = Custom Cruiser
R = Cutlass Supreme Int'l
T = Cutlass Convertible
V = Toronado Trofe'o
W = 98 Touring Sedan
W = 98 Regency Elite
X = 98 Regency (FWD)
Y = 88 Royale LS
Z = Toronado

6th POSITION BODY TYPE
1 = 2 Door Coupe
3 = 2 Door Convertible
5 = 4 Door Sedan
8 = 4 Door Wagon

7th POSITION RESTRAINT SYSTEM
1 = Manual Belts
2 = Manual Belts (Dual Air Bags)
3 = Manual Belts (Driver Air Bag)
4 = Automatic Belts
5 = Automatic Belts (Driver Air Bag)
6 = Automatic Belts (Dual Air Bags)

8th POSITION ENGINE CODE
A = 2.3-L4, MFI
D = 2.3-L4, MFI
E = 5.0-V8, MFI
L = 3.8-V6, MFI
M = 3.1-V6, MFI
N = 3.3-V6, MFI
R = 2.5-L4, TBI
X = 3.4-V6, MFI
1 = 3.8-V6, MFI
3 = 2.3-L4, MFI
4 = 2.2-L4, MFI
7 = 5.7-V8, TBI

9th POSITION CHECK DIGIT

10th POSITION MODEL YEAR
P = 1993
R = 1994

11th POSITION ASSEMBLY PLANT
B = Lansing, MI
C = Lansing, MI
D = Doraville, GA
E = Linden, NJ
F = Flint, MI
G = Framingham, MA
K = Leeds, MO
M = Lansing, MI
R = Arlington, TX
U = Hamtramck, MI
W = Willow Run, MI
X = Fairfax, KS
Y = Wilmington, DE
Z = Fremont, Ca
1 = Wentzville, MO
1 = Oshawa #2, Canada
2 = Ste. Therese, Canada
4 = Orion, MI
7 = Lordstown, OH
9 = Oshawa #1, Canada

12th Thru 17th POSITION PRODUCTION SEQUENCE NUMBER

1994 PONTIAC V.I.N. DEFINED

1st POSITION COUNTRY
1 = United States
2 = Canada

2nd POSITION MANUFACTURER
G = General Motors

3rd POSITION DIVISION
2 = Pontiac
7 = GM of Canada

4th POSITION CARLINE CODE
F = Firebird/Formula
H = Bonneville
J = Sunbird & Convertible
N = Grand Am
W = Grand Prix

5th POSITION CARLINE SERIES
B = Sunbird SE & Convertible
E = Grand Am SE
J = Grand Prix SE
L = Sunbird SE
M = Grand Prix
S = Firebird
V = Formula & Convertible
W = Grand Am GT
X = Bonneville SE
Z = Bonneville SSE

6th POSITION BODY TYPE
1 = 2 Door Coupe
2 = 2 Door Coupe
3 = 2 Door Convertible
5 = 4 Door Sedan

7th POSITION RESTRAINT SYSTEM
1 = Manual Belts
2 = Manual Belts (Dual Air Bags)
3 = Manual Belts (Driver Air Bag)
4 = Automatic Belts
5 = Automatic Belts (Driver Air Bag)
6 = Automatic Belts (Dual Air Bags)

8th POSITION ENGINE CODE
A = 2.3-L4, MFI
C = 3.8-V6, MFI
H = 2.0-L4, MFI
L = 3.8-V6, MFI
P = 5.7-V8, MFI
S = 3.4-V6, MFI
T = 3.1-V6, MFI
X = 3.1-V6, MFI
1 = 3.8-V6, MFI
3 = 2.3-L4, MFI

9th POSITION CHECK DIGIT

10th POSITION MODEL YEAR
R = 1994

11th POSITION ASSEMBLY PLANT

12th Thru 17th POSITION PRODUCTION SEQUENCE NUMBER

1991-93 PONTIAC V.I.N. DEFINED

1st POSITION COUNTRY
1 = United States
2 = Canada
K = Korea

2nd POSITION MANUFACTURER
G = General Motors
L = Daewoo Motors

3rd POSITION DIVISION
2 = Pontiac
7 = GM of Canada

4th POSITION CARLINE CODE
A = 6000
B = Parisienne/Safari
F = Firebird
G = Grand Prix Brougham
H = Bonneville
J = Sunbird, 2000 & Conv.
L = Tempest
M = Firefly
N = Grand Am
P = Fiero
T = T-1000/Lemans
W = Grand Prix

5th POSITION CARLINE SERIES
B = Sunbird, J2000
B = Sunbird LE
B = Sunbird SE & Conv.
C = Sunbird, J2000 LE
D = Sunbird, J2000 SE
D = Sunbird GT
E = Fiero/Grand Am/6000 SE
E = Grand Am LE
F = Fiero SE/6000 LE
G = 6000 LE/Fiero GT
H = 6000 STE
J = Grand Prix LE
J = Grand Prix LE & SE
J = 6000 SE
L = T1000/Parisienne
M = Fiero Sport Coupe
N = Bonneville/Parisienne Brougham
N = Lemans
N = Lemans SE Aero Cpe & Sedan
P = Grand Prix Brougham & SE
P = Grand Prix GT/GTP
R = Bonneville Brougham
R = Firefly
R = Lemans SE
S = Firebird/Bonneville
S = Lemans GSE
T = Grand Prix STE
T = Parisienne Brougham
T = Tempest
U = Sunbird GT/Parisienne Export
V = Grand Am LE
V = Formula
W = Firebird Trans Am
W = Grand Am SE & GT
X = Firebird SE/Bonneville LE
X = Bonneville SE

5th POSITION (CONTINUED)
X = Lemans, Lemans GSE
X = Lemans Aero Coupe
Y = Bonneville SSE, SSEi
Z = Bonneville LE, SE & SSE

6th & 7th POSITION, 1985-86 BODY TYPE
19 = 4 Door Sedan
27 = 2 Door Coupe
35 = 4 Door Wagon
37 = 2 Door Coupe
47 = 2 Door Coupe
57 = 2 Door Coupe
67 = 2 Door Convertible
69 = 4 Door Sedan
77 = 2 Door Hatchback
87 = 2 Door Coupe

6th POSITION, 1987-93 BODY TYPE
2 = 2 Door Coupe
2 = 2 Door Hatchback
2 = 2 Door Coupe
3 = 2 Door Convertible
5 = 4 Door Sedan
5 = 3 Door Cargo Van
6 = 4 Door Sedan
6 = 4 Door Hatchback
6 = 3 Door Van
8 = 4 Door Wagon

7th POSITION, 1987-93 RESTRAINT SYSTEM
1 = Manual Belts
2 = Manual Belts (Built In Safety)
2 = Manual Belts (Dual Air Bags)
3 = Manual Belts (Driver Air Bag)
4 = Automatic Belts
5 = Automatic Belts (Driver Air Bag)

8th POSITION, 1985-88 ENGINE CODE
A = 3.8-V6, 2 barrel
B = 3.8-V6, 2 barrel
C = 1.6-L4, 2 barrel
D = 1.8-L4, Diesel
E = 5.0-V8, Fuel Injected
F = 5.0-V8, Fuel Injected
G = 5.0-V8, 4 barrel
H = 5.0-V8, 4 barrel
J = 1.8-L4, MFI
J = 3.0-V6, MFI
N = 5.7-V8, Diesel
P = 2.0-L4, EFI
R = 2.5-L4, TBI
S = 2.8-V6, MFI
U = 4.3-V6, Diesel
V = 4.3-V6, Diesel
W = 2.8-V6, MFI
Z = 4.3-V6, TBI
0 = 1.8-L4, TBI
2 = 2.5-L4, TBI
6 = 1.6-L4, 2 barrel
6 = 1.6-L4, TBI
9 = 2.8-V6, MFI

8th POSITION, 1989-93 ENGINE CODE
A = 2.3-L4, MFI
C = 3.8-V6, MFI
D = 2.3-L4, MFI
E = 5.0-V8, TBI
F = 5.0-V8, MFI
K = 2.0-L4, TBI
L = 3.8-V6, MFI
M = 2.0-L4, MFI
N = 3.3-V6, MFI
P = 5.7-V8, MFI
R = 2.5-L4, TBI
S = 2.8-V6, MFI
S = 3.4-V6, MFI
T = 3.1-V6, MFI
U = 2.5-L4, TBI
V = 3.1-V6, MFI
W = 2.8-V6, MFI
X = 3.4-V6, MFI
Y = 5.0-V8, 4 Barrel
Z = 4.3-V6, TBI
3 = 2.3-L4, MFI
7 = 3.8-V6, MFI
8 = 5.7-V8, MFI

9th POSITION CHECK DIGIT

10th POSITION MODEL YEAR
F = 1985
G = 1986
H = 1987
J = 1988
K = 1989
L = 1990
M = 1991
N = 1992
P = 1993

11th POSITION ASSEMBLY PLANT
A = Lakewood, GA
B = Lansing, MI
B = Korea
C = Lansing, MI
F = Flint, MI
L = Van Nuys, CA
M = Lansing, MI
N = Norwood, OH
P = Pontiac, MI
U = Hamtramck, MI
W = Willow Run, MI
X = Fairfax, KS
Y = Wilmington, DE
Z = Wentzville, MO
1 = Oshawa #2, Canada
2 = Ste. Therese, Quebec, Canada
5 = Bowling Green, KY
6 = Oklahoma City, OK
7 = Lordstown, OH
9 = Oshawa #1, Canada

12th Thru 17th POSITION PRODUCTION SEQUENCE NUMBER

SATURN

V.I.N. DEFINED

1st POSITION
COUNTRY
1 = United States

2nd POSITION
MANUFACTURER
G = General Motors

3rd POSITION
DIVISION
8 = Saturn

4th POSITION
CARLINE CODE
Z = SL, SL1&2, SC
Z = SC1&2, SW1&2

5th POSITION
CARLINE SERIES
E = SC1
F = SL, SC1
G = SL1, SC, SC2, SW1
H = SL1, SC, SC2, SW1
J = SL2, SW2
K = SL2, SW2

6th POSITION
BODY TYPE
1 = 2 Door Coupe
5 = 4 Door Sedan
8 = 5 Door Wagon

7th POSITION
RESTRAINT SYSTEM
4 = Automatic Belts
5 = Passive W/Driver Air Bag

8th POSITION
ENGINE CODE
7 = 1.9-L4, MFI
9 = 1.9-L4, TBI

9th POSITION
CHECK DIGIT

10th POSITION
MODEL YEAR
M = 1991
N = 1992
P = 1993
R = 1994

11th POSITION
ASSEMBLY PLANT
Z = Spring Hill

12th Thru 17th POSITION
PRODUCTION SEQUENCE NUMBER

SERVICE REMINDER & WARNING LAMP RESET PROCEDURES

TABLE OF CONTENTS

Fig. 1 Driver Information Center. 1986–92 Cadillac Eldorado & Seville

ANTI-LOCK WARNING LAMP

This lamp will be illuminated when the ignition switch is placed in the ON position. The lamp may be illuminated for as long as 30 seconds as a bulb and system check. If lamp remains illuminated or comes on while operating the vehicle, a problem in the anti-lock brake system is indicated. When lamp is illuminated, place ignition switch in OFF position, then restart engine. If lamp still remains illuminated, the anti-lock brake system should be serviced. The brake system will remain functional, but without the anti-lock function. After servicing the anti-lock brake system the lamp will automatically reset. On some models it may be necessary to operate vehicle at a speed over 18 MPH to reset lamp.

AIRBAG WARNING LAMP

On models equipped with an airbag system, if the airbag warning lamp illuminates and stays on, diagnosis and repair of the airbag system will be necessary to reset the lamp.

CHANGE OIL OR CHANGE OIL NOW MESSAGE

CADILLAC

When the engine oil life index has reached zero, the Change Engine Oil message will be indicated on the Driver Information Display. After performing the engine oil change, the engine Oil Life Index may be reset as follows:

1989–91 Eldorado & Seville

Press and hold the ENG DATA and RANGE buttons, **Fig. 1**, for a minimum of 5 seconds.

1991–92 DeVille & Fleetwood

Press RANGE and FUEL USED buttons simultaneously to display oil life index, then press the RANGE and RESET buttons until "Change Oil Soon" light flashes (approximately five seconds). The oil life index will not remain displayed.

1992–93 Eldorado & Seville

Press the INFORMATION button until oil life index is displayed, then press STORE/RECALL until oil life index resets to 100 (approximately five seconds).

1993 DeVille, Fleetwood (FWD) & Sixty Special

Reset the Engine Oil Life Index (EOLI) after each oil change by pressing the RANGE and RESET keys on the Fuel Data Center for 5-50 seconds. The "Change Oil Soon" lamp will flash four times to indicate that the index has been reset.

Fig. 2 Driver Information Center. 1988–91 Oldsmobile except Toronado

Fig. 3 Information Center. 1986–89 Oldsmobile Toronado

1993 RWD Fleetwood

1. Turn ignition switch to On position, without starting engine.
2. Press accelerator pedal to wide open throttle (WOT) position and release three times within five seconds.
3. If "Change Oil" warning indicator goes out, system has been reset.
4. If "Change Oil" warning indicator does not reset, turn ignition switch Off and repeat procedure.

OLDSMOBILE
Except Toronado

When the engine oil life index has reached 10 or less, the Driver Information System display will indicate distance to oil change and sound a beep, when ignition switch is placed in the Run or Accessory position for the first time each day. When the engine oil life index has reached 0, the Driver Information System display will indicate Change Oil Now and sound a beep, when ignition switch is placed in the Run or Accessory position for the first time each day. After engine oil change has been performed, the oil life index may be reset by depressing and holding the Oil and Reset buttons for approximately 5 seconds, **Fig. 2.**

1986–89 Toronado

When the engine oil life index has reached 0, the Information System display will indicate Change Oil. After engine oil change has been performed, the oil life index may be reset by depressing and holding the Engine Data and Gauge buttons until Oil Index 100 message appears in Information Display panel, **Fig. 3.**

1990–92 Toronado

When the engine oil life index has reached 0, the Information System display will indicate Change Oil. After engine oil change has been performed, the oil life index may be reset by depressing and holding the reset button for at least five seconds.

1992–93 Eighty-Eight & Ninety-Eight

When the engine oil life index has reached 10 or less, the Driver Information System display will indicate distance to oil

change and sound a beep when the ignition switch is placed in the RUN or ACC position for the first time each day. When the engine oil life index has reached zero, the Driver Information System display will indicate "Change Oil Now" and sound a beep, when ignition switch is placed in the RUN or ACC position for the first time each day. After engine oil change has been performed, the oil life index may be reset as follows:

1. Depress the TEST button and release.
2. Depress OIL button and release.
3. Depress and hold the RESET button for approximately seven seconds.

BUICK
1991–93 LeSabre & Park Avenue

The reset button is located under the passenger side of the instrument panel. With the ignition in the ON position, but the engine not started, use a pencil to push reset button, holding it for five seconds. After this, the "Change Oil Soon" light will flash four times. This indicates that the Oil Life Monitor System has acknowledged the oil change.

PONTIAC
6000 & BONNEVILLE

After changing engine oil and filter, if necessary, reset service interval indicator by depressing and releasing the service reminder button until the desired item is displayed. When the desired item is displayed, do not release service reminder button. After button has been depressed for approximately 10 seconds, the service interval mileage display will begin to count down in 500 mile intervals. When desired service interval mileage is reached, release button. The service interval reminder indicates miles to service, not miles from last service.

CHEVROLET
1990–91 Corvette

After changing engine oil and filter, if necessary, reset service interval indicator as follows:

1. Turn ignition On, press ENG/MET button and release, then press ENG/MET button again within five seconds.
2. Within five seconds of step 1, press and hold the RANGE button until the "Change Oil" indicator begins to flash.

Hold RANGE button until indicator stops flashing and goes out, approximately 10 seconds.

3. If indicator was not successfully reset, turn ignition Off and repeat reset procedure.

1992–93 Corvette

1. Turn ignition key to On position, without starting engine.
2. Press ENG MET button on the trip monitor and release, then press and release again within five seconds.
3. Within five seconds of step 2, press and hold GAUGES button on trip monitor. "Change Oil" lamp will flash.
4. Hold GAUGES button until "Change Oil" lamp stops flashing and goes out.
5. When light goes out, the engine oil life monitor is reset. If it does not reset, turn ignition switch Off and repeat procedure.

CHECK ENGINE INDICATOR LAMP (DIESEL ENGINE)

MODELS w/DIESEL ELECTRONIC CONTROL SYSTEM

The check engine lamp will be illuminated when the ignition switch is placed in the On position. When the engine is started, the lamp should go off. If the lamp remains On after the engine is started, the self diagnosis system has detected a problem and has stored a code in the system Electronic Control Module (ECM). After diagnosis and repair, the ECM memory can be cleared of codes when the ignition switch has been placed in the Off position. To clear codes, disconnect battery ground cable for approximately 30 seconds. It should be noted, when battery ground cable is disconnected to clear codes, components such as clocks, electronically tuned radios etc., will have to be reset.

CHECK ENGINE OR SERVICE NOW/SOON ENGINE INDICATOR LAMPS (GASOLINE ENGINES w/ELECTRONIC ENGINE CONTROLS OR EFI)

EXCEPT CHEVROLET SPECTRUM & SPRINT, GEO & PONTIAC LEMANS

The check engine lamp will be illuminated when the ignition switch is placed in the On position. When the engine is started, the lamp should go off. If the lamp remains On for 10 seconds or constantly after the engine is started, the self diagnosis system has detected a problem and has stored a code in the system Electronic Control Module (ECM). After diagnosis and repair, the ECM memory can be cleared of codes as follows:

On models except Cadillac with DEFI and 1986-88 Buick Reatta/Riviera and Oldsmobile Toronado/Trofeo, remove the ECM fuse or disconnect the battery ground cable for approximately 30 seconds, with ignition switch in the Off

position. It should be noted, if battery ground cable is disconnected to clear codes, components such as clocks, electronically tuned radios etc., will have to be reset.

On vehicle that are equipped as such, the ECM power feed is connected by a pigtail, inline fuse holder, at the positive battery terminal. To clear codes within the ECM system and protect the components that need resetting, disconnect the inline fuse.

On 1980-85 Cadillac models with DEFI engines, depress Electronic Climate Control Off and Hi buttons to clear codes. On 1986-92 Cadillac DeVille and Fleetwood models, depress Off and Lo button on the Electronic Climate Control to clear stored BCM codes. Depress Off and Hi to clear stored ECM codes.

On Cadillac Eldorado and Seville and 1986-88 Buick Reatta/Riviera and Oldsmobile Toronado/Trofeo models, the stored codes are cleared during the self-diagnostic procedure.

CHEVROLET SPECTRUM

The check engine lamp will be illuminated when the ignition switch is in the On position with engine not operating. When engine is started, the Check Engine lamp should go off. If lamp remains on, a code has been stored by the Electronic Control Module (ECM). After diagnosis and repair, place ignition switch in Off position, then clear codes stored in the ECM memory by removing the Emission or ECM fuse, located in the fuse box under the instrument panel on the lefthand side, for approximately 10 seconds.

CHEVROLET SPRINT
1987–88 Models Less Turbo Engine

The check engine lamp will be illuminated when the ignition switch is in the On position with engine not operating. When engine is started, the Check Engine lamp should go off. If lamp remains on, a code has been stored by the Electronic Control Module (ECM) memory. After diagnosis and repair, with diagnosis switch in Off position, start engine and allow to reach operating temperature. After engine has reached operating temperature, the Check Engine lamp should be off while engine is operating.

1987–88 Models w/Turbo Engine

The check engine lamp will be illuminated when the ignition switch is in the On position with engine not operating. When engine is started, the Check Engine lamp should go off. If lamp remains on, a code has been stored by the Electronic Control Module (ECM) memory. After diagnosis and repair, place ignition switch in Off position, then clear codes stored in the ECM memory by disconnecting the battery ground cable, for approximately 20 seconds.

GEO METRO

The check engine lamp will be illuminated when the ignition switch is in the On position with engine not operating. When engine is started, the Check Engine lamp should go off. If lamp remains on, a code has been stored by the Electronic

Control Module (ECM) memory. After diagnosis and repair, place ignition switch in Off position, then clear codes stored in the ECM memory by disconnecting the battery ground cable, for approximately 20 seconds.

GEO PRIZM

The check engine lamp will be illuminated when the ignition switch is in the On position with engine not operating. When engine is started, the Check Engine lamp should go off. If lamp remains on, a code has been stored by the Electronic Control Unit (ECU) memory. After diagnosis and repair, place ignition switch in Off position, then clear codes stored in the ECU memory by removing the Stop Fuse. The Stop fuse is located in a fuse panel, in the passenger compartment, on driver's side, behind kick panel, **Fig. 4**. The fuse must be removed for 10 seconds or longer, depending on ambient temperature. The lower the ambient temperature, the longer the fuse will have to be removed.

GEO STORM

The check engine lamp will be illuminated when the ignition switch is in the On position with engine not operating. When engine is started, the Check Engine lamp should go off. If lamp remains on, a code has been stored by the Electronic Control Module (ECM) memory. After diagnosis and repair, place ignition switch in Off position, then clear codes stored in the ECM memory by disconnecting the battery ground cable for approximately 30 seconds.

GEO SPECTRUM

The check engine lamp will be illuminated when the ignition switch is in the On position with engine not operating. When engine is started, the Check Engine lamp should go off. If lamp remains on, a code has been stored by the Electronic Control Module (ECM) memory. After diagnosis and repair, place ignition switch in Off position, then clear codes stored in the ECM memory by disconnecting the battery ground cable for approximately 30 seconds.

PONTIAC LEMANS

The check engine lamp will be illuminated when the ignition switch is placed in the On position. When the engine is started, them should go off. If the lamp remains On for 10 seconds or constantly after the engine is started, the self diagnosis system has detected a problem and has stored a code in the system Electronic Control Module (ECM). After diagnosis and repair, the ECM memory can be cleared of codes, by disconnecting battery ground cable for 10 seconds, with ignition switch in the off position.

CHECK INFO CENTER WARNING LAMP

1986–92 CADILLAC ELDORADO & SEVILLE

This lamp will be illuminated for a few seconds when the ignition switch is placed in the On position as a bulb check. If

Fig. 4 Stop fuse location. Geo Prizm

lamp remains illuminated, a message is store in the Driver Information Center. Refer to "Driver Information Center."

CHOKE OR OIL/CHOKE WARNING LAMP

MODELS WITH CARBURETED ENGINE

On models less gauges, the oil/choke warning indicator lamp should be illuminated when the ignition switch is in the Run or Start position. When the engine is started, the choke warning indicator lamp should go off. If the lamp fails to illuminate with ignition switch in Run or Start position with engine not operating, a burned bulb or fuse or defect in choke electrical system is indicated. If lamp remains on after engine has been started, a problem in the engine oil pressure system or electrical choke system exist.

On models equipped with gauges, the choke warning indicator lamp should be illuminated when the ignition switch is in the Run or Start position. When the engine is started, the choke warning indicator lamp should go off. If fails to illuminate with ignition switch in Run or Start position with engine not operating, a burnt out bulb or fuse or defect in choke electrical system is indicated. If lamp remains on after engine has been started, a problem in the alternator circuit is indicated.

After service has been completed, the lamp operation should return to normal.

DRIVER INFORMATION CENTER

CADILLAC

1986–88 Cadillac Eldorado & Seville

This system, **Fig. 1,** incorporates a warning lamp, located on the instrument cluster, that is illuminated when the ignition switch is in the On position. After a few seconds the lamp should go off, unless a message in The Driver Information System is present. The driver information center will display the following messages:

A/C Overheated—A/C Compressor Off—This message is displayed when excessive pressure in the refrigerant system is encountered. When this condition is encountered, the A/C compressor clutch will be de-energized and cool air will not be delivered to the vehicle interior. The message will continue to appear and the A/C compressor clutch will continue to be de-energized until the system pressure returns to normal range. If this message frequently appears, the A/C system should be serviced.

A/C Sensor Fault—This message will be displayed when the sensor controlling A/C compressor clutch cycling has failed. When this sensor has failed, the A/C compressor will not operate and the A/C system will emit warmer air. After servicing system and replacing sensor, the display message will be cancelled.

Battery Volts High—This message will appear when the charging system is overcharging the battery. After completing charging system diagnosis and repair, the message will be cancelled when battery voltage returns to 11.5 to 15.5 volts with engine operating. Battery voltage can be displayed on the Drive Information Center Display by depressing the Eng-Data button three times.

Battery Volts Low—If this message is displayed while driving the vehicle or after vehicle has been started, a problem in the charging system is present or battery has been drained. After diagnosing charging system or electrical system for cause of battery drain, the message will be cancelled when engine is operating and battery voltage is between 11.5 to 15.5 volts. Battery voltage can be displayed on the Drive Information Center Display by depressing the Eng-Data button three times.

Engine Hot—A/C Compressor Off—This message will appear when A/C system is on Auto or Defrost and engine coolant temperature is excessive. The A/C compressor clutch will be automatically de-energized when excessive engine coolant temperatures are encountered. When engine coolant temperature returns to normal, the A/C compressor clutch will be energized and the message on the display will be cancelled.

Front Or Rear Door Ajar—This message will appear when the transmission selector lever is moved out of the Park position and a door is not properly closed. The message can be cancelled by properly closing the indicated door.

Fuel Level Very Low—When low fuel level conditions are encountered this message will appear. To cancel message, add fuel.

Headlamps Or Parking Lamps On—This message will be displayed when the headlamp switch is On, vehicle is moving and the sensed level of outside light indicates that headlamps should not be illuminated. This message may be cancelled by placing the headlamp switch in the Off position.

Low A/C Refrigerant—A/C Compressor Off—This message will be displayed when the A/C system detects a refrigerant charge low enough to cause compressor damage. When this condition is encountered, the A/C compressor clutch is de-energized and the A/C system is switched from Auto to Econ. The system will remain in Econ until necessary repairs are made and system is recharged. After completing necessary repairs and recharging the system, A/C system operation will return to normal and the message on the display will be cancelled.

Low A/C Refrigerant—Service A/C Soon—This message will be displayed when the A/C system detects that refrigerant charge is low enough to cause a reduction in cooling capacity. This message will be displayed until system has been recharged.

Low Washer Fluid—This message will appear when windshield washer fluid level is low. To cancel message, refill windshield washer fluid reservoir.

Service Electrical System—This message will appear when a problem in the charging system is present. After repairing charging system, the message will be automatically cancelled.

Service Now Or Service Soon—This message will be displayed when a problem in one the engine monitored systems is present. After diagnosis and repair the message will be automatically cancelled.

System Problem—Service Car Soon—This message will be displayed when one or more of the vehicle computers supplying information to the Driver Information Center become defective. After diagnosis and repair of the defective computer, the message will be automatically cancelled.

Theft System Problem/Car May Not Start—This message will appear when the vehicle security system senses an improper ignition key has been placed in the ignition switch. After removal of key from ignition switch, the Driver Information Center display will indicate "Wait 3 Minutes," "Wait 2 Minutes," "Wait 1 Minute" and then "Start Car." When the "Start Car" message appears, insert ignition key and attempt to start vehicle. If message appears again, check ignition key for damage and replace as necessary. If key appears to be satisfactory, clean pellet contacts with a soft cloth and attempt to restart vehicle.

Trunk Open—This message will appear when the ignition switch is the Run position and the trunk is not properly closed. The message can be cancelled by properly closing the trunk.

1989—92 Cadillac Eldorado & Seville

This system incorporates a warning lamp, located on the instrument cluster, that is illuminated when the ignition switch is in the On position. After a few seconds the lamp should go off, unless a message in The Driver Information System is present. The driver information center will display the following messages:

A/C Overheated—A/C Compressor Off—This message is displayed when excessive pressure in the refrigerant system is encountered. When this condition is encountered, the A/C Compressor clutch will be de-energized and cool air will not be delivered to the vehicle interior. The message will continue to appear and the A/C compressor clutch will continue to be de-energized until the system pressure returns to normal range. If this message frequently appears, the A/C system should be serviced.

A/C Sensor Fault—This message will be displayed when the sensor controlling A/C compressor clutch cycling has failed. When this sensor has failed, the A/C compressor will not operate and the A/C system will emit warmer air. After servicing system and replacing sensor, the display message will be cancelled.

Battery Volts High—This message will appear when the charging system is overcharging the battery. After completing charging system diagnosis and repair, the message will be cancelled when battery voltage returns to 11.5 to 15.5 volts with engine operating. Battery voltage can be displayed on the Drive Information Center Display by depressing the Eng-Data button three times.

Battery Volts Low—If this message is displayed while driving the vehicle or after vehicle has been started, a problem in the charging system is present or battery has been drained. After diagnosing charging system or electrical system for cause of battery drain, the message will be cancelled when engine is operating and battery voltage is between 11.5 to 15.5 volts. Battery voltage can be displayed on the Drive Information Center Display by depressing the Eng-Data button three times.

Change Engine Oil—When the engine oil life index has reached 0, the Change Engine Oil message will be indicated. After performing the engine oil change, the engine Oil Life Index may be reset by depressing and holding the Engine Data and Range buttons for at least 5 seconds

Cooling Fan Fault—This message will appear when the engine cooling fan system inoperative. After repairing cooling fan system the message will be automatically cancelled.

Engine Hot—A/C Compressor Off—This message will appear when A/C system is Auto or Defrost and engine coolant temperature is excessive. The A/C compressor clutch will be automatically de-energized when excessive engine coolant temperatures are encountered. When engine coolant temperature returns to normal, the A/C compressor clutch will be energized and the message on the display will be cancelled.

Front Or Rear Door Ajar—This message will appear when the transmission selector lever is moved out of the Park position and a door is not properly closed. The message can be cancelled by properly closing the indicated door.

Fuel Level Very Low—When low fuel level conditions are encountered this message will appear. To cancel message, add fuel.

Gear Select Problem—This message will appear if a problem in the transaxle gear select system is encountered while operating vehicle. After performing necessary service, the message will automatically be cancelled.

Headlamps Or Parking Lamps On—This message will be displayed when the headlamp switch is On, vehicle is moving and the sensed level of outside light indicates that headlamps should not be illuminated. This message may be cancelled by placing the headlamp switch in the Off position.

Headlamps Suggested—This message will be displayed when the Twilight Sentinel is in the Off position, vehicle is moving and the sensed level of outside light indicates that headlamps should be illuminated. This message may be cancelled by activating the Twilight Sentinel System.

Low A/C Refrigerant—A/C Compressor Off—This message will be displayed when the A/C system detects a refrigerant charge low enough to cause compressor damage. When this condition is encountered, the A/C compressor

Fig. 5 Driver Information Center. 1988–90 Pontiac 6000 STE & Bonneville SSE

clutch is de-energized and the A/C system is switched from Auto to Econ. The system will remain in Econ until necessary repairs are made and system is recharged. After completing necessary repairs and recharging the system, A/C system operation will return to normal and the message on the display will be cancelled.

Low A/C Refrigerant—Service A/C Soon—This message will be displayed when the A/C system detects that refrigerant charge is low enough to cause a reduction in cooling capacity. This message will be displayed until system has been recharged.

Low Washer Fluid—This message will appear when windshield washer fluid level is low. To cancel message, refill windshield washer fluid reservoir.

Oil Life Index—The oil life index is a series of numerals ranging from 0 to 100. The 100 is indicated when engine oil has been drained and replacement engine oil has been installed. The 0 is an indication that the engine oil should be changed. The oil life index is accessed by depressing the Engine Data button four times.

Service Electrical System—This message will appear when a problem in the charging system is present. After repairing charging system, the message will be automatically cancelled.

Set Timing Mode—This message will appear if ignition timing is improperly set. After performing necessary service, the message will be automatically cancelled.

Starting Disabled/Due to Theft System/Remove Ignition Key—This message is an indication of a problem in the vehicle security system that may prohibit the vehicle from being restarted after the ignition switch has been placed in the Off position. After servicing the vehicle security system the message will be automatically cancelled.

System Ok—This message will be displayed for approximately 5 seconds after ignition switch has been placed in the On position, unless a problem in the system has been detected. After approximately 5 seconds the display will return to the last display function selected.

System Problem—Service Car Soon—This message will be displayed when one or more of the vehicle computers supplying information to the Driver Information Center become defective. After diagnosis and repair of the defective computer, the message will be automatically cancelled.

Theft System Problem/Car May Not Start—This message will appear when the vehicle security system senses an improper ignition key has been placed in the ignition switch. After remove key from ignition switch, the Driver Information Center display will indicate "Wait 3 Minutes," "Wait 2 Minutes," "Wait 1 Minute" and then "Start Car." When the "Start Car" message appears, insert ignition key and attempt to start vehicle. If message appears again, check ignition key for damage and replace as necessary. If key appears to be satisfactory, clean pellet contacts with a soft cloth and attempt to restart vehicle.

Trunk Open—This message will appear when the ignition switch is the Run position and the trunk is not properly closed. The message can be cancelled by properly closing the trunk.

PONTIAC 6000 & BONNEVILLE

The Driver Information Center Display, **Fig. 5,** is located on the instrument panel. When the ignition switch is placed in the On position, the display will go through a bulb check, in which the vehicle graph and message title will be displayed in sequence. After the sequence has been completed, all messages and vehicle graph will remain illuminated for approximately 2 seconds. After approximately 2 seconds, if all monitored systems are functioning properly, the message titles should go off and only the vehicle outline should be illuminated. If a problem in any of the monitored systems is present, the particular title for the monitored system will be illuminated and its approximate location on the vehicle graphic display will be illuminated. The following messages will be displayed:

1. **Function Monitor**—The coolant level, fuel level and windshield washer levels are monitored when ignition switch is the On position.
   a. Coolant Level—This message will be indicated when engine coolant level in the radiator drops below a pre-determined level. To cancel message, check cooling system, then add coolant to bring system to proper level.
   b. Fuel Level—This message will be indicated when fuel level is 5 gallons or less. To cancel message add fuel to fuel tank.
   c. Washer Fluid—This message will be indicated when windshield washer fluid is at about 40% of capacity. To cancel message, add washer fluid to reservoir.
2. **Lamp Check**—The headlamps, tail lamps, brake lamps and turn signal lamps will be checked whenever the lamp system is activated. To cancel this message, replace bulb or check and repair electrical system as necessary for lamp system indicated.
3. **Security**—Door, Hood Or Trunk Ajar are monitored. This message will appear when the indicated component is open or improperly closed. To cancel message, properly close indicated component.

4. **Service Reminder**—Oil change, oil filter change, engine tune-up and tire rotation intervals are monitored.
   a. After the bulb check sequence has been completed, the service interval can be checked by depressing the service reminder button. Depressing the button once will display the Change Oil indication and mileage remaining to service interval. Depressing the button a second time, will display the Change Oil Filter indication and mileage remaining to service interval. Depressing the button a third time will display the Rotate Tires and mileage to service interval. Depressing the button a fourth time will display Tune-Up indication and mileage to service interval.
   b. After completing the required service, reset service interval indicator by depressing and releasing the service reminder button until the desired item is displayed. When the desired item is displayed, do not release service reminder button. After button has been depressed for approximately 10 seconds, the service interval mileage display will begin to count down in 500 mile intervals. When desired service interval mileage is reached, release button. The service interval reminder indicates miles to service, not miles from last service.

EMISSION OR SENSOR MAINTENANCE REMINDER FLAG

1980 MODELS & 1981–83 CADILLAC LIMOUSINE & COMMERCIAL CHASSIS

At 30,000 mile intervals, a Emission or Sensor reminder flag, if equipped, will appear across the odometer to indicate the need for oxygen sensor replacement. After performing the required service, the flag must be reset for the next 30,000 mile interval.

On models except Cadillac, this is accomplished by gaining access to the speedometer head and removing the speedometer lens. Using a suitable pointed tool, rotate edge of flag wheel detents downward, until flag wheel can no longer be rotated. Flag wheel alignment mark should center in odometer.

On Cadillac models, remove lower steering column cover, then lightly pull sensor reset cable to reset flag. The sensor reset cable is located to the left of the speedometer cluster.

ENGINE CONTROL SYSTEM WARNING LAMP

1986–88 CADILLAC ELDORADO & SEVILLE

This lamp will be illuminated for a few seconds when the ignition switch is placed in On position as a bulb check. If lamp remains on, a problem in one of the emission control systems is indicated. The Driver Information Center should indicate a Service Soon or Service Now message. Refer to "Driver Information Center."

SERVICE REMINDER & WARNING LAMP RESET PROCEDURES

LOW COOLANT LAMP

This lamp will be illuminated when engine coolant level in the radiator drops below a pre-determined level. To turn lamp off, check cooling system, then add coolant to bring system to proper level.

OXYGEN SENSOR MAINTENANCE REMINDER LAMP

1985–86 CHEVROLET SPRINT

A Sensor lamp is located on the instrument panel to indicate proper operation of the oxygen sensor feedback circuit. Every 30,000 miles of vehicle operation, the lamp will begin to flash. When the lamp begins to flash, the feedback circuit should be checked and the lamp reset using the following procedure.

1. Ensure that ignition switch is off, remove fuse panel cover and move cancel switch to on position, **Fig. 6**.
2. Turn ignition switch to On position and observe Sensor lamp. If lamp does not light (without flashing), check for defective bulb or open feed circuit and repair as needed.
3. After illumination of lamp is confirmed, start engine and run until it reaches normal operating temperature.
4. Run engine at 1500-2000 RPM while observing lamp.
5. If lamp flashes, system is operating properly. If lamp does not flash, a problem in the Computer Controlled Emission Control System may be indicated.
6. After proper system operation has been verified, place cancel switch in off position to reset automatic indicator system.

SERVICE AIR COND LAMP

CADILLAC

This lamp will be illuminated when the A/C system detects a low refrigerant charge. The lamp will be illuminated for approximately 2 seconds after ignition switch has been placed in the On position as a bulb check.

If while operating vehicle, the lamp illuminates for approximately 60 seconds and then goes off, the refrigerant level is low enough to cause reduced cooling capacity. At this point the blower motor will increase speed to try to offset the loss in cooling capacity. The lamp will be automatically reset after system has been checked and refrigerant charge has been brought to proper level.

If lamp is illuminated for approximately 60 seconds after engine start up, the refrigerant charge may be low enough to cause A/C compressor damage. When this condition is encountered, the A/C compressor clutch is de-energized and the A/C system is switched from Auto to Econ. The system will remain in Econ until necessary repairs are made and system is recharged. After completing necessary repairs and recharging the system, A/C system operation will return to normal and the lamp will be automatically reset.

1. CANCEL SWITCH
2. FUSES
3. FUSE CASE COVER
4. STEERING WHEEL

Fig. 6   Oxygen sensor indicator lamp cancel switch. 1985–86 Chevrolet Sprint

SERVICE ELECTRICAL SYSTEM LAMP

CADILLAC

This lamp will be illuminated when a problem in the charging system is present. The lamp will be illuminated during engine starting as a bulb check. If lamp is illuminated while engine is operating, the charging system should be checked. After repairing charging system, the lamp will be automatically reset.

WATER IN FUEL OR DRAIN FUEL FILTER WARNING LAMP

MODELS w/DIESEL ENGINE

The water in fuel indicator will be illuminated when excessive water has entered the fuel system. As the fuel filter becomes plugged, a low pressure sensor activates the lamp. The lamp will be illuminated during engine starting as a bulb check. Once the engine has started, the lamp should go off. If the lamp is illuminated intermittently, drain fuel filter. If lamp remains illuminated, drain fuel filter. If the lamp still remains on after fuel filter has been drained, replace fuel filter. If lamp is illuminated during high speed operation or during heavy acceleration, replace fuel filter. If after starting, the engine stalls and will not restart and lamp remains illuminated, check for plugged fuel filter or fuel lines. If this condition occurs immediately after refueling, check fuel tank for large concentration of water in fuel, and if necessary purge fuel tank and replace fuel filter. After performing the required service, the increased fuel pressure through the fuel filter will reset the water in fuel lamp.

VEHICLE LIFT POINTS

INDEX

FRT

FRAME CONTACT HOIST

FLOOR JACK

SUSPENSION CONTACT HOIST

Fig. 1   Century, Cutlass Calais, Cutlass Ciera, Cutlass Cruiser, 1991–92 Grand Am, Skylark & 1992 Achieva

FRAME CONTACT HOIST   FLOOR JACK   SUSPENSION CONTACT HOIST

FRAME CONTACT HOIST
(REARWARD OF FRONT TIRE)

FRAME CONTACT HOIST
(FORWARD OF REAR TIRE)

SUSPENSION CONTACT HOIST
(UNDER FRONT LOWER CONTROL ARM)

WHEN USING FLOOR JACK, LIFT
ON CENTER OR REAR TORQUE ARM

SUSPENSION CONTACT HOIST
(LIFTING ON REAR TIRES)

Fig. 2 1993 Achieva, Beretta, Corsica, Grand Am & Skylark

FRT ▶

FRAME CONTACT HOIST
FLOOR JACK
SUSPENSION CONTACT HOIST

USING FLOOR JACK UNDER
REAR CONTROL ARM

WHEN USING FLOOR JACK, LIFT
ON CENTER OF FRONT CROSSMEMBER

WHEN USING FLOOR JACK, LIFT ON
REAR SUSPENSION CENTER SUPPORT

FRAME CONTACT HOIST
(REARWARD OF FRONT TIRE)

FRAME CONTACT HOIST
(FORWARD OF REAR TIRE)

SUSPENSION CONTACT HOIST
(UNDER FRONT LOWER CONTROL ARM)

SUSPENSION CONTACT HOIST
(LIFTING ON REAR TIRES)

**Fig. 3 Bonneville, DeVille, Eighty-Eight, Electra, Fleetwood, LeSabre, Ninety-Eight, Park Avenue
& 1992 Beretta & Corsica**

FRAME CONTACT HOIST

FLOOR JACK

SUSPENSION CONTACT HOIST

◀FRT

Fig. 4   Caprice, Custom Cruiser, Estate Wagon, Roadmaster & Safari

FRT▶

FRAME CONTACT HOIST   FLOOR JACK   SUSPENSION CONTACT HOIST

Fig. 5   Eldorado & Seville, Riviera & Reatta, Toronado & Trofeo

CAUTION: Use jacking pad only for raising the vehicle with a floor jack. Do not use lateral links, trailing arm or jacking pad for pulling or towing the vehicle.

1 WHEN USING FLOOR JACK, LIFT ON CENTER OF FRONT CROSSMEMBER

2 WHEN USING FLOOR JACK, LIFT ON REAR JACK PAD

Fig. 6 Cutlass Supreme, Grand Prix, Regal & Lumina (Part 1 of 2)

3 FRAME CONTACT HOIST
(REARWARD OF FRONT TIRE)

4 FRAME CONTACT HOIST
(FORWARD OF REAR TIRE)

5 SUSPENSION CONTACT HOIST
(LIFTING ON REAR TIRES)

6 SUSPENSION CONTACT HOIST
(UNDER FRONT LOWER CONTROL ARM)

Fig. 6   Cutlass Supreme, Grand Prix, Regal & Lumina (Part 2 of 2)

FRAME CONTACT HOIST   FLOOR JACK   SUSPENSION CONTACT HOIST

Fig. 7   Cavalier, Sunbird & 1991 Beretta & Corsica

—USING FRAME CONTACT HOIST—
—REARWARD OF FRONT TIRE—

—USING FRAME CONTACT HOIST—
—FORWARD OF REAR TIRE—

—USING SUSPENSION CONTACT HOIST—
—UNDER FRONT LOWER CONTROL ARM—

—USING SUSPENSION CONTACT HOIST—
—LIFTING ON REAR AXLE—

Fig. 8   1991–92 Camaro & Firebird

FRAME CONTACT HOIST
FLOOR JACK
SUSPENSION CONTACT HOIST

FRT

RIGHT SIDE
FRAME CONTACT HOIST
REARWARD OF FRONT WHEEL

LEFT SIDE
FRAME CONTACT HOIST
REARWARD OF FRONT WHEEL

RIGHT SIDE
FRAME CONTACT HOIST
FORWARD OF REAR WHEEL

LEFT SIDE
FRAME CONTACT HOIST
FORWARD OF REAR WHEEL

DRIVETRAIN AND FRONT
SUSPENSION FRAME

FLOOR JACK - FRONT

Fig. 9   Corvette

■ DRIVE ON HOIST   ▩ TWIN POST SUSPENSION HOIST   ▦ FRAME ENGAGING HOIST

SUPPORTS MUST BE POSITIONED SO AS TO DISTRIBUTE LOAD AND SUPPORT CAR IN A STABLE MANNER. CARE MUST BE EXERCISED TO ENSURE THAT PLACEMENT OF SUPPORTS DOES NOT DAMAGE BRAKE LINES, FUEL LINES, PARKING BRAKE CABLE, OR EXHAUST SYSTEM.

Fig. 10   Brougham

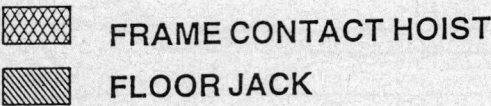

FRAME CONTACT HOIST

FLOOR JACK

Fig. 11   1993 Camaro & Firebird

WHEN USING FRAME CONTACT HOIST:

1. LEFT FRONT TIRE
2. LEFT FRONT FENDER
3. LEFT DOOR

FRONT SUPPORT LOCATION

WHEN USING FLOOR JACK:

FRONT SUPPORT LOCATION

1. TRAILING ARM
2. TRAILING ARM BOLT
3. REAR TIRE

REAR SUPPORT LOCATION

1. REAR AXLE

REAR SUPPORT LOCATION

Fig. 12   Metro

← Front

▨ SUSPENSION CONTACT HOIST

■ FRAME CONTACT HOIST/SAFETY STAND

● FLOOR JACK
FRONT. . .ENGINE LOWER CROSSMEMBER
REAR . . .REAR SUBFRAME

Fig. 13 Prizm

← FRONT

FLOOR JACK
FRONT... ENGINE LOWER CROSSMEMBER
REAR... REAR SUBFRAME

FRAME CONTACT HOIST/SAFETY STAND

SUSPENSION CONTACT HOIST

Fig. 14 Storm

FRT ▶

FRAME CONTACT HOIST

FLOOR JACK

SUSPENSION CONTACT HOIST

Fig. 15 LeMans

Jack Stand Support Points and Floor Jack Lift Points

Floor Jack Lift Points

A. Lower Control Arms
B. Rocker Flange, Front
C. Rocker Flange, Rear
D. Rear Suspension Crossmember

Do not lift the vehicle at the front tension strut.

Fig. 16   Saturn

VEHICLE MAINTENANCE SCHEDULES

INDEX

1991–92 Cadillac Brougham & Fleetwood

SCHEDULE I

Follow Schedule I if your car is MAINLY operated under one or more of the following conditions:
- When most trips are less than 4 miles (6 kilometers).
- When most trips are less than 10 miles (16 kilometers) and outside temperatures remain below freezing.
- Idling and/or low speed operation in stop-and-go traffic.
- Towing a trailer. ***
- Operating in dusty areas.

Schedule I should also be followed if the vehicle is used for livery service or other commercial applications.

ITEM NO.	TO BE SERVICED	When To Perform Miles (Kilometers) Or Months Whichever Occurs First	The Services Shown In This Schedule Up To 48,000 Miles (80,000 Km) Are To Be Performed After 48,000 Miles At The Same Intervals															
		MILES (000)	3	6	9	12	15	18	21	24	27	30	33	36	39	42	45	48
		KILOMETERS (000)	5	10	15	20	25	30	35	40	45	50	55	60	65	70	75	80
1	Engine Oil & Oil Filter Change*	Every 3,000 Mi. (5,000 Km) Or 3 Mos.	●	●	●	●	●	●	●	●	●	●	●	●	●	●	●	●
2	Chassis Lubrication	Every Other Oil Change		●		●		●		●		●		●		●		●
3	Throttle Boot Mounting Bolt Torque *	At 6,000 Mi (10,000 Km) Only		●**														
4	Tire & Wheel Inspection & Rotation	At 6,000 Mi. (10,000 Km) And Then Every 15,000 (25,000 Km)		●					●					●				
5	Engine Accessory Drive Belt Inspection *	Every 30,000 Mi. (50,000 Km) Or 24 Mos.										●**						
6	Cooling System Service *											●						
7	Wheel Bearing Repack (Brougham Only)																	
8	Transmission/Transaxle Service																	
9	Spark Plug Replacement	Every 30,000 Mi. (50,000 Km)										●**						
10	Spark Plug Wire Inspections*											●**						
11	PCV Valve Inspection *											●						
12	EGR System Service *											●						
13	Air Cleaner, PCV Filter & A.I.R. Filter Replacement *											●**						
14	Engine Timing Check *											●						
15	Fuel Tank, Cap & Lines Inspection *											●						
16	Throttle Body Inspection											●						

SCHEDULE II

Follow Schedule II ONLY IF NONE of the driving conditions specified in Schedule 1 apply:

ITEM NO.	TO BE SERVICED	When To Perform Miles (Kilometers) Or Months Whichever Occurs First	The Services Shown In This Schedule Up To 45,000 Miles (75,000 Km) Are To Be Performed After 45,000 Miles At The Same Intervals					
		MILES (000)	7.5	15	22.5	30	37.5	45
		KILOMETERS (000)	12.5	25	37.5	50	62.5	75
1	Engine Oil & Oil Filter Change*	Every 7,500 Mi. (12,500 Km) Or 12 mos.	●	●	●	●	●	●
	Oil Filter Change *	At first and then every other oil change or 12 mos.	●		●		●	
2	Chassis Lubrication	Every 7,500 Mi. (12,500 Km) Or 12 mos.	●	●	●	●	●	●
3	Throttle Body Mounting Bolt Torque *	At 7,500 Mi (12,500 Km) Only	●**					
4	Tire & Wheel Inspection & Rotation	At 7,500 Mi. (12,500 Km) And Then Every 15,000 (25,000 Km)	●		●		●	
5	Engine Accessory Drive Belt Inspection *	Every 30,000 Mi. (50,000 Km) Or 24 mos.				●**		
6	Cooling System Service *					●		
7	Wheel Bearing Repack (Brougham Only)	Every 30,000 Mi. (50,000 Km)				●		
8	Transmission/Transaxle Service							
9	Spark Plug Replacement	Every 30,000 Mi. (50,000 Km) Or 36 Mos.				●**		
10	Spark Plug Wire Inspections*					●**		
11	PCV Valve Inspection *					●		
12	EGR System Service *					●		
13	Air Cleaner, PCV Filter & A.I.R. Filter Replacement *					●**		
14	Engine Timing Check *					●		
15	Fuel Tank, Cap & Lines Inspection *					●		
16	Throttle Body Inspection *					●		

* An Emission Control Service
** The U.S. Environmental Protection Agency has determined that failure to perform this maintenance item will not nullify the emission warranty or limit recall liability prior to the completion of vehicle useful life. General Motors, however, urges that all Emission Control Maintenance Services shown be performed at the indicated intervals and the maintenance be recorded.
†Schedule 1 should also be followed if the car is used for livery service or commercial application
*** Trailer pulling is not recommended for some models. See Owner's Manual for details.
The services shown in these schedules up to 48,000 miles (80,000 km) are to be performed after 48,000 miles at the same intervals.

1991–92 Cadillac Except Brougham & Fleetwood

SCHEDULE I

Follow Schedule I if your car is MAINLY operated under one or more of the following conditions:
- When most trips are less than 4 miles (6 kilometers).
- When most trips are less than 10 miles (16 kilometers) and outside temperatures remain below freezing.
- Idling and/or low speed operation in stop–and–go traffic.
- Towing a trailer. ***
- Operating in dusty areas.

Schedule I should also be followed if the vehicle is used for livery service or other commercial applications.

ITEM NO.	TO BE SERVICED	When To Perform Miles (Kilometers) Or Months Whichever Occurs First	The Services Shown In This Schedule Up To 48,000 Miles (80,000 Km) Are To Be Performed After 48,000 Miles At The Same Intervals															
		MILES (000)	3	6	9	12	15	18	21	24	27	30	33	36	39	42	45	48
		KILOMETERS(000)	5	10	15	20	25	30	35	40	45	50	55	60	65	70	75	80
1	Engine Oil & Oil Filter Change*	Every 3,000 Mi. (5,000 Km) Or 3 Mos.	•	•	•	•	•	•	•	•	•	•	•	•	•	•	•	•
2	Chassis Lubrication	Every Other Oil Change		•		•		•		•		•		•		•		•
3	Throttle Boot Mounting Bolt Torque *	At 6,000 Mi (10,000 Km) Only		•**														
4	Tire & Wheel Inspection & Rotation	At 6,000 Mi. (10,000 Km) And Then Every 15,000 (25,000 Km)		•					•					•				
5	Engine Accessory Drive Belt Inspection *	Every 30,000 Mi. (50,000 Km) Or 24 Mos.										•**						
6	Cooling System Service *											•						
7	Front Wheel Bearing Repack (Brougham Only)																	
8	Transmission/Transaxle Service																	
9	Spark Plug Replacement ****	Every 30,000 Mi. (50,000 Km)										•**						
10	Spark Plug Wire Inspection**											•						
11	EGR System Check *											•						
12	Air Cleaner Filter & A.I.R. Filter (Brougham Only) Replacement *											•**						
13	Engine Timing Check *											•						
14	Fuel Tank, Cap & Lines Inspection *											•						
15	Throttle Body Inspection											•						

SCHEDULE II

Follow Schedule II ONLY IF NONE of the driving conditions specified in Schedule I apply:

ITEM NO.	TO BE SERVICED	When To Perform Miles (Kilometers) Or Months Whichever Occurs First	The Services Shown In This Schedule Up To 45,000 Miles (75,000 Km) Are To Be Performed After 45,000 Miles At The Same Intervals					
		MILES (000)	7.5	15	22.5	30	37.5*	45
		KILOMETERS(000)	12.5	25	37.5	50	62.5	75
1	Engine Oil & Oil Filter Change*	Every 7,500 Mi. (12,500 Km) Or 12 mos.	•	•	•	•	•	•
	Oil Filter Change *	At first and then every other oil change or 12 mos.	•		•		•	
2	Chassis Lubrication	Every 7,500 Mi. (12,500 Km) Or 12 mos.	•	•	•	•	•	•
3	Throttle Body Mounting Bolt Torque *	At 7,500 Mi (12,500 Km) Only	•**					
4	Tire & Wheel Inspection & Rotation	At 7,500 Mi. (12,500 Km) And Then Every 15,000 (25,000 Km)	•		•		•	
5	Engine Accessory Drive Belt Inspection *	Every 30,000 Mi. (50,000 Km) Or 24 mos.				•**		
6	Cooling System Service *					•		
7	Front Wheel Bearing Repack (Brougham Only)	Every 30,000 Mi. (50,000 Km)				•		
8	Transmission/Transaxle Service							
9	Spark Plug Replacement ****	Every 30,000 Mi. (50,000 Km) Or 36 Mos.				•**		
10	Spark Plug Wire Inspection**					•**		
11	EGR System Check *					•		
12	Air Cleaner Filter & A.I.R. Filter (Brougham Only) Replacement *					•**		
13	Engine Timing Check *					•		
14	Fuel Tank, Cap & Lines Inspection *					•		
15	Throttle Body Inspection *					•		

*   An Emission Control Service

**   The U.S. Environmental Protection Agency has determined that failure to perform this maintenance item will not nullify the emission warranty or limit recall liability prior to the completion of vehicle useful life. General Motors, however, urges that all Emission Control Maintenance Services shown be performed at the indicated intervals and the maintenance be recorded.
     1Schedule 1 should also be followed if the car is used for livery service or commercial application

***   Trailer pulling is not recommended for some models. See Owner's Manual for details.

**** .. BROUGHAM ONLY. Replace on all other carlines every 100,000 miles (160,000 km).

The services shown in these schedules up to 48,000 miles (80,000 km) are to be performed after 48,000 miles at the same intervals.

VEHICLE MAINTENANCE SCHEDULES
1993 Cadillac

SCHEDULE I

Follow Schedule I if your car is MAINLY operated under one or more of the following conditions:

- When most trips are less than 4 miles (6 kilometers).
- When most trips are less than 10 miles (16 kilometers) and outside temperatures remain below freezing.
- Idling and/or low speed operation in stop-and-go traffic.
- Towing a trailer. ***
- Operating in dusty areas.

Schedule I should also be followed if the vehicle is used for livery service or other commercial applications.

ITEM NO.	TO BE SERVICED	When To Perform Miles (Kilometers) Or Months Whichever Occurs First	The Services Shown In This Schedule Up To 48,000 Miles (80,000 Km) Are To Be Performed After 48,000 Miles At The Same Intervals														
		MILES (000)	3	6	9	12	15	18	21	24	27	30	33	36	39	42	45	48
		KILOMETERS (000)	5	10	15	20	25	30	35	40	45	50	55	60	65	70	75	80
1	Engine Oil & Oil Filter Change*	Every 3,000 Mi. (5,000 Km) Or 3 Mos.	●	●	●	●	●	●	●	●	●	●	●	●	●	●	●	●
2	Chassis Lubrication	Every Other Oil Change		●		●		●		●		●		●		●		●
3	Throttle Boot Mounting Bolt Torque *	At 6,000 Mi (10,000 Km) Only		●**														
4	Tire & Wheel Inspection & Rotation	At 6,000 Mi. (10,000 Km) And Then Every 15,000 (25,000 Km)		●					●					●				
5	Engine Accessory Drive Belt Inspection *	Every 30,000 Mi. (50,000 Km) Or 24 Mos.										●**						
6	Cooling System Service *											●						
7	Front Wheel Bearing Repack (Brougham Only)																	
8	Transmission/Transaxle Service																	
9	Throttle Body Inspection	Every 30,000 Mi. (50,000 Km)										●**						
10	Spark Plug Wire Inspection *, **											●**						
11	EGR System Check *, **											●						
12	Air Cleaner, Filter Replacement *											●**						
13	Engine Timing Check *											●						
14	Fuel Tank, Cap & Lines Inspection *, **											●						
15	Spark Plug Replacement	Every 100,000 Mi. (160,000 Km)																

SCHEDULE II

Follow Schedule II ONLY IF NONE of the driving conditions specified in Schedule I apply:

ITEM NO.	TO BE SERVICED	When To Perform Miles (Kilometers) Or Months Whichever Occurs First	The Services Shown In This Schedule Up To 45,000 Miles (75,000 Km) Are To Be Performed After 45,000 Miles At The Same Intervals					
		MILES (000)	7.5	15	22.5	30	37.5*	45
		KILOMETERS (000)	12.5	25	37.5	50	62.5	75
1	Engine Oil & Oil Filter Change*	Every 7,500 Mi. (12,500 Km) Or 12 mos.	●	●	●	●	●	●
	Oil Filter Change *	At first and then every other oil change or 12 mos.	●		●		●	
2	Chassis Lubrication	Every 7,500 Mi. (12,500 Km) Or 12 mos.	●	●	●	●	●	●
3	Throttle Body Mounting Bolt Torque *	At 7,500 Mi (12,500 Km) Only	●**					
4	Tire & Wheel Inspection & Rotation	At 7,500 Mi. (12,500 Km) And Then Every 15,000 (25,000 Km)	●		●		●	
5	Engine Accessory Drive Belt Inspection *	Every 30,000 Mi. (50,000 Km) Or 24 mos.				●**		
6	Cooling System Service *					●		
7	Front Wheel Bearing Repack (Brougham Only)	Every 30,000 Mi. (50,000 Km)				●		
8	Transmission/Transaxle Service							
9	Throttle Body Inspection *	Every 30,000 Mi. (50,000 Km) Or 36 Mos.				●**		
10	Spark Plug Wire Inspection *, **					●**		
11	EGR System Check *, **					●		
12	Air Cleaner, PCV Filter & A.I.R. Filter Replacement *					●**		
13	Engine Timing Check *					●		
14	Fuel Tank, Cap & Lines Inspection *, **					●		
15	Spark Plug Replacement	Every 100,000 Mi. (160,000 Km)						

*   An Emission Control Service

**   The U.S. Environmental Protection Agency has determined that failure to perform this maintenance item will not nullify the emission warranty or limit recall liability prior to the completion of vehicle useful life. General Motors, however, urges that all Emission Control Maintenance Services shown be performed at the indicated intervals and the maintenance be recorded.

    ¹Schedule 1 should also be followed if the car is used for livery service or commercial application

***   Trailer pulling is not recommended for some models. See Owner's Manual for details.

The services shown in these schedules up to 48,000 miles (80,000 km) are to be performed after 48,000 miles at the same intervals.

All Except Cadillac, LeMans, Metro, Prizm & Storm

SCHEDULED MAINTENANCE SERVICES

SCHEDULE I

Follow Schedule I if your vehicle is MAINLY driven under one or more of the following conditions:
- When most trips are less than 6 kilometers (4 miles).
- When most trips are less than 16 kilometers (10 miles) and outside temperatures remain below freezing.
- When most trips include extended idling and/or frequent low-speed operation as in stop-and-go traffic.†
- Towing a trailer.**
- Operating in dusty areas.

The services shown in this schedule up to 80 000 km (48,000 miles) are to be performed after 80 000 km (48,000 miles) at the same intervals.

ITEM NO.	TO BE SERVICED	WHEN TO PERFORM — Kilometers (Miles) or Months, Whichever Occurs First	KM 5 / MI 3	10 / 6	15 / 9	20 / 12	25 / 15	30 / 18	35 / 21	40 / 24	45 / 27	50 / 30	55 / 33	60 / 36	65 / 39	70 / 42	75 / 45	80 / 48
1.	Engine Oil & Oil Filter Change*	Every 5 000 km (3,000 mi.) or 3 mos.	•	•	•	•	•	•	•	•	•	•	•	•	•	•	•	•
2.	Chassis Lubrication	Every other oil change		•		•		•		•		•		•		•		•
3.	Throttle Body Mounting Bolt Torque*	At 10 000 km (6,000 mi.) only		•														
4.	Tire & Wheel Inspection & Rotation	At 10 000 km (6,000 mi.) and then every 25 000 km (15,000 mi.)		•					•					•				
5.	Engine Accessory Drive Belt Inspection	Every 50 000 km (30,000 mi.) or 24 mos.										•						
6.	Cooling System Service*											•						
7.	Front Wheel Bearing Repack										•							
8.	Transmission Service										•							
9.	Spark Plug Replacement*										•							
10.	Spark Plug Wire Inspection*‡										•							
11.	PCV Valve Inspection*‡										•							
12.	Thermostatically Controlled Air Cleaner Inspection	Every 50 000 km (30,000 mi.).										•						
13.	EGR System Inspection*‡										•							
14.	Air Cleaner Filter Replacement*										•							
15.	Engine Timing Check*										•							
16.	Fuel Tank, Cap & Lines Inspection*‡										•							

† Note: Schedule I should also be followed if the vehicle is used for delivery service, police, taxi or other commercial applications.

‡ The U.S. Environmental Protection Agency has determined that the failure to perform this maintenance item will not nullify the emission warranty or limit recall liability prior to the completion of vehicle useful life. General Motors, however, urges that all recommended maintenance services be performed at the indicated intervals and the maintenance be recorded in section C of the owner's maintenance schedule.

* An Emission Control Service

** Trailering is not recommended for some models. See your Owner's Manual for details.

All Except Cadillac, LeMans, Metro, Prizm & Storm

SCHEDULED MAINTENANCE SERVICES

SCHEDULE II

Follow Schedule II ONLY if none of the driving conditions specified in Schedule I apply.

The services shown in this schedule up to 75 000 km (45,000 miles) are to be performed after 75 000 km (45,000 miles) at the same intervals.

ITEM NO.	TO BE SERVICED	WHEN TO PERFORM Kilometers (Miles) or Months, Whichever Occurs First	KILOMETERS (000) 12.5 / MILES 7.5	25 / 15	37.5 / 22.5	50 / 30	62.5 / 37.5	75 / 45
1.	Engine Oil Change*	Every 12 500 km (7,500 mi.) or 12 mos.	•	•	•	•	•	•
	Oil Filter Change†	At first and then every other oil change or 12 mos.	•		•		•	
2.	Chassis Lubrication	Every 12 500 km (7,500 mi.) or 12 mos.	•	•	•	•	•	•
3.	Throttle Body Mounting Bolt Torque	At 12 500 km (7,500 mi.) only	•					
4.	Tire & Wheel Inspection & Rotation	At 12 500 km (7,500 mi.) and then every 25 000 km (15,000 mi.)	•		•		•	
5.	Engine Accessory Drive Belt Inspection	Every 50 000 km (30,000 mi.) or 24 mos.				•		
6.	Cooling System Service*	Every 50 000 km (30,000 mi.)				•		
7.	Front Wheel Bearing Repack	Every 50 000 km (30,000 mi.)				•		
8.	Transmission Service					•		
9.	Spark Plug Replacement*					•		
10.	Spark Plug Wire Inspection*‡					•		
11.	PCV Valve Inspection*‡					•		
12.	Thermostatically Controlled Air Cleaner Inspection					•		
13.	EGR System Inspection*‡	Every 50 000 km (30,000 mi.).				•		
14.	Air Cleaner Filter Replacement*					•		
15.	Engine Timing Check*					•		
16.	Fuel Tank, Cap & Lines Inspection*‡					•		

‡ The U.S. Environmental Protection Agency has determined that the failure to perform this maintenance item will not nullify the emission warranty or limit recall liability prior to the completion of vehicle useful life. General Motors, however, urges that all recommended maintenance services be performed at the indicated intervals and the maintenance be recorded in section C of the owner's maintenance schedule.

* An Emission Control Service

LeMans

Select and follow Schedule I or Schedule II based on how you use your car:

SCHEDULE I

Follow Schedule I if your car is mainly operated under one or more of the following conditions:

- When most trips are less than 4 miles (6 kilometers).
- When most trips are less than 10 miles (16 kilometers) and outside temperatures remain below freezing.
- Idling and/or low speed operation in stop-and-go traffic.
- Operating in dusty areas.

Schedule I should also be followed if the car is used for delivery service, police, taxi or other commercial applications.

ITEM NO.	TO BE SERVICED	WHEN TO PERFORM Miles (kilometers) or Months, Whichever Occurs First	The services shown in this schedule up to 48,000 miles (80 000 km) are to be performed after 48,000 miles at the same intervals.															
		MILES (000)	3	6	9	12	15	18	21	24	27	30	33	36	39	42	45	48
		KILOMETERS (000)	5	10	15	20	25	30	35	40	45	50	55	60	65	70	75	80
1	Engine Oil & Oil Filter Change*	Every 3,000 miles (5 000 km) or 3 months	•	•	•	•	•	•	•	•	•	•	•	•	•	•	•	•
2	Throttle Body Mounting Bolt Torque*	At 6,000 miles (10 000 km) only		•														
3	Tire & Wheel Rotation	At 6,000 miles (10 000 km), and then every 15,000 miles (25 000 km)		•						•				•				
4	Drive Belt Inspection*	Every 30,000 miles (50 000 km) or 24 months										•						
5	Cooling System Service*											•						
6	Brake System Service	See Explanation on Page 1																
7	Transaxle Service																	
8	Spark Plug Service*	Every 30,000 miles (50 000 km)										•						
9	Spark Plug Wire Inspection*											•						
10	Fuel Micro-Filter Replacement*	Every 30,000 miles (50 000 km) or 36 months										•						
11	Air Cleaner Element Replacement*											•						
12	Engine Timing Check*											•						
13	Fuel Tank, Cap & Lines Inspection*	Every 30,000 miles (50 000 km)										•						
14	Thermostatically Controlled Air Cleaner Inspection*											•						

SCHEDULE II

Follow Schedule II **only** if none of the driving conditions specified in Schedule I apply.

ITEM NO.	TO BE SERVICED	WHEN TO PERFORM Miles (kilometers) or Months, Whichever Occurs First	The services shown in this schedule up to 45,000 miles (75 000 km) are to be performed after 45,000 miles at the same intervals					
		MILES (000)	7.5	15	22.5	30	37.5	45
		KILOMETERS (000)	12.5	25	37.5	50	62.5	75
1	Engine Oil & Oil Filter Change*	Every 7,500 miles (12 500 km) or 12 months	•	•	•	•	•	•
2	Throttle Body Mounting Bolt Torque*	At 7,500 miles (12 500 km) only	•					
3	Tire & Wheel Rotation	At 7,500 miles (12 500 km) and then every 15,000 miles (25 000 km)	•		•		•	
4	Drive Belt Inspection*	Every 30,000 miles (50 000 km) or 24 months				•		
5	Cooling System Service*					•		
6	Brake System Service	See Explanation on Page 1						
7	Transaxle Service							
8	Spark Plug Service*	Every 30,000 miles (50 000 km)				•		
9	Spark Plug Wire Inspection*					•		
10	Fuel Micro-Filter Replacement*	Every 30,000 miles (50 000 km) or 36 months				•		
11	Air Cleaner Element Replacement*					•		
12	Engine Timing Check*					•		
13	Fuel Tank, Cap & Lines Inspection*	Every 30,000 miles (50 000 km)				•		
14	Thermostatically Controlled Air Cleaner Inspection*					•		

FOOTNOTES:

* An Emission Control Service.

Metro

SCHEDULED MAINTENANCE SERVICES
SCHEDULE I

Follow Schedule I if your vehicle is MAINLY operated under one or more of the following conditions:
- When most trips are less than 4 miles (6 kilometers).
- When most trips are less than 10 miles (16 kilometers) and outside temperatures remain below freezing.
- When most trips include extended idling and/or frequent low-speed operation as in stop-and-go traffic.
- Operating in dusty areas.

Schedule I should also be followed if the vehicle is used for delivery service, police, taxi or other commercial applications.

The services shown in this schedule up to 60 000 miles (100 000 km) are to be performed after 60 000 miles at the same intervals.

WHEN TO PERFORM — Miles (kilometers) or Months, Whichever Occurs First (Also, See Explanation of Services Pages 6-7)

Column headers: MILES (000) / KILOMETERS (000)

#	TO BE SERVICED	WHEN TO PERFORM	3/5	6/10	9/15	12/20	15/25	18/30	21/35	24/40	27/45	30/50	33/55	36/60	39/65	42/70	45/75	48/80	51/85	54/90	57/95	60/100
1	Engine Oil and Oil Filter Change*	Every 3 000 Miles (5 000 km) or 3 Months	•	•	•	•	•	•	•	•	•	•	•	•	•	•	•	•	•	•	•	•
2	Chassis Lubrication	Every Other Oil Change		•		•		•		•		•		•		•		•		•		•
3	Tire and Wheel Inspection and Rotation	Every 6 000 Miles (10 000 km)		•		•		•		•		•		•		•		•		•		•
4	Water Pump Belt Inspection*	Every 30 000 Miles (50 000 km) or 30 Months										•										•
5	Cooling System Service*	See Explanation of Scheduled Maintenance Services										•										•
6	Brake Fluid Inspection	Every 15 000 Miles (25 000 km) or 15 Months					•					•					•					•
7	Transaxle Service	See Explanation of Scheduled Maintenance Services										•										•
8	Spark Plug Replacement*	Every 30 000 Miles (50 000 km)										•										•
9	Spark Plug Wires, Replacement*	Every 60 000 Miles (100 000 km) or 60 Months																				•
10	Air Cleaner Element Replacement*	Every 30 000 Miles (50 000 km) or 30 Months										•										•
11	Fuel Tank, Cap and Lines—Inspection*‡	Every 15 000 Miles (25 000 km) or 15 Months					•					•					•					•

* An Emission Control Service.

‡ The U.S. Environmental Protection Agency has determined that the failure to perform this maintenance item will not nullify the emission warranty or limit recall liability prior to the completion of vehicle useful life. General Motors, however, urges that all recommended maintenance services be performed at the indicated intervals and the maintenance be recorded in the Maintenance Schedule Booklet.

Metro

SCHEDULED MAINTENANCE SERVICES
SCHEDULE II

Follow Schedule II only if none of the driving conditions specified in Schedule I apply.

The services shown in this schedule up to 60 000 miles (100 000 km) are to be performed after 60 000 miles at the same intervals.

TO BE SERVICED	WHEN TO PERFORM Miles (kilometers) or Months, Whichever Occurs First (Also, See Explanation of Services Pages 6–7)	MILES (000) 7.5 / KILOMETERS (000) 12.5	15 / 25	22.5 / 37.5	30 / 50	37.5 / 62.5	45 / 75	52.5 / 87.5	60 / 100
1 Engine Oil and Oil Filter Change*	Every 7 500 Miles (12 500 km) or 7.5 Months	•	•	•	•	•	•	•	•
2 Chassis Lubrication	Every 7 500 Miles (12 500 km) or 7.5 Months	•	•	•	•	•	•	•	•
3 Tire and Wheel Inspection and Rotation	At 7 500 Miles (12 500 km) and Then Every 15 000 Miles (25 000 km)	•		•		•		•	
4 Water Pump Belt Inspection*	Every 30 000 Miles (50 000 km) or 30 Months				•				•
5 Cooling System Service*	See Explanation of Scheduled Maintenance Services								
6 Brake Fluid Inspection	Every 15 000 Miles (25 000 km) or 15 Months		•		•		•		•
7 Transaxle Service	See Explanation of Scheduled Maintenance Services								
8 Spark Plug Replacement*	Every 30 000 Miles (50 000 km)				•				•
9 Spark Plug Wires, Replacement*	Every 60 000 Miles (100 000 km) or 60 Months								•
10 Air Cleaner Element Replacement*	Every 30 000 Miles (50 000 km) or 30 Months				•				•
11 Fuel Tank, Cap and Lines—Inspection ‡	Every 15 000 Miles (25 000 km) or 15 Months		•		•		•		•

* An Emission Control Service

‡ The U S Environmental Protection Agency has determined that the failure to perform this maintenance item will not nullify the emission warranty or limit recall liability prior to the completion of vehicle useful life General Motors however urges that all recommended maintenance services be performed at the indicated intervals and the maintenance be recorded in the Maintenance Schedule Booklet.

Prizm

THE SERVICES SHOWN IN THIS SCHEDULE UP TO 60,000 MILES (100 000 km) ARE TO BE PERFORMED AFTER 60,000 MILES (100 000 km) AT THE SAME INTERVALS

TO BE SERVICED	WHEN TO PERFORM MILES (KILOMETERS) OR MONTHS WHICHEVER OCCURS FIRST	3.75 / 6 200	7.5 / 12 500	11.25 / 18 700	15 / 25 000	18.75 / 31 250	22.5 / 37 500	26.25 / 43 750	30 / 50 000	33.75 / 56 250	37.5 / 62 500
ENGINE OIL & FILTER CHANGE*	EVERY 3,750 mi. (6 200 km) OR 6 mos. FIRST AND EVERY OTHER OIL CHANGE.	•	•	•	•	•	•	•	•	•	•
CHASSIS LUBRICATION	EVERY OTHER OIL CHANGE.		•		•		•		•		•
VALVE CLEARANCE ADJUSTMENT	EVERY 60,000 mi. (100 000 km) OR 72 mos.										
ENGINE TIMING BELT REPLACEMENT											
ENGINE IDLE SPEED ADJUSTMENT	AT 7,500 mi. (12 500 km) OR 12 mos. AND THEN EVERY 15,000 mi. (25 000 km) OR 24 mos.		•				•				•
TIRE & WHEEL INSPECTION AND ROTATION	AT 6,000 mi. (10 000 km) AND THEN EVERY 15,000 mi. (25 000 km).										
ENGINE ACCESSORY DRIVE BELT(S) INSPECTION*											
COOLING SYSTEM SERVICE*											
TRANSAXLE SERVICE											
SPARK PLUG REPLACEMENT (VIN 5)*	EVERY 60,000 mi. (100 000 km) OR 72 mos.										
SPARK PLUG REPLACEMENT (VIN 6)*	EVERY 30,000 mi. (50 000 km) OR 36 mos.								•		
CHARCOAL CANISTER INSPECTION*	SEE EXPLANATION FOR SERVICE INTERVAL.										
AIR CLEANER FILTER SERVICE*	SEE EXPLANATION FOR SERVICE INTERVAL.										
FUEL TANK, CAP & LINES INSPECTION*††	EVERY 30,000 mi. (50 000 km) OR 36 mos.								•		
FUEL TANK, CAP GASKET REPLACEMENT											

FOOTNOTES: * AN EMISSION CONTROL SERVICE

†† THE U.S. ENVIRONMENTAL AGENCY HAS DETERMINED THAT THE FAILURE TO PERFORM THIS MAINTENANCE ITEM WILL NOT NULLIFY THE EMISSION WARRANTY OR LIMIT RECALL LIABILITY PRIOR TO THE COMPLETION OF VEHICLE'S USEFUL LIFE. GENERAL MOTORS, HOWEVER, URGES THAT ALL RECOMMENDED MAINTENANCE SERVICES BE PERFORMED AT THE INDICATED INTERVALS AND THE MAINTENANCE BE RECORDED IN SECTION E OF THE OWNER'S MAINTENANCE SCHEDULE.

** TRAILERING IS NOT RECOMMENDED FOR SOME MODELS, SEE THE OWNER'S MANUAL FOR DETAILS.

Prizm

THE SERVICES SHOWN IN THIS SCHEDULE UP TO 60,000 MILES (100 000 km) ARE TO BE PERFORMED AFTER 60,000 MILES (100 000 km) AT THE SAME INTERVALS.

TO BE SERVICED	WHEN TO PERFORM MILES (KILOMETERS) OR MONTHS WHICHEVER OCCURS FIRST	MILES (000) 7.5 / KM 12.54	15 / 25	22.5 / 37.5	30 / 50	37.5 / 62.5	45 / 75	52.5 / 87.5	60 / 100
ENGINE OIL & OIL FILTER CHANGE*	EVERY 7,500 mi. (12 500 km) OR 12 mos.	•	•	•	•	•	•	•	•
CHASSIS LUBRICATION	EVERY OTHER OIL CHANGE.		•		•		•		•
VALVE CLEARANCE ADJUSTMENT	EVERY 60,000 mi. (100 000 km) OR 72 mos.								•
ENGINE IDLE SPEED ADJUSTMENT	AT 7,500 mi. (12 500 km) OR 12 mos. AND THEN EVERY 15,000 mi. (25 000 km) OR 24 mos.	•		•		•		•	
COOLING SYSTEM SERVICE	AT 45,000 mi. (75 000 km) OR 36 mos. AND THEN EVERY 30,000 mi. (50 000 km) OR 24 mos.						•		
CHARCOAL CANISTER INSPECTION									
TIRE & WHEEL INSPECTION AND ROTATION	AT 7,500 mi. (12 500 km) AND THEN EVERY 15,000 mi. (25 000 km).	•		•		•		•	
ENGINE ACCESSORY DRIVE BELT(S) INSPECTION*									
FUEL TANK CAP GASKET REPLACEMENT									
TRANSAXLE SERVICE									
SPARK PLUG REPLACEMENT (VIN 5)*	EVERY 60,000 mi. (100 000 km) OR 72 mos.								•
SPARK PLUG REPLACEMENT (VIN 6)*	EVERY 30,000 mi. (50 000 km) OR 36 mos.				•				•
EGR SYSTEM INSPECTION*††	EVERY 30,000 mi. (50 000 km) OR 36 mos.				•				•
AIR CLEANER FILTER REPLACEMENT*	EVERY 30,000 mi. (50 000 km) OR 36 mos.				•				•
FUEL TANK, CAP & LINES INSPECTION*††	EVERY 30,000 mi. (50 000 km) OR 36 mos.				•				•
PCV SYSTEM INSPECTION*									

FOOTNOTES: * AN EMISSION CONTROL SERVICE

†† THE U.S. ENVIRONMENTAL AGENCY HAS DETERMINED THAT THE FAILURE TO PERFORM THIS MAINTENANCE ITEM WILL NOT NULLIFY THE EMISSION WARRANTY OR LIMIT RECALL LIABILITY PRIOR TO THE COMPLETION OF VEHICLE'S USEFUL LIFE. GENERAL MOTORS, HOWEVER, URGES THAT ALL RECOMMENDED MAINTENANCE SERVICES BE PERFORMED AT THE INDICATED INTERVALS AND THE MAINTENANCE BE RECORDED IN SECTION E OF THE OWNER'S MAINTENANCE SCHEDULE.

Storm

SCHEDULED MAINTENANCE SERVICES
SCHEDULE I

Follow Schedule I if your car is MAINLY operated under one or more of the following conditions:
- When most trips are less than 4 miles (6 kilometers).
- When most trips are less than 10 miles (16 kilometers) and outside temperatures remain below freezing.
- When most trips include extended idling and/or frequent low-speed operation as in stop-and-go traffic.
- Towing a trailer.#
- Operating in dusty areas.

Schedule I should also be followed if the car is used for delivery service, police, taxi or other commercial applications.

The services shown in this schedule up to 60 000 miles (100 000 km) are to be performed after 60 000 miles at the same intervals.

	TO BE SERVICED	WHEN TO PERFORM — Miles (kilometers) or Months, Whichever Occurs First	3/5	6/10	9/15	12/20	15/25	18/30	21/35	24/40	27/45	30/50	33/55	36/60	39/65	42/70	45/75	48/80	51/85	54/90	57/95	60/100	100
1	Engine Oil Replacement*	Every 3 000 Miles (5 000 km) or 3 Months	•	•	•	•	•	•	•	•	•	•	•	•	•	•	•	•	•	•	•	•	•
	Oil Filter Replacement*	At First and Then Every Other Oil Change	•		•		•		•		•		•		•		•		•		•		•
2	Chassis and Body Lubrication	Every Other Oil Change		•		•		•		•		•		•		•		•		•		•	
3	Valve Clearance Adjustment* VIN 6	Every 15 000 Miles (25 000 km)					•					•					•					•	
	VIN 5	Every 60 000 Miles (100 000 km)																				•	
4	Timing Belt Replacement	Every 60 000 Miles (100 000 km)																				•	
5	Tire and Wheel Inspection and Rotation	At 6 000 Miles (10 000 km) and Then Every 15 000 Miles (25 000 km)		•					•					•					•				
6	Drive Belt Inspection*	Every 30 000 Miles (50 000 km)										•										•	
7	Cooling System Inspection*	Every 15 000 Miles (25 000 km)					•					•					•					•	
	Cooling System Refill*	Every 30 000 Miles (50 000 km)										•										•	
8	Manual Transaxle Fluid Replacement	Every 15 000 Miles (25 000 km)					•					•					•					•	
	Automatic Transaxle Fluid Replacement	Every 15 000 Miles (25 000 km)					•					•					•					•	
9	Spark Plug Replacement*	Every 30 000 Miles (50 000 km)										•										•	
10	Power Steering Fluid Replacement	Every 21 000 Miles (35 000 km) or 24 Months							•							•							
11	Power Steering Hose Inspection	Every 42 000 Miles (70 000 km)														•							
12	Air Cleaner Element Replacement*	See Explanation of Scheduled Maintenance Services																					
13	Fuel Cap, Lines and Tank Inspection*‡	Every 15 000 Miles (25 000 km)					•					•					•					•	
14	PCV Valve Inspection*‡	Every 30 000 Miles (50 000 km)										•										•	

MILES (000) / KILOMETERS (000)

* An Emission Control Service.

‡ The U.S. Environmental Protection Agency has determined that the failure to perform this maintenance item will not nullify the emission warranty or limit recall liability prior to the completion of vehicle useful life. General Motors, however, urges that all recommended maintenance services be performed at the indicated intervals and the maintenance be recorded in Section C of the Owner's Maintenance Schedule.

Trailering is not recommended for some models. See your Owner's Manual for details.

Storm

SCHEDULED MAINTENANCE SERVICES
SCHEDULE II

Follow Schedule II only if none of the driving conditions specified in Schedule I apply.

The services shown in this schedule up to 60 000 miles (96 000 km) are to be performed after 60 000 miles at the same intervals.

#	TO BE SERVICED	WHEN TO PERFORM (Miles (kilometers) or Months, Whichever Occurs First)	3/5	6/10	7.5/12.5	9/15	12/20	15/25	18/30	21/35	22.5/37.5	24/40	27/45	30/50	33/55	36/60	37.5/62.5	39/65	42/70	45/75	48/80	51/85	52.5/87.5	54/90	57/95	60/100
1	Engine Oil Replacement*	Every 7 500 Miles (12 500 km) or 12 Months			•			•			•			•			•			•			•			•
	Oil Filter Replacement*	At First and Then Every Other Oil Change			•						•						•						•			
2	Chassis and Body Lubrication	Every 7 500 Miles (12 500 km) or 12 Months			•			•			•			•			•			•			•			•
3	Valve Clearance Adjustment* VIN 6	Every 15 000 Miles (25 000 km)						•						•						•						•
	VIN 5	Every 60 000 Miles (100 000 km)																								•
4	Timing Belt Replacement	Every 60 000 Miles (100 000 km)																								•
5	Tire and Wheel Inspection and Rotation	At 7 500 Miles (12 500 km) and Then Every 15 000 Miles (25 000 km)			•						•						•						•			
6	Drive Belt Inspection*	Every 30 000 Miles (50 000 km)												•												•
7	Cooling System Inspection*	Every 15 000 Miles (25 000 km)						•						•						•						•
	Cooling System Refill*	Every 30 000 Miles (50 000 km)												•												•
8	Manual Transaxle Fluid Replacement	Every 30 000 Miles (50 000 km)												•												•
	Automatic Transaxle Fluid Replacement	Every 30 000 Miles (50 000 km)												•												•
9	Spark Plug Replacement*	Every 30 000 Miles (50 000 km)												•												•
10	Power Steering Fluid Replacement	Every 22 500 Miles (37 500 km) or 24 Months									•									•						
11	Power Steering Hose Inspection	Every 45 000 Miles (75 000 km)																		•						
12	Air Cleaner Element Replacement*	Every 30 000 Miles (50 000 km)												•												•
13	Fuel Cap, Lines and Tank Inspection* ‡	Every 15 000 Miles (25 000 km)						•						•						•						•
14	PCV Valve Inspection* ‡	Every 30 000 Miles (50 000 km)												•												•

* An Emission Control Service.

‡ The U.S. Environmental Protection Agency has determined that the failure to perform this maintenance item will not nullify the emission warranty or limit recall liability prior to the completion of vehicle useful life. General Motors, however, urges that all recommended maintenance services be performed at the indicated intervals and the maintenance be recorded in Section C of the Owner's Maintenance Schedule.

Saturn

Follow Schedule I if the car is usually operated under one or more of the following conditions:
- Most trips are less than 8 Km (5 miles).
- It's below freezing outside, day and night.
- It's very humid outside.
- Your engine is often idling or running at low speed, as in heavy traffic.
- You're towing a trailer.
- You drive in dusty places.
- Your Saturn is used for delivery service, police, taxi or other commercial purposes.

Service	Kilometers x 1000 (Miles x 1000)	5 (3)	10 (6)	15 (9)	20 (12)	25 (15)	30 (18)	35 (21)	40 (24)	45 (27)	50 (30)	55 (33)	60 (36)	65 (39)	70 (42)	75 (45)	80 (48)	85 (51)	90 (54)	95 (57)	100 (60)
1. Change engine oil and filter. * Every 3 mos. or 5,000 km (3,000 mi).		●	●	●	●	●	●	●	●	●	●	●	●	●	●	●	●	●	●	●	●
2. Inspect axle boots, suspension bushings and ball joint seals. Every 6 mos. or 10,000 km (6,000 mi).			●		●		●		●		●		●		●		●		●		●
3. Inspect exhaust system and shields. Every 6 mos. or 10,000 km (6,000 mi).			●		●		●		●		●		●		●		●		●		●
4. Inspect and rotate tires and wheels. At 10,000 km (6,000 mi) and then every 25,000 km (15,000 mi).			●					●					●					●			
5. Service manual transaxle, change fluid. At 10,000 km (6,000 mi) only.			●																		
6. Service automatic transaxle, change fluid. Every 50,000 km (30,000 mi).											●										●
7. Change automatic transaxle pressure filter. At 50,000 km (30,000 mi) and then every 100,000 km (60,000 mi).											●										
8. Replace spark plugs. * Every 50,000 km (30,000 mi).											●										●
9. Inspect vacuum line/hose. * # Every 24 mos. or 50,000 km (30,000 mi).											●										●
10. Inspect EGR system. * # Every 24 mos. or 50,000 km (30,000 mi).											●										●
11. Inspect fuel tank, cap, and pipe/hoses. * # Every 24 mos. or 50,000 km (30,000 mi).											●										●
12. Inspect engine accessory drive belt and coolant hoses. Every 24 mos. or 50,000 km (30,000 mi).											●										●
13. Replace engine air filter. * Every 36 mos. or 50,000 km (30,000 mi).											●										●
14. Flush cooling system, change coolant and check pressure cap. * Every 36 mos. or 60,000 km (36,000 mi).													●								
15. Replace fuel filter. Every 48 mos. or 100,000 km (60,000 mi).																					●

Saturn

Schedule II should only be followed if none of the conditions for Schedule I apply.

- If trips are more than 8 km (5 miles), more than half or these miles should include non-stop highway driving.

Kilometers x 1000 (Miles x 1000)	5 (3)	10 (6)	15 (9)	20 (12)	25 (15)	30 (18)	35 (21)	40 (24)	45 (27)	50 (30)	55 (33)	60 (36)	65 (39)	70 (42)	75 (45)	80 (48)	85 (51)	90 (54)	95 (57)	100 (60)
1. Change engine oil and filter. * Every 6 mos. or 10,000 km (6,000 mi).	■	■	■	■	■	■	■	■	■	■	■	■	■	■	■	■	■	■	■	■
2. Inspect axle boots, suspension bushings and ball joint seals. Every 6 mos. or 10,000 km (6,000 mi).	■	■	■	■	■	■	■	■	■	■	■	■	■	■	■	■	■	■	■	■
3. Inspect exhaust system and shields. Every 6 mos. or 10,000 km (6,000 mi).	■	■	■	■	■	■	■	■	■	■	■	■	■	■	■	■	■	■	■	■
4. Inspect and rotate tires and wheels. At 10,000 km (6,000 mi) and then every 30,000 km (18,000 mi).		■						■						■						■
5. Service manual transaxle, change fluid. At 10,000 km (6,000 mi).		■																		
6. Service automatic transaxle, change fluid. Every 50,000 km (30,000 mi).										■										■
7. Change automatic transaxle pressure filter. At 50,000 km (30,000 mi) and then every 100,000 km (60,000 mi).										■										
8. Replace spark plugs. * Every 50,000 km (30,000 mi).										■										■
9. Inspect vacuum line/hose. * # Every 24 mos. or 50,000 km (30,000 mi).										■										■
10. Inspect EGR system. * # Every 24 mos. or 50,000 km (30,000 mi).										■										■
11. Inspect fuel tank, cap, and pipe/hoses. * # Every 24 mos. or 50,000 km (30,000 mi).										■										■
12. Inspect engine accessory drive belt and coolant hoses. Every 24 mos. or 50,000 km (30,000 mi).										■										■
13. Replace engine air filter. * Every 36 mos. or 50,000 km (30,000 mi).										■										■
14. Flush cooling system, change coolant and check pressure cap. * Every 36 mos. or 60,000 km (36,000 mi).												■								
15. Replace fuel filter. Every 48 mos. or 100,000 km (60,000 mi).																				■

* An emission control service.

The U.S. Environmental Protection Agency has determined that the failure to perform the maintenance item will not nullify the emission warranty or limit recall liability prior to the completion of vehicle useful life. Saturn, however, urges that all recommended maintenance services be performed at the indicated intervals and the maintenance be recorded in Section C of the owner's maintenance booklet.

ELECTRICAL SYMBOL IDENTIFICATION

Fig. 1   Symbol Identification (Part 1 of 4). All Except Geo, LeMans, Electra, LeSabre, Park Avenue & Saturn

CONNECTOR REFERENCE NUMBER FOR COMPONENT LOCATION TABLE

INSULATION COLOR IS BOTH SHOWN AND LABELED

TABLE ALSO SHOWS TOTAL NUMBER OF TERMINALS POSSIBLE: C103 (6 CAVITIES)

SPLICES ARE SHOWN AND NUMBERED

CIRCUIT NUMBER IS SHOWN TO HELP IN TRACING CIRCUITS

.5 RED 2

S200

.5 RED 2

5 CAVITY CONNECTOR (5 OUT OF 5 CAVITIES ARE USED)

GROMMETS ARE SHOWN AND NUMBERED

.8 PNK/BLK 239

P404

.8 PNK/BLK 239

5 CAVITY CONNECTOR (4 OUT OF 5 CAVITIES ARE USED)

A WAVY LINE MEANS A WIRE IS TO BE CONTINUED

.5 RED 2

CONNECTOR ATTACHED TO COMPONENT

WIRE INSULATION IS ONE COLOR WITH ANOTHER COLOR STRIPE (RED WITH YELLOW)

2 RED/YEL

19

FUSIBLE LINK

WIRE SIZE AND INSULATION COLOR ARE LABELED

1 RED 2

CONNECTOR ON COMPONENT LEAD (PIGTAIL)

Fig. 1   Symbol Identification (Part 2 of 4). All Except Geo, LeMans, Electra, LeSabre, Park Avenue & Saturn

RESISTOR

VARIABLE RESISTOR

POTENTIOMETER

CAPACITOR

BRUSH

MOTOR

CRYSTAL

MULTI-POSITION SWITCH

SWITCH CONTACTS THAT MOVE TOGETHER

DASHED LINE SHOWS A MECHANICAL CONNECTION BETWEEN SWITCH CONTACTS

RELAY COIL

RELAY SHOWN WITH NO CURRENT FLOWING THROUGH COIL

WHEN CURRENT FLOWS THROUGH COIL, CONTACT MOVES TO NORMALLY OPEN POSITION

NORMALLY OPEN CONTACT

NORMALLY CLOSED CONTACT

HEAT ACTUATED CONTACT

HEATING ELEMENT

HORN OR SPEAKER

SOLENOID OR COIL

A WAVY LINE MEANS A WIRE IS TO BE CONTINUED

A CURRENT PATH IS CONTINUED AS LABELED. ARROW SHOWS THE DIRECTION OF CURRENT FLOW AND IS REPEATED WHERE CURRENT PATH CONTINUES

A WIRE WHICH CONNECTS TO ANOTHER CIRCUIT. THE WIRE IS SHOWN AGAIN IN THAT CIRCUIT. ARROW SHOWS DIRECTION OF CURRENT FLOW

COMPONENT CASE IS DIRECTLY ATTACHED TO METAL PART OF CAR (GROUNDED)

WIRE IS ATTACHED TO METAL PART OF CAR (GROUNDED)

GROUND IS NUMBERED

WIRE IS INDIRECTLY CONNECTED TO GROUND

BROKEN WIRE INDICATES THAT CIRCUITRY IS NOT SHOWN IN COMPLETE DETAIL BUT IS COMPLETE IN THE INDICATED CELL. ARROW SHOWS DIRECTION OF CURRENT FLOW

SEE GROUND DISTRIBUTION 14

.5 RED 2

1 YEL 5

A

TO GENERATOR 30

1 DK GRN 19

EXTERIOR LIGHTS 110

G103

GROUND DISTRIBUTION 14

G101

150

3 BLK

G200

Fig. 1 Symbol Identification (Part 3 of 4). All Except Geo, LeMans, Electra, LeSabre, Park Avenue & Saturn

Fig. 1 Symbol Identification (Part 4 of 4). All Except Geo, LeMans, Electra, LeSabre, Park Avenue & Saturn

VACUUM CHECK VALVE

VACUUM SOURCE (SHOWN WITH NO VACUUM)

EASY FLOW DIRECTION

NO FLOW DIRECTION

VACUUM ACTUATOR (SINGLE DIAPHRAGM, TWO POSITION)

VACUUM

NO VACUUM

PARTIAL VACUUM

VACUUM ACTUATOR (SERVO, MULTIPLE POSITION)

VACUUM ACTUATOR (DOUBLE DIAPHRAGM, THREE POSITIONS)

NO VACUUM

NO VACUUM

ENGINE CONTROL MODULE (ECM) SOLID STATE

BAT

5 VOLTS

5 VOLTS

5 VOLTS

REGULATOR

A

B

"SOLID STATE" IDENTIFIES MODULE AS ELECTRONIC. SIMPLIFIED COMPONENTS WITHIN THE MODULE SHOW HOW EACH CIRCUIT IS COMPLETED

TRANSISTOR SHOWN AS SWITCH

INDICATES PULSING OUTPUT

WITH NO LOAD ON THIS CIRCUIT, 5 VOLTS WILL BE MEASURED USING A HIGH IMPEDANCE DIGITAL VOLTMETER

5 VOLTS WILL BE PRESENT WHEN BATTERY VOLTAGE IS APPLIED BETWEEN TERMINALS "A" AND "B"

VACUUM TANK

VACUUM JUNCTION

HOSE COLOR

BROWN

BLUE

RED

"BRAKE" INDICATOR (RED)

INDICATOR WHICH DISPLAYS THE LIGHTED WORD "BRAKE"

LIGHT EMITTING DIODE

PHOTO SENSITIVE TRANSISTOR

DIODE CURRENT FLOWS ONLY IN DIRECTION OF ARROW

COMPONENT "A"

COMPONENT "B"

SLIP RING ASSEMBLY

SPRING LOADED BRUSH

SLIP RING

WIRE SIZE AND INSULATION COLOR ARE BOTH SHOWN AND LABELED

SPLICES ARE SHOWN AND NUMBERED

A WAVY LINE MEANS A WIRE IS TO BE CONTINUED ON ADJACENT PAGE

WIRE INSULATION IS ONE COLOR WITH ANOTHER COLOR STRIPE (RED WITH YELLOW)

WIRE SIZE AND INSULATION COLOR ARE LABELED

CURRENT PATH IS CONTINUED AS LABELED. THE ARROW SHOWS THE DIRECTION OF CURRENT FLOW AND IS REPEATED WHERE CURRENT PATH CONTINUES

A WIRE WHICH CONNECTS TO ANOTHER CIRCUIT. THE WIRE IS SHOWN AGAIN ON THAT CIRCUIT

5.0 RED

S200

5.0 RED

5.0 RED

2.0 RED/YEL

FUSIBLE LINK

1.0 RED

1.0 YEL

A

1.0 DK GRN

SEE EXTERIOR LIGHTS

CONNECTOR REFERENCE NUMBER FOR COMPONENT LOCATION LIST

TABLE ALSO SHOWS TOTAL NUMBER OF TERMINALS POSSIBLE: C103 (6 CAVITIES)

5 CAVITY CONNECTOR (5 OUT OF 5 CAVITIES ARE USED)

5 CAVITY CONNECTOR (4 OUT OF 5 CAVITIES ARE USED)

CONNECTOR ATTACHED TO COMPONENT

CONNECTOR ON COMPONENT LEAD (PIGTAIL)

FEMALE TERMINAL

MALE TERMINAL

C103

0.5 GRA

GRA

ENTIRE COMPONENT SHOWN

PART OF A COMPONENT SHOWN

NAME OF COMPONENT

DETAILS ABOUT COMPONENT OR ITS OPERATION

COMPONENT CASE IS DIRECTLY ATTACHED TO METAL PART OF CAR (GROUNDED)

WIRE IS ATTACHED TO METAL PART OF CAR (GROUNDED)

GROUND IS NUMBERED FOR REFERENCE ON COMPONENT LOCATION LIST

WIRE IS INDIRECTLY CONNECTED TO GROUND

WIRE MAY HAVE ONE OR MORE SPLICES BEFORE IT IS GROUNDED

PARK BRAKE SWITCH CLOSED WITH PARKING BRAKE ON

G103

SEE GROUND DISTRIBUTION

G101

Fig. 2 Symbol Identification (Part 1 of 3). LeMans, Metro, Prizm & Storm

Fig. 2 Symbol Identification (Part 2 of 3). LeMans, Metro, Prizm & Storm

SERVO MOTOR → PARTIAL VACUUM

COMPONENT IS SENSITIVE TO ELECTROSTATIC DISCHARGE.

SINGLE DIAPHRAGM MOTOR

VACUUM

NO VACUUM

VACUUM TANK

EASY FLOW DIRECTION

VACUUM CHECK VALVE

NO FLOW DIRECTION

DOUBLE DIAPHRAGM MOTOR

NO VACUUM

NO VACUUM

1.0 YEL

0.5 YEL

0.8 YEL

3 WIRES ARE SHOWN CONNECTED TOGETHER WITH A PIGGYBACK CONNECTOR

HOSE COLOR

VACUUM JUNCTION

BROWN

BLUE

RED

MECHANICAL VACUUM VALVE

VENT

VACUUM SOURCE

A

B

IN THE "AT REST" POSITION SHOWN, THE VALVE DOES THE FOLLOWING:
PORT A IS SEALED
PORT B IS VENTED TO THE ATMOSPHERE

WHEN THE VALVE IS MOVED TO THE "OPERATED" POSITION VACUUM FROM PORT A IS CONNECTED TO PORT B

SOLENOID VACUUM VALVE

VENT

VACUUM SOURCE

A

B

THE SOLENOID VACUUM VALVE USES THE SOLENOID TO MOVE THE VALVE

Fig. 2 Symbol Identification (Part 3 of 3). LeMans, Metro, Prizm & Storm

Fig. 3 Symbol Identification. Electra & LeSabre

Fig. 4 Symbol Identification (Part 1 of 2). Park Avenue

- **Other Electrical Symbols**

Circuit breakers open circuits to protect against high current. They reset automatically. The positive temperature coefficient (PTC) type requires removal of supply voltage before it will reset.

Resistor.

Capacitor.

Light emitting diode.

Circuit breaker (PTC).

Fuse.

Solenoid or coil.

Potentiometer.

Crystal.

Diode. Positive current flows in arrow direction.

Horn or speaker.

Variable resistor.

Motor.

Indicator light. Illuminates a symbol or word(s) (in quotes) in the specified color.

"BRAKE-INDICATOR" Red

Choice bracket. Shows differences in wiring for options.

INDICATORS CLUSTER A7   GAGES CLUSTER C200

- **Wires, Grounds, Splices, and Grommets**

Wire indirectly connected to ground; may have one or more splices in line.

G200

Wire attached to car for ground.

G200

Component case grounded to car.

- **Connectors**

Female terminal. Male terminal.

Connector on component lead (pigtail).

Piggyback connector.

C401

Connector attached to component.

C

Junction block connector.

C323

Two terminals in same connector; dashed line shows physical connection.

E4 C206

E3

- **Switches and Relays**

Ganged switch contacts. Dashed line shows mechanical connection.

Normally open switch.

Heat-actuated switch. When element heats up, it pulls contact arm to change its position.

Relay shown with no current through relay coil. When current flows through coil, contact arm changes position.

- **Components**

Only part of component shown; remainder shown elsewhere.

Entire component shown.

• Vacuum Motors

• Vacuum motors operate like electrical solenoids. When vacuum is applied, the shaft is pulled in. When no vacuum is applied, a spring pushes the shaft out all the way.

• Bi-directional motors can be operated by vacuum in two directions. When there is no vacuum, the motor is in its center at-rest position.

• A servo (vacuum) motor is operated by a control valve which applies a variable amount of vacuum to the motor. The higher the vacuum level, the greater the motor arm retraction.

No vacuum

Vacuum

Partial vacuum

Servo motors.

No vacuum

No vacuum

Bi-directional motor.

• Diagnostic Tools

Multimeter. Symbol inside meter window indicates meter setting.
V = voltage
A = amperes
Ω = resistance

Fused jumper.

Test lamp.

Lit test lamp.

• Wires, Grounds, Splices, and Grommets (continued)

G200

Dashed line means circuit not shown complete but is complete where indicated.

Arrow means wire connects to another circuit. Shows direction of current flow.

S200

Splice. (welded)

S201 (IDC)

Splice. (Insulation Displacement Connection)

P100

Grommet.

A

Circuit is continued where indicated; arrow shows direction of current flow and is repeated where circuit continues.

2 RED/YEL
19

Wire insulation is one color with another color stripe. (Shown, red wire with yellow stripes.)

• Vacuum

Vacuum junction.

Vacuum tank.

Easy flow direction.

No flow direction.

Vacuum check valve.

ENGINE VACUUM SOURCE

VENT

A

B

Mechanical vacuum valve. When valve is at rest, port B is vented; vacuum at port A has no effect.

ENGINE VACUUM SOURCE

VENT

Solenoid vacuum valve. A solenoid is used to move the valve.

Fig. 4 Symbol Identification (Part 2 of 2). Park Avenue

Fig. 5   Symbol Identification. Saturn

WIRE COLOR CODE IDENTIFICATION

Wire Color	Abbreviation
Black	BLK
Blue	BLU
Brown	BRN
Dark Blue	DK BLU
Dark Green	DK GRN
Gray	GRY
Green	GRN
Light Blue	LT BLU
Light Green	LT GRN
Orange	ORN
Pink	PNK
Purple	PPL
Red	RED
Tan	TAN
White	WHT
Yellow	YEL

BUICK ROADMASTER, CADILLAC BROUGHAM & FLEETWOOD (RWD), CHEVROLET CAPRICE & OLDSMOBILE CUSTOM CRUISER

(B & D Cars)

INDEX OF SERVICE OPERATIONS

NOTE: Refer To Rear Of This Manual For Vehicle Manufacturer's Special Tool Suppliers.

INDEX OF SERVICE OPERATIONS-Continued

Specifications

GENERAL ENGINE SPECIFICATIONS

Year	Engine CID/Liter	Engine VIN Code①	Fuel System	Bore & Stroke	Compression Ratio	Net Brake H.P. @ RPM②	Maximum Torque	Normal Oil Pressure, psi
1991	5.0L/V8-305	E	TBI	3.74 x 3.48	9.3	170 @ 4200	255 @ 2400	③
	5.7L/V8-350	7	TBI	4.00 x 3.48	9.8	185 @ 3800	300 @ 2400	③
1992	4.3L/V6-262	Z	TBI	4.00 x 3.48	9.3	145 @ 4200	225 @ 2000	③
	5.0L/V8-305	E	TBI	3.74 x 3.48	9.3	170 @ 4200	255 @ 2400	③
	5.7L/V8-350	7	TBI	4.00 x 3.48	9.8	185 @ 3800	300 @ 2400	③
1993	4.3L/V6-262	Z	TBI	4.00 x 3.48	9.3	145 @ 4200	225 @ 2000	③
	5.0L/V8-305	E	TBI	3.74 x 3.48	9.1	170 @ 4100	255 @ 2400	③
	5.7L/V8-350	7	TBI	4.00 x 3.48	9.8	185 @ 3800	300 @ 2400	③
1994⑤	5.7L/V8-350	P	TBI	4.00 x 3.48	10.5	260 @ 5000	⑥	④

TBI—Throttle Body Fuel Injection.
①—The eighth digit of the VIN denotes engine code.
②—Ratings are net, as installed in vehicle.
③—Minimum w/engine hot, 6 psi. @ 1000 RPM; 18 psi. @ 2000 RPM; 24 psi. @ 4000 RPM.
④—Minimum 6 psi @ 1000 RPM, 18 psi @ 2000 RPM & 24 psi @ 4000 RPM.
⑤—Fleetwood (RWD) & Roadmaster.
⑥—Fleetwood (RWD), 335 @ 2400 RPM; Roadmaster, 330 @ 3200 RPM.

TUNE UP SPECIFICATIONS

| Year & Engine/VIN Code ① | Spark Plug Gap, Inch | Ignition Timing | | | Curb Idle Speed, RPM ④ | Fast Idle Speed, RPM ④ | Fuel Pump Pressure, psi |
		Firing Order Fig. ②	Degrees BTDC ③	Mark Fig.			
1991							
5.0L/V8-305/E	.035	A	TDC ⑧	B	⑥	⑥	9–13 ⑦
5.7L/V8-350/7	.035	A	TDC ⑩	B	⑥	⑥	9–13 ⑦
1992–93							
4.3L/V6-262/Z	.035	C	TDC ⑤	B	⑥	⑥	9–13 ⑦
5.0L/V8-305/E	.035	A	TDC ⑧	B	⑥	⑥	9–13 ⑦
5.7L/V8-350/7	.035	A	TDC ⑩	B	⑥	⑥	9–13 ⑦
1994							
5.7L/V8-350/P	.050	D ⑨	TDC ⑩	B	⑧	⑥	⑦

① —The eighth digit of the VIN denotes engine code.

② —Before removing wires from distributor cap, determine location of No. 1 wire in cap, as distributor position may have been altered from that shown at the end of this chart.

③ —BTDC: Before Top Dead Center.

④ —D: Drive. When adjusting idle speed set parking brake & block drive wheels.

⑤ —Disconnect set timing by-pass connector (tan/black wire) when adjusting ignition timing. The timing by-pass connector breaks out of the engine wiring harness on the righthand side of the engine compartment. After completing adjustment, reconnect set timing connector. With engine off, clear trouble code from ECM memory by removing battery voltage to the ECM for 30 seconds.

⑥ —Idle speed is controlled by IAC (Idle Air Control) or ILC (Idle Load Compensator).

⑦ —Wrap shop towel around fuel hose to steel line connection in engine compartment to prevent fuel spillage. Disconnect hose from steel line & install suitable fuel pressure gauge between hose & line. Ensure gauge connections are tight, then start engine & check fuel pressure readings.

⑧ —Disconnect EST bypass electrical connector when checking ignition timing. The bypass connector is located on the AIR control valve tube. After completing adjustment, reconnect EST bypass electrical connector.

⑨ —1-8-4-3-6-5-7-2.

⑩ —Computer controlled, no adjustment.

Fig. A

Fig. B

Fig. C

1 DISTRIBUTOR ASSEMBLY, IGNITION

Fig. D

FRONT WHEEL ALIGNMENT SPECIFICATIONS

Model	Year	Caster Angle, Degrees		Camber Angle, Degrees		Toe, Degrees
		Limits	Desired	Limits	Desired	
Brougham	1991–92	+2 to +4	+3	−.5 to +.5	0	0
Caprice	1991–92	+3 to +4	+3.5	+.3 to +1.3	+.8	+.16①
	1993	+2.5 to +4.5	+3.5	−.8 to +.8	0	0①
Custom Cruiser	1991–92	+3 to +4	+3.5	+.3 to +1.3	+.8	+.16①
Fleetwood (RWD)	1993–94	+2 to +4	+3	−.5 to +.5	0	0
Roadmaster	1991–92	+3 to +4	+3.5	+.3 to +1.3	+.8	+.16①
	1993–94	+2.5 to +4.5	+3.5	−.8 to +.8	0	0①

①—Total toe.

REAR WHEEL ALIGNMENT SPECIFICATIONS

Year	Model	Camber Angle, Degrees				Total Toe, Degrees
		Limits		Desired		
		Left	Right	Left	Right	
1991–94	All	−.05 to +.05①	−.05 to +.05①	0①	0①	−.05 to +.05①

①—Not adjustable. If out of specifications, check for worn, bent or damaged axle housing, frame or suspension arm.

COOLING SYSTEM & CAPACITY DATA

Make & Year	Model	Engine Liter/ CID ①	Cooling System Capacity, Qts.	Radiator Cap Relief Pressure, psi	Thermo. Opening Temp. °F	Fuel Tank, Gals.	Engine Oil, Qts. ②	Auto. Trans. Qts. ③	Rear Axle, Pts.
BUICK									
1991	Roadmaster	5.0L/V8-305	16.7	15	195	22	4④	⑨	4.25
1992	Roadmaster	5.0L/V8-305	⑩	15	195	23	4④	⑨	4.25
1993	Roadmaster	5.0L/V8-305	⑩	15	195	23	4④	⑨	4.25
1994	Roadmaster	5.7L/V8-350	—	15	195	23	4④	5⑰	4.2
CADILLAC									
1991	Brougham	5.0L/V8-305	16.5	15	195	25	4④	⑬	4.2
		5.7L/V8-350	16.5	15	195	25	4④	⑬	4.2
1992	Brougham	5.0L/V8-305	16.5	15	195	25	4④	⑦	4.2
		5.7L/V8-350	16.5	15	195	25	4④	⑦	4.2
1993	Fleetwood (RWD)	5.7L/V8-350	⑤	15	195	23	4④	⑦	4.2
1994	Fleetwood (RWD)	5.7L/V8-350	⑫	15	185	23	4④	⑨	4.2
CHEVROLET									
1991	Caprice Sedan	5.0L/V8-305	⑩	15	195	23	4④	⑨	⑧
	Caprice Wagon	5.7L/V8-350	14.6	15	195	23	4④	⑨	⑧
1992	Caprice Sedan	4.3L/V6-262	⑯	15	195	23	4⑮	⑪	⑭
		5.0L/V8-305	⑩	15	195	23	4④	⑪	⑭
	Caprice Wagon	5.7L/V8-350	14.6	15	195	22	4④	⑪	⑭
1993	Caprice Sedan	4.3L/V6-262	⑥	15	195	23	4⑮	⑨	⑭
		5.0L/V8-305	⑥	15	195	23	4⑮	⑨	⑭
	Caprice Wagon	5.7L/V8-350	14.6	15	195	22	4⑮	⑨	⑭
OLDSMOBILE									
1991	Custom Cruiser	5.0L/V8-305	⑩	15	195	23	4④	⑨	4.25
		5.7L/V8-350	⑩	15	195	23	4④	⑨	4.25
1992	Custom Cruiser	5.0L/V8-305	⑩	15	195	23	4④	⑨	4.25
		5.7L/V8-350	⑩	15	195	23	4④	⑨	4.25

① —CID: Cubic Inch Displacement.
② —Approximate, additional oil may be required.
③ —Approximate, make final check w/dipstick.
④ —Add 1 qt. w/filter change.
⑤ —Less heavy duty radiator, 15 qts., w/heavy duty radiator, 15.7 qts.
⑥ —Police option w/heavy duty radiator 15.1 qts.
⑦ —Drain & refill, 5 qts., total capacity, 11 qts.
⑧ —7½ inch ring gear, 3.5 pts., 7⅝ inch ring gear, 3.5 pts., 8½ inch ring gear, 4.25 pts.
⑨ —Drain & refill, 5 qts.; total capacity, 11.2 qts.
⑩ —Less heavy duty radiator, 16.7 qts., w/heavy duty radiator, 17.3 qts.
⑪ —Drain & refill, 5.3 qts., total capacity, 11 qts.
⑫ —Less heavy duty radiator, 14.3 qts., w/heavy duty radiator, 14.6 qts.
⑬ —Drain & refill, 4.5 qts., total capacity, 10 qts.
⑭ —7½ inch ring gear, 2.9 pts., 8½ inch ring gear, 3.5 pts.
⑮ —Add ½ qt. w/filter change.
⑯ —Less heavy duty radiator, 12.6 qts., w/heavy duty radiator, 13.2 qts.
⑰ —Refill only.

LUBRICANT DATA

Year	Models	Lubricant Type					
		Transmission		Transfer Case	Rear Axle ①	Power Steering	Brake System
		Manual	Automatic				
1991–94	All	—	DEXRON IIE	—	SAE 80W–90 GL–5	Power Steering Fluid	DOT 3

① —If equipped w/limited slip, friction modifier will also be required except on 1994 Fleetwood (RWD).

Electrical
INDEX

PRECAUTIONS
AIRBAG SYSTEM DISARMING
1993–94 Fleetwood (RWD)

The diagnostic energy reserve module (DERM) can maintain voltage to cause a system deployment for up to ten minutes after the ignition switch is turned off and the battery is disconnected. Servicing the SIR system during this period may result in accidental deployment and personal injury.
1. Ensure front wheels are pointed straight ahead.
2. Turn ignition switch to Lock position and remove SIR fuse from fuse block.
3. Remove left side sound insulator.
4. Remove Connector Position Assurance (CPA), then disconnect yellow two-way SIR electrical connector form both connectors, located near steering column base.

Caprice, Custom Cruiser & Roadmaster

The diagnostic energy reserve mod-

ule (DERM) can maintain voltage to cause a system deployment for up to ten minutes after the ignition switch is turned off and the battery is disconnected. Servicing the SIR system during this period may result in accidental deployment and personal injury.

1. Ensure front wheels are pointed straight ahead.
2. Turn ignition switch to Lock position and remove SIR fuse from fuse block.
3. Remove Connector Position Assurance (CPA), then disconnect yellow two-way SIR electrical connector at base of steering column.

AIRBAG SYSTEM ARMING
1993–94 Fleetwood (RWD)

1. Connect both yellow two-way SIR electrical connector near the steering column base and corresponding Connector Position Assurance (CPA).
2. Install left side sound insulator.
3. Install SIR fuse into fuse block, turn ignition switch to RUN position and ensure that "Inflatable Restraint" lamp flashes 7 times and then shuts off.

Caprice, Custom Cruiser & Roadmaster

1. Connect yellow two-way SIR electrical connector at base of column, then install Connector Position Assurance (CPA).
2. Install SIR fuse into fuse block, turn ignition switch to RUN position and ensure that "Inflatable Restraint" lamp flashes 7 to 9 times and then shuts off.

FUSE PANEL & FLASHER LOCATIONS

The primary fuse panel is located behind behind the lefthand side of the instrument panel near the shroud. On Police models, the auxiliary fuse panel is located behind the lefthand side of the instrument panel, near the lefthand side of the steering column.

On Brougham and Fleetwood (RWD), the hazard warning flasher is located on the fuse panel. On Caprice, Custom Cruiser and Roadmaster the hazard warning flasher is located on the convenience center near the instrument panel fuse panel.

Fig. 1   Ignition lock installation

On Roadmaster, the turn signal flasher is located on the convenience center near the fuse panel. On Brougham and Fleetwood (RWD), the turn signal flasher is located on a bracket behind the instrument panel to the right of the steering column. On Caprice, the turn signal flasher is located on the convenience center next to the auxiliary fuse block. On Custom Cruiser, the turn signal flasher is located on the convenience center near the fuse panel.

STARTER
REPLACE

If shims are used between starter and engine block, they should be placed in their original location during installation.

1. **On models equipped with airbags,** disable airbag system as described under "Airbag System Disarming."
2. **On all models,** disconnect battery ground cable.
3. Raise and support vehicle.
4. Remove starter to engine brace and starter heat shields, if equipped.
5. Remove flywheel housing cover.
6. Remove starter mounting bolts and lower starter. Note position of shims, if used.
7. Disconnect solenoid wires and the battery cable.
8. Remove starter from vehicle.
9. Reverse procedure to install.
10. Rearm airbag system as described under "Airbag System Arming."

DISTRIBUTOR
REPLACE
EXCEPT 1994 FLEETWOOD (RWD)
Removal

1. **On models equipped with airbags,** disable airbag system as described under "Airbag System Disarming."
2. **On all models,** disconnect battery ground cable.
3. Disconnect ignition switch feed and tachometer leads from distributor cap. Screwdriver or other tools should not be used to release lead connector locking tab.
4. Remove distributor cap attaching screws, then position cap out of way.
5. Disconnect four terminal ECM electrical connector from distributor electrical connector.
6. Remove distributor hold down clamp and bolt. Mark position of distributor rotor to distributor housing and position of distributor housing to engine for use during installation.
7. Lift distributor upward until rotor stops rotating and mark position of rotor to distributor housing for use during installation.
8. Remove distributor from engine.

Installation

1. Position rotor to mark on distributor housing, then insert distributor into engine aligning rotor to housing and housing to engine marks made during removal.
2. If engine was was disturbed while distributor was removed, proceed as follows:
   a. Remove spark plug from No. 1 cylinder.
   b. With transmission in Neutral or Park and parking brake applied, position finger over spark plug opening in cylinder head, then slowly crank engine until compression is felt.
   c. Align crankshaft pulley with TDC (0) mark on timing indicator.
   d. Locate distributor rotor contact between No. 1 and 8 spark plug firing positions on distributor.
   e. Insert distributor into engine.
3. Install distributor hold clamp and bolt. Hand tighten bolt.
4. Connect ECM four terminal electrical connector to distributor.
5. Install distributor cap, then connect ignition switch and tachometer lead connector to cap.
6. Connect battery ground cable, then check and adjust ignition timing as necessary. Torque distributor hold down bolt to 27 ft. lbs.
7. Rearm airbag system as described under "Airbag System Arming."

1994 FLEETWOOD (RWD)
Removal

1. Ensure ignition switch is Off and in Lock position.
2. Remove water pump as outlined under "Water Pump, Replace".

3. Remove crankshaft balancer assembly as outlined under "Crankshaft Balancer Assembly & Hub."
4. Disconnect spark plug wire harness assemblies and four-terminal PCM connector from distributor, then vacuum harness from distributor.
5. Remove distributor bolts/screws, then distributor. Pull distributor assembly forward until coupling disengages from end of camshaft.

Installation

1. Install distributor. Rotate distributor coupling until camshaft sprocket pin slot aligns with camshaft sprocket pin. Slide distributor onto end of camshaft until fully seated on engine front cover.
2. **Do not attempt to fully seat distributor using bolts/screws. If distributor will not seat by hand, it is not properly aligned with camshaft. Rotate crankshaft until engine is at No. 1 cylinder TDC (camshaft at nine o'clock position). Rotate distributor coupling until camshaft sprocket pin slot aligns with distributor base timing mark. Install distributor using hand pressure to fully seat.**
3. Install distributor bolts/screws. **Torque** to 106 inch lbs.
4. Connect four-terminal connector, vacuum harness and spark plug harness assemblies to distributor.
5. Install crankshaft balancer and hub assembly, then **torque** to specifications.
6. Install water pump, then **torque** to specifications.

IGNITION LOCK
REPLACE

1. **On models equipped with airbags,** disable airbag system as described under "Airbag System Disarming," then remove steering wheel as described under " Steering Wheel, Replace."
2. **On all models,** remove turn signal switch as described under "Turn Signal Switch, Replace," then remove buzzer switch.
3. Place ignition switch in Run position, then remove lock cylinder retaining screw and lock cylinder.
4. Install by rotating lock cylinder to stop while holding housing, **Fig. 1.** Align cylinder key with keyway in housing, then push lock cylinder assembly into housing until fully seated.
5. Install lock cylinder retaining screw.
6. Install buzzer switch, turn signal switch and steering wheel.
7. Rearm airbag system as described under "Airbag System Arming."

IGNITION SWITCH
REPLACE
EXCEPT 1994 FLEETWOOD (RWD)

The ignition switch is mounted on top of

Fig. 2   Ignition switch

Fig. 5   Mechanical neutral safety system. Models w/standard column

73 JACKET ASM, STRG COL
74 RETAINER, CABLE
75 SCREW, WASH HD (#10-24X.25)
77 SCREW, HEX WASH HD TAP
78 NUT, HEXAGON
79 SWITCH ASM, IGNITION
80 STUD, DIMR & IGN SWITCH MTG
81 SWITCH ASM, DIMMER
82 BRACKET, SOLENOID
83 SOLENOID ASM, INTERLOCK
84 SCREW, HEX WASH HD (10-24X.25)
85 SPRING, BALL JOINT
86 ACTUATOR ASM, IGN SWITCH

Fig. 3   Exploded view of ignition switch, dimmer switch and solenoid. 1994 Fleetwood (RWD)

Fig. 4   Mechanical neutral safety system. Models w/tilt column

Fig. 6   Mechanical neutral safety system in Park position

the mast jacket inside the brake pedal support and is actuated by a rod and rack assembly.

1. **On models equipped with airbags,** disable airbag system as described under "Airbag System Disarming."
2. **On all models,** disconnect battery ground cable.
3. Disconnect and lower steering column. **It may be necessary, on some models, to remove the upper column mounting bracket if it hinders servicing of switch. Use extreme care when lowering steering column to prevent damage to column assembly. Only lower steering column a sufficient distance to perform ignition switch service.**
4. Rotate ignition lock to Off unlocked position.
5. If lock cylinder has been removed, pull switch actuator rod up to stop, then push rod down to second detent to place switch in Off unlocked position, **Fig. 2.**
6. Remove column mounted dimmer switch, if equipped, then remove switch retaining screws and switch.
7. Reverse procedure to install, noting the following:
   a. Place gear shift lever in neutral.
   b. Place lock cylinder and switch in Off locked position, **Fig. 2.**
   c. Fit actuator rod into hole in switch slider and secure switch with retaining screws, ensuring switch does not move out of detent.
   d. Install and adjust dimmer switch, if removed, as outlined in "Dimmer

Switch, Replace."
8. Rearm airbag system as described under "Airbag System Arming."

1994 FLEETWOOD (RWD)

Refer to **Fig. 3** when performing this procedure.
1. Disable airbag system as described under "Airbag System Disarming."
2. Disconnect battery ground cable.
3. Disconnect steering column from vehicle.
4. Remove solenoid cable from interlock solenoid assembly and solenoid bracket. Remove balljoint spring.
5. Remove washer head screw, then interlock solenoid assembly.
6. Remove hexagon head tapping screw and hexagon nut, then solenoid bracket.
7. Remove washer head screw, then dimmer switch assembly.
8. Remove dimmer and ignition switch mounting stud and ignition switch, then disconnect ignition switch from wire harness.
9. Reverse procedure to install noting the following:
   a. Remove plastic pin after switch is assembled to column. Failure to do so may cause switch damage.
   b. Adjust ignition switch by moving slider to extreme right position, then move switch slider one detent to left OFF-LOCK position. Install $3/32$ inch drill bit in hole on switch to limit travel.
   c. **Torque** dimmer and ignition mounting stud to 35 ft. lbs., then remove drill bit from ignition switch.
   d. Adjust dimmer switch by installing $3/32$ inch drill bit in hole on switch to limit travel. Position switch on column and push to remove all lash. Remove drill bit.

   e. **Torque** washer screw and hexagon nut to 35 inch lbs.
   f. **Torque** hexagon washer tap screw to 22 inch lbs.
   g. **Torque** hexagon washer screw to 35 inch lbs.
   h. Rearm airbag system as described under "Airbag System Arming."

NEUTRAL START SWITCH
REPLACE

Actuation of the ignition switch is prevented by a mechanical lockout system, **Figs. 4 and 5,** which prevents the lock cylinder from rotating when the selector lever is out of Park or Neutral. When the selector lever is in Park or Neutral, the slots in the bowl plate and the finger on the actuator rod align, allowing the finger to pass through the bowl plate in turn actuating the ignition switch, **Fig. 6.** If the selector lever is in any position other than Park or Neutral, the finger contacts the bowl plate when the lock cylinder is rotated, thereby preventing full travel of the lock cylinder.

On all models incorporating an electric neutral start switch, the start switch, back-up light switch and parking brake vacuum release valve are combined into one unit. This unit is mounted on the steering column under the instrument panel.

HEADLAMP SWITCH
REPLACE

ROADMASTER

1. **On models equipped with airbags,**

25	HEADLAMP SWITCH INDICATOR LAMP (WITH TWILIGHT SENTINEL)
26	PANEL LAMP DIMMER SWITCH CONNECTOR
27	SWITCH
28	SCREW
29	TWILIGHT SENTINEL SWITCH CONNECTOR
30	HEADLAMP SWITCH CONNECTOR

Fig. 7 Headlamp switch replacement. Caprice, Custom Cruiser & Roadmaster

A CONNECTOR, ELECTRICAL
B LOCK TANG
C ACCESS HOLE
27 SWITCH ASSEMBLY, HEADLAMP
75 PANEL ASSEMBLY, INSTRUMENT

Fig. 9 Headlamp switch replacement. 1993–94 Fleetwood (RWD)

disable airbag system as described under "Airbag System Disarming."
2. **On all models,** disconnect battery ground cable.
3. Remove lower steering column trim panel attaching screws, then pull downward to remove.
4. Through glove compartment, unsnap righthand molding.
5. Loosen steering column support bracket to instrument panel carrier attaching bolts. **Do not remove bolts.**
6. Gently lower steering column assembly. **Use extreme care when lowering steering to prevent damage to column assembly.**
7. Remove lefthand trim plate to instrument panel carrier assembly six attaching screws, then unsnap lefthand trim assembly.
8. Remove headlamp switch attaching screws.

A	WITH TWILIGHT SENTINEL
B	WITHOUT TWILIGHT SENTINEL
1	SWITCH
2	BRACKET
3	LENS
4	ESCUTCHEON
5	KNOB AND ROD
6	WASHER
7	SLEEVE
8	KNOB
9	SPRING WASHER
10	LEVER
11	NUT
12	POTENTIOMETER
13	BUTTON, ROD RETAINING

Fig. 8 Headlamp switch replacement. 1991–92 Brougham

9. Pull switch rearward, then disconnect switch electrical connectors and remove, **Fig. 7.**
10. Reverse procedure to install.
11. Rearm airbag system as described under "Airbag System Arming."

1991–92 BROUGHAM

1. Disconnect battery ground cable.
2. Remove lefthand instrument panel insert.
3. Remove three screws attaching light switch to instrument panel, **Fig. 8.**
4. **On vehicles equipped with Cruise Control and Twilight Sentinel,** remove two screws retaining Cruise Control switch to instrument panel.
5. Slide Cruise Control switch forward to remove headlamp switch.
6. Disconnect electrical connector from headlamp switch.
7. While depressing rod retaining button, pull switch knob and rod from switch, **Fig. 8.**
8. Remove nut from switch lens housing, then remove switch.
9. Reverse procedure to install.

1993–94 FLEETWOOD (RWD)

1. Disable airbag system as outlined under "Airbag System Disarming."
2. Remove instrument panel left sound insulator assembly.
3. Remove instrument panel driver knee bolster deflector.
4. Using suitable flat bladed tool, pry headlamp switch from instrument panel, **Fig. 9.**
5. Disconnect switch electrical connector, then remove switch.
6. Reverse procedure to install. Rearm airbag system as outlined under "Airbag System Arming."

CAPRICE

Refer to "Roadmaster," for headlamp

Fig. 10 Lock plate retaining ring removal

switch replacement procedure.

CUSTOM CRUISER
1991–92

Refer to "Roadmaster" for headlamp switch replacement procedure.

STOP LIGHT SWITCH REPLACE

The stop light switch has a slip fit in the mounting sleeve which permits positive adjustment by pulling the brake pedal up firmly against the stop. The pedal arm forces the switch body to slip in the mounting sleeve bushing to position the switch properly.

1. **On models equipped with airbags,** disable airbag system as described under "Airbag System Disarming."
2. **On all models,** disconnect wires from switch and remove switch from bracket.
3. Position replacement switch in bracket and push inward until fully seated.

Fig. 11   Taping turn signal electrical connector & wiring

Fig. 12   Lifting turn signal switch from column bowl

Fig. 13   Turn signal switch replacement

Fig. 14   Column mounted dimmer switch installation

Brake pedal arm moves switch to correct distance on rebound. Check if pedal is in full return position by lifting slightly by hand.
4. Connect switch electrical connector.
5. Rearm airbag system as described under "Airbag System Arming."

TURN SIGNAL SWITCH
REPLACE

1. **On models equipped with airbags,** disable airbag system as described under "Airbag System Disarming."
2. **On all models,** disconnect battery cable, then remove steering wheel and column to instrument panel trim cover.
3. **On models with telescoping column,** remove bumper spacer and snap ring retainer. On all other models, remove cover from lock plate.
4. **On all models,** using a suitable tool, compress lock plate (horn contact carrier on tilt models) and remove snap ring (C-ring on tilt models), **Fig. 10.**
5. Remove lock plate, cancelling cam, upper bearing preload spring, thrust washer and signal lever.
6. Remove turn signal lever or actuating arm screw, if equipped, or on models with column mounted wiper switch, pull lever straight out of detent. Depress hazard warning button, then unscrew button.
7. Pull connector from bracket and wrap upper part of connector with tape to prevent snagging the wires during removal, **Fig. 11.** On Tilt models, posi-

tion shifter housing in Low position. Remove harness cover.
8. Remove retaining screws and remove switch, **Figs. 12 and 13.**
9. Reverse procedure to install.
10. Rearm airbag system as described under "Airbag System Arming."

DIMMER SWITCH
REPLACE

1. **On models equipped with airbags,** disable airbag system as described under "Airbag System Disarming."
2. **On all models,** disconnect battery ground cable.
3. Remove instrument panel lower trim and on models with A/C, remove A/C duct extension at column.
4. Disconnect shift indicator from column and remove toe-plate cover screws.
5. Remove two nuts from instrument panel support bracket studs and lower steering column, resting steering wheel on front seat.
6. Remove dimmer switch retaining screws and the switch. Tape actuator rod to column and separate switch from rod.
7. Reverse procedure to install. To adjust switch, depress dimmer switch slightly and install a 3/32 inch twist drill to lock the switch to the body, **Fig. 14.** Force switch upward to remove lash between switch and pivot, then remove tape from actuator rod. Remove twist drill and check for proper operation.
8. Rearm airbag system as described under "Airbag System Arming."

STEERING WHEEL
REPLACE
Mark position of steering wheel in relation to shaft prior to removal to ensure correct installation.

EXCEPT 1991–92 BROUGHAM & 1993–94 FLEETWOOD (RWD)
Less Airbag

1. Disconnect battery ground cable.

Fig. 15   Steering wheel. Less airbag, except 1991–92 Brougham

2. Remove horn pad attaching screws.
3. Pull pad reward, then turn horn lead insulator in counterclockwise direction to disconnect horn lead.
4. Remove steering wheel attaching nut and retainer, **Fig. 15.**
5. Using suitable steering wheel puller, remove steering wheel.
6. Reverse procedure to install.

With Airbag

1. Disable airbag system as described under "Airbag System Disarming."
2. Disconnect battery ground cable.
3. Using suitable 30 Torx driver, or equivalent, loosen airbag inflator module attaching screws until module can be released from steering wheel, **Fig. 16.**
4. Pull module rearward, then disconnect coil, connector position assurance and horn lead connectors, then remove module. **Do not carry module by connectors or wires, when placing live module on bench, place bag and trim cover upward.**
5. Remove steering wheel attaching nut.
6. Using suitable steering wheel puller, remove steering wheel and horn contact.
7. Reverse procedure to install.
8. Rearm airbag system as described under "Airbag System Arming."

1991–92 BROUGHAM

1. Disconnect battery ground cable.
2. Remove steering wheel pad attaching

A	TERMINAL FROM INFLATABLE RESTRAINT MODULE
B	MOUNTING POST
C	CLIP
D	TERMINAL FROM COIL ASSEMBLY
E	CONNECTOR POSITION ASSURANCE
1	INFLATOR MODULE
2	STEERING WHEEL
60	SCREW

Fig. 16 Steering wheel. With airbag, except 1991–92 Brougham

19	CLUSTER
20	SCREW
21	ADAPTER
22	ADAPTER

Fig. 17 Instrument cluster replacement. Caprice, Custom Cruiser & Roadmaster

1	CRUISE CONTROL SWITCH
2	LOWER STEERING COLUMN FILLER
3	STEERING COLUMN COLLAR
4	LEFT-HAND INSTRUMENT PANEL TRIM PLATE
5	HEADLAMP SWITCH
6	WINDSHIELD WIPER SWITCH
7	SHIFT INDICATOR CABLE
8	SPEEDOMETER CLUSTER

VIEW A

Fig. 18 Instrument cluster replacement. 1991–92 Brougham

ing wheel assembly, use only specified steering wheel puller. Under no conditions should the end of the steering shaft be hammered on, as hammering could loosen the plastic injections which maintain steering column rigidity. When attaching J 1859-A steering wheel puller bolts and J 38720 steering wheel puller to steering wheel puller, use care to prevent threading bolts all then way through the steering wheel hub into the coil and damaging the airbag coil.

3. Remove steering wheel.
4. Reverse procedure to install noting the following:
   a. Align block tooth on steering wheel with block tooth on steering shaft within one female serration.
   b. **Torque** steering wheel nut to 30 ft. lbs.
   c. Rearm airbag system as described under "Airbag System Arming."

INSTRUMENT CLUSTER REPLACE

ROADMASTER

1. **On models equipped with airbags,** disable airbag system as described under "Airbag System Disarming."
2. **On all models,** disconnect battery ground cable.
3. Remove lower steering column trim panel attaching screws, then pull downward to remove.
4. Through glove compartment, unsnap righthand molding.
5. Loosen steering column support bracket to instrument panel carrier attaching bolts. **Do not remove bolts.**
6. Gently lower steering column assem-

screws.
3. Pull pad rearward, then remove horn contact from plastic tower by pushing wire inward and turning counterclockwise.
4. Turn ignition switch to On position.
5. **On models equipped with tilt and telescope wheel,** remove telescoping locking lever to adjuster attaching screws, then remove adjuster.
6. **On models equipped with standard wheel,** remove locking lever assembly.
7. **On all models,** scribe steering wheel

with installation alignment mark.
8. Remove steering wheel attaching nut.
9. Using suitable steering wheel puller tool, remove steering wheel.
10. Reverse procedure to install.

1993–94 FLEETWOOD (RWD)

1. Disable airbag system as described under "Airbag System Disarming," then remove inflatable restraint steering wheel module assembly.
2. Remove nut. **When removing steer-**

19 CLUSTER ASSEMBLY, INSTRUMENT
20 BOLT/SCREW, INSTRUMENT CLUSTER, 1.9 N·m (17 LB. IN.)
75 PANEL ASSEMBLY, INSTRUMENT

Fig. 19 Instrument cluster replacement. 1993–94 Fleetwood (RWD)

bly. **Use extreme care when lowering steering to prevent damage to column assembly.**

7. Remove lefthand trim plate to instrument panel carrier assembly six attaching screws, then unsnap lefthand trim assembly.
8. Remove instrument cluster attaching screws.
9. Pull cluster rearward, then disconnect shift indicator cable.
10. Pull instrument cluster from panel carrier, **Fig. 17,** then remove.
11. Reverse procedure to install.
12. Rearm airbag system as described under "Airbag System Arming."

1991–92 BROUGHAM
Less Digital Cluster

1. Disconnect battery ground cable.
2. Remove cluster bezel, then with shift lever in the Park position, remove the screw securing shift indicator cable to steering column.
3. Remove four screws securing cluster to instrument horizontal support, **Fig. 18.** On vehicles equipped with speed control sensor, disconnect sensor from cluster before completely removing cluster assembly. This will prevent connector from damaging cluster during removal.
4. Disengage speedometer cable at neck by pulling cluster straight out and depressing retaining spring. **To remove cluster, place shift lever in Low range and on models with tilt wheel, place wheel in lowest position.**
5. Rotate cluster downward, disconnect printed circuit connector, then remove cluster.
6. Reverse procedure to install.

Digital Cluster

1. Disconnect battery ground cable.
2. Loosen outlet grille directional knob Allen key, located at bottom of knob,

then remove knob.
3. Remove lower steering column cover attaching screws.
4. Remove lefthand trim panel six attaching screws, then place shift level in Park position.
5. Remove lefthand trim panel from instrument column.
6. With shift lever in Park position, remove steering column shift indicator clip.
7. Remove instrument cluster four attaching screws, then tilt steering wheel downward, remove cluster.
8. Reverse procedure to install.

1993–94 FLEETWOOD (RWD)

1. Disable airbag system as outlined under "Airbag System Disarming."
2. Remove instrument panel left sound insulator assembly.
3. Remove instrument panel driver knee bolster deflector.
4. Remove steering column tilt lever assembly.
5. Remove cluster trim plate.
6. Disconnect transmission shift indicator cable.
7. Remove instrument cluster attaching screws, **Fig. 19,** then remove cluster.
8. Reverse procedure to install. Rearm airbag system as outlined under "Airbag System Arming."

CAPRICE

Refer to "Roadmaster" for instrument cluster removal procedure.

CUSTOM CRUISER
1991–92 Models

Refer to "Roadmaster" for instrument cluster removal procedure.

RADIO
REPLACE

When installing radio, be sure to adjust antenna trimmer for peak reception. Also, be sure to connect speaker before applying power to radio.

ROADMASTER

1. Disable airbag system as described under "Airbag System Disarming."
2. Disconnect battery ground cable.
3. Remove steering column lower trim panel, then remove lefthand trim panel.
4. Remove radio bracket to instrument carrier attaching screws, then pull radio and bracket assembly outward.
5. Disconnect radio and antenna electrical connectors.
6. Remove radio to bracket attaching nuts, then remove radio.
7. Reverse procedure to install.

1991–92 BROUGHAM
Radio Control Head

1. Disconnect battery ground cable.

1 BRACKET LEDGE FOR FULLY SEATED REMOTE CHASSIS
2 REAR CONNECTOR (2) HARNESS ROUTES THROUGH SIDE SLOT IN BRACKET
3 REAR CONNECTORS (2)
4 FRONT CONNECTORS (3)
5 REMOTE RADIO CHASSIS

Fig. 20 Radio receiver replacement. 1991–92 Brougham

2. Remove set screws at bottom of each A/C vent on/off lever heads, then pull lever heads forward and off.
3. Remove two screws from lower portion of instrument panel trim plate, then remove trim plate from instrument panel.
4. Remove center 7 mm black screw from upper center radio control head upper bracket.
5. Remove two screws from lower ends of bottom radio control bracket.
6. Carefully pull radio control forward.
7. Disconnect electrical connectors from radio control, then remove radio control and bracket.
8. Reverse procedure to install.

Radio Receiver

The radio receiver is located behind the lefthand side of the instrument panel.
1. Disconnect battery ground cable.
2. Remove 4 screws and one wing nut from lefthand side hush panel, then remove panel.
3. Remove attaching screw from lefthand A/C duct, then pull duct down and outward.
4. Remove attaching screw from righthand A/C duct, then pull duct down and outward.
5. Remove two mounting bolts and ground strap from chime module mounting bracket.
6. Remove nut from bottom of radio receiver.
7. Position chime module, bracket and wiring downward and out of way.
8. Disconnect antenna lead from radio receiver.
9. Carefully pull radio receiver downward and toward front of vehicle, then disconnect gray and black electrical connectors from rear of receiver, **Fig. 20.**
10. Carefully pull radio receiver from behind instrument panel, then disconnect blue, white and black electrical

A HARNESS ASSEMBLY, INSTRUMENT PANEL WIRING
B CONNECTOR, ELECTRICAL
40 RADIO ASSEMBLY
41 BOLT/SCREW, RADIO CONTROL
42 BRACKET, RADIO UPPER
43 BRACKET, RADIO LOWER

44 NUT, RADIO CONTROL, 2.8 N·m (25 LB. IN.)
45 BOLT/SCREW, RADIO UPPER BRACKET, 1.9 N·m
    (17 LB. IN.)
46 BOLT/SCREW, RADIO LOWER BRACKET, 1.9 N·m
    (17 LB. IN.)
75 PANEL ASSEMBLY, INSTRUMENT

**Fig. 21   Radio receiver
replacement. 1993–94
Fleetwood (RWD)**

connectors from front radio receiver.
11. Remove radio receiver.
12. Reverse procedure to install.

1993–94 FLEETWOOD (RWD)

1. Disable airbag system as outlined under "Airbag System Disarming."
2. Remove instrument panel righthand molding assembly.
3. Remove instrument panel righthand trim plate assembly.
4. Remove radio to instrument panel attaching screws, **Fig. 21.**
5. Pull radio assembly slightly rearward, then disconnect radio electrical connector.
6. Remove upper and lower radio to bracket attaching nuts, then remove radio attaching bolts and screws.
7. Reverse procedure to install. Rearm airbag system as outlined under "Airbag System Arming."

CAPRICE

Refer to "Roadmaster," for radio replacement procedure.

CUSTOM CRUISER
1991–92

Refer to "Roadmaster," for radio replacement procedure.

WIPER MOTOR REPLACE

1991–92 BROUGHAM

1. Raise hood and remove cowl screen or grille.
2. Disconnect wiring and washer hoses.
3. Reaching through cowl opening, loosen transmission drive link attaching nuts to motor crankarm.
4. Disconnect drive link from motor

**Fig. 24   Windshield wiper
switch actuator pivot pin
replacement**

crankarm.
5. Remove motor attaching screws.
6. Remove motor while guiding crankarm through hole.
7. Reverse procedure to install.

CAPRICE, CUSTOM CRUISER, ROADMASTER & 1993–94 FLEETWOOD (RWD)

1. Disable airbag system as described under "Airbag System Disarming."
2. Disconnect battery ground cable.
3. Remove righthand wiper arm and hose.
4. Remove lefthand cowl vent screen, then righthand screen.
5. Remove wiper linkage access hole cover attaching screws, then remove hole cover.
6. Disconnect wiper motor drive link from motor crank arm.
7. Disconnect wiper motor electrical connectors.
8. Remove motor attaching bolts, then remove motor guiding crank arm through access hole.
9. Reverse procedure to install.
10. Rearm airbag system as described under "Airbag System Arming."

**Fig. 22   Windshield wiper
switch. Standard steering
column**

**Fig. 23   Windshield wiper
switch. Tilt steering column**

WIPER TRANSMISSION REPLACE

1991–92 BROUGHAM

1. Raise hood and remove wiper arm assemblies.
2. Remove lower windshield reveal molding and cowl vent screen.
3. Place suitable lever between drive link and motor crankarm, then pry drive link from crankarm.
4. Remove screws securing transmission pivot retainers to body, then withdraw transmission assembly through plenum opening.
5. Reverse procedure to install.

CAPRICE, CUSTOM CRUISER, ROADMASTER & 1993–94 FLEETWOOD (RWD)

1. Disable airbag system as described under "Airbag System Disarming."
2. Disconnect battery ground cable.
3. Remove right and lefthand wiper arm and hose.
4. Remove lefthand cowl vent screen, then righthand screen.
5. Disconnect plastic nozzle hose from rubber washer hose.
6. Remove wiper linkage access hole cover attaching screws, then remove cover.
7. Disconnect drive link from motor crank arm.
8. Remove linkage to body attaching screws, then remove linkage through access hole.

9. Reverse procedure to install.
10. Rearm airbag system as described under "Airbag System Arming."

WIPER SWITCH
REPLACE

EXCEPT 1991–92 BROUGHAM & 1993–94 FLEETWOOD (RWD)

1. **On models equipped with airbags,** disable airbag system as described under "Airbag System Disarming."
2. **On all models,** disconnect battery ground cable and remove turn signal switch as outlined.
3. Remove ignition lock, ignition switch and dimmer switch as outlined.
4. Remove ignition lock housing retaining screws and housing, **Figs. 22 and 23.**
5. Remove pivot bolt and wiper switch from lock housing, **Fig. 24.**
6. Reverse procedure to install.
7. Rearm airbag system as described under "Airbag System Arming."

1991–92 BROUGHAM

1. Disconnect battery ground cable.
2. Remove lefthand climate control outlet grille.
3. Remove screw securing switch to instrument panel.
4. Pull control switch and electrical connector out, then disconnect from panel.
5. Reverse procedure to install.

1993–94 FLEETWOOD (RWD)

The wiper/washer switch is non-replaceable component of the multi-function lever. The multi-function lever must be replaced as an assembly.

BLOWER MOTOR
REPLACE

1991–92 BROUGHAM

1. **On models equipped with airbags,** disable airbag system as described under "Airbag System Disarming."
2. **On all models,** disconnect battery ground cable.
3. Disconnect blower motor lead wire, then the cooling tube, if equipped.
4. Remove blower motor to case attaching screws, then remove blower motor, **Fig. 25 and 26.**
5. Reverse procedure to install.
6. Rearm airbag system as described under "Airbag System Arming."

CAPRICE, CUSTOM CRUISER, ROADMASTER & 1993–94 FLEETWOOD (RWD)

1. **On models equipped with airbags,**

1	HEATER MODULE
44	RESISTOR ASSEMBLY
50	HEATER WIRING HARNESS
61	BLOWER COVER HOUSING
62	SCREW

Fig. 25   Blower motor & heater core. Less A/C

6	BLOWER
7	EVAPORATOR
8	HEATER
88	SEAL
89	SCREEN
90	SCREW
91	SCREW
92	UPPER CASE
93	LOWER CASE

Fig. 26   Blower motor, heater core & evaporator core. With A/C, except Caprice, Custom Cruiser, Roadmaster & 1993 Fleetwood (RWD)

disable airbag system as described under "Airbag System Disarming."
2. **On all models,** disconnect battery ground cable.
3. Remove righthand instrument panel sound insulator attaching screws, then pull panel rearward disengaging attaching studs.
4. Disconnect blower assembly electrical connector.
5. Remove righthand hinge pillar trim finish panel.
6. Remove secondary ECM bracket attaching screw, then position secondary ECM and bracket aside.
7. Support blower motor assembly, then remove blower motor assembly attaching screws.
8. Remove blower motor assembly.
9. Reverse procedure to install.
10. Rearm airbag system as described under "Airbag System Arming."

HEATER CORE
REPLACE
LESS A/C

1. **On models equipped with airbags,** disable airbag system as described under "Airbag System Disarming."
2. **On all models,** disconnect battery ground cable and drain cooling system.
3. Disconnect heater hoses from heater core. Plug core outlets to prevent coolant spillage.
4. Disconnect electrical connections at blower motor and resistor.
5. Detach heater wiring from clip at blower housing cover.
6. Remove blower housing cover attaching screws, then remove blower housing cover, **Fig. 25.**
7. Remove heater core.

1	MODULE
7	EVAPORATOR
8	HEATER
27	VACUUM TANK
41	CASE

Fig. 27   Heater core & evaporator core. Caprice, Custom Cruiser, Roadmaster & 1993 Fleetwood (RWD)

8. Reverse procedure to install.
9. Rearm airbag system as described under "Airbag System Arming."

WITH A/C
1991–92 Brougham

1. **On models equipped with airbags,** disable airbag system as described under "Airbag System Disarming."
2. **On all models,** disconnect battery ground cable and drain cooling system.
3. Disconnect heater hoses at heater core. Cap core outlets to prevent coolant spillage.
4. Pull hood seal from A/C module flange and area above air screen.
5. Remove air inlet screen attaching screws and air inlet screen.
6. Remove righthand windshield wiper arm.
7. Detach A/C module ground strap from dash panel.
8. Disconnect electrical connectors from A/C module upper case components.
9. Remove upper A/C module attaching screws, then remove A/C module upper case, **Fig. 26.**
10. Remove heater core tube seal, then remove heater core retaining clamp and lift heater core from case.
11. Reverse procedure to install.
12. Rearm airbag system as described under "Airbag System Arming."

Caprice, Custom Cruiser, Roadmaster & 1993–94 Fleetwood (RWD)

1. **On models equipped with airbags,** disable airbag system as described under "Airbag System Disarming."
2. **On all models,** disconnect battery ground cable, then drain cooling system.
3. Remove heater outlet attaching screw.
4. Disconnect heater core pipe fittings, then disengage pipe from fitting.
5. Remove righthand instrument insulator panel attaching screws, then pull panel rearward to disconnect.
6. Remove instrument panel lower reinforcement attaching nut and screw.
7. Disconnect lower evaporator case vacuum electrical connectors.
8. Remove righthand pillar trim finish panel, then roll carpet back to gain access.
9. Remove seven lower evaporator case attaching screws, then remove lower evaporator case.
10. Remove heater core attaching straps and screws, then pull heater core rearward working heater tubes out of seal, **Fig. 27.**
11. Reverse procedure to install.
12. Rearm airbag system as described under "Airbag System Arming."

EVAPORATOR CORE
REPLACE
1991–92 BROUGHAM

1. **On models equipped with airbags,** disable airbag system as described under "Airbag System Disarming."
2. **On all models,** disconnect battery ground cable and discharge refrigerant from A/C system.
3. Disconnect evaporator core inlet and outlet refrigerant lines. Cap lines and outlets.

4. Remove expansion tube from evaporator inlet pipe using tool No. J26549-D or equivalent.
5. Pull hood seal from A/C module flange and area above air screen.
6. Remove air inlet screen attaching screws and air inlet screen.
7. Remove righthand windshield wiper arm.
8. Detach A/C module ground strap from dash panel.
9. Disconnect electrical connectors from A/C module upper case components.
10. Remove upper A/C module attaching screws, then remove A/C module upper case, **Fig. 26.**
11. Remove evaporator core clamp, then lift evaporator core from case.
12. Reverse procedure to install. When installing, ensure evaporator core seal remain properly positioned. After completing installation, add three ounces of refrigerant oil and recharge A/C system, refer to "Air Conditioning" section.
13. Rearm airbag system as described under "Airbag System Arming."

CAPRICE, CUSTOM CRUISER, ROADMASTER & 1993–94 FLEETWOOD (RWD)

1. Disable airbag system as described under "Airbag System Disarming."
2. Disconnect battery ground cable and discharge refrigerant from A/C system.
3. Disconnect evaporator core inlet and outlet refrigerant lines. Cap lines and outlets.
4. Remove righthand instrument insulator panel attaching screws, then pull panel rearward to disconnect.
5. Remove instrument panel lower reinforcement attaching nut and screw.
6. Disconnect lower evaporator case vacuum electrical connectors.
7. Remove righthand pillar trim finish panel, then roll carpet back to gain access.
8. Remove seven lower evaporator case attaching screws, then remove lower evaporator case.
9. Remove evaporator core attaching screw and bracket, **Fig. 27.**
10. Pull heater core rearward and down to remove.
11. Reverse procedure to install.
12. Rearm airbag system as described under "Airbag System Arming."

4.3L/V6-262, 5.0L/V8-305 & 5.7L/V8-350

INDEX

PRECAUTIONS

AIRBAG SYSTEM DISARMING

1993–94 Fleetwood (RWD)

The diagnostic energy reserve module (DERM) can maintain voltage to cause a system deployment for up to ten minutes after the ignition switch is turned off and the battery is disconnected. Servicing the SIR system during this period may result in accidental deployment and personal injury.
1. Ensure front wheels are pointed straight ahead.
2. Turn ignition switch to Lock position and remove SIR fuse from fuse block.
3. Remove left side sound insulator.
4. Remove Connector Position Assurance (CPA), then disconnect yellow two-way SIR electrical connector form both connectors, located near steering column base.

Caprice, Custom Cruiser & Roadmaster

The diagnostic energy reserve module (DERM) can maintain voltage to cause a system deployment for up to ten minutes after the ignition switch is turned off and the battery is disconnected. Servicing the SIR system during this period may result in accidental deployment and personal injury.
1. Ensure front wheels are pointed straight ahead.
2. Turn ignition switch to Lock position and remove SIR fuse from fuse block.

3. Remove Connector Position Assurance (CPA), then disconnect yellow two-way SIR electrical connector at base of steering column.

AIRBAG SYSTEM ARMING

1993–94 Fleetwood (RWD)

1. Connect both yellow two-way SIR electrical connector near the steering column base and corresponding Connector Position Assurance (CPA).
2. Install left side sound insulator.
3. Install SIR fuse into fuse block, turn ignition switch to RUN position and ensure that "Inflatable Restraint" lamp flashes 7 times and then shuts off.

Caprice, Custom Cruiser & Roadmaster

1. Connect yellow two-way SIR electrical connector at base of column, then install Connector Position Assurance (CPA).
2. Install SIR fuse into fuse block, turn ignition switch to RUN position and ensure that "Inflatable Restraint" lamp flashes 7 to 9 times and then shuts off.

FUEL SYSTEM PRESSURE RELIEF

1. Turn ignition Off, then disconnect battery ground cable.
2. Loosen fuel filler cap to relieve fuel tank pressure. Do not tighten until service has been completed.
3. Connect fuel pressure gauge.
4. Install bleed hose into approved container an open valve to bleed system pressure.
5. Drain any fuel remaining in gauge into approved container.

ENGINE MOUNTS
REPLACE

1. **On models equipped with airbag,** disable airbag system as described under "Airbag System Disarming."
2. **On all models,** remove mount retaining bolt from below frame mounting bracket, **Fig. 1.**
3. Raise front of engine and remove mount to engine bolts and mount. On 4.3L/V6-262 engines, the righthand mount may be removed by loosening the trough bolt. **Raise engine only enough to provide sufficient clearance for mount removal. Check for interference between rear of engine and cowl panel which could result in distributor damage.**
4. Reverse procedure to install.
5. Rearm airbag system as described under "Airbag System Arming."

ENGINE
REPLACE

EXCEPT LT1

1. **On models equipped with airbag,** disable airbag system as described under "Airbag System Disarming."
2. **On all models,** disconnect battery cable from battery, then remove air cleaner assembly.
3. Drain cooling system, then disconnect

A	ENGINE ASSEMBLY
B	TRANSMISSION ASSEMBLY
1	ENGINE MOUNT
2	BOLT
3	BOLT
4	WASHER
5	BRACKET
6	SHIM
7	TRANSMISSION MOUNT
8	WASHER
9	BOLT
10	WASHER
11	NUT
91	BRACKET
92	NUT
93	BOLT
94	NUT

Fig. 1 Engine & transmission mounting

radiator and heater hoses.
4. Remove upper fan shroud, then remove engine cooling fan.
5. Remove power steering pump from bracket and position aside with hoses attached.
6. Remove A/C compressor from mounting and position aside with hoses attached.
7. Disconnect accelerator and T.V. cables from throttle body.
8. Remove radiator from vehicle.
9. Disconnect electrical wiring and vacuum hoses as necessary to permit engine removal. Tag electrical wiring and vacuum hoses so they may be installed at the same locations.
10. **On all models,** disconnect ground strap at engine bulkhead.
11. Scribe alignment marks on hinges, then remove hood.
12. **On 1991-93 models,** remove distributor, wiper motor and MAP sensor.
13. **On all models,** disconnect cruise control cable, if equipped.
14. Disconnect battery ground cable from

cylinder head.
15. Raise and support vehicle, then drain crankcase.
16. Disconnect electrical wiring from starter motor.
17. Remove exhaust crossover pipe and catalytic convertor as an assembly.
18. Remove flywheel cover, then remove flywheel to converter attaching bolts.
19. Remove engine mount through bolts.
20. **On TBI models,** wrap shop towel around fuel hose to steel line connection to prevent fuel spillage, then disconnect fuel hoses from fuel lines. On carbureted engines, disconnect fuel line from fuel pump.
21. **On all models,** disconnect converter clutch wiring at transmission.
22. Detach transmission oil cooler lines from clip at oil pan.
23. **On 1992-93 4.3L/V6-262 engine,** remove converter AIR pipe from exhaust manifold.
24. **On all models,** remove transmission to engine attaching bolts.
25. Lower vehicle, then support transmis-

sion using a suitable jack.
26. Install a suitable engine lifting fixture to engine, then remove engine from vehicle.
27. Reverse procedure to install.
28. Rearm airbag system as described under "Airbag System Arming."

LT1

This engine is equipped with a sequential multiport fuel injection system. Fuel injector connectors **must** be positioned onto the correct fuel injectors or engine performance and exhaust emissions may be seriously affected. Fuel injector connectors are numbered to match the correct injector for that cylinder.
1. Disconnect battery ground cable, then recover R134a refrigerant. Refer to "Air Conditioning" section.
2. Drain coolant into suitable container(s), then remove air cleaner resonator bracket nuts and resonator assembly by loosening clamp at air intake duct and sliding resonator assembly off studs.
3. Remove air intake duct.
4. Disconnect fuel lines at fuel rail.
5. **On models equipped with mechanical fan,** remove radiator fan upper shroud.
6. **On models equipped with mechanical fan,** remove fan blade clutch nuts and fan blade with clutch attached.
7. **On models equipped with mechanical fan,** remove fan pulley.
8. **On all models,** disconnect heater hoses from water pump.
9. Disconnect accelerator control cable at throttle body.
10. Disconnect radiator inlet and outlet hoses from water pump and engine, then coolant hose at throttle body.
11. Raise and support vehicle, then remove engine oil filter adapter hose assemblies, if equipped, and drain engine oil.
12. Remove warm up three-way catalytic converters and gaskets from exhaust manifolds.
13. Remove converter cover bolts/screws, then cover.
14. Remove converter bolts/screws.
15. Remove serpentine drive belt as outlined.
16. Remove air conditioning hose from compressor, then plug open ends of lines and fittings.
17. Disconnect transmission fluid cooler lines from engine clips.
18. **On models equipped with mechanical fan,** remove radiator fan lower shroud.
19. **On all models,** remove electric engine cooling fans.
20. Disconnect electrical connectors from starter motor, knock sensor, oxygen sensor, engine oil level switch and fuel pump switch/engine oil pressure gage sensor.
21. Lower vehicle, then disconnect power steering inlet and outlet hoses at pump. Siphon fluid from reservoir to prevent excessive spillage.
22. Disconnect brake booster vacuum hose and generator wiring from gen-

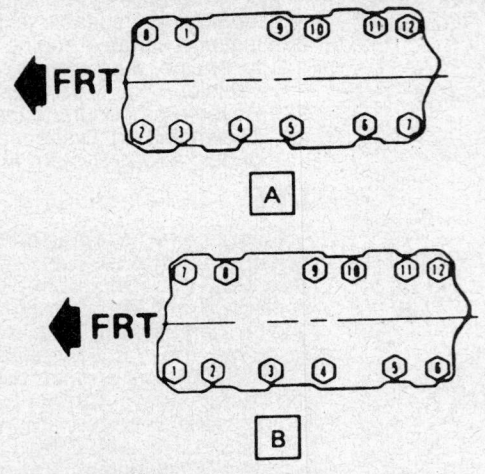

A — INITIAL TIGHTENING SEQUENCE

B — FINAL TIGHTENING SEQUENCE

Fig. 2 Intake manifold bolt tightening sequence. 4.3L/V6-262

Fig. 3 Intake manifold bolt tightening sequence. 5.0L/V8-305 & 5.7L/V8-350 except LT1

erator.

23. Disconnect engine wiring harness connectors and ground straps, then raise and support vehicle.
24. Remove transmission-to-engine bolts/screws, then transmission filler tube bolt/screw at rear of right hand cylinder head.
25. Remove engine mount through-bolts/screws, then lower vehicle.
26. Disconnect engine wiring harness support at left front corner of intake manifold.
27. Install engine lifting device to boss at left front corner of intake manifold using a 3/8-16 NC standard thread bolt. Bolt should be long enough to thread into intake manifold at least one inch. Install other end of engine lifting device to fourth studded bolt on right side of intake manifold. Use a 3/8-16 NC nut to secure lifting device to studded bolt.
28. Remove engine.
29. Reverse procedure to install.

INTAKE MANIFOLD
REPLACE

EXCEPT LT1

1. **On models equipped with airbag,** disable airbag system as described under "Airbag System Disarming."
2. **On all models,** disconnect battery ground cable, drain cooling system and remove air cleaner.
3. Disconnect accelerator, transmission and cruise control linkages, as equipped.
4. Disconnect fuel line from carburetor or TBI unit and remove fuel line clips as needed, then remove carburetor or throttle body from intake manifold.
5. Disconnect necessary vacuum hoses and electrical connectors, noting position for installation.

6. Disconnect upper radiator and heater hoses from manifold.
7. **On Brougham and 1993 Fleetwood (RWD) models,** remove thermostat and housing.
8. **On all models,** remove distributor as described in "Electrical" section under "Distributor, Replacement."
9. Remove ignition coil, AIR pump, cruise control servo and brackets, as needed.
10. Remove alternator upper mounting bracket and EGR solenoids.
11. Remove manifold retaining bolts and the manifold.
12. Reverse procedure to install, noting the following:
    a. Ensure surfaces are clean and dry, then apply 3/16 bead of RTV sealer on each block ridge and apply suitable sealer around water outlets, install gaskets and secure gasket position by extending bead of sealer approximately 1/2 inch onto gasket ends.
    b. Install manifold and retaining bolts, ensuring areas between case ridges and manifold are completely sealed.
    c. Torque manifold bolts to specifications in sequence shown in **Figs. 2 and 3.**
    d. After installing carburetor or TBI unit, check to ensure no fuel leakage is present.
13. Rearm airbag system as described under "Airbag System Arming."

LT1

This engine is equipped with a sequential multiport fuel injection system. Fuel injector connectors must be positioned onto the correct fuel injectors or engine performance and exhaust emissions may be seriously affected. Fuel injector connectors are numbered to match the correct injector for that cylinder.

1. Disable airbag system as described

under "Airbag System Disarming."
2. Disconnect battery ground cable, then drain coolant into suitable container(s).
3. Remove air cleaner resonator bracket nuts and resonator assembly by loosening clamp at air intake duct and sliding resonator assembly off studs.
4. Remove throttle body air duct.
5. Disconnect fuel injector wiring harness connectors.
6. Disconnect left and right wiring harness clips, then position aside.
7. Remove accelerator control cable bracket bolts/screws and bracket from throttle body.
8. Relieve fuel system pressure as outlined.
9. Disconnect fuel pipe connectors from fuel rail, then remove fuel rail bolts/screws.
10. Remove resonator bracket with canister purge solenoid attached.
11. Disconnect fuel pressure regulator vacuum tube, then remove fuel rail from intake manifold and position aside.
12. Disconnect vacuum and crankcase vent hoses.
13. Remove EGR control valve relay nut, then control valve relay.
14. Remove EGR valve pipe nuts, bolt/screw, pipe and gasket. Discard gasket.
15. Disconnect engine wiring harness and remove nuts at left front corner of intake manifold.
16. Disconnect coolant hoses from throttle body, then remove throttle body bolts/screws, throttle body and gasket.
17. Remove intake manifold bolts/screws and studs, then intake manifold and gaskets. Discard gaskets.
18. Reverse procedure to install, noting the following:
    a. Ensure surfaces are clean and dry, then apply 3/16 bead of RTV sealer to front and rear of engine block. Extend bead approximately 1/2 inch up each cylinder head.
    b. Install manifold and retaining bolts, ensuring areas between case ridges and manifold are completely sealed.
    c. Torque manifold bolts to specifications

6 MANIFOLD ASSEMBLY, INTAKE

Fig. 4   Intake manifold bolt tightening sequence. 1994 Fleetwood (RWD)

16 MANIFOLD ASSEMBLY, EXHAUST
17 GASKET, EXHAUST MANIFOLD
18 GASKET, EXHAUST MANIFOLD
19 MANIFOLD ASSEMBLY, EXHAUST
20 STUD, EXHAUST MANIFOLD
21 BOLT/SCREW, EXHAUST MANIFOLD
245 SPACER, EXHAUST MANIFOLD

Fig. 6   Exhaust manifold installation. 1994 Fleetwood (RWD)

17 CYLINDER HEAD
18 EXHAUST MANIFOLD (V8)
19 WASHER
20 LOCK
21 BOLTS
22 STUDS

Fig. 5   Exhaust manifold installation. Except 1994 Fleetwood (RWD)

Fig. 7   Cylinder head bolt tightening sequence. 4.3L/V6-262

Fig. 8   Cylinder head bolt tightening sequence. 5.0L/V8-305 & 5.7L/V8-350 except LT1

tions in sequence shown in **Fig. 4**.
19. Rearm airbag system as described under "Airbag System Arming."

EXHAUST MANIFOLD
REPLACE
EXCEPT LT1

1. **On models equipped with airbag,** disable airbag system as described under "Airbag System Disarming."
2. **On all models,** disconnect battery ground cable, then raise and support vehicle.
3. Disconnect cross-over pipe from exhaust manifold.
4. Lower vehicle, then remove air cleaner, if necessary.
5. Disconnect spark plug wires and diverter valve, if necessary.
6. Remove hoses, brackets and pipes as necessary to permit exhaust manifold

removal. Tag hoses so they can be installed in the same locations.
7. Remove exhaust manifold attaching bolts and studs, then remove exhaust manifold and gasket, **Fig. 5**.
8. Reverse procedure to install.
9. Rearm airbag system as described under "Airbag System Arming."

LT1

1. Disable airbag system as described under "Airbag System Disarming."
2. Remove warm up three-way catalytic converter and gasket from exhaust manifold.
3. Remove oil level indicator tube.
4. Remove secondary air injection pipe fitting from exhaust manifold.
5. Remove generator rear lower braces.
6. Remove exhaust manifold bolts/screws, studs and spacers, **Fig. 6**.
7. Remove exhaust manifold and gasket.
8. Reverse procedure to install.
9. Rearm airbag system as described under "Airbag System Arming."

CYLINDER HEAD
REPLACE
EXCEPT LT1

1. Disconnect battery ground cable, then drain cooling system and engine block.
2. Remove intake manifold and exhaust manifolds.
3. Remove rocker arm covers.

4. **On all models,** remove alternator lower mounting bolt and position alternator aside.
5. Remove dipstick tube and bracket.
6. If equipped with A/C, remove compressor and forward mounting bracket and position aside.
7. Remove power steering pump and bracket, position aside.
8. Remove rocker arm cover, rocker arms and push rods. **Keep rocker arm, rocker arm balls and push rods in order so they can be installed in the same position.**
9. Remove diverter valve, if equipped.
10. Remove cylinder head bolts and cylinder head.
11. Reverse procedure to install. Apply suitable sealer to cylinder head bolts and gradually torque bolts to specifications in sequence shown in **Figs. 7 and 8**.

LT1
Left

1. Raise and support vehicle, then drain coolant into suitable container(s).
2. Remove three-way catalytic converter and gasket from exhaust manifold, then lower vehicle.
3. Remove intake manifold as outlined.
4. Disconnect secondary air injection pipe from check valve.
5. Disconnect coolant air bleed pipe bolt/screw from left cylinder head using a back up wrench on pipe fitting.
6. Remove ignition coil bolts/screws and coil assembly as follows:
   a. Disconnect four-terminal PCM connector at ignition coil module.

A GASKET TAB (YELLOW SIDE UP)
B BOLT TIGHTENING SEQUENCE
34 HEAD ASSEMBLY, CYLINDER
67 BLOCK, ENGINE
81 BOLT/SCREW, CYLINDER HEAD
82 GASKET, CYLINDER HEAD

Fig. 9   Cylinder head bolt tightening sequence. 1994 Fleetwood (RWD)

34	OIL LEVEL INDICATOR
37	ROCKER ARM
41	PUSH ROD

Fig. 10   Adjusting valve lash

b. Disconnect ignition coil wiring connectors, then coil harness.

c. Remove studs, then ignition coil. Do not wipe silicone grease from bottom of ignition coil assembly if it is to be reinstalled.

7. Remove left exhaust manifold as outlined.

8. Disconnect spark plug wire harness from clips, then from spark plugs.

9. Remove spark plugs.

10. Disconnect coolant temperature sensor.

11. Remove rocker arm cover bolts/screws, then cover.

12. Remove rocker arm nuts, rocker arms and pushrods.

13. Remove cylinder head bolts/screws, then cylinder head and gasket. Discard gasket.

14. Reverse procedure to install. Apply suitable sealer to cylinder head bolts and gradually torque bolts to specifications in sequence shown in **Fig. 9.**

Right

1. Raise and support vehicle, then drain coolant into suitable container(s).

2. Remove serpentine drive belt and belt tensioner as outlined.

3. Disconnect transmission fluid level indicator tube bracket from transmission housing and rear of right cylinder head.

4. Remove air conditioning compressor rear brace bolt/screw from engine block, then disconnect compressor electrical connector.

5. Remove air conditioning compressor front mounting bolts/screws and position compressor aside.

6. Remove three-way catalytic converter and gasket from exhaust manifold, then lower vehicle.

7. Remove right exhaust manifold as outlined.

8. Remove generator.

9. Remove right rocker arm cover.

10. Remove intake manifold as outlined, then disconnect coolant air bleed pipe bolt/screw from both cylinder heads using a back up wrench on pipe fittings.

11. Disconnect radiator outlet hose and heater hoses from water pump and reposition.

12. Remove power steering pump as outlined. Refer to "Front Suspension & Steering" section.

13. Remove generator, powr steering pump and air conditioning compressor bracket assembly.

14. Disconnect spark plug wiring harness from spark plugs, then remove spark plugs.

15. Remove rocker arms and pushrods.

16. Disconnect engine coolant temperature sensor electrical connector on side of cylinder head.

17. Remove cylinder head bolts/screws, then cylinder head and gasket. Discard gasket.

18. Reverse procedure to install. Apply suitable sealer to cylinder head bolts and gradually torque bolts to specifications in sequence shown in **Fig. 9.**

VALVE LASH SPECIFICATIONS

Year	Engine/VIN	Valve Lash
1991–93	5.0L/V8-305/E	1 Turn①
1991–94	5.7L/V8-350/P	1 Turn①
1992–93	4.3L/V6-262/Z	¾ Turn②

① —Turn rocker arm stud nut until all lash is eliminated, then tighten nut the additional turn listed in ¼ turn increments. Refer to "Valve Lash, Adjust" procedure.

② —Turn down from zero lash.

VALVE ARRANGEMENT

FRONT TO REAR

4.3L/V6-262

Right. . . . . E-I-I-E-I-E
Left . . . . E-I-E-I-I-E

5.0L/V8-305 & 5.7L/V8-350

All . . . . E-I-I-E-E-I-I-E

VALVE LIFT SPECIFICATIONS

Engine/VIN	Year	Int.	Exh.
5.0L/V8-305/E	1991–93	.350	.385
5.7L/V8-350/7	1991	.413	.428
4.3L/V6-262/Z	1992–93	.350	.385
5.7L/V8-350/7	1992–93	①	①
5.7L/V8-350/P	1994	.418	.430

① —Except police models, intake .350 inch, exhaust .385 inch. Police models, intake .413 inch, exhaust .428 inch.

CAMSHAFT LIFT SPECIFICATIONS

Engine/VIN	Year	Int.	Exh.
5.0L/V8-305/E	1991–92	.234	.257
5.7L/V8-350/7	1991	.257	.269
4.3L/V6-262/Z	1992	.234	.257
5.7L/V8-350/7	1992	①	①
All	1993	.233	.257
5.7L/V8-350/P	1994	.279	.286

① —Except police models, intake .233 inch, exhaust .256 inch. Police models, intake .257 inch, exhaust .269 inch.

VALVE LASH ADJUST

After the engine has been thoroughly warmed up the valves may be adjusted, **Fig. 10,** with the engine shut off as follows: With engine in position to fire No. 1 cylinder the following valves may be adjusted: V6-262, Exhaust 1-5-6, intake 1-2-3. V8's, Exhaust 1-3-4-8, intake 1-2-5-7. Then crank the engine one more complete revolution which will bring No. 4 cylinder on V6-262, engine and No. 6 cylinder on V8 engines, to the firing position at which time the following valves may be adjusted: V6-262, Exhaust 2-3-4, intake 4-5-6. V8's, Exhaust 2-5-6-7, intake 3-4-6-8.

The following procedure, performed with the engine running, should be done only in case readjustment is required.

1. After engine has been warmed up to

17	CYLINDER HEAD
32	ROCKER ARM STUD

Fig. 11   Rocker arm stud removal

Fig. 12   Rocker arm stud installation

1—ROLLER
2—LIFTER BODY
3—PLUNGER SPRING
4—BALL CHECK RETAINER
5—BALL CHECK SPRING
6—BALL CHECK
7—PLUNGER
8—OIL METERING VALVE
9—PUSH ROD SEAT
10—RETAINER RING

Fig. 13   Exploded view of hydraulic valve lifter

operating temperature, remove valve cover and install a new valve cover gasket.

2. With engine running at idle speed, back off valve rocker arm nut until rocker arm starts to clatter.
3. Turn rocker arm nut down slowly until the clatter just stops. This is the zero lash position.
4. Turn nut down 1/4 additional turn and pause 10 seconds until engine runs smoothly. Repeat additional 1/4 turns, pausing 10 seconds each time, until nut has been turned down the number of turns listed in the "Valve Lash Specifications" chart from the zero lash position. **This preload adjustment must be done slowly to allow the lifter to adjust itself to prevent the possibility of interference between the valve head and top of piston, which might result in internal damage and/or bent push rods. Noisy lifters should be replaced.**

ROCKER ARMS

When replacing rocker arms or rocker arm balls, bearing surfaces of rocker arms and balls should be coated with pre-lube 3755008 or equivalent.

ROCKER ARM STUDS
REPLACE

If studs are loose in cylinder head, .003 inch or .013 inch oversize studs may be installed after reaming holes with a proper size reamer.

1. Remove the old stud by placing a suitable spacer, **Fig. 11**, over stud. Install nut and flat washer and remove stud by turning nut.
2. Ream hole for oversize stud.
3. Coat press-fit area of stud with rear axle lube. Then install new stud, **Fig. 12**. If tool shown is used, it should bottom on the head.

PUSHRODS

On engines that use push rods with a hardened insert at one end, the hardened end is identified by a color stripe and should always be installed toward the rocker arm during assembly.

VALVE GUIDES

On all engines valves operate in guide holes bored in the head. If clearance becomes excessive, use the next oversize valve and ream the bore to fit. Valves with oversize stems are available in .003, .015 and .030 inch.

HYDRAULIC VALVE LIFTERS
REPLACE

Valve lifters can be lifted from their bores after removing rocker arms and push rods and intake manifold. Adjustable pliers with protected jaws may be used to remove lifters which are stuck due to carbon or varnish deposits. **Fig. 13** illustrates the type of valve lifter used.

FRONT COVER
REPLACE

On all engines the cover oil seal may be replaced without taking off the timing gear cover. After removing the vibration damper, pry out the old seal with a screwdriver. Install the new seal with the lip or open end toward inside of cover and drive it into position.

1. **On models equipped with airbag,** disable airbag system as described under "Airbag System Disarming."
2. **On 1994 Fleetwood (RWD) models, remove water pump as outlined.**
3. **On 1994 Fleetwood (RWD) models, remove crankshaft balancer and hub as outlined.**
4. **On 1994 Fleetwood (RWD) models, remove distributor as outlined.**
5. **On models except 1994 Fleetwood (RWD),** disconnect battery ground cable and drain cooling system, then remove vibration damper and water pump.
6. **On all models,** remove oil pan and gasket as outlined.
4. Remove front cover retaining screws and the front cover.
5. Reverse procedure to install.
6. Rearm airbag system as described under "Airbag System Arming."

CRANKSHAFT BALANCER & HUB
LT1

1. Raise and support vehicle if equipped with mechanical fan.
2. Remove serpentine drive belt as outlined.
3. Remove crankshaft pulley bolts/screws and pulley, if equipped with mechanical fan.
4. Remove balancer bolts/screws and balancer.
5. Match mark crankshaft hub to engine front cover. **Do not crank engine over after matching crankshaft hub and front cover. Rotating crankshaft will misalign installation of crankshaft hub and balancer to crankshaft, possibly resulting in engine imbalance.**
6. Remove crankshaft hub bolt/screw and washer, crankshaft hub using crankshaft hub remover and installer.
7. Reverse procedure to install. If engine is accidentally turned over, the crankshaft hub can be installed after match marking the hub and front cover using the following procedure:
   a. Set No. 1 piston to TDC. When No. 1 piston is at TDC, crankshaft keyway should be in position shown in Fig. 14.
   b. Install crankshaft hub with cast arrow on hub in 12 o'clock position.

TIMING CHAIN
REPLACE

EXCEPT LT1

1. Remove engine front cover as outlined previously.
2. Remove crankshaft oil slinger.
3. Crank engine until timing marks on sprockets are in alignment, **Fig. 15.**
4. Remove three camshaft to sprocket bolts.
5. Remove camshaft sprocket and timing chain together. Sprocket is a light press fit on camshaft for approximately 1/8 inch. If sprocket does not come off easily, a light blow with a plastic hammer on the lower edge of the sprocket should dislodge it.

A TIMING MARKS
B KEYWAY
56 BOLT/SCREW, CAMSHAFT SPROCKET
57 SPROCKET, CAMSHAFT
58 BOLT/SCREW, CAMSHAFT RETAINER
59 RETAINER, CAMSHAFT
60 CAMSHAFT ASSEMBLY
61 CHAIN ASSEMBLY, TIMING
62 SPROCKET, CRANKSHAFT
63 DRIVESHAFT ASSEMBLY, WATER PUMP
64 BOLT/SCREW, WATER PUMP DRIVESHAFT BEARING
RETAINER

**Fig. 14 Camshaft assembly, sprockets & sprocket alignment,
water pump driveshaft assembly & timing marks. 1994
Fleetwood (RWD)**

A   TIMING MARKS
38   CYLINDER BLOCK
58   TIMING CHAIN
59   CRANKSHAFT SPROCKET
101 CAMSHAFT SPROCKET

**Fig. 15 Valve timing marks.
Except LT1**

A   5/16 INCH 18 × 4 INCH BOLTS
38 CYLINDER BLOCK
60 CAMSHAFT

**Fig. 16 Camshaft from
cylinder block removal**

6. If crankshaft sprocket is to be replaced, remove it with a suitable gear puller. Install new sprocket, aligning key and keyway.
7. Install chain on camshaft sprocket. Hold sprocket vertical with chain hanging below and shift around to align the timing marks on sprockets.
8. Align dowel in camshaft with dowel hole in sprocket and install sprocket on camshaft. Do not attempt to drive sprocket on camshaft as welch plug at rear of engine can be dislodged.
9. Draw sprocket onto camshaft, using the three mounting bolts. Tighten to specifications.
10. Lubricate timing chain with engine oil and install cover.

TIMING CHAIN, CRANKSHAFT & CAMSHAFT SPROCKETS & WATER PUMP DRIVESHAFT
REPLACE
LT1

1. Remove water pump as outlined.
2. Remove front cover as outlined.
3. Rotate crankshaft until timing marks punched on crankshaft sprocket and camshaft sprocket are aligned as shown in **Fig. 14.**
4. Remove camshaft sprocket bolts/screws, then camshaft sprocket and timing chain.
5. **Do not turn crankshaft after timing chain has been removed to prevent damage to pistons or valves.**

6. Remove water pump bearing retainer bolts/screws and water pump driveshaft using a suitable driven gear assembly remover. Remove and discord seal from water pump driveshaft.
7. Remove crankshaft sprocket using a suitable crankshaft gear remover, then remove key, if necessary.
8. Reverse procedure to install.

CAMSHAFT
REPLACE
EXCEPT LT1

1. Remove intake manifold as described under "Intake Manifold, Replace."
2. Remove valve covers, rocker arms and push rods. Keep rocker arms and push rods in order so they can be installed in the same locations.
3. Remove accessory drive belt(s), then remove upper fan shroud.
4. **On 1991 models,** disconnect oil cooler lines.
5. **On all models,** remove radiator. On models equipped with A/C, discharge refrigerant system and remove condenser.
6. Remove timing chain as described under "Timing Chain, Replace."
7. **On carbureted engine,** remove fuel pump.
8. **On TBI engines,** disconnect fuel hose from front fuel line. Position shop towel around fuel hose to fuel line connection to prevent fuel spillage.
9. **On all models,** remove grille.
10. Remove valve lifters. Keep valve lifters in order so they can be installed in the same locations.
11. Install two 5/16-18 x 4 bolts in cam-

shaft bolt holes, then carefully remove camshaft, **Fig. 16.**
12. Reverse procedure to install.

LT1

1. Recover R134a refrigerant.
2. Remove intake manifold as outlined.
3. Remove valve covers, rocker arms and push rods. Keep rocker arms and push rods in order so they can be installed in the same locations.
4. Remove bolt/screw and oil pump driveshaft.
5. Remove water pump as outlined.
6. Remove front cover as outlined.
7. Remove camshaft sprocket as outlined under "Timing Chain, Crankshaft & Camshaft Sprockets & Water Pump Driveshaft"
8. Remove lifters.
9. Remove radiator as follows:
   a. Disconnect battery ground cable, then remove air intake duct and resonator.
   b. Drain coolant into suitable containers through valve located in left radiator end tank.

Fig. 17   Piston & rod assembly. 4.3L/V6-262

Fig. 18   Piston & rod assembly. 5.0L/V8-305 & 5.7L/V8-350 except LT1

A   FLANGES OF CONNECTING RODS MUST FACE TO THE FRONT IN THE LEFT BANK AND TO THE REAR IN THE RIGHT BANK
B   ARROW TO BE ORIENTED TO FRONT OF ENGINE
98   CRANKSHAFT ASSEMBLY
99   CAP, CONNECTING ROD
100   NUT, CONNECTING ROD
101   BEARING, CONNECTING ROD
102   BOLT/SCREW, CONNECTING ROD
103   PISTON ASSEMBLY
104   ROD ASSEMBLY, CONNECTING

Fig. 19   Piston & rod assembly. LT1

A   SEAL REMOVAL NOTCHES
85   REAR CRANKSHAFT SEAL RETAINER

Fig. 20   Crankshaft rear oil seal retainer notch locations

Fig. 21   Crankshaft rear oil seal installation

c. Disconnect engine coolant hoses from radiator, then remove engine cooling fans.
d. Disconnect and plug transmission cooler and engine oil cooler lines.
e. Disconnect coolant recovery reservoir, then remove upper mounting panel if not equipped with mechanical fan.
f. Remove radiator.
10. Remove air conditioning condenser.
11. Remove camshaft retainer bolts/screws and camshaft retainer.
12. Remove camshaft as follows:
 a. Install three ⁵/₁₆-18 x 4 bolts in camshaft bolt holes, then carefully remove camshaft, **Fig. 14.**
13. Reverse procedure to install.

PISTON & ROD ASSEMBLY

Assemble pistons to connecting rods as shown in **Figs. 17 through 19.**

Upon installation, measure the connecting rod side clearance using a suitable feeler gauge. Refer to "Engine Rebuilding Specifications" for connecting rod side clearance.

PISTON PINS & RINGS

Pistons are available in standard and oversizes of .010 and .030 inch.
Piston rings are available in standard and oversizes of .030 inch.

MAIN & ROD BEARINGS

Connecting rod bearings are available in standard and undersizes of .001, .002, .010 and .020 inch.
Main bearings are available in standard and undersizes of .001, .002, .009, .010 and .020 inch.

CRANKSHAFT REAR OIL SEAL

REPLACE

These engines are equipped with a one-piece, lip type seal mounted in a separate seal retainer. Seal replacement requires removal of the transmission.

1. **On models equipped with airbag,** disable airbag system as described under "Airbag System Disarming."
2. **On all models,** raise and support vehicle, then remove transmission and flywheel.
3. Pry seal from retainer, inserting screwdriver in notches provided in seal retainer, **Fig. 20.**
4. Lubricate inner and outer diameters of replacement seal with engine oil, then mount seal on tool J-35621 or equivalent, **Fig. 21.**
5. Mount tool on rear of crankshaft, tightening screws snugly to ensure seal will be installed squarely on crankshaft.
6. Tighten wing nut on tool until it bottoms, then remove tool from crankshaft.
7. Reverse remaining procedure to complete installation.
8. Rearm airbag system as described under "Airbag System Arming."

ENGINE OIL PRESSURE 10 LBS.
MINIMUM AT 500 RPM AND 30-55
LBS. AT 2000 RPM.
OIL FILTER BY-PASS VALVE
OPERATES AT 9- TO 11 LBS.
PRESSURE.

1. GASKET
2. REINFORCEMENT
3. OIL PAN
4. RETAINER
5. 72-130 IN. LBS. (13)
6. 150-250 IN. LBS.

Fig. 22 Oil pan & gasket assembly. 4.3L/V6-262

ENGINE OIL PRESSURE 10 LBS.
MINIMUM AT 500 RPM AND 30-55
LBS. AT 2000 RPM.
OIL FILTER BY-PASS VALVE
OPERATES AT 9- TO 11 LBS.
PRESSURE.

1. GASKET
2. REINFORCEMENT
3. OIL PAN
4. RETAINER
5. 150-250 IN. LBS.
6. 72-130 (14)

Fig. 23 Oil pan & gasket assembly. 5.0L/V8-305 & 5.7L/V8-350 except LT1

61	IDLER GEAR
62	PUMP BODY
63	PICKUP SCREEN AND PIPE
64	DRIVESHAFT
65	RETAINING PIN
66	SPRING
67	PRESSURE REGULATOR VALVE
68	PLUG
69	DRIVE GEAR AND SHAFT
70	RETAINER
71	COVER
72	COVER BOLT

Fig. 24 Exploded view of oil pump

OIL PAN
REPLACE

EXCEPT LT1

1. **On models equipped with airbag,** disable airbag system as described under "Airbag System Disarming."
2. **On all models,** disconnect battery ground cable, then remove air cleaner.
3. **On 1991-93 models with 5.0L/V8-305, 5.7L/V8-350 and 1992-93 4.3L/V6-262 engines,** remove distributor cap and wires.
4. **On all models,** remove upper fan shroud.
5. Raise and support vehicle, then disconnect AIR pipe at exhaust manifold.
6. Disconnect AIR hose at converter pipe.
7. Drain crankcase.
8. Disconnect exhaust pipe at exhaust manifold.
9. Remove flywheel cover.
10. **On 1991-93 models,** remove transmission dipstick tube assembly.
11. **On all models,** detach transmission oil cooler lines from oil pan clips.
12. Remove attaching bolts, then remove starter motor.
13. **On 1991-93 models with 5.0L/V8-305 and 5.7L/V8-350 engines,** remove oil level sensor electrical connector, then remove oil level sensor.
14. **On all models,** remove both left and righthand engine mount through bolts.
15. Remove oil pan attaching nuts and bolts, then lower oil pan, **Fig. 22 and 23.**
16. Position forward crankshaft counterbalance weight and throw to permit oil pan removal.
17. Raise engine slightly to permit oil pan removal.
18. Remove oil pan and gasket.
19. Reverse procedure to install. Apply a small quantity of sealer 1052914 or equivalent to front cover and engine

block junction and rear seal retainer and engine block junction.
20. Rearm airbag system as described under "Airbag System Arming."

LT1

1. Disable airbag system as described under "Airbag System Disarming."
2. Disconnect battery ground cable, then remove air cleaner, resonator and air intake duct.
3. Remove radiator upper fan shroud if equipped with a mechanical fan.
4. Disconnect windshield wiper motor electrical connector.
5. Raise and support vehicle, then drain engine oil.
6. Disconnect oil level sensor connector, then remove oil level sensor.
7. Remove warm up three-way catalytic converters from exhaust manifolds, then catalytic converter support-to-transmission bolts/screws and washers.
8. Remove engine oil filter adapter, then disconnect transmission fluid cooler lines from clip at oil pan.
9. Remove starter, then converter cover bolt/screws and cover.
10. Rotate crankshaft until arrow on crankshaft balancer is pointing straight down (six o'clock).
11. Remove engine mount through-bolts/screws and nuts, then raise engine with jacking fixture.
12. Remove oil pan bolts/screws, studs, nuts, then oil pan, reinforcements and gaskets.
13. Reverse procedure to install. Apply a small quantity of sealer 1052914 or equivalent to front cover and engine block junction and rear seal retainer and engine block junction.
14. Rearm airbag system as described under "Airbag System Arming."

OIL PUMP
REPLACE

1. Remove oil pan as described previously.

2. Remove pump to rear main bearing cap bolt and remove pump and extension shaft.
3. Reverse procedure to install. Make sure that installed position of oil pump screen is with bottom edge parallel to oil pan rails.

OIL PUMP SERVICE

1. Remove oil pump as described previously.
2. Remove pump cover screws and pump cover, **Figs. 24.**
3. Mark gear teeth so they can be reassembled with same teeth indexing, then remove drive gear, idler gear and shaft.
4. Remove pressure regulator valve retaining pin, pressure regulator valve and related parts.
5. If pickup screen and pipe require replacement, mount pump in a soft-jawed vise and extract pipe from pump.
6. Wash all parts in cleaning solvent and dry with compressed air.
7. Inspect pump body and cover for cracks and excessive wear.
8. Inspect pump gears for damage or excessive wear.
9. Check drive gear shaft for looseness in pump body.
10. Inspect inside of pump cover for wear that would allow oil to leak past the ends of the gears.
11. Inspect pickup screen and pipe assembly for damage to screen, pipe or relief grommet.

A	ROTATE TENSIONER IN DIRECTION SHOWN TO INSTALL OR REMOVE BELT
37	A C COMPRESSOR OR BELT IDLER PULLEY
38	BELT TENSIONER
39	GENERATOR ASSEMBLY PULLEY
40	SERPENTINE BELT
41	P S PUMP PULLEY
42	WATER PUMP PULLEY
43	AIR PUMP PULLEY
50	CRANKSHAFT PULLEY

Fig. 25 Serpentine drive belt routing. Except 1994 Fleetwood (RWD)

A	COOLING SYSTEM WITHOUT MECHANICAL FAN
B	COOLING SYSTEM WITH MECHANICAL FAN
C	INDICATOR MARK
D	ACCEPTABLE OPERATING RANGE
E	UNACCEPTABLE OPERATING RANGE
40	TENSIONER ASSEMBLY, DRIVE BELT (WITH MECHANICAL FAN)
41	PULLEY, FAN
42	BALANCER ASSEMBLY, CRANKSHAFT
146	PUMP ASSEMBLY, POWER STEERING
147	GENERATOR ASSEMBLY
148	BELT, SERPENTINE DRIVE
149	COMPRESSOR ASSEMBLY, AIR CONDITIONING
192	PULLEY, CRANKSHAFT
198	BELT, FAN
253	TENSIONER ASSEMBLY, DRIVE BELT

Fig. 26 Serpentine drive belt routing. 1994 Fleetwood (RWD)

12. Check pressure regulator valve for fit in pump housing.
13. Reverse procedure to assemble. Turn drive shaft by hand to check for smooth operation. **The pump gears and body are not serviced separately. If the pump gears or body are damaged or worn, the pump assembly should be replaced. Also, if the pick-up screen and pump assembly was removed, it should be replaced with a new one as loss of the press fit condition could result in an air leak and loss of oil pressure.**

BELT TENSION DATA

Year	New Lbs.	Used Lbs.
A/C Compressor		
1991–94	105–125	105–125

SERPENTINE DRIVE BELTS

BELT ROUTING

Refer to **Figs. 25 and 26,** for serpentine belt routing diagrams.

BELT, REPLACE

Except 1994 Fleetwood (RWD)

1. **On models equipped with airbag,** disable airbag system as described under "Airbag System Disarming."
2. **On all models,** disconnect battery ground cable.

3. Using suitable 1/2 inch breaker bar, push belt tensioner upward, then remove belt.
4. Reverse procedure to install.
5. Rearm airbag system as described under "Airbag System Arming."

1994 Fleetwood (RWD)

1. Disable airbag system as described under "Airbag System Disarming."
2. Disconnect battery ground cable.
3. Remove fan belt from tensioner, if equipped with mechanical fan. Use 13 mm wrench to rotate tensioner pulley clockwise while sliding belt from tensioner pulley.
4. Remove fan belt from pulleys, if equipped with mechanical fan.
5. Remove radiator outlet nuts at air conditioning compressor, if equipped with mechanical fan.
6. Remove serpentine drive belt from tensioner. Us 9/16 off-set wrench to rotate tensioner pulley clockwise while sliding belt from tensioner.
7. Reverse procedure to install.

BELT TENSIONER, REPLACE

1. **On models equipped with airbag,** disable airbag system as described under "Airbag System Disarming."
2. **On all models,** disconnect battery ground cable.
3. Remove serpentine belt as previously outlined.
4. Remove belt tensioner attaching bolt, then belt tensioner.
5. Reverse procedure to install.
6. Rearm airbag system as described under "Airbag System Arming."

COOLING SYSTEM BLEED

These engines do not require a specific bleed procedure. After filling cooling system, start engine and allow to reach operating temperature with radiator cap removed. Air in system will then be automatically bled through cap opening.

THERMOSTAT
REPLACE

1. **On models equipped with airbag,** disarm airbag system as described under "Airbag System Disarming."
2. **On all models,** disconnect battery negative cable.
3. If necessary, remove air cleaner assembly.
4. With engine cool, drain engine coolant below thermostat level.
5. Disconnect radiator hose from thermostat housing.
6. Remove thermostat housing retaining bolts, then the housing, gasket and thermostat.
7. Reverse procedure to install noting the following:
   a. Ensure thermostat gasket sealing surface is clean.
   b. Install thermostat with new gasket.
   c. Tighten thermostat housing retaining bolts to specifications.
   d. Refill and bleed cooling system as needed.
   e. Rearm airbag system as described under "Airbag System Arming."

A	ALIGNMENT REFERENCE MARK	4	NUT
1	COOLANT PUMP	5	FAN CLUTCH
2	COOLANT PUMP HUB	6	COOLING FAN
3	BOLT	7	STUD

Fig. 27 Water pump replacement. Except LT1

WATER PUMP
REPLACE

EXCEPT LT1

1. **On models equipped with airbag,** disable airbag system as described under "Airbag System Disarming."
2. **On all models,** disconnect battery ground cable and drain cooling system.
3. Remove upper fan shroud, then remove accessory drive belts.
4. Remove fan and pulley from water pump hub.
5. Remove power steering pump, A/C compressor and AIR pump brackets, as required.
6. Remove radiator lower hose and heater hose from water pump.
7. Remove water pump attaching bolts and the pump, **Fig. 27.** Note position of bolts for assembly reference.
8. Reverse procedure to install.
9. Rearm airbag system as described under "Airbag System Arming."

A	WITHOUT MECHANICAL FAN	128	STUD, WATER PUMP
B	WITH MECHANICAL FAN	129	BOLT/SCREW, WATER PUMP
37	PUMP ASSEMBLY, WATER	130	BRACKET, COOLANT FAN PULLEY
38	GASKET, WATER PUMP	131	STUD, COOLANT FAN PULLEY BRACKET
39	COUPLING, WATER PUMP DRIVESHAFT	132	NUT, COOLANT FAN PULLEY BRACKET
41	PULLEY, FAN	156	SEAL, WATER PUMP DRIVESHAFT
50	COVER ASSEMBLY, ENGINE FRONT	247	NUT, FAN BLADE CLUTCH
63	DRIVESHAFT ASSEMBLY, WATER PUMP	248	STUD, FAN BLADE CLUTCH
127	BOLT/SCREW, WATER PUMP	249	BLADE ASSEMBLY, FAN

Fig. 28   Water pump replacement. 1994 Fleetwood (RWD)

LT1

1. Drain cooling system into suitable container(s).
2. **If equipped with mechanical fan,** remove air cleaner bracket, air cleaner, resonator and air intake duct.
3. **If equipped with mechanical fan,** remove upper radiator fan shroud, fan belt from tensioner and fan blade with clutch.
4. **On all models,** disconnect engine coolant and heater hoses from water pump.
5. **If equipped with mechanical fan,** remove fan pulley, pulley bracket and nuts.
6. **On all models,** disconnect electrical connector from coolant sensor.
7. Remove secondary air injection pump and bracket.
8. Remove water pump bolts/screws and stud, then water pump, gasket and water pump driveshaft coupling and seals, **Fig. 28.** Discard seals.
9. Reverse procedure to install.

FUEL PUMP
REPLACE

1. **On models equipped with airbag,** disable airbag system as described under "Airbag System Disarming."
2. **On all models,** remove fuel tank filler cap, then disconnect battery ground cable.
3. Drain fuel tank.
4. Remove fuel tank as follows:

a. Raise and support vehicle.
b. Disconnect electrical connectors.
c. Disconnect hoses from sending unit.
d. Support fuel tank, then disconnect retaining straps.
e. Lower tank and remove from vehicle.
5. Remove fuel level sending unit and pump assembly by turning cam lock ring counterclockwise.
6. Remove fuel pump from level sending unit by pulling fuel pump up and outward, away from bottom support, **Fig. 29.**
7. Reverse procedure to install.
8. Rearm airbag system as described under "Airbag System Arming."

FUEL GAGE SENDING UNIT
WITH FUEL PUMP

1. SPLASH CUP LIQUID VAPOR SEPARATOR
2. FUEL TUBE
3. RETURN TUBE
4. RUBBER COUPLER AND SOUND ISOLATOR
5. FUEL LEVEL SENDER
6. ELECTRIC FUEL PUMP
7. FUEL FILTER

Fig. 29   Intake electric fuel pump & fuel gauge sending unit

FUEL FILTER
REPLACE

1. Relieve fuel system pressure as outlined.
2. Remove fuel filter bracket attaching bolt.
3. Grasp filter and one fuel line fitting, twist quick connect fitting 1/4 turn in each direction to loosen within fitting, repeat for other fitting.
4. Depress quick connect fitting plastic tabs of male end connector, then pull connector apart, repeat for other fitting.
5. Remove fuel filter.
6. Reverse procedure to install.

TIGHTENING SPECIFICATIONS
5.0L/V8-305, 5.7L/V8-350 (EXCEPT LT1) & 1992–93 4.3L/V6-262 ENGINES

Year	Component	Torque/Ft. Lbs.	Year	Component	Torque/Ft. Lbs.
1991-93	AIR Crossover Pipe	24⑦	1991-93 —Cont'd	Oil Filter Adapter Bolt	18
	Alternator Bracket	37		Oil Gallery Plug	113①
	Belt Tensioner Bolt	37		Oil Pan Attaching Bolts	101①
	Camshaft Retainer Bolt	105①		Oil Pan Attaching Nuts	17
	Camshaft Sprocket	21		Oil Pump	77
	Connecting Rod Cap Bolt	44		Oil Pump Cover	80①
	Cooling Fan Shroud	53①		Rear Seal Retainer	11
	Crankshaft Pulley Bolt	43		Rocker Arm Cover	95
	Cylinder Head Bolt	④		Spark Plug	⑥
	Engine Block Coolant Drain Plug	16		Thermostat Housing	21
	Engine Cooling Fan Bolts	18		Throttle Body To Intake Manifold	16
	Engine Front Cover	100①		Torque Converter To Flywheel Bolts	35
	Exhaust Crossover Pipe Nut	15		Transmission Mount Bolt To Engine	70
	Exhaust Manifold Bolt	②		Transmission Mount Nut To Engine	35
	Flywheel To Crankshaft	74		Valve Lifter Retainer Bolt	12
	Flywheel Housing Cover	89①		Vibration Damper	70
	Front Engine Mount Bracket Bolts	70		Water Pump	⑤
	Front Engine Mount Bracket Nut	49			
	Front Engine Mount Bolts	33			
	Front Engine Mount Nut	30			
	Fuel Feed/Return Pipes	20			
	Fuel Pump & Sender Assembly Nut	27①			
	Fuel Pump Lower Cover Bolt	105①			
	Fuel Pump Upper Cover Bolt	25			
	Fuel Tank Cross Strap Nut	11			
	Fuel Tank Front Strap Bolt	24			
	Fuel Tank Rear Strap Nut	18			
	Ignition Distributor Clamp	27			
	Intake Manifold Bolt	⑧			
	Main Bearing Cap Bolt	③			

①—Inch lbs.
②—Bolt 26 ft. lbs.; stud, 20 ft. lbs.
③—Except 1991–92 Brougham, 77 ft. lbs., 1991–92 Brougham, 75 ft. lbs.
④—Except Brougham, 68 ft. lbs., 1991–92 Brougham, 70 ft. lbs., 1993 Fleetwood (RWD), 65 ft. lbs.
⑤—Except 1991–92 Brougham, 30 ft. lbs., 1991–92 Brougham, to block 22 ft. lbs., to front cover 10 ft. lbs.
⑥—Except 1992 Caprice & 1993 models, 22 ft. lbs., 1992 Caprice & 1993 models, 11 ft. lbs.
⑦—4.3L/V6-262 engine.
⑧—Tighten in two steps, first to 124 inch lbs., then to 35 ft. lbs.

Continued

TIGHTENING SPECIFICATIONS—Continued
5.0L/V8-305, 5.7L/V8-350 (EXCEPT LT1) & 1992–93 4.3L/V6-262 ENGINES

Year	Component	Torque/Ft. Lbs.
1994	Accelerator Control Cable Bracket Bolt/Screw	90①
	Camshaft Retainer Bolt/Screw	108①
	Camshaft Sprocket Bolt/Screw	21
	Connecting Rod Nut	47
	Crankshaft Balancer Bolt/Screw	60
	Crankshaft Balancer Hub Bolt/Screw	75
	Crankshaft Bearing Cap Bolt/Screw & Stud	78
	Crankshaft Rear Oil Seal Housing Nut & Bolt/Screw	11
	Cylinder Head Bolt	②
	Distributor Bolt/Screw	106①
	EGR Control Valve Relay Nut	16
	EGR Valve Nut	16
	EGR Valve Pipe Bolt/Screw & Nut	18
	Engine Coolant Air Bleed Pipe Bolt/Screw	30
	Exhaust Manifold Stud & Bolt/Screw	26
	Fan Pulley Bracket Nut	26
	Front Cover Bolts/Screws	100①
	Fuel Pump Switch & Oil Pressure Gage Sensor	108①
	Fuel Rail Bolt/Screw	89①
	Generator Bracket Bolt/Screw	30
	Ignition Coil Studs	24
	Intake Manifold	②
	Oil Filter Adapter Bolt/Screw	17

Year	Component	Torque/Ft. Lbs.
1994 -Cont'd	Oil Gallery Plug	18
	Oil Level Indicator Nut	100①
	Oil Level Switch Sensor	26
	Oil Pan Corner Bolt/Screw And Nut Or Stud	15
	Oil Pan Drain Plug	16
	Oil Pan Side Rail Bolt/Screw Or Stud	100①
	Oil Pump Bolt/Screw To Rear Crankshaft Bearing Cap	65
	Oil Pump Cover Bolt/Screw	80①
	Oil Pump Driveshaft Bolt/Screw	13
	Rocker Arm Cover Bolt/Screw	100①
	Rocker Arm Stud	50
	Secondary Air Injection Pipe Fitting To Exhaust Manifold	25
	Secondary Air Injection Pump Bracket Bolt/Screw	18
	Spark Plug	11
	Starter Motor Bolt/Screw	35
	Throttle Body Bolt/Screw	19
	Valve Lifter Guide Retainer Bolt/Screw	15
	Water Pump Bolt/Screw & Stud	30
	Water Pump Driveshaft Bearing Retainer Bolt/Screw	108①

①—Inch lbs.
②—In two passes: First pass, 71 inch lbs; second pass, 35 ft. lbs.

Rear Axle & Suspension
INDEX

DESCRIPTION

In these rear axles, the rear axle housing and differential carrier are cast into an integral housing assembly. The drive pinion assembly is mounted in two opposed tapered roller bearings. The pinion bearings are preloaded by a spacer behind the front bearing. The pinion is positioned by a washer between the head of the pinion and the rear bearing. The differential is supported in the carrier by two tapered roller side bearings. These bearings are preloaded by spacers located between the bearings and carrier housing. The differential assembly is positioned for proper ring

gear and pinion backlash by varying these spacers. The differential case houses two side gears in mesh with two pinions mounted on a pinion shaft which is held in place by a lockpin. The side gears and pinions are backed by thrust washers. A limited slip rear axle, available on most models, uses disc or cone type clutches which are splined to the side gears to lock the axle shafts to the case or in effect to each other. Therefore, if one drive wheel is on a slippery surface, the other wheel must develop more torque than on a standard type differential before the differential case will allow wheel spin. However, axle shaft torques produced during cornering are sufficient to overcome the clutch action, allowing axles to rotate at different speeds.

REAR AXLE REPLACE

Construction of the axle assembly is such that service operations may be performed with the housing installed in the vehicle or with the housing removed and installed in a holding fixture. The following procedure is necessary only when the housing requires replacement.
1. Raise and support vehicle, then support rear axle with a suitable jack.
2. **On models equipped with anti-lock brake systems**, remove rear axle speed sensor as follows:
   a. Disconnect speed sensor electrical harness.

| 26 | LOCK BOLT |
| 31 | AXLE SHAFT "C" LOCK |

Fig. 1   Pinion shaft lock bolt & C-lock removal

A	5 DEGREES MAXIMUM REARWARD
B	15 DEGREES MAXIMUM FORWARD
C	ARROW POINTING TO LEFT SIDE OF CAR, PERPENDICULAR TO CENTERLINE OF CHASSIS
D	COIL LEG
1	REAR SPRING
3	SHOCK ABSORBER
11	WASHER
12	NUT
13	INSULATOR

Fig. 3   Coil spring installation

3	SHOCK ABSORBER
11	WASHER
12	NUT
21	BOLT
22	NUT

Fig. 2   Shock absorber replacement

b. Remove speed sensor harness bracket attaching bolt.
c. Remove speed sensor to rear axle attaching bolt, then remove speed sensor and bracket assembly and position aside.
d. Reverse procedure to install. Wheel speed sensors are to installed by hand. **Do not hammer sensors into position, as damage may result.**
3. **On all models,** disconnect shock absorbers from lower mountings.
4. Remove propeller shaft.
5. Disconnect upper control arms from axle housing attachments.
6. Disconnect brake line from axle housing junction block and the parking brake cable.
7. Disconnect lower control arms from axle housing attachments.
8. Lower axle slowly until springs can be moved. Roll axle assembly out from under vehicle.
9. Reverse procedure to install.

AXLE SHAFT
REPLACE

1. Raise vehicle and remove wheel and brake drum or rotor.
2. Drain lube from carrier and remove cover.
3. Remove differential pinion shaft lock bolt and remove differential pinion shaft, **Fig. 1.**

4. Pull flanged end of axle shaft toward center of vehicle and remove C-lock from button end of shaft.
5. Remove axle shaft from housing, being careful not to damage seal.
6. Reverse procedure to install the axle shaft.

PROPELLER SHAFT
REPLACE

1. Raise and support vehicle.
2. Mark position of shaft in relation to pinion flange for reassembly.
3. Remove straps securing universal joint to pinion flange, then disconnect shaft from flange. **Tape bearing cups to universal joint to prevent loss of needle bearings.**
4. Slide yoke out of transmission and remove propeller shaft. Insert suitable plug in transmission to prevent fluid loss.
5. Reverse procedure to install.

SHOCK ABSORBER
REPLACE

1. If equipped with Superlift shock absorbers, disconnect air lines from shock absorber fittings.
2. With rear axle properly supported, disconnect shock absorber from upper and lower mountings, **Fig. 2.**
3. Reverse procedure to install.

COIL SPRINGS
REPLACE

If more than one coil spring is being replaced, remove and install one spring at a time to prevent axle assembly from slipping or twisting out of position.
1. Support vehicle at frame and rear axle.
2. **On models equipped with anti-lock brake systems,** remove rear axle speed sensor as follows:
   a. Disconnect speed sensor electrical harness.
   b. Remove speed sensor harness bracket attaching bolt.
   c. Remove speed sensor to rear axle attaching bolt, then remove speed sensor and bracket assembly and position aside.

| 2 | UPPER CONTROL ARM | 14 | BOLT |
| 5 | LOWER CONTROL ARM | 15 | NUT |

Fig. 4   Control arm replacement

d. Reverse procedure to install. Wheel speed sensors are to installed by hand. **Do not hammer sensors into position, as damage may result.**
3. **On all models,** disconnect shock absorbers at lower mountings.
4. Disconnect upper control arms from axle housing.
5. Disconnect stabilizer bar from either right or lefthand side of control arm, if equipped.
6. **On models equipped with electronic suspension,** disconnect height sensor arm link.
7. **On all models,** remove brake hose support bolt and support without disconnecting the brake lines.
8. Lower axle until spring can be removed, then remove spring and insulator.
9. Reverse procedure to install. Springs must be installed with an insulator between upper seat and spring and positioned properly, **Fig. 3.**

CONTROL ARMS & BUSHINGS
REPLACE

If more than one control arm is being replaced, remove and install one arm at a time to prevent axle assembly from slipping or twisting out of position.

| A | THRUST BEARING (HIDDEN INSIDE J 21474-5) |
| 10 | REAR AXLE HOUSING BUSHING |

Fig. 5 Upper control arm rear bushing (differential carrier bushing) removal

A	THRUST BEARING
B	J 21474-19 (HIDDEN INSIDE J 21474-5)
10	REAR AXLE HOUSING BUSHING

Fig. 6 Upper control arm rear bushing (differential carrier bushing) installation

| A | PRESS   J 25317-2 |
| 9 | CONTROL ARM BUSHING |

Fig. 7 Control arm bushing removal

CONTROL ARMS, REPLACE

1. Raise vehicle and support at frame pads. Support nose of axle housing to prevent assembly from twisting when control arm is removed.
2. **On models equipped with anti-lock brake systems,** remove rear axle speed sensor as follows:
   a. Disconnect speed sensor electrical harness.
   b. Remove speed sensor harness bracket attaching bolt.
   c. Remove speed sensor to rear axle attaching bolt, then remove speed sensor and bracket assembly and position aside.
   d. Reverse procedure to install. Wheel speed sensors are to installed by hand. **Do not hammer sensors into position, as damage may result.**
3. **On all models,** if lower control arm is being replaced, remove bolts securing stabilizer bar to control arm, if equipped.
4. Remove bolts securing control arm to chassis and rear axle, and the control arm, **Fig. 4.**
5. Reverse procedure to install, lower vehicle and torque control arm bolts to specifications, with vehicle at normal ride height. **All torque prevailing type fasteners must be torqued at the nut, not at the bolt, to ensure proper clamping force.**

| A | PRESS |
| 9 | CONTROL ARM BUSHING |

Fig. 8 Control arm bushing installation

BUSHING REPLACEMENT
Differential Carrier Bushings (Upper Control Arm Rear Bushing)

The upper control arm rear bushing, which is pressed into the differential carrier, can be replaced using the following procedure:
1. Raise vehicle and support at frame pads, and support nose of axle housing to prevent assembly from twisting.
2. Lower rear axle to obtain clearance, disconnect upper control arm from

axle and position aside.
3. Install suitable bushing removal tool as shown in **Fig. 5,** tighten puller screw and press bushing out of housing.
4. To install replacement bushing, reverse position of removal tool and pull bushing into position by tightening screw, **Fig. 6.**

Control Arm Bushings

1. Raise and support vehicle and remove control arm as outlined previously.
2. Press bushings out of control arm using suitable tools as shown in **Fig. 7.**
3. Reverse procedure to install, ensuring bushing is properly seated in control arm, **Fig. 8.** If replacement bushing fits loosely in control arm, or if mounting areas are damaged or deformed, control arm must be replaced.

STABILIZER BAR REPLACE

1. Support vehicle at rear axle.
2. Remove bolts securing stabilizer bar to lower control arms.
3. Reverse procedure to install. Use spacer shims, if needed, placed equally on each side of stabilizer bar. Tighten attaching bolts with vehicle at curb height.

TIGHTENING SPECIFICATIONS

Year	Component	Torque/ Ft. Lbs.	Year	Component	Torque/ Ft. Lbs.
1991-94 —Cont'd	Brake Assembly To Rear Axle	35	1991-94 —Cont'd	Upper Control Arm Front Bushing Nut ③	92
	Lower Control Arm Bushing Bolt ③	122		Upper Control Arm Rear Bushing Bolt ③	80
	Lower Control Arm Bushing Nut ③	92		Upper Control Arm Rear Bushing Nut ③	70
	Lower Control Arm To Frame Bolt ④	89		Upper Control Arm To Axle Housing Bolt ④	85
	Lower Control Arm To Frame Nut ④	92		Upper Control Arm To Axle Housing Nut ④	70
	Propeller Shaft Rear Universal Joint To Pinion Yoke	16		Upper Control Arm To Frame Bolt ④	89
	Rear Axle Filler Plug	26		Upper Control Arm To Frame Nut ④	92
	Shock Absorber Lower Attachment	48		Wheel Lug Nuts	②
	Shock Absorber Upper Attachment	①			
	Stabilizer Bar To Mounting Bracket	52			
	Stabilizer Mounting Bracket To Control Arm	21			
	Upper Control Arm Front Bushing Bolt ③	122			

①—Upper bolt, 20 ft. lbs.; upper nut, 12 ft. lbs..
②—1991–93, except sedan, 100 ft. lbs., sedan, 81 ft. lbs.
③—Except Brougham.
④—Brougham.

Front Suspension & Steering

INDEX

PRECAUTIONS

AIRBAG SYSTEM DISARMING

1993—94 Fleetwood (RWD)

The diagnostic energy reserve module (DERM) can maintain voltage to cause a system deployment for up to ten minutes after the ignition switch is turned off and the battery is disconnected. Servicing the SIR system during this period may result in accidental deployment and personal injury.

1. Ensure front wheels are pointed straight ahead.
2. Turn ignition switch to Lock position and remove SIR fuse from fuse block.
3. Remove left side sound insulator.
4. Remove Connector Position Assurance (CPA), then disconnect yellow two-way SIR electrical connector form both connectors, located near steering column base.

Caprice, Custom Cruiser & Roadmaster

The diagnostic energy reserve module (DERM) can maintain voltage to cause a system deployment for up to ten minutes after the ignition switch is turned off and the battery is disconnected. Servicing the SIR system during this period may result in accidental deployment and personal injury.

1. Ensure front wheels are pointed straight ahead.
2. Turn ignition switch to Lock position and remove SIR fuse from fuse block.
3. Remove Connector Position Assurance (CPA), then disconnect yellow two-way SIR electrical connector at base of steering column.

AIRBAG SYSTEM ARMING

1993—94 Fleetwood (RWD)

1. Connect both yellow two-way SIR electrical connector near the steering column base and corresponding Connector Position Assurance (CPA).
2. Install left side sound insulator.

3. Install SIR fuse into fuse block, turn ignition switch to RUN position and ensure that "Inflatable Restraint" lamp flashes 7 times and then shuts off.

Caprice, Custom Cruiser & Roadmaster

1. Connect yellow two-way SIR electrical connector at base of column, then install Connector Position Assurance (CPA).
2. Install SIR fuse into fuse block, turn ignition switch to RUN position and ensure that "Inflatable Restraint" lamp flashes 7 to 9 times and then shuts off.

DESCRIPTION

All models use a Short-Long Arm (SLA) type front suspension with independent coil springs riding on lower control arms, **Fig. 1.** Ball joints link upper and lower control arms to a spindle assembly, and tubular shock absorbers are used to dampen spring action. On some models, a spring steel stabilizer shaft is connected between the chassis and lower control arms to control side roll.

WHEEL BEARINGS
ADJUST

1. While rotating wheel forward, torque spindle nut to 12 ft. lbs., **Fig. 2**
2. Back off nut until just loose then hand tighten nut and back it off again until either hole in spindle lines up with hole in nut. **Do not back off nut more than 1/2 flat.**
3. Install new cotter pin. With wheel bearing properly adjusted, there will be .001–.005 inch end play.

WHEEL BEARINGS
REPLACE

1. Raise car and remove front wheels.
2. **On models equipped with anti-lock brake systems,** remove right and left wheel speed sensors as follows:

a. Under vehicle hood, disconnect speed sensor electrical harness.
b. Raise and support vehicle, then remove speed sensor harness bracket attaching bolt.
c. Remove speed sensor to steering knuckle attaching bolt, then remove speed sensor and bracket assembly and position aside.
d. Reverse procedure to install. Wheel speed sensors are to installed by hand. **Do not hammer sensors into position, as damage may result.**
3. **On all models,** remove bolts holding brake caliper to its mounting and insert a fabricated block (1 1/16 x 1 1/16 x 2 inches in length) between the brake pads as the caliper is being removed. Once removed, the caliper can be wired or secured in some manner away from the disc.
4. Remove spindle nut and hub and disc assembly. Grease retainer and inner wheel bearing can now be removed, **Fig. 3.**
5. Reverse procedure to install.

BALL JOINT INSPECTION

UPPER BALL JOINT

1. Raise and support vehicle. Position jack stands under lower control arm as close to lower ball joint as possible.
2. Position a suitable dial indicator against wheel rim, **Fig. 4.**
3. Grasp wheel at top and bottom, then pull top of wheel outward, while pushing inward on bottom of wheel. Note dial indicator reading.
4. Pull bottom of wheel outward, while pushing inward on top of wheel. Note dial indicator reading.
5. Deflection reading on dial indicator should not exceed .125 inch.
6. If reading exceeds .125 inch replace upper ball joint.

LOWER BALL JOINT

All models have a wear indicator built into the lower ball joint, **Fig. 5.** When inspecting wear indicator, vehicle must be supported in a normal manner on wheels to properly load ball joint.

1. RETAINER, Upper Cont Arm Bush
2. BUSHING, Upper Cont Arm
3. ARM, Frt Suspension Upper Cont Arm
4. BUSHING, Front
5. NUT, Hex (5/8"-18)
6. RIVET, Strg Knu Upr Cont Arm Ball Stud
7. FITTING, Lubrication
8. BALL JOINT KIT, Upper Cont Arm
9. NUT, Hex (3/8"-16)
10. RETAINER, Frt Shk Abs to Upr Arm Brkt
11. BUMPER, Upper Strg Knu Upr Cont Arm
12. GROMMET, Frt Shk Abs to Upr Arm Brkt
13. BOLT, Upr Arm Shaft to Frame Brkt
14. INSULATOR, Frt Spring
15. SPRING, Frt Coil
16. SHOCK ABSORBER, Frt
17. BUSHING, Lower Cont Arm Rear
18. NUT, Hex (1/2"-13)
19. ARM, Frt Suspension Lwr Cont Arm
20. NUT, Strg Knu Cont Arm Ball Stud
21. PIN, Cotter (1/8" x 1-1/4")
22. BALL JOINT KIT, Lwr Cont Arm
23. BOLT, Caliper Asm
24. CALIPER, Frt Brake
25. FITTINGS, Ball Joint
26. KNUCKLE, Steering
27. GASKET, Frt Brake Supt to Knu
28. SHIELD, Frt Disc Brake
29. NUT, Ball Joint to Strg Knu
30. WHEEL, Frt Suspension
31. NUT, Wheel Bolt (1/2"-20)
32. LINK KIT, Frt Stablizer
33. RETAINER, Frt Stab Link Grommet
34. GROMMET, Frt Stab Link
35. PIN, Cotter (1/4" x 1-1/4")
36. CAP, Wheel Bearing Grease
37. NUT, Steering Knuckle (3/4"-20)
38. WASHER, Strg Knu Spindle
39. BEARING, Hub & Disc
40. HUB, W/Disc Frt Wheel
41. BEARING, Frt Wheel Inner
42. BOLT, Shield to Knuckle
43. WASHER, Flat (9/16")
44. SEAL, Frt Wheel Hub Oil
45. BOLT, Frt Wheel Hub
46. BUMPER, Strg Knu Lwr Cont Arm
47. NUT, Bumper Asm (3/8"-16)
48. NUT, Frt Shk Abs to Lwr Cont Arm
49. BUSHING, Strg Knu Lwer Cont Arm
50. BOLT, Frt Susp Lwr Cont Arm to Frm (M12 x 1.75 x 110)
51. SPACER, Frt Stab Link Bolt Grommet
52. SCREW, Frt Stab Shaft Brkt
53. BRACKET, Frt Stab Shaft
54. BUSHING, Frt Stab to Frame
55. SHAFT, Frt Stab
56. NUT, Frt Stab Link (5/16"-18)
57. NUT, Stab Brkt to Frame (3/8"-16)
58. SHIM, Upper Cont Arm Shaft
59. SHAFT KIT, Upper Cont Arm
60. NUT, Upper Cont Arm to Frame Brkt (1/2"-13)
61. BOLT, Frt Shk Abs to Lwr Cont Arm Nut

Fig. 1   Front suspension

SUSPENSION & STEERING LINKAGE CHECK

1. Raise vehicle with jack placed under frame torque box behind front wheel.
2. Lock steering wheel with wheels in straight ahead position, then mount dial indicator on a suitable stand with pointer bearing against outer rim of wheel, **Fig. 6.**
3. Move wheel in and out at front and rear, without moving steering wheel, while observing gauge.
4. If gauge reading exceeds .108 inches, check steering linkage and suspension for excessive wear or damage and wheel bearings for proper adjustment.

BALL JOINT REPLACE

UPPER BALL JOINT

1. Raise vehicle and support with stands at outer ends of lower control arms.
2. Remove wheel and tire.
3. Remove cotter pin and retaining nut, then separate ball joint stud from knuckle using a suitable tool, **Fig. 7.**
4. Support upper control arm in a raised position.

5. Remove heads of rivets securing joint to arm, then drive out rivets to remove joint.
6. Position replacement joint on top of control arm, insert retaining bolts supplied with joint from under arm, install nuts and torque to specifications, **Fig. 8.**
7. Remove upper control arm support, assemble ball joint to steering knuckle, install washer, if equipped, and retaining nut.
8. Torque retaining nut to specifications.
9. Tighten retaining nut up to an additional 1/16 turn, if necessary, to align hole in ball stud with nut, then install cotter pin.

1. HAND SPIN WHEEL

3. BACK OFF NUT UNTIL JUST LOOSE POSITION.

2. TIGHTEN THE NUT TO 16 N·m (12 FT. LBS.) FULLY SEAT BEARINGS– THIS OVERCOMES ANY BURRS ON THREADS

4. HAND "SNUG-UP" THE NUT

5. LOOSEN NUT UNTIL EITHER HOLE IN THE SPINDLE LINES UP WITH A SLOT IN THE NUT– THEN INSERT COTTER PIN.

NOTICE BEND ENDS OF COTTER PIN AGAINST NUT, CUT OFF EXTRA LENGTH TO PREVENT INTERFERENCE WITH DUST CAP.

6. WHEN THE BEARING IS PROPERLY ADJUSTED THERE WILL BE FROM .03-.13mm (.001-.005 INCHES) END-PLAY (LOOSENESS)

Fig. 2 Front wheel bearing adjustment

1 SUPPORT FRONT LOWER CONTROL ARM ASSEMBLY AS FAR OUTBOARD AS POSSIBLE

2 POSITION DIAL INDICATOR TO CHECK MOVEMENT AT THIS POINT

3 ROCK WHEEL AND TIRE ASSEMBLY IN AND OUT AT TOP AND BOTTOM

Fig. 4 Upper ball joint wear inspection

FRT

A POSITION DIAL INDICATOR TO CHECK MOVEMENT AT THIS POINT

B MOVE WHEEL IN AND OUT AT FRONT AND BACK

Fig. 6 Suspension & steering linkage check

STEERING KNUCKLE — SHIELD — DISC — COTTER PIN — WASHER

GASKET — SEAL — RACE — RACE — BEARING — NUT — CAP

INNER BEARING

Fig. 3 Hub & wheel bearing replacement

FRONT SUSPENSION BALL JOINT WEAR INDICATOR

WORN — NEW

SINTERED IRON BEARING

WEAR SURFACES

WHEN BALL JOINT WEAR CAUSED WEAR INDICATOR SHOULDER TO BE BELOW SURFACE, REPLACEMENT IS REQUIRED.

1.27mm (.050")

HOUSING SOCKET

RUBBER PRESSURE RING

WEAR INDICATOR (OUT WHEN NEW)

Fig. 5 Lower ball joint wear indicator

J 23742

Fig. 7 Disconnecting upper ball joint from steering knuckle

Fig. 8 Upper ball joint installation

LOWER BALL JOINT

1. Raise vehicle and support at frame, and remove wheel and tire.
2. Position a suitable jack under lower control arm spring seat, and raise jack to compress coil spring. **Jack must remain in place during ball joint replacement to hold spring and lower control arm in position.**
3. Remove cotter pin and nut securing ball joint stud to steering knuckle, then disconnect joint from knuckle using a suitable tool, **Fig. 9.**
4. Lift knuckle assembly from ball stud, guiding control arm out of splash shield, then support knuckle aside to allow clearance for joint removal.
5. Remove grease fitting, then press ball joint assembly out of lower control arm using a suitable tool, **Fig. 10.**
6. Press replacement joint into arm using suitable tools, **Fig. 11.** Fit spindle over ball stud, install washer, if equipped, and retaining nut.
7. Torque retaining nut to specifications.
8. Tighten nut up to an additional 1/16 turn, if necessary, to align hole in ball stud with nut, then install cotter pin.

SHOCK ABSORBER REPLACE

1. Raise and support vehicle as needed, and remove wheel and tire.
2. Hold shock absorber shaft with a suitable wrench and remove upper retaining nut, washer and bushing.

Fig. 9 Disconnecting lower ball joint from steering knuckle

Spring to be installed with tape at lowest position. Bottom of spring is coiled helical, and the top is coiled flat with a gripper notch near end of wire.

After assembly, end of spring coil must cover all or part of one inspection drain hole. The other hole must be partly exposed or completely uncovered.

Minimum Compressed Height
241.3 mm

Fig. 12 Coil spring positioning

3. Remove lower retaining bolts and shock absorber.
4. Reverse procedure to install. Torque upper retaining nut and lower mounting bolts to specifications.

COIL SPRING
REPLACE

1. Raise and support front of vehicle, then remove wheel and tire assembly. Support vehicle by frame so control arms hang free.

Fig. 10 Pressing lower ball joint from lower control arm

2. **On models equipped with anti-lock brake systems,** remove right and left wheel speed sensors as follows:
   a. Under vehicle hood, disconnect speed sensor electrical harness.
   b. Raise and support vehicle, then remove speed sensor harness bracket attaching bolt.
   c. Remove speed sensor to steering knuckle attaching bolt, then remove speed sensor and bracket assembly and position aside.
   d. Reverse procedure to install. Wheel speed sensors are to installed by hand. **Do not hammer sensors into position, as damage may result.**
3. **On all models,** remove stabilizer to lower control arm attachment.
4. Disconnect tie rod end from from steering knuckle.
5. Install a suitable coil spring compressor, then compress coil spring.
6. Remove lower control arm to frame bolts, then pivot lower control arm rearward.
7. Carefully loosen coil spring compressor and remove coil spring from vehicle.
8. Reverse procedure to install. Position coil spring as shown in **Fig. 12.** Install front pivot bolt first. **To ensure adequate suspension clearance, install front pivot bolt from front, with nut toward rear of vehicle. Rear bolt can be installed from either direction.**
9. Torque pivot bolts to specifications.

POWER STEERING GEAR
REPLACE

1. **On models equipped with airbags,** disable airbag system as described under "Airbag System Disarming."
2. **On all models,** disconnect battery ground cable.

Fig. 11 Pressing lower ball joint into lower control arm

5	POWER STEERING GEAR
29	WASHER
30	BOLT

Fig. 13 Power steering gear mount

3. Disconnect pressure and return hoses from power steering gear. Position hoses in upward direction to prevent fluid drainage. Cap lines and fittings.
4. Disconnect intermediate steering shaft from steering gear stub shaft.
5. Disconnect Pitman arm from steering gear.
6. **On models equipped with ABS brake systems,** remove ABS modulator bracket attaching nut from steering gear.
7. **On all models,** remove steering attaching bolts and washers, then remove steering gear, **Fig. 13.**
8. Reverse procedure to install. Tighten attaching bolts to specifications.
9. Rearm airbag system as described under "Airbag System Arming."

A	FUEL INJECTED 4.3L, 5.0L and 5.7 ENGINES	25	BOLT
B	CARBURATED 5.0L ENGINE	26	BOLT
1	PUMP	27	SPACER
2	PULLEY	28	NUT
24	BOLT		

Fig. 14   Power steering pump mount

5 PUMP ASSEMBLY, POWER STEERING
12 BOLT/SCREW, POWER STEERING PUMP BRACKET
13 BOLT/SCREW, GENERATOR BRACKET
14 PULLEY, POWER STEERING PUMP
15 BRACKET, POWER STEERING PUMP
17 BOLT/SCREW, POWER STEERING PUMP
18 BRACKET ASSEMBLY, GENERATOR AND POWER
   STEERING PUMP

Fig. 15   Exploded view of power steering pump

POWER STEERING PUMP REPLACE

EXCEPT 1994 FLEETWOOD (RWD)

1. **On models equipped with airbags,** disable airbag system as described under "Airbag System Disarming."
2. **On all models,** disconnect battery ground cable.
3. Disconnect hoses at power steering pump, then plug pump parts and hoses.
4. Loosen pump adjusting bolt and remove pump drive belt.
5. Remove pump to support bracket at-taching bolts and the pump, **Fig. 14.**
6. Reverse procedure to install. Torque attaching bolts to specifications.
7. Rearm airbag system as described under "Airbag System Arming."

1994 FLEETWOOD (RWD)

1. Siphon power steering fluid from reservoir to prevent excess spillage.
2. Drain engine cooling system into suitable container(s), then, if equipped with mechanical fan, remove engine cooling fan bracket.
3. Disconnect heater inlet and outlet hoses from water pump.
4. Remove heater inlet and outlet hose clip bolt/screw from generator and power steering pump bracket, **Fig. 15,** then position aside.
5. Remove drive belt from power steering pump as outlined under "Belt, Replace."
6. Disconnect power steering gear inlet hose from power steering pump, **Fig. 16.**
7. Disconnect power steering fluid reservoir hose from power steering pump by squeezing clamp and sliding away from pump, then rotating and sliding hose away from power steering pump, **Fig. 16.**
8. Remove pump bracket bolts/screws and generator bracket bolt/screw, then pump and pulley.
9. Reverse procedure to install.

A INSULATOR
2 RESERVOIR ASSEMBLY, POWER STEERING FLUID
3 CLAMP, POWER STEERING GEAR OUTLET HOSE
4 HOSE ASSEMBLY, POWER STEERING GEAR INLET
5 PUMP ASSEMBLY, POWER STEERING
6 HOSE ASSEMBLY, POWER STEERING GEAR OUTLET
7 SWITCH ASSEMBLY, IDLE SPEED CONTROL POWER STEERING
8 GEAR ASSEMBLY, POWER STEERING
9 BOLT/SCREW, POWER STEERING HOSE CLAMP
10 CLAMP, POWER STEERING HOSE
11 HOSE ASSEMBLY, POWER STEERING FLUID RESERVOIR
16 CLAMP, POWER STEERING FLUID RESERVOIR HOSE

Fig. 16 Power steering gear inlet & outlet hose locations

TIGHTENING SPECIFICATIONS

Year	Component	Torque/ Ft. Lbs.	Year	Component	Torque/ Ft. Lbs.
1991–93	ABS Modulator Bracket	18	1991–93 —Cont'd	Steering Knuckle Hub Nut	125
	Idler Arm To Frame Nut	61		Tie Rod Clamp Nuts	14
	Intermediate Shaft Coupling Flange Bolt	52		Tie Rod End To Steering Knuckle Stud Nut	35
	Lower Ball Joint To Knuckle Stud Nut	83		Upper Ball Joint To Knuckle Stud Nut	60
	Lower Control Arm To Frame Nuts	92		Upper Control Arm Bushing Nuts	85
	Pitman Shaft Nut	179		Upper Control Arm To Frame Nuts	72
	Power Steering Inlet/Outlet Hose Fitting	21		Wheel Bearing Nut	12
	Power Steering Outlet Hose Clamp	12①		Wheel Lug Nuts	②
	Power Steering Pump Bracket To Engine	24	1994	Generator Bracket Bolt/Screw	37
	Power Steering Pump To Bracket	37		Heater Inlet & Outlet Hose Clip Bolt/Screw	17①
	Shock Absorber Lower Attachment	20		Power Steering Hose Clamp Bolt/Screw	44①
	Shock Absorber Upper Attachment	97①		Power Steering Pump Bolt/Screw	37
	Splashshield Bolt	124①		Power Steering Pump Bracket Bolt/Screw	30
	Stabilizer Bar Bracket To Frame	24		Power Steering Gear Inlet Hose Fitting To Power Steering Gear	21
	Stabilizer Bar To Idler Arm Nut	40		Power Steering Gear Inlet Hose Fitting To Power Steering Pump	21
	Stabilizer Bar To Inner Tie Rod Nut	40		Power Steering Gear Outlet Hose Fitting To Power Steering Gear	21
	Stabilizer Bar To Pitman Arm Nut	44			
	Stabilizer Link Nut	13			
	Steering Gear To Frame Bolts	70			

① —Inch lbs.
② —1991–93, except sedan, 100 ft. lbs.,
sedan, 81 ft. lbs.

Wheel Alignment

INDEX

Fig. 1   Caster & camber adjustments

Fig. 2   Toe-in adjustment

CAMBER, ADJUST

Camber adjustments are made by means of shims between the upper control arm inner support shaft and the support bracket attached to the frame, **Fig. 1.** Shims may be added, subtracted or transferred to change the readings.

Change shims at both the front and rear of the shaft. Adding an equal number of shims at both front and rear of the support shaft will decrease positive camber. One shim (1/32 inch) at each location will move camber approximately 1/6 degree.

TOE-IN, ADJUST

Toe-in can be adjusted by loosening the clamp bolts at each end of each tie rod and turning each tie rod to increase or decrease its length as necessary until proper toe-in is secured and the steering gear is on the high point for straight-ahead driving, **Fig. 2.**

PRELIMINARY CHECK

1. Inspect tires for proper inflation and similar tread wear.
2. Inspect hub and bearing for excessive wear, repair as required.
3. Inspect ball joints.
4. Inspect tie rod ends for excessive looseness.
5. Check wheel and tire runout.
6. Inspect vehicle ride height.
7. Inspect rack and pinion for looseness at frame.
8. Ensure proper strut operation.
9. Check suspension and steering components for damage, replace as required.

FRONT WHEEL ALIGNMENT

CASTER, ADJUST

Caster adjustments are made by means of shims between the upper control arm inner support shaft and the support bracket attached to the frame, **Fig. 1.** Shims may be added, subtracted or transferred to change the readings.

Transfer shims from front to rear or rear to front. The transfer of one shim to the front bolt from the rear bolt will decrease positive caster. One shim (1/32 inch) transferred from the rear bolt to the front bolt will change caster about 1/2 degree.

VEHICLE RIDE HEIGHT

EXCEPT CADILLAC

Refer to **Figs. 3 and 4,** for ride height measurements and specifications.

CADILLAC

Refer to **Figs. 5 and 6,** for ride height measurements and specifications.

TRIM HEIGHTS CHART

VEHICLE	SUSPENSION	TIRE	J		K		P		R	
			mm	INCH	mm	INCH	mm	INCH	mm	INCH
SEDAN	FEI	205-75	252.00	9.92	264.00	10.39	742.00	29.52	539.00	21.22
		225-70	252.00	9.92	264.00	10.39	742.00	29.52	539.00	21.22
	FE2	225-70	252.00	9.92	264.00	10.39	742.00	29.52	539.00	21.22
		205-75	252.00	9.92	264.00	10.39	742.00	29.52	539.00	21.22
	Police	225-75*	252.00	9.92	264.00	10.39	742.00	29.52	539.00	21.22
		235-70*	252.00	9.92	264.00	10.39	742.00	29.21	539.00	21.22
WAGON	ALL	225-75	252.00	9.92	264.00	10.39	742.00	29.21	550.00	21.65
		225-70	252.00	9.92	264.00	10.39	742.00	29.21	550.00	21.65

*Speed Rated Tires

Fig. 3 Vehicle riding height measurement locations & specifications 1991 Buick, Chevrolet & Oldsmobile

MODEL	SUSPENSION	TIRE	J		K		P		R		D		Z	
			mm	INCH	mm	INCH	mm	INCH	mm	INCH	mm	INCH	mm	INCH
SEDAN	FE1	215-75	252	9.9	264	10.4	742	29.2	540	21.3	151	5.9	61	2.4
		225-70	252	9.9	264	10.4	742	29.2	540	21.3	152	6.0	62	2.4
	FE2/F41	225-70	252	9.9	264	10.4	742	29.2	539	21.2	152	6.0	63	2.5
WAGON	F40	225-75	252	9.9	264	10.4	742	29.2	550	21.7	133	5.2	63	2.5
		225-75	252	9.9	264	10.4	742	29.2	550	21.7	122	4.8	53	2.1
POLICE	783	215-75	252	9.9	264	10.4	742	29.2	539	21.2	148	5.8	59	2.3
		225-70	252	9.9	264	10.4	742	29.2	539	21.2	151	5.9	62	2.4
TAXI	783	235-70	252	9.9	264	10.4	742	29.2	539	21.2	144	5.7	54	2.1
		225-70	252	9.9	264	10.4	742	29.2	539	21.2	151	5.9	62	2.4

NOTE: Trim heights should be within ± 10mm (0.4 inch).

Fig. 4 Vehicle riding height measurement locations & specifications 1992–93 Buick, Chevrolet & Oldsmobile

		SUSPENSION		ROCKER PANEL		WHEEL OPENING	
		Z	D	J	K	P	R
BROUGHAM	mm	55	160	268	277	736	613
	in.	2.17	6.30	10.55	10.91	28.98	24.13

Fig. 5 Vehicle ride height measurement. 1991–92 Cadillac Fleetwood (RWD)

MODEL	SUSPENSION	TIRE	J		K		P		R		D		Z	
			mm	INCH	mm	INCH	mm	INCH	mm	INCH	mm	INCH	mm	INCH
SEDAN	FE1	235-70	252	9.9	264	10.4	737	29.0	546	21.5	147	5.8	56	2.2
	FE2/F41	225-70	252	9.9	264	10.4	737	29.0	546	21.5	152	6.0	61	2.4

NOTE: Trim heights should be within ± 10 mm (0.4 inch).

Fig. 6 Vehicle ride height measurement. 1993–94 Cadillac Fleetwood (RWD)

CHEVROLET CAMARO & PONTIAC FIREBIRD (F Cars)

INDEX OF SERVICE OPERATIONS

NOTE: Refer To The Rear Of This Manual For Vehicle Manufacturer's Special Tool Suppliers.

INDEX OF SERVICE OPERATIONS-Continued

Specifications

GENERAL ENGINE SPECIFICATIONS

Year	Engine Liter/CID	VIN Code ①	Fuel System	Bore & Stroke	Compression Ratio	Net Brake H.P. @ RPM ②	Maximum Torque	Normal Oil Pressure, psi
1991	3.1L/V6-191	T	MFI	3.50 x 3.31	8.5	140 @ 4400	180 @ 3600	③
	5.0L/V8-305	E	TBI	3.74 x 3.48	9.3	170 @ 4000	255 @ 2400	④
	5.0L/V8-305 ⑤	F	TPI	3.74 x 3.48	9.3	205 @ 4200	285 @ 3200	④
	5.0L/V8-305 ⑥	F	TPI	3.74 x 3.48	9.3	230 @ 4200	300 @ 3200	④
	5.7L/V8-350	8	TPI	4.00 x 3.48	9.3	245 @ 4400	345 @ 3200	④
1992	3.1L/V6-191	T	MFI	3.50 x 3.31	8.5	140 @ 4400	180 @ 3200	⑦
	5.0L/V8-305	E	TBI	3.74 x 3.48	9.3	170 @ 4000	255 @ 2400	④
	5.0L/V8-305	F	TPI	3.74 x 3.48	9.3	205 @ 4200	285 @ 3200	④
	5.7L/V8-350 ⑤	8	TPI	4.00 x 3.48	9.8	245 @ 4400	345 @ 3200	④
	5.7L/V8-350 ⑥	8	TPI	4.00 x 3.48	9.3	230 @ 4400	300 @ 3200	④
1993-94	3.4L/V6-207	S	MFI	3.62 x 3.31	9.0	160 @ 4600	200 @ 3600	⑧
	5.7L/V8-350	P	MFI	4.00 x 3.48	10.5	275 @ 5000	325 @ 2400	④

MFI: Multi-Port Fuel Injection.
TBI: Throttle Body Injection.
TPI: Tune Port Injection.
① —The eighth digit of the VIN denotes engine code.
② —Ratings are net-as installed in vehicle.
③ —10 psi @ 500 RPM minimum; 51 to 55 psi @ 2000 RPM.
④ —Minimum, 6 psi @ 1000 RPM; 18 psi @ 2000 RPM; 24 psi @ 4000 RPM.
⑤ —Auto. trans.
⑥ —Manual trans.
⑦ —8 psi @ 600 RPM minimum.
⑧ —50 to 65 psi @ 2400 RPM & oil temperature at 240°F.

TUNE UP SPECIFICATIONS

Year & Engine Liter/CID (VIN code) ①	Spark Plug Gap	Firing Order Fig. ④	Ignition Timing BTDC ② Man. Trans.	Ignition Timing BTDC ② Auto. Trans.	Mark Fig.	Curb Idle Speed ③ Man. Trans.	Curb Idle Speed ③ Auto. Trans.	Fast Idle Speed Man. Trans.	Fast Idle Speed Auto. Trans.	Fuel Pump Pressure, psi
1991-92										
3.1L/V6-191(T)	.045	A	10⑤	10⑤	B	800⑥	650D⑥	⑥	⑥	34-47⑦
5.0L/V8-305(E) EFI	.035	C	—	TDC⑧	B	—	600D⑥	—	⑥	9-13⑨
5.0L/V8-305(F) TPI	.035	C	6⑧	6⑧	B	800⑥	800N	⑥	⑥	34-47⑦
5.7L/V8-350(8)	.035	C	—	6⑧	D	—	800N⑥	—	⑥	34-47⑦
1993-94										
3.4L/V6-207(S)	.045	⑩	⑤	⑤	⑪	⑥	⑥	⑥	⑥	41-47⑫
5.7L/V8-350(P)	.050	G	⑤	⑤	E	⑥	⑥	⑥	⑥	41-47⑦

① —The eighth digit of Vehicle Identification Number (VIN) denotes engine code.
② —BTDC: Before Top Dead Center.
③ —D: Drive. N: Neutral. When adjusting idle speed, set parking brake & block drive wheels.
④ —Before disconnecting wires from distributor cap, determine location of No. 1 wire in cap, as distributor position may have been altered from that shown at the end of this chart.
⑤ —Computer controlled, no adjustment.
⑥ —Idle speed is controlled by an Idle Speed Control (ISC) motor, Idle Air Control (IAC) valve or Idle Load Compensator (ILC).
⑦ —With shop towel wrapped around fuel pressure valve to prevent fuel spillage, connect a suitable fuel pressure gauge to fuel pressure valve. Check fuel pressure with ignition switch On, engine not running.
⑧ —Disconnect set timing bypass connector (tan/black wire) near the brake booster when adjusting ignition timing. After completing adjustment, reconnect set timing connector. With engine off, clear trouble code from Electronic Control Module memory (ECM) by removing battery voltage to ECM for 30 seconds.
⑨ —Wrap shop towel around fuel hose to steel line connection in engine compartment to prevent fuel spillage. Disconnect hose from steel line & install a suitable fuel pressure gauge between hose & line. Ensure gauge connections are tight, then start engine & check fuel pressure readings.
⑩ —Cylinder numbering front to rear, left bank 2, 4, 6; right bank, 1, 3, 5. Firing order 1-2-3-4-5-6. Refer to Fig. F for spark plug wire connections at coil unit.
⑪ —Equipped with crankshaft sensor.
⑫ —With ignition switch in the off position, disconnect battery ground cable. Loosen fuel tank filler cap. Disconnect fuel line quick connect fittings, then install a suitable fuel pressure test gauge. Tighten fuel tank filler cap & connect battery ground cable. Place ignition switch in On position & check for leaks at gauge connections. With ignition switch in On position note fuel pressure reading.

Continued

Fig. A

FIRING ORDER 1-2-3-4-5-6

Fig. B

Fig. C

FIRING ORDER 1-8-4-3-6-5-7-2

SCREW

Fig. D

Fig. E

COMPUTER CONTROLLED COIL IGNITION

Fig. F

Fig. G

WHEEL ALIGNMENT SPECIFICATIONS
FRONT WHEEL

Year	Model	Caster Angle, Degrees		Camber Angle, Degrees		Toe, Degrees
		Limits	Desired	Limits	Desired	
1991	All	+4.5 to +5.5	+5	−.2 to +.8	+.3	0
1992	All	+4.3 to +5.3	+4.8	−.2 to +.8	+.3	0
1993–94	All	+3.9 to +4.9	+4.4	−.1 to +.9	+.4	0

Continued

WHEEL ALIGNMENT SPECIFICATIONS—Continued
REAR WHEEL

Year	Model	Camber Angle, Degrees ①		Total Toe, Degrees ①	
		Limits	Desired	Limits	Desired
1991–92	All	−.5 to +.5	0	−.3 to +.3	0
1993–94	All	−.6 to +.6	0	−.3 to +.3	0

① —Not adjustable. If out of specification, check for worn, bent or damaged axle housing, frame or suspension components.

COOLING SYSTEM & CAPACITY DATA

Year	Model Or Engine Liter/CID (VIN) ①	Cooling System Capacity, Qts.		Radiator Cap Relief Pressure, psi	Thermo. Opening Temp. °F	Fuel Tank, Gals.	Engine Oil Refill Qts.	Transmission Oil		Rear Axle, Pts.
		Less A/C	With A/C					Man Trans., Pts.	Auto. Trans., Qts. ②	
1991	3.1L/V6-191(T)	14.7	14.7	15	195	15.5	4③	5.9	④	3.6
	5.0L/V8-305(E)	17.3	18	15	195	15.5	4⑤	5.9	⑥	3.6
	5.0L/V8-305(F)	17.1	17.3	15	195	15.5	4⑤	5.9	⑥	3.6
	5.7L/V8-350(8)	16.4	16.4	15	195	15.5	4⑤	—	⑥	3.6
1992	3.1L/V6-191(T)	14.7	14.8	15	195	15.5	4③	5.9	④	3.6
	5.0L/V8-305(E)	17.4	18	15	195	15.5	4⑤	5.9	⑥	3.6
	5.0L/V8-305(F)	17.9	18	15	195	15.5	4⑤	5.9	⑥	3.6
	5.7L/V8-350(8)	16.6	16.7	15	195	15.5	4⑤	—	⑥	3.6
1993–94	3.4L/V6-207(S)	12.5	12.5	15	195	15.5	4③	5.9	④	2.9
	5.7L/V8-350(P)	15.3	15.3	15	180	15.5	4⑤	8.2	⑥	2.9

① —The eighth digit of Vehicle Identification Number (VIN) denotes engine code.
② —Approximate. Make final check with dipstick.
③ —Additional oil may be required to bring oil level to full mark when changing filter.
④ —Total capacity, 8.35 qts; pan only, 5 qts.
⑤ —Add 1 qt. with filter change.
⑥ —Total capacity, 11.2 qts; pan only, 5 qts.

LUBRICANT DATA

Year	Model	Lubricant Type				
		Transmission		Rear Axle	Power Steering System	Brake System
		Manual	Automatic			
1991	All	Dexron II/IIE	Dexron II/IIE	80W–90 GL-5 ①	Power Steering Fluid ②	DOT 3
1992–94	All	Dexron IIE	Dexron IIE	80W–90 GL-5 ①	Power Steering Fluid ②	DOT 3

① —Limited slip differentials also require 4 oz. of lubricant additive (GM part No. 1052358 or equivalent).
② —Meeting GM specification 9985010.

Electrical

INDEX

PRECAUTIONS

AIRBAG SYSTEM DISARMING

The diagnostic energy reserve module (DERM) can maintain voltage to cause a system deployment for up to ten minutes after the ignition switch is turned off and the battery is disconnected. Servicing the SIR system during this period may result in accidental deployment and personal injury.

1. Ensure front wheels are pointed straight ahead.
2. Turn ignition switch to Lock position and remove SIR or AIRBAG fuse.
3. Remove left sound insulator. **Remove courtesy lamp from sound insulator, if necessary.**
4. Remove Connector Position Assurance (CPA), then disconnect yellow two-way SIR electrical connector at base of steering column.

AIRBAG SYSTEM ARMING

1. Connect yellow two-way SIR electrical connector, then install Connector Position Assurance (CPA).
2. Install left sound insulator. **Install courtesy lamp to sound insulator, if applicable.**
3. Install SIR fuse to fuse block, turn ignition switch to Run position and ensure that "Inflatable Restraint" lamp flashes 7 to 9 times, then shuts off.

FUSE PANEL & FLASHER LOCATION

1991-92

The fuse panel is located behind the left hand side of the instrument panel. The hazard warning flasher is located behind the instrument panel to the right of the steering column, in the convenience center. The turn signal flasher is located behind the left hand side of the instrument panel, clipped to the fuse block bracket.

1993-94

The instrument panel fuse block is located on the lefthand side of the instrument panel carrier, on the side. The underhood electrical center is located on the lefthand side of the engine compartment, forward of the wheelhouse. The convenience center is located on the lefthand side of the steering column, mounted to the bottom of the instrument panel carrier. The hazard warning flasher is located in the convenience center. The turn signal flasher is mounted to a bracket on the righthand side of the steering column, above the data link.

STARTER REPLACE

1991-92

If shims are used between starter and engine block, they should be placed in their original location during installation. If starter is noisy during cranking, remove one .015 inch double shim or add one .015 single shim to the outer bolt. If starter makes a high pitched whine after firing, add .015 inch double shims until noise ceases.

On 1991 models with 5.0L/V8-305 (VIN E) engine, if a clicking or rattling noise is present in the flywheel area with engine running, check for interference between starter motor and torque converter cover. This interference may cause converter cover to contact flywheel. The noise may be more noticeable when engine is cold. To correct this condition, remove torque converter cover and check cover opening, Fig 1. The width of the starter motor opening should be 2.8 inches. If opening is less than 2.8 inch, remove sufficient material from cover with a utility knife to increase opening width to 2.8 inches, Fig. 1. Reinstall torque converter cover.

1. Disconnect battery ground cable.
2. Raise and support vehicle.
3. Remove starter to engine brace and starter heat shields, if equipped.
4. Remove flywheel housing cover.
5. Remove starter mounting bolts and lower starter. Note position of shims, if used, **Fig. 2.**
6. Disconnect solenoid wires and the battery cable.
7. Remove starter from vehicle.
8. Reverse procedure to install.

Fig. 1 Torque converter cover modification. 1991 w/5.0L/V8-305 (VIN E) engines

A V6 ENGINES
B V8 ENGINES

1	STARTER MOTOR	4	BRACKET
2	BOLT	5	NUT	8	DOUBLE SHIM
3	SHIM	6	WASHER	9	SINGLE SHIM
		7	BOLT		

Fig. 2 Starter motor replacement. 1991-92

A 5.7L LT1 ENGINE
B 3.4L L32 ENGINE
13 SHIM, STARTER MOTOR SINGLE
14 SHIM, STARTER MOTOR DOUBLE
15 MOTOR ASSEMBLY, STARTER
16 BOLT/SCREW, STARTER MOTOR, 47 N·m (35 LB. FT.)
17 BOLT/SCREW, STARTER MOTOR, 47 N·m (35 LB. FT.)
18 SHIM, STARTER MOTOR SINGLE
19 SHIM, STARTER MOTOR DOUBLE
20 MOTOR ASSEMBLY, STARTER
21 BOLT/SCREW, STARTER MOTOR, 47 N·m (35 LB. FT.)

Fig. 3 Starter motor replacement. 1993-94

1993-94

This vehicle was designed for starter mounting without shims. If single or double shims have been added to correct a noise or engagement problem, they should be reinstalled in their original positions to ensure proper pinion to flywheel assembly engagement.

Removal

1. Disconnect battery ground cable, then raise and support vehicle.

A INSERT 0.5 mm (0.20") WIRE GAGE HERE TO CHECK
84 FLYWHEEL ASSEMBLY
85 PINION, STARTER DRIVE

Fig. 4 Flywheel assembly to pinion clearance check. 1993-94

2. Disconnect exhaust crossover pipe at manifolds, then remove starter motor mounting bolts and lower starter motor assembly, **Fig. 3.**
3. Disconnect electrical connectors from starter motor assembly, then remove starter motor assembly.

Installation

Before connecting electrical connectors, tighten inner nuts on the solenoid terminals. If the nuts are not tight, the solenoid cap may be damaged during installation of connectors. Torque inner nut of BAT terminal to 80 inch lbs.

1. Connect electrical connectors to starter motor assembly, then **torque BAT terminal nut to 80 inch lbs. and S terminal nut to 22 inch lbs.**
2. Install starter motor assembly and **torque** mounting bolts to 35 ft. lbs.
3. Measure pinion to flywheel clearance, **Fig. 4**, adding shims if necessary.
4. Connect exhaust crossover pipe to manifolds, then lower vehicle and connect battery ground cable.

DISTRIBUTOR
REPLACE

1991-92
Removal

1. Disconnect battery ground cable.
2. Disconnect ignition switch feed and tachometer leads from distributor cap. Screwdriver or other tools should not be used to release lead connector locking tab.
3. Remove distributor cap attaching screws, then position cap out of way.
4. Disconnect four terminal ECM electrical connector from distributor electrical connector.
5. Remove distributor hold-down clamp and bolt. Mark position of distributor rotor to distributor housing and position of distributor housing to engine for use during installation.
6. Lift distributor upward until rotor stops rotating and mark position of rotor to distributor housing for use during installation.
7. Remove distributor from engine.

1 DISTRIBUTOR ASSEMBLY
3 BOLT/SCREW, DISTRIBUTOR
4 DRIVESHAFT, DISTRIBUTOR

Fig. 5   Distributor replacement. 1993—94 5.7L/V8-350 engines

Installation

1. Position rotor to mark on distributor housing, then insert distributor into engine aligning rotor to housing and housing to engine marks made during removal.
2. If engine was was disturbed while distributor was removed, proceed as follows:
   a. Remove spark plug from No. 1 cylinder.
   b. With transmission in Neutral or Park and parking brake applied, position finger over spark plug opening in cylinder head, then slowly crank engine until compression is felt.
   c. Align crankshaft pulley with TDC (0) mark on timing indicator.
   d. Locate distributor rotor contact between spark plug firing positions No. 1 and 6 on V6 engines, No. 1 and 8 on V8 engines, on distributor.
   e. Insert distributor into engine.
3. Install distributor hold clamp and bolt. Hand tighten bolt.
4. Connect ECM four terminal electrical connector to distributor.
5. Install distributor cap, then connect ignition switch and tachometer lead connector to cap.
6. Connect battery ground cable, then check and adjust ignition timing as necessary. **Torque** distributor hold-down bolt to 27 ft. lbs.

1993–94
Removal

1. Ensure ignition switch is in Off or Lock position, then remove water pump assembly as described under "Water Pump, Replace" in the "5.0L/V8-305 & 5.7L/V8-350 Engines" section.
2. Remove crankshaft balancer assembly as described under "Crankshaft Balancer Assembly & Hub, Replace" in the "5.0L/V8-305 & 5.7L/V8-350 Engines" section.
3. Disconnect spark plug wire assemblies and the four-terminal ECM connector from distributor assembly.
4. Remove distributor assembly bolts, then pull distributor assembly forward

1	GENERATOR	
2	BRACKET	
3	BOLT	
4	BRACE	
5	SCREW	
6	BELT TENSIONER	
7	STUD	
8	NUT	
9	STUD	
10	NUT	
11	NUT	
12	STUD	
13	BOLT	
14	REAR BRACKET	
15	BOLT	
16	NUT	
17	NUT	
18	SUPPORT	
19	BOLT	

Fig. 6   Alternator replacement. 3.1L/V6-191 engines

4	BRACKET ASSEMBLY	16	BOLT
5	GENERATOR	17	BOLT
9	BOLT	18	NUT
10	BRACE	19	STUD
11	BRACE	20	BOLT
12	NUT	21	BOLT
13	BOLT	22	SCREW
14	STUD	23	NEGATIVE BATTERY CABLE
15	NUT		

Fig. 7   Alternator replacement. 1991–92 5.0L/V8-305 & 5.7L/V8-350 engines

until driveshaft disengages from end of camshaft assembly, **Fig. 5.**
5. Mark top surface of driveshaft for alignment during installation.

Installation

1. Turn driveshaft until alignment mark made during removal is on top, then

1 BRACE, GENERATOR REAR INNER
2 NUT, GENERATOR BRACE, 25 N·m (18 LB. FT.)
5 GENERATOR ASSEMBLY
7 BRACKET, ACCESSORY MOUNTING
9 BOLT/SCREW, GENERATOR REAR BRACE,
  25 N·m (18 LB. FT.)
17 BOLT/SCREW, GENERATOR, 50 N·m (37 LB. FT.)
21 BOLT/SCREW, GENERATOR, 50 N·m (37 LB. FT.)
25 NUT, GENERATOR, 50 N·m (37 LB. FT.)

Fig. 8 Alternator replacement. 3.4L/V6-207 engines

5 GENERATOR ASSEMBLY
7 BRACKET, ACCESSORY MOUNTING
9 BOLT/SCREW, GENERATOR REAR BRACE,
  50 N·m (37 LB. FT.)
10 BRACE ASSEMBLY, GENERATOR REAR OUTER
12 NUT, GENERATOR REAR BRACE, 33 N·m (24 LB. FT.)
17 BOLT/SCREW, GENERATOR, 50 N·m (37 LB. FT.)
21 BOLT/SCREW, GENERATOR, 25 N·m (18 LB. FT.)

Fig. 9 Alternator replacement. 1993–94 5.7L/V8-350 engines

install distributor assembly.
2. Install and **torque** distributor bolts to 97 inch lbs.
3. Connect four-terminal ECM connector and spark plug wire assemblies to distributor assembly.
4. Install crankshaft balancer assembly as described under "Crankshaft Balancer Assembly & Hub, Replace" in the "5.0L/V8-305 & 5.7L/V8-350 Engines" section.
5. Install water pump assembly as described under "Water Pump, Replace" in the "5.0L/V8-305 & 5.7L/V8-350 Engines" section.

ALTERNATOR
REPLACE

Disconnect battery ground cable. Refer to **Figs. 6 through 9** for alternator replacement.

IGNITION LOCK
REPLACE

1. Disable airbag system as described under "Precautions."
2. Remove steering wheel as described under "Steering Wheel, Replace."
3. Remove turn signal switch as described under "Turn Signal Switch, Replace."
4. Remove buzzer switch retaining clip, then the buzzer switch.

18 LOCK RETAINING SCREW
20 VATS LOCK CYLINDER SET

Fig. 10 Ignition lock cylinder replacement

5. Place ignition switch in Lock position.
6. Remove lock cylinder retaining screw, **Fig. 10.**
7. Disconnect terminal electrical connector at bulkhead connection to provide slack.
8. Remove wiring connector from steering column.
9. Attach a suitable length of mechanic wire to ignition lock electrical connector for use during installation. Detach wire retaining clip, then carefully pull ignition lock wiring through housing shroud, steering column and lock

housing cover.
10. Remove lock cylinder.
11. Reverse procedure to install. Ensure lock cylinder wiring is properly routed through steering column. **Torque** lock cylinder retaining screw to 22 inch lbs.
12. Rearm airbag system as described under "Precautions."

IGNITION SWITCH
REPLACE

1991–92

The ignition switch is mounted on top of the mast jacket inside the brake pedal support and is actuated by a rod and rack assembly.
1. Disable airbag system as described under "Precautions."
2. Disconnect battery cable.
3. Remove steering column as described in "Steering Columns" section.
4. Rotate ignition lock to Off unlocked position.
5. If lock cylinder has been removed, pull switch actuator rod up to stop, then pushrod down to second detent to place switch in Off unlocked position, **Fig. 11.**
6. Remove column mounted dimmer switch, if equipped, then remove switch retaining screws and switch.

A MOVE SWITCH SLIDER TO EXTREME RIGHT
   POSITION AND THEN MOVE SLIDER ONE
   DETENT TO THE LEFT (OFF LOCK)

84 IGNITION SWITCH

Fig. 11 Ignition switch positioning

1   INSTRUMENT PANEL
23 CLUSTER TRIM PLATE
25 ELECTRICAL CONNECTOR
26 SWITCH
27 SWITCH KNOB
28 NUT

Fig. 12 Headlamp switch replacement. 1991–92 Camaro

7. Reverse procedure to install, noting the following:
   a. Place gear shift lever in neutral.
   b. Place lock cylinder and switch in Off unlocked position, **Fig. 6.**
   c. Fit actuator rod into hole in switch slider and secure switch with retaining screws, ensuring switch does not move out of detent.
   d. Install and adjust dimmer switch, if removed, as described in "Dimmer Switch, Replace."
8. Rearm airbag system as described under "Precautions."

1993–94
Removal

1. Disable airbag system as described under "Precautions," then disconnect battery ground cable.
2. Remove lefthand instrument panel sound insulator assembly, then the instrument panel driver knee bolster assembly and deflector.
3. Ensure steering column lock and ignition switch are in Lock position, then remove steering column upper support nuts and lower column assembly.

A CONNECTOR, INSTRUMENT PANEL WIRING HARNESS
   FOG LAMP ELECTRICAL
B CONNECTOR, INSTRUMENT PANEL WIRING HARNESS
   ELECTRICAL
C CONNECTOR, INSTRUMENT PANEL WIRING HARNESS
   DIMMER SWITCH ELECTRICAL
5 BEZEL ASSEMBLY, INSTRUMENT PANEL CLUSTER
   TRIM PLATE
75 CARRIER, INSTRUMENT PANEL
83 SWITCH ASSEMBLY, HEADLAMP AND INSTRUMENT
   PANEL LAMP DIMMER

Fig. 13 Headlamp switch replacement. 1993–94 Camaro

4. Disconnect electrical connectors from dimmer switch assembly and ignition switch, then remove dimmer switch actuator rod.
5. Remove dimmer switch assembly, then the ignition switch actuator rod.
6. Remove ignition switch, then disconnect automatic transmission park lock cable assembly, if equipped.

Installation

1. Connect automatic transmission park lock cable assembly, if equipped, then ensure ignition switch, steering column lock and ignition cylinder assembly are in LOCK position.
2. Install ignition switch to jacket, then connect ignition switch actuator rod to ignition switch.
3. **Torque** ignition switch mounting screws to 22 inch lbs.
4. Install dimmer switch assembly, then adjust by pressing switch mechanism slightly to insert a 3/32 inch drill bit and moving dimmer switch assembly to remove tool.
5. **Torque** dimmer switch mounting screws to 35 inch lbs.
6. Install dimmer switch actuator rod, then connect electrical connectors to dimmer switch assembly and ignition switch.
7. Raise column assembly and install upper support nuts.
8. Install instrument panel driver knee bolster assembly and deflector, then the lefthand instrument panel sound insulator assembly.
9. Rearm airbag system as described under "Precautions."

LIGHT SWITCH
REPLACE
CAMARO
1991–92

1. Disable airbag system as described under "Precautions."
2. Disconnect battery ground cable.
3. Open screw covers, then remove knee bolster attaching screws and knee bolster.
4. From under instrument panel, depress release button on light switch, then remove switch knob and shaft assembly from switch, **Fig. 12.**
5. Remove instrument cluster trim plate,

---

1 BOLT/SCREW
2 HEADLAMP/PARKING
   LAMP SWITCH

Fig. 14 Headlamp switch replacement. 1991–92 Firebird

then remove switch retaining nut.
6. Lower switch and disconnect electrical connector, then remove switch.
7. Reverse procedure to install.
8. Rearm airbag system as described under "Precautions."

1993–94

1. Remove switch assembly from bezel assembly, **Fig. 13.**
2. Disconnect electrical connector from switch assembly.
3. Reverse procedure to install.

FIREBIRD
1991–92

1. Disable airbag system as described under "Precautions."
2. Disconnect battery ground cable.
3. Remove left and right hand lower instrument panel trim covers.
4. Remove instrument cluster trim plate.
5. Remove switch attaching screws, then depress switch side tangs and pull switch from instrument panel, **Fig. 14.**
6. Disconnect electrical connector and remove switch.
7. Reverse procedure to install.
8. Rearm airbag system as described under "Precautions."

1993–94

1. Remove switch assembly from carrier, **Fig. 15.**
2. Disconnect electrical connector from switch assembly.
3. Reverse procedure to install.

A CONNECTOR, INSTRUMENT PANEL WIRING HARNESS ELECTRICAL
B CONNECTOR, INSTRUMENT PANEL WIRING HARNESS ELECTRICAL
75 CARRIER, INSTRUMENT PANEL
83 SWITCH ASSEMBLY, HEADLAMP AND INSTRUMENT PANEL LAMP DIMMER

Fig. 15 Headlamp switch replacement. 1993-94 Firebird

A MANUAL TRANSMISSION
B AUTOMATIC TRANSMISSION
C CONNECTOR, ELECTRICAL
D CONNECTOR, ELECTRICAL
E CONNECTOR, ELECTRICAL
F CONNECTOR, ELECTRICAL
G CONNECTOR, ELECTRICAL
H WITH 3.4L L32 ENGINE
J WITH 5.7L LT1 ENGINE
5 PEDAL ASSEMBLY, BRAKE AND ACCELERATOR AND CLUTCH (WITH BRACKET)
6 PEDAL ASSEMBLY, BRAKE AND ACCELERATOR (WITH BRACKET)
25 SWITCH ASSEMBLY, CRUISE CONTROL CLUTCH
26 SWITCH ASSEMBLY, STOPLAMP AND TORQUE CONVERTER CLUTCH
27 SWITCH ASSEMBLY, CRUISE CONTROL RELEASE
28 SWITCH ASSEMBLY, CRUISE CONTROL CLUTCH ANTICIPATE
29 SWITCH ASSEMBLY, CLUTCH START

Fig. 17 Stop lamp switch replacement. 1993-94

1 BRAKE PEDAL
2 SWITCH – WITHOUT CRUISE CONTROL
3 SWITCH – WITH CRUISE CONTROL
4 CLIP

Fig. 16 Stop lamp switch replacement. 1991-92

STOP LIGHT SWITCH
REPLACE

1991-92

1. Disable airbag system as described under "Precautions."
2. Remove left hand side hush panel.
3. Working from underneath instrument panel, disconnect wire connector from switch at brake pedal support.
4. Remove switch from mounting bracket, Fig. 16.
5. Depress brake pedal and install new switch into clip, until switch body bottoms out against clip.
6. Release brake pedal, then pull pedal rearward against internal stop. The switch is properly positioned when no clicks are noticed when brake pedal is against internal stop. Ensure brake lamps remain Off when brake pedal is in the released position, if readjust switch.
7. Rearm airbag system as described under "Precautions."

1993-94

1. Remove lefthand instrument panel sound insulator assembly, then disconnect electrical connectors, Fig. 17.
2. Remove release switch assembly, stoplamp and TCC switch assembly and clutch switch assembly, or clutch anticipate switch assembly, if equipped, from pedal assembly with bracket.
3. Install release switch assembly, stoplamp and TCC switch assembly and clutch switch assembly, or clutch anticipate switch assembly, if equipped, to pedal assembly with bracket.
4. Connect electrical connectors, then adjust switches as follows:
   a. Depress brake pedal assembly or clutch pedal assembly and insert release switch assembly, stoplamp and TCC switch assembly and clutch switch assembly, or clutch anticipate switch assembly into pedal assembly with bracket until retainer is fully seated.
   b. Slowly pull brake or clutch pedal assembly rearward with a force of 50 lbs. until click sounds can no longer be heard.
   c. Measure release switch assembly and stoplamp and TCC switch assembly contacts, should be open 1 inch or less of pedal assembly travel, and should occur at the same time or before onset of braking.
5. Install lefthand instrument panel sound insulator assembly.

CLUTCH START SWITCH
REPLACE

1991-92

1. Disable airbag system as described under "Precautions."

817 SWITCH
818 CARRIER TANG
819 BOLTS
820 GAGE PIN
821 SHIFT CONTROL LEVER
822 NEUTRAL NOTCH
823 PARK NOTCH
824 TANG SLOT
825 DETENT PLATE

Fig. 18 Neutral safety switch replacement

2. Disconnect battery ground cable.
3. Disconnect wire connector at switch.
4. Remove retaining nut, if so equipped and unscrew switch from bracket.
5. To install, depress clutch pedal, then insert and push switch into clip until shoulder bottoms out.
6. Plug connector on switch and check for proper operation.
7. Rearm airbag system as described under "Precautions."

1993-94

Refer to "Stop Light Switch, Replace."

NEUTRAL SAFETY SWITCH
REPLACE

1. Disconnect batter ground cable.

2 RETAINING RING
3 COIL ASSEMBLY
4 WAVE WASHER

Fig. 19 Coil assembly removal

J-23653

Fig. 20 Lock plate retaining ring removal

A 6 O'CLOCK POSITION: HARNESS THROUGH HERE
3 COIL ASSEMBLY
12 TURN SIGNAL AND HAZARD WARNING SWITCH
26 WIRING PROTECTOR

Fig. 21 Turn signal switch removal

STYLE A
LOCKING TAB
SPRING
COIL HUB
HUB DIRECTION

STYLE B
COIL HOUSING
LOCKING TAB
SPRING
COIL HUB
HUB DIRECTION

Perform the following steps to center coil assembly:

A. Remove coil assembly.
B. Hold coil assembly with clear bottom up to see coil ribbon.
C. NOTE: There are two different styles of coils. One rotates clockwise and the other rotates counterclockwise.
D. While holding coil assembly, depress spring lock to rotate hub in direction of arrow until it stops.
E. The coil ribbon should be wound up snug against center hub.
F. Rotate coil hub in opposite direction approximately two and a half (2-1/2) turns. Release spring lock between locking tabs in front of arrow.

Fig. 22 Centering coil assembly

2. Remove floor console, then disconnect electrical connectors from switch.
3. Place shift lever in Neutral position of detent plate, then remove switch attaching screws and switch, **Fig. 18**.
4. To install, ensure the shift lever is in Neutral, then position switch on shift lever making sure pin on shaft is in slot of switch.
5. If reinstalling existing switch, rotate switch to align service adjustment hole with carrier tang hole. Insert a 3/32 inch gauge pin and rotate switch until pin drops in to a depth of 19/32 inch. **Torque** switch attaching nut to 18 inch lbs., then remove gauge pin.
6. If installing a new switch, **torque** attaching nuts to 18 inch lbs., then move

shift lever out of Neutral to shear pin which is part of new switch.
7. Reconnect electrical connectors to switch, then apply parking brake and start engine. Check back-up lights and seat belt warning system for proper operation and ensure engine will start only in Park or Neutral.
8. Turn ignition off and install floor console.

TURN SIGNAL SWITCH REPLACE

1. Disable airbag system as described under "Precautions."
2. Remove steering wheel as described under "Steering Wheel, Replace."
3. Place ignition switch in Lock position to retain coil assembly in the centered position.
4. Disconnect battery ground cable.
5. Remove coil assembly retaining ring, **Fig. 19**.
6. Lift coil assembly from from steering shaft and allow to hang from wire, then remove wave washer.
7. Using a suitable tool, compress lock plate and remove snap ring (C-ring on tilt models), **Fig. 20**.
8. Remove lock plate, turn signal canceling cam and upper bearing spring, inner race seat and inner race.
9. Place turn signal lever in right hand turn position, then remove multi-function lever and hazard warning flasher knob.
10. Remove turn signal switch lever attaching screw, then remove lever.
11. Remove turn signal switch attaching screws.
12. Disconnect turn signal switch electrical connector at lower portion of steering column.
13. Remove turn signal switch wiring protector cover from steering column, **Fig. 21**.
14. Carefully pull turn signal switch wiring up and out of steering column.
15. Reverse procedure to install. If coil assembly has become uncentered, refer to **Fig. 22** for centering procedure.
16. Rearm airbag system as described under "Precautions."

86
A

A 3/32 INCH DRILL BIT
86 DIMMER SWITCH

Fig. 23 Column mounted dimmer switch installation

DIMMER SWITCH REPLACE

1991-92

1. Disable airbag system as described under "Precautions."
2. Disconnect battery ground cable.
3. Remove instrument panel lower trim.
4. **On models with A/C,** remove A/C duct extension at column.
5. **On all models,** remove steering column as described in "Steering Columns" section.
6. Remove dimmer switch retaining screw(s) and the switch. Tape actuator rod to column and separate switch from rod.
7. Reverse procedure to install. To adjust switch, depress dimmer switch slightly and install a 3/32 inch twist drill to lock the switch to the body, **Fig. 23**. Force switch upward to remove lash. **Torque** retaining screws to 35 inch lbs. and remove tape from actuator rod. Remove twist drill and check for proper operation.
8. Rearm airbag system as described under "Precautions."

1993-94

Refer to "Ignition Switch, Replace."

1	INSTRUMENT PANEL
36	INSTRUMENT PANEL CLUSTER
37	SCREW

Fig. 24   Instrument cluster. 1991–92 Camaro

STEERING WHEEL
REPLACE

1991–92
Removal

1. With steering wheel in straight ahead position, place ignition switch in Lock position.
2. Remove Airbag (SIR) fuse from fuse panel.
3. Remove lower left hand trim panel, then remove connector position assurance and disconnect yellow two way Supplemental Inflatable Restraint connector at base of steering column.
4. Disconnect battery ground cable and tape cable end.
5. Remove inflator module attaching screws from rear of steering wheel.
6. Lift inflator module from steering wheel, then disconnect electrical connectors from inflator module.
7. Remove steering wheel retaining nut.
8. Using puller J-1859-03 or equivalent, pull steering wheel from steering shaft.
9. Disconnect horn electrical connect and remove steering wheel.

Installation

1. Connect horn electrical connector.
2. Align block tooth on steering wheel with block tooth on steering shaft, then install steering wheel.
3. Install steering wheel retaining nut and **torque** to 30 ft. lbs.
4. Connect SIR coil electrical connector to inflator module, then install connector position assurance.
5. Position inflator module to steering wheel, then install new mounting screws. **Torque** mounting screws to 25 inch lbs.
6. Ensure ignition switch is in Lock position.
7. Connect yellow SIR two way electrical

connector and install connector position assurance at base of steering column.
8. Install lower left hand trim panel.
9. Install Airbag (SIR) fuse into fuse panel.
10. Connect battery ground cable.
11. Place ignition switch in Run position and note operation of inflatable Restraint warning lamp. Warning lamp should flash 7 to 9 times and then turn off. If not, refer to "Passive Restraint" section for diagnostic system check.

1993–94
Removal

When removing steering wheel, use only specified puller. Do not hammer on end of steering column shaft. Hammering on shaft may damage plastic injections, affecting column assembly rigidity.

When attaching specified puller to steering wheel, use caution to prevent threading bolts through steering wheel hub into SIR coil assembly, damaging coil assembly.

1. Disable airbag system as described under "Precautions," then disconnect battery ground cable.
2. Remove screws from back of steering wheel assembly using a No. 30 TORX driver, then the inflatable restraint steering wheel module assembly from steering wheel assembly.
3. Disconnect SIR coil assembly electrical connector and retainer from inflatable restraint steering wheel module assembly.
4. **On Firebird models,** disconnect radio control switch electrical connector from inflatable restraint steering wheel module assembly, if equipped.
5. **On all models,** disconnect horn lead from column assembly.
6. Remove steering wheel using steering wheel puller J 1859-A and steering wheel puller bolts J 38720.

Installation

1. Route SIR coil assembly electrical connector to steering wheel, then install steering wheel, aligning block tooth on steering wheel with block tooth on steering column shaft within one female serration.
2. Install nut and **torque** to 32 ft. lbs.
3. Connect horn lead to column assembly.
4. **On Firebird models,** connect radio control switch electrical connector from inflatable restraint steering wheel module assembly, if equipped.
5. **On all models,** connect SIR coil assembly electrical connector and retainer to inflatable restraint steering wheel module assembly.
6. Secure SIR coil assembly electrical connector to steering wheel by inserting thick section of wire into existing retainers.
7. Position inflatable restraint steering wheel module assembly to steering wheel, ensuring wiring is not exposed or trapped between module assembly and steering wheel.
8. Install inflatable restraint steering wheel module assembly screws and **torque** to 25 inch lbs.
9. Rearm airbag system as described under "Precautions."

INSTRUMENT CLUSTER
REPLACE

1991–92 CAMARO

1. Disable airbag system as described under "Precautions."
2. Disconnect battery ground cable.
3. Remove instrument cluster trim panel.
4. Remove cluster retaining screws, then pull cluster back and disconnect speedometer cable and electrical connectors, as equipped, **Fig. 24.**
5. Reverse procedure to install.
6. Rearm airbag system as described under "Precautions."

1991–92 FIREBIRD

1. Disable airbag system as described under "Precautions."
2. Disconnect battery ground cable, then remove knee bolster.
3. Remove instrument cluster trim plate.
4. Remove cluster attachment screws, **Fig. 25,** pull cluster back and disconnect necessary electrical connections.
5. Remove trip odometer reset knob, if equipped, then cluster lens.
6. Reverse procedure to install.
7. Rearm airbag system as described under "Precautions."

1993–94

1. Disable airbag system as described under "Precautions," then disconnect battery ground cable.
2. Disconnect instrument panel upper trim panel assembly from lower windshield support, then remove from carrier.

1—INSTRUMENT CLUSTER

2—SCREW

Fig. 25 Instrument cluster. 1991–92 Firebird

A CONNECTOR, INSTRUMENT CLUSTER WIRING HARNESS ELECTRICAL
75 CARRIER, INSTRUMENT PANEL
78 CLUSTER ASSEMBLY, INSTRUMENT
79 BOLT/SCREW, INSTRUMENT CLUSTER, 2.2 N•m (20 LB. IN.)

Fig. 26 Instrument cluster. 1993–94 Camaro

75 CARRIER, INSTRUMENT PANEL
78 CLUSTER ASSEMBLY, INSTRUMENT
79 BOLT/SCREW, INSTRUMENT CLUSTER, 2.2 N•m (20 LB. IN.)

Fig. 27 Instrument cluster. 1993–94 Firebird

A CRANK ARM DRIVE PIN IN CAM POCKET
12 SCREW (3), 10 N•m (7.5 LB. FT.)
13 LINKAGE ASSEMBLY, RH
14 SCREW, 10 N•m (7.5 LB. FT.)
15 LINKAGE ASSEMBLY, LH
16 BRACKET, WIPER MOTOR
17 MOTOR ASSEMBLY, WIPER
18 PAD, LOCATOR (2)
19 SCREW, 10 N•m (7.5 LB. FT.)
20 NUT, 10 N•m (7.5 LB. FT.)

Fig. 28 Windshield wiper motor/transmission assembly. 1993–94

3. Remove instrument cluster assembly carrier, **Fig. 26 and 27**, then disconnect electrical connector from cluster assembly.
4. Reverse procedure to install.
5. Rearm airbag system as described under "Precautions."

WIPER MOTOR
REPLACE

1991–92

1. Raise hood, then remove wiper arms and cowl cover.
2. Disconnect wiring and washer hoses.
3. Reaching through cowl opening, loosen transmission drive link attaching nuts to motor crankarm.
4. Disconnect drive link from motor crankarm.
5. Remove motor attaching screws.
6. Remove motor while guiding crankarm through hole.
7. Reverse procedure to install.

1993–94
Removal

1. Remove wiper arm and blade assemblies as follows:
   a. Operate wipers at lowest delay setting, then shut Off wipers at inner wipe (end of sweep) position.
   b. Mark windshield at tip of blade assembly to aid installation, then lift wiper arm nut cover and remove nut.
   c. Remove wiper arm from linkage drive shaft using wiper arm puller J 39637.
2. Disconnect battery ground cable, then remove lefthand cowl panel and hood seal.
3. Disconnect washer hose assembly from lefthand cowl panel, then the electrical connector from wiper motor assembly.
4. Remove screw and nut from lefthand linkage assembly, **Fig. 28,** then disconnect socket of righthand linkage assembly from ball of lefthand linkage assembly using wiper linkage separator J39232.
5. Remove lefthand linkage assembly, then the screw from wiper motor assembly.
6. Pull wiper motor assembly free from slots of bracket, then disconnect socket of righthand linkage assembly from crank arm ball of wiper motor assembly using wiper linkage separator.

Installation

When installing wiper motor assembly, ensure that crank arm is in inner wipe position. Crank arm drive pin must be engaged in cam pocket.
1. Press socket of righthand linkage assembly into engagement with crank arm ball of wiper motor assembly using wiper linkage installer J 39529.
2. Install wiper motor assembly with two locator pads pressed fully into slots of bracket, then the mounting screw and **torque** to 7.5 ft. lbs.
3. Install lefthand linkage assembly without attaching parts, then press socket of righthand linkage assembly into engagement with ball of lefthand linkage assembly using wiper linkage installer.
4. Attach lefthand linkage assembly with screw and nut and **torque** to 7.5 ft. lbs.
5. Connect electrical connector to wiper motor assembly, then the washer hose assembly to lefthand cowl panel and washer nozzle.
6. Install lefthand cowl panel and hood seal, then connect battery ground cable.
7. Install wiper arm and blade assemblies as follows:
   a. Install wiper arm and blade assembly onto linkage drive shaft, with tip of blade assembly aligned with mark made at removal.
   b. Install nut on linkage drive shaft and **torque** to 24 ft. lbs. while holding wiper arm.
   c. Close nut cover, then run wipers and check for proper wipe pattern. Shut Off wipers and check for correct park position.

WIPER TRANSMISSION
REPLACE
1991–92

1. Ensure motor is in park position.
2. Raise hood and remove wiper arm assemblies.
3. Remove cowl vent screen.
4. Loosen nuts securing pivot at motor crankarm, then disconnect transmission rod from crankarm.
5. Remove retaining nuts or screws securing transmission to body, then withdraw transmission assembly through cowl opening.
6. Reverse procedure to install.

1993–94
Removal

1. Remove wiper arm and blade assemblies as follows:
   a. Operate wipers at lowest delay setting, then shut Off wipers at inner wipe (end of sweep) position.
   b. Mark windshield at tip of blade assembly to aid installation, then lift wiper arm nut cover and remove nut.
   c. Remove wiper arm from linkage drive shaft using wiper arm puller J 39637.
2. Remove lefthand cowl panel and hood seal, then disconnect washer hose assembly from lefthand cowl panel.
3. Remove screw and nut from lefthand linkage assembly, **Fig. 28**, then disconnect socket of righthand linkage assembly from ball of lefthand linkage assembly using wiper linkage separator J39232.
4. Remove lefthand linkage assembly, then the screws securing righthand linkage assembly.
5. Disconnect socket of righthand linkage assembly from crank arm ball of wiper motor assembly using wiper linkage separator, then remove righthand linkage assembly from slotted plenum access hole.

Installation

1. Install righthand linkage assembly from slotted plenum access hole, then the screws securing righthand linkage assembly finger tight.
2. Align righthand linkage assembly, then press socket of righthand linkage assembly into engagement with crank arm ball of wiper motor assembly using wiper linkage installer J 39529.
3. Install lefthand linkage assembly without attaching parts, then press socket of righthand linkage assembly into engagement with ball of lefthand linkage assembly using wiper linkage installer.
4. Attach lefthand linkage assembly with screw and nut and **torque** to 7.5 ft. lbs.
5. Connect washer hose assembly to lefthand cowl panel and washer nozzle.
6. Install lefthand cowl panel and hood

seal, then connect battery ground cable.
7. Install wiper arm and blade assemblies as follows:
   a. Install wiper arm and blade assembly onto linkage drive shaft, with tip of blade assembly aligned with mark made at removal.
   b. Install nut on linkage drive shaft and **torque** to 24 ft. lbs. while holding wiper arm.
   c. Close nut cover, then run wipers and check for proper wipe pattern. Shut Off wipers and check for correct park position.

WINDSHIELD WIPER SWITCH
REPLACE
1991–92

1. Disable airbag system as described under "Precautions."
2. Disconnect battery ground cable.
3. Remove ignition lock cylinder as described under "Ignition Lock, Replace."
4. Remove housing cover end cap.
5. **On models with cruise control,** unplug connector from housing cover end base plate, then remove multi-function lever.
6. **On all models,** remove lock housing cover screws.
7. Remove housing cover end base plate and dimmer switch rod actuator from lock housing cover, then pull wiper switch wire harness through steering column.
8. Remove wiper switch pivot pin, then the wiper/pivot switch.
9. Reverse procedure to install.
10. Rearm airbag system as described under "Precautions."

1993–94

1. **On models with cruise control,** remove tilt wheel release lever and access cover, then disconnect electrical connectors.
2. **On all models,** remove wiper switch by grasping firmly and pulling straight out.
3. Reverse procedure to install, noting the following:
   a. Ensure wiper switch is in Off position before installing.
   b. Position tilt lever ±5° from centerline of column assembly.

RADIO
REPLACE

When installing radio, be sure to adjust antenna trimmer for peak reception. Also, be sure to connect speaker before applying power to radio.
1. Disable airbag system as described under "Precautions."
2. Disconnect battery ground cable.
3. Remove accessory trim plate, then radio to console attaching screws.

4. Pull radio outward and disconnect electrical connector, then remove radio.
5. Reverse procedure to install.
6. Rearm airbag system as described under "Precautions."

BLOWER MOTOR
REPLACE
1991–92

1. Disconnect battery ground cable.
2. Remove fender brace at rear right hand corner of engine compartment, if necessary.
3. Disconnect blower motor and resistor wires.
4. Disconnect cooling tube, if equipped.
5. Remove blower motor retaining screws and motor/cage assembly from case.
6. While holding blower motor cage, remove cage retaining screw and slide cage from motor shaft.
7. Reverse procedure to install.

1993–94

1. Ensure ignition switch is in Off position, then remove righthand instrument panel sound insulator assembly and side trim panel.
2. Remove blower motor mounting bolts, then the blower motor.
3. reverse procedure to install. **Torque** mounting bolts to 20 inch lbs.

HEATER CORE
REPLACE
1991–92

1. Disable airbag system as described under "Precautions."
2. Disconnect battery ground cable and drain cooling system.
3. Disconnect heater hoses from heater core tubes.
4. Remove instrument panel and center console.
5. Remove heater case, **Fig. 29**.
6. Remove heater core shroud screws, then separate heater case assembly.
7. Remove core mounting strap, then the core.
8. Reverse procedure to install.
9. Rearm airbag system as described under "Precautions."

1993–94

1. Open instrument panel compartment by pushing in on sides of compartment to release it.
2. Drain coolant.
3. Remove heater module bolts, then the heater module assembly cover, **Fig. 30**.
4. Remove heater core bolt and heater core clamp, then the hose pipe clamp bolt and hose pipe clamp.
5. Disconnect hose heater hose assem-

8	HEATER	73	CLAMP
9	MODULE	74	STRAP
37	SEAL	75	SEAL
41	SCREW	76	SHROUD
42	SCREW	77	REAR CASE

Fig. 29   Heater core replacement. 1991–92

A   SEALS
1   MODULE ASSEMBLY, HEATER
14   CORE, HEATER
41   BOLT/SCREW, HEATER MODULE
42   BOLT/SCREW, HEATER CORE
43   CLAMP, HEATER CORE
44   CLAMP, HEATER HOSE PIPE
45   BOLT/SCREW, HEATER HOSE PIPE

Fig. 30   Heater core replacement. 1993–94

7	EVAPORATOR
90	SCREW
91	CASE
92	SEAL
93	SEAL

Fig. 31   Evaporator core replacement. 1991–92

bly from heater hose pipes, then carefully pull heater core toward you to remove.
6. Reverse procedure to install, noting the following:
   a. Ensure seals around heater pipes stay in place when installing core.
   b. **Torque** hose pipe clamp bolt and heater core bolt to 16 inch lbs. and heater module bolts to 18 inch lbs.
   c. Operate engine and check for coolant leaks, then check coolant level, adding coolant as necessary.

EVAPORATOR CORE
REPLACE

1991–92

1. Disable airbag system as described under "Precautions."
2. Disconnect battery ground cable.
3. Discharge A/C refrigerant system, then remove the accumulator.
4. Remove blower motor resistor assembly.
5. Remove blower motor relay and bracket.

6. Remove upper evaporator case attaching screws, then remove upper evaporator case and seal, **Fig. 31.**
7. Disconnect refrigerant line from lower fitting of evaporator. Cap refrigerant line and evaporator fitting.
8. Remove evaporator and seal.
9. Reverse procedure to install.
10. Rearm airbag system as described under "Precautions."

1993–94

1. Discharge refrigerant into a recovery station, then drain coolant.
2. Remove righthand instrument panel sound insulator panel assembly, then disconnect heater hoses at heater core assembly.
3. Remove instrument panel compartment, then the heater core as previously described.
4. Remove evaporator temperature sensor assembly, **Fig. 32,** then disconnect temperature control cable assembly at temperature valve case assembly.
5. Remove bolts from temperature valve

case assembly, then the temperature valve case assembly by sliding case assembly downward to disengage upper case clip.
6. Remove thermostatic expansion valve assembly.
7. Using a small hand saw, remove perforated section of evaporator module assembly as one piece and retain for reuse.
8. Remove bolts retaining evaporator, then the evaporator from module assembly by sliding evaporator to left and pulling out through opening cut in module.
9. Reverse procedure to install, noting the following:
   a. If replacing evaporator, transfer condensate screen to new evaporator.
   b. If replacing evaporator, add 3 fluid ounces of polyalkylene glycol (PAG) synthetic refrigerant oil to new evaporator.
   c. Apply sealer 3012078 between evaporator upper and lower case just behind thermostatic expansion valve assembly to prevent air entry from engine compartment.
   d. Use epoxy glue to adhere perforated section of module assembly to module assembly.
   e. Fill radiator and bleed cooling system.
   f. Partially charge system and perform a leak test, then recover refrigerant and evacuate and charge system.

3 EVAPORATOR, AIR CONDITIONING
4 CORE ASSEMBLY, HEATER
25 SENSOR ASSEMBLY, AIR CONDITIONING
   EVAPORATOR TEMPERATURE
41 BOLT/SCREW, AIR CONDITIONING EVAPORATOR
42 CASE ASSEMBLY, TEMPERATURE VALVE
43 CLAMP, HEATER CORE TUBE
44 CASE, AIR CONDITIONING EVAPORATOR UPPER
45 CASE, AIR CONDITIONING EVAPORATOR LOWER
46 CASE, AIR DISTRIBUTOR UPPER
47 COVER, HEATER AND AIR CONDITIONING
   EVAPORATOR CASE
48 BOLT/SCREW, TEMPERATURE VALVE CASE ASSEMBLY
49 BOLT/SCREW, HEATER AND AIR CONDITIONING
   EVAPORATOR CASE COVER
59 BOLT/SCREW, HEATER CORE TUBE CLAMP
65 CLAMP, AIR CONDITIONING EVAPORATOR

**Fig. 32 Evaporator core replacement.
1993–94**

3.1L/V6-191 & 3.4L/V6-207 Engines

INDEX

PRECAUTIONS

AIRBAG SYSTEM DISARMING

The diagnostic energy reserve module (DERM) can maintain voltage to cause a system deployment for up to ten minutes after the ignition switch is turned off and the battery is disconnected. Servicing the SIR system during this period may result in accidental deployment and personal injury.

1. Ensure front wheels are pointed straight ahead.
2. Turn ignition switch to Lock position and remove SIR or AIRBAG fuse.
3. Remove left sound insulator. **Remove courtesy lamp from sound insulator, if necessary.**
4. Remove Connector Position Assurance (CPA), then disconnect yellow two-way SIR electrical connector at base of steering column.

AIRBAG SYSTEM ARMING

1. Connect yellow two-way SIR electrical connector, then install Connector Position Assurance (CPA).
2. Install left sound insulator. **Install courtesy lamp to sound insulator, if applicable.**
3. Install SIR fuse to fuse block, turn ignition switch to Run position and ensure

that "Inflatable Restraint" lamp flashes 7 to 9 times, then shuts off.

FUEL SYSTEM PRESSURE RELIEF

Failure to relieve system pressure prior to disconnecting fuel system components may cause fire or personal injury. Remove fuel tank filler cap to release fuel tank pressure. Connect pressure gauge J-34730-1 or equivalent to pressure tap on fuel rail, position bleed hose into suitable container and slowly relieve fuel system pressure. Prior to disconnecting fuel line, position shop towel over fitting.

ENGINE MOUNTS
REPLACE

FRONT MOUNT

3.1L/V6-191 Engines

1. Disconnect battery ground cable.
2. Remove upper half of fan shroud, if necessary.
3. Raise and support vehicle.
4. Remove engine mount through bolt, then raise front of engine to release weight from mount.
5. Remove mount to engine bolts and mount, **Fig. 1. Raise engine only**

enough to provide sufficient clearance for mount removal. Check for interference between rear of engine and cowl panel which could result in distributor damage.
6. Reverse procedure to install.

3.4L/V6-207 Engines

1. Raise and support vehicle, then disconnect exhaust crossover pipe.
2. Remove engine mount through bolt and nut, then raise engine with a jack.
3. Remove engine mount, then the engine bracket, if necessary.
4. Reverse procedure to install. Tighten fasteners to specifications.

REAR MOUNT

3.1L/V6-191 Engines

1. Disconnect battery ground cable.
2. Raise and support vehicle, then remove crossmember to transmission mount nuts and washers.
3. **On models with automatic transmission,** raise transmission slightly for clearance, then remove crossmember to transmission support nuts, bolts and insulators and transmission support.
4. **On all models,** remove transmission mount attaching bolts, then remove mount, **Fig. 1.**
5. Reverse procedure to install.

Fig. 1 Engine mounting. 3.1L/V6-191 engines

3.4L/V6-207 Engines

Refer to "Front Mount" for procedures.

ENGINE
REPLACE

3.1L/V6-191 ENGINES

1. Disable airbag system as described under "Precautions."
2. Disconnect battery ground cable, then remove air cleaner duct.
3. Scribe alignment marks on hood and hood hinge, then remove hood.
4. Remove serpentine drive belt.
5. Remove A/C compressor from bracket and position out of way with refrigerant hoses attached.
6. Drain cooling system, then disconnect upper and lower radiator hoses, coolant recovery hose and heater hose at water pump and valve.
7. Disconnect throttle linkage and cruise control cable, if equipped.
8. Disconnect vacuum hose from power brake unit.
9. Remove distributor cap and position aside with wiring attached.
10. Remove power steering pump from bracket and position out of way with hoses attached.
11. Disconnect and tag all electrical wiring and hoses that may interfere with engine removal.
12. Raise and support vehicle, then detach transmission oil cooler lines at oil pan clips, if equipped.
13. Disconnect exhaust crossover pipe at exhaust manifolds.
14. **On models with automatic transmission,** remove converter housing cover, then remove torque converter to driveplate attaching bolts.
15. **On all models,** disconnect wiring from starter motor.
16. **On models with manual transmission,** remove bellhousing to engine bolts.

17. **On all models,** remove engine mount through bolts, then lower vehicle.
18. Relieve fuel system pressure as described under "Precautions," then disconnect fuel lines.
19. Support transmission using a transmission jack or other suitable support.
20. Attach a suitable engine lifting device to engine, then remove engine from vehicle. When removing engine, detach wire from bracket at left hand rear of engine.
21. Reverse procedure to install.
22. Rearm airbag system as described under "Precautions."

3.4L/V6-207 ENGINES

1. Disable airbag system and relieve fuel system pressure as described under "Precautions," then disconnect battery ground cable.
2. Raise and support vehicle, then remove wheels.
3. Drain coolant, then disconnect exhaust crossover pipe assembly from intermediate pipe.
4. **On vehicles with automatic transmission,** remove converter cover bolts and converter bolts.
5. **On all vehicles,** remove front fascia lower deflectors, stabilizer bar bolts and the serpentine drive belt.
6. **On vehicles with automatic transmission,** disconnect transmission cooler lines from radiator.
7. **On all vehicles,** disconnect lower radiator hose from radiator and heater hoses from pipes at engine, then the electrical ground straps from right side of engine block and electrical connections from starter motor.
8. Disconnect electrical connectors from knock sensor, oxygen sensor, coolant temperature sensor, camshaft sensor, crankshaft sensor and wheel speed sensor.
9. Disconnect electrical connectors from engine oil level switch and fuel pump switch/engine oil pressure gauge sensor assemblies.

10. Disconnect right front brake line from caliper brake hose, then the wiring harness from transmission.
11. Disconnect shift linkage from transmission, then the propeller shaft from transmission. **Scribe alignment marks on propeller shaft before disconnecting.**
12. Disconnect torque arm from transmission, then the intermediate steering shaft from rack and pinion assembly.
13. Disconnect electrical ground straps from left side of frame rail, then lower vehicle.
14. Remove air intake duct, then the fuel pipe assembly.
15. Disconnect cruise and accelerator control cables from throttle body, then he upper radiator hose from intake manifold and lower radiator hose from front cover.
16. Disconnect radiator fan electrical connections, then remove radiator fan assembly.
17. Disconnect brake booster vacuum hose, then the Y brace from right exhaust manifold.
18. Remove alternator and A/C compressor bracket and reposition, then disconnect engine wiring harness connectors and reposition.
19. Remove brake master cylinder and reposition, then the upper bolts and nuts from strut assemblies.
20. Disconnect right front brake line from modulator valve assembly and clips, then raise and support vehicle.
21. Place a lift table under engine and engine frame assembly, then remove engine frame and transmission support bolts.
22. Raise vehicle from engine, transmission and engine frame assemblies, then secure strut assemblies to engine frame.
23. Disconnect transmission TV cable from throttle body, then remove transmission assembly.
24. **On vehicles with manual transmission,** remove clutch housing and clutch assembly.
25. **On all vehicles,** disconnect power steering lines from power steering pump.
26. Remove engine mount through bolts, then the engine assembly from engine frame.
27. Reverse procedure to install, noting the following:
    a. Tighten fasteners to specifications.
    b. Bleed brake and power steering systems.
    c. Align wheels.
    d. Rearm airbag system as described under "Precautions."

INTAKE MANIFOLD
REPLACE

3.1L/V6-191 ENGINES

1. Disconnect battery ground cable, remove air cleaner and drain cooling system.
2. Relieve fuel system pressure as described under "Precautions."

1	PLENUM TO MANIFOLD BOLT	4	INTAKE MANIFOLD
2	INTAKE PLENUM	5	FUEL RAIL ASSEMBLY
3	GASKET	6	FUEL RAIL ATTACHING BOLT

Fig. 2 Fuel rail & plenum replacement. 3.1L/V6-191 engines

3. Disconnect air inlet duct, electrical connectors, coolant hoses and vacuum hoses from throttle body, noting position for installation.
4. Disconnect accelerator, cruise control and transmission cables, as equipped.
5. Remove throttle body retaining bolts and the throttle body.
6. Remove EGR pipe retaining bolts and throttle cable bracket.
7. Remove bolts securing plenum to manifold and the plenum, **Fig. 2.**
8. Disconnect fuel lines from fuel rail and remove cold start valve.
9. Disconnect vacuum hose from pressure regulator and remove fuel rail retaining bolts.
10. Disconnect injector harness connectors and remove fuel rail assembly, **Fig. 2.**
11. Disconnect high tension leads from spark plugs and disconnect wiring from coil.
12. Remove distributor cap and plug wire assembly.
13. Rotate crankshaft until No. 1 cylinder is at TDC on compression stroke, mark position of distributor rotor and remove distributor.
14. Remove air injection hose, if equipped, disconnect canister hoses and remove pipe bracket from front of left valve cover.
15. Remove left valve cover and air management bracket, then remove right valve cover.
16. Disconnect upper radiator and heater hoses from manifold.
17. Disconnect coolant switches and remove manifold retaining bolts.
18. Remove manifold and thoroughly clean old gasket and sealer from mating surfaces.

A APPLY A SMOOTH CONTINUOUS BEAD APPROX 2.0-3.0 MM (0.08-0.12-INCH) WIDE AND 3.0-5.0 MM (0.12-INCH-0.2-INCH) THICK ON BOTH SURFACES. BEAD CONFIGURATION MUST INSURE COMPLETE SEALING OF WATER AND OIL. SURFACE MUST BE FREE OF OIL AND DIRT TO INSURE ADEQUATE SEAL.

TORQUE INTAKE MANIFOLD BOLTS TO 26 N·m (19 FT. LBS.)

Fig. 3 Intake manifold replacement & bolt tightening sequence. 3.1L/V6-191 engines

19. Ensure surfaces are clean and dry, then apply 3/16 bead of RTV sealer on each block ridge, install gaskets and secure gasket position by extending bead of sealer approximately 1/4 inch onto gasket ends. **New gaskets must be cut to fit behind pushrods. When installing gaskets, note left and right side markings.**
20. Install manifold and retaining bolts, ensuring areas between case ridges and manifold are completely sealed.
21. Torque manifold bolts to specifications in sequence shown in **Fig. 3,** then reverse remaining procedure to complete installation.

UPPER INTAKE MANIFOLD REPLACE

3.4L/V6-207 ENGINES

1. Disable airbag system and relieve fuel system pressure as described under "Precautions," then disconnect battery ground cable.
2. Drain coolant, then disconnect throttle body air duct.
3. Disconnect fuel rail injector wiring harness connectors, then the wiring harness retaining nut and set harness aside.
4. Remove accelerator cable bracket bolts, then disconnect bracket and cables from throttle body assembly.
5. Disconnect fuel pipe connectors, then remove fuel pipe assembly and reposition.
6. Disconnect coolant hoses from throttle body assembly, then remove fuel rail stud.
7. Disconnect fuel pressure regulator vacuum hose, then the electrical connectors from IAC, TPS, MAP sensor and evaporative emissions canister purge solenoid valve.
8. Blow dirt out of injector bores with compressed air, then remove fuel rail assembly.
9. Disconnect vacuum harness assembly, then then EGR flexible pipe assembly from upper intake manifold and reposition.
10. Remove upper intake manifold assembly.
11. Reverse procedure to install, noting the following:
   a. Tighten fasteners to specifications.
   b. Apply teflon sealant 1052080 to threads of EGR flexible pipe assembly bolts and fuel pipe hold down plate bolts.
   c. Lightly lubricate fuel injector O-rings with clean engine oil.
   d. Rearm airbag system as described under "Precautions."

LOWER INTAKE MANIFOLD REPLACE

3.4L/V6-207 ENGINES

1. Disable airbag system and relieve fuel

Fig. 4 Lower intake manifold bolt tightening sequence. 3.4L/V6-207 engines

ALL 25-42 N·m (18-30 FT LBS)

Fig. 5 Exhaust manifold replacement. 3.1L/V6-191 engines

system pressure as described under "Precautions," then disconnect battery ground cable.

2. Remove upper intake manifold as previously described, then the rocker arm covers.
3. Disconnect upper radiator hose and heater hose from lower intake manifold assembly, then the wiring harness ground leads.
4. Remove lower intake manifold assembly.
5. Reverse procedure to install, noting the following:
   a. Tighten manifold bolts in sequence shown in **Fig. 4**, to specifications.
   b. Tighten other fasteners to specifications.
   c. Apply sealant 12345739 at engine block to manifold mating surface. Bead should be 0.08–0.12 inch wide by 0.12–0.20 inch thick.

EXHAUST MANIFOLD REPLACE

LEFT SIDE

3.1L/V6-191 Engines

1. Disconnect battery ground cable.
2. Raise and support vehicle.
3. Disconnect exhaust crossover pipe from exhaust manifold, then lower vehicle.
4. Remove power steering pump rear bracket.
5. Remove exhaust manifold attaching bolts and nut, then remove exhaust manifold and gasket, **Fig. 5**.
6. Reverse procedure to install.

3.4L/V6-207 Engines

1. Disconnect battery ground cable, then raise and support vehicle.
2. Disconnect exhaust crossover pipe from manifold, then lower vehicle.
3. Disconnect oxygen sensor electrical connector.
4. **On vehicles with manual transmission,** remove secondary air injection check valve pipe bracket nut and reposition pipe.
5. **On all vehicles,** remove exhaust manifold.
6. Reverse procedure to install. Tighten fasteners to specifications.

RIGHT SIDE

3.1L/V6-191 Engines

1. Disconnect battery ground cable, then remove throttle body air duct.
2. Disconnect EGR transfer tube at plenum, then remove EGR valve with adapter and shield from exhaust manifold.
3. Remove serpentine drive belt, then remove AIR pump pulley.
4. Remove AIR pump upper bracket, then disconnect AIR hose from check valve.
5. Raise and support vehicle, then remove exhaust crossover pipe nuts from exhaust manifold.
6. Disconnect vacuum line and electrical connector from diverter valve, then lower vehicle.
7. Remove AIR pump to lower bracket attaching bolt, then remove AIR pump with diverter valve.
8. Disconnect AIR pipe from exhaust manifold.
9. Remove alternator brace, then remove exhaust manifold attaching bolts and exhaust manifold, **Fig. 5**.
10. Reverse procedure to install.

3.4L/V6-207 Engines

1. Disconnect battery ground cable, then raise and support vehicle.
2. Disconnect exhaust crossover pipe from manifold, then remove transmission filler tube.
4. Remove A/C compressor rear bracket bolts, then the two rear exhaust manifold bolts.
5. Lower vehicle, then remove serpentine drive belt.
6. Disconnect oxygen sensor electrical connector, then remove alternator.
7. Remove A/C compressor from bracket and reposition, then the alternator rear Y brace.
8. Remove EGR valve, adapter, and flexible pipe.
9. **On vehicles with manual transmis-**

sion, disconnect secondary air injection pipe assembly from exhaust manifold.
10. **On all vehicles,** remove exhaust manifold.
11. Reverse procedure to install. Tighten fasteners to specifications.

CYLINDER HEAD REPLACE

LEFT SIDE

3.1L/V6-191 Engines

1. Remove intake manifold as described under "Intake Manifold, Replace."
2. Remove spark plugs.
3. Raise and support vehicle, then drain coolant from engine block.
4. Drain crankcase and remove oil filter.
5. Lower vehicle and remove engine oil dipstick and tube.
6. Remove exhaust manifold as described under "Exhaust Manifold, Replace."
7. Remove serpentine drive belt.
8. Remove A/C compressor and bracket and position aside with refrigerant hose attached.
9. Remove engine lift bracket, if equipped.
10. Disconnect engine ground cable from rear of cylinder head.
11. Remove power steering pump and bracket and position aside with hoses attached.
12. Loosen rocker arm nuts until pushrods can be removed.
13. Remove cylinder head attaching bolts, then remove cylinder head.
14. Reverse procedure to install. Prior to installation, coat cylinder head bolts with sealer 1052080 or equivalent. Torque cylinder bolts in sequence shown in **Fig. 6**.

3.4L/V6-207 Engines

1. Raise and support vehicle and drain coolant, then lower vehicle.

HEAD TORQUE SEQUENCE

Coat thread with sealer before installing. Using a 12" clicker torque wrench torque to 55 N·m (40 Lbs. Ft.). Rotate wrench an additional 90 (1·4 turn).

Fig. 6 Cylinder head replace & bolt tightening sequence. 3.1L/V6-191 engines

2. Remove upper intake manifold, lower intake manifold and left exhaust manifold as previously described.
3. Remove oil dipstick and tube assembly, then the serpentine drive belt.
4. Disconnect coolant temperature sensor electrical connector, then the spark plug wires from spark plugs.
5. Remove spark plugs, engine lift bracket, wiring harness clip from rear of cylinder head and secondary air injection pipe bracket bolt.
6. Remove power steering pump assembly and brackets and set aside, then loosen rocker arms until pushrod assemblies can be removed.
7. Remove cylinder head bolts, then the cylinder head.
8. Reverse procedure to install, noting the following:
   a. Tighten fasteners to specifications.
   b. Coat threads of cylinder head bolts with sealing compound 1052080 and **torque** in sequence shown in **Fig. 7**, to 41 ft. lbs., then in sequence an additional 90 degrees using torque angle meter J 36660.
   c. Adjust valves.

RIGHT SIDE

3.1L/V6-191 Engines

1. Remove intake manifold as described under "Intake Manifold, Replace."
2. Remove spark plugs.
3. Remove exhaust manifold as described under "Exhaust Manifold, Replace."
4. Raise and support vehicle, then drain coolant from engine block.
5. Drain crankcase and remove oil filter.
6. Lower vehicle.
7. Loosen rocker arms until pushrods can be removed.
8. Remove serpentine drive belt, then remove belt tensioner.
9. Remove alternator and brackets.
10. Disconnect engine ground cable from rear of cylinder head.
11. Remove cylinder head attaching bolts, then remove cylinder head.

32 ROCKER ARM NUT

Fig. 8 Adjusting valve lash

12. Reverse procedure to install. Prior to installation, coat cylinder head bolts with sealer 1052080 or equivalent. Torque cylinder bolts in sequence shown in **Fig. 6**.

3.4L/V6-207 Engines

1. Raise and support vehicle and drain coolant, then lower vehicle.
2. Remove serpentine drive belt tensioner assembly.
3. Remove upper intake manifold, lower intake manifold and right exhaust manifold as previously described.
4. Remove alternator and brackets, then disconnect spark plug wires from spark plugs.
5. Loosen rocker arms until pushrod assemblies can be removed.
6. Remove cylinder head bolts, then the cylinder head.
7. Reverse procedure to install, noting the following:
   a. Tighten fasteners to specifications.
   b. Coat threads of cylinder head bolts with sealing compound 1052080 and **torque** in sequence shown in

◀ FRT

Fig. 7 Cylinder head bolt tightening sequence. 3.4L/V6-207 engines

Fig. 7, to 41 ft. lbs., then in sequence an additional 90 degrees using torque angle meter J 36660.
c. Adjust valves.

VALVE LASH SPECIFICATIONS

Year	Engine (VIN)	Valve Lash
1991–92	3.1L/V6-191(T)	1½ Turns ①
1993–94	3.4L/V6-207(S)	1½ Turns ①

①—Turn rocker arm stud nut until all lash is eliminated, then tighten nut the additional turn listed.

VALVE ARRANGEMENT

FRONT TO REAR

Right . . . . E-I-E-I-E
Left . . . . E-I-I-E-I-E

CAMSHAFT LOBE LIFT SPECIFICATIONS

Engine (VIN)	Int.	Exh.
3.1L/V6-191(T)	.2626	.2732
3.4L/V6-207(S)	.2626	.2732

VALVES

ADJUST

After the engine has been thoroughly warmed up the valves may be adjusted, **Fig. 8**, with the engine shutoff as follows: With engine in position to fire No. 1 cylinder the following valves may be adjusted: exhaust 1-2-3, intake 1-5-6. Then crank the engine one more complete revolution which will bring No. 4 cylinder to the firing position at which time the following valves may be adjusted: exhaust 4-5-6, intake 2-3-4.

The following procedure, performed with the engine running, should be done only in case readjustment is required.

1. After engine has been warmed up to operating temperature, remove valve cover and install a new valve cover gasket.
2. With engine running at idle speed, back off valve rocker arm nut until rocker arm starts to clatter.
3. Turn rocker arm nut down slowly until the clatter just stops. This is the zero lash position.

221. Lifter Body	226. Plunger
222. Plunger Spring	227. Metering Valve
223. Check Ball Retainer	228. Pushrod Seat
224. Check Ball Spring	229. Retainer
225. Check Ball	

Fig. 11 Hydraulic valve lifter

[A] NUT
[B] FLAT WASHER
[40] ROCKER ARM STUD

Fig. 9 Removing pressed-in type rocker arm stud

4. Turn nut down ¼ additional turn and pause 10 seconds until engine runs smoothly. Repeat additional ¼ turns, pausing 10 seconds each time, until nut has been turned down the number of turns listed in the Valve Lash Specifications Chart from the zero lash position. **This preload adjustment must be done slowly to allow the lifter to adjust itself to prevent the possibility of interference between the intake valve head and top of piston, which might result in internal damage and/or bent pushrods. Noisy lifters should be replaced.**

ROCKER ARM STUDS
REPLACE

If studs are loose in cylinder head, .003 inch or .013 inch oversize studs may be installed on all engines with pressed-in type studs, after reaming holes with a proper size reamer. On engines with threaded rocker studs, looseness can be corrected by installing the proper size Heli-Coil insert, or by replacing cylinder head. Replace damaged pressed-in rocker arm studs using the following procedure:
1. Remove the old stud by placing a suitable spacer, **Fig. 9,** over stud. Install nut and flat washer and remove stud by turning nut.
2. Ream hole for oversize stud.
3. Coat press-fit area of stud with rear axle lube. Then install new stud, **Fig. 10.** If tool shown is used, it should bottom on the head.

PUSHRODS

On engines that use pushrods with a hardened insert at one end, the hardened end is identified by a color stripe and should always be installed toward the rocker arm during assembly. When installing, ensure pushrods are seated properly in hydraulic lifters.

VALVE GUIDES

Valves operate in guide holes bored in the head. If clearance becomes excessive, use the next oversize valve and ream the

Fig. 10 Installing pressed-in type rocker arm stud

bore to fit. Valves with oversize stems are available in .003, .015 and .030 inch.

HYDRAULIC LIFTERS
REPLACE

Some engine may be equipped with standard and over size lifters. Lifter bosses where oversize lifters are installed will be marked by dab of white paint or stamped .25 mm O.S.

Valve lifters can be lifted from their bores after removing rocker arms and pushrods and intake manifold. Adjustable pliers with protected jaws may be used to remove lifters which are stuck due to carbon or varnish deposits. Tag lifters so they can be installed at the same location as removed. If new lifters are being installed, coat lifter foot with Molykote or equivalent. **Fig. 11** illustrate types of valve lifter used.

FRONT COVER
REPLACE

3.1L/V6-191 ENGINES
1. Remove oil pan as described under "Oil Pan, Replace."
2. Remove power steering pump and bracket.
3. Disconnect heater hose, then remove water pump as described under "Water Pump, Replace."
4. Remove vibration damper, then disconnect lower radiator hose from front cover.
5. Remove front cover retaining bolts and cover.
6. Thoroughly clean sealing surfaces of front cover and engine block surface.
7. Reverse procedure to install.

3.4L/V6-207 ENGINES
1. Disconnect throttle body air duct, then remove serpentine drive belt.
2. Remove water pump as described under "Water Pump, Replace," then the crankshaft balancer assembly using torsional damper remover J 24420.

3. Remove power steering pump and bracket, then the oil pan assembly as described under "Oil Pan, Replace."
4. Disconnect lower radiator hose from front cover assembly, then remove crankshaft sensor.
5. Remove front cover assembly.
6. Reverse procedure to install, noting the following:
   a. Tighten fasteners to specifications.
   b. Coat both sides of lower tabs of front cover gasket with sealer 1052080.
   c. Install crankshaft balancer assembly using torsional damper installer J 29113.

FRONT COVER OIL SEAL
REPLACE

The front cover oil seal may be replaced without taking off the front cover. After removing the vibration damper, pry out the old seal with a screwdriver. Install the new seal with the lip or open end toward inside of cover and drive it into position using tool No. J35468 or equivalent.

TIMING CHAIN
REPLACE

3.1L/V6-191 ENGINES
1. Remove front cover as described previously.
2. Remove crankshaft oil slinger.
3. Crank engine until timing marks on sprockets are in alignment, **Fig. 12.**
4. Remove camshaft to sprocket bolts.
5. Remove camshaft sprocket and timing chain together. If sprocket does not come off easily, a light blow with a plastic hammer to the sprocket should dislodge it.
6. If crankshaft sprocket is to be replaced, remove it with a suitable gear puller.
7. Apply Molykote or equivalent to sprocket thrust surfaces.
8. Install crankshaft sprocket, aligning key and keyway, if removed.
9. Install chain on camshaft sprocket. Hold sprocket vertical with chain hanging below and shift around to align the timing marks on sprockets.

Fig. 12 Valve timing marks. 3.1L/V6-191 engines

A ALIGNMENT MARKS
25 CHAIN ASSEMBLY, TIMING
26 SPROCKET, CRANKSHAFT
71 ENGINE BLOCK
97 BOLT/SCREW, CAMSHAFT SPROCKET
98 SPROCKET, CAMSHAFT
100 CAMSHAFT ASSEMBLY

Fig. 13 Valve timing marks. 3.4L/V6-207 engines

Fig. 14 Front cover, timing chain & camshaft. 3.1L/V6-191 engines

10. Align dowel in camshaft with dowel hole in sprocket and install sprocket on camshaft. Do not attempt to drive sprocket on camshaft as welch plug at rear of engine can be dislodged.
11. Draw sprocket onto camshaft, using the mounting bolts. Tighten to specifications.
12. Lubricate timing chain with engine oil and install front cover.

3.4L/V6-207 ENGINES

1. Remove front cover assembly as previously described, then rotate crankshaft until timing marks on crankshaft sprocket and camshaft sprocket are aligned to marks on engine block or timing chain dampener, Fig. 13.
2. Remove camshaft sprocket bolts, then the camshaft sprocket and timing chain assembly.
3. Remove crankshaft sprocket using crankshaft sprocket remover J 23444-A, then the timing chain dampener.
4. Remove crankshaft sprocket key, if necessary.
5. Reverse procedure to install, noting the following:
   a. Tighten fasteners to specifications.
   b. Install crankshaft sprocket using crankshaft sprocket installer J 38612.
   c. When installing camshaft sprocket and timing chain assembly, ensure timing marks are aligned as previously described.
   d. Coat crankshaft and camshaft sprockets with engine oil.

CAMSHAFT
REPLACE

3.1L/V6-191 ENGINES

1. Remove valve lifters and engine front cover.
2. Remove grille, radiator and condenser.
3. Remove timing chain as described previously.
4. Remove camshaft from engine using care not to damage camshaft bearings, Fig. 14.
5. Reverse procedure to install. Coat camshaft journals with engine oil. If installing a new camshaft, coat camshaft lobes with GM ESO or equivalent prior to installation.

3.4L/V6-207 ENGINES

1. Remove upper intake manifold assembly, then the lower intake manifold assembly as previously described.
2. Remove rocker arm covers, then the rocker arm nuts and balls.
3. Remove rocker arms and pushrod assemblies. **Place rocker arms, balls and pushrod assemblies in a rack so that they may be reinstalled in same locations from which they were removed.**
4. Remove oil pump drive assembly, then the front cover assembly as previously described.
5. Remove camshaft sprocket as described under "Timing Chain, Replace," then the valve lifter assemblies.
6. Discharge A/C refrigerant into a recovery station, then remove A/C compressor.
7. Disconnect A/C condenser hose and receiver and dehydrator hose from condenser, then remove radiator assembly with A/C condenser.
8. Install three 5/16 - 18 x 4 inch bolts in camshaft bolt holes, then carefully rotate and pull camshaft assembly out of bearings.

NOTCH TO FRONT OF ENGINE

Fig. 15 Piston & rod assembly (numbers on rod & cap must be on same side). 3.1L/V6-191 engines

9. Reverse procedure to install, noting the following:
   a. Tighten fasteners to specifications.
   b. If installing new camshaft, coat camshaft lobes with Molykote.
   c. If installing new camshaft, replace all valve lifter assemblies.
   d. Lubricate all camshaft journals and oil pump drive assembly with engine oil.
   e. Lubricate oil pump drive gear with prelube 1052365.

PISTON & ROD ASSEMBLY

3.1L/V6-191 ENGINES

Assemble pistons to connecting rods as shown in Fig. 15.
Upon installation, measure the connecting rod side clearance using a suitable feeler gauge. Refer to "Engine Rebuilding Specifications" for connecting rod side clearance.

3.4L/V6-207 ENGINES

When installing piston and connecting rod assemblies, stamped arrow on piston assembly must point to front of engine

Fig. 16   Crankshaft rear oil seal removal

Fig. 17   Crankshaft rear oil seal installation

while flange on connecting rod must face toward front of piston on lefthand assembly and face toward rear of piston on righthand assembly.

PISTONS, PINS & RINGS

Pistons and piston rings are available in standard and oversizes of .010 and .030 inch.

MAIN & ROD BEARINGS

Connecting rod bearings are available in standard and undersizes of .001, .002, .010 and .020 inch.

Main bearings are available in standard and undersizes of .001, .002, .009, .010 and .020 inch.

CRANKSHAFT REAR OIL SEAL
REPLACE

1. Raise and support vehicle.
2. Support engine as needed, then remove transmission.
3. Remove clutch and pressure plate, if equipped, then remove flywheel or flex plate.
4. Insert screwdriver through seal lip and pry seal from bore, taking care not to damage crankshaft, **Fig. 16.**
5. Clean seal bore and crankshaft, then inspect for burrs, nicks and wear, and repair as needed.
6. Lightly lubricate replacement seal lip with engine oil, mount seal on installer J-34686 or equivalent and seat dust lip of seal squarely against collar.
7. Lubricate outer diameter of seal with engine oil, align dowel pin of tool with dowel pin hole in crankshaft, mount tool on crankshaft and **torque** to 24 to 60 inch lbs., **Fig. 17.**
8. Rotate T handle of tool clockwise, pressing seal into bore until collar is tight against engine case to ensure seal is fully seated.
9. Rotate T handle of tool counterclockwise to stop, then remove tool and ensure seal is seated squarely in bore.
10. Reverse remaining procedure to complete installation.

OIL PAN
REPLACE
3.1L/V6-191 ENGINES

1. Disconnect battery ground cable.
2. Raise and support vehicle, then remove catalytic converter hanger bolts.
3. Detach transmission oil cooler lines from oil pan clips, if equipped.
4. Place crankshaft damper timing mark at the 7 O'clock position.
5. Drain crankcase, then remove flywheel dust cover, if equipped.
6. Disconnect exhaust crossover pipe from exhaust manifolds.
7. Remove engine mount through bolts, then raise engine slightly permit oil pan removal using a suitable lifting device.
8. Remove oil pan attaching bolts, then remove oil pan, **Fig. 18.**
9. Reverse procedure to install.

3.4L/V6-207 ENGINES

1. Disconnect battery ground cable, then remove air intake duct.
2. Raise and support vehicle, then drain engine oil.
3. Remove wiring harness clips from left side of oil pan assembly, then disconnect oil level sensor connector.
4. Remove oil level sensor assembly, then disconnect exhaust crossover pipes from exhaust manifold assemblies.
5. Remove exhaust pipe hanger bolt and reposition pipe, then disconnect transmission cooler lines from clip at oil pan assembly, if equipped.
6. Remove starter motor assembly, then the converter cover, if equipped.
7. Remove engine mount through bolts, then raise engine with a jacking fixture.
8. Remove oil pan bolts, studs, nuts and reinforcements, then the oil pan assembly.
9. Reverse procedure to install, noting the following:
   a. Tighten fasteners to specifications.
   b. Apply a small amount of sealer 12345739 where oil pan gasket tabs seat on rear crankshaft bearing cap groove.

Fig. 18   Oil pan replacement. 3.1L/V6-191 engines

OIL PUMP
OIL PUMP, REPLACE
3.1L/V6-191 Engines

1. Remove oil pan as described previously.
2. Remove pump to rear main bearing cap bolt and remove pump and extension shaft.
3. Reverse procedure to install. Make sure that installed position of oil pump screen is with bottom edge parallel to oil pan rails. Prime oil pump prior to installation.

3.4L/V6-207 Engines

1. Remove oil pan as previously described, then the oil pump assembly and driveshaft.
2. Reverse procedure to install, noting the following:
   a. Tighten fasteners to specifications.
   b. Align slot on end of intermediate shaft with drive tang on oil pump drive assembly.

OIL PUMP SERVICE
3.1L/V6-191 Engines

1. Remove oil pump as described previously.
2. Remove pump cover screws and pump cover, **Fig. 19.**
3. Mark gear teeth so they can be reassembled with same teeth indexing, then remove drive gear, idler gear and shaft.
4. Remove pressure regulator valve retaining pin, pressure regulator valve and related parts.
5. If pickup screen and pipe require replacement, mount pump in a soft-jawed vise and extract pipe from pump.
6. Wash all parts in cleaning solvent and dry with compressed air.
7. Inspect pump body and cover for

69	SHAFT EXTENSION	75	PRESSURE REGULATOR SPRING
70	PUMP BODY	76	RETAINING PIN
71	DRIVE GEAR AND SHAFT	77	SCREW
72	IDLER GEAR	78	PICKUP SCREEN AND PIPE
73	PUMP COVER		
74	PRESSURE REGULATOR VALVE		

Fig. 19 Exploded view of oil pump. 3.1L/V6-191 engines

cracks and excessive wear.

8. Inspect pump gears for damage or excessive wear.
9. Check drive gear shaft for looseness in pump body.
10. Inspect inside of pump cover for wear that would allow oil to leak past the ends of the gears.
11. Inspect pickup screen and pipe assembly for damage to screen, pipe or relief grommet.
12. Check pressure regulator valve for fit in pump housing.
13. Reverse procedure to assemble. Turn driveshaft by hand to check for smooth operation. **The pump gears and body are not serviced separately. If the pump gears or body are damaged or worn, the pump assembly should be replaced. Also, if the pick-up screen and pump assembly was removed, it should be replaced with a new one as loss of the press fit condition could result in an air leak and loss of oil pressure.**

3.4L/V6-207 Engines

1. Remove oil pump as previously described, then drain oil from pump.
2. Remove drive shaft, then the pump cover.
3. Remove pump gears, then the cotter pin, spring and pressure regulator valve. **Pressure regulator valve spring is under pressure in some models, use extreme caution when removing retaining pin. If valve is stuck, soak pump housing in carburetor cleaning solvent.**
4. Clean all parts of sludge, oil and varnish.
5. Inspect for foreign material, pump housing and cover for cracks, scoring, casting imperfections and damaged threads.
6. Inspect idler gear shaft. If loose in housing, replace pump.
7. Inspect pressure regulator valve for scoring and sticking and pressure regulator spring for loss of tension or bending.
8. Inspect suction pipe and screen assembly for looseness or broken wire mesh or screen. If suction pipe is loose, bent or broken, pump body cover and suction pipe must be replaced.
9. Inspect gears for chipping, galling or wear and drive shaft and drive shaft extension for looseness or wear.
10. Measure gear lash, pump housing gear pocket, gears, gear side clearance and gear end clearance. When deciding pump serviceability based on end clearance, consider depth of wear pattern in pump cover.
11. Reverse steps 1 through 3 to assemble pump. Tighten fasteners to specifications.

BELT TENSION DATA

Engine (VIN)	Year	Less A/C, Lbs. ①	With A/C, Lbs. ②
3.1L/V6-191(T)	1991-92	95-140	85-110

① —Checked between tensioner & power steering pump.
② —Checked between tensioner & A/C compressor.

1. GENERATOR	5. WATER PUMP
2. TENSIONER	6. CRANKSHAFT
3. BELT	7. A.I.R. PUMP
4. P/S PUMP	8. A/C COMPRESSOR

Fig. 20 Serpentine drive belt routing. 3.1L/V6-191 engines

A	INDICATOR MARK
B	READING FOR REPLACING BELT IN SERVICE
C	DEFECTIVE PARTS CHECK RANGE
D	MAXIMUM TOLERANCE BELT READING
E	MINIMUM TOLERANCE BELT READING
28	PULLEY, CRANKSHAFT
50	PULLEY, WATER PUMP
145	TENSIONER ASSEMBLY, DRIVE BELT
147	GENERATOR ASSEMBLY
148	BELT, SERPENTINE DRIVE
149	COMPRESSOR ASSEMBLY, AIR CONDITIONING
150	PULLEY ASSEMBLY, DRIVE BELT IDLER
229	PULLEY, POWER STEERING PUMP

Fig. 21 Serpentine drive belt routing. 3.4L/V6-207 engines

SERPENTINE DRIVE BELT
REPLACE

1. Disconnect battery ground cable.
2. Lift belt tensioner off belt using a socket and breaker bar.
3. Remove drive belt.
4. Reverse procedure to install. Refer to **Figs. 20 and 21** for serpentine belt routing. Start and operate engine for 5 minutes. Check belt tension using a suitable belt tension gauge. **On models less A/C,** check belt tension between tensioner and power steering pump. **On models with A/C,** check belt tension between tensioner and A/C compressor. Refer to "Belt Tension Data" for specifications. Operate engine 30 seconds, then recheck belt tension. If tension is not with in limits, check belt and tensioner and replace as necessary.

Fig. 22 Thermostat & housing replacement. 3.1L/V6-191 engines

Fig. 23 Water pump bolt tightening specifications. 3.1L/V6-191 engines

1   "O" RING
2   FUEL FILTER BRACKET
3   FUEL FEED PIPE
4   FUEL FILTER

Fig. 24 Fuel filter replacement. 3.1L/V6-191 engines

a. Tighten fasteners to specifications.
b. Bleed cooling system.

THERMOSTAT
REPLACE

3.1L/V6-191 ENGINES

1. Disconnect battery ground cable, then drain cooling system, until coolant lever is below level of thermostat.
2. Remove air cleaner and air duct, as necessary.
3. Relieve fuel system pressure as described under "Precautions."
4. Remove throttle body and plenum.
5. Disconnect radiator from thermostat housing.
6. Remove thermostat housing attaching bolts, then remove housing and thermostat, **Fig. 22.**
7. Reverse procedure to install.

3.4L/V6-207 ENGINES

1. Disconnect battery ground cable, then drain cooling system, until coolant lever is below level of thermostat.
2. Remove air cleaner, then disconnect radiator inlet hose from thermostat assembly.
3. Remove thermostat housing attaching bolts, then remove housing and thermostat.
4. Reverse procedure to install. Tighten fasteners to specifications.

COOLING SYSTEM BLEED

After filling cooling system, start engine and allow to reach operating temperature with radiator cap removed. Air in system is bleed through radiator cap opening. Add coolant as necessary to bring to proper level, then install radiator cap and check coolant level in recovery reservoir.

WATER PUMP
REPLACE

3.1L/V6-191 ENGINES

1. Disconnect battery ground cable and drain cooling system.
2. Remove intake duct, then remove serpentine drive belt.
3. Disconnect heater hose from water pump.

1   THREADED FITTING
2   IN-LINE FUEL FILTER
3   QUICK-CONNECT FITTING
4   IN-LINE FUEL FILTER BRACKET

Fig. 25 Fuel filter replacement. 3.4L/V6-207 engines

4. Disconnect radiator hose from thermostat housing.
5. Remove power steering pump and bracket and position aside with hoses attached.
6. Remove water pump attaching bolts, then remove water pump and gasket.
7. Reverse procedure to install. Prior to installation, coat water pump bolt threads with a suitable sealer. Refer to **Fig. 23,** for water pump attaching bolt torque.

3.4L/V6-207 ENGINES

1. Drain cooling system, then disconnect air duct and electrical connector.
2. Disconnect top coil of coil pack, then loosen tensioner pulley bolt.
3. Disconnect heater hose from pump, then loosen water pump pulley bolts.
4. Remove power steering bracket bolts, then the serpentine drive belt.
5. Remove water pump pulley, then the power steering pump bracket and pump.
6. Remove water pump.
7. Reverse procedure to install, noting the following:

FUEL PUMP
REPLACE

3.1L/V6-191 ENGINES

1. Disconnect battery ground cable, then disconnect engine harness connector at ignition distributor.
2. Relieve fuel system pressure as described under "Precautions."
3. Drain fuel tank. Place fuel in an approved container.
4. Remove filler neck shield.
5. Remove tires, then raise and support vehicle.
6. Remove track bar and brace.
7. Support axle, then disconnect lower shock mount.
8. Remove exhaust from converter back, then the heat shield.
9. Disconnect brake cables from S clips, then from retainers on frame rails.
10. Remove stabilizer bar links.
11. Lower axle, then remove rear springs.
12. Disconnect fuel lines and wires.
13. Support fuel tank and remove straps.
14. Remove fuel tank from vehicle.
15. Remove fuel level sending unit and pump assembly by turning cam lock ring counterclockwise.
16. Remove fuel pump from level sending unit by pulling fuel pump upward and outward, away from bottom support.
17. Reverse procedure to install.

3.4L/V6-207 ENGINES

1. Relieve fuel system pressure as described under "Precautions," then drain fuel tank. Place fuel in an approved container.
2. Remove fuel tank as follows:
   a. Raise and support vehicle, then remove fuel filler neck shield.
   b. Remove rear axle assembly as described in "Rear Axle & Suspension" section.

c. Remove exhaust pipe and muffler and muffler heat shield.

d. Clean all fuel pipe and hose connections, then disconnect rear fuel feed pipe assembly from fuel sender/pump assembly, fuel return, vapor and vent hoses at fuel sender/pump assembly.

e. Disconnect electrical connector from fuel sender assembly, then remove fuel tank.

3. Remove fuel sender/pump retaining nuts and retaining ring, then the fuel sender/pump assembly.

4. Reverse procedure to install. Tighten fasteners to specifications.

FUEL FILTER
REPLACE

3.1L/V6-191 ENGINES

1. Relieve fuel system pressure as described under "Precautions."
2. Raise and support vehicle.
3. Clean all fuel filter connections and surrounding areas.
4. Disconnect fuel feed pipes from filter, **Fig. 24**, then drain remaining fuel into suitable container.
5. Remove filter mounting screw, then the fuel filter.

6. Reverse procedure to install.

3.4L/V6-207 ENGINES

1. Relieve fuel system pressure as described under "Precautions," then raise and support vehicle.
2. Clean both fuel feed pipe connections and surrounding areas, then remove fuel filter bracket.
3. Disconnect quick-disconnect fitting at fuel filter inlet, **Fig. 25**, then the threaded outlet fitting from chassis fuel pipe.
4. Remove fuel filter.
5. Reverse procedure to install. Tighten fittings to specifications.

TIGHTENING SPECIFICATIONS

Year	Component	Torque/ Ft. Lbs.
3.1L/V6-191 ENGINES		
1991–92	Camshaft Rear Cover	89①
	Camshaft Sprocket	21
	Clutch Housing Cover	53①
	Clutch Housing To Engine	70
	Clutch Pressure Plate To Flywheel	15
	Connecting Rod Cap	39
	Crankshaft Damper	70
	Crankshaft Pulley	37
	Cylinder Head	③
	Distributor Hold-Down Bolt	25
	Drive Belt Tensioner Brace To Alternator Bracket	26
	Drive Belt Tensioner Brace To Engine	18
	Engine Coolant Drain Plugs	15
	Engine Front Cover Bolts	15
	Engine Mount Nut	30
	Engine Mount Through Bolt & Nut	50
	Exhaust Crossover Pipe Nut	15
	Exhaust Manifold	25
	Flywheel to Crankshaft	52
	Fuel Line Nuts & Bolts	20
	Fuel Rail	18
	Intake Manifold (Center)	15
	Intake Manifold (Lower)	19
	Intake Plenum Bolts & Studs	15
	Main Bearing Cap	73
	Oil Dipstick Tube Nut	27
	Oil Filter Adapter Bolts	63
	Oil Pan Drain Plug	18
	Oil Pan Rear Two Bolts	18
	Oil Pan Except Rear Two Bolts	89①
	Oil Pump	30
	Rocker Arm Cover	10
	Spark Plug	25
	Starter Motor Mounting Bolts	35
	Thermostat Housing	18
	Throttle Body Bolts	20

Year	Component	Torque/ Ft. Lbs.
3.1L/V6-191 ENGINES-Continued		
1991–92 —Cont'd	Timing Chain Damper	15
	Torque Converter to Flywheel Bolts (Automatic)	46
	Torque Housing Cover (Automatic)	89①
	Transmission to Crossmember Nut	35
	Transmission Mount to Support Bolt (Manual)	40
	Transmission Mount To Support Nut	35
	Transmission Mount to Transmission	40
	Transmission Support to Frame	40
	Transmission to Engine (Automatic)	35
	Transmission to Flywheel Housing (Manual)	55
	Water Pump	②
3.4L/V6-207 ENGINES		
1993–94	Accelerator Cable Bracket Bolt	90①
	Camshaft Sprocket Bolts	18
	Connecting Rod Nuts	37
	Crankshaft Balancer Bolt	58
	Crankshaft Bearing Cap Bolts	37④
	Crankshaft Pulley Bolts	37
	Cylinder Head	②
	Dipstick Tube Nut	15
	EGR Flexible Pipe Bolts	19
	EGR Valve Adapter Bolt & Stud	23
	Engine Mount Bolts	43
	Engine Mount Through Bolt	70
	Engine Mount Through Bolt Nut	59
	Engine Oil Level Sensor	16
	Exhaust Manifold Bolts	18
	Flywheel Bolts	61
	Front Cover Bolts	15
	Fuel Filter Fitting	20
	Fuel Pipe Bracket-To-Front Brace Bolt	71①
	Fuel Pipe Bracket-To-Intake Manifold Assembly Bolt	89
	Fuel Pipe Hold Down Plate Bolt	18
	Fuel Rail Stud	19
	Fuel Sender Retaining Nuts	63①

Continued

Year	Component	Torque/ Ft. Lbs.
3.4L/V6-207 ENGINES-Continued		
1993-94 -Cont'd	Fuel Tank Strap Attaching Bolts	25
	Lower Intake Manifold Bolts & Nuts	22
	Oil Pan Front Corner Nuts	24
	Oil Pan Rear Corner Bolts	18
	Oil Pan Side Rail Bolts	89①
	Oil Pan Studs	53①
	Oil Pump Bolts	30
	Oil Pump Drive Clamp Bolt	25
	Secondary Air Injection Check Valve Pipe Bracket Nut	18
	Serpentine Drive Belt Idler Pulley Bolts	37
	Serpentine Drive Belt Tensioner Bolts	24
	Spark Plugs	11

Year	Component	Torque/ Ft. Lbs.
3.4L/V6-207 ENGINES-Continued		
1993-94 -Cont'd	Thermostat Housing Bolts	21
	Timing Chain Dampener Bolts	15
	Upper Intake Manifold Bolts	18
	Valve Rocker Arm Cover Reinforcement Nuts	89①
	Water Pump Bolts, Large	33
	Water Pump Bolts, Small	89①

①—Inch lbs.
②—Refer to text.
③—Torque to 40 ft. lbs., then tighten an additional 90° (¼
④—Plus an additional 77° using torque angle meter J 36660.

5.0L/V8-305 & 5.7L/V8-350 Engines

NOTE: For Procedures Related To The 5.7L/V8-350 (VIN P) Engines Not Found In This Section, Refer To The 1992-93 5.7L/V8-350 Single Cam 16 Valve Engine (VIN P) Engine Section In The Chevrolet Corvette Chapter.

INDEX

PRECAUTIONS
AIRBAG SYSTEM DISARMING

The diagnostic energy reserve module (DERM) can maintain voltage to cause a system deployment for up to ten minutes after the ignition switch is turned off and the battery is disconnected. Servicing the SIR system during this period may result in accidental deployment and personal injury.

1. Ensure front wheels are pointed straight ahead.
2. Turn ignition switch to Lock position and remove SIR or AIRBAG fuse.
3. Remove left sound insulator. **Remove courtesy lamp from sound insulator, if necessary.**
4. Remove Connector Position Assurance (CPA), then disconnect yellow two-way SIR electrical connector at base of steering column.

AIRBAG SYSTEM ARMING

1. Connect yellow two-way SIR electrical connector, then install Connector Position Assurance (CPA).
2. Install left sound insulator. **Install courtesy lamp to sound insulator, if applicable.**
3. Install SIR fuse to fuse block, turn ignition switch to Run position and ensure that "Inflatable Restraint" lamp flashes 7 to 9 times, then shuts off.

FUEL SYSTEM PRESSURE RELIEF

5.0L/V8-305 (VIN E) TBI Engine

Remove fuel tank filler cap to release fuel tank pressure. The fuel injection system incorporates an internal constant bleed which releases fuel system pressure whenever engine is off.

5.0L/V8-305 (VIN F) & 5.7/V8-350 Engines

Failure to relieve system pressure prior to disconnecting fuel system components may cause fire or personal injury. Remove fuel tank filler cap to release fuel tank pressure. Connect pressure gauge J-34730-1 or equivalent to pressure tap on fuel rail, position bleed hose into suitable container and slowly relieve fuel system pressure. Prior to disconnecting fuel line, position shop towel over fitting.

ENGINE MOUNTS

REPLACE

Do not raise or support engine by positioning jack under oil pan, crankshaft damper or other sheet metal components. Raise engine only enough to provide sufficient clearance for mount removal. Check for interference between rear of engine and cowl panel which could result in distributor damage.

FRONT MOUNT

1. Disconnect battery ground cable.
2. Raise and support vehicle.
3. Remove engine mount through bolt, then raise front of engine to release weight from mount.
4. Remove mount to engine bolts and mount, **Fig. 1.**
5. Reverse procedure to install.

REAR MOUNT

Except 5.7L/V8-350 (VIN P) Engines

1. Disconnect battery ground cable.
2. Support rear of engine to relieve weight on rear mount.
3. Remove mount to crossmember nut and washer.
4. Remove mount to transmission attaching bolt, then raise rear of engine slightly and remove mount, **Fig. 1.**
5. Reverse procedure to install.

A	FRONT CROSSMEMBER
B	REAR CROSSMEMBER
C	WELD NUT
D	TRANSMISSION ASSEMBLY
1	MOUNT
2	NUT
4	BOLT
5	WASHER
6	THROUGH-BOLT
7	BRACKET
8	NUT
9	REAR MOUNT
10	BOLT
11	NUT
12	WASHER
13	BOLT
14	WASHER

Fig. 1 Engine mounting. Except 5.7L/V8-350 (VIN P) engines

ENGINE

REPLACE

EXCEPT 5.7L/V8-350 (VIN P) ENGINES

Do not raise or support engine by positioning jack under oil pan, crankshaft damper or other sheet metal components. Raise engine only enough to provide sufficient clearance for mount removal. Check for interference between rear of engine and cowl panel which could result in distributor damage.

1. Disable airbag system as described under "Precautions."
2. Disconnect battery ground cable.
3. Scribe alignment marks on hood and hood hinge, then remove hood.
4. Remove air cleaner assembly, then raise and support vehicle.
5. Drain crankcase and cooling system, then disconnect lower radiator hose.
6. Remove lower fan attaching bolts, then disconnect electrical connectors and remove clips from fan.
7. Lower vehicle, then disconnect upper radiator hose.
8. Remove upper shroud and fan assembly.
9. Disconnect transmission oil cooler lines, if equipped, then remove radiator.
10. Remove serpentine drive belt.
11. Disconnect throttle linkage and cruise control cable, if equipped.
12. Remove plenum extension attaching screws and plenum extension, if equipped.
13. Disconnect and tag spark plug leads and wiring at distributor, then remove distributor.
14. Remove ignition coil, if equipped with external coil.
15. Disconnect all electrical wiring and vacuum hoses which would interfere with engine removal.
16. **On 5.0L/V8-305 VIN F and 5.7L/V8-350 engines,** relieve fuel system pressure as described under "Precautions."
17. **On all models,** disconnect fuel hoses at fuel lines.
18. Remove power steering pump pulley, then remove power steering pump.
19. Discharge A/C refrigerant system, then remove A/C compressor.
20. Disconnect battery ground cable from engine block.

VIEW A

VIEW B

C	RTV SEALER
15	STUDS
16	BOLTS
17	INTAKE MANIFOLD
18	GASKET (LEFT)
19	GASKET (RIGHT)
20	CYLINDER HEAD

Fig. 2   Intake manifold replace. Except 5.7L/V8-350 (VIN P) engines

21. Disconnect AIR hoses and pipe.
22. Raise and support vehicle, then disconnect crossover pipe from exhaust manifolds.
23. **On models with automatic transmission,** remove torque converter housing cover, then remove torque converter to flywheel attaching bolts. Also detach oil cooler lines at oil pan.
24. **On all models,** remove starter motor.
25. Remove engine mount bolts.
26. Support transmission using a transmission jack or other suitable fixture, then remove transmission crossmember bolts.
27. Lower transmission, then remove bellhousing to engine attaching bolts.
28. Raise transmission and install and tighten two transmission crossmember mounting bolts.
29. Remove transmission support device and lower vehicle.
30. Attach suitable a suitable engine lifting device to engine.
31. Position suitable support under transmission.
32. Disconnect ground wires and remove catalytic converter support bracket from rear of cylinder head.
33. Reverse engine from vehicle. Prior to removing engine, ensure all electrical wiring and hoses which would interfere with engine removal are disconnected.
34. Reverse procedure to install.
35. Rearm airbag system as described under "Precautions."

5.7L/V8-350 (VIN P) ENGINES

1. Disable airbag system and relieve fuel system pressure as described under "Precautions," then disconnect battery ground cable.
2. Remove air intake duct, then raise and support vehicle and remove wheels.

3. Drain coolant and engine oil, then remove exhaust crossover pipe assembly.
4. **On vehicles with automatic transmission,** remove converter cover and converter bolts.
5. **On all vehicles,** remove front fascia lower deflectors, stabilizer bar bolts and the serpentine drive belt.
6. Remove secondary air injection pump assembly, then disconnect A/C hose assembly from condenser and compressor.
7. **On vehicles with automatic transmission,** disconnect transmission cooler lines from radiator.
8. **On all vehicles,** disconnect lower radiator hose from radiator and lower heater hose from water pump, then the electrical ground straps from right side of engine block and electrical connections from starter motor.
9. Disconnect electrical connectors from knock sensor, oxygen sensor, coolant temperature sensor, wheel speed sensor, engine oil level switch and fuel pump switch/engine oil pressure gauge sensor assemblies.
10. Disconnect left front brake line from caliper brake hose, then the wiring harness from transmission.
11. Disconnect shift linkage from transmission, then the propeller shaft from transmission. **Scribe alignment marks on propeller shaft before disconnecting.**
12. Disconnect torque arm from transmission, then the intermediate steering shaft from rack and pinion assembly.
13. Disconnect electrical ground straps from left side of engine block and frame rail, then lower vehicle.
14. Disconnect fuel lines from fuel rail assembly.
15. Disconnect cruise and accelerator control cables from throttle body, then the upper and lower radiator hoses and upper heater hose from water pump.
16. Disconnect coolant air bleed pipe hose from radiator assembly.

17. Disconnect brake booster vacuum hose, then the alternator.
18. Disconnect engine wiring harness connectors and reposition harness.
19. Disconnect A/C receiver and dehydrator hose from condenser, A/C hose from expansion tube, then the power steering reservoir and reposition.
20. Remove brake master cylinder and reposition, then the upper bolts and nuts from strut assemblies.
21. Disconnect right front brake line from modulator valve assembly and clips, then raise and support vehicle.
22. Place a lift table under engine and engine frame assembly, then remove engine frame and transmission support bolts.
23. Raise vehicle from engine, transmission and engine frame assemblies, then secure strut assemblies to engine frame.
24. Disconnect transmission TV cable from throttle body, then remove transmission assembly.
25. **On vehicles with manual transmission,** remove clutch housing and clutch assembly.
26. **On all vehicles,** disconnect hose assemblies from A/C compressor, then remove compressor.
27. Disconnect power steering lines from power steering pump.
28. Remove engine mount through bolts, then the engine assembly from engine frame.
29. Reverse procedure to install, noting the following:
    a. Tighten fasteners to specifications.
    b. Bleed brake and power steering systems.
    c. Align wheels.
    d. Rearm airbag system as described under "Precautions."

INTAKE MANIFOLD REPLACE

5.0L/V8-305 TBI (VIN E)

1. Disconnect battery ground cable, drain cooling system and remove air cleaner.
2. Disconnect accelerator, transmission and cruise control linkages, as equipped.
3. Disconnect fuel line from TBI unit and remove fuel line clips as needed.
4. Remove throttle body.
5. Disconnect ECM control wiring harness and position aside.
6. Disconnect upper radiator and heater hoses from manifold.
7. Disconnect electrical wiring and hoses as necessary to permit intake manifold removal.
8. Remove accelerator cable bracket.
9. Remove distributor cap, rotate crankshaft until No. 1 cylinder is at TDC on compression stroke, mark position of distributor rotor, then remove distributor.
10. Remove ignition coil.

Fig. 3 Intake manifold bolt tightening sequence. Except 5.7L/V8-350 (VIN P) engines

11. Remove coolant temperature sensor.
12. Remove intake manifold retaining bolts and the manifold, **Fig. 2**.
13. Ensure surfaces are clean and dry, then apply 3/16 bead of RTV sealer on each block ridge and apply suitable sealer around water outlets, install gaskets and secure gasket position by extending bead of sealer approximately 1/2 inch onto gasket ends.
14. Install manifold and retaining bolts, ensuring areas between case ridges and manifold are completely sealed.
15. Torque manifold bolts to specifications in sequence shown in **Fig. 3**, then reverse remaining procedure to complete installation.

5.0L/V8-305 (VIN F) TPI & 5.7L/V8-350 (VIN 8)

1. Disconnect battery ground cable, drain cooling system and remove air intake duct.
2. Disconnect accelerator, cruise control and transmission cables, as equipped.
3. Disconnect air inlet duct and heater hoses at throttle body.
4. Disconnect and tag electrical connectors and vacuum hoses at throttle body and intake manifold.
5. Relieve fuel system pressure as described under "Precautions," then disconnect fuel lines.
6. Remove vent valve assembly and hoses.
7. Remove vapor pipe assembly.
8. Remove plenum extension.
9. Disconnect and tag spark plug wires at distributor cap.
10. Rotate crankshaft until No. 1 cylinder is at TDC on compression stroke, remove distributor cap and mark position of distributor rotor, then remove distributor.
11. Loosen fuel rail retaining bolts and raise rail assembly.
12. Remove remaining manifold runners and the fuel rail assembly.
13. Remove ignition coil and EGR solenoid.
14. Disconnect upper radiator hose, then remove thermostat housing and gasket.
15. Remove EGR valve and pipe.
16. Disconnect all necessary electrical connectors and vacuum hoses, then remove manifold retaining bolts and the manifold, **Fig. 2**.
17. Ensure surfaces are clean and dry, then apply 3/16 bead of RTV sealer on

22	WASHER
23	STUD
24	BOLT
25	STUD
26	BOLT (L03 ENGINE)
27	EXHAUST MANIFOLD

Fig. 4 Exhaust manifold replace. Except 5.7L/V8-350 (VIN P) engines

each block ridge and apply suitable sealer around water outlets, install gaskets and secure gasket position by extending bead of sealer approximately 1/2 inch onto gasket ends.
18. Install manifold and retaining bolts, ensuring areas between case ridges and manifold are completely sealed.
19. Torque manifold bolts to specifications in sequence shown in **Fig. 3**, then reverse remaining procedure to complete installation.

EXHAUST MANIFOLD REPLACE

EXCEPT 5.7L/V8-350 (VIN P) ENGINES

1. Disconnect battery ground cable.
2. If necessary, disconnect spark plug wires from spark plugs.
3. Remove AIR pipes and AIR valve.
4. Raise and support vehicle.
5. Disconnect exhaust crossover pipe from exhaust manifold, then lower vehicle.
6. Remove exhaust manifold attaching bolts, then remove exhaust manifold

and gasket, **Fig. 4**.
7. Reverse procedure to install.

CYLINDER HEAD REPLACE

EXCEPT 5.7L/V8-350 (VIN P) ENGINES

1. Disconnect battery ground cable, then drain cooling system and engine block.
2. Remove intake manifold and exhaust manifolds.
3. Remove alternator lower mounting bolt and position alternator aside.
4. Remove dipstick tube and bracket.
5. If equipped with A/C, remove compressor and forward mounting bracket and position aside.
6. Remove power steering pump and bracket, position aside.
7. Remove rocker arm cover, rocker arms and pushrods. **Keep rocker arm, rocker arm balls and pushrods in order so they can be installed in the same position.**
8. Remove diverter valve, if equipped.

20	CYLINDER HEAD
57	BOLTS
58	BOLTS
59	CYLINDER BLOCK
60	GASKET

Fig. 5 Cylinder head replace & bolt tightening sequence. Except 5.7L/V8-350 (VIN P) engines

9. Remove cylinder head bolts and cylinder head, **Fig. 5.**
10. Reverse procedure to install. Apply suitable sealer to cylinder head bolts and gradually torque bolts to specifications in sequence shown in **Fig. 5.**

VALVE LASH SPECIFICATIONS

Year & Engine (VIN)	Valve Lash
5.0L/V8-305(E & F)	1 Turn ①
5.7L/V8-350(8)	1 Turn ①

① —Turn rocker arm stud nut until all lash is eliminated, then tighten nut the additional turn listed.

VALVE ARRANGEMENT

FRONT TO REAR

5.0L/V8-305 & 5.7L/V8-350 (VIN 8)

All . . . . E-I-I-E-E-I-I-E

CAMSHAFT LOBE LIFT SPECIFICATIONS

Engine (VIN)	Int.	Exh.
5.0L/V8-305(E)	.234	.257
5.0L/V8-305(F)	.275	.285
5.7L/V8-350(8)	.275	.285

VALVE LIFT SPECIFICATIONS

Engine (VIN)	Int.	Exh.
5.0L/V8-305(E)	.350	.385
5.0L/V8-305(F)	.413	.428
5.7L/V8-350(8)	.413	.428

A	NUT
B	FLAT WASHER
40	ROCKER ARM STUD

Fig. 7 Removing pressed-in type rocker arm stud. Except 5.7L/V8-350 (VIN P) engines

VALVES
ADJUST

EXCEPT 5.7L/V8-350 (VIN P) ENGINES

After the engine has been thoroughly warmed up the valves may be adjusted, **Fig. 6,** with the engine shutoff as follows: With engine in position to fire No. 1 cylinder the following valves may be adjusted: exhaust 1-3-4-8, intake 1-2-5-7. Then crank the engine one more complete revolution which will bring No. 6 cylinder on V8 engines, to the firing position at which time the following valves may be adjusted: exhaust 2-5-6-7, intake 3-4-6-8.

The following procedure, performed with the engine running, should be done only in case readjustment is required.

1. After engine has been warmed up to operating temperature, remove valve cover and install a new valve cover gasket.
2. With engine running at idle speed, back off valve rocker arm nut until rocker arm starts to clatter.
3. Turn rocker arm nut down slowly until

32	ROCKER ARM NUT

Fig. 6 Adjusting valve lash. Except 5.7L/V8-350 (VIN P) engines

the clatter just stops. This is the zero lash position.

4. Turn nut down ¼ additional turn and pause 10 seconds until engine runs smoothly. Repeat additional ¼ turns, pausing 10 seconds each time, until nut has been turned down the number of turns listed in the "Valve Lash Specifications Chart" from the zero lash position. **This preload adjustment must be done slowly to allow the lifter to adjust itself to prevent the possibility of interference between the intake valve head and top of piston, which might result in internal damage and/or bent pushrods. Noisy lifters should be replaced.**

ROCKER ARM STUDS
REPLACE

EXCEPT 5.7L/V8-350 (VIN P) ENGINES

If studs are loose in cylinder head, .003 inch or .013 inch oversize studs may be installed on all engines with pressed-in type studs, after reaming holes with a proper size reamer. On engines with threaded rocker studs, looseness can be corrected by installing the proper size Heli-Coil insert, or by replacing cylinder head. Replace damaged pressed-in rocker arm studs using the following procedure:

1. Remove the old stud by placing a suitable spacer, **Fig. 7,** over stud. Install nut and flat washer and remove stud by turning nut.
2. Ream hole for oversize stud.
3. Coat press-fit area of stud with rear axle lube. Then install new stud, **Fig. 8.** If tool shown is used, it should bottom on the head.

Fig. 8 Installing pressed-in type rocker arm stud. Except 5.7L/V8-350 (VIN P) engines

221. Lifter Body	226. Plunger
222. Plunger Spring	227. Metering Valve
223. Check Ball Retainer	228. Pushrod Seat
224. Check Ball Spring	229. Retainer
225. Check Ball	230. Roller

Fig. 9 Hydraulic valve lifters. Except 5.7L/V8-350 (VIN P) engines

PUSHRODS
EXCEPT 5.7L/V8-350 (VIN P) ENGINES

On engines that use pushrods with a hardened insert at one end, the hardened end is identified by a color stripe and should always be installed toward the rocker arm during assembly.

VALVE GUIDES
EXCEPT 5.7L/V8-350 (VIN P) ENGINES

Valves operate in guide holes bored in the head. If clearance becomes excessive, use the next oversize valve and ream the bore to fit. Valves with oversize stems are available in .003, .015 and .030 inch.

HYDRAULIC LIFTERS
REPLACE
EXCEPT 5.7L/V8-350 (VIN P) ENGINES

Valve lifters can be lifted from their bores after removing rocker arms and pushrods and intake manifold. Adjustable pliers with protected jaws may be used to remove lifters which are stuck due to carbon or varnish deposits. **Fig. 9** illustrate types of valve lifters used.

FRONT COVER
REPLACE
EXCEPT 5.7L/V8-350 (VIN P) ENGINES

The cover oil seal may be replaced without taking off the front cover. After removing the vibration damper, pry out the old seal with a screwdriver. Install the new seal with the lip or open end toward inside of cover and drive it into position.
1. Disconnect battery ground cable and drain cooling system.

A BOLTS
55 CAMSHAFT

Fig. 11 Removing camshaft. Except 5.7L/V8-350 (VIN P) engines

2. Remove vibration damper and water pump.
3. Remove oil pan and gasket as described.
4. Remove timing cover retaining screws and the timing cover.
5. Reverse procedure to install.

TIMING CHAIN
REPLACE
EXCEPT 5.7L/V8-350 (VIN P) ENGINES

1. Remove timing chain cover as described previously.
2. Remove crankshaft oil slinger.
3. Crank engine until timing marks on sprockets are in alignment, **Fig. 10.**
4. Remove three camshaft to sprocket bolts.

Fig. 10 Valve timing marks. Except 5.7L/V8-350 (VIN P) engines

5. Remove camshaft sprocket and timing chain together. Sprocket is a light press fit on camshaft for approximately 1/8 inch. If sprocket does not come off easily, a light blow with a plastic hammer on the lower edge of the sprocket should dislodge it.
6. If crankshaft sprocket is to be replaced, remove it with a suitable gear puller. Install new sprocket, aligning key and keyway.
7. Install chain on camshaft sprocket. Hold sprocket vertical with chain hanging below and shift around to align the timing marks on sprockets.
8. Align dowel in camshaft with dowel hole in sprocket and install sprocket on camshaft. Do not attempt to drive sprocket on camshaft as welch plug at rear of engine can be dislodged.
9. Draw sprocket onto camshaft, using the three mounting bolts. Tighten to specifications.
10. Lubricate timing chain and install cover.

CAMSHAFT
REPLACE
EXCEPT 5.7L/V8-350 (VIN P) ENGINES

1. Remove valve lifters and engine front cover.
2. Remove grille, radiator, oil cooler and condenser.
3. Remove timing chain as described previously.
4. Install two 5/16-18x4 bolts in camshaft bolt holes, **Fig. 11.**
5. Remove camshaft from engine using care not to damage camshaft bearings.
6. Reverse procedure to install.

PISTON & ROD
ASSEMBLE
EXCEPT 5.7L/V8-350 (VIN P) ENGINES

Assemble pistons to connecting rods as shown in **Fig. 12.**

Upon installation, measure the connecting rod side clearance using a suitable feeler gauge. Refer to "Engine Rebuilding Specifications" for connecting rod side clearance.

Fig. 12 Piston & rod assemble. Except 5.7L/V8-350 (VIN P) engines

Fig. 13 Low friction, light weight piston. Except 5.7L/V8-350 (VIN P) engines

Fig. 14 Crankshaft rear oil seal removal. Except 5.7L/V8-350 (VIN P) engines

PISTONS, PINS & RINGS

EXCEPT 5.7L/V8-350 (VIN P) ENGINES

Pistons are available in standard and oversizes of .010 and .030 inch.

Piston rings are available in standard and oversizes of .030 inch.

A low friction light weight piston and new design ring pack are used. The low friction light weight piston can be identified by a raised notch on the bottom of the piston pin bore located toward rear of engine, Fig. 13.

MAIN & ROD BEARINGS

EXCEPT 5.7L/V8-350 (VIN P) ENGINES

Connecting rod bearings are available in standard and undersizes of .001, .002, .010 and .020 inch.

Main bearings are available in standard and undersizes of .001, .002, .009, .010 and .020 inch.

CRANKSHAFT REAR OIL SEAL

REPLACE

EXCEPT 5.7L/V8-350 (VIN P) ENGINES

These engines are equipped with a one-piece, lip type seal mounted in a separate seal retainer. Seal replacement requires removal of the transmission.

1. Raise and support vehicle, then remove transmission, clutch assembly and flywheel, as equipped.
2. Pry seal from retainer, inserting screwdriver in notches provided in seal retainer, **Fig. 14.**
3. Lubricate inner and outer diameters of replacement seal with engine oil, then mount seal on tool J-35621 or equivalent.
4. Mount tool on rear of crankshaft, tightening screws snugly to ensure seal will be installed squarely on crankshaft.
5. Tighten wing nut on tool until it bottoms, then remove tool from crankshaft.
6. Reverse remaining procedure to complete installation.

OIL PAN

REPLACE

EXCEPT 5.7L/V8-350 (VIN P) ENGINES

1. Disconnect battery ground cable, then remove fan shroud.
2. **On models with TBI,** remove air cleaner.
3. **On all models,** remove plenum extension, if equipped.
4. Disconnect and tag spark plug wires at distributor, then remove distributor cap.
5. Remove A/C compressor and position aside with refrigerant lines attached.
6. Raise and support vehicle, then drain crankcase.
7. Remove AIR pipe, if equipped, and hanger bolts from catalytic converter. On some models it may be necessary to disconnect exhaust crossover pipe at exhaust manifolds.
8. Remove starter motor attaching bolts and position starter motor aside.
9. Remove engine mount through bolts, then raise engine.
10. Remove oil pan attaching bolts and oil pan, **Fig. 15. If oil pan removal is hampered by the forward crankshaft throw and/or counterweight extending downward, turn crankshaft as needed to put throw in a horizontal position.**
11. Reverse procedure to install, using a new gasket and seals.

61	BOLT
62	NUT
63	OIL PAN
64	GASKET
65	REINFORCEMENT
66	RETAINER
67	CLIP
68	STUD (LB9 AND L98)

Fig. 15 Oil pan replace. Except 5.7L/V8-350 (VIN P) engines

69	SHAFT EXTENSION	75	PRESSURE REGULATOR SPRING
70	PUMP BODY	76	RETAINING PIN
71	DRIVE GEAR AND SHAFT	77	SCREW
72	IDLER GEAR	78	PICKUP SCREEN AND PIPE
73	PUMP COVER		
74	PRESSURE REGULATOR VALVE		

Fig. 16 Exploded view of oil pump. Except 5.7L/V8-350 (VIN P) engines

OIL PUMP

OIL PUMP, REPLACE

Except 5.7L/V8-350 (VIN P) Engines

1. Remove oil pan as described previously.
2. Remove pump to rear main bearing cap bolt and remove pump and extension shaft.
3. Reverse procedure to install. Make sure that installed position of oil pump screen is with bottom edge parallel to oil pan rails.

OIL PUMP SERVICE

Except 5.7L/V8-350 (VIN P) Engines

1. Remove oil pump as described previously.
2. Remove pump cover screws and pump cover, **Fig. 16**.
3. Mark gear teeth so they can be reassembled with same teeth indexing, then remove drive gear, idler gear and shaft.
4. Remove pressure regulator valve retaining pin, pressure regulator valve and related parts.
5. If pickup screen and pipe require replacement, mount pump in a soft-jawed vise and extract pipe from pump.
6. Wash all parts in cleaning solvent and dry with compressed air.
7. Inspect pump body and cover for cracks and excessive wear.
8. Inspect pump gears for damage or excessive wear.
9. Check drive gear shaft for looseness in pump body.
10. Inspect inside of pump cover for wear that would allow oil to leak past the ends of the gears.
11. Inspect pickup screen and pipe assembly for damage to screen, pipe or relief grommet.
12. Check pressure regulator valve for fit in pump housing.
13. Reverse procedure to assemble. Turn driveshaft by hand to check for smooth operation. **The pump gears and body are not serviced separately. If the pump gears or body are damaged or worn, the pump assembly should be replaced. Also, if the pick-up screen and pump assembly was removed, it should be replaced with a new one as loss of the press fit condition could result in an air leak and loss of oil pressure.**

BELT TENSION DATA

Engine	Year	Belt Tension, Lbs.
All	1991–92	99–121

SERPENTINE DRIVE BELT
REPLACE

EXCEPT 5.7L/V8-350 (VIN P) ENGINES

1. Disconnect battery ground cable.
2. Using a breaker bar, lift tensioner upward and off drive belt.
3. Remove serpentine drive belt from pulleys.
4. Reverse procedure to install. Refer to **Fig. 17** for serpentine belt routing.

COOLING SYSTEM BLEED

EXCEPT 5.7L/V8-350 (VIN P) ENGINES

After filling cooling system, start engine and allow to reach operating temperature with radiator cap removed. Air in system is bleed through radiator cap opening. Add coolant as necessary to bring to proper level, then install radiator cap and check coolant level in recovery reservoir.

THERMOSTAT
REPLACE

EXCEPT 5.7L/V8-350 (VIN P) ENGINES

1. Disconnect battery ground cable, then drain cooling system, until coolant lever is below level of thermostat.
2. Remove air cleaner and air duct, as necessary.
3. Relieve fuel system pressure as described under "Precautions."
4. Remove throttle body.
5. Disconnect radiator hose from thermostat housing.
6. Remove thermostat housing attaching bolts, then remove housing and thermostat, **Fig. 18**.
7. Reverse procedure to install.

WATER PUMP
REPLACE

EXCEPT 5.7L/V8-350 (VIN P) ENGINES

1. Disconnect battery ground cable and drain cooling system.
2. Remove intake air duct assembly.
3. Remove fan shroud or upper radiator support, as applicable, then remove accessory drive belts.

1	TENSIONER ASSEMBLY
2	ROTATE TENSIONER IN DIRECTION SHOWN TO INSTALL OR REMOVE BELT
3	GENERATOR ASSEMBLY
4	ACCESSORY DRIVE BELT
5	P/S PUMP
6	WATER PUMP
7	CRANKSHAFT
8	AIR PUMP
9	A/C COMPRESSOR OR BELT IDLER

Fig. 17   Serpentine drive belt routing. Except 5.7L/V8-350 (VIN P) engines

4. Remove pulley from water pump hub.
5. Remove radiator lower hose and heater hose from water pump.
6. Remove water pump attaching bolts and the pump, **Fig. 19**, noting position of bolts for assembly reference.
7. Reverse procedure to install.

FUEL PUMP
REPLACE

EXCEPT 5.7L/V8-350 (VIN P) ENGINES

1. Disconnect battery ground cable, then disconnect engine harness connector at ignition distributor.
2. **On models with port fuel injection,** relieve fuel system pressure as described under "Precautions."
3. **On all models,** drain fuel tank. Place fuel in an approved container.

Fig. 18   Thermostat replacement. Except 5.7L/V8-350 (VIN P) engines

1	"O" RING
2	FUEL FILTER BRACKET
3	FUEL FEED PIPE
4	FUEL FILTER

Fig. 20   Fuel filter replacement. Except 5.7L/V8-350 (VIN P) engines

4. Remove gas cap and filler neck shield.
5. Remove tires, then raise and support vehicle.
6. Remove track bar and brace.
7. Support axle, then disconnect lower shock mount.
8. Remove exhaust from converter back, then the heat shield.
9. Disconnect brake cables from S clips, then from retainers on frame rails.
10. Remove stabilizer bar links.
11. Lower axle, then remove rear springs.
12. Disconnect fuel lines and wires.

Fig. 19   Water pump replace. Except 5.7L/V8-350 (VIN P) engines

13. Support fuel tank and remove straps.
14. Remove fuel tank from vehicle.
15. Remove fuel level sending unit and pump assembly by turning cam lock ring counterclockwise.
16. Remove fuel pump from level sending unit by pulling fuel pump up and outward, away from bottom support.
17. Reverse procedure to install.

5.7L/V8-350 (VIN P) ENGINES

Refer to "3.4L/V6-207 Engines" in the "3.1L/V6-191 & 3.4L/V6-207 Engines" section.

FUEL FILTER
REPLACE

EXCEPT 5.7L/V8-350 (VIN P) ENGINES

1. Relieve fuel system pressure as described under "Precautions."
2. Raise and support vehicle.
3. Clean all fuel filter connections and surrounding areas.
4. Disconnect fuel feed pipes from filter, **Fig. 20,** then drain remaining fuel into suitable container.
5. Remove filter mounting screw, then the fuel filter.
6. Reverse procedure to install.

5.7L/V8-350 (VIN P) ENGINES

Refer to "3.4L/V6-207 Engines" in the "3.1L/V6-191 & 3.4L/V6-207 Engines" section.

TIGHTENING SPECIFICATIONS

Year	Component	Torque/Ft. Lbs.	Year	Component	Torque/Ft. Lbs.
1991–92	Camshaft Retainer Nuts	106①	1991–92 —Cont'd	Drive Belt Idler Pulley (Long Bolt)	61
	Camshaft Sprocket Bolts	21		Drive Belt Idler Pulley (Short Bolt)	37
	Clutch Pressure Plate To Flywheel Bolts	30		Drive Belt Tensioner	37
	Connecting Rod Cap Nuts	44		Engine Bracket Bolt	38
	Crankshaft Damper Bolt	70		Engine Coolant Drain Plug	15
	Crankshaft Pulley To Damper	43		Engine Front Cover	97①
	Crankshaft Rear Oil Seal Retainer	11		Engine Mount Nut	30
	Cylinder Head Bolts	68		Engine Mount Through Bolt	50
	Distributor Clamp Bolt	27		Engine Oil Cooler Retainer	17

Continued

TIGHTENING SPECIFICATIONS—Continued

Year	Component	Torque/ Ft. Lbs.	Year	Component	Torque/ Ft. Lbs.
1991-92 —Cont'd	Exhaust Crossover Pipe To Exhaust Manifold Nuts	15	1991-92 —Cont'd	Spark Plug	20
	Exhaust Manifold Bolt & Stud (Center)	20		Starter Motor Mounting Bolts	35
	Exhaust Manifold Bolt & Stud (Outer)	26		Thermostat Housing (5.0L/V8-305 TBI VIN E)	21
	Flywheel To Crankshaft Bolts	74		Thermostat Housing (5.0L/V8-305 TPI VIN F & 5.7L/V8-350)	25
	Fuel Line Nuts	20		Torque Converter Cover Bolts	89①
	Fuel Pump Cover Lower Bolt	106①		Torque Converter To Flywheel Attaching Bolts	46
	Fuel Pump Cover Upper Bolt	25		Throttle Body Attaching Bolts (5.0L/V8-305 TBI VIN E)	16
	Fuel Rail Attaching Bolts (5.0L/V8-305 TPI VIN F & 5.7L/V8-350)	15		Throttle Body Attaching Bolts (5.0L/V8-305 TPI VIN F & 5.7L/V8-350)	18
	Ignition Coil Bracket Bolt (5.0L/V8-305 TBI VIN E)	16		Throttle Body Fuel Inlet Line (5.0L/V8-305 TBI VIN E)	30
	Ignition Coil Bracket Bolt (5.0L/V8-305 TPI VIN F & 5.7L/V8-350)	50 ①		Throttle Body Fuel Outlet Line (5.0L/V8-305 TBI VIN E)	21
	Intake Manifold Bolt & Stud	②		Transmission Rear Mount Bolt	40
	Main Rod Cap Bolts	77		Transmission Rear Mount Nut	35
	Oil Filter Adapter Bolt	18		Transmission To Bellhousing Bolts (Manual)	55
	Oil Galley Plug	115①		Transmission To Engine Bolts (Automatic)	35
	Oil Level Dipstick Tube Bracket Bolt	25		Valve Cover Bolts	97①
	Oil Pan Drain Plug	16		Valve Lifter Retainer Bolt	15
	Oil Pan To Engine Bolts	97①		Water Pump Bolts	30
	Oil Pan To Engine Nuts	17			
	Oil Pump Cover Screws	80①			
	Oil Pump To Rear Main Bearing Cap	65			
	Runner To Manifold Bolts (5.0L/V8-305 TPI VIN F & 5.7L/V8-350)	25			

①—Inch Lbs.
②—Torque bolts & studs to 89 inch lbs., then tighten to final torque of 35 ft. lbs.

Clutch & Manual Transmission
INDEX

HYDRAULIC CLUTCH SYSTEM BLEEDING

1991-92

1. Clean area around clutch fluid reservoir, then remove cap and add DOT 3 type brake fluid as necessary to bring to proper level, **Fig. 1.**
2. At clutch actuator, fully loosen bleeder screw located near fluid inlet line connection.
3. Allow system to gravity bleed until a steady stream of fluid is expelled from bleeder valve. Maintain reservoir level during gravity bleeding operation.
4. After air has been expelled from slave cylinder, tighten bleeder screw.
5. Push clutch fork lightly toward actuator, then open bleeder screw. While maintaining light force on clutch fork, tighten bleeder screw.
6. Push clutch fork lightly toward actuator with bleeder screw closed. This will force any remaining air into reservoir.
7. Check clutch system by starting vehicle, then select reverse gear with clutch pedal fully depressed. If gears do not grate, system is satisfactory. If gears do grate, repeat bleeding procedure.
8. Check actuator output rod travel. Minimum travel should be .43 inch for V6 engines, .57 inch for V8 engines.

1993-94

1. Loosen clutch master cylinder nuts to end of threads on U-bolt, then clean dirt and grease from reservoir cap, **Figs. 2 and 3.**
2. Remove reservoir cap and diaphragm, then wrap a piece of mechanics wire around lefthand hood strut bracket ensuring wire is accessible from underside of vehicle.
3. Raise and support vehicle, then remove actuator cylinder and retain in engine compartment using mechanics wire previously installed.
4. Lower vehicle, then grasp actuator cylinder and depress pushrod approximately .787 inch (20 mm) into cylinder bore and hold.
5. Install diaphragm and reservoir cap while holding in actuator pushrod, then release actuator pushrod.
6. Hold actuator cylinder vertically with pushrod facing down, then press pushrod into actuator cylinder bore with short .390 inch (10 mm) strokes while inspecting master cylinder res-

1	FLUID RESERVOIR
2	CLUTCH MASTER CYLINDER
3	BOOT
4	CLUTCH MASTER CYLINDER INPUT ROD
5	SHIPPING STRAP
6	BOOT
7	ACTUATOR

Fig. 1   Clutch hydraulic system. 1991–92

ervoir for air bubbles. **Actuator cylinder should be lower than master cylinder.**

7. Continue stroking cylinder until air bubbles are no longer entering reservoir, then raise and support vehicle.
8. Remove actuator cylinder from mechanics wire, then install actuator cylinder and tighten to specifications.
9. Lower vehicle, then remove mechanics wire from lefthand hood strut bracket.
10. Install clutch master cylinder nuts and tighten to specifications, then inspect fluid level, adding fluid if necessary.

CLUTCH ACTUATOR
REPLACE

1991–92

1. Disconnect battery ground cable.
2. Disconnect input rod from clutch master cylinder, **Fig. 1.** This will prevent damage to actuator if clutch pedal is depressed while actuator is removed.
3. Raise and support vehicle, then disconnect hydraulic hose from clutch actuator.

4. Remove actuator and heat shield attaching bolts, then remove actuator and heat shield.
5. Reverse procedure to install. After completing installation, bleed clutch hydraulic system.

CLUTCH MASTER & ACTUATOR CYLINDER
REPLACE

1993–94

1. Disconnect battery ground cable, then remove instrument panel driver knee bolster assembly.
2. Disconnect clutch master cylinder pushrod from clutch pedal assembly, then remove clutch master cylinder nuts from dash panel assembly.
3. Remove clutch master cylinder U-bolt from dash panel assembly, then the clutch master cylinder from dash panel assembly.
4. Remove clutch master cylinder reservoir retainer, then the clutch master cylinder reservoir from lefthand hood strut bracket.
5. Raise and support vehicle, then remove clutch actuator cylinder from clutch housing.

6. Remove clutch master and actuator cylinder assembly from vehicle.
7. Reverse procedure to install, noting the following:
    a. Tighten fasteners to specifications.
    b. Bleed hydraulic clutch system.

CLUTCH
REPLACE

1991–92

1. Support engine and remove transmission as described further on.
2. Remove slave cylinder heat shield and cylinder from flywheel housing. Prior to removing slave cylinder, disconnect pushrod from clutch master cylinder.
3. Remove flywheel housing, **Fig. 4.**
4. Slide clutch fork from ball stud and remove fork from dust boot. **Look for X mark on flywheel and on clutch cover. If X mark is not evident, prick punch marks on flywheel and clutch cover for indexing purposes during installation.**
5. Loosen clutch to flywheel attaching bolts evenly one turn at a time until spring pressure is released. Then remove bolts and clutch assembly.
6. Reverse procedure to install. Prior to installation, lubricate pilot bearing sparingly with machine oil. Also apply wheel bearing lubricant 1051344 or equivalent to clutch fork ball socket and fingers and release bearing collar recesses. Use a suitable pilot tool to center clutch disc. Tighten clutch cover bolts evenly and gradually to avoid distorting cover.

1993–94

1. Disconnect battery ground cable, then remove instrument panel driver knee bolster assembly.
2. Disconnect clutch master cylinder pushrod from clutch pedal assembly, then raise and support vehicle.
3. Remove transmission assembly, then the clutch actuator cylinder and retain with mechanics wire.
4. Remove transmission brace, then the flywheel housing cover and flywheel housing assembly, **Figs. 5 and 6.**
5. Remove clutch pressure plate, then the clutch disc.
6. Reverse procedure to install, noting the following:
    a. Tighten fasteners to specifications.
    b. Align clutch disc and pressure plate using clutch alignment arbor J 33169 for 5-speed transmission or J 38836 for 6-speed transmission.
    c. Check for proper clutch fork to clutch release bearing engagement.

MANUAL TRANSMISSION
REPLACE

1991-92

It may be necessary to remove the catalytic converter and its support bracket to facilitate transmission removal.

1. Disconnect battery ground cable.
2. Raise and support vehicle, then drain lubricant from transmission.
3. Remove propeller shaft.
4. Support left hand side of rear axle with a suitable lifting device.
5. Remove torque arm rear attaching bolts, then remove front torque arm bracket and torque arm.
6. Disconnect speed sensor and backup lamp switch electrical connectors.
7. Remove catalytic converter hanger bracket.
8. Support engine using a suitable jack stand, then remove transmission mount nuts at support.
9. Remove transmission support bolts, then remove support.
10. Lower transmission just enough to provide access to shift control assembly.
11. Remove shift control assembly attaching bolts, then disconnect shift control from extension housing.
12. Remove transmission to flywheel housing attaching bolts, the remove transmission from vehicle.
13. Reverse procedure to install. Apply a 1/8 bead of sealant 12345739 or equivalent to extension sealing surface.

1993-94

5-Speed Transmission

1. Disconnect battery ground cable, then remove front floor console trim plate assembly.
2. Raise and support vehicle, then drain fluid from transmission.
3. Disconnect propeller shaft assembly, then support rear axle assembly with a jack stand.
4. Remove rear axle torque arm assembly, then the catalytic converter hanger assembly.
5. Disconnect electrical connectors from backup lamp switch and speed sensor, then support engine assembly with a jack stand.
6. Remove transmission support and mount assembly, then lower transmission enough to reach control bolts.
7. Remove transmission control bolts, then lower transmission and remove control assembly. **Control must be held while lowering transmission as control is not retained in vehicle and could drop damaging component.**
8. Remove transmission assembly.
9. Reverse procedure to install, noting the following:
   a. Tighten fasteners to specifications.
   b. Apply a continuous 1/8 inch bead of RTV sealant 12345739 to exten-

A RESERVOIR, CLUTCH MASTER CYLINDER
B MASTER CYLINDER, CLUTCH
C ACTUATOR CYLINDER, CLUTCH
1 CYLINDER ASSEMBLY, CLUTCH MASTER AND ACTUATOR
2 BRACKET, HOOD STRUT LEFT-HAND
3 RETAINER, CLUTCH MASTER CYLINDER RESERVOIR
4 HOSE CLIP, CLUTCH MASTER CYLINDER AND ACTUATOR
5 NUT, CLUTCH ACTUATOR CYLINDER, 20 N·m (15 LB. FT.)

Fig. 2 Clutch hydraulic system. 1993-94 5-Speed

A RESERVOIR, CLUTCH MASTER CYLINDER
B MASTER CYLINDER, CLUTCH
C ACTUATOR CYLINDER, CLUTCH
6 CYLINDER ASSEMBLY, CLUTCH MASTER AND ACTUATOR
7 RETAINER, CLUTCH MASTER CYLINDER RESERVOIR
8 BRACKET, HOOD STRUT LEFT-HAND
9 HOSE CLIP, CLUTCH MASTER CYLINDER AND ACTUATOR
10 NUT, CLUTCH ACTUATOR CYLINDER, 20 N·m (15 LB. FT.)
11 NUT, TRANSMISSION BRACE, 50 N·m (37 LB. FT.)
12 COVER, FLYWHEEL HOUSING
13 BRACE, TRANSMISSION
14 BOLT/SCREW, TRANSMISSION BRACE, 50 N·m (37 LB. FT.)

Fig. 3 Clutch hydraulic system. 1993-94 6-Speed

1. CLUTCH HOUSING COVER
2. FLYWHEEL
3. CLUTCH DISC
4. PRESSURE PLATE ASSEMBLY
5. CLUTCH RELEASE BEARING
6. CLUTCH FORK
7. CLUTCH HOUSING
8. CLUTCH BALL STUD

Fig. 4 Clutch disc, pressure plate & housing assembly. 1991—92

12 COVER, FLYWHEEL HOUSING
29 FLYWHEEL ASSEMBLY, ENGINE
30 PLATE ASSEMBLY, CLUTCH PRESSURE (WITH COVER)
31 BEARING ASSEMBLY, CLUTCH RELEASE
32 STUD, CLUTCH FORK BALL
33 WASHER, CLUTCH FORK BALL STUD
34 HOUSING ASSEMBLY, FLYWHEEL
35 BOOT, CLUTCH FORK
36 FORK ASSEMBLY, CLUTCH
37 PLATE ASSEMBLY, CLUTCH DRIVEN
38 BEARING, CLUTCH PILOT
49 PIN, FLYWHEEL HOUSING LOCATOR
50 BOLT/SCREW, FLYWHEEL, 83 N·m (61 LB. FT.)
51 BOLT/SCREW, CLUTCH PRESSURE PLATE AND COVER,
   20 N·m (15 LB. FT.) PLUS 30 DEGREES
52 PIN, FLYWHEEL GROOVE
53 BOLT/SCREW, FLYWHEEL HOUSING COVER, 8.5 N·m
   (75 LB. IN.)
54 TRANSMISSION ASSEMBLY, MANUAL (5-SPEED)
65 BOLT/SCREW, FLYWHEEL HOUSING, 75 N·m
   (55 LB. FT.)

**Fig. 5 Clutch disc, pressure plate & housing
assembly. 1993–94 5-Speed**

39 PLATE ASSEMBLY, CLUTCH PRESSURE (WITH COVER)
40 BEARING ASSEMBLY, CLUTCH RELEASE
41 T-STUD, CLUTCH FORK
42 TRANSMISSION ASSEMBLY, MANUAL (6-SPEED)
43 SPACER, CLUTCH ACTUATOR CYLINDER
44 HOUSING ASSEMBLY, FLYWHEEL
45 FORK ASSEMBLY, CLUTCH
46 FLYWHEEL ASSEMBLY, ENGINE
47 PLATE ASSEMBLY, CLUTCH DRIVEN
48 COVER, FLYWHEEL HOUSING
55 PIN, FLYWHEEL HOUSING LOCATOR
56 COVER, FLYWHEEL HOUSING
57 BOLT/SCREW, CLUTCH PRESSURE PLATE AND COVER
   30 N·m (22 LB. FT.)
58 RETAINER, CLUTCH RELEASE BEARING
59 BOLT/SCREW, FLYWHEEL, 100 N·m (74 LB. FT.)
60 PIN, FLYWHEEL GROOVE
61 BOLT/SCREW, FLYWHEEL HOUSING COVER,
   8.5 N·m (75 LB. IN.)
62 BOLT/SCREW, FLYWHEEL HOUSING, 47 N·m
   (35 LB. FT.)
63 BOLT/SCREW, CLUTCH FORK T-STUD, 24 N·m
   (18 LB. FT.)
64 BOLT/SCREW, TRANSMISSION, 35 N·m (26 LB. FT.)

**Fig. 6 Clutch disc, pressure plate & housing
assembly. 1993–94 6-Speed**

sion housing to control assembly sealing surface.

6-Speed Transmission

1. Disconnect battery ground cable, then remove front floor console trim plate assembly.
2. Remove control lever handle, then raise and support vehicle.
3. Drain fluid from transmission, then support rear axle assembly with a jack stand.
4. Disconnect propeller shaft assembly, then remove rear axle torque arm.
5. Remove catalytic converter hanger assembly, then disconnect electrical connectors from backup lamp switch and reverse lockout solenoid.
6. Disconnect clutch master cylinder pushrod from clutch pedal assembly, then remove clutch actuator cylinder and retain with mechanics wire.
7. Remove actuator spacer, then pull clutch fork assembly down to disengage release bearing.
8. Disconnect electrical connector from electronic speed sensor, then support engine assembly with a jack stand.
9. Support transmission assembly with a jack stand, then remove transmission support and mount assembly.
10. Remove transmission assembly.
11. Reverse procedure to install. Tighten fasteners to specifications.

TIGHTENING SPECIFICATIONS

Year	Component	Torque/Ft. Lbs.
1991–92	Actuator (Slave Cylinder) To Housing	15
	Clutch Housing To Engine (V6)	70
	Clutch Housing To Engine (V8)	35
	Clutch Pedal Mounting Bracket	26
	Extension Housing Bolt	22
	Flywheel To Crankshaft (V6)	52
	Flywheel To Crankshaft (V8)	74
	Heat Shield To Clutch Housing	15
	Master Cylinder To Cowl	115①
	Neutral Safety Switch	19①
	Pressure Plate To Flywheel (V6)	15
	Pressure Plate To Flywheel (V8)	30
	Reservoir To Mounting Bracket	53①
	Shift Control Lever Bolt	13
	Transmission Drain & Fill Plugs	20
	Transmission To Flywheel Housing Bolt	55

Year	Component	Torque/Ft. Lbs.
1993–94	Actuator Cylinder Nuts	15
	Clutch Master Cylinder Nuts	20
	Flywheel Housing Bolts, 5-Speed	55
	Flywheel Housing Bolts, 6-Speed	35
	Flywheel Housing Cover Bolts	75①
	Pressure Plate To Flywheel, 5-Speed	15②
	Pressure Plate To Flywheel, 6-Speed	22
	Shift Control Lever Bolt, 5-Speed	13
	Shift Control Lever Bolt, 6-Speed	18
	Transmission Brace Nut & Bolt, 5-Speed	37
	Transmission To Flywheel Housing Bolt, 5-Speed	55
	Transmission To Flywheel Housing Bolt, 6-Speed	26

①—Inch lbs.
②—Plus an additional 30 degrees.

Rear Axle & Rear Suspension

INDEX

REAR AXLE
REPLACE

Construction of the axle assembly is such that service operations may be performed with the housing installed in the vehicle or with the housing removed and installed in a holding fixture. The following procedure is necessary only when the housing requires replacement.

1. Raise and support vehicle, then support rear axle with a suitable jack.
2. Disconnect shock absorbers from lower mountings.
3. Remove track bar.
4. Disconnect brake line from axle housing junction block and the parking brake cable.
5. Disconnect lower control arms from axle housing attachments.
6. Remove propeller shaft.
7. Lower axle slowly until springs can be moved. Roll axle assembly out from under vehicle.
8. Reverse procedure to install.

AXLE SHAFT
REPLACE

BORG WARNER AXLE

1. Raise and support rear of vehicle, then remove wheel and tire assembly.
2. Remove brake caliper, then remove brake rotor.
3. Remove four nuts attaching axle shaft bearing retainer to axle housing.
4. Using puller and adapter J-21579 and J-2619-01 or equivalent, pull axle shaft from housing, Fig. 1.
5. To replace axle shaft bearing, split inner retainer with a suitable chisel, then remove retainer from axle shaft, Fig. 2. Using Tool No. J-22912-01 or equivalent, press bearing and seal from axle shaft.
6. Reverse procedure to install. When replacing oil seals, it should be noted right hand seal is identified by black bands, while left hand seal is identified

Fig. 1   Removing axle shaft. Borg Warner axle

by gold bands. Prior to installation, seal lips should be lightly coated with a suitable grease. When pressing bearing and seal onto axle shaft, use tool No. J-8853-01 or equivalent. Position chamfer on outer diameter of bearing retainer toward bearing. **On models with limited slip,** both axle shaft splines should be fully engaged before axle shaft is rotated to maintain spline alignment.

GM AXLE

1. Raise vehicle and support vehicle, then remove wheel and brake drum or rotor.
2. Drain lube from carrier and remove cover.
3. Remove differential pinion shaft lock screw and remove differential pinion shaft, **Fig. 3.**
4. Pull flange end of axle shaft toward center of vehicle and remove C-lock from button end of shaft, **Fig. 3.**
5. Remove axle shaft from housing, being careful not to damage seal.
6. Reverse procedure to install the axle shaft.

PROPELLER SHAFT
REPLACE

1991–92

1. Raise and support vehicle.
2. Mark position of shaft in relation to pinion flange for reassembly.
3. Remove straps securing universal joint to pinion flange, then disconnect shaft from flange. **Tape bearing cups to universal joint to prevent loss of needle bearings.**
4. Slide yoke out of transmission and remove propeller shaft. Insert suitable plug in transmission to prevent fluid loss.
5. Reverse procedure to install.

1993–94

1. Raise and support vehicle, then mark relationship of propeller shaft assembly to pinion gear yoke.
2. **On two-piece propeller shafts,** remove bolts from center support bearing.
3. Remove center support bearing and washers from torque arm assembly.
4. **On all propeller shafts,** remove bolts and retainers, then the propeller shaft.
5. Reverse procedure to install, noting the following:
   a. Tighten fasteners to specifications.
   b. Lubricate slip yoke with .6 ounces of propeller shaft slip yoke lubri-

2	SEAL
3	BEARING CONE
4	BEARING CUP

Fig. 2   Removing axle shaft bearing retainer nuts. Borg Warner axle

cant 1050169.
   c. Align marks on pinion gear yoke and propeller shaft.

SHOCK ABSORBER
REPLACE

1991–92

1. Raise vehicle and support rear axle.
2. Pull back carpeting, then remove shock absorber upper mounting nut.
3. Remove shock absorber lower mounting nut, then remove shock absorber, **Fig. 4.**
4. Reverse procedure to install.

1993–94

1. Fold down seat back frame, then remove quarter trim panel.
2. Pull folding carpet back, then raise and support vehicle.
3. Support rear axle, then remove shock absorber.
4. Reverse procedure to install. Tighten fasteners to specifications.

COIL SPRINGS
REPLACE

1991–92

1. Raise and support vehicle and support rear axle with a suitable adjustable jack.
2. Remove track bar mounting bolt from axle and loosen track bar bolt at body brace, **Fig. 4.**
3. Disconnect rear brake hose clip at underbody, then disconnect shock absorbers at lower mountings.
4. Carefully lower rear axle and remove springs and insulators.
5. Reverse procedure to install.

1993–94

1. Raise and support vehicle, then support rear axle with an adjustable lifting device. **Do not use twin post type hoist.**
2. Remove shock absorber nuts from rear axle, then lower rear axle.
3. Remove upper insulator assembly,

| 5 | LOCK SCREW |
| 40 | C-LOCK |

Fig. 3   Pinion shaft lock screw & axle shaft C-lock. GM axle

then the rear spring.
4. Reverse procedure to install. Tighten fasteners to specifications.

LOWER CONTROL ARM & BUSHINGS
REPLACE

LOWER CONTROL ARM

If both control arms are to be removed, remove one control arm at a time to prevent axle from slipping or rolling.

1. Raise vehicle and support at frame pads. Support nose of axle housing to prevent assembly from twisting when control arm is removed.
2. Remove bolts securing control arm to chassis and rear axle, and the control arm, **Fig. 4.**
3. Reverse procedure to install.

CONTROL ARM BUSHINGS

1. Raise and support vehicle and remove control arm as described previously.
2. Press bushings out of control arm using suitable tools as shown in **Fig. 5.**
3. Reverse procedure to install, ensuring bushing is properly seated in control arm, **Fig. 6. If replacement bushing fits loosely in control arm, or if mounting areas are damaged or deformed, control arm must be replaced.**

STABILIZER BAR
REPLACE

1. Raise and support vehicle.
2. Remove link bolt nuts, washers, bushings, spacers and link bolts securing stabilizer to chassis, **Fig. 7.**
3. Remove clamps securing stabilizer shaft to rear axle and stabilizer shaft.
4. Reverse procedure to install. Torque link bolts and U-bolt nuts to specifications.

WITH RR DISC BRAKES

1. RAIL
2. JOUNCE BUMPER
3. SPRING INSULATOR ASSEMBLY
4. COIL SPRING
5. OPTIONAL STABILIZER BAR
6. LOWER CONTROL ARM
7. UNDERBODY
8. TORQUE ARM
9. PROP SHAFT
10. SHOCK ABSORBER
11. TRACK BAR
12. TRACK BAR BRACE

Fig. 4   Exploded view of rear suspension

1. PRESS
2. J 22222-5
3. J 25317-2
4. J 21465-8

Fig. 5   Control arm bushing removal

1. PRESS
2. J 25317-2
3. J 22222-5
4. J 25317-1

Fig. 6   Control arm bushing installation

TRACK BAR/REAR AXLE TIE ROD & BRACE REPLACE

1. Raise vehicle and support rear axle at curb height.
2. Remove track bar/rear axle tie rod mounting bolt and nut from rear axle and from body bracket, then remove track bar/rear axle tie rod, **Fig. 4.**
3. Remove heat shield attaching screws from track bar brace.
4. Remove three track bar/rear axle tie rod brace to body brace screws.
5. Remove nut and bolt from body bracket, then remove track bar/rear axle tie rod brace.
6. Reverse procedure to install.

(R.H. SHOWN L.H. OPPOSITE)

1. SADDLE
2. AXLE ASSEMBLY
3. 27 N·m (20 FT. LB.)
4. UNDERBODY PANEL ASSEMBLY
5. 22 N·m (16 FT. LB.)
6. 47 N·m (35 FT. LB.)

Fig. 7   Stabilizer bar installation

TIGHTENING SPECIFICATIONS

Year	Component	Torque/ Ft. lbs.
1991–92	Control Arm To Rear Axle	85
	Control Arm To Underbody	85
	Rear Axle Housing Cover To Axle	22
	Rear Axle Pinion Shaft Lock Screw	27
	Shock Absorber Lower Mounting	66
	Shock Absorber Upper Mounting	13
	Stabilizer Bracket To Body	35
	Stabilizer Clamp To U-Bolt	18
	Stabilizer Shaft To Body Bracket	13
	Torque Arm Outer Bracket	30
	Torque Arm To Rear Axle	98
	Track Bar To Axle	77
	Track Bar To Body Bracket	59
	Track Bar Brace To Body Bracket Nut	61
	Track Bar Brace To Body Bracket Screw	35
	Universal Joint Strap Bolt	16

Year	Component	Torque/ Ft. lbs.
1991–92	Wheel Lug Nuts	100
1993–94	Control Arm Bolts	74
	Control Arm Nuts	60
	Differential Pinion Gear Shaft Lock Bolt	27
	Shock Absorber Lower Nut	66
	Shock Absorber Upper Nut	13
	Stabilizer Link	16
	Stabilizer Shaft Bracket Bolts	17
	Stabilizer Shaft Nuts	18
	Torque Arm To Rear Axle Bolts	96
	Torque Arm To Rear Axle Nuts	97
	Torque Arm To Transmission Center Bolt	20
	Torque Arm To Transmission Lower & Upper Bolts	37
	Torque Arm To Transmission Nuts	30
	Wheel Lug Nuts	100

Front Suspension & Steering

INDEX

DESCRIPTION

1991–92

A modified strut type suspension is used on Camaro and Firebird, **Fig. 1**. Each wheel is independently connected to the chassis by a lower control arm, spindle and a strut assembly which locates the spindle and controls ride by dampening spring action. Coil springs are mounted between the lower control arm and crossmember, and a stabilizer shaft is connected between the chassis and control arms to control side roll.

1993–94

The short/long arm (SLA) front suspension assembly, **Fig. 2**, is designed to allow each wheel to compensate for changes in road surface level without significantly affecting the opposite wheel. Each wheel is independently connected to the frame by a steering knuckle, wheel hub, shock absorber and spring, upper and lower ball studs and upper and lower control arms.

WHEEL BEARINGS
ADJUST

1991–92

1. While rotating wheel forward, **torque** spindle nut to 12 ft. lbs., **Fig. 3**.
2. Back off nut until just loose then hand tighten nut and back it off again until either hole in spindle lines up with hole in nut. **Do not back off nut more than ½ flat.**
3. Install new cotter pin. With wheel bearing properly adjusted, there will be .001-.005 inch endplay.

1993–94

These vehicles use a maintenance-free wheel bearing, which does not require adjustment.

WHEEL BEARINGS
REPLACE

1991–92

1. Raise and support vehicle, then remove wheel and tire assembly.
2. Remove disc brake caliper. Once removed, the caliper can be wired or secured in some manner away from the disc. Do not allow caliper to hang from brake hose.
3. Remove spindle nut and hub and disc assembly. Grease retainer and inner wheel bearing can now be removed.
4. Reverse procedure to install.

1993–94

These vehicles use a maintenance-free wheel bearing, which is serviced as an assembly with the wheel hub.

SUSPENSION & STEERING LINKAGE CHECK

1991-92

1. Raise vehicle with jack placed under frame torque box behind front wheel.
2. Lock steering wheel with wheels in straight ahead position, then mount dial indicator on a suitable stand with pointer bearing against outer rim of wheel, **Fig. 4.**
3. Move wheel in and out at front and rear, without moving steering wheel, while observing gauge.
4. If gauge reading exceeds .108 inches, check steering linkage and suspension for excessive wear or damage.

LOWER BALL JOINT INSPECTION

Ball joint seals should be checked for cuts and tears. If cuts and tears are present, replace ball joint.

On 1993-94 vehicles, the lower ball joint has a visual wear indicator. Proceed as follows to inspect:
1. Ensure vehicle is supported by wheel assemblies so weight of vehicle is properly loading ball joints, then wipe grease fitting free of dirt and grease.
2. Wear is indicated by position of 1/2 inch diameter nipple in which grease fitting is threaded. If nipple is flush or inside cover surface, replace ball joint.

UPPER BALL JOINT INSPECTION

1993-94

1. Raise front end of vehicle and position floor stands under both lower control arms as near to ball joints as possible.
2. Position a dial indicator against wheel rim as shown in **Fig. 5.** Push in on bottom of tire while pulling out at top, then reverse procedure.
3. Deflection on dial indicator should not exceed .125 inch. If deflection exceeds specification, replace ball joint.
4. If ball joint is disconnected from steering knuckle, check for looseness or see if ball joint can be twisted in its socket using your fingers.
5. If either of the above conditions exist, replace ball joint.

LOWER BALL JOINT REPLACE

1. Raise vehicle and support at frame, and remove wheel and tire.
2. Position a suitable jack under lower control arm spring seat, and raise jack to compress coil spring. **Jack must remain in place during ball joint replacement to hold spring and lower control arm in position.**

1	FRONT CROSSMEMBER
2	UPPER MOUNT
3	STRUT
4	COIL SPRING
5	KNUCKLE
6	HUB AND DISC
7	LOWER CONTROL ARM

Fig. 1   Front suspension exploded view. 1991-92

Fig. 2   Front suspension exploded view. 1993-94

Fig. 3 Wheel bearing adjustment. 1991–92

FRT

A CHECKING LINKAGE WEAR — VIEWED FROM ABOVE.

B POSITION DIAL INDICATOR TO CHECK MOVEMENT AT THIS POINT

C MOVE WHEEL IN AND OUT AT FRONT AND BACK

Fig. 4 Suspension & steering linkage check. 1991–92

1 SUPPORT FRONT LOWER CONTROL ARM ASSEMBLY AS FAR OUTBOARD AS POSSIBLE

2 POSITION DIAL INDICATOR TO CHECK MOVEMENT AT THIS POINT

3 ROCK WHEEL AND TIRE ASSEMBLY IN AND OUT AT TOP AND BOTTOM

Fig. 5 Upper ball joint check. 1993–94

STRUT
REPLACE
1991–92

1. Raise and support vehicle.
2. Remove wheel and support lower control arm with a suitable jack.
3. Remove brake hose bracket and two strut to knuckle bolts, **Fig. 7**.
4. Remove upper mounting assembly cover.
5. Remove nut from upper end of strut, then the strut and shield.
6. Reverse procedure to install.

COIL SPRING
REPLACE
1991–92

1. Raise and support vehicle, then remove wheel and tire assembly.
2. Remove stabilizer link and bushings from lower control arm.
3. Remove cotter pin and nut from tie rod end.
4. Using tool J-24292-B or equivalent, disconnect tie rod end from steering knuckle.
5. Using a suitable spring compressor, compress coil spring, **Fig. 8**.
6. Remove lower control arm pivot bolt, then pivot control arm rearward.
7. Remove spring compressor and coil spring.
8. Reverse procedure to install. When installing, position coil spring as shown in **Fig. 8**. Lower control arm must be positioned at dimension A, **Fig. 9**, when torquing bolts.

SHOCK ABSORBER & SPRING
REPLACE
1993–94

1. Remove brake master cylinder nuts, then move master cylinder aside.
2. Remove upper shock absorber mounting nuts and bolts, then raise and support vehicle.
3. Remove wheel, then disconnect stabilizer shaft link.
4. Remove lower shock absorber mounting nuts and bolts, then separate lower ball joint from steering knuckle.

J 9519-18
J 9519-23
J 9519-7
LOWER CONTROL ARM

INSTALLING BALL JOINT
LOWER CONTROL ARM
J 9519-23
J 9519-9
J 9519-18

Fig. 6 Lower ball joint replacement

3. Remove cotter pin and nut securing ball joint stud to steering knuckle, then disconnect joint from knuckle using a suitable tool.
4. Lift knuckle assembly from ball stud, guiding control arm out of splash shield, then support knuckle aside to allow clearance for joint removal.
5. Remove grease fitting, then press ball joint assembly out of lower control arm using a suitable tool, **Fig. 6**.
6. Press replacement joint into arm by reversing removal tools, fit spindle over ball stud, install washer, if equipped, and retaining nut.
7. Torque retaining nut to specifications.
8. Tighten nut up to an additional 1/16 turn, if necessary, to align hole in ball stud with nut, then install cotter pin.

UPPER BALL JOINT
REPLACE
1993–94

1. Raise and support vehicle, then remove wheel.

2. Place a floor jack under shock absorber mounting location on lower control. **Jack must remain in place during ball joint replacement to hold spring and lower control arm in position.**
3. Loosen ball joint from steering knuckle, then remove cotter pin and nut.
4. Support steering knuckle with floor stands, then disconnect ball joint from upper control arm using ball joint/tie rod separator J 39549.
5. With upper control arm in raised position, drill out four rivets approximately 1/4 inch deep using a 1/8 inch drill bit.
6. Drill off rivet heads using a 1/2 inch drill bit, then punch out rivets using a small punch and remove ball joint.
7. Position new ball joint and install bolts and nuts supplied with new ball joint.
8. Remove support from steering knuckle, then connect ball joint to steering knuckle.
9. tighten nut enough to align slot with stud hole, then tighten nut to specifications and install cotter pin.

5. Mark lower mount location relative to upper mount location, then remove shock absorber and spring assembly.
6. Proceed as follows to disassemble shock absorber assembly:
   a. Install modular shock assembly compressor adapter J 34013-114 onto strut spring compressor J 34013-B, using wing nuts to secure tool to mounting holes C-H in lower left corner and P in upper right corner for driver side shock absorber assembly, **Figs. 10 and 11**, or to holes A-X-P in upper left corner and C-H in lower right corner for passenger side shock absorber assembly, **Fig. 12**.
   b. Install strut compressor adapter J 34013-88 and modular shock support J-34013-218 onto strut spring compressor, **Fig. 13. Ensure strut compressor adapter and modular shock support are aligned so that they can open and close together. If tools are not properly aligned, they will not open.**
   c. Install shock absorber assembly to top of modular shock assembly compressor adapter, **Figs. 14 and 15. Ensure top of shock absorber assembly is flat against modular shock assembly compressor adapter. Shock absorber assembly will not be aligned properly if it does not lay flat against tool.**
   d. Install shock absorber assembly into strut compressor adapter and modular shock support, **Fig. 16**, then close strut compressor adapter and modular shock support and install locking pin. **Ensure mounting ears of shock absorber assembly are facing downward toward rear of strut spring compressor or shock absorber assembly will not align properly.**
   e. Turn screw on strut spring compressor counterclockwise to raise shock absorber assembly up to modular shock assembly compressor adapter. Ensure studs go through guide holes in modular shock assembly compressor adapter and top of shock absorber assembly is flat against tool.
   f. Compress front spring assembly approximately ½ inch or three or four complete turns of screw on modular shock assembly compressor adapter. **Do not over compress front spring assembly. Severe overloading may cause tool failure, possibly resulting in personal injury.**
   g. Insert J 39642-1 from modular shock nut removal set J 39642 on shock absorber nut, then insert J 39642-2 from modular shock nut removal set J 39642 through J 39642-1 to hold shock absorber rod in place.
   h. Remove shock absorber nut and discard, then turn strut spring compressor clockwise to relieve spring pressure.

Fig. 7 Front suspension strut replacement. 1991–92

7. Proceed as follows to assemble shock absorber assembly:
   a. Install shock absorber to strut compressor adapter and modular shock support. **Ensure mounting ears of shock absorber assembly are facing downward toward rear of strut spring compressor or shock absorber assembly will not align properly.**
   b. Close strut compressor adapter and modular shock support and install locking pin, then ensure upper and lower spring seats are positioned correctly.
   c. Assemble shock absorber assembly to top of modular shock assembly compressor adapter. **Ensure top of shock absorber assembly is flat against modular shock assembly compressor adapter. Shock absorber assembly will not be aligned properly if it does not lay flat against tool.**
   d. Turn screw on strut spring compressor counterclockwise to raise shock absorber assembly up to modular shock assembly compressor adapter without compressing spring assembly. Ensure studs on shock absorber assembly go through guide holes in modular shock assembly compressor adapter. **Only turn screw until shock absorber assembly is held in strut spring compressor by itself. Do not load spring assembly.**
   e. Place modular shock assembly alignment rod J 34013-115 down through top of strut spring compressor, through top of shock absorber assembly and onto shock absorber rod, **Fig. 17. Ensure shock assembly alignment rod is straight with shock absorber assembly. If shock assembly alignment rod is angled, repeat steps 7a through 7d until tool is straight.**
   f. Turn operating screw clockwise to compress spring assembly until threaded portion of shock absorber rod is through top of shock absorber assembly. **Do not over compress front spring assembly. Severe overloading may cause tool failure, possibly resulting in personal injury.**
   g. Remove modular shock assembly alignment rod, then insert a new shock absorber nut on shock absorber rod. **Always replace shock absorber nut. Do not turn shock absorber rod when tightening nut or shock absorber assembly could be damaged. Retain shock absorber rod in a stationary position when tightening nut.**
   h. Place J 39642-1 from modular shock nut removal set J 39642 on shock absorber nut, then insert J 39642-2 from modular shock nut removal set J 39642 through J 39642-1 to hold shock absorber rod in place and tighten nut to specifications.
   i. Remove shock absorber assembly from strut spring compressor.
8. Reverse steps 1 through 5 to install. Tighten fasteners to specifications

J 23028

FRONT CROSSMEMBER

LOWER CONTROL ARM

SPRING

SPRING TO BE INSTALLED WITH TAPE AT LOWEST POSITION BOTTOM OF SPRING IS COILED HELICAL, AND THE TOP IS COILED FLAT WITH A GRIPPER NOTCH NEAR END OF WIRE.

AFTER ASSEMBLY, END OF SPRING COIL MUST COVER ALL OR PART OF ONE INSPECTION DRAIN HOLE. THE OTHER HOLE MUST BE PARTLY EXPOSED OR COMPLETELY UNCOVERED.

VIEW A

BOLT MUST BE INSTALLED IN DIRECTION SHOWN.

NUT (90 N·m)

NUT (90 N·m)

FRONT CROSSMEMBER

BOLT MUST BE INSTALLED IN DIRECTION SHOWN.

BUMPER

NUT (28 N·m)

FRONT CROSSMEMBER

INSULATOR

LOWER CONTROL ARM

SPRING

VIEW B

INSTALL THE FRONT LEG OF THE LOWER CONTROL ARM INTO THE CROSSMEMBER PRIOR TO INSTALLING THE REAR LEG.

CONTROL ARM MUST BE POSITIONED TO "Z" CURB HEIGHT DIMENSION WHEN BOLTS ARE TORQUED.

Fig. 8   Coil spring replacement. 1991–92

CENTER OF LOWER CONTROL ARM FRONT BUSHING BOLT HEAD

A

LOWEST POINT OF BALL STUD ASM (EXCLUDING GREASE FITTING)

Fig. 9   Lower control arm dimension A measurement location (Part 1 of 2). 1991–92

Fig. 10   Modular shock absorber assembly compressor mounting hole locations. 1993–94

J 34013-B

J 34013-114

Fig. 11   Modular shock absorber assembly compressor adapter, driver side. 1993–94

Year	Model	Suspension (Option Code)	Dimension A, Inches
1991–92	Camaro Coupe	Soft Ride (FE1)	1.220
		Ride & Handling (FE2) ①	1.181
		Ride & Handling (FE2) ②	.906
	Firebird Coupe	Soft Ride (FE1)	1.102
		Ride & Handling (FE2)	1.220
		Special Heavy Duty (FE41)	1.181
	Camaro & Firebird Convertible	Soft Ride (FE1)	1.299
		Ride & Handling (FE2) ①	1.220
		Ride & Handling (FE2) ②	.945

① —With 15 inch wheels.
② —With 16 inch wheels.

Fig. 9   Lower control arm dimension A specifications (Part 2 of 2). 1991–92

Fig. 12   Modular shock absorber assembly compressor adapter, passenger side. 1993–94

A   MATCHING ANGLE BETWEEN SHOCK ABSORBER ASSEMBLY AND J 34013-114
23   SPRING ASSEMBLY, FRONT
24   ABSORBER ASSEMBLY, FRONT SHOCK

Fig. 15   Installing upper passenger side shock absorber assembly to strut spring compressor. 1993–94

Fig. 13   Mounting strut compressor adapter & modular shock support to strut spring compressor. 1993–94

23   SPRING ASSEMBLY, FRONT
24   ABSORBER ASSEMBLY, FRONT SHOCK

Fig. 16   Installing shock absorber assembly to strut spring compressor. 1993–94

A   MATCHING ANGLE BETWEEN SHOCK ABSORBER ASSEMBLY AND J 34013-114
23   SPRING ASSEMBLY, FRONT
24   ABSORBER ASSEMBLY, FRONT SHOCK

Fig. 14   Installing upper driver side shock absorber assembly to strut spring compressor. 1993–94

A   ROD, FRONT SHOCK ABSORBER
23   SPRING ASSEMBLY, FRONT
24   ABSORBER ASSEMBLY, FRONT SHOCK

Fig. 17   Installing modular shock assembly alignment rod. 1993–94

STABILIZER SHAFT
REPLACE

1. Raise and support vehicle.
2. Remove nut from link bolt located at each side, then remove bolt, grommets and bushings, **Fig. 18.**
3. Remove stabilizer shaft to body bolts, then remove stabilizer bar.
4. Reverse procedure to install.

POWER STEERING GEAR
REPLACE

1991–92

1. Disconnect pressure hose and cooling pipe from power steering gear. Position pressure hose in upward position to prevent fluid drainage.
2. Disconnect intermediate steering shaft from power steering gear stub shaft.
3. Disconnect Pitman arm from power steering gear.
4. Remove steering gear attaching bolts, then remove power steering gear, **Fig. 19.**
5. Reverse procedure to install.

1993–94

1. Raise and support vehicle, then re-move wheels.
2. Disconnect inlet and outlet hoses from steering gear, then the steering linkage outer tie rods from steering knuckles.
3. Disconnect steering gear coupling shaft from steering gear, then remove steering gear.
4. Reverse procedure to install, noting the following:
   a. Tighten fasteners to specifications.
   b. Adjust steering gear so that it aligns as straight as possible with steering gear coupling shaft.
   c. Refill and bleed power steering system.

POWER STEERING PUMP
REPLACE

1991–92

1. Remove serpentine drive belt.
2. Remove pulley from power steering pump shaft, **Figs. 21 and 22.**
3. Disconnect hoses at power steering pump, then plug pump ports and hoses.
4. Remove pump to support bracket attaching bolts and the pump.
5. Reverse procedure to install. Torque attaching bolts to specifications.

1993–94
3.4L/V6-207 Engines

1. Remove serpentine belt, then the front air intake duct.
2. Disconnect inlet and outlet hoses from pump, then remove pump pulley using pump pulley remover J 25034-B.
3. Remove pump support from pump, then the pump.
4. Reverse procedure to install, noting the following:
   a. Tighten fasteners to specifications.

OBTAIN TORQUE BY RUNNING
NUT TO UNTHREADED PORTION
OF BOLT/SCREW.

INSULATOR
NUT (22 N·m)
RETAINER
STABILIZER SHAFT
KNUCKLE & HUB ASM
SPACER
RETAINER
INSULATOR
INSULATOR
RETAINER
BOLT

BOLT MUST BE INSTALLED IN
DIRECTION SHOWN.

STABILIZER SHAFT
INSULATOR
INSTALL STABILIZER SHAFT INSULATOR WITH SLIT TOWARD FRONT OF VEHICLE AS SHOWN.
BRACKET
BOLT (53 N·m)
SIDE RAIL
HOLD STABILIZER SHAFT AT APPROX. 55.0 FROM BOTTOM OF SIDE RAIL WHEN TIGHTENING STABILIZER SHAFT INSULATORS.
VIEW A

Fig. 18   Stabilizer shaft replacement

1 GEAR ASSEMBLY, POWER STEERING
8 KNUCKLE ASSEMBLY, STEERING
26 NUT, STEERING GEAR
27 BOLT/SCREW, STEERING GEAR, 85 N·m (63 LB. FT.)
34 CROSSMEMBER ASSEMBLY, FRONT

Fig. 20   Power steering gear installation. 1993–94

5	POWER STEERING GEAR
15	BOLT
29	WASHER

Fig. 19   Power steering gear installation. 1991–92

1	PUMP
2	PULLEY
24	BOLT
26	BRACE
28	NUT
30	BOLT

Fig. 21   Power steering pump installation. 3.1L/V6-191

b. Install pump pulley using pump pulley installer J 25033-B. Face of pulley hub must be flush with end of pump shaft before applying load to pulley hub. Load required to press pulley hub onto pump shaft must be greater than 1500 lbs., but less than 7000 lbs.
c. Refill and bleed power steering system.

5.7L/V8-350 Engines

1. Raise and support vehicle, then drain engine coolant.
2. Remove serpentine belt, then lower vehicle.
3. Remove front air intake duct, then the alternator.
4. Disconnect radiator outlet hose from engine, heater inlet and outlet hoses from water pump, then the throttle body heater return hose from heater outlet hose.
5. Remove pump mounting bolts, then disconnect inlet and reservoir hoses from pump and remove pump.
6. Reverse procedure to install, noting the following:
   a. Tighten fasteners to specifications.
   b. Refill and bleed power steering system.

1	PUMP
2	PULLEY
24	BOLT
25	NUT
26	BRACE
27	NUT

Fig. 22 Power steering pump installation. 5.0L/V8-305 & 1991–92 5.7L/V8-350

4 PUMP ASSEMBLY, POWER STEERING
17 SUPPORT, POWER STEERING PUMP
18 BOLT/SCREW, POWER STEERING PUMP REAR BRACKET, 50 N·m (37 LB. FT.)
19 NUT, POWER STEERING PUMP SUPPORT, 50 N·m (37 LB. FT.)
20 BOLT/SCREW, POWER STEERING PUMP, 50 N·m (37 LB. FT.)
35 BRACE ASSEMBLY, POWER STEERING PUMP REAR

Fig. 23 Power steering pump installation. 3.4L/V6-207

4 PUMP ASSEMBLY, POWER STEERING
11 HOSE ASSEMBLY, POWER STEERING FLUID RESERVOIR
21 BOLT/SCREW, POWER STEERING PUMP, 25 N·m (18 LB. FT.)
36 BRACKET ASSEMBLY, GENERATOR AND AIR CONDITIONER COMPRESSOR AND POWER STEERING PUMP AND DRIVE BELT TENSIONER

Fig. 24 Power steering pump installation. 1993–94 5.7L/V8-350

TIGHTENING SPECIFICATIONS

Year	Component	Torque/Ft. Lbs.
1991–92	Idler Arm To Frame Nut	63
	Lower Control Arm Ball Joint Stud	80
	Lower Control Arm Pivot Bolt	61
	Pitman Arm Nut	184
	Power Steering Gear Mounting Bolts	73
	Power Steering Pump Brace To Pump Nut (V6 Engine)	18
	Power Steering Pump Brace To Pump Nut (V8 Engine)	37
	Power Steering Pump Bracket To Engine Bolt	24

Year	Component	Torque/Ft. Lbs.
1991–92 —Cont'd	Power Steering Pump Bracket To Engine Stud Nut	24
	Relay Rod To Inner Tie Rod Nut	40
	Relay Rod To Pitman Arm Nut	35
	Stabilizer Bracket Bolt	39
	Stabilizer Link Nut	①
	Strut To Steering knuckle	②
	Strut Bottom Upper Nut	40
	Strut Upper Mount To Wheel Housing Tower	14
	Tie Rod Adjuster Clamp Nut	13
	Tie Rod End To Steering Knuckle	35

Continued

TIGHTENING SPECIFICATIONS—Continued

Year	Component	Torque/ Ft. Lbs.
1991-92	Tie Rod (Outer) To Steering Arm Nut	35
	Wheel Lug Nuts	100
1993-94	Lower Ball Joint Nut	81
	Lower Shock Absorber Nuts	48
	Power Steering Gear Mounting Bolts	63
	Power Steering Pump Bolts (V6 Engine)	37
	Power Steering Pump Bolts (V8 Engine)	18
	Power Steering Pump Support To Pump Nuts & Bolts (V6 Engine)	37

Year	Component	Torque/ Ft. Lbs.
1993-94 -Cont'd	Stabilizer Bracket To Frame Bolts	41
	Stabilizer Clamp To Stabilizer Bracket Bolts	41
	Stabilizer Link Nut	17
	Upper Ball Joint Nut	39
	Upper Shock Absorber Mount To Strut Tower Bolts	37
	Upper Shock Absorber Mount To Strut Tower Nuts	32
	Wheel Lug Nuts	100

①—Less ride & handling suspension, 13 ft. lbs.; w/ride & handling suspension, 18 ft. lbs.

②—Torque nuts to 125 ft. lbs., then tighten each nut an additional 120°.

Ensure total torque reading exceeds 148 ft. lbs.

Wheel Alignment

INDEX

Fig. 1   Caster adjustment. 1991–92

Fig. 2   Front caster & camber adjustment tool installation. 1991–92

FRONT WHEEL ALIGNMENT

Prior to checking or adjusting front suspension alignment, inspect suspension components for damage or excessive wear, and replace as needed. Ensure tire pressures and wheel bearings are properly adjusted, then raise and release front bumper several times to allow vehicle to assume normal ride height.

CASTER

1991-92

Caster adjustments are made by moving the position of the upper strut mount assembly, **Fig. 1**. To make adjustment, remove dust cap and fender bolt and attach tool J-29724 to original fender bolt, **Fig. 2**. Tighten the turnbuckle and loosen the three strut mount attaching nuts.

Adjust caster by lightly tapping the mount assembly forward or rearward.

Move mount forward to decrease caster, or rearward to increase caster, **Fig. 1**.

1993-94

1. Jounce front bumper three times to allow vehicle to return to normal ride height, then raise and support vehicle.
2. Loosen front lower control arm nuts, then install camber/caster adjuster J 38658 to slot holes in lower control arm and front crossmember, **Fig. 3**.
3. Adjust caster to specifications by rotating turnbuckle on camber/caster adjuster. Clockwise increases caster, counterclockwise decreases caster.
4. Remove camber/caster adjuster, then **torque** front lower control arm nuts to 96 ft. lbs.

CAMBER

1991-92

Camber adjustments are made by mov-

ing the position of the upper strut mount assembly, **Fig. 4**. To make adjustment, remove dust cap and fender bolt and attach tool J-29724 to original fender bolt, **Fig. 2**. Tighten the turnbuckle and loosen the three strut mount attaching nuts.

Adjust camber by rotating the turnbuckle to move mount assembly inward or outward. Move mount inboard to decrease camber, or outboard to increase camber, **Fig. 4**.

1993-94

1. Jounce front bumper three times to allow vehicle to return to normal ride height, then raise and support vehicle.
2. Loosen front lower control arm nuts, then install camber/caster adjuster J 38658 to slot holes in lower control arm and front crossmember, **Fig. 5**.
3. Adjust camber to specifications by rotating turnbuckle on camber/caster adjuster. Clockwise increases caster,

2 CROSSMEMBER ASSEMBLY, FRONT
3 ARM ASSEMBLY, FRONT LOWER CONTROL

Fig. 3 Front caster adjustment tool installation. 1993–94

Fig. 4 Front camber adjustment

2 CROSSMEMBER ASSEMBLY, FRONT
3 ARM ASSEMBLY, FRONT LOWER CONTROL

Fig. 5 Front camber adjustment tool installation. 1993–94

counterclockwise decreases caster.
4. Remove camber/caster adjuster, then **torque** front lower control arm nuts to 96 ft. lbs.

TOE-IN

1991–92

1. Loosen clamp bolts at each end of tie rod adjustable sleeves.
2. Set steering wheel in straight-ahead position, then turn tie rods as necessary until toe-in is within specifications.
3. After adjustment is complete, ensure threads exposed on each end of sleeve are equal and tie rod end

NOTE EQUAL WITHIN THREE THREADS MUST BE VISIBLE AT INNER & OUTER ENDS OF ADJUSTER SLEEVE WHEN ASSEMBLED TO STEERING KNUCKLE.

TIE ROD-INNER

CAUTION CLAMP MUST BE BETWEEN & CLEAR OF DIMPLES BEFORE TORQUING NUT.

TIE ROD-OUTER

ADJUSTER SLEEVE SLOT

HORIZONTAL LINE 50°

10°

FRT

REARWARD ROTATION VIEW A

NOTE SLOT IN ADJUSTER SLEEVE MUST NOT BE WITHIN THIS AREA OF CLAMP JAWS.

FRT

GAP

CAUTION CLAMP ENDS MAY TOUCH WHEN NUTS ARE TORQUED TO SPECIFICATION BUT GAP MUST BE VISIBLE ADJACENT TO ADJUSTER SLEEVE.

TORQUE:
⚠ 19 N•M (14 FT.LBS.)

VIEW B TIGHT

Fig. 6 Tie rod clamp & sleeve positioning

A ADJUSTMENT SLOTS
B MACHINED FLATS
C SOCKET INSTALLED ON HEAD OF PIVOT BOLT
14 RELAY ROD
25 LOWER CONTROL ARM
26 FRONT CROSSMEMBER

Fig. 7 Relay rod height adjustment

housings are at right angles to steering arm.
4. Position tie rod clamps and sleeves as shown, **Fig. 6,** then tighten nuts.

1993–94

Toe adjustments are made separately at each individual wheel.
1. Ensure steering wheel is set in a straight ahead position within ± 3.5 degrees.
2. Loosen nut on inner tie rod, then adjust toe to specifications. Left and right toe adjustment should be equal within ± .2 degrees.
3. Ensure steering gear boot is not twisted, then **torque** inner tie rod nut to 35 ft. lbs.

RELAY ROD HEIGHT ADJUSTMENT

1991–92

Relay rod height should be equal (plus or minus .039 inch) from side to side. If relay rod height is not within specifications, steering and handling problem could be encountered. Relay rod height is adjusted at the idler arm to frame attachment.
1. Raise and support vehicle.
2. Using a suitable wire brush, clean both flats of relay rod.
3. Position tool J33093 or equivalent on flat of relay rod at Pitman arm end.
4. Position a socket on pivot bolt of left hand lower control arm.

A RIGHT SIDE OF REAR AXLE IS FORWARD (TOE-OUT OF LEFT WHEEL, AND TOE-IN OF RIGHT WHEEL).

B RIGHT SPINDLE IS NOT PERPENDICULAR TO CENTERLINE OF VEHICLE (TOE-OUT OF RIGHT WHEEL).

C AXLE SAG (NEGATIVE CAMBER).

Fig. 8   Rear wheel alignment check. 1991-92

A RIGHT SIDE OF REAR AXLE ASSEMBLY IS FORWARD (TOE-OUT OF LEFT TIRE AND WHEEL ASSEMBLY AND TOE-IN OF RIGHT TIRE AND WHEEL ASSEMBLY)
B RIGHT SPINDLE IS NOT PERPENDICULAR TO CENTERLINE OF VEHICLE
C REAR VIEW OF REAR AXLE ASSEMBLY SAG
D TOP VIEW
E CENTERLINE OF TIRE AND WHEEL ASSEMBLY
F PERPENDICULAR TO CENTERLINE OF VEHICLE
G PARALLEL TO CENTERLINE OF VEHICLE
H DEVIATION OF TOE FROM CENTERLINE OF VEHICLE
J NEGATIVE CAMBER ANGLE
13 FRONT TIRE AND WHEEL ASSEMBLY
14 REAR TIRE AND WHEEL ASSEMBLY

Fig. 9   Rear wheel alignment check. 1993-94

5. Measure distance between bottom socket and tool and note, **Fig. 7.**
6. Loosen idler arm to frame nuts just enough to allow idler arm to slide upward and downward.
7. Position tool J33093 or equivalent on flat of relay rod at idler arm end.
8. Position a socket on pivot bolt of right hand lower control arm.
9. Measure distance between bottom socket and tool and note, **Fig. 7.**
10. Both reading should be with in .039 inch of each other. If not, adjust position of idle arm at frame until readings are within limits.
11. **Torque** idler arm to frame nuts to 52 ft. lbs., then remove tool and socket and lower vehicle.
12. Check and adjust toe as necessary.

REAR WHEEL ALIGNMENT

After front wheel alignment has been checked or adjusted, rear wheel alignment angles should be checked if vehicle still does not track properly or if excessive rear tire wear is present. Rear wheels should be parallel to and the same distance from the vehicle centerline, **Fig. 8 and 9.**

Rear wheel alignment is not adjustable. If alignment angles are not within specification, check for bent or damaged suspension arms, axle housing or frame.

THRUST ANGLE

1991-92

The vehicle is steered by the front wheels. The path which the rear wheels follow is the thrust angle, **Fig. 10.** In an ideal setting, the thrust angle would be aligned with that of the vehicle center line.

1993-94

If the thrust angle is not within specifications, inspect upper and lower control arms for damage. If control arms are not damaged, check frame dimensions.

VEHICLE RIDE HEIGHT
1991-92

Refer to **Fig. 11** for vehicle ride height measurements and specifications. When checking vehicle ride height measurements, fuel tank should be full, tires at should be correct pressure, front seat should be rearward position, truck should be empty except for spare tire and jack and vehicle should be on level ground. If fuel tank is not full, add weight to trunk to compensate for amount fuel vehicle is below the full level.

Prior to checking ride height, lift front bumper upward approximately 1.5 inches and gently release (3 times), then check front ride height. Push front bumper downward approximately 1.5 inches and gently release (3 times), then recheck front ride height. Average of both readings to determine vehicle ride height. Check rear ride height in same manner, lifting and pushing rear bumper.

A — THRUST ANGLE
B — THRUST LINE-OFF CENTER
C — REAR TOE-OUT CONDITION
D — GEOMETRIC CENTERLINE

Fig. 10   Thrust angle check

Fig. 11   Vehicle ride height measurement locations & specifications (Part 1 of 2)

| Year | Make & Model | Suspension (Option Code) | Riding Height Measurements, Inches ① | | |
			Dimension D	Dimension J	Dimension K
1991–92	Camaro Coupe	Soft Ride (FE1)	4.409	8.346	8.307
		Ride & Handling (FE2) ②	4.370	8.346	8.307
		Ride & Handling (FE2) ③	4.331	8.031	8.110
	Firebird Coupe	Soft Ride (FE1)	4.370	8.228	8.268
		Ride & Handling (FE2) ③	4.449	8.228	8.268
		Special Heavy Duty (F41) ④	4.370	8.228	8.268
		Special Heavy Duty (F41) ⑤	4.409	8.228	8.268
	Camaro & Firebird Convertibles	Soft Ride (FE1)	4.449	8.346	8.307
		Ride & Handling (FE2) ②	4.370	8.346	8.307
		Ride & Handling (FE2) ③	4.331	8.031	8.110

TBI: Throttle Body Injection.
TPI: Tuned Port Injection.

①—Plus or minus .4 inch.
②—With 15 inch wheels.
③—With 16 inch wheels.

④—With 5.0L/V8-305 TBI engine.
⑤—With 5.0L/V8-305 TPI engine.

Fig. 11   Vehicle ride height measurement locations & specifications (Part 2 of 2)

CHEVROLET CORVETTE
(Y Car)
INDEX OF SERVICE OPERATIONS

NOTE: Refer To The Rear Of This Manual For Vehicle Manufacturer's Special Tool Suppliers.

Continued

Specifications
GENERAL ENGINE SPECIFICATIONS

Year	Engine Liter/CID	VIN Code ①	Fuel System	Bore & Stroke	Compression Ratio	Net Brake H.P. @ RPM ②	Maximum Torque	Normal Oil Pressure psi
1991	5.7L/V8-350 ③ ⑧	8	TPI	4.00 x 3.48	9.5	245 @ 4000	340 @ 3200	④
	5.7L/V8-350 ⑤ ⑧	8	TPI	4.00 x 3.48	9.5	250 @ 4400	345 @ 3200	④
	5.7L/V8-350 ⑥	J	TPI	3.90 x 3.66	11.0	375 @ 5800	370 @ 4800	⑦
1992-94	5.7L/V8-350 ⑧	P	TPI	4.00 x 3.48	10.2	300 @ 5000	330 @ 4000	④
	5.7L/V8-350 ⑥	J	TPI	3.90 x 3.66	11.0	375 @ 5800	370 @ 4800	⑦

CID—Cubic Inch Displacement.
TPI—Tune Port Injection.
①—The eighth digit of the VIN denotes engine code.
②—Ratings are net, as installed in vehicle.

③—Models w/single outlet mufflers.
④—With engine hot, minimum oil pressure at 1000 RPM, 6 psi.; at 2000 RPM, 18 psi.; at 4000 RPM, 24 psi.
⑤—Models w/dual outlet sport mufflers.

⑥—4 Cam 32 valve engine (ZR-1).
⑦—With engine hot, minimum oil pressure, at idle speed, 12 psi.; above 3000 RPM, 40 psi.
⑧—Single cam 16 valve engine.

TUNE UP SPECIFICATIONS

Year & Engine (VIN code) ①	Spark Plug Gap	Firing Order Fig. ③	Ignition Timing BTDC ② Man. Trans.	Auto. Trans.	Mark Fig.	Curb Idle Speed ④ Man. Trans.	Auto. Trans.	Fast Idle Speed Man. Trans.	Auto. Trans.	Fuel Pump Pressure psi
1991										
5.7L/V8-350(8) ⑩	.035	A	6⑤	6⑤	B	⑥	⑥	⑥	⑥	40.5-47 ⑦
5.7L/V8-350(J) ⑧	.035	C	6⑨	—	D	⑥	—	⑥	—	48-55 ⑦
1992-94										
5.7L/V8-350(P) ⑩	.050	E	⑨	⑨	—	⑥	⑥	⑥	⑥	41-47 ⑦
5.7L/V8-350(J) ⑥	.035	C	⑨	—	D	⑥	—	⑥	—	48-55 ⑦

①—The eighth digit of the VIN denotes engine code.
②—BTDC: Before Top Dead Center.
③—Before removing from distributor cap, determine location of No. 1 wire in cap, as distributor position may have been altered from that shown at the end of this chart.
④—When checking idle speed, set parking brake & block drive wheels.
⑤—Disconnect set timing by-pass

connector (tan/black wire), which breaks out of the engine wiring harness conduit. After completing ignition timing check, reconnect timing bypass connector. With engine off, clear ECM memory by removing battery voltage to ECM for 30 seconds.
⑥—Idle speed is controlled by an idle speed control motor.

⑦—With shop towel wrapped around fuel pressure fitting to prevent fuel spillage, connect a suitable fuel pressure gauge. Check fuel pressure with ignition switch in ON position, engine not running.
⑧—4 Cam 32 valve engine (ZR-1).
⑨—Computer controlled, no adjustment.
⑩—Single cam 16 valve engine.

Continued

Fig. A

Fig. B

Fig. C

Fig. D

Fig. E

WHEEL ALIGNMENT SPECIFICATIONS
FRONT WHEEL

Year	Model	Caster Angle, Degrees		Camber Angle, Degrees		Toe Per Wheel, Degrees		Steering Wheel Angle, Degrees
		Limits	Desired	Limits	Desired	Limits	Desired	
1991-94	All	+5.5 to +6.5	+6	0 to +1	+.5	−.10 to +.10	0	−1 to +1

WHEEL ALIGNMENT SPECIFICATIONS—Continued

REAR WHEEL

Year	Model	Camber Angle, Degrees		Toe Per Wheel, Degrees		Thrust Angle, Degrees	
		Limits	Desired	Limits	Desired	Limits	Desired
1991-94	All	−.5 to +.5	0	−.1 to +.1	0	−.1 to +.1	0

COOLING SYSTEM & CAPACITY DATA

Year	Model Or Engine (VIN)①	Cooling System Capacity, Qts.	Radiator Cap Relief Pressure, psi.	Thermo. Opening Temp.	Fuel Tank, Gals.	Engine Oil, Qts.②		Transmission Oil			Rear Axle Pts.
						Less Filter Change	With Filter Change	Man Trans. Pts.	Auto. Trans. Qts.③		
									Drain & Refill	Total Capacity	
1991	5.7L/V8-350(8)⑧	17.8	15	195	20	4④	5④	4.4	5	11.2	3.75
	5.7L/V8-350(J)⑦	14.7	15	180	20	⑤	⑤	4.4	—	—	3.75
1992-94	5.7L/V8-350(P)⑧	17.8	15	195	20	4⑥	5⑥	4.4	5	11.2	3.75
	5.7L/V8-350(J)⑦	14.7	15	180	20	⑤	⑤	4.4	—	—	3.75

①—The eighth digit of the VIN denotes engine code.
②—After refilling, recheck oil level.
③—Approximate, make final check w/dipstick.
④—Recommended engine oil SG SAE 5W-30.

⑤—Recommended engine oil SG SAE 10W-30. Less filter change, 7.6 qts.; with filter change 8.6 qts. With oil cooler drain & flush, less filter change, 9.6 qts.; with filter change, 10.6 qts. Total system capacity with filter removed & oil pan dry, 11.6 qts.

⑥—Recommended engine oil SG SAE 5W-30 synthetic engine oil meeting GM specification GM4718M.
⑦—4 cam 32 valve engine (ZR-1).
⑧—Single cam 16 valve engine.

LUBRICANT DATA

Year	Lubricant Type				
	Transmission		Rear Axle	Power Steering System	Brake System
	Automatic	Manual			
1991	Dexron II	5W-30①	②	Power Steering Fluid ③	DOT 3 Brake Fluid
1992-94	Dexron IIE	5W-30①	②	Power Steering Fluid ④	DOT 3 Brake Fluid

①—Manual transmission fluid, GM part No. 1052931 or equivalent.
②—Use 80W-90 GL-5 gear lubricant & lubricant additive (GM part No. 1052358 or equivalent).
③—Meeting GM specification 9985010.
④—Meeting GM specification 9985835.

Electrical

INDEX

PRECAUTIONS

AIRBAG SYSTEM DISARMING

The diagnostic energy reserve module (DERM) can maintain voltage to cause a system deployment for up to ten minutes after the ignition switch is turned off and the battery is disconnected. Servicing the SIR system during this period may result in accidental deployment and personal injury.

1. Ensure front wheels are pointed straight ahead.
2. Turn ignition switch to Lock position and remove SIR or AIRBAG fuse.
3. Remove left sound insulator. **Remove courtesy lamp from sound insulator, if necessary.**
4. Remove Connector Position Assurance (CPA), then disconnect yellow two-way SIR electrical connector at base of steering column.

AIRBAG SYSTEM ARMING

1. Connect yellow two-way SIR electrical connector, then install Connector Position Assurance (CPA).
2. Install left sound insulator. **Install courtesy lamp to sound insulator, if applicable.**
3. Install SIR fuse to fuse block, turn ignition switch to RUN position and ensure "Inflatable Restraint" lamp flashes 7 to 9 times, then shuts off.

FUSE PANEL & FLASHER LOCATION

The fuse panel is located behind the far righthand corner of the instrument panel. The hazard warning flasher is located behind the righthand side of the instrument

1	LONG SHIM
2	SHORT SHIM
3	STARTER MOTOR
4	OUTBOARD BOLT
5	INBOARD BOLT

Fig. 1 Starter motor replacement. 5.7L/V8-350 single cam 16 valve engine .MDUL/.MDNM/

panel near radio receiver. The turn signal flasher is located behind the below left-hand side of the instrument panel to the left of the steering column.

STARTER
REPLACE

If shims are used between starter and engine block, they should be placed in their original location during installation. If starter is noisy during cranking, remove one .015 inch double shim or add one .015 single shim to the outer bolt. If starter

makes a high pitched whine after firing, add .015 inch double shims until noise ceases.

5.7L/V8-350 SINGLE CAM 16 VALVE ENGINE

1. Disconnect battery ground cable.
2. Raise and support vehicle, then disconnect starter wiring.
3. Remove starter to engine brace and starter heat shields, if equipped.
4. Remove starter mounting bolts and lower starter, **Fig. 1.** Note position of shims, if used.

Fig. 2 Starter motor replacement. 5.7L/V8-350 4 cam 32 valve (ZR-1) engine

1	MOTOR, STARTER
2	BOLT, STARTER MOTOR MOUNTING
3	CASE, CYLINDER

1	GENERATOR MOUNTING BRACKET
2	GENERATOR UPPER MOUNTING BOLT
3	GENERATOR
4	GENERATOR LOWER MOUNTING BOLT
5	POWER STEERING PUMP BRACKET
6	BOLT, 50 N·m (37 lb. ft.)
7	GENERATOR REAR BRACE
8	GENERATOR BRACE BOLT
9	ENGINE STUD
10	NUT, 33 N·m (24 lb. ft.)

Fig. 3 Alternator mounting. 1991 5.7L/V8-350 single cam 16 valve engine

1	GENERATOR
2	GENERATOR MOUNTING BRACE
3	BOLT - TIGHTEN TO 33 N·m (24 lb. ft.)
4	BOLT - TIGHTEN TO 50 N·m (37 lb. ft.)
5	BOLT - TIGHTEN TO 33 N·m (24 lb. ft.)
6	GENERATOR REAR BRACE
7	GENERATOR, A/C COMPRESSOR AND POWER STEERING PUMP BRACKET
8	BOLT - TIGHTEN TO 50 N·m (37 lb. ft.)
9	BOLT
10	NUT - TIGHTEN TO 50 N·m (37 lb. ft.)

Fig. 4 Alternator mounting. 1992-94 5.7L/V8-350 single cam 16 valve engine

5. Disconnect solenoid wires and the battery cable.
6. Remove starter from vehicle.
7. Reverse procedure to install. **Torque** starter mounting bolts to 34 ft. lbs.

5.7L/V8-350 4 CAM 32 VALVE (ZR-1) ENGINE

1. Disconnect battery ground cable, then drain cooling system.

2. Remove intake plenum assembly. Refer to the "5.7L/V8-350 4 Cam 32 Valve Engine" section, "Intake Plenum Assembly, Replace" procedure.
3. Remove ignition coil pack described under "Ignition Coil Pack, Replace."
4. Disconnect battery positive cable and electrical leads from starter motor.
5. Remove starter motor to engine block attaching bolts, then remove starter motor, **Fig. 2**.
6. Reverse procedure to install. Prior to installation, coat threads of starter mounting bolts with Loctite 262 or equivalent. **Torque** starter mounting bolts to 38 ft. lbs.

ALTERNATOR
REPLACE
5.7L/V8-350 SINGLE CAM 16 VALVE ENGINE

1. Disconnect battery ground cable, then remove intake air duct.
2. Disconnect regulator electrical connector and battery lead from rear of alternator.
3. **On 1991 models**, rotate serpentine belt tensioner using a 1/2 inch breaker bar to release belt tension, then remove serpentine drive belt.
4. **On 1992-94 models**, using a suitable socket and handle on tensioner pulley bolt, lift tensioner upward in the clockwise direction, then remove serpentine drive belt.
5. **On all models**, remove alternator rear mounting bolt and nut, then re-

1	GENERATOR SUPPORT BRACKET
2	GENERATOR
3	GENERATOR LOWER SUPPORT BRACKET
4	GENERATOR LOWER MOUNTING BOLT
5	GENERATOR BRACKET BOLT
6	GENERATOR UPPER SUPPORT BRACKET BOLT

Fig. 5 Alternator mounting. 5.7L/V8-350 four cam 32 valve engine

move alternator rear mounting bracket, **Figs. 3 and 4.**

6. Remove two bolts from alternator upper mounting, then remove upper mounting bracket.
7. Remove two bolts from alternator lower mounting, then remove lower mounting bracket.
8. Remove alternator from vehicle.
9. Reverse procedure to install, noting the following:
   a. Do not tighten alternator mounting bolts until all mounting brackets and bolts have been installed.
   b. **Torque** alternator lower and upper mounting bolts to 37 ft. lbs.
   c. **Torque** alternator rear mounting bolt to 17 ft. lbs. and rear mounting nut to 24 ft. lbs.
   d. **On 1991 models,** position serpentine drive belt over pulleys, then rotate tensioner using a ½ breaker bar.
   e. **On 1992-94 models,** lift tensioner using a suitable socket and handle on pulley bolt, then position serpentine drive belt over pulleys and release tensioner.
   f. **On 1991 models,** check serpentine drive belt tension using a suitable belt tension gauge. Belt tension should be 60 to 90 lbs. on 1991 models. If not replace serpentine drive belt or tensioner as necessary.
   g. **On 1992-94 models,** check to ensure belt tension indicator marks are within limit lines on belt tensioner indicator.

5.7L/V8-350 4 CAM 32 VALVE (ZR-1) ENGINE

1. Disconnect battery ground cable, then remove intake air duct.
2. Remove throttle body extension.
3. Using a ½ inch breaker bar, rotate serpentine drive belt tensioner to release belt tension.

4. Remove serpentine drive belt from water pump pulley, then remove belt.
5. Remove alternator lower support bolts and bracket, **Fig. 5.**
6. Remove rear support bracket to alternator retaining bolt.
7. Remove alternator upper support bolts and bracket.
8. Disconnect electrical connector, then remove oil sender unit.
9. Disconnect electrical connectors from alternator, then remove alternator from vehicle.
10. Reverse procedure to install, noting the following:
    a. Apply Loctite 565 or equivalent to threads of alternator mounting bolts prior to installation. **Torque** alternator mounting bolts to 19 ft. lbs.
    b. When installing serpentine drive belt, position belt over A/C compressor pulley. Retract belt tensioner using a ½ inch drive ratchet and route belt over alternator, crankshaft and power steering pump pulleys, then position belt behind water pump pulley. Ensure belt is properly positioned on pulleys, then pull belt forward onto water pump pulley. Release belt tensioner.
    c. **Torque** throttle body extension attaching bolts to 53 inch lbs.

DISTRIBUTOR REPLACE

1991 5.7L/V8-350 SINGLE CAM 16 VALVE ENGINE
Removal

1. Disconnect battery ground cable.
2. Remove intake manifold plenum extension.
3. Disconnect ignition switch feed and tachometer leads from distributor cap. Screwdriver or other tools should not be used to release lead connector locking tab.
4. Remove distributor cap attaching screws, then position cap out of way.
5. Disconnect four terminal ECM electrical connector from distributor electrical connector.
6. Remove distributor hold-down clamp and bolt. Mark position of distributor rotor to distributor housing and position of distributor housing to engine for use during installation.
7. Lift distributor upward until rotor stops rotating in counterclockwise direction and mark position of rotor to distributor housing for use during installation.
8. Remove distributor from engine.

Installation

1. Position rotor to mark on distributor housing, then insert distributor into engine aligning rotor to housing and housing to engine marks made during removal.
2. If engine was was disturbed while distributor was removed, proceed as follows:

47	BOLT
48	DRIVESHAFT
49	DISTRIBUTOR

Fig. 6 Distributor replacement. 1992-94 5.7L/V8-350 single cam 16 valve engine

   a. Remove spark plug from No. 1 cylinder.
   b. With transmission in Neutral or Park and parking brake applied, position finger over spark plug opening in cylinder head, then slowly crank engine until compression is felt.
   c. Align crankshaft pulley with TDC (0) mark on timing indicator.
   d. Locate distributor rotor contact between No. 1 and 8 spark plug firing positions on distributor.
   e. Insert distributor into engine.
3. Install distributor hold clamp and bolt. Hand tighten bolt.
4. Connect ECM four terminal electrical connector to distributor.
5. Install distributor cap, then connect ignition switch and tachometer lead connector to cap.
6. Connect battery ground cable, then check and adjust ignition timing as necessary. **Torque** distributor hold-down bolt to 25 ft. lbs.

1992-94 5.7L/V8-350 SINGLE CAM 16 VALVE ENGINE
Removal

1. Disconnect battery ground cable.
2. Disconnect intake air temperature sensor harness connector.
3. Using a suitable socket and handle on serpentine drive belt tensioner pulley bolt, lift tensioner upward in the clockwise direction, then remove serpentine drive belt.
4. Drain coolant from engine.
5. Disconnect coolant hoses from water pump, then disconnect coolant sensor electrical connector.
6. Remove water pump as described under "Water Pump, Replace."
7. Remove crankshaft pulley attaching bolts, then remove pulley.
8. Remove crankshaft damper as described under "Crankshaft Damper, Replace."
9. Disconnect spark plug cables from

Fig. 7 Coil pack electrical & spark plug wire connections. 5.7L/V8-350 4 cam 32 valve (ZR-1) engine

B (IGN)
A (IGN)

A (1·6)
B (8·5)
C (3·2)
D (4·7)

distributor, then disconnect four terminal ECM connector at distributor. Note location of spark plug wires in distributor cap for use during installation.
10. Remove distributor attaching bolts, then pull distributor forward until shaft disengages from engine, **Fig. 6.**

Installation

1. Position distributor shaft in engine and place alignment mark at top shaft. Remove distributor shaft from engine and position in distributor. Rotate shaft until alignment mark is located at top.
2. Position distributor and shaft assembly to engine and install, **Fig. 6.** **Torque** distributor to engine attaching bolts to 8 ft. lbs.
3. Connect ECM four terminal connector at distributor, then connect spark plug wires to distributor cap terminals.
4. Install crankshaft damper as described under "Crankshaft Damper, Replace."
5. Install crankshaft pulley.
6. Install water pump assembly as described under "Water Pump, Replace."
7. Connect coolant sensor electrical connector.
8. Connect coolant hoses to water pump, then fill cooling system.
9. Install serpentine drive belt and air intake duct.
10. Connect intake air temperature sensor harness connector and battery ground cable.

IGNITION COIL PACK REPLACE

5.7L/V8-350 4 CAM 32 VALVE (ZR-1) ENGINE

1. Disconnect battery ground cable.

18 SCREW, LOCK RETAINING
20 LOCK CYLINDER SET, STRG COL PASS KEY

Fig. 8 Ignition lock replacement

2. Remove intake plenum assembly. Refer to the "5.7L/V8-350 4 Cam 32 Valve Engine" section, "Intake Plenum Assembly, Replace" procedure.
3. Note position of spark plug wires to coils, **Fig. 7.**
4. Disconnect spark plug wires from coils.
5. Disconnect electrical connectors from ignition coil pack terminals.
6. Remove four coil pack retaining bolts, then remove coil pack.
7. Reverse procedure to install. **Torque** coil pack M6-16 retaining bolts to 89 inch lbs. and M8-20 retaining bolts to 19 ft. lbs.

IGNITION LOCK REPLACE

1. Disarm airbag system as outlined under "Precautions."
2. Disconnect battery ground cable.
3. Remove steering wheel as described under "Steering Wheel, Replace."
4. Remove turn signal switch as described under "Turn Signal Switch, Replace."
5. Place ignition switch in Lock position.
6. Remove lock cylinder retaining screw.
7. Disconnect terminal electrical connector at bulkhead connection to provide slack.
8. Remove wiring connector from steering column.
9. Attach a suitable length of mechanic wire to ignition lock electrical connector for use during installation. Detach wire retaining clip, then carefully pull ignition lock wiring through housing shroud, steering column and lock housing cover, **Fig. 8.**
10. Remove lock cylinder.
11. Reverse procedure to install. Ensure lock cylinder wiring is properly routed through steering column. **Torque** lock cylinder retaining screw to 22 inch lbs.
12. Rearm airbag system as outlined under "Precautions."

IGNITION SWITCH REPLACE

The ignition switch is mounted on top of the mast jacket inside the brake pedal support and is actuated by a rod and rack assembly.

MOVE SWITCH SLIDER TO EXTREME RIGHT POSITION AND THEN MOVE SLIDER ONE DETENT TO THE LEFT (OFF LOCK)

80

80 SWITCH ASM. IGNITION

Fig. 9 Ignition switch adjustment

1. Disarm airbag system as outlined under "Precautions."
2. Disconnect battery ground cable.
3. Remove steering column from vehicle as outlined in the "Steering Columns" section.
4. Remove hex nut and washer head screw.
5. Remove horn pad ground wiring assembly from dimmer and ignition switch mounting stud. Remove wiring assembly from slot D of turn signal switch connector body, if necessary.
6. Remove cable bracket, then the dimmer switch from actuator rod.
7. Remove dimmer and ignition switch mounting stud.
8. Remove ignition switch assembly from switch actuator assembly, then disconnect wiring harness from switch assembly.
9. Reverse procedure to install, noting the following:
   a. Place lock cylinder and switch in OFF-LOCKED position, **Fig. 9.** A new ignition switch will be pinned in OFF-LOCKED position. Remove plastic pin after switch is assembled to column.
   b. Install and adjust dimmer switch as outlined under "Dimmer Switch, Replace."
10. Rearm airbag system as outlined under "Precautions."

CLUTCH START SWITCH REPLACE

1. Disarm airbag system as outlined under "Precautions."
2. Disconnect battery ground cable and set parking brake.
3. Remove hush panel from under instrument panel.
4. Remove clip securing clutch start switch actuating lever to clutch pedal, then disengage lever from pedal arm, **Fig. 10.**
5. Remove clutch start switch to pedal bracket retaining screw, then disconnect electrical connector and remove switch.
6. Reverse procedure to install.
7. Rearm airbag system as outlined under "Precautions."

Fig. 10 Clutch start switch replacement

1	CLUTCH PEDAL ASSEMBLY BRACKET
2	TRANSMISSION CLUTCHSTART SWITCH
3	INSTRUMENT PANEL WIRING HARNESS
4	CLUTCH START SWITCH ROD
5	CLUTCH PEDAL
6	CLUTCH START SWITCH ROD RETAINER

NEUTRAL START SWITCH
REPLACE

1. Disarm airbag system as outlined under "Precautions."
2. Remove floor console cover, then disconnect electrical connectors from switch.
3. Place shift lever in Neutral position of detent plate, then remove switch attaching nuts and switch, **Fig. 11.**
4. To install, ensure the shift lever is in Neutral, then position switch on shift lever making sure pin on shaft is in slot of switch.
5. If reinstalling existing switch, rotate switch to align service adjustment hole with carrier tang hole. Insert a .094 inch gauge pin and rotate switch until pin drops in to a depth of .59 inch. **Torque** switch attaching nut to 26 inch lbs., then remove gauge pin.
6. If installing a new switch, **torque** attaching nuts to 26 inch lbs., then move shift lever out of Neutral to shear pin which is part of new switch.
7. Reconnect electrical connectors to switch, then apply parking brake and start engine. Check back-up lights and seat belt warning system for proper operation and ensure engine will start only in Park or Neutral.
8. Turn ignition off and install floor console.
9. Rearm airbag system as outlined under "Precautions."

HEADLAMP SWITCH
REPLACE

1. Disarm airbag system as outlined under "Precautions."

2. Disconnect battery ground cable.
3. Remove instrument cluster bezel as described under "Instrument Cluster, Replace."
4. Remove attaching screws from right-hand side of switch, **Fig. 12.**
5. Remove switch trim plate attaching screws.
6. Disconnect electrical connectors, then remove switch.
7. Reverse procedure to install.
8. Rearm airbag system as outlined under "Precautions."

STOP LAMP SWITCH
REPLACE

1. Disarm airbag system as outlined under "Precautions."
2. Remove lefthand lower trim panel as follows:
   a. Remove retainer securing lower trim panel to stud on steering column.
   b. Remove trim panel mounting screws, then the trim panel.
   c. Remove DLC connector assembly mounting screw, then disconnect courtesy lamp electrical connector.
3. Remove stop lamp electrical connectors, then the vacuum hose for cruise control switch.
4. Depress retainer tabs and remove switch from bracket.
5. Reverse procedure to install, noting the following:
   a. With brake pedal depressed, insert switch assembly into bracket until seated. Audible clicks can be heard as threaded portion is pushed through bracket toward brake pedal.
   b. Pull brake pedal fully rearward against pedal stop until click sounds are not heard. Switch will move in retainer, providing adjustment.
   c. Repeat steps a and b until click sounds are not heard.
6. Rearm airbag system as outlined under "Precautions."

TURN SIGNAL SWITCH
REPLACE

1. Disarm airbag system as outlined under "Precautions."
2. Remove steering wheel as described under "Steering Wheel, Replace."
3. Place ignition switch in Lock position to retain coil assembly in the centered position.
4. Disconnect battery ground cable.
5. Remove coil assembly retaining ring, **Fig. 13.**
6. Lift coil assembly from from steering shaft and allow to hang from wire.
7. Using a suitable tool, compress lock plate and remove retaining ring, **Fig. 14.**
8. Remove lock plate, turn signal canceling cam and upper bearing spring, inner race seat and inner race.
9. Place turn signal lever in righthand

Fig. 11 Neutral safety switch replacement

1	NEUTRAL START AND BACKUP LAMP SWITCH
2	GAGE PIN
3	NUT
4	CARRIER TANG
5	MOUNTING STUD
6	DETENT PLATE

turn position, then remove multi-function lever and hazard warning flasher knob.
10. Remove turn signal switch lever attaching screw, then remove lever.
11. Remove turn signal switch attaching screws.
12. Disconnect turn signal switch electrical connector at lower portion of steering column.
13. Remove turn signal switch wiring protector cover from steering column.
14. Carefully pull turn signal switch wiring up and out of steering column, **Fig. 15.**
15. Reverse procedure to install. If coil assembly has become uncentered, refer to **Fig. 16** for centering procedure.
16. Rearm airbag system as outlined under "Precautions."

DIMMER SWITCH
REPLACE

1. Disarm airbag system as outlined under "Precautions."
2. Disconnect battery ground cable.
3. Remove steering column from vehicle as outlined in the "Steering Columns" section.
4. Remove hex nut and washer head screw.
5. Remove horn pad ground wiring assembly from dimmer and ignition switch mounting stud. Remove wiring assembly from slot D of turn signal switch connector body, if necessary.
6. Remove cable bracket, then the dimmer switch assembly from actuator rod.
7. Disconnect wiring harness from dimmer switch.
8. Reverse procedure to install. Adjust dimmer switch as follows:
   a. Install a 3/32 inch twist drill, to limit switch travel, **Fig. 17.**

1. INSTRUMENT PANEL
2. HEADLAMP DIMMER AND ACCESSORY SWITCH
3. SCREW
4. SWITCH LOCATOR
5. I/P HARNESS CONNECTOR
6. INSTRUMENT PANEL LOCATOR
7. SWITCH TRIM PLATE

Fig. 12 Headlamp switch replacement

2. RING, RETAINING
3. COIL ASM. INFL RESTRAINT
4. WASHER, WAVE

Fig. 13 Coil assembly removal

J-23653

Fig. 14 Lock plate retaining ring removal

Fig. 15 Turn signal switch removal

PERFORM THE FOLLOWING STEPS TO CENTER COIL ASSEMBLY:
A. REMOVE COIL ASSEMBLY.
B. HOLD COIL ASSEMBLY WITH CLEAR BOTTOM UP TO SEE COIL RIBBON.
C. NOTE: THERE ARE TWO DIFFERENT STYLES OF COILS. ONE ROTATES CLOCKWISE AND THE OTHER ROTATES COUNTERCLOCKWISE.
D. WHILE HOLDING COIL ASSEMBLY, DEPRESS SPRING LOCK TO ROTATE HUB IN DIRECTION OF ARROW UNTIL IT STOPS.
E. THE COIL RIBBON SHOULD BE WOUND UP SNUG AGAINST CENTER HUB.
F. ROTATE COIL HUB IN OPPOSITE DIRECTION APPROXIMATELY TWO AND A HALF (2-1/2) TURNS. RELEASE SPRING LOCK BETWEEN LOCKING TABS IN FRONT OF ARROW.

Fig. 16 Centering coil assembly

SWITCH ASM, DIMMER

3/32" DRILL BIT

Fig. 17 Column mounted dimmer switch installation

b. Position switch on column and push against dimmer switch rod to remove all lash.
c. Remove drill bit and check for proper operation.
9. Rearm airbag system as outlined under "Precautions."

STEERING WHEEL
REPLACE

Mark position of steering wheel in relation to shaft prior to removal to ensure correct installation.

1. CONNECTOR
2. STEERING WHEEL
3. INFLATOR MODULE
4. TORX SCREW

Fig. 18 Removing inflator module from steering wheel

REMOVAL

1. Disarm airbag system as outlined under "Precautions."
2. Disconnect battery ground cable.
3. Remove inflator module attaching screws from rear of steering wheel, **Fig. 18.**
4. Lift inflator module from steering wheel, then disconnect electrical connectors and connector position assurance from inflator module. **To lessen chances of personal injury, when carrying an inflator module, position bag and trim cover away you.**

Never carry module by wiring or electrical connector. Also when placing inflator module on work bench or other surface, face bag and trim cover upward, away from surface.

5. Remove steering wheel retaining nut, then disconnect horn electrical connector.
6. Using puller J-1859-03 or equivalent, pull steering wheel from steering shaft, **Fig. 19.**

INSTALLATION

1. Connect horn electrical connector.
2. Position steering wheel spline alignment marks to alignment marks of steering shaft splines, then install steering wheel.
3. Install steering wheel retaining nut and **torque** to 30 ft. lbs.
4. Connect SIR coil electrical connector to inflator module, then install connector position assurance.

1	J 1859 – 03 STEERING WHEEL PULLER
2	STEERING WHEEL
3	J38720 PULLER SIDE SCREWS

Fig. 19 Steering wheel removal

1	INSTRUMENT PANEL CARRIER
2	INSTRUMENT PANEL CLUSTER BEZEL
3	SCREWS

Fig. 20 Instrument cluster bezel replacement

5. Position inflator module to steering wheel, then install new mounting screws, **Fig. 18. Torque** mounting screws to 87 inch lbs.
6. Ensure ignition switch is in OFF position, then connect battery ground cable.
7. Rearm airbag system as outlined under "Precautions."

INSTRUMENT CLUSTER
REPLACE
1991

1. Disarm airbag system as outlined under "Precautions."
2. Disconnect battery ground cable.
3. Remove transmission shift lever knob.
4. Remove console trim plate attaching screws, then disconnect electrical connectors and remove trim plate.
5. Remove center air duct attaching screws.
6. Remove accessory trim plate attaching screws, clips and trim plate.
7. Remove lefthand lower trim plate attaching screws and retainers. Remove screw attaching ALDL connector to trim panel, then disconnect courtesy lamp electrical connector and remove trim panel.
8. Remove drivers side knee booster attaching screws.
9. Remove steering column tilt lever.
10. Remove steering column upper attaching bolts, then carefully lower steering column.
11. Remove instrument cluster bezel at-

taching screws, then remove bezel, **Fig. 20.**
12. Remove instrument cluster attaching screws, then disconnect electrical connectors and remove instrument cluster, **Fig. 21.**
13. Reverse procedure to install.
14. Rearm airbag system as outlined under "Precautions."

1992-94

1. Disarm airbag system as outlined under "Precautions."
2. Remove lefthand lower trim panel as follows:
   a. Remove retainer securing lower trim panel to stud on steering column.
   b. Remove trim panel mounting screws, then the trim panel.
   c. Remove DLC connector assembly mounting screw, then disconnect courtesy lamp electrical connector.
3. Remove driver's knee bolster as follows:
   a. Pull down carpet from upper corner of lefthand console side trim panel.
   b. Remove screws from flip down access door. Bend door down to access bolster retaining screws.
   c. Remove screws from knee bolster brackets, then the knee bolster.
4. Remove steering column support bolts, then lower steering column.
5. Remove cluster bezel attaching screws, then the bezel, **Fig. 20.**
6. Remove cluster mounting screws, **Fig. 21,** then disconnect cluster electrical connectors.
7. Remove instrument cluster from vehicle.
8. Reverse procedure to install, noting the following:
   a. **Torque** cluster mounting screws to 16 inch lbs.
   b. **Torque** bezel mounting screws to 29 inch lbs.
   c. Rearm airbag system as outlined under "Precautions."

1	I/P CARRIER ASSEMBLY
2	SCREW
3	I/P CLUSTER ASSEMBLY
4	U – NUT

Fig. 21 Instrument cluster replacement

A	MULTI-FUNCTION LEVER
19	COVER ASM. LOCK HOUSING
21	ACTUATOR. DIMMER SWITCH ROD
24	BASE PLATE. COL HSG COVER END
25	CAP. COL HSG COVER END
77	ROD. DIMMER SWITCH

Fig. 22 Multi-function lever replacement

RADIO
REPLACE

When installing radio, be sure to adjust antenna trimmer for peak reception. Also, be sure to connect speaker before applying power to radio.

RADIO CONTROL

1. Disarm airbag system as outlined under "Precautions."
2. Disconnect battery ground cable.
3. Remove transmission gear selector knob.
4. Remove console trim plate attaching screws from under ash tray.
5. Disconnect electrical connectors from console trim plate components, then remove trim plate.
6. Remove screw attaching center air outlet to instrument panel carrier, then remove outlet.
7. Remove screws attaching accessory trim plate to instrument panel.
8. Disconnect electrical connector to engine power switch, then remove accessory trim plate.
9. Remove console door.
10. Remove screws attaching console righthand side trim panel to instru-

1	SLOTS FOR CLIPS		6	TRIM PAD CLIPS
2	RETAINING BRACKETS		7	UPPER TRIM PAD
3	LOWER WINDSHIELD ASSEMBLY		8	BOLT/SCREW RIGHT SIDE
4	INSTRUMENT PANEL		9	BOLT/SCREW AIR OUTLET
5	BOLT/SCREWS TO RETAINING BRACKETS		10	BOLT/SCREWS TO I/P

Fig. 23   Instrument panel trim pad removal

ment panel and console. Remove passenger seat from vehicle to gain access to screws at side of trim panel. After all attaching screws have been removed, remove side trim panel.
11. Remove screws attaching radio control to instrument panel.
12. Pull radio control outward, then disconnect electrical connectors and remove radio control.
13. Reverse procedure to install.
14. Rearm airbag system as outlined under "Precautions."

RADIO RECEIVER
1991-92

1. Disarm airbag system as outlined under "Precautions."
2. Disconnect battery ground cable.
3. Remove screws attaching lower righthand trim panel to instrument panel and support.
4. Disconnect courtesy lamp electrical connector and air duct, then remove lower righthand trim panel.
5. Remove radio receiver front attaching nut and loosen side mounting nuts.
6. Slide radio receiver forward to release tab, then disconnect electrical connectors and antenna lead.
7. Remove radio receiver.
8. Reverse procedure to install.
9. Rearm airbag system as outlined under "Precautions."

1993-94

1. Disarm airbag system as outlined under "Precautions."
2. Disconnect battery ground cable.
3. Open right rear floor storage compartment door, then remove tray.
4. Remove radio receiver by pulling firmly on receiver to separate hook and loop fastener.
5. Disconnect antenna cable extension and electrical connectors.
6. Reverse procedure to install.
7. Rearm airbag system as outlined under "Precautions."

WIPER MOTOR
REPLACE

1. Disconnect battery ground cable.
2. Remove wiper arms, if necessary.
3. Disconnect wiper motor upper electrical connectors.
4. Remove lefthand plenum screen.
5. Remove left and righthand wiper transmission attaching nuts.
6. Remove left and righthand wiper transmission sockets.
7. **On ZR1 models,** disconnect vacuum booster supply hose at plenum.
8. **On all models,** remove wiper motor attaching bolts, then carefully lift wiper motor from mounting.
9. Disconnect wiper motor lower electrical connectors and remove wiper motor.
10. Reverse procedure to install.

WIPER TRANSMISSION
REPLACE

1. Ensure motor is in park position.
2. Raise hood and remove wiper arm assemblies.
3. Remove lefthand cowl vent screen.
4. Loosen nuts securing pivot at motor crankarm, then disconnect transmission rod from crankarm.
5. Remove retaining nuts or screws securing transmission to body, then withdraw transmission assembly through cowl opening.
6. Reverse procedure to install.

WIPER SWITCH
REPLACE

1. Disarm airbag system as outlined under "Precautions."
2. Pull column housing end toward from of vehicle and remove cover, **Fig. 22.**
3. Disconnect electrical connector and grommet.

4. Pull outward on multi-function lever to release from detent.
5. Reverse procedure to install. When installing, position lever in off position, then align lever tab with mounting slot.
6. Rearm airbag system as outlined under "Precautions."

BLOWER MOTOR
REPLACE

1. Disconnect battery ground cable.
2. Remove right front wheel housing rear panel, and push housing aside.
3. Remove motor cooling tube and screws securing relay, and set relay aside.
4. Remove motor retaining screws, motor and impeller.
5. Reverse procedure to install.

HEATER CORE
REPLACE

1. Disarm airbag system as outlined under "Precautions."
2. Remove lower righthand trim panel as follows:
   a. Remove fuse box cover, then instrument panel side trim panel.
   b. Remove lower trim panel mounting screw, then the trim panel.
   c. Disconnect courtesy lamp harness connector.
3. Remove glovebox as follows:
   a. Remove screws from glovebox lower hinge, then from latch striker.
   b. Remove glovebox from upper trim pad, then disconnect glovebox lamp switch connector.
4. Remove righthand outer air outlet mounting screws, then the air outlet.
5. Remove center air outlet mounting screws, then the air outlet.
6. Remove console trim plate as follows:
   a. **On models with automatic transmission,** Pry up shifter button, then remove shifter button retainer, snap ring and shift knob.
   b. **On models with manual transmission,** Pry up shifter button, then remove shifter button, retainer, shift knob, setscrew and reverse inhibitor.
   c. **On all models,** disconnect electrical connectors for lighter, rear compartment lid release switch and gear indicator lamp, if equipped. Unclip accessory plug harness.
   d. Pry locking tabs on underside of shifter boot from groove in shaft, then remove console trim plate with boot.
7. Remove accessory trim plate mounting screw, then the trim plate. On ZR-1 models, disconnect engine power switch from trim plate.
8. Remove windshield defroster grill by prying up on rear edge, the disconnect sun load sensor connector.
9. Remove lefthand outer air outlet mounting screws, then the air outlet.

10. Remove upper trim pad mounting screws, **Fig. 23**, then the upper trim pad.
11. Drain cooling system, then remove in vehicle temperature sensor aspirator hose.
12. Disconnect in vehicle temperature sensor connector, the remove floor heat deflector mounting screws.
13. Remove righthand knee bolster brace, then the floor heat deflector.
14. Remove relays from multi use relay bracket, then loosen wiring harness retainer to radio receiver mounting nuts.
15. Remove wiring harness retainer, then the harnesses from wiring harness retainer.
16. Remove carrier nuts from righthand pillar.
17. Remove console righthand side trim panel as follows:
    a. Remove righthand seat, then trim panel to tunnel mounting screws.
    b. Remove console door, then the remaining side trim panel mounting screws.
18. Remove lower trim panel support as follows:
    a. Remove bolts mounting lower trim panel support to passenger inner knee bolster bracket.
    b. Remove bolts mounting trim panel support to passenger knee bolster outer bracket.
    c. Remove lower trim panel support.
19. Remove four passenger knee bolster inner bracket fasteners.
20. Remove bolts mounting passenger knee bolster inner bracket to lower instrument panel support.
21. Remove bolts mounting passenger knee bolster inner bracket to bulkhead, then remove passenger knee bolster inner bracket.
22. Remove passenger knee bolster outer bracket as follows:
    a. Remove bolts mounting outer bracket to lower windshield frame assembly.
    b. Remove bolts mounting outer bracket to pillar assembly, then the outer bracket.
23. Remove side window defroster duct mounting clip, then duct hose from knee bolster brace.
24. Pull carrier back and remove passenger knee bolster brace.
25. Disconnect radio receiver electrical connectors.
26. Remove multi use relay bracket and disconnect cruise control module electrical connectors.
27. Remove screws attaching side window defroster duct to rear of heater case.
28. Remove fuse block from carrier, then disconnect vacuum hose from actuator.
29. Remove vacuum line retainer tape on heater, then the harness from retainer clip on bottom of rear heater case.

1. HEATER CORE/HOUSING
2. CORE HOUSING TO DUCT GASKET
3. HEATER CORE TO BLOWER EVAP. MODULE GASKET (BULKHEAD)
4. SEAL
5. TEMPERATURE DOOR MOTOR
6. INSIDE TEMPERATURE SENSOR ASPIRATOR ASSEMBLY

Fig. 24 Heater core housing

1. AIR CONDITIONING WIRING HARNESS BRACKET
2. BLOWER MOTOR AND EVAPORATOR MODULE BOLT
3. ELECTRONIC SPARK CONTROL BRACKET
4. AIR CONDITIONING EVAPORATOR AND BLOWER MOTOR MODULE
5. AIR CONDITIONING EVAPORATOR AND BLOWER MOTOR MODULE GASKET
6. BLOWER MOTOR AND EVAPORATOR MODULE NUT

Fig. 25 Evaporator core housing

30. Remove side window defroster center duct extension (in heater case).
31. Remove rear heater case attaching screw, then the rear heater case half, **Fig. 24**.
32. Remove height fill reservoir, then heater hose from heater core.
33. Remove heater core from case.
34. Reverse procedure to install.
35. Rearm airbag system as outlined under "Precautions."

EVAPORATOR CORE
REPLACE

1. Disconnect battery ground cable.
2. Discharge A/C refrigerant system
3. Drain cooling system.
4. Remove front wheel house rear panel and seal.
5. Disconnect electrical connectors from blower motor.
6. Disconnect evaporator outlet hose.
7. Remove pressure cycling switch.
8. Disconnect heater hoses and evaporator inlet hose, then expansion tube.
9. Disconnect vapor pipe bracket from evaporator case.
10. Remove attaching bolt from upper righthand fender apron.
11. Remove nuts and bolts attaching evaporator core and blower housing to dash panel, **Fig. 25**.
12. Remove evaporator housing from vehicle, then separate housing and remove evaporator core.
13. Reverse procedure to install.

INDEX

PRECAUTIONS

AIRBAG SYSTEM DISARMING

The diagnostic energy reserve module (DERM) can maintain voltage to cause a system deployment for up to ten minutes after the ignition switch is turned off and the battery is disconnected. Servicing the SIR system during this period may result in accidental deployment and personal injury.

1. Ensure front wheels are pointed straight ahead.
2. Turn ignition switch to Lock position and remove SIR or AIRBAG fuse.
3. Remove left sound insulator. **Remove courtesy lamp from sound insulator, if necessary.**
4. Remove Connector Position Assurance (CPA), then disconnect yellow two-way SIR electrical connector at base of steering column.

AIRBAG SYSTEM ARMING

1. Connect yellow two-way SIR electrical connector, then install Connector Position Assurance (CPA).
2. Install left sound insulator. **Install courtesy lamp to sound insulator, if applicable.**
3. Install SIR fuse to fuse block, turn ignition switch to RUN position and ensure "Inflatable Restraint" lamp flashes 7 to 9 times, then shuts off.

FUEL SYSTEM PRESSURE RELIEF

Failure to relieve system pressure prior to disconnecting fuel system components may cause fire or personal injury. Remove fuel tank filler cap to release fuel tank pressure. Connect pressure gauge J-34730-1 or equiva-

1	MOUNT, ENGINE
2	BOLT
3	NUT, ENGINE MOUNT BOLT
4	FRAME, DRIVETRAIN AND FRONT SUSPENSION
5	BOLT, ENGINE MOUNT
6	BRACE, SUPPORT
7	BLOCK, ENGINE

Fig. 1   Engine mounts

lent to pressure tap on fuel rail, position bleed hose into suitable container and slowly relieve fuel system pressure. Prior to disconnecting fuel line, position shop towel over fitting.

ENGINE MOUNTS
REPLACE

1. Disconnect battery ground cable, then disconnect air intake duct from air cleaner.
2. Raise and support vehicle, then remove Electronic Spark Control sensor shield.
3. Support engine and remove mount through bolt, **Fig. 1.**
4. Raise engine sufficiently to provide clearance for mount bolt removal.
5. Remove bolts securing engine mount to block and the mount.

6. Position replacement mount on engine, lower engine into position and install retaining bolts.
7. Reverse procedure to install.

ENGINE
REPLACE

1. Disarm airbag system as outlined under "Precautions."
2. Disconnect battery ground cable, then drain cooling system.
3. Disconnect throttle, cruise control and TV cables.
4. Remove plenum extension from plenum.
5. Disconnect EGR pipe from intake and exhaust manifolds.
6. Remove ignition distributor from engine. Refer to "Distributor, Replace" procedure in the "Electrical" section.
7. Disconnect electrical connector from oil pressure switch.
8. Disconnect windshield wiper motor electrical connector, then remove wiper motor cover.
9. Remove air intake duct.
10. Disconnect power brake unit vacuum hose.
11. Disconnect fuel vapor canister hoses.
12. Disconnect electrical connectors from cooling fan control switch, alternator, EGR solenoid, coolant temperature sensor, AIR switch and control valve, throttle position sensor, idle air control valve, A/C compressor and manifold air temperature sensor. Also disconnect fuel injector wiring harness from left and righthand sides.
13. Disconnect vapor hose from intake manifold. Also disconnect cruise control and A/C vacuum connectors.
14. Disconnect heater hose at throttle body.
15. Disconnect upper radiator hose at thermostat housing.

Fig. 2   Intake manifold bolt tightening sequence

16. Remove water pump damper, then remove serpentine drive belt and water pump pulley.
17. Remove AIR switch, control and mounting bracket.
18. Relieve fuel system pressure as described under "Fuel System Pressure Relief," then disconnect and cap fuel lines at fuel rail.
19. Remove A/C accumulator clamping bolt.
20. Remove lower righthand side wheel housing center panel.
21. Remove A/C compressor brace, then remove A/C compressor and accumulator from mounting brackets and position aside with refrigerant hoses attached.
22. Remove A/C compressor front mounting brace, then remove belt tensioner.
23. Disconnect heater hose from water pump.
24. Remove A/C compressor lower brace and fuel line clamp.
25. Remove alternator, then remove AIR pump with mounting brackets and pipe as an assembly.
26. Remove A/C compressor mounting bracket and AIR system muffler.
27. Disconnect lower radiator hose from water pump, then disconnect hose from engine oil cooler pipe.
28. Remove crankshaft pulley.
29. Remove power steering pump with bracket and position aside with hoses attached.
30. Raise and support vehicle.
31. Disconnect AIR pipe from righthand exhaust manifold.
32. Disconnect exhaust cross-over pipe at exhaust manifolds.
33. Disconnect electrical connectors from oil temperature sensor, starter motor, ESC sensor and righthand side coolant temperature sensor. Also disconnect battery ground cable at engine block.
34. Remove flywheel cover, then remove starter motor.
35. Drain crankcase, then remove oil filter.
36. **On models with manual transmission,** remove transmission and clutch assembly.
37. **On models with automatic transmission,** remove transmission to engine and torque converter to flywheel attaching bolts.
38. **On all models,** remove engine mount through bolts and nuts.
39. Lower vehicle.

40. **On models with automatic transmission,** use suitable transmission jack to support transmission.
41. **On all models,** install suitable engine lifting fixture, then ensure all wiring and hoses that would interfere with engine removal are disconnected.
42. Carefully lift engine from vehicle.
43. Reverse procedure to install.
44. Rearm airbag system as outlined under "Precautions."

INTAKE MANIFOLD
REPLACE

1. Disarm airbag system as outlined under "Precautions."
2. Disconnect battery ground cable, then drain cooling system.
3. Disconnect throttle, TV and cruise control cables from throttle body and brackets.
4. Remove bracket from plenum.
5. Disconnect electrical connectors from coolant temperature sensor, throttle position sensor, manifold air temperature sensor, idle air control and manifold absolute pressure sensor.
6. Disconnect air inlet duct from throttle body.
7. Disconnect and tag vacuum hoses from plenum and throttle body.
8. Disconnect heater hoses from throttle body.
9. Disconnect power brake unit vacuum hose from plenum fitting.
10. Remove plenum to runner attaching bolts, then remove plenum from engine.
11. Disconnect vacuum hose, then remove EGR solenoid from thermostat housing.
12. Remove EGR valve from intake manifold.
13. Remove injector wiring harness attaching bolts.
14. Relieve fuel system pressure as described under "Fuel System Pressure Relief," then disconnect and cap fuel lines at fuel rail.
15. Remove fuel rail and injector assemblies.
16. Remove ignition distributor, refer to "Distributor, Replace" procedure in the "Electrical" section.
17. Disconnect upper radiator hose from thermostat housing.
18. Remove AIR pump brace.
19. Disconnect EGR valve pipe and position aside.
20. Disconnect hose from PCV valve and crankcase vent tube from intake manifold.
21. Remove intake manifold attaching bolts and intake manifold.
22. Ensure gasket surfaces are clean and dry, then install gaskets on cylinder head with blocked openings toward rear of engine.
23. Bend gasket tabs flush with front face with cylinder head, then apply a .2 inch bead of RTV sealer to front and rear ridges of cylinder block.
24. Apply sealant 1052080 or equivalent to manifold bolts.

1	GASKET, EXHAUST MANIFOLD CENTER
2	GASKET, EXHAUST MANIFOLD
3	MANIFOLD, EXHAUST
4	BOLT
5	STUD
6	VALVE, CHECK
7	HEAD, CYLINDER
8	TUBE, OIL LEVEL INDICATOR
9	NUT
10	BLOCK, ENGINE

Fig. 3   Exhaust manifold replacement

25. Install manifold and torque bolts to specifications in sequence shown in **Fig. 2,** then reverse remaining procedure to complete installation.
26. Rearm airbag system as outlined under "Precautions."

EXHAUST MANIFOLD
REPLACE

LEFT SIDE

1. Disconnect battery ground cable.
2. Disconnect AIR hose at check valve, then remove alternator brace.
3. Disconnect spark plug wires from spark plugs and brackets and position aside, then remove spark plugs after engine has cooled.
4. Raise and support vehicle.

5. Disconnect exhaust cross-over pipe at exhaust manifold.
6. Lower vehicle, then remove exhaust manifold attaching bolts and remove exhaust manifold, **Fig. 3**.
7. Reverse procedure to install.

RIGHT SIDE

1. Disconnect battery ground cable.
2. Disconnect EGR valve pipe and position aside.
3. Remove A/C compressor brace, then remove oil level dipstick and tube.
4. Disconnect AIR hose at check valve.
5. Disconnect temperature sending unit electrical connector.
6. Disconnect spark plug wire from spark plugs and brackets, then remove spark plugs after engine has cooled.
7. Raise and support vehicle.
8. Remove AIR pipe clamp at manifold.
9. Disconnect exhaust cross-over pipe at exhaust manifolds.
10. Lower vehicle.
11. Remove exhaust manifold attaching bolts, then remove exhaust manifold, **Fig. 3**.
12. Reverse procedure to install.

CYLINDER HEAD
REPLACE

1. Disarm airbag system as outlined under "Precautions."
2. Disconnect battery ground cable and remove air cleaner.
3. Drain cooling system and engine block, then remove intake manifold.
4. Disconnect AIR hose from exhaust manifold check valve, and if right cylinder head is to be removed, disconnect AIR hose from converter pipe.
5. If right cylinder head is to be removed, remove A/C compressor as follows:
   a. Remove lower compressor mounting bolt and nuts securing bracket to water pump.
   b. Move compressor assembly forward, remove upper mounting bolt and disconnect electrical connector, and secure compressor aside.
   c. Disconnect electrical connectors to high pressure switch, then remove high pressure switch and EGR solenoid.
   d. Disconnect EFI harness from rocker cover clamp.
6. If left cylinder head is to be removed, remove alternator and brace.
7. Remove valve cover retaining bolts, bend plug wire bracket away from cover for clearance, and remove cover.
8. Remove spark plugs and temperature sending unit from cylinder head.
9. Raise and support vehicle, and disconnect exhaust pipe from manifold. If right cylinder head is to be replaced, remove 2 rear manifold bolts and dipstick tube bolt.
10. Lower vehicle and remove exhaust manifold.

Fig. 4   Cylinder head tightening sequence

11. If left cylinder head is to be removed, remove AIR pump upper bracket and power steering reservoir, and set aside.
12. Remove spark plug wire bracket and bolts securing ground straps to cylinder head.
13. Loosen rocker arm nuts and remove pushrods.
14. Remove head bolts and cylinder head.
15. Reverse procedure to install, noting the following:
    a. Ensure gasket surfaces are clean and free of nicks or deep scratches, and bolt and block threads are clean.
    b. Coat both sides of head gasket with a thin even coat of sealer, and ensure gasket is properly positioned over dowel pins.
    c. Coat cylinder head bolt threads with GM sealer No. 1052080 or equivalent, then install all bolts finger tight.
    d. Torque cylinder head bolts to specifications in sequence shown in **Fig. 4**.
    e. Install intake manifold gaskets on head with blocked openings toward rear, bend gasket tabs flush with rear face of cylinder head, and apply a .2 inch bead of RTV sealer on front and rear cylinder block ridges.
    f. Install manifold, apply sealant 1052624 or equivalent to manifold bolts, and torque bolts to specifications in sequence shown in **Fig. 2**.
16. Rearm airbag system as outlined under "Precautions."

VALVE ADJUSTMENT

After the engine has been thoroughly warmed up the valves may be adjusted with the engine shutoff as follows: With engine in position to fire No. 1 cylinder the following valves may be adjusted: Exhaust 1-3-4-8, intake 1-2-5-7. Then crank the engine one more complete revolution which will bring No. 6 cylinder to the firing position at which time the following valves may be adjusted: Exhaust 2-5-6-7, intake 3-4-6-8.

The following procedure, performed with the engine running, should be done only in case readjustment is required.

1. After engine has been warmed up to operating temperature, remove valve cover and install a new valve cover gasket.
2. With engine running at idle speed, back off valve rocker arm nut until rocker arm starts to clatter.

3. Turn rocker arm nut down slowly until the clatter just stops. This is the zero lash position.
4. Turn nut down 1/4 additional turn and pause 10 seconds until engine runs smoothly. Repeat additional 1/4 turns, pausing 10 seconds each time, until nut has been turned down the number of turns listed in the Valve Clearance Specifications Chart from the zero lash position. **This preload adjustment must be done slowly to allow the lifter to adjust itself to prevent the possibility of interference between the intake valve head and top of piston, which might result in internal damage and/or bent pushrods. Noisy lifters should be replaced.**

VALVE ADJUSTMENT SPECIFICATIONS

Engine/VIN	Valve Clearance
5.7L/V8-350	1 Turn ①

① —Turn rocker arm stud nut until all lash is eliminated, then tighten nut one additional turn.

VALVE ARRANGEMENT
FRONT TO REAR

All . . . . E-I-I-E-E-I-I-E

CAMSHAFT LIFT SPECIFICATIONS

Engine	Int.	Exh.
5.7L/V8-350	.2750	.2856

ROCKER ARMS

When replacing rocker arms or rocker arm balls, bearing surfaces of rocker arms and balls should be coated with pre-lube 12345501 or equivalent.

ROCKER ARM STUDS

Rocker arm studs with damaged threads should be replaced. Threads of replacement rocker arms studs should be coated with sealing compound 1052080 or equivalent prior to installation. Looseness can be corrected by installing the proper size Heli-Coil insert, or by replacing cylinder head.

PUSHRODS

On engines that use pushrods with a hardened insert at one end, the hardened end is identified by a color stripe and should always be installed toward the rocker arm during assembly.

1 BODY, LIFTER
2 SPRING, BALL CHECK
3 CHECK, BALL
4 VALVE, OIL METERING
5 RING, RETAINER
6 SEAT, PUSHROD
7 PLUNGER
8 RETAINER, BALL CHECK
9 SPRING, PLUNGER
10 ROLLER

Fig. 5 Roller type hydraulic lifter

A MALLET
1 COVER, ENGINE FRONT
2 SEAL, FRONT COVER

Fig. 7 Engine front cover seal installation

VALVE GUIDES

Valves operate in guide holes bored in the head. If clearance becomes excessive, use the next oversize valve and ream the bore to fit. Valves with oversize stems are available in .003, .015 and .030 inch.

HYDRAULIC VALVE LIFTERS
REPLACE

Valve lifters, **Fig. 5** can be lifted from their bores after removing rocker arms, pushrods, intake manifold and valve lifter retainer. When removing, position valve lifters in rack so they may be installed at the same location. Adjustable pliers with protected jaws may be used to remove lifters which are stuck due to carbon or varnish deposits. When installing replacement valve lifters, coat roller with pre-lube 12345501 or equivalent.

FRONT COVER
REPLACE

1. Disconnect battery ground cable and drain cooling system.
2. Remove vibration damper and water pump.
3. Remove oil pan and gasket as outlined.

1 BOLT
2 WASHER
3 PULLEY, CRANKSHAFT
4 DAMPER, TORSIONAL
5 SEAL, FRONT COVER
6 COVER, ENGINE FRONT
7 GASKET, FRONT COVER
8 BLOCK, ENGINE
9 CAMSHAFT
10 KEY
11 CRANKSHAFT
12 RETAINER, CAMSHAFT
13 CHAIN, TIMING
14 SPROCKET, CAMSHAFT
15 SPROCKET, CRANKSHAFT
16 PIN

Fig. 6 Front cover & timing chain components

4. Remove AIR control valve, check valve pipe and silencer as an assembly.
5. Remove fuel inlet and return lines.
6. Remove A/C compressor mounting bracket.
7. Remove water pump as described under "Water Pump, Replace."
8. Remove front cover retaining screws and the front cover, **Fig. 6.**
9. Reverse procedure to install. Apply sealant 1052080 or equivalent approximately 1 inch in either direction at front cover to engine junction and at point where rear seal retainer meets case prior to installation of oil pan.

FRONT COVER OIL SEAL
REPLACE

WITH FRONT COVER INSTALLED

1. Disconnect battery ground cable.
2. Remove serpentine drive belt.
3. Remove water pump damper and crankshaft pulley.
4. Disconnect power steering gear line, if necessary.
5. Remove attaching bolts, then using puller J-23523 or equivalent, remove crankshaft damper.
6. Carefully pry oil seal from front cover.
7. Using tool No. J-35468, position oil to front cover with open side of seal toward inside of front cover.
8. Tap seal into front cover until properly seated.
9. Using puller J-23523 or equivalent, install crankshaft damper and install attaching bolt.
10. Connect power steering line, if removed. After completing installation check power steering fluid lever in reservoir.
11. Install crankshaft pulley and water pump damper.
12. Install serpentine drive belt and connect battery ground cable.

A TIMING MARK, CAMSHAFT SPROCKET
B TIMING MARK, CRANKSHAFT SPROCKET
C SPROCKET CENTER LINE

Fig. 8 Aligning timing chain sprocket timing marks

WITH FRONT COVER REMOVED

1. Remove front cover as described under "Front Cover, Replace.
2. From rear of front cover, tap out oil seal.
3. Properly support front cover in seal area.
4. Using tool No. J-35468 or equivalent, install oil seal. Position open end of oil seal toward inside of front cover, **Fig. 7.**
5. Install engine front cover.

TIMING CHAIN
REPLACE

1. Remove front cover as outlined previously.
2. Remove crankshaft oil slinger.
3. Crank engine until timing marks on sprockets are in alignment, **Fig. 8.**
4. Remove three camshaft to sprocket bolts, **Fig. 6.**

Fig. 9   Piston & rod assembly

C	ARROW, TO BE ORIENTED TO FRONT OF ENGINE
1	CRANKSHAFT
2	CAP. CONNECTING ROD
3	NUT. CONNECTING ROD
4	INSERT. BEARING
5	BLOCK. CYLINDER
6	BOLT. CONNECTING ROD
7	PISTON
8	ROD. CONNECTING

Fig. 10   Low friction, light weight piston

5. Remove camshaft sprocket and timing chain together. Sprocket is a light press fit on camshaft for approximately 1/8 inch. If sprocket does not come off easily, a light blow with a plastic hammer on the lower edge of the sprocket should dislodge it.
6. If crankshaft sprocket is to be replaced, remove it with a suitable gear puller. Install new sprocket, aligning key and keyway.
7. Install chain on camshaft sprocket. Hold sprocket vertical with chain hanging below and shift around to align the timing marks on sprockets.
8. Align dowel in camshaft with dowel hole in sprocket and install sprocket on camshaft. Do not attempt to drive sprocket on camshaft as welch plug at rear of engine can be dislodged.
9. Draw sprocket onto camshaft, using the three mounting bolts. Tighten to specifications.

10. Lubricate timing chain with engine oil, then install cover.

CAMSHAFT REPLACE

1. Remove valve lifters and engine front cover.
2. Remove grille, radiator and A/C condenser.
3. Remove timing chain as outlined previously.
4. Remove camshaft retainer bolts and retainer, **Fig. 6**.
5. Install two 5/16-18x4 bolts in camshaft bolt holes, then remove camshaft.
6. Reverse procedure to install. Prior to installing camshaft, coat lobes and distributor drive gear with pre-lube 12345501 or equivalent.

PISTON & ROD ASSEMBLY

Assemble pistons to connecting rods as shown in **Fig. 9**.

Upon installation, measure the connecting rod side clearance using a suitable feeler gauge. Refer to "Engine Rebuilding Specifications" for connecting rod side clearance.

PISTON PINS & RINGS

Pistons are available in standard and oversizes of .010 and .030 inch.

Piston rings are available in standard and oversizes of .030 inch.
Refer to Fig. 10, for piston installation.

MAIN & ROD BEARINGS

Connecting rod bearings are available in standard and undersizes of .001, .002, .010 and .020 inch.

Main bearings are available in standard and undersizes of .001, .002, .009, .010 and .020 inch.

CRANKSHAFT REAR OIL SEAL REPLACE

These engines are equipped with a one-piece, lip type seal mounted in a separate seal retainer. Seal replacement requires removal of the transmission.

1. Raise and support vehicle, then remove transmission, clutch assembly and flywheel, as equipped.
2. Pry seal from retainer, inserting screwdriver in notches provided in seal retainer, **Fig. 11**.
3. Lubricate inner and outer diameters of replacement seal with engine oil, then mount seal on tool J-35621 or equivalent, **Fig. 12**.
4. Mount tool on rear of crankshaft, tightening screws snugly to ensure seal will be installed squarely on crankshaft.

A	NOTCH, SEAL RETAINER
1	RETAINER, REAR SEAL
2	SEAL, CRANKSHAFT REAR

Fig. 11   Crankshaft rear seal retainer notch locations

1	RETAINER, SEAL
2	SEAL, CRANKSHAFT REAR
3	CRANKSHAFT

Fig. 12   Crankshaft rear seal installation

1	BOLT	4	SHAFT, INTERMEDIATE
2	BAFFLE	5	CAP, MAIN BEARING
3	PUMP, OIL	6	RETAINER, SHAFT

Fig. 14   Oil pump & baffle replacement

Fig. 15   Oil pump exploded view

10. Reverse procedure to install. Torque oil pan retaining bolts to specifications.

OIL PUMP
REPLACE

1. Remove oil pan as described previously.
2. Remove oil pan baffle nuts, then remove baffle.
3. Remove pump to rear main bearing cap bolt and remove pump and extension shaft, **Fig. 14.**
4. Reverse procedure to install. Prime oil pump with clean engine oil prior to installation. Make sure that installed position of oil pump screen is with bottom edge parallel to oil pan rails.

OIL PUMP SERVICE

1. Remove oil pump as described previously.
2. Remove pump cover screws and pump cover, **Fig. 15.**
3. Mark gear teeth so they can be reassembled with same teeth indexing, then remove drive gear, idler gear and shaft.
4. Remove pressure regulator valve retaining pin, pressure regulator valve and related parts.
5. If pickup screen and pipe require replacement, mount pump in a soft-jawed vise and extract pipe from pump.

1	STUD
2	BOLT
3	NUT
4	PAN, OIL
5	GASKET, OIL PAN
6	BAFFLE
7	REINFORCEMENT, OIL PAN

Fig. 13   Oil pan replacement

6. Wash all parts in cleaning solvent and dry with compressed air.
7. Inspect pump body and cover for cracks and excessive wear.
8. Inspect pump gears for damage or excessive wear.
9. Check drive gear shaft for looseness in pump body.
10. Inspect inside of pump cover for wear that would allow oil to leak past the ends of the gears.
11. Inspect pickup screen and pipe assembly for damage to screen, pipe or relief grommet.
12. Check pressure regulator valve for fit in pump housing.
13. Reverse procedure to assemble. Turn driveshaft by hand to check for smooth operation. **The pump gears and body are not serviced separately. If the pump gears or body are damaged or worn, the pump**

5. Tighten wing nut on tool until it bottoms, then remove tool from crankshaft.
6. Reverse remaining procedure to complete installation.

OIL PAN
REPLACE

1. Disconnect battery ground cable.
2. Raise and support vehicle, then drain crankcase.
3. Disconnect transmission oil cooler lines at flywheel cover.
4. Disconnect catalytic converter AIR pipe clamps at manifold and exhaust pipe.
5. Disconnect starter motor electrical connectors, then remove starter motor.
6. Remove oil filter, then disconnect oil cooler adapter at block.
7. Remove flywheel cover, then disconnect oil cooler line at oil pan.
8. Remove ESC shield, then the front crossmember braces.
9. Remove oil pan attaching bolts, **Fig. 13,** then rotate crankshaft and remove oil pan.

1	PUMP, A.I.R.
2	PULLEY, GENERATOR
3	PULLEY, POWER STEERING PUMP
4	BELT, SERPENTINE
5	PULLEY, CRANKSHAFT
6	TENSIONER, BELT
7	COMPRESSOR, AIR CONDITIONING
8	PULLEY, COOLANT PUMP
9	DAMPER, COOLANT PUMP PULLEY VIBRATION

Fig. 16 Serpentine drive belt routing

1	PUMP, COOLANT
2	GASKET, COOLANT PUMP
3	HOUSING, THERMOSTAT
4	BOLT, THERMOSAT HOUSING
5	GASKET, THERMOSTAT HOUSING
6	THERMOSTAT
7	BOLT, COOLANT PUMP
8	STUD, COOLANT PUMP

Fig. 17 Thermostat & water pump replacement

1	GASKET
2	FUEL LEVEL METER ASSEMBLY
3	FILER NECK HOUSING
4	FUEL FILER CAP
5	NIPPLE
6	DRAIN HOSE
7	SCREW ASSEMBLY (WITH O – RING) 4.5 N·m (40 LB. IN.)
8	FILLER DOOR BEZEL
9	SCREW

Fig. 18 Fuel meter & pump assembly replacement

assembly should be replaced. Also, if the pick-up screen and pump assembly was removed, it should be replaced with a new one as loss of the press fit condition could result in an air leak and loss of oil pressure.

BELT TENSION DATA

Engine/VIN	New Lbs.①	Used Lbs.①
5.7L/V8-350	60-90	60-90

①—Checked between alternator & AIR pump.

SERPENTINE DRIVE BELT
REPLACE

To remove serpentine drive belt, rotate tensioner using a 1/2 inch breaker bar to release belt tension, then remove serpentine drive belt. To install, position serpentine drive belt over pulleys, then rotate tensioner using breaker bar. Refer to Fig. 16 for serpentine belt routing.

COOLING SYSTEM BLEED

After filling cooling system, start engine and allow to reach operating temperature with radiator cap removed. Air in system will be bled through radiator cap opening. Add coolant as necessary to bring level to bottom of high fill reservoir neck, then install radiator cap and check coolant level in recovery reservoir.

THERMOSTAT
REPLACE

1. Disconnect battery ground cable.
2. Remove air cleaner and intake duct assembly.
3. Remove surge tank pressure cap, then drain cooling system.
4. Disconnect upper radiator hose from coolant outlet.
5. Disconnect coolant hose at throttle body.
6. Disconnect electrical and vacuum connectors at EGR solenoid.
7. Remove thermostat housing attaching bolts, then remove housing and thermostat, Fig. 17.
8. Reverse procedure to install.

WATER PUMP
REPLACE

1. Disconnect battery ground cable, and drain cooling system.
2. Remove air cleaner and duct assembly.

3. Rotate belt tensioner counterclockwise to release tension, and remove drive belt.
4. Remove water pump and AIR pump pulleys, and disconnect air management valve adapter from AIR pump.
5. Remove AIR pump, then disconnect fuel supply and return lines. **Relieve fuel system pressure before disconnecting fuel hoses.**
6. Remove A/C compressor rear braces and lower mounting bolt.
7. Remove nuts securing A/C compressor and idler pulley bracket to water pump and disconnect electrical connector from compressor.
8. Move compressor bracket forward, remove upper mounting bolt and compressor, and secure aside.
9. Disconnect AIR hoses at check valves and AIR pipe at intake manifold and power steering bracket.
10. Remove power steering reservoir bracket and upper alternator mounting bolt.
11. Remove lower AIR pump bracket, then disconnect hoses from water pump.
12. Remove mounting bolts, then the water pump, Fig. 17.
13. Reverse procedure to install.

FUEL PUMP
REPLACE

The fuel pump is an electric in tank design attached to the fuel level sending unit. Replace fuel pump as follows:
1. Disconnect battery ground cable.
2. Connect pressure gauge J-34370-1 or equivalent to pressure tap on fuel rail, position bleed hose in suitable container and slowly relieve fuel system pressure. **Failure to relieve system pressure prior to disconnecting fuel system components may cause fire or personal injury.**

3. Drain fuel tank. Drain fuel into an approved fuel storage container.
4. Remove fuel filler door bezel attaching screws, then remove bezel, **Fig. 18.**
5. Remove fuel filler cap, then lift fuel filler neck housing and disconnect drain hose.
6. Remove fuel meter and pump attaching screws.
7. Disconnect fuel lines, hoses and electrical connectors from fuel meter and pump assembly. Tag hoses and electrical connectors so they may be installed at the same location.
8. Carefully remove fuel meter and pump assembly.
9. Reverse procedure to install.

1	FUEL FEED PIPES	5	FUEL FILTER SHIELD
2	O-RINGS (2)	6	FILTER SHIELD ATTACHING SCREWS (2)
3	IN-LINE FUEL FILTER	7	RIGHT SIDE FRAME
4	FUEL FILTER ATTACHING SCREW		

Fig. 19 Fuel filter replacement

FUEL FILTER
REPLACE

1. Relieve fuel system pressure as outlined under "Fuel System Pressure Relief."
2. Raise and support vehicle.
3. Remove filter shield attaching screws, then the shield, **Fig. 19.**
4. Clean all fuel filter connections and surrounding areas.
5. Disconnect fuel feed pipes from filter, then drain remaining fuel into suitable container.
6. Remove filter mounting screw, then the fuel filter.
7. Reverse procedure to install.

TIGHTENING SPECIFICATIONS

Year	Component	Torque/ Ft. Lbs.	Year	Component	Torque/ Ft. Lbs.
1991	Camshaft Gear	15	1991 —Cont'd	Oil Pan Bolts (Front & Rear Corners)	16
	Clutch Pressure Plate To Flywheel Bolts	30		Oil Pan Bolts (Side Rails)	8
	Connecting Rod	45		Oil Pan Drain Plug	16
	Crankshaft Pulley	32		Oil Pump Bolt	65
	Crankshaft Rear Seal Retainer	11		Rocker Arm Cover	90②
	Crankshaft Vibration Damper	70		Rocker Arm Stud	50
	Cylinder Head Bolts	67		Spark Plugs	22
	Distributor Clamp Bolt	25		Thermostat Housing	25
	Engine Front Cover	98②		Torque Converter To Flywheel Bolts	46
	Engine Mount To Engine	41		Transmission To Engine Bolts (Auto. Trans.)	35
	Engine Mount Through Bolt	40		Transmission To Flywheel Housing Bolts (Man. Trans.)	37
	Exhaust Manifold	19			
	Flywheel Attaching Bolts	74		Valve Lifter Retainer	12
	Intake Manifold Runner	25		Water Pump	30
	Intake Manifold	①			
	Main Bearings	80			
	Oil Cooler	13			
	Oil Pan Baffle Nuts	25			

①—Except tightening sequence positions 1 & 4, 35 ft. lbs.; tightening sequence positions 1 & 4, 45 ft. lbs.
②—Inch lbs.

1992-94 5.7L/V8-350 Single Cam 16 Valve Engine (VIN P)

INDEX

PRECAUTIONS
AIRBAG SYSTEM DISARMING

The diagnostic energy reserve module (DERM) can maintain voltage to cause a system deployment for up to ten minutes after the ignition switch is turned off and the battery is disconnected. Servicing the SIR system during this period may result in accidental deployment and personal injury.
1. Ensure front wheels are pointed straight ahead.
2. Turn ignition switch to Lock position and remove SIR or AIRBAG fuse.
3. Remove left sound insulator. **Remove courtesy lamp from sound insulator, if necessary.**
4. Remove Connector Position Assurance (CPA), then disconnect yellow two-way SIR electrical connector at base of steering column.

AIRBAG SYSTEM ARMING

1. Connect yellow two-way SIR electrical connector, then install Connector Position Assurance (CPA).
2. Install left sound insulator. **Install courtesy lamp to sound insulator, if applicable.**
3. Install SIR fuse to fuse block, turn ignition switch to RUN position and ensure "Inflatable Restraint" lamp flashes 7 to 9 times, then shuts off.

FUEL SYSTEM PRESSURE RELIEF

Failure to relieve system pressure prior to disconnecting fuel system components may cause fire or personal injury. Remove fuel tank filler cap to release fuel tank pressure. Connect pressure gauge J-34730-1 or equivalent to pressure tap on fuel rail, position bleed hose into suitable container and slowly relieve fuel system pressure. Prior to disconnecting fuel line, position shop towel over fitting.

ENGINE MOUNTS
REPLACE

Check engine mounts for damage to rubber components or mounting stud and fluid loss, and replace as necessary.
1. Disconnect battery ground cable.
2. Raise and support vehicle.
3. Remove engine mount nuts (128), **Fig. 1,** at each side.
4. Disconnect catalytic converters from exhaust manifolds. Position catalytic out of way.
5. Using a suitable engine lifting device, raise engine just enough so that mount studs clear crossmember.
6. Remove engine mount through bolt.
7. Remove engine mount, heat shield and spacers, if equipped.
8. Remove engine bracket attaching bolts, then remove bracket.
9. Reverse procedure to install.

ENGINE
REPLACE

1. Disarm airbag system as outlined under "Precautions."
2. Disconnect battery ground cable, then drain cooling system.
3. Remove air intake duct, then disconnect electrical connectors and vacuum lines from upper part of engine.
4. Disconnect upper radiator hose at water pump and throttle body coolant hose at radiator tee.
5. Disconnect lower radiator hose and heater hose from water pump.
6. Disconnect coolant hose from right-hand side of throttle body.
7. Disconnect pressure hose from power steering pump.
8. Remove alternator upper brace.
9. Remove center panel from lefthand wheelwell.
10. Remove serpentine drive belt.
11. Remove A/C compressor from mounting bracket and position aside with refrigerant lines attached.
12. Disconnect electrical connector from windshield wiper motor, then remove cover.
13. Disconnect hose from AIR diverter valve.
14. Relieve fuel system pressure as described under "Fuel System Pressure Relief," then disconnect and cap fuel lines at fuel rail.
15. Disconnect hose from power steering reservoir.
16. Disconnect accelerator, cruise control, throttle valve and traction control cables.
17. Raise and support vehicle, then disconnect wiring from starter motor.
18. Disconnect catalytic converters from exhaust manifolds.
19. **On models with manual transmission,** remove transmission as described under transmission replace.
20. **On models with automatic transmission,** driveplate to converter attaching bolts.
21. **On models with manual transmission,** remove pressure plate and clutch disk, then remove flywheel.
22. **On all models,** disconnect ground leads at rear of engine.
23. Disconnect electrical connectors from coolant temperature sensor, oil pressure sender, oil level indicator and knock sensor.

A DRIVETRAIN AND FRONT
SUSPENSION FRAME
B FRONT SIDE MEMBER
124 BRACKET
125 NUT
126 BOLT
127 MOUNT
128 NUT
129 HEAT SHIELD
130 THROUGH-BOLT
131 SPACER

Fig. 1 Engine mount replacement

24. Remove nuts from engine mount studs, then lower vehicle.
25. Install suitable engine lifting device.
26. Ensure all components that would interfere with engine removal are detached, then lift engine from vehicle.
27. Reverse procedure to install.
28. Rearm airbag system as outlined under "Precautions."

INTAKE MANIFOLD
REPLACE

1. Disarm airbag system as outlined under "Precautions."
2. Disconnect battery ground cable, then drain cooling system.
3. Remove throttle body air duct, then disconnect electrical connectors from fuel injectors.
4. Disconnect left and righthand wiring harness and position aside.
5. Remove accelerator cable bracket and disconnect cable from throttle body.

1	BOLT
2	FUEL RAIL
3	THROTTLE BODY
4	BOLT
5	GASKET
6	INTAKE MANIFOLD
7	VACUUM HOSE

Fig. 2 Fuel rail & throttle body replacement

6. Disconnect hoses from AIR diverter valve.
7. Disconnect ground strap from intake manifold.
8. Remove retaining bolts from fuel rail.
9. Disconnect vacuum hose from fuel pressure regulator.
10. Relieve fuel system pressure as described under "Fuel System Pressure Relief," then disconnect and cap fuel lines at fuel rail.
11. Remove fuel injectors and fuel rail from intake manifold and position aside, **Fig. 2.**
12. Disconnect vacuum and PCV hoses from intake manifold.
13. Remove EGR solenoid bracket and fuel vapor canister purge solenoid bracket.
14. Remove EGR valve.
15. Disconnect air pipe from intake manifold and righthand exhaust manifold.
16. Remove alternator brace.
17. Disconnect coolant hoses from throttle body.
18. Remove throttle body to intake manifold mounting bolts, then remove throttle body and gasket, **Fig. 2.**
19. Remove intake manifold to engine block attaching bolts and studs, then remove intake manifold and gasket, **Fig. 3.**
20. Reverse procedure to install. Prior to installation, apply a $3/16$ inch bead of sealer 1052366 or equivalent to front and rear of engine block. Extend bead of sealer $1/2$ inch up each cylinder head to seal and retain gaskets. Install manifold and torque bolts to specifications in sequence shown in **Fig. 4.**
21. Rearm airbag system as outlined under "Precautions."

EXHAUST MANIFOLD
REPLACE

LEFT SIDE

1. Disconnect battery ground cable.
2. Raise and support vehicle, then disconnect catalytic converter from exhaust manifold.
3. Lower vehicle, then remove air intake duct.
4. Remove serpentine drive belt.
5. Remove center panel front lefthand

A	SEALER
6	INTAKE MANIFOLD
8	BOLT
9	STUD
10	GASKET

Fig. 3 Intake manifold replacement

Fig. 4 Intake manifold bolt tightening sequence

6 INTAKE MANIFOLD

wheelwell.

6. Remove alternator and A/C compressor upper brace.
7. Remove A/C compressor and position aside with refrigerant hoses attached.
8. Disconnect air pipe, check valve and hose as an assembly from exhaust manifold.
9. Disconnect spark plug wires from spark plugs and wire clips from supports.
10. Remove accessory and A/C compressor bracket braces.
11. Remove spark plug wire supports, then remove spark plugs from cylinder head.
12. Remove exhaust manifold attaching bolts and studs, **Fig. 5.**
13. Remove heat shields, exhaust manifold and gasket.
14. Reverse procedure to install.

RIGHT SIDE

1. Disconnect battery ground cable.
2. Raise and support vehicle, then disconnect catalytic converter from exhaust manifold.
3. Lower vehicle, then disconnect electrical connectors from fuel injectors.
4. Disconnect vacuum hose from fuel pressure regulator.
5. Relieve fuel system pressure as described under "Fuel System Pressure Relief," then disconnect and cap fuel lines at fuel rail.
6. Remove fuel rail to intake manifold attaching bolts, then remove fuel injectors and rail.
7. Remove spark plug wires from spark plugs and wire clips from supports.
8. Remove spark plugs from cylinder head, then remove front spark plug wire bracket and bolt.
9. Remove oil level dipstick and tube.
10. Disconnect air pipe, gasket and check valve as an assembly from intake and exhaust manifolds and cylinder head.
11. Remove exhaust manifold attaching bolts and studs, **Fig. 5.**
12. Remove heat shields, exhaust manifold and gasket.
13. Reverse procedure to install. Prior to installing oil level dipstick and tube, apply sealer 1052080 or equivalent around tube approximately 1/2 inch below bead.

CYLINDER HEAD
REPLACE

LEFT SIDE

1. Disarm airbag system as outlined under "Precautions."
2. Disconnect battery ground cable.
3. Raise and support vehicle, then disconnect catalytic converter from exhaust manifold.
4. Drain cooling system, then lower vehicle.
5. Disconnect upper radiator hose, then remove serpentine drive belt.
6. Remove intake manifold as described under "Intake Manifold, Replace."
7. Remove center panel from lefthand wheelwell.
8. Remove A/C compressor and position aside with refrigerant hoses attached.
9. Remove alternator and A/C compressor brace.
10. Remove spark plug wire bracket, then disconnect spark plug wires from spark plugs.
11. Remove spark plugs from cylinder head.
12. Remove lefthand exhaust manifold as describe under "Exhaust Manifold, Replace."
13. Remove alternator and brace.
14. Disconnect AIR diverter valve hose.
15. Remove valve cover, then remove drive belt tensioner and idler pulley.
16. Remove power steering pump attaching bolts, then disconnect hoses and remove power steering pump.
17. Disconnect spark plug wires and coil wire at distributor.
18. Remove accessory mounting bracket.
19. Remove rocker arms and pushrods. Tag rocker arms and pushrods so they can be installed in the same positions.
20. Remove cylinder head attaching bolts, then remove cylinder head and gasket.
21. Reverse procedure to install. When installing cylinder head gasket, position over dowel pins with bead facing upward. Prior to installing cylinder head bolts, coat threads with sealer 1052080 or equivalent. Tighten cylinder head bolts to torque list under tighten specification in sequence shown in **Fig. 6.**
22. Rearm airbag system as outlined under "Precautions."

RIGHT SIDE

1. Disarm airbag system as outlined under "Precautions."
2. Disconnect battery ground cable.
3. Raise and support vehicle, then disconnect catalytic converter from exhaust manifold.
4. Drain cooling system, then lower vehicle.
5. Disconnect lower radiator and heater hoses.
6. Remove power steering pump reservoir from cylinder head and position out of way.

16	EXHAUST MANIFOLD
17	GASKET
18	GASKET
19	EXHAUST MANIFOLD
20	STUD
21	BOLT

Fig. 5 Exhaust manifold replacement

7. Remove coil and bracket.
8. Remove intake manifold as described under "Intake Manifold, Replace."
9. Remove spark plug wires from clips, then remove front spark plug wire bracket.
10. Remove oil level dipstick and tube.
11. Disconnect spark plug wire, then remove spark plugs from cylinder head.
12. Remove righthand exhaust manifold as describe under "Exhaust Manifold, Replace."
13. Remove cylinder head rear vent pipe and valve cover.
14. Remove power steering pump attaching bolts, then disconnect hoses and remove power steering pump.
15. Remove rocker arms and pushrods. Tag rocker arms and pushrods so they can be installed in the same positions.
16. Remove cylinder head attaching bolts, then remove cylinder head and gasket.
17. Reverse procedure to install. When installing cylinder head gasket, position over dowel pins with bead facing upward. Prior to installing cylinder head bolts, coat threads with sealer 1052080 or equivalent. Tighten cylinder head bolts to torque list under tighten specification in sequence shown in **Fig. 6.**
18. Rearm airbag system as outlined under "Precautions."

34	CYLINDER HEAD
67	CYLINDER BLOCK
81	BOLT
82	GASKET

Fig. 6   Cylinder head bolt tightening sequence

27	PUSHROD	34	CYLINDER HEAD
32	BOLT	35	RESTRICTOR
33	RETAINER	36	LIFTERS

Fig. 7   Valve lifter replacement

VALVE ADJUSTMENT

After the engine has been thoroughly warmed up the valves may be adjusted with the engine shutoff as follows: With engine in position to fire No. 1 cylinder the following valves may be adjusted: Exhaust 1-3-4-8, intake 1-2-5-7. Then crank the engine one more complete revolution which will bring No. 6 cylinder to the firing position at which time the following valves may be adjusted: Exhaust 2-5-6-7, intake 3-4-6-8.

The following procedure, performed with the engine running, should be done only in case readjustment is required.
1. After engine has been warmed up to operating temperature, remove valve cover and install a new valve cover gasket.
2. With engine running at idle speed, back off valve rocker arm nut until rocker arm starts to clatter.
3. Turn rocker arm nut down slowly until the clatter just stops. This is the zero lash position.
4. Turn nut down ¼ additional turn and pause 10 seconds until engine runs smoothly. Repeat additional ¼ turns, pausing 10 seconds each time, until nut has been turned down the number of turns listed in the Valve Clearance Specifications Chart from the zero lash position. **This preload adjustment must be done slowly to allow the lifter to adjust itself to prevent the possibility of interference between the intake valve head and top of piston, which might result in internal damage and/or bent pushrods. Noisy lifters should be replaced.**

VALVE ADJUSTMENT SPECIFICATIONS

Engine/VIN	Year	Valve Clearance
5.7L/V8-350(P)	1992-94	1 Turn ①

①—**Turn rocker arm stud nut until all lash is eliminated, then tighten nut the additional turn listed, plus or minus ¼ turn.**

42	DAMPER	77	WEIGHT
43	BOLT		
44	WASHER		
45	HUB		
46	BOLT		

Fig. 8   Crankshaft damper & hub

VALVE ARRANGEMENT
FRONT TO REAR

All . . . . E-I-I-E-E-I-I-E

CAMSHAFT LIFT SPECIFICATIONS

Engine	Year	Int.	Exh.
5.7L/V8-350	1992-94	.300	.300

ROCKER ARMS

Tag rocker arms and components during remove so they can be installed in the same positions. When replacing rocker arms or rocker arm balls, bearing surfaces of rocker arms and balls should be coated with pre-lube 1052365 or equivalent.

ROCKER ARM STUDS

Rocker arm studs with damaged threads should be replaced. Threads of replacement rocker arms studs should be coated with sealing compound 1052080 or equivalent prior to installation. Looseness can be corrected by installing the proper size Heli-Coil insert, or by replacing cylinder head.

PUSHRODS

Tag pushrods during remove so they can be installed in the same positions. When installing, ensure pushrod is seated in lifter sockets.

VALVE GUIDES

Valves operate in guide holes bored in the head. If clearance becomes excessive, use the next oversize valve and ream the bore to fit. Valves with oversize stems are available in .003, .015 and .030 inch.

HYDRAULIC VALVE LIFTERS
REPLACE

Valve lifters, **Fig. 7** can be lifted from their bores after removing rocker arms, pushrods, intake manifold and valve lifter retainer. When removing, position valve lifters in rack so they may be installed at the same location. Adjustable pliers with protected jaws may be used to remove lifters which are stuck due to carbon or varnish deposits. When installing replacement valve lifters, coat roller with pre-lube 1052365 or equivalent.

CRANKSHAFT DAMPER & HUB
REPLACE

1. Disconnect battery ground cable.
2. Remove air intake duct, then remove serpentine drive belt.
3. Raise and support vehicle, then remove engine mount nuts.
4. Remove power steering fluid cooler.
5. Attach suitable engine lifting device, then raise engine slightly to provide tool access to damper attaching bolts.
6. Remove damper to hub attaching bolts, then remove damper, **Fig. 8.**

Fig. 9 Engine front cover replacement

50	FRONT COVER
51	GASKET
52	BOLT
74	PIN

A	TIMING MARKS		
B	KEYWAY	60	CAMSHAFT
56	BOLT	61	TIMING CHAIN
57	SPROCKET	62	SPROCKET
58	BOLT	63	DRIVEN GEAR
59	RETAINER	64	BOLTS

Fig. 10 Camshaft, sprockets & timing chain

7. Disconnect power steering line from steering gear.
8. Place alignment marks on damper hub and front cover for use during installation. **After placing alignment marks on hub and front cover do not rotate crankshaft, as an engine imbalance may result.**
9. Remove crankshaft hub bolt and washer, then remove crankshaft hub using tool No. J39046 or equivalent.
10. Reverse procedure to install. If crankshaft was accidentally rotated after placing alignment marks, position No. 1 cylinder at top dead center, then install hub with arrow casting at 12 O'clock position. If a replacement damper is to be installed, balance weights of the same size as the original damper must be install in the same locations on the new damper.

FRONT COVER
REPLACE

1. Disconnect battery ground cable and drain cooling system.
2. Remove throttle body air duct.
3. Remove water pump as described under "Water Pump, Replace."
4. Remove crankshaft damper and hub as described under "Crankshaft Damper and Hub, Replace."
5. Remove ignition distributor as described under "Distributor, Replace" in the Electrical Section of this chapter.
6. Remove oil pan as described under "Oil Pan, Replace."
7. Remove front cover retaining screws and the front cover, **Fig. 9.**
8. Reverse procedure to install.

FRONT COVER OIL SEAL
REPLACE

1. Remove front cover as described under "Front Cover, Replace.
2. Remove oil seal for crankshaft, water pump shaft and distributor shaft as necessary.
3. Properly support front cover in seal area.
4. Using tool No. J-35468 or equivalent, install crankshaft oil seal.
5. Using tool No. J-39090 or equivalent, install distributor shaft oil seal.
6. Using tool No. J-39088 or equivalent, install water pump oil seal.
7. Install engine front cover.

TIMING CHAIN
REPLACE

1. Remove front cover as outlined previously.
2. Remove crankshaft oil slinger.
3. Rotate engine until timing marks on sprockets are in alignment, **Fig. 10.**
4. Remove camshaft to sprocket bolts, **Fig. 10.**
5. Remove camshaft sprocket and timing chain together. Do not rotate crankshaft after timing chain has been removed.
6. If crankshaft sprocket is to be replaced, remove it with a suitable gear puller. Install new sprocket, aligning key and keyway.
7. If water pump driven gear is to be replaced, remove mounting bolts, then remove gear using a suitable gear puller. Install new gear using tool No. J3092 or equivalent, then install mounting bolts.
8. Install chain on camshaft sprocket. Hold sprocket vertical with chain hanging below and shift around to align the timing marks on sprockets. Align dowel in camshaft with dowel hole in sprocket and install sprocket on camshaft. **When installing camshaft sprocket onto camshaft, ensure teeth camshaft sprocket and water pump driven gear mesh. Do not attempt to drive sprocket on camshaft as welch plug at rear of engine can be dislodged.**
9. Using tool No. J39089, install water pump driven gear O-ring.
10. Lubricate timing chain with engine oil, then install front cover.

CAMSHAFT
REPLACE

1. Disconnect battery ground cable, then remove surge tank cap and drain cooling system.
2. Remove engine front cover as described under "Front Cover, Replace."
3. Remove intake manifold as described under "Intake Manifold, Replace."
4. Remove oil pump stub shaft retaining bolt, then remove stub shaft, **Fig. 11.**
5. Remove valve covers, rocker arms and pushrods. Tag rocker arms and pushrods so they can be installed in the same locations.

| 65 | SHAFT ASSEMBLY |
| 66 | BOLT |

Fig. 11 Oil pump stub shaft location

6. Remove camshaft sprocket and timing chain as described under "Timing Chain, Replace."
7. Remove air cleaner assembly, then disconnect reservoir hose from radiator.
8. From lefthand side of radiator support, remove relay bracket.
9. Remove AIR pump inlet duct, then remove AIR pump mounting bolts and position AIR pump out of way.
10. Disconnect electrical connectors from engine cooling fans.
11. Remove bolt retaining accumulator bracket to upper radiator support.
12. Remove fan shroud to radiator upper support attaching screws.
13. Remove access plug from upper part of radiator.
14. Disconnect radiator bleed hose, then remove bolts and nuts retaining upper radiator support to front side member.
15. Remove screws attaching upper radiator support to lower support, then remove upper radiator support.
16. Disconnect hoses from radiator. **On models with automatic transmission,** disconnect transmission fluid cooler lines from radiator.
17. Remove radiator from vehicle.
18. Raise and support vehicle, then remove lower fan shroud attaching bolts.
19. Lower vehicle, then remove fan shroud and fans.
20. Detach A/C condenser line bracket from front crossmember.
21. Remove engine mount stud nuts, then using a suitable engine lifting fixture, raise front of engine slightly to provide clearance for camshaft removal.
22. Remove camshaft retainer bolts and retainer, **Fig. 10.**
23. Install three ⁵⁄₁₆ 18 x 4 inch bolts into camshaft bolt holes, **Fig. 12.**
24. Carefully rotate and pull camshaft from engine. Use care when removing camshaft to prevent damage to camshaft bearings.

| A | ⁵⁄₁₆-18 x 4" BOLTS |
| 60 | CAMSHAFT |

Fig. 12 Removing camshaft from engine

25. Reverse procedure to install. Prior to installation, coat camshaft and bearings with engine oil. If installing a new camshaft, coat lobes with Molykote or equivalent. When installing a new camshaft, roller lifters should also be replaced.

PISTON & ROD ASSEMBLY

Assemble pistons to connecting rods as shown in **Fig. 13.**

Upon installation, measure the connecting rod side clearance using a suitable feeler gauge. Refer to "Engine Rebuilding Specifications" for connecting rod side clearance.

PISTON PINS & RINGS

Pistons are available in standard and oversizes of .010 and .030 inch.

Piston rings are available in standard and oversizes of .030 inch.

MAIN & ROD BEARINGS

Connecting rod bearings are available in standard and undersizes of .001, .002, .010 and .020 inch.

Main bearings are available in standard and undersizes of .001, .002, .009, .010 and .020 inch.

CRANKSHAFT REAR OIL SEAL
REPLACE

This engine is equipped with a one-piece, lip type seal mounted in a separate seal retainer. Seal replacement requires removal of the transmission.

1. Raise and support vehicle, then remove transmission, clutch assembly and flywheel, as equipped.
2. Pry seal from retainer, inserting

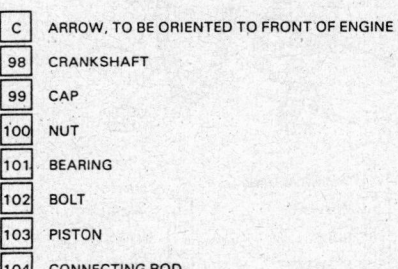

C	ARROW, TO BE ORIENTED TO FRONT OF ENGINE
98	CRANKSHAFT
99	CAP
100	NUT
101	BEARING
102	BOLT
103	PISTON
104	CONNECTING ROD

Fig. 13 Piston & rod assembly

screwdriver in notches provided in seal retainer, **Fig. 14.**
3. Lubricate replacement seal with engine oil, then mount seal on tool J-35621 or equivalent, **Fig. 15.**
4. Mount tool on rear of crankshaft, tightening screws snugly to ensure seal will be installed squarely on crankshaft.
5. Tighten wing nut on tool until it bottoms, then remove tool from crankshaft.
6. Reverse remaining procedure to complete installation.

OIL PAN
REPLACE

1. Disconnect battery ground cable.
2. Raise and support vehicle, then drain crankcase.
3. Disconnect oil level sensor electrical connector, then remove oil level sensor, **Fig. 16.**

A SEAL REMOVAL NOTCHES

114 REAR CRANKSHAFT SEAL RETAINER

Fig. 14   Crankshaft rear oil seal removal

89 INTERMEDIATE SHAFT
95 RETAINER
118 OIL PUMP
119 BAFFLE
120 BOLT

Fig. 17   Oil pump replacement

4. Remove oil filter.
5. Remove starter motor, then remove flywheel cover.
6. Disconnect catalytic converters at exhaust manifolds.
7. Remove nuts from engine mount studs.
8. Remove oil pan attaching bolts, nuts and studs, then remove oil pan.
9. Reverse procedure to install. Prior to installation apply a small amount of sealer 1052914 or equivalent to front cover to engine mating surface and rear seal retainer to engine mating surface. Apply sealer 1 inch in each direction of the radius cavity of these mating surfaces. Torque oil pan retaining bolts to specifications.

OIL PUMP
REPLACE

1. Remove oil pan as described previously.

J 35621

Fig. 15   Crankshaft rear oil seal installation

86 IDLER GEAR
87 PUMP BODY
88 PICKUP SCREEN AND PIPE
89 INTERMEDIATE SHAFT
90 RETAINING PIN
91 SPRING
92 PRESSURE REGULATOR VALVE
93 PLUG
94 DRIVE GEAR AND SHAFT
95 RETAINER
96 COVER
97 BOLT

Fig. 18   Exploded view of oil pump

2. Remove oil pan baffle nuts.
3. Remove pump to rear main bearing cap bolt and remove oil pan baffle, pump intermediate shaft and retainer, **Fig. 17.**
4. Reverse procedure to install. Prime oil pump with clean engine oil prior to installation.

OIL PUMP SERVICE

1. Remove oil pump as described previously.
2. Remove pump cover screws and pump cover, **Fig. 18.**
3. Mark gear teeth so they can be reassembled with same teeth indexing, then remove drive gear, idler gear and shaft.
4. Remove pressure regulator valve retaining pin, pressure regulator valve and related parts.
5. If pickup screen and pipe require replacement, mount pump in a

---

VIEW A

A	AUTO TRANSMISSION	**83**	STUD
B	MANUAL TRANSMISSION	**84**	BOLT
53	REINFORCEMENT	**85**	NUT
54	OIL PAN	**118**	OIL LEVEL SENSOR
55	GASKET		

Fig. 16   Oil pan installation

soft-jawed vise and extract pipe from pump.
6. Wash all parts in cleaning solvent and dry with compressed air.
7. Inspect pump body and cover for cracks and excessive wear.
8. Inspect pump gears for damage or excessive wear.
9. Check drive gear shaft for looseness in pump body.
10. Inspect inside of pump cover for wear that would allow oil to leak past the ends of the gears.
11. Inspect pickup screen and pipe assembly for damage to screen, pipe or relief grommet.
12. Check pressure regulator valve for fit in pump housing.
13. Reverse procedure to assemble. Turn driveshaft by hand to check for smooth operation. **The pump gears and body are not serviced separately. If the pump gears or body**

A MINIMUM BELT
LENGTH MARK
B MAXIMUM BELT
LENGTH MARK
C BELT REPLACEMENT MARK
D MOVABLE INDICATOR
42 DAMPER
145 TENSIONER
146 POWER STEERING PULLEY
147 GENERATOR
148 DRIVE BELT
149 A/C COMPRESSOR
150 IDLER PULLEY

Fig. 19   Serpentine drive belt replacement

1	THERMOSTAT HOUSING
2	AIR BLEED VALVE
3	THROTTLE BODY ASSEMBLY
4	THROTTLE BODY NIPPLE
5	CLAMP - THROTTLE BODY
6	THROTTLE BODY HOSE

Fig. 20   Cooling system bleed valve locations

are damaged or worn, the pump assembly should be replaced. Also, if the pick-up screen and pump assembly was removed, it should be replaced with a new one as loss of the press fit condition could result in an air leak and loss of oil pressure.

BELT TENSION DATA

Engine (VIN)	Year	New Lbs.①	Used Lbs.
5.7L/V8-350(P)	1992-94	①	①

①—Indicator located on tensioner housing.

SERPENTINE DRIVE BELT
REPLACE

1. Using a suitable socket and handle on tensioner pulley bolt, lift tensioner upward in the clockwise direction, then remove serpentine drive belt, **Fig. 19.**
2. Reverse procedure to install. Check to ensure belt tension indicator marks are within limit lines on belt tensioner indicator.

COOLING SYSTEM BLEED

Open bleed valves, **Fig. 20,** on thermostat housing and throttle body prior to adding coolant. Add coolant through radiator surge tank opening until level is at base of tank neck. Close each bleed valve as solid flow of coolant is emitted from valve. Start engine and operate with surge tank cap removed until engine coolant level is maintained at base of surge tank neck. Add coolant as necessary, then install surge tank cap with arrows facing overflow tube. Fill coolant recovery reservoir to proper le-

vel. Start engine and allow reach operating temperature. Turn engine off and allow to cool, then recheck coolant level.

THERMOSTAT
REPLACE

1. Disconnect battery ground cable.
2. Disconnect intake air temperature sensor electrical connector.
3. Remove air cleaner and intake duct assembly.
4. Remove pressure cap from surge tank, then drain cooling system.
5. Disconnect lower radiator hose from thermostat housing on water pump.
6. Remove thermostat housing attaching bolts, then remove housing, **Fig. 21.**
7. Remove thermostat and seal.
8. Reverse procedure to install. When installing thermostat seal, position seal with taper facing upward. Bleed cooling system as described under "Cooling System Bleed."

WATER PUMP
REPLACE

1. Disconnect battery ground cable.
2. Disconnect intake air temperature sensor electrical connector.
3. Remove air cleaner and duct assembly.
4. Remove radiator surge tank cap, then drain cooling system and remove knock sensor.
5. Disconnect upper and lower radiator hose, heater hose and coolant sensor electrical connector from water pump.
6. Remove coolant sensor wire retainer from front of water pump.
7. Using a ⁵/₈ inch box wrench on ser-

pentine drive belt tensioner, left tensioner upward and remove belt from alternator pulley.
8. Remove six water pump to engine attaching bolts, then remove water pump, **Fig. 21.**.
9. Reverse procedure to install. Prior to assembling coupling to pump, apply a light coat of grease seals and splines. When installing coupling, white band should face toward engine, **Fig. 21.** Install water pump gaskets with tabs facing upward. After installation bleed cooling system.

FUEL PUMP
REPLACE

The fuel pump is an electric in tank design attached to the fuel level sending unit. Replace fuel pump as follows:
1. Disconnect battery ground cable.
2. Connect pressure gauge J-34370-1 or equivalent to pressure tap on fuel rail, position bleed hose in suitable container and slowly relieve fuel system pressure. **Failure to relieve system pressure prior to disconnecting fuel system components may cause fire or personal injury.**
3. Remove fuel tank filler cap, then drain fuel tank. Drain fuel into an approved fuel storage container.
4. Remove fuel filler door bezel attaching screws, then remove bezel, **Fig. 22.**
5. Lift fuel filler neck housing and disconnect drain hose.
6. Remove fuel meter and pump attaching screws.

1	FUEL FEED PIPE	
2	IN-LINE FUEL FILTER	
3	FUEL RETURN PIPE	
4	FUEL FILTER ATTACHING SCREW	
5	FUEL FILTER BRACKET	
6	FUEL PIPE O-RING	
7	RIGHT SIDE FRAME	

Fig. 23   Fuel filter replacement

1	COOLANT PUMP		9	GASKET (INSTALL TAB UP)
2	O-RING SEAL		10	BOLT (SHORT)
3	COOLANT PUMP SHAFT		11	COOLANT SENSOR
4	COUPLING		12	BOLT (LONG)
5	WHITE BAND (TOWARD ENGINE)		13	THERMOSTAT
6	DRIVEN GEAR SHAFT		14	SEAL (INSTALL TAPER UP)
7	TIMING CHAIN FRONT COVER		15	THERMOSTAT HOUSING
8	BOLTS - RETAINER PLATE		16	AIR BLEED VALVE

Fig. 21   Water pump & thermostat replacement

1	GASKET
2	FUEL LEVEL METER ASSEMBLY
3	FILER NECK HOUSING
4	FUEL FILER CAP
5	NIPPLE
6	DRAIN HOSE
7	SCREW ASSEMBLY (WITH O-RING) 4.5 N·m (40 lb. in.)
8	FILLER DOOR BEZEL
9	SCREW

Fig. 22   Fuel pump/sending unit replacement

7. Disconnect fuel lines, hoses and electrical connectors from fuel meter and pump assembly. Tag hoses and electrical connectors so they may be installed at the same location.
8. Carefully remove fuel meter and pump assembly.
9. Reverse procedure to install. Prior to installation, position gasket on fuel tank with notch facing forward in right-hand corner of fuel tank. Carefully fold strainer to fit through fuel tank opening. Strainer must unfold when positioned inside tank.

FUEL FILTER REPLACE

1. Relieve fuel system pressure as outlined under "Precautions."
2. Raise and support vehicle.
3. Clean all fuel filter connections and surrounding areas.
4. Disconnect fuel feed pipes from filter, **Fig. 23**, then drain remaining fuel into suitable container.
5. Remove filter mounting screw, then the fuel filter.
6. Reverse procedure to install.

TIGHTENING SPECIFICATIONS

Year	Component	Torque/ Ft. Lbs.	Year	Component	Torque/ Ft. Lbs.
1992-94	Accessory Bracket Bolt	25	1992-94 —Cont'd	Catalytic Converter To Exhaust Manifold Nuts	21
	Camshaft Retainer Bolt	105①		Coolant Sensor	17
	Camshaft Sprocket Bolt	21		Crankshaft Damper To Hub Bolts	60
	Connecting Rod Cap Nut	47		Crankshaft Hub Bolt	70
	Camshaft Sprocket Bolt	21			

Continued

TUNE UP SPECIFICATIONS-Continued

Year	Component	Torque/ Ft. Lbs.
1992-94 —Cont'd	Crankshaft Rear Seal Retainer Bolt & Nut	11
	Cylinder Head Bolt	65
	EGR Solenoid Bracket Nut	25
	EGR Valve Bolt	16
	Engine Front Cover Bolt	100①
	Engine Mount Stud Nuts	40
	Engine Mount Through Bolts	77
	Engine Oil Galley Plug	18
	Exhaust Manifold Bolt/Stud	26
	Flywheel Bolt	74
	Fuel Pump/Sending Unit To Fuel Tank	45①
	Fuel Rail Bolt	15
	Ignition Distributor Bolt	100①
	Intake Manifold Bolt/Stud	35
	Knock Sensor	14
	Main Bearing Cap Bolt	②
	Oil Filter Adapter Bolt	17
	Oil Level Sensor	16
	Oil Pan	③

Year	Component	Torque/ Ft. Lbs.
1992-94 —Cont'd	Oil Pan Baffle Nut	25
	Oil Pan Drain Plug	16
	Oil Pressure Fittings (Plus Alignment)	89①
	Oil Pressure Sensor/Switch	105①
	Oil Pump To Rear Main Bearing Cap	65
	Oil Pump Cover	80①
	Oil Pump Stub Shaft Bolt	13
	Oil Temperature Sensor	108①
	Purge Solenoid Bracket Nut	25
	Rocker Arm Stud	50
	Spark Plug	11
	Starter Motor Mounting Bolts	34
	Thermostat Housing To Water Pump	8
	Throttle Body To Intake Manifold	19
	Valve Lifter Retainer	15
	Valve Rocker Arm Cover	75①
	Water Pump To Engine Bolt	35
	Water Pump Driven Gear Retainer	105①

①—Inch lbs.

5.7L/V8-350 4 CAM 32 Valve (ZR-1) Engine

INDEX

PRECAUTIONS

AIRBAG SYSTEM DISARMING

The diagnostic energy reserve mod-ule (DERM) can maintain voltage to cause a system deployment for up to ten minutes after the ignition switch is turned off and the battery is disconnected. Servicing the SIR system during this period may result in accidental deployment and personal injury.

1. Ensure front wheels are pointed straight ahead.
2. Turn ignition switch to Lock position and remove SIR or AIRBAG fuse.
3. Remove left sound insulator. **Remove courtesy lamp from sound insulator, if necessary.**

A LOCATION PEG
1 BRACKET, ENGINE MOUNT
2 NUT, ENGINE MOUNT/BRACKET
3 BOLT, ENGINE MOUNT BRACKET/ENGINE
4 MOUNT, ENGINE HYDRAULIC
5 NUT, ENGINE MOUNT/FRAME
6 HEAT SHIELD, ENGINE MOUNT
7 BOLT, ENGINE MOUNT/BRACKET
8 SIDE MEMBER, FRONT
9 FRAME, DRIVETRAIN AND FRONT SUSPENSION
10 SPACER, ENGINE MOUNT

Fig. 1 Engine mount replacement

4. Remove Connector Position Assurance (CPA), then disconnect yellow two-way SIR electrical connector at base of steering column.

AIRBAG SYSTEM ARMING

1. Connect yellow two-way SIR electrical connector, then install Connector Position Assurance (CPA).
2. Install left sound insulator. **Install courtesy lamp to sound insulator, if applicable.**
3. Install SIR fuse to fuse block, turn ignition switch to RUN position and ensure "Inflatable Restraint" lamp flashes 7 to 9 times, then shuts off.

FUEL SYSTEM PRESSURE RELIEF

Failure to relieve system pressure prior to disconnecting fuel system components may cause fire or personal injury. Remove fuel tank filler cap to release fuel tank pressure. Connect pressure gauge J-34730-1 or equivalent to pressure tap on fuel rail, position bleed hose into suitable container and slowly relieve fuel system pressure. Prior to disconnecting fuel line, position shop towel over fitting.

ENGINE MOUNTS
REPLACE

Check engine mounts for damage to rubber components or mounting stud and fluid loss, and replace as necessary.
1. Disconnect battery ground cable.
2. Remove exhaust manifold from side on engine mount is to be replaced. Refer to "Exhaust Manifold, Replace."
3. Remove nut attaching engine mount to engine and frame, **Fig. 1.**
4. Support engine.
5. Raise engine slightly to permit removal of engine mount to bracket nut and

bolt, then remove nut and bolt.
6. Remove engine mount and heat shield from vehicle.
7. If necessary, remove bolts attaching mount bracket to engine, then remove bracket.
8. Reverse procedure to install.

ENGINE
REPLACE

1. Disarm airbag system as outlined under "Precautions."
2. Disconnect battery ground cable.
3. Raise and support vehicle.
4. Drain cooling system and crankcase.
5. Remove exhaust system from vehicle.
6. Remove driveshaft from vehicle.
7. Position suitable support under transmission.
8. Remove drive line support member from vehicle.
9. Remove transmission from vehicle, refer to "Transmission, Replace."
10. Remove clutch assembly, refer to "Clutch, Replace."
11. Install engine lifting hook J-37307 or equivalent, to rear of engine.
12. Detach AIR tube center section from AIR hose and oil pan.
13. Remove oxygen sensors.
14. Detach lower power steering hose from oil cooler.
15. Disconnect battery ground cable from engine.
16. Remove engine mount to engine and frame attaching nut.
17. Lower vehicle, then remove air cleaner assembly and duct.
18. Disconnect oil cooler lines from oil filter housing.
19. Raise rear of engine.
20. Remove fuel tank filler cap.
21. Relieve fuel system pressure as described under "Fuel System Pressure Relief."
22. Disconnect fuel lines at fuel rail.
23. Remove evaporator housing panel

and restrictor.
24. Remove righthand firewall wiring harness connector retaining bolts.
25. Disconnect engine righthand wiring harness connector.
26. Remove righthand lower instrument panel sound insulator, then disconnect right firewall connector wiring harness from under instrument.
27. Disconnect air bleed hose from at plenum.
28. Disconnect radiator upper and lower hoses.
29. Disconnect vacuum lines from power steering pump.
30. Discharge A/C refrigerant system.
31. Disconnect A/C suction and discharge line flange from A/C compressor.
32. Disconnect A/C compressor to accumulator line at accumulator.
33. Remove A/C accumulator from bracket and position aside, then remove accumulator bracket from vehicle.
34. Disconnect power steering pressure line at power steering gear.
35. Disconnect accelerator and cruise control cables from throttle body and plenum retainers.
36. Install lifting hook J-37307-1 or equivalent, to front of engine.
37. Disconnect electrical connectors from ECM.
38. Remove left front fender from vehicle.
39. Disconnect battery positive cable and remove battery hold-down, then remove battery from vehicle.
40. Disconnect engine lefthand firewall electrical connector.
41. Disconnect engine wiring harness fusible links at junction block.
42. Disconnect electrical connectors from secondary injector modules, battery positive cable junction block, differential pressure switch, A/C cut-out relay, A/C high blower relay, transmission shift solenoid relay, fuel pump fuse and forward lamp link.
43. Disconnect battery positive lead, then disconnect electrical connectors at blower motor resistor, blower motor, A/C pressure sensors, A/C cooling fan switch, windshield washer pump, low coolant sensor and ESC knock sensor and sensor relay.
44. Disconnect vacuum pump hose.
45. Disconnect front and rear vacuum connectors.
46. Position engine wiring harness out of way.
47. Disconnect engine ground strap from lefthand frame rail.
48. Position battery positive out of way.
49. Remove lefthand plenum screen.
50. Disconnect vacuum hose from power brake unit.
51. Remove windshield wiper motor.
52. Remove MAP sensor and bracket from plenum.
53. Disconnect AIR hose from lefthand exhaust manifold.
54. Ensure all electrical connector and vacuum hoses that would interfere with engine removal are disconnected.

Fig. 2 Plenum assembly bolt tightening sequence

| A | PLENUM |
| B | BOLT, PLENUM |

| 1 | GASKET, PLENUM |
| 2 | HOUSING, INJECTOR |

Fig. 3 Injector housing & gasket

55. Attach suitable engine lifting fixture and remove engine from vehicle.
56. Reverse procedure to install.
57. Rearm airbag system as outlined under "Precautions."

PLENUM ASSEMBLY REPLACE

1. Disarm airbag system as outlined under "Precautions."
2. Disconnect battery ground cable.
3. Drain cooling system, then remove air intake duct.
4. Remove cable shield, then disconnect control cables at throttle body.
5. Remove cable hold-down clamps from plenum.
6. Disconnect fresh air hoses from throttle body extension.
7. Disconnect electrical connectors from TPS, IAC and MAT.
8. Disconnect air bleed hose from plenum.
9. Disconnect power brake unit vacuum hose at plenum.
10. Disconnect vacuum hose located between plenum and fuel pressure regulator.
11. Disconnect vacuum hoses at mid-plenum.
12. Disconnect vacuum hose from MAP sensor and plenum, then disconnect electrical connector from MAP sensor.
13. Relieve fuel system pressure as described under "Fuel System Pressure Relief," then disconnect and cap fuel lines at fuel rail.
14. Remove bolts attaching plenum assembly to injector housing.
15. Disconnect electrical connectors from ignition module.
16. Disconnect PCV and purge canister vacuum hoses from plenum.
17. Disconnect vacuum hose from lower portion of throttle body extension.
18. Remove plenum assembly. Cover injector housing openings.

19. Reverse procedure to install. Tighten plenum assembly attaching bolts in sequence shown in **Fig. 2.**
20. Rearm airbag system as outlined under "Precautions."

INJECTOR HOUSING REPLACE

1. Disarm airbag system as outlined under "Precautions."
2. Disconnect battery ground cable, then drain cooling system.
3. Remove plenum assembly as described under "Plenum Assembly, Replace."
4. Remove fuel tank filler cap.
5. Relieve fuel system pressure as described under "Fuel System Pressure Relief."
6. Disconnect fuel lines at righthand fuel rail.
7. Disconnect electrical connectors from injectors.
8. Remove bolts attaching fuel rail to injector housing, then remove injectors from housing and remove fuel rail.
9. Disconnect coolant outlet pipe from injector housing being removed.
10. If lefthand injector housing is to be removed, remove bolt retaining outlet pipe bracket to power steering pump bracket.
11. If righthand injector housing is to be removed, remove oil pressure sensor from oil filter housing.
12. Remove PCV grommet from injector housing, then disconnect ventilation hose.
13. If lefthand injector housing is to be removed, disconnect electrical connectors from coolant temperature and cooling fan switches.
14. If righthand injector housing is to be replaced, remove bolt attaching alternator rear support bracket and ventilation pipe bracket to injector housing, then remove ventilation pipe and

bracket.
15. Remove injector housing to cylinder head attaching bolts, then remove injector housing and gasket, **Fig. 3.**
16. Reverse procedure to install.
17. Rearm airbag system as outlined under "Precautions."

EXHAUST MANIFOLD REPLACE

LEFT SIDE
1991

1. Disconnect battery ground cable.
2. Raise and support vehicle, then remove wheel and tire assembly.
3. Remove wheel housing lower rear and center panels.
4. Disconnect AIR hose from exhaust manifold, then remove exhaust manifold to cylinder head attaching bolts and nut.
5. Remove gasket from exhaust manifold.
6. Raise and support vehicle.
7. Disconnect catalytic converter oxygen sensor electrical connector.
8. Remove catalytic converter heat shield attaching screws, then remove heat shields.
9. Remove bolts attaching exhaust pipe to converter, then remove exhaust manifold and converter assembly, **Fig. 4.**
10. Reverse procedure to install. If exhaust stud was removed or is loose, apply Loctite 620 or equivalent to stud threads.

1992-94

1. Disconnect battery ground cable.
2. Raise and support vehicle, then remove wheel and tire assembly.
3. Remove wheel housing lower rear and center panels.
4. Remove exhaust system as follows:
   a. Remove underbody braces, if equipped.
   b. Remove bolt attaching exhaust pipe flange to lefthand catalytic converter.
   c. Loosen clamp securing exhaust pipe to righthand catalytic converter.

NOTE: LEFT EXHAUST MANIFOLD SHOWN, RIGHT EXHAUST MANIFOLD BOLT LOCATIONS ARE THE SAME.

1	STUD, EXHAUST MANIFOLD	5	BOLT W/SPACER, EXHAUST MANIFOLD/CONVERTER
2	FLANGE, EXHAUST	6	GASKET, EXHAUST MANIFOLD/CONVERTER
3	MANIFOLD/CONVERTER, EXHAUST	7	HEAD, CYLINDER
4	NUT, EXHAUST MANIFOLD STUD	8	BRACKET, BOLT

Fig. 4 Exhaust manifold & converter assembly. 1991

d. Support exhaust system, then remove bolts attaching resonator assembly to front spring hanger.
e. Remove bolts attaching resonator assembly to rear spring hanger.
f. Remove nuts attaching mufflers to hanger brackets, then remove exhaust system from vehicle.
5. Remove lefthand floor heat shield, then remove lefthand frame heat shield.
6. Remove engine heat shield, then disconnect oxygen sensor electrical connector.
7. Remove AIR check valves, housings and tubes.
8. Remove manifold outer heat shield.
9. Remove catalytic converter from exhaust manifold.
10. Remove exhaust manifold attaching bolts, nut and spacers, then remove exhaust manifold and gasket, **Fig. 5.**
11. Reverse procedure to install.

RIGHT SIDE

1991

1. Disconnect battery ground cable.
2. Raise and support vehicle, then remove wheel and tire assembly.
3. Remove wheel housing lower rear and center panels.
4. Remove engine level dipstick and tube.
5. Remove front exhaust manifold to cylinder head attaching bolts, then remove center stud nut.
6. Disconnect oxygen sensor electrical connector. It may be necessary to remove ignition timing and oxygen sensor electrical connector bracket attaching bolts to gain access to connector.
7. Disconnect AIR hose from exhaust manifold.

8. Remove converter heat shield attaching screws, then remove heat shield.
9. Remove exhaust pipe to converter attaching bolts.
10. Remove exhaust manifold to cylinder head rear attaching bolts, then remove gasket and manifold and converter assembly, **Fig. 4.**
11. Reverse procedure to install. If exhaust stud was removed or is loose, apply Loctite 620 or equivalent to stud threads.

1992-94

1. Disconnect battery ground cable.
2. Raise and support vehicle, then remove wheel and tire assembly.
3. Remove wheel housing lower rear and center panels.
4. Remove manifold outer heat shields.
5. Remove exhaust system as follows:
   a. Remove underbody braces, if equipped.
   b. Remove bolt attaching exhaust pipe flange to lefthand catalytic converter.
   c. Loosen clamp securing exhaust pipe to righthand catalytic converter.
   d. Support exhaust system, then remove bolts attaching resonator assembly to front spring hanger.
   e. Remove bolts attaching resonator assembly to rear spring hanger.
   f. Remove nuts attaching mufflers to hanger brackets, then remove exhaust system from vehicle.
6. Remove engine block heat shield.
7. Remove catalytic converter from exhaust manifold.
8. Disconnect oxygen sensor electrical connector.
9. Remove exhaust manifold rear attaching bolts, spacers and nut.
10. Lower vehicle, then remove AIR check valve and hoses from manifold.
11. Remove oil level dipstick tube retaining bolt.
12. Remove remaining exhaust manifold attaching bolts and spacers, then remove exhaust manifold and gasket, **Fig. 5.**
13. Reverse procedure to install.

CYLINDER HEAD
REPLACE

LEFT SIDE

1. Disarm airbag system as outlined under "Precautions."
2. Disconnect battery ground cable.
3. Remove lefthand injector housing as described under "Injector Housing, Replace."
4. Disconnect vacuum hose from throttle valve actuator secondary port.
5. Remove power brake unit.
6. Remove valve lash adjusters from lefthand side as described under "Hydraulic Valve Lash Adjusters, Replace."
7. Disconnect AIR control valve hoses and electrical connectors.
8. Remove camshaft position sensor.

9. Remove lefthand exhaust manifold to cylinder head attaching bolts. Refer to "Exhaust Manifold, Replace" procedure. It is not necessary to remove exhaust manifold from vehicle.
10. Remove access plug from front of cylinder head, then remove upper bolt attaching secondary timing chain fixed guide.
11. Remove cylinder head attaching bolts, then remove cylinder head and gasket.
12. Reverse procedure to install. Prior to installation of cylinder head bolts, coat threads and washers with engine oil. Tighten cylinder head attaching bolts in sequence shown in **Fig. 6.** Prior to installation of secondary timing chain fixed guide upper attaching bolt, apply Loctite 262 or equivalent to bolt threads.
13. Rearm airbag system as outlined under "Precautions."

RIGHT SIDE

1. Disarm airbag system as outlined under "Precautions."
2. Disconnect battery ground cable.
3. Remove righthand injector housing as described under "Injector Housing, Replace."
4. Remove valve lash adjusters from righthand side as described under "Hydraulic Valve Lash Adjusters, Replace."
5. Remove alternator.
6. Remove righthand exhaust manifold to cylinder head attaching bolts. Refer to "Exhaust Manifold, Replace" procedure. It is not necessary to remove exhaust manifold from vehicle.
7. Remove fuel filter heat shield.
8. Disconnect vacuum hose from throttle valve actuator secondary port.
9. Remove access plug from front of cylinder head, then remove upper bolt attaching secondary timing chain fixed guide.
10. Remove cylinder head attaching bolts, then remove cylinder head and gasket.
11. Reverse procedure to install. Prior to installation of cylinder head bolts, coat threads and washers with engine oil. Tighten cylinder head attaching bolts in sequence shown in **Fig. 6.** Prior to installation of secondary timing chain fixed guide upper attaching bolt, apply Loctite 262 or equivalent to bolt threads.
12. Rearm airbag system as outlined under "Precautions."

VALVE ADJUSTMENT

This engine is equipped with hydraulic valve lash adjusters, which require no adjustment.

1 GASKET	6 HEAT SHIELD, OUTER LEFT	
2 BOLT W/SPACER	7 HEAT SHIELD, LEFT	
3 EXHAUST MANIFOLD, RIGHT	8 HEAT SHIELD, OUTER RIGHT	
4 SCREW	9 HEAT SHIELD, OUTER RIGHT FRONT	
5 WASHER	10 HEAT SHIELD, INNER	

Fig. 5   Exhaust manifold & converter assembly. 1992-94

VALVE ADJUSTMENT SPECIFICATIONS

Year	Engine (VIN)	Valve Clearance
1991-94	5.7L/V8-350(J)	①

①—Equipped w/hydraulic valve lash adjusters, no adjustment.

VALVE ARRANGEMENT

Exhaust valve are located on the exhaust manifold side of the cylinder head. Intake valve are located on the plenum side of the cylinder head.

CAMSHAFT LIFT SPECIFICATIONS

Engine (VIN)	Year	Int.①	Exh.①
5.7L/V8-350(J)	1991-94	.3898	.3898

①—Plus or minus .002 inch.

HYDRAULIC VALVE LASH ADJUSTERS REPLACE

1. Disconnect battery ground cable.
2. Remove camshaft(s) as described under "Camshaft, Replace."
3. Remove valve lash adjusters from cylinder head, **Fig. 7.**. Note position of lash adjusters during removal so they may be reinstalled into the same bore.
4. Check lash adjuster contact surfaces for concave wear using a straight-edge and replace as necessary. If camshaft lobe is worn, replace lash adjusters and camshaft as an assembly.
5. Reverse procedure to install. Apply engine oil to lash adjusters and bores prior to installation.

1 BOLT, CYLINDER HEAD
2 HEAD, CYLINDER-RH
3 HEAD, CYLINDER-LH

Fig. 6 Cylinder head bolt tightening sequence

1 LIFTER, INTAKE VALVE
2 HEAD, CYLINDER
3 CAMSHAFT, EXHAUST-RH

Fig. 7 Hydraulic valve lifter installation

1 COVER, CAMSHAFT
2 BOLT, CAMSHAFT COVER

Fig. 8 Camshaft cover bolt tightening sequence

1 GASKET, ENGINE FRONT COVER
2 COVER, ENGINE FRONT
3 SEAL, ENGINE FRONT COVER
4 BOLT, ENGINE FRONT COVER
5 STUD, ENGINE FRONT COVER
6 NUT, ENGINE FRONT COVER STUD

Fig. 9 Engine front cover & gasket

CAMSHAFT COVER REPLACE

LEFT SIDE

1. Disconnect battery ground cable.
2. Remove power steering pump.
3. Discharge A/C refrigerant system, then disconnect suction and discharge hoses from A/C compressor. Cap refrigerant lines and A/C compressor openings.
4. Disconnect spark plug wires from spark plugs.
5. Disconnect ventilation hose from camshaft cover.
6. Remove hold-down clamps retaining throttle and cruise control cables to plenum.
7. Remove throttle body extension and coolant outlet tube.
8. **On 1991 models,** disconnect vacuum hose from power brake unit.
9. **On 1992-94 models,** remove power brake booster from vehicle.
10. **On all models,** remove bolts attaching camshaft cover to cylinder head, then remove cover.
11. Reverse procedure to install. Apply Permabond A136 or equivalent to camshaft cover prior to installation. Apply Loctite 565 to end plugs. Prior to installation, ensure camshaft end

plugs and spark plug bore O-rings are properly position. Also insert the two rear lower camshaft cover bolts prior to placing cover on cylinder head. Tighten camshaft cover attaching bolts in sequence shown in **Fig. 8.**

RIGHT SIDE

1. Disconnect battery ground cable, then drain cooling system.
2. Disconnect spark plug wires from spark plugs.
3. Disconnect blower motor resistor electrical connectors.
4. Remove evaporator housing panel attaching screws, then remove panel.
5. Remove oil pressure sensor from oil filter housing.
6. Remove bolt attaching coolant outlet pipe to alternator bracket.
7. Remove screws attaching coolant outlet to injector housing, then position coolant outlet aside.
8. Remove bolt attaching fresh air pipe bracket to injector housing.
9. Remove camshaft cover to cylinder head attaching bolts, then remove cover.
10. Reverse procedure to install. Apply Permabond A136 or equivalent to camshaft cover prior to installation. Apply Loctite 565 to end plugs. Prior to installation, ensure camshaft end plugs and spark plug bore O-rings are

properly position. Tighten camshaft cover attaching bolts in sequence shown in **Fig. 8.** When installing coolant outlet pipe bracket bolt and oil pressure sensor, apply Loctite 565 or equivalent to threads.

FRONT COVER & SEAL REPLACE

REMOVAL

1. Disconnect battery ground cable.
2. Remove water pump as described under "Water Pump, Replace."
3. Discharge A/C refrigerant system, then remove A/C compressor.
4. Remove steering gear, if necessary.
5. Remove serpentine drive belt.
6. Remove crankshaft damper to crankshaft retaining bolt and washer, then remove damper using puller J-24420-C or equivalent.
7. Remove key from crankshaft keyway.
8. Remove front cover attaching screws and nuts, then remove front cover, **Fig. 9.**
9. Using tool No. J-29077-A, remove seal from front cover.

5.7L/V8-350 4 CAM 32 VALVE (ZR-1) ENGINE

INSTALLATION

1. Apply Loctite 262 or equivalent to front cover stud threads. Apply Loctite 565 or equivalent to front cover bolt threads.
2. Position front cover and gasket to engine, then install attaching bolts and nuts finger tight.
3. Lubricate front cover seal with engine oil, then install seal using installation tool No. J-37309 or equivalent, **Fig. 10.** Torque front cover attaching bolts and nuts to specification, then remove seal installation tool.
4. Install water pump and A/C compressor.
5. Apply engine oil to seal surface of crankshaft damper, then position damper to crankshaft.
6. Apply Loctite 262 or equivalent to crankshaft damper attaching bolt, then install bolt and tighten to specification.
7. Install serpentine drive belt and connect battery ground cable.

TIMING CHAIN
REPLACE

PRIMARY TIMING CHAIN

1. Disconnect battery ground cable.
2. Remove engine front cover as described under "Front Cover, Replace."
3. Remove left and righthand intake camshafts as described under "Camshaft, Replace."
4. Remove bolts attaching primary timing chain guide to oil pump, then remove chain guide.
5. Remove idler sprocket assembly attaching bolts, **Fig. 11.**
6. Detach primary timing chain from idler sprocket and crankshaft sprocket, then remove timing chain from engine.
7. Reverse procedure to install. Apply Loctite 262 or equivalent to idle sprocket attaching and primary timing guide bolt threads prior to installation. When installing primary timing chain guide, use only finger pressure to remove slack from chain.

SECONDARY TIMING CHAINS

Removal

1. Disconnect battery ground cable.
2. Remove camshafts as described under "Camshaft, Replace."
3. Remove primary timing chain as described previously.
4. Disengage left and righthand secondary timing chains from idler sprocket.
5. Remove idler sprocket attaching bolts, then remove idle sprocket, **Fig. 11.**
6. Remove left and righthand secondary timing chains.

Installation

1. Install longer outer secondary timing chain through lefthand cylinder head

J 37309

1	PAN, OIL
2	COVER, ENGINE FRONT
3	PLATE, ENGINE TIMING INDICATOR

Fig. 10   Engine front cover seal installation

1	SPROCKET ASSEMBLY, CAMSHAFT TIMING CHAIN IDLER
2	GUIDE, CAMSHAFT SECONDARY TIMING CHAIN FIXED - RH
3	GUIDE, CAMSHAFT SECONDARY TIMING CHAIN PIVOT - LH
4	CHAIN, CAMSHAFT SECONDARY TIMING
5	GUIDE, CAMSHAFT SECONDARY TIMING CHAIN FIXED - LH
6	CHAIN, CAMSHAFT PRIMARY TIMING
7	SPROCKET, CRANKSHAFT
8	PUMP, OIL
9	GUIDE, CAMSHAFT TIMING CHAIN PIVOT - RH

Fig. 11   Primary & secondary timing chains & guides

NOTE: SHORT SHOULDER OF SPROCKET MUST FACE FORWARD.

VIEW A

1	CRANKCASE
2	PAN, OIL
3	SPROCKET, CRANKSHAFT
4	SEAT, OIL PUMP SEAL

Fig. 12   Crankshaft sprocket installation

1	HEAD, CYLINDER
2	CASE, CYLINDER
3	CRANKCASE
4	PAN, OIL

Fig. 13   Installing tool No. J-38098 into crankshaft position sensor opening

1	CAMSHAFT
2	RETAINER, CAMSHAFT
3	WASHER, CAMSHAFT THRUST
4	SPROCKET, CAMSHAFT
5	PLATE, CAMSHAFT SPROCKET TIMING
6	PIN, CAMSHAFT SPROCKET
7	WASHER, CAMSHAFT SPROCKET
8	BOLT, CAMSHAFT SPROCKET

Fig. 14   Camshafts, sprocket & retainers

and hold in position with retainer J-38099 or equivalent, then place chain on inner idler sprocket.

2. Install shorter inner secondary timing chain through righthand cylinder head and hold in position with retainer J-38099 or equivalent, then place chain on outer idler sprocket.
3. Install primary timing chain as described previously.
4. Install camshafts as described under "Camshaft, Replace."
5. Connect battery ground cable.

CRANKSHAFT SPROCKET
REPLACE

1. Disconnect battery ground cable.
2. Remove primary timing chain as described under "Timing Chain, Replace."
3. Using tool No. J-38211 and J-24420-C, remove crankshaft sprocket from crankshaft.
4. Remove key and oil pump seal seat from crankshaft.
5. Reverse procedure to install. Position sprocket to crankshaft with short shoulder toward front, **Fig. 12.** Use tool J-38132 or equivalent to install crankshaft sprocket.

CAMSHAFT
REPLACE

REMOVAL

1. Disconnect battery ground cable.
2. If camshaft(s) is to be removed from lefthand cylinder head, remove A/C compressor.
3. If camshaft(s) is to be removed from righthand cylinder head, remove oil filter housing.
4. Remove camshaft cover as described under "Camshaft Cover, Replace."
5. Raise and support vehicle.
6. Disconnect electrical connector from crankshaft position sensor, then remove crankshaft position sensor from engine.
7. Install tool No. J-38098 or equivalent into crankshaft position sensor opening. Ensure tool properly positioned in sensor opening, **Fig. 13.**

8. Lower vehicle, then remove secondary timing chain tensioner housing to cylinder head attaching bolts.
9. Remove secondary timing chain tensioner housing, O-ring and tensioner.
10. Position a suitable wrench at rear of camshaft on hex, then remove camshaft sprocket attaching bolt(s) and washer(s), **Fig. 14.**
11. Remove camshaft timing plates and pins, then remove camshaft retainers and thrust washers.
12. Remove camshaft and sprocket. Use tool No. J-38099 or equivalent to retain secondary timing chain, **Fig. 15.**

INSTALLATION

If a replacement camshaft is to be installed, the hydraulic valve lash adjusters should also be replaced to aid in preventing premature camshaft wear.

1. Position camshaft sprocket to secondary timing chain while removing retaining tool(s).

2. Note position of alignment hole for timing pin tool, then slide camshaft into camshaft sprocket. Position camshaft so that no valves are open.
3. Lubricate camshaft lobes, journals, thrust washers and retainers with engine oil.
4. Install camshaft retainers, thrust washers and bolts, **Fig. 14.**
5. If both camshafts where removed, repeat steps 1 through 4 for other camshaft.
6. Install timing pin(s) J-37326 or equivalent into camshaft retainers and alignment hole on camshaft. Use a suitable wrench on hex at rear of camshaft to position camshaft alignment holes, **Fig. 16.**
7. Install secondary timing chain pre-tensioning tool No. J-37305 or equivalent, then tighten tool until slack is removed from timing chain, **Fig. 17.**
8. Install timing plate and pin. If holes are not aligned on timing plate, reverse plate.
9. Apply Loctite 262 or equivalent to a new camshaft sprocket retaining bolt threads. Apply engine oil to camshaft sprocket washer.
10. Position a suitable wrench on hex at rear of camshaft to prevent rotation, then install camshaft sprocket bolt and washer and **torque** to 19 ft. lbs. Using tool No. J-36660 or equivalent, tighten bolt an additional 80° to 85°.
11. Remove timing pins from camshaft retainer(s) and alignment hole(s).
12. Remove pre-tensioning tool from secondary timing chain.
13. Lubricate a new secondary timing chain tensioner exterior with engine oil.
14. Install secondary timing chain tensioner, housing, O-ring and bolts. Ensure oil hole in tensioner piston is in vertical position and fork at end of tensioner is properly engaged on chain guide.
15. Raise and support vehicle.
16. Remove tool from crankshaft position sensor opening, then install crankshaft position sensor and connect electrical connector.
17. Lower vehicle, then install camshaft cover.
18. If camshaft was removed lefthand cylinder head, install A/C compressor.
19. If camshaft was removed righthand cylinder head, install oil filter housing.
20. Connect battery ground cable.

PISTON & ROD ASSEMBLY

Assemble pistons to connecting rods as shown in **Fig. 18.** When install piston and rod assembly, arrow on piston head must face front of engine.

Upon installation, measure the connecting rod side clearance using a suitable feeler gauge. Connecting rod side clearance should be .008 to .028 inch.

1	HEAD, CYLINDER
2	CHAIN, CAMSHAFT SECONDARY TIMING
3	LIFTER, VALVE

Fig. 15   Secondary timing chain retaining tool installation

1	CAMSHAFT, INTAKE RH
2	HEAD, CYLINDER

Fig. 16   Camshaft timing pin installation

1	CHAIN, CAMSHAFT SECONDARY TIMING
2	HEAD, CYLINDER
3	CASE, CYLINDER
4	CHAIN, CAMSHAFT PRIMARY TIMING

Fig. 17   Secondary timing chain tension tool installation

PISTON PINS & RINGS

Pistons, pins, rings and cylinder liners are replaced in matched sets as an assembly.

MAIN & ROD BEARINGS

Main and rod bearing are of the precision insert type and must be replaced in a

1 | CASE, CYLINDER
2 | LINER, CYLINDER

Fig. 19 Cylinder liner retainer installation

NOTE: LARGE CHAMFERS ON CONNECTING RODS MUST FACE CRANKSHAFT COUNTERWEIGHTS.

VIEW A

1 | PISTON
2 | ROD, CONNECTING - LH
3 | BEARING, CONNECTING ROD
4 | ROD, CONNECTING - RH
5 | CAP, CONNECTING ROD BEARING
6 | BOLT, CONNECTING ROD BEARING CAP
7 | CRANKSHAFT

Fig. 18 Piston & rod assembly

APPLY BAND OF SEALER 12 mm (0.47 in.) WIDE AND 25.4 mm (1.0 in.) FROM BASE OF CYLINDER LINER, AROUND ENTIRE CIRCUMFERENCE.

12.0 mm (0.47 in.)

25.4 mm (1.0 in.)

Fig. 21 Applying sealer to cylinder liner outer surface

Fig. 20 Cylinder liner removal

complete set of upper and lower halves. If main or rod bearing are found to be worn or out of round, the crankshaft must be replaced.

CYLINDER LINER
REPLACE
REMOVAL

1. Disconnect battery ground cable.
2. Remove engine from vehicle as described under "Engine, Replace."
3. Remove flywheel attaching bolts, then remove flywheel from crankshaft.
4. Remove crankshaft rear oil seal housing.
5. Remove cylinder heads from engine.
6. Remove oil pump from engine.
7. Install cylinder liner retainers J-37330 or equivalent, **Fig. 19.**

8. Invert engine, then remove oil pan.
9. Rotate crankshaft until piston is located at bottom of cylinder liner bore.
10. Remove connecting rod bearing cap bolts, then remove cap and bearing. Mark side of rod cap so they can be installed in the same position.
11. Remove piston and rod assemblies from cylinder liner.
12. Remove bolts and washers attaching crankcase at main bearing journals.
13. Remove bolts attaching crankcase to cylinder case, then remove crankcase from cylinder case.
14. Remove crankshaft, then remove main bearing inserts. Tag bearing insert so they can be installed in the same locations.
15. Remove cylinder liner retaining tool, then remove cylinder liner using tool Nos. J-38124 and J-8092 or equiva-

lent, **Fig. 20.**

INSTALLATION

1. Position cylinder liners into cylinder case. Flats on liners should face front and rear of cylinder case.
2. Check cylinder liner protrusion. Distance between cylinder case deck and lower ridge at top of liner should be .001 to .003 inch. If protrusion is not within limits, check liner ridge and cylinder case seat for burrs, damage or debris and clean as necessary. If protrusion is still not within limits, replace cylinder liner.
3. After proper cylinder liner protrusion has been obtained, remove liner. Apply a bead of Loctite 565 or equivalent, approximately .47 inch wide, around circumference of liner, 1 inch from liner bottom edge, **Fig. 21.**

1 CASE, CYLINDER
2 CRANKCASE
3 BOLT, MAIN BEARING
4 BOLT, CRANKCASE
5 NUT/BOLT, CRANKCASE

Fig. 22 Crankcase to cylinder case bolt tightening sequence

1 CASE, CYLINDER
2 CRANKCASE
3 PAN, OIL
4 SEAL, CRANKSHAFT REAR
5 HOUSING, REAR OIL SEAL
6 CRANKSHAFT
7 PIPE, CYLINDER CASE "VEE" DRAIN

Fig. 23 Crankshaft rear seal & housing

4. Position liner into cylinder case and install liner retainer J37330 or equivalent, **Fig. 19.**
5. Lubricate main bearing insert with engine oil. Insert upper main bearing insert into cylinder case bores. Insert lower main bearing inserts into crankcase bores.
6. Position crankshaft on cylinder case.
7. Apply Permabond A136 or equivalent to crankcase on cylinder case sealing surfaces. Be sure to rout sealant around bolt holes.
8. Install crankcase on cylinder case.
9. Coat new bolts and washers located at main bearing journals with engine oil. Do not coat other crankcase to cylinder case attaching bolts.
10. Install all crankcase to cylinder case bolts finger tight. Do not rotate crankshaft until bolts have been tighten to final torque reading.
11. Torque crankcase to cylinder case attaching bolts to specified torque in sequence shown in **Fig. 22.** Torque bolts listed in numbered sequence first, then tighten bolts listed in lettered sequence.
12. Lubricate pistons, connecting rod bearings, cylinder liner bores and crank pin journals with engine oil.
13. Using a suitable ring compressor install piston and rod assemblies into cylinder liner bores and locate rod and bearing on crankshaft.
14. Install connecting rod bearings and caps. **Torque** new connecting bolts to 22 ft. lbs., then tighten bolts an additional 80° to 85° using tool No. J-36660 or equivalent. Rotate crankshaft as necessary to install piston and connecting rod assemblies.
15. Install oil pan and gasket, then invert engine. Apply Loctite 242 or equivalent to all oil pan attaching screws.
16. Remove cylinder liner retainers, then install oil pump.
17. Install cylinder heads.
18. Install crankshaft rear oil seal housing.

1 OIL PAN GASKET
2 OIL PAN BAFFLE
3 OIL PAN
4 OIL PAN PICKUP SPACER
5 OIL PAN BOLT
6 OIL PAN STUD BOLT
7 OIL PICKUP PIPE AND SCREEN ASSEMBLY
8 OIL LEVEL SENSOR

TORQUE SEQUENCE

7 5 1 3 9 11
15 ← FRT 13
16 14
17
8 4 2 6 10 12

Fig. 24 Oil pan, baffle & gasket

19. Apply Loctite 262 or equivalent to flywheel attaching bolt threads, then install flywheel. Flywheel must be installed with crankshaft dowel pin at the 6 o'clock position.
20. Install engine in vehicle.

CRANKSHAFT REAR OIL SEAL
REPLACE

1. Disconnect battery ground cable.
2. Remove transmission and clutch assembly.

3. Remove flywheel from crankshaft.
4. Remove oil seal housing to cylinder block attaching screws.
5. Remove seal housing assembly from crankshaft, then remove seal from housing, **Fig. 23.**
6. Reverse procedure to install. Using tool J-37312 or equivalent, install seal into housing until it is 1 to 1.5 mm below housing surface. Lubricate seal lip with engine oil prior to installation.

OIL PAN
REPLACE

1. Disconnect battery ground cable.
2. Remove oil level dipstick from tube.
3. Raise and support vehicle, then drain oil from crankcase.
4. Remove flywheel housing cover attaching bolts, then remove cover.
5. Disconnect low oil level sensor electrical connector, then remove oil level sensor, if equipped.
6. Remove bolts attaching AIR pipe bracket to oil pan.
7. Remove converter heat shield attaching screws, then remove heat shields.
8. Remove engine mount retaining nuts at front crossmember rear brace from left and righthand sides.
9. Remove bolts attaching front crossmember rear braces to front crossmember and side crossmembers, then remove braces.
10. Remove bolts attaching oil pan to engine block, then remove oil pan, **Fig. 24.**
11. Disassemble oil pan, if necessary, as follows:
    a. Remove baffle to oil pan attaching bolts, then remove baffle.
    b. Remove bolt and spacer attaching oil pickup assembly to oil pan, then remove pickup assembly. Clean oil pickup assembly with suitable solvent and dry with compressed air.

1	PLATE, OIL PUMP
2	GEAR, OUTER
3	GEAR, INNER
4	O-RING, OIL PUMP BODY
5	BOLT, OIL PUMP
6	SEAL, OIL PUMP CRANKSHAFT
7	BODY, OIL PUMP
8	O-RING, OIL PRESSURE REGULATION VALVE
9	HOUSING, OIL PRESSURE REGULATION VALVE
10	O-RING, OIL PRESSURE REGULATION VALVE
11	VALVE, OIL PRESSURE REGULATION
12	SPRING, OIL PRESSURE REGULATION VALVE OUTER
13	SPRING, OIL PRESSURE REGULATION VALVE INNER
14	STOP, OIL PRESSURE REGULATION VALVE
15	RETAINER, OIL PRESSURE REGULATION VALVE
16	RETAINER, OIL PRESSURE REGULATION VALVE
17	O-RING, OIL FILTER FEED RETURN
18	O-RING, OIL FILTER FEED RETURN
19	SCREW, OIL PUMP PLATE
20	O-RING, OIL PUMP CRANKSHAFT

NOTE: CHAMFER ON INNER GEAR MUST FACE TO THE REAR (TOWARD ENGINE) SO AS TO ACCOMMODATE CRANKSHAFT O-RING 20.

Fig. 25 Exploded view of oil pump

12. Assemble oil pan, if necessary, as follows:
   a. Install oil pickup assembly to oil pan. Prior to installation, apply Loctite 565 or equivalent to oil pan and oil pickup assembly joint. Also apply Loctite 262 or equivalent to oil pickup assembly mounting bolt threads.
   b. Install baffle to oil pan. Prior to installation, apply Loctite 262 or equivalent to bolt threads.
13. Reverse procedure to install. Apply Loctite 242 or equivalent to all oil pan attaching screws. Tighten bolts in sequence shown in **Fig. 24.**

OIL PUMP
REPLACE
REMOVAL

1. Disconnect battery ground cable.
2. Remove crankshaft sprocket as described under "Crankshaft Sprocket, Replace."
3. Remove bolts attaching oil pump to engine block, then remove oil pump.
4. Remove O-ring from crankshaft.
5. Remove oil pump shaft seal using tool No. J-29077-A or equivalent.

INSTALLATION

1. Position O-ring on crankshaft.
2. Apply Loctite 262 or equivalent to oil pump attaching bolt threads.
3. Position oil pump to engine, aligning flats on oil pump drive gear with flats on crankshaft.
4. Install oil pump to engine block attaching bolts and finger tighten.
5. Using tool No. J-38383 or equivalent, align oil pump on crankshaft, then tighten oil pump to engine block attaching bolts.
6. Install oil pump shaft seal using tool Nos. J-38135 and J-38463 or equivalent.
7. Install crankshaft sprocket.

OIL PUMP SERVICE
DISASSEMBLE

1. Remove oil pump plate to pump housing attaching screws, then remove plate, **Fig. 25.**
2. Remove inner and outer gears from pump housing.
3. Remove snap ring retaining pressure regulator valve to pump housing, then remove pressure regulator valve.
4. Remove snap ring from pressure regulator valve and disassembly valve, if necessary.
5. Remove oil pump shaft seal using tool No. J-29077-A or equivalent, if not removed during disassembly.
6. Remove O-rings from pump housing.

ASSEMBLE

1. Install O-rings into pump housing, **Fig. 25.**
2. Assemble pressure regulator valve and install snap ring.
3. Position pressure regulator valve into pump housing, then install snap ring.
4. Position inner and outer gears into pump housing. Place inner gear into pump housing with chamfer facing rear of pump housing (toward engine). Place outer pump gear in housing with chamfer facing toward recess in pump housing.
5. Position pump plate to pump housing, then install attaching screws.

OIL FILTER HOUSING
REPLACE

1. Disconnect battery ground cable.
2. Drain cooling system.
3. Remove air intake duct.
4. Disconnect hoses from coolant outlets and radiator inlet.
5. Remove clamps from inlet pipe, then remove inlet pipe and hose assembly.
6. Rotate serpentine belt tensioner, then slip belt behind water pump pulley.
7. Release belt tensioner, then remove belt from pulleys.
8. Remove serpentine drive belt tensioner attaching bolt and tensioner.
9. Remove oil filter.
10. Disconnect electrical connectors from oil pressure, oil temperature and low oil pressure switches.
11. Remove oil pressure sensor from filter housing.
12. Remove bolt attaching outlet pipe to alternator bracket.
13. Disconnect oil cooler lines from oil filter housing.
14. Remove oil filter housing to engine block attaching bolts, then remove oil filter housing, **Fig. 26.**
15. Reverse procedure to install. Apply Loctite 565 or equivalent to threads of oil pressure sensor and outlet pipe bracket to alternator bracket bolt.

OIL COOLER
REPLACE

1. Disconnect battery ground cable.
2. Drain cooling system.
3. Remove air cleaner assembly.
4. Remove radiator upper air deflector.
5. Disconnect electrical connectors from cooling fan relays.
6. Remove accumulator bracket to upper radiator support attaching bolts.
7. Remove fan shroud to upper radiator attaching screws.
8. Remove rubber access plug from upper part of radiator, then disconnect radiator air bleed hose.

9. Remove bolts and nuts attaching upper radiator support to frame side member.
10. Remove oil cooler line to oil cooler attaching bolts, then remove seal retainers and seals from oil cooler and A/C lines.
11. Remove AIR pump.
12. Remove AIR rear bracket bolt and loosen front bracket bolt.
13. Remove AIR pump intake duct, then remove bolt attaching upper radiator support to lower support.
14. Remove upper radiator support from vehicle.
15. Disconnect upper and lower radiator hoses from radiator, then remove radiator from vehicle.
16. Disconnect oil cooler lines from oil cooler. Cap oil cooler lines and fittings.
17. Remove oil cooler to condenser attaching screws, then remove cooler, **Fig. 27.**
18. Reverse procedure to install. Ensure oil cooler O-rings are properly positioned prior to installation.

CYLINDER CASE VENTILATION COVER & BAFFLE
REPLACE

1. Disconnect battery ground cable.
2. Remove plenum as described under "Plenum Assembly, Replace."
3. Discharge A/C system, then remove A/C compressor.
4. Disconnect spark plug wires from coil pack, then remove bolts attaching ignition coil pack to ventilation cover and cylinder case.
5. Disconnect electrical connectors, then remove ignition coil pack assembly.
6. Disconnect vacuum hoses from vacuum reservoir, then remove reservoir attaching nuts and reservoir.
7. Disconnect vacuum hoses and electrical connector from vacuum solenoid, then remove vacuum solenoid attaching screw and vacuum solenoid.
8. Disconnect vacuum hoses from secondary port throttle actuators, then remove actuator to bracket attaching nuts and retaining clips and remove actuators.
9. Remove actuator bracket to control cover attaching screws, then remove covers.
10. Disconnect links from lever assemblies.
11. Disconnect electrical connectors from coolant temperature sensor and cooling fan switch, then remove sensor and switch from injector housing.
12. Disconnect hoses from ventilation cover, then remove ventilation cover attaching screws and ventilation cover, **Fig. 28.**
13. Remove cylinder case ventilation baffle attaching screws, then remove baffle, **Fig. 29.**
14. Reverse procedure to install. Prior to

1	FILTER, OIL	14	VALVE, OIL TEMPERATURE CONTROL
2	BRACKET, OIL FILTER HOUSING	15	O-RING, OIL TEMPERATURE CONTROL VALVE
3	CAP, OIL COOLER BYPASS SEAL	16	DISC, OIL TEMPERATURE CONTROL VALVE SEAL
4	RETAINER, OIL COOLER BYPASS VALVE	17	RETAINER, OIL TEMPERATURE CONTROL VALVE
5	O-RING, OIL COOLER BYPASS VALVE	18	RETAINER, OIL FILTER BYPASS VALVE
6	SPRING, OIL COOLER BYPASS VALVE	19	CAP, OIL FILTER BYPASS VALVE SEAL
7	VALVE, OIL COOLER BYPASS	20	O-RING, OIL FILTER BYPASS VALVE
8	HOUSING, OIL FILTER	21	SPRING, OIL FILTER BYPASS VALVE
9	BOLT, OIL FILTER HOUSING	22	VALVE, OIL FILTER BYPASS
10	SENSOR, OIL TEMPERATURE	23	ADAPTER, OIL FILTER
11	ADAPTER, OIL COOLER	24	SENSOR, OIL PRESSURE
12	SPRING, OIL TEMPERATURE CONTROL VALVE		
13	SLEEVE, OIL TEMPERATURE CONTROL VALVE		

Fig. 26 Oil filter housing assembly

1	O-RING, ENGINE OIL COOLER
2	PIPE, ENGINE OIL COOLER
3	COOLER, ENGINE OIL
4	BOLT, ENGINE OIL COOLER
5	HOSE, ENGINE OIL COOLER

Fig. 27 Oil cooler assembly replacement

A | PASSAGE. CYLINDER CASE VENTILATION COVER
1 | COVER. CYLINDER CASE VENTILATION
2 | HOSE, CYLINDER CASE VENTILATION - LEFT HAND
3 | HOSE, CYLINDER CASE VENTILATION - RIGHT HAND

Fig. 28   Cylinder case ventilation cover

1 | CASE, CYLINDER
2 | BAFFLE, CYLINDER CASE VENTILATION
3 | HEAD, CYLINDER
4 | RAIL, FUEL

Fig. 29   Cylinder case ventilation baffle

1 | SERPENTINE DRIVE BELT
2 | BELT TENSIONER

Fig. 30   Serpentine drive belt routing

installing coolant sensor and cooling fan switch, apply Loctite 565 or equivalent to threads.

BELT TENSION DATA

Engine (VIN)	Year	New Lbs. ①	Used Lbs. ①
5.7L/V8-350(J)	1991-94	①	①

① —Controlled by belt tensioner.

SERPENTINE DRIVE BELT
REPLACE

1. Disconnect battery ground cable.
2. Remove air intake duct from throttle body extension.
3. Using a 1/2 inch ratchet, retract serpentine drive belt tensioner.
4. Lift belt rearward, off water pump pulley, then remove belt from vehicle.
5. Reverse procedure to install. Refer to **Fig. 30.** for serpentine belt routing.

COOLING SYSTEM BLEED

After filling cooling system, start engine and allow to reach operating temperature with radiator cap removed. Air in system will be bled through radiator cap opening. Add coolant as necessary to bring level to bottom of high fill reservoir neck, then install radiator cap and check coolant level in recovery reservoir.

THERMOSTAT
REPLACE

1. Disconnect battery ground cable.
2. Remove surge tank cap, then drain cooling system.
3. Raise and support vehicle.
4. Remove bolts attaching thermostat housing sections, **Fig. 31.**
5. Loosen bolts attaching housing bracket to front side member.
6. Remove thermostat and seal, **Fig. 32.**
7. Reverse procedure to install. Thermostat should be installed with taper toward radiator. Ensure seal is properly in housing.

WATER PUMP
REPLACE

1. Disconnect battery ground cable.
2. Drain cooling system.
3. Remove air intake duct.
4. Remove throttle body extension attaching screws, then remove extension from throttle body.
5. Disconnect hoses from coolant inlets and outlet and radiator upper hose.
6. Remove hose and inlet pipe assembly from vehicle.
7. Remove serpentine drive belt.
8. Remove bolt attaching serpentine drive belt tensioner to water pump, then remove tensioner.
9. Disconnect engine to water pump hose.
10. Remove bolts attaching lower alternator mounting bracket, then remove bracket. Note length and location of bolts for installation.

1 | THERMOSTAT BRACKET
2 | RADIATOR OUTLET HOSE
3 | THERMOSTAT HOUSING

Fig. 31   Thermostat housing location

11. Remove water pump to front cover attaching bolts, **Fig. 33.**
12. Remove bolt attaching A/C compressor to water pump.
13. Remove water pump from engine.
14. Reverse procedure to install. Apply Loctite 565 or equivalent to alternator lower bracket attaching bolt threads prior to installation.

FUEL PUMP
REPLACE

The fuel is an electric in tank design attached to the fuel level sending unit. Replace fuel pump as follows:
1. Disconnect battery ground cable.
2. Connect pressure gauge J-34370-1 or equivalent to pressure tap on fuel rail, position bleed hose in suitable

A	QUICK CONNECT FITTING	2	BOLT
B	ORIENTATION TAB	3	THERMOSTAT SEAL
C	GROOVE	4	THERMOSTAT
E	RELEASE TAB	5	SEAL
1	THERMOSTAT HOUSING		

Fig. 32 Thermostat assembly

1	ENGINE FRONT COVER	2	COOLANT PUMP GASKET	3	COOLANT PUMP

Fig. 33 Water pump installation & bolt locations

1	FUEL FEED PIPE
2	IN-LINE FUEL FILTER
3	FUEL RETURN PIPE
4	FUEL FILTER ATTACHING SCREW
5	FUEL FILTER BRACKET
6	FUEL PIPE O-RING
7	RIGHT SIDE FRAME

Fig. 35 Fuel filter replacement

1	GASKET
2	FUEL LEVEL METER ASSEMBLY
3	FILLER NECK HOUSING
4	FUEL FILLER CAP
5	NIPPLE
6	DRAIN HOSE
7	SCREW ASSEMBLY (WITH O – RING) 4.5 N·m (40 LB. IN.)
8	FILLER DOOR BEZEL
9	SCREW

Fig. 34 Fuel pump replacement

container and slowly relieve fuel system pressure. **Failure to relieve system pressure prior to disconnecting fuel system components may cause fire or personal injury.**

3. Drain fuel tank. Drain fuel into an approved fuel storage container.
4. Remove fuel filler door bezel attach-

ing screws, then remove bezel, **Fig. 34.**
5. Remove fuel filler cap, then lift fuel filler neck housing and disconnect drain hose.
6. Remove fuel meter and pump attaching screws.
7. Disconnect fuel lines, hoses and elec-

trical connectors from fuel meter and pump assembly. Tag hoses and electrical connectors so they may be installed at the same location.
8. Carefully remove fuel meter and pump assembly.
9. Reverse procedure to install.

FUEL FILTER REPLACE

1. Relieve fuel system pressure as outlined under "Fuel System Pressure Relief."
2. Raise and support vehicle.
3. Clean all fuel filter connections and surrounding areas.
4. Disconnect fuel feed pipes from filter, **Fig. 35,** then drain remaining fuel into suitable container.
5. Remove filter mounting screw, then the fuel filter.
6. Reverse procedure to install.

TIGHTENING SPECIFICATIONS

Year	Component	Torque/ Ft. Lbs.
1991	AIR Pipe Bracket To Oil Pan	20
	Belt Tensioner To Water Pump	45
	Camshaft Cover To Cylinder Head Bolt (M6)	89①
	Camshaft Cover To Cylinder Head Bolt (M8)	15
	Camshaft Position Sensor	71①
	Camshaft Retainer Bolt	89①
	Camshaft Sprocket Bolt	②
	Connecting Rod Cap Bolts	③
	Coolant Outlet Cover To Injector Housing	53①
	Coolant Outlet Cover Pipe Bracket To Alternator Bracket	38
	Coolant Outlet Cover Pipe Bracket To Power Steering Pump Bracket	20
	Crankcase To Cylinder Case Bolts	④
	Crankshaft Damper Bolt	148
	Crankshaft Position Sensor	71①
	Crankshaft Rear Seal Housing To Cylinder Case	89①
	Cylinder Case Ventilation Baffle To Cylinder Case	89①
	Cylinder Case Ventilation Cover To Cylinder Case	89①
	Cylinder Head Bolts	118
	Engine Front Cover Bolt	20
	Engine Front Cover Stud Nut	21
	Engine Front Cover Stud	97①
	Engine Mount To Engine Bolts	38
	Engine Mount To Drivetrain & Frame Nut	40
	Engine Mount To Front Crossmember Nut	40
	Engine Timing Plate To Front Cover Bolts	89①
	Exhaust Manifold To Cylinder Head Bolt & Stud Nut	11
	Exhaust Manifold To Stud	22
	Engine Mount Bracket To Cylinder Case Bolt	38
	Exhaust Pipe To Converter Flange	15
	Flywheel To Crankshaft	74
	Front Crossmember Rear Brace To Crossmember Bolt	59
	Front Crossmember Rear Brace To Side Member	46
	Fuel Rail To Injector Housing Bolt	20
	Ignition Coil Pack Bracket To Cylinder Case Ventilation Cover	89①
	Injector Housing To Cylinder Head	20
	Low Oil Pressure Switch	9
	MAP Sensor Bracket (1991)	89①
	Oil Dipstick Tube To Exhaust Manifold	11
	Oil Filter Housing To Cylinder Case	20
	Oil Pan Baffle To Oil Pan Bolt	89①
	Oil Pan To Crankcase	20
	Oil Pick-up Tube To Oil Pan Bolt	89①
	Oil Pressure Sensor	9
	Oil Pump Plate To Housing	27①
	Oil Pump To Cylinder Case	20
	Plenum To Injector Housing	20

Year	Component	Torque/ Ft. Lbs.
1991 —Cont'd	Secondary Timing Chain Pivot Guide To Cylinder Case	20
	Spark Plug	15
	Thermostat Housing Bolt	18
	Throttle Body Extension To Throttle Body	53①
	Throttle Body To Plenum	11
	Timing Chain Idler Sprocket Bolts	20
	Timing Chain Tensioner	89①
	Transmission To Clutch Housing Bolts	37
	Water Pump Pulley To Hub	89①
	Water Pump To Cylinder Case	20
1992-94	AIR Pipe Bracket To Oil Pan	19
	Belt Tensioner To Water Pump	45
	Camshaft Cover To Cylinder Head Bolt (M6)	89①
	Camshaft Cover To Cylinder Head Bolt (M8)	15
	Camshaft Position Sensor	71①
	Camshaft Retainer Bolt	89①
	Camshaft Sprocket Bolt	②
	Connecting Rod Cap Bolts	③
	Coolant Outlet Cover To Injector Housing	89①
	Coolant Outlet Cover Pipe Bracket To Alternator Bracket	38
	Coolant Outlet Cover Pipe Bracket To Power Steering Pump Bracket	19
	Crankcase To Cylinder Case Bolts	④
	Crankshaft Damper Bolt	148
	Cylinder Case Ventilation Baffle To Cylinder Case	89①
	Cylinder Case Ventilation Cover To Cylinder Case	89①
	Cylinder Head Bolts	118
	Engine Front Cover Bolt	19
	Engine Front Cover Stud Nut	21
	Engine Front Cover Stud	97①
	Engine Mount To Engine Bolts	38
	Engine Mount To Drivetrain & Frame Nut	40
	Engine Mount To Front Crossmember Nut	40
	Engine Timing Plate To Front Cover Bolts	89①
	Exhaust Manifold To Cylinder Head Bolt & Stud Nut	18
	Exhaust Manifold To Stud	22
	Exhaust Pipe To Converter Flange	15
	Flywheel To Crankshaft	66
	Front Crossmember Rear Brace To Crossmember Bolt	59
	Front Crossmember Rear Brace To Side Member	46
	Fuel Rail To Injector Housing Bolt	19
	Ignition Coil Pack Bracket To Cylinder Case Ventilation Cover	89①
	Injector Housing To Cylinder Head	19
	MAT Sensor Bracket	71①
	Oil Dipstick Tube To Exhaust Manifold	11
	Oil Filter Housing To Cylinder Case	19
	Oil Pan Baffle To Oil Pan Bolt	89①

Continued

Year	Component	Torque/ Ft. Lbs.
1992-94 —Cont'd	Oil Pan To Crankcase	23
	Oil Pick-up Tube To Oil Pan Bolt	89①
	Oil Pressure Sensor	9
	Oil Pump Plate To Housing	26①
	Oil Pump To Cylinder Case	19
	Plenum To Injector Housing	19
	Secondary Timing Chain Pivot Guide To Cylinder Case	19
	Spark Plug	15
	Thermostat Housing Bolt	18
	Throttle Body Extension To Throttle Body	53①
	Throttle Body To Plenum	11
	Timing Chain Idler Sprocket Bolts	20

Year	Component	Torque/ Ft. Lbs.
1992-94 —Cont'd	Timing Chain Tensioner	89①
	Transmission To Clutch Housing Bolts	37
	Water Pump Pulley To Hub	89①
	Water Pump To Cylinder Case	20

① —Inch Lbs.
② —Torque to 19 ft. lbs., then tighten an additional 80° to 85°.
③ —Torque to 22 ft. lbs., then tighten an additional 80° to 85°.
④ —Torque M12 bolts (at main bearing journal Nos. 1, 3 & 5) to 30 ft. lbs. then tighten an additional 45° to 50°. Torque M10 bolts (at main bearing journal Nos. 2 & 4) to 15 ft. lbs., then tighten an additional 77.5° to 82.5°. Torque remaining crankcase to cylinder case bolts to 20 ft. lbs.

Clutch & Manual Transmission
INDEX

ADJUSTMENTS
CLUTCH PEDAL

The clutch release mechanism on these models is hydraulically operated, and is not adjustable. When the clutch pedal is depressed, the pedal pushrod contacts a plunger in the clutch master cylinder bore. The plunger first closes off the master cylinder fluid return port, then when moved further, forces fluid under pressure into the clutch actuating cylinder. As pressure is applied to the actuating cylinder, the actuating cylinder piston is forced outward activating the clutch release fork. To diagnose malfunctions in the clutch release system, proceed as follows:

SHIFT LINKAGE

The gear shift lever assembly is floor mounted and located on top of extension housing. The shift assembly does not require adjustment.

HYDRAULIC SYSTEM SERVICE
INSPECTION

1. With engine running at normal operating temperature and brakes applied, hold clutch pedal in fully depressed position and move transmission selector between 1st and reverse several times.

1	CLUTCH HOUSING
2	CLUTCH ACTUATOR CYLINDER STUD NUT
3	HYDRAULIC LINE
4	BLEED SCREW
5	CLUTCH ACTUATOR CYLINDER
6	CLUTCH ACTUATOR CYLINDER STUD

Fig. 1 Clutch actuating cylinder replacement

2. If transmission selector can be moved without binding or gear clash, clutch is releasing properly.
3. If shifter cannot be moved or if gear clash is evident, inspect clutch pedal bushings for damage and wear, and replace as needed.
4. If bushings are satisfactory, check clutch pedal travel.
5. Clutch pedal travel should be 6.25 inch.

BLEEDING

1. Fill clutch master cylinder reservoir with clutch hydraulic fluid 12345347 or DOT 3 brake fluid. It may be necessary to remove ECM from mounting bracket to gain access to reservoir. If a squeaking noise is present in clutch master cylinder, drain DOT 3 brake fluid from clutch hydraulic system and fill with clutch hydraulic fluid 12345347 or equivalent.
2. Raise and support vehicle.
3. Remove actuating cylinder attaching bolts and lower cylinder to a point below the catalytic converter, then remove bleeder screw cap.
4. Hold cylinder in horizontal position with bleeder screw vertical.
5. Fully depress and hold clutch pedal, then open bleeder screw.
6. Close bleeder screw, then release clutch pedal.
7. Repeat steps 4 and 5 until all air has been purged from system, remount actuating cylinder and repeat inspection. **Check and fill master cylinder reservoir, as needed, to ensure no air is drawn into system during bleeding.**

CLUTCH ACTUATING CYLINDER, REPLACE

1. Disconnect battery ground cable.
2. Raise and support vehicle, then remove actuating cylinder stud nuts.

1. CRANKSHAFT
2. CLUTCH HOUSING COVER
3. DUAL MASS FLYWHEEL
4. CLUTCH DRIVEN PLATE
5. RELEASE BEARING
6. CLUTCH PRESSURE COVER (W/PLATE)
7. CLUTCH COVER AND PRESSURE PLATE BOLT
8. RELEASE BEARING RETAINER
9. CLUTCH FORK
10. CLUTCH HOUSING
11. CLUTCH HOUSE BOLT
12. SPECIAL BALL STUD LOCKING SCREW
13. CLUTCH FORK BALL STUD
14. DUAL MASS FLYWHEEL BOLT
15. CLUTCH HOUSING COVER BOLT
16. CRANKSHAFT DOWEL PIN

Fig. 2 Exploded view of clutch assembly

SEALER
APPLY A BEAD OF SEALER AROUND THE TOP AND BOTTOM MATING SURFACES OF DRIVELINE TO AXLE AND TRANSMISSION EXTENSION AT POINTS D AND ALSO TO THE CAVITY AROUND THE BOLTS AT POINTS E. USE URETHANE IN CAULKING KIT (P/N 963067) OR EQUIVALENT.

INSULATOR
REMOVE INSULATOR WITH FLAT BLADE SCRAPER AND CLEAN SURFACE. INSTALL INSULATOR BY REMOVING THE BACKING ON THE INSULATOR AND PRESSING THE INSULATOR AS SHOWN IN VIEW C TO OBTAIN ADHESION TO SUPPORT BEAM. TRIM OFF ANY OVERHANG.

1. DRIVELINE SUPPORT FRONT WASHER
2. SELF-LOCKING NUT
3. DRIVELINE SUPPORT
4. WASHER
5. HEX SELF-LOCKING NUT
6. REAR AXLE CARRIER
7. HEX BOLT
8. PROPELLER SHAFT RETAINER
9. PROPELLER BOLT
10. PROPELLER SHAFT
11. TRANSMISSION EXTENSION HOUSING

Fig. 3 Driveline support installation & sealer application locations

3. Detach hydraulic line from retaining clip. Note position of line for use during installation.
4. Remove actuating cylinder and pushrod from clutch housing. Do not allow actuating cylinder to be suspended from hydraulic line.
5. Disconnect hydraulic line and remove actuating cylinder, **Fig. 1.**
6. Reverse procedure to install. Bleed clutch hydraulic system.

CLUTCH
REPLACE

On models less ZR-1 engine, a magnesium clutch housing may be used. On these models aluminum spacer plates will be installed between clutch housing and engine and clutch housing and transmission.

1. Disconnect battery ground cable.
2. Remove exhaust system from vehicle.
3. Remove transmission from vehicle as described under "Transmission, Replace."
4. **On models except ZR-1,** disconnect ground connection at lefthand side of clutch housing.
5. **On all models,** remove nuts attaching actuating cylinder to clutch housing, then position actuating cylinder aside. Support actuating cylinder so that hydraulic hose does not become damaged.
6. Remove starter motor from vehicle.
7. **On ZR-1 models,** remove nut attaching lefthand side catalytic converter shield to converter housing.
8. **On all models,** remove clutch cover from clutch housing.
9. Remove bolts attaching clutch housing to engine. **On ZR-1 models,** also remove bolt attaching righthand catalytic converter heat shield to clutch housing.
10. Remove clutch housing. Align fork with two flats on release bearing, push fork away from bearing. **On some models,** it may be necessary to loosen ball stud locking screw and ball stud to remove housing.
11. Place align marks on clutch cover and flywheel for use during installation.
12. Alternately and evenly loosen clutch cover to flywheel attaching bolts one turn at a time until spring tension is relieved.
13. Remove clutch cover and clutch disc, **Fig. 2.**
14. Check flywheel for signs of lubricant leakage. Also check flywheel friction surfaces for burned or heat checked metal. Flywheel should be checked for internal looseness. Slight movement is normal. If any of the above conditions are present, replace flywheel. The flywheel should not be machines.
15. Reverse procedure to install. When installing clutch cover to flywheel, align marks made during removal. When installing clutch cover attaching bolts, tighten alternately and evenly in a side to side-cross pattern. Lubricate clutch fork ball and release bearing inner and outer circumference with lubricant 1052356 or equivalent.

MANUAL TRANSMISSION
REPLACE

On models less ZR-1 engine, a magnesium clutch housing may be used. On these models aluminum spacer plates will be installed between clutch housing and engine and clutch housing and transmission.

It may be necessary to remove the catalytic converter and its support bracket to facilitate transmission removal.

1. Disconnect battery ground cable.
2. Remove shift lever.
3. Remove complete exhaust system.
4. Remove front cross over hanger from transmission.
5. Remove propeller shaft.
6. Support transmission with a suitable jack, then remove driveline support beam.
7. Disconnect electrical connectors.
8. Remove transmission to clutch housing attaching bolts, then the transmission from vehicle.
9. Reverse procedure to install. When installing driveline support, apply sealer at locations shown in **Fig. 3.**

TIGHTENING SPECIFICATIONS

Year	Component	Torque/ Ft. Lbs.
1991–94	Clutch Actuating Cylinder Bolts Or Nuts	19
	Clutch Cover To Flywheel	30
	Clutch Fork Ball Stud Nut	33
	Clutch Fork Ball Stud Locking Screw	20
	Clutch Housing To Engine	37
	Clutch Master Cylinder Bolts	12
	Clutch Pedal Pivot Bolt Or Nut	13
	Flywheel Bolt To Crankshaft	①
	Hydraulic Hose Fittings At Clutch Actuating Cylinder	13

Year	Component	Torque/ Ft. Lbs.
1991-94 —Cont'd	Hydraulic Hose Fittings At Clutch Master Cylinder	13
	Support Beam To Differential Carrier Bolt	60
	Support Beam To Transmission Bolt	37
	Transmission Drain Plug	34
	Transmission Fill Plug	34
	Transmission To Clutch Housing Bolt	37

① —Except 1992 ZR-1 engine, 74 ft. lbs.;
  1992 ZR-1 engine, 66 ft. lbs.

Rear Axle & Suspension

INDEX

REAR AXLE
REPLACE

1. Raise and support vehicle, and remove spare tire, tire cover and underbody braces, as required.
2. Remove exhaust system assembly as follows:
   a. Disconnect AIR pipe at converter and AIR pipe clamps at manifold.
   b. Disconnect electrical connector from oxygen sensor.
   c. Support exhaust system, remove bolts securing mufflers to hangers, and remove converter bracket.
   d. Disconnect exhaust pipes at manifolds and remove exhaust system.
3. Disconnect leaf spring from spindle support knuckles, then remove bolts securing spring to differential carrier and spring.
4. Scribe mark between cam bolts and brackets, then remove cam bolts and mounting bracket from carrier.
5. Disconnect tie rods from left and right spindle support knuckles.
6. Remove straps securing driveshaft universal joints to differential side yokes, push wheel and tire assemblies outward, and disconnect driveshafts from side yokes. **Tape**

A COVER TO BODY ATTACHMENT   **B** CARRIER TO SUPPORT BEAM

Fig. 1 Differential carrier attachment

bearing cups to universal joint yokes to prevent loss of needle bearings.
7. Remove straps securing propeller shaft universal joint to pinion flange, push propeller shaft forward into transmission and tie shaft to support beam.
8. Support transmission and remove bolts securing differential carrier beam to frame brackets, **Fig. 1.**
9. Remove mounting bolts at front of differential carrier and carrier assembly.
10. Reverse procedure to install. When installing driveline support, apply sealer at locations shown in **Fig. 2.** Check rear suspension alignment.

REAR WHEEL SHAFT
REPLACE

1. Remove center cap from wheel.
2. Remove cotter pin, spindle nut and washer from spindle, **Fig. 3.**
3. Raise and support vehicle, and remove wheel and tire.
4. Disconnect tie rod and spring from spindle support knuckle.
5. Scribe a reference mark between cam bolt and bracket, remove cam bolt and

SEALER
APPLY A BEAD OF SEALER AROUND THE TOP AND BOTTOM MATING SURFACES OF DRIVELINE TO AXLE AND TRANSMISSION EXTENSION AT POINTS D AND ALSO TO THE CAVITY AROUND THE BOLTS AT POINTS E. USE URETHANE IN CAULKING KIT (P/N 963067) OR EQUIVALENT.

INSULATOR
REMOVE INSULATOR WITH FLAT BLADE SCRAPER AND CLEAN SURFACE. INSTALL INSULATOR BY REMOVING THE BACKING ON THE INSULATOR AND PRESSING THE INSULATOR AS SHOWN IN VIEW C TO OBTAIN ADHESION TO SUPPORT BEAM. TRIM OFF ANY OVERHANG.

1 DRIVELINE SUPPORT FRONT WASHER	5 HEX SELF-LOCKING NUT	9 PROPELLER BOLT
2 SELF-LOCKING NUT	6 REAR AXLE CARRIER	10 PROPELLER SHAFT
3 DRIVELINE SUPPORT	7 HEX BOLT	11 TRANSMISSION EXTENSION HOUSING
4 WASHER	8 PROPELLER SHAFT RETAINER	

Fig. 2 Driveline support installation & sealer application locations

1 AXLE SHAFT
2 U-JOINT SHAFT RETAINER BOLT
3 U-JOINT SHAFT RETAINER
4 SPINDLE
5 COTTER PIN
6 WHEEL NUT RETAINER
7 SPINDLE NUT
8 SPINDLE WASHER
9 WHEEL HUB
10 CALIPER MOUNTING PLATE
11 WHEEL SPINDLE WASHER
12 ANTI-LOCK BRAKE TOOTH RING
13 WASHER
14 WHEEL HUB BOLT
15 SUSPENSION KNUCKLE

Fig. 3 Rear wheel hub, bearing & spindle

separate spindle support rod from bracket.
6. Remove straps securing inner universal joint to drive yoke, pull knuckle assembly outward, and disconnect shaft from yoke. **Tape bearing cups to universal joint yoke to prevent loss of needle bearings.**
7. Pull spindle out of hub and remove rear wheel shaft.
8. Reverse procedure to install, torquing cam bolt and spindle nut to specifications.

HUB & BEARING
REPLACE

1. Remove rear wheel shaft assembly as outlined in "Rear Wheel Shaft, Replace."
2. Remove wheel speed sensor.
3. Remove bolts securing brake caliper bracket to support knuckle, secure caliper aside, then remove brake rotor.
4. Remove hub and bearing retaining bolts, **Fig. 3.**
5. Remove cotter pin, wheel nut retainer, nut and washer from spindle.
6. Remove hub and bearing assembly.
7. Reverse procedure to install. Install spindle washer with flat portion against should of wheel spindle and with lip of washer facing spindle splines. Do not allow vehicle to rest on tires until after wheel spindle nut has been tightened to the specified torque.

SPINDLE SUPPORT ROD
REPLACE

1. Raise and support vehicle, and remove wheel and tire.
2. Scribe mark between cam bolt and bracket for reassembly.
3. Remove cam bolt and disconnect support rod from bracket, **Fig. 4.**
4. Remove bolt securing spindle support rod to knuckle and rod.
5. Reverse procedure to install, then check rear suspension alignment. Torque retaining bolt at knuckle and cam bolt to specifications.

SPINDLE SUPPORT KNUCKLE
REPLACE

1. Remove center cap from wheel, cotter pin and spindle nut.
2. Raise and support vehicle, and remove wheel and tire, then remove wheel speed sensor.
3. Remove bolts securing brake caliper to knuckle, brake caliper assembly and brake rotor.
4. Disconnect tie rod, leaf spring and stabilizer shaft from knuckle as outlined previously.
5. Disconnect shock absorber and support rod from knuckle, using a back-up wrench on shock mounting stud.
6. Disconnect spindle rod from knuckle.
7. Remove bolts securing control arms to knuckle, lower knuckle assembly and slide spindle out of hub and bearing.
8. Reverse procedure to install, then check rear suspension alignment. Torque all bolts to specifications.

REAR WHEEL SPINDLE
REPLACE

1. Raise and support vehicle, then remove wheel and tire assembly.

2. Remove wheel speed sensor.
3. Detach rear spring from knuckle.
4. Remove axle outer socket from knuckle.
5. Remove spindle rod from spindle bracket.
6. Remove cotter pin, wheel nut retainer, nut and washer from spindle.
7. Remove rear wheel shaft.
8. Remove spindle from hub and bearing, then remove washer from spindle.
9. Reverse procedure to install. Install spindle washer with flat portion against should of wheel spindle and with lip of washer facing spindle splines. Do not allow vehicle to rest on tires until after wheel spindle nut has been tightened to the specified torque.

PROPELLER SHAFT
REPLACE

1. With transmission in neutral and parking brake released, raise and support vehicle, then remove underbody braces, as required.
2. Remove exhaust system as follows:
   a. Disconnect AIR pipe from catalytic converter and exhaust pipe.
   b. Disconnect electrical connector to oxygen sensor.
   c. Remove bolts securing muffler to hangers, disconnect exhaust pipes from manifolds and remove exhaust system as an assembly.
3. Support transmission, remove support beam retaining bolts and support beam.
4. Mark position of shaft in relation to pinion flange for installation.
5. Remove straps securing universal joint to pinion flange, then disconnect shaft from flange. **Tape bearing cups to universal joint to prevent loss of needle bearings.**
6. Slide yoke out of transmission and remove propeller shaft. Insert suitable plug in transmission to prevent fluid loss.
7. Reverse procedure to install. When installing driveline support, apply sealer at locations shown in **Fig. 2**.

SHOCK ABSORBER
REPLACE

If shock absorber is to be discarded, position shock absorber in a suitable vise with piston facing downward. Measure .40 to .60 inch from bottom of shock absorber and drill a .20 inch hole to release gas pressure from shock absorber. Measure 5.5 to 6 inches from gas pressure release drill hole and drill another .20 inch hole to drain oil from shock absorber.

MODELS LESS SELECTIVE RIDE CONTROL

1. Raise and support vehicle.
2. Using a suitable jack stand, support knuckle.

1	DIFFERENTIAL CARRIER
2	HEX NUT
3	SPINDLE ROD ADJUSTMENT CAM
4	SPINDLE ROD ADJUSTMENT NUT
5	HEX NUT
6	SPINDLE ROD BRACKET
7	SPINDLE ROD BRACKET STUD
8	WHEEL SPINDLE ROD ADJUSTMENT BOLT
9	HEX NUT
10	SPINDLE ROD WASHER
11	SPINDLE ROD
12	SUSPENSION KNUCKLE
13	HEX BOLT
14	WHEEL SPINDLE LOWER CONTROL ROD
15	SPINDLE CONTROL ROD BRACKET
16	WHEEL SPINDLE ROD BOLT
17	HEX BOLT
18	WHEEL SPINDLE UPPER CONTROL ROD
19	SPINDLE ROD WASHER
20	SPINDLE ROD BOLT

Fig. 4 Knuckle & control arm

3. Disconnect shock absorber from upper and lower mountings, **Fig. 5**.
4. Reverse procedure to install.

MODELS WITH SELECTIVE RIDE CONTROL
Removal

1. Disconnect battery ground cable.
2. Raise and support vehicle.
3. Using a suitable jack stand, support knuckle.
4. Disconnect shock absorber from upper and lower mountings, **Fig. 6**. Do not allow shock absorber to hang from wiring harness.
5. Remove retaining clip, then remove electrical actuator from shock absorber.
6. Remove shock absorber from vehicle.

Installation

1. Install retaining clip onto cup assembly retainer, **Fig. 7**.
2. Install electrical actuator into cup retainer with electrical lead facing toward front of vehicle. A click should be noted when actuator is properly seated. Selector gear should be located a minimum of .20 inch top of retainer, **Fig. 8**.
3. Ensure actuator is properly seated in cup retainer, then position shock absorber to lower mounting.
4. Position shock absorber to upper mounting.
5. Position vehicle at proper trim height using jack stands, then tighten upper shock absorber attaching bolts.
6. Install shock absorber lower attaching nut and washer.
7. Lower vehicle and connect battery ground cable.

1	SHOCK ABSORBER
2	HEX NUT
3	SHOCK ABSORBER WASHER
4	SHOCK ABSORBER STUD
5	SHOCK ABSORBER WASHER
6	HEX NUT
7	SUSPENSION KNUCKLE
8	SHOCK ABSORBER BRACKET BOLT
9	WELD NUT
10	HEX NUT
11	SHOCK ABSORBER INSULATION RETAINER
12	SHOCK ABSORBER UPPER BRACKET
13	SHOCK ABSORBER INSULATION RETAINER
14	SHOCK ABSORBER UPPER GROMMET
15	SHOCK ABSORBER UPPER INSULATOR

Fig. 5 Shock absorber replacement. Models less Selective Ride Control

1	SELECTIVE RIDE CONTROL SHOCK ABSORBER
2	HEX NUT
3	SHOCK ABSORBER WASHER
4	SHOCK ABSORBER STUD
5	SHOCK ABSORBER BRACKET BOLT
6	CUP ASSEMBLY RETAINER
7	ACTUATOR RETAINING CLIP
8	SHOCK ABSORBER ELECTRICAL ACTUATOR
9	ACTUATOR ELECTRICAL CONNECTOR
10	WIRING HARNESS CONNECTOR
11	WELD NUT

Fig. 6 Shock absorber replacement. Models w/Selective Ride Control

1	CUP ASSEMBLY RETAINER
2	ACTUATOR RETAINING CLIP

Fig. 7 Installing actuator clip. Models w/Selective Ride Control

1	HEX PREVAILING TORQUE NUT
2	CUP ASSEMBLY RETAINER
3	SELECTOR GEAR

Fig. 8 Positioning selector gear. Models w/Selective Ride Control

LEAF SPRING
REPLACE

When servicing, use care not to scratch the fiber glass leaf spring. Also do not use any cleaning solvent on spring.
1. Raise and support vehicle and remove wheel and tire assembly.
2. Using tool No. J-33432 or equivalent to compress spring.
3. Remove cotter pin, retaining nuts, bushings and link bolts securing spring to spindle support knuckles, **Fig. 9.**
4. Release spring and remove compressing tool J-33432 or equivalent.
5. Remove bolts securing spring anchor plate to rear axle carrier, **Fig. 10.**
6. Reverse procedure to install.

CONTROL ARM
REPLACE

1. Raise and support vehicle, and remove wheel and tire assembly.
2. Remove bolts securing control arm to spindle support knuckle, **Fig. 4.**
3. Remove control arm bolt at mounting bracket and control arm.
4. Reverse procedure to install. Torque control arm to bracket bolt and control arm to knuckle bolt to specifications.

TIE ROD
REPLACE

1. Raise and support vehicle, then remove wheel and tire.
2. Loosen o uter tie rod jam nuts, then remove cotter pin and nut securing tie rod to spindle support knuckle, **Fig. 11.**
3. Press tie rod from knuckle using tool J-24319-01 or equivalent.
4. Remove tie rod from adjusting sleeve, counting number of turns necessary.
5. Reverse procedure to install, then check rear suspension alignment. Torque tie rod nut specifications.

STABILIZER SHAFT
REPLACE

1. Raise and support vehicle, then remove wheel and tire assemblies.
2. Remove spare tire and carrier.
3. Remove bolts and nuts attaching stabilizer shaft links to stabilizer shaft link brackets, **Fig. 12.**
4. Remove nuts attaching fuel tank safety straps to stabilizer shaft brackets, then remove safety straps.
5. Remove stabilizer shaft bracket nuts, brackets and insulators.
6. Remove nuts, then detach mufflers from hanger brackets.
7. Remove stabilizer shaft from vehicle.
8. Reverse procedure to install. Torque bushing retaining nuts and bolts securing stabilizer links to knuckles to specifications, and bolts securing links to stabilizer shaft to specifications.

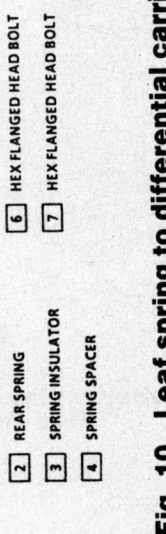

1	DIFFERENTIAL CARRIER	5	SPRING ANCHOR PLATE
2	REAR SPRING	6	HEX FLANGED HEAD BOLT
3	SPRING INSULATOR	7	HEX FLANGED HEAD BOLT
4	SPRING SPACER		

Fig. 10 Leaf spring to differential carrier attachment

1	COTTER PIN	6	SUSPENSION KNUCKLE
2	REAR SPRING	7	WHEEL SPINDLE UPPER CONTROL ROD
3	SLOTTED SPRING NUT	8	SUSPENSION BUMPER
4	SPRING INSULATOR	9	HEX NUT
5	SPRING BOLT		

Fig. 9 Leaf spring to knuckle attachment

RIGHT SIDE SHOWN (LEFT SIDE TYPICAL)

SQUARED-OFF UPPER CORNER (BOTH ENDS)

VIEW B

INSTALLED "A" MOUNTING HOLE

VIEW C

MAIN

VIEW A

1	SUSPENSION KNUCKLE	8	STABILIZER SHAFT INSULATOR
2	STABILIZER SHAFT LINK NUT	9	STABILIZER SHAFT BRACKET SUPPORT
3	STABILIZER SHAFT LINK BRACKET	10	STABILIZER SHAFT BRACKET
4	STABILIZER SHAFT LINK	11	HEX FLANGED NUT
5	STABILIZER SHAFT LINK INSULATOR	12	HEX BOLT
6	STABILIZER SHAFT	13	REAR CROSSMEMBER
7	STABILIZER SHAFT LINK BOLT		

Fig. 12 Stabilizer bar replacement

Fig. 11 Tie rod replacement

1	DIFFERENTIAL CARRIER	7	HEX NUT
2	AXLE TIE ROD	8	SUSPENSION KNUCKLE
3	AXLE TIE BOLT	9	DIFFERENTIAL CARRIER BOLT
4	WASHER	10	AXLE OUTER SOCKET
5	AXLE TIE ROD NUT	11	JAM NUT
6	COTTER PIN		

TIGHTENING SPECIFICATIONS

Year	Component	Torque/Ft. Lbs.	Year	Component	Torque/Ft. Lbs.
1991	Cam Bolt To Spindle Rod	187	1992-94	Cam Bolt To Spindle Rod	187
	Control Rods To Knuckle	140		Control Rods To Knuckle	140
	Control Rods To Spindle Control Rod	63		Control Rods To Spindle Control Rod	63
	Differential Cover To Body	89		Differential Cover To Body	89
	Hub & Bearing To Knuckle	66		Hub & Bearing To Knuckle	66
	Shock Absorber To Body Bolt	22		Shock Absorber To Body Bolt	22
	Shock Absorber To Knuckle	61		Shock Absorber To Knuckle	61
	Shock Absorber Stud To Knuckle Nut	89		Shock Absorber Stud To Knuckle Nut	89
	Spindle Nut	164		Spindle Nut	164
	Spindle Rod To Differential Carrier	60		Spindle Rod To Differential Carrier	60
	Spindle Rod To Knuckle	107		Spindle Rod To Knuckle	107
	Stabilizer Shaft To Body	18		Stabilizer Shaft To Body	18
	Stabilizer Shaft To Link Bracket To Knuckle	18		Stabilizer Shaft To Link Bracket To Knuckle	18
	Stabilizer Link To Bracket & Shaft	39		Stabilizer Link To Bracket & Shaft	39
	Support Beam To Differential Carrier Bolt	59		Support Beam To Differential Carrier Bolt	59
	Support Beam To Transmission	37		Support Beam To Transmission	37
	Tie Rod End To Knuckle	37		Tie Rod End To Knuckle	33
	Tie Rod Jam Nut	46		Tie Rod Jam Nut	50
	Tie Rod To Differential Carrier	55		Tie Rod To Differential Carrier	54
	Transverse Spring To Differential Carrier	37		Transverse Spring To Differential Carrier	37
	Trunnion Strap (Pinion)	17		Trunnion Strap (Pinion)	17
	Trunnion Strap (Yoke)	26		Trunnion Strap (Yoke)	26
	Wheel Lug Nuts	100		Wheel Lug Nuts	100

Front Suspension & Steering

INDEX

WHEEL BEARING REPLACE

The wheel bearing and hub assembly is a sealed unit. If endplay exceeds .005 inch, or if noise or roughness is detected, the unit must be replaced as an assembly.
1. Raise and support vehicle, and remove wheel and tire. Prior to raising vehicle, remove tie offs and grommets to provide ABS sensor wire to lower control arm clearance.
2. Remove bolts securing brake caliper bracket to steering knuckle and se-cure caliper assembly aside, then remove brake rotor.
3. Disconnect electrical connector from speed sensor, then remove speed sensor cable bracket.
4. Remove bolts securing hub to knuckle and hub assembly, **Fig. 1.**
5. Reverse procedure to install.

BALL JOINT INSPECTION

UPPER BALL JOINT

1. Raise and support front of vehicle, then position jack stands under lower control arms.
2. Position a suitable dial indicator against wheel rim, **Fig. 2.**
3. Move wheel inward and outward, while observing dial indicator reading. Indicator reading should not exceed .125 inch.
4. Replace upper ball joint if looseness is indicated.

LOWER BALL JOINT

Lower ball joints are equipped with with visual wear indicators. When checking, vehicle must be supported by wheel and tire assemblies to maintain load on ball joints. Refer to **Fig. 3.**

Fig. 1   Hub & bearing assembly replacement

1   HEX FLANGE TORQUE NUT

2   STEERING KNUCKLE

3   WHEEL HUB BOLT

4   WHEEL HUB

A   SPEED SENSOR CONNECTOR MUST BE FACING THE REAR OF THE VEHICLE

Fig. 2   Upper ball joint inspection

C. ROCK WHEEL IN AND OUT AT TOP AND BOTTOM

B. POSITION DIAL INDICATOR TO CHECK MOVEMENT AT THIS POINT

A. SUPPORT L.C. ARM AS FAR OUTBOARD AS POSSIBLE

DISCONNECTING LOWER BALL JOINT J 33436

Fig. 3   Lower ball joint inspection

WORN

NEW

SINTERED IRON BEARING

WEAR SURFACES

HOUSING SOCKET

RUBBER PRESSURE RING

WEAR INDICATOR (OUT WHEN NEW)

1.27 mm (.050 in.)

WHEN BALL JOINT WEAR CAUSES THIS SHOULDER TO RETREAT BELOW THE SURFACE, REPLACEMENT IS REQUIRED.

(A) CENTER PUNCH RIVET   (B) DRILL PILOT HOLE

(C) DRILL RIVET HEAD   (D) PUNCH OUT RIVET

1   UPPER CONTROL ARM

2   UPPER CONTROL ARM BALL STUD

3   STEERING KNUCKLE

4   LOWER CONTROL ARM BALL STUD

5   LOWER CONTROL ARM

Fig. 4   Upper ball joint removal

BALL JOINT
REPLACE

UPPER BALL JOINT

1. Raise vehicle and support with stands at outer ends of lower control arms.
2. Support upper control arm in a raised position.
3. Remove wheel and tire assembly.
4. Remove cotter pin and retaining nut, then separate ball joint stud from knuckle using a suitable tool, **Fig. 4.**
5. Remove heads of rivets securing joint to arm, then drive out rivets to remove joint, **Fig. 4.**
6. Position replacement joint on top of control arm, insert retaining bolts supplied with joint from under arm, install nuts and torque to specifications, **Fig. 5.**
7. Remove upper control arm support, assemble ball joint to steering knuckle, install washer, if equipped, and retaining nut.
8. Torque retaining nut to specifications.
9. Tighten retaining nut up to an additional 1/16 turn, if necessary, to align hole in ball stud with nut, then install cotter pin. Cotter pin must be installed in direction from rear to front of vehicle.

LOWER BALL JOINT

1. Raise vehicle and support front of vehicle.
2. Support lower control using a suitable jack stand, then remove wheel and tire assembly.
3. Remove cotter pin and nut securing ball joint stud to steering knuckle, then disconnect joint from knuckle using a suitable tool, **Fig. 6.**
4. Lift knuckle assembly from ball stud, guiding control arm out of splash shield, then support knuckle aside to allow clearance for joint removal.
5. Remove grease fitting, then press ball joint assembly out of lower control arm using a suitable tool, **Fig. 6.**
6. Press replacement joint into arm by reversing removal tools, fit spindle over ball stud, install washer, if equipped, and retaining nut, **Fig. 7.**
7. Torque retaining nut to specifications.
8. Tighten nut up to an additional 1/16 turn, if necessary, to align hole in ball stud with nut, then install cotter pin. Cotter pin must be installed in direction from rear to front of vehicle.

SHOCK ABSORBER
REPLACE

If shock absorber is to be discarded, position shock absorber in a suitable vise with piston facing downward. Measure approximately .50 inch from bottom of shock absorber and drill a .20 inch hole to release gas pressure from shock absorber. Measure 5.5 to 6 inches from gas pressure release drill hole and drill another .20 inch hole to drain oil from shock absorber.

1. UPPER CONTROL ARM BALL STUD
2. UPPER CONTROL ARM
3. BOLTS MUST BE MOUNTED IN THE DIRECTION SHOWN
4. COTTER PIN
5. UPPER CONTROL ARM BALL STUD NUT
6. UPPER CONTROL ARM BALL STUD MUST BE REPLACED WASHER
7. STEERING KNUCKLE

Fig. 5 Upper ball joint installation

1. UPPER CONTROL ARM
2. UPPER CONTROL ARM BALL STUD
3. STEERING KNUCKLE
4. LOWER CONTROL ARM BALL STUD
5. LOWER CONTROL ARM

Fig. 6 Lower ball joint removal

1. COTTER PIN
2. HEX SLOTTED NUT
3. LOWER CONTROL ARM BALL STUD MUST BE REPLACED WASHER
4. STEERING KNUCKLE
5. LOWER CONTROL ARM
6. LOWER CONTROL ARM BALL STUD
7. INSTALL ZERK FITTING AS SHOWN

Fig. 7 Lower ball joint installation

MODELS LESS SELECTIVE RIDE CONTROL

1. Raise and support vehicle as needed, and remove wheel and tire.
2. Remove shock absorber from upper and lower attachments, **Fig. 8.** If upper retaining nut is difficult to remove, remove wheel housing lower center panel to gain access to nut.
3. Reverse procedure to install.

MODELS w/SELECTIVE RIDE CONTROL

1. Disconnect battery ground cable.
2. Raise and support front of vehicle, then remove wheel and tire assembly.
3. Support lower control arm with suitable jack stand.
4. Remove actuator retaining clip, then remove actuator from cup retainer. Note position of electrical connector for use during installation.
5. Remove shock absorber upper retaining nut, then remove cup retainer, **Fig. 9.**
6. Remove shock absorber retainer and upper insulator.
7. Remove shock absorber lower attaching nuts and bolts, then compress shock absorber and remove from vehicle.
8. Reverse procedure to install, noting the following:
   a. When installing actuator, a click should be noted when actuator is properly seated.
   b. **On 1991 models,** selector gear should be located a minimum of

.20 inch top of retainer, **Fig. 10.**
   c. **On 1992-94 models,** selector gear should be located a minimum of .178 inch top of retainer, **Fig. 10.**
   d. **On all models,** a minimum clearance of .315 inch should be maintained between wheel housing lower center panel and actuator electrical lead, **Fig. 9.** Electrical connector should be positioned as noted during removal.

LEAF SPRING
REPLACE

When servicing, use care not to scratch the fiber glass leaf spring. Also do not use any cleaning solvent on spring.
1. Disconnect battery ground cable.
2. Raise and support vehicle, and remove front wheel and tire assembly.
3. Remove shock absorber to lower control arm attachments.
4. Remove bolts and nuts attaching stabilizer shaft links to lower control arms.
5. **On models with Selective Ride Control,** disconnect electrical connector and detach sensor cable from bracket.
6. **On all models,** disconnect wheel speed sensor electrical connector and sensor cable from bracket.
7. **On all models,** remove both spring protectors, **Fig. 11.**
8. Install spring compressor J-33432 or equivalent, **Fig. 12.**
9. Disconnect lower ball joints from steering knuckles.
10. Compress spring by rotating turnbuckle on spring compressor.

11. Remove bolts securing shock brackets to lower control arms and spring mounting bolts.
12. Release tension on spring compressor and remove compressor.
13. Remove spring and retainer shims, if equipped. Note number of shims removed.
14. Reverse procedure to install. Prior to installation, lubricate spring pads with a suitable rubber lubricant. If equipped, install spring retainer shims. The number of spring retaining shims can be determined by the color code located on the spring. If color code is blue, no shims are required; yellow or white, 1 shim; green, 2 shims. Torque spring mounting bolts to specifications, with vehicle on ground.

CONTROL ARM
REPLACE

UPPER CONTROL ARM

1. Disconnect battery ground cable.
2. Raise and support vehicle, then remove wheel and tire assembly.
3. Remove wheel housing seal and lower center panel.
4. **On models equipped with Selective Ride Control,** disconnect shock absorber actuator electrical connector.
5. **On all models,** using a suitable jack stand, support lower control arm.
6. Disconnect wheel speed sensor electrical connector and detach speed sensor cable from bracket.

1	SHOCK ABSORBER TOWER	7	CUP ASSEMBLY RETAINER
2	HEX PREVAILING TORQUE NUT	8	SHOCK ABSORBER ELECTRICAL ACTUATOR
3	SHOCK ABSORBER INSULATOR RETAINER	9	ACTUATOR RETAINING CLIP
4	SHOCK ABSORBER UPPER INSULATOR	10	ROSEBUD CLIP
5	SHOCK ABSORBER LOWER INSULATOR	11	ACTUATOR ELECTRICAL CONNECTOR
6	SHOCK (SELECTIVE RIDE) ABSORBER	12	FRONT WHEELHOUSE LOWER CENTER PANEL

Fig. 9 Shock absorber replacement. Models w/Selective Ride Control

1	SHOCK ABSORBER TOWER
2	HEX PREVAILING TORQUE NUT
3	SHOCK ABSORBER INSULATOR RETAINER
4	SHOCK ABSORBER UPPER INSULATOR
5	SHOCK ABSORBER LOWER INSULATOR
6	SHOCK ABSORBER
7	HEX FLANGE HEAD BOLT
8	LOWER CONTROL ARM
9	HEX FLANGE NUT

Fig. 8 Shock absorber replacement. Models less Selective Ride Control

7. Using tool No. J-33436 or equivalent, detach upper ball joint from steering knuckle.
8. Remove upper control arm to frame member attaching bolts and shims, **Fig. 13**. Note location and number of shims for installation.
9. Remove upper control arm from vehicle.
10. Reverse procedure to install. Install shims in same location as removed. Install upper ball joint stud cotter pin from rear to front of vehicle. After completing installation, check wheel alignment and adjust as necessary.

LOWER CONTROL ARM

1. Disconnect battery ground cable.
2. Raise and support vehicle, then remove wheel and tire assembly.
3. Remove both spring protectors, then install spring compressor J-33432 or equivalent.
4. Compress front spring with tool, then

support lower control arm with suitable jack stand.
5. Disconnect shock absorber and stabilizer shaft link from lower control arm.
6. Disconnect front wheel speed sensor electrical connector, then detach speed sensor cable from bracket.
7. Disconnect lower ball joint from steering knuckle.
8. Remove lower control arm to frame member attaching bolts, then remove lower control arm, **Fig. 14**.
9. Reverse procedure to install. When installing, position lower ball joint stud so that cotter pin can be installed from rear to front of vehicle. When tightening stabilizer shaft link, lower control arm and shock absorber lower attaching bolts and nuts, use jack stands to hold suspension at proper trim height.

STEERING KNUCKLE REPLACE

1. Disconnect battery ground cable.
2. Raise and support vehicle, then remove wheel and tire assembly.
3. Remove brake caliper and rotor.
4. Disconnect wheel speed sensor electrical connector, then detach speed sensor cable from bracket.
5. Remove hub assembly attaching bolts and nuts, then remove hub assembly.
6. Support lower control arm using a suitable jack stand.
7. Disconnect upper and lower control arms from steering knuckle, **Fig. 15**.
8. Disconnect tie rod end from steering knuckle.

1	HEX PREVAILING TORQUE NUT
2	CUP ASSEMBLY RETAINER
3	SELECTOR GEAR

Fig. 10 Positioning selector gear

9. Remove steering knuckle.
10. Reverse procedure to install. When installing, position ball joint studs so that cotter pins can be installed from rear to front of vehicle. When installing wheel hub, speed sensor cable should be facing rearward.

STABILIZER SHAFT REPLACE

1. Raise and support vehicle, then remove wheel and tire assembly.
2. Support lower control arm with a suitable jack stand.
3. Remove stabilizer shaft attaching bolts, insulator clamps and brackets from frame, **Fig. 16**.
4. Remove stabilizer shaft from vehicle.
5. Reverse procedure to install. When tightening stabilizer shaft link attaching bolts and nuts, use jack stands to hold suspension at proper trim height. Refer to **Fig. 16**, for bolt installation direction.

CHEVROLET CORVETTE

RACK & PINION STEERING GEAR REPLACE

1. Disconnect battery ground cable.
2. Position drain pan under vehicle, then disconnect inlet and outlet hoses from steering gear.
3. Disconnect power steering fluid cooling pipes, if equipped.
4. Disconnect intermediate steering shaft from power steering gear.
5. Raise and support vehicle, and remove wheel and tire assemblies.
6. Disconnect outer tie rods from steering knuckles, **Fig. 17.**
7. Remove power steering fluid oil cooler, if equipped.
8. Remove stabilizer shaft from vehicle as describe under "Stabilizer Shaft, Replace."
9. Remove steering gear to frame attaching bolts and nuts, then remove steering gear.
10. Reverse procedure to install. Top off fluid reservoir, bleed system and check for leaks. After completing installation, check front toe setting.

POWER STEERING PUMP REPLACE

EXCEPT ZR-1

1991

1. Disconnect battery ground cable.
2. Position suitable drain pan under vehicle.
3. Remove serpentine drive belt.
4. **On models with automatic transmission,** remove water pump damper.
5. Loosen power steering reservoir and bracket attaching bolts, then position reservoir and bracket to permit power steering pump pulley removal.
6. Remove cap from power steering pump pulley, then remove pulley using a suitable puller.
7. Disconnect hoses from power steering pump.
8. Remove bolts attaching power steering pump rear bracket to brace, **Fig. 18.**
9. Remove engine mount bolt, then remove power steering pump rear brace.
10. Remove power steering pump attaching bolts, then remove power steering pump and rear bracket.
11. Reverse procedure to install.

1992-94

1. Disconnect battery ground cable.
2. Position suitable drain pan under vehicle.
3. Remove serpentine drive belt.
4. Remove cap from power steering pump pulley, then remove pulley using a suitable puller.

Fig. 11 Front leaf spring replacement

SPRING SHIM REQUIREMENTS

SPRING COLOR CODE	NUMBER OF SHIMS REQUIRED PER SIDE
BLUE	0
YELLOW	1
GREEN	2

1 SPRING RETAINING BOLT
2 DRIVETRAIN AND SUSPENSION FRAME
3 MULTI-THREAD "U" NUT
4 SPRING PROTECTOR TO FRAME BOLT 25 N·m (18 lb. ft.)
5 SPRING PROTECTOR
6 FRONT TRANSVERSE SPRING
7 SPRING RETAINER NUT
8 FRONT SPRING RETAINER
9 SPRING PAD
10 APPLY RUBBER LUBRICANT

Fig. 12 Compressing front leaf spring

1 DRIVETRAIN AND SUSPENSION FRAME
2 SPRING
3 TOOL - J 33432
4 TOOL ADAPTERS - J 33432-88

5. Disconnect power steering hoses from pump.
6. Remove power steering pump mounting bolts, then remove power steering pump and front bracket, **Fig. 19.**
7. Reverse procedure to install.

ZR-1

1. Disconnect battery ground cable.
2. Drain cooling system, then remove air intake duct.
3. Drain power steering fluid.
4. Remove vacuum hose retainer from power steering fluid reservoir, then disconnect and position hoses aside.
5. Remove lefthand coolant outlet housing and hose.
6. Remove serpentine drive belt.
7. Remove power steering pump to cylinder head bracket attaching bolts, **Fig. 20.**
8. Remove power steering pump to A/C compressor bracket bolt.
9. Disconnect power steering fluid cooler hose from reservoir.
10. Disconnect power steering gear inlet hose from power steering pump.
11. Remove power steering pump from vehicle.
12. Reverse procedure to install.

1. DRIVETRAIN AND SUSPENSION FRAME
2. UPPER CONTROL ARM WASHER
3. UPPER CONTROL ARM
4. UPPER CONTROL ARM BALL STUD
5. UPPER CONTROL ARM BALL STUD NUT
6. COTTER PIN
7. UPPER CONTROL ARM BALL STUD WASHER
8. HEX FLANGE PREVAILING TORQUE NUT
9. STEERING KNUCKLE
10. UPPER CONTROL ARM SHIM
11. UPPER CONTROL ARM BOLT

Fig. 13   Upper control arm replacement

1. DRIVETRAIN AND SUSPENSION FRAME
2. SHOCK ABSORBER
3. HEX FLANGE HEAD BOLT
4. COTTER PIN
5. HEX SLOTTED NUT
6. LOWER CONTROL ARM BALL STUD WASHER
7. STEERING KNUCKLE
8. LOWER CONTROL ARM
9. HEX FLANGE NUT
10. HEX FLANGE PREVAILING TORQUE NUT
11. LOWER CONTROL ARM WASHER
12. LOWER CONTROL ARM BOLT

Fig. 14   Lower control arm replacement

1	DRIVETRAIN AND SUSPENSION FRAME
2	UPPER CONTROL ARM
3	UPPER CONTROL ARM BALL STUD NUT
4	COTTER PIN
5	UPPER CONTROL ARM BALL STUD WASHER
6	HEX SLOTTED NUT
7	LOWER CONTROL ARM BALL STUD WASHER
8	STEERING KNUCKLE
9	LOWER CONTROL ARM
10	STEERING GEAR TIE ROD BALL STUD

Fig. 15   Steering knuckle replacement

1	DRIVETRAIN AND SUSPENSION FRAME
2	LOWER CONTROL ARM
3	HEX NUT
4	STABILIZER SHAFT LINK
5	HEX BOLT
6	STABILIZER SHAFT LINK UPPER INSULATOR
7	STABILIZER SHAFT
8	BOLT
9	STABILIZER SHAFT INSULATOR CLAMP
10	STABILIZER SHAFT INSULATOR
11	STABILIZER SHAFT BRACKET
12	STABILIZER SHAFT LINK LOWER INSULATOR

Fig. 16   Stabilizer shaft replacement

1 POWER STEERING GEAR
2 BOLT
3 OUTER TIE ROD
4 NUT
5 DRIVETRAIN AND SUSPENSION FRAME
6 BOLT
7 NUT
8 STEERING GEAR TO FRAME CLAMP

Fig. 17 Steering gear attachment

1	POWER STEERING PUMP MOUNTING BOLTS	7	GENERATOR/POWER STEERING PUMP BRACKET
2	BRACKET MOUNTING BOLT	8	POWER STEERING PUMP REAR BRACKET
3	HUB CAP	9	POWER STEERING PUMP REAR BRACE
4	PUMP PULLEY	10	ENGINE MOUNT BOLT
5	AIR INJECTION BRACKET STUD	11	REAR BRACE MOUNTING BOLT
6	POWER STEERING PUMP		

Fig. 18 Power steering pump installation. 1990–91 except ZR-1

Fig. 20 Power steering pump installation. ZR-1

1 POWER STEERING PUMP MOUNTING BRACKET
2 POWER STEERING RESERVOIR
3 CLAMPS
4 POWER STEERING RESERVOIR HOSE
5 COOLER ASSEMBLY OUTLET HOSE
6 POWER STEERING GEAR INLET HOSE ASSEMBLY
7 POWER STEERING PUMP

Fig. 19 Power steering pump installation. 1992 except ZR-1

1 PUMP PULLEY
2 POWER STEERING PUMP
3 GENERATOR MOUNTING BOLTS AND NUT
4 GENERATOR/AC COMPRESSOR AND POWER STEERING PUMP BRACKET
5 GENERATOR MOUNTING BRACKET SPACER
6 REAR INNER SUPPORT BRACE
7 REAR SUPPORT BRACE
8 OUTER SUPPORT BRACE
9 TENSIONER ASSEMBLY
10 IDLER SHIELD
11 IDLER PULLEY ASSEMBLY
12 POWER STEERING BRACKET
13 REAR INNER SUPPORT BRACE BOLTS
14 REAR SUPPORT BRACE BOLT/NUT
15 BOLTS
16 BRACKET MOUNTING BOLTS

TIGHTENING SPECIFICATIONS

Component	Torque/ Ft. Lbs.	Component	Torque/ Ft. Lbs.
Hub & Bearing Assembly To Steering Knuckle Bolts	46	Stabilizer Shaft To Link Bolt	35
Lower Ball Joint Stud Nut	50	Steering Gear Clamp Bolts	18
Lower Control Arm Shaft To Frame Member	82	Steering Gear To Crossmember	30
Power Steering Pump & Bracket Mounting Bolts (Except ZR-1)	18	Tie Rod End To Steering Knuckle Stud Nut	33
Power Steering Pump & Bracket Mounting Bolts (ZR-1)	19	Tie Rod Jam Nut	50
		Upper Ball Joint Stud Nut	33
Shock Absorber Lower Attaching Bolt	19	Upper Ball Joint To Control Arm Bolts	②
Shock Absorber Upper Attaching Nut	①	Upper Control Arm Shaft To Frame Member	37
Spring Protector To Crossmember Bolt	18	Wheel Lug Nuts	100
Spring Retainer Bolts	48		
Stabilizer Shaft Clamp Bolts	40		
Stabilizer Shaft Link To Lower Control Arm Bolt	35		

① —Models less Selective Ride Control, 19 ft. lbs.; with Selective Ride Control, 31 ft. lbs.
② —1991, 18 ft. lbs.; 1992-94, 13 ft. lbs.

Wheel Alignment

INDEX

UPPER CONTROL ARM SHAFT IS OUTBOARD TO THE FRAME

A ADD SHIMS HERE TO INCREASE POSITIVE CASTER
B SUBTRACT SHIMS HERE TO INCREASE POSITIVE CASTER
C ADD SHIMS EQUALLY TO INCREASE POSITIVE CAMBER
1 UPPER CONTROL ARM SHAFT
2 DRIVETRAIN AND FRONT SUSPENSION FRAME

Fig. 1 Front caster & camber adjustments

FRONT WHEEL ALIGNMENT

Prior to checking or adjusting front suspension alignment, inspect suspension components and wheel bearings for damage or excessive wear, and replace as needed. Ensure tire pressure is properly adjusted, then raise and release front bumper several times to allow vehicle to assume normal ride height.

CASTER, ADJUST

Caster adjustments are made by means of shims between the upper control arm shaft and the support bracket attached to the frame. Shims may be added, subtracted or transferred to change the readings.

Transfer shims from front to rear or rear to front. The transfer of one shim to the front bolt from the rear bolt will decrease positive caster. One shim transferred from the rear bolt to the front bolt will change caster about .36°. Refer to **Fig. 1**, and note the effect of shim placement.

CAMBER, ADJUST

Camber adjustments are made by means of shims between the upper control arm shaft and the support bracket attached to the frame, **Fig. 1**. Shims may be added, subtracted or transferred to change the readings.

Change shims at both the front and rear

LOOSEN LOCK NUT

ADJUST TOE BY ROTATING TIE ROD

Fig. 2 Toe-in adjustment

A | NEGATIVE CAMBER ANGLE

B | VERTICAL

C | CENTERLINE OF WHEEL

1 | SPINDLE ROD

2 | WHEEL SPINDLE ROD ADJUSTMENT BOLT

Fig. 3 Rear camber adjustment

Fig. 4 Vehicle thrust angle

of the shaft. Adding an equal number of shims at both front and rear of the support shaft will decrease positive camber.

TOE-IN, ADJUST

Toe-in can be adjusted by loosening the clamp bolts at each end of each tie rod and turning each tie rod to increase or decrease its length as necessary until proper toe-in is secured and the steering gear is on the high point for straight-ahead driving, **Fig. 2**.

REAR WHEEL ALIGNMENT

Rear wheel alignment should be checked and adjusted periodically, when rear tires indicate abnormal wear, or when suspension components are replaced. Prior to rear wheel alignment, check suspension components for damage or excessive wear and repair as needed. Also ensure tires are properly inflated, and wheel bearing endplay is within specifications.

CAMBER, ADJUST

Camber is adjusted by rotating the eccentric cam and bolt located at the inboard end of the spindle support rod, **Fig. 3**. To check and adjust camber, proceed as follows:

Vertical heights: "Z" and "J" dimensions-lift front bumper of vehicle up approximately 38.0 mm. Gently remove hands and let vehicle settle on its own. Repeat twice for a total of 3 times. Measure "Z" and "J" dimensions. Push front bumper of vehicle down approximately 38.0 mm. Gently remove hands and let vehicle rise on its own. Repeat twice for a total of 3 times. Measure "Z" and "J" dimensions. True heights are the average of the high and low measurements.

"D" and "K" dimensions - same procedure as "Z" and "J" dimensions using rear bumper.

Recommended tire pressure: Trim height. Set tire pressure to agree with vehicle's tire pressure sticker for loading "up to vehicle capacity."

NOTE: Load Conditions:
Shipping Weight-Vehicle is built to parts list specifications including coolant to capacity and 20.8 liters (5.5 gallons) of gasoline.

Curb Weight-Vehicle is built to parts list specifications including coolant to capacity and full tank of gasoline.

Fig. 5 Ride height measurement locations. 1991

MODEL	SUSP.	ENG.	Z		D		J		K	
			SHIPPED	CURB	SHIPPED	CURB	SHIPPED	CURB	SHIPPED	CURB
1YY07	FE1	L98	55.5	57.2	62.8	55.6	197.0	196.2	205.7	199.7
1YY07	FE7	L98	52.7	54.2	56.2	50.8	193.0	192.6	199.6	195.2
1YY07	FE1	LT5	43.7	45.4	62.8	55.6	187.9	187.1	203.2	197.3
1YY07	FE7	LT5	41.5	43.0	57.1	51.7	184.6	184.2	198.1	193.6
1YY67	FE1	L98	64.5	66.2	70.1	62.9	204.5	203.8	212.3	206.3
1YY67	FE1	LT5	52.5	54.2	70.4	63.2	195.3	194.5	210.0	204.1
1YZ07	FE7	LT5	42.1	43.6	57.4	52.0	185.2	184.7	198.4	193.9

NOTE: All dimensions in mm.
Dimension "Z", "J", "K", and "D" . . . Vertical to ground and apply to all vehicles.

**Fig. 6   Ride height specifications. 1991
(FE1=Soft Ride Suspension; FE7=Heavy Duty
Suspension; L98=V8-350/5.7L Single Cam
Engine; LT5=V8-350/5.7L 4 Cam Engine;
1YY07=Hatchback; 1YY67=Convertible;
1YZ07=ZR-1 Hatchback)**

VERTICAL HEIGHTS: "Z" AND "J" DIMENSIONS - LIFT FRONT BUMPER OF VEHICLE UP APPROXIMATELY 38.0 mm. GENTLY REMOVE HANDS AND LET VEHICLE SETTLE ON ITS OWN. REPEAT TWICE FOR A TOTAL OF 3 TIMES. MEASURE "Z" AND "J" DIMENSIONS. PUSH FRONT BUMPER OF VEHICLE DOWN APPROXIMATELY 38.0 mm. GENTLY REMOVE HANDS AND LET VEHICLE RISE ON ITS OWN. REPEAT TWICE FOR A TOTAL OF 3 TIMES. MEASURE "Z" AND "J" DIMENSIONS. TRUE HEIGHTS ARE THE AVERAGE OF THE HIGH AND LOW MEASUREMENTS.

"D" AND "K" DIMENSIONS - SAME PROCEDURE AS "Z" AND "J" DIMENSIONS USING REAR BUMPER.

RECOMMENDED TIRE PRESSURE: TRIM HEIGHT. SET TIRE PRESSURE TO AGREE WITH VEHICLE'S TIRE PRESSURE STICKER FOR LOADING "UP TO VEHICLE CAPACITY."

NOTE: LOAD CONDITIONS: SHIPPING WEIGHT - VEHICLE IS BUILT TO PARTS LIST SPECIFICATIONS INCLUDING COOLANT TO CAPACITY AND 20.8 LITERS (5.5 GALLONS) OF GASOLINE. CURB WEIGHT - VEHICLE IS BUILT TO PARTS LIST SPECIFICATIONS INCLUDING COOLANT TO CAPACITY AND FULL TANK OF GASOLINE.

Fig. 7   Ride height measurement locations. 1992-94

1. Place rear wheels of vehicle on suitable alignment equipment following manufacturer's instructions, then check camber reading.
2. If wheel camber is not within specifications, loosen cam bolt retaining nut.
3. Rotate cam bolt, **Fig. 3**, until camber reading is within specifications listed at the front of this chapter.

TOE-IN ADJUST

Toe-in is adjusted by loosening locknuts on tie rod ends and rotating adjuster sleeves until desired setting is obtained, **Fig. 2.**

THRUST ANGLE

The vehicle is steered by the front wheels. The path which the rear wheels follow is the thrust angle, **Fig. 4.** In an ideal setting, the thrust angle would be aligned with that of the vehicle center line.

VEHICLE RIDE HEIGHT

Refer to **Figs. 5 through 8** for ride height measurements and specifications.

MODEL	SUSP.	ENG.	Z		D		J		K	
			SHIPPED	CURB	SHIPPED	CURB	SHIPPED	CURB	SHIPPED	CURB
1YY07	FE1	VIN P	55.5	57.2	62.8	55.6	197.0	196.2	205.7	199.7
1YY07	FE7	VIN P	52.7	54.2	56.2	50.8	193.0	192.6	199.6	195.2
1YY67	FE1	VIN P	64.5	66.2	70.1	62.9	204.5	203.8	212.3	206.3
1YZ07	FE1	VIN J	42.1	43.6	57.4	52.0	185.2	184.7	198.4	193.9

NOTE: All dimensions in mm.
Dimension "Z", "J", "K", and "D"... Vertical to ground and apply to all vehicle.

Fig. 8   Ride height specifications. 1992-94 (FE1=Soft Ride Suspension; FE7=Heavy Duty Suspension; VIN P=V8-350/5.7L Single Cam Engine; VIN J=V8-350/5.7L 4 Cam Engine; 1YY07=Hatchback; 1YY67=Convertible; 1YZ07=ZR-1 Hatchback)

BUICK CENTURY, OLDSMOBILE CUTLASS CIERA & CUTLASS CRUISER & PONTIAC 6000 (A Cars)

INDEX OF SERVICE OPERATIONS

NOTE: Refer To The Rear Of This Manual For Vehicle Manufacturer's Special Service Tool Suppliers.

Specifications
GENERAL ENGINE SPECIFICATIONS

Year	Engine Liter/CID ①	Engine VIN Code ②	Fuel System	Bore & Stroke	Compression Ratio	Net H.P. @ RPM ③	Maximum Torque Ft. Lbs. @ RPM	Normal Oil Pressure psi
1991	2.5L/4-151	R	TBI ⑤	4.00 x 3.00	8.3	110 @ 5200	135 @ 3200	50
	3.1L/V6-189	T	MPFI ⑥	3.50 x 3.31	8.8	135 @ 4400	180 @ 3600	⑨
	3.3L/V6-204	N	SFI ④	3.70 x 3.16	9.0	160 @ 5200	185 @ 2000	45 ⑦
1992	2.5L/4-151	R	TBI ⑤	4.00 x 3.00	8.3	110 @ 5200	135 @ 3200	50
	3.3L/V6-204	N	SFI ④	3.70 x 3.16	9.0	160 @ 5200	185 @ 2000	45 ⑦
1993	2.2L/4-134	4	MPFI ⑥	3.50 x 3.46	8.85	110 @ 5200	130 @ 3200	56 ⑧
	3.3L/V6-204	N	SFI ④	3.70 x 3.16	9.0	160 @ 5200	185 @ 2000	45 ⑦
1994	2.2L/4-134	MPFI ⑥	3.50 @ 3.46	9.0	120 @ 5200	130 @ 4000	12-20 ⑨
	3.1L/V6-191	N	MPFI ⑥	3.50 x 3.31	9.6	160 @ 5200	185 @ 4000	40-52 ⑩

① —CID-cubic inch displacement.
② —The eighth digit denotes engine code.
③ —Ratings are net-as installed in vehicle.
④ —Sequential-port fuel injection.
⑤ —Throttle body injection.
⑥ —Multi-port fuel injection
⑦ —psi @ 2000 RPM.
⑧ —psi @ 3000 RPM.
⑨ —15 psi @ 1100 RPM or 50-65 @ 2400 RPM.
⑩ —psi @ 2400 RPM.

TUNE UP SPECIFICATIONS

Engine Liter/CID	Engine VIN Code ①	Spark Plug Gap	Ignition Timing BTDC Firing Order Fig.	Ignition Timing BTDC Auto. Trans.	Ignition Timing BTDC Mark Fig.	Curb Idle Speed	Fast Idle Speed	Fuel Pump Pressure
1991								
2.5L/4-151	R	.060	⑦	③	④	⑤	⑤	9-13 ⑥
3.1L/V6-189	T	.045	⑧	③	④	⑤	⑤	41-47 ⑩
3.3L/V6-204	N	.060	②	③	④	⑤	⑤	41-47 ⑩
1992								
2.5L/4-151	R	.060	⑦	③	④	⑤	⑤	9-13 ⑥
3.3L/V6-204	N	.060	②	③	④	⑤	⑤	41-47 ⑩
1993-94								
2.2L/4-134	4	.045	⑨	③	④	⑤	⑤	41-47 ⑥
3.1L/V6-191	N	—	—	—	—	—	—	—
3.3L/V6-204	N	.060	②	③	④	⑤	⑤	41-47 ⑩

① —The eighth digit of the Vehicle identification Number (V.I.N.) denotes engine code.
② —Refer to Fig. A for cylinder numbering. Firing order is 1-6-5-4-3-2.
③ —No adjustment.
④ —Equipped with crankshaft position sensor.
⑤ —Idle speeds are controlled by the idle air control (IAC) valve or idle speed control (ISC) motor.
⑥ —Wrap shop towel around fuel hose to steel line connection to prevent fuel spillage. Disconnect fuel hose from steel line & connect suitable fuel pressure gauge. Ensure pressure gauge connections are tight, then start engine & note fuel pressure reading.
⑦ —Refer to Fig. B for cylinder numbering. Firing order 1-3-4-2.
⑧ —Refer to Fig. C for cylinder numbering. Firing order 1-2-3-4-5-6.
⑨ —Refer to Fig. D for cylinder numbering. Firing order 1-3-4-2.
⑩ —With shop towel wrapped around fuel pressure valve to prevent fuel spillage, connect a suitable fuel pressure gauge to fuel pressure valve. Check fuel pressure with ignition switch On, engine not running.

Fig. A

Fig. B

Fig. C

Fig. D

FRONT WHEEL ALIGNMENT SPECIFICATIONS

Year	Model	Caster Angle, Degrees		Camber Angle, Degrees				Toe-In Inch
				Limits		Desired		
		Limits	Desired	Left	Right	Left	Right	
1991	All	+1.0 to +2.4 ①	+1.7 ①	−.5 to +.5	−.5 to +.5	0	0	0
1992–93	All	+.7 to +2.7	+1.7	−.5 to +.5	−.5 to +.5	0	0	0
1994	All	+2.3 to +3.7	3.0	−.5 to +.5	−.5 to +.5	0	0	0

REAR WHEEL ALIGNMENT SPECIFICATIONS

Year	Model	Camber Angle, Degrees				Toe-In Inch
		Limits		Desired		
		Left	Right	Left	Right	
1991-94	All	−.3 to +.3	−.3 to +.3	0	0	0

COOLING SYSTEM & CAPACITY DATA

Year	Engine		Cooling Capacity, Qts.		Radiator Cap Relief Pressure, Lbs.	Thermo. Opening Temp. °F	Fuel Tank Gals.	Engine Oil Refill Qts. ②	Automatic Transaxle Oil, Qts. ①
	Liter/CID	VIN	Less A/C	With A/C					
1991	2.5L/4-151	R	9.7	9.9	15	195	15.7	4.0	⑤
	3.1L/V6-189	T	③	③	15	195	15.7	4.0	⑤
	3.3L/V6-204	N	12.9	13.2	15	195	15.7	4.0	⑤
1992	2.5L/4-151	R	9.7	9.9	15	195	15.7	4.0	④
	3.3L/V6-204	N	12.9	13.2	15	195	15.7	4.0	④
1993	2.2L/4-134	4	7.6	7.6	15	195	16.5	4.0	④
	3.3L/V6-204	N	12.9	13.2	15	195	16.5	4.0	④
1994	2.2L/4-134	4	—	8.7	15.9	192	16.5	4.0	④
	3.1L/V6-191	N	—	11.6	15	195	16.5	4.0	④

① —Approximate, make final check w/dipstick.
② —Additional oil may be required to bring oil level to full mark when changing oil filter.
③ —Three speed trans., 13.1 qts; Four speed trans., 12.8 qts.
④ —Oil pan only, 4 qts. w/3T40 trans. or 6 qts. w/4T60 trans.; Total capacity, 7 qts. w/3T40 trans. or 8 qts. w/4T60 trans.
⑤ —Oil pan only, 7 qts. w/3T40 trans. or 6 qts. w/4T60 trans.; Total capacity, 9 qts. w/3T40 trans. or 6 qts. w/4T60 trans.

LUBRICANT DATA

Year	Model	Lubricant Type			
		Automatic	Rear Axle	Power Steering ①	Brake System
1991	All	Dexron II	—	GM Power Steering	DOT 3
1992-94	All	Dexron IIE	—	GM Power Steering	DOT 3

①—An equivalent fluid meeting GM requirements can be used.

Electrical

INDEX

PRECAUTIONS

AIRBAG SYSTEM DISARMING

The diagnostic energy reserve module (DERM) can maintain voltage to cause a system deployment for up to ten minutes after the ignition switch is turned off and the battery is disconnected. Servicing the SIR system during this period may result in accidental deployment and personal injury.

1. Ensure front wheels are pointed straight ahead.
2. Turn ignition switch to Lock position and remove SIR fuse from fuse block.
3. Remove Connector Position Assurance (CPA), then disconnect yellow two-way SIR electrical connector at base of steering column.

AIRBAG SYSTEM ARMING

1. Connect yellow two-way SIR electrical connector at base of column, then install Connector Position Assurance (CPA).
2. Install SIR fuse into fuse block, turn ig-nition switch to RUN position and ensure that "Inflatable Restraint" lamp flashes 7 to 9 times and then shuts off.

FUSE PANEL & FLASHER LOCATION

CENTURY

The fuse panel is located behind the righthand side of the instrument panel, in or near the glove box.

The hazard flasher is located in the convenience center behind the instrument panel, to the left of the steering column and the turn signal flasher is located on the accelerator pedal bracket.

CUTLASS CIERA, CUTLASS CRUISER & 6000

The fuse panel is located behind the righthand side of the instrument panel, in or near the glove box.

The hazard flasher is located in the convenience center behind the righthand side of instrument panel and the turn signal flasher is located on the instrument panel brace to the right side of the steering column.

STARTER REPLACE

Upon removal of starter, note if any shims are used. If shims are used, they should be reinstalled in their original location during installation.

If starter is noisy during cranking, remove one .015 inch double shim or add one .015 inch single shim to the outer bolt. If starter makes a high pitched whine after firing, add .015 inch double shims until noise ceases.

2.2L/4-134 ENGINE

1. Disable airbag system as described under "Airbag System Disarming."
2. Disconnect battery ground cable.
3. Remove engine torque strut bracket pencil brace.
4. Raise and support vehicle.
5. Remove bolts from flexplate inspection cover, then the cover.
6. Remove starter attaching bolts, then carefully lower starter. Note position of shims, if used.
7. Disconnect starter wiring.
8. Reverse procedure to install.
9. Rearm airbag system as described under "Airbag System Arming."

2.5L/4-151 ENGINE

1. Disconnect battery ground cable.
2. Raise and support vehicle.
3. Remove all electrical wiring from starter.
4. Remove dust cover attaching bolts, then dust cover.
5. Remove starter motor attaching bolts, then the nut securing starter bracket to rear of starter.
6. Remove starter from vehicle. **If starter needs additional room, remove engine brace and roll engine rearward.**
7. Reverse procedure to install, **torque** starter motor attaching bolts to 32 ft. lbs.

3.1L/V6-189 ENGINE

1. Disconnect battery negative cable, then remove air cleaner.
2. Raise and support vehicle, then remove nut from brace at A/C compressor.
3. Remove nut from brace at engine and brace, then electrical connector from oil pressure sending unit.
4. Remove oil pressure sending unit, then oil filter.
5. Remove dust cover attaching bolts, then dust cover.
6. Remove starter attaching bolts, then lower starter.
7. Remove all electrical wiring from starter, then remove starter from vehicle.
8. Reverse procedure to install.

3.3L/V6-204 ENGINE

This procedure has been revised by technical service bulletin No. 90-6D-1.
1. **On models equipped with airbag,** disable airbag system as described under "Airbag System Disarming."
2. Disconnect battery ground cable.
3. Raise and support vehicle.
4. Remove flywheel cover attaching bolts, then the cover.
5. Disconnect all electrical wires from starter.
6. Remove starter motor attaching bolts, then the motor by rotating the solenoid side toward the vehicle.
7. Reverse procedure to install. **Torque** starter attaching bolts to 32 ft. lbs. and inspection cover bolts to 89 inch lbs.
8. Rearm airbag system as described under "Airbag System Arming."

IGNITION LOCK
REPLACE

1. **On models equipped with airbag,** disable airbag system as described under "Airbag System Disarming."
2. Remove turn signal switch as outlined under "Turn Signal Switch, Replace."
3. Remove buzzer switch and spring clip. Ignition key must be removed from lock to remove buzzer switch. Switch and spring clip are one assembly.
4. Turn lock cylinder to Run position,

Fig. 1 Ignition & dimmer switch replacement . Fixed column.

then remove lock cylinder retaining screw and the lock cylinder.
5. To install, rotate lock cylinder to the stop while holding housing. Align cylinder key with keyway in housing, then push lock cylinder into housing until fully seated. Lock cylinder must be in Run position to install buzzer switch.
6. Install lock cylinder retaining screw, then the buzzer switch, turn signal switch and steering wheel.
7. Rearm airbag system as described under "Airbag System Arming."

IGNITION & DIMMER SWITCHES
REPLACE

FIXED COLUMN

1. **On models equipped with airbag,** disable airbag system as described under "Airbag System Disarming."
2. Remove ignition lock as outlined under "Ignition Lock, Replace."
3. Refer to **Fig. 1**, for ignition and dimmer switch replacement procedures.
4.
4. Rearm airbag system as described under "Airbag System Arming."

TILT COLUMN

1. **On models equipped with airbag,** disable airbag system as described under "Airbag System Disarming."
2. Remove ignition lock as outlined under "Ignition Lock, Replace."
3. Remove housing as follows:
   a. Reinstall tilt lever and place column in full Up position.
   b. Pull upward on tilt lever and pull housing upward until it stops.

   c. Move housing to right to disengage rack from actuator, then remove housing from steering column.
4. Refer to **Fig. 2**, for ignition and dimmer switch replacement procedures.
5. Install housing as follows:
   a. While holding up on tilt lever to disengage lock shoes install over steering shaft.
   b. Move rack downward and hold. Tip housing to the left until rack engages pin on actuator rod.
   c. Push housing down until pivot pin holes are in alignment.
6. Rearm airbag system as described under "Airbag System Arming."

NEUTRAL START SWITCH
REPLACE

REMOVAL

1. **On models equipped with airbag,** disable airbag system as described under "Airbag System Disarming."
2. Disconnect battery ground cable.
3. Apply parking brake and block wheels, then place transaxle in the NEUTRAL position.
4. Disconnect shift linkage from transmission, then the electrical connector from the neutral switch, **Fig. 3.**
5. Remove two switch mounting bolts, then the switch.

INSTALLATION

1. Place shift shaft in neutral.
2. Align flats in shift shaft with flats in switch.
3. Install mounting bolts, if bolt holes will not align with mounting boss on the

Fig. 2   Ignition & dimmer switch replacement. Tilt column

Fig. 3   Neutral switch removal & adjustment

[1] HARNESS CLIP
[2] WIRING RETAINER
[3] NEUTRAL START SWITCH
[4] BRACKET, NEUTRAL START SWITCH
[5] BOLT/SCREW
[6] MANUAL SHAFT
[7] SERVICE ADJUSTMENT HOLE
[8] 3/32 INCH DRILL BIT OR 2.34 DIA. GAGE PIN

transmission, proceed as follows:
a. Ensure shift shaft is in neutral position. **Do not rotate switch. Switch is pinned in a neutral position.**
b. Install mounting bolts loosely.
c. Align slot in support with slot in

back and insert a 3/32 drill bit horizontally into both pieces.
4. **Torque** mounting bolts to 18 ft. lbs.
5. Remove drill bit, if used, then reconnect electrical connector and shift linkage.

Fig. 4   Stoplamp switch replacement

6. Verify that engine will start only in neutral or park position, if engine starts in any other position, adjust switch as follows:
   a. Place shifter in NEUTRAL position, then loosen switch attaching screws.
   b. Rotate switch on shifter assembly to align service adjustment hole with carrier tang hole, **Fig. 3.**
   c. Insert a 3.32 inch gauge pin to a depth of 5/8 inch.
   d. **Torque** mounting bolts to 18 ft. lbs., then remove gauge pin.
7. Release parking brake and remove wheel blocks.
8. Rearm airbag system as described under "Airbag System Arming."

HEADLAMP SWITCH
REPLACE
CENTURY

1. **On models equipped with airbag,** disable airbag system as described under "Airbag System Disarming."
2. Disconnect battery ground cable.
3. Remove left instrument panel trim plate as follows:
   a. Remove screws holding ALDL connector, then lower connector.
   b. Remove filler panel attaching screws, then lap vent hose.
   c. Remove filler panel by swinging down and pulling out.
   d. Remove steering column opening filler attaching screws, then opening filler.
   e. Remove left trim plate attaching screw, then trim plate. On vehicles with column shift, shift transaxle to First gear.
4. Remove switch trim plate attaching screws, then trim plate.
5. Remove switch attaching screws, then switch.
6. Reverse procedure to install.
7. Rearm airbag system as described under "Airbag System Arming."

6000

1. Disconnect battery ground cable.
2. Remove headlight rod and knob assembly, then left trim plate.
3. Remove switch/bracket assembly attaching screws, then disconnect electrical connector.

Tighten nut until tool slightly depresses lock plate

Fig. 5   Compressing lock plate

Fig. 6   Left trim plate removal. Century

1- CLUSTER ASM
2- INSTRUMENT PNL

Fig. 7   Instrument cluster removal. Century

4. Remove switch/bracket assembly. Loosen bezel and remove switch from bracket.
5. Reverse procedure to install.

CUTLASS CIERA & CRUISER

1. **On models equipped with airbag,** disable airbag system as described under "Airbag System Disarming."
2. Disconnect battery ground cable, then remove upper console, if equipped.
3. Remove accessory trim plate as follows:
   a. Pry steering column collar rearward, using a suitable tool, and remove.
   b. Remove outer air deflectors, then the two screws behind the deflector openings.
   c. Remove screw from behind steering column collar.
   d. **On models less console,** open ashtray and remove trim plate attaching screws.
   e. **On models with console,** remove four screws from ashtray trim cover, then ashtray trim cover. Remove trim plate attaching screws.
   f. **On all models,** pull trim plate rearward to release clips, then remove trim plate.
4. Remove 3 switch to panel attaching screws.
5. Pull switch rearward and remove from panel.
6. Reverse procedure to install.
7. Rearm airbag system as described under "Airbag System Arming."

STOP LAMP SWITCH
REPLACE

1. **On models equipped with airbag,** disable airbag system as described under "Airbag System Disarming."
2. Disconnect battery ground cable.
3. Disconnect electrical connector from stop lamp switch.
4. Remove stop lamp switch from brake pedal support bracket, **Fig. 4.**
5. Reverse procedure to install.
6. Rearm airbag system as described under "Airbag System Arming."

STOP LAMP SWITCH
ADJUST

Insert switch into tubular clip until the switch body seats on the tube clip. Pull the brake pedal rearward against internal pedal stop. This will properly position switch in tubular clip.

TURN SIGNAL SWITCH
REPLACE

1. **On models equipped with airbag,** disable airbag system as described under "Airbag System Disarming."
2. Disconnect battery ground cable.
3. Remove steering wheel as outlined under "Steering Wheel, Replace" procedure.
4. Using a screwdriver, pry cover from housing.
5. Using lock plate compressing No. J-23653 or equivalent, compress lock plate, and pry snap ring from groove on shaft, **Fig. 5.** Slowly release lock plate compressing tool, then remove tool and lock plate from shaft end.
6. Slide canceling cam and upper bearing preload spring from end of shaft.
7. Remove turn signal (multi-function) lever.
8. Remove hazard warning knob retaining screw, button, spring and knob.
9. Remove pivot arm.
10. Wrap upper part of electrical connector with tape to prevent snagging of wires during switch removal.
11. Remove switch retaining screws and pull switch up from column, guiding wire harness through column.
12. Reverse procedure to install.
13. Rearm airbag system as described under "Airbag System Arming."

STEERING WHEEL
REPLACE

1. **On models equipped with airbag,** disable airbag system as described under "Airbag System Disarming."
2. Disconnect battery ground cable.
3. Remove horn button or pad.
4. Disconnect horn pad and lead by pushing down and turning counterclockwise.

5. Remove retainer and steering wheel retaining nut.
6. Using steering wheel puller No. J-1859-03 or equivalent, remove steering wheel. With steering wheel controls, puller bolts should not be turned in more than five complete turns.
7. Reverse procedure to install.
8. Rearm airbag system as described under "Airbag System Arming."

INSTRUMENT CLUSTER
REPLACE

CENTURY

1. **On models equipped with airbag,** disable airbag system as described under "Airbag System Disarming."
2. Disconnect battery ground cable.
3. Remove steering column filler panel as follows:
   a. Remove ALDL connector attaching screws, then lower ALDL connector.
   b. Remove filler panel attaching screws, then lap vent hose.
   c. Remove filler panel by swinging down and pulling out.
4. Remove left trim plate as follows:
   a. Remove steering column opening filler attaching screws, then opening filler.
   b. Remove ashtray, then trim plate attaching screws, **Fig. 6.**
   c. Pull trim panel straight forward to release two retaining clips in center of panel, then remove panel.
5. Disconnect speedometer cable from transmission. If two piece cable is used, disconnect in engine compartment to ensure there is cable slack.
6. Remove shift indicator clip from steering column shift bowl, then cluster attaching screws, **Fig. 7.**
7. Pull cluster assembly out far enough to reach behind and disconnect speedometer cable.
8. Remove cluster.
9. Reverse procedure to install.
10. Rearm airbag system as described under "Airbag System Arming."

CUTLASS CIERA & CRUISER

1. **On models equipped with airbag,** disable airbag system as described under "Airbag System Disarming."
2. Disconnect battery ground cable, then

1. TRIM PLATE
2. I.P.
3. SPEAKER OPENING
4. DUCT

VIEW A

1. CLUSTER TRIM PLATE
2. SPEAKER OPENING
3. CLUSTER
4. RADIO

**Fig. 9   Cluster trim plate
removal. Cutlass Ciera &
Cruiser**

**Fig. 8   Accessory trim plate removal. Cutlass
Ciera & Cruiser**

1. I.P. HARNESS ASSEMBLY
2. INSTRUMENT PANEL
3. CLUSTER ASSEMBLY

**Fig. 10   Instrument cluster
removal. Cutlass Ciera &
Cruiser**

remove upper console, if equipped.
3. Remove accessory trim plate as follows:
   a. Pry steering column collar rearward, using a suitable tool, and remove.
   b. Remove outer air deflectors, then the two screws behind the deflector openings.
   c. Remove screw from behind steering column collar.
   d. **On models less console,** open ashtray and remove trim plate attaching screws.
   e. **On models with console,** remove four screws from ashtray trim cover, then ashtray trim cover. Remove trim plate attaching screws.
   f. **On all models,** pull trim plate rearward to release clips, then remove accessory trim plate, **Fig. 8.**
4. Remove screws attaching cluster trim plate, then trim plate, **Fig. 9.**
5. Remove steering column trim collar and trim plate.
6. Disconnect shift indicator clip from steering column shift bowl.
7. Remove cluster assembly attaching bolts, **Fig. 10,** then pull cluster rearward.
8. Disconnect speedometer cable from cluster.
9. Remove cluster assembly.
10. Reverse procedure to install.
11. Rearm airbag system as described under "Airbag System Arming."

6000

1. Call up and record maintenance reminder mileage, if equipped w/driver information center (DIC).
2. Disconnect battery ground cable.
3. Remove center and lefthand lower instrument panel trim plates.

4. Remove cluster pad, **Fig. 11,** then air duct.
5. Remove cluster attaching screws, then pull cluster rearward, this will disengage two cluster connectors.
6. Disconnect DIC connector, located in a cable about one foot from cluster, if equipped.
7. Remove cluster from vehicle.
8. Reverse procedure to install.

RADIO
REPLACE
CENTURY

1. **On models equipped with airbag,** disable airbag system as described under "Airbag System Disarming."
2. Disconnect battery ground cable.
3. Remove steering column filler panel as follows:
   a. Remove ALDL connector attaching screws, then lower ALDL connector.
   b. Remove filler panel attaching screws, then lap vent hose.
   c. Remove filler panel by swinging down and pulling out.
4. Remove left trim plate as follows:
   a. Remove steering column opening filler attaching screws, then opening filler.
   b. Remove ashtray, then trim plate attaching screws, **Fig. 6.**
   c. Pull trim panel straight forward to release two retaining clips in center of panel, then remove panel.
5. Remove right cluster trim plate attaching screws, then trim plate.
6. Remove radio assembly attaching screws, then pull out radio.
7. Disconnect all electrical connectors from radio, then remove radio.

8. Reverse procedure to install.
9. Rearm airbag system as described under "Airbag System Arming."

CUTLASS CIERA &
CRUISER

1. **On models equipped with airbag,** disable airbag system as described under "Airbag System Disarming."
2. Disconnect battery ground cable, then remove upper console, if equipped.
3. Remove accessory trim plate as follows:
   a. Pry steering column collar rearward, using a suitable tool, and remove.
   b. Remove outer air deflectors, then the two screws behind the deflector openings.
   c. Remove screw from behind steering column collar.
   d. **On models less console,** open ashtray and remove trim plate attaching screws.
   e. **On models with console,** remove four screws from ashtray trim cover, then ashtray trim cover. Remove trim plate attaching screws.
   f. **On all models,** pull trim plate rearward to release clips, then remove accessory trim plate, **Fig. 8.**
4. Remove screws attaching cluster trim plate, then trim plate, **Fig. 9.**
5. Remove radio attaching bolts, then pull out radio.

1 – CLUSTER PAD
2 – SHIFT INDICATOR
3 – PAD ASSY.
4 – SHIFT INDICATOR LIGHT

Fig. 11 Cluster pad removal. 6000

Fig. 13 Housing & wiper switch replacement. Fixed column

Fig. 12 Wiper motor transmission removal

Fig. 14 Cover & wiper switch replacement. Tilt column

6. Disconnect all electrical connectors from radio, then remove radio.
7. Reverse procedure to install.
8. Rearm airbag system as described under "Airbag System Arming."

6000

1. Disconnect battery ground cable.
2. Remove right side instrument panel trim plate.
3. Remove four radio attaching screws, then disconnect electrical and antenna connections.
4. Remove radio from vehicle.
5. Reverse procedure to install.

WIPER MOTOR TRANSMISSION REPLACE

1. **On models equipped with airbag,** disable airbag system as described under "Airbag System Disarming."
2. Raise hood, then remove right and left wiper arm and blade assemblies.
3. Loosen, but do not remove nuts securing transmission drive link to motor crank arm.

4. Remove air inlet panel attaching screw, then panel.
5. Disconnect transmission drive link from motor crank arm, **Fig. 12.**
6. Remove wiper transmission to body attaching screw.
7. Carefully guide transmission assembly through access hole in upper shroud panel to remove.
8. Reverse procedure to install. **Torque** transmission drive link nuts to 53-75 inch lbs.
9. Rearm airbag system as described under "Airbag System Arming."

WIPER MOTOR REPLACE

FRONT

1. **On models equipped with airbag,** disable airbag system as described under "Airbag System Disarming."
2. Raise hood, then remove right and left wiper arm and blade assemblies.
3. Remove shroud grille to body attaching screws, then shroud grille.
4. Loosen, but do not remove nuts securing transmission drive link to motor

crank arm, then disconnect drive link.
5. Disconnect wiring connectors and washer hoses.
6. Remove 3 screws attaching wiper motor to firewall.
7. Remove motor while guiding crank arm through hole.
8. Reverse procedure to install. Motor

must be in "Park" position before assembling transmission drive link to crank arm. **Torque** transmission drive link to 48-75 inch lbs.

9. Rearm airbag system as described under "Airbag System Arming."

REAR

1. Remove wiper arm, then nut on transmission shaft.
2. Remove liftgate glass opening upper finishing molding, the disconnect electrical connector from motor.
3. Remove upper mounting screw (second screw is a dowel).
4. Rotate motor assembly to 12 o'clock position, guide motor pivot out of tailgate assembly.
5. Reverse procedure to install.

WIPER SWITCH
REPLACE

FRONT
Fixed Column

1. **On models equipped with airbag, disable airbag system as described under "Airbag System Disarming."**
2. Remove ignition and dimmer switches as outlined under "Ignition & Dimmer Switches," Replace."
3. Refer to **Fig. 13,** for wiper switch replacement.
4. Rearm airbag system as described under "Airbag System Arming."

Tilt Column

1. **On models equipped with airbag, disable airbag system as described under "Airbag System Disarming."**
2. Remove ignition lock as outlined under "Ignition Lock, Replace."
3. Refer to **Fig. 14,** for wiper switch replacement.
4. Rearm airbag system as described under "Airbag System Arming."

REAR

1. Disconnect battery ground cable.
2. Remove lefthand trim panel, then right side switch trim cover.

3. Remove switch attaching screws, then switch.
4. Reverse procedure to install.

BLOWER MOTOR
REPLACE

EXCEPT CENTURY

1. Disconnect battery ground cable.
2. Disconnect blower motor electrical connections.
3. Remove blower motor attaching screws, then blower motor. **On models with A/C it may be necessary to dismount alternator and move away from module.**
4. Reverse procedure to install.

CENTURY

1. **On models equipped with airbag, disable airbag system as described under "Airbag System Disarming."**
2. Disconnect battery ground cable.
3. Remove wiper arms, then cowl panel.
4. Disconnect blower motor electrical connectors and vent tube, then remove blower motor attaching screws.
5. Remove fan retaining nut from blower motor shaft.
6. Holding fan securely, remove fan from blower motor while removing blower motor from vehicle. **Failure to hold fan securely can cause fan to fall into heater A/C module.**
7. Reverse procedure to install.
8. Rearm airbag system as described under "Airbag System Arming."

HEATER CORE
REPLACE

LESS A/C

1. **On models equipped with airbag, disable airbag system as described under "Airbag System Disarming."**
2. Drain cooling system.
3. Disconnect heater inlet and outlet hoses.
4. Remove lower instrument panel sound insulator, then radio noise suppression strap.
5. Remove cover retaining screws and cover.

6. Remove heater core strap, then heater core.
7. Reverse procedure to install.
8. Rearm airbag system as described under "Airbag System Arming."

WITH A/C

1. **On models equipped with airbag, disable airbag system as described under "Airbag System Disarming."**
2. Drain cooling system.
3. Disconnect heater inlet and outlet hoses.
4. Remove lower instrument panel sound insulator, then heater floor outlet duct.
5. Remove heater core cover screws and clips securing cover to air valve housing, then heater core cover.
6. Remove heater core retaining straps, then heater core.
7. Reverse procedure to install.
8. Rearm airbag system as described under "Airbag System Arming."

EVAPORATOR CORE
REPLACE

1. **On models equipped with airbag, disable airbag system as described under "Airbag System Disarming."**
2. Disconnect battery ground cable, then discharge A/C system.
3. Remove air cleaner assembly.
4. Disconnect A/C heater module electrical connectors, then harness straps. Move harness aside.
5. If equipped, remove heater hose routing bracket and resistor from cover, then vacuum tank.
6. Disconnect liquid line at evaporator inlet and low pressure line at evaporator outlet.
7. Dismount alternator and move away from module, if necessary.
8. Remove evaporator core cover retaining screws (loosen bottom screws only), then remove evaporator core cover.
9. Remove evaporator core.
10. Reverse procedure to install.
11. Rearm airbag system as described under "Airbag System Arming."

2.2L/4-134 Engine

NOTE: For Procedures Not Found In This Section, Refer To The 2.2L/4-134 Engine Section In The Chevrolet Cavalier & Pontiac Sunbird Chapter.

INDEX

PRECAUTIONS

AIRBAG SYSTEM DISARMING

The diagnostic energy reserve module (DERM) can maintain voltage to cause a system deployment for up to ten minutes after the ignition switch is turned off and the battery is disconnected. Servicing the SIR system during this period may result in accidental deployment and personal injury.

1. Ensure front wheels are pointed straight ahead.
2. Turn ignition switch to Lock position and remove SIR fuse from fuse block.
3. Remove Connector Position Assurance (CPA), then disconnect yellow two-way SIR electrical connector at base of steering column.

AIRBAG SYSTEM ARMING

1. Connect yellow two-way SIR electrical connector at base of column, then install Connector Position Assurance (CPA).
2. Install SIR fuse into fuse block, turn ignition switch to RUN position and ensure that "Inflatable Restraint" lamp flashes 7 to 9 times and then shuts off.

FUEL SYSTEM PRESSURE RELIEF

Whenever the fuel lines are to be disconnected for engine service on fuel injected engines, relieve fuel system pressure following the procedures outlined below. Failure to follow these procedures exactly, may result in personal injury.

1. Disconnect battery ground cable, then loosen filler cap to relieve tank vapor pressure.
2. Connect fuel pressure gauge No. J-34730-1 or equivalent to fuel pressure valve. Wrap a shop towel around fitting while connecting gauge to avoid spillage.
3. Install bleed hose into an approved container and open valve to bleed system pressure. Fuel connections are now safe for servicing.
4. Drain any fuel remaining in gauge into approved container.

ENGINE MOUNT
REPLACE

1. Install engine support tool Nos. J-28467-A and J-36462, or equivalent, then remove engine mount strut.
2. Raise and support vehicle, then remove right wheel and tire assembly.
3. Remove right engine splash shield.
4. Remove engine mount nuts from frame.
5. Lower vehicle,.
6. Using tool No J-28467-A or equivalent, raise engine off mount.
7. Remove nut attaching engine bracket to mount, then remove mount assembly, **Fig. 1.**
8. Reverse procedure to install.

ENGINE
REPLACE

1. Disconnect battery ground cable and drain cooling system.
2. Open hood to full position, then remove gas support at cowl.
3. Remove air cleaner and duct assembly.
4. Remove throttle control cable bracket at intake and rocker cover.
5. Relieve fuel pressure as follows:
   a. Loosen fuel tank filler cap to relieve tank pressure.
   b. Raise and support vehicle, then disconnect fuel pump electrical connector.
   c. Lower vehicle.
   d. Start and operate engine until fuel supply is consumed.
   e. Crank engine for approximately 3 seconds to relieve remaining pressure.
   f. Disconnect battery ground cable, then reconnect fuel pump connector.
6. Disconnect fuel line, then the vacuum, radiator and heater hoses.
7. Remove engine mount strut and bracket pencil brace, then disconnect engine electrical connector.

8. Rotate engine forward.
9. Remove power steering pump and electrical connectors at rear of engine.
10. Disconnect transaxle fluid level indicator, then remove transaxle engine bolts except two upper bolts.
11. Rotate engine rearward, then raise and support vehicle.
12. Remove front wheel and tire assembly.
13. Remove right side engine splash shield, then disconnect exhaust pipe from crossover.
14. Remove flywheel cover and starter motor.
15. Remove engine mount to frame nuts.
16. Remove converter to flywheel bolts.
17. Disconnect A/C compressor, leaving hoses attached, then position compressor aside.
18. Disconnect front exhaust pipe support bracket at transaxle.
19. Remove transaxle support bracket to transaxle bolt, then lower vehicle.
20. Rotate engine forward and rearward, then remove rear and front transaxle attaching bolts to engine.
21. Attach suitable lifting device to engine.
22. Remove engine.
23. Reverse procedure to install.

FUEL FILTER
REPLACE

1. Relieve fuel system pressure as outlined under "Fuel System Pressure Relief."
2. Raise and support vehicle.
3. Remove bracket attaching screw and filter bracket, **Fig. 2.**
4. Grasp filter and fuel line fitting. Twist quick-connect fitting 1/4 turn in each direction to loosen any dirt within fitting.
5. Using compressed air, blow out dirt from quick-connect fitting.
6. Remove feed pipe nut from fuel filter, then drain any remaining fuel into a suitable container.
7. Remove fuel filter.
8. Reverse procedure to install.

1 ASSEMBLY, ENGINE
2 BRACKET A/C COMPRESSOR
3 BOLT
4 NUT
5 MOUNT, ENGINE
6 BRACKET, ENGINE
7 ASSEMBLY, CROSSMEMBER
8 WASHER

Fig. 1   Engine mounts

1   FUEL SENDER
2   FUEL TANK
3   QUICK CONNECT FITTINGS
4   IN-LINE FUEL FILTER BRACKET
5   FILTER BRACKET ATTACHING SCREW

Fig. 2   Fuel filter replacement

2.5L/4-151 Engine

INDEX

Fig. 1 Engine mounts

PRECAUTIONS

FUEL SYSTEM PRESSURE RELIEF

Whenever the fuel lines are to be disconnected for engine service on fuel injected engines, relieve fuel system pressure following the procedures outlined below. Failure to follow these procedures exactly, may result in personal injury.

1. Place transmission in Park or Neutral.
2. Disconnect fuel pump at rear body connector or remove fuel pump inline fuse located in the engine compartment, behind righthand headlights.
3. Start engine and allow to run until engine stalls.
4. After engine stalls, engage starter for approximately three seconds to relieve any residual pressure remaining in system.
5. Turn ignition switch off, then reconnect fuel pump connector or replace fuel pump inline fuse.

ENGINE MOUNTS
REPLACE

1. Raise and support front of vehicle, then remove chassis to mount attaching nuts, **Fig. 1.**
2. Remove forward torque rod attaching bolts at radiator support panel.
3. Raise engine slightly using a suitable engine lifting device. Raise engine only enough to provide clearance for mount removal.
4. Remove two upper mount to engine support bracket attaching nuts and remove engine mount.
5. Reverse procedure to install.

ENGINE
REPLACE

1. Disconnect cables from battery, then drain cooling system.
2. Remove air cleaner assembly, then disconnect engine electrical harness connector.
3. Remove hood support, then prop hood up.
4. Disconnect all external vacuum hose connections, then remove radiator and heater hoses.
5. **On models equipped with A/C,** disconnect compressor and position aside. Do not disconnect refrigerant lines from compressor.
6. **On all models,** remove alternator

Fig. 2 Intake manifold tightening sequence

and alternator bracket, then engine torque strut.
7. Remove throttle and transaxle linkages at the throttle body assembly and intake manifold.
8. Remove all transaxle-to-engine attaching bolts except the top two bolts.
9. Remove front engine mount-to-cradle nuts, then front exhaust pipe.
10. Remove flywheel inspection cover, then torque converter-to-flywheel attaching bolts.
11. Remove starter motor.
12. **On models equipped with power steering,** remove power steering pump and bracket and position aside.
13. **On all models,** disconnect fuel feed line. Refer to "Fuel System Pressure Relief" for fuel pressure bleed procedure.
14. Remove 2 rear transaxle support bracket bolts.
15. Using a suitable jack and a block of wood placed under transaxle, raise engine and transaxle until engine front mount studs clear cradle bracket.
16. Attaching suitable lifting equipment to engine. Put tension on engine and remove 2 remaining transaxle to engine attaching bolts.
17. Slide engine assembly forward and lift from vehicle.
18. Reverse procedure to install.

**Fig. 4   Cylinder head
tightening sequence**

Fig. 3   Exhaust manifold tightening sequence

1 ROLLER	**6**	BALL CHECK
2 LIFTER BODY	**7**	PLUNGER
3 PLUNGER SPRING	**8**	OIL METERING VALVE
4 BALL CHECK RETAINER	**9**	PUSH ROD SEAT
5 BALL CHECK SPRING	**10**	RETAINER RING

**Fig. 5   Exploded view of roller type hydraulic
lifter**

INTAKE MANIFOLD
REPLACE

1. Disconnect battery ground cable, then remove air cleaner.
2. Disconnect PCV valve and hose at TBI unit, then drain cooling system.
3. Disconnect fuel line and all vacuum hoses that will interfere with manifold removal. **Refer to "Fuel System Pressure Relief" for fuel pressure bleed procedure.**
4. Disconnect all electrical connections and throttle linkage from TBI unit.
5. Disconnect downshift and cruise control linkage, if applicable.
6. Disconnect throttle linkage and TV cables, position cables aside.
7. Disconnect heater hose.
8. Remove intake manifold attaching bolts, then the intake manifold.
9. Reverse procedure to install. Torque bolts to specification in sequence shown in **Fig. 2.**

EXHAUST MANIFOLD
REPLACE

1. Remove air cleaner, then torque rod strut.
2. Remove oxygen sensor connector, then dipstick tube.
3. Raise and support vehicle, then remove exhaust pipe from manifold.
4. Lower vehicle, then remove exhaust manifold attaching bolts and washers.
5. Remove exhaust manifold and gasket.
6. Reverse procedure to install, **torquing** exhaust manifold bolts 1,2,6 and 7 to 28 ft. lbs. and bolts 3,4 and 5 to 37 ft. lbs. in sequence shown in **Fig. 3.**

CYLINDER HEAD
REPLACE

1. Disconnect battery ground cable, then drain cooling system.
2. Raise and support vehicle, then disconnect exhaust pipe from exhaust manifold.
3. Disconnect oxygen sensor connector, then lower vehicle.
4. Remove battery (auxiliary) ground cable, then oil dipstick tube and air cleaner.

5. Disconnect wire connectors, throttle linkage and fuel lines from TBI unit. **Refer to "Fuel System Pressure Relief" for fuel pressure bleed procedure.**
6. Disconnect heater hose from intake manifold, then all wiring connections from intake manifold and cylinder head.
7. Remove all vacuum lines that will interfere with manifold or cylinder head removal.
8. Remove engine torque strut rod bolts from upper support, then serpentine drive belt.
9. Remove alternator brackets and position alternator aside.
10. **On vehicles equipped w/top mounted A/C compressor,** remove compressor brackets and position compressor aside.
11. **On vehicles equipped w/top mounted power steering pump,** remove pump upper bracket.
12. **On all models,** remove radiator hoses, then rocker arm and push rod covers.
13. Remove rocker arms, push rods, then cylinder head attaching bolts.
14. Lift cylinder head with intake and exhaust manifolds as an assembly from cylinder block.
15. Reverse procedure to install. Coat heads and threads of cylinder bolts with a suitable sealing compound, then install bolts finger tight.
16. Tighten cylinder head bolts in sequence shown in **Fig. 4** as follows:
    a. **Torque** all bolts to 18 ft. lbs.
    b. **Torque** all bolts except No. 9 to 26 ft. lbs. **Torque** No. 9 bolt to 18 ft. lbs.
    c. Repeat sequence again, turning all bolts an additional 90 degrees or (1/4 turn).
17. Tighten intake manifold bolts in sequence shown in **Fig. 2,** if necessary.
18. Tighten exhaust manifold bolts in sequence shown in **Fig. 3,** if necessary.

ROCKER ARM STUDS

Rocker arm studs that are cracked or have damaged threads can be removed from the cylinder head using a deep well socket. Install and torque new rocker arm stud to specifications.

TIGHTEN IN PROPER SEQUENCE "A" THROUGH "G".

1 BOLT
2 FRONT COVER

Fig. 6 Front cover tightening sequence. 1991–92 models

10 TIMING MARKS TO BE ALIGNED AS SHOWN WHEN ENGINE IS ROTATED TO T.D.C.

Fig. 7 Aligning timing marks. 1991–92 models

1 BALANCER ASSEMBLY
2 BAFFLE
3 10 N·m (90 LB. IN.)
* CIRCLED NUMBERS SHOW BOLT POSITION (SEE TEXT FOR TIGHTENING SEQUENCE)

Fig. 8 Force balancer tightening sequence

VALVE CLEARANCE SPECIFICATIONS

These engines are equipped with hydraulic lifters, no provision for adjustment is provided.

VALVE ARRANGEMENT

FRONT TO REAR

2.5L/4-151 . . . . I-E-I-E-E-I-E-I

CAM LOBE LIFT SPECIFICATIONS

Engine	Year	Int.	Exh.
2.5L/4-151	1991–92	.248	.248

VALVE GUIDES

Valve guides are an integral part of the cylinder head and are not removable. If valve stem clearance becomes excessive, the valve guide should be reamed to the next oversize and the appropriate oversize valves installed. Valves are available in .003 and .005 inch oversizes.

VALVE LIFTERS

Failure of a hydraulic valve lifter, **Fig. 5,** is generally caused by an inadequate oil supply or dirt. An air leak at the intake side of the oil pump or too much oil in the engine will cause air bubbles in the oil supply to the lifters, causing them to collapse. This is a probable cause of trouble if several lifters fail to function, but air in oil is an unlikely cause of failure of a single unit.

Valve lifters can be removed after removing rocker arm cover, intake manifold, pushrod cover and pushrod retainer and guide, if applicable. Loosen rocker arm stud nut and rotate rocker arm so that pushrod can be removed, then remove valve lifter. It may be necessary to use lifter remover No. J-3049 or equivalent to facilitate lifter removal.

FRONT COVER
REPLACE
1991–92

1. Disconnect battery ground cable, then remove serpentine drive belt tensioner and drive belt.
2. Raise and support vehicle, then remove right hand wheel assembly.
3. Remove right fender splash shield, then flywheel cover. Install suitable tool to prevent flywheel from rotating.
4. Remove crankshaft harmonic balancer attaching bolt, then balancer and key.
5. Remove front cover attaching screws, then front cover.
6. Using flathead screwdriver, remove oil seal. Do not distort cover.
7. Reverse procedure to install, noting the following:
   a. Position centering tool No. J-34995 or equivalent, into cover, then install and partially tighten two opposing cover screws.
   b. Torque bolts to specifications in sequence shown in **Fig. 6.**

TIMING CHAIN
REPLACE
1991–92

1. Remove front cover as outlined under "Front Cover, Replace."
2. Loosen but do not remove camshaft bolt.
3. Align timing marks on camshaft and crankshaft gears, then remove camshaft bolt.
4. Remove timing chain and sprocket.
5. Reverse procedure to install, noting the following:
   a. Align timing marks as shown in **Fig. 7.**

CAMSHAFT
REPLACE
1991–92
With Engine In Vehicle

1. Disconnect battery ground cable, then drain cooling system.
2. Remove air cleaner assembly, PCV hose, EGR valve, spark plug wires and clips.
3. Remove fuel line bracket and fuel lines. **Refer to "Fuel System Pressure Relief" for fuel pressure bleed procedure.**
4. Remove vacuum hoses including power brake booster hose.
5. Remove all wiring and throttle linkage from TBI assembly.
6. Remove transaxle downshift bracket, then heater hose from intake manifold.
7. Remove serpentine drive belt, then tensioner to engine attaching bolts. Position tensioner/power steering pump assembly aside.
8. Remove intake manifold, pushrod cover and valve lifters.
9. Disconnect electrical connections from DIS assembly, then remove DIS assembly.
10. Remove bolt from torque strut at engine bracket, then swing strut aside.
11. Install engine lift bracket, then engine support fixtures No. J-28467-A and J-36462.
12. Raise and support vehicle, then remove both front wheel assemblies.
13. Drain engine oil, then move steering column intermediate shaft cover aside.

1	RING — PISTON COMP. UPR.
2	RING — PISTON COMP. LWR.
3	SEGMENT — OIL CNTR. RING
4	SPACER — OIL CNTR. RING
5	PISTON ASM.
6	BOLT SCREW
7	ROD — CONNECTING
8	PIN — PISTON

Fig. 9   Piston & rod assembly

1	OIL RING SPACER GAP (TANG IN HOLE OR SLOT WITH ARC)
2	OIL RING RAIL GAPS
3	2ND COMPRESSION RING GAP
4	TOP COMPRESSION RING GAP

Fig. 10   Locating pin ring gaps

14. Remove steering shaft to steering gear pinch bolt, then right front lower ball joint pinch bolt.
15. Remove right front ball joint from knuckle, then lower air deflector.
16. Remove right front wheelhouse engine splash shield.
17. Remove flywheel cover, then crankshaft balancer retaining bolt. **Have an assistant hold flywheel from turning while removing bolt.**
18. Remove crankshaft balancer, then front cover.
19. Remove frame bolts and insulators, then brake line to frame bracket and bolt.
20. Remove oil filter, then lower frame/powertrain assembly with support fixtures. **Lower passenger side just enough to access camshaft gear area.**
21. Align timing marks on camshaft and crankshaft sprockets, then remove camshaft sprocket bolt.
22. Remove timing chain and sprockets, then camshaft thrust plate.
23. Remove camshaft. Use care not to damage camshaft bearings.
24. Reverse procedure to install, noting the following:
   a. Ensure crankshaft and camshaft

APPLY RTV SEALANT AS SPECIFIED

1–3/8 " WIDE X 3/16 " THICK

2–3/16 " WIDE X 1/8 " THICK

3–1/8 " BEAD IN AREAS SHOWN

BLOCK   PAN

Fig. 11   Oil pan sealer application

timing marks on gears are aligned, **Fig. 7.**
   b. Torque all bolts/nuts to specifications.

With Engine Removed From Vehicle

1. Remove engine from vehicle as outlined under "Engine, Replace."
2. Remove rocker arm cover, then push rods.
3. Remove pushrod cover, then valve lifters.
4. Remove crankshaft harmonic balancer, then front cover.
5. Remove camshaft sprocket bolt, then timing chain and sprockets.
6. Remove camshaft thrust plate, then pull camshaft from engine block. Use care not to damage camshaft bearings.
7. Reverse procedure to install, noting the following:
   a. Ensure crankshaft and camshaft timing marks on gears are aligned, **Fig. 7.**
   b. Torque all bolts/nuts to specifications.

FORCE BALANCER ASSEMBLY REPLACE

1. Remove oil pan as outlined further on.
2. Remove balancer assembly to crankcase attaching bolts, then balancer assembly.
3. To install, proceed as follows:
   a. Position No. 1 and No. 4 cylinders at TDC (crank counterweights at BDC). **When installing balancer, the end of the housing without dowel pins must remain in contact with block surface. If it loses contact, gear engagement may be lost and permanent damage to either the crank or balancer gears may result.**
   b. Install balancer onto crankshaft with balance weights at BDC (plus or minus one half gear tooth).
   c. **Torque** bolt in sequence, 3-1-2-4, (circled numbers shown in **Fig. 8**).
   d. Following sequence shown in step

   c. **torque** short bolts to 11 ft. lbs. plus 75° and long bolts to 11 ft. lbs. plus 90°.
   e. Rotate crankshaft four times and check for clearance between the fourth counterweight and balancer weights.
   f. Reinstall oil pan.

PISTON & ROD ASSEMBLE

Assemble piston to rod with mark on piston and rod both facing toward front of engine. Rod may not be marked, **Fig. 9.**

PISTONS, PINS & RINGS

Install rings on pistons as shown in **Fig. 10.**

Pistons, pins and rings are available in standard and oversizes.

MAIN & ROD BEARINGS

Main and rod bearings are available in standard size and undersizes.

OIL PAN REPLACE

1. Disconnect battery ground cable, then remove coolant reservoir bottle.
2. Remove engine torque strut, then air cleaner assembly.
3. Remove air inlet, then serpentine drive belt.
4. Remove A/C compressor from brackets and set aside, then engine oil level indicator.
5. Support engine using support fixture No. J-28467-A, then raise and support vehicle.
6. Drain engine oil, then remove starter and support bracket. Position starter aside.
7. Remove flywheel covers, then turn front wheels to full right position.
8. Remove engine wiring harness retainer screws under both sides of oil pan.
9. Remove right side engine splash shield, then front engine mount bracket bolts/nuts.

1 BOLT
2 OUTLET
3 THERMOSTAT ASSEMBLY
4 HOUSING
5 BOLT
6 GASKET

Fig. 12 Thermostat & housing assembly

10. Remove transaxle mount nuts.
11. Using support fixture installed in step 5, raise engine approximately two inches, then remove front engine mount and bracket.
12. Loosen frame bolts, then remove oil pan attaching bolts.
13. Remove oil pan.
14. Reverse procedure to install, noting the following:
    a. Apply RTV sealant as shown in **Fig. 11.**
    b. Torque all bolts/nuts to specifications.

OIL PUMP SERVICE
REMOVAL & DISASSEMBLY

The oil pump can be serviced without removing the balancer assembly.
1. Remove oil pan as outlined under "Oil Pan, Replace."
2. Remove restrictor, oil filter, oil pump cover assembly and gears, then the pressure regulator plug or pin, spring and valve. **Use caution when removing plug or pin, since spring pressure can cause personal injury.**

CLEANING & INSPECTION

1. Clean all parts in solvent and dry with compressed air.
2. Inspect pump housing, cover assembly, regulator valve and spring and screen assembly for excessive wear or damage.
3. Inspect depth of wear pattern in gear housing pocket and face of oil pump cover assembly, then the gear thickness. Gear pocket depth should be .514-.516 inch, while gear thickness should be .511-.512 inch.

ASSEMBLY & INSTALLATION

1. Lubricate all internal parts with engine oil.
2. Pack all pump cavities with petroleum jelly, then install gears.
3. Install oil pump cover assembly, then the pressure regulator valve, spring and pin or plug. Torque pump cover attaching bolts to specifications.
4. Clean intake screen, then install oil filter and restrictor.

REAR MAIN BEARING OIL SEAL
REPLACE

The rear main oil seal is a one piece unit and is replaced without removing the oil pan or crankshaft.
1. Remove transaxle and flywheel.
2. **On models equipped w/manual transaxle,** remove pressure plate and disc.
3. Using a suitable screwdriver, remove rear main bearing oil seal. Use care not to scratch crankshaft.
4. Lubricate inside and outside diameters of replacement seal with engine oil. Install seal using seal installer No. J34924-A onto rear crankshaft flange with helical lip side facing toward engine. Ensure seal is firmly and evenly seated.
5. Install flywheel and transaxle.

COOLING SYSTEM BLEED

This engine does not require a specified bleed procedure. After filling cooling system, run engine to operating temperature with radiator/pressure cap off. Air will then be automatically bled through cap opening.

THERMOSTAT
REPLACE

Refer to **Fig. 12** when performing the following procedure.
1. Disconnect battery ground cable.
2. If necessary, remove air cleaner assembly.
3. With engine cool, drain engine coolant below thermostat level. **Never open cooling system with engine hot.**
4. Disconnect radiator hose from thermostat housing.
5. Remove thermostat housing retaining bolts, then the housing, gasket and thermostat.
6. Reverse procedure to install, noting the following:
    a. Ensure thermostat gasket area is thoroughly clean.
    b. Install thermostat with new gasket.
    c. Apply a suitable sealer to thermostat housing retaining bolts. Install and **torque** bolts to 20 ft. lbs.
    d. Refill and bleed cooling system as necessary.

1 COOLANT PUMP
2 BOLT/SCREW
3 GASKET, COOLANT PUMP INLET
4 INLET, COOLANT PUMP
5 BOLT/SCREW
6 GASKET, COOLANT PUMP

Fig. 13 Water pump removal

WATER PUMP
REPLACE

1. Disconnect battery ground cable, then drain cooling system.
2. Remove alternator, then disconnect radiator and heater hoses from inlet.
3. Remove water pump attaching bolts **Fig. 13**, then water pump and pulley assembly.
4. Separate pulley and water pump.
5. Reverse procedure to install, torquing all bolts/nuts to specifications.

FUEL PUMP
REPLACE

1. Relieve fuel pressure as outlined under "Fuel System Pressure Relief," then disconnect battery ground cable.
2. Remove fuel tank.
3. Remove fuel pump assembly by turning cam lock ring counterclockwise. Lift assembly from fuel tank and remove fuel pump from fuel tank sending unit.
4. Reverse procedure to install.

FUEL FILTER
REPLACE

1. Relieve fuel system pressure as outlined under "Fuel System Pressure Relief."
2. Raise and support vehicle.
3. Remove bracket attaching screw and filter bracket, **Fig. 12.**
4. Grasp filter and fuel line fitting. Twist quick-connect fitting 1/4 turn in each direction to loosen any dirt within fitting.
5. Using compressed air, blow out dirt from quick-connect fitting.
6. Remove feed pipe nut from fuel filter, then drain any remaining fuel into an suitable container.
7. Remove fuel filter.
8. Reverse procedure to install.

1	**FUEL SENDER**
2	**FUEL TANK**
3	**QUICK CONNECT FITTINGS**
4	**IN-LINE FUEL FILTER BRACKET**
5	**FILTER BRACKET ATTACHING SCREW**

Fig. 14   Fuel filter replacement

1. ROUTING WITHOUT AIR CONDITIONING
2. ROUTING WITH AIR CONDITIONING
3. TENSIONER – ROTATE DRIVE BELT TENSIONER IN DIRECTION OF ARROW TO INSTALL OR REMOVE DRIVE BELT.

Fig. 15   Serpentine drive belt routing

Fig. 16   Drive belt tensioner removal

SERPENTINE DRIVE BELT

BELT ROUTING

Refer to **Fig. 15**, for routing of serpentine drive belt.

TENSIONER INSPECTION

1. Run engine, with no accessories on, until normal operating temperature is reached. Shut engine off and read belt tension using belt tension gauge J-23600-B or equivalent. Place gauge halfway between alternator and power steering pump.

2. Start engine, with accessories off, and allow system to stabilize for 15 seconds. Turn engine off. Using a 15 mm socket, apply clockwise force to tensioner pulley bolt. Release force and immediately take a tension reading without disturbing belt tensioner position.

3. Using 15 mm socket, apply counter-clockwise force to tensioner pulley bolt, raise pulley to eliminate all tension. Slowly lower pulley to belt and take a tension reading without disturbing belt tensioner position.

4. Average three readings. If average is not between 50-70 lbs. and belt is within tensioner's operating range, replace belt tensioner.

TENSIONER, REPLACE

1. Partially drain cooling system, then remove serpentine drive belt.
2. Remove power steering pump bolt from tensioner. Position pump aside.
3. Remove tensioner attaching bolts, then tensioner, **Fig. 16**.
4. Reverse procedure to install, torquing all bolts/nuts to specifications.

TIGHTENING SPECIFICATIONS

Year	Component	Torque/Ft. Lbs.	Year	Component	Torque/Ft. Lbs.
1991-92	Belt Tensioner Bolt	37	1991-92 —Cont'd	Exhaust Manifold Bolt	①
	Camshaft Thrust Plate Bolt	7.5		Flywheel To Crankshaft Bolt (Automatic)	55
	Connecting Rod Nuts	29		Flywheel To Crankshaft Bolt (Manual)	69
	Cylinder Head Bolts	①		Force Balancer to Block Bolts	①
	EGR Valve To Manifold Bolt	16		Front Cover Bolt	7.5
	Engine Bracket To Engine Bolt	40		Harmonic Balancer Bolt	162
	Engine Lift Brackets	37		Intake Manifold Bolt	25 ③
	Engine Mount To Bracket Nut	35		Main Bearing To Block Bolt	65
	Engine Mount To Frame Nut	35		Oil Filter Access Plug	②
	Engine Torque Strut Bolt/Nut	41		Oil Indicator Fill Tube Nut	17
	Engine Torque Strut Bracket Bolt	17			

Continued

TIGHTENING SPECIFICATIONS—Continued

Year	Component	Torque/ Ft. Lbs.	Year	Component	Torque/ Ft. Lbs.
1991-92 —Cont'd	Oil Pan Bolt	7.5	1991-92 —Cont'd	Throttle Body Injection Assembly	18
	Oil Pan Drain Plug	25		Transaxle Mount To Bracket Nut	33
	Oil Pump Cover Bolt	7.5		Transaxle Mount To Frame Nut	33
	Pushrod Cover Nut	7.5		Water Outlet Housing Bolt	20
	Rocker Arm Bolt	20		Water Pump To Block	25
	Rocker Arm Cover Bolt	6.6			
	Stud Roller Lifter Guide Retainer To Block	7.5			
	Thermostat Housing Bolt	20			

①—Refer to text.
②—Finger tight, then an additional ¼ turn.
③—Refer to text.

3.1L/V6-189 Engine

INDEX

PRECAUTIONS

AIRBAG SYSTEM DISARMING

The diagnostic energy reserve module (DERM) can maintain voltage to cause a system deployment for up to ten minutes after the ignition switch is turned off and the battery is disconnected. Servicing the SIR system during this period may result in accidental deployment and personal injury.

1. Ensure front wheels are pointed straight ahead.
2. Turn ignition switch to Lock position and remove SIR fuse from fuse block.
3. Remove Connector Position Assurance (CPA), then disconnect yellow two-way SIR electrical connector at base of steering column.

AIRBAG SYSTEM ARMING

1. Connect yellow two-way SIR electrical connector at base of column, then install Connector Position Assurance (CPA).
2. Install SIR fuse into fuse block, turn ignition switch to RUN position and ensure that "Inflatable Restraint" lamp flashes 7 to 9 times and then shuts off.

FUEL SYSTEM PRESSURE RELIEF

Whenever the fuel lines are to be disconnected for engine service on fuel injected engines, relieve fuel system pressure following the procedures outlined below. Failure to follow these procedures exactly, may result in personal injury.

1. Disconnect battery ground cable, then loosen filler cap to relieve tank vapor pressure.
2. Connect fuel pressure gauge No. J-34730-1 or equivalent to fuel pressure valve. Wrap a shop towel around fitting while connecting gauge to avoid spillage.
3. Install bleed hose into an approved container and open valve to bleed system pressure. Fuel connections are now safe for servicing.
4. Drain any fuel remaining in gauge into approved container.

ENGINE MOUNTS REPLACE

1. Disconnect battery ground cable, then remove mount retaining nuts from below frame mounting bracket.
2. Remove transaxle mount nuts, then install suitable engine support fixture.

3. Raise engine only enough to provide clearance for mount removal.
4. Remove mount to engine bracket nuts, then mount **Fig. 1**.
5. Reverse procedure to install, torquing bolts/nuts to specifications.

ENGINE REPLACE

1. Disconnect battery cables, then drain cooling system.
2. Remove air cleaner assembly, including air flow duct from throttle body, then all necessary wiring.
3. Remove hood, then disconnect throttle, T.V. and cruise control cables.
4. Remove fuel lines. Refer to "Fuel System Pressure Relief" for fuel pressure bleed procedure.
5. Remove crossover pipe from manifolds, then serpentine drive belt.
6. Remove radiator and heater hoses from engine, then A/C bolts at front bracket.
7. Remove power steering pump and position aside, then remove alternator, if necessary.
8. Remove brake booster vacuum supply line, then EGR at exhaust, if equipped.

Fig. 1   Engine mounts

1	PLENUM	4	GASKET
2	BOLT (9)	5	BOLT (4)
3	FUEL RAIL ASM		

Fig. 2   Plenum & fuel rail removal

9. Raise and support vehicle, then remove A/C compressor bolts at rear bracket. Position compressor aside.
10. Remove A.I.R. pump, if equipped, then flywheel cover.
11. Remove starter, then torque converter bolts.
12. Remove transaxle bracket. then exhaust pipe from manifold.
13. Remove engine front mount retaining nuts, then lower vehicle.
14. Remove engine torque strut(s), then bulkhead connector.
15. Support transaxle, then remove transaxle attaching bolts.
16. Attach suitable lifting device to engine, then remove engine from vehicle.
17. Reverse procedure to install, torquing all bolts/nuts to specifications.

INTAKE MANIFOLD
REPLACE

1. Remove air cleaner assembly, including air flow duct from throttle body, then disconnect battery ground cable.
2. Remove all cables at throttle body, then disconnect brake vacuum pipe at plenum.
3. Remove cable bracket at plenum, then all necessary vacuum lines.
4. Remove EGR valve, throttle body and ignition wire plastic shield bolts from plenum.

1	TIGHTEN IN PROPER SEQUENCE	2	INTAKE MANIFOLD
		3	GASKET
		4	CYLINDER HEAD
		5	SEALER

⑦ ④ ③ ⑥
⑧ ① ② ⑤

Fig. 3   Intake manifold tightening sequence

5. Remove plenum attaching bolts, then plenum, **Fig. 2.**
6. Remove fuel lines at fuel rail. Refer to "Fuel System Pressure Relief" for fuel pressure bleed procedure.
7. Remove serpentine drive belt, then al-

ternator. Position alternator aside.
8. Remove power steering lines at alternator bracket, then power steering pump mounting bolts. Position pump aside.
9. Remove wiring from fuel injectors, then drain cooling system.
10. Remove bypass hose at water pump and cylinder head.
11. Remove PCV hose, then front valve cover.
12. Remove alternator brace and bracket, then rear valve cover.
13. Remove upper radiator hose, then all necessary wiring.
14. Remove coolant sensor, then fuel lines at bracket.
15. Remove throttle body heater hose, then heater pipe at intake.
16. Remove intake manifold attaching bolts, then intake manifold. **Ensure washers are retained in their original positions on four center bolts.**
17. Loosen rocker arms, then remove pushrods. **Intake and exhaust pushrods are different lengths with exhaust pushrods being longer of the two.**
18. Reverse procedure to install, noting the following:
    a. Place 3 mm bead of suitable RTV sealer on each ridge where front and rear of intake manifold contacts the block.
    b. **Torque** intake manifold attaching bolts to 15 ft. lbs. in sequence shown in **Fig. 3**, then retighten to 24 ft. lbs. in sequence shown in **Fig. 3**.
    c. Torque all bolts/nuts to specifications.

RH EXHAUST MANIFOLD
1 RH EXHAUST MANIFOLD
2 GASKET
4 LH EXHAUST MANIFOLD
5 SHIELD
7 CROSSOVER

Fig. 4   Removal of exhaust manifolds

1 COAT THREADS WITH SEALER
TIGHTEN IN PROPER SEQUENCE
2 CYLINDER HEAD
3 GASKET
4 CYLINDER BLOCK

TIGHTENING SEQUENCE

**Fig. 5   Cylinder head
tightening sequence**

EXHAUST MANIFOLD
REPLACE
LEFT

1. Remove battery ground cable, then air cleaner assembly.
2. Remove coolant recovery bottle, then serpentine drive belt.
3. Remove A/C compressor. Position compressor aside.
4. Remove right side torque strut, then strut mounting bracket.
5. Remove heat shield, then crossover pipe at manifolds.
6. Remove exhaust manifold attaching bolts, then manifold, **Fig. 4.**
7. Reverse procedure to install, torquing all bolts/nuts to specifications.

RIGHT

1. Remove battery ground cable, then air cleaner assembly.
2. Raise and support vehicle, then remove exhaust pipe from manifold.
3. Lower vehicle, then remove breather and mass air flow sensor.
4. Remove heat shield, then crossover at manifold.
5. Remove throttle and T.V. cables from throttle body, then throttle and T.V. cable bracket at plenum.
6. Remove oxygen sensor, then exhaust manifold attaching bolts.
7. Remove exhaust manifold, **Fig. 4.**
8. Reverse procedure to install, torquing all bolts/nuts to specifications.

CYLINDER HEAD
REPLACE
LEFT

1. Remove intake manifold as outlined under "Intake Manifold, Replace."
2. Remove left exhaust manifold as outlined under "Exhaust Manifold, Replace."
3. Remove oil level indicator, then plug wires from left cylinder head.
4. Loosen rocker arms, then remove pushrods. **Intake and exhaust pushrods are different lengths with exhaust pushrods being longer of the two.**

|0.25 OS|

**Fig. 6   Oversize valve lifter
marking**

5. Remove cylinder head attaching bolts, then cylinder head, **Fig. 5.**
6. Reverse procedure to install, noting the following:
   a. Coat cylinder head bolt threads with a suitable sealing compound.
   b. **Torque** cylinder head attaching bolts to 33 ft. lbs. in sequence shown in **Fig. 5.**
   c. Turn bolts and additional 1/4 turn in sequence shown in **Fig. 5.**
   d. Torque all bolts/nuts to specifications.

RIGHT

1. Remove intake manifold as outlined under "Intake Manifold, Replace."
2. Remove right exhaust manifold as outlined under "Exhaust Manifold, Replace."
3. Remove plug wires from right cylinder head.
4. Loosen rocker arms, then remove pushrods. **Intake and exhaust pushrods are different lengths with exhaust pushrods being longer of the two.**
5. Remove cylinder head attaching bolts, then cylinder head, **Fig. 5.**
6. Reverse procedure to install, noting the following:
   a. Coat cylinder head bolt threads with a suitable sealing compound.
   b. **Torque** cylinder head attaching bolts to 33 ft. lbs. in sequence shown in **Fig. 5.**
   c. Turn bolts and additional 1/4 turn in sequence shown in **Fig. 5.**
   d. Torque all bolts/nuts to specifications.

VALVE ARRANGEMENT
FRONT TO REAR

Left . . . . E-I-I-E-I-E
Right . . . . E-I-E-I-I-E

VALVE LIFTERS

Some engines will be equipped with both standard and .010 inch oversize valve lifters. The cylinder case will be marked where the oversize valve lifters are installed with a dab of white paint and .25 mm. O.S. will be stamped on the valve lifter boss, **Fig. 6.**

Failure of a hydraulic valve lifter is generally caused by an inadequate oil supply or dirt. An air leak at the intake side of the oil pump or too much oil in the engine will cause air bubbles in the oil supply to the lifters, causing them to collapse. This is a probable cause of trouble if several lifters fail to function, but air in oil is an unlikely cause of failure of a single unit.

Valve lifters can be removed after removing rocker arm covers, intake manifold, rocker stud nuts, rocker arm balls, rocker arms and pushrods.

VALVE ADJUSTMENT

1. Crank engine until mark on torsional damper is aligned with TDC mark on timing tab. Check to ensure engine is in the No. 1 cylinder firing position by placing fingers on No. 1 cylinder rocker arms as mark on damper comes near TDC mark on timing tab. If valves are not moving, the engine is in the No. 1 firing position. If valves move as damper mark nears TDC mark on timing tab, engine is in the No. 4 cylinder firing position and should be rotated one revolution to reach the No. 1 cylinder firing position.
2. With engine in the No. 1 cylinder firing position, adjust the following valves:

Fig. 7   Front cover assembly removal

1	FRONT COVER
2	GASKET
3	27 N·m (20 LB. FT.)
4	38 N·m (28 LB. FT.)
5	SEALER

Fig. 9   Piston & rod assembly

1	RING PISTON COMP UPR
2	RING — PISTON COMP LWR
3	SEGMENT — OIL CNTR RING
4	SPACER — OIL CNTR RING
5	PISTON ASM
6	BOLT SCREW
7	ROD — CONNECTING
8	PIN — PISTON

Exhaust-1, 2,3; Intake-1, 5, 6. To adjust valves, back off adjusting nut until lash is felt at push rod, then tighten adjusting nut until all lash is removed. This can be determined by rotating the push rod while tightening the adjusting nut. When all lash has been eliminated, turn adjusting nut an additional 1 1/2 turns.

3. Crank engine one revolution until mark on torsional damper and TDC mark are again aligned. This is the No. 4 cylinder firing position. With engine in this position, the following valves can be adjusted: Exhaust-4, 5 & 6; Intake-2, 3 & 4.
4. Install rocker arm covers, then start engine and check timing and idle speed.

ROCKER ARM STUDS

Rocker arm studs that are cracked or have damaged threads can be replaced. If threads in cylinder head are damaged or stripped, the head can be retapped and a helical type insert added. When installing a new rocker arm stud, torque stud to specifications.

VALVE GUIDES

Valve guides are an integral part of the cylinder head and are not removable. If valve stem clearance becomes excessive,

the valve guide should be reamed to the next oversize and the appropriate oversize valves installed. Valves are available in oversizes of .003, .015 and .030 inch.

FRONT COVER
REPLACE

1. Disconnect battery ground cable, then drain cooling system.
2. Remove serpentine drive belt, then drive belt tensioner.
3. Remove alternator and power steering pump. Position pump aside.
4. Raise and support vehicle, then remove inner splash shield.
5. Remove flywheel cover at transaxle, then starter.
6. Remove harmonic balancer as follows:
   a. Remove balancer retaining bolt. Have an assistant keep flywheel from turning.
   b. Using harmonic balancer puller No. J-24420-B, remove balancer.
7. Remove serpentine belt idler pulley, then lower oil pan.
8. Remove lower cover bolts, then lower vehicle.
9. Remove radiator hose at water pump, then heater hose at cooling system fill pipe.
10. Remove bypass and overflow hoses, then canister purge hose.
11. Remove upper cover bolts, then front cover, **Fig. 7**.
12. Reverse procedure to install, torquing all bolts/nuts to specifications.

TIMING CHAIN
REPLACE

1. Remove front cover as outlined under "Front Cover, Replace."
2. Place No. 1 piston at top dead center with marks on camshaft and crankshaft sprockets aligned, **Fig. 8**.
3. Remove camshaft sprocket bolts, then remove sprocket and timing chain. If sprocket does not come off easily, tap lower edge of sprocket with a plastic mallet.
4. If crankshaft sprocket is to be replaced, remove sprocket using a suitable puller. Install new sprocket, aligning key and keyway.
5. Install timing chain on camshaft sprocket. Hold sprocket vertically with chain hanging down and align marks on camshaft and crankshaft sprockets.

Fig. 8   Aligning timing marks

1	OIL RING SPACER GAP (TANG IN HOLE OR SLOT WITH ARC)
2	OIL RING RAIL GAPS
3	2ND COMPRESSION RING GAP
4	TOP COMPRESSION RING GAP

Fig. 10   Locating pin ring gaps

6. Align dowel pin hole in sprocket with dowel pin on camshaft, then install sprocket on camshaft.
7. Using camshaft sprocket attaching bolts, draw sprocket on camshaft. Torque bolts to specifications.
8. Lubricate timing chain with engine oil, then install front cover as outlined previously.

CAMSHAFT
REPLACE

1. Remove engine from vehicle as described under "Engine, Replace."
2. Remove pushrods and valve lifters.
3. Remove front cover as outlined under "Front Cover, Replace."
4. Remove timing chain and sprocket as outlined under "Timing Chain, Replace."
5. Withdraw camshaft from engine, using care not to damage camshaft bearings.
6. Reverse procedure to install. When installing timing chain, align valve timing marks as shown in **Fig. 8**.

PISTON & ROD
ASSEMBLY

Assemble piston to rod with mark on piston and rod both facing toward front of engine, **Fig. 9**. Rod may not be marked.

2 OIL PUMP DRIVE

3 OIL PUMP

Fig. 11 Oil pump removal

Fig. 12 Oil pump exploded view

Fig. 13 Rear main bearing oil seal installation

PISTONS, PINS & RINGS

Install rings on pistons as shown in **Fig. 10**.

Pistons, pins and rings are available in standard and oversizes.

MAIN & ROD BEARINGS

Main and rod bearings are available in standard size and undersizes.

OIL PAN
REPLACE

1. Remove battery ground cable, then serpentine drive belt and tensioner.
2. Support vehicle using support fixtures No. J-28467-A and J-36462 or equivalent.
3. Raise and support vehicle, then drain engine oil from crankcase.
4. Remove right side wheel assembly, then right side splash shield.
5. Remove steering gear pinch bolt. **Failure to disconnect intermediate shaft from rack and pinion stub shaft can result in damage to steering gear and/or intermediate shaft.**
6. Remove transaxle mount retaining nut, then engine to frame mount nuts.
7. Remove front engine mount bracket from block, then outboard flywheel/starter plastic shield.
8. Remove inboard flywheel metal shield, then start.
9. Place jack stand under frame front center crossmember, then loosen rear frame bolts. **Do not remove rear frame bolts.**
10. Remove front frame bolts, then lower front of frame.
11. Disconnect DIS sensor wire, then remove oil pan retaining bolts.
12. Remove oil pan retaining nuts, then oil pan.
13. Reverse procedure to install, torquing all bolts/nuts to specifications.

1. WATER OUTLET
2. THERMOSTAT
3. INLET MANIFOLD
4. BLEEDER
5. 25 N·m (18 LB. FT.)

Fig. 14 Thermostat & housing assembly

OIL PUMP SERVICE
REMOVAL

1. Remove oil pan as described under "Oil Pan, Replace."
2. Remove pump to rear main bearing cap bolt and remove pump and extension shaft, **Fig. 11.**

DISASSEMBLY

1. Remove pump cover attaching bolts and pump cover, **Fig. 12.**
2. Mark drive and idler gear teeth so they can be installed in the same position, then remove idler and drive gear and shaft from pump body.
3. Remove pin, spring and pressure regulator valve from pump cover.
4. If pickup tube and screen assembly are to be replaced, mount pump cover in a soft jawed vise and remove pickup tube from cover. Do not remove screen from pickup tube, these components are serviced as an assembly.

INSPECTION

1. Inspect pump body and cover for excessive wear and cracks.
2. Inspect pump gear for damage or excessive wear. If pump gears are damaged or worn, the entire pump assembly must be replaced.
3. Check drive gear shaft for looseness in pump body.
4. Inspect pump cover for wear that would allow oil to leak past gear teeth.
5. Inspect pickup tube and screen assembly for damage.
6. Check pressure regulator valve for fit in pump cover.

ASSEMBLY

1. If pickup tube and screen were removed, apply sealer to end of pickup tube, then mount pump cover in a soft jawed vise and using mounting tool No. J-8369 or equivalent, tap pickup tube into position using a plastic mallet. **Whenever the pickup tube and screen assembly has been removed, a new pickup tube and screen assembly should be installed. Use care when installing pickup tube and screen assembly so that tube does not twist, shear or collapse. Loss of a press fit condition could result in an air leak and a loss of oil pressure.**
2. Install pressure regulator valve, spring and pin, **Fig. 12.**
3. Install drive gear and shaft in pump body.
4. Align marks made during disassembly, then install idler gear.
5. Install pump cover gasket, cover and attaching bolts. Torque bolts to specifications.
6. Rotate pump drive shaft by hand and check pump for smooth operation.

INSTALLATION

1. Assemble pump and extension shaft with retainer to rear main bearing cap, aligning extension shaft with drive gear.
2. Install pump to rear main bearing cap bolt.
3. Install oil pan as described under "Oil Pan, Replace."

1—WATER PUMP

2—GASKET

3—BOLTS

4—LOCATOR · MUST BE VERTICAL

**Fig. 15 Water pump assembly
replacement**

REAR MAIN BEARING OIL SEAL
REPLACE

1. Remove transaxle and flywheel.
2. Using a screwdriver, pry out old seal. Use care to avoid damaging crankshaft. File all burrs or nicks as required.
3. Install new seal using seal installer No. J34686 or equivalent, as follows:
   a. Apply a light coat of engine oil to I.D. and O.D. of oil seal.
   b. Slide seal over tool mandrel until dust lip bottoms squarely against collar of tool.
   c. Align dowel pin of tool with dowel pin hole in crankshaft, **Fig. 13,** then attach tool to crankshaft with screw provided.
   d. Turn handle of tool until seal is pushed into bore and collar is positioned firmly against case. Remove tool.
4. Install flywheel and transmission, then start engine and check for leaks.

COOLING SYSTEM BLEED

These engines do not require a specified bleed procedure. After filling cooling system, run engine to operating temperature with radiator/pressure cap off. Air will then be automatically bled through cap opening.

Open air bleed vent on bypass pipe three turns when draining system. The engine has two engine drain plug.

THERMOSTAT
REPLACE

Refer to **Fig. 14** when performing the following procedure.

1   FUEL SENDER
2   FUEL TANK
3   QUICK CONNECT FITTINGS
4   IN-LINE FUEL FILTER BRACKET
5   FILTER BRACKET ATTACHING SCREW

Fig. 16   Fuel filter replacement

1. Disconnect battery ground cable.
2. With engine cool, drain engine coolant below thermostat level. **Never open cooling system with engine hot.**
3. Disconnect radiator hose from thermostat housing.
4. Remove thermostat housing retaining bolts, then the housing, gasket and thermostat.
5. Reverse procedure to install, noting the following:
   a. Ensure thermostat gasket area is thoroughly clean.
   b. Install thermostat with new gasket.
   c. Apply a suitable sealer to thermostat housing retaining bolts. Install and **torque** bolts to 18 ft. lbs.
   d. Refill and bleed cooling system as necessary.

WATER PUMP
REPLACE

1. Disconnect battery ground cable, then drain cooling system.
2. Remove vacuum line from top of coolant pump.
3. Remove serpentine drive belt, then water pump pulley.
4. Remove water pump attaching bolts, then water pump **Fig. 15.**
5. Reverse procedure to install. Torque all bolts/nuts to specifications.

FUEL PUMP
REPLACE

1. Relieve fuel pressure as outlined under "Fuel System Pressure Relief,"

then disconnect battery ground cable.
2. Remove fuel tank.
3. Remove fuel pump assembly by turning cam lock ring counterclockwise. Lift assembly from fuel tank and remove fuel pump from fuel tank sending unit.
4. Reverse procedure to install.

FUEL FILTER
REPLACE

1. Relieve fuel system pressure as outlined under "Fuel System Pressure Relief."
2. Raise and support vehicle.
3. Remove bracket attaching screw and filter bracket, **Fig. 16.**
4. Grasp filter and fuel line fitting. Twist quick-connect fitting 1/4 turn in each direction to loosen any dirt within fitting.
5. Using compressed air, blow out dirt from quick-connect fitting.
6. Remove feed pipe nut from fuel filter, then drain any remaining fuel into an suitable container.
7. Remove fuel filter.
8. Reverse procedure to install.

SERPENTINE DRIVE BELT

BELT ROUTING

Refer to **Fig. 17,** for routing of serpentine drive belt.

A INSERT BREAKER BAR HERE
1 GENERATOR
2 SERPENTINE BELT
3 WATER PUMP
4 AIR CONDITIONING COMPRESSOR
5 CRANKSHAFT
6 BELT TENSIONER
7 POWER STEERING PUMP

Fig. 17 Serpentine drive belt routing

TENSIONER INSPECTION

1. Run engine, with no accessories on, until normal operating temperature is reached. Turn engine off and read belt tension using belt tension gauge J-23600-B or equivalent. Place gauge halfway between alternator and power steering pump.
2. Start engine, with accessories off, and allow system to stabilize for 15 seconds. Turn engine off. Using a 15 mm socket, apply clockwise force to tensioner pulley bolt. Release force and immediately take a tension reading without disturbing belt tensioner position.
3. Using a 15 mm socket, apply counterclockwise force to tensioner pulley bolt, raise pulley to eliminate all tension. Slowly lower pulley to belt and take a tension reading without disturbing belt tensioner position.
4. Average three readings. If average is not between 50-70 lbs. and belt is within tensioner's operating range, replace belt tensioner.

TENSIONER, REPLACE

1. Remove serpentine drive belt.
2. Remove tensioner attaching bolts, then tensioner, **Fig. 18.**

THE INDICATOR MARK ON THE MOVEABLE PORTION OF THE TESNIONER MUST BE WITHIN THE LIMITS OF THE SLOTTED AREA ON THE STATIONARY PORTION OF THE TENSIONER. ANY READING OUTSIDE THESE LIMITS INDICATES EITHER A DEFECTIVE BELT OR TENSIONER.

Fig. 18 Belt tensioner replacement

3. Reverse procedure to install, torquing all bolts/nuts specifications.

TIGHTENING SPECIFICATIONS

Year	Component	Torque/ Ft. Lbs.
1991-93	Camshaft Sprocket Bolt	21
	Connecting Rod Nut	39
	Cylinder Head Bolt	②
	Drive Belt Tensioner Bolt	37
	Engine Bracket To Engine Bolt	81
	Engine Bracket To Engine Mount Nut	34
	Engine Mount To Frame Nut	34
	Engine Strut Bracket To Engine Bolt	17
	Engine Strut To Tie Bar Bracket	41
	Engine Strut To Upper Tie Bar	17
	Exhaust Crossover Nut	18
	Exhaust Manifold Heat Shield Nut	89①
	Exhaust Manifold To Cylinder Head Bolt	18
	Flywheel Bolt	52
	Front Cover Bolt	③
	Intake Manifold Bolt	②
	Main Bearing Cap Bolt	73
	Oil Filter	11
	Oil Filter Adapter Connector	50

Year	Component	Torque/ Ft. Lbs.
1991-93 —Cont'd	Oil Level Indicator Retaining Nut	18
	Oil Pan Bolt	89①
	Oil Pan Nut	89①
	Oil Pan Rear Bolts (2)	18
	Oil Pan Stud To Cylinder Block	89①
	Oil Pump Drive Bolt	25
	Oil Pump Mounting Bolt	30
	Oxygen Sensor	31
	Rocker Arm Cover Bolt	89①
	Rocker Arm Nut	18
	Spark Plug	10-25
	Thermostat Housing	15-23
	Timing Chain Dampener Bolt	15
	Torsional Dampener (Harmonic Balancer)	76
	Water Pump	89①

①—Inch lbs.
②—Refer to text.
③—Refer to Fig. 7.

3.3L/V6-204 Engine

INDEX

PRECAUTIONS

AIRBAG SYSTEM DISARMING

The diagnostic energy reserve module (DERM) can maintain voltage to cause a system deployment for up to ten minutes after the ignition switch is turned off and the battery is disconnected. Servicing the SIR system during this period may result in accidental deployment and personal injury.

1. Ensure front wheels are pointed straight ahead.
2. Turn ignition switch to Lock position and remove SIR fuse from fuse block.
3. Remove Connector Position Assurance (CPA), then disconnect yellow two-way SIR electrical connector at base of steering column.

AIRBAG SYSTEM ARMING

1. Connect yellow two-way SIR electrical connector at base of column, then install Connector Position Assurance (CPA).
2. Install SIR fuse into fuse block, turn ignition switch to RUN position and ensure that "Inflatable Restraint" lamp flashes 7 to 9 times and then shuts off.

FUEL SYSTEM PRESSURE RELIEF

Whenever the fuel lines are to be disconnected for engine service on fuel injected engines, relieve fuel system pressure following the procedures outlined below. Failure to follow these procedures exactly, may result in personal injury.

1. Disconnect battery ground cable, then loosen filler cap to relieve tank vapor pressure.
2. Connect fuel pressure gauge No. J-34730-1 or equivalent to fuel pressure valve. Wrap a shop towel around fitting while connecting gauge to avoid spillage.
3. Install bleed hose into an approved

1	BRACKET
2	BOLT
3	MOUNT
4	NUT
5	BOLT
6	HEAT SHIELD
7	BRACKET

VIEW A

Fig. 1   Engine mount removal

container and open valve to bleed system pressure. Fuel connections are now safe for servicing.
4. Drain any fuel remaining in gauge into approved container.

ENGINE MOUNTS REPLACE

1. Attach suitable engine lifting fixture to engine.
2. Raise and support front of vehicle.
3. Remove mount to engine mount bracket nuts. Raise engine slightly

and remove mount to frame nuts. Remove mount, **Fig. 1**.
4. Reverse procedure to install, torquing all bolts/nuts to specifications.

ENGINE REPLACE

1. Remove hood, then disconnect battery ground cable.
2. Drain cooling system, then remove radiator and heater hoses.
3. Remove upper engine torque strut, then engine cooling fan.
4. Remove air intake duct from throttle body, then vacuum hosing to all non-engine mounted components.
5. Remove fuel lines. Refer to "Fuel System Pressure Relief" for fuel pressure bleed procedure.
6. Remove all cables from throttle body, then cable bracket.
7. Remove serpentine drive belt, then disconnect all necessary electrical connections.
8. Remove power steering pump from mounting bracket. Position pump aside.
9. Remove upper transaxle to engine bolts, then raise and support vehicle.
10. Remove A/C compressor. Position compressor aside.
11. Remove engine mount to frame nuts, then exhaust pipe from exhaust manifold.
12. Remove flywheel dust cover, then flywheel to converter bolts. Mark torque converter and flywheel to assure proper assembly.
13. Remove lower engine to transaxle bolts. **One bolt is located between transaxle case and engine block and is installed in the opposite direction.**
14. Lower car, then install engine lift fixture.
15. Remove engine.
16. Reverse procedure to install, torquing all bolts/nuts to specifications.

Fig. 2 Intake manifold tightening sequence

Fig. 3 Cylinder head tightening sequence

1—ROLLER
2—LIFTER BODY
3—PLUNGER SPRING
4—BALL CHECK RETAINER
5—BALL CHECK SPRING
6—BALL CHECK
7—PLUNGER
8—OIL METERING VALVE
9—PUSH ROD SEAT
10—RETAINER RING

Fig. 4 Exploded view of roller type hydraulic valve lifter

INTAKE MANIFOLD
REPLACE

1. Disconnect battery ground cable, then drain cooling system.
2. Remove serpentine drive belt, then alternator and bracket.
3. Remove power steering pump braces, then coolant bypass hose.
4. Remove air inlet duct, heater pipe and upper radiator hose.
5. Remove throttle cable bracket and cables from throttle body.
6. Remove vacuum lines and wiring connectors as necessary.
7. Remove fuel lines. Refer to "Fuel System Pressure Relief" for fuel pressure bleed procedure.
8. Remove heater hose from throttle body.
9. Remove intake manifold attaching bolts, then intake manifold.
10. Reverse procedure to install, noting the following:
    a. Apply suitable sealer to ends of manifold seals.
    b. Apply thread lock compound No. 12345493 or equivalent, to intake manifold bolt threads before assembly.
    c. **Torque** intake manifold bolts twice to 89 inch lbs., in sequence shown in **Fig. 2.**

EXHAUST MANIFOLD
REPLACE
LEFT

1. Disconnect battery ground cable, then remove air cleaner inlet duct.
2. Remove spark plug wires, then ex-

haust crossover pipe to manifold attaching bolts.
3. Remove engine lift hook, then manifold heat shield.
4. Remove oil level indicator tube, then manifold studs.
5. Remove exhaust manifold.
6. Reverse procedure to install, torquing all studs/nuts to specifications.

RIGHT

1. Disconnect battery ground cable, then remove spark plug wires.
2. Disconnect oxygen sensor lead, then remove throttle cable bracket and cables from throttle body.
3. Remove brake booster hose from manifold, then exhaust crossover pipe to manifold attaching bolts.
4. Remove exhaust pipe from manifold, then engine lift hook.
5. Remove transaxle oil level indicator tube, then manifold heat shield.
6. Remove manifold studs, then exhaust manifold.
7. Reverse procedure to install, torquing all studs/nuts to specifications.

CYLINDER HEAD
REPLACE

1. Remove intake manifold as outlined under "Intake Manifold, Replace."
2. Remove exhaust manifolds as outlined under "Exhaust Manifold, Replace."
3. Remove valve covers.
4. **For left cylinder head removal,** remove alternator bracket with ignition module and coils attached.
5. Remove A/C compressor bracket bolt, then power steering pump. Position pump aside.
6. **For right cylinder head removal,** remove serpentine drive belt, then tensioner assembly.
7. **For either cylinder head removal,** remove spark plug wires, rocker arm assemblies, guide plate and pushrods.
8. Remove cylinder head attaching bolts, then cylinder head.

9. Reverse procedure to install, noting the following:
   a. Apply sealant No. 1052080 or equivalent to underside of cylinder head bolt heads.
   b. Apply thread locker No. 12345382 or equivalent to bolt threads.
   c. Using sequence shown in **Fig. 3, torque** cylinder head bolts to 35 ft. lbs.
   d. Rotate each bolt an additional 130° using sequence shown in **Fig. 3,** then rotate the center four bolts 30° using the same sequence.
   e. Apply thread locker No. 12345493 or equivalent to rocker arm pedestal bolts before assembly.
   f. Torque all bolts/nuts to specifications.

VALVE ARRANGEMENT
FRONT TO REAR

Left side..................... E-I-E-I-I-E
Right side .... E-I-I-E-I-E

VALVE LIFTERS

Failure of an hydraulic valve lifter, **Fig. 4,** is generally caused by dirt or an inadequate oil supply. An air leak at the intake side of the oil pump or too much oil in the engine will cause air bubbles in the oil supply to the lifters, causing them to collapse. This is a probable cause of trouble if several lifters fail to function, but air in the oil is an unlikely cause of failure of a single unit.

The valve lifters may be lifted out of their bores after removing the rocker arms, pushrods and intake manifold. Adjustable pliers with taped jaws may be used to remove lifters that are stuck due to varnish, carbon, etc. Roller type lifters are used to reduce friction and improve performance. The lifters are cylindrical with the exception of two parallel flats milled into the upper part of the body. Slotted guides which hold the lifters in pairs fit over the milled area to keep the lifters from turning in their bores.

Fig. 5   Adjusting crankshaft sensor

ROCKER ARMS

Rocker arms are mounted to the cylinder head via individual iron pedestals and are retained by hardened steel bolts.

To install rocker arms, position pedestal retainer, rocker arm and pedestal onto cylinder head. Install retaining bolts and torque to specification.

VALVE CLEARANCE SPECIFICATIONS

These engines are equipped with hydraulic lifters. No provision for adjustment is provided.

VALVE GUIDES

The valve guides are an integral part of the cylinder head and cannot be replaced.

If valve stem clearance is excessive, the valve guide must be reamed and an oversize valve installed. Valves are available in oversize of .010 inch.

FRONT COVER
REPLACE

1. Disconnect battery ground cable and drain cooling system.
2. Remove serpentine drive belt, then heater hoses.
3. Disconnect lower radiator and coolant bypass hoses from cover.
4. Raise and support vehicle, then remove right front wheel.
5. Remove right inner fender splash shield.
6. Remove torque converter cover, then prevent flywheel from turning using suitable tool.
7. Remove balancer bolt and washer, then remove balancer assembly.
8. Disconnect electrical connections at camshaft, crankshaft and oil pressure sensors.
9. Remove bolts attaching front cover to cylinder block, then oil pan to front cover bolts.
10. Remove front cover assembly and gasket.

11. Reverse procedure to install, noting the following:
    a. Adjust crankshaft sensor using tool shown in **Fig. 5**.
    b. When reinstalling front cover bolts, apply a suitable sealer to the threads to prevent leakage.
    c. Torque all bolts/nuts to specifications.

TIMING CHAIN
REPLACE

1. Remove front cover as outlined under "Front Cover, Replace."
2. Temporarily install balancer bolt and washer in end of crankshaft. Turn crankshaft so timing marks on sprockets are as close together as possible. Remove balancer bolt and washer using a sharp blow on wrench handle, so bolt can be removed without changing position of sprockets.
3. Remove timing chain dampener, then and camshaft sprocket bolts.
4. Using two large screwdrivers, alternately pry off sprockets and chain.
5. Reverse procedure to install. Assemble timing chain on sprockets and slide sprockets and chain assembly onto camshaft and crankshaft with timing marks aligned as shown in **Fig. 6.**
6. Torque all bolts and nuts to specifications.

CAMSHAFT
REPLACE

1. Remove engine as outlined under "Engine, Replace."
2. Remove intake manifold as outlined under "Intake Manifold, Replace."
3. Remove rocker arm covers.
4. Remove rocker arms, pushrods and valve lifters.
5. Remove front cover as outlined under "Front Cover, Replace."
6. Align timing marks of camshaft and crankshaft sprocket. Remove timing chain and sprockets.
7. Remove cam sensor magnet assembly and camshaft thrust plate if applicable.

Fig. 6   Valve timing marks

8. Slide camshaft forward out of bearing bores, using care so as not to damage bearing surfaces.
9. Reverse procedure to install, noting the following:
    a. Ensure crankshaft and camshaft timing marks as shown in **Fig. 6.**
    b. Torque all bolts/nuts to specifications.

PISTON & ROD ASSEMBLE

Pistons can be installed on connecting rod in either direction.

Piston/connecting rod assembly must be installed in engine as shown in **Fig. 7.**

PISTONS, PINS & RINGS

Install rings on piston as shown in **Fig. 8.**

Pistons are available in standard sizes and oversize of .010 inch. Rings are available in standard sizes and oversize of .010 inch. Piston pins are supplied with piston and available only in standard sizes.

MAIN & ROD BEARINGS

Main and connecting rod bearings are available in standard sizes and undersizes of .0005, .0010 and .0015 inch.

OIL PAN
REPLACE

1. Disconnect battery ground cable, then raise and support vehicle.
2. Drain engine oil, then remove flywheel cover.
3. Remove starter, then oil filter.
4. Remove oil pan attaching bolts, then oil pan.
5. Remove and discard old oil pan gasket.

Fig. 7 Piston and rod assembly

1—OIL RING SPACER GAP
  (TANG IN HOLE OR SLOT WITH ARC)
2—OIL RING RAIL GAPS
3—2ND COMPRESSION RING GAP
4—TOP COMPRESSION RING GAP

Fig. 8 Piston ring end gap locations

Fig. 9 Oil pump and housing assembly

Fig. 10 Checking inner gear tip clearance

6. Reverse procedure to install, torquing all bolts/nuts to specifications.

OIL PUMP SERVICE
REMOVAL & INSPECTION

1. Remove front cover, then the oil filter adapter, pressure regulator valve and valve spring.
2. Remove oil pump cover attaching screws, cover and gears, **Fig. 9**.
3. Inspect pump cover and housing for cracks, scoring, porosity and damaged threads, pressure regulator valve and spring for sticking, scoring or tension loss and gears for chipping, galling or excessive wear. Replace as necessary.
4. Check gear clearance as follows:
   a. Check inner gear tip clearance with feeler gauge as shown in **Fig. 10**. Maximum clearance should not exceed .006 inch.
   b. Check outer gear diameter clearance with feeler gauge as shown in **Fig. 11**. Clearance should be .008-.015 inch.
   c. Check gear end clearance (gear drop in housing) as shown in **Fig. 12**. Clearance should be .001-.0035 inch.
5. Replace parts as necessary.

ASSEMBLY & INSTALLATION

1. Lubricate gears with petroleum jelly, then install into oil pump housing.
2. Pack gear cavity with petroleum jelly, then install pump cover and attaching screws. Torque attaching screws to specifications.

Fig. 11 Checking outer gear diameter clearance

3. Install pressure regulator valve spring and valve.
4. Install oil filter adapter using new gasket. Torque adapter bolts to specifications.
5. Reinstall front cover onto engine.

REAR MAIN BEARING OIL SEAL REPAIR

1. Remove transaxle and flywheel.
2. Using a screwdriver, pry out old seal. Use care to avoid damaging crankshaft. File all burrs or nicks as required.
3. Install new seal using seal installer No. J38196 or equivalent, as follows:
   a. Apply a light coat of engine oil to I.D. and O.D. of oil seal.
   b. Slide seal over tool mandrel until dust lip bottoms squarely against collar of tool.
   c. Align dowel pin of tool with dowel pin hole in crankshaft, **Fig. 13**, then attach tool to crankshaft with screw provided.
   d. Turn handle of tool until seal is pushed into bore and collar is positioned firmly against case. Remove tool.
4. Install flywheel and transmission, then start engine and check for leaks.

COOLING SYSTEM BLEED

These engines do not require a specified bleed procedure. After filling cooling

Fig. 12 Checking gear end clearance

system, run engine to operating temperature with radiator pressure cap off. Air will then be automatically bled through cap opening.

THERMOSTAT
REPLACE

Refer to **Fig. 14** when performing the following procedure.
1. Disconnect battery negative cable.
2. If necessary, remove air cleaner assembly.
3. With engine cool, drain engine coolant below thermostat level. **Never open cooling system with engine hot.**
4. Disconnect radiator hose from thermostat housing.
5. Remove thermostat housing retaining bolts, then the housing, gasket and thermostat.
6. Reverse procedure to install noting the following:
   a. Ensure thermostat gasket area is thoroughly clean.
   b. Install thermostat with new gasket.
   c. Apply a suitable sealer to thermostat housing retaining bolts. Install and **torque** bolts to 20 ft. lbs.
   d. Refill and bleed cooling system as necessary.

WATER PUMP
REPLACE

1. Disconnect battery ground cable.
2. Drain cooling system, then remove

Fig. 13   Rear main seal installation

1	INTAKE MANIFOLD	5	27 N·m (20 LB. FT.)
2	THROTTLE BODY	6	CLAMP 3 N·m (27 LB. IN.)
3	THERMOSTAT	7	OUTLET HOSE
4	OUTLET ASM.		

Fig. 14   Thermostat & housing assembly

1. WATER PUMP
2. ENGINE FRONT COVER ASM.
3. GASKET
4. 11 N·m (97 LBS. IN.)
5. 39 N·m (29 LBS. FT.)

Fig. 15   Water pump removal & installation

1   FUEL SENDER
2   FUEL TANK
3   QUICK CONNECT FITTINGS
4   IN-LINE FUEL FILTER BRACKET
5   FILTER BRACKET ATTACHING SCREW

Fig. 16   Fuel filter replacement

Fig. 17   Serpentine drive belt routing

1. DRIVE BELT TENSIONER

Fig. 18   Replacing tensioner

serpentine drive belt.
3. Remove lower radiator hose and heater hose at pump.
4. Remove water pump pulley attaching bolts. Long bolt is removed through access hole located in the body side rail.
5. Remove water pump pulley.
6. Remove water pump attaching bolts, then the water pump, **Fig. 15.**
7. Reverse procedure to install, torquing bolts to specifications.

FUEL PUMP
REPLACE

1. Relieve fuel pressure as outlined under "Fuel System Pressure Relief," then disconnect battery ground cable.
2. Remove fuel tank.
3. Remove fuel pump assembly by turn-

ing cam lock ring counterclockwise. Lift assembly from fuel tank and remove fuel pump from fuel tank sending unit.
4. Reverse procedure to install.

FUEL FILTER
REPLACE

1. Relieve fuel system pressure as outlined under "Fuel System Pressure Relief."
2. Raise and support vehicle.
3. Remove bracket attaching screw and filter bracket, **Fig. 16.**
4. Grasp filter and fuel line fitting. Twist quick-connect fitting 1/4 turn in each direction to loosen any dirt within fitting.
5. Using compressed air, blow out dirt from quick-connect fitting.
6. Remove feed pipe nut from fuel filter,

then drain any remaining fuel into an suitable container.
7. Remove fuel filter.
8. Reverse procedure to install.

SERPENTINE DRIVE BELT
BELT ROUTING

Refer to **Fig. 17,** for routing of serpentine drive belt.

TENSIONER INSPECTION

1. Run engine, with no accessories on, until normal operating temperature is reached. Turn engine off and read belt

tension using belt tension gauge J-23600-B or equivalent. On models equipped with A/C, place gauge half-way between alternator and A/C compressor. On models less A/C, place gauge halfway between power steering pump and crankshaft pulley.

2. Start engine, with accessories off, and allow system to stabilize for 15 seconds. Turn engine off. Using a 18 mm socket, apply clockwise force to ten-

sioner pulley bolt. Release force and immediately take a tension reading without disturbing belt tensioner position.

3. Using a 18 mm socket, apply counter-clockwise force to tensioner pulley bolt, raise pulley to eliminate all tension. Slowly lower pulley to belt and take a tension reading without disturbing belt tensioner position.

4. Average three readings. If average is

lower than 67 lbs. and belt is within tensioner's operating range, replace belt tensioner.

TENSIONER, REPLACE

1. Remove serpentine drive belt.
2. Remove tensioner attaching bolts, then tensioner, **Fig. 18.**
3. Reverse procedure to install, torquing all bolts/nuts specifications.

TIGHTENING SPECIFICATIONS

Year	Component	Torque/ Ft. Lbs.
1991–93	Alternator Support To Cylinder Head	37
	Alternator Support Through Generator	37
	Balancer Assembly To Crankshaft	219
	Camshaft Sensor To Front Cover	80③
	Camshaft Sprocket Bolt	26
	Camshaft Thrust Plate Bolt	11③
	Connecting Rod Bolts	①
	Coolant Temperature Sensor To Intake	15
	Crankshaft Bearing Caps To Cylinder Block	90
	Crankshaft Sensor To Front Cover	22
	Crankshaft Sensor Clamp Bolt	40③
	Cylinder Block Drain Plug	25
	Cylinder Head To Block	②
	Engine Mount Bracket To Cylinder Block	44
	Engine Mount To Cylinder Block	70
	Engine Mount To Frame	33
	Engine Mount To Engine Mount Bracket	33
	ESC Knock Sensor To Cylinder Block	13
	Exhaust Manifold To Cylinder Head	30
	Flywheel Cover To Transaxle	48③
	Flywheel To Crankshaft	61
	Front Cover To Block	22
	Fuel Feed & Return Pipes TO Fuel Rail	22
	Fuel Rail To Intake Manifold	11
	Heater Hose Pipe To Throttle Body	20
	Ignition Module To Alternator Support	18
	Intake Manifold To Cylinder Head	②
	Oil Filter Adapter To Front Cover	24

Year	Component	Torque/ Ft. Lbs.
1991–93 —Cont'd	Oil Filter Assembly To Filter Adapter	18
	Oil Galley Plugs	25
	Oil Pan Drain Plug	30
	Oil Pan To Cylinder Block	10.3
	Oil Pan To Front Cover	10.3
	Oil Pressure Switch To Oil Filter Adapter	24
	Oil Pump Cover To Timing Chain Cover	8
	Oil Screen Housing To Cylinder Block	9.5
	Oxygen Sensor To Exhaust Manifold	31
	Rocker Arm Cover To Cylinder Head	7.3
	Rocker Arm Pedestal To Cylinder Head	28
	Serpentine Belt Tensioner To Cylinder Head	37
	Spark Plug	20
	Starting Motor To Cylinder Block	35
	Strut Bracket To Manifold Studs	24
	Strut Bracket To Cylinder Head	37
	Thermostat Housing To Intake Manifold	20
	Throttle Body To Intake Manifold	20
	Throttle Cable Bracket To Throttle Body	36③
	Timing Chain Dampener	14
	Torque Converter To Flywheel	46
	Transaxle To Cylinder Block	46
	Vacuum Harness To Intake Manifold	9.5
	Valve Lifter Guide Retainer Bolts	27
	Water Pump To Front Cover	7
	Water Pump Pulley To Hub	9.5

① —20 ft. lbs., plus an additional 50°.
② —Refer to text.
③ —Inch lbs.

Rear Axle & Suspension

INDEX

1 UNDERBODY
2 INSULATOR UPPER
3 SPRING
4 LOWER INSULATOR ON A SERIES ONLY
5 TRACK BAR

Fig. 1   Rear axle & suspension

REINFORCEMENT
CONTROL ARM
CONTROL ARM BRACKET (REF)
VIEW B (TYPICAL BOTH SIDES)
POSITION CONTROL ARM BRACKETS AS SHOWN PRIOR TO INSTALLING AXLE ASM. TO UNDERBODY AND TIGHTEN NUT TO SPECIFIED TORQUE
"FRONT"
AXLE ASM.
CONTROL ARM (WELDED TO AXLE ASM.)
L.H. SIDE SHOWN (TYPICAL BOTH SIDES)

Fig. 2   Control arm bracket installation

UNDERBODY
± 15°
INSULATOR
SPRING
POSITION LEG OF UPPER COIL ON SPRINGS PARALLEL TO AXLE ASM. & TOWARDS L.H. SIDE OF VEHICLE WITHIN LIMITS SHOWN.
AXLE ASM.
± 15°
"FRONT"
LOWER SPRING INSULATOR ON "A" SERIES ONLY

Fig. 3   Coil spring & insulator installation

Fig. 4   Control arm bushing removal

DESCRIPTION

The rear suspension, **Fig. 1**, consists of a rear axle assembly, control arms, coil springs, shock absorbers, track bar and a track bar brace. The rear axle is trailing arm type design. A non-serviceable stabilizer bar is welded to the inside of the axle housing and is an integral part of the axle assembly. A single unit hub and bearing assembly is bolted to each end of the axle assembly. The hub and bearing assembly is a sealed unit and must be replaced as an assembly.

REAR AXLE, REPLACE

When removing rear axle assembly, do not use twin-post type hoist. The swing arc tendency of this axle may cause it to slip from hoist. Perform axle removal on floor if necessary.
1. Raise rear of vehicle and support rear axle using a jack.

2. Remove rear wheel assembly and brake drum. **Do not hammer on brake drum since damage to bearings may result.**
3. Disconnect parking brake cable from equalizer, then remove brake line brackets from frame.
4. Disconnect shock absorber from lower mountings on axle housing.
5. Remove track bar attaching nut and bolt, then disconnect track bar. **Do not suspend rear axle by brake hoses, otherwise damage to hoses may result.**
6. Carefully lower rear axle assembly, then remove coil spring and insulators.
7. Disconnect brake lines from control arm attachments.
8. Remove parking brake cable from rear axle attachments.
9. Remove hub attaching bolts, then the hub and bearing assembly. Position backing plate out of way.

10. Remove control arm bracket to underbody attaching bolts (four each side), then lower axle assembly and remove from vehicle.
11. Reverse procedure to install, noting the following:
   a. If control arm brackets were removed from control arms, install control arm bracket at a 40-44° angle as shown in **Fig. 2.**
   b. Torque all bolts/nuts to specifications.

HUB & BEARING ASSEMBLY, REPLACE

1. Raise and support rear of vehicle, then remove wheel and tire assembly and brake drum. **Do not hammer on brake drum since damage to bearing may result.**
2. Remove hub and bearing assembly attaching bolts, then hub and bearing assembly. Do not support brake assembly by brake line.
3. Reverse procedure to install, torquing bolts/nuts to specifications.

Fig. 5 Control arm bushing installation

COIL SPRING, REPLACE

1. Raise rear of vehicle and support rear axle using a jack.
2. Remove right and left brake line bracket attaching bolts from frame and allow brake lines to hang freely.
3. Remove track bar attaching nut and bolt at rear axle, then disconnect track bar.
4. Disconnect shock absorbers at lower mountings. **Do not suspend rear axle by brake hoses since damage to hoses may result.**
5. Carefully lower rear axle assembly, then remove springs and insulators.
6. Reverse procedure to install, **Fig. 3**.

CONTROL ARM BUSHING, REPLACE

1. Raise rear of vehicle and support rear axle under front side of spring seat using a jack.

2. If right hand side bushing is to be replaced, disconnect parking brake cable from equalizer.
3. Remove parking brake cables from bracket attachment, then position out of way.
4. Disconnect brake line bracket from frame.
5. Disconnect shock absorber from lower mounting, then pull spring out of way.
6. Remove four control arm to underbody attaching bolts, then allow control arm to rotate downward.
7. Remove nut and bolt from bracket attachment, then remove bracket.
8. The bushing can now be replaced using tools shown in **Figs. 4 and 5.** When installing bushing, cut-outs on rubber portion of bushing must face front and rear of vehicle. Press bushing in until end of bushing is aligned with scribed line on tool No. J-28685-2, **Fig. 5.**
9. Reverse procedure to install control arm. Install bracket to control arm as shown in **Fig. 2.**

TRACK BAR, REPLACE

1. Raise rear of vehicle and support rear axle using a jack.
2. Remove nut and bolt attaching track bar to axle housing and underbody, then remove track bar, **Fig. 6.**
3. Reverse procedure to install, torquing bolts/nuts to specifications.

SHOCK ABSORBER REPLACE

1. Open deck lid and remove trim cover,

1	UNDERBODY BRACKET
3	TRACK BAR
4	AXLE ASM.
6	TRACK BAR BRACE (WAGON ONLY)

Fig. 6 Track bar installation

then remove shock absorber upper attaching nut.
2. Raise rear of vehicle and support rear axle using a jack.
3. Disconnect shock absorber from lower attachment and remove shock absorber from vehicle.
4. Reverse procedure to install, torquing bolts/nuts to specifications.

TIGHTENING SPECIFICATIONS

Year	Component	Torque/ Ft. Lbs.
1991–94	Brake Line Bracket Screw	8
	Control Arm Bracket To Underbody	28
	Control Arm To Bracket Nut	84
	Hub & Bearing Assembly Bolts	44
	Shock Absorber Lower Nut	44
	Shock Absorber Mount To Body	16
	Shock Absorber Upper Nut	16
	Track Bar Bolt At Axle	44
	Track Bar Nut At Brace Or Underbody Bracket	35
	Wheel Lug Nuts	92

Front Suspension & Steering

INDEX

Fig. 1   Front suspension

Fig. 2   Front wheel bearing & hub assembly removal

1 HUB AND BEARING ASSEMBLY   4 WASHER
2 STEERING KNUCKLE   6 SEAL
3 SHIELD   8 O-RING

Fig. 3   Exploded view of hub, bearing and seal assembly

Fig. 4   Front wheel bearing seal installation

HUB, BEARING & SEAL REPLACE

Hub and bearing are replaced as an assembly.
1. Loosen hub nut with vehicle on ground.
2. Raise and support vehicle, then remove front wheel.
3. Install drive axle seal protectors. **These protectors should be used any time service is performed on or near drive axle. Failure to use them may result in interior joint or seal damage.**
4. Remove, then discard hub nut and washer.
5. Remove brake caliper from support and suspend caliper from frame with a length of wire. **Do not suspend caliper by the brake hose.** Remove rotor.
6. Using tool No. J-28733, or equivalent, separate hub and drive axle, **Fig. 2.**
7. Remove hub and bearing attaching bolts, then shield, hub and bearing assembly and O-ring, **Fig. 3.**
8. To remove factory seal, tap seal toward engine. When seal is removed from steering knuckle, cut it off drive axle using side cutters. **Factory seal is installed from engine side of steering knuckle. Replacement seal is installed from wheel side of steering knuckle.**
9. Reverse procedure to install, noting the following:
   a. Lubricate seal, then install using seal installer No. J-28671 or equivalent, **Fig. 4.**
   b. Torque bolts/nuts to specifications.

2 STUD DO NOT REMOVE
3 CONTROL ARM
4 STABILIZER SHAFT BUSHING
5 BUSHING CLAMP

Fig. 5   Control arm replacement

BALL JOINT INSPECTION

1. Raise and support front of vehicle allowing suspension to hang free.
2. Grasp tire at the top and bottom, then move top of tire in an in-and-out motion.
3. Check for any horizontal movement of the knuckle relative to the control arm.
4. If any movement or looseness is detected in the joint or if the joint seal is cut, the ball joint must be replaced.

DESCRIPTION

The front suspension, **Fig. 1,** on these vehicles is a MacPherson strut design. The lower control arms pivot from the engine cradle. This engine cradle has isolation mounts to the body and conventional rubber bushings are used for the lower control arm pivots. The upper end of the strut is isolated by a rubber mount incorporating a bearing for wheel turning. The lower end of the steering knuckle pivots on a ball stud which is retained in the lower control arm with rivets and is clamped to the steering knuckle. Sealed wheel bearings are used and are bolted to the steering knuckle.

REMOVE LOWER CONTROL ARM BUSHING

INSTALL LOWER CONTROL ARM BUSHING

1	J 21474-18-NUT	5	J 21474-19-BOLT
2	BEARING	6	J 21474-25-SPACER
3	J 21068-12 (BUSHING REMOVER)	7	J 35561-3 (BUSHING INSTALLER)
4	J 21474-5 (BUSHING RECEIVER)		

Fig. 6   Control arm bushings replacement

1 FRAME
2 STABILIZER SHAFT FRAME BUSHING
3 STABILIZER SHAFT
4 REINFORCEMENT PLATE
A INSTALL INSULATOR WITH SLIT TOWARD FRONT OF VEHICLE AS SHOWN.

Fig. 8   Stabilizer bar replacement

LOWER BALL JOINT
REPLACE

1. Raise and support vehicle, then place jack stands under suspension.
2. Lower vehicle slightly so weight of vehicle rests on jack stands, then remove wheel assembly.
3. Install drive axle seal protectors. **These protectors should be used any time service is performed on or near drive axle. Failure to use them may result in interior joint or seal damage.**
4. Remove pinch bolt, then ball joint from steering knuckle.
5. Drill out three rivets retaining ball joint. Use a 1/8 inch drill to make a pilot hole through rivets. Finish drilling rivets with 1/2 inch drill bit.
6. Loosen stabilizer shaft bushing assembly nut, then remove ball joint from control arm.
7. Reverse procedure to install, torquing bolts/nuts to specifications.

LOWER CONTROL ARM & BUSHINGS
REPLACE

1. Raise and support vehicle, then place jack stands under suspension.

1. Refer to front wheel bearing removal.
2. Remove clamp bolt. Disconnect knuckle from ball stud.
3. Remove both through bolts holding strut-to-knuckle. Remove knuckle.

NOTICE: Whenever separating the ball joint from the knuckle, be careful not to cut or tear the ball joint seal, or damage to the ball joint could occur. If the seal is cut or torn, the ball joint MUST be replaced.

INSTALL

1. Install knuckle to ball joint.
2. Loosely install knuckle to strut.
3. Refer to front wheel bearing installation.
4. Place jackstand under hub and rotor assembly and lower hoist to load control arm. Then place cam in position as noted and tighten nuts.
5. Install parts as shown.

KNUCKLE
BOLT SHOULD EASILY GO IN PLACE. IF NOT, CHECK STUD ALIGNMENT
190 N·m (140 FT. LBS.)
STRUT
TIE ROD
KNUCKLE
50 N·m (40 FT. LBS.)
CONTROL ARM
54 N·m (40 FT. LBS.)

J-6627 or BT-7101
REMOVE TIE ROD END

J-22269-01
27mm or 1-1/8" SOCKET
TIE ROD END
INSTALL TIE ROD END

Fig. 7   Steering knuckle replacement

1 STRUT ASSEMBLY
3 KNUCKLE AND HUB ASSEMBLY
4 LOWER CONTROL ARM
5 FRAME
6 BOLT/SCREW
8 MOUNT WASHER
9 SHOCK TOWER
VIEW A

Fig. 9   Strut assembly replacement

2. Lower vehicle slightly so weight of vehicle rests on jack stands, then remove wheel assembly.
3. Install drive axle seal protectors. **These protectors should be used any time service is performed on or near drive axle. Failure to use them may result in interior joint or seal damage.**
4. Remove pinch bolt holding ball joint to steering knuckle, then control arm mounting bolts.
5. Remove control arm from vehicle, **Fig. 5.**
6. Refer to **Fig. 6,** for bushing replacement procedure.
7. Reverse procedure to install, noting the following:
   a. Weight of vehicle must be supported by control arms when tight-

DISASSEMBLE AND ASSEMBLE STRUT

DISASSEMBLY	ASSEMBLY
NOTICE: Care should be taken to avoid chipping or cracking the spring coating when handling the front suspension coil spring.	
1. Mount Strut Compressor J-34013 in Holding Fixture J-3289-20.	1. Install bearing cap into Strut Compressor if previously removed.
2. Mount strut into Strut Compressor. Notice that Strut Compressor has strut mounting holes drilled for specific car lines.	2. Mount strut into Strut Compressor using bottom locking pin only. Extend dampener shaft and install clamp J-34013-20 on dampener shaft.
3. Compress strut approx. ½ its height after initial contact with top cap. NEVER BOTTOM SPRING OR DAMPENER ROD.	3. Install spring over dampener and swing assembly up so upper locking pin can be installed. Install upper insulator, shield, bumper, and upper spring seat. Be sure flat on upper spring seat is facing in proper direction. The spring seat flat should be 10° forward of the centerline of strut assembly spindle.
4. Remove the nut from the strut dampener shaft and place the J-34013-27 Guiding Rod on top of the dampener shaft. Use this rod to guide the dampener shaft straight down through the bearing cap while decompressing the spring. Remove components.	4. Install Guiding Rod and turn forcing screw while Guiding Rod centers the assembly. When threads on dampener shaft are visable, remove Guiding Rod and install nut.
5. Perform services as required.	5. Tighten nut to a torque of 85 N·m (65 lbs. ft.). Use a crowsfoot line wrench while holding dampener shaft with socket.
	6. Remove clamp.

Fig. 10   Disassembly & assembly of strut

1	STERING GEAR
2	BUSHING
3	BOLT
4	NUT –
5	NUT –
6	COTTER PIN
7	SLEEVE

Fig. 11   Steering gear replacement

1 PUMP ASSEMBLY, POWER STEERING
2 BOLT/SCREW, POWER STEERING PUMP
3 BRACKET ASSEMBLY, POWER STEERING PUMP
4 BOLT/SCREW, POWER STEERING PUMP BRACKET
5 BOLT/SCREW, POWER STEERING PUMP BRACE
6 BRACE, POWER STEERING PUMP BRACKET
7 BOLT/SCREW, POWER STEERING PUMP BRACKET

Fig. 12   Power steering pump replacement. 2.2L/4-134 engine

ening control arm mounting nuts.
b. Torque bolts/nuts to specifications.

STEERING KNUCKLE REPLACE

For removal and installation procedures, refer to **Fig. 7.**

STABILIZER BAR & BUSHINGS REPLACE

1. Raise and support vehicle.
2. Remove stabilizer shaft insulator clamp and insulator at control arms. Do not remove studs from control arms.
3. Remove plates from frame, then stabilizer bar and insulator bushings, **Fig. 8.**
4. Reverse procedure to install, torquing bolts/nuts to specifications.

STRUT ASSEMBLY REPLACE

1. Remove strut top attaching nuts, then raise and support vehicle.
2. Place jack stands under suspension support, the lower vehicle slightly so weight of vehicle rests on jack stands.
3. Remove wheel assemblies, then install drive axle seal protectors.
4. Disconnect front wheel sensor, if equipped w/anti-lock brakes.
5. Remove brake line bracket from strut assembly, then strut to steering knuckle attaching bolts.
6. Remove strut from vehicle, **Fig. 9.**
7. Reverse procedure to install, torquing bolts/nuts to specifications.

STRUT ASSEMBLY SERVICE

Refer to **Fig. 10,** for strut assembly service.

STEERING GEAR REPLACE

1. Install engine support fixture No. J-28467-A or equivalent.
2. Raise and support vehicle, then remove both front wheel assemblies.
3. Remove intermediate shaft lower pinch bolt, then intermediate shaft from stub shaft.
4. Disconnect tie rod ends from steering knuckles.
5. If equipped, remove brake line retaining bolts from heat shield, then heat shield.
6. Support engine frame at rear with jack stand, then remove engine mounts to frame attaching bolts.
7. Remove rear engine frame retaining bolts, then loosen front engine retaining bolts. **Do not remove front engine retaining bolts.**

1. POWER STEERING PUMP
2. BOLT
3. TENSIONER ASSY.
4. PULLEY

**Fig. 13   Power steering pump
replacement. 2.5L/4-151
engine**

1. POWER STEERING PUMP
2. BOLT
3. PULLEY
4. COVER

**Fig. 14   Power steering pump
replacement. 3.1L/V6-189
engine**

1	BELT TENSIONER ASM.
2	POWER STEERING PUMP
3	BOLT SCREW
4	BELT TENSIONER BRACE
5	PULLEY
6	ACCESSORY DRIVE BELT
7	BOLT

**Fig. 15   Power steering pump
replacement. 3.3L/V6-204
engine**

8. Lower engine frame at rear 4 to 5 inches. **Do not lower frame more than specified, as damage to engine components may result.**
9. Remove steering gear heat shield, then line retaining clip from steering gear.

10. Disconnect and cap pump lines at steering gear.
11. Remove steering gear assembly mounting bolts, **Fig. 11**, then steering gear assembly through left wheel opening.
12. Reverse procedure to install, torquing all bolts/nuts to specifications.

POWER STEERING PUMP REPLACE

1. Remove serpentine drive belt from

pulley, then disconnect power steering lines at pump.
2. Remove pump retaining bolts, then pump, **Figs. 12 through 15.**
3. Reverse procedure to install, torquing bolts/nuts to specifications.

TIGHTENING SPECIFICATIONS

Year	Component	Torque/Ft. Lbs.
1991–94	Ball Joint Pinch Bolt Nut	33
	Brake Line Bracket Bolt	13
	Control Arm Pivot Bolt Nut	61
	Caliper Bolt	38
	Hub & Bearing Retaining Bolt	①
	Hub Nut	②
	Insulator Clamp Nut	33
	Reinforcement Plate To Frame Bolt	40
	Stabilizer Shaft Bushing Clamp Nut	33
	Steering Knuckle To Strut Assembly Bolt	140
	Strut Assembly To Body Nut	18
	Strut Dampener Shaft Nut	65
	Wheel Lug Nut	92

① —Standard brakes, 63 ft. lbs.; heavy duty brakes, 70 ft. lbs.
② —1991, 192 ft. lbs.

Wheel Alignment

INDEX

Page No.

Fig. 1   Measurement location points

MODEL	SUSPENSION	TIRE SIZE	Z (CURB)	D (CURB)	J (CURB)	K (CURB)
WAGON	FE1-F40	P185-75R14	−8mm (−.31 IN.)	185mm (7.28 IN.)	228mm (8.98 IN.)	234mm (9.21 IN.)
WAGON	FE1-F40	P195-75R14	−8mm (−.31 IN.)	185mm (7.28 IN.)	239mm (9.40 IN.)	244mm (9.60 IN.)
SEDAN	FE1	P185-75R14	−8mm (−.31 IN.)	185mm (7.28 IN.)	228mm (8.97 IN.)	234mm (9.21 IN.)
SEDAN	FE2	P195-70R15	−8mm (−.31 IN.)	185mm (7.28 IN.)	239mm (9.41 IN.)	245mm (9.64 IN.)
SEDAN	FE2	P195-70R15	−8mm (−.31 IN.)	185mm (7.28 IN.)	238mm (9.37 IN.)	245mm (9.64 IN.)
SEDAN	F40	P185-75R14	−8mm (−.31 IN.)	185mm (7.28 IN.)	229mm (9.01 IN.)	234mm (9.21 IN.)

Fig. 2   Vehicle ride height specifications. 1991 6000

MODEL	SUSPENSION	TIRE SIZE	Z (CURB)	D (CURB)	J (CURB)	K (CURB)
WAGON	FE1	P185-75R14	−1mm (−.04 IN.)	191mm (7.52 IN.)	236mm (9.29 IN.)	240mm (9.44 IN.)
WAGON	FE1	P195-75R14	−1mm (−.04 IN.)	191mm (7.52 IN.)	242mm (9.53 IN.)	246mm (9.69 IN.)
COUPE	FE1	P185-75R14	−1mm (−.04 IN.)	191mm (7.52 IN.)	236mm (9.29 IN.)	242mm (9.53 IN.)
SEDAN	FE1	P185-75R14	−1mm (−.04 IN.)	191mm (7.52 IN.)	236mm (9.29 IN.)	242mm (9.53 IN.)
SEDAN	F41	P195-75R14	−1mm (−.04 IN.)	191mm (7.52 IN.)	243mm (9.57 IN.)	249mm (9.80 IN.)

Fig. 3   Vehicle ride height specifications. Century

MODEL	SUSPENSION	TIRE SIZE	Z (CURB)	D (CURB)	J (CURB)	K (CURB)
WAGON	FE1	P185-75R14	−1mm (−.04 IN.)	191mm (7.52 IN.)	234mm (9.21 IN.)	238mm (9.37 IN.)
WAGON	FE1	P195-75R14	−1mm (−.04 IN.)	191mm (7.52 IN.)	234mm (9.21 IN.)	246mm (9.68 IN.)
WAGON	FE1	P195-70R14	−1mm (−.04 IN.)	191mm (7.52 IN.)	232mm (9.13 IN.)	237mm (9.33 IN.)
COUPE/SEDAN	FE1	P185-75R14	−1mm (−.04 IN.)	191mm (7.52 IN.)	234mm (9.21 IN.)	240mm (9.45 IN.)
COUPE/SEDAN	FE1	P195-75R14	−1mm (−.04 IN.)	191mm (7.52 IN.)	241mm (9.48 IN.)	247mm (9.72 IN.)
COUPE/SEDAN	FE1	P195-70R14	−1mm (−.04 IN.)	191mm (7.52 IN.)	232mm (9.13 IN.)	238mm (9.68 IN.)
SEDAN	FE3	P195-75R14	−1mm (−.04 IN.)	191mm (7.52 IN.)	241mm (9.48 IN.)	248mm (9.76 IN.)

Fig. 4   Vehicle ride height specifications. 1991–92 Cutlass Ciera & Cruiser

MODEL	SUSPENSION	TIRE SIZE	Z (CURB)	D (CURB)	J (CURB)	K (CURB)
WAGON	FE1	P185-75R14	−1mm (−.04 IN.)	191mm (7.52 IN.)	239mm (9.41 IN.)	246mm (9.69 IN.)
WAGON	FE1	P195-75R14	−1mm (−.04 IN.)	191mm (7.52 IN.)	245mm (9.65 IN.)	252mm (9.92 IN.)
SEDAN	FE1	P185-75R14	−1mm (−0.4 IN.)	191mm (7.52 IN.)	239mm (9.41 IN.)	247mm (9.72 IN.)
SEDAN	FE1	P195-75R14	−1mm (−0.4 IN.)	191mm (7.52 IN.)	245mm (9.65 IN.)	253mm (9.97 IN.)

Fig. 5   Vehicle ride height specifications. 1993 Cutlass Ciera & Cruiser

Camber and toe-in are the only adjustments that can be performed on these vehicles.

FRONT WHEEL ALIGNMENT

CAMBER

The camber angle is adjusted by loosening the strut cam bolt and the through bolt, then rotating the cam bolt to move the upper portion of the steering knuckle inward or outward. When correct camber angle is obtained, **torque** cam and through bolts to 140 ft. lbs.

When performing this adjustment, the top through bolt must be loosened to prevent damage to the outer cam guide.

TOE-IN

Toe-in is controlled by tie rod position. Adjustment is made by loosening the nuts at the steering knuckle end of the tie rods and rotating the rods to obtain proper toe-in setting. When adjusting toe-in, the tie rod boot clamps must be removed. After correct toe-in setting is obtained, **torque** tie rod nuts to 45 ft. lbs.

VEHICLE RIDE HEIGHT

Refer to **Figs. 1 through 5,** for vehicle ride height specifications and measurement location points.

BUICK LESABRE & PARK AVE., CADILLAC CONCOURS, DEVILLE & FLEETWOOD (FWD), OLDSMOBILE EIGHTY EIGHT & NINETY EIGHT & PONTIAC BONNEVILLE
(C & H Cars)
INDEX OF SERVICE OPERATIONS

NOTE: Refer To The Rear Of This Manual For Vehicle Manufacturer's Special Service Tool Suppliers.

INDEX OF SERVICE OPERATIONS-Continued

Specifications
GENERAL ENGINE SPECIFICATIONS

Year	Engine Liter/CID	Engine VIN Code ①	Fuel System	Bore and Stroke	Compression Ratio	Net H.P. @ RPM ②	Maximum Torque Ft. Lbs. @ RPM	Normal Oil Pressure Psi
1991	3800/V6-231	C	Fuel Injection	3.80 x 3.40	8.5	165 @ 5200	210 @ 2000	37
	3800/V6-231	L	Fuel Injection	3.80 x 3.40	8.5	170 @ 5200	220 @ 3200	37
	4.9L/V8-300	B	Fuel Injection	3.62 x 3.62	9.5	200 @ 4100	275 @ 3000	⑤
1992	3800/V6-231	L	Fuel Injection	3.80 x 3.40	8.5	170 @ 4800	220 @ 2000	60⑥
	3800/V6-231③	1	Fuel Injection	3.80 x 3.40	8.5	205 @ 4400	260 @ 2800	60⑥
	4.9L/V8-300	B	Fuel Injection	3.62 x 3.62	9.5	200 @ 4400	275 @ 3000	④
1993	3800/V6-231	L	Fuel Injection	3.80 x 3.40	9.0	170 @ 4800	225 @ 3200	60⑥
	3800/V6-231③	1	Fuel Injection	3.80 x 3.40	9.0	205 @ 4400	260 @ 2600	60⑥
	4.9L/V8-300	B	Fuel Injection	3.62 x 3.62	9.5	200 @ 4400	275 @ 3000	④
1994	3800/V6-231	L	Fuel Injection	3.80 x 3.40	9.0	170 @ 4800	225 @ 3200	60⑥
	3800/V6-231③	1	Fuel Injection	3.80 x 3.40	9.0	205 @ 4400	260 @ 2600	60⑥
	4.6L/V8-279	Y	Fuel Injection	3.66 x 3.31	10.3	270 @ 5600	—	35⑦
	4.9L/V8-300	B	Fuel Injection	3.62 x 3.62	9.5	200 @ 4400	275 @ 3000	④

① —The eighth digit denotes engine code.
② —Ratings are net-as installed in vehicle.
③ —Supercharged.
④ —11 psi at idle, 53 psi at 2000 RPM.
⑤ —9 psi at idle, 26 psi at 1500 RPM.
⑥ —At 1850 RPM.
⑦ —At 2000 RPM.

TUNE UP SPECIFICATIONS

Year & Engine/VIN Code ①	Spark Plug Gap	Ignition Timing Firing Order Fig. ②	Ignition Timing °BTDC	Ignition Timing Mark Fig.	Curb Idle Speed	Fast Idle Speed	Fuel Pump Pressure		
1991									
3800/V6-231/C	.060	⑥	⑦	⑧	③	③	40-47⑤		
3800/V6-231/L	.060	⑥	⑦	⑧	③	③	40-47⑤		
4.9L/V8-300/B	.060	A	10④	B	③	③	32-38⑨		
1992-93									
3800/V6-231/1	.060	⑥	⑦	⑧	③	③	40-47⑤		
3800/V6-231/L	.060	⑥	⑦	⑧	③	③	40-47⑤		
4.9L/V8-300/B	.060	A	10④	B	③	③	32-38⑨		
1994									
3800/V6-231/1	.060	⑥	⑦	⑧	③	③	40-47⑤		
3800/V6-231/L	.060	⑥	⑦	⑧	③	③	40-47⑤		
4.6L/V8-279/Y	.050	⑩	10⑦	—	③	③	—		
4.9L/V8-300/B	.060	A	10④	B	③	③	32-38⑨		

① —The eighth digit of the Vehicle Identification Number (VIN) denotes engine code.

② —Before removing wires from distributor cap, determine location of No. 1 wire in cap, as distributor position may have been altered from that shown at the end of this chart.

③ —Idle speed is controlled by an idle speed control (ISC) motor or an idle air control (IAC) valve.

④ —Connect jumper wire between ALCL connector terminals A & B. The ALCL connector is located under the instrument panel to the right of the steering column. After completing adjustment, disconnect jumper wire from between terminals A & B. With engine off, clear trouble code from Electronic Control Module (ECM) memory by removing battery voltage from ECM for 30 seconds.

⑤ —With shop towel wrapped around fuel pressure valve to prevent fuel spillage, connect a suitable fuel pressure gauge to fuel pressure valve. Check fuel pressure with ignition switch in the On position, engine not running.

⑥ —Cylinder numbering left to right as viewed from front of vehicle, front bank, 1, 3, 5; rear bank, 2, 4, 6. Firing order 1-6-5-4-3-2. Two different types computer controlled coil ignition systems are used. Refer to Figs. C & D for spark plug wire connections at coil unit.

⑦ —Computer controlled, no adjustment.

⑧ —Equipped with crankshaft position sensor.

⑨ —With shop towel wrapped around fitting to prevent spillage, connect a suitable fuel pressure gauge to fuel line service fitting. Check fuel pressure while cranking engine.

⑩ —Cylinder numbering from left to right as viewed from front of vehicle, front bank, 2, 4, 6, 8; rear bank, 1, 3, 5, 7. Firing order 1-2-7-3-4-5-6-8. Refer to Fig. E for plug wire connections at the coil unit.

Continued

FIRING ORDER 1-8-4-3-6-5-7-2

FRONT OF ENGINE

FRONT OF VEHICLE

Fig. A

Fig. B

COMPUTER CONTROLLED COIL IGNITION

Fig. C

COMPUTER CONTROLLED COIL IGNITION

Fig. D

Fig. E

FRONT WHEEL ALIGNMENT SPECIFICATIONS

| Year | Model | Caster Angle, Degrees | | Camber Angle, Degrees | | | | Total Toe, Degree |
| | | | | Limits | | Desired | | |
		Limits	Desired	Left	Right	Left	Right	
1991	Bonneville	+2.5 to +3.5	+3	−.3 to +.7	−.3 to +.7	+.2	+.2	0
	DeVille & Fleetwood (FWD)	+2.5 to +3.5	+3	−1 to 0	0 to +1	−.5	+.5	0
	LeSabre	+2.5 to +3.5	+3	−.3 to +.7	−.3 to +.7	+.2	+.2	0
	Park Avenue	+2.5 to +3.5	+3	−.3 to +.7	−.3 to +.7	+.2	+.2	0
	Eighty-Eight & Ninety-Eight	+2.5 to +3.5	+3	−.3 to +.7	−.3 to +.7	+.2	+.2	0
1992	Bonneville	+2.5 to +3.5	+3	−.3 to +.7	−.3 to +.7	+.2	+.2	0
	DeVille & Fleetwood (FWD)	+2.5 to +3.5	+3	−1 to 0	0 to +1	−.5	+.5	0
	LeSabre	+2.5 to +3.5	+3	−.3 to +.7	−.3 to +.7	+.2	+.2	0
	Park Avenue	+2.5 to +3.5	+3	−.3 to +.7	−.3 to +.7	+.2	+.2	0
	Eighty-Eight & Ninety-Eight	+2.5 to +3.5	+3	−.3 to +.7	−.3 to +.7	+.2	+.2	0
1993	Bonneville	+2.5 to +3.5	+3	−.55 to +.95	−.3 to +.7	+.2	+.2	0
	DeVille & Sixty Special	+2.5 to +3.5	+3	−1 to 0	0 to +1	−.5	+.5	0
	LeSabre	+2.5 to +3.5	+3	−.55 to +.95	−.3 to +.7	+.2	+.2	0
	Park Avenue	+2.5 to +3.5	+3	−.55 to +.95	−.3 to +.7	+.2	+.2	0
	Eighty-Eight & Ninety-Eight	+2.5 to +3.5	+3	−.55 to +.95	−.3 to +.7	+.2	+.2	0
1994	Bonneville	+2.5 to +3.5	+3	−.55 to +.95	−.3 to +.7	+.2	+.2	0
	Concours	+2.5 to +3.5	+3	−1 to 0	0 to +1	−.5	+.5	0
	DeVille	+2.5 to +3.5	+3	−1 to 0	0 to +1	−.5	+.5	0
	LeSabre	+2.5 to +3.5	+3	−.55 to +.95	−.3 to +.7	+.2	+.2	0
	Park Avenue	+2.5 to +3.5	+3	−.55 to +.95	−.3 to +.7	+.2	+.2	0
	Eighty-Eight & Ninety-Eight	+2.5 to +3.5	+3	−.55 to +.95	−.3 to +.7	+.2	+.2	0

REAR WHEEL ALIGNMENT SPECIFICATIONS

Year	Model	Camber Angle, Degrees		Total Toe, Degrees
		Limits	Desired	
1991–92	Bonneville	−.8 to +.2	−.3	+.1
	DeVille & Fleetwood (FWD)	−.8 to +.2	−.3	+.1
	LeSabre	−.8 to +.2	−.3	+.1
	Park Avenue	−.8 to +.2	−.3	+.1
	Eighty-Eight & Ninety-Eight	−.8 to +.2	−.3	+.1
1993	Bonneville	−1.05 to +.45	−.3	+.1
	DeVille & Sixty Special	−.8 to +.2	−.3	+.1
	LeSabre	−1.05 to +.45	−.3	+.1
	Park Avenue	−1.05 to +.45	−.3	+.1
	Eighty-Eight & Ninety-Eight	−1.05 to +.45	−.3	+.1
1994	Bonneville	−1.05 to +.45	−.3	+.1
	Concours	−.8 to +.2	−.3	+.1
	DeVille	−.8 to +.2	−.3	+.1
	LeSabre	−1.05 to +.45	−.3	+.1
	Park Avenue	−1.05 to +.45	−.3	+.1
	Eighty-Eight & Ninety-Eight	−1.05 to +.45	−.3	+.1

COOLING SYSTEM & CAPACITY DATA

Year	Model	Engine/VIN	Cooling Capacity, Qts.	Radiator Cap Relief Pressure, Lbs.	Thermo. Opening Temp.	Fuel Tank Gals.	Engine Oil Refill Qts.	Auto. Transaxle Qts.①
1991	Bonneville	3800/V6-231/C	13	15	195	18	4②	③
	DeVille/Fleetwood (FWD)	4.9L/V8-300/—	13.2	15	195	18	5②	③
	LeSabre	3800/V6-231/C	13	15	195	18	4②	③
	Park Avenue/Park Avenue Ultra	3800/V6-231/L	13	15	195	18	4②	③
	Eighty-Eight	3800/V6-231/C	13	15	195	18	4②	③
	Ninety-Eight	3800/V6-231/L	13	15	195	18	4②	③
1992–93	Bonneville SE & SSE	3800/V6-231/L	13	15	195	19	4②	③
	Bonneville SSEi	3800/V6-231/1⑥	—	13.5–18.0	—	19	—	8⑤
	DeVille/Fleetwood (FWD)	4.9L/V8-300/B	13.2	15	195	19	5④	③
	LeSabre	3800/V6-231/C	13	15	195	19	4②	③
	Park Avenue	3800/V6-231/L	13	15	195	19	4②	③
	Park Avenue Ultra	3800/V6-231/1⑥	—	13.5–18.0	—	19	—	8⑤
	Eighty-Eight	3800/V6-231/L	13	15	195	18	4②	③
	Ninety-Eight Regency	3800/V6-231/L	13	15	195	18	4②	③
	Ninety-Eight Touring Sedan	3800/V6-231/1⑥	—	13.5–18.0	—	18	—	8⑤
1994	Bonneville	3800/V6-231/L,1	12.5	15	195	18	4④	⑦
	Concours	4.6L/V8-279/Y	13.2	15	195	—	7④	⑥
	DeVille	4.9L/V8-300/B	13.2	15	195	19	5④	⑤
	LeSabre	3800/V6-231/C	13	15	195	19	4②	③
	Park Avenue	3800/V6-231/L	13	15	195	19	4②	③
	Park Avenue Ultra	3800/V6-231/1⑥	—	13.5–18.0	—	19	—	8⑤
	Eighty-Eight	3800/V6-231/L	13	15	195	18	4②	③
	Ninety-Eight Regency	3800/V6-231/L	13	15	195	18	4②	③
	Ninety-Eight Touring Sedan	3800/V6-231/1⑥	—	13.5–18.0	—	18	—	8⑤

①—Approximate, make final check with dipstick.
②—Additional oil may be required to bring oil level to full mark when changing oil filter.
③—Oil pan capacity, 6 qts.; total capacity, 11 qts.
④—Add ½ qt. w/filter change.
⑤—Drain & refill.
⑥—Supercharged.
⑦—Oil pan capacity, 8 qts.; total capacity, 11 qts.
⑧—Oil pan capacity, 8 qts.; total capacity, 12.6 qts.

LUBRICANT DATA

		Lubricant Type			
		Transaxle			
Year	Model	Manual	Automatic	Power Steering	Brake System
1991	All	—	Dexron II	Power Steering Fluid	DOT 3
1992–94	All	—	Dexron IIE	Power Steering Fluid	DOT 3

Electrical

INDEX

PRECAUTIONS

AIRBAG SYSTEM DISARMING

1991 Park Avenue

When carrying a live inflator module, ensure bag and trim cover are pointed away from you. Never carry inflator module by the wires or connector on underside of module.

The diagnostic energy reserve module (DERM) can maintain voltage to cause a system deployment for up to ten minutes after the ignition switch is turned off and the battery is disconnected. Servicing the SIR system during this period may result in accidental deployment and personal injury.

1. Turn ignition switch to Off position, then disconnect and tape battery ground cable terminal.
2. Remove SIR fuse from fuse block, then the left sound insulator.
3. Remove Connector Position Assurance (CPA), then disconnect yellow two-way SIR electrical connector at base of steering column.
4. Remove screws and/or nuts from back of steering wheel, then the inflator module from steering wheel.
5. Remove Connector Position Assurance (CPA), then disconnect coil assembly connector and horn lead.
6. Place inflator module on a bench or other surface with bag and trim cover facing up.

1991 Eighty-Eight & Ninety-Eight

The diagnostic energy reserve module (DERM) can maintain voltage to cause a system deployment for up to ten minutes after the ignition switch is turned off and the battery is disconnected. Servicing the SIR system during this period may result in accidental deployment and personal injury.

1. Turn ignition switch to Off position, then remove I/P fuse 7 from fuse block.
2. Disconnect yellow two-way SIR electrical connector at base of steering column.

1991-94 DeVille, Concours, Fleetwood (FWD), Sixty Special & 1992-94 Bonneville, LeSabre, Park Avenue, Eighty-Eight & Ninety-Eight

The diagnostic energy reserve module (DERM) can maintain voltage to cause a system deployment for up to ten minutes after the ignition switch is turned off and the battery is disconnected. Servicing the SIR system during this period may result in accidental deployment and personal injury.

1. Ensure front wheels are pointed straight ahead.
2. Turn ignition switch to Lock position and remove SIR or AIRBAG fuse.
3. Remove left sound insulator. **Remove courtesy lamp from sound insulator, if necessary.**
4. **On models with passenger side airbag,** open trap door at rear of glove box.
5. **On all models,** remove Connector Position Assurance (CPA), then disconnect yellow two-way SIR electrical connectors at base of steering column and behind glove box trap door.

AIRBAG SYSTEM ARMING

1991 Park Avenue

1. Turn ignition switch to Off position, connect horn lead and coil assembly connector, then install Connector Position Assurance (CPA).
2. Install inflator module and secure to steering wheel with new screws and/or nuts.

Fig. 1 — TO ASSEMBLE, ROTATE TO STOP WHILE HOLDING CYLINDER.
LOCK CYLINDER
LOCK RETAINING SCREW
CLIP
KEY WARNING BUZZER SWITCH
HOUSING

Fig. 1   Lock cylinder removal

66
64
65
74
68

64. SCREW, WASH. HD (#10-24 x .25)
65. STUD, DIMR & IGN SW MOUNTING
66. SWITCH ASM, IGN & BEAM CHANGE
68. SWITCH, DIMMER
74. NUT, HEXAGON (#10-24 x .25)

Fig. 2   Ignition switch removal. Standard column

3. **Torque** screws and/or nuts to 25 inch lbs.
4. Connect yellow two-way SIR electrical connector at base of steering column, then install Connector Position Assurance (CPA).
5. Install left sound insulator, then the SIR fuse into fuse block.
6. Connect battery ground cable.
8. Turn ignition switch to RUN position and ensure that "Inflatable Restraint" indicator flashes 7 to 9 times, then shuts Off.

1991 Eighty-Eight & Ninety-Eight

1. Connect yellow two-way SIR electrical connector at base of steering column.
2. Install I/P fuse 7 into fuse block, turn ignition switch to RUN position and ensure that "Inflatable Restraint" indicator flashes 7 to 9 times, then shuts Off.

1991-94 DeVille, Fleetwood, Concours, Sixty Special & 1992-94 Bonneville, LeSabre, Park Avenue, Eighty-Eight & Ninety-Eight

1. Connect yellow two-way SIR electrical connector(s), then install Connector Position Assurance (CPA).
2. Install left sound insulator. **Install courtesy lamp to sound insulator, if applicable.**
3. Install SIR fuse to fuse block, turn ignition switch to Run position and ensure that "Inflatable Restraint" lamp flashes 7 to 9 times, then shuts off.

40. ROD, DIMMER SWITCH ACTUATOR
41. SWITCH ASSY, DIMMER
42. SCREW, WASHER HEAD
45. NUT, HEXAGON

Fig. 3   Dimmer switch removal. Standard column

FUSE PANEL & FLASHER LOCATION

The instrument panel fuse panel is located under the lefthand side of the instrument panel. The engine compartment fuse panel is located at the rear fo the engine compartment at the bulkhead.

On Cadillac and all 1991 models, the turn signal flasher is located behind the lefthand side of the instrument panel on the lefthand side of the steering column. On all 1992-94 models except Cadillac, the turn signal flasher is located below the instrument panel on top of the left hand shroud. On Park Avenue models, the hazard flasher is located behind the lefthand side of the instrument panel at the lefthand side of the steering column. On 1991 Buick LeSabre models, the hazard flasher is located below the lefthand side of the instrument panel near the brake pedal. On Cadillac models, the hazard flasher is located below the lefthand side of the instrument panel at the top of the brake pedal support. On Oldsmobile and Pontiac models, the hazard flasher is located behind the lefthand side of the instrument panel on the righthand side of the steering column support.

STARTER REPLACE

When removing starter, note if any shims are used between the starter and mounting surface. If shims are found, reinstall in original locations.

If starter is noisy during cranking, remove one .015 inch double shim or add one .015 inch single shim to the outer bolt. If starter makes a high pitched whine after engine start, add .015 inch double shims until noise ceases.

1. Disarm airbag system as described under "Precautions."
2. Disconnect battery ground cable and raise and support vehicle.
3. Remove starter braces, shields or other components that may hinder starter removal.
4. Support starter and remove mounting bolts.
5. Lower starter and disconnect solenoid wires and battery cable.
6. Remove starter from vehicle.
7. Reverse procedure to install.
8. Rearm airbag system as described under "Precautions."

44
43

43. STUD, DIMMER & IGNITION SWITCH MOUNTING
44. SWITCH ASSY, IGNITION

Fig. 4   Ignition & dimmer switch removal. Tilt column & column w/SIR

TERMINAL CONNECTOR
VIEW FROM BACK OF BULKHEAD CONNECTOR
PUSH UP ON LOCKING TAB OF CONNECTOR WITH SCREWDRIVER AND REMOVE WIRE CONNECTOR FROM BULKHEAD CONNECTOR.
TAN
GREEN
YELLOW

A BULKHEAD CONNECTOR
B POSITIVE ASSURANCE TERMINAL CONNECTOR

Fig. 5   Disconnecting dimmer switch from bulkhead connector

IGNITION LOCK REPLACE

1. Disable airbag system as described under "Precautions."
2. Remove steering wheel as described in "Steering Wheel, Replace."
3. Remove turn signal switch as described in "Turn Signal Switch, Replace."
4. Remove key from lock cylinder, then remove buzzer switch from column housing.
5. Reinsert key and turn lock cylinder to LOCK position, then remove lock cylinder retaining screw and lock cylinder, **Fig. 1.**
6. To install, rotate lock cylinder to the stop while holding housing. Align cylinder key with keyway in housing, then push lock cylinder into housing until fully seated.
7. Install lock cylinder retaining screw.
8. Install buzzer switch, turn signal switch and steering wheel.
9. Rearm airbag system as described under "Precautions."

IGNITION & DIMMER SWITCHES REPLACE

1. Disable airbag system as described under "Precautions."
2. Remove turn signal switch as outlined under "Turn Signal Switch, Replace" procedure.

1 I/P CARRIER 3 HEADLAMP SWITCH
2 INTERIOR LIGHT 4 TWILIGHT SENTINEL
   DIMMER   SWITCH

Fig. 6 Headlamp switch removal. Buick except Park Avenue

Fig. 7 Headlamp switch removal. Park Avenue

Fig. 8 Headlamp switch removal. DeVille & Fleetwood (FWD)

1. HEADLAMP SWITCH
2. FULLY DRIVEN, SEATED AND NOT STRIPPED
3. PLUG FIBER OPTIC INTO REAR OF SWITCH ASM.

Fig. 9 Headlamp switch removal. Oldsmobile except Ninety-Eight & 1992–94 Eighty-Eight

3. Refer to **Figs. 2 through 4,** to remove ignition and dimmer switches.
4. Refer to **Fig. 5** to disconnect dimmer switch from bulkhead connector.
5. When installing dimmer switch, depress switch slightly to install a $3/32$ inch twist drill. Force switch upward to remove lash and tighten retaining screw.
6. Rearm airbag system as described under "Precautions."

PARK/NEUTRAL & BACK-UP LAMP SWITCH
REPLACE

1. Disable airbag system as described under "Precautions."
2. Disconnect battery ground cable.
3. Disconnect shift cable from transaxle.
4. Disconnect electrical connector from switch.
5. Remove two switch mounting bolts and the switch.
6. Align flats on switch with flats on transaxle shaft and push switch over shaft and fully seat on transaxle.
7. Install and **torque** switch mounting bolts to 20 ft. lbs. **If switch was rotated and the pin broken, the switch will be automatically reset to the neutral position as follows:**
   a. Place transaxle shaft in neutral position.
   b. Install switch on transaxle as out-

1 SCREW
2 CONNECTORS
3 HEADLIGHT SWITCH

Fig. 10 Headlamp switch removal. Ninety-Eight & 1992–94 Eighty-Eight

1 CONNECTORS
2 SCREW
3 HEADLAMP SWITCH

Fig. 12 Headlamp switch removal. 1992–94 Bonneville

lined previously and loosely install mounting bolts.
c. Insert a $3/32$ inch gauge pin into service adjustment hole of switch.

1. Headlamp Switch Assembly
2. Switch Assembly Attaching Screws
3. I/P Lamp Dimmer Control
4. Headlamp Switch
5. Twilight Sentinel Control

Fig. 11 Headlamp switch removal. 1991 Bonneville

d. Rotate switch until pin drops in detent.
e. **Torque** mounting bolts to 20 ft. lbs.
f. Rearm airbag system as described under "Precautions."

HEADLAMP SWITCH
REPLACE

Disable airbag system as described in "Precautions" prior to working on or near the steering column. After completion of repairs, rearm airbag system as described under "Precautions."

BUICK

Refer to **Figs. 6 and 7,** for switch replacement.

CADILLAC

Refer to **Fig. 8,** for switch replacement.

OLDSMOBILE

Refer to **Figs. 9 and 10,** for switch replacement.

PONTIAC

Refer to **Figs. 11 and 12,** for switch replacement.

TURN SIGNAL SWITCH
REPLACE

1. Disable airbag system as described under "Precautions."

9 SCREW, BINDING HD CROSS RECESS
10 SCREW, RD WASH HD (M4.2X1.41)
11 ARM ASM. SIGNAL SWITCH
12 SWITCH ASM. TURN SIGNAL
B MULTI-FUNCTION LEVER
C HAZARD KNOB ASSEMBLY

Fig. 13 Multi-function lever & hazard knob assembly removal

1 CAM TOWER	6 NUT
2 CONNECTOR, SWITCH	7 BOLT/SCREW
3 HORN CONTACT LEAD	8 CONNECTOR, SIR INFLATOR MODULE
4 INFLATOR MODULE	9 RETAINER, CPA
5 SWITCH ASM	10 BOLT/SCREW

VIEW A

Fig. 15 Inflator module assembly

26 PROTECTOR, WIRING
79 NUT, HEXAGON (#10-24)
82 STRAP, WIRE HARNESS
107 MODULE ASM. E & C INTERFACE

TURN SIGNAL SWITCH CONNECTOR

Fig. 14 Turn signal switch removal

2. Remove steering wheel as described in "Steering Wheel, Replace."
3. Using lock plate compressor tool No. J 23653-C or equivalent, push down shaft lock and remove shaft lock retaining ring.
4. Remove shaft lock, turn signal cancelling cam assembly, upper bearing spring, upper bearing inner race seat and inner race.
5. Set turn signal to RIGHT TURN position, then remove multi-function lever and hazard knob assembly, **Fig. 13.**
6. Remove signal switch arm retaining screw and switch arm.
7. Remove turn signal switch attaching screws, then signal switch as follows:
   a. Disconnect turn signal switch connector from bulkhead connector and wire harness strap, **Fig. 14.**
   b. Disconnect E & C module connector from signal switch harness.
   c. Remove wiring protector, then nut holding ground wire to stud.
   d. Gently pull wire harness through column.
8. Reverse procedure to install.
9. Rearm airbag system as described under "Precautions."

STEERING WHEEL REPLACE

EXCEPT MODELS W/INFLATABLE RESTRAINT SYSTEM
STANDARD & TILT WHEEL

1. Disconnect battery ground cable.
2. **On models with control pad assembly,** pry out control pad using a thin bladed tool.
3. **On models less control pad assembly,** remove two steering wheel pad retaining screws.
4. **On all models,** disconnect horn wire from cam tower.
5. **On models with control pad assembly,** pry rocker button and push button from control pad.
6. **On all models,** remove steering wheel nut retainer.
7. Remove steering wheel retaining nut.
8. Using a suitable puller, remove steering wheel.
9. Reverse procedure to install.

TELESCOPING WHEEL
Except Cadillac

1. Disconnect battery ground cable.
2. Remove two steering wheel pad retaining screws.
3. Disconnect horn wire from steering wheel pad.
4. Remove steering shaft lock knob bolt positioning screws, then the lock knob bolt from steering shaft.
5. Remove steering wheel nut retainer and the steering wheel nut. Using a suitable puller, remove steering wheel.
6. Reverse procedure to install.

Cadillac

1. Disconnect battery ground cable.
2. Remove two steering wheel pad retaining screws.

3. Disconnect horn wire from steering wheel pad.
4. Remove three screws from telescoping adjusting lever.
5. Remove steering shaft lock knob from steering shaft.
6. Remove steering wheel nut.
7. Using a suitable puller, remove steering wheel.
8. Reverse procedure to install.

MODELS w/INFLATABLE RESTRAINT SYSTEM

1. Disable airbag system as described under "Precautions."
2. Remove module retaining screws from back of steering wheel.
3. Remove module from steering wheel, then disconnect horn contact, by pushing slightly and twisting counterclockwise.
4. Remove connector position assurance, then disconnect coil assembly connector, **Fig. 15.**
5. Remove steering wheel retaining nut.
6. Using suitable steering wheel puller, remove wheel.
7. Reverse procedure to install.
8. Rearm airbag system as described under "Precautions."

INSTRUMENT CLUSTER REPLACE

BUICK
Except Park Avenue

1. Disable airbag system as described under "Precautions."
2. Disconnect battery ground cable.
3. Remove upper trim pad, **Fig. 16,** as follows:
   a. Remove defroster grille, then the A/C outlets from upper trim pad.
   b. Remove instrument panel trim plates, then 10 instrument panel pad retaining screws.
   c. **On models equipped with twi-**

1 I/P TOP COVER (PAD) **3** A/C OUTLET SEALS
2 I/P CARRIER

Fig. 16 Instrument panel top cover pad removal. Buick except 1991 Park Avenue

1 INSTRUMENT PANEL **3** TRIM COVER
2 STEERING COLUMN **4** A/C OUTLET HOSE

Fig. 17 Steering column cover to disconnect shift cable removal. Buick except Park Avenue

1 CLUSTER HOUSING ASM. **2** I/P CARRIER

Fig. 18 Cluster removal. Buick except Park Avenue

Fig. 19 I/P trim pad & trim panels removal. Park Avenue

Fig. 20 Instrument cluster removal. Park Avenue

light sentinel, pop up photocell retainer, then remove photocell by turning counterclockwise.
  d. **On all models,** slide panel pad out far enough to disconnect aspirator tube and in-car temperature sensor electrical connector.
  e. Remove pad.
4. **On models with analog cluster,** Remove steering column filler panel, **Fig. 17,** then disconnect shift indicator cable from steering column.
5. **On all models,** remove five instrument cluster attaching screws, then the cluster, **Fig. 18.**
6. Rearm airbag system as described under "Precautions."

Park Avenue

1. Disable airbag system as described

under "Precautions."
2. Disconnect battery ground cable.
3. Remove right and left side sound insulators.
4. Remove instrument panel lower trim plates, **Fig. 19.**
5. Remove air vent deflectors, then three glove box attaching bolts.
6. Remove five instrument panel trim plate attaching screws, then trim plate.
7. Remove seven lower instrument panel trim pad to instrument panel attaching screws.
8. Slide rubber collar up steering column, then slide clip off with gear selector as shown in **Fig. 20.**
9. Remove five instrument cluster to instrument panel attaching bolts, then pull cluster straight out.
10. Reverse procedure to install.

11. Rearm airbag system as described under "Precautions."

CADILLAC

1. Disable airbag system as described under "Precautions."
2. Disconnect battery ground cable.
3. Remove upper trim pad as follows:
  a. Remove A/C outlets from upper trim pad.
  b. Remove screws locations 2 and 3 from both side of pad, **Fig. 21.**
  c. Remove upper trim pad.
4. Remove screw (88) and plate (87), **Fig. 22.**
5. Remove cluster attaching screws.
6. Disconnect wiring from rear of cluster and remove cluster from vehicle.
7. Reverse procedure to install.
8. Rearm airbag system as described under "Precautions."

OLDSMOBILE

1991 Eighty-Eight

1. Disable airbag system as described under "Precautions."
2. Disconnect battery ground cable.
3. Remove center trim plate, **Fig. 23.**
4. Remove three cluster trim plate attaching screws, then the cluster trim plate, **Fig. 24.**
5. Remove five instrument cluster retaining screws, then disconnect shift indicator cable, if equipped.
6. Disconnect cluster electrical connectors.
7. Remove cluster assembly.

1	CHART — PAD ASSEMBLY
2	SCREW
3	SCREW
4	NUT
5	GRILLE
6	NUT
23	OUTLET

Fig. 21 Upper trim pad assembly. DeVille & Fleetwood (FWD)

37	CLUSTER ASSEMBLY
38	SCREW
39	NUT
87	PLATE
88	SCREW
89	NUT

Fig. 22 Cluster removal. DeVille & Fleetwood (FWD)

VIEW A

1. CENTER TRIM PLATE
2. FULLY DRIVEN, SEATED AND NOT STRIPPED
3. NUT

Fig. 23 Center instrument panel trim plate. Oldsmobile except Ninety-Eight & 1992-94 Eighty-Eight

8. Reverse procedure to install.
9. Rearm airbag system as described under "Precautions."

Ninety-Eight & 1992-94 Eighty-Eight

1. Disable airbag system as described under "Precautions."
2. Disconnect battery ground cable.
3. Remove cluster trim plate to instrument panel attaching screws, **Fig. 25.**
4. Tilt trim plate rearward and disconnect driver information display and defogger/heated windshield connectors.
5. Remove cluster trim plate, then cluster to instrument panel attaching screws, **Fig. 26.**
6. Pull cluster rearward, then disconnect cluster electrical connector and PRNDL cable.
7. Remove cluster assembly.
8. Reverse procedure to install.
9. Rearm airbag system as described under "Precautions."

PONTIAC
1991

1. Disable airbag system as described under "Precautions."
2. Disconnect battery ground cable.
3. **On models with tilt wheel,** place wheel in lowest position.

4. **On all models,** place selector lever in position "1."
5. lightly pry around perimeter of trim plate, then remove trim plate.
6. Remove IP trimplate, then the speaker, side defogger and defroster grilles.
7. Remove speaker attaching screws and electrical connectors.
8. Remove I/P pad.
9. Remove 5 attaching screws, **Fig. 27,** then disconnect PRNDL cable from steering column bowl.
10. Remove instrument cluster.
11. Reverse procedure to install.
12. Rearm airbag system as described under "Precautions."

1992-94

1. Disable airbag system as described under "Precautions."
2. Disconnect battery ground cable.
3. Remove steering column lower filler attaching screws, then remove.
4. Remove steering column support attaching bolts, then carefully lower steering column and cover to prevent damage.
5. Remove instrument panel trim plate attaching screws.
6. Pull headlamp dimmer and twilight sentinel control knob rearward.
7. Pull panel cluster plate rearward to remove.
8. Remove headlamp switch attaching screws, pull rearward, then remove dimmer and twilight sentinel control knob from switch.
9. Remove instrument panel cluster trim plate.
10. Remove instrument cluster attaching screws, then pull righthand side of cluster rearward, **Fig. 28.**
11. Depress cluster electrical connector locking tab through top right side of assembly.
12. Pull bottom of cluster rearward, then rotate cluster to face upward, then pull rearward to remove.
13. Reverse procedure to install.
14. Rearm airbag system as described under "Precautions."

1. CLUSTER TRIM PLATE
2. NUT (3)
3. FULLY DRIVEN, SEATED AND NOT STRIPPED
4. WEDGE TRIM PLATE EXISTING CLIPS AND I.P. PAD ASSEMBLY

Fig. 24 Cluster removal. Oldsmobile except Ninety-Eight & 1992-94 Eighty-Eight

RADIO
REPLACE
BUICK
LeSabre

1. Disable airbag system as described under "Precautions."
2. Remove lower RH trim plate.
3. Remove four radio retaining screws, then pull radio out of dash and disconnect electrical connectors and antenna lead.
4. Remove radio, **Fig. 29.**
5. Reverse procedure to install.
6. Rearm airbag system as described under "Precautions."

Park Avenue

1. Disable airbag system as described under "Precautions."
2. Disconnect battery ground cable.
3. Remove instrument panel lower trim plates and four air vent deflectors by prying gently.
4. Remove bolts and screws that attach the glove box to the instrument panel, **Fig. 30.**
5. Remove five instrument panel trim plate attaching screws.

1	IP CLUSTER TRIM PLATE
2	SCREW

Fig. 25 Cluster trim plate removal. Ninety-Eight & 1992–94 Eighty-Eight

1—CLUSTER

2—FULLY DRIVEN, SEATED, NOT STRIPPED

Fig. 27 Cluster removal. 1991 Bonneville

1	CLUSTER CONNECTOR
2	WINDSHIELD DEFROSTER GRILLE
3	PRNDL CABLE
4	BOLT
5	CLUSTER ASSEMBLY

Fig. 26 Cluster removal. Ninety-Eight & 1992–94 Eighty-Eight

VIEW A

1	SCREW
2	CLUSTER ASSEMBLY
3	CLUSTER ASSEMBLY CONNECTORS

Fig. 28 Cluster removal. 1992–94 Bonneville

1	RADIO	3	COVER IF NO RADIO
2	BRACKET	4	I/P CARRIER

Fig. 29 Radio installation. Buick except Park Avenue

OLDSMOBILE

1991 Eighty-Eight

1. Disable airbag system as described under "Precautions."
2. Remove center and lower trim plates.
3. Remove four radio retaining screws, then slide radio rearward and disconnect electrical connectors and antenna lead.
4. Remove radio, **Fig. 32.**
5. Reverse procedure to install.
6. Rearm airbag system as described under "Precautions."

Ninety-Eight & 1992–94 Eighty-Eight

1. Disable airbag system as described under "Precautions."

6. Remove five radio to instrument panel attaching bolts and nuts, **Fig. 30.**
7. Pull radio straight back and disconnect electrical connectors and antenna.
8. Reverse procedure to install.
9. Rearm airbag system as described under "Precautions."

CADILLAC

1. Disable airbag system as described under "Precautions."

2. Disconnect battery ground cable.
3. Remove radio trim plate, **Fig. 31.**
4. Open ashtray and remove one screw from rear support bracket.
5. Remove two screws from front of radio, then pull radio straight out and disconnect electrical connectors and antenna.
6. Remove four bracket retaining nuts and brackets.
7. Reverse procedure to install.
8. Rearm airbag system as described under "Precautions."

Fig. 30   Radio removal & installation. Park Avenue

1—LOCATOR PIN
2—UPPER MOUNTING BRACKET
3—LOWER MOUNTING BRACKET
4—NUT; 53 LB.IN. / 6 N·m
5—BOLT/SCREW; 13 LB.IN. / 1.4 N·m
6—I/P TIE BAR
7—SUPPORT BRACKET
8—RADIO
9—SIDE WINDOW DEFOGGER DUCT
10—ANTENNA CABLE (BODY)
11—ANTENNA CABLE (RADIO)
12—STRAP (TO PREVENT RATTLES)
13—IP ENGAGEMENT TABS
14—17 LB.IN/ 1.9 N·m

Fig. 33   Radio replace. 1991 Bonneville

1. NUT; 4N·M (35 LB-IN)
2. BRACKET
3. NUT
4. BOLT/SCREW 1.9 N·M (17 LB-IN)
5. RADIO

Fig. 31   Radio installation. DeVille & Fleetwood (FWD)

1. RADIO
2. L.H. BRACKET
3. BOLT/SCREW ASSEMBLY
4. FULLY DRIVEN, SEATED AND NOT STRIPPED
5. INSULATOR

Fig. 32   Radio replace. 1991 Eighty-Eight

2. Remove instrument cluster trim plate as described in "Instrument Cluster, Replace."
3. Remove five radio to instrument panel attaching screws.
4. Pulling radio rearward, disconnect electrical connectors and antenna.
5. Remove radio mounting brackets.
6. Reverse procedure to install.
7. Rearm airbag system as described under "Precautions."

PONTIAC

1991

1. Disable airbag system as described under "Precautions."
2. Remove instrument panel trim plate.
3. Disconnect two wires from lighter, then remove ashtray.
4. Remove radio upper mounting bracket retaining screws.
5. Remove rear support bracket retaining screw.
6. Press on instrument panel engagement tabs, **Fig. 33**, then pull radio from instrument panel.
7. Disconnect electrical connectors, then remove radio.
8. Reverse procedure to install.
9. Rearm airbag system as described under "Precautions."

1992—94

1. Disable airbag system as described under "Precautions."

18. SECTOR ASSY, SWITCH ACTUATOR
20. BEARING ASSY
21. BUSHING, BEARING RETAINING

22. CONTACT HORN CIRCUIT
23. RETAINER, UPPER BEARING
28. COVER, HOUSING
29. SCREW, BINDING HEAD

Fig. 35 Lock housing cover removal. Standard column

VIEW A

1 RADIO BRACKET ALIGNMENT PIN
2 RADIO
3 SCREW
4 RADIO MOUNTING BRACKET
5 IP RADIO MOUNT BRACKET

Fig. 34 Radio replace. 1992–94 Bonneville

19 COVER ASM, LOCK HOUSING
22 PIN, SWITCH ACTUATOR PIVOT
23 SWITCH ASM, PIVOT & (PULSE)

Fig. 38 Wiper switch removal. Tilt column & columns w/SIR

2. Remove turn signal switch as outlined under "Turn Signal Switch, Replace" procedure.
3. Refer to **Figs. 35 through 38,** for switch replacement.
4. Rearm airbag system as described under "Precautions."

24. SWITCH ASSY, PIVOT &
33. PIN, SWITCH ACTUATOR PIVOT

Fig. 36 Wiper switch removal. Standard column

19 COVER ASM, LOCK HOUSING
21 ACTUATOR, DIMMER SW ROD
24 BASE PLATE, COL HSG CVR END
25 CAP, COL HSG COVER END
77 ROD, DIMMER SWITCH
B MULTI-FUNCTION LEVER
F CRUISE CONTROL PLUG

Fig. 37 Lock housing cover removal. Tilt column & columns w/SIR

BLOWER MOTOR REPLACE

1. Disable airbag system as described under "Airbag System Disarming," then disconnect battery ground cable.
2. Disconnect cooling tube and blower motor electrical connector.
3. Remove blower motor attaching screws and the blower motor.
4. Reverse procedure to install.
5. Rearm airbag system as described under "Precautions."

HEATER CORE REPLACE

EXCEPT CADILLAC

1. Disable airbag system as described under "Precautions."
2. Disconnect battery ground cable.
3. Drain cooling system.
4. Remove right sound insulator.
5. Remove center and lower instrument panel trim plates.
6. **On models with automatic climate control,** remove speaker grille and speaker for access to programmer attaching bolt.
7. Disconnect wiring and hoses from programmer.
8. Remove programmer linkage cover and disconnect linkage.
9. Remove programmer attaching bolt and the programmer.

2. Disconnect battery ground cable.
3. Carefully pry instrument panel trim panel, pull panel upward, then rearward to remove.
4. Remove radio attaching screws, then pull rearward.
5. Disconnect electrical connector and antenna lead.
6. Remove radio assembly, **Fig. 34.**
7. Reverse procedure to install.
8. Rearm airbag system as described under "Precautions."

WINDSHIELD WIPER MOTOR REPLACE

1. Disable airbag system as described under "Precautions."
2. Remove wiper arms.
3. **On 1991 models,** remove cowl cover.
4. **On 1992-94 models,** remove air inlet screen assembly.
5. **On all models,** disconnect wiper arm drive link from crank arm.
6. Disconnect motor electrical connectors.
7. Remove wiper motor attaching screws, then remove motor guiding cranking arm through hole.

WINDSHIELD WIPER TRANSMISSION REPLACE

1. Disable airbag system as described under "Precautions."
2. **On 1992-94 models,** disconnect washer hoses.
3. **On all models,** remove wiper arms.
4. Remove air inlet screen assembly.
5. Disconnect drive link from motor crank arm.
6. Remove linkage attaching screws, the pull transmission through access hole in shroud upper panel.
7. Reverse procedure to install.
8. Rearm airbag system as described under "Precautions."

WINDSHIELD WIPER SWITCH REPLACE

1. Disable airbag system as described under "Precautions."

8. Reverse procedure to install.
9. Rearm airbag system as described under "Precautions."

1. BOLT/SCREW; 3 N•M (27 LB-IN)
2. EVAPORATOR AND BLOWER MODULE
3. GASKET
4. BOLT/SCREW; 3.4 N•M (30 LB-IN)
5. BLOWER MOTOR
6. SHIELD
7. BOLT/SCREW; 1.9 N•M (17 LB-IN)
8. DASH PANEL
9. CATALYTIC CONVERTER HEAT SHIELD
10. 13.0 MM (APPROXIMATELY)

Fig. 39 Evaporator removal. DeVille, Fleetwood (FWD) & Sixty Special

1. BOLT/SCREW; 3 N•M (27 LB-IN)
2. EVAPORATOR AND BLOWER MODULE
3. GASKET
4. BOLT/SCREW; 3.4 N•M (30 LB-IN)
5. BLOWER MOTOR
6. SHIELD
7. BOLT/SCREW; 1.9 N•M (17 LB-IN)
8. DASH PANEL
9. CATALYTIC CONVERTER HEAT SHIELD
10. 13.0 MM (APPROXIMATELY)

Fig. 40 Evaporator/heater module assembly. Park Avenue

10. **On all models,** remove heater core cover, then the splash cover for access to heater hoses.
11. Disconnect heater hoses from heater core.
12. Remove heater core cover, then the heater core.
13. Reverse procedure to install.
14. Rearm airbag system as described under "Precautions."

CADILLAC

1. Disable airbag system as described under "Precautions."
2. Disconnect battery ground cable.
3. Remove glove box attaching screws, then the glove box.
4. Remove lower sound insulator attaching screws and nuts, then the lower sound insulator.
5. Remove programmer as follows:
   a. Remove programmer shield attaching screws, then the programmer shield.
   b. Disconnect threaded rod from programmer.
   c. Disconnect programmer electrical and vacuum connector, then remove programmer.
6. Disconnect body control module electrical connector, then remove module attaching screws and module.
7. Remove relay panel from module assembly, then the module assembly heater core cover.
8. Disconnect heater hoses from heater core.

9. Remove two heater core attaching screws, then the heater core.
10. Reverse procedure to install.
11. Rearm airbag system as described under "Precautions."

EVAPORATOR CORE REPLACE

CADILLAC

1. Disable airbag system as described under "Precautions."
2. Disconnect battery ground cable.
3. Drain coolant, then remove front dash cover and vacuum tank.
4. Remove relay pack, EGR solenoid valve and related parts.
5. Loosen wiring harness from front of dash and position aside.
6. Disconnect heater hoses from evaporator module.
7. Remove MAP sensor, sensor bracket and attaching rods from dash panel.
8. Remove wiring harness brackets from lift cover and position out of the way.
9. Discharge A/C system.
10. Remove washer reservoir, then disconnect all accumulator lines.
11. Disconnect upper hose from power steering pump and position aside.
12. Remove blower motor and exhaust manifold heat shield, **Fig. 39.**
13. Disconnect all wiring and connectors

attached to evaporator and blower module.
14. Remove all brackets around barrier insulator, then all screws and bolts around insulator.
15. Raise and support vehicle.
16. Cut barrier insulator on mark line, located on right side of barrier insulator.
17. Remove evaporator core.
18. Reverse procedure to install.
19. Rearm airbag system as described under "Precautions."

PARK AVENUE

Brazed fittings are used on the condenser and evaporator. These fittings cannot be turned. It is important that the service technician recognize which fitting is to be turned and use backup wrenches. The brazed fitting that should not be turned is always the same color as the pipe it is brazed to.

1. Disconnect battery ground cable.
2. Discharge A/C system, then remove vacuum tank.
3. Remove rear sight shield, then disconnect positive battery booster cable from underhood fuse block.
4. Remove underhood fuse block from relay bracket and position aside.
5. Remove relay bracket from dash panel, then the blower resistor from top of evaporator/heater module casing.
6. Disconnect A/C module to accumulator tube from accumulator.
7. Disconnect A/C compressor and condenser hose from the accumulator.
8. Remove clamp from accumulator, then disconnect electrical connector from the pressure cycling switch.
9. Disconnect evaporator to condenser

tube from evaporator case and condenser.

10. Disengage tube from clips holding evaporator tube to fender, then remove tube from vehicle.
11. Remove blower motor, the all brackets from evaporator/heater module, **Fig. 40.**
12. Remove heat shield from bottom of evaporator/heater module, then the three screws attaching bottom of module to dash panel.
13. Remove five screws attaching top and side of module to the dash panel.
14. Cut insulator on module along line indicated, **Fig. 41.**
15. Remove four module to insulator attaching screws, located behind insulator.
16. Remove Electronic Brake Control Module (EBCM) as follows:
    a. Remove two screws attaching the Assembly Line Diagnostic Link (ALDL) connector to the righthand side sound insulator.
    b. Remove push-on nuts and attaching bolts from left and right sound insulators, **Fig. 41.**
    c. Remove righthand footwell courtesy light and oil life module from right side sound insulator, then the insulator from vehicle.
    d. Remove left footwell courtesy light from left side sound insulator, then the insulator from the vehicle.
    e. Remove two floor outlet assembly to instrument panel attaching screws.
    f. Remove four EBCM bracket to instrument panel attaching screws.
    g. Pull bracket away from the instrument panel and remove EBCM to bracket attaching bolt, then slide EBCM out of bracket.
17. Pull down rug and padding, then remove dash panel to evaporator/heater module case attaching screw.
18. Pull module case away from dash panel and remove evaporator.
19. Reverse procedure to install.

BUICK LESABRE, OLDSMOBILE & PONTIAC

Brazed fittings are used on the con-

Fig. 41 Electronic Brake Control Module (EBCM) assembly removal. Park Avenue

denser and evaporator. These fittings cannot be turned. It is important that the service technician recognize which fitting is to be turned and use backup wrenches. The brazed fitting that should not be turned is always the same color as the pipe it is brazed to.

1. Disconnect battery ground cable.
2. Discharge A/C system, then remove engine rear sight shield.
3. Disconnect electrical connector from pressure cycling switch.
4. Remove accumulator clamp screw.
5. Disconnect accumulator inlet and outlet connections, then remove accumulator from the vehicle.
6. Remove blower motor resistor, then the vacuum tank.

7. Remove engine coolant reservoir, then the evaporator tube from condenser outlet.
8. Disconnect A/C lines from clamp near the shock tower, then remove evaporator tube from vehicle.
9. Remove blower motor, then the brackets and heat shield from blower module assembly.
10. Cut blower module assembly along indicated line, then remove bolts attaching blower module assembly to front of dash (driver's side only).
11. Remove large piece of blower module assembly insulation.
12. Remove screws from evaporator cover, then the evaporator.
13. Reverse procedure to install.

3800/V6-231 Engines

INDEX

PRECAUTIONS
AIRBAG SYSTEM DISARMING
1991 Park Avenue

When carrying a live inflator module, ensure bag and trim cover are pointed away from you. Never carry inflator module by the wires or connector on underside of module.

The diagnostic energy reserve module (DERM) can maintain voltage to cause a system deployment for up to ten minutes after the ignition switch is turned off and the battery is disconnected. Servicing the SIR system during this period may result in accidental deployment and personal injury.

1. Turn ignition switch to Off position, then disconnect and tape battery ground cable terminal.
2. Remove SIR fuse from fuse block, then the left sound insulator.
3. Remove Connector Position Assurance (CPA), then disconnect yellow two-way SIR electrical connector at base of steering column.
4. Remove screws and/or nuts from back of steering wheel, then the inflator module from steering wheel.
5. Remove Connector Position Assurance (CPA), then disconnect coil assembly connector and horn lead.
6. Place inflator module on a bench or other surface with bag and trim cover facing up.

1991 Eighty-Eight & Ninety-Eight

The diagnostic energy reserve module (DERM) can maintain voltage to cause a system deployment for up to ten minutes after the ignition switch is turned off and the battery is disconnected. Servicing the SIR system during this period may result in accidental deployment and personal injury.

1. Turn ignition switch to Off position, then remove I/P fuse 7 from fuse block.

2. Disconnect yellow two-way SIR electrical connector at base of steering column.

1992-94 Bonneville, LeSabre, Park Avenue, Eighty-Eight & Ninety-Eight

The diagnostic energy reserve module (DERM) can maintain voltage to cause a system deployment for up to ten minutes after the ignition switch is turned off and the battery is disconnected. Servicing the SIR system during this period may result in accidental deployment and personal injury.

1. Ensure front wheels are pointed straight ahead.
2. Turn ignition switch to Lock position and remove SIR or AIRBAG fuse.
3. Remove left sound insulator. **Remove courtesy lamp from sound insulator, if necessary.**
4. **On models with passenger side airbag,** open trap door at rear of glove box.
5. **On all models,** remove Connector Position Assurance (CPA), then disconnect yellow two-way SIR electrical connectors at base of steering column and behind glove box trap door.

AIRBAG SYSTEM ARMING
1991 Park Avenue

1. Turn ignition switch to Off position, connect horn lead and coil assembly connector, then install Connector Position Assurance (CPA).
2. Install inflator module and secure to steering wheel with new screws and/or nuts.
3. **Torque** screws and/or nuts to 25 inch lbs.
4. Connect yellow two-way SIR electrical connector at base of steering column, then install Connector Position Assurance (CPA).
5. Install left sound insulator, then the SIR fuse into fuse block.
6. Connect battery ground cable.
8. Turn ignition switch to RUN position and ensure that "Inflatable Restraint"

indicator flashes 7 to 9 times, then shuts Off.

1991 Eighty-Eight & Ninety-Eight

1. Connect yellow two-way SIR electrical connector at base of steering column.
2. Install I/P fuse 7 into fuse block, turn ignition switch to RUN position and ensure that "Inflatable Restraint" indicator flashes 7 to 9 times, then shuts Off.

1992-94 Bonneville, LeSabre, Park Avenue, Eighty-Eight & Ninety-Eight

1. Connect yellow two-way SIR electrical connector(s), then install Connector Position Assurance (CPA).
2. Install left sound insulator. **Install courtesy lamp to sound insulator, if applicable.**
3. Install SIR fuse to fuse block, turn ignition switch to Run position and ensure that "Inflatable Restraint" lamp flashes 7 to 9 times, then shuts off.

FUEL SYSTEM PRESSURE RELIEF

After relieving fuel system pressure, a small amount of fuel may be released when servicing fuel pipes or connections. In order to reduce the risk of personal injury, cover fuel pipe fittings with a suitable shop towel before disconnecting to catch any fuel that may leak.

1. Disarm airbag system as described under "Precautions."
2. Disconnect battery ground cable, then loosen fuel filler cap to relieve tank pressure.
3. Connect fuel pressure gauge tool No. J 34370-1 or equivalent to fuel pressure connection. Wrap fitting in suitable shop towel.
4. Install bleed hose to suitable container, then open valve and bleed off pressure.
5. Disconnect fuel pressure gauge, then

Fig. 1   Engine mount. VIN C

drain gauge in suitable container.

6. Rearm airbag system as described under "Precautions."

ENGINE MOUNTS
REPLACE

3800/V6-231 VIN C

1. Disable airbag system as described under "Precautions."
2. Raise and support front of vehicle.
3. Attach suitable engine lifting equipment to engine.
4. Remove mount to engine bracket nuts. Raise engine slightly and remove mount to frame nuts.
6. Remove engine mount, **Fig. 1.**
7. Reverse procedure to install.
8. Rearm airbag system as described under "Precautions."

3800/V6-231 VIN L & 1

1. Disable airbag system as described under "Airbag System Disarming," then disconnect battery ground cable.
2. Attach suitable lifting equipment to engine, then raise engine slightly to remove weight from engine mounts.
3. Remove accessory drive belt.
4. Remove through bolt from front engine mount, **Fig. 2.**
5. Lift engine until power steering reservoir touches strut tower cross brace, then loosen bottom two bolts on front engine mount.
6. Remove A/C line clip, then the top two bolts from front engine mount and remove mount.
7. Reverse procedure to install.
8. Rearm airbag system as described under "Precautions."

ENGINE
REPLACE

1. Disable airbag system as described under "Precautions."
2. Relieve fuel pressure as outlined under "Fuel System Pressure Relief."

1	CROSS BRACE	4	NUT 70 N·m (52 LB. FT.)
2	BOLT 87 N·m (65 LB. FT.)	5	BRACKET
3	FRONT MOTOR MOUNT (TORQUE AXIS) MOUNTING BRACKET		

Fig. 2   Engine mount. VIN L & 1

3. Scribe hood installation alignment marks, then remove hood.
4. Disconnect battery leads, then drain engine coolant.
5. **On VIN L engines,** remove strut tower cross brace.
6. **On all models,** disconnect windshield washer, radiator and heater supply hoses.
7. Disconnect starter electrical connector and wiring.
8. Disconnect main engine harness and battery harness electrical connectors at relay center.
9. Remove accessory drive belt.
10. Remove power steering pump and position aside.
11. Remove air intake duct and air cleaner assembly.
12. Remove throttle cable from linkage bracket, then other applicable cables.
13. Disconnect the following electrical connectors and position aside:
    a. **On VIN L engines,** MAT sensor.
    b. **On all models,** throttle position switch.
    c. Idle air control valve.
    d. Oxygen sensor.
14. Remove ignition coil ground strap attaching screws.
15. Disconnect fuel feed and return lines from fuel rail and pressure regulator.
16. Disconnect throttle body canister hoses.
17. Disconnect brake booster and heater control hoses from engine vacuum connection.
18. Raise and support vehicle.
19. Remove exhaust pipe from right manifold.
20. Disconnect cruise control servo vacuum hoses.
21. Install suitable engine lifting equipment, then raise engine slightly.
22. Remove A/C compressor and position aside.
23. Disconnect engine oil cooler lines, if equipped.

Fig. 3   Intake manifold tightening sequence

24. Remove front engine mount.
25. Remove right front engine to transaxle bracket.
26. Using suitable jack stands, support transaxle, then remove engine to transaxle attaching bolts.
27. Remove flywheel cover.
28. Scribe flywheel installation alignment mark, then remove torque converter to flywheel attaching bolts.
29. Separate engine from transaxle, then remove engine assembly.
30. Reverse procedure to install.
31. Rearm airbag system as described under "Precautions."

INTAKE MANIFOLD
REPLACE

1. Disable airbag system as described under "Precautions."
2. Relieve fuel pressure as outlined under "Fuel System Pressure Relief."
3. Remove plastic engine cover and air intake duct, then remove fuel rail, then exhaust manifold heat shield.
4. Disconnect righthand side spark plug wires and position aside.
5. Remove cable bracket to cylinder head mounting bolt, then the power steering pump support bracket.
6. Loosen alternator and move to obtain clearance.
7. Remove alternator bracket, heater pipes and bypass hose.
8. Remove intake manifold attaching bolts, then the manifold.
9. Reverse procedure to install, noting the following:
    a. Clean cylinder block, heads and intake manifold sealing surface of all oil using a suitable solvent.
    b. Remove adhesive compound from intake manifold bolts and bolt holes.
    c. Apply thread lock compound part No. 12345493 or equivalent to intake manifold bolt threads prior to installation.
    d. Tighten intake manifold bolts in two steps to specifications in sequence shown in **Fig. 3.**
    e. Rearm airbag system as described under "Precautions."

1 SUPERCHARGER
2 GASKET, SUPERCHARGER
3 LOWER INTAKE MANIFOLD
4 BOLTS, SUPERCHARGER (8)
5 LOCATOR PINS
6 O-RINGS, COOLANT PASSAGE (2)
7 STUD, TENSIONER BRACKET TO SUPERCHARGER

Fig. 4 Supercharger. VIN 1

1 BOLT
2 INTAKE MANIFOLD UPPER
3 INTAKE MANIFOLD LOWER
4 INTAKE MANIFOLD GASKET
5 INTAKE MANIFOLD SEAL

Fig. 5 Upper intake manifold. VIN L

SUPERCHARGER
REPLACE

1. Disable airbag system as described under "Precautions."
2. Relieve fuel pressure as outlined under "Fuel System Pressure Relief."
3. Disconnect battery ground cable.
4. Remove accessory drive belt.
5. Remove fuel injector sight shield.
6. Disconnect fuel pipe from fuel rail.
7. Disconnect pressure regulator vacuum hose.
8. Disconnect injector electrical connectors.
9. Remove fuel rail attaching bolts, then remove rail with injectors.
10. Disconnect idle air control, throttle position switch, MAF, EGR and boost control solenoid electrical connectors, then position aside.
11. Remove air intake duct.
12. Disconnect throttle and cruise control cables.
13. Remove cable bracket.
14. Remove tensioner bracket to supercharger mounting stud with suitable stud removal tool or install two 8 mm nut together on stud, then install suitable wrench to inner nut and turn counterclockwise to remove stud.
15. Remove supercharger to intake manifold attaching bolts, **Fig. 4,** then remove and discard gasket and O-rings.
16. Reverse procedure to install.
17. Rearm airbag system as described under "Precautions."

UPPER INTAKE MANIFOLD
REPLACE

3800/V6-231 VIN L

1. Disable airbag system as described under "Airbag System Disarming," then relieve fuel pressure as outlined under "Fuel System Pressure Relief."

2. Disconnect battery ground cable.
3. Remove fuel injector sight shield and air intake duct.
4. Remove spark plug wires on right (rear) side of engine and position aside.
5. Remove fuel rail, then the exhaust manifold heat shield.
6. Remove cable bracket to cylinder head mounting bolt.
7. Remove upper intake manifold attaching bolts, then the manifold, **Fig. 5.**
8. Reverse procedure to install.
9. Rearm airbag system as described under "Precautions."

EXHAUST MANIFOLD
REPLACE

LEFT SIDE (FRONT)
3800/V6-231 VIN C & L

1. Disable airbag system as described under "Airbag System Disarming," then relieve fuel pressure as outlined under "Fuel System Pressure Relief."
2. Disconnect battery ground cable, then remove two crossover pipe to manifold attaching bolts.
3. Disconnect spark plug wires at spark plugs.
4. Remove manifold attaching bolts.
5. Remove oil dipstick tube and dipstick.
6. Remove manifold.
7. Reverse procedure to install.
8. Rearm airbag system as described under "Precautions."

3800/V6-231 VIN 1

1. Disable airbag system as described under "Precautions."
2. Relieve fuel pressure as outlined under "Fuel System Pressure Relief."
3. Disconnect battery ground cable.
4. Remove two flange bolts.
5. Remove manifold to bracket attaching nut.

6. Remove manifold to engine studs, then remove manifold.
7. Reverse procedure to install.
8. Rearm airbag system as described under "Precautions."

RIGHT SIDE (REAR)

1. Disable airbag system as described under "Precautions."
2. Relieve fuel pressure as outlined under "Fuel System Pressure Relief."
3. Disconnect battery ground cable, then disconnect spark plug wires from spark plugs and position aside.
4. Remove throttle cable bracket, then the crossover pipe heat shield.
5. Remove transaxle dipstick and dipstick tube.
6. Disconnect oxygen sensor lead, then remove EGR pipe.
7. Remove two exhaust pipe to manifold attaching bolts.
8. Remove plastic vacuum tank mounted on cowl, then raise and support vehicle.
9. Remove catalytic converter heat shield and pipe hanger.
10. Remove front exhaust pipe to manifold attaching nuts, then the pipe from manifold.
11. Lower vehicle, then remove engine lift bracket.
12. Remove exhaust manifold attaching nuts, then the manifold.
13. Reverse procedure to install.
14. Rearm airbag system as described under "Precautions."

Fig. 6 Cylinder head tightening sequence

CYLINDER HEAD
REPLACE

1. Disable airbag system as described under "Precautions."
2. Relieve fuel pressure as outlined under "Fuel System Pressure Relief."
3. Disconnect battery ground cable, then remove intake and exhaust manifolds as described previously.
4. To remove left (front) valve cover, proceed as follows:
   a. Disconnect C³I and spark plug wires.
   b. Remove alternator bracket.
   c. Remove A/C compressor bracket bolt.
5. To remove right (rear) valve cover, proceed as follows:
   a. Remove power steering pump.
   b. Remove belt tensioner assembly.
   c. Remove fuel line heat shield.
6. Remove rocker arm assemblies, guide plate and pushrods.
7. Remove cylinder head attaching bolts, then remove.
8. Reverse procedure to install, noting the following:
   a. Clean all gasket mating surfaces and cylinder head bolt holes in block.
   b. Clean threads in block with appropriate tap.
   c. Apply suitable sealant to bolt threads.
   d. **Torque** cylinder head bolts to 35 ft. lbs. in sequence, **Fig. 6.**
   e. Tighten each bolt an additional 130° in sequence.
   f. Tighten center four bolts an additional 30° in sequence.
   g. Rearm airbag system as described under "Precautions."

VALVE ARRANGEMENT
FRONT TO REAR
Left Side
3800/V6-231 VIN C & L . . . . . . E-I-E-I-I-E

Right Side
3800/V6-231 VIN C & L . . . . . . E-I-I-E-I-E

CAM LOBE LIFT SPECIFICATIONS

Engine/VIN	Year	Int.	Exh.
3800/V6-231/C & L	1991–94	.250	.255

24	DOWEL PIN
143	HEAD GASKET
148	LIFTER GUIDE
149	VALVE LIFTER
150	PUSHROD GUIDE
151	ROCKER ARM
152	ROCKER ARM PIVOT
154	PUSHROD
155	LIFTER GUIDE RETAINER
201	BOLT
202	BOLT
203	HEAD BOLT

Fig. 7 Rocker arm assembly

ROCKER ARMS

Rocker arms are pedestal mounted, over support plates, **Fig. 7.** To replace rocker arms, remove valve cover, pedestal retaining bolt(s), pedestal and the rocker arm. Replace rocker arms and pedestals as an assembly if they are damaged or excessively worn. If rocker arms are to be reused, they must be installed in original position.

VALVE GUIDES

The valve guides are an integral part of the cylinder head and cannot be replaced. If excessive valve stem clearance is noted, the valve guide must be reamed and an oversize valve guide installed. Valves are available in an oversize of .010 inch.

FRONT COVER
REPLACE

1. Disable airbag system as described under "Airbag System Disarming," then relieve fuel pressure as outlined under "Fuel System Pressure Relief."
2. Disconnect battery ground cable.
3. **On Vin L and 1 engines,** remove torque axis mount.
4. **On all engines,** remove serpentine belt.
5. Using pulling tool No. J38197 or equivalent, remove crankshaft pulley.
6. Remove crankshaft sensor shield, then oil pan to front cover attaching bolts.
7. Remove front cover attaching bolts, then the front cover.
8. Reverse procedure to install, noting the following:
   a. Inspect timing chain for in and out movement, movement should not exceed 1 inch.
   b. Check timing chain sprockets for any signs of wear.

c. Clean gasket mating surfaces at timing chain cover and cylinder block.
d. Apply sealant part No. 1052080 or equivalent to bolt threads prior to installation.
e. Adjust crankshaft sensor using tool No. J37087 or equivalent as shown in **Fig. 8.**
f. Rearm airbag system as described under "Precautions."

TIMING CHAIN
REPLACE

1. Remove front cover as outlined under "Front Cover, Replace."
2. **On Vin C engines,** remove camshaft thrust button.
3. **On all engines,** align timing marks on sprockets, **Fig. 9,** so that they are as close together as possible.
4. Remove timing chain dampener.
5. Remove camshaft sprocket bolts, **Figs. 10 and 11.**
6. Remove camshaft sprocket and chain, then the crankshaft sprocket.
7. Reverse procedure to install, noting the following:
   a. Ensure No. 1 piston is at TDC.
   b. Ensure camshaft and balance shaft timing marks are straight down, **Fig. 9.**
   c. Assemble timing chain on sprockets with their timing marks in their closest together position.
   d. Torque camshaft sprocket bolts specifications.

CAMSHAFT
REPLACE

1. Disable airbag system as described under "Airbag System Disarming," then relieve fuel pressure as outlined under "Fuel System Pressure Relief."

Fig. 8 Crankshaft sensor adjustment

Fig. 9 Timing balance shaft & camshaft marks

1	37 N•M (27 LBS. FT.)
2	TIMING CHAIN
3	CAMSHAFT SPROCKET
4	CAMSHAFT GEAR
5	KEY
6	DAMPER
7	BOLT (SPECIAL) 19 N•M (14 LBS. FT.)
8	SPRING
9	CRANKSHAFT SPROCKET

Fig. 10 Timing chain & sprockets. VIN C

2. Disconnect battery ground cable, then remove intake manifold as described previously.
3. Remove valve cover, rocker arms, pushrods and valve lifters.
4. Remove crankshaft pulley and crankshaft sensor cover.
5. Remove front cover, timing chain and sprockets.
6. Remove camshaft thrust plate and camshaft. **When removing or installing camshaft, avoid marring the bearing surface.**
7. Reverse procedure to install, coating camshaft and valve lifters with prelube part No. 1052365 or equivalent prior to installation.
8. Rearm airbag system as described under "Precautions."

BALANCE SHAFT
REPLACE
REMOVAL

1. Remove engine as previously described.
2. Remove flywheel, then the intake manifold.
3. Remove lifter guide retainer, then the front cover.
4. Remove balance shaft drive gear bolt, **Fig. 12,** then the camshaft sprocket and timing chain.
5. Remove balance shaft retainer bolts, retainer and gear.
6. Using tool J-6125-B, remove balance shaft. **The balance shaft and both bearings are serviced as a complete package. Use only the correct tools for bearing and shaft removal and installation. Inspect balance shaft drive gear and the camshaft drive gear for nicks and burrs.**
7. Remove balance shaft rear plug.
8. Using tool J-36995-5, remove balance shaft rear bearing.

INSTALLATION

1. Dip balance shaft rear bearing in clean engine oil, then, using tool J-36995-1, install bearing with rolled edge facing into engine and manufacturer's markings facing flywheel side.
2. Dip front balance shaft bearing into clean engine oil, then, using tool J-36996, install balance shaft into block.

63	KEY
78	DAMPER ASSEMBLY
79	CRANKSHAFT SPROCKET
84	BOLT
85	TIMING CHAIN
87	CAMSHAFT SPROCKET
88	CAMSHAFT GEAR

Fig. 11 Timing chain & sprockets. VIN L & 1

3. Temporarily install balance shaft bearing retainer and bolts.
4. Install balance shaft drive gear, then apply suitable sealant to and install bolt, tightening to specifications.
5. Install balance shaft rear plug.
6. Measure balance shaft endplay, **Fig. 13.**. Endplay should be 0–.008 inch.
7. Measure balance shaft radial play at both front and rear, **Figs. 14 and 15.** Front radial play should be 0–.0011 inch and rear radial play should be .0005–.0047 inch.
8. Turn camshaft so, with camshaft sprocket temporarily installed, timing mark is straight down.
9. With camshaft sprocket and camshaft gear removed, turn balance shaft so that the timing mark on gear points straight down.
10. Install camshaft gear, aligning marks on balance shaft gear and camshaft gear by turning balance shaft, **Fig. 9.**
11. Turn crankshaft so that No. 1 piston is at TDC.
12. Install timing chain and camshaft sprocket.
13. Measure gear lash, **Fig. 16,** at four places, every ¼ turn. Lash should be .002–.005 inch.
14. Install balance shaft front bearing retainer and bolts, then tighten to specifications.
15. Install front cover, then the lifter guide retainer.
16. Install intake manifold, then the fly-

wheel. Torque flywheel bolts to specifications.
17. Install engine in vehicle.

PISTON & ROD, ASSEMBLE

Pistons should be assembled to rods and installed as shown in **Fig. 17.**

After piston and rod installation, measure connecting rod side clearance. Side clearance should be .003–.015 inch.

PISTONS, PINS & RINGS

Pistons and ring are available in standard sizes and oversizes of .010. Piston pins are supplied with the piston and are available in standard size only.

To check piston fit in bore, measure bore diameter using suitable telescoping gauges and record reading. Measure piston across skirt at a point ¾ inch below piston pin center line and record reading. Subtract piston diameter from bore diameter and compare to specified clearance.

MAIN & ROD BEARINGS

Main bearings are available in standard sizes and undersizes of .001 and .002 inch. Rod bearings are available in standard size and an undersize of .008 inch.

CRANKSHAFT OIL SEAL
REPLACE

1. Remove flexplate and confirm rear seal leak.
2. Insert a screwdriver through oil seal dust lip and pry seal out towards end of crankshaft pilot.
3. Reverse procedure to install, noting the following:

REMOVING SHAFT

INSTALLING REAR BEARING

REMOVING REAR BEARING

INSTALLING SHAFT

2	BOLT	7	RETAINER
3	BALANCE SHAFT GEAR	8	PLUG
5	PIN	9	BEARING
6	BOLT	214	WASHER

215 NUT

Fig. 12   Balance shaft service

Fig. 13   Measuring balance shaft endplay

Fig. 14   Measuring balance shaft front radial play

Fig. 15   Measuring balance shaft rear radial play

a. Check inside of bore and crankshaft for nicks or burrs. Repair or replace as required.

b. Apply engine oil to inside and outside surfaces of the new seal, then slide seal over seal installation tool No. J38196 or equivalent as shown in **Fig. 18**, until seal bottoms squarely against bottom of tool.

c. Align dowel pin of tool with dowel pin in crankshaft and attach tool to crankshaft by hand and tighten attaching screws to 60 inch lbs, **Fig. 19.**

d. Turn T-handle of tool so that collar pushes seal into bore, turn handle until collar is tight against case.

e. Loosen T-handle, remove attaching screws and the tool.

OIL PAN
REPLACE

1. Disable airbag system as described under "Airbag System Disarming," then relieve fuel pressure as outlined under "Fuel System Pressure Relief."
2. Raise and support vehicle, then drain engine oil.
3. **On 1992-94 models,** disconnect oil level sensor electrical connector.
4. **On all models,** remove oil pan retaining bolts, then the oil pan.
5. Remove old oil pan gasket and discard.
6. Reverse procedure to install.
7. Rearm airbag system as described under "Precautions."

OIL PUMP SERVICE
REMOVAL & INSPECTION

1. Remove front cover, refer to "Front Cover, Replace" procedure.
2. Remove oil filter adapter, pressure regulator valve and spring.
3. Remove oil pump cover attaching screws, then the cover and gears, **Fig. 20.**
4. Check pump cover and housing for cracks, scoring, porous or damaged casting, damaged threads or excessive wear or galling. Replace as required.
5. Check pressure regulator valve for scoring, burrs or sticking in valve bore. Replace as required.

Fig. 16 Measuring balance shaft gear lash

RIDGE(S)

RIDGE(S) TOWARD FRONT OF ENGINE

FRONT OF ENGINE

Fig. 17 Piston installation direction

SPRING SIDE
DUST LIP SIDE
J 38196

SEAL BORE TO SEAL SURFACE TO BE LUBRICATED WITH ENGINE OIL BEFORE ASSEMBLY

Fig. 18 Crankshaft rear oil seal (rear main) & tool

1	ALIGNMENT HOLE
2	DUST LIP
3	DOWEL PIN
4	COLLAR
5	MANDRIL
6	ATTACHING SCREWS
7	SEAL

Fig. 19 Crankshaft rear oil seal installation (rear main)

59 PUMP OUTER GEAR
59 PUMP INNER GEAR
60 OIL PUMP COVER
64 SCREW
72 FRONT COVER

Fig. 20 Oil pump

Fig. 21 Measuring oil pump inner gear tip clearance

Fig. 23 Measuring oil pump gear end clearance

2. Measure oil pump outer gear diameter clearance, **Fig. 22**. Clearance should be .008-.015 inch.
3. Measure oil pump gear end clearance with gear dropped in housing, **Fig. 23**. Clearance should be .0010-.0035 inch.
4. Measure pressure regulator valve for valve to bore clearance of .0015-.003 inch.
5. Lubricate all gears with clean motor oil, then install gears in housing.
6. Pack pump cavity with suitable petroleum jelly.
7. Install pump cover and cover attaching screws. Tighten cover attaching screws to specifications.
8. Install pressure regulator valve and spring.
9. Install oil filter adapter using a new gasket. Torque oil filter adapter attaching bolts to specifications.
10. Install front cover on engine. During front cover installation, ensure inner pump gear is properly engaged on crankshaft sprocket.

BELT TENSION DATA

Belt Serpentine	New Lbs. ①	Used Lbs. ①

① —Equipped with auto-tensioner.

Fig. 22 Measuring oil pump outer gear diameter clearance

6. Check pressure regulator valve spring for tension loss or bending. Replace spring as required.
7. Check gears for chipping galling or excessive wear. Replace as required.

ASSEMBLY & INSTALLATION

1. Measure oil pump inner gear tip clearance, **Fig. 21**. Maximum clearance should be .006 inch.

SERPENTINE DRIVE BELTS

BELT ROUTING

Refer to **Figs. 24** and **25**, for serpentine drive belt routing.

BELT TENSIONER, REPLACE

3800/V6-231 VIN C & L

1. Disable airbag system as described under "Precautions."
2. Disconnect battery ground cable.
3. Remove accessory drive, **Fig. 24**.
4. Remove tensioner pulley attaching bolt, then remove pulley.

Fig. 24 Serpentine belt routing & replacement. VIN C & L

5. Remove power steering pump from bracket and position aside.
6. Loosen, but do not remove, alternator attaching bolts, then remove alternator to tensioner attaching bolt.
7. Remove tensioner attaching bolt and studs, then remove.
8. Reverse procedure to install.
9. Rearm airbag system as described under "Precautions."

3800/V6-231 VIN 1

1. Disable airbag system as described under "Precautions."
2. Disconnect battery ground cable.
3. Remove inner and outer accessory drive belts, Fig. 25.
4. Remove alternator attaching bolts, then position aside.
5. Drain engine coolant.
6. Disconnect heater hoses from pipes and pipes from engine.
7. Raise and support vehicle.
8. Remove lower bracket to transaxle bracket attaching bolt.
9. Drain power steering fluid, then disconnect power steering hoses.
10. Remove power steering pump attaching bolts, then position aside.
11. Lower vehicle.
12. Remove tensioner bracket attaching bolts, supercharger to bracket attaching nut, then remove tensioner and bracket.
13. Reverse procedure to install.
14. Rearm airbag system as described under "Precautions."

BELT, REPLACE

1. Disable airbag system as described under "Precautions."
2. Disconnect battery ground cable.
3. **On VIN C and L engines,** refer to **Fig. 24.**
4. **On VIN 1 engines,** refer to **Fig. 25.**
5. **On all models,** reverse procedure to install.
6. Rearm airbag system as described under "Precautions."

COOLING SYSTEM BLEED

1. Fill cooling system and leave radiator cap off.
2. Turn A/C-heater control to any A/C mode and set temperature to the highest setting.
3. Start engine and allow engine to idle until bottom radiator hose is hot.
4. Cycle engine speed up to 3000 RPM and back to idle five times. This should expel any trapped air in the system.
5. Refill radiator and install pressure cap.
6. Allow engine to return to outside temperature, then fill coolant reservoir to FULL COLD mark.

THERMOSTAT REPLACE

1. Disable airbag system as described under "Airbag System Disarming," then disconnect battery negative cable.
2. With engine cool, drain engine coolant below thermostat level. **Never open cooling system with engine hot. Failure to follow this warning may cause personal injury.**
3. Disconnect radiator hose from thermostat housing.
4. Remove thermostat housing retaining bolt(s), then the housing, gasket and thermostat.
5. Reverse procedure to install noting the following:
   a. Prior to installation, ensure thermostat gasket area is thoroughly clean.
   b. Install thermostat with new gasket.
   c. Tighten thermostat housing retaining bolt(s) to specifications.
   d. Refill and bleed cooling system as needed.
   e. Rearm airbag system as described under "Precautions."

WATER PUMP REPLACE

1. Disconnect battery ground cable and drain cooling system.
2. Remove drive belts and disconnect radiator hoses and heater hoses from pump.
3. Remove water pump pulley attaching bolts, **Fig. 26.** The long bolt is accessed through hole in body side rail. Remove pump pulley.
4. Remove water pump attaching bolts

Fig. 25 Serpentine belt routing & replacement. VIN 1
and the water pump.
5. Reverse procedure to install.

FUEL PUMP REPLACE

1. Disable airbag system as described under "Airbag System Disarming," then relieve fuel pressure as outlined under "Fuel System Pressure Relief."
2. Disconnect battery ground cable.
3. Drain fuel tank and disconnect tank unit wire from connector in rear compartment.
4. Remove ground wire retaining screw from underbody.
5. Disconnect hoses from tank unit.
6. Support fuel tank and release the two retaining straps. Lower tank from vehicle.
7. Remove fuel gauge sender and pump assembly by turning cam lock counterclockwise, then remove.
8. Remove pump from sending unit.
9. Reverse procedure to install.
10. Rearm airbag system as described under "Precautions."

FUEL FILTER REPLACE

1. Disable airbag system as described under "Airbag System Disarming," then relieve fuel pressure as outlined under "Fuel System Pressure Relief."
2. Raise and support vehicle.
3. Disconnect fuel pipe inlet connector, then loosen filter from bracket, **Fig. 27.**

1. WATER PUMP
2. ENGINE FRONT COVER ASM.
3. GASKET
4. 11 N•m (97 LBS. IN.)
5. 39 N•m.(29 LBS. FT.)

Fig. 26 Water pump assembly

| 1 FUEL FILTER | 3 BOLT/SCREW |
| 2 QUICK CONNECTOR | 4 FUEL FILTER BRACKET |

Fig. 27 Fuel filter replacement

4. Disconnect outlet connector, then remove filter.
5. Reverse procedure to install.
6. Rearm airbag system as described under "Precautions."

TIGHTENING SPECIFICATIONS

Year	Component	Torque/Ft. Lbs.
1991-94	Balance Shaft Gear Bolt	14 ①
	Balance Shaft Retainer	22
	Boost Control Solenoid To Bypass Actuator	22 ⑲
	Bypass Actuator To Supercharger	22 ⑲
	Camshaft Sensor To Front Cover	75 ②
	Camshaft Sprocket Bolts	⑥
	Connecting Rod Bolts	⑦
	Coolant Temperature Sensor To Intake	15
	Crankshaft Bearing Caps	⑧
	Crankshaft Sensor To Front Cover	22
	Crankshaft Sensor Clamp Bolt	40 ②
	Cylinder Block Drain Plug	15
	Cylinder Head To Block	③
	EGR Pipe To Exhaust Manifold	15
	EGR Pipe To EGR Valve	20
	EGR Valve To Intake Manifold Adapter	20
	Engine Mount To Cylinder Block	70
	ESC Knock Sensor	13
	Exhaust Manifold To Cylinder Head	⑩
	Flywheel Cover To Transaxle	48 ②
	Flywheel To Crankshaft	⑪
	Front Cover To Block	22
	Fuel Feed & Return Pipes To Fuel Rail	22
	Fuel Rail To Intake Manifold	⑫
	Generator Support To Cylinder Head	36
	Generator Support Through Generator	36
	Heater Hose Fitting To Intake	11
	Ignition Module To Generator Support	18
	Intake Manifold To Cylinder Head	88 ②
	Intake Manifold (Upper) To Lower Manifold	⑳

Year	Component	Torque/Ft. Lbs.
1991-94 —Cont'd	Oil Filter Adapter To Front Cover	⑬
	Oil Galley Plugs	25
	Oil Level Sensor To Oil Pan	16 ⑱
	Oil Pan Drain Plug	⑭
	Oil Pan To Block	124 ②
	Oil Pan To Front Cover	124 ②
	Oil Pressure Switch	24
	Oil Pump Cover To Front Cover	97 ②
	Oil Screen Housing To Cylinder Block	⑮
	Oxygen Sensor	31
	Pulley Assembly To Crankshaft	⑨
	Rocker Arm Cover	88 ②
	Rocker Arm Pedestal	28
	Spark Plug	⑯
	Starter Motor	35
	Supercharger To Lower Intake Manifold	19-22 ⑲
	Thermostat Housing	20
	Throttle Body Adapter To Intake	20
	Throttle Body To Throttle Body Adapter	20
	Throttle Cable Bracket	35 ②
	Timing Chain Damper	④
	Torque Converter To Flywheel	46
	Transaxle To Cylinder Block	55
	Valve Lifter Guide Bolts	⑤
	Water Pump Cover To Timing Chain Cover	⑰
	Water Pump Pulley	114 ②

①—Tighten bolt an additional 35°.
②—Inch lbs.
③—Refer to text for procedure.
④—1991, 14 ft. lbs., 1992-94, 16 ft. lbs.
⑤—1991, 27 ft. lbs., 1992-94, 22 ft. lbs.

Continued

TIGHTENING SPECIFICATIONS—Continued

⑥ —1991, 27 ft. lbs., 1992–94, 74 ft. lbs. then tighten an additional 105°.
⑦ —20 ft. lbs., then tighten an additional 50°.
⑧ —26 ft. lbs., then tighten an additional 50°.
⑨ —1991, 105 ft. lbs., then tighten an additional 56°, 1992–94, 110 ft. lbs., then tighten an additional 76°.
⑩ —1991, 41 ft. lbs., 1992–94, 38 ft. lbs.
⑪ —1991, 61 ft. lbs., 1992–94, 11 ft. lbs., then tighten an additional 50°.

⑫ —1991, 120 inch lbs., 1992–94, 11 ft. lbs.
⑬ —1991, 24 ft. lbs., 1992–94, 22 ft. lbs.
⑭ —1991, 18 ft. lbs., 1992–94 30 ft. lbs.
⑮ —1991, 73 inch lbs., 1992–94, 11 ft. lbs.
⑯ —1991, 20 ft. lbs., 1992–94, 12 ft. lbs.
⑰ —1991, 126 inch lbs., 1992–94, 11 ft. lbs.
⑱ —1992–94 models.
⑲ —VIN 1, supercharged.
⑳ —1992–94, 22 ft. lbs.

4.6L/V8-279 Engine

NOTE: Refer To The 4.6L/V8-279 Engine Section In The Buick Reatta & Riviera: Cadillac Eldorado & Seville: Oldsmobile Toronado & Trofeo Section For Repair Procedures On This Engine.

4.9L/V8-300 Engines

INDEX

PRECAUTIONS
AIRBAG SYSTEM DISARMING

The diagnostic energy reserve module (DERM) can maintain voltage to cause a system deployment for up to ten minutes after the ignition switch is turned off and the battery is disconnected. Servicing the SIR system during this period may result in accidental deployment and personal injury.

1. Ensure front wheels are pointed straight ahead.
2. Turn ignition switch to Lock position and remove SIR or AIRBAG fuse.
3. Remove left sound insulator. **Remove courtesy lamp from sound insulator, if necessary.**
4. Remove Connector Position Assurance (CPA), then disconnect yellow two-way SIR electrical connector at base of steering column.

AIRBAG SYSTEM ARMING

1. Connect yellow two-way SIR electrical connector, then install Connector Position Assurance (CPA).
2. Install left sound insulator. **Install courtesy lamp to sound insulator, if applicable.**
3. Install SIR fuse to fuse block, turn ignition switch to Run position and ensure that "Inflatable Restraint" lamp flashes 7 to 9 times, then shuts off.

FUEL SYSTEM PRESSURE RELIEF

After relieving fuel system pressure, a small amount of fuel may be released when servicing fuel pipes or connections. In order to reduce the risk of personal injury, cover fuel pipe fittings with a suitable shop towel before disconnecting to catch any fuel that may leak.

1. Disarm airbag system as outlined under "Precautions."
2. Disconnect battery ground cable, then loosen fuel filler cap to relieve tank pressure.
3. Connect fuel pressure gauge tool No. J 34370-1 or equivalent to fuel pressure connection. Wrap fitting in suitable shop towel.
4. Install bleed hose to suitable container, then open valve and bleed off pressure.
5. Disconnect fuel pressure gauge, then drain gauge in suitable container.
6. Rearm airbag system as outlined under "Precautions."

Fig. 1   Engine & transaxle mounts

ENGINE MOUNTS
REPLACE
RIGHT SIDE

1. Disarm airbag system as outlined under "Precautions."
2. Relieve fuel pressure as outlined under "Fuel System Pressure Relief."
3. Open hood, then remove engine bracket to engine brace.
4. Remove engine bracket to mount attaching nuts.
5. Raise and support vehicle.
6. Using suitable jack stands, support vehicle at each front frame horn.
7. Remove two engine mount to frame attaching nut, **Fig. 1.**
8. Remove two transaxle bracket to mount attaching nuts.
9. Install engine support tool No. J 28467 or equivalent, then raise engine until bracket is clear of mounts.
10. Remove bracket to block stud and bolts, then pull mount and bracket forward to remove.
11. Remove transaxle mount bracket, then mount assembly.
12. Reverse procedure to install.

13. Rearm airbag system as outlined under "Precautions."

LEFT FRONT TRANSAXLE MOUNT

1. Disarm airbag system as outlined under "Precautions."
2. Relieve fuel pressure as outlined under "Fuel System Pressure Relief."
3. Raise and support vehicle.
4. Using suitable jack stands, support vehicle at each front frame horn.
5. Remove mount to transaxle bracket and frame attaching nuts.
6. Install engine support tool No. J 28467 or equivalent, raise engine, then remove bracket to transaxle attaching bolts.
7. Raise engine assembly until brackets are clear.
8. Pull mount and bracket upward to remove.
9. Reverse procedure to install.
10. Rearm airbag system as outlined under "Precautions."

LEFT REAR TRANSAXLE MOUNT

1. Disarm airbag system as outlined under "Precautions."
2. Relieve fuel pressure as outlined under "Fuel System Pressure Relief."
3. Raise vehicle hood, install engine support tool No. J 28467 or equivalent, then raise and support vehicle.
4. Remove rack and pinion three right-hand attaching bolts.
5. Remove mount attaching nuts and bolts.
6. While moving rack and pinion up and forward, remove mount assembly.
7. Reverse procedure to install.
8. Rearm airbag system as outlined under "Precautions."

ENGINE
REPLACE

1. Disarm airbag system as outlined under "Precautions."
2. Relieve fuel pressure as outlined under "Fuel System Pressure Relief."
3. Disconnect battery ground cable.
4. Drain engine coolant and oil.
5. Remove air cleaner assembly.
6. Mark hood installation alignment mars, then remove.
7. Remove cooling fan.
8. Remove accessory drive belt.
9. Remove upper radiator and heater hoses from thermostat housing.
10. Disconnect and position aside the following electrical connectors:
    a. Oil pressure switch.
    b. distributor.
    c. EGR solenoid.
    d. Engine temperature switch.
    e. Idle speed control (ISC).
    f. Throttle position sensor (TPS).
    g. Coolant temperature sensor and fuel injectors at rail connector.
    h. MAT sensor.
    i. Oxygen sensor.
    j. Alternator.
    k. Ground wire at alternator bracket.
11. Disconnect throttle cable from throttle lever.
12. Disconnect cruise control diaphragm with bracket and position aside.
13. Remove exhaust crossover pipe.
14. Disconnect oil and transmission cooler lines at radiator.
15. Remove radiator.
16. Disconnect oil and transmission cooler lines from oil filter adapter, then remove lines.
17. Remove oil cooler line bracket at transmission, then air cleaner bracket.
18. Remove oil filter housing adapter.
19. Remove strut tower crosscar brace.
20. Remove right front heater hose.
21. Remove power steering line bracket from right cylinder head.
22. Disconnect power steering tensioner assembly and position aside.
23. Discharge A/C system, then disconnect accumulator and condenser lines.
24. Disconnect fuel rail fuel lines, then remove fuel line bracket to transmission

BOLT TIGHTENING SEQUENCE

1. TIGHTEN BOLTS 1, 2, 3, & 4 IN SEQUENCE TO 12.0 N·m (8 FT-LBS).
2. TIGHTEN BOLTS 5 THRU 16 IN SEQUENCE TO 12.0 N·m (8 FT-LBS).
3. RETIGHTEN ALL BOLTS IN SEQUENCE TO 16.0 N·m (12 FT-LBS).
4. REPEAT STEP 3 UNTIL TORQUE LEVEL IS MAINTAINED.

BOLT POSITION	BOLT LENGTH (MM)	BOLT POSITION	BOLT LENGTH (MM)
1	55	9	40
2	55	10	40
3	55	11	40
4	55	12	55
5	30	13	40 W/Studhead
6	30	14	40
7	30	15	55
8	30	16	40

Fig. 2   Intake manifold bolt size & bolt torque sequence

Fig. 3   Cylinder head bolt tightening sequence

25. Disconnect vacuum modulator line and power brake vacuum line and position aside.
26. Raise and support vehicle.
27. Remove starter heat shield.
28. Disconnect starter electrical connectors and engine block ground wires.
29. Disconnect exhaust pipe to converter at RH manifold.
30. Remove starter, then two flexplate covers.
31. Remove three flexplate attaching bolts, then remove.
32. Remove A/C compressor lower dust shield.
33. Remove right front wheel and tire assembly.
34. Remove wheelwell plastic shield.
35. Remove right rear transaxle to engine mount.
36. Remove lower engine mount attaching nut.
37. Remove front engine mount attaching nuts, then right rear transaxle mount attaching bolts.
38. Disconnect oxygen sensor electrical connector and heater bypass bracket front righthand side of vehicle.
39. Lower vehicle, then remove five upper engine to transaxle attaching bolts.
40. Install suitable engine lifting equipment, ensuring A/C accumulator line clearance.
41. Support transmission using suitable jack stand, then remove engine to transmission attaching bolts, then remove engine assembly.
42. Reverse procedure to install.
43. Rearm airbag system as outlined under "Precautions."

INTAKE MANIFOLD
REPLACE

1. Disarm airbag system as outlined under "Precautions."
2. Relieve fuel pressure as outlined un-

der "Fuel System Pressure Relief."
3. Disconnect battery ground cable.
4. Remove air cleaner assembly, then drain engine coolant.
5. Remove cross car brace, then accessory drive belt.
6. Disconnect power steering and tensioner bracket assembly and position aside.
7. Remove alternator and bracket.
8. Disconnect throttle cable from throttle body.
9. Disconnect the following electrical connectors and position aside:
   a. Distributor.
   b. Oil pressure switch.
   c. Coolant sensor.
   d. EGR solenoid.
   e. ISC motor.
   f. TP sensor.
   g. Fuel injectors.
   h. MAT sensor.
10. Remove MAP hoses.
11. Disconnect thermostat housing attaching hoses.
12. Remove A/C hose bracket.
13. Remove distributor cap, spark plug wire protectors and position aside.
14. Mark distributor rotor installation alignment, then remove rotor.
15. Disconnect fuel lines at transmission bracket.
16. Disconnect throttle body fuel and vacuum lines.
17. Disconnect throttle body and transmission modulator line vacuum supply lines.
18. Loosen vacuum line clip at lift bracket.
19. Remove valve covers.
20. Mark pushrods with installation positions, then remove rocker arms and pushrods. **Ensure pushrods are installed in original positions.**
21. Remove bracket at power steering.
22. Remove right front and rear lift brackets.
23. Remove intake manifold attaching bolts, then remove.
24. Reverse procedure to install. Refer to **Fig. 2,** for torque specifications and

tightening sequence.
25. Rearm airbag system as outlined under "Precautions."

EXHAUST MANIFOLD
REPLACE
RIGHT SIDE

1. Disarm airbag system as outlined under "Precautions."
2. Relieve fuel pressure as outlined under "Fuel System Pressure Relief."
3. Disconnect battery ground cable, then remove air cleaner assembly.
4. Disconnect oxygen sensor and coolant temperature sensor electrical connectors.
5. Remove two forward, upper exhaust manifold to cylinder head attaching bolts.
6. Raise and support vehicle.
7. Remove manifold to converter exhaust pipe attaching bolts.
8. Using suitable jack stands, support engine cradle.
9. Remove rear engine cradle bolts, loosen, but do not remove, front cradle bolts.
10. Lower engine cradle slightly, then remove exhaust manifold attaching bolts, remove manifold.
11. Reverse procedure to install.
12. Rearm airbag system as outlined under "Precautions."

LEFT SIDE

1. Disarm airbag system as outlined under "Precautions."
2. Relieve fuel pressure as outlined under "Fuel System Pressure Relief."
3. Disconnect battery ground cable.
4. Remove both cooling fans.
5. Remove exhaust crossover pipe.
6. Remove accessory drive belt.
7. Remove power steering and tensioner covering manifolds.
8. Remove manifold attaching bolts, then remove.
9. Reverse procedure to install.
10. Rearm airbag system as outlined under "Precautions."

CYLINDER HEAD
REPLACE

1. Disarm airbag system as outlined un-

Fig. 4   Rocker arm support, rocker arms & pivots

Fig. 6   RTV sealant application

PLUNGER AND BODY ARE FITTED PAIRS AND MUST NOT BE MISMATED.

Fig. 5   Hydraulic valve lifter

der "Airbag System Disarming," then relieve fuel pressure as outlined under "Fuel System Pressure Relief."

2. Disconnect battery ground cable, then drain cooling system.
3. Remove intake manifold as outlined under "Intake Manifold, Replace" procedure.
4. If removing left side cylinder head, remove the two cooling fans.
5. Remove appropriate exhaust manifold as outlined under "Exhaust Manifold, Replace," procedure.
6. Remove dipstick tube when lefthand cylinder head is to be replaced.
7. Remove ten cylinder head bolts.
8. Reverse procedure to install, referring to **Fig. 3**, for bolt tightening sequence. Torque cylinder head bolts in 3 steps as follows:
   a. **Torque** all bolts to 38 ft. lbs. in specified sequence.
   b. **Torque** all bolts to 68 ft. lbs. in specified sequence.
   c. **Torque** bolts 1, 3 and 4 to 90 ft. lbs.
9. Rearm airbag system as outlined under "Precautions."

VALVE LIFT SPECIFICATIONS

Engine	Year	Int.	Exh.
All	1991–92	.384	.396

VALVE TIMING

INTAKE OPENS BEFORE TDC

Engine	Year	Degrees
4.9L/V8-300	1991–92	21

ROCKER ARM SUPPORT, ROCKER ARM & PIVOT REPLACE

1. Remove rocker arm covers.
2. Remove rocker arm support retaining nuts from stud headed cylinder head

bolts, **Fig. 4**. Removing the rocker arm support with the rocker arms and pivots attached is recommended since the pivot assemblies may be damaged if pivot bolt torque is not removed evenly against valve spring pressure.
3. Secure support in a suitable vise and remove rocker arms and pivots.
4. Reverse procedure to install. Torque pivot bolts to specifications.

VALVE GUIDES

Check valve stem to valve guide clearance. Clearance should be .005 inch or less. Service valves are available in standard size (.343 inch) or oversizes of .003 and .006 inch. If clearance is excessive, ream valve guide to accommodate next oversize valve. Some engines are factory fitted with .003 inch oversize valve guides and valves and are identified by a "3" stamped on the cylinder head gasket surface in-line with the oversize valve.

HYDRAULIC VALVE LIFTERS REPLACE

Valve lifters may be removed from their bores after the intake manifold, rocker arms and pushrods are removed. Adjustable pliers with taped jaws may be used to remove lifters that are stuck due to var-

nish, carbon, etc. **Fig. 5**, illustrates the type of lifter used.

FRONT COVER REPLACE

1. Disconnect battery ground cable.
2. Drain cooling system.
3. Remove air cleaner.
4. Remove drive belt.
5. Remove alternator and position aside.
6. Remove A/C accumulator from bracket and position aside.
7. Remove idler pulley, water pump pulley and water pump.
8. Raise and support vehicle.
9. Remove crankshaft puller and hub.
10. Remove cover attaching bolts and the cover.
11. Reverse procedure to install. When installing, place a bead of RTV sealer on the front cover lip on the oil pan sealing surface and a ¼ inch bead of RTV sealer on the oil pan where the oil pan, cylinder block and cover join together, **Fig. 6**. The ¼ inch bead is needed because the cover has a rounded corner instead of a square corner. If the extra RTV is not applied an oil leak may occur.

FRONT COVER OIL SEAL REPLACE

1. Remove crankshaft pulley and vibration damper.
2. Remove oil seal with tools J-1859-03 and J-23129 or equivalents, **Fig. 7**.
3. Lubricate new oil seal with engine oil and install with tool J-29662 or equivalent.
4. Install crankshaft puller and vibration damper.

Fig. 7   Timing case oil seal removal

Fig. 8   Camshaft timing marks

Fig. 9   Piston & rod assembly

Fig. 10   Measuring piston diameter

Fig. 11   Piston ring end gap location

TIMING CHAIN
REPLACE

1. Remove front cover as outlined under "Front Cover, Replace."
2. Remove oil slinger from crankshaft.
3. Rotate crankshaft to align camshaft and crankshaft sprocket timing marks, **Fig. 8.**
4. Remove screw attaching camshaft sprocket to camshaft, then the camshaft and crankshaft sprockets with the timing chain attached.
5. Reverse procedure to install. Ensure that timing marks are aligned, **Fig. 8.**

CAMSHAFT
REPLACE

1. Remove engine as outlined under "Engine, Replace" procedure.
2. Remove front cover and timing chain.
3. Remove intake manifold and valve lifters.
4. Slide camshaft forward carefully from engine.
5. Reverse procedure to install.

PISTON & ROD
ASSEMBLE

Assemble pistons to rods as shown in **Fig. 9.** Measure connecting rod side clearance with a suitable feeler gauge after installation. Clearance should be .008 to .020 inch.

PISTONS

When measuring piston diameter, place micrometer 1¼ inch below crown (top) of piston, perpendicular to piston pin, **Fig. 10.**

Cylinder liner diameter is measured two inches down from top of liner and perpendicular to the cylinder centerline. The difference between the two readings should be .0004–.0020 inch. Cylinder bore out of round should not exceed .0008 inch. If any reading is not within specifications, the piston and cylinder liner must be replaced. No attempt should be made to rebore or hone the cylinder liner. Refer to "Cylinder Liner, Replace" procedure.

PISTON PINS

Piston pins are a matched fit with the piston and are not available for separate replacement. Piston pins are pressed into the connecting rods and will not become loose enough to cause a knock or tapping until after very high mileage.

PISTON RINGS

On these engines, replacement rings are available in standard size only. If piston ring clearance is excessive, the piston and cylinder liner must be replaced. Refer to "Cylinder Liner, Replace" procedure. Arrange piston rings as shown in **Fig. 11.**

MAIN & ROD BEARINGS

Main and rod bearings are supplied in standard sizes only.

CYLINDER LINER
REPLACE

1. Remove cylinder heads, pistons and connecting rods must be removed before replacing cylinder liner. After removing cylinder heads, install tool J-29775 to retain the cylinder liners not being replaced.
2. If original liners are to be reinstalled, mark position of cylinder liner in cylinder block and keep piston with original liner for reference during installation.
3. Pull cylinder liner from cylinder block. Discard O-ring from base of liner.
4. Check cylinder liner and cylinder block mating surfaces.
5. If original cylinder liner is to be installed and engine has not experienced overheating, install new O-ring onto bottom of liner. Align reference marks made during removal and install liner into cylinder block.
6. If new liner is being installed or if original liner is being installed and the engine has experienced overheating, then cylinder liner height must be measured as follows:
   a. Place liner in cylinder block without O-ring.
   b. Place gauge J-29776 or equivalent on cylinder liner. Check that spring-loaded guide pins fit into liner with machined pads resting on edge of liner and dial indicator plunger contacting block deck face. Apply moderate pressure to

Fig. 12 Oil pan removal & installation

1	SUPPLY TUBE	7	PUMP COVER
2	PRESSURE RELIEF VALVE	8	"O" RING
3	PUMP BODY	9	DRIVE SHAFT
4	PICKUP	10	NUT
5	OUTER ROTOR	11	BOLT
6	INNER ROTOR		

Fig. 13 Oil pump assembly

1	GENERATOR	5	AIR CONDITIONER COMPRESSOR
2	TENSIONER	6	CRANKSHAFT
3	STEERING GEAR	7	COOLANT PUMP
4	ACCESSORY DRIVE BELT	8	IDLER PULLEY

Fig. 14 Serpentine drive belt routing

gauge until dial indicator stops moving. Record this reading. If reading is on the + side of dial indicator, cylinder liner is higher than block face. If reading is on the − side, the liner is lower than the block face.

c. Repeat step b at two other locations on the liner. Use average of the three readings as actual liner height.

d. Cylinder liner height should be 0–.003 inch above cylinder deck face.

e. Check liner-to-liner height with tool J-29766 or equivalent. Install adjacent liners with O-ring. Liner-to-liner height should be −.002 to +.002 inch. Mark liners in measured positions.

7. When installing liners into block, check alignment marks. Be sure to install O-ring onto liner.

CRANKSHAFT REAR OIL SEAL
REPLACE

Before replacing the crankshaft oil seal, be sure that the apparent oil seal leak is not actually a leak between the sides of the rear main cap and crankcase.

1. Remove transaxle, then the flex plate from crankshaft.
2. Remove old seal with tool J-26868 or equivalent.
3. Lubricate new seal lip with wheel bearing grease and place on crankshaft with spring facing inside of engine.
4. Press seal into position with tool J-34604 or equivalent. Seal is fully installed when flush with block or slightly below. The use of the tool is recommended since the seal must fit squarely on the crankshaft, otherwise an oil leak could result.

OIL PAN
REPLACE

1. Disarm airbag system as outlined under "Airbag System Disarming," then disconnect battery ground cable.
2. Raise and support vehicle.

3. Drain oil pan.
4. Remove two flexplate covers.
5. Remove oil pan attaching bolts and the two nuts from studs.
6. Remove oil pan, **Fig. 12**.
7. Reverse procedure to install. RTV sealer is used to seal the oil pan.
8. Rearm airbag system as outlined under "Precautions."

OIL PUMP
REPLACE

1. Remove oil pan as outlined under "Oil Pan, Replace" procedure.
2. Remove bolts securing oil pump to engine, **Fig. 13**.
3. Remove oil pump.
4. Reverse procedure to install.

OIL PUMP SERVICE

1. Remove oil pump cover to housing attaching screws, **Fig. 13**.
2. Remove inlet and outlet pipes attaching screws, then remove and discard O-rings.
3. Slide inner and outer rotors from housing. **Pressure relief valve is not removable.**
4. Inspect pump housing for damage that may cause a leak or binding condition in rotor pocket.
5. Inspect drive and driven rotors for nicks and burrs.
6. Inspect interior pump surface for excessive wear or scoring.
7. Inspect pump housing cover, inlet and

outlet pipes for flatness.
8. Inspect inlet screen and pipe for debris.
9. Inspect pump driveshaft for wear or twisting.
10. Ensure pressure relief valve closes by filling housing valve cavity with suitable light oil, not oil leakage should be indicated.
11. Install outer rotor in rotor pocket with slots toward bottom of pump.
12. Slide inner rotor inside driven rotor with internal hex towards top of pump, then rotate gears ensuring not binding or roughness.
13. Install pump cover, tighten to specifications.
14. Install inlet pipe to housing, tighten to specifications.
15. Temporarily install driveshaft to pump, then rotate gears ensuring no binding or roughness.

BELT TENSION DATA

Engine	Year	Lbs.
4.9L/V8-300	1991–92	120

SERPENTINE DRIVE BELTS
BELT ROUTING

Refer to **Fig. 14**, for serpentine drive belt routing.

BELT, REPLACE

1. Disarm airbag system as outlined under "Precautions."
2. Using suitable 1/2 inch breaker bar, rotate belt tensioner upward from drive belt, **Fig. 15**.

1 DRIVE BELT TENSIONER

2 ACCESSORY DRIVE BELT

Fig. 15   Drive belt removal

1 WATER PUMP ASSEMBLY

2 WATER PUMP GASKET

3 FRONT COVER

4 WATER PUMP INLET GASKET

5 WATER PUMP INLET

Fig. 16   Water pump assembly

FRT

KEY	FASTENER TYPE	QTY.	TORQUE	
			N·m	FT. LBS.
A	TORX SCREW	4	40	30
B	NUT	7	7	5
C	STUD	1	40	30
D	HEX SCREW	7	7	5

Fig. 17   Water pump tightening sequence & specifications

3. Remove accessory drive belt.
4. Reverse procedure to install.
5. Rearm airbag system as outlined under "Precautions."

COOLING SYSTEM BLEED

1. Fill cooling system and leave radiator cap off.
2. Start engine, then and push front "DEF" button and increase temperature to 90°.
3. Run engine at 2000 RPM for approximately 10 minutes, then refill radiator until full and install radiator cap with engine running.
4. Fill coolant reservoir to the "FULL" mark.

THERMOSTAT
REPLACE

1. Disarm airbag system as outlined under "Airbag System Disarming," then disconnect battery negative cable.
2. With engine cool, drain engine coolant below thermostat level. **Never open cooling system with engine hot. Failure to follow this warning may cause personal injury.**
3. Remove two thermostat housing retaining bolts, then the upper thermostat housing.
4. Remove thermostat and gasket from lower housing, then clean both mating surfaces.
5. Reverse procedure to install. Replace gasket and tighten thermostat housing retaining bolts to specifications.

1	FUEL FILTER	3	BOLT/SCREW
2	QUICK CONNECTOR	4	FUEL FILTER BRACKET

Fig. 18   Fuel filter replacement

6. With installation done, ensure that draincock is closed, refill radiator with proper coolant mixture, replace pressure cap and start engine. Check for leaks.
7. Rearm airbag system as outlined under "Precautions."

WATER PUMP
REPLACE

1. Disarm airbag system as outlined under "Airbag System Disarming," then disconnect battery ground cable and drain cooling system.
2. Remove A/C accumulator from bracket and position aside.
3. Remove A/C accumulator bracket from wheel house.
4. Remove right hand cross-car brace.
5. Remove drive belt as outlined previously.
6. Remove drive belt idler puller and bracket.

7. Remove water pump pulley.
8. Remove water pump attaching bolts and the water pump, **Fig. 16.**
9. Reverse procedure to install. Tightening to specifications in sequence shown in, **Fig. 17.**
10. Rearm airbag system as outlined under "Precautions."

FUEL PUMP
REPLACE

1. Remove fuel tank.
2. Remove cam lock with tool J-24187 or equivalent.
3. Remove fuel sending unit and fuel pump assembly from tank.
4. Remove fuel pump from sending unit.
5. Reverse procedure to install.

FUEL FILTER
REPLACE

1. Release fuel system pressure as outlined under "Fuel System Pressure Relief."
2. Raise and support vehicle.
3. Twist quick-connect fitting 1/4 turn in each direction to loosen dirt within fitting.
4. Using compressed air, clean quick-connect fitting at ends of filter.
5. Disconnect quick-connect fittings by squeezing plastic tabs of male end connector and pulling apart.
6. Remove filter from bracket, then the fuel filter, **Fig. 18.**
7. Reverse procedure to install.

TIGHTENING SPECIFICATIONS
4.9L/V8-300 ENGINE

Year	Component	Torque/Ft. Lbs.
1991-94	Connecting Rod Bolts	25
	Coolant Fan To Radiator Support Bolts	84 ①
	Coolant Hose Clamps	15 ①
	Coolant Temperature Sensor	15
	Cylinder Head Bolts	②
	Damper To Crankshaft	70
	Distributor Hold-Down Nut	20
	Distributor Hold-Down Stud	26
	EGR Valve Screws	18
	Exhaust Manifold Bolts	16
	Exhaust Outlet Flange Studs	15
	Flywheel To Crankshaft	70
	Front Cover Screws (Lower 4)	17
	Front Cover Screws (Upper 4)	30
	Intake Manifold Bolts	②
	Lift Bracket To Cylinder Head	29
	Main Bearing Caps	85
	MAT Sensor	20
	Oil Filter Adapter To Block	14
	Oil Gallery Plug At Rear Of Block	32
	Oil Pan Bolts	14
	Oil Drain Plug	22

Year	Component	Torque/Ft. Lbs.
1991-94 —Cont'd	Oil Pressure Switch	10
	Oil Pump Cover Screws	7
	Oil Pump Mounting Nut To Stud	22
	Oil Pump Mounting Screws To Block	14
	Oxygen Sensor	30
	Radiator	88 ①
	Rocker Arm Cover Screws	8
	Rocker Arm Pivot To Support	22
	Rocker Arm Support To Head Bolts	36
	Spark Plugs	23
	Thermostat Housing To Intake Manifold	23
	Timing Sprocket To Camshaft	36
	Transaxle Oil Cooler Fittings	20
	Upper Thermostat Housing To Lower Housing	19
	Water Passage Plugs	5
	Water Pump Pulley To Pump Bolts	115 ①
	Water Pump To Block	29
	Water Pump To Front Cover Bolts	97 ①

① —Inch lbs.
② —Refer to text.

Rear Suspension

INDEX

DESCRIPTION

These vehicles use an independent rear suspension consisting of lower control arms, coil springs, toe links, suspension knuckles, superlift struts and stabilizer bar, **Fig. 1.** The hub and wheel bearing is an assembly and does not require periodic lubrication.

HUB & BEARING ASSEMBLY
REPLACE

1. Raise and support rear of vehicle. Remove wheel assembly and brake drum. **Do not hammer on drum since damage to bearing may occur.**
2. Remove four hub and bearing assem-

bly to axle attaching bolts and the assembly from axle, **Fig. 2.**
3. Reverse procedure to install. Torque attaching bolts to specifications.

COIL SPRING
REPLACE

1. Support vehicle so the rear wheel and control arm hang free. Remove rear wheel.
2. Disconnect rear stabilizer bar from knuckle bracket.
3. Disconnect electronic level control height sensor link if removing right control arm.
4. Disconnect parking brake cable clip from frame if removing left control arm.
5. Place tool J-23028-01 in position to cradle control arm bushings, **Fig. 3.**

Tool J-23028-01 should be secured to a suitable jack, otherwise, personal injury could result.
6. Raise jack to relieve tension from control arm pivot bolts.
7. Place a chain around spring and control for safety.
8. Remove rear control arm pivot bolt and nut, **Fig. 4.**
9. Slowly lower jack until front bolt and nut can be removed.
10. Remove coil spring. **Do not apply force on lower arm and ball joint to remove spring. Maneuver spring to remove.**
11. Reverse procedure to install, noting the following:
   a. Replace spring insulators that are damaged or if vehicle has been in service for more than 50,000 miles.
   b. Install springs so that end of spring is as shown in **Fig. 5.**

1	SUPERLIFT* STRUT	4	SUSPENSION ADJUSTMENT LINK
2	STABILIZER BAR	5	LOWER CONTROL ARM
3	COIL SPRING		

Fig. 1 Rear suspension

1 PIVOT BOLT
2 PIVOT NUT
3 INSULATOR
4 COIL SPRING
5 CONTROL ARM

Fig. 4 Coil spring replacement

c. Tighten suspension fasteners sufficiently to retain position of components, lower vehicle so that it rests on the wheels at normal ride height, then torque fasteners as follows: 1-Torque control arm pivot nuts to specifications. 2-Torque control arm pivot bolts to specifications. 3-Torque stabilizer shaft link bolt to specifications. **Failure to torque fasteners to specifications in listed sequence may adversely affect ride and handling.**

REAR TIE ROD/ADJUSTMENT LINK REPLACE

1. Raise and support vehicle.

Fig. 2 Hub & bearing assembly

Fig. 5 Rear spring positioning

1	WASHER		
2	NUT, RETAINING	7	BOOT, LEFT SIDE ONLY
3	CONTROL ARM	8	NUT
4	KNUCKLE	9	LINK, SUSPENSION ADJUSTMENT
5	COTTER PIN	10	SPACER
		6	NUT, CASTELLATED

Fig. 6 Tie rod/adjustment link installation

2. Remove wheel assembly, cotter key and castle nut, **Fig. 6.**
3. Using tool J-24319-01, disconnect outer tie rod/adjustment from knuckle. **When disconnecting the tie rod/adjustment from knuckle, do not use a wedge since seal damage will occur.**
4. Remove rod/link assembly retaining nut and retainer.
5. Remove rod/link assembly from lower control arm.
6. Reverse procedure to install. **Torque** link retaining nut to specifications and castellated nut securing ball stud to 37 ft. lbs. Install cotter pin retaining

Fig. 3 Installing tool J-23028-01

Fig. 7 Ball joint inspection

castellated nut, tightening nut as needed to insert pin through hole in stud. Do not loosen nut to align slots with hole.

BALL JOINT INSPECTION

The ball joint has a visual wear indicator. Checking the condition of the ball joint is a simple procedure but must be followed accurately to prevent unnecessary ball joint replacement.

The vehicle must be supported by the wheels during inspection to ensure that the vehicle weight is properly loading the ball joints.

The ball joint is inspected for wear by visual observation alone. Wear is indicated by retraction of the 1/2 inch diameter nipple into the ball joint cover (the ball joint grease fitting is threaded into this nipple).

The nipple protrudes .050 inch beyond the surface of the ball joint cover on a new unworn joint. Normal wear will result in the surface of this nipple retracting very slowly inward. The ball joint should be replaced if the nipple is flush or below the cover surface, **Fig. 7.**

Ball stud tightness in the knuckle boss should also be checked when inspecting the ball joint. This may be done by shaking the wheel and feeling for movement of the stud end or castellated nut at the knuckle boss.

Checking the fastener tightness at the castellated nut is an alternative method of inspecting (a loose nut can indicate a bent stud or an "opened up" hole in the knuckle boss). If worn, the ball joint and knuckle must be replaced.

REMOVE CASTELLATED NUT AND REINSTALL WITH FLAT SIDE FACING UPWARD.

PLACE J-34505 INTO POSITION AS SHOWN. LOOSEN NUT AND BACK OFF UNTIL . . .

VIEW A

. . THE NUT CONTACTS THE TOOL. CONTINUE BACKING OFF THE NUT UNTIL THE NUT FORCES THE BALL STUD OUT OF THE KNUCKLE.

VIEW B

VIEW C

5	REAR CONTROL ARM
24	KNUCKLE
43	COTTER PIN
44	CASTELLATED NUT
45	BALL JOINT
46	SPECIAL TOOL J-34505
47	SPECIAL TOOL J-9519-23 (CLAMP)
47A	SPECIAL TOOL J-9519-18 (SCREW)
48	SPECIAL TOOL J-9519-7
48A	SPECIAL TOOL J-9519-16
49	SPECIAL TOOL J-9519-17

Fig. 8 Ball joint replacement

1	STABILIZER SHAFT	7	BOLT
2	BOLT	8	INSULATOR
3	NUT	9	BOLT
4	BRACKET	10	STABILIZER SHAFT BRACKET
5	NUT	11	LINK
6	RETAINER	12	BOLT

Fig. 9 Stabilizer bar & bushing assembly

If the ball joint is separated from the knuckle for suspension service, the ball joint seal should be inspected for damage. A damaged seal will cause joint failure. If seal damage is found the ball joint should be replaced.

LOWER CONTROL ARM BALL JOINT
REPLACE

1. Raise and support vehicle.
2. Remove wheel assembly, cotter key and castle nut.
3. Disconnect outer tie rod/adjustment link from knuckle as outlined previously.
4. Disconnect electronic level control height sensor link from right side control arm.
5. Support control arm with a suitable jack.
6. Remove ball joint cotter pin and nut.
7. Using tool J-29330, disconnect ball joint from knuckle, **Fig. 8.**
8. Using tool J-9519-7, remove ball joint from control arm.
9. Reverse procedure to install.

STABILIZER BAR
REPLACE

1. Remove rear wheels and tires.
2. Remove stabilizer shaft support bolt,

nut, retainer and insulators from knuckle bracket, **Fig. 9.**
3. Remove bushing clip bolt.
4. Bend open end of support assembly downward.
5. Remove stabilizer shaft and bushings.

LOWER CONTROL ARM
REPLACE

1. Remove coil spring as outlined under "Coil Spring, Replace" procedure.
2. Remove control arm front pivot bolt.
3. Remove control arm from vehicle.
4. Reverse procedure to install.

REAR STRUT
REPLACE

1. Raise and support vehicle.
2. Remove trunk side cover.
3. Remove wheel assembly.
4. Disconnect air tube from superlift strut, **Fig. 10.**
5. Remove two strut tower mount nuts.
6. Remove two strut anchor bolts, washers and nuts from knuckle, then the knuckle bracket.
7. Remove strut from vehicle.
8. Reverse procedure to install.

CONTROL ARM BUSHINGS
REPLACE

These vehicles incorporate control arm

configuration with two different sized bushings, **Fig. 11.** These bushings are not interchangeable, and require different combinations of special tools for removal and installation. The following service procedure refer to these bushings as A and B.

REMOVAL

1. Remove control arm from vehicle.
2. Place control arm onto a suitable work bench, up side down.
3. For bushing A, install spacer tool J-22222-5, for bushing B, install spacer tool J-33793-5 onto control arm.
4. Position receiver tube J-25317-2 and cap tool J-29376-7 on outer side of control arm. Ensure receiver tube does not contact the bushing flange.
5. Coat threaded area of long bolt J-21474-19 with extreme pressure lubricant J-23444-A, then install bolt through receiver, cap and bushing.
6. Install remover tool J-22222-2 for bushing A or tool J-28685-2 for bushing B onto bolt at inner side of control arm. Position remover so small diameter portion contacts bushing.
7. Place bearing on bolt and install long nut tool J21474-18. Bearing must be installed between nut and remover.
8. Draw bushing out of control arm by tightening the nut.

INSTALLATION

1. With control arm up side down on

1 NUT
2 STRUT
3 STABILIZER SHAFT BRACKET
4 BOLT
5 KNUCKLE
6 NUT

Fig. 10   Strut assembly

Fig. 11   Control arm bushing removal/installation

work bench, position new bushing into control arm. **When installing new bushings, the flanged end of the bushing must face outward when installed in the control arm.**

2. Install spacer tool J-22222-5 for bushing A or tool J-33793-5 for bushing B.
3. Position receiver tube J-25317-2 and cap tool J-29376-7 onto inner side of control arm. Receiver tube should be centered over the hole.
4. Coat threaded area of long bolt with extreme pressure lubricant J-23444-A and install through receiver, cap and bushing.
5. Position installer J-28685-2 onto bolt at outer side of control arm. Installer should be positioned with large diameter end contacting bushing flange.
6. Place bearing on bolt and install long nut J-21474-18. Bearing must be positioned between nut and installer.
7. Draw bushing into control arm by tightening nut. Tighten nut until bushing flange seats firmly against control arm.
8. Install control arm into vehicle, adjust rear wheel alignment, if necessary.

TIGHTENING SPECIFICATIONS

Year	Component	Torque/Ft. Lbs.	Year	Component	Torque/Ft. Lbs.
1991-94	**Ball Joint Nut**	88①②	1991-94 —Cont'd	**Strut Mount To Underbody**	18–19
	Control Arm Pivot Bolts	138		**Strut Tower Mounting Nut**	35
	Control Arm Pivot Nuts	85		**Suspension Adjustment Link At Knuckle**	33
	Hub & Bearing Assembly Bolts	52		**Suspension Adjustment Link At Control Arm**	63
	Stabilizer Shaft Bushing Assembly Nut	35–37		**Suspension Adjustment Link Locknut**	48
	Stabilizer Shaft Bushing Clip Bolt	37		**Wheel Lug Nuts**	100
	Stabilizer Shaft Link Bolt	13-14			
	Stabilizer Shaft Mounting Bracket Bolt	14			
	Stabilizer Shaft Support Nut	14			
	Strut To Knuckle Bolts	③			

①—Inch lbs.
②—Tighten nut an additional ⅔ of a turn.
③—1991, 180 ft. lbs., 1992-94, 140 ft. lbs.

Front Suspension & Steering

INDEX

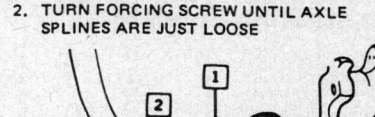

1. J-28733
2. TURN FORCING SCREW UNTIL AXLE SPLINES ARE JUST LOOSE

Fig. 2   Separating drive axle from hub

MANDATORY COTTER PIN INSTALLATION

Fig. 1   Front suspension

1. HUB AND BEARING ASSEMBLY
2. STEERING KNUCKLE
3. SHIELD
4. WASHER
5. HUB NUT 245 N·m (180 LBS. FT.)
6. SEAL
7. HUB AND BEARING RETAINING BOLT (55 TORX) 95 N·m (70 LBS. FT.)
8. "O" RING

Fig. 3   Hub & bearing assembly

DESCRIPTION

The front suspension is of the MacPherson design, **Fig. 1.** The control arm pivots from the cradle and is mounted in rubber bushings. The upper end of the strut is isolated by a rubber mount and contains a non-serviceable bearing to allow for rotation. The lower end of the steering knuckle pivots on a ball joint riveted to the control arm. The ball joint is fastened to the steering knuckle with a castle nut and cotter pin.

HUB & BEARING REPLACE

1. Raise and support vehicle and remove wheel assembly.
2. Install drive axle boot protector tool J-28712 on outer joints and J-34754 on inner joints.

3. Insert a suitable drift through opening in caliper into rotor cooling fins to prevent assembly from rotating, then remove hub nut and washer.
4. Remove caliper bracket mounting bolts and the caliper and bracket assembly, then secure assembly aside taking care not to stretch brake hose. Use care not to damage brake hose.
5. Disconnect ABS front wheel speed sensor connector and unclip connector from dust shield.
6. Remove rotor, then press drive axle from hub using J-28733 or equivalent, **Fig. 2.**
7. Remove hub assembly retaining bolts, shield, hub and bearing assembly, and O-ring, **Fig. 3.**
8. Reverse procedure to install. Fill area between seal and bearing assembly with GM lubricant part NO. 1052497 or equivalent. Torque hub attaching bolts to specifications, caliper bolts and hub nut to specifications.

BALL JOINT INSPECTION

Ball joints must be replace if any looseness is detected or ball joint seal is cut or damaged.

To inspect ball joints, raise the front of the vehicle, allowing suspension to hang freely. Grasp the tire at the top and bottom, an move the top of the tire in an in and out motion. Check for any horizontal movement of the knuckle relative to the control arm. If the ball stud is disconnected from the knuckle and looseness is detected, or if the ball stud can be twisted using finger pressure, replace the ball joint.

Ball stud tightness in the knuckle boss

1. J 36226 BALL JOINT SEPARATOR

Fig. 4   Separating ball joint from steering knuckle

1. Stabilizer Bar
2. Control Arm
3. Insulator (4)
4. Retainer (4)
5. Bolt
6. Nut 17 N·m (13 LBS. FT.)

Fig. 7   Stabilizer bar bushing assembly

1. SERVICE BALL JOINT
2. BALL JOINT MOUNTING BOLTS MUST FACE DOWN
3. STEERING KNUCKLE
4. CONTROL ARM
5. BALL JOINT MOUNTING NUTS 68 N·m (50 LBS. FT.)
6. BALL JOINT TO STEERING KNUCKLE NUT 110 N·m (81 LBS. FT.) BEFORE COTTER PIN INSTALLATION
7. COTTER PIN

Fig. 5   Service ball joint attachment

1. STABILIZER BAR
2. STABILIZER BAR MOUNTING BRACKET
3. STABILIZER BAR MOUNTING BUSHING
4. 50 N·m (37 LBS. FT.)
5. FRAME WELDED NUTS
6. FRAME

VIEW A

1. CONTROL ARM
2. FRAME
3. FRAME MOUNTED BUSHING
4. CONTROL ARM MOUNTED BUSHING
5. FRAME MOUNTED BUSHING NUT 190 N·m (140 LBS. FT.)
6. CONTROL ARM MOUNTED BUSHING NUT 123 N·m (90 LBS. FT.)
7. WASHER

Fig. 6   Control arm assembly

1. STABILIZER BAR
2. STEERING KNUCKLE
3. TIE ROD

Fig. 9   Stabilizer bar replacement

should also be inspected. This may be done by shaking the wheel and feeling for movement of the stud end or nut at the knuckle boss. Worn or damaged ball joints and knuckles must be replaced.

BALL JOINT
REPLACE

1. Raise and support vehicle and place jackstands under cradle. Vehicle weight should not be placed on the control arms.
2. Remove wheel assembly.
3. Install drive axle boot protectors.
4. Remove cotter key from ball joint nut and, using tool J-34505, separate ball joint from steering knuckle, **Fig. 4.**
5. Drill out ball joint retaining rivets.
6. Remove stabilizer bar bushing to control arm bolt.
7. Pull control arm downward and remove ball joint from steering knuckle and control arm.
8. Reverse procedure to install. **Torque** new ball joint attaching nuts to specifications, **Fig. 5.**

Fig. 8   Stabilizer bar mounting

CONTROL ARM
REPLACE

1. Raise and support vehicle and place jackstands under cradle. Vehicle weight should not be placed on the control arms.
2. Remove wheel assembly.
3. Install drive axle boot protectors.
4. Remove cotter key from ball joint nut and, using tool J-34505, separate ball joint from steering knuckle.

5. Remove stabilizer bar bushing to control arm bolt.
6. Remove control arm mounting bolts and the control arm, **Fig. 6.**
7. Reverse procedure to install. When installing control arms, install but do not torque control arm mounting bolts. Sufficiently tighten bolts to assure security but final torque is applied when vehicle weight is supported by control arms. Torque rear arm bolt and front bolt to specifications.

STABILIZER BAR
REPLACE

1. Raise and support vehicle and place jackstands under cradle. Vehicle weight should not be placed on the control arms.
2. Remove wheel assembly.
3. Install drive axle boot protectors.
4. Remove nuts, washers, bushings and bolt securing stabilizer shaft to each control arm, **Fig. 7.**
5. Remove stabilizer bar mounting bolts, two bolts from each side, **Fig. 8.**
6. Disconnect tie rods from steering knuckles.

1. STRUT ASSEMBLY
2. STRUT TO BODY NUTS 24 N·m (18 LBS. FT.)
3. BRAKE LINE BRACKET BOLT 17 N·m (13 LBS. FT.)
4. STRUT TO STEERING KNUCKLE NUTS 195 N·m (144 LBS. FT.)
5. Retain STEERING KNUCKLE with wire once STRUT ASSEMBLY is removed

Fig. 10 Strut assembly

7. Remove exhaust pipe between exhaust manifold and catalytic converter.
8. Rotate right side strut assembly completely to the right.
9. Slide stabilizer bar to the right over the steering knuckle and pull downward on left side until stabilizer bar clears the cradle, **Fig. 9.**
10. Reverse procedure to install.

STRUT ASSEMBLY REPLACE

1. Remove three nuts attaching top of strut to body, **Fig. 10.**
2. Raise and support vehicle and place jackstands under cradle. Vehicle weight should not be placed on the control arms.
3. Remove wheel assembly.
4. Install drive axle boot protectors.
5. Remove brake line bracket bolt from strut assembly.
6. Remove strut to steering knuckle attaching bolts.
7. Remove strut assembly from vehicle.
8. Reverse procedure to install. Torque strut mounting bolts to specifications.

STRUT SERVICE

Refer to **Figs. 11 and 12** when performing the following procedure.
1. Remove strut as outlined under "Strut

1. STRUT ASSEMBLY
2. STRUT COMPRESSOR J-34013
3. Install LOCKING PINS through STRUT ASSEMBLY
4. Tighten NUTS till flush with STRUT COMPRESSOR
5. COMPRESSOR FORCING SCREW

Fig. 11 Disassembling strut

1 BOLT
  TIGHTEN IN SEQUENCE A THRU E.
2 STEERING GEAR
3 NUT; 47 N·m (35 LB. FT.). MAXIMUM PERMISSIBLE TORQUE TO ALIGN COTTER PIN SLOT IS 70 N·m (52 LB. FT.).
4 WASHER
5 STEERING KNUCKLE

Fig. 13 Steering gear replacement

Assembly, Replace" procedure.
2. Mount strut in compressor tool J-34013 and holding fixture J-3289-20.
3. Rotate compressor forcing screw until spring compresses slightly.
4. Hold damper shaft from rotating and remove nut from top of strut assembly.
5. Use tool J-34013-30 to guide damper shaft from assembly.
6. Loosen compressor forcing screw while guiding damper shaft from as-

Fig. 12 Exploded view of strut assembly

sembly. Continue to loosen nut until strut damper and spring can be removed.
7. Reverse procedure to assemble. When assembling spring, the flat on upper spring seat must face outward 90 degrees from centerline of vehicle or when mounted in the strut compressor, the seat faces in the same direction as the steering knuckle mounting flange.

POWER STEERING GEAR REPLACE

1. Raise and support vehicle with weight resting on suspension.
2. Remove front wheel assemblies.
3. Disconnect intermediate shaft from steering gear stub shaft.
4. Disconnect both tie rod ends from steering knuckles.
5. Remove line retainers and disconnect hydraulic lines from steering gear.
6. Remove five steering gear attaching bolts, **Fig. 13.**
7. Remove steering gear from vehicle by sliding out to the side.
8. Reverse procedure to install. Refer to **Fig. 13,** for tightening sequence.

POWER STEERING PUMP
REPLACE

3800/V6-231 ENGINE

1. Disconnect battery ground cable.
2. Remove air cleaner, if necessary.
3. Remove alternator drive belt and alternator.
4. Raise and support vehicle.

5. Disconnect hydraulic lines from pump.
6. Remove rear pump adjustment bracket to pump nut.
7. Remove pump drive belt.
8. Lower vehicle.
9. Remove pump rear adjustment bracket.
10. Remove power steering pump from vehicle.
11. Reverse procedure to install.

4.9L/V8-300 ENGINES

1. Disconnect battery ground cable.
2. Remove pump drive belt and the pulley.
3. Disconnect hydraulic lines from pump.
4. Remove two pump mounting bolts.
5. Remove power steering pump from vehicle.
6. Reverse procedure to install.

TIGHTENING SPECIFICATIONS

Year	Component	Torque/Ft. Lbs.	Year	Component	Torque/Ft. Lbs.
1991-94	Ball Joint To Knuckle	88 ① ②	1991-94 —Cont'd	Service Ball Joint To Control Arm	50
	Brake Caliper To Knuckle	38		Stabilizer Shaft Bushing Nut	13
	Brake Line Bracket To Underbody	13		Stabilizer Shaft Mounting Bracket	37
	Control Arm Mounting Nut (Front)	140-144		Steering Knuckle To Strut Bolts	140-144
	Control Arm Mounting Nut (Rear)	88-90		Strut Assembly To Body Nuts	18
	Drive Axle Shaft Nut	③		Strut Mount Nut	55
	Hub & Bearing To Knuckle	70		Tie Rod To Knuckle	35 ④
	Power Steering Gear	50		Wheel Lug Nut	100
	Power Steering Gear Inlet Hose To Pump	20			
	Power Steering Gear Lines To Gear	70 ①			
	Power Steering Pump	20			

① —Inch lbs.
② —Tighten an additional 120°.
③ —1991, 192 ft. lbs., 1992–94, 107 ft. lbs.
④ —Tighten to align cotter pin.

Wheel Alignment

INDEX

PRELIMINARY CHECK

1. Inspect tires for proper inflation and similar tread wear.
2. Inspect hub and bearing for excessive wear, repair as required.
3. Inspect ball joints.
4. Inspect tie rod ends for excessive looseness.
5. Check wheel and tire runout.
6. Inspect vehicle ride height.
7. Inspect rack and pinion for looseness at frame.
8. Ensure proper strut operation.
9. Inspect control arm bushings.
10. Inspect stabilizer shaft for loose or missing parts.
11. Check suspension and steering components for damage, replace as required.

FRONT WHEEL ALIGNMENT
CASTER, ADJUST

1. **On 1991 Bonneville, Eighty-Eight and LeSabre models,** remove three strut to body attaching nuts, **Fig. 1.**
2. **On all models except 1991 Bonneville, Eighty-Eight and LeSabre models,** proceed as follows:
   a. Loosen cross brace assembly through bolts, **Fig. 2.**
   b. Remove inboard strut nuts, then the brace assembly.
   c. Remove remaining nut over oval strut mounting hole, **Fig. 1.**
3. **On all models,** lift front of vehicle by body to separate strut from inner wheelhouse.
4. Drill two 11/32 inch holes at front and rear of oval strut mounting hole.
5. File excess metal to elongate original holes, then paint exposed metal with primer.
6. Lower front of vehicle.
7. **On 1991 Bonneville, Eighty-Eight and LeSabre models,** install three strut to body attaching nuts.
8. **On all models except 1991 Bonneville, Eighty-Eight and LeSabre models,** place cross brace assembly on inboard strut studs and install strut attaching nuts.
9. **On all models,** set caster to specifications by moving strut forward or rearward as necessary.
10. **Torque** strut attaching nuts to 18 ft. lbs.
11. **On all models except 1991 Bonneville, Eighty-Eight and LeSabre models,** torque cross brace bar through bolts to 21 ft. lbs.

CAMBER, ADJUST

1. Loosen both strut to knuckle attaching nuts, **Fig. 3.**
2. Install camber adjusting tool J-29862.
3. Set camber to specifications.
4. Remove adjusting tool and **torque** strut to knuckle attaching nuts to 144 ft. lbs.
5. Recheck camber.

TOE, ADJUST

1. Loosen locknuts on both inner tie rods, **Fig. 4.**
2. Adjust toe to specifications by rotating inner tie rod.

1. WASHER
2. COVER
3. ATTACHING NUT 25 N·m (18 LB. FT.)
4. STRUT ASSEMBLY
5. DRILL 11/32 INCH HOLES

Fig. 1 Caster adjustment

1. NUT, STRUT INBOARD STUD
2. THROUGH–BOLTS
3. STUD, STRUT INBOARD
4. BAR ASM, CROSS BRACE

Fig. 2 Cross brace removal

1. INNER TIE ROD - TURN TO ADJUST TOE
2. NUT 70 N·m (50 LBS. FT.) LOOSEN TO ADJUST TOE
3. BOOT - READJUST AFTER SETTING TOE
4. NUT 195 N·m (144 LBS. FT.)
5. J-29862
6. STRUT ASSEMBLY
7. KNUCKLE
8. WASHER

Fig. 3 Camber adjustment

1. TURN TO ADJUST TOE
2. RE-ADJUST BOOTS
3. LOOSEN NUT TO ADJUST TOE, RE-TIGHTEN TO 70 N·m (50 LBS. FT.)

Fig. 4 Toe adjustment

1. TURN TIE ROD TO ADJUST TOE
2. LOCK NUT, TORQUE TO 65 N·m (48 LBS. FT.)
3. J-29862
4. WASHERS
5. NUT 195 N·m (144 LBS. FT.)

Fig. 5 Rear camber & toe adjustments

Fig. 6 Ride height measurements. 1991

3. **Torque** locknuts to 50 ft. lbs.
4. Recheck toe setting.

REAR WHEEL ALIGNMENT

When checking rear wheel alignment, the electronic leveling system must have the superlift struts inflated with residual pressure only.

Place a weight in trunk and turn ignition on and move transmission selector from Park to Reverse position and back. This will activate the compressor. Turn ignition off and remove weight from trunk. Wait 30 seconds for the system to exhaust. Roll vehicle forward one complete wheel rotation. Jounce vehicle before checking alignment.

CAMBER, ADJUST

1. Loosen strut to knuckle attaching nuts.

2. Install camber adjusting tool J-29862, **Fig. 5.**
3. Move strut to set camber to specifications.
4. Remove camber adjusting tool and **torque** strut to knuckle nuts to 144 ft. lbs.
5. Recheck camber setting.

Fig. 7   Ride height measurements. 1992–94

Make & Model	Year	Riding Height Measurements In Inches					
		Dimension Z	Dimension D	Dimension P	Dimension R	Dimension J	Dimension K
BUICK							
LeSabre	1991	2–2^{13}/$_{16}$	3^1/$_8$–3^7/$_8$	27^1/$_2$ –28^5/$_{16}$	27^1/$_2$–28^5/$_{16}$	9–9^{13}/$_{16}$	9^5/$_{16}$–10^1/$_{16}$
	1992–94	1^{15}/$_{16}$–2^3/$_4$	2^{11}/$_{16}$–3^7/$_{16}$	—	—	9–9^{13}/$_{16}$	9^5/$_{16}$–10^1/$_{16}$
Park Avenue	1991	2–2^{13}/$_{16}$	2^{11}/$_{16}$–3^7/$_{16}$	27 ^{1}/$_2$–28^5/$_{16}$	27^3/$_{16}$–28	8^{15}/$_{16}$–9^3/$_4$	9^1/$_{16}$–9^{13}/$_{16}$
	1992–94	1^{15}/$_{16}$–2^3/$_4$	2^{11}/$_{16}$–3^7/$_{16}$	—	—	9–9^{13}/$_{16}$	9^1/$_{16}$–9^{27}/$_{32}$
CADILLAC							
Concours/DeVille/Fleetwood (FWD)/Sixty Special	1991	2–2^{13}/$_{16}$	2^{11}/$_{16}$–3^7/$_{16}$	27^1/$_2$–28^5/$_{16}$	27 ^{3}/$_{16}$–28	8^{15}/$_{16}$–9^3/$_4$	9^1/$_{16}$–9^{13}/$_{16}$
	1992–94	1^{15}/$_{16}$–2^3/$_4$	2^{11}/$_{16}$–3^7/$_{16}$	—	—	9–9^{13}/$_{16}$	9^1/$_{16}$–9^{27}/$_{32}$
OLDSMOBILE							
Eighty-Eight	1991	2^1/$_{16}$–2^{13}/$_{16}$	3^1/$_8$–3^7/$_8$	27^{11}/$_{16}$–28^1/$_2$	28–28^3/$_4$	9–9^{13}/$_{16}$	9^5/$_{16}$–10^1/$_{16}$
	1992–94	1^{15}/$_{16}$–2^3/$_4$	2^{11}/$_{16}$–3^7/$_{16}$	—	—	9–9^{13}/$_{16}$	9^5/$_{16}$–10^1/$_{16}$
Ninety-Eight	1991	2–2^3/$_4$	2^{11}/$_{16}$–3^7/$_{16}$	27^1/$_2$–28^5/$_{16}$	27^3/$_{16}$–28	9–9^3/$_4$	9^1/$_{16}$–9^{13}/$_{16}$
	1992–94	1^{15}/$_{16}$–2^3/$_4$	2^{11}/$_{16}$–3^7/$_{16}$	—	—	9–9^{13}/$_{16}$	9^1/$_{16}$–9^{27}/$_{32}$
PONTIAC							
Bonneville	1991	2^1/$_{16}$–2^7/$_8$	2^3/$_4$–3^9/$_{16}$	27^7/$_8$–28^{11}/$_{16}$	27^7/$_8$–28^3/$_4$	9 ^{1}/$_8$–9^7/$_8$	9^1/$_8$–9^7/$_8$
	1992 ①	1^{15}/$_{16}$–2^3/$_4$	2^{11}/$_{16}$–3^7/$_{16}$	—	—	9–9^{13}/$_{16}$	9^5/$_{16}$–10^1/$_{16}$
	1992 ②	1^{15}/$_{16}$–2^3/$_4$	2^{11}/$_{16}$–3^7/$_{16}$	—	—	9–9^{13}/$_{16}$	9^1/$_{16}$–9^{27}/$_{32}$
	1993–94	1^{15}/$_{16}$–2^3/$_4$	2^{11}/$_{16}$–3^7/$_{16}$	—	—	9–9^{13}/$_{16}$	9^5/$_{16}$–10^1/$_{16}$

① —SE.
② —Except SE

Fig. 8   Ride height specifications

TOE, ADJUST

Toe adjustment is made by loosening the locknut at tie rod end and turning inner tie rod to set toe to specifications, **Fig. 5.**

VEHICLE RIDE HEIGHT

Refer to **Figs. 6, 7 and 8,** for ride height specifications and measurement loca-

tions. Check ride height as follows:
1. Ensure vehicle is on level ground.
2. Ensure tires are inflated to proper pressures.
3. Fuel tank should be full to obtain accurate readings.
4. Trunk should be empty except for spare tire and jack.
5. Place the front seat in the far rearward position, then turn ignition to On position to activate the electronic level

control, if equipped.
6. Bounce the car three times at the front and rear to normalize suspension.
7. Measure from lowest point on the ball joint housing to control arm bolt centerline, "D" and "Z" positions.
8. Measure from level floor to rocker panel at "J" and "K" positions.
9. **On 1991 models,** measure from level floor to wheel opening at "P" and "R" positions.

BUICK REATTA & RIVIERA: CADILLAC ELDORADO & SEVILLE: OLDSMOBILE TORONADO & TROFEO
(E & K Cars)
INDEX OF SERVICE OPERATIONS

NOTE: Refer To Rear Of This Manual For Vehicle Manufacturer's Special Service Tool Suppliers.

INDEX OF SERVICE OPERATIONS-Continued

Specifications
GENERAL ENGINE SPECIFICATIONS

Year	Engine Liter/CID [1]	Engine VIN Code [2]	Fuel Injection System	Bore & Stroke	Compression Ratio	Net H.P. @ RPM [3]	Maximum Torque Ft. Lbs. @ RPM	Normal Oil Pressure Pounds
1991	3.8L/V6-231	C	SPFI [4]	3.80 X 3.40	8.5	165 @ 4800	210 @ 2000	40 [6]
	4.9L/V8-300	B	MPI [8]	3.62 x 3.62	9.5	200 @ 4400	275 @ 3000	—
1992	3.8L/V6-231	L	TPI [5]	3.80 X 3.40	8.5	170 @ 4800	220 @ 3200	60 [7]
1993	3.8L/V6-231	L	TPI [5]	3.80 X 3.40	8.5	170 @ 4800	220 @ 3200	60 [7]
	4.6L/V8-279	9	MPI [8]	3.66 x 3.31	10.3	295 @ 6000	290 @ 4400	35 [9]
	4.6L/V8-279	Y	MPI [8]	3.66 x 3.31	10.3	270 @ 5600	—	35 [9]
	4.9L/V8-300	B	MPI [8]	3.62 x 3.62	9.5	200 @ 4400	275 @ 3000	—
1994	4.6L/V8-279	9	MPI [8]	3.66 x 3.31	10.3	295 @ 6000	290 @ 4400	35 [9]
	4.6L/V8-279	Y	MPI [8]	3.66 x 3.31	10.3	270 @ 5600	—	35 [9]

[1]—CID-Cubic inch displacement.
[2]—The eighth digit denotes engine code.

[3]—Ratings are net-as installed in vehicle.
[4]—Sequential-Port Fuel Injection.
[5]—Tuned Port Fuel Injection.

[6]—At 1850 RPM, w/5W-30 engine oil.
[7]—At 1850 RPM, w/10W-30 engine oil.
[8]—Multi-Port Fuel Injection.
[9]—At 2000 RPM.

TUNE UP SPECIFICATIONS

| Year & Engine/VIN Code ① | Spark Plug Gap | Ignition Timing | | | Curb Idle Speed ③ | Fast Idle Speed | Fuel Pump Pressure, Psi |
		Firing Order Fig. ④	Degrees BTDC ②	Mark Fig.			
1991							
3.8L/V6-231(C)	.060	⑪	⑤	⑩	⑥	⑥	40–47⑦
4.9L/V8-300(B)	.060	C	10⑧	D	⑥	⑥	32–38⑨
1992							
3.8L/V6-231(L)	.060	⑪	⑤	⑩	⑥	⑥	41–47⑦
4.9L/V8-300(B)	.060	C	10⑧	D	⑥	⑥	40–50⑨
1993							
3.8L/V6-231(L)	.060	⑪	⑤	⑩	⑥	⑥	41–47⑦
4.6L/V8-279(9)	.050	⑫	10⑤	—	⑥	⑥	—
4.6L/V8-279(Y)	.050	⑫	10⑤	—	⑥	⑥	—
4.9L/V8-300(B)	.060	C	10⑧	D	⑥	⑥	40–50⑨
1994							
4.6L/V8-279(9)	.050	⑫	10⑤	—	⑥	⑥	—
4.6L/V8-279(Y)	.050	⑫	10⑤	—	⑥	⑥	—

①—The eighth digit of the Vehicle Identification Number (VIN) denotes engine code.
②—BTDC: Before Top Dead Center.
③—On auto. trans. models, idle speed is adjusted in Drive. When adjusting idle speed, set parking brake & block drive wheels.
④—Before disconnecting wires from distributor cap, determine location of No. 1 wire in cap, as distributor position may have been altered from that shown at the end of this chart.
⑤—Computer controlled, no adjustment.
⑥—Idle speed is controlled by an idle speed control (ISC) motor or an idle air control (IAC) valve.
⑦—With shop towel wrapped around fuel pressure valve to prevent fuel

spillage, connect a suitable fuel pressure gauge to fuel pressure valve. Check fuel pressure with ignition switch in the On position, engine not running.
⑧—Connect jumper wire between ALCL connector terminals A & B. The ALCL connector is located under the instrument panel to the right of the steering column. After completing adjustment, disconnect jumper wire from between terminals A & B. With engine off, clear trouble code from Electronic Control Module (ECM) by removing battery voltage to ECM for 30 seconds.
⑨—Wrap shop towel around fuel hose to steel line connection in engine compartment to prevent fuel spillage. Disconnect fuel hose from

steel line & connect a suitable fuel pressure gauge between hose & line. Ensure gauge connections are tight, then start engine & check fuel pressure readings.
⑩—Equipped with crankshaft position sensor.
⑪—Cylinder numbering from left to right as viewed from front of vehicle, front bank, 1, 3, 5; rear bank, 2, 4, 6. Firing order 1-6-5-4-3-2. Refer to Figs. A & B for spark plug wire connections at coil unit.
⑫—Cylinder numbering from left to right as viewed from front of vehicle, front bank, 2, 4, 6, 8; rear bank, 1, 3, 5, 7. Firing order 1-2-7-3-4-5-6-8. Refer to Fig. E for spark plug wire connections at coil unit.

COMPUTER CONTROLLED COIL IGNITION
Fig. A

Fig. D

Fig. B

Fig. E

FIRING ORDER 1·8·4·3·6·5·7·2
FRONT OF ENGINE
Fig. C

FRONT WHEEL ALIGNMENT SPECIFICATIONS

Year	Model	Caster Angle, Degrees		Camber Angle, Degrees					Total Toe Degrees
				Limits		Desired			
		Limits	Desired	Left	Right	Left	Right		
1991	Eldorado & Seville	+1.3 to +3.3	+2.3	−.8 to +.8	−.8 to +.8	0	0		+.2
	Reatta	+1.8 to +3.8	+2.8	−.8 to +.8	−.8 to +.8	0	0		+.2
	Riviera	+1.3 to +3.3	+2.3	−.8 to +.8	−.8 to +.8	0	0		+.2
	Toronado & Trofeo	+1.3 to +3.3	+2.3	−.8 to +.8	−.8 to +.8	0	0		+.2
1992	All	+1.3 to +3.3	+2.3	−.8 to +.8	−.8 to +.8	0	0		+.2
1993	All	+1.3 to +3.3	+2.3	0 to −1.0	0 to +1.0	−.5	+.5		+.2
1994	All	+1.3 to +3.3	+2.3	0 to −1.0	0 to +1.0	−.5	+.5		+.2

REAR WHEEL ALIGNMENT SPECIFICATIONS

Year	Model	Camber Angle, Degrees				Total Toe Degrees
		Limits		Desired		
		Left	Right	Left	Right	
1991	Eldorado & Seville	−.4 to +.2	−.4 to +.2	−.1	−.1	+.2
	Reatta	−.6 to +.4	−.6 to +.4	−1	−1	+.2
	Riviera	−.5 to +.5	−.5 to +.5	0	0	+.2
	Toronado & Trofeo	−.7 to +.3	−.7 to +.3	−.2	−.2	+.2
1992	All	—	—	—	—	+.2
1993	All	+.5 to −.5	+.5 to −.5	0	0	+.2
1994	All	+.5 to −.5	+.5 to −.5	0	0	+.2

COOLING SYSTEM & CAPACITY DATA

Year	Liter/CID/VIN	Cooling Capacity, Qts.	Radiator Cap Relief Pressure, Lbs.	Thermo. Opening Temp.°F	Fuel Tank Gals	Engine Oil Refill Qts. [2]	Auto Transaxle Qts. [1]	
							Drain & Refill	Overhaul
1991	3.8L/V6-231/C	13	15	195	18	4	6.5	11
	4.9L/V8-300/B	12.1	15	195	18.8	5	6	8
1992	3.8L/V6-231/L	13	15	195	18	4	6	11
	4.9L/V8-300/B	12.1	15	195	18.8	5	6	8
1993	3.8L/V6-231/L	13	15	195	18	4	—	11
	4.6L/V8-279/9 or Y	12.5	15	195	—	7	—	15
	4.9L/V8-300/B	12.1	15	195	18.8	5	6	8
1994	4.6L/V8-279/9 or Y	12.5	15	195	—	7	—	15

① —Approximate. Make final check w/dipstick.

② —Additional oil will be necessary when changing filter.

LUBRICANT DATA

Year	Model	Lubricant Type		
		Automatic Transaxle	Power Steering	Brake System
1991	Eldorado, Seville	Dexron II ①	GM Power Steering Fluid ②	Dot 3
	Reatta	Dexron II ①	GM Power Steering Fluid ②	Dot 3
	Riviera	Dexron II ①	GM Power Steering Fluid ②	Dot 3
	Toronado, Trofeo	Dexron II ①	GM Power Steering Fluid ②	Dot 3
1992	Toronado, Trofeo	Dexron II ①	GM Power Steering Fluid ②	Dot 3
	Eldorado, Seville	Dexron II ①	GM Power Steering Fluid ②	Dot 3
	Riviera	Dexron II ①	GM Power Steering Fluid ②	Dot 3
1993	Eldorado, Seville	Dexron II ①	GM Power Steering Fluid ②	Dot 3
	Riviera	Dexron II ①	GM Power Steering Fluid ②	Dot 3
1994	Eldorado, Seville	Dexron II ①	GM Power Steering Fluid ②	Dot 3

① —Reatta, Riviera, Toronado, Trofeo &
1992-94 Eldorado and Seville use
Dexron IIE.

② —Or equivalent, meeting GM
requirements 9985010.

Electrical

INDEX

PRECAUTIONS
AIRBAG SYSTEM DISARMING

The diagnostic energy reserve module (DERM) can maintain voltage to cause a system deployment for up to ten minutes after the ignition switch is turned off and the battery is disconnected. Servicing the SIR system during this period may result in accidental deployment and personal injury.

1. Ensure front wheels are pointed straight ahead.
2. Turn ignition switch to Lock position and remove SIR or AIRBAG fuse.
3. Remove left sound insulator. **Remove courtesy lamp from sound insulator, if necessary.**
4. Remove Connector Position Assurance (CPA), then disconnect yellow two-way SIR electrical connector at base of steering column.
5. **On 1993-94 Eldorado and Seville,** open trap door in rear of glove box. Remove Connector Position Assurance (CPA), then disconnect yellow two-way SIR electrical connector for passenger inflator module.

AIRBAG SYSTEM ARMING

1. Connect yellow two-way SIR electri-

PART OF
BATTERY
NEGATIVE
CABLE ASM.

FRONT
OF
CAR

1. RETAINING NUT (6)
2. STAR WASHER (3)
3. STARTER MOTOR SOLENOID
4. SHIELD
5. POSITIVE BATTERY CABLE
6. ENGINE WIRING
   HARNESS ASM.

**Fig. 1   Starter wiring.
Eldorado & Seville
w/4.9L/V8-300**

cal connector(s), then install Connector Position Assurance (CPA).
2. Install left sound insulator. **Install courtesy lamp to sound insulator, if applicable.**
3. Install SIR fuse to fuse block, turn ignition switch to Run position and ensure that "Inflatable Restraint" lamp flashes 7 to 9 times, then shuts off.

FUSE PANEL & FLASHER LOCATION

On Reatta, Riviera, Toronado and Trofeo models, the fuse panel is located inside the glove compartment. On Eldorado and Seville models, the fuse panel is located behind the center of the instrument panel, behind the glove box door.

On Toronado and Trofeo models, the hazard flasher and turn signal flasher are located behind the instrument panel, on the righthand side of the steering column support. On Eldorado, Reatta, Riviera and Seville models, the turn/hazard module is located behind the lefthand side of the instrument panel above the steering column.

STARTER MOTOR
REPLACE

If shims are used between starter and engine block, they should be placed in original position during installation. If starter is noisy during cranking, remove double .015 inch shim or add .015 inch shim at outer bolt only. If high pitched whine is observed after engine starts, add double .015 inch shims (to maximum of .045 inch) until noise is corrected.

ELDORADO & SEVILLE
4.9L/V8-300 Engine

1. Disconnect battery ground cable, then

raise and support vehicle.
2. Remove nuts securing starter shield and the shield.
3. Disconnect front and rear exhaust pipe if necessary.
4. Remove nuts securing solenoid wires and battery cable, then disconnect wiring, **Fig. 1.**
5. Remove starter brace, mounting bolts and the starter motor.
6. Reverse procedure to install.

4.6L/V8-279 Engine

1. Disarm airbag system as outlined under "Precautions."
2. Remove intake manifold as outlined under "Intake Manifold, Replace" in "4.6L/V8-279 Engine" section.
3. Remove starter electrical connectors, then starter mounting bolts.
4. Remove starter from vehicle.
5. Reverse procedure to install.
6. Rearm airbag system as outlined under "Precautions."

REATTA, RIVIERA, TORONADO & TROFEO

1. Disconnect battery ground cable, then raise and support vehicle.
2. Remove flywheel inspection cover, then starter splash shield, if equipped.
3. Remove two bolts securing starter to engine block, then lower starter motor.
4. Remove retaining nuts and disconnect electrical connectors, noting position for installation.
5. Reverse procedure to install.

DISTRIBUTOR
REPLACE

ELDORADO & SEVILLE

1. Remove distributor appearance cover and retainer.
2. Disconnect ignition switch battery feed wire from distributor cap.
3. Disconnect coil connections from cap. **Do not use a screwdriver or other tool to release locking tabs.**
4. Remove four bolts from distributor cap, note position of cap ignition coil then move cap aside.
5. Disconnect six terminal ECM harness from distributor.
6. Remove distributor clamp nut and hold-down clamp. Use tool No. J29791 or equivalent to remove hold-down nut.
7. Note position of rotor. Pull distributor up until rotor stops turning counterclockwise, then note position of rotor.
8. Remove distributor. **A thrust washer is used between distributor drive gear and crankcase. This washer may stick to bottom of distributor when removed. Before replacing distributor, ensure thrust washer is located in crankcase at bottom of distributor bore.**
9. Reverse procedure to install, noting the following:
   a. If distributor position was lost, or set incorrectly, remove No. 1 spark

18. SCREW, LOCK RETAINING
20. LOCK CYLINDER SET, STRG COL PASS KEY

Fig. 2   Lock cylinder set removal

plug wire.
b. Place a finger over No. 1 spark plug hole while an assistant slowly cranks engine until compression is felt.
c. Align timing mark on pulley with 0 mark on timing indicator.
d. Turn rotor to point between No. 1 and No. 8 spark plug towers on distributor cap.
e. Install distributor.

IGNITION LOCK
REPLACE

1. Disarm airbag system as outlined under "Precautions."
2. Disconnect battery ground cable, then remove steering wheel as outlined under "Horn Sounder & Steering Wheel Replace."
3. Remove turn signal switch as outlined under 'Turn Signal Switch Replace."
4. Remove key from lock, then the buzzer switch assembly.
5. Place key in "Lock" position, then remove lock retaining screw, **Fig. 2.**
6. Disconnect electrical connector, retaining clip from housing cover, then withdraw lock cylinder assembly from column.
7. Reverse procedure to install. **Torque lock retaining screw to 22 inch lbs.**
8. Rearm airbag system as outlined under "Precautions."

IGNITION & DIMMER SWITCH
REPLACE

REMOVAL

1. Disarm airbag system as outlined under "Precautions."
2. Disconnect battery ground cable.
3. **On models with floor shift,** place transmission selector in park and rotate ignition lock to "Run" position.
4. **On all models,** remove left hush panel, lower steering column cover, insulator at toe plate, and the lower steering column mounting screws.
5. Remove nuts securing upper steering column bracket to instrument panel, then carefully lower column. **Disconnect shift indicator cable and electrical connectors, as needed, prior to lowering column. Do not force**

1. POSITION OF LOCKING PIN AND CAM WITH SHIFT LEVER IN "PARK".
2. CAM
3. LOCKING PIN

**Fig. 3   Park-lock cable.
Models w/floor shift**

column down as it may be damaged.

6. Remove dimmer switch mounting nut, screw and the dimmer switch, then tape actuator rod to steering column.
7. **On models with floor shift,** insert screwdriver into slot in ignition switch inhibitor, depress park-lock cable latch and disconnect cable from inhibitor, **Fig. 3. Ignition switch must be in "Run" position. Do not attempt to disconnect park-lock cable with switch in any other position.**
8. Rotate ignition key to "Off-Lock" position.
9. **On all models,** remove ignition switch stud bolt, disconnect electrical connector, then remove switch assembly.

INSTALLATION

1. Move ignition switch slider to extreme right, then one detent to the left to place switch in "Off-Lock" position.
2. Connect electrical connector to ignition switch, install switch assembly on column ensuring actuator is properly engaged, and **torque** stud bolt to 35 inch lbs.
3. Install dimmer switch assembly, depress switch against actuator and insert 3/32 inch drill into adjustment slot, **Fig. 4,** then **torque** nut and retaining screw to 35 inch lbs.
4. **On models with floor shift,** rotate ignition lock to "Run" position, then install shift-lock cable on inhibitor.
5. **On all models,** reverse remaining procedure to complete installation. **Torque** upper column bracket bolts to 20 ft. lbs and lower column bolts to 25 ft. lbs.
6. Rearm airbag system as outlined under "Precautions."

HORN SOUNDER & STEERING WHEEL
REPLACE

If the airbag has been deployed, inspect coil for signs of scorching, melting, or other damage. Coil must be replaced if damaged.
1. Disarm airbag system as outlined under "Precautions."

DIMMER SWITCH
DIMMER SWITCH ACTUATOR ROD
3/32" Drill

ADJUST DIMMER SWITCH

**Fig. 4   Dimmer switch
installation**

2. Turn ignition switch to the Off position, disconnect battery ground cable.
3. Remove Torx screws from back of steering wheel.
4. Remove inflator module from wheel. **Always carry live inflator modules with the trim cover facing away from you. Never carry module by the wiring. Always place module on a flat surface with the trim cover facing up.**
5. Remove horn contact by pushing slightly and twisting counterclockwise.
6. Disconnect Connector Position Assurance (CPA) and coil assembly connector from inflator module.
7. Remove steering column shaft nut.
8. Remove steering wheel using puller No. J 1859-03 or equivalent. **Do not thread puller bolts too far in steering wheel. Threading puller bolts too far into steering wheel could damage SIR coil assembly. Four turns is sufficient.**
9. Reverse procedure to install, noting the following:
   a. **Torque** steering wheel shaft nut to 30 ft. lbs.
   b. **Torque** SIR module retaining screws to 27 inch lbs.
   c. Rearm airbag system as outlined under "Precautions."

TURN SIGNAL SWITCH
REPLACE

1. Disarm airbag system as outlined under "Precautions."
2. Disconnect battery ground cable, then remove steering wheel and inflator module (if equipped), as described under "Steering Wheel Replace."
3. Remove lower steering column trim cover.
4. Mount spring compressor J 23653 or equivalent on steering shaft, **Fig. 5.**
5. Remove lock plate retaining ring and telescoping wheel components, as equipped, then remove spring compressor.
6. Remove lock plate, canceling cam, upper bearing spring, then upper bearing inner race and seat.
7. Remove multi-function lever.
8. Remove turn signal switch retaining screws, then the switch assembly.
9. Reverse procedure to install.
10. Rearm airbag system as outlined under "Precautions."

SHAFT LOCK COVER
RETAINING RING
SHAFT LOCK
CANCELLING CAM ASSEMBLY
SPRING
COVER
SHAFT LOCK RETAINER
CARRIER SNAP RING RETAINER
SPACERS
RETRACTED STRG SHAFT BUMPER

*ON TELESCOPE STEERING ONLY

Pry out at these locations to remove cover
Screwdriver
REMOVE SHAFT LOCK COVER

J-23653
J-23653-4
RETAINING RING
Tighten nut until tool slightly depresses shaft lock
REMOVE AND INSTALL RETAINING RING

**Fig. 5   Lock plate & cancelling
cam removal**

WINDSHIELD WIPER SWITCH
REPLACE

1991 ELDORADO & SEVILLE

1. Remove A/C vent and radio trim plate from instrument cluster bezel.
2. Remove seven screws securing instrument cluster bezel and the bezel.
3. Remove two screws securing right switch module and pull module from instrument panel socket.
4. Reverse procedure to install.

1992-94 ELDORADO & SEVILLE

1. Disarm airbag system as outlined under "Precautions."
2. Remove steering wheel as outlined under "Steering Wheel Replace."
3. Slide connector cover toward front of vehicle, then unplug electrical connector.
4. Push lever in and rotate clockwise 1/4 turn and pull out switch.
5. Reverse procedure to install.
6. Rearm airbag system as outlined under "Precautions."

REATTA & RIVIERA

1. Disarm airbag system as outlined under "Precautions."
2. Remove steering wheel as outlined under "Steering Wheel Replace."
3. Remove access cover from steering column housing.
4. Disconnect electrical connectors, pull lever straight out of switch.
5. Reverse procedure to install.
6. Rearm airbag system as outlined under "Precautions."

3 TRANSAXLE ASSEMBLY	14 SERVICE ADJUSTMENT SLOT
12 TRANS MANUAL SHAFT	15 SERVICE GAGE PIN (2.34 MM — 3/32 IN.)
13 NEUTRAL START & BACK UP LAMP SW.	16 NUT (27 N·m/20 FT. LBS.)

Fig. 6 Back-up/neutral safety switch replacement. Eldorado & Seville

1 LOCKTAB
2 SHIFT CONTROL CABLE ASM
3 NUT
4 LINKAGE BRACKET
5 BOLT (2)
6 NEUTRAL START SWITCH
7 ELECTRICAL CONNECTOR
8 BRACKET, SHIFT CONTROL CABLE
9 MANUAL SHAFT
10 2.34 MM DIA. GAGE PIN, OR 3/32 IN. DRILL BIT

Fig. 7 Back-up/neutral safety switch replacement. Reatta, Riviera, Toronado & Trofeo

TORONADO & TROFEO

1. Disarm airbag system as outlined under "Precautions."
2. Remove steering wheel as outlined under "Steering Wheel Replace."
3. Remove access cover from steering column housing.
4. Disconnect electrical connectors, pull lever straight out of switch. **The switch must be in the OFF position before removing lever and do not extend lever wire beyond its normal length.**
5. Reverse procedure to install.
6. Rearm airbag system as outlined under "Precautions."

BACK-UP LAMP/NEUTRAL SAFETY SWITCH
REPLACE
ELDORADO & SEVILLE

1. Remove shift linkage, electrical connector and vacuum hose.
2. Remove attaching nut and shift lever, then the fuel line bracket.
3. Remove switch attaching screws, then the switch **Fig. 6**.
4. Reverse procedure to install, noting the following:
   a. **Torque** Attaching screws to 20 ft. lbs.
   b. Adjust switch as outlined under "Adjustments."

REATTA, RIVIERA, TORONADO & TROFEO

1. Set parking brake, place gear selector in "Neutral" position.
2. Remove linkage bracket attaching nut, then the linkage bracket, **Fig. 7.**
3. Remove switch attaching bolts, then the switch.
4. Reverse procedure to install, noting the following:
   a. **Torque** switch attaching bolts to 20 ft. lbs.
   b. Adjust switch as described under "Adjustments."

BACK-UP LAMP/NEUTRAL SAFETY SWITCH
ADJUST
ELDORADO & SEVILLE

1. Position transaxle shifter assembly in N notch in detent plate, then loosen switch attaching screws.
2. Rotate switch on shifter assembly until adjustment hole aligns with carrier tang hole.
3. Insert 3/32 inch gauge pin into adjustment hole to a depth of 15/32 inch.
4. Tighten switch mounting bolts, then remove gauge pin.

REATTA, RIVIERA, TORONADO & TROFEO

1. Place transaxle control shifter in the "Neutral" notch in detent plate.
2. Loosen switch attaching bolts, then rotate switch on shifter assembly to align service adjustment slot.
3. Insert 3/32 drill bit into service slots, then **torque** attaching bolts to 20 ft. lbs.
4. Remove drill bit.

LIGHT SWITCH
REPLACE
ELDORADO & SEVILLE
1991 Models

1. Disarm airbag system as outlined under "Precautions."
2. Disconnect battery ground cable.
3. Remove A/C vent and radio bezel from instrument cluster bezel.
4. Remove seven screws securing instrument cluster bezel, then the bezel.
5. Remove screws securing switch module, then pull module from socket in instrument panel.
6. Reverse procedure to install.
7. Rearm airbag system as outlined under "Precautions."

1992-94 Models

1. Disarm airbag system as outlined under "Precautions."
2. Disconnect battery ground cable.
3. Remove headlamp switch module from instrument panel by firmly pulling outward on headlamp switch knob, **Fig. 8.**
4. Disconnect electrical connector from switch.
5. Reverse procedure to install.
6. Rearm airbag system as outlined under "Precautions."

REATTA & RIVIERA

1. Disarm airbag system as outlined under "Precautions."
2. Turn ignition switch to the Off position.
3. Remove two upper panel cluster attaching screws, then pull trim plate out of lower retaining clips.
4. Remove two switch attaching screws, then the switch assembly, **Fig. 9.**
5. Disconnect electrical connectors.
6. Reverse procedure to install.
7. Rearm airbag system as outlined under "Precautions."

TORONADO & TROFEO

1. Disarm airbag system as outlined under "Precautions."

FRONT OF CAR

1. HEADLAMP SWITCH
2. TWILIGHT SENTINEL/DRL MODULE

Fig. 8   Headlamp switch replacement. 1992-94 Eldorado & Seville

1. HEADLAMP SWITCH ASSEMBLY
2. SCREW (2)
3. ELECTRICAL CONNECTOR
4. I/P CLUSTER HOUSING

Fig. 9   Headlamp switch replacement. Reatta & Riviera

1. DIGITAL DISPLAY FILTER LENSE
2. WARNING LIGHT LENSE
3. TRIP ODOMETER RESET BUTTON
4. DIGITAL INSTRUMENT CLUSTER ASSEMBLY

Fig. 10   Instrument cluster removal. 1991 Eldorado & Seville

1. INSTRUMENT CLUSTER
2. SCREW
3. INSTRUMENT PANEL
4. PRNDL ASSEMBLY (COLUMN SHIFT ONLY)
5. PRNDL ASSEMBLY RETAINING SCREWS

Fig. 11   Instrument cluster removal. 1992-94 Eldorado & Seville

2. Disconnect battery ground cable.
3. Remove left side insulator and knee bolster.
4. Remove switch attaching screws, then pull switch assembly from electrical connector.
5. Reverse procedure to install.
6. Rearm airbag system as outlined under "Precautions."

INSTRUMENT CLUSTER REPLACE

ELDORADO & SEVILLE

1991 Models

1. Disarm airbag system as outlined under "Precautions."
2. Disconnect battery ground cable.
3. Remove A/C duct and radio trim plate from instrument cluster bezel.
4. Remove seven screws securing instrument panel cluster from housing.

5. Remove digital display, warning lamp lenses and trip odometer reset button, **Fig. 10.**
6. Remove two screws securing cluster, then pull cluster from instrument panel socket.
7. Reverse procedure to install, noting the following:
   a. Ensure electrical connector pins are properly aligned when cluster is pressed into instrument panel.
   b. Rearm airbag system as outlined under "Precautions."

1992-94 Models

1. Disarm airbag system as outlined under "Precautions."
2. Remove fuses A5 and B5 from rear compartment fuse panel and fuse A3 from engine compartment fuse panel.
3. Using a small flat-bladed tool, remove defroster grill.
4. Remove sunload and headlamp auto control sensors from defroster grill.

5. Remove three upper trim panel retaining screws, through defroster grill opening.
6. Remove heater and A/C vents from instrument panel.
7. Remove four upper trim panel retaining screws, through vent openings.
8. Remove upper trim panel.
9. Disconnect two electrical connectors from top of instrument panel.
10. Remove four instrument cluster to instrument panel attaching screws, **Fig. 11.**
11. Raise cluster, remove two screws securing PRNDL mechanism on digital clusters.
12. Remove instrument cluster.
13. Reverse procedure to install.
14. Rearm airbag system as outlined under "Precautions."

REATTA & RIVIERA

1. Disarm airbag system as outlined under "Precautions."
2. Place ignition switch in Off position.
3. Remove left-side sound insulator retaining screws and nuts.
4. Remove courtesy lamp from sound insulator, then the lefthand side sound insulator from the vehicle.
5. Disconnect Connector Position Assurance (CPA) and yellow two-way connector from base of the steering column.
6. Disconnect battery ground cable.
7. Remove four trim plate retaining screws, then pull trim plate from lower retaining clips, **Fig. 12.**
8. Remove center air duct assembly.
9. Remove 13 screws retaining housing to back of instrument panel.
10. Remove two screws from front of instrument panel.
11. Reverse procedure to install.
12. Rearm airbag system as outlined under "Precautions."

TORONADO & TROFEO

1. Disarm airbag system as outlined under "Precautions."
2. Disconnect battery ground cable.
3. Remove two front retaining screws, two rear retaining nuts, then the courtesy lamp from lefthand side sound insulator.
4. Remove sound insulator from vehicle.

5. Remove two retaining screws from knee bolster, then the bolster from the vehicle.
6. Remove trim plate retaining screws, then the trim plate from vehicle.
7. Remove screws retaining cluster to instrument panel.
8. Pull cluster forward enough to disconnect electrical connectors, then remove cluster from vehicle.
9. Reverse procedure to install.
10. Rearm airbag system as outlined under "Precautions."

CATHODE RAY TUBE (CRT) REPLACE

CRT's are located in the center of the instrument panel assembly and may also be known as a visual information center (VIC), driver information display (DID), electronic control center (ECC), or a graphic control center (GCC).

Some of the CRT's have a controller built in. For those which do not, refer to "CRT Controller, Replace."
1. Disconnect battery ground cable.
2. Remove instrument panel trim plate attaching screws, then the trim plate.
3. Remove four attaching bolts securing CRT to instrument panel and mounting bracket assembly.
4. Carefully pull out CRT, then disconnect electrical connector from rear of CRT assembly.
5. Reverse procedure to install.

CRT CONTROLLER REPLACE
TORONADO & TROFEO

1. Disconnect battery ground cable.
2. Remove console compartment retaining screws, then the compartment.
3. Gently pry off compact disc trim plate, if equipped.
4. Disconnect console trim plate electrical connectors, then remove console trim plate.
5. Remove compact disc player, if equipped.
6. Remove screws and nuts retaining console assembly to the floor.
7. Disconnect electrical connectors, then remove console.
8. Remove four nuts retaining controller to retaining bracket.
9. Disconnect electrical connectors, then remove controller from vehicle.
10. Reverse procedure to install.

RADIO
REPLACE
LESS CRT
1991 ELDORADO & SEVILLE

1. Disarm airbag system as outlined under "Precautions."
2. Disconnect battery ground cable.
3. Remove radio trim plate from instru-

1. I/P CLUSTER HOUSING (CLUSTER REMOVED)
2. I/P CLUSTER TRIM PLATE
3. SCREW (4)

Fig. 12 Trim plate retaining screw locations. Reatta & Riviera.

1. RADIO TRIM PLATE
2. UPPER CONSOLE TRIM PLATE
3. RADIO CONTROL HEAD
4. CONTROL HEAD HARNESS ASSEMBLY

VIEW A

Fig. 13 Radio removal. 1992-94 Eldorado & Seville w/console shift

ment cluster bezel.
4. Twist lefthand A/C vent to remove.
5. Remove seven screws (six Phillips and one Torx) securing instrument panel trim plate.
6. Loosen lower two mounting nuts under radio (top nuts do not have to be loosened), then pull radio away from instrument panel.
7. Disconnect electrical connectors and antenna lead, then remove radio assembly.
8. Reverse procedure to install.
9. Rearm airbag system as outlined under "Precautions."

1992-94 ELDORADO & SEVILLE
With Console Shift

1. Disarm airbag system as outlined under "Precautions."

2. Using a putty knife, remove radio trim plate, **Fig. 13.**
3. Remove console trim plate by pulling up the upper edge first.
4. Remove two nuts from bottom of control head.
5. Position control head so that the right side is removed first, to clear connectors on left side.
6. Disconnect electrical connectors, then remove radio.
7. Reverse procedure to install.
8. Rearm airbag system as outlined under "Precautions."

With Column Shift

1. Disarm airbag system as outlined under "Precautions."
2. Remove radio trim, then the four screws from side bracket, **Fig. 14.**
3. Remove control head, then discon-

1	RADIO TRIM PLATE
2	RADIO CONTROL HEAD
3	CONTROL HEAD BRACKETS
4	HARNESS

Fig. 14 Radio removal. 1992-94 Eldorado & Seville w/column shift

1	PROGRAMMER
2	PROG. MTG. SCREW (3 REQ'D)
3	THREADED ROD

Fig. 15 Programmer mounting bolt locations

nect electrical connectors.
4. Reverse procedure to install.
5. Rearm airbag system as outlined under "Precautions."

REATTA & RIVIERA

1. Disarm airbag system as outlined under "Precautions."
2. Disconnect battery ground cable.
3. Remove top of instrument panel plate, then the screws retaining radio and ECC bracket.
4. Remove bracket from radio and disconnect electrical connector.
5. Reverse procedure to install.
6. Rearm airbag system as outlined under "Precautions."

TORONADO & TROFEO
Radio

1. Disarm airbag system as outlined under "Precautions."
2. Disconnect battery ground cable.
3. Remove screws securing instrument cluster bezel, then pull bezel away from instrument panel to disengage retaining clips.
4. Disconnect electrical connectors and remove cluster bezel.
5. Remove screws securing ECC panel and radio brackets to instrument panel and pull assembly away from panel.
6. Disconnect electrical connectors, noting position for installation, then remove ECC panel and radio assembly.
7. Remove nuts securing radio to brackets, then the radio.
8. Reverse procedure to install.
9. Rearm airbag system as outlined under "Precautions."

Console Mounted Tape Player & Booster

1. Disarm airbag system as outlined under "Precautions."
2. Disconnect battery ground cable, then carefully pull trim plate from console.
3. Lift out shift indicator assembly and disconnect bulbs from indicator.
4. Remove screws securing console mounting plate.
5. Disconnect electrical connectors, then remove mounting plate assembly.

6. Remove nuts securing tape player or booster to mounting plate, then the components as required.
7. Reverse procedure to install, pressing console trim plate into retaining clip until trim plate is secured.
8. Rearm airbag system as outlined under "Precautions."

WITH CRT

1. Disarm airbag system as outlined under "Precautions."
2. Disconnect battery ground cable.
3. Pull shift indicator trim plate up and out slowly. Place selector in neutral if necessary.
4. Remove indicator lamp bulbs.
5. Remove lumbar/bolster control switch, if equipped.
6. Remove outer console trim plate.
7. Remove attaching screws securing graphic equalizer and tape mounting plate.
8. Remove mounting plate.
9. Disconnect electrical connector from tape deck and graphic equalizer.
10. Pull tape holder out of console bucket.
11. Remove screws at bottom of console compartment liner and screws at top of liner, then pull liner out.
12. Remove nuts attaching console to floor pan.
13. Pull console upward and slide back toward rear seat.
14. Pull radio remote chassis out to the right.
15. Disconnect radio chassis electrical connectors.
16. Reverse procedure to install.
17. Rearm airbag system as outlined under "Precautions."

BLOWER MOTOR
REPLACE

1. Disconnect battery ground cable, then remove strut tower cross brace (two nuts each side).
2. Remove cowl relay center bracket (two nuts), then disconnect electrical connector and cooling hose from blower motor.
3. **On Eldorado and Seville models,**

Remove MAP sensor mounting bracket.
4. **On all models,** remove blower motor retaining screws, then tilt blower motor in case to allow fan removal. **Fan must be removed prior to blower motor to prevent fan from being bent.**
5. Remove fan retainer and fan from blower motor, then remove blower motor.
6. Remove blower fan from case.
7. Reverse procedure to install.

HEATER CORE
REPLACE

ELDORADO & SEVILLE

1. Disarm airbag system as outlined under "Precautions."
2. Disconnect battery ground cable, then drain cooling system.
3. Remove screws securing glove box module and the glove box, then the righthand lower sound insulator.
4. Remove programmer as follows:
   a. Remove two ECM bracket mounting screws, then position ECM aside to gain access to rear programmer mounting screw.
   b. Remove threaded rod, then the vacuum connector retaining nut from programmer.
   c. Disconnect electrical and vacuum connectors from programmer assembly, then remove three mounting screws and programmer, **Fig. 15.**
5. **On 1991 models,** disconnect electrical connections from BCM, then remove BCM and mounting bracket from vehicle.
6. Disconnect electrical connections from ECM, then remove the ECM and mounting bracket from vehicle.
7. **On all models,** remove heater core cover, then disconnect heater hoses from heater core.
8. Remove two heater core retaining screws, then the heater core.

9. Reverse procedure to install. Prior to installing glove box module, adjust air mix door link rod as follows:
   a. Set temperature control for 90°F and allow 1-2 minutes for programmer arm to travel to maximum heat position, **Fig. 16**.
   b. Disconnect air mix door link rod from programmer and ensure air mix door operated freely.
   c. Preload air mix door in maximum heat position by pulling rod to seat door against seal, then snap rod into connector on programmer arm, taking care not to disturb position of arm or air mix door.
   d. Set control for 60°F and ensure programmer arm and air mix door travel to maximum cooling position.
10. Rearm airbag system as outlined under "Precautions."

REATTA & RIVIERA

1. Disarm airbag system as outlined under "Precautions."
2. Disconnect negative battery cable, then drain the cooling system.
3. Turn ignition to the Off position, then remove fuse No. 14 from fuse panel.
4. Remove left side sound insulator retaining screws and nuts.
5. Disconnect courtesy lamp from insulator panel and remove from vehicle.
6. Remove instrument panel cluster trim plate retaining screws, then remove plate from vehicle.
7. Remove center air duct assembly.
8. Remove 13 instrument panel cluster retaining screws, then pull cluster outward from instrument panel.
9. Remove two headlamp switch to instrument panel retaining screws, then disconnect headlamp switch electrical connector and remove from vehicle.
10. Remove four electronic climate control head retaining screws, if equipped.
11. Remove climate control electrical connector then the climate control assembly.
12. **On models equipped with integral radio unit,** proceed as follows:
    a. Remove radio/ECC retaining screws.
    b. Remove radio bracket to radio retaining nuts.
    c. Disconnect radio electrical connectors and remove radio from vehicle.
13. **On models equipped with cassette tape/compact disc,** remove holder from rear console storage compartment.
14. Remove two outer and three inner console trim plate retaining screws, then the trim plate.
15. **On models equipped with CD player,** proceed as follows:
    a. Remove CD trim plate from instrument panel.
    b. Disconnect two CD player electrical connectors accessed through ashtray.
    c. Remove two T-15 Torx retaining screws to CD mounting bracket,

1	PROGRAMMER	4	THREADED ROD
2	OUTPUT ARM	5	MAX. A/C POSITION
3	RETAINER	6	MAX. HEAT POSITION

Fig. 16 Programmer linkage positioning

then pull player and bracket forward.
   d. Remove two 10mm bracket to CD retaining nuts.
16. **On all models,** remove two front storage compartment retaining screws, then the storage compartment.
17. Remove right side sound insulator retaining screws and nuts.
18. Disconnect courtesy lamp from panel and remove sound insulator from vehicle.
19. Remove six knee bolster retaining screws, then remove bolster from vehicle.
20. Remove four steering column reinforcement plate retaining screws, then remove plate from vehicle.
21. Remove glove box door and glove box unit retaining screws.
22. Remove three upper trim pad retaining screws, then pull trim pad up and out of retaining clips to remove from vehicle.

23. Remove lower left side instrument panel retaining bolt.
24. Remove hood release retaining screws.
25. Remove two instrument panel brace retaining screws, then the brace.
26. Remove four inflator module retaining screws located on back of steering wheel assembly.
27. Remove inflator module from vehicle. **When carrying a live inflator, ensure the bag and trim cover are pointed away in case of accidental deployment. Do not carry inflator module by wires of connector on underside of module. When placing a live inflator module on a bench or other surface, ensure the bag and trim cover faces in a upward direction. Never rest steering column assembly on the steering wheel with the inflator module face down and column vertical. This is necessary in case of accidental deployment. Otherwise, personal injury may result.**
28. Disconnect ignition wiring and multi-function switch electrical connectors.
29. Remove pinch bolt from intermediate shaft.
30. Remove upper and lower steering column support brackets, then remove steering column from vehicle.
31. Remove lower right instrument panel retaining bolt and three upper instrument panel retaining screws.
32. Disconnect instrument panel electrical connectors, then remove instrument panel from vehicle.
33. Disconnect programmer electrical connectors, then remove programmer from vehicle, **Fig. 15.**
34. Disconnect BCM electrical connectors, then remove BCM and mounting bracket from vehicle.
35. Disconnect ECM electrical connectors, then remove ECM and mounting bracket from vehicle.
36. Remove heater core cover, then the hoses from heater core.
37. Remove two heater core retaining screws, then the heater core from vehicle.
38. Reverse procedure to install.
39. Rearm airbag system as outlined under "Precautions."

TORONADO & TROFEO

1. Disarm airbag system as outlined under "Precautions."
2. Disconnect battery ground cable and drain cooling system, then remove righthand sound insulator.
3. Remove knee bolster, then the instrument panel column reinforcement plate.
4. Remove instrument panel cluster trim plate, then the lefthand side switch assembly.
5. Remove righthand side switch plate assembly, then the instrument panel cluster.
6. Remove climate control head, if equipped.
7. Remove four bolts retaining driver in-

formation display (DID), then the DID.
8. Remove center A/C deflectors, then unsnap and remove defroster grille.
9. Remove upper, then the lower-left instrument panel mounting screws and bolts.
10. Remove hood release assembly, retaining bolts and center instrument panel brace.
11. Remove steering column, then the glove box.
12. Remove lower-right instrument panel retaining bolt, then the fuse box retaining screws and fuse box.
13. Remove console, then the instrument panel. Disconnect instrument panel electrical connectors.
14. Disconnect programmer electrical connectors, then remove programmer, **Fig. 16.**
15. Disconnect BCM electrical connections, then remove BCM and mounting bracket.
16. Disconnect ECM electrical connections, then remove ECM and mounting bracket.
17. Remove heater core from housing, then the hoses from the core.
18. Remove two heater core retaining screws, then the heater core from vehicle.
19. Reverse procedure to install.
20. Rearm airbag system as outlined under "Precautions."

EVAPORATOR CORE
REPLACE

ELDORADO & SEVILLE

1. Discharge refrigerant from system.

Refer to "A/C Refrigerant Recovery" in "Air Conditioning" chapter.
2. Drain radiator and cooling system.
3. Remove two bolts from each side of cross-tower support bracket.
4. Remove two nuts from cowl relay center bracket, then position relay bracket aside.
5. Disconnect electrical connectors from power module, blower motor and blower motor resistor.
6. Disconnect both heater core hoses from heater core.
7. Remove evaporator line retaining bracket.
8. Remove evaporator core refrigerant lines. **Cap all open fittings to prevent contamination of system.**
9. Remove heater hose T-connector.
10. Remove two heat shield screws from engine compartment.
11. Raise and support vehicle, then remove the remaining two heat shield retaining screws from under the vehicle.
12. Remove heat shield, then the two A/C module retaining screws (one 7 mm and one 10 mm).
13. Lower vehicle and remove MAP sensor bracket.
14. Remove diverter valve from righthand side valve cover.
15. Remove two harness hold-down brackets from valve cover.
16. Remove power module, blower motor and sound insulator.
17. Remove A/C module cover screws, module cover, sound insulator and the seal.
18. Remove evaporator retaining clamp, then pull evaporator core from evaporator case.

19. Reverse procedure to install, noting the following:
    a. **Torque** module cover retaining screws to 27 inch lbs.
    b. **Torque** line fitting bolt to 18 ft. lbs.
    c. Leak test all refrigerant connections.

REATTA, RIVIERA, TORONADO & TROFEO

1. Discharge refrigerant from system. Refer to "A/C Refrigerant Recovery" in "Air Conditioning" chapter.
2. Drain cooling system, remove cross tower support bracket attaching nuts and bolts.
3. Remove relay center, set aside.
4. Remove heater hoses from heater core, then the evaporator core retaining bracket.
5. Disconnect refrigerant inlet and outlet lines from evaporator.
6. Remove heater hose T connector.
7. Remove two engine compartment heat shield attaching screws, then raise vehicle and remove two remaining heat shield attaching screws from under the vehicle. Remove heat shield.
8. Remove two A/C module attaching screws, then lower vehicle.
9. Disconnect electrical connectors from power module and blower motor.
10. Remove power module, then the blower motor.
11. Remove module cover, sound insulator, seal and evaporator core.
12. Reverse procedure to install.
13. Rearm airbag as outlined under "Precautions."

3.8L/V6-231 & 4.9L/V8-300 Engines

NOTE: For Service Procedures Not Found In This Section, Refer To 3.8L/V6-231 & 4.9L/V8-300 Engine Section in the Buick LeSabre & Park Avenue, Cadillac DeVille & Fleetwood, Oldsmobile Eighty Eight & Ninety Eight & Pontiac Bonneville Chapter.

INDEX

PRECAUTIONS
AIRBAG SYSTEM
DISARMING

The diagnostic energy reserve mod-
ule (DERM) can maintain voltage to cause a system deployment for up to ten minutes after the ignition switch is turned off and the battery is disconnected. Servicing the SIR system during this period may result in accidental

deployment and personal injury.
1. Ensure front wheels are pointed straight ahead.
2. Turn ignition switch to Lock position and remove SIR or AIRBAG fuse.
3. Remove left sound insulator. **Remove**

courtesy lamp from sound insulator, if necessary.
4. Remove Connector Position Assurance (CPA), then disconnect yellow two-way SIR electrical connector at base of steering column.
5. **On 1993-94 Eldorado and Seville,** open trap door in rear of glove box.
6. Remove Connector Position Assurance (CPA), then disconnect yellow two-way SIR electrical connector for passenger inflator module.

AIRBAG SYSTEM ARMING

1. Connect yellow two-way SIR electrical connector(s), then install Connector Position Assurance (CPA).
2. Install left sound insulator. **Install courtesy lamp to sound insulator, if applicable.**
3. Install SIR fuse to fuse block, turn ignition switch to Run position and ensure that "Inflatable Restraint" lamp flashes 7 to 9 times, then shuts off.

RELIEVING FUEL SYSTEM PRESSURE

1. Loosen fuel filler cap, then connect gauge J-34730-1 to fuel pressure connection. Wrap shop towel around fitting while connecting gauge.
2. Install bleed hose into approved container, then open valve on gauge to bleed system pressure.

ENGINE MOUNTS
REPLACE
ELDORADO & SEVILLE

RIGHT SIDE ENGINE & TRANSAXLE MOUNT

Removal

Refer to **Fig. 1,** for engine and transaxle mount position.
1. Open hood, then remove brace between engine bracket and engine.
2. Remove two nuts securing mount to engine bracket.
3. Raise vehicle on a hoist and support with stands at each front frame horn.
4. Remove two nuts securing engine mount to frame.
5. Remove two nuts securing transaxle bracket to mount.
6. Remove two nuts securing transaxle mount to frame bracket.
7. Raise engine using support J-28467 or equivalent, lifting engine until bracket is free from engine and transaxle mounts.
8. Remove stud and two bolts securing bracket to block, then the bracket and mount by pulling forward.
9. Remove transaxle mounting bracket from transaxle, then the mount.

Installation

Refer to **Fig. 1,** for engine and transaxle mount position.
1. Position engine mount and bracket between block and frame, then tighten bracket bolts and stud to specifications.

2. Position transaxle mount and bracket between transaxle and frame, then tighten bracket retaining bolts to specifications.
3. Guide mounts into position while lowering engine and reverse remaining procedure to complete installation, tighten all fasteners to specifications.

LEFT ENGINE MOUNT

Refer to **Fig. 1,** for engine and transaxle mount position.
1. Disconnect battery ground cable, then remove air cleaner assembly.
2. Remove serpentine drive belt, then discharge A/C system and recover coolant. Refer to "A/C Coolant Recovery" in 'Air Conditioning."
3. Install engine support tool No. J-28467 or equivalent.
4. Remove lower center exhaust manifold nut, then the top nut from engine damper.
5. Raise and support vehicle, remove right engine splash shield and A/C splash shield.
6. Remove engine damper.
7. Remove two A/C compressor brackets, then the A/C compressor.
8. Remove water pipe bracket bolt.
9. Remove bolts securing engine mount bracket to block and cradle.
10. Remove engine mount and bracket assembly through right wheelhell.
11. Remove engine mount from bracket.
12. Reverse procedure to install, tighten engine mount bolts and nuts to specifications.

REATTA, RIVIERA, TORONADO & TROFEO

1. Support engine using tool J-28467 or equivalent.
2. Raise and support vehicle.
3. Remove nuts securing engine mount to bracket, **Figs. 2 and 3,** then raise engine slightly.
4. Remove nuts securing mount to frame and engine mount.
5. Reverse procedure to install. Tighten mount fasteners to specifications as shown in **Figs. 2 and 3.**

ENGINE
REPLACE

ELDORADO & SEVILLE

1. Disarm airbag system and relieve fuel system pressure as described under "Precautions."
2. Disconnect battery ground cable.
3. Drain cooling system.
4. Remove air cleaner assembly.
5. Mark position of hood hinges, disconnect necessary electrical connectors, then remove hood hinge bolts and the hood.
6. Remove engine cooling fan and serpentine drive belt.
7. Disconnect upper radiator and heater hoses from thermostat housing.
8. Disconnect and mark the electrical connectors from the following components:

a. Oil pressure switch.
b. Coolant temperature sensor.
c. Distributor.
d. EGR solenoid.
e. Engine temperature switch.
f. ISC motor.
g. Throttle position switch.
h. Injectors.
i. MAT sensor.
j. Oxygen sensor.
k. Throttle body base warmer.
l. Alternator and ground wiring at alternator bracket.
m. Electric EFE grid.
9. Release engine harness from retainers and secure aside.
10. Disconnect accelerator, cruise control and transmission cables from throttle body.
11. Remove cruise control diaphragm brackets and secure assembly aside.
12. Disconnect oil and transmission cooler lines from radiator.
13. Disconnect remaining hoses and remove radiator.
14. Disconnect oil cooler lines at filter adapter and remove lines.
15. Remove oil cooler line bracket at transaxle and the air cleaner bracket.
16. Remove oil filter adapter housing.
17. Disconnect AIR tubes from diverter valve, if equipped.
18. Remove front right and rear body cross braces.
19. Disconnect and remove right front heater hose and coolant reservoir.
20. Remove AIR filter box and bracket, if equipped.
21. Disconnect power steering line bracket from right cylinder head, remove power steering pump and tensioner retaining bolts and secure assembly aside.
22. Discharge A/C system, disconnect A/C lines at accumulator and condenser, plug lines and fittings.
23. Disconnect fuel lines at throttle body and fuel line bracket from transaxle, then position fuel lines aside.
24. Remove EGR lines and brackets.
25. Disconnect vacuum modulator line, then the power brake vacuum line.
26. Raise and support vehicle, remove starter shield, then disconnect starter wiring and block ground straps.
27. Remove exhaust crossover pipe and starter motor.
28. Remove both flexplate dust shields, then the three bolts securing torque converter to flexplate.
29. Remove A/C compressor dust shield.
30. Remove right front tire and wheel, then the outer wheelhouse plastic shield.
31. Remove right rear engine to transaxle mounting bolt and lower engine damper nut.
32. Remove front (left) engine mount nuts and right rear engine/transaxle mount bolts, **Fig. 1.**
33. Disconnect alternator and oxygen sensor wiring, then remove heater bypass bracket from right side of vehicle.
34. Remove right engine brace, then lower vehicle.

Fig. 1 Engine & transaxle mounts. Eldorado & Seville

1	BRACKET
2	NUT 41 N·M (30 LBS. FT.)
3	MOUNT ASSEMBLY
4	WASHER
5	NUT 41 N·M (30 LBS. FT.)
6	BOLT 90 N·M (66 LBS. FT.)
7	BOLT 28 N·M (21 LBS. FT.)

Fig. 2   Front engine mount. Reatta, Riviera, Toronado & Trofeo

1	THROTTLE BODY INLET COOLANT HOSE
2	MANIFOLD COOLANT OUTLET
3	BOLT
4	O-RING
5	THERMOSTAT
6	RADIATOR HOSE

Fig. 5   Thermostat replacement. Riviera, Reatta, Toronado & Trofeo

35. Remove five top engine to transaxle mounting bolts.
36. Install lift equipment and support transaxle with a jack.
37. Raise engine, separate engine from transaxle, then remove engine from vehicle.
38. Reverse procedure to install.
39. Rearm airbag system as described under "Precautions."

REATTA, RIVIERA, TORONADO & TROFEO

1. Disarm airbag system and relieve fuel system pressure as described under "Precautions."
2. Disconnect battery ground cable.
3. Remove air intake duct.

1	95 N·m (70 LBS. FT.)
2	67 N·m (50 LBS. FT.)
3	67 N·m (50 LBS. FT.)

Fig. 3   Rear engine mount. Reatta, Riviera, Toronado & Trofeo

4. Remove throttle cable bracket and throttle cables from throttle body.
5. Drain engine coolant.
6. Raise and support vehicle.
7. Remove exhaust pipe from rear exhaust manifold, then the engine mount bolts.
8. Disconnect starter wiring, then remove starter.
9. Remove A/C compressor and secure aside.
10. Disconnect power steering hoses at steering gear.
11. Remove lower transaxle-to-engine bolts. **Note location and direction of bolts for assembly reference.**
12. Remove torque converter dust shield, then scribe an alignment mark between converter and flexplate, remove converter bolts.
13. Remove engine support bracket at transaxle.
14. Lower vehicle, then disconnect radiator hoses and heater hoses at engine.
15. Disconnect vacuum modulator and canister purge lines.
16. Disconnect engine wiring harness, then remove remaining transaxle to engine bolts.
17. Attach lifting equipment to engine and support transaxle.
18. Raise engine, separate engine from transaxle and remove engine from vehicle.
19. Reverse procedure to install.
20. Rearm airbag system as described under "Precautions."

COOLING SYSTEM BLEED

To be performed after cooling system has been drained, flushed and is ready to be refilled.
1. Fill cooling system with a 50/50 mixture of antifreeze and water, to just below the filler neck.
2. Fill coolant recovery reservoir to specified fill mark on outside of reservoir.
3. Run engine with radiator cap removed until normal operating temperature is achieved.
4. With engine running at idle, add coolant to radiator, until it reaches the bottom of the filler neck.
5. Cycle the engine to 5000 RPM, then

1	UPPER HOUSING
2	GASKET
3	THERMOSTAT ASSEMBLY
4	LOWER HOUSING
5	GASKET

Fig. 4   Thermostat replacement. Eldorado & Seville

1	FUEL FILTER	6	ENGINE FUEL RETURN PIPE
2	FUEL FEED LINE	7	FILTER RETAINER BRACKET
3	FUEL RETURN LINE	8	FUEL VAPOR LINE
4	JUMPER ASM. FILTER TO ENGINE FEED PIPE	9	L.H. FRAME SIDE RAIL
5	ENGINE FUEL FEED PIPE		

Fig. 6   Fuel filter replacement. 1991 models

back to idle at least five times. This will help expel any air trapped in the system.
6. Replace radiator cap. **Arrows on the cap must line up with the coolant recovery reservoir hose.**

THERMOSTAT
REPLACE
ELDORADO & SEVILLE

1. Drain coolant level below that of ther-

[1] FUEL FILTER **[3]** FUEL RETURN PIPE **[5]** FILTER RETAINER BRACKET
[2] FUEL FEED PIPE **[4]** FUEL VAPOR PIPE

Fig. 7 Fuel filter replacement. 1992-93 models

mostat housing.
2. Remove upper air filter assembly if necessary.
3. Remove upper thermostat housing attaching bolts, **Fig. 4.**
4. Remove upper thermostat housing, then thermostat and gasket from lower housing.
5. Reverse procedure to install, noting the following:
   a. Tighten upper thermostat attaching bolts to specifications.
   b. Fill cooling system, bleed system as outlined under "Cooling System Bleed."

RIVIERA, REATTA, TORONADO & TROFEO

1. Drain coolant until level is below that of the thermostat housing.
2. Remove fuel rail cover from engine.
3. Remove thermostat upper housing attaching bolt, **Fig. 5.**
4. Remove upper thermostat housing, then the thermostat.
5. Reverse procedure to install, noting the following:
   a. Install new rubber O-ring on upper thermostat housing, lubricate with coolant.

b. Tighten thermostat attaching bolt to specifications.
c. Fill cooling system, then bleed system as outlined under "Cooling System Bleed."

FUEL FILTER
REPLACE

1. Disconnect battery ground cable.
2. Release fuel system pressure as described under "Relieving Fuel System Pressure."
3. Disconnect fuel filter bracket release tabs.
4. Twist quick-connect fitting 1/4 turn in each direction to loosen dirt within fitting.
5. Using compressed air, clean quick-connect fitting at ends of filter.
6. Disconnect quick-connect fittings by squeezing plastic tabs of male end connector and pulling apart.
7. Remove fuel filter, **Figs. 6 and 7.**
8. Reverse procedure to install.

SERVICE BULLETINS
OIL LEAK DIAGNOSIS

When diagnosing oil leaks from rear of engine, use of a high intensity black light is the recommended procedure. This will help eliminate improper diagnosis, as various seals at rear of engine, if leaking, may appear to be a defective rear main seal.

TIGHTENING SPECIFICATIONS

Torque Specifications Are For Clean And Lightly Lubricated Threads Only. Dry Or Dirty Threads Produce Increased Friction Which Prevents Accurate Measurement Of Tightness.

3.8L/V6-231 ENGINE

Year	Component	Torque/Ft. Lbs.
1991-93	Alternator Support To Cylinder Head	36
	Alternator Support Through Alternator	36
	Engine Mount To Cylinder Block	70
	Flywheel To Crankshaft	61
	Heater Hose Fitting To Intake	11
	Ignition Module To Alternator Support	18
	Oil Level Switch To Oil Pan	40
	Oil Pan Drain Plug	18
	Oxygen Sensor To Exhaust Manifold	31
	Spark Plug To Cylinder Head	20
	Starter Motor To Cylinder Block	35
	Thermostat Housing To Intake Manifold	10
	Water Pump Cover To Timing Chain Cover	7
	Water Pump Pulley To Hub	12

4.9L/V8-300 ENGINE

Year	Component	Torque/Ft. Lbs.
1991-93	Air Pipe To Cylinder Head	22
	Coolant Temperature Sensor	22
	Distributor Hold-Down Nut	18
	Distributor Hold-Down Stud	26
	Engine Metal Temperature Switch	6
	Flywheel To Crankshaft	70
	Heater Water Valve	22
	Lower Thermostat Housing To Water Pump Bolt	7
	Lower Thermostat Housing To Water Pump Stud	30
	MAT Sensor	22
	Oil Filter Adapter To Block Screws	15
	Oil Pressure Switch	10
	Oxygen Sensor	30
	Spark Plugs	11
	Thermal Vacuum Switch (TVS)	15
	Upper Thermostat Housing To Lower Thermostat Housing Screws	20

4.6L/V8-279 Engine

INDEX

PRECAUTIONS

AIRBAG SYSTEM DISARMING

The diagnostic energy reserve module (DERM) can maintain voltage to cause a system deployment for up to ten minutes after the ignition switch is turned off and the battery is disconnected. Servicing the SIR system during this period may result in accidental deployment and personal injury.

1. Ensure front wheels are pointed straight ahead.
2. Turn ignition switch to Lock position and remove SIR or AIRBAG fuse.
3. Remove left sound insulator. **Remove courtesy lamp from sound insulator, if necessary.**
4. Remove Connector Position Assurance (CPA), then disconnect yellow two-way SIR electrical connector at base of steering column.
5. Open trap door in rear of glove box.
6. Remove Connector Position Assurance (CPA), then disconnect yellow two-way SIR electrical connector for passenger inflator module.

AIRBAG SYSTEM ARMING

1. Connect yellow two-way SIR electrical connector(s), then install Connector Position Assurance (CPA).
2. Install left sound insulator. **Install courtesy lamp to sound insulator, if applicable.**
3. Install SIR fuse to fuse block, turn ignition switch to Run position and ensure that "Inflatable Restraint" lamp flashes 7 to 9 times, then shuts off.

RELIEVING FUEL SYSTEM PRESSURE

1. Remove fuel pump fuse B1 in console fuse block.
2. Loosen fuel filler cap, then connect gauge J-34730-1 to fuel pressure connection. Wrap shop towel around fitting while connecting gauge.
3. Install bleed hose into approved container, then open valve on gauge to bleed system pressure.

THROTTLE POSITION (TP) SENSOR LEARN PROCEDURE

Ensure nothing is touching or obstructing the accelerator or brake pedals during this procedure.
1. Turn ignition to On (engine Off) position.
2. Depress OFF and WARMER buttons of the Electronic Climate Control (ECC) until all segments of the display are illuminated.
3. Turn ignition switch Off, then wait 20 seconds.
4. Repeat steps 1 through 3 two more times.

IDLE LEARN PROCEDURE

This procedure must be performed after throttle position sensor learn procedure.
Air temperature must be at least 50°F to perform this test.
1. Start and run engine until coolant temperature is 176°F, then allow to idle for an additional 5 minutes.
2. Apply brakes and place transaxle in Drive range.
3. Turn ECC to Off position and allow engine to idle for 30 seconds.
4. Turn ECC to Auto position and allow engine to idle for another 30 seconds.
5. Place transaxle in Park range and turn ignition to Off position.

ENGINE FRONT MOUNT REPLACE

1. Remove righthand cooling fan, then the lefthand fan.
2. Remove right and left torque struts, **Fig. 1.**
3. Install engine support fixture No. J-28467-A. Use only one support at left rear engine bracket.
4. Raise and support vehicle, then remove nuts securing mount to engine cradle, **Fig. 2.**
5. Remove bolts securing motor mount bracket to crankcase, then lower vehicle.
6. Remove bolts securing mount to cylinder head and bracket.
7. Raise engine by tightening support chain until mount and bracket can be separated and removed.
8. Reverse procedure to install.

ENGINE REPLACE

1. Disarm airbag system as outlined under "Airbag System Disarming."
2. Release fuel system pressure as outlined under "Relieving Fuel System Pressure."
3. Remove hood, then disconnect both battery cables.
4. Remove air cleaner inlet duct, then drain cooling system.
5. Remove left and right torque struts. Reinstall bolts in torque strut bracket at left front of engine as this will be used as an engine lift point.
6. Disconnect radiator hoses from water crossover.
7. Remove both engine cooling fans, then the serpentine drive belt.
8. Disconnect cruise control servo connections, then ISC electrical connector.
9. Disconnect throttle cable from throttle body cam.

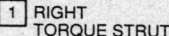

1 RIGHT
TORQUE STRUT

2 LEFT
TORQUE STRUT

3 REAR
TRANSMISSION
HYDROMOUNT

4 TRANSMISSION
HYDROMOUNT

5 ENGINE
HYDROMOUNT

Fig. 3   Bellhousing mounting bolt locations

Fig. 1   Engine/transaxle mounts

30 N•m (25 LBS. FT) — NUT

Fig. 2   Front engine mount replacement

10. Disconnect shift cable from park/neutral switch and cable bracket at transmission. Remove park/neutral switch.
11. Disconnect power brake vacuum hose, then the cylinder head temperature switch.
12. Remove bellhousing bolts, **Fig. 3**, then the ignition coils and spark plug wires.
13. Raise and support vehicle, then remove oil pan to transmission brace.
14. Remove torque converter splash shield, then converter to flywheel bolts.
15. Disconnect oil cooler lines at oil filter adapter.
16. Remove A/C compressor. Position compressor aside leaving lines attached.
17. disconnect electrical connections from harness along lefthand side of engine, **Fig. 4**. Move harness out from

behind exhaust manifold.
18. Remove nuts securing motor mount to engine cradle front crossmember, then the exhaust pipe.
19. Remove right front wheel, then the crankcase to transmission bracket at transmission tail shaft.
20. Disconnect knock sensor, then remove bolts from transmission to cylinder head brace at cylinder head.
21. Lower vehicle, then using fuel line remover No. J-37088 or equivalent, disconnect fuel lines.
22. Disconnect injector harness connector, then the hoses from coolant reservoir. Remove coolant reservoir.
23. Disconnect cam position sensor, then the heater hoses from water pipes at front of right cylinder head.
24. Disconnect battery cable from junction block, then remove retainer at cylinder head.
25. Disconnect starter cable from junction

block, then the power steering pump line at pump.
26. Remove power steering line retainer at right front of crankcase, then disconnect rear oxygen sensor connector.
27. Remove screws securing wiring harness retainer to right cam cover. Position harness aside.
28. Connect suitable engine lifting fixture to engine using support hooks at left rear and right rear of engine. Use torque strut bracket at left front of engine for third lift point.
29. Remove engine from vehicle.
30. Reverse procedure to install.
31. Rearm airbag system as outlined under "Airbag System Arming."

INTAKE MANIFOLD REPLACE

1. Remove air intake duct from throttle body.
2. Disconnect and plug coolant hoses at throttle body and coolant reservoir.
3. Disconnect electrical connectors from intake manifold, TP sensor, ISC motor, EEC solenoid and cruise control servo.
4. Disconnect vacuum hoses from brake booster, fuel pipe bundle and body.
5. Disconnect pcv hose at manifold, then the accelerator cable at throttle body. Position cable aside.
6. Release fuel system pressure as outlined under "Relieving Fuel System Pressure."
7. Disconnect fuel pipe quick connects at fuel pipe bundle in engine compartment.
8. Remove EEC solenoid bracket at rear cam cover, then reposition transaxle range control cable away from cruise control servo.
9. Remove intake manifold bolts, then the intake manifold/throttle body assembly.
10. Reverse procedure to install. Tighten manifold bolts to specifications in sequence shown in **Fig. 5**.

Fig. 5 Intake manifold tightening sequence

1	COMPRESSOR CLUTCH
2	GENERATOR CONN
3	RIGHT PULLER FAN
4	OIL PRESSURE SWITCH
5	LEFT PULLER FAN
6	O₂ SENSOR
7	CRANKSHAFT POSITION SENSORS (2)
8	TRANSMISSION
9	GROUND
10	OIL LEVEL SWITCH
11	KNOCK SENSOR
12	STARTER
13	MAT SENSOR
14	COOLANT TEMPERATURE SENSOR
15	VEHICLE SPEED SENSOR
16	POWER STEERING PRESSURE SWITCH
17	CAM POSITION SENSOR
18	PCM & DIS GROUNDS
19	MAP SENSOR
20	IDLE SPEED CONTROL
21	THROTTLE POSITION SENSOR
22	CRUISE CONTROL SERVO
23	EGR
24	PARK/NEUTRAL SAFETY SWITCH
25	BRAKE BOOSTER SENSOR
26	SPEED SENSING SWITCH
27	CANISTER PURGE SOLENOID
28	DIS MODULE
29	BATTERY/STARTER JUNCTION BOX
30	POWERTRAIN CONTROL MODULE

Fig. 4 Engine electrical connection locations

THROTTLE BODY
REPLACE

1. Remove intake manifold/throttle body assembly as outlined under "Intake Manifold, Replace."
2. Disconnect vacuum manifold at throttle body, then the vacuum hoses at cruise control servo.
3. Disconnect cruise control cable at servo. Cable can be removed at servo blade without removing plastic retainer.
4. Remove cruise control servo and bracket from throttle body, then disconnect cruise control cable at throttle body.
5. Remove throttle position sensor, then disconnect fuel pipe retainer at ISC bracket.
6. Remove throttle body from intake manifold, then the ISC motor and bracket from throttle body.
7. Reverse procedure to install.

8. Reverse procedure to install. **Perform TP sensor learn and idle learn procedures.**

EXHAUST MANIFOLD
REPLACE
LEFT SIDE

1. Remove motor mount as outlined under "Engine Front Mount, Replace."
2. Remove rear alternator bracket, then remove two bolts at manifold outlet flange.
3. Disconnect oxygen sensor electrical connector, then remove manifold attaching bolts.
4. Remove exhaust manifold, then the oxygen sensor.
5. Reverse procedure to install. Coat oxygen sensor threads with high temperature anti-seize compound.

RIGHT SIDE

1. Disconnect both battery cables, then

the rear oxygen sensor and harness clip.
2. Raise and support vehicle, then disconnect exhaust pipe from catalytic converter.
3. Disconnect suspension position sensor at both lower control arms.
4. Support rear crossmember of engine cradle with suitable screw jack, then remove 4 cradle to body bolts.
5. Carefully lower rear of engine cradle.
6. Remove pipe to exhaust manifold and crossover exhaust pipe mounting bolts.
7. Remove exhaust manifold mounting nuts, then the exhaust manifold.
8. Reverse procedure to install. Coat oxygen sensor threads with high temperature anti-seize compound.

CAM COVERS
REPLACE

LEFT SIDE

1. Disconnect both battery cables, then partially drain cooling system.
2. Disconnect upper radiator hose at water crossover, then the spark plug wires.
3. Remove right cooling fan, then disconnect PCV fresh air tube from cam cover.
4. Remove right and left torque struts, then disconnect water pump drive belt.
5. Remove water pump pulley using tools shown in **Fig. 6.**
6. Remove camshaft seal retainer screws, then seal.
7. Disconnect battery cable retainer at front of cam cover, then remove cam cover retaining screws.
8. Remove cam cover as shown in **Fig. 7.**
9. Reverse procedure to install.

RIGHT SIDE

1. Disconnect both battery cables, then remove tower to tower brace.
2. Disconnect DIS wiring connectors and mounting bolts, then remove DIS and right bank spark plug wires.
3. Disconnect PCV valve, then remove purge canister solenoid from rear of cover.

J-38825 PULLEY REMOVER   J-38823 PULLEY INSTALLER

Fig. 6   Water pump pulley replacement

REMOVAL

CRITICAL:
AREAS FOR
SEAL DAMAGE

STEP 1
LIFT END STRAIGHT
UP 10"

STEP 2
FORCE EXHAUST
EDGE UP 1 1/2"
AGAINST DIPSTICK TUBE

STEP 3
SWING FILL-CAP END
OVER INTAKE MANIFOLD
WHILE SLIDING ENTIRE
COVER OVER SHAFT

INSTALLATION

CRITICAL:
AVOID DAMAGE TO SEAL
AT SHAFT HOLE CORNER
FROM DRAGGING SEAL
ACROSS CYLINDER HEAD

STEP 1
DIP AND TWIST HOLE
CORNER PAST TENSIONER
AND OVER CAMSHAFT

STEP 2
WITH FINGERS GUIDING
SEAL, SWING COVER UNTIL
SQUARE WITH CYLINDER
HEAD, AND FORCED AGAINST
DIPSTICK TUBE

STEP 3
SLIDE COVER LEFT
AND DOWN ON HEAD
SIMULTANEOUSLY

Fig. 7   Cam cover replacement

4. Remove wiring harness from cover, then the cam cover mounting screws.
5. Support front of engine cradle and remove front cradle mounting screws.
6. Remove right and left torque struts.
7. Lower engine cradle to provide clearance at rear of engine compartment.
8. Remove cam cover.
9. Reverse procedure to install.

HARMONIC BALANCER
REPLACE

1. Release tension from accessory drive belt, then raise and support vehicle.
2. Remove right front wheel, then the splash shields from wheelwell.
3. Remove brace between engine oil pan and transmission case, then in-

FRT

Fig. 8   Removing chain guide access plugs

stall flywheel holder No. J-39411 or equivalent.
4. Remove balancer bolt, then support engine cradle with suitable jack screw and remove 3 engine cradle bolts at right side of cradle.
5. Disconnect RSS sensor from right-hand lower control arm, then lower engine cradle to obtain clearance below body rail for balancer puller.
6. Install pilot No. J-39344-2 into end of crankshaft.
7. Using puller No. J-38416 or equivalent, remove harmonic balancer.
8. Reverse procedure to install.

CYLINDER HEAD
REPLACE

1. Remove intake manifold as described under "Intake Manifold, Replace."
2. Remove cam covers as described under "Cam Covers, Replace."
3. Remove harmonic balancer as described under "Harmonic Balancer, Replace."
4. Remove front cover as described under "Front Cover, Replace."
5. Remove oil pump as described under "Oil Pump, Replace."
6. Remove chain tensioner from timing chain for cylinder head being removed.
7. Remove cam sprockets from head being removed. **Timing chains should remain in chain case.**
8. Remove timing chain guide retaining screws through access plugs at front of cylinder head, **Fig. 8.**
9. Remove water crossover, then the exhaust manifold as described under "Exhaust Manifold, Replace."
10. Remove cylinder head bolts, then the cylinder head and gasket. When camshafts remain in the cylinder head some valves will be open at all times. Do not rest the cylinder head on a flat surface with cylinder face down.
11. Reverse procedure to install. Using tightening sequence shown in **Fig. 9,** tighten cylinder head bolts as follows:
   a. **Torque** ten M11 bolts to 22 ft. lbs.

Fig. 9   Cylinder head bolt tightening sequence

Fig. 10   Holding drive chain tension

1	UPPER CRANKCASE
2	GASKET
3	FRONT COVER
4	SEAL
5	DOWEL PIN
6	10 N·m (7 LBS. FT.)

Fig. 11   Front cover replacement

plus an additional 90°.
   b. Repeat sequence and tighten an additional 90°.
   c. **Torque M6** bolts to 10 ft. lbs.

CAMSHAFT PRIMARY CHAIN
REPLACE

1. Remove engine assembly as described under "Engine, Replace," then place engine assembly on a suitable stand.
2. Remove serpentine drive belt, idler pulley and belt tensioner.
3. Remove front cover as described under "Front Cover, Replace."
4. Remove oil pump assembly as described under "Oil Pump, Replace."
5. Remove cam covers as described under "Cam Covers, Replace."
6. Remove three timing chain tensioners, then all four camshaft sprockets.
7. Remove secondary drive chains from around intermediate shaft sprocket.
8. Remove one bolt from intermediate shaft sprocket and slide gears and primary drive chain off crankshaft and intermediate shaft.
9. Reverse procedure to install, time camshafts as described under "Setting Camshaft Timing."

CAMSHAFT SECONDARY DRIVE CHAIN
REPLACE

1. Remove front cover as described under "Front Cover, Replace."
2. Remove lefthand cam cover as described under "Cam Covers, Replace."
3. Remove lefthand secondary chain tensioner.
4. Remove lefthand chain guide as described under "Cylinder Head, Replace."
5. Remove lefthand cam sprocket bolts and sprockets.
6. Remove lefthand secondary drive chain, **Fig. 10.**
7. To remove righthand secondary drive chain, refer to steps 2 through 6 and substitute righthand for lefthand.
8. Reverse procedure to install, time camshafts as described under "Setting Camshaft Timing."

CAMSHAFT
REPLACE

REMOVAL

1. Remove cam cover as described in "Cam Covers, Replace."
2. Secure cam sprocket to timing chain by installing tyraps through sprocket holes. Use two tyraps per sprocket. **The sprocket-chain relationship must be maintained throughout this procedure or camshaft timing will be lost and require further engine disassembly to time.**
3. Install cam chain holder tool No. J 38815 or equivalent behind camshaft sprockets so that it is positioned between chain tensioner and chain guide, **Fig. 10.** Apply tension to tool by tightening tension adjusting screw.
4. Remove both camshaft sprocket bolts. **Note location of cam drive pins in end of camshafts.**
5. Work sprockets off of cams using play in chain.
6. Loosen cam bearing cap bolts a few turns at a time until all valve spring

pressure has been released.
7. Remove bolts and bearing caps, then the camshaft.

INSTALLATION

1. Apply camshaft prelube part No. 1052365 or equivalent to face of each cam lobe.
2. Install camshaft, then position cam bearing caps to cylinder head noting the following:
   a. Arrow on top pf bearing cap points towards front of engine.
   b. The "E" mark on top of bearing cap indicates a cap for the exhaust cam.
   c. The "I" mark on top of bearing cap indicates a cap for the intake cam.
   d. The No. "1" mark on top of the bearing cap should be towards front of engine.
3. Loosely install cam bearing cap bolts, then alternately tighten each bearing cap bolt a few turns at a time against valve spring pressure until all bolts are snug.
4. Tighten bearing cap bolts to specification.
5. Rotate camshaft until drive pins are in position to engage cam sprockets over cams, then install retaining bolts. Tighten sprocket bolts to specification.
6. Remove chain holder tool, then the tyraps from cam sprockets.
7. Install cam cover.

FRONT COVER
REPLACE

1. Remove serpentine drive belt.
2. Remove harmonic balancer as outlined under "Harmonic Balancer, Replace."
3. Remove belt tensioner, then the belt idler pulley.
4. Remove front cover mounting bolts, **Fig. 11,** then the front cover.
5. Reverse procedure to install.

FRONT COVER SEAL
REPLACE

1. Remove harmonic balancer as out-

Fig. 12   Rotating tensioner release lever

1 RELEASE TO FIRST CLICK
2 INSTALL LOCK PIN

Fig. 13   Locking tensioner in collapsed position

1   INTAKE POSITION
2   EXHAUST POSITION
3   TIMING MARKS

Fig. 14   Setting camshaft timing

lined under "Harmonic Balancer, Replace."

2. Using screwdriver behind front cover seal, pry out seal. Do not score cover bore for seal or crankshaft.
3. Lubricate seal lips with engine oil and position seal to front cover with garter spring side toward engine.
4. Using seal installer No. J-38818 and harmonic balancer installer No. J-39344 or equivalents, push seal into front cover until it bottoms on cover.
5. Install harmonic balancer.

CAMSHAFT DRIVE CHAIN TENSIONER
REPLACE

1. Remove front cover as described in "Front Cover, Replace."
2. Remove two tensioner mounting bolts, then the tensioner.
3. Collapse new tensioner as follows:
   a. Rotate ratchet release lever counter clockwise and hold, **Fig. 12.**
   b. Collapse tensioner shoe and hold.
   c. Release ratchet lever and slowly release pressure on shoe.
   d. As ratchet lever moves to first click hold tensioner shoe inward and insert a pin through hole in release lever, **Fig. 13.**
4. Install tensioner and bolts, tighten bolts to specification.
5. Remove retaining pin allowing tensioner shoe to extend.

6. Install front cover.

SETTING CAMSHAFT TIMING

Setting camshaft timing is necessary whenever the cam drive system has been disturbed such that the relationship between any chain and sprocket has been lost.

1. Remove cam covers as described under "Cam Covers, Replace."
2. Remove front cover as described under "Front Cover, Replace."
3. Remove or retract three chain tensioners. **Tensioners may be in their installed positions but must be fully retracted as described under "Camshaft Drive Chain Tensioner, Replace."**
4. Remove oil pump assembly as described in "Oil Pump, Service."
5. Rotate crankshaft until sprocket drive key is at approximately the 1 o'clock position.
6. Install crankshaft and intermediate shaft sprockets to primary drive chain with their timing marks aligned as shown in **Fig. 14.**
7. Install crank and intermediate shaft sprockets over their respective shafts.
8. Rotate crankshaft so that crankshaft key engages the sprocket without changing timing mark position.
9. Install intermediate sprocket retaining bolt, tighten bolt to specification.
10. Install primary chain tensioner and release tensioner shoe. Tighten tensioner mounting bolts to specification.
11. Install flywheel holder tool No. J-

39411 or equivalent to lock crankshaft in this position.
12. Route secondary drive chain for right-hand cylinder head over inner row of intermediate shaft teeth.
13. Route secondary drive chain over chain guide and install exhaust cam sprocket to chain so that the camshaft drive pin engages sprocket marked "RE" (right head exhaust). There should be no slack in lower section of chain and cam drive pin must be perpendicular to cylinder head face as shown in **Fig. 14. RE cam sprocket must contain cam position sensor pickup.**
14. Install intake cam sprocket into chain so that sprocket notch marked "RI" (right head intake) engages cam drive pin while pin remains perpendicular to cylinder head face as shown in **Fig. 14.**
15. A hex is cast into camshafts so that an open end wrench can be used to provide minor repositioning of the cams.
16. Loosely install exhaust and intake cam sprocket bolts.
17. Install chain tensioner and release tension on shoe, then tighten tensioner mounting bolts to specification.
18. Tighten cam sprocket bolts to specification.
19. Route secondary drive chain for left-hand cylinder head over outer row of intermediate shaft teeth and repeat steps 13 through 18 for lefthand cams.

MAIN BEARINGS

Shell type main bearings of steel backed

Fig. 15   Main bearing cap bolt tightening sequence

aluminum are used at all positions. The upper halves are all interchangeable, as are all of the lower halves except for the thrust bearings in the No. 3 position. If bearing clearance is greater than .003 inch and new bearings do not reduce the clearance to .0005-.002 inch, a new crankshaft will be required. Undersized bearing are not available and crankshaft grinding is not allowed. When installing main bearing bolts, **torque** bolts in to 15 ft. lbs. plus an additional 65° using sequence shown in **Fig. 15**. Maximum crankshaft endplay is .019 inch.

1 PISTON ARROW TOWARD CHAIN CASE ON BOTH SIDES
2 PISTON
3 ROD CAP
4 LOCATER LUGS INDICATE PISTON FRONT TOWARDS ENGINE FRONT
5 BEARING CAP ARROWS POINT TOWARD EACH OTHER ON PAIRED RODS
6 ROD CAPS
7 BEARING CAP ARROWS POINT TOWARD EACH OTHER ON PAIRED RODS

Fig. 16   Piston & rod assembly

PISTON & ROD ASSEMBLY

Refer to **Fig. 16** for correct piston and rod assembly installation.

OIL PAN
REPLACE

1. Remove engine assembly and place on suitable engine stand.
2. Drain engine oil.
3. Remove oil pan bolts, then the pan.
4. Reverse procedure to install, noting the following:
   a. Gasket is reusable unless damaged. **Do not remove gasket from oil pan groove unless replacement is required.**
   b. Using sequence shown in **Fig. 17**, tighten oil pan bolts to specification.

OIL PUMP
SERVICE
REMOVAL

1. Remove front cover as described in "Front Cover, Replace."
2. Remove three oil pump mounting bolts, **Fig. 18**.
3. Remove pump and drive spacer.

DISASSEMBLE

1. Remove drive spacer from pump housing, **Fig. 19**.
2. Remove two screws holding pump housing halves together.
3. Remove inner and outer rotors from housing. **Mark mating surfaces.**
4. Remove pressure relief valve.

Fig. 17   Oil pan bolt tightening sequence

INSPECTION

1. Inspect pump housing for nicks, burrs, chips or debris that may cause a leak or binding condition in rotor pocket.
2. Inspect drive or driven rotors for nicks or burrs.
3. Check pump cover and interior surface for excessive wear or score marks.

ASSEMBLE

1. Install inner and outer rotors to pump cover. **Align marks made during pump disassemble procedure.**
2. Install pressure relief valve seat, spring and pilot in pump housing.
3. Assemble housing and cover over locating dial.
4. Insert a ³/₈ inch drill bit in pump mounting hole on opposite side to aid in alignment of housing and cover.
5. Install two bolts and **torque** to 9 ft. lbs.

INSTALLATION

1. Install oil pump drive spacer into oil pump from rear so that drive flat engages pump rotor.
2. Position pump over crankshaft, then loosely install bolts.
3. Holding pump up as high as possible, **torque** pump retaining bolts to 7 ft. lbs. plus an additional 35°.
4. Install front cover assembly as described in "Front Cover, Replace."

REAR MAIN SEAL
REPLACE

1. Remove transaxle assembly, refer to "Automatic Transmissions/Transaxles."
2. Remove eight flywheel mounting bolts, then the flywheel.
3. Drill a ¹/₈ inch hole into metal body of rear main seal, then remove seal using a slide hammer.
4. Place a small dab of RTV sealant at crankcase split line across end of upper/lower crankcase seal.
5. Lubricate new oil seal with engine oil, then slide seal over arbor of seal installation tool No. J 38817 or equivalent.
6. Thread seal-installer tool No. J 38818 in crankshaft flange and install seal by turning handle until tool bottoms against crankcase, **Fig. 20**.
7. Install flywheel and transaxle assembly.

COOLING SYSTEM BLEED

This engine does not require a specified bleed procedure. After filling cooling sys-

1 ENGINE UPPER CRANKCASE
2 OIL PUMP DRIVE SPACER
3 OIL PUMP
4 BOLT (3)
5 LOWER CRANKCASE

Fig. 18   Removing oil pump

1 GEROTOR ASSEMBLY
2 OUTER GEAR
3 INNER GEAR
4 HOUSING
5 DRIVE SPACER
6 RELIEF VALVE
7 COVER

Fig. 19   Exploded view of oil pump

1 J 38817

**Fig. 20   Installing rear main
seal**

tem, run engine to operating temperature with radiator/pressure cap off. Air will then be automatically bled through cap opening.

SERPENTINE DRIVE BELT
REPLACE

1. Rotate drive belt tensioner mechanism upward, away from drive belt using a ½ inch breaker bar.
2. Remove serpentine drive belt.
3. Reverse procedure to install. Refer to **Fig. 21**, for serpentine drive belt routing.

WATER PUMP
REPLACE

1. Drain cooling system, then remove air cleaner.
2. Remove water pump housing retaining bolts, then the water pump housing, **Fig. 22**.
3. Remove water pump drive belt, then

1 DRIVE BELT TENSIONER
2 SERPENTINE DRIVE BELT

**Fig. 21   Serpentine drive belt
routing**

the water pump.
4. Reverse procedure to install.

THERMOSTAT
REPLACE

1. Drain cooling system, then remove front end beauty panel and air cleaner.
2. Remove thermostat housing mounting bolts, then the housing, **Fig. 23**.
3. Remove thermostat and O-ring from housing.
4. Reverse procedure to install.

FUEL FILTER
REPLACE

1. Disconnect battery ground cable.
2. Release fuel system pressure as outlined under "Relieving Fuel System Pressure."

1 WATER PUMP ASM.
2 O-RING SEAL
3 WATER PUMP HOUSING ASM.

**Fig. 22   Water pump assembly
& housing**

1 THERMOSTAT
2 THERMOSTAT HOUSING

**Fig. 23   Thermostat
replacement**

3. Disconnect fuel filter bracket release tabs.
4. Twist quick-connect fitting ¼ turn in each direction to loosen dirt within fitting.
5. Using compressed air, clean quick-connect fitting at ends of filter.
6. Disconnect quick-connect fittings by squeezing plastic tabs of male end connector and pulling apart.
7. Remove fuel filter.
8. Reverse procedure to install.

TIGHTENING SPECIFICATIONS

Year	Component	Torque/ Ft. Lbs.
1993-94	Belt Tensioner	35
	Cam Cover	7
	Camshaft Bearing Cap	9
	Camshaft Drive Chain Tensioner	20
	Camshaft Seal Retainer To Cover	10 ①
	Camshaft Sprocket	90
	Coolant Drain Plug	6
	Cooling Fan Mounting Bolts	88 ①
	Cylinder Head Bolts	③
	Engine To Transmission	35
	Exhaust Manifold To Cylinder Head Bolt	20
	Exhaust Manifold To Cylinder Head Locknut	25
	Flywheel	11 ⑤
	Flywheel Housing Cover	12 ①
	Front Cover	7
	Fuel Filter Bolt	88 ①
	Intake Manifold Bolts	71 ① ②
	Intake Manifold Cover Bolts	106 ①
	Main Bearing Cap Bolts	③

Year	Component	Torque/ Ft. Lbs.
1993-94 —Cont'd	Oil Filter Adpater	20
	Oil Pan	7
	Oil Pan Drain Plug	15
	Oil Pump To Lower Crankcase	7 ⑥
	Oil Pump To Suction Pipe	7
	Oxygen Sensor	30
	Thermostat Housing Bolts	18
	Throttle Body Bolts	106 ①
	Torque Strut Bracket To Cylinder Head	35
	Torque Strut Bracket To Water Manifold	20
	Torsional Damper	105 ④
	Transmission Brace	35
	Water Pump Housing	20
	Water Pump Pulley Mounting Bolts	22
	Water Pump Stud Nuts	62 ①

①—Inch pounds.
②—Plus an additional ⅓ turn (120°).
③—Refer to text.
④—Plus an additional 120°.
⑤—Plus an additional 50°.
⑥—Plus an additional 35°.

Rear Suspension

INDEX

DESCRIPTION

All rear suspension components are mounted on a suspension support assembly, **Fig. 1,** which is attached to the body at four points. The transverse leaf spring is fully isolated from the crossmember and is held in position by left and right retainers and insulators. On their inboard end, the control arms pivot on the suspension support, allowing each end of the leaf spring to act directly on the control arm surface. A suspension knuckle pivots on the outboard end of each control arm, and each knuckle contains a sealed hub and wheel bearing assembly. Each knuckle is located at the top by an air adjustable strut assembly which is connected to the suspension support.

On some models, a stabilizer shaft is used to further locate the knuckle assemblies and provide increased roll stiffness. Strut charging is controlled by an Electronic Level Control (ELC) system, which maintains a standard rear trim height under a variety of load conditions.

HUB & BEARING REPLACE

1. Raise and support vehicle.
2. Remove tire and wheel assembly.
3. Remove brake caliper attaching bolts and position caliper aside. **Do not suspend caliper by brake line.**
4. Remove rotor retainers, if equipped. Retainers may be discarded after removal.
5. Remove rotor.
6. Remove four hub mounting bolts, then the hub and bearing assembly.
7. Reverse procedure to install, torquing to specifications.

STRUT REPLACE

1. Raise and support vehicle on frame contact type hoist, then remove wheel and tire assembly.
2. If left strut is to be replaced, disconnect ELC height sensor link.
3. Reinstall two wheel nuts to retain brake rotor, then remove stabilizer shaft mounting bolt at strut, if equipped.
4. Remove brake caliper as outlined, then secure aside leaving hoses connected.
5. Loosen, but do not remove, knuckle pivot bolt at outboard end of control arm. **Support outboard end of control arm with a jackstand to slightly compress spring. Jackstand must be of adequate strength to support vehicle weight and be properly positioned to prevent personal injury.**
6. Remove upper strut rod cap, mounting nut and insulator, **Fig. 2.**
7. Slowly remove jackstand to relieve spring pressure, compress strut by hand, then remove lower insulator.
8. Rotate strut and knuckle assembly outward, remove pinch bolt, then separate strut from knuckle.
9. Reverse procedure to install, ensuring strut is fully seated with tang on strut bottomed in steering knuckle slot.

1	UNDERBODY ASSEMBLY
2	SUSPENSION SUPPORT INSULATORS
3	UPPER STRUT MOUNTING NUT
4	STRUT MOUNT INSULATORS
5	STRUT
6	KNUCKLE
7	HUB AND BEARING ASSEMBLY
8	CONTROL ARM
9	SPRING RETAINER
10	SPRING INSULATORS
11	SINGLE LEAF SPRING
12	STABILIZER SHAFT
13	SUSPENSION SUPPORT
14	TRIM HEIGHT ADJUSTMENT SPACER (OPTIONAL)

Fig. 1   Rear suspension exploded view. Left side

1	STRUT ROD CAP	8	LOWER PINCH BOLT 55 N·m (40 LBS. FT.)
2	NUT 88 N·m (65 LBS. FT.)	9	KNUCKLE
3	RETAINER	10	LOCATING SLOT
4	UPPER INSULATOR	11	CONTROL ARM
5	SUSPENSION SUPPORT	12	SPRING
6	LOWER INSULATOR	13	TRIM HEIGHT ADJUSTMENT SPACER (OPTIONAL)
7	STRUT		

Fig. 2   Rear strut replacement

When suspension is fully assembled, torque bolts to specifications.

KNUCKLE
REPLACE

Left and right knuckles are not interchangeable. When replacing knuckles, check knuckle for the L or R designation stamped on knuckle.
1. Raise and support vehicle on frame contact type hoist, then remove wheel and tire assembly.
2. If left knuckle is to be replaced, disconnect ELC height sensor link.
3. Remove stabilizer shaft mounting bolt from strut, if equipped.
4. Remove brake caliper as outlined, and secure aside leaving hoses connected.
5. Remove brake rotor, hub retaining bolts and the hub and bearing assembly.
6. Loosen, but do not remove, knuckle pivot bolt at outboard end of control arm.
7. Support outboard end of control arm with a proper jackstand. **Jack stand must be securely positioned or personal injury may result.**
8. Remove upper strut rod cap, mounting nut and insulator, **Fig. 2.**
9. Compress strut by hand and remove lower insulator.
10. Rotate strut and knuckle assembly outward, remove pinch bolt, then separate strut from knuckle.
11. Remove speed sensor from knuckle if

LEFT (L) OR RIGHT (R)
DESIGNATION HERE

VIEW A

1	KNUCKLE
2	NUT (80 N·m/59 FT. LBS.)
3	RETAINER
4	PIVOT BOLT
5	CONTROL ARM

Fig. 3   Knuckle replacement

equipped with anti-lock brakes.
12. Remove knuckle pivot bolt and the knuckle, **Fig. 3.**
13. Reverse procedure to install, ensuring strut is fully seated with tang on strut bottomed in steering knuckle slot. When suspension is fully assembled, torque bolts and wheel lug nut to specifications.

CONTROL ARM
REPLACE

1. Raise and support vehicle on frame contact type hoist, then remove wheel and tire assembly.
2. If left control arm is to be replaced, disconnect ELC height sensor link.
3. Remove stabilizer shaft mounting bolt from strut, if equipped.
4. Reinstall two wheel nuts to retain brake rotor, then remove brake caliper as outlined and secure aside leaving hoses connected.
5. Loosen, but do not remove, knuckle pivot bolt at outboard end of control arm.
6. Support outboard end of control arm with a proper jackstand.
7. Remove upper strut rod cap, mounting nut and insulator, **Fig. 2.**
8. Slowly remove jackstand to relieve spring pressure.
9. Compress strut by hand and remove lower insulator.
10. Remove wheel speed sensor from knuckle if equipped with anti-lock brakes.
11. Support knuckle assembly, remove knuckle pivot bolt, then remove strut, knuckle, hub, bearing and rotor as an assembly.
12. Remove both inner control arm bolts, then the control arm, **Fig. 4.**
13. Reverse procedure to install, ensuring strut is fully seated with tang on strut bottomed in steering knuckle slot. When suspension is fully assembled, torque bolts to specifications.

1 SUSPENSION CROSSMEMBER ASSEMBLY
2 INNER CONTROL ARM BOLTS
3 CONTROL ARM
4 NUTS (90 N·m/66 FT. LBS.)

Fig. 4 Lower control arm replacement

1 J-21474-18 NUT
2 J-21474-19 BOLT
3 BEARING (PART OF J-21474-19)
4 J-21474-5
5 J-21474-23
6 J-28576-1
7 J-35739-3
8 J-35739-1 SPACER — USE WIDER SIDE ON OUTER BUSHINGS. NARROW SIDE ON INNER BUSHINGS
9 J-35739-2

Fig. 5 Control arm bushings replacement

CONTROL ARM BUSHINGS
REPLACE
OUTER
Removal

If inner control arm bolts are not loosened, or removed, alignment will not be disturbed and it will not be necessary to perform wheel alignment after outer bushing replacement.

1. Outer control arm bushings can be replaced without removing control arm from vehicle after performing steps 1–12 of "Control Arm, Replace" procedure.
2. Insert spacer between control arm flanges. Special tool No. J-35739-1 or equivalent, is a combination of two spacers. **The wide spacer must be used for outer bushing removal and installation.**
3. Coat the threads of tool No. J-21474-19 bolt with high pressure lubricant J-23444-A, or equivalent, to prevent thread damage.
4. Install tool Nos. J-35739-2 remover, J-21474-5 receiver, bearing, J-21474-18 nut and J-21474-19 bolt or equivalents as shown in **Fig. 5.**
5. Remove bushing from control arm by tightening nut.

Installation

1. Position new bushing for installation on control arm. Bushing must be installed from the outside of the control arm, then drawn inward toward the control arm centerline.
2. Insert wide end of J-35739-1 spacer between control arm flanges.
3. Coat threads of bolt J-21474-19 with high pressure lubricant J-23444-A.
4. Install bushing installer J-28576-1, receiver J-35739-3, bearing, nut J-21474-18 and bolt J-21474-19, **Fig. 5.**

5. Draw bushing into control arm by tightening nut. Tighten nut until bushing flange seats firmly against control arm.
6. Refer to "Control Arm, Replace" for suspension assembly.

INNER

Control arm must be removed from vehicle to replace inner control arm bushings. After replacing inner bushings, check wheel alignment as outlined.

1. Remove control arm as described under "Control Arm, Replace."
2. Insert spacer between control arm flanges. Special tool No. J-35739-1 or equivalent is a combination of two spacers. **The narrow spacer must be used for inner bushing removal and installation.**
3. Coat the threads of bolt No. J-21474-19 with high pressure lubricant J-23444-A to prevent thread damage.
4. Install remover J-21474, receiver J-21474-5, bearing, nut J-21474-18 and bolt J-21474-19, **Fig. 5.**
5. Remove bushing from control arm by tightening nut.

Installation

1. Position new bushing on control arm. **Bushing must be installed from the outside of the control arm, then drawn inward to the control arm centerline.**
2. Insert narrow end of spacer J-35739-1 between control arm flanges, then coat threads of bolt J-21474-19 with high pressure lubricant J-23444-A.
3. Install bushing installer J-28576-1, receiver J-21474-5, bearing, nut J-21474-18 and bolt J-21474-19, **Fig. 5.**
4. Draw bushing into control arm by tightening nut. **Tighten nut until bushing flange seats firmly against control arm.**
5. Refer to "Control Arm, Replace," for suspension assembly.

SPRING & INSULATORS
REPLACE

Removal of rear spring requires disassembly of either left or right side of the sus-

1. SPRING
2. SPRING RETAINER
3. SUSPENSION CROSSMEMBER ASSEMBLY
4. RETAINER BOLTS (28 N·m/21 FT. LBS.)
5. LOWER OUTBOARD INSULATOR
6. JACKSTAND

Fig. 6 Spring replacement

pension while leaving opposite side intact. Spring may be removed from either side of vehicle.

1. Remove lower control arm as outlined.
2. Place a support under outboard end of spring as shown in **Fig. 6**, then lower vehicle so weight of vehicle compresses spring. **Ensure jack stand can support weight of vehicle and is properly positioned under spring.**

3. Remove three spring retainer bolts, retainer and lower insulator, **Fig. 7**, from end of spring nearest support stand.
4. Slowly raise vehicle, allowing spring to deflect downward until spring no longer exerts force on stand.
5. Remove retainer bolts, retainer and insulator from opposite end of spring, then withdraw spring from crossmember.
6. Remove upper spring insulators.
7. Inspect spring insulators and retainers and replace as needed.
8. Install center and upper outboard insulators in crossmember, then torque bolts to specifications. **Ensure arrows on upper outboard insulators point toward centerline of vehicle.**
9. Position spring in suspension support by inserting through disassembled side of suspension. Ensure outboard and center insulator bands are centered on spring insulators.
10. Install lower insulator and retainer on side opposite disassembled portion of suspension, torque retaining bolts to specifications, then place a stand under free end of spring, **Fig. 6.**
11. Lower vehicle, allowing weight to load spring and deflect free end of spring into position in suspension support.
12. Install lower insulator and spring retainer on disassembled side of suspension support, then torque bolts to specifications.

1. CENTER INSULATOR
2. CENTER INSULATOR NUTS (28 N·m/21 FT. LBS.)
3. OUTBOARD INSULATOR NUTS (28 N·m/21 FT. LBS.)
4. SUSPENSION CROSSMEMBER ASSEMBLY
5. UPPER OUTBOARD INSULATOR
6. OUTBOARD INSULATOR LOCATING BAND
7. SPRING
8. SPRING RETAINER
9. RETAINER BOLTS (28 N·m/21 FT. LBS.)
10. LOWER OUTBOARD INSULATOR
11. CENTER INSULATOR LOCATING BAND

Fig. 7 Exploded view of spring

13. Raise vehicle and remove stand.
14. Reverse remaining procedure to complete installation.

TIGHTENING SPECIFICATIONS

Year	Component	Torque/ Ft. Lbs.
1991-94	**Caliper Mounting Bracket Bolts**	83
	Center Insulator Nuts	21
	Hub Mounting Bolts	52
	Inner Control Arm To Suspension Support	66
	Knuckle Pinch Bolt	40
	Knuckle Pivot Bolt	59
	Spring Retainer Bolts	21
	Stabilizer Shaft Bracket Bolt	43
	Stabilizer Shaft Mounting Bolt	43
	Stabilizer Shaft Mounting Nut	43
	Strut Bracket Bolt	43
	Suspension Support Forward Arm Bolts	66
	Suspension Support Upper Mounting Bolts	66
	Upper Outboard Insulator Nuts	21
	Upper Strut Nut	65
	Wheel Lug Nuts	100

Front Suspension & Steering

INDEX

FRONT OF CAR

1. INSULATOR – INSTALL WITH SLIT TO REAR OF CAR
2. STABILIZER SHAFT
3. STABILIZER LINK
4. BRACKET
5. BOLT – 47 N·m (35 lbs. ft.)
6. WASHER
7. NUT – 65 N·m (48 lbs. ft.)
8. SPRING & STRUT ASSEMBLY
9. FRAME

Fig. 1   Stabilizer shaft replacement

1. CONTROL ARM
2. BOLT – 140 N·m (100 FT. LBS.) TIGHTEN WITH CAR AT PROPER TRIM HEIGHT
3. NUT – 123 N·m (91 FT. LBS.) TIGHTEN WITH CAR AT PROPER TRIM HEIGHT
4. INSULATOR
5. RETAINER
6. NUT – 70 N·m (52 FT. LBS.)
7. PIN
8. NUT – TIGHTEN NUT TO 10 N·m (88 IN. LBS.) CONTINUE TIGHTENING BY ROTATING NUT AN ADDITIONAL 120°, DURING WHICH A MINIMUM TORQUE OF 50 N·m (37 FT. LBS.) MUST BE OBTAINED. INSTALL COTTER PIN
9. KNUCKLE
10. BALL JOINT ATTACHMENT RIVETS
11. BUSHING

Fig. 2   Lower control arm replacement

STABILIZER SHAFT REPLACE

1. Raise vehicle and support with weight of vehicle resting on frame, not the lower control arms.
2. Remove right front wheel and tire.
3. **On models with road sensing suspension,** disconnect position sensor from lower control arm.
4. **On all models,** remove left and right insulators, retainers, spacers and bolts, **Fig. 1.**
5. Remove left and right bracket bolts, brackets and insulators.
6. Disconnect exhaust pipe from rear manifold, raise pipe to gain clearance, then withdraw stabilizer shaft.
7. Reverse procedure to install.

BALL JOINT REPLACE

1. Raise and support vehicle.
2. Remove tire and wheel assembly.
3. **On models with road sensing suspension,** disconnect position sensor from lower control arm.
4. **On all models,** remove ball joint from knuckle.
5. Drill out three rivets retaining ball joint. Start with a 1/4 inch drill bit, then use a 1/2 inch bit.
6. Remove ball joint.
7. Reverse procedure to install, noting the following:
   a. **Torque** ball joint to control arm nut to 84 inch lbs. using 90° adapter J-35551 or equivalent.
   b. Tighten nut an additional 120°, noting torque reading.
   c. Tighten nut up to an additional 60° to align holes and install cotter pin. **When tightening nut, minimum torque (as listed in "Tightening Specifications") must be obtained. If minimum torque cannot be obtained, check for stripped threads and repair as needed. If threads are satisfactory, replace ball joint and steering knuckle.**

CONTROL ARM REPLACE

Care must be taken not to overextend driveshaft Tri-Pot joints when replacing suspension components. Overextending joint could cause separation of internal joint components, resulting in failure of the joint.

1. Remove ball joint from steering knuckle as outlined under "Ball Joint, Replace."
2. Remove control arm bushing bolt and brake reaction rod nut, retainer and insulator, **Fig. 2.**
3. Remove control arm from frame.
4. Install control arm on frame.
5. Install control arm bushing bolt and nut, retainer and insulator but do not tighten bolt.
6. Install lower ball joint in steering knuckle as outlined.
7. Reverse remaining procedure to complete installation. Torque bolts to specifications as shown in **Figs. 1 and 2.**

CONTROL ARM BUSHINGS REPLACE

When replacing lower control arm bush-

1	J-35561-1
2	J-35561-2
3	J-35561-3
4	BUSHING
5	LOWER CONTROL ARM
6	PRESS

REMOVE BUSHING

INSTALL BUSHING

Fig. 3   Lower control arm bushings replacement

ings, refer to **Fig. 3.**

1. Remove lower control arm as outlined under "Control Arm, Replace."
2. Install driver, tool No. J-35561-1, receiver No. J-35561-2 and installing cup No. J-35561-3, or equivalents.
3. Press out bushing.
4. Lubricate new bushing with rubber lube.
5. Install tools, then press in new bushing.
6. Install lower control arm.

HUB & BEARING ASSEMBLY
REPLACE

1. Siphon 2/3 of the brake fluid from master cylinder, then raise vehicle and support frame with stands.
2. Remove wheel and tire assembly.
3. Insert a drift through rotor and remove hub nut and washer.
4. Remove caliper boots, lift caliper off rotor and bracket, then secure caliper aside.
5. Remove bolts securing caliper bracket, bracket and the brake rotor. **Prevailing torque bolts used to secure mounting bracket cannot be reused. If bolts become loose or are removed, bolts must be replaced.**
6. Mount tool J-28733 or equivalent on hub, **Fig. 4,** then tighten screw just enough to separate drive axle from hub.
7. Remove hub retaining bolts and the hub and bearing assembly, **Fig. 5.**
8. If seal is being replaced, drive seal toward engine, then cut seal off drive axle.
9. Lubricate seal lip and install using a driver, install O-ring and fill cavity between seal and bearing with grease.
10. Install hub and bearing assembly over drive axle and torque bolts to specifications.
11. Install rotor and caliper mounting bracket and torque new bracket bolts to specifications.

1	NUT 245 N·m (180 FT. LBS.)
2	WASHER
3	ROTOR
4	BOLT 95 N·m (70 FT. LBS.)
5	FRONT BRACE SHIELD
6	HUB AND BEARING
7	KNUCKLE
8	SEAL

Fig. 5   Hub & bearing assembly replacement

12. Install caliper ensuring insulators are properly positioned, coat mounting bolt shafts with silicone grease and torque to specifications.
13. Install hub nut and washer, insert drift through rotor and tighten nut securely.
14. Remove drift, install wheel and tire assembly and lower vehicle, then torque hub nut to specifications.

STEERING KNUCKLE
REPLACE

1. Remove hub and bearing assembly as outlined under "Hub & Bearing Assembly, Replace."
2. Remove nut securing tie rod, then separate tie rod from knuckle.
3. Cut inner tabs from boot protector tool No. J-34754 or equivalent and install protector over drive axle outer joint.
4. Remove cotter pin and nut securing lower ball joint and separate ball stud from steering knuckle.
5. Remove bolts securing strut to steer-

1	NUT 245 N·m (180 FT. LBS.)
2	WASHER
3	ROTOR
4	BOLT 95 N·m (70 FT. LBS.)
5	FRONT BRACE SHIELD
6	HUB AND BEARING
7	KNUCKLE
8	SEAL

Fig. 4   Drive axle from hub separation

ing knuckle, **Fig. 6,** and the steering knuckle.
6. Reverse procedure to install.

STRUT ASSEMBLY
REPLACE

Care must be taken not to overextend driveshaft Tri-Pot joints when replacing suspension components. Overextending joint could cause separation of internal joint components, resulting in failure of the joint.

1. Remove nuts securing top of strut assembly to body, **Fig. 6.**
2. Raise vehicle and support frame with stands, then remove wheel and tire.
3. Scribe reference marks between strut and steering knuckle as follows:
   a. Scribe strut along lower outboard strut radius (A), **Fig. 7.**
   b. Scribe strut flange on inboard side along curve of knuckle (B).
   c. Scribe mark along strut/knuckle interface (C).
4. Disconnect brake line bracket from strut.
5. Remove bolt securing strut to stabilizer link, then the stabilizer link.
6. Remove bolts securing strut to steering knuckle, support knuckle with wire and remove strut.
7. Reverse procedure to install, aligning scribe marks made during disassembly. Torque nuts and bolts to specifications, then check alignment.

STRUT SERVICE

1. Place strut assembly in strut compressor J-34013, **Fig. 8.**
2. Turn compressor forcing screw until spring compresses slightly.
3. Keep dampener shaft from turning with a T-50 Torx bit and remove nut from top of dampener shaft.
4. Using tool J-34013-38 or equivalent, guide dampener shaft out of assembly.

1	COVER
2	NUT 24 N·m (18 FT. LBS.)
3	WASHER
4	STRUT AND SPRING ASSEMBLY
5	WASHER
6	NUT 184 N·m (136 FT. LBS.)
7	KNUCKLE
8	BOLT — INSTALL IN DIRECTION SHOWN

Fig. 6   Steering knuckle & strut replacement

5. Loosen compressor screw while guiding dampener shaft out of assembly, continually loosening compressor screw till strut dampener and spring can be removed. **Be careful to avoid chipping or cracking the spring coating when handling the front suspension coil spring.**
6. Install strut dampener in strut compressor J-34013 with clamp J-34013-20 clamped on dampener shaft.
7. Install spring over strut in correct position and move assembly upright in strut compressor and install upper locking pin. **Flat on upper spring seat must face out from centerline of vehicle, Fig. 9, or when mounted in strut compressor spring seat faces same direction as steering knuckle mounting flange.**
8. Install rod J-34013-38 or equivalent into strut assembly to guide dampener shaft on reassembly of strut.
9. Start turning compressor screw clockwise on J-34013 while guiding J-34013-38 which will center dampener shaft in the assembly.
10. Continue turning compressor screw until dampener shaft threads are visible through top of strut assembly.
11. Install washer and nut, then remove J-34013-20 from dampener shaft.
12. Hold dampener shaft with socket, then torque dampener shaft nut to specifications.
13. Remove three nuts securing strut assembly to strut compressor, the two locking pins at bottom of strut compressor and the strut assembly.

POWER STEERING PUMP REPLACE

ELDORADO & SEVILLE

1. Remove serpentine drive belt.

Fig. 7   Steering knuckle & strut alignment marking

1	ROD J-34013-38 INSTALLED
2	CLAMP J-34013-20 INSTALLED
3	FLAT ON SPRING SEAT MUST FACE SAME DIRECTION AS STEERING KNUCKLE FLANGE
4	BOTH LOCKING PINS INSTALLED
5	COMPRESSOR FORCING SCREW

Fig. 9   Flat on upper spring seat alignment

2. Remove pump pulley using a puller, **Fig. 10.**
3. Disconnect pressure and return lines from pump, noting position for installation.
4. Remove two pump mounting bolts, **Fig. 11,** and the pump.
5. Reverse procedure to install.

REATTA, RIVIERA, TORONADO & TROFEO

1. Remove drive belt.
2. Disconnect pressure and return lines from pump.
3. Remove pump mounting bolts, **Fig. 12,** and the pump.
4. Reverse procedure to install.

POWER STEERING GEAR REPLACE

1. Raise vehicle and support vehicle on frame contact hoist, then remove front wheels.

1	STRUT ASSEMBLY
2	STRUT COMPRESSOR J-34013
3	INSTALL LOCKING PINS THROUGH STRUT ASSEMBLY
4	TIGHTEN NUTS TILL FLUSH WITH STRUT COMPRESSOR
5	COMPRESSOR FORCING SCREW
6	HOLDING FIXTURE J3289-20

Fig. 8   Strut assembly installation in strut compressor

INSTALL POWER STEERING PUMP PULLEY

FLAT WASHER MUST BE USED TO POSITION PULLEY FLUSH WITH END OF SHAFT.

Fig. 10   Power steering pump pulley removal. Eldorado & Seville

2. Remove pinch bolt and disconnect intermediate shaft from steering gear.
3. Disconnect tie rods from steering knuckles.
4. Remove power steering line retainer, then disconnect pressure and return lines from steering gear.
5. Remove steering gear mounting bolts, **Figs. 13 and 14,** then withdraw gear through wheel opening.
6. Reverse procedure to install. Tighten tie rod nuts to specifications. After tightening nut as specified, continue tightening nut to align cotter pin holes, then install new cotter pins.

1. POWER STEERING PUMP
2. BOLT – 27 N·m (20 LBS. FT.)
3. PULLEY
4. BELT TENSIONER
5. CLAMP
6. 27 N·m (20 LBS. FT.)

Fig. 12   Power steering pump installation. Reatta, Riviera, Toronado & Trofeo

1. STEERING GEAR
2. BOLT – 68 N·m (50 LBS. FT.) AFTER SECOND REUSE OF BOLT, LOCKTITE THREAD LOCKING KIT NO. 1052624 MUST BE USED.
3. WASHER
4. RETAINER
5. NUT – TIGHTEN NUT TO 10 N·m (7 LBS. FT.) THEN TIGHTEN NUT AN ADDITIONAL 120 DEGREES (2 FLATS) DURING WHICH A MINIMUM TORQUE OF 45 N·m (33 LBS. FT.) IS TO BE OBTAINED. IF 45 N·m (33 LBS. FT.) IS NOT OBTAINED, INSPECT FOR STRIPPED THREADS. IF THREADS ARE SATISFACTORY, REPLACE KNUCKLE.
6. PIN
7. KNUCKLE
8. FRAME
9. RTV SEALER AROUND INSERTS

Fig. 13   Power steering gear installation. Reatta, Riviera, Toronado & Trofeo

1	PUMP
2	PUMP MOUNTING BOLTS (25 N·m/18 FT. LBS.)
3	PUMP AND TENSIONER BRACKET
4	BRACE
5	BOLTS (45 N·m/33 FT. LBS.)
6	NUT (45 N·m/33 FT. LBS.)
7	NUT (25 N·m/18 FT. LBS.)

Fig. 11   Power steering pump installation. Eldorado & Seville

1	BOLT 68 N·m (50 LBS. FT.) AFTER SECOND REUSE OF BOLT, LOCTITE THREAD LOCKING KIT, #1052624 MUST BE USED.
2	STEERING GEAR
3	FRAME
4	NUT. SEE INSTALLATION PROCEDURE FOR TORQUE SPECIFICATION.
5	RETAINER
6	WASHER
7	STEERING KNUCKLE
8	RTV SEALER AROUND INSERTS

Fig. 14   Power steering gear installation. Eldorado & Seville

TIGHTENING SPECIFICATIONS

Year	Component	Torque/ Ft. Lbs
1991-94	Adjuster Plug Locknut	50
	Ball Joint To Control Arm	50
	Ball Joint To Knuckle	37
	Brake Reaction Rod To Frame	58
	Caliper Attaching Bolts	63
	Caliper Mounting Bracket	83
	Control Arm Bushing Nuts	103
	Cylinder Line Fittings	15
	Dampener Shaft	55
	Hub & Bearing To Knuckle	70
	Hub To Drive Axle	180
	Inner Tie Rod Housing To Rack	70
	Intermediate Shaft Pinch Bolts	35
	Outer Tie Rod Jam Nut	30
	Pinion Locknut	26
	Pinion Preload	1.4
	Power Steering Line Fittings	20
	Stabilizer Bracket To Frame	35
	Stabilizer Link Nut	48
	Strut Mount To Body	18
	Strut To Knuckle	136
	Strut To Strut Top Mount	①
	Tie Rod Nuts	②
	Tie Rod Pinch Bolts	41
	Wheel Lug Nuts	100

①—Tighten old design (flanged) nut to 75 ft. lbs. & new design (non-flanged) nut to 55 ft. lbs.
②—Tighten to 7.5 ft. lbs., then an additional ⅓ turn.

Wheel Alignment

INDEX

Fig. 1 Front end alignment angles

FRONT WHEEL ALIGNMENT

Steering and vibration complaints are not always the result of improper alignment. Another possibility is tire "lead" due to worn or improperly manufactured tires. "Lead" is the vehicles's deviation from a straight path on a level road without pressure on the steering wheel.

Before making any adjustment affecting wheel alignment, make the following checks to ensure correct alignment readings and alignment adjustments.

1. Check all tires for proper inflation

pressures and ensure all tires have approximately equal tread wear.
2. Check hub and bearing assemblies for excessive wear, correcting as necessary.
3. Check ball joints and tie rod ends. If they are excessively loose, correct before making adjustment.
4. Check runout of wheels and tires.
5. Check vehicle trim height, correcting as necessary before adjusting alignment.
6. Check for proper operation of the Electronic Level Control system.
7. Check strut dampers for proper operation.

8. Check control arms for loose bushings.
9. Check stabilizer bar for loose or missing parts.

Consideration must also be given to excess loads, such as tool boxes or sample cases. If these items are normally carried in the vehicle, they should remain in the vehicle during alignment adjustments. Consideration should be given to condition of equipment being used to adjust alignment. Be sure to follow equipment manufacturer's instructions. Regardless of equipment being used, vehicle must be on level surface, both fore and aft and sideways.

MEASURING FRONT ALIGNMENT ANGLES

Install alignment equipment following equipment manufacturer's instructions. Measure alignment angles, **Fig. 1**, and record the readings. If adjustments are necessary, they must be made in order; caster first, camber second and toe third. Jounce front and rear bumpers three times to normalize suspension prior to measuring angles.

CASTER ADJUSTMENT

1. With car supported by its wheels, remove the three top strut mounting nuts and washers, **Fig. 2**.
2. Lift front of car by the body to separate top strut mount from inner wheelhouse. **Do not raise control arms or tires.**
3. Drill two ~11/32 inch holes at the front and rear of outboard strut mounting holes. Use a rat-tail file to slot the outboard hole.
4. Paint any bare metal areas with a corrosion protective primer or paint.
5. Reposition strut mount in holes, then lower front of car.
6. Reinstall washers and nuts.
7. Set caster to specifications by moving top of strut forward or rearward as required. 1 mm of movement is equivalent to 0.1° of caster.
8. **Torque** top strut mounting bolts to 18 ft. lbs.

CAMBER ADJUSTMENT

1. Loosen both strut to knuckle bolts just enough to allow movement.
2. Adjust camber by turning camber adjustment bolt, **Fig. 3**.
3. **Torque** strut to knuckle nuts to 136 ft. lbs.
4. **Torque** camber adjustment bolt to 7 ft. lbs.

1. NUT 24 N·m (18 LBS. FT.)
2. WASHER
3. STRUT ASSY.
4. COVER
5. DRILL 8.731mm (11/32") HOLES
6. FILE HERE THEN PAINT
   WITH PRIMER

Fig. 2   Front wheel caster adjustment

1. NUT 185 N·m (145 LBS. FT.)
2. BOLT
3. WASHER
4. CAMBER ADJUSTMENT BOLT

Fig. 3   Front wheel camber adjustment

TOE ADJUSTMENT

1. Loosen locknut on inner tie rods, **Fig. 4.**
2. Adjust toe by turning inner tie rods.
3. Adjust boots so that they are not twisted.
4. **Torque** locknuts to 45 ft. lbs.

REAR WHEEL ALIGNMENT

Rear wheel toe is the only adjustable angle. If camber is not within specifications, inspect for worn or damaged rear suspension components.

Before checking rear trim height or measuring rear alignment angles, the following

1. INNER TIE ROD
2. LOCK NUT — 60 N·m (45 LBS. FT.)
3. BOOT — READJUST AFTER SETTING TOE

Fig. 4   Front wheel toe adjustment

procedure should be performed to ensure the rear air-adjustable struts are filled with residual pressure only.

1. Place a weight of at least 300 lbs. in vehicle trunk.
2. Turn ignition On, then wait for the Car Is Leveling light to illuminate.
3. Turn ignition Off and remove weight from trunk.
4. Wait at least 30 seconds for ELC system to exhaust.
5. Roll car forward or backward several complete tire rotations to eliminate the effects of tire camber change.
6. Jounce front and rear bumpers 3 times to normalize suspension prior to measuring angles.

TOE ADJUSTMENT

1. Loosen front and rear inside control arm mounting bolts, **Fig. 5.**

1 BOLT
2 CONTROL ARM
3 SCREW DRIVER OR PRY BAR
4 SLOTTED HOLE

Fig. 5   Rear toe adjustment

2. Insert a screwdriver or pry bar between the inside rear control arm mounting bolt and rear support assembly, then move control arm to set toe to specifications.
3. **Torque** inside front and rear control arm mounting bolt to 66 ft. lbs.

Fig. 6   Ride height measurement locations. 1991–93 Reatta & Riviera

Fig. 7   Ride height measurement locations. 1991–92 Eldorado, Seville; 1991–92 Toronado & Trofeo

Fig. 8   Ride height measurement locations. 1993-94 Eldorado & Seville

RIDE HEIGHT

Refer to **Figs. 6 through 8**, for ride height measurements and **Fig. 9**, for specifications. When checking ride height measurements, fuel tank should be full, tires at should be correct pressure, front seat should be rearward position, truck should be empty except for spare tire and jack and vehicle should be on level ground. If fuel tank is not full, add weight to trunk to compensate for amount fuel vehicle is below the full level.

Prior to checking ride height, lift front bumper upward approximately 1.5 inches and gently release (3 times), then check front ride height. Push front bumper downward approximately 1.5 inches and gently release (3 times), then recheck front ride height. Average of both readings to determine vehicle ride height. Check rear ride height in same manner, lifting and pushing rear bumper.

Model	Year	Engine Liter/CID(VIN)	Ride Height Measurements In Inches					
			Dimension Z	Dimension D	Dimension J	Dimension K	Dimension P	Dimension R
Eldorado	1991	All	2.05	1.14	9.02	9.09	28.27	27.95
	1992	All	2.05	1.18	8.78	8.70	28.23	28.19
	1993	4.9L/V8-300(B)	2.01	1.46	8.78	8.70	28.23	28.19
		4.6L/V8-279(Y)	2.09	1.46	8.78	8.70	28.23	28.19
		4.6L/V8-279(9)	2.09	1.14	8.78	8.70	28.23	28.19
	1994	4.6L/V8-279(Y)	2.09	1.46	8.78	8.70	28.23	28.19
		4.6L/V8-279(9)	2.09	1.14	8.78	8.70	28.23	28.19
Reatta	1991	All	2.09	1.38	8.50	8.62	28.86	29.33
Riviera	1991-93	All	1.81	1.10	8.62	8.74	27.40	27.76
Seville	1991	All	2.01	1.18	9.02	9.09	28.23	28.50
	1992	All	2.21	1.34	9.65	9.65	28.68	28.68
	1993	4.9L/V8-300(B)	2.05	1.46	9.49	9.49	28.43	28.43
	1993-94	4.6L/V8-279(9)	2.09	1.46	9.49	9.49	28.43	28.43
Seville STS	1992	All	2.05	1.22	9.49	9.49	28.43	28.43
Toronado	1991	All	1.81	.95	—	—	—	—
	1992	All	2.24	1.34	9.09	9.09	27.80	28.27
Trofeo	1991	All	1.81	.95	—	—	—	—
	1992	All	2.24	1.34	9.09	9.09	27.80	28.27

Fig. 9 Vehicle ride height specifications

CHEVROLET CAVALIER & PONTIAC SUNBIRD (J Cars)

INDEX OF SERVICE OPERATIONS

NOTE: Refer To The Rear Of This Manual For Manufacturer's Special Service Tool Suppliers.

Continued

Specifications
GENERAL ENGINE SPECIFICATIONS

Year	Engine Liter/CID ①	Engine VIN Code ②	Fuel System	Bore & Stroke	Compression Ratio	Net H.P. @ RPM ③	Maximum Torque Ft. Lbs @ RPM	Normal Oil Pressure psi
1991	2.0L/4-121 OHC ④	K	EFI	3.38 x 3.38	8.8	96 @ 4800	118 @ 3600	65
	2.2L/4-134 OHV ⑤	G	EFI	3.50 x 3.46	9.0	95 @ 5200	120 @ 3200	63-77
	3.1L/V6-192	T	EFI	3.50 x 3.31	8.8	140 @ 4500	180 @ 3600	50-65
1992-94	2.0L/4-121 OHC ④	H	EFI	3.38 x 3.38	9.2	110 @ 5200	123 @ 3600	65
	2.2L/4-134 OHV ⑤	4	EFI	3.50 x 3.46	9.0	120 @ 5200	130 @ 4000	56
	3.1L/V6-192	T	EFI	3.50 x 3.31	8.9	140 @ 4200	185 @ 3200	50-65

① —CID-cubic inch displacement.
② —The eighth digit denotes engine code.
③ —Ratings are net as installed in vehicle.
④ —Overhead cam engine.
⑤ —Overhead valve engine.

TUNE UP SPECIFICATIONS

Year & Engine/ VIN Code ①	Spark Plug Gap	Firing Order Fig. ②	Ignition Timing BTDC Man. Trans.	Ignition Timing BTDC Auto. Trans.	Mark Fig.	Curb Idle Speed ③ Man. Trans.	Curb Idle Speed ③ Auto Trans.	Fast Idle Speed Man. Trans.	Fast Idle Speed Auto. Trans.	Fuel Pump Pressure
1991										
2.0L/4-121(K) OHC	.045	A	8	8	B	④	④	④	④	9-13 ⑤
2.2L/4-134(G)	.035	⑧	⑨	⑨	⑩	④	④	④	④	9-13 ⑦
3.1L/V6-192(T)	.045	⑪	⑨	⑨	⑩	④	④	④	④	40.5-47 ⑥
1992-94										
2.0L/4-121(H) OHC	.045	⑫	⑨	⑨	⑩	④	④	④	④	41-47 ⑬
2.2L/4-134(4)	.045	⑧	⑨	⑨	⑩	④	④	④	④	41-47 ⑬
3.1L/V6-192(T)	.045	⑪	⑨	⑨	⑩	④	④	④	④	41-47 ⑥

① —The eighth digit of the Vehicle Identification Number (VIN) denotes engine code.
② —Before removing wires from distributor cap, determine location of No. 1 wire in cap, as distributor position may have been altered from that shown at the end of this chart.
③ —Not adjustable.
④ —Idle speeds are controlled by the idle air control (IAC) valve.
⑤ —To relieve fuel pressure, remove fuel pump fuse from fuse panel, then start engine & allow to run until fuel supply is deleted. When engine has stopped, engage starter for 3 seconds to dissipate remaining fuel system pressure. Remove air cleaner & plug Thermac port on throttle body unit. Install a suitable fuel pressure gauge on throttle body side of fuel filter at rear of vehicle near fuel tank. Start engine & note fuel pressure reading. Before removing fuel gauge, relieve fuel system pressure.

⑥ —With shop towel wrapped around fuel pressure valve to prevent fuel spillage, connect a suitable fuel pressure gauge to fuel pressure valve. Check fuel pressure with ignition switch in the On position, engine not running.
⑦ —Wrap shop towel around fuel hose to steel line connection in engine compartment to prevent fuel spillage. Disconnect fuel hose from steel line and connect a suitable fuel gauge between hose & line. Ensure gauge connections are tight, then start engine & check fuel pressure.
⑧ —Cylinder numbering from front of engine to rear of engine, 1, 2, 3, 4. Firing order 1-3-4-2. Refer to Fig. C for spark plug wire connections at coil unit.
⑨ —No adjustment.
⑩ —Equipped with crankshaft sensor.
⑪ —Cylinder numbering left to right as viewed from front of vehicle, front bank, 2, 4, 6; rear bank, 1, 3, 5. Firing

order 1-2-3-4-5-6. Refer to Fig.D for spark plug wire connections at coil unit.
⑫ —Cylinder numbering from front of engine to rear of engine, 1, 2, 3, 4. Firing order 1-3-4-2. Refer to Fig. E for spark plug wire connection at coil unit.
⑬ —To relieve fuel pressure, loosen fuel tank filler cap. Remove fuel pup fuse from fuse panel, then start engine and allow to run until fuel supply is deleted. When engine has stopped, engage starter for 3 seconds to dissipate remaining fuel system pressure. Disconnect battery ground cable. Locate fuel feed quick connect fitting in engine compartment. Install a suitable fuel pressure gauge between fuel feed quick connect fittings. Connect battery ground cable. Start engine and note fuel pressure reading. Before removing fuel gauge, relieve fuel system pressure.

Continued

Fig. A

Fig. B

Fig. C

Fig. D

Fig. E

FRONT WHEEL ALIGNMENT

Year	Model	Caster Angle, Degrees		Camber Angle, Degrees				Total Toe, Degrees
				Limits		Desired		
		Limits	Desired	Left	Right	Left	Right	
1991-94	All	+.7 to +2.7	+1.7	−.7 to +.7	−.7 to +.7	0	0	0

REAR WHEEL ALIGNMENT

Year	Model	Camber Angle, Degrees ①	Thrust Angle, Degrees ①	Total Toe, Degrees ①
1991-94	All	−.82 to +.32	−.31 to +.31	+.25

①—Non-adjustable, for inspection purposes only.

COOLING SYSTEM & CAPACITY DATA

Year	Model or Engine/VIN	Cooling Capacity, Qts.		Radiator Cap Relief Pressure, Lbs.	Thermo. Opening Temp.	Fuel Tank Gals.	Engine Oil Refill Qts.	Transaxle Oil	
		Less A/C	With A/C					Manual Transaxle Pts.	Auto. Transaxle Qts. ①
1991	Cavalier 2.2L/4-134/G	11.7	11.7	15	195	13.6	4②	④	③
	Cavalier 3.1L/V6-192/T	14.2	14.2	15	195	13.6	4②	④	③
	Sunbird 2.0L/4-121/K	11.7	11.7	15	195	13.6	4②	④	③
	Sunbird 3.1L/V6-192/T	14.2	14.2	15	195	13.6	4②	④	③
1992-94	Cavalier 2.2L/4-134/4	9.2	9.2	15	195	15.2	4②	4	③
	Cavalier 3.1L/V6-192/T	13.1	13.1	15	195	15.2	4②	4	③

Continued

TUNE UP SPECIFICATIONS-Continued

Year	Model or Engine/VIN	Cooling Capacity, Qts. Less A/C	Cooling Capacity, Qts. With A/C	Radiator Cap Relief Pressure Lbs.	Thermo. Opening Temp.	Fuel Tank Gals.	Engine Oil Refill Qts.	Transaxle Oil Manual Transaxle Pts.	Transaxle Oil Auto. Transaxle Qts. ①
1992-94 —Cont'd	Sunbird 2.0L/4-121/H	11.7	11.7	15	195	15.2	4②	4	③
	Sunbird 3.1L/V6-192/T	14.2	14.2	15	195	15.2	4②	4	③

①—Approximate, make final check with dipstick.
②—When changing engine oil filter additional oil may be required.
③—Oil pan only, 4 qts. After overhaul, less torque converter drain, 6 qts.; with torque converter drain, 9 qts.
④—Isuzu 5 speed, 5.4 pts.; Muncie 5 speed, 4 pts.

LUBRICANT DATA

Year	Model	Lubricant Type Transaxle Manual	Lubricant Type Transaxle Automatic	Power Steering	Brake System
1991	All	①	DEXRON II	②	DOT-3
1992-93	All	①	DEXRON IIE	②	DOT-3
1994	All	Syncromesh Transmission Fluid (STF)	DEXRON IIE	②	DOT-3

①—Manual transmission fluid GM part No. 12345349 or equivalent.
②—Power steering fluid GM part No. 9985010 or equivalent.

Electrical
INDEX

FUSE PANEL & FLASHER LOCATION

The fuse panel is located on the left side of the instrument panel. To gain access to the panel, pivot access door downward.

The hazard flasher is located under dash panel, left side of steering column.

The turn signal flasher is located under dash panel, right side of steering column.

STARTER REPLACE

2.2L/4-134 ENGINE

1. Disconnect battery ground cable.
2. Raise and support vehicle, then remove remove bolts attaching starter motor and bracket to engine.
3. Lower starter motor and disconnect leads at solenoid.
4. Remove starter motor from vehicle. Note position of shims for installation, if used.
5. Reverse procedure to install.

2.0L/4-121 ENGINE NON-TURBOCHARGED
Manual Transaxle

1. Disconnect battery ground cable.
2. Remove wiring strap from upper starter mounting bolt.
3. Disconnect shifter cables at selector lever.
4. Remove upper and lower transaxle control lever cable bracket and cables.
5. Remove drive axle support brace.
6. Disconnect wiring from starter motor, then remove starter motor mounting bolts and starter motor.
7. Reverse procedure to install.

Automatic Transaxle

1. Disconnect battery ground cable.
2. Remove blower motor as described under "Blower Motor, Replace."
3. Disconnect wiring from starter motor.
4. Remove starter motor bracket, then disconnect wiring loom from upper starter mounting bolt and remove bolt.
5. Remove starter motor lower mounting bolt, then remove starter motor through blower motor opening.
6. Reverse procedure to install.

Fig. 1 Lock cylinder removal

2.0L/4-121 TURBOCHARGED ENGINE

1. Disconnect battery ground cable.
2. Remove intake manifold support brace.
3. Disconnect wire harness clamp at motor mount, then the upper starter to engine block attaching bolt.
4. Raise and support vehicle.
5. **On models equipped with automatic transaxle,** remove transaxle rear strut.
6. **On all models,** remove fuel line to support bracket attaching bolt, then loosen fuel lines 1/2 turn to gain access to starter. **Place shop towel over fuel line and fitting when disconnecting.**
7. Remove rear starter brace attaching bolts, then the rear starter brace.
8. Remove lower starter to engine block attaching bolt.
9. Disconnect starter motor electrical connectors, then remove starter motor.
10. Reverse procedure to install.

3.1L/V6-192 ENGINE

1. Disconnect battery ground cable, then raise and support vehicle.
2. Remove starter motor to engine attaching bolts.
3. Disconnect starter electrical connectors, then lower starter out of vehicle.
4. Note installation position of starter shim, if equipped.
5. Reverse procedure to install.

DISTRIBUTOR
REPLACE

2.0L/4-121 ENGINE

1. Disconnect battery ground cable.
2. Remove distributor cap and spark plug wires from distributor.
3. Disconnect coil and EST electrical connectors.
4. Remove distributor to cam carrier nuts, then mark distributor tang drive and cam shaft for installation.
5. Remove distributor assembly.
6. Reverse procedure to install. **Torque** distributor to cam carrier nuts to 13 ft. lbs.

Fig. 2 Ignition & dimmer switch removal. Models less tilt column

Fig. 3 Ignition & dimmer switch removal. Models with tilt column

IGNITION LOCK
REPLACE

1. Remove steering wheel as outlined under "Steering Wheel, Replace" procedure.
2. Remove turn signal switch as outlined under "Turn Signal Switch, Replace" procedure.
3. Re move buzzer switch.
4. Turn lock cylinder to "Run" position, then remove the lock cylinder retaining screw and lock cylinder, **Fig. 1.**
5. To install, rotate lock cylinder to stop while holding housing. Align cylinder key with keyway in housing, then push cylinder into housing until fully seated.
6. Install lock cylinder retaining screw.
7. Install buzzer switch, turn signal switch and steering wheel.

1 BOLT
2 SWITCH ASM.
3 TRANS. SHAFT
4 SERVICE ADJUSTMENT HOLE
5 3/32 INCH DRILL BIT OR 2.34 DIA. GAGE PIN

VIEW A

Fig. 4 Back-up light/neutral start switch replacement

J-23653-4 J-23653 SNAP RING

Fig. 6 Compressing lock plate

1 INSTRUMENT PANEL ASM.
2 BOLT/SCREW – FULLY DRIVEN, SEATED AND NOT STRIPPED
3 HEADLAMP/FOGLAMP SWITCH ASM.
4 SCREW – FULLY DRIVEN, SEATED AND NOT STRIPPED
5 HEADLAMP SWITCH PANEL HOUSING

Fig. 5 Headlamp/fog lamp switch replacement. Sunbird

IGNITION & DIMMER SWITCHES
REPLACE
CAVALIER

1. Remove steering wheel as outlined under "Steering Wheel, Replace" procedure.
2. Remove turn signal switch as outlined under "Turn Signal Switch, Replace" procedure.
3. Remove windshield wiper switch as outlined under "Windshield Wiper Switch, Replace" procedure.
4. Remove ignition switch to ignition switch housing attaching screws.
5. Depress ignition switch locking tab, then disconnect switch electrical connector s.
6. Reverse procedure to install, noting the following:
   a. Ensure lock cylinder shaft aligns with slotted opening on ignition switch.
   b. **Torque** ignition switch attaching screws to 21 inch lbs.

SUNBIRD

1. Remove steering wheel as outlined under "Steering Wheel, Replace" procedure, then the turn signal switch and lock cylinder as previously described.
2. Refer to **Figs. 2 and 3** to remove ignition and dimmer switches.
3. When installing dimmer switch, depress switch slightly and install a 3/32 drill into switch. Force switch upward to remove lash and tighten retaining screw.

CLUTCH START SWITCH
REPLACE

1. Disconnect clutch switch electrical connector.
2. Remove clutch bracket and switch attaching nuts, then remove switch.
3. Reverse procedure to install. **Torque** switch attaching nuts to 53 inch lbs .

NEUTRAL START SWITCH
REPLACE

On vehicles equipped with automatic transmission, the neutral start and back-up light switches are combined into one unit and must be replaced as an assembly.

MANUAL TRANSMISSION

For neutral start switch refer to "Clutch Start Switch, Replace." Back-up light switch replacement is as follows:
1. Disconnect battery ground cable.
2. Disconnect back-up lamp electrical connector.
3. Unscrew back-up light switch assembly from transaxle assembly.
4. Reverse procedure to install, noting the following:
   a. Apply pipe sealant GM P/N 1052080 or equivalent to threaded switch.
   b. **Torque** back-up lamp switch to 24 ft. lbs.

AUTOMATIC TRANSMISSION

1. Disconnect battery ground cable and shift linkage.

2. Disconnect electrical connector from switch.
3. Remove switch mounting bolts, then switch assembly, **Fig. 4.**
4. If same switch is to be reinstalled, proceed as follows:
   a. Place shift shaft in Neutral position.
   b. Align flats of shift shaft with switch, then install switch.
   c. Loosely install mounting bolts.
   d. Insert gauge pin, **Fig. 4**, in service adjustment hole and rotate switch until pin drops in to a depth of 9 mm (9/64 inch).
   e. **On 1991 models, torque** mounting bolts to 22 ft. lbs.
   f. **On 1992-94 models, torque** mounting bolts to 18 ft. lbs.
5. If a new switch is to be installed, proceed as follows:
   a. Place shift shaft in Neutral position.
   b. Align flats of shift shaft with switch, then install switch.
   c. If bolt holes do not align with mounting boss on transaxle, verify shift shaft is in Neutral position, do not rotate switch. Switch is pinned in Neutral position. If switch has been rotated and the pin broken, use procedure outlined in step 4.
   d. **On 1991 models, torque** mounting bolts to 22 ft. lbs.
   e. **On 1992-94 models, torque** mounting bolts to 18 ft. lbs.
6. Verify engine will only start in Park or Neutral positions.

HEADLAMP SWITCH
REPLACE
CAVALIER

The headlamp switch is part of the turn

1 INSTRUMENT PANEL
2 SCREW - 2 N.m (19 LBS. IN.)
3 I.P. CLUSTER ASM.

Fig. 7 Instrument cluster. Cavalier

Fig. 8 Instrument cluster. Sunbird

1 HEADLAMP/TURN SIGNAL/CRUISE CONTROL HAZZARD SWITCH
2 WINDSHIELD WIPER/WASHER SWITCH
3 TILT LEVER (IF EQUIPPED)

Fig. 9 Wiper switch removal. Cavalier

1 INSTRUMENT PANEL ASSEMBLY
2 SCREW – FULLY DRIVEN, SEATED AND NOT STRIPPED
3 SWITCH, WINDSHIELD WIPER
4 HOUSING, WINDSHIELD WIPER SWITCH
5 REAR WINDOW DEFOGGER/CONVERTIBLE TOP SWITCH

Fig. 10 Windshield wiper switch removal. Sunbird

3. Disconnect switch electrical connector.
4. Remove switch from brake pedal support bracket.
5. Reverse procedure to install.

STOPLIGHT SWITCH
ADJUST

Insert stop lamp switch in retainer until switch body seats on retainer. Pull brake pedal upward against internal pedal stop. Switch will be moved in retainer providing proper adjustment.

Proper switch adjustment is achieved when no audible clicks are heard when the pedal is pulled upward and the brake lights do not remain on without brake application.

TURN SIGNAL SWITCH
REPLACE

SUNBIRD

1. Disconnect battery ground cable.
2. Remove steering wheel as outlined under "Steering Wheel, Replace" procedure.
3. Using a suitable screwdriver, pry cover from housing.
4. Using lock plate compr essing tool J-23653-4, compress lock plate and pry snap ring from groove on steering shaft, **Fig. 6.** Slowly release compressing tool, then remove tooland lock plate from shaft.
5. Slide canceling cam and bearing preload spring from steering shaft.
6. Remove turn signal (multi-function) lever.
7. Remove hazard warning knob retaining screw, button, spring and knob.
8. Remove actuator arm screw and actuator arm.
9. Remove switch retaining screws and pull switch upward from column, guiding wire harness through column.
10. Reverse procedure to install.

CAVALIER

1. Disconnect battery ground cable.
2. Remove steering wheel as outlined under "Steering Wheel, Replace."
3. Remove lower steering column cover

signal lever assembly and is not serviceable. The headlamp switch, turn signal lever and cruise control switch must be replaced as an assembly.

SUNBIRD

1. Disconnect battery ground cable.
2. Remove left hand sound insulator.
3. Remove two screws attaching left hand trim panel, then remove trim panel by gently prying from instrument panel.
4. Remove screw attaching headlamp switch to housing, then disconnect electrical connector and remove switch, **Fig. 5.**
5. Reverse procedure to install.

STOPLIGHT SWITCH
REPLACE

1. Disconnect battery ground cable.
2. Remove drivers' side hash panel.

upper and lower attaching bolts, then remove lower steering column cover.
4. Separate rose bud fastener, integral to wiring harness, from jacket assembly.
5. Remove turn signal switch attaching screws, the depress locking tab and remove turn signal switch electrical connectors.
6. Reverse procedure to install. **Torque** turn signal switch attaching screws to 48 inch lbs.

STEERING WHEEL
REPLACE

1. Disconnect battery ground cable.
2. Remove steering wheel center pad attaching screws.
3. Disconnect horn electrical connector, then remove steering wheel center pad.
4. Remove steering wheel retaining nut and retainer.
5. Remove steering dampener, if equipped.
6. Scribe alignment marks on steering wheel and shaft to aid installation.
7. Using tool J-1859-03 or BT-61-9 or equivalent, remove steering wheel

1	HEATER & EVAPORATOR
2	DRAIN TUBE
3	BLOWER ASSEMBLY

NOTICE: WHEN REMOVING THE HEATER & EVAPORATOR ASSEMBLY, PULL ASSEMBLY STRAIGHT TOWARD INTERIOR OF CAR UNTIL PLASTIC DRAIN TUBE CLEARS COWL. IF ASSEMBLY IS TILTED IN ANY DIRECTION BEFORE THE TUBE CLEARS THE COWL, THE TUBE MAY BREAK.

Fig. 11 Heater core & blower motor

from shaft.
8. Reverse procedure to install. **Torque** steering wheel attaching nut to 30 ft. lbs.

INSTRUMENT CLUSTER
REPLACE

CAVALIER

1. Disconnect battery ground cable.
2. Remove steering column opening filler attaching screws, then remove steering opening filler.
3. Pull down slightly on steering column cover to remove bottom cluster extension attaching screws, then remove cluster extension.
4. Disconnect instrument panel dimmer and interior lamp control switches electrical connectors.
5. Remove instrument cluster top attaching screws, **Fig. 7.**
6. Pull instrument cluster rearward to remove.
7. Reverse procedure to install. **Torque** instrument cluster attaching bolts to 19 inch lbs.

SUNBIRD

1. Disconnect battery ground cable.
2. Remove four screws attaching instrument cluster trim plate to instrument panel, then pull trim plate outward to remove.
3. Remove four screws attaching instrument cluster to instrument panel, **Fig. 8.**
4. Remove steering column cover, then remove instrument cluster from instrument panel.
5. Reverse procedure to install. **Torque** instrument cluster attaching bolts to 12 inch lbs.

WIPER MOTOR TRANSMISSION
REPLACE

1. Remove wiper arms from transmission spindle shafts.
2. Remove shroud top vent grille panel and screen.
3. Loosen, but do not remove, transmission drive link to motor crank arm attaching nuts then pull drive link from motor crank arm.
4. Remove transmission to cowl panel attaching screws and the transmission assembly.
5. Reverse procedure to install. **Torque** wiper transmission attaching screws and nuts to 64 inch lbs. on 1991 models or 71 inch lbs. for 1992-94 models.

WIPER MOTOR
REPLACE

1. Disconnect battery ground cable.
2. Remove wiper arms from transmission spindle shafts.
3. Remove shroud top vent grille panel and screen.
4. Loosen, but do not remove, transmission drive link to motor crank arm attaching nuts, then pull drive link out of motor crank arm.
5. Disconnect wiper motor electrical connections and remove wipermotor attaching bolts.
6. Rotate wiper motor upward and outward, and remove from vehicle.
7. Reverse procedure to install. **Torque** wiper motor attaching bolts to 48 inch lbs. on 1991 models or 80 inch lbs. for 1992-94 models.

WIPER SWITCH
REPLACE
CAVALIER

1. Disconnect battery ground cable.
2. Remove horn pad and steering wheel as described under "Steering Wheel, Replace."
3. Remove tilt lever from column, if equipped, **Fig. 9.**
4. Remove upper and lower steering column covers.
5. Remove dampener assembly, then the headlight switch assembly.
6. Remove windshield wiper switch assembly.
7. Reverse procedure to install.

SUNBIRD

1. Disconnect battery ground cable.
2. Remove right trim plate from instrument panel.
3. Remove attaching screw from wiper switch housing, **Fig. 10.**
4. Disconnect wiring harness connector and remove wiper switch.
5. Reverse procedure to install.

BLOWER MOTOR
REPLACE

1. Disconnect battery ground cable.
2. Disconnect blower motor electrical connections.
3. **On 3.1L/V6-192 engines,** remove tower to tower brace assembly.
4. **On all models,** remove blower motor retaining screws and blower motor.
5. Reverse procedure to install.

HEATER CORE
REPLACE

1. Disconnect battery ground cable and drain cooling system.
2. Raise and support vehicle.
3. Remove rear lateral transaxle strut and mount, if equipped.
4. Disconnect heater case drain tube, then disconnect heater core heater hoses.
5. Lower vehicle and remove right and left hush panels, steering column trim cover and glove compartment.
6. Remove heater duct retaining screw and heater duct.
7. Remove heater core cover attaching screws, then gently pull cover rearward and out of vehicle, **Fig. 11.** When removing heater core assembly, pull assembly straight toward interior of vehicle until plastic drain tube clears cowl. If assembly is tilted in any direction before tube clears cowl, the drain tube may break.
8. Remove heater core retaining clamps and heater core from case.
9. Reverse procedure to install.

EVAPORATOR CORE
REPLACE

1. Disconnect battery ground cable.
2. Discharge air conditioning system, then drain cooling system.
3. Raise and support vehicle.
4. Remove rear lateral transaxle strut and mount, if equipped.
5. Disconnect heater core heater hoses.
6. Disconnect evaporator lines at evaporator core.
7. Disconnect heater and evaporator assembly drain tube.
8. Lower vehicle and remove right and left hush panels, steering column trim cover and glove compartment.
9. Remove heater duct retaining screw and heater duct.
10. Remove heater core cover attaching screws, then gently pull cover rearward and out of vehicle, **Fig. 11.** When removing heater core assembly, pull assembly straight toward interior of vehicle until plastic drain tube clears cowl. If assembly is tilted in any direction before tube clears cowl, the drain tube may break.
11. Remove heater core retaining clamps and heater core from case.
12. Remove defroster vacuum actuator to module case attaching screw.
13. Remove evaporator cover and core.
14. Reverse procedure to install.

2.0L/4-121 Engine

INDEX

PRECAUTIONS

FUEL SYSTEM PRESSURE RELIEF

Non-Turbocharged Engines

1. Loosen fuel filler cap, then remove the fuel pump fuse.
2. Start engine and run until remaining fuel is consumed.
3. Engage starter for approximately three seconds, to ensure relief of any reaming pressure.
4. Disconnect battery ground cable to avoid possible fuel discharge if any attempt is made to start the engine.

Turbocharged Engines

1. Disconnect battery ground cable.
2. Loosen fuel filler cap, then connect gauge tool No. J 34730-1 or equivalent to fuel pressure connection. **Wrap a towel around gauge fitting to avoid any fuelspillage.**
3. Install bleed hose into a container and open valve to bleed system pressure.
4. Drain any fuel remaining in gauge.

ENGINE MOUNTS
REPLACE

FRONT

1. Disconnect battery ground cable.
2. Support engine using tool No. J28467-A or equivalent, then remove two mount to bracket attaching bolts, Fig. 1.

1.	BOLTS - 64 N·m (47 Lbs. Ft.)	
2.	SIDE FRAME	
3.	BRACKET	
4.	MOUNT ASSEMBLY	
5.	NUT	
6.	BOLTS - 68 N·m (50 Lbs. Ft.)	
7.	BOLTS - 73 N·m (54 Lbs. Ft.)	
8.	BOLT - 83 N·m (61 Lbs. Ft.)	

Fig. 1 Front engine mounts

3. Remove two top mount attaching bolts, then raise and support vehicle.
4. Remove lower mount attaching bolt, then the engine mount.
5. Reverse procedure to install. Torque front engine mount attaching bolts to specifications.

REAR

1. Disconnect battery ground cable.
2. Support engine using tool No. J28467-A or equivalent, then remove two mount to bracket attaching bolts, Fig. 2.

3. Raise and support vehicle.
4. Remove two lower mount attaching nuts and reinforcement, then the engine mount.
5. Reverse procedure to install. Torque rear engine mount attaching bolts to specifications.

ENGINE
REPLACE

1. Relieve fuel system pressure as outlined under "Fuel System Pressure Relief."

1. ENGINE MOUNT
2. RIGHT ENGINE COMPARTMENT RAIL
3. ENGINE COMPARTMENT COWL. ASSEMBLY
4. BRACKET
5. BOLT - 61 N.M (45 LBS. FT.)

6. NUT - 24 N.M (18 LBS. FT.)
7. REINFORCEMENT BRACKET
8. ENGINE MOUNT BRACKET
9. BOLTS - 54 N.M (40 LBS. FT.)
10. BOLT - 54 N.M (40 LBS. FT.)

Fig. 2   Rear engine mounts

2. Disconnect battery cables and engine ground wire, then drain cooling system.
3. Remove battery and battery tray.
4. Remove air cleaner.
5. Disconnect engine electrical harness connectors at bulkhead, brake cylinder, wiper motor, cooling fan, relays and grounds.
6. Disconnect throttle cable from bracket and throttle body assembly.
7. Disconnect vacuum hoses from throttle body assembly, then disconnect power steering high pressure hose at cut-off switch.
8. Disconnect vacuum hoses at map sensor and canister, then disconnect air conditioning relay cluster switches.
9. Disconnect power steering return hose at power steering pump.
10. Disconnect ECM electrical connectors, then pull harness through bulkhead and position harness over engine.
11. Disconnect upper and lower radiator hoses from engine, then disconnect wire connector at temperature switch on thermostat housing.
12. Disconnect transmission shift cable at transmission, then raise and support vehicle.
13. Disconnect vehicle speed sensor electrical connector.
14. Disconnect exhaust pipe at exhaust manifold and remove exhaust pipe from converter.
15. Remove heater hoses from heater core, fuel lines at flex hoses and transmission cooler lines at flex hoses. **Place shop towel over fuel line and fitting when disconnecting.**
16. Remove front wheels, right hand spoiler section and splash shield.
17. Remove and support right and left brake calipers.
18. Discharge A/C system, disconnect electrical connectors at A/C com-

pressor, then remove A/C compressor and mounting brackets. Using a piece of wire, support compressor in wheel opening.
19. Remove center front suspension support attachment bolts, then remove one bolt at each end, then loosen remaining bolt.
20. **On automatic transaxle vehicles,** remove rear transaxle lateral strut.
21. **On all models,** remove front transaxle strut.
22. Lower vehicle and support front end by placing jack stands under core support.
23. Using a suitable hoist, position front post of hoist to rear ofcowl.
24. Using a suitable piece of wood (4 inch x 4 inch x 6 ft.), position onto front post of hoist.
25. Raise vehicle slightly and remove jack stands from front end.
26. Position a suitable dolly under engine and transaxle assembly.
27. Position three pieces of wood (4 inch x 4 inch x 12 inch) under engine and transaxle assembly only.
28. Slightly lower vehicle onto dolly and remove right and left front suspension support remaining bolts.
29. Remove transaxle mount to bracket attaching bolt.
30. Remove front and rear engine mount to bracket attaching bolts.
31. Remove right and left steering knuckle to strut attaching bolts.
32. Remove engine and transaxle as an assembly.
33. Position engine and transaxle assembly into vehicle.
34. Loosely install transaxle and left front mounts to side rail bolts.
35. Install right rear mount to body bolts.
36. Position a suitable jack under control arms and raise struts into position, then install retaining nuts.
37. Reverse procedure to complete installation. Tighten all nuts, bolts and screws to specifications.

INTAKE MANIFOLD
REPLACE

NON-TURBOCHARGED ENGINES
1991 Models

1. Relieve fuel system pressure as outlined under "Fuel System Pressure Relief" procedure.
2. Disconnect battery ground cable.
3. Remove air cleaner, then drain cooling system.
4. Remove alternator and bracket at camshaft carrier.
5. Disconnect power steering pump and position aside.
6. Remove power steering bracket at intake manifold.
7. Remove ignition coil and bracket assembly, then the throttle cable from intake manifold bracket.
8. Remove throttle cable and TV cable from TBI unit.
9. Remove TBI unit electrical connector.
10. Remove vacuum brake hose, coolant hoses and fuel lines. **Place shop towel over fuel line and fitting when disconnecting.**
11. Remove ECM harness, then the intake manifold attaching nuts and manifold.
12. Reverse procedure to install. Refer to **Fig. 3,** for manifold nut tightening sequence.

1992-94

1. Disconnect battery ground cable.
2. Remove air cleaner duct from manifold.
3. Remove direct ignition unit, then drain engine coolant.
4. Disconnect coolant and vacuum hoses from manifold.
5. Remove throttle body, gasket, fuel injectors and fuel rail.
6. Remove EGR and PCV hose from manifold.
7. Remove generator and generator bracket at camshaft carrier.
8. Remove power steering bracket from intake manifold, then set power steering and bracket assembly aside.
9. Remove ECM harness to gain access to intake manifold lower retaining nuts.
10. Remove intake manifold attaching nuts, then the manifold.
11. Reverse procedure to install, using sequence shown in **Fig. 3** tighten manifold attaching nuts to specification.

TURBOCHARGED ENGINES

1. Relieve fuel system pressure as outlined under "Fuel System Pressure Relief" procedure.
2. Remove induction tube and hoses.
3. Disconnect ignition coil, throttle body, MAP sensor and wastegate electrical connectors.
4. Remove PCV hose and throttle body vacuum hose.
5. Remove throttle cable and cruise

INTAKE MANIFOLD NUT TIGHTENING SEQUENCE

1	INTAKE MANIFOLD GASKET	4	WASHER
2	INTAKE MANIFOLD STUDS	5	NUT
3	INTAKE MANIFOLD		

Fig. 3 Intake manifold replacement & tightening sequence

control cable, if equipped.
6. Remove fuel line from throttle cable support bracket. **Place shop towel over fuel line and fitting when disconnecting.**
7. Remove ignition coil bracket attaching screws, then remove ignition coil bracket.
8. Remove vacuum hoses at rear of manifold.
9. Remove transmission filler tube bracket.
10. Remove manifold support bracket attaching bolts, then remove bracket.
11. Remove heater tube support bracket on lower side of manifold.
12. Disconnect fuel injector electrical connectors.
13. Remove coolant recovery tank and accessory drive belt.
14. Remove power steering and alternator front adjusting bracket.
15. Remove power steering pump bracket to engine head.
16. Remove fuel line to fuel rail inlet, then remove fuel return line from regulator outlet. **Place shop towel over fuel line and fitting when disconnecting.**
17. Remove intake manifold attaching nuts and washers, then remove manifold.
18. Reverse procedure to install. Torque intake manifold attaching bolts to specifications.

EXHAUST MANIFOLD REPLACE

NON-TURBOCHARGED ENGINES

1. Disconnect battery ground cable.
2. Remove air cleaner, then remove spark plug wires and retainers.
3. Remove oil dipstick tube and breather.
4. Disconnect oxygen sensor electrical connectors.

5. Remove exhaust pipe, then remove exhaust manifold attaching nuts.
6. Remove exhaust manifold and gasket.
7. Reverse procedure to install. Refer to **Fig. 4,** for manifold bolt tightening sequence. Tighten attaching nuts to specifications.

TURBOCHARGED ENGINES

1. Disconnect battery ground cable.
2. Remove spark plug wires.
3. Remove turbocharger as follows:
   a. Raise and support vehicle.
   b. Remove lower fan attaching screw.
   c. Remove exhaust pipe to manifold attaching nuts, then remove exhaust pipe.
   d. Remove rear A/C support bracket attaching bolt, then loosen remaining A/C support bracket bolts.
   e. Remove turbo support bracket to engine attaching bolt.
   f. Remove oil drain hose at turbo, then remove water return pipe.
   g. Lower vehicle, then disconnect coolant recovery pipe and position to one side.
   h. Remove oxygen sensor.
   i. Remove oil and water feed pipes.
   j. Remove air intake duct and vacuum hose at actuator.
   k. Remove exhaust manifold attaching nuts, then remove exhaust manifold and turbocharger assembly.
4. Remove turbocharger to exhaust manifold attaching bolts, then remove exhaust manifold and gasket.
5. Reverse procedure to install. Refer to **Fig. 5,** for exhaust manifold attaching bolt sequence. Torque attaching nuts and bolts to specifications.

CYLINDER HEAD REPLACE

Cylinder head bolts should only be loosened when engine is cold. Do not reuse cylinder head bolts.
1. Relieve fuel system pressure as outlined under "Fuel System Pressure Relief."
2. Disconnect battery ground cable and drain coolant.
3. Remove air filter housing assembly.
4. **On turbocharged models,** remove turbo induction tube.
5. **On all models,** remove coolant reservoir tank.
6. Remove fuel vapor pipe assembly. **Place shop towel over fuel line and fitting when disconnecting.**
7. Remove serpentine belt and front timing cover upper attaching bolts.
8. Loosen serpentine belt tensioner and position aside.
9. Raise and support vehicle, then remove righthand inner splash shield and lower righthand splash shield.
10. Remove air conditioning belt.
11. Remove crankshaft pulley as outlined under "Crankshaft Pulley, Replace."
12. Remove flywheel inspection cover.

1	NUT
2	EXHAUST MANIFOLD GASKET
3	EXHAUST MANIFOLD

TORQUE #2 AND #3 MANIFOLD RUNNERS PRIOR TO #1 AND #4

Fig. 4 Exhaust manifold replacement. Non-turbocharged models

13. Remove front timing belt cover lower attaching bolts, then remove cover, then align timing marks.
14. Loosen water pump attaching bolts and release timing belt tension using tool No. J-33039-A or equivalent, then remove timing belt.
15. **On turbocharged models,** remove exhaust pipe from turbo assembly, then disconnect oil and coolant lines to turbo assembly, then remove lower turbo assembly brace.
16. **On non-turbocharged models,** remove exhaust pipe to manifold.
17. **On all models,** lower vehicle and remove fuel vapor pipe. **Place shop towel over fuel line and fitting when disconnecting.**
18. Remove rear timing cover attaching bolts, then remove rear timing cover.
19. Remove PCV attaching hose.
20. Disconnect intake manifold and cylinder head electrical connectors.
21. Remove exhaust manifold attaching bolts.
22. **On turbocharged models,** remove exhaust manifold and turbo assembly.
23. **On all models,** remove power steering pump pressure and return lines.
24. Remove alternator and alternator bracket with power steering pump.
25. Disconnect front and rear engine lift brackets, then remove coil assembly.
26. **On turbocharged models,** remove turbo boost solenoid.
27. **On all models,** remove breather tube bracket and breather tube.
28. Remove accelerator linkage and bracket, then remove attaching fuel lines. **Place shop towel over fuel line and fitting when disconnecting.**
29. Remove cylinder head and intake manifold electrical connectors and attaching hoses and coolant lines.
30. Remove cylinder head and camshaft carrier attaching bolts in sequence shown in **Fig. 6.**
31. Remove camshaft carrier, them remove rocker arms, lash compensators and thrust pieces.

1 – GASKET
2 – EXPANSION JOINTS FACE OUTWARD
3 – MANIFOLD ASM.
4 – STUD. 27 N•M (20 LB. FT.)
5 – NUT. 22 N•M (16 LB. FT.)

TORQUE NO. 2 & 3 MANIFOLD RUNNERS PRIOR TO NO. 1 & 4 RUNNERS

Fig. 5 Exhaust manifold bolt tightening sequence. Turbocharged models

Fig. 6 Cylinder head & camshaft carrier bolt loosening sequence

Fig. 7 Cylinder head & camshaft carrier bolt tightening sequence

32. Remove cylinder head and intake manifold.
33. Reverse procedure to install. Refer to **Fig. 7**, for cylinder head and camshaft carrier attaching bolt tightening sequence. Tighten attaching bolts to specifications.

VALVE ADJUSTMENT

Valve lash is obtained through the use of hydraulic valve lash compensators. No provision for adjustment is provided.

CAMSHAFT LIFT SPECIFICATIONS

Year	Int.	Exh.
1991	.237	.237
1992-94	.263	.263

ROCKER ARMS
REPLACE

1. Disconnect battery ground cable.
2. Remove camshaft carrier cover.
3. Using tool No. J-33302-25 or equivalent, **Fig. 8**, compress valve springs and remove rocker arms. Place rocker arms in a suitable rack so they can be installed in the same location.
4. Remove hydraulic lash compensators and place them in a rack so they can be installed in the same location.
5. Reverse procedure to install. **The preload of the hydraulic valve lash compensator is automatic and ser-**

vicing of the compensator requires only care and cleanliness be exercised in the handling of these components.

HYDRAULIC VALVE LASH COMPENSATORS
REPLACE

Refer to "Rocker Arms, Replace" for replacement procedures.

VALVE SPRING & VALVE STEM OIL SEAL
REPLACE

REMOVAL

1. Disconnect battery ground cable.
2. Remove camshaft carrier cover as described under "Camshaft Carrier Cover, Replace."
3. Remove rocker arms and spark plugs.
4. Install air line adapter tool No. J-22794 or equivalent, into spark plug port and apply compressed air to hold valves in place.
5. Using tool No. J-33302-25 or equivalent, **Fig. 8**, compress valve spring and remove rocker guides, valve locks, caps and valve spring.
6. Remove valve stem oil seal.

INSTALLATION

1. Using clean engine oil, lubricate valve stem and install new valve stem oil seal over valve stem and seat onto valve guide.
2. Position valve spring and cap over valve stem. Using tool No. J-33302-25 or equivalent, compress valve spring and install valve locks.
3. Install rocker guides and rocker arms, then remove tool No. J-33302-25.
4. Remove air line adapter tool and install spark plugs.
5. Install camshaft carrier cover. Torque bolts to specifications.

VALVE GUIDES

Valve guides are an integral part of the cylinder head. If valve stem to guide clearance is excessive, the guide should be reamed to the next oversize and the appropriate oversize valve installed. Valves

Fig. 8 Using tool No. 33302 to compress valve spring

are available in standard sizes and oversizes of .00295 inch, .0059 inch and .00984 inch.

VALVE SEATS

Using a suitable dial indicator measure valve seat concentricity. Valve seat should be concentric to within .002 inch of total indicator reading. Ensure valve guide bores are free from carbon or dirt to allow proper seating of the pilot in the valve guide. When reconditioning the valve seats, use a 45° stone to rough the valve seat and another stone with the same angle to finish the valve seat. Narrow down the valve seats to the proper width, .0050 -.0701 inch for both intake and exhaust.

CRANKSHAFT PULLEY
REPLACE

1. Disconnect battery ground cable.
2. Remove inner fender shield.
3. Remove air conditioning belt, if equipped, then remove serpentine belt.
4. Remove crankshaft pulley bolts and pulley.
5. Reverse to install, noting the following:
   a. Using a suitable sealer, coat threads of pulley bolts and install onto pulley.
   b. Torque bolts to specifications.

1. TENSIONER ARM
2. HOLE IN BASE
3. HIGH TORQUE STOP

Fig. 9 Timing belt tensioner positions

Fig. 10 Camshaft sprocket removal

Fig. 11 Crankshaft front oil seal installation

FRONT COVER
REPLACE

1. Remove serpentine belt.
2. Loosen serpentine belt tensioner attaching bolt, then allow tensioner to swing downward.
3. Remove timing cover attaching bolts and nut, then remove cover.
4. Reverse procedure to install.

TIMING BELT
REPLACE

1. Disconnect battery ground cable.
2. Remove serpentine belt, then remove timing belt cover as outlined under "Timing Belt Front Cover, Replace" procedure.
3. Loosen water pump attaching bolts and release tension with tool No. J33039-A or equivalent.
4. Raise and support vehicle.
5. Lower vehicle, then remove timing belt.
6. Reverse procedure to install, noting the following:
   a. Turn crankshaft and camshaft gears clockwise to align timing marks on gears with timing marks on rear cover.
   b. Install timing belt, ensuring portion between camshaft gear and crankshaft gear is in tension.
   c. Using tool No. J33039-A or equivalent, turn water pump eccentric clockwise until tensioner arm contacts high torque stop, **Fig. 9**. Torque water pump attaching screws slightly.
   d. Turn engine by crankshaft gear bolt 720° clockwise to seat belt to gear teeth.
   e. Turn water pump eccentric counterclockwise until hole in tensioner arm aligns with hole in base. Perform operation with engine at room temperature, approximately 68°F.
   f. Torque water pump attaching bolts to specifications ensuring tensioner holes remain as adjusted.

REAR COVER
REPLACE

1. Disconnect battery ground cable.
2. Remove timing belt as described under "Timing Belt, Replace."
3. Remove camshaft and crankshaft sprockets as described under "Camshaft Sprocket, Replace" and "Crankshaft Sprocket, Replace."
4. Remove timing belt tensioner assembly.
5. Remove timing belt rear cover bolts and cover.
6. Reverse procedure to install. Torque bolts to specifications.

CAMSHAFT CARRIER COVER
REPLACE

1. Remove air cleaner and disconnect breather hoses.
2. **On turbocharged models,** remove turbo induction tube.
3. **On all models,** remove cover bolts and cover.
4. Reverse procedure to install. Torque camshaft carrier cover bolts to specification.

CAMSHAFT SPROCKET
REPLACE

1. Disconnect battery ground cable.
2. Remove camshaft carrier cover as outlined under "Camshaft Carrier Cover, Replace."
3. Remove timing belt as outlined under "Timing Belt, Replace."
4. Using a suitable tool, secure camshaft and remove camshaft sprocket bolt, washer and sprocket, **Fig. 10**.
5. Reverse procedure to install. Tighten camshaft sprocket bolt and camshaft carrier cover to specification.

CAMSHAFT
REPLACE
REMOVAL

1. Disconnect battery ground cable.
2. Remove camshaft carrier cover.
3. Using tool No. J-33302-25 or equivalent, **Fig. 8,** compress valve springs and remove rocker arms.
4. Remove camshaft sprocket as described under "Camshaft Sprocket, Replace."
5. Remove washer fluid container assembly.
6. Disconnect spark plug wires from spark plugs, then remove distributor from engine.
7. Remove camshaft thrust plate from rear of camshaft carrier.
8. Slide camshaft rearward and remove camshaft from carrier.

INSTALLATION

1. Install new front oil seal onto camshaft carrier using fingers.
2. Position camshaft into carrier. **Ensure not to damage front oil seal when installing camshaft.**
3. Install camshaft thrust plate and bolts. Torque bolts to specifications.
4. Check camshaft endplay. Endplay should be within .016 to .064 inch.
5. Install distributor, camshaft sprocket, timing belt and timing belt front cover.
6. Using tool No. J-33302-25 or equivalent, **Fig. 8,** compress valve springs and install rockerarms.
7. Install camshaft carrier cover. Torque bolts to specifications.

CRANKSHAFT SPROCKET
REPLACE

1. Disconnect battery ground cable.
2. Remove timing belt as described under "Timing Belt, Replace."
3. Remove crankshaft sprocket bolt, washer and sprocket.
4. Reverse procedure to install.

ARROW TOWARD FRONT OF ENGINE

NUMBERED SIDE OF ROD TOWARD INTAKE MANIFOLD SIDE OF ENGINE

Fig. 12   Piston & rod assembly

RTV

RTV

SECTION AA

Fig. 13   Oil pan installation

Fig. 14   Disassembled view of oil pump

CRANKSHAFT FRONT OIL SEAL
REPLACE

1. Disconnect battery ground cable.
2. Remove crankshaft sprocket as described under "Crankshaft Sprocket, Replace."
3. Remove key and rear thrust washer from end of crankshaft.
4. Remove rear timing cover as described under "Timing Belt Rear Cover, Replace."
5. Using a suitable tool, remove crankshaft front oil seal.
6. During installation of crankshaft front oil seal, position tool No. J-33083 or equivalent, **Fig. 11**, onto crankshaft. Lubricate front oil seal lip and install onto crankshaft.
7. Reverse procedure to complete installation.

PISTON & ROD ASSEMBLY

Assemble piston to rod, with arrow on piston facing toward front of engine and numbered side toward intake manifold side of engine, **Fig. 12**. Upon installation, measure connecting rod side clearance using a suitable feeler gauge. Side clearance should be .0028 to .0095 inch.

PISTONS PINS & RINGS

Pistons and rings are available in standard size and oversize of .020 inch (.5 mm). Piston pins are available in standard size only.

MAIN & ROD BEARINGS

Main and rod bearings are available in standard sizes and undersizes of .010 inch (.25 mm) and .020 inch (.5 mm).

CRANKSHAFT REAR OIL SEAL
REPLACE

1. Remove transaxle from vehicle as described under "Transaxle, Replace."
2. Remove flywheel attaching bolts and flywheel or flexplate.
3. **On models with manual transaxle,** remove pressure plate and clutch disc.
4. **On all models,** using a suitable tool, pry crankshaft rear oil seal from bore.
5. Clean engine block and crankshaft to seal mating surfaces.
6. Lubricate crankshaft rear oil seal.
7. Use seal installer J-36227 to press seal evenly into position.
8. **On models with manual transaxle,** torque flywheel attaching bolts to specifications.
9. **On models with automatic transaxle,** torque flexplate attaching bolts to specifications.
10. **On models with manual transaxle,** install clutch disc and pressure plate.
11. **On all models,** install transaxle assembly.

OIL PAN
REPLACE

1. Disconnect battery ground cable.
2. Raise and support vehicle.
3. Drain engine oil.
4. Disconnect exhaust pipe from exhaust manifold or wastegate, as required.

5. Remove flywheel cover attaching bolts.
6. Remove oil pan bolts and oil pan.
7. Reverse procedure to install. Apply sealer to oil pan and oil pan gasket as shown in **Fig. 13**. Also coat threads of oil pan bolts with sealer. Torque bolts to specifications.

OIL PUMP SCREEN & PICKUP TUBE
REPLACE

1. Disconnect battery ground cable.
2. Remove oil pan as described under "Oil Pan, Replace."
3. Remove pickup tube support bolts, pickup tube to oil pump bolts, pickup tube and O-ring.
4. Reverse procedure to install. **Torque** pickup tube to oil pump bolts to 71 inch lbs. and pickup tube support to block bolt to 53 inch lbs.

OIL PUMP SERVICE
REMOVAL

1. Disconnect battery ground cable and drain engine oil.
2. Remove crankshaft sprocket as outlined under "Crankshaft Sprocket, Replace."
3. Remove timing belt rear cover as outlined under "Timing Belt Rear Cover, Replace."
4. Disconnect engine oil pressure switch electrical connector from the switch.
5. Remove oil pan and oil filter.
6. Remove pickup tube to engine block bolts, pickup tube and oil pump.

DISASSEMBLE

1. Remove five screws and rear cover from oil pump, **Fig. 14**.
2. Remove gears, plug, pressure regulator valve plunger and spring.
3. If necessary, remove pickup tube and O-ring from oil pump body.

INSPECTION

After disassembling the oil pump, thoroughly clean all oil pump components and check them for excessive wear and damage.

Fig. 15   Checking drive gear to oil pump housing clearance

1	THERMOSTAT HOUSING CAP
2	THERMOSTAT
3	THERMOSTAT HOUSING ASM.
4	CYLINDER HEAD

Fig. 17   Thermostat & housing assembly

1. Using a suitable straightedge and feeler gauge, **Fig. 15**, check oil pump clearances.
2. Check clearances for the following oil pump components:
   a. Clearance between idler gear and oil pump body should be .004-.007 inch.
   b. Clearance between drive gear and oil pump body should be .014-.018 inch.
   c. End clearance should be .001-.004 inch.
3. If clearances obtained are not within specified limits, replace worn or damaged oil pump components.

ASSEMBLE

1. Install valve plunger and spring.
2. Using a suitable sealer, coat threads of pressure regulator valve plunger plug and install. Torque plug and attaching bolts to specifications.
3. Install oil pump gears into oil pump body.

INSTALLATION

1. Install gasket and oil pump onto engine. Torque oil pump bolts specifications.
2. Install pickup tube and bolts. Refer to "Oil Pump Screen & Pickup Tube, Replace" for torque specifications.

1. GENERATOR
2. SERPENTINE DRIVE BELT
3. POWER STEERING PUMP
4. SERPENTINE TENSIONER
5. CRANKSHAFT PULLEY
6. A/C TENSIONER
7. A/C COMPRESSOR
8. A/C "V" BELT

Fig. 16   Serpentine belt routing

3. Install oil pan and oil filter.
4. Connect engine oil pressure switch electrical connector to switch.
5. Install timing belt rear covers and crankshaft sprocket.

BELT TENSION DATA

Year	Belt	New Lbs.	Used Lbs.
1991-94	—	225-236	112-124

SERPENTINE DRIVE BELT
REPLACE

1. Disconnect battery ground cable, then remove coolant recovery tank.
2. Using 19 mm wrench, pivot tensioner and remove belt from alternator.
3. Raise and support vehicle, then remove inner fender splash shield.
4. Remove A/C belt, if equipped.
5. Remove serpentine drive belt.
6. Reverse procedure to install. Refer to **Fig. 16**, for drive belt routing.

BELT TENSIONER
REPLACE

1. Remove drive belt from alternator.
2. Remove bolt from rear of tensioner, then the tensioner.
3. Reverse procedure to install, tighten bolt to specifications.

COOLING SYSTEM BLEED

To ensure sufficient engine cooling, freezing and corrosion protection, maintain

1—BOLT · 28 N·m (21 LB. FT.)

2—WATER PUMP

3—SEAL RING

Fig. 18   Water pump removal & installation

the protection level at −34°F or lower. Use a solution of antifreeze and water, ensuring solution is no more than 70 percent antifreeze.

1. Fill surge tank or radiator to base of filler neck, then install pressure cap.
2. Block the drive wheel and apply parking brake.
3. **On models equipped with automatic transaxle,** place shifter in Park position.
4. **On models equipped with manual transaxle,** place transaxle in Neutral position.
5. **On all models,** start engine and allow to run until upper radiator hose is hot.
6. Turn engine Off, check level of coolant in surge tank or radiator.
7. Allow engine to cool, then add coolant as necessary.

VIEW A

VIEW B

30 mm (1.2 IN.)
MINIMUM CLEARANCE

1. BAR
2. PIPE, FUEL FEED
3. FITTING BACK-UP
   WRENCH REQUIRED AT THIS ATTACHMENT
4. SEAL, O-RING
5. BRACKET, FUEL FILTER
6. FILTER, FUEL
7. SCREW – FULLY DRIVEN, SEATED AND
   NOT STRIPPED
8. PIPE ASM., FUEL
9. SEAT SPRING

Fig. 19 Fuel filter replacement. 1991

THERMOSTAT
REPLACE

Refer to **Fig. 17** when performing the following procedure.
1. Disconnect battery negative cable.
2. With engine cool, drain engine coolant below thermostat level. **Never open cooling system with engine hot. Failure to follow this warning may cause personal injury.**
3. Remove thermostat housing cap, then the thermostat.
4. Reverse procedure to install.

WATER PUMP
REPLACE

1. Disconnect battery ground cable.
2. Drain cooling system, then remove timing belt. Refer to "Timing Belt, Replace" for procedure.
3. Remove timing belt rear protective covers, as required.

4. Remove lower radiator hose from water pump.
5. Remove water pump attaching bolts then the water pump and sealing ring, **Fig 18.**
6. Clean engine block and water pump sealing surfaces, then apply a $3/32$ inch of RTV sealant to sealing surfaces. While RTV sealant is still wet, install water pump. Tighten attaching bolts finger tight.
7. Install lower radiator hose on water pump, then timing belt rear protective covers.
8. Install timing belt. Refer to "Timing Belt, Replace" for procedure.

FUEL PUMP
REPLACE

1. Depressurize fuel system as outlined under "Fuel System Pressure Relief."
2. Disconnect battery ground cable.
3. Raise and support vehicle.
4. Remove fuel tank as follows:
   a. Drain fuel tank. **Place shop towel over fuel line and fitting when disconnecting.**
   b. Disconnect tank meter assembly harness from body harness electrical connectors.
   c. Remove tank filler hoses and vent pipes. **Place shop towel over fuel line and fitting when disconnecting.**
   d. Support fuel tank with suitable equipment, then disconnect fuel tank attaching straps.
   e. Carefully lower fuel tank, if required remove fuel tank meter assembly and seal using tool No. J-24187 or equivalent.
5. Remove fuel tank sending unit and pump assembly by turning cam lock ring counterclockwise.
6. Remove fuel meter pump assembly from fuel tank and fuel pump from fuel sending unit.
7. Pull fuel pump upward into fuel hose while pulling outward away from bottom support. **Do not damage rubber insulator and strainer during fuel pump removal.**
8. After fuel pump assembly is clear of bottom support, pull pump assembly out of rubber connector and from vehicle.
9. Reverse procedure to install.

1. HOSE-PART OF FUEL SENDER
2. FUEL VAPOR PIPE
3. FUEL RETURN PIPE
4. FUEL FEED PIPE
5. FUEL FEED PIPE NUT
6. HOSE-PART OF FUEL SENDER
7. ABS AND FUEL SENDER HARNESS

Fig. 20 Fuel filter replacement. 1992-94

FUEL FILTER
REPLACE
1991

1. Release fuel system pressure as outlined under "Fuel System Pressure Relief."
2. Raise and support vehicle.
3. Disconnect fuel lines from filter, then remove filter, **Fig. 19.**
4. Reverse procedure to install.

1992-94

1. Release fuel system pressure as outlined under "Fuel System Pressure Relief."
2. Raise and support vehicle.
3. Using back-up wrench, remove filter fitting. If nylon fuel lines become kinked and cannot be straightened, they must be replaced.
4. Twist quick-connect fitting $1/4$ turn in each direction to loosen dirt within fitting.
5. Using compressed air, clean quick-connect fitting at ends of filter.
6. Disconnect quick-connect fittings by squeezing plastic tabs of male end connector and pulling apart.
7. Remove fuel filter, **Fig. 20.**
8. Reverse procedure to install.

TIGHTENING SPECIFICATIONS

Component	Torque/Ft. Lbs.	Component	Torque/Ft. Lbs.
Camshaft Carrier & Cylinder Head	①	Crankshaft Sprocket	114
Camshaft Carrier Cover	71⑥	Cylinder Head	①
Camshaft Sprocket	33	Distributor To Cylinder Head	13②
Camshaft Rear Thrust Plate	71⑥	Engine Mount (Front)	⑨
Connecting Rod Cap	26③	Engine Mount (Rear)	⑦
Coolant Pipe To Block	20②	Exhaust Manifold Attaching Nuts	⑧
Crankshaft Pulley To Sprocket	13	Exhaust Manifold Studs	20②

TIGHTENING SPECIFICATIONS—Continued

Component	Torque/Ft. Lbs.
Exhaust Manifold To Turbocharger	18②
Exhaust Pipe To Manifold	19
Exhaust Pipe To Manifold	26②
Flexplate, Auto. Trans.	48
Flywheel, Manual Trans.	48⑤
Fuel Tank Strap Bolt (Front)	25
Fuel Tank Strap Nut (Rear)	106⑥
Heater Pipe To Intake	18
Intake Manifold	18②
Intake Manifold	15-20
Main Bearing Caps	44④
Oil Pan	44⑥
Oil Pan Drain Plug	34
Oil Pump	62⑥
Oil Pump Cover	71⑥
Oil Pump Drive	15-22
Oil Pump Pressure Regulating Valve	22
Oil Pump Suction Tube Bolts	71⑥
Pressure Plate To Flywheel	18
Serpentine Drive Belt Tensioner	35
Spark Plug	15
Suspension Support (Front)	65
Thermostat Housing	20
Throttle Body Assembly	17②
Throttle Body Injector Assembly	16
Timing Belt Front Cover	89⑥

Component	Torque/Ft. Lbs.
Timing Belt Rear Cover	89⑥
Timing Belt Tensioner	18
Transaxle Mount Bolt	22⑩
Transaxle To Engine	55⑩
Transaxle Strut To Body Bolt (Front)	40
Transaxle Strut To Body Bolt (Rear)	23
Transaxle Strut To Transaxle (Front	50
Turbo Injection Tube Clamps	3②
Water Inlet	15-22
Water Outlet To Cam Carrier	11
Water Pump	18
Wheel And Tire Assembly	100

① —Torque cylinder head & camshaft carrier bolts to 18 ft. lbs., then tighten bolts an additional 180° in 60° increments. Start engine & allow to reach operating temperature, then tighten bolts an additional 30° to 50°.
② —Turbocharged engine.
③ —Plus an additional 40–45°.
④ —Plus an additional 40–50°.
⑤ —Plus an additional 30°.
⑥ —Inch lbs.
⑦ —Refer to Fig. 2, for specifications.
⑧ —Torque to 16 ft. lbs. for turbocharged and non-turbo models.
⑨ —Refer to Fig. 1, for specifications.
⑩ —Vehicles equipped with automatic transmission.

2.2L/4-134 Engine
INDEX

PRECAUTIONS
FUEL SYSTEM PRESSURE RELIEF

1. Loosen fuel filler cap, then remove the fuel pump fuse.

2. Start engine and run until remaining fuel is consumed.
3. Engage starter for approximately three seconds, to ensure relief of any reaming pressure.
4. Disconnect battery ground cable to avoid possible fuel discharge if any attempt is made to start the engine.

ENGINE MOUNTS
REPLACE
FRONT MOUNT

1. Disconnect battery ground cable.
2. Remove upper engine mount to body bolts, **Fig. 1.**

Fig. 1 Front engine mount

Fig. 2 Rear engine mount

3. Remove upper engine mount to engine bracket bolt.
4. Raise and support vehicle.
5. Using a suitable jack, support engine assembly.
6. Remove inner fender shield.
7. Remove lower engine mount to body bolt.
8. Remove lower engine mount to engine mount bracket bolt, then remove mount.
9. Reverse procedure to install, torque bolts and nuts to specifications.

REAR MOUNT

1. Disconnect battery ground cable.
2. Raise and support vehicle.
3. Remove engine mount retaining bolts and nuts, **Fig. 2,** then remove mount.
4. Reverse procedure to install, torque bolts and nuts to specifications.

ENGINE
REPLACE

Refer to **Figs. 3 and 4,** when performing the following procedure.
1. Disconnect battery ground cable.
2. Loosen fuel filler cap to relieve tank vapor pressure.
3. Drain engine coolant, ,then disconnect hood lamp wiring.
4. Mark position of hood for assembly reference, then remove hood retaining bolts and remove hood.
5. Remove throttle body intake duct, then rear sight shields.

6. Remove the battery, then air cleaner housing.
7. Remove upper radiator hose, then disconnect brake booster vacuum hose.
8. Remove alternator top brace, then disconnect wiring.
9. Disconnect upper engine wiring harness from engine.
10. Discharge A/C system, then remove compressor to condenser and accumulator lines.
11. Raise and support vehicle.
12. Remove left splash shield, then disconnect exhaust system from the engine.
13. Disconnect lower engine wiring, then remove flywheel inspection cover.
14. Remove front wheels and lower radiator hose.
15. Disconnect heater hoses from the heater core, then remove brake calipers from the steering knuckle. Use wire to support brake calipers.
16. Disconnect tie rod ends from struts, then lower the vehicle.
17. Remove left side sound insulator from under dash panel, then disconnect the clutch master cylinder pushrod from the clutch pedal.
18. Remove clutch slave cylinder retaining nuts at front of dash and disconnect remote reservoir, if equipped.
19. Disconnect fuel feed and return lines, **Fig. 5. Place shop towel over fuel line and fitting when disconnecting.**

20. Disconnect transaxle linkage at the transaxle.
21. Disconnect accelerator, cruise control and TV cables from throttle body.
22. **On models equipped with automatic transaxle,** disconnect transmission cooling lines from the transaxle.
23. **On all models,** disconnect power steering hoses from the power steering pump.
24. Remove four center carriage support bolts, then align dolly under frame and lower vehicle to dolly and add support under engine.
25. Support rear of vehicle, then remove upper transaxle mount.
26. Remove upper strut bolts and nuts.
27. Remove front engine mount, then rear engine mount.
28. Remove four rear, then four front carriage retaining bolts.
29. Wire front carriage bolt holes together to prevent axle separation.
30. Raise vehicle and remove engine and transaxle assembly on dolly.
31. Reverse procedure to install.

CYLINDER HEAD
REPLACE

1. Disconnect battery ground cable, then loosen fuel filler cap to relieve tank vapor pressure.
2. Remove air cleaner assembly, then drain cooling system.
3. Disconnect attaching vacuum hoses, electrical connectors and accelerator cable.
4. Remove coolant reservoir tank.

1 NUT, Air Cleaner	21 FITTING, Heater Coolant Hose	40 NUT	61 STUD, Intake Manifold
2 AIR CLEANER ASM.	22 SEAL, Valve Stem Oil	41 BRACKET, Engine Lift	62 STUD, Intake Manifold
3 CLAMP	23 SPRING, Valve	42 BOLT, Cylinder Head	63 GASKET, Intake Manifold
4 SEAL, Throttle Body	24 CAP, Valve Spring	43 STUD, Exhaust Manifold	64 MANIFOLD, Intake
5 BOLT	25 KEY, Valve Stem	44 GASKET, Exhaust Manifold	65 FITTING, Vacuum Power Brake
6 SUPPORT, Spark Plug Wire Front	26 PLUG, Spark	45 MANIFOLD, Exhaust	66 FITTING, Intake Manifold Vacuum
7 SUPPORT, Spark Plug Wire Rear	27 WIRE, Spark Plug	46 BOLT	67 TUBE, EGR Vacuum & Evaporator Canister
8 BOLT	28 NUT	47 SENSOR, Oxygen	68 GASKET, TBI
9 SUPPORT, Ignition Wire	29 VALVE, EGR	48 VALVE, Inlet	69 INJECTOR, Throttle Body
10 BOLT, Valve Rocker Cover	30 GASKET, EGR Valve	49 GASKET, Cylinder Head	70 BOLT, TBI
11 TUBE, Crankcase Vent	31 PLUG, Water Outlet	50 HEAD, w Guide and Insert	71 PIPE, Fuel Injection (Return)
12 BOLT, Valve Rocker Cover	32 SENSOR, Coolant Temperature	51 BOLT, Cylinder Head (Short)	72 PIPE, Fuel Injection (Feed)
13 COVER, Valve Rocker	33 STUD, EGR Valve	52 BOLT, Cylinder Head (Long)	73 VALVE, Positive Crankcase Ventilation
14 GASKET, Valve Rocker Cover	34 ADAPTER, Collant Outlet	54 BRACKET, Drive Belt Tensioner	74 SEAL, PCV Cap
15 NUT, Valve Rocker Arm	35 THERMOSTAT, Engine Coolant Outlet	55 BOLT	75 DUCT, Air Cleaner Intake
16 BALL, Rocker Arm	36 OUTLET, Coolant	56 STUD	76 HOSE, PCV
17 ARM, Valve Rocker	37 STUD	57 BRACKET, Accelerator Control Cable	77 CAP, PCV
18 STUD, Valve Rocler Arm Ball	38 NUT	58 STUD	78 SEAL, PCV
19 GUIDE, Push Rod	39 GASKET, Coolant Outlet	59 NUT	79 SEAL, PCV
20 SEAT, Valve Spring		60 STUD	

Fig. 3   Exploded view of cylinder head assembly. 1991

No.	Description	No.	Description
1	PCV HOSE	42	COOLANT OUTLET
2	PCV VALVE CAP	43	NUT
3	PCV CAP O-RING	44	STUD
4	PCV VALVE UPPER O-RING	45	NUT
5	PCV VALVE LOWER O-RING	46	NUT
6	PCV VALVE LOWER O-RING	47	OXYGEN
10	BOLT	48	ENGINE LIFT BRACKET
17	CRANK CASE VENT TUBE	49	STUD
18	ROCKER COVER AND GASKET	50	STUD
19	BRACKET	51	STUD
20	SPARK PLUG	52	EXHAUST MANIFOLD
21	BOLT	53	EXHAUST MANIFOLD GASKET
22	BRACKET	54	HOSE NIPPLE
23	BOLT	55	EXHAUST VALVE
24	SECONDARY IGNITION CABLES	56	INTAKE VALVE
25	KEY	57	CYLINDER HEAD GASKET
26	VALVE SPRING	58	CYLINDER HEAD
27	VALVE STEM OIL SEAL	59	COOLANT JACKET PLUG
28	VALVE SPRING SEAT	60	BOLT
29	ROCKER ARM STUD	61	BOLT
30	PUSHROD GUIDE	62	SERPENTINE DRIVE BELT TENSIONER
31	COOLANT OUTLET GASKET	74	ROCKER ARM
32	COOLANT PIPE ADAPTER	75	ROCKER ARM BALL
33	COOLANT OUTLET ADAPTER	76	NUT
34	STUD	77	UPPER INTAKE MANIFOLD ASSEMBLY
35	VALVE SPRING CAP	78	STUD
36	NUT	79	EGR VALVE SOLENOID
37	EGR VALVE	80	BOLT
38	EGR VALVE GASKET	81	STUD
39	PLUG	82	UPPER INTAKE MANIFOLD ASSEMBLY GASKET
40	COOLANT SENSOR	83	LOWER INTAKE MANIFOLD
41	THERMOSTAT	84	EGR VALVE INJECTOR

Fig. 4   Exploded view of cylinder head assembly. 1992-94

1. HOSE, FUEL FEED
2. HOSE, FUEL RETURN
3. FITTING – BACK-UP WRENCH REQUIRED AT THESE LOCATIONS
4. SEAL – O-RING
5. FITTING – 27 N·m (20 LBS. FT.)
6. PIPE, FUEL RETURN
7. PIPE, FUEL FEED

Fig. 5   Engine fuel hoses & pipes

5. Remove serpentine belt, then remove alternator.
6. Loosen power steering pump attaching bolts, then position away.
7. Remove serpentine belt tensioner.
8. Remove ignition wires, then remove canister purge line beneath manifold.
9. Remove upper radiator hose, then remove upper and lower heater hose at manifold.
10. Remove throttle body cables from bracket.
11. Remove cylinder head coolant inlet hose.
12. Remove intake manifold brace to power steering bracket attaching bolts.
13. Remove attaching fuel lines. **Place shop towel over fuel line and fitting when disconnecting.**
14. Remove rocker arm cover attaching bolts, then remove rocker arm cover.
15. Remove rocker arms and pushrods.
16. Remove ignition cable bracket.
17. Disconnect exhaust pipe at exhaust manifold.
18. Remove cylinder head attaching bolts.
19. **On models equipped with automatic transaxle,** remove transaxle fluid level indicator bracket.
20. **On all models,** remove cylinder head assembly.
21. Reverse procedure to install. Refer to **Fig. 6,** for cylinder head bolt tightening sequence. Torque attaching bolts to specifications.

Fig. 6 Cylinder head bolt tightening sequence

1	FITTING
2	STUD
3	INTAKE MANIFOLD
4	GASKET
5	NUT

Fig. 7 Intake manifold bolt tightening sequence. 1991

1	STUD
2	GASKET
3	INTAKE MANIFOLD
4	NUT
5	CLIP

Fig. 8 Intake manifold bolt tightening sequence. 1992-94

INTAKE MANIFOLD
REPLACE

1991

1. Disconnect battery ground cable, then remove fuel filler cap to relieve fuel tank pressure.
2. Remove air cleaner assembly, then drain engine coolant.
3. Disconnect vacuum lines and wires from the intake as necessary.
4. Disconnect fuel feed and return lines, **Fig. 5.**
5. Disconnect TBI linkage and TBI assembly, then remove the power steering pump and position aside.
6. Disconnect coolant hose to intake manifold.
7. Raise and support vehicle.
8. Disconnect accelerator and T.V. cables, then remove the bracket.
9. Remove lower intake manifold retaining nuts, then lower the vehicle.
10. Remove upper intake manifold retaining bolts and nuts, then remove intake manifold.
11. Reverse procedure to install, torque bolts to specifications in sequence shown in **Fig. 7.**

1992-94

1. Remove air intake duct.
2. Drain coolant and disconnect all attaching vacuum lines and wires.
3. Disconnect throttle linkage, then remove MAP sensor and EGR solenoid valve.
4. Remove the power steering pump and position aside.
5. Remove upper intake manifold assembly, EGR valve injector, fuel injector retainer bracket, regulator injectors and fuel lines.
6. Disconnect accelerator and TV cables, then remove cable bracket.
7. Raise and support vehicle.
8. Remove intake manifold lower nuts, then lower vehicle.
9. Remove intake manifold upper nuts.
10. Remove lower intake manifold and gasket.
11. Reverse procedure to install, torque bolts to specifications in sequence shown in **Fig. 8.**

EXHAUST MANIFOLD
REPLACE

1. Disconnect battery ground cable.
2. Disconnect oxygen sensor lead, then remove serpentine belt.
3. Remove alternator and position aside.
4. Raise and support vehicle.
5. Disconnect exhaust pipe from the exhaust manifold, then lower the vehicle.
6. Remove exhaust manifold attaching bolts and oil fill tube, then remove exhaust manifold.
7. Reverse procedure to install, torque manifold retaining bolts to specifications.

VALVE ADJUSTMENT

Valve lash is obtained through the use of hydraulic valve lifters. No adjustment is possible.

VALVE GUIDES

Valve guides are an integral part of the cylinder head and are not removable. If valve stem clearance becomes excessive, the valve guide should be reamed to the next oversize and the appropriate oversize valves installed. Valves are available in .00295, .0059 and .00984 inch oversizes.

Fig. 9 Valves, valve seals & valve springs

1	LOCKS
2	CAP
3	SPRING
4	SEAL (EX)
5	SPRING SEAT
6	VALVE (EX)
7	VALVE (IN)
8	SEAL (IN)
9	STUD
10	GUIDE

HYDRAULIC VALVE LIFTERS
REPLACE

1. Remove rocker cover as described previously.
2. Loosen rocker arm nut and swing rocker arm aside.
3. Remove pushrod, then using a flexible magnetic wand remove lifter.
4. Inspect lifter for any signs of damage or wear, replacing as necessary.
5. Reverse procedure to install.

VALVE SPRING & VALVE STEM OIL SEAL
REPLACE

REMOVAL

1. Disconnect battery ground cable, then remove rocker cover.
2. With engine cold, remove spark plug and clean debris from plug recess.
3. Remove rocker arm and pushrod on cylinders to be serviced.
4. Install air line adapter tool No. J 23590 or equivalent in spark plug thread and apply compressed air to hold valves in place.
5. With valve spring compressor tool No. J 5892-C or equivalent, compress valve spring and remove valve lock and cap, **Fig. 9**.
6. Remove spring, valve stem oil seal and shim.

INSTALLATION

1. Install shim if required, then new valve stem oil seal.
2. Set valve spring and cap in place.
3. Using valve spring compressor tool No. J 5892-C or equivalent, compress valve spring.
4. Install valve locks and release compressor. **Make sure locks seat properly in the upper groove of the valve stem. Grease may be used to hold the locks in place while releasing the compressor tool.**
5. Install spark plug, pushrods, rocker arms and rocker cover.

CRANKSHAFT PULLEY & HUB
REPLACE

REMOVAL

Refer to **Fig. 10**, when performing the following any procedures.
1. Disconnect battery ground cable.
2. Remove serpentine belt, then raise and support vehicle.
3. Remove wheel and tire assembly, then inner fender splash shield.
4. Remove three crankshaft pulley retaining bolts.
5. Remove crankshaft pulley hub bolt, then the crankshaft pulley.
6. Install crankshaft pulley puller tool No. J 24420-B or equivalent on hub.
7. Turn puller screw and remove hub.

INSTALLATION

1. Coat front cover seal contact area with engine oil.
2. Apply RTV sealer No. 1052917 or equivalent, to keyway in pulley hub.
3. Place crankshaft pulley hub into position over key on crankshaft.
4. Install crankshaft pulley installer No. J 29113 into crankshaft so that at least ¼ inch of thread is engaged.
5. Pull pulley hub into position and remove tool from crankshaft.
6. Install crankshaft pulley, then three pulley retaining bolts.
7. Install inner slash shield, then wheel and tire assembly.
8. Lower vehicle and install serpentine belt.
9. Connect battery ground cable.

FRONT COVER
REPLACE

1. Disconnect battery ground cable.
2. Remove serpentine belt, then the belt tensioner.
3. Raise and support vehicle, then remove oil pan as described in "Oil Pan, Replace."
4. Remove crankshaft pulley and hub as described in "Crankshaft Pulley and Hub, Replace."
5. Remove front cover retaining bolts, then remove front cover.
6. Reverse procedure to install.

TIMING CHAIN & SPROCKETS
REPLACE

1. Disconnect battery ground cable, then remove crankcase front cover as described in "Front Cover, Replace."
2. Align marks on crankshaft sprocket and camshaft sprocket, **Fig. 11**.
3. Remove timing chain tensioner upper bolt, then loosen timing chain tensioner Torx as far as possible, but do not remove.
4. Remove camshaft sprocket and timing chain.
5. Using puller tool No. J 22888-20 or equivalent, remove crankshaft sprocket.
6. Reverse procedure to install, noting the following:
   a. Compress tensioner spring, then install a cotter pin or nail into hole A as shown in **Fig. 12**.
   b. Lube timing chain and sprockets with engine oil, lube thrust thrust surface with camshaft assembly lube No. 1052365 or equivalent.
   c. Align marks on camshaft and crankshaft sprockets with tabs on tensioner as shown in **Fig. 12**.
   d. Align dowel in camshaft with dowel hole camshaft sprocket.
   e. Draw camshaft sprocket onto camshaft using the mounting bolt. Torque to specifications.

Fig. 10 Exploded view of cylinder block assembly

1. RING, Piston
2. PISTON, w Pin
3. BOLT, Connecting Rod
4. BEARING, Connecting Rod
5. PIN, Cylinder Head Dowel
6. PLUG, Cylinder Water Jacket Hole
7. PIN, Clutch Housing
8. CORD, Engine Block Heater
9. HEATER, Engine Block
10. RETAINER
11. CAP, Oil Fil & Gage
12. BOLT
13. TUBE, Oil Fil
14. SEAL, Oil Fil Tube
15. BOLT
16. PLUG
17. COVER, Camshaft Rear
18. BOLT
19. PLUG
20. CLAMP
21. HOSE, Coolant Inlet
22. BOLT
23. INLET, Coolant
24. GASKET, Coolant Inlet
25. PLUG

26. ENGINE, Partial
27. NUT, Connecting Rod
28. BEARING, Crankshaft
29. SEAL, Crankshaft Rear Oil
30. BOLT, Flywheel
31. RETAINER, Flywheel
32. FLYWHEEL, Crankshaft
33. BOLT, Clutch Cover & Pressure Plate
34. WASHER, Spring Lock
35. COVER, Plate, Clutch Pressure
36. PLATE, Clutch Driven
37. SEALANT
38. BOLT, Crankshaft Bearing Cap
39. CAP, Crankshaft Bearing
40. SEALER
41. BOLT
42. DRIVE, Oil Pump
43. SHAFT, Distributor to Oil Pump
44. RETAINER
45. PUMP, w Screen
46. BOLT, Oil Pump & Screen
47. STUD
48. SEAL, Oil Pan Rear
49. PAN, Oil
50. NUT

51. BOLT
52. GASKET, Oil Pan Drain Screw
53. SCREW, Oil Pan Drain
54. SHIM, Starter Motor
55. MOTOR, Starter
56. BOLT, Starter Motor Outboard
57. BOLT, Starter Motor Inboard
58. BOLT
59. NUT
60. WASHER, Flat
61. BRACKET, Starter Motor
62. HUB, Crankshaft Pulley
63. WASHER
64. PULLEY, Crankshaft
65. SEAL, Crankshaft Front Oil
66. SCREW, Hex
67. COVER, Crankcase Front End
68. CHAIN, Camshaft Timing
69. SPROCKET, Crankshaft
70. KEY
71. CRANKSHAFT, Engine
72. GASKET, Water Pump
73. PUMP, Coolant
74. PULLEY, Water Pump
75. BOLT
76. BOLT

77. BOLT, Tensioner Timing Chain
78. TENSIONER, Timing Chain
79. BOLT, Hex
80. WASHER, Camshaft Sprocket
81. SPROCKET, Camshaft
82. SCREW, Camshaft Thrust Plate
83. PLATE, Camshaft Thrust
84. PIN
85. BEARING, Camshaft
86. CAMSHAFT, Engine
87. SWITCH, Fuel Pump
88. VALVE, Oil Filter By-pass
89. FILTER, Oil (PF52)
90. CONNECTOR, Oil Filter Adapter
91. ADAPTER, Oil Filter
92. GASKET, Oil Filter Adapter
93. LIFTER, Hydraulic Valve
94. ROD, Push
95. COIL, w Module Ignition
96. BOLT
97. STUD, Ignition coil
98. SENSOR, Crankshaft
99. GASKET
100. BOLT, Crankshaft Pulley Hub
101. BOLT, Crankshaft Pulley
102. CONNECTING ROD

1. 105 N·m (77 LB.FT.)
2. TENSIONER
3. CAMSHAFT SPROCKET
4. CRANKSHAFT SPROCKET
5. 12 N·m (106 LB.IN.)
6. 24 N·m (18 LB.FT.)

NOTE— ALIGN TABS ON TENSIONER WITH MARKS ON CAMSHAFT & CRANKSHAFT SPROCKETS.

#4 CYLINDER TDC COMPRESSION STROKE

Fig. 11   Timing chain & sprockets

A

DIRECTION OF TENSION TO BE APPLIED

Fig. 12   Timing chain tensioner

Fig. 13   Installing piston

CAMSHAFT
REPLACE
REMOVAL

1. Remove engine assembly as described in "Engine, Replace."
2. Drain engine oil and remove oil filter.
3. Remove valve lifters and crankcase front cover as described previously.
4. Remove oil pump drive, then remove timing chain and camshaft sprocket.
5. Remove camshaft thrust plate and camshaft. Use care not to damage camshaft bearings with the camshaft when withdrawing the camshaft.
6. Inspect camshaft for wear, galling, wear, gouges and overheating. If any of these problems exist, replace the camshaft.

INSTALLATION

1. Install camshaft and thrust plate. **Coat camshaft lobes and bearings with camshaft lube No. 1051396 or equivalent. Insert camshaft with extreme care to avoid personal injury and gouging of the camshaft bearings.**
2. Torque thrust plate specifications, then install camshaft sprocket and timing chain.
3. Install crankcase front cover.
4. Replace valve lifters. Lifters must be installed in the same bores from which they were removed. **If a new camshaft is installed, replace all valve lifters. Some lifters may be oversized, verify marking near the lifter bore.**
5. Install valve mechanism, parts must be reinstalled in the same position and with the same mating surfaces from which they were removed.
6. Install rocker cover, then the oil pump drive.
7. Replace oil filter, then install engine assembly.

PISTON & ROD ASSEMBLY

Assemble piston to rod, with arrow on piston facing toward front of engine **Fig. 13**. Upon installation measure connecting rod side clearance using a feeler gauge. Side clearance should be .0039 to .0149 inch.

PISTON PINS & RINGS

Pistons are available in standard size and oversize of .020 inch (.5mm). Piston pins are available in standard size only.

CRANKSHAFT REAR OIL SEAL
REPLACE

1. Remove transaxle from vehicle as described in "Transaxle, Replace."
2. **On models with manual transaxle,** remove pressure plate and clutch disc.
3. **On all models,** remove flywheel attaching bolts and flywheel.
4. Insert a screwdriver or similar tool in through the dust lip as shown in **Fig. 14,** pry out seal.
5. Reverse procedure to install, noting the following:
   a. Lubricate seal bore to seal surface with engine oil.
   b. Using seal installation tool No. J 34686 or equivalent, align dowel pin of tool with dowel pin hole in crankshaft and attach tool to crankshaft.
   c. **Torque** tool attaching screws to 27-62 inch lbs., then tighten tool T handle to push seal into bore. Continue to tighten until tool is flush against block.

OIL PAN
REPLACE

1. Disconnect battery ground cable.
2. Raise and support vehicle, then disconnect exhaust pipe from the exhaust manifold.
3. Drain engine oil, then remove starter bracket at block.

Fig. 14   Crankshaft rear seal removal

1. PICK UP TUBE AND SCREEN.
2. PUMP COVER.
3. DRIVE GEAR AND SHAFT.
4. IDLER GEAR.
5. PUMP BODY.
6. PRESSURE REGULATOR SPRING.
7. PRESSURE REGULATOR VALVE.
8. RETAINING PIN.
9. GASKET.
10. ATTACHING BOLTS.

Fig. 15   Exploded view of oil pump

Fig. 16   Measuring oil pump gear lash

Fig. 17   Measuring gear side clearance

Fig. 18   Measuring oil pump gear pocket

4. Remove starter and position aside, then remove flywheel cover.
5. Remove four right side engine support bolts, then lower support slightly to gain clearance for oil pan removal.
6. **On models with automatic transaxle,** remove oil filter and extension.
7. **On all models,** remove oil pan retaining bolts and oil pan.
8. Reverse procedure to install, noting the following:
   a. Apply a 1/16 inch diameter bead of GM 1052914 RTV or equivalent, on oil pan to block sealing flanges.
   b. Apply RTV sealer or equivalent to oil pan surface which fits to engine front cover.
   c. Using a new oil pan rear seal, apply a thin coat of RTV sealer or equivalent on ends down to ears, install pan against cylinder case and install bolts.
   d. **On models with automatic transaxle,** replace oil filter adapter seal and install oil filter adapter.

OIL PUMP SERVICE

REMOVAL

1. Remove oil pan as described previously.
2. Remove pump to rear main bearing cap bolt, then remove pump and extension shaft.

Fig. 19   Measuring oil pump end clearance

DISASSEMBLY

1. Drain oil from pump, then remove driveshaft, **Fig. 15.**
2. Remove pump cover, **Do not remove pickup tube from cover unless loose or broken.**
3. Remove pump gears, then the pressure regulator valve. **The pressure regulator valve spring is under pressure. Exercise caution when removing the retaining pin, as bodily injury may result.**

4. Remove plug, spring and valve. If valve is stuck, soak the pump housing in carburetor cleaning solvent.

INSPECTION

Thoroughly clean all oil pump components and check them for excessive wear or damage.

1. Using a straightedge and feeler gauge, check oil pump clearances as shown in **Figs. 16 through 19.**
2. Install gears and measure in several places, gear lash should be within .004-.008 inch.
3. Measure depth and diameter of oil pump gear pocket, depth should be 1.195-1.198 inch and diameter should be 1.503-1.506 inch.
4. Measure gear side clearance, side clearance should be .0015-.004.
5. Measure gear end clearance, end clearance should be .002-.006. When deciding pump serviceability based on end clearance, consider depth of wear pattern in the pump cover and/or cover plate.

ASSEMBLY

1. Lubricate all internal parts with engine

WITHOUT A/C   WITH A/C

1	GENERATOR
2	P/S PUMP
3	TENSIONER
4	CRANKSHAFT
5	WATER PUMP
6	A/C

Fig. 20   Serpentine drive belt routing

1	BOLT - 10 Nm (8 LBS. FT.)
2	THERMOSTAT AND HOUSING
3	GASKET
4	THERMOSTAT
5	HOUSING
6	STUD - 10 Nm (90 LBS. IN.)
7	NUT - 10 Nm (90 LBS. IN.)

Fig. 21   Thermostat & housing assembly

oil during assembly.
2. Install pump gears. **To avoid engine damage, all pump cavities must be packed with petroleum jelly before installing gears to assure priming.**
3. Install oil pump cover and gasket.
4. Install pressure regulator valve, spring and retaining pin.
5. Torque pump cover bolts to specifications. Whenever the oil pump is overhauled, clear the oil pan of oil and sludge, replace oil filter and fill crankcase with clean oil.

INSTALLATION

1. Install pump and extension shaft, then torque main bearing cap bolt to specification.
2. Install oil pan.

SERPENTINE DRIVE BELT
REPLACE

1. Remove coolant reservoir.
2. Rotate tensioner clockwise with a 15 mm wrench and slide belt from generator pulley. Release tensioner and remove belt.
3. Reverse procedure to install, routing belt as shown in **Fig. 20.**

SERPENTINE DRIVE BELT TENSIONER
REPLACE

1. Disconnect negative battery cable and remove coolant reservoir.
2. Remove serpentine belt as described under "Serpentine Drive Belt, Replace."
3. Remove two generator bolts.
4. Remove power steering pump and position aside.
5. Remove tensioner bolts and tensioner.

1. BOLT — 25 N·m (18 LBS. FT.)

Fig. 22   Water pump installation

6. Reverse procedure to install, **Torquing** tensioner bolts to 37 ft. lbs.

COOLING SYSTEM BLEED

To ensure sufficient engine cooling, freezing and corrosion protection, maintain the protection level at −34°F or lower. Use a solution of antifreeze and water, ensuring solution is no more than 70 percent antifreeze.

1. Fill surge tank or radiator to base of filler neck, then attach pressure cap.
2. Block the drive wheel and apply parking brake.
3. **On models equipped with automatic transaxle,** place shifter in Park position.
4. **On models equipped with manual transaxle,** place transaxle in Neutral position.
5. **On all models,** start engine and allow to run until upper radiator hose is hot.
6. Turn engine Off, check level of coolant in surge tank or radiator.
7. Allow engine to cool, then add coolant as necessary.

THERMOSTAT
REPLACE

Refer to **Fig. 21** when performing the following procedure.
1. Disconnect battery negative cable.
2. Remove air intake duct.
3. With engine cool, drain engine coolant below thermostat level. **Never open cooling system with engine hot. Failure to follow this warning may cause personal injury.**
4. Disconnect radiator hose from thermostat housing.
5. Remove thermostat housing retaining nuts, then the housing, gasket and thermostat.
6. Reverse procedure to install noting the following:
   a. Prior to installation, ensure thermostat gasket area is thoroughly clean.
   b. Install thermostat with new gasket.
   c. **Torque** thermostat housing retaining nuts to 89 inch lbs.
   d. Refill and bleed cooling system as needed.

WATER PUMP
REPLACE

1. Disconnect battery ground cable, then drain cooling system.
2. Remove serpentine drive belt, then the alternator and bracket.
3. Remove water pump pulley attaching bolts, then remove the pulley, **Fig. 22.**
4. Remove water pump attaching bolts, then the water pump.
5. Reverse procedure to install.

FUEL PUMP
REPLACE

1. Disconnect battery ground cable, then drain fuel tank.
2. Raise and support vehicle.
3. Disconnect tank meter assembly harness from body harness connector.
4. Remove ground wire retaining screw from underbody, then disconnect hos-

7. Remove tank assembly.
8. Remove fuel tank sending unit and pump assembly by turning cam lock ring counter clockwise.
9. Lift assembly from fuel tank and remove fuel pump from fuel tank sending unit.
10. Pull fuel pump up into attaching hose while pulling outward away from bottom support. Take care to prevent damage to rubber insulator and strainer during removal. After pump assembly is clear of bottom support, pull pump assembly out of rubber connector for removal.
11. Reverse procedure to install.

FUEL FILTER REPLACE

1991

1. Release fuel system pressure as outlined under "Fuel System Pressure Relief."
2. Raise and support vehicle.
3. Disconnect fuel lines from filter, then remove filter, **Fig. 23.**
4. Reverse procedure to install.

1992-94

1. Release fuel system pressure as outlined under "Fuel System Pressure Relief."
2. Raise and support vehicle.
3. Using back-up wrench, remove filter

30 mm (1.2 IN.) MINIMUM CLEARANCE

VIEW A

VIEW B

1. BAR
2. PIPE, FUEL FEED
3. FITTING   BACK-UP WRENCH REQUIRED AT THIS ATTACHMENT
4. SEAL, O-RING
5. BRACKET, FUEL FILTER
6. FILTER, FUEL
7. SCREW – FULLY DRIVEN, SEATED AND NOT STRIPPED
8. PIPE ASM., FUEL
9. SEAT SPRING

Fig. 23 Fuel filter replacement. 1991 models

es from fuel meter assembly.
5. Disconnect hoses at tank from filler and vent pipes.
6. Support fuel tank with jack, then disconnect two fuel tank retaining straps.

1. HOSE-PART OF FUEL SENDER
2. FUEL VAPOR PIPE
3. FUEL RETURN PIPE
4. FUEL FEED PIPE
5. FUEL FEED PIPE NUT
6. HOSE-PART OF FUEL SENDER
7. ABS AND FUEL SENDER HARNESS

Fig. 24 Fuel filter replacement. 1992-94 models

fitting. If nylon fuel lines become kinked and cannot be straightened, they must be replaced.
4. Twist quick-connect fitting 1/4 turn in each direction to loosen dirt within fitting.
5. Using compressed air, clean quick-connect fitting at ends of filter.
6. Disconnect quick-connect fittings by squeezing plastic tabs of male end connector and pulling apart.
7. Remove fuel filter, **Fig. 24.**
8. Reverse procedure to install.

TIGHTENING SPECIFICATIONS

Component	Torque/Ft. Lbs.	Component	Torque/Ft. Lbs.
Brake Booster Vacuum Fitting	10	Main Bearing Cap Bolts	70
Battery Ground Cable	13	Oil Fill Tube To Cylinder Block	18
Camshaft Pulley	77	Oil Filter Adapter To Cylinder Block	18
Camshaft Thrust Plate	106③	Oil Pan	71③
Coolant Drain Plug (Cylinder Block)	11	Oil Pump Cover Bolts	89③
Coolant Outlet To Cylinder Head	8	Oil Pump Drive Assembly Bolt	18
Crankcase Front Cover Bolts	97③	Oil Pump To Bearing Cap	32
Crankshaft Pulley & Hub To Crankshaft	77	Pressure Plate To Flywheel	15
Crankshaft Pulley To Hub	37	Rear Engine Lift Bracket	32
Cylinder Head Bolts	②	Rocker Arm Cover	89③
DIS Coil Assembly	18	Rocker Arm Nuts	22
Exhaust Manifold Nuts	115③	Rod Bearing Cap Nut	38
Exhaust Manifold Studs	9-10	Serpentine Tensioner Assembly	37
Exhaust Pipe To Manifold	18	Spark Plugs	11
Engine Mount Bracket To Engine, Front	50	Timing Chain Cover	8
Engine Mount, Lower, To Bracket, Rear	18	Timing Chain Tensioner	18
Engine Mount To Bracket, Front	74	Water Pump	18
Engine Mount To Bracket, Rear	50	Water Pump Inlet	18
Flywheel To Crankshaft, Auto. Trans.	52	Wheel Lug Nuts	100
Flywheel To Crankshaft, Manual Trans.	55		
Intake Manifold	①		

① —1991, 18 ft. lbs.; 1992-94, 22 ft. lbs.
② —Torque long bolts to 46 ft. lbs. and short bolts to 43 ft. lbs. Tightening all bolts an additional 90° in sequence.
③ —Inch lbs.

INDEX

PRECAUTIONS

FUEL SYSTEM PRESSURE RELIEF

1. Loosen fuel filler cap, then remove the fuel pump fuse.
2. Start engine and run until remaining fuel is consumed.
3. Engage starter for approximately three seconds, to ensure relief of any reaming pressure.
4. Disconnect battery ground cable to avoid possible fuel discharge if any attempt is made to start the engine.

IDLE LEARN PROCEDURE

On models with 3.1L/V6-192 port fuel injected (PFI) engine, any time vehicle power has been interrupted the programed position of the IAC valve pintle is lost. The following procedure must be performed to update the ECM memory with the correct IAC valve pintle position for the vehicle and provide a stable idle speed.

1. Restore vehicle power.
2. Place transaxle in Park or Neutral position.
3. Connect TECH I scan tool to ALDL connector located under the left hand side of the dash panel.
4. Select "IAC System."
5. Select "Idle Learn" in the "Misc. Test" mode.
6. Proceed as directed.

ENGINE MOUNTS
REPLACE
FRONT MOUNT

1. Disconnect battery ground cable.

2. Remove engine mount nuts, then raise and support vehicle .
3. Support engine with suitable jack.
4. Remove inner fender shiel d.
5. Remove and discard engine mount bolts, **Fig. 1.**
6. Remove engine mount from vehicle.
7. Reverse procedure to install, using new engine mount bolts. Remove alignment bolt. Refer to **Fig. 1,** for tightening specifications. **If excessive force is required to remove alignment bolt, loosen transaxle adjusting bolts to align power train components.**

REAR MOUNT

1. Disconnect battery ground cable, then raise and support vehicle.
2. Support engine with suitable jack.
3. Remove motor mount nuts and attaching bolts, **Fig. 2.**
4. Reverse procedure to install. Refer to **Fig. 2,** for tightening specifications.

ENGINE
REPLACE

1. Disconnect battery ground cable and drain cooling system.
2. Remove air cleaner and duct assembly.
3. Remove exhaust crossover heat shield and the exhaust crossover pipe.
4. Remove serpentine belt, tensioner and idler, if equipped.
5. Disconnect radiator hose at engine.
6. Disconnect accelerator and T.V. cables at throttle valve.
7. Remove alternator and disconnect wiring harness at engine .
8. Loosen fuel filler cap to relieve tank vapor pressure, then disconnect fuel hoses and the coolant bypass and

overflow hoses at engine.
9. Raise and support vehicle, then remove right inner fender splash shield.
10. Remove harmonic balance and the flywheel cover.
11. Remove starter attaching bolts, disconnect electrical connectors at starter and remove starter.
12. Remove A/C compressor and its mounting bracket(s).
13. Disconnect exhaust pipe at rear of manifold.
14. Remove flex plate to torque converter attaching bolts and the transaxle to engine brace bolts.
15. Remove front and rear engine mount to frame attaching bolts.
16. Disconnect shift cable bracket at transaxle.
17. Remove lower bellhousing bolts and lower vehicle.
18. Disconnect heater hoses at engine.
19. Install suitable engine lifting device and support transaxle with suitable jack.
20. Remove transaxle attaching bolts.
21. Remove engine from vehicle.
22. Reverse procedure to install.

CYLINDER HEAD
REPLACE
REMOVAL

1. Disconnect battery ground cable.
2. Remove intake manifold and plenum assembly as described under "Intake Manifold, Replace."
3. Remove exhaust manifold as described under "Exhaust Manifold, Replace."
4. Disconnect wiring harness at cylinder head.
5. Remove spark plug wires and the spark plugs.

Fig. 1 references:

1	73 N·m (54 LB. FT.)
2	ENGINE MOUNT
3	83 N·m (61 LB. FT.)
4	ENGINE MOUNT BRACKET
5	64 N·m (47 LB. FT.)
6	100 N·m (74 LB. FT.)
7	68 N·m (50 LB. FT.)

Fig. 1   Front engine mount

Fig. 2 references:

1	61 N·m (45 LB. FT.)
2	R.H. BODY RAIL
3	COWL PANEL
4	ENGINE MOUNT BRACKET
5	ENGINE MOUNT BRACKET
6	54 N·m (40 LB. FT.)

Fig. 2   Rear engine mount

Head Torque Sequence

Fig. 3   Installing cylinder head

6. Remove rocker arm covers, rocker arm nuts, rocker arm balls, rocker arms and pushrods.
7. Remove cylinder head attaching bolts and the cylinder head.

INSTALLATION

Gasket surfaces on cylinder head and case must be clean and free of nicks or heavy scratches. Cylinder bolt threads in case and threads on cylinderhead bolts must be clean to obtain true torque.
1. Place gasket in position over dowel pins with note "This Side Up" showing and install cylinder head.
2. Coat cylinder head bolt threads with suitable sealant and install bolts.
3. Torque bolts in proper sequence, **Fig. 3.**
4. Install pushrods and loosely retain with rocker arms, ensuring lower ends of pushrods are in lifter seats.
5. Install spark plugs and wires.
6. Install intake and exhaust manifolds, then adjust valves as necessary.

INTAKE MANIFOLD
REPLACE

1. Disconnect battery ground cable.

2. Disconnect accelerator and T.V. cable bracket at plenum.
3. Disconnect brake vacuum pipe and plug harness at plenum.
4. Disconnect throttle body at plenum.
5. Disconnect EGR pipe at EGR valve, then remove plenum.
6. Disconnect fuel inlet and return pipes at fuel rail.
7. Remove serpentine belt, then disconnect alternator assembly and position aside.
8. Remove power steering lines at alternator bracket, then remove power steering pump attaching bolts and position aside.
9. Loosen alternator bracket attaching bolts.
10. Remove idle air to throttle body vacuum hose, then disconnect fuel injector electrical connectors.
11. Remove fuel rail and breather tube.
12. Remove plug wires at intake manifold.
13. Remove rocker arm covers and drain cooling system.
14. Remove radiator hose at thermostat outlet.
15. Disconnect coolant sensor and oil sending switch electrical connectors, then remove coolant sensor.

16. Remove filler neck to cylinder head bypass hose, then remove heater inlet pipe at manifold.
17. Remove intake manifold attaching bolts, then remove intake manifold.
18. Reverse procedure to install. Refer to **Fig. 4,** for intake manifold tightening sequence and specifications.

EXHAUST MANIFOLD
REPLACE

LEFT SIDE

1. Disconnect battery ground cable and remove air cleaner and inlet hose.
2. Drain cooling system, then remove coolant bypass pipe.
3. Disconnect crossover pipe at manifold, then remove manifold attaching bolts and the manifold.
4. Reverse procedure to install.

RIGHT SIDE

1. Disconnect battery ground cable and remove air cleaner.
2. Raise and support vehicle, then remove heat shield.
3. Remove exhaust pipe at crossover,

1	TIGHTEN IN PROPER SEQUENCE TO 20 N·m (15 LB. FT.), THEN RETIGHTEN TO 33 N·m (24 LB. FT.)
2	INTAKE MANIFOLD
3	GASKET
4	CYLINDER HEAD
5	SEALER

⑦ ④ ③ ⑥
⑧ ① ② ⑤

Fig. 4   Intake manifold installation

then lower the vehicle.
4. Disconnect oxygen sensor electrical connector.
5. Remove exhaust manifold attaching bolts, then remove manifold.
6. Reverse procedure to install, torque attaching nuts, bolts and screws to specifications.

ROCKER ARM COVERS
REPLACE

LEFT SIDE

1. Disconnect battery ground cable and drain cooling system.
2. Loosen bypass tube at intake, then remove rocker arm cover to air inlet attaching tube.
3. Remove rocker arm cover attaching bolts, then remove rocker arm cover.
4. Reverse procedure to install. Torque rocker arm cover attaching bolts to specifications.

RIGHT SIDE

1. Disconnect battery ground cable.
2. Remove brake booster vacuum line at bracket, then remove cable bracket at plenum.
3. Remove vacuum line bracket at cable bracket, then remove lines at alternator bracket stud.
4. Remove rear alternator attaching brace, then remove serpentine belt.
5. Remove alternator attaching bolts and position alternator aside.
6. Remove PCV valve, then remove rocker arm cover attaching bolts.

7. Remove spark plug wires, then remove rocker arm cover assembly.
8. Reverse procedure to install. Torque attaching bolts to specifications.

VALVE ADJUSTMENT

Vehicles are equipped with a non-adjustable rocker arm studs. If valve reconditioning is required, the non-adjustable rocker arm stud must be replaced with an adjustable rocker arm stud and the following procedure must be performed.
1. Remove rocker arm covers.
2. Crank engine until mark on torsional damper lines up with O mark on timing tab. The engine should also be in the No . 1 firing position. This can be determined by placing fingers on No. 1 rocker arms as mark on damper approaches O mark.
3. If valves are not moving, engine is in No. 1 firing position. If valves move as the mark comes up to the timing tab, engine is in No. 4 firing position and should be rotated one revolution to reach No. 1 position.
4. With engine in No. 1 firing position, adjust exhaust valves 1, 2 and 3 and intake valves 1, 5 and 6, as follows:
   a. Back out adjusting nut until lash is felt at pushrod, then turn in adjusting nut until all lash is removed.
   b. When lash has been removed, turn adjusting nut in additional 1 1/2 turns to center lifter plunger.
5. Crank engine one revolution until timing tab O mark and torsional damper

mark are again in alignment.
6. With the engine in this, the No. 4 firing position. adjust exhaust valves 4, 5 and 6 and intake valves 2, 3 and 4 as previously described.
7. Install rocker arm covers, then start engine and check timing and idle speed.

VALVE ARRANGEMENT
FRONT TO REAR

Right . . . . E-I-E-I-I-E
Left . . . . E-I-I-E-I-E

CAMSHAFT LIFT SPECIFICATIONS

Engine	Intake	Exhaust
3.1/V6-192	.2626	.2732

VALVE STEM OIL SEAL & VALVE SPRING
REPLACE

REMOVAL

1. Remove rocker arm cover, then the spark plug, rocker arm and pushrod oncylinder(s) being serviced.
2. Install air line adapter tool No. J-22794 or equivalent to spark plug port and apply compressed air to hold valves in place.
3. Using valve spring compressor tool No. J-26513-A or equivalent to compress valve spring, remove valve locks, valve caps, oil seal and valve spring and damper.
4. Remove valve stem oil seal.

INSTALLATION

1. Set valve spring and damper around valve guide boss.
2. Install a valve stem seal over the valve stem and valve guide base-inlet only.
3. Drop an oil seal and valve rotator over the exhaust, and a valve spring cap over the valve spring.
4. Compress spring using valve spring compressor tool No. J-26513-A or equivalent, install oil seal in lower groove of stem, ensuring seal is flat and not twisted.
5. Install valve locks and release compressor tool, ensuring locks seat properly in upper groove of valve stem. Use suitable grease as necessary to hold locks in place while releasing compressor tool.
6. Using tool J-23994 or equivalent, apply vacuum to valvecap to ensure no air leaks past seal.
7. Install spark plug, torquing to specifications.
8. Install and adjust valve mechanism.

Fig. 5   Installing front cover

Fig. 6   Valve timing marks

VALVE GUIDES

Valve guides are an integral part of the cylinder head and are not removable. If valve stem clearance becomes excessive, the valve guide should be reamed to the next oversize and the appropriate oversize valves installed. Valves are available in .003, .015 and .030 inch over sizes.

HYDRAULIC VALVE LIFTERS
REPLACE

1. Remove intake manifold as previously described.
2. Remove valve mechanism, then the valve lifters.
3. Install valve lifters. When installing new lifters, coat foot of valve lifters with Molykote or equivalent, ensuring lifter foot is convex.
4. Install intake manifold as previously described.
5. Install and adjust valve mechanism.

FRONT COVER
REPLACE

1. Disconnect battery ground cable and drain cooling system.
2. Remove serpentine belt and tensioner.
3. Disconnect alternator and position aside.
4. Disconnect power steering pump and position aside.
5. Raise and support vehicle, then re-

move inner splash shield.
6. Remove flywheel cover attaching bolts at transaxle, then remove flywheel cover.
7. Remove harmonic balancer with pulling tool No. J 24420-B or equivalent.
8. Remove starter assembly.
9. Remove serpentine belt idler pulley.
10. Remove oil pan as outlined under "Oil Pan, Replace."
11. Remove front cover lower attaching bolts.
12. Lower vehicle, then remove water pump attaching radiator hose.
13. Remove heater hose at cooling system fill pipe, then remove bypass and overflow hoses.
14. Remove water pump pulley, the remove spark plug wire shield at water pump.
15. Remove canister purge hose.
16. Remove upper front cover attaching bolts, then remove front cover, **Fig. 5.**
17. Reverse to install. Torque all attaching nuts, bolts or screws to specifications.

FRONT COVER OIL SEAL
REPLACE

1. Remove front wheel and tire assemblies.
2. Remove inner splash shield and torsional damper, then pry seal from cover using a suitable screwdriver. **Use caution not to damage crankshaft surface during seal removal.**

3. Install new seal using tool No. J 35468 or equivalent, so open end faces toward inside of cover, then drive seal into position using suitable tool.

TIMING CHAIN & SPROCKET
REPLACE

1. Remove crankcase front cover, refer to "Front Cover, Replace" procedure.
2. Place No. 1 cylinder at TDC and align timing marks on crankshaft and camshaft sprockets, **Fig. 6.**
3. Remove camshaft sprocket attaching bolts. Tap lower edge of sprocket with plastic mallet and remove sprocket and timing chain.
4. Align timing marks, **Fig. 6,** and install timing chain on sprockets.
5. Align dowel on camshaft with dowel hole on camshaft sprocket, then install sprocket to camshaft, using attaching bolts to to draw sprocket fully to camshaft. Torque attaching bolts to specification.
6. Lubricate timing chain with engine oil, then install front cover.

CAMSHAFT
REPLACE

1. Remove engine from vehicle, refer to "Engine, Replace" procedure.
2. Remove valve lifters, refer to "Hydraulic Valve Lifters, Replace" procedure.
3. Remove crankcase front cover, refer to "Front Cover, Replace" procedure.
4. Remove fuel pump and pushrod, then the timing chain and sprocket. Refer to "Timing Chain & Sprocket, Replace" procedure.
5. Remove camshaft. **Use caution not to damage bearings during camshaft removal.**
6. Reverse procedure to install. Coat camshaft lobes with GM EOS 1052367 or other suitable lubricant before installation.

Fig. 7 Piston & rod assembly

Fig. 8 Removing oil seal

Fig. 10 Oil pump assembly

Fig. 9 Installing oil seal

PISTON & ROD ASSEMBLY

There is a machined hole or cast notch in the top of all pistons. The piston assemblies should always be installed with the hole or notch toward front of engine, **Fig. 7.**

PISTON PINS & RINGS

Pistons and rings are available in standard and oversize. Piston pins are available in standard size only.

MAIN & ROD BEARINGS

Main and rod bearing are available in standard sizes and undersizes.

REAR MAIN BEARING OIL SEAL
REPLACE

1. Support engine using tool No. J 28467-A or equivalent, then remove transaxle assembly.
2. Remove flywheel assembly.
3. Remove oil seal as shown in **Fig. 8.** Use caution not to damage crankshaft surface with removal tool.
4. Check inside diameter of bore and crankshaft for nicks or burrs. Repair as required.
5. Apply oil to inside diameter of new seal, then install seal on mandrel of tool No. J-34686 until back of seal bottoms squarely against collar of tool, **Fig. 9.**
6. Align dowel pin of tool with dowel pin of crankshaft, then attach tool to crankshaft. **Torque** attaching screws to 45 inch lbs.
7. Turn "T" handle of tool so collar pushes seal into bore. Ensure seal is properly seated.
8. Loosen "T" handle of tool until it comes to a stop, then remove tool attaching screws. Ensure seal is seated squarely in bore.
9. Install flywheel and transaxle assembly.

OIL PAN
REPLACE

1. Disconnect battery ground cable.
2. Remove serpentine belt and belt tensioner.
3. Raise and support vehicle, then drain engine oil.
4. Remove starter assembly, then remove outer plastic flywheel and starter shield.
5. Remove inner metal flywheel shield.
6. Remove engine to frame mount attaching nuts as outlined under "Engine Mounts, Replace."
7. Lower vehicle and support engine using tool No. J 28467-A or equivalent.
8. Raise and support vehicle, then remove inner fender splash shield.
9. Remove oil pan attaching nuts and bolts, then remove oil pan.
10. Reverse procedure to install. Torque attaching nuts and bolts to specifications.

OIL PUMP SERVICE
REMOVAL

1. Remove oil pan, refer to "Oil Pan, Replace" procedure.
2. Remove pump to rear main bearing attaching bolt, then the pump and extension shaft.

DISASSEMBLE

1. Remove pump cover attaching bolts (7), **Fig. 10,** and pump cover (3). **Mark gear teeth to ensure correct position during assembly.**

2. Remove idler gear and drive gear (2), then the shaft from pump body (1).
3. Remove pressure regulator valve retaining pin (6), pressure regulator spring (5) and valve (4).
4. If pickup screen and pipe assembly need to be replaced, mount pump in a suitable vise, then remove pipe from pump cover. **Do not remove pickup screen from pipe. This is serviced as an assembly.**

CLEANING & INSPECTION

1. Wash all parts in suitable cleaning solvent, then dry with compressed air.
2. Inspect pump body and cover for cracks or excessive wear.
3. Inspect pump gears for damage or excessive wear. Pump gears and body are not serviced separately. If pump gears are defective, replace entire oil pump assembly.
4. Check drive gear shaft for looseness in the pump body.
5. Inspect in side of pump cover for wear that would permit oil to leak past ends of gears.
6. Inspect pickup screen and pipe assembly for looseness or damage.
7. Check pressure regulator valve for damage and proper fit.
8. Using a straightedge and feeler gauge, check clearances as shown in **Figs. 11 through 14.**
9. Install gears and measure in several places, gear lash should be within .0037-.0077 inch.
10. Measure depth and diameter of oil pump gear pocket, depth should be 1.202-1.20 5 inch and diameter should be 1.504-1.506 inch.
11. Measure gear side clearance, gear side clearance should be .003-.004 inch.
12. Measure gear end clearance, gear end clearance should be .002-.006 inch. **When determining pump serviceability based on end clearance, consider depth of wear pattern in pump cover.**

ASSEMBLY

1. Lubricate all internal parts with engine oil during assembly.
2. Install pump gears.
3. Prime engine oil galleries by removing

Fig. 11   Measuring oil pump gear lash

Fig. 12   Measuring gear side clearance

1	DEPTH OF POCKET
2	DIAMETER OF POCKET

Fig. 13   Measuring oil pump gear pocket

Fig. 14   Measuring oil pump end clearance

engine oil pump drive unit and rotate oil pump using suitable drill motor, socket and extension.
4. Install oil pump cover and gasket.
5. Install pressure regulator valve and spring, then install cotter pin or plug, if equipped.
6. If pipe assembly was removed, it should be replaced with a new part. Mount pump in suitable vise and apply suitable sealer to outside diameter of swaged end of pipe, then tap pipe in place using a suitable tool. **Loss of press fit condition could result in an air leak and loss of oil pressure. Also use caution not to twist, shear or collapse pipe during installation.**
7. Turn driveshaft by hand to ensure smooth operation.

INSTALLATION

1. Install pump and extension shaft with retainer to rear main bearing cap, aligning top end of hexagon extension shaft with hexagon socket of distributor drive gear.
2. Install pump to rear bearing cap bolt and torque to specifications.
3. Install oil pan, refer to "Oil Pan, Replace" procedure.

WATER PUMP
REPLACE

1. Disconnect battery ground cable, then

drain cooling system.
2. Disconnect serpentine belt at the water pump pulley.
3. Remove water pump pulley, then the water pump, **Fig. 15.**
4. Reverse procedure to install.

SERPENTINE DRIVE BELT
REPLACE

1. Remove belt guard.
2. Lift or rotate tensioner using a 1/2 inch breaker bar.
3. Remove serpentine drive belt.
4. Reverse procedure to install, routing belt as shown in **Fig. 16.**

SERPENTINE DRIVE BELT TENSIONER
REPLACE

1. Remove serpentine belt as described under "Serpentine Drive Belt, Replace."
2. Raise and support vehicle.
3. Remove inner splash shield, tensioner bolt and tensioner.
4. Reverse procedure to install, **Torquing** tensioner bolt to 35 ft. lbs.

COOLING SYSTEM BLEED

To ensure sufficient engine cooling, freezing and corrosion protection, maintain the protection level at −34°F or lower. Use a solution of antifreeze and water, ensuring solution is no more than 70 percent antifreeze.
1. Fill surge tank or radiator to base of filler neck, then attach pressure cap.
2. Block the drive wheel and apply parking brake.
3. **On models equipped with automatic transaxle,** place shifter in Park position.
4. **On models equipped with manual transaxle,** place transaxle in Neutral position.
5. **On all models,** start engine and allow to run until upper radiator hose is hot.
6. Stop engine, check level of coolant in surge tank or radiator.

Fig. 15   Water pump mounting

7. Allow engine to cool, then add coolant as necessary.

THERMOSTAT
REPLACE

1. Disconnect negative battery cable.
2. Drain coolant and remove air cleaner assembly.
3. Remove coolant outlet to inlet manifold attaching bolt and nut, coolant outlet and thermostat.
4. Reverse procedure to install.

FUEL PUMP
REPLACE

1. Loosen fuel filler cap to relieve tank vapor pressure, then disconnect battery ground cable.
2. Remove fuel tank as follows:
   a. Drain fuel tank, then raise and support vehicle. **Ensure additional support to the opposite end from which components are being replaced, to avoid personal injury.**
   b. Disconnect fuel tank harness from body harness electrical connectors.
   c. Remove ground wire attaching screw, if equipped.
   d. Remove tank meter assembly, filler and vent pipe hoses.
   e. Support fuel tank with suitable tool, then disconnect fuel tank attaching straps.
   f. Lower fuel tank, then remove fuel

A	INSERT BREAKER BAR HERE
1	GENERATOR
2	SERPENTINE BELT
3	WATER PUMP
4	AIR CONDITIONING COMPRESSOR
5	CRANKSHAFT
6	BELT TENSIONER
7	POWER STEERING PUMP

Fig. 16 Serpentine belt routing

1. BAR
2. PIPE, FUEL FEED
3. FITTING   BACK-UP
   WRENCH REQUIRED AT THIS ATTACHMENT
4. SEAL, O-RING
5. BRACKET, FUEL FILTER
6. FILTER, FUEL
7. SCREW — FULLY DRIVEN, SEATED AND
   NOT STRIPPED
8. PIPE ASM., FUEL
9. SEAT SPRING

Fig. 17 Fuel filter replacement. 1991

1. HOSE-PART OF FUEL SENDER
2. FUEL VAPOR PIPE
3. FUEL RETURN PIPE
4. FUEL FEED PIPE
5. FUEL FEED PIPE NUT
6. HOSE-PART OF FUEL SENDER
7. ABS AND FUEL SENDER HARNESS

Fig. 18 Fuel filter replacement. 1992-94

tank meter assembly and gasket using tool No. J 24187 or equivalent.

g. Remove sound insulators.

3. Remove fuel lever sending unit and pump assembly by turning cam lock ring counterclockwise. Lift assembly from fuel tank, then remove fuel pump from fuel lever sending unit.

4. Pull fuel pump up to attaching hose or pulsator while pulling outward away from bottom support. After pump assembly is clear of bottom support, remove assembly from rubber connector or pulsator. **Use caution not to damage rubber insulator and strainer during removal.**

5. Reverse procedure to install.

FUEL FILTER
REPLACE

1991

1. Release fuel system pressure as outlined under "Fuel System Pressure Relief."

2. Raise and support vehicle.

3. Disconnect fuel lines from filter, then remove filter, **Fig. 17.**

4. Reverse procedure to install.

1992-94

1. Release fuel system pressure as outlined under "Fuel System Pressure Relief."

2. Raise and support vehicle.

3. Using back-up wrench, remove filter fitting. If nylon fuel lines become kinked and cannot be straightened, they must be replace.

4. Twist quick-connect fitting 1/4 turn in each direction to loosen dirt within fitting.

5. Using compressed air, clean quick-connect fitting at ends of filter.

6. Disconnect quick-connect fittings by squeezing plastic tabs of male end connector and pulling apart.

7. Remove fuel filter, **Fig. 18.**

8. Reverse procedure to install.

TIGHTENING SPECIFICATIONS

Component	Torque/Ft. Lbs.
Camshaft Rear Cover	6-9
Camshaft Sprocket	21
Connecting Rod Nut	39
Crankshaft Balancer	76
Cylinder Head	③
Distributor hold-down	20-31
Drive Belt Tensioner Bolt	35
Engine Mount Bracket To Body Lower Bolt	74
Exhaust Crossover To Right Manifold	18
Exhaust Manifold	18
Front Cover	①
Front Engine Mount To Bracket Bolt	50
Front Engine Mount To Frame Bolt (Top)	54
Front Engine Mount To Bracket Bolt (Bottom)	61
Front Engine Mount Bracket Body Upper Bolt	74
Heat Shield	89④
Intake Manifold	13-25
Main Bearing Cap	63-83
Negative Battery Cable	11
Oil Level Indicator Nut	18

Component	Torque/Ft. Lbs.
Oil Pan	②
Oil Pump Drive	25
Oil Pump To Rear Bearing Cap	30
Rear Engine Mount To Engine Bolt	40
Rear Engine Bracket To Body Bolt	45
Rocker Arm Covers	89④
Rocker Arm Nuts	18
Spark Plugs	18
Thermostat Housing	15-23
Timing Chain Dampener	15
Torsional Dampener	67-85
Water Pump Pulley To Pump Bolts	15
Water Pump To Block	18
Water Pump To Front Cover Bolts	90④

①—8 mm bolts, 20 ft. lbs.; 10 mm bolts, 28 ft. lbs.
②—6 mm bolts, 71 inch lbs; 8 mm bolts, 18 ft.lbs.
③—Torque bolts in sequence to 33 ft. lbs., then turn an additional 90°.
④—Inch Lbs.

Clutch & Manual Transaxle

INDEX

ADJUSTMENTS

CLUTCH PEDAL

On these models, a hydraulic clutch system is used, **Fig. 1**. The system consists of a dash mounted master cylinder with integral reservoir, a transmission mounted slave cylinder and high pressure tubing to connect the two components.

The hydraulic clutch system provides automatic clutch adjustment, therefore, there is no provision for adjustment.

SHIFT CABLE

Isuzu Transaxle

Refer to **Fig. 2**, for exploded view of shifter cables.

Muncie Transaxle

Refer to **Fig. 3** for exploded view of shifter cables.

HYDRAULIC SYSTEM SERVICE

BLEEDING HYDRAULIC SYSTEM

1. Fill reservoir with a suitable DOT 3 type brake fluid.
2. Fully loosen bleeder screw located on slave cylinder near inlet connection.
3. While maintaining reservoir fluid level, allow fluid to flow from bleeder valve until a steady stream of fluid with no air bubbles is present, then tighten bleeder screw.
4. Fill reservoir to proper level, then start engine.
5. Depress clutch for approximately ten seconds, then select reverse gear. If no gear clash is present, system is satisfactory. If gear clash is present, repeat bleeding procedure.

INSPECTION

1. While observing clutch slave cylinder pushrod travel, have an assistant depress clutch pedal.
2. If slave cylinder pushrod moves .433 inch or more, hydraulic system is operating properly.
3. If slave cylinder pushrod did not move .433 inch, proceed as follows:
   a. Check clutch master cylinder fluid level. The clutch slave cylinder must be installed during this operation. Refill as necessary.
   b. If master cylinder requires fluid, check hydraulic system components for leakage. Remove rubber boots from cylinders and check for leakage past pistons. A slight wetting of piston and walls urfaces is acceptable.
   c. If excessive leakage is indicated, entire hydraulic system must be replaced.

Fig. 1 Hydraulic clutch assembly

1. LOCKING PIN
2. LEVER, TRANS.
3. 10 N·m (90 LBS. IN.)
4. 25 N·m (19 LBS. FT.)
5. CABLE ASM.
6. TRANSAXLE CONTROL ASM.

Fig. 2 Isuzu five speed manual transaxle shift cable adjustment

CLUTCH MASTER & ACTUATOR CYLINDERS, REPLACE

FOUR CYLINDER ENGINE
Removal

1. Disconnect negative battery cable.
2. Remove sound insulator from inside of vehicle.
3. Disconnect clutch master cylinder pushrod from clutch pedal.
4. Remove clutch master cylinder retaining nuts at front of dash and disconnect remote reservoir, if equipped.
5. Remove actuator retaining nuts at transaxle.
6. Remove hydraulic system as a unit from vehicle.

Installation

1. Install actuator cylinder to transaxle support bracket aligning pushrod into pocket on lever. **Torque** nuts evenly to 16 ft. lbs.
2. Install clutch master cylinder to front of dash. **Torque** nuts evenly to 16 ft. lbs. **Do not remove plastic pushrod retainer from actuator cylinder. Retainer will break off on first clutch pedal application.**
3. Connect remote reservoir, if equipped.
4. Remove pedal restrictor from pushrod, then lubricate pushrod bushing on clutch pedal.
5. Connect pushrod with clutch pedal and install retaining clip.
6. Install sound insulator.
7. Press clutch pedal down several times. This will break plastic retaining straps on actuator cylinder pushrod. **Do not remove plastic button on pushrod.**
8. Connect negative battery cable.

SIX CYLINDER ENGINE
Removal

1. Remove air intake duct from air cleaner.
2. Disconnect negative and positive battery cables from battery.
3. Remove left fender brace and battery.
4. Disconnect MAT sensor lead at air cleaner.
5. Disconnect mass air flow sensor lead, then remove PCV retaining clamp from air intake duct.
6. Remove clamp retaining air intake duct to throttle body.
7. Remove mass air flow mounting bolt and air cleaner bracket mounting bolts at battery tray.
8. Remove air cleaner, mass air flow sensor and air intake duct as an assembly.
9. Disconnect electrical lead at washer bottle, then remove attaching bolts and washer bottle.
10. Remove cruise control mounting bracket retaining nuts from strut tower, if equipped.
11. Remove sound insulator from inside of vehicle.
12. Disconnect clutch master cylinder pushrod from clutch pedal.
13. Remove clutch master cylinder retaining nuts at front of dash.
14. Remove actuator cylinder retaining nuts at transaxle.
15. Remove hydraulic system as a unit from vehicle.

Installation

1. Install actuator cylinder to transaxle support bracket aligning pushrod into pocket on lever. **Do not remove plastic pushrod retainer from actuator cylinder. Retainer will break off on first clutch pedal application. Torque** nuts evenly to 16 ft. lbs.
2. Install clutch master cylinder to front of dash. **Torque** nuts evenly to 16 ft. lbs.
3. Remove pedal restrictor from pushrod. Lubricate pushrod bushing on clutch pedal, then connect pushrod to clutch pedal and install retaining clip.
4. Check cruise control switch adjustment at clutch pedal. **If adjustment is necessary, do not exert an upward force on clutch pedal pad of more than 20 ft. lbs. or damage to master cylinder pushrod retaining ring may result.**
5. Install sound insulator.
6. Press clutch pedal down several

times. This will break plastic retaining straps on actuator cylinder pushrod. **Do not remove plastic button on pushrod.**

7. Install washer bottle.
8. Install air cleaner, mass air flow sensor and air intake duct.
9. Install clamp retaining air intake duct to throttle body.
10. Install PCV pipe retaining clamp.
11. Connect mass air flow and MAT sensor leads.
12. Install battery and left fender brace.
13. Connect positive and negative battery cables, then air intake duct to air cleaner.

CLUTCH
REPLACE

1. Disconnect battery ground cable.
2. Re move hush panel from driver's foot well, as required, then disconnect clutch master cylinder pushrod from clutch pedal.
3. Remove transaxle as outlined under "Manual Transaxle, Replace" procedure.
4. Mark position of pressure plate to flywheel to aid reassembly.
5. Gradually loosen pressure plate to flywheel attaching bolts until spring tension is relieved.
6. Support pressure plate and remove attaching bolts, pressure plate and driven disc, **Fig. 4.**
7. Clean pressure plate and flywheel mounting surfaces. Inspect bearing retainer outer surface of the transaxle.
8. Place pressure plate and driven disc in position and support with tool No. J-29074, **Fig. 5. The driven disc is installed with the damper springs offset toward the transaxle. Stamped letters found on the driven disc identify the "Flywheel Side."**
9. Install and gradually tighten the pressure plate to flywheel attaching bolts. Remove support tool.
10. Lubricate the release bearing outside diameter groove and inside diameter recess with lubricant 1051344 or equivalent.
11. Install transaxle.

MANUAL TRANSAXLE
REPLACE
FOUR CYLINDER ENGINE

1. Disconnect battery ground cable.
2. Install engine support fixture J-28467-A or equivalent, then raise engine enough to take pressure off motor mounts, **Fig. 6.**
3. Remove left sound insulator.
4. Remove clutch master cylinder pushrod from clutch pedal.
5. Remove wire harness at mount bracket.
6. Remove clutch slave cylinder from transaxle support bracket and position aside.

1. SHIFT CABLE
2. SELECTOR CABLE
3. CLIP
4. SCREW – 2 N·m (18 LBS. IN.)
5. GROMMET
6. CABLE CLAMP
7. NUT – 10 N·m (90 LBS. IN.)
8. STUD
9. NUT – 25 N·m (19 LBS. FT.)
10. LOCKING PIN

Fig. 3   Muncie five speed manual transaxle shift cable assembly

FLYWHEEL
DRIVEN PLATE ASSEMBLY
PRESSURE PLATE AND COVER ASSEMBLY
CLUTCH RELEASE BEARING
TRANSAXLE

Fig. 4   Clutch assembly

7. Remove transaxle mount and mount bracket attaching bolts.
8. Remove shift cables and retaining clamp at transaxle.
9. Remove ground cable at transaxle attaching bolts, then disconnect back-up switch electrical connector.
10. Raise and support vehicle, then drain transaxle fluid.
11. Remove left front wheel and inner splash shield.
12. Remove transaxle front strut and front strut bracket.
13. Remove clutch housing cover attaching bolts, then the vehicle speed sensor at transaxle.
14. Remove stabilizer shaft at left suspension support and control arm.
15. Remove left suspension support attaching bolts and swing aside.
16. Remove drive axles and left shaft at transaxle.
17. Position suitable jack under transaxle, then remove transaxle to engine attaching bolts.
18. Slide transaxle towards drivers side, away from engine, then lower transaxle from vehicle while guiding right drive axle out of transaxle.

19. Reverse procedure to install. When installing transaxle, carefully guide right hand drive axle shaft into transaxle bore as transaxle is being raised. The right hand drive axle shaft cannot be installed once the transaxle has been connected to the engine.

SIX CYLINDER ENGINE

1. Disconnect battery ground cable.
2. Install engine support fixture J-28467-A or equivalent, then raise engine enough to take pressure off motor mounts, **Fig. 6.**
3. Remove left sound insulator.
4. Remove clutch master cylinder pushrod from clutch pedal.
5. Remove air cleaner and air intake duct assembly.
6. Remove clutch slave cylinder from transaxle support bracket and position aside.
7. Remove transaxle mount through bolt, then raise and support vehicle.
8. Remove exhaust crossover bolts at RH manifold, then lower vehicle.
9. Remove left hand exhaust manifold, then the transaxle mount bracket.

Fig. 5   Aligning clutch disc & pressure plate

1. TOOL J-28467
2. THREAD ONTO STRUT ATTACHING BOLTS ABOVE NUTS — 3 PER SIDE

Fig. 6   Engine support fixture installation

10. Remove transaxle shift cables, then the upper transaxle to engine attaching bolts.
11. Remove transaxle vent tube
12. Raise and support vehicle, then remove left front tire and inner splash shield.
13. Remove transaxle strut and bracket.
14. Drain transaxle, then remove clutch housing cover attaching bolts.
15. Remove speedometer cable, then the stabilizer shaft at left suspension support and control arm.
16. Remove left hand suspension support attaching bolts and swing aside.
17. Remove left hand drive axle from transaxle.
18. Remove intermediate shaft housing to transaxle attaching bolts, then slide housing away from transaxle. Using a suitable tool, disconnect intermediate shaft from transaxle.
19. Position suitable jack under transaxle, then remove remaining transaxle to engine attaching bolts.
20. Lower transaxle assembly from vehicle.
21. Reverse procedure to install. When installing transaxle, carefully guide right hand drive axle shaft into transaxle bore as transaxle is being raised. The right hand drive axle shaft cannot be installed once the transaxle has been connected to the engine.

TIGHTENING SPECIFICATIONS

Component	Torque/Ft. Lbs.
Back-up Switch Assembly To Transaxle	24
Clutch Bleed Screw	17①
Clutch Cover To Flywheel	②
Clutch Cover To Transaxle	115①
Clutch Master Cylinder	16
Clutch Slave Cylinder Nut	16
Clutch Release Lever (Isuzu)	37
Front Transaxle Strut To Transaxle	50
Front Transaxle To Body Bolt	40
Rear Mount Bracket To Transaxle	40
Rear Transaxle Mount To Body	23
Shift Cable Grommet To Shroud	18①
Shift Control Box To Transaxle (Isuzu)	13
Shift Control To Floor	18

Component	Torque/Ft. Lbs.
Shift Linkage Retainer To Transaxle Case	17
Shift Retainer To Transaxle Case (Isuzu)	18
Shift Shaft Lever Nut	61
Speedometer/VSS Housing To Transaxle	84①
Transaxle Mount To Transaxle	37
Transaxle Shift Cable Bracket To Cables	90①
Transaxle Shift Lever To Cable Stud	18
Transaxle To Engine Bolts and Studs (Isuzu)	55
Transaxle To Engine Nut	55
Transaxle To Engine Stud	106①
Transaxle To Engine Stud/Bolts	55
Wheel Lug Nuts	100

①—Inch lbs.
②—1991, 22 ft. lbs.; 1992-94, 18 ft. lbs. plus 30° turn.

Rear Axle & Suspension

INDEX

1	CONTROL ARM BUSHING
2	AXLE ASSEMBLY
3	SPRING INSULATOR
4	SHOCK ABSORBER

Fig. 1   Rear suspension

DESCRIPTION

The rear suspension, **Fig. 1**, is a semi-independent type suspension consisting of an axle assembly with trailing arms and twisting cross beam, coil springs and double action shock absorbers. A stabilizer bar is available and is attached to the inside of the axle beam and to the lower end of the control arms. A single unit hub and bearing assembly is bolted to each end of the axle assembly. The hub and bearing assembly is a sealed, non-serviceable unit and must be replaced as an assembly.

REAR AXLE
REPLACE

1. Raise vehicle and support vehicle. Support rear suspension with suitable jack.
2. Disconnect stabilizer bar at axle assembly, if equipped, **Fig. 2.**
3. Remove rear wheel assembly and brake drum. Do not hammer on brake drum since damage to bearings may result.
4. Remove shock absorber to lower mounting bracket attaching bolts, then disconnect shock absorbers from axle assembly, **Fig. 2.**
5. Disconnect parking brake cable and brake lines at axle brackets.
6. Carefully lower rear axle assembly and remove coil springs and insulators.

7. Remove control arm to underbody bracket bolts, then lower the axle assembly and remove from vehicle.
8. Remove hub to rear axle attaching bolts, then the hubs, bearings and backing plates from rear axle assembly.
9. Reverse procedure to install and bleed brake system.

1. STABILIZER SHAFT	9. NUT	17. NUT — 83 N·m (61 LBS. FT.)
2. INSULATOR	10. BOLT — 18 N·m (13 LBS. FT.)	18. TAB NUT
3. CLAMP	11. AXLE	19. BOLT — 47 N·m (35 LBS. FT.)
4. UPPER SPACER	12. BUMPER	20. SHOCK ABSORBER
5. LOWER SPACER	13. SPRING	21. MOUNT
6. BOLT	14. INSULATOR	22. RETAINER
7. NUT — 22 N·m (16 LBS. FT.)	15. UNDERBODY	23. NUT — 29 N·m (21 LBS. FT.)
8. CLAMP	16. WASHER	24. NUT — 17 N·m (13 LBS. FT.)

Fig. 2   Exploded view of rear suspension

HUB & BEARING
REPLACE

1. Raise and support vehicle, then remove wheel and tire assembly and brake drum. **Do not hammer brake drum since damage to bearing may result.**

1	CENTER BRAKE PIPE	5	SPRING INSULATOR
2	BRAKE HOSE	6	SPRING
3	BRAKE PIPE BRACKET	7	COMPRESSION BUMPER
4	UNDERBODY	8	AXLE ASM.
		9	15mm MAX. (.594")
		10	SPRING
		11	SPRING STOP PART OF SPRING SEAT.

VIEW A (BOTH SPRINGS)

Fig. 3 Coil spring installation

1. J-29376-1
2. J-29376-2
3. J-29376-4
4. J-29376-6
5. J-29376-7
6. J-21474-18
7. J-21474-19
8. SLOT SOLID BUSHINGS WITH HACKSAW TO ALLOW J-29376-6 TO ENGAGE BUSHINGS.
9. REAR AXLE ASSEMBLY
10. CONTROL ARM BUSHING
11. TO PROPERLY INDEX BUSHING ON INSTALLATION, ALIGN ARROWS ON J-29376-1 AND J-29376-4

Fig. 4 Control arm bushing removal & installation

2. Remove four hub/bearing assembly to rear axle attaching bolts, then the hub/bearing assembly from axle. **The upper rear hub attaching bolt may not clear brake shoe when removing hub and bearing assembly. Partially remove hub and bearing assembly prior to removing this bolt.**
3. Reverse procedure to install. Torque hub attaching bolts to specification. **Use care not to drop hub/bearing assembly since damage to bearing may result.**

SHOCK ABSORBER
REPLACE

1. Open deck lid, then remove trim cover and shock absorber upper retaining nut.
2. Raise rear of vehicle and support rear axle using a suitable jack.
3. Remove shock absorber lower attaching bolt, then disconnect shock absorber from mounting bracket, **Fig. 2.** Remove shock absorber from vehicle.

4. Reverse procedure to install. Torque attaching bolt to specification.

COIL SPRING
REPLACE

1. Raise and support rear of vehicle. Support rear axle using a suitable jack.
2. Remove wheel and tire assemblies.
3. Remove brake line bracket attaching bolts from frame, **Fig. 2,** and allow brake lines to hang freely.
4. Remove shock absorber to lower mounting bracket bolts, then disconnect shock absorbers from axle assembly. **Do not suspend rear axle by brake hoses since damage to hoses may result.**
5. Carefully lower rear axle assembly and remove springs and insulators.
6. Reverse procedure to install. Position ends of upper coil in seat of body and within limits shown in **Fig. 3.**

CONTROL ARM BUSHING
REPLACE

1. Raise rear of vehicle and support rear axle under front side of spring seat using a suitable jack.
2. Remove wheel and tire assembly.
3. If right hand side bushing is to be replaced, disconnect brake line bracket from body. If left hand side bushing is to be replaced, disconnect brake line bracket from frame and parking brake cable at hook guide.
4. Remove control arm to mounting bracket attaching nut, bolt and washer, then allow control arm to rotate downward.
5. The bushing can now be replaced using tools shown in **Fig. 4.** When installing bushing, the arrow on the installer must align with arrow on the receiver, **Fig. 4.**
6. Reverse procedure to complete installation. **The control arm attaching bolt must be torqued after vehicle is lowered to floor and is in its standing height position.** Torque attaching bolt to specifications.

TIGHTENING SPECIFICATIONS

Component	Torque/Ft. Lbs.	Component	Torque/Ft. Lbs.
Axle To Body Bracket	68	Shock Absorber Mount To Body	13
Brake Line Bracket To Axle	11	Shock Absorber To Mount	21
Brake Line Bracket To Frame	8	Stabilizer Shaft Clamp Bolts At Axle	13
Hub & Bearing Assembly	37	Stabilizer Shaft Clamp Nuts	16
Shock Absorber Bolt At Axle	35	Wheel Lug Nuts	100

Front Suspension & Steering

INDEX

DESCRIPTION

The front suspension, **Fig. 1**, on these vehicles is of the MacPherson strut design. The lower control arms pivot from the lower side rails through rubber bushings. The upper end of the strut is isolated by a rubber mount incorporating a non-serviceable bearing for wheel turning. The tie rods connect to the steering arm on the strut, below the spring seat. The lower end of the steering knuckle pivots on a ball stud which is retained to the lower control arm by rivets and is secured to the steering knuckle with a nut and cotter pin. The sealed wheel bearings are integral with the hub and are serviced as an assembly.

WHEEL BEARING REPLACE

REMOVAL

1. Raise and support vehicle.
2. Remove tire and wheel assembly, then install modified outer seal protector No. J34754 or equivalent, **Fig. 2.**
3. Insert a drift punch through the rotor, **Fig. 3,** then remove axle shaft nut and washer.
4. Remove ball joint, then using tool No. J 28733-A or equivalent, disengage axle from hub and bearing assembly.
5. **On all models,** move axle shaft inward, then remove caliper attaching bolts and support caliper.
6. Remove brake rotor, then hub and bearing assembly attaching bolts.
7. Remove hub and bearing assembly.

INSTALLATION

1. Install hub and bearing assembly, torque attaching bolts to specification.
2. Install hub and bearing seal, then the brake rotor.
3. Install caliper, torque attaching bolts to specification.
4. Move axle shaft outward, then insert drift punch through rotor, **Fig. 3.**
5. Install washer and new shaft nut, torque shaft nut to specification.
6. Install ball joint, then remove drift punch and seal protector.
7. Install tire and wheel assembly, then lower vehicle.

1.	COVER	13.	NUT	25.	BOLT	37.	SUPPORT
2.	NUT	14.	PIN	26.	COVER	38.	BOLT
3.	NUT	15.	SEAL	27.	BOLT	39.	NUT
4.	MOUNT	16.	HUB	28.	BALL JOINT	40.	BOLT
5.	SEAT	17.	SHIELD	29.	RIVET	41.	WASHER
6.	INSULATOR	18.	BOLT	30.	GROMMET	42.	AXLE
7.	BUMPER	19.	WASHER	31.	WASHER	43.	SPACER
8.	SPRING	20.	NUT	32.	BOLT	44.	NUT
9.	INSULATOR	21.	WASHER	33.	ARM	45.	SHAFT
10.	STRUT	22.	ROTOR	34.	BUSHING	46.	NUT
11.	NUT	23.	KNUCKLE	35.	BOLT	47.	INSULATOR
12.	SEAL	24.	CALIPER	36.	BOLT	48.	CLAMP

Fig. 1 Exploded view of front suspension

BALL JOINT INSPECTION

1. Raise and support vehicle so that suspension is allowed to hang free.
2. Grasp wheel and tire assembly at top and bottom, then rock top of wheel and tire assembly inward and outward.
3. While rocking wheel and tire assembly, observe movement between steering knuckle and control arm. If

[1] REMOVE TABS
[2] J 34754 DRIVE AXLE SEAL PROTECTOR

Fig. 2 Modified outer seal protector

1. DRIFT PUNCH
2. 6 POINT DEEP WELL SOCKET

Fig. 3 Removing and installing shaft nut

BOLT MUST BE INSTALLED IN DIRECTION SHOWN

Fig. 4 Assembling lower ball joint to lower control arm

1. CONTROL ARM
2. SUSPENSION SUPPORT
3. BOLT – 83 N·m (61 LBS. FT.)
4. WASHER
5. NUT
6. BOLT – 90 N·m (66 LBS. FT.) TIGHTEN FIRST
7. BOLT – 88 N·m (65 LBS. FT.) TIGHTEN SECOND
8. BOLT – 88 N·m (65 LBS. FT.) TIGHTEN THIRD

Fig. 5 Replacing lower control arm

any horizontal movement is present, replace ball joint.
4. If ball joint is disconnected from steering knuckle, use finger to try to twist ball joint in its socket. If ball joint can be twisted in its socket, replace ball joint.

BALL JOINT
REPLACE

1. Raise and support vehicle, then remove wheel and tire.
2. Install modified tool No. J 34754 or equivalent, then remove ball joint attaching cotter pin.
3. Remove ball joint stud retaining nut, then, using tool No. J-38892, or equivalent, separate ball joint from steering knuckle.

4. Using a 1/8 inch drill, drill pilot holes completely through the rivets. Using a 1/2 inch drill, drill final holes through rivets to ensure fitting of new ball joint.
5. Loosen stabilizer shaft assembly bushing attaching nut.
6. Remove ball joint from steering knuckle and control arm.
7. Assemble new ball joint to lower control arm with bolts provided in service package, **Fig. 4**. Torque bolts to specification.
8. Insert ball joint stud into steering knuckle and torque nut to specifications.
9. Install wheel and tire.

CONTROL ARM
REPLACE

1. Raise and support vehicle, then re-

move wheel and tire.
2. Disconnect stabilizer bar at lower control arm and control arm support.
3. Install modified seal protector tool No. J 34754 or equivalent.
4. Using tool No. No. J 38892, or equivalents, separate ball joint from steering knuckle.
5. Remove control arm support to chassis retaining bolts and remove control arm support and control arm as an assembly.
6. Separate control arm from support, then using tool Nos. J29792-1 and J29792-2 or equivalent, remove bushings from control arm.
7. Lubricate new bushings and install into control arm using tool Nos. J29792-1, J29792-2 and J29792-3 or equivalent.
8. Attach lower control arm to control arm support. **Torque** pivot bolts to 61 ft. lbs.
9. Install control arm support to chassis. Refer to **Fig. 5**, for attaching bolt torques.
10. Reverse procedure to complete installation. Check toe setting and adjust as required.

STEERING KNUCKLE
REPLACE

1. Raise and support vehicle, then remove wheel and tire.
2. Remove front hub and bearing as outlined under "Wheel Bearing, Replace" procedure.
3. Using tool No. J-38892, or equivalent, separate ball joint from steering knuckle.
4. Remove strut to steering knuckle attaching bolts, then disconnect strut from steering knuckle.
5. Assemble strut to new steering knuckle and install attaching bolts finger tight.
6. Insert ball joint stud into steering knuckle and torque stud nut to specification.
7. Torque strut to steering knuckle bolts to specification.
8. Reverse removal procedure to complete installation.

1. STABILIZER SHAFT
2. CLAMP
3. INSULATOR
4. NUT
5. SUSPENSION SUPPORT
6. BOLT
7. WASHER
8. GROMMET
9. SPACER
10. NUT
11. CONTROL ARM

Fig. 6   Stabilizer bar installation

1. STRUT ASSEMBLY
2. STEERING KNUCKLE
3. BOLT
4. NUT - 180 N.m (133 LBS. FT.)
5. SUPPORT
6. STRUT MOUNT COVER
7. NUT - 24 N.m (18 LBS. FT.)

Fig. 7   Installing strut assembly

STABILIZER BAR
REPLACE

1. Raise and support vehicle, allowing control arms to hang freely.
2. Remove left front wheel and tire assembly.
3. Disconnect stabilizer bar at control arms and control arm supports.
4. Disconnect stabilizer bar from control arms, **Fig. 6**.
5. Loosen front and remove rear and center bolts from suspension support

assembly. Lower support enough to allow stabilizer bar removal.
6. Remove stabilizer bar with insulators.
7. Reverse procedure to install. Torque suspension support assembly in a manner which will allow front suspension to hang free.

STRUT ASSEMBLY
REPLACE

1. Raise hood and remove strut protective cap and three strut to body attaching nuts.
2. Raise and support vehicle, support suspension using suitable jack stands.
3. Remove wheel and tire assembly, then install modified inner drive joint boot protector tool No. J-347 54
4. Using tool J-24319, disconnect tie rod from strut assembly.
5. Remove strut to steering knuckle attaching bolts, **Fig. 7**, then remove strut from vehicle.
6. Reverse procedure to install.

STRUT ASSEMBLY
SERVICE

DISASSEMBLY

1. Position strut compressor tool No. J-34013 in holding fixture tool No.

Fig. 8   Assembling strut unit

J-3289-20, or equivalents.
2. Position strut in strut compressor, then compress strut approximately $1/2$ of its height. Use care not to bottom spring or damper rod.
3. Remove nut from strut dampener shaft, then position guide rod J-34013-27 on dampener shaft. Use guide rod J-34013-27 to position dampener shaft down through bearing cap while compressing coil spring.

1. STEERING GEAR ASSEMBLY
2. L.H. CLAMP – HORIZONTAL SLOT AT TOP
3. R.H. CLAMP – HORIZONTAL SLOT AT TOP
4. NUT – 30 N·m (22 LBS. FT.) – HAND START ALL NUTS. TIGHTEN LEFT SIDE CLAMP NUTS FIRST, THEN TIGHTEN RIGHT SIDE NUTS.
5. STUD – 20 N·m (15 LBS. FT.) AFTER SECOND REUSE OF STUD, THREAD LOCKING KIT NO. 1052624 MUST BE USED.
6. NUT – 50 N·m (35 LBS. FT.)
   75 N·m (50 LBS. FT.) MAXIMUM TO INSTALL COTTER PIN.
7. COTTER PIN

Fig. 9   Power rack & pinion steering gear removal

4. Remove components from coil strut unit.

ASSEMBLY

1. Position bearing cap on strut compressor.
2. Position strut to strut compressor and install compressor bottom locking pin.
3. Extend dampener shaft and install clamp tool No. J-34013-20 or equivalent, to hold shaft in position, **Fig. 8.**
4. Position spring over dampener, then position strut to strut compressor upper locking pin hole and install pin.
5. Install upper insulator, shield, bumper and upper spring seat. The flat on the upper spring seat should face in the same direction as the centerline of the strut assembly spindle, **Fig. 8.**
6. Install guide rod J-34013-27 onto dampener shaft, the compress strut unit until dampener shaft threads are visible. Remove guide rod and install retaining nut.
7. While holding dampener shaft in position with a suitable wrench, torque retaining nut to specification. After tightening nut, remove clamp from dampener shaft clamp J-34013-20.

POWER STEERING GEAR
REPLACE

1. Disconnect battery ground cable .
2. Remove left hand sound insulator.
3. From under instrument panel, pull downward on steering column seal, then remove upper pinch bolt from flexible coupling.
4. Disconnect pressure line from steering gear and remove screw attaching line bracket to cowl.

5. Raise and support front of vehicle, then remove both front wheel and tire assemblies.
6. Disconnect tie rods from struts using tool No. J24319-01, then lower vehicle.
7. Remove steering gear mounting clamps, **Fig. 9.**
8. Move steering gear slightly forward, then disconnect return line from gear and drain power steering fluid.
9. Remove lower pinch bolt from flexible coupling, then detach coupling from steering gear stub shaft and remove dash seal.
10. Raise and support front of vehicle, then remove splash shield from left inner fender.
11. Place steering knuckle and hub assembly into the full left turn position, then remove steering gear through access hole in left hand inner fender.
12. Reverse procedure to install, noting the following:
    a. If steering gear mounting clamps have backed out during removal, install double nuts on stud and **Torque** to 22 ft. lbs.
    b. **Torque** coupling to stub shaft pinch bolt to 30 ft. lbs.
    c. Torque pressure and return line fittings to specifications.

POWER STEERING PUMP
REPLACE

1. Disconnect battery ground cable.
2. Remove serpentine belt.
3. Remove power steering pump attaching pressure lines.

4. Remove power steering pump attaching bolts.
5. Remove pump assembly, then transfer power steering pump pulley.
6. Reverse to install. Torque attaching bolts to specifications.

MANUAL STEERING GEAR
REPLACE

1. Disconnect battery ground cable.
2. Remove left hand sound insulator.
3. From under instrument panel, pull downward on steering column seal, then remove upper pinch bolt from flexible coupling.
4. Raise and support front of vehicle, then remove both front wheel and tire assemblies.
5. Disconnect tie rods from struts using tool No. J24319-01, then lower vehicle.
6. Remove steering gear mounting clamps, **Fig. 9.**
7. Move steering gear assembly slightly forward, then remove lower pinch bolt from flexible coupling and detach coupling from steering gear stub shaft.
8. Remove dash panel seal from steering gear.
9. Raise and support front of vehicle, then remove splash shield from left inner fender.
10. Place left hand knuckle and hub assembly in the full left turn position, then remove steering gear through access hole in left hand inner fender.
11. Reverse procedure to install. Torque attaching nuts, bolts and screws to specifications.

TIGHTENING SPECIFICATIONS

Component	Torque/Ft. Lbs.
Ball Joint To Knuckle	41-50
Caliper Bolts	38
Control Arm Pivot Bolt	61
Hub & Bearing Assembly	70
Hub Nut	185
Inner Tie Rod End Bolts	65
Power Coupling To Steering Column	30
Power Coupling To Stub Shaft	30
Power Rack & Pinion Mounts	22
Power Steering Return Lines	19
Stabilizer Shaft To Control Arm	13
Stabilizer To Support Assembly	16
Steering Knuckle To Strut Assembly	133
Strut Assembly To Body	18
Strut Cartridge Retaining Nut	65
Suspension Support Assembly	①
Tie Rod Pinch Bolts	41
Tie Rod To Steering Knuckle	37
Tie Rod To Strut	37
Wheel Lug Nuts	100

① —Torque suspension support
assembly center bolts to 66 ft. lbs.;
then front bolts to 65 ft. lbs; then
rear bolts to 65 ft. lbs.

Wheel Alignment

INDEX

FRONT WHEEL ALIGNMENT

CASTER ADJUSTMENT

Caster is not adjustable. If caster angle is not within specifications, inspect for suspension support misalignment or front suspension damage.

CAMBER ADJUSTMENT

Toe setting is the only adjustment normally required. However, in special circumstances, such as damage due to road hazard or collision, camber may be adjusted by modifying the strut assembly.

1. Secure bottom of strut assembly in a suitable vise.
2. Enlarge bottom holes in outer flanges with a round file until holes in outer flanges match slots in inner flanges, **Fig. 1.**
3. Connect strut to steering knuckle and install bolts finger tight.
4. Grasp top of tire firmly, then move tire inboard or outboard until correct camber reading is obtained. Tighten retaining bolts enough to secure camber setting.
5. Remove wheel and tire and tighten strut to steering knuckle retaining bolts. **Torque** strut to steering knuckle attaching bolt to 133 ft. lbs.

TOE-OUT ADJUSTMENT

Toe-out is controlled by tie rod position. Adjustment is made by loosening the clamp bolts at the steering knuckle end of the tie rods and rotating the rods to obtain proper toe setting, **Fig. 2.** After correct toe setting is obtained, tighten clamp bolts. **Torque** clamp bolts to 41 ft. lbs.

VEHICLE RIDE HEIGHT

Refer to **Figs. 3 and 4,** for ride height measurements and **Fig. 5,** for specifications. When checking ride height measurements, fuel tank should be full, tires should be at correct pressure, front seat should be rearward position, truck should be empty except for spare tire and jack and vehicle should be on level ground. If fuel tank is not full, add weight to trunk to compensate for amount fuel vehicle is below the full level.

Prior to checking ride height, lift front bumper upward approximately 1.5 inches and gently release (3 times), then check front ride height. Push front bumper downward approximately 1.5 inches and gently release (3 times), then recheck front ride height. Average of both readings to determine vehicle ride height. Check rear ride height in same manner, lifting and pushing rear bumper.

Fig. 1 Modifying strut bracket to adjust camber

A ADJUST TOE SETTING HERE

B LOOSEN CLAMP BOLTS TO ADJUST TOE. RETIGHTEN TO 47 N·m (35 LB. FT.)

1 OUTER TIE ROD

2 STRUT DAMPER

Fig. 2 Adjusting toe

Fig. 3 Vehicle ride height measurement locations. 1991 models

Fig. 4 Vehicle ride height measurement locations. 1992-94 models

Year	Make & Model	Tire Size	Engine Liter/CID	Ride Height Measurements In Inches ①		
				Dimension Z	Dimension J	Dimension K
1991-94	Cavalier Station Wagon	185/75R14	2.2L/4-134	3.62	9.53	9.65
		195/70R14	2.2L/4-134	3.78	9.53	9.65
		195/70R14	3.1L/V6-192	3.82	9.53	9.65
	Cavalier Coupe & Sedan	185/75R14	2.2L/4-134	3.42	9.26	9.13
		195/70R14	2.2L/4-134	3.58	9.26	9.13
		195/70R14	3.1L/V6-192	3.62	9.26	9.13
	Cavalier Z34	205/60R15	3.1L/V6-192	3.58	9.26	9.13
	Sunbird LE Coupe & Sedan, Sunbird S Coupe	185/75R14	2.0L/4-121	3.42	9.26	9.13
		195/70R14	2.0L/4-121	3.58	9.26	9.13
		195/70R14	3.1L/V6-192	3.62	9.26	9.13
	Sunbird LE Convertible	185/75R14	2.0L/4-121	3.46	9.26	9.13
		195/70R14	2.0L/4-121	3.62	9.26	9.13
		195/70R14	3.1L/V6-192	3.66	9.26	9.13
	Sunbird GT	215/60R14	3.1L/V6-192	3.86	9.26	9.13
		205/60R15	3.1L/V6-192	3.58	9.26	9.13
	Cavalier Station Wagon	185/75R14	2.2L/4-134	9/32	9.53	9.65
		195/70R14	2.2L/4-134	7/16	9.53	9.65
		195/70R14	3.1L/V6-192	31/64	9.53	9.65
	Cavalier Convertible	185/75R14	All	5/64	9.26	9.13
	Cavalier Coupe & Sedan	195/70R14	All	5/64	9.26	9.13
	Cavalier Z34	205/60R15	3.1L/V6-192	15/64	9.26	9.13
	Sunbird Except GT Series	185/75R14	All	5/64	9.26	9.13
		195/70R14	All	13/64	9.26	9.13
		195/65R15	All	9/32	9.26	9.13
	Sunbird GT	205/60R15	All	15/64	9.26	9.13

①—Maximum variation side to side and
front to rear is ¾ inch.

Fig. 5 Vehicle ride height specifications

CHEVROLET BERETTA & CORSICA (L Cars)

INDEX OF SERVICE OPERATIONS

NOTE: Refer To The Rear Of This Manual For Vehicle Manufacturer's Special Service Tool Suppliers.

INDEX OF SERVICE OPERATIONS-Continued

Specifications
GENERAL ENGINE SPECIFICATIONS

Year	Engine Liter/CID ①	Engine VIN Code ②	Fuel System	Bore & Stroke	Compression Ratio	Net H.P. @ RPM	Maximum Torque Ft. Lbs. @ RPM	Normal Oil Pressure, psi
1991	2.2L/4-134	G	MPFI	3.50 x 3.46	9.0	95 @ 5200	120 @ 3200	63-77
	2.3L/4-138	A	MPFI	3.62 x 3.35	10.0	180 @ 6200	160 @ 5000	15-30
	3.1L/V6-192	T	MPFI	3.50 x 3.31	8.8	135 @ 4200	180 @ 3600	15④
1992-93	2.2L/4-134	4	MPFI	3.50 x 3.46	8.85	—	—	63-77③
	2.3L/4-138	A	MPFI	3.62 x 3.35	10.0	180 @ 6200	160 @ 5000	15-30
	3.1L/V6-192	T	MPFI	3.50 x 3.31	8.8	140 @ 4200	185 @ 3600	15④
1994	2.2L/4-134	4	MPFI	3.50 x 3.46	9.0	120 @ 5200	130 @ 4000	63-77⑤
	2.3L/4-138	A	MPFI	3.63 x 3.35	10.0	170 @ 6200	150 @ 5200	30⑥
	3.1L/V6-192	T	MPFI	3.50 x 3.31	9.6	160 @ 5200	185 @ 4000	—

①—CID-cubic inch displacement.
②—The eighth digit denotes engine code.
③—At 1200 RPM.
④—At 1100 RPM.
⑤—At 2000 RPM.

TUNE UP SPECIFICATIONS

Year & Engine/ V.I.N. Code ①	Spark Plug Gap	Ignition Timing BTDC				Curb Idle Speed ③		Fast Idle Speed		Fuel Pump, psi
		Firing Order Fig. ②	Man. Trans.	Auto. Trans.	Mark Fig.	Man. Trans.	Auto. Trans.	Man. Trans.	Auto. Trans.	
1991										
2.2L/4-134/G	.035	④	③	③	⑥	⑦	⑦	⑦	⑦	9–13⑧
2.3L/4-138/A	.035	C	⑤	—	⑥	⑦	—	⑦	—	51⑩
3.1L/V6-192/T	.045	⑨	③	③	⑥	⑦	⑦	⑦	⑦	40.5–47⑩
1992-93										
2.2L/4-134/4	.035	④	③	③	⑥	⑦	⑦	⑦	⑦	43–47
2.3L/4-138/A	.035	C	⑤	—	⑥	⑦	—	⑦	—	51⑩
3.1L/V6-192/T	.045	⑨	③	③	⑥	⑦	⑦	⑦	⑦	40.5–47⑩
1994										
2.2L/4-134/4	.035	④	③	③	⑥	⑦	⑦	⑦	⑦	43–44
2.3L/4-138/A	.035	C	⑤	—	⑥	⑦	—	⑦	—	43
3.1L/V6-192/T	.045	⑨	③	③	⑥	⑦	⑦	⑦	⑦	—

① —The eighth digit of Vehicle Identification Number (V.I.N.) denotes engine code.

② —Before removing wires from distributor cap, determine location of No. 1 wire in cap, as distributor position may have been altered from that shown at the end of this chart.

③ —Not adjustable.

④ —Cylinder numbering front to rear, 1, 2, 3, 4. Firing order 1-3-4-2. Refer to Fig. A for spark plug wire connections at coil unit.

⑤ —Computer controlled, no adjustment.

⑥ —Equipped w/crankshaft position sensor.

⑦ —Idle speeds are controlled by the idle air control assembly.

⑧ —Wrap shop towel around fuel hose to steel line connection in engine compartment to prevent fuel spillage. Disconnect fuel hose from steel line and connect suitable fuel pressure gauge. Ensure gauge connections are tight, then start engine & check fuel pressure readings.

⑨ —Cylinder numbering left to right as viewed from front of vehicle, front bank 2, 4, 6; rear bank 1, 3, 5. Firing order, 1-2-3-4-5-6. Refer to Fig. B for spark plug wire connections at coil unit.

⑩ —With shop towel wrapped around fuel pressure valve to prevent fuel spillage, connect a suitable fuel pressure gauge to fuel pressure valve. Check fuel pressure with ignition switch On, engine not running.

Fig. A

Fig. B

IGNITION COIL AND MODULE ASM.

FIRING ORDER 1—3—4—2

Fig. C

WHEEL ALIGNMENT SPECIFICATIONS
FRONT WHEEL

Year	Model	Caster Angle, degrees		Camber Angle, degrees				Toe degrees
		Limits	Desired	Limits		Desired		
				Left	Right	Left	Right	
1991–92	①	+.4 to +1.9	+1.15	+.6 to +.8	+.6 to +.8	+.7	+.7	0
	②	+.4 to +1.9	+1.15	-.8 to +.4	-.8 to +.4	-.2	-.2	0
1993–94	①	+.2 to +2.2	+1.2	−.7 to +.7	−.7 to +.7	0	0	0
	③	+.2 to +2.2	+1.2	−.85 to +.55	−.85 to +.55	−.15	−.15	0

① —Except GTZ.
② —GTZ.

REAR WHEEL

Year	Model	Camber Angle, Degrees				Toe Degrees ①
		Limits		Desired		
		Left	Right	Left ①	Right ①	
1991	Beretta	−.8 to +.3	−.8 to + .3	−.25	−.25	.9 to 1.6
	Corsica	−.9 to +.4	−9 to + .4	−.25	−.25	.1 to .4
1992	Beretta	−.89 to +.39①	−.89 to + .39①	−.25	.25	.20
	Corsica	−.82 to +.32①	−.82 to + .32	−.25	−.25	.25
1993–94	All	−.85 to +.35①	−.85 to + .35①	−.25	−.25	0

① —Not adjustable.

COOLING SYSTEM & CAPACITY DATA

Year	Model or Engine/VIN	Cooling Capacity, Qts.		Radiator Cap Relief Pressure, psi	Thermo. Opening Temp. °F	Fuel Tank Gals.	Engine Oil Refill Qts. ④	Transaxle Oil	
		Less A/C	With A/C					Manual Transaxle Pts.	Auto. Transaxle Qts. ①
1991	2.2L/4-134/G	8.5	8.5	15	195	15.6	4	4.2	③
	2.3L/4-138/A	9.2	9.2②	15	192	15.6	4	4.2	—
	3.1L/V6-192/T	12.5	12.5	15	195	15.6	4	4.2	6
1992-93	2.2L/4-134/4	8.7	8.7	15	195	15.6	4	4.2	③
	2.3L/4-138/A	9.2	9.2	15	192	15.6	4	4.2	③
	3.1L/V6-192/T	13.1	13.1	15	195	15.6	4	4.2	②
1994	2.2L/4-134/4	9.2	9.2	15	195	15.2	4	4.2	③
	2.3L/4-138/A	10.4	10.4	15	192	15.2	4	4.2	③
	3.1L/V6-192/T	12.7	12.7	15	195	15.2	4	4.2	③

① —Approximate, make final check with dipstick.
② —With heavy duty radiator, 9.4 qts.
③ —Oil pan only, 4 qts. After overhaul, less torque converter drain, 6 qts.; with torque converter drain, 9 qts.
④ —When changing engine oil filter additional oil may be required.

LUBRICANT DATA

Model	Lubricant Type			
	Transaxle		Power Steering	Brake System
	Manual	Automatic		
All	Manual Transmission Fluid ①	Dexron IIE	Power Steering Fluid ②	DOT 3

① —GM part No. 12345349 or equivalent.
② —Meeting requirements of GM 9985010.

Electrical

INDEX

PRECAUTIONS

AIRBAG SYSTEM DISARMING

The diagnostic energy reserve module (DERM) can maintain voltage to cause a system deployment for up to ten minutes after the ignition switch is turned off and the battery is disconnected. Servicing the SIR system during this period may result in accidental deployment and personal injury.

1. Ensure front wheels are pointed straight ahead.
2. Turn ignition switch to Lock position and remove SIR or AIRBAG fuse.
3. Remove left sound insulator. **Remove courtesy lamp from sound insulator, if necessary.**
4. Remove Connector Position Assurance (CPA), then disconnect yellow two-way SIR electrical connector at base of steering column.

AIRBAG SYSTEM ARMING

1. Connect yellow two-way SIR electrical connector, then install Connector Position Assurance (CPA).
2. Install left sound insulator. **Install courtesy lamp to sound insulator, if applicable.**
3. Install SIR fuse to fuse block, turn ignition switch to Run position and ensure that "Inflatable Restraint" lamp flashes 7 to 9 times, then shuts off.

FUSE PANEL & FLASHER LOCATION

The fuse panel is located behind the lefthand side of the instrument panel, near the shroud.

The hazard warning flasher is located behind the lefthand side of the instrument panel in the convenience center. The turn signal flasher is located next to the convenience center.

STARTER
REPLACE

2.2L/4-134 ENGINE

1. Disconnect battery ground cable.
2. Raise and support front of vehicle.
3. Disconnect solenoid wires and battery cable at starter motor.
4. Disconnect wiring clamp at starter support bracket, then remove the support bracket to engine attaching bolt.
5. Remove starter attaching bolts, then carefully lower starter. Note position of shims, if used.
6. Reverse procedure to install.

2.3L/4-138 ENGINE

1. Disconnect battery ground cable, then remove serpentine drive belt.
2. Remove coolant reservoir.
3. Disconnect A/C line rail clip.
4. Remove alternator, then the oil fill tube and dipstick assembly.
5. Remove alternator bracket, then the air cleaner assembly.
6. Place a suitable drain pan under engine oil pan, then remove oil filter.
7. Remove starter as follows:
  a. Remove upper and lower starter mounting bolts.
  b. Position starter for access to solenoid wiring, then disconnect wiring.
  c. Remove starter from near front of engine between intake manifold and engine block.
8. Reverse procedure to install.

3.1L/V6-192 ENGINE

1. Remove air cleaner assembly.
2. Disconnect battery ground cable.
3. Raise and support front of vehicle.
4. **On models with engine oil cooler,** remove oil filter, then position oil cooler hose out of the way.
5. **On all models,** remove A/C compressor brace attaching nuts, then the starter support brace-to-engine attaching nut.

6. Remove flywheel inspection cover attaching bolts, then the cover.
7. Remove starter attaching bolts, then carefully lower starter. Note position of shims, if used.
8. Disconnect starter wiring at solenoid.
9. Reverse procedure to install. On models with engine oil cooler, check engine oil level after installing filter.

IGNITION LOCK
REPLACE

1. Disarm airbag as outlined in "Precautions." Failure to do so may result in accidental deployment of airbag, possibly causing personal injury.
2. Remove Steering wheel as outlined in "Steering wheel Replace."
3. Disconnect battery ground cable, remove coil assembly retaining clip, then coil assembly. Let coil assembly hang freely.
4. Remove wave washer, then on standard columns remove spacer shaft lock.
5. Attach tool No. J-23563-C or equivalent, compress shaft lock, then pry off retaining ring.
6. Remove shaft lock, then turn signal canceling cam assembly.
7. Remove upper bearing spring, then place turn signal to right turn position.
8. Remove multifunction lever, then hazard knob assembly.
9. **On models with tilt and cruise control,** remove signal switch arm assembly.
10. **On all models** remove turn signal switch attaching screws, then turn signal switch.
11. Remove buzzer switch assembly, then ignition lock retaining screw.
12. Place cylinder lock in "Lock" position, then remove cylinder lock.
13. Reverse procedure to install noting the following:
  a. After cylinder lock is installed place lock in "Run" position.
  b. After all work has been completed, rearm airbag as outlined in "Precautions."

1. 3/32" INCH DRILL BIT
2. IGNITION SWITCH ASSEMBLY
3. SWITCH SLIDER
4. IGNITION SWITCH ROD

Fig. 1   Ignition switch adjustment

1. DIMMER SWITCH
2. 3/32" INCH DRILL BIT

Fig. 2   Dimmer switch adjustment

1. SMALL KNOB
2. LARGE KNOB
3. SWITCH

ASSEMBLY SEQUENCE   SECTION B-B

Fig. 4   Headlamp & windshield wiper assembly switch

1. HEADLIGHT SWITCH KNOB
2. HEADLIGHT SWITCH
3. SCREW
4. BEZEL
5. WIPER SWITCH
6. WIPER SWITCH KNOB
7. CLIP

VIEW A

Fig. 3   Instrument cluster bezel removal

IGNITION SWITCH
REPLACE

1. Disarm airbag as outlined in "Precautions." Failure to do so may result in accidental deployment of airbag, possibly causing personal injury.
2. Place ignition switch in the "Off-Lock" position.
3. Remove steering column support bracket bolts, then flexible coupling bolts.
4. Remove upper and lower steering column bolts, then lower steering column.
5. Remove electrical connectors from ignition and dimmer switch.
6. Remove hex nut from stud, dimmer switch actuator rod, then dimmer switch.
7. Remove ignition switch stud, then actuator rod.
8. Remove park lock cable from ignition switch, then ignition switch.
9. Reverse position to install noting the following:
   a. When installing ignition switch place slider in far left position and move back one detent to the right. Insert a 3/32 drill bit in adjustment hole **Fig. 1** to hold switch slider in proper position when installing ignition switch.
   b. When installing dimmer switch place and 3/32 drill bit into hole on switch to limit travel **Fig. 2**, then position switch onto column and push against dimmer switch rod to remove lash. Tighten down switch.
   c. After all work has been completed, rearm airbag as outlined in "Airbag Arming."

DIMMER SWITCH
REPLACE

Refer to "Ignition Switch, Replace" for dimmer switch replacement.

HEADLAMP, REAR WINDOW DEFOGGER OR WINDSHIELD WIPER/WASHER SWITCH
REPLACE

Refer to **Figs. 3 and 4** when performing the following procedure.
1. Disarm airbag as outlined in "Precautions." Failure to do so may result in accidental deployment of airbag, possibly causing personal injury.
2. Disconnect battery ground cable.
3. Remove instrument cluster bezel.
4. Squeeze small switch knob at side and pull straight out.
5. Insert a suitable flat blade screwdriver into slots adjacent to center of inner knob and disengage knob from switch.
6. Remove switch to bezel screws, then switch.
7. Reverse procedure to install noting the following:
   a. When positioning inner knob to switch, make certain tabs align with slots, then press to secure.
   b. Position outer knob on switch and align "D" shaped hole in knob to shaft on switch, then press to secure.
   c. After all work has been completed, rearm airbag as outlined in "Precautions."

STOP LAMP SWITCH
ADJUST

Insert stop lamp switch into tubular clip above brake pedal until switch body seats fully into clip. Pull brake pedal rearward against internal pedal stop. The switch will be properly positioned in the tubular clip automatically. **Rotate switch 1/2 turn counterclockwise to ensure that switch does not hold brake pedal down after adjustment.**

NEUTRAL START SWITCH
REPLACE

1. Disconnect battery ground cable.
2. Disconnect shift linkage from transaxle.
3. Disconnect electrical connector from neutral start switch.
4. Remove neutral start switch attaching screws, then the switch.
5. Ensure transaxle shift shaft is in Neutral position.
6. If installing new switch, align new back-up light/neutral start switch flats with flats of shift shaft, then install switch. **Torque** attaching bolts to 22 ft. lbs.
7. If used switch is being installed, proceed as follows:
   a. Align back-up light/neutral start switch flats with flats of shift shaft, then install switch. Loosely install attaching bolts.

1	INSTRUMENT PANEL
2	CLUSTER
3	BOLT
4	CLIP
5	BEZEL
6	WIPER SWITCH
7	SCREW
8	HEADLIGHT SWITCH

Fig. 5 Instrument cluster removal

b. Insert 3/32 inch drill in service adjustment hole, then rotate switch until drill drops to a depth of 9/64 inch.
c. **Torque** attaching bolts to 22 ft. lbs.
8. With either new or used switch, ensure engine will only start in Neutral and Start positions.

CLUTCH START SWITCH
REPLACE

1. **On models equipped with airbag,** disarm airbag as outlined in "Precautions." Failure to do so may result in accidental deployment of airbag, possibly causing personal injury.
2. **On all models,** disconnect battery ground cable.
3. Disconnect wiring connector from switch located on clutch pedal support above clutch pedal.
4. Disconnect switch link from pedal, then remove switch retaining link and switch.
5. Reverse procedure to install.
6. Reactivate airbag as described under "Precautions."

TURN SIGNAL SWITCH
REPLACE

1. Disarm airbag as outlined in "Precautions." Failure to do so may result in accidental deployment of airbag, possibly causing personal injury.
2. Remove Steering wheel as outlined in "Steering wheel Replace."
3. Disconnect battery ground cable, remove coil assembly retaining clip, then coil assembly. Let coil assembly hang freely.
4. Remove wave washer, then on standard columns remove spacer shaft lock.
5. Attach tool No. J-23563-C or equivalent, compress shaft lock, then pry off retaining ring.
6. Remove shaft lock, then turn signal canceling cam assembly.
7. Remove upper bearing spring, then place turn signal to right turn position.
8. Remove multifunction lever, then hazard knob assembly.
9. **On models with tilt and cruise control,** remove signal switch arm assembly.

10. **On all models** remove turn signal switch attaching screws, then turn signal switch.
11. Reverse procedure to install noting the following:
    a. After all work has been completed, rearm airbag as outlined in "Precautions."

STEERING WHEEL
REPLACE

1. Disarm airbag as outlined in "Precautions." Failure to do so may result in accidental deployment of airbag, possibly causing personal injury.
2. Disconnect battery ground cable.
3. Remove four Torx screw from back of steering wheel, then connector position assurance (CPA) electrical connector from rear of inflator module.
4. Remove horn slip ring connectors, then horn ring.
5. Remove steering column locknut.
6. Using puller J 1859-03 or equivalent, remove steering wheel.
7. Reverse procedure to install noting the following:
    a. **Torque** steering wheel locknut to 31 ft. lbs.
    b. After all work has been completed, rearm airbag as outlined in "Precautions."

INSTRUMENT CLUSTER
REPLACE

Disarm airbag as outlined in "Precautions." Failure to do so may result in accidental deployment of airbag, possibly causing personal injury. After all work has been completed, rearm airbag as outlined in "Precautions."

Refer to **Fig. 5** for instrument cluster replacement procedures.

RADIO
REPLACE

Refer to **Fig. 6,** for replacement of radio.

1	INSTRUMENT PANEL PAD
2	TRIM BEZEL
3	RETAINERS

Fig. 6 Radio removal

WIPER MOTOR
REPLACE

1. Disconnect battery ground cable.
2. Remove left side wiper arm using following procedure:
    a. Remove plastic cap from end of wiper arm shaft.
    b. Remove nut from end of wiper arm shaft.
    c. Using suitable tool, pry wiper arm from wiper arm shaft.
3. Remove wiper drive link from crank arm.
4. Disconnect electrical connectors and washer hoses from wiper motor.
5. Remove wiper motor attaching bolts, then remove wiper motor, guiding crank arm through drive hole.
6. Reverse procedure to install.

WIPER MOTOR TRANSMISSION
REPLACE

1. Disconnect battery ground cable.
2. Remove left and right side wiper arms using following procedure:
    a. Remove plastic cap from end of wiper arm shaft.
    b. Remove nut from end of wiper arm shaft.
    c. Using suitable tool, pry wiper arm from wiper arm shaft.
3. Loosen, but do not remove, transmission drive link(s) to wiper motor crank arm attaching screws.
4. Remove air inlet screen.
5. Disconnect transmission drive link(s) from wiper motor crank arm.
6. Remove wiper transmission to body attaching bolts.
7. Remove wiper transmission by guiding it through shroud upper panel access hole.
8. Reverse procedure to install.

BLOWER MOTOR
REPLACE
LESS A/C

On Models with 3.1L/V6-192 engines it is necessary to remove the serpentine belt and alternator to prior to performing the following procedure.
1. Disarm airbag system as outlined under "Precautions."
2. Disconnect blower motor and blower motor resistor electrical connections.
3. Remove plastic water shield from right side of cowl.
4. Remove blower motor attaching screws, then the blower motor.
5. Remove blower motor cage attaching nut, then the cage.
6. Reverse procedure to install. Rearm airbag system as outlined under "Precautions."

WITH A/C

On Models with 3.1L/V6-192 engines it is necessary to remove the serpentine belt and alternator to prior to performing the following procedure.
1. **On all models,** disconnect battery ground cable.
2. Disconnect blower motor electrical connections.
3. Disconnect blower motor attaching screws, then pull blower motor and cage out.
4. Remove plastic water shield from right side of cowl.
5. Remove blower motor.
6. Remove blower cage attaching nut, then the blower cage.
7. Reverse procedure to install.

HEATER CORE
REPLACE
LESS A/C

1. Disarm airbag as outlined in "Precautions." Failure to do so may result in accidental deployment of airbag, possibly causing personal injury.
2. Remove radio assembly, through opening of radio release heater core cover retaining clips.
3. Remove screw attaching floor outlet, turning clockwise and to the right release rear floor air outlet.
4. Drain engine coolant, raise and support vehicle, then disconnect hoses from heater core.
5. Remove elbow tube from heater core case, then lower vehicle.
6. Remove heater core cover screws, then cover.
7. Remove heater core attaching screws, clamps, then heater core from vehicle.
8. Reverse procedure to install noting the following:
   a. After all work has been completed, rearm airbag as outlined in "Precautions."

WITH A/C

1. Disarm airbag as outlined in "Precautions." Failure to do so may result in accidental deployment of airbag, possibly causing personal injury.
2. Disconnect battery ground cable, then drain cooling system.
3. Raise and support vehicle, then disconnect drain tube from heater core.
4. Remove heater hoses from heater core, then lower vehicle.
5. Remove console if equipped, then right and left sounder insulator.
6. Remove steering column opening filler, then floor air outlet duct.

7. Remove heater core cover, heater core mounting clamps, then heater core.
8. Reverse procedure to install noting the following:
   a. After all work has been completed, rearm airbag as outlined in "Precautions."

EVAPORATOR CORE
REPLACE

1. Disarm airbag as outlined in "Precautions." Failure to do so may result in accidental deployment of airbag, possibly causing personal injury.
2. Discharge and recover refrigerant, as outlined in "Discharging & Evacuating System" in the "Air Conditioning" section.
3. Disconnect battery ground cable, then raise and support vehicle.
4. Remove front exhaust shield, then three cradle cross brace attaching bolts and swing brace to the side.
5. Remove A/C lines from evaporator, then lower vehicle.
6. Remove under dash insulator panel from right side.
7. Remove electrical junction box from heater core cover, then left side insulator panel.
8. Remove steering column filler, then partially remove shift console if equipped.
9. Remove floor duct, heater core cover, shroud, then straps.
10. Remove evaporator assembly.
11. Reverse procedure to install noting the following:
    a. After all work has been completed, rearm airbag as outlined in "Precautions."
    b. Evacuate and recharge system.

NOTE: Refer To 2.2L/4-134 Engine Section In The "Chevrolet Cavalier & Pontiac Sunbird" Chapter For Service Procedures Not Covered In This Section.

INDEX

Fig. 1 Front engine mount assembly

3. Remove left sound insulator. **Remove courtesy lamp from sound insulator, if necessary.**
4. Remove Connector Position Assurance (CPA), then disconnect yellow two-way SIR electrical connector at base of steering column.

AIRBAG SYSTEM ARMING

1. Connect yellow two-way SIR electrical connector, then install Connector Position Assurance (CPA).
2. Install left sound insulator. **Install courtesy lamp to sound insulator, if applicable.**
3. Install SIR fuse to fuse block, turn ignition switch to Run position and ensure that "Inflatable Restraint" lamp flashes 7 to 9 times, then shuts off.

1. 54 N·m (40 LB.FT.)
2. 24 N·m (18 LB.FT.)
3. ENGINE MOUNT BRACKET
4. ENGINE MOUNT
5. POWER STEERING PUMP BRACKET

Fig. 2 Rear engine mount assembly

PRECAUTIONS

AIRBAG SYSTEM DISARMING

The diagnostic energy reserve module (DERM) can maintain voltage to cause a system deployment for up to ten minutes after the ignition switch is turned off and the battery is disconnected. Servicing the SIR system during this period may result in accidental deployment and personal injury.
1. Ensure front wheels are pointed straight ahead.
2. Turn ignition switch to Lock position and remove SIR or AIRBAG fuse.

ENGINE MOUNTS
REPLACE

FRONT

Refer to **Fig. 1** when performing the following procedure.
1. Disconnect battery ground cable.
2. Remove two bolts retaining upper engine mount to body.
3. Remove bolt retaining upper engine mount to engine bracket.
4. Raise and support vehicle.
5. Support the engine.
6. Remove inner fender shield.
7. Remove bolt retaining lower engine mount to body.
8. Remove bolt retaining lower engine mount to engine mount bracket, then remove the mount.

9. Reverse procedure to install noting the following:
  a. Clean threads of all bolts removed. Prior to installation apply a suitable lock compound to bolt threads.
  b. Refer to **Fig. 1** for torque values.

REAR

Refer to **Fig. 2** when performing the following procedure.

Removal

1. Disconnect battery ground cable.
2. Raise and support vehicle.
3. Remove engine mount nuts and bolts, then the engine mount.
4. If necessary, remove engine mount bracket.

Installation

1. Clean threads of all bolts removed. Prior to installation apply a suitable lock compound to bolt threads.
2. Install engine mount bracket if removed. Do not tighten bracket bolts at this time.
3. Slightly raise engine and transaxle.
4. Install engine mount. Refer to **Fig. 2** for torque values.
5. Lower vehicle.
6. Install battery ground cable.

ENGINE
REPLACE

1. Disconnect battery cables, then remove the battery.
2. Relieve fuel tank vapor pressure by loosening the fuel filler cap.
3. Drain cooling system.
4. Disconnect hood lamp wiring. Remove the hood.
5. Remove throttle body intake duct.
6. Remove rear sight shields.
7. Remove air cleaner housing.
8. Remove upper radiator hose.
9. Disconnect vacuum hose from brake booster.
10. Disconnect alternator electrical connector, then remove the top brace, **Fig. 3**.
11. Remove upper engine wiring harness from engine.
12. Properly discharge A/C system. Refer to "Air Conditioning" in the "General Services" section for procedure.
13. Remove compressor-to-condenser, and accumulator refrigerant lines.
14. Raise and support vehicle.
15. Remove left splash shield.
16. Remove exhaust system.
17. Remove lower engine wiring harness.
18. Remove flywheel inspection cover.
19. Remove front wheels.
20. Remove lower radiator hose.
21. Disconnect heater hoses from heater core.
22. Remove calipers from steering knuckle. Properly support calipers.
23. Remove tie rod ends from struts.
24. Lower the vehicle.
25. **On models with manual transaxle,** remove clutch slave cylinder as follows:
    a. Remove slave cylinder to transaxle attaching bolts.
    b. Using Hydraulic Line Separating Tool No. J-36221 or equivalent, disconnect hydraulic line quick connect fitting.
    c. Remove the slave cylinder.
26. **On all models,** ensure engine compartment fuel line connections are clean, then using Connector Tool Set No. J-37088 or equivalent, disconnect the fuel line quick connect fittings. Plug all fittings.
27. Disconnect linkage from transaxle.
28. Disconnect accelerator, cruise control, and T.V. cables from the TBI unit.
29. **On models with automatic transaxle,** disconnect cooling lines from transaxle.

30. **On all models,** disconnect hoses from power steering pump.
31. Remove four center carriage bolts.
32. Position a dolly with added engine support under the vehicle, then lower vehicle onto the dolly.
33. Support rear of vehicle.
34. Remove upper transaxle mount.
35. Remove upper strut mounting nuts and bolts.
36. Remove front and rear engine mounts as described previously.
37. Remove eight front and rear carriage bolts. **To prevent axle separation, wire front carriage bolt holes together.**
38. Raise the vehicle.
39. Remove engine and transaxle assembly on the dolly.
40. Reverse procedure to install noting the following:
    a. **On models with manual transaxle,** bleed the hydraulic clutch system as described in "Clutch And Manual Transaxle" section.
    b. **On all models,** replenish all fluids as needed.
    c. When recharging the A/C system refer to "Air Conditioning" in the "General Services" section for procedure.
    d. Check wheel Alignment, refer to "Wheel Alignment" section in this chapter.

INTAKE MANIFOLD
REPLACE

1991 MODELS

1. Disconnect battery ground cable.
2. Relieve fuel tank vapor pressure by loosening the fuel filler cap.
3. Remove air cleaner assembly.
4. Drain cooling system.
5. Disconnect all wiring and vacuum lines necessary to facilitate manifold removal.
6. Ensure engine compartment fuel line connections are clean, then using

Fig. 3 Alternator assembly

1	31 N·m (23 LB. FT.)
2	BRACE
3	3.3 N·m (29 LB. IN.)
4	SHIELD
5	NUT
6	43 N·m (32 LB. FT.)
7	BRACKET
8	GENERATOR

Connector Tool Set No. J-37088 or equivalent, disconnect fuel line quick connect fittings. Plug all fittings.
7. Disconnect TBI linkage, then remove TBI assembly.
8. Remove power steering pump as follows:
    a. Disconnect return and pressure hoses from the pump.
    b. Loosen drive belt tensioner. Separate belt from power steering pulley.
    c. Remove three front pump retaining bolts, **Fig. 4**. Bolts can be accessed through hole in the pulley.
    d. Remove one retaining bolt from rear of the pump, then remove the pump.
9. Remove coolant hose from intake manifold.
10. Raise and support vehicle.
11. Unscrew coolant pipe retaining nut at top of D.I.S. Move the pipe rearward.
12. Disconnect accelerator and T.V. cables, then remove attaching bracket.
13. Remove six lower intake manifold retaining nuts, **Fig. 5**.
14. Lower the vehicle.
15. Remove the remaining intake manifold retaining bolts and nuts, then the manifold and gasket.
16. Reverse procedure to install noting the following:
    a. Prior to installation, thoroughly clean manifold mating surfaces.
    b. Install intake manifold with new gasket. Refer to **Fig. 5** for tightening sequence and torque values.
    c. When installing power steering pump, refer to **Fig. 4** for bolt tightening sequence and torque values.
    d. When installing serpentine drive belt, refer to "Belt Tension Data" in this section.

1992-94 MODELS

1. Relieve fuel system pressure, then remove air intake duct.
2. Drain engine coolant, then disconnect vacuum line and electrical wires as necessary.

Fig. 4   Power steering pump assembly

Fig. 5   Intake manifold replacement

Fig. 6   Upper intake manifold replacement

3. Remove throttle linkage, then power steering pump.
4. Remove MAP sensor and EGR solenoid valve.

5. Remove upper intake manifold assembly, then EGR valve injector, **Fig. 6.**
6. Remove fuel injector retainer bracket,

regulator, then injectors.
7. Remove accelerator and T.V. cables, then cable bracket.
8. Raise and support vehicle, then remove intake manifold lower attaching bolts.
9. Lower vehicle, remove intake manifold upper attaching nuts, then intake manifold and gasket.
10. Reverse procedure to install noting the following:
    a. Tighten intake manifold attaching nut in sequence as shown in **Fig. 7.**
    b. **Torque** intake manifold attaching nut to 22 inch lbs.
    c. **Torque** accelerator bracket attaching bolts to 18 inch lbs.

EXHAUST MANIFOLD
REPLACE

1. Disconnect battery ground cable.
2. Disconnect oxygen sensor.
3. Loosen drive belt tensioner and remove drive belt.
4. Remove alternator, **Fig. 3.**
5. Raise and support vehicle.
6. Disconnect exhaust pipe from manifold.
7. Lower the vehicle.
8. Remove eight exhaust manifold retaining bolts, **Fig. 8.**
9. Remove oil filler tube.
10. Remove exhaust manifold and gasket.
11. Reverse procedure to install noting the following:
    a. Install exhaust manifold with new gasket. Refer to **Fig. 8** for torque values.
    b. When installing alternator, refer to **Fig. 3** for torque values.
    c. When installing serpentine drive belt, refer to "Belt Tension Data" in this section.

CYLINDER HEAD
REPLACE
1991 MODELS

1. Disconnect battery ground cable.
2. Remove air cleaner assembly.
3. Relieve fuel tank vapor pressure by loosening the fuel filler cap.
4. Drain cooling system.
5. Remove TBI cover.
6. Remove coolant reservoir.
7. Raise and support vehicle.
8. Disconnect exhaust pipe from manifold.
9. Remove coolant hose from intake manifold.
10. Disconnect accelerator and T.V. cables, then remove attaching bracket.
11. Lower the vehicle.
12. Disconnect vacuum lines at intake manifold.
13. Disconnect all wiring necessary to facilitate cylinder head removal.
14. Remove upper radiator hose from thermostat housing.

1 STUD
2 GASKET
3 INTAKE MANIFOLD
4 NUT
5 CLIP

Fig. 7 Intake manifold tightening sequence

INTAKE MANIFOLD NUT
TIGHTENING SEQUENCE

1 5-15 N·m (3-11 FT. LBS.)
2 8-18 N·m (6-13 FT. LBS.)

Fig. 8 Exhaust manifold replacement

1 8-12 N·m (6-9 FT. LBS.)
2 15-25 N·m (11-18 FT. LBS.)

Fig. 9 Rocker cover, rocker arm & pushrod assemblies

15. Remove serpentine belt, then belt tensioner.
16. Remove power steering pump as follows:
    a. Disconnect return and pressure hoses from the pump.
    b. Loosen drive belt tensioner. Separate belt from power steering pulley.
    c. Remove three front pump retaining bolts, **Fig. 4**. Bolts can be accessed through hole in the pulley.
    d. Remove one retaining bolt from rear of the pump, then remove the pump.
17. Ensure engine compartment fuel line connections are clean, then using Connector Tool Set No. J-37088 or equivalent, disconnect fuel line quick connect fittings. Plug all fittings.
18. Remove alternator and rear brace, **Fig. 3**.
19. Remove rocker arm cover, **Fig. 9**, then the rocker arms and pushrods. **Keep rocker arms and pushrods in order so they can be reinstalled in position they were removed from.**
20. Remove cylinder head attaching bolts, then the cylinder head and gasket, intake and exhaust manifolds, and TBI unit as an assembly.
21. Reverse procedure to install noting the following:
    a. Ensure cylinder head mating surfaces are thoroughly clean. Install cylinder head with a new gasket.
    b. Refer to **Fig. 10** for tightening sequence and torque specifications.
    c. When installing rocker arms, and rocker cover, refer to **Fig. 9** for torque values.
    d. When installing alternator, refer to **Fig. 3** for torque values.
    e. When installing power steering pump, refer to **Fig. 4** for bolt tightening sequence and torque values.

f. When installing serpentine drive belt, refer to "Belt Tension Data" in this section.

1992-94 MODELS

1. Relieve fuel pressure, then remove air inlet duct.
2. Disconnect vacuum lines and electrical connectors.
3. Remove accelerator linkage, then coolant reservoir.
4. Remove serpentine belt, alternator, power steering pump, then serpentine drive belt tensioner.
5. Remove secondary ignition wires, then canister purge line from under manifold.
6. Remove upper radiator hose, throttle body cables from bracket, then coolant inlet hose on cylinder head.
7. Remove intake manifold brace from power steering bracket, then fuel lines.
8. Remove rocker arm cover, rocker arms, then pushrods, **Fig. 9**. **When valve train components are removed they should be kept in order. Install in same location with same mating surfaces as when removed.**
9. Remove secondary ignition cable bracket, engine lift bracket, then front exhaust pipe.
10. Remove head bolts, then on models equipped with automatic transaxle remove fluid level indicator bracket.
11. Remove cylinder head.
12. Reverse procedure to install noting the following:
    a. Ensure mating surfaces are clean, then install head using new gasket.
    b. Refer to **Fig. 10** for cylinder head bolts tightening sequence and tighten specifications.
    c. Tighten rocker arms to specifications.

CRANKSHAFT PULLEY & HUB
REPLACE
REMOVAL

1. Disconnect battery ground cable.
2. Loosen drive belt tensioner and remove drive belt.
3. Raise and support vehicle.
4. Remove wheel and tire assembly.
5. Remove inner fender shield.
6. Remove three crankshaft pulley bolts, **Fig. 11**, the pulley and hub bolt, then the pulley.
7. Install Crankshaft Pulley Puller Tool No. J-24420-B or equivalent to hub. Remove hub by turning the puller screw.

INSTALLATION

1. Apply clean engine oil to contact area of front cover seal.
2. Apply a suitable sealer to pulley hub keyway.
3. Position pulley hub over key on crankshaft.
4. Install Crankshaft Pulley Installer Tool No. J-29113 or equivalent, to crank-

1 LONG BOLTS
2 SHORT BOLTS
3 STUD
4 NUMBERS ON GASKET INDICATE TORQUE SEQUENCE.

CYLINDER HEAD BOLT TORQUE PROCEDURE

1. TIGHTEN BOLTS IN SEQUENCE (ITEM 4) TO:
   • LONG BOLTS; 63 N·M (46 LB-FT)
   • SHORT BOLTS; 58 N·M (43 LB-FT)
2. TIGHTEN ALL BOLTS AN ADDITIONAL ANGLE OF 90° IN SEQUENCE (ITEM 4) USING J 36660 OR EQUIVALENT.

Fig. 10   Cylinder head tightening sequence & torque specifications

1 90-120 N·m (66-88 FT. LBS)
2 40-60 N·m (30-44 FT. LBS)

Fig. 11   Crankshaft pulley and hub replacement

1 8-14 N·m (6-10 FT. LBS)

Fig. 14   Front cover replacement

1 8 N·m (6 FT. LBS) MIN.

Fig. 12   Oil pan replacement

1 40-60 N·m (30-44 FT. LBS.)

NOMINAL BELT
INSTALL BELT
REPLACE BELT
TO RELEASE TENSION
INDICATOR MARK
VIEW A

THE INDICATOR MARK ON THE MOVEABLE PORTION OF THE TENSIONER MUST BE WITHIN THE LIMITS OF THE SLOTTED AREA ON THE STATIONARY PORTION OF THE TENSIONER. ANY READING OUTSIDE THESE LIMITS INDICATES EITHER A DEFECTIVE BELT OR TENSIONER.

Fig. 13   Drive belt tensioner assembly

6. Remove flywheel inspection cover.
7. Remove four right side support bolts, then slightly lower the support.
8. **On models with automatic transaxle**, remove oil filter and extension.
9. **On all models**, remove twelve bolts and two nuts retaining the oil pan, **Fig. 12.**
10. Remove oil pan and gasket.

INSTALLATION

1. Ensure oil pan mating surfaces are thoroughly clean.
2. Apply a 1/8 inch diameter bead of suitable sealer on the oil pan to engine block sealing flanges.
3. Apply suitable sealer on the oil pan to front cover mating surface.
4. Apply suitable sealer on ends to the ears of a new oil pan rear seal.

shaft. Ensure a minimum of 1/4 inch of threads are engaged. Pull pulley hub into position, then remove the tool.
5. Install crankshaft pulley, then the pulley and hub bolts. Refer to **Fig. 11** for torque values.
6. Install inner fender shield.
7. Install wheel and tire assembly.
8. Lower the vehicle.
9. When installing serpentine drive belt, refer to "Belt Tension Data" in this section.
10. Reconnect battery ground cable.

OIL PAN
REPLACE
REMOVAL

1. Disconnect battery ground cable.
2. Disconnect exhaust pipe from manifold.
3. Raise and support vehicle.
4. Drain the crankcase.
5. Remove starter bracket, and the starter.

5. Install oil pan to engine block. Refer to **Fig. 12** for torque values.
6. **On models with automatic transaxle**, install oil filter adapter with a new seal, then the oil filter.
7. **On all models**, install exhaust pipe to manifold.
8. Install right side support with attaching bolts.
9. Install starter.
10. Lower the vehicle.
11. Refill crankcase.
12. Connect battery ground cable.

OIL PUMP
REPLACE

1. Remove oil pan as previously described.
2. Remove pump to rear main bearing cap bolt, then the pump and extension shaft.
3. Remove extension shaft and retainer.
4. Reverse procedure noting the following:
   a. Heat retainer in hot water prior to assembling extension shaft.
   b. **Torque** oil pump bolt to 32 ft. lbs.

FRONT COVER
REPLACE

1. Disconnect battery ground cable.
2. Loosen drive belt tensioner and remove drive belt.
3. Remove tensioner, **Fig. 13.**

WITHOUT A/C   WITH A/C

1 GENERATOR
2 P/S PUMP
3 TENSIONER
4 CRANKSHAFT
5 WATER PUMP
6 A/C

Fig. 15 Serpentine drive belt routing

2 PULLEY

WATER PUMP

1 BOLTS;
30 N•M (22 LB-FT)

Fig. 16   Water pump pulley installation

4. Raise and support vehicle.
5. Remove oil pan as described previously.
6. Remove crankshaft pulley and hub as described previously.
7. Remove eight front cover attaching bolts, **Fig. 14,** then the front cover and gasket.
8. Reverse procedure to install noting the following:
   a. Ensure front cover mating surfaces are thoroughly clean.
   b. Install front cover with new gasket. Refer to **Fig. 14** for torque values.
   c. Clean tensioner bolts and prior to installation apply a suitable lock compound to bolt threads. Refer to **Fig. 13** for torque values.
   d. When installing serpentine drive belt, refer to "Belt Tension Data" in this section.

BELT TENSION DATA

1. Check belt tensioner indicator marks, **Fig. 13,** to ensure belt is in operating range. Replace belt as needed, refer to **Fig. 15** for belt routing.
2. With all accessories Off, run engine until operating temperature is achieved.
3. Turn ignition switch to Off.
4. Position Belt Tensioner Tool No. J-23600 or equivalent, on the drive belt between power steering pump and alternator. Note reading, and remove the tool.
5. Run engine for 15 seconds, then turn the ignition switch to Off.
6. Using a 15 mm socket, apply counterclockwise force to tensioner pulley bolt. Release the pulley, then take a reading as described in step 4.
7. Using a 15 mm socket, apply clockwise force to tensioner pulley bolt until the install position is reached. Slowly release pulley to rest position, then take a reading as described in step 4. Use caution not to disturb the belt tensioner position.
8. If average of the three readings taken is 63–77 lbs., and the belt is in the ten-

1. BOLT — 25 N•m (18 LBS. FT.)

Fig. 17   Water pump replacement

sioners operating range, replace the belt tensioner as described in this section.

SERPENTINE DRIVE BELT

BELT ROUTING

Refer to **Fig. 15** for serpentine drive belt routing.

PRECAUTIONS

When installing or removing the drive belt, never exceed 30 ft. lbs. torque on the tensioner center bolt, **Fig. 13.** Care should also be taken to avoid bending or twisting the tensioner. If the belt tensioner or idler assembly produces a whining noise, inspect for bearing failure. If the drive belt becomes frayed, check belt tensioner assembly alignment and ensure belt edge does not contact the tensioner pulley flange.

Serpentine drive belt performance will not be impaired by cracks in the belt ribs. However belt replacement will be required if any of the following conditions occur: Belt ribs are missing, the belt slips or is frayed, or the belt tensioner runs out of travel before adjustment is proper.

BELT TENSIONER REPLACEMENT

1. Disconnect battery ground cable.
2. Remove coolant reservoir.
3. Loosen drive belt tensioner and remove drive belt.
4. Remove two alternator bolts.
5. Remove belt tensioner pulley.
6. Remove power steering pump as follows:
   a. Disconnect return and pressure hoses from the pump.
   b. Loosen drive belt tensioner. Separate belt from power steering pulley.
   c. Remove three front pump retaining bolts, **Fig. 4.** Bolts can be accessed through hole in the pulley.
   d. Remove one retaining bolt from rear of the pump, then remove the pump.
7. Remove four tensioner retaining bolts, **Fig. 13,** then the tensioner.
8. Reverse procedure to install noting the following:
   a. Clean tensioner bolts and prior to installation apply a suitable lock compound to bolt threads. Refer to **Fig. 13** for torque values.
   b. When installing power steering pump, refer to **Fig. 4** for bolt tightening sequence and torque values.
   c. When installing alternator bolts, refer to **Fig. 3** for torque values.
   d. When installing serpentine drive belt, refer to **Fig. 15** for belt routing.

COOLING SYSTEM BLEED

These engines do not require a specified bleed procedure. After filling cooling system, run engine to operating temperature with radiator pressure cap off. Air will then be automatically bled through cap opening.

THERMOSTAT
REPLACE

1. Remove air cleaner duct, then disconnect battery ground cable.
2. Drain cooling system below level of thermostat housing.
3. Remove radiator hose from water out-

Fig. 18 Exhaust assembly

1	EXHAUST PIPE	5	EXHAUST PIPE RUBBER HANGERS (2)
2	FUEL TANK RETAINING STRAP	6	MUFFLER
3	FUEL TANK	7	MUFFLER HANGER ATTACHING BOLTS (2)
4	HEAT SHIELD	8	HEAT SHIELD ATTACHING SCREWS (3)

Fig. 19 Fuel tank removal

1	ELECTRICAL CONNECTOR	5	FUEL VAPOR TUBE
2	FUEL VENT TUBE	6	FUEL TANK STRAP BOLTS (2)
3	FUEL FEED TUBE	7	FUEL TANK STRAPS (2)
4	FUEL RETURN TUBE	8	FUEL TANK

let, then remove three water outlet attaching nuts.
4. Remove outlet, then thermostat.
5. Reverse procedure to install. **Torque** water outlet attaching nut to 89 inch lbs.

WATER PUMP
REPLACE

1. Disconnect battery ground cable.
2. Drain cooling system.
3. Loosen drive belt tensioner and remove drive belt.
4. Remove water pump pulley attaching bolts, **Fig. 16**, then the pulley.
5. Remove alternator, **Fig. 3.**
6. Remove alternator side bracket.
7. Remove water pump attaching bolts, **Fig. 17**, then the pump and gasket.
8. Reverse procedure to install noting the following:
   a. Ensure water pump mating surface is thoroughly clean.
   b. Install water pump with new gasket. Refer to **Figs. 16 and 17** for torque values.
   c. When installing alternator, refer to **Fig. 3** for torque values.
   d. When installing serpentine drive belt, refer to "Belt Tension Data" in this section.

FUEL FILTER
REPLACE

1. Raise and support vehicle.
2. Grasp filter and one nylon fuel connecting line fitting. Twist quick connect fitting ¼ turn in each direction to loosen any dirt within fitting.
3. Repeat Step 2 for the other connector.
4. Remove fuel filter retaining screw, then squeeze plastic tabs of male end connector of filter connections and pull apart.
5. Using compressed air, blow the quick connectors clean or dirt. **Safety glasses must be worn during this procedure.**
6. Remove protective caps from new filter.
7. Apply a few drops of clean engine oil to the male tubes ends of the filter assembly.
8. Push connectors together to cause the retaining tabs/fingers to snap into place.
9. Once installed, pull on both ends of each connection to ensure they are secure.
10. Turn the ignition switch to the On Position, engine Off, for two seconds.
11. Turn ignition switch to the Off position for ten seconds, then to the ON position. Check fuel filter for leaks.

FUEL PUMP
REPLACE

1. Disconnect battery ground cable.
2. Relieve fuel tank vapor pressure by

loosening the fuel filler cap.

3. Using a suitable syphon, drain the fuel tank.

4. Remove fuel tank as follows:
   a. Raise and support vehicle.
   b. Remove two rubber exhaust pipe hangers, **Fig. 18.**
   c. Remove two muffler hanger retaining bolts.
   d. Remove three heat shield attaching screws, then the heat shield.
   e. Remove fuel tank filler tube, vent tube, vent hose, and clamps.
   f. Disconnect electrical connector, **Fig. 19.**
   g. Disconnect fuel level meter vapor hose.
   h. Ensure fuel line connections are clean. Disconnect fuel return quick connect fitting by squeezing plastic tab on male end of the fitting. Using Fuel Line Separator Tool Set No. J-37088 or equivalent, disconnect fuel line quick connect fitting. Plug all fittings.
   i. Properly support tank.
   j. Remove two rear retaining strap attaching bolts, then the fuel tank and retaining straps.

5. Thoroughly clean fuel level meter assembly connection and surrounding area, **Fig. 20.**

6. Using Fuel Sender Spanner Wrench tool No. J-35731, remove fuel level meter assembly lock ring. Remove assembly from tank, and discard the O-ring.

7. Disassemble fuel level meter assembly as follows:
   a. Note orientation of fuel filter for proper installation.
   b. To remove fuel filter, rotate it while pulling fuel pump in opposite direction, **Fig. 21.**
   c. Disconnect fuel pump electrical connector.
   d. Position fuel level meter assembly upside down on work area.
   e. Pull downward on fuel pump to separate it from mounting bracket. Tilt pump outward and remove it from pulsator.

8. Reverse procedure to install noting the following:

a. Never run fuel pump unless submerged in fuel.
b. Always replace fuel filter when installing fuel pump.
c. Always use new O-ring when installing fuel level meter assembly.

1	ELECTRICAL CONNECTOR	7	DEFLECTOR
2	FUEL LEVEL METER	8	FUEL PUMP FILTER
3	PULSATOR	9	MOUNTING BRACKET
4	RUBBER BUMPER	10	FUEL PUMP ELECTRICAL CONNECTOR
5	FUEL PUMP	11	INLET TUBE
6	RUBBER INSULATOR		

Fig. 20 Fuel level meter assembly

1	INSULATOR
2	TAPE
3	HARNESS ASM.
4	RETAINER (SENDER)
5	FUEL LEVEL SENDER UNIT
6	LOCKING CAM
7	GASKET, O-RING
8	FUEL TANK ASM.

NOTE: HARNESS MUST BE ROUTED BELOW FUEL PIPES

Fig. 21 Fuel tank assembly

TIGHTENING SPECIFICATIONS

Year	Component	Torque/ Ft. Lbs.	Year	Component	Torque/ Ft. Lbs.
1991–94	Accelerator Cable Mounting Bracket	18	1991–94 —Cont'd	EGR Valve	16
	Camshaft Pulley	77		Exhaust Manifold Nuts	16
	Camshaft Thrust Plate	9		Exhaust Manifold Studs	9–10
	Coolant Drain Plug (Cylinder Block)	11		Flywheel To Crankshaft	52
	Coolant Outlet To Cylinder Head	8		Heater Hose To Intake Manifold	24
	Crankcase Front Cover Bolts	97②		Intake Manifold	18
	Crankshaft Pulley & Hub To Crankshaft	85		Main Bearing Cap Bolts	70
	Crankshaft Pulley To Hub	37		Oil Fill Tube To Cylinder Block	18
	Crankshaft Sensor	80②		Oil Filter Adapter To Cylinder Block	18
	Cylinder Head Bolts	①		Oil Pan	7–8
	DIS Coil Assembly	18		Oil Pump Drive Assembly Bolt	18

Year	Component	Torque/ Ft. Lbs.
1991–94	Oil Pump To Bearing Cap	31
	Oxygen Sensor	31
	PCV Valve Cap	89 ②
	Power Brake Hose Vacuum Fitting	115 ②
	Pressure Plate To Flywheel	15
	Rear Engine Lift Bracket	32
	Rocker Arm Cover	7-8
	Rocker Arm Nuts	22
	Rod Bearing Cap Nut	38
	Serpentine Tensioner Assembly	37
	Spark Plugs	11

Year	Component	Torque/ Ft. Lbs.
1991–94 —Cont'd	Timing Chain Cover	8
	Timing Chain Tensioner	18
	Water Pump	18
	Water Pump Inlet	18

① —On 1991 41 ft. lbs., plus three additional steps; 1st step, all bolts an additional 45°; 2nd step, all bolts an additional 45°; 3rd step, long bolts (8, 4, 1, 5, & 9) an additional 20°, short bolts (7, 3, 2, 6 & 10) an additional 10°. 1992–94 cylinder head torque specifications, refer to text.
② —Inch lbs.

2.3L/4-138 Engine

NOTE: Refer To 2.3L/4-138 Engine Section In The "Buick Skylark, Oldsmobile Achieva & Cutlass Calais & Pontiac Grand Am" Chapter For Service Procedures Not Covered In This Section.

INDEX

PRECAUTIONS
AIRBAG SYSTEM DISARMING

The diagnostic energy reserve module (DERM) can maintain voltage to cause a system deployment for up to ten minutes after the ignition switch is turned off and the battery is disconnected. Servicing the SIR system during this period may result in accidental deployment and personal injury.
1. Ensure front wheels are pointed straight ahead.
2. Turn ignition switch to Lock position and remove SIR or AIRBAG fuse.
3. Remove left sound insulator. **Remove courtesy lamp from sound insulator, if necessary.**
4. Remove Connector Position Assurance (CPA), then disconnect yellow two-way SIR electrical connector at base of steering column.

AIRBAG SYSTEM ARMING

1. Connect yellow two-way SIR electrical connector, then install Connector

Position Assurance (CPA).
2. Install left sound insulator. **Install courtesy lamp to sound insulator, if applicable.**
3. Install SIR fuse to fuse block, turn ignition switch to Run position and ensure that "Inflatable Restraint" lamp flashes 7 to 9 times, then shuts off.

ENGINE MOUNTS
REPLACE

1991 MODELS
Front Mount

Refer to **Fig. 1** when performing the following procedure.
1. Disconnect battery ground cable.
2. Remove upper retaining nut from mount.
3. Using Engine Support tool or equivalent, **Fig. 2,** lift engine from mount.
4. Raise and support vehicle.
5. Remove two lower retaining nuts from mount.
6. Lower the vehicle.
7. Remove the mount.
8. Remove nut retaining battery cable

clip to mount bracket stud. Separate cable clip from stud.
9. Remove the stud, two retaining bolts, then the mount bracket.
10. Reverse procedure to install. Refer to specifications for torque values.

Rear Mount

Refer to **Fig. 3** when performing the following procedure.
1. Disconnect battery ground cable.
2. Disconnect vacuum lines and pull vacuum harness through front lift bracket.
3. Using Engine Support tool or equivalent, **Fig. 2,** lift rear of engine slightly.
4. Remove lower right splash shield.
5. Remove nut from engine mount through bolt.
6. Remove four bracket-to-body retaining bolts, then the bracket and mount assembly.
7. Remove three mount-to-bracket retaining nuts. Separate bracket from mount.
8. Reverse procedure to install. Refer to specifications for torque values.

Fig. 1 Front engine mount assembly

121. BRACKET
122. WASHER
123. STUD
124. BOLT/SCREW (2)
125. NUT
126. MOUNT ASM.
127. NUT (2)

1. TOOL J 28467
2. THREAD ONTO STRUT ATTACHING BOLTS ABOVE NUTS – 3 PER SIDE
3. POWER STEERING PIVOT BOLT

Fig. 2 Engine support tool

1 BOLT/SCREW – 12 N·m (9 LBS. FT.)
2 THROTTLE CABLE BRACKET
3 THROTTLE BODY
4 NUT – 26 N·m (19 LBS. FT.)

Fig. 5 Accelerator cable bracket

128. BOLT/SCREW
129. BRACKET
130. BOLT/SCREW (3)
131. NUT
132. TRANSAXLE SUPPORT (PARTIAL VIEW)
133. BRACKET ASM.
134. BOLT/SCREW (4)
135. MOUNT ASM.
136. NUT (3)
137. ENGINE COMPARTMENT R.H. RAIL ASM.
138. COWL ASM.

Fig. 3 Rear engine mount assembly

1. MOUNT
2. BOLT - 75 N·m (55 LBS. FT.)
3. TRANSAXLE ASSEMBLY

Fig. 4 Transaxle mount

1992–94 MODELS

Right Mount

1. Disconnect battery ground cable.
2. Install Engine Support tool No. J-28467-A or equivalent **Fig. 2**, then raise engine off mount.
3. Raise and support vehicle, remove right side wheel, then right side splash shield.
4. Remove two front engine mount lower attaching bolts.
5. Lower vehicle, remove nut holding lower mounting bolt.
6. Remove bracket to mount attaching nut, then mount assembly.
7. Reverse procedure to install.

Engine Mount Strut

1. Disconnect battery ground cable, then raise and support vehicle.
2. Remove bolts attaching engine mount strut to body and engine mount strut bracket.
3. Remove engine mount strut.
4. Reverse procedure to install.

Transaxle Mount

1. Disconnect battery ground cable.
2. Install Engine Support tool No. J-28467-A or equivalent **Fig. 2**, then raise engine off mount.
3. Remove through bolt at transaxle mount, then bolts attaching mount to transaxle, **Fig. 4**.
4. Remove mount.
5. Reverse procedure to install.

ENGINE
REPLACE

1. Relieve fuel system pressure as follows:
    a. Disconnect battery negative cable.
    b. Relieve fuel tank vapor pressure by loosening the fuel filler cap.
    c. Install Fuel Pressure Gauge Tool, No. J-34730 or equivalent, to fuel pressure valve. **To avoid spilling fuel when connecting the gauge wrap fitting with a towel.**
    d. Position end of bleed hose into a suitable container. Open the bleeder valve until system pressure is gone.
2. Drain cooling system.
3. Raise and support vehicle.
4. Remove front wheels.
5. Remove air cleaner assembly.
6. Disconnect heater hoses.
7. Remove upper radiator hose.
8. Remove coolant fan.
9. Properly discharge A/C system. Refer to "Air Conditioning" in the "General Services" section for procedure.
10. Remove oil filter.
11. Remove A/C compressor to condenser refrigerant line.
12. Disconnect all electrical connectors and vacuum lines necessary to facilitate engine removal.
13. Remove battery ground cable to engine block retaining bolt, then the battery cable.
14. Separate shift cable from bracket.

Fig. 6 Power steering pump assembly

15. Disconnect vacuum hose from brake booster.
16. Disconnect accelerator cable, then remove the bracket, **Fig. 5.**
17. Remove power steering pump assembly with hoses attached, **Fig. 6,** and position aside.
18. Remove oil/air separator.
19. Disconnect engine compartment fuel lines.
20. **On models with manual transaxle,** remove clutch actuator.
21. **On all models,** disconnect engine oil cooler lines from adapter.
22. Remove exhaust manifold as described later in this section.
23. Remove front engine mount retaining nut, **Fig. 1.**
24. Remove lower radiator hose and heater hose.
25. Install Engine Support Tool No. J-28467 or equivalent, **Fig. 2.**
26. Remove splash shields.
27. Separate ball joints from steering knuckles, then stabilizer shafts from both control arms.
28. Remove drive axles as described in the "Front Wheel Drive" section.
29. Remove suspension support.
30. Remove ground strap from block.
31. Remove rear engine mount assembly as described previously.
32. Remove transaxle mount through bolt.
33. Lower the engine.
34. Disconnect starter wires.
35. **On models equipped with manual transmission,** the throttle body coolant pipes must be removed before engine is removed. **Do not bent coolant pipes to gain clearance.**
36. Remove engine and transaxle assembly.
37. Reverse procedure to install noting the following:
    a. **On models with manual transaxle,** bleed the hydraulic clutch system as described in "Clutch And Manual Transaxle" section.
    b. Replenish all fluids as needed.

c. When recharging the A/C system refer to "Air Conditioning" in the "General Services" section for procedure.
d. Check wheel Alignment, refer to "Wheel Alignment" section in this chapter.

INTAKE MANIFOLD
REPLACE

1. Disconnect battery ground cable.
2. Drain cooling system.
3. Disconnect MAP sensor electrical connector and vacuum hose.
4. Disconnect MAT sensor, purge solenoid, and fuel injector harness electrical connectors.
5. Disconnect intake manifold vacuum hoses.
6. Disconnect fuel regulator, and purge solenoid-to-canister hoses.
7. Remove throttle body-to-air cleaner duct, then separate vent tube from the duct.
8. Remove accelerator cable bracket, **Fig. 5.**
9. Remove brake booster vacuum hose, along with retaining bracket to power steering bracket.
10. Disconnect throttle body coolant lines.
11. Remove oil/air separator with hoses, **Fig. 7.** Disconnect hoses from the oil filler, chain cover, intake duct, and intake manifold.
12. Remove oil filler cap/level indicator assembly from filler tube, **Fig. 7.**
13. Remove bolt/screw retaining the oil filler tube to engine. Pull tube upward to separate it from the block.
14. Disconnect injector harness electrical connector.
15. Remove oil filler tube by pulling upward while rotating it between intake tubes and fuel rail electrical harness. Discard oil filler tube O-ring.
16. Remove intake manifold support

320. SEPARATOR – OIL/AIR
321. HOSE (INTAKE DUCT TO SEPR.)
322. HOSE (INTAKE MANIF. TO SEPR.)
323. BOLT/SCREW (2)
324. HOSE (FILL TUBE TO SEPR.)
325. HOSE (CHAIN CVR. TO SEPR.)
326. OIL FILL CAP & INDICATOR ASM.
327. OIL FILL TUBE
328. O-RING SEAL
329. GUIDE, OIL LEVE INDICATOR
     HOLES IN GUIDE MUST FACE OUTBOARD
     90° ±5° DEGREES FROM CENTERLINE OF
     CRANKSHAFT. (IN LINE WITH OIL FILTER)
329A. POSITION TOP OF GUIDE 18 mm – 19 mm
     (2 3/32" – 3/4") DOWN FROM SURFACE OF
     BLOCK.
330. CLAMP
331. BOLT/SCREW (1)

Fig. 7 Crankcase ventilation components

brace, **Fig. 8.**
17. Remove five bolts and two nuts retaining the intake manifold, **Fig. 9.**
18. Remove intake manifold and gasket.
19. Reverse procedure to install noting the following:
    a. Install intake manifold with new gasket. Ensure numbers stamped on the gasket face the manifold surface. Refer to **Fig. 9** for tightening sequence, and to specifications for torque values.
    b. Install a new O-ring to oil filler tube. Refer to **Fig. 7** when installing oil filler tube to engine.

1. BRACE, INTAKE MANIFOLD
2. BOLT/SCREW - 25 N.m (18 LBS. FT.)
3. NUT - 54 N.m (40 LBS. FT.)
4. STUD - 54 N.m (40 LBS. FT.)
5. WASHER
6. SPACER

Fig. 8   Intake manifold support brace

99. STUD
100. INTAKE MANIFOLD GASKET
103. INTAKE MANIFOLD
104. BOLT
105. NUT

Fig. 9   Intake manifold replacement

183. BRACE
185. NUT

Fig. 10   Exhaust manifold brace

314. EXHAUST MANIFOLD
315. HEAT SHIELD
317. SEAL
318. STUD
319. EXHAUST PIPE
320. SPRING NUT ASM.

Fig. 11   Exhaust pipe installation

EXHAUST MANIFOLD
REPLACE

1. Disconnect battery ground cable.
2. Disconnect oxygen sensor.
3. Raise and support vehicle.
4. Remove exhaust manifold brace, **Fig. 10.**
5. Remove exhaust pipe from manifold, **Fig. 11.**
6. Lower the vehicle.
7. Remove exhaust manifold heat shields, **Fig. 12.**
8. Remove exhaust manifold and gasket, **Fig. 13.**
9. Reverse procedure to install noting the following:
   a. Install exhaust manifold with new gasket. Refer to specifications for

314. EXHAUST MANIFOLD
315A. HEAT SHIELD - UPPER
315B. HEAT SHIELD - LOWER
316. NUT - 22 N.m (16 LBS. FT.)
317. BOLT, STUD END - 26 N.m (19 LBS. FT.)
318. BOLT - 14 N.m (10 LBS. FT.)
319. NUT - 42 N.m (31 LBS. FT.)

Fig. 12   Exhaust manifold heat shield installation

   torque values.
   b. Coat threads of Oxygen sensor with suitable anti-seize compound before installing.

OIL PAN
REPLACE

1. Disconnect battery ground cable.
2. Drain engine oil.

110. STUD, EXHAUST MANIFOLD TO CYL. HEAD
158. MANIFOLD ASM. (VIN D)
160. NUT (7) SEE "TIGHTENING SEQUENCE"
176. GASKET
314. MANIFOLD ASM. (VIN A)

Fig. 13   Exhaust manifold replacement

1. ROTATE TENSIONER IN DIRECTION OF ARROW TO REMOVE OR INSTALL BELT.

Fig. 14   Serpentine drive belt routing

3. Remove flywheel cover, then the exhaust manifold brace.
4. Disconnect radiator outlet pipe to oil pan bolt, then transaxle to oil pan nut.
5. Remove oil pan to transaxle stud, then the oil pan bolts.
6. Remove oil pan.
7. Reverse procedure to install.

1. BOLT; 50 N•M (37 LB-FT)
2. BRACKET
3. BOLT; 26 N•M (20 LB-FT)
4. BOLT; 26 N•M (20 LB-FT)
5. GENERATOR
6. LOWER ALTERNATOR BRACKET
7. BRACKET
8. BOLT; 50 N•M (37 LB-FT)
9. A/C COMPRESSOR

Fig. 15   Alternator assembly

146. BRACKET ASM.
147. BRACE – FRONT
148. BOLT (M10 X 1.5 X 40) (5)
149. BOLT (M8 X 1.25 X 20)
150. NUT
151. IDLER PULLEY
152. BRACE
153. BOLT/SCREW
156. SPACER
157. BOLT/SCREW (3)

A. BOLTS INSTALLED AT THESE TWO LOCATIONS FIRST

Fig. 16   Tensioner bracket assembly

OIL PUMP
REPLACE

1. Remove oil pan as previously described.
2. Remove oil pump assembly bolts.
3. Remove oil pump assembly.
4. Reverse procedure to install.

SERPENTINE DRIVE BELT
BELT ROUTING

Refer to **Fig. 14** for serpentine drive belt routing.

PRECAUTIONS

When installing or removing the drive belt care should be taken to avoid bending or twisting the tensioner. Inspect bearings if belt tensioner or idler assembly produce a whining noise. If the drive belt becomes frayed, check belt tensioner assembly alignment and ensure belt edge does not contact the tensioner pulley flange.

Serpentine drive belt performance will not be impaired by cracks in the belt ribs. However belt replacement will be required if any of the following conditions occur: Belt ribs are missing, the belt slips or is frayed, or the belt tensioner runs out of travel before adjustment is proper.

TENSIONER BRACKET REPLACEMENT

1. Disconnect battery ground cable.
2. Loosen drive belt tensioner and remove drive belt.
3. Remove alternator assembly, **Fig. 15**.
4. **On models with A/C,** remove oil filter.
5. **On models with A/C,** remove rear compressor bracket.
6. **On models less A/C,** remove bolts retaining the idle pulley brace. Remove the brace.
7. **On all models,** raise and support vehicle.
8. Remove right splash shield.
9. **On models with A/C,** remove front compressor mounting bolts and position compressor aside.
10. **On all models,** remove chain housing to belt tensioner bracket brace, **Fig. 16**.
11. Remove five bolts retaining bracket to block.
12. Remove bracket from wheel opening.
13. Reverse procedure to install. Refer to specifications for torque values.

BELT TENSION DATA

1. Check belt tensioner indicator marks, **Fig. 17**, to ensure belt is in operating range. Replace belt as needed, refer to **Fig. 14** for belt routing.
2. With all accessories Off, run engine until operating temperature is achieved.
3. Turn ignition switch to Off.
4. Position Belt Tensioner Tool No. J-36018 or equivalent, on the drive belt between idler pulley and alternator (models less A/C), or between A/C compressor and alternator (models with A/C). Note reading, and remove the tool.
5. Run engine for 15 seconds, then turn the ignition switch to Off.
6. Using a 13 mm socket, apply clockwise force to tensioner pulley bolt. Release the pulley, then take a reading as described in step 4.
7. Using a 13 mm socket, apply counter-

THE INDICATOR MARK ON THE STATIONARY PORTION OF THE TENSIONER MUST BE WITHIN THE LIMITS OF THE SLOTTED AREA ON THE MOVEABLE PORTION OF THE TENSIONER. ANY READING OUTSIDE THESE LIMITS INDICATES EITHER A FAULTY BELT OR TENSIONER.

1. MINIMUM BELT LENGTH
2. NOMINAL BELT LENGTH
3. MAXIMUM (REPLACE) BELT LENGTH

Fig. 17 Drive belt tensioner indicator marks

1. TIMING CHAIN HOUSING
2. GASKET, TIMING CHAIN HOUSING TO WATER PUMP BODY
3. NUT (3)
4. WATER PUMP BODY ASM.
5. GASKET, WATER PUMP BODY TO WATER PUMP COVER
6. WATER PUMP COVER
7. BOLT (M6 X 1 X 65) — 3 LOWER POSITIONS
8. BOLT (M6 X 1 X 25)
9. BOLT (M6 X 1 X 90)
10. GASKET, WATER PUMP COVER TO BLOCK
11. BOLTS, WATER PUMP COVER TO BLOCK (2)

Fig. 18 Water pump replacement

clockwise force to tensioner pulley bolt until the Install position is reached. Slowly release pulley to Rest position, then take a reading as described in step 4. Use caution not to disturb the belt tensioner position.
8. If average of the three readings taken is 50 lbs., and the belt is in the tensioners operating range, replace the tensioner bracket assembly as described in this section.

COOLING SYSTEM BLEED

These engines do not require a specified bleed procedure. After filling cooling system, run engine to operating temperature with radiator/pressure cap off. Air will then be automatically bled through cap opening.

THERMOSTAT
REPLACE

1. Disconnect battery ground cable, then drain coolant until level is below that thermostat housing.
2. Remove upper radiator hose and heater hose from housing, place aside.
3. Remove electrical connector from coolant sensor, then throttle body coolant hose.
4. Remove two thermostat housing attaching bolts, thermostat housing, then thermostat.
5. Reverse procedure to install. **Torque** thermostat housing attaching bolts to 19 ft. lbs.

WATER PUMP
REPLACE

1. Disconnect negative battery cable.
2. Drain cooling system.
3. Raise and support vehicle.
4. Disconnect oxygen sensor connector, then the exhaust pipe from exhaust manifold.
5. Remove radiator outlet pipe from oil pan and transaxle.
6. Lower vehicle.
7. Remover upper and lower exhaust manifold heat shields.

8. Remove exhaust manifold to cylinder head retaining nuts, then the exhaust manifold seals and gaskets.
9. Disconnect radiator outlet pipe assembly to coolant pump cover bolts.
10. Remove coolant cover to cylinder block bolts, then coolant pump assembly to timing chain housing nuts, **Fig. 18.**
11. Remove coolant pump and cover assembly.
12. Reverse procedure to install noting the following:
    a. Ensure water pump mating surfaces are clean.
    b. Lube O-ring on radiator outlet pipe with coolant prior to installing.

FUEL FILTER
REPLACE

1. Loosen fuel filler cap to relieve tank pressure. Do not tighten at this time.
2. Raise and support vehicle, then disconnect fuel pump electrical connector from fuel tank.
3. Lower vehicle.
4. Start engine and run until fuel supply remaining in fuel lines is consumed. Engage starter for 3.0 seconds to ensure relief of any remaining pressure.
5. Raise and support vehicle, then connect fuel tank electrical connector.
6. Grasp filter and one nylon fuel connecting line fitting. Twist quick connect fitting 1/4 turn in each direction to loosen any dirt within fitting.
7. Repeat Step 2 for the other connector.
8. Remove fuel filter retaining screw, then squeeze plastic tabs of male end connector of filter connections and pull apart.
9. Using compressed air, blow the quick connectors clean or dirt. **Safety glasses must be worn during this procedure.**
10. Remove protective caps from new filter.
11. Apply a few drops of clean engine oil to the male tubes ends of the filter assembly.
12. Push connectors together to cause the retaining tabs/fingers to snap into place.
13. Once installed, pull on both ends of each connection to ensure they are secure.

14. Turn the ignition switch to the On Position, engine Off, for two seconds.
15. Turn ignition switch to the Off position for ten seconds, then to the ON position. Check fuel filter for leaks.

FUEL PUMP
REPLACE

1. Disconnect battery ground cable.
2. Relieve fuel tank vapor pressure by loosening the fuel filler cap.
3. Using a suitable syphon, drain the fuel tank.
4. Remove fuel tank as follows:
    a. Raise and support vehicle.
    b. Remove two rubber exhaust pipe hangers, **Fig. 19.**
    c. Remove two muffler hanger retaining bolts.
    d. Remove three heat shield attaching screws, then the heat shield.
    e. Remove fuel tank filler tube, vent tube, vent hose, and clamps.
    f. Disconnect electrical connector, **Fig. 20.**
    g. Disconnect fuel level meter vapor hose.
    h. Ensure fuel line connections are clean. Disconnect fuel return quick connect fitting by squeezing plastic tab on male end of the fitting. Using Fuel Line Separator Tool Set No. J-37088 or equivalent, disconnect fuel line quick connect fitting. Plug all fittings.
    i. Properly support tank.
    j. Remove two rear retaining strap attaching bolts, then the fuel tank and retaining straps.
5. Thoroughly clean fuel level meter assembly connection and surrounding area, **Fig. 21.**
6. Using Fuel Sender Spanner Wrench tool No. J-35731 or equivalent, remove fuel level meter assembly lock ring. Remove assembly from tank, and discard the O-ring.
7. Disassemble fuel level meter assembly as follows:
    a. Note orientation of fuel filter for proper installation.
    b. To remove fuel filter, rotate it while pulling fuel pump in opposite direction, **Fig. 22.**
    c. Disconnect fuel pump electrical connector.

FRT

FRT

FRT

FRT

1 EXHAUST PIPE	5 EXHAUST PIPE RUBBER HANGERS (2)
2 FUEL TANK RETAINING STRAP	6 MUFFLER
3 FUEL TANK	7 MUFFLER HANGER ATTACHING BOLTS (2)
4 HEAT SHIELD	8 HEAT SHIELD ATTACHING SCREWS (3)

Fig. 19   Exhaust assembly

1 ELECTRICAL CONNECTOR	5 FUEL VAPOR TUBE
2 FUEL VENT TUBE	6 FUEL TANK STRAP BOLTS (2)
3 FUEL FEED TUBE	7 FUEL TANK STRAPS (2)
4 FUEL RETURN TUBE	8 FUEL TANK

Fig. 20   Fuel tank removal

d. Position fuel level meter assembly upside down on work area.

e. Pull downward on fuel pump to separate it from mounting bracket. Tilt pump outward and remove it from pulsator.

8. Reverse procedure to install noting the following:

a. Never run fuel pump unless submerged in fuel.

b. Always replace fuel filter when installing fuel pump.

c. Always use new O-ring when installing fuel level meter assembly.

Fig. 21 Fuel tank assembly

1	INSULATOR
2	TAPE
3	HARNESS ASM.
4	RETAINER (SENDER)
5	FUEL LEVEL SENDER UNIT
6	LOCKING CAM
7	GASKET, O – RING
8	FUEL TANK ASM.

NOTE: HARNESS MUST BE ROUTED BELOW FUEL PIPES

Fig. 22 Fuel level meter assembly

1	ELECTRICAL CONNECTOR	7	DEFLECTOR
2	FUEL LEVEL METER	8	FUEL PUMP FILTER
3	PULSATOR	9	MOUNTING BRACKET
4	RUBBER BUMPER	10	FUEL PUMP ELECTRICAL CONNECTOR
5	FUEL PUMP	11	INLET TUBE
6	RUBBER INSULATOR		

TIGHTENING SPECIFICATIONS

Year	Component	Torque/ Ft. Lbs.	Year	Component	Torque/ Ft. Lbs.
1991–94	Camshaft Rear Cover	10	1991–94 —Cont'd	Front Engine Mount To Cylinder Block Bracket	55 ③
	Camshaft Sprocket To Cam Bolt	⑤		Front Engine Mount To Engine Mount Crossmember	30 ③
	Coolant Outlet To Cylinder Head	19		Fuel Rail To Camshaft Housing	19
	Crankshaft Position Sensor To Block	80 ①		Ignition Coil And Module Assembly To Camshaft Housing	15
	Cylinder Head Threaded Plug	⑥		Intake Manifold Brace Bolts	19
	Engine Mount Strut Bracket Attaching Bolt	49 ④		Intake Manifold To Cylinder Head	18
	Engine Mount Strut Through Bolt	89 ④		Oil/Air Separator To Intake Manifold	71 ①
	ESC Knock Sensor	15		Oil Cooler lines To Oil Cooler Adapter	26
	Exhaust Manifold To Cylinder Head Nuts	27		Oil Filter Connector To Block	21
	Exhaust Manifold To Cylinder Head Studs	106 ①		Oil Fill Tube Bolt	72 ①
	Exhaust Manifold To Exhaust Pipe	22		Oil Filter To Block	②
	Exhaust Manifold To Oil Pan Brace	19			
	Exhaust Manifold Studs To Manifold	22			
	Front Cover To Timing Chain Housing	106 ①			
	Front Engine Mount Bracket To Block	40 ③			

Continued

2.3L/4-138 ENGINE

TIGHTENING SPECIFICATIONS—Continued

Year	Component	Torque/ Ft. Lbs.
1991-94	Oil Pan Baffle Bolts	30
	Oil Pan Bolts	17
	Oil Pan Drain Plug	19
	Oil Pump To Block	40
	Oil Pump Cover To Oil Pump Body	106①
	Rear Crankshaft Seal Housing To Block	106①
	Rear Engine Mount Bracket To Body	40③
	Rear Engine Mount Bracket To Engine	44③
	Rear Engine Mount To Body Bracket	55③
	Rear Engine Mount Through Bolt Nut	55③
	Right Engine Mount Attaching Bolt	42④
	Spark Pugs To Cylinder Head	17
	Starter To Block Bolt	71
	Tensioner Bracket Assembly Bracket To Block	40
	Tensioner Bracket Assembly Bracket To Front Brace	19
	Tensioner Bracket Assembly Bracket To Idler	40

Year	Component	Torque/ Ft. Lbs.
1991-94 —Cont'd	Tensioner Bracket Assembly Rear Brace To Block Or Idler	40
	Timing Chain Housing To Block	19
	Timing Chain Tensioner To Housing	⑦
	Throttle Body To Intake Manifold	19
	Transaxle Mount To Body	40
	Water Pump To Timing Chain Housing	19
	Water Pump To Water Pump Cover	10

① —Inch lbs.
② —¾ to one turn after initial gasket contact.
③ —1991 models.
④ —1992-94 models.
⑤ —1991-92 models, 40 ft. lbs.; 1993-94 models, 52 ft. lbs.
⑥ —1991-92 models, 19 ft. lbs.; 1993-94 models, 40 ft. lbs.
⑦ —1991-92 models, 115 inch lbs.; 1993-94 models, 89 inch lbs.

3.1L/V6-192 Engine

NOTE: Refer To 3.1L/V6-192 Engine Section In "Buick Regal, Chevrolet Lumina, Oldsmobile Cutlass Supreme & Pontiac Grand Prix" Chapter For Service Procedures Not Covered In This Section.

INDEX

PRECAUTIONS

AIRBAG SYSTEM DISARMING

The diagnostic energy reserve module (DERM) can maintain voltage to cause a system deployment for up to ten minutes after the ignition switch is turned off and the battery is disconnected. Servicing the SIR system during this period may result in accidental deployment and personal injury.

1. Ensure front wheels are pointed straight ahead.
2. Turn ignition switch to Lock position and remove SIR or AIRBAG fuse.
3. Remove left sound insulator. **Remove courtesy lamp from sound insulator, if necessary.**
4. Remove Connector Position Assurance (CPA), then disconnect yellow two-way SIR electrical connector at base of steering column.

AIRBAG SYSTEM ARMING

1. Connect yellow two-way SIR electri-

cal connector, then install Connector Position Assurance (CPA).
2. Install left sound insulator. **Install courtesy lamp to sound insulator, if applicable.**
3. Install SIR fuse to fuse block, turn ignition switch to Run position and ensure that "Inflatable Restraint" lamp flashes 7 to 9 times, then shuts off.

IDLE LEARN PROCEDURE

Any time vehicle power has been interrupted (battery disconnected), the programed position of the IAC valve pintle is lost. The following procedure

CHEVROLET BERETTA & CORSICA

must be performed to update the ECM memory with the correct IAC valve pintle position, enabling the ECM to provide a stable idle speed.

1. Restore vehicle power.
2. Connect suitable scan tool to ALDL connector, located under the lefthand side of the dash panel.
3. Select "IAC System."
4. Select "Idle Learn" in the "Misc. Test" mode.
5. Proceed as directed by scan tool.

ENGINE MOUNT
REPLACE

FRONT MOUNT

1. Disconnect battery ground cable.
2. Remove two engine mount to body bracket bolts, then the upper engine mount to engine bracket bolt. Raise and support vehicle.
3. Support engine with suitable jack.
4. Remove inner fender shield.
5. Remove lower engine mount to body bracket bolt, **Fig. 1.**
6. Remove lower engine mount to engine bracket bolt, then remove mount.
7. Reverse procedure to install. Clean all bolts with suitable solvent and apply suitable locking compound to threads prior to installation. Torque bolts to specifications given in **Fig. 1.**

REAR MOUNT

1. Disconnect battery ground cable, then raise and support vehicle.
2. Support engine with suitable jack.
3. Remove motor mount nuts and attaching bolts, **Fig. 2.**
4. Reverse procedure to install.

ENGINE
REPLACE

1. Relieve fuel system pressure as follows:
   a. Disconnect battery ground cable.
   b. Relieve fuel tank vapor pressure by loosening fuel filler cap.
   c. Install Fuel Pressure Gauge tool No. J-34730 or equivalent, to fuel pressure valve. **To avoid spilling fuel when connecting the gauge, wrap fitting with a shop towel.**
   d. Position end of bleed hose into a suitable container, then open bleeder valve until system pressure is relieved.
2. Removed air cleaner assembly.
3. Remove battery cables and battery.
4. Drain cooling system, then disconnect transaxle cooler lines at radiator.
5. Disconnect transaxle fluid level indicator.
6. Disconnect upper and lower radiator hoses from engine.
7. Disconnect heater outlet hose from water pump, then the heater inlet hose at rear of engine.
8. Remove serpentine belt.
9. Disconnect shift cable linkage and ca-

Fig. 1 Engine front mount

Fig. 2   Engine rear mount

HEAD TORQUE SEQUENCE

Coat thread with sealer before installing. Using a 12" clicker torque wrench torque to 45 N·m (33 Lbs. Ft.). Rotate wrench an additional 90° (1/4 turn).

Fig. 3   Cylinder head installation

ble from mounting bracket. It may be necessary to place transaxle in low gear.

10. Disconnect accelerator and cruise control cable, if equipped, from throttle linkage.
11. Disconnect A/C pressure switch electrical connector.
12. Disconnect vacuum check valve from power brake booster, then the canister purge vacuum line from the engine.
13. Disconnect upper engine electrical connectors, then the vacuum hose from vacuum reservoir.
14. Raise and support vehicle.
15. Remove front wheel and tire assemblies.
16. Remove righthand splash shield, then the oil filter.
17. Disconnect lower engine electrical connectors.
18. Disconnect A/C compressor, leaving hoses and rear bracket attached, then secure compressor out of the way.
19. Disconnect exhaust pipe from crossover.
20. Disconnect brake hose bracket at strut, then the brake calipers.
21. Disconnect tie rods from strut assemblies.
22. Place suitable engine table under front of vehicle, then lower vehicle enough to place engine and transaxle assembly onto table.
23. Lower table with engine and transaxle assembly, then raise vehicle.
24. Reverse procedure to install.

CYLINDER HEAD
REPLACE

LEFT SIDE

1. Disconnect battery ground cable.

2. Drain engine coolant into suitable container, then remove rocker arm cover.
3. Remove intake manifold. Refer to "Intake Manifold, Replace" for procedure.
4. Remove exhaust crossover at right side exhaust manifold.
5. Remove oil dipstick tube bracket.
6. Loosen rocker arm nuts until pushrods can be removed. **Keep pushrods in order they are removed so they can be installed in their original position.**
7. Remove cylinder head attaching bolts, then the cylinder head.
8. Reverse procedure to install, noting the following:
   a. Clean cylinder head bolts and cylinder head bolt holes with suitable solvent.
   b. Apply GM 1052080 sealer or equivalent to cylinder head bolt threads prior to installation.
   c. Position new head gasket on deck surface over dowel pins with "This Side Up" facing up, then install cylinder head.
   d. Tighten bolts in sequence shown to specifications, **Fig. 3.**

RIGHT SIDE

1. Raise and support vehicle, then remove right side exhaust manifold.
2. Lower vehicle, then remove rocker arm cover.
3. Remove intake manifold. Refer to "Intake Manifold, Replace" for procedure.
4. Loosen rocker arm nuts until pushrods can be removed. **Keep pushrods in order they are removed so they can be installed in their original position.**
5. Remove cylinder head attaching bolts, then the cylinder head.
6. Reverse procedure to install, noting the following:
   a. Clean cylinder head bolts and cylinder head bolt holes with suitable solvent.
   b. Apply GM 1052080 sealer or equivalent to cylinder head bolt threads prior to installation.
   c. Position new head gasket on deck surface over dowel pins with "This Side Up" facing up, then install cylinder head.
   d. Tighten bolts in sequence shown to specifications, **Fig. 3.**

INTAKE MANIFOLD
REPLACE

1. Disconnect battery ground cable.
2. Disconnect accelerator and T.V. cable bracket at plenum.
3. Disconnect throttle body at plenum.

Fig. 4 Exhaust manifold installation

1	CYLINDER HEAD	5	10 N·m (89 LB. IN.)
2	GASKET	6	HEAT SHIELD
3	MANIFOLD (RIGHT)	7	MANIFOLD (LEFT)
4	25 N·m (18 LB. FT.)		

4. Disconnect EGR pipe at EGR valve, then remove plenum.
5. Disconnect fuel inlet and return pipes at fuel rail.
6. Remove auxiliary drive belt.
7. Remove power steering pump and position aside.
8. Remove alternator with wiring attached and position aside.
9. Loosen alternator bracket.
10. Disconnect idle air vacuum hose at throttle body and the electrical connectors at injectors.
11. Remove fuel rail, breather tube and the runners.
12. Remove both rocker arm covers.
13. Drain cooling system into suitable container.
14. Disconnect radiator hose at thermostat outlet.
15. Disconnect coolant sensor and oil sender switch electrical connectors.
16. Remove coolant sensor, then disconnect cooling system bypass hose and heater inlet pipe at manifold.
17. Remove intake manifold attaching bolts, then the intake manifold.
18. Loosen rocker arm nuts until pushrods can be removed. **Keep pushrods in order they are removed so they can be installed in their original position.**
19. Reverse procedure to install, noting the following:
    a. When installing gaskets, install only on right or left side as marked.
    b. Clean cylinder case sealing surface front and rear ridges and apply a 3/16 inch bead of suitable RTV sealant on each cylinder block ridge.
    c. Install new intake gaskets on cylinder heads, then install pushrods. Tighten rocker arm attaching nuts to specifications.
    d. When installing intake manifold, ensure areas between case ridges and manifold are completely sealed.
    e. Install manifold retaining bolts and nuts, tighten to specifications.

EXHAUST MANIFOLD
REPLACE
LEFT SIDE

1. Remove air cleaner assembly.
2. Disconnect negative battery cable.
3. Remove coolant fan, then the heat shield.
4. Remove exhaust crossover pipe at manifold.
5. Remove exhaust manifold bolts, then the exhaust manifold, **Fig. 4.**
6. Reverse procedure to install.

RIGHT SIDE

1. Remove air cleaner assembly.
2. Disconnect negative battery cable.
3. Raise and support vehicle.
4. Remove exhaust pipe at crossover, then lower vehicle.
5. Remove heatshield, then the crossover at manifold.
6. Disconnect accelerator and T.V. cables, then remove bracket.
7. Remove oxygen sensor.
8. Remove exhaust manifold bolts, then the exhaust manifold, **Fig. 4.**
9. Reverse procedure to install.

VALVE ADJUSTMENT

1. Remove rocker arm covers.
2. Crank engine until assembly alignment mark on front face of torsional damper lines up with the arrow on the front cover. The engine should also be in the No. 1 firing position. This can be determined by placing fingers on No. 1 rocker arms as mark on torsional damper approaches arrow on front cover.
3. If valves are not moving, engine is in No. 1 firing position. If valves move as the mark comes up to the arrow on front cover, engine is in No. 4 firing position and should be rotated one revolution to reach No. 1 position.
4. With engine in No. 1 firing position, adjust exhaust valves 1, 2 and 3 and intake valves 1, 5 and 6, as follows:

a. Back out adjusting nut until lash is felt at pushrod, then turn in adjusting nut until all lash is removed.
b. When lash has been removed, turn adjusting nut in additional 1 1/2 turns to center lifter plunger.
5. Crank engine one revolution until arrow on front cover and torsional damper mark are again in alignment.
6. With the engine in this, the No. 4 firing position, adjust exhaust valves 4, 5 and 6 and intake valves 2, 3 and 4 as previously described.
7. Install rocker arm covers.

VALVE ARRANGEMENT
FRONT TO REAR

Right . . . . E-I-E-I-I-E
Left . . . . E-I-I-E-I-E

CAMSHAFT LIFT SPECIFICATIONS

Engine	Int.	Exh.
3.1L/V6-192	.2626	.2732

VALVE STEM OIL SEAL & VALVE SPRING
REPLACE

1. Remove rocker arm cover, then the spark plug, rocker arm and pushrod on cylinder(s) being serviced. **Keep valve train parts in order they are removed so they can be installed in their original position.**
2. Install Air Line Adapter tool No. J-23590 or equivalent, to spark plug port and apply compressed air to hold valves in place.
3. Using Valve Spring Compressor tool No. J-5892 or equivalent, to compress valve spring, remove valve locks, valve caps, valve spring and seat.
4. Remove valve stem oil seal.
5. Reverse procedure to install.

A INSERT BREAKER BAR HERE
1 GENERATOR
2 SERPENTINE BELT
3 WATER PUMP
4 AIR CONDITIONING COMPRESSOR
5 CRANKSHAFT
6 BELT TENSIONER
7 POWER STEERING PUMP

Fig. 13   Serpentine drive belt routing

NOTE: PUMP MUST ROTATE FREELY AFTER INSTALLATION

1 WATER PUMP
2 GASKET
3 8-12 N·m (6-9 FT. LBS.)

Fig. 15   Water pump installation

INSTALLATION

1. Align oil pump extension shaft drive gear socket and pump housing, then install pump assembly. Tighten pump assembly retaining bolts to specifications.
2. Install oil pan as previously described.

SERPENTINE DRIVE BELTS

BELT ROUTING

Refer to **Fig. 13** for serpentine drive belt routing.

1 TENSIONER
2 48-60 N·m (35-44 FT. LBS.)
3 20-30 N·m (14-22 FT. LBS.)

TO RELEASE TENSION

NOMINAL BELT   REPLACE BELT

INSTALL BELT

VIEW A   INDICATOR MARK

THE INDICATOR MARK ON THE MOVEABLE PORTION OF THE TENSIONER MUST BE WITHIN THE LIMITS OF THE SLOTTED AREA ON THE STATIONARY PORTION OF THE TENSIONER. ANY READING OUTSIDE THESE LIMITS INDICATES EITHER A DEFECTIVE BELT OR TENSIONER.

Fig. 14   Belt tensioner operating range

BELT TENSIONER ADJUSTMENT

Belt tension is maintained by a spring loaded belt tensioner. To remove or install drive belt, rotate tensioner with with a 3/4 inch socket. If belt tension is not satisfactory, ensure belt tensioner is within operating limits, **Fig. 14**. If belt tensioner is allowed to operate outside its operating limits, damage to belt tensioner may result.

BELT TENSIONER REPLACEMENT

1. Remove serpentine belt guard, **Fig. 13.**
2. Lift or rotate tensioner using a 1/2 inch breaker bar.
3. Remove serpentine belt, then the tensioner bolt.
4. Remove tensioner.
5. Reverse procedure to install.

COOLING SYSTEM BLEED

These engines do not require a specified bleed procedure. After filling cooling system, run engine to operating temperature with radiator/pressure cap off. Air will then be automatically bled through cap opening.

THERMOSTAT REPLACE

1. Disconnect battery ground cable.
2. Drain engine coolant below level of thermostat housing.
3. **On 3.1L/V6-192 engine,** remove crankcase vent tube.
4. **On all models,** remove upper radiator hose from housing.
5. Remove housing attaching bolts, water outlet, then thermostat.
6. Reverse procedure to install. **Torque** attaching bolts to 19 ft. lbs.

WATER PUMP
REPLACE

1. Disconnect battery ground cable, then drain cooling system.
2. Remove accessory drive belt.
3. Remove water pump pulley, then the water pump, **Fig. 15.**
4. Reverse procedure to install.

FUEL FILTER
REPLACE

1. Disconnect battery ground cable.
2. Loosen fuel filler cap to relieve tank pressure. Do not tighten at this time.
3. Connect Fuel Pressure Gage tool No. J-34730-1 or equivalent to fuel pressure valve. **Wrap a shop towel around fitting while connecting gage to avoid spillage.**
4. Install bleed hose into approved container and open valve to bleed system pressure.
5. Drain any fuel remaining in gage into an approved container.
6. Raise and support vehicle.
7. Grasp filter and one nylon fuel connecting line fitting. Twist quick connect fitting 1/4 turn in each direction to loosen any dirt within fitting.
8. Repeat Step 2 for the other connector.
9. Remove fuel filter retaining screw, then squeeze plastic tabs of male end connector of filter connections and pull apart.
10. Using compressed air, blow the quick connectors clean of dirt. **Safety glasses must be worn during this procedure.**
11. Remove protective caps from new filter.
12. Apply clean engine oil to the male tubes ends of the filter assembly.
13. Push connectors together to cause the retaining tabs/fingers to snap into place.
14. Once installed, pull on both ends of each connection to ensure they are secure.
15. Turn the ignition switch to the On position for two seconds.
16. Turn ignition switch to the Off position for ten seconds, then to the ON position. Check fuel filter for leaks.

FUEL PUMP
REPLACE

1. Disconnect battery ground cable.
2. Raise and support vehicle.
3. Drain, then remove fuel tank as follows:
   a. Raise and support vehicle.
   b. Remove two rubber exhaust pipe hangers, **Fig. 16.**
   c. Remove two muffler hanger retaining bolts.
   d. Remove three heat shield attaching screws, then the heat shield.
   e. Remove fuel tank filler tube, vent

1	EXHAUST PIPE	5	EXHAUST PIPE RUBBER HANGERS (2)
2	FUEL TANK RETAINING STRAP	6	MUFFLER
3	FUEL TANK	7	MUFFLER HANGER ATTACHING BOLTS (2)
4	HEAT SHIELD	8	HEAT SHIELD ATTACHING SCREWS (3)

Fig. 16   Exhaust assembly

1	ELECTRICAL CONNECTOR	5	FUEL VAPOR TUBE
2	FUEL VENT TUBE	6	FUEL TANK STRAP BOLTS (2)
3	FUEL FEED TUBE	7	FUEL TANK STRAPS (2)
4	FUEL RETURN TUBE	8	FUEL TANK

Fig. 17   Fuel tank removal

tube, vent hose, and clamps.

f. Disconnect electrical connector, **Fig. 17.**

g. Disconnect fuel level meter vapor hose.

h. Ensure fuel line connections are clean. Disconnect fuel return quick connect fitting by squeezing plastic tab on male end of the fitting. Using Connector Tool Set No. J-37088 or equivalent, disconnect fuel line quick connect fitting. Plug all fittings.

i. Properly support tank.

j. Remove two rear retaining strap attaching bolts, then the fuel tank and retaining straps.

4. Rotate fuel sender/pump assembly cam lock ring, then lift out fuel sender/pump assembly.

5. Remove fuel pump from fuel sender by pulling fuel pump up into attaching hose while pulling outwards from lower support.

6. Reverse procedure to install noting the following:

a. Install new fuel sender/pump assembly O-ring onto fuel tank before installation.

b. Always replace fuel filter when installing new pump.

c. Never run fuel pump unless submerged in fuel.

TIGHTENING SPECIFICATIONS

Year	Component	Torque/Ft. Lbs.
1991–94	Camshaft Rear Cover	7
	Camshaft Sprocket	18
	Connecting Rod Cap	37
	Cylinder Head	①
	Drive Belt Tensioner Belt	37
	Engine Strut Bracket To Engine	34
	Exhaust Crossover Nut	18
	Exhaust Manifold	21
	Exhaust Manifold To Heat Shield	89 ③
	Flywheel to Crankshaft	52
	Intake Manifold	18
	Main Bearing Cap	④
	Oil Filter	11
	Oil Filter Adapter Connector	46
	Oil Level Indicator Retaining Nut	18
	Oil Pan	②
	Oil Pump	⑤
	Oil Pump Cover	8
	Rocker Arm Nuts	20

Year	Component	Torque/Ft. Lbs.
1991–94	Rocker Arm Stud	47
	Rocker Arm Cover	6-9
	Spark Plugs	10-25
	Strut Brackets To Upper Tie Bar	16
	Strut To Tie Bar Brackets	32
	Thermostat Housing	19
	Timing Chain Dampener Pulley	15
	Vibration Damper or Pulley	67-85
	Water Pump	7

① —Torque to 33 ft. lbs., then tighten an additional 90°.

② —1991–92 models, torque 6mm bolts to 6-9 ft. lbs. and 8 mm bolts to 15-23 ft. lbs.; 1993–94 models, torque to 89 inch lbs.

③ —Inch lbs.

④ —1991–92 models, 63-83 ft. lbs.; 1993–94 models, 37 ft. lbs. plus an additional 77° turn.

⑤ —1991–92 models, 25-38 ft. lbs.; 1993–94 models, 30 ft. lbs.

Clutch & Manual Transaxle

INDEX

ADJUSTMENTS

CLUTCH

On these models, a hydraulic clutch system is used, **Fig. 1.** The system consists of a dash mounted master cylinder with integral reservoir, a transmission mounted slave cylinder and high pressure tubing to connect the two components.

The hydraulic clutch system provides automatic clutch adjustment, therefore, there is no provision for adjustment.

CLUTCH
REPLACE

INSPECTION

1. While observing clutch slave cylinder pushrod travel, have an assistant depress clutch pedal. Brake pedal should travel approximately 7.4 inches.

2. If slave cylinder pushrod moves .433 inch or more, hydraulic system is operating properly.

3. If slave cylinder pushrod did not move .433 inch, proceed as follows:

a. Check clutch master cylinder fluid level. The clutch slave cylinder must be installed during this operation. Refill as necessary.

b. If master cylinder requires fluid, check hydraulic system components for leakage. Remove rubber boots from cylinders and check for leakage past pistons. A slight wetting of piston and wall surfaces is acceptable.

c. If excessive leakage is indicated, entire hydraulic system must be replaced.

REPLACEMENT

1. Disconnect battery ground cable.
2. Remove hush panel from driver's footwell, then disconnect clutch master cylinder pushrod from clutch pedal.
3. Remove transaxle as outlined under "Manual Transaxle, Replace" procedure.
4. Mark position of pressure plate to flywheel to aid reassembly.
5. Gradually loosen pressure plate to flywheel attaching bolts until spring tension is relieved.
6. Support pressure plate and remove attaching bolts, pressure plate and driven disc, **Fig. 2.**
7. Clean pressure plate and flywheel mounting surfaces. Inspect bearing retainer outer surface of the transaxle.
8. Place pressure plate and driven disc in position and support with clutch Alignment Arbor tool No. J-29074 or equivalent, **Fig. 3. The driven disc is installed with the damper springs offset toward the transaxle. Stamped letters found on the driven disc identify the "Flywheel Side."**
9. Install and gradually **torque** the pressure plate to flywheel attaching bolts to 15 ft. lbs. Remove support tool.
10. Lubricate the clutch throwout fork where it contacts the release bearing and pack the release bearing inside diameter recess with suitable grease.
11. Install transaxle and hush panel, then connect battery ground cable.

HYDRAULIC SYSTEM SERVICE
CLUTCH BLEED

1. Clean dirt and grease from the cap to ensure no foreign substances enter the system.
2. Remove cap and diaphragm and fill reservoir to the top with hydraulic clutch fluid No. 12345347 or an equivalent fluid that meets Dot 3 specifications.
3. Loosen bleed screw which is located on the slave cylinder body next to the inlet connection.
4. Fluid will now begin to move from the master cylinder down the tube to the slave. It is important that for efficient gravity fill, the reservoir must be kept full all the time.
5. It will be noticeable at this point, that bubbles will appear at the bleed screw outlet. This means that air is being expelled from the system. When the slave is full, a steady stream of fluid will come from the slave outlet. At this point, tighten bleed screw.
6. Assemble diaphragm and cap to the reservoir, fluid in reservoir should be level with step.
7. The hydraulic system should now be fully bled and should release the clutch. Check vehicle by starting the engine, pushing clutch pedal to the floor and selecting reverse gear. There should be no grating of gears,

Fig. 1 Hydraulic clutch assembly

Fig. 2 Clutch assembly

if there is, the hydraulic system still contains air. If this is the case, repeat bleed procedure.

SHIFT CABLES
REPLACE

Refer to **Figs. 4 and 5,** when replacing manual shift cables.
1. Disconnect battery ground cable.
2. Remove clamp and nut from each transaxle shift lever.
3. Remove shift knob, console and shift boot.
4. Remove shift cables from shifter control assembly by twisting between cable socket and control lever with suitable screwdriver.
5. Remove spring clips retaining cables to control assembly.
6. Remove right front sill plate, then pull back carpet to gain access to shift cables.
7. Remove shift cable grommet cover attaching screws, then remove cable cover at floor pan and remove shift cables.
8. Reverse procedure to install.

SHIFT CONTROL ASSEMBLY
REPLACE

1. Disconnect battery ground cable.
2. Remove shift knob, console and shift boot.
3. Remove shift cables from shifter control assembly by twisting between cable socket and control lever with suitable screwdriver.
4. Remove spring clips retaining cables to control assembly.
5. Remove shift control assembly.
6. Reverse procedure to install.

MANUAL TRANSAXLE
REPLACE
ISUZU TRANSAXLE

1. Disconnect battery ground cable.
2. Install engine support fixture, **Fig. 6.** Connect fixture hook to engine lift ring and raise engine enough to relieve weight from engine mounts. The engine support fixture must be posi-

Fig. 3   Clutch disc & pressure plate alignment

1. TOOL J-28467
2. THREAD ONTO STRUT ATTACHING BOLTS, ABOVE NUTS – 3 PER SIDE

Fig. 6   Engine support fixture installation

1	SHIFT CABLE
2	SELECTOR CABLE
3	CLIP
4	SCREW - 2 N.m (18 LBS. FT.)
5	GROMMET
6	CABLE CLAMP
7	NUT - 25 N.m (18 LBS. FT.)
8	STUD
9	NUT 25 N.m (19 LBS. FT.)
10	LOCKING PIN

Fig. 4   Shift cable replacement. Muncie

1	LOCKING PIN
2	TRANSMISSION LEVER
3	NUT - 28 N.m (21 LBS. FT.)
4	NUT - 25 N.m (18 LBS. FT.)
5	CABLE ASSEMBLY
6	TRANSAXLE CONTROL ASSEMBLY

Fig. 5   Shift cable replacement. Isuzu

tioned in the center of the cowl and the attaching parts properly tightened before supporting engine.
3. Remove left sound insulator from under instrument panel, then disconnect clutch master cylinder pushrod from clutch pedal.

4. Remove clutch slave cylinder from transaxle support and position aside.
5. Remove transaxle mount attaching bolts.
6. Remove transaxle mount bracket attaching bolts and nuts.
7. Disconnect shift cables and remove

retaining clips at transaxle.
8. Disconnect ground cable at transaxle mounting stud, then the shift light wiring.
9. Raise and support vehicle, then remove left front wheel.
10. Remove left front inner splash shield retaining screws and the splash shield.
11. Remove transaxle front strut and front strut bracket.
12. Remove clutch housing cover attaching bolts, then disconnect speedometer cable at transaxle.
13. Disconnect stabilizer bar at the left suspension support and control arm.
14. Remove left side support attaching bolts, then swing support aside.
15. Install boot protectors at drive axles, then disengage both drive axles at transaxle. Remove left drive axle from transaxle housing bore.
16. Attach the transaxle case to a suitable jack, then remove transaxle to engine mounting bolts.
17. Slide transaxle away from engine, lower jack and guide right drive axle from transaxle housing bore. Remove transaxle from vehicle.
18. Reverse procedure to install. **When installing transaxle, guide the right drive axle into transaxle bore as transaxle is being raised. The right drive axle cannot be installed after the transaxle is connected to engine.**

MUNCIE TRANSAXLE (NEW VENTURE)

1. Disconnect battery ground cable.
2. Install engine support fixture, **Fig. 6.** Connect fixture hook to engine lift ring and raise engine enough to relieve weight from engine mounts. The engine support fixture must be positioned in the center of the cowl and the attaching parts properly tightened before supporting engine.
3. Remove left sound insulator from un-

der instrument panel, then disconnect clutch master cylinder pushrod from clutch pedal.

4. Remove air cleaner and air intake duct assembly.
5. Remove clutch slave cylinder from transaxle brace and position aside.
6. Remove transaxle mount through bolt.
7. Raise and support vehicle, then remove two exhaust crossover bolts from right side manifold.
8. Lower vehicle, then remove left side exhaust manifold.
9. Remove shift cables, then upper transaxle to engine attaching bolts.
10. Raise and support vehicle, then remove left tire and wheel assembly.

11. Remove left front inner splash shield, then the transaxle strut and bracket.
12. Drain transaxle into suitable container, then remove clutch housing cover bolts.
13. Disconnect speedometer wire connector.
14. Remove stabilizer bar from left side suspension support and control arm.
15. Remove left side suspension support attaching bolts, then swing support aside.
16. Install boot protectors at drive axles, then disengage both drive axles at transaxle. Remove left drive axle from transaxle housing bore.
17. **On models equipped with manual transmission and 2.3L/4-138 en-**

gine, the throttle body coolant pipes must be removed before engine is removed. **Do not bent coolant pipes to gain clearance.**
18. **On all Models,** attach the transaxle case to a suitable jack, then remove transaxle to engine mounting bolts.
19. Slide transaxle away from engine, lower jack and guide right drive axle from transaxle housing bore. Remove transaxle from vehicle.
20. Reverse procedure to install. **When installing transaxle, guide the right drive axle into transaxle bore as transaxle is being raised. The right drive axle cannot be installed after the transaxle is connected to engine.**

TIGHTENING SPECIFICATIONS

Year	Component	Torque/ Ft. Lbs.
1991–94	Actuator Cylinder Support To Transaxle	37
	Alternate Oil Level Check/Fill Plug	18
	Back-Up Lamp Switch Assembly To Transaxle	①
	Clutch Actuator Cylinder Nut	16
	Clutch Cover To Flywheel Bolt	③
	Clutch Housing Cover To Transaxle	89②
	Clutch Master Cylinder Nut	20
	Clutch Pedal Bracket Nut	20
	Clutch Start Switch Nuts	53②
	Electronic Speed Sensor Retainer	7
	Fluid Drain Plug	18
	Fluid Reservoir Bolt	80②
	Fluid Reservoir Bracket Bolt	16
	Flywheel To Crankshaft	52
	Front Transaxle Strut To Body Bolt	44
	Front Transaxle Strut To Transaxle	44
	Rear Mount Bracket To Mount	72
	Rear Mount Bracket To Transaxle	44
	Rear Transaxle Mount To Body Bolt	41
	Rear Transaxle Mount To Body Nuts	24
	Shift Cable Grommet To Shroud	12②
	Shift Control To Floor	18
	Shift Control Box To Transaxle	13
	Shift Linkage Retainer To Transaxle Case	17
	Shift Retainer To Transaxle Case	90②
	Shift Shaft To Lever Nut	61
	Speedometer To Vehicle Speed Sensor	84②
	Transaxle Shift Cable Bracket To Cables	18
	Transaxle Shift Lever To Cable Stud	18
	Transaxle To Engine Bolts	55

①—Muncie, 24 ft. lbs.; Isuzu, 7 ft. lbs.
②—Inch lbs.
③—Except 2.3L/4-138, 18 ft. lbs.;
    2.3L/4-138, 22 ft. lbs.

Rear Axle & Suspension

INDEX

Fig. 1 Rear suspension. Corsica

Fig. 2 Rear suspension. Beretta

then disconnect shock absorbers from axle assembly, **Figs. 1 and 2.**
5. Disconnect parking brake cable and brake lines at axle brackets.
6. Carefully lower rear axle assembly and remove coil springs and insulators.
7. Remove control arm to underbody bracket bolts, then lower the axle assembly and remove from vehicle.
8. Remove hub to rear axle attaching bolts, then the hubs, bearings and backing plates from rear axle assembly.
9. Reverse procedure to install and bleed brake system.

HUB & BEARING
REPLACE

1. Raise and support vehicle, then remove wheel and tire assembly and brake drum. **Do not hammer brake drum since damage to bearing may result.**
2. Remove four hub/bearing assembly to rear axle attaching bolts, then the hub/bearing assembly from axle. **The upper rear hub attaching bolt may not clear brake shoe when removing hub and bearing assembly. Partially remove hub and bearing assembly prior to removing this bolt.**
3. Reverse procedure to install. Tighten hub to axle attaching bolts to specifications. **Use care not to drop hub/bearing assembly since damage to bearing may result.**

SHOCK ABSORBER
REPLACE

1. Open deck lid, then remove trim cover (if equipped) and shock absorber upper retaining nut.
2. Raise rear of vehicle and support rear axle using a suitable jack.
3. Remove shock absorber lower attaching bolt, then disconnect shock absorber from mounting bracket, **Figs. 1 and 2.** Remove shock absorber from vehicle.
4. Reverse procedure to install. Tighten attaching bolts to specifications.

COIL SPRING
REPLACE

1. Raise and support rear of vehicle. Support rear axle using a suitable jack.

DESCRIPTION

This rear suspension is a semi-independent type suspension consisting of an axle assembly with trailing arms and twisting cross beam, coil springs and double action shock absorbers. A stabilizer bar is available and is attached to the inside of the axle beam and to the lower end of the control arms. A single unit hub and bearing assembly is bolted to each end of the axle assembly. The hub and bearing assembly is a sealed, non-serviceable unit and must be replaced as an assembly.

REAR AXLE
REPLACE

1. Raise vehicle and support vehicle. Support rear suspension with suitable jack.
2. Disconnect stabilizer bar at axle assembly, if equipped.
3. Remove rear wheel assembly and brake drum. **Do not hammer on brake drum since damage to bearings may result.**
4. Remove shock absorber to lower mounting bracket attaching bolts,

Fig. 3   Coil spring & brake line installation

1	CENTER BRAKE PIPE
2	BRAKE HOSE
3	BRAKE PIPE BRACKET
4	UNDERBODY
5	SPRING INSULATOR
6	SPRING
7	COMPRESSION BUMPER
8	AXLE ASM.

VIEW A (BOTH SPRINGS)

9	15mm MAX. (.594")
10	SPRING
11	SPRING STOP PART OF SPRING SEAT.

1	PLATE—J-29376-7	3	NUT—J-21474-18
2	REMOVER—J-29376-6	4	RECEIVER—J-29376-1

Fig. 4   Control bushing removal

2. Remove wheel and tire assemblies.
3. Remove brake line bracket attaching bolts, **Fig. 3**, from frame and allow brake lines to hang freely.
4. Remove shock absorber to lower mounting bracket bolts, then disconnect shock absorbers from axle assembly. **Do not suspend rear axle by brake hoses since damage to hoses may result.**
5. Carefully lower rear axle assembly and remove springs and insulators.
6. Reverse procedure to install. Position ends of upper coil in seat of body and within limits shown in **Fig. 3**.

CONTROL ARM BUSHING
REPLACE

1. Raise and support rear of vehicle.
2. Remove wheel and tire assembly, then support body with suitable jack stands
3. Remove brake line bracket to body attaching screws from both sides.
4. Remove control arm to mounting bracket attaching nut, bolt and washer, then allow control arm to rotate downward.
5. The bushing can now be replaced using tools shown in **Figs. 4 and 5**. When installing bushing, the arrow on the installer must align with arrow on the receiver, **Fig. 4**.
6. Reverse procedure to complete installation. **The control arm attaching bolt must be torqued to specifications after vehicle is lowered to floor and is in its standing height position.**

STABILIZER BAR
REPLACE

1. Raise vehicle on hoist and support body with jack stands.
2. Remove nuts and bolts at both the axle and control arm attachments and remove bracket, insulator and stabilizer shaft, **Figs. 6 and 7**.
3. Reverse procedure to install.

1	RECEIVER J29376-1	3	NUT J-21474-18	5	BUSHING MUST BE INDEXED IN INSTALLER, AND INSTALLER ARROW MUST ALIGN WITH ARROW ON RECEIVER FOR PROPER BUSHING INSTALLATION.
2	PLATE J29376-7	4	INSTALLER J29376-4		

Fig. 5   Control arm bushing installation

Fig. 6   Stabilizer assembly. Beretta

1	SHAFT ASM
2	NUT
3	CLAMP ASSY
4	INSULATOR
5	SPACER — LOWER
6	SPACER — UPPER
7	NUT
8	INSULATOR
9	CLAMP
10	BOLT SCREW

36.0mm SPACER AS INSTALLED MUST NOT INTERFERE WITH WELD BEAD ON INSERT-CROSSMEMBER.

16 N·m (12 FT. LBS)
18 N·m (13 FT. LBS)

W INSULATORS 4 & 8 MUST BE INSTALLED AS SHOWN.
Y TAB MUST BE INSERTED INTO SLOT BEFORE TORQUING NUT.
T CLAMP 3 MUST BE INSTALLED AS SHOWN.
Z HOLD NUT 2 & TORQUE BOLT SCREW.

TYPICAL L & RH

TORQUE:

$\triangle_1$ 18 N·m (13 FT. LBS.)

$\triangle_2$ 22 N·m (16 FT. LBS.)

BRACE

SPACER

VIEW A

SPACER MUST CONTACT BRACE WHEN
SPACER & PARTS ARE INSTALLED.

AXLE ASM

FRT

1	NUT
2	CLAMP ASM
3	BOLT, SCREW
4	INSULATOR
5	CLAMP
6	NUT
7	SPACER — LOWER
8	SHAFT
9	SPACER — UPPER

TAB MUST BE INSERTED INTO
SLOT BEFORE TORQUING NUT.
OR BOLT.

Fig. 7 Stabilizer assembly. Corsica

TIGHTENING SPECIFICATIONS

Year	Component	Torque/ Ft. Lbs.
1991–94	Brake Line Bracket To Control Arm	11
	Brake Line Bracket To Frame	8
	Control Arm Pivot Bolts	66 ①
	Control Arm To Underbody Attaching Nut	③
	Hub To Axle	④
	Shock Absorber Lower Attaching Bolt	35
	Shock Absorber Upper Shaft Nut	22
	Stabilizer Bar To Axle	16
	Stabilizer Bar To Control Arm	16
	Stabilizer Shaft To Rear Axle Assembly Nut ②	103
	Upper Shock Mount	21
	Upper Shock Mount Bolt To Body	13
	Wheel Lug Nuts	100

① —Torque control arm attaching bolt
after vehicle is lowered to floor and
is in its' standing height position.

② —Beretta.

③ —52 ft. lbs., plus 120° rotation.

④ —1991–92 models, 38 ft. lbs.; 1993–94
models, 43 ft. lbs.

Front Suspension & Steering

INDEX

DESCRIPTION

The front suspension, **Figs. 1 through 3**, on these vehicles is of the MacPherson strut design. The lower control arms pivot from the lower side rails through rubber bushings. The upper end of the strut is isolated by a rubber mount incorporating a non-serviceable bearing for wheel turning. The tie rods connect to the steering arm on the strut, below the spring seat. The lower end of the steering knuckle pivots on a ball stud which is retained to the lower control arm by rivets and is secured to the steering knuckle with a nut and cotter pin. The sealed wheel bearings are integral with the hub and are serviced as an assembly.

Fig. 1 Front suspension

WHEEL BEARING
REPLACE

REMOVAL

1. Loosen hub nut with vehicle on ground.
2. Raise and support vehicle, then remove front wheel.
3. Install Drive Axle Protective Boot Cover tool No. J-28712 or equivalent.
4. Remove hub nut.
5. Remove brake caliper from support and suspend caliper from flame with a length of wire. Do not suspend caliper by brake hose.
6. Remove brake rotor.
7. Remove three hub and bearing attaching bolts, then the splash shield. If the old bearing is being reinstalled, mark attaching bolts and corresponding holes for reinstallation, **Fig 4.**
8. Using Front Hub Spindle Remover tool No. J-28733 or equivalent, remove bearing from steering knuckle, **Fig. 5. If excessive corrosion is present, ensure that bearing is loose in the knuckle before using puller tool.**
9. If installing new bearing, replace steering knuckle seal. **Do not move drive axle until hub nut is installed and tighten to specifications.**

INSTALLATION

1. Clean and inspect bearing mating surfaces and steering knuckle bore for dirt, nicks and burrs.
2. If installing new steering knuckle seal, apply grease to seal and knuckle bore, then press seal into steering knuckle.
3. Push bearing onto axle shaft, then install splash shield and hub to steering knuckle attaching bolts. Tighten attaching bolts to specifications. Install hub to axle retaining nut and apply a partial **torque** of 74 ft. lbs., **Fig. 6.**
4. Install rotor, brake caliper and wheel assembly.
5. Lower vehicle and **torque** hub nut to 191 ft. lbs.

BALL JOINT
REPLACE

LOWER

1. Raise and support vehicle, then remove wheel and tire.
2. Locate center of rivet body and mark with a center punch.
3. Using a 1/8 inch drill, drill pilot holes completely through the rivets. Using a 1/2 inch drill, drill final holes through rivets to ensure fitting of new ball joint.
4. Remove ball joint stud retaining nut, then, using Ball Joint Separator tool No. J-29330 or equivalent, separate ball joint from steering knuckle. Re-

Fig. 3   Exploded view of front suspension. GTZ models

31	BOLT	38	PLATE, FRONT ENGINE MOUNT CROSSMEMBER
32	CONTROL ARM	39	CROSSMEMBER, FRONT ENGINE MOUNT
33	BOLT	40	SUSPENSION SUPPORT
34	BUSHING, CONTROL ARM	41	NUT
35	BOLT	42	WASHER
36	NUT	43	BOLT
37	BOLT		

16	LOWER SPRING INSULATOR	24	SEAL (PART OF)
17	STRUT	25	STEERING KNUCKLE
18	BRACKET, STABILIZER LINK	26	NUT, BALL JOINT
19	NUT	27	COTTER PIN
20	DISK BRAKE SPLASH SHIELD	28	HUB AND BEARING SEAL
21	WASHER	29	NUT
22	BOLT	30	BALL JOINT
23	HUB AND BEARING ASSEMBLY		

1	CLAMP, STABILIZER SHAFT	9	NUT
2	INSULATOR, STABILIZER SHAFT	10	NUT, STRUT DAMPENER SHAFT
3	NUT	11	STRUT MOUNT
4	STABILIZER SHAFT	12	SPRING SEAT
5	STABILIZER LINK	13	UPPER SPRING INSULATOR
6	NUT	14	STRUT BUMPER AND SHIELD
7	BOLT	15	SPRING
8	COVER, STRUT MOUNT		

Fig. 2   Exploded view of front suspension. Except GTZ models

29	INSULATOR, STABILIZER LINK	36	NUT
30	WASHER, STABILIZER LINK	37	SUSPENSION SUPPORT
31	BOLT, STABILIZER LINK	38	NUT
32	CONTROL ARM	39	WASHER
33	BOLT	40	BOLT
34	BUSHING, CONTROL ARM	41	SPACER, STABILIZER LINK
35	BOLT	42	NUT STABILIZER LINK

15	STRUT	22	STEERING KNUCKLE
16	NUT	23	NUT, BALL JOINT
17	DISK BRAKE SPLASH SHIELD	24	COTTER PIN
18	WASHER	25	HUB AND BEARING SEAL
19	BOLT	26	NUT
20	HUB AND BEARING ASSEMBLY	27	BALL JOINT
21	SEAL (PART OF 25)	28	BOLT

1	CLAMP, STABILIZER SHAFT	8	COVER, STRUT MOUNT
2	INSULATOR, STABILIZER SHAFT	9	NUT
3	NUT	10	NUT, STRUT DAMPENER SHAFT
4	STABILIZER SHAFT	11	STRUT MOUNT
5	BOLT	12	SPRING SEAT
6	NUT	13	UPPER SPRING INSULATOR
7	NUT	14	STRUT BUMPER AND SHIELD
			SPRING
			LOWER SPRING INSULATOR

Fig. 4 Front hub & wheel bearing assembly

TOOL J-28733

Fig. 5 Front hub & bearing assembly removal

TEMPORARILY INSTALL LONG BOLT

Fig. 6 Hub nut installation

BOLT MUST BE INSTALLED IN DIRECTION SHOWN 68 N·m (50 FT. LBS.)

INSTALL BALL JOINT TO CONTROL ARM

Fig. 7 Lower ball joint to lower control arm installation

CONTROL ARM — J 29792-1

TO REMOVE, INSERT J 29792-1 INTO BUSHING, SUPPORT CONTROL ARM ON J 29792-2, AND PRESS AS SHOWN.

J 29797-2

SUPPORT PLATE

CONTROL ARM — J 29792-2

TO INSTALL, SUPPORT CONTROL ARM ON J 29792-3, PLACE BUSHING INTO J 29792-2, AND PRESS BUSING INTO CONTROL ARM USING J 29792-1. LUBRICATE BUSHING.

J 29792-3

SUPPORT PLATE

Fig. 8 Lower control arm bushing replacement

move ball joint from lower control arm.
5. Assemble new ball joint to lower control arm with bolts provided in service package, **Fig. 7**, and tighten bolts to specifications.
6. Insert ball joint stud into steering knuckle and tighten nut to specifications.
7. Install wheel and tire, check toe setting and adjust as required.

CONTROL ARM
REPLACE
LOWER

1. Raise and support vehicle, then remove wheel and tire.
2. Disconnect stabilizer bar at lower control arm and control arm support.
3. Using Ball Joint Separator tool No. J-29330 or equivalent, separate ball joint from steering knuckle.
4. Remove control arm support to chassis retaining bolts and remove control arm support and control arm as an assembly.
5. Separate control arm from support, then using tools shown in **Fig. 8**, remove bushings from control arm.
6. Lubricate new bushings and install into control arm using tools shown in **Fig. 8**.
7. Attach lower control arm to control arm support and tighten pivot bolts to specifications.

EXCEPT GTZ

GTZ

1 SUSPENSION SUPPORT	5 CONTROL ARM	9 PLATE, ENGINE MOUNT CROSSMEMBER
2 BOLT	6 NUT	10 ENGINE MOUNT CROSSMEMBER
3 WASHER	7 BOLT-TIGHTEN SECOND	11 NUT
4 BOLT-TIGHTEN FIRST	8 BOLT-TIGHTEN THIRD	

Fig. 9 Lower control arm replacement

8. Install control arm support to chassis, using attaching bolt tightening sequence shown in **Fig. 9**. Tighten bolts to specifications.
9. Reverse procedure to complete installation. Check wheel alignment.

CONTROL ARM BUSHING
REPLACE

Refer to "Control Arm, Replace" for control arm bushing replacement procedure.

STEERING KNUCKLE
REPLACE

1. Raise and support vehicle, then re-

move wheel and tire.
2. Remove front hub and bearing as outlined under Wheel Bearing, Replace procedure.
3. Using Ball Joint Separator tool No. J-29330 or equivalent, separate ball joint from steering knuckle.
4. Remove strut to steering knuckle attaching bolts, then disconnect strut from steering knuckle.
5. Assemble strut to new steering knuckle and install attaching bolts finger tight.
6. Insert ball joint stud into steering knuckle and tighten stud nut to specifications.
7. Tighten strut to steering knuckle attaching bolts to specifications.
8. Reverse removal procedure to complete installation.

Fig. 10 Stabilizer bar installation

1 BOLT	6 NUT
2 BOLT	7 STEERING KNUCKLE
3 NUT	8 BRACKET, STABILIZER LINK
4 COVER, STRUT MOUNT	9 NUT
5 STRUT ASSEMBLY	10 STABILIZER LINK

Fig. 11 Strut assembly mounting

STABILIZER BAR
REPLACE

1. Disconnect battery ground cable.
2. Install Engine Support tool No. J-28467 or equivalent.
3. Raise and support vehicle, allowing control arms to hang free.
4. Remove left front tire and wheel assembly.
5. Disconnect stabilizer bar from arms, then from support assemblies.
6. Loosen front support attaching bolts, then remove rear and center support bolts. Allow supports to drop down enough to remove stabilizer bar, **Fig. 10.**
7. Reverse procedure to install. Before tightening any attaching bolts, ensure stabilizer bar is centered in chassis. Refer to **Fig. 10**, for tighten specifications.

STABILIZER BUSHINGS
REPLACE

Refer to "Stabilizer Bar, Replace" for stabilizer bushing replacement.

STRUT
REPLACE

1. Raise hood and remove strut protec-

tive cap and three strut to body attaching nuts **Fig. 11.**
2. Raise and support vehicle, allowing suspension to hang freely.
3. Remove wheel and tire, then install Drive Axle Protective Cover tool No. J-28712 or equivalent.
4. Using Steering Linkage Puller tool No. J-24319 or equivalent, disconnect tie rod from strut assembly.
5. Remove strut to steering knuckle attaching bolts, then remove strut from vehicle.
6. Reverse procedure to install. Position flats of strut mounting bolts as shown in **Fig. 12.** Tighten all nuts and bolts to specifications.

STRUT SERVICE
DISASSEMBLY

Care must be taken not to damage special coating on coil springs. If special coating is damaged, coil spring damage could occur.
1. Clamp Strut Compressor tool No. J-26584 or equivalent in a suitable vise.
2. Place strut assembly in compressor tool and install Bottom Adapter tool No. J-26584-400 or equivalent, making sure that adapter captures strut and locating pins are fully engaged, **Fig. 13.**
3. Position Top Adapter tool No.

J-26584-430 or equivalent on strut cap, aligning mounting holes as necessary.
4. Rotate compressor forcing screw clockwise until top support flange contacts top adapter. Continue rotating forcing screws until strut spring is compressed to approximately 1/2 its height. **Do not bottom the spring or strut damper rod.**
5. Remove damper top nut, then place alignment rod on strut shaft. Use alignment rod to guide shock shaft through spring cap during removal.
6. Remove strut components, then relieve compressor tension.

ASSEMBLY

1. Perform Steps 1 & 2 as outlined in the Disassembly procedure.
2. Position spring on strut, making sure spring is properly seated on bottom spring plate.
3. Install shields, bumpers and insulators on spring seat, then install coil spring seat on top of spring, **Fig. 14.**
4. Install bearing cap on spring seat, ensuring they are centered together and properly aligned.
5. Rotate spring as necessary to have upper end of spring located within 10 mm from end of groove in upper insulator and lower end of spring located 10-15 mm from end of groove in lower insulator.
6. Position Top Adapter tool No. J-26584-430 or equivalent on strut cap, then engage compressor slightly. Pull up strut rod to its full extension and clamp in place with Clamp tool No. J-34013-20 or equivalent.
7. Insert Alignment Rod tool No. J-34013-27 or equivalent through bearing and spring cap and position on top of strut rod. Compress spring slowly while guiding strut rod through bearing cap with alignment rod.
8. Continue compressing spring until one inch of strut rod is above bearing cap. Install strut attaching nut and tighten to specifications.
9. Remove strut rod clamp, then release

NOTE: THE UPPER SPRING SEAT FLAT MUST BE ALIGNED WITH THE LOWER STRUT TO KNUCKLE ATTACHMENT.

Fig. 12 Strut assembly installation

tension on coil spring and remove compressor.

POWER STEERING GEAR REPLACE

1. Disconnect battery ground cable.
2. Remove lefthand sound insulator.
3. Remove steering column coupling upper pinch bolt.
4. Remove hydraulic line retainer, then disconnect pump pressure and return lines from steering gear.
5. Raise and support vehicle.
6. Remove front wheel and tire assemblies.

Fig. 13 Damper & coil spring from strut removal

7. Disconnect tie rods from steering knuckles.
8. Lower vehicle, then remove steering gear mounting clamps.
9. Move steering gear forward, then remove steering column coupling lower pinch bolt.
10. Remove steering column coupling and dash seal from steering gear.
11. Raise and support vehicle, then remove steering gear through left front wheel opening.
12. Reverse procedure to install. Tighten all bolts to specifications noting the following:
    a. When installing steering gear, attach clamps and finger tighten all attaching nuts prior to tightening. Ensure dash seal is indexed and flush with steering gear.

POWER STEERING PUMP REPLACE

EXCEPT 2.3L/4-138 ENGINE

1. Disconnect battery ground cable.
2. Place suitable container under pump to catch fluid.

Fig. 14 Strut coil spring & upper mounting installation

3. Disconnect pressure and return lines at pump, then plug open ends at hoses and pump.
4. Remove auxiliary drive belt.
5. Working through holes in pump pulley, remove pump attaching bolts.
6. Remove power steering pump.
7. Reverse procedure to install.

2.3L/4-138 ENGINE

1. Disconnect negative battery cable.
2. Remove air cleaner assembly, then the pump drive belt.
3. Disconnect power brake booster vacuum line, then the power steering pressure switch electrical connector.
4. Remove pump bracket bolts and bracket.
5. Disconnect pressure and return lines at pump, then plug open ends at hoses and pump.
6. Remove pump pivot bracket bolts and bracket.
7. Remove power steering pump.
8. Reverse procedure to install.

TIGHTENING SPECIFICATIONS

Year	Component	Torque/Ft. Lbs.
1991–92	Ball Joint To Control Arm	50
	Ball Joint To Steering Knuckle Nuts	26①
	Control Arm Pivot Bolts	63
	Control To Suspension Support Bolts	44①
	Front Engine Mount Lower Nuts	30
	Front Engine Mount Upper Nut	55
	Gear Inlet & Outlet Pipes To Rack & Pinion Steering Gear	20
	Gear Inlet Pipe To Pump	18
	Hub & Bearing Assembly Bolts	70
	Hub To Axle Nut	192
	Hub To Steering Knuckle	70

Year	Component	Torque/Ft. Lbs.
1991–92 —Cont'd	Inner Tie Rod To Rack & Pinion Steering Gear Bolts	66
	Outer Tie Rod End Nuts	55
	Pinion Locknut	26
	Pivot Bracket To Power Steering Pump Bolts ④	23
	Power Steering Pump O-Ring Union Fitting	55
	Rack & Pinion Steering Gear Mounting Stud	15
	Stabilizer Link Nuts	③
	Stabilizer Shaft Clamp Nuts	17
	Steering Column Pinch Bolts	②
	Steering Gear Clamps	28

Continued

TIGHTENING SPECIFICATIONS—Continued

Year	Component	Torque/ Ft. Lbs.
1991-92 —Cont'd	Strut Assembly To Body Bolts	18
	Strut Rod To Bearing Cap	60
	Strut To Steering Knuckle	129
	Tie Rod To Steering Knuckle	44
	Wheel Lug Nuts	100
1993-94	Ball Joint To Control Arm	50
	Ball Joint To Steering Knuckle Nuts	55 ①
	Control Arm Pivot Bolts	63
	Control To Suspension Support Bolts	61
	Front Engine Mount Lower Nuts	30
	Front Engine Mount Upper Nut	55
	Gear Inlet & Outlet Pipes To Rack & Pinion Steering Gear	20
	Gear Inlet Pipe To Pump	18
	Hub And Bearing Assembly Bolts	70
	Hub To Axle Nut	192
	Hub To Steering Knuckle	70

Year	Component	Torque/ Ft. Lbs.
1993-94 —Cont'd	Inner Tie Rod To Rack & Pinion Steering Gear Bolts	65
	Outer Tie Rod End Nuts	55
	Pinion Locknut	26
	Pivot Bracket To Power Steering Pump Bolts ④	23
	Power Steering Pump O-Ring Union Fitting	55
	Rack & Pinion Steering Gear Mounting Stud	15
	Stabilizer Link Nuts	15
	Stabilizer Shaft Clamp Nuts	15
	Steering Column Pinch Bolts	②
	Steering Gear Clamps	22
	Strut Assembly To Body	19
	Strut Rod To Bearing Cap	60
	Strut To Steering Knuckle	133
	Tie Rod To Steering Knuckle	44
	Wheel Lug Nuts	100

① —Plus 60° rotation.
② —Torque upper pinch bolt to 29 ft. lbs., torque lower pinch bolt to 37 ft. lbs.
③ —Except GTZ models; 13 ft. lbs., GTZ models; 70 ft. lbs.
④ —2.3L/4-138 models.

Wheel Alignment

INDEX

PRELIMINARY INSPECTION

1. Inspect tires for proper inflation and similar tread wear.
2. Inspect hub and bearing for excessive wear, repair as required.
3. Inspect ball joints.
4. Inspect tie rod ends for excessive looseness.
5. Check wheel and tire runout.
6. Inspect vehicle ride height.
7. Inspect rack and pinion for looseness at frame.
8. Ensure proper strut operation.
9. Check suspension and steering components for damage, replace as required.

FRONT WHEEL ALIGNMENT

Toe setting is the only adjustment normally required. However, in special circumstances, such as damage due to road hazard or collision, camber may be adjusted by modifying the strut assembly. Caster is not adjustable.

CAMBER

1. Secure bottom of strut assembly in a suitable vise.
2. Enlarge bottom holes in outer flanges with a round file until holes in outer flanges match slots in inner flanges, **Fig. 1.**
3. Connect strut to steering knuckle and install bolts finger tight.
4. Grasp top of tire firmly, then move tire inboard or outboard until correct camber reading is obtained. Tighten retaining bolts enough to secure camber setting.
5. Remove wheel and tire and **torque** strut to steering knuckle retaining bolts to 133 ft. lbs.

TOE-IN

Toe is controlled by tie rod position. Adjustment is made by loosening the clamp bolts at the steering knuckle end of the tie rods and rotating the adjuster to obtain proper toe setting. After correct toe setting is obtained, **torque** clamp bolts to 35 ft. lbs.

REAR WHEEL ALIGNMENT

There are no adjustments to be made on this rear suspension. If alignment is outside specifications, check for broken or bent parts and replace as necessary.

VEHICLE RIDE HEIGHT

Refer to **Fig. 2,** for ride height specifications and measurement locations. Check ride height as follows:
1. Ensure vehicle is on level ground.
2. Ensure tires are inflated to proper pressures.
3. Fuel tank should be full to obtain accurate readings.
4. Trunk should be empty except for spare tire and jack.
5. Bounce the car three times at the front

Fig. 1   Strut bracket modification

and rear to normalize suspension.

6. Measure from lowest point on the ball joint housing to control arm bolt centerline, "D" and "Z" positions.

7. Measure from level floor to rocker panel at "J" and "K" positions.

TIRE SIZE	SERIES	Z		D		J		K	
		SHIPPED	CURB	SHIPPED	CURB	SHIPPED	CURB	SHIPPED	CURB
P185–75R14	CORSICA	21	19	185	175	246	242	260	251
P195–70R14	CORSICA	23	21	187	177	246	242	260	251
P205–55R16	BERETTA	2	0	167	157	233	229	249	238
P205–60R15	CORSICA	8	6	173	163	233	229	246	238
P195–70R14	BERETTA	18	16	183	173	243	239	257	248
P205–60R15	BERETTA	8	6	172	164	232	229	246	235
P205–55VR16	BERETTA	2	0	168	159	233	229	253	243

Fig. 2   Vehicle ride height measurements & specifications

NOTE: Refer To Rear Of This Manual For Vehicle Manufacturer's Special Service Tool Suppliers.

Continued

INDEX OF SERVICE OPERATIONS-Continued

Specifications
GENERAL ENGINE SPECIFICATIONS

Year	Engine Liter/CID ①	Engine VIN Code ②	Fuel Injection System	Bore & Stroke	Compression Ratio	Net H.P. @ RPM ③	Maximum Torque Ft. Lbs. @ RPM	Normal Oil Pressure psi.
1991	2.3L/4-138	D	MFI	3.62 x 3.35	9.5	160 @ 6200	155 @ 5200	④
	2.3L/4-138 HO	A	MFI	3.62 x 3.35	10.0	180 @ 6200	160 @ 5200	④
	2.5L/4-151	U	TBI	4.00 x 3.00	8.3	110 @ 5200	135 @ 3200	26 ⑥
	3.3L/V6-204 (3300)	N	MFI	3.70 x 3.16	9.0	160 @ 5200	185 @ 2000	30 ⑤
1992–93	2.3L/4-138	3	MFI	3.62 x 3.35	9.5	120 @ 5200	140 @ 3200	④
	2.3L/4-138	D	MFI	3.62 x 3.35	9.5	160 @ 6200	155 @ 5200	④
	2.3L/4-138 HO	A	MFI	3.62 x 3.35	10.0	180 @ 6200	160 @ 5200	④
	3.3L/V6-204 (3300)	N	MFI	3.70 x 3.16	9.0	160 @ 5200	185 @ 2000	60 ⑦
1994	2.3L/4-138	3	MFI	3.62 x 3.35	9.5	115 @ 5200	140 @ 3200	④
	2.3L/4-138	D	MFI	3.62 x 3.35	9.5	155 @ 6200	150 @ 5200	④
	2.3L/4-138 HO	A	MFI	3.62 x 3.35	10.0	175 @ 6200	155 @ 5200	④

MFI: Multi-Port Fuel Injection.
TBI: Throttle Body Fuel Injection.
① —CID-Cubic inch displacement.
② —The eighth digit denotes engine code.
③ —Ratings are net-as installed in vehicle.
④ —At 900 RPM, 15 psi. minimum; at 2000 RPM, 30 psi. minimum.
⑤ —At 1850 RPM, with engine at operating temperature using SAE 10W-30 engine oil.
⑥ —At 800 RPM, With engine at operating temperature.
⑦ —At 1850 RPM, with engine at operating temperature.

TUNE UP SPECIFICATIONS

Year & Engine (V.I.N. Code) ①	Spark Plug Gap Inch	Firing Order Fig. ②	Ignition Timing Deg. BTDC Man. Trans.	Ignition Timing Deg. BTDC Auto. Trans.	Mark Fig.	Curb Idle Speed RPM ③ Man. Trans.	Curb Idle Speed RPM ③ Auto. Trans.	Fast Idle Speed RPM Man. Trans.	Fast Idle Speed RPM Auto. Trans.	Fuel Pump Pressure, psi
1991										
2.3L/4-138(D)	.035	⑩	⑦	⑦	⑧	④	④	④	④	40.5–47 ⑨
2.3L/4-138(A) HO	.035	⑩	⑦	—	⑧	④	—	④	—	40.5–47 ⑨
2.5L/4-151(U)	.060	⑩	⑦	⑦	⑧	④	④	④	④	9–13 ⑤
3.3L/V6-204(N)	.060	⑥	—	⑦	⑧	—	④	—	④	41–47 ⑨
1992										
2.3L/4-138(3)	.035	⑩	⑦	⑦	⑧	900 ④	700D ④	④	④	41–47 ⑨
2.3L/4-138(D)	.035	⑩	⑦	⑦	⑧	900 ④	700D ④	④	④	41–47 ⑨
2.3L/4-138(A) HO	.035	⑩	⑦	—	⑧	900 ④	—	④	—	41–47 ⑨
3.3L/V6-204(N)	.060	⑥	—	⑦	⑧	—	675D ④	—	④	41–47 ⑨
1993										
2.3L/4-138(3)	.035	⑩	⑦	⑦	⑧	900 ④	700D ④	④	④	41–47 ⑪
2.3L/4-138(D)	.035	⑩	⑦	⑦	⑧	900 ④	700D ④	④	④	41–47 ⑪
2.3L/4-138(A) HO	.035	⑩	⑦	—	⑧	900 ④	—	④	—	41–47 ⑪
3.3L/V6-204(N)	.060	⑥	—	⑦	⑧	—	675D ④	—	④	41–47 ⑨
1994										
2.3L/4-138(3)	.035	⑩	⑦	⑦	⑧	900 ④	700D ④	④	④	41–47 ⑪
2.3L/4-138(D)	.035	⑩	⑦	⑦	⑧	900 ④	700D ④	④	④	41–47 ⑪
2.3L/4-138(A) HO	.035	⑩	⑦	—	⑧	900 ④	—	④	—	41–47 ⑪

① —The eighth digit of the Vehicle Identification Number (V.I.N.) denotes engine code.
② —Before removing wires from distributor cap, determine location of No. 1 wire in cap, as distributor position may have been altered from that shown at the end of this chart.
③ —P: Park. When adjusting idle speed, set parking brake & block drive wheels.
④ —Idle speed is controlled by an idle air control (IAC) valve or an idle speed control (ISC) motor.
⑤ —Loosen fuel tank filler cap to relieve pressure in tank. Remove fuel pump fuse, then start engine & operate until engine stalls. Crank engine for

Continued

TUNE UP SPECIFICATIONS—Continued

approximately 3 seconds. Disconnect battery ground cable. Wrap shop towel around around fuel hose to steel line connection in engine compartment to prevent fuel spillage. Disconnect fuel hose from steel line & install a suitable fuel pressure gauge between hose & line. Connect battery ground cable & install fuel pump fuse. Ensure gauge connections are tight, then start engine & check fuel pressure readings.

⑥—Cylinder numbering left to right as viewed from front of vehicle, front bank, 1, 3, 5; rear bank, 2, 4, 6. Firing order, 1-6-5-4-3-2. Two different types of coil units are used, refer to Figs. A & B for spark plug wire connections at coil unit.

⑦—Computer controlled, no adjustment.

⑧—Equipped with crankshaft position sensor.

⑨—With shop towel wrapped around fuel pressure valve to prevent fuel spillage, connect a suitable fuel pressure gauge to fuel pressure valve. Check fuel pressure with ignition switch in the On position, engine not running.

⑩—Cylinder numbering front to rear, 1, 2, 3, 4. Firing order 1-3-4-2. Refer to Fig. C for spark plug wire connections at coil unit.

⑪—Loosen fuel tank filler cap, then raise vehicle & disconnect fuel pump electrical connector. Start engine & operate until fuel supply is depleted. Crank engine for approximately 3 seconds, then place ignition switch in off position. Connect fuel pump electrical connector, then disconnect battery ground cable. Disconnect fuel line quick connect fittings, then install a suitable fuel pressure test gauge. Tighten fuel tank filler cap & connect battery ground cable. Place ignition switch in On position & check for leaks at gauge connections. With ignition switch in On position note fuel pressure reading.

COMPUTER CONTROLLED COIL IGNITION

Fig. A

COMPUTER CONTROLLED COIL IGNITION

Fig. B

Fig. C

FRONT WHEEL ALIGNMENT SPECIFICATIONS

Year	Model	Caster Angle, Degrees		Camber Angle, Degrees		Total Toe Deg.
		Limits	Desired	Limits	Desired	
1991–92	All	+.7 to +2.7	+1.7	−.7 to +.7	0	−.2 to +.2
1993–94	All	+.45 to +2.45	+1.45	−.7 to +.7	0	−.2 to +.2

REAR WHEEL ALIGNMENT SPECIFICATIONS

Year	Model	Camber Angle, Degrees		Total Toe Deg.	Thrust Angle Deg.
		Limits	Desired		
1991–92	All	−.82 to +.32	−.25	−.06 to +.56	−.31 to +.31
1993–94	All	−.85 to +.35	−.25	−.35 to +.35	−.35 to +.35

COOLING SYSTEM & CAPACITY DATA

Year	Model or Engine (VIN)	Cooling Capacity, Qts. Less A/C	With A/C	Surge Tank Cap Relief Pressure, psi.	Thermo. Opening Temp. Deg. F	Fuel Tank Gals.	Engine Oil Refill Qts. ②	Transaxle Oil Manual Transaxle Pts.	Auto. Transaxle Qts. ①
1991	2.3L/4-138(D)	10.4	10.4	15	195	13.6	4	4	③
	2.3L/4-138(A) HO	10.4	10.4	15	195	13.6	4	4	③
	2.5L/4-151(U)	10.7	10.7	15	195	13.6	4	4	③
	3.3L/V6-204(N)	12.7	12.7	15	195	13.6	4	4	③
1992–93	2.3L/4-138(3, A & D)	9.5	9.5	18	195	13.6	4	4	③
	3.3L/V6-204(N)	12.7	12.7	18	195	13.6	4	4	③
1994	2.3L/4-138(3, A & D)	9.5	9.5	18	195	13.6	4	4	③

① —Approximate; make final check with dipstick.　② —When changing filter, additional oil may be required.　③ —Oil pan capacity, 4 qts; total capacity, 6 qts.

LUBRICANT DATA

Year	Model	Lubricant Type Transaxle Automatic	Manual	Clutch Hydraulic System	Power Steering System	Brake System
1991	All	Dexron II/IIE	①	DOT 3 Brake Fluid	Power Steering Fluid②	DOT 3 Brake Fluid
1992–93	All	Dexron IIE	①	DOT 3 Brake Fluid	Power Steering Fluid②	DOT 3 Brake Fluid

① —Synchromesh transaxle fluid (GM part No. 12345349 or equivalent).
② —Meeting GM specification 9985010.

Electrical

INDEX

Fig. 1 Starter motor replacement. 2.3L/4-138

FUSE PANEL & FLASHER LOCATION

The fuse panel is located behind left side of instrument panel.

On 1991 models, flashers are located above the fuse panel.

On 1992-94 models, the turn signal flasher is located behind the instrument panel on right hand side of steering column bracket. The hazard warning flasher is located on the convenience center, behind the left hand side of the instrument panel to the left of the steering column.

STARTER REPLACE

2.3L/4-138 ENGINE

1. Disconnect battery ground cable.
2. Remove air induction tube as necessary.
3. Disconnect coolant fan connector and remove coolant fan.
4. Remove oil filter and intake manifold brace.
5. Remove starter bolts and pull starter motor towards the passenger side of vehicle, **Fig. 1.**
6. Disconnect electrical connections and remove starter by lifting out between intake manifold and radiator.
7. Reverse procedure to install.

2.5L/4-151 ENGINE

1. Disconnect battery ground cable.
2. Raise and support vehicle, if necessary.
3. Remove starter motor mounting bolts, then lower the starter motor, **Fig. 2.**
4. Remove nuts/bolts that hold the starter bracket to the starter and engine.
5. Disconnect starter leads and remove starter from vehicle.
6. Reverse procedure to install.

3.3L/V6-204 ENGINE

1. Disconnect battery ground cable.
2. Raise and support vehicle, if necessary.

Fig. 2 Starter motor replacement. 2.5L/4-151

3. Remove starter motor mounting bolts, then lower the starter motor, **Fig. 3.**
4. Disconnect starter leads and remove starter from vehicle.
5. Reverse procedure to install.

IGNITION COIL MODULE REPLACE

2.3L/4-138 ENGINE

1. Disconnect battery ground cable.

1. STARTER MOTOR
2. BOLT

Fig. 3   Starter motor replacement. 3.3L/V6-204

1	#2/3 IGN COIL	4	CRANKSHAFT SENSOR
2	#1/4 IGN COIL	5	BOLT (3)
3	IGN MODULE		

Fig. 6   Ignition coil module replacement. 2.5L/4-151

2. Disconnect electrical connector at ignition coil module.
3. Remove four IDI ignition coil module attaching bolts, then pull straight upward to remove module, **Figs. 4 and 5.** Use tool No. J36011 to remove connector assemblies still attached to spark plugs. Twist tool, then pull upward to remove connector from spark plug.
4. Reverse procedure to install. On connector boots which remained on spark plugs during removal, ensure spring terminal is properly positioned in boot. Prior to installation, apply a suitable release compound to porcelain area of spark plug which is in contact with connector boot. When installing IDI ignition coil module, position over spark plugs, then push straight down. Apply sealant 1052080 or equivalent to the four IDI ignition coil module attaching bolts prior to installation. Torque IDI ignition coil module attaching bolts to 15 ft. lbs.

2.5L/4-151 ENGINE

1. Disconnect battery ground cable.
2. Disconnect electrical connectors at ignition coil module.
3. Disconnect and tag spark plug wires at coils.
4. Remove ignition coil module to engine attaching bolts, then remove module, **Fig. 6.**

NOTE: SHOWN WITH INTAKE CAM CARRIER REMOVED FOR ILLUSTRATIVE PURPOSES.

1	I.D.I. COVER ASSEMBLY
2	CONNECTOR ASSEMBLY (INCLUDING SPRING TERMINAL, BOOT AND BOOT RETAINER)
3	SPARK PLUG

Fig. 4   IDI ignition coil module replacement. 2.3L/4-138 (VIN A & D)

Fig. 7   Ignition coil module replacement. 3.3L/V6-204

5. Reverse procedure to install. **Torque** coil to ignition coil module to engine attaching bolts to 20 ft. lbs.

3.3L/V6-204 ENGINE

1. Disconnect battery ground cable.
2. Disconnect 14 terminal electrical connector at ignition coil module.
3. Disconnect and tag spark plug wires at coils.
4. Remove nuts and washers attaching ignition coil module to bracket, then remove module, **Fig. 7.**
5. If necessary, remove bolts attaching coils to ignition coil module, then remove coils.
6. Reverse procedure to install. **Torque** coil to ignition coil module attaching bolts to 27 inch lbs.

1. I.D.I. COVER ASSEMBLY
2. CONNECTOR ASSEMBLY (INCLUDING SPRING TERMINAL, BOOT AND BOOT RETAINER)
3. SPARK PLUG

Fig. 5   IDI ignition coil module replacement. 1992-94 2.3L/4-138 (VIN 3)

ALTERNATOR
REPLACE

2.5L/4-151 & 3.3L/V6-204 ENGINES

1. Disconnect battery ground cable.
2. Disconnect electrical leads from alternator.
3. Remove alternator drive belt.
4. Remove alternator to mounting bracket attaching bolts, then remove alternator, **Figs. 8 and 9.**
5. Reverse procedure to install.

2.3L/4-138 ENGINE

1. Disconnect battery ground cable.
2. Remove serpentine drive belt, refer to Serpentine Drive Belt, Replace." in the "2.3L/4-138 Engine" section.
3. Disconnect oil/air separator hose, then vacuum harness bracket and position vacuum harness aside.
4. Remove two (one 10 mm and one 13 mm head) lower mounting bolts at rear of alternator **Fig. 10. Use care not to damage radiator core when removing lower mounting bolts.**
5. Remove alternator front mounting bolt, then disconnect electrical leads and remove alternator.
6. Reverse procedure to install.

Fig. 8   Alternator mounting. 2.5L/4-151

1	SUPPORT, GENERATOR
2	BOLT – 50 N·m (36 LBS. FT.)
3	BRACE, GENERATOR REAR
4	BOLT – 27 N·m (17 LBS. FT.)
5	GENERATOR
6	NUT
7	BRACE, GENERATOR FRONT

Fig. 9   Alternator mounting. 3.3L/V6-204

1. GENERATOR ASM.
2. GENERATOR SUPPORT
3. BOLT - 27 N·m (20 LBS. FT.)
4. GENERATOR BRACKET
5. GENERATOR SUPPORT
6. BOLT - 27 N·m (20 LBS. FT.)
7. TENSIONER ASM.
8. BOLT - 27 N·m (20 LBS. FT.)

1. GENERATOR
2. 26 N·m (20 LBS. IN.)
3. 50 N·m (37 LBS. IN.)
4. BRACE
5. SPACER (USED W/O A/C)

Fig. 10   Alternator mounting. 2.3L/4-138

Fig. 11   Ignition lock replacement. 1991

4-RING, RETAINING
6-CAM ASM, TURN SIGNAL CANCEL
33-SHAFT ASM, STEERING COLUMN

Fig. 12   Upper plate snap ring removal. 1992–94

12-BOLT, SHEAR (M6X1.0) WITH WASHER
14-HOUSING ASM, BRG & STRG
16-HOUSING ASM, LOCK CYL A/TRNS

Fig. 13   Ignition lock cylinder housing replacement. 1992–94

IGNITION LOCK
REPLACE

1991

1. Disconnect battery ground cable.
2. Remove steering wheel as described under "Steering Wheel, Replace."
3. Remove turn signal switch as described under "Turn Signal Switch, Replace," then remove buzzer switch.
4. Place ignition switch in Run position, then remove lock cylinder retaining screw and lock cylinder, **Fig. 11.**
5. Install by rotating lock cylinder to stop while holding housing, **Fig. 11.** Align cylinder key with keyway in housing, then push lock cylinder assembly into housing until fully seated.
6. Install lock cylinder retaining screw.
7. Install buzzer switch, turn signal switch and steering wheel.

1992-94

1. Disconnect battery ground cable.
2. Remove steering wheel as described under "Steering Wheel, Replace," then remove upper steering column covers.
3. Remove windshield wiper switch as described under "Windshield Wiper Switch, Replace."
4. Using tool No. J23653 or equivalent, compress plate cam, then remove snap ring, plate cam and upper bearing spring, **Fig. 12.**
5. Remove thrust washer, then remove upper bearing.
6. Disconnect steering column shaft from coupling and remove column to mounting bracket bolts.
7. Remove steering column from vehicle.
8. With ignition lock in Run position, use a 1/4 inch drill bit to remove heads of shear bolts, **Fig. 13.**
9. Remove lock cylinder housing.
10. Using locking type pliers , remove threaded portion of shear bolts from lock cylinder housing.
11. Reverse procedure to install. Clean metal particles from steering column. Ignition lock should be Run position during installation. When installing lock cylinder, heads of bolts should shear at approximately 97 inch lbs. of torque.

Fig. 14 Ignition & dimmer switch replacement. 1991 less tilt column

Fig. 15 Ignition & dimmer switch replacement. 1991 w/tilt column

IGNITION & DIMMER SWITCH
REPLACE
1991

1. Disconnect battery ground cable.
2. Remove ignition lock as described under "Ignition Lock, Replace."
3. Refer to **Figs. 14 and 15 to remove** ignition and dimmer switches.
4. Reverse procedure to install. To adjust dimmer switch, depress switch slightly and install a 3/32 inch twist drill to lock the switch to the body, **Figs. 14 and 15.** Force switch upward to remove lash between switch and pivot, then tighten retaining screws.

IGNITION SWITCH
REPLACE
1992-94

1. Disconnect battery ground cable.
2. Remove steering wheel and covers as described under "Steering Wheel, Replace."
3. Place ignition key in the Off/Lock position.
4. Remove two ignition switch mounting screws, then disconnect electrical connectors and remove switch, **Fig. 16.**
5. Reverse procedure to install.

HEADLAMP, HAZARD WARNING, REAR DEFOGGER & WINDSHIELD WIPER/WASHER SWITCHES
REPLACE
1991

The headlamp, hazard flasher, rear defogger and windshield wiper/washer controls are incorporated into switch modules mounted on either side of the instrument cluster.

1. Disconnect battery ground cable.
2. Remove steering column collar, if equipped, then the steering column filler plate screws and filler plate or lap duct assembly.
3. Remove instrument cluster trim plate attaching screws, then the trim plate.
4. **On Skylark models,** remove switch bezel retaining screws and the bezels.
5. **On all models,** remove switch retaining screws, pull switch assembly away from instrument panel, **Figs. 17 through 20,** and disconnect electrical connectors as needed to complete removal.
6. Reverse procedure to install.

**Fig. 16 Ignition switch &
electrical connections.
1992-94**

**Fig. 17 Satellite switch
removal. 1991 Skylark**

1. HEADLIGHT SWITCH
2. HEADLIGHT SWITCH CONNECTORS
3. FULLY DRIVEN, SEATED AND NOT STRIPPED

**Fig. 18 Satellite switch
removal. 1991 Cutlass Calais**

1. INSTRUMENT PANEL
2. SWITCH, HEADLAMP
3. SCREW, 1.5 N·m (13 LBS. IN.)
4. NUT

**Fig. 19 Headlamp defroster
switch removal. 1991 Grand
Am**

1. INSTRUMENT PANEL
2. CONNECTOR, WINDSHIELD WASHER SWITCH
3. SWITCH, WINDSHIELD WASHER
4. SCREW — 1.5 N·m (13 LBS. IN.)
5. NUT

**Fig. 20 Windshield
wiper/washer switch removal.
1991 Grand Am**

Tighten nut until tool slightly
depresses shaft lock.

**Fig. 21 Shaft lock retaining
ring removal. 1991**

**Fig. 22 Turn signal
replacement. 1991**

TURN SIGNAL SWITCH
REPLACE

1991

1. Disconnect battery cable, then remove steering wheel and column to
   instrument panel trim cover.
2. Remove lock cover, then using a suitable tool, compress lock plate and remove snap ring, **Fig. 21**.
3. Remove lock plate, cancelling cam,
   upper bearing preload spring.
4. Remove turn signal lever by pulling
   lever straight out of detent. If equipped
   with cruise control, use mechanics
   wire to disconnect electrical connector and remove harness from column.
5. Depress hazard warning button, then
   unscrew button.
6. Remove turn signal switch wiring protector.
7. Remove retaining screws and remove

switch, **Fig. 22**. Carefully guide switch
wiring up through steering column.
8. Reverse procedure to install.

HEADLAMP, HAZARD
WARNING, TURN SIGNAL
& CRUISE CONTROL
SWITCH
REPLACE

1992-94

1. Disconnect battery ground cable.
2. Remove horn pad and steering wheel
   as described under "Steering Wheel,
   Replace."
3. Remove tilt lever from steering column, if equipped. If necessary position
   spark plug boot or other suitable device over tilt lever (to prevent damage), then remove tilt lever using locking pliers.
4. Remove steering column upper and
   lower covers, then remove dampener
   assembly.
5. Remove switch assembly attaching
   screw, then remove switch, **Fig. 23**.
6. Reverse procedure to install.

WINDSHIELD
WIPER/WASHER SWITCH
REPLACE

1992-94

1. Disconnect battery ground cable.
2. Remove headlamp, hazard warning,

1. HEADLAMP/TURN SIGNAL/CRUISE CONTROL/
   HAZZARD SWITCH
2. WINDSHIELD WIPER/WASHER SWITCH
3. TILT LEVER (IF EQUIPPED)

**Fig. 23 Column mounted
switch replacement. 1992-94**

turn signal and cruise control switch
as described previously.
3. Remove windshield wiper/washer to
   steering column attaching screws,
   then remove switch, **Fig. 23**.
4. Reverse procedure to install.

1. BOLT - 24 N.m (18 LBS. FT.)
2. SWITCH ASM.
3. TRANS. SHAFT
4. SERVICE ADJUSTMENT HOLE
5. 3/32 INCH DRILL BIT OR 2.34 DIA. GAGE PIN

VIEW A

Fig. 24 Neutral safety/back-up lamp switch replacement

1. CLUSTER ASSEMBLY
2. CLUSTER CONNECTORS
3. FULLY DRIVEN. SEATED AND NOT STRIPPED

Fig. 25 Instrument cluster removal. 1991 Cutlass Calais

1—INSTRUMENT PANEL
2—CLUSTER ASM.
3—TRIM PLATE
4—BOLT/SCREW—USE TORQUE CONTROL TOOL 800 RPM MAX.

Fig. 26 Instrument cluster installation. 1991 Grand Am

NEUTRAL SAFETY SWITCH REPLACE

AUTOMATIC TRANSAXLE
Removal

1. Disconnect battery ground cable.
2. Disconnect shift linkage.
3. Disconnect switch electrical connector, then remove switch mounting screws and switch, **Fig. 24.**

Installation

1. Place shift shaft in Neutral position, then align flats on shaft with flats on switch.
2. Loosely install switch.
3. If original switch is being installed, insert a 3/32 inch drill bit into switch adjustment hole, **Fig. 24.** Move switch until drill bit drops to depth of 9/64 inch, then tighten switch mounting screws and remove drill bit.
4. New switches are pinned in Neutral position. If installation is difficult, ensure shift shaft is Neutral. Do not rotate switch. Tighten switch mounting screws.

BACK-UP LAMP SWITCH REPLACE

MANUAL TRANSAXLE

1. Disconnect battery ground cable.
2. Disconnect back-up lamp switch electrical connector.
3. Remove back-up lamp switch from top of transaxle case.
4. Reverse procedure to install. Prior to installation, apply sealant 1052080 or equivalent to switch threads.

CLUTCH START SWITCH REPLACE

1. Disconnect battery ground cable.
2. Disconnect switch electrical connector.
3. Remove nuts attaching switch to mounting, then remove switch.
4. Reverse procedure to install. After installation, check switch for proper operation.

STOP LAMP SWITCH REPLACE

1. Disconnect battery ground cable.
2. Disconnect electrical connectors from switch, then pull switch out of retaining clip on brake pedal support.
3. Depress brake pedal and push replacement switch into retainer until switch shoulder is bottomed against bracket.
4. Adjust switch by pulling brake pedal back against stop.
5. Ensure switch has continuity when pedal is depressed from normal rest position and when pedal fully returns to rest position stop lamps are off.

INSTRUMENT CLUSTER REPLACE

1991

1. Disconnect battery ground cable.
2. Remove steering column collar, if equipped and the steering column opening filler plate or lap duct assembly.
3. Remove instrument cluster trim plate attaching screws, then the trim plate.
4. Remove screws attaching steering column support to lower steering column assembly.
5. Remove instrument cluster to instrument panel attaching screws, then pull cluster assembly rearward, **Figs. 25 through 27.** On models with electronic instrument cluster, note warning printed on front of cluster and do not touch electronic components as static electricity may damage components.
6. Reverse procedure to install.

1992-94
Achieva

1. Disconnect battery ground cable.
2. Remove steering wheel as outlined under "Steering Wheel, Replace."
3. Remove steering column covers.
4. Remove instrument cluster trim plate eight attaching screws, **Fig. 28.**
5. Pull trim plate rearward to disconnect electrical connectors, then remove plate.
6. Remove instrument cluster four attaching screws, them remove cluster.
7. Reverse procedure to install. **Torque** instrument cluster trim plate attaching screws to 17 inch lbs.

Grand Am

1. Disconnect battery ground cable.
2. Remove three lower left hand sound insulator attaching screws.
3. Disconnect cruise control module electrical connector and lamp, then remove lower left hand sound insulator panel.
4. Remove ALDL connector attaching screws, then remove steering column filler panel attaching screws and filler panel.
5. Carefully pull driver's side air deflectors rearward.
6. In a rocking motion, alternately and carefully pry left and right hand instrument panel cover retaining clips up-

1	CLUSTER FACE PLATE
2	INSTRUMENT CLUSTER
3	ODOMETER
4	BULB COVER

* WHEN CLUSTER IS
REPLACED, ODOMETER
MUST BE TRANSFERRED
TO NEW CLUSTER
(IF SO EQUIPPED)

Fig. 27 Instrument cluster installation. 1991 Skylark

1 SCREWS (6) 2 N·m (17 LBS. IN.)
2 I/P CLUSTER TRIM PLATE
3 INSTRUMENT PANEL

**Fig. 28 Instrument cluster
trim plate removal. 1992–94
Achieva**

1. SCREW - 2 N·m (17 LBS. IN.)
2. INSTRUMENT PANEL
3. INSTRUMENT PANEL CLUSTER

**Fig. 29 Instrument cluster
installation. 1992–94 Grand
Am**

ward, then remove instrument panel cover.
7. Remove fuse panel cover, then remove left hand instrument panel trim plate. Pull trim plate rearward to disengage retaining clips.
8. Open upper instrument panel compartment door, then remove four compartment to instrument panel attaching screws.
9. Remove upper instrument panel compartment from instrument panel.
10. Press release tab upward, then remove lower instrument panel compartment door.
11. Remove lower instrument panel compartment to instrument panel attaching screws, then disconnect electrical connector and remove compartment.
12. Remove right hand instrument panel trim plate attaching screws.
13. Carefully pull right hand instrument panel trim plate rearward to disengage retaining clips, then remove trim panel.
14. Remove instrument cluster attaching screws, then pull cluster forward and disconnect electrical connectors.
15. Remove instrument cluster, **Fig. 29.**
16. Reverse procedure to install.

Skylark

1. Disconnect battery ground cable.
2. Remove instrument panel trim plate two attaching screws, **Fig. 30.**
3. Pull trim plate rearward to disengage plate clips, then remove plate.
4. Remove instrument cluster four attaching screws.
5. Pull top of cluster rearward to remove.
6. Reverse procedure to install. **Torque** instrument cluster trim plate attaching screws to 17 inch lbs.

STEERING WHEEL
REPLACE

1. Disconnect battery ground cable, then remove the attaching screws for the steering pad.
2. Remove the pad and horn lead, then remove the steering wheel retainer and nut.
3. **On 1991 models,** remove the dampener, if equipped.
4. **On all models,** remove the steering wheel with a suitable steering wheel puller.
5. Reverse procedure to install.

RADIO
REPLACE

ACHIEVA

1. Disconnect battery ground cable.
2. Remove steering wheel as outlined under "Steering Wheel, Replace."
3. Remove steering column covers.
4. Remove instrument cluster trim plate eight attaching screws, **Fig. 28.**
5. Pull trim plate rearward to disconnect electrical connectors, then remove plate.
6. Remove two radio to radio bracket attaching nuts.
7. Pull radio rearward to disconnect antenna and electrical connectors, then remove radio assembly.

1. INSTRUMENT PANEL
2. I/P CLUSTER TRIM PLATE
3. SCREWS - 2 N·m (17 LBS. IN.)

**Fig. 30 Instrument cluster
trim plate removal. 1992–94
Skylark**

8. Reverse procedure to install. **Torque** radio to radio bracket attaching nuts to 35 inch lbs.

CUTLASS CALAIS
Models w/Auto Calculator

1. Disconnect battery ground cable.
2. Remove radio trim plate attaching screws, then the trim plate.
3. Remove radio mounting bracket attaching screws, then disconnect antenna lead and electrical connector(s) from radio.
4. Remove radio.
5. Reverse procedure to install.

Models Less Auto
Calculator

1. Disconnect battery ground cable, then open ashtray and remove insert.
2. Depress tab on each ashtray locking tang, pull ashtray out to second stop, depress tabs again and remove ashtray. **There is a locking tang on each side of ashtray and each tang has a tab on the right side, Fig. 31.**
3. Remove 2 screws securing upper ashtray bracket and the bracket and trim plate assembly.
4. Remove radio mounting screws and withdraw radio.

1. TRIM PLATE
2. LOWER ASHTRAY HOUSING
3. RADIO
4. FULLY DRIVEN, SEATED AND NOT STRIPPED
5. LOCKING TANG
6. TAB
7. UPPER ASHTRAY HOUSING

Fig. 31   Radio installation. Cutlass Calais

Fig. 32   Radio installation. 1991 Skylark

5. Disconnect antenna lead and electrical connectors, then remove radio.
6. Reverse procedure to install.

GRAND AM

1991

1. Disconnect battery ground cable.
2. Remove right console extension panel and rear main plate.
3. Remove radio mounting screws.
4. Disconnect antenna lead and electrical connectors, then remove radio.
5. Reverse procedure to install.

1992-94

1. Disconnect battery ground cable.
2. Remove three lower left hand sound insulator attaching screws.
3. Disconnect cruise control module electrical connector and lamp, then remove left hand sound insulator panel.
4. Remove ALDL connector attaching screws, then remove steering column filler panel attaching screws and filler panel.
5. Open upper instrument panel compartment door, then remove four compartment to instrument panel attaching screws.
6. Remove upper instrument panel compartment from instrument panel.
7. Press release tab upward, then remove lower instrument panel compartment door.
8. Remove lower instrument panel compartment to instrument panel attaching screws, then disconnect electrical

connector and remove compartment.
9. Remove right hand instrument panel trim plate attaching screws.
10. Carefully pull right hand instrument panel trim plate rearward to disengage retaining clips, then remove trim panel.
11. Remove radio upper retaining nuts.
12. Pull radio rearward and disconnect electrical connectors and antenna lead.
13. Remove radio from instrument panel.
14. Reverse procedure to install.

SKYLARK

1991

1. Disconnect battery ground cable.
2. Remove console extensions, lower instrument panel trim and face plates, as needed, to gain access to components and mounting hardware.
3. Remove necessary screws and nuts, **Fig. 32**, disconnect electrical connectors and antenna lead if necessary, then remove components.
4. Reverse procedure to install.

1992-94

1. Disconnect battery ground cable.
2. Remove instrument panel trim plate two attaching screws, **Fig. 30**.
3. Pull trim plate rearward to disengage plate clips, then remove plate.
4. Remove two radio to radio bracket attaching nuts.
5. Pull radio rearward to disconnect antenna and electrical connectors, then remove radio assembly.

6. Reverse procedure to install. **Torque** radio to radio bracket attaching nuts to 35 inch lbs.

WINDSHIELD WIPER MOTOR
REPLACE

1. Disconnect battery ground cable.
2. Remove wiper arm and blades assemblies.
3. Remove cowl cover assembly, then disconnect drive link from crank arm.
4. Disconnect wiper motor electrical connectors.
5. Remove wiper motor attaching bolts, then remove wiper motor.
6. Reverse procedure to install.

WINDSHIELD WIPER LINKAGE
REPLACE

1. Disconnect battery ground cable.
2. Remove wiper arm and blades assemblies.
3. Remove cowl cover assembly, then disconnect drive link from crank arm.
4. Remove windshield wiper transmission to body attaching screws, then guide linkage out through access hole.
5. Reverse procedure to install.

BLOWER MOTOR
REPLACE

1991

1. Disconnect battery ground cable.
2. **On with 2.5L & 3.3L engines,** remove power steering pressure hose from power steering pump.
3. **On all models,** remove blower motor mounting screws.
4. Disconnect electrical connectors from blower motor.
5. Remove blower motor assembly.
6. Reverse procedure to install.

1992-94

1. Disconnect battery ground cable.
2. **On models with 3.3L/V6-204 engines**, remove power steering pump from mounting bracket and position aside with hoses attached.
3. **On all models**, disconnect electrical connectors from blower motor.
4. Partially cut blower motor case cover as indicated in **Fig. 33**. The cutting pattern is also indicated on the blower case cover. Cover thickness is approximately 1/8 inch. Cut just through thickness of cover. Any cut deeper than thickness of cover may cause damage to cooling tube.
5. Move cut portion of cover downward and disconnect blower motor cooling tube.
6. Remove blower motor retaining screws and blower motor.
7. Reverse procedure to install. Use three retaining clips to attach cut portion of blower motor cover.

HEATER CORE REPLACE

1991

1. Disconnect battery ground cable.
2. Drain cooling system.
3. Raise and support vehicle.
4. Disconnect heater hoses from heater core assembly.
5. Remove drain tube.
6. Lower vehicle.
7. Remove instrument panel sound insulator.
8. Remove heater duct and hose assembly and position aside.
9. Remove 2 heater core cover attaching screws, then the covers.
10. Remove heater core from vehicle.
11. Reverse procedure to install.

1992-94

1. Disconnect battery ground cable.
2. Drain cooling system.
3. Raise and support vehicle.
4. Disconnect heater hoses from heater core assembly.
5. Remove drain tube.
6. Lower vehicle.
7. If equipped, remove console as follows:
   a. Apply parking brake and block drive wheels.
   b. Position transaxle shift lever in Neutral.
   c. **On models with automatic transaxle**, remove clip retaining shift lever handle to lever, then remove shift lever handle.
   d. **On models with manual transaxle**, turn shift lever handle counter-clockwise to remove from lever.

CUT INSULATOR ON INDENTATION AS SHOWN

NOTE: DO NOT CUT IN THIS AREA

Fig. 33 Cutting pattern for blower motor removal. 1992–94 models

   e. Carefully pry upward on outer edges of console trim plate.
   f. Disconnect electrical connectors and ashtray lamp from console trim plate, then remove trim plate from console.
   g. Remove console to mounting bracket attaching screws, then remove console.
8. Remove three lower left hand sound insulator attaching screws.
9. Disconnect cruise control module electrical connector and lamp, then remove left hand sound insulator panel.
10. Remove two lower right hand sound insulator attaching screws and two nuts.
11. Disconnect EVO controller electrical connector and lamp, then remove right hand sound insulator panel.
12. Remove ALDL connector attaching screws, then remove steering column filler panel attaching screws and filler panel.
13. Remove floor outlet duct.
14. Remove heater core cover attaching screws, then remove heater core cover.
15. Remove heater core mounting clamps, then remove heater core.
16. Reverse procedure to install.

EVAPORATOR CORE REPLACE

1991

1. Disconnect battery ground cable, then discharge A/C system.
2. Drain cooling system, then raise and support vehicle.
3. Remove heater hoses at the heater core, then remove the drain tube.
4. Remove block fitting at the evaporator and discard O-ring seals, then lower vehicle.
5. Remove sound insulators, then the floor air outlet duct and hoses from duct.
6. Remove console assembly, if equipped, then heater core covers.
7. Remove heater core, then evaporator core covers and evaporator core.
8. Reverse procedure to install. Install new O-rings at block fitting and evacuate and recharge system.

1992-94

1. Discharge and recover refrigerant from A/C system.
2. Disconnect battery ground cable.
3. Raise and support vehicle, then remove front exhaust system heat shield.
4. Remove three attaching bolts, then swing cradle cross brace aside.
5. Disconnect refrigerant lines from evaporator, then lower vehicle.
6. Remove under dash insulator panel from right hand side.
7. Disconnect electrical connector at heater core cover on heater A/C module.
8. Remove steering column filler panel.
9. Remove center console to gain access to floor duct and heater core cover.
10. Remove heater core shroud and straps. Use care when removing evaporator core, as heater heater core is only suspended by heater core pipes.
11. Remove evaporator core from vehicle.
12. Reverse procedure to install. When connecting refrigerant lines, use new O-rings.

2.3L/4-138 Engine

INDEX

PRECAUTIONS

FUEL SYSTEM PRESSURE RELIEF

Failure to relieve system pressure prior to disconnecting fuel system components may cause fire or personal injury.

1. Loosen fuel tank filler cap to relieve tank pressure.
2. Raise and support vehicle, then disconnect fuel pump electrical connector.
3. Start and operate engine until fuel supply is consumed.
4. Crank engine for approximately 3 seconds to relieve remaining pressure.
5. Disconnect battery ground cable, then reconnect fuel pump connector.

ENGINE MOUNTS
REPLACE

1991
Front Mount

1. Disconnect battery ground cable.
2. Remove front mount upper retaining nut, **Fig. 1.**
3. Using tool No. J-28467 or equivalent, raise engine off mount.
4. Raise and support vehicle, then remove front engine mount lower retaining nuts.
5. Lower vehicle and remove mount assembly.
6. Reverse procedure to install.

Rear Mount

1. Disconnect battery ground cable.
2. Using engine support No. J-28467 or equivalent, relieve engine weight from rear mount.

119.	BRACKET
120.	WASHER
121.	STUD
122.	BOLT/SCREW (2)
123.	NUT
124.	MOUNT ASM.
125.	NUT (2)

Fig. 1   Engine front mount. 1991

3. Raise and support vehicle, then remove right hand lower splash shield.
4. Remove rear engine mount through bolt and nut, then remove four bracket to body attaching bolts, **Fig. 2.**
5. Remove bracket assembly and mount from vehicle, then remove three mount to bracket attaching nuts and separate mount from bracket.
6. Reverse procedure to install.

1992-94
Front Mount

1. Disconnect battery ground cable.
2. Using tool No. J-28467-A or equivalent, raise engine off mount.
3. Raise and support vehicle, then remove right hand wheel and tire assembly.
4. Remove right hand splash shield.
5. Remove two front engine mount lower attaching bolts.
6. Lower vehicle, then remove nut attaching mount to body.
7. Remove nut attaching engine bracket to mount, then remove mount assembly, **Fig. 3.**
8. Reverse procedure to install.

Engine Mount Strut

1. Disconnect battery ground cable.
2. Raise and support vehicle.
3. Remove bolts attaching engine mount strut to body and engine mount strut bracket, **Fig. 4.**
4. Remove engine mount strut.
5. Reverse procedure to install.

ENGINE
REPLACE

1. Disconnect battery ground cable, then drain cooling system.
2. Disconnect heater hose at thermostat housing, then upper radiator hose.
3. Disconnect air cleaner to throttle body duct.
4. Remove upper radiator support.
5. Remove engine cooling fan.
6. **On models equipped with A/C,** discharge A/C system, then disconnect hoses from A/C compressor and discard O-rings.
7. **On all models,** disconnect two vacuum lines at front of engine.

126. BOLT/SCREW
127. BRACKET
128. BOLT/SCREW (3)
129. NUT
130. TRANSAXLE SUPPORT (PARTIAL VIEW)
131. BRACKET ASM.
132. BOLT/SCREW (4)
133. MOUNT ASM.
134. NUT (3)
135. ENGINE COMPARTMENT R.H. RAIL ASM.
136. COWL ASM.

Fig. 2 Engine rear mount. 1991

1. BOLT - 66 N•m (42 LBS. FT.) (TIGHTEN FIRST)
2. BOLT - 66 N•m (42 LBS. FT.) (TIGHTEN SECOND)
3. NUT - 42 N•m (31 LBS. FT.) (TIGHTEN LAST)
4. BOLT
5. RIGHT ENGINE MOUNT
6. BOLTS - 62 N•m (46 LBS. FT.)
7. BOLTS - 80 N•m (59 LB. FT.)
8. ENGINE MOUNT

Fig. 3 Right engine mount. 1992–94

1. BOLT - 35 N•m (26 LBS. FT.)
2. BODY
3. UPPER ENGINE MOUNT STRUT (EXCEPT MANUAL TRANS.)
4. BOLT - 35 N•m (26 LBS. FT.)
5. BOLT - 120 N•m (89 LBS. FT.)
6. LOWER ENGINE MOUNT STRUT
7. BOLT - 120 N•m (89 LBS. FT.)
8. ENGINE MOUNT STRUT BRACKET
9. BOLTS - 66 N•m (49 LBS. FT.)

VIEW A

Fig. 4 Engine mount & strut. 1992–94

8. Disconnect electrical connectors from alternator, A/C compressor (if equipped), injector harness, idle air control and throttle position sensor at throttle body and position aside.
9. Disconnect electrical connections from starter motor solenoid.
10. Disconnect ground connections at engine front mount and battery ground cable at transaxle.
11. Disconnect electrical connectors at ignition coil and module assembly, both coolant sensors, oil pressure switch, power steering switch, knock sensor, oxygen sensor, crankshaft position sensor, vehicle speed sensor, neutral safety or backup lamp switch and starter solenoid connector.
12. Disconnect power brake unit vacuum hose from throttle body and power brake unit vacuum tube to check valve hose from tube.
13. Disconnect throttle cable and remove throttle cable bracket.
14. Remove power steering pump rear bracket and power brake vacuum tube as an assembly.
15. Remove power steering pivot bolt, pump and drive belt. Position pump aside with lines attached.
16. De-pressurize fuel system, then disconnect fuel lines.
17. **On models with manual transaxle,** disconnect shift cables, then remove clutch slave cylinder.
18. **On models with automatic transaxle,** disconnect shift cable, throttle valve cables and transaxle oil cooler lines.
19. **On all models,** remove exhaust manifold and heat shield, then lower radiator hose.
20. Remove nut from front engine mount, then install tool J-28467 or other suitable engine lifting fixture.
21. Raise and support vehicle, then remove front wheel and tire assemblies.
22. Remove right hand lower splash shield and radiator air deflector.
23. Separate ball joints from steering knuckles.
24. Using a suitable holding fixture, support front suspension, then remove suspension support attaching bolts. Remove suspension supports, crossmember and stabilizer bar as an assembly. Then remove heater outlet hose from radiator outlet pipe.
25. Position tool J-34754 or equivalent on drive axle boots, then remove axle shafts from transaxle and position aside.
26. Remove transaxle rear mount through bolt nut, then remove nut from engine rear mount through bolt.
27. Remove rear engine mount body bracket, then position suitable support under engine and lower vehicle to engine support.
28. Remove transaxle mount through bolt.
29. Mark engine support fixture hook

93. BOLT - 35 N.m (26 LBS. FT.) PLUS 110 DEGREES
111. BOLT - 35 N.m (26 LBS. FT.) PLUS 100 DEGREES

Fig. 5 Cylinder head bolt tightening sequence. 1991

threads so that engine can be returned to this position for installation, then remove engine support fixture.

30. Slowly and carefully raise vehicle off engine and transaxle assembly. It may be necessary to move engine and transaxle assembly slightly rearward to provide for intake manifold clearance.
31. Separate engine from transaxle.
32. Reverse procedure to install.

CYLINDER HEAD
REPLACE

1. Disconnect battery ground cable, then drain cooling system.
2. Disconnect upper radiator hose, heater hose and throttle body heater hoses from coolant outlets.
3. Remove exhaust manifold as described under "Exhaust Manifold, Replace."
4. **On DOHC engine,** remove intake camshaft housing. **On SOHC engine,** remove camshaft housing. Refer to "Camshaft, Housing and Valve Lash Adjusters, Replace."
5. **On DOHC engine,** remove exhaust camshaft housing as described under "Camshaft, Housing and Valve Lash Adjusters, Replace."
6. **On all models,** remove engine oil filler cap and dipstick from engine.
7. Pull oil fill tube upward to unseat from engine.
8. Disconnect injector wiring harness.
9. Remove oil fill tube out top rotating as necessary to gain clearance for oil/air separator nipple, located between intake manifold tubes.
10. Remove air cleaner to throttle body duct.
11. Disconnect power brake unit vacuum hose from throttle body.
12. Remove throttle cable bracket.
13. Remove throttle body from intake manifold and position aside with throttle cable, coolant hoses and electrical connectors attached.
14. Disconnect MAP sensor vacuum hose at intake manifold.
15. Remove intake manifold brace, then disconnect electrical connectors from the MAP sensor, MAT sensor and purge solenoid.

16. Disconnect upper radiator hose from water outlet.
17. Disconnect both coolant temperature sensor electrical connectors.
18. Loosen cylinder head attaching bolts in reverse order of tightening sequence, **Figs. 5 and 6.**
19. Remove cylinder head and gasket.
20. Reverse procedure to install. Tighten cylinder head attaching bolts using torque angle meter J-36660 or equivalent, as follows:
    a. **On 1991 models,** tighten cylinder head attaching bolts to specification in sequence, **Fig. 5,** then rotate bolts 7 and 9 additional 100° and bolts 1, 2, 3, 4, 5, 6, 8 and 10 an additional 100°.
    b. **On 1992 models, torque** cylinder head bolts 1 through 6 to 26 ft. lbs, bolts 7 and 8 to 15 ft. lbs. and bolts 9 and 10 to 22 ft. lbs. in sequence, **Fig. 6,** then tighten all bolts in sequence an additional 90°. In sequence, loosen each bolt one turn and retighten to specifications, then tighten all cylinder head bolts an additional 90°.
    c. **On 1993-94 VIN A and D engines, torque** cylinder head bolts 1 through 6 to 18 ft. lbs, bolts 7 and 8 to 22 ft. lbs. and bolts 9 and 10 to 26 ft. lbs. in sequence, **Fig. 6.** Tighten cylinder head bolts 1 through 6 in sequence an additional 90°, then tighten bolts 7 through 10 in sequence an additional 60°. In sequence, loosen each bolt one turn and retighten to torque specifications, then tighten cylinder head bolts 1 through 6 an additional 90° and bolts 7 through 10 an additional 60°.
    d. **On 1993-94 VIN 3 engines, torque** cylinder head bolts 1 through 6 to 18 ft. lbs, bolts 7 and 8 to 26 ft. lbs. and bolts 9 and 10 to 30 ft. lbs. in sequence, **Fig. 6.** Tighten cylinder head bolts 1 through 6 in sequence an additional 90°, then tighten bolts 7 through 10 in sequence an additional 60°. In sequence, loosen each bolt one turn and retighten to torque specifications, then tighten cylinder head bolts 1 through 6 an additional 90° and bolts 7 through 10 an additional 60°.

INTAKE MANIFOLD
REPLACE

1. Disconnect battery ground cable, then drain coolant to appropriate level.
2. Disconnect vacuum hose and electrical connector from MAP sensor.
3. Disconnect electrical connectors from the MAP sensor, MAT sensor, purge solenoid and fuel injector harness and position aside, then disconnect hoses from intake manifold and hose at fuel regulator and purge solenoid to canister.

Fig. 6 Cylinder head bolt tightening sequence. 1992–94

4. Disconnect air cleaner to throttle body duct.
5. Disconnect vent tube to air cleaner duct.
6. Remove throttle cable bracket, then disconnect power brake unit vacuum hose with retaining bracket to power steering bracket and position aside.
7. Disconnect coolant lines from throttle body.
8. Remove oil/air separator, leaving hoses attached to the separator. Disconnect hoses from the oil fill, chain housing, chain cover, intake duct and intake manifold and remove as an assembly.
9. Remove oil fill cap and dipstick assembly, then pull oil fill tube upward to unseat from engine block.
10. Disconnect injector wiring harness connector.
11. Remove oil fill tube out top, rotating as necessary to gain clearance for oil/air separator nipple between intake tubes and fuel rail electrical harness.
12. Remove intake manifold support bracket, **Figs. 7 and 8.**
13. Remove remaining intake manifold attaching bolts and nuts, then remove intake manifold and gasket.
14. Reverse procedure to install. Tighten intake manifold bolts in sequence shown in **Figs. 9 and 10.**

EXHAUST MANIFOLD
REPLACE

1. Disconnect battery ground cable.
2. Disconnect electrical connector from oxygen sensor.
3. Remove heat shield, then raise and support vehicle.
4. Remove exhaust manifold brace to manifold bolt.
5. Remove manifold to exhaust pipe spring loaded nuts, then pull down and back on exhaust pipe to disengage from manifold.
6. Lower vehicle and remove exhaust manifold to cylinder head retaining nuts, then manifold seals and gaskets.
7. Reverse procedure to install. Tighten exhaust manifold attaching bolts in sequence shown in **Figs. 11 and 12.**

100. STUD, BOLT, INTAKE MANIFOLD TO CYLINDER HEAD
159. BRACE — INTAKE MANIFOLD
160. BOLT/SCREW — BRACE TO BLOCK
161. BOLT SCREW — BRACE TO INTAKE MANIFOLD
162. NUT — BRACE TO INT. MANIFOLD STUD

Fig. 7 Intake manifold brace removal. 1991

400. INTAKE MANIFOLD BRACE
401. BOLTS - 26 N.m (19 LBS. FT.)

Fig. 8 Intake manifold brace removal. 1992–94

CAMSHAFT LIFT SPECIFICATIONS

Year & Engine (VIN)	Int.	Exh.
1991–94		
2.3L/4-138(A)	.410	.410
2.3L/4-138(D)	.375	.375
1992–94		
2.3L/4-138(3)	.410	.410

VALVE ADJUSTMENT

These engines are equipped with hydraulic valve lash adjusters, which do not require adjustment.

VALVE GUIDES

Valve guides are an integral part of the cylinder head and are not removable. If valve stem clearance becomes excessive, the valve guide should be reamed to the next oversize and the appropriate oversize valves installed. Valves are available in .010 inch oversize.

VALVE LASH ADJUSTERS

These engines use hydraulic valve lash adjusters. The valve lash adjusters can replaced after the intake camshaft and housing or exhaust camshaft and housing on DOHC engine, or camshaft and camshaft housing on SOHC engine, are removed. Refer to the appropriate "Camshaft, Housing and Valve Lash Adjusters, Replace" procedure.

TIGHTENING SEQUENCE

99. STUD
100. INTAKE MANIFOLD GASKET
101. INTAKE MANIFOLD
102. STUD/BOLT
103. BOLT
104. NUT

Fig. 9 Intake manifold installation & bolt tightening sequence. 1991

TIGHTENING SEQUENCE

99. STUD - 11 N.m (96 LBS. IN.)
100. INTAKE MANIFOLD GASKET
103. INTAKE MANIFOLD
104. BOLT - 25 N.m (18 LBS. FT.)
105. NUT - 25 N.m (18 LBS. FT.)

Fig. 10 Intake manifold installation & bolt tightening sequence. 1992-94

FRONT COVER
REPLACE

1. Disconnect battery ground cable, then remove coolant reservoir.
2. Remove serpentine drive belt.
3. **On 1992-94 models,** remove alternator from mounting bracket and position aside. Reinstall alternator mount through bolt and attach engine support fixture.
4. **On all models,** remove upper front cover attaching screws.
5. **On DOHC engine,** remove cover vent hose.

6. **On 1991 models,** remove engine lift bracket.
7. **On 1992-94 models,** remove right hand front engine mount and engine lift bracket. On automatic transaxle models, also remove upper engine strut.
8. **On all models,** raise and support vehicle, then remove right hand wheel and tire assembly.
9. Remove right hand lower splash shield.
10. Using harmonic balancer tool No. J-38122 to hold crankshaft balancer in position, remove retaining bolt, then remove balancer using puller No. J-24420-B.
11. Remove fasteners attaching lower portion of front cover, then lower vehicle.
12. Remove front cover and gaskets.
13. Reverse procedure to install.

TIMING CHAIN
REPLACE
REMOVAL

1. Remove front cover as described under "Front Cover, Replace."
2. Remove crankshaft oil slinger.
3. Rotate crankshaft in clockwise direction until camshaft and crankshaft timing marks are aligned, **Figs. 13 and 14.**
4. Remove three timing chain guides.
5. Raise and support vehicle.
6. **On early production engines,** gently pry off timing chain tensioner spring retainer and remove spring, **Fig. 15.**

107. STUD, EXHAUST MANIFOLD TO CYL. HEAD
156. MANIFOLD ASM.
158. NUT (7) SEE INSERT FOR TIGHTENING SEQUENCE
172. BRACE ASM. – EXHAUST MANIFOLD
173. BOLT/SCREW (2)
174. GASKET

Fig. 11 Exhaust manifold installation & bolt tightening sequence. 1991

(HEAT SHIELD REMOVED FOR ILLUSTRATION PURPOSES)

TIGHTENING SEQUENCE

110. STUD - 12 N.m (106 LBS. IN)
160. NUT (7) - 42 N.m (31 LBS. FT.) SEE TIGHTENING SEQUENCE
176. GASKET
314. MANIFOLD ASSEMBLY

Fig. 12 Exhaust manifold installation & bolt tightening sequence. 1992-94

7. **On all models,** removing timing chain tensioner shoe retainer.
8. Ensure slack in timing chain is above tensioner shoe, then remove chain tensioner shoe. The timing chain must be disengaged from grooves in tensioner shoe to permit removal of shoe. Position a suitable screwdriver under timing chain while pulling shoe outward to disengage. If difficulty is encountered in removing tensioner shoe, proceed as follows:
   a. Lower vehicle, then while holding intake camshaft sprocket in position with camshaft sprocket wrench No. J-36013, remove sprocket bolt and washer.
   b. Remove washer, then re-install bolt into camshaft by hand.
   c. Position a suitable three jaw puller into intake camshaft sprocket relief holes and remove sprocket. Do not pry on camshaft sprocket as damage to sprocket or timing chain housing may result.
9. Remove tensioner assembly attaching bolts and tensioner assembly. Use care when removing, as tensioner is spring loaded.
10. Remove timing chain tensioner shoe pivot stud, then remove timing chain.

INSTALLATION

1. While holding camshaft sprocket in position with tool No. J-36013, install attaching and washer, if removed. Torque to specifications.
2. Install timing pins J-36008 or equivalent through holes in camshaft sprockets into holes in timing chain housing to position camshafts for proper timing, **Figs. 13 and 14.** If camshafts are out of position and must be rotated more that 1/8 turn to insert timing pins, the crankshaft should be rotated in the clockwise direction to a position 90° off TDC. After camshafts have been positioned and timing pins have been installed rotate crankshaft in counterclockwise direction to TDC.
3. **On DOHC engine,** place timing chain cover exhaust camshaft sprocket, idler sprocket and crankshaft sprocket.
4. Remove timing pin from intake camshaft and attach tool J-36013 to camshaft sprocket. Using camshaft sprocket wrench, rotate camshaft sprocket counterclockwise until timing chain can be installed over sprocket. Release tool after timing chain has been installed over sprock-

et. The timing chain tension between intake and exhaust camshaft sprockets should tighten. The timing pin should easily fit through intake camshaft sprocket timing hole into timing chain housing timing hole. If timing pin does not fit easily, repeat procedure.
5. **On SOHC engine,** remove timing pin from camshaft and attach tool J-36013 to camshaft sprocket. Using camshaft sprocket wrench, rotate camshaft sprocket counterclockwise until timing chain can be installed over sprocket. Release tool after timing chain has been installed over sprocket. The timing chain tension should tighten. The timing pin should easily fit through camshaft sprocket timing hole into timing chain housing timing hole. If timing pin does not fit easily, repeat procedure.
6. **On all engines,** with timing pins installed, raise and support vehicle.
7. With slack removed from timing chain between intake camshaft sprocket on DOHC engine, camshaft sprocket on SOHC engine, and crankshaft sprocket, timing marks on crankshaft and engine block should be aligned. If crankshaft timing marks are not aligned, move timing chain one tooth forward or rearward to align marks.
8. Install timing chain tensioner shoe pivot.
9. Reset timing chain tensioner, **Fig. 16,** as follows:
   a. Position restraint cylinder, spring and nylon plug into plunger. Align slot in restraint cylinder with peg in plunger. Rotate restraint cylinder in a clockwise direction and push into plunger until it is bottomed. Keep rotating restraint cylinder clockwise, until spring force pushes the restraint cylinder away from the plunger. The plunger peg will lock the restraint cylinder in the loaded position.

A. CAMSHAFT TIMING ALIGNMENT PIN LOCATIONS
B. CRANKSHAFT GEAR TIMING MARKS

53. SHOE AND TENSIONER ASSEMBLY
55. TIMING CHAIN
69. GUIDE - R.H. TIMING CHAIN
70. GUIDE - L.H. TIMING CHAIN
76. SPROCKET, CAMSHAFT

Fig. 13 Valve timing marks. SOHC engine

* REMOVE ANTI-RELEASE FROM TENSIONER AND DEPRESS SHOE ASM. ONCE TO RELEASE TENSIONER

51. SHOE ASM., TIMING CHAIN TENSIONER
54. TENSIONER, TIMING CHAIN
56. SPRING, TIMING CHAIN TENSIONER
    A. INSTALLED POSITION
57. RETAINER, TIMING CHAIN SPRING TENSIONER

56 AND 57 ARE EARLY PRODUCTION. DO NOT REINSTALL, NOT NEEDED.

Fig. 15 Timing chain tensioner spring & retainer

b. Position timing chain tensioner spacer tool J-36589 on plunger assembly.
c. Position plunger assembly into tensioner body, so that long end of plunger will be toward crankshaft when installed.
10. Install timing chain tensioner assembly with long end of plunger toward crankshaft. Torque to specifications.
11. Install timing chain tensioner shoe and retainer.
12. Remove tool J-36589 from timing chain tensioner, then press timing chain tensioner plunger into tensioner body to unload plunger.
13. Lower vehicle to point where timing pins can be removed from camshaft sprockets, then rotate crankshaft two revolutions in the clockwise direction. Align crankshaft timing marks, then re-insert timing pins through camshaft

A. CAMSHAFT TIMING ALIGNMENT PIN LOCATIONS
B. CRANKSHAFT GEAR TIMING MARKS
51. SHOE ASM. TIMING CHAIN TENSIONER
53. TIMING CHAIN
54. TENSIONER, TIMING CHAIN
67. GUIDE — R.H. TIMING CHAIN
68. GUIDE — L.H. TIMING CHAIN
69. GUIDE — UPPER TIMING CHAIN
73. SPROCKET, EXHAUST CAMSHAFT
74. SPROCKET, INTAKE CAMSHAFT

Fig. 14 Valve timing marks. DOHC engine

sprockets into timing chain housing timing holes. Timing pins should slide easily through timing holes. If timing pins cannot be insert easily, repeat procedure to properly time engine.
14. Install three timing chain guides, then install crankshaft oil slinger.
15. Install engine front cover.

CAMSHAFT, HOUSING & HYDRAULIC VALVE LASH ADJUSTERS REPLACE

Whenever camshaft housing to cylinder head attaching bolts are loosened, the camshaft housing to cylinder head gasket must be replaced.

DOHC INTAKE OR SOHC CAMSHAFT HOUSING

1. Disconnect battery ground cable, then disconnect ignition coil and module electrical connectors.
2. Remove four bolts attaching ignition coil and module assembly to camshaft housings, then pull upward on assembly to remove, **Figs. 17 and 18**. If connectors are stuck to spark plugs,

LATE PRODUCTION SHOWN
EARLY PRODUCTION SIMILAR

54. TENSIONER, TIMING CHAIN ASM.
    A. PLUNGER ASM.
    B. LONG END
    C. PEG
    D. NYLON PLUG
    E. SPRING
    F. RESTRAINT CYLINDER
    G. J 36589 ANTI-RELEASE DEVISE
    H. TENSIONER BODY

Fig. 16 Timing chain tensioner

use spark plug connector remover J-36011 to remove.
3. Disconnect power steering idle speed switch electrical connector.

77. IGNITION COIL AND MODULE ASM.
78. BOLTS, IGNITION COIL AND MODULE ASM. TO CAMSHAFT HOUSINGS
81. COVER, CAMSHAFT HOUSING (INTAKE SHOWN)
90. SPARK PLUG

Fig. 17   Ignition coil & module assembly removal. DOHC engine

79. IGNITION COIL
80. BOLTS - 22 N·m (16 LBS. FT.)
125. BOLTS - 22 N·m (16 LBS. FT.)

Fig. 18   Ignition coil & module assembly removal. SOHC engine

4. Remove power steering pump and position aside with hoses attached.
5. Using power steering pulley J-36014 and J-29785-A, remove power steering pump drive pulley from camshaft.
6. Remove oil/air separator assembly.
7. Disconnect vacuum line from fuel pressure regulator, then disconnect injector wiring harness.
8. Remove fuel line bracket from top of intake camshaft housing.
9. De-pressurize fuel system, then remove fuel rail retaining bolts and fuel rail. Leave fuel lines attached and position fuel rail over master cylinder. Cover openings in cylinder head and injector nozzles.
10. Disconnect timing chain housing as follows:
   a. Remove coolant recovery tank, then serpentine drive belt.
   b. Raise and support vehicle, then remove right front wheel and tire assembly.
   c. Remove right lower splash shield, then balancer bolt using tool No. J 37086 or equivalent to prevent crankshaft rotation when loosening bolt.
   d. Remove balancer using tool No. J24420-B or equivalent, then front cover lower bolts and nut.
   e. Lower vehicle, then remove water pump assembly to timing chain housing nuts. If not previously removed.
   f. Remove front cover upper bolts and nuts, then front cover.
   g. Remove timing chain as described under "Timing Chain, Replace."
   h. Remove chain housing to belt tensioner bracket brace.
   i. Remove timing chain housing to block lower fasteners, then four oil pan to front cover bolts.
   j. Remove oil/air separator hose from chain housing.
   k. Remove camshaft sprocket retaining bolts and washers while holding sprockets with tool No. J36013 or equivalent camshaft sprocket wrench.
   l. Remove camshaft sprockets. Note: sprockets are identical and interchangeable, no marking is necessary.
   m. Remove chain housing to camshaft housing bolts, then timing chain housing and gaskets.
11. Remove camshaft housing cover at-

taching bolts, **Fig. 19.**
12. Loosen camshaft housing to cylinder head attaching bolts in reverse order of tightening sequence, **Fig. 20.**
13. Leave two camshaft housing to cylinder head attaching bolts loosely installed. Thread four of the camshaft housing to cylinder head bolts into tapped holes on camshaft housing cover to separate cover from housing.
14. Remove the two camshaft housing to cylinder head bolts and remove camshaft housing cover.
15. Note position of timing chain sprocket dowel pin for re-assembly, then remove camshaft, using care not to damage journals.
16. Remove oil seal from camshaft. This seal must be replaced any time the cover and camshaft housing are separated.
17. Remove valve lash adjuster. Keep valve lash adjusters in order for re-assembly. Store valve lash adjusters in the upside down position in clean engine oil to prevent lifter bleed down.
18. Remove camshaft housing and gasket from cylinder head.
19. Reverse procedure to install. Prior to installation, lubricate camshaft journals and valve lash adjusters with lubricant No. 1052365 or equivalent. Apply suitable sealant to threads of camshaft housing and cover retaining bolts and ignition coil and module assembly attaching bolts. When installing camshaft housing cover to camshaft housing, refer to **Fig. 21 for seal positioning. Torque camshaft housing and cover bolts in sequence shown in Fig. 20.** Torque bolts in position 1 through 10, **Fig. 20,** to 11 ft. lbs., then tighten an additional 75°. Tighten bolts in positions 11 and 12, **Fig. 20,** to 11 ft. lbs, then tighten an additional 25°. Torque timing chain housing to engine and camshaft housing fasteners to specifications.

81. SEALS, CAMSHAFT HOUSING TO CAMSHAFT HOUSING COVER (EACH SEAL IS DIFFERENT)
82A. BOLT, CAMSHAFT HOUSING TO CYLINDER HEAD
82B. BOLT, CAMSHAFT HOUSING COVER TO CAMSHAFT HOUSING
83. COVER, CAMSHAFT
90. CAMSHAFT HOUSING (INTAKE SHOWN)
91. GASKET, CAMSHAFT HOUSING TO CYLINDER HEAD
117. DOWEL PIN (2)

Fig. 19 Camshaft housing & cover

Fig. 20 Camshaft housing bolt tightening sequence

81A. SEAL-INNER (EXHAUST, RED)
81B. SEAL-OUTER (EXHAUST, RED)
81C. SEAL-OUTER (INTAKE, BLUE)
81D. SEAL-INNER (INTAKE, BLUE)

Fig. 21 Camshaft housing cover seal installation & identification

DOHC EXHAUST

1. Disconnect battery ground cable, then disconnect ignition coil and module electrical connectors.
2. Remove four bolts attaching ignition coil and module assembly to camshaft housings, then pull upward on assembly to remove, **Fig. 17.** If connectors are stuck to spark plugs, use tool J-36011 to remove.
3. Disconnect oil pressure switch electrical connector.
4. Remove transaxle dipstick and tube assembly from camshaft cover and position aside.
5. Remove exhaust camshaft cover and gasket.
6. Disconnect timing chain housing as follows:
   a. Remove coolant recovery tank, then serpentine drive belt.
   b. Raise and support vehicle, then remove right front wheel and tire as-sembly.
   c. Remove right lower splash shield, then balancer bolt using tool No. J 37086 or equivalent to prevent crankshaft rotation when loosening bolt.
   d. Remove balancer using tool No. J 24420-B or equivalent, then front cover lower bolts and nut.
   e. Lower vehicle, then remove water pump assembly to timing chain housing nuts. If not previously removed.
   f. Remove front cover upper bolts and nuts, then front cover.
   g. Remove timing chain as described under "Timing Chain, Replace."
   h. Remove chain housing to belt tensioner bracket brace.
   i. Remove timing chain housing to block lower fasteners, then four oil pan to front cover bolts.
   j. Remove oil/air separator hose from chain housing.
   k. Remove camshaft sprocket retaining bolts and washers while holding sprockets with tool No. J 36013 or equivalent camshaft sprocket wrench.
   l. Remove camshaft sprockets. Note: sprockets are identical and interchangeable, no marking is necessary.
   m. Remove eight chain housing to camshaft housing bolts, then timing chain housing and gaskets.
7. Loosen camshaft housing to cylinder head attaching bolts in reverse order of tightening sequence, **Fig. 20.**
8. Leave two camshaft housing to cylinder head attaching bolts loosely installed. Thread four of the camshaft housing to cylinder head bolts into tapped holes on camshaft housing cover to separate cover from housing.
9. Remove the two camshaft housing to cylinder head bolts and remove camshaft housing cover.

7. PISTON
7A. ORIENTATION ARROW – TOWARDS FRONT OF ENGINE
10. CONNECTING ROD
10A. OIL SQUIRT HOLE – TOWARDS EXHAUST SIDE
11. BEARING CONNECTING ROD
43. NUT, CONNECTING ROD CAP TO CONNECTING ROD
44. CAP, CONNECTING ROD

Fig. 22   Piston & rod assembly

10. Note position of timing chain sprocket dowel pin for re-assembly, then remove camshaft, using care not to damage journals.
11. Remove oil seal from camshaft. This seal must be replaced any time the cover and camshaft housing are separated.
12. Remove valve lash adjuster. Keep valve lash adjusters in order for re-assembly. Store valve lash adjusters in the upside down position in clean engine oil to prevent lifter bleed down.
13. Remove camshaft housing and gasket from cylinder head.
14. Reverse procedure to install. Prior to installation, lubricate camshaft journals and valve lash adjusters with lubricant No. 1052365 or equivalent. Apply suitable sealant to threads of camshaft housing and cover retaining bolts and ignition coil and module assembly attaching bolts. When installing camshaft housing cover to camshaft housing, refer to **Fig. 21 for seal positioning. Torque camshaft housing and cover bolts in sequence shown in Fig. 20.** Torque bolts to 11 ft. lbs., then tighten an additional 75°. Torque timing chain housing to engine and camshaft housing fasteners to 19 ft. lbs.

PISTON & ROD ASSEMBLY

Assemble piston to rod with arrow on piston toward front of engine and oil squirt hole on rod toward exhaust side of engine, **Fig. 22.**

Upon installation, measure connecting rod side clearance using a suitable feeler gauge. Connecting rod side clearance should be .0059 to .0177 inch.

PISTON PINS & RINGS

Pistons and rings are available in standard size and oversize of .010 inch. Piston pins and pistons are serviced as an assembly.

21. SEAL, REAR CRANKSHAFT
22. BOLT, REAR CRANKSHAFT SEAL HOUSING TO BLOCK (6)
23. HOUSING, REAR CRANKSHAFT SEAL
24. GASKET, REAR CRANKSHAFT SEAL HOUSING TO BLOCK
25. DOWEL PIN, REAR CRANKSHAFT SEAL HOUSING TO BLOCK
35. OIL PAN
36C. BOLT, TO SEAL HOUSING

Fig. 23   Crankshaft rear oil seal replacement

MAIN & ROD BEARINGS

Main and rod bearings are available in standard size only.

CRANKSHAFT REAR OIL SEAL
REPLACE

1. Remove transaxle assembly as described under "Transaxle, Replace."
2. **On models with manual transaxle,** remove clutch as described under "Clutch, Replace."
3. **On all models,** remove flywheel to crankshaft attaching bolts, then remove flywheel.
4. Remove oil pan to crankshaft rear seal housing attaching bolts.
5. Remove crankshaft rear seal housing to engine attaching screws, then remove housing and gasket, **Fig. 23.**
6. Support crankshaft rear seal housing on two wooden blocks of equal thickness with crankshaft side facing upward, then drive seal out through transaxle side of housing.
7. Press replacement seal into housing using rear crankshaft seal installer No. J-36005.
8. Reverse procedure to install. Lubricate seal lips with engine oil prior to installing housing. Torque crankshaft rear seal housing to specifications.

OIL PAN
REPLACE
1991

1. Disconnect battery ground cable, then drain crankcase.
2. Remove flywheel housing inspection cover, then remove splash shield to suspension support bolt.
3. **On models with manual transaxle,** remove exhaust manifold brace.
4. **On all models,** remove radiator outlet pipe to oil pan bolt.
5. Remove transaxle to oil pan nut, then remove stud using a 7 mm socket.
6. Carefully pry out spacer located between oil pan and transaxle.
7. Remove oil pan to transaxle stud, then remove oil pan to engine attaching bolts.
8. Remove oil pan and gasket. It may be necessary to rotate crankshaft to provide clearance for oil pan removal.
9. Reverse procedure to install. Install and torque oil pan attaching bolts as shown in **Fig. 24.**

1992–94

1. Disconnect battery ground cable.
2. Drain crankcase and cooling system.
3. Remove flywheel housing cover.
4. Remove right hand front wheel and tire assembly, then remove splash shield.
5. Relieve serpentine drive belt tension.
6. Remove engine mount strut from strut bracket.

39A. BOLT (4) (M6 x 1.25 x 25) TO CHAIN HOUSING
12 N.m (106 LBS. IN.)
39B. BOLT (12) (M8 x 1.25 x 22) TO CYLINDER BLOCK
24 N.m (17 LBS. FT.)
39C. BOLT (2) (M6 x 1.25 x 25) TO REAR CARRIER
12 N.m (106 LBS. IN.)

Fig. 24 Oil pan bolt identification & locations. 1991

39A. BOLT (4) (M6 X 1.0 X 25) - 12 N.m (106 LBS. IN.)
39B. BOLT (10) (M8 X 1.25 X 22) - 24 N.m (18 LBS. FT.)
39C. BOLT (10) (M6 X 1.0 X 25) - 12 N.m (106 LBS. IN.)
39D. STUD OR BOLT (2) (M8 X 1.25 X 22) -
26 N.m (19 LBS. FT.)

Fig. 25 Oil pan bolt identification & locations. 1992–94

27. SHIM
29. BOLT (2)
30. OIL PUMP AND SCREEN
31. NUT – SCREEN TO BLOCK

Fig. 26 Oil pump removal

28. OIL PUMP
28A. DRIVEN GEAR COVER – OIL PUMP
28B. BOLT/SCREW (3)
30. SCREEN ASM. – OIL PUMP
30A. GASKET – SCREEN TO PUMP
30B. BOLT/SCREW (2)

Fig. 27 Removing oil cover

26. OIL PUMP DRIVE GEAR
28. OIL PUMP – COVER REMOVED
28A. OIL PUMP DRIVEN GEAR

Fig. 28 Measuring oil pump gear backlash

1 ROTATE TENSIONER IN DIRECTION OF ARROW TO REMOVE OR INSTALL BELT.

Fig. 29 Serpentine drive belt replacement

1. OUTLET ASM. – WATER
2. GASKET
3. THERMOSTAT ASM.
4. BOLT (2) (M8 X 1.25 X 30)
5. PLUG – WATER OUTLET
6. SENSOR, COOLANT

Fig. 30 Thermostat replacement

7. Remove A/C compressor from bracket and support with refrigerant hoses attached.
8. Remove engine mount strut bracket bolts and position bracket aside.
9. Remove radiator outlet pipe bolts, then detach A/C and radiator outlet pipes from suspension supports.
10. Remove exhaust manifold brace.
11. Remove oil pan to flywheel cover nut and bolt.
12. Remove radiator outlet pipe from lower radiator hose and oil pan.
13. Disconnect oil level sensor electrical connector.
14. Remove oil pan attaching bolts and oil pan.
15. Reverse procedure to install. Refer to **Fig. 25**, for oil pan bolt identification and tighten specifications.

OIL PUMP SERVICE
REPLACEMENT

1. Remove oil pan as described under "Oil Pan, Replace."

2. Remove oil pump attaching bolts, then remove oil pump and shims, if equipped, **Fig. 26.**
3. Reverse procedure to install. Torque oil pump to engine attaching bolts to specifications. Torque oil pump screen to engine attaching nut to specifications.

1. TIMING CHAIN HOUSING
2. GASKET, TIMING CHAIN HOUSING TO WATER PUMP BODY
3. NUT (3)
4. WATER PUMP BODY ASM.
5. GASKET, WATER PUMP BODY TO WATER PUMP COVER
6. WATER PUMP COVER
7. BOLT (M6 X 1 X 65) — 3 LOWER POSITIONS
8. BOLT (M6 X 1 X 25)
9. BOLT (M6 X 1 X 90)
10. GASKET, WATER PUMP COVER TO BLOCK
11. BOLTS, WATER PUMP COVER TO BLOCK (2)

Fig. 31 Water pump replacement

OIL PUMP GEAR BACKLASH ADJUSTMENT

1. Remove oil pump as described under "Oil Pump, Replace."
2. Remove four attaching bolts, then separate the driven gear cover and screen assembly from the oil pump, **Fig. 27.**
3. Position oil pump housing to engine with original shim(s), then install attaching bolts and torque to specifications.
4. Using dial indicator assembly, measure oil pump driven gear to drive gear backlash, **Fig. 28.** Crankshaft should not move during check. Backlash should be .0091 to .0201 inch. To decrease backlash, remove shims. To increase backlash, add shims.
5. After obtaining proper backlash setting, rotate crankshaft 180° and recheck backlash setting.
6. Remove oil pump from engine.
7. Install oil pump cover and pickup tube to oil pump housing. Torque oil pump cover to oil pump housing attaching screws to specifications.
8. Install oil pump and shims.

BELT TENSION DATA

Year	Engine	Belt Tension, Lbs.①
1991-94	2.3L/4-138	50

①—On models less A/C, take reading between alternator & idler pulley. On models with A/C, take reading between alternator & A/C compressor. If reading is less than listed, replace belt tensioner.

SERPENTINE DRIVE BELT
REPLACE

Refer to **Fig. 29.** for serpentine drive belt replacement.

1 HOSE — PART OF FUEL SENDER
2 FUEL VAPOR PIPE
3 FUEL RETURN PIPE
4 FUEL FEED PIPE
5 FUEL FEED PIPE NUT — 27 N·m (20 LBS. FT.)
6 HOSE — PART OF FUEL SENDER
7 ABS AND FUEL SENDER HARNESS

Fig. 32 Fuel filter replacement

COOLING SYSTEM BLEED
1991

After filling cooling system, start engine and allow to reach operating temperature with surge tank pressure cap installed. Stop engine, then position shop towel over surge tank pressure cap. Slowly and carefully remove surge tank cap. Add coolant as necessary to bring to proper level, then install surge tank pressure cap.

1992–94

After filling cooling system, start engine and allow to reach operating temperature with surge tank pressure cap removed. Air will bleed through surge cap opening. Add coolant as necessary to bring to proper level, then install surge tank pressure cap.

THERMOSTAT
REPLACE

1. Disconnect battery ground cable.
2. Drain cooling to level below thermostat.
3. Disconnect radiator hose and heater hose from thermostat housing.
4. Disconnect electrical connector from coolant sensor.
5. Remove throttle body cooling hose.
6. Remove thermostat housing attaching bolts, then remove thermostat housing and thermostat, **Fig. 30.**
7. Reverse procedure to install.

WATER PUMP
REPLACE

1. Disconnect battery ground cable, then drain cooling system. Note: disconnect heater hose from thermostat housing for more complete coolant drain.
2. Disconnect electrical connector from oxygen sensor.
3. Remove upper and lower exhaust manifold heat shields.
4. Remove bolt attaching exhaust manifold brace to exhaust manifold.
5. Loosen exhaust manifold to exhaust pipe spring loaded bolts using a 13mm wrench.
6. Remove radiator outlet pipe to water pump cover bolts.
7. Raise and support vehicle.
8. Remove manifold to exhaust pipe spring loaded nuts.
9. Pull down and back on exhaust pipe to disengage from manifold bolts.
10. Remove radiator outlet pipe from oil pan and transaxle. On vehicles equipped with manual transaxle, exhaust manifold brace must be removed.

11. Leave the lower radiator hose attached and pull down gently on the radiator outlet pipe to disengage it from the water pump. Leave outlet pipe to hang.
12. Lower vehicle, then remove exhaust manifold to cylinder head retaining nuts and exhaust manifold, seals and gaskets.
13. Remove water pump cover to cylinder block bolts.
14. Remove water pump assembly to timing chain housing nuts. Note: on early production models it may be necessary to loosen and reposition the rear engine mount, mount to engine block bracket to gain clearance.
15. Remove water pump and cover assembly.
16. Remove water pump cover to water pump assembly, **Fig. 31.**
17. Reverse procedure to install. Torque water pump to water pump cover attaching bolts to specifications. Torque water pump to engine and timing chain cover attaching bolts to specifications.

FUEL PUMP
REPLACE

1. Disconnect battery ground cable, then drain fuel tank.
2. Disconnect tank unit harness connector.
3. Remove ground wire retaining screw from underbody.
4. Disconnect hoses from tank meter assembly, then hoses at tank from filler and vent pipes.
5. Support fuel tank and disconnect the two fuel tank retaining straps.
6. Remove fuel tank from vehicle.
7. Remove fuel tank sending unit and pump assembly by turning cam lock ring counterclockwise. Lift assembly from fuel tank and remove pump from sending unit.
8. Pull fuel pump up into attaching hose while pulling outward away from bottom support. Take care to prevent damage to rubber insulator and strainer during removal.
9. After pump assembly is clear of bottom support, pull pump assembly out of rubber connector for removal.
10. Reverse procedure to install.

FUEL FILTER
REPLACE

The fuel filter is located below the rear of the vehicle, rearward of the fuel tank.
1. Relieve fuel system pressure as outlined under "Precautions."
2. Raise and support vehicle.
3. Using suitable back-up wrench, remove fuel filter fitting, **Fig. 32.**
4. Grasp filter and one nylon fuel connection line fitting, twist quick connect fitting 1/4 turn in each direction to loosen dirt in fitting.
5. Using compressed air, clean dirt from quick connect fitting.
6. Depress quick connect fitting plastic tabs of male end connector and pull apart.
7. Remove fuel filter.
8. Reverse procedure to install.

TIGHTENING SPECIFICATIONS

Year	Component	Torque/ Ft. Lbs.
1991	Camshaft Housing & Cover To Cylinder Head	11①
	Camshaft Sprocket To Cam Bolt	40
	Connecting Rod Nuts	②
	Coolant Outlet To Cylinder Head	19
	Crankshaft Balancer To Crankshaft	74③
	Crankshaft Bearing Cap Bolts	15③
	Crankshaft Position Sensor To Block	80④
	Cylinder Head Bolts	⑤
	Exhaust Camshaft Housing Cover	10
	Exhaust Manifold To Cylinder Head Nuts	31
	Exhaust Manifold To Cylinder Head Studs	106④
	Exhaust Manifold To Exhaust Pipe	18
	Exhaust Manifold To Oil Pan	19
	Exhaust Manifold Studs To Manifold	22
	Flywheel To Clutch Cover	22
	Flywheel To Converter	46
	Flywheel To Crankshaft	22⑥
	Front Cover To Timing Chain Housing	106④
	Fuel Rail To Camshaft Housing	19
	Ignition Coil & Module Assembly To Camshaft Housing	13
	Intake Manifold To Cylinder Head Nuts	18
	Intake Manifold To Cylinder Head Studs	96④
	Oil/Air Separator To Intake Manifold	71④
	Oil Filter Connector To Block	21
	Oil Filter To Block	⑦
	Oil Pan Bolts	⑤
	Oil Pan Drain Plug	19
	Oil Pump To Block	40
	Oil Pump Cover To Oil Pump Body	106④
	Oil Pump Screen To Pump	30

Year	Component	Torque/ Ft. Lbs.
1991 —Cont'd	Rear Crankshaft Seal Housing To Block	106④
	Spark Plugs To Cylinder Head	17
	Starter To Block Or Transaxle To Starter	71
	Thermostat Housing	19
	Throttle Body To Intake Manifold	19
	Timing Chain Housing To Block Or Camshaft Housing	19
	Timing Chain Housing To Block Stud	19
	Timing Chain Tensioner To Housing & Block	115④
	Transaxle Mount To Body	40
	Water Pump To Timing Chain Housing	19
	Water Pump To Water Pump Cover	10
	Water Pump Cover To Block	19
1992	Camshaft Housing & Cover To Cylinder Head	11①
	Camshaft Sprocket To Cam Bolt	40
	Connecting Rod Nuts	②
	Coolant Outlet To Cylinder Head	19
	Crankshaft Balancer To Crankshaft	74③
	Crankshaft Bearing Cap Bolts	15③
	Crankshaft Position Sensor To Block	80④
	Cylinder Head Bolts	⑤
	Exhaust Camshaft Housing Rear Cover	10
	Exhaust Manifold Lower Heat Shield Bolt	120④
	Exhaust Manifold To Cylinder Head Nuts	31
	Exhaust Manifold To Cylinder Head Studs	106④
	Exhaust Manifold To Exhaust Pipe	19
	Exhaust Manifold To Oil Pan	19
	Exhaust Manifold Studs To Manifold	19
	Flywheel To Clutch Cover	22
	Flywheel To Converter	46
	Flywheel To Crankshaft	22⑥

Continued

TIGHTENING SPECIFICATIONS—Continued

Year	Component	Torque/ Ft. Lbs.
1992 —Cont'd	Front Cover To Timing Chain Housing	106④
	Fuel Pipe Bracket To Camshaft Housing	⑧
	Fuel Rail To Camshaft Housing	19
	Ignition Coil & Module Assembly To Camshaft Housing	15
	Intake Manifold Brace Bolts	19
	Intake Manifold To Cylinder Head Nuts	18
	Intake Manifold To Cylinder Head Studs	96④
	Oil/Air Separator To Intake Manifold	72④
	Oil Filter Connector To Block	21
	Oil Filter To Block	⑦
	Oil Pan Bolts	⑤
	Oil Pan Drain Plug	19
	Oil Pump To Block	40
	Oil Pump Cover To Oil Pump Body	106④
	Oil Pump Screen To Pump	30
	Rear Crankshaft Seal Housing To Block	106④
	Spark Plugs To Cylinder Head	17
	Starter To Block Or Transaxle To Starter	71
	Thermostat Housing	19
	Throttle Body To Intake Manifold	19
	Timing Chain Housing To Block Or Camshaft Housing	19
	Timing Chain Housing To Block Stud	19
	Timing Chain Tensioner To Housing & Block	84④
	Water Pump To Timing Chain Housing	19
	Water Pump To Water Pump Cover	10
	Water Pump Cover To Block	10
1993-94	Camshaft Housing & Cover To Cylinder Head	11③
	Camshaft Sprocket To Cam Bolt	52
	Connecting Rod Nuts	②
	Coolant Outlet To Cylinder Head	19
	Crankshaft Balancer To Crankshaft	110③
	Crankshaft Bearing Cap Bolts	15③
	Crankshaft Position Sensor To Block	80④
	Cylinder Head Bolts	⑤
	Exhaust Camshaft Housing Rear Cover	10
	Exhaust Manifold Lower Heat Shield Bolt	124④
	Exhaust Manifold To Cylinder Head Nuts	31
	Exhaust Manifold To Cylinder Head Studs	106④

Year	Component	Torque/ Ft. Lbs.
1993-94 —Cont'd	Exhaust Manifold To Exhaust Pipe	19
	Exhaust Manifold To Oil Pan	19
	Exhaust Manifold Studs To Manifold	19
	Flywheel To Clutch Cover	22
	Flywheel To Converter	46
	Flywheel To Crankshaft	22⑥
	Front Cover To Timing Chain Housing	106④
	Fuel Pipe Bracket To Camshaft Housing	⑧
	Fuel Rail To Camshaft Housing	19
	Ignition Coil & Module Assembly To Camshaft Housing	16
	Intake Manifold Brace Bolts	19
	Intake Manifold To Cylinder Head Nuts	18
	Intake Manifold To Cylinder Head Studs	96④
	Oil/Air Separator To Intake Manifold	71④
	Oil Filter Connector To Block	21
	Oil Filter To Block	⑦
	Oil Pan Bolts	⑤
	Oil Pan Drain Plug	19
	Oil Pump To Block	40
	Oil Pump Cover To Oil Pump Body	106④
	Oil Pump Screen To Pump	30
	Rear Crankshaft Seal Housing To Block	106④
	Spark Plugs To Cylinder Head	16
	Starter To Block Or Transaxle To Starter	71
	Thermostat Housing	19
	Throttle Body To Intake Manifold	19
	Timing Chain Housing To Block Or Camshaft Housing	19
	Timing Chain Housing To Block Stud	19
	Timing Chain Tensioner To Housing & Block	84④
	Water Pump To Timing Chain Housing	19
	Water Pump To Water Pump Cover	124④
	Water Pump Cover To Block	19

① —Plus an additional 75°.
② —18 ft. lbs. plus an additional 80°.
③ —Plus an additional 90°.
④ —Inch lbs.
⑤ —Refer to text.
⑥ —Plus an additional 45°.
⑦ —¾ to one turn after initial gasket contact.
⑧ —11 ft. lbs. plus an additional 25°.

2.5L/4-151 Engine
INDEX

PRECAUTIONS
FUEL SYSTEM PRESSURE RELIEF

Failure to relieve system pressure prior to disconnecting fuel system components may cause fire or personal injury.

1. Loosen fuel tank filler cap to relieve tank pressure.
2. Raise and support vehicle, then disconnect fuel pump electrical connector.
3. Start and operate engine until fuel supply is consumed.
4. Crank engine for approximately 3 seconds to relieve remaining pressure.
5. Disconnect battery ground cable, then reconnect fuel pump connector.

ENGINE MOUNTS
REPLACE
FRONT MOUNT

1. Support engine using fixture No. J 28467-A or equivalent.
2. Raise and support vehicle.
3. Remove engine mount to chassis attaching bolts, **Fig. 1.**, then engine mount to bracket nuts from rear mount, **Fig. 2.**
4. Remove engine mount to engine bracket bolts.
5. Remove engine mount.
6. Reverse procedure to install.

REAR MOUNT

1. Support engine using fixture No. J 28467-A or equivalent.
2. Raise and support vehicle.
3. Remove engine mount to chassis bracket nuts, **Fig. 2.**
4. Remove engine mount to engine bracket bolts.
5. Remove engine mount.
6. Reverse procedure to install.

Fig. 1   Front engine mount

1—R.H. RAIL ASM.

2—COWL ASM.

3—ENGINE ASM.

4—DEFLECTOR

5—ENGINE ASM.

6—DEFLECTOR

7—TRANSAXLE ASM.

Fig. 2   Rear engine mount

ENGINE
REPLACE

1. Disconnect battery cables, then drain cooling system and remove air cleaner assembly.
2. Disconnect ECM electrical connectors. Route electrical harness through bulkhead and position aside.
3. Disconnect engine wiring harness

Fig. 3 Cylinder head bolt tightening sequence

1	INTAKE MANIFOLD GASKET
2	INTAKE MANIFOLD
3	34 N·m (25 LB. FT.)

Fig. 4 Intake manifold bolt tightening sequence.

and position aside.

4. Disconnect all vacuum and coolant hoses necessary for engine removal.
5. **On models equipped with A/C,** unfasten A/C compressor and position aside, leaving refrigerant lines attached.
6. **On models equipped with power steering,** unfasten power steering pump and position aside, leaving hoses attached.
7. **On all models,** remove front and rear transaxle struts.
8. Disconnect fuel lines from throttle body.
9. **On models equipped with automatic transaxle,** disconnect transaxle cooler lines, then the transaxle shift linkage and downshift cable.
10. **On all models,** disconnect throttle cable from throttle body.
11. Disconnect redundant ground wire, then remove multi-relay bracket.

12. Raise and support vehicle.
13. **On models equipped with power steering,** remove power steering line bracket from engine.
14. **On all models,** remove front wheels.
15. Remove brake calipers and rotors.
16. Remove 2 steering knuckle to strut attaching bolts from each side.
17. Disconnect exhaust pipe from exhaust manifold and position aside.
18. Remove 2 body to frame attaching bolts from lower control arm on each side.
19. Loosen 8 remaining body to frame attaching bolts.
20. Remove one bolt from each end of frame side, leaving one bolt per corner.
21. Position suitable jack stands under front of body, then move hoist back to body pan with a 6 foot long 4 x 4 inch block of wood between hoist and vehicle.

22. Raise hoist and remove jack stands, then place dolly under engine with 4 x 4 inch blocks to maintain position on dolly.
23. Lower vehicle, allowing engine to rest on dolly, then remove engine mount bolts and right front bracket.
24. Remove 4 remaining frame to body bolts, then raise vehicle off engine/transaxle assembly.
25. Separate engine from transaxle.
26. Reverse procedure to install.

CYLINDER HEAD
REPLACE

1. Disconnect battery ground cable, then drain cooling system.
2. Remove exhaust manifold as described under "Exhaust Manifold, Replace."
3. Remove oil level indicator tube, then the air cleaner assembly.
4. Disconnect electrical connectors, throttle linkage and fuel lines from throttle body unit, then disconnect heater hose from intake manifold.
5. Disconnect electrical connectors from intake manifold and cylinder head.
6. Disconnect vacuum lines from cylinder head.
7. **On models equipped with A/C,** unfasten A/C compressor and position aside, leaving refrigerant lines attached (if top mounted).
8. **On all models,** position alternator brackets aside, then remove upper power steering pump bracket.
9. Remove upper power steering pump bracket (if top mounted).
10. Remove rocker arm cover, then the rocker arms and pushrods.
11. Remove cylinder head attaching bolts, then the cylinder head.
12. Reverse procedure to install. **Torque** cylinder head attaching bolts in the following sequence:
    a. **Torque** all bolts in sequence, **Fig. 3,** to 18 ft. lbs.
    b. Repeat sequence, bringing **torque** to 26 ft. lbs. on all bolts except No. 9. Retorque No. 9 to 18 ft. lbs.
    c. Repeat sequence, turning all bolts 90° (1/4 turn).

INTAKE MANIFOLD
REPLACE

1. Disconnect battery ground cable.
2. Remove air cleaner assembly.
3. Disconnect PCV valve and hose from throttle body unit.
4. Drain engine coolant, then disconnect fuel lines from throttle body.
5. Disconnect vacuum lines, then disconnect electrical connectors and throttle linkage from throttle body unit.
6. Disconnect transaxle downshift cable and cruise control linkage, if equipped.
7. Unfasten throttle linkage and throttle valve cable and position aside.
8. Disconnect heater hose from manifold.

BOLT TIGHTENING SEQUENCE
TIGHTEN BOLT POSITION NUMBER IN SEQUENCE AS FOLLOWS: 3-5-6-2-1-7-4 OR BY USING ALPHA GROUPS "A" AND "B": "A" BEING FIRST AND "B" LAST. BOLT AT POSITION 4 TO BE INSTALLED WITH OIL LEVEL INDICATOR ASM.

Fig. 5 Exhaust manifold bolt tightening sequence

1	RETAINER SPRING
2	PUSH ROD SEAT
3	ROCKER FEED METERING VALVE
4	PLUNGER
5	BALL CHECK VALVE
6	BALL CHECK VALVE SPRING (HIGH BALL LIFTER ONLY)
7	BALL CHECK VALVE RETAINER
8	PLUNGER SPRING
9	LIFTER BODY

Fig. 6 Hydraulic valve lifter components

1 – BALANCER ASSEMBLY
2 – RESTRICTOR
3 – FILTER
4 – OIL PAN
5 – GASKET
6 – PLUG
7 – BOLT

Fig. 7 Balance shaft/oil pump assembly removal

9. Remove intake manifold attaching bolts and the manifold.
10. Reverse procedure to install. Torque attaching bolts to specifications in sequence shown in **Fig. 4.**

EXHAUST MANIFOLD
REPLACE

1. Disconnect battery ground cable.
2. Remove air cleaner assembly.
3. Unfasten alternator upper mounting brackets and position aside.
4. Disconnect oxygen sensor electrical connector.
5. Raise and support vehicle.
6. Disconnect exhaust pipe from exhaust manifold, then lower vehicle.
7. Remove exhaust manifold attaching bolts, then the manifold and gasket.
8. Reverse procedure to install. **Torque** attaching bolts in sequence, **Fig. 5. Torque** bolts 1, 2, 6 and 7 to 26 ft. lbs. and bolts 3, 4 and 5 to 37 ft. lbs.

VALVE ADJUSTMENT

These engines are equipped with hydraulic valve lifters. No provision for adjustment is provided.

VALVE ARRANGEMENT
FRONT TO REAR

2.5L/4-151 . . . . I-E-I-E-I-E-I

VALVE TIMING
Intake Opens Before TDC

Engine	Year	Degrees
2.5L/4-151	1991	33

CAMSHAFT LIFT SPECIFICATIONS

Engine	Year	Int.	Exh.
2.5L/4-151	1991	.248	.248

VALVE GUIDES

Valve guides are an integral part of the cylinder head and are not removable. If valve stem clearance becomes excessive, the valve guide should be reamed to the next oversize and the appropriate oversize valves installed. Valves are available in .003 and .005 inch oversizes.

HYDRAULIC VALVE LIFTERS

Hydraulic roller valve lifters are used on these engines. Lifter retainers and guide plates are used to keep the lifter from rotating on the camshaft. Failure of a hydraulic valve lifter, **Fig. 6**, is generally caused by an inadequate oil supply or dirt. An air leak at the intake side of the oil pump or too much oil in the engine will cause air bubbles in the oil supply to the lifters causing

them to collapse. This is a probable cause of trouble if several lifters fail to function, but air in oil is an unlikely cause of failure of a single unit.

Valve lifters can be removed after removing rocker arm cover and pushrod cover. Loosen rocker arm bolt and rotate rocker arm so that pushrod can be removed, then remove lifter guide, retainer and the valve lifter. It may be necessary to use tool No. J-3049 to facilitate lifter removal.

BALANCE SHAFT ASSEMBLY
REPLACE
REMOVAL

1. Remove oil pan attaching bolts and the oil pan.
2. Remove balance shaft assembly attaching bolts and the balance shaft assembly, **Figs. 7 and 8.**

INSTALLATION

When installing the balancer, the end of the housing without dowel pins must remain in contact with the block surface. if it loses contact, gear engagement may be lost and permanent damage to either the crankshaft or the balancer gears may result.

1. Rotate crankshaft until the fourth counterweight from the front is positioned exactly at B.D.C.
2. Install balancer onto block with balance weights at exactly B.D.C. plus or minus 1/2 gear tooth.
3. Install balancer bolts and **torque** to 107 inch lbs. in sequence, 3-1-2-4 **Fig. 9.**

Fig. 8 Exploded view of balance shaft/oil pump assembly

1 – SPLASH GUARD
2 – BALANCER
3 – GEROTOR OIL PUMP
4 – FILTER BODY
5 – PRESSURE REGULATOR VALVE
6 – RESTRICTOR
7 – FILTER
8 – COUNTERWEIGHTED BALANCE SHAFT
9 – COUNTERWEIGHTED BALANCE SHAFT GEAR
10 – GEROTOR OIL PUMP DRIVE

1 | BALANCER ASSEMBLY
2 | BAFFLE
3 | 10 N·m (90 LB. IN.)
* CIRCLED NUMBERS SHOW BOLT POSITION (SEE TEXT FOR TIGHTENING SEQUENCE)

Fig. 9 Balance shaft installation

4. Following the same sequence, **torque** the short bolts to 11 ft. lbs. plus 75° and the long bolts to 11 ft. lbs. plus 90°
5. Rotate crankshaft at least four complete turns while observing for adequate clearance between the fourth crankshaft counterweight and the balancer weights.

6. Install oil pan and torque bolts to specifications.

FRONT COVER
REPLACE
REMOVAL

1. Remove drive belts, then power steering pump bolts and lay pump aside.
2. Raise and support vehicle, then remove right front wheel and tire assembly.
3. Remove inner fender splash shield, then right hand cover.
4. Remove flywheel cover using a suitable tool to prevent flywheel rotation.
5. Remove bolt and washer, then balancer and key.
6. Remove front cover attaching bolts, then front cover and oil seal.

INSTALLATION

1. Apply a ³/₈ inch wide by ³/₁₆ inch thick bead of RTV sealant to joint at oil pan and front cover.
2. Apply a ¼ inch wide by ⅛ inch thick bead of RTV sealant to front cover at cylinder block mating surfaces.
3. Install oil seal to front cover using tool No. J-34995 or equivalent and leave installed in front cover oil seal bore.
4. Install front cover and partially tighten 2 opposing front cover screws with tool in place.
5. Install remaining cover to block screws and **torque** to 89 inch lbs., then remove tool.
6. Install key, balancer, washer and bolt using a suitable tool to prevent flywheel rotation and **torque** bolt to 162 ft. lbs.
7. Install flywheel cover, then right hand cover.
8. Install inner fender splash shield, then right front wheel and tire assembly.
9. Lower vehicle, then install power steering pump.
10. Install drive belts.

TIMING CHAIN & GEARS
REPLACE

1. Remove front cover as described under "Front Cover, Replace."
2. Loosen camshaft bolt, this will aid in preventing camshaft from moving off timing marks.
3. Align cam and crankshaft timing marks, engine at T.D.C., **Fig. 10.**
4. Remove camshaft bolt, then timing chain and sprockets.
5. Reverse procedure to install, **torquing** camshaft bolt to 43 ft. lbs.

CAMSHAFT
REPLACE

1. Remove engine from vehicle as described under "Engine, Replace."
2. Remove rocker arm cover, pushrods, pushrod cover and valve lifters.
3. Remove crankshaft balancer, then front cover as described under "Front Cover, Replace."
4. Align timing marks with engine at T.D.C. **Fig. 10.**
5. Remove cam sprocket bolt, then timing chain and sprockets.
6. Remove camshaft thrust plate, then slide camshaft out through front of block. Use care not to damage camshaft bearings.

Fig. 10 Valve timing marks

Fig. 11 Piston & rod assembly

7. Reverse procedure to install aligning marks on cam and crank gears as shown in **Fig. 10.**

PISTON & ROD ASSEMBLY

Assemble piston to rod with notch on piston facing toward front of engine and the raised notch side of rod at bearing end facing toward rear of engine, **Fig. 11.**

Upon installation, measure the connecting rod side clearance using a suitable feeler gauge. Clearance should be .006 to .024 inch.

PISTON PINS & RINGS

Pistons and rings are available in standard and oversizes of .010, .020 and .030 inch. Piston pins are available in oversizes of .001 and .003 inch.

MAIN & ROD BEARINGS

Main and rod bearings are available in standard size and undersizes of .001, .002 and .010 inch.

OIL PAN
REPLACE

1. Disconnect battery ground cable, then raise and support vehicle.
2. Drain engine oil, then disconnect exhaust pipe at manifold and hanger and swing out of the way.
3. Remove starter cover, then flywheel cover.
4. Remove starter, then oil pan attaching bolts and the oil pan.
5. Reverse procedure to install.

OIL PUMP SERVICE
REMOVAL

It is not necessary to remove the balance shaft assembly to service the oil pump or pressure regulator valve.

Fig. 12 Exploded view of balance shaft/oil pump assembly

1. Drain crankcase, then remove oil pan as described under "Oil Pan, Replace" and oil filter.

DISASSEMBLE

1. Remove oil pump cover assembly, then oil pump gears. **Figs. 8 and 12.**
2. Remove pressure regulator valve, plug or pin, spring and valve. If valve is stuck, clean valve and pump housing with carburetor cleaner.

INSPECTION

Inspect pump components and should any of the following conditions be found, the oil pump assembly should be replaced.

1. Inspect pump housing and cover assembly for cracks, scoring or casting imperfections.
2. Inspect pressure regulator valve for scoring or sticking, burrs may be removed with a fine oil stone.
3. Inspect pressure regulator valve spring for loss of tension or bending, if in doubt replace spring.
4. Inspect screen assembly for looseness or broken wire mesh or screen.
5. Inspect oil pump for chipping, galling or wear.
6. Measure pump housing pocket depth and gear thickness, refer to "Engine Rebuilding Specifications" for specifications.

ASSEMBLY

To avoid engine damage, all pump cavities must be packed with petroleum jelly before installing the gears to assure priming.

1. Lubricate all internal parts with engine oil.
2. Install pump gears, then oil pump cover assembly.
3. Install pressure regulator valve and spring, then plug or pin. Make sure pin is properly secured.
4. **Torque** oil pump cover assembly bolts to 89 inch lbs.

INSTALLATION

1. Clean oil pump screen and oil pan.

1. HOUSING OUTLET
2. THERMOSTAT
3. THERMOSTAT HOUSING
4. BOLT/SCREW — 10 N·m (90 LBS. IN.)

Fig. 13 Thermostat replacement

2. Install oil filter.
3. Install oil pan and fill crankcase with clean engine oil.

BELT TENSION DATA

Year & Engine (VIN)	Belt	New Belt, Lbs.	Used Belt, Lbs.
1991			
2.5L/4-151(U)	Alternator	165	90
	PS/Water Pump	180	90
	A/C	165	90

COOLING SYSTEM BLEED

After filling cooling system, start engine and allow to reach operating temperature with surge tank pressure cap installed. Stop engine, then position shop towel over surge tank pressure cap. Slowly and carefully remove surge tank cap. Add coolant as necessary to bring to proper level, then install surge tank pressure cap.

THERMOSTAT
REPLACE

1. Disconnect battery ground cable.
2. Drain cooling system until level is below thermostat.
3. Remove air cleaner assembly.
4. Remove thermostat housing attaching bolts, then remove thermostat housing and thermostat, **Fig. 13**.
5. Reverse procedure to install.

WATER PUMP
REPLACE

REMOVAL

1. Disconnect battery ground cable, then drain cooling system.
2. Remove drive belts.
3. Remove water pump attaching bolts, then remove water pump from cover assembly, **Fig. 14**.

Fig. 14 Water pump assembly

VIEW A   VIEW B

30 mm (1.2 IN.) MINIMUM CLEARANCE

1. BAR
2. PIPE, FUEL FEED
3. FITTING — 27 N·m (20 LBS. FT.) BACK-UP WRENCH REQUIRED AT THIS ATTACHMENT
4. SEAL, O-RING
5. BRACKET, FUEL FILTER
6. FILTER, FUEL
7. SCREW — FULLY DRIVEN, SEATED AND NOT STRIPPED
8. PIPE ASM., FUEL
9. SEAT SPRING

Fig. 15 Fuel pump replacement

4. If installing a new pump use the pulley from the old unit.

INSTALLATION

1. Apply a 1/8 inch bead of red RTV sealant or equivalent, on the water pump sealing surface.

2. Coat water pump bolts with RTV sealant to avoid coolant leaks.
3. While the sealant is still wet, install the pump and **torque** bolts to 25 ft. lbs.
4. Install drive belts, then fill cooling system and connect battery ground cable.
5. Inspect cooling system for leaks.

FUEL PUMP
REPLACE

1. Disconnect battery ground cable, then drain fuel tank.
2. Disconnect tank unit harness connector.
3. Remove ground wire retaining screw from underbody.
4. Disconnect hoses from tank meter assembly, then hoses at tank from filler and vent pipes.
5. Support fuel tank and disconnect the two fuel tank retaining straps.
6. Remove fuel tank from vehicle.
7. Remove fuel tank sending unit and pump assembly by turning cam lock ring counterclockwise. Lift assembly from fuel tank and remove pump from sending unit.
8. Pull fuel pump up into attaching hose while pulling outward away from bottom support. Take care to prevent damage to rubber insulator and strainer during removal.
9. After pump assembly is clear of bottom support, pull pump assembly out of rubber connector for removal.
10. Reverse procedure to install.

FUEL FILTER REPLACE

The fuel filter is located below the rear of the vehicle, forward of the fuel tank.

1. Relieve fuel system pressure as outlined under "Precautions."
2. Raise and support vehicle.
3. Using suitable back-up wrench, remove fuel filter fittings, **Fig. 15.**
4. Remove fuel filter.
5. Reverse procedure to install. Ensure feed line is angled at 30°.

TECHINCAL SERVICE BULLETINS
CAM SERVICING

On some models, when servicing the cam or crank gears, it is recommended that a new gear set kit be used to replace individual gears (part No. 10101789).

TIGHTENING SPECIFICATIONS

Year	Component	Torque/ Ft. Lbs.
1991	Balancer To Block Short Bolts	15①
	Balancer To Block Long Bolts	11②
	Camshaft Sprocket Bolt	43
	Camshaft Thrust Plate To Block	89③
	Connecting Rod Nut	29
	Crankshaft Dampener Bolt	162
	Cylinder Head Bolts	④
	Engine Front Mount To Engine Bolt	41
	Engine Front Mount To Engine Bracket	15
	Engine Front Mount To Chassis Bottom Bolt	61
	Engine Front Mount To Chassis Top Bolt	54
	Engine Rear Mount To Chassis Bracket Nut	18
	Engine Rear Mount To Engine Bracket	43
	Engine Rear Bracket To Engine Bolt (MT)	47
	Engine Rear Bracket To Engine Bolt (AT)	37
	Exhaust Manifold Inner Bolt	26
	Exhaust Manifold Outer Bolt	37
	Flywheel To Crankshaft Bolt (A/T)	55
	Flywheel To Crankshaft Bolt (M/T)	69
	Intake Manifold Bolt	25
	Main Bearing Cap Bolt	65
	Oil Filter Access Plug Bolt	⑤
	Oil Pan Drain Plug Bolt	25
	Oil Pan To Block	89③
	Pushrod Cover To Block Bolt	89③
	Rocker Arm Bolt	20
	Rocker Arm Cover Bolt	80③
	Spark Plugs	11
	Starter Motor Bracket To Engine	37
	Starter Motor To Engine	32
	Starter Motor To Starter Retaining Nut	44
	Thermostat Housing Bolt	20
	Throttle Body Attaching Bolts	18
	Throttle Inlet & Outlet Nuts	30
	Timing Gear Cover To Block Bolt	89③
	Torque Converter To Flywheel (AT)	46
	Water Pump To Block	25

①—Plus an additional 75°
②—Plus an additional 90°
③—Inch lbs.
④—Refer to text.
⑤—Hand tighten plus ¼ turn.

3.3L/V6-204 Engine

INDEX

VIEW A

1 A/C COMPRESSOR & ENGINE MOUNTING BRACKET
2 BOLTS-90 N•M (66 LBS-FT)
3 BOLTS-20 N•M (15 LBS-FT)
4 LOCATING BOLT (REMOVE AFTER MOUNT IS INSTALLED)
5 BOLT-70 N•M (52 LBS-FT)
6 BOLT-73 N•M (54 LBS-FT)
7 BOLT - 83 N•m (61 LBS. FT.)

Fig. 1   Front engine mount. 1991

PRECAUTIONS

FUEL SYSTEM PRESSURE RELIEF

Failure to relieve system pressure prior to disconnecting fuel system components may cause fire or personal injury. Remove fuel tank filler cap to release fuel tank pressure. Connect pressure gauge J-34730-1 or equivalent to pressure tap on fuel rail, position bleed hose into suitable container and slowly relieve fuel system pressure. Prior to disconnecting fuel line, position shop towel over fitting.

ENGINE MOUNTS
REPLACE

1991
Front Mount

1. Support engine using fixture No. J-28467 or equivalent.
2. Load the fixture slightly to remove the weight of the engine from the mount.
3. Remove mount to engine bracket bolts, then raise the engine.
4. Remove mount to engine compartment bolts, then the mount, **Fig. 1**.
5. Reverse procedure to install.

Rear Mount

1. Support engine using fixture No. J-28467 or equivalent.
2. Raise and support vehicle.
3. Remove mount to engine mount bracket nuts.
4. Raise engine slightly, then remove mount to frame bracket nuts and the mount, **Fig. 2**.
5. Reverse procedure to install.

1992-93
Right Engine Mount

1. Disconnect battery ground cable.
2. Support engine using tool J28476-A or equivalent.
3. Raise and support vehicle, then remove mount to engine mount bracket nuts.
4. Raise engine slightly, then remove mount to frame nuts.
5. Remove engine mount, **Fig. 3**.
6. Reverse procedure to install.

Engine Mount Strut

1. Disconnect battery ground cable.
2. Raise and support vehicle.
3. Remove bolts attaching engine mount strut to body.

VIEW A

1 NUT 45 N•M (33 LBS FT)
2 MOUNT
3 BRACKET
4 BOLT 54 N•M (40 LBS FT)
5 BOLT 95 N•M (70 LBS FT)
6 BOLT 56 N•M (41 LBS FT)
7 WASHER
8 BOLT 56 N•M (41 LBS FT)
9 PLATE
10 NUTS 24 N•M (18 LBS FT)

Fig. 2   Rear engine mount. 1991

4. Remove engine mount strut, **Fig. 4**.
5. Reverse procedure to install.

ENGINE
REPLACE

1. Remove hood and cover fenders.
2. Depressurize and disconnect fuel lines from fuel rail.
3. Disconnect battery ground cable, then drain engine coolant.
4. Remove radiator and heater hoses,

A. BRACKET - PART OF BODY ASM.
B. ENGINE ASM.
C. ENGINE MOUNT STRUT BRACKET

1. ENGINE MOUNT ASM.
2. ENGINE MOUNT BRACKET
3. BOLT - 66 N·m (49 LBS. FT.)
4. BOLT - 62 N·m (46 LBS. FT.)
5. NUT & BOLT 42 N·m (31 LBS. FT.)
6. BOLT - 50 N·m (37 LBS. FT.) PLUS 70° TURN
7. BOLT & NUT - 50 N·m (37 LBS. FT.)
8. ENGINE MOUNT BRACE

Fig. 3   Right engine mount. 1992–93

A. FRONT SUSPENSION SUPPORT
B. ENGINE ASM.

1. ENGINE MOUNT STRUT ASSEMBLY
2. ENGINE MOUNT STRUT BRACKET ASM.
3. A/C COMPRESSOR BRACKET ASM.
4. STUD - 50 N·m (37 LBS. FT.)
5. BOLT - 120 N·m (89 LBS. FT.)
6. BOLT - 90 N·m (66 LBS. FT.)

Fig. 4   Engine mount strut & bracket. 1992–93

then engine cooling fan.

5. Remove air intake duct from throttle body, then vacuum lines from the brake power booster and evaporative canister purge.
6. Remove cable bracket and cables from throttle body, then the drive belt.
7. Remove power steering pump and position aside, then disconnect electrical connectors.
8. Remove upper transaxle to engine bolts, then raise and support vehicle.
9. **On models with A/C,** remove A/C compressor and position aside.
10. **On all models,** remove rear engine mount to mount bracket bolts.
11. Remove flywheel dust cover, then flywheel to torque converter bolts. Use a scribe to mark flywheel to torque converter relationship to ensure proper reassembly.
12. Remove lower engine to transaxle bolts. One bolt is located between the transaxle case and engine block and is installed in the opposite direction.
13. Lower vehicle, then remove front engine mount to bracket bolts, then engine assembly.
14. Reverse procedures to install.

INTAKE MANIFOLD
REPLACE

1. Depressurize and disconnect fuel lines from fuel rail, then disconnect battery ground cable.
2. Remove serpentine drive belt, then the alternator and braces.
3. Remove power steering pump and braces and position aside.
4. Remove coolant bypass hose, then the heater hose.
5. Remove upper radiator hose, then the air inlet duct.
6. Remove throttle cable bracket and cables from throttle body.
7. Disconnect vacuum hoses, then electrical connectors.

Fig. 5   Intake manifold bolt tightening sequence

8. Remove the fuel rail, then disconnect the vapor canister purge line.
9. Remove heater hose from the throttle body, then disconnect the rear spark plug wires.
10. Remove the intake manifold bolts, then the manifold.
11. Reverse procedure to install noting the following:
   a. Clean the intake manifold bolts and bolt holes of adhesive compound.
   b. Apply sealant 12345336 or equivalent, to the ends of the manifold seals.
   c. Apply thread lock compound 12345493 or equivalent, to the manifold bolt threads.
   d. Torque the manifold bolts following the sequence in **Fig. 5,** to specifications.
   e. Lubricate throttle body coolant and heater pipe O-rings with anti-freeze before assembly.

EXHAUST MANIFOLD
REPLACE
FRONT

1. Disconnect battery ground cable.

2. Remove air cleaner inlet duct, then disconnect spark plug wires at spark plugs. Tag spark plug wires so they can be installed at the same location.
3. Disconnect exhaust crossover pipe from exhaust manifold.
4. Remove engine lifting hook.
5. Remove heat shield from exhaust manifold.
6. Remove engine oil dipstick and tube.
7. Remove exhaust manifold attaching studs, then remove exhaust manifold.
8. Reverse procedure to install.

REAR

1. Disconnect battery ground cable.
2. Disconnect spark plug wires at spark plugs. Tag spark plug wires so they can be installed in the same locations.
3. Disconnect electrical connector at oxygen sensor.
4. Disconnect throttle cables at throttle body, then remove throttle cable bracket.
5. Disconnect power brake unit vacuum hose at intake manifold.
6. Disconnect exhaust crossover pipe and exhaust pipe from exhaust manifold.
7. Remove engine lifting hook.
8. Remove transaxle dipstick and tube.
9. Remove heat shield from exhaust manifold.
10. Remove exhaust manifold attaching studs and bolt, then remove exhaust manifold.
11. Reverse procedure to install.

CYLINDER HEAD
REPLACE

1. Disconnect battery ground cable.
2. Remove intake manifold as described under "Intake Manifold, Replace."
3. Remove exhaust manifold as described under "Exhaust Manifold, Replace."

Fig. 6 Cylinder head bolt tightening sequence

5	PUSHROD GUIDE
6	ROCKER ARM
7	ROCKER ARM PIVOT
8	BOLT 51 N•M (37 LBS. FT.)
9	HEAD GASKET
10	HEAD BOLT

Fig. 7 Rocker arm installation

1	ROLLER	6	BALL CHECK
2	LIFTER BODY	7	PLUNGER
3	PLUNGER SPRING	8	OIL METERING VALVE
4	BALL CHECK RETAINER	9	PUSH ROD SEAT
5	BALL CHECK SPRING	10	RETAINER RING

Fig. 8 Hydraulic roller valve lifter

1	OIL SEAL
2	CAM BUTTON
3	CAM BUTTON SPRING

Fig. 9 Engine front cover replacement

4. Remove valve covers, then disconnect spark plug wires.
5. If right hand cylinder is to be removed, proceed as follows:
   a. Remove power steering pump and position aside with hose attached.
   b. Remove belt tensioner assembly.
6. If left hand cylinder head is to be removed, proceed as follows:
   a. Remove alternator bracket with ignition module and coil units attached.
   b. Remove A/C compressor mounting bolt from cylinder head.
7. Remove rocker arm assemblies, guide plate and pushrods.
8. Remove cylinder head attaching bolts and cylinder heads.
9. Reverse procedure to install noting the following:
   a. Clean threads in the block using a $7/16$-14 tap, then clean bolt threads.
   b. Apply sealant 1052080 or equivalent, to the underside of the bolt heads.
   c. Apply thread locker 12345382 or equivalent, to the bolt threads.
   d. Install cylinder head bolts and tighten in sequence shown in **Fig. 6**. Torque each cylinder head bolt to 35 ft. lbs., then tighten an additional 130° using torque angle meter No. J-36660. Tighten the center four cylinder head attaching bolts an additional 30° using torque angle meter J-36660.

ROCKER ARMS

1. Remove valve cover.
2. Remove rocker arm pedestal retaining bolts.

3. Remove pedestal and rocker arm assembly, **Fig. 7**. Keep rocker arms and pedestals together and note installation position. Components that are to be reused should be installed in original position.
4. Reverse procedure to install, **torquing** pedestal retaining bolts to 28 ft. lbs. Clean bolt threads and apply thread locking compound 112345493 to bolt threads prior to installation.

VALVE ADJUSTMENT

These engines are equipped with hydraulic valve lifters. No provision for adjustment is provided.

VALVE GUIDES

The valve guides are an integral part of the cylinder head and cannot be replaced.

If the valve stem clearance is excessive, the valve guide must be reamed and an oversize valve installed. Valves are available in oversize of .010 inch.

HYDRAULIC VALVE LIFTERS

Failure of an hydraulic valve lifter, **Fig. 8**, is generally caused by dirt or an inadequate oil supply. An air leak at the intake side of the oil pump or too much oil in the engine will cause air bubbles in the oil supply to the lifters, causing them to collapse. This is a probable cause of trouble if several lifters fail to function, but air in the oil is an unlikely cause of failure of a single unit.

The valve lifters may be lifted out of their

bores after removing the rocker arms, pushrods and intake manifold. Adjustable pliers with taped jaws may be used to remove lifters that are stuck due to varnish, carbon, etc.

FRONT COVER
REPLACE

1. Disconnect battery ground cable, then drain cooling system.
2. Remove serpentine drive belt, then the heater pipes. Remove lower radiator and coolant bypass hoses from front cover.
3. **On 1991 models,** remove alternator and position aside, then the power steering pump.
4. **On all models,** raise and support vehicle.
5. Remove right front wheel and tire assembly, then remove inner fender splash shield.
6. **On 1991 models,** remove right front axle, then support engine using fixture No. J-28467 or equivalent.
7. **On 1991 models,** remove engine mount, then tensioner bracket.
8. **On all models,** remove torque converter cover, then install flywheel holding tool J-37096 or equivalent to hold fly wheel in position.

Fig. 10   Valve timing marks

Fig. 11   Timing chain replacement. 1991

Fig. 13   Piston installation direction.

63	KEY
78	DAMPER ASSEMBLY
79	CRANKSHAFT SPROCKET
84	BOLT
85	TIMING CHAIN
87	CAMSHAFT SPROCKET
88	CAMSHAFT GEAR

Fig. 12   Timing chain replacement. 1992–93

9. Remove crankshaft balancer bolt, then remove balancer.
10. Remove crankshaft sensor shield.
11. Disconnect electrical connectors at camshaft and crankshaft sensors and oil pressure sender switch.
12. Remove oil pan to front cover attaching bolts.
13. Remove front cover to engine attaching bolts, then remove front cover, **Fig. 9.**
14. Reverse procedure to install. Apply sealant 1052080 or equivalent, to front cover bolt threads. Adjust crankshaft sensor using tool No. J-37087 or equivalent. Hold flywheel in place using tool No. J-37096 or equivalent, when tightening balancer bolt.

TIMING CHAIN
REPLACE

1. Remove front cover as described under "Front Cover, Replace."
2. Align timing marks on sprockets so they are as close together as possible, **Fig. 10.**
3. Remove camshaft sprocket attaching bolts, then the camshaft sprocket, chain and crankshaft sprocket, **Figs. 11 and 12.**
4. Reverse procedure to install. Install chain with No. 1 piston at TDC, timing mark on camshaft sprocket facing straight down and timing marks on sprockets as close together as possible, **Fig. 10.**

CAMSHAFT
REPLACE

1. Disconnect battery ground cable, then remove engine as described in "Engine, Replace."
2. Remove intake manifold as described in " Intake Manifold, Replace."
3. Remove valve covers, then rocker arms, pushrods and valve lifters.
4. Remove crankshaft balancer assembly.
5. Remove crankshaft sensor shield.
6. Remove front cover as described in "Front Cover, Replace."
7. Remove timing chain and sprockets.
8. Slide camshaft forward out of bearing bores, using care so as not to damage bearing surfaces.
9. Reverse procedure to install noting the following:
   a. Prior to installation, coat camshaft and dip valve lifters in lubricant No. 12345501 or equivalent.
   b. When installing camshaft, align crankshaft and camshaft timing marks as shown in **Fig. 10.**

PISTON & ROD ASSEMBLY

When installing piston and connecting rod in cylinder bore, ridge on the outer diameter of the piston pin bore on the inside of the piston must face toward front of engine as shown in Fig. 13.

Measure connecting rod side clearance using a suitable feeler gauge. Clearance should be .003 to .015 inch.

PISTON PINS & RINGS

Pistons are available in standard sizes and oversizes of .010 and .020 inch. Rings are available in standard sizes and oversizes of .010 and .020 inch. Piston pins are supplied with piston and available only in standard sizes.

MAIN & ROD BEARINGS

Main bearings are available in standard sizes and undersize of .001 inch. Rod bearings are available in standard sizes and in undersize of .008 inch.

OIL PAN
REPLACE

1991

1. Disconnect battery ground cable.
2. Raise and support vehicle, then drain oil.
3. Remove transaxle converter cover, then remove starter motor.
4. Remove oil filter, then remove oil pan retaining bolts and oil pan.
5. Reverse procedure to install.

1992–93

1. disconnect battery ground cable.
2. Raise and support vehicle, then drain crankcase.
3. Remove lower splash shield and flap.
4. Remove crankshaft pulley and crankshaft sensor cover.
5. Disconnect A/C compressor electrical connector and hose support from suspension support.
6. Remove A/C compressor from mounting bracket and position aside with refrigerant hoses attached.
7. Remove right hand suspension support front bolts.
8. Loosen all suspension support attaching bolts so that support will drop approximately 1.5 inches at front.
9. Remove oil lever sensor from oil pan.
10. Remove flywheel housing cover.
11. Remove oil pan attaching bolts and oil pan. Move A/C refrigerant line as necessary to obtain clearance for oil pan removal.
12. Reverse procedure to install.

1. 11 N·m (88 IN. LBS.)
2. OIL PUMP COVER
3. PUMP OUTER GEAR
4. PUMP INNER GEAR
5. FRONT COVER

Fig. 14   Oil pump & housing assembly

Inner Gear Tip Clearance

Fig. 15   Checking inner gear tip clearance

Outer Gear Dia. Clearance

Fig. 16   Checking outer gear diameter clearance

Gear End Clearance

Fig. 17   Checking gear end clearance

OIL PUMP SERVICE

REMOVAL & INSPECTION

1. Remove engine front cover as described under "Front Cover, Replace," then the oil filter adapter, pressure regulator valve and valve spring.
2. Remove oil pump cover attaching screws, cover and gears, **Fig. 14.**
3. Inspect pump cover and housing for cracks, scoring, porosity and damaged threads, pressure regulator valve and spring for sticking, scoring or tension loss and gears for chipping, galling or excessive wear. Replace as necessary.
4. Check gear clearance as follows:
   a. Check inner gear tip clearance with feeler gauge as shown in **Fig. 15.** Maximum clearance should not exceed .006 inch.
   b. Check outer gear diameter clearance with feeler gauge as shown in **Fig. 16.** Clearance should be .008-.015 inch.
   c. Check gear end clearance (gear drop in housing) with suitable dial indicator as shown in **Fig. 17.** Clearance should be .001-.0035 inch.
5. Replace parts as necessary.

ASSEMBLY & INSTALLATION

1. Lubricate gears with petroleum jelly, then install into oil pump housing.
2. Pack pump cavity with petroleum jelly, then install pump cover and attaching screws. **Torque** attaching screws to 97 inch lbs.

3. Install pressure regulator valve spring and valve.
4. Install oil filter adapter using new gasket. **Torque** adapter to 24 ft.lbs.
5. Reinstall front cover onto engine.

REAR MAIN BEARING OIL SEAL
REPLACE

1. Remove flywheel, then confirm rear seal leak.
2. Insert a screwdriver or similar tool in through the dust lip at any angle and pry seal out by moving the handle of the tool towards the end of the crankshaft pilot. Repeat as required around the seal until seal is removed. Care must be taken not to damage crankshaft OD surface or chamfer with pry tool.
3. Using tool No. J-38196 or equivalent, apply engine oil to the ID and OD of new seal. Slide new seal over mandrel until back of seal bottom squarely fits against collar.
4. Install seal as follows:
   a. Align dowel pin of tool with dowel pin in crankshaft and attach tool to crankshaft by hand, or **torque** attaching screws to 60 inch lbs.
   b. Turn T-handle of tool so that collar pushes seal into bore, turn the handle until the collar is tight against the case. This will ensure the seal is seated properly.
   c. Loosen the T-handle of the tool until it comes to a stop, then remove attaching screws.
5. Install flywheel.

BELT TENSION DATA

Year	Engine (VIN)	Belt Tension, Lbs. ①
1991-93	3.3L/V6-204(N)	67

①—On models less A/C, take reading between power steering pump & crankshaft pulley. On models with A/C, take reading between alternator & A/C compressor. If reading is less than listed, replace belt tensioner.

POWER STEERING
GENERATOR
Position for belt replacement.
Lift tensioner pulley with a 18 MM box end wrench on pulley nut.
WATER PUMP
A/C COMPRESSOR
CRANKSHAFT BALANCER
MINIMUM TENSION
BELT TENSION INDICATOR
MAXIMUM TENSION
BELT
BELT TENSIONER PULLEY

Fig. 18   Serpentine belt routing

SERPENTINE DRIVE BELT

Refer to **Fig. 18.** for serpentine drive belt replacement. The right front engine mount must be removed to replace serpentine drive belt.

COOLING SYSTEM BLEED
1991

After filling cooling system, start engine and allow to reach operating temperature with surge tank pressure cap installed. Stop engine, then position shop towel over surge tank pressure cap. Slowly and carefully remove surge tank cap. Add coolant as necessary to bring to proper level, then install surge tank pressure cap.

1. OUTLET
2. BOLT — 27 N·m (20 LBS. FT.)
3. STUD — 27 N·m (20 LBS. FT.)
4. GASKET
5. THERMOSTAT

Fig. 19   Thermostat replacement

1. WATER PUMP
2. ENGINE FRONT COVER ASM.
3. GASKET
4. 11 N·m (97 LBS. IN.)
5. 39 N·m (29 LBS. FT.)

Fig. 20   Water pump replacement

30 mm (1.2 IN.) MINIMUM CLEARANCE

VIEW A

VIEW B

1. BAR
2. PIPE, FUEL FEED
3. FITTING — 27 N·m (20 LBS. FT.) BACK-UP WRENCH REQUIRED AT THIS ATTACHMENT
4. SEAL, O-RING
5. BRACKET, FUEL FILTER
6. FILTER, FUEL
7. SCREW — FULLY DRIVEN, SEATED AND NOT STRIPPED
8. PIPE ASM., FUEL
9. SEAT, SPRING

Fig. 21   Fuel filter replacement. 1991

1992–93

After filling cooling system, start engine and allow to reach operating temperature with surge tank pressure cap removed. Air will bleed through surge cap opening. Add coolant as necessary to bring to proper level, then install surge tank pressure cap.

THERMOSTAT
REPLACE

1. Disconnect battery ground cable.
2. Drain cooling system until level is below thermostat.
3. Remove air cleaner assembly.
4. Remove thermostat housing and thermostat, **Fig. 19**.
5. Reverse procedure to install. Apply sealer to bolt threads prior to installation.

WATER PUMP
REPLACE

1. Disconnect battery ground cable.
2. Drain cooling system, then remove serpentine belt.
3. Remove idler pulley bolt, then water pump pulley bolts and remove pulley.
4. Remove water pump attaching bolts, then the water pump, **Fig. 20**.
5. Reverse procedure to install.

FUEL PUMP
REPLACE

1. Disconnect battery ground cable, then drain fuel tank.
2. Disconnect tank unit harness connector.
3. Remove ground wire retaining screw from underbody.
4. Disconnect hoses from tank meter as-

1. HOSE-PART OF FUEL SENDER
2. FUEL VAPOR PIPE
3. FUEL RETURN PIPE
4. FUEL FEED PIPE
5. FUEL FEED PIPE NUT - 27 N·m (20 LBS. FT.)
6. HOSE-PART OF FUEL SENDER
7. ABS AND FUEL SENDER HARNESS

Fig. 22   Fuel filter replacement. 1992-93

sembly, then hoses at tank from filler and vent pipes.
5. Support fuel tank and disconnect the two fuel tank retaining straps.
6. Remove fuel tank from vehicle.
7. Remove fuel tank sending unit and pump assembly by turning cam lock ring counterclockwise. Lift assembly from fuel tank and remove pump from sending unit.
8. Pull fuel pump up into attaching hose while pulling outward away from bottom support. Take care to prevent damage to rubber insulator and strainer during removal.
9. After pump assembly is clear of bottom support, pull pump assembly out of rubber connector for removal.
10. Reverse procedure to install.

FUEL FILTER
REPLACE
1991

The fuel filter is located below the rear of

the vehicle, forward of the fuel tank.
1. Relieve fuel system pressure as outlined under "Precautions."
2. Raise and support vehicle.
3. Using suitable back-up wrench, remove fuel filter fittings, **Fig. 21**.
4. Remove fuel filter.
5. Reverse procedure to install. Ensure feed line is angled at 30°.

1992-93

The fuel filter is located below the rear of the vehicle, rearward of the fuel tank.
1. Relieve fuel system pressure as outlined under "Precautions."
2. Raise and support vehicle.
3. Using suitable back-up wrench, remove fuel filter fitting, **Fig. 22**.
4. Grasp filter and one nylon fuel connection line fitting, twist quick connect fitting 1/4 turn in each direction to loosen dirt in fitting.
5. Using compressed air, clean dirt from quick connect fitting.
6. Depress quick connect fitting plastic tabs of male end connector and pull apart.
7. Remove fuel filter.
8. Reverse procedure to install.

TIGHTENING SPECIFICATIONS

Year	Component	Torque/ Ft. Lbs.
1991	Balance Assembly To Crankshaft	105④
	Camshaft Sprocket Bolts	52⑤
	Connecting Rod Bolts	20①
	Coolant Temperature Sensor To Intake	15
	Crankshaft Bearing Caps To Cylinder Block	26⑥
	Cylinder Block Drain Plug	25
	Cylinder Head To Block	②
	ESC Knock Sensor To Cylinder Block	13
	Exhaust Manifold To Cylinder Head	41
	Flywheel Cover To Transaxle	53③
	Front Cover To Block	22
	Intake Manifold To Cylinder Head	89③
	Oil Pan Drain Plug	30
	Oil Pan To Cylinder Block	124③
	Oil Pan To Front Cover	124③
	Oil Pump Cover To Timing Chain Cover	97③
	Oxygen Sensor To Exhaust Manifold	31
	Rocker Arm Pedestal To Cylinder Head	28
	Serpentine Belt Tensioner To Cylinder Head	38
	Spark Plug To Cylinder Head	20
	Starting Motor To Cylinder Block	35
	Thermostat Housing	20
	Timing Chain Dampener	14
	Torque Converter To Flywheel	46
	Transaxle To Cylinder Block	46
	Valve Lifter Guide Retainer Bolts	27
	Water Pump Pulley To Hub	115③
1992	Balance Shaft Gear Bolt	14⑦
	Balance Shaft Retainer	22
	Camshaft Sprocket Bolts	74⑧
	Connecting Rod Bolts	20①
	Coolant Temperature Sensor To Intake	15
	Crankshaft Bearing Caps To Cylinder Block	26①
	Cylinder Block Drain Plug	22
	Cylinder Head To Block	②
	ESC Knock Sensor To Cylinder Block	13
	Exhaust Manifold To Cylinder Head	38
	Flywheel Cover To Transaxle	48③
	Front Cover To Block	22
	Intake Manifold To Cylinder Head	88③
	Oil Pan Drain Plug	30
	Oil Pan To Cylinder Block	124③
	Oil Pan To Front Cover	124③
	Oil Pump Cover To Timing Chain Cover	97③
	Oxygen Sensor To Exhaust Manifold	31
	Rocker Arm Pedestal To Cylinder Head	88③
	Serpentine Belt Tensioner To Cylinder Head	38
	Spark Plug To Cylinder Head	12
	Starting Motor To Cylinder Block	35
	Thermostat Housing	20
	Timing Chain Dampener	16
	Torque Converter To Flywheel	46
	Transaxle To Cylinder Block	55

Year	Component	Torque/ Ft. Lbs.
1992	Valve Lifter Guide Retainer Bolts	22
	Water Pump To Front Cover	11
	Water Pump Pulley To Hub	114③
1993	Alternator Bracket To Cylinder Head	36
	Alternator Through Bolt	36
	Balancer To Crankshaft	111⑩
	Camshaft Sprocket Bolts	74⑨
	Connecting Rod Bolts	20①
	Coolant Temperature Sensor To Intake	15
	Crankshaft Bearing Caps To Cylinder Head	26①
	Crankshaft Sensor To Front Cover	22
	Crankshaft Sensor Clamp Bolt	40③
	Cylinder Block Drain Plug	15
	Cylinder Head Bolts	②
	Engine Mount To Cylinder Block	70
	ESC Knock Sensor To Cylinder Block	13
	Exhaust Manifold To Cylinder Head	38
	Flywheel Cover To Transaxle	48③
	Flywheel To Crankshaft	11①
	Front Cover To Block	22
	Fuel Feed & Return Pipes To Fuel Rail	22
	Fuel Rail To Intake Manifold	11
	Heater Hose Fitting To Intake	11
	Ignition Module To Alternator Bracket	18
	Intake Manifold To Cylinder Head	89③
	Oil Drain Plug	30
	Oil Filter Adapter To Front Cover	22
	Oil Gallery Plugs	25
	Oil Level Sensor To Oil Pan	16
	Oil Pan	124③
	Oil Pressure Switch	24
	Oil Pump Cover To Front Cover	97③
	Oil Screen Housing To Cylinder Block	11
	Oxygen Sensor To Exhaust Manifold	31
	Rocker Arm Pedestal To Cylinder Head	18⑪
	Spark Plug	20
	Starter Motor To Cylinder Head	35
	Thermostat Housing	20
	Throttle Body To Intake Manifold	21
	Throttle Body Cable Bracket To Throttle Body	35③
	Timing Chain Damper	16
	Torque Converter To Flywheel	46
	Transaxle To Cylinder Block	55
	Valve Cover	89③
	Valve Lifter Guide Bolts	22
	Water Pump To Front Cover	11⑫
	Water Pump Pulley To Hub	114③

① —Plus an additional 50°.
② —Refer to text.
③ —Inch lbs.
④ —Plus an additional 56°.
⑤ —Plus an additional 110°.
⑥ —Plus an additional 45°.
⑦ —Plus an additional 35°.
⑧ —Plus an additional 105°.
⑨ —Plus an additional 90°.
⑩ —Plus an additional 76°.
⑪ —Plus an additional 70°.
⑫ —Plus an additional 80°.

Clutch & Manual Transaxle

NOTE: For Service Procedure Refer To Clutch & Manual Transaxle Section In Buick Skyhawk, Chevrolet Cavalier & Pontiac Sunbird Chapter.

Rear Axle & Suspension

INDEX

DESCRIPTION

The rear suspension, **Figs. 1 and 2,** is a semi-independent type suspension consisting of an axle assembly with trailing arms and cross beam, coil springs and shock absorbers. A stabilizer bar is available and is attached to the inside of the axle beam and to the lower end of the control arms. A single unit hub and bearing assembly is bolted to each end of the axle assembly. The hub and bearing assembly is a sealed, non-serviceable unit and must be replaced as an assembly.

REAR AXLE
REPLACE

1. Raise vehicle and support vehicle. Support rear suspension with suitable jack.
2. Remove rear wheel and tire assembly assembly.
3. Disconnect brake lines from axle brackets.
4. Disconnect stabilizer bar at axle assembly, if equipped, **Figs. 1 and 3.**
5. Remove shock absorber to lower mounting bracket attaching bolts, then disconnect shock absorbers from axle assembly, **Figs. 1 and 2.**
6. Disconnect parking brake cable.
7. Carefully lower rear axle assembly and remove coil springs and insulators.
8. If equipped, disconnect ABS electrical connector and mount clip.
9. Disconnect brake lines at left and right hand wheels.
10. Remove control arm to underbody bracket bolts, then lower the axle assembly and remove from vehicle.
11. Reverse procedure to install and bleed brake system.

HUB & BEARING
REPLACE

1. Raise and support vehicle, then remove wheel and tire assembly and brake drum. **Do not hammer brake drum since damage to bearing may result.**

1.	STABILIZER SHAFT	9.	NUT	17.	NUT
2.	INSULATOR	10.	BOLT	18.	TAB NUT
3.	CLAMP	11.	AXLE	19.	BOLT
4.	UPPER SPACER	12.	BUMPER	20.	SHOCK ABSORBER
5.	LOWER SPACER	13.	SPRING	21.	MOUNT
6.	BOLT	14.	INSULATOR	22.	RETAINER
7.	NUT	15.	UNDERBODY	23.	NUT
8.	CLAMP	16.	WASHER	24.	NUT

Fig. 1 Rear suspension. 1990–91

NOTE COVER MUST BE INSTALLED SO THAT ARROW POINTS TO LEFT HAND OF VEHICLE

1	COVER (MUST BE INSTALLED WITH ARROW POINTING TO LEFT OF VEHICLE.)
2	NUT
3	REINFORCEMENT
4	UPPER SHOCK ABSORBER MOUNT
5	SHOCK ABSORBER
6	WASHER
7	WASHER
8	NUT
9	BOLT
10	NUT

Fig. 2   Rear suspension. 1992–94

1	REAR AXLE ASSEMBLY
2	BOLT
3	WASHER
4	NUT
5	STABILIZER SHAFT

Fig. 3   Stabilizer bar attachments. 1992–94

A SLOT SOLID BUSHINGS WITH HACKSAW TO ALLOW J 29376-6 TO ENGAGE BUSHINGS.

B TO PROPERLY INDEX BUSHING ON INSTALLATION, ALIGN ARROWS ON J 29376-1 AND J 29376-4

1 REAR AXLE ASSEMBLY

2 CONTROL ARM BUSHING

Fig. 4   Control arm bushing installation

2. Remove four hub/bearing assembly to rear axle attaching bolts, then the hub/bearing assembly from axle. **The upper rear hub attaching bolt may not clear brake shoe when removing hub and bearing assembly. Partially remove hub and bearing assembly prior to removing this bolt. Also if equipped, disconnect ABS wheel sensor electrical connector.**

3. Reverse procedure to install. Torque hub attaching bolts to specification. **Use care not to drop hub/bearing assembly since damage to bearing may result.**

SHOCK ABSORBER
REPLACE

1. Open deck lid, then remove trim cover and shock absorber upper retaining nut.

2. Raise rear of vehicle and support rear axle using a suitable jack.

3. Remove shock absorber lower attaching bolt, then disconnect shock absorber from mounting bracket, **Figs. 1 and 2.** Remove shock absorber from vehicle.

4. Reverse procedure to install. Torque attaching bolt to specification. **When installing upper shock absorber attachment components, refer to Figs. 1 and 2,** for proper installation order.

COIL SPRING
REPLACE

1. Raise and support rear of vehicle. Support rear axle using a suitable jack.

2. Remove wheel and tire assemblies.

3. Remove brake line bracket attaching bolts from body and allow brake lines to hang freely.

4. Remove shock absorber to lower mounting bracket bolts, then disconnect shock absorbers from axle assembly. **Do not suspend rear axle by brake hoses since damage to hoses may result.**

5. Carefully lower rear axle assembly and remove springs and insulators.

6. Reverse procedure to install. Upper ends of spring must be properly positioned in spring seat and with in $9/16$ inch of spring stop.

CONTROL ARM BUSHING
REPLACE

1. Raise rear of vehicle and support rear axle under front side of spring seat using a suitable jack.

2. Remove stabilizer bar from axle.

3. Remove wheel and tire assembly.

4. If right hand side bushing is to be replaced, disconnect brake line bracket from body. If left hand side bushing is to be replaced, disconnect brake line bracket from body and parking brake cable at hook guide.

5. Remove control arm to mounting bracket attaching nut, bolt and washer, then allow control arm to rotate downward.

6. The bushing can now be replaced using tools shown in **Fig. 4.** When installing bushing, the arrow on the installer must align with arrow on the receiver, **Fig. 4.**

7. Reverse procedure to complete installation. **The control arm attaching bolt must be torqued after vehicle is lowered to floor and is in its standing height position. Torque attaching bolt to specifications.**

STABILIZER BAR
REPLACE

1. Raise and support vehicle. Support vehicle body with jack stands.
2. Remove stabilizer bar attachments to axle and control arms, then remove stabilizer bar, **Figs. 1 and 3.**
3. Reverse procedure to install.

TIGHTENING SPECIFICATIONS

Year	Component	Torque/ Ft. Lbs.
1991	**Axle To Body Bracket**	68
	Hub & Bearing To Axle Bolts	37
	Shock Absorber Upper Mounting Bolt To Body	13
	Shock Absorber Upper Mounting Nut	21
	Shock Absorber Lower Mounting Bolt To Axle	35
	Stabilizer Bar To Axle Clamp Nuts To Axle	13
	Stabilizer Bar To Control Arm Clamp Nuts	16
	Wheel Lug Nuts	100
1992-94	**Axle To Body Bracket**	68
	Control Arm To Underbody Nuts	①

Year	Component	Torque/ Ft. Lbs.
1992-94	**Hub & Bearing To Axle Bolts**	37
	Shock Absorber Upper Mounting Bolt To Body	13
	Shock Absorber Upper Mounting Nut	21
	Shock Absorber Lower Mounting Bolt To Axle	35
	Stabilizer Bar To Axle Clamp Nuts To Axle	13
	Stabilizer Bar To Axle Nuts	103
	Stabilizer Bar To Control Arm Clamp Nuts	16
	Wheel Lug Nuts	100

①—Torque to 52 ft. lbs., then tighten an additional 120°.

Front Suspension & Steering

INDEX

DESCRIPTION

The front suspension, **Fig. 1,** on these vehicles is of the strut and spring design. The lower control arms pivot from the lower side rails through rubber bushings. The upper end of the strut is isolated by a rubber mount incorporating a bearing for wheel turning. The tie rods connect to the steering arm on the strut, below the spring seat. The lower end of the steering knuckle pivots on a ball stud which is retained to the lower control arm by rivets and is secured to the steering knuckle with a nut and cotter pin. The sealed wheel bearings are integral with the hub and are serviced as an assembly.

WHEEL BEARING
REPLACE

REMOVAL

1. Raise and support vehicle.
2. Remove wheel and tire assembly, then install modified outer seal protector No. J34754 or equivalent, **Fig. 2.**
3. Insert a drift punch through the rotor, **Fig. 3,** then remove axle shaft nut and washer.
4. Remove lower ball joint cotter pin and nut, then loosen ball joint from steering knuckle using tool No. J29330 or equivalent.
5. If left hand drive axle shaft is being remove, turn wheel to right. If right hand drive axle shaft is being removed, turn wheel left.
6. Position a suitable pry bar between suspension support and lower control arm and separate lower ball joint from steering knuckle. On some models, it may be necessary to remove nut attaching link to stabilizer shaft.
7. Use tool No. J28733-A to separate drive axle shaft from hub and bearing assembly, **Fig. 4.**
8. Separate drive axle shaft from hub and wheel bearing assembly, then move strut and knuckle assembly rearward. Use wire or rope to suspend drive axle shaft from underbody. Use care not to over-extend driveshaft joints.
9. Remove caliper attaching bolts and brake caliper with brake hose attached. Use wire to suspend caliper from underbody. Do not allow caliper to hang from brake hose.
10. Remove brake rotor, then hub and bearing assembly attaching bolts, **Fig. 5.**
11. Remove hub and bearing assembly.

INSTALLATION

1. Install hub and bearing assembly, **Fig. 5,** torque attaching bolts to specification.
2. Install brake rotor, then install caliper and torque attaching bolts to specification.
3. Install hub and bearing seal into steering knuckle. Lubricate inner diameter of seal lips and fill cavity hub and bearing and seal with grease 09985254 or equivalent.
4. Install modified outer seal protector No. J34754 or equivalent, **Fig. 2,** then insert drive axle shaft into hub and bearing assembly.
5. Position lower ball joint to steering knuckle, then install lower ball joint stud nut and cotter pin.
6. Insert drift punch through rotor, **Fig. 3.**
7. Install washer and new shaft nut,

1. COVER	13. NUT	25. BOLT	37. SUPPORT
2. NUT	14. PIN	26. COVER	38. BOLT
3. NUT	15. SEAL	27. BOLT	39. NUT
4. MOUNT	16. HUB	28. BALL JOINT	40. BOLT
5. SEAT	17. SHIELD	29. RIVET	41. WASHER
6. INSULATOR	18. BOLT	30. GROMMET	42. AXLE
7. BUMPER	19. WASHER	31. WASHER	43. SPACER
8. SPRING	20. NUT	32. BOLT	44. NUT
9. INSULATOR	21. WASHER	33. ARM	45. SHAFT
10. STRUT	22. ROTOR	34. BUSHING	46. NUT
11. NUT	23. KNUCKLE	35. BOLT	47. INSULATOR
12. SEAL	24. CALIPER	36. BOLT	48. CLAMP

Fig. 1   Exploded view of front suspension

Fig. 2   Modified outer seal protector

Fig. 3   Drive axle shaft nut replacement

A. TURN FORCING SCREW UNTIL AXLE SPLINES ARE JUST LOOSE

Fig. 4   Drive axle shaft from hub removal

torque shaft nut to specification.
8. Remove drift punch and seal protector.
9. Install tire and wheel assembly, then lower vehicle and check front wheel alignment.

BALL JOINT
REPLACE

1. Raise and support vehicle.
2. Remove tire and wheel assembly, then install modified outer seal protector No. J34754 or equivalent, **Fig. 2.**
3. Remove lower ball joint cotter pin and nut, then loosen ball joint from steering knuckle using tool No. J29330 or equivalent.
4. Position a suitable pry bar between suspension support and lower control arm and separate lower ball joint from steering knuckle. On some models, it may be necessary to remove nut attaching link to stabilizer shaft.
5. Locate center of rivet body and mark

with a center punch.
6. Using a ⅛ inch drill, drill pilot holes completely through the rivets. Using a ½ inch drill, drill final holes through rivets to ensure fitting of new ball joint.
7. Remove ball joint from lower control arm.
8. Assemble new ball joint to lower control arm with bolts provided in service package, **Fig. 6.** Torque bolts to specification.
9. Insert ball joint stud into steering knuckle and torque nut to specifications, then install cotter pin.
10. Install wheel and tire, check front wheel alignment.

CONTROL ARM
REPLACE

1. Raise and support vehicle, then remove wheel and tire assembly.
2. Disconnect stabilizer bar at lower control arm and control arm support.
3. Using tool J-29330, separate ball joint from steering knuckle.

4. Position a suitable pry bar between suspension support and lower control arm and separate lower ball joint from steering knuckle. On some models, it may be necessary to remove nut attaching link to stabilizer shaft.
5. Remove control arm support to chassis retaining bolts and remove control arm support and control arm as an assembly, **Fig. 7.**
6. Separate control arm from support, then using tool No. J29792 or equivalent, remove bushings from control arm. Coat threads of tool with extreme pressure lubricant.
7. Lubricate new bushings and install into control arm using tool Nos. J29792 or equivalent. Coat threads of tool with extreme pressure lubricant.

1. HUB AND BEARING ASSEMBLY
2. STEERING KNUCKLE
3. WASHER
4. DRIVE AXLE NUT
5. WHEEL BEARING SEAL
6. HUB AND BEARING RETAINING BOLT

**Fig. 5   Front hub & wheel
bearing assembly**

1. SERVICE BALL JOINT
2. BALL JOINT MOUNTING BOLTS
3. NUT
4. LOWER CONTROL ARM
5. STEERING KNUCKLE

**Fig. 6   Lower ball joint to
lower control arm assembly**

8. Reverse procedure installation. Check front wheel alignment and adjust as required.

STEERING KNUCKLE
REPLACE

1. Raise and support vehicle, then remove wheel and tire.
2. Remove front hub and bearing as outlined under "Wheel Bearing, Replace" procedure.
3. Remove strut to steering knuckle attaching bolts, then disconnect strut from steering knuckle.
4. Assemble strut to steering knuckle and install attaching bolts finger tight.
5. Insert ball joint stud into steering knuckle and torque stud nut to specification, then install cotter pin.
6. Torque strut to steering knuckle bolts to specification.
7. Reverse removal procedure to complete installation.

STABILIZER BAR
REPLACE

1. Raise and support vehicle, allowing

DIRECT ACTING STABILIZER SUSPENSION

BASE SUSPENSION

1. SUSPENSION SUPPORT
2. BOLT
3. WASHER
4. BOLT
5. CONTROL ARM

6. NUT
7. BOLT
8. BOLT

Fig. 7   Lower control arm replacement

control arms to hang freely.
2. Remove left front wheel and tire assembly.
3. Disconnect stabilizer bar at control arms and suspension support assemblies, **Figs. 8 and 9.**
4. Loosen front and remove rear and center bolts from suspension support assembly. Lower support enough to allow stabilizer bar removal.
5. Remove stabilizer bar with insulators.
6. Reverse procedure to install.

STRUT ASSEMBLY
REPLACE

1. Raise hood and remove strut protective cap and three strut to body attaching nuts.
2. Raise and support vehicle, allowing suspension to hang freely.
3. Remove wheel and tire, then install modified outer seal protective J-34754.
4. Remove tie rod end cotter pin and nut, then using tool J-24319-01, disconnect tie rod from strut assembly.
5. Scribe alignment marks on strut flange, **Fig. 10.**
6. Remove strut to steering knuckle attaching bolts, then remove strut from vehicle, **Fig. 11.** Use care not to damage spring coating.
7. Reverse procedure to install. Align marks on strut flange and steering knuckle made during removal, then torque bolts to specification.

STRUT ASSEMBLY
SERVICE

DISASSEMBLE

1. Position strut compressor J-34013 in holding fixture J-3289-20. Use care not to damage spring coating.
2. Position strut in strut compressor, then compress strut approximately ½ of its height. Use care not to bottom spring or damper rod.
3. Remove nut from strut dampener

1. STABILIZER SHAFT
2. CLAMP
3. INSULATOR, STABILIZER SHAFT
4. NUT
5. WASHER
6. INSULATOR, STABILIZER LINK
7. SPACER
8. BOLT
9. NUT

**Fig. 8   Stabilizer bar
installation. Less direct acting
stabilizer system**

shaft, then position guide rod J-34013-27 on dampener shaft. Use guide rod J-34013-27 to position dampener shaft down through bearing cap while compressing coil spring.
4. Remove components from coil strut unit, **Fig. 12.**

ASSEMBLE

1. Position bearing cap on strut compressor.
2. Position strut to strut compressor and install compressor bottom locking pin.
3. Extend dampener shaft and install clamp J-34013-20 to hold shaft in position.
4. Position spring over dampener, then position strut to strut compressor upper locking pin hole and install pin. Use care not to damage spring coating.
5. Install upper insulator, shield, bumper and upper spring seat. The flat on the upper spring seat should face in the same direction as the centerline of the strut assembly spindle, **Fig. 13.**

1. STABILIZER SHAFT
2. CLAMP, STABILIZER SHAFT
3. INSULATOR, STABILIZER SHAFT
4. STABILIZER LINK
5. NUT

6. NUT
7. BOLT
8. STRUT
9. BRACKET, STABILIZER LINK

Fig. 9 Stabilizer bar installation. With direct acting stabilizer system

A SCRIBE KNUCKLE ALONG LOWER OUTBOARD STRUT RADUIS
B SCRIBE STRUT FLANGE ON INBOARD SIDE ALONG CURVE OF KNUCKLE
C SCRIBE ACROSS STRUT/KNUCKLE INTERFACE

Fig. 10 Strut & knuckle alignment marks

BASE SUSPENSION

DIRECT ACTING STABILIZER SUSPENSION

1. BOLT
2. BOLT
3. NUT
4. COVER, STRUT MOUNT
5. STRUT ASSEMBLY

6. NUT
7. STEERING KNUCKLE
8. BRACKET, STABILIZER LINK
9. NUT
10. STABILIZER LINK

Fig. 11 Strut assembly replacement

1 STRUT MOUNT NUT
2 STRUT MOUNT
3 SPRING SEAT
4 SPRING UPPER INSULATOR
5 JOUNCE BUMPER
6 STRUT DUST SHIELD
7 SPRING
8 SPRING LOWER INSULATOR
9 STRUT

Fig. 12 Exploded view of strut assembly

6. Install guide rod J-34013-27 onto dampener shaft, the compress strut unit until dampener shaft threads are visible. Remove guide rod and install retaining nut.
7. While holding dampener shaft in position with a suitable wrench, torque retaining nut to specification. After tightening nut, remove clamp from dampener shaft clamp J-34013-20.

POWER STEERING GEAR
REPLACE

1. Disconnect battery ground cable.
2. Remove left hand sound insulator.
3. From under instrument panel, pull downward on steering column seal, then remove upper pinch bolt from flexible coupling.
4. Remove line retainer.
5. Raise and support front of vehicle, then remove both front wheel and tire

assemblies.
6. Disconnect tie rods from struts using tool No. J24319-01, then lower vehicle.
7. Remove steering gear mounting clamps, **Fig. 14.**
8. Disconnect power steering hydraulic lines form steering gear.
9. Move steering gear slightly forward and remove lower pinch bolt from flexible coupling, then detach coupling from steering gear stub shaft and remove dash seal.
10. Remove steering gear through left hand wheel opening.
11. Reverse procedure to install. If steering gear mounting clamp studs have backed out during removal, reinstall studs to cowl and tighten until stud is fully seated. Torque should nut exceed 15 ft. lbs. After second reuse of studs, thread locking kit 1052624 must be used.

POWER STEERING PUMP
REPLACE
2.3L/4-138 ENGINE

1. Disconnect pressure and return lines from power steering pump. Allow fluid to drain into a suitable container.

1 FLAT ON SPRING SEAT MUST FACE SAME DIRECTION AS STRUT ASSEMBLY SPINDLE

2 BOTH LOCKING PINS INSTALLED

3 COMPRESSOR FORCING SCREW

Fig. 13   Assembling strut unit

1 POWER STEERING PUMP
2 DRIVE BELT
3 ADJUSTMENT SCREW
4 FRONT BRACKET
5 BOLT - 26 N.m (19 LBS. FT.)
6 BOLT - 91 N.m (67 LBS. FT.)
7 BOLT/STUD - 54 N.m (40 LBS. FT.)
8 BOLT - 54 N.m (40 LBS. FT.)
9 REAR SUPPORT
10 FRONT SUPPORT
11 PULLEY - NOTE: WHEN TENSIONING BELT TIGHTEN REAR BRACKET ADJUSTMENT BELT FIRST, THEN THE BOLT JUST BELOW IT. TIGHTEN BOLT **6** LAST.

VIEW B

Fig. 15   Power steering pump mounting. 2.3L/4-138

1. RACK AND PINION.
2. L.H. CLAMP - HORIZONTAL SLOT AT TOP
3. R.A. CLAMP HORIZONTAL SLOT AT TOP
4. NUT - 30 N•m (22 LBS.FT.) - HAND START ALL NUTS. TIGHTEN LEFT HAND SIDE CLAMP NUTS FIRST, THEN TIGHTEN RIGHT SIDE NUTS.
5. STUD - 20 N•m (15 LBS.FT.) AFTER SECOND REUSE OF STUD, THREAD LOCKING KIT NO.1052624 MUST BE USED.
6. NUT
7. COTTER PIN

Fig. 14   Power rack & pinion steering gear mounting

2. Loosen adjusting stud, then remove outer bracket.
3. Remove drive belt from pump pulley and position aside.
4. Remove bracket to pump bolts, **Fig. 15.**
5. Remove pump and bracket assembly from vehicle. Separate pump from bracket as necessary.
6. Reverse procedure to install.

1. REAR ADJ. BRACKET
2. POWER STEERING PUMP
3. FRONT ADJ. BRACKET
4. BOLT — 50 N•m (38 LBS. FT.)
5. BOLT — 27 N•m (20 LBS. FT.)
6. PULLEY
7. SPACER
8. WASHER

Fig. 16   Power steering pump mounting. 2.5L/4-151

2.5L/4-151 ENGINE

1. Remove drive belt.
2. Disconnect pressure and return lines from power steering pump. Allow fluid to drain into a suitable container.
3. Front adjusting bracket to rear adjusting bracket bolt.
4. Front adjusting bracket to engine bolt and spacer, **Fig. 16.**
5. Remove pump with front adjusting bracket. Separate pump from front adjusting bracket as necessary.
6. Reverse procedure to install.

1 POWER STEERING PUMP
2 BOLT - 25 N.m (18 LBS. FT.)
3 PULLEY
4 COVER

Fig. 17   Power steering pump mounting. 3.3L/V6-204

3.3L/V6-204 ENGINE

1. Remove drive belt.
2. Remove pump mounting bolts, **Fig. 17.**
3. Remove pump from mounting bracket.
4. Disconnect pressure and return lines from power steering pump, then remove pump. Allow fluid to drain into a suitable container.
5. Reverse procedure to install.

TIGHTENING SPECIFICATIONS

Year	Component	Torque/ Ft. Lbs.
1991–94	Disc Brake Caliper Bolts	38
	Driveshaft Hub Nut	185
	Control Arm Pivot Bolt	61
	Hub & Bearing Assembly	70
	Lower Ball Joint To Knuckle	41–50
	Power Steering Line Fittings	19
	Stabilizer Shaft To Control Arm	13
	Stabilizer To Support Assembly	16
	Steering Gear Mounting Clamp	22
	Steering Coupling To Steering Column	30
	Steering Coupling To Stub Shaft	30

Year	Component	Torque/ Ft. Lbs.
1991–94	Steering Knuckle To Strut Assembly	133
	Strut Assembly To Body	18
	Suspension Support Assembly	①
	Strut Cartridge Retaining Nut	65
	Tie Rod End To Steering Knuckle	37
	Tie Rod (Inner) Bolts	65
	Tie Pinch Bolts	41
	Wheel Lug Nuts	100

①—Torque suspension support assembly center bolts to 66 ft. lbs.; then front bolts to 65 ft. lbs; then rear bolts to 65 ft. lbs.

Wheel Alignment

INDEX

Fig. 1   Caster, camber & toe angles

Fig. 2   Modifying strut bracket to adjust camber

PRELIMINARY INSPECTION

Before measuring and setting front wheel alignment, rest front wheels on turn plates.

Before setting rear toe, rest rear wheels on slider plates or turn plates. Before setting any alignment angle, jounce the vehicle three times at each end to establish trim height.

Special adapters are available for using a magnetic hub gauge at rear wheels. Depending on type of equipment used, these may not be necessary. After removing hub cap and bearing cap, hub gauge will snap into place on brake drum. Magnetic mounting toe gauges may also be installed in the same manner.

Always perform wheel alignment on a level alignment rack. Before doing align-

Fig. 3 Toe adjustment

Fig. 4 Thrust angle

A	THRUST ANGLE
B	THRUST LINE — OFF CENTER
C	REAR TOE-OUT CONDITION
D	GEOMETRIC CENTERLINE

Fig. 5 Vehicle ride height measurement locations. 1991 models

Fig. 6 Vehicle ride height measurement locations. 1992-94 models

Make & Model	Year	Riding Height Measurements In Inches			
		Tire Size	Dimension Z	Dimension J	Dimension K
BUICK					
Skylark	1991	185/75R14	3.70	9.41	9.21
		195/70R14	3.86	9.41	9.21
		215/60R14	4.05	9.41	9.21
	1992-94	185/75R14	13/32	9.30	9.40
		195/65R15	23/64	9.30	9.40
		205/55R16	9/32	9.30	9.40
OLDSMOBILE					
Achieva	1992-94	185/75R14	13/32	9.30	9.40
		195/70R14	9/16	9.30	9.40
		195/65R15	①	9.30	9.40
		205/55R16	1/4	9.30	9.40
Cutlass Calais	1991	185/75R14	3.74	9.49	9.37
		195/70R14	3.90	9.49	9.37
		215/60R14	4.02	9.37	9.26
		205/60R15	3.86	9.49	9.37
		205/55R16	3.54	9.49	9.37
PONTIAC					
Grand Am	1991	185/75R14	3.78	9.57	9.61
		195/70R14	3.94	9.57	9.61
		205/55R16	3.58	9.57	9.61
	1992-94	185/75R14	7/16	9.30	9.40
		195/70R14	19/32	9.30	9.40
		195/65R15	5/16	9.30	9.40
		205/55R16	1/4	9.30	9.40

① —Achieva S models, 5/16; Achieva SL models, 15/16.

Fig. 7 Vehicle ride height specifications

ment, check the following.
1. Worn suspension parts.
2. Standing curb height.
3. Remove heavy weights from trunk.
4. Wheel bearings.
5. Full tank of gas.
6. Place front seats in full rear position.
7. Check rear toe adjustment.
8. Always road test vehicle after adjusting alignment. If vehicle still pulls, switch front tires. If vehicle still pulls in same direction, check alignment and rear tracking. If vehicle pulls in opposite direction, rotate tires, then road test again.

FRONT WHEEL ALIGNMENT

CASTER

Caster angle is not adjustable. If caster angle, **Fig. 1,** is not with in specifications, check suspension support for improper alignment and suspension components for damage. Replace damaged components as necessary.

CAMBER

Toe setting is the only adjustment nor-
mally required. However, in special circumstances, such as damage due to road hazard or collision, camber angle, **Fig. 1,** may be adjusted by modifying the strut assembly.
1. If strut is on vehicle, disconnect strut from steering knuckle. If strut is off vehicle, secure bottom of strut assembly in a suitable vise.
2. Enlarge bottom holes in outer flanges with a round file, until holes in outer flanges match slots in inner flanges, **Fig. 2.**
3. Install or connect strut to steering knuckle and install bolts finger tight.
4. Grasp top of tire firmly, then move tire inboard or outboard until correct camber reading is obtained. Tighten retaining bolts enough to secure camber setting.
5. Remove wheel and tire assembly, if necessary, then tighten strut to steering knuckle retaining bolts to 133 ft. lbs.

TOE

Toe, **Fig. 1,** is controlled by tie rod position. Adjustment is made by loosening the clamp bolts at the steering knuckle end of
the tie rods and rotating the rods to obtain proper toe setting, **Fig. 3.** After correct toe setting is obtained, tighten clamp bolts. **Torque** clamp bolts to 41 ft. lbs.

REAR WHEEL ALIGNMENT

After front wheel alignment has been checked or adjusted, rear wheel alignment angles should be checked if vehicle still does not track properly or if excessive rear tire wear is present. Rear wheels should be parallel to and the same distance from the vehicle centerline.

Rear wheel alignment is not adjustable. If alignment angles are not within specification, check for bent or damaged suspension arms, components or underbody.

THRUST ANGLE

The vehicle is steered by the front wheels. The path which the rear wheels follow is the thrust angle, **Fig. 4.** In an ideal setting, the thrust angle would be aligned with that of the vehicle center line.

VEHICLE RIDE HEIGHT

Refer to **Figs. 5 and 6,** for vehicle ride height measurements and **Fig. 7,** for specifications. When checking ride height measurements, fuel tank should be full, tires at should be correct pressure, front seat should be in the rearward position, trunk should be empty except for spare tire and jack and vehicle should be on level ground. If fuel tank is not full, add weight to trunk to compensate for amount fuel the vehicle is below the full level.

Prior to checking ride height, lift front bumper upward approximately 1.5 inches and gently release (3 times), then check front ride height. Push front bumper downward approximately 1.5 inches and gently release (3 times), then recheck front ride height. Average of both readings to determine vehicle ride height. Check rear ride height in same manner, lifting and pushing rear bumper.

BUICK REGAL, CHEVROLET LUMINA, OLDSMOBILE CUTLASS SUPREME & PONTIAC GRAND PRIX
(W Cars)
INDEX OF SERVICE OPERATIONS

NOTE: Refer To Rear Of This Manual For Vehicle Manufacturer's Special Service Tool Suppliers.

Continued

INDEX OF SERVICE OPERATIONS—Continued

Specifications

GENERAL ENGINE SPECIFICATIONS

Year	Engine Liter/CID ①	Engine VIN Code ②	Fuel System	Bore and Stroke	Compression Ratio	Net H.P. @ RPM ③	Maximum Torque Ft. Lbs. @ RPM	Normal Oil Pressure, Psi
1991—92	2.5L/4-151	R	MFI ⑪	4.00 x 3.00	8.30	110 @ 5200	135 @ 3200	26 ④
	3.1L/V6-192	T	MFI ⑪	3.50 x 3.31	8.80	135 @ 4400	180 @ 3600	15 ⑤
	3.4L/V6-204	X	MFI ⑪	3.62 x 3.31	9.25–9.50	⑩	215 @ 4000	15 ⑤
	3800/V6-231	L	MFI ⑪	3.80 x 3.40	8.50	170 @ 4800	220 @ 3200	60 ⑥
1993	2.2L/4-134	4	MFI ⑪	3.50 x 3.46	8.85	110 @ 5200	130 @ 3200	56 ⑦
	3.1L/V6-192	T	MFI ⑪	3.50 x 3.31	8.80	135 @ 4400	180 @ 3600	15 ⑤
	3.4L/V6-204	X	MFI ⑪	3.62 x 3.31	9.25–9.50	⑩	215 @ 4000	15 ⑤
	3800/V6-231	L	MFI ⑪	3.80 x 3.40	8.50	170 @ 4800	220 @ 3200	60 ⑥
1994	3.1L/V6-192	T	SFI ⑫	3.50 x 3.31	9.60	165 @ 5200	190 @ 4000	40-52 ⑧
	3.1L/V6-192	T	MFI ⑪	3.50 x 3.31	8.90	140 @ 4400	185 @ 3200	50-65 ⑩
	3.4L/V6-204	X	SFI ⑫	3.62 x 3.31	9.25	210 @ 5200	215 @ 4000	40 ⑧

① —CID-Cubic inch displacement.
② —The eighth digit of the VIN denotes engine code.
③ —Ratings are net-as installed in vehicle.
④ —At 800 RPM.
⑤ —At 1100 RPM.
⑥ —At 1850 RPM.
⑦ —At 3000 RPM.
⑧ —At 2000 RPM.
⑨ —At 2400 RPM.
⑩ —210 net H.P. @ 5200 RPM with manual transaxle; 200 net H.P. @ 5000 RPM with automatic transaxle.
⑪ —Multi-Port fuel injection.
⑫ —Sequential-Port fuel injection.

TUNE UP SPECIFICATIONS

Year & Engine, VIN Code ①	Spark Plug Gap	Ignition Timing BTDC ② Firing Order Fig. ④	Ignition Timing BTDC ② Man. Trans.	Ignition Timing BTDC ② Auto. Trans.	Ignition Timing BTDC ② Mark Fig.	Curb Idle Speed ③ Man. Trans.	Curb Idle Speed ③ Auto Trans.	Fast Idle Speed Man. Trans.	Fast Idle Speed Auto. Trans.	Fuel Pump Pressure, Psi
1991-92										
2.5L/4-151,R	.060	⑩	—	⑤	⑥	—	⑦	—	⑦	26–32 ⑪
3.1L/V6-192,T	.045	⑫	—	⑤	⑥	⑦	⑦	⑦	⑦	40–46 ⑧
3.4L/V6-204,X	.045	⑫	⑤	⑤	⑥	⑦	⑦	⑦	⑦	40–47 ⑧
3800/V6-231,L	.060	⑨	—	⑤	⑥	—	⑦	—	⑦	40–47 ⑧
1993										
2.2L/4-134,4	.045	⑩	—	⑤	⑥	—	⑦	—	⑦	41–47 ⑧
3.1L/V6-192,T	.045	⑫	—	⑤	⑥	⑦	⑦	⑦	⑦	40–46 ⑧
3.4L/V6-204,X	.045	⑫	⑤	⑤	⑥	⑦	⑦	⑦	⑦	40–47 ⑧
3800/V6-231,L	.060	⑨	—	⑤	⑥	—	⑦	—	⑦	40–47 ⑧
1994										
3.1L/V6-192,T	.045	⑫	—	⑤	⑥	⑦	⑦	⑦	⑦	40–46 ⑧
3.4L/V6-204,X	.045	⑫	⑤	⑤	⑥	⑦	⑦	⑦	⑦	40–47 ⑧

① —The eighth digit of Vehicle Identification Number (VIN) denotes engine code.
② —BTDC: Before Top Dead Center.
③ —Idle speed on manual transmission models is adjusted in neutral. On automatic transmission models, idle is adjusted in drive. When adjusting idle speed, set parking brake and block drive wheels. Where two idle speeds are listed, the higher speed is with the idle or A/C solenoid energized.
④ —Before removing wires from distributor cap, determine location of No. 1 wire in cap, as distributor position may have been altered from that shown at the end of this chart.

⑤ —Computer controlled, no adjustment.
⑥ —Equipped with a crankshaft position sensor.
⑦ —Idle speed is controlled by an idle air control (IAC) valve or idle speed control (ISC) motor.
⑧ —With shop towel wrapped around fuel pressure valve to prevent fuel spillage, connect a suitable fuel pressure gauge to fuel pressure valve. Check fuel pressure with ignition switch On, engine not running.
⑨ —Cylinder numbering as viewed from front of vehicle, front bank, 1, 3, 5; rear bank, 2, 4, 6. Firing order 1-6-5-4-3-2. Two different types of

computer controlled coil ignition systems are used. Refer to Figs. B and C for spark plug wire connections at coil unit.
⑩ —Cylinder numbering from front of engine, 1, 2, 3, 4. Firing order 1-3-4-2. Refer to Fig. D for spark plug wire connections at coil unit.
⑪ —Wrap shop towel around fuel hose to steel line connection in engine compartment to prevent fuel spillage. Disconnect fuel hose from steel line and install a suitable fuel pressure gauge between hose and line. Ensure gauge connections are tight, then start engine and check fuel pressure readings.

Continued

TUNE UP SPECIFICATIONS—Continued

⑫—Cylinder numbering left to right as
viewed from front of vehicle, front
bank, 2, 4, 6; rear bank, 1, 3, 5. Firing
order 1-2-3-4-5-6. Refer to Fig. A for
spark plug wire connections at coil
unit.

Fig. A

COMPUTER CONTROLLED
COIL IGNITION

Fig. B

COMPUTER CONTROLLED
COIL IGNITION

Fig. C

Fig. D

WHEEL ALIGNMENT SPECIFICATIONS

Year	Model	Caster Angle, Degrees		Camber Angle, Degrees		Toe-In Degrees
		Limits	Desired	Limits	Desired	
Front						
1991	Cutlass Supreme & Lumina	+1.3 to +2.3	+1.8	+.20 to +1.2	+.7	0
	Grand Prix & Regal	+1.5 to +2.5	+2.0	+.20 to +1.2	+.7	0
1992–94	All	+1.5 to +2.5	+2.0	+.20 to +1.2	+.7	0
Rear						
1991	Cutlass Supreme & Lumina	—	—	−.10 to −.20	−.15	−.1
	Grand Prix & Regal	—	—	−.5 to −.15	−.10	−.1
1992–94	All①	—	—	+.5 to +1.5	+.1	−.1
	Lumina②	—	—	+.27 to +.37	+.32	−.1
	Grand Prix②	—	—	+.5 to +.15	+.10	−.1

①—Models w/15 & 16 inch tires.
②—Models w/14 inch tires.

COOLING SYSTEM & CAPACITY DATA

Year	Model or Engine/VIN	Cooling Capacity, Qts.		Radiator Cap Relief Pressure, Psi.	Thermo. Opening Temp.	Fuel Tank Gals.	Engine Oil Refill Qts. ①	Transaxle Oil	
		Less A/C	With A/C					Manual Transaxle Pts.	Auto. Transaxle Qts. ②
1991	2.5L/4-151,R	9.4	9.4	15	195	16.0	4③	4.2	④
	3.1L/V6-192,T	12.6	12.6	15	195	16.0	4③	4.2	⑤
	3.4L/V6-204,X	12.8	12.8	15	195	16.0	4③	4.2	⑦
	3800/V6-231,L	11.1	11.1	15	195	16.0	4③	—	⑦

Continued
SPECIFICATIONS

COOLING SYSTEM & CAPACITY DATA—Continued

Year	Model or Engine/ VIN	Cooling Capacity, Qts.		Radiator Cap Relief Pressure, Psi.	Thermo. Opening Temp.	Fuel Tank Gals.	Engine Oil Refill Qts. ①	Transaxle Oil	
		Less A/C	With A/C					Manual Transaxle Pts.	Auto. Transaxle Qts. ②
1992	2.5L/4-151,R	9.1	9.1	15	195	16.0	4③	4.2	⑧
	3.1L/V6-192,T	12.0	12.0	15	195	16.0	4③	4.2	⑧
	3.4L/V6-204,X	12.6	12.6	15	195	16.0	6⑨	4.2	⑧
1993	2.2L/4-134,4	11.7	11.7	15	195	17.1	4③	—	⑥
	3.1L/V6-192,T	12.0	12.0	15	195	16.0	4③	4.2	⑧
	3.4L/V6-204,X	12.6	12.6	15	195	16.0	6⑨	4.2	⑧
	3800/V6-231,L	11.1	11.1	15	195	16.0	4③	—	⑦
1994	3.1L/V6-192,T	12.0	12.0	15	195	16.0	4⑤	4.2	⑧
	3.4L/V6-204,X	12.6	12.6	15	195	16.0	6⑨	4.2	⑧

①—The eight digit of vehicle identification number (VIN) denotes engine code.

②—Capacity approximate. Make final check with dipstick and add fluid as necessary.

③—Additional oil may be required to bring oil level to full mark when changing oil filter.

④—Drain & refill, 7 qts.; total capacity, 9 qts.

⑤—THM 3T40 transaxle, drain & refill, 7 qts.; total capacity, 9 qts.; THM 4T60, drain & refill, 6 qts.; total capacity, 8 qts.

⑥—Drain & refill, 6 qts.; total capacity, 9 qts.

⑦—Drain & refill, 6 qts.; total capacity, 8 qts.

⑧—THM 3T40 transaxle, drain & refill, 4 qts.; total capacity, 7 qts.; THM 4T60, drain & refill, 6 qts.; total capacity, 8 qts.; THM 4T60-E, drain & refill, 7.4 qts.; total capacity, 10 qts.

⑨—With filter change.

LUBRICANT DATA

Year	Model	Lubricant Type			
		Transaxle		Power Steering	Brake System
		Manual	Automatic		
1991–94	All	GM Synchromesh Transmission Fluid	Dexron IIE	GM Type Power Steering Fluid	DOT 3

Electrical

INDEX

FUSE PANEL & FLASHER LOCATION

On all models, the fuse panel is located behind the instrument panel, under the glove compartment. The turn signal flasher is located under the instrument panel, to the right of the steering column. The hazard warning flasher is located in the convenience center, under the glove box assembly.

IGNITION LOCK REPLACE

On 1994 models equipped with airbags, disable airbag system prior to performing service operation as possible airbag deployment may cause personal injury.

1. Disconnect battery ground cable.
2. Remove steering column from vehicle. On vehicles with tilt column, column should be tilted to the full up position for removal.
3. Remove and discard two lower spring retainers.
4. Remove lower bearing spring and lower bearing seat.
5. Remove nut retainer and jam nut, then the steering wheel.
6. Remove cancel cam assembly, then the hazard knob screw and hazard warning knob.
7. Position turn signal switch so that turn signal switch screws and housing screw can be removed through opening in switch.
8. Remove housing screw and column housing cover, then the turn signal switch screws.
9. Remove wiring protector from opening in instrument panel bracket on jacket assembly and separate from wires.
10. Disconnect pivot/pulse switch connector then remove the pivot screw and pivot/pulse switch assembly.
11. Disconnect turn signal switch connector from ignition and dimmer switch assembly connector.
12. Disconnect 17 way secondary lock from turn signal connector.
13. Using terminal remover tool No. J-35689-A or equivalent, disconnect wires on buzzer switch from turn signal connector and wrap wire ends with tape.
14. Remove turn signal switch assembly from column.
15. Remove and discard two lower spring retainers.
16. Remove lower bearing spring and seat.
17. Remove adapter screws then the adapter and bearing assembly.
18. **On models with tilt columns,** proceed as follows:
    a. Insert Phillips head screwdriver into square opening in spring retainer, push down and turn left to release retainer and wheel tilt spring.
    b. Remove spring retainer, tilt spring and tilt spring guide.
    c. Using pivot pin remover tool No. J-21854-01 or equivalent, remove two pivot pins.
19. **On all models,** place lock cylinder in Run position.
20. **On models with tilt column,** pull tilt lever to release steering column housing. Remove the steering shaft assembly and steering column housing as a complete unit.
21. **On non-tilt models,** proceed as follows:
    a. Place opening in retaining ring over flat on steering shaft.
    b. Remove retaining ring using a suitable screwdriver.
    c. Remove thrust washer, upper bearing spring and washer.
    d. Remove steering shaft from lower

end of jacket and bowl assembly.
    e. Remove housing screws and steering column housing.
    f. Remove housing spacer the the bearing using a suitable drift. Discard bearing.
22. **On all models,** place lock cylinder in Off-Lock position and remove key.
23. Remove buzzer switch by lifting switch tab with screwdriver and pulling gently on wires.
24. Remove lock retaining screw and the lock cylinder.
25. Reverse procedure to install, noting the following:
    a. **Torque** lock retaining screw to 22 inch lbs.
    b. **Torque** steering column housing screws to 88 inch lbs.
    c. **Torque** turn signal switch and column housing cover screws to 35 inch lbs.
    d. **Torque** hazard knob screw to 7 inch lbs.
    e. **Torque** jam nut to 30 ft. lbs.
    f. Install new lower spring retainers, compressing spring until retainers are positioned 1.14 inch from lower end of steering shaft.

STARTER REPLACE

2.2L/4-134 & 2.5L/4-151 ENGINE

1. Disconnect battery ground cable.
2. Raise and support vehicle.
3. Remove flywheel cover attaching bolts, then the cover.
4. Remove stud from starter motor bracket.
5. Remove starter motor attaching bolts, lower starter and disconnect starter wiring.
6. Remove starter motor, then the bracket from starter.
7. Reverse procedure to install, noting the following:
    a. When removing starter, note if any shims are used between starter and mounting surface. If shims are found, reinstall in original location.
    b. **Torque** starter motor attaching bolts to 32 ft. lbs.
    c. **Torque** starter motor bracket stud to 18 ft. lbs.

3.1L/V6-192 ENGINE

1. Disconnect battery ground cable.
2. Remove air cleaner assembly.
3. Raise and support vehicle.
4. **On models with engine oil cooler,** proceed as follows:
    a. Position a suitable drain pan under vehicle, then remove oil filter.
    b. Position hose next to starter motor aside.
5. **On all models,** remove nut attaching starter brace to A/C compressor.
6. Remove nut attaching starter brace to engine, then the brace.
7. Remove bolts attaching flywheel inspection cover, then the cover.
8. Remove starter motor attaching bolts,

lower starter and disconnect starter wiring.
9. Remove starter motor and shims (if used).
10. Reverse procedure to install, noting the following:
    a. When removing starter, note if any shims are used between starter and mounting surface. If shims are found, reinstall in original location.
    b. **Torque** starter motor attaching bolts to 32 ft. lbs.
    c. **Torque** starter brace nuts to 23 ft. lbs.
    d. **On models with oil cooler,** check engine oil level, adding oil as necessary.

3.4L/V6-204 ENGINE
Manual Transaxle

1. Disconnect battery ground cable.
2. Remove air cleaner assembly.
3. Raise and support vehicle.
4. Place a suitable drain pan under vehicle and remove oil filter.
5. Disconnect electrical connections from oil pressure sensor.
6. Disconnect the crank sensor wire from ignition module.
7. Remove oil cooler adapter stud and set oil cooler aside.
8. Disconnect starter electrical connections.
9. Remove starter mounting bolts and starter.
10. Reverse procedure to install, **Torquing** starter bolts to 32 ft. lbs.

Automatic Transaxle

1. Disconnect battery ground cable.
2. Remove air cleaner assembly.
3. Raise and support vehicle.
4. Place a suitable drain pan under vehicle and remove oil filter.
5. Disconnect electrical connections from oil pressure sensor.
6. Disconnect the crank sensor wire from ignition module.
7. Remove oil cooler adapter stud and set oil cooler aside.
8. Remove wiring harness from bellhousing clamp and lower radiator tie bar.
9. Disconnect power steering oil cooler lines from front crossmember.
10. Remove flywheel inspection cover.
11. Disconnect electrical connections from starter. **Disconnect and move electrical connections on cooling fan if necessary to gain access.**
12. Remove starter mounting bolts and starter assembly from vehicle.
13. Reverse procedure to install, **Torquing** starter mounting bolts to 32 ft. lbs.

3800/V6-231 ENGINE

1. Disconnect battery ground cable.
2. Remove right side cooling fan.
3. Remove serpentine drive belt.
4. Remove A/C compressor upper support brace.
5. Lay A/C compressor in fan opening.
6. Raise and support vehicle.
7. Disconnect engine oil cooler lines at flex connection.

8. Remove bolts from flywheel inspection cover.
9. Remove bolts from starter.
10. Disconnect starter motor wiring.
11. Remove starter motor.
12. Reverse procedure to install, **Torquing** starter motor attaching bolts to 32 ft. lbs.

PIVOT & PULSE SWITCH & TURN SIGNAL SWITCH ASSEMBLIES
REPLACE

On 1994 models equipped with airbags, disable airbag system prior to performing service operation as possible airbag deployment may cause personal injury.

1. Disconnect battery ground cable.
2. Remove nut retainer and jam nut, then the steering wheel.
3. Remove turn signal cancel cam assembly.
4. Remove hazard knob screw and the hazard warning knob.
5. Position turn signal switch so that turn signal switch screws and housing screw can be removed through openings in switch.
6. Remove housing screw and the column housing cover.
7. **On models with tilt columns,** remove shoe pin retainer cap.
8. **On all models,** remove pivot switch screw and the pivot and pulse switch assembly.
9. Remove turn signal switch screws.
10. Remove wiring protector from opening in instrument panel bracket on jacket assembly and separate from wires.
11. Disconnect turn signal switch connector from ignition and dimmer switch assembly connector.
12. Disconnect 17 way lock from turn signal connector.
13. Using terminal remover tool No. J-35689-A or equivalent, disconnect wires on buzzer switch assembly from turn signal connector.
14. Remove turn signal switch assembly from column.
15. Reverse procedure to install, noting the following:
    a. **Torque** turn signal switch and column housing cover screws to 35 inch lbs.
    b. **Torque** pivot switch screw to 20 inch lbs.
    c. **Torque** hazard knob screw to 7 inch lbs.
    d. **Torque** jam nut to 30 ft. lbs.

IGNITION & DIMMER SWITCH ASSEMBLY
REPLACE
REMOVAL

On 1994 models equipped with airbags, disable airbag system prior to performing service operation as possible airbag deployment may cause personal injury.

1. Place shift lever in P position and the lock cylinder in Off-Lock position.
2. Disconnect battery ground cable.
3. Remove steering column from vehicle.
4. Disconnect turn signal switch connector from ignition and dimmer switch assembly connector.
5. Disconnect pivot and pulse switch connector from ignition and dimmer switch connector.
6. Remove bowl shield screw, bowl shield nut and the bowl shield.
7. Remove dimmer and ignition switch assembly as follows:
    a. Remove dimmer switch nut, then the upper mounting stud.
    b. Remove dimmer switch, then the dimmer switch actuator rod.
    c. Remove lower mounting stud, then the ignition switch from ignition switch actuator rod.

INSTALLATION

Lock cylinder set must be in the Off-Lock position when installing ignition switch to insure proper switch slider positioning.

1. Place ignition switch slider in far left position and move back one detent to right, then insert a $3/32$ inch drill bit in adjustment hole on ignition switch to hold switch slider in proper position during installation.
2. Install ignition switch to switch rod.
3. Install ignition switch to steering column jacket assembly with lower mounting stud, **Torquing** to 35 inch lbs.
4. Remove adjustment tool from ignition switch.
5. Install dimmer switch actuator rod through hole in instrument panel bracket and into hole in dimmer switch rod cap.
6. Install dimmer switch assembly on lower mounting stud with dimmer switch nut and upper mounting stud but do not tighten.
7. To adjust dimmer switch, insert a $3/32$ inch drill bit and push switch against actuator rod to remove all lash.
8. **Torque** dimmer switch nut and upper mounting stud to 35 inch lbs., then remove adjustment tool from dimmer switch.
9. Install bowl shield to column bowl and upper mounting stud, then install shield screw, **Torquing** to 35 inch lbs.
10. Install bowl shield nut, **Torquing** to 35 inch lbs.
11. Connect turn signal switch connector to ignition and dimmer switch assembly connector and snap in place.
12. Connect pivot and pulse switch connector to ignition and dimmer switch connector.
13. Install steering column and connect battery ground cable.

RADIO
REPLACE

On 1994 models equipped with airbags, disable airbag system prior to performing service operation as possible airbag deployment may cause personal injury.

CUTLASS SUPREME

1. Disconnect battery ground cable.
2. Remove radio mounting screws.
3. Pull radio out far enough to disconnect antenna, speaker and electrical connectors, then remove radio.
4. Reverse procedure to install.

GRAND PRIX

1. Remove steering column trim cover as follows:
    a. Disconnect ALDL connector from trim cover.
    b. Remove attaching screws from bottom of trim cover.
    c. Remove cover by carefully pulling rearward to disengage from three retaining clips on top of cover.
2. Remove bolts from left side of accessory trim plate.
3. Open glove compartment door, remove bolts from right side of accessory trim plate, then the trim plate.
4. Remove bolts attaching top of radio and nuts attaching bottom of radio.
5. Pull radio out and disconnect electrical and antenna connectors, then remove radio.
6. Reverse procedure to install.

LUMINA

1. Remove right side instrument panel trim plate by unsnapping from instrument panel carrier.
2. Remove two screws retaining radio and pull out far enough to disconnect antenna, speaker and electrical connectors, then remove radio.
3. Reverse procedure to install.

REGAL

1. Disconnect battery ground cable.
2. Remove right sound insulator.
3. Remove bolt holding courtesy lamp, then courtesy lamp and connector.
4. Remove radio receiver mounting screws, then disconnect electrical and antenna connectors.
5. Remove radio receiver.
6. Reverse procedure to install.

STEERING WHEEL
REPLACE

On 1994 models equipped with airbags, disable airbag system prior to performing service operation as possible airbag deployment may cause personal injury.

The following procedure has been modified by technical service bulletin No. 90-9-1.

1. Disconnect battery ground cable.
2. Remove trim plate and retainer.
3. Disconnect horn wire from cam tower.
4. Turn ignition switch to On position.
5. Scribe an alignment mark on steering wheel hub inline with slash mark on steering shaft.
6. Loosen steering wheel nut, positioning it flush with end of shaft.
7. Using a suitable puller, loosen steering wheel. **When removing a steering wheel with accessory controls**

in the hub, use caution to avoid damaging the electronic circuits. Steering wheel puller bolts should be turned in no more than four to six threads to avoid contact with the electronic circuits.

8. Remove steering shaft nut and steering wheel.
9. Reverse procedure to install, aligning scribe mark and **Torquing** steering shaft nut to 30 ft. lbs.

BLOWER MOTOR
REPLACE

On 1994 models equipped with airbags, disable airbag system prior to performing service operation as possible airbag deployment may cause personal injury.

1. Disconnect battery ground cable.
2. Remove right sound insulator panel from under instrument panel.
3. Remove rear retaining screws from electrical convenience center, then loosen front screw and slide convenience center out.
4. Disconnect electrical connector at motor and remove harness from clip.
5. remove blower motor mounting screws and the blower motor.
6. Reverse procedure to install.

HEATER CORE
REPLACE

On 1994 models equipped with airbags, disable airbag system prior to performing service operation as possible airbag deployment may cause personal injury.

WITH A/C

1. Disconnect battery ground cable and drain cooling system.
2. Remove upper dash weatherstripping and the upper secondary cowl.
3. Disconnect heater hoses from heater core.
4. Remove sound insulator, rear seat duct adapter and the heater duct, **Fig. 1.**
5. Remove heater core cover and the heater core.
6. Reverse procedure to install.

LESS A/C

1. Disconnect battery ground cable and drain cooling system.
2. **On models with 2.5L engine,** rotate engine as follows:
   a. Position transaxle in N.
   b. Remove coolant reservoir and position aside. It is not necessary to disconnect coolant reservoir hoses.
   c. Remove torque strut-to-engine bracket nut and bolt.
   d. Using a prybar at engine torque strut bracket, rotate engine and transaxle assembly forward.
   e. Align slave hole in torque strut with engine bracket hole.
   f. Retain engine in this position using torque strut-to-engine bracket bolt.

1. SEAL
2. DUCT ASSEMBLY
3. 1.5 N·m (12 LBS. IN.)
4. ADAPTER
5. 3.3 N·m (29 LBS. IN.)
6. COVER
7. TRANS CABLES
8. REAR SEAT DUCT
9. MODULE

Fig. 1   Removing heater core

3. **On models with 3.1L engines,** rotate engine as follows:
   a. Position transaxle in N.
   b. Remove torque strut-to-engine bracket bolts and position strut aside.
   c. Install passenger side torque strut-to-engine bracket bolt in engine bracket.
   d. Remove coolant reservoir and position aside. It is not necessary to disconnect coolant reservoir hoses.
   e. Place a pry bar in bracket so that it contacts bracket and bolt.
   f. Rotate engine by pulling forward on pry bar.
   g. Align slave hole in driver side torque strut with engine bracket hole.
   h. Retain engine in this position using torque strut-to-engine bracket bolt.
4. **On all models,** remove upper secondary cowl panel.
5. Remove heater hose retaining bracket nuts.
6. Remove upper nut securing lower secondary cowl panel.
7. Disconnect heater hoses from heater core.
8. Blow air through heater core nipples to remove coolant from core.
9. Remove lower right sound insulator panel.
10. Remove rear seat duct adapter, then the heater floor duct, **Fig. 1.**
11. Remove lower left sound insulator panel.
12. Remove heater core cover attaching screws, then the cover, **Fig. 1.**
13. Remove heater core retaining bolt, then the heater core.
14. Reverse procedure to install.

EVAPORATOR CORE
REPLACE

On 1994 models equipped with airbags, disable airbag system prior to performing service operation as possible airbag deployment may cause personal injury.

1. Disconnect battery ground cable and discharge A/C system.
2. Drain cooling system.
3. Remove upper weatherstrip from body and upper secondary cowl.
4. Remove lower secondary cowl upper nut.
5. Disconnect evaporator core block connections at cowl.
6. Disconnect heater hoses from heater core.
7. Remove right lower instrument panel sound insulator panel.
8. Remove rear seat duct adapter and lower heater duct.
9. Remove lower left instrument panel sound insulator panel.
10. Remove heater core cover screws and heater core.
11. Remove evaporator core cover and evaporator core.
12. Reverse procedure to install.

INSTRUMENT CLUSTER
REPLACE

On 1994 models equipped with airbags, disable airbag system prior to performing service operation as possible airbag deployment may cause personal injury.

CUTLASS SUPREME

1. Disconnect battery ground cable.
2. Remove five Phillips head screws at top of trim plate and pull top of trim plate out.
3. Starting at either side, carefully pull bottom of trim plate to release five spring clips.
4. Remove trim plate.
5. Disconnect shift indicator cable, if equipped.
6. Remove four bolts attaching cluster to carrier.
7. Pull cluster forward and disconnect cluster connector.
8. Remove cluster.
9. Reverse procedure to install.

GRAND PRIX

1. Disconnect battery ground cable.

2. Remove two screws at top of instrument cluster trim plate.
3. Remove two Phillips head screws from under glove compartment.
4. remove two Phillips head screws connecting door hinges to instrument panel.
5. Open glove compartment door, holding at bottom, then lift door up and pull out to release door stops.
6. Remove three Phillips head screws at top of glove compartment.
7. Remove two Phillips head screws holding plastic clips under compartment.
8. Slide glove compartment out of instrument panel.
9. Disconnect electrical connectors for light and trunk release switch.
10. Remove one screw above glove compartment, then lift front of pad and pull rearward to release clips.
11. Remove four instrument cluster attaching screws.
12. Lift cluster and disconnect electrical connector, then remove cluster.
13. Reverse procedure to install.

LUMINA
1. Disconnect battery ground cable.
2. Remove instrument panel pad as follows:
   a. Remove five screws from under lower edge of instrument panel pad.
   b. Remove pad by lifting front and pulling rearward to release, then lifting up and out.
3. Disconnect electrical connectors from cluster.
4. Remove three cluster attaching screws, disconnect shift indicator cable, then remove cluster assembly.
5. Reverse procedure to install.

REGAL
1991-92
1. Disconnect battery ground cable.
2. Carefully pry off speaker grilles.
3. Remove screw from under each speaker grille.
4. Remove five screws from under lower edge of instrument panel pad.
5. Remove pad by lifting front and pulling rearward to release, then lifting up and out.
6. Remove cluster trim plate attaching screw and the trim plate.
7. Disconnect electrical connector at cluster.
8. Remove six cluster attaching bolts and the cluster.
9. Reverse procedure to install.

1993-94
1. Disconnect battery ground cable.
2. Remove air cleaner assembly.
3. Remove instrument pad cover and instrument cluster trim plate.
4. Remove LH sound insulator.
5. Remove steering column trim panel.
6. Remove shift control cable at bracket and lever.
7. Remove shift indicator cable.
8. Disconnect electrical connectors, then remove cluster mounting bolts and instrument cluster.
9. Reverse procedure to install. **Torque cluster mounting bolts to 18 inch lbs.**

1- INSTRUMENT PANEL CARRIER
2- HEADLIGHT SWITCH

Fig. 2 Headlamp switch removal. 1993-94 Regal

HEADLIGHT SWITCH
REPLACE

On 1994 models equipped with airbags, disable airbag system prior to performing service operation as possible airbag deployment may cause personal injury.

CUTLASS SUPREME
1. Disconnect battery ground cable.
2. Remove five Phillips head screws at top of trim plate and pull top of trim plate out.
3. Starting at either side, carefully pull bottom of trim plate to release five spring clips.
4. Remove trim plate.
5. Remove two screws securing left air outlet trim plate.
6. Remove left air outlet trim plate by pulling carefully at bottom to release spring clips.
7. Disconnect electrical connector.
8. Remove headlight switch retaining screws and the switch.
9. Reverse procedure to install.

GRAND PRIX
1. Remove screw from instrument panel, under switch.
2. Remove switch assembly by carefully pulling out to release two spring clips at top.
3. Reverse procedure to install.

LUMINA
1. Disconnect battery ground cable.
2. Remove left instrument panel trim plate by pulling rearward to disengage retaining clips.
3. Remove two switch assembly attaching screws, pull switch out far enough to disconnect wiring connectors, then remove switch assembly.
4. Reverse procedure to install.

REGAL
1991-92
1. Disconnect battery ground cable.
2. Carefully pry off speaker grilles.
3. Remove screw from under each speaker grille.
4. Remove five screws from under lower edge of instrument panel pad.
5. Remove pad by lifting front and pulling rearward to release, then lifting up and out.
6. Remove cluster trim plate attaching screw and the trim plate.
7. Remove four switch assembly attaching bolts and the switch assembly.
8. Reverse procedure to install.

1993-94
1. Disconnect battery ground cable.
2. Remove instrument panel trim plate.
3. Remove headlight switch mounting bolts, then the switch, **Fig. 2.**
4. Reverse procedure to install.

WINDSHIELD WIPER SWITCH
REPLACE

Refer to procedure outlined under "Pivot & Pulse Switch & Turn Signal Switch Assembly, Replace."

STOP LIGHT SWITCH
REPLACE

On 1994 models equipped with airbags, disable airbag system prior to performing service operation as possible airbag deployment may cause personal injury.

The following procedure has been modified by technical service bulletin No. 90-159-5.
1. Disconnect battery ground cable.
2. Remove left side sound insulator panel.
3. Slide steering shaft protective sleeve toward front of dash.
4. Disconnect air distribution tube and pull down.
5. Remove retainer pin which holds stop light switch to steering column bracket.
6. Disconnect switch arm from pedal by pushing arm over and off of brake pedal pin.
7. Release switch by pulling down and releasing top snap clip.
8. Remove connector position assurance locking pins from four wire and two wire connector.
9. Disconnect two wire and four wire connectors.
10. Reverse procedure to install, then adjust switch as follows:
    a. Depress brake pedal as far as possible and hold.
    b. Using a stiff wire with a hooked end, gently pull on switch set lever and listen for an audible click.
11. Install left sound insulator panel.

NEUTRAL SAFETY SWITCH
REPLACE

On 1994 models equipped with airbags, disable airbag system prior to performing service operation as possible airbag deployment may cause personal injury.

1. Place vehicle in N.
2. Disconnect battery ground cable, then raise and support vehicle.
3. Disconnect electrical connector.
4. Remove switch harness from two retention clips, then lower vehicle.
5. Disconnect vacuum lines and electrical connector at cruise control servo, if equipped.
6. Detach servo, if equipped, and position out of way.

Fig. 3 Placing crank arm in inner wipe position

7. Disconnect shift lever at transaxle. Do not disconnect lever from cable.
8. Remove switch.
9. Reverse procedure to install, noting the following:
   a. Align groove on inner sleeve of switch with groove on switch body.
   b. **Torque** switch attaching bolts to 18 ft. lbs.
   c. **Torque** shift lever attaching nut to 15 ft. lbs.
   d. **Torque** cruise control servo retaining nut to 27 inch lbs.

WINDSHIELD WIPER MODULE
REPLACE

1992–94

The windshield wiper module consists of both the wiper motor and the wiper transmission.
1. Disconnect battery ground cable.
2. Raise hood and remove washer hose, protective cap and nut from each wiper arm.
3. Lift each wiper arm and insert a suitable pin or pop rivet completely through the two holes located next to pivot of arm, then, using wiper arm removal tool No. J-8966 or equivalent, lift each arm off its transmission shaft.
4. Remove lower reveal molding attaching screws, then lower hood and remove lower reveal molding upward and rearward.
5. Raise hood, then remove air inlet panel screws, underhood lamp switch (if equipped) and the air inlet panel. **Attach holding wire or string to upper portion of switch before removing retaining nut to prevent switch from falling between panels.**
6. Disconnect wiring harness connectors at motor and the washer hose at firewall.
7. If motor is inoperative, motor crank arm must be rotated to inner wipe position, **Fig. 3.** Engage upper jaw of pliers against top edge of crank arm and lower jaw against crank arm nut, **Fig. 4.**

8. Remove three screws from bellcrank housing, then lower transmission.
9. Remove wiper module from vehicle.
10. Reverse procedure to install.

WINDSHIELD WIPER TRANSMISSION
REPLACE

1991

1. With wipers in park position, disconnect washer hose from plastic connector.
2. Remove protective cap.
3. Lift wiper arm and insert a suitable pin completely through the two holes located next to pivot of arm.
4. Remove wiper arm retaining nut.
5. Lift arm off its driveshaft using an up and down rocking motion.
6. Remove top vent screen shroud.
7. Disconnect transmission drive linkage assembly in cowl area.
8. Remove transmission to body attaching screws.
9. Remove transmission and linkage from vehicle.
10. Reverse steps 6 through 9 to install transmission.
11. Install wiper arms one inch below park position.
12. Remove pin and lower wiper arm into position.
13. **Torque** a new wiper arm retaining nut to 14.7-17.7 ft. lbs.
14. Run wiper system and ensure correct operation.
15. Replace washer hose and install protective cap.

1992–94

1. Remove module as previously outlined.
2. Remove two transmission socket screws, then remove socket from link ball.
3. Remove righthand, lefthand, and bellcrank mounting screws and remove transmission from module.
4. Connect new transmission to module.
5. Ensure wiper motor is in inner wipe position, **Fig. 3.**
6. Using suitable tool, align holes in module and bellcrank and install transmission socket screws.
7. Ensure body seal is in proper place on righthand side of module and install wiper module as previously described.
8. Install passenger side wiper arm and blade. Measure from tip of blade to bottom edge of glass, ensuring distance is approximately 9 1/8 inches (231 mm), then tighten nut install protective cap and reconnect washer hose.
9. Install driver side wiper arm and blade. Measure from tip of blade to bottom edge of glass, ensuring distance is ap-

Fig. 4 Moving crank arm to inner wipe position

proximately 2 inches (53 mm), then tighten nut, install protective cap and reconnect washer hose.
10. Run wiper at high and low speeds with wet and tacky windshield, ensuring wiper parks properly and there is no interference between blades.

WINDSHIELD WIPER MOTOR
REPLACE

1991

1. With wipers in park position, disconnect washer hose from plastic connector.
2. Remove protective cap.
3. Lift wiper arm and insert a suitable pin completely through the two holes located next to pivot of arm.
4. Remove wiper arm retaining nut.
5. Lift arm off its driveshaft using an up and down rocking motion.
6. Remove top vent screen shroud.
7. Disconnect wiper arm drive link from crank arm.
8. Disconnect wiper motor electrical connections.
9. Remove wiper motor attaching bolts then wiper motor guiding crank arm through hole.
10. Reverse steps 6 through 9 to install.
11. Install wiper arms one inch below park position.
12. Remove pin and lower wiper arm into position.
13. **Torque** a new wiper arm retaining nut to 14.7-17.7 ft. lbs.
14. Run wiper system and ensure correct operation.
15. Replace washer hose and install protective cap.

1992–94

1. Remove module as previously outlined.
2. Remove crank arm from motor. **Do not remove crank arm from transmission.**
3. Reverse procedure to install, **Torquing** crank arm nut to 25-38 ft. lbs.

2.2L/4-134 Engine

NOTE: For Procedures Not Found In This Section, Refer To The 2.2L/4-134 Engine Section In The Chevrolet Cavalier & Pontiac Sunbird Chapter.

INDEX

1. FUEL VAPOR
2. FUEL SENDER ASSEMBLY
3. FUEL TANK
4. CHASSIS FUEL FEED PIPE
5. IN-LINE FUEL FILTER
6. QUICK-CONNECT FITTINGS
7. FUEL RETURN PIPE
8. FUEL FEED

Fig. 1 Fuel filter replacement

PRECAUTIONS

FUEL SYSTEM PRESSURE RELIEF

To reduce the risk of fire and personal injury, it is necessary to relieve the fuel system pressure before servicing fuel system components.
1. Disconnect battery ground cable.
2. Loosen fuel tank filler cap to relieve tank pressure.
3. Connect fuel pressure gage tool No. J-34730-1, or equivalent, to the fuel pressure valve. Wrap a shop towel around fitting while connection gage to avoid spillage.
4. Install bleed hose into an approved container and open valve to bleed system pressure.

ENGINE MOUNT
REPLACE

1. Remove air cleaner duct assembly.
2. Disconnect engine torque struts.
3. Install engine support tool Nos. J-28467-A, J-28467-90, J-35953 and J-36462, or equivalent, then raise and support vehicle.
4. Remove engine mount nuts at frame.
5. Lower vehicle and raise engine.
6. Remove upper engine mount nuts at mount.

7. Remove mount.
8. Reverse procedure to install.

ENGINE
REPLACE

On 1994 models equipped with airbags, disable airbag system prior to performing service operation as possible airbag deployment may cause personal injury.
1. Disconnect battery ground cable.
2. Mark and remove hood assembly.
3. Remove air cleaner and duct assembly.
4. Drain cooling system, then disconnect engine torque strut completely.
5. Remove air intake silencer assembly.
6. Remove coolant recovery reservoir, then disconnect upper and lower radiator hose at engine.
7. Disconnect brake booster vacuum hose at intake manifold and throttle control cable at throttle body.
8. Remove serpentine drive belt, then disconnect electrical connectors and remove retaining screws at engine cooling fan.
9. Remove power steering pump and position aside.

10. Disconnect fuel lines from engine.
11. Remove alternator heat shield, then disconnect electrical connections at alternator and exhaust oxygen sensor.
12. Remove engine torque strut mount at engine lift bracket.
13. Raise and support vehicle.
14. Remove flywheel and torque converter cover.
15. Remove motor mounts as outlined under "Engine Mount," Replace.
16. Disconnect front exhaust pipe from exhaust manifold.
17. Lower vehicle.
18. Rotate engine, then install strut to bolt hole in engine lift bracket and torque strut mount bracket. This holds engine forward and gives access to rear of engine.
19. Disconnect electrical connectors at starter motor and ground wires at engine block in front of starter.
20. Remove A/C compressor bolts at bracket, then position compressor aside.
21. Remove engine to transaxle bracket at transaxle.
22. Disconnect vacuum hose at intake manifold.
23. Disconnect electrical connectors at speed sensor, knock sensor, engine block ground wires and wire harness clamp nut under intake manifold.
24. Disconnect electrical connectors at throttle body and injector harness. Leave harness on injectors and pull harness from manifold.
25. Remove bellhousing to engine attaching bolts.
26. Remove engine torque struts.
27. Install engine lifting device, then disconnect electrical connectors from electronic ignition module.
28. Remove engine from vehicle.
29. Reverse procedure to install.

FUEL PUMP
REPLACE

1. Disconnect battery ground cable.
2. Relieve fuel system pressure as outlined under "Fuel System Pressure Relief."
3. Drain fuel tank, then remove fuel tank assembly.
4. Remove fuel sender assembly.
5. Reverse procedure to install.

FUEL FILTER
REPLACE

1. Relieve fuel system pressure as outlined under "Fuel System Pressure Relief."
2. Raise and support vehicle.
3. Remove bracket attaching screw and filter bracket, **Fig. 1.**
4. Grasp filter and fuel line fitting. Twist quick-connect fitting ¼ turn in each direction to loosen any dirt within fitting.
5. Using compressed air, blow out dirt from quick-connect fitting.
6. Remove feed pipe nut from fuel filter, then drain any remaining fuel into a suitable container.
7. Remove fuel filter.
8. Reverse procedure to install.

2.5L/4-151 Engine

NOTE: For Procedures Not Found In This Section, Refer To The 2.5L/4-151 Engine Section In The Buick Century, Chevrolet Celebrity, Oldsmobile Cutlass Ciera/Cutlass Cruiser & Pontiac 6000 Chapter.

3.1L/V6-192 Engine

INDEX

IDLE LEARN PROCEDURE

On models with 3.1L/V6-192 engine, any time vehicle power has been interrupted the programed position of the IAC valve pintle is lost. The following procedures must be performed to update the ECM memory with the correct IAC valve pintle position for the vehicle and provide a stable idle speed.
1. Restore vehicle power.
2. Connect TECH I scan tool to ALDL connector located under the lefthand side of the dash panel.
3. Select "IAC System."
4. Select "Idle Learn" in the "Misc. Test" mode.
5. Proceed as directed.

PRECAUTIONS
FUEL SYSTEM PRESSURE RELIEF

To reduce the risk of fire and personal injury, it is necessary to relieve the fuel system pressure before servicing fuel system components.
1. Disconnect battery ground cable.
2. Loosen fuel tank filler cap to relieve tank pressure.
3. Connect fuel pressure gage tool No. J-34730-1, or equivalent, to the fuel pressure valve. Wrap a shop towel around fitting while connection gage to avoid spillage.
4. Install bleed hose into an approved container and open valve to bleed system pressure.

MOUNTS
REPLACE
ENGINE MOUNT

1. Disconnect battery ground cable.
2. Remove mount retaining nuts from below cradle mounting bracket, **Fig. 1.**
3. Raise engine enough to provide clearance, then remove mount to engine bracket attaching nuts and the mount.
4. Reverse procedure to install, torquing nuts and bolts to specifications.

TRANSAXLE MOUNT

1. Disconnect battery ground cable.
2. Support transaxle with suitable jack.
3. Remove crossmember to mount attaching nuts, **Fig. 2.**

Fig. 1 Engine mount

1	ENGINE MOUNT
3	FRAME
4	BRACKET

| 1 | MOUNT |
| 2 | BRACKET |

| 7 | SUPPORT |

Fig. 2 Transaxle mount

4. Remove bracket to transaxle attaching bolts.
5. Remove mount and bracket assembly.
6. Separate mount from bracket.
7. Reverse procedure to install, torquing nuts and bolts to specifications.

ENGINE
REPLACE

> On 1994 models equipped with airbags, disable airbag system prior to performing service operation as possible airbag deployment may cause personal injury.

1. Disconnect battery ground cable, then drain coolant.
2. Scribe alignment marks, then remove hood.
3. Remove air flow tube from air cleaner and throttle valve, then the air cleaner assembly. On turbocharged models, remove turbocharger assembly.
4. Disconnect necessary electrical wiring, then the throttle and T.V. cables.
5. Relieve fuel pressure as follows:
   a. Connect fuel pressure gauge tool No. J-34730-1 or equivalent to fuel pressure connection. Wrap shop cloth around fitting while connecting gage.
   b. Insert bleed hose into suitable container and open valve to bleed system pressure.
6. Disconnect fuel lines.

7. Remove AIR pump belt, then the serpentine drive belt cover and belt.
8. Disconnect radiator hoses at engine.
9. Remove A/C compressor bolts from front bracket.
10. Remove power steering pump and position aside.
11. Disconnect heater hoses from engine.
12. Disconnect brake booster vacuum supply line.
13. Disconnect EGR from exhaust.
14. Raise and support vehicle.
15. Remove A/C compressor bolts at rear bracket, then position compressor aside.
16. Remove flywheel cover, then disconnect starter and position aside.
17. Remove torque converter bolts, then the transaxle bracket.
18. Remove engine front mount retaining nuts.
19. Disconnect exhaust pipe at crossover, then lower vehicle.
20. Remove engine torque struts, then the coolant recovery bottle.
21. Disconnect crossover pipe at left manifold.
22. **On except Lumina models,** pull engine assembly forward and support in this position.
23. **On all models,** disconnect crossover pipe at right manifold.
24. Disconnect bulkhead connector.
25. **On except Lumina models,** remove engine support and allow engine to roll to normal position.
26. **On all models,** remove engine to transaxle attaching bolts, attach lifting

device to engine and support transaxle.
27. Remove engine assembly.
28. Reverse procedure to install.

ROCKER ARM COVER
REPLACE

LEFT

1. Disconnect battery ground cable and drain coolant.
2. Disconnect ignition wire clamps from coolant tube, then loosen coolant tube below thermostat housing at engine block.
3. Disconnect coolant tube at each end.
4. Disconnect coolant tube hose at water pump.
5. Remove coolant tube.
6. Remove tube from between rocker cover and air inlet hose.
7. Remove ignition wire guide.
8. Remove cover attaching bolts and the cover. **If cover adheres to cylinder head, shear off by bumping end of cover with palm of hand or soft rubber mallet. If cover still will not come loose, carefully pry until loose. Do not distort sealing flange.**
9. Reverse procedure to install, noting the following:
   a. Clean sealing surfaces on cylinder head and cover.
   b. Use new gasket, ensuring gasket is seated properly in rocker cover groove.

c. Apply suitable sealer in notch in cylinder head.

d. Torque attaching bolts to specifications.

RIGHT

1. Disconnect battery ground cable and drain coolant.
2. Disconnect vacuum hoses at plenum.
3. Remove air cleaner assembly.
4. Disconnect EGR tube at crossover pipe.
5. Remove ignition wire guide, then disconnect ignition wire harness at plenum and spark plugs.
6. Disconnect two coolant hoses at throttle base.
7. Disconnect necessary electrical connectors at plenum.
8. Disconnect throttle, TV and cruise control cables.
9. Disconnect bracket at right side of plenum.
10. Disconnect brake booster vacuum supply hose from plenum.
11. Remove serpentine belt cover and the belt.
12. Detach coolant recovery bottle and position out of way.
13. Remove engine struts, then pull engine forward and secure in forward position, using slave feature on strut.
14. Remove alternator attaching bolts and position alternator out of way.
15. Remove PCV valve.
16. Remove cover attaching bolts and the cover. **If cover adheres to cylinder head, shear off by bumping end of cover with palm of hand or soft rubber mallet. If cover still will not come loose, carefully pry until loose. Do not distort sealing flange.**
17. Reverse procedure to install, noting the following:
    a. Clean sealing surfaces on cylinder head and cover.
    b. Use new gasket, ensuring gasket is seated properly in rocker cover groove.
    c. Apply suitable sealer in notch in cylinder head.
    d. Torque attaching bolts to specifications.

INTAKE MANIFOLD REPLACE

1991–92

1. Disconnect battery ground cable.
2. Remove accelerator cable and T.V. cable bracket, throttle body and EGR valve, then the plenum.
3. Relieve fuel pressure as follows:
   a. Connect fuel pressure gauge tool No. J-34730-1 or equivalent to fuel pressure connection. Wrap shop cloth around fitting while connecting gage.
   b. Insert bleed hose into suitable container and open valve to bleed system pressure.
4. Disconnect fuel inlet and return pipes from fuel rail.
5. Remove serpentine belt cover and belt.

VIEW A

1	22 N·m (16 LB. FT.) THEN 32 N·m (23 LB. FT.) RETORQUE 32 N·m (23 LB. FT.) IN SEQUENCE	**2** INTAKE MANIFOLD
		3 GASKET
		4 33 N·m (24 LB. FT.)
		5 SEALER

⑦ ④ ③ ⑥
⑧ ① ② ⑤

Fig. 3 Installing intake manifold

6. Detach power steering pump and alternator and position out of way.
7. Remove alternator bracket.
8. Disconnect idle air vacuum hose at throttle body.
9. Disconnect wires at injectors and remove fuel rail.
10. Remove breather tube and runners, then the rocker arm covers.
11. Drain cooling system.
12. Disconnect radiator hose from thermostat outlet.
13. Disconnect wires at coolant sensor and oil sending switch, then remove coolant sensor.
14. Disconnect bypass hose at fill neck and head.
15. Disconnect heater inlet pipe from manifold.
16. Remove manifold attaching bolts and the manifold. **Retain Belleville washers in same positions on four center bolts.**
17. Reverse procedure to install, noting the following:
    a. Remove old gasket material and the loose sealant from front and rear ridges of cylinder block, then clean sealing surfaces.
    b. Apply bead of suitable sealant as shown, **Fig. 3.**
    c. Torque intake manifold nuts and bolts to specification, **Fig. 3.**

1993–94

On 1994 models equipped with airbags, disable airbag system prior to performing service operation as possible airbag deployment may cause personal injury.
1. Disconnect battery ground cable.
2. Remove air cleaner assembly.
3. Remove strut bolts and nuts at engine brackets, and pull struts up out of the way.
4. Drain cooling system, then remove throttle body and EGR valve at plenum.
5. Remove brake booster valve at plenum, then the plenum.

6. Relieve fuel pressure as follows:
   a. Connect fuel pressure gauge tool No. J-34730-1 or equivalent to fuel pressure connection. Wrap shop cloth around fitting while connecting gage.
   b. Insert bleed hose into suitable container and open valve to bleed system pressure.
7. Remove fuel line bracket, then disconnect fuel lines at fuel rail.
8. Rotate engine assembly forward and remove generator bolts. Support generator aside.
9. Remove power steering line clamp nut at generator bracket.
10. Remove secondary air injection pump and position aside.
11. Remove generator mounting bracket.
12. Remove rear engine lift bracket studs and lift bracket.
13. Remove power steering pump and position aside.
14. Remove power brake booster pipe bracket at rear of cylinder head.
15. Disconnect spark plug wires from rear cylinder head.
16. Remove rear valve cover bolts, cover and gasket.
17. Rotate engine assembly back.
18. Remove upper radiator hose clamp and disconnect hose from engine.
19. Remove coolant bypass pipe retaining bolts and bracket nut, then remove coolant bypass pipe and gasket.
20. Remove front cover bolts, cover and gasket.
21. Disconnect fuel injector and intake manifold electrical connectors.
22. Remove coolant sensor, then disconnect heater inlet pipe from intake manifold and cylinder head.
23. Remove intake manifold bolts, then disconnect necessary vacuum hoses.
24. Remove manifold attaching bolts and the manifold. **Retain Belleville washers in same positions on four center bolts.**
25. Reverse procedure to install, noting the following:
    a. Remove old gasket material and the loose sealant from front and rear ridges of cylinder block, then clean sealing surfaces.
    b. Apply bead of suitable sealant as shown, **Fig. 3.**
    c. Torque intake manifold nuts and bolts to specification, **Fig. 3.**

EXHAUST MANIFOLD REPLACE

On 1994 models equipped with airbags, disable airbag system prior to performing service operation as possible airbag deployment may cause personal injury.

LEFT

1. Disconnect battery ground cable.
2. Remove air cleaner and breather hose.

1–LIFTER BODY
2–PLUNGER SPRING
3–BALL CHECK RETAINER
4–BALL CHECK SPRING
5–BALL CHECK
6–PLUNGER
7–OIL METERING VALVE
8–PUSH ROD SEAT
9–RETAINER RING

Fig. 4 Exploded view of valve lifter

Fig. 5 Oversize lifter marking

Coat thread with sealer before installing. Using a 12" clicker torque wrench torque to 45 N·m (33 Lbs. Ft.). Rotate wrench an additional 90° (1/4 turn).

Fig. 6 Installing cylinder head

3. **On models with turbocharged engines,** remove turbocharger.
4. **On all models,** disconnect torque struts from engine.
5. Remove coolant recovery bottle, then the serpentine belt cover and belt.
6. Remove A/C compressor, then the A/C strut and bracket.
7. Remove heat shield, then disconnect exhaust crossover pipe.
8. Remove manifold attaching bolts, then the manifold.
9. Reverse procedure to install, torquing manifold attaching bolts to specifications.

RIGHT

1. Disconnect battery ground cable, then raise and support vehicle.
2. Disconnect exhaust pipe from exhaust manifold, then lower vehicle.
3. **On models with turbocharged engines,** remove turbocharger.
4. **On all models,** disconnect engine torque struts, then remove coolant recovery bottle.
5. Pull engine forward and secure in forward position.
6. Remove air cleaner and breather hose, then the mass air flow sensor.
7. Remove heat shield, then disconnect crossover pipe at manifold.
8. Disconnect accelerator and T.V. cable at throttle lever, then remove accelerator and T.V. cable bracket from plenum and position out of way.
9. Remove manifold attaching bolts and the manifold.
10. Reverse procedure to install, torquing manifold attaching bolts to specifications.

VALVE MECHANISM
REPLACE

1. Remove rocker arm covers and rocker arms, identifying components so that they can be installed in same location.
2. Remove rocker arm pivot balls and rocker arms, then the pushrods. Intake and exhaust pushrods are different lengths (exhaust pushrods are longer). Intake pushrods are marked orange, exhaust pushrods are marked blue.

3. Reverse procedure to install, noting the following:
   a. Ensure pushrods seat in lifter.
   b. Coat bearing surfaces of rocker arms and pivot balls with Molykote or equivalent lubricant.
   c. Torque rocker arm nuts to specifications.

VALVES
ADJUST

1. Crank engine until mark on torsional damper is aligned with TDC mark on timing tab. Check to ensure engine is in the No. 1 cylinder firing position by placing fingers on No. 1 cylinder rocker arms as mark on damper comes near TDC mark on timing tab. If valves are not moving, the engine is in the No. 1 firing position. If valves move as damper mark nears TDC mark on timing tab, engine is in the No. 4 cylinder firing position and should be rotated one revolution to reach the No. 1 cylinder firing position.
2. With engine in the No. 1 cylinder firing position, adjust the following valves: Exhaust-1, 2,3; Intake-1, 5, 6. To adjust valves, back off adjusting nut until lash is felt at pushrod, then tighten adjusting nut until all lash is removed. This can be determined by rotating the pushrod while tightening the adjusting nut. When all lash has been eliminated, turn adjusting nut an additional 1 1/2 turns.
3. Crank engine one revolution until mark on torsional damper and TDC mark are again aligned. This is the No. 4 cylinder firing position. With engine in this position, the following valves can be adjusted: Exhaust-4, 5 & 6; Intake-2, 3 & 4.
4. Install rocker arm covers, then start engine and check timing and idle speed.

VALVE STEM OIL SEAL AND/OR VALVE SPRING
REPLACE

1. Remove rocker arm cover, then the spark plug.
2. Remove rocker arm and pushrod.
3. Install air line adapter tool No. J-23590 or equivalent to spark plug port and apply compressed air to hold valves in place.

4. Using valve spring compressor tool No. J-5892 or equivalent, compress valve spring and disassemble valve assembly.
5. Remove valve stem oil seal.
6. Reverse procedure to install, noting the following:
   a. When assembling valve assembly, use plastic seat provided and press over valve guide boss.
   b. If necessary, use grease to retain valve locks.

VALVE LIFTERS

Roller type valve lifters, **Fig. 4,** are used in this engine. Valve lifters must be replaced whenever camshaft is replaced.

Valve lifters should be kept in order so that they will be reinstalled in their original positions. Some engines will have both standard and .010 inch oversize valve lifters.

Where oversize lifters are used, the cylinder case will be marked "0.25 OS" with white paint on the lifter boss, **Fig. 5.**

If lifters are removed, they must be installed in their original location. If replacement is necessary, use lifters with a narrow flat ground along the lower 3/4 of the lifter. These flats provide additional oil to the cam lobe and lifter surfaces.

VALVE ARRANGEMENT
FRONT TO REAR

Cowl side . . . . E-I-E-I-E
Radiator side . . . . E-I-I-E-I-E

CYLINDER HEAD
REPLACE

LEFT

The following procedure has been modified by technical service bulletin No. 90-53-6.

1. Disconnect battery ground cable, then drain coolant.
2. Remove rocker covers and intake manifold as previously outlined.
3. Remove exhaust crossover, then the oil lever indicator bracket.
4. Remove left exhaust manifold as previously outlined.
5. Disconnect plug wires at left head, then remove pushrods. Intake and ex-

Fig. 7 Installing timing cover

1	FRONT COVER
2	GASKET
3	18-36 N·m (13-26 FT. LBS.)
4	27-48 N·m (20-35 FT. LBS.)
5	SEALER #1052080 OR EQUIVALENT

haust pushrods are different lengths (exhaust pushrods are longer). Intake pushrods are marked orange and are 6 inches long, exhaust pushrods are marked blue and are 6³/₈ inches long.
6. Remove cylinder head attaching bolts, then the cylinder head.
7. Reverse procedure to install, noting the following:
   a. Clean gasket surfaces on head, cylinder block and intake manifold, cylinder block bolt threads and the cylinder head bolts.
   b. Place gasket in position over dowel pins with "This Side Up" marking facing upward.
   c. Coat cylinder head bolt threads with suitable sealant.
   d. Torque cylinder head bolts to specifications in proper sequence, **Fig. 6.**
   e. Torque rocker arm nuts to specifications.

RIGHT

The following procedure has been modified by technical service bulletin No. 90-53-6.
1. Disconnect battery ground cable, then drain cooling system.
2. Raise and support vehicle and disconnect exhaust from crossover, then lower vehicle.
3. Disconnect torque struts from engine.
4. Detach coolant recovery bottle and position aside.
5. Pull engine forward and secure.
6. Remove exhaust crossover heat shield and disconnect crossover from right manifold.
7. Remove right exhaust manifold as previously outlined.
8. Disconnect spark plug wires from right cylinder head.
9. Remove rocker covers and intake manifold as previously outlined.
10. Remove pushrods. Intake and exhaust pushrods are different lengths (exhaust pushrods are longer). Intake pushrods are marked orange and are 6 inches long, exhaust pushrods are marked blue and are 6³/₈ inches long.

Fig. 8 Aligning timing marks

11. Remove cylinder head attaching bolts, then the cylinder head.
12. Reverse procedure to install, noting the following:
   a. Clean gasket surfaces on head, cylinder block and intake manifold, cylinder block bolt threads and the cylinder head bolts.
   b. Place gasket in position over dowel pins with "This Side Up" marking facing upward.
   c. Coat cylinder head bolt threads with suitable sealant.
   d. Torque cylinder head bolts to specification in proper sequence, **Fig. 6.**
   e. Torque rocker arm nuts to specifications.

TIMING COVER
REPLACE

1. Disconnect battery ground cable and drain cooling system.
2. Remove serpentine drive belt tensioner, then the alternator.
3. Remove serpentine drive belt cover, then the drive belt.
4. Detach power steering pump and position aside.
5. Raise and support vehicle.
6. Remove inner splash shield, then the flywheel cover.
7. Remove starter, then, using torsional dampener remover tool No. J-24420 or equivalent, the crankshaft balancer.
8. Remove serpentine drive belt idler pulley, then the oil pan.
9. Remove lower timing cover attaching bolts, then lower vehicle.
10. Disconnect radiator hose at water pump and heater coolant hose from cooling system fill pipe.
11. Disconnect bypass, overflow and canister purge hoses.
12. Remove upper timing cover attaching bolts, then the cover.
13. Reverse procedure to install, noting the following:
   a. Clean sealing surfaces on front cover and cylinder block.
   b. Use new gasket and be careful not to damage sealing surfaces.
   c. Apply sealant and torque timing cover attaching bolts as shown, **Fig. 7.**

NOTE—ALIGN TIMING MARKS ON CAM & CRANK SPROCKETS USING ALIGNMENT MARKS ON DAMPER STAMPING OR CAST ALIGNMENT MARKS ON CYL & CASE.

1	TIMING CHAIN	4	DAMPER
2	CRANK SPROCKET	5	20-27 N·m (15-20 FT. LBS.)
3	CAMSHAFT SPROCKET	6	18-24 N·m (13-18 FT. LBS.)

Fig. 9 Replacing timing chain & sprockets

FRONT COVER OIL SEAL
REPLACE

1. Remove inner splash shield.
2. Using torsional dampener remover tool No. J-24420 or equivalent, remove crankshaft balancer.
3. Using suitable tool, pry out seal, being careful not to damage crankshaft.
4. Reverse procedure to install, noting the following:
   a. Lubricate new seal with clean engine oil and insert in front cover with lip facing engine.
   b. Use front cover alignment and oil seal installer tool No. J-35468 or equivalent to drive seal into place.

TIMING CHAIN & SPROCKETS
REPLACE
REMOVAL

1. Remove timing cover as previously outlined.
2. Position No. 1 piston at TDC with marks on camshaft and crankshaft sprockets aligned, **Fig. 8.**
3. Remove camshaft sprocket and chain. If sprocket does not come off easily, a light blow on lower edge of sprocket should dislodge it.
4. Remove crankshaft sprocket.

INSTALLATION

1. Install crankshaft sprocket.
2. Apply Molykote or equivalent to sprocket thrust surface.
3. Hold sprocket with chain hanging down and align marks on camshaft and crankshaft sprockets, **Fig. 9.**
4. Align dowel in camshaft with dowel hole in camshaft sprocket.
5. Draw camshaft sprocket onto camshaft using attaching bolts, then torque bolts to specification, **Fig. 9.**
6. Lubricate timing chain with engine oil.
7. Install timing cover.

[1] 25 N·m (18 LB. FT.)
[2] 17 N·m (13 LB. FT.)
ALL OTHERS 10 N·m (89 LB. IN.)
[3] SEALER (1052917)

Fig. 10   Installing oil pan

[1] PISTON
[2] ARROW TOWARDS FRONT OF ENGINE

Fig. 11   Piston marking

DUST LIP

Fig. 12   Removing rear main seal

CAMSHAFT
REPLACE

1. Remove engine as previously outlined.
2. Remove valve lifters, then the timing cover as previously outlined.
3. Remove timing chain and sprocket as previously outlined, then the camshaft.
4. Reverse procedure to install, noting the following:
   a. If installing new camshaft, coat camshaft lobes with GM E.O.S. 1052367 or equivalent.
   b. Lubricate camshaft journals with engine oil.

CAM LOBE LIFT SPECIFICATIONS

Intake..............................2626
Exhaust..........................2732

OIL PAN
REPLACE

1. Disconnect battery ground cable, then remove serpentine drive belt cover, drive belt and belt tensioner.
2. Using engine support fixture tool No. J-28467 or equivalent, and an extra support leg, support engine.
3. Raise and support vehicle, then drain engine oil.
4. Remove right wheel and tire assembly, then the right splash shield.
5. Remove steering gear pinch bolt, then the transaxle mount retaining nuts. **Failure to disconnect intermediate shaft from rack and pinion stub shaft may cause damage to steer-**

ing gear and/or intermediate shaft. **This damage may cause loss of steering control.**
6. Remove engine to cradle mount retaining nuts.
7. Remove front engine horse collar bracket from block.
8. Remove outboard flywheel/starter plastic shield, then the inboard flywheel metal shield.
9. Detach starter and allow to hang from body.
10. Place jack under cradle front center crossmember.
11. Loosen rear cradle bolts. **Do not remove.**
12. Remove front cradle bolts and lower front of cradle.
13. Disconnect DIS sensor wire.
14. Remove eight oil pan retaining bolts and four oil pan retaining nuts, then the oil pan.
15. Reverse procedure to install, noting the following:
   a. Clean oil pan flanges, oil pan rail, front cover, rear main bearing cap and the threaded holes.
   b. Use new gasket.
   c. Apply suitable sealant as shown and torque nuts and bolts to specification, **Fig. 10.**

PISTON & ROD ASSEMBLY

When installing piston and rod assemblies into cylinder block, ensure arrow on top of piston faces toward front of engine, **Fig. 11.**

REAR MAIN SEAL
REPLACE

REMOVAL

1. Disconnect battery ground cable.
2. Using engine support fixture tool No. J-28467 or equivalent, and an extra support leg, support engine, then remove transaxle.
3. Remove flywheel.

4. Using suitable tool, remove seal by inserting tool in through dust lip at an angle, **Fig. 12,** and pry seal out by moving handle of tool toward end of crankshaft pilot, repeating around circumference of seal as necessary. **Be careful not to damage crankshaft O.D. surface.**

INSTALLATION

1. Check I.D. of bore for nicks or burrs and repair as required.
2. Inspect crankshaft for burrs or nicks on surface which contacts seal, repairing or replacing crankshaft as necessary.
3. Install seal as follows:
   a. Apply engine oil to I.D. and O.D. of new seal, then slide seal over mandrel until back of seal bottoms squarely against collar of rear main bearing seal installer tool No. J-34686 or equivalent, **Fig. 13.**
   b. Align dowel pin of tool with dowel pin in crankshaft by hand, or by **Torquing** attaching screws to 45 inch lbs., **Fig. 13.**
   c. Turn "T" handle of tool so that collar pushes seal into bore, turning handle until collar is tight against case.
   d. Loosen "T" handle of tool until it comes to a stop, then remove attaching screws.
   e. Ensure seal is seated squarely in bore.
4. Install flywheel, then the transaxle.

OIL PUMP SERVICE
REMOVAL

1. Remove oil pan as previously described.
2. Remove pump and driveshaft extension.

DISASSEMBLY

1. Drain oil from pump.
2. Remove pump cover and pump gears, **Fig. 14.**
3. Remove pressure regulator valve. If valve is stuck, sock pump housing in carburetor cleaning solvent. **Pressure regulator valve spring may be under pressure. Remain retaining pin carefully.**

Fig. 13 Installing rear main seal

Fig. 14 Exploded view of oil pump

1. PUMP BODY
2. IDLER GEAR AND DRIVE GEAR
3. PUMP COVER
4. PRESSURE REGULATOR VALVE
5. PRESSURE REGULATOR SPRING
6. RETAINING PIN
7. BOLTS

Fig. 15 Measuring oil pump gear lash

1 CHECK CLEARANCE BETWEEN GEAR TEETH AND SIDE WALL

1—DEPTH OF POCKET
2—DIAMETER OF POCKET

Fig. 16 Measuring oil pump gear pocket

1—LENGTH OF GEAR
2—DIAMETER OF GEAR

Fig. 17 Measuring oil pump gears

Fig. 18 Measuring gear side clearance

4. Clean sludge, oil and/or varnish from all parts. Varnish may be removed by soaking in carburetor or cleaning solvent.

INSPECTION

1. Inspect pump housing and cover for cracks or damaged threads, replacing as necessary. **Do not attempt to repair pump housing.** Replace spring as necessary.
2. Inspect idler gear shaft. If loose in housing, replace pump.
3. Inspect pressure regulator valve for scoring or sticking. Burrs may be removed with a fine oil stone.
4. Inspect pressure regulator valve spring for loss of tension or bending.
5. Inspect suction pipe and screen assembly for looseness if permanently pressed into pump body. If pipe is loose or has been removed, pump body cover must be replaced. Check for broken wire mesh or screen.
6. Inspect gears for chipping, galling or wear.
7. Measure gear lash in several positions, **Fig. 15**. Gear lash should be .0037-.0077 inch.
8. Measure pump housing gear pocket depth, **Fig. 16**. as follows:
   a. **On models with an aluminum pump body,** pump depth should be 1.195-1.198 inches.

   b. **On models with a cast pump body,** pump depth should be 1.202-1.205 inches.
9. Measure pump housing gear pocket diameter, **Fig. 16**. Pump housing diameter should be 1.503-1.506 inches.
10. Measure pump gear diameters, **Fig. 17**. Gear diameter should be 1.498-1.500 inches.
11. Measure pump gear side clearance, **Fig. 18**. Gear side clearance should be .003-.004 inches.
12. Measure oil pump end clearance, **Fig. 19**, as follows:
   a. **On models with an aluminum pump body except 1990 Lumina,** end clearance should be .0016-.0067 inch.
   b. **On models with a cast pump body,** end clearance should be .002-.006 inch.

ASSEMBLY

1. Lubricate all internal parts with engine oil.
2. Install pump gears.
3. Prime engine oil galleries by removing engine oil pump drive unit and rotating oil pump, using drill motor, appropriate socket and extension.
4. Install cover and gasket. **Use only original equipment gaskets as gasket thickness is critical to proper pump operation.**

5. Install pin, ensuring it is properly secured.
6. **Torque** pump cover attaching bolts to 89 inch. lbs.

INSTALLATION

1. Apply sealer No. 1050026, Fel-Pro set and seal, or equivalents to new pipe and tap into place with a plastic hammer, using oil suction pipe installer tool No. J-21182 or equivalent.
2. Install oil pump and driveshaft extension, engaging driveshaft extension into drive gear.
3. Install pump to rear bearing cap bolt, torquing to specifications.
4. Clean oil pan of oil and sludge and replace oil filter.
5. Install oil pan, then fill crankcase and check oil pressure. If pressure does not build up almost immediately, remove oil pan and check oil pump suction pipe attachment to pump. If necessary, disassemble oil pump, fill all cavities with petroleum jelly and reassemble. **Running engine without measurable oil pressure will cause extensive damage.**

CONNECTING RODS & MAIN BEARINGS

Engine bearings are of the precision insert type. They are available for service

Fig. 19   Measuring oil pump end clearance

Fig. 20   Main bearing insert markings

use in standard and various undersizes, **Fig. 20.**

To determine correct replacement insert size, bearing clearance must be measured as follows:

1. Measure crankshaft journal diameter in several places, approximately 90° apart and average the measurements.
2. Measure taper and run-out, which should be .0002 inch (maximum).
3. Install bearing inserts and torque rod and main bearing cap bolts to specification, then measure I.D. with an inside micrometer. Measure connecting rod I.D. in same direction as length of rod.
4. Select a suitable set of inserts to provide specified clearance limits. **Do not mix inserts of different nominal size in same bearing bore.** If clearance limits cannot be met, crankshaft journal must be reconditioned and undersized bearing inserts installed.

THERMOSTAT
REPLACE

1. Drain coolant.
2. Disconnect radiator hose from thermostat housing.
3. Remove thermostat housing bolts, thermostat housing and thermostat.
4. Reverse procedure to install.

WATER PUMP
REPLACE

1. Disconnect battery ground cable and drain engine coolant.
2. Remove serpentine drive belt, then disconnect radiator and heater hose.
3. Remove water pump attaching bolts, then the water pump, **Fig. 21.**
4. Reverse procedure to install. noting the following:
   a. Clean water pump mating surfaces.
   b. **Torque** water pump attaching bolts to 89 inch lbs.

COOLING SYSTEM BLEED

1. Open vent valves located on the thermostat housing and throttle body return pipe above the water pump, **Fig. 22.** Turn both vents screws two to three turns.

1	WATER OUTLET
2	26 N·m (19 LB. FT.)
3	GASKET
4	THERMOSTAT
5	COOLANT SENSOR
6	PLUG

Fig. 22   Cooling system bleed vent

2. Fill cooling system to the base of the radiator neck.
3. Close both vent valves. **Do not over tighten vent valves.**
4. **On all models,** install radiator cap.
5. Add sufficient coolant to the recovery tank.
6. Start engine and observe low coolant warning lamp.
7. If lamp remains On, repeat bleed procedure.

FUEL PUMP
REPLACE

1. Disconnect battery ground cable.
2. Relieve fuel system pressure as outlined under "Fuel System Pressure Relief."
3. Drain fuel tank, then remove fuel tank assembly.
4. Remove fuel sender assembly.
5. Reverse procedure to install.

FUEL FILTER
REPLACE

1. Relieve fuel system pressure as outlined under "Fuel System Pressure Relief."

1. WATER PUMP
2. GASKET
3. 10 N·m (89 LB. IN.)
4. LOCATOR – MUST BE VERTICAL

Fig. 21   Water pump mounting

2. Raise and support vehicle.
3. Remove bracket attaching screw and filter bracket, **Fig. 23.**
4. Grasp filter and fuel line fitting. Twist quick-connect fitting ¼ turn in each direction to loosen any dirt within fitting.
5. Using compressed air, blow out dirt from quick-connect fitting.
6. Remove feed pipe nut from fuel filter, then drain any remaining fuel into a suitable container.
7. Remove fuel filter.
8. Reverse procedure to install.

TURBOCHARGER
REPLACE

On 1994 models equipped with airbags, disable airbag system prior to performing service operation as possible airbag deployment may cause personal injury.

1. Disconnect battery ground cable, then drain cooling system.
2. Remove intercooler-to-intake manifold duct attaching bolt from thermostat housing, then the duct.
3. Remove air cleaner-to-turbocharger duct from turbocharger.
4. Remove air cleaner inlet duct, then the air cleaner and duct assembly.
5. Remove turbocharger-to-intercooler duct from turbocharger.
6. Remove turbocharger heat shields.
7. Disconnect oxygen sensor electrical connector, then remove oxygen sensor.
8. Remove water return line from turbocharger.
9. Remove oil supply line from turbocharger.
10. Disconnect vacuum line from turbocharger compressor outlet, then the vacuum line from actuator assembly.
11. Remove actuator arm-to-wastegate retaining clip, then the actuator arm from wastegate.

1 FUEL VAPOR
2 FUEL SENDER ASSEMBLY
3 FUEL TANK
4 CHASSIS FUEL FEED PIPE
5 IN-LINE FUEL FILTER
6 QUICK-CONNECT FITTINGS
7 FUEL RETURN PIPE
8 FUEL FEED

Fig. 23   Fuel filter replacement

Fig. 24   Turbocharger mounting

A INSERT BREAKER BAR HERE
1 GENERATOR
2 SERPENTINE BELT
3 WATER PUMP
4 AIR CONDITIONING COMPRESSOR
5 CRANKSHAFT
6 BELT TENSIONER
7 POWER STEERING PUMP

Fig. 25   Serpentine drive belt routing

12. Remove wastegate actuator from turbocharger.
13. **On models with cruise control,** remove cruise control servo and position aside.
14. Remove turbocharger downpipe from turbocharger.
15. Loosen turbocharger water supply hose clamp, then remove hose.
16. Remove turbocharger oil drain hose from drain pipe.
17. Remove turbocharger-to-exhaust crossover attaching bolts, then the turbocharger, **Fig. 24.**
18. Reverse procedure to install, noting the following:
    a. Transfer oil and water lines.
    b. Torque nuts and bolts to specifications.
    c. Prime turbocharger with oil before

starting the engine. Crank engine with fuel pump fuse removed until normal operating oil pressure is reached.

SERPENTINE BELT REPLACE

On 1994 models equipped with airbags, disable airbag system prior to performing service operation as possible airbag deployment may cause personal injury.

1. Remove belt guard.
2. Lift or rotate tensioner using a 1/2 inch breaker bar.
3. Remove serpentine belt.
4. Reverse procedure to install, routing drive belt as shown in **Fig. 25.**

TIGHTENING SPECIFICATIONS

Year	Component	Torque/Ft. Lbs.	Year	Component	Torque/Ft. Lbs.
1991–94	Camshaft Rear Cover	7	1991–94	Exhaust Manifold Bolts	19
	Camshaft Sprocket	21		Exhaust Manifold Heat Shield	90①
	Connecting Rod Bearing Cap Nuts	39		Flywheel Bolts	60
	Crankshaft Balancer	77		Fuel Filter	22
	Crossover/Turbocharger Support Bracket	19		Fuel Tank Bolts	35
	Cylinder Head Bolts	②		Intake Manifold Bolts	24
	Drive Belt Tensioner Bolt	⑤		Intake Manifold Nuts	23
	Engine Bracket To Engine Bolt	④		Intake Manifold Studs	23
	Engine Mount Bracket To Engine	63		Intercooler To Support	89①⑥
	Engine Mount To Engine Mount Bracket	32		Main Bearing Cap Bolts	73
	Engine Mount To Frame	32		Oil Cooler Connector	29
	Engine Strut Bracket To Engine	34		Oil Filter	11
	Exhaust Crossover Nut	18		Oil Level Indicator Retainer Nut	18
	Exhaust Downpipe Bracket To Cylinder Head	35⑥		Oil Pan	③
	Exhaust Downpipe Bracket To Downpipe	18⑥		Oil Pump Drive Bolt	25
	Exhaust Downpipe To Turbocharger	17		Oil Pump	25–35
				Oxygen Sensor	31

Continued

TIGHTENING SPECIFICATIONS—Continued

Year	Component	Torque/Ft. Lbs.
1991–94	Rocker Arm Adjusting Nuts	14–20
	Rocker Arm Covers	7
	Spark Plugs	20
	Strut Bracket To Upper Tie Bar	16
	Strut To Engine Bracket Bolt	41
	Strut To Tie Bar Bracket	32
	Thermostat Housing	19
	Timing Chain Cover	③
	Timing Chain Dampener	15
	Transaxle Bracket To Transaxle	60
	Transaxle Mount To Frame	38
	Transaxle Mount To Transaxle Bracket	30
	Transaxle Mount To Transaxle Mount Support	38

Year	Component	Torque/Ft. Lbs.
1991–94	Turbocharger Coolant Feed	21
	Turbocharger Coolant Return	21
	Turbocharger Oil Feed	15
	Turbocharger Oil Return	30
	Turbocharger To Exhaust Manifold Crossover	17
	Water Pump	19

① —Inch lbs.
② —Torque in sequence to 33 ft. lbs. then turn an additional 90°.
③ —Refer to text.
④ —Bracket side bolts, 59 ft. lbs.; bracket front bolts, 81 ft. lbs.
⑤ —1991 models, 32 ft. lbs.; 1992–94 models, 37 ft. lbs.
⑥ —Turbocharged engines.

3.4L/V6-204 ENGINE

INDEX

IDLE LEARN PROCEDURE

On models with 3.4L/V6-204 engine, any time vehicle power has been interrupted the programed position of the IAC valve pintle is lost. The following procedures must be performed to update the ECM memory with the correct IAC valve pintle position for the vehicle and provide a stable idle speed.
1. Restore vehicle power.
2. Connect TECH I scan tool to ALDL connector located under the lefthand side of the dash panel.
3. Select "IAC System."
4. Select "Idle Learn" in the "Misc. Test" mode.
5. Proceed as directed.

PRECAUTIONS
FUEL SYSTEM PRESSURE RELIEF

To reduce the risk of fire and personal injury, it is necessary to relieve the fuel system pressure before servicing fuel system components.
1. Disconnect battery ground cable.
2. Loosen fuel tank filler cap to relieve tank pressure.
3. Connect fuel pressure gage tool No. J-34730-1, or equivalent, to the fuel pressure valve. Wrap a shop towel around fitting while connection gage to avoid spillage.
4. Install bleed hose into an approved

1 103 N·m (76 LB. FT.)
2 BRACKET
3 MOUNT
4 58 N·m (43 LB. FT.)
5 BRACKET ASSEMBLY, ENGINE MOUNTING
6 43 N·m (32 LB. FT.)

Fig. 1   Front engine mounting bracket

container and open valve to bleed system pressure.

ENGINE MOUNTS
REPLACE

On 1994 models equipped with airbags, disable airbag system prior to performing service operation as possible airbag deployment may cause personal injury.

FRONT

1. Remove air cleaner assembly.
2. Disconnect engine torque strut.
3. Install engine support tool Nos. J-28467, J-28467-90 and J-36462, or equivalent.
4. Raise and support vehicle.
5. Remove right front tire and wheel assembly.
6. Remove righthand engine splash shield.
7. Drain engine oil into a suitable container and remove oil filter.
8. Remove front engine mount nuts at mount bracket and frame, **Fig. 1.**
9. Install drive axle boot protector and lower vehicle.
10. Raise engine.
11. Raise and support vehicle.
12. Remove front mount.
13. Reverse procedure to install.

REAR

1. Remove air cleaner assembly and disconnect engine torque strut.
2. Install engine support tool Nos. J-28467, J-28467-90 and J-36462, or equivalent, then raise and support vehicle.
3. Remove right front tire and wheel assembly, righthand engine and drive axle splash shields.
4. Install drive axle boot protector.
5. Remove engine mount nuts at frame, **Figs. 2 and 3.**
6. Lower vehicle and raise engine.
7. Raise and support vehicle.

1 47 N·m (35 LB. FT.)
2 BRACKET
3 MOUNT
4 43 N·m
5 ENGINE MOUNTING BRACKET ASSEMBLY
6 85 N·m (61 LB. FT.)
7 BRACE

Fig. 2   Rear engine mounting bracket. Manual transaxles

1 ENGINE MOUNT BRACKET ASSEMBLY
2 47 N·m (35 LB. FT.)
3 TRACE BRACKET
4 BRACKET
5 MOUNT

DISASSEMBLED VIEW

Fig. 3   Rear engine mounting bracket. Automatic transaxles

8. Remove power rack and pinion mounting bolts and hang rack on frame.
9. Disconnect right ball joint from lower control arm.
10. Install a suitable jack under righthand side of frame.
11. Remove righthand frame mounting bolts.
12. Loosen lefthand frame mounting bolts.
13. Lower righthand side of frame approximately three inches.
14. Remove upper engine mount nuts at mount.
15. Remove mount.
16. Reverse procedure to install.

ENGINE
REPLACE

On 1994 models equipped with airbags, disable airbag system prior to performing service operation as possible airbag deployment may cause personal injury.

MANUAL TRANSAXLES

1. Disconnect battery cables and remove battery jump terminal.
2. Remove air cleaner and duct assembly.
3. Drain cooling system and remove coolant recovery tank.
4. Disconnect control cables at throttle body.
5. Remove serpentine drive belt as outlined under "Serpentine Drive Belt."
6. Disconnect wiring harness cover and upper engine wire connectors at right strut tower.
7. Disconnect engine ground near air cleaner bracket.
8. Relieve fuel system pressure as outlined under 'Fuel System Pressure Relief'' then disconnect fuel lines at fuel rail.
9. Disconnect heater hose quick connect at intake manifold and bracket.
10. Disconnect and remove engine torque strut.
11. Remove upper and lower radiator hoses.
12. Disconnect heater hoses at water pump.
13. Remove engine torque strut bracket at frame.
14. Remove right and left engine coolant fan retaining screws.
15. Remove upper radiator support.
16. Remove both engine cooling fans.
17. Disconnect electrical bulkhead connector at right fire wall.
18. Disconnect ECM and set on engine.
19. Remove convenience center, wiring harness cover, harness clips and low coolant sensor connector and position entire harness assembly on top of engine.
20. Discharge A/C system and disconnect A/C lines near accumulator.
21. Remove shift control cable at lever bracket.
22. Mark then disconnect all necessary vacuum lines.
23. Raise and support vehicle.
24. Remove both front tire and wheel assemblies.
25. Remove both flywheel covers.
26. Drain engine oil into a suitable container.

27. Remove starter motor.
28. Remove flywheel to converter bolts.
29. Remove right and left engine splash shields.
30. Disconnect front brake ABS electrical connectors, if equipped.
31. Disconnect front exhaust pipe and converter assembly.
32. Remove both front brake calipers and support on body.
33. Disconnect steering column intermediate shaft pinch bolt and remove shaft from stub.
34. Position transaxle jack under power train.
35. Disconnect and plug transaxle cooler lines.
36. Remove frame bolts.
37. Lower powertrain from vehicle.
38. Disconnect electrical connectors and harness from left lower side of engine.
39. Remove A/C compressor with lines attached.
40. Disconnect electrical, alternator and sensor connectors and ground connections from rear of engine.
41. Remove exhaust crossover pipe.
42. Remove right axle from from transaxle as outlined under "Drive Axle, Replace" in the "Front Wheel Drive Axles" section.
43. Remove drive axle shield.
44. Remove engine mounts as outlined under "Mounts, Replace."
45. Remove power steering pump assembly.
46. Remove transaxle to engine bolts.
47. Install engine lifting device and remove engine assembly from transaxle.
48. Reverse procedure to install.

AUTOMATIC TRANSAXLES

1. Relieve fuel system pressure as outlined under "Fuel System Pressure Relief."
2. Remove air cleaner assembly.
3. Mark and remove hood assembly.
4. Disconnect battery ground cable and drain cooling system.
5. Discharge A/C system and remove coolant recovery tank.
6. Remove heater hoses from engine.
7. Disconnect engine torque strut mount and stud.
8. Disconnect and remove engine cooling fans.
9. Remove radiator hoses from engine.
10. Disconnect control cables from bracket and throttle body.
11. Disconnect bulkhead connections from cowl.
12. Disconnect fuel lines from engine.
13. Remove exhaust crossover pipe.
14. Remove lower transaxle to engine bolts including ground wires.
15. Remove power steering pump from engine and position aside.
16. Disconnect EGR pipe from EGR valve.
17. Raise and support vehicle.
18. Remove right tire and wheel assembly then the right splash shield.
19. Disconnect A/C manifold from A/C compressor.

20. Remove flywheel and steel torque converter inspection covers then starter.
21. Remove front exhaust pipe and converter.
22. Disconnect motor mounts as outlined under "Mounts, Replace."
23. Disconnect electrical connections at front and rear of engine then from alternator.
24. Remove torque converter bolts.
25. Remove right ball joint bolt and separate joint from control arm.
26. Remove drive axle assembly.
27. Lower vehicle.
28. Support transaxle using a suitable jack and install lifting device on engine.
29. Disconnect quick connects near ECM.
30. Remove remaining transaxle to engine bolts.
31. Disconnect necessary vacuum lines from rear of engine.
32. Remove engine assembly.
33. Reverse procedure to install.

INTAKE PLENUM REPLACE

On 1994 models equipped with airbags, disable airbag system prior to performing service operation as possible airbag deployment may cause personal injury.

1. Relieve fuel system pressure as outlined under "Fuel System Pressure Relief."
2. Remove air cleaner assembly.
3. Disconnect battery ground cable and drain cooling system.
4. Remove control cables at throttle body.
5. Disconnect fuel rail cover bolts and remove fuel pipes at fuel rail.
6. Disconnect heater hose at intake manifold.
7. Disconnect vacuum lines from PVC valve and throttle body of plenum.
8. Disconnect AIR solenoid, EGR valve, canister purge solenoid, MAP sensor and throttle position sensor connectors.
9. Remove EGR bolts and EGR valve.
10. Disconnect fuel line bracket and heater hose at throttle body of plenum.
11. Disconnect all necessary vacuum lines at plenum.
12. Remove wire loom bracket for rear bank of spark plug wires.
13. Remove nuts at plenum and plenum bracket.
14. Remove plenum from vehicle.
15. Reverse procedure to install.

INTAKE MANIFOLD REPLACE

On 1994 models equipped with airbags, disable airbag system prior to performing service operation as possible airbag deployment may cause personal injury.

1. Relieve fuel system pressure as outlined under "Fuel System Pressure Relief."

2. Disconnect fuel rail as follows:
   a. Remove intake manifold plenum as outlined under "Intake Plenum, Replace."
   b. Remove fuel line bracket bolts.
   c. Disconnect fuel lines at fuel rail using a suitable back-up wrench on the fuel rail fittings.
   d. Disconnect vacuum lines at pressure regulator.
   e. Remove fuel rail bolts.
   f. Disconnect injector electrical connectors.
   g. Remove fuel rail from vehicle.
3. Disconnect heater hose pipe bracket from thermostat housing.
4. Remove temperature sensor from intake manifold.
5. Disconnect radiator hose from thermostat housing.
6. Remove intake manifold bolts and intake manifold.
7. Reverse procedure to install, inserting rubber isolators fully into manifold flange before tightening fasteners to specifications.

EXHAUST MANIFOLD REPLACE

On 1994 models equipped with airbags, disable airbag system prior to performing service operation as possible airbag deployment may cause personal injury.

FRONT

1. Remove air cleaner assembly.
2. Remove exhaust crossover pipe.
3. Remove engine torque strut bracket to frame bolts and lift strut out of the way.
4. Remove upper radiator shroud, right side cooling fan heat shield and right cooling fan assembly.
5. On models with manual transaxles, remove front hose from air pipe.
6. On all models, remove exhaust manifold nuts then the manifold and heat shield.
7. Reverse procedure to install.

REAR

Automatic Transaxles

1. Remove rear cam carrier as outlined under "Camshaft Carrier, Replace."
2. Remove exhaust crossover pipe.
3. Raise and support vehicle.
4. Disconnect front exhaust pipe at manifold.
5. Lower vehicle.
6. Disconnect oxygen sensor connector.
7. Remove exhaust manifold nuts then the manifold and heat shield.
8. Reverse procedure to install.

Manual Transaxles

1. Remove air cleaner assembly.
2. Disconnect battery ground cable.
3. Remove exhaust crossover pipe.
4. Raise and support vehicle.
5. Disconnect front exhaust manifold pipe.
6. Disconnect and remove oxygen sensor.

1. HEAD BOLT — REFER TO TEXT FOR TORQUING PROCEDURE
2. CYLINDER HEAD
3. GASKET
4. PIN
5. ENGINE BLOCK

TIGHTENING SEQUENCE

6 2 3 7
5 1 4 8

Fig. 4 Cylinder head bolt tightening sequence

7. Remove exhaust manifold heat shield and disconnect EGR pipe at manifold.
8. Remove exhaust manifold nuts then the exhaust manifold.
9. Reverse procedure to install.

VALVE STEM OIL SEAL & VALVE SPRING
REPLACE
HEAD ON ENGINE

1. Remove camshaft carrier as outlined under "Camshaft Carrier, Replace."
2. Remove spark plugs and install spark plug port adapter tool No. J-22794, or equivalent, and apply compressed air to hold valves in place.
3. Compress valve spring using valve spring compressor tool No. J-38606, or equivalent.
4. Remove valve stem locks and release spring tension.
5. Remove valve cap, valve spring and valve stem oil seal. **Wrap tape over valve lock grooves to prevent damage to valve seals.**
6. Reverse procedure to install.

HEAD OFF ENGINE

1. Compress valve spring using valve spring compressor tool No. J-38606, or equivalent.
2. Remove valve stem locks and release spring tension.
3. Remove valve cap, valve spring and valve stem oil seal. **Wrap tape over valve lock grooves to prevent damage to valve seals.**
4. Reverse procedure to install.

VALVE LIFTERS

1. Remove camshaft carrier as outlined under "Camshaft Carrier, Replace."

2. Remove six lifter hold-down hoses.
3. Remove lifters.
4. Reverse procedure to install.

CYLINDER HEAD
REPLACE

On 1994 models equipped with airbags, disable airbag system prior to performing service operation as possible airbag deployment may cause personal injury.

FRONT

1. Relieve fuel system pressure as outlined under "Fuel System Pressure Relief."
2. Remove intake manifold, camshaft carrier and exhaust manifold as outlined under "Intake Manifold, Replace," " Camshaft Carrier, Replace" and "Exhaust Manifold, Replace."
3. Remove right cooling fan assembly.
4. Remove oil level indicator tube.
5. Disconnect temperature sending unit connector.
6. Remove cylinder head bolts then the cylinder head.
7. Reverse procedure to install, noting the following:
   a. Install cylinder head gasket with metal tabs between cylinders facing up.
   b. **Torque** cylinder head bolts in sequence shown in **Fig. 4** to 33 ft. lbs. plus an additional 90° turn using torque/angle meter tool No. J-36660, or equivalent.

REAR

1. Relieve fuel system pressure as outlined under "Fuel System Pressure Relief."
2. Remove intake manifold, camshaft carrier and exhaust manifold as outlined under "Intake Manifold, Replace," " Camshaft Carrier, Replace" and "Exhaust Manifold, Replace."
3. Disconnect oxygen sensor connector.
4. Remove rear timing belt tensioner bracket.
5. Remove cylinder head bolts then the cylinder head and gasket.
6. Reverse procedure to install, noting the following:
   a. Install cylinder head gasket with metal tabs between cylinders facing up.
   b. **Torque** cylinder head bolts in sequence shown in **Fig. 4** to 33 ft. lbs. plus an additional 90° using torque/angle meter tool No. J-36660, or equivalent.

SECONDARY TIMING BELT SERVICE
COVER, REPLACE
Right

1. Disconnect battery ground cable.
2. Remove secondary timing belt right cover bolts then the belt cover, **Fig. 5.**
3. Reverse procedure to install.

1. TIMING BELT COVER (RIGHT)
2. 10 N·m (89 LB. IN.)
3. TIMING BELT COVER (LEFT)
4. TIMING BELT COVER (CENTER)
5. FRONT COVER

Fig. 5 Timing belt covers

Left

1. Disconnect battery ground cable.
2. Remove spark plug cover as follows:
   a. Disconnect vacuum hose from camshaft carrier cover.
   b. Remove spark plug cover bolts then the cover.
3. Remove secondary timing belt left cover bolts then the cover, **Fig. 5.**
4. Reverse procedure to install.

Center

1. Disconnect battery ground cable.
2. Remove ECM harness cover.
3. Remove serpentine belt tensioner as outlined under "Serpentine Drive Belt."
4. Remove secondary timing belt right and left covers as outlined under "Secondary Timing Belt, Service."
5. Disconnect power steering pipe retaining clip nut at alternator stud.
6. Remove secondary timing belt center cover bolts then the belt cover, **Fig. 5.**
7. Reverse procedure to install.

TENSIONER PLATE & ACTUATOR, REPLACE
Removal

1. Remove power steering pump as outlined under "Power Steering Pump, Replace" in the "Front Suspension & Steering" section.
2. Remove secondary timing belt center cover as outlined under "Secondary Timing Belt, Service."
3. Rotate engine clockwise to align timing marks on camshaft sprockets, **Fig. 6.**
4. Verify tensioner pulley position to determine if length of belt is satisfactory as follows:
   a. Insert a flat, narrow .02 inch thick ruler along the tensioner pulley and engage the steps in the tensioner base and note the reading at the top of the tensioner pulley, **Fig. 7.**

1	RH EXHAUST CAMSHAFT SPROCKET
2	RH INTAKE CAMSHAFT SPROCKET
3	LH INTAKE CAMSHAFT SPROCKET
4	LH EXHAUST CAMSHAFT SPROCKET
5	PERMANENT MARKS PAINTED DOTS REMOVE PREVIOUS MARKS IF TIMING IS BEING CHANGED AND MARK AGAIN IN THESE LOCATIONS.
6	CRANKSHAFT DAMPER
7	INTERMEDIATE SHAFT SPROCKET

NOTE: THIS TDC #1 EXHAUST. INTERMEDIATE SHAFT BELT SPROCKET TIMING MARK IS AT 8 O'CLOCK (POINTING TOWARDS DRAIN NOTCH)

Fig. 6   Engine timing marks

Fig. 7   Actuator measurement

1	50 N·m (37 LB. FT.)	8	SECONDARY TIMING BELT TENSIONER BRACKET
2	PULLEY ASSEMBLY	9	CYLINDER HEAD
3	SECONDARY TIMING BELT	10	DRIVEN SPROCKET
4	50 N·m (37 LB. FT.)	11	DRIVE SPROCKET
5	ACTUATOR	12	IDLER ASSEMBLY
6	LOCK PIN (PAPER CLIP)	13	CRANKSHAFT REFERENCE MARKS
7	SIDE PLATE	14	25 N·m (18 LB. FT.)

Fig. 8   Secondary timing belt system

b. If reading is 1.56-1.68 inch, belt is in acceptable range.
c. If reading is 1.70-1.84 inch, belt is to be replaced.
5. Loosely clamp two camshaft sprockets on each side of engine together using clamping pliers, or equivalent. **Do not mar camshaft sprockets with clamping device.**
6. Hold belt to righthand exhaust camshaft sprocket with a C-clamp and a wide pad on belt. **No deflection of camshaft sprocket should be noted, if deflection is noted, loosen clamping device.**
7. Remove tensioner side plate retaining bolts from tensioner and remove the side plate from the actuator and base, **Fig. 8.**
8. Rotate actuator assembly around the arm pivot and out of the mounting base. Removal of tensioner from base allows it to extend to its maximum travel. **Do not lose or damage ta-**

pered bushing when removing tensioner assembly.
9. Set actuator on table in vertical position to allow oil to drain to boot end, for 5 minutes prior to refilling.
10. Form a double loop in a .032 inch diameter paper clip leaving a 1.85 inch straight length as shown in **Fig. 9.**
11. Remove rubber end plug from rear of tensioner assembly. The assembly is filled with oil and removal of plug may allow oil to escape.
12. Insert paper clip through center hole in vent plug and into pilot hole.
13. Insert a small screwdriver into screw slot inside end of tensioner.
14. Retract tensioner plunger by rotating screw in a clockwise direction while pushing rod tip against the table top, until fully retracted.
15. Rotate screw slot to align with vent hole, and push the straight section of paper clip into screw slot to retain plunger in retracted position.
16. If tensioner oil has been lost, fill tensioner with SAE 5W 30 Mobil 1, or equivalent, engine oil through end hole. Fill to bottom of plug hole only when plunger is fully retracted and pin is installed.

Installation

1. Install rubber end plug to rear of actuator assembly.
2. Insert actuator bushing into side plate.
3. Install actuator assembly onto mounting base by inserting tapered trunnion of tensioner into matching hole of bushing in bracket and installing side plate bolts. Ensure installed actuator assembly rotates freely.
4. Gently rotate tensioner pulley 11 ft. lbs. counterclockwise into belt using square lug in arm and engage actuator shaft in arm socket.
5. Pull out paper clip and allow pulley to move into belt.
6. Remove sprocket clamp and any other belt holding device.
7. Repeat step 4 and applying 12-15 ft. lbs. of torque to set initial tension on belt.

1	PAPER CLIP
2	DOUBLE LOOP

Fig. 9   Reworked paper clip

8. Rotate engine clockwise three times to seat belt. Ensure sprocket reference marks are aligned properly.
9. Verify tensioner pulley position to determine if length of belt is satisfactory as follows:
   a. Insert a flat, narrow .02 inch thick ruler along the tensioner pulley and engage the steps in the tensioner base and note the reading at the top of the tensioner pulley, **Fig. 7.**
   b. If reading is 1.56-1.68 inch, belt is in acceptable range.
   c. If reading is 1.70-1.84 inch, belt is to be replaced.
10. Install secondary timing belt center cover as outlined under "Secondary Timing Belt, Service."
11. Install power steering pump as outlined under "Power Steering Pump, Replace" in the "Front Suspension & Steering" section.

BELT, REPLACE
Removal

1. Remove secondary timing belt actuator as outlined under "Secondary Timing Belt, Service."
2. If belt is to be reused, mark rotation direction on timing belt.
3. Remove tensioner pulley/arm assembly as outlined under "Secondary Timing Belt, Service."
4. Remove timing belt, by carefully sliding it off pulleys.

Installation

1. Install actuator and side plate. **Ensure**

1	INTERMEDIATE SHAFT SPROCKET
2	TIMING CHAIN
3	CRANKSHAFT SPROCKET
4	TIMING CHAIN TENSIONER
5	25 N·m (18 LB. FT.)
A	SPRING PIN HOLE
B	CHAMFER AND COUNTER BORE INWARD
C	SPROCKETS OUTWARD

Fig. 10 Timing chain assembly

reference marks on sprockets are properly aligned.

2. Install timing belt by routing it around idlers and sprockets as follows, **Fig. 8.**
   a. Start at intermediate camshaft sprocket and work counterclockwise.
   b. Ensure belt is installed in direction of rotation.
   c. Engage teeth into sprockets, place rubber hose behind belt at intermediate sprocket and accumulate slack at tensioner location.
3. Install tensioner pulley to mounting base as follows:
   a. Use a flat magnet, tape or cup plug to hold pivot tube in pulley during this step.
   b. After starting pivot bolt, rotate arm counterclockwise to position square lug at 6 o'clock position.
   c. **Torque** pivot bolt to 37 ft. lbs.
4. Install actuator as outlined under "Secondary Timing Belt, Replace."

TENSIONER PULLEY, ARM & BRACKET, REPLACE

1. Remove secondary timing belt tensioner plate and actuator as outlined under "Secondary Timing Belt, Service."
2. Remove tensioner pulley bolt and pulley/arm assembly.
3. Remove mounting bracket bolts then the mounting bracket.
4. Reverse procedure to install, ensuring correct replacement color code on bracket is used.

TIMING CHAIN & SPROCKETS
REPLACE

1. Raise and support vehicle.
2. Remove starter and flywheel cover.

3. Remove oil pan as outlined under "Oil Pan, Replace."
4. Remove engine as outlined under "Engine, Replace."
5. Remove front cover as outlined under "Front Cover, Replace."
6. Mark reference points on the intermediate sprocket, chain link, front face of cylinder and crankshaft sprocket, **Fig. 10.**
7. Retract timing chain tensioner as outlined under "Timing Chain Tensioner, Replace."
8. Remove timing chain and crankshaft sprocket using universal puller bridge tool No. J-8433, or equivalent, and special legs and protector tool No. J-38611, or equivalent. If intermediate gear does not slide off easily with timing chain, rotate crankshaft back and forth to help loosen gear.
9. Reverse procedure to install, noting the following:
   a. Aligning marks made during disassembly.
   b. Large chamfer and counterbore of crankshaft sprocket are installed toward the crankshaft.
   c. Intermediate shaft sprocket spline sockets are installed away from the case.
   d. Crankshaft sprocket must be pressed on for the final .31 inch to seated position using crankshaft gear installer tool No. J-38612, or equivalent.

TIMING CHAIN TENSIONER
REPLACE

1. Remove timing chain as outlined under "Timing Chain, Replace."
2. Retract tensioner shoe using tensioner retractor tool No. J-33875, or equivalent, as follows, **Fig. 11.**
   a. Insert tool on both sides of tensioner. Pull on thru pin in tensioner arm to retract spring located in tensioner arm.
   b. While compressing spring, use a suitable tool and insert in hole to retain spring.
3. Remove timing chain and sprockets as outlined under "Timing Chain & Sprockets, Replace."
4. Remove tensioner mounting bolts then the tensioner.
5. Inspect tensioner for wear, cracks or other damage.
6. With tensioner shoe retracted, install tensioner to engine block.
7. Lightly coat tensioner chain surfaces with oil.
8. Install timing chain as outlined under "Timing Chain, Replace."

CAMSHAFT CARRIER COVER
REPLACE
FRONT

1. Disconnect oil/air breather hose from cover.

1	TENSIONER
2	PIN

Fig. 11 Retracting timing chain tensioner

2. Remove spark plug wires from plugs.
3. Remove rear spark plug wire cover.
4. Remove camshaft carrier cover bolts then the cover and O-ring.
5. Reverse procedure to install, ensuring bolt isolators are fully seated into cover before tightening cover bolts.

REAR

1. Remove intake plenum as outlined under "Intake Plenum, Replace."
2. Remove secondary timing belt right cover as outlined under "Secondary Timing Belt, Service."
3. Remove spark plug wires and oil/air separator hose at camshaft cover.
4. Remove camshaft cover bolts then the camshaft cover and gaskets.
5. Reverse procedure to install, ensuring bolt isolators are fully seated into cover before tightening cover bolts.

CAMSHAFT CARRIER
REPLACE
FRONT

1. Remove left camshaft carrier cover as outlined under "Camshaft Carrier Cover, Replace."
2. Remove secondary timing belt as outlined under "Secondary Timing Belt, Service."
3. Install fuel line hoses under camshaft and between lifters to hold lifters in carrier as shown in **Fig. 12.**
4. Remove exhaust crossover pipe.
5. Remove engine torque strut and strut bracket on engine.
6. Remove camshaft carrier bolts and nut then the camshaft carrier and gasket.
7. Reverse procedure to install, noting the following:
   a. Remove oil from camshaft carrier to cylinder head bolt holes, **Fig. 13.**
   b. Use petroleum jelly in lifter bores, along with hoses to keep lifters in place.

REAR

1. Remove right camshaft carrier cover as outlined under "Camshaft Carrier Cover, Replace."

Fig. 12 Lifter and camshaft hold-down tool

2. Remove secondary timing belt as outlined under "Secondary Timing Belt, Service."
3. Install fuel line hoses under camshaft and between lifters to hold lifters in carrier as shown in **Fig. 12.**
4. Remove front engine lift hook.
5. Remove camshaft carrier bolts and nut then the camshaft carrier and gasket.
6. Reverse procedure to install, noting the following:
   a. Remove oil from camshaft carrier to cylinder head bolt holes **Fig. 13.**
   b. Use petroleum jelly in lifter bores, along with hoses to keep lifters in place.

CAMSHAFT SPROCKET
REPLACE
REMOVAL

1. Remove camshaft carrier covers as outlined under "Camshaft Carrier Cover, Replace."
2. Remove secondary timing belt and covers as outlined under "Secondary Timing Belt, Service."
3. Remove clamping device from sprocket.
4. Rotate camshafts so flats on camshaft to be serviced are facing up, **Fig. 13.**
5. Install camshaft hold-down tool No. J-38613, or equivalent, and **Torque** bolt to 22 ft. lbs., **Fig. 12.**
6. Remove camshaft sprocket bolt and washer using camshaft holding tool Nos. J38613 and J-38614, or equivalent.
7. Remove camshaft sprocket using sprocket remover tool No. J-38616, or equivalent.
8. Remove flat ring from sprocket bore.

INSTALLATION

1. Install new flat ring to large bore of sprocket.

Fig. 13 Camshaft carrier components

1	SEAL
2	LH CAMSHAFT CARRIER
3	LIFTER
4	CAM HOLD DOWN TOOL
5	CAMSHAFT PLUG
6	THRUST PLATE
7	10 N·m (89 LB. IN.)
8	GASKET
9	THRUST PLATE COVER
10	CAMSHAFT OIL SEAL
11	CAMSHAFT
12	OIL GALLERY PLUG
13	RH CAMSHAFT CARRIER
14	INTAKE CAMSHAFT "FLATS"
15	EXHAUST CAMSHAFT "FLATS"
16	BEFORE INSTALLING CAM CARRIER TO CYLINDER HEAD, REMOVE OIL FROM THESE BOLT HOLES.

2. Wipe camshaft noses with a light coat of oil.
3. Install camshaft sprocket on camshaft.
4. Install lock ring far enough to minimize tipping.
5. Lightly oil camshaft sprocket bolt threads and washer before using. Install bolt and washer into camshaft and seat bolt finger tight then back off 1/4–1/2 turn. **Final torque specification will be reached after performing procedure outlined under "Camshaft Timing."**
6. Repeat steps 1 through 5 for remaining camshafts.
7. Check each sprocket for binding by rotating it around the camshaft.
8. Install secondary timing belt as outlined under "Secondary Timing Belt, Service."
9. Set camshaft timing as outlined under "Camshaft Timing."

CAMSHAFT
REPLACE

1. Remove camshaft carrier as outlined under "Camshaft Carrier, Replace."
2. Remove lifters as outlined under "Lifter, Replace."
3. Install cam shaft hold-down tool No. J-38613, or equivalent.
4. Remove camshaft sprockets as outlined under "Camshaft Sprocket, Replace."

5. Remove camshaft carrier thrust plate cover, **Fig. 13.**
6. Remove thrust plate and bolts, **Fig. 13.**
7. Remove camshaft hold-down tool.
8. Remove camshaft by carefully removing it out the back of the carrier. **All camshaft journals are the same diameter and care must be taken when removing camshaft to avoid damage to bearing surfaces.**
9. Reverse procedure to install, noting the following:
   a. Coat camshaft lobes and journals with GM engine oil supplement (EOS), or equivalent.
   b. Adjust camshaft timing as outlined under "Camshaft Timing."

CAMSHAFT OIL SEAL
REPLACE

1. Remove camshaft as outlined under "Camshaft, Replace."
2. Remove camshaft seal by prying seal out with a suitable screwdriver.
3. Reverse procedure to install, using seal installation tool No. J-38619, or equivalent.

CAMSHAFT TIMING

If only one bank is to be timed, ensure bank to bank camshaft timing relationship is one revolution apart. Timing flats should be 180° opposite when finally timed.

1. Remove spark plugs.
2. Remove camshaft sprockets as outlined under "Camshaft Sprocket, Replace."
3. Rotate camshaft flats Up and install camshaft hold-down tool No. J-38613, or equivalent. **Torque** tool bolt to 22 ft. lbs.
4. Install secondary timing belt and tensioner pulley arm assembly as outlined under "Secondary Timing Belt, Service."
5. Ensure freeness of rotation of tensioner pulley arm assembly.
6. Rotate tensioner pulley 11 ft. lbs. counterclockwise into the belt using cast square lug on body and engage ball end of actuator into socket on pulley arm.
7. Remove tensioner lockpin, using needle nose pliers, or equivalent, allowing tensioner shaft to extend and the pulley to move into belt.
8. Remove sprocket and belt holding devices, then rotate tensioner pulley counterclockwise applying 12-15 ft. lbs. of torque.
9. Rotate engine clockwise three times to seat belt. Align crankshaft reference marks during final rotation to TDC.
10. Set lock ring on right exhaust and intake camshaft into bore by threading in attaching bolt as follows:
    a. Hold sprocket from turning using sprocket holding tool No. J-38614, or equivalent.
    b. Running **Torque**, before seating, of bolt should be 44-66 ft. lbs.
    c. If less torque is required before seating, the shim and lock rings must be replaced and inspect nose of camshaft for foreign material.
    d. If more torque is required before seating, the shim and lock rings must be replaced and inspect bolt threads for burrs and/or foreign material.
    e. Seating of lock ring is accomplished when edge of ring is flush with sprocket hub.
    f. **Torque** sprocket bolt to 81 ft. lbs. to complete this step.
11. Remove camshaft holding tool.
12. Rotate engine clockwise an odd number of revolutions and realign the intermediate shaft marks at TDC. Ensure timing marks on damper lines up with front cover marks.
13. Repeat steps 2 through 9 for left intake and exhaust camshaft then repeat step 10.
14. Remove holding tools then the old timing marks.
15. Mark the position of each sprocket at TDC of number one exhaust position with permanent paint, **Fig. 6.**
16. Install secondary timing belt and covers as outlined under "Secondary Timing Belt, Service."
17. Install camshaft carrier covers as outlined under "Camshaft Carrier Cover, Replace."

CAM LOBE LIFT SPECIFICATIONS

Intake 370inch
Exhaust 370inch

INTERMEDIATE SHAFT BELT SPROCKET & OIL SEAL
REPLACE
REMOVAL

1. Verify the relationship of intermediate sprocket to front cover.
2. Raise and support vehicle.
3. Remove starter motor and install flywheel holding tool No. J-37096, or equivalent.
4. Lower vehicle.
5. Rotate engine and position to factory alignment marks. Remove sprocket bolt and washer.
6. Mark position of sprocket on nose end of intermediate shaft.
7. Remove secondary timing belt as outlined under "Secondary Timing Belt, Service."
8. Reverse center bolt and engage self-tapping screws of sprocket remover tool No. J-38616, or equivalent, into three equally spaced holes on belt sprocket and remove intermediate shaft timing belt sprocket.
9. Remove intermediate shaft belt sprocket oil seal.

INSTALLATION

1. Install oil seal using seal installer tool No. J-38619, or equivalent.
2. Lubricate seal surfaces of intermediate shaft sprocket.
3. Align timing marks and install sprocket into position engaging locating tangs of sprocket into mating sockets of chain sprocket.
4. Verify engagement by measuring from face of belt sprocket to front cover. If measurement is more than 1.65 inches, tangs are not engaged.
5. Install O-ring in position on end of intermediate shaft.
6. Lightly lubricate threads of sprocket bolt and torque bolt to specification.
7. Raise and support vehicle. Remove flywheel holding tool and install starter assembly.
8. Lower vehicle and install secondary timing belt and covers.

INTERMEDIATE SHAFT & BEARINGS
REPLACE

1. Remove engine assembly as outlined under "Engine, Replace."
2. Remove oil pump drive assembly as outlined under "Oil Pump, Service."
3. Remove timing chain as outlined under "Timing Chain & Sprockets, Replace."

4. Remove intermediate shaft thrust plate and screws.
5. Remove intermediate shaft. **All intermediate shaft journals are the same diameter and care should be taken not to damage bearings or journals during removal.**
6. Remove intermediate shaft bearing using bearing remover/installer tool No. J-33049, or equivalent.
7. Reverse procedure to install, noting the following:
    a. Align oil holes in bearing with oil holes in cylinder block. Install oil feed holes at 4 and 7 o'clock for front bearing and 4 o'clock for bearings 2, 3 and 4.
    b. Apply oil to intermediate shaft journals prior to installation.
    c. Replace O-ring seal after sprocket installation.

INTERMEDIATE SHAFT REAR COVER
REPLACE

1. Remove transaxle assembly as outlined under "Transaxle, Replace" in the "Clutch & Manual Transaxle" or the "Automatic Transaxle" section.
2. Remove intermediate shaft rear cover bolts then the cover and gasket.
3. Reverse procedure to install.

CRANKSHAFT PULLEY & DAMPER
REPLACE

1. Remove serpentine drive belt as outlined under "Serpentine Drive Belt."
2. Raise and support vehicle.
3. Remove right tire and wheel assembly then the engine splash shield.
4. Remove starter as outlined under "Starter, Replace" in the "Electrical" section.
5. Remove crankshaft damper bolt using flywheel holding tool No. J-37096, or equivalent.
6. Remove crankshaft pulley bolt and pulley.
7. Remove crankshaft damper using crankshaft damper removal tool No. J-24430, or equivalent.
8. Reverse procedure to install, noting the following:
    a. Coat front cover oil seal with engine oil.
    b. Install suitable sealant to keyway of damper before installation.
    c. Install damper using crankshaft damper installer tool No. J-29113, or equivalent.

FRONT COVER
REPLACE

1. Remove secondary timing belt tensioner mounting bracket and idler pulleys as outlined under "Secondary Timing Belt, Service."
2. Remove engine front lift hook.

1 FRONT COVER
2 SEALER
3 GASKET
4 LOCATING PINS
5 ENGINE BLOCK
6 47 N·m (35 LB. FT.)
7 27 N·m (20 LB. FT.)
8 FRONT COVER OIL SEAL
9 INTERMEDIATE SHAFT SEAL

Fig. 14   Front cover & oil seal

1 ENGINE BLOCK
2 PISTON
3 ARROW FACES TOWARDS FRONT OF ENGINE

Fig. 15   Piston marking

3. Remove engine torque strut bracket from frame and pull strut and bracket out of the way.
4. Remove upper radiator support.
5. Remove righthand cooling fan heat shield then the cooling fan assembly.
6. Remove lower radiator hose from coolant pump.
7. **On models with manual transaxles,** remove front air hose at air pipe.
8. **On all models,** remove heater hose at front cover and heater pipe bracket at frame.
9. Raise and support vehicle.
10. Remove right tire and wheel assembly then the engine splash shield.
11. Remove crankshaft pulley and damper as outlined under "Crankshaft Pulley & Damper, Replace."
12. Drain engine oil into a suitable container and remove oil filter.
13. Remove A/C compressor mounting bolts.
14. Remove lower front cover bolts, **Fig. 14.**
15. **On models with automatic transaxles,** remove drive axle assembly.
16. **On all models,** remove rear alternator bracket then the starter motor.
17. Lower vehicle.
18. Remove intermediate timing belt sprocket as outlined under "Intermediate Shaft Belt Sprocket & Oil Seal, Replace."
19. Remove upper alternator retaining bolts.
20. Remove forward lamp relay center screws and position relay center aside.
21. Remove oil cooler hose from front cover.
22. Remove water pump pulley.
23. Remove front cover upper bolts then the front cover and gasket.
24. Reverse procedure to install, noting the following:
   a. Apply GM sealer part No. 1052080, or equivalent, to lower edges od sealing surface of front cover.

1 AMOUNT UNDERSIZE STAMPED AT EITHER END (.016, .032)

Fig. 16   Bearing marking

   b. Apply suitable thread sealant to large bolts.
   c. Tighten attaching bolts to specifications.

FRONT COVER OIL SEAL
REPLACE

1. Remove crankshaft pulley and damper as outlined under "Crankshaft Pulley & Damper, Replace."
2. Pry out seal using a suitable pry tool.
3. Reverse procedure to install, lubricate seal with oil and install using seal installer tool No. J-34995, or equivalent.

PISTON & CONNECTING RODS

When installing piston and rod assemblies into cylinder block, ensure arrow on top of piston faces toward the front of the engine, **Fig. 15.**

CONNECTING RODS & MAIN BEARINGS

Connecting rod and main bearing are of the precision insert type. They are available for service use in standard and two undersizes of .016 and .032 inch. Bearing undersize amount is stamped at either end of the bearing, **Fig. 16.**

OIL DISTRIBUTION COVER
REPLACE

1. Remove intake manifold as outlined under "Intake Manifold, Replace."
2. Remove oil distribution cover mounting bolts then the cover and gasket.
3. Reverse procedure to install.

OIL PAN & BAFFLE
REPLACE

1. Remove air cleaner assembly.
2. Install engine support fixture tool Nos. J-28467-A, J-28467-90 and J-36462, or equivalent.
3. Raise and support vehicle.
4. Remove right tire and wheel assembly and steering gear heat shield.
5. Remove steering gear bolts then hang steering gear from frame.
6. Separate ball joints from control arms.
7. Remove power steering cooler line clips from frame.
8. Disconnect engine mounts at frame as outlined under "Mounts, Replace."
9. Support frame assembly and remove frame bolts then remove frame assembly.
10. Disconnect and remove starter assembly.
11. Remove flywheel cover.
12. Remove oil pan nuts and bolts then the oil pan and gasket.
13. Remove oil baffle nuts. Rotate pick up tube and remove oil baffle.
14. Reverse procedure to install, tightening oil pan bolts to specifications shown in **Fig. 17.**

OIL PUMP
REPLACE

1. Remove oil pan and baffle as outlined under "Oil Pan & Baffle, Replace."
2. Remove oil pump bolt then the oil pump and driveshaft extension.
3. Install shaft extension on oil pump, engage shaft extension into drive gear.
4. Tighten oil pump bolt to specification.
5. Install oil pan and baffle.

Fig. 17 Oil pan assembly

1	10 N·m (89 LB. IN.)
2	REINFORCEMENT
3	OIL PAN
4	25 N·m (18 LB. FT.)
5	GASKET
6	ENGINE BLOCK
7	IGNITION SENSOR WIRE CLIP

VIEW A

Fig. 18 Removing rear main seal

DUST LIP

1	FUEL VAPOR
2	FUEL SENDER ASSEMBLY
3	FUEL TANK
4	CHASSIS FUEL FEED PIPE
5	IN-LINE FUEL FILTER
6	QUICK-CONNECT FITTINGS
7	FUEL RETURN PIPE
8	FUEL FEED

Fig. 19 Water pump assembly

1	LOCATOR — MUST BE IN VERTICAL POSITION
2	FRONT COVER
3	GASKET
4	COOLANT PUMP
5	10 N·m (89 LB. IN.)

FRT

Fig. 20 Fuel filter replacement

VIEW A

Fig. 21 Serpentine drive belt routing

1	SERPENTINE BELT
2	BELT TENSIONER

1	45 N·m (33 LB. FT.)
2	DRIVE BELT TENSIONER

Fig. 22 Serpentine drive belt tensioner

OIL PUMP DRIVE
REPLACE

1. Remove rear cylinder head as outlined under "Cylinder Head, Replace."
2. Remove oil pump drive bolt and clamp.
3. Remove oil pump drive assembly and O-ring.
4. Reverse procedure to install.

REAR MAIN SEAL
REPLACE

1. Remove transaxle assembly as outlined under "Transaxle, Replace" in the "Clutch & Manual Transaxle" or the "Automatic Transaxle" section.

2. Remove flywheel assembly.
3. Remove oil seal using a suitable pry tool as shown in **Fig. 18.**
4. Reverse procedure to install, using seal installer tool No. J-34686, or equivalent.

WATER PUMP
REPLACE

1. Remove air cleaner assembly.
2. Disconnect battery ground cable.
3. Drain engine coolant into a suitable container.
4. Remove serpentine drive belt as outlined under "Serpentine Drive Belt."
5. Remove water pump pulley.
6. Remove water pump bolts then the water pump and gasket, **Fig. 19.**
7. Reverse procedure to install.

COOLING SYSTEM BLEED

1. Open air bleed vents on thermostat housing and heater water inlet pipe.
2. Add 3.6 quarts of engine antifreeze through the radiator neck.
3. Add clean water slowly to the system until level of coolant has reached base of radiator neck.

4. Close bleed vents and add clean water if necessary to bring coolant level to the base of radiator neck.

THERMOSTAT
REPLACE

1. Remove air cleaner and duct assembly.
2. Drain coolant.
3. Remove engine torque strut bolt at engine.

4. Disconnect upper radiator hose at thermostat housing.
5. Release fuel pressure as previously described under "Fuel System Pressure Relief."
6. Disconnect fuel lines at fuel rail.
7. Remove heater hose bracket at thermostat housing stud.
8. Disconnect heater hose at throttle body.
9. Remove thermostat housing bolts, thermostat housing and thermostat.
10. Reverse procedure to install.

FUEL PUMP
REPLACE

1. Disconnect battery ground cable.
2. Relieve fuel system pressure as outlined under "Fuel System Pressure Relief."
3. Drain fuel tank, then remove fuel tank assembly.
4. Remove fuel sender assembly.
5. Reverse procedure to install.

FUEL FILTER
REPLACE

1. Relieve fuel system pressure as outlined under "Fuel System Pressure Relief."
2. Raise and support vehicle.
3. Remove bracket attaching screw and filter bracket, **Fig. 20.**
4. Grasp filter and fuel line fitting. Twist quick-connect fitting 1/4 turn in each direction to loosen any dirt within fitting.
5. Using compressed air, blow out dirt from quick-connect fitting.
6. Remove feed pipe nut from fuel filter, then drain any remaining fuel into a suitable container.
7. Remove fuel filter.

8. Reverse procedure to install.

SERPENTINE DRIVE BELT

BELT, REPLACE

1. Remove coolant recovery reservoir.
2. Rotate tensioner clockwise using a box end wrench.
3. Remove serpentine belt.
4. Reverse procedure to install, routing belt as shown in **Fig. 21.**

BELT TENSIONER, REPLACE

1. Remove serpentine drive belt as outlined under "Serpentine Drive Belt."
2. Remove tensioner bolt then the tensioner, **Fig. 22.**
3. Reverse procedure to install.

TIGHTENING SPECIFICATIONS

Year	Component	Torque/Ft. Lbs.
1991–94	A/C Compressor To Front Cover Bolt	37
	AIR Pipe	15
	Camshaft Carrier Bolt	18
	Camshaft Carrier Cover Bolt	89①
	Camshaft Carrier Thrust Plate Bolt	89①
	Camshaft Sprocket Bolt	81
	Clutch Cover Bolt	18
	Upper Radiator Mounting Panel Bolt	89①
	Cooling Fan Attaching Bolt	89①
	Connecting Rod Cap Nut	39
	Crankshaft Damper Mounting Bolt	78
	Crankshaft Main Cap Bolt	②
	Crankshaft Pulley To Crankshaft Damper Bolt	37
	Crankshaft Sensor Bolt	14
	Cylinder Head Bolt	③
	EGR Tube Assembly Bolt	18
	EGR VAlve Assembly Bolt	18
	Engine Mount To Bracket Nut	35
	Engine Mounting Bracket To Engine Bolt	61④
	Exhaust Crossover Nut	18
	Exhaust Heat Shield Nut	116①
	Exhaust Mounting Nut	116①
	Exhaust Stud	13
	Flywheel To Engine Bolt	61
	Front Cover Bolts (Large)	35
	Front Cover Bolts (Small)	18
	Front Engine Mounting Bracket To Engine Bolt	63
	Fuel Filter	22
	Fuel Pipe Clip Bolt	53①
	Fuel Pipe Retaining Screw	89①
	Fuel Rail Bolt	89①
	Fuel Tank Bolts	35
	Idler Pulley Bolt	37

Year	Component	Torque/Ft. Lbs.
1991–94	Ignition Coil Bolt	18
	Ignition Coil Nut	125①
	Intake Manifold Bolt	18
	Intake Plenum Bolt	18
	Intake Plenum Nut	89①
	Intermediate Shaft Thrust Plate Screw	89①
	Intermediate Shaft Belt Sprocket Bolt	95⑥
	Knock Sensor	71①
	Oil Cooler Connector	24
	Oil Cooler Fitting	13
	Oil Distribution Cover Bolt	18
	Oil Level Indicator Bolt	89①
	Oil Pan Baffle Nut	18
	Oil Pan Bolt	89①⑤
	Oil Pan Bolt	18⑥
	Oil Pan Nut	89①
	Oil Pump Drive Bolt	35⑨
	Oil Pump To Rear Main Bolt	40
	Power Steering Pump To Bracket Bolt	25
	Rear Camshaft Cover Bolt	89①
	Rear Engine Mounting Brace To Bracket Bolt	61
	Rear Engine Mounting Brace To Bracket Nut	35④
	Secondary Timing Belt Idler Bolt	37
	Secondary Timing Belt Tensioner Bracket Bolt	37
	Secondary Timing Belt Tensioner Pulley Bolt	37
	Secondary Timing Belt Tensioner Side Plate Bolt	18
	Serpentine Drive Belt Tensioner Bolt	33
	Spark Plug	11
	Starter Mounting Bolt	32
	Tensioner Mounting Bolt	18
	Timing Belt Cover Bolt	89①

Continued

TIGHTENING SPECIFICATIONS—Continued

Year	Component	Torque/Ft. Lbs.
1991–94	**Timing Chain Tensioner Bolt**	18
	Torque Strut and Engine Lift Bracket Bolt	52
	Trace Bracket To Rear Engine Mounting Bracket Bolt	35⑦
	Water By-Pass Nut	18
	Water Outlet Bolt	18
	Water Pump Bolt	89①

① —Inch lbs.
② —Torque to 37 ft. lbs plus an additional ¾ turn.
③ —Refer to text.
④ —Manual Transaxle.
⑤ —Except two rear bolts.
⑥ —Two rear bolts.
⑦ —Automatic Transaxle.
⑧ —1992–94, 80 ft. lbs.
⑨ —1992–94, 27 ft. lbs.

3800/V6-231 ENGINE

NOTE: For Procedures Not Found In This Section, Refer To The 3800/V6-231 Engine Section In The Buick Electra, Lesabre & Park Ave., Cadillac Deville & Fleetwood, Oldsmobile Eighty Eight & Ninety Eight & Pontiac Bonneville Chapter.

INDEX

PRECAUTIONS

FUEL SYSTEM PRESSURE RELIEF

To reduce the risk of fire and personal injury, it is necessary to relieve the fuel system pressure before servicing fuel system components.
1. Disconnect battery ground cable.
2. Loosen fuel tank filler cap to relieve tank pressure.
3. Connect fuel pressure gage tool No. J-34730-1, or equivalent, to the fuel pressure valve. Wrap a shop towel around fitting while connection gage to avoid spillage.
4. Install bleed hose into an approved container and open valve to bleed system pressure.

MOUNT
REPLACE

ENGINE MOUNT

1. Disconnect battery ground cable.
2. Remove mount nuts from below frame mounting bracket.
3. Raise and support engine to gain clearance using engine support fixture tool Nos. J-28467-A, J-28467-90 and J-35953, or equivalent.

1	FUEL VAPOR
2	FUEL SENDER ASSEMBLY
3	FUEL TANK
4	CHASSIS FUEL FEED PIPE
5	IN-LINE FUEL FILTER
6	QUICK-CONNECT FITTINGS
7	FUEL RETURN PIPE
8	FUEL FEED

Fig. 1   Fuel filter replacement

4. Remove mount to engine nuts then the mount.
5. Reverse procedure to install, **Torquing** nuts to 32 ft. lbs and bolts to 70 ft. lbs.

TRANSMISSION MOUNT

1. Disconnect battery ground cable.
2. Remove engine torque strut from engine.
3. Raise and support vehicle.
4. Remove left tire and wheel assembly and lower splash shield.
5. Support transaxle using a suitable jack.
6. Remove mount nuts then the mount.

7. Reverse procedure to install, noting the following:
   a. **Torque** upper bracket to engine bolts to 61 ft. lbs.
   b. **Torque** lower bracket to engine bolts to 35 ft. lbs.
   c. **Torque** upper bracket to engine mount nuts to 22 ft. lbs.
   d. **Torque** lower bracket to frame bolts to 38 ft. lbs.
   e. **Torque** frame bracket to mount nuts to 35 ft. lbs.

ENGINE
REPLACE

1. Mark and remove hood assembly.
2. Disconnect battery ground cable.
3. Remove air cleaner assembly.
4. Relieve fuel system pressure as follows:
   a. Disconnect battery ground cable.
   b. Loosen fuel filler cap.
   c. Connect fuel pressure gauge tool No. J-34730-1, or equivalent, to the fuel pressure valve.
   d. Place bleed hose into a suitable container.
   e. Open valve and relieve fuel system pressure.
5. Remove fuel lines from rail and mounting bracket.
6. Remove coolant bottle and inner fender electrical cover.
7. Remove fuel injector sight cover.
8. Remove throttle cables, bracket and vacuum line from throttle body.
9. Remove heat shield from exhaust crossover pipe then then crossover pipe.

10. Remove engine torque strut from engine.
11. Remove the engine cooling fan.
12. Remove vacuum line from transaxle module.
13. Remove serpentine drive belt.
14. Remove power steering pump and alternator from engine.
15. Disconnect all necessary electrical connectors.
16. Remove upper and lower radiator and heater hoses from engine.
17. Remove transaxle to engine bolts and ground wire harness with bolt.
18. Raise and support vehicle.
19. Remove right tire and wheel assembly and inner splash shield.
20. Remove flywheel cover and scribe torque convertor to flywheel for installation.
21. Remove flywheel to convertor bolts.
22. Disconnect wire harness clamps from frame near radiator.
23. Remove A/C compressor and position aside.
24. Remove starter motor.
25. Remove transaxle to engine bolt through wheelwell using suitable extension.
26. Disconnect engine mount to frame nuts.
27. Remove oil filter.
28. Disconnect front exhaust pipe from manifold.
29. Disconnect oil cooler piper from hose connections.
30. Lower vehicle.
31. Install lifting device and remove engine assembly.
32. Reverse procedure to install, noting the following:

a. Align engine with transaxle dowel pins.
b. **Torque** torque strut bolts to 41 ft. lbs.
c. **Torque** flywheel to convertor bolts to 46 ft. lbs.

FUEL PUMP
REPLACE

1. Disconnect battery ground cable.
2. Relieve fuel system pressure as outlined under "Fuel System Pressure Relief."
3. Drain fuel tank, then remove fuel tank assembly.
4. Remove fuel sender assembly.
5. Reverse procedure to install.

FUEL FILTER
REPLACE

1. Relieve fuel system pressure as outlined under "Fuel System Pressure Relief."
2. Raise and support vehicle.
3. Remove bracket attaching screw and filter bracket, **Fig. 1.**
4. Grasp filter and fuel line fitting. Twist quick-connect fitting 1/4 turn in each direction to loosen any dirt within fitting.
5. Using compressed air, blow out dirt from quick-connect fitting.
6. Remove feed pipe nut from fuel filter, then drain any remaining fuel into a suitable container.
7. Remove fuel filter.
8. Reverse procedure to install.

Clutch & Manual Transaxle

INDEX

DESCRIPTION

The hydraulic system components (master cylinder and clutch actuator) **Fig. 1** can be serviced separately. If a component fails, that component may be replaced. The clutch hydraulic system is serviced as two major assemblies, the master cylinder and actuator assemblies. Each assembly has been bled of air and filled with brake fluid. Individual components of these assemblies are not available separately.

Whenever powertrain components are lowered for any reason (removal or access

to other components), the clutch actuator must be removed from the transaxle case. Refer to procedure outlined under "Clutch Actuator." **Failure to remove actuator may result in hydraulic system damage.**

Prior to any operation that requires removal of the actuator, the clutch master cylinder pushrod must be disconnected from the clutch pedal. **Failure to disconnect pushrod will result in permanent damage to the actuator if the clutch pedal is depressed without resistance from clutch loads.** Master cylinder pushrod bushing must also be replaced when-

ever it has been removed from the clutch pedal.

CLUTCH HYDRAULIC SYSTEM SERVICE

MASTER CYLINDER

1. Disconnect battery ground cable.
2. Remove sound insulator, then disconnect master cylinder pushrod from clutch pedal.
3. Remove two nuts attaching master cylinder reservoir to strut tower.

4. Remove anti-rotational screw located next to master cylinder flange at pedal support plate.
5. Using wrench flats on front end of master cylinder, twist master cylinder counterclockwise to release twist lock to plate attachment. **Do not twist hose connections on top of master cylinder body.**
6. Remove two nuts attaching clutch actuator to transaxle case, then the actuator from transaxle housing with pushrod attached forward out of pedal plate.
7. Pull master cylinder assembly. Lift reservoir off strut tower studs, then remove complete hydraulic assembly from vehicle.
8. Reverse procedure to install, noting the following:
   a. Install master cylinder into opening in pedal plate and rotate 45° by applying torque on wrench flats only.
   b. **Torque** anti-rotational screw to 18 inch lbs.
   c. **Torque** reservoir attaching nuts to 36 inch lbs.
   d. Install actuator on transaxle housing. Actuator pushrod busing and retaining straps should be left assembled. Actuator straps will break during normal operation. Pushrod bushing must enter pocket in internal fork housing as actuator is installed on housing studs.
   e. **Torque** actuator attaching nuts evenly to 18 ft. lbs.
   f. Install new bushing in master cylinder pushrod. Lubricate bushing prior to installation.
   g. Connect master cylinder pushrod to clutch pedal, with bushing tangs snapped into pedal pin groove.
   h. Press clutch pedal down several times, ensuring pedal effort is normal and firm.
   i. **On models equipped with cruise control,** adjust cruise control clutch switch. Refer to procedure outlined under "Cruise Control, Adjust" in the "Cruise Control" section.

ACTUATOR
Removal

Whenever powertrain components are lowered for any reason (removal or access to other components), the clutch actuator must be removed from the transaxle case. **Failure to remove actuator may result in hydraulic system damage.**
1. Disconnect battery ground cable.
2. Remove air cleaner assembly and sound insulator.
3. Disconnect master cylinder pushrod from clutch pedal, **Fig. 2.**
3. Disconnect hydraulic system at quick connect fitting using tool J-36221.
4. Remove two bolts holding canister bracket to transaxle.
5. Remove two actuator attaching nuts, then the actuator from transaxle housing.

1	CLUTCH RESERVOIR	6	ACTUATOR
2	MASTER CYLINDER	7	38 N·m (28 FT. LB.)
3	HYDRAULIC LINE — MUST NOT BE BENT OR DAMAGED	8	25 N·m (18 FT. LB.)
4	QUICK CONNECT FITTING	9	2 N·m (18 IN. LB.)
5	CANISTER	10	4 N·m (36 IN. LB.)
		11	SHOCK TOWER STUD

Fig. 1   Clutch hydraulic system.

1	PEDAL BRACKET
2	PEDAL BUSHING
3	PUSH ROD BUSHING
4	PUSH ROD
5	CLUTCH PEDAL
6	SPACER
7	PEDAL BRACKET BOSSES
8	31 N·m (23 FT. LB.)
9	PIVOT BOLT

Fig. 2   Clutch pedal assembly

Installation

1. Inspect actuator pushrod for lever bushing and replace if missing.
2. Install actuator on transaxle housing studs with pushrod centered in pocket of internal lever in housing. An axial load on pushrod may be required to compress actuator piston spring.
3. Install actuator attaching nuts, **Torquing** nuts evenly to 18 ft. lbs.
4. Install new bushing in master cylinder pushrod. Lubricate bushing prior to installation.
5. Connect master cylinder pushrod to clutch pedal, with bushing tangs snapped into pedal pin groove, **Figs. 2 & 3.**

6. Press clutch pedal down several times, ensuring pedal effort is normal and firm.
7. **On models equipped with cruise control,** adjust cruise control clutch switch. Refer to procedure outlined under "Cruise Control, Adjust."
8. Install sound insulator and air cleaner, then connect battery ground cable.

MASTER CYLINDER BLEED
Manual Method

During this procedure, fluid level in master cylinder must be maintained.

Use a maximum of 50 lbs. pedal pressure to check pedal firmness.

1. Disconnect quick connect fittings in clutch hydraulic line. Insert quick disconnect tool No. J-36221 or equivalent and depress white plastic sleeve to separate connection.
2. Remove cap and diaphragm, and fill reservoir with DOT 3 brake fluid.
3. Remove lefthand upper secondary cowl, then remove air from supply hose by squeezing it until no more air bubbles are seen in reservoir.
4. Pump clutch pedal slowly by hand until slight resistance is felt.
5. Holding pedal pressure, bleed air from system by depressing internal valve at quick connect fitting. **Do not use a sharp object.**
6. Repeat steps 4 and 5 until pedal is firm and no air bubbles are seen.
7. Reconnect clutch hydraulic line, then replace reservoir cap and diaphragm.

Pressure Method

During this procedure, fluid level in master cylinder must be maintained.

1. Disconnect quick connect fittings in clutch hydraulic line. Insert quick disconnect tool No. J-36221, or equivalent, and depress white plastic sleeve to separate connection.
2. Remove cap and diaphragm, and fill reservoir with DOT 3 brake fluid.
3. Install pressure bleed adapter cap No. J-36234 or equivalent to reservoir and connect pressure bleeder.
4. Apply pressure not to exceed 30 lbs., to hydraulic system.
5. Depress internal valve at quick connect fitting. **Do not use a sharp object.**
6. Release internal valve when air is no longer visible.
7. Open internal valve and slowly depress clutch pedal. **Close internal valve before releasing clutch pedal.**
8. Repeat this procedure until air is no longer visible.
9. Reconnect clutch hydraulic line, then replace reservoir cap and diaphragm.

CLUTCH
ADJUST

This clutch is equipped with a hydraulic slave cylinder (actuator) and there is no provision for adjustment.

A 3 TANGS ON BUSHING MUST BE IN GROOVE ON PIN
1 BUSHING
2 PIN

Fig. 3 Bushing tang engagement

CLUTCH
REPLACE
REMOVAL

Prior to any operation that requires removal of the actuator, the master cylinder pushrod must be disconnected from the clutch pedal. **Failure to disconnect pushrod will result in permanent damage to the actuator if the clutch pedal is depressed without resistance from clutch loads.** Master cylinder pushrod bushing must also be replaced whenever it has been removed from the clutch pedal.

1. Disconnect battery ground cable.
2. Remove sound insulator from inside vehicle, then disconnect clutch master cylinder pushrod from clutch pedal.
3. Disconnect quick connect fittings in clutch hydraulic line. Insert tool No. J-36221 or equivalent and depress white plastic sleeve to separate connection.
4. Remove actuator to transaxle attaching nuts, then the actuator.
5. Remove transaxle assembly. Refer to procedure outlined under "Transaxle, Replace."
6. Place alignment marks on clutch cover assembly and flywheel to ensure reassembly in same position.
7. Loosen attaching bolts one turn at a time, until spring pressure is relieved.
8. Support clutch cover, then remove bolts.
9. Remove clutch cover and driven disc.

INSTALLATION

1. Position clutch disc and clutch cover, matching light side of clutch cover (marked with paint) with heavy side of flywheel (stamped with an X). Stamped letters on clutch disc identify "flywheel side." Support clutch disc and clutch cover with clutch alignment arbor tool No. J-35822 or equivalent.
2. Install clutch cover to flywheel bolts in three holes marked "L," then install remaining clutch cover to flywheel bolts, remove tool and **Torque** bolts to 21 ft. lbs. in two steps on 1991 models and 15 ft. lbs. plus a 30° turn on 1992-94 models.
3. Lightly lubricate clutch fork ends which contact bearing and completely

pack I.D. recess of release bearing with suitable grease. Levers on clutch fork shaft must bear on large ears of release bearing. Levers fit between large ears and small tangs on bearing. Fork shaft must move freely with bearing in place.

4. Tie actuator lever through actuator hole to studs, holding release bearing in position.
5. Install transaxle assembly. **Clutch lever must not be moved toward flywheel until transaxle is bolted to engine.**
6. Align actuator and master cylinder quick connect fittings in hydraulic line and insert master cylinder fitting into actuator fitting until it locks in place.
7. **On all models,** remove tie from actuator lever.
8. Inspect actuator rod for lever bushing and replace if missing.
9. Install actuator on housing studs with pushrod bushing centered in pocket of internal lever in housing. It may require an axial load on the pushrod to compress the actuator piston spring.
10. Install actuator retaining nuts, **Torquing** evenly to 18 ft. lbs.
11. Install new bushing in master cylinder pushrod, lubricating before installation.
12. Connect master cylinder pushrod to clutch pedal, with bushing tangs snapped into pedal pin groove.
13. Depress clutch pedal several times, ensuring effort is normal and firm.
14. Readjust cruise control, if necessary, by pulling upward on clutch pedal with a force of not more than 20 lbs.
15. Install sound insulator and connect battery ground cable.

TRANSAXLE
REPLACE

On 1994 models equipped with airbags, disable airbag system prior to performing service operation as possible airbag deployment may cause personal injury.

Prior to any operation that requires removal of the actuator, the master cylinder pushrod must be disconnected from the clutch pedal. **Failure to disconnect pushrod will result in permanent damage to the actuator if the clutch pedal is depressed without resistance from clutch loads.** Master cylinder pushrod bushing must also be replaced whenever it has been removed from the clutch pedal.

1. Disconnect battery ground cable.
2. Install engine support fixture tool No. J-28467-A, or equivalent, together with support leg tool No. J-36462 or equivalent.
3. Remove air cleaner housing and air intake tube.
4. Remove clutch actuator from transaxle. Refer to procedure outlined under "Clutch Hydraulic System, Service."
5. Disconnect electrical connector at speedometer driven gear sensor.
6. Remove nut and retaining clamp securing shift and select cables to transaxle.
7. Remove two nuts from cable ball

8. Disconnect exhaust crossover pipe at left exhaust manifold.

9. Disconnect EGR tube from crossover pipe.

10. Remove crossover to exhaust pipe connecting bolts.

11. Loosen crossover to right exhaust manifold clamp.

12. Swing crossover upward to gain access to top transaxle bolts.

13. Remove two upper transaxle mounting bolts and two upper transaxle mounting studs, leaving one lower mounting bolt and one lower mounting stud attached.

14. Disconnect electrical connector at back-up lamp switch.

15. Raise and support vehicle, then remove drain plug to drain transaxle fluid.

16. Remove four clutch housing cover retaining screws.

17. Remove both front tire and wheel assemblies, then the left and right wheelhouse splash shields.

18. Disconnect power steering cooler lines from frame, then remove power steering rack and pinion heat shield.

19. Disconnect power steering rack and pinion at frame.

20. Disconnect ball joints at steering knuckle.

21. Remove transaxle mount upper retaining bolts, then the engine mount lower retaining nuts.

22. Remove subframe retaining bolts from body, then remove subframe from vehicle.

23. Remove drive axles from transaxle and support from body.

24. Detach starter assembly and support from body.

25. Securely attach transaxle to suitable jack, then remove remaining transaxle mounting bolt and stud and remove transaxle.

26. Reverse procedure to install, noting the following:

   a. **Torque** transaxle to engine attaching bolts and studs to 55 ft. lbs.

   b. Using frame or lower control arm for leverage, seat drive axle into transaxle, using screwdriver/pry bar at groove provided on inner joint.

   c. Verify that axle snap ring is seated by tapping on inner groove with screwdriver. Also, grasp inner housing and pull outboard. **Do not pull on axle shaft.** If snap ring is seated, axle will remain in place.

   d. After positioning frame with body mount bolts installed but not tightened, align frame to body by inserting two 19 mm (.74 inch) diameter by 203 mm (8 inch) long pins in alignment holes on right side of frame, then **Torque** body mount bolts to 100 ft. lbs. **Alignment pins must not be removed until all body mount bolts are torqued to specification. Alignment pins must be kept perpendicular to frame. Right side body mounts (nearest alignment pins) should be tightened first to maintain correct front wheel alignment.**

   e. **Torque** clutch housing cover retaining screws to 115 inch lbs.

TIGHTENING SPECIFICATIONS

Year	Component	Torque/ Ft. Lbs.
1991–94	**Back-Up Lamp Switch**	25
	Cable Ball Stud Nut	18
	Cable Retaining Clamp Nut	89①
	Clutch Actuator Nut	18
	Clutch Canister Bracket Bolts	28
	Clutch Cover To Flywheel	②
	Clutch Fluid Reservoir Nut	36①
	Clutch Housing Cover Screw	116①
	Clutch Master Cylinder Anti-Rotation Screw	18①
	Clutch Pedal Pivot Nut	23

Year	Component	Torque/ Ft. Lbs.
1991–94 —Cont'd	**Control Assembly Bolt**	18
	Flywheel To Crankshaft Bolt	③
	Shift Lever Nut	61
	Shift Linkage Bracket Bolt	17
	Speedometer Signal Assembly Bolt	80①
	Transaxle Mount To Frame Nut	42
	Transaxle Mount To Transaxle Bolt	35
	Transaxle Mounting Bolt	55

①—Inch lbs.
②—1991 models, 21 ft. lbs.; 1992–94 models, 15 ft. lbs. plus 30°.
③—1991 models, 52 ft. lbs.; 1992–94 models, 61 ft. lbs.

Rear Axle & Suspension

INDEX

DESCRIPTION

These vehicles use a tri-link independent rear suspension system with a transverse leaf spring and tubular struts with large lateral links attached to the body crossmember. The three mounting points are the crossmember, strut tower and trailing arm. The crossmember is stamped steel and the composite fiberglass mono leaf spring is transversely mounted to the under side of the crossmember, with its padded ends free riding on the cast knuckle assembly.

REAR HUB & BEARING ASSEMBLY REPLACE

The rear hub and bearing assembly is

2	BOLT 46 N•m (34 lbs. ft.)
3	REAR STRUT
4	KNUCKLE ASSEMBLY
17	AUXILIARY SPRING ASSEMBLY
20	BOLT
28	NUT 180 N•m (133 lbs. ft.)
109	BRACKET-STABILIZER SHAFT

Fig. 1 Auxiliary spring replacement

1	STABILIZER SHAFT	4	TRAILING ARM
2	CALIPER ASSEMBLY	5	SPINDLE ROD (REAR)
3	90 N•m +90° (66 LB. FT.) -90°	6	AUXILIARY SPRING

Fig. 2 Compressing auxiliary spring

not serviceable. If the hub and/or bearing is damaged, the complete assembly must be replaced.

1. Raise and support vehicle, then remove tire and wheel assembly.
2. Remove brake caliper, leaving hose attached, and suspend out of way.
3. Remove brake rotor.
4. Disconnect anti-lock brake system electrical harness connector, if equipped.
5. Remove hub and bearing assembly mounting bolts, then the assembly.
6. Reverse procedure to install, torquing hub and bearing assembly mounting bolts to specifications.

AUXILIARY SPRING ASSEMBLY
REPLACE

1. Raise and support vehicle, then remove wheel and tire assembly.
2. Remove leaf spring rear retention plate bolt.
3. Remove leaf spring retention bolt only enough to rotate plate clear of rod.
4. Install rear auxiliary spring compressor tool No. J-37956 or equivalent ensuring pin in stationary end of clamp is inserted in hole of upper auxiliary spring bracket, **Figs 1 and 2.**
5. Remove plug from upper bracket, then seat rod in tool channel and hand tighten.
6. Remove rod-to-knuckle bolt, then loosen tool forcing screw to allow spring to expand.
7. Remove auxiliary spring attaching bolts, then the spring and tool. **When removing auxiliary spring, ensure rod/bushing clears transverse spring and boss on knuckle.**
8. Reverse procedure to install, noting the following:
   a. Compress auxiliary spring with spring compressor tool enough to install rod-to-knuckle bolt.

J 35778

Fig. 3 Removing transverse spring assembly

   b. Install rod-to-knuckle bolt, using Loctite or equivalent. Torque to specifications.
   c. Properly position leaf spring retention plate, install bolt and torque to specifications.

TRANSVERSE SPRING ASSEMBLY
REPLACE

Do not use corrosive cleaning agents, engine degreaser or solvents on or near the fiberglass leaf spring.

1. Raise and support vehicle.
2. Remove three jack pad attaching bolts and the pad.
3. Remove left and right spring retention plate attaching bolts.
4. Remove right side trailing link to knuckle attaching nut and bolt.
5. Disconnect anti-lock brake system electrical harness connector, if equipped.
6. Assemble rear spring leaf spring compressor tool No. J-35778 or equivalent to transverse spring.
7. Loosen tool handle to base of tool shank.
8. Hang center shank of tool at spring center. It is not necessary to separate

tool body and shank. **Attach from front side of vehicle only.**
9. Attach tool body to spring. **Always center spring on roller of tool.**
10. Fully compress spring, then slide spring to left side. It may be necessary to pry the spring, using a screwdriver/pry bar, to the opposite side, using the wheel for leverage.
11. Relax the spring until removal clearance is achieved, then remove spring, **Fig. 3.**
12. Reverse procedure to install, noting the following:
   a. Torque trailing link to knuckle attaching bolt to specifications.
   b. Torque spring retention plate mounting bolts to specifications. **Rear spring retention plates are designed with tabs on one end. Tabs must be aligned with support assembly.**
   c. Torque jack pad mounting bolts to specifications.

STABILIZER SHAFT ASSEMBLY
REPLACE

1. Raise and support vehicle, then remove rear wheel and tire assemblies.
2. Remove right and lefthand stabilizer shaft link bolts, then open brackets to remove insulator.
3. Remove right and lefthand strut to knuckle to stabilizer shaft nuts, **Fig. 4. Do not remove strut to knuckle bolts.**
4. Remove insulator brackets from bolts and from stabilizer shaft, then the stabilizer shaft.
5. Reverse procedure to install, noting the following:
   a. It may be necessary to pry stabilizer shaft to one side for installation clearance at strut. Use caution when prying.
   b. Torquing stabilizer shaft link bolts

1 BODY
99 NUT 25 N•m (18 lbs. ft.)
101 NUT
102 BRACKET-STABILIZER SHAFT
103 BOLT 25 N•m (18 lbs. ft.)
104 BOLT-STABILIZER SHAFT LINK
105 BOLT 50 N•m (57 lbs. ft.)
106 LINK—STABILIZER SHAFT
107 INSULATOR
108 STABILIZER SHAFT

Fig. 4 Stabilizer shaft assembly replacement

and strut to knuckle bolts to specifications.

TRI-LINK SUSPENSION ASSEMBLY REPLACE

TRAILING LINK

1. Raise and support vehicle.
2. Disconnect anti-lock brake system electrical harness connector, if equipped.
3. Remove trailing link to knuckle attaching nut and bolt, then the trailing link to body attaching nut and bolt, **Figs. 5 and 6.**
4. Remove trailing link.
5. Reverse procedure to install, torquing trailing link to body nut and trailing link to knuckle nut to specifications.

FRONT LATERAL LINK

1. Raise and support vehicle, then remove tire and wheel assembly.
2. Remove rod to knuckle bolt, then the exhaust pipe heat shield.
3. Lower to fuel tank to gain access.
4. Remove lateral link to knuckle attaching bolt.
5. Remove lateral link to suspension crossmember attaching nut and bolt, then the lateral link.
6. Reverse procedure to install, **Torquing** lateral link to suspension crossmember nut to 140 ft. lbs. and the lateral link to knuckle attaching bolt to 157 ft. lbs.

REAR LATERAL LINK

1. Raise and support vehicle, then remove tire and wheel assembly.
2. Remove transverse spring as previously outlined.
3. Remove lower auxiliary spring bracket from rod.
4. Remove rear lateral link attaching nut from crossmember.
5. Push bolt forward enough to provide

3 REAR STRUT
4 KNUCKLE ASSEMBLY
8 TRAILING ARM
12 FRONT LATERAL LINK
13 REAR LATERAL LINK
17 AUXILIARY SPRING
20 BOLT
21 BOLT 213 N•m (157 lbs. ft.)
22 WASHER
23 WASHER
24 BOLT 213 N•m (157 lbs. ft.)
25 BOLT
26 WASHER
27 NUT 260 N•m (192 lbs ft.)
28 NUT 180 N•m (133 lbs. ft.)
108 STABILIZER SHAFT
109 BRACKET-STABILIZER SHAFT
110 INSULATOR

Fig. 5 Exploded view of tri-link suspension assembly

clearance for link removal, then remove rear lateral link.
6. Reverse procedure to install, **Torquing** lateral link to crossmember attaching nut to 157 ft. lbs. and the rear lateral link to knuckle attaching bolt to 140 ft. lbs.

KNUCKLE ASSEMBLY REPLACE

The following procedure has been added by technical service bulletin No. 89-3-23.
1. Raise and support vehicle, then remove tire and wheel assembly.
2. Place scribe marks on strut and knuckle to ensure installation in same position.
3. Remove jack pad.
4. Install rear leaf spring compressor tool No. J-35778 or equivalent onto

transverse spring assembly and tighten to hold spring pressure. **Do not remove spring or retention plates.**
5. Remove auxiliary spring as previously outlined.
6. Disconnect front link from knuckle.
7. Remove brake caliper, leaving hose attached, and suspend caliper out of way.
8. Remove brake rotor, then the hub and bearing assembly as previously described.
9. Disconnect anti-lock brake system electrical harness connector, if equipped.
10. Remove hub and bearing assembly.
11. Disconnect trailing link from knuckle, **Fig. 5.**
12. Remove strut to knuckle attaching nuts, then the stabilizer shaft bracket.
13. Remove strut to knuckle attaching bolts, then the knuckle.
14. Reverse procedure to install, torquing strut to knuckle attaching bolts and trailing link retaining nut to specifications.

STRUT ASSEMBLY
REPLACE

The following procedure has been modified by technical service bulletin No. 89-3-23.
1. Remove upper strut mount cover from inside rear compartment, then raise and support vehicle and remove tire and wheel assembly.
2. Place scribe marks on strut and knuckle to ensure installation in same position.
3. Remove jack pad.
4. Install rear leaf spring compressor tool No. J-35778 or equivalent onto

transverse spring assembly and tighten to hold spring pressure. **Do not remove spring or retention plates.**
5. Remove auxiliary spring as previously outlined.
6. Remove brake hose bracket at strut.
7. Remove upper strut attaching bolts at body and allow assembly to drop down.
8. Remove stabilizer shaft bracket by removing strut to knuckle attaching nuts.
9. Remove strut to knuckle attaching bolts, then the strut assembly.
10. Reverse procedure to install, torquing upper strut attaching bolts to specifications.

4 KNUCKLE ASSEMBLY
8 TRAILING LINK
9 65 N•m (48 lbs. ft.)
10 BOLT
25 BOLT
26 WASHER
27 NUT 260 N•m (192 lbs ft.)

Fig. 6 Exploded view of trailing link

TIGHTENING SPECIFICATIONS

Year	Component	Torque/Ft. Lbs.	Year	Component	Torque/Ft. Lbs.
1991–94	Caliper Bleeder Valve	62①	1991–94 —Cont'd	Strut To Knuckle Nut	133
	Front Caliper Mounting Bolt	79		Suspension Crossmember To Body Bolt	85
	Front Caliper Mounting Bracket To Knuckle	148		Trailing Arm To Knuckle	192
	Jack Pad Bolt	18		Trailing Link To Body Nut	48
	Proportioning Valve Caps	20		Upper Strut Bolt	34
	Rear Caliper Mounting Bolt	92		Wheel/Hub/Bearing To Knuckle Bolt	52
	Rod To Knuckle	66②		Wheel Lug Nuts	100
	Rod To Support Crossmember	81③			
	Spring Retention Plate Bolt	15			
	Stabilizer Shaft Link Bolt	40			
	Stabilizer Shaft Link To Body Bracket Nut	18			

① —Inch lbs.
② —Turn an additional 90° after reaching specified torque.
③ —Turn an additional 60° after reaching specified torque.

Front Suspension & Steering

INDEX

DESCRIPTION

The front suspension system on these vehicles is of the MacPherson strut design. This design incorporates MacPherson struts with coil springs and a one piece configuration with lower control arms. The use of tapered top coil springs on top of the struts provides a well controlled ride and allows a lower hood profile.

STRUT CARTRIDGE
REPLACE

Do not service strut unless weight of vehicle is on suspension.

REMOVAL

1. Scribe alignment marks on cover plate, remove cover plate retaining

nuts, then the cover plate.
2. Using No. 50 Torx bit and strut rod remover/installer tool No. J-35669, or equivalents, remove strut shaft.
3. Remove strut mount bushing by prying with suitable tool.
4. Using strut mount plate wrench tool No. J-35670 or equivalent, remove jounce bumper retainer.
5. Attach strut extension rod tool No. J-35668 or equivalent to strut shaft

and compress shaft down into cartridge, then remove tool and pull out jounce bumper.

6. Attach strut extension rod tool No. J-35668 or equivalent to strut shaft and extend shaft, then remove tool and, using strut cap nut wrench tool No. J-35671 or equivalent, unscrew closure nut.
7. Remove strut cartridge.
8. Remove oil from strut tube using suction device.

INSTALLATION

1. Using strut cap nut wrench tool No. J-35671 or equivalent, install self contained replacement cartridge.
2. Install jounce bumper, then using strut mount plate wrench tool No. J-35670 or equivalent, the jounce bumper retainer.
3. Install strut mount bushing. If necessary, use strut extension rod tool No. J-35668 or equivalent after bushing is partially installed and position strut shaft as required. Lubricate bushing with a soap solution to ease installation.
4. Using No. 50 Torx bit and strut rod remover/installer tool No. J-35669, or equivalents, install strut shaft nut, torquing to specifications.
5. Install strut mount cover, aligning scribe marks. Torque cover plate nuts to specifications.

HUB & BEARING ASSEMBLY REPLACE

1. Remove wheel cover, then loosen drive axle shaft nut and washer one turn. **Do not remove nut at this time. Failure to follow proper removal sequence may cause bearing damage.**
2. Raise and support vehicle, then remove wheel and tire assembly.
3. Remove brake caliper and bracket assembly, then the brake rotor, **Fig. 1.**
4. Remove drive axle shaft nut and washer.
5. Loosen hub and bearing assembly to knuckle attaching bolts.
6. Using front hub spindle remover tool No. J-28733-A or equivalent, push axle splines back out of hub and bearing assembly.
7. Remove hub and bearing assembly to knuckle attaching bolts.
8. **On models with anti-lock brakes (ABS),** remove ABS sensor mounting bolt and position sensor aside.
9. **On all models,** remove hub and bearing assembly. **Protect axle boots from damage during handling.**
10. Reverse procedure to install, **Torquing** all bolts to specifications.

17	KNUCKLE/STRUT ASSEMBLY
101	70 N·m 52 LB. FT.)
102	HUB/BEARING ASSEMBLY
103	ROTOR
104	CALIPER AND BRACKET ASSEMBLY
105	DRIVE AXLE
106	WASHER
107	250 N·m (184 LB. FT.)

Fig. 1   Removing hub & bearing assembly

21	WELD NUTS
22	LOWER CONTROL ARM
25	FRAME
26	CLAMP BOLT
27	CLAMP
28	INSULATOR
29	STABILIZER SHAFT
30	BOLT 47 N·m (35 lbs. ft.)
31	CLAMP
32	INSULATOR
34	NUT 47 N·m (35 lbs. ft.)

Fig. 2   Replacing stabilizer shaft & insulators

STABILIZER SHAFT & INSULATORS REPLACE

1. Raise and support vehicle, then remove wheel and tire assembly.
2. Move steering shaft dust shield to gain access to pinch bolt.
3. Remove pinch bolt from lower intermediate steering shaft.
4. Loosen all insulator clamp attaching nuts and bolts, **Fig. 2.**
5. Place suitable jack under center of rear frame crossmember.
6. Loosen two front frame to body bolts four turns.
7. Remove two rear frame to body bolts.
8. Lower rear of frame just enough to gain access for stabilizer shaft removal.
9. Remove insulators and clamps from frame and control arms.
10. Pull stabilizer shaft rearward, swing down and remove from left side of vehicle.
11. Reverse procedure to install, noting the following:
    a. Coat new insulators with rubber lu-

1. COVER PLATE NUT
2. COVER PLATE
3. SHOCK TOWER
4. STRUT SHAFT NUT
6. JOUNCE BUMPER RETAINER
7. STRUT MOUNT
8. JOUNCE BUMPER
9. SPRING INSULATOR
10. DUST SHIELD
11. SPRING
12. SPRING INSULATOR
13. SPRING SEAT AND BEARING
15. CLOSURE NUT
17. KNUCKLE STRUT ASSEMBLY
18. BALL JOINT

**Fig. 3   Cross-sectional view of
strut & knuckle assembly**

bricant.
b. Torque clamp to frame nuts and clamp to lower control arm bolts to specifications.
c. **Torque** frame attaching bolts to 100 ft. lbs.
d. **Torque** pinch bolt to specifications.
e. **Torque** lug nuts to 100 ft. lbs.

STRUT & KNUCKLE ASSEMBLY SERVICE

REMOVAL

1. Disconnect battery ground cable.
2. Scribe alignment marks on cover plate, then loosen three cover plate retaining nuts.
3. Raise and support vehicle, then remove wheel and tire assembly.
4. Remove brake caliper and bracket assembly, leaving hose attached, and support caliper out of way.
5. Remove brake rotor, then the hub and bearing to knuckle attaching bolts.

6. **On models with anti-lock brakes (ABS),** remove ABS sensor mounting bolt and position sensor aside.
7. **On all models,** separate axle from transaxle and carefully remove drive axle assembly.
8. Remove tie rod to knuckle attaching nut.
9. Using tie rod puller/ball joint remover tool No. J-35917 or equivalent, separate tie rod from knuckle.
10. Remove lower ball joint to knuckle attaching nut.
11. Using tool No. J-35917 or equivalent, separate ball joint from lower control arm.
12. Remove ball joint heat shield, then the cover plate retaining nuts.
13. Remove strut and knuckle assembly.

SERVICE

Springs are under high tension. Do not remove strut shaft nut without using a suitable spring compressing tool.
1. Mount strut and knuckle assembly into strut spring compressor tool No. J-34013-A and strut compressor adapter tool No. J-34013-88, or equivalents, then compress spring with compressor forcing screw just enough to release tension from upper spring insulator.
2. Using Torx bit and strut rod nut remover/installer tool No. J-35669, or equivalents, remove strut shaft nut.
3. Relieve all spring tension, then remove spring and strut components, **Fig. 3.**
4. Install spring seat and bearing.
5. Install lower spring insulator. Lower spring coil end must be visible between the step and the first retention tab of insulator.
6. Install front suspension spring.
7. Install dust shield to lower spring seat.
8. Install jounce bumper.
9. Install upper spring insulator. Upper spring coil end must be between step and location mark on insulator.
10. Using strut mount plate wrench tool No. J-35670 or equivalent, install jounce bumper retainer to strut mount.
11. Install strut mount and upper strut mount bushing.
12. Using strut spring compressor and strut compressor adapter tools Nos. J-34013-A and J-34013-88, or equivalents, compress strut assembly.
13. Align strut cartridge shaft with strut extension rod tool No. J-35668 or equivalent.
14. Using strut rod nut remover/installer tool No. J-35669 or equivalent and Torx bit, install strut shaft nut, torquing to specifications.

INSTALLATION

1. Install strut mount cover plate and upper strut mount to body attaching nuts. Do not tighten nuts until vehicle is lowered to floor.
2. Install ball joint heat shield.
3. Install lower ball joint to control arm attaching nut, **Torquing** to 15 ft. lbs., then tighten an addition 90°.

J 21474-8 (TO REMOVE LARGE BUSHING)
J 21474-23 (TO REMOVE SMALL BUSHING)
J 21474-18   BEARING   J 21474-5
J 21474-19
J 37267

REMOVE LOWER CONTROL ARM BUSHING

J 21474-19   J 21474-5   J 21474-13
J 21474-18
BEARING
J 37267

INSTALL LOWER CONTROL ARM BUSHING

**Fig. 4   Replacing lower
control arm bushings**

4. Further tighten to next slot in nut with cotter pin hole in stud and install new cotter pin. **Do not tighten more than an additional 60° to align with hole and do not loosen nut at any time during installation.**
5. Install tie rod to knuckle attaching nut, torquing to specifications, and install cotter pin.
6. Carefully install drive axle assembly through opening in knuckle and insert drive axle into transaxle.
7. Install hub and bearing to knuckle attaching bolts, torquing to specifications.
8. **On models with anti-lock brakes (ABS),** position ABS sensor and install mounting bolt.
9. **On all models,** install brake rotor, then the brake caliper and bracket assembly.
10. Install wheel and tire assembly and lower vehicle.
11. **Torque** lug nuts to 100 ft. lbs. and the cover plate nuts to specifications.
12. Connect battery ground cable.

LOWER CONTROL ARM
REPLACE

1. Raise and support vehicle, then remove wheel and tire assembly.
2. **On 3.4L engine models,** Remove engine splash shields.
3. **On all models,** remove stabilizer shaft to lower control arm insulator bracket bolts.
4. Remove lower ball joint cotter pin and nut, then, using tie rod puller/ball joint remover tool No. J-35917 or equivalent, separate ball joint from lower control arm.
5. Remove lower control arm to frame attaching nuts and bolts, then the lower control arms.
6. If bushing replacement is necessary, refer to **Fig. 4.** Coat threads of control arm bushing service tool set No. J-21474-19 or equivalent with an ex-

treme pressure lubricant. To facilitate installation, coat outer casing of bushing with suitable lubricant.

7. Reverse procedure to install, noting the following:
   a. Lower control arm to frame bolts must be installed as shown, **Fig. 5.**
   b. Torque lower control arm to frame bolts to specifications.
   c. **Torque** lower ball joint nut 15 ft. lbs. and tighten an additional 90°, then further tighten to align next slot in nut with cotter pin hole in stud. **Do not tighten more than 60° to align with hole and do not loosen nut at any time during installation.**
   d. Torque stabilizer shaft bolts to specifications.
   e. **Torque** lug nuts to 100 ft. lbs.

22	LOWER CONTROL ARM
24	70 N·m (52 LB. FT.)
25	FRAME ASSEMBLY
33	BOLT

Fig. 5 Installing lower control arm

STEERING GEAR REPLACE

On 1994 models equipped with airbags, disable airbag system prior to performing service operation as possible airbag deployment may cause personal injury.

2.2L, 2.5L, 3.1L & 3800 ENGINES

1. Remove air cleaner, then raise and support vehicle. **Provide additional support at rear of vehicle.**
2. Remove front wheel and tire assemblies.
3. Remove intermediate shaft lower pinch bolt at steering gear.
4. Remove intermediate shaft from stub shaft. **Failure to disconnect intermediate shaft from rack and pinion shaft stub may result in damage to steering gear and/or intermediate shaft. This damage can cause loss of steering control.**
5. Disconnect electrical connector at switch.
6. Using tie rod puller/ball joint remover tool No. J-35917 or equivalent, disconnect tie rod ends from knuckle and strut assembly.
7. Support body with suitable stands, then remove rear frame mounting bolts and lower rear frame no more than five inches. **Do not lower rear of frame too far. Damage to engine components nearest to cowl may result.**
8. Remove heat shield, then the pipe retaining clip from steering gear.
9. Disconnect inlet pipes and outlet line from power steering gear.
10. Remove remaining brackets and clips.
11. Remove rack and pinion mounting nuts and bolts, then the rack and pinion assembly through the left wheel opening.
12. Reverse procedure to install, noting the following:
    a. Torque rack and pinion mounting bolts to specifications.
    b. Replace O-rings as necessary.
    c. Torque power steering line fitting to specifications.

d. Torque heat shield attaching screws to specifications.
e. **Torque** rear frame attaching bolts to 100 ft. lbs.
f. Torque tie rod end castle nuts to specifications.
g. Torque intermediate shaft lower pinch bolt to specifications.
13. After completing installation, bleed power steering system as follows:
    a. Turn wheels all the way to left.
    b. Add power steering to Cold mark on fluid level indicator.
    c. Start engine and run at fast idle, then add fluid, if necessary, to bring level to Cold mark.
    d. Bleed system by turning wheels from side to side without hitting stops. Keep fluid level at Cold mark.
    e. Return wheels to center position and continue running engine for 2-3 minutes.
    f. Road test vehicle to ensure steering functions normally and is free of noise.
    g. Check fluid level and ensure level is at Hot mark after system has stabilized at its normal operating temperature.

3.4L ENGINE

1. Remove air cleaner and duct assembly.
2. Install engine support tools J-28467-A, J-28467-90 and J-36462 or equivalents.
3. Raise and support vehicle, then remove both front wheel and tire assemblies.
4. Loosen right side engine splash shield.
5. Disconnect both left and right tie rods from steering knuckles.
6. Remove intermediate shaft from stub shaft. **Failure to disconnect intermediate shaft from rack and pinion shaft stub may result in damage to steering gear and/or intermediate shaft. This damage can cause loss of steering control.**

7. Disconnect electrical connector at pressure switch.
8. Remove exhaust pipe and catalytic converter assembly.
9. Support frame at center rear using jack stands.
10. Remove frame retaining bolts, then lower frame three inches.
11. Remove power steering gear heat shield.
12. Remove power steering line clamp at steering gear.
13. Remove both power steering gear mounting bolts, then disconnect pressure and return lines at steering gear.
14. Remove steering gear through left wheel opening.
15. Replace stub shaft seals.
16. Reverse procedure to install, noting the following:
    a. Torque rack and pinion mounting bolts to specifications.
    b. Replace O-rings as necessary.
    c. Torque power steering line fitting to specifications.
    d. Torque heat shield attaching screws to specifications.
    e. **Torque** rear frame attaching bolts to 100 ft. lbs.
    f. Torque tie rod end castle nuts to specifications.
    g. Torque intermediate shaft lower pinch bolt to specifications.
17. After completing installation, bleed power steering system as follows:
    a. Turn wheels all the way to left.
    b. Add power steering to Cold mark on fluid level indicator.
    c. Start engine and run at fast idle, then add fluid, if necessary, to bring level to Cold mark.
    d. Bleed system by turning wheels from side to side without hitting stops. Keep fluid level at Cold mark.
    e. Return wheels to center position and continue running engine for 2-3 minutes.
    f. Road test vehicle to ensure steering functions normally and is free of noise.
    g. Check fluid level and ensure level is at Hot mark after system has stabilized at its normal operating temperature.

POWER STEERING PUMP REPLACE

On 1994 models equipped with airbags, disable airbag system prior to performing service operation as possible airbag deployment may cause personal injury.

1. Disconnect battery ground cable.
2. Disconnect inlet and outlet hoses from pump.
3. Remove serpentine belt guard as necessary.
4. Remove belt from pulley, using 1/2 inch breaker bar.
5. Remove coolant recovery bottle as necessary.
6. Remove pump assembly.
7. Transfer pulley as necessary.
8. Reverse procedure to install, them bleed power steering system as follows:
   a. Turn wheels all the way to left.
   b. Add power steering to Cold mark on fluid level indicator.
   c. Start engine and run at fast idle, then add fluid, if necessary, to bring level to Cold mark.
   d. Bleed system by turning wheels from side to side without hitting stops. Keep fluid level at Cold mark.
   e. Return wheels to center position and continue running engine for 2-3 minutes.
   f. Road test vehicle to ensure steering functions normally and is free of noise.
   g. Check fluid level and ensure level is at Hot mark after system has stabilized at its normal operating temperature.

TIGHTENING SPECIFICATIONS

Year	Component	Torque/ Ft. Lbs.
1991–94	Adjuster Plug Locknut	50
	Ball Joint Heat Shield Retaining Nuts	54①
	Cylinder End Fittings	20
	Drive Axle Nut	184
	Engine Torque Strut Bracket Bolt	40
	Front Bracket To Engine Bolt	67
	Front Strut Closure Nut	82
	Front Strut Piston Shaft Nut	72
	Front Wheel Hub/Bearing To Knuckle Bolts	52
	Heat Shield Screws	54①
	Idle Speed Power Steering Pressure Switch	116①
	Inner Tie Rod To Rack	70
	Intermediate Shaft Pinch Bolt	35
	Lower Ball Joint Nut	②
	Lower Control Arm To Frame Bolts	56
	Pinion Locknut	26
	Pinion Preload	16①③

Year	Component	Torque/ Ft. Lbs.
1991–94	Power Steering Cooler Pipe Retaining Screw	71①
	Pump Mounting Bolt	21
	Pump To Front Or Rear Bracket Bolt	19
	Rack And Pinion Fittings	20
	Rack And Pinion Mounting Bolts	59
	Stabilizer Bar Insulator Clamp To Frame Nuts	35
	Stabilizer Bar Insulator Clamp To Lower Control Arm Bolt	39
	Strut Mount Cover Plate Nuts	18
	Tie Rod End Jam Nut	50
	Tie Rod End Nuts	40
	Union Fitting To Hydraulic Pump Housing	55
	Valve End Fittings	12
	Wheel Lug Nuts	100

①—Inch lbs.
②—Refer to text.
③—Maximum.

Wheel Alignment

INDEX

PRELIMINARY CHECK

1. Ensure tires are inflated to correct pressure, and check for uneven wear.
2. Check front wheel bearings and related suspension components for damage and replace as necessary, to eliminate improper alignment due to faulty components.
3. Check ball joints and tie rods.
4. Check vehicle trim heights.
5. Check steering gear for looseness at frame.
6. Check struts for improper operation.
7. Check for loose control arms.
8. Check for loose or missing stabilizer shaft attachments.

ADJUSTMENTS

When adjusting wheel alignment, always adjust both front and rear alignment, proceeding in the following order.
1. Rear wheel camber
2. Rear wheel toe and tracking
3. Front wheel camber and toe.

CAMBER

FRONT

1. Open hood and remove three strut cover plate nuts and the cover plate.
2. Lift front of vehicle just to the point that strut stud clears strut tower and cover top of strut. **Do not over extend drive axle. Do not lift by suspension.**
3. Use strut alignment templet tool No. J-36892 or equivalent to mark holes, then file three holes. File inboard or outboard of existing hole depending or camber requirement. Do not file more than .2 inch in either direction. **Paint exposed metal with red oxide primer and, after primer has dried, paint area with paint matching body color.**
4. Lower front of vehicle and guide strut studs into slotted holes.
5. Install three strut cover plate nuts.
6. Set camber to specifications by moving strut, then **Torque** strut cover plate nuts to 17 ft. lbs.

REAR

Refer to **Fig. 1** when adjusting rear wheel alignment.
1. Raise and support vehicle.
2. Remove tire and wheel assembly.
3. Remove auxiliary spring as outlined under "Auxiliary Spring Assembly, Replace."

CHECK AND SET ALIGNMENT WITH A FULL FUEL TANK.

VEHICLE MUST BE JOUNCED 3 TIMES BEFORE CHECKING ALIGNMENT TO ELIMINATE FALSE READINGS

FRONT AND REAR SUSPENSION ARE HELD TO DIMENSIONS INDICATED IN "TRIM HEIGHTS" SEE SECTION 3.

TOE LEFT AND RIGHT SIDE TO BE SET SEPARATELY PER WHEEL TO ACHIEVE SPECIFIED TOTAL TOE AND THRUST ANGLE.

(A) TOTAL TOE.

Fig. 1 Checking & adjusting rear alignment

Fig. 2 Ride height measurement location

MODEL		Z	D	J	K
SUSP	TIRE SIZE	CURB	CURB	CURB	CURB
FE1 (A)	P195-75-R14	84 mm (3.31 in.)	104 mm (4.09 in.)	249 mm (9.80 in.)	249 mm (9.80 in.)
FE1 (E)	P195-75-R14	85 mm (3.35 in.)	105 mm (4.13 in.)	249 mm (9.80 in.)	249 mm (9.80 in.)
FE1 (A)	P205-70-R15	72 mm (2.83 in.)	93 mm (3.66 in.)	249 mm (9.80 in.)	249 mm (9.80 in.)
FE1 (E)	P205-70-R15	73 mm (2.87 in.)	93 mm (3.66 in.)	249 mm (9.80 in.)	249 mm (9.80 in.)
FE3 (A)	P215-65-R15	74 mm (2.91 in.)	95 mm (3.70 in.)	249 mm (9.80 in.)	249 mm (9.80 in.)
FE3 (D)	P215-65-R15	75 mm (2.95 in.)	96 mm (3.78 in.)	249 mm (9.80 in.)	249 mm (9.80 in.)
FE3 (E)	P215-65-R15	75 mm (2.95 in.)	95 mm (3.70 in.)	249 mm (9.80 in.)	249 mm (9.80 in.)
FE3 (C, B and F)	P225-60-R16	67 mm (2.64 in.)	87 mm (3.43 in.)	249 mm (9.80 in.)	249 mm (9.80 in.)
FE3 (D and G)	P225-60-R16	67 mm (2.64 in.)	88 mm (3.46 in.)	249 mm (9.80 in.)	249 mm (9.80 in.)

A. 2.3L and 3.1L Coupe w/o Z7Q/Z7S
B. 3.4L Coupe w/o Z7Q/Z7S
C. 3.1L and 3.4L Coupe w/Z7Q
D. 3.1L Coupe w/Z7S
E. 2.3L and 3.1L Sedan w/o Z7Q/Z7S
F. 3.4L Sedan w/o Z7Q/Z7S
G. 3.1L and 3.4L Sedan w/Z7Q

Fig. 3   Ride height specification chart. 1991 Cutlass Supreme

MODEL			Z	D	J	K
ENG	SUSP	TIRE SIZE	CURB	CURB	CURB	CURB
3.1L	FE1** ‡	P205-70-R14	86mm (3.39 in.)	106mm (4.22 in.)	249mm (9.80 in.)	249mm (9.80 in.)
	FE1**	P205-70-R15	73mm (2.87 in.)	94mm (3.70 in.)	249mm (9.80 in.)	249mm (9.80 in.)
	FE1‡	P205-70-R15	73mm (2.87 in.)	93mm (3.66 in.)	249mm (9.80 in.)	249mm (9.80 in.)
	FE3**	P225-60-R16	67mm (2.64 in.)	87mm (3.43 in.)	249mm (9.80 in.)	249mm (9.80 in.)
	FE3‡	P225-60-R16	66mm (2.60 in.)	87mm (3.43 in.)	249mm (9.80 in.)	249mm (9.80 in.)
3.8L	FE1** ‡	P205-70-R15	73mm (2.87 in.)	93mm (3.66 in.)	249mm (9.80 in.)	249mm (9.80 in.)
	FE3**	P225-60-R16	67mm (2.64 in.)	87mm (3.43 in.)	249mm (9.80 in.)	249mm (9.80 in.)
	FE3‡	P225-60-R16	66mm (2.60 in.)	87mm (3.43 in.)	249mm (9.80 in.)	249mm (9.80 in.)

**Buick Sedan   ‡Buick Coupe

Fig. 4   Ride height specification chart. 1991 Regal

MODEL		Z	D	J	K
SUSP	TIRE SIZE	CURB	CURB	CURB	CURB
FE1 (A)	P205-70-R15	73 mm (2.87 in.)	103 mm (4.06 in.)	251 mm (9.88 in.)	257 mm (10.12 in.)
FE1 (C)	P205-70-R15	72 mm (2.83 in.)	102 mm (4.02 in.)	251 mm (9.88 in.)	257 mm (10.12 in.)
FE3 (A)	P215-65-R15	74 mm (2.91 in.)	105 mm (4.13 in.)	251 mm (9.88 in.)	257 mm (10.12 in.)
FE3 (D)	P215-65-R15	75 mm (2.95 in.)	104 mm (4.09 in.)	251 mm (9.88 in.)	257 mm (10.12 in.)
FE3 (B and E)	P215-60-R16	73 mm (2.87 in.)	103 mm (4.06 in.)	251 mm (9.88 in.)	257 mm (10.12 in.)
FE3 (D)	P225-60-R16	66 mm (2.60 in.)	97 mm (3.82 in.)	251 mm (9.88 in.)	257 mm (10.12 in.)
FE3 (E)	P225-60-R16	67 mm (2.64 in.)	97 mm (3.82 in.)	251 mm (9.88 in.)	257 mm (10.12 in.)

A. 2.3L and 3.1L Sedan w/o Z 7m/Z 7N
B. 3.1L and 3.4L Sedan w/Z 7M
C. 2.3L and 3.12 Coupe w/o Z 7M/Z 7N
D. 3.1L and 3.4L Coupe w/o Z 7M/Z 7N
E. 3.1L and 3.4L Coupe w/Z 7M

Fig. 5   Ride height specification chart. 1991 Grand Prix

MODEL		Z	D	J	K
SUSP	TIRE SIZE	CURB	CURB	CURB	CURB
FE1 (Coupe)	P195-75R14	83mm (3.27 in.)	104 mm (4.09 in.)	249mm (9.80 in.)	249 mm (9.80 in.)
FE1 (Sedan)	P195-75R14	84mm (3.31 in.)	105 mm (4.13 in.)	249mm (9.80 in.)	249 mm (9.80 in.)
F-41	P205-70R15	73mm (2.87 in.)	92 mm (3.62 in.)	249mm (9.80 in.)	249 mm (9.80 in.)
F41	P225-60R16	66mm (2.60 in.)	86 mm (3.39 in.)	249mm (9.80 in.)	249 mm (9.80 in.)
FE3	P225-60R16	67mm (2.64 in.)	87 mm (3.43 in.)	249mm (9.80 in.)	249 mm (9.80 in.)

Fig. 6   Ride height specification chart. 1991 Lumina

4. Remove strut/upper auxiliary spring bracket/stabilizer shaft bracket, if equipped.
5. Place strut in vise.
6. File lower strut to knuckle attaching hole oblong.
7. Place auxiliary spring assembly in vise.
8. File lower strut attaching hole oblong.
9. Place stabilizer bracket in vise.
10. File lower stabilizer bracket to strut at-taching hole oblong.
11. Attach strut assembly/stabilizer shaft bracket/upper auxiliary spring brack-et to knuckle.
12. Install strut to body bolts and break hose bracket.
13. Install auxiliary spring and install tire and wheel assembly.
14. Adjust camber then **Torque** strut to knuckle nuts to 136 ft. lbs.
15. Check and adjust toe if necessary.

TOE
FRONT

1. Remove small seal clamps.
2. With steering wheel in straight ahead position, loosen jam nuts on tie rods.
3. Rotate inner tie rod to obtain proper toe angle, then ensure that number of threads showing on each tie rod is ap-proximately equal.
4. Ensure tie rod ends are square, then **Torque** jam nuts to 46 ft. lbs.
5. Ensure seals are not twisted and in-stall seal clamps.

REAR

1. Install rear toe adjusting tool No. J-38118, or equivalent, after lubricat-ing threads.
2. Hand tighten turnbuckle portion of tool in direction of adjustment. Equal amounts of threads should be show-ing on both sides of turnbuckle.
3. Loosen rear rod nut at crossmember a minimum of four turns.
4. Rotate turnbuckle portion of tool to reach correct toe specification.
5. **Torque** rear rod to crossmember nut to 81 ft. lbs. plus an additional 60° turn.
6. Remove tool.

RIDE HEIGHT

Check ride height as follows, refer to **Fig. 2** for ride height location and **Figs. 3 through 14** for specification charts:
1. Ensure vehicle is on level ground.
2. Ensure tires are inflated to proper pressures.
3. Fuel tank should be full to obtain ac-curate readings.
4. Trunk should be empty except for spare tire and jack.
5. Bounce the car three times at the front and rear to normalize suspension.
6. Measure from lowest point on the ball joint housing to control arm bolt centerline, "D" and "K" positions.

MODEL		Z	D	J	K
SUSP	TIRE SIZE	CURB	CURB	CURB	CURB
FE1 (A)	P205/70R15/N	72 mm (2.83 in.)	93 mm (3.66 in.)	249 mm (9.80 in.)	249 mm (9.80 in.)
FE1 (A)	P215/60R16/N	71 mm (2.79 in.)	93 mm (3.66 in.)	249 mm (9.80 in.)	249 mm (9.80 in.)
FE1 (B)	P205/70R15/N	73 mm (2.87 in.)	94 mm (3.70 in.)	249 mm (9.80 in.)	249 mm (9.80 in.)
FE1 (B)	P215/60R16/N	72 mm (2.83 in.)	93 mm (3.66 in.)	249 mm (9.80 in.)	249 mm (9.80 in.)
FE3 (A)	P225/60R16/N	66 mm (2.60 in.)	87 mm (3.43 in.)	249 mm (9.80 in.)	249 mm (9.80 in.)
FE3 (C)	P225/60R16/N	66 mm (2.60 in.)	88 mm (3.46 in.)	249 mm (9.80 in.)	249 mm (9.80 in.)
FE3 (D)	P225/60R16/N	66 mm (2.60 in.)	88 mm (3.46 in.)	249 mm (9.80 in.)	249 mm (9.80 in.)
FE3 (E)	P225/60R16/N	67 mm (2.64 in.)	88 mm (3.46 in.)	249 mm (9.80 in.)	249 mm (9.80 in.)

A. Coupe
B. Sedan
C. Convertible
D. 3.1L (LHO) Engine — Sedan
E. 3.4L (LQI) Engine — Sedan

Fig. 7   Ride height specification chart. 1992 Cutlass Supreme

MODEL		Z	D	J	K
SUSP	TIRE SIZE	CURB	CURB	CURB	CURB
FE1 (A)	P195/75R14/N	83 mm (3.27 in.)	104 mm (4.09 in.)	249 mm (9.80 in.)	249 mm (9.80 in.)
FE1 (B)	P195/75R14/N	83 mm (3.27 in.)	105 mm (4.13 in.)	249 mm (9.80 in.)	249 mm (9.80 in.)
FE2 (A)	P205/70R15/N	72 mm (2.83 in.)	92 mm (3.62 in.)	249 mm (9.80 in.)	249 mm (9.80 in.)
FE2 (B)	P205/70R15/N	73 mm (2.87 in.)	93 mm (3.66 in.)	249 mm (9.80 in.)	249 mm (9.80 in.)
F41 (A)	P215/60R16/N	71 mm (2.80 in.)	92 mm (3.62 in.)	249 mm (9.80 in.)	249 mm (9.80 in.)
F41 (B)	P215/60R16/N	72 mm (2.83 in.)	92 mm (3.62 in.)	249 mm (9.80 in.)	249 mm (9.80 in.)
FE3 (A, B)	P225/60R16/N	67 mm (2.64 in.)	86 mm (3.39 in.)	249 mm (9.80 in.)	249 mm (9.80 in.)

A. Coupe   B. Sedan

Fig. 8   Ride height specification chart. 1992 Lumina

SUSP	MODEL	ENG	STYLE	TIRE SIZE	Z	D	J	K
FE1	SE	LHO	2 DR	P205/70R15/N	73 mm (2.87 in.)	93 mm (3.66 in.)	249 mm (9.80 in.)	249 mm (9.80 in.)
FE1	SE	LHO	2 DR	P215/60R16/N	72 mm (2.83 in.)	92 mm (3.62 in.)	249 mm (9.80 in.)	249 mm (9.80 in.)
FE1	SE	LHO	4 DR	P205/70R15/N	73 mm (2.87 in.)	92 mm (3.62 in.)	249 mm (9.80 in.)	249 mm (9.80 in.)
FE1	SE	LHO	4 DR	P215/65R15/N	75 mm (2.95 in.)	95 mm (3.70 in.)	249 mm (9.80 in.)	249 mm (9.80 in.)
FE1	SE	LHO	4 DR	P215/60R16/N	72 mm (2.83 in.)	92 mm (3.62 in.)	249 mm (9.80 in.)	249 mm (9.80 in.)
FE1	LE	LHO	4 DR	P205/70R15/N	73 mm (2.87 in.)	92 mm (3.62 in.)	249 mm (9.80 in.)	249 mm (9.80 in.)
FE1	LE	LHO	4 DR	P215/65R15/N	75 mm (2.95 in.)	95 mm (3.70 in.)	249 mm (9.80 in.)	249 mm (9.80 in.)
FE3	SE	LHO	4 DR	P215/65R15/N	75 mm (2.95 in.)	95 mm (3.70 in.)	249 mm (9.80 in.)	249 mm (9.80 in.)
FE3	SE	LQ1	4 DR	P225/60R16/N	68 mm (2.68 in.)	87 mm (3.43 in.)	249 mm (9.80 in.)	249 mm (9.80 in.)
FE3	LE	LHO	4 DR	P205/70R15/N	73 mm (2.87 in.)	92 mm (3.62 in.)	249 mm (9.80 in.)	249 mm (9.80 in.)
FE3	LE	LHO	4 DR	P215/65R15/N	75 mm (2.95 in.)	95 mm (3.70 in.)	249 mm (9.80 in.)	249 mm (9.80 in.)
FE3	LE	LQ1	4 DR	P225/60R16/N	68 mm (2.68 in.)	87 mm (3.43 in.)	249 mm (9.80 in.)	249 mm (9.80 in.)
FE3	STE	LHO	4 DR	P225/60R16/N	67 mm (2.64 in.)	87 mm (3.43 in.)	249 mm (9.80 in.)	249 mm (9.80 in.)
FE3	STE	LQ1	4 DR	P225/60R16/N	68 mm (2.68 in.)	87 mm (3.43 in.)	249 mm (9.80 in.)	249 mm (9.80 in.)
FE3	SE	LHO	2 DR	P215/65R15/N	74 mm (2.91 in.)	95 mm (3.70 in.)	249 mm (9.80 in.)	249 mm (9.80 in.)
FE3	SE	LHO	2 DR	P225/60R16/N	66 mm (2.60 in.)	87 mm (3.43 in.)	249 mm (9.80 in.)	249 mm (9.80 in.)
FE3	SE	LQ1	2 DR	P225/60R16/N	67 mm (2.64 in.)	87 mm (3.43 in.)	249 mm (9.80 in.)	249 mm (9.80 in.)
FE3	GT/GTP	LHO	2 DR	P225/60R16/N	67 mm (2.64 in.)	87 mm (3.43 in.)	249 mm (9.80 in.)	249 mm (9.80 in.)
FE3	GT/GTP	LQ1	2 DR	P225/60R16/N	67 mm (2.64 in.)	87 mm (3.43 in.)	249 mm (9.80 in.)	249 mm (9.80 in.)
FE3	GT/GTP	LQ1	2 DR	P245/50ZR16/N	76 mm (2.99 in.)	97 mm (3.82 in.)	249 mm (9.80 in.)	249 mm (9.80 in.)

Fig. 9   Ride height specification chart. 1992 Grand Prix

MODEL		Z	D	J	K
SUSP	TIRE SIZE	CURB	CURB	CURB	CURB
FE1	P205/70R14/N	86 mm (3.39 in.)	106 mm (4.22 in.)	249 mm (9.80 in.)	249 mm (9.80 in.)
FE1	P205/70R15/N	73 mm (2.87 in.)	93 mm (3.66 in.)	249 mm (9.80 in.)	249 mm (9.80 in.)
FE3	P225/60R16/N	66 mm (2.60 in.)	87 mm (3.43 in.)	249 mm (9.80 in.)	249 mm (9.80 in.)

Fig. 10   Ride height specification chart. 1992 Regal

SUSP	MODEL	ENGINE	STYLE	TIRE	Z (CURB)	D (CURB)
FE1	Z7P w/o BYP	LHO	2 DR.	P205/70R15	72.2 mm (2.84 in.)	92.3 mm (3.63 in.)
FE1	Z7P with BYP	LHO	2 DR.	P215/60R16	71.3 mm (2.81 in.)	92.3 mm (3.63 in.)
FE1	Z7P with BYP	L82	2 DR.	P215/60R16	71.3 mm (2.81 in.)	92.3 mm (3.63 in.)
FE3	Z7P w/o BYP	LQ1	2 DR.	P225/60R16	66.1 mm (2.60 in.)	87.4 mm (3.44 in.)
FE3	Z7P with BYP	LQ1	2 DR.	P225/60R16	66.1 mm (2.60 in.)	87.4 mm (3.44 in.)
FE3	Z7Q w/o BYP	LHO	2 DR.	P225/60R16	65.7 mm (2.59 in.)	87.4 mm (3.44 in.)
FE3	Z7Q w/o BYP	LQ1	2 DR.	P225/60R16	66.9 mm (2.63 in.)	87.4 mm (3.44 in.)
FE3	Z7S w/o BYP	LHO	2 DR.	P225/60R16	66.4 mm (2.62 in.)	89.0 mm (3.50 in.)
FE3	Z7S withBYP	LQ1	2 DR.	P225/60R16	67.7 mm (2.67 in.)	89.0 mm (3.50 in.)
FE1	Z7P w/o BYP	LHO	4 DR.	P205/70R15	72.8 mm (2.87 in.)	93.5 mm (3.68 in.)
FE1	Z7P with BYP	LHO	4 DR.	P215/60R16	71.9 mm (2.83 in.)	93.3 mm (3.67 in.)
FE1	Z7P with BYP	L82	4 DR.	P215/60R16	71.9 mm (2.83 in.)	93.3 mm (3.67 in.)
FE3	Z7P w/o BYP	LQ1	4 DR.	P225/60R16	66.9 mm (2.63 in.)	87.9 mm (3.46 in.)
FE3	Z7P with BYP	LQ1	4 DR.	P225/60R16	66.9 mm (2.63 in.)	87.9 mm (3.46 in.)
FE3	Z7Q w/o BYP	LHO	4 DR.	P225/60R16	66.5 mm (2.62 in.)	88.0 mm (3.46 in.)
FE3	Z7Q w/o BYP	LQ1	4 DR.	P225/60R16	66.9 mm (2.63 in.)	87.9 mm (3.46 in.)

- NOTE: All measurements are ± 10 mm (0.39 in.)
- NOTE: "J" and "K" curb heights are 249 mm (9.80 in.) for all model combinations

Fig. 11 Ride height specification chart. 1993–94 Cutlass

SUSP	MODEL	ENGINE	STYLE	TIRE	Z (CURB)	D (CURB)
FE1	LUMINA	LHO	2 DR.	P195/75R14	83.8 mm (3.30 in.)	103.9 mm (4.09 in.)
FE1	LUMINA	LN2/LHO	4 DR.	P195/75R14	83.2 mm (3.28 in.)	104.5 mm (4.11 in.)
FE2	EUROSPORT	LHO	2 DR.	P205/70R15	72.7 mm (2.86 in.)	92.3 mm (3.63 in.)
FE2	LUMINA 9C6	LN2	4 DR.	P205/70R15	71.4 mm (2.81 in.)	92.8 mm (3.65 in.)
FE2	LUMINA	LHO	4 DR.	P205/70R15	72.7 mm (2.86 in.)	92.8 mm (3.65 in.)
FE3	LUMINA Z34	LQ1	2 DR.	P225/60R16	66.8 mm (2.63 in.)	86.0 mm (3.39 in.)
FE3	EUROSPORT Z34	LQ1	4 DR.	P225/60R16	66.8 mm (2.63 in.)	86.0 mm (3.39 in.)
F41	LUMINA	LHO	2 DR.	P215/60R16	71.7 mm (2.82 in.)	91.6 mm (3.61 in.)
F41	EUROSPORT	LHO	2 DR.	P215/60R16	71.7 mm (2.82 in.)	91.7 mm (3.61 in.)
F41	LUMINA	LN2/LHO	4 DR.	P215/60R16	71.0 mm (2.80 in.)	92.1 mm (3.63 in.)
F41	LUMINA B4C	LHO	4 DR.	P205/70R15	72.6 mm (2.86 in.)	92.3 mm (3.63 in.)
F41	LUMINA B4C	LHO	4 DR.	P215/65R15	73.8 mm (2.91 in.)	94.3 mm (3.71 in.)
F41	EUROSPORT	LHO	4 DR.	P215/60R16	71.7 mm (2.82 in.)	92.2 mm (3.63 in.)

- NOTE: All measurements are ± 10 mm (0.39 in.)
- NOTE: "J" and "K" curb heights are 249 mm (9.80 in.) for all model combinations

Fig. 12 Ride height specification chart. 1993–94 Lumina

SUSP	MODEL	ENGINE	STYLE	TIRE	Z (CURB)	D (CURB)
FE1	SE w/o B4U	LHO	4 DR.	P205/70R15	73.4 mm (2.89 in.)	92.3 mm (3.63 in.)
FE1	SE w/o B4U	LHO	4 DR.	P215/65R15	75.2 mm (2.96 in.)	94.8 mm (3.73 in.)
FE1	SE w/o B4U	LHO	4 DR.	P215/60R16	72.4 mm (2.85 in.)	92.2 mm (3.63 in.)
FE3	SE w/o B4U	LHO	4 DR.	P215/65R15	75.2 mm (2.96 in.)	94.8 mm (3.73 in.)
FE3	SE w/o B4U	LQ1	4 DR.	P215/65R15	76.7 mm (3.02 in.)	94.7 mm (3.73 in.)
FE3	SE w/o B4U	LQ1	4 DR.	P225/60R16	68.4 mm (2.69 in.)	86.7 mm (3.41 in.)
FE1	LE w/o B4U	LHO	4 DR.	P205/70R15	74.1 mm (2.92 in.)	92.3 mm (3.63 in.)
FE3	LE w/o B4U	LQ1	4 DR.	P225/60R16	68.4 mm (2.69 in.)	87.3 mm (3.44 in.)
FE3	STE w/o B4U	LHO	4 DR.	P225/60R16	67.1 mm (2.64 in.)	86.9 mm (3.42 in.)
FE3	STE w/o B4U	LQ1	4 DR.	P225/60R16	68.5 mm (2.70 in.)	86.7 mm (3.41 in.)
FE1	LE EXPORT	LHO	4 DR.	P205/70R15	74.1 mm (2.92 in.)	92.3 mm (3.63 in.)
FE1	LE EXPORT	LHO	4 DR.	P215/65R15	75.2 mm (2.96 in.)	94.8 mm (3.73 in.)
FE3	LE EXPORT	LHO	4 DR.	P205/70R15	74.1 mm (2.92 in.)	92.3 mm (3.63 in.)
FE3	LE EXPORT	LHO	4 DR.	P215/65R15	75.2 mm (2.96 in.)	94.8 mm (3.73 in.)
FE3	LE EXPORT	LQ1	4 DR.	P225/60R16	68.4 mm (2.69 in.)	87.3 mm (3.44 in.)
FE1	SE w/o B4U	LHO	2 DR.	P205/70R15	73.6 mm (2.90 in.)	92.5 mm (3.64 in.)
FE1	SE w/o B4U	LHO	2 DR.	P215/60R16	72.6 mm (2.86 in.)	92.4 mm (3.64 in.)
FE3	SE w/o B4U	LHO	2 DR.	P215/65R15	74.7 mm (2.94 in.)	94.5 mm (3.72 in.)
FE3	SE w/o B4U	LHO	2 DR.	P225/60R16	66.5 mm (2.62 in.)	86.5 mm (3.41 in.)
FE3	SE with B4U	LHO	2 DR.	P225/60R16	66.5 mm (2.62 in.)	86.5 mm (3.41 in.)
FE3	SE w/o B4U	LQ1	2 DR.	P225/60R16	67.7 mm (2.67 in.)	86.2 mm (3.39 in.)
FE3	SE with B4U	LQ1	2 DR.	P225/60R16	67.7 mm (2.67 in.)	86.2 mm (3.39 in.)
FE3	GT w/o B4U	LHO	2 DR.	P225/60R16	67.2 mm (2.65 in.)	87.0 mm (3.43 in.)
FE3	GT with B4U	LHO	2 DR.	P225/60R16	67.2 mm (2.65 in.)	87.0 mm (3.43 in.)
FE3	GT w/o B4U	LQ1	2 DR.	P225/60R16	67.8 mm (2.67 in.)	86.9 mm (3.42 in.)
FE3	GT with B4U	LQ1	2 DR.	P245/50ZR16	76.4 mm (3.01 in.)	96.6 mm (3.80 in.)
FE3	GT with B4U	LQ1	2 DR.	P225/60R16	67.8 mm (2.67 in.)	86.9 mm (3.42 in.)

- NOTE: All measurements are ± 10 mm (0.39 in.)
- NOTE: "J" and "K" curb heights are 249 mm (9.80 in.) for all model combinations

Fig. 13 Ride height specification chart. 1993–94 Grand Prix

SUSP	MODEL	ENGINE	STYLE	TIRE	Z (CURB)	D (CURB)
FE1	REGAL	LH0	4 DR.	P205/70R15	72.7 mm (2.86 in.)	93.4 mm (3.68 in.)
FE1	REGAL	LHO	4 DR.	P205/70R14	86.2 mm (3.39 in.)	106.3 mm (4.19 in.)
FE3	REGAL	LHO	4 DR.	P225/60R16	66.7 mm (2.63 in.)	87.2 mm (3.43 in.)
FE1	REGAL	L27	4 DR.	P205/70R15	73.4 mm (2.89 in.)	93.4 mm (3.68 in.)
FE1	REGAL	LHO	2 DR.	P205/70R15	72.7 mm (2.86 in.)	92.9 mm (3.66 in.)
FE1	REGAL	LHO	2 DR.	P205/70R14	86.2 mm (3.39 in.)	105.7 mm (4.16 in.)
FE3	REGAL	LHO	2 DR.	P225/60R16	65.9 mm (2.59 in.)	87.2 mm (3.43 in.)
FE1	REGAL	L27	2 DR.	P205/70R15	73.4 mm (2.89 in.)	92.9 mm (3.66 in.)

Fig. 14   Ride height specification chart. 1993–94 Regal

GEO PRIZM
(S Car)
INDEX OF SERVICE OPERATIONS

NOTE: Refer To Rear Of This Manual For Vehicle Manufacturer's Special Service Tool Suppliers.

Continued

Specifications

GENERAL ENGINE SPECIFICATIONS

Year	Engine		Fuel System	Bore & Stroke	Compression Ratio	Net H.P. @ RPM③	Maximum Torque Ft. Lbs. @ RPM	Normal Oil Pressure Pounds
	Liter/CID①	VIN Code②						
1991-92	1.6L/4-97	5	Fuel Injection	3.19 x 3.08	9.4	108 @ 6600	97 @ 4800	④
	1.6L/4-97	6	Fuel Injection	3.19 x 3.08	9.5	102 @ 5800	101 @ 4800	④
1993-94	1.6L/4-97	6	Fuel Injection	3.19 x 3.08	9.5	105 @ 5800	100 @ 4800	④
	1.8L/4-107.5	8	Fuel Injection	3.19 x 3.37	9.5	115 @ 5600	115 @ 2800	—

①—Cubic inch displacement.
②—The eighth digit of the VIN denotes engine code.
③—Ratings are net-as installed in vehicle.
④—At idle, 4.3 psi; At 3000 RPM, 36-71 psi.

TUNE UP SPECIFICATIONS

Year & Engine/VIN①	Spark Plug Gap	Ignition Timing BTDC				Curb Idle Speed③		Fast Idle Speed		Fuel Pump Pressure
		Firing Order Fig.②	Man. Trans.	Auto. Trans.	Mark Fig.	Man. Trans.	Auto Trans.	Man. Trans.	Auto. Trans.	
1991-92										
1.6L/4-97 (5)	.031	A	10°⑤	10°⑤	B	700	700N	④	④	38-44
1.6L/4-97 (6)	.031	⑥	10°⑤	10°⑤	C	800	800N	④	④	38-44
1993-94										
1.6L/4-97 (6)	.031	⑦	10°⑥	10°⑥	F	700	700N	④	④	38-44
1.8L/4-107.5 (8)	.031	⑦	10°⑥	10°⑥	F	700	700N	④	④	38-44

①—The eighth digit of the Vehicle Identification Number (VIN) denotes engine code.
②—Before removing wires from distributor cap, determine location of No. 1 wire in cap, as distributor position may have been altered from that shown at the end of this chart.
③—N:Neutral, D:Drive. When adjusting idle speed, set parking brake & block drive wheels.
④—Electronically controlled.
⑤—At 700 RPM with jumper wire connected between terminals of check engine connector. The check engine connector is located in the engine compartment on the left hand inner fender.
⑥—Cylinder numbering front of engine to rear 1, 2, 3, 4. Firing, 1-3-4-2. Refer to Fig. D for spark plug wire connections at distributor cap.
⑦—Cylinder numbering front of engine to rear 1, 2, 3, 4. Firing, 1-3-4-2. Refer to Fig. E for spark plug wire connections at distributor cap.

FIRING ORDER: 1-3-4-2

Fig. A

Fig. B

Fig. C

Fig. D

Fig. E

Fig. F

WHEEL ALIGNMENT SPECIFICATIONS

FRONT WHEEL ALIGNMENT

Year	Model	Caster Angle, Degrees		Camber Angle, Degrees				Toe-In, Inch	Toe Out on Turns, Degrees	
		Limits	Desired	Limits		Desired			Outer Wheel	Inner Wheel
				Left	Right	Left	Right			
1991–92	Except GSi	+.61 to +2.11	+1.36	−.9 to +.6	−.9 to +.6	−.15	−.15	.04	—	—
	GSi ①	+.7 to +2.2	+1.45	−.95 to +.55	−.95 to +.55	−.20	−.20	.04	—	—
	GSi ②	+.61 to +2.11	+1.36	−1.02 to +.48	−1.02 to +.48	−.27	−.27	.04	—	—
1993–94	All	+.58 to +2.08	+1.33	−.92 to +.58	−.92 to +.58	−.17	−.17	.08	33	37–41

① —Models w/automatic transaxle.   ② —Models w/manual transaxle.

REAR WHEEL ALIGNMENT

Year	Model	Camber Angle, Degrees				Toe-In, Inch
		Limits		Desired		
		Left	Right	Left	Right	
1991-92	Except GSi	−1.33 to +.17	−1.33 to +.17	−.58	−.58	.04
	GSi	−1.43 to +.07	−1.43 to +.07	−.68	−.68	.04
1993-94	All	−1.67 to −.17	−1.67 to −.17	−.92	−.92	.24

COOLING SYSTEM & CAPACITY DATA

Year	Engine (VIN)	Cooling Capacity, Qts.		Radiator Cap Relief Pressure, Lbs.	Thermo. Opening Temp.	Fuel Tank Gals.	Engine Oil Refill Qts.	Transaxle Oil	
		Manual Trans.	Auto. Trans.					Man. Transaxle Qts.	Auto. Transaxle Qts. ①
1991-92	1.6L/4-97 (5)	6.0	③	14.2	180	13.2	3.6④	2.7	⑤
	1.6L/4-97 (6)	6.0	③	14.2	180	13.2	3.2②	2.7	⑤
1993-94	1.6L/4-97 (6)	6.3	6.2	13.1	180	13.2	3.3②	1.5	⑥
	1.8L/4-107.5 (8)	6.6	6.4	13.1	180	13.2	4.1②	1.5	⑥

① —Approximate make final check w/dipstick.
② —With filter change add .2 qt.
③ —With 3 speed automatic transaxle, 5.8 qts.; with 4 speed automatic transaxle, 6.1 qts.
④ —With filter change add .3 qt.
⑤ —With 3 speed automatic transaxle, 5.8 qts.; with 4 speed automatic transaxle, 7.6 qts.
⑥ —With 3 speed automatic transaxle, 2.6 qts.; with 4 speed automatic transaxle, 3.5 qts.

LUBRICANT DATA

Year	Model	Lubricant Type			
		Transmission Or Transaxle		Power Steering	Brake System
		Manual	Automatic		
1991-92	All	75W-90 GL-5	Dexron II/IIE	Dexron II/IIE	DOT-3
1993-94	All	75W-90 GL-4	Dexron II/IIE	Power Steering Fluid ①	DOT-3

① —Meeting GM specification 9985010.

Electrical

INDEX

PRECAUTIONS

1994 Models are equipped with a passenger side airbag which must be disabled before beginning component service.

AIRBAG SYSTEM DISARMING

1. Position steering wheel in a straight ahead position.
2. Remove IGN, CIG and RADIO fuses from junction block No. 1.
3. Remove Connector Position Assurance (CPA) and disconnect lower steering column (yellow two-cavity) connector, **Fig. 1**, at base of steering column.

AIRBAG SYSTEM ARMING

1. Turn ignition switch to the Lock position.
2. Connect lower steering column connector and secure with Connector Position Assurance (CPA).
3. Ensure no one is inside vehicle and install IGN, CIG and RADIO fuses.
4. Turn ignition switch to the ACC or ON positions and ensure airbag indicator illuminates steadily for approximately six seconds and then turns off.
5. If the airbag indicator does not illuminate as specified, airbag system has a malfunction.

FUSE PANEL & FLASHER LOCATION

1991 MODELS

There are three fuse blocks; the first is on the left front kick panel, the second is on the right front kick panel and the third is behind the battery. The flasher is located under the instrument panel, left of the steering column.

1992 MODELS

There are four fuse blocks; the first is

937

926

927

926 INSTRUMENT PANEL
927 KNEE BOLSTER
937 LOWER STEERING COLUMN CONNECTOR

Fig. 1 Connector Position Assurance (CPA)

behind the left front kick panel, the second is behind the right front kick panel, the third is left of the battery and the fourth is in the lefthand corner of the engine compartment. The flasher is located under the instrument panel, left of the steering column.

1993-94 MODELS

There are three fuse blocks; the first is behind the left front kick panel, the second is behind the right front kick panel and the third is left of the air cleaner at the lefthand front of the engine compartment. The flasher is located under the instrument panel, left of the steering column.

STEERING WHEEL REPLACE

1991-92

1. Disconnect battery ground cable.
2. Remove steering column center cover and pad assembly.
3. Mark the end of the steering shaft in relation to steering wheel so the

wheel and shaft can be aligned properly during installation.
4. Remove steering wheel retaining nut.
5. Using Steering Wheel Puller tool No. J-1859-03, or equivalent, remove steering wheel.
6. Reverse procedure to install, ensuring proper position of steering wheel.

1993-94

1. Disarm airbag as outlined under "Airbag System Disarming."
2. Place front wheels in a straight ahead position.
3. Remove two side trim covers from steering column, **Fig. 2**.
4. Remove two Torx head screws, release Connector Position Assurance (CPA) and disconnect upper steering column connector, **Fig. 3**.
5. Remove airbag from steering wheel.
6. Disconnect horn connector.
7. Remove steering wheel retaining nut.
8. Mark the end of the steering shaft in relation to steering wheel so the wheel and shaft can be aligned properly during installation.
9. Remove steering wheel retaining nut.
10. Using Steering Wheel Puller tool No. J-1859-03, or equivalent, remove steering wheel.
11. Reverse procedure to install, noting the following:
    a. Install airbag module and **torque** Torx head screws to 78 inch lbs.
    b. Ensure proper position of steering wheel.
    c. **Torque** steering wheel nut to 25 ft. lbs.
    d. Arm airbag system as outlined under "Airbag System Arming."

IGNITION LOCK REPLACE

1. Disarm airbag system as outlined under "Airbag System Disarming."
2. Remove steering wheel as outlined under "Steering Wheel, Replace."

311 INFLATOR MODULE
314 UPPER STEERING COLUMN CONNECTOR
323 CONNECTOR POSITION ASSURANCE (CPA)

Fig. 3 Airbag module removal. 1993–94

306 KNEE BOLSTER
308 UPPER STEERING COLUMN COVER
309 COMBINATION SWITCH
310 SIDE TRIM COVERS

311 INFLATOR MODULE
312 LOWER STEERING COLUMN COVER
313 SRS COIL ASSEMBLY
322 STEERING WHEEL

Fig. 2 Steering column assembly. 1993–94

Fig. 5 Ignition cylinder removal

b. Rearm airbag as outlined under "Airbag System Arming."

IGNITION SWITCH
REPLACE

1. Remove ignition lock as outlined under "Ignition Lock, Replace."
2. Remove ignition switch from ignition switch housing.
3. Reverse procedure to install.

STARTER
REPLACE

EXCEPT GSI MODELS

1. Disconnect battery ground cable.
2. Disconnect electrical connectors from starter motor, **Fig. 6.**
3. Remove starter motor retaining bolts.
4. Remove starter motor.
5. Reverse procedure to install.

GSI MODELS

1. Disconnect battery ground cable.
2. Remove rear cooling fan.
3. Raise and support vehicle.
4. Remove right and left splash shields.
5. Disconnect oxygen sensor connector.
6. Disconnect forward exhaust pipe.
7. Disconnect electrical connections from starter assembly.
8. Remove starter assembly attaching bolts.
9. Remove starter assembly from vehicle.
10. Reverse procedure to install.

1 COLUMN HOLE COVER
2 INTERMEDIATE SHAFT
3 IGNITION HARNESS CONNECTOR
4 LOCK CYLINDER ASSEMBLY
5 UPPER COLUMN COVER
6 MULTI-FUNCTION SWITCH

7 WHEEL PAD
8 STEERING WHEEL
9 STEERING COLUMN TUBE
10 LOWER COLUMN COVER
11 LOWER INSTRUMENT FINISH PANEL

Fig. 4 Steering column assembly. 1991–92

3. Remove upper and lower steering column covers, **Figs. 2 and 4.**
4. Disconnect ignition switch electrical connections.
5. Using a center punch, mark center of tapered-head bolts securing lock cylinder housing.
6. Drill into tapered-head bolts using a .12-.16 inch (3-4 mm) drill bit.

7. Remove tapered-head bolts using a bolt extractor.
8. Place ignition switch in ACC position.
9. Push down stop key and remove cylinder, **Fig. 5.**
10. Reverse procedure to install, noting the following:
   a. Tighten new tapered-head bolts until bolt heads break off.

Fig. 6   Starter motor installation

A   ALIGNMENT MARKS
313   SRS COIL ASSEMBLY

**Fig. 8   SRS coil alignment.
1993—94**

4. Mark distributor housing and rotor position.
5. Remove distributor mounting bolts.
6. Remove distributor and O-ring from engine.
7. Reverse procedure to install.

COMBINATION SWITCH
REPLACE

1991—92

1. Disconnect battery ground cable.
2. Remove steering wheel cover and steering wheel as previously outlined under "Steering Wheel, Replace."
3. Remove instrument lower finish panel, air duct and column upper and lower covers.
4. Disconnect electrical connector from ignition/turn signal switch, **Fig. 7.**
5. Remove combination switch assembly.
6. Reverse procedure to install.

1993—94

1. Disarm airbag system as outlined under "Airbag System Disarming."
2. Remove steering wheel as outlined under "Steering Wheel Replace."
3. Remove upper and lower steering column covers.
4. Unclip and set aside left front carpet retainer.
5. Disconnect hood release lever.
6. Remove knee bolster.
7. Untape SRS coil assembly harness from combination switch harness.
8. Disconnect connector from SRS coil.
9. Remove SRS coil assembly from combination switch.
10. Disconnect electrical connector from ignition/turn signal switch, **Fig. 2.**
11. Remove combination switch assembly.
12. Align the SRS coil prior to installation as follows:
    a. Ensure front wheels are in a straight ahead position.
    b. Turn SRS coil counterclockwise by hand until it becomes harder to turn.
    c. Turn the SRS coil clockwise about three turns to align the red marks, **Fig. 8.**
    d. Install and connect the SRS coil.

306   KNEE BOLSTER
308   UPPER STEERING COLUMN COVER
309   COMBINATION SWITCH
310   SIDE TRIM COVERS
311   INFLATOR MODULE
312   LOWER STEERING COLUMN COVER
315   STEERING COLUMN ASSEMBLY
316   IGNITION SWITCH

Fig. 7   Instrument panel switch installations

DISTRIBUTOR
REPLACE

1. Disconnect battery ground cable.

2. Disconnect distributor electrical connectors.
3. Remove distributor cap and spark plug cables and position aside.

Fig. 9 Heater case. 1993–94

13. Reverse procedure to install, arming the airbag as outlined under "Airbag System Arming."

RADIO
REPLACE

1. Disable airbag as outlined under "Airbag System Disarming."
2. Remove steering column covers.
3. Remove console trim bezel.
4. Disconnect rear wiper/washer, cruise control and defogger electrical connections.
5. Remove radio attaching screws.
6. Remove radio from console.
7. Disconnect radio connections and antenna cable.
8. Reverse procedure to install. Rearm airbag as outlined under "Airbag System Arming."

HEATER CORE
REPLACE

1991–92

1. Remove steering wheel as outlined under "Steering Wheel, Replace."
2. Remove trim bezel, instrument panel assembly, cluster assembly, center console and all console trim as outlined under "Instrument Panel Pad/Cluster, Replace."
3. Remove cup holder from console.
4. Remove radio as outlined under "Radio, Replace."
5. Drain cooling system.
6. Disconnect all cables and ducts from heater case.
7. Disconnect blower switch harness and heater control assembly.
8. Remove two center console support braces.
9. Remove heater hoses from case and grommets from cowl.
10. Remove mounting bolts, nuts and clips from heater and air distribution cases.
11. Remove heater and air distribution cases.
12. Remove screws and clips from case, separate case halves.
13. Remove heater core from case.
14. Reverse procedure to install.

1993–94

1. Disarm airbag system as outlined under "Airbag System Disarming."
2. Disconnect battery ground cable.
3. Remove evaporator case assembly as outlined under "Evaporator Core,

1	AMPLIFIER	6	DRAIN HOSE
2	UPPER UNIT CASE	7	WIRE HARNESS
3	EVAPORATOR	8	THERMISTOR
4	EXPANSION VALVE	9	CLIPS
5	LOWER UNIT CASE	10	SCREW

Fig. 10 Evaporator case. 1991–92

102 EVAPORATOR CASE
132 GLOVE BOX
133 RIGHT-SIDE KICK PANEL

Fig. 11 Evaporator case. 1993–94

Replace."
4. Drain cooling system into a suitable container.
5. Loosen and remove heater core hoses.
6. Remove heater core pipe grommet from vehicle.
7. Remove instrument panel as outlined under "Instrument Panel Pad/Cluster, Replace."
8. Remove right and left instrument panel brace.
9. Remove left and center ventilation ducts.
10. Remove heater case from vehicle, **Fig. 9.**

11. Remove two heater core brackets then slide the heater core from vehicle.
12. Reverse procedure to install, rearming airbag as outlined under "Airbag System Arming."

EVAPORATOR CORE
REPLACE

1991–92

1. Disconnect battery ground cable.
2. Discharge refrigeration system.
3. Remove and cap suction and liquid tube from evaporator case outlet and

WITH A/C

WITH CASSETTE BOX

1	DEFROSTER GRILLE	12	INSTRUMENT CLUSTER	23	TRIM BEZEL
2	DEFROSTER DUCT	13	CLUSTER BEZEL	24	CENTER CONSOLE TRIM
3	CENTER VENTILATION DUCT	14	GLOVE BOX AND TRIM ASSEMBLY	25	HOOD RELEASE LEVER
4	RIGHT VENTILATION DUCT	15	CASSETTE BOX	26	LEFT LOWER DASH TRIM
5	BRACE	16	REAR CONSOLE	27	SCUFF PLATE
6	"A" PILLAR TRIM	17	SHIFT LEVER BOOT (M/T)	28	COWL SIDE TRIM
7	A/C DUCT	18	REAR CONSOLE	29	INSTRUMENT PANEL
8	LOWER A/C DEFLECTOR	19	FRONT CONSOLE	30	"A" PILLAR TRIM
9	RIGHT VENTILATION DEFLECTOR	20	ASHTRAY	31	LEFT WINDOW DEFLECTOR
10	RIGHT WINDOW DEFLECTOR	21	RETAINER	32	LEFT VENTILATION DUCT
11	COWL SIDE TRIM	22	CUP HOLDER		

Fig. 12 Instrument panel & related components. 1991–92

inlet fittings.
4. Remove right lower instrument panel trim assembly as outlined under Instrument Panel, Replace."
5. Remove grommets from inlet and outlet fittings.
6. Remove glove box compartment.
7. Disconnect wiring harness connectors.
8. Remove case attaching screws and remove evaporator case from behind instrument panel.
9. Separate upper and lower case halves, **Fig. 10.**
10. Disconnect liquid tube from inlet fitting of the expansion tube.
11. Remove packing and heat sensing tube from suction tube of evaporator.
12. Remove expansion valve.
13. Reverse procedure to install.

1993–94

1. Disarm airbag system as outlined under "Airbag System Disarming."
2. Discharge air conditioning system using a suitable A/C recovery system.
3. Disconnect battery ground cable.
4. Remove right side kick panel and glove box assembly.
5. Disconnect evaporator outlet and inlet pipe and plug hoses and evaporator openings.
6. Disconnect hold-down brackets for inlet and outlet pipes.
7. Remove air conditioning amplifier electrical connector then the amplifier.
8. Disconnect evaporator thermistor connector.
9. Remove evaporator case from vehicle, **Fig. 11.**
10. Separate evaporator case halves then remove thermister from evaporator.
11. Remove evaporator from case.
12. Reverse procedure to install, rearming airbag as outlined under "Airbag System Arming."

BLOWER MOTOR
REPLACE

The blower motor is located underneath the instrument panel at the far right side of the vehicle. It is accessible from below the instrument panel.
1. Disconnect battery ground cable.
2. Disconnect rubber air duct running between motor and heater assembly.
3. Disconnect blower motor electrical connectors.
4. Remove blower motor attaching screws.
5. Remove blower motor from under instrument panel.
6. Reverse procedure to install.

WIPER MOTOR
REPLACE
FRONT

1. Disconnect battery ground cable.
2. Disconnect wiper motor electrical connection.
3. Remove wiper motor attaching bolts.
4. Disconnect wiper linkage from wiper motor output arm.
5. Remove wiper motor.
6. Reverse procedure to install.

REAR

1. Disconnect battery ground cable.
2. Remove wiper arm assembly.
3. Remove liftgate trim panel.
4. Disconnect wiper motor electrical connector.
5. Remove wiper motor attaching bolts.
6. Remove rear wiper motor assembly.
7. Reverse procedure to install.

INSTRUMENT PANEL PAD/CLUSTER
REPLACE

CLUSTER, REPLACE
1991–92

1. Disconnect battery ground cable.
2. Disconnect hood release lever.
3. Remove lefthand lower dash trim panel screws and pull out trim, **Fig. 12.**
4. Disconnect speaker connector.
5. Remove A/C duct from lower A/C register, if equipped.
6. Remove lefthand lower trim panel.
7. Remove upper and lower steering column covers.
8. Remove center console trim panel screws and pull out trim.
9. **On 1991 models,** disconnect and remove cruise control/defogger and rear wiper/washer switches from trim panel.
10. **On all models,** disconnect and remove cigar lighter lamp from trim panel.
11. Remove center trim panel.
12. Remove cluster bezel attaching screws.

A   CLIP LOCATIONS
805 INSTRUMENT PANEL

Fig. 14   Instrument panel removal. 1993–94

801	CENTER CONSOLE TRIM BEZEL
802	KNEE BOLSTER
803	ASHTRAY
804	INSTRUMENT PANEL LEFT-SIDE OUTLET TRIM BEZEL
805	INSTRUMENT PANEL
806	HEATER CONTROL ASSEMBLY
807	GLOVE BOX ASSEMBLY
808	CENTER CONSOLE
809	CENTER CONSOLE LOWER TRAY
810	REAR CENTER CONSOLE
811	ARM REST/STORAGE COMPARTMENT

Fig. 13   Instrument panel & related components. 1993–94

13. Disconnect hazard flasher and dimmer switch electrical connections.
14. Remove cluster bezel.
15. Remove instrument cluster attaching screws.
16. Disconnect speedometer cable and electrical connectors from cluster.
17. Remove instrument cluster.
18. Reverse procedure to install.

1993–94

1. Disarm airbag system as outlined under "Airbag System Disarming."
2. Disconnect battery ground cable.
3. Remove instrument cluster bezel screws, then the bezel by disengaging two lower clips.
4. Remove instrument cluster screws then the cluster disconnecting three electrical connectors.
5. Reverse procedure to install, rearming airbag as outlined under "Airbag System Arming."

INSTRUMENT PANEL, REPLACE

1991–92

1. Disconnect battery ground cable.
2. Remove steering wheel as outlined under "Steering Wheel, Replace."
3. Remove instrument cluster as outlined under "Cluster, Replace."
4. Remove cup holder.
5. Remove radio as outlined under "Radio, Replace."
6. **On 1991 models,** remove glove box and trim assembly.
7. **On all models,** remove four attaching screws from heater and A/C control unit.
8. Remove instrument panel to center console trim.
9. Remove five bolts retaining instrument panel to vehicle.
10. **On 1992 models,** pry off left and right side window deflectors.
11. **On all models,** disconnect three

electrical connectors and relay unit on the lefthand side of instrument panel.
12. Disconnect the electrical connector on the lefthand side of instrument panel.
13. Detach defroster duct retainers and remove instrument panel.
14. Reverse procedure to install.

1993–94

1. Disarm airbag system as outlined under "Airbag System Disarming."
2. Disconnect battery ground cable.
3. Remove right and left A-pillar lower trim panel.
4. Remove kick panels.
5. Remove steering wheel as outlined under "Steering Wheel, Replace."
6. Remove steering column upper and lower trim panels.
7. Remove center console as follows:
   a. Remove ashtray, disconnect the center console trim bezel, **Fig. 13.**
   b. Remove cigar lighter, rear defogger and hazard switch connectors.
   c. Disconnect cigar lighter and ashtray lamp from center console bezel then remove the bezel from the vehicle.
   d. Remove the radio as outlined under "Radio, Replace."
   e. Remove glove box assembly.
   f. Remove knee bolster cover plates then the knee bolster and hood release cable.
   g. Remove screws securing center console to rear console.
   h. **On models with manual transmissions,** remove gear shift lever upper boot.
   i. **On models with automatic transmissions,** remove center console lower tray by prying gently with a screwdriver.
   j. **On all models,** Remove screws from rear tray of rear console.
   k. Set parking brake and remove rear and center console from vehicle.
8. Remove instrument cluster assembly as outlined under "Cluster, Replace."

9. Remove light control knob then the light switch nut.
10. Remove instrument panel left side outlet trim bezel.
11. Disconnect light switch connector

then remove switch.
12. Remove bolts and screws shown in **Fig. 14**, then remove instrument panel from vehicle by pulling toward rear

to disengage five clips.
13. Reverse procedure to install, rearming airbag as outlined under "Airbag System Arming."

1.6L/4-97 & 1.8L/4-107.5 Engines
INDEX

PRECAUTIONS

1994 Models are equipped with a passenger side airbag which must be disabled before beginning component service.

AIRBAG SYSTEM DISARMING

1. Position steering wheel in a straight ahead position.
2. Remove IGN, CIG and RADIO fuses from junction block No. 1.
3. Remove Connector Position Assurance (CPA) and disconnect lower steering column (yellow two-cavity) connector, at base of steering column.

AIRBAG SYSTEM ARMING

1. Turn ignition switch to the Lock position.
2. Connect lower steering column connector and secure with Connector Position Assurance (CPA).
3. Ensure no one is inside vehicle and install IGN, CIG and RADIO fuses.
4. Turn ignition switch to the ACC or ON positions and ensure airbag indicator illuminates steadily for approximately six seconds and then turns off.
5. If the airbag indicator does not illuminate as specified, airbag system has a malfunction.

FUEL SYSTEM PRESSURE RELEASE

1991-92
1. Loosen fuel filler cap to release fuel

tank pressure.
2. Disconnect battery ground cable.
3. Wrap a shop towel around the fuel supply fitting.
4. Slowly loosen fuel fitting.
5. Close fuel fitting.

1993-94

1. Loosen fuel filler cap to release fuel tank pressure.
2. Remove radio as outlined under "Radio, Replace" in the "Electrical" section.
3. Disconnect circuit opening relay connector.
4. Start engine and allow to stall.
5. Crank engine for an additional three seconds to release remaining fuel pressure.
6. Disconnect battery ground cable.
7. Connect circuit opening relay connector.
8. Install radio and tighten fuel fuller cap.

ENGINE MOUNT REPLACE

1991-92 MODELS

1. Disconnect battery ground cable.
2. Using Engine Support Fixture tool No. J-28467-A or equivalent, support engine assembly.
3. Raise and support vehicle.
4. Remove right lower stone shield.
5. Remove two lower engine mount to

engine bracket nuts.
6. Lower vehicle.
7. Remove bolts and right engine mount support.
8. Remove upper bolt from engine mount to engine bracket.
9. Remove windshield washer reservoir.
10. Remove right engine mount through bolt and engine mount.
11. Reverse procedure to install.

1993-94 MODELS

1. Disconnect battery ground cable.
2. Using Engine Support Fixture tool No. J-28467-A or equivalent, support engine assembly.
3. Remove cruise control actuator and position aside.
4. Remove cruise control actuator bracket.
5. Disconnect two piece air conditioning pipe bracket.
6. Remove bolts from engine mount bracket and engine mount.
7. Raise and support vehicle.
8. Remove engine splash shields.
9. Remove nuts from underside of engine mount bracket.
10. Lower vehicle.
11. Remove insulator from engine mount bracket.
12. Remove engine mount and bracket from vehicle, moving A/C pipe to gain clearance.
13. Remove mount through bolt and the engine mount, **Fig. 1**
14. Reverse procedure to install.

ENGINE
REPLACE
1991–92 MODELS

1. Disconnect battery ground and positive cables, then remove battery and engine compartment hood.
2. Remove right and left side engine undercovers.
3. Drain engine oil into suitable container.
4. Drain coolant from radiator and engine block into suitable container.
5. **On models equipped with manual transaxle**, drain transaxle fluid into suitable container.
6. **On all models**, remove air cleaner assembly and coolant reservoir tank.
7. Remove radiator and coolant fan as an assembly.
8. Disconnect heater hoses from coolant inlet housing.
9. Disconnect fuel pressure hose from fuel filter, then the heater and air hoses from air valve.
10. Disconnect fuel return hose from fuel pressure regulator.
11. **On models equipped with manual transaxle**, remove clutch slave cylinder without disconnecting hydraulic line and position aside.
12. **On all models**, disconnect vacuum hose from charcoal canister.
13. Disconnect transaxle shift control cables from transaxle.
14. Disconnect speedometer cable, then the cruise control cable (if equipped), accelerator cable and accelerator link.
15. **On models equipped with cruise control**, remove cruise control actuator.
16. Disconnect engine main electrical harness from all related sensors and switches.
17. **On all models**, disconnect brake booster hose from intake manifold.
18. Remove A/C compressor and power steering pump (if equipped) with lines attached and position aside.
19. Disconnect oxygen sensor electrical connector, then remove oxygen sensor.
20. Disconnect oil cooler hoses from oil cooler.
21. Raise and support vehicle, then disconnect catalytic converter clamp, engine pipe clamp and engine pipe from exhaust manifold.
22. Disconnect front and rear engine mounts to center member attaching bolts, then remove front mount through bolt and mount.
23. Remove center member to frame attaching bolts, then the center member.
24. Remove axle to side gear shaft attaching bolts, then disconnect right side lower arm from steering knuckle and separate. Remove axle shafts from side gear shafts and position aside with suitable wire.
25. Lower vehicle to ground level.
26. Attach suitable lifting equipment to engine and transaxle assembly, then

A   THROUGH BOLT PART OF ENGINE MOUNT
B   BOLT A HOLE
C   BOLT B HOLE
B   BOLT C HOLES   662   ENGINE MOUNT
661   ENGINE MOUNT BRACKET   663   TANG
                                664   INSULATOR

Fig. 1   Engine mount replace. 1993–94 models

remove right and left side mounts.
27. Carefully lift engine and transaxle assembly from vehicle and place on suitable stand.
28. Remove radiator fan temperature switch connector and cold start injector time switch connector.
29. Disconnect vacuum hoses from Bi-Metal Vacuum Switching Valves (BVSV), then remove coolant inlet housing attaching bolts and nut.
30. Disconnect hoses from coolant bypass tubes, then remove coolant inlet housing.
31. Disconnect back-up lamp switch connector, water temperature sensor connector and water temperature switch connector.
32. **On models equipped with automatic transaxle**, neutral start switch connectors and transaxle solenoid connector.
33. **On models equipped with automatic transaxle**, rotate crankshaft as necessary to gain access to and remove six torque converter attaching bolts.
34. **On all models**, remove starter assembly, then separate transaxle from engine.
35. Reverse procedure to install.

1993–94 MODELS

1. Release fuel system pressure as outlined under "Fuel System Pressure Release."
2. Disconnect and remove battery.
3. Drain cooling system, engine and transaxle oil into suitable containers.
4. Mark hood hinge position on hood, then remove hood assembly.
5. Remove two splash shields.
6. Disconnect accelerator and kickdown cables.
7. Remove radiator and engine cooling fan assembly.
8. Disconnect necessary electrical harness and vacuum hose connections.
9. Remove air cleaner hose and air cleaner upper and lower cases.
10. Remove coolant reservoir bracket.
11. Remove washer reservoir.

12. Remove cruise control actuator.
13. Disconnect heater hose from thermostat housing and coolant inlet pipe.
14. Disconnect fuel feed pipe from the fuel rail and intake manifold.
15. Disconnect fuel return hose from fuel pressure regulator.
16. **On models with manual transmission**, remove clutch release cylinder.
17. **On all models**, disconnect transaxle control cables.
18. Remove left and right scuff plates.
19. Remove shift lever knob.
20. Remove knee bolster, glove box door, instrument panel trim bezel, front and rear console and lefthand cowl side trim panel.
21. Remove radio as outlined under "Radio, Replace" in the "Electrical" section.
22. Disconnect and remove engine control module.
23. Disconnect cowl panel harness connector and pull harness from the cowl panel.
24. Remove air conditioner compressor and power steering oil pump leaving hoses attached and position in a out of the way location. **Do not allow compressor or oil pump to be supported by the hoses.**
25. Raise and support vehicle.
26. Disconnect front exhaust pipe, exhaust pipe support brackets and oxygen sensor.
27. Disconnect front drive axles as outlined in the "Front Wheel Drive" section.
28. Lower vehicle.
29. Attach an engine lifting device to the engine then disconnect engine and transaxle mounts.
30. Ensure all electrical, vacuum and fuel hoses connections are disconnected.
31. Remove engine with transaxle attached from vehicle.
32. Reverse procedure to install.

CYLINDER HEAD
REPLACE
1991–92
Except GSi

1. Disconnect battery ground cable.
2. Drain coolant into a suitable container.
3. Raise and support vehicle.
4. Remove righthand lower stone shield.
5. Disconnect two mount nut and stud protectors, then remove two rear transaxle mount to main crossmember mount nuts.
6. Remove two center mount to center crossmember nuts.
7. Lower vehicle.
8. Remove air cleaner assembly.
9. Disconnect throttle, cruise control and transaxle kickdown cables.
10. Mark then disconnect all necessary electrical and vacuum connections.
11. Disconnect fuel inlet line.
12. Disconnect cold start injector pipe and the fuel rail.
13. Remove heater hoses water outlet

Fig. 2 **Cylinder head & related components. Except GSi models**

1 CAMSHAFT SNAP RING	13 VALVE KEEPERS	24 EXHAUST MANIFOLD UPPER INSULATOR
2 WAVE WASHER	14 VALVE SPRING RETAINER	25 EXHAUST MANIFOLD GASKET
3 CAMSHAFT SUB-GEAR	15 VALVE SPRING	26 EXHAUST MANIFOLD
4 CAMSHAFT GEAR SPRING	16 VALVE SPRING SEAT	27 EXHAUST MANIFOLD LOWER INSULATOR
5 CYLINDER HEAD COVER	17 VALVE STEM OIL SEAL	28 CENTER TIMING BELT COVER
6 SPARK PLUG TUBE GASKET	18 VALVE GUIDE BUSHING	29 UPPER TIMING BELT COVER
7 CYLINDER HEAD COVER GASKET	19 VALVE	30 CAMSHAFT TIMING GEAR
8 CAMSHAFT BEARING CAP	20 DISTRIBUTOR	31 FUEL RAIL
9 CAMSHAFT (INTAKE)	21 WATER INLET HOUSING	32 COLD-START INJECTOR PIPE
10 CAMSHAFT (EXHAUST)	22 WATER OUTLET HOUSING	33 INTAKE MANIFOLD GASKET
11 ADJUSTING SHIM	23 HEAD GASKET	34 INTAKE MANIFOLD
12 VALVE LIFTER		

1	CAMSHAFT GEAR HOLE
2	EXHAUST CAMSHAFT CAP MARK

Fig. 3 **Camshaft gear hole alignment. Except GSi models**

Fig. 4 **Cylinder bolt removal sequence. Except GSi models**

cal" section.

30. Place No. 1 cylinder at TDC on its compression stroke. Turn crankshaft pulley and align its groove with the "0" mark of timing belt cover. **Ensure that camshaft gear hole is aligned with exhaust camshaft cap mark, Fig. 3.**
31. Remove plug from lower timing belt cover and place alignment marks on camshaft timing gear and belt.
32. Loosen idler pulley mount bolt and push idler pulley toward left then tighten temporarily.
33. Remove timing belt from camshaft timing gear. **Support timing belt so meshing of crankshaft timing gear and belt do not shift. Do not allow oil, water or dust to come in contact with timing belt.**
34. Remove cylinder head bolts in sequence shown in **Fig. 4.**
35. Remove cylinder head with intake and exhaust manifolds attached.
36. Reverse procedure to install, noting the following:
    a. Apply a light coat of clean engine oil to cylinder head bolt threads and under the bolt head before installation.
    b. **Torque** cylinder head bolts in four steps in sequence shown in **Fig. 5** ending with a final torque of 44 ft. lbs.

and inlet housings, **Fig. 2.**
14. Remove spark plugs and PVC valve.
15. Remove cylinder head cover.
16. Loosen the A/C compressor, power steering pump and alternator brackets then remove accessory drive belts.
17. Remove A/C idler pulley.
18. Remove cruise control actuator and bracket.
19. Remove windshield washer reservoir.
20. Support engine using Engine Support Fixture tool No. J-28467-A, or equivalent.
21. Remove right engine mount through bolt and raise engine.
22. Remove water pump pulley and lower engine.
23. Remove engine wiring harness from upper timing belt cover.
24. Raise and support vehicle.
25. Remove cylinder head to cylinder block bracket then the exhaust manifold support bracket.
26. Disconnect exhaust pipe from exhaust manifold.
27. Remove upper and center timing belt covers.
28. Remove right engine mount bracket.
29. Remove distributor as outlined under "Distributor, Replace" in the "Electri-

Fig. 5 Cylinder bolt tightening sequence. Except GSi models

GSi

1. Disconnect battery ground cable.
2. Drain cooling system into a suitable container.
3. Remove air cleaner assembly, then disconnect cruise control cable (if equipped), accelerator cable and link.
4. Disconnect heater hose from rear cylinder head cover.
5. Mark position of vacuum hoses for assembly, then disconnect vacuum hoses from throttle body.
6. Remove cruise control actuator (if equipped), ignition coil and coolant outlet hose.
7. Remove ignition coil.
8. Remove water outlet hose and outlet from cylinder head, **Fig. 6.**
9. Remove brake booster vacuum hose, then the PCV hose.
10. Remove EGR valve and tubes, then the cold start injector pressure hose.
11. Disconnect water by-pass hoses from auxiliary air valve.
12. Remove vacuum pipe and cylinder rear cover.
13. Remove distributor as outlined under "Distributor, Replace" in the "Electrical" section.
14. Disconnect exhaust manifold from cylinder head as outlined under "Intake & Exhaust Manifold, Replace."
15. Remove delivery pipe with injectors.
16. Remove intake manifold as outlined under "Intake & Exhaust Manifold, Replace."
17. Remove power steering and alternator drive belts.
18. Remove cylinder head cover and spark plugs.
19. Set crankshaft pulley at TDC of compression stroke. **Ensure valve lifters for No. 1 cylinder are loose. If not, rotate crankshaft pulley an additional 360° to set engine at TDC compression.**
20. Disconnect right engine mount.
21. Remove water pump pulley then timing belt covers and timing belt as outlined under "Timing Belt Cover, Replace" and "Timing Belt & Camshaft Timing Pulley, Replace."
22. Remove camshaft as outlined under "Camshaft, Replace."
23. Remove cylinder head bolts in sequence shown in **Fig. 7.**
24. Remove cylinder head from engine

Fig. 6 Cylinder head & related components. GSi models

block.
25. Reverse procedure to install, **torque cylinder head bolts to 44 ft. lbs. in sequence shown in Fig. 8.**

1993–94

1. Remove camshafts as described under "Camshaft Replace."
2. Remove vacuum hoses from intake chamber.
3. Remove A/C actuator electrical connector, if equipped.
4. Disconnect EGR solenoid vacuum valve electrical connector, vacuum hose from EGR, mounting bolt, then EGR solenoid valve, if equipped.
5. Remove engine wire clamp, intake manifold brace attaching bolts, then brace.
6. Remove fuel return hose from pressure regulator.
7. Remove EGR valve and EGR vacuum modulator, if equipped.
8. Disconnect throttle body position sensor electrical connector, remove accelerator bracket mounting bolts, accelerator bracket, throttle body mounting bolts, then throttle body.
9. Remove fuel inlet hose clamp bolt, then air intake chamber brace and gasket.

10. Remove PCV valves, vacuum hose from pressure regulator, air intake chamber cover nuts and bolts, then air intake chamber cover.
11. Remove union bolt, two gaskets, then fuel inlet pipe from fuel rail.
12. Remove injector electrical connectors, fuel rail attaching bolts, then fuel rail with injectors attached.
13. Remove four insulators, then two spacers from cylinder head.
14. Remove intake manifold attaching bolts, then intake manifold.
15. Remove oxygen sensor electrical connector, front pipe to manifold attaching nuts and bolts, then upper heat insulator.
16. Remove exhaust manifold brace, if equipped.
17. Remove cylinder head bolts in sequence as shown in **Fig. 4**, using a 10 MM 12 point socket. **Note bolt lengths and location when removing bolts from head.**
18. Remove cylinder head from dowels.
19. Reverse procedure to install noting the following:
   a. Install head bolts in proper location, **Torque** bolts in several passes and in sequence shown in **Fig. 5** to 22 ft lbs., tighten head bolts in

A CYLINDER HEAD

Fig. 8 Cylinder head bolt tightening sequence. GSi models

Fig. 9 First valve clearance adjustment

Fig. 7 Cylinder head bolt loosening sequence. GSi model

sequence an additional 90°, then in sequence again an additional 90°.
  b. Tighten all attaching nuts and bolts to specification.

INTAKE & EXHAUST MANIFOLDS REPLACE

INTAKE MANIFOLD

1991–92

1. Disconnect battery ground cable.
2. Drain cooling system.
3. Remove air cleaner assembly.
4. **On GSi models,** remove upper radiator hose.
5. **On all models,** disconnect throttle and accelerator cables.
6. Mark then remove all necessary vacuum hoses.
7. **On except GSi models,** proceed as follows:
  a. Disconnect throttle position, cold start, air control valve and vacuum sensors and injector electrical connectors.
  b. Remove cold start injector pipe.
  c. Remove water hose from air valve.
8. **On GSi models,** proceed as follows:
  a. Remove fuel delivery pipe and injectors then the temperature sensor connector.
  b. Remove water outlet bypass pipe.
9. **On all models,** raise and support vehicle.
10. Remove intake manifold bracket.
11. Lower vehicle.
12. Remove intake manifold attaching bolts.
13. Remove intake manifold.
14. Reverse procedure to install.

1993–94

1. Release fuel system pressure as follows:
  a. Loosen fuel filler cap to fuel tank pressure.
  b. Remove radio as outlined under "Radio Replace" in the "Electrical" section.
  c. Disconnect circuit opening relay electrical connector.
  d. Start engine and allow to stall.
  e. Crank engine for an additional 3 seconds to release any remaining fuel pressure.
  f. Disconnect battery ground cable.
  g. Reconnect circuit opening relay connector.
  h. Install radio and tighten filler cap.
2. Disconnect vacuum hoses from vacuum sensor on fuel filter, brake booster and A/C actuator hoses.
3. Disconnect exhaust gas recirculation (EGR) solenoid valve, vacuum hose from EGR valve then remove the EGR valve.
4. Remove intake manifold brace.
5. Disconnect fuel return hose from pressure regulator.
6. Disconnect TPS sensor and accelerator bracket then remove the throttle body from intake manifold.
7. Remove air intake chamber brace and gasket.
8. Disconnect PCV hoes from cylinder head cover.
9. Remove air intake chamber cover and gasket.
10. Disconnect fuel inlet pipe from fuel rail.
11. Disconnect injector electrical connectors.
12. Remove fuel rail with injectors attached.
13. Remove intake manifold bolts and the intake manifold.
14. Reverse procedure to install.

EXHAUST MANIFOLD

1. Disconnect battery ground cable.
2. Remove exhaust manifold heat shield or insulator.
3. Raise and support vehicle.
4. Disconnect front exhaust pipe.
5. **On except GSi models,** remove exhaust manifold support bracket.

6. **On all models,** lower vehicle.
7. **On except GSi models,** disconnect oxygen sensor.
8. **On all models,** remove exhaust manifold attaching bolts then exhaust manifold.
9. Reverse procedure to install.

VALVE ADJUSTMENT

Measure and adjust valve clearance while the engine is cold.
1. Disconnect battery ground cable.
2. Remove cylinder head cover.
3. Set No. 1 cylinder at TDC on the compression stroke.
4. Turn crankshaft to align groove in crankshaft pulley with "0" mark on No. 1 timing belt cover. **Ensure that valve lifters on No. 1 cylinder have freeplay. If not, rotate crankshaft pulley 360° and align the "0" mark on timing belt cover.**
5. Measure and record valve lash clearance between the cam lobe and the adjusting shim on cylinders shown in **Fig. 9.**
6. Rotate crankshaft 360° and align groove with "0" mark timing belt cover.
7. Measure and record valve lash clearance between the cam lobe and the adjusting shim on cylinders shown in **Fig. 10.**
8. If clearance is not within specifications, obtain the Valve Clearance Adjustment Set tool No. J-37141-A, or equivalent.
9. Insert Valve Spring Compression Tool No. J-37141-1, or equivalent, between the camshaft and lifter adjusting shim. This action will compress the valve spring and push lifter down.
10. Insert Lifter Holding Tool No. J-37141-2A, or equivalent, between camshaft and lifter. Position bottom edge of tool on lifter and not on adjusting shim. The lifter appears to be a sleeve around the adjusting shim. This action will hold the lifter away from camshaft, **Fig. 11.**
11. Remove Spring Compression Tool No. J-37141-1. Lifter Holding Tool No. J-37141-2A should hold lifter down away from camshaft.
12. Remove adjusting shim with a small screwdriver and magnetic finger, **Fig. 12.**
13. Measure thickness of removed shim.

Fig. 10 Second valve clearance adjustment

AVAILABLE SHIMS

Shim No.	Thickness	Shim No.	Thickness
02	2.500 (0.0984)	20	2.950 (0.1161)
04	2.550 (0.1004)	22	3.000 (0.1181)
06	2.600 (0.1024)	24	3.050 (0.1201)
08	2.650 (0.1043)	26	3.100 (0.1220)
10	2.700 (0.1063)	28	3.150 (0.1240)
12	2.750 (0.1083)	30	3.200 (0.1260)
14	2.800 (0.1102)	32	3.250 (0.1280)
16	2.850 (0.1122)	34	3.300 (0.1299)
18	2.900 (0.1142)		

Intake valve clearance (cold):
0.15 — 0.25 mm (0.006 — 0.010 in.)

Example: A 2.800 mm shim is installed and the measured clearance is 0.450 mm. Replace the 2.800 mm shim with shim No. 24 (3.050 mm).

Fig. 13 Valve shim size chart

14. Calculate thickness of new shim required by using the following formula:
   a. T = Thickness of shim removed.
   b. A = Valve clearance measured.
   c. N = Thickness of shim required.
   d. For intake valves use formula; N = T + (A - .008 inch (.20 mm)).
   e. For exhaust valves use formula; N = T + (A - .010 inch (.25 mm)).
   f. Select a shim from **Fig. 13** with a thickness as close as possible to the calculated valve.
15. Install new adjusting shims as required.
16. Depress valve spring using Spring Compressor tool No. J-37141-1 and remove the Lifter Holding tool No. J-37141-2A.
17. Install cylinder head cover and connect battery ground cable.

VALVE ADJUSTMENT SPECIFICATIONS

Year	Engine	Intake Inches	Exhaust Inches
1991–94	1.6L/4-97	.006–.010	.008–.012

TIMING BELT COVER
REPLACE
1991–92
GSi Models

1. Disconnect battery ground cable.

Fig. 11 Depressing valve spring

Fig. 12 Removing adjusting shim

1	GASKET	8 TIMING BELT GUIDE
2	IDLER PULLEY	9 NO. 1 TIMING BELT COVER
3	INTAKE CAMSHAFT PULLEY	10 CRANKSHAFT PULLEY
4	EXHAUST CAMSHAFT TIMING PULLEY	11 DRIVE BELT
5	CRANKSHAFT TIMING PULLEY	12 WATER PUMP PULLEY
6	TIMING BELT	13 NO. 2 TIMING BELT COVER
7	TENSION SPRING	14 NO. 3 TIMING BELT COVER

Fig. 14 Timing belt components. 1991–92 GSi models

2. Remove righthand wheel and lower splash shield.
3. Drain coolant.
4. Disconnect accelerator and cruise control cables.
5. Remove cruise control actuator and ignition coil.
6. Remove water outlet hose.
7. Remove accessory drive belts.
8. Remove spark plugs.
9. Set No. 1 cylinder at TDC on the compression stroke. Turn crankshaft pulley to align its groove with idler pulley bolt. Remove oil filter cap and ensure that you see hole in camshaft. **If hole cannot be seen, turn crankshaft 360° and check again.**
10. Disconnect righthand engine mount.
11. Remove water pump pulley.
12. Remove crankshaft pulley using Holder tool No. J-8614-0, or equivalent and Puller tool No.J-1859-03, or equivalent.
13. Remove timing belt cover attaching

screws and belt covers, **Fig. 14.**
14. Reverse procedure to install.

Except GSi Models
1. Disconnect battery ground cable.
2. Raise and support vehicle.
3. Remove right lower stone shield.
4. Lower vehicle.
5. Disconnect engine wiring harness from upper timing belt cover.
6. Remove accessory drive belts.
7. Remove crankshaft pulley using Puller tool No. J-1859-03, or equivalent.
8. Remove cylinder head cover and windshield washer reservoir.
9. Support engine using Engine Support Fixture tool No. J-28467-A, or equivalent.
10. Remove right engine mount through bolt.
11. Raise and support vehicle.
12. Remove two rear transaxle mount to main crossmember nuts.
13. Remove two center transaxle mount

Fig. 16 Camshaft timing pulley alignment. 1991–92 GSi models

Fig. 17 Belt & pulley alignment. 1991–92 GSi models

1	UPPER TIMING BELT COVER	6	CAMSHAFT TIMING PULLEY	11	CRANKSHAFT PULLEY
2	BOLT	7	CRANKSHAFT TIMING GEAR	12	BOLT
3	IDLER PULLEY	8	TENSION SPRING	13	INSPECTION PLUG
4	TIMING BELT	9	TIMING BELT GUIDE	14	CENTER TIMING BELT COVER
5	BOLT	10	LOWER TIMING BELT COVER	15	BOLT

Fig. 15 Timing belt components. 1991–92 Except GSi models

to center crossmember nuts.
14. Lower vehicle.
15. Raise engine and remove water pump pulley.
16. Remove timing belt covers attaching screws and timing belt covers, **Fig. 15.**
17. Reverse procedure to install.

TIMING BELT & CAMSHAFT TIMING PULLEY REPLACE

1991—92

GSI MODELS

Removal

1. Disconnect battery ground cable, then remove right front wheel and engine undercover.
2. Drain radiator coolant, then disconnect cruise control cable (if equipped), accelerator cable and link.
3. Remove cruise control actuator (if equipped), then the ignition coil and coolant outlet hose.
4. Remove accessory drive belts, then the spark plugs.
5. Turn crankshaft pulley and align groove with "0" mark on the No. 1 timing belt cover, then remove oil filler cap and ensure cavity in camshaft is visible indicating TDC compression. If camshaft cavity is not visible, rotate crankshaft an additional 360° to set engine at TDC compression.
6. Raise engine with suitable jack, then remove right side engine mount through bolt and the mount. **Insert suitable piece of wood between**

jack and engine to prevent damage.
7. Remove crankshaft pulley using suitable tools.
8. Remove timing belt covers and gaskets, then the timing belt guide from crankshaft sprocket.
9. Loosen idler pulley bolt, then push idler pulley as far left as possible and temporarily tighten idler pulley bolt.
10. Remove timing belt, idler pulley bolt, pulley and tension spring. **If timing belt is to reused, mark direction and belt-to-sprocket reference marks to ensure correct position during installation.**
11. Remove cylinder head covers, then using suitable wrench positioned on camshaft flats, remove camshaft sprocket attaching bolts and sprockets.

Installation

1. Install camshaft sprockets, aligning marks as shown in **Fig. 16.** Install sprocket attaching bolts and torque to specifications.
2. Install cylinder head covers, then the crankshaft sprocket, idler pulley and tension spring. Pry idler pulley towards the left as far as possible and temporarily tighten attaching bolt.
3. Install timing belt. **If belt is being reused, ensure it is installed in the same position as removed.**
4. Slowly loosen timing belt idler bolt, then temporarily install crankshaft pulley bolt.
5. Turn crankshaft two complete revolutions clockwise from TDC of compression stroke to TDC of compression stroke.
6. Check valve timing. Ensure each

sprocket is aligned as shown in **Fig. 17.**
7. Tighten timing belt idler pulley bolt to 27 ft. lbs.
8. Measure timing belt deflection as shown in **Fig. 18.** If deflection is not .16 inch with 4.4 lbs. of pressure, readjust as necessary with idler pulley.
9. Remove crankshaft pulley bolt, then install timing belt guide. Ensure guide cup side is facing outward.
10. Install timing belt covers and gaskets.
11. Reverse steps 1 through 5 of removal procedure to complete installation. When installing crankshaft pulley torque pulley bolt to specification.

EXCEPT GSI MODELS

Removal

1. Disconnect battery ground cable.
2. Remove timing belt covers as outlined under "Timing Belt Covers, Removal." **If timing belt is to be reused, mark direction and belt-to-sprocket reference marks to ensure correct position during installation.**
3. Remove timing belt guide from crankshaft sprocket.
4. Loosen idler pulley bolt, then push idler pulley as far left as possible and temporarily tighten idler pulley bolt.
5. Remove timing belt, idler pulley bolt, pulley and tension spring.
6. Remove idler pulley bolt, pulley and return spring.
7. Remove crankshaft timing pulley.
8. Remove camshaft timing gear by securing the camshaft with a wrench and removing the bolt, **Fig. 19.** Ensure not to damage cylinder head or camshaft with wrench.

Fig. 18   Measuring belt deflection. 1991–92 GSi models

610   EXHAUST CAMSHAFT
630   CAMSHAFT TIMING GEAR

Fig. 21   Camshaft timing gear replacement. 1993–94 models

Installation

1. Install camshaft timing gear.
2. Install crankshaft timing gear.
3. Position No. 1 cylinder at TDC.
4. Align camshaft timing gear hole with the exhaust camshaft cap mark, **Fig. 3.**
5. Install idler pulley, mount bolt and tensioner spring. Pry idler to left and temporarily tighten.
6. Install timing belt. If reusing original timing belt, align points made during disassembly with arrow pointing in proper direction.
7. Loosen timing belt idler pulley mount bolt.
8. Temporarily install crankshaft pulley bolt and turn crankshaft 2 revolutions from TDC to TDC. **Always turn the crankshaft clockwise.**
9. Ensure all components are properly aligned.
10. Install the timing belt idler pulley bolt.
11. Ensure timing belt deflection is .20–.24 inch. If belt is not within specification, the idler pulley must be adjusted.
12. Reverse remaining removal procedure to complete procedure.

1993–94

Removal

1. Disconnect battery ground cable.
2. Remove wiper reservoir, cruise control actuator cover and cable.
3. Remove cruise control actuator.
4. Raise and support engine.
5. Remove right tire and wheel assembly then the wheel housing.

1 CAMSHAFT TIMING GEAR

Fig. 19   Camshaft timing gear. 1991–92 Except GSi models

6. Remove accessory drive belts.
7. Lower vehicle.
8. Remove A/C compressor keeping hoses attached. Position in a out of the way location.
9. Remove A.C compressor bracket.
10. Remove power steering pump keeping hoses attached. Position in a out of the way location.
11. Disconnect alternator and oil pressure switch electrical connections.
12. Remove wiring harness cover and harness from cylinder head.
13. Remove spark plug wires and plugs.
14. Remove PCV hoses from cylinder head covers.
15. Remove cylinder head covers and gaskets.
16. Turn crankshaft to position No. 1 cylinder at TDC on its compression stroke. Valve lifters for No. 1 cylinder should be loose.
17. Disconnect engine ground wire from right fender apron.
18. Disconnect engine mounts as outlined under "Engine Mount Replace."
19. Remove water pump and crankshaft pulleys using puller tool No. J 1859-03 or equivalent.
20. Remove timing belt cover bolts and the timing belt covers.
21. Slide timing belt guide from crankshaft.
22. Ensure timing marks are aligned, **Fig. 20.**
23. If timing belt is to reused, mark timing belt with arrow showing direction of engine rotation.
24. Remove idler pulley bolt, idler pulley and tension spring.
25. Remove timing belt from camshaft and crankshaft timing gears.
26. Remove camshaft timing gear while holding camshaft by the hexagonal wrench head section, **Fig. 21.**
27. Remove crankshaft timing gear using two flat blade screwdrivers to pry off.

Installation

1. Install camshaft and crankshaft timing gear aligning keyways on shafts.

630   CAMSHAFT TIMING GEAR
669   CRANKSHAFT TIMING GEAR

Fig. 20   Engine timing marks. 1993–94 models

A   20N (4.4 lbs.)
B   5 – 6 mm (0.20 – 0.24")
630   CAMSHAFT TIMING GEAR
669   CRANKSHAFT TIMING GEAR

Fig. 22   Timing belt tension check. 1993–94 models

2. Tighten camshaft timing gear while holding camshaft by the hexagonal wrench head section, **Fig. 21.**
3. Install idler pulley and idler pulley spring.
4. Push idler pulley to its extreme left travel and tighten idler pulley.
5. Install timing belt to camshaft and crankshaft timing gears and idler pulley.
6. Loosen idler pulley bolt allowing spring to pull pulley to the right.
7. Temporarily install crankshaft pulley bolt and turn crankshaft two complete revolutions clockwise.
8. Ensure timing marks are still aligned.
9. Measure timing belt deflection as shown in **Fig. 22.** Belt deflection should be .20-.24 inch with 4.4 lbs. of pressure applied.
10. Replace timing belt if not with specification.
11. If timing belt is within specification, tighten idler pulley.
12. Install timing belt guide, facing cupped side outward.
13. Install timing belt covers starting with the lowest cover to the highest.
14. Install crankshaft pulley and secure with one bolt.
15. Install engine mount to body.
16. Raise and support vehicle.
17. Install mounting brackets to engine mount.
18. Install right side wheelhousing and tire and wheel assembly.
19. Lower vehicle.
20. Install A/C pipe bracket and engine ground wire to right front fender.
21. Install new cylinder cover gasket and

A I = INTAKE   E = EXHAUST
B I = INTAKE   E = EXHAUST
C FRONT MARK
D I.D. FOR BEARING
   NO. 2 THRU NO. 5

Fig. 23   Camshaft bearing caps installation. GSi models

1 INTAKE BEARING CAP BOLT
2 EXHAUST BEARING CAP BOLT

Fig. 26   Number 1 bearing cap bolts. Except GSi models

cover.
22. Install PCV hoses, spark plugs and wires.
23. Install engine wiring harness and cover.
24. Connect alternator and oil pressure switch electrical connectors.
25. Install power steering oil pump and air conditioner compressor.
26. Install and adjust accessory drive belts.
27. Install cruise control actuator and windshield washer reservoir.
28. Connect battery ground cable.

CAMSHAFT REPLACE

GSI MODELS

Removal

1. Disconnect battery ground cable.
2. Remove cylinder head cover.
3. Remove timing belt covers as outlined under "Timing Belt Cover, Replace."
4. Remove timing belt as outlined under "Timing Belt & Camshaft Timing Pulley, Replace."
5. Remove camshaft bearing caps.
6. Remove camshaft.

A CAMSHAFT

Fig. 24   Camshaft bearing caps tightening sequence. GSi models

1 SERVICE BOLT
2 SUB-GEAR
3 MAIN GEAR

Fig. 27   Fastening sub-gear to main gear. Except GSi models

Installation

1. Install camshaft(s). Exhaust camshaft has distributor drive gear.
2. Install camshaft bearing caps on each journal with arrows pointed toward the front, **Fig. 23.**
3. Torque cap bolts in three passes to specification in sequence shown in **Fig. 24.**
4. Install timing belt and covers as previously described.
5. Install cylinder head cover and connect battery ground cable.

EXCEPT GSI MODELS

Removal

1. Disconnect battery ground cable.
2. Remove cylinder head cover.
3. Remove timing belt covers as outlined under "Timing Belt Cover, Replace."
4. Remove timing belt as outlined under "Timing Belt & Camshaft Timing Pulley, Replace."
5. Remove camshaft timing gear by holding the camshaft with a wrench and removing the camshaft bolt. **Use caution not to damage camshaft or cylinder head with wrench.**

1 SERVICE BOLT HOLE (INTAKE CAMSHAFT)

Fig. 25   Service bolt hole alignment. Except GSi models

Fig. 28   Intake camshaft removal sequence. Except GSi models

6. With the No. 1 cylinder in TDC position, the service bolt hole of the intake camshaft gear should be in position as shown in **Fig. 25.**
7. Alternately loosen the No. 1 (front) intake and exhaust camshaft bearing cap bolts in several steps, **Fig. 26.**
8. Remove No. 1 bearing caps.
9. Fasten the intake camshaft sub-gear to the main gear with a service bolt, **Fig. 27.**
10. Uniformly loosen each intake camshaft bearing cap bolt in several steps in sequence shown in **Fig. 28.**
11. Remove intake camshaft bearing caps and camshaft. **The camshaft must be held level while it is being removed. If the camshaft is not kept level, the portion of the cylinder head receiving the shaft trust may crack or be damaged. If the camshaft cannot be lifted out straight and level, retighten the No. 3 bearing cap and alternately loosen the bolts of the bearing cap in several steps while pulling up on the camshaft gear.**
12. Rotate exhaust camshaft 105°, using a suitable wrench.
13. Place lockpin in position shown in **Fig. 29.**
14. Uniformly loosen each exhaust camshaft bearing cap bolt in several steps in sequence shown in **Fig. 30.**
15. Remove exhaust camshaft bearing caps and camshaft.
16. Disassemble intake camshaft by inserting pins into service holes in camshaft sub-gear, **Fig. 31.**
17. Using a screwdriver, turn sub-gear clockwise and remove pin C.
18. Remove snap ring, wave washer, camshaft sub gear, and camshaft gear spring.
19. Remove exhaust camshaft oil seal.

1 KNOCKPIN POSITION

Fig. 29   Knockout pin position. Except GSi models

Fig. 32   Exhaust camshaft tightening sequence. Except GSi models

Cylinder Block No.	1	2	3	1	2	3	1	2	3
Crankshaft No.	0	0	0	1	1	1	2	2	2
Bearing No.	1	2	3	2	3	4	3	4	5

Fig. 35   Main & rod bearing identification. GSi models

Installation

1. Install ring, wave washer, camshaft sub-gear and camshaft gear spring.
2. Install pins A and B, **Fig. 31**, into service holes of camshaft sub-gear.
3. Using a screwdriver, align holes of camshaft drive gear and sub-gear by turning camshaft sub-gear clockwise.
4. Install pin C.
5. Install the exhaust camshaft on cylinder head so that No. 1 and No. 3 cam lobes push their valves lifters evenly.
6. Install bearing caps on journals with arrows pointing toward the crankshaft pulley.
7. Tighten each bearing cap to specification in several steps in sequence shown in **Fig. 32**.
8. Apply multi-purpose grease to a new exhaust camshaft oil seal and install oil seal using Seal Installer tool No. J-35403 or equivalent.
9. Position lockpin of exhaust camshaft so that No. 4 cylinder cam lobes push their lifters.
10. Engage intake camshaft gear with exhaust camshaft gear by matching alignment marks.
11. Roll camshaft into position keeping timing gears engaged.
12. Install intake camshaft bearing cap No. 2 through No. 5 with arrows pointing toward the crankshaft pulley. No. 1 bearing cap will be install later in this procedure.
13. Tighten intake camshaft bearing cap

610   EXHAUST CAMSHAFT

Fig. 30   Exhaust camshaft removal sequence. Except GSi models

609   INTAKE CAMSHAFT

Fig. 33   Intake camshaft tightening sequence. Except GSi models

BEARING SELECTION TABLE

Crankshaft Block Mark	1	2	3	1	2	3	1	2	3
Crankshaft Mark	0	0	0	1	1	1	2	2	2
Bearing Mark	1	2	3	3	2	4	3	4	5

Fig. 36   Main & rod bearing identification. Except GSi models

bolts to specifications in several steps in sequence shown in **Fig. 33**.
14. Remove pins from intake camshaft sub-gear.
15. Install No. 1 bearing cap. If No. 1 bearing cap does not fit properly, push the camshaft gear backward by prying apart the cylinder head and camshaft gear with a suitable pry tool.
16. Turn exhaust camshaft one revolution from TDC to TDC of No. 1 cylinder.
17. Ensure alignment marks on exhaust and intake gear align.
18. Install camshaft timing gear and secure camshaft and install timing gear bolt, **Fig. 19**.
19. Install timing belt as outlined under "Timing Belt & Camshaft Timing Pulley, Replace."
20. Install timing belt covers as outlined under "Timing Belt Cover, Replace."
21. Install cylinder head cover and connect battery ground cable.

PISTONS & RODS ASSEMBLE

Assemble pistons to connecting rods as shown in **Fig. 34**.

MAIN & ROD BEARINGS

Main and rod service bearings are available in 5 standard sizes, marked 1

1 PIN A
2 PIN B
3 PIN C

Fig. 31   Exploded view of intake camshaft. Except GSi models

FRONT

ALIGN

Fig. 34   Piston & rod assembly

through 5. If replacing a bearing, replace with one having the same number. If the number of the bearing cannot be determined, select a bearing according to the numbers imprinted on the cylinder block and crankshaft then refer to **Fig. 35** and **36** for proper bearing number.

CRANKSHAFT REAR OIL SEAL
REPLACE

1. Remove transaxle and flywheel assembly.
2. Remove rear end plate.
3. Remove rear main oil seal retainer.
4. Carefully knock out oil seal from retainer.
5. Replace old oil seal with a new one, then apply a suitable lubricant.
6. Assemble retainer, rear end plate onto engine, then insert and securely tighten attaching bolts.
7. Assemble flywheel assembly to engine, then install transaxle.

1	DRIVE GEAR
2	DRIVEN GEAR

Fig. 37 Oil pump gear to housing clearance check

1	DRIVE GEAR
2	DRIVEN GEAR

Fig. 38 Oil pump gear to gear clearance check

1	OIL PUMP HOUSING
2	DRIVE GEAR
3	DRIVEN GEAR

Fig. 39 Oil pump side clearance check

1	WATER PUMP ASSEMBLY
2	O RING
3	WATER PUMP PULLEY

Fig. 40 Water pump removal

OIL PAN
REPLACE
GSi MODELS

1. Disconnect battery ground cable.
2. Raise and support vehicle.
3. Drain engine oil.
4. Remove righthand undercover.
5. Disconnect front exhaust pipe and bracket.
6. Remove oil pan bolts.
7. Remove oil pan.
8. Reverse procedure to install.

EXCEPT GSi MODELS

1. Disconnect battery ground cable.
2. Raise and support vehicle.
3. Drain engine oil.
4. Remove right and left stone covers.
5. Disconnect oxygen sensor connector.
6. Disconnect exhaust pipe from catalytic converter.
7. Disconnect exhaust pipe from exhaust manifold.
8. Remove oil pan bolts and pan.
9. Reverse procedure to install.

OIL PUMP
REPLACE

1. Disconnect battery ground cable.
2. Remove timing belt as outlined under "Timing Belt Cover, Replace" and "Timing Belt & Camshaft Timing Pulley, Replace."
3. Raise and support vehicle.
4. Remove crankshaft timing gear pulley.
5. Remove oil pan as outlined under "Oil Pan, Replace."
6. Remove oil pump bolts and oil pump assembly.
7. Reverse procedure to install, noting the following:
   a. Using feeler gauge, measure driven gear to housing clearance, **Fig. 37.** If clearance is greater than .0078 inch, replace the oil pump.
   b. Using feeler gauge, measure drive gear to driven gear clearance, **Fig. 38.** If clearance is greater than .0012 inch, replace the gear set.
   c. Using feeler gauge, measure oil pump body to gear clearance, **Fig. 39.** If clearance is greater than .004 inch replace the oil pump.

WATER PUMP
REPLACE
1991–92

1. Drain cooling system.
2. Raise and support engine.
3. Remove nut for rear engine mount.
4. Lower vehicle.
5. Remove windshield washer reservoir, cruise control module and bracket.
6. Remove through bolt from right engine mount.
7. With a suitable jack, raise engine.
8. Loosen water pump pulley bolts.
9. Remove accessory drive belts.
10. Remove water pump pulley.
11. Lower engine into place.
12. Disconnect water inlet and by-pass hoses from water inlet pipe.
13. Remove water inlet pipe and O-ring.
14. Remove and plug oil dipstick.
15. Remove upper timing belt cover as outlined under "Timing Belt Cover, Removal."
16. Remove water pump bolts and water pump, **Fig. 40.**
17. Reverse procedure to install.

1993–94

1. Disconnect battery ground cable, then drain cooling system.
2. Raise and support engine using tool No. J 28467-A or equivalent.
3. Remove right engine mount and insulator as outlined under "Engine Mount, Replace."
4. Remove timing covers, then on models equipped with power steering remove front transaxle mount from vehicle.
5. Remove radiator fan motor assembly, then engine wiring harness retainer clip from engine.
6. Remove oil level indicator from guide tube, guide tube mounting bolt, then guide tube.
7. Remove engine coolant temperature sending unit electrical connector, then two nut attaching engine coolant inlet pipe to cylinder block.
8. Loosen hose clamp, remove coolant inlet pipe from vehicle, then inlet hose from water pump.
9. Raise engine on vehicles equipped with power steering.

1	UNION BOLT	6	GASKET
2	GASKET	7	FUEL LINE
3	FUEL LINE	8	GASKET
4	GASKET	9	UNION BOLT
5	FILTER		

Fig. 41 Fuel filter replacement. 1991-92 models

10. Remove water pump attaching bolts, water pump, then O-ring.
11. Reverse procedure to install.

COOLING SYSTEM BLEED

These engines do not require a specified bleed procedure. After filling cooling system, run engine to operating temperature with radiator/pressure cap off. Air will then be automatically bled through cap opening.

THERMOSTAT
REPLACE

1991–92

1. Drain coolant.
2. Remove water inlet housing and thermostat.
3. Thoroughly clean gasket surfaces.
4. Install thermostat with air bleed valve on top and aligned with protrusion on water inlet.
5. Install water inlet housing and new gasket, then **torque** bolts to 20 ft. lbs.
6. Fill radiator with coolant, then start engine and check for leaks.

1993–94

1. Drain engine coolant, then disconnect engine coolant switch electrical connector.
2. Remove thermostat housing attaching nuts, thermostat housing, then thermostat and gasket.
3. Reverse procedure to install, tighten thermostat housing to specifications.

BELT TENSION DATA

Year	Engine Code	Belt	New Ft. Lbs.	Used Ft. Lbs.
1991–92	5 & 6	A/C	140–180	80–120
	5	Alt.	170–180	95–135
	6	Alt.	140–180	110–150
1993–94	6 & 8	Alt.	①②	—
	6 & 8	A/C	①③	—
	6 & 8	P.S.	①③	—

①—With 22 lbs. exerted.
②—Deflection of 0.24–0.35 inches.
③—Deflection of 0.20–0.32 inches.

FUEL PUMP
REPLACE

1991–92

1. Drain fuel tank.
2. Disconnect all fuel and electrical connections.
3. Raise and support vehicle.
4. Support fuel tank with a suitable jack.
5. Loosen and remove fuel tank support straps.
6. Lower fuel tank from vehicle.
7. Remove fuel tank bracket from fuel tank.
8. Remove fuel pump from fuel tank bracket.
9. Remove fuel pump filter from pump.
10. Reverse procedure to install, noting the following:
    a. **Torque** fuel tank bracket bolts to 30 inch lbs.
    b. **Torque** fuel tank flare nut to 22 ft. lbs.

1993–94

1. Relieve fuel system pressure as outlined in "Fuel System Pressure Release."
2. Remove rear seat cushion, floor service hole cover attaching screws, then cover.
3. Disconnect fuel sender electrical connector, then fuel feed hose from sender assembly.
4. Remove fuel return hose from sender assembly, fuel sender attaching bolts, then fuel sender.
5. Remove fuel pump from fuel pump bracket by pulling off lower side of fuel pump from fuel pump bracket, then fuel pump electrical connector.
6. Remove rubber cushion from fuel pump, then fuel pump strainer from fuel pump.
7. Reverse procedure to install.

FUEL FILTER
REPLACE

1991–92

The fuel filter is located in the engine

604 FUEL FILTER
605 FUEL FILTER BRACKET
606 FUEL FILTER BRACKET BOLT

Fig. 42 Fuel filter replacement. 1993-94 models

compartment, below the power brake vacuum booster assembly.

1. Relieve fuel system pressure as follows:
   a. Remove fuel filler cap, then disconnect circuit opening relay located under instrument panel near Engine Control Module (ECM).
   b. Start engine and allow to stall, then crank engine for an additional ten seconds.
   c. Slowly loosen and remove cold start injector valve line bolt at fuel rail. Cover lines to be removed with shop towel.
   d. Disconnect battery ground cable.
2. Remove air intake duct, then fuel line union bolt from filter outlet (upper connection), **Fig. 41.**
3. Raise and support vehicle.
4. Remove fuel line union bolt from filter lower fitting.
5. Loosen filter bracket retaining bolt, then remove filter and bracket assembly from vehicle.
6. Reverse procedure to install. **Torque** fuel line banjo fittings to 21 ft. lbs.

1993–94

1. Relieve fuel system pressure as outlined in "Fuel System Pressure Release."
2. Remove intake air temperature sensor electrical connector, then loosen air cleaner (ACL) hose clamp bolt.
3. Remove four cap clips from ACL, then ACL hose and cap from vehicle.
4. Remove evaporative emission hose (EVAP) from EVAP canister, EVAP mounting bolt, EVAP canister.
5. Remove fuel feed outlet and outlet lines from fuel filter, fuel filter mounting bolts, then fuel filter, **Fig. 42.**
6. Reverse procedure to install.

TIGHTENING SPECIFICATIONS

Year	Component	Torque/Ft. Lbs.
1991–92	Camshaft Bearing Cap Bolts ② ③	115 ①
	Camshaft Timing Gear Bolt ②	43
	Camshaft Timing Pulley Bolt ③	34
	Cold Start Injector Pipe Union Bolt ②	13
	Connecting Rod Bearing Cap Nuts	36
	Crankshaft Pulley Bolt ②	105
	Crankshaft Pulley Bolt ③	87
	Cylinder Head Bolts ②	44
	Cylinder Head Cover Cap Nuts ②	15
	Engine Mount Support Bolts ③	35
	Engine Mount Through Bolt ③	64
	Engine Mount To Bracket Bolt ③	45
	Engine Mount To Engine Bracket Nuts ③	45
	Exhaust Manifold Nuts And Bolts ②	18
	Exhaust Manifold Nuts ③	18
	Exhaust Manifold Support Bolts ②	18
	Exhaust Manifold Insulator Bolts ②	18
	Exhaust Pipe To Exhaust Manifold Bolts ②	18
	Flywheel To Crankshaft Attaching Bolts (Automatic)	47
	Flywheel To Crankshaft Attaching Bolts (manual)	58
	Idler Pulley Bolt ③	27
	Intake Manifold Bolts ②	14
	Intake Manifold Bolts ③	20
	Intake Manifold Bracket Bolts ③	20
	Main Bearing Cap Bolts	44
	Oil Cooler Center Bolts ③	20
	Oil Pan Bolts ③	53 ①
	Oil Pan Nuts And Bolts ②	44 ①
	Oil Pump Bolts ②	16
	Oil Pump Bolts ③	89 ①
	Oil Pump Cover Screws	89 ①
	Oil Strainer/Pick Up Assembly Bolts And Nuts ②	89 ①
	Pressure Regulator Bolts ②	65
	Rear End Plate Bolts ②	89 ①
	Rear Main Oil Seal Retainer Bolts ②	84 ①
	Rear Main Seal Retainer Bolts ③	89 ①
	Relief Valve Plug ③	27
	Right Engine Mount Through Bolt ②	64
	Spark Plugs	13
	Timing Belt Cover Bolt	44 ①
	Timing Belt Idler Pulley Bolt ②	27
	Transaxle Mount To Center Crossmember Nuts	45
	Transaxle Mount To Main Crossmember Nuts	45
1993–94	Accelerator Bracket Bolts	11
	A/C Compressor Flexible Hose Mounting Bolts	89 ①
	A/C Pipe Bracket Bolt	89 ①
	Actuator Bolt	19
	Air Cleaner (ACL) Lower Case Bolt	89 ①
	Air Intake Chamber Brace Bolt	21

Year	Component	Torque/Ft. Lbs.
1993–94 —Cont'd	Air Intake Chamber Cover Nuts & Bolts	14
	Air Pipe Nut & Bolt	80 ①
	Alternator Bracket Bolts	23
	Camshaft Bearing Cap Bolts	115 ①
	Camshaft Timing Gear Bolt	43
	Center Support Bearing	45
	Connecting Rod Bearing Cap Nuts	22 ④
	Coolant Pump Bolts	124 ①
	Coolant Pump Pulley Bolts	18
	Coolant Reservoir Mounting Bolts	11
	Crankshaft Pulley Bolts	87
	Cruise Control Actuator Bracket Bolts	19
	Cylinder Head Bolts	22 ⑤
	EGR Solenoid Valve Mounting Bolt	115 ①
	EGR Valve To EGR Pipe Nut & Bolts	43
	EGR Valve To Intake Manifold Nuts & Bolts	115 ①
	Engine Hanger Bolt	20
	Engine Mount Bracket Mounting Nuts	38
	Engine Mount Through Nut & Bolts	47
	Engine Mount To Body Bolts	19
	Engine Mount To Cylinder Block Brake Bolts	38
	Engine Mount To Engine Bracket "A" Bolts	19
	Engine Mount To Engine Bracket "B" Bolts	47
	Engine Mount To Engine Bracket "C" Bolts	47
	Engine Oil Pan Nuts & Bolts	44 ①
	Exhaust Manifold Brace Bolts	29
	Exhaust Manifold Nuts	25
	Flywheel Bolts (Automatic Transaxles)	47
	Flywheel Bolts (Manual Transaxles)	58
	Front Pipe Hanger Bolts	14
	Front Pipe Support Bolts	14
	Front Pipe To Catalytic Converter	32
	Front Pipe To Exhaust Manifold Nuts & Bolts	46
	Fuel Feed Pipe Connector	22
	Fuel Inlet Hose Clamp Bolt	89 ①
	Fuel Rail Bolts	11
	Guide Tube Bolts	80 ①
	Idler Pulley Mounting Bolts	27
	Insulator Bolt	47
	Intake Manifold Brace Bolts	14
	Intake Manifold Nuts And Bolts	14
	Lower Engine Reinforcement Brace To Cylinder Block Bolts ⑥	47
	Lower Engine Reinforcement Brace To Transaxle Bolts ⑥	47
	Lower Heat Insulator Bolts	80 ①
	Main Bearing Bolt Caps	44
	Mounting Bracket To Engine Mounting Bolt	47
	Mounting Bracket To Engine Mounting Nuts	38
	Oil Drain Plug	97 ①
	Oil Pressure Switch	115 ①
	Oil Pump Bolts	16

1.6L/4-97 & 1.8L/4-107.5 ENGINES

TIGHTENING SPECIFICATIONS—Continued

Year	Component	Torque/Ft. Lbs.
1993-94 —Cont'd	Oil Strainer Bolts	62①
	Power Steering Pump Bracket Bolts	32
	Rear End Plate Bolts	89①
	Rear Main Seal Bolts	89①
	Rotor Plate Screw	89①
	Splash Shield Bolts	44①
	Throttle Body Nuts & Bolts	17
	Timing Belt Cover Bolts	62①
	Transaxle To Engine Mounting Bolts	17

Year	Component	Torque/Ft. Lbs.
1993-94 —Cont'd	Union Bolts	22
	Upper Heat Insulator Bolts	80①
	Wheelhousing Bolts	11
	Wiring Harness Cover Bolts	53①

① —Inch lbs.
② —Except GSi models.
③ —GSi models.
④ —Plus an additional 90°.
⑤ —Plus 90°, plus an additional 90°.
⑥ —1.6L/4-97 engine.

Clutch & Manual Transaxle

INDEX

ADJUSTMENTS

CLUTCH PEDAL, ADJUST

1. Check height as shown in **Fig. 1.**
2. If it is necessary to adjust pedal height, remove instrument lower finish panel and air duct.
3. Loosen locknut and turn stopper bolt until the height is correct, then tighten locknut.
4. Push in on clutch pedal until resistance is felt, then check pushrod and pedal freeplay. Pushrod play should be .039-.197 inch, while freeplay should be .20-.59 inch.
5. To adjust, loosen locknut and turn pushrod until freeplay and pushrod play are within specification, then tighten locknut.
6. Recheck pedal height and adjust as necessary.
7. Reinstall air duct and lower finish panel.

SHIFT LEVER FREEPLAY, ADJUST

Shift cables on these models are not adjustable. If cables are out of adjustment, replacement of the defective cable(s) will be required.

HYDRAULIC SYSTEM SERVICE

CLUTCH ACTUATOR, REPLACE

1. Disconnect negative battery cable.

PUSH ROD PLAY AND FREEPLAY ADJUST POINT
PEDAL HEIGHT ADJUST POINT
1.0-5.0mm (0.039-0.197 in.) PUSH ROD PLAY
PEDAL HEIGHT

Fig. 1 Clutch pedal adjustment

2. Raise and support vehicle.
3. Disconnect clutch hydraulic line.
4. Remove two mounting bolts and actuator.
5. Reverse procedure to install. Bleed as follows:
   a. Clean top and sides of reservoir to ensure no foreign material enters system.
   b. Remove cap and fill reservoir with suitable brake fluid.
   c. Connect one end of a clear vinyl tube to bleeder screw and insert other end of tube into a half filled container of brake fluid.
   d. Slowly pump clutch pedal several times.
   e. While pumping clutch pedal, loosen bleeder screw until fluid starts to runout.
   f. Tighten bleeder screw.
   g. Repeat procedure until no air bubbles exist in escaping fluid.

CLUTCH
REPLACE

1. Remove transaxle assembly from vehicle.
2. Loosen each set bolt one turn at a time until spring tension is released.
3. Remove attaching bolts and pull off clutch assembly, **Fig. 2.**
4. Remove release bearing fork and boot from the transaxle.
5. Reverse procedure to install. Torque bolts to specifications.

MANUAL TRANSAXLE
REPLACE

1. Disconnect battery ground and positive cables.
2. Support engine using Engine Support Fixture tool No. J-28467-A, or equivalent.
3. Remove battery and battery tray.
4. Remove air cleaner assembly.
5. Disconnect back-up switch.
6. Disconnect ground cable at transaxle.
7. Remove two actuator mounting bolts.
8. Remove actuator line bracket.
9. Remove shift cable retainers, end clips and cables from bracket and lay aside.
10. Remove left transaxle mount cover, brace and through bolt.
11. Remove two upper transaxle to engine bolts.
12. Remove starter assembly.
13. Disconnect speedometer cable.
14. Raise and support vehicle.
15. Remove right and left stone shields.
16. Drain transaxle oil.

1. 78N•m (58 FT-LBS)
2. FLYWHEEL
3. CLUTCH DISC
4. CLUTCH COVER
5. 19N•m (14 FT-LBS)
6. RELEASE BEARING AND HUB

7. RELEASE FORK
8. BOOT

Fig. 2 Clutch assembly

17. Remove drive axles.
18. Remove three center crossmember to radiator support bolts.
19. Remove front and center mount bolt shields.
20. Remove front, center and rear mount nuts.
21. Remove two center crossmember to main crossmember bolts.
22. Remove exhaust hangers.
23. Support main crossmember using a suitable jack.
24. Remove eight main crossmember to underbody bolts.

25. Remove two lower A-frame bracket to underbody bolts. **Lower main crossmember slowly while holding onto the center crossmember. Center crossmember will be free to fall at this time and could cause serious bodily injury.**
26. Remove front through bolt and mount.
27. Remove front mount bracket from transaxle.
28. Remove center mount from transaxle.
29. Remove transaxle inspection cover.
30. Remove two lower transaxle bracket to mount bolts.

31. Lower vehicle.
32. Remove remaining transaxle mount to bracket bolts.
33. Lower transaxle using Engine Support tool No. J-28467, or equivalent to gain clearance to remove transaxle.
34. Remove transaxle mount.
35. Raise and support vehicle.
36. Support transaxle using a suitable jack.
37. Remove front and rear lower transaxle to engine bolts.
38. Lower transaxle from vehicle.
39. Reverse procedure to install.

TIGHTENING SPECIFICATIONS

Year	Component	Torque/ Ft. Lbs.
1991–94	Actuator Assembly Bolts	106 ①
	Back-Up Light Switch	30
	Bleeder Screw	97 ①
	Clutch Cover Bolts	14
	Clutch Line Tube	11
	Flywheel Bolts	58
	Master Cylinder Nuts	11
	Pedal Assembly Bracket To Instrument Panel Bolts	11
	Transaxle Case Cover Bolts	13
	Transaxle Case Bolts	22

① —Inch lbs.

Rear Axle & Suspension

INDEX

KNUCKLE
REPLACE

1991-92

1. Raise and support vehicle.
2. Support suspension using a suitable jack. Place jack under suspension supports, not the suspension arms.
3. Lower vehicle slightly so weight rests on jack.
4. Remove tire and wheel assembly.
5. **On except GSi models,** remove brake drum assembly.
6. **On GSi models,** remove rear disc brake assembly.
7. **On all models,** remove rear axle hub as outlined under "Rear Axle Hub, Replace," **Fig. 1.**
8. **On except GSi models,** disconnect brake line from brake hose and backing plate.
9. **On GSi models,** disconnect brake hose from caliper assembly.
10. **On all models,** remove strut rod from knuckle as outlined under "Strut Rod, Replace."
11. Remove front and rear suspension arms from knuckle as outlined under "Suspension Arm, Replace."
12. Disconnect strut assembly as outlined under "Strut/Coil Spring, Replace."
13. Remove knuckle.
14. Reverse procedure to install, torquing attaching bolts to specifications.

1993-94

1. Remove rear hub as described under "Rear Axle & Axle Carrier, Replace" found in this section.
2. Remove brake lines and hoses, then backing plate from rear suspension hub.
3. Remove nut, bolt, and strut rod from knuckle.
4. Remove nut, bolt, and both lateral links from knuckle.
5. Remove two nuts, bolts, and strut assembly from knuckle.
6. Remove rear suspension knuckle from vehicle.

1	FUEL TANK BAND	
2	STRUT TOWER COVER	
3	STRUT ROD PISTON NUT	
4	STRUT ASSEMBLY	
5	REAR TOE ADJUSTMENT BOLT	
6	NO. 2 SUSPENSION ARM-TO-BODY BOLT	
7	STABILIZER BAR LINK-TO-STRUT ASSEMBLY NUT	
8	NO. 2 SUSPENSION ARM	
9	STRUT ASSEMBLY-TO-KNUCKLE NUT	
10	NO. 2 SUSPENSION ARM-TO-KNUCKLE BOLT	
11	BRAKE LINE	
12	REAR DISC BRAKE ASSEMBLY	
13	REAR SUSPENSION KNUCKLE	

14	STRUT ROD	
15	STRUT ROD-TO-KNUCKLE BOLT	
16	STRUT ROD-TO-BODY BOLT	
17	NO. 1 SUSPENSION ARM-TO-KNUCKLE BOLT	
18	NO. 1 SUSPENSION ARM	
19	NO. 1 SUSPENSION ARM-TO-BODY BOLT	
20	STABILIZER BRACKET BOLT	
21	STABILIZER BAR BRACKET	
22	BUSHING	
23	STABILIZER BAR LINK	
24	STABILIZER BAR LINK NUT	
25	STABILIZER BAR	

Fig. 1   Rear suspension assembly

7. Reverse procedure to install noting the following:
  a. When replacing rear suspension knuckle, **torque** attaching nuts and bolts to specifications.
  b. Bleed brakes, then check rear wheel alignment.

REAR AXLE HUB
REPLACE
1991-92

1. Raise and support vehicle.
2. Support suspension using a suitable

1. WHEEL BEARING LOCKNUT
2. BEARING INNER RACE
3. BEARING OUTER RACE
4. AXLE SHAFT
5. HUB BOLT
6. OIL SEAL
7. AXLE HUB
8. BEARING

Fig. 2   Rear axle hub assembly

Fig. 3   Removing axle shaft from hub

1. SUSPENSION SUPPORT
2. STRUT LOWER BRACKET

Fig. 4   Aligning suspension support plate

jack. Place jack under suspension supports, not the suspension arms.
3. Lower vehicle slightly so weight rests on jack.
4. Remove tire and wheel assembly.
5. **On except GSi models,** remove brake drum assembly.
6. **On GSi models,** remove rear disc brake assembly.
7. **On all models,** remove axle hub and rear suspension knuckle mounting bolts, **Fig. 2.**
8. Reverse procedure to install, using a new O-ring seal when installing.

REAR AXLE HUB & AXLE CARRIER
REPLACE

1993-94

1. Raise and support vehicle. Place jack stand under suspension support, not suspension arms.
2. Lower vehicle, remove rear wheels, then rear drums.
3. Check hub bearing endplay using tools No. J 26900-13 or equivalent magnetic base and tool No. J 8001 or equivalent dial indicator. If endplay exceeds 0.020 inches replace axle hub bearing on vehicles without ABS or rear axle hub on vehicles with ABS.
4. Remove bolt attaching ABS speed sensor, if equipped.
5. Remove axle hub and rear suspension knuckle mounting bolts, then axle hub from vehicle.
6. Remove O-ring from backing plate.
7. Reverse procedure to install.

REAR AXLE HUB
SERVICE

1. Remove rear axle hub as outlined under "Rear Axle Hub, Replace."
2. Unstake wheel bearing locknut and remove.
3. Remove axle shaft from hub assembly using a Bearing Removal tool Nos. J-22912, J-38278 and J-8433, or equivalents, **Figs. 2 and 3.**
4. Remove bearing inner and outer race.

5. Remove oil seal from axle shaft using Seal Installer/Remover tool No. J-26941, or equivalent, and slide hammer.
6. Reverse procedure to install, using a new bearing locknut.

STRUT/COIL SPRING ASSEMBLY
REPLACE

1991-92

1. Raise and support vehicle.
2. Support suspension using a suitable jack. Place jack under suspension supports, not the suspension arms.
3. Lower vehicle slightly so weight rests on jack.
4. Remove tire and wheel assembly.
5. Disconnect brake hose from brake hose bracket.
6. Disconnect stabilizer bar link from strut assembly as outlined under "Stabilizer Bar, Replace."
7. Disconnect strut assembly mounting bolts from knuckle.
8. Remove seat back side cushion (sedan) or rear sill side panel (hatchback).
9. Disconnect strut assembly mounting nuts holding strut support.
10. Remove strut assembly from vehicle.
11. Reverse procedure to install.

1993-94

1. Raise and support vehicle. Place jack stand under suspension support, not suspension arms.
2. Remove rear wheels, brake lines from brake hoses and backing plate.
3. Remove brake clip from brake line, then brake hose from hose bracket.
4. Remove ABS wire harness attaching bolt, if equipped.
5. Remove stabilizer bar link attaching nut from strut assembly.
6. Remove strut assembly mounting bolts and nuts from rear suspension knuckle.
7. Remove strut top mounting nuts, then strut assembly from vehicle.
8. Reverse procedure to install.

STRUT/COIL SPRING ASSEMBLY SERVICE
DISASSEMBLY

1. Remove strut assembly as outlined under "Strut/Coil Spring Assembly, Replace."
2. Mount strut assembly in Strut Holding/Spring Compression tool No. J-34013, or equivalent.
3. Remove strut piston rod to suspension support nut.
4. Remove suspension support, coil spring, insulator and bumper.

ASSEMBLY

1. Mount strut in Holding/Spring Compression tool No. J-34013, or equivalent.
2. Align coil spring end with lower seat hollow and install coil spring.
3. Install spring bumper and insulator.
4. Align suspension support with piston rod and install.
5. Align suspension support with strut lower bracket as shown in **Fig. 4.**
6. Compress spring slightly, install a new strut rod piston nut and torque to specification.

SUSPENSION ARM
REPLACE
1991–92
Rear
1. Raise and support vehicle.
2. Remove bolt and nut attaching rear suspension arm to axle carrier.
3. Remove cam and bolt attaching rear suspension arm to body, then the rear suspension arm.
4. Note location of cam plate mark before removing bolt and cam.
5. Reverse procedure to install.

Front
1. Raise and support vehicle.
2. Remove bolt and nut attaching front suspension arm to axle carrier.
3. Remove bolt and nut attaching front suspension arm to the body, then the front suspension arm.
4. Reverse procedure to install.

STRUT ROD
REPLACE
1991–92
1. Raise and support vehicle.
2. Remove bolt and nut attaching strut rod to axle carrier.
3. Remove bolt and nut attaching strut rod to body, then the strut rod assembly from the vehicle.
4. Reverse procedure to install.

LATERAL LINK & STRUT ROD
REPLACE
1993–94
1. Raise and support vehicle. Place jack stand under suspension support, not suspension arms, remove two strut rod nut and bolts, then strut rod.
2. Remove resonator/intermediate pipe assembly from catalytic converter.
3. Remove resonator/intermediate pipe assembly from muffler/tail pipe assembly.
4. Remove muffler/tail pipe assembly attaching bolts, then muffler/tail pipe assembly from hanger.
5. Remove intermediate pipe heat shield, then six crossmember to body attaching bolts.
6. Remove front lateral link with the two bolts and four washers.
7. Reverse procedure to install, tighten nuts and bolts to specifications.

STABILIZER ARM
REPLACE
1991–92
1. Support fuel tank with a suitable jack.
2. Disconnect fuel tank straps.
3. Disconnect stabilizer bar links from strut assemblies, **Fig. 1.**
4. Disconnect stabilizer bar bracket mounting bolts.
5. Remove stabilizer bar from vehicle.
6. Reverse procedure to install.

STABILIZER BAR
REPLACE
1993–94
1. Raise and support vehicle. Place jack stand under suspension support, not suspension arms.
2. Remove rear wheels, then left and right stabilizer bar links.
3. Remove right and left stabilizer bar bushing retainers. Scribe marks between stabilizer bar bushings, stabilizer, and body.
4. Remove stabilizer bushings.
5. Remove resonator/intermediate pipe assembly from catalytic converter.
6. Remove resonator/intermediate pipe assembly from muffler/tail pipe assembly.
7. Remove muffler/tail pipe assembly attaching bolts, then muffler/tail pipe assembly from hanger.
8. Remove intermediate pipe heat shield, then right fuel tank band.
9. Support crossmember with jack, then remove six bolts attaching crossmember to body.
10. Remove stabilizer bar.
11. Reverse procedure to install, tighten all nuts and bolts to specifications.

TIGHTENING SPECIFICATIONS

Year	Component	Torque/ Ft. Lbs.
1991–92	Axle Hub Mounting Bolts	59
	Brake Line To Backing Plate	11
	Stabilizer Bar Bracket Mounting Bolts	14
	Stabilizer Bar Link To Strut Assembly	26
	Stabilizer Bar Links To Strut Assembly	26
	Stabilizer Bar To Stabilizer Bar Links Nuts	26
	Strut Assembly To Body Nuts	29
	Strut Assembly To Knuckle Nuts	105
	Strut Rod Piston Nut	36
	Strut Rod To Body Nut	87
	Strut Rod To Knuckle Nuts	87
	Suspension Arm Bolts	87
	Wheel Bearing Locknut	90
	Wheel Lug Nuts	76
1993–94	ABS Speed Sensor Bolt	69①
	ABS Wire Harness Bolt	48①
	Axle Hub To Rear Knuckle Mounting Bolts	59
	Brake Line Fittings	11

Year	Component	Torque/ Ft. Lbs.
1993–94 —Cont'd	Fuel Tank Band Bolts	29
	Intermediate Pipe Heat Shield Bolt	48①
	Lateral Link Nut & Bolts	87
	Muffler/Tail Pipe Assembly To Body Bolts	115①
	Resonator/Intermediate Pipe Assembly To Muffler/Tail Pipe Bolts	14
	Resonator/Intermediate Pipe Assembly To Catalytic Converter Bolts	32
	Stabilizer Bar Bushing Retainer Bolts	14
	Stabilizer Bar Link To Stabilizer Bar Bolts	26
	Stabilizer Bar Link To Strut Assembly Nut	32
	Stabilizer Assembly To Rear Suspension Knuckle Mounting Nuts & Bolts	105
	Stabilizer Assembly To Strut Support Mounting Nuts	29
	Strut Rod Nuts & Bolts	67
	Wheel Bearing Locknut	90
	Wheel Lug Nuts	76

①—Inch lbs.

Front Suspension & Steering

INDEX

DESCRIPTION

The front suspension, **Figs. 1 and 2**, on this vehicle is a MacPherson strut design. The upper end of the strut is anchored to the body by a strut support. The strut and strut support are isolated by a rubber mount. The lower end of the strut is connected to the upper end of the steering knuckle. The lower end of the knuckle is attached to the ball joint, which is attached to the suspension control arm assembly. Movement of the steering wheel is transmitted to the tie-rod end and then to the knuckle, turning the wheel and tire assembly.

STRUT/COIL SPRING REPLACE

1. Raise and support vehicle.
2. Support suspension using a suitable jack. Place jack under suspension supports, not the control arm.
3. Lower vehicle slightly so weight rests on jack.
4. Install a Drive Joint Seal Protector tool No. J-34754, or equivalent.
5. Remove brake hose from disc brake caliper.
6. Remove clip from brake hose.
7. Remove brake hose from brake hose bracket.
8. Remove bolts and nuts attaching strut assembly to steering knuckle.
9. Remove strut assembly mounting nuts holding suspension support plate.
10. Remove strut assembly.
11. Reverse procedure to install.

STRUT/COIL SPRING SERVICE

1. Using Strut Holding/Spring Compression tool No. J-34013-A, or equivalent, compress spring slightly. **Ensure spring seat is secure and will not turn.**
2. Remove strut rod piston nut.
3. Remove suspension support, dust seal, spring seat and insulator and bumper.
4. Reverse procedure to assemble.

1 STRUT ROD PISTON NUT	12 STRUT MOUNTING NUT AND BOLT
2 SUSPENSION SUPPORT	13 BRAKE HOSE CLIP
3 DUST SEAL	14 COTTER PIN
4 SPRING SEAT	15 BALL JOINT CASTLE NUT
5 UPPER INSULATOR	16 BALL JOINT
6 COIL SPRING	17 BALL JOINT MOUNTING NUT AND BOLT
7 SPRING BUMPER	18 CROSSMEMBER MOUNTING NUTS
8 LOWER INSULATOR	19 CROSSMEMBER-TO-CONTROL-ARM BOLT
9 SHOCK ABSORBER	20 CROSSMEMBER MOUNTING BOLTS
10 BRAKE LINE GASKETS	21 SUSPENSION CROSSMEMBER
11 BRAKE LINE-TO-CALIPER BOLT	

Fig. 1 Disassembled view of front suspension. Except GSi models

LOWER CONTROL ARM
REPLACE

1. Raise and support vehicle.
2. Remove lower control arm attaching nuts and bolts.
3. **On models with stabilizer bar,** disconnect stabilizer bar links.
4. **On all models,** remove the six bolts and two nuts and remove the suspension crossmember with control arms attached.
5. Remove control arm mounting bolts and nuts. Remove control arm from crossmember.
6. Reverse procedure to install. Torque control arm to body front nuts and bolts to specifications.

LOWER CONTROL ARM BUSHING
REPLACE

1. Remove control arm as outlined under "Lower Control Arm, Replace."
2. Using a suitable tool, remove lower control arm bushing from lower control arm.
3. Reverse procedure to install. Torque bushing nut to specifications.

LOWER BALL JOINT
REPLACE

1. Raise and support vehicle.
2. Support suspension using a suitable jack. Place jack under suspension supports, not the control arm.
3. Lower vehicle slightly so weight rests on jack.
4. Loosen wheel lug nuts.
5. Remove tire and wheel assembly.
6. Install Inner Drive Joint Seal Protector tool No. J-34754, or equivalent. **Care must be taken not to allow tri-pot joints to over extend. Over extended tri-pot joints could result in separation of internal components and possible join failure.**
7. Using Ball Joint Removal tool No. J-35413 or equivalent, separate ball joint from knuckle assembly.
5. Remove two nuts and bolts attaching ball joint and control arm.
6. Remove ball joint.
7. Reverse procedure to install. Torque knuckle to ball joint nut to specifications. During installation, always replace a self-locking nut with a new one.

STEERING KNUCKLE
REPLACE

1. Remove locknut cap and bearing locknut.
2. Remove brake caliper and support with wire.
3. Remove disc brake rotor.
4. Separate tie rod from steering knuckle using Tie Rod Puller tool No. J-6627-A, or equivalent.

5. Remove lower ball joint bolt and nuts and separate it from lower control arm.
6. Remove two strut to steering knuckle nuts.
7. Install Drive Joint Protector tool No. J-34754, or equivalent.
8. Tap driveshaft with a plastic hammer and drive out driveshaft.
9. Remove two strut to steering knuckle bolts.
10. Remove steering knuckle assembly.
11. Reverse procedure to install.

HUB
REPLACE

1. Remove knuckle from vehicle and mount into a suitable vise.
2. Using a suitable screwdriver, remove dust deflector.

1	STABILIZER BAR	17	BRAKE LINE-TO-CALIPER BOLT
2	STABILIZER BAR BRACKET BOLT	18	REAR BRACKET BOLT
3	STABILIZER BAR BRACKET	19	REAR BRACKET
4	STABILIZER BAR BUSHING	20	REAR BRACKET BOLT
5	STRUT ROD PISTON NUT	21	BALL JOINT CASTLE NUT
6	SUSPENSION SUPPORT	22	BALL JOINT
7	DUST SEAL	23	BALL JOINT RETAINING NUTS AND BOLT
8	SPRING SEAT	24	CROSSMEMBER MOUNTING BOLT
9	UPPER INSULATOR	25	CROSSMEMBER MOUNTING BOLT
10	COIL SPRING	26	CONTROL MOUNTING NUTS
11	SPRING BUMPER	27	CONTROL ARM THROUGH BOLT
12	LOWER INSULATOR	28	CROSSMEMBER MOUNTING BOLT
13	SHOCK ABSORBER	29	CROSSMEMBER MOUNTING BOLT
14	BRAKE LINE GASKETS	30	CROSSMEMBER MOUNTING BOLT
15	BRAKE HOSE CLIP	31	STABILIZER LINK NUTS
16	STRUT MOUNTING NUT AND BOLT	32	STABILIZER LINK

Fig. 2 Disassembled view of front suspension. GSi models

PARTS LIST

1 DEFLECTOR. DUST	3 RACE. INNER BEARING	5 BEARING. AXLE HUB
2 SEAL. INNER GREASE	4 RING. SNAP	6 KNUCKLE. STEERING FRONT

7 SHIELD. DUST	9 RACE. OUTER BEARING
8 SEAL. OUTER GREASE	10 HUB. DRIVE AXLE

Fig. 3   Disassembled view of hub & bearing assembly

3. Using Seal Remover tool No. J-26941 or equivalent, remove inner grease seal from knuckle, **Fig. 3.**
4. Remove inner bearing snap ring and disc brake dust shield.
5. Push out hub using Hub REmover tool Nos. J-25287 and J-35378 or equivalents.
6. Using tools mentioned in step 5, remove outer bearing race from hub.
7. Using Seal Remover tool No. J-26941 or equivalent, remove outer grease seal.
8. Using Bearing Remover tool Nos. J-35399 and J-35379 or equivalents, remove bearing assembly.
9. Reverse procedure to install. Use Bearing Installation tool Nos. J-8092 and J-35411 to install hub bearing assembly. Use Seal Installation tool No. J-35737 to install outer grease seal. Install hub using tool Nos. J-8092 and J-35399. Use tool No. J-35737 to install inner grease seal. Use Ring Installation tool No. J-35379 to install dust deflector ring. Ensure dust deflector ring faces down (open end down).

STABILIZER BAR
REPLACE

1. Raise and support vehicle.
2. Disconnect stabilizer bar links from lower control arms.
3. Remove stabilizer bar brackets from body.

4. Disconnect exhaust pipe from manifold and/or catalytic converter.
5. Remove stabilizer bar from vehicle.
6. Reverse procedure to install.

MANUAL STEERING GEAR
REPLACE

1. Disconnect battery ground cable.
2. Remove intermediate shaft cover.
3. Loosen upper pinch bolt. Remove lower pinch bolt from pinion shaft.
4. Loosen wheel lug nuts.
5. Raise and support vehicle.
6. Remove both front wheel and tire assemblies.
7. Remove cotter pins from tie rod ends.
8. Disconnect both tie rod ends from steering knuckles. Using Tie Rod End Remover tool No. J-24319-01, or equivalent only, to separate tie rod joints.
9. Remove steering gear to body mounting nuts and bolts.
10. Remove steering assembly from vehicle.
11. Reverse procedure to install.

POWER STEERING GEAR
REPLACE

1. Remove intermediate steering shaft protector.
2. Loosen upper, and remove lower intermediate shaft pinch bolts.

3. Open hood and place drain pan under gear assembly.
4. Loosen wheel lug nuts.
5. Raise and support vehicle.
6. Remove both front wheel and tire assemblies.
7. Using tie rod remover J-24319-01 or equivalent, remove both tie rod ends from knuckles.
8. Support transaxle with a suitable jack.
9. Remove rear center engine mounting member to body mounting bolts.
10. Remove rear engine mount to mount bracket attaching nut and bolt. Raise and lower rear of transaxle to gain access to steering gear to body attaching nuts and bolts.
11. Disconnect pressure and return lines at steering gear.
12. Remove four gear to body mounting nuts and bolts.
13. Remove gear through access opening.
14. Reverse procedure to install.

POWER STEERING PUMP
REPLACE

1. Remove air cleaner assembly.
2. Remove return hose clamp.
3. Disconnect and cap pressure and return lines from pump.
4. Loosen pump pulley and remove.
5. Remove adjusting bolt, pivot bolt and drive belt.
6. Remove pump assembly.
7. Reverse procedure to install.

TIGHTENING SPECIFICATIONS

Year	Component	Torque/ Ft. Lbs.
1991–92	Ball Joint To Knuckle Nuts	94
	Ball Joint To Lower Control Arm Nuts	105
	Brake Caliper Bolts	65
	Brake Line Bracket Bolts	22
	Control Arm Rear Bracket To Crossmember Nuts	14
	Lower Control Arm Bushing Nuts	101
	Lower Control Arm Front Lower Arm Bolt	152
	Lower Control Arm Rear Bracket Bolts	94
	Rear Bracket To Crossmember Bolt	14
	Stabilizer Bar Link Nuts	26
	Stabilizer Bar To Body Bolts	29
	Stabilizer Bracket Bolts	94
	Stabilizer Bracket Nuts & Bolts	94
	Strut Piston Nut	34
	Strut To Body Nuts	29
	Strut To Knuckle Nuts & Bolts	194
	Tie Rod To Knuckle Nuts	36
	Wheel Bearing Locknuts	137
	Wheel Lug Nuts	76
1993–94	ABS Hose Bolt	21
	ABS Speed Sensor Bolt	69 [1]
	ABS Wire Harness Bolt	48 [1]
	Brake Caliper To Steering Knuckle Set Bolt	65
	Ball Joint To Control Arm Nuts & Bolts	105
	Ball Joint To Steering Knuckle Nut	87
	Control Arm Rear Bushing Retaining Nut	101
	Control Arm To Suspension Crossmember Bolt	161
	Dust Cover Bolts	73 [1]
	Driveshaft Locknut	159
	Engine Crossmember To Suspension Crossmember Nut A	35
	Engine Crossmember To Suspension Crossmember Bolt B	45
	Engine Crossmember To Suspension Crossmember Nut C	35
	Left & Right Rear Control Arm Bushing Retaining Bracket Bolt A	108
	Left & Right Rear Control Arm Bushing Retaining Bracket Bolt	37
	Left & Right Rear Control Arm Bushing Retaining Bracket Nut C	14
	Steering Knuckle To Strut Assembly Nuts	203
	Strut Assembly Mounting Nuts	29
	Suspension Crossmember To Body Bolts	152
	Tie Rod End Nut	36
	Wheel Lug Nuts	76

[1] —Inch lbs.

Wheel Alignment

INDEX

Fig. 1   Front toe adjustment

REAR TOE   ADJUSTMENT MECHANISM

Rear suspension arm No. 2 is equipped with toe   adjustment cams.

Toe-Out   Toe-In

Standard Center Line

Toe   Adjustment

(1) Measure the distance and find the difference between the left and right disc wheels and the centerline of the adjustment cam. (If the difference is not within standard specifications, check each part for deformation.)

(2) Turn each cam an equal amount in the opposite direction. (Toe   changes about 2 mm for each turn of the cam on each side.)

Cam Center

Measure at the Same Height on Both Left and Right Sides

Fig. 2   Rear toe adjustment

FRONT WHEEL ALIGNMENT

CASTER & CAMBER

Caster and camber cannot be adjusted. Should caster be found out of specification, locate cause first. If components are damaged, bent, loose, dented or worn, they should be replaced. To prevent an incorrect reading of camber or caster, jounce the bumper three times before checking.

TOE-IN

Toe-in is adjusted by changing tie rod length. Loosen boot clamps and slide from the boot assembly. Loosen right and left tie rod end locknuts, then turn right and left tie rods to align toe-in to specification. Right and left tie rods must be equal in length, **Fig. 1.**

After adjustment, install boot clamps, tighten nuts to specification and ensure rack boots are not twisted.

Torque strut-to-knuckle nut to specifications, and tie rod locking nut to 41 ft. lbs.

Fig. 3   Ride height. Front

Fig. 4   Ride height. Rear

	TIRE SIZE	FRONT	REAR
4A-LC	P175/70 R 13	192 mm	258 mm
	P155/80 R 13	191 mm	257 mm
4A-GE	P175/70 HR 13	183 mm	259 mm

Fig. 5   Ride height measurement chart

REAR WHEEL ALIGNMENT

REAR TOE ADJUSTMENT
1991–92

Toe-in can be adjusted by rotating the cam located on the rear lower control arm. Loosen bolt and rotate nut to give the correct specification. Measure distance between left and right wheel discs and centerline of adjustment cam, **Fig. 2.**

1993–94
1. Loosen left and right lateral link locknuts.
2. Adjust total rear toe to 0.08–0.40° by turning lateral link adjusting tubes. One revolution of adjusting tube will adjust rear to approximately 1.2°.
3. Check difference between left and right lateral link length, the right link length must be less than 0.039 inches difference.
4. **Torque** lateral link locknuts to 41 ft. lbs.

REAR CAMBER & CASTER ADJUSTMENT

Rear caster and camber cannot be adjusted. Should camber be found out of specification, locate cause first. If components are damaged, bent loose, dented or worn, they should be replaced. To prevent an incorrect reading of camber, jounce the bumper three times before checking. If a tie rod or tie rod end is replaced, check toe and steering angle with turning radius gages. If steering angle is not correct, check right and left tie rods for equal length. If tie rod length is change to correct steering, reinspect toe.

RIDE HEIGHT

Refer to **Figs. 3 and 4** for vehicle height and **Fig. 5,** for specification chart.

GEO METRO
(M Car)
INDEX OF SERVICE OPERATIONS

NOTE: Refer To The Rear Of This Manual For Vehicle Manufacturer's Special Tool Suppliers.

Continued

INDEX OF SERVICE OPERATIONS-Continued

Specifications

GENERAL ENGINE SPECIFICATIONS

Year	Engine Liter/CID①	Engine VIN Code②	Fuel System	Bore & Stroke Inches	Comp. Ratio	Net. H.P. @ RPM③	Maximum Torque, Ft. Lbs. @ RPM	Normal Oil Pressure, psi @ 3000 RPM
1991-94	1.0L/3-61	6	EFI④	2.91 x 3.03	9.5	55 @ 5700	58 @ 3300	42.7-54

①—CID: Cubic Inch Displacement.
②—The eighth digit of the VIN denotes engine code.
③—As installed in-vehicle.
④—Electronic Port Fuel Injection.

TUNE UP SPECIFICATIONS

Year & Engine/ VIN Code	Spark Plug Gap	Ignition Timing BTDC① Firing Order Fig.	Ignition Timing BTDC① Man. Trans.	Ignition Timing BTDC① Auto. Trans.	Ignition Timing BTDC① Mark Fig.	Curb Idle Speed, RPM Man. Trans.	Curb Idle Speed, RPM Auto. Trans. ⑥	Fast Idle Speed, RPM Man. Trans.	Fast Idle Speed, RPM Auto. Trans.	Fuel Pump Pressure, psi ⑤
1991-94										
1.0L/3-61/5⑦	.041	②	⑧	⑧	B	⑩	850N	③	③	13-20
1.0L/3-61/5⑨	.041	②	④	④	B	800/900	850N	③	③	13-20

①—BTDC: Before Top Dead Center.
②—Cylinder numbering front of engine to rear 1, 2, 3. Firing, 1-3-2. Refer to Fig. A for spark plug wire connections at distributor cap.
③—Controlled by an idle speed control motor.
④—With distributor vacuum advance hose disconnected, 6° BTDC; w/distributor vacuum advance hose connected, 12° BTDC.
⑤—To relieve fuel system pressure, remove fuel pump relay from main fuse panel located in engine compartment. Operate engine until it stalls, then crank engine several times in three second intervals. Remove fuel tank filler cap to release vapor pressure, then reinstall cap. Place ignition switch in off position, then install fuel pump relay. After fuel pressure has been relieved, attach a suitable fuel pressure gauge to fuel feed hose. Start engine, then check fuel pressure w/engine idling.
⑥—N: Neutral.
⑦—Except LS models.
⑧—When checking ignition timing, connect a jumper wire between diagnostic connector terminals C & D. The diagnostic connector is located next to the ignition coil. Refer to vehicle emission control information label for ignition timing setting.
⑨—LS models.
⑩—Metro, 800/900 RPM; Metro XFI, 700 RPM; Metro Convertible, 850/900 RPM.

Continued

Fig. A

Fig. B

FRONT WHEEL ALIGNMENT SPECIFICATIONS

| Year | Models | Caster Angle, Degrees | | Camber Angles, Degrees | | Toe-In, Inch | Turning Angle, Degrees | |
		Limits	Desired	Limits	Desired		Inner Wheel	Outer Wheel
1991-94	All	+1 to +5	+3	−1 to +1	0	0	38	32

REAR WHEEL ALIGNMENT SPECIFICATIONS

| | Camber Angles, Degrees | | | | |
| | Limits | | Desired | | |
Year	Left	Right	Left	Right	Toe-In, Inch
1991-94	−1 to +1	−1 to +1	0	0	.079

COOLING SYSTEM & CAPACITY DATA

| Year | Engine | Cooling System | | | Fuel Tank Gals. | Engine Oil Qts. ① | Transaxle | |
		Capacity, Qts.	Radiator Cap Relief Pressure, psi	Thermostat Open Temp. °F			Man. Pints	Auto. Qts. ①
1991-94	1.0L/3-61	4.1	12.8	190	10.6	3.7②	5	5.2③

① —Make final check w/dipstick.
② —Additional oil may be required to bring oil level to full mark when changing oil filter.
③ —Total capacity.

LUBRICANT DATA

| Year | Model | Lubricant Type | | | |
| | | Transaxle | | Power Steering | Brake System |
		Manual	Automatic		
1991-94	All	SAE 75W (GL-5)	Dexron II	—	DOT 3

Electrical

INDEX

PRECAUTIONS

AIRBAG SYSTEM DISARMING

The diagnostic energy reserve module (DERM) can maintain voltage to cause a system deployment for up to ten minutes after the ignition switch is turned off and the battery is disconnected. Servicing the SIR system during this period may result in accidental deployment and personal injury.

1. **On 1991 models,** turn ignition switch to Off position.
2. **On 1992-94 models,** place steering wheel so that wheels are pointing straight ahead, then turn ignition switch to LOCK position.
3. **On all models,** remove SIR IG fuse from SIR fuse block.
4. Remove rear plastic access cover from inflator module housing.
5. Remove Connector Position Assurance (CPA), then disconnect yellow two-way SIR electrical connector inside inflator module housing.

AIRBAG SYSTEM ARMING

1. **On 1991 models,** turn ignition switch to Off position.
2. **On 1992-94 models,** turn ignition switch to LOCK position.
3. **On all models,** connect yellow two-way SIR electrical connector inside inflator module housing, then install Connector Position Assurance (CPA).
4. Install SIR IG fuse into SIR fuse block, then the rear plastic access cover onto inflator module housing.
5. Turn ignition switch to RUN position and ensure that "Inflatable Restraint" lamp flashes 7 to 9 times and then shuts off.

| 1 | CENTER PUNCH (WITH SHARP POINT) |
| 2 | IGNITION SWITCH MOUNTING BOLTS |

Fig. 1 Removing ignition lock retaining bolts

FUSE PANEL & FLASHER LOCATION

The main fuse panel (alternator and ignition switch fuses and main fuse for junction fuse panel) is located in the engine compartment on the left hand fender apron. The junction fuse panel (fuses for other components) is located under the left hand side of the instrument panel.

The turn signal and hazard flasher is located under the left hand side of the instrument panel near the fuel panel.

STARTER REPLACE

1. Disconnect battery ground cable.
2. Disconnect solenoid lead and battery cable from starter terminals.
3. Remove two starter mounting bolts, then starter.
4. Reverse procedure to install. **Torque** starter mounting bolts to 17 ft. lbs.

DISTRIBUTOR REPLACE

1. Remove negative battery cable.
2. Disconnect electrical connectors and vacuum lines.
3. Remove distributor cap, then mark rotor position on housing assembly.
4. Mark distributor housing assembly position on engine.
5. Remove distributor flange bolts, then remove distributor from engine.
6. Reverse procedure to install. Ensure alignment marks match.

IGNITION LOCK REPLACE

REMOVAL

1. **On models with airbag,** disarm airbag as described under "Airbag System Disarming."
2. **On all models,** remove turn signal/dimmer switch as described under "Turn Signal Switch, Replace."
3. Disconnect ignition switch and key warning electrical connectors.
4. Lift up floor mat at steering shaft and remove steering column coupling cover cover.
5. Remove upper steering shaft coupling bolt, then connect ignition switch and key warning electrical connectors.
6. Remove steering column attaching nuts, then remove column assembly.
7. Using a center punch, loosen and remove steering lock attaching bolts, **Fig. 1.**
8. Place ignition switch in ACC or ON position and remove from steering column.

INSTALLATION

1. Position oblong hole on steering shaft at center of hole in steering column, **Fig. 2.**

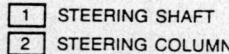

1 STEERING SHAFT
2 STEERING COLUMN

Fig. 2 Aligning steering shaft & column

Fig. 3 Ignition lock retaining bolt installation

1 LOWER JOINT ASSEMBLY
2 UPPER JOINT ASSEMBLY

Fig. 4 Steering shaft to coupling alignment

1. NEUTRAL SAFETY SWITCH
2. NEUTRAL SAFETY SWITCH JOINT

Fig. 5 Positioning neutral safety switch

1. NEUTRAL SAFETY SWITCH
2. BOLT

Fig. 6 Installing neutral safety switch to manual lever

A 0.5-1.0 mm (0.02-0.04 in)

Fig. 7 Stop lamp switch adjustment

2. Place ignition switch in ACC or ON position.
3. Position ignition switch to steering column, then place switch in LOCK position.
4. Align ignition switch hub with oblong hole on steering shaft, then rotate steering shaft to ensure it locks.
5. Install replacement ignition switch attaching bolts. Tighten bolts until bolt head breaks off, **Fig. 3.**
6. Place ignition switch in ON or ACC and check for smooth steering shaft rotation. Also check steering shaft lock for proper operation.
7. Insert steering shaft into coupling, aligning flat on end of steering shaft with bolt hole on coupling, **Fig. 4.**
8. Position steering column mounting brackets to mounting studs, then install and **torque** attaching nuts to 10 ft. lbs.
9. Install steering shaft coupling bolt and **torque** to 18 ft. lbs.
10. Install steering shaft coupling cover.
11. Install turn signal/dimmer switch as described under "Turn Signal Switch, Replace."
12. **On models with airbag,** rearm airbag as described under "Airbag System Arming."

IGNITION SWITCH
REPLACE

Refer to "Ignition Lock, Replace" procedure.

CLUTCH START SWITCH
ADJUST

1. Disconnect battery ground cable.
2. Disconnect electrical connector at clutch start switch.
3. Loosen switch locknut, then back-off switch adjustment.
4. Connect an ohmmeter between switch terminals.
5. Position clutch pedal at approximately .6 to 1.2 inches from floor and hold.
6. Rotate switch into bracket until ohmmeter just indicates continuity, then tighten locknut. **Torque** locknut to 10 ft. lbs.
7. Connect switch electrical connector and battery ground cable.

NEUTRAL SAFETY SWITCH
REPLACE

1. Disconnect battery ground cable.
2. Remove attaching bolt, then remove neutral safety switch from transaxle.
3. Place shift lever in Neutral position.
4. Using a screwdriver, position neutral safety switch a shown in **Fig. 5. Switch should click at this position.**
5. Install neutral safety switch to manual shift shaft and loosely install attaching bolt.
6. Rotate switch slightly until a click is heard, then tighten attaching bolt to 9.5 to 16.5 ft. lbs., **Fig. 6.**
7. Connect electrical connector to switch and battery ground cable to battery, then check switch for proper operation.

HEADLAMP SWITCH
REPLACE

1. Disconnect battery ground cable.
2. Remove steering column trim panel.
3. Lower steering column.
4. Remove instrument cluster bezel screws and pull bezel out.
5. Remove headlamp switch from bezel.
6. Remove cluster to instrument panel attaching screws.
7. Pull cluster rearward to reach and disconnect headlamp switch connector.
8. Remove headlamp switch.
9. Reverse procedure to install.

STOPLIGHT SWITCH
ADJUST

Pull up brake pedal and adjust switch position so that clearance between end of thread and brake pedal contact plate A is .02-.04 inch, **Fig. 7.** Tighten locknut.

TURN SIGNAL SWITCH
REPLACE

1. **On models with airbag,** disarm airbag as described under "Airbag System Disarming."
2. **On all models,** remove steering wheel, refer to "Steering Wheel, Replace."
3. Remove steering column covers, **Fig. 8.**
4. Disconnect turn signal/dimmer switch electrical connector.

1. STEERING JOINT COVER
2. UPPER COLUMN COVER
3. LOWER COLUMN COVER
4. TURN SIG./DIMMER SWITCH

Fig. 8 Turn signal/dimmer switch removal

5. Remove turn signal/dimmer switch attaching screws, then remove switch, **Fig. 8.**
6. Reverse procedure to install.
7. **On models with airbag,** rearm airbag as described under "Airbag System Arming."

DIMMER SWITCH
REPLACE

Replace dimmer switch as an assembly with the turn signal switch. Refer to "Turn Signal Switch, Replace" for replacement procedure.

STEERING WHEEL
REPLACE

1. **On models with airbag,** disarm airbag as described under "Airbag System Disarming."
2. Remove airbag inflator module as described in the "Passive Restraints" section.
3. **On all models,** remove steering wheel nut, then place alignment marks on steering shaft and wheel for use during installation.
4. Remove steering wheel using a suitable puller tool.
5. Reverse procedure to install. When installing steering wheel, align marks made during removal. **Torque** steering wheel nut to 24 ft. lbs.
6. **On models with airbag,** rearm airbag as described under "Airbag System Arming."

1. CLUSTER LENS
2. SPEEDOMETER WINDOW RETAINER
3. CLUSTER HOUSING MOUNTING SCREW
4. TACHOMETER
5. WATER TEMPERATURE GAGE
6. CLUSTER HOUSING
7. CLUSTER INDICATOR BULB (12V. 1.4W)
8. BULB SOCKET
9. BULB SOCKET
10. CLUSTER ILLUMINATION BULB (12V. 3.4W)
11. CLUSTER PRINTED CIRCUIT BOARD
12. CLUSTER HOUSING ATTACHING BRACKET
13. FUEL GAGE
14. SPEEDOMETER HEAD ASSEMBLY
15. TRIP ODOMETER KNOB
16. SPEEDOMETER CABLE ASSEMBLY

Fig. 9 Instrument cluster assembly

INSTRUMENT CLUSTER
REPLACE

1. Disconnect battery ground cable.
2. Remove four screws attaching cluster switch panel to instrument panel.
3. Disconnect electrical connectors from switches, then pull instrument cluster bezel and switch panel slightly outward as an assembly.
4. Remove six screws attaching cluster bezel to switch panel.
5. Remove front wiper switch and headlamp and hazard warning lamp switch from switch panel.
6. Remove four instrument cluster housing attaching screws from switch housing.
7. Disconnect instrument cluster electrical connectors and speedometer cable.
8. Remove instrument cluster, **Fig. 9.**
9. Reverse procedure to install.

INSTRUMENT CLUSTER
PRINTED CIRCUIT
REPLACE

1. Disconnect battery ground cable.
2. Remove instrument cluster as described under "Instrument Cluster, Replace."

3. Remove eight gauge and speedometer to cluster housing attaching screws.
4. Remove indicator lamps from cluster housing.
5. Remove printed circuit from cluster housing.
6. Reverse procedure to install.

RADIO
REPLACE

1991

1. Disconnect battery ground cable.
2. Remove one attaching bolt from rear of radio, then disconnect antenna lead.
3. Using radio removal forks or other suitable tool at hole on each side of radio face plate, pull radio assembly outward from instrument panel.
4. Disconnect electrical connector from radio, then remove radio from vehicle.
5. Reverse procedure to install. Radio removal forks or other suitable tool is not necessary for radio installation.

1992-94

1. Disconnect battery ground cable.
2. Remove three screws and center console bezel.
3. Remove four screws from radio face.

1	WIPER BLADE
2	WIPER ARM
3	WIPER MOTOR
4	WASHER PUMP
5	WASHER FLUID RESERVOIR
6	WASHER HOSE
7	WASHER NOZZLE AND SEAL

Fig. 10 Front windshield wiper/washer motor & linkage assembly

1	REAR WIPER BLADE ASSEMBLY	9	REAR WIPER MOTOR ASSEMBLY
2	REAR WIPER ARM	10	REAR WIPER MOTOR MOUNTING SCREW
3	REAR WIPER ARM ATTACHING NUT	11	REAR WIPER MOTOR GROUND SCREW
4	REAR WIPER ARM ATTACHING NUT COVER	12	REAR WIPER WASHER HOSES
5	REAR WIPER LINKAGE ASSEMBLY	13	REAR WIPER WASHER HOSE GROMMETS
6	REAR WIPER LINKAGE ATTACHING BOLT	14	REAR WIPER WASHER NOZZLE
7	REAR WIPER PIVOT CAP	15	REAR WIPER WASHER NOZZLE SEAL
8	REAR WIPER WASHER HOSE CONNECTORS	16	REAR WIPER CRANKING ARM AND ATTACHING NUT

Fig. 11 Rear windshield wiper/washer motor & linkage assembly

4. Remove one bolt at rear of radio.
5. Pull radio out of instrument panel, then disconnect electrical and antenna connections before completely removing radio from vehicle.
6. Reverse procedure to install.

WIPER SWITCH
REPLACE

FRONT

1. Disconnect battery ground cable.
2. Remove steering column trim panel.
3. Lower steering column.
4. Remove instrument cluster bezel screws and pull bezel out.
5. Remove wiper switch from bezel.
6. Remove cluster to instrument panel attaching screws.
7. Pull cluster rearward to reach and disconnect wiper switch connector.
8. Remove wiper switch.
9. Reverse procedure to install.

REAR
1991

1. Disconnect battery ground cable.
2. Remove switch by pushing forward.
3. Disconnect electrical connector, then remove switch.
4. Reverse procedure to install.

1992-94

1. Disconnect battery ground cable.
2. Remove lower steering column trim cover.
3. Remove both steering column mounting nuts and lower steering column.
4. Remove instrument panel cluster trim bezel.
5. Remove rear wiper switch from bezel.
6. Reverse procedure to install.

WIPER MOTOR
REPLACE

FRONT

1. Disconnect battery ground cable.
2. Disconnect connect electrical connector from wiper motor.
3. Remove three wiper motor attaching screws, then remove nut and washer attaching wiper linkage to motor, **Fig. 10**.
4. Remove wiper motor from vehicle.
5. Reverse procedure to install.

REAR

1. Disconnect battery ground cable.
2. Remove left and right hand speaker grilles from rear lid, if equipped.
3. Disconnect electrical connector from

rear speakers, then remove speakers, if equipped.
4. Remove nine push pins from lid access panel, then remove panel.
5. Disconnect wiper motor electrical connector.
6. Remove wiper motor ground screw, then remove wiper linkage arm to wiper motor attaching nut, **Fig. 11**.
7. Remove three wiper motor attaching screws, then remove wiper motor.
8. Reverse procedure to install.

WIPER LINKAGE
REPLACE

FRONT

1. Disconnect battery ground cable.
2. Remove both wiper arm and blade assemblies.
3. Remove five push pins and left hand cowl panel.
4. Remove three push pins and left hand cowl panel.
5. Remove front wiper motor from vehicle as described under "Wiper Motor, Replace."
6. Remove four nuts attaching wiper motor linkage, then remove wiper motor linkage through left hand cowl cover opening, **Fig. 10**.
7. Reverse procedure to install.

Fig. 12 Blower motor case attaching screw locations

Fig. 14 Instrument panel attaching screw locations

1	BLOWER MOTOR CASE
2	BLOWER MOTOR RESISTER
3	BLOWER FAN
4	GASKET
5	MOTOR ASSEMBLY
6	AIR HOSE

Fig. 13 Blower motor & case assembly

| 1 | MOUNTING BOLTS |
| 2 | MOUNTING NUTS |

Fig. 15 Heater case attaching bolt & nut locations

1	HEATER CASE
2	CONTROL DOOR (DAMPER)
3	HEATER CORE
4	HEATER CASE
5	CONTROL LEVEL LINKAGE
6	CONTROL SHAFT

Fig. 16 Exploded view of heater case assembly

REAR

1. Disconnect battery ground cable.
2. Remove wiper blade and arm assembly, **Fig. 11.**
3. Remove rear wiper motor as described under "Wiper Motor, Replace."
4. Remove two nuts attaching wiper linkage to rear lid.
5. Remove linkage trough left hand side of rear lid.
6. Reverse procedure to install.

BLOWER MOTOR
REPLACE

1. Disconnect battery ground cable.
2. Remove two screws attaching glove compartment striker to instrument panel.
3. Remove one screw attaching rear of glove compartment upper panel, then remove upper panel.
4. Disconnect blower motor and blower resistor electrical connectors.
5. Disconnect fresh air control cable from blower motor housing.
6. Remove three blower motor housing attaching bolt, then remove blower motor housing, **Fig. 12.**
7. Remove air hose, then remove three attaching screws and separate blower motor from housing, **Fig. 13.**
8. Reverse procedure to install.

HEATER CORE
REPLACE

1. Disconnect battery ground cable.
2. Drain cooling system, then disconnect heater hoses from heater core.
3. **On models equipped with automatic transaxle, remove console**

as follows:

a. Position shift control lever in Low position.
b. Remove four console attaching screws, then carefully pull console outward at bottom to disengage retaining pins.
c. Move front seats fully forward, then remove two attaching screws and parking brake lever cover.
d. Remove four screws attaching shift control lever to console.
e. Remove Park lock out knob from shift control console, if equipped.
f. Remove console from vehicle.
4. Remove Instrument cluster as described under "Instrument Cluster, Replace."
5. Remove turn signal/dimmer switch as described under "Turn Signal Switch, Replace."
6. Remove ashtray and bracket, then remove cigar lighter assembly.
7. Disconnect electrical connector, then carefully remove A/C switch through front of instrument panel bezel, if equipped.
8. Remove radio as described under "Radio, Replace."
9. Remove knobs from heater control.
10. Remove two instrument panel bezel to instrument panel attaching screws, then remove bezel.
11. Remove two screws attaching heater control panel, then pull control panel slightly outward and disconnect blower switch electrical connector.
12. Remove screw attaching hood re-

lease lever to instrument panel.
13. Remove two attaching screws from left and right hand side of instrument panel, **Fig. 14.**
14. Remove four attaching screws from instrument panel support member.
15. Remove two attaching screws from heater control assembly.
16. Remove attaching screw from rear glove of compartment upper panel.
17. Remove instrument panel access cover, then remove attaching screw at panel.
18. Remove radio speaker trim covers, then remove one speaker to instrument panel attaching screw from each speaker.
19. Remove left and right hand kick panels, then remove one instrument panel attaching screw from behind each

kick panel.
20. Disconnect electrical connectors from radio speakers.
21. Disconnect electrical connectors from instrument panel, then remove instrument panel.
22. Remove two mounting bolts and two mounting nuts attaching heater case to dash panel, **Fig. 15**.
23. Remove heater case from vehicle.
24. Remove heater case retaining clips and two attaching screws.
25. Separate heater case halves, then carefully remove heater core, **Fig. 16**.
26. Reverse procedure to install.

EVAPORATOR CORE
REPLACE

1. Disconnect battery ground cable.
2. Discharge refrigerant from A/C system.
3. Remove glove compartment striker, then one attaching screw from rear of glove compartment upper panel and remove panel.
4. Remove blower motor, then disconnect blower resistor electrical connectors.
5. Remove fresh/recirc control cable

from blower case assembly.
6. Remove blower case from vehicle.
7. Disconnect air conditioner and evaporator thermistor electrical connectors.
8. Remove compressor suction line and receiver/dryer outlet line from evaporator. **Cap hose and fittings immediately.**
9. Remove evaporator case from vehicle.
10. Remove A/C amplifier from evaporator case by releasing two lower lock tabs, then slide amplifier upward to disengage from evaporator case.
11. Reverse procedure to install.

Engine
INDEX

PRECAUTIONS
AIRBAG SYSTEM DISARMING

The diagnostic energy reserve module (DERM) can maintain voltage to cause a system deployment for up to ten minutes after the ignition switch is turned off and the battery is disconnected. Servicing the SIR system during this period may result in accidental deployment and personal injury.
1. **On 1991 models,** turn ignition switch to Off position.
2. **On 1992-94 models,** place steering wheel so that wheels are pointing straight ahead, then turn ignition switch to LOCK position.
3. **On all models,** remove SIR IG fuse from SIR fuse block.
4. Remove rear plastic access cover from inflator module housing.
5. Remove Connector Position Assurance (CPA), then disconnect yellow two-way SIR electrical connector inside inflator module housing.

AIRBAG SYSTEM ARMING

1. **On 1991 models,** turn ignition switch to Off position.

2. **On 1992-94 models,** turn ignition switch to LOCK position.
3. **On all models,** connect yellow two-way SIR electrical connector inside inflator module housing, then install Connector Position Assurance (CPA).
4. Install SIR IG fuse into SIR fuse block, then the rear plastic access cover onto inflator module housing.
5. Turn ignition switch to Run position and ensure that "Inflatable Restraint" lamp flashes 7 to 9 times and then shuts Off.

ENGINE MOUNTS
REPLACE
FRONT

1. Disconnect battery ground cable.
2. Remove engine mount nut, then raise and support vehicle.
3. Support engine using an engine support fixture.
4. Remove engine mount and frame bracket, then remove mount from bracket.
5. Reverse procedure to install.

REAR

1. Disconnect battery ground cable.
2. Remove engine mount nut, then raise and support vehicle.
3. Remove nut retaining mount to body bracket.
4. Support engine using an engine support fixture.
5. Remove frame bracket, then remove mount.
6. Reverse procedure to install.

ENGINE
REPLACE

1. Relieve fuel system pressure as follows:
   a. Remove fuel pump relay from main fuse panel located in engine compartment, **Fig. 1.**
   b. Operate engine until it stalls, then crank engine several times in three second intervals.
   c. Remove fuel tank filler cap to release vapor pressure, then reinstall cap.
   d. Place ignition switch in off position, then install fuel pump relay.

1. MAIN FUSE BOX
2. LOCK TABS
3. FUEL PUMP RELAY ELECTRICAL CONNECTOR
4. FUEL PUMP RELAY

Fig. 1 Fuel pump relay location

2. Disconnect battery ground cable.
3. Disconnect windshield washer hose, then remove hood.
4. Remove air cleaner assembly.
5. Drain cooling system, then remove radiator and engine cooling fan.
6. Disconnect high tension lead from ignition coil.
7. Disconnect electrical connector from distributor.
8. Disconnect electrical connectors from coolant temperature sender, engine coolant temperature sensor, engine cooling fan switch and engine oil pressure sender.
9. Disconnect electrical connector from EGR vacuum switching valve.
10. Disconnect electrical connectors from idle speed control valve, throttle position switch, fuel injector and pressure sensor.
11. Disconnect electrical connectors and wiring from alternator and starter motor.
12. Disconnect electrical connector from oxygen sensor.
13. Disconnect battery ground cable from transaxle.
14. **On models with manual transaxle,** disconnect electrical connector from back-up lamp switch.
15. **On models with automatic transaxle,** disconnect electrical connectors from neutral safety switch, speed sensor and direct clutch and second brake solenoids.
16. **On all models,** disconnect intake manifold to power brake unit vacuum hose.
17. Disconnect evaporative emission canister hoses from intake manifold and tube connections.
18. Disconnect fuel hoses from throttle body.
19. Disconnect heater hoses from engine.
20. Disconnect accelerator cable from throttle body.
21. **On models with manual transaxle,** disconnect clutch cable from from fork and housing.
22. **On models with automatic transaxle,** disconnect shift control and fluid

pressure control cables from transaxle.
23. **On all models,** disconnect speedometer cable from transaxle.
24. Raise and support vehicle, then disconnect exhaust pipe from exhaust manifold.
25. Drain engine crankcase, then drain fluid from transaxle.
26. **On models with manual transaxle,** disconnect control shaft and extension rod from transaxle.
27. **On all models,** separate drive axles from transaxle. Support drive axles from chassis using wire.
28. **On models with automatic transaxle,** remove engine torque rod bracket from transaxle.
29. Lower vehicle and install an engine lifting fixture.
30. Remove engine and transaxle mounting bolts, then remove engine and transaxle assembly from vehicle.
31. Reverse procedure to install.

CYLINDER HEAD REPLACE

1. Relieve fuel system pressure as follows:
   a. Remove fuel pump relay from main fuse panel located in engine compartment, **Fig. 1.**
   b. Operate engine until it stalls, then crank engine several times in three second intervals.
   c. Remove fuel tank filler cap to release vapor pressure, then reinstall cap.
   d. Place ignition switch in off position, then install fuel pump relay.
2. Disconnect battery ground cable.
3. Drain cooling system, then remove air cleaner assembly.
4. Disconnect coil wire from distributor cap.
5. Disconnect electrical connector from distributor.
6. Disconnect electrical connectors from coolant temperature sender, engine coolant temperature sensor and engine cooling fan switch.
7. Disconnect electrical connector from EGR vacuum switching valve.
8. Disconnect electrical connectors from idle speed control valve, throttle position switch and fuel injector.
9. Disconnect oxygen sensor electrical connector, then detach wiring harness from clamps.
10. Disconnect ground wires from intake manifold.
11. Disconnect heater hose from intake manifold and radiator hose from thermostat housing.
12. Disconnect fuel hoses from throttle body.
13. Disconnect MAP sensor hose from intake manifold.
14. Disconnect evaporative emission hoses from intake manifold and tube.
15. Disconnect power brake unit vacuum hose from intake manifold.

Fig. 2   Cylinder head bolt tightening sequence

16. Disconnect accelerator cable from throttle body.
17. Raise and support vehicle, then disconnect exhaust pipe from exhaust manifold.
18. Lower vehicle, then remove cylinder head cover.
19. Remove cylinder head attaching bolts, then remove cylinder head.
20. Reverse procedure to install. **Torque** cylinder head bolts to specification listed at the end of this section in sequence shown in **Fig. 2.**

INTAKE MANIFOLD REPLACE

1. Relieve fuel system pressure as follows:
   a. Remove fuel pump relay from main fuse panel located in engine compartment, **Fig. 1.**
   b. Operate engine until it stalls, then crank engine several times in three second intervals.
   c. Remove fuel tank filler cap to release vapor pressure, then reinstall cap.
   d. Place ignition switch in off position, then install fuel pump relay.
2. Disconnect battery ground cable.
3. Drain cooling system, then remove air cleaner assembly.
4. Disconnect electrical connectors from coolant temperature sender, engine and coolant temperature sensor.
5. Disconnect electrical connector from EGR vacuum switching valve.
6. Disconnect electrical connectors from idle speed control valve, throttle position switch and fuel injector.
7. Disconnect ground wires from intake manifold.
8. Disconnect fuel hoses from throttle body.
9. Disconnect coolant hoses from intake manifold.
10. Disconnect MAP sensor hose from intake manifold.
11. Disconnect evaporative emission hoses from intake manifold and tube.
12. Disconnect power brake unit vacuum hose from intake manifold.
13. Disconnect PCV valve hose from cylinder head cover.
14. Disconnect accelerator cable from throttle body.

1. CYLINDER HEAD COVER
2. GASKET
3. CYLINDER HEAD
4. CAMSHAFT HOUSING NO. 1
5. CAMSHAFT HOUSING NO. 2
6. CAMSHAFT HOUSING NO. 3
7. CAMSHAFT
8. OIL SEAL
9. VALVE LASH ADJUSTER

Fig. 3   Camshaft & hydraulic valve lash adjusters

1. INTAKE ROCKER ARM SHAFT
2. EXHAUST ROCKER ARM SHAFT
3. SCREW
4. CAMSHAFT
5. CAMSHAFT OIL SEAL
6. ROCKER ARM SPRING
7. LOCK NUT
8. VALVE ADJUSTING SCREW
9. ROCKER ARM
10. VALVE COTTER
11. VALVE SPRING RETAINER
12. VALVE STEM SEAL
13. VALVE SPRING
14. VALVE SPRING SEAT
15. VALVE GUIDE
16. INTAKE VALVE
17. EXHAUST VALVE

Fig. 5   Timing belt & cover assembly

15. Disconnect all other electrical connectors and hoses to permit intake manifold and throttle body removal.
16. Remove intake manifold to cylinder head attaching nuts and bolts, then remove intake manifold and throttle body as an assembly.
17. Reverse procedure to Install.

EXHAUST MANIFOLD
REPLACE

1. Disconnect battery ground cable.
2. Disconnect oxygen sensor electrical connector, then release wiring harness from clamps.
3. Disconnect exhaust pipe from exhaust manifold.
4. Remove exhaust manifold attaching bolts and nuts, then remove exhaust manifold from cylinder head.
5. Reverse procedure to install.

VALVE ADJUSTMENT

These engines are equipped with hydraulic valve lash adjusters and no adjustment is required.

VALVE ARRANGEMENT
FRONT TO REAR

1.0L/3-61 . . . . I-E-I-E-I-E

VALVE GUIDES

Valves and valve guides are available in standard size only. The Valve guide can be driven from cylinder bore using Valve Guide Remover tool No. J-37968-1 or equivalent. The valve guide should be driven from the combustion chamber side of the cylinder head out through the valve spring side.

1. CYLINDER HEAD
2. OIL HOLE

Fig. 4   Applying engine oil to camshaft oil holes

The cylinder head valve guide bore should be reamed with an 11 mm reamer prior to valve guide installation. Heat cylinder head to 176 to 212°F, then drive valve guide into cylinder head bore using Valve Guide Remover tool No. J-37968-1 and Valve Guide Installer tool No. J-37968-2 or equivalent. Valve guide should be driven in until tool contacts cylinder head. Valve guide protrusion should be .45 inch from cylinder head surface. After installation, ream valve guide with a 5.5 mm reamer.

HYDRAULIC VALVE LASH ADJUSTER SERVICE

Hydraulic valve lash adjusters should not be disassembled.

1. Remove camshaft as described under "Camshaft, Replace."
2. Remove hydraulic valve lash adjusters from cylinder head, **Fig. 3**.
3. Check hydraulic valve lash adjusters for wear and damage and replace as necessary.
4. Using a micrometer, measure outside diameter of hydraulic valve lash adjuster. Outside diameter should be 1.2188 to 1.2194 inches.
5. Measure hydraulic valve lash adjuster bore in cylinder head. Bore diameter should be 1.2205 to 1.2214 inches.
6. To determine hydraulic valve lash adjuster to cylinder head bore clearance, subtract adjuster outside diameter from cylinder head adjuster bore diameter. Adjuster to bore clearance should be .0010 to .0025 inch. If clearance is greater than .0059 inch, replace adjuster or cylinder head as necessary.
7. Place valve lash adjuster in clean engine oil prior to installation. Also pour engine oil through camshaft journal oil holes, until oil is emitted from hydraulic valve lash adjuster oil holes, **Fig. 4**.
8. Apply engine oil to valve lash adjuster, then position adjuster in cylinder head bore and install camshaft.

TIMING BELT & COVER
REPLACE
REMOVAL

1. Disconnect battery ground cable, then raise and support vehicle.

1. "V" MARK ON CYLINDER HEAD COVER

2. TIMING MARK ON CAMSHAFT TIMING BELT GEAR

3. ARROW MARK ON OIL PUMP CASE

4. PUNCH MARK ON CRANKSHAFT TIMING BELT GEAR

Fig. 6   Aligning camshaft & crankshaft sprocket timing marks

1. TENSIONER PLATE
2. TENSIONER
3. LUG
4. HOLE

Fig. 7   Tensioner assembly

1. CAMSHAFT TIMING BELT GEAR
2. ROD
3. SHOP CLOTH
4. CAMSHAFT

Fig. 10   Camshaft sprocket bolt removal & installation

1. TENSIONER BOLT
2. TENSIONER STUD
3. TENSIONER PLATE
4. TENSIONER
5. SPRING

Fig. 8   Checking tensioner plate movement

1. CRANKSHAFT TIMING BELT GEAR
2. KEY

Fig. 9   Positioning crankshaft sprocket key

2. Remove fender apron extension from right hand side of vehicle.
3. Remove water pump drive belt, then remove water pump pulley.
4. Remove four attaching bolts and crankshaft pulley.
5. Remove outer timing belt cover, **Fig. 5.**
6. Align camshaft and crankshaft timing marks, **Fig. 6.**
7. Remove timing belt tensioner, tensioner plate, spring and damper.
8. Remove timing belt.

INSPECTION

Check timing belt for wear and cracks and replace as necessary. Check timing belt tensioner for smoothness of rotation and replace as necessary.

INSTALLATION

1. Position lug on tensioner plate to hole in tensioner, **Fig. 7.**
2. Position tensioner and tensioner plate to engine, then install and hand tighten attaching bolt. Ensure that tensioner and tensioner plate move in the same direction, **Fig. 8.** If movement is

not as indicated, remove tensioner and reinsert tensioner plate lug into tensioner.
3. Ensure camshaft and crankshaft timing marks are aligned, **Fig. 6.**
4. With tensioner plate pushed upward, install timing belt over camshaft and crankshaft pulleys. **Arrow on timing belt should face toward direction of crankshaft rotation. When installing timing belt, keep drive side of belt free of slack.**
5. Install tensioner spring and damper, then hand tighten tensioner stud.
6. Rotate crankshaft two revolutions clockwise direction to remove slack from belt. **Ensure slack is removed from drive belt and that camshaft and crankshaft timing marks are aligned.**
7. Tighten tensioner stud, then tighten tensioner bolt to torque listed at the end of this section.
8. Install timing belt outer cover and crankshaft pulley. **Ensure seal is between oil pump housing and water pump.**
9. Install water pump pulley and drive belt.
10. Install right hand side fender apron

extension, then lower vehicle and connect battery ground cable.

CAMSHAFT REPLACE

REMOVAL

1. Disconnect battery ground cable.
2. Remove air cleaner assembly, then remove cylinder head cover.
3. Remove distributor from cylinder head.
4. Remove timing belt as described under "Timing Belt, Replace."
5. After timing belt has been remove, position crankshaft sprocket key as shown in, **Fig. 9.**
6. Hold camshaft in position by inserting a rod into .39 inch hole in camshaft, then remove camshaft sprocket retaining bolt, **Fig. 10.** Place shop cloth under rod to prevent damage to cylinder head surface.
7. Remove camshaft housings to cylinder head attaching bolts and studs, **Fig. 3.**
8. Remove camshaft from cylinder head. **Hydraulic valve lash adjusters should also be removed and placed in engine oil until installation.**

INSTALLATION

1. Pour engine oil into camshaft journal oil holes until oil is emitted from hy-

1 TIMING BELT GEAR PIN HOLE

Fig. 11   Position camshaft sprocket pin hole

Fig. 14   Camshaft housing bolt tightening sequence

1 APPLY SEALANT

Fig. 12   Camshaft housing to cylinder head surface sealant application

1. PISTON
2. ARROW MARK
3. CONNECTING ROD
4. OIL HOLE

Fig. 15   Piston & connecting rod assembly

1 NO. 1 HOUSING
2 NO. 2 HOUSING
3 NO. 3 HOUSING

Fig. 13   Camshaft housing locations

1. OIL PAN
2. OIL PUMP STRAINER
3. SEAL
4. DRAIN PLUG GASKET
5. DRAIN PLUG

Fig. 16   Oil pan & pick-up tube

draulic valve lash adjuster holes, **Fig. 4.**
2. Lubricate valve lash adjusters with engine oil and install on cylinder head.
3. Lubricate camshaft with engine oil, then position on cylinder head with sprocket pin hole positioned as shown in **Fig. 11.**
4. Lubricate camshaft journal bores in camshaft housing with engine oil.
5. Apply sealant to cylinder head mating surface of camshaft housings No. 1 and No. 3, **Fig. 12.**
6. Position camshaft housings over camshaft and onto cylinder head mating surface. **Arrow on camshaft housing should face camshaft sprocket side of cylinder head.** Camshaft housings are numbered from 1 to 3. The housings are positioned on the cylinder head in numerical order, starting with No. 1 at camshaft sprocket side of cylinder head, **Fig. 13.**
7. Apply engine oil to camshaft housing attaching bolts and studs, then loosely install bolts and studs. Tighten bolts and studs in sequence shown in **Fig. 14.** to specifications.
8. Apply engine oil to camshaft oil seal lip, then install seal. Seal surface should be flush with housing surface.
9. Hold camshaft in position by inserting a rod into .39 inch hole in camshaft, then install and tighten camshaft sprocket retaining bolt, **Fig. 10.** Place shop cloth under rod to prevent damage to cylinder head surface.
10. Install cylinder head cover.
11. Install timing belt as described under "Timing Belt, Replace."

12. Install ignition distributor, then install air cleaner assembly.
13. Connect battery ground cable, then adjust ignition timing.

PISTON & ROD ASSEMBLY

Refer to **Fig. 15** when assembling piston and connecting rod. When installing piston and connecting rod, arrow on piston head should face front of engine and oil hole in connecting rod should face intake manifold. When installing connecting rod cap, arrow on cap should face front of engine.

Measure rod bearing side clearance using a feeler gauge. Connecting rod bearing side clearance should be .0039 to .0078 inch.

PISTON PINS & RINGS

Pistons and rings are available in standard size and oversizes of .010 and .020 inch. Piston pins are supplied with pistons in matched sets.

MAIN & ROD BEARINGS

Main and rod bearings are available in standard size and under size of .010 inch. Crankshaft thrust bearings are available in standard size and under size of .005 inch.

CRANKSHAFT REAR OIL SEAL
REPLACE

1. Remove transaxle as described under "Transaxle, Replace" in the "Automat-

ic Transaxle" or "Clutch & Manual Transaxle" sections.
2. **On models with manual transaxle,** remove pressure plate and clutch disc.
3. **On all models,** remove flywheel.
4. Remove seal retainer, then remove seal from retainer.
5. Reverse procedure to install.

OIL PAN
REPLACE

1. Disconnect battery ground cable.
2. Raise and support vehicle.
3. Drain oil pan.
4. Remove flywheel dust cover.
5. Disconnect exhaust pipe at manifold.
6. Remove oil pan bolts and pan, **Fig. 16.**
7. Remove oil pump screen.
8. Reverse procedure to install. Apply continuous bead of silicon type sealer to oil pan flange inside bolt holes. When tightening oil pan attaching bolts, start at center and working outward. **Torque** bolts to specification listed at the end of this section.

OIL PUMP
REPLACE

REMOVAL

1. Refer to "Timing Belt, Replace" procedure to remove timing belt.

1. GEAR PLATE
2. INNER GEAR
3. OUTER GEAR
4. GASKET
5. PIN
6. PIN
7. RELIEF VALVE
8. SPRING
9. RETAINER
10. RETAINER RING

Fig. 17 Rotor type (Trochoid) oil pump

1. OIL PUMP
2. RUBBER SEAL
3. WATER PUMP

Fig. 20 Rubber seal installation

2. Refer to "Oil Pan, Replace" procedure to remove oil pan.
3. Remove crankshaft timing belt sprocket.
4. Remove alternator mounting bracket, if necessary.
5. Remove A/C compressor mounting bracket, if so equipped.
6. Remove alternator adjusting bolt and upper cover bolt, if necessary.
7. Remove oil pump bolts and pump, **Figs. 17.**

INSTALLATION

1. Install oil pump pins and gasket on engine block.
2. Install Oil Seal Guide tool No. J-34853 or equivalent, onto crankshaft to prevent damage to oil seal lip, **Fig. 18.** Apply engine oil to your special tool.
3. Install oil pump onto crankshaft and engine block. Note location of mounting bolts, **Fig. 19. No. 1 bolts are shorter then No. 2 bolts** in length. Install bolts as shown in **Fig. 19,** then **torque** to specification listed at the end of this section.

1. CRANKSHAFT
2. J-34853

Fig. 18 Crankshaft oil seal guide tool installation

1. OUTER GAUGE
2. CRESCENT
3. CLEARANCE

Fig. 21 Checking oil pump gear radial clearance. Rotor type similar

4. After installing oil pump, check that oil seal lip is not twisted, then remove tool.
5. Install rubber seal between oil pump and water pump, **Fig. 20.**
6. If necessary, trim edges of oil pump seal flush with oil pan mating surface.
7. Install timing belt guide, key and crankshaft timing sprocket. Note that timing belt guide must be installed so that curved side faces oil pump.
8. Install timing belt and tensioner components.
9. Adjust water pump belt tension.
10. Fill crankcase.
11. Connect battery ground cable.
12. Run engine to check that oil pressure is correct.

OIL PUMP SERVICE

1. Remove dipstick tube from oil pump.
2. Remove gear/rotor plate screws and gear plate.
3. Remove outer and inner gears/rotors.
4. Inspect oil seal lip for damage and replace as necessary.
5. Inspect outer and inner gears/rotors, gear/rotor plate, and oil pump case for excessive wear or damage.
6. Using feeler gauge, check radial clearance between outer gear/rotor and crescent, **Fig. 21.** If clearance exceeds .0122 inch, replace outer gear/rotor.

1. NO. 1 BOLTS (SHORT)
2. NO. 2 BOLTS (LONG)

Fig. 19 Oil pump bolt location

Fig. 22 Checking oil pump gear side clearance. Rotor type similar

7. Using straightedge and feeler gauge, measure side clearance which should not exceed .0059 inch, **Fig. 22.**
8. Wash, clean and dry all oil pump parts.
9. Apply light coat of engine oil to inner and outer gears/rotors, oil seal lip portion, and inside surfaces of oil pump case and plate.
10. Install outer and inner gears/rotors in pump case.
11. Install gear/rotor plate and tighten screws securely. Check that gears turn smoothly by hand.
12. Install O-ring in pump case, then dipstick tube.

BELT TENSION DATA

Belt & Year	Belt Deflection Inch ①
A/C Compressor	
1991-94	.20-.25
Alternator & Water Pump	
1991-94 New	.20-.27
1991-94 Used	.24-.31

①—With thumb pressure applied.

COOLING SYSTEM BLEED

These engines do not require a specified bleed procedure. After filling cooling system, run engine to operating temperature with radiator/pressure cap off. Air will then be automatically bled through cap opening.

1. RUBBER SEAL

Fig. 23 Installing rubber seals

THERMOSTAT
REPLACE

1. Disconnect battery ground cable.
2. Drain cooling system.
3. Remove radiator inlet hose at thermostat housing.
4. Remove thermostat housing and thermostat.
5. Clean both gasket surfaces thoroughly.
6. Reverse procedure to install.

WATER PUMP
REPLACE

1. Disconnect battery ground cable.
2. Drain cooling system.
3. Remove drive belt, water pump pulley, crankshaft pulley, timing belt outside cover, timing belt and timing belt tensioner.
4. Remove water pump mounting bolts and nuts, and water pump.
5. Install water pump on engine block.
6. Install rubber seals between water pump and oil pump, and between water pump and cylinder head, **Fig. 23.**
7. Install timing belt tensioner, timing belt, timing belt outside cover, crankshaft pulley, water pump pulley and drive belt.

8. Tighten drive belt so it deflects .25-.35 inch on span between water pump pulley and crankshaft pulley.
9. Install valve cover and air cleaner.
10. Fill cooling system.
11. Connect battery ground cable.

FUEL PUMP
REPLACE

1. Relieve fuel system pressure as follows:
   a. Remove fuel pump relay from main fuse panel located in engine compartment, **Fig. 1.**
   b. Operate engine until it stalls, then crank engine several times in three second intervals.
   c. Remove fuel tank filler cap to release vapor pressure, then reinstall cap.
   d. Place ignition switch in off position, then install fuel pump relay.
2. Disconnect battery ground cable.
3. Remove rear seat cushion, then disconnect fuel pump and sending unit electrical connectors, then push harness through floor pan grommet.
4. Drain fuel tank, then disconnect inlet hose from fuel filter.
5. Disconnect fuel filler hose from fuel tank.
6. Disconnect vapor hoses and fuel feed and return hoses at fuel tank and pump.
7. Remove fuel tank mounting bolts, then lower fuel tank from vehicle.
8. Remove fuel pump to fuel tank attaching bolts, then remove fuel pump, **Fig. 24.**
9. Separate fuel; pump from motor and sending unit as necessary.
10. Reverse procedure to install.

FUEL FILTER
REPLACE

The fuel filter is located at the lefthand front corner of the fuel tank assembly.
1. Relieve fuel system pressure as follows:

1	SENDING UNIT
2	FUEL PUMP
3	FUEL TANK
4	FUEL FILTER

Fig. 24 Electric fuel pump & sending unit removal

a. Remove fuel pump relay from main fuse panel located in engine compartment, **Fig. 1.**
b. Start engine and allow to run until it stalls, then crank engine several times in three second intervals.
c. Remove fuel tank filler cap to release vapor pressure, then reinstall cap.
d. Place ignition switch in off position, then install fuel pump relay.
2. Disconnect battery ground cable.
3. Raise and support vehicle, then place approved fuel holding container under fuel filter.
4. Disconnect fuel filter inlet hose clamp and hose from filter. **A small amount of fuel may be released after the fuel hose is disconnected. In order to reduce the chance of personal injury, cover the fittings with a shop towel.**
5. Disconnect fuel filter outlet hose clamp and hose from filter.
6. Remove mounting bracket and filter as an assembly.
7. Reverse procedure to install.

TIGHTENING SPECIFICATIONS

Torque specifications are for clean and lightly lubricated threads only. Dry or dirty threads produce increased friction which prevents accurate measurement of tightness.

Component	Torque/Ft. Lbs.	Component	Torque/Ft. Lbs.
Alternator Mounting Bolts & Nuts	17	**Flywheel To Crankshaft**	45
Camshaft Housing To Cylinder Head	8	**Ignition Distributor To Cylinder Head**	10
Camshaft Sprocket Bolt	44	**Intake Manifold To Cylinder Head**	17
Connecting Rod Cap Bolts	26	**Main Bearing Cap Bolts**	40
Crankshaft Pulley Bolts	8	**Oil Pan Drain Plug**	26
Crankshaft Sprocket Bolt	81	**Oil Pan To Engine**	8
Cylinder Head Bolts	54	**Oil Pressure Switch**	10
Cylinder Head Cover	4	**Oil Pump Pickup Tube Bolts**	8
Exhaust Manifold To Cylinder Head	17		

Continued

TIGHTENING SPECIFICATIONS—Continued

Component	Torque/Ft. Lbs.	Component	Torque/Ft. Lbs.
Oil Pump Rotor Plate Screws	8	Timing Belt Cover Nuts & Bolts	8
Oil Pump To Engine	8	Timing Belt Tensioner Bolt	20
Spark Plug	18	Timing Belt Tensioner Stud	8
Starter Mounting Bolts	17	Water Pump To Engine	7.5-9

Clutch & Manual Transaxle

INDEX

A	FREE TRAVEL 2–4 MM (0.08–0.15 IN.)
1	RELEASE LEVER
2	CLUTCH CABLE
3	JOINT NUT

Fig. 1   Clutch cable adjustment

ADJUSTMENTS

CLUTCH PEDAL HEIGHT

Using clutch pedal stop bolt, adjust height of clutch pedal so it is even with brake pedal.

CLUTCH RELEASE ARM PLAY

1. Measure clutch pedal freeplay. Clutch pedal freeplay should be .6 to .8 inch.
2. If clutch pedal freeplay is not within specifications, adjust clutch cable joint nut to provide a free travel of .08 to .15 inch at release lever, **Fig. 1.**

SHIFT LINKAGE

Check gear shift control lever vertical endplay. Vertical endplay should be 0 to .007 inch. Check distance between instrument panel and gear shift control lever, with transaxle in neutral, **Fig. 2.** Distance should be approximately 10.6 inches, if not adjust.

CLUTCH
REPLACE

1. Refer to "Manual Transaxle, Replace" procedure to remove transaxle.
2. Install suitable tool into pilot bearing to support clutch assembly during removal.
3. Check for X mark or white painted letter on pressure plate and corresponding mark stamped on flywheel. If no markings are found, mark flywheel and pressure plate for assembly purposes.
4. Loosen pressure plate to flywheel mounting bolts 1 turn at a time until spring pressure is released, **Fig. 3.** It may be necessary to use Flywheel Holder tool No. J-35271 or equivalent to hold flywheel in position when loosening bolts.
5. Remove bolts, pressure plate and clutch disc.
6. Reverse procedure to install. Lubricate splines of transaxle input shaft and pilot bearing surface and release bearing with lithium wheel bearing grease. **Torque** pressure plate attaching bolts to 17 ft. lbs.

CLUTCH CABLE
REPLACE

1. Disconnect battery ground cable at battery.
2. Remove clutch cable joint nut, then disconnect cable from release arm.
3. Remove clutch cable bracket bolts and bracket.
4. Remove cable retaining bolts at clutch pedal.
5. Remove clutch cable from vehicle.
6. Reverse procedure to install. Refer to "Adjustments" to adjust cable.

MANUAL TRANSAXLE
REPLACE

1. Disconnect battery ground cable.

A	CONTROL LEVER POSITION DISTANCE
1	INSTRUMENT PANEL
2	CONSOLE BOX
3	CONTROL LEVER HOUSING NUT
4	BOOT COVER
5	CONTROL LEVER KNOB
6	CONTROL LEVER BOOT
7	BOOT NO. 2
8	SHIFT CONTROL LEVER COVER

Fig. 2   Positioning gearshift control lever

2. Disconnect clutch cable from release lever and bracket.
3. Disconnect electrical connectors from transaxle, then remove wiring harness to transaxle retaining brackets.
4. Disconnect speedometer cable from transaxle.
5. Remove upper transaxle attaching bolts.
6. Remove starter motor as described under "Starter Motor, Replace."
7. Disconnect vacuum hose from pressure sensor.
8. Install an engine support fixture, then raise and support vehicle.

1. FLYWHEEL
2. DISC
3. CLUTCH COVER
4. LOCK WASHER
5. BOLT
6. RELEASE BEARING
7. RELEASE FORK PIN
8. NO. 2 BUSHING
9. RELEASE SHAFT
10. RETURN SPRING
11. NO. 1 BUSHING
12. SHAFT SEAL
13. SHAFT COVER

Fig. 3   Clutch assembly

| 1 | DRIVEAXLE (LH.) |
| 2 | SCREWDRIVER |

Fig. 4   Front drive axle snap ring removal

9. Drain lubricant from transaxle.
10. Disconnect gear shift control lever from gear shift shaft.
11. Remove extension rod nut, then remove extension rod with washers.
12. Remove attaching nuts and bolts, then remove exhaust pipe.
13. Remove clutch housing lower cover.
14. Remove left front wheel and tire assembly.
15. Disconnect left tie rod end and ball joint from steering knuckle.
16. Separate drive axles from transaxle, **Fig. 4.** Support drive axles from chassis using wire.
17. Remove lower transaxle to engine attaching bolts and nuts.
18. Support transaxle using a jack.
19. Remove two rear engine mounting nuts, then remove transaxle left hand mounting bracket attaching nuts and bolts and bracket.
20. Lower transaxle and engine assembly to disconnect assembly from stud bolts at rear engine mounting, the pull transaxle outward toward left hand side to disconnect input shaft from clutch assembly.
21. Lower transaxle, then remove from vehicle.
22. Reverse procedure to install. Lubricate splines of transaxle input shaft and pilot bearing surface and release bearing with lithium wheel bearing grease. When installing transaxle, guide right drive axle into transaxle as it is raised into vehicle. **Torque** transaxle to engine bolts to 37 ft. lbs.

TIGHTENING SPECIFICATIONS

Component	Torque/Ft. Lbs.	Component	Torque/Ft. Lbs.
Cable Bracket Bolts	17	Gear Shift Control Shaft Bolts And Nuts	13
Clutch Cable Outer Bolts	53①	Release Arm Bolt	10
Clutch Cover Bolts	17	Switch locknut	10
Extension Rod Nut	13	Transmission Case Bolts	14
Extension Rod Stud Bolt	24	Transmission To Engine Bolts	37
Flywheel Bolts	45		

① —Inch lbs.

Rear Axle & Suspension

INDEX

WHEEL BEARING
REPLACE

1. Raise and support rear of vehicle, then remove wheel and tire assembly.
2. Remove wheel bearing dust cap from brake drum.
3. Using a chisel, unstake wheel bearing nut, then remove wheel bearing nut and washer.
4. Loosen parking brake cable adjusting nuts, then remove plug from backing plate and back off drum brake adjustment.
5. Using a suitable puller, remove brake drum.
6. Using a brass drift, remove wheel bearings from brake drum.
7. Reverse procedure to install, noting the following:
   a. Fill Hub cavity (A), **Fig. 1,** with lithium wheel bearing grease.
   b. Install wheel bearings and spacer using Bearing and Hub Installer tool Nos. J-7079-2 and J-34842 or equivalents. **Wheel bearing should be installed with sealed side facing outward, Fig. 1.**
   c. Install brake drum on spindle.

Torque wheel bearing nut to specification listed at the end of this section, then stake nut in position.
   d. After completing installation, adjust drum brake and parking brake.
   e. Bleed and check brake system for proper operation prior to moving vehicle.

STRUT
REPLACE

1. Raise and support rear of vehicle, then remove wheel and tire assembly.

| 1 | BRAKE DRUM | 3 | SEALED SIDE |
| 2 | SPACER | 4 | WHEEL BEARING |

Fig. 1 Wheel bearing installation

| 1 | SUPPORT NUT |
| 2 | STRUT |

Fig. 2 Strut upper attaching nuts

1	STRUT
2	MOUNT BOLT
3	KNUCKLE

Fig. 3 Strut lower mounting bolt

| 1 | STRUT |
| 2 | KNUCKLE |

Fig. 4 Position strut to rear suspension knuckle

1	CONTROL ROD	4	WASHER
2	INSIDE NUT	5	CAR BODY
3	LOCK WASHER

Fig. 5 Control rod inner bolt

Fig. 6 Removing coil spring

2. Support suspension using a jack.
3. Remove strut upper support nuts, then push downward on strut, **Fig. 2**.
4. Remove strut lower mounting bolt, **Fig. 3**.
5. Separate strut from rear suspension knuckle, by compressing strut. **If strut is difficult to remove, open slit on knuckle just enough to allow strut removal.**
6. Reverse procedure to install. When installing strut, align projection on strut with slit on rear suspension knuckle, **Fig. 4**.

COIL SPRING
REPLACE

1. Raise and support rear of vehicle, then remove wheel and tire assembly.
2. Place alignment marks on control rod and control rod washer (A), **Fig. 5**, for setting toe during installation.
3. Remove control rod to body attaching bolt, then separate control rod from bracket.
4. From wheel side of control rod, remove nut from rear suspension knuckle stud, then disconnect control rod.
5. Loosen, but do not remove suspension arm rear attaching nut.
6. Loosen rear suspension knuckle lower mounting nut. Position a jack under suspension arm, then remove knuckle lower mounting nut.

7. Raise lower arm slightly to allow removal of rear suspension knuckle lower mounting bolt.
8. Disengage rear suspension knuckle from suspension arm, then carefully lower suspension arm and remove coil spring, **Fig. 6**.
9. Remove remaining suspension arm attaching bolts and nuts and remove suspension arm, if necessary.
10. Reverse procedure to install. When installing spring, position spring end to stepped portion of suspension arm, **Fig. 7**. When installing control rod to body bracket, align marks made on washer and control rod during removal. **Do not torque control rod or suspension arm attaching nuts and bolts until after vehicle has been lowered.**

CONTROL ROD
REPLACE

1. Raise and support rear of vehicle, then remove wheel and tire assembly.
2. Remove E-ring, then detach brake hose from control rod.
3. Place alignment marks on control rod and control rod washer at body bracket for setting toe during installation, **Fig. 5**.
4. Remove control rod to rear suspension knuckle attaching nut, **Fig. 8**.
5. Remove control rod to body bracket bolt, then remove control rod.

6. Reverse procedure to install. Position control rod to vehicle as shown in **Fig. 9**. When installing control rod to body bracket, align marks made on washer and control rod during removal. **Do not torque control rod attaching nuts and bolts until after vehicle has been lowered.**

REAR SUSPENSION KNUCKLE
REPLACE

1. Raise and support rear of vehicle, then remove wheel and tire assembly.
2. Remove brake drum, then disconnect brake hose from rear suspension knuckle bracket.
3. Disconnect brake line from wheel cylinder. Cap brake line and wheel cylinder fitting bore.
4. Remove brake backing plate attaching bolts, then remove brake backing plate.

1 SUSPENSION ARM
2 STEPPED PART
3 SPRING END

Fig. 7 Positioning coil spring to suspension arm

1 CONTROL ROD
2 OUTSIDE NUT
3 INSIDE NUT

Fig. 8 Control arm installation

1 LEFT SIDE CONTROL ROD
2 RIGHT SIDE CONTROL ROD
3 BRAKE HOSE MOUNTING BRACKET

Fig. 9 Positioning control arm to vehicle

5. Position a jack under suspension arm.
6. Place alignment marks on control rod and control rod washer at body bracket for setting toe during installation.
7. Remove control rod to body bracket attaching nut and washer.
8. Remove control rod to rear suspension knuckle stud nut, then remove control rod.
9. Remove strut to rear suspension knuckle attaching bolt.
10. Remove strut to suspension arm attaching bolt, then separate rear suspension knuckle from suspension arm and strut. **If strut is difficult to remove, open slit on knuckle just enough to allow strut removal.**
11. Reverse procedure to install. When installing control rod to body bracket, align marks made on washer and control rod during removal. **Do not torque control rod or suspension arm attaching nuts and bolts until after vehicle has been lowered.** Prior to installation, apply sealer to mat-

ing surface of brake backing plate and rear suspension knuckle. When installing brake drum, **torque** wheel bearing nut to specification listed at the end of this section, then stake nut in place using a chisel. After completing installation, adjust and bleed brake system, then check for proper brake operation before moving vehicle.

SUSPENSION ARM
REPLACE

Refer to "Coil Spring, Replace" for replacement procedure.

TIGHTENING SPECIFICATIONS

Component	Torque/Ft. Lbs.
Brake Backing Plate Retaining Nuts	17
Brake Line Fitting To Wheel Cylinder	12
Control Rod Nuts	59
Rear Suspension Knuckle Arm Lower Mounting Nut	37
Suspension Arm Front Nut	44
Suspension Arm Mounting Bracket Bolt	33

Component	Torque/Ft. Lbs.
Suspension Arm Rear Nut	37
Strut Lower Mounting Bolt	44
Strut Support Nut	24
Strut Upper Nut	37
Wheel Lug Nuts	44
Wheel Bearing Retaining Nut	74①

①—Tighten nut, then stake in position.

Front Suspension & Steering
INDEX

HUB & BEARING
REPLACE

When checking wheel bearings, raise and support front of vehicle, then rotate wheel and tire assembly to check bearing for smoothness of rotation and noise. Also check wheel bearing endplay with a dial indicator. Wheel bear-

ing endplay should not exceed .016 inch.
1. Raise and support vehicle, then remove front wheel and tire assembly.
2. Unstake, then remove hub retaining nut.
3. Remove caliper bolts, then caliper with brake line attached. Suspend caliper from chassis with wire.

4. Refer to **Fig. 1,** and measure dimension A for assembly reference. Pull hub out of knuckle.
5. Disconnect tie rod end from knuckle with Tie Rod End Remover tool No. J-21687-02 or equivalent.
6. Remove strut to knuckle bolts and then ball joint stud pinch bolt, **Fig. 2.**
7. Remove knuckle.

NOTE DIMENSION "A" AS SHOWN BEFORE HUB REMOVAL AS AN AID IN INSTALLATION.

Fig. 1   Checking dimension "A" to assure proper installation of hub

1. STRUT
2. TIE ROD END
3. KNUCKLE
4. STRUT BRACKET NUT
5. BALL STUD NUT
6. TIE ROD END CASTLE NUT
7. BALL STUD

Fig. 2   Steering knuckle removal

1. STEERING KNUCKLE
2. SPACER
3. WHEEL BEARING
4. APPLY GM WHEEL BEARING LUBRICANT #1051344

Fig. 3   Steering knuckle hub bearings & seal

8. Using a drift, remove outer, then inner bearing from knuckle.
9. Apply suitable grease to balls and oil seal lips of wheel bearings. Fill area A, **Fig. 3**, to approximately 40 percent of capacity with suitable grease.
10. Install wheel bearings using Bearing Installer tool No. J-34856 or equivalent. **Install wheel bearings with sealed side facing outward. Also ensure spacer is spacer is snug and centered between inner and outer bearings.**
11. Install wheel bearing seal (5), **Fig. 3**, using Seal Installer tool No. J-34881 or equivalent.
12. Install spacer on hub with bevel side first, **Fig. 4.**
13. Check that wheel bearing spacer bore is aligned with bearing bores. If not, move spacer until aligned.
14. Using plastic hammer, tap hub lightly into knuckle, taking care that alignment is maintained.
15. Using Wheel Hub Installer tool No. J-34856 and Handle tool No. J-7079-2 or equivalent, drive hub until dimension A, noted in step 4, is obtained.
16. Install brake caliper.
17. Torque caliper bolts to specification listed at the end of this section.
18. Torque driveshaft castle nut to speci-

fication listed at the end of this section.
19. Stake nut in position.
20. Install wheel and tire assembly, then lower vehicle.

CONTROL ARM
REPLACE

1. Raise and support vehicle, then remove wheel and tire assembly.
2. Remove ball joint stud to steering knuckle pinch bolt, **Fig. 5.**
3. Remove control arm bracket nut, then remove bracket bolts.
4. Remove control arm and bracket.
5. If control arm bushing are to be replaced, proceed as follows:
   a. Remove lower control arm as described under "Lower Control Arm, Replace."
   b. Press rear bushing from control arm, **Fig. 5.**
   c. Cut flange off front bushing, then press front bushing from control arm, **Fig. 6.**
   d. Apply soap and water to outer surface of front bushing, then press front bushing into control arm until it is centered.
   e. Position rear bushing to control arm, then drive bushing into control arm, **Figs. 7 and 8.**
6. Reverse procedure to install.

STRUT
REPLACE

1. Raise and support vehicle allowing front suspension to hang free.
2. Remove front wheel and tire assembly.
3. Remove E-clip from brake hose and disengage hose from strut bracket, **Fig. 9.**
4. Support lower control arm and knuckle assembly, then remove strut to knuckle bolts.
5. Remove upper strut mount nuts, then remove strut from vehicle.
6. Reverse procedure to install.

STRUT SERVICE

1. Mount strut in a spring compressor.

1. SPACER
2. BRAKE DISC
3. WHEEL HUB

Fig. 4   Wheel hub spacer installation

2. Compress spring approximately 1/2 inch.
3. Remove nut from strut shaft and remove components, **Fig. 10.**
4. Reverse procedure to assemble. Compress spring so strut shaft protrudes through cap by about 1 inch. Torque nut to specification listed at the end of this section.

MANUAL STEERING GEAR
REPLACE

1. Slide driver's seat rearward.
2. Pull off front part of floor mat on driver's side, then remove steering shaft joint cover.
3. Loosen steering shaft upper joint bolt without removing, **Fig. 11.**
4. Remove steering shaft lower joint bolt and disconnect lower joint from pinion.
5. Raise and support vehicle.
6. Remove front wheel and tire assemblies.
7. Remove cotter pins and castle nuts from tie rod ends.
8. Using tie rod end remover J-21687-02 or equivalent, disconnect tie rods from knuckles.
9. Remove steering gear housing mounting bolts, brackets and steering gear, **Fig. 12.**
10. Reverse procedure to install.

1	BALL STUD BOLT
2	KNUCKLE
3	BRACKET NUT
4	WASHER
5	SUSPENSION ARM BRACKET
6	SUSPENSION ARM BRACKET BOLTS
7	SUSPENSION ARM BUSHING
8	SUSPENSION ARM REAR BRACKET
9	SUSPENSION ARM REAR BRACKET BOLT
10	SUSPENSION ARM
11	SUSPENSION ARM FRONT BUSHING
12	BALL STUD

Fig. 5   Lower control arm replacement

1	FRONT BUSHING
2	SUSPENSION ARM

Fig. 6   Cutting flange from control arm front bushing

1	REAR BUSHING
2	SUSPENSION ARM

Fig. 7   Rear bushing to control arm installation

A	5mm ±1
1	REAR BUSHING
2	SUSPENSION ARM

Fig. 8   Rear bushing positioning

1	STRUT SUPPORT NUTS
2	STRUT BRACKET BOLTS

Fig. 9   Strut attaching nut bolt locations

Fig. 11 Steering shaft upper & lower joint bolts

1. UPPER JOINT BOLT
2. LOWER JOINT BOLT

1 NUT	10 BEARING LOWER WASHER
2 WASHER	11 BEARING SPACER
3 STOPPER	12 COIL SPRING UPPER SEAT
4 INNER SPACER	13 COIL SPRING SEAT
5 SUPPORT COMP.	14 STRUT COVER
6 BEARING SEAT	15 BUMP STOPPER
7 BEARING UPPER WASHER	16 COIL SPRING
8 BEARING SEAL	17 STRUT
9 BEARING	

Fig. 10 Exploded view of strut assembly

1. CAR BODY
2. STEERING GEAR CASE
3. CASE MOUNT BOLT
4. PINION SIDE BRACKET
5. RACK SIDE BRACKET

Fig. 12 Steering gear attaching bolts & brackets

TIGHTENING SPECIFICATIONS

Component	Torque/Ft. Lbs.	Component	Torque/Ft. Lbs.
Ball Joint Stud Nut	44	Strut Bracket Nut	59
Control Arm Bracket Bolt	69	Strut Nut	37
Control Arm Bracket Nut	92	Strut Support Nut	20
Control Arm Rear Bracket Bolt	32	Tie Rod End Castle Nut	32
Hub Bearing Nut	129 ①	Tie Rod End Locknut	33
Steering Gear Mounting Bracket Bolts	18	Wheel Lug Nuts	44
Steering Shaft Coupling Bolts	18	① —After tightening, stake nut in position.	

Wheel Alignment

INDEX

Fig. 1   Suspension geometry

35 — 55 N·m
(3.5 — 5.5 kg-m)
(25.5 — 39.5 lb.-ft.)

Fig. 2   Front wheel toe adjustment

DESCRIPTION

Wheel alignment, is the angular relationship between the wheels, suspension attaching parts and ground. The angle of the knuckle away from the vertical, pointing in or out of wheels, tilt of the wheels from vertical (when viewed from front of vehicle) and tilt of suspension members from vertical (when viewed from side of vehicle), all of these are involved in proper alignment, Fig. 1.

CASTER

Caster is tilting of the front steering axis either forward or backward from the vertical (when viewed from side of vehicle). A backward tilt is positive (+) and a forward tilt is negative (−). On short and long arm type suspensions you cannot see a caster angle without using a special instrument, but if you look straight down from the top of the upper control arm to the ground you would find that ball joints do not line up (fore and aft) when a caster angle other than 0° is present.

CAMBER

Camber is the tilting of front and rear wheels from the vertical when viewed from front of vehicle. When wheels tilt outward at top, camber is positive (+). When wheels tilt inward, camber is negative (MI). Amount of tilt is measured in degrees from the vertical and this is camber angle.

TOE

Toe is the turning in or out of wheels. The purpose of toe is to ensure parallel rolling of wheels. Excessive toe-in or toe-out may increase tire wear. Toe also serves to offset small deflections of the suspension which occurs when vehicle is moving.

PRELIMINARY INSPECTION

Steering and vibration problems are not always the result of alignment. An additional problem to be checked is tire lead due to worn or improperly manufactured tires. "Lead" is the deviation of the vehicle from a straight path on a level road without hand pressure on the steering wheel.

To insure correct alignment readings and alignment specifications, the following checks and inspections should be made.
1. Check tire for proper inflation and thread wear.
2. Check for loose ball joints and tie rod ends. If excessive looseness is noted, replace defective parts before adjusting toe.
3. Check for wheel and tire assembly run-out.
4. Check trim heights. If not within specifications, correct before adjusting toe.
5. Check for loose control arms.
6. Check for loose or missing stabilizer bar components.

7. Consideration must be given to excess loads, such as tool boxes, kegs, etc. If excess load is normally carried in vehicle, it should remain during alignment checks.

FRONT WHEEL ALIGNMENT

CAMBER & CASTER ADJUSTMENT

1. Position vehicle on an alignment fixture following manufacturer's instructions and check caster and camber angles. Bumper should be bounced three times before inspection, to prevent incorrect reading.

2. Camber and caster cannot be adjusted. Should either be found out of specification, locate the cause first.
3. If improper alignment is caused by damaged, worn or loose suspension parts, they should be replaced. If vehicle body or chassis is damaged, it should be repaired.

TOE ADJUSTMENT

1. Loosen right and left tie rod end locknuts, **Fig. 2**.
2. Apply grease between tie rods and rack boots.
3. Turn right and left tie rods by the same amount to align toe to specification. **Right and left tie rods should become equal in length.**
4. After adjustment, tighten locknuts and ensure rack boots are not twisted.

70–90 N·m
(51.0–65.0 lb-ft)

1 INSIDE NUT
2 INSIDE BOLT (CAM BOLT)
3 CONTROL ROD

Fig. 3   Rear wheel toe adjustment.

STEERING ANGLE

When a tie rod or tie rod end is replaced, check toe and steering angle with turning radius gages. If steering angle is not correct, check right and left tie rods for equal length.

REAR WHEEL ALIGNMENT

CAMBER

Camber cannot be adjusted. Should camber be found out of specification, locate the cause. If improper alignment is caused by damaged, worn or loose suspension parts, they should be replaced. If vehicle body or chassis is damaged, it should be repaired.

TOE

The rear wheel toe is adjusted by the inner control arm cam bolt, **Fig. 3**. If toe is found to out of specification, loosen left and right inner control arm cam bolt nuts, then rotate cam bolts by equal amounts to correct toe setting. After completing adjustment, torque cam bolt nuts to 51 to 65 ft. lbs.

GEO STORM
(R Car)
INDEX OF SERVICE OPERATIONS

NOTE: Refer To The Rear Of This Manual For Vehicle Manufacturer's Special Tool Suppliers.

Continued

INDEX OF SERVICE OPERATIONS—Continued

Specifications

GENERAL ENGINE SPECIFICATIONS

Year	Engine Liter/CID ①	Engine VIN Code ②	Fuel System	Bore & Stroke	Comp. Ratio	Net HP @ RPM ③	Maximum Torque Ft. Lbs. @ RPM	Normal Oil Pressure psi
1991	1.6L/4-97 ④	6	MFI	3.15 x 3.11	9.1	95 @ 5800	97 @ 4800	43.5–72.5 ⑥
	1.6L/4-97 ⑤	5	MFI	3.15 x 3.11	9.8	130 @ 7000	102 @ 5800	51.2–80.4 ⑥
1992–93	1.6L/4-97 ④	6	MFI	3.15 x 3.11	9.1	95 @ 5800	97 @ 4800	43.5–72.5 ⑥
	1.8L/4-110 ⑤	8	MFI	3.15 x 3.54	9.7	140 @ 6400	120 @ 4600	71 ⑥

①—CID: Cubic Inch Displacement.
②—The eighth digit of the VIN denotes engine code.
③—Ratings are net, as installed in vehicle.
④—Single overhead cam.
⑤—Double overhead cams.
⑥—At 3000 RPM.

TUNE UP SPECIFICATIONS

Year & Engine/ VIN Code	Spark Plug Gap	Ignition Timing BTDC ① Firing Order Fig.	Ignition Timing BTDC ① Man. Trans.	Ignition Timing BTDC ① Auto. Trans.	Mark Fig.	Curb Idle Speed Man. Trans.	Curb Idle Speed Auto. Trans.	Fast Idle Speed Man. Trans.	Fast Idle Speed Auto. Trans.	Fuel Pump Pressure psi
1991										
1.6L/4-97(6)	.041	A	②	②	B	850 ③	940N ③	③	③	④
1.6L/4-97(5)	.041	A	②	②	B	850 ③	940N ③	③	③	④
1992–93										
1.6L/4-97(6)	.041	A	②	②	B	850 ③	940N ③	③	③	④
1.8L/4-110(8)	.041	A	⑤	⑤	B	850 ③	940N ③	③	③	④

①—BTDC: Before Top Dead Center.
②—Ignition timing should be 9–11° BTDC with jumper wire connected between ALDL connector terminals 1 & 3. Refer to Fig. C for ALDL connector location. If a large fluctuation in ignition timing is present, decrease fluctuation by increasing engine speed to 1500–2000 RPM.
③—Idle speeds are ECM controlled.
④—25–30 psi w/vacuum hose connected to pressure regulator and 35–42 psi w/vacuum hose disconnected.
⑤—Set timing to specification on under hood decal.

TUNE UP SPECIFICATIONS—Continued

Fig. A

Fig. B

Fig. C

| 1 | ALDL CONNECTOR C-52 |
| 2 | JUMPER WIRE |

WHEEL ALIGNMENT SPECIFICATIONS

FRONT

Year	Model	Caster Angle, Degrees ①		Camber Angle, Degrees ①		Toe In Inch	
		Limits	Desired	Limits	Desired	Limits	Desired
1991	All	+2 to +4	+3	−1.5 to +.5	−.5	−.039 to +.039	0
1992–93	All	+4 to +5	+4.5	−1.5 to +.5	−.5	−.039 to +.039	0

① —Not adjustable

REAR

Year	Model	Camber Degrees				Toe
		Limits		Desired		
		Left	Right	Left	Right	
1991–93	All	−1.5 to +.5	−1.5 to +.5	−.5	−.5	.16

COOLING SYSTEM & CAPACITY DATA

Year	Engine (VIN)	Cooling Capacity Qts.		Radiator Cap Relief Pressure, Lbs.	Thermo. Opening Temp. °F.	Fuel Tank Gals.	Engine Oil w/Filter Qts. ③	Transaxle Oil	
		Automatic Transmission	Manual Transmission					Manual Transaxle, Pts.	Auto Transaxle, Qts. ①
1991	1.6L/4-97 (5)	7.8	7.3	4.3–14.2	180°	12.4	4③	4	②
	1.6L/4-97 (6)	7.7	7.2	4.3–14.2	180°	12.4	3.2③	4	②
1992–93	1.6L/4-97 (6)	7.7	7.2	4.3–14.2	180°	12.4	3.2③	4	②
	1.8L/4-110 (8)	8	7.5	4.3–14.2	170°	12.4	4③	4	6.6

① —Approximate, make final check w/dipstick.
② —3 speed, 6.9 qts., 4 speed, 7 qts.
③ —Includes filter.

LUBRICANT DATA

Year	Model	Lubricant Type			Brake System
		Transaxle		Power Steering	
		Manual	Automatic		
1991–93	All	GM Syncromesh Transmission Fluid	Dexron II	GM Type Power Steering Fluid	DOT 3

Electrical

INDEX

Fig. 1   Fuse panel location

Fig. 2   Distributor assembly

PRECAUTIONS

AIRBAG SYSTEM DISARMING

1991

The diagnostic energy reserve module (DERM) can maintain voltage to cause a system deployment for up to ten minutes after the ignition switch is turned off and the battery is disconnected. Servicing the SIR system during this period may result in accidental deployment and personal injury.

1. Turn ignition switch to Off position, then disconnect battery ground cable.
2. Remove fuses C-22 and C-23 from fuse box, then disconnect orange three-way connector at the base of the steering column.

1992-93

The diagnostic energy reserve module (DERM) can maintain voltage to cause a system deployment for up to ten minutes after the ignition switch is turned off and the battery is disconnected. Servicing the SIR system during this period may result in accidental deployment and personal injury.

1. Place steering wheel so that wheels are pointing straight ahead, then turn ignition switch to LOCK position.
2. Remove fuses C-22 and C-23 from fuse block.
3. Remove switch bezel from instrument panel, then disconnect electrical connector from switches.
4. Remove cigar lighter bezel from instrument panel, then disconnect cigar lighter electrical connectors.
5. Remove two screws and hood latch release handle from knee bolster, then the three screws, three bolts and two nuts retaining knee bolster.
6. Disconnect lap cooler air duct from knee bolster, then remove knee bolster from vehicle.
7. Remove Connector Position Assurance (CPA), then disconnect orange three-way connector at the base of the steering column.

AIRBAG SYSTEM ARMING

1991

1. Turn ignition switch to Off position, then connect orange three-way connector at the base of the steering column.
2. Install fuses C-22 and C-23 into fuse box, then connect battery ground cable.

1992-93

1. Turn ignition switch to Off position, then connect orange three-way connector at the base of the steering column.
2. Connect lap cooler air duct to knee bolster, then install knee bolster.
3. **Torque** knee bolster bolts and nuts to 89 inch lbs.
4. Install hood latch release handle to knee bolster.
5. Connect cigar lighter electrical connector, then snap cigar lighter bezel into place on instrument panel.
6. Connect switch bezel electrical connectors, then snap switch bezel into place on instrument panel.

FUSE PANEL & FLASHER LOCATION

The fuse panel is located below lefthand side of instrument panel, **Fig. 1.**

Turn signal and hazard flasher is located above fuse panel, under lefthand side of instrument panel.

STARTER REPLACE

1. Disconnect battery ground cable, then battery positive cable from starter.
2. **On models with manual transaxle,** disconnect ignition switch lead from starter solenoid.
3. **On models with automatic transaxle,** disconnect ignition switch lead from starter solenoid pigtail.
4. **On all models,** remove two starter motor mounting bolts, then the motor.
5. Reverse procedure to install, **torque** starter attaching bolts to 29 ft. lbs. and battery positive cable nut to 26 ft. lbs.

DISTRIBUTOR REPLACE

1. Disconnect battery ground cable.
2. Remove all distributor electrical connections, then distributor cap.
3. Mark distributor housing position on engine, and the rotor position on distributor housing assembly.

1. Steering wheel
2. Knee pad
3. Steering wiring connector
4. Coil assembly
5. Retaining ring
6. Cushion rubber
7. Steering lock fixing blot
8. Steering lock assembly

Fig. 3 Steering column assembly

Fig. 4 Ignition switch assembly

Fig. 5 SIR module removal

Fig. 6 Steering wheel removal

10. Remove turn signal switch retaining screws, then turn signal switch.
11. Reverse procedure to install.
12. **On all models equipped with the SIR or inflatable restraint systems,** enable system as described under "Precautions."

DIMMER SWITCH
REPLACE

Refer to "Turn Signal Switch, Replace," for dimmer switch replacement.

IGNITION LOCK
REPLACE

1. **On all models equipped with the SIR or inflatable restraint systems,** disable system as described under "Precautions" before performing any repair procedures on or near steering column.
2. Disconnect battery ground cable.
3. Remove steering wheel as described in "Steering Wheel, Replace."
4. Remove turn signal assembly as described in "Turn Signal/Dimmer Switch, Replace."
5. Turn key to Off position, depress retaining pin, then remove ignition lock cylinder from switch.
6. Reverse procedure to install.
7. **On all models equipped with the SIR or inflatable restraint systems,** enable system as described under "Precautions."

IGNITION SWITCH
REPLACE

1. **On all models equipped with the SIR or inflatable restraint systems,** disable system as described under "Precautions" before performing any repair procedures on or near steering column.
2. Disconnect battery ground cable.
3. Remove steering wheel as described in "Steering Wheel, Replace."

4. Remove distributor mounting bolt, **Fig. 2,** then distributor from engine.
5. Remove O ring from distributor shaft.
6. Reverse procedures to install, using new O-ring gaskets.

TURN SIGNAL SWITCH
REPLACE

1. **On all models equipped with the SIR or inflatable restraint systems,** disable system as described under "Precautions" before performing any repair procedures on or near steering column.
2. Disconnect battery ground cable.
3. Remove steering wheel as described in "Steering Wheel, Replace."
4. Remove lower switch panel, dash lighter panel and hood release cable.
5. Remove lap air deflector attaching screws, then the lap air reflector.
6. Remove left lower dash trim panel attaching screws, then lower dash trim panel.
7. Remove upper steering column mounting bolts and lower column.
8. Remove two piece steering column cover attaching screws and cover.
9. Disconnect coil assembly wiring harness from turn signal switch, then remove four retaining screws and coil assembly, **Fig. 3.**

4. Remove turn signal assembly as described in "Turn Signal/Dimmer Switch, Replace."
5. Remove ignition lock as described in "Ignition Lock, Replace."
6. Disconnect electrical connector from ignition switch, then remove snap ring and spacer collar from steering shaft, **Fig. 4.**
7. Disconnect back drive cable from ignition switch, then remove ignition switch retaining bolts and ignition switch from steering column.
8. Reverse procedure to install.
9. **On all models equipped with the SIR or inflatable restraint systems,** enable system as described under "Precautions."

STEERING WHEEL
REPLACE

1. **On all models equipped with the SIR or inflatable restraint systems,** disable system as described under "Precautions" before performing any repair procedures on or near steering column.
2. Disconnect battery ground cable.
3. Remove SIR module mounting screws and SIR module, **Fig. 5.**
4. Remove steering wheel retaining nut.
5. Using Steering Wheel Puller tool No.

Fig. 7 Horn harness connector

Fig. 8 Headlamp control switch

1. METER HOOD
2. METER ASSEMBLY
3. FRONT COVER HOLE COVER
4. FRONT COVER
5. INSTRUMENT PANEL ASSEMBLY

6. GLOVE BOX
7. CIGAR LIGHTER BEZEL
8. SWITCH BEZEL
9. KNEE PAD ASSEMBLY

Fig. 9 Instrument panel

J-1859-03 or equivalent, remove steering wheel from column, **Fig. 6.**
6. Remove horn switch retaining screws and horn switch from steering wheel, **Fig. 7.**
7. Remove rear steering wheel cover attaching screws, then the cover.
8. Reverse procedure to install, **torque steering wheel nut to 25 ft. lbs.**
9. **On all models equipped with the SIR or inflatable restraint systems,** enable system as described under "Precautions."

HEADLAMP SWITCH
REPLACE

1. **On all models equipped with the SIR or inflatable restraint systems,** disable system as described under "Precautions" before performing any repair procedures on or near steering column.
2. Disconnect battery ground cable.
3. Refer to "Dash Panel Service" to remove meter hood.
4. Remove meter cluster from meter hood, then two clips attaching headlamp control harness.
5. Remove four headlamp control switch retaining screws, then the headlamp control switch with illumination box, **Fig. 8.**

6. Disconnect electrical connector, then two illumination box retaining screws and illumination box.
7. Reverse procedure to install.
8. **On all models equipped with the SIR or inflatable restraint systems,** enable system as described under "Precautions."

INSTRUMENT CLUSTER
REPLACE

1. **On all models equipped with the SIR or inflatable restraint systems,** disable system as described under "Precautions" before performing any repair procedures on or near steering column.
2. Disconnect battery ground cable.
3. Refer to "Dash Panel Service," then remove meter hood.
4. Remove four dash gauge retaining screws, then disconnect electrical connectors and speedometer cable, **Fig. 9.**
5. Remove dash gauge assembly.
6. Reverse procedure to install, ensuring that all electrical connectors are securely connected.
7. **On all models equipped with the SIR or inflatable restraint systems,** enable system as described under "Precautions."

WINDSHIELD WIPER SWITCH
REPLACE
FRONT

1. **On all models equipped with the SIR or inflatable restraint systems,** disable system as described under "Precautions" before performing any repair procedures on or near steering column.
2. Disconnect battery ground cable.
3. Remove meter hood as described in "Dash Panel Service."
4. Remove meter cluster, then the two attaching clips from wiper/washer switch harness.
5. Remove four switch attaching screws, then the switch with illumination bulb.
6. Reverse procedure to install.
7. **On all models equipped with the SIR or inflatable restraint systems,** enable system as described under "Precautions."

REAR

1. Disconnect battery ground cable.
2. Remove trim bezel.
3. Remove rear wiper switch, then disconnect electrical connector.
4. Reverse procedure to install.

Fig. 11   Evaporator assembly

#	
1	THERMOSTATIC SWITCH
2	SENSOR
3	GROMMET
4	UPPER CASE
5	EXPANSION VALVE
6	EVAPORATOR CORE
7	LINING
8	RESISTOR
9	LOWER CASE
10	CLIP
11	RETAINING SCREW

Fig. 10   Heater assembly

#	
1	SIDE DEFROSTER DUCT
2	DEFROSTER NOZZLE
3	VENTILATOR DUCT
4	HEATER HOSES
5	BLOWER ASSEMBLY
6	DUCT
7	HEATER UNIT

CLUTCH START SWITCH
REPLACE

1. Disconnect battery ground cable.
2. Disconnect electrical connector from clutch switch that is mounted above clutch pedal.
3. Remove front locknut, then the switch.
4. Remove rear locknut.
5. Reverse the procedure to install. Adjust clutch start switch as follows:
   a. Loosen clutch switch locknut, then rotate clutch switch until threaded portion bottoms on switch bracket, then tighten locknut.

STOP LAMP SWITCH
REPLACE

1. Remove stop lamp switch locknut, then the stop lamp switch.
2. Reverse procedure to install. Adjust stop lamp switch as follows:
   a. Loosen stop lamp switch locknut. Thread stop lamp switch into bracket until tip of switch is gently resting on pedal arm. Carefully thread stop lamp switch inward, until freeplay between brake pedal and pushrod is eliminated, then tighten locknut.

RADIO
REPLACE

1. Remove four heater control knobs, then four radio bezel screws from radio bezel, **Fig. 9.**
2. Disconnect illumination lamp and harness from radio bezel.
3. Remove three righthand side panel retaining screws, then four radio bracket retaining screws.
4. Remove radio from I/P, then disconnect electrical and antenna connectors.
5. Reverse procedure to install.

HEATER CORE
REPLACE

1. Disconnect battery ground cable.
2. Drain cooling system, then disconnect heater hoses at engine compartment.
3. Remove instrument panel assembly, referring to "Dash Panel Service" for procedure.
4. Remove evaporator assembly as described in "Evaporator Core, Replace."
5. Remove duct between blower assembly and heater unit, **Fig. 10,** then the center ventilation duct.
6. Remove four heater unit retaining nuts, then the heater unit.
7. Remove three duct mounting screws, then the five mode control to heater core case retaining screws.
8. Remove mode control case, but do not remove the link assembly at this time.
9. Remove five screws so that two halves of the heater core case may be separated, **Fig. 10.**
10. Remove heater core.
11. Reverse procedure to install.

BLOWER MOTOR
REPLACE

1. Disconnect battery ground cable.
2. Disconnect blower motor electrical connector.
3. Remove four blower motor attaching screws, then the blower motor, **Fig. 10.**
4. Reverse procedure to install.

EVAPORATOR CORE
REPLACE

1. Disconnect battery ground cable.
2. Discharge A/C system as described in "Air Conditioning."
3. Remove A/C lines from expansion valve, capping all fittings immediately to keep moisture out of system.
4. Remove retaining clip and expansion valve from the evaporator.
5. Remove glove box assembly from I/P, then the lower dash reinforcement bracket.
6. Disconnect electrical connector from thermostat switch and blower motor resistor.
7. Remove air inlet cable from blend door, then retaining nuts from evaporator case.
8. Remove evaporator assembly from dash, then retaining clip from evaporator case.
9. Remove four case retaining screws, then separate case, **Fig. 11.**
10. Remove evaporator core and evaporator grommet from case.
11. Reverse procedure to install.

1.6L/4-97 & 1.8L/4-110 Engines

INDEX

1	RIGHT MOUNT BOLT
2	RIGHT MOUNT NUT

Fig. 1 Right engine mount

PRECAUTIONS

AIRBAG SYSTEM DISARMING

1991

The diagnostic energy reserve module (DERM) can maintain voltage to cause a system deployment for up to ten minutes after the ignition switch is turned off and the battery is disconnected. Servicing the SIR system during this period may result in accidental deployment and personal injury.

1. Turn ignition switch to Off position, then disconnect battery ground cable.
2. Remove fuses C-22 and C-23 from fuse box, then disconnect orange three-way connector at the base of the steering column.

1992–93

The diagnostic energy reserve module (DERM) can maintain voltage to

cause a system deployment for up to ten minutes after the ignition switch is turned off and the battery is disconnected. Servicing the SIR system during this period may result in accidental deployment and personal injury.

1. Place steering wheel so that wheels are pointing straight ahead, then turn ignition switch to LOCK position.
2. Remove fuses C-22 and C-23 from fuse block.
3. Remove switch bezel from instrument panel, then disconnect electrical connectors from switches.
4. Remove cigar lighter bezel from instrument panel, then disconnect cigar lighter electrical connectors.
5. Remove two screws and hood latch release handle from knee bolster, then the three screws, three bolts and two nuts retaining knee bolster.
6. Disconnect lap cooler air duct from knee bolster, then remove knee bolster from vehicle.
7. Remove Connector Position Assurance (CPA), then disconnect orange three-way connector at the base of the steering column.

AIRBAG SYSTEM ARMING

1991

1. Turn ignition switch to Off position, then connect orange three-way connector at the base of the steering column.
2. Install fuses C-22 and C-23 into fuse box, then connect battery ground cable.

1992–93

1. Turn ignition switch to Off position, then connect orange three-way con-

1	TORQUE ROD BRACKET
2	TORQUE ROD BOLT

Fig. 2 Torque rod engine mount

nector at the base of the steering column.
2. Connect lap cooler air duct to knee bolster, then install knee bolster.
3. **Torque** knee bolster bolts and nuts to 89 inch lbs.
4. Install hood latch release handle to knee bolster.
5. Connect cigar lighter electrical connector, then snap cigar lighter bezel into place on instrument panel.
6. Connect switch bezel electrical connectors, then snap switch bezel into place on instrument panel.

ENGINE MOUNTS
REPLACE

RIGHT MOUNT

1. Disconnect battery ground cable.
2. Using Engine Support Fixture tool No. J28467-A or equivalent, support engine.

3. Raise and support vehicle.
4. Remove bolt and nut from mounting bridge bracket, **Fig. 1.**
5. Remove engine mount through bolt, then the engine mount.
6. Reverse procedure to install.

TORQUE ROD

1. Disconnect battery ground cable, then raise and support vehicle.
2. Remove torque rod bracket attaching nut and bolts, **Fig. 2.**
3. Remove torque rod center bolt and nut, then remove torque rod and bracket assembly.
4. Reverse procedure to install.

REAR MOUNT

1. Disconnect battery ground cable.
2. Support engine using Engine Support Fixture tool No. J-28467-A or equivalent.
3. Raise and support vehicle.
4. Remove dampener weight from the engine mounting, then the bolt from transaxle case.
5. Remove center bolts from the center beam, then the rear engine mount.
6. Reverse procedure to install.

LEFT MOUNT

1. Disconnect battery cables, then remove battery.
2. Remove cover plate, then the left engine mount bolts from transaxle case.
3. Remove left engine mount center bolt, then left engine mount.
4. Reverse procedure to install.

ENGINE
REPLACE

1. Disconnect battery cables.
2. Remove battery, battery tray and hood.
3. Drain engine coolant, then remove accelerator cable from throttle valve.
4. Remove breather hose from intake air duct, then intake air duct from throttle valve.
5. Remove air cleaner assembly.
6. Disconnect MAP sensor hose from MAP sensor, then the brake booster vacuum hose and two canister hoses from pipes of the common chamber.
7. Remove two cable harness connectors near LH shock tower.
8. Disconnect ignition coil electrical connectors, then the ignition coil and bracket as an assembly.
9. Disconnect engine harness ground cable from LH inner fender, then the chassis harness terminal from relay and fuse box.
10. Disconnect cooling fan and oxygen sensor harness connectors.
11. Disconnect ground cable terminal at rear of cylinder head cover and four connectors from automatic transaxle control system harness.
12. **On models with manual transaxle,** disconnect clutch cable by loosening two adjusting nuts.

13. Remove two transaxle shift cables by disconnecting cotter pin and removing clip from shift cable bracket.
14. **On models with automatic transaxle,** disconnect transaxle shift cable by removing cotter pin, then the joint from shift cable lever.
15. **On all models,** remove two heater hoses from engine, speedometer cable from transaxle and upper radiator hose from radiator.
16. Remove fuel feed pipe and fuel return hose near the filter, then the coolant coolant recovery tank with bracket as an assembly.
17. Remove power steering belt, power steering pump and bracket.
18. Remove cooling fan and shroud, then raise and support vehicle.
19. Remove righthand and lefthand undercovers, then the lower radiator hose.
20. Remove two transaxle oil cooler lines from transaxle.
21. Remove two air conditioning compressor bracket bolts from engine and set aside.
22. Remove front tire and wheel assemblies, then the drive axles.
23. Remove front exhaust pipe from exhaust manifold, then lower vehicle.
24. Lower vehicle and attach a suitable engine hoist to the lifting bracket, applying slight pressure.
25. Remove engine and transaxle mounts.
26. Remove engine and transaxle as an assembly.
27. Remove transaxle from engine.
28. Reverse procedure to install.

INTAKE MANIFOLD
REPLACE
SOHC ENGINE

Refer to **Figs. 3, 4 and 5** for SOHC engine breakdown.
1. Remove battery ground cable, then ignition coil wires.
2. Remove accelerator cable from throttle valve and common chamber, then two cable harness connectors at lefthand shock tower.
3. Disconnect cable harness from intake air control valve, MAT and TPS sensors.
4. Remove breather hose from intake air duct, then intake air duct from throttle valve and PCV hose from the cylinder head cover.
5. Remove EGR valve and canister vacuum hoses from throttle valve, then the EGR pipe from EGR valve and exhaust manifold.
6. Remove common chamber bracket and throttle valve assembly attaching bolts, then the throttle valve.
7. Remove coolant bypass pipe clip bolt and MAP sensor from common chamber.
8. Remove brake booster and canister vacuum hoses from common chamber and throttle valve.
9. Remove pressure regulator and EGR vacuum hoses from common chamber.

10. Remove engine hanger bolt, then the common chamber retaining nuts and bolts.
11. Remove common chamber from engine assembly.
12. Reverse procedure to install.

DOHC ENGINE

Refer to **Figs. 6 through 9,** when working on DOHC engines.
1. Disconnect battery ground cable.
2. Remove accelerator cable clip and PCV hose from intake air duct, then the intake air duct from vehicle.
3. Remove accelerator cable from throttle valve, then MAP sensor hose from MAP sensor.
4. Remove vacuum hose from brake booster and two canister hoses from pipes on common chamber, then remove canister pipe bracket.
5. Remove fuel pressure regulator vacuum hose, then remove induction control valve vacuum hose.
6. Remove throttle valve from common chamber, then disconnect alternator harness clip and three fuel injector harness cable clips.
7. Loosen EGR pipe bracket at exhaust manifold and loosen EGR clip at thermostat housing.
8. Remove two common chamber bracket bolts on lefthand side of engine and engine hanger bolt on righthand side of common chamber.
9. Remove ten bolts and two nuts from common chamber induction control valve assembly, then the common chamber.
10. Reverse procedure to install.

INDUCTION CONTROL
VALVE ASSEMBLY
REPLACE

1. Disconnect battery ground cable, then ignition coil wires.
2. Remove common chamber as described in ""Common Chamber/Intake Manifold, Replace.""
3. Remove two oil cooler pipe clip nuts from studs located under induction control valve.
4. Remove fuel feed pipe and return fuel hose, then two fuel rail retaining bolts.
5. Remove two fuel injector harness bracket retaining bolts, then the fuel injector harness and fuel rail with fuel injectors attached from injection control valve assembly.
6. Disconnect VSV harness connector from induction control valve.
7. Remove seven bolts and two nuts from induction control valve assembly, then the induction control assembly.
8. Reverse procedures to install, **torquing** induction control valve retaining bolts to 17 ft. lbs.

EXHAUST MANIFOLD
REPLACE

1. Disconnect battery ground cable

nuts and bolts, then the exhaust manifold.
5. Reverse procedure to install.

CYLINDER HEAD REPLACE

SOHC ENGINE

1. Disconnect battery ground cable, then drain coolant.
2. Disconnect accelerator cable from throttle valve.
3. Remove breather hose from intake air duct, then the intake air duct from the throttle valve.
4. Remove MAP sensor hose from MAP sensor, then the brake booster vacuum hose.
5. Remove two canister hoses and EGR vacuum hoses from common chamber.
6. Disconnect oxygen sensor harness from oxygen sensor, ignition coil ground from thermostat housing flange and coolant temperature sensor from thermo unit harness.
7. Remove cable harness clip from bracket at coolant outlet pipe, then two cable harness connectors near lefthand strut tower.
8. Remove two heater hoses from engine and upper radiator hose from radiator.
9. Remove fuel feed hose and return hose, then raise and support vehicle.
10. Remove righthand undercover and exhaust pipe from exhaust manifold, then lower vehicle.
11. Remove right side engine mount, then the alternator and power steering belts.
12. Remove engine mounting bracket from timing cover, timing cover and timing belt.
13. Remove cylinder head center cover, cylinder head bolts, then the cylinder head.
14. Reverse procedure to install, noting the following:
    a. Using tightening sequence shown in **Fig. 10, torque** cylinder head bolts in two steps. First to 29 ft. lbs, then to 58 ft. lbs.
    b. Install timing belt as described in "Timing Belt Replace."

DOHC ENGINE

1. Disconnect battery ground cable, then drain coolant.
2. Disconnect accelerator cable from intake air duct, then accelerator cable clips from cylinder head cover and common chamber.
3. Disconnect accelerator cable from throttle valve and remove PCV hose from intake duct side.
4. Remove intake air duct from throttle valve, then MAP sensor hose from MAP sensor.
5. Remove brake booster vacuum hose from brake booster, then two canister hoses from pipes on common chamber.

Fig. 3 SOHC engine cylinder head components

1	CENTER COVER	21	EXHAUST VALVE
2	RETAINING BOLT	22	VALVE STEM SEAL
3	RETAINING BOLT	23	UPPER SPRING SEAT
4	CYLINDER HEAD COVER	24	TAPPET
5	OIL FILLER CAP	25	INTAKE VALVE
6	DISTRIBUTOR	26	LOWER SPRING SEAT
7	CAMSHAFT (INTAKE CAM)	27	VALVE SPRING
8	CAMSHAFT (EXHAUST CAM)	28	SPLIT COLLAR
9	CAMSHAFT OIL SEAL	29	ADJUSTER (SHIM)
10	CYLINDER HEAD BOLT	30	INDUCTION CONTROL VALVE GASKET
11	SPARK PLUG	31	CYLINDER HEAD
12	VALVE GUIDE (EXHAUST)	32	VALVE GUIDE (INTAKE)
13	CAMSHAFT BRACKET	33	TIMING PULLEY (INTAKE CAM)
14	OXYGEN SENSOR	34	TIMING PULLEY (EXHAUST CAM)
15	HEAT PROTECTOR	35	INDUCTION CONTROL VALVE ASSEMBLY
16	EXHAUST MANIFOLD	36	FUEL INJECTOR
17	EXHAUST MANIFOLD GASKET	37	FUEL RAIL
18	SEAT INSERT (INTAKE)	38	COMMON CHAMBER GASKET
19	SEAT INSERT (EXHAUST)	39	GASKET
20	CYLINDER HEAD GASKET	40	COMMON CHAMBER

2. Remove heat protector, then disconnect oxygen sensor electrical connector.
3. Remove the EGR pipe from exhaust manifold and EGR valve, then the front exhaust pipe from exhaust manifold.
4. Remove exhaust manifold retaining

6. Remove two canister pipes and MAP sensor pipe from common chamber, then canister pipe support bracket.
7. Disconnect oxygen sensor harness connector, ignition coil ground cable from thermostat housing flange, coolant temperature sensor and thermo unit harness connector at thermostat housing.
8. Disconnect two ground cable terminals from right side of common chamber, then ground cable from rear RH side of common chamber.
9. Disconnect starter and alternator cable clip.
10. Remove two heater hoses from engine, then upper radiator hose.
11. Remove throttle valve heating hose from coolant bypass pipe, then coolant bypass pipe bracket from cylinder head and fuel feed pipe and return fuel hose.
12. Raise and support vehicle, then remove righthand side undercover.
13. Remove front exhaust pipe from exhaust manifold, then lower vehicle.
14. Remove right side engine mount, then cylinder head center cover.
15. Remove spark plug wires from spark plugs and clips, then PCV hose from cylinder head cover.
16. Remove upper timing cover and cylinder head cover.
17. Remove timing belt, then cylinder head bolts as shown in **Fig. 11.**
18. Raise cylinder head and remove oil cooler pipe from oil cooler.
19. Remove cylinder head.
20. Reverse procedure to install, using tightening sequence shown in **Fig. 12, torque** cylinder head bolts in two steps. First to 29 ft. lbs., then to 58 ft. lbs.

1	CANISTER HOSE TO COMMON CHAMBER
2	COMMON CHAMBER
3	EGR HOSE: THROTTLE VALVE TO VSV
4	EGR HOSE: VSV TO TRANSDUCER
5	EGR VSV
6	MAP SENSOR HOSE
7	EGR TRANSDUCER
8	EGR HOSE: EGR VALVE TO TRANSDUCER
9	MAP SENSOR
10	ACCELERATOR CABLE
11	EGR HOSE: TRANSDUCER TO EGR VALVE
12	EGR VALVE
13	THROTTLE VALVE
14	EGR PIPE
15	AIR DUCT
16	AIR CLEANER
17	FUEL FILTER
18	FUEL FEED HOSE
19	IGNITION COIL
20	PCV HOSE: CYLINDER HEAD COVER TO AIR DUCT
21	FUEL RETURN PIPE
22	DISTRIBUTOR
23	FUEL RAIL
24	OXYGEN SENSOR
25	CYLINDER HEAD COVER
26	PCV HOSE: CYLINDER HEAD COVER TO COMMON CHAMBER
27	VACCUM HOSE: PRESSURE REGULATOR TO COMMON CHAMBER
28	CANISTER HOSE: TO THROTTLE VALVE
29	CANISTER HOSE
30	CANISTER

Fig. 4   SOHC engine air intake system

CAMSHAFT LIFT SPECIFICATIONS

SOHC ENGINE

Year	Liter/CID	Intake & Exhaust
1991–93	1.6L/4-97	1.426①

①—Minimum height.

DOHC ENGINE

Year	Liter/CID	Intake & Exhaust
1991	1.6L/4-97	1.503①
1992–93	1.8L/4-110	1.531①

①—Minimum height.

VALVE CLEARANCE SPECIFICATIONS

SOHC ENGINE

Year	Engine	Intake Inch	Exhaust Inch
1991–93	1.6L/4-97	.006	.010

DOHC ENGINE

Year	Engine	Intake Inch	Exhaust Inch
1991	1.6L/4-97	.004–.008 ①	.008–.012 ①
1992–93	1.8L/4-110	①	①

①—Equipped w/hydraulic lifters, no adjustments necessary.

VALVES

ADJUST

SOHC ENGINE

1. Set number one cylinder at TDC on the compression stroke, then turn crankshaft pulley to align its notched line with the 0 mark on timing cover.
2. Ensure that valves on No. 1 cylinder have play and valves No. 4 cylinder do not. If not as specified, turn crankshaft pulley 360° and align the 0 mark on lower timing cover, **Fig. 13.**
3. Measure valve lash between rocker arm and valve stem as follows:
   a. Intake and exhaust valves on No. 1 cylinder.
   b. Intake valve on No. 2 cylinder.
   c. Exhaust valves on No. 3 cylinder.
4. Valve lash should be 0.006 inch on intake and 0.010 on exhaust valves.
5. If lash is not as specified, adjust valve lash by loosening adjustment screw locknut and turn adjustment screw until lash is within specifications, **Fig. 14.**
6. Tighten adjustment locknut, then rotate crankshaft 360° and measure lash as follows:
   a. Intake and exhaust valves on No. 4 cylinder.
   b. Intake valves on No. 3 cylinder.
   c. Exhaust valves on No. 2 cylinder.

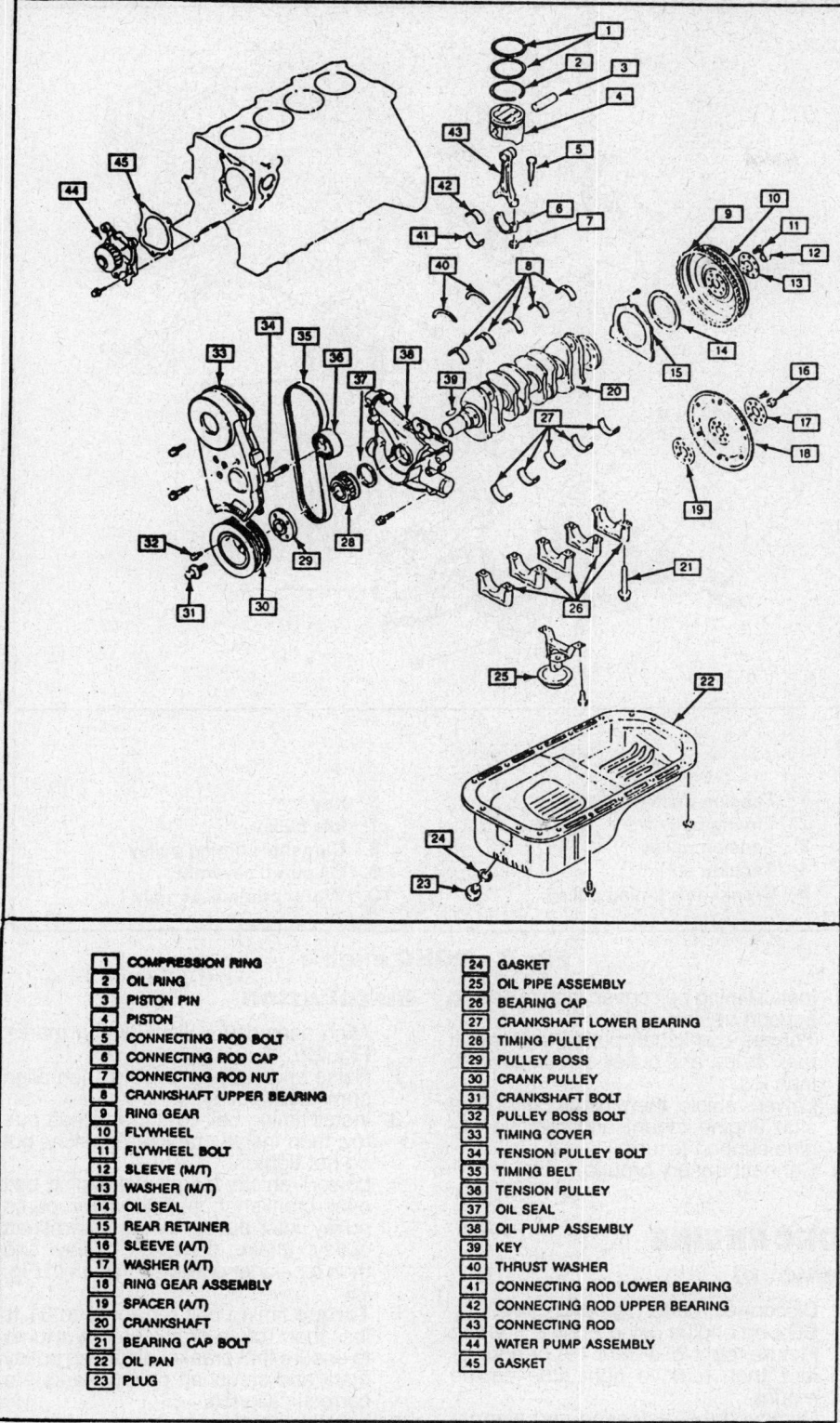

Fig. 5 SOHC cylinder block components

1	COMPRESSION RING	24	GASKET
2	OIL RING	25	OIL PIPE ASSEMBLY
3	PISTON PIN	26	BEARING CAP
4	PISTON	27	CRANKSHAFT LOWER BEARING
5	CONNECTING ROD BOLT	28	TIMING PULLEY
6	CONNECTING ROD CAP	29	PULLEY BOSS
7	CONNECTING ROD NUT	30	CRANK PULLEY
8	CRANKSHAFT UPPER BEARING	31	CRANKSHAFT BOLT
9	RING GEAR	32	PULLEY BOSS BOLT
10	FLYWHEEL	33	TIMING COVER
11	FLYWHEEL BOLT	34	TENSION PULLEY BOLT
12	SLEEVE (M/T)	35	TIMING BELT
13	WASHER (M/T)	36	TENSION PULLEY
14	OIL SEAL	37	OIL SEAL
15	REAR RETAINER	38	OIL PUMP ASSEMBLY
16	SLEEVE (A/T)	39	KEY
17	WASHER (A/T)	40	THRUST WASHER
18	RING GEAR ASSEMBLY	41	CONNECTING ROD LOWER BEARING
19	SPACER (A/T)	42	CONNECTING ROD UPPER BEARING
20	CRANKSHAFT	43	CONNECTING ROD
21	BEARING CAP BOLT	44	WATER PUMP ASSEMBLY
22	OIL PAN	45	GASKET
23	PLUG		

7. Valve lash measurement for intake valves should be 0.006 inch and 0.010 on exhaust valves.

8. If lash is not as specified, adjust valve lash by loosening adjustment screw locknut and turn adjustment screw until lash is within specifications.

9. Install cylinder head cover.

1.6L DOHC ENGINE

The DOHC engine is not equipped with rocker arms. Valve adjustment is performed by using selective shims. Measure valve lash when engine is cold.

1. Disconnect battery ground cable.
2. Remove cylinder head cover and camshafts as described in "Cylinder Head Cover, Replace" and "Camshafts, Replace."
3. Remove selective shims and tappets. **Be sure to arrange shims and tappets in order of removal to ensure proper installation.**
4. Valve lash adjustment must be done while engine is cold. Use Valve Lash Spring Spacer tool No. J-38413-2 (left) and tool No. J-38413-3 (right) or equivalents to make adjustments.
5. Set No. 1 cylinder to TDC, then align crankshaft pulley to 0 mark on the timing cover.
6. Ensure valves on No. 1 cylinder have play and valves on No. 4 cylinder do not have play. If valves are not set as above, rotate crankshaft pulley 360° and align with 0 mark on timing cover, then recheck valves.
7. Measure and record valve lash between cam lobe and selective shim as follows:
   a. On No. 1 cylinder, intake and exhaust valves.
   b. On No. 2 cylinder, intake valves.
   c. On No. 3 cylinder, exhaust valves.
8. Rotate crankshaft pulley 360° and ensure that rear camshaft bearing caps are removed so that selective shims may be removed.
9. Measure and record valve lash between cam lobe and selective shim as follows:
   a. On No. 4 cylinder, intake and exhaust valves.
   b. On No. 3 cylinder, intake valves.
   c. On No. 2 cylinder, exhaust valves.
10. Valve clearance on the exhaust valve must be between 0.008-0.012 inch. If clearance is not as specified, replace shim by turning the camshaft lobe downward and inserting tool No. J-38413-2 (Left) or tool No. J-38413-3 (Right) between camshaft journal and the cam lobe next to selective shim. Turn cam lobe upward and remove selective shim, **Fig. 15 and 16.**
11. Refer to **Fig. 17,** for available exhaust shims.
12. Valve clearance on the intake valve must be between 0.004-0.008 inch. If clearance is not as specified, replace shim by turning the camshaft lobe downward and inserting tool No. J-38413-2 (Left) or tool No. J-38413-3 (Right) or equivalents, between camshaft journal and the cam lobe next to selective shim. Turn cam lobe upward and remove selective shim.
13. Refer to **Fig. 17,** for available intake shims.
14. Install cylinder head cover.

VALVE GUIDES
REPLACE

Using Valve Guide Remover tool No.

J-37985 or equivalent, drive valve guides from cylinder head with a hammer. Install valve guides using Installer tool No. J-38462 with Valve Guide Remover tool No. J-37985 or equivalents.

ROCKER ARMS
REPLACE

SOHC ENGINE

1. Disconnect battery ground cable.
2. Remove PCV hoses and spark plug wires from the clip.
3. Remove two bolts from timing belt cover, then loosen lower timing belt cover bolts.
4. Remove cylinder head cover bolts, then cylinder head cover.
5. Remove rocker arm bracket bolts in order shown in **Fig. 18.**
6. Remove rocker arm shaft and rocker arm assembly, then remove rocker arms from shafts.
7. Reverse procedure to install, noting the following:
   a. Apply GM 1052942 sealant or equivalent to No. 1 and No. 5 rocker brackets.
   b. Using tightening sequence shown in **Fig. 19, torque** bolts to 22 ft. lbs.
   c. Make necessary valve lash adjustments.

TIMING BELT
REPLACE

SOHC ENGINE
Removal

1. Disconnect battery ground cable.
2. Remove alternator and power steering belts, then support engine using Engine Support Fixture tool No. J-28467-A or equivalent.
3. Remove right side engine mount, then the timing belt cover.
4. Rotate crankshaft until No. 4 cylinder is at TDC compression stroke, then place camshaft pulley timing mark at the 9 o'clock position, **Fig. 20.**
5. Remove crankshaft pulley bolt, then raise and support vehicle.
6. Remove crankshaft pulley, then lower vehicle.
7. Loosen tension pulley retaining bolt 1/2 turn and remove timing belt.

Installation

1. Ensure camshaft pulley timing marks are aligned as shown in **Fig. 20.**
2. Install timing belt over, camshaft pulley, water pump pulley and tensioner pulley in order as shown in **Fig. 21.**
3. **Torque** timing belt tensioner to 31 ft. lbs., then rotate crankshaft two turns to ensure that crankshaft timing mark and camshaft pulley marks are correct.

4. Install timing belt cover, then raise and support vehicle.
5. **Torque** crankshaft pulley center bolt to 87 ft. lbs. and pulley side bolts to 89 inch lbs.
6. Lower vehicle, then install belts, right side engine mount and remove engine support fixture.
7. Connect battery ground cable.

DOHC ENGINE
Removal

1. Disconnect battery ground cable.
2. Support engine using Engine Support Fixture tool No. J-28467-A or equivalent, then remove right side engine mount.
3. Remove power steering and alternator drive belts, then upper timing belt cover.
4. Raise and support vehicle, then remove crankshaft pulley bolt and crankshaft pulley.
5. Lower vehicle and remove lower timing cover.
6. Align crankshaft pulley to TDC, then loosen tension pulley retaining bolt 1/2 turn and remove timing belt.

1. Tension pulley lock bolt
2. Timing belt
3. Tension pulley
4. Tension spring
5. Crankshaft timing pulley
6. Key
7. Idle pulley
8. Camshaft timing pulley
9. Oil pump assembly
10. Water pump assembly

Fig. 6   DOHC engine

Installation

1. Align camshaft pulleys timing marks, **Fig. 22.**
2. Raise and support vehicle, then align crankshaft pulley to TDC.
3. Install timing belt over crankshaft pulley, then install crankshaft pulley, but do not tighten.
4. Lower vehicle, then install timing belt over crankshaft pulley, water pump pulley, idler pulley, exhaust camshaft pulley, intake camshaft pulley and then tensioner pulley as shown in **Fig. 23.**
5. **Torque** timing belt tensioner to 31 ft. lbs., then rotate crankshaft two turns to ensure that crankshaft timing pulley mark and camshaft pulley marks are correctly aligned.
6. Install lower timing cover.
7. Raise and support vehicle, then **torque** crankshaft pulley bolt to 87 ft. lbs. on 1.6L engines and 108 ft. lbs. on 1.8L engines.
8. Lower vehicle and install upper timing cover.
9. Install alternator and power steering belts, then right side engine mount.
10. Remove engine support and install battery ground cable.

CAMSHAFT
REPLACE
SOHC ENGINE
Removal

1. Disconnect battery ground cable.
2. Remove PCV hoses and spark plug wires from the clip.
3. Remove two bolts from the timing belt cover, then loosen lower timing belt cover bolts.
4. Remove cylinder head cover bolts, then cylinder head cover.
5. Rotate crankshaft to TDC on compression stroke by aligning the camshaft pulley timing marks, **Fig. 22.**
6. Loosen timing belt tensioner, then remove timing belt.
7. Remove distributor, camshaft bearing cap retaining bolts and covers.
8. Remove camshaft and camshaft seal.

Installation

1. Install camshaft in cylinder head with dowel pin in the upright position.
2. Install camshaft bearing caps, but do not tighten.
3. Apply GM 1052942 sealant or equivalent to No. 1 and No. 5 camshaft bearing caps.
4. **Torque** camshaft bearing caps to 89 inch lbs.
5. Install new camshaft oil seal using Seal Installation tool No. J-5268 or equivalent.
6. Install distributor, camshaft timing pulley and timing belt, referring to "Timing Belt Replace" for procedure.
7. Install cylinder head cover, then battery ground cable.

DOHC ENGINE
Removal

1. Disconnect battery ground cable.
2. Remove cylinder head cover, then rotate crankshaft to TDC by aligning camshaft pulley timing marks.
3. Loosen timing belt tensioner, then remove camshaft pulleys from camshaft.
4. Remove distributor, then camshaft bearing caps bolts. **Bolts must be kept in the order they were taken out. To ensure that they will be installed into the same threaded hole.**
5. Remove the camshaft, then the camshaft seals.

Installation

1. Install camshaft into cylinder head, ensuring that dowel pin is in the up position and distributor drive slot is at end of exhaust camshaft, **Fig. 24.**
2. Install bearing caps and bolts in order that they were removed, but do not tighten at this time.
3. Apply GM 1052942 sealant or equivalent to No. 1 and No. 5 camshaft bearing caps, **Fig. 25.**
4. **Torque** camshaft bearing cap bolts to 89 inch lbs. using sequence shown in **Fig. 26.**

1	COMPRESSION RING
2	OIL RING
3	PISTON PIN
4	PISTON
5	CONNECTING ROD
6	CONNECTING ROD BOLT
7	CONNECTING ROD CAP
8	CONNECTING ROD NUT
9	UPPER BEARING (CRANKSHAFT)
10	RING GEAR (M/T)
11	FLYWHEEL (M/T)
12	FLYWHEEL BOLT
13	SLEEVE (M/T)
14	WASHER (M/T)
15	OIL SEAL
16	REAR RETAINING GASKET
17	SLEEVE (M/T)
18	WASHER (M/T)
19	REAR GEAR ASSEMBLY (A/T)
20	SPACER (A/T)
21	CRANKSHAFT
22	BEARING CAP BOLT
23	OIL PAN
24	GASKET
25	PLUG
26	OIL PIPE ASSEMBLY
27	BEARING CAP
28	LOWER BEARING (CRANKSHAFT)
29	CRANKSHAFT TIMING PULLEY
30	CRANKSHAFT PULLEY
31	CRANKSHAFT BOLT
32	LOWER TIMING COVER
33	IDLE PULLEY BOLT
34	TENSION PULLEY BOLT
35	TENSION PULLEY
36	TENSION SPRING
37	TIMING BELT
38	IDLE PULLEY
39	OIL SEAL
40	OIL PUMP ASSEMBLY
41	KEY
42	THRUST WASHER
43	LOWER BEARING (CONNECTING ROD)
44	UPPER BEARING (CONNECTING ROD)
45	UPPER TIMING COVER
46	WATER PUMP ASSEMBLY
47	GASKET

Fig. 7   DOHC cylinder block components

Fig. 9 DOHC intake & exhaust components

1	MAP SENSOR HOSE: CYLINDER HEAD COVER TO PIPE
2	CANISTER HOSE: TO THROTTLE VALVE
3	CANISTER HOSE: TO PIPE
4	THROTTLE VALVE
5	MAP SENSOR HOSE: PIPE TO MAP SENSOR
6	EGR VALVE
7	EGR HOSE: PIPE TO EGR VALVE
8	EGR PIPE
9	MAP SENSOR
10	EGR HOSE: THROTTLE VALVE TO PIPE
11	AIR DUCT
12	EGR HOSE: TRANSDUCER TO EGR VALVE
13	AIR CLEANER
14	FUEL FILTER
15	FUEL FEED PIPE
16	FUEL RETURN PIPE
17	THROTTLE VALVE HEATING HOSE: THERMOSTAT HSG TO T-VALVE
18	CANISTER HOSE: PIPE TO THROTTLE VALVE
19	PCV HOSE: CYLINDER HEAD COVER TO AIR DUCT
20	EGR HOSE: VSV TO TRANSDUCER
21	VSV: EGR
22	EGR HOSE: PIPE TO VSV
23	EGR HOSE: EGR VALVE TO TRANSDUCER
24	EGR HOSE: TRANSDUCER TO PIPE
25	EGR TRANSDUCER
26	THROTTLE VALVE HEATING HOSE: T-VALVE TO BYPASS PIPE
27	PCV HOSE: CYLINDER HEAD COVER TO AIR DUCT
28	CANISTER HOSE
29	CANISTER
30	VACUUM HOSE: FUEL PRESSURE REGULATOR TO COMMON CHAMBER

Fig. 8 DOHC cylinder head components

1	COOLANT PIPE (TO OIL COOLER)
2	COOLANT HOSE (TO OIL COOLER)
3	COOLANT TEMPERATURE SENSOR
4	GASKET
5	THERMO VACUUM SWITCH
6	THERMOSTAT HOUSING
7	GASKET
8	COOLANT OUTLET PIPE
9	THERMOSTAT
10	BYPASS PIPE
11	INLET PIPE COOLANT
12	GASKET
13	CENTER BOLT
14	COOLANT HOSE (TO CYLINDER BLOCK)
15	GASKET
16	GASKET
17	OIL COOLER
18	OIL FILTER
19	COOLANT HOSE (FROM BYPASS PIPE)
20	COOLANT PIPE BOLT

Fig. 10 SOHC cylinder head tightening sequence

Fig. 11 DOHC cylinder head bolt removal sequence

Fig. 12 DOHC cylinder head tightening sequence

Fig. 13 SOHC crankshaft pulley timing mark

Fig. 14 SOHC clearance adjustment

Fig. 15 DOHC lash service. 1.6L engine

Fig. 16 DOHC clearance adjustment. 1.6L engine

NO in Chart	Thickness (mm)	NO in Chart	Thickness (mm)
1	2.55	11	3.05
2	2.60	12	3.10
3	2.65	13	3.15
4	2.70	14	3.20
5	2.75	15	3.25
6	2.80	16	3.30
7	2.85	17	3.35
8	2.90	18	3.40
9	2.95	19	3.45
10	3.00		

Note; Thickness mark is printed on the surface to be contacted with tappet.

Fig. 17 Valve shim chart. 1.6L engine

Fig. 18 Rocker arm shaft removal. SOHC Engine

Fig. 19 Rocker arm shaft tightening sequence. SOHC Engine

Fig. 20 SOHC cam pulley timing mark

Fig. 21   SOHC timing belt

Fig. 22   DOHC cam pulley timing mark

Fig. 23   DOHC timing belt

Fig. 24   Distributor drive slot

Fig. 25   Camshaft bearing cap sealant

Fig. 26   Camshaft bearing cap tightening sequence

Fig. 27   Piston mark location. 1.6L engine

Fig. 28   Piston mark location. 1.8L engine

5. Install new camshaft oil seal using Oil Seal Installer tool No. J-35268 or equivalent.
6. Install distributor, camshaft timing pulleys, then the timing belt.
7. Install cylinder head cover, then battery ground cable.

PISTON & ROD ASSEMBLY

Align front marks on piston and rod assemblies, **Figs. 27 & 28.**. Ensure that mark is facing front of engine when installing into cylinder block.

PISTON, PINS & RINGS

There are three standard size pistons and two oversized pistons. When installing

piston rings, ensure that code marks are facing upwards. Install pin into piston and rod as shown in **Fig. 29**.

MAIN & ROD BEARINGS

Rod bearings come in three standard sizes and two oversize, 0.0098 inch and 0.0196 inch. If after replacing rod bearing, thrust clearance is still excessive, replace crankshaft. Connecting rod bearing cap nuts should be **torqued** in three steps to 36 ft. lbs. on 1.6L engine and 18 ft. lbs. plus 100° on 1.8L engine.

When replacing a main bearing, always replace it with one that has the same number. If you can not read number, refer to **Figs. 30 & 31**, for sizes of main bearings. When servicing the crankshaft, inspect all

Fig. 29   Piston pin remover & installer

① Size mark	Main Bearing Bore Diameter (mm)	Crank Shaft Main Journal Diameter (mm)	② Size Mark	Crank Shaft Bearing Size Mark (Upper Side)	Crank Shaft Bearing Size Mark (Lower Side)	Oil Clearance (mm) (Reference)
1	55.992-56.000	51.918-51.928	— —	Blue	Blue	0.022-0.048
		51.929-51.938	—	Black	Black	0.020-0.046
2	55.984-55.991	51.918-51.928	— —			0.022-0.048
		51.929-51.938	—	Brown	Brown	0.020-0.046
3	55.976-55.983	51.918-51.928	— —			0.022-0.048
		51.929-51.938	—	Green	Green	0.020-0.046
Under Size 0.25	55.976-56.000	51.668-51.688		Stamp of Size	Stamp of Size	0.020-0.088
Under Size 0.50		51.418-51.438				

Fig. 30   Main bearing selection table. 1.6L engine

SIZE MARK	MAIN BEARING BORE DIAMETER (mm)	CRANKSHAFT MAIN JOURNAL DIAMETER (mm)	SIZE MARK	CRANKSHAFT BEARING SIZE MARK (UPPER SIDE)	CRANKSHAFT BEARING SIZE MARK (LOWER SIDE)	OIL CLEARANCE (mm) (REFERENCE)
1	55.992–56.000	51.918–51.928	— —	BLUE	BLUE	0.023–0.048
		51.929–51.938	—	BLACK	BLACK	0.020–0.046
2	55.984–55.991	51.918–51.928	— —			0.023–0.048
		51.929–51.938	—	BROWN	BROWN	0.020–0.046
3	55.976–55.983	51.918–51.928	— —			0.023–0.048
		51.929–51.938	—	GREEN	GREEN	0.020–0.046

Fig. 31   Main bearing selection table. 1.8L engine

Fig. 34   Measuring oil pump drive to driven gear

journals for wear or damage. Install upper half of bearings into cylinder block, and the lower half into main bearing caps. If oil clearance can not be brought within specifications using a standard bearing, regrind crankshaft for next oversize bearing.

CRANKSHAFT REAR OIL SEAL
REPLACE

1. Disconnect battery ground cable, then raise and support vehicle.
2. Remove right and left undercovers, then the oil pan as described in "Oil Pan, Replace."

3. Remove transaxle as described in "Transaxle, Replace" in "Clutch & Manual Transaxle" section.
4. Mark flywheel and engine position for installation reference, then remove flywheel.
5. Remove flywheel spacer and rear main seal retainer.
6. Remove rear main seal from retainer, **Fig. 32**.
7. Reverse procedure to install.

OIL PAN
REPLACE

1. Disconnect battery ground cable.
2. Raise and support vehicle, then drain crankcase oil.
3. Remove righthand undercover, then exhaust pipe from exhaust manifold.
4. Remove torque rod and flywheel dust cover.
5. Remove stiffener from cylinder block, then oil pan.
6. Reverse procedure to install. Use new oil pan gasket, applying GM 1052942 sealant or equivalent to gasket surface. **Torque** stiffener bolts to 50 ft. lbs.

OIL PUMP SERVICE
REMOVAL

1. Disconnect battery ground cable.
2. Remove timing belt cover, alternator and power steering belts, then raise

Fig. 32   Rear main oil seal retainer

Fig. 33   Oil pump removal

Fig. 35   Measuring oil pump driven gear to housing

and support vehicle.
3. Remove crankshaft pulley, then oil pump attaching bolts and oil pump, **Fig. 33**.

INSPECTION

1. Measure oil pump driven gear to housing clearance, **Fig. 34**, using suitable feeler gauge. If clearance is more than 0.078 inch, replace oil pump.
2. Measure oil pump drive gear to driven gear clearance, **Fig. 35**. If the clearance is more than 0.012 inch, replace the gear set.
3. Measure oil pump body to gear clearance, **Fig. 36**, using a feeler gauge and precision straightedge. If the clearance is more than 0.004 inch, replace oil pump.

Fig. 36 Measuring oil pump body to gear clearance

1. OIL PUMP HOUSING
2. DRIVE GEAR
3. DRIVEN GEAR

J 26900-9

INSTALLATION

1. Apply GM 1052942 sealant or equivalent to oil pump gasket surface.
2. Install oil pump, **torque** oil pump to block bolts to 89 inch lbs.
3. Install crankshaft pulley, then lower vehicle.
4. Install timing belt cover, then the power steering and alternator belts.
5. Connect battery ground cable.

WATER PUMP
REPLACE

SOHC ENGINE

1. Disconnect battery ground cable, then drain coolant system.
2. Remove power steering belt, then timing belt cover and timing belt. See "Timing Belt Replace."
3. Remove water pump to block retaining bolts, then water pump.
4. Reverse procedure to install.

DOHC ENGINE

1. Disconnect battery ground cable, then drain cooling system.
2. Remove right front engine mount as outlined under "Engine Mount, Replace."
3. Remove engine mount bridge.
4. Remove upper timing belt cover assembly.
5. Remove power steering belt.
6. Remove lower timing belt cover assembly.
7. Loosen timing belt tensioner, then remove timing belt at water pump pulley.
8. Remove water pump attaching bolts, then remove water pump.
9. Reverse procedure to install.

COOLING SYSTEM BLEED

These engines do not require a specified bleed procedure. After filling cooling system, run engine to operating temperature with radiator/pressure cap off. Air will then be automatically bled through cap opening.

6003 — 6004
6002
6002 — 6005
6006
628

VEHICLES NOT EQUIPPED WITH AIR CONDITIONING

6004
6003
6002
6005
6006
6007

VEHICLES EQUIPPED WITH AIR CONDITIONING

628 CRANKSHAFT PULLEY
6002 SERPENTINE DRIVE BELT
6003 SERPENTINE DRIVE BELT TENSIONER PULLEY
6004 POWER STEERING PUMP PULLEY
6005 GENERATOR PULLEY
6006 SERPENTINE DRIVE BELT IDLER PULLEY
6007 AIR CONDITIONING COMPRESSOR PULLEY

Fig. 37 Serpentine belt routing

THERMOSTAT
REPLACE

SOHC ENGINE

1. Drain cooling System.
2. Disconnect radiator hose from thermostat housing cap.
3. Remove thermostat housing cap and thermostat from thermostat housing.
4. Clean both gasket surfaces thoroughly.
5. Reverse procedure to install.

DOHC ENGINE

1. Disconnect battery ground cable.
2. Drain cooling system.
3. Disconnect ignition wire from ignition coil.
4. Remove distributor cap from distributor and set aside.
5. Disconnect lower radiator hose from thermostat housing cap.
6. Disconnect EGR pipe bracket from thermostat housing.
7. Disconnect EGR pipe from exhaust manifold.
8. Disconnect upper radiator hose from thermostat housing.
9. Remove thermostat housing cap and thermostat from thermostat housing.
10. Clean both gasket surfaces thoroughly.
11. Reverse procedure to install.

SERPENTINE DRIVE BELT

REMOVAL

1. Rotate serpentine belt tensioner pulley clockwise to release tension from belt using a 3/8 drive socket wrench.
2. Remove serpentine belt from pulleys.

INSTALLATION

1. Route serpentine belt around all pulleys as shown in **Fig. 37**.
2. Rotate tensioner pulley away from drive belt and install drive belt to tensioner pulley.
3. Return tensioner to its original position and remove socket wrench.

BELT TENSION DATA

Engine	Belt	Tension Lbs. (New)	Tension Lbs. (Used)
1991			
1.6L/4-97	Alternator	140–180	110–150
	Power Steering	①	—
1992–93			
1.6L/4-97	Alternator	140–180	110–150
	Power Steering	①	—
1.8L/4-110	Alternator	70–110	—
	Power Steering	130–160	120–150

①—On models w/A/C, tension gauge should read 145 lbs; on models less A/C - gauge should read 90 lbs.

FUEL FILTER
REPLACE

The fuel filter is located in the engine compartment, below the power brake vacuum booster assembly.

1. Relieve fuel system pressure as follows:
   a. Remove fuel filler cap, then fuel pump relay from underhood relay center.
   b. Start engine and allow to run until it stalls, then crank engine for an additional ten seconds.
   c. Disconnect battery ground cable.
2. Remove air intake duct, then disconnect fuel line from filter outlet (upper connection).
3. Raise and support vehicle.
4. Disconnect fuel line lower fitting from filter, then cap the ends of the fuel line fittings.
5. Loosen filter bracket clamp bolt, then remove filter from bracket.

6. Reverse procedure to install, noting the following:
   a. Apply clean engine oil to sealing surface of fuel lines.
   b. **Torque** fuel line fittings to 25 ft. lbs.

FUEL PUMP
REPLACE

1. Disconnect battery ground cable, then loosen fuel filler cap to relieve tank vapor pressure.
2. Disconnect fuel fitting, wrapping a shop towel around fitting to prevent spraying.
3. Siphon or pump fuel into approved container.
4. Raise and support vehicle with suitable floor jacks.
5. Remove exhaust pipe from catalytic converter, then fuel filler neck hose from fuel tank.
6. Remove fuel overflow pipe hose from fuel tank.
7. Disconnect fuel gauge sending unit and fuel pump electrical connectors.
8. Remove fuel vapor, fuel supply and fuel return hose from the fuel tank.
9. Support fuel tank using a suitable transaxle jack or equivalent, then remove six tank retaining bolts and tank.
10. Remove eight fuel pump mounting screws, then fuel pump/bracket from fuel tank.
11. Remove fuel pump supply hose extension from bracket, gasket from pump bracket or tank and filter from pump pick-up tube.
12. Disconnect electrical connector wires from pump.
13. Remove pump from bracket, then outlet hose from pump.
14. Reverse procedure to install.

TIGHTENING SPECIFICATIONS

Year	Component	Torque/ Ft. Lbs.
1991	Camshaft Bearing Caps	89①
	Camshaft Pulley Retaining Bolts	43
	Common Chamber Bolts & Nuts	17
	Connecting Rod Bearing Cap Nuts	36
	Crankshaft Pulley Center Bolt	87
	Cylinder Head Bolts	②
	Cylinder Head Cover Bolts	③
	EGR Pipe Bracket Bolts	32
	Exhaust Manifold Bolts & Nuts	30
	Flexplate Retaining Bolts	47
	Flywheel Retaining Bolts	58
	Fuel Pump Screws	30①
	Fuel Pump Supply Hose Fitting	25
	Fuel Tank Bolts	25
	Induction Port Retaining Bolts	17
	Left Engine Mount Center Bolt	50
	Left Engine Mount To Transaxle Case Bolts	35
	Main Bearing Cap Bolts	44
	Mounting Bridge Bracket Bolt	29
	Oil Pan Bolts & Nuts	89①
	Oil Pump Bolts	89①
	Oil Pump Cover Screws	89①
	Rear Main Seal Retainer Bolts	89①
	Rear Mount Center Bolt	76
	Rear Mount Transaxle Case Bolt	37
	Relief Valve Plug	27
	Right Mount Through Bolt	50
	Rocker Arm Bracket Bolts	16
	Stiffener Bolts	50
	Throttle Valve Bolts	17
	Timing Belt Tensioner	31
	Torque Rod Center Bolt	50
	Torque Rod Bracket Bolts & Nut	28
	Water Pump Bolts (DOHC)	17
	Water Pump Bolts (SOHC)	17.4
1992–93	Accelerator Cable Bracket Bolts	89①
	Air Conditioning Compressor Mounting Bolts	30
	Air Conditioning Compressor Mounting Bracket Bolts	15

Year	Component	Torque/ Ft. Lbs.
1992-93 —Cont'd	Battery Cable To Battery Terminal Retainers	11
	Battery Retainer Bolt	44①
	Battery Retainer Nut	72①
	Camshaft Bearing Cap Bolts	89①
	Center Crossmember Bolts	45
	Common Chamber Bolts & Nuts	17
	Connecting Rod Bearing Cap Nuts	18④
	Crankshaft Pulley Center Bolt	108
	Cylinder Head Bolts	53②
	Cylinder Head Cover Bolts	53①
	EGR Pipe Nut	11
	EGR Pipe Bracket Bolt	89①
	EGR Pipe To Exhaust Manifold	11
	Engine Lift Bracket Bolts	18
	Engine Wiring Harness Conduit Bolt	53①
	Exhaust Camshaft Timing Pulley Bolt	44
	Exhaust Manifold Nuts	29
	Exhaust Manifold To Cylinder Block Brace Bolts	15
	Flywheel Bolts	22
	Forward Exhaust Pipe Nuts	46
	Fuel Pipe Bracket Bolt	89①
	Ground Cable Bolt	71①
	Guide Tube Bolt	11
	Heat Shield Bolts	11
	Hood Bolts	15
	Intake Camshaft Timing Pulley Bolt	44
	Oil Cooler Center Bolt	32
	Oil Cooler Pipe Bolt	89①
	Oil Pan Bolts & Nuts	89①
	Oil Pressure Switch	10
	Oil Pump Bolts	89①
	Main Bearing Cap Bolts (Three Passes)	65
	Power Steering Pump Mounting Bolts	15
	Power Steering Pump Fluid Pressure Pipe Union Bolt	15
	Rear Crankshaft Seal Retaining Bolts	89①
	Rear Engine Mount Through Bolt	37
	Rear Engine Mount To Cylinder Block Bolts	75
	Relief Valve Plug	27

Continued

TIGHTENING SPECIFICATIONS—Continued

Year	Component	Torque/Ft. Lbs.	Year	Component	Torque/Ft. Lbs.
1992-93 —Cont'd	Right Engine Mount Bracket Nut & Bolt	30	1992-93 —Cont'd	Torque Rod Nut	94
	Right Engine Mount Bridge Bolt	37		Torque To Center Crossmember Through Bolt & Nut	51
	Right Engine Mount Through Bolt	50		Timing Belt Cover Bolts	89 ①
	Right Side Intake Manifold Brace Nut & Bolt	15		Timing Belt Tensioner Pulley Bolt	31
	Serpentine Belt Idler Pulley Bolt	22		Vacuum Switching Valve Bolts	89 ①
	Serpentine Belt Tensioner Center Bolt	30			
	Spark Plugs	21			
	Starter Motor Nut & Bolt	29			
	Suspension To Rear Engine Mount Brace Bolt & Nut	15			
	Torque Rod Bolts	14			

① —Inch lbs.
② —Refer to text.
③ —On vehicles w/VIN Code 5 tighten to 26 inch lbs., on vehicles with VIN Code 6 tighten to 89 inch lbs.
④ —Plus 100°.

Clutch & Manual Transaxle
INDEX

| Clutch lever free play (M) | 2±1 (0.08±0.04) |
| Clutch pedal free play (L) | 10±5 (0.39±0.20) |

Fig. 1 Clutch cable adjustment

ADJUSTMENTS
CLUTCH CABLE

1. Measure clutch pedal freeplay, **Fig. 1**, to confirm adjustments are within specifications.
2. If freeplay is not within specifications, turn adjustment nut clockwise or counterclockwise to adjust cable.
3. Repeat step 2 so that play between clutch release arm and clutch cable is within

SHIFT CABLE

1. Place transaxle in "Neutral" position.
2. Turn adjusting nuts (2) until change lever (1) is at right angle to pivot case, as viewed from side of gear control, **Fig. 2**.
3. Turn adjusting nuts (4) until change lever (1) is at a right angle to pivot case as viewed from rear of gear control, **Fig. 3**.
4. After making adjustments, tighten adjusting nuts (2) and (4). specifications shown in **Fig. 1**.

CLUTCH
REPLACE

1. Remove transaxle assembly as outlined under "Transaxle, Replace."
2. Mark clutch cover assembly position to flywheel for installation alignment.
3. Remove clutch cover bolts evenly, releasing spring tension.
4. Remove clutch cover and disc.
5. Reverse procedure to install. Torque clutch cover bolts to specifications.

MANUAL TRANSAXLE
REPLACE
REMOVAL

1. Disconnect battery cables, then remove battery and battery tray.
2. Drain transaxle fluid, then remove air cleaner assembly.
3. Disconnect wire connectors and ground cable.
4. Disconnect engine wiring harness clip, then remove ignition coil ground cable.

Fig. 2   Shift cable adjustment

5. Remove battery bracket and ignition coil assembly.
6. Remove speedometer cable, clutch cable and shifter cable, then using Engine Support Fixture tool No. J 28467-A or equivalent, support engine assembly.
7. Raise and support vehicle, then remove wheel and tire assembly.
8. Remove front undercovers, then remove ball joints at steering knuckles.
9. Remove front drive axles, then remove front exhaust pipe.
10. Remove torque rod and bracket, then left transaxle mount.
11. Remove front transaxle through bolt, then center beam with rear transaxle mount.
12. Remove engine stiffener and flywheel dust cover.
13. Using suitable jacks, support transaxle, then remove transaxle attaching bolts.
14. Remove transaxle assembly.

INSTALLATION

1. Install transaxle assembly, then

1. Inter cooler (DOHC-Turbo)
2. Air duct and air cleaner element
3. Snap pin
4. Clip
5. Front console panel and floor console
6. Nut ; shift cable
7. Snap pin
8. Adjusting nut
9. Nut ; shift cable clip
10. Nut ; harness clip
11. Cable cover and grommet
12. Shift cable
13. Select cable

Fig. 3 Shift cable assembly

torque attaching bolts to specifications.
2. Remove transaxle support, then install flywheel dust cover.
3. Install engine stiffener, then install center beam with rear transaxle mount, then install front and left transaxle mount through bolts.
4. Torque bolts to specifications.
5. Install torque rod, bracket and front exhaust pipe.
6. Install right drive axle assemblies, then install ball joints.
7. Install front undercovers, then wheel and tire assembly, then lower vehicle.
8. Remove engine support fixture.
9. Install shift cable, clutch cable and speedometer cable.
10. Install battery bracket, ignition coil assembly and ignition coil ground cable.
11. Install engine electrical harness clamp, then connect ground cable.
12. Connect electrical connectors, battery, battery tray and battery cables.

TIGHTENING SPECIFICATIONS

Year	Component	Torque/ ft. lbs.	Year	Component	Torque/ Ft. Lbs.
1991–93	Clutch Cover Bolts	13	1991–93 —Cont'd	Transaxle Front Retaining Nut	45
	Clutch Flywheel Bolts	58		Transaxle Left Axle Mount Bolts	29
	Transaxle Center Crossmember Bolts	45		Transaxle Left Through Bolt	64
	Transaxle Filler Plug	20		Transaxle Rear Mount Bolt	29
	Transaxle Front Mount Bracket	45		Transaxle To Engine Bolts	55

Rear Axle & Suspension

INDEX

HUB & BEARING
REPLACE

1. Disconnect battery ground cable.
2. Raise and support vehicle, then remove wheel and tire assembly.
3. Using suitable jack stands, support rear suspension, then remove rear brake drum assembly.
4. Check hub axial play at hub flange, **Fig. 1**, using suitable dial indicator. If axial play is greater then 0.020 inch, replace hub assembly.
5. Remove four hub to knuckle bolts, then the hub assembly.
6. Reverse procedures to install.

Fig. 1   Measuring hub axial play

LATERAL LINK
REPLACE

1. Place vehicle on level surface, then

disconnect battery ground cable.
2. Raise and support vehicle, then remove tire and wheel assemblies. Refer to **Figs. 2 and 3** when servicing lateral links.
3. Remove lateral link bolt on lefthand side and push crossmember down to prevent interference with fuel tank.
4. Remove righthand side lateral link mounting bolts from rear crossmember and rear suspension knuckle.
5. Remove lateral links.
6. Reverse procedures to install.

STRUT
REPLACE

1. Place vehicle on level surface, then disconnect battery ground cable.

Fig. 2   Lateral link adjustment

Fig. 3   Lateral link replacement

Fig. 4   Strut tower cover removal

Fig. 5   Upper strut nut removal

Fig. 7   Stabilizer bar connection

Fig. 6   Trailing link removal

1. Bolts
2. Trailing link

2. Raise and support vehicle, then remove tire and wheel assemblies.
3. Support suspension with jackstands, then lower vehicle slightly so weight rest on jackstands and not suspension arms.
4. Remove flexible brake hose and clip at strut.
5. Remove stabilizer bar link from strut, then strut to knuckle bolts.
6. Open rear hatch and remove strut tower cover, then loosen nuts for strut mount and remove strut assemblies, **Figs. 4 and 5,**.
7. Reverse procedure to install.

TRAILING LINK
REPLACE

1. Place vehicle on level surface, then disconnect battery ground cable.
2. Raise and support vehicle, then remove tire and wheel assemblies.
3. Remove trailing link bolts, then trailing link, **Fig. 6.**
4. Reverse procedure to install, noting the following:

Fig. 8   Stabilizer brackets

a. It will be necessary to reset trim height before you torque trailing link bolts. Refer to "Trim Height, Adjust" in "Wheel Alignment" section.
b. **Torque** trailing link bolts to 94 ft. lbs.

STABILIZER BAR
REPLACE

Refer to **Figs. 7 and 8** when replacing stabilizer bar.

1. Disconnect battery ground cable, then raise and support vehicle.
2. Place jack stands under suspension support, then lower vehicle slightly so that vehicle weight rests on support not on suspension arms.
3. Remove bracket with rubber bushing from body, then the stabilizer bar.
4. Reverse procedure to install.

SPINDLE KNUCKLE
REPLACE

1. Raise and support vehicle, then remove tire and wheel assemblies.
2. Place jack stands under suspension support, then lower vehicle slightly so that vehicle weight rests on support not on suspension arms.
3. Remove rear brake drum, then hub unit assembly as described in "Hub Assembly, Replace."
4. Remove backing plate with brake assembly and set aside.
5. Remove through bolt from lateral link at axial side.
6. Remove suspension knuckle from strut.
7. Reverse procedure to install.

TIGHTENING SPECIFICATIONS

Year	Component	Torque/Ft. Lbs.	Year	Component	Torque/Ft. Lbs.
1991–93	Crossmember Bolts	94	1991–93 —Cont'd	Strut Rod Piston Nut	36
	Hub Assembly	49		Strut To Knuckle Bolts	116
	Lateral Link Bolts	94		Strut Tower Nuts	50
	Link Bolts	19		Trailing Link Bolts	94
	Stabilizer Bar Brackets	71		Wheel Lug Nuts	87
	Stabilizer Bar Link	19			

Front Suspension & Steering

INDEX

317 FRONT DISC BRAKE CALIPER
319 STRUT ASSEMBLY
320 BRAKE HOSE
321 BRAKE HOSE RETAINING CLIP

Fig. 1 Front brake hose removal

1. Brake hose
2. Speed sensor cable (If equipped with ABS)
3. Bolt
4. Nut
5. Strut assembly

Fig. 2 Front strut assembly

STRUT
REPLACE

1. Disconnect battery ground cable.
2. Raise and support vehicle, then remove wheel and tire assembly.
3. Using suitable jack stands, support front suspension.
4. Disconnect front caliper brake hose, clip and bracket, then drain brake fluid, **Fig. 1.**
5. Cap brake hose to prevent fluid leakage and dirt from entering system.
6. Remove strut assembly lower attaching bolts and nuts, **Fig. 2.**
7. Remove upper strut mount attaching nuts, **Fig. 3,** then remove strut assembly.
8. Reverse procedure to install. Torque attaching nuts and bolt to specifications.

322 STRUT ASSEMBLY NUTS
323 STRUT MOUNT

Fig. 3 Upper strut mount

CONTROL ARM ASSEMBLY
REPLACE
LOWER

1. Disconnect battery ground cable.

2. Raise and support vehicle, then remove wheel and tire assembly.
3. Remove stabilizer bar link to control arm assembly.
4. Remove lower ball joint attaching nuts, **Fig. 4.**
5. Remove control arm front bushing attaching bolt.
6. Remove control arm rear bushing attaching bolts, then remove control arm assembly.
7. Reverse procedure to install. Torque attaching nuts and bolt to specifications.

STABILIZER BAR
REPLACE

1. Disconnect battery ground cable.
2. Using Engine Support Fixture tool No. J28467-A or equivalent, support engine assembly.
3. Raise and support vehicle, then using suitable jack stands, support front suspension.
4. Remove wheel and tire assembly, then remove front exhaust pipe.

1. Ball joint
2. Pinch bolt
3. Bolt
4. Bolt
5. Lower control arm (LCA)

Fig. 4   Lower control arm assembly

314   INTERMEDIATE SHAFT
315   INTERMEDIATE SHAFT-TO-STEERING JOINT PINCH BOLT
316   STEERING JOINT

Fig. 6   Steering shaft

1. Exhaust pipe, front
2. Pipes ; power steering
3. Nut ; boot
4. Steering shaft
5. Ball joint
6. Tie rod
7. Crossmember assembly
8. Steering unit assembly
9. Stabilizer bar

Fig. 5   Front crossmember assembly

J 21687-02

Fig. 7   Tie rod removal

5. Disconnect power steering gear lines, **Fig. 5.**
6. Remove steering shaft and boot inside vehicle, **Fig. 6.**
7. Remove lower ball joint assemblies.
8. Using Tie Rod End Removal tool No. J-21687-02 or equivalent, remove tie rod at steering knuckle, **Fig. 7.**
9. Remove engine torque rod center beam attaching nut and bolt.
10. Remove rear engine mount.
11. Remove center beam attaching bolts, then remove crossmember attaching bolts.
12. Remove center beam, crossmember, steering gear and stabilizer bar assembly.
13. Remove steering gear assembly, then remove stabilizer bar.
14. Reverse procedure to install. Torque attaching nuts and bolts to specifications.

HUB, BEARING & STEERING KNUCKLE REPLACE

REMOVAL

1. Disconnect battery ground cable.
2. Raise and support vehicle, then remove wheel and tire assembly.

Fig. 8   Wheel hub & steering knuckle assembly

1. Brake caliper
2. Rotor
3. Hub nut
4. Tie rod
5. Pinch bolt
6. Ball joint
7. Bolt
8. Hub knuckle assembly

3. Remove brake caliper attaching bolts, support caliper and position aside, **Fig. 8.**
4. Remove brake rotor assembly.
5. Using suitable gauge measure hub bearing endplay. If endplay exceeds .0002 inch, replace hub bearing.
6. Stake hub axle attaching nut, then remove hub axle attaching nut.
7. Using tool No. J-34866 and tool No. J-2619-01 or equivalents, remove hub assembly.

8. Using Tie Rod End Remover tool No. J-21687-02 or equivalent, remove tie rod, **Fig. 7.**
9. Remove lower ball joint assembly.
10. Remove lower strut to steering knuckle attaching nuts and bolts, then remove steering knuckle.

INSTALLATION

1. Install knuckle assembly into driveshaft and snug hub nuts. **Ensure**

that seals are not damaged when installing the shaft into the knuckle. If hub and knuckle assemblies are disassembled, seals, inter and outer must be replaced with new seals.

2. Install ball joint of lower control arm to knuckle. Do not loosen boot on ball joint.
3. Install lower ball joint. Torque to specifications
4. Install tie rod. Torque to specifications.
5. Install hub nut and torque to specifications, then stake hub nut.
6. Install rotor, then brake caliper, torque caliper bolts to specifications.

POWER STEERING GEAR REPLACE

1. Remove intermediate steering shaft cover, then remove dust boot ring attaching nuts.
2. Raise and support vehicle, then remove wheel and tire assembly.
3. Remove dust boot from bulkhead, then position drain pan under vehicle.
4. Remove intermediate steering shaft pinch bolt.
5. Using Tie Rod End Remover tool No. J-21687-02 or equivalent, disconnect tie rod ends at steering knuckles.
6. Remove power steering fluid line hold-down bracket.
7. Disconnect power steering high pressure line, drain power steering fluid, then remove rack to crossmember attaching bolts.
8. Remove steering gear bracket attaching nut and bolt, then position steering gear from mounts.
9. Disconnect power steering return line, then disconnect intermediate shaft knuckle.
10. Remove steering gear through right side of vehicle.
11. Reverse procedure to install.

POWER STEERING PUMP REPLACE

1. Raise and support vehicle, then place drain pan underneath vehicle.
2. Loosen power steering pump adjusting and pivot bolts, then remove drive belt.
3. Disconnect power steering pump high pressure and return lines, cap lines to prevent contamination.
4. Remove adjusting and pivot bolts, then remove power steering pump and bracket assembly.
5. Reverse procedure to install.

TIGHTENING SPECIFICATIONS

Year	Component	Torque/ Ft. Lbs.
1991–93	Ball Joint To Control Arm	115
	Ball Joint To Steering Knuckle	49
	Brake Caliper Bolt	72
	Control Arm To Crossmember	117
	Crossmember Assembly to Frame Bolt	137
	Engine Torque Rod To Center Beam Bolt	37
	Hub Assembly Nut	137
	Inner Tire Rod	65
	Knuckle To Strut Bolts	116
	Lower Control Arm Front Bushing	95
	Lower Control Arm Rear Bushing	51
	Lower Strut To Knuckle Bolt	115

Year	Component	Torque/ Ft. Lbs.
1991–93 —Cont'd	Outer Tie Rod Nut To Steering Knuckle	40
	Pinch Bolt To Ball Joint Of Lower Control Arm	48
	Power Steering Pump Adjusting Bolt	15
	Power Steering Pump Pivot Bolt	15
	Stabilizer Bar To Control Arm	19
	Stabilizer Bar To Crossmember	12
	Stabilizer Link Bolt	19
	Steering Gear To Crossmember	41
	Strut Rod Piston Nut	34
	Tie Rod Nut To Lower Control Arm	19
	Upper Strut Mounting Nuts	50
	Wheel Lug Nuts	87

Wheel Alignment

INDEX

DESCRIPTION

Wheel alignment is the angular relationship between the wheels, suspension attaching parts and ground, **Fig. 1.** The angle of the knuckle away from the vertical, pointing in or out of wheels, tilt of the wheels from vertical (when viewed from front of vehicle) and tilt of suspension members from vertical (when viewed from side of vehicle), all of these are involved in proper alignment.

CASTER

Caster is tilting of the steering axis either forward or backward from the vertical (when viewed from side of vehicle). A backward tilt is positive (+) and a forward tilt is negative (-). On short and long arm type suspension you cannot see a caster angle without using a special instrument, but if you look straight down from the top of the upper control arm to the ground, you would find that ball joints do not line up

what a caster angle other than 0° is present.

CAMBER

Camber is the tilting of front and rear wheels from the vertical when viewed from front of vehicle. When wheels tilt outward at top, camber is positive (+). When wheels tilt inward, camber is negative (-). Amount of tilt is measured in degrees from the vertical and this is camber angle.

Fig. 1   Front alignment angles

Fig. 2   Vehicle ride height

Fig. 5   Vehicle ride height center

Fig. 3   Vehicle ride height, bushing center

Fig. 4   Vehicle ride height, wheel level

TOE

Toe is the turning in or out of wheels. The purpose of toe is to ensure parallel rolling of wheels. Excessive toe-in or toe-out may increase tire wear. Toe also serves to offset small deflections of the suspension which occurs when vehicle is moving.

PRELIMINARY INSPECTION

Steering and vibration problems are not always the results of poor alignment. An additional problem to be checked is tire lead due to worn or improperly manufactured tires. ""Lead" is the deviation of the vehicle from a straight path on a level road without hand pressure on the steering wheel.

Refer to "Front Wheel Alignment Specifications" and "Rear Wheel Alignment Specifications" located in the front of this chapter, to insure correct specifications, if vehicle is within specification the following checks and inspections should be performed.

1. Check tires for proper inflation and tread wear.
2. Check for loose ball joints and tie rod ends. If excessive looseness is noted, replace defective parts before adjusting toe.
3. Check for wheel and tire assembly run-out.
4. Check trim heights. If not within specifications, correct before adjusting toe.
5. Check for loose control arms.

6. Check for loose or missing stabilizer bar components.
7. Consideration must be given to excess loads. If excess load is normally carried in vehicle, it should remain during alignment checks.

FRONT WHEEL ALIGNMENT

CAMBER & CASTER

Camber and caster are not adjustable. If during inspection, either is found to be out of specifications, locate the cause. Check for damaged, loose, bent or worn front suspension parts. Replace worn or damaged parts as needed. To prevent any incorrect reading during inspection, bounce front bumper three or more times.

TOE-IN

1. Loosen right and left tie rod end locknuts.
2. Apply grease between tie rods and rack boots.
3. Turn right and left tie rods by the same amount to align toe to specification. **Right and left tie rods should become equal in length.**
4. After adjustment, tighten locknuts and ensure rack boots are not twisted.

REAR WHEEL ALIGNMENT

CAMBER

Camber cannot be adjusted. Should

camber be found out of specification, locate the cause and replace vehicle parts to correct the damage. If the body or chassis is found to be damaged, the damaged area must be corrected to provide proper alignment.

TOE

1. Loosen jam nuts on rear support rod.
2. Turn hex screw in center to obtain proper toe angle.
3. Tighten jam nuts. **Torque** jam nuts to 65 ft. lbs.

VEHICLE RIDE HEIGHT

FRONT

When reattaching the control arm, hold the position of wheel center to keep distance of 3 inches at bushing center (B) height, **Fig. 2.** Bushing will twist if the wheel center height is too high or low. If bushing does twist, bushing will suffer premature damage.

Measure height (B) at front bushing center and set point at height of (B) plus 3 inches, **Figs. 3 and 4.** Move front rotor assembly by using a suitable floor jack until reaching specification height (A), then tighten the bushing bolts at this time.

REAR

Refer to **Fig. 5** when adjusting vehicle ride height.

1. Hold the position of wheel center to keep distance of 1.3 inch height from rear bushing center of lateral link.
2. Measure height of bushing center at rear side of crossmember. Set point at height of B + 1.299 inch.
3. Raise up rear wheel using a jack until it reaches specified height.
4. Tighten lateral or trailing links bolts to specifications.

PONTIAC LEMANS
(T Car)
INDEX OF SERVICE OPERATIONS

NOTE: Refer To The Rear Of This Manual For Vehicle Manufacturer's Special Tool Suppliers.

Continued

INDEX OF SERVICE OPERATIONS—Continued

Specifications

GENERAL ENGINE SPECIFICATIONS

Year	Engine Liter/CID①	Engine VIN Code②	Fuel System	Bore x Stroke Inches	Compression Ratio	Net HP @ RPM③	Maximum Torque Ft. Lbs. @ RPM	Oil Pressure, psi
1991	1.6L/4-98	6	TBI	3.11 x 3.21	8.6	74 @ 5600	90 @ 2800	4.35–21.75
	2.0L/4-121	K	TBI	3.39 x 3.39	8.8	96 @ 4800	118 @ 3600	—
1992–93	1.6L/4-98	6	TBI	3.11 x 3.21	8.5	74 @ 5600	90 @ 2800	4.35–21.75

①—CID: Cubic Inch Displacement.
②—The eighth digit of the VIN denotes engine code.
③—Ratings are net as installed in vehicle.

TUNE UP SPECIFICATIONS

Year & Engine/VIN Code ①	Spark Plug Gap	Ignition Timing BTDC ②				Curb Idle Speed ③		Fast Idle Speed		Fuel Pump Pressure psi
		Firing Order ④	Man. Trans.	Auto. Trans.	Mark Fig.	Man. Trans.	Auto. Trans.	Man. Trans.	Auto. Trans.	
1991										
1.6L/4-98/6	.060	1-3-4-2	8⑦	8⑦	A	600⑥⑧	500⑥⑧	⑧	⑧	9–13⑤
2.0L/4-121/K	.060	B	8⑦	8⑦	C	600⑥⑧	500⑥⑧	⑧	⑧	9–13⑤
1992–93										
1.6L/4-98/6	.060	1-3-4-2	8⑦	8⑦	A	600⑥⑧	500⑥⑧	⑧	⑧	9–13⑤

① —The eighth digit of the Vehicle Identification Number (VIN) denotes engine code.
② —BTDC: Before Top Dead Center.
③ —N: Neutral.
④ —Before disconnecting wires from distributor cap, determine location of No. 1 wire in cap, as distributor position may have been altered from that shown at the end of this chart.

⑤ —Remove fuel pump fuse from fuse panel, then start engine & operate until engine stops. Crank engine for approximately 3 seconds to relieve fuel pressure from lines. Disconnect fuel supply hose, then connect a suitable fuel pressure gauge between hose & tube. Operate engine at idle & note gauge reading.
⑥ —Minimum.

⑦ —Align notch on crankshaft pulley with pointer. Prior to checking ignition timing, connect a jumper wire between terminals A & B of ALDL diagnostic connector. The ALDL diagnostic connector is located under the righthand side of the instrument panel.
⑧ —Idle speed is controlled by the IAC (Idle Air Control) assembly.

Fig. A

Fig. B

Fig. C

WHEEL ALIGNMENT SPECIFICATIONS
FRONT WHEEL

Year	Model	Caster Angle, degrees		Camber Angle, degrees				Toe-In, degrees
		Limits	Desired	Limits		Desired		
				Left	Right	Left	Right	
1991	All	+.75 to +2.75	+1.75①	+.45 to −1.05	+.45 to −1.05	−.3	−.3	−.16 to +.16
1992–93	All	+.75 to +2.75	+1.75①	+.25 to −1.25	+.25 to −1.25	−.75	−.75	−.33 to 0

① —Deviation from left to right side of vehicle: 1° maximum.

REAR WHEEL

Year	Model	Camber Angle, degrees		Toe-In, degrees
		Limits	Desired	
All	All	−1.25 to −.75	−1①	−.67 to −.17

① —Variation from left to right side of vehicle: .25° maximum.

COOLING SYSTEM & CAPACITY DATA

Year	Engine (VIN)	Cooling Capacity Qts.		Radiator Cap Relief Pressure, psi.	Thermo. Opening Temp.	Fuel Tank Gals.	Engine Oil Refill Qts.	Transaxle Oil	
		Less A/C	With A/C					Man. Trans. Pts.	Auto. Trans. Qts. ①
1991	2.0L/4-121 (K)	8.1	8.1	15	195	13	4②	4.4	③
1991–93	1.6L/4-98 (6)	8.1	8.1	15	195	13	4②	3.4	③

①—Approximate, make final check with dipstick.
②—Additional oil maybe required with filter change.
③—Oil pan only, 4 qts.; total capacity, 6 qts.

LUBRICANT DATA

Year	Model	Lubricant Type			
		Transaxle		Power Steering	Brake System
		Manual	Automatic		
1991–93	All	80W	Dexron IIE	GM Type Power Steering Fluid	DOT 3

Electrical

INDEX

FUSE PANEL & FLASHER LOCATION

The fuse panel is located under the left-hand side of the instrument panel.

The flasher is located on the fuse panel under the lefthand side of the i nstrument panel.

1. SET SCREW
2. DETENT SPRING

Fig. 1 Ignition lock replacement

STARTER REPLACE

1. Disconnect battery ground cable.
2. Disconnect wiring at starter motor, then remove upper and lower starter attaching bolts.
3. Remove starter motor from vehicle.
4. Reverse procedure to install. **Torque** starter bolts to 33 ft. lbs.

DISTRIBUTOR REPLACE

1. Disconnect battery ground cable.
2. Remove ignition coil and spark plug wires at distributor cap.
3. Disconnect coil and EST electrical connectors.

4. **On models with 1.6L/4-98 engine,** remove distributor clamp attaching bolt.
5. **On models with 2.0L/1-121 engine,** remove distributor cam carrier attaching nuts.
6. **On all models,** mark distributor tang drive and camshaft for correct assembly, then remove distributor.
7. Reverse procedure to install.

IGNITION LOCK REPLACE

1. Disconnect battery ground cable.
2. Remove lower instrument cluster trim.
3. Remove turn signal and wiper switch cover attaching screws and the cover.
4. Turn ignition key to position "Il."
5. Depress detent spring, **Fig. 1,** then slide lock cylinder out of steering column.
6. Reverse procedure to install.

14- HOUSING ASM, IGN SWITCH
15- SWITCH ASM, IGNITION
16- SCREW, IGN SWITCH RETAINING

Fig. 2.   Ignition switch replacement

1 OFFSET SCREWDRIVER
2 RETAINER

Fig. 5   Headlamp switch replacement

Fig. 3   Turn signal & wiper switch replacement

1. RETAINING RING
2. CABLE AT SUPPORT

Fig. 4   Neutral start switch replacement

206 SCREW-TRIMPLATE
207 TRIMPLATE-INSTRUMENT PANEL

Fig. 6   Instrument cluster trim plate screw locations

IGNITION SWITCH
REPLACE

1. Disconnect battery ground cable.
2. Remove lower instrument cluster trim.
3. Remove turn signal and wiper switch cover attaching screws and the cover.
4. Disconnect electrical connector from ignition switch.
5. Remove ignition switch setscrew, then remove ignition switch, **Fig. 2.**
6. Reverse procedure to install.

TURN SIGNAL SWITCH
REPLACE

1. Disconnect battery ground cable.
2. Remove lower instrument cluster trim.
3. Remove screws from both sides of upper cover panel. Rotate steering wheel as necessary to gain access to all screws.
4. Remove three lower panel attaching screws, then pull handle from lock release lever and remove tilt lever, if equipped.
5. Depress switch release tabs, **Fig. 3,** then disconnect electrical connector and remove switch.
6. Reverse procedure to install.

STEERING WHEEL
REPLACE

1. Disconnect battery ground cable.
2. Remove steering wheel horn cap, then disconnect horn electrical leads.

3. Remove steering wheel retaining nut and retainer, then place alignment marks on steering wheel and steering shaft.
4. Remove steering wheel using Steering Wheel Puller tool No. J-36541 or equivalent.
5. Unclip steering wheel contact ring, if required.
6. Reverse procedure to install. When installing steering wheel, align marks placed on steering wheel and steering shaft. Also the turn signal cancelling cam on the steering wheel should be to the left. **Torque** steering wheel attaching nut to 13 ft. lbs.

NEUTRAL START SWITCH
REPLACE

1. Disconnect battery ground cable.
2. Disconnect shift linkage and electrical connector from switch, **Fig. 4.**
3. Remove switch attaching bolts and the switch.
4. Reverse procedure to install. Adjust switch prior to tightening attaching bolts, as follows:
   a. Shift transaxle into Neutral.
   b. Loosen switch attaching bolts, then rotate switch on shift assembly to align adjustment hole with carrier tang hole. Insert a 3/32 drill bit into adjustment hole on switch to a depth of 3/8 inch.
   c. **Torque** attaching bolts to 22 ft. lbs., then remove drill bit.

HEADLAMP SWITCH
REPLACE

1. Disconnect battery ground cable.
2. Depress switch retaining clips using a suitable screwdriver, **Fig. 5.**
3. Disconnect electrical connector and remove switch.
4. Reverse procedure to install.

INSTRUMENT CLUSTER
REPLACE

1. Disconnect battery ground cable.
2. Remove turn signal switch housing

attaching screws and the housing. Rotate steering wheel as necessary to gain access to all screws.
3. Remove two instrument panel trim plate attaching screws and the trim plate, **Fig. 6.**
4. Depress speedometer cable retainer spring and disconnect cable from cluster.
5. Remove instrument cluster attaching screws.
6. Disconnect electrical connectors from cluster, then remove cluster from vehicle, **Fig. 7.**
7. Reverse procedure to install.

RADIO
REPLACE

1. Disconnect battery ground cable.
2. Place ignition switch in On position, then set transaxle selector lever in the 1 position.
3. Using a suitable pointed plastic tool, remove package panel, **Fig. 8.**
4. Remove front center console attaching screws from under ashtray and plastic cap, **Fig. 9.**
5. **On models with automatic transaxle,** remove selector lever, then pull indicator strap from cover. Remove retaining clips and trim cover.
6. **On models with manual transaxle,** remove shift knob, trim plate and boot.
7. **On all models,** remove front console.
8. Remove four console upper attaching

1. SERVICE ENGINE SOON INDICATOR
2. FASTEN BELTS INDICATOR
3. BRAKE INDICATOR
4. TURN INDICATOR
5. CHARGE INDICATOR
6. LOW OIL PRESSURE INDICATOR
7. HIGH BEAM INDICATOR
8. UPSHIFT INDICATOR
9. CLUSTER ILLUMINATION

Fig. 7 Instrument cluster replacement

A POINTED PLASTIC TOOL
113 CONSOLE-FRONT CENTER
405 PACKAGE PANEL

Fig. 8 Package panel removal

A REMOVE SCREWS
B REMOVE SCREW (UNDER CAP)
113 CONSOLE-FRONT CENTER

Fig. 9 Front console attaching screw location

Fig. 10 Radio replacement

screws, then slide console toward rear of vehicle.
9. Remove radio from instrument panel, **Fig. 10.**

WIPER MOTOR
REPLACE

1. Disconnect battery ground cable.
2. Remove cowl vent grille attaching screws and the grille.
3. Disconnect wiper motor electrical connectors.
4. Remove crank arm to wiper motor attaching nut.
5. Remove wiper motor attaching bolts and the wiper motor.
6. Reverse procedure to install.

BLOWER MOTOR
REPLACE
LESS A/C

1. Disconnect battery ground cable.
2. Remove wiper arm attaching nuts, then slide arms off splined shafts.

3. Remove four wind deflector attaching screws and the deflector halves.
4. Remove washer nozzle hoses from washer nozzles.
5. Remove seal from dash panel and clip, then the right side wiper bearing attaching nut.
6. Remove water deflector, then disconnect electrical connector from blower motor housing.
7. Remove blower motor housing attaching screws and the housing.
8. Remove housing cover attaching cover screws and the cover.
9. Remove blower motor from housing.
10. Reverse procedure to install.

WITH A/C

1. Disconnect battery ground cable.
2. Disconnect blower motor electrical connectors.
3. Disconnect air hose from lower housing.
4. Remove blower motor to case attaching screws.
5. Remove blower motor and fan assembly from housing.
6. Remove blower fan retaining nut and the fan from motor.
7. Reverse procedure to install.

HEATER CORE
REPLACE
LESS A/C

1. Disconnect battery ground cable, then drain cooling system.
2. Block off heater hoses with spring clips, then mark hoses for installation reference.
3. Disconnect heater hoses from heater core.
4. Remove package panel, then move heater control levers to lowest position.
5. Disconnect temperature control cable from actuating lever and air distributor.
6. Remove kick panel from under glove box.
7. Disconnect temperature valve linkage from righthand air distributor.
8. Lift carpeting, then remove air distributor cover attaching screws and the cover.
9. Remove heater core attaching screws, then the heater core and

bracket assembly. Move temperature valve as necessary to gain access to all screws.
10. Reverse procedure to install.

WITH A/C

1. Disconnect battery ground cable.
2. Block off heater hoses with spring clips, then disconnect the hoses from heater core.
3. Disconnect evaporator drain hose from heater case.
4. **On models equipped with manual transaxle,** remove gear shift boot.
5. **On all models,** remove package

shelf, then the front floor console shift plate and front center console.
6. Remove glove box attaching screws and straps, then the glove box.
7. Remove hush panel retainers and the hush panel.
8. Remove outer heater case cover retainers, then bend back tab and remove the cover.
9. Remove heater case cover retaining clips and the cover.
10. Remove heater core cover attaching screws and the cover.
11. Remove heater core clamps and the heater core.
12. Reverse procedure to install.

EVAPORATOR CORE
REPLACE

1. Disconnect battery ground cable.
2. Discharge air conditioning system.
3. Remove heater core as previously outlined.
4. Disconnect accumulator to evaporator pipe and orifice tube to evaporator at dash panel.
5. Remove evaporator cover attaching screws, then remove evaporator cover.
6. Remove evaporator bracket attaching screws, then remove pipe clamps.
7. Remove evaporator core.
8. Reverse procedure to install.

1.6L/4-98 Engine
INDEX

ENGINE MOUNTS
REPLACE

1. Disconnect battery ground cable.
2. Install engine support fixture No. J28467-A with fixture adapters J28467-70 or equivalents. **Support tool must be positioned in center of cowl and properly tightened prior to supporting engine and transaxle assembly.**
3. Remove engine mount attaching bolts and the mount, **Fig. 1.**
4. Reverse procedure to install. Tighten mount attaching bolts to torque listed at the end of this section.

ENGINE
REPLACE

1. Relieve fuel system pressure as follows:
  a. Remove fuel pump fuse from fuse panel.
  b. Start engine. After engine stalls, crank for ten seconds to relieve residual pressure from fuel system.
  c. Turn ignition off and install fuel pump fuse.

2. Disconnect battery cables and engine ground wire.
3. Disconnect lower radiator hose and drain cooling system into a suitable container.
4. Remove air cleaner assembly.
5. Disconnect upper radiator hose and heater hose from engine.
6. Disconnect cable from throttle body.
7. Label and disconnect the following vacuum hoses; brake servo, vacuum sensor, intake manifold to vapor canister and throttle valve body to vapor canister.
8. **On models equipped with automatic transaxle,** disconnect transaxle shift cable from throttle body.
9. **On all models,** disconnect fuel lines from throttle body. **Place shop towel over fuel line and fitting when disconnecting.**
10. Disconnect electrical connectors from the following components: oxygen sensor, oil pressure switch, intake manifold temperature sensor, speed sensor, injector nozzle, back-up lamp switch, neutral start switch, throttle valve, idle air control motor and distributor.
11. Disconnect instrument panel harness connector, ground wires from camshaft housing and intake manifold and

wiring harness retaining strap.
12. Remove ignition coil plugs and cable.
13. Disconnect bulkhead wiring harness connector.
14. **On models equipped with automatic transaxle,** disconnect torque converter clutch electrical connector.
15. **On all models,** raise and support vehicle.
16. Remove splash shield.
17. Remove exhaust pipe and catalytic converter.
18. Pull driveshaft out of transaxle, then remove closure plug from transaxle case.
19. Disconnect interference suppression cable from transaxle.
20. Remove clutch cover plate, then remove clutch housing to engine block lower attaching bolts.
21. Lower vehicle, then attach suitable lifting equipment to engine lift hooks.
22. Support transaxle with a suitable jack, then remove right front and left front engine mount attaching bolts and the mount, then remove rear engine mount attaching bolts..
23. Remove clutch housing to engine block upper attaching bolts.
24. Separate engine from clutch housing, then carefully lift engine from vehicle.
25. Reverse procedure to install.

201	BRACKET-ENGINE REAR
202	BOLT-REAR MOUNT
203	MOUNT-ENGINE REAR
204	WASHER
205	NUT
206	WASHER
207	BOLT
208	MOUNT-ENGINE FRONT LEFT
209	WASHER
210	BOLT
211	BRACKET-ENGINE MOUNT FRONT LEFT
212	BOLT
213	BOLT
214	BRACKET-ENGINE MOUNT-FRONT RIGHT
215	BOLT
216	MOUNT-ENGINE FRONT RIGHT
217	SUPPORT-ENGINE FRONT MOUNT
218	WASHER
219	NUT

Fig. 1   Engine mounts

70	MANIFOLD-INTAKE
79	THROTTLE BODY INJECTION (TBI)
165	NUT-TORQUE TO 22 N•m (16 Lbs. Ft.)
166	BOLT-TORQUE TO 22 N•m (16 Lbs. Ft.)
	LOOSENING SEQUENCE: C-G-B-H-D-F-E-I-A
	TIGHTENING SEQUENCE: A-I-E-F-D-H-B-G-C

Fig. 2   Intake manifold tightening sequence

INTAKE MANIFOLD REPLACE

1. Relieve fuel system pressure as follows:
   a. Remove fuel pump fuse from fuse panel.
   b. Start engine. After engine stalls, crank for ten seconds to relieve residual pressure from fuel system.
   c. Turn ignition off and install fuel pump fuse.
2. Disconnect battery ground cable.
3. Remove air cleaner assembly, then drain cooling system.
4. Unfasten alternator and position aside.
5. Disconnect throttle cable from intake manifold bracket.
6. Disconnect throttle and throttle valve cables from throttle body.
7. Disconnect electrical connectors from throttle body.
8. Disconnect fuel inlet and return lines, then the coolant hoses from intake manifold. **Place shop towel over fuel line and fitting when disconnecting.**
9. Remove manifold attaching bolts and the manifold, **Fig. 2.**
10. Reverse procedure to install. Clean manifold and cylinder head mating surfaces and install a new gasket prior to installation. Tighten intake manifold attaching nuts and bolts in sequence shown in **Fig. 2.**

27	WIRE-SPARK PLUG
35	MANIFOLD-EXHAUST
37	NUTS-TORQUE TO 22 N•m (16 LBS. FT)
	LOOSENING SEQUENCE: H-A-E-D-F-C-G-B
	TIGHTENING SEQUENCE: B-G-C-F-D-E-A-H

Fig. 3   Exhaust manifold tightening sequence

EXHAUST MANIFOLD REPLACE

1. Remove air cleaner assembly.
2. Disconnect spark plug wires and the oxygen sensor electrical connector.
3. Remove pre-heater from exhaust manifold.
4. Disconnect exhaust pipe from manifold, then remove manifold attaching nuts and the manifold, **Fig. 3.**

5. Reverse procedure to install. Clean manifold and cylinder head mating surfaces and install a new gasket prior to installation. Tighten exhaust manifold attaching nuts to specifications and in sequence shown in **Fig. 3.**

CYLINDER HEAD REPLACE

1. Relieve fuel system pressure as follows:
   a. Remove fuel pump fuse from fuse panel.
   b. Start engine. After engine stalls, crank for ten seconds to relieve residual pressure from fuel system.
   c. Turn ignition off and install fuel pump fuse.
2. Disconnect battery ground cable.
3. Remove air cleaner assembly, then drain cooling system.
4. Unfasten alternator and position aside.
5. Remove distributor and ignition wires.
6. Disconnect cables from intake manifold bracket, throttle body and downshift cable.
7. Disconnect ECM electrical connectors at the throttle body and intake manifold.
8. Disconnect fuel inlet and return lines, then the coolant and heater hoses

Fig. 4   Cylinder head bolt loosening sequence

Fig. 5   Compressing valve springs

Fig. 6   Cylinder head bolt tightening sequence

anerobic sealant to cam carrier sealing surface.
c. Install new cylinder head gasket.
d. Tighten cylinder head attaching bolts to torque listed at the end of this section in sequence shown in **Fig. 6.**

VALVE CLEARANCE SPECIFICATIONS

This engine is equipped with hydraulic lash adjusters. If valve lash is present, check for worn rocker arm, stuck hydraulic valve lash adjuster plunger or defective valve lash adjuster.

VALVE GUIDES

Valve guides are an integral part of the cylinder head. If stem to guide clearance becomes excessive, the valve guide should be reamed to the next oversize and the appropriate oversize valve should be installed. Valve are available in oversizes of .003, .006 and .010 inch.

CAMSHAFT LIFT SPECIFICATIONS

Engine	Year	Int. Inch	Exh. Inch
1.6L/4-98	All	.220	.241

FRONT COVER
REPLACE

1. Disconnect battery ground cable.
2. Remove alternator and A/C compressor drive belts.
3. Remove power steering pump.
4. Unsnap upper to lower portions of cover, then remove cover from engine.
5. Reverse procedure to install. Snap lower portion of cover in first.

TIMING BELT
REPLACE

1. Remove front cover as outlined under "Front Cover, Replace."
2. Remove air cleaner assembly, then disconnect breather hoses from valve cover.
3. Remove valve cover attaching bolts and the cover.
4. Remove timing belt.
5. Align camshaft sprocket mark with

1 CAMSHAFT TIMING MARK – AT 12 O'CLOCK POSITION
2 CAMSHAFT SPROCKET
3 TIMING BELT
4 CRANKSHAFT TIMING MARK
5 POINTER
6 OIL PAN
7 CRANKSHAFT PULLEY

Fig. 7   Timing mark alignment

from intake manifold and water outlet. **Place shop towel over fuel line and fitting when disconnecting.**
9. Disconnect breather and PCV hoses at camshaft carrier.
10. Remove upper radiator hose.
11. Disconnect exhaust pipe from manifold, then disconnect oxygen sensor electrical connector.
12. Disconnect engine wiring harness and the thermostat housing electrical connector.
13. Remove timing belt as described under "Timing Belt, Replace."
14. Loosen cylinder head attaching bolts

gradually in sequence, **Fig. 4,** until all bolts are removed.
15. Remove valve cover, then compress valve springs using a suitable tool, **Fig. 5,** and remove rocker arms and valve lash compensators. **Identify components for installation reference.**
16. Remove cylinder head as an assembly with intake and exhaust manifolds.
17. Reverse procedure to install, noting the following:
a. Clean all cylinder head, valve cover and block mating surfaces.
b. Apply a continuous bead (3 mm) of

Fig. 8 Camshaft gear removal

rear timing belt cover mark, **Fig. 7.**
6. Reverse procedure to install.

CAMSHAFT & CRANKSHAFT SPROCKETS REPLACE

1. Remove timing belt cover as previously described.
2. Remove air cleaner assembly, then disconnect breather hoses from valve cover.
3. Remove valve cover attaching bolts and the cover.
4. Remove timing belt.
5. Hold camshaft with a suitable wrench, then remove bolt, washer and camshaft sprocket, **Figs. 8 through 10.**
6. Remove retaining bolt and washer, then the crankshaft pulley and sprocket.
7. Reverse procedure to install, noting the following:
   a. Align mark on camshaft sprocket with mark on rear timing belt cover.
   b. Tighten camshaft gear attaching bolt and crankshaft sprocket retaining bolt to torque listed at the end of this section.

REAR COVER REPLACE

1. Remove camshaft sprocket as previously described.
2. Remove rear cover attaching bolts and the cover. Guide cover over water pump rear cover.
3. Reverse procedure to install.

CRANKSHAFT PULLEY REPLACE

1. Disconnect battery ground cable.
2. Loosen and remove alternator and A/C compressor drive belts.
3. Remove crankshaft pulley attaching bolt and the pulley.
4. Reverse procedure to install. Torque attaching bolt to specification listed at the end of this section.

1 LEVER-ACCELERATOR CONTROL	45 ROTO CAP-EXHAUST VALVE
2 ROD-THROTTLE CONTROL	46 SEAL-VALVE
3 BRACKET-ACCELERATOR CONTROL	47 LOCK (COLLAR)-VALVE STEM
4 FILTER-FUEL	48 ADJUSTER-HYDRAULIC VALVE LASH
5 BOLT	49 ARM-VALVE ROCKER
6 BOLT	50 VALVE-THRUST PIECE
7 BRACKET-FUEL FILTER	51 CAP-VALVE SPRING
8 SEAL-FUEL FEED LINE O-RING	52 SPRING-INTAKE AND EXHAUST VALVE
9 PIPE-FUEL TANK TO FILTER	53 RING-SEAL
10 BRACKET-ENGINE LIFT	54 THERMOSTAT (92 DEGREE)
11 CAP-OIL	55 HOUSING-COOLING THERMOSTAT
12 SEAL-OIL CAP	56 BOLT-SPROCKET
13 BOLT	57 BELT-TIMING
14 BOLT-CAMSHAFT CARRIER HOUSING	58 COVER-TIMING BELT LOWER REAR
15 WASHER	59 COVER-TIMING BELT LOWER FRONT
16 COVER-CAMSHAFT HOUSING	60 COVER-TIMING BELT UPPER FRONT
17 BOLT	61 BOLT
18 COIL	62 WASHER-TIMING GEAR
19 GASKET-CAMSHAFT CARRIER COVER	63 SPROCKET-CAMSHAFT TIMING
20 DISTRIBUTOR	64 BALL
21 NUT	65 SEAL-CAMSHAFT OIL
22 BOLT	66 PIN
23 BOLT	67 CAMSHAFT
24 PLATE-CAMSHAFT PRESS	68 GASKET-INTAKE MANIFOLD
25 TUBE-PCV	69 CONNECTOR-FUEL GAGE
26 HOUSING-CAMSHAFT CARRIER	70 MANIFOLD-INTAKE
27 WIRE-SPARK PLUG	71 CONNECTOR-INTAKE MANIFOLD
28 SUPPORT-SPARK PLUG WIRE	72 BRACKET-GENERAL MOUNTING
29 VALVE-CYLINDER HEAD BYPASS	73 INSERT-INTAKE MANIFOLD TBI
30 ADAPTER	74 GASKET-E.G.R.
31 SENSOR-COOLANT TEMPERATURE	75 VALVE-E.G.R.
32 CAP	76 SENSOR-INTAKE MANIFOLD COOLANT TEMPERATURE
33 PLUG-SPARK	77 GASKET-TBI
34 GASKET-EXHAUST MANIFOLD	78 STUD
35 MANIFOLD-EXHAUST	79 THROTTLE BODY INJECTOR (TBI)
36 STOVE-EXHAUST MANIFOLD HEAT	80 GASKET-AIR CLEANER
37 NUT	81 HOSE-HEAT STOVE
38 STUD	82 CLAMP
39 GASKET-CYLINDER HEAD	83 HOSE-CYLINDER BLOCK VENT
40 VALVE-EXHAUST	84 AIR CLEANER
41 VALVE-INTAKE	85 SEAL-AIR CLEANER CAP NUT
42 HEAD-CYLINDER	86 WASHER-AIR CLEANER CAP NUT
43 GUIDE	87 NUT-AIR CLEANER
44 WASHER-INTAKE VALVE SPRING SEAT	

Fig. 9 Cylinder head & components

Fig. 10 Cylinder block & components

101 INDICATOR (ROD)-OIL LEVEL	133 RING-OIL PUMP PRESSURE RELIEF VALVE
102 TUBE-OIL	134 SPRING-OIL PUMP PRESSURE RELIEF VALVE
103 BLOCK-ENGINE CYLINDER	135 PLUNGER-OIL PUMP PRESSURE RELIEF VALVE
104 SLEEVE-TRANSMISSION	136 PUMP-OIL
105 PLUG-CLIP TYPE	137 FILTER-OIL
106 SLEEVE-CYLINDER TO CYLINDER BLOCK	138 CONNECTOR-OIL FILTER
107 PLUG-IGNITION TIMING BUSHING	139 VALVE-OIL PUMP BYPASS
158 BUSHING-IGNITION TIMING	140 RING-OIL PUMP SEAL
109 SLEEVE-OIL PLUG	141 WASHER
110 BOLT	142 GEAR-CRANKSHAFT TIMING
111 BOLT	143 WASHER-CRANKSHAFT PULLEY
112 WASHER	144 BOLT-CRANKSHAFT TIMING GEAR
113 COVER-CLUTCH PRESSURE WITH PLATE	145 BOLT-CRANKSHAFT PULLEY
114 PLATE (DISC)-CLUTCH DRIVEN (M/T)	146 PULLEY-CRANKSHAFT
115 FLYWHEEL	147 SCREW-REAR TIMING BELT COVER
116 RING-REAR CRANKSHAFT OIL SEAL	148 COVER-TIMING BELT UPPER REAR
117 BEARING	149 BOLT
118 CRANKSHAFT	150 GASKET-OIL PUMP
119 BEARING SET-CRANKSHAFT	151 PLUG
120 BEARING-CRANKSHAFT MAIN	152 BOLT-COOLANT PUMP
121 CAP-CRANKSHAFT MAIN BEARING	153 PUMP-COOLANT
122 BOLT	154 RING-COOLANT PUMP SEAL
123 GASKET-OIL PAN	155 NECK-CYLINDER BLOCK COOLANT INLET
124 PAN-OIL	156 GASKET-CYLINDER BLOCK VENT PIPE
125 BOLT-OIL PAN DRAIN	157 PIPE-CYLINDER BLOCK VENT
126 GASKET (RING)-OIL PAN DRAIN BOLT	158 HOSE-CYLINDER BLOCK VENT
127 BOLT	159 BOLT-CONNECTING ROD
128 KEY-CRANKSHAFT	160 CAP-CONNECTING ROD BEARING
129 PIPE-OIL PUMP SUCTION	161 BEARING SET-CONNECTING ROD
130 RING-OIL PUMP SUCTION PIPE	162 ROD-CONNECTING
131 BRACKET	163 PISTON WITH PIN
132 BOLT-OIL PUMP PRESSURE RELIEF VALVE	164 PISTON RINGS

CAMSHAFT
REPLACE

1. Remove air cleaner assembly, then disconnect breather hoses from valve cover.
2. Remove valve cover attaching bolts and the cover.
3. Apply compressed air to spark plug hole using a suitable adapter to hole valves in place.
4. Compress valve springs using a suitable tool, **Fig. 5**, then remove rocker arms and valve lash compensators. **Identify components for installation reference.**
5. Remove camshaft gear attaching bolt and the gear.
6. Remove distributor, then the camshaft thrust plate and camshaft.
7. Reverse procedure to install, noting following:
   a. Tighten camshaft thrust plate attaching bolts to torque listed at the end of this section.
   b. Ensure camshaft endplay measures .0035-.0083 inch.

CRANKSHAFT FRONT OIL SEAL
REPLACE

1. Remove crankshaft gear as previously described.
2. Remove crankshaft key and rear thrust washer.
3. Remove timing belt rear cover, then pry front seal out of groove.
4. Lubricate, then install new seal using Seal Installer tool No. J36534 or equivalent, **Fig. 11.**

CRANKSHAFT REAR OIL SEAL
REPLACE

1. Remove transaxle assembly.
2. Remove flywheel attaching bolts and the flywheel.
3. **On models equipped with manual transaxle,** remove clutch pressure plate and disc.
4. **On all models,** pry rear seal out of groove.
5. Lubricate outer surface of new seal, then install the seal using Seal Installer tool No. J36792 or equivalent.

PISTON & ROD ASSEMBLY

Assemble piston to rod, with notch on piston head toward front of engine, **Fig. 12.** Upon installation, measure rod bearing side clearance using a suitable feeler gauge. Rod bearing side clearance should be .0028-.0095 inch.

PISTONS, PINS & RINGS

Pistons and rings are available in stan-

136

J 36534

136 PUMP-OIL

Fig. 11 Crankshaft front seal installation

NOTCH TOWARD FRONT OF ENGINE

Fig. 12 Piston & rod assembly

Fig. 13 Oil pan sealant application

170

169

136

136 PUMP-OIL
169 SWITCH-OIL PRESSURE
170 BOLTS-OIL PUMP

Fig. 14 Oil pump replacement

1. PUMP, OIL
2. PLUG
3. RING, SEAL
4. GEAR, OIL PUMP DRIVE
5. GEAR, OIL PUMP DRIVEN
6. COVER, OIL PUMP
7. BOLT (M6 x 1 x 16)
8. GASKET
9. SLEEVE
10. VALVE, BYPASS
11. BOLT, PRESS. REL. VLV.
12. RING, PRESS. REL. VLV.
13. SPRING PRESS. REL. VLV.
14. PLUNGER, PRESS. REL. VLV.
15. BOLT (6 x 1 x 25)
     WASHER

Fig. 15 Exploded view of oil pump assembly

dard size and oversize of .020 inch. Pistons and pins are supplied in matched sets.

MAIN & ROD BEARINGS

Main and rod bearings are available in standard sizes and undersizes of .010 and .020 inch.

OIL PAN
REPLACE

1. Disconnect battery ground cable.
2. Raise and support vehicle.
3. Remove right splash shield.
4. Drain engine oil, then disconnect exhaust pipe from exhaust manifold.
5. **On models equipped with manual transaxle,** remove clutch cover plate attaching bolts, then remove clutch cover plate.
6. **On all models,** remove oil pan attaching bolts and the oil pan.
7. Reverse procedure to install. Apply suitable sealant to bolt threads and oil pan seams, **Fig. 13.**

OIL PUMP
REPLACE
REMOVAL

1. Remove crankshaft gear and timing belt rear cover as previously described.
2. Disconnect electrical connector from oil pressure switch.
3. Remove oil pan as previously described.
4. Remove oil filter, then the pickup tube and oil pump, **Fig. 14.**
5. Remove crankshaft front oil seal.

INSTALLATION

1. Install oil pump using a new gasket.
2. Install pickup tube and support using a new O-ring.
3. Install oil pan, then a new front seal using Seal Installer tool No. J36534 or equivalent.
4. Install new oil filter, then reconnect oil pressure switch electrical connector.
5. Install rear timing belt cover and crankshaft gear.

OIL PUMP SERVICE
DISASSEMBLY

1. Drain oil from pump, then remove suction pipe and screen assembly.
2. Remove oil pump cover and gears, **Fig. 15.**
3. Carefully remove pressure regulator valve plug or cotter pin, then the valve spring and valve.

INSPECTION

1. Clean all pump components in suitable solvent.
2. Inspect pump housing and cover for damage or casting imperfections. Replace housing if necessary.
3. Inspect idler gear shaft fit in housing. If shaft fits loosely, replace pump or timing chain cover as needed.
4. Inspect pressure regulator valve for damaging or sticking. Small burrs may be removed with an oil stone.
5. Install pressure regulator valve spring for loss of tension or damage and replace as necessary.
6. Inspect suction pipe and screen for looseness or damage and replace as necessary.

7. Inspect gears for damage and replace as necessary.
8. Inspect driveshaft for looseness or excessive wear and replace as necessary.

ASSEMBLY

1. Lubricate all internal components with clean engine oil.
2. Pack all pump cavities with petroleum jelly, then install the gears. **Ensure mark on gears faces timing cover.**
3. Install cover and gasket, then the pressure regulator valve and spring.
4. Apply Loctite sealant to pressure regulator valve plug threads, then install the plug and torque to specifications listed at the end of this section.

WATER PUMP
REPLACE

1. Disconnect lower radiator hose and drain coolant into a suitable container.
2. Remove front cover, timing belt and rear cover as previously described.
3. Remove water pump attaching bolts and the water pump.
4. Reverse procedure to install. Apply silicone grease to pump sealing surface and new seal ring prior to installation.

COOLING SYSTEM BLEED

These engines do not require a specified bleed procedure. After filling cooling system, run engine to operating temperature with radiator/pressure cap off. Air will then be automatically bled through cap opening.

THERMOSTAT
REPLACE

1. Drain radiator through lower hose.
2. Remove timing belt front cover as described under "Timing Belt Front Cover, Replace."
3. Remove timing belt described under "Timing Belt, Replace."
4. Remove timing belt rear cover as described under "Timing Belt Rear Cover, Replace."
5. Remove thermostat housing and thermostat.
6. Clean sealing surfaces on both head and thermostat housing.
7. Reverse procedure to install.

BELT TENSION DATA

Year	Belt	Lbs. New	Lbs. Used
All	A/C Comp.	155	80
	Alt. & P/S	①	①

① —.5–.75 inch deflection.

FUEL PUMP
REPLACE

1. Relieve fuel system pressure as follows:
   a. Remove fuel pump fuse from fuse panel.
   b. Start engine. After engine stalls, crank for ten seconds to relieve residual pressure from fuel system.
   c. Turn ignition off and install fuel pump fuse.
2. Disconnect battery ground cable.

3. Raise rear seat, then remove cover from floor pan.
4. Disconnect electrical fuel pump connector and fuel line from fuel pump.
5. Remove fuel pump attaching bolts and the fuel pump.
6. Reverse procedure to install.

FUEL FILTER
REPLACE

The inline filters can be found on the rear crossmember of the vehicle. Always use a backup wrench anytime the filter is removed or installed.

1. Relieve fuel system pressure as follows:
   a. Remove fuel pump fuse from fuse panel.
   b. Start engine. After engine stalls, crank for ten seconds to relieve residual pressure from fuel system.
   c. Turn ignition off and install fuel pump fuse.
2. Remove fuel pump fuse from fuse panel located in the passenger compartment.
3. Crank engine, engine will start and run until fuel supply remaining in the fuel lines is consumed.
4. Engage starter for 3.0 seconds to ensure relief of any remaining pressure in the system.
5. Turn the ignition switch to the Off position, then replace the fuel pump fuse.
6. Raise and support the vehicle, then disconnect the front and rear fuel lines from the filter assembly.
7. Remove retaining bolt and clamp assembly.
8. Reverse procedure to install. **Torque fuel line fittings to 22 ft. lbs.**

TIGHTENING SPECIFICATIONS

Torque specifications are for clean & lightly lubricated threads only. Dry or dirty threads increase friction which prevents accurate measurement of tightness.

Year	Component	Torque/Ft. Lbs.
1991–93	A/C Compressor Nuts & Bolts	18
	Camshaft Carrier & Cylinder Head Bolts	18①
	Camshaft Carrier Cover Bolts	18
	Camshaft Sprocket Bolt	33
	Crankshaft Pulley Bolt	41
	Crankshaft Sprocket Bolt	33
	Connecting Rod Cap Bolts	18④
	Exhaust Manifold Heat Stove Bolts	89②
	Exhaust Manifold Nuts	16
	Exhaust Pipe Nuts	115②
	Flywheel Bolts	26⑤
	Generator Bolts	18
	Intake Manifold Nuts & Bolts	16
	Left Front Engine Mount	37
	Left Front Mounting Bracket To Block	30

Year	Component	Torque/Ft. Lbs.
1991–93 —Cont'd	Left Front Mounting Bracket To Engine Mount	30
	Lower Timing Belt Front Cover Bolts	71②
	Main Bearing Cap Bolts	37③
	Oil Pan Bolts	71②
	Oil Plug	33
	Oil Pump Bolts	62②
	Power Steering Pump Bolts	18
	Power Steering Pump Pulley Bolts	20
	Pressure Relief Valve Bolt	22
	Rear Engine Mount Bolts	37
	Rear Mounting Bracket Nut & Bolt	30
	Right Front Engine Mount Nuts	37
	Right Front Mounting Bracket To Block Bolts	30
	Right Front Mounting Bracket To Engine Mount Bolt	30

TIGHTENING SPECIFICATIONS—Continued

Year	Component	Torque/ Ft. Lbs.	
1991-93 —Cont'd	Rear Thrust Plate Bolts	71②	①—Plus 2 turns of 60° each & 1 turn of 30°.
	Timing Belt Rear Cover Bolts	89②	②—Inch Lbs. ③—Plus 1 turn of 45° to 60°.
	Upper Timing Belt Front Cover Bolts	71②	④—Plus 1 turn of 30°. ⑤—Plus 1 turn of 30° to 45°.

2.0L/4-121 Engine

INDEX

1—BOLT/SCREW
2—SIDE FRAME
3—BRACKET
4—MOUNT ASM.
5—NUT

Fig. 1   Front engine mounting

1—BOLT/SCREW
2—R.H. RAIL
3—MOUNT ASM.
4—COWL ASM.
5—REINFORCEMENT
6—NUT
7—NUT
8—BRACKET ASM.
9—TENSIONER

Fig. 2   Rear engine mounting

ENGINE MOUNTS
REPLACE

1. Disconnect battery ground cable.
2. Support engine using Engine Support Brace tool No. J-28467-A or equivalent.
3. Remove mount to bracket attaching bolts, then remove mount to engine upper attaching bolts, **Figs. 1 and 2.**
4. Raise and support vehicle, then remove mount to engine lower attaching bolts and engine mount.
5. Reverse procedure to install. Apply Loctite in kit No. 1052624 or other suitable thread locking compound to bolt threads prior to installation.

ENGINE
REPLACE

1. On all models, remove fuel pump fuse from fuse panel, then start and operate engine until it stalls. After stalling, crank engine for approximately 3 seconds to deplete

Fig. 3 Intake manifold tightening sequence

INLET MANIFOLD NUT TIGHTENING SEQUENCE

TORQUE #2 AND #3 MANIFOLD RUNNERS PRIOR TO #1 AND #4.

Fig. 4 Exhaust manifold tightening sequence

Fig. 5 Cylinder head bolt loosening sequence

fuel pressure in fuel lines.

2. Disconnect battery ground cable and engine ground strap.
3. Drain cooling system, then disconnect radiator and heater hoses.
4. Remove air cleaner assembly.
5. Disconnect engine wiring harness at bulkhead connector.
6. Disconnect electrical connectors at brake cylinder, cooling fan relay, cooling fan motor, windshield wiper motor and coolant temperature switch. Also disconnect electrical connectors at A/C compressor clutch and A/C relay, if equipped.
7. Disconnect electrical connector from ECM (Electronic Control Module) and pull harness through bulkhead connector.
8. Remove vacuum hoses at fuel injection, MAP sensor and canister.
9. Disconnect throttle cable at bracket and throttle body.
10. Disconnect shift control cable at transaxle.
11. Disconnect power steering hoses at pump.
12. Raise and support front of vehicle, then disconnect exhaust pipe from exhaust manifold and position aside.
13. **On models equipped with automatic transaxle,** disconnect transmission fluid cooler lines.
14. **On all models,** disconnect fuel lines. **Place shop towel over fuel line and fitting when disconnecting.**
15. Remove heater hoses at heater core.
16. Remove front wheel and tire assemblies.
17. Remove front brake calipers with brake hoses attached and suspend from wheel opening with suitable wire.
18. Discharge A/C system, then disconnect refrigerant lines from A/C compressor, then disconnect A/C compressor electrical connectors.
19. Ensure vehicle is properly supported, then remove two center bolts from suspension support. Remove one bolt from each end of suspension support, then loosen the remaining bolts.
20. **On models with automatic transaxle,** remove transaxle rear strut.
21. **On all models,** remove transaxle front strut.
22. Support front vehicle by positioning jack stands under radiator support.
23. Position suitable jack and a wooden board (4 x 4 inches x 6 foot) across width of vehicle at rear of cowl.

24. Raise vehicle slightly and remove jack stands positioned under radiator support.
25. Position a suitable dolly with 3 wooden blocks (4 x 4 x 12 inches) as supports, under engine and transaxle assembly.
26. Carefully lower vehicle to position engine and transaxle assembly on dolly.
27. Remove remaining bolt at left and righthand sides of the front suspension supports.
28. Scribe line indicating position of strut to steering knuckle. This scribe line is used during installation to reset camber adjustment.
29. Remove engine and transaxle mount to bracket attaching bolts, then steering knuckle to strut bolts.
30. Raise vehicle, allowing engine, transaxle and suspension to remain on dolly. Prior to raising vehicle, ensure all necessary electrical wiring, cables, linkages and hoses are disconnected to permit engine and transaxle removal.
31. Separate engine from transaxle.
32. Reverse procedure to install. When installing strut to steering knuckle, align scribe lines made during removal.

INTAKE MANIFOLD REPLACE

1. Remove fuel pump fuse from fuse panel, then start and operate engine until it stalls. After stalling, crank engine for approximately 3 seconds to deplete fuel pressure in fuel lines.
2. Disconnect battery ground cable, then drain cooling system.
3. Remove air cleaner and serpentine belt.
4. Remove alternator and bracket from camshaft carrier.
5. Remove power steering pump bracket to intake manifold attaching bolts, then position pump and bracket aside with hoses attached.
6. Remove ignition coil and bracket assembly.
7. Disconnect throttle cable from intake manifold bracket and throttle body.
8. Disconnect TV cable and electrical connectors from throttle body.
9. Disconnect power brake unit vacuum hose at filter.
10. Disconnect fuel lines at throttle body. **Place shop towel over fuel line and**

fitting when disconnecting.

11. Disconnect water pump to intake manifold coolant bypass hose and inlet tube.
12. Disconnect ECM electrical connector to provide access to intake manifold lower attaching nuts.
13. Remove intake manifold attaching nuts and intake manifold.
14. Reverse procedure to install. Tighten intake manifold attaching nuts in sequence shown in **Fig. 3.**

EXHAUST MANIFOLD REPLACE

1. Disconnect battery ground cable, then remove air cleaner assembly.
2. Tag, then remove spark plug wires and retainers.
3. Remove oil dipstick tube and breather.
4. Disconnect electrical connector from oxygen sensor.
5. Disconnect exhaust pipe from exhaust manifold.
6. Remove exhaust manifold attaching nuts, then remove exhaust manifold.
7. Reverse procedure to install. Tighten exhaust manifold attaching nuts in sequence shown in **Fig. 4.**

CYLINDER HEAD REPLACE

1. Remove fuel pump fuse from fuse panel, then start and operate engine until it stalls. After stalling, crank engine for approximately 3 seconds to deplete fuel pressure in fuel lines.
2. Disconnect battery ground cable, then remove air cleaner assembly.
3. Drain cooling system, then remove serpentine drive belt.
4. Remove alternator and bracket assembly, then remove ignition coil.
5. Mark position of distributor rotor to distributor body and distributor body to cylinder head, then remove distributor.
6. Disconnect cables from intake manifold brackets.
7. Disconnect throttle and TV cables from throttle body.
8. Disconnect electrical connectors from throttle body and intake manifold.
9. Disconnect power brake unit vacuum hose at filter.

PONTIAC LEMANS

Fig. 6 Cylinder head bolt tightening sequence

Fig. 7 Compressing valve springs

Fig. 9 Timing belt & components

1	ROCKER ARM
2	THRUST PIECE
3	LASH ADJUSTER
4	VALVE STEM LOCK
5	VALVE SPRING CAP
6	VALVE SPRING
7	VALVE SEAL
8	EXHAUST ROTO CAP
9	INLET SPRING WASHER

Fig. 8 Rocker arms assemblies

2. Disconnect breather hoses from camshaft carrier cover.
3. Remove camshaft carrier cover attaching bolt, then remove cover.
4. Using Valve Spring Compressing Fixture tool No. J-33302-B or equivalent, compress valve and springs, **Fig. 7**, then remove remove rocker arms, thrust pieces and hydraulic valve lash adjusters, **Fig. 8.** Tag components so they can be installed in the same position.
5. Reverse procedure to install.

VALVE SPRING & VALVE STEM OIL SEAL REPLACE

1. Remove camshaft carrier cover attaching bolts, then remove carrier cover.
2. Remove rocker arm and hydraulic valve lash adjuster for cylinder being serviced as described under "Rocker Arms and Hydraulic Valve Lash Adjusters, Replace."
3. Remove spark plug, then position adapter J-22794 or equivalent into spark plug hole. Connect a suitable compressed air source to adapter to hold valve in position.
4. Using tool No. J-33302-25 or equivalent, **Fig. 7**, compress valve springs and remove valve locks, caps, springs, spring washers, exhaust valve rotators and valve stem oil seals, **Fig. 8.**
5. Reverse procedure to install. Lubricate valve stem oil seal with engine oil prior to installation. When installing valve stem oil seal, use a suitable plastic sleeve to position seal over valve stem.

CRANKSHAFT PULLEY REPLACE

1. Disconnect battery ground cable, then

10. Disconnect fuel lines from throttle body unit. **Place shop towel over fuel line and fitting when disconnecting.**
11. Disconnect radiator, heater and bypass hoses from cylinder head and intake manifold.
12. Disconnect breather hose from camshaft carrier cover.
13. Disconnect exhaust pipe from exhaust manifold.
14. Disconnect electrical connectors from oxygen sensor, wiring harness, thermostat housing, coolant temperature switch and other components to permit cylinder head, intake manifold and exhaust manifold to be removed as an assembly.
15. Remove timing belt, as described under "Timing Belt, Replace," then remove timing belt rear cover.
16. With engine cold, loosen cylinder head/camshaft carrier attaching bolts in sequence shown in **Fig. 5.**
17. Remove camshaft carrier, rocker arms and hydraulic valve lash adjusters.
18. Remove cylinder head, intake manifold and exhaust manifold as an assembly. If necessary, separate intake and exhaust manifolds from cylinder head after removal from engine.
19. Reverse procedure to install. Prior to installation, the intake and exhaust manifolds must be assembled to cylinder head, if removed. Apply a continuous bead (3 mm) of anerobic sealant

1052942 or equivalent to cam carrier sealing surface prior to installation. Tighten cylinder head bolts to torque listed at the end of this section in sequence shown in **Fig. 6.**

VALVE CLEARANCE SPECIFICATIONS

This engine is equipped with hydraulic lash adjusters. If valve lash is present, check for worn rocker arm, stuck hydraulic valve lash adjuster plunger or defective valve lash adjuster.

VALVE GUIDES

Valve guides are an integral part of the cylinder head. If stem to guide clearance becomes excessive, the valve guide should be reamed to the next oversize and the appropriate oversize valve should be installed. Valves are available in oversizes of .003, .006 and .010 inch.

CAMSHAFT LIFT SPECIFICATIONS

Engine	Year	Int, Inch	Exh, Inch
2.0L/4-121	All	.2366	.2515

ROCKER ARMS REPLACE

1. Disconnect battery ground cable, then remove air cleaner assembly.

Fig. 10 Water pump eccentric adjusting tool modification

Fig. 11 Camshaft sprocket replacement

Fig. 13 Crankshaft front seal installation

Fig. 12 Piston & rod assembly

remove serpentine drive belt.
2. Remove inner fender shield.
3. Remove A/C compressor drive belt, if equipped.
4. Remove crankshaft pulley attaching bolt and remove pulley.
5. Reverse procedure to install. Prior to installation of crankshaft pulley attaching bolt, apply Loctite 242 or equivalent to bolt threads, then torque bolt to specification listed at the end of this section.

FRONT COVER
REPLACE

1. Disconnect battery ground cable, then remove serpentine drive belt.
2. Loosen serpentine drive belt tensioner bolt and allow tensioner arm to swing downward.
3. Remove timing belt cover attaching bolts and nuts, then remove timing belt cover, **Fig. 9.**
4. Reverse procedure to install.

TIMING BELT
REPLACE
REMOVAL

1. Disconnect battery ground cable, then remove A/C belt, if equipped, then remove serpentine drive belt.
2. Remove power steering pump, bracket and serpentine drive belt tensioner as an assembly.
3. Remove timing timing belt cover attaching bolts, then remove timing belt cover, **Fig. 9.**
4. Loosen water pump attaching bolts, then using tool No. J-33039-A or equivalent, **Fig. 10,** on water pump eccentric, release tension.
5. Remove crankshaft pulley as described under "Crankshaft Pulley, Replace."
6. Remove timing belt from camshaft and crankshaft sprockets, **Fig. 9.**

INSTALLATION

1. Align timing marks on camshaft and crankshaft sprockets with timing marks on timing belt rear cover.
2. Position timing belt to camshaft and crankshaft sprockets and tensioner, **Fig. 9.**

3. Using tool No. 33039-A or equivalent, **Fig. 10,** rotate water pump eccentric clockwise until tensioner contacts high torque stop, then tighten water pump attaching bolts slightly.
4. Rotate crankshaft pulley 2 revolutions in clockwise direction to seat timing belt on sprockets.
5. With engine at room temperature, rotate water pump eccentric counterclockwise until hole in tensioner arm is inline with hole in base. Using Cam Drive Belt Tension Adjustment Wrench tool No. 33039-A or equivalent to rotate water pump eccentric.
6. Tighten water pump attaching bolts to torque listed at the end of this section. Ensure tensioner holes remain aligned.
7. Install crankshaft pulley, then install timing belt cover.
8. Install power steering pump, bracket and serpentine drive belt tensioner.
9. Install and tension A/C belt, if equipped, and serpentine drive belt, then connect battery ground cable.

CAMSHAFT SPROCKET
REPLACE

1. Disconnect battery ground cable.
2. Remove camshaft cover carrier attaching bolts, then remove camshaft cover carrier.
3. Remove timing belt as described under "Timing Belt, Replace."
4. While holding camshaft in position with a suitable open end wrench, remove camshaft sprocket attaching bolts, then remove washer and sprocket, **Fig. 11.**
5. Reverse procedure to install. While holding camshaft in position with an

open end wrench, tighten camshaft sprocket attaching bolt to torque listed at the end of this section.

CRANKSHAFT SPROCKET
REPLACE

1. Disconnect battery ground cable.
2. Remove timing belt as described under "Timing Belt, Replace."
3. Remove crankshaft sprocket attaching bolt and washer, then remove crankshaft sprocket.
4. Reverse procedure to install. When installing crankshaft sprocket, ensure it is proper positioned on crankshaft key. Tighten crankshaft sprocket attaching bolt to torque listed at the end of this section.

REAR COVER
REPLACE

1. Disconnect battery ground cable.
2. Remove timing belt as described under "Timing Belt, Replace."
3. Remove camshaft and crankshaft sprockets as described previously.
4. Remove timing belt tensioner assembly.
5. Remove timing belt rear cover attaching bolts, then remove cover, **Fig. 9.**
6. Reverse procedure to install. Tighten timing belt rear cover attaching bolts to torque listed at the end of this section.

CAMSHAFT
REPLACE

1. Disconnect battery ground cable.
2. Remove rocker arms and hydraulic valve lash adjusters as described under, "Rocker Arms and Hydraulic Valve Lash Adjusters, Replace."
3. Remove camshaft sprocket as de-

Fig. 14 Oil pan & gasket

1	PUMP-OIL		
2	PLUG	9	SLEEVE-OIL PUMP
3	RING-SEAL OIL PUMP	10	VALVE-BYPASS
4	GEAR-OIL PUMP DRIVE	11	BOLT-PRESSURE RELIEF VALVE
5	GEAR-OIL PUMP DRIVEN	12	RING-PRESSURE RELIEF VALVE
6	COVER-OIL PUMP	13	SPRING-PRESSURE RELIEF VALVE
7	BOLT (M6 x 1 x 16)	14	PLUNGER-PRESSURE RELIEF VALVE
8	GASKET-OIL PUMP	15	BOLT (6 x 1 x 25)

Fig. 15 Exploded view of oil pump assembly

scribed under "Camshaft Sprocket, Replace."
4. Remove distributor from engine.
5. Remove rear thrust plate, then slide camshaft from rear of engine.
6. Reverse procedure to install. Lubricate camshaft front carrier oil seal with engine oil prior to camshaft installation. Tighten camshaft rear thrust plate attaching bolts to torque listed at the end of this section. Camshaft endplay should be .0016-.0064 inch.

PISTON & ROD ASSEMBLY

Assemble piston to rod, with notch on piston head toward front of engine and numbered side of rod toward intake manifold side of engine, **Fig. 12.** Upon installation, measure rod bearing side clearance using a feeler gauge. Rod bearing side clearance should be .0039-.0149 inch.

PISTONS, PINS & RINGS

Pistons and rings are available in standard size only.

MAIN & ROD BEARINGS

Main and rod bearings are available in standard sizes and undersizes of .005 and .010 inch.

CRANKSHAFT FRONT OIL SEAL
REPLACE

1. Disconnect battery ground cable.
2. Remove crankshaft pulley as described under "Crankshaft Pulley, Replace."
3. Remove key and thrust washer from crankshaft.

4. Remove timing belt rear cover as described under "Timing Belt Rear Cover, Replace."
5. Pry crankshaft front seal from oil pump.
6. Reverse procedure to install. Prior to installation, lubricate seal lip with engine oil. Using Front Crankshaft Seal Installer tool No. J-33083 or equivalent to install seal, **Fig. 13.**

CRANKSHAFT REAR OIL SEAL
REPLACE

1. Remove transaxle assembly as described under "Transaxle, Replace."
2. Remove flywheel attaching bolts and flywheel.
3. **On models with manual transaxle,** remove pressure plate and clutch disc.
4. **On all models,** pry crankshaft rear oil seal from engine.
5. Reverse procedure to install. Prior to installation, lubricate seal lip with engine oil. Using Rear Crankshaft Seal Installer tool No. J-36227 or equivalent, to install seal.

OIL PAN
REPLACE

1. Disconnect battery ground cable.
2. Raise and support front of vehicle, then drain crankcase.
3. Disconnect exhaust pipe from exhaust manifold.
4. Remove flywheel cover attaching bolts and flywheel cover.
5. Remove oil pan attaching bolts, then remove oil pan, **Fig. 14.**
6. Reverse procedure to install. Apply sealant to oil pan gasket as shown in **Fig. 14.** Prior to installation, apply Loctite to oil pan attaching bolts. Tighten oil pan attaching bolts to torque listed at the end of this section.

OIL PUMP
REPLACE

1. Disconnect battery ground cable.
2. Remove crankshaft sprocket as described under "Crankshaft Sprocket, Replace."
3. Remove timing belt rear cover as described under "Timing Belt Rear Cover, Replace."
4. Disconnect oil pressure sender electrical connector.
5. Remove oil pan as described under "Oil Pan, Replace."
6. Remove oil filter.
7. Remove oil pump attaching bolts, then oil filter and pickup tube assembly.
8. Pry crankshaft front oil seal from oil pump.
9. Reverse procedure to install. Tighten oil pump attaching bolts to torque listed at the end of this section. After installing oil pump and oil pan, lubricate crankshaft front oil seal lip with engine oil, then install seal using Front Crankshaft Seal Installer tool No. J-33083 or equivalent, **Fig. 13.**

OIL PUMP SERVICE
DISASSEMBLY

1. Drain oil from pump into a suitable container.
2. Remove pump driveshaft, then remove pickup tube and screen assembly.
3. Remove pump cover attaching screws, then remove pump cover and gears, **Fig. 15.**
4. Carefully remove regulator valve plug, spring and valve from pump housing. If valve is difficult to remove, soak pump housing in a suitable carburetor cleaning solvent.

A WATER PUMP BOLTS
B LOWER REAR TIMING
  BELT COVER

Fig. 16   Water pump attaching bolt locations

CLEANING & INSPECTION

1. Clean components in a suitable carburetor cleaning solvent.
2. Check all component wear and damage.
3. Check regulator valve spring for loss of tension and distortion.
4. Using a feeler gauge measure oil pump gear lash. Gear lash should be .004-.008 inch.
5. Check clearance between idler gear and oil pump body. Clearance should be .0043-.0074 inch.
6. **On all models,** check clearance between drive gear and oil pump housing. Clearance should be .014-.018 inch.
7. Using a straightedge and feeler gauge, check clearance between gears and pump cover. Clearance should be .001 to .004 inch.
8. Measure oil pump housing gear pocket depth and diameter. Gear pocket depth should be .395-.397 inch. Gear depth pocket should be 3.231-3.234 inch.
9. Measure drive and idler gear length and diameter. Drive and idler gear length should be .393-.394 inch. Drive gear diameter should be 1.612-1.613 inches. Idler gear diameter should be 3.2248-3.2269 inches.
10. **On all models,** replace any components that are found to be unsatisfactory.

ASSEMBLY

1. Lubricate all components with engine oil and pack pump all cavities with petroleum jelly prior to assembly.
2. Position gears in pump body, with gear mark facing timing cover, **Fig. 15.**
3. Install pump cover and gasket, then install and tighten attaching bolts to torque listed at the end of this section.
4. Install pressure regulator valve and spring, then install plug and torque to specification listed at the end of this section. Prior to installing plug, coat threads with Loctite 573 or equivalent.
5. Install pump pickup tube and screen.

A WATER PUMP REMOVED FROM ENGINE
  BLOCK SHOWING IMPELLER
B SEAL-WATER PUMP

Fig. 17   Water pump seal installation

47 HOSE-FUEL PUMP
52 PUMP-FUEL
54 ELECTRICAL CONNECTOR-
   FUEL PUMP

Fig. 19   Fuel pump replacement

WATER PUMP
REPLACE

1. Disconnect battery ground cable.
2. Disconnect lower radiator hose and allow cooling system to drain.
3. Remove timing belt as described under "Timing Belt, Replace."
4. Remove timing belt lower rear cover.
5. Remove water pump attaching bolts and water pump, **Fig. 16.**
6. Reverse procedure to install. Prior to installation, coat water pump seal and sealing surface with suitable silicone grease, **Fig. 17.**

COOLING SYSTEM BLEED

These engines do not require a specified bleed procedure. After filling cooling system, run engine to operating temperature with radiator/pressure cap off. Air will then be automatically bled through cap opening.

THERMOSTAT
REPLACE

1. Drain coolant through lower radiator hose.

1. GENERATOR
2. SERPENTINE DRIVE BELT
3. POWER STEERING PUMP
4. SERPENTINE TENSIONER
5. CRANKSHAFT PULLEY
6. A/C TENSIONER
7. A/C COMPRESSOR
8. A/C "V" BELT

Fig. 18   Serpentine drive belt routing

2. Remove upper radiator hose.
3. Remove thermostat housing and thermostat.
4. Clean sealing surfaces on head and thermostat housing.
5. Reverse procedure to install.

BELT TENSION DATA

Belt tension is controlled automatically by the belt tensioner.

SERPENTINE DRIVE BELT
BELT ROUTING

Refer to **Fig. 18,** for serpentine drive belt routing.

FUEL PUMP
REPLACE

1. Remove fuel pump fuse from fuse panel, then start and operate engine until it stalls. After stalling, crank engine for approximately 3 seconds to deplete fuel pressure in fuel lines.
2. Disconnect battery ground cable.
3. Raise rear seat, then lift cover from vehicle floor pan.
4. Disconnect electrical connector and fuel line from fuel pump, **Fig. 19.**
5. Remove fuel pump to fuel tank attaching bolts, then remove fuel pump.
6. Reverse procedure to install.

FUEL FILTER
REPLACE

The inline filters can be found on the rear crossmember of the vehicle. Always use a backup wrench anytime the filter is removed or installed.

1. Relieve fuel system pressure as follows:

a. Remove fuel pump fuse from fuse panel.
b. Start engine. After engine stalls, crank for ten seconds to relieve residual pressure from fuel system.
c. Turn ignition off and install fuel pump fuse.
2. Remove fuel pump fuse from fuse panel located in the passenger compartment.
3. Crank engine, engine will start and run until fuel supply remaining in the fuel lines is consumed.
4. Engage starter for 3.0 seconds to ensure relief of any remaining pressure in the system.
5. Turn the ignition switch to the Off position, then replace the fuel pump fuse.
6. Raise and support the vehicle, then disconnect the front and rear fuel lines from the filter assembly.
7. Remove retaining bolt and clamp assembly.
8. Reverse procedure to install. **Torque** fuel line fittings to 22 ft. lbs.

TIGHTENING SPECIFICATIONS

Torque specifications are for clean & lightly lubricated threads only. Dry or dirty threads increase friction which prevents accurate measurement of tightness.

Year	Component	Torque/Ft. Lbs.
1991	A/C Compressor Mounting Bracket To Engine	69
	A/C Compressor To Engine Mounting Bracket (Front)	69
	A/C Compressor To Engine Mounting Bracket (Rear)	50
	A/C Compressor To Rear Bracket	23
	Alternator Brace To Manifold	23
	Alternator To Bracket (Long Bolts)	32
	Alternator To Bracket (Short Bolts)	23
	Camshaft Carrier Cover Bolts	6
	Camshaft Rear Cover	7.5
	Camshaft Sprocket Bolt	33
	Camshaft Thrust Plate Bolts	6
	Connecting Rod Cap Bolts	38
	Coolant Inlet	18
	Crankshaft Pulley Bolts	20
	Crankshaft Sprocket	114
	Cylinder Head/Camshaft Carrier Bolts	①
	EGR Valve	15
	Engine Mount Bolts & Nuts	40
	Exhaust Manifold Bolts	16
	Exhaust Pipe To Exhaust Manifold	②
	Flexplate To Crankshaft Bolts	52
	Flywheel To Crankshaft Bolts	55
	Front Cover	8
	Fuel Pump Screw Fittings	15
	Idler Pulley Bolts	23
	Intake Manifold Bolts	16
	Main Bearing Cap Bolts	70
	Oil Filter Adapter, Auto. Trans.	13
	Oil Filter Adapter, Man. Trans.	26

Year	Component	Torque/Ft. Lbs.
1991 —Cont'd	Oil Pan Bolts	3.7
	Oil Pan Drain Plug	33
	Oil Pump Cover	7
	Oil Pump Pressure Regulating Valve Plug	22
	Oil Pump Pick-Up Tube To Engine Bolt	4.4
	Oil Pump Pick-Up Tube To Oil Pump Bolts	6
	Oil Pump To Engine Bolts	32
	Oxygen Sensor	31
	Serpentine Drive Belt Tensioner	18
	Spark Plug	18
	Starter Motor To Engine	32
	Starter Motor To Front Bracket	9
	Thermostat Adapter	8
	Thermostat Housing	7.5
	Thermostat Outlet	9
	Throttle Body Fuel Lines	20
	Throttle Body To Intake Manifold Bolt	12
	Timing Belt Front Cover	7.5
	Timing Belt Rear Cover	7.3
	Timing Belt Tensioner	18
	Transaxle (Auto.) Torque Converter to Flexplate Bolts	44
	Transaxle To Engine Bolts	55
	Water Pump Bolts	18
	Water Pump Pulley	23

①—Torque bolts to 18 ft. lbs., then advance each bolt an additional 180° in 60° increments. Start engine & allow to reach operating temperature, then tighten bolts an additional 30 to 50°.
②—Torque to 19 ft. lbs.

Clutch & Manual Transaxle

INDEX

Fig. 1   Clutch pedal adjustments

1. ALIGNMENT ARROW
2. NOTCH

Fig. 4   Shift linkage adjustment hole plug

ADJUSTMENTS

CLUTCH PEDAL

1. Measure and record distance between outer edge of steering wheel and center of clutch pedal, **Fig. 1.**
2. Fully depress clutch pedal and repeat measurement made in step 1.
3. Determine clutch pedal travel by subtracting first measurement from second measurement.
4. If clutch pedal travel is not 5.43–5.71 inches, remove clip and adjust cable nut as necessary, then install clip.

SHIFT LINKAGE

1. Disconnect battery ground cable.
2. Place gearshift lever in Neutral position, then loosen rod clamp bolt, **Fig. 2.**
3. Remove adjustment hole plug from shift lever cover, **Fig. 3,** then turn shift rod to the left until a ³/₁₆ inch gauge pin can be inserted into adjustment hole in intermediate shift lever.

10. ROD CLAMP BOLT

Fig. 2   Clutch assembly

4. Remove shift boot from console, then unfasten console and lift upward to gain access to shift control lever mechanism.
5. Move gearshift lever to 1st/2nd gear position while still in Neutral.
6. Ensure lever is against stop and arrow is aligned with notch, **Fig. 4,** then **torque** rod clamp bolt to 10 ft. lbs. plus an additional 90–180°.
7. Measure clearance between catch "A," **Fig. 5,** and stop "B" with lever in neutral position. Clearance should measure .12 inch.
8. Remove gauge pin and install plug.
9. Adjust dimension "C," **Fig. 5,** to .449–.465 inch by turning adjusting nut "D" as necessary. **Bend back two locking tabs at nut prior to adjustment.**
10. Install boot then the console assembly.
11. Reconnect battery ground cable.

CLUTCH
REPLACE
REMOVAL

1. Disconnect battery ground cable.
2. Remove clip and nut, then disconnect clutch cable from release lever. **Prior to disconnecting, measure threaded end of clutch cable at clutch release lever, so that cable may be set in the same position during installation.**
3. Raise and support vehicle.
4. Remove left front wheel and tire assembly.
5. Remove 17 mm plug from transaxle cover.

1. ADJUSTMENT HOLE PLUG

Fig. 3   Shift rod clamp bolt

1. CATCH "A"
2. STOP "B"
3. DIMENSION "C"
4. ADJ. NUT "D"

Fig. 5   Shift lever alignment

6. Mark relationship between input shaft and cluster gear, then remove snap ring from end of input shaft.
7. Remove screw at end of input shaft using Input Shaft Retaining Screw Remover & Installer tool No. J-36668 or equivalent.
8. Screw Input Shaft Remover & Installer tool No. J-36644 and Slide Hammer tool No. J-6125-B or equivalents into end of input shaft, then pull input shaft out of cluster gear.
9. Remove clutch cover attaching bolts and the cover.
10. Push back clutch release lever, then install Pressure Plate Spring Clamps tool No. J-36554 or equivalent on pressure plate.
11. Rotate flywheel 120° and install a second clamp, then rotate an additional 120° and install a third clamp. **Pressure plate and clutch disc cannot be removed without the three spring clamps properly installed.**
12. Support pressure plate and remove

attaching bolts, pressure plate and clutch disc, **Fig 6.**

INSTALLATION

1. Position new pressure in a suitable press and apply enough pressure to install three spring clamps.
2. Install pressure plate and clutch disc, noting the following:
   a. Ensure long portion of clutch disc hub faces transaxle.
   b. Apply suitable grease to clutch disc spline and release bearing.
   c. Ensure reference marks on flywheel and pressure plate are properly aligned.
   d. Install two pressure plate bolts. Align clutch disc splines with input shaft splines and marks on input shaft with marks on cluster gear, then install remaining bolts and torque all to specifications.
3. Seat input shaft in cluster gear using Input Shaft Remover & Installer tool No. J-36644 and Slide Hammer tool No. J-6125-B or equivalents.
4. Install screw at end of input shaft using Input Shaft Retaining Screw Remover & Installer tool No. J-36668 or equivalent, then torque to specifications.
5. Install snap ring onto input shaft. **Ensure sharp end of snap ring faces cover.**
6. Apply suitable Teflon pipe thread sealant to transaxle cover plug threads, then install the plug and torque to specifications.
7. Remove spring clamps, then install clutch cover and torque attaching bolts to specifications.
8. Lower vehicle, then connect clutch cable to release lever. Set threaded portion of clutch to measurement noted during removal and adjust as necessary.

1. FLYWHEEL
2. DISC
3. PRESSURE PLATE
4. RELEASE BEARING

Fig. 6 Shift lever measurements

MANUAL TRANSAXLE REPLACE

If only the transaxle is to be removed, the transaxle end shield along with the main shaft and driveshaft should be removed from the transaxle casing.

1. Disconnect battery ground cable.
2. Remove air cleaner.
3. Remove clutch cable at release lever attaching clip and nut.
4. Remove universal joint attaching clip and bolt.
5. Disconnect speedometer cable, speed sensor and back-up lamp electrical connectors.
6. Loosen shift rod clamp attaching bolt.
7. Remove upper transaxle to engine attaching bolts.
8. Install Engine Support Fixture tool No. J28467-A or equivalent.
9. Raise and support vehicle.
10. Remove front wheel and tire assemblies.
11. Remove splash shield.
12. Disconnect interference suppression capacitor cable at transaxle.
13. Press both ball joints from steering knuckle.
14. Disengage axle shafts from transaxle casing.
15. Remove transaxle cover at end shield.
16. Disengage both drive axles at transaxle using Drive Axle Remover tool No. J-36639 or equivalent.
17. Mark relationship between transaxle driveshaft and cluster gear, then remove snap ring from end of input shaft.
18. Pull out left drive axle and support.
19. Support transaxle using suitable jack.
20. Remove left front mount bracket attaching bolts, then remove bracket.
21. Remove left rear mount bracket to transaxle attaching bolts.
22. Remove lower transaxle to engine attaching bolts.
23. Lower jack while guiding right drive axle out of transaxle and remove transaxle from vehicle.
24. Reverse procedure to install. Torque all attaching points to specifications.

TIGHTENING SPECIFICATIONS

Year	Component	Torque/Ft. Lbs.
1991-93	**Ball Joint Nut**	50
	Clutch Cover Plug	36
	Clutch Fork To Release Lever Shaft Bolt	26
	Flywheel Bolts	26②
	Flywheel Cover Bolts	62①
	Front Mount Bracket To Mount	55
	Front Mount Bracket To Transaxle	48
	Input Shaft Attaching Screw	11
	Pressure Plate To Flywheel	11
	Rear Mount Bracket To Transaxle	55
	Release Bearing Guide Sleeve Bolts	45①
	Upper & Lower Transaxle To Engine	55
	Wheel Lug Nuts	66

①—**Inch lbs.**
②—**Plus 1 turn of 30° to 45°.**

Rear Axle & Suspension

INDEX

1	COVER-TRIM
2	NUT-SHOCK UPPER
3	WASHER-SHOCK UPPER
4	BUMPER-SHOCK UPPER
5	GROMMET-SHOCK UPPER
6	WASHER-SHOCK UPPER
7	ABSORBER-SHOCK
8	BOLT-HEX
9	NUT-HEX
10	RING-SEAL
11	BEARING-WHEEL HUB INNER
12	HUB-WHEEL
13	BEARING-WHEEL HUB OUTER
14	WASHER-HUB LOCKING
15	PIN-COTTER
16	NUT-SPINDEL
17	CAP-HUB DUST
18	NUT-STABILIZER SHAFT
19	WASHER
20	BOLT-STABILIZER SHAFT
21	NUT-BUSHING HEX
22	BUSHING-AXLE SUPPORT
23	BOLT-AXLE SUPPORT
24	INSULATOR-STABILIZER SHAFT
25	SHAFT-STABILIZER
26	SUPPORT-REAR AXLE
27	BUMPER-SPRING LOWER
28	SPRING SET-COIL
29	RING-SPRING UPPER INSULATOR

Fig. 1   Exploded view of rear axle & suspension assembly

REAR AXLE
REPLACE
REMOVAL

1. Raise and support vehicle.
2. Remove rear wheel and tire assemblies.
3. Remove exhaust heat shield from vehicle underbody.
4. Measure and record length of thread on parking brake lever pushrod.
5. Remove self-locking nut from parking brake lever pushrod and the lock plate from brake cable compensation yoke.
6. Disconnect parking brake cable from brake cable compensation yoke.
7. Disconnect parking brake cable from guides on transaxle tunnel and plastic sleeves on fuel tank and position toward muffler.
8. Raise one rear axle arm using a suitable jack.
9. Disconnect brake lines from brake pressure hoses on rear axle bracket and remove lock clips. **Cap brake line fittings.**

10. Disconnect brake pressure hoses from bracket.
11. Remove shock absorbers as described under "Shock Absorber, Replace."
12. Remove rear axle arm attaching bolt, then lower the arm and remove coil spring. If necessary, depress rear axle arm using a pry bar positioned in shock absorber bracket.
13. Repeat step 12 on opposite side.
14. Support center of rear axle assembly using a suitable jack.
15. Remove rear axle attaching bolts and carefully lower axle assembly from vehicle, **Fig. 1.**
16. If rear axle assembly is to be replaced, proceed as follows:
    a. Remove brake drum setscrew and the drum.
    b. Remove dust cap from wheel hub.
    c. Remove wheel hub retaining nut and the wheel hub.
    d. Bend open brake line retaining clamps.
    e. Remove brake anchor plates and paper seal from rear axle arm.
    f. Remove stabilizer bar attaching

bolts and the stabilizer bar.
    g. Disconnect parking brake cable from mounting.

INSTALLATION

1. If rear axle assembly is being replaced, proceed as follows:
    a. Attach stabilizer bar to rear axle and tighten attaching bolts to torque listed at the end of this section.
    b. Apply suitable sealant to brake anchor plate, then position new paper seals on plate.
    c. Apply suitable locking compound to anchor plate attaching bolts, then install the bolts and tighten to torque listed at the end of this section.
    d. Position brake lines in rear axle clamps and bend clamps closed.
    e. Apply suitable grease to wheel spindle, then install wheel hub and **torque** attaching nut to 12 ft. lbs.
    f. Adjust wheel bearings as described under "Wheel Bearings, Adjust."
    g. Install brake drums and setscrew.
    h. Position parking brake cable over exhaust muffler.
2. Raise rear axle assembly and secure to vehicle underbody. Raise one rear axle arm slightly using a suitable jack.
3. Install coil spring, ensuring lower rubber damper is properly positioned in spring seat.
4. Raise axle arm and install shock absorber. Tighten attaching bolts to torque listed at the end of this section.
5. Repeat steps 3 and 4 on opposite side.
6. Fasten brake pressure hoses to rear axle bracket and retaining clips.
7. Attach brake pressure lines to pressure hoses.
8. Install parking brake cable and adjust to dimension recorded at removal.
9. Install rear wheel and tire assemblies, then adjust wheel bearings as described under "Wheel Bearings, Adjust."
10. Tighten rear axle attaching bolts to torque listed at the end of this section, with weight of vehicle on wheels.
11. Bleed brake system, then adjust parking brake as necessary.

WHEEL BEARING
ADJUST

1. Raise and support rear of vehicle.
2. Remove hub dust cap, then the spin-

A = 9mm (0.36 in.)

Fig. 2 Shock absorber upper nut installation

1. J-29376-1
2. J29376-11
3. J29376-6A
4. J29376-12
5. J-21474-18
6. J-21474-22
7. SLOT SOLID BUSHINGS WITH HACKSAW TO ALLOW J-29376-6A TO ENGAGE BUSHINGS.
8. REAR AXLE ASSEMBLY
9. CONTROL ARM BUSHING
10. TO PROPERLY INDEX BUSHING ON INSTALLATION, ALIGN ARROWS ON J-29376-1 AND J-29376-11

REMOVE LEFT SIDE

INSTALL LEFT SIDE

VIEW A

VIEW B

LEFT HAND

Fig. 3 Control arm bushing removal & installation

dle nut cotter pin and nut.
3. **Torque** spindle nut to 18 ft. lbs. while turning wheel assembly forward by hand.
4. Back off spindle nut until just loose, then hand-tighten the nut.
5. Loosen spindle nut until either hole in spindle aligns with slot in nut, then install new cotter pin. **Do not loosen nut more than ½ turn.**
6. Ensure bearing endplay measures .001 to .005 inch, then install dust cap on hub.

SHOCK ABSORBER
REPLACE

1. Open deck lid and remove trim cover, if equipped.
2. Remove upper shock absorber attaching nut.
3. Raise rear of vehicle and support rear axle using a suitable jack.
4. Remove lower attaching bolt and nut and the shock absorber. **Do not remove both shock absorbers at the same time.**
5. Reverse procedure to install, noting the following:
   a. Tighten lower attaching bolt to torque listed at the end of this section.
   b. Tighten upper attaching nut until thread extends .36 inch above the nut, **Fig. 2.**

STABILIZER BAR
REPLACE

1. Raise and support rear of vehicle.
2. Remove one rear wheel and tire assembly.
3. Remove stabilizer bar attaching bolts and nuts from both sides of axle, then remove stabilizer bar toward side of vehicle less wheel.
4. Reverse procedure to install. Tighten stabilizer bar attaching bolts to torque listed at the end of this section.

COIL SPRING
REPLACE

1. Raise and support rear of vehicle. Support control arms with suitable jackstands.

Fig. 4 Control arm bushing alignment

45° ± 5°

2. Remove brake line clips from body bracket and allow brake line to hang free.
3. Disconnect parking brake cable at equalizer.
4. Disconnect brake hoses and cap fittings.
5. Remove right and left shock absorber lower attaching bolts.
6. Carefully lower rear axle and remove springs and insulators.
7. Reverse procedure to install, noting the following:
   a. Prior to installing springs, secure upper insulators to body with suitable adhesive.
   b. Tighten shock absorber lower attaching bolts to torque listed at the end of this section.

CONTROL ARM BUSHING
REPLACE

1. Raise and support rear of vehicle.
2. Raise one rear axle arm using a suitable jack and remove shock absorber lower attaching bolt.
3. Raise opposite rear axle arm and remove shock absorber lower attaching bolt.

4. Lower axle arm slightly and remove coil spring with rubber damper, then raise axle and install shock absorber lower attaching bolt.
5. Repeat step 4 on opposite side of axle.
6. Support center of rear axle assembly using a suitable jack.
7. Remove brake line retaining clips from vehicle underbody and position brake lines in underbody recess.
8. Remove rear axle attaching bolts, then lower axle slightly and support with Hangar tool No. J-29376-13 or equivalent.
9. Heat control arm bushings to 122-158°F, then remove the bushings using tools shown in **Fig. 3.**
10. Install new bushings as shown in **Fig. 3.**
11. Reverse remainder of removal procedure to complete installation. Ensure bushings are properly aligned, **Fig. 4.**

HUB & BEARING
REPLACE

1. Raise and support rear of vehicle.
2. Remove wheel and tire assembly.
3. Remove brake drum setscrew and the drum. If necessary, loosen parking brake cable and press parking brake lever in with a screwdriver.
4. Remove dust cap from hub, then the spindle nut cotter pin and nut.
5. Remove wheel hub and lockwasher.
6. Remove seal from wheel hub using a suitable screwdriver.
7. Remove inner tapered roller bearing from hub.
8. Drive inner and outer bearing outer races out of wheel hub using a suitable drift.
9. Reverse procedure to install, noting the following:
   a. Press bearing outer races into hub using Rear Hub Inner and Outer

Bearing Race Installer tool No. J-6791 and Driver Handle tool No. J-8092 or equivalents.

b. Pack wheel bearings, seal lip and wheel hub with suitable wheel bearing grease.

c. Following completion of installation, adjust wheel bearings and parking brake as needed.

TIGHTENING SPECIFICATIONS

Year	Component	Torque/Ft. Lbs.
1991-93	Brake Anchor Plate Bolt To Rear Axle Arm	21
	Brake Pipe To Brake Hose Cap Screws	8
	Control Arm To Body Bracket Nut	70
	Rear Axle To Underbody Nut & Bolt	76
	Rear Axle To Underbody Nut & Bolt w/New Control Arm Bushing	70
	Rear Axle Wheel Spindle Nut	18
	Shock Absorber To Body Mount	①
	Shock Absorber To Axle Bolt	51
	Stabilizer Shaft To Axle Nuts	59
	Wheel Lug Nuts	66

①—Tighten until .36 inch of thread is exposed above top of nut.

Front Suspension & Steering

INDEX

STEERING KNUCKLE REPLACE

1. Loosen two upper strut to body attaching nuts, **Fig. 1.**
2. Loosen wheel lug nuts, then remove drive axle shaft retaining pin, nut and washer.
3. Raise and support front of vehicle. Support vehicle on suitable jackstands.
4. Remove wheel and tire assembly.
5. Install modified outer seal protector J-28712 or equivalent.
6. Remove brake caliper and position aside, leaving brake line attached.
7. Remove brake disc attaching screws and the disc.
8. Remove outer tie rod to steering arm attaching nuts, then separate tie rod from arm using Tie Rod Remover tool No. J-24319-01 or equivalent.
9. Remove lower ball joint retaining clip and stud nut, then separate ball joint from steering knuckle using Ball Joint Separator tool No. J-36226 or equivalent. **Disregard "This Side Towards Wheel" marking on tool. Tool must be turned to opposite position when used on these vehicles.**
10. Support drive axle, then separate the axle from front wheel hub using Drive

Axle Separator tool No. J-37105 or equivalent and remove two strut to body attaching nuts and steering knuckle and strut assembly from vehicle.
11. Reverse procedure to install, noting the following:
    a. Torque strut to body attaching nuts to specification listed at the end of this section.
    b. Torque lower ball joint nut to specification listed at the end of this section.
    c. Torque tie rod attaching nut to specification listed at the end of this section.
    d. Torque disc to wheel hub bolt to specification listed at the end of this section.
    e. With weight of vehicle on wheels, **torque** new drive axle to hub nut to 74 ft. lbs., then back off nut and retorque to 15 ft. lbs. Tighten nut an additional 1/4 turn, then install cotter pin. If necessary, loosen nut slightly to align cotter pin holes.

STRUT REPLACE

Refer to "Steering Knuckle, Replace," for strut replacement procedure.

STRUT SERVICE

1. Secure strut assembly in Spring Compressor tool No. J-34013 with Adapter tool No. J-34013-87 or equivalents, **Fig. 2.**
2. Turn compressor forcing screw to compress spring slightly, then remove upper bearing dust cover.
3. Remove dampener shaft nut while using a suitable socket to prevent shaft from turning.
4. Guide dampener shaft out of strut assembly while loosening compressor screw.
5. Continue to loosen compressor screw, then remove strut dampener and spring.
6. Remove thrust washer, upper strut mount, raised edge washer and plastic mount from top of strut, **Fig. 1.**
7. Remove strut shield, upper spring insulator, spring, strut bumper and front brake shield.
8. Remove strut cartridge nut and the cartridge using Strut Cartridge Nut Wrench tool No. J-36804 or equivalent. **Exercise extreme caution as strut cartridge nut is under high torque pressure.**
9. Reverse procedure to assemble, noting the following:

1. CLIP, RETAINING
2. NUT
3. BOLT
4. CLAMP, FRT STAB SHF
5.
6. BALL JOINT, LOWER CONT ARM
7.
8. BOLT
9. WASHER
10. GROMMET, STAB SHF LINK
11. BOLT
12. WASHER
13. ARM, LOWER CONTROL
14. BUSHING, LOWER CONTROL REAR
15. BUSHING, LOWER CONTROL FRONT
16. WASHER
17. NUT
18. GROMMET, STAB SHF LINK
19. WASHER
20. SPACER

21. WASHER
22. GROMMET, STAB SHF LINK
23.
24. BOLT
25. CLAMP
26. INSULATOR, STAB SHF
27. SHAFT, FRONT STAB
28. GROMMET, STAB SHF LINK
29. WASHER
30. NUT
31. NUT, STRUT CARTRIDGE CLOSURE
32. CARTRIDGE, STRUT
33. KNUCKLE/SUPT TUBE
34. WASHER, THRUST
35. NUT, PISTON ROD
36. COVER, UPPER BEARING DUST
37. NUT
38. WASHER
39. MOUNT (BEARING) UPPER STRUT
40. WASHER, RAISED EDGE

41. MOUNT (PLASTIC)
42. SHIELD, STRUT
43. INSULATOR, UPPER SPRING
44. SPRING
45. BUMPER, STRUT
46. SHIELD, FRONT BRAKE
47. RING, SNAP
48. BEARING, FRONT WHEEL
49. RING, SNAP
50. HUB, FRONT WHEEL
51. DISC, BRAKE
52. WASHER
53. PIN, COTTER
54. NUT, DRIVE SHAFT
55. SCREW, STOP
56. CALIPER, FRONT BRAKE
57. SCREW
58. WASHER

Fig. 1   Exploded view of front suspension

Fig. 3   Spring mount alignment

Lug on plastic front spring mount serves as installation guide: looking in direction of travel, lug points forwards on spring strut for left side of vehicle; on spring strut for right side of vehicle, lug points backwards.

Fig. 4   Control arm rear bushing removal

1. STRUT COMPRESSOR J 34013
2. INSTALL LOCKING PINS THROUGH STRUT ASSEMBLY
3. TIGHTEN NUTS TILL FLUSH WITH STRUT COMPRESSOR (SEE VIEW A)
4. COMPRESSOR FORCING SCREW
5. CLAMPING TOOL J 34013-87 (SEE VIEW B)
33. STRUT ASSEMBLY
35. NUT, PISTON ROD

Fig. 2   Strut disassembly

a. Install new strut cartridge nut and tighten to torque listed at the end of this section. Do not remove wax lubricant from nut.
b. Apply suitable lubricant to upper strut bearings prior to assembly.
c. Position spring as shown, **Fig. 3**, and move assembly upright in strut compressor before installing upper locking pin.
d. Tighten dampener shaft nut to torque listed at the end of this section, while preventing nut from turning.

CONTROL ARM
REPLACE

1. Raise and support front of vehicle. Support vehicle on suitable jackstands placed under frame.

2. Remove wheel and tire assembly.
3. Disconnect stabilizer bar from control arm.
4. Install modified outer seal protector J-28712 or equivalent.
5. Remove ball joint retaining clip and stud nut, then separate ball joint from steering knuckle using Ball Joint Separator tool No. J-36226 or equivalent. **Disregard "This Side Towards Wheel" marking on tool. Tool must be turned to opposite position when used on these vehicles.**
6. Remove control arm attaching bolts and the control arm.
7. If necessary, replace control arm bushings as shown in **Figs. 4 through 7.**
8. Reverse procedure to install. Tighten attachments to torque listed at the end of this section.

BALL JOINT INSPECTION

1. Raise and support front of vehicle so that suspension is allowed to hang free.
2. Grasp wheel and tire assembly at 6 and 12 o'clock positions, then rock top of wheel and tire assembly inward and outward.
3. While rocking wheel and tire assembly, observe movement between steering knuckle and control arm. If

Fig. 5   Control arm front bushing removal

any horizontal movement is present, replace ball joint.
4. If ball joint is disconnected from steering knuckle, use finger pressure to try to twist ball joint in its socket. If ball joint can be twisted in its socket, replace ball joint.

BALL JOINT
REPLACE

1. Remove control arm as previously described.
2. Drill heads off ball joint rivets, then

Fig. 6 Control arm rear bushing installation

Fig. 7 Control arm front bushing installation

Fig. 8 Stabilizer bar attaching nut installation

A NUT
B BOLT
C BEARING
33 KNUCKLE AND SUPPORT TUBE
50 HUB

Fig. 9 Hub from steering knuckle removal

punch out rivets using a suitable drift and remove ball joint.
3. Reverse procedure to install. Tighten ball joint retaining nuts from below the control arm to torque listed at the end of this section.

STABILIZER BAR REPLACE

1. Raise vehicle and support so that front suspension hangs free.
2. Remove front wheel and tire assemblies.
3. Disconnect stabilizer bar link assemblies from control arms, **Fig. 1**.
4. Remove stabilizer bar bracket attaching bolts, then the bushings, brackets and stabilizer bar.
5. Reverse procedure to install. Tighten stabilizer bar to body bolts to torque listed at the end of this section and the stabilizer bar to control arm nuts to a length of 1¹⁵/₃₂ inch, **Fig. 8**.

HUB & BEARING REPLACE

1. Remove steering knuckle as previously described.
2. Remove hub from steering knuckle and wheel bearing using Drive Axle Separator tool No. J-37105-1 or Front Wheel Hub Remover tool No.

50 HUB-FRONT WHEEL
63 INNER RACE

Fig. 10 Bearing inner race removal

J-37105-3 or equivalent, **Fig. 9**.
3. Using Inner Bearing Race Remover Legs tool No. J-22888-35 and Inner Bearing Race Remover Support Bracket tool No. J-22888-36 or equivalents, remove bearing race from hub, **Fig. 10**.
4. Remove snap rings retaining bearing to steering knuckle, then remove bearing using tool J-37105-1 or J-37105-3 or equivalent, **Fig. 11**.
5. Position snap ring into steering knuckle bore, then install bearing using tool No. J-37105-1 or J-37105-3 or equivalent.
6. Using tool No. J-37105-1 or J-37105-3 or equivalent, pull hub onto bearing assembly and steering knuckle, then install snap ring.

STEERING GEAR REPLACE

1. Disconnect battery ground cable.
2. **On models equipped with manual steering,** remove both pinch bolts from coupling assembly, then slide coupling up on steering spindle. Position steering wheel straight ahead as shown in **Fig. 12**.

J37105-2 (REMOVAL) AS SHOWN
J37105-2 (INSTALLATION) REVERSE TOOL

A BOLT
B NUT
C BEARING
33 KNUCKLE AND SUPPORT TUBE
47 RING-SNAP-MUST BE REMOVED FOR BEARING REMOVAL. INSTALL AFTER HUB (50) INSTALLATION
48 BEARING-FRONT WHEEL
49 RING-SNAP-MUST BE INSTALLED FOR BEARING INSTALLATION AND REMOVED FOR BEARING REMOVAL.

Fig. 11 Bearing from steering knuckle bore removal

3. **On all models,** remove air cleaner assembly.
4. Loosen both tie rods from center of steering gear housing, then pry lock plate in half, then remove both tie rod bolts from center of steering gear housing.
5. Remove steering damper brackets and mounting clamps, then remove steering damper, then push flex coupling upward on steering spindle, as equipped.
6. **On models equipped with power steering gear,** disconnect fluid lines from gear.
7. **On models equipped with power steering,** remove steering gear and pinion flexible coupling clamp attaching bolts.
8. **On models equipped with manual steering,** remove left and right mounting clamp bolt and nut, then remove clamp.
9. **On all models,** Remove instrument panel seal from gear, then remove steering gear through righthand wheel opening.
10. Reverse procedure to install, noting the following:

STEERING. POSITION STRAIGHT AHEAD

After all necessary operations on the steering gear or the steering column assembly are completed (removing and reinstalling, disassembling and re-assembling), the exact straight ahead position of the steering is to be checked in each case

- The straight ahead position is achieved when reference dimension A = 325 mm/12.8 in

MEASURING GAGE J36666

To make check, place Measuring Gage J36666 between end of tie rod and left hand mounting recess for steering gear (looking in direction of travel)

Hold steering wheel in this exact straight ahead position

The following conditions must be fulfilled

1 The steering spindle clamp flange bolt must be lying horizontally on top

2 The steering wheel must be centered on the steering spindle

(Steering wheel spokes centered diagonally and pointing downwards)

TOP HORIZONTAL POSITION

MEASURING GAGE J36666

1a If clamp flange bolt is slanted pinion is displaced one tooth on rack (assembly error) — steering pinion position must be corrected

2a If steering wheel is off center by more than ± 5° (clamp flange bolt must lie horizontally on top), pull steering wheel off of steering spindle using J36541 and center on spindle splines.

ASSEMBLY ERROR

Fig. 12 Steering wheel position adjustment

a. After second reuse of mounting clamp studs, thread locking kit No. 1052624 or equivalent must be used.
b. Tighten mounting clamp attaching nuts to torque listed at the end of this section.
c. Tighten coupling to steering column attaching bolts to torque listed at the end of this section.

POWER STEERING PUMP
REPLACE
1.6L/4-98 ENGINE

1. Disconnect battery ground cable.
2. Remove power steering pump drive belt, then three attaching bolts and power steering pulley.
3. Disconnect fluid lines from pump.
4. Remove pump to upper timing belt cover attaching clips, then remove clips.
5. Remove power steering pump mounting bolts, then remove pump from vehicle.
6. Reverse procedure to install. After completing installation, bleed system by cycling steering wheel from side to side without contacting stops. Keep fluid at proper level during bleeding procedure.

2.0L/4-121 ENGINE

1. Disconnect battery ground cable.
2. Remove power steering pump drive belt, then disconnect fluid lines from pump.
3. Remove power steering pump to bracket attaching bolts through holes in pulley.
4. Remove power steering pump from vehicle.
5. Reverse procedure to install. After completing installation, bleed system by cycling steering wheel from side to side without contacting stops. Keep fluid at proper level during bleeding procedure.

TIGHTENING SPECIFICATIONS

Year	Component	Torque/Ft. Lbs.
1991-93	Ball Joint To Strut/Knuckle Assembly Nut	50
	Control Arm Front Mounting Bolts	100
	Control Arm Rear Mounting Bolts	50
	Disc Brake Rotor To Hub Screw	3
	Flex Coupling To Steering Shaft Clamp Bolt	16
	Flex Coupling To Stub Shaft Clamp Bolt	16
	Hub & Bearing Nut	①
	Inner Tie Rod To Steering Gear	66
	Power Steering Fluid Line Fittings	20
	Power Steering Pump Attaching Bolts	18
	Power Steering Pump Pulley Attaching Bolts	20
	Stabilizer Bar To Body Clamp Bolts	29
	Steering Damper Bracket To Steering Gear Bolts	16

Year	Component	Torque/Ft. Lbs.
1991-93 —Cont'd	Steering Gear Mounting Clamp Bolts & Nuts	28
	Steering Gear Retaining Bracket Nuts	16
	Strut To Body Nuts	18
	Strut Cartridge Retaining Nut	145
	Strut PushRod Nut	40
	Tie Rod End To Steering Knuckle Assembly Nut	45
	Tie Rod Pinch Bolts	16
	Wheel Lug Nuts	66

① —With weight of vehicle on wheels, torque new drive axle to hub nut to 74 ft. lbs., then back off nut and retorque to 15 ft. lbs. Tighten nut an additional ¼ turn, then install cotter pin. If required, loosen nut slightly to align cotter pin holes.

Wheel Alignment

INDEX

PRELIMINARY INSPECTION

1. Inspect tires for proper inflation and similar tread wear.
2. Inspect hub and bearing for excessive wear, repair as required.
3. Inspect ball joints.
4. Inspect tie rod ends for excessive looseness.
5. Check wheel and tire runout.
6. Inspect vehicle ride height.
7. Inspect rack and pinion for looseness at frame.
8. Ensure proper strut operation.
9. Check suspension and steering components for damage, replace as required.

FRONT WHEEL ALIGNMENT

CASTER & CAMBER

Front caster and camber angles are not adjustable. If caster or camber is found to be out of specifications, inspect suspension and related body components for

A   ADJUST TOE
    SETTING HERE

B   LOOSEN CLAMP BOLTS
    ADJUST TOE.

1   TIE ROD-OUTER
2   DAMPER-STRUT

Fig. 1   Front toe adjustment

damage and repair or replace as necessary.

TOE

1. Loosen right and left tie rod end clamps, **Fig. 1.**
2. Turn right and left tie rod adjusters as necessary to bring toe within specifications.
3. Ensure right and left tie rods are equal in length, then **torque** clamp bolts to 15 ft. lbs.

REAR WHEEL ALIGNMENT

CASTER & CAMBER

Rear caster and camber angles are not adjustable. If caster or camber is found to be out of specifications, inspect suspension and related body components for damage and repair or replace as necessary.

TOE

Rear toe is not adjustable. If toe is found to be out of specifications, inspect rear axle assembly and wheel spindle for damage and correct as necessary.

VEHICLE RIDE HEIGHT

Vehicle trim height is measured from the rocker panel to ground. From rocker panel front to ground should be 7.7 inches. From rocker panel rear to ground, trim height should be 7.5 inches. If trim height is not within limits, check control arms, struts and ball joints for wear and damage.

AIR CONDITIONING
TABLE OF CONTENTS

System Testing
INDEX

GENERAL PRECAUTIONS

R-12 SYSTEMS

The Freon refrigerant used is also known as R-12. It is colorless and odorless both as a gas and a liquid. Since it boils (vaporizes) at −21.7°F, it will usually be in a vapor state when being handled in a repair shop. But if a portion of the liquid coolant should come in contact with the hands or face, note that its temperature momentarily will be at least −22°F.

Protective goggles should be worn when opening any refrigerant lines. If liquid coolant does touch the eyes, bathe the eyes quickly in cold water, then apply a bland disinfectant oil to the eyes. See an eye doctor.

When checking a system for leaks with a torch type leak detector, do not breathe the vapors coming from the flame. Do not discharge refrigerant in the area of a live flame. A poisonous phosgene gas is produced when R-12 is burned. While the small amount of gas produced by a leak detector is not harmful unless inhaled directly at the flame, the quantity of refrigerant released into the air when a system is purged can be extremely dangerous if allowed to come into contact with an open flame.

Never allow the temperature of refrigerant drums to exceed 125°F. The excessive increase in temperature will cause a corresponding increase in pressure which may cause the safety plug to release or the drum to burst.

If it is necessary to heat a drum of refrigerant when charging a system, the drum should be placed in water no hotter than 125°F. Never use a blow torch or other open flame. If possible, a pressure release mechanism should be attached before the drum is heated.

When connecting and disconnecting service gauges on an A/C system, ensure that gauge hand valves are fully closed and that compressor service valves, if equipped, are in the back-seated (fully counterclockwise) position. Do not disconnect gauge hoses from service port adapters, if used, while gauges are connected to A/C system. To disconnect hoses, always remove adapter from service port. Do not disconnect hoses from gauge manifold while connected to A/C system, as refrigerant will be rapidly discharged.

After disconnecting gauge lines, check the valve areas to be sure service valves are correctly seated and Schraeder valves, if used, are not leaking.

R-134a SYSTEMS

R-134a refrigerant is a non toxic, non-flammable, clear colorless odorless liquified gas.

R-134a refrigerant is not compatible with R-12 refrigerant. Even small amounts of R-12 in a R-134a system will cause lubricant contamination, compressor failure or improper A/C performance. Never add R-12 to a R-134a system.

Avoid breathing R-134a refrigerant and lubricant vapor or mist. Exposure may irritate eyes, nose and throat. Use only approved service equipment to discharge R-134a systems.

EXERCISE SYSTEM

An important fact most owners ignore is that A/C units must be used periodically. Manufacturers caution that when the air conditioner is not used regularly, particularly during the cold months, it should be turned on for a few minutes once every two or three weeks while the engine is running. This keeps the system in good operating condition.

Checking out the system for the effects of disuse before the onset of summer is one of the most important aspects of A/C servicing.

First clean out the condenser core, mounted in all cases at the front of the radiator. All obstructions, such as leaves, bugs or dirt, must be removed, as they will reduce heat transfer and impair the efficiency of the system. Make sure the space between the condenser and the radiator also is free of foreign matter.

Make certain the evaporator water drain is open. The evaporator cools and dehumidifies the air before it enters the passenger compartment; there, the refrigerant is changed from a liquid to a vapor. As the core cools the air, moisture condenses on it but is prevented from collecting in the evaporator by the water drain.

PERFORMANCE TEST

The system should be operated for at least 15 minutes to allow sufficient time for all parts to become completely stabilized. Determine if the system is fully charged by the use of test gauges and sight glass if one is installed on system. Head pressure will read from 180 psi to 220 psi or higher, depending upon ambient temperature and the type unit being tested. The sight glass should be free of bubbles if a glass is used in the system. Low side pressures should read approximately 15 psi to 30 psi, again depending on the ambient temperature and the unit being tested. It is not feasible to give a definite reading for all types of systems used, as the type control and component installation used on a particular system will directly influence the pressure readings on the high and low sides, Fig. 1.

Evaporator Pressure Gauge Reading	Evaporator Temperature F°	High Pressure Gauge Reading	Ambient Temperature
0	-21°	45	20°
0.6	-20°	55	30°
2.4	-15°	72	40°
4.5	-10°	86	50°
6.8	- 5°	105	60°
9.2	0°	126	70°
11.8	5°	140	75°
14.7	10°	160	80°
17.1	15°	185	90°
21.1	20°	195	95°
22.5	22°	220	100°
23.9	24°	240	105°
25.4	26°	260	110°
26.9	28°	275	115°
28.5	30°	290	120°
37.0	40°	305	125°
46.7	50°	325	130°
57.7	60°		
70.1	70°		
84.1	80°		
99.6	90°		
116.9	100°		
136.0	110°		
157.1	120°		
179.0	130°		

Fig. 1   Pressure-temperature relationship. Conditions equivalent to 30 mph or 1750 engine RPM

Fig. 2   Manifold gauge set hose connections

The high side pressure will definitely be affected by the ambient or outside air temperature. A system that is operating normally will indicate a high side gauge reading between 150-170 psi with an 80°F ambient temperature. The same system will register 210-230 psi with an ambient temperature of 100°. No two systems will register exactly the same, therefore, allowance for variations in head pressures must be considered. Following are the most important normal readings likely to be encountered during the season.

Ambient Temp.	High Side Pressure
80	150-170
90	175-195
95	185-205
100	210-230
105	230-250
110	250-270

RELATIVE TEMPERATURE OF HIGH AND LOW SIDES

The high side of the system should be uniformly hot to the touch throughout. A difference in temperature will indicate a partial blockage of liquid or gas at this point.

The low side of the system should be uniformly cool to the touch with no excessive sweating of the suction line or low side service valve. Excessive sweating or frosting of the low side service valve usually indicates an expansion valve is allowing an excessive amount of refrigerant into the evaporator.

EVAPORATOR OUTPUT

At this point, provided all other inspection tests have been performed, and components have been found to operate as they should, a rapid cooling down of the interior of the vehicle should result. The use of a thermometer is not necessary to determine evaporator output. Bringing all units to the correct operating specifications will insure that the evaporator performs as intended.

DISCHARGING & EVACUATING SYSTEM

REFRIGERANT RECOVERY

The refrigerant system must be discharged using an air conditioning refrigerant recovery and recycling system J-38100-C. After completing any necessary repairs the refrigerant system can then be evacuated and charged using air conditioning service charging station J-23500-A or equivalent, or manifold gauge set J-23500-A or equivalent. Service fitting caps are color coded for easy reference. Red cap indicates high side port. Blue cap indicates low side port.

Failure to check for residual oil from previous recovery can result in adding extra oil to the current vehicle being serviced. This will result in reduced performance and possible compressor damage.

1. Start vehicle and run with the A/C On for two minutes, then attach manifold gauge set to the A/C system, **Fig. 2.** Attach recovery station inlet hose to center fitting of manifold gauge set.
2. Open both valves of manifold gauge set. Ensure refrigerant tank vapor valve and liquid valve are open.
3. Turn main power switch On.
4. Depress compressor start switch. The amber "Compressor On" light will come on and the compressor will start. The compressor will shutoff automatically when recovery is complete. Wait two minutes and check for pressure rise. If pressure rise occurs, depress compressor start switch to repeat recovery procedure.
5. To drain receiver dehydrator of A/C system oil, open receiver dehydrator pressurizing valve for 15 seconds to allow some compressor discharge pressure back into receiver dehydrator. Open oil drain valve slowly and drain receiver dehydrator. When oil stops draining, close oil drain valve. **Do not allow receiver dehydrator to completely depressurize.**

REFRIGERANT RECYCLING

1. Turn main power switch On.
2. Open both valves on recovery tank.
3. Turn "Recycle Start" switch On. The amber "Recycle On" light will come on and the refrigerant pump will start.
4. Refrigerant will be seen going through the "Moisture Indicator" at start up. If there is a sufficient supply of refrigerant, bubbles will clear after a few seconds. When bubbles clear from "Moisture Indicator," refrigerant pump is operating at maximum efficiency.

USING J 5420 ADAPTER

OPEN DURING EVACUATION AND CHARGING

THIS HI-PRESS. VALVE IS CLOSED & LINE DISCONNECTED DURING DISCHARGING & CHARGING

LOW-SIDE   HIGH-SIDE

VALVE   VALVE

ACCUMULATOR

VACUUM PUMP

J 23575-01 MANIFOLD GAUGE SET

THIS HIGH PRESSURE VALVE IS OPEN & VAC. PUMP LINE CONNECTED ONLY DURING EVACUATION

MULTI-CAN DISPENSING UNIT USING J 6271-01 SINGLE CAN OR J 6272-02 MULTI CAN OPENER-VALVE

30 LB. DRUM HAS OWN OPENER-VALVE

DECREASE OF WEIGHT ON SCALE INDICATES CHARGE ADDED

14 OZ. CANS

NOTICE: MAKE SURE OUTLET VALVE ON OPENER IS CLOSED (CLOCKWISE) BEFORE INSTALLING OPENER TO R-12 CONTAINER TO PREVENT LOSS OF REFRIGERANT.

OPEN AND INVERTED DURING CHARGING CLOSED DURING EVACUATION

USING J 23390 OPENER-VALVE FOR 12 LB. CAN

Fig. 3   Charging A/C system

5. Allow station to operate until dot in center of "Moisture Indicator" turns green. "Moisture Indicator Dot" should change to a shade indicated on the reference decal. Always run recycling system a minimum of 30 minutes. If "Moisture Indicator" starts out yellow, it could take as long as two hours to turn green, depending on moisture content of refrigerant.

6. Turn Off station when recycling is complete.

REFRIGERANT RECOVERY & RECYCLING OPERATING HINTS

1. When using recovery station in conjunction with a charging station, attach center port hose of manifold gauge set to inlet port of recovery station, then follow normal operating procedures for recovery/recycling station.

2. When using recovery station in conjunction with an automatic charging station, attach exhaust hose to inlet of recovery station. On automatic A/C service stations, a hole has been added at rear of cabinet for access to exhaust hose. On older type stations, open front doors of cabinet to reach exhaust hose.

3. After attaching exhaust hose to recovery station, depress main power switch on automatic charging station. Depress exhaust switch. Then follow normal operating procedures for recovery station.

4. Air is automatically vented from recovery tank during recycling. This feature eliminated the need to purge hoses before recovering refrigerant.

5. Operating engine with A/C Off during recovery may reduce recovery time.

6. To help prevent escape of refrigerant to the atmosphere, the recovery sta-

tion can be attached to a "Dial A Charge" cylinder top vent port when filling the cylinder.

7. Always check the recovery station for residual oil from previous recovery.

EVACUATE SYSTEM
With Vacuum Pump

Vacuum pumps suitable for removing air and moisture from A/C systems are commercially available. A specification for system pump-down used here is 28-29½ inches vacuum. This reading can be attained at or near sea level only. For each 1000 feet of altitude this operation is being performed, the reading will be 1 inch vacuum lower. As an example, at 5000 feet elevation, only 23-24½ inch of vacuum can be obtained. **The system must be completely discharged before it can be evacuated. Damage to vacuum pump may result if pressurized refrigerant is allowed to enter.**

1. With hand gauges connected into system, remove cap from vacuum hose connector. Install hand gauge manifold center hose to vacuum pump connector. Open low side gauge manifold hand valve only.

2. Ensure low side gauge is calibrated correctly. It should be reading zero. If not, adjust calibration.

3. Evacuate system with the vacuum pump until the low pressure gauge reads at least 28 inches of vacuum. Continue evacuating system for an additional 15 minutes for routine system servicing or 20 to 30 minutes, if any parts have been replaced.

4. When system evacuation is complete, close low side gauge manifold hand valve, then turn vacuum pump off.

5. Check ability of system to hold vacuum. Watch low side gauge to see that gauge does not rise at a faster rate than 1 inch vacuum every 4 to 5 minutes. If low side gauge rises at too rap-

id a rate, install partial charge and leak test. Evacuate system again.

6. If system holds vacuum, charge system with refrigerant.

Using Charging Station

A vacuum pump is built into the charging station and is constructed to withstand repeated and prolonged use without damage. Complete moisture removal from the system is possible only with a vacuum pump constructed for the purpose.

The system must be completely discharged before it can be evacuated. Damage to the vacuum pump may result if pressurized refrigerant is allowed to enter.

1. Connect hose to vacuum pump, if system was discharged through charging station.

2. Open low side gauge hand valve of charging station.

3. Connect station into 110 volt current.

4. Turn vacuum pump on according to instructions for specific station being used.

5. Evacuate system with the vacuum pump until the low pressure gauge reads at least 28 inches of vacuum. Continue evacuating system for an additional 15 minutes for routine system servicing or 20 to 30 minutes, if any parts have been replaced.

6. Close low side gauge hand valve, then turn vacuum pump off.

7. Check ability of system to hold vacuum. Watch low side gauge to see that gauge does not rise at a faster rate than 1 inch vacuum every 4 to 5 minutes. If low side gauge rises at too rapid a rate, install partial charge and leak test. Then evacuate system again.

8. If system holds vacuum, charge system with refrigerant.

CHARGING THE SYSTEM
USING CHARGING STATION J-23500-01

Use instructions provided with charging station with the following exceptions:

1. Do not connect high pressure line to A/C system.

2. Always keep high pressure valve closed on charging station.

3. Perform all evacuation and charging through accumulator low-side pressure service fitting.

Use of these procedures will prevent charging station from being accidentally exposed to high-side vehicle system pressure.

USING DISPOSABLE CANS OR REFRIGERANT DRUM

Never use these cans to charge into the high pressure side of the system (compressor discharge port) or into a system that is at high temperature, because the high system pressures could be transferred into the charging can causing it to explode.

If R-12 drum is used, place on scale and

note total weight before charging. During charging, watch scale to determine amount of R-12 used.

If 14 ounce R-12 cans are used, close tapping valve, then attach cans following instructions included with manifold adapter.

Charging Of System

1. Start and run engine until normal operating temperature is reached.and allow to warm up (choke off, normal idle). Set A/C control lever to OFF.
2. With R-12 drum or cans inverted, open R-12 supply valve and allow 1 lb. of liquid R-12 to flow into system through low-side service fitting on accumulator, **Fig. 3.**
3. **On all models except Cadillac w/display diagnosis,** when 1 lb. of

refrigerant has entered system, engage compressor by setting A/C lever to NORM and blower switch to HI to draw in remainder of charge.
4. **On Cadillac models w/display diagnosis,** when 1 lb. of refrigerant has entered system, engage compressor by setting climate control panel to AUTO and blower switch to HI to draw in remainder of charge. If system switches to ECON when AUTO is pressed, low refrigerant is indicated, and the compressor will not operate. To obtain compressor operation, clear diagnostic trouble codes and select AUTO again.
5. **On all models,** cooling condenser with a large fan will speed up charging procedure by maintaining condenser temperature below charging cylinder temperature.

6. Close refrigerant supply valve and run engine for 30 seconds to clear lines and gauges.
7. With engine running, remove charging low side hose adapter from accumulator service fitting. Unscrew rapidly to avoid excessive refrigerant loss. **Do not remove a gauge line from its adapter when line is connected to A/C system. To disconnect line, always remove line adapter from service fitting. Do not remove charging hose at gauge set while attached to accumulator, as system will be discharged due to depressed Schraeder valve.**
8. Replace protective cap on accumulator fitting and turn engine off.
9. Check system for leaks.
10. Start engine and check for proper system pressures.

Troubleshooting

INDEX

SYMPTOM DIAGNOSIS CHARTS

CLUTCH CYCLING ORIFICE TUBE SYSTEM

When diagnosing specific air conditioning system symptoms, refer to **Figs. 1 through 4.**

VARIABLE DISPLACEMENT ORIFICE TUBE SYSTEM

When diagnosing specific air conditioning system symptoms, refer to **Figs. 5 through 11.**

THERMAL EXPANSION VALVE SYSTEM

When diagnosing specific air conditioning system symptoms, refer to **Figs. 12 through 19.**

LEAK TESTS

Testing the refrigerant system for leaks is one of the most important phases of troubleshooting. One or more of the methods outlined will prove useful in detecting leaks or checking connections if service work is performed. Before beginning any leak test, attach a manifold gauge set and note pressure. If little or no pressure is indicated, a partial charge must be installed. Check all connections, compressor head

gasket, oil filler plug and compressor shaft seal for leaks.

ELECTRONIC LEAK DETECTORS

There are a number of electronic leak detectors available to perform leak tests. Current versions of the electronic leak detectors have three settings, one for R-12, one for R-134a and one for gross. The gross setting is for isolating very large leaks already found in one of the other two settings. Refer to operating instructions for the unit being used and observe these general procedures.
1. Move detector probe one inch per second in areas of suspected leaks.
2. Position probe below test point, as refrigerant gas is heavier than air.
3. Be sure to check service access gauge port valve fittings, particularly when valve caps are missing, as dirt accumulations can destroy the sealing area of valve core when manifold gauge set is attached. Replace missing valve caps after cleaning valve core area. **Valve caps should only be finger tightened. Using pliers to tighten valve caps may distort sealing surface of valve.**
4. Check for leaks in manifold gauge set and hoses, as well as the rest of the system.

FLAME-TYPE (HALIDE) LEAK DETECTORS

1. Adjust detector flame as low as possi-

ble to obtain maximum sensitivity. Be sure copper element is cherry red and not burned away. The flame will be almost colorless.
2. Slowly move detector along areas of suspected leaks. A slight leak will cause the flame to change to a bright yellow-green color. A significant leak will be indicated by a brilliant blue flame. Position flame under areas being tested as refrigerant gas is heavier than air. **The presence of dust in the pickup hose may cause a change in the color of the flame. If not recognized, a false diagnosis could be made. Store leak detector in a clean place and ensure hose is free of dust before leak testing.**
3. Check for leaks in the manifold gauge set and hoses, as well as the rest of the system.
4. Use a small fan to ventilate areas where the leak detector indicates refrigerant constantly. These areas are contaminated with refrigerant and must be ventilated before leak can be pinpointed.

FLUID LEAK DETECTORS

Apply leak detector solution around joints to be tested. A cluster of bubbles will form immediately if there is a leak. A white foam that forms after a short while will indicate an extremely small leak. In some confined areas such as sections of the evaporator and condenser, electronic leak detectors will be more useful.

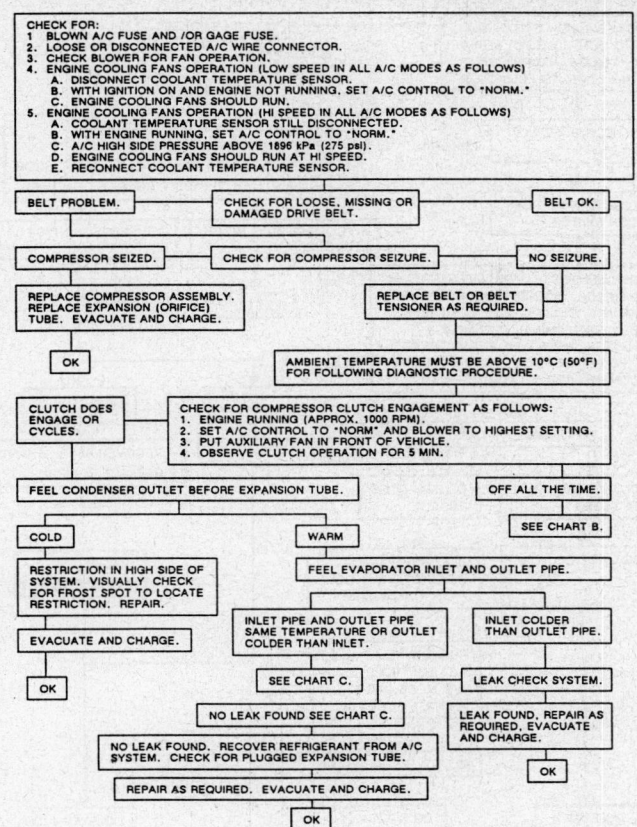

Fig. 1   Troubleshooting chart A. Clutch cycling orifice tube system

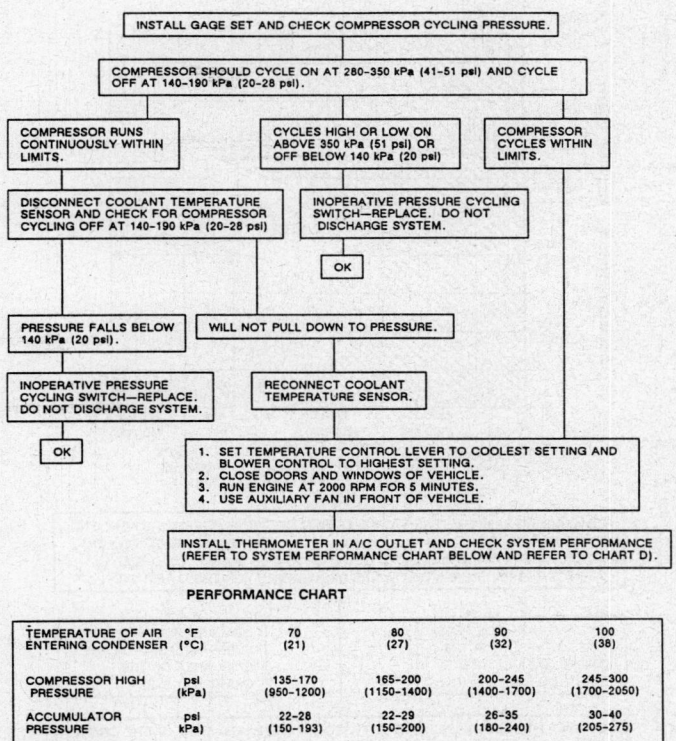

PERFORMANCE CHART

TEMPERATURE OF AIR ENTERING CONDENSER	°F (°C)	70 (21)	80 (27)	90 (32)	100 (38)
COMPRESSOR HIGH PRESSURE	psi (kPa)	135-170 (950-1200)	165-200 (1150-1400)	200-245 (1400-1700)	245-300 (1700-2050)
ACCUMULATOR PRESSURE	psi kPa	22-28 (150-193)	22-29 (150-200)	26-35 (180-240)	30-40 (205-275)
AVERAGE A/C AIR DISCHARGE	°F (°C)	36-43 (2.2-6.0)	36-43 (2.2-6.0)	36-43 (2.2-6.0)	42-48 (5.50-9.0)

Fig. 3   Troubleshooting chart C. Clutch cycling orifice tube system

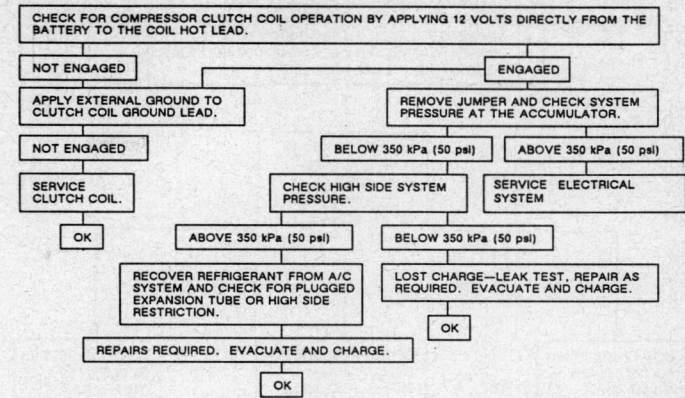

Fig. 2   Troubleshooting chart B. Clutch cycling orifice tube system

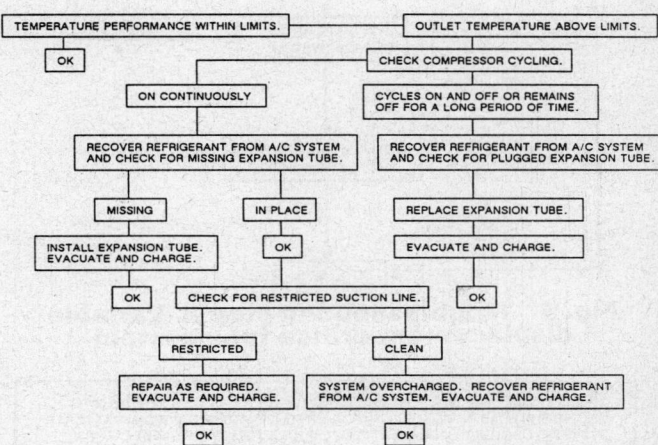

Fig. 4   Troubleshooting chart D. Clutch cycling orifice tube system

Diagnostic Procedures
For
Variable Displacement Orifice Tube (VDOT)
Systems

The procedures in the following charts will help you diagnose V5 compressor and VDOT refrigerant system problems causing insufficient cooling. They must be used in conjunction with other appropriate   manual information.

The V5 compressor is a variable displacement compressor which matches air conditioning demand by changing its stroke, instead of cycling its clutch. A control valve located in the rear head of the compressor senses compressor low side pressure and causes the compressor mechanism to change stroke. Because the V5 compressor always runs and the system does not cycle, these diagnostic procedures differ from those used for fixed displacement systems. By using these procedures, you will avoid needlessly replacing A/C components.

STEP 1--*Preliminary Checks*

Repair the following as necessary. If discharge air temperature with A/C on is normal after making the following repairs, the system is operating properly.

- A/C fuse
- A/C blower operation.
- Temperature door. Move temp. door lever rapidly from cold to hot. Listen for temp. door hitting at each end. Adjust as necessary. (Cable operated temp. door only.).
- Clutch coil and rear head switch(es) connections.
- Compressor belt. Adjust or replace if damaged or missing.
- Engine cooling fan operation.
- Condenser – Check for restricted air flow.

Fig. 5   Troubleshooting step 1. Variable displacement orifice tube system

Fig. 6 Troubleshooting step 2. Variable displacement orifice tube system

Fig. 7 Troubleshooting step 3. Variable displacement orifice tube system

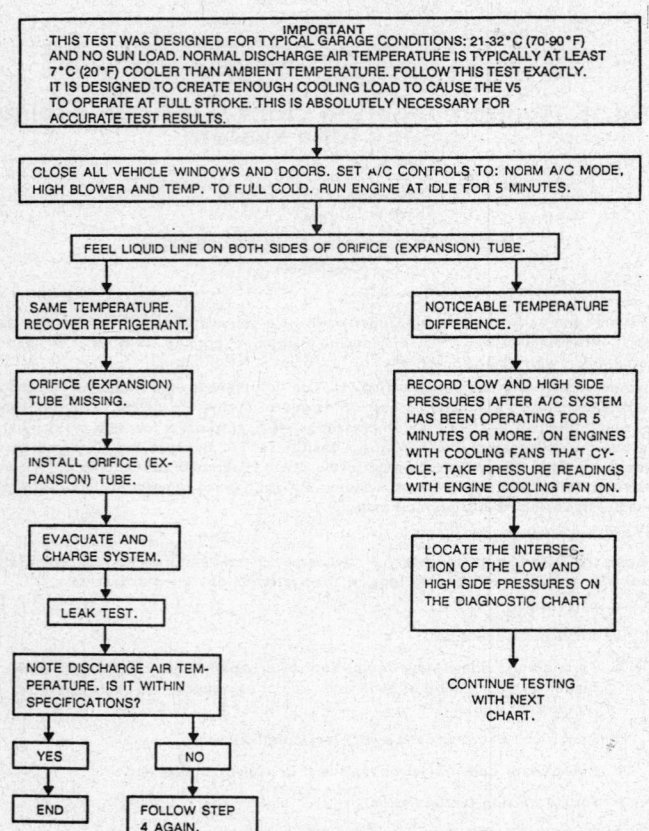

Fig. 8 Troubleshooting step 4 (Part 1 of 2). Variable displacement orifice tube system

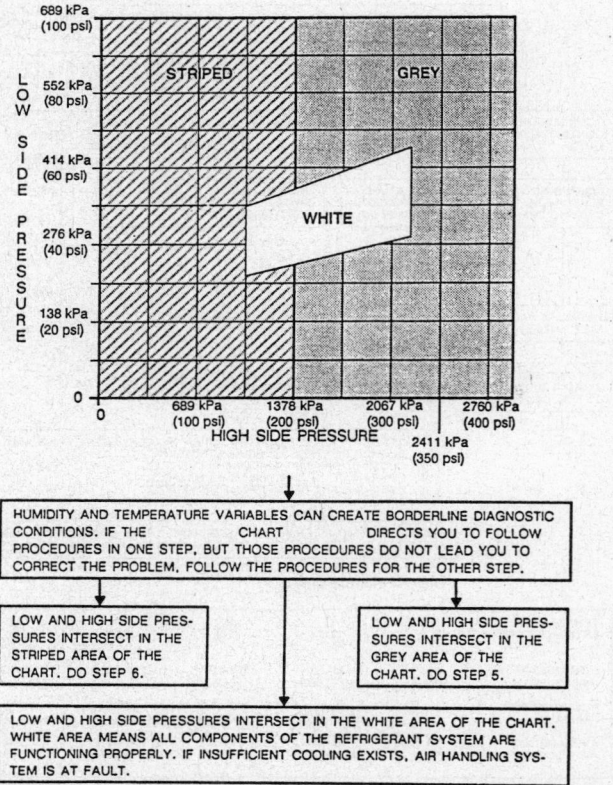

Fig. 8 Troubleshooting step 4 (Part 2 of 2). Variable displacement orifice tube system

Fig. 9 Troubleshooting step 5. Variable displacement orifice tube system

Fig. 10 Troubleshooting step 6. Variable displacement orifice tube system

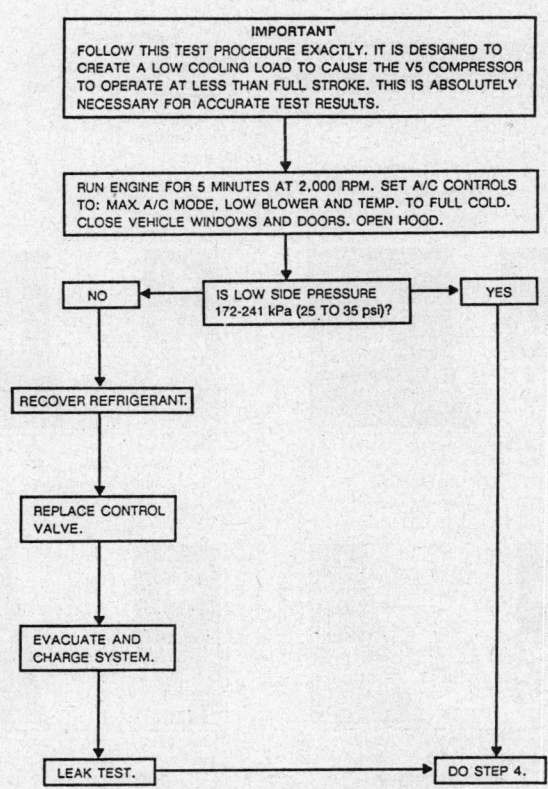

Fig. 11 Troubleshooting step 7. Variable displacement orifice tube system

V5/TXV SYSTEM DIAGNOSTICS

Diagnostic Flow Chart

This chart is the starting point for verifying and diagnosing all air conditioning and HVAC control related complaints. It represents the correct path to follow from a customer complaint or condition through delivery of the vehicle back to the customer.

Preliminary Checks

This step covers all physical and visual inspections of interior and underhood components. Many problems can be detected by a thorough inspection. Failure to perform this step could result in wasted time proceeding further down the flow chart.

Vehicle Set Up and Performance Test

To run an air conditioning performance test the vehicle must be set-up according to instructions. The instructions include manifold gauge set installation and controller settings. Improper vehicle set up will result in inaccurate pressure and temperature readings.

General and Specific System Condition Charts

These charts were developed in a wind tunnel by producing known system problems and recording pressures and temperatures at various ambient temperatures. The tests were then validated using the same vehicle set up in a service environment. To find your system problem, compare the performance test readings to the readings on the charts for your ambient temperature and humidity. When all pressure and temperature readings fall within the limits of a given chart, use that chart to repair the vehicle. There is some variance in readings between systems of different vehicles; however the target areas have been developed to accommodate these changes.

Compressor Control Test

This is designed to evaluate the compressor's ability to change displacement with varying heat loads.

Step 1 — *Preliminary Checks*

Repair the following as necessary. If discharge temperature with A/C on is normal after making the following repairs, the system is operating properly.

- A/C fuse
- A/C blower operation
- Temperature door. Move temperature door lever rapidly from cold to hot. Listen for temperature door hitting at each end. Adjust as necessary. (Cable operated door only)
- Clutch coil connection
- Transducer connection
- Compressor belt. Replace if damaged or missing
- Engine cooling fan operation (at idle, cooling fan must be on at any A/C mode) cooling fan must be operating in correct direction (drawing outside air through the condenser toward engine)
- Condenser — Check for restricted air flow
- Dealer technical bulletins for updates on A/C system

Fig. 12 Troubleshooting step 1. Thermal expansion valve system

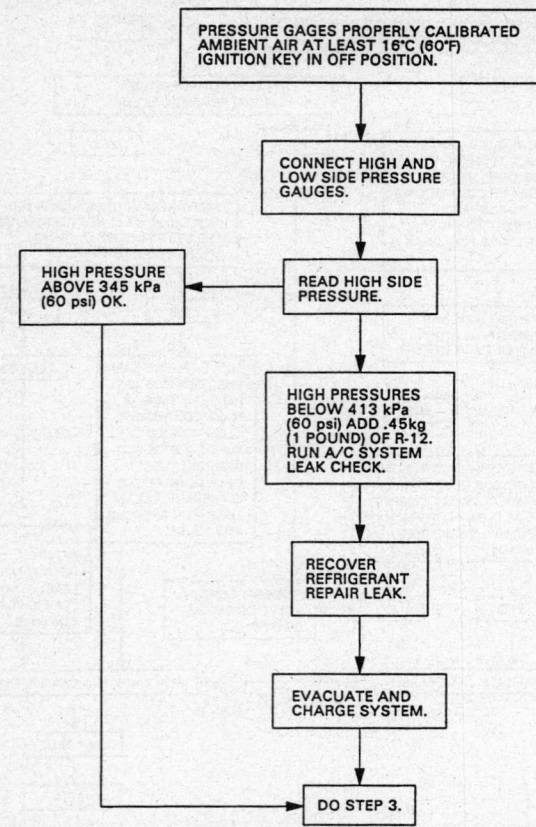

Fig. 13   Troubleshooting step 2. Thermal expansion valve system

Fig. 14   Troubleshooting step 3. Thermal expansion valve system

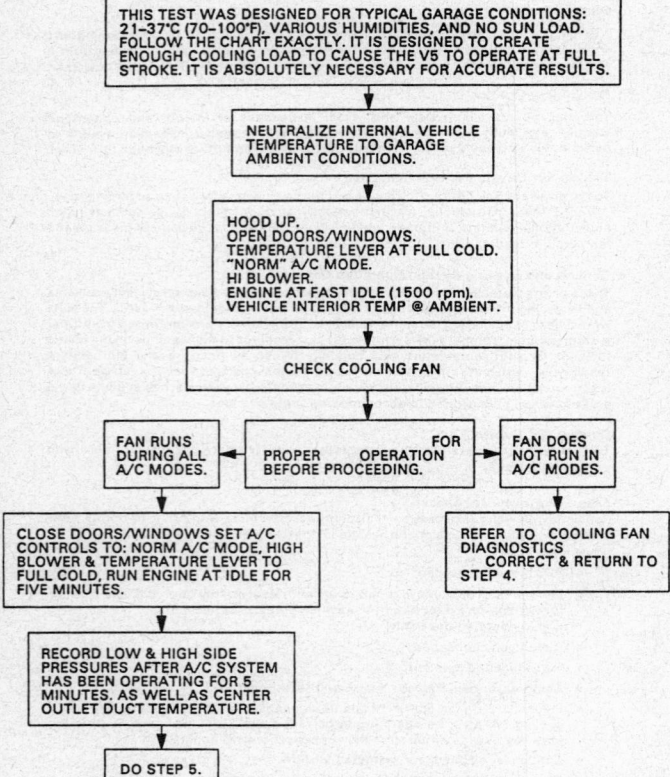

Fig. 15   Troubleshooting step 4. Thermal expansion valve system

Fig. 16   Troubleshooting step 5. Thermal expansion valve system

Step 6 — Diagnostic Code Procedures

Refer to appropriate diagnostic code chart for ambient garage conditions. NOTE: High humidity is above 60% relative. (Obtain humidity level from local radio weather report.)

A – NORMAL SYSTEM PERFORMANCE

AMBIENT TEMPERATURE – OUTLET TEMP RANGES:		ADDITIONAL INDICATORS
70 LOW HUMIDITY	45 – 50	SYSTEM WITHIN SPECS.
HI HUMIDITY	51 – 56	
80 LOW HUMIDITY	50 – 57	NOTE: IF LOW SIDE PRESSURE IS LESS THAN 172 kPa (25 psi), MAY INDICATE POSSIBLE CONTROL VALVE PROBLEM — GO TO STEP 8.
HI HUMIDITY	58 – 65	
90 LOW HUMIDITY	60 – 65	
HI HUMIDITY	66 – 70	
100 LOW HUMIDITY	67 – 75	
HI HUMIDITY	76 – 80	

B – LOW REFRIGERANT CHARGE

AMBIENT TEMPERATURE – OUTLET TEMP RANGES:		
70 LOW HUMIDITY	63 – 70	SYSTEM SLIGHTLY COOLER THAN AMBIENT DEPENDING UPON REMAINING CHARGE.
HI HUMIDITY	63 – 77	
80 LOW HUMIDITY	64 – 75	
HI HUMIDITY	74 – 81	
90 LOW HUMIDITY	75 – 85	CONFIRM BY TOUCHING COMPRESSOR SUCTION/DISCHARGE PIPE. SUCTION PIPE WILL BE COOL TO WARM & DISCHARGE WARM TO HOT. LEAK CHECK, RECOVER REPAIR & RECHARGE. REPEAT STEP 4.
HI HUMIDITY	81 – 88	
100 LOW HUMIDITY	85 – 102	
HI HUMIDITY	90 – 105	

C – REFRIGERANT OVERCHARGE OR RESTRICTED RECEIVER/DRYER	CONFIRM BY TOUCHING R/D INLET/ OUTLET IF TEMP DIFFERENCE R&R RD & RETURN TO STEP 4.
COMPLAINT WILL BE POOR OR INTERMEDIATE COOLING AT HIGH AMBIENTS (TRANSDUCER SHUTS SYSTEM DOWN BECAUSE OF EXCESSIVE HIGH SIDE SYSTEM PRESSURE)	CONFIRM BY TOUCHING COMPRESSOR SUCTION/DISCHARGE PIPE — IT WILL BE COOL & DISCHARGE PIPE WILL BE HOT.
D – TXV STUCK CLOSED OUTLET TEMPERATURE COOL TO WARM	CONFIRM BY THOROUGH PHYSICAL INSPECTION OF ALL LINES AND COMPONENTS. PRIOR TO FRONT OF DASH. IF INLET LINE IS COOL AT FOD CHECK FOR RESTRICTION ON HIGH SIDE. (NOTICEABLE WARM/COLD TEMPERATURE DIFFERENCE AT GIVEN POINT ON LIQUID LINE OR RD) IF NO RESTRICTION FOUND, CONFIRM BY LISTENING FOR 'HISS' ON NORM A/C, LOW BLOWER. VERIFY BY RUNNING ENGINE AT 2000 rpm; IF PRESSURES DO NOT CHANGE BY MORE THAN 20 psi AND OUTLET AIR DOESN'T FEEL COOL, REPLACE TXV.
E – TXV STUCK OPEN SYSTEM APPEARS TO PERFORM NORMALLY, BUT MAY GO WARM TEMPORARILY ON EXTENDED DRIVES AND RECORRECT ITSELF AFTER VEHICLE SHUT DOWN. MAY ALSO CAUSE COMPRESSOR "SLUGGING" — NOISE	RUN HI BLOWER, NORMAL A/C FAST IDLE FOR 2 MIN. ENGINE OFF FOR 3 MIN. RESTART ENGINE WITH A/C OFF. LET ENGINE RPM STABALIZE. ON LOW BLOWER RUN A/C AND LISTEN FOR SLUGGING. REPLACE TXV. HOOD SHOULD BE LOWERED FOR THIS PROCEDURE.
F – COMPRESSOR NO PUMP OUTLET TEMPERATURE IS AMBIENT	CONFIRM BY FOLLOWING STEP 7.

NOTE: IF NONE OF THE ABOVE CONDITIONS CAN BE VERIFIED, RECOVER, EVACUATE AND RECHARGE WITH PROPER CHARGE AND PREFORM STEP 4 AGAIN.

Fig. 17   Troubleshooting step 6. Thermal expansion valve system

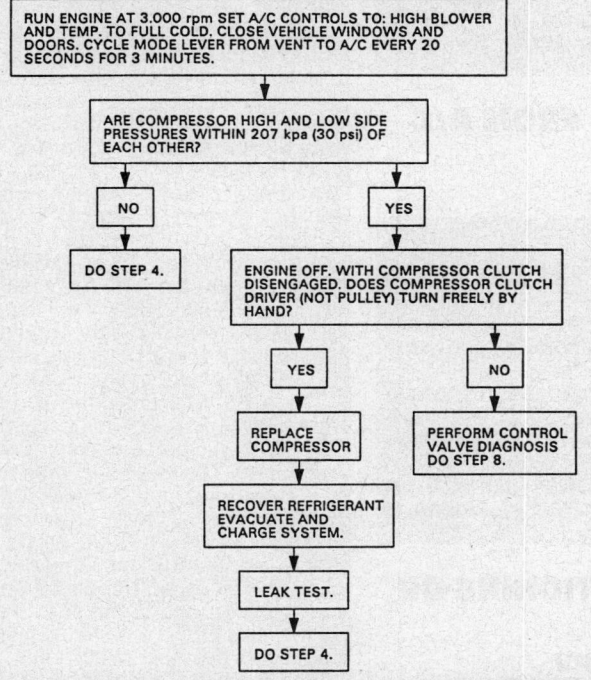

Fig. 18   Troubleshooting step 7. Thermal expansion valve system

NOTE: FAILED TXV CAN CAUSE INTERNAL COMPRESSOR FAILURE. AFTER REPLACING FAILED COMPRESSOR, PAY PARTICULAR ATTENTION TO TXV OPERATION. IF PROBLEM INDICATED, PERFORM APPROPRIATE REPAIR PROCEDURE.

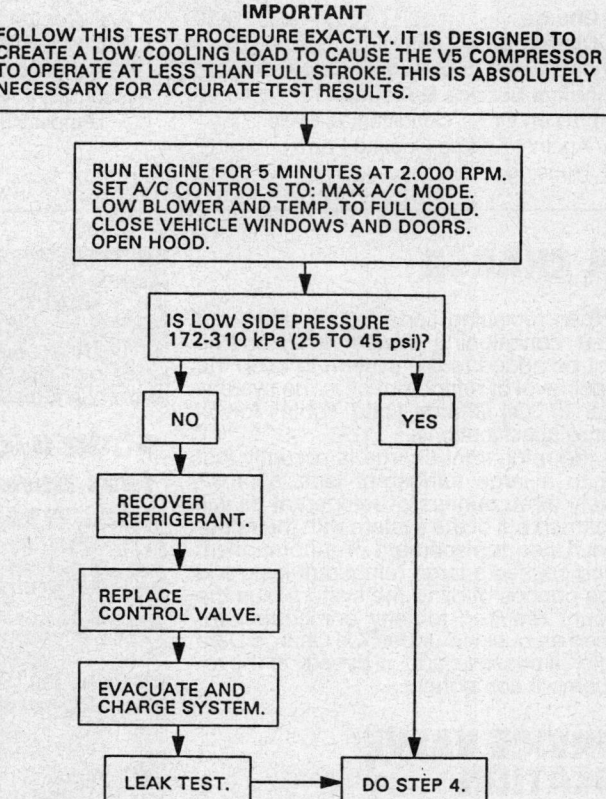

Fig. 19   Troubleshooting step 8. Thermal expansion valve system

FLUORESCENT LEAK DETECTORS

R-12 Refrigerant

To test for leaks with this method, add fluorescent leak detection additive J-36790 or equivalent to the refrigeration system following manufacturers instructions. Scan all accessible areas of refrigeration system with tester No. J-28428-D. The additive can remain in the refrigeration system as it is not harmful to system components.

R-134a Refrigerant

No fluorescent detection additive is currently approved by General Motors for use in R-134a systems.

System Service

INDEX

OIL CHARGE

When replacing certain components of an air conditioning system a oil charge must be added to the system to keep the proper level of refrigerant oil in the system. Refer to "Oil Charge Data Table" for oil charge specifications.

If the refrigerant charge is abruptly lost due to a large refrigerant leak, approximately three ounces of refrigerant oil will be carried out of the system with the refrigerant. Upon replacement of a component which caused a large refrigerant leak, add three ounces of oil to the system plus the amount required for any component replaced as outlined under "Oil Charge Data Table." If possible, add oil directly to the replacement component.

SERVICE VALVE LOCATION

The high pressure charging valve is located either on the high pressure line or the muffler, and the low pressure charging valve is located either on the accumulator or low pressure line.

TECHNICAL SERVICE BULLETINS

ABRASION OF AIR CONDITIONING HOSE AGAINST ENGINE COOLING FAN HOUSING
1991 Beretta & Corsica w/3.1L/V6-192 Engine

Some of these models have shown evidence of the air conditioning suction hose rubbing against the bottom brace of the engine cooling fan. If the plastic insulator that protects the hose is not in the proper position and the weight of the hose against the brace is heavy enough to damage the hose and could cause a refrigerant leak. The surface of the brace's edge is formed to produce a sharp 90° angle. This condition, in combination with the plastic insulation not being in proper position, may cause a cut in the hose.

To correct this condition, use a standard flat file to file both the leading and trailing edges of the brace to create a rounded edge. In addition, reposition the plastic insulator against the metal crimp connection on the hose. Secure both ends of the insulator to the air conditioner hose using common black electrical tape.

POOR A/C PERFORMANCE
1991 Beretta & Corsica

Some of these models may experience a condition of an inoperative engine cooling fan, which may result in engine overheating or poor air conditioning performance (if equipped). This condition may occur if engine cooling fan wiring leads have rubbed against the transaxle case in between the point of "breaking out" of the main engine harness and the connector at the fan.

To correct this condition, repair wiring and install a protective plastic conduit to insulate the wiring from direct contact on the transaxle case. **Refer to MOTOR'S WIRING DIAGRAM for proper wiring repair.**

WATER LEAKS FROM A/C MODULE
1991 Caprice

On some of these models, water may leak from the A/C module lower evaporator case when making right turns or rapid lane changes.
This condition is caused by inadequate sealing of the lower evaporator case to the air conditioning module.

To correct this problem, remove the lower evaporator case and reseal using silicone sealant (part No. RTV 1052915) and a foam filter (part No. 52453695). **Refer to MOTOR'S AIR CONDITIONING & HEATER MANUAL for replacement procedures.**

NO AIR CONDITIONING OR COOLING
1992 Lumina APV w/3800/V6-231 PFI Engine

Some of these models may experience no air conditioning or no cooling operation from the air conditioning system. This condition may be caused by the Engine Control Module (ECM) retaining a code 66. Code 66 is stored in the ECM to protect the compressor from engaging when the system is low on refrigerant. The ECM monitors the A/C request line for a switching voltage controlled by the pressure cycling switch. If voltage is present at the ECM for less than 1.5 seconds, ten consecutive times, code 66 will set and the ECM will not provide a ground for the A/C relay for the rest of the ignition cycle. If code 66 is set three times, the ECM will never engage the A/C relay until code 66 is cleared.

To correct this condition, check system for leakage and/or low refrigerant charge. Repair as necessary, then disconnect battery ground cable from battery to clear code 66 from ECM memory.

NO AIR CONDITIONING
1992 Lumina APV w/3800/V6-231 Engine

On vehicles that experience no air conditioning check for ECM code 66 first. Code 66 is stored in the ECM to protect compressor from engaging when the system is low on refrigerant. The ECM monitors A/C request line (circuit 67) for a switching voltage controlled by the pressure cycling switch. If voltage is present at ECM for less than 1.5 seconds, 10 successive times, code 66 will set and the ECM will not provide a ground for A/C relay (circuit 366) for the rest of the ignition cycle. If code 66 is set 3 times, the ECM will never engage the A/C relay until code 66 is cleared. A code 66 will not illuminate the service engine soon light and can only be cleared with a scan tool or by disconnecting battery power to the ECM.

Code 66 was designed to protect the compressor from damage by preventing its operation when the system was low on refrigerant. The ECM assumes the system is low on refrigerant if it sees the pressure cycling switch cycling more rapidly than normal, just like a system will do when it is low on refrigerant. Based on this rapid cycling, the ECM sets code 66 and will not provide a ground to the A/C clutch relay. CAMS and TECH 1 will also be unable to command the A/C clutch relay On when code 66 is set. Do not replace the ECM if it fails to ground the A/C clutch relay, make sure there is no Code 66 set first. The A/C compressor will start working when a new ECM is installed, as disconnecting the ECM clears the codes.

Fig. 1 Vacuum line installation

1. HOSE-OUTLET
2. CLAMP ASM
3. HOSE-ASM-INLET
4. VALVE, WATER HEATER
5. 3/32 RUBBER VACUUM HOSE
6. LUBRICANT, RUBBER (4 PLACES)
△ TORQUE CLAMPS TO 1.4-2.0 Nm (12-18 Lb-in)

Fig. 2 Vacuum line & antenna cable routing

Fig. 3 Tee coupling

1. TEE
2. SLEEVING, 3/32 RUBBER VACUUM HOSE
3. LUBRICANT, RUBBER (3 PLACES)

To correct this condition, follow normal diagnostic procedures for code 66. **Refer to MOTOR'S TRUCK ENGINE TUNE UP & ELECTRONICS MANUAL for diagnostic procedures.**

A/C CONTROL BUTTON STICKS
1991 Cutlass Supreme

On these models, the select buttons on the A/C control may stick when the control is twisted, trying to meet irregular instrument panel mounting surfaces.

To correct this problem, proceed as follows:
1. Remove instrument panel trim. **Refer to MOTOR'S AUTO REPAIR MANUAL for removal procedures.** Loosen control mounting screws. If control has three screws, move lower right screw to upper right.
2. Loosen control's mounting screws, then remove lower right screw. **Note that some 1990 models were built with only three mounting screws, none at the upper right.**
3. **Torque** mounting screws to 13 inch lbs. Tighten lower screws before upper and begin with right-hand side.
4. Install instrument panel trim.

A/C BLOWS WARM AIR AFTER VEHICLE IS PARKED 2–5 HOURS
1991 Ninety-Eight

Some of these models may experience a condition where the HVAC does not immediately control the temperature properly. This condition may be caused by programmers with software versions 01 through 06 that prohibit the outside temperature from updating until five hours have elapsed after the ignition switch is turned off. Vehicles with these software versions must be driven above 10 mph for the outside temperature to update. It may take up to ten minutes to fully update at 50 mph.

To correct this condition, install a new Programmer (part No. 16165978). This programmer has a new software version 07 and will allow a temperature update after the ignition switch has been turned off for 2½ hours.

INSUFFICIENT A/C COOLING AT HIGH TEMPERATURE
1991 Bravada

Some vehicles may experience insufficient cooling in high ambient temperatures.

To correct this condition, proceed as follows:
1. Install coolant shutoff valve as follows:
   a. Drain engine coolant.
   b. Cut heater both heater hoses 3½ inches from the cowl. If may be necessary to cut about 1 inch out of each hose to allow water heater valve to be inserted. The exact amount of hose will depend on hose routing for different engine configuration.
   c. Insert heater water valve, (part No. 14044414), in hoses and install hose clamps. **Torque** clamps to 12-18 inch lbs. If wiring for blower relay will interference with valve, add convoluted conduit to protect wires.
   d. Install plastic vacuum line on water valve fitting and add a 3/32 inch rubber sleeve for coupling, **Fig. 1.** Route vacuum line with antenna cable to grommet into dash area, **Fig. 2.**
   e. Punch a hole in grommet. Do not puncture antenna cable.
   f. Route vacuum line under dash to the glove box area, **Fig. 3.**
   g. Open glove box and remove rear panel, then remove insulator assembly under dash. Locate Max A/C line going to the plenum valve and air recirculation door valve. The line is black plastic with and orange stripe.
   h. Cut line and insert tee coupling (part No. 6272766). Use 3/32 inch rubber vacuum line for couplings, **Fig. 3.** Install added vacuum line to bottom leg of tee.
   i. Install under dash insulator and rear panel of glove box door.
   j. Refill cooling system.
   k. Install upper and lower insulators, part Nos. 1562121 and 15612120, on the A/C accumulator assembly. The insulator is designed for a

G-Van and must be modified for Bravada accumulator.

l. Install and tighten clamp (part No. 15530486) on overlapped portion of insulators.

m. Start engine and check for cooling system leaks.

n. Place climate control lever in Max A/C position. Ensure water valve is operating properly.

2. Install underbody shield as follows:

a. Raise and support vehicle.

b. Place shield (part No. 15564769) so that back edge rests on front crossmember and front outer edges rest on frame rails.

c. Align shield mounting holes with pre-drilled threaded holes on front crossmember and frame rails.

d. **Torque** mounting bolts to 8.5 ft. lbs.

e. Lower vehicle.

NO A/C COOLING
1991—92 BONNEVILLE

On these models, if a no A/C or no cooling condition exists, always check for a trouble code 66 first. Trouble code 66 is stored in the ECM to protect the compressor from engaging when the system is low on refrigerant. The ECM monitors the A/C request line (ckt 67) for a switching voltage controlled by the pressure cycling switch. If voltage is present at the ECM for less than 1.5 seconds, 10 successive times, trouble code 66 will set and the ECM will not provide a ground for the A/C relay for the rest of the ignition cycle.

If trouble code 66 is set three times, the ECM will never engage the A/C relay until the code is cleared from memory. Code 66 will not illuminate the service engine soon lamp and can only be detected with a scan tool or by disconnecting battery power to the ECM.

Trouble code 66 was designed to protect the compressor from damage by preventing its operation when the system was low on refrigerant. The ECM assumes the system is low on refrigerant if it sees the pressure cycling switch cycling more rapidly than normal, just like a system will do when it is low on refrigerant. Based on this rapid cycling, the ECM sets code 66 and will not provide a ground to the A/C clutch relay.

CAMS and TECH1 scan tools will also be unable to command the A/C clutch relay On when code 66 is stored. Do not replace the ECM if it fails to ground the A/C clutch relay. Ensure code 66 is not set first. The A/C compressor will start working when a new ECM is installed, as disconnecting the ECM clears all codes. However, the malfunction has not been found.

OIL CHARGE DATA TABLE

Model	Year	Compressor Model	Compressor	Evaporator	Condenser	Accumulator	Receiver
	Application		**Oil Charge (Fl. Oz.) When replacing component**				
BUICK							
Century	1991-93	⑨	③	3	1	3.5	—
LeSabre	1991-93	HR-6②	③	3	1	3.5	—
Park Avenue	1991-93	HR-6②	③	3	1	3.5	—
Reatta	1991	HR-6②	③	3	1	3.5	—
Regal	1991-93	⑬	③	3	1	3.5	—
Riviera	1991-93	HR-6②	③	3	1	3.5	—
Roadmaster	1991-93	R-4②	③	3	1	3.5	—
Skylark	1991-93	V-5①	③	3	1	3.5	—
CADILLAC							
Brougham	1991-92	HR100T/HR110T②	⑪	3	1	⑤	—
DeVille	1991-93	HR-6HE②	③	3	1	3.5	—
Eldorado	1991-93	HR-6HE②	③	3	1	3.5	—
Fleetwood	1991-93	HR-6HE②	③	3	1	3.5	—
Seville	1991-93	HR-6HE②	③	3	1	3.5	—
CHEVROLET							
Beretta	1991	V-5①	④	2	1	⑤	—
	1992-93	V-5①	③	2	1	—	3.5
Camaro	1991-92	R-4②	③	3	1	3.5	—
	1993	HR-6HE②	③	3	1	3.5	—
Caprice	1991-92	R-4②	③	3	1	3.5	—
	1993	HR100T/HR110T②	3	1	3.5	—	
Cavalier	1991-93	V-5①	③	3	1	3.5	—
Corsica	1991	V-5①	④	2	1	⑤	—
	1992-93	V-5①	③	2	1	—	3.5
Corvette	1991-93	10PA20②	⑥	3	1	3.5	—
	1991-93	10PA17⑭②	⑥	3	1	3.5	—
Lumina	1991-93	V-5①	③	3	1	3.5	—
GEO							
Metro	1991-93	⑮	⑧	.7-1.0	.7-1.0	—	.4
Prizm	1991	—	⑫	1.4–1.7	1.4–1.7	—	.7
	1992-93	—	③	3	⑦	—	3.5
Storm	1991	KC-50	—	1.7	1	—	1
	1992-93	KC-50	⑩	1.7	1	—	1
OLDSMOBILE							
Achieva	1992-93	V-5①	③	3	1	—	3.5
Custom Cruiser	1991-93	R-4②	③	3	1	3.5	—
Cutlass Calais	1991	V-5①	③	3	1	3.5	—
Cutlass Ciera	1991-92	⑨	③	3	1	3.5	—
	1993	⑯	③	3	1	3.5	—
Cutlass Cruiser	1991-92	⑨	③	3	1	3.5	—
	1993	⑯	③	3	1	3.5	—
Cutlass Supreme	1991-93	V-5①	③	3	1	3.5	—
Toronado	1991-92	HR-6②	③	3	1	3.5	—
Trofeo	1991-92	HR-6②	③	3	1	3.5	—
88	1991-93	HR-6②	③	3	1	3.5	—
98	1991-93	HR-6②	③	3	1	3.5	—

Continued

OIL CHARGE DATA TABLE-Continued

	Application		Oil Charge (Fl. Oz.) When replacing component				
Model	Year	Compressor Model	Compressor	Evaporator	Condenser	Accumulator	Receiver
PONTIAC							
Bonneville	1991-93	HR-6②	③	3	1	3.5	—
Firebird	1991-92	R-4②	③	3	1	3.5	—
	1993	HR100T/HR110T③	③	3	1	3.5	—
Grand Am	1991-93	V-5①	③	3	1	3.5	—
Grand Prix	1991-93	V-5①	③	3	1	3.5	—
LeMans	1991-93	V-5①	③	3	1	3.5	—
Sunbird	1991-93	V-5①	③	3	1	3.5	—
6000	1991	V-5①	③	3	1	3.5	—

① —Variable displacement compressor.
② —Fixed displacement compressor.
③ —Drain oil from old compressor and measure, then drain new compressor. If more than one ounce is drained from old compressor, add same amount to new compressor. If less than one ounce is drained from compressor, add two ounces.
④ —Drain oil from old compressor and measure, then drain new compressor. Add same amount of oil to new compressor as drained from old compressor.
⑤ —Drain oil from accumulator and measure. Add same amount of oil to new accumulator, plus two ounces. If no oil is drained, add two ounces to new accumulator.
⑥ —Drain oil from old compressor and measure, then drain new compressor. Add same amount to new compressor as drained from old compressor, plus one ounce.
⑦ —Drain oil from old condenser and measure. If more than .5 ounce is drained from old condenser, add same amount to new condenser. If less than .5 ounce is drained from condenser, add .5 ounce.
⑧ —Replacement compressors contain 2.7 ounces. Drain 1.4 ounces from new compressor before installing.
⑨ —2.5L engine is equipped with V-5 compressors. 3.3L engine is equipped with HR-6 compressor.
⑩ —Replacement compressors contain 5.1 ounces. Drain 2.4 ounces from new compressor before installing.
⑪ —Drain oil from old compressor and measure, then drain new compressor. Amount drained from old compressor should not be more than five ounces. Add same amount of oil to new compressor as drained from old compressor, plus enough extra oil to equal a total of six ounces.
⑫ —Drain oil from old compressor and measure, then drain new compressor. Add same amount of oil to new compressor as drained from old compressor, plus .7 ounce.
⑬ —3.1L engine is equipped with V-5 compressor. 3.8L engine is equipped with HR-6 compressor.
⑭ —ZR-1 engine.
⑮ —Nippondenso 10 cylinder compressor.
⑯ —2.2L engine is equipped with V-5 compressors. 3.3L engine is equipped with HR-6 compressor.

A/C Data Table

				Refrigeration Oil		Compressor Clutch Air Gap Inch
Model	Year	Refrigerant Capacity, Lbs.	Viscosity	Total System Capacity, Ounces	Compressor Oil Level	
BUICK						
Century	1991	2.75	525	8	①	.020-.030
	1992	2.40	525	8	①	.020-.030
	1993	2.375	525	9	①	.020-.030
LeSabre	1991	2.87	525	8	①	.020-.030
	1992-93	2.42	525	8	①	.020-.030
Park Avenue	1991	2.87	525	8	①	.015-.025
	1992	2.42	525	8	①	.020-.030
Reatta	1991	2.40	525	8	①	.020-.030
Regal	1991-92	②	525	8	①	.020-.030
	1993	②	525	9	①	.020-.030
Riviera	1991-93	2.40	525	8	①	.020-.030
Roadmaster	1991	3.12	525	8	①	.020-.040
	1992	3.12	525	8	①	.020-.030
	1993	3.125	525	6	①	.020-.030
Skylark	1991	2.25	525	8	①	.015-.025
	1992-93	2.65	525	8	①	.020-.030

A/C DATA TABLE–Continued

| Model | Year | Refrigerant Capacity, Lbs. | Refrigeration Oil | | | Compressor Clutch Air Gap Inch |
			Viscosity	Total System Capacity, Ounces	Compressor Oil Level	
CADILLAC						
Brougham	1991-92	3.30	525	8	①	.020-.030
	1993	3.30	525	6	①	.020-.030
Deville	1991-93	2.42	525	8	①	.020-.030
Eldorado	1991-93	2.40	525	8	①	.020-.030
Fleetwood	1991-92	2.42	525	8	①	.020-.030
Seville	1991-93	2.40	525	8	①	.020-.030
CHEVROLET						
Beretta	1991	2.25	525	8	①	.015-.025
	1992-93	2.63	525	8	①	.020-.030
Camaro	1991	2.25	525	6	①	.020-.040
	1992-93	3.12	525	6	①	.020-.030
Caprice	1991	3.12	525	6	①	.020-.040
	1992-93	3.12	525	6	①	.020-.030
Cavalier	1991	2.25	525	8	①	.015-.025
	1992-93	2.25	525	8	①	.020-.030
Corsica	1991	2.25	525	8	①	.015-.025
	1992-93	2.63	525	8	①	.020-.030
Corvette	1991-93	2.25	500	8	①	.014-.026
Lumina	1991	2.25	525	8	①	.015-.025
	1992-93	2.25	525	9	①	.020-.030
GEO						
Metro	1991-93	1.10	525	2.7	①	.016-.028
Prizm	1991	1.4-1.7	—	—	①	.014-.026
	1992-93	1.4-1.7	525	6	①	.014-.026
Storm	1991	1.3-1.7	—	6.7	①	.010-.020
	1992-93	1.2-1.4	—	5.1	①	.010-.020
OLDSMOBILE						
Achieva	1992-93	2.65	525	8	①	.020-.030
Custom Cruiser	1991	3.10	525	6	①	.020-.040
	1992-93	3.12	525	6	①	.020-.030
Cutlass Calais	1991	2.25	525	8	①	.015-.025
Cutlass Ciera	1991	2.75	525	8	①	.020-.030
	1992	2.40	525	8	①	.020-.030
	1993	2.40	525	9	①	.020-.030
Cutlass Cruiser	1991	2.75	525	8	①	.020-.030
	1992	2.40	525	8	①	.020-.030
	1993	2.40	525	9	①	.020-.030
Cutlass Supreme	1991	2.25	525	8	①	.015-.025
	1992	2.25	525	9	①	.020-.030
Toronado	1991-92	2.40	525	8	①	.020-.030
Trofeo	1991-92	2.40	525	8	①	.020-.030
88	1991-93	2.42	525	8	①	.020-.030
98	1991-93	2.42	525	8	①	.020-.030
PONTIAC						
Bonneville	1991-93	2.42	525	8	①	.020-.030
Firebird	1991-93	3.12	525	6	①	.020-.030
Grand Am	1991	2.25	525	8	①	.015-.025
	1992-93	2.65	525	8	①	.020-.030

A/C DATA TABLE–Continued

| Model | Year | Refrigerant Capacity, Lbs. | Refrigeration Oil | | | Compressor Clutch Air Gap Inch |
			Viscosity	Total System Capacity, Ounces	Compressor Oil Level	
PONTIAC-Continued						
Grand Prix	1991	2.25	525	8	①	.015-.025
	1992-93	2.25	525	9	①	.020-.030
LeMans	1991	2.20	525	8	①	.015-.025
	1992-93	2.20	525	8	①	.020-.030
Sunbird	1991	2.25	525	8	①	.015-.025
	1992-93	2.25	525	8	①	.020-.030
6000	1991	2.40	525	8	①	.015-.025

① —Note that "Oil Level" cannot be checked. Refer to total capacity in ounces.

② —Models less 3800 engine, 2.25 lbs.; models with 3800 engine, 2.75 lbs.

COOLING FANS
TABLE OF CONTENTS

Variable Speed Fans
INDEX

Fig. 1   Typical variable-speed fan installed

Fig. 2   Variable-speed fan w/flat bi-metal thermostatic spring

Fig. 3   Variable-speed fan w/coiled bi-metal thermostatic spring

DESCRIPTION

The fan drive clutch, **Fig. 1,** is a fluid coupling containing silicone oil. Fan speed is regulated by the torque-carrying capacity of the silicone oil. The more silicone oil in the coupling the greater the fan speed, and the less silicone oil the slower the fan speed.

Two types of fan drive clutches are in use. On one, **Fig. 2,** a bi-metallic strip and control piston on the front of the fluid coupling regulates the amount of silicone oil entering the coupling. The bi-metallic strip bows outward with an increase in surrounding temperature and allows a piston to move outward. The piston opens a valve regulating the flow of silicone oil into the coupling from a reserve chamber. The silicone oil is returned to the reserve chamber through a bleed hole when the valve is closed.

On the other type of fan drive clutch, **Fig. 3,** a heat-sensitive, bi-metal spring connected to an opening plate brings about a similar result. Both units cause the fan speed to increase with a rise in temperature and to decrease as the temperature goes down.

In some cases a Flex-Fan is used instead of a Fan Drive Clutch. Flexible blades vary the volume of air being drawn through the radiator, automatically increasing the pitch at low engine speeds.

FAN DRIVE CLUTCH TEST

Do not operate the engine until the fan has been first checked for possible cracks and separations.

Run the engine at a fast idle speed (1000 RPM) until normal operating temperature is reached. This process can be speeded up by blocking off the front of the radiator with cardboard. Regardless of temperatures, the unit must be operated for at least five minutes immediately before being tested.

Stop the engine and, using a glove or a cloth to protect the hand, immediately check the effort required to turn the fan. If considerable effort is required, it can be assumed that the coupling is operating satisfactorily. If very little effort is required to turn the fan, it is an indication that the coupling is not operating properly and should be replaced.

If the clutch fan is the coiled bi-metal spring type, it may be tested while the vehicle is being driven. To check, disconnect the bi-metal spring, **Fig. 4**, and rotate 90° counterclockwise. This disables the temperature-controlled free-wheeling feature and the clutch performs like a conventional fan. If this cures the overheating condition, replace the clutch fan.

SERVICE PROCEDURE

To prevent silicone fluid from draining into fan drive bearing, do not store or place drive unit on bench with rear of shaft pointing downward.

Fig. 4   Disconnecting bi-metal spring

The removal procedure for either type of fan clutch assembly is generally the same for all cars. Merely unfasten the unit from the water pump and remove the assembly from the car.

The type of unit shown in **Fig. 2** may be partially disassembled for inspection and cleaning. Take off the capscrews that hold the assembly together and separate the fan from the drive clutch. Next remove the metal strip on the front by pushing one end of it toward the fan clutch body so it clears the retaining bracket. Then push the strip to the side so that its opposite end will spring out of place. Now remove the small control piston underneath it.

Check the piston for free movement of the coupling device. If the piston sticks, clean it with emery cloth. If the bi-metal strip is damaged, replace the entire unit. These strips are not interchangeable.

When reassembling, install the control piston so that the projection on the end of it will contact the metal strip. Then install the metal strip. After reassembly, clean the clutch drive with a cloth soaked in solvent. Avoid dipping the clutch assembly in any type of liquid. Install the assembly in the reverse order of removal.

The coil spring type of fan clutch cannot be disassembled, serviced or repaired. If it does not function properly it must be replaced with a new unit.

Electric Cooling Fans

NOTE: Wire Code Identification And Symbol Identification Located In The Front Of This Manual Can Be Used As An Aid When Using Wiring Circuits Found In This Section.

INDEX

Continued
VARIABLE SPEED FANS

INDEX-Continued

Continued

PRECAUTIONS

AIRBAG SYSTEM DISARMING

1991 Park Avenue

When carrying a live inflator module, ensure bag and trim cover are pointed away from you. Never carry inflator module by the wires or connector on underside of module.

The diagnostic energy reserve module (DERM) can maintain voltage to cause a system deployment for up to ten minutes after the ignition switch is turned off and the battery is disconnected. Servicing the SIR system during this period may result in accidental deployment and personal injury.

1. Turn ignition switch to OFF position, then disconnect and tape battery ground cable terminal.
2. Remove Connector Position Assurance (CPA), then disconnect yellow two-way SIR electrical connector at base of steering column.
3. Remove screws and/or nuts from back of steering wheel, then the inflator module from steering wheel.
4. Remove Connector Position Assurance (CPA), then disconnect coil assembly connector and horn lead.
5. Place inflator module on a bench or other surface with bag and trim cover facing Up.

1991 88 & 98

The diagnostic energy reserve module (DERM) can maintain voltage to cause a system deployment for up to ten minutes after the ignition switch is turned off and the battery is disconnected. Servicing the SIR system during this period may result in accidental deployment and personal injury.

1. Turn ignition switch to OFF position, then remove I/P fuse 7 from fuse block.
2. Disconnect yellow two-way SIR electrical connector at base of steering column.

Beretta, Bonneville w/Single Airbag, Camaro, Corsica, Corvette, DeVille, Eldorado, Firebird, Fleetwood (FWD), Fleetwood (RWD), LeSabre, Reatta, Riviera, Seville & Toronado/Trofeo & 1992–93 Park Avenue, 88 & 98

The diagnostic energy reserve module (DERM) can maintain voltage to cause a system deployment for up to ten minutes after the ignition switch is turned off and the battery is disconnected. Servicing the SIR system during this period may result in accidental deployment and personal injury.

1. Ensure front wheels are pointed straight ahead.
2. Turn ignition switch to LOCK position and remove SIR or AIRBAG fuse.
3. Remove left sound insulator. **Remove courtesy lamp from sound insulator, if necessary.**
4. Remove Connector Position Assurance (CPA), then disconnect yellow two-way SIR electrical connector at base of steering column.

Bonneville w/Dual Airbags

The diagnostic energy reserve module (DERM) can maintain voltage to cause a system deployment for up to ten minutes after the ignition switch is turned off and the battery is disconnected. Servicing the SIR system during this period may result in accidental deployment and personal injury.

1. Ensure front wheels are pointed straight ahead.
2. Turn ignition switch to OFF position and remove SIR fuse from fuse panel.
3. Remove left and right sound insulators.
4. Remove Connector Position Assurance (CPA), then disconnect yellow two-way SIR electrical connector at base of steering column.
5. Remove Connector Position Assurance (CPA), then disconnect yellow two-way passenger inflator module connector at base of right side instrument panel, clipped to knee bolster.

Metro

The diagnostic energy reserve module (DERM) can maintain voltage to cause a system deployment for up to ten minutes after the ignition switch is turned off and the battery is disconnected. Servicing the SIR system during this period may result in accidental deployment and personal injury.

1. **On 1992-93 models,** place steering wheel so that wheels are pointing straight ahead, then turn ignition switch to LOCK position.
2. **On 1991 models,** turn ignition switch to OFF position.
3. **On all models,** remove SIR IG fuse from SIR fuse block.
4. Remove rear plastic access cover from inflator module housing.
5. Remove Connector Position Assurance (CPA), then disconnect yellow two-way SIR electrical connector inside inflator module housing.

1991 Storm

The diagnostic energy reserve module (DERM) can maintain voltage to cause a system deployment for up to ten minutes after the ignition switch is turned off and the battery is disconnected. Servicing the SIR system during this period may result in accidental deployment and personal injury.

1. Turn ignition switch to OFF position, then disconnect battery ground cable.
2. Remove fuses C-22 and C-23 from fuse box, then disconnect orange three-way connector at the base of the steering column.

1992–93 Storm

The diagnostic energy reserve module (DERM) can maintain voltage to cause a system deployment for up to ten minutes after the ignition switch is turned off and the battery is disconnected. Servicing the SIR system during this period may result in accidental deployment and personal injury.

1. Place steering wheel so that wheels are pointing straight ahead, then turn ignition switch to LOCK position.
2. Remove fuses C-22 and C-23 from fuse block.
3. Remove switch bezel from instrument panel, then disconnect electrical connector from switches.
4. Remove cigar lighter bezel from instrument panel, then disconnect cigar lighter electrical connectors.
5. Remove two screws and hood latch release handle from knee bolster, then the three screws, three bolts and two nuts retaining the knee bolster.
6. Disconnect lap cooler air duct from knee bolster, then remove knee bolster from vehicle.
7. Remove Connector Position Assurance (CPA), then disconnect orange three-way connector at the base of the steering column.

1993 Prizm

1. Ensure front wheels are pointed straight ahead, then turn ignition switch to LOCK position.
2. Remove IGN and CIG & RADIO fuse from junction block No. 1.

3. Remove Connector Position Assurance (CPA) and disconnect lower steering column (yellow two-cavity) connector at base of steering column.

AIRBAG SYSTEM ARMING

1991 Park Avenue

1. Turn ignition switch to OFF position, connect horn lead and coil assembly connector, then install Connector Position Assurance (CPA).
2. Install inflator module and secure to steering wheel using new screws and/or nuts.
3. **Torque** screws and/or nuts to 25 inch lbs.
4. Connect yellow two-way SIR electrical connector at base of steering column, then install Connector Position Assurance (CPA).
5. Install left sound insulator, then the SIR fuse into fuse block.
6. Turn ignition switch to RUN position and ensure that "Inflatable Restraint" indicator flashes 7 to 9 times, then turns off.

1991 88 & 98

1. Connect yellow two-way SIR electrical connector at base of steering column.
2. Install I/P fuse 7 into fuse block, turn ignition switch to RUN position and ensure that "Inflatable Restraint" indicator flashes 7 to 9 times, then turns off.

Beretta, Bonneville w/Single Airbag, Camaro, Corsica, Corvette, DeVille, Eldorado, Firebird, Fleetwood (FWD), Fleetwood (RWD), LeSabre, Reatta, Riviera, Seville, Toronado, Trofeo & 1992–93 Park Avenue, 88 & 98

1. Connect yellow two-way SIR electrical connector, then install Connector Position Assurance (CPA).
2. Install left sound insulator. **Install courtesy lamp to sound insulator, if applicable.**
3. Install SIR fuse to fuse block, turn ignition switch to RUN position and ensure that "Inflatable Restraint" lamp flashes 7 to 9 times, then turns off.

Bonneville w/Dual Airbags

1. Connect yellow two-way passenger inflator module connector at base of right side instrument panel, clipped to knee bolster, then install Connector Position Assurance (CPA).
2. Connect yellow two-way SIR electrical connector at base of steering column, then install Connector Position Assurance (CPA).
3. Install left and right sound insulators, then the SIR fuse into fuse panel.
4. Turn ignition switch to RUN position and ensure that "Inflatable Restraint" lamp flashes 7 to 9 times, then turns off.

Metro

1. Turn ignition switch to LOCK position.
2. Connect yellow two-way SIR electrical connector inside inflator module housing, then install Connector Position Assurance (CPA).
3. Install SIR IG fuse into SIR fuse block, then the rear plastic access cover onto inflator module housing.
4. Turn ignition switch to RUN position and ensure that "Inflatable Restraint" lamp flashes 7 to 9 times and then turns off.

1991 Storm

1. Turn ignition switch to OFF position, then connect orange three-way connector at the base of the steering column.
2. Install fuses C-22 and C-23 into fuse box, then connect battery ground cable.

1992–93 Storm

1. Turn ignition switch to OFF position, then connect orange three-way connector at the base of the steering column.
2. Connect lap cooler air duct to knee bolster, then install knee bolster.
3. **Torque** knee bolster bolts and nuts to 89 inch lbs.
4. Install hood latch release handle to knee bolster.
5. Connect cigar lighter electrical connector, then snap cigar lighter bezel into place on instrument panel.
6. Connect switch bezel electrical connectors, then snap switch bezel into place on instrument panel.

1993 Prizm

1. Turn ignition switch to LOCK position.
2. Connect lower steering column yellow two-cavity connector.
3. Install IGN and CIG & RADIO fuses.
4. Turn ignition switch to ACC or ON positions and verify that the airbag indicator illuminates steady for approximately six seconds and then turns off.

METRO
DESCRIPTION
Radiator Fan

When ignition switch is in On position, system voltage is applied through ignition fuse to radiator fan switch. Fan switch closes when engine coolant temperature reaches 208°F. With fan switch closed, voltage is applied to radiator fan motor. Since fan motor is permanently grounded, fan operates as soon as voltage is applied. When temperature falls below 199°F, fan switch opens and voltage to fan motor is interrupted.

A/C Condenser Fan

When ignition switch is in On position, system voltage is applied to dual pressure switch through heater fuse on vehicles equipped w/automatic transaxle, or ignition fuse on vehicles equipped w/manual

Fig. 1   Coolant fan wiring circuit (engine cooling fan). 1991 Metro

transaxle. Dual pressure switch remains closed as long as refrigerant pressure is between 30-383 psi. With dual pressure switch closed, voltage is applied to A/C clutch relay. A/C clutch relay is energized when A/C amplifier grounds coil of relay. With A/C clutch relay energized, voltage is applied through A/C fuse and closed contacts of A/C clutch relay to coil of A/C condenser fan relay. Since A/C condenser fan relay is permanently grounded, relay energizes, contacts close, and voltage is applied to condenser fan. Since condenser fan is permanently grounded, fan operates as soon voltage is applied.

TROUBLESHOOTING

1. Using a suitable fuse tester, check A/C, IG and radiator fan fuses, also fusible link B.
2. Check engine coolant level.
3. Check A/C system for proper charge.
4. Ensure all system grounds are clean and tight.

DIAGNOSIS

Refer to **Figs. 1 through 4** when performing diagnostic procedures.

Engine Cooling Fan

1. Start and run engine, ensure that engine coolant temperature is below 199°F. If fan operates, proceed to step 3.
2. If fan motor operates, run engine until coolant temperature is above 208°F. If fan continues to operate, system is functioning properly. If fan does not operate, proceed to step 6.

3. Disconnect fan switch connector, if fan stops running, replace fan switch.
4. If fan continues to run, connect a suitable test lamp from fan switch connector cavity 2 to ground. If lamp lights, repair short to voltage in blue wire.
5. If lamp does not light, disconnect fan relay connector. If fan stops running, replace fan relay. If fan continues running, repair short to voltage in blue/red wire.
6. Disconnect fan relay connector and connect a fused jumper wire between cavities 2 and 4 on connector. If fan does not operate, proceed to step 11.
7. If fan operates, connect a suitable digital ohmmeter from fan relay connector cavity 3 to ground and measure resistance. If resistance is greater than .3 ohms (1991) or 1.0 ohms (1992-93), repair black wire between fan relay and ground.
8. If resistance is less than .3 ohms, connect test lamp from fan relay connector cavity 1 to ground. If test lamp lights, replace fan relay.
9. If test lamp does not light, backprobe fan switch connector with test lamp from cavity 2 to ground. If test lamp lights, repair open in blue wire.
10. If test lamp does not light, backprobe fan switch connector with test lamp from cavity 1 to ground. If test lamp lights, replace fan switch. If test lamp does not light, repair open in black/white wire between fan switch and junction block.
11. Connect test lamp from fan relay con-

nector cavity 2 to ground. If test lamp does not light, repair open in white/green wire between fuse and relay box fan relay.
12. If lamp lights, reinstall relay and disconnect fan motor connector. Connect an ohmmeter from connector cavity 1 to ground and measure resistance. If resistance is greater than .3 ohms (1991) or 1.0 ohms (1992-93), repair black wire between fan motor and ground G200 on 1991 XFi, base, LSi and 1992-93 convertible models or black wire between fan motor and ground G101 on 1991 convertible and 1992-93 hardtop models.
13. If resistance is less than .3 ohms (1991) or 1.0 ohms (1992-93), connect test lamp from fan motor connector cavity 2 to ground. If lamp lights, replace fan motor. If lamp does not light, repair open in blue/red wire.

1991 A/C Condenser Fan

1. Turn ignition switch to On position and press A/C switch. If condenser fan does not operate, proceed to step 3.
2. If fan operates, press A/C switch Off. If fan stops, system is functioning properly. If fan continues to operate, proceed to step 16.
3. Disconnect fan motor connector and connect a suitable test lamp between cavities 1 and 2. If lamp lights, replace condenser fan motor.
4. If lamp does not light, connect a suitable digital ohmmeter from fan motor connector cavity 1 to ground and

Fig. 2   Coolant fan wiring circuit (A/C condenser fan). 1991 Metro

Fig. 3   Coolant fan wiring circuit (A/C condenser fan). 1992–93 Metro

Fig. 4 Coolant fan wiring circuit (engine cooling fan). 1992—93 Metro

measure resistance. If resistance is greater than .3 ohms, repair black wire between fan motor and ground G104.

5. If resistance is less than .3 ohms, backprobe fan relay connector with test lamp from cavity 4 to ground. If lamp lights, repair open in blue/black wire.

6. If lamp does not light, disconnect fan relay connector and connect test lamp from cavity 2 to ground. If lamp does not light, repair open in red wire.

7. If lamp lights, connect an ohmmeter from fan relay connector cavity 3 to ground and measure resistance. If resistance is greater than .3 ohms, repair black wire between fuse and relay box and S117.

8. If resistance is less than .3 ohms, connect test lamp from fan relay connector cavity 1 to ground. If lamp lights, replace fan relay.

9. If lamp does not light, backprobe A/C clutch relay with test lamp from cavity 4 to ground. If lamp lights, repair open in black/white wire between clutch relay and fan relay.

10. If lamp does not light, disconnect clutch relay connector and connect an ohmmeter from cavity 3 to ground and measure resistance. If resistance is greater than .3 ohms, proceed to step 15.

11. If resistance is less than .3 ohms, connect test lamp from clutch relay connector cavity 1 to ground. If lamp lights, replace clutch relay.

12. If lamp does not light, backprobe dual pressure switch connector with test lamp from cavity 1 to ground. If lamp lights, repair open in yellow wire.

13. If lamp does not light, disconnect dual pressure switch connector and con-

nect test lamp from cavity 2 to ground. If lamp lights, replace dual pressure switch.

14. If lamp does not light, backprobe junction block connector C7 with test lamp from cavity 1 to ground. If lamp lights, repair open in black/white wire between junction block and dual pressure switch. If lamp does not light, replace junction block.

15. Disconnect A/C controller connector and connect an ohmmeter from controller connector cavity 7 to clutch relay connector cavity 3 and measure resistance. If resistance is greater than .3 ohms, repair open in pink wire. If resistance is less than .3 ohms, problem is in compressor control system.

16. Disconnect fan relay connector. if fan continues to operate, repair short to voltage in blue/black wire.

17. If fan stops, connect test lamp from fan relay connector cavity 1 to ground. If lamp does not light, replace fan relay.

18. If lamp lights, disconnect clutch relay connector and connect test lamp from connector cavity 4 to ground. If lamp lights, repair short to voltage in black/white wire between clutch relay and fan relay.

19. If lamp does not light, connect an ohmmeter from clutch relay connector cavity 3 to ground and measure resistance. Is resistance is infinite, replace clutch relay. If resistance is less than infinite, problem is in compressor control system.

1992—93 A/C Condenser Fan

1. Turn ignition switch to On position and press A/C switch. If condenser

fan does not operate, proceed to step 3.

2. If fan operates, press A/C switch Off. If fan stops, system is functioning properly. If fan continues to operate, proceed to step 16.

3. Disconnect fan motor connector and connect a suitable test lamp between cavities 1 and 2. If lamp lights, replace condenser fan motor.

4. If lamp does not light, connect a suitable digital ohmmeter from fan motor connector cavity 1 to ground and measure resistance. If resistance is greater than 3 ohms, repair black wire between fan motor and ground G104.

5. If resistance is less than 3 ohms, backprobe fan relay connector with test lamp from cavity 4 to ground. If lamp lights, repair open in blue/black wire.

6. If lamp does not light, disconnect fan relay connector and connect test lamp from cavity 2 to ground. If lamp does not light, repair open in red wire.

7. If lamp lights, connect an ohmmeter from fan relay connector cavity 3 to ground and measure resistance. If resistance is greater than 1.0 ohms, repair black wire between fuse and relay box and G104.

8. If resistance is less than 1.0 ohms, connect test lamp from fan relay connector cavity 1 to ground. If lamp lights, replace fan relay.

9. If lamp does not light, backprobe A/C clutch relay with test lamp from cavity 4 to ground. If lamp lights, repair open in light green/red wire between clutch relay and fan relay.

10. If lamp does not light, disconnect clutch relay connector and connect a test lamp from cavity 3 to battery posi-

tive. If test lamp lights, replace condenser fan relay. If test lamp does not light, go to step 14.

11. Connect test lamp from A/C compressor clutch relay connector cavity 1 to chassis ground. If test lamp lights, replace A/C compressor clutch relay.

12. If lamp does not light, disconnect dual pressure switch connector. Connect test lamp from cavity 2 to ground. If lamp does not light, repair open in black/white wire between S105 and dual pressure switch.

13. If lamp lights, connect a fused jumper from dual pressure switch connector cavity 2 to cavity 1 and reconnect all relays. If condenser fan operates, replace dual pressure switch. If condenser fan does not operate, repair open in yellow wire between dual pressure switch and compressor clutch relay.

14. Disconnect A/C amplifier connector, then connect an ohmmeter from amplifier connector cavity 7 to clutch relay connector cavity 3 and measure resistance. If resistance is greater than 1.0 ohms, repair open in pink wire. If resistance is less than 1.0 ohms, problem is in A/C amplifier system.

15. Disconnect condenser fan relay connector, if fan continues to operate, repair short to voltage in blue/black wire.

16. If fan stops, connect test lamp from fan relay connector cavity 1 to ground. If lamp does not light, replace fan relay.

17. If lamp lights, disconnect clutch relay connector and connect test lamp from connector cavity 4 to ground. If lamp lights, repair short to voltage in light green/red wire between compressor clutch relay and condenser fan relay.

18. If lamp does not light, connect an ohmmeter from clutch relay connector cavity 3 to ground and measure resistance. Is resistance is infinite, replace clutch relay. If resistance is less than infinite, problem is in A/C amplifier system.

COOLING FAN, REPLACE

1. Disconnect battery ground cable.
2. Drain cooling system and disconnect upper radiator hose from radiator.
3. Disconnect fan motor electrical connector.
4. Raise and support vehicle, then remove one lower mounting bolt from fan shroud.
5. Lower vehicle and remove two upper cooling fan mounting bolts, then remove fan from vehicle.
6. Reverse procedure to install.

THERMO SWITCH, REPLACE

1. Disconnect battery ground cable, then drain cooling system.
2. Remove air cleaner and air inlet tube.
3. Disconnect switch electrical lead,

then remove switch from thermostat cap.

4. Reverse procedure to install, wrapping switch threads with sealing tape before installation.

BERETTA & CORSICA

SYSTEM DESCRIPTION

Voltage is available at all times through fusible link A to coolant fan relay contacts. With ignition switch in Run position, voltage is available through fuse 9 to coolant fan relay coil. When the ECM receives a signal from coolant temperature sensor, ground is provided for coolant fan relay by module's coolant fan terminal. Voltage is applied through fuse 9 to coolant fan relay coil. When ECM grounds the circuit, coolant fan relay contacts close and voltage is applied through coolant fan relay contacts to coolant fan and the fan runs.

When refrigerant pressure opens coolant fan pressure switch on 3.1/V6-192 (VIN T models, the ECM responds by energizing coolant fan relay which turns coolant fan On.

TROUBLESHOOTING

1. If coolant fan does not operate, check fuse No. 9 and Fuse Link A.
2. If coolant fan runs with ignition switch in the OFF position, replace the coolant fan relay.
3. Ensure that ground G101 is clean and tight.

SYSTEM CHECK

1. With engine cold and at idle speed, move A/C selector switch to the NORM position, coolant fan should come on. Move the A/C selector to the OFF position, coolant fan should turn off.
2. Run engine at fast idle for several minutes, coolant fan should come on before coolant temperature indicator comes on or if equipped with temperature gauge before gauge reads H.
3. If coolant fan does not operate as described above refer to "Coolant Fan Does Not Run At All" or "Coolant Fan Does Not Turn Off With Ignition Switch In Run."

DIAGNOSIS

Refer to **Figs. 5 through 10** when performing diagnostic procedures.

1991

Coolant Fan Does Not Run At All

1. Connect a fused jumper wire between the Assembly Line Diagnostic Link (ALDL) connector terminal B and ground.
2. Turn ignition switch to the RUN position. If coolant fan does not run, proceed to step 3. If coolant fan runs, problem is ECM related.
3. With ignition switch in RUN position, backprobe with fused jumper wire between coolant fan relay terminal F and

ground. If coolant fan does not run, proceed to step 5. If coolant fan runs, locate and repair open circuit in dark green/white wire No. 335.

4. Disconnect coolant fan relay connector, connect a test lamp between terminal D pink/black wire and ground. If test lamp lights, proceed to step 7. If test lamp does not light, check fuse 9 and pink/black wire for open circuit.

5. Connect test lamp between terminals D pink/black wire and F dark green/white wire. If test lamp lights, proceed to step 7. If test lamp does not light, check dark green/white wire for an open circuit, repair if necessary. If circuit is satisfactory, problem is ECM related.

6. Connect test lamp to terminal A red wire and ground. If test lamp lights, proceed to step 7. If test lamp does not light, check fusible link and red wire for open circuit.

7. With coolant fan relay connector disconnected, connect a fused jumper wire between terminal A red wire and terminal E black/red wire. If coolant fan does not run, proceed to step 8. If coolant fan runs, replace coolant fan relay.

8. With ignition switch in RUN and jumper wire connected as in step 7, connect a test lamp between terminal B black/red wire and ground. If test lamp lights, replace coolant fan. If test lamp does not light, locate and repair open circuit in black/red wire.

9. Connect test lamp between terminal B black/red wire and terminal A black wire. If test lamp lights, replace coolant fan. If test lamp does not light, locate and repair open circuit in black wire.

Coolant Fan Does Not Turn Off With Ignition Switch In Run

1. Turn ignition switch to Run position, then disconnect coolant fan relay. If coolant fan does not shut off, check black/red wire for short to voltage.

2. If coolant fan shuts Off, connect a test lamp between terminals D (pink/black) and F (dark green/white) of coolant fan relay connector. If lamp does not light, replace coolant fan relay. If lamp lights, check dark green/white wire for short to ground. If wire is satisfactory, problem is ECM related.

1992

Coolant Fan Does Not Run At All

1. Connect a jumper wire between the Assembly Line Diagnostic Link (ALDL) connector terminal B and ground.
2. Turn ignition switch to the RUN position. If coolant fan does not run, proceed to step 3. If coolant fan runs, problem is ECM related.
3. With ignition switch in RUN position, connect a fused jumper wire between ECM connector terminal C3 and ter-

Fig. 5 Coolant fan wiring circuit. 1991 Beretta & Corsica

minal E8 (VIN A & T) or terminal C1 and terminal C13 (VIN 4). If coolant fan does not run, proceed to step 4. If coolant fan runs, problem is ECM related.

4. With ECM connector terminal C3 and terminal E8 (VIN A & T) or terminal C1 and terminal C13 (VIN 4) grounded, disconnect coolant fan relay connector and connect a volt meter between terminal D (pink/black wire) and ground. If battery voltage is present, proceed to step 5. If battery voltage is not present, repair open in circuit 39.

5. With ECM connector terminal C3 and terminal E8 (VIN A & T) or terminal C1 and terminal C13 (VIN 4) grounded, disconnect coolant fan relay connector and connect a volt meter between terminal D (pink/black wire) and terminal F (dark green/white). If battery voltage is present, proceed to step 6. If battery voltage is not present, repair open in circuit 335.

6. Connect a volt meter to terminal A (red wire) and terminal E (black/red wire) of coolant fan relay connector. If battery voltage is not present, proceed to step 7. If battery voltage is present, repair open in circuit 2.

7. With coolant fan relay connector disconnected, connect a fused jumper wire between terminal A red wire and terminal E black/red wire. If coolant fan does not run, proceed to step 8. If coolant fan runs, replace coolant fan relay.

8. With ignition switch in RUN and jump-

er wire connected as in step 7, connect a volt meter between terminal B black/red wire and ground. If battery voltage is not present, repair open in circuit 702. If battery voltage is present proceed to step 9.

9. With ignition switch in RUN and jumper wire connected as in step 7, connect a volt meter between terminal B black/red wire and terminal A black wire of coolant fan connector. If battery voltage is not present, repair open in circuit 150. If battery voltage is present replace coolant fan motor.

Coolant Fan Does Not Turn Off With Ignition Switch In Run

1. Turn ignition switch to Run position, then disconnect coolant fan relay.
2. Connect a test lamp between terminals D (pink/black) and F (dark green/white) of coolant fan relay connector. If lamp does not light, replace coolant fan relay. If lamp lights, check circuit 335 for short to ground. If wire is satisfactory, problem is ECM related.

1993

For cooling fan system diagnosis on these models, refer to **Figs. 11 through 13.**

COOLING FAN, REPLACE
2.3L/4-138 Engine

1. Disconnect battery ground cable.

2. Disconnect electrical connectors from motor and fan frame.
3. Remove fan assembly from radiator.
4. Reverse procedure to install. **Torque** attaching bolts to 7 ft. lbs.

2.2L/4-134 & 3.1L/V6-192 Engines

1. Disconnect battery ground cable.
2. Remove air cleaner, intake ductwork and bracket.
3. Disconnect electrical connectors, then remove upper and lower mounting bolts.
4. Remove fan assembly.
5. Reverse procedure to install. **Torque** mounting bolts to 8 ft. lbs.

6000
SYSTEM DESCRIPTION
2.5L/4-151 Engine

Voltage is available at all times through fusible link A to the coolant fan relay contacts. With ignition switch in RUN position, voltage is available through the C/H fuse to the coolant fan relay coil.

Depending on coolant temperature, the coolant switch fan contact will be open or closed.

With the coolant fan switch contact closed, voltage is applied through the C/H fuse to the coolant fan relay coil, and the coolant fan relay contacts close. Voltage is applied through fusible link A to the coolant fan relay contacts and the coolant fan to ground. The coolant fan operates.

Fig. 7 Coolant fan wiring circuit. 1992 Beretta & Corsica w/2.2L/4-135 engine

Fig. 6 Coolant fan wiring circuit. 1992 Beretta & Corsica w/3.1L/V6-192 & 2.3L/4-138

Fig. 9 Coolant fan wiring circuit. 1993 Beretta & Corsica w/2.3L/4-138

Fig. 8 Coolant fan wiring circuit. 1993 Beretta & Corsica w/2.2L/4-135

Fig. 10 Coolant fan wiring circuit. 1993 Beretta & Corsica w/3.1L/V6-192

The coolant fan is energized when the A/C compressor operates. This ensures adequate air flow over the A/C condenser.

The coolant fan runs when the function selector is in MAX, NORM or BI-LEVEL position, the A/C low pressure cut-out switch is closed, and the ECM completes a voltage path to ground.

3.1L/V6-192 (VIN T) Engine

Voltage is available at all times through the battery junction block and fusible link F to the coolant fan relay contacts. With ignition switch in RUN position, voltage is available through C/H fuse to the coolant fan relay coil.

When the ECM receives a signal from the coolant temperature sensor, ground is provided for the coolant fan relay between the module's coolant fan control terminal and ground terminal. Voltage is applied through the C/H fuse to the coolant fan relay coil, and the ECM to ground. The coolant fan relay contacts close. Voltage is applied through the battery junction block to the coolant fan relay contacts, and the coolant fan to ground. The coolant fan operates.

The coolant fan is energized when the A/C compressor operates. This ensures adequate air flow over the A/C condenser.

The coolant fan runs when the A/C high pressure switch closes and the ECM provides ground between the module's coolant fan control terminal and ground terminal.

TROUBLESHOOTING

1. Check FAN/ALT fuse.
2. Replace coolant fan relay if coolant fan runs with ignition switch off.

SYSTEM CHECK

1. With engine cold and idling, move A/C selector, if equipped, to NORM. Coolant fan should run.
2. With engine coolant below operating temperature, move A/C selector to OFF. Coolant fan should turn off.
3. With engine warm, run engine at fast idle for several minutes. Coolant fan should turn on before coolant temperature indicator comes on or coolant temperature gauge needle reaches H.

DIAGNOSIS

Refer to **Figs. 14 and 15** when performing diagnostic procedures on this system.

Coolant Fan Does Not Run

1. Connect fused jumper between ALDL connector terminal B and ground and turn ignition switch to RUN position. If coolant fan runs, problem is ECM related.
2. If coolant fan does not run, connect fused jumper between dark green/white wire of ECM connector C1 (VIN R) or C3 (VIN W) and ground and turn ignition switch to RUN position. If coolant fan runs, problem is ECM related.
3. If coolant fan does not run, leave fused jumper connected as in step 2, disconnect coolant fan relay connector, turn ignition switch to RUN position and connect test lamp between terminals as follows:
   a. Between D wire terminal and ground. If lamp does not illuminate, check C/H fuse and brown/white wire for open.
   b. Between D and F wire terminals. If lamp does not illuminate, check dark green/white wire for open.
   c. Between red wire terminal and ground. If lamp does not illuminate, check red wire and fusible link A for open.
4. If lamp illuminates in steps a, b and c, disconnect coolant fan relay connector and connect fused jumper between A and E wire terminals. If coolant fan runs, replace coolant fan.
5. If coolant fan does not run, leave fused jumper connected as in step 4, disconnect coolant fan connector and connect test lamp between terminals as follows:
   a. Between B wire terminal and ground. If lamp does not illuminate, check black/red wire (VIN R and T) or yellow wire (VIN W and T) for open.
   b. Between B and black wire terminals. If lamp does not illuminate, check black wire for open.
   c. If lamp illuminates in steps a and b, replace coolant fan.

Coolant Fan Runs Continuously

1. Place ignition switch in RUN position, disconnect coolant fan relay. If coolant fan does not turn off, check black/red wire for short to voltage. If coolant fan turns off, proceed to step 2.
2. Disconnect coolant fan relay connector and connect test lamp between terminals D (brown) and F (dark green/white) of connector. If test lamp does not light, replace coolant fan relay. If test lamp lights, check dark green/white wire for short to ground. If wire is satisfactory, problem is ECM related.

CHART C-12
COOLING FAN CONTROL DIAGNOSIS
2.2L

Circuit Description:

Battery voltage to operate the cooling fan motor is supplied to relay by CKT 2. Ignition voltage to energize the cooling fan control is supplied by CKT 39. When the ECM grounds CKT 335, the relay is energized and the cooling fan is turned "ON."

When the engine is running, the ECM will turn the engine cooling fan "ON" for any of the following reasons:

- Diagnostic Trouble Code (DTC) 14 is set.
- Coolant temperature is 106°C (223°F) or greater.
- A/C refrigerant pressure is 189 psi or greater with A/C selected and a Diagnostic Trouble Code (DTC) 66 is not set.

Once the cooling fan is enabled, the ECM will turn the fan "OFF" when:

- Engine is turned "OFF."
- Coolant temperature drops to 99°C (203°F) or less.
- A/C refrigerant pressure drops to 38 psi or less with A/C selected.

Diagnostic Aids:

If the owner complained of an overheating problem, it must be determined if the complaint was due to an actual boil over, or the hot light, or temperature gage indicated overheating.

If the gage or light indicates overheating, but no boil over is detected, the gage circuit should be checked. The gage accuracy can also be checked by checking the engine coolant temperature reading using a scan tool and comparing its display with the instrument cluster gage.

If the engine is actually overheating and the gage indicates overheating, but the cooling fan is not coming "ON," the ECT sensor has probably shifted out of calibration and should be replaced.

IF ECM IS FAULTY AND MUST BE REPLACED, THE NEW ECM MUST BE PROGRAMMED.

COOLING FAN CONTROL RELAY CONNECTOR

Fig. 11   Chart C-12, cooling fan diagnosis. 1993 Beretta & Corsica w/2.2L/4-135

CHART C-12
COOLANT FAN FUNCTIONAL CHECK
2.3L (VIN A) "L" CARLINE

Circuit Description:

The electric coolant fan is controlled by the Engine Control Module (ECM) through the fan relay based on inputs from the engine coolant and intake air temperature sensors, the A/C control switch, A/C refrigerant pressure sensor and the vehicle speed sensor. The ECM controls the coolant fan by grounding CKT 335 which turns "ON" the fan relay.

The fan relay will be commanded "ON" when:

- Engine coolant temperature 103°C (217°F) - 106°C (223°F) or more.
- A/C clutch requested.
- Vehicle speed is less than 35 mph.

The fan relay will be commanded "ON" regardless of vehicle speed when:

- DTC 14 or 15 are set.
- Engine coolant temperature 115°C (239°F) - 118°C (224°F) or more.
- A/C refrigerant pressure is high.

The coolant fan may be commanded "ON" when the engine is not running under fan "Run-ON" conditions described previously in this section.

Test Description: Number(s) below refer to circled number(s) on the diagnostic chart.

1. With the field service mode activated, the coolant fan control driver should close, which should energize the fan control relay.
2. Test to see if fault is in wiring to the fan or the fan/relay connection.

Diagnostic Aids:

If the owner complained of an overheating problem, it must be determined if the complaint was due to an actual boil over, or the "Temp" light, or temperature gage indicated overheating.

If the gage, or light, indicates overheating, but no boil over is detected, the gage or light circuit should be checked. The gage accuracy can also be checked by comparing the coolant sensor reading using a scan tool with the gage reading.

If the engine is actually overheating, and the gage indicates overheating, but the coolant fan is not coming "ON," the Engine Coolant Temperature (ECT) sensor has probably shifted out of calibration and should be replaced.

If the engine is overheating, and the coolant fan is "ON," the cooling system should be checked.

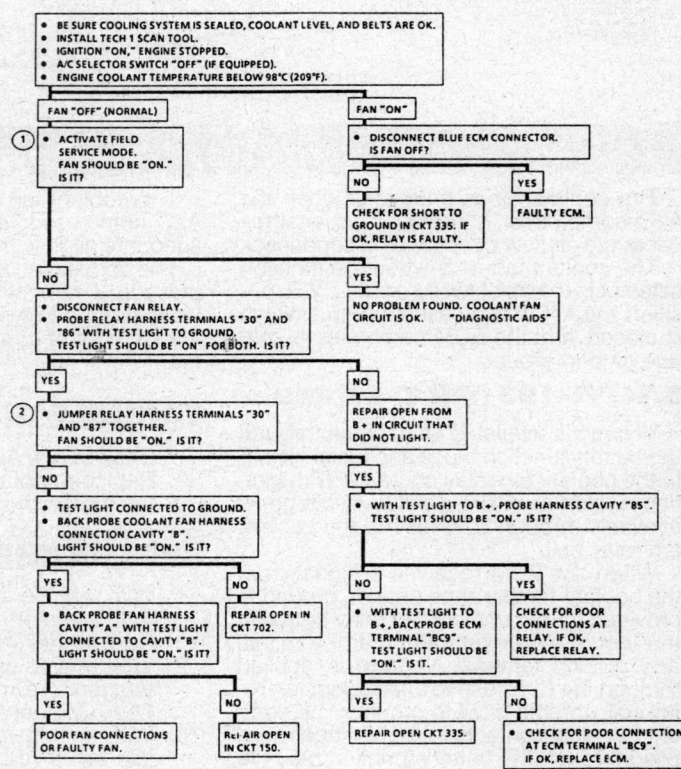

Fig. 12   Chart C-12, cooling fan diagnosis. 1993 Beretta & Corsica w/2.3L/4-138

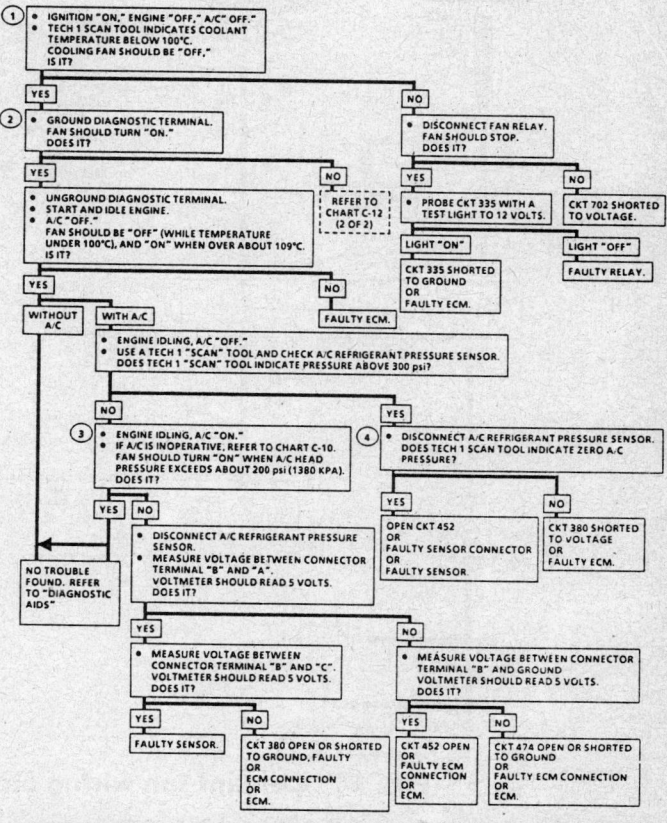

CHART C-12

(Page 1 of 2)
COOLING FAN CONTROL DIAGNOSIS
3.1L (VIN T) "L" CARLINE (MFI)

Circuit Description:

The electric cooling fan is controlled by the ECM, based on inputs from the engine coolant temperature sensor, the A/C refrigerant pressure sensor and vehicle speed. The ECM controls the fan by grounding CKT 335 which energizes the fan control relay. Battery voltage is then supplied to the fan motor.

The ECM grounds CKT 335 when coolant temperature is over about 109°C (228°F), or when A/C has been requested and the A/C refrigerant pressure sensor indicates high A/C pressure, 200 psi (1380 kPa). Once the ECM turns the relay "ON," it will keep it "ON" for a minimum of 25 seconds, or until vehicle speed exceeds 70 mph.

Also, if DTC 14 or 15 sets or the ECM is in back up, the fan will run at all times.

Test Description: Number(s) below refer to circled number(s) on the diagnostic chart.
1. With the diagnostic terminal grounded, the cooling fan control driver will close, which should energize the fan control relay.
2. If the A/C fan control switch or circuit is open, the fan would run whenever A/C is requested.
3. With A/C compressor clutch engaged, the A/C fan control switch should open when A/C refrigerant pressure exceeds 200 psi (1380 kPa). This signal should cause the ECM to energize the fan control relay.
4. Disconnecting the A/C refrigerant pressure sensor will cause a DTC 66 to set. After finishing this step, be sure to clear DTC(s).

Diagnostic Aids:

If the owner complained of an overheating problem, it must be determined if the complaint was due to an actual boil over, or the hot light (temperature gage) indicated overheating.

If the gage (light) indicates overheating, but no boil over is detected, the gage circuit should be checked. The gage accuracy can also be checked by comparing the engine coolant temperature sensor reading using a scan tool and comparing its reading with the gage reading.

If the engine is actually overheating, and the gage indicates overheating, but the cooling fan is not coming "ON," the engine coolant temperature sensor has probably shifted out of calibration and should be replaced.

If the engine is overheating, and the cooling fan is "ON," the cooling system should be checked.

Fig. 13   Chart C-12, cooling fan diagnosis (Part 1 of 2). 1993 Beretta & Corsica w/3.1L/V6-192

CHART C-12

(Page 2 of 2)
COOLING FAN CONTROL DIAGNOSIS
3.1L (VIN T) "L" CARLINE (MFI)

Test Description: Number(s) below refer to circled number(s) on the diagnostic chart.
1. 12 volts should be available to both terminals "A" and "D" when the ignition is "ON."
2. This test checks the ability of the ECM to ground CKT 335. The MIL (Service Engine Soon) should also be flashing at this point.
3. If the fan does not turn "ON" at this point, CKT 702 or CKT 150 is open or the cooling fan motor is faulty.

Fig. 13   Chart C-12, cooling fan diagnosis (Part 2 of 2). 1993 Beretta & Corsica w/3.1L/V6-192

Fig. 14   Coolant fan wiring circuit. 1991 6000 w/2.5L/4-151 engine

Fig. 15   Coolant fan wiring circuit. 1991 6000 w/3.1L/V6-192 engine

COOLANT FAN, REPLACE

1. Disconnect battery ground cable.
2. Disconnect wiring harness from fan motor and fan frame.
3. Remove fan assembly from radiator support.
4. Reverse procedure to install.

SERVICE BULLETINS

Cooling Fan Runs Battery Dead

If this problem occurs and the cooling fan relay is found to have failed because of its' contact points sticking together, the cause of the problem may either be the air conditioning system or the cooling fan temperature switch.

If the cooling fan motor is operating within acceptable current draw limits (20 amps on low speed or 35 amps on high speed), check A/C high side pressure with system operating. High side pressure should be stable. If high speed pressure shows a rapidly vibrating needle on the gauge, this will cause the A/C cooling fan pressure switch to cycle on and off as rapidly as the gauge needle is moving. This will cause the relay terminals to arc and eventually weld themselves together, which will leave the fan in operation with ignition key turned off. Check the fan pressure switch or check the A/C system for an internal failure.

The other cause of this condition may be the cooling fan temperature switch. To check the switch, touch one end of a test light to the positive battery terminal and the other end to the temperature switch located on the intake manifold. With the engine running, if the test light flickers on and off rapidly, the temperature switch may cause the cooling fan relay to fail in a similar manner as described above.

In either case, after the problem has been corrected, replace the coolant fan relay.

CUTLASS CALAIS

SYSTEM DESCRIPTION

2.3L/4-138 (VIN A & D) Engine

A two speed coolant fan is used with the VIN D engine. The coolant fan is turned on and off by the coolant fan relays.

For low speed operation, the low speed relay coil is grounded through the ECM when vehicle speed is less than 45 mph and the engine coolant reaches 208°F, or when the A/C is turned on. The contacts close and voltage is applied through the coolant fan resistor to the coolant fan. The fan runs at low speed.

For high speed operation, the high speed relay coil is grounded through the ECM when the coolant temperature reaches 228°F. The contacts close and voltage is applied to the coolant fan. The fan runs at high speed. The coolant fan will continue to run at high speed after the ignition switch is turned off until the coolant temperature lowers.

2.5L/4-151 (VIN U) & 3.3L/V6-204 (VIN N) Engines

The coolant fan is controlled by the coolant fan relay. The coolant fan relay is electrically operated by the ECM. The ECM receives input signals from the coolant temperature sensor, the vehicle speed sensor and the A/C mode selector. The ECM activates the coolant fan relay when the engine coolant, which is sensed by the coolant temperature sensor, is above 227°F, when the A/C is turned on or when the coolant temperature sensor fails. Any of these input signals causes the ECM to ground circuit 335 when vehicle speed is less than 35 mph. With circuit 335 grounded, the coolant fan relay is energized and its contacts close, turning the coolant fan on.

TROUBLESHOOTING

1. If coolant fan does not operate, check fusible link F.
2. On **2.5L/4-151 VIN U and 3.3L/V6-204 VIN N,** if coolant fan does not operate, check HTR/A/C fuse.
3. If coolant fan operates with ignition switch in Off position, replace coolant fan relay.

SYSTEM CHECK

1. With ambient air temperature above 70°F, open all doors, start vehicle and set A/C mode selector, if equipped, to MAX. Coolant fan should turn on in a short period of time.
2. With engine coolant below operating temperature, move A/C mode selector to OFF position. Coolant fan should turn off in a short period of time.
3. Run engine at fast idle for several minutes. The coolant fan should turn on before coolant temperature indicator comes on or coolant temperature gage needle reaches HOT.
4. On **2.5L/4-151 VIN U and 3.3L/V6-204 VIN N,** when ignition switch is turned to Off position, coolant fan shuts Off.
5. On **2.3L/4-138 VIN A and D,** when ignition switch is turned to Off position, coolant fan continues to run until engine temperature lowers.

DIAGNOSIS

Refer to **Figs. 16 through 18** when performing the following diagnostic procedures.

Coolant Fan Does Not Turn On

1. With ignition switch in RUN position, ground terminal B (white VIN N & U) or (white/black VIN A & D) of ALDL connector. If coolant fan runs, problem is ECM related.
2. If coolant fan does not run, ground terminal C1/C21 (dark green/white VIN U) or C3/E8 (dark green VIN N) or (light green/black VIN A & D) of ECM with fused jumper. If coolant fan runs, problem is ECM related.

3. If coolant fan does not run, leave fused jumper connected as in step 2, disconnect coolant fan relay connector and measure voltage from terminal 5 (brown VIN U) or 2 (brown VIN N) or (red VIN A & D) to ground. If no voltage is present, check brown wire and HTR/A/C fuse for an open (VIN N & U) or red wire and fusible link F (VIN A & D).
4. If battery voltage is present, leave fused jumper connected as in step 2, measure voltage between terminals 5 (brown) and 2 (dark green/white) (VIN U) or 2 (brown VIN N) or (red VIN A & D) and 5 (dark green VIN N) or (light green/black VIN A & D). If no voltage is present, check dark green/white, dark green or light green/black wire for open.
5. If battery voltage is present, measure voltage from terminal 1 (red) to ground. If no voltage is present, check red wire and fusible link F for open.
6. If battery voltage is present, connect a 20 amp fused jumper between terminals 1 (red) and 4 (black/red). If coolant fan runs, replace coolant fan relay.
7. If coolant fan does not run, leave fused jumper connected as in step 6, disconnect coolant fan connector and measure voltage from terminal B (black/red) to ground. If no voltage is present, check black/red wire for open.
8. If battery voltage is present, leave fused jumper connected as in step 6 and measure voltage between Terminals B (black/red) and A (black).
9. If no voltage is present, check black wire for open.
10. If battery voltage is present, replace coolant fan motor.

Coolant Fan Does Not Turn Off With Engine Coolant Cool, A/C Mode Selector Off & Ignition Switch in RUN Position

1. Turn ignition switch to RUN position, disconnect coolant fan relay connector and connect test lamp between terminals 5 (brown/white) and 2 (dark green/white) (VIN U) or 2 (brown VIN N) or (red VIN A & D) and 5 (dark green VIN N) or (light green/black VIN A & D). If lamp does not illuminate, replace coolant fan relay.
2. If lamp illuminates, check dark green/white, dark green or light green/black wire for short to ground. If wire is satisfactory, problem is ECM related.

Coolant Fan Does Not Turn On With A/C Mode Selector On, And Head Pressure Above 150 psi, But Does Turn On With Engine Hot

1. Turn ignition switch to RUN position and place A/C mode selector in MAX position. Measure voltage between terminal C1/24 (dark green/white) (VIN U) or C1/C9 (light green) (VIN A, D & N) of the ECM and ground.

Fig. 16 Coolant fan wiring circuit. Cutlass Calais w/2.3L/4-138 Fig. 17 Coolant fan wiring circuit. Cutlass Calais w/2.5L/4-151 engine

Fig. 18   Coolant fan wiring circuit. Cutlass Calais w/3.3L/V6-204 engine

CUTLASS CIERA & CUTLASS CRUISER

SYSTEM DESCRIPTION

2.2L/4-135 ENGINE

The coolant fan is turned on and off by the ECM based on inputs from the ECT sensor, vehicle speed sensor and the A/C system. Battery voltage is applied at all times to terminal "A" of the coolant fan relay and when the ignition switch is in the RUN position, battery voltage is applied to terminal "D" of the relay. The ECM energizes the coolant fan relay by grounding the dark green (535) wire. The relay energizes and battery voltage is applied to the coolant fan. The ECM opens circuit (535) to de-energize the relay and turn off the coolant fan. The ECM will turn the coolant fan on when the A/C is turned on and vehicle speed is less than 35 mph, coolant temperature is above 225°F (104°C) and vehicle speed is less than 35 mph, or the ECT sensor fails.

2.5L/4-151 ENGINE

The coolant fan is turned on and off by the ECM based on inputs from the coolant temperature sensor, vehicle speed sensor and the A/C system. Battery voltage is applied at all times to terminal E of the coolant fan relay and when the ignition switch is in RUN position, battery voltage is applied to terminal C of the relay. The ECM energizes the coolant fan relay by grounding the dark green/white wire. The relay energizes and battery voltage is applied to the cooling fan. THe ECM opens circuit 335 to de-energize the relay and turn off the coolant fan. The ECM will turn on the coolant fan when A/C is on and vehicle speed is less than 35 mph or when coolant temperature is above approximately 225°F and vehicle speed is less than 35 mph.

3.3L/V6-204 ENGINE
1991—92

Two types of coolant fans are used with this engine. The coolant fans are turned on and off either by the coolant fan relay, the coolant fan delay relay, the pusher coolant fan relay or the puller coolant fan relay depending on the specific application or engine requirement.

For operation without A/C, the coolant fan relay is controlled by the coolant fan switch or the ECM. For operation with A/C, the coolant fan relay is controlled by the coolant fan switch, the A/C high pressure switch and the ECM.

When one of these components grounds the coil of the coolant fan relay, the contacts close and the fan comes on.

THe heavy duty coolant system, used on some models, consists of two coolant fans. The puller coolant fan is controlled by the puller coolant fan relay. This relay is controlled by the ECM, the puller contacts of the A/C dual pressure switch and the coolant fan switch. The pusher coolant fan is controlled by the pusher coolant fan relay. This relay is controlled by the coolant fan switch and the pusher contacts of the

2. If battery voltage is present, problem is ECM related.
3. If no voltage is present, check dark green/white or light green wire for an open.

COOLANT FAN, REPLACE

Except 2.3L/4-138 (VIN A & D) Engine

1. Disconnect battery ground cable.
2. Remove wiring harness from fan motor and fan frame.
3. Remove fan guard and hose support as necessary.
4. Remove fan assembly from radiator support.
5. Reverse procedure to install.

2.3L/4-138 (VIN A & D) Engine

1. Disconnect battery ground cable.
2. Remove air cleaner to throttle body duct.
3. Disconnect electrical connectors from

throttle position sensor, IAC and MAP sensor and position harness aside.
4. Remove vacuum harness assembly from throttle body and position aside.
5. Disconnect MAP sensor vacuum hose at intake manifold.
6. Remove coolant fan shroud attaching bolts and the shroud together with MAP sensor.
7. Remove coolant fan to upper radiator support attaching bolt, remaining upper radiator support bolt and the upper radiator support.
8. Remove electrical connector from coolant fan.
9. Lift fan assembly out of two lower insulators, rotate bracket so two lower bracket legs point upward, move fan assembly toward driver's side until fan blade overlaps radiator tank to core seam by approximately one inch and remove fan assembly upward. **Because of minimum clearance, care must be taken not to damage lock tang on throttle position sensor with fan bracket.**
10. Reverse procedure to install.

A/C high pressure switch. When any one of these components grounds the coil of one of the relays, that particular fan runs.

When a ground path is provided for the pusher coolant fan relay, the puller coolant fan relay also receives the ground path. When the pusher coolant fan runs, so does the puller coolant fan.

On all vehicles, the coolant fan delay relay operates the coolant fan(s) for a short period of time after the engine is turned off. A solid state timer relay removes the path to ground for the coolant fan delay relay coil to turn off the fan.

1993

The coolant fan is controlled by the coolant fan relay. The coolant fan relay is electrically operated by the ECM. The ECM receives input signals from the ECT sensor, the vehicle speed sensor and the A/C mode selector. The ECM will activate the coolant fan relay when the engine coolant temperature reaches 212°F (100°C), the A/C is turned on and vehicle speed is below 40 mph, or the ECT sensor fails. Any of these input signals causes the ECM to ground circuit (535). When circuit (535) is grounded, the coolant fan relay is energized and its contacts close, turning the coolant fan on.

TROUBLESHOOTING

1. **On 1991-92 models,** check FAN/ALT fuse.
2. **On 1993 models,** check ENG/A/C fuse.
3. If coolant fan runs with ignition switch off, replace coolant fan relay.

SYSTEM CHECK

1. With ambient air temperature above 60°F, start engine and set A/C mode selector, if equipped, to MAX. Coolant fan should turn on.
2. With engine coolant below operating temperature, move A/C mode selector to OFF position. Coolant fan should turn off in a short period of time.
3. Run engine at fast idle until engine coolant becomes hot. The coolant fan should turn on before coolant temperature indicator comes on or coolant temperature gage needle reaches HOT.

SYSTEM DIAGNOSIS

Refer to **Figs. 19 through 22** when performing the following diagnostic procedures.

1991–92 MODELS
Coolant Fan Does Not Turn On

1. With ignition switch in RUN position, ground terminal B (white/black) wire of ALDL connector. If coolant fan runs, problem is ECM related.
2. If coolant fan does not run, ground terminal C1/21 (VIN R) or C3/E8 (VIN N) of ECM connector with a fused jumper. If coolant fan runs, problem is ECM related.

3. If coolant fan does not run, leave fused jumper connected as in step 2, disconnect coolant fan relay connector and measure voltage from brown wire terminal to ground. If no voltage is present, check FAN/ALT fuse and brown wires for open.
4. If battery voltage is present, leave fused jumper connected as in step 2, measure voltage between brown and dark green (VIN N) or dark green/white (VIN R) wire terminals. If no voltage is present, check dark green or dark green/white wire for open.
5. If battery voltage is present, disconnect coolant fan relay connector and measure voltage from terminal A (red) wire to ground. If no voltage is present, check red wire and fusible link for open.
6. If battery voltage is present, connect a 20 amp fused jumper between terminals A and E of coolant fan relay connector. If coolant fan runs, replace coolant fan relay.
7. If coolant fan does not run, leave fused jumper connected as in step 6, disconnect connector from coolant fan and measure voltage between terminal B and ground. If no voltage is present, check black/red (VIN R) or black/pink (VIN N) wire for open.
8. If battery voltage is present, leave fused jumper connected as in step 6 and measure voltage between terminals B and A of coolant fan connector.
9. If no voltage is present, check black wire for open.
10. If battery voltage is present, replace coolant fan motor.

Coolant Fan Does Not Turn Off With Engine Coolant Cool, A/C Off & Ignition Switch In Run Position

1. Turn ignition switch to RUN position, disconnect coolant fan relay connector and connect test lamp between terminals F and D .
2. If lamp does not illuminate, replace coolant fan relay.
3. If lamp illuminates, check dark green/white (VIN R) or dark green (VIN N) wire for short to ground. If wire is satisfactory, problem is ECM related.

1993
Coolant Fan Does Not Turn On

1. Turn ignition switch to the RUN position and ground terminal "B" of the DLC connector. If coolant fan does not run, refer to step 2. If coolant fan runs, check for possible ECM failure.
2. Using a fused jumper, ground ECM terminals (C1/D13) on 2.2L/4-135 engines or (C3/E8) on 3.3L/V6-204 engines. If coolant fan does not run, refer to step 3. If coolant fan runs, check for possible ECM failure.
3. Leaving fused jumper grounded at ECM, disconnect coolant fan relay connector. Measure voltage from

brown wire to ground. If battery voltage is present, refer to step 4. If battery voltage is not present, check ENG/A/C fuse and pink/black wire for an open circuit.
4. With fused jumper still connected at the ECM, measure voltage between pink/black and dark green wires. If battery voltage is present, refer to step 5. If battery voltage is not present, check dark green wire for an open circuit.
5. Measure voltage from terminal "A" (red) to ground at coolant fan relay connector. If battery voltage is present, proceed to step 6. If battery voltage is not present, check red wire and fusible link for an open circuit.
6. Connect a fused jumper with a 20 amp fuse between terminals "A" and "E" of the coolant fan relay connector. If coolant fan does not run, refer to step 7. If coolant fan runs, replace coolant fan relay.
7. Leaving fused jumper connected at the coolant fan relay connector, disconnect connector from coolant fan. Measure voltage between terminal "B" of the coolant fan connector and ground. If battery voltage is present, refer to step 8. If battery voltage is not present, check black/pink wire for an open circuit.
8. Leaving fused jumper connected at the coolant fan relay connector. Measure voltage between terminals "B" and "A" of the coolant fan connector. If battery voltage is present, replace coolant fan motor. If battery voltage is not present, check black wire for an open circuit.

Coolant Fan Does Not Turn Off With Engine Coolant Cool, A/C Off & Ignition Switch In Run

1. Turn ignition switch to the RUN position and disconnect coolant fan relay connector.
2. Connect a test lamp between terminals "F" and "D" of the coolant fan relay connector.
3. If test lamp lights, proceed to step 4. If test lamp does not light, replace coolant fan relay.
4. Check dark green wire of relay for a short to ground. If wire is satisfactory, problem is ECM related. If wire is not satisfactory, repair or replace as required.

COOLANT FAN, REPLACE

1. Disconnect battery ground cable.
2. Remove engine strut brace bolts from upper tie bar and rotate strut and brace rearward. **To prevent shearing of rubber bushing(s) loosen bolt(s) on strut before rotating.**
3. Disconnect wiring harness from motor and the fan frame.
4. Remove fan frame attaching bolts, then the fan assembly.
5. Reverse procedure to install.

Fig. 19   Coolant fan wiring circuit. 1991–92 Cutlass Ciera & Cutlass Cruiser w/2.5L/4-151 engine

Fig. 20   Coolant fan wiring circuit. 1991–92 Cutlass Ciera & Cutlass Cruiser w/3.3L/V6-204 engine

Fig. 21 Coolant fan wiring circuit. 1993 Cutlass Ciera & Cutlass Cruiser w/2.2L/4-135 engine

Fig. 22 Coolant fan wiring circuit. 1993 Cutlass Ciera & Cutlass Cruiser w/3.3L/V6-204 engine

Fig. 23   Coolant fan wiring circuit (less auxiliary cooling fan). 1991 Camaro & Firebird w/5.0L/V8-305 (VIN F) & 5.7L/V8-350 (VIN 8) engines

SERVICE BULLETINS

Cooling Fan Runs Battery Dead

Refer to "Service Bulletins" in "6000" for diagnosis and repair of this condition.

CAMARO & FIREBIRD

SYSTEM DESCRIPTION

3.1L/V6-192 (VIN T), 3.4L/V6-204 (VIN S), 5.0L/V8-305 (VIN F) & 5.7L/V8-350 (VIN 8) Engines

The coolant fan is controlled by the ECM. In the 6 cylinder, the coolant fan is also controlled by the redundant cooling fan switch. When the ECM grounds circuit 335, the coolant fan relay is energized and battery voltage is applied to the coolant fan. If the ECM fails on the 6 cylinder engine, the redundant coolant fan switch will ground the 335 circuit and energize the coolant fan relay. The ECM will ground the coolant fan relay when the coolant temperature sensor indicates the coolant temperature is greater than 222°F or when A/C control head pressure is greater than 233 psi and vehicle speed is less than 40 mph.

The auxiliary coolant fan, used on the 8 cylinder engines, is controlled by the fan pressure switch and the auxiliary coolant fan switch. If one of these switches closes, the auxiliary coolant fan relay is turned on. When a switch is closed, terminal D11 of

ECM connector C2 is grounded. This tells the ECM that the auxiliary coolant fan should be on.

5.0L/V8-305 (VIN E) Engine

The coolant fan is activated by the coolant fan switch. The switch closes when coolant temperature is over 238°F completing a path to ground through the coolant fan relay windings. The relay contacts then close and voltage is applied to the coolant fan. When the coolant temperature drops to 214°F, the switch opens and the coolant fan stops.

In A/C equipped vehicles, the A/C control head completes a path to ground for the coolant fan relay. Voltage is then applied to the coolant fan.

5.7L/V8-350 (VIN P) Engine

The coolant fan is controlled by the ECM based on various inputs. Battery voltage is supplied to the primary fan relay on terminals "D1" and "F4" of the secondary fan relay. Ignition voltage is supplied to terminal "D5" of the primary fan relay and "F2" of the secondary fan relay. Grounding circuit 335 will energize the primary cooling fan relay and supply battery voltage to the secondary fan motor. Grounding circuit 473 will energize the secondary cooling fan relay and supply battery voltage to the secondary fan motor.

TROUBLESHOOTING

1. Check FAN/FP fuse if coolant fan does not run.
2. Check that ground G118 (3.1L/V6-192), G112 (5.0L/V8-305

VIN E), G104 (5.0L/V8-305 VIN F and 5.7L/V8-350 VIN 8) or G106 (3.4L/V6-204 and 5.7L/V8-350 VIN P) is clean and tight.
3. Check fusible link.
4. If coolant fan runs with ignition switch off, replace coolant fan relay.

SYSTEM CHECK

1. With engine cold and idling, turn A/C selector, if equipped, to NORM. On VIN E, coolant fan should turn on. On VINs T, F and 8, coolant fan, and auxiliary coolant fan, should turn on when A/C control head pressure exceeds 233 psi.
2. With engine coolant below operating temperature, move A/C selector to off. On VIN E, coolant fan should turn off. On VIN T, F and 8, coolant fan, and auxiliary coolant fan if equipped, should turn off when A/C control head pressure falls below 233 psi.
3. With engine warm, run engine at fast idle foe several minutes. Ensure coolant fan turns on before coolant temperature indicator lights or before coolant temperature gage needle indicates hot.
4. Turn ignition switch to OFF position. Coolant fan, and auxiliary coolant fan if equipped, should turn off.

1991–92 SYSTEM DIAGNOSIS & TESTING

Refer to **Figs. 23 through 30** when performing the following diagnostic procedures.

Fig. 24 Coolant fan wiring circuit (auxiliary cooling fan). 1991 Camaro & Firebird w/5.0L/V8-305 (VIN F) & 5.7L/V8-350 (VIN 8) engine

Fig. 25 Coolant fan wiring circuit. 1991 Camaro & Firebird w/5.0L/V8-305 (VIN E) engine

Fig. 26   Coolant fan wiring circuit. 1991 Camaro & Firebird w/3.1L/V6-192 (VIN T) engine

Fig. 27   Coolant fan wiring circuit (less auxiliary cooling fan). 1992 Camaro & Firebird w/5.0L/V8-305 (VIN F) & 5.7L/V8-350 (VIN 8) engine

Fig. 28   Coolant fan wiring circuit (auxiliary cooling fan). 1992 Camaro & Firebird w/5.0L/V8-305 (VIN F) & 5.7L/V8-350 (VIN 8) engine

Fig. 29   Coolant fan wiring circuit. 1992 Camaro & Firebird w/5.0L/V8-305 (VIN E) engine

Fig. 30   Coolant fan wiring circuit. 1992 Camaro & Firebird w/3.1L/V6-192 (VIN T) engine

3.1L/V6-192 (VIN T) ENGINE

If coolant fan does not run at all, perform test A. If coolant fan does not turn off with engine coolant cool, A/C Off and ignition switch in RUN position, perform test B. If coolant fan does not turn On with A/C On and head pressure above 223 psi, but does turn On with engine hot, perform test C.

Test A: Coolant Fan Open Test

1. Connect fused jumper between ALDL connector terminal B and ground and turn ignition switch to RUN position. If coolant fan runs, problem is ECM related.
2. If coolant fan does not run, connect fused jumper to coolant fan relay connector between dark green/white wire and ground and turn ignition switch to RUN position. If coolant fan runs, check dark green/white wire for open. If wire is satisfactory, problem is ECM related.
3. If coolant fan does not run, disconnect coolant fan relay connector, turn ignition switch to run position and connect test lamp between terminals as follows:
   a. Connect between terminal D and ground. If lamp does not illuminate, check C/H-FAN fuse, tan/white wire for open.
   b. Connect between red wire terminal and ground. If lamp does not illuminate, check fusible link J and red wire for open.

4. If lamp illuminates in steps a and b, disconnect coolant fan relay connector and connect fused jumper between red and black/red wire terminals. If coolant fan runs, replace coolant fan relay.
5. If coolant fan does not run, leave fused jumper connected as in step 4, disconnect coolant fan connector and connect test lamp between terminals as follows:
   a. Connect between black/red wire terminal and ground. If lamp does not illuminate, check black/red wire for open.
   b. Connect between black/red and black wire terminals. If lamp does not illuminate, check black wire for open.
   c. If lamp illuminates in steps a and b, replace coolant fan.

Test B: Coolant Fan Does Not Turn Off With Engine Coolant Cool, A/C Off And Ignition Switch In RUN Position

1. Disconnect coolant fan relay, connect a test lamp between terminals D and F of the fan relay connector. If lamp does not light, replace coolant fan relay.
2. If test lamp lights, check and repair dark green/white wire for a short to ground. If wire is satisfactory, connect a fused jumper between terminal C2/D12 of the ECM and ground.
3. After waiting two minutes if fan contin-

ues to run, problem is ECM related.
4. If fan stops, disconnect fan A/C pressure switch connector and connect a fused jumper between terminal B and ground.
5. After two minutes if fan continues to run, check dark blue wire for an open.
6. If fan stops, connect a fused jumper between terminals B and A of the fan A/C pressure switch connector. If fan continues to run, Repair open in black/white wire.
7. If fan stops, replace fan A/C pressure switch.

Test C: Coolant Fan Does Not Turn On With A/C On And Head Pressure Above 223 psi, But Does Turn On With Engine Hot

1. With ignition switch in RUN position and A/C mode selector in MAX position, disconnect fan A/C pressure switch connector. Measure voltage between terminal B and ground. If no voltage is present, repair short to ground in dark green/white wire.
2. If battery voltage is present, problem is ECM related.

5.0L/V8-305 (VIN F) & 5.7L/V8-350 (VIN 8) ENGINES

If coolant fan does not turn on, perform test A. If coolant fan does not turn off with engine cool, A/C mode selector OFF and ignition switch in RUN position, perform test B. If coolant fan does not turn on with A/C mode selector ON and head pressure above 233psi, but does run with engine hot, perform test C and, if only auxiliary coolant does not turn on, perform test D.

Test A: Coolant Fan Does Not Turn On

1. Turn ignition switch to On position, then ground terminal B (white/black) of ALDL connector. If coolant fan runs, problem is ECM related.
2. If coolant fan does not run, ground terminal C3/E8 (dark green/white) of ECM with a fused jumper wire. If coolant fan runs, problem is ECM related.
3. If coolant fan does not run, leave terminal C3/E8 grounded as in step 2. Disconnect coolant fan relay connector and measure voltage from terminal D (brown) of coolant fan relay connector to ground. If no voltage is present, check brown wire and FAN/FP fuse for open.
4. If battery voltage is present, lamp illuminates in steps a and b, disconnect coolant fan relay connector and connect fused jumper between orange and black/red wire terminals. If coolant fan runs, replace coolant fan relay.
5. If coolant fan does not run, leave terminal C3/E8 grounded as in step 2. Measure voltage between terminals D (brown) and F (dark green/white) of coolant fan relay connector. If no voltage is present, check dark green/white wire for open.
6. If battery voltage is present, measure voltage from terminal E (orange) of coolant fan relay connector to ground. If no voltage is present, check orange wire and fusible link D for open.
7. If battery voltage is present, disconnect coolant fan relay connector and connect a 20 amp fused jumper wire between terminals E (orange) and A (red/black). If coolant fan runs, replace relay.
8. If coolant fan does not run, leave jumper wire connected as in step 7. Measure voltage between terminal B (black/red) of coolant fan connector and ground. If no voltage is present, check black/red wire for open.
9. If battery voltage is present, leave jumper wire connected as in step 7. Measure voltage between terminals B (black/red) and A (red) of coolant fan connector. If no voltage is present, check black wire for open.
10. If battery voltage is present, replace coolant fan motor.

Test B: Coolant Fan Does Not Turn Off With Engine Coolant Cool, A/C Mode Selector OFF & Ignition Switch In RUN Position

1. With ignition switch in RUN position, disconnect coolant fan relay connector and connect test lamp between terminals D (brown) and F (dark green/white) of coolant fan relay connector. If lamp does not light, replace coolant fan relay.
2. If lamp lights, check dark green/white wire for short to ground. If wire is satisfactory, problem is ECM related.

Test C: Coolant Fan Does Not Turn On With A/C Mode Selector ON & Head Pressure Above 233 psi, But Does Run With Engine Hot

1. Turn ignition switch to On position, set A/C mode selector to MAX, disconnect fan A/C pressure switch connector, then measure voltage between terminal B (gray) of fan A/C pressure switch and ground. If no voltage is present, check gray wire for open.
2. If battery voltage is present, measure voltage between terminal B (gray) and A (black/white) of A/C pressure switch connector. If no voltage is present, check black/white wire for open.
3. If battery voltage is present, connect a fused jumper wire between terminal B (gray) and A (black/white) of A/C pressure switch connector. If coolant fans do not run, problem is ECM related.
4. If coolant fans run, replace fan A/C pressure switch.

Test D: Coolant Fan & Auxiliary Coolant Fan Open Test

1. With ignition switch in RUN position, disconnect auxiliary coolant fan relay and connect a suitable voltmeter between terminal E (orange) and ground. If battery voltage is not obtained, check fusible link D and orange wire for open, then connect voltmeter between terminal D (brown) and ground. If battery voltage is not obtained, check FAN/FP fuse and brown wire for open. If battery voltage was obtained, proceed to step 2.
2. With auxiliary coolant fan relay connector disconnected, connect a 20 amp fused jumper wire between terminals E (orange) and A (black/pink). If coolant fan runs, proceed to step 4. If coolant fan does not run, leave jumper in place and proceed to step 3.
3. Disconnect auxiliary coolant fan connector, then connect a voltmeter between terminal D (black/pink) and ground. If battery voltage is not obtained, check black/pink wire for open, then connect voltmeter between terminals B (black/pink) and A (black). If battery voltage is not obtained, check black wire for open. If battery voltage was obtained, repair or replace coolant fan.
4. Reconnect coolant fan relay and connect a fused jumper wire from auxiliary coolant fan switch connector to ground. If coolant fan runs, check or replace coolant fan switch. If coolant fan does not run, check gray and black wires for open. If wires are satisfactory, check or replace coolant fan relay.

5.0L/V8-305 (VIN E) ENGINE

If coolant fan does not run at all or if coolant fan does not run with high engine temperature, perform test A. If coolant fan

does not turn On with A/C on, perform test B. If coolant fan will not turn Off, perform test C.

Test A: Coolant Fan Open Test

1. Turn ignition switch to On position, then disconnect coolant fan relay connector and connect a suitable voltmeter between terminal E (red) and ground. If battery voltage is not obtained, check fusible link E and red wire for open, then connect voltmeter between terminal D (brown) and ground. If battery voltage is not obtained, check FAN/FP fuse and brown wire for open. If battery voltage was obtained, proceed to step 2.
2. With coolant fan relay disconnected, connect a 20 amp fused jumper wire between terminals E (red) and A (black/red). If coolant fan runs, proceed to step 4. If coolant fan does not run, leave jumper in place and proceed to step 3.
3. Disconnect coolant fan connector, then connect voltmeter between terminal B (black/red) and ground. If battery voltage is not obtained, check black/red wire for open, then connect voltmeter between terminals B (black/red) and A (black). If battery voltage is not obtained, check black wire for open. If battery voltage was obtained, repair or replace coolant fan.
4. Reconnect coolant fan relay, then connect fused jumper from coolant fan switch connector to ground. If coolant fan runs, check or replace coolant fan switch. If coolant fan does not run, check dark green/white wires for open. If wires are satisfactory, check or replace coolant fan relay.

Test B: Coolant Fan A/C Open

1. Turn ignition switch to On position, then disconnect A/C control head connector and connect fused jumper wire between terminal B (dark green) and ground. If coolant fan does not run, check dark green/white and dark green wires for open, then connect jumper between terminals B (dark green) and A (black). If coolant fan does not run, check black wire for open. If coolant fan runs, repair or replace A/C control head.

Test C: Coolant Fan Does Not Turn Off

1. If coolant fan runs with ignition in Off position, replace coolant fan relay.
2. With ignition in RUN position and A/C Off, disconnect coolant fan switch. If coolant fan turns Off, check or replace coolant fan switch. If coolant fan continues to run, check dark green/white and dark green wires and A/C control head for short to ground.

1993 SYSTEM DIAGNOSIS & TESTING

To perform diagnosis and testing procedures on these systems, refer to charts Figs. 31 and 32, and wiring diagrams Figs. 33 and 34.

CHART C-12
(Page 1 of 2)
COOLING FAN CONTROL CIRCUIT DIAGNOSIS

Circuit Description:

The electric cooling fan is controlled by the ECM, based on inputs from the Engine Coolant Temperature (ECT) sensor, the A/C control switches, vehicle speed, and state of the A/C refrigerant pressure sensor. The ECM controls the fan by grounding CKT 335 which energizes the fan control relay. Battery voltage is then supplied to the fan motor.

The ECM grounds CKT 335 when engine coolant temperature is over about 109°C (228°F), or when A/C has been requested and the A/C refrigerant pressure is about 1655 kPa (240 psi). Once the ECM turns the relay "ON," it will keep it "ON" for a minimum of 30 seconds, or until vehicle speed exceeds 113 km/h (70 mph).

Also, if DTC 14 or 15 sets or the ECM is in back up, the primary fan will run at all time.

Test Description: Number(s) below refer to circled number(s) on the diagnostic chart.

1. With the diagnostic terminal grounded, the cooling fan control driver(s) will close, which should energize the fan control relay(s).
2. If the A/C pressure is above 240 psi (1655 kPa) or circuit is open, the fan would run whenever A/C is requested.
3. With A/C clutch engaged and the A/C refrigerant pressure sensor is functioning properly, the fan should come "ON" when pressure exceeds about 20 psi. Under very cold ambient conditions, the fan will remain "OFF." This signal should cause the ECM to energize the cooling fan control relay.
4. This will determine if the A/C refrigerant pressure sensor is faulty or if the ECM or circuitry is faulty.

Diagnostic Aids:

If the owner complained of an overheating problem, it must be determined if the complaint was due to an actual boilover, a hot light or temp. gage indicated over heating.

If the gage or light indicates overheating, but no boilover is detected, the gage circuit should be checked.

Fig. 31   Chart C-12, coolant fan diagnosis (Part 1 of 2). 1993 Camaro & Firebird w/3.4L/V6-204 (VIN S) engine

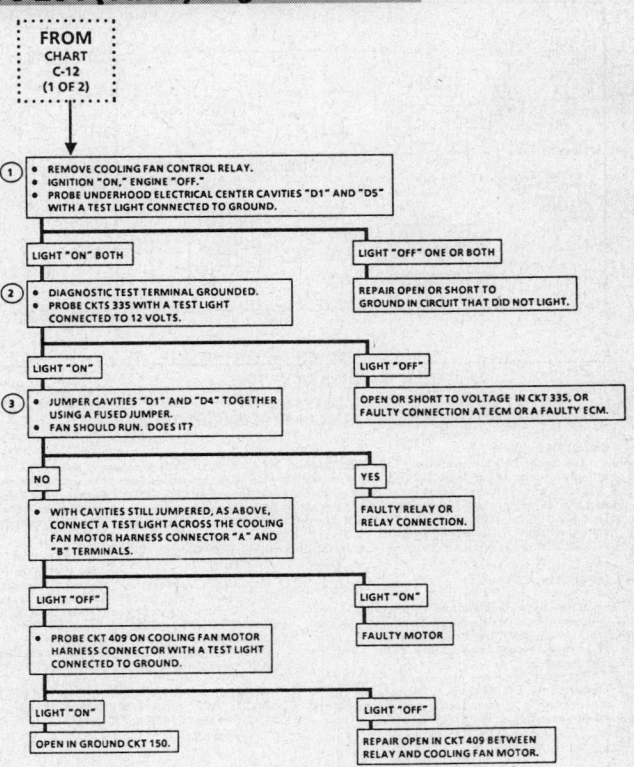

CHART C-12
(Page 2 of 2)
COOLING FAN CONTROL CIRCUIT DIAGNOSIS

Test Description: Number(s) below refer to circled number(s) on the diagnostic chart.

1. 12 volts should be available to CKT 541 and CKT 402 of the relay when the ignition is "ON."
2. This test checks the ability of the ECM to ground CKT 335.

The Malfunction Indicator Lamp (MIL) "Service Engine Soon" should also be flashing at this point.

3. If the fan does not turn "ON" at this point, CKT 409 or CKT 150 is open, or the cooling fan motor is faulty.

Fig. 31   Chart C-12, coolant fan diagnosis (Part 2 of 2). 1993 Camaro & Firebird w/3.4L/V6-204 (VIN S) engine

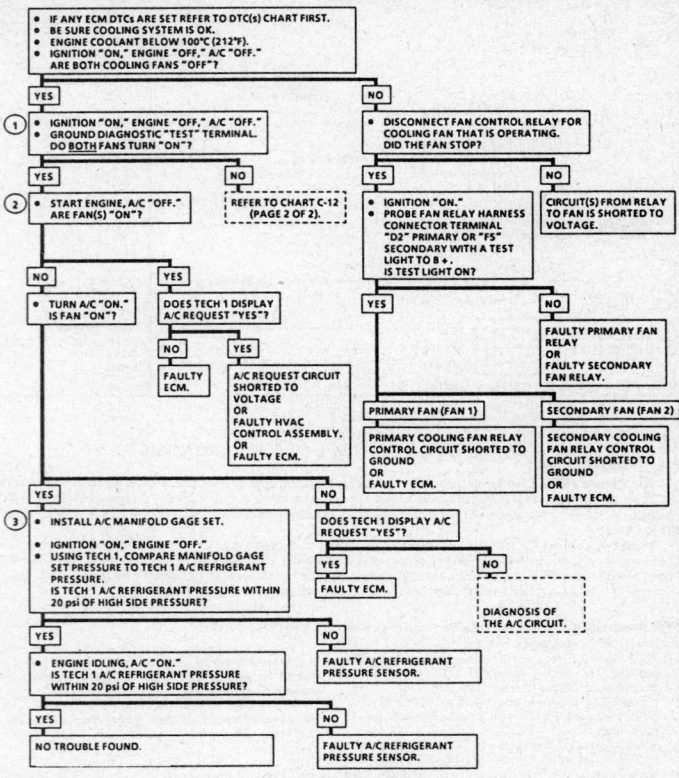

CHART C-12 (Page 1 of 2)
ELECTRIC COOLING FAN CONTROL CIRCUIT DIAGNOSIS

Circuit Description:

The cooling fans are controlled by the ECM based on various inputs. Battery voltage is supplied to the primary fan relay on terminals "D1" and "F4" of the secondary fan relay. Ignition voltage is supplied to terminal "D5" of the primary fan relay and "F2" of the secondary fan relay. Grounding CKT 335 (relay terminal "D2") will energize the primary cooling fan relay (Fan 1) and supply battery voltage to the primary cooling fan motor. Grounding CKT 473 (relay terminal "F5") will energize the secondary cooling fan relay (Fan 2) and supply battery voltage to the secondary fan motor.

When certain Diagnostic Trouble Codes (DTCs) are set, the ECM will enable the cooling fans.

Test Description: Number(s) below refer to circled number(s) on the diagnostic chart.

1. With the diagnostic "test" terminal grounded, the cooling fan control driver(s) will close, which should energize the fan control relay(s).
2. The cooling fans should come "ON" anytime A/C system is operating.
3. Comparing Tech 1 pressure and manifold gage set pressure will determine if the A/C refrigerant pressure sensor is out of range. An out of range A/C refrigerant pressure sensor can cause the cooling fans to operate at the wrong times.

Diagnostic Aids:

If the owner complained of an overheating problem, it must be determined if the complaint was due to an actual boil over, or the warning indicator light, or engine coolant temperature gage indicated overheating.

The gage accuracy can also be checked by comparing the Engine Coolant Temperature (ECT) sensor reading using a Tech 1 and comparing its reading with the gage reading.

If the engine is actually overheating and the gage indicated overheating, but the cooling fan is not coming "ON," the Engine Coolant Temperature (ECT) sensor has probably shifted out of calibration and should be replaced.

If the engine is overheating and the cooling fans are "ON," the cooling system should be checked,

The ECM will command fan 1 "ON" at 108°C (226°F) and "OFF" at 105°C (221°F), and fan 2 "ON" at 113°C (235°F) and "OFF" at 110°C (230°F).

Fig. 32   Chart C-12, coolant fan diagnosis (Part 1 of 2). 1993 Camaro & Firebird w/5.7L/V8-350 (VIN P) engine

CHART C-12
(Page 2 of 2)
ELECTRIC COOLING FAN CONTROL CIRCUIT DIAGNOSIS

Circuit Description:

The cooling fans are controlled by the ECM based on various inputs. Battery voltage is supplied to the primary fan relay on terminals "D1" and "F4" of the secondary fan relay. Ignition voltage is supplied to terminal "D5" of the primary fan relay and "F2" of the secondary fan relay. Grounding CKT 335 (relay terminal "D2") will energize the primary cooling fan relay (Fan 1) and supply battery voltage to the primary cooling fan motor. Grounding CKT 473 (relay terminal "F5") will energize the secondary cooling fan relay (Fan 2) and supply battery voltage to the secondary fan motor.

The ECM will enable the cooling fans, when certain Diagnostic Trouble Codes (DTCs) are set.

Diagnostic Aids:

If the owner complained of an overheating problem, it must be determined if the complaint was due to an actual boil over, the warning indicator light, or engine coolant temperature gage indicated overheating.

The gage accuracy can also be checked by comparing the Engine Coolant Temperature (ECT) sensor reading using a Tech 1 and comparing its reading with the gage reading.

If the engine is actually overheating and the gage indicated overheating, but the cooling fan is not coming "ON," the Engine Coolant Temperature (ECT) sensor has probably shifted out of calibration and should be replaced.

If the engine is overheating and the cooling fans are "ON," the cooling system should be checked.

The ECM will command fan 1 "ON" at 108°C (226°F) and "OFF" at 105°C (221°F) and an 2 "ON" at 113°C (235°F) and "OFF" at 110°C (230°F).

Fig. 32   Chart C-12, coolant fan diagnosis (Part 2 of 2). 1993 Camaro & Firebird w/5.7L/V8-350 (VIN P) engine

Fig. 34 Coolant fan wiring circuit. 1993 Camaro & Firebird w/5.7L/V8-350 (VIN P) engine

Fig. 33 Coolant fan wiring circuit. 1993 Camaro & Firebird w/3.4L/V6-204 (VIN S) engine

COOLANT FAN, REPLACE

1. Disconnect battery ground cable, then remove air cleaner top, if equipped.
2. Disconnect wire harness.
3. Remove cooling fan to radiator support bolts.
4. Remove cooling fan assembly.
5. Reverse procedure to install.

BONNEVILLE

SYSTEM DESCRIPTION

1991

A two speed coolant fan is turned on and off by the low and high speed coolant fan relays.

For low speed operation, the low speed relay coil is grounded through the ECM. The ECM grounds the coil when engine coolant is above 213°F. When the vehicle speed is greater than 47 mph, the ECM will turn off the low speed coolant fan if it is operating.

With the low speed relay coil grounded, its contacts close. Voltage is applied through the coolant fan resistor to the coolant fan. The resistor reduces voltage supplied to the fan so the fan runs at low speed.

For high speed operation, the high speed relay coil is grounded through the high speed contacts in the A/C dual pressure switch or by the ECM. The A/C dual pressure switch high speed contacts close at a refrigerant pressure above 275 psi. The ECM switch closes when coolant temperature rises above 226°F.

With high speed coil grounded, its contacts close. Battery voltage is applied to the coolant fan. The fan runs at high speed.

The coolant fan with heavy duty, if equipped, operates whenever coolant fan runs at high speed. The A/C dual pressure switch and ECM also control the auxiliary coolant fan relay which supplies battery voltage to the auxiliary coolant fan when energized.

1992–93

Two coolant fans, wired in parallel, operate whenever cooling is required.

The powertrain control module (PCM) has two coolant fan control terminals, one for high speed and one for low speed. When the PCM's low speed control closes at connector C3, terminal C4, it grounds the low speed coolant fan relay coil. When the ignition switch is in the run position and relay contacts close, voltage is supplied to the coolant fans. The coolant fan resistors drop the voltage to the lefthand coolant fan, causing it to run in low speed. The righthand coolant fan runs also, but at high speed because the coolant fan resistors are bypassed. The PCM's low speed output is turned on when coolant temperature reaches 212°F.

High speed operation is similar to low speed, when the coolant temperature reaches 226°F, the PCM's high speed control closes at connector C3, terminal C3, grounding the high speed coolant relay coil. The relay contacts close and both fans run at high speed since the PCM's low speed control remains closed. When A/C head pressure reaches 210 psi, the A/C pressure fan switch closes, grounding PCM connector C1, terminal D9. This also causes the PCM high speed control to close, and both coolant fans run at high speed.

TROUBLESHOOTING

1991

1. Visually inspect fuse 6.
2. Visually inspect lefthand underhood fuse block fuse 4.
3. If either fan runs with ignition switch off, replace associated coolant fan relay.

1992–93

1. Visually inspect fuse 16.
2. Visually inspect lefthand underhood fuse block fuse 4.
3. When only one coolant fan does not run check coolant fan motor for mechanical binding or wiring to suspect coolant fan. If satisfactory, replace coolant fan motor.
4. If either fan runs with ignition switch off, replace associated coolant fan relay.

SYSTEM CHECK

1991

1. With engine cold and idling, move A/C selector switch, if equipped, to NORM. The coolant fan should run for 60 seconds at low speed. When A/C head pressure exceeds 275 psi, coolant fan runs at high speed and auxiliary coolant fan runs.
2. With engine coolant below operating temperature, move A/C selector switch to OFF. Coolant fan should turn off in a short period of time.
3. Run engine at fast idle for several minutes. When coolant temperature exceeds 213°F, ECM turns coolant fan on at low speed. When coolant temperature exceeds 226°F, coolant fan runs at high speed and auxiliary coolant fan runs.

1992–93

1. With ambient temperature above 60°F and engine cold and idling, set A/C mode selector to On. Lefthand coolant fan should run at low speed and righthand coolant fan should run at high speed.
2. Set A/C mode selector to off. Coolant fans should turn off after about one minute.
3. Run engine at fast idle for several minutes. Lefthand coolant fan should run at low speed and righthand coolant fan should run at high speed.
4. Restrict air flow through radiator by covering half of the grill side of radiator. Both coolant fans should operate at high speed after a few minutes.

1991 SYSTEM DIAGNOSIS

Refer to **Fig. 35** when performing diagnostic procedures on these systems.

Coolant Fan Does Not Run In Low Or High Speed

1. Disconnect high speed coolant fan relay connector and connect a 20 amp fused jumper between terminals 1 (red) and 4 (black/pink). If coolant fan runs, proceed to "Coolant Fan Does Not Run In Low Speed" and "Coolant Fan Does Not Run In High Speed."
2. If coolant fan does not run, leave fused jumper connected as in step 1, disconnect coolant fan connector and measure voltage from terminal B (black/pink) to ground. If no voltage is present, check underhood fuse 4 and red and black/pink wires for open.
3. If battery voltage is present, leave fused jumper connected as in step 1 and measure voltage between terminals B (black/pink) and C (black) at coolant fan connector. If no voltage is present, check black wire for open.
4. If battery voltage is present, check related coolant fan wiring. If satisfactory, replace coolant fan motor.

Coolant Fan Does Not Run In Low Speed

1. Disconnect low speed coolant fan relay connector and connect a fused jumper between terminals 1 (red) and 4 (black/red). If coolant fan does not run at low speed, check red and black/red wires and coolant fan resistor and wiring.
2. If coolant fan runs at low speed, remove fused jumper and turn ignition switch to RUN position. Measure voltage between terminal 2 (brown) and ground at low speed coolant fan relay connector. If no voltage is present, check fuse 6 and brown wire for open.
3. If battery voltage is present, reconnect low speed coolant fan relay and place ignition switch in RUN position. Ground terminal E2 of ECM connector C3 with a fused jumper. If coolant fan runs at low speed, problem is ECM related.
4. If coolant fan does not run at low speed, check dark green wire for open. Check low speed coolant fan relay terminal contact. If satisfactory, replace low speed coolant fan relay.

Coolant Fan Does Not Run In High Speed

1. Place ignition switch in RUN position and ground terminal B of the ALDL connector with a fused jumper.
2. If coolant fan runs, problem is ECM related.
3. If coolant fan does not run at high speed, remove fused jumper from ALDL connector, then disconnect high speed coolant fan relay and connect a 20 amp fused jumper between terminals 1 (red) and 4 (black/pink). If coolant fan does not run, check red, black/pink wires and coolant fan assembly wiring for an open.
4. If coolant fan runs on high speed, remove fused jumper and place ignition switch in RUN position. Measure voltage between terminal 2 ((brown) and

Fig. 35 Coolant fan wiring circuit. 1991 Bonneville

ground at the high speed coolant fan relay connector. If no voltage is present, check brown wire for an open.

5. If battery voltage is present, reconnect high speed coolant fan relay and place ignition switch in RUN position. Ground terminal B5 of ECM connector C2 with a fused jumper. If coolant fan does not run at high speed, check light green/black wire for an open. Check condition of the high speed coolant fan relay terminal contact. If satisfactory, replace high speed coolant fan relay.

6. If coolant fan runs at high speed, problem is ECM related.

Auxiliary Coolant Fan Does Not Run

1. If coolant fan does not operate in high speed, refer to "Coolant Fan Does Not Run In High Speed."

2. If coolant fan runs in high speed, disconnect auxiliary cooling fan relay connector and place ignition switch in RUN position. Measure voltage between terminal 2 (brown) and ground. if no voltage is present, check brown wire for an open.

3. If battery voltage is present, measure voltage between terminal 1 (red) and ground. If no voltage is present, check red wire for an open.

4. If battery voltage is present, discon-

nect auxiliary coolant fan relay connector and connect a 20 amp fused jumper between terminals 1 (red) and 4 (black/pink). If auxiliary coolant fan runs, check auxiliary coolant fan relay connector terminal contact. Check light green/black wire for open. If satisfactory, replace auxiliary cooling fan relay.

5. If auxiliary cooling fan does not run, leave jumper wire connected as in step 4. Disconnect the connector from the auxiliary cooling fan and measure voltage between terminal B (black/pink) and ground. If no voltage is present, check black/pink wire for open.

6. If Battery voltage is present, leave jumper wire connected as in step 4 and measure voltage between terminals B (black/pink) and A (black). If no voltage is present, check black wire for an open.

7. If battery voltage is present, check auxiliary cooling fan connector terminals. if satisfactory, replace the auxiliary cooling fan motor.

Coolant Fan Runs Continuously In Low Speed With Ignition Switch In RUN Position, Engine Coolant Cool & A/C Off

1. Place ignition switch in RUN position and disconnect low speed coolant fan

relay connector, connect test lamp between terminals 2 (brown) and 5 (dark green).

2. If test lamp does not light, replace low speed coolant fan relay.

3. If test lamp lights, check dark green wire for short to ground. if wire is satisfactory, problem is ECM related.

Coolant Fan Runs Continuously In High Speed And/Or Auxiliary Coolant Fan Runs Continuously With Ignition Switch IN RUN Position, Engine Coolant Cool & A/C Off

1. Turn ignition switch to RUN position and disconnect A/C coolant fan pressure switch connector. If coolant fan(s) stops, replace A/C coolant fan pressure switch.

2. If coolant fan(s) runs, place ignition switch in RUN position and disconnect high speed coolant relay connector and/or auxiliary coolant fan relay connector.

3. Connect a test lamp between terminals 2 (brown) and 5 (light green/black). If test lamp does not light, replace suspected relay.

4. If test lamp lights, check light green/black wires for a short to ground. If wires are satisfactory, problem is ECM related.

Fig. 36 Coolant fan wiring circuit. 1992–93 Bonneville

Low Speed Coolant Fan Does Not Operate Immediately After Selecting A/C

1. Disconnect ECM connector C1, turn ignition switch to RUN position, place A/C selector at NORM position and measure voltage at terminal C9 of connector C1 at ECM.
2. If no voltage is present, problem is in A/C compressor controls.
3. If battery voltage is present, problem is ECM related.

High Speed Coolant Fan And/Or Auxiliary Coolant Fan Do Not Operate With A/C Pressure Above 275 psi.

1. Turn ignition switch to RUN position and disconnect connector from A/C coolant fan pressure switch. Connect a fused jumper wire between terminals A (black) and B (light green/black). If high speed and/or auxiliary coolant fan(s) do not operate, check light green/black and black wires for open.
2. If high speed and/or auxiliary coolant fan(s) run, check switch terminal contacts. If satisfactory, replace A/C coolant fan pressure switch.

1992–93 SYSTEM DIAGNOSIS

Refer to **Fig. 36** when performing diagnostic procedures on these systems.

Coolant Fan Input Test

1. Turn ignition to run, then connect terminals B and A of ALDL connector. If coolant fan does not turn On, proceed to step 2. If coolant fan turns On, problem is PCM related.
2. Turn ignition switch off and remove jumper wire from ALDL connector, then disconnect righthand coolant fan motor connector and measure resistance between connector C123 terminal A and ground.
3. If resistance is less than 50 ohms, repair black/red wire for short to ground, and inspect low speed coolant fan relay for damage.
4. If resistance is more than 50 ohms, reconnect righthand coolant fan motor connector and measure resistance between connector C123 terminal B and ground.
5. If resistance is less than 50 ohms, repair pink/black wire for short to ground and inspect high speed coolant fan relay for damage. If resistance is more than 50 ohms, proceed to step 6.

6. Turn ignition switch to RUN and reconnect terminals A and B of ALDL connector. Measure voltage from connector C123 terminal A to ground.
7. If battery voltage is not measured, perform "Low Speed Coolant Fan Test." If battery voltage is measured, keep ALDL terminals connected and measure voltage from connector C123 terminal B to ground.
8. If battery voltage is not measured, turn ignition switch off, disconnect jumper wire from ALDL, reconnect connector C123 and perform "High Speed Coolant Fan Input Test."
9. If battery voltage is not measured, keep ALDL terminals connected and measure voltage from connector C123 terminal B to terminal C. If battery voltage is not measured, turn ignition switch off and check black wire for and open.
10. If battery voltage is measured, turn ignition switch off and check wiring within coolant fan assembly. If wiring is good, replace coolant fan motor.

Low Speed Coolant Fan Input Test

1. Disconnect low speed coolant fan relay and turn ignition switch to run, then measure voltage from relay connector terminal 2 to ground. If battery

voltage is not measured, check brown wire for an open or short to ground and replace fuses where necessary. If battery voltage is measured, proceed to step 2.

2. Turn ignition switch off and measure voltage from terminal 1 to ground. If battery voltage is not measured, check red wire for an open or short to ground and replace fuses where necessary. If battery voltage is measured proceed to step 3.

3. Connect terminals A and B of ALDL connector and connect a test lamp between relay connector terminal 1 and terminal 5, then turn ignition switch to Run. If test light does not light check gray/black wire for open circuit. If wiring is good, problem is PCM related. If test lamp lights, proceed to step 4.

4. Turn ignition switch off and connect a fused jumper between relay connector terminal 1 and terminal 4. Lefthand coolant fan should run at low speed and righthand coolant fan should run at high speed.

5. If fan does not run as specified, check black/red wire and coolant fan resistor for an open. If fan does run as specified, replace low speed coolant fan relay.

High Speed Coolant Fan Input Test

1. Disconnect high speed coolant relay and turn ignition switch to run. Measure voltage from terminal 2 to ground. If battery voltage is not present, check brown wire for an open or short to ground and replace fuses where necessary. If battery voltage is present, proceed to step 2.

2. Turn ignition switch off and measure voltage from relay connector terminal 1 to ground. If battery voltage is not present, check red wire for open or short to ground and replace fuses where necessary. If battery voltage is present, proceed to step 3.

3. Connect terminals A and B of ALDL connector and connect a test lamp between relay connector terminal 1 and terminal 5, then turn ignition to run. If test lamp does not light, check dark green/white wire for an open. If satisfactory, problem is PCM related. If test lamp lights, proceed to step 4.

4. Turn ignition switch off and connect a fused jumper between relay connector terminal 1 and terminal 4, then turn ignition switch back to RUN. If coolant fan runs at high speed, replace high speed coolant fan relay. If coolant fan does not run at high speed, check black/pink wire and coolant fan resistor for an open.

LH Coolant Fan Runs Continuously In Low Speed w/Ignition Switch At Run, Engine Coolant Cool & A/C Off

1. Turn ignition switch off and disconnect low speed coolant fan relay, then

measure resistance between relay connector terminal 5 and ground.

2. If infinite ohms resistance is measured, replace low speed coolant fan relay.

3. If infinite ohms resistance is not measured, check gray/black wire for short to ground. If satisfactory, problem is PCM related.

LH Coolant Fan Runs Continuously In High Speed w/Ignition Switch At Run, Engine Coolant Cool & A/C Off

1. Turn ignition switch off and disconnect high speed coolant fan relay, then measure resistance between relay connector terminal 5 and ground.

2. If resistance is present, check dark green/white wire for short to ground. If satisfactory, problem is PCM related. If resistance is not present, proceed to step 3.

3. Measure resistance between high speed coolant fan relay terminals 1 and 4. If resistance is present, replace high speed coolant fan relay. If resistance is not present, proceed to step 4.

4. Disconnect A/C pressure fan switch and measure continuity between connector terminal A and ground. If continuity does not exist, replace A/C pressure fan switch. If continuity does exist proceed to step 5.

5. Check dark green/white wire for a short to ground. If satisfactory, problem is PCM related.

LH Coolant Fan Does Not Operate In High Speed w/A/C Head Pressure Above 210 psi

1. Turn ignition switch off and disconnect A/C pressure fan switch connector, then measure resistance from terminal B to ground. If more than 2 ohms was measured, check black/white wire for an open. If less than 2 ohms was measured, proceed to step 2.

2. Connect a jumper wire between terminal A and terminal B of switch connector, then turn ignition switch to RUN. If coolant fan does not run at high speed, check dark green/white wire for an open If satisfactory, problem is PCM related. If coolant fan does run at high speed, proceed to step 3.

3. Reconnect A/C pressure fan switch connector and install pressure gauge set, then perform "System Check" while monitoring A/C head pressure.

4. If pressure does not rise above 210 psi, repair A/C system. If pressure does rise above 210 psi, replace A/C pressure fan switch.

COOLANT FAN, REPLACE

1. Disconnect battery ground cable.
2. Remove harness from fan motor and fan frame.
3. Remove fan guard and hose support if necessary, then frame to radiator support attaching bolts.

4. Remove fan and frame assembly.
5. Reverse procedure to install.

SERVICE BULLETINS
Cooling Fan Runs Battery Dead

Refer to "Service Bulletins" in "6000" for diagnosis and repair of this condition.

CAVALIER
SYSTEM DESCRIPTION
1991

The coolant fan is turned on and off by the ECM based on inputs from the coolant temperature sensor, vehicle speed sensor and the A/C system, if equipped. Battery voltage is applied at all times to terminal 1 of the coolant fan relay and, when the ignition switch is in RUN position, battery voltage ia applied to terminal 5 of the relay. The ECM energizes the coolant fan relay by grounding circuit 335. The relay energizes and battery voltage is applied to the coolant fan.

1992–93

Refer to "Circuit Description" in **Figs. 37 and 38** for coolant fan operation.

TROUBLESHOOTING

1. If coolant fan does not operate, check the following:
   a. **On 1991 models,** check fusible link L.
   b. **On 1992-93 models,** check fusible link C.
   c. **On all models,** check HTR/A/C fuse.
2. If coolant fan runs with ignition switch off, replace coolant fan relay.

SYSTEM CHECK

1. With ambient temperature above 70°F, open all doors, start engine and set mode selector, if equipped to MAX. Coolant fan should turn on.
2. With engine coolant below operating temperature, move mode selector to OFF position. Coolant fan should turn off in a short period of time.
3. Run engine at fast idle for several minutes, coolant fan should turn on before coolant temperature indicator comes on or coolant temperature display shows H.
4. Turn ignition switch to Off position, coolant fan should turn off.

DIAGNOSIS
1991 MODELS

Refer To **Figs. 39 and 40** when performing diagnostic procedures on these systems.

Coolant Fan Does Not Turn On

1. Turn ignition switch to RUN position, then ground terminal B (white/black) of ALDL connector. If coolant fan runs, problem is ECM related.

CHART C-12
COOLING FAN CONTROL
2.2L

Circuit Description:

Battery voltage to operate the cooling fan motor is supplied to relay by CKT 2. Ignition voltage to energize the relay is supplied to relay by CKT 650. When the ECM grounds CKT 335, the relay is energized and the cooling fan is turned "ON." When the engine is running, the ECM will turn the cooling fan "ON" if:
- A/C is "ON."

When the engine is running, the ECM will turn the engine cooling fan "ON" for any of the following reasons:
- Diagnostic Trouble Code (DTC) 14 is set.
- Engine coolant temperature is 106°C (223°F) or greater.
- A/C refrigerant pressure is 51 psi or greater with A/C selected and a Diagnostic Trouble Code (DTC) 66 is not set.

Once the cooling fan is enabled, the ECM will turn the fan "OFF" when:
- Engine is turned "OFF."
- Engine coolant temperature drops to 99°C (210°F) or less.
- A/C refrigerant pressure drops to 41 psi or less with A/C selected.

Diagnostic Aids:

If the owner complained of an overheating problem, it must be determined if the complaint was due to an actual boil over, or the hot light, or temperature gage indicated overheating.

If the gage or light indicates overheating, but no boil over is detected, the gage circuit should be checked. The gage accuracy can also be checked by checking the engine coolant temperature display using a scan tool and comparing its display with the instrument cluster gage.

If the engine is actually overheating and the gage indicates overheating, but the cooling fan is not coming "ON," the ECT sensor has probably shifted out of calibration and should be replaced.

IF ECM IS FAULTY AND MUST BE REPLACED, THE NEW ECM MUST BE PROGRAMMED.

COOLING FAN CONTROL RELAY CONNECTOR

Fig. 37   Chart C-12, coolant fan diagnosis. 1992–93 Cavalier w/2.2L/4-135 engine

---

2. If coolant fan does not run, ground terminal C1/21 (VIN G), C1/C13 (VIN 4) or C3/E8 (VIN T) of ECM with fused jumper wire. If coolant fan runs, problem is ECM related.

3. If coolant fan does not run, leave terminal grounded as in step 2 and disconnect coolant fan relay connector. Measure voltage from terminal 5 (brown/white) to ground. If no voltage is present, check brown and brown/white wire and HTR/A/C fuse for open.

4. If battery voltage is present, leave terminal grounded as in step 2 and measure voltage between terminals 5 (brown/white) and 2 (dark green/white) of coolant fan relay connector. If no voltage is present, check dark green/white wire for open.

5. If battery voltage is present, measure voltage from terminal 1 (red) of coolant fan relay connector to ground. If no voltage is present, check red wire and fusible link L (1991) or fusible link C (1992) for an open.

6. If battery voltage is present, disconnect coolant fan relay connector and connect a 20 amp fused jumper between terminals 1 (red) and 4 (black/red). If coolant fan runs, replace coolant fan relay.

7. If coolant fan does not run, leave fused jumper in place as in step 6 and disconnect connector from coolant fan. Measure voltage from terminal B (black/red) of coolant fan connector to ground. If no voltage is present, check black/red wire for open.

8. If battery voltage is present, leave fused jumper in place as in step 6 and measure voltage between terminals B (black/red) and A (black) of coolant fan connector. If no voltage is present, check black wire for open.

9. If battery voltage is present, replace coolant fan motor.

Coolant Fan Does Not Turn Off With Engine Cool, A/C Mode Selector Off & Ignition Switch In RUN

1. Turn ignition switch to RUN position, then disconnect coolant fan relay connector and connect test lamp between terminals 5 (brown/white) and 2 (dark green/white) of coolant fan relay connector. If lamp does not light, replace coolant fan relay.

2. If lamp lights, check dark green/white wire for short to ground. If wire is satisfactory, problem is ECM related.

1992–93 MODELS

To perform diagnosis and testing procedures on these systems, refer to charts **Figs. 37 and 38**, and wiring diagrams **Figs. 41 and 42.**

COOLANT FAN, REPLACE
2.2L/4-135 Engine

1. Disconnect battery ground cable.
2. Remove air cleaner duct, then disconnect wiring harness from motor and fan frame.
3. Remove fan assembly from radiator support.
4. Reverse procedure to install.

3.1L/V6-192 Engine

1. Disconnect battery ground cable.
2. Remove air cleaner duct, then air cleaner assembly.
3. Mark latch position for reassembly, then remove primary hood latch.
4. Drain engine coolant to a level below radiator inlet hose, then disconnect radiator inlet hose at radiator and position aside.
5. **On models with automatic transmission,** disconnect trans cooler lines and position aside.
6. **On all models,** disconnect wiring harness connector at coolant fan, then remove fan assembly from radiator support.
7. Reverse procedure to install.

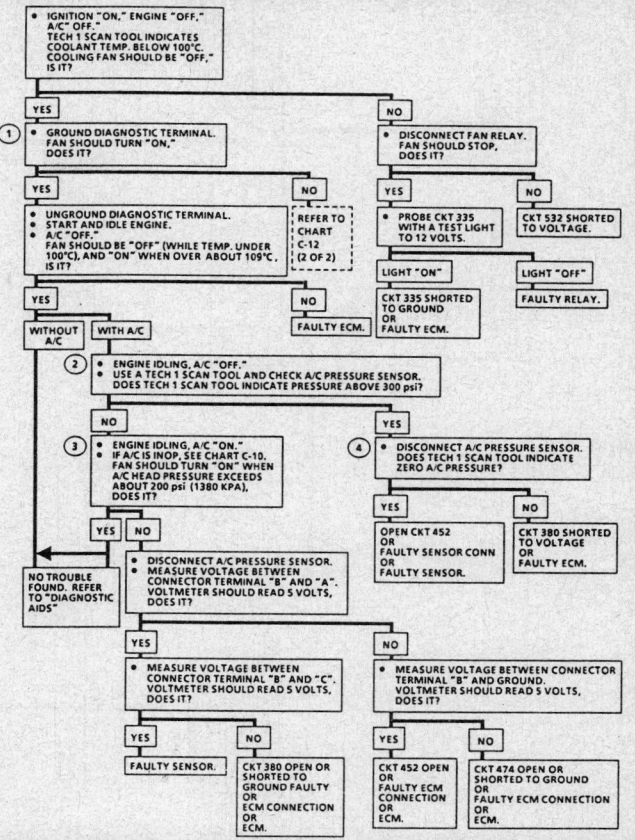

CHART C-12
(Page 1 of 2)
COOLANT FAN CONTROL DIAGNOSIS

Circuit Description:

The electric cooling fan is controlled by the ECM based on inputs from the engine coolant temperature sensor, the A/C pressure sensor and vehicle speed. The ECM controls the fan by grounding CKT 335, which energizes the fan control relay. Battery voltage is then supplied to the fan motor.

The ECM grounds CKT 335 when engine coolant temperature is over about 109°C (228°F) or when A/C has been requested and the A/C pressure sensor indicates high A/C pressure, 200 psi (1380 kPa). Once the ECM turns the relay "ON," it will keep it "ON" for a minimum of 25 seconds or until vehicle speed exceeds 70 mph.

Also, if DTC 14 or 15 sets or the ECM is in back up, the fan will run at all times.

Test Description: Number(s) below refer to circled number(s) on the diagnostic chart.

1. With the diagnostic terminal grounded, the cooling fan control driver will close, which should energize the fan control relay.
2. If the A/C fan control switch or circuit is open, the fan would run whenever A/C is requested.
3. With A/C clutch engaged, the A/C fan control switch should open when A/C high pressure exceeds about 200 psi (1380 kPa). This signal should cause the ECM to energize the fan control relay.
4. Disconnecting the A/C pressure sensor will cause a DTC 66 to set. After finishing this step, be sure to clear DTC(s).

Diagnostic Aids:

If the owner complained of an overheating problem, it must be determined if the complaint was due to an actual boilover or the hot light (temperature gage) indicated over heating.

If the gage (light) indicates overheating but no boilover is detected, the gage circuit should be checked. The gage accuracy can also be checked by comparing the coolant sensor reading using a Tech 1 scan tool and comparing its reading with the gage reading.

If the engine is actually overheating and the gage indicates overheating but the cooling fan is not coming "ON," the ECT sensor has probably shifted out of calibration and should be replaced.

If the engine is overheating and the cooling fan is "ON," the cooling system should be checked.

Fig. 38   Chart C-12, coolant fan diagnosis (Part 1 of 2). 1992–93 Cavalier w/3.1L/V6-192 (VIN T) engine

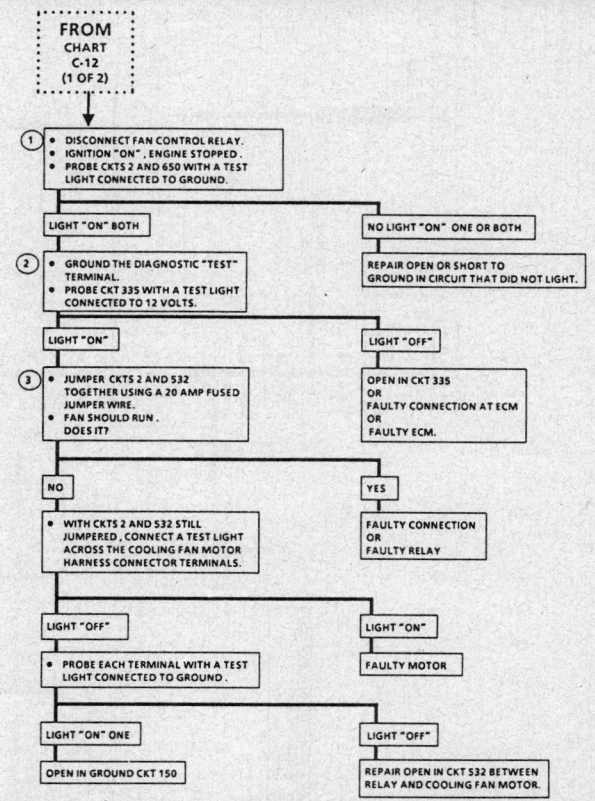

CHART C-12
(Page 2 of 2)
COOLANT FAN CONTROL DIAGNOSIS

Test Description: Number(s) below refer to the diagnostic chart.

1. 12 volts should be available to both terminal "2" and CKT 532 when the ignition is "ON."
2. This test checks the ability of the ECM to ground CKT 335.

The Malfunction Indicator Lamp (MIL) should also be flashing at this point.

3. If the fan does not turn "ON" at this point, CKT 532 or CKT 150 is open or the cooling fan motor is faulty.

Fig. 38   Chart C-12, coolant fan diagnosis (Part 2 of 2). 1992–93 Cavalier w/3.1L/V6-192 (VIN T) engine

Fig. 40 Coolant fan wiring circuit. 1991 Cavalier w/3.1L/V6-192 engine

Fig. 39 Coolant fan wiring circuit. 1991 Cavalier w/2.2L/4-135 engine

Fig. 42 Coolant fan wiring circuit. 1992–93 Cavalier w/3.1L/V6-192 engine

Fig. 41 Coolant fan wiring circuit. 1992–93 Cavalier w/2.2L/4-135 engine

CUTLASS SUPREME, GRAND PRIX & REGAL

SYSTEM DESCRIPTION

ALL MODELS EXCEPT REGAL W/3800/V6-231 (VIN L) ENGINE

Each coolant fan is turned on and off by separate coolant fan relays.

The primary coolant fan relay coil is grounded through the ECM when vehicle speed is less than a speed determined by the ECM and engine coolant reaches 227°F with A/C off and 223°F with A/C on. The contacts close and voltage is applied through the primary coolant fan relay to the primary coolant fan. The primary coolant fan runs until the ignition switch is turned off, or coolant temperature decreases to 220°F with A/C off or 216°F with A/C on.

The secondary coolant fan relay coil is grounded through the ECM when the coolant temperature reaches 245°F. The contacts close and voltage is applied to the coolant fan. The fan runs at high speed. The coolant fan will continue to run at high speed in RUN position until coolant temperature lowers to 238°F.

REGAL W/3800/V6-231 (VIN L) ENGINE

Low Speed Operation

When coolant temperature is greater than 212°F, ECM provides a ground signal to coil of fan relay No. 1. Relay energizes and voltage is applied to primary and secondary cooling fans, which are connected in series through normally closed contacts of relay No. 3. ECM will continue to energize fan relay No. 1 for two minutes when ignition is shut off if coolant temperature is above 230°F and inlet air temperature is above 104°F. Also, ECM will energize fan relay No. 1 if A/C is required.

High Speed Operation

When coolant temperature is greater than 226°F, ECM provides a ground signal to fan relay No. 2 and 3. Relays energize and cooling fans are now connected in parallel and fans now run at high speed. Relays remain energized until coolant temperature drops below 225°F. ECM will also energize fan relays 2 and 3 if A/C is requested and fan A/C pressure switch closes.

If cooling fans are operating in low speed mode and vehicle is travelling at 50 mph or greater, ECM will de-energize fan relay No. 1. If cooling fans are operating in high speed mode, ECM will not de-energize relay.

TROUBLESHOOTING

1991

1. If both coolant fans do not operate, check IGN fuse. On 1991 Regal models, check FAN fuse also.

2. If a coolant fan does not operate, check fusible links N and L.
3. If coolant fan runs with ignition switch in OFF position, replace suspect coolant fan relay.

1992—93

1. Visually inspect IGN fuses and fusible elements.
2. If coolant fan runs with ignition switch in OFF position, check black/red (702 and 532) wires for a short to battery, or dark green/white (335) or dark blue/white (473) wires for short to ground. If wires are satisfactory, replace suspect coolant fan relay.

DIAGNOSIS

Refer To **Figs. 43 through 50** when performing diagnostic procedures on these systems.

1991—92 MODELS EXCEPT REGAL W/3800/V6-231 (VIN L) ENGINE

Primary Coolant Fan Does Not Run

1. With ignition switch in RUN position, ground terminal B (white/black) of ALDL connector. If primary coolant fan runs, problem is ECM related.
2. If primary coolant fan does not run, turn ignition switch to RUN position and ground terminal A9 (dark green/white) at ECM with fused jumper. If primary coolant fan runs, problem is ECM related.
3. If primary coolant fan does not run, turn ignition switch to RUN position, leave fused jumper connected as in step 2, disconnect primary coolant fan relay connector and measure voltage from terminal 3 (red) to ground. If no voltage is present, check for open in red wire.
4. If battery voltage is present, turn ignition switch to RUN position, leave fused jumper connected as in step 2 and measure voltage between terminals 3 (red) and 1 (dark green/white). If no voltage is present, check dark green/white wire for an open.
5. If battery voltage is present, disconnect primary coolant fan relay connector and measure voltage from terminal 2 (red VIN D & X), (brown/white VIN T) or (pink/black early production regal VIN T) to ground at RS electrical center. If no voltage is present, check brown/white, red or pink/black wire for open.
6. If battery voltage is present, disconnect primary coolant fan relay connector and connect a 20 amp fused jumper between terminals 3 (red) and 5 (black/red) at RS electrical center. If primary coolant fan runs, check for satisfactory contact between primary coolant fan relay and RS electrical center. If satisfactory, replace primary coolant fan relay.
7. If primary coolant fan does not run, leave fused jumper connected as in

step 6, disconnect primary coolant fan connector and measure voltage from terminal B (black/red) to ground. If no voltage is present, check black/red wire for open.
8. If battery voltage is present, leave fused jumper in place as in step 6 and measure voltage between terminals B (black/red) and A (black).
9. If no voltage is present, check black wire for open.
10. If battery voltage is present, check primary coolant fan connector terminals for cleanness and tightness and, if satisfactory, replace primary coolant fan.

Secondary Coolant Fan And/Or Generator Coolant Fan (VIN X) Does Not Run

1. With ignition switch in RUN position, ground terminal A3 (dark blue/white) at ECM with fused jumper. If coolant fan runs, problem is ECM related.
2. If coolant fan does not run, leave fused jumper connected as in step 1, disconnect secondary coolant fan relay connector, turn ignition switch to RUN position and measure voltage at RS electrical center terminal 2 (brown) or (pink/black early production Regal VIN T) to ground. If no voltage is present, check brown or pink/black wire for open.
3. If battery voltage is present, leave fused jumper connected as in step 1, turn ignition switch to RUN position and measure voltage between terminals 2 (brown) or (pink/black early production Regal VIN T) and 1 (dark blue/white). If no voltage is present, check dark blue/white wire for open.
4. If battery voltage is present, measure voltage between terminal 3 (red) and ground. If no voltage is present, check red wire for open.
5. If battery voltage is present, disconnect secondary coolant fan relay connector and connect 20 amp fused jumper between terminals 3 (red) and 5 (black/red) at RS electrical center.
6. If secondary and/or generator coolant fan (VIN X) runs, check secondary coolant fan relay connector terminal contact at RS electrical center. If satisfactory, replace secondary coolant fan relay.
7. If secondary and/or generator coolant fan (VIN X) does not run, leave fused jumper connected as in step 5, then disconnect secondary and/or generator coolant fan connector (VIN X) and measure voltage between terminal B (except VIN X) or terminal A (VIN X) (black/red) and ground. If no voltage is present, check black/red wire for open.
8. If battery voltage is present, leave fused jumper connected as in step 5 and measure voltage between terminals B (black/red) and A (black) or terminals A (black/red) and B (black) (VIN X). If no voltage is present, check black wire for open.

9. If battery voltage is present, check suspect coolant fan connector and ensure terminals are clean and tight. If satisfactory, replace suspect coolant fan.

Primary Coolant Fan Runs Continuously With Engine Coolant Cool & A/C Mode Selector Off

1. Disconnect primary coolant fan relay at RS electrical center, turn ignition switch to RUN position and connect test lamp between terminals 3 (red) and 1 (dark green/white).
2. If lamp does not illuminate, replace primary coolant fan relay.
3. If lamp illuminates, check dark green/white wire for short to ground. If wire is satisfactory, problem is ECM related.

Secondary Coolant Fan And/Or Generator Coolant Fan Runs Continuously With Engine Coolant Cool & A/C Mode Selector Off

1. Disconnect secondary coolant fan relay at RS electrical center, turn ignition switch to RUN position and connect test lamp between terminals 3 (red) and 1 (dark blue/white).
2. If lamp does not illuminate, replace secondary coolant fan relay.
3. If lamp illuminates, check dark blue/white wire for short to ground. If wire is satisfactory, problem is ECM related.

1991–92 REGAL W/3800/V6-231 (VIN L) ENGINE

Cooling Fan Isolation Test

1. Turn ignition switch to RUN position, then connect a fused jumper wire between terminal B of ALDL connector and ground. If both cooling fans run at low speed for several seconds and then at high speed, problem is ECM related.
2. If both cooling fans do not run at low speed for several seconds and then at high speed, observe if both fans run at low speed.
3. If both fans run at low speed, proceed to step 7.
4. If both fans do not run at low speed, observe if they run at high speed.
5. If both fans run at high speed, refer to "Cooling Fans Run At High Speed Only." If both fans do not run at high speed, observe if either fan runs at high speed.
6. If secondary (righthand) does not run, refer to "Secondary Cooling Fan Does Not Run." If primary (lefthand) does not run, refer to "Primary Cooling Fan Does Not Run."
7. If both fans run at low speed, observe if they run at high speed.
8. If both fans run at high speed, system is operating normally.

9. If both fans do not run at high speed, observe if either fan runs at high speed.
10. If neither fan runs, refer to "No Cooling Fans Operate At High Speed." If secondary (righthand) does not run, refer to "Secondary Cooling Fan Does Not Run At High Speed." If primary (lefthand) does not run, refer to "Primary Cooling Fan Does Not Run At High Speed."

Cooling Fan Runs At High Speed Only

1. Disconnect fan relay No. 3, then connect a fused jumper wire at RS electrical center from terminal 3 to 4. Ground terminal A8 at ECM connector with a fused jumper, then observe if both cooling fans run at low speed.
2. If both cooling fans do not run at low speed, check black/red wire for open.
3. If both cooling fans run at low speed, replace fan relay No. 3.

Secondary Cooling Fan Does Not Run

1. Disconnect fan relay No. 1, then connect a fused jumper wire at RS electrical center from terminal 3 to 5. Observe if primary (lefthand) cooling fan runs.
2. If primary cooling fan runs, check black/red wires for short to ground.
3. If primary cooling fan does not run, leave jumper connected as in step 1 and disconnect fan relay No. 3. Connect a fused jumper from terminal 3 to terminal 4 and observe if secondary (righthand) cooling fan runs.
4. If secondary cooling fan runs, replace fan relay No. 3.
5. If secondary cooling fan does not run, leave jumper connected as in step 1 and disconnect secondary cooling fan connector. Connect test lamp from terminal B to ground. If lamp does not light, check black/red wire for open.
6. If lamp lights, leave jumper connected as in step 1 and connect test lamp between terminals B and A. If lamp does not light, check black wire for open.
7. If lamp lights, replace secondary cooling fan.

Primary Cooling Fan Does Not Run

1. Disconnect fan relay No. 1, then turn ignition switch to RUN position and connect a test lamp at RS electrical center from terminal 2 to ground. If lamp does not light, check fan fuse and orange wire.
2. If lamp lights, set heater and A/C control selector to NORM and connect test lamp from terminals 2 to 1 of fan relay No. 1. If lamp does not light, check dark green wire for open. If wire is satisfactory, problem Is ECM related.

3. If lamp lights, connect test lamp from terminal 3 of fan relay No. 1 to ground. If lamp does not light, check fusible link N and red wire for open.
4. If lamp lights, connect fused jumper between terminals 3 and 5 of fan relay No. 1 and observe if both cooling fans run.
5. If both cooling fans run, replace fan relay No. 1.
6. If both cooling fans do not run, leave jumper connected as in step 4 and disconnect primary cooling fan connector. Connect test lamp from terminal B to ground. If lamp does not light, check black/pink (1991) or black/red (1992) wire for an open.
7. If lamp lights, leave jumper connected as in step 4 and connect test lamp between terminals B and A. If lamp lights, replace primary cooling fan.
8. If lamp does not light, reconnect primary cooling fan connector and disconnect fan relay No. 3. Leave jumper connected as in step 4 and connect fused jumper from terminal 3 of fan relay No. 3 to ground. If primary cooling fan runs at high speed, replace fan relay No. 3.
9. If primary cooling fan does not run at high speed, check black/red (1991) or black/pink (1992) wire for open.

Secondary Cooling Fan Does Not Run At High Speed

1. Disconnect fan relay No. 2, then turn ignition switch to RUN position and connect two test lamps from terminals 2 and 3 of fan relay to ground. If one or both lamps do not light, check fusible link M and red wire or IGN fuse and pink/black (1991 regular production and all 1992) or brown (1991 early production) for open.
2. If lamps light, connect fused jumper between terminals 3 and 5 of fan relay No. 2. If secondary cooling fan runs at high speed, replace fan relay No. 2.
3. If secondary cooling fan does not run at high speed, check black/red wire for open circuit.

Primary Cooling Fan Does Not Run At High Speed

1. Disconnect fan relay No. 3, then turn ignition switch to RUN position and connect test lamp from terminal 2 of fan relay to ground. If lamp does not light, check pink/black (1991 regular production and all 1992) or brown (1991 early production) wire for open.
2. If lamp lights, connect test lamp between terminals 2 and 5. If lamp does not light, check black wire for open.
3. If lamp lights, connect terminal B of ALDL to ground and wait 10 seconds. Connect test lamp between terminals 2 and 1. If lamp does not light, check light green/black wire for open.
4. If lamp lights, replace fan relay No. 3.

Continued on page 16-48

Fig. 43   Coolant fan wiring circuit (Part 1 of 3). 1991 Cutlass Supreme & Grand Prix w/3.1L/V6-192 & 3.4L/V6-204 engines

Fig. 43   Coolant fan wiring circuit (Part 2 of 3). 1991 Cutlass Supreme & Grand Prix w/2.3L/4-138 engine

Fig. 43   Coolant fan wiring circuit (Part 3 of 3). 1991 Cutlass Supreme & Grand Prix w/2.3L/4-138, 3.1L/V6-192 & 3.4L/V6-204 engines

Fig. 44   Coolant fan wiring circuit (Part 1 of 2). 1991 Regal w/3.1L/V6-192 engine (early production models)

Fig. 44 Coolant fan wiring circuit (Part 2 of 2). 1991 Regal w/3.1L/V6-192 engine (early production models)

Fig. 45 Coolant fan wiring circuit (Part 1 of 2). 1991 Regal w/3.1L/V6-192 engine (regular production models)

Fig. 45   Coolant fan wiring circuit (Part 2 of 2). 1991 Regal w/3.1L/V6-192 engine (regular production models)

Fig. 46   Coolant fan wiring circuit (Part 1 of 2). 1991 Regal w/3800/V6-231 engine

Fig. 46   Coolant fan wiring circuit (Part 2 of 2). 1991 Regal w/3800/V6-231 engine

Fig. 47   Coolant fan wiring circuit (Part 1 of 2). 1992 Cutlass Supreme & Grand Prix

Fig. 47   Coolant fan wiring circuit (Part 2 of 2). 1992 Cutlass Supreme & Grand Prix

Fig. 48   Coolant fan wiring circuit (Part 1 of 2). 1992 Regal

Fig. 48   Coolant fan wiring circuit (Part 2 of 2). 1992 Regal

No Cooling Fans Operate At High Speed

1. Disconnect fan relay No. 2, then turn ignition switch to RUN position and connect test lamp from terminal 2 of fan relay to ground. If lamp does not light, check IGN fuse and pink/black (1991 regular production and all 1992) or brown (1991 early production) wire for open.
2. If lamp lights, connect terminal B of ALDL to ground and wait 10 seconds. Connect test lamp between terminals 2 and 1. If lamp does not light, check light green/black wire for open. If wire is satisfactory, problem is ECM related.
3. If lamp lights, system is operating normally. Check for intermittent faults.

1993 ALL MODELS
Primary Coolant Fan Does Not Run

1. Turn ignition switch to the RUN position and connect a fused jumper between DLC connector terminal "B" and ground. If coolant fan does not run, proceed to step 2. If coolant fan runs, problem is ECM related.
2. Remove primary coolant fan relay and connect a test light between primary coolant fan relay connector terminal "3" and ground. Then connect the test light between terminal "2" and ground. If test light comes on in both cases, proceed to step 3. If test light does not come in both cases, check for faulty connection. If connection is satisfactory, check circuits 650 and 1444 for an open.
3. Connect a fused jumper between primary coolant fan relay connector terminals "3" and "5." If coolant fan does not run, proceed to step 4. If coolant fan runs, check for the following:
   a. Circuit 335 for an open or short to battery.
   b. Poor connection.
   c. If connection and circuit are satisfactory, replace primary coolant fan relay.
4. Leaving fused jumper attached between terminals "3" and "5," disconnect primary coolant fan relay connector and connect a test light between coolant fan connector terminal "B" and ground. If test light comes on, proceed to step 5. If test light does not come on, check for poor connection or an open in circuit (702).
5. Leave fused jumper attached between terminals "3" and "5." Connect a test light between primary coolant fan connector terminals "A" and "B," then proceed as follows:
   a. If test lamp comes on, check for poor connection. If connection is satisfactory, replace primary coolant fan motor.
   b. If test lamp does not come on, check for poor connection or an open circuit 150 between primary coolant fan and splice (S105).

Secondary Coolant Fan Does Not Run

1. Attach a fused jumper between secondary coolant fan relay terminal "1" and ground, then turn ignition switch to RUN. If coolant fan does not run, proceed to step 2. If coolant fan runs, check for an open in circuit (473) or poor connection at ECM. If circuit and connection are satisfactory, problem is ECM related.
2. Remove fused jumper and secondary coolant fan relay. Connect a test light between secondary coolant fan relay connector terminal "3" and ground, then between terminal "2" and ground. If test light comes on in both cases, proceed to step 3. If test light does not come on in both cases, check for a poor connection. If connection is satisfactory, check for an open in circuits (250) and (1442) on engines except 3800/V6-231 or circuit (1445) on 3800/V6-231.
3. Connect a fused jumper between secondary coolant fan relay connector terminals "3" and "5." If secondary coolant fan does not run, proceed to step 4. If secondary coolant fan runs, check circuit (473) for an open or short to battery. If circuit is satisfactory, replace coolant fan relay.
4. Leave fused jumper attached between terminals "3" and "5." Disconnect secondary coolant fan connector, then connect a test light between

Continued on page 16-60

secondary coolant fan connector terminal "B" and ground. If test lamp lights, proceed to step 5. If test lamp does not light, check for a poor connection or open in circuit (532).

5. Connect a test lamp between secondary coolant fan connector terminals "A" and "B." If test lamp lights, check for poor connection. If connection is satisfactory, replace secondary coolant fan motor. If test lamp does not light, check for poor connection or open in circuit (150).

Primary Coolant Fan Runs Continuously With Engine Coolant Cool & A/C Mode Selector Off

1. Disconnect primary coolant fan relay number "1." If coolant fan stops running, proceed to step 2. If coolant fan continues to run, check circuit (702) for a short to battery.
2. Turn ignition switch to the RUN position and connect a test lamp between primary coolant fan relay terminals "1" and "3." If test lamp lights, check circuit (335) for a short to ground. If circuit (335) is satisfactory, problem is ECM related. If test lamp does not light, replace primary coolant fan relay.

Secondary Coolant Fan Runs Continuously With Engine Coolant Cool & A/C Mode Selector Off

1. Disconnect secondary coolant fan relay number "2." If coolant fan stops running, proceed to step 2. If coolant fan continues to run, check circuit (532) for a short to battery.
2. Turn ignition switch to the RUN position and connect a test lamp between secondary coolant fan relay terminals "1" and "3." If test lamp lights, check circuit (473) for a short to ground. If circuit (473) is satisfactory, problem is ECM related. If test lamp does not light, replace secondary coolant fan relay.

COOLANT FAN, REPLACE

1. Disconnect battery ground cable, then remove air cleaner assembly.
2. **On VIN A & D models,** remove lower bolt from engine strut to body brace.
3. **On all models,** remove engine strut brace bolts from upper tie bar and rotate strut(s) and brace(s) rearward. **To prevent shearing of rubber bushing(s), loosen bolt(s) on engine strut(s) before rotating.**
4. Remove coolant bottle.
5. Disconnect harness from fan motor and fan frame.
6. Remove fan frame to radiator support attaching bolts.
7. Remove fan and frame assembly.
8. Reverse procedure to install.

CORVETTE
SYSTEM DESCRIPTION
1991

The coolant fan is turned on and off by the ECM based on inputs from the coolant temperature sensor, the vehicle speed sensor and the A/C coolant fan switch, if equipped. Battery is applied at all times to terminal E of the coolant fan relay and, when ignition switch is in RUN position, battery voltage is applied to terminal D of relay. The ECM energizes the coolant fan by grounding circuit 409. The relay energizes, and battery voltage is applied to the coolant fan motor.

The secondary coolant fan is turned on and off by the ECM based on input from the A/C coolant fan switch. When the A/C coolant fan switch is open (above 190 psi), the switch removes ground to the A/C coolant fan switch input at the ECM. The ECM then grounds the secondary coolant fan relay coil, closing the relay contacts and turning on the secondary coolant fan motor.

Battery voltage is applied at all times to the secondary coolant fan relay contacts by fusible link E. Voltage is supplied to the secondary coolant fan relay coil when ignition switch is in the Run, Bulb Test or Start position.

1992–93 VIN P

The primary and secondary coolant fans are turned on and off by the ECM based on inputs from the coolant temperature sensor, the vehicle speed sensor and the A/C pressure sensor, if equipped. Battery is applied at all times to terminal E of the coolant fan relay and when ignition switch is in RUN position, battery voltage is applied to terminal D of the relays. The ECM energizes the coolant fan by grounding circuit 335. The relay energizes, and battery voltage is applied to the primary coolant fan motor.

The secondary coolant operates similar to the primary coolant fan. Voltage is supplied at all times to the secondary coolant fan relay contacts by fusible link E. Voltage is supplied to the secondary coolant fan relay coil when ignition switch is in the Run, Bulb Test or Start position.

If ECM codes are set or if the ECM is running in fuel-mode back-up, the fans will be On at all times.

1992–93 VIN J

Operation is similar to the VIN P engine except the secondary coolant fan is operated by the A/C coolant fan switch instead of the A/C pressure sensor.

When the A/C coolant fan switch is open (above 240 psi), the switch removes ground to the A/C coolant fan switch input at the ECM. The ECM then grounds the secondary coolant fan relay coil, closing the relay contacts and turning on the secondary coolant fan motor.

If ECM codes are set or if the ECM is running in fuel-mode back-up, the fans will be On at all times.

TROUBLESHOOTING

1. Check for an open Gauges fuse.
2. Check for an open fusible link D or E.
3. Check for corrosion on coolant fan and coolant fan relay terminals.
4. Ensure grounds are clean and tight.

DIAGNOSIS

Refer to wiring diagrams **Figs. 51 through 56** when performing diagnostic procedures on these systems.

1991 MODELS

Refer to **Figs. 57 and 58** for system diagnostic charts.

1992 MODELS

Refer to **Figs. 59 and 60** for system diagnostic charts.

1993 MODELS

Refer to **Figs. 61 and 62** for system diagnostic charts.

COOLANT FAN, REPLACE
5.7L/V8-350 (VIN 8) ENGINE
Primary (Left) Fan

1. Disconnect battery ground cable, then remove air intake duct.
2. Remove power steering pump reservoir to front crossmember bolts and position reservoir aside.
3. Disconnect electrical connector from fan motor, then remove bolts retaining fan assembly to fan shroud.
4. Remove end cap from power steering pump pulley, then the fan assembly.
5. Reverse procedure to install.

Secondary (Right) Fan

1. Disconnect battery ground cable, then remove upper righthand bolt retaining fan assembly to fan shroud.
2. Raise and support vehicle, then disconnect electrical connector from fan motor.
3. Remove remaining bolts retaining fan assembly to fan shroud, then the fan assembly from vehicle.
4. Reverse procedure to install.

5.7L/V8-350 (VIN J) ENGINE
Primary (Left) Fan

1. Disconnect battery ground cable, then remove radiator pressure cap and drain coolant.
2. Remove air intake duct, then clamps and hoses from coolant outlets, radiator inlet and inlet pipe.
3. Remove hose and inlet pipe assembly from vehicle, then disconnect electrical connector from fan motor.
4. Remove screws retaining fan motor to motor support, then bolt retaining A/C discharge line clamp to crossmember.
5. Remove bolts retaining fan assembly to fan shroud, then end cap from power steering pulley.
6. Remove fan assembly from vehicle.
7. Reverse procedure to install.

Continued on page 16-60

Fig. 50 Cooling fan wiring circuit. 1993 Regal w/3800/V6-231 engine

Fig. 49 Cooling fan wiring circuit. 1993 Cutlass Supreme, Grand Prix & Regal except 3800/V6-231 engine

Fig. 51 Coolant fan wiring circuit. 1991 Corvette w/5.7L/V8-350 (VIN 8) engine

Fig. 52 Coolant fan wiring circuit. 1991 Corvette ZR1 w/5.7L/V8-350 (VIN J) engine

Fig. 54 Coolant fan wiring circuit. 1992 Corvette ZR1 w/5.7L/V8-350 (VIN J) engine

Fig. 53 Coolant fan wiring circuit. 1992 Corvette w/5.7L/V8-350 (VIN P) engine

Fig. 56 Coolant fan wiring circuit. 1993 Corvette ZR1 w/5.7L/V8-350 (VIN J) engine

Fig. 55 Coolant fan wiring circuit. 1993 Corvette w/5.7L/V8-350 (VIN P) engine

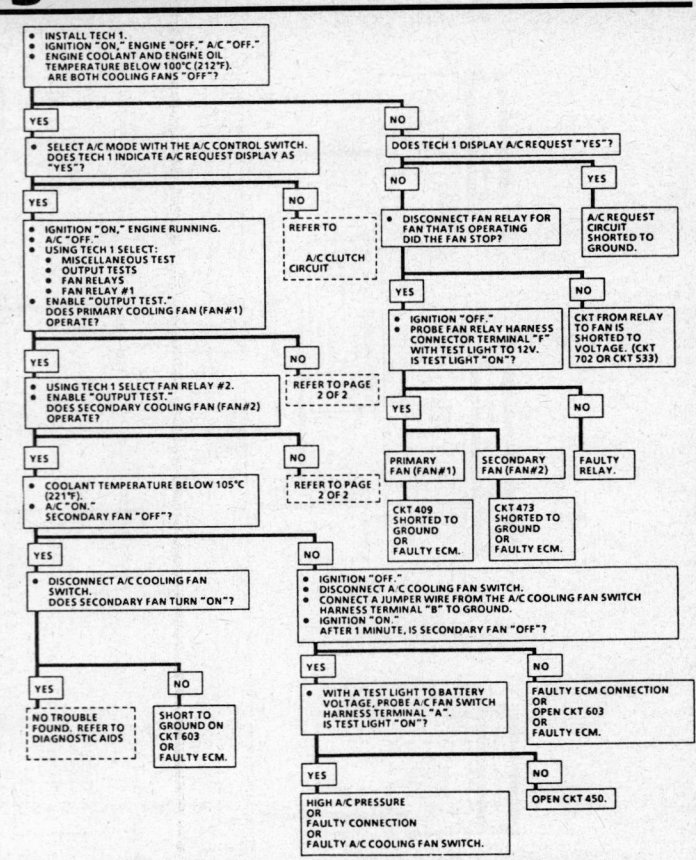

CHART C-12
(Page 1 of 2)
ELECTRIC COOLING FAN CONTROL CIRCUIT DIAGNOSIS
5.7L   "Y" CARLINE (PORT)

Circuit Description:

The cooling fans are controlled by the ECM based on various inputs. Battery voltage is supplied to the fan relays on terminal "E" and ignition voltage to terminal "D". Grounding CKT 409 (relay terminal "F") will energize the primary cooling fan relay (Fan 1) and supply battery voltage to the primary cooling fan motor. Grounding CKT 473 (relay terminal "F") will energize the secondary cooling fan relay (Fan 2) and supply battery voltage to the secondary fan motor.

The A/C cooling fan switch, mounted in the A/C high pressure line, will open when head pressure is approximately 1655 kPa (240 psi) and this input will cause the ECM to ground CKT 473 or CKT 409 if other criteria are met.

If a Code 14, 15, 52 or 62 are set or the ECM is operating in the fuel back-up mode, the ECM will turn "ON" both the cooling fans.

Diagnostic Aids:

If the owner complained of an overheating problem it must be determined if the complaint was due to an actual boil over, or the warning indicator light, or engine coolant temperature gage indicated overheating.

The gage accuracy can also be checked by comparing the Coolant Temperature Sensor (CTS) reading using a "Scan" tool and comparing its reading with the gage reading.

If the engine is actually overheating and the gage indicates overheating, but the cooling fan is not coming "ON," the Coolant Temperature Sensor (CTS) has probably shifted out of calibration and should be replaced.

If the engine is overheating and the cooling fans are "ON," the cooling system should be checked.

Fig. 57   Chart C-12, coolant fan diagnosis (Part 1 of 2). 1991 Corvette w/5.7L/V8-350 (VIN 8) engine

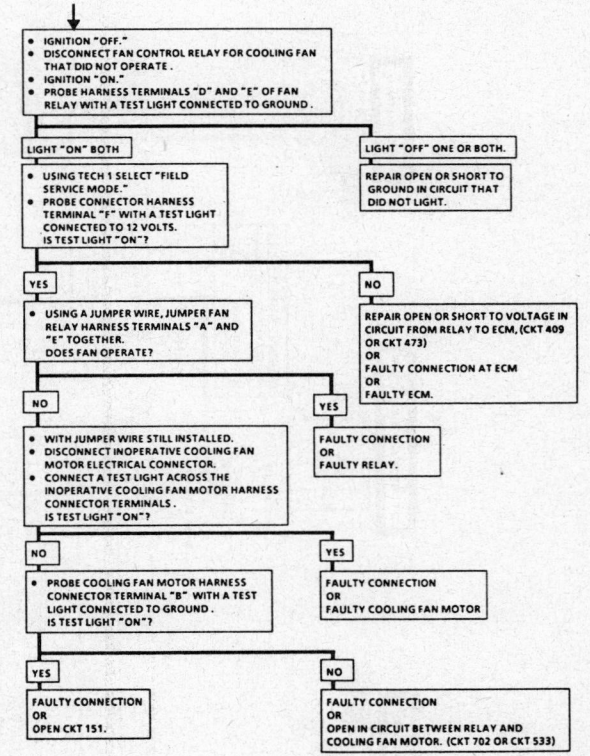

CHART C-12
(Page 2 of 2)
ELECTRIC COOLING FAN CONTROL CIRCUIT DIAGNOSIS
5.7L   "Y" CARLINE (PORT)

Circuit Description:

The cooling fans are controlled by the ECM based on various inputs. Battery voltage is supplied to the fan relays on terminal "E" and ignition voltage to terminal "D". Grounding CKT 409 (relay terminal "F") will energize the primary cooling fan relay (Fan 1) and supply battery voltage to the primary cooling fan motor. Grounding CKT 473 (relay terminal "F") will energize the secondary cooling fan relay (Fan 2) and supply battery voltage to the secondary fan motor.

The A/C cooling fan switch, mounted in the A/C high pressure line, will open when head pressure is approximately 1655 kPa (240 psi). This input will cause the ECM to ground CKT 473 or CKT 409 if other criteria are met.

If a Code 14, 15, 52 or 62 are set or the ECM is operating in the fuel back-up mode, the ECM will turn "ON" both the cooling fans.

Diagnostic Aids:

If the owner complained of an overheating problem, it must be determined if the complaint was due to an actual boil over or the warning indicator light or engine coolant temperature gage indicated overheating.

The gage accuracy can also be checked by comparing the Coolant Temperature Sensor (CTS) reading using a "Scan" tool and comparing its reading with the gage reading.

If the engine is actually overheating and the gage indicates overheating, but the cooling fan is not coming "ON." the Coolant Temperature Sensor (CTS) has probably shifted out of calibration and should be replaced.

If the engine is overheating and the cooling fans are "ON," the cooling system should be checked.

Fig. 57   Chart C-12, coolant fan diagnosis (Part 2 of 2). 1991 Corvette w/5.7L/V8-350 (VIN 8) engine

CHART C-12
(Page 1 of 2)
ELECTRIC COOLING FAN CONTROL CIRCUIT DIAGNOSIS
5.7L "Y" CARLINE (PORT)

Circuit Description:

The cooling fans are controlled by the ECM based on various inputs. Battery voltage is supplied to the fan relays on terminal "E" and ignition voltage to terminal "D". Grounding CKT 409 (relay terminal "F") will energize the primary cooling fan relay (Fan 1) and supply battery voltage to the primary cooling fan motor. Grounding CKT 473 (relay terminal "F") will energize the secondary cooling fan relay (Fan 2) and supply battery voltage to the secondary fan motor.

The A/C cooling fan switch, mounted in the A/C high pressure line, will open when head pressure exceeds 1655 kPa (240 psi). This input causes the ECM to ground CKT 473 or CKT 409 if other criteria are met.

If a Code 14, or 15 sets or the ECM is operating in the fuel back-up mode, the ECM will turn "ON" the cooling fans.

Diagnostic Aids:

If the owner complained of an overheating problem, it must be determined if the complaint was due to an actual boil over, or the warning indicator light, or engine coolant temperature gage indicated overheating.

The gage accuracy can also be checked by comparing the Coolant Temperature Sensor (CTS) reading using a Tech 1 and comparing its reading with the gage reading.

If the engine is actually overheating and the gage indicated overheating, but the cooling fan is not coming "ON," the Coolant Temperature Sensor (CTS) has probably shifted out of calibration and should be replaced.

If the engine is overheating and the cooling fans are "ON," the cooling system should be checked

The ECM will command Fan 1 "ON" at 108°C (226°F) and "OFF" at 105°C (221°F) and, Fan 2 "ON" at 113°C (235°F) and "OFF" at 108°C (226°F).

Fig. 58   Chart C-12, coolant fan diagnosis (Part 1 of 2). 1991 Corvette ZR1 w/5.7L/V8-350 (VIN J) engine

CHART C-12
(Page 2 of 2)
ELECTRIC COOLING FAN CONTROL CIRCUIT DIAGNOSIS
5.7L "Y" CARLINE (PORT)

Circuit Description:

The cooling fans are controlled by the ECM based on various inputs. Battery voltage is supplied to the fan relays on terminal "E" and ignition voltage to terminal "D". Grounding CKT 409 (relay terminal "F") will energize the primary cooling fan relay (Fan 1) and supply battery voltage to the primary cooling fan motor. Grounding CKT 473 (relay terminal "F") will energize the secondary cooling fan relay (Fan 2) and supply battery voltage to the secondary fan motor.

The A/C cooling fan switch, mounted in the A/C high pressure line, will open when head pressure exceeds 1655 kPa (240 psi) and this input causes the ECM to ground CKT 473 or CKT 409 if other criteria are met.

If a Code 14, or 15 sets or the ECM is operating in the fuel back-up mode, the ECM will turn "ON" the cooling fans.

Diagnostic Aids:

If the owner complained of an overheating problem, it must be determined if the complaint was due to an actual boil over, or the warning indicator light, or engine coolant temperature gage indicated overheating.

The gage accuracy can also be checked by comparing the Coolant Temperature Sensor (CTS) reading using a Tech 1 and comparing its reading with the gage reading.

If the engine is actually overheating and the gage indicated overheating, but the cooling fan is not coming "ON," the Coolant Temperature Sensor (CTS) has probably shifted out of calibration and should be replaced.

If the engine is overheating and the cooling fans are "ON," the cooling system should be checked

Fig. 58   Chart C-12, coolant fan diagnosis (Part 2 of 2). 1991 Corvette ZR1 w/5.7L/V8-350 (VIN J) engine

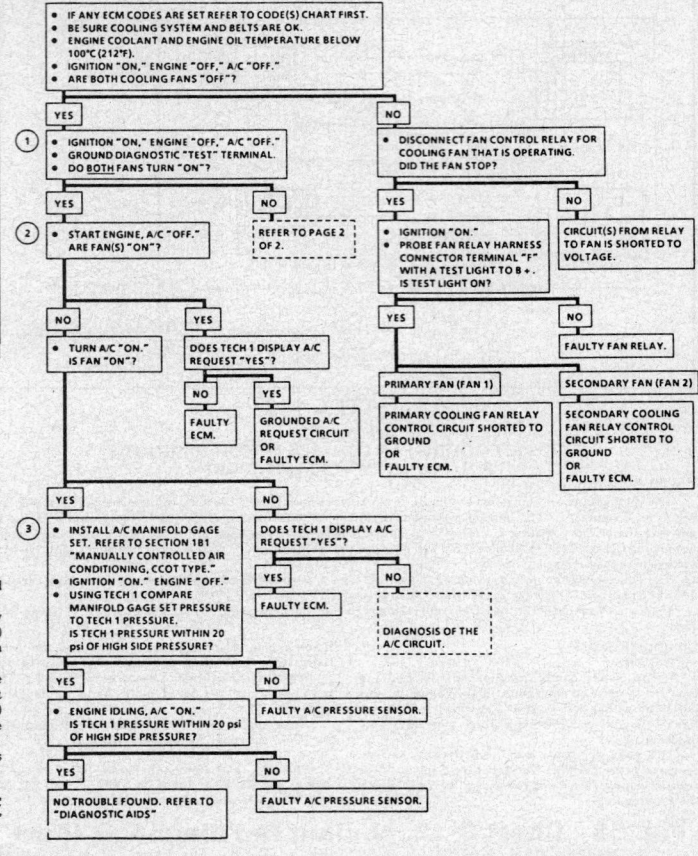

CHART C-12

(Page 1 of 2)

ELECTRIC COOLING FAN CONTROL CIRCUIT DIAGNOSIS
5.7L "Y" CARLINE (PORT)

Circuit Description:

The cooling fans are controlled by the ECM based on various inputs. Battery voltage is supplied to the fan relays on terminal "E" and ignition voltage to terminal "D". Grounding CKT 409 (relay terminal "F") will energize the primary cooling fan relay (Fan 1) and supply battery voltage to the primary cooling fan motor. Grounding CKT 473 (relay terminal "F") will energize the secondary cooling fan relay (Fan 2) and supply battery voltage to the secondary fan motor.

If any ECM codes are set or the ECM is operating in the fuel back-up mode, the ECM will turn "ON" the cooling fans.

Test Description: Number(s) below refer to circled number(s) on the diagnostic chart.

1. With the diagnostic "test" terminal grounded, the cooling fan control driver(s) will close, which should energize the fan control relay(s).
2. The cooling fans should come "ON" anytime A/C system is operating.
3. Comparing Tech 1 pressure and manifold gage set pressure will determine if the A/C pressure sensor is out of range. An out of range A/C pressure sensor can cause the cooling fans to operate at the wrong times.

Diagnostic Aids:

If the owner complained of an overheating problem, it must be determined if the complaint was due to an actual boil over, or the warning indicator

light, or engine coolant temperature gage indicated overheating.

The gage accuracy can also be checked by comparing the Coolant Temperature Sensor (CTS) reading using a Tech 1 and comparing its reading with the gage reading.

If the engine is actually overheating and the gage indicated overheating, but the cooling fan is not coming "ON," the Coolant Temperature Sensor (CTS) has probably shifted out of calibration and should be replaced.

If the engine is overheating and the cooling fans are "ON," the cooling system should be checked

The ECM will command Fan 1 "ON" at 108°C (226°F) and "OFF" at 105°C (221°F) and, Fan 2 "ON" at 113°C (235°F) and "OFF" at 108°C (226°F).

Fig. 59   Chart C-12, coolant fan diagnosis (Part 1 of 2). 1992 Corvette w/5.7L/V8-350 (VIN P) engine

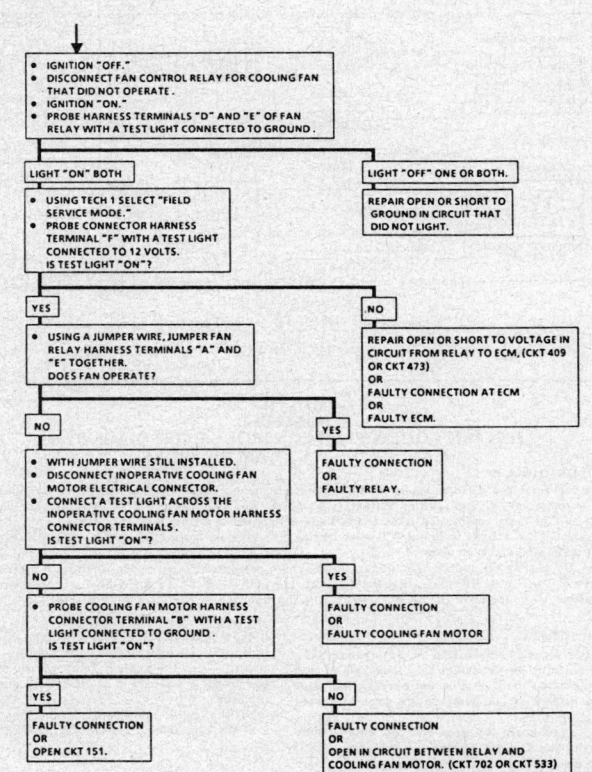

CHART C-12

(Page 2 of 2)

ELECTRIC COOLING FAN CONTROL CIRCUIT DIAGNOSIS
5.7L "Y" CARLINE (PORT)

Circuit Description:

The cooling fans are controlled by the ECM based on various inputs. Battery voltage is supplied to the fan relays on terminal "E" and ignition voltage to terminal "D". Grounding CKT 409 (relay terminal "F") will energize the primary cooling fan relay (Fan 1) and supply battery voltage to the primary cooling fan motor. Grounding CKT 473 (relay terminal "F") will energize the secondary cooling fan relay (Fan 2) and supply battery voltage to the secondary fan motor.

If any ECM codes are set or the ECM is operating in the fuel back-up mode, the ECM will turn "ON" the cooling fans.

Diagnostic Aids:

If the owner complained of an overheating problem, it must be determined if the complaint was due to an actual boil over, or the warning indicator light, or engine coolant temperature gage indicated overheating.

The gage accuracy can also be checked by comparing the Coolant Temperature Sensor (CTS) reading using a Tech 1 and comparing its reading with the gage reading.

If the engine is actually overheating and the gage indicated overheating, but the cooling fan is not coming "ON," the Coolant Temperature Sensor (CTS) has probably shifted out of calibration and should be replaced.

If the engine is overheating and the cooling fans are "ON," the cooling system should be checked

Fig. 59   Chart C-12, coolant fan diagnosis (Part 2 of 2). 1992 Corvette w/5.7L/V8-350 (VIN P) engine

CHART C-12

(Page 1 of 2)
ELECTRIC COOLING FAN CONTROL CIRCUIT DIAGNOSIS
5.7L "Y" CARLINE (PORT)

Circuit Description:

The cooling fans are controlled by the ECM based on various inputs. Battery voltage is supplied to the fan relays on terminal "E" and ignition voltage to terminal "D". Grounding CKT 335 (relay terminal "F") will energize the primary cooling fan relay (Fan 1) and supply battery voltage to the primary cooling fan motor. Grounding CKT 473 (relay terminal "F") will energize the secondary cooling fan relay (Fan 2) and supply battery voltage to the secondary fan motor.

The A/C cooling fan switch, mounted in the A/C high pressure line, will open when head pressure is approximately 1655 kPa (240 psi) and this input will cause the ECM to ground CKT 473 or CKT 335 if other criteria are met.

If a Codes 14, 15, 52 or 62 are set or the ECM is operating in the fuel back-up mode, the ECM will turn "ON" both the cooling fans.

Diagnostic Aids:

If the owner complained of an overheating problem it must be determined if the complaint was due to an actual boil over, or the warning indicator light, or engine coolant temperature gage indicated overheating.

The gage accuracy can also be checked by comparing the Coolant Temperature Sensor (CTS) reading using a "Scan" tool and comparing its reading with the gage reading.

If the engine is actually overheating and the gage indicates overheating, but the cooling fan is not coming "ON," the Coolant Temperature Sensor (CTS) has probably shifted out of calibration and should be replaced.

If the engine is overheating and the cooling fans are "ON," the cooling system should be checked

Fig. 60   Chart C-12, coolant fan diagnosis (Part 1 of 2). 1992 Corvette ZR1 w/5.7L/V8-350 (VIN J) engine

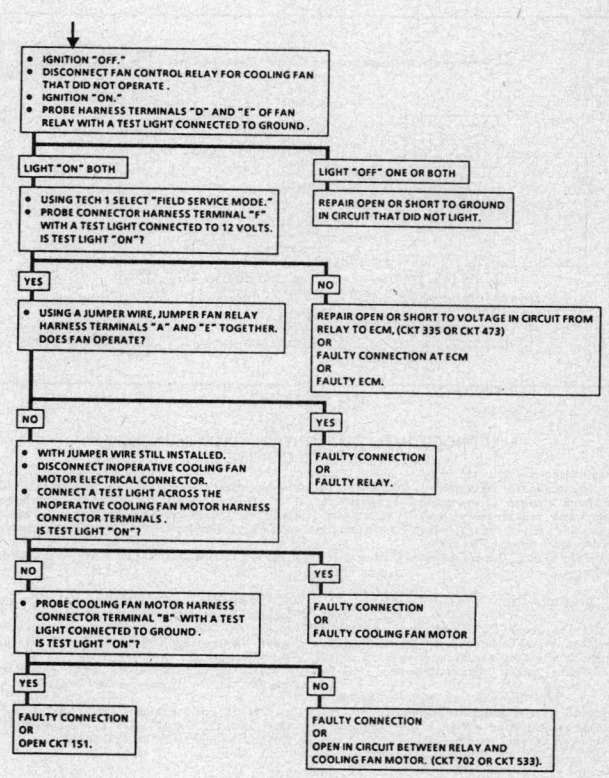

CHART C-12

(Page 2 of 2)
ELECTRIC COOLING FAN CONTROL CIRCUIT DIAGNOSIS
5.7L "Y" CARLINE (PORT)

Circuit Description:

The cooling fans are controlled by the ECM based on various inputs. Battery voltage is supplied to the fan relays on terminal "E" and ignition voltage to terminal "D". Grounding CKT 335 (relay terminal "F") will energize the primary cooling fan relay (Fan 1) and supply battery voltage to the primary cooling fan motor. Grounding CKT 473 (relay terminal "F") will energize the secondary cooling fan relay (Fan 2) and supply battery voltage to the secondary fan motor.

The A/C cooling fan switch, mounted in the A/C high pressure line, will open when head pressure is approximately 1655 kPa (240 psi). This input will cause the ECM to ground CKT 473 or CKT 335 if other criteria are met.

If a Codes 14, 15, 52 or 62 are set or the ECM is operating in the fuel back-up mode, the ECM will turn "ON" both the cooling fans.

Diagnostic Aids:

If the owner complained of an overheating problem, it must be determined if the complaint was due to an actual boil over or the warning indicator light or engine coolant temperature gage indicated overheating.

The gage accuracy can also be checked by comparing the Coolant Temperature Sensor (CTS) reading using a "Scan" tool and comparing its reading with the gage reading.

If the engine is actually overheating and the gage indicates overheating, but the cooling fan is not coming "ON," the Coolant Temperature Sensor (CTS) has probably shifted out of calibration and should be replaced.

If the engine is overheating and the cooling fans are "ON," the cooling system should be checked

Fig. 60   Chart C-12, coolant fan diagnosis (Part 2 of 2). 1992 Corvette ZR1 w/5.7L/V8-350 (VIN J) engine

ELECTRIC COOLING FANS

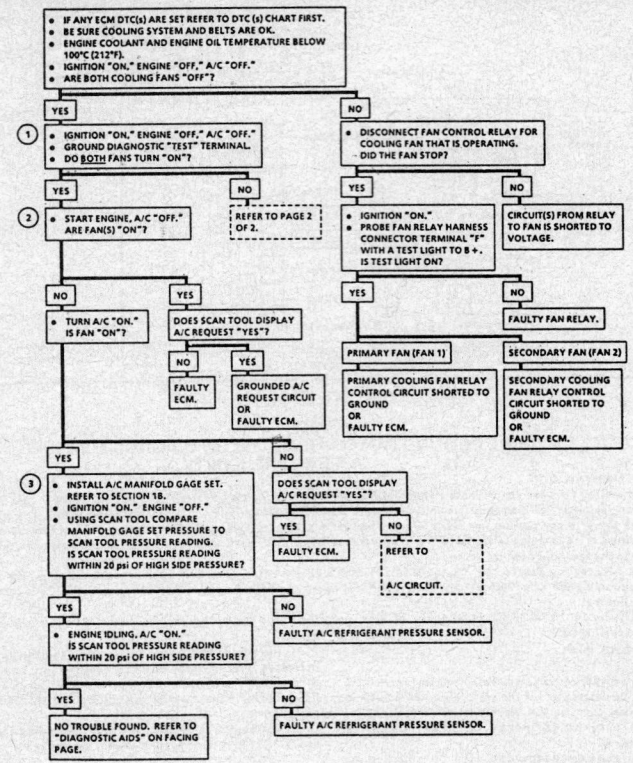

CHART C-12

(Page 1 of 2)

ELECTRIC COOLING FAN CONTROL CIRCUIT DIAGNOSIS
5.7L (VIN P) "Y" CARLINE (MFI)

Circuit Description:

The cooling fans are controlled by the ECM based on various inputs. Battery voltage is supplied to the fan relays on terminal "E" and ignition voltage to terminal "D". Grounding CKT 335 (relay terminal "F") will energize the primary cooling fan relay (Fan 1) and supply battery voltage to the primary cooling fan motor. Grounding CKT 473 (relay terminal "F") will energize the secondary cooling fan relay (Fan 2) and supply battery voltage to the secondary fan motor.

If any ECM DTC(s) are set or the ECM is operating in the fuel back-up mode, the ECM will turn "ON" the cooling fans.

Test Description: Number(s) below refer to circled number(s) on the diagnostic chart.

1. With the diagnostic "test" terminal grounded, the cooling fan control driver(s) will close, which should energize the fan control relay(s).
2. The cooling fans should come "ON" anytime A/C system is operating.
3. Comparing Tech 1 pressure and manifold gage set pressure will determine if the A/C refrigerant pressure sensor is out of range. An out of range A/C refrigerant pressure sensor can cause the cooling fans to operate at the wrong times.

Diagnostic Aids:

If the owner complained of an overheating problem, it must be determined if the complaint was due to an actual boil over, or the warning indicator light, or engine coolant temperature gage indicated overheating.

The gage accuracy can also be checked by comparing the Engine Coolant Temperature (ECT) sensor reading using a Tech 1 and comparing its reading with the gage reading.

If the engine is actually overheating and the gage indicated overheating, but the cooling fan is not coming "ON," the Engine Coolant Temperature (ECT) sensor has probably shifted out of calibration and should be replaced.

If the engine is overheating and the cooling fans are "ON," the cooling system should be checked,

The ECM will command fan 1 "ON" at 108°C (226°F) and "OFF" at 105°C (221°F) and, fan 2 "ON" at 113°C (235°F) and "OFF" at 108°C (226°F).

Fig. 61   Chart C-12, coolant fan diagnosis (Part 1 of 2). 1993 Corvette w/5.7L/V8-350 (VIN P) engine

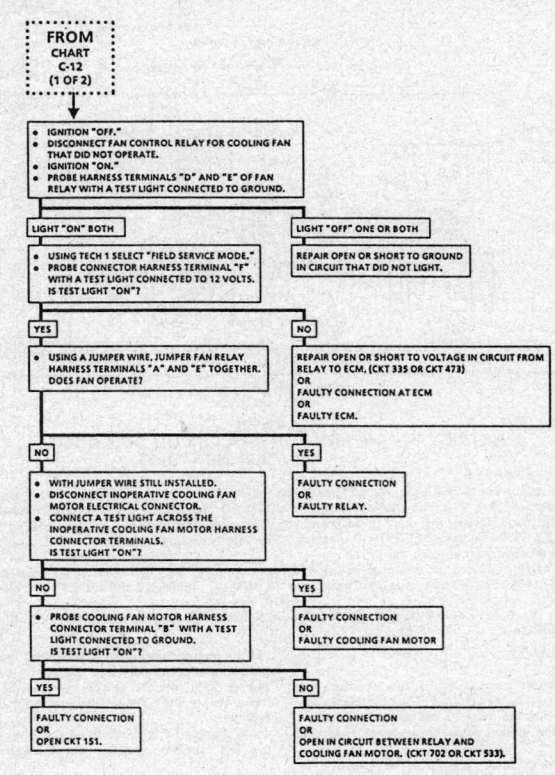

CHART C-12

(Page 2 of 2)

ELECTRIC COOLING FAN CONTROL CIRCUIT DIAGNOSIS
5.7L (VIN P) "Y" CARLINE (MFI)

Circuit Description:

The cooling fans are controlled by the ECM based on various inputs. Battery voltage is supplied to the fan relays on terminal "E" and ignition voltage to terminal "D". Grounding CKT 335 (relay terminal "F") will energize the primary cooling fan relay (Fan 1) and supply battery voltage to the primary cooling fan motor. Grounding CKT 473 (relay terminal "F") will energize the secondary cooling fan relay (Fan 2) and supply battery voltage to the secondary fan motor.

If any ECM DTC(s) are set or the ECM is operating in the fuel back-up mode, the ECM will turn "ON" the cooling fans.

Diagnostic Aids:

If the owner complained of an overheating problem, it must be determined if the complaint was due to an actual boil over, or the warning indicator light, or engine coolant temperature gage indicated overheating.

The gage accuracy can also be checked by comparing the Engine Coolant Temperature (ECT) sensor reading using a Tech 1 and comparing its reading with the gage reading.

If the engine is actually overheating and the gage indicated overheating, but the cooling fan is not coming "ON," the Engine Coolant Temperature (ECT) sensor has probably shifted out of calibration and should be replaced.

If the engine is overheating and the cooling fans are "ON," the cooling system should be checked,

The ECM will command fan 1 "ON" at 108°C (226°F) and "OFF" at 105°C (221°F) and, fan 2 "ON" at 113°C (235°F) and "OFF" at 108°C (226°F).

Fig. 61   Chart C-12, coolant fan diagnosis (Part 2 of 2). 1993 Corvette w/5.7L/V8-350 (VIN P) engine

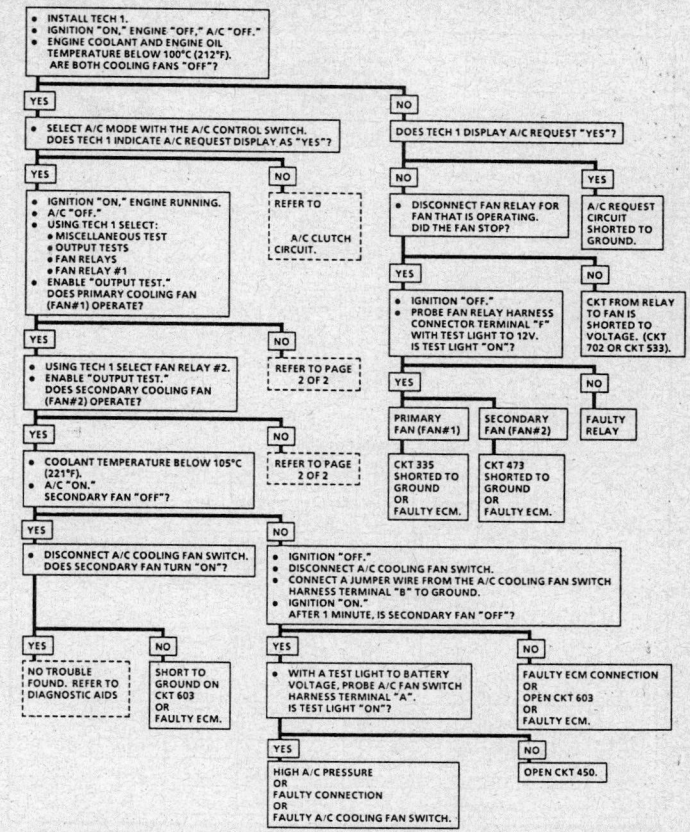

CHART C-12
(Page 1 of 2)
ELECTRIC COOLING FAN CONTROL CIRCUIT DIAGNOSIS
5.7L (VIN J) "Y" CARLINE (SFI)

Circuit Description:

The cooling fans are controlled by the ECM based on various inputs. Battery voltage is supplied to the fan relays on terminal "E" and ignition voltage to terminal "D". Grounding CKT 335 (relay terminal "F") will energize the primary cooling fan relay (Fan 1) and supply battery voltage to the primary cooling fan motor. Grounding CKT 473 (relay terminal "F") will energize the secondary cooling fan relay (Fan 2) and supply battery voltage to the secondary fan motor.

The A/C cooling fan switch, mounted in the A/C high pressure line, will open when head pressure is approximately 1655 kPa (240 psi) and this input will cause the ECM to ground CKT 473 or CKT 335 if other criteria are met.

If DTCs 14, 15, 52 or 62 are set or the ECM is operating in the fuel back-up mode, the ECM will turn "ON" both the cooling fans.

Diagnostic Aids:

If the owner complained of an overheating problem it must be determined if the complaint was due to an actual boil over, or the warning indicator light, or engine coolant temperature gage indicated overheating.

The gage accuracy can also be checked by comparing the Engine Coolant Temperature (ECT) sensor reading using a scan tool and comparing its reading with the gage reading.

If the engine is actually overheating and the gage indicates overheating, but the cooling fan is not coming "ON," the Engine Coolant Temperature (ECT) sensor has probably shifted out of calibration and should be replaced.

If the engine is overheating and the cooling fans are "ON," the cooling system should be checked.

The ECM will command Fan 1 "ON" when coolant temperature is greater than 108°C (226°F) and "OFF" at 103°C (217°F) and, Fan 2 "ON" at 112°C (234°F) and "OFF" at 110°C (230°F). The ECM will also enable the cooling fans when ECM DTCs 14, 15, 52 and 62 are set, engine oil temperature is too high or A/C head pressure is too high.

Fig. 62   Chart C-12, coolant fan diagnosis (Part 1 of 2). 1993 Corvette ZR1 w/5.7L/V8-350 (VIN J) engine

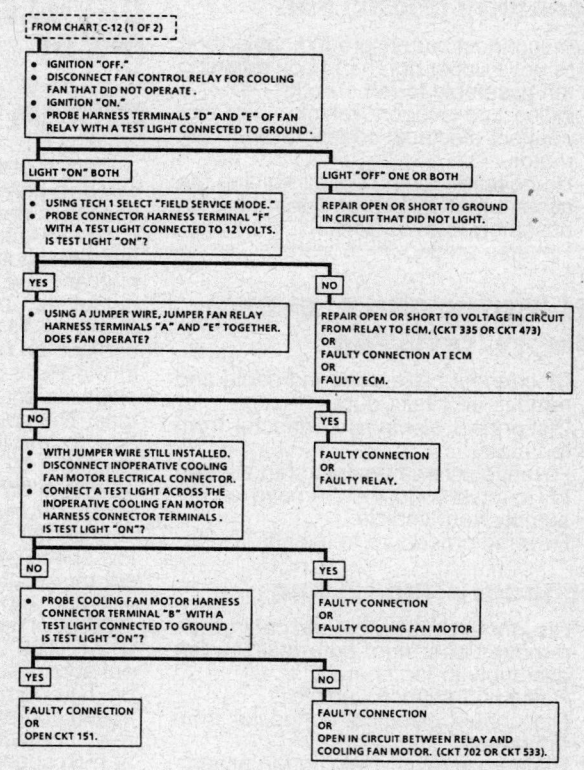

CHART C-12
(Page 2 of 2)
ELECTRIC COOLING FAN CONTROL CIRCUIT DIAGNOSIS
5.7L (VIN J) "Y" CARLINE (SFI)

Circuit Description:

The cooling fans are controlled by the ECM based on various inputs. Battery voltage is supplied to the fan relays on terminal "E" and ignition voltage to terminal "D". Grounding CKT 335 (relay terminal "F") will energize the primary cooling fan relay (Fan 1) and supply battery voltage to the primary cooling fan motor. Grounding CKT 473 (relay terminal "F") will energize the secondary cooling fan relay (Fan 2) and supply battery voltage to the secondary fan motor.

The A/C cooling fan switch, mounted in the A/C high pressure line, will open when head pressure is approximately 1655 kPa (240 psi). This input will cause the ECM to ground CKT 473 or CKT 335 if other criteria are met.

If DTCs 14, 15, 52 or 62 are set or the ECM is operating in the fuel back-up mode, the ECM will turn "ON" both the cooling fans.

Diagnostic Aids:

If the owner complained of an overheating problem, it must be determined if the complaint was due to an actual boil over or the warning indicator light or engine coolant temperature gage indicated overheating.

The gage accuracy can also be checked by comparing the Engine Coolant Temperature (ECT) sensor reading using a scan tool and comparing its reading with the gage reading.

If the engine is actually overheating and the gage indicates overheating, but the cooling fan is not coming "ON," the Engine Coolant Temperature (ECT) sensor has probably shifted out of calibration and should be replaced.

If the engine is overheating and the cooling fans are "ON," the cooling system should be checked.

The ECM will command Fan 1 "ON" when coolant temperature is greater than 108°C (226°F) and "OFF" at 103°C (217°F) and, Fan 2 "ON" at 112°C (234°F) and "OFF" at 110°C (230°F). The ECM will also enable the cooling fans when ECM DTCs 14, 15, 52 and 62 are set, engine oil temperature is too high or A/C head pressure is too high.

Fig. 62   Chart C-12, coolant fan diagnosis (Part 2 of 2). 1993 Corvette ZR1 w/5.7L/V8-350 (VIN J) engine

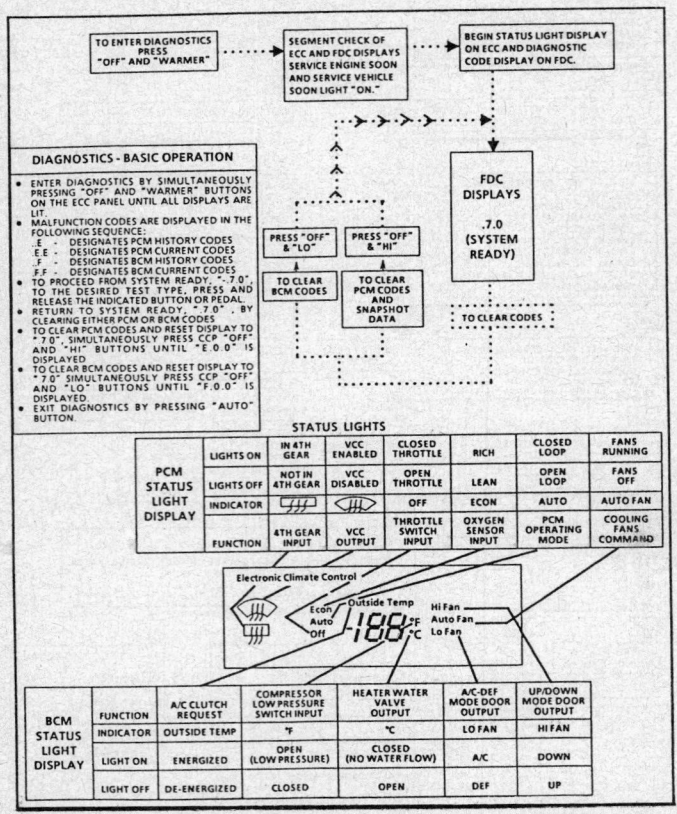

Fig. 63   Diagnostic flow diagram (Part 1 of 3). 1991 DeVille & Fleetwood (FWD)

Fig. 63   Diagnostic flow diagram (Part 2 of 3). 1991 DeVille & Fleetwood (FWD)

Secondary (Right) Fan

1. Disconnect battery ground cable, then remove upper righthand bolt retaining fan assembly to fan shroud.
2. Raise and support vehicle, then disconnect electrical connector from fan motor.
3. Remove remaining bolts retaining fan assembly to fan shroud, then the fan assembly from vehicle.
4. Reverse procedure to install.

5.7L/V8-350 (VIN P) ENGINE

Primary (Left) Fan

1. Disconnect battery ground cable and remove air intake duct.
2. Disconnect electrical connector from fan motor.
3. Remove screws retaining fan assembly to fan shroud, then remove fan assembly from vehicle.
4. Reverse procedure to install.

Secondary (Right) Fan

1. Disconnect battery ground cable, then remove upper right bolt retaining fan assembly to fan shroud.
2. Raise and support vehicle.
3. Disconnect electrical connector from fan motor.
4. Remove screws retaining fan assembly to fan shroud, then remove fan assembly from vehicle.
5. Reverse procedure to install.

DEVILLE & FLEETWOOD (FWD)

SYSTEM DESCRIPTION

This system uses two coolant fans, wired in parallel, both fans run whenever cooling is required.

The Powertrain Control Module (PCM) has two coolant fan outputs, one each for high and low speed. When PCM low speed output is turned on at connector C2 (terminal 11), it grounds the low speed coolant fan relay's coil. If ignition switch is in the RUN position, the relay's contacts close, completing the circuit to the cooling fans. The coolant fan resistor lowers voltage to the left side coolant fan, which causes it to run at low speed. Since the right side coolant fan is wired in parallel, it also runs, but at high speed because the coolant fan resistor is bypassed. The PCM low speed output is turned on when coolant temperature reaches 208°F (98°C).

If coolant temperature reaches 226°F (106°C) or refrigerant temperature reaches 212°F (100°C), the PCM's high speed output at connector C2 (terminal B8) is turned on. This output grounds the coil of the high speed coolant fan relay, which causes the relay contacts to close, and both fans run at high speed.

The PCM controls its outputs based on signals received from the Coolant Temperature Sensor (CTS) and Refrigerant High Side Temperature Sensor. The CTS is wired directly to the PCM and the refrigerant temperature sensor is wired to the BCM. The BCM processes the signal from the sensor and sends it to the PCM through a Serial Data Line.

TROUBLESHOOTING

If only one coolant fan fails to operate, check wires to that coolant fan. If wires are satisfactory, replace coolant fan.

ENTERING DIAGNOSTIC MODE

To enter and display diagnostics, refer to diagnostic flow diagram shown in **Fig. 63**.

SYSTEM CHECK

1. Start engine and let idle. Left side coolant fans should run at low speed and right side fan should run at high speed after a few minutes.
2. With engine idling, restrict air flow through radiator by covering half of grill side of the radiator. Coolant fans should run at high speed after a few minutes.
3. Uncover radiator. Left side coolant fans should return to low speed and right side coolant fan should continue to run at high speed.

SYSTEM DIAGNOSIS

Refer to **Fig. 64** when performing diagnostic procedures on these systems.

PCM SWITCH TESTS	
DIAGNOSTIC DISPLAY	CIRCUIT TEST
SWITCH CRUISE "ON" BEFORE TESTING	
E.7.0	CRUISE BRAKE SWITCH
E.7.1	VCC BRAKE SWITCH
E.7.2	THROTTLE SWITCH
E.7.3	PARK/NEUTRAL
E.7.4	CRUISE "ON/OFF"
E.7.5	CRUISE "SET/COAST"
E.7.6	CRUISE "RESUME/ACCEL."
E.7.7	POWER STEERING PRESSURE
E.7.8	SWITCH (ENGINE RUNNING)

PCM OUTPUT OVERRIDES	
DIAGNOSTIC DISPLAY	OVERRIDE
E.5.0	NO OVERRIDE
E.5.1	VCC
E.5.2	EGR
E.5.3	ISC
E.5.4	INJECTORS (1-8)
E.5.5	FUEL PUMP RELAY
E.5.7	CRUISE SERVO
E.5.8	COOLANT FANS
E.5.9	FIXED SPARK
E.6.0	INJECTOR FLOW
E.6.1	TRANSAXLE SHIFTING

PRESSING "WARMER" WILL INCREASE OR ACTIVATE
PRESSING "COOLER" WILL DECREASE OR DEACTIVATE

FDC DISPLAY OF PCM DATA		DISPLAY	
PARAMETER NUMBER	PARAMETER	RANGE	UNITS
P.0.1	THROTTLE POSITION	-10.0 TO 90.0	DEGREES
P.0.2	MAP	14 TO 109	KPA
P.0.3	COMPUTED BARO	60 TO 102	KPA
P.0.4	COOLANT TEMPERATURE	-40 TO 151	°C
P.0.5	MAT	-40 TO 151	°C
P.0.6	SPARK ADVANCE	0 TO 90	DEGREES
P.0.7	BATTERY VOLTAGE	0 TO 25	VOLTS
P.0.8	ENGINE SPEED	0 TO 637	RPM/10
P.0.9	VEHICLE SPEED	0 TO 255	MPH
P.1.2	INJECTOR PULSE WIDTH	0 TO 99.6	MILLISECONDS
P.1.4	O_2 SENSOR VOLTAGE	0 TO .99	VOLTS
P.1.6	O_2 CROSS COUNTS	0 TO 255	COUNTS/SEC
P.1.8	FUEL INTEGRATOR	0 TO 255	COUNTS
P.2.0	BLOCK LEARN	0 TO 255	COUNTS
P.2.1	CRUISE SERVO POSITION	0 TO 100	PERCENT
P.2.2	PRNDL (CKT 772, 773)	00 TO 11	0 = SW. CLOSED
P.2.3	PRNDL (CKT 771, 776)	00 TO 11	0 = SW. CLOSED
P.2.4	IGNITION CYCLES	0 TO 255	KEY CYCLES
P.2.5	PROM ID	0 TO 999	•CODE

PCM OUTPUT CYCLING	
PARAMETER NUMBER	PARAMETER
E.0.0	CYCLE NONE
E.0.1	CANISTER PURGE SOLENOID
E.0.2	VCC SOLENOID
E.0.3	EGR SOLENOID
E.0.6	ISC MOTOR
E.0.7	CRUISE VENT SOLENOID
E.0.8	CRUISE VAC SOLENOID
E.0.9	SHIFT SOLENOID "A"
E.1.0	SHIFT SOLENOID "B"
E.1.1	A/C CLUTCH RELAY
E.1.2	CYCLE ALL

FDC DISPLAY OF BCM DATA		DISPLAY	
PARAMETER NUMBER	PARAMETER	RANGE	UNITS
P.2.0	COMMANDED BLOWER VOLTAGE	-3.3 TO 18.0	VOLTS
P.2.1	COOLANT TEMPERATURE	-40 TO 151	°C
P.2.2	COMMANDED AIR MIX DOOR POSITION	0 TO 100	%
P.2.3	ACTUAL AIR MIX DOOR POSITION	0 TO 100	%
P.2.4	AIR DELIVERY MODE	0 TO 8	CODE □
P.2.5	IN-VEHICLE TEMPERATURE	-39 TO 102	°C
P.2.6	ACTUAL OUTSIDE TEMPERATURE	-40 TO 93	°C
P.2.7	HIGH SIDE TEMPERATURE (CONDENSER OUT)	-15 TO 215	°C
P.2.8	LOW SIDE TEMPERATURE (EVAPORATOR IN)	-40 TO 93	°C
P.2.9	ACTUAL FUEL LEVEL	.8 TO 18.1	GALLONS
P.3.0	IGNITION CYCLE COUNTER	0 TO 99	KEY CYCLES
P.3.1	OIL LIFE FORWARD ODOMETER	0 TO 70	(x 100) MILES
P.3.2	SUN LOAD SENSOR READING	0 TO 255	COUNTS
P.3.3	BCM PROM I.D.	0 TO 255	•CODE

• PROM ID

PROM ID CODE NUMBER IDENTIFIES AN INDIVIDUAL CALIBRATION AND IS PERIODICALLY UPDATED;

□ AIR DELIVERY MODE

BCM AIR DELIVERY MODE IS PARAMETER (P.2.4) OF BCM DATA AND IS DISPLAYED AS A NUMERICAL CODE AS FOLLOWS:

CODE NO.	MODE	CODE NO.	MODE
0	MAX. A/C	4	HEATER
1	A/C	5	OFF
2	BI-LEVEL	6	NORMAL PURGE
3	HEATER/DEFROST	7	COLD PURGE
		8	FRONT DEFOG

Fig. 63   Diagnostic flow diagram (Part 3 of 3). 1991 DeVille & Fleetwood (FWD)

Coolant Fans Do Not Operate

1. Enter diagnostics and turn coolant fans on using PCM override. If coolant fans turn on, proceed to step 2. If coolant fans do not turn on, proceed to step 3.
2. Start engine, turn on A/C and idle engine for a few minutes. Read PCM Data-Coolant Temperature Sensor (CTS) and read BCM Data-Refrigerant Temperature Sensor. If both readings are above ambient and rising parameters, replace PCM. If readings are not above ambient and rising parameters, check wiring to suspect sensor, if wiring is satisfactory, replace sensor.
3. Disconnect high speed coolant fan relay and measure voltage between relay terminal No. 1 (red) and ground. If battery voltage is indicated, proceed to step 4. If battery voltage is not indicated, check red wire from relay connector to left side underhood fuse block for an open circuit.
4. Turn ignition switch to the RUN position, measure voltage between high speed relay terminal No. 2 (brown) and ground. If battery voltage is indicated, repair open circuit in coolant fan ground (black) wire. If battery voltage is not indicated, check brown wire from relay connector to instrument panel fuse block for an open circuit.

Coolant Fans Do Not Operate At Low Speed

The right side coolant fan runs at high speed when activated.

1. Enter diagnostics and turn coolant fans on low speed using PCM override. If coolant fans turn on, proceed to step 2. If coolant fans do not turn on, proceed to step 3.
2. Start engine, turn on A/C and idle engine for a few minutes. Read PCM Data-Coolant Temperature Sensor (CTS) and read BCM Data-Refrigerant Temperature Sensor. If both readings are above ambient and rising, replace PCM. If readings are not above ambient and rising, check wiring to suspect sensor, if wiring is satisfactory, replace sensor.
3. Leave PCM connected and turn ignition to the RUN position, connect a fused jumper between PCM connector C2 (terminal A11, gray/black) and ground. If coolant fans run, replace PCM. If coolant fans do not run, proceed to step 4.
4. Leaving fused jumper in place at the PCM connector, check voltages at low speed coolant fan relay as follows:
   a. From terminal No. 1 (red) to ground. If battery voltage is indicated proceed to step b. If battery voltage is not indicated, repair open circuit in red wire.

b. From terminal No. 1 (red) to terminal 5 (gray/black). If battery voltage is indicated, proceed to step c. If battery voltage is not indicated, repair open circuit in gray/black wire.
   c. From terminal No. 2 (brown) to ground. If battery voltage is indicated, proceed to step 5. If battery voltage is not indicated, repair open circuit in brown wire.
5. Connect a fused jumper between low speed coolant fan relay terminal No. 2 (brown) and terminal No. 4 (black/red). If coolant fans do not run, check red/black wire for an open circuit, if wire is satisfactory, check coolant fan resistors and wiring. If coolant fans run, replace low speed coolant fan relay.

Coolant Fans Do Not Operate At High Speed

1. Enter diagnostics and turn coolant fans on high speed using PCM override. If coolant fans turn on, proceed to step 2. If coolant fans do not turn on, proceed to step 3.
2. Start engine, turn on A/C and idle engine for a few minutes. Read PCM Data-Coolant Temperature Sensor (CTS) and read BCM Data-Refrigerant Temperature Sensor. If both readings are above ambient and rising, replace PCM. If readings are not above ambient and rising, check wiring to suspect sensor, if wiring is satisfactory, replace sensor.
3. Leave PCM connected and turn ignition to the RUN position, connect a fused jumper between PCM connector C2 (terminal B8, dark green/white) and ground. If coolant fans run, replace PCM. If coolant fans do not run, proceed to step 4.
4. Leaving fused jumper in place at the PCM connector, check voltages at high speed coolant fan relay as follows:
   a. From terminal No. 1 (red) to ground. If battery voltage is indicated proceed to step b. If battery voltage is not indicated, repair open circuit in red wire.
   b. From terminal No. 1 (red) to terminal 5 (dark green/white). If battery voltage is indicated, proceed to step c. If battery voltage is not indicated, repair open circuit in gray/black wire.
   c. From terminal No. 2 (brown) to ground. If battery voltage is indicated, proceed to step 5. If battery voltage is not indicated, repair open circuit in brown wire.
5. Connect a fused jumper between high speed coolant fan relay terminal No. 2 (brown) and terminal No. 4 (black/pink). If coolant fans do not run, check black/pink wire for an open circuit. If coolant fans run, replace low speed coolant fan relay.

Fig. 64   Coolant fan wiring circuit. DeVille & Fleetwood (FWD)

COOLANT FAN, REPLACE

1. Disconnect battery ground cable.
2. Raise and support vehicle.
3. Disconnect fan electrical connectors.
4. Remove fan to lower cradle attaching screws.
5. Lower vehicle.
6. For right fan, remove A/C accumulator from bracket and position out of the way.
7. Remove air cleaner intake duct.
8. Remove fan to upper radiator mounting panel attaching screws.
9. Remove upper radiator mounting panel.
10. Remove cooling fan(s).
11. Reverse procedure to install.

FLEETWOOD (RWD)
DESCRIPTION

The primary and secondary coolant fans are turned on and off by the ECM based on inputs from A/C head pressure, engine coolant temperature, vehicle speed and A/C request signals.

The primary coolant fan is turned on when vehicle speed is below 35 mph, diagnostic trouble codes (DTC) 14 or 15 are set, coolant temperature is greater than 226°F or high A/C pressure is indicated.

The secondary coolant fan is controlled by the ECM through the engine coolant temperature sensor. The A/C cooling fan switch on the A/C high pressure line is grounded when head pressure exceeds

200-300 psi, enabling the secondary fan motor. The secondary fan is also turned on when DTC's 14 or 15 are set or coolant temperature is greater than 231°F.

DIAGNOSIS & TESTING

Refer to wiring diagram **Fig. 65** and diagnosis chart **Fig. 66** when performing system diagnosis.

COOLANT FAN, REPLACE
Less Heavy Duty Cooling System

1. With ignition switch in off position, disconnect battery ground cable.
2. Disconnect coolant fan electrical connectors.
3. Remove fan assembly attaching bolts, then lift fan upward from radiator support slot.
4. Remove motor to fan attaching nuts.
5. Reverse procedure to install.

With Heavy Duty Cooling System

1. With ignition switch in off position, disconnect battery ground cable.
2. Remove radiator fan shroud attaching bolts, then the upper fan shroud.
3. Remove fan blade assembly attaching nuts, then the fan blade and clutch assembly.
4. Remove clutch to fan blade attaching bolts, then the clutch from fan blade. **Place clutch in a upright position to prevent fluid leakage.**
5. Reverse procedure to install.

ELDORADO & SEVILLE
1991

SYSTEM DESCRIPTION
Circuit Operation

The ECM controls both coolant fans by controlling three relays through two outputs. There are two modes of coolant fan operation. One mode is the series mode where only coolant fan relay B is energized by the ECM and both coolant fans run at low speed. The second mode is parallel mode where all three of the coolant fan relays are energized by the ECM and both coolant fans run at high speed. Coolant fan operation is only possible when the ignition switch is in the RUN position.

The coolant fans will run at slow speed when circuit 535 is grounded by the ECM at terminal 2A11. Coolant fan relay B is energized and voltage is applied to both coolant fans.

The coolant fans run at high speed when circuits 535 and 536 are grounded by the ECM. Grounding circuit 535 energizes coolant fan relay B and battery voltage is applied to the pusher fan. When circuit 536 is grounded coolant fan relays C and D are energized. Coolant fan relay C provides a ground for the pusher fan through circuit 804. Battery voltage is applied through coolant fan relay D to the puller fan.

Fig. 65 Coolant fan wiring circuit. Fleetwood (RWD)

Series Mode

The BCM will request the ECM to turn On the coolant fans at low speed when A/C high side temperature is greater than 140°F and will request the ECM to turn the coolant fans Off when A/C high side temperature drops below 122°F.

The BCM will also request the ECM to turn the coolant fans On at lo speed when vehicle speed is less than 20 mph, A/C compressor clutch engagement is possible or the outside air temperature is greater than 113°F.

The ECM will turn On the coolant fans at low speed when coolant temperature is greater than 212°F and turn the coolant fans Off when coolant temperature falls below 208°F.

Parallel Mode

The BCM will request the ECM to turn the coolant fans On at high speed when A/C high side temperature is above 158°F or an A/C high side temperature sensor failure is current and A/C clutch engagement is possible. The BCM will request the ECM to turn the coolant fans Off when A/C high side temperature drops below

138°F.

The ECM will turn the coolant fans On at high speed if coolant temperature is above 226°F or a coolant temperature sensor failure is current. The ECM will switch the coolant fans Off when coolant temperature drops below 222°F.

TROUBLESHOOTING

1. If both coolant fans do not operate, check fusible link L by operating the horn.
2. If there is also a problem with A/C compressor clutch engagement, check coolant fan fuse 1 in the underhood relay center.
3. If both coolant fans operate in low speed with ignition switch OFF, check for a short to battery voltage on circuit 532. If circuit is satisfactory, replace coolant fan relay B.
4. If both coolant fans operate in high speed but not in low speed, check the 533 circuit between coolant fan relay C and S161 for an open. Also check continuity of coolant fan relay C between terminals 1 and 3.

5. For a continuous low speed operation with ignition switch in RUN only, check circuit 535 for a short to ground. If circuit is satisfactory, problem is ECM related.
6. If puller fan runs continuously with ignition switch in ON or OFF position, check circuit 533 for a short to battery voltage If circuit is satisfactory, replace coolant fan relay D.
7. If puller fan run continuously with ignition switch in RUN position only, check circuit 536 for a short to ground. If circuit is satisfactory, problem is ECM related.
8. If a no low speed,no high speed puller fan condition exists, check circuit 533 between S161 and puller fan for an open. Check circuit 804 between puller fan and S112 for and open. Check puller fan and terminal contacts.
9. If a no low speed or pusher fan runs in high speed when in system test ES08, check circuit 533 for a short to ground between pusher fan and coolant fan relay C. If circuit is satisfactory, replace coolant fan relay C.

ENTERING DIAGNOSTIC MODE

Refer to **Fig. 67** when entering diagnostic mode.

Turn ignition On, then depress OFF and WARMER buttons on the Climate Control Panel (CCP), **Fig. 68**. Hold buttons until all display panel segments illuminate, indicating beginning of diagnostic readout. **The two display panels must be illuminated to ensure all segments are operating. Do not attempt diagnosis unless all segments appear, as a misdiagnosis could result. If any segments are inoperative, the display panel must be replaced.**

After all ECM and BCM codes have been displayed, "ECM" will be displayed. At this point pressing the OFF button will return to diagnostic codes. Pressing the LO button will display the next system and pressing the HI button will proceed to the first test type for the system selected.

Having selected a system, the first available test type will be displayed. While selecting a specific test type, the OFF button will stop the test type and return the display to the next available system. Pressing the LO button will display the next available test type and pressing the HI button will select the displayed test type.

After selecting the test type, the first available test will be displayed. If dashes ever appear, this test is not allowed while vehicle is running. While selecting a specific test, pressing the OFF button will stop the test selection process and return the display to the next available test type. Pressing the LO button will display the next smaller test number for the selected test type. Pressing the HI button will display the next larger test number for the selected test type.

Pressing the RESET/RECALL button will halt diagnostics and return to normal display and operation.

CHART C-12 (Page 1 of 3)
ELECTRIC COOLING FAN CONTROL CIRCUIT DIAGNOSIS

Circuit Description:
The cooling fans are controlled by the ECM based on various inputs. The primary cooling fan relay is energized by the cooling fan control relay when the cooling fan control relay is de-energized. The primary fan relay will be energized and supply battery voltage to the primary cooling fan relay. Grounding CKT 473 (relay terminal "2") will energize the secondary cooling fan relay (Fan 2) and supply battery voltage to the secondary fan motor.

The A/C cooling fan switch, mounted in the A/C high pressure line, will be grounded when head pressure exceeds 1800 kPa-2070 kPa (200-300 psi) and enable the secondary cooling fan motor.

If a DTC 14, or 15 sets or the ECM is operating in the fuel back-up mode, the ECM will turn "ON" the cooling fans.

Diagnostic Aids:
If the owner complained of an overheating problem, it must be determined if the complaint was due to an actual boil over, or the warning indicator light, or engine coolant temperature gage indicated overheating.

The gage accuracy can also be checked by comparing the Engine Coolant Temperature (ECT) sensor reading using a Tech 1 and comparing its reading with the gage reading. If the engine is actually overheating and the gage indicated

overheating, but the cooling fan is not coming "ON," the Engine Coolant Temperature (ECT) sensor has probably shifted out of calibration and should be replaced.

If the engine is overheating and the cooling fans are "ON," the cooling system should be checked.

The ECM will command Fan 1 "ON" at 108°C (226°F) and "OFF" at 105°C (221°F) and, Fan 2 "ON" at 111°C (231°F) and "OFF" at 107°C (225°F).

Fig. 66   Chart C-12, coolant fan diagnosis (Part 1 of 3). Fleetwood (RWD)

CHART C-12 (Page 2 of 3)
ELECTRIC COOLING FAN CONTROL CIRCUIT DIAGNOSIS

Circuit Description:
The cooling fans are controlled by the ECM based on various inputs. The primary cooling fan relay is energized by the cooling fan control relay when the cooling fan control relay is de-energized. The primary fan relay will be energized and supply battery voltage to the primary cooling fan motor. Grounding CKT 473 (relay terminal "2") will energize the secondary cooling fan relay (Fan 2) and supply battery voltage to the secondary fan motor.

The A/C cooling fan switch, mounted in the A/C high pressure line, will be grounded when head pressure exceeds 1800 kPa-2070 kPa (200-300 psi) and enable the secondary cooling fan motor.

If a DTC 14, or 15 sets or the ECM is operating in the fuel back-up mode, the ECM will turn "ON" the cooling fans.

Diagnostic Aids:
If the owner complained of an overheating problem, it must be determined if the complaint was due to an actual boil over, or the warning indicator light, or engine coolant temperature gage indicated overheating.

The gage accuracy can also be checked by comparing the Engine Coolant Temperature (ECT) sensor reading using a Tech 1 and comparing its reading with the gage reading. If the engine is

actually overheating and the gage indicated overheating, but the cooling fan is not coming "ON," the Engine Coolant Temperature (ECT) sensor has probably shifted out of calibration and should be replaced.

If the engine is overheating and the cooling fans are "ON," the cooling system should be checked,

Fig. 66   Chart C-12, coolant fan diagnosis (Part 2 of 3). Fleetwood (RWD)

CHART C-12 (Page 3 of 3)
ELECTRIC COOLING FAN CONTROL CIRCUIT DIAGNOSIS

Circuit Description:

The cooling fans are controlled by the ECM based on various inputs. The primary cooling fan relay is energized by the cooling fan control relay when the cooling fan control relay is de-energized. The primary fan relay will be energized and supply battery voltage to the primary cooling fan motor. Grounding CKT 473 (relay terminal "2") will energize the secondary cooling fan relay (Fan 2) and supply battery voltage to the secondary fan motor.

The A/C cooling fan switch, mounted in the A/C high pressure line, will be grounded when head pressure exceeds 1800 kPa-2070 kPa (200-300 psi) and enable the secondary cooling fan motor.

If a DTC 14, or 15 sets or the ECM is operating in the fuel back-up mode, the ECM will turn "ON" the cooling fans.

Diagnostic Aids:

If the owner complained of an overheating problem, it must be determined if the complaint was due to an actual boil over, or the warning indicator light, or engine coolant temperature gage indicated overheating.

The gage accuracy can also be checked by comparing the Engine Coolant Temperature (ECT) sensor reading using a Tech 1 and comparing its reading with the gage reading. If the engine is actually overheating and the gage indicated overheating, but the cooling fan is not coming "ON," the Engine Coolant Temperature (ECT) sensor has probably shifted out of calibration and should be replaced.

If the engine is overheating and the cooling fans are "ON," the cooling system should be checked.

The ECM will command Fan 1 "ON" at 108°C (226°F) and "OFF" at 105°C (221°F) and, Fan 2 "ON" at 111°C (231°F) and "OFF" at 107°C (225°F).

Fig. 66   Chart C-12, coolant fan diagnosis (Part 3 of 3). Fleetwood (RWD)

SYSTEM CHECK

1. Enter diagnostics as outlined under "Entering Diagnostic Mode."
2. Enter ECM override and select ES08, coolant fan output override mode.
3. Operate the COOLER and WARMER buttons as indicated in **Fig. 69** to check the operation of the coolant fan system.
4. If all the results in **Fig. 69** are correct the coolant fans, relays and wiring are satisfactory. If a system still exists proceed to "Diagnosis."

DIAGNOSIS

Refer To **Fig. 70** when performing diagnostic procedures on these systems.

Both Coolant Fans Do Not Operate At All

1. If horn operate, proceed to step 2. If horns do not operate, check the following:
   a. Check fusible link L for an open.
   b. Check circuits 2, 532 and 533 for a short to ground before replacing fusible link.
   c. Check circuit 2 to S160 and circuit 804 between S112 and G100 for an open.
2. Measure voltage between underhood relay center position B terminal 2 to ground with the relay removed and ignition switch in RUN position. If battery voltage is not present, check circuit 850 and coolant fan fuse 1 for an open.
3. If battery voltage is present, check wiring to both coolant fans and the fan terminal contacts. If wiring or terminal contact is unsatisfactory, repair/replace as necessary.
4. If wiring and terminal contacts are satisfactory, check circuits 535 and 536 for an open. If both circuits are satisfactory, problem is ECM related.
5. If one or both circuits are unsatisfactory, repair/replace as necessary.

No Low Speed, No High Speed Pusher Fan

1. Disconnect coolant fan relay B from the underhood relay center. Turn ignition switch in RUN position and measure voltage between terminal 1 and ground then terminal 2 and ground of the relay center position B. If no voltage is present at one or both terminals, check circuits 2 and/or 850 for an open.
2. If battery voltage is present, enter diagnostics and select ECM override ES08 as outlined under "Diagnosis," set the display to 10. Connect a test lamp between terminals 2 and 5 at position B of the relay center. If test lamps does not light, check circuit 535 for an open or short to battery voltage. If wiring is satisfactory, problem is ECM related.
3. If test lamps lights, connect a fused jumper between terminals 1 and 4 at position B of relay center. If coolant fan runs at low speed, check or replace coolant fan relay B.
4. If the coolant fan does not run at high speed, leave jumper in place and disconnect coolant fan relay C. If coolant fan runs at high speed, check/replace relay C.
5. If pusher fan does not run at high speed, check circuits 532 and 533 for an open to pusher fan. Also check pusher fan terminal contact. If satisfactory, replace pusher fan.

No High Speed Pusher Fan

1. Disconnect coolant relay C from the underhood relay center and with the ignition switch in RUN position, measure voltage between terminals 2 and 4.
2. If battery voltage is present, check terminal contact at relay C. If satisfactory, replace coolant fan relay C.
3. If no voltage is present, check circuit 804 for an open.

Fig. 67 How to operate Service Mode. 1991 Eldorado & Seville

Fig. 68   Climate Control/Driver Information Center (CCDIC) Display. 1991 Eldorado & Seville

Fig. 69   System check table. 1991 Eldorado & Seville

Cooler (output #1, ECM terminal 2A11)	warmer (output #2, ECM terminal 2B8)	
Diagnostic Display	Diagnostic Display	Correct Result
0	0	Both Fans off
0	1	Puller Fan high speed Pusher Fan off
1	0	Both Fans low speed
1	1	Both Fans high speed

Fig. 70   Coolant fan wiring circuit (Part 1 of 2). 1991 Eldorado & Seville

Fig. 70   Coolant fan wiring circuit (Part 2 of 2). 1991 Eldorado & Seville

No High Speed Puller Fan

1. Disconnect coolant fan relay D from the underhood relay center. With the ignition switch in RUN position, measure voltage between terminal 1 and ground then between terminal 2 and ground of the relay center position D. If battery voltage is not present at one or both terminals, check circuits 2 and 850 for an open.
2. If battery voltage is present at both terminals, enter diagnostics and select ECM override ES08 and set display to 01. Connect a test lamp between terminals 2 and 5 of the relay center position D. If lamp does not light, check circuit 536 for an open.
3. If test lamp lights, connect a fused jumper between terminals 1 and 4 of the relay center position D. If puller fan does not run, check circuit 533 for an open.
4. If the puller fan runs at high speed, check terminal contact at relay D. If satisfactory, replace coolant fan relay D.

No High Speed Both Fans

1. Disconnect coolant fan relays C and D. Turn ignition switch to RUN position, measure voltage between terminal 2 and ground at position C then between terminals 2 and 1 at position D. If battery voltage is not present at one or both terminals, check associated circuit for an open.
2. If battery voltage is present at both terminals, check circuit 536 for an open or short to battery voltage. If circuit 536 is satisfactory, problem is ECM related.
3. If circuit 635 is not satisfactory, repair/replace as necessary.

1992–93

DESCRIPTION

The powertrain control module (PCM) controls both cooling fans by controlling three relays through two outputs. There are two modes of cooling fan operation, low speed and high speed. In the low speed mode the cooling fans are powered in series, cooling fan relay 1 is energized by the PCM and both cooling fans run at low speed. In the high speed mode the cooling fans are powered in parallel which allows the fans to run at high speed. Cooling fans operate only when the ignition is in run.

DIAGNOSIS & TESTING

Refer To **Fig. 71** when performing diagnostic procedures on these systems.

Low Speed Conditions, 4.9L/V8-300 Engine

The PCM will turn on the cooling fans at low speed when the engine coolant temperature exceeds 223°F. The cooling fans will be turned off when the coolant temperature drops below 208°F. The PCM monitors engine coolant temperature using the coolant temperature sensor at terminal 3E16 through circuit 410.

The heater and A/C (HVAC) programmer will request the PCM to turn on the cooling fans at low speed through the UART data line when the A/C high side refrigerant temperature exceeds 140°F. The HVAC programmer will request that the cooling fans be turned off once the A/C high side refrigerant temperature falls below 122°F.

The HVAC programmer also will request low cooling fan speed operation when all of the following conditions are met:

1. Vehicle speed is below 20 mph.
2. A/C compressor clutch engagement is possible.
3. Outside air temperature is greater than 45°F.

Low Speed Conditions, 4.6L/V8-279 Engine

The PCM will turn on the cooling fans at low speed when engine coolant temperature exceeds 222°F. The cooling fans will be turned off when the coolant temperature drops below 215°F. The PCM monitors engine coolant temperature using the coolant temperature sensor at terminal "1B5" through circuit (585).

The PCM will also activate low speed operation if the transaxle temperature exceeds 239°F. The cooling fans will be turned off when the transaxle temperature falls below 230°F. The PCM monitors transaxle temperature using the transaxle temperature sensor input at terminal "1B14" through circuit (585).

The heater and A/C programmer will request the PCM to turn on the cooling fans at low speed through the UART data line. The PCM will turn on the cooling fans at low speed if a low coolant level is detected and the engine engine coolant temperature exceeds 176°F. The cooling fans will be turned off when the coolant temperature drops below 113°F. The PCM monitors coolant level using the coolant level switch input at terminal "1B16" through circuit (1478).

Low Speed Operation, 4.9L/V8-300 Engine

Low speed cooling fan operation will occur when the PCM grounds coolant fan relay number 1's coil through circuit 1269 at terminal 2A11. With only cooling fan relay 1 energized, voltage is applied to both pusher and puller cooling fans. The voltage path to the fans is through cooling fan number 1's contacts, circuits 532 and 533, and the cooling fan relay number 2's contacts. The two fans are connected to each other through a series circuit. This causes the voltage being applied by fuse 6 to be divided between the two fans. The division of voltage causes the fans to operate at a lower speed. In the series mode the fans are grounded through circuit 804 and ground G104.

Low Speed Operation, 4.6L/V8-279 Engine

Low speed cooling fan operation will occur when the PCM grounds coolant fan relay No. 1. The PCM grounds the relay through circuit (1269) at terminal "3F8." When coolant fan relay No. 1 is energized,

voltage is applied to both left and right fans. The voltage path to the fans is through relay No. 1 contacts, circuits (532) and (533), and cooling fan relay No. 2 contacts. The two fans are connected to each other through a series circuit. This causes the voltage that is applied through fuse 6 to be divided between the two fans. The division of voltage causes the fans to operate at a lower speed. In the series mode the fans are grounded through circuit (804) and ground (G107).

High Speed Conditions, 4.9L/V8-300 Engine

The PCM will turn on the cooling fans at high speed when the engine coolant temperature exceeds 226°F or if the coolant temperature sensor circuit has failed. The PCM will switch the cooling fans to low speed operation when the coolant temperature falls below 223°F.

The HVAC programmer will request the PCM to turn on the cooling fans at high speed through the UART data line if the A/C high side refrigerant temperature exceeds 158°F or an A/C high side temperature sensor circuit failure occurs. The HVAC programmer will request that the cooling fans be switched to low speed operation when the high side refrigerant temperature falls below 138°F.

High Speed Conditions, 4.6L/V8-279 Engine

The PCM will turn on the cooling fans at high speed when the coolant temperature exceeds 230°F or if the coolant temperature sensor circuit has failed. The PCM will switch the cooling fans to low speed operation when the coolant level temperature falls below 221°F.

The PCM will request high speed operation if the transaxle temperature exceeds 248°F. The PCM will switch to low speed operation once the transaxle temperature falls below 239°F. The PCM will turn on the cooling fans at high speed if a low coolant level is detected and coolant temperature exceeds 185°F. The PCM will switch to low speed operation once the coolant temperature drops below 176°F.

The heater and A/C programmer can request the PCM to turn on the cooling fans at high speed through the UART data line.

High Speed Operation, 4.9L/V8-300 Engine

The cooling fans run at high speed when cooling fan relays 1, 2 and 3 are grounded by PCM terminals 2B8 and 2A11 through circuits 1269 and 1270. With coolant fan relay number 1 energized, battery voltage is applied to the pusher fan through the relay contacts. The pusher fan runs at high speed because now the fan is grounded directly through the contacts of coolant fan relay number 2.

Since cooling fan relay number 3 is also energized during high speed operation, battery voltage is applied directly to the puller cooling fan through the closed contacts of the relay. The fan will run at high speed since it is no longer in series with the pusher fan.

Fig. 71 Coolant fan wiring circuit (Part 2 of 2). 1992 Eldorado & Seville

Fig. 71 Coolant fan wiring circuit (Part 1 of 2). 1992 Eldorado & Seville

Fig. 72 Coolant fan wiring circuit (Part 2 of 2).
1993 Eldorado & Seville w/4.6L/V8-279 engine

Fig. 72 Coolant fan wiring circuit (Part 1 of 2).
1993 Eldorado & Seville w/4.6L/V8-279 engine

Fig. 73 Coolant fan wiring circuit (Part 2 of 2). 1993 Eldorado & Seville w/4.9L/V8-300 engine

Fig. 73 Coolant fan wiring circuit (Part 1 of 2). 1993 Eldorado & Seville w/4.9L/V8-300 engine

High Speed Operation, 4.6L/V8-279 Engine

The cooling fans run at high speed when cooling fan relays 1, 2 and 3 are grounded by PCM terminals "3F8" and "3F7" through circuits (1269) and (1270). With coolant fan relay No. 1 energized, battery voltage is applied to the left cooling fan motor through the relay contacts. The left cooling fan runs at high speed because the fan is grounded directly through the contacts of cooling fan relay No. 2, circuit (150) and ground (G109).

Since cooling fan relay No. 3 is also energized during high speed operation, battery voltage is applied directly to the right cooling fan through the closed contacts of the relay. The fan will run at high speed since it is no longer in series with the left cooling fan.

COOLANT FAN, REPLACE

1991

1. Disconnect battery ground cable.
2. **On front cooling fan,** proceed as follows:
   a. Remove radiator cover panel.
   b. Disconnect and remove fan control module and bracket.
   c. Remove front grill.
3. **On rear coolant fan,** proceed as follows:
   a. Remove air cleaner duct.
   b. Remove A/C hose bracket.
4. **On both fans,** disconnect electrical connections.
5. Remove cooling fan(s).
6. Reverse procedure to install.

1992–93

1. Disconnect battery ground cable.
2. **On front cooling fan,** proceed as follows:
   a. Remove plastic radiator cover.
   b. Disconnect fan electrical connector.
   c. Remove right headlamp bracket.
   d. Remove three bolts and cooling fan from vehicle.
3. **On rear coolant fan,** proceed as follows:
   a. Remove upper engine to radiator support torque strut.
   b. Disconnect fan electrical connector.
   c. Disconnect oil cooler bracket from fan.
   d. Remove two upper and lower bolts and fan from vehicle.
4. **On both fans,** reverse procedure to install.

EIGHTY-EIGHT & NINETY-EIGHT

SYSTEM DESCRIPTION

1991 Eighty Eight

A two speed coolant fan is turned on and off by the low and high speed coolant fan relays.

For low speed operation, the low speed relay coil is grounded through the ECM. The ECM grounds the coil when engine coolant is above 213°F, and vehicle speed is below 47 mph or the A/C system has been turned on.

With low speed relay coil grounded, its contacts close. Voltage is applied through the coolant fan resistor to the coolant fan. The resistor reduces voltage supplied to the fan so the fan runs at low speed.

For high speed operation, the high speed relay coil is grounded through the A/C coolant fan pressure switch or by the ECM when coolant temperature is above 226°F. The A/C coolant fan pressure switch high speed contacts close at a refrigerant pressure above 275 psi.

With the high speed coil grounded, its contacts close. Battery voltage is applied to the coolant fan. The fan runs at high speed.

The heavy duty coolant fan, if equipped, operates whenever the coolant fan runs at high speed. The A/C coolant fan pressure switch and ECM also control the auxiliary coolant fan relay, if equipped, which supplies battery voltage to the auxiliary coolant fan when energized.

Ninety Eight & 1992–93 Eighty Eight

Two coolant fans, wired in parallel, operate whenever cooling is required.

The powertrain control module (PCM) has two coolant fan control terminals : one for high speed and one for low speed. When the PCM's low speed control closes at connector C3, terminal C4, it grounds the low speed coolant relay coil. When the ignition switch is in the RUN position and the relay contacts close, voltage is supplied to the coolant fans. The coolant fan resistors drop the voltage to the lefthand coolant fan, causing it to run in low speed. The righthand coolant fan also runs, but at high speed because the coolant fan resistors are bypassed. The PCM's low speed output is turned on when coolant temperature reaches 212°F.

High speed operation is similar to low speed. When coolant temperature reaches 226°F, the PCM's high speed control closes at connector C3, terminal C3, grounding the high speed coolant relay coil. The relay contacts close and both fans run at high speed since the PCM's low speed control remains closed. When A/C head pressure reaches 210 psi, the A/C pressure fan switch closes, grounding PCM input connector C1, terminal D9. This also causes the PCM high speed control to close, and both coolant fans run at high speed.

TROUBLESHOOTING

1991 Eighty Eight

1. Visually inspect fuse 6.
2. Check fusible link D.
3. If either fan runs with ignition switch in OFF position, replace associated coolant fan relay.

Ninety Eight & 1992–93 Eighty Eight

1. Visually inspect instrument panel fuse No. 16 and lefthand underhood fuse block fuse 4.
2. If only one coolant fan does not run, proceed as follows:
   a. Check fan for mechanical binding.
   b. Check wiring to suspect coolant fan.
   c. If wiring is satisfactory, replace coolant fan motor.
3. If coolant fan runs continuously with ignition switch off, remove both coolant fan relays one at a time. replace relay that caused fans to stop.

SYSTEM CHECK

1991 Eighty Eight

1. With ambient temperature above 60°F and engine cold and idling, move A/C selector switch, if equipped, to NORM. Coolant fan should run at low speed. When A/C head pressure exceeds 275 psi, coolant fan should run at high speed and auxiliary coolant fan should run.
2. With engine coolant below 208°F, move A/C selector switch to OFF position. Coolant fan(s) should turn off.
3. Run engine at fast idle for several minutes. When engine temperature exceeds 208°F, ECM should turn coolant fan on and coolant fan should run at low speed. When engine temperature exceeds 226°F, coolant fan should run at high speed and auxiliary coolant fan should run.

Ninety Eight & 1992–93 Eighty Eight

1. With ambient temperature above 60°F and engine cold and idling, set A/C mode selector to NORM. Lefthand coolant fan should run at low speed. Righthand coolant fan should run at high speed.
2. With engine cold, move A/C mode selector to OFF. Coolant fans should turn off after about one minute.
3. Run engine at fast idle for several minutes. Lefthand coolant fan runs at low speed and righthand coolant fan runs at high speed.
4. Restrict air flow through radiator by covering half of grill side of radiator. After a few minutes both coolant fans should run at high speed.

DIAGNOSIS

Refer To **Figs. 74 and 75** when performing diagnostic procedures on these systems.

1991 EIGHTY EIGHT

Coolant Fan Does Not Run In Low Or High Speed

1. Disconnect high speed coolant fan relay connector and connect a 20 amp fused jumper between terminals 1 (red) and 4 (black/pink) wire terminals. If coolant fan runs, proceed to "Coolant Fan Does Not Run In High Speed."

Fig. 74   Coolant fan wiring circuit. 1991 88 w/3800/V6-231 (VIN C) engine

Fig. 75   Coolant fan wiring circuit. 98 & 1992–93 88

2. If coolant fan does not run, leave fused jumper connected as in step 1, disconnect connector C123 and measure voltage from terminal B (black/pink) wire terminal to ground. If battery voltage is not present, check lefthand underhood fuse block fuse 4, red wire and black/pink wire for open.

3. If battery voltage is present, leave fused jumper connected as in step 1, and measure voltage between terminals B (black/pink) and C (black) wire terminals. If battery voltage is not present, check black wire for open.

4. If battery voltage is present, check wiring between terminals B (pink/black) and C (black) and, if satisfactory, replace coolant fan assembly.

Coolant Fan Does Not Run In Low Speed

1. Disconnect low speed coolant fan relay connector and connect a 20 amp fused jumper between terminals 1 (red) and 4 (black/pink) wire terminals. If coolant fan does not run at low speed, check red and black/red wires and coolant fan resistor.

2. If coolant fan does not run, remove fused jumper connected in step 1, turn ignition switch to RUN and measure voltage from terminal B (brown) wire terminal to ground at low speed coolant relay connector. If battery voltage is not present, check instrument panel fuse block fuse 6, and brown wire for open.

3. If battery voltage is present, reconnect low speed coolant fan relay and turn ignition switch to RUN. Ground terminal E2 of ECM connector C3 with a fused jumper. If coolant fan runs at low speed, problem is ECM related.

4. If coolant fan does not run at low speed, check dark green wire for an open and check low speed coolant fan relay terminal contact. If satisfactory, replace low speed coolant fan relay.

Coolant Fan Does Not Run In High Speed

1. Turn ignition switch to RUN position and ground terminal B of ALDL connector with a fused jumper. If coolant fan runs at high speed, problem is ECM related.

2. If coolant fan does not run, at high speed, removed fused jumper connected in step 1 and remove high speed coolant fan relay. Connect a 20 amp fused jumper between terminals 1 (red) and 4 (pink/black) of high speed coolant fan relay connector. If coolant fan does not run at high speed, check red, black/pink and black wires for an open.

3. If coolant fan runs at high speed, remove fused jumper connected in step 2, turn ignition switch to RUN and measure voltage between terminal 2 (brown) and ground at high speed coolant fan relay connector. If battery voltage is not present, check brown wire for an open.

4. If battery voltage is present, reconnect high speed coolant fan relay and turn ignition switch to RUN. Ground terminal B5 of ECM connector C2 with a fused jumper. If coolant fan runs at high speed, problem is ECM related.

5. If coolant fan does not run at high speed, check light green/black wire for open and check high speed coolant fan relay terminal contact. If satisfactory, replace high speed coolant fan relay.

Heavy Duty Coolant Fan Does Not Run

1. If coolant fan does not run in high speed, proceed to "Coolant Fan Does Not Run In High Speed."

2. If coolant fan runs in high speed, disconnect heavy duty coolant fan relay connector, turn ignition switch to RUN position and measure voltage from terminal 2 (brown) wire terminal to ground. If battery voltage is not present, check brown wire for open.

3. If battery voltage is present, measure voltage between terminal 1 (red) wire terminal and ground. If battery voltage is not present, check red wire for open.

4. If battery voltage is present, connect a 20 amp fused jumper between terminals 1 (red) and 4 (black/pink) at heavy duty coolant fan relay connector If heavy duty coolant fan runs, check auxiliary coolant fan relay connector terminal contact and the light green/black wire to splice S119 and, if satisfactory, replace auxiliary coolant fan relay.

5. If auxiliary coolant fan does not run, leave fused jumper connected as in step 4, disconnect connector from heavy duty coolant fan and measure voltage between terminal B (black/pink) wire terminal and ground. If battery voltage is not present, check black/pink wire for open.

6. If battery voltage is present, leave fused jumper connected as in step 4, and measure voltage between terminals B (black/pink) and A (black) wire terminals.

7. If battery voltage is not present, check black wire for open.

8. If battery voltage is present, check heavy duty coolant fan connector terminals and, if satisfactory, replace auxiliary coolant fan motor.

Coolant Fan Runs Continuously In Low Speed With Ignition Switch In Run Position, Engine Coolant Cool & A/C Off

1. Disconnect low speed coolant fan relay connector, turn ignition switch to RUN position and connect test lamp between terminals 2 (brown) and 5 (dark green) wire terminals at low speed coolant fan relay connector.

2. If lamp does not illuminate, replace low speed coolant fan relay.

3. If lamp illuminates, check dark green wire for short to ground. If wire is satisfactory, problem is ECM related.

Coolant Fan Runs Continuously In High Speed And/Or Auxiliary Coolant Fan Runs Continuously With Ignition Switch In RUN Position, Engine Coolant Cool & A/C Off

1. Turn ignition switch to RUN position and disconnect A/C coolant fan pressure switch connector. If coolant fan(s) stop(s), replace A/C coolant fan pressure switch.

2. If coolant fan(s) run(s), turn ignition switch to RUN position, disconnect high speed coolant fan relay connector and/or heavy duty coolant fan relay connector and connect test lamp between terminals 2 (brown) and 5 (light green/black) wire terminals.

3. If lamp does not illuminate, replace suspect relay.

4. If lamp illuminates, check light green/black wires for short to ground and, if wires are satisfactory, problem is ECM related.

Coolant Fan And/Or Heavy Duty Fan Does Not Run With A/C On, But Does Operate Normally With Engine Hot

1. If coolant fan does not operate in low speed with A/C on problem is ECM related.

2. If coolant fan operates in high speed with A/C on, check whether coolant fan operates at high speed and auxiliary coolant fan runs when A/C pressure is above 275 psi.

3. If fan does not operate at high speed with A/C On, check A/C coolant fan pressure switch and light green black wire and black wire to A/C coolant fan pressure switch.

NINETY EIGHT & 1992–93 EIGHTY EIGHT
Both Coolant Fans Do Not Run

1. Turn ignition switch to RUN, connect a fused jumper between ALDL terminals A and B. If coolant fans run, problem is PCM related. If coolant fans do not run, proceed to step 2.

2. Leave jumper connected as in step 1 and disconnect connector (C123). Measure voltage between terminal A (black/red) and ground. If battery voltage is not present, refer to "Lefthand Coolant Fan Does Not Operate In Low Speed." If battery voltage is present, proceed to step 3.

3. With jumper still connected, measure voltage between terminal B (black/pink) and ground. If battery voltage is not present, refer to "Lefthand Coolant Fan Does Not Operate In High Speed." If battery voltage is present, proceed to step 4.

4. Jumper still connected to ALDL, measure voltage from terminal B (black/pink) to terminal C (black). If battery voltage is not present, check black wire for an open circuit. If battery voltage is present, check wiring within coolant fan assembly. If wiring is satisfactory, replace fan motor.

Lefthand Coolant Fan Does Not Operate In Low Speed

1. Disconnect low speed coolant fan relay and turn ignition switch to RUN. Measure voltage from relay connector terminal No. 2 (brown) to ground. If battery voltage is not present, check brown wire for an open circuit. If battery voltage is present, proceed to step 2.
2. Measure voltage from terminal No. 1 (red) to ground. If battery voltage is not present, check red wire for an open circuit. If battery voltage is present, proceed to step 3.
3. Connect a test lamp between relay connector terminal Nos. 1 (red) and 5 (gray/black), then connect a jumper between ALDL terminals A and B. If test lamp does not light, check gray/black wire for an open circuit. If circuit is satisfactory, problem is PCM related. If test lamp lights, proceed to step 4.
4. Connect a fused jumper between relay connector terminal Nos. 1 (red) and 4 (black). If lefthand coolant fan runs in low speed, replace low speed coolant fan relay. If coolant fan does not run in low speed, check black/red wire and coolant fan resistor for an open circuit.

Lefthand Coolant Fan Does Not Operate In High Speed

1. Disconnect high speed coolant fan relay and turn ignition switch to RUN. Measure voltage from relay connector terminal 2 (brown) to ground. If battery voltage is present, proceed to step 2. If battery voltage is not present, check brown wire for an open circuit.
2. Measure voltage from terminal 1 (red) to ground. If battery voltage is present, proceed to step 3. If battery voltage is not present, check red wire for an open circuit.
3. Connect a test lamp between relay connector terminal Nos. 1 (red) and 5 (dark green/white). If test lamp lights, proceed to step 4. If test lamp does not light, check dark green/white wire for an open. If wire is satisfactory, problem is PCM related.
4. Connect a fused jumper between relay connector terminal Nos. 1 (red) and 4 (black/pink). If coolant fan runs in high speed, replace high speed coolant fan relay. If coolant fan does not run, check black/red wire and coolant fan resistor for an open circuit.

Lefthand Coolant Fan Runs Continuously In Low Speed With Ignition Switch At RUN, Engine Coolant Cool & A/C Off

1. Disconnect low speed coolant fan relay and turn ignition switch to RUN.
2. Connect a test lamp between terminal Nos. 2 (brown) and 5 (gray/black) at low speed coolant fan connector.
3. If test lamp lights, check gray/black wire for a short to ground. If wire is satisfactory, problem is PCM related.

4. If test lamp does not light, replace low speed coolant fan relay.

Lefthand Coolant fan Runs Continuously In High Speed With Ignition Switch At RUN, Engine Coolant Cool & A/C Off

1. Disconnect high speed coolant fan relay and turn ignition switch to RUN.
2. Connect a test lamp between terminal Nos. 2 (brown) and 5 (dark green/white) at high speed relay connector.
3. If test lamp lights, check dark green/white wire for a short to ground. If wire is satisfactory, problem is PCM related.
4. If test lamp does not light, replace high speed coolant fan relay.

Coolant Fans Do Not Operate In High Speed With A/C Head Pressure Above 210 psi

1. Disconnect A/C pressure fan switch connector.
2. Measure resistance from terminal B (black/white) to ground.
3. If resistance is zero, refer to step 4. If resistance is not zero, check black/white wire for an open circuit.
4. Connect a jumper between terminals A (dark green/white) and B (black/white) of switch connector and turn ignition switch to RUN.
5. If coolant fans run in high speed, replace A/C pressure fan switch. If coolant fans do not run in high speed, check dark green/white wire for an open circuit. If wire is satisfactory, problem is PCM related.

COOLANT FAN, REPLACE

1. Disconnect battery ground cable.
2. Remove wiring harness from fan motor and fan frame.
3. Remove fan guard and hose support as necessary.
4. Remove fan assembly from radiator support.
5. Reverse procedure to install.

SERVICE BULLETINS
Cooling Fan Runs Battery Dead

Refer to "Service Bulletins" in "6000" for diagnosis and repair of this condition.

GRAND AM

SYSTEM DESCRIPTION
1991 2.5L/4-151 (VIN U) & All 1992–93 Engines

The coolant fan is controlled by the coolant fan relay. The coolant fan relay is electrically operated by the ECM. The ECM receives input signals from the coolant temperature sensor, the vehicle speed sensor and the A/C mode selector. The ECM activates the coolant fan relay when the engine coolant, which is sensed by the coolant temperature sensor, is above

227°F, when the A/C is turned on or when the coolant temperature sensor fails. Any of these input signals causes the ECM to ground circuit 335 (1991) and 535 or 536 (1992-93) when vehicle speed is less than 35 mph. With circuit 335 (1991) and 535 or 536 (1992-93) grounded, the coolant fan relay is energized and its contacts close, turning the coolant fan on.

1991 2.3L/4-138 (VIN A & D) Engine

A two speed heavy duty coolant fan is used with this engine. The coolant fan is turned on and off by the coolant fan relays.

For low speed operation, the low speed relay coil is grounded through the ECM when vehicle speed is less than 45 mph and the engine coolant reaches 208°F, or when the A/C is turned on. The contacts close and voltage is applied through the coolant fan resistor to the coolant fan. The fan runs at low speed.

For high speed operation, the high speed relay coil is grounded through the ECM when the coolant temperature reaches 228°F. The contacts close and voltage is applied to the coolant fan. The fan runs at high speed.

TROUBLESHOOTING
1991

1. If coolant fan does not operate on VINs U and D, check fusible link F and H-AC fuse.
2. If coolant fan runs with ignition switch in OFF position on VIN U, replace coolant fan relay.
3. If coolant fan runs in high speed with ignition switch in OFF position on VIN D, replace high speed coolant fan relay.
4. If coolant fan runs in low speed with ignition switch in OFF position on VIN D, replace low speed coolant fan relay.

1992–93

If coolant fan runs with ignition switch in Off position, replace coolant fan relay.

SYSTEM CHECK

1. With ambient air temperature above 70°F, open all doors, start vehicle and set A/C mode selector, if equipped, to MAX position. Coolant fan should turn on in a short period of time.
2. With engine coolant below operating temperature, move A/C selector to OFF position. Coolant fan should turn off in a short period of time.
3. Run engine at fast idle for several minutes. Coolant fan should turn on before coolant temperature indicator comes on or coolant temperature gage needle reaches HOT.
4. Turn ignition switch to OFF position. Coolant fan should turn off when engine temperature lowers.

DIAGNOSIS

Refer to **Figs. 76 through 78** when performing diagnostic procedures on these systems.

Fig. 77 Coolant fan wiring circuit. 1991 Grand Am w/2.3L/4-138 (VIN D & A) engine

Fig. 76 Coolant fan wiring circuit. 1991 Grand Am w/2.5L/4-151 (VIN U) engine

Fig. 78   Coolant fan wiring circuit. 1992–93 Grand Am

Coolant Fan Does Not Turn Off With Engine Cool, A/C Mode Selector Off & Ignition Switch In RUN Position

1. Turn ignition switch to RUN position, disconnect coolant fan relay connector and connect test lamp between brown and dark green/white wire terminals. If lamp does not illuminate, replace coolant fan relay.
2. If lamp illuminates, check dark green/white wire for short to ground. If wire is satisfactory, problem is ECM related.

Coolant Fan Does Not Turn On With A/C Mode Selector On And Head Pressure Above 150 psi, But Does Run With Engine Hot

1. Place ignition in RUN position and A/C mode selector in MAX position. Measure voltage between terminal C1/24 of the ECM and ground.
2. If no voltage is present, check dark green/white wire for an open.
3. If battery voltage is present, problem is ECM related

1991 2.3L/4-138 (VIN A & D) ENGINE

Coolant Fan Does Not Turn On

1. Place ignition switch in RUN position. Ground terminal B of the ALDL connector. If coolant fan runs, problem is ECM related.
2. If coolant fan does not run, ground terminal C3/E8 of the ECM connector with a fused jumper. If coolant fan runs, problem is ECM related.
3. If coolant fan does not run and terminal C3/E8 is still grounded, disconnect coolant fan relay connector. Measure voltage between terminal 2 of the coolant fan relay connector to ground. If no voltage is present, check red wire and fusible link F for and open.
4. If battery voltage is present and terminal C3/E8 is still grounded, measure voltage between red wire terminal and ground of the relay connector. If no voltage is present, check red wire and fusible link F for an open.
5. If battery voltage is present, connect a fused jumper between terminals 1 and 4 of the coolant fan relay. If coolant fan runs, replace coolant fan relay.
6. If coolant fan does not run, leave jumper on relay connector and measure voltage between terminal B of the coolant fan connector to ground. If no voltage is present, check black/red wire for an open.
7. If battery voltage is present, leave jumper on relay connector and measure voltage between terminals B and A on coolant fan connector. If no voltage is present, check black wire for an open.
8. If battery voltage is present, Replace coolant fan motor.

1991 2.5L/4-151 (VIN U) ENGINE

Coolant Fan Does Not Turn On

1. With ignition switch in RUN position, ground terminal B of ALDL connector. If coolant fan runs, problem is ECM related.
2. If coolant fan does not run, turn ignition switch to RUN position and ground ECM C1 connector dark green/white wire terminal with fused jumper. If coolant fan runs, problem is ECM related.
3. If coolant fan does not run, leave fused jumper connected as in step 2, turn ignition switch to RUN position, disconnect coolant fan relay connector and measure voltage from brown wire terminal to ground. If battery voltage is not present, check brown and brown/white wires for open.
4. If battery voltage is present, leave fused jumper connected as in step 2, turn ignition switch to RUN position and measure voltage between brown and dark green/white wire terminals. If battery voltage is not present, check dark green/white wire for open.
5. If battery voltage is present, disconnect coolant fan relay connector and measure voltage from red (1) wire terminal to ground. If battery voltage is not present, check red (2) wire and fusible link F for open.
6. If battery voltage is present, disconnect coolant fan relay connector and connect fused jumper with 20 amp fuse between red (1) and black/red wire terminals. If coolant fan runs, replace coolant fan relay.
7. If coolant fan does not run, leave fused jumper connected as in step 6, disconnect coolant fan connector and measure voltage between black/red wire terminal and ground. If battery voltage is not present, check black/red wire for open.
8. If battery voltage is present, leave fused jumper connected as in step 6, and measure voltage between black/red and black wire terminals of coolant fan connector.
9. If battery voltage is not present, check black wire for open.
10. If battery voltage is present, replace coolant fan.

Coolant Fan Runs Continuously With Engine Coolant Cool & A/C Mode Selector Off

1. Disconnect coolant fan relay connector.
2. Connect a test lamp between terminals 2 and 5 of the relay connector. If lamp does not light, replace coolant fan relay.
3. If test lamp lights, check and repair green/ black wire for a short to ground. If wire is satisfactory, problem is ECM related.

Coolant Fan Does Not Turn On With A/C Mode Selector On And Head Pressure Above 150 psi, But Does Run With Engine Hot

1. Place ignition in RUN position and A/C mode selector in MAX position. Measure voltage between terminal C1/C9 of the ECM and ground.
2. If no voltage is present, check light green wire for an open.
3. If battery voltage is present, problem is ECM related

1992–93
Coolant Fan Does Not Turn On

1. With ignition switch in RUN position, ground terminal B of ALDL connector. If coolant fan runs, problem is ECM related.
2. If coolant fan does not run, turn ignition switch to RUN position and jump ECM C3, terminal E8 to ground with a fused jumper. If coolant fan runs, problem is ECM related.
3. If coolant fan does not run, leave fused jumper connected as in step 2, turn ignition switch to RUN position, disconnect coolant fan relay connector and measure voltage from terminal 2 (red) wire terminal to ground. If battery voltage is not present, repair open in circuit 2.
4. If battery voltage is present, leave fused jumper connected as in step 2, turn ignition switch to RUN position, disconnect coolant fan relay connector and measure voltage between terminal 2 (red) and terminal 5 (dark green or light green/black) wire terminals of coolant fan relay connector. If battery voltage is not present, repair open in circuit 535 or 536.
5. If battery voltage is present, disconnect coolant fan relay connector and measure voltage from red (1) wire terminal to ground. If battery voltage is not present, repair open in circuit 2.
6. If battery voltage is present, disconnect coolant fan relay connector and connect fused jumper with 20 amp fuse between terminals 1 (red) and 4 (black/red) wire terminals. If coolant fan runs, replace coolant fan relay.
7. If coolant fan does not run, leave fused jumper connected as in step 6, disconnect coolant fan connector and measure voltage between terminal B (black/red) wire terminal and ground.

If battery voltage is not present, repair open in circuit 532.
8. If battery voltage is present, leave fused jumper connected as in step 6, and measure voltage between terminals B (black/red) and A (black) wire terminals of coolant fan connector.
9. If battery voltage is not present, repair open in circuit 151.
10. If battery voltage is present, replace coolant fan motor.

Coolant Fan Does Not Turn Off With Engine Cool, A/C Mode Selector Off & Ignition Switch In RUN Position

1. Turn ignition switch to RUN position, disconnect coolant fan relay connector and connect test lamp between terminals 2 (red) and 5 (dark green or light green/black) wire terminals. If lamp does not illuminate, replace coolant fan relay.
2. If lamp illuminates, check circuit 535 or 536 for a short to ground. If wire is satisfactory, problem is ECM related.

COOLANT FAN, REPLACE
2.5L/4-151 (VIN U) Engine

1. Disconnect battery ground cable.
2. Remove wiring harness from fan motor and fan frame.
3. Remove fan guard and hose support as necessary.
4. Remove fan assembly from radiator support.
5. Reverse procedure to install.

1991 2.3L/4-138 (VIN A & D) Engine

1. Disconnect battery ground cable.
2. Remove air cleaner to throttle body duct.
3. Disconnect electrical connectors from throttle position sensor, IAC and MAP sensor and position harness aside.
4. Remove vacuum harness assembly from throttle body and position aside.
5. Disconnect MAP sensor vacuum hose at intake manifold.
6. Remove coolant fan shroud attaching bolts and the shroud together with MAP sensor.
7. Remove coolant fan to upper radiator support attaching bolt, remaining upper radiator support bolt and the upper radiator support.
8. Remove electrical connector from coolant fan.
9. Lift fan assembly out of two lower insulators, rotate bracket so two lower bracket legs point upward, move fan assembly toward driver's side until fan blade overlaps radiator tank to core seam by approximately one inch and remove fan assembly upward. **Because of minimum clearance, care must be taken not to damage lock tang on throttle position sensor with fan bracket.**
10. Reverse procedure to install.

1992–93 2.3L/4-138 (VIN A, D & 3) Engine

1. Disconnect battery ground cable and remove air intake duct assembly.
2. Remove coolant fan mounting bolt and disconnect electrical connector from fan motor.
3. Remove coolant fan assembly out through bottom.
4. Reverse procedure to install.

3.3L/V6-204 Engine

1. Disconnect battery ground cable and remove air intake duct assembly.
2. Partially drain cooling system and disconnect upper radiator hose from radiator.
3. Disconnect wiring harness from cooling fan motor and fan frame.
4. Remove fan guard and hose support if necessary.
5. Remove fan assembly from radiator support.
6. Reverse procedure to install.

LEMANS

SYSTEM DESCRIPTION
Models Less A/C

Cooling fan operation is controlled by an engine temperature switch. When engine temperature reaches 221°F, the switch closes and the fan is energized. As the engine cools, the engine temperature switch opens and the cooling fan stops.

Models With A/C

Operation of the two-speed cooling fan is controlled by high and low speed cooling fan relays. When the A/C system is turned on, voltage is supplied to the A/C compressor relay, the ECM grounds the compressor relay coil and the low speed fan relay is energized. Voltage is then transferred from fuse No. 14, through the cooling fan resistor and to the fan.

When the ECM determines that the engine should be cooled, it will ground the high speed fan relay to apply voltage directly from the fuse to the fan motor.

DIAGNOSIS

Refer to **Figs. 79 through 81** when performing diagnostic procedures on this system.

MODELS LESS A/C
Coolant Fan Does Not Run

1. Check fuses 11 and 12, replace as necessary.
2. Connect a fused jumper wire between terminal B of the Assembly Line Diagnostic Link Connector (ALDL) and ground, then turn the ignition switch to the RUN position. If coolant fan does not run, proceed to step 3. If coolant fan runs, problem is ECM related.
3. Disconnect ECM C2 connector, then connect a fused jumper wire between C1 green/white connector and ground. Turn ignition switch to RUN, If coolant fan does not run, proceed to

Fig. 79 Coolant fan wiring circuit (less A/C). LeMans

Fig. 80 Coolant fan wiring circuit (Part 1 of 2). 1991 LeMans w/A/C

Fig. 80 Coolant fan wiring circuit (Part 2 of 2). 1991 LeMans w/A/C

**Fig. 81 Coolant fan wiring circuit (Part 1 of 2).
1992–93 LeMans w/A/C**

Fig. 81 Coolant fan wiring circuit (Part 2 of 2). 1992–93 LeMans w/A/C

step 4. If coolant fan runs, problem is ECM related.

4. Leaving jumper wire connected from the previous step, disconnect coolant fan relay connector. Turn ignition switch to RUN, then using a Test lamp proceed as follows:
   a. Connect test lamp between terminal 1 (brown) wire and ground. If test lamp lights, proceed to step b. If test lamp does not light, locate and repair open in brown wire.
   b. Connect test lamp between terminal 3 (red/yellow) wire and ground. If test lamp lights, proceed to step c. If test lamp does not light, locate and repair open in red/yellow wire.
   c. Connect test lamp between terminal 1 (brown) and terminal 4 (green/white) wires. If test lamp lights, proceed to step d. If test lamp does not light, locate and repair open in green/white wire.
   d. Connect test lamp between terminal 1 (brown) and terminal 2 (red/white) wires. If test lamp lights, replace high speed coolant fan relay. If test lamp does not light, proceed to step 5.
5. With coolant fan relay connector disconnected, connect fused jumper wire between terminal 2 (red/white) and terminal 3 (red/yellow).
6. Check voltage between red/white terminal and ground. If battery voltage is indicated, proceed to step 7. If battery voltage is not indicated, locate and repair open circuit in red/white wire.
7. Check voltage between red/white and black wires. If battery voltage is indicated, replace coolant fan. If battery voltage is not indicated, locate and repair open circuit in black wire.

Coolant Fan Runs Constantly When Ignition Switch Is In Run

1. Disconnect ECM connector C2, then turn ignition switch to the RUN position.
2. If coolant fan is off, problem is ECM related.
3. If coolant fan is on, locate and repair short to ground in green/white wire.

Coolant Fan Does Not Run At Low Speed

1. Disconnect Connector C1 from ECM, then turn ignition switch to the RUN position.
2. Connect a fused jumper wire between terminal A4 (blue) wire and ground. If coolant fan does not run, proceed to step 3. If coolant fan runs, problem is ECM related.
3. With ignition switch in RUN and jumper wire connected as in step 2. Disconnect low speed coolant fan relay connector and proceed as follows:
   a. Connect a test lamp between connector terminal 1 (red/yellow) and ground. If test lamp lights, proceed to step b. If test lamp does not light, locate and repair open in red/yellow wire.
   b. Connect a test lamp between con-

nector terminals 1 (red/yellow) and 4 (black). If test lamp lights, replace low coolant fan relay. If test lamp does not light, locate and repair open in black wire.

1991 MODELS w/A/C
Coolant Fan Does Not Run At All

1. Disconnect low speed coolant fan relay connector, turn ignition switch to the RUN position and the A/C to the NORM mode.
2. Using a test light, proceed as follows:
   a. Connect test lamp between terminal 1 (red/yellow) wire and ground. If test lamp lights, proceed to step b. If test lamp does not light, locate and repair open circuit in red/yellow wire.
   b. Connect test lamp between terminal 1 (red/yellow) wire and black wire. If test lamp lights, proceed to step c. If test lamp does not light, locate and repair open circuit in black wire.
   c. Connect test lamp between terminal 3 (red/yellow) wire and ground. If test lamp lights, proceed to step 3. If test lamp does not light, locate and repair open circuit in either one of the red/yellow wires.
3. Connect a fused jumper wire between terminal 3 (red/yellow) and terminal 2 (red/yellow) wires. If coolant fan does not run at low speed, proceed to step 4. If coolant fan runs at low speed, replace low speed coolant fan relay.
4. Leaving fused jumper connected from step 3, disconnect coolant fan connector.
5. Connect a test lamp between terminal A (red/yellow) wire of the coolant fan connector and ground. If test lamp lights, proceed to step 6. If test lamp does not light, locate and repair open circuit in either the red/yellow or the red/white wires in the coolant fan resistor.
6. Connect a test lamp between terminal A (red/yellow) and terminal B (Black) wires of the coolant fan connector. If test lamp lights, replace coolant fan. If test lamp does not light, locate and repair open circuit in the black wire.

Coolant Fan Runs Constantly With Ignition Switch Off

1. With ignition switch off, disconnect high speed coolant fan relay.
2. If fan stops replace high speed coolant fan relay. If fan does not stop replace low speed coolant fan relay.

Coolant Fan Does Not Run At Low Speed

1. Disconnect connector C1 from ECM., then turn ignition switch to the run position.
2. Connect a fused jumper wire between terminal A4 (blue) wire and ground. If coolant fan does not run, proceed to step 3. If coolant fan runs, problem is ECM related.

3. With ignition switch in RUN and jumper wire connected as in step 2. Disconnect low speed coolant fan relay connector and proceed as follows:
   a. Connect a test lamp between terminal 1 (red/yellow) and ground. If test lamp lights, proceed to step b. If test lamp does not light, locate and repair open in red/yellow wire.
   b. Connect a test lamp between terminal 1 (red/yellow) and terminal 4 (black). If test lamp lights, replace low coolant fan relay. If test lamp does not light, locate and repair open in black wire.

1992–93 MODELS w/A/C

Refer to Fig. 82 when performing diagnostic procedures on this system.

COOLING FAN, REPLACE

1. Disconnect battery ground cable.
2. Disconnect fan motor electrical connectors.
3. Remove oxygen sensor plug from air shroud.
4. Remove fan frame-to-radiator support attaching bolts, then then fan and frame assembly. A bent or damaged fan assembly must be replaced.
5. Reverse procedure to install.

SKYLARK
SYSTEM DESCRIPTION

The coolant fan is controlled by the coolant fan relay. The coolant fan relay is electrically operated by the ECM. The ECM receives input signals from the coolant temperature sensor, vehicle speed sensor and A/C mode selector. The ECM will activate the coolant fan relay when engine temperature is above 227°F, air conditioning is turned on, or the coolant temperature sensor fails. Any of these input signals causes the ECM to ground circuit 335 on 2.5L/4-151 VIN U engines, circuit 536 on 2.3L/4-138 VIN D and VIN 3 engines and circuit 535 on 3.3L/V6-204 VIN N engines, when vehicle speed is less than 35 mph. When circuits are grounded, the coolant fan relay is energized and its contacts close, turning the coolant fan on.

TROUBLESHOOTING
1991

1. If the coolant fan does not run, check fusible link F.
2. **On 2.5L/4-151 VIN U and 3.3L/V6-204 VIN N engines,** if coolant fan does not operate, check HTR-A/C fuse.
3. **On 2.5L/4-151 VIN U and 3.3L/V6-204 VIN N engines,** if coolant fan runs with ignition switch off, replace coolant fan relay.

1992–93

If coolant fan runs with ignition switch Off, replace coolant fan relay.

Fig. 82   Chart C-12, cooling fan diagnosis chart (Cooling fan circuit check Part 1 Of 2). 1992–93 LeMans w/A/C

Fig. 82   Chart C-12, cooling fan diagnosis chart (Cooling fan circuit check Part 2 Of 2). 1992–93 LeMans w/A/C

SYSTEM CHECK

1. With ambient air temperature above 70°F, open all doors, start car and set A/C mode selector on MAX. Coolant fan should turn on.
2. With engine coolant below operating temperature, move A/C mode selector to OFF. Coolant fan should turn off in a short period of time.
3. Run engine at fast idle for several minutes. Coolant fan should come on before the coolant temperature indicator comes on or the coolant temperature display shows H.
4. **On 1991 VIN D and all 1992-93 models,** turn ignition switch Off. Coolant fan turns off when engine temperature lowers.

SYSTEM DIAGNOSIS

Refer to **Figs. 83 through 86** when performing diagnostic procedures on these systems.

2.5L/4-151 (VIN U) ENGINE
Coolant Fan Does Not Turn On

1. Turn ignition switch to the RUN position, ground terminal B white wire of the ALDL connector.
2. If coolant fan runs, problem is ECM related.
3. If coolant fan does not run, ground terminal C1/21 dark green/white of the ECM with a fused jumper.
4. If coolant fan runs, problem is ECM related.
5. If coolant fan does not run, leaving terminal C1/21 of the ECM grounded,

disconnect coolant fan relay connector. Measure voltage from terminal 5 brown wire of the coolant fan relay connector to ground.
6. If no voltage is indicated, check brown wire and HTR-A/C fuse for an open circuit.
7. If battery voltage is indicated, measure voltage between terminals 5 brown wire and 2 dark green/white of the coolant fan relay connector.
8. If no voltage is indicated, check dark green/white wire for an open circuit.
9. If battery voltage is indicated, measure voltage from terminal 1 red of the coolant fan relay connector to ground.
10. If no voltage is indicated, check red wire and fusible link F for an open circuit.
11. If battery voltage is indicated, connect a fused jumper with a 20 amp fuse between terminals 1 red wire and 4 black/red wire of the disconnected coolant fan relay connector.
12. If coolant fan runs, replace coolant fan relay.
13. If coolant fan does not run, disconnect connector from coolant fan and measure voltage from terminal B black/red of the coolant fan connector to ground.
14. If no voltage is indicated, check black/red wire for an open circuit.
15. If battery voltage is indicated, measure voltage between terminals B black/red wire and A black wire of the coolant fan connector.
16. If no voltage is indicated, check black wire for an open circuit.
17. If battery voltage is indicated, replace coolant fan motor.

Coolant Fan Does Not Turn Off With Engine Coolant Cool, A/C Mode Selector Off & Ignition Switch In Run

1. Turn ignition switch to the RUN position, then disconnect the coolant fan relay connector.
2. Connect a test lamp between terminals 5 brown wire and 2 dark green/white wire of the coolant fan relay connector.
3. If test lamp does not light, replace coolant fan relay.
4. If test lamp lights, check dark green/white wire for an open circuit.
5. If wire is satisfactory, problem is ECM related.

Coolant Fan Does Not Turn On With A/C Mode Selector On & Head pressure Above 150 psi, But Does Run With Engine Hot

1. Turn ignition switch to run, and switch A/C mode selector to MAX position.
2. Measure voltage between terminal C1/24 dark green/white wire of the ECM and ground.
3. If no voltage is indicated, check dark green/white wire for an open circuit.
4. If battery voltage is indicated, problem is ECM related.

1991 2.3L/4-138 (VIN D) ENGINE
Coolant Fan Does Not Turn On

1. Turn ignition switch to RUN position, ground terminal B white wire of the ALDL connector.
2. If coolant fan runs, problem is ECM related.
3. If coolant fan does not run, ground terminal C3/F7 light green/black wire of the ECM with a fused jumper.
4. If coolant fan runs, problem is ECM related.

Fig. 84 Coolant fan wiring circuit. 1991 Skylark w/2.3L/4-138 engine

Fig. 83 Coolant fan wiring circuit. 1991 Skylark w/2.5L/4-151 (VIN U) engine

Fig. 86 Coolant fan wiring circuit. 1992–93 Skylark

Fig. 85 Coolant fan wiring circuit. 1991 Skylark w/3.3L/V6-204 engine

5. If coolant fan does not run, leaving terminal C3/F7 grounded, disconnect coolant fan relay connector.
6. Measure voltage from terminal 2 red wire of the coolant fan relay connector and ground.
7. If no voltage is indicated, check red wire and fusible link F for an open circuit.
8. If battery voltage is indicated, measure voltage between terminals 2 red wire and 5 light green/black wire of the coolant fan relay connector.
9. If no voltage is indicated, check light green/black wire for an open circuit.
10. If battery voltage is indicated, measure voltage from terminal 1 red wire of the coolant fan relay connector to ground.
11. If no voltage is indicated, check red wire and fusible link F for an open circuit.
12. If battery voltage is indicated, connect a fused jumper with a 20 amp fuse between terminals 1 red wire and 4 black/red wire of the coolant fan relay connector.
13. If coolant fan runs, replace coolant fan relay.
14. If coolant fan does not run, leave fused jumper connected at coolant fan relay connector.
15. Disconnect connector from the coolant fan, measure voltage from terminal B black/red wire of the coolant fan connector and ground.
16. If no voltage is indicated, check black/red wire for an open circuit.
17. If battery voltage is indicated, leave fused jumper connected at the coolant fan relay connector.
18. Measure voltage between terminals B black/red wire and A black wire of the coolant fan connector.
19. If no voltage is indicated, check black wire for an open circuit.
20. If battery voltage is indicated, replace coolant fan motor.

Coolant Fan Does Not Turn Off With Engine Coolant Cool & A/C Mode Selector Off

1. Disconnect coolant relay connector, then connect a test lamp between terminals 2 red wire and 5 light green/black wire of the coolant fan relay connector.
2. If test lamp does not light, replace coolant fan relay.
3. If test lamp lights, check light green/black wire for a short to ground.
4. If wire is satisfactory, problem is ECM related.

Coolant Fan Does Not Turn On With A/C Mode Selector On & Head pressure Above 150 psi, But Does Run With Engine Hot

1. Turn ignition switch to the RUN position, switch A/C mode selector to MAX.

2. Measure voltage between terminal C1/C9 light green wire of the ECM and ground.
3. If no voltage is indicated, check light green wire for an open circuit.
4. If battery voltage is indicated, problem is ECM related.

1991 3.3L/V6-204 (VIN N) ENGINE

A/C Coolant Fan Does Not Turn

1. Turn ignition switch to the RUN position, then ground terminal B white wire of the ALDL connector.
2. If coolant fan runs, problem is ECM related.
3. If coolant fan does not run, ground terminal C3/E8 dark green wire of the ECM with a fused jumper.
4. If coolant fan runs, problem is ECM related.
5. If coolant fan does not run, with terminal C3/E8 dark green wire of the ECM grounded disconnect coolant fan relay connector.
6. Measure voltage from terminal 2 brown wire of the coolant fan relay to ground.
7. If no voltage is indicated, check brown wire and HTR-A/C fuse for an open circuit.
8. If battery voltage is indicated, with ECM still grounded, measure voltage between terminals 2 brown wire and 5 dark green wire of the coolant fan relay connector.
9. If no voltage is indicated, check dark green wire for an open circuit.
10. If battery voltage is indicated, measure voltage from terminal 1 red wire of the coolant fan relay connector to ground.
11. If no voltage is indicated, check red wire for an open circuit.
12. If battery voltage is indicated, connect a fused jumper with a 20 amp fuse between terminals 1 red wire and 4 black/red wire of the coolant fan relay connector.
13. If coolant fan runs, replace coolant fan relay.
14. If coolant fan does not run, with fused jumper still connected at coolant fan relay connector, measure voltage between terminals B black/red wire and A black wire of the coolant fan connector.
15. If no voltage is indicated, check black wire for an open circuit.
16. If battery voltage is indicated, replace coolant fan motor.

Coolant Fan Does Not Turn Off With Engine Coolant Cool, A/C Mode Selector Off & Ignition Switch In Run

1. Turn ignition switch to the RUN position, then disconnect coolant fan relay connector.
2. Connect a test lamp between terminals 2 brown wire and 5 dark green wire of the coolant fan relay connector.

3. If test lamp does not light, replace coolant fan relay.
4. If test lamp lights, check dark green wire for a short to ground.
5. If wire is satisfactory, problem is ECM related.

Coolant Fan Does Not Turn On With A/C Mode Selector On & Head pressure Above 150 psi, But Does Run With Engine Hot

1. Turn ignition switch to the RUN position and switch A/C mode selector to the MAX position.
2. Measure voltage between terminal C1/C9 light green of the ECM and ground.
3. If no battery voltage is indicated, check light green wire for an open circuit.
4. If battery voltage is indicated, problem is ECM related.

1992—93

Coolant Fan Does Not Turn On

1. Turn ignition switch to RUN position, ground terminal B of the ALDL connector.
2. If coolant fan runs, problem is ECM related.
3. If coolant fan does not run, jump connector C3, terminal E8, to ground.
4. If coolant fan runs, problem is ECM related.
5. If coolant fan does not run, leave terminal E8 grounded and disconnect coolant fan relay connector.
6. Measure voltage from terminal 2 red wire of the coolant fan relay connector and ground.
7. If no voltage is indicated, repair open in circuit 2.
8. If battery voltage is indicated, leave terminal E8 grounded and measure voltage between terminals 2 (red) wire and 5 (dark green or light green/black) wire of the coolant fan relay connector.
9. If no voltage is indicated, repair open in circuit 535 or 536.
10. If battery voltage is indicated, measure voltage from terminal 1 (red) wire of the coolant fan relay connector to ground.
11. If no voltage is indicated, repair open in circuit 2.
12. If battery voltage is indicated, connect a fused jumper with a 20 amp fuse between terminals 1 (red) wire and 4 (black/red) wire of the coolant fan relay connector.
13. If coolant fan runs, replace coolant fan relay.
14. If coolant fan does not run, leave fused jumper connected at coolant fan relay connector.
15. Disconnect connector from the coolant fan, measure voltage from terminal B (black/red) wire of the coolant fan connector and ground.
16. If no voltage is indicated, repair open in circuit 532.

17. If battery voltage is indicated, leave fused jumper connected at the coolant fan relay connector.
18. Measure voltage between terminals B (black/red) wire and A (black) wire of the coolant fan connector.
19. If no voltage is indicated, repair open in circuit 151.
20. If battery voltage is indicated, replace coolant fan motor.

Coolant Fan Does Not Turn Off With Engine Coolant Cool & A/C Mode Selector Off & ignition switch in RUN

1. Turn ignition switch to RUN and disconnect coolant relay connector, then connect a test lamp between terminals 2 red wire and 5 (dark green or light green/black) wire of the coolant fan relay connector.
2. If test lamp does not light, replace coolant fan relay.
3. If test lamp lights, check circuit 535 and 536 for a short to ground.
4. If wire is satisfactory, problem is ECM related.

COOLING FAN, REPLACE

1991 Except 2.3L/4-138 (VIN D) Engine

1. Disconnect battery ground.
2. Disconnect cooling fan motor and fan frame electrical connectors.
3. Remove fan guard and hose support, as required.
4. Remove fan assembly attaching bolts, then remove.
5. Reverse procedure to install.

1991 2.3L/4-138 (VIN D) Engine

1. Disconnect battery ground cable.
2. Remove air cleaner to throttle body attaching duct.
3. Remove TPS, IAC and MAP sensor electrical connectors, then position harness aside.
4. Disconnect throttle body vacuum hose assembly, then position aside.
5. Disconnect MAP sensor vacuum hose from intake manifold.
6. Remove fan shroud attaching bolts, then remove.
7. Remove upper radiator support attaching bolts, then remove.
8. Disconnect cooling fan electrical connectors.
9. Lift fan assembly from lower insulators, then rotate bracket so lower bracket legs point upward.
10. Move fan assembly toward LH side of engine compartment to remove. **Do not damage lock tang on TPS sensor with fan bracket.**
11. Reverse procedure to install.

1992–93 2.3L/4-138 (VIN 3) Engine

1. Disconnect battery ground cable and remove air intake duct assembly.
2. Remove coolant fan mounting bolt and disconnect electrical connector from coolant fan.

3. Remove coolant fan out through bottom.
4. Reverse procedure to install.

1992–93 3.3L/V6-204 Engine

1. Disconnect battery ground cable and remove air intake duct assembly.
2. Partially drain cooling system and disconnect upper radiator hose from radiator.
3. Disconnect wiring harness from fan motor and fan frame.
4. Remove fan guard and hose support, if necessary.
5. Remove fan assembly from radiator support.
6. Reverse procedure to install.

SUNBIRD

SYSTEM DESCRIPTION

The coolant fan is controlled by the coolant fan relay. The coolant fan relay is electrically operated by the ECM. The ECM receives input signal from the coolant temperature sensor, vehicle speed sensor and the A/C mode selector. The ECM activates the coolant fan relay when engine coolant, which is sensed by the coolant temperature sensor, is above 227°F, when A/C is turned on and when coolant temperature sensor fails. Any of these input signals causes the ECM to ground circuit 335. With circuit 335 grounded, the coolant fan relay is energized and its contacts close. The battery runs with battery voltage across its terminals.

TROUBLESHOOTING

2.0L/4-121 (VIN K) Engine

1. If coolant fan does not operate, check C-H fuse.
2. If coolant fan runs with ignition switch off, replace coolant fan relay.

2.0L/4-121 (VIN M) Engine

1. If coolant fan does not operate, check fusible link C.
2. If coolant fan runs with engine on but does not run with ignition switch off and engine coolant hot, problem is ECM related.

3.1L/V6-192 (VIN T) & 2.0L/4-121 (VIN H) Engines

1. If coolant fan does not operate, check fusible link C and HTR-A/C fuse.
2. If coolant fan runs with ignition switch in OFF position, replace coolant fan relay.

SYSTEM CHECK

1. With ambient temperature air temperature above 70°F, open all doors, start vehicle and set A/C mode selector to MAX. Coolant fan should turn on.
2. With engine coolant below operating temperature, move A/C mode selector to OFF. Coolant fan should turn off in a short time.
3. With engine warm, run engine at a fast idle for several minutes. Coolant fan should turn on before coolant temperature indicator shows H.

4. Turn ignition switch off. On VINs K, T and H coolant fan should turn off. On VIN M, coolant fan should run until engine coolant temperature lowers.

DIAGNOSIS

Refer to **Figs. 87 through 89** when performing diagnostic procedures on these systems.

1991 MODELS

Coolant Fan Does Not Turn On

1. Turn ignition switch to ON position, ground terminal B (WHT/BLK) of ALDL connector.
2. If coolant fan does not operate, go to step 3. If fan does operate, problem is ECM related.
3. Ensure terminal C1/21 (VIN K), or C3/E8 (VIN T) are grounded at ECM, disconnect fan relay connector, the measure voltage from coolant fan relay terminal 5 (BRN/WHT) and ground. If no voltage, check 650 (BRN/WHT) and 50 (BRN) wires and HTR-A/C fuse for open.
4. If battery voltage is present, ensure terminal C1/21 (VIN K) or C3/E8 (VIN T) are grounded at ECM, then measure voltage between coolant fan relay terminals 5 (BRN/WHT) and 2 (DK GRN/WHT). If no voltage, check 355 (DK GRN/WHT) wire for open.
5. If battery voltage is present, measure voltage from terminal 1 (RED) to ground. If no voltage, check 2 (RED) wire and fusible link C for open.
6. If battery voltage is present, disconnect coolant fan relay, then connect 20 amp fused jumper between terminals 1 (RED) and 4 (BLK/RED). If coolant fan runs, replace coolant fan.
7. If coolant fan does not operate, ensure fused jumper is connected as in step 6, disconnect coolant fan connector, then measure voltage between terminals B (BLK/RED) and ground. If no voltage, check 532 (BLK/RED) wire for open.
8. If battery voltage is present, ensure fused jumper is connected as in step 6, then measure voltage between terminals B (BLK/RED) and A (BLK). If no voltage, check 150 (BLK) wire for open.
9. If battery voltage is present, replace coolant fan motor.

Coolant Fan Does Not Turn Off w/Engine Coolant Cool, A/C Mode Selector Off & Ignition Switch in Run

1. Turn ignition switch to RUN position, disconnect coolant fan relay, then connect test lamp between coolant fan relay terminals 5 (BRN/WHT) and 2 (DK GRN/WHT). If test lamp does not light, replace coolant fan relay.
2. If test lamp lights, check 335 (DK GRN/WHT) wire for short to ground. If wire is shorted, repair or replace if necessary.
3. If wire is good, problem is ECM related.

Fig. 88 Coolant fan wiring circuit. 1992–93 Sunbird w/2.0L/4-122 (VIN H) engine

Fig. 87 Coolant fan wiring circuit. 1991 Sunbird w/2.0L/4-122 (VIN K) engine

1992-93 MODELS
Coolant Fan Does Not Turn On

1. Turn ignition switch to ON position, ground terminal B (WHT/BLK) of ALDL connector.
2. If coolant fan does not operate, go to step 3. If fan does operate, problem is ECM related.
3. Ground terminal B2/C2 (VIN H), or E8/C3 (VIN T) of engine control module with a fused jumper. If coolant fan does not run, go to step 4. If fan runs, problem is ECM related.
4. With terminals grounded as in step 3, disconnect coolant fan relay connector and measure voltage from terminal 5 (brown/white) wire of coolant fan relay to ground. If battery voltage is present, go to step 5. If battery voltage is not present, check brown/white wire and HTR-A/C fuse for an open.
5. With terminals grounded as in step 3, measure voltage from terminals 5 (brown/white) wire and 2 (dark green/white) of coolant fan relay connector. If battery voltage is present, go to step 6. If battery voltage is not present, check dark green/white wire for an open.
6. Measure voltage from terminal 1 (red) wire of coolant fan relay to ground. If battery voltage is present, go to step 7. If battery voltage is not present, check red wire and fusible link C for an open.
7. Connect 20 amp fused jumper between terminals 1 (red) wire and 4 (black/red) wire of coolant fan relay connector. If coolant fan does not run, go to step 8. If coolant fan runs, replace coolant fan relay.
8. With fused jumper connected as in step 7, disconnect coolant fan connector, then measure voltage between terminals B (black/red) and ground. If battery voltage is present, go to step 9. If battery voltage is not present, check black/red wire for open.
9. With fused jumper connected as in step 7, then measure voltage between terminals B (black/red) and A (black) of coolant fan connector. If battery voltage is present, replace coolant fan motor. If battery voltage is not present, check 150 (black) wire for open.

Coolant Fan Does Not Turn Off w/Engine Coolant Cool, A/C Mode Selector Off & Ignition Switch In Run

1. Turn ignition switch to RUN position, disconnect coolant fan relay, then connect test lamp between coolant fan relay terminals 5 (brown/white) and 2 (dark green/white). If test lamp does not light, replace coolant fan relay.
2. If test lamp lights, check 335 (dark green/white) wire for short to ground. If wire is shorted, repair or replace if necessary.
3. If wire is good, problem is ECM related.

Fig. 89 Coolant fan wiring circuit. Sunbird w/3.1L/V6-192 (VIN T) engine

COOLANT FAN, REPLACE
1991

1. Disconnect battery ground cable.
2. Remove air cleaner to throttle body duct.
3. Remove electrical connector from coolant fan.
4. Lift fan assembly out of two lower insulators, rotate bracket so two lower bracket legs point upward, move fan assembly toward driver's side until fan blade overlaps radiator tank to core seam by approximately one inch and remove fan assembly upward. **Because of minimum clearance, care must be taken not to damage lock tang on throttle position sensor with the fan bracket.**
5. Reverse procedure to install.

1992-93

1. Disconnect battery ground cable.
2. Remove air cleaner duct and air cleaner assembly.
3. **On 4 cylinder engine models,** remove wiring harness from motor and fan frame, then remove fan assembly from radiator support.
4. **On V6 engine models,** remove primary hood latch.
5. Drain engine coolant, then disconnect upper radiator hose at radiator and position aside.
6. Disconnect transaxle cooler lines at radiator and position aside, then disconnect wiring harness connector at coolant fan and remove fan assembly from radiator support.
7. **On all models,** reverse procedure to install.

PARK AVENUE & LESABRE

SYSTEM DESCRIPTION

A two speed coolant fan is turned on and off by the low and high speed coolant fan relays.

For low speed operation, the low speed coolant fan relay coil is grounded through the ECM or the low speed contacts of the A/C dual pressure switch. The ECM grounds the coil when vehicle speed is less than 35 mph and the engine coolant is warmed up. The A/C dual pressure switch low speed contacts close with high refrigerant pressure above 260 psi.

CONDITIONS:
- Ignition switch: RUN (engine idling)
- Engine: cold (below normal operating temperature)
- Ambient temperature: above 16°C (60°F)

ACTION	NORMAL RESULT
Set heater and A/C control assembly to NORM.	Coolant fan turns on.
Set heater and A/C control assembly to OFF.	Coolant fan turns off.
Run engine at fast idle for several minutes.	Coolant fan turns on.
Disconnect Low Speed Coolant Fan Relay and run engine at fast idle for several minutes.	Coolant fan runs at high speed and auxiliary coolant fan turns on before engine overheats.

Fig. 90   System check. 1991 LeSabre

SYSTEM CHECK - NORMAL OPERATION

CONDITIONS:
- Ignition switch: RUN (engine idling)
- Engine: cold (below normal operating temperature)
- Ambient temperature: above 16°C (60°F)

ACTION	NORMAL RESULT
Set heater and A/C control assembly to A/C mode.	LH coolant fan runs in low speed; RH coolant fan runs in high speed.
Set heater and A/C control assembly to OFF.	Coolant fans turn off after about a minute.
Run engine at fast idle for several minutes.	LH coolant fan runs in low speed; RH coolant fan runs in high speed.
Restrict air flow through radiator by covering half of grille side of radiator.	Both coolant fans runs at high speed after a few minutes.

Fig. 91   System check. Park Avenue & 1992–93 LeSabre

With the low speed relay coil grounded, its contacts close. Voltage is applied through the coolant fan resistor to the coolant fan. The resistor reduces battery voltage supplied to the fan so that the fan runs at a low speed.

For high speed operation, the high speed coolant fan relay coil is grounded through the high speed contacts in the A/C dual pressure switch or by the temperature switch. The pressure switch high speed contacts close at a refrigerant pressure above 300 psi. The temperature switch closes when coolant temperature rises above 230°F.

With the high speed relay coil grounded, its contacts close. Battery voltage is applied to the coolant fan. The fan runs at high speed.

The heavy duty coolant fan is turned on and off by the heavy duty coolant fan relay. The heavy duty coolant fan relay is grounded through the high speed contacts in the A/C dual pressure switch or by the temperature switch. With the heavy duty relay coil grounded, its contacts close. Battery voltage is applied to the heavy duty coolant fan. The fan runs at high speed.

SYSTEM CHECK

For system check refer to **Figs. 90 and 91.**

DIAGNOSIS

Refer to **Figs. 92 through 115** when performing diagnostic procedures on this system.

COOLANT FAN, REPLACE

1. Disconnect battery ground cable.
2. Disconnect electrical connector from fan motor and frame.
3. Remove frame to radiator support attaching bolts.
4. Remove fan assembly.
5. Reverse procedure to install.

SERVICE BULLETINS
Cooling Fan Runs Battery Dead

Refer to "Service Bulletins" in "6000" for diagnosis and repair of this condition.

CENTURY
SYSTEM DESCRIPTION
2.2L/4-135 (VIN 4) Engine

The coolant fan is turned on and off by the ECM based on inputs from the ECT sensor, vehicle speed sensor and the A/C system. Battery voltage is applied at all times to terminal "A" of the coolant fan relay. When the ignition switch is in the RUN position, battery voltage is applied to terminal "D" of the relay. The ECM energizes the coolant fan relay by grounding circuit (535) dark green wire of the relay. When the relay is energized it supplies battery voltage to the coolant fan. The relay is de-energized when the ECM opens circuit (535). The ECM turns on the coolant fan when the A/C is on and vehicle speed is less than 35 mph, coolant temperature is above 225°F (107°C) and vehicle speed is less than 35 mph or the ECT sensor fails.

2.5L/4-151 (VIN R) Engine

The coolant fan is turned on and off by the ECM, based on inputs from the coolant temperature sensor, vehicle speed sensor and the A/C system. Battery voltage is applied at all times to terminal A of the coolant fan relay and when the ignition switch is turned to the RUN position, voltage is applied to terminal D of the relay. The ECM energizes the coolant fan relay by grounding the dark green/yellow wire circuit (335). The relay energizes and battery voltage is applied to the coolant fan. The ECM opens circuit 335 to de-energize the relay and turn off the coolant fan.

3.3L/V6-204 Engine

The coolant fan is controlled by the coolant fan relay. The coolant fan relay is electrically operated by the ECM. The ECM receives input signals from the coolant temperature sensor, vehicle speed sensor and A/C mode selector. The ECM activates the coolant fan relay when either the engine coolant temperature is above 202°F, when A/C is turned on, or when coolant temperature sensor fails. Any of these signals will cause the ECM to ground circuit 535, turning the coolant fan on.

TROUBLESHOOTING

1. **On 1991-92 models,** check FAN/ELECT fuse.
2. **On 1993 models,** check ENG/A/C fuse.
3. **On all models,** if coolant fan runs with ignition off, replace the coolant fan relay.

SYSTEM CHECK
Models Less Heavy Duty Cooling

1. With ambient temperature above 60°F, start car and set A/C mode selector to the MAX position. Coolant fan should turn on.
2. With engine coolant below operating temperature, move A/C mode selector to OFF. Coolant fan should turn off in a short time period.
3. Run engine at fast idle until engine coolant becomes hot. Coolant fan should come on and run before coolant temperature indicator comes on or the coolant temperature gage reads hot.

Continued on page 16-96

Fig. 92   Coolant fan wiring circuit. 1991 LeSabre

	DIAGNOSIS									
SYMPTOM	Check 67 wire for an open, see Air Conditioning. If OK, ECM diagnosis.	Check I/P Fuse Block Fuse 6 by visual inspection.	Check LH Underhood Fuse Block Fuse 4.	Do Coolant Fan Input Test A.	Do High Speed Coolant Fan Input Test B.	Do Low Speed Coolant Fan Input Test C.	Do Auxiliary Coolant Fan Input Test D.	Do Test E.	Do A/C Pressure Signal Test F.	Do Relay Ground Short Test G.
Coolant fan does not run.		• Do 1st	• Do 2nd	• Do 3rd						
Coolant fan does not run at low speed.						•				
Coolant fan does not run at high speed.					•					
Coolant fan does not run at low speed after selecting A/C.	•									
Coolant fan runs continuously in low speed with ignition switch at RUN, engine coolant cool, and A/C off.								•		
Auxiliary coolant fan does not run, but coolant fan operates normally.							•			
Coolant fan runs continuously in high speed and/or auxiliary coolant fan runs with ignition switch at RUN, engine coolant cool, and A/C off.										•
High speed coolant fan and/or auxiliary coolant fan do not operate with A/C pressure above 1896 kPa (275 psi).									•	

Fig. 93   Symptom diagnosis guide. 1991 LeSabre

A: COOLANT FAN INPUT TEST
- Ignition switch: RUN
- Jumper ALDL Connector terminal B to ground.
- If coolant fan(s) turn(s) on at this point, check Coolant Temperature Sensor (CTS).
- Connector C130: disconnected

Battery voltage. If not, do Test C.
Battery voltage. If not, do Test B.
0 ohms. If not, check 151 wire for an open.

BLK
C130

- If all measurements are correct, check related wiring within the coolant fan assembly before replacing Coolant Fan Motor.

Fig. 94   Coolant fan test A. 1991 LeSabre

B: HIGH SPEED COOLANT FAN INPUT TEST
- Ignition switch: RUN
- High Speed Coolant Fan Relay connector: disconnected

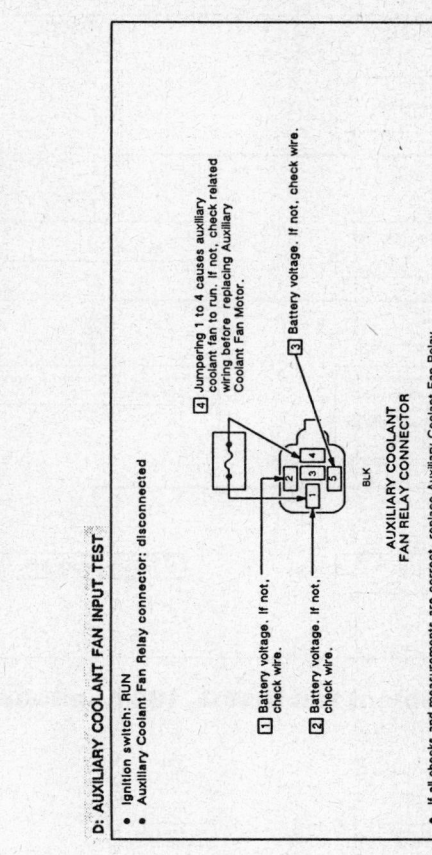

1. Battery voltage. If not, check wire.
2. Battery voltage. If not, check wire.
3. Jumper ALDL Connector terminal B to ground. Test lamp lights. If not, check 451 wire.
4. Jumpering 1 to 4 causes coolant fan to run. If not, check wiring before replacing Coolant Fan Motor.

BLK
HIGH SPEED COOLANT FAN RELAY CONNECTOR

- If all checks and measurements are correct, replace High Speed Coolant Fan Relay.

Fig. 95   Coolant fan test B. 1991 LeSabre

C: LOW SPEED COOLANT FAN INPUT TEST
- Ignition switch: RUN
- Low Speed Coolant Fan Relay connector: disconnected

1. Battery voltage. If not, check wire.
2. Battery voltage. If not, check wire.
3. Jumper ALDL Connector terminal B to ground. Test lamp lights. If not, check related wiring.
4. Jumpering 1 to 4 causes coolant fan to run. If not, check wiring and Coolant Fan Resistor before replacing Coolant Fan Motor.

BLK
LOW SPEED COOLANT FAN RELAY CONNECTOR

- If all checks and measurements are correct, replace Low Speed Coolant Fan Relay.

Fig. 96   Coolant fan test C. 1991 LeSabre

D: AUXILIARY COOLANT FAN INPUT TEST
- Ignition switch: RUN
- Auxiliary Coolant Fan Relay connector: disconnected

1. Battery voltage. If not, check wire.
2. Battery voltage. If not, check wire.
3. Battery voltage. If not, check wire.
4. Jumpering 1 to 4 causes auxiliary coolant fan to run. If not, check related wiring before replacing Auxiliary Coolant Fan Motor.

BLK
AUXILIARY COOLANT FAN RELAY CONNECTOR

- If all checks and measurements are correct, replace Auxiliary Coolant Fan Relay.

Fig. 97   Coolant fan test D. 1991 LeSabre

E: COOLANT FAN RUNS CONTINUOUSLY
- Ignition switch: RUN
- ECM connector C3: disconnected
- Low Speed Coolant Fan Relay connector: disconnected

If test lamp lights, check related wiring for a short to ground.

If test lamp does not light, replace Low Speed Coolant Fan Relay.

BLK
LOW SPEED COOLANT FAN RELAY CONNECTOR

Fig. 98   Coolant fan test E. 1991 LeSabre

F: A/C PRESSURE SIGNAL TEST
- A/C Coolant Fan Pressure Switch connector: disconnected
- Ignition switch: RUN

1. 0 ohms. If not, check wire.
2. Jumpering terminals A and B causes coolant fan and auxiliary coolant fan (if equipped) to run. If not, check wiring.

BLK
A/C COOLANT FAN PRESSURE SWITCH CONNECTOR

- If both checks are correct, check A/C Coolant Fan Pressure Switch connector terminals. They should be clean and tight.

Fig. 99   Coolant fan test F. 1991 LeSabre

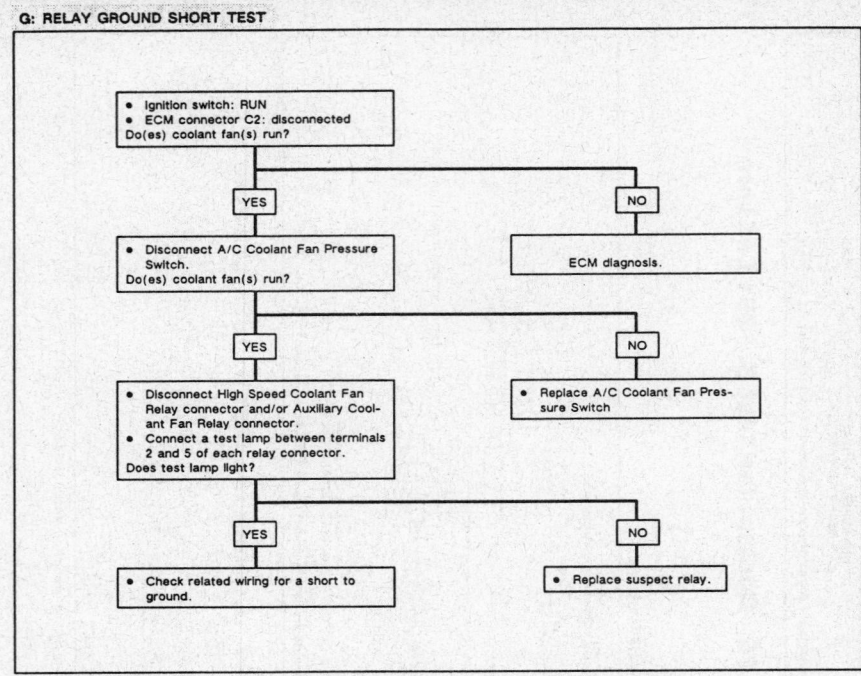

Fig. 100   Coolant fan test G. 1991 LeSabre

Fig. 101   Coolant fan wiring circuit. 1991 Park Avenue

B: HIGH SPEED COOLANT FAN INPUT TEST

- Ignition switch: RUN
- High Speed Coolant Fan Relay connector: disconnected

[1] Battery voltage. If not, check wire.

[2] Battery voltage. If not, check wire.

[4] Jumpering 1 to 4 causes coolant fans to run. If not, check related wiring.

[3] Jumper ALDL Connector terminal B to ground. Test lamp lights. If not, check wiring.

BLK

HIGH SPEED COOLANT FAN RELAY CONNECTOR

- If all checks and measurements are correct, replace High Speed Coolant Fan Relay.

Fig. 103 Coolant fan test B. 1991 Park Avenue

D: LH COOLANT FAN RUNS CONTINUOUSLY IN HIGH SPEED

- Ignition switch: RUN
- PCM connector C3: disconnected
- High Speed Coolant Fan Relay connector: disconnected

If test lamp lights, check related wiring for a short to ground.

If test lamp does not light, replace High Speed Coolant Fan Relay.

BLK

HIGH SPEED COOLANT FAN RELAY CONNECTOR

Fig. 105 Coolant fan test D. 1991 Park Avenue

F: A/C PRESSURE SIGNAL TEST

- A/C Pressure Fan Switch connector: disconnected
- Ignition switch: RUN

[1] 0 ohms. If not, check wire.

[2] Coolant fans run. If not, check wiring.

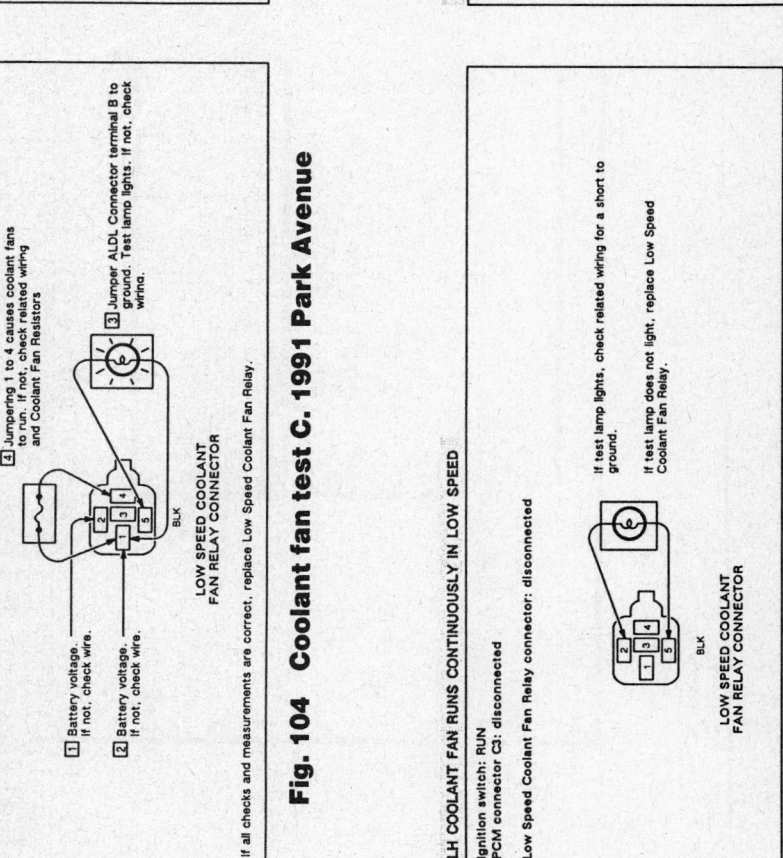

B A

BLK

A/C PRESSURE FAN SWITCH CONNECTOR

- If both checks are correct, check A/C Pressure Fan Switch connector terminals. They should be clean and tight.
- If terminals OK, replace A/C Pressure Fan Switch.

Fig. 107 Coolant fan test F. 1991 Park Avenue

A: COOLANT FAN INPUT TEST

- Ignition switch: RUN
- Jumper ALDL Connector terminal B to ground.
- If coolant fans turn on at this point, PCM diagnosis.
- Connector C130: disconnected

Battery voltage. If not, do Test C.

Battery voltage. If not, do Test B.

0 ohms. If not, check 151 wire for an open.

BLK

C130

- If all measurements are correct, check related wiring within the coolant fan assembly before replacing Coolant Fan Motor.

Fig. 102 Coolant fan test A. 1991 Park Avenue

C: LOW SPEED COOLANT FAN INPUT TEST

- Ignition switch: RUN
- Low Speed Coolant Fan Relay connector: disconnected

[1] Battery voltage. If not, check wire.

[2] Battery voltage. If not, check wire.

[4] Jumpering 1 to 4 causes coolant fans to run. If not, check related wiring and Coolant Fan Resistors.

[3] Jumper ALDL Connector terminal B to ground. Test lamp lights. If not, check wiring.

BLK

LOW SPEED COOLANT FAN RELAY CONNECTOR

- If all checks and measurements are correct, replace Low Speed Coolant Fan Relay.

Fig. 104 Coolant fan test C. 1991 Park Avenue

E: LH COOLANT FAN RUNS CONTINUOUSLY IN LOW SPEED

- Ignition switch: RUN
- PCM connector C3: disconnected
- Low Speed Coolant Fan Relay connector: disconnected

If test lamp lights, check related wiring for a short to ground.

If test lamp does not light, replace Low Speed Coolant Fan Relay.

BLK

LOW SPEED COOLANT FAN RELAY CONNECTOR

Fig. 106 Coolant fan test E. 1991 Park Avenue

Fig. 108 Coolant fan wiring circuit (Part 2 of 2). 1992-93 LeSabre & Park Avenue

Fig. 108 Coolant fan wiring circuit (Part 1 of 2). 1992-93 LeSabre & Park Avenue

SYMPTOM	DIAGNOSIS		
	● Do 1st	● Do 2nd	● Do 3rd
Both coolant fans do not run.	Check I/P fuse block fuse 16 by visual inspection.	Check LH underhood fuse block fuse 4 by visual inspection.	Do Coolant Fan Input Test A.
LH coolant fan does not operate in low speed.	Do Low Speed Coolant Fan Input Test C.		
LH coolant fan does not operate in high speed.	Do High Speed Coolant Fan Input Test B.		
LH coolant fan runs continuously in low speed with ignition switch at RUN, engine coolant cool, and A/C off.	Do LH Coolant Fan Runs Continuously in Low Speed Test E.		
LH coolant fan runs continuously in high speed with ignition switch at RUN, engine coolant cool, and A/C off.	Do LH Coolant Fan Runs Continuously in High Speed Test D.		
LH coolant fan does not operate at high speed with A/C head pressure above 1445 kPa (210 psi).	Do A/C Pressure Signal Test F.		
Only one coolant fan does not run.	Check coolant fan and motor for mechanical bindings.	Check wiring to suspect coolant fan; check coolant fan connector for proper terminal contact.	Replace coolant fan motor, see ③ or ④ .

Fig. 109   Symptom diagnosis guide. 1992–93 LeSabre & Park Avenue

Fig. 110   Coolant fan test A (Coolant fan input). 1992–93 LeSabre & Park Avenue

Fig. 111   Coolant fan test B (High speed coolant fan input). 1992–93 LeSabre & Park Avenue

Models w/Heavy Duty Cooling

1. With ambient temperature above 60°F, start car and set A/C mode selector to the MAX position. Puller coolant fan should turn on.
2. With engine coolant below operating temperature, move A/C mode selector to OFF. Puller coolant fan should turn off in a short time period.
3. Run engine at fast idle until engine coolant becomes hot. Puller coolant fan should come on when coolant temperature reaches 202°F and the pusher coolant fan should come on when coolant temperature reaches 226°F.

SYSTEM DIAGNOSIS

Refer to **Figs. 116 through 119** when performing diagnostic procedures on these systems.

1991–92

Coolant Fan Does Not Turn On

1. With ignition switch in the RUN position, ground terminal B white/black wire of the DLC (ALDL) connector. If coolant fan does not run, proceed to step 2. If coolant fan runs, problem is ECM related.
2. With ignition switch in the RUN position, use a fused jumper wire and ground ECM terminal C1/21 (VIN R), or terminal C3/E38 (VIN N). If coolant fan does not run, proceed to step 3. If coolant fan runs, problem is ECM related.
3. Leaving fused jumper connected and ignition in the RUN position, disconnect coolant fan relay connector.
4. Measure voltage from the brown/white wire of the coolant fan relay connector to ground. If voltage is equal to battery voltage, proceed to step 5. If there is no voltage indicated, check FAN/ELECT fuse, brown and brown/white wires for an open circuit.
5. Fused jumper still connected and ignition switch still in RUN position, measure voltage as follows:
   a. On **2.5L/4-151 engines**, measure between brown/white and dark green/white wires.
   b. On **3/3L/V6-204 engines**, measure between brown/white and dark green wires.
6. If battery voltage is indicated, proceed to step 7. If no voltage is indicated, check dark green/white (2.5L/4-151), or dark green (3.3L/V6-204) wire, for an open circuit.
7. With coolant fan relay disconnected, measure voltage between terminal A (red wire) of the connector and ground. If battery voltage is indicated, proceed to step 8. If battery voltage is not indicated, check red wire or fusible link for an open.
8. Connect a fused jumper with a 20 amp fuse between terminals A and E at the coolant fan relay connector. If coolant fan does not run, proceed to step 9. If coolant fan runs, replace coolant fan relay.

- Ignition switch: OFF
- Connector C130: connected
- Low speed coolant fan relay connector: disconnected
- Ignition switch: RUN

[1] Battery voltage.
If not: check wiring for an open or short to ground and replace fuse when necessary.

[2] Battery voltage.
If not: check wiring for an open or short to ground and replace fuse when necessary.

[4] Jumpering 1 to 4 causes coolant fans to run.
If not: check in-line connector C130 for proper terminal contact; check related wiring and coolant fan resistors for an open, see [5].

[3] Jumper data link connector DLC terminal B to terminal A. Test lamp lights. If not: check wiring for an open; check PCM connector C3 (terminal C4) for proper terminal contact.

LOW SPEED COOLANT FAN RELAY CONNECTOR

- If all checks and measurements are correct: replace low speed coolant fan relay.

Fig. 112   Coolant fan test C (Low speed coolant fan input). 1992–93 LeSabre & Park Avenue

- Ignition switch: OFF
- High speed coolant fan relay connector: disconnected

[2] Infinite ohms. If not: replace high speed coolant fan relay.

[1] Greater than 5 ohms. If not: check wiring for a short to ground.

HIGH SPEED COOLANT FAN RELAY

HIGH SPEED COOLANT FAN RELAY CONNECTOR

- If both measurements are correct: go to Test F steps [2] and [3].

Fig. 114   Coolant fan test E (Lefthand coolant fan runs continuously in low speed). 1992–93 LeSabre & Park Avenue

- Ignition switch: OFF
- Low speed coolant fan relay connector: disconnected

Greater than 5 ohms. If not: check wiring for a short to ground.

LOW SPEED COOLANT FAN RELAY CONNECTOR

- If measurement is correct: replace low speed coolant fan relay.

Fig. 113   Coolant fan test D (Lefthand coolant fan runs continuously in high speed). 1992–93 LeSabre & Park Avenue

[1] Install pressure gage set. Repeat "System Check" while monitoring A/C head pressure. If pressure does not exceed 1445 kPa (210 psi): see   Air Conditioning

[2]
- Ignition switch: OFF
- A/C pressure fan switch connector: disconnected
Less than 5 ohms.
If not: check wiring for an open.

[3]
- Ignition switch: RUN
5 volts. If not: check wiring for an open or short to ground; check in-line connector C265 (terminal N6) and PCM connector C1 (terminal D9) for proper terminal contact.

A/C PRESSURE FAN SWITCH CONNECTOR

- If all checks are correct: check A/C pressure fan switch connector for proper terminal contact; replace A/C pressure fan switch, see [1].

Fig. 115   Coolant fan test F (A/C pressure signal). 1992–93 LeSabre & Park Avenue

Fig. 116 Coolant fan wiring circuit. Century w/2.5L/4-151 engine

Fig. 117 Coolant fan wiring circuit. 1991–92 Century w/3.3L/V6-204 engine

Fig. 118   Coolant fan wiring circuit. 1993 Century w/2.2L/4-135 engine

Fig. 119   Coolant fan wiring circuit. 1993 Century w/3.3L/V6-204 engine

9. Leaving fused jumper wire connected from step 8, disconnect connector from the coolant fan.
10. Measure voltage between terminal B of the connector and ground. If battery voltage is indicated, proceed to step 11. If battery voltage is not indicated, check for an open circuit in black/red (2.5L/4-151), or pink/black (3.3L/V6-204) wire.
11. Leaving fused jumper connected at the coolant fan relay connector, measure voltage between terminals A and B of the coolant fan connector. If battery voltage is indicated, replace coolant fan motor. If no voltage is indicated, check black wire for an open circuit.

Coolant Fan Does Not Turn Off With Engine Coolant Cool, A/C Off & Ignition Switch In Run

1. Turn ignition switch off, then disconnect coolant fan relay connector.
2. Connect a test lamp between terminals F and D of the coolant fan relay connector. If test lamp lights, proceed to step 3. If test lamp does not light, replace coolant fan relay.
3. Check wires for a short to ground as follows:
   a. On **2.5L/4-151 engines**, check dark green/white wire.
   b. On **3.3L/V6-204 engines**, check dark green wire.
4. If all wires are satisfactory, problem is ECM related.

Coolant Fan Does Not Turn On With A/C On

1. Turn ignition switch to run, put A/C mode selector in the MAX position.
2. Measure voltage between terminal C1/24 (2.5L/4-151) or C1/C9 (3.3L/V6-204) and ground.
3. If battery voltage is indicated, problem si ECM related.
4. If no voltage is indicated, check light blue/black wire or light blue wire for an open circuit.

Coolant Fan Does Not Turn On With A/C On & A/C Head Pressure Above 200 psi

1. Disconnect ECM connector C1, measure resistance from C1/D12 dark green/white wire to ground.
2. If resistance is zero, proceed to step 3. If resistance is infinite, proceed as follows:
   a. Check dark green/white wire for an open circuit, repair if necessary.
   b. If wire is satisfactory, check that coolant fan A/C pressure switch is closed.
   c. If switch is closed, problem is ECM related.
   d. If switch is open, replace switch.
3. Leaving ECM C1 connector disconnected, turn ignition switch to RUN position.
4. Switch A/C mode selector to the MAX position, measure voltage between

terminal C1/C9 light green/white wire of the ECM to ground.
5. If battery voltage is indicated, problem is ECM related.
6. If no voltage is indicated, check light green/white wire for an open circuit.
7. If wire is satisfactory, problem is in A/C system.

1993
Coolant Fan Does Not Turn On

1. Turn ignition switch to the RUN position, then ground terminal "B" of the DLC. If coolant fan does not run, proceed to step 2. If coolant fan runs, problem is ECM related.
2. Ground terminal the following terminals:
   a. On **2.2L/4-135 engine**, ground terminal "C1/D13" of the ECM with a fused jumper and proceed to step 3.
   b. On **3.3L/V6-204 engine**, ground terminal "C3/E8" of the ECM with a fused jumper and proceed to step 3.
3. If coolant fan does not run, proceed to step 4. If coolant fan runs, problem is ECM related.
4. Leaving fused jumper connected at the ECM, disconnect coolant fan relay connector and measure voltage from brown wire to ground. If battery voltage is indicated, proceed to step 5. If battery voltage is not indicated, check ENG/A/C fuse and pink/black wire (639) for an open.
5. With fused jumper still grounded at the ECM, measure voltage as follows:
   a. On **2.2L/4-135 engine**, measure between pink/black wire (639) and dark green/white wire (535).
   b. On **3.3L/V6-204 engine**, measure between pink/black wire (639) and dark green wire (535).
6. If battery voltage is indicated, proceed to step 7. If zero voltage is indicated, check dark green/white wire (2.2L/4-135) or dark green wire (3.3L/V6-204) for an open circuit.
7. Measure voltage from terminal "A" of the coolant fan relay connector to ground. If battery voltage is indicated, proceed to step 8. If zero voltage is indicated, check red wire (2) and fusible link for an open.
8. Connect a fused jumper with a 20 amp fuse between terminals "A" and "E" at the coolant fan relay connector. If coolant fan does not run, proceed to step 9. If coolant fan runs, replace coolant fan relay.
9. Leaving fused jumper connected at the coolant fan relay connector, disconnect connector from the coolant fan. Measure voltage between terminal "B" of the connector and ground. If battery voltage is indicated, proceed to step 10. If zero voltage is indicated, check black/pink wire for an open.
10. With fused jumper connected at the coolant fan relay connector, measure voltage between terminals "B" and "A" of the coolant fan connector. If

battery voltage is indicated, replace coolant fan motor. If zero voltage is indicated, check black wire (150) for an open.

Coolant Fan Does Not Turn Off With Engine Coolant Cool, A/C Off & Ignition Switch In Run

1. With ignition switch in the RUN position, disconnect coolant fan relay connector.
2. Connect a test lamp between terminals "F" and "D" of the coolant fan relay connector. If test lamp lights, proceed to step 3. If test lamp does not light, replace coolant fan relay.
3. Check dark green/white wire (2.2L/4-135) or dark green wire (3.3L/V6-204) for a short to ground. If wire is satisfactory, problem is ECM related. If wire is not satisfactory, replace or repair as necessary.

SERVICE BULLETINS
Cooling Fan Runs Battery Dead

Refer to "Service Bulletins" in "6000" for diagnosis and repair of this condition.

REATTA, RIVIERA, TORONADO & TROFEO

SYSTEM DESCRIPTION

The coolant fans on these models consists of a fan located behind the radiator, and a fan mounted in front of the radiator.

The rear fan operates on two speeds, while the front fan operates only on high speed. Both fans are activated any time the coolant fans are in the high speed mode.

The fans will be activated by the ECM, when the engine coolant temperature sensor or the A/C high pressure sensor reach calibration points.

DIAGNOSIS

Refer to wiring circuits **Figs. 120 through 123** when performing diagnostic procedures on these systems. Refer to C-12 charts **Figs. 124 through 128** for fan system diagnosis. When diagnosing a fan system malfunction, remember that fans are ECM controlled only.

COOLANT FAN, REPLACE

1. Disconnect battery ground cable.
2. Remove wiring harness from fan motor and fan frame.
3. Remove fan assembly.
4. Reverse procedure to install.

Continued on page 16-107

Fig. 120 Coolant fan wiring circuit (Part 1 of 2). 1991 Riviera

Fig. 120 Coolant fan wiring circuit (Part 1 of 2). 1991 Reatta

Fig. 120   Coolant fan wiring circuit (Part 2 of 2). 1991 Riviera & Reatta

Fig. 121   Coolant fan wiring circuit (Part 1 of 2). 1991 Toronado & Trofeo

Fig. 121 Coolant fan wiring circuit (Part 2 of 2). 1991 Toronado & Trofeo

Fig. 122 Coolant fan wiring circuit (Part 1 of 2). 1992–93 Riviera

Fig. 122   Coolant fan wiring circuit (Part 2 of 2). 1992–93 Riviera

Fig. 123   Coolant fan wiring circuit (Part 1 of 2). 1992 Toronado & Trofeo

Fig. 123 Coolant fan wiring circuit (Part 2 of 2). 1992 Toronado & Trofeo

CHART C-12A

COOLING FAN FUNCTIONAL CHECK
3800 (VIN L) "E" CARLINE (TPI)

Circuit Description:

The PCM and three relays are used to control the two cooling fans.

LO Speed Fans Operation- Low speed of both fans are controlled by the PCM. The PCM energizes cooling fan relay "G" through terminal "GC4" when the coolant temperature exceeds 101°C (214°F) or when A/C high side refrigerant temperature exceeds 50°C (122°F).

High Speed Fans Operation- High speed of both fans are controlled by the PCM. The PCM energizes all three relays when coolant temperature exceeds 108°C (226°F) or when A/C high side refrigerant temperature exceeds 65°C (149°F).

Test Description: Number(s) below refer to circled number(s) on the diagnostic chart.
1. Codes 14 or 15 could mean coolant system or sensor operation is not normal so fan(s) operation can't be checked correctly.
2. Selecting output tests, Fan 1 with the Tech 1 grounds fan relay "G" through the PCM fans should cycle "ON" and run at low speed.
3. Selecting output tests Fan 2 should cause the PCM to energize fan relays "G", "C", and "D". Both fans should run at high speed.

Diagnostic Aids:

An intermittent may be caused by a poor connection, rubbed through wire insulation, or a wire broken inside the insulation.

Check For:
- Poor Connection or Damaged Harness Inspect PCM harness connectors for backed out terminals "GC4" or "GC3", improper mating, broken locks, improperly formed or damaged terminals, poor terminal to wire connection, and damaged harness.
- Intermittent Test If connections and harness check OK, a digital voltmeter connected from affected terminal to ground while moving related connectors and wiring harness. If the failure is induced, the voltage reading will change.
- Mis-Scaled Coolant Temperature Sensor (CTS)
- Basic Cooling System Problem

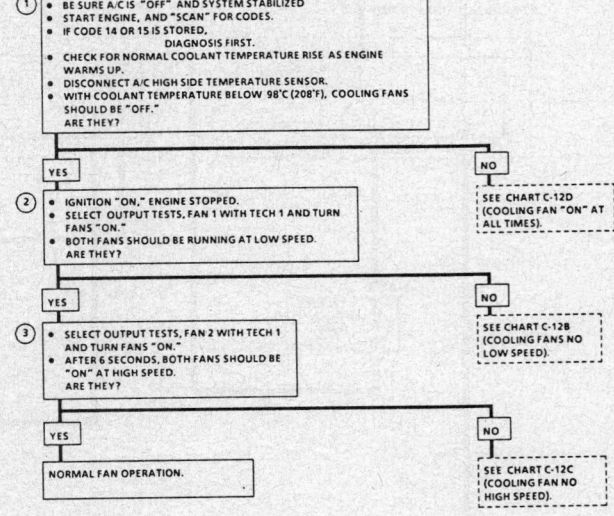

Fig. 124 Chart C-12A (Cooling fan functional check). Reatta, Riviera, Toronado & Trofeo

CHART C-12B
COOLING FAN NO LOW SPEED
3800 (VIN L) "E" Carline (TPI)

Circuit Description:

The PCM and three relays are used to control the two cooling fans.

<u>LO Speed Fans Operation</u> - Low speed of both fans are controlled by the PCM. The PCM energizes cooling fan relay "G" through terminal "GC4" when the coolant temperature exceeds 101°C (214°F) or when A/C high side refrigerant temperature exceeds 50°C (122°F).

<u>High Speed Fans Operation</u> - High speed of both fans are controlled by the PCM. The PCM energizes all three relays, when coolant temperature exceeds 108°C (226°F) or when A/C high side refrigerant temperature exceeds 65°C (149°F).

NOTICE: Mechanization drawing above reflects only those circuits used for low speed fans.

Test Description: Number(s) below refer to circled number(s) on the diagnostic chart.
1. Test light should be "ON" because harness terminal "2" has B+ with ignition switch turned "ON." Terminal "4" has B+ all the time.
2. Test light "ON" validates relay "C", CKTs 1593, 1594, 1595 and 804.
3. Jumpering "1" to "4" of relay "G", removing relay "C" and touching a test light to terminal "1" validates the circuit up to relay "C". If light is "OFF", it is CKT 1593 or CKT 1595 to the front fan.
4. Test light "ON" validates CKTs 804 and 1594 to rear fan.

Fig. 125   Chart C-12B (Cooling fan no low speed). Reatta, Riviera, Toronado & Trofeo

CHART C-12C-A
COOLING FAN NO HIGH SPEED REAR FAN
3800 (VIN L) "E" Carline (TPI)

Circuit Description:

The PCM and three relays are used to control the two cooling fans.

<u>LO Speed Fans Operation</u> - Low speed of both fans are controlled by the PCM. The PCM energizes cooling fan relay "G" through terminal "GC4" when the coolant temperature exceeds 101°C (214°F) or when A/C high side refrigerant temperature exceeds 50°C (122°F).

<u>High Speed Fans Operation</u> - High speed of both fans are controlled by the PCM. The PCM energizes all three relays when coolant temperature exceeds 108°C (226°F) or when A/C high side refrigerant temperature exceeds 65°C (149°F).

Test Description: Number(s) below refer to circled number(s) on the diagnostic chart.
1. Test light should be "ON" because harness terminal "5" has B+ with ignition switch turned "ON." Terminal "1" has B+ all the time.
2. Test light should be "ON" with output tests, Fan-2 selected and cycled "ON" with the Tech 1.
3. Jumpering harness terminals "1" and "4" bypasses the relay. If fan runs, the relay is faulty.
4. Test light "ON" proves CKTs 1594 and 804 are OK, so fan motor is faulty.

Fig. 126   Chart C-12C-A (Cooling fan no high speed rear fan). Reatta, Riviera, Toronado & Trofeo

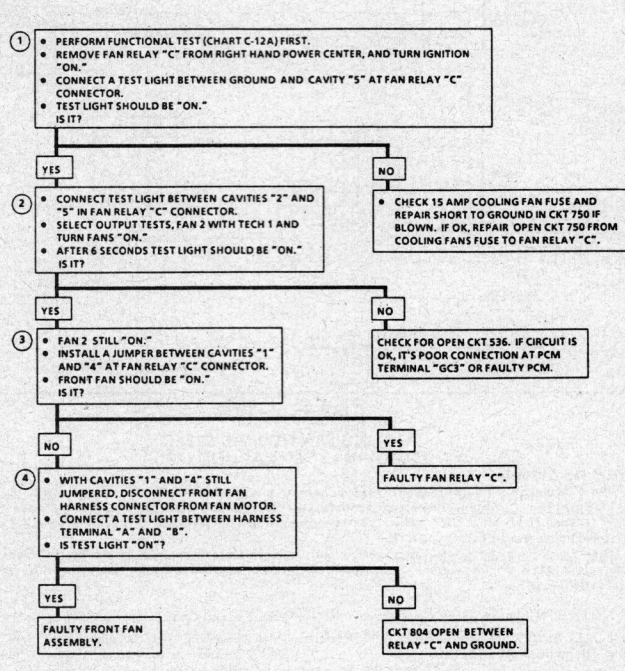

CHART C-12C-B

COOLING FAN NO HIGH SPEED FRONT FAN
3800 (VIN L) "E" CARLINE (TPI)

Circuit Description:

The PCM and three relays are used to control the two cooling fans.

LO Speed Fans Operation - Low speed of both fans are controlled by the PCM. The PCM energizes cooling fan relay "G" through terminal "GC4" when the coolant temperature exceeds 101°C (214°F) or when A/C high side refrigerant temperature exceeds 50°C (122°F).

High Speed Fans Operation - High speed of both fans are controlled by the PCM. The PCM energizes all three relays when coolant temperature exceeds 108°C (226°F) or when A/C high side refrigerant temperature exceeds 65°C (149°F).

Test Description: Numbers below refer to circled numbers on the diagnostic chart.

1. Test light should be "ON" because harness terminal "5" has B+ with ignition switch turned "ON."
2. Test light "ON" validates circuit 536 from PCM to relay "C".
3. Jumpering "1" to "4" of relay "C" bypasses fan relay.
4. Test light "ON" validates all circuits. If light is "ON," front fan motor is faulty. If light is "OFF," it is a problem with the ground CKT 804.

Fig. 127 Chart C-12C-B (Cooling fan no high speed front fan). Reatta, Riviera, Toronado & Trofeo

CHART C-12D

COOLING FAN(S) "ON" AT ALL TIMES
3800 (VIN L) "E" CARLINE (TPI)

Circuit Description:

The PCM and three relays are used to control the two cooling fans.

LO Speed Fans Operation - Low speed of both fans are controlled by the PCM. The PCM energizes cooling fan relay "G" through terminal "GC4" when the coolant temperature exceeds 101°C (214°F) or when A/C high side refrigerant temperature exceeds 50°C (122°F).

High Speed Fans Operation - High speed of both fans are controlled by the PCM. The PCM energizes all three relays when coolant temperature exceeds 108°C (226°F) or when A/C high side refrigerant temperature exceeds 65°C (149°F).

Test Description: Number(s) below refer to circled number(s) on the diagnostic chart.

1. Fans run when key is "OFF."
2. Fans should not run when engine coolant temperature is below 101°C (214°F).
3. Disconnecting the A/C high side temperature sensor will disable the BCM to PCM request due to the A/C high side temperature.
4. Defines fan operation based on coolant temperature only.

Diagnostic Aids:

Cooling fans should be "OFF" if:
1. Coolant temperature is less than 98°C (208°F).
2. A/C high side temperature is less than 50°C (122°F).

NOTE: On-board diagnostics may assist in diagnosing; monitor the following parameters: ED04 and BD21 are coolant temperature.

BD27 is A/C high side temperature sensor.

Disconnecting the A/C high side temperature sensor should result in BD27 reading less than –30°C (–30°F).

Disconnecting the coolant temperature sensor should cause BD21 to read less than –30°C (–30°F) also. If not, see Code 14 or 15.

BD27 should read about 50°C (122°F) when A/C system high side pressure is approximately 160 psi. Comparing these might isolate a bad sensor.

NOTE: Normal cooling fan operation requires low speed if: Engine is running, vehicle speed is less than 45 mph and coolant temperature exceeds 101°C (214°F) or A/C high side temperature is greater than 50°C (122°F).

Fig. 128 Chart C-12D (Cooling fan/fans on at all times). Reatta, Riviera, Toronado & Trofeo

LUMINA

SYSTEM DESCRIPTION

1991–92 Models

Each coolant fan is controlled by individual cooling fan relays. The primary cooling fan relay coil is grounded through the ECM when vehicle speed is less than the speed set by the ECM and the coolant temperature reaches 227°F with the A/C off, and 223°F with A/C on. The primary cooling fan runs until the ignition switch is turned off, or coolant temperature decreases to 220°F with A/C off, or 216°F with A/C on.

The secondary cooling fan relay coil is grounded through the ECM when the coolant temperature reaches 245°F. The contacts close and voltage is applied to the secondary cooling fan, and on models with the V6 VIN X engine, the generator cooling fan. The fan runs at high speed and will continue with the ignition in RUN position until the coolant temperature lowers to 238°F.

1993

Each coolant fan is turned on and off by a separate coolant fan relay.

The primary coolant fan relay coil is grounded by the ECM when vehicle speed is less than a speed determined by and engine coolant temperature reaches 227°F (108°C) with A/C off or 223°F (106°C) with A/C on. The relay contacts close and voltage is applied through the primary coolant fan relay to the primary coolant fan. The primary coolant fan will run until the ignition switch is turned off or engine coolant temperature decreases to 220°F (104°C) with A/C off 216°F (102°C) with A/C on.

The secondary coolant fan relay coil is grounded by the ECM when the engine coolant temperature reaches 245°F (118°C). The relay contacts close and voltage is applied to the secondary coolant fan. The fan runs at high speed until engine coolant temperature lowers to 238°F (114°C).

TROUBLESHOOTING

1991–92

1. If coolant fan does not operate, check IGN fuse.
2. If coolant fan runs with ignition switch in the OFF position, replace the coolant fan relay.

1993

1. Check IGN fuses and fusible elements "L" and "N."
2. If coolant fan runs with ignition switch in the off position, check the following:
   a. Circuits (702) and (532) for a short to battery.
   b. Circuits (335) and (473) for a short to ground.
   c. Check for broken or partially broken wires inside of the insulation which could cause failure but prove good in a continuity/voltage check.
   d. Check for proper installation of aftermarket equipment.

e. If circuits are satisfactory and equipment is installed correctly, replace coolant fan relay.

DIAGNOSIS

Refer to **Figs. 129 through 132** when performing diagnostic procedures on this system.

1991–92 MODELS

Primary Cooling Fan Does Not Run

1. With ignition switch in RUN position, ground terminal B (WHT/BLK) of the ALDL connector. If coolant fan runs, problem is ECM related.
2. If coolant fan does not run, ground terminal A9 (DK GRN/WHT) at the ECM with a fused jumper. If coolant fan runs, problem is ECM related.
3. If coolant fan does not run, ignition switch in RUN position, leave jumper from step 2 installed and disconnect coolant fan relay connector. Measure voltage between terminal 3 (RED) and ground. If no voltage is present, check red wire for an open.
4. If battery voltage is present, ensure ignition switch in RUN position, measure voltage between terminal 3 (RED) and terminal 1 (DK GRN/WHT). If no voltage is present, check 335 (DK GRN/WHT) wire for an open.
5. If battery voltage is present, disconnect primary coolant fan relay then measure voltage from terminal 2 (RED) (VIN X, VIN T) or 2 (BRN/WHT) (VIN R) to ground at RS electrical center. If no voltage is present, check 650 (BRN/WHT) or 1444 (RED) for open.
6. If battery voltage is present, with primary coolant fan relay disconnected connect a fused jumper with 20 amp fuse between terminals 3 (RED) and 5 (BLK/RED) at RS electrical center. If coolant fan runs, check terminal contact between primary cooling fan relay and RH electrical center, if good, replace primary cooling fan relay.
7. If primary coolant fan does not run, leave jumper installed from step 6 then disconnect the primary coolant fan connector and measure voltage between terminal B (BLK/RED) and ground. If no voltage is present, check 702 (BLK/RED) wire for an open.
8. If battery voltage is present, measure voltage between terminals B (BLK/RED) and A (BLK). If no voltage is present, check 150 (BLK) wire for an open.
9. If battery voltage is present, check primary cooling fan connector, if good, replace primary coolant fan.

Secondary Cooling Fan Does Not Run

1. Turn ignition switch to RUN position, ground terminal A3 (DK BLU/WHT) at

ECM with fused jumper. If cooling fan runs, problem is ECM related.
2. If cooling fan does not run, disconnect secondary cooling fan relay, leave fused jumper at ECM, ensure ignition switch in RUN position, then measure voltage at RH electrical center terminal 2 (BRN) to ground. If no voltage, check 250 (BRN) wire for open.
3. If battery voltage is present, leave ignition switch in RUN position and fused jumper at ECM, then measure voltage between terminals 2 (BRN) and 1 (DK BLU/WHT). If no voltage, check 473 (DK BLU/WHT) wire for open.
4. If battery voltage is present, measure voltage between terminal 3 (RED) and ground. If no voltage, check 1442 (RED) wire for open.
5. If battery voltage is present, disconnect secondary cooling fan relay, then connect fused jumper between terminals 3 (RED and 5 (BLK/RED) at RH electrical center. If secondary cooling and generator run, check secondary cooling fan relay terminals, if good, replace secondary cooling fan relay.
6. If secondary cooling and generator fan do not run, ensure fused jumper in place, measure voltage from secondary cooling fan relay terminal B (BLK/RED) to ground or generator cooling fan relay terminal A (BLK/RED) to ground. If no voltage, check 532 (BLK/RED) wire for open.
7. If battery voltage is present, ensure fused jumper in place, then measure voltage between secondary cooling fan relay terminals B (BLK/RED) and A (BLK) or generator cooling fan connector terminals a (BLK/RED) and B (BLK). If no voltage, check 150 (BLK) wire for open.
8. If battery voltage is present, check cooling fan connector terminals, if good replace cooling fan.

Primary Cooling Fan Runs Continuously w/Engine Coolant Cool & A/C Mode Selector Off

1. Disconnect primary fan relay at RH electrical center, turn ignition switch to RUN position, then connect test lamp between terminals 3 (RED) and 1 (DK GRN/WHT). If test lamp does not light, replace primary coolant fan relay.
2. If test lamp lights, check 335 (DK GRN/WHT) wire for short to ground, if good, problem is ECM related.

Secondary Cooling Or Generator Fan Runs Continuously w/Engine Coolant Cool & A/C Mode Selector Off

1. Turn ignition switch to RUN position, disconnect secondary cooling fan relay at RH electrical center, then connect test lamp between terminals 3 (RED) and 1 (DK BLU/WHT). If test lamp does not light, replace secondary cooling fan relay.
2. If test lamp lights, check 473 (DK BLU/WHT) wire for short to ground, if good, problem is ECM related.

Fig. 129   Coolant fan wiring circuit (Part 1 of 2). 1991 Lumina

Fig. 129   Coolant fan wiring circuit (Part 2 of 2). 1991 Lumina

Fig. 130   Coolant fan wiring circuit. 1992 Lumina less A/C

Fig. 131   Coolant fan wiring circuit (Part 1 Of 2). 1992 Lumina w/A/C

Fig. 131   Coolant fan wiring circuit (Part 2 Of 2). 1992 Lumina w/A/C

1993

Primary Coolant Fan Does Not Run

1. With ignition switch in the RUN position, connect a fused jumper between DLC connector terminal "B" and ground. If coolant fan does not run, proceed to step 2. If coolant fan runs, problem is ECM related.
2. Remove primary coolant fan relay. Connect a test light between primary coolant fan relay connector terminal "3" and ground, then terminal "2" and ground. If test light comes on in both cases, proceed to step 3. If test light does not come on in both cases, check for a poor connection. If connection is satisfactory, check circuits (650) and (1444) for an open.
3. Connect a fused jumper between coolant fan relay connector terminals "3" and "5." If primary coolant fan does not run, proceed to step 4. If coolant fan runs, check circuit (335) for an open or short to battery. If circuit (335) is satisfactory, check for a poor connection. If connection is satisfactory, replace coolant fan relay.
4. Leave fused jumper attached and disconnect primary coolant fan electrical connector. Connect a test light between coolant fan connector terminal "B" and ground. If test light comes on, proceed to step 5. If test lamp does not come on, check for poor connection or an open in circuit (702).
5. With fused jumper still attached, connect a test light between primary coolant fan connector terminals "A" and "B." If test light does not come on, check for a poor connection or open

in primary coolant fan circuit (150). If test light does come on, check for poor connection. If connection is satisfactory, replace coolant fan motor.

Secondary Coolant Fan Does Not Run

1. Attached a fused jumper between secondary coolant fan relay terminal "1" and ground, then turn ignition switch to the RUN position. If secondary coolant fan does not run, proceed to step 2. If secondary coolant fan runs, check for an open in circuit (473) or a poor connection at ECM connector "A" terminal "3." If circuit and connection are satisfactory, problem is ECM related.
2. Remove fused jumper and secondary coolant fan relay. Connect a test light between secondary coolant fan relay connector terminal "3" and ground, then between terminal "2" and ground. If test light comes on in both cases, proceed to step 3. If test light does not come on in both cases. Check for a poor connection or an open in circuits (250) or (1442).
3. Connect a fused jumper between secondary coolant fan relay connector terminals "3" and "5." If coolant fan does not run, proceed to step 4. If coolant fan runs, check circuit (473) for an open or short to battery. If circuit is satisfactory, check for a poor connection. If connection is satisfactory, replace coolant fan relay.
4. Leave fused jumper attached at the coolant fan relay connector. Disconnect secondary coolant fan connector, then connect a test light between secondary coolant fan connector ter-

minal "B" and ground. If test light comes on, proceed to step 5. If test light does not come on, check for a poor connection or an open in circuit (532).
5. Connect a test light between secondary coolant fan connector terminals "A" and "B." If test light does not come on, check for a poor connection or open in circuit (150). If test light comes on, check for a poor connection. If connection is satisfactory, replace secondary coolant fan motor.

Primary Coolant Fan Runs Continuously With Engine Coolant Cool & A/C Off

1. Disconnect primary coolant fan relay No. 1. If coolant fan stops running, proceed to step 2. If coolant fan continues to run, check circuit (702) for a short to battery.
2. Turn ignition switch to the RUN position, then connect a test light between primary coolant fan relay connector terminals "1" and "3." If test light does not come on, replace primary coolant fan relay. If test light comes on, check circuit (335) for a short to ground. If circuit is satisfactory, problem is ECM related.

Secondary Coolant Fan Runs Continuously With Engine Coolant Cool & A/C Off

1. Disconnect secondary coolant fan relay No. 2. If coolant fan stops running, proceed to step 2. If coolant fan continues to run, check circuit (532) for a short to battery.
2. Turn ignition switch to the RUN position, then connect a test light between secondary coolant fan relay connector terminals "1" and "3." If test light

Fig. 132 Coolant fan wiring circuit. 1993 Lumina

2. With engine coolant below operating temperature, move A/C mode selector to OFF. Coolant fan should turn off in a short time period.
3. Run engine at fast idle until engine coolant becomes hot. Coolant fan should come on and run before coolant temperature indicator comes on or the coolant temperature gage reads 280°F or temperature indicator light comes on.
4. Turn ignition switch OFF. Coolant fan turns off when engine temperature lowers.

DIAGNOSIS

Refer to **Fig. 133** when performing diagnostic procedures on this system.

Coolant Fan Does Not Turn On

1. With ignition switch in RUN position, ground terminal B of the ALDL connector. If coolant fan runs, problem is ECM related.
2. If coolant fan does not run, ground ECM connector C3, terminal E8 with a fused jumper. If coolant fan runs, problem is ECM related.
3. If coolant fan does not run, leave jumper from step 2 installed and disconnect coolant fan relay connector. Measure voltage between terminal 2 (red) wire and ground. If no voltage is present, repair open in circuit 2.
4. If battery voltage is present, leave jumper from step 2 installed measure voltage between terminals 2 (red) and 5 (dark green or light green/black) of coolant fan relay connector. If no voltage is present, repair open in circuit 535 or 536.
5. If battery voltage is present, measure voltage between terminal 1 (red) wire and ground on the relay connector. If no voltage is present, repair open in circuit 2.
6. If battery voltage is present, connect a 20 amp fused jumper between terminals 1 (red) wire and 4 (black/red) at relay connector. If coolant fan runs, replace coolant fan relay.
7. If coolant fan does not run, leave jumper installed from step 6 then disconnect the coolant fan connector and measure voltage between terminal B (black/red) wire and ground. If no voltage is present, repair open in circuit 532.
8. If battery voltage is present, measure voltage between terminals B (black/red) wire and A (black) wire of coolant fan connector. If no voltage is present, repair open in circuit 151.
9. If battery voltage is present, replace coolant fan.

Coolant Fan Does Not Turn Off w/Engine Coolant Cool, A/C Mode Selector Off And Ignition Switch In Run.

1. With ignition switch in RUN position, disconnect coolant fan relay connector and connect a test lamp between

does not come on, replace secondary coolant fan relay. If test light does come on, check circuit (473) for a short to ground. If circuit is satisfactory, problem is ECM related.

COOLANT FAN, REPLACE

1. Disconnect battery ground cable.
2. Remove air cleaner assembly.
3. Remove coolant reservoir.
4. Remove engine strut brace bolts from upper tie bar and rotate strut(s) and brace(s) rearward. **Loosen strut retaining bolts on both ends to prevent damage to strut(s).**
5. Disconnect wiring harness from fan motor(s) and fan frame(s).
6. Remove fan frame attaching bolts.
7. Remove fan assembly.
8. Reverse procedure to install.

ACHIEVA
SYSTEM DESCRIPTION

The coolant fan is controlled by the engine control module (ECM) via the coolant

fan relay. The ECM receives input signals from the coolant temperature sensor (CTS), vehicle speed sensor and the A/C mode selector. The ECM activates the coolant fan relay when the engine coolant temperature exceeds 227°F, the air conditioning is turned on or if the coolant temperature sensor fails when vehicle speed is below 35 mph by grounding circuit 535 or 536. When circuit 535 or 536 is grounded, the coolant fan relay energizes, applying battery voltage to the coolant fan. The coolant fan will continue to run after the ignition switch is turned OFF, until the engine coolant temperature lowers.

TROUBLESHOOTING

If coolant fan continues to run with ignition switch in the Off position after engine coolant temperature lowers, replace coolant fan relay.

SYSTEM CHECK

1. With ambient temperature above 70°F, start car, open all doors and set A/C mode selector to the MAX position. Coolant fan should turn on.

terminals 2 (red) and 5 (dark green or light green/black). If test lamp does not light, replace coolant fan relay.

2. If test lamp lights, check circuit 535 or 536 for a short to ground. If satisfactory, problem is ECM related.

COOLANT FAN, REPLACE

3.3L/V6-204 Engine

1. Disconnect battery ground cable.
2. Remove air intake duct assembly up to air cleaner.
3. Partially drain cooling system and disconnect upper radiator hose from radiator.
4. Disconnect wiring harness from motor and fan frame.
5. Remove fan guard and hose support as necessary.
6. Remove fan assembly from radiator support.
7. Reverse procedure to install.

2.3L/4-138 Engine

1. Disconnect battery ground cable.
2. Remove air intake duct assembly.
3. Remove coolant fan mounting bolt.
4. Disconnect electrical connector from coolant fan.
5. Remove coolant fan assembly out through bottom.
6. Reverse procedure to install.

PRIZM

SYSTEM DESCRIPTION

When the ignition switch is in either the RUN or START positions, system voltage is applied to the coils of the main engine relay and to fan relay 1. Because the main relay is grounded at G108, the relay is energized, its contacts close, and battery voltage is applied through the relay and the radiator fan fusible link to the contacts of fan relay 1.

When engine coolant temperature is below 194°F, the coolant fan temperature switch provides a ground for relay 1, the relay energizes and its contacts are pulled open.

Whenever engine coolant temperature reaches or exceeds 194°F, the coolant fan temperature switch opens, fan relay 1 is de-energized, its contacts close, and system voltage is applied through the relay to the coolant fan motor. Since the fan motor is grounded at G108, it start to operate as soon as voltage is applied.

When engine coolant temperature drops below 194°F, the coolant fan temperature switch closes to ground, fan relay 1 is energized the relay contacts are pulled open and system voltage is no longer applied to the fan motor.

TROUBLESHOOTING

1. Check the IGN fuse by turning the ignition switch to RUN and noting indicator lamp operation.
2. Check the ECM/IG fuse with a fuse tester.
3. Check the A/C fuse with a fuse tester.
4. Check all relays in junction blocks 2 and 5 are mounted securely.

Fig. 133 Coolant fan wiring circuit. Achieva

5. Check radiator fan fusible link for an open.
6. Check, clean and tighten body grounds G102 and G203.

DIAGNOSIS

1991

Refer to wiring circuits **Fig. 134 and 135** when performing diagnostic procedures on this system.

Less A/C

1. Start engine, ensure coolant temperature is below 194°F. If coolant fan does not operate, go to step 2. If coolant does operate, go to step 3.
2. Run engine until temperature reach and exceed 194°F, if coolant operates, system is normal. If coolant fan does not operate, go to step 7.
3. Remove coolant fan temperature switch connector, then connect fused jumper between connector and ground. If coolant fan stop running, replace coolant fan temperature switch. If coolant fan continues to run, go to step 4.
4. Turn ignition switch OFF, with suitable multimeter, backprobe junction block

2 connector C3 and chassis ground. If resistance is more than 0.3 ohms repair open in light green wire between junction block 2 and coolant temperature switch. If resistance is more than 0.3 ohms, go to step 5.
5. Remove jumper. Reconnect coolant fan switch connector, then turn ignition switch ON. Remove fan relay 1 from junction block 2. If coolant fan continues to run, repair short in BLK/RED wire between junction block 2 and coolant fan motor. If coolant fan stops running, go to step 6.
6. Disconnect junction block 2 connector C3, then connect multimeter between C3 and fan relay 1 and connector cavity 2. Measure resistance, if less the 0.3 ohms, replace junction block 2. If more than 0.3 ohms, replace fan relay 1.
7. Disconnect coolant temperature switch. If coolant fan starts running, replace coolant fan temp switch. If coolant fan does not run, go to step 8.
8. Disconnect junction block 2 connector C3, then connect multimeter from coolant temp switch to ground. Measure resistance, if less than infinite, repair short in LT GRN wire between

Fig. 134   Coolant fan wiring circuit. 1991 Prizm less A/C

Fig. 135   Coolant fan wiring circuit (Part 1 of 2). 1991 Prizm w/A/C

Fig. 135   Coolant fan wiring circuit (Part 2 of 2). 1991 Prizm w/A/C

junction block 2 and temp switch. If infinite, go to step 9.

9. Disconnect fan relay 1, then connect multimeter to connector cavity 2 and ground. Measure resistance, if less than infinite, replace junction block 2. If infinite, go to step 10.
10. Connect test lamp between fan relay 1 connector cavity 1 and ground. If test lamp does not light, replace junction block 2. If test lamp does light, go to step 11.
11. Connect test lamp between fan relay 1 connector cavity 4 and ground. If test lamp does not light, check coolant fan fusible link, if good, replace junction block 2. If test lamp lights, go to step 12.
12. Reconnect coolant temp switch, fan relay 1 and junction block 2 connector C3. Backprobe fan relay 1 with test lamp from cavity 3 to ground. If test lamp does not light, replace fan relay 1. If test lamp lights, go to step 13.
13. Backprobe junction block 2 connector C5, from cavity 11 to ground. If test lamp does not light, replace junction block 2. If test lamp lights, go to step 14.
14. Disconnect coolant fan motor connector, then connect test lamp from cavity 1 to ground. If test lamp does not light, repair BLK/RED wire open. If test lamp lights, go to step 15.
15. Connect multimeter between coolant fan connector cavity 2 and ground. Measure resistance, if more than 0.3 ohms, repair BLK/WHT ground between coolant fan motor and G102. If less than 0.3 ohms, replace coolant fan motor.

With A/C

1. Start engine, ensure coolant temperature is below 194°F. If coolant and condenser fan motors do not operate, go to step 2. If coolant fan operates at full speed, go to step 4. If condenser fan operates at full speed, go to step 7. If coolant and condenser fans operate at half speed, got to step 11. If coolant and condenser fans operate at full speed, go to step 32.
2. Press A/C switch ON, move blower to any position except OFF. If coolant and condenser fans operate at half speed, go to step 3. If coolant and condenser fans do not operate, go to step 12.
3. Run engine until temperature is 194°F or above, turn A/C and blower switch OFF. If coolant and condenser fans operate at full speed, all systems are normal. If coolant and condenser fans do not operate at full speed, go to step 29. If coolant fan does not operate, go to step 36. If condenser fan does not operate, go to step 42.
4. Connect multimeter between fan relay 1 cavity 2 to ground. Measure resistance, if more than 0.3 ohms, replace junction block 2. If less than 0.3 ohms, go to step 5.
5. Connect test lamp from fan relay 1 cavity 3 to ground. If test lamp does not light, replace fan relay 1. If test lamp lights, go to step 6.
6. Connect test lamp between junction block 2 connector C2 cavity 11 to ground. If test lamp lights, repair short

in BLK/RED wire. If test lamp does not light, replace junction block 2.
7. Connect multimeter between A/C fan relay 2 cavity 2 to ground. Measure resistance, if more than 0.3 ohms, go to step 8. If less than 0.3 ohms, go to step 9.
8. Back probe junction block 2 connector C5 cavity 8 to ground. Measure resistance, if less than 0.3 ohms, repair BLU/BLK wire open. If more then 0.3 ohms, replace junction block 2.
9. Connect test lamp from A/C fan relay 2 cavity 6 to ground. If test lamp does not light, repair BLK/ORN wire open. If test lamp lights, go to step 10.
10. Connect test lamp from A/C relay 2 cavity 1 to ground. If test lamp lights, replace WHT wire. If test lamp does not light, replace A/C fan relay 2.
11. Connect test lamp between A/C fan relay 3 cavity 1 to ground. If test lamp lights, repair BLK/WHT wire short. If test lamp does not light, replace A/C fan relay 3.
12. Connect fused jumper between coolant temp switch connector and ground. Connect multimeter between coolant fan motor cavity 2 to ground. Measure resistance, if more than 0.3 ohms, repair WHT/BLK ground wire between coolant fan and G102. If less than 0.3 ohms, go to step 13.
13. Connect fused jumper between coolant fan cavity 1 and ground. If condenser fan operates at full speed, replace coolant fan motor. If condenser fan does not operate, go to step 14.
14. With fused jumper, backprobe A/C fan relay 3 cavity 1 to ground. If condenser fan operates at full speed, re-

pair BLK/RED wire open. If condenser fan does not operate, go to step 15.

15. Connect test lamp between A/C fan relay 3 cavity 1 to ground. If test lamp does not light, repair open in BLK/WHT wire. If test lamp lights, go to step 16.

16. Connect multimeter between A/C fan relay 3 cavity 3 to ground. Measure resistance, if more than 0.3 ohms, repair WHT/BLK ground between A/C fan relay 3 and G102. If less than 0.3 ohms, go to step 17.

17. Connect fused jumper from A/C fan relay cavity 2 to ground. If condenser fan operates at full speed, replace A/C fan relay 3. If condenser fan does not operate, go to step 18.

18. With fused jumper, backprobe A/C fan relay 2 cavity 4 to ground. If condenser fan operates at full speed, repair open in WHT/RED wire. If condenser fan does not operate, go to step 19.

19. Connect test lamp from A/C fan relay 2 cavity 6 to ground. If test lamp does not light, repair open in BLK/ORN wire. If test lamp lights, go to step 20.

20. Connect multimeter from A/C fan relay 2 cavity 2 to ground. Measure resistance, if more than 0.3 ohms, go to step 21. If less than 0.3 ohms, go to step 25.

21. Connect multimeter, backprobe between junction block 2 connector C5 cavity 2 to ground. Measure resistance, if less than 0.3 ohms, go to step repair open in BLU/BLK wire. If more, go to step 22.

22. Connect multimeter, backprobe between junction block connector C3 cavity 2 to ground. Measure resistance, if less then 0.3 ohms, replace junction block 2, If more, got to step 23.

23. Connect multimeter, backprobe between refrigerant pressure switch cavity 1 and ground. Measure resistance, if less than 0.3 ohms, repair open in GRN/BLK wire. If more, go to step 24.

24. Connect multimeter, backprobe between refrigerant pressure switch cavity 2 and ground. Measure resistance, if less than 0.3 ohms, replace refrigerant pressure switch. If more, repair open in LT GRN wire.

25. Connect fused jumper from A/C fan relay cavity 1 to ground. If condenser fan operates at full speed, replace A/C fan relay 2. If not, go to step 26.

26. With fused jumper, backprobe condenser fan connector cavity 1 to ground. If condenser fan operates at full speed, repair open in WHT wire. If not, go to step 27.

27. With test lamp, backprobe condenser fan cavity 2 to ground. If test lamp lights, replace condenser fan motor. If not, go to step 28.

28. With test lamp, backprobe junction block connector C5 cavity 3 to ground. If test lamp lights, repair open in BLU/RED or BLU wire, junction block 5 or condenser fan fusible link. If not, replace junction block 5.

29. Disconnect coolant temp switch connector. If coolant fan begins to rotate, replace coolant temp switch. If coolant and condenser fans do not operate at full speed, go to step 30.

30. Disconnect refrigerant pressure switch connector. If coolant and condenser fans operate at full speed, repair short in LT GRN wire between refrigerant pressure switch and coolant temp switch. If not, go to step 31.

31. Disconnect junction block 2 connector C3. If coolant and condenser fans operate at full speed, repair short to ground in LT GRN/BLK wire. If not, replace junction block 2.

32. Connect fused jumper between coolant temp switch connector and ground. If coolant and condenser fans stop operating, replace coolant temp switch. If continue operation, go to step 33.

33. Backprobe refrigerant pressure switch with fused jumper between cavity 2 and ground. If coolant and condenser fans stop, repair open in LT GRN wire. If not, go to step 34.

34. Backprobe refrigerant pressure switch with fused jumper between cavity 1 and ground. If coolant and condenser fan stop, replace refrigerant switch. If operates, go to step 35.

35. Backprobe junction block 2 connector C3 with fused jumper from cavity 2 to ground. If coolant and condenser fans stop, repair open in LT GRN/BLK wire. If operates, replace junction block 2.

36. Connect multimeter between coolant fan connector cavity 2 and ground. Measure resistance, if more than 0.3 ohms, repair WHT/BLK ground between coolant fan and G102. If less, go to step 37.

37. Connect test lamp from condenser fan connector cavity 1 to ground. If test lamp lights, replace coolant fan motor. If not, go to step 38.

38. Backprobe junction block 2 connector C5 cavity 11 to ground with test lamp. If test lamp lights, repair open in BLK/RED wire between junction block 2 and coolant fan. If not, go to step 39.

39. With test lamp, backprobe fan relay 1 cavity 3 to ground. If test lamp lights, replace junction block 1. If not, go to step 40.

40. Connect multimeter between fan relay cavity 1 and ground. Measure resistance, if less than 0.3 ohms, replace junction block 2. If more, go to step 41.

41. Connect test lamp from fan relay cavity 4 to ground. If test lamp does not light, check coolant fan fusible link, if good, replace junction block 2. If test lamp lights, replace fan relay 1.

42. Connect test lamp between condenser fan cavities 1 and 2. If test lamp lights, replace condenser fan motor. If not, go to step 43.

43. Connect test lamp between condenser fan connector cavity 2 and ground. If test lamp does not light, go to step 44. If test lamp lights, go to step 45.

44. With test lamp, backprobe junction

block 2 connector C5 cavity 3 to ground. If test lamp lights, repair open in BLU or BLU/RED wire or condenser fan fusible link. If not, replace junction block 2.

45. With multimeter, backprobe A/C fan relay 2 cavity 1 to ground. Measure resistance, if less than 0.3 ohms, repair open in WHT wire. If more, go to step 46.

46. Connect multimeter between A/C fan relay 2 cavity 3 and ground. Measure resistance, if more than 0.3 ohms, repair open in WHT/BLK wire between A/C fan relay and G102. If less, go to step 47.

47. Connect multimeter between A/C fan relay 2 cavity 2 to ground. Measure resistance, if more the 0.3 ohms, replace A/C fan relay 2. If less, go to step 48.

48. With multimeter, backprobe junction block 2 connector C5 cavity 8 to ground. Measure resistance, if less than 0.3 ohms, repair open in BLU/BLK wire. If more, replace junction block 2.

1992

Refer to **Figs. 136 through 139** to perform diagnostic procedures on this system.

1993

Refer to wiring diagrams **Figs. 140 and 141** and diagnostic charts **Figs. 142 through 144** when performing diagnostic procedures on this system.

COOLANT FAN, REPLACE

1. Disconnect battery ground cable.
2. Disconnect coolant fan electrical harness.
3. Remove coolant fan from vehicle.
4. Reverse procedure to install.

STORM

SYSTEM DESCRIPTION

With the engine running, the generator applies voltage to the restart relay. The voltage passes through the closed contacts of the restart relay to the condenser fan relay and the radiator fan relay. The triple switch closes when the refrigerant pressure is above 214 psi. When the triple switch closes, the condenser fan and radiator fan relays energize.

The condenser fan receives battery voltage from fuse E-4 through the closed contacts of the condenser fan relay. The radiator fan receives battery voltage from fusible link FL-4 through the radiator fan relay.

The thermo switch closes when the coolant temperature is above 179°F. When the thermo switch closes, the radiator fan and condenser fan operate in the same manner as when the triple switch closes.

When the ignition switch is turned to START, the restart relay is energized, the contacts are opened and the fans will not operate.

Continued on page 16-124

Fig. 136 Coolant fan wiring circuit. 1992 Prizm less A/C

COOLANT FANS: WITHOUT AIR CONDITIONING		DIAGNOSTIC CHART A
TEST	**RESULT**	**ACTION**
A1. Start and run the engine. Make certain that engine coolant temperature is below 90°C (194°F).	RADIATOR FAN MOTOR does not operate.	GO TO **A2.**
	RADIATOR FAN MOTOR operates below 90°C (194°F).	GO TO **A3.**
A2. Run the engine until operating temperature reaches 90°C (194°F).	Radiator fan motor operates at 90°C (194°F) and above.	All systems diagnosed are functioning normally.
	Radiator fan motor does not operate at 90°C (194°F) or above.	GO TO **A7.**
A3. Remove the COOLANT TEMPERATURE SWITCH connector. Connect a fused jumper between the connector cavity and chassis ground.	RADIATOR FAN MOTOR stops running.	Replace COOLANT TEMPERATURE SWITCH.
	RADIATOR FAN MOTOR continues to run.	GO TO **A4.**
A4. Turn ignition switch to "OFF." Backprobe JUNCTION BLOCK 2 connector C3 with a digital multimeter from cavity 2 to chassis ground. Measure resistance.	More than 1.0 ohm.	Repair open in LT GRN wire or LT GRN/BLK wire between JUNCTION BLOCK 2 and COOLANT TEMPERATURE SWITCH.
	Less than 1.0 ohm.	GO TO **A5.**
A5. Remove jumper. Reconnect COOLANT TEMPERATURE SWITCH connector. Turn ignition switch to "ON." Remove Fan Relay 1 from JUNCTION BLOCK 2.	RADIATOR FAN MOTOR continues to run.	Repair short to voltage in BLK/RED wire between JUNCTION BLOCK 2 and RADIATOR FAN MOTOR.
	RADIATOR FAN MOTOR stops running.	GO TO **A6.**
A6. Disconnect JUNCTION BLOCK 2 connector C3. Connect a digital multimeter from JUNCTION BLOCK 2 connector C3 terminal 2 (JUNCTION BLOCK 2 side) to Fan Relay 1 connector cavity 2. Measure resistance.	Less than 1.0 ohm.	Replace Fan Relay 1.
	More than 1.0 ohm.	Replace JUNCTION BLOCK 2.
A7. Disconnect COOLANT TEMPERATURE SWITCH connector.	RADIATOR FAN MOTOR starts running.	Replace COOLANT TEMPERATURE SWITCH.
	RADIATOR FAN MOTOR does not operate.	GO TO **A8.**

Fig. 137 System diagnosis chart (Part 1 of 2). 1992 Prizm less A/C

	TEST	RESULT	ACTION
	COOLANT FANS: WITHOUT AIR CONDITIONING		DIAGNOSTIC CHART A (CONT'D)
A8.	Disconnect JUNCTION BLOCK 2 connector C3. Connect a digital multimeter from cavity 2 to chassis ground. Measure resistance.	Less than infinite.	Repair short to ground in LT GRN or LT GRN/BLK wire between JUNCTION BLOCK 2 and COOLANT TEMPERATURE SWITCH.
		Infinite.	GO TO A9.
A9.	Disconnect Fan Relay 1 connector. Connect a digital multimeter from connector cavity 2 to chassis ground. Measure resistance.	Less than infinite.	Replace JUNCTION BLOCK 2.
		Infinite.	GO TO A10.
A10.	Connect a test lamp from Fan Relay 1 connector cavity 1 to chassis ground.	Test lamp does not light.	Replace JUNCTION BLOCK 2.
		Test lamp lights.	GO TO A11.
A11.	Connect a test lamp from Fan Relay 1 connector cavity 4 to chassis ground.	Test lamp does not light.	Check Radiator Fan Fusible Link if good, replace JUNCTION BLOCK 2.
		Test lamp lights.	GO TO A12.
A12.	Reconnect COOLANT TEMPERATURE SWITCH, Fan Relay 1 and JUNCTION BLOCK 2 connector C3. Backprobe Fan Relay 1 connector with a test lamp from cavity 3 to chassis ground.	Test lamp does not light.	Replace Fan Relay 1.
		Test lamp lights.	GO TO A13.
A13.	Backprobe JUNCTION BLOCK 2 connector C5 with a test lamp from cavity 11 to chassis ground.	Test lamp does not light.	Replace JUNCTION BLOCK 2.
		Test lamp lights.	GO TO A14.
A14.	Disconnect RADIATOR FAN MOTOR connector. Connect a test lamp from connector cavity 1 to chassis ground.	Test lamp does not light.	Repair open in BLK/RED wire.
		Test lamp lights.	GO TO A15.
A15.	Connect a digital multimeter from RADIATOR FAN MOTOR connector cavity 2 to chassis ground. Measure resistance.	More than 3.0 ohms.	Repair WHT/BLK ground wire between RADIATOR FAN MOTOR and G102.
		Less than 3.0 ohms.	Replace RADIATOR FAN MOTOR.

Fig. 137   System diagnosis chart (Part 2 of 2). 1992 Prizm less A/C

Fig. 138   Coolant fan wiring circuit (Part 1 Of 2). 1992 Prizm w/A/C

Fig. 138 Coolant fan wiring circuit (Part 2 Of 2). 1992 Prizm w/A/C

COOLANT FANS: WITH AIR CONDITIONING		DIAGNOSTIC CHART B
TEST	**RESULT**	**ACTION**
B1. Start and run the engine. Make certain that engine coolant temperature is below 90°C (194°F).	RADIATOR FAN MOTOR and CONDENSER FAN MOTOR do not operate.	GO TO **B2.**
	RADIATOR FAN MOTOR operates at full speed.	GO TO **B4.**
	CONDENSER FAN MOTOR operates at full speed.	GO TO **B7.**
	RADIATOR FAN MOTOR and CONDENSER FAN MOTOR operate at half speed.	GO TO **B11.**
	RADIATOR FAN MOTOR and CONDENSER FAN MOTOR operate at full speed.	GO TO **B29.**
B2. Press A/C switch to ON. Move blower switch to any position except "OFF."	RADIATOR FAN MOTOR and CONDENSER FAN MOTOR operate at half speed.	GO TO **B3.**
	RADIATOR FAN MOTOR and CONDENSER FAN MOTOR do not operate.	GO TO **B12.**
B3. Run the engine until operating temperature reaches 90°C (194°F). Press A/C switch to OFF. Move blower switch to "OFF."	RADIATOR FAN MOTOR and CONDENSER FAN MOTOR operate at full speed.	All systems diagnosed are functioning normally.
	RADIATOR FAN MOTOR and CONDENSER FAN MOTOR do not operate at full speed.	GO TO **B27.**
	RADIATOR FAN MOTOR does not operate.	GO TO **B31.**
	CONDENSER FAN MOTOR does not operate.	GO TO **B37.**
B4. Disconnect Fan Relay 1 connector. Connect a digital multimeter from cavity 2 to chassis ground. Measure resistance.	More than 1.0 ohm.	Replace JUNCTION BLOCK 2.
	Less than 1.0 ohm.	GO TO **B5.**

Fig. 139 System diagnosis chart (Part 1 of 6). 1992 Prizm w/A/C

COOLANT FANS: WITH AIR CONDITIONING		DIAGNOSTIC CHART B (CONT'D)
TEST	**RESULT**	**ACTION**
B5. Connect a test lamp from Fan Relay 1 connector cavity 3 to chassis ground.	Test lamp does not light.	Replace Fan Relay 1.
	Test lamp lights.	GO TO **B6**.
B6. Disconnect JUNCTION BLOCK 2 connector C5. Connect a test lamp from cavity 11 to chassis ground.	Test lamp lights.	Repair short to voltage in BLK/RED wire.
	Test lamp does not light.	Replace JUNCTION BLOCK 2.
B7. Disconnect A/C Fan Relay 2 connector. Connect a digital multimeter from cavity 2 to chassis ground. Measure resistance.	More than 1.0 ohm.	GO TO **B8**.
	Less than 1.0 ohm.	GO TO **B9**.
B8. Backprobe JUNCTION BLOCK 2 connector C5 with a digital multimeter from cavity 8 to chassis ground. Measure resistance.	Less than 1.0 ohm.	Repair open in BLU/BLK wire.
	More than 1.0 ohm.	Replace JUNCTION BLOCK 2.
B9. Connect a test lamp from A/C Fan Relay 2 connector cavity 6 to chassis ground.	Test lamp does not light.	Repair open in BLK/ORN wire.
	Test lamp lights.	GO TO **B10**.
B10. Connect a test lamp from A/C Fan Relay 2 connector cavity 1 to chassis ground.	Test lamp lights.	Repair short to voltage in WHT wire.
	Test lamp does not light.	Replace A/C Fan Relay 2.
B11. Disconnect A/C Fan Relay 3 connector. Connect a test lamp from cavity 1 to chassis ground.	Test lamp lights.	Repair short to voltage in BLK/WHT wire.
	Test lamp does not light.	Replace A/C Fan Relay 3.
B12. Disconnect COOLANT TEMPERATURE SWITCH connector. Connect a fused jumper from connector cavity to chassis ground. Disconnect RADIATOR FAN MOTOR connector. Connect a digital multimeter from cavity 2 to chassis ground. Measure resistance.	More than 3.0 ohms.	Repair WHT/BLK ground wire between RADIATOR FAN MOTOR and G102.
	Less than 3.0 ohms.	GO TO **B13**.
B13. Connect a fused jumper from RADIATOR FAN MOTOR connector cavity 1 to chassis ground.	CONDENSER FAN MOTOR operates at full speed.	Replace RADIATOR FAN MOTOR.
	CONDENSER FAN MOTOR does not operate.	GO TO **B14**.

Fig. 139   System diagnosis chart (Part 2 of 6). 1992 Prizm w/A/C

COOLANT FANS: WITH AIR CONDITIONING		DIAGNOSTIC CHART B (CONT'D)
TEST	**RESULT**	**ACTION**
B14. Backprobe A/C Fan Relay 3 connector with a fused jumper from cavity 4 to chassis ground.	CONDENSER FAN MOTOR operates at full speed.	Repair open in BLK/RED wire between A/C Fan Relay 3 and Junction Block 2.
	CONDENSER FAN MOTOR does not operate.	GO TO **B15**.
B15. Disconnect A/C FAN RELAY 3 connector. Connect a test lamp from cavity 1 to chassis ground.	Test lamp does not light.	Repair open in BLK/WHT wire.
	Test lamp lights.	GO TO **B16**.
B16. Connect a digital multimeter from A/C FAN RELAY 3 connector cavity 3 to chassis ground. Measure resistance.	More than 1.0 ohm.	Repair WHT/BLK ground wire between A/C Fan Relay 3 and G102.
	Less than 1.0 ohm.	GO TO **B17**.
B17. Connect a fused jumper from A/C Fan Relay 3 connector cavity 2 to chassis ground.	CONDENSER FAN MOTOR operates at full speed.	Replace A/C Fan Relay 3.
	CONDENSER FAN MOTOR does not operate.	GO TO **B18**.
B18. Backprobe A/C Fan Relay 2 connector with a fused jumper from cavity 4 to chassis ground.	CONDENSER FAN MOTOR operates at full speed.	Repair open in WHT/RED wire.
	CONDENSER FAN MOTOR does not operate.	GO TO **B19**.
B19. Disconnect A/C Fan Relay 2 connector. Connect a test lamp from cavity 6 to chassis ground.	Test lamp does not light.	Repair open in BLK/ORN wire.
	Test lamp lights.	GO TO **B20**.
B20. Connect a digital multimeter from A/C Fan Relay 2 connector cavity 2 to chassis ground. Measure resistance.	More than 1.0 ohm.	GO TO **B21**.
	Less than 1.0 ohm.	GO TO **B23**.
B21. Backprobe JUNCTION BLOCK 2 connector C5 with a digital multimeter from cavity 8 to chassis ground. Measure resistance.	Less than 1.0 ohm.	Repair open in BLU/BLK wire.
	More than 1.0 ohm.	GO TO **B22**.
B22. Backprobe JUNCTION BLOCK 2 connector C3 with a digital multimeter from cavity 2 to chassis ground. Measure resistance.	Less than 1.0 ohm.	Replace JUNCTION BLOCK 2.
	More than 1.0 ohm.	Repair open in LT GRN or LT GRN/BLK wire.

Fig. 139   System diagnosis chart (Part 3 of 6). 1992 Prizm w/A/C

COOLANT FANS: WITH AIR CONDITIONING		DIAGNOSTIC CHART B (CONT'D)
TEST	**RESULT**	**ACTION**
B23. Connect a fused jumper from A/C Fan Relay 2 connector cavity 1 to chassis ground.	CONDENSER FAN MOTOR operates at full speed.	Replace A/C Fan Relay 2.
	CONDENSER FAN MOTOR does not operate.	GO TO **B24.**
B24. Backprobe CONDENSER FAN MOTOR connector with a fused jumper from cavity 1 to chassis ground.	CONDENSER FAN MOTOR operates at full speed.	Repair open in WHT wire.
	CONDENSER FAN MOTOR does not operate.	GO TO **B25.**
B25. Backprobe CONDENSER FAN MOTOR connector with a test lamp from cavity 2 to chassis ground.	Test lamp lights.	Replace CONDENSER FAN MOTOR.
	Test lamp does not light.	GO TO **B26.**
B26. Backprobe JUNCTION BLOCK 2 connector C5 with a test lamp from cavity 3 to chassis ground.	Test lamp lights.	Repair open in BLU/RED or BLU wire between JUNCTION BLOCK 2 and CONDENSOR FAN MOTOR, JUNCTION BLOCK 5 or Condenser Fan Fusible Link.
	Test lamp does not light.	Replace JUNCTION BLOCK 5.
B27. Disconnect COOLANT TEMPERATURE SWITCH connector.	RADIATOR FAN MOTOR begins to operate.	Replace COOLANT TEMPERATURE SWITCH.
	RADIATOR FAN MOTOR and CONDENSER FAN MOTOR do not operate at full speed.	GO TO **B28.**
B28. Disconnect JUNCTION BLOCK 2 connector C3.	RADIATOR FAN MOTOR and CONDENSER FAN MOTOR operate at full speed.	Repair short to ground in LT GRN/BLK or LT GRN wire.
	RADIATOR FAN MOTOR and CONDENSER FAN MOTOR do not operate at full speed.	Replace JUNCTION BLOCK 2.
B29. Disconnect COOLANT TEMPERATURE SWITCH connector. Connect a fused jumper from connector cavity to chassis ground.	RADIATOR FAN and CONDENSER FAN MOTOR stop operating.	Replace COOLANT TEMPERATURE SWITCH.
	RADIATOR FAN and CONDENSER FAN MOTOR continue to operate.	GO TO **B30.**

Fig. 139   System diagnosis chart (Part 4 of 6). 1992 Prizm w/A/C

COOLANT FANS: WITH AIR CONDITIONING		DIAGNOSTIC CHART B (CONT'D)
TEST	**RESULT**	**ACTION**
B30. Backprobe JUNCTION BLOCK 2 connector C3 with a fused jumper from cavity 2 to chassis ground.	RADIATOR FAN MOTOR and CONDENSER FAN MOTOR stop operating.	Repair open in LT GRN or LT GRN/BLK wire.
	RADIATOR FAN MOTOR and CONDENSER FAN MOTOR continue to operate.	Replace JUNCTION BLOCK 2.
B31. Disconnect RADIATOR FAN MOTOR connector. Connect a digital multimeter from cavity 2 to chassis ground. Measure resistance.	More than 3.0 ohms.	Repair WHT/BLK ground wire between RADIATOR FAN MOTOR and G102.
	Less than 3.0 ohms.	GO TO **B32.**
B32. Connect a test lamp from RADIATOR FAN MOTOR connector cavity 1 to chassis ground.	Test lamp lights.	Replace RADIATOR FAN MOTOR.
	Test lamp does not light.	GO TO **B33.**
B33. Backprobe JUNCTION BLOCK 2 connector C5 with a test lamp from cavity 11 to chassis ground.	Test lamp lights.	Repair open in BLK/RED wire between JUNCTION BLOCK 2 and RADIATOR FAN MOTOR.
	Test lamp does not light.	GO TO **B34.**
B34. Backprobe Fan Relay 1 with a test lamp from cavity 3 to chassis ground.	Test lamp lights.	Replace JUNCTION BLOCK 2.
	Test lamp does not light.	GO TO **B35.**
B35. Disconnect Fan Relay 1 connector. Connect a digital multimeter from cavity 2 to chassis ground. Measure resistance.	Less than 1.0 ohm.	Replace JUNCTION BLOCK 2.
	More than 1.0 ohm.	GO TO **B36.**
B36. Connect a test lamp from Fan Relay 1 connector cavity 4 to chassis ground.	Test lamp does not light.	Check Radiator Fan Fusible Link. If good, replace JUNCTION BLOCK 2.
	Test lamp lights.	Replace Fan Relay 1.
B37. Disconnect CONDENSER FAN MOTOR connector. Connect a test lamp from cavity 1 to cavity 2.	Test lamp lights.	Replace CONDENSER FAN MOTOR.
	Test lamp does not light.	GO TO **B38.**
B38. Connect a test lamp from CONDENSER FAN MOTOR connector cavity 2 to chassis ground.	Test lamp does not light.	GO TO **B39.**
	Test lamp lights.	GO TO **B40.**

Fig. 139   System diagnosis chart (Part 5 of 6). 1992 Prizm w/A/C

	TEST	RESULT	ACTION
COOLANT FANS: WITH AIR CONDITIONING			**DIAGNOSTIC CHART B (CONT'D)**
B39.	Backprobe JUNCTION BLOCK 2 connector C5 with a test lamp from cavity 3 to chassis ground.	Test lamp lights.	Repair open in BLU wire between JUNCTION BLOCK 2 and CONDENSER FAN MOTOR or BLU/RED wire or Condenser Fan Fusible Link.
		Test lamp does not light.	Replace JUNCTION BLOCK 2.
B40.	Backprobe A/C Fan Relay 2 with a digital multimeter from cavity 1 to chassis ground. Measure resistance.	Less than 3.0 ohms.	Repair open in WHT wire.
		More than 3.0 ohms.	GO TO **B41**.
B41.	Disconnect A/C Fan Relay 2 connector. Connect a digital multimeter from cavity 3 to chassis ground. Measure resistance.	More than 1.0 ohm.	Repair open in WHT/BLK wire between A/C Fan Relay 2 and G102.
		Less than 1.0 ohm.	GO TO **B42**.
B42.	Connect a digital multimeter from A/C Fan Relay 2 cavity 2 to chassis ground. Measure resistance.	More than 1.0 ohm.	GO TO **B43**.
		Less than 1.0 ohm.	Replace A/C Fan Relay 2.
B43.	Backprobe JUNCTION BLOCK 2 connector C5 with a digital multimeter from cavity 8 to chassis ground. Measure resistance.	Less than 1.0 ohm.	Repair open in BLU/BLK wire.
		More than 1.0 ohm.	Replace JUNCTION BLOCK 2.

Fig. 139   System diagnosis chart (Part 6 of 6). 1992 Prizm w/A/C

Fig. 140   Coolant fan wiring circuit. 1993 Prizm less A/C

Fig. 141   Coolant fan wiring circuit (Part 2 of 2). 1993 Prizm w/A/C

Fig. 141   Coolant fan wiring circuit (Part 1 of 2). 1993 Prizm w/A/C

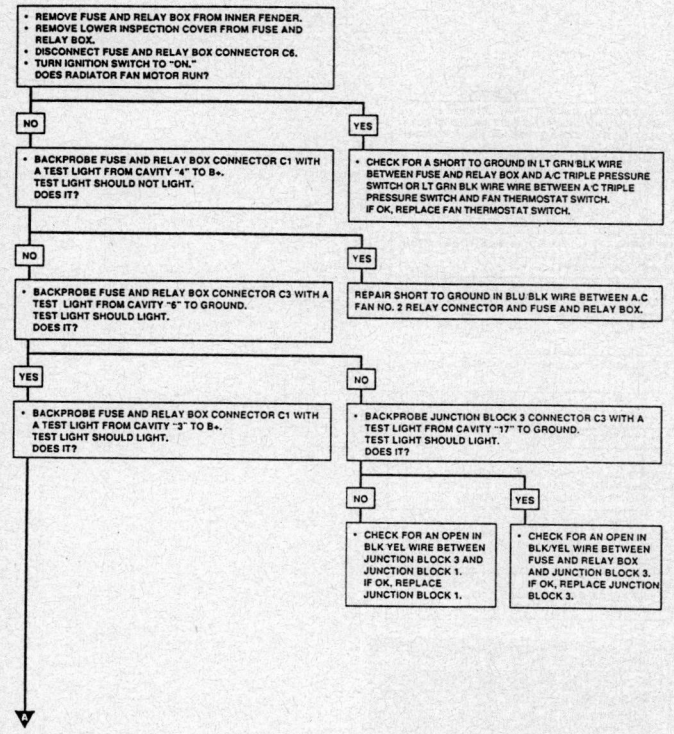

Fig. 142   Coolant fan system diagnosis (Radiator fan motor does not run, part 1 of 2). 1993 Prizm

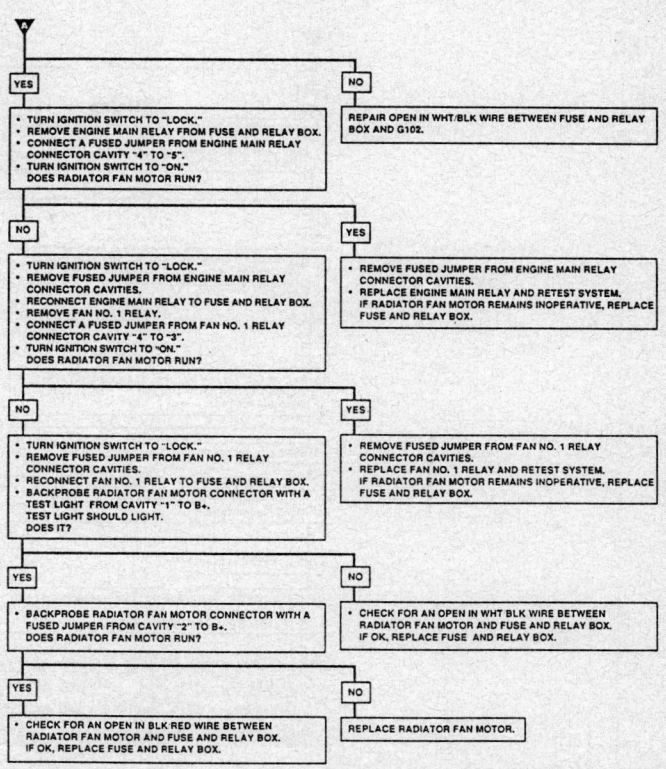

Fig. 142   Coolant fan system diagnosis (Radiator fan motor does not run, part 2 of 2). 1993 Prizm

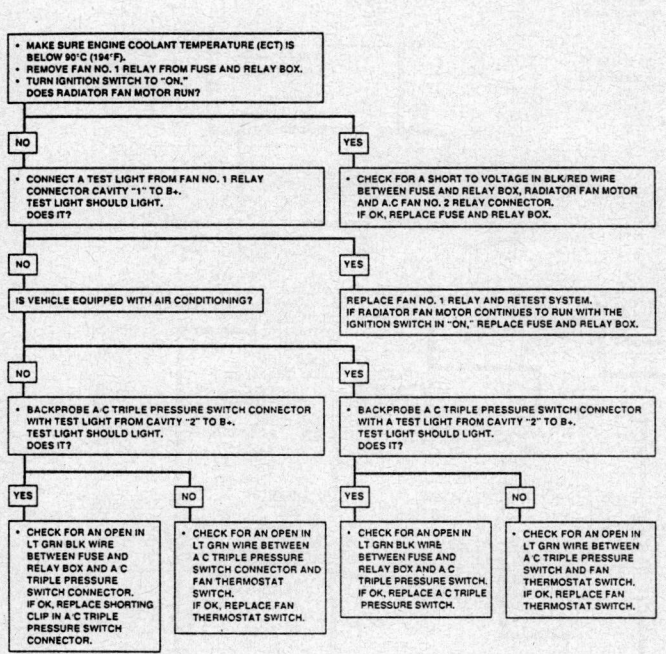

Fig. 143   Coolant fan system diagnosis (Radiator fan motor runs continuously with ignition switch on). 1993 Prizm

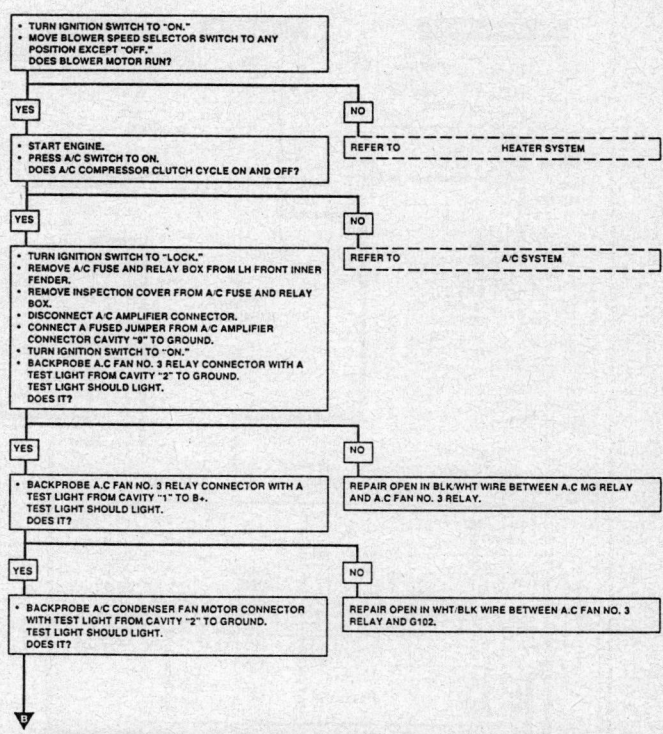

Fig. 144   Coolant fan system diagnosis (Radiator fan motor & A/C condenser fan motor do not run at half speed during A/C system operation, part 1 of 2). 1993 Prizm

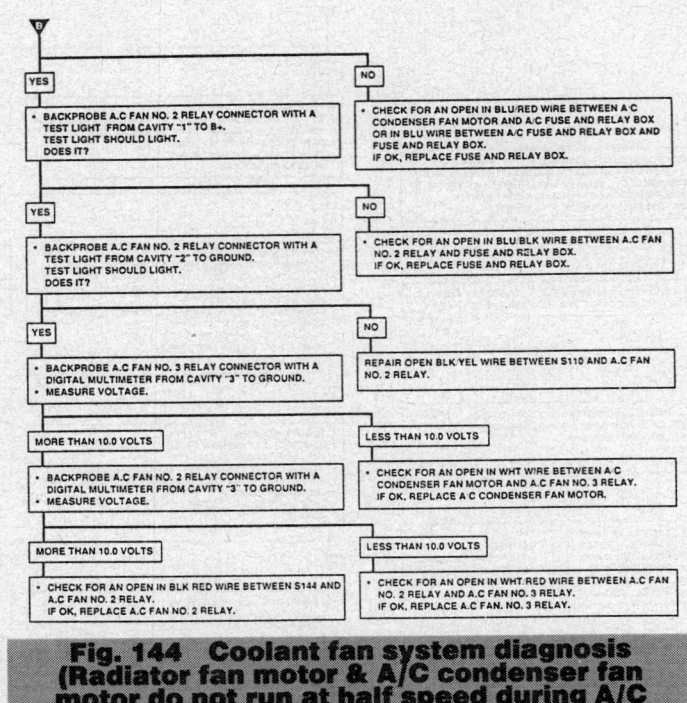

Fig. 144 Coolant fan system diagnosis (Radiator fan motor & A/C condenser fan motor do not run at half speed during A/C system operation, part 2 of 2). 1993 Prizm

Fig. 145 Coolant fan wiring circuit. 1991 Storm

COOLANT FANS	DIAGNOSTIC CHART A		
	TEST	RESULT	ACTION
A1.	Start and run the engine until coolant temperature reaches 82°C (179°F).	RADIATOR FAN MOTOR and CONDENSER FAN MOTOR operate.	GO TO A2.
		Neither fan operates.	GO TO A4.
		RADIATOR FAN MOTOR only operates.	GO TO A7.
		CONDENSER FAN MOTOR only operates.	GO TO A13.
A2.	Disconnect RADIATOR FAN THERMO SWITCH connector. Run engine with air conditioning operating for 5 minutes.	RADIATOR FAN MOTOR and CONDENSER FAN MOTOR both operate at least once during the 5 minute test.	GO TO A3.
		Neither fan operates at all during the 5 minute test.	GO TO A17.
A3.	Turn ignition switch to "OFF."	Both fans stop operating.	All systems diagnosed are functioning normally.
		Both fans continue to operate.	GO TO A24.
		CONDENSER FAN MOTOR continues to operate.	GO TO A25.
		RADIATOR FAN MOTOR continues to operate.	GO TO A26.
A4.	Connect a fused jumper from COOLANT FAN CHECK CONNECTOR to chassis ground while engine is running.	Both fans operate.	GO TO A5.
		Neither fan operates.	GO TO A19.
A5.	Disconnect RADIATOR FAN THERMO SWITCH connector. Connect a fused jumper between terminals 1 and 2 with engine running.	Both fans operate.	Replace RADIATOR FAN THERMO SWITCH.
		Neither fan operates.	GO TO A6.
A6.	Remove jumper. Connect a digital multimeter from RADIATOR FAN THERMO SWITCH connector terminal 2 to chassis ground. Measure resistance.	More than 0.3 ohms.	Repair BLK ground wire between RADIATOR FAN THERMO SWITCH and G102.
		Less than 0.3 ohms.	Repair open in WHT wire between RADIATOR FAN THERMO SWITCH and S138.

Fig. 146 System diagnosis chart (Part 1 of 4). 1991 Storm

COOLANT FANS	DIAGNOSTIC CHART A (CONT'D.)		
	TEST	RESULT	ACTION
A7.	Remove Condenser Fan Relay and Radiator Fan Relay from FUSE AND RELAY BOX. Connect a digital multimeter from Condenser Fan Relay connector cavity 3 to chassis ground. Measure resistance.	More than 0.3 ohms.	Repair open in WHT wire between Radiator Fan Relay and Condenser Fan Relay.
		Less than 0.3 ohms.	Reinstall relays and GO TO A8.
A8.	Backprobe Condenser Fan Relay connector with a test lamp from cavity 1 to chassis ground.	Test lamp does not light.	Repair open in WHT/RED wire between Condenser Fan Relay and Radiator Fan Relay.
		Test lamp lights.	GO TO A9.
A9.	Backprobe Condenser Fan Relay connector with a test lamp from cavity 2 to chassis ground.	Test lamp does not light.	Repair open in BLU/ORN wire between Fuse E-4 and Condenser Fan Relay.
		Test lamp lights.	GO TO A10.
A10.	Backprobe Condenser Fan Relay connector with a test lamp from cavity 4 to chassis ground.	Test lamp does not light.	Replace Condenser Fan Relay.
		Test lamp lights.	GO TO A11.
A11.	Backprobe CONDENSER FAN MOTOR connector with a test lamp from cavity 1 to chassis ground.	Test lamp does not light.	Repair open in BLU wire between CONDENSER FAN MOTOR and FUSE AND RELAY BOX.
		Test lamp lights.	GO TO A12.
A12.	Disconnect CONDENSER FAN MOTOR connector. Connect a digital multimeter from cavity 2 to chassis ground. Measure resistance.	Less than 0.3 ohms.	Replace CONDENSER FAN MOTOR.
		More than 0.3 ohms.	Repair BLK ground wire between CONDENSER FAN MOTOR and G103.
A13.	Backprobe Radiator Fan Relay with a test lamp from cavity 2 to chassis ground.	Test lamp does not light.	Repair open in BLK/GRN wire between FL-4 and Radiator Fan Relay.
		Test lamp lights.	GO TO A14.
A14.	Backprobe Radiator Fan Relay connector with a test lamp from cavity 4 to chassis ground.	Test lamp does not light.	Replace Radiator Fan Relay.
		Test lamp lights.	GO TO A15.
A15.	Backprobe RADIATOR FAN MOTOR connector with a test lamp from cavity 1 to chassis ground.	Test lamp does not light.	Repair open in BLK/BLU wire between FUSE AND RELAY BOX and RADIATOR FAN MOTOR.
		Test lamp lights.	GO TO A16.

Fig. 146 System diagnosis chart (Part 2 of 4). 1991 Storm

COOLANT FANS		DIAGNOSTIC CHART A (CONT'D.)	
	TEST	**RESULT**	**ACTION**
A16.	Disconnect RADIATOR FAN MOTOR connector. Connect a digital multimeter from connector terminal 2 to chassis ground. Measure resistance.	Less than 0.3 ohms.	Replace RADIATOR FAN MOTOR.
		More than 0.3 ohms.	Repair BLK ground wire between RADIATOR FAN MOTOR and G102.
A17.	Disconnect TRIPLE SWITCH connector and remove Condenser Fan Relay from FUSE AND RELAY BOX. Connect a digital multimeter from TRIPLE SWITCH connector terminal 2 to Condenser Fan Relay connector cavity 3. Measure resistance.	More than 0.3 ohms.	Repair open in WHT wire between S138 and TRIPLE SWITCH.
		Less than 0.3 ohms.	GO TO **A18**.
A18.	Connect a digital multimeter from TRIPLE SWITCH connector terminal 1 to chassis ground. Measure resistance.	More than 0.3 ohms.	Repair BLK ground wire between TRIPLE SWITCH and G103.
		Less than 0.3 ohms.	Replace TRIPLE SWITCH. IMPORTANT: Receiver/Dryer Assembly must be replaced as a unit in order to replace TRIPLE SWITCH.
A19.	Remove Condenser Fan Relay and Radiator Fan Relay from FUSE AND RELAY BOX. Connect a digital multimeter from Radiator Fan Relay connector cavity 3 to RADIATOR FAN THERMO SWITCH connector terminal 1. Measure resistance.	More than 0.3 ohms.	Repair open in WHT wire between FUSE AND RELAY BOX and S138.
		Less than 0.3 ohms.	GO TO **A20**.
A20.	Backprobe GENERATOR connector with a test lamp from cavity 1 to chassis ground.	Test lamp does not light.	A fault exists within the GENERATOR or related circuitry. Refer to Starter and Charging System Diagnosis
		Test lamp lights.	GO TO **A21**.
A21.	Backprobe Restart Relay connector with a test lamp from cavity 4 to chassis ground.	Test lamp does not light.	Repair open in WHT/BLU wire between GENERATOR and FUSE AND RELAY BOX.
		Test lamp lights.	GO TO **A22**.
A22.	Backprobe Restart Relay connector with a test lamp from cavity 5 to chassis ground.	Test lamp does not light.	Replace Restart Relay.
		Test lamp lights.	GO TO **A23**.

Fig. 146   System diagnosis chart (Part 3 of 4). 1991 Storm

COOLANT FANS		DIAGNOSTIC CHART A (CONT'D.)	
	TEST	**RESULT**	**ACTION**
A23.	Backprobe Heater and A/C Relay connector with a test lamp from cavity 1 to chassis ground.	Test lamp does not light.	Repair open in WHT/RED wire between Restart Relay and Heater and A/C Relay.
		Test lamp lights.	Repair open in WHT/RED wire between Heater and A/C Relay and Radiator Fan Relay.
A24.	Remove Restart Relay from FUSE AND RELAY BOX.	Fans stop operating.	Repair short to voltage in WHT/BLU wire between GENERATOR and FUSE AND RELAY BOX.
		Fans continue to operate.	Repair short to voltage in WHT/RED wire between Restart Relay and Condenser Fan Relay.
A25.	Remove Condenser Fan Relay from FUSE AND RELAY BOX.	CONDENSER FAN MOTOR stops operating.	Replace Condenser Fan Relay.
		CONDENSER FAN MOTOR continues to operate.	Repair short to voltage in BLU wire between FUSE AND RELAY BOX and CONDENSER FAN MOTOR.
A26.	Remove Radiator Fan Relay from FUSE AND RELAY BOX.	RADIATOR FAN MOTOR stops operating.	Replace Radiator Fan Relay.
		RADIATOR FAN MOTOR continues to operate.	Repair short to voltage in BLK/BLU wire between FUSE AND RELAY BOX and RADIATOR FAN MOTOR.

Fig. 146   System diagnosis chart (Part 4 of 4). 1991 Storm

Fig. 147 Coolant fan wiring circuit (Part 1 Of 2). 1992–93 Storm

Fig. 147 Coolant fan wiring circuit (Part 2 Of 2). 1992–93 Storm

COOLANT FANS	DIAGNOSTIC CHART A	
TEST	**RESULT**	**ACTION**
A1. Start and run engine until coolant temperature reaches 82°C (179°F).	RADIATOR FAN MOTOR and CONDENSER FAN MOTOR operate.	GO TO **A2.**
	Neither fan operates.	GO TO **A4.**
	RADIATOR FAN MOTOR only operates.	GO TO **A7.**
	CONDENSER FAN MOTOR only operates.	GO TO **A13.**
A2. Shut off engine. Disconnect RADIATOR FAN THERMO SWITCH connector. Start engine. Operate air conditioning for five minutes.	RADIATOR FAN MOTOR and CONDENSER FAN MOTOR both operate at least once during the five minute test.	GO TO **A3.**
	Neither fan operates at all during the five minute test.	GO TO **A17.**
A3. Turn ignition switch to "OFF."	Both fans stop operating.	All systems diagnosed are functioning normally.
	Both fans continue to operate.	GO TO **A24.**
	CONDENSER FAN MOTOR continues to operate.	GO TO **A25.**
	RADIATOR FAN MOTOR continues to operate.	GO TO **A26.**
A4. Connect a fused jumper from RADIATOR COOLING FAN CHECK CONNECTOR to chassis ground.	Both fans operate.	GO TO **A5.**
	Neither fan operates.	GO TO **A19.**
A5. Shut off engine. Disconnect RADIATOR FAN THERMO SWITCH connector. Connect a fused jumper between terminals 1 and 2. Start engine.	Both fans operate.	Replace RADIATOR FAN THERMO SWITCH.
	Neither fan operates.	GO TO **A6.**
A6. Shut off engine. Remove jumper from RADIATOR FAN THERMO SWITCH. Connect a digital multimeter from connector terminal 2 to chassis ground. Measure resistance.	More than 0.4 ohms.	Repair BLK ground wire between RADIATOR FAN THERMO SWITCH and G102.
	Less than 0.4 ohms.	Repair open in WHT wire between RADIATOR FAN THERMO SWITCH and S138.

Fig. 148 System diagnosis chart (Part 1 of 4). 1992–93 Storm

COOLANT FANS	DIAGNOSTIC CHART A (CONT'D)	
TEST	**RESULT**	**ACTION**
A7. Shut off engine. Remove Condenser Fan Relay and Radiator Fan Relay from FUSE AND RELAY BOX. Connect a digital multimeter from Condenser Fan Relay connector cavity 3 to chassis ground. Measure resistance.	More than 2.0 ohms.	Repair open in WHT wire between Radiator Fan Relay and Condenser Fan Relay.
	Less than 2.0 ohms.	Reinstall Radiator Fan Relay and GO TO **A8.**
A8. Connect a test lamp from Condenser Fan Relay connector cavity 1 to chassis ground. Start engine.	Test lamp does not light.	Repair open in WHT/RED wire between Condenser Fan Relay and Radiator Fan Relay.
	Test lamp lights.	GO TO **A9.**
A9. Connect a test lamp from Condenser Fan Relay connector cavity 2 to chassis ground.	Test lamp does not light.	Repair open in BLU/ORN wire between Fuse E-4 and Condenser Fan Relay.
	Test lamp lights.	GO TO **A10.**
A10. Shut off engine. Disconnect CONDENSER FAN MOTOR connector. Connect a digital multimeter from Condenser Fan Relay connector cavity 4 to CONDENSER FAN MOTOR connector cavity 1. Measure resistance.	Less than 2.0 ohms.	Reconnect CONDENSER FAN MOTOR connector and GO TO **A11.**
	More than 2.0 ohms.	Repair open in BLU wire between CONDENSER FAN MOTOR and FUSE AND RELAY BOX.
A11. Reinstall Condenser Fan Relay. Backprobe CONDENSER FAN MOTOR with a test lamp from connector cavity 1 to chassis ground.	Test lamp does not light.	Replace Condenser Fan Relay.
	Test lamp lights.	GO TO **A12.**
A12. Disconnect CONDENSER FAN MOTOR connector. Connect a digital multimeter from cavity 2 to chassis ground. Measure resistance.	Less than 3.0 ohms.	Replace CONDENSER FAN MOTOR.
	More than 3.0 ohms.	Repair BLK ground wire between CONDENSER FAN MOTOR and G103.
A13. Shut off engine. Remove Radiator Fan Relay from FUSE AND RELAY BOX. Connect a test lamp from connector cavity 2 to chassis ground. Start engine.	Test lamp does not light.	Repair open in BLK/GRN wire between FL-4 and Radiator Fan Relay.
	Test lamp lights.	GO TO **A14.**
A14. Shut off engine. Disconnect RADIATOR FAN MOTOR connector. Remove Radiator Fan Relay from FUSE AND RELAY BOX. Connect a digital multimeter from connector cavity 4 to RADIATOR FAN MOTOR connector cavity 1. Measure resistance.	Less than 3.0 ohms.	Reconnect RADIATOR FAN MOTOR connector. GO TO **A15.**
	More than 3.0 ohms.	Repair open in BLK/BLU wire between RADIATOR FAN MOTOR and FUSE AND RELAY BOX.

Fig. 148 System diagnosis chart (Part 2 of 4). 1992–93 Storm

COOLANT FANS	DIAGNOSTIC CHART A (CONT'D)	
TEST	**RESULT**	**ACTION**
A15. Reinstall Radiator Fan Relay. Backprobe RADIATOR FAN MOTOR connector cavity 1 with a test lamp to chassis ground. Start engine.	Test lamp does not light.	Replace Radiator Fan Relay.
	Test lamp lights.	GO TO **A16.**
A16. Shut off engine. Disconnect RADIATOR FAN MOTOR connector. Connect a digital multimeter from connector terminal 2 to chassis ground. Measure resistance.	Less than 3.0 ohms.	Replace RADIATOR FAN MOTOR.
	More than 3.0 ohms.	Repair BLK ground wire between RADIATOR FAN MOTOR and G102.
A17. Shut off engine. Disconnect TRIPLE SWITCH connector and remove Condenser Fan Relay from FUSE AND RELAY BOX. Connect a digital multimeter from TRIPLE SWITCH connector cavity 1 to Condenser Fan Relay connector cavity 3. Measure resistance.	More than 2.0 ohms.	Repair open in WHT wire between S138 and TRIPLE SWITCH.
	Less than 2.0 ohms.	GO TO **A18.**
A18. Connect a digital multimeter from TRIPLE SWITCH connector terminal 3 to chassis ground. Measure resistance.	More than 2.0 ohms.	Repair BLK ground wire between TRIPLE SWITCH and G103.
	Less than 2.0 ohms.	Check for poor connection at TRIPLE SWITCH. If OK, replace TRIPLE SWITCH. IMPORTANT: Receiver/Dryer Assembly must be replaced as a unit in order to replace TRIPLE SWITCH.
A19. Shut off engine. Remove Condenser Fan Relay and Radiator Fan Relay from FUSE AND RELAY BOX. Connect a digital multimeter from Radiator Fan Relay connector cavity 3 to RADIATOR FAN THERMO SWITCH connector terminal 1. Measure resistance.	More than 2.0 ohms.	Repair open in WHT wire between FUSE AND RELAY BOX and S138.
	Less than 2.0 ohms.	GO TO **A20.**
A20. Backprobe GENERATOR connector with a test lamp from cavity 1 to chassis ground.	Test lamp does not light.	A fault exists within the GENERATOR or related circuitry. Refer to Starter and Charging System Diagnosis
	Test lamp lights.	GO TO **A21.**
A21. Shut off engine. Remove Restart Relay from FUSE AND RELAY BOX. Connect a test lamp from connector cavity 4 to chassis ground. Start engine.	Test lamp does not light.	Repair open in WHT/BLU wire between GENERATOR and FUSE AND RELAY BOX.
	Test lamp lights.	GO TO **A22.**

Fig. 148   System diagnosis chart (Part 3 of 4). 1992–93 Storm

COOLANT FANS	DIAGNOSTIC CHART A (CONT'D)	
TEST	**RESULT**	**ACTION**
A22. Shut off engine. Remove Heater and A/C Relay from FUSE AND RELAY BOX. Connect a digital multimeter from connector cavity 1 to Restart Relay connector cavity 5. Measure resistance.	Less than 2.0 ohms.	Reinstall Restart Relay. GO TO **A23.**
	More than 2.0 ohms.	Repair open in WHT/RED wire between Restart Relay and Heater and A/C Relay.
A23. Connect a test lamp from Heater and A/C Relay connector cavity 1 to chassis ground. Start engine.	Test lamp does not light.	Replace Restart Relay.
	Test lamp lights.	Repair open in WHT/RED wire between Heater and A/C Relay and Radiator Fan Relay.
A24. Remove Restart Relay from FUSE AND RELAY BOX.	Fans stop operating.	Repair short to voltage in WHT/BLU wire between GENERATOR and FUSE AND RELAY BOX.
	Fans continue to operate.	Repair short to voltage in WHT/RED wire between Restart Relay and Condenser Fan Relay.
A25. Remove Condenser Fan Relay from FUSE AND RELAY BOX.	CONDENSER FAN MOTOR stops operating.	Replace Condenser Fan Relay.
	CONDENSER FAN MOTOR continues to operate.	Repair short to voltage in BLU wire between FUSE AND RELAY BOX and CONDENSER FAN MOTOR.
A26. Remove Radiator Fan Relay from FUSE AND RELAY BOX.	RADIATOR FAN MOTOR stops operating.	Replace Radiator Fan Relay.
	RADIATOR FAN MOTOR continues to operate.	Repair short to voltage in BLK/BLU wire between FUSE AND RELAY BOX and RADIATOR FAN MOTOR.

Fig. 148   System diagnosis chart (Part 4 of 4). 1992–93 Storm

TROUBLESHOOTING

1991

1. Check fuse C-21 and E-4 using a fuse tester.
2. Check fusible link FL-4 using a fuse tester.
3. Be sure that grounds G102 and G103 are clean and tight.
4. Check that A/C system is properly charged.

1992—93

1. Check fuse C-21, C11 and E-4 using a fuse tester.

2. Be sure that grounds G102 and G103 are clean and tight.
3. Check that A/C system is properly charged.

DIAGNOSIS

1991

Refer to **Figs. 145 and 146** to perform diagnostic procedures on this system.

1992—93

Refer to **Figs. 147 and 148** to perform diagnostic procedures on this system.

COOLANT FAN, REPLACE

1. Disconnect battery ground cable.
2. Drain coolant from radiator.
3. Remove upper radiator hose.
4. Disconnect electrical connections from coolant fan motor.
5. Disconnect cable form thermo switch.
6. Remove coolant fan assembly from vehicle.
7. Reverse procedure to install.

GENERAL TESTING

Gauge failures are often caused by defective wiring or grounds. The first step in locating a trouble should be a thorough inspection of all wiring, terminals and printed circuits. If wiring is secured by clamps, check to see whether the insulation has been severed thereby grounding the wire. In the case of a fuel gauge installation, rust may cause failure by corrosion at the ground connection of the tank unit.

GAUGES

VARIABLE VOLTAGE GAUGES

The variable voltage type dash gauge consists of two magnetic coils to which battery voltage is applied. The coils act on the gauge pointer and pull in opposite directions. One coil is grounded directly to the chassis, while the other coil is grounded through a variable resistor within the sending unit. Resistance through the sending unit determines current flow through its coil, and therefore pointer position.

When resistance is high in the sending unit, less current is allowed to flow through its coil, causing the gauge pointer to move toward the directly grounded coil. When resistance in the sending unit decreases, more current is allowed to pass through its coil, increasing the magnetic field. The gauge pointer is then attracted toward the coil which is grounded through the sending unit.

A special tester is required to diagnose this type gauge. Follow manufacturers instructions included with the tester.

VOLTMETER

The voltmeter is a gauge which measures the electrical flow from the battery to indicate whether the battery output is within tolerances. The voltmeter reading can range from 13.5-14.0 volts under normal operating conditions. If an undercharge or overcharge condition is indicated for an extended period, the battery and charging system should be checked.

TROUBLESHOOTING

To check voltmeter, turn key and headlights on with engine off. Pointer should move to 12.5 volts. If no needle movement is observed, check connections from battery to circuit breaker. If connections are tight and meter shows no movement, check wire continuity. If wire continuity is satisfactory, the meter is inoperative and must be replaced.

ELECTRICAL TEMPERATURE GAUGES

This temperature indicating system consists of a sending unit, located on the cylinder head, electrical temperature gauge and an instrument voltage regulator. As engine temperature increases or decreases, the resistance of the sending unit changes, in turn controlling current flow through the gauge. When engine temperature is low sending unit resistance is high, current flow through the gauge is restricted, and the gauge pointer remains against the stop or moves very little. As engine temperature increases sending unit resistance decreases and current flow through the gauge increases, resulting in increased pointer movement.

TROUBLESHOOTING

Troubleshooting for the electrical temperature indicating system is the same as for the electrical oil pressure indicating system.

ELECTRICAL OIL PRESSURE GAUGES

This oil pressure indicating system incorporates an instrument voltage regulator, electrical oil pressure gauge and a sending unit which are connected in series. The sending unit consists of a diaphragm, contact and a variable resistor. As oil pressure increases or decreases, the diaphragm actuated the contact on the variable resistor, in turn controlling current flow through the gauge. When oil pressure is low, the resistance of the variable resistor is high, restricting current flow to the gauge, in turn indicating low oil pressure. As oil pressure increases, the resistance of the variable resistor is lowered, permitting an increased current flow to the gauge, resulting in an increased gauge reading.

TROUBLESHOOTING

Disconnect the oil pressure gauge lead from the sending unit, connect a 12 volt test lamp between the gauge lead and the ground and turn ignition on. If test lamp flashes, the instrument voltage regulator is functioning properly and the gauge circuit is not broken. If the test lamp remains lit, the instrument voltage regulator is defective and must be replaced. If the test lamp does not light, check the instrument voltage regulator for proper ground or an open circuit. Also, check for an open in the instrument voltage regulator to oil pressure gauge wire or in the gauge itself. **If test lamp flashes and gauge is not accurate, the gauge may be out of calibration, requiring replacement.**

FUEL GAUGES

The fuel gauge system consists of a sending unit, instrument voltage regulator and an electric fuel gauge. The sending unit is a variable resistor that is controlled by a float. Corresponding to actual fuel level, the float will rise or fall. When the ignition is turned to the On position, voltage is applied to the gauge through the voltage regulator, completing the gauge ground circuit through the sending unit.

When the tank is full and the float is raised, maximum resistance (approximately 90 ohms) is produced by the sending unit, current flow through the gauge is decreased, and the gauge pointer moves slightly. As the tank empties and the float drops resistance in the sending unit decreases, current flow through the gauge increases and the gauge pointer moves toward empty.

Most analog fuel gauges are of the free floating type, which means that the gauge pointer does not remain against the full stop when the ignition is off. Rather, the pointer floats to a mid-position when no voltage is applied to the gauge.

TROUBLESHOOTING
Gauge Reads Empty When Tank Is Full

This condition is generally caused by a short in the fuel tank unit circuit.
1. Disconnect electrical connector to sending unit, then turn ignition switch to ON position.
2. If gauge reads past full, test gauge

with tester BT-6508 or equivalent. If gauge reads empty, disconnect main body harness connector, near the fuse block.

3. If gauge still shows empty, check for short in printed circuit or defective gauge. If gauge reads beyond full, reconnect front body harness connector and disconnect rear body harness connector (in left wheel house).

4. If gauge shows empty, locate and repair grounded wire in harness between front and rear body harness connectors. If gauge reads beyond full, check for short between rear body harness connector, damaged float or defective sending unit.

Gauge Reads Full Or Beyond At All Times

This condition is generally caused by an open in the tank unit circuit.
1. Check tank unit ground for proper contact with body or chassis and repair as needed.
2. If tank unit ground is satisfactory, disconnect electrical connector to tank unit and connect harness side of connector to suitable ground with jumper wire, then turn on ignition.
3. If gauge reads empty, remove fuel tank and inspect wiring to sending unit. If wiring and connections are satisfactory, replace tank unit.
4. If gauge still shows full, disconnect front body harness connector and ground fuel gauge wire terminal in instrument panel side of connector.
5. If gauge still reads full, check for loose connection in cluster, open (crack) in printed circuit or defective gauge. If gauge reads empty, locate and repair open or poor connection between front body connector and tank unit connector.

Fuel Gauge Inaccurate

Tester BT-6508 or equivalent must be used to diagnose dash gauge malfunction.
1. Ensure battery is fully charged, disconnect electrical connector to tank unit and connect tester to between harness connector and suitable ground following manufacturer's instructions.
2. Set tester on empty then turn on ignition. Gauge should read empty or below.
3. Set tester on full. Gauge should read full or above.
4. If gauge does not respond to tester input, replace dash gauge. If gauge responds correctly, check for poor connections at tank unit, poor tank unit ground or defective tank unit.

FUEL USAGE GAUGE
BUICK & CADILLAC
Operation

This system consists of green and amber indicator lights located on the fuel gauge or telltale lamp cluster, a switch mounted on the instrument panel behind the gauges and an interconnecting vacuum hose and tee. The system operates on engine vacuum through a dual contact vacuum sensing switch. When the accelerator is operated slowly and smoothly, engine vacuum remains high and the switch passes current to the green indicator light which indicates economical fuel consumption. When the accelerator pedal is depressed rapidly, vacuum decreases and the switch passes current to the amber indicator light, which indicates high fuel consumption. The amber indicator light will glow when the ignition switch is in the On position with the engine stopped.

Functional Test

1. With ignition switch in the on position, ground each terminal at the economy switch. Both green and amber indicator lights should glow. If not check for burned out bulbs.
2. With ignition switch in On position, amber indicator light should glow. If not, check for loose or disconnected wires at fuel economy switch or for poor ground. If amber indicator light still does not glow replace switch.
3. Start engine and allow to idle, the green indicator light should glow. If not, check for leaking, plugged or kinked vacuum hose between vacuum source and fuel economy switch. Check for loose or disconnected wires at economy switch or poor ground. If green indicator lamp still does not glow, replace switch.

WARNING LAMPS
ALTERNATOR INDICATOR LAMP
DELCOTRON CHARGING SYSTEM

The CS generator uses a new type of regulator which has a built in fault detection. The CS generator does not have a diode trio or test hole. This generator uses only two connections, battery positive and an "L" terminal to the charge indicator bulb. Use of "P," "F" and "S" terminals is optional. The "P" terminal is connected to the stator and may be connected to a tachometer or other device. The "F" terminal is connected internally to field positive and is used in service diagnostics. The "S" terminal may be connected externally to a voltage source, such as battery voltage.

Troubleshooting

If charge indicator light works abnormally, perform the following test procedure:
1. Visually check belt and wiring.
2. With engine control switch ON and engine stopped, charge indicator lamp should be on. If lamp is not on, detach wiring harness at generator and ground "L" terminal. If lamp lights, generator is faulty. If lamp does not light, locate open circuit between grounding lead and ignition switch and check for a faulty bulb.
3. With engine control switch ON and engine running at a moderate speed, charge indicator lamp should be off. If lamp is not off, detach wiring harness at generator. If lamp goes off, generator is faulty. If lamp stays on, check for grounded "L" terminal in wire harness.

OIL PRESSURE INDICATOR LAMP

Many cars utilize a warning light on the instrument panel in place of the conventional dash indicating gauge to warn the driver when the oil pressure is dangerously low. The warning light is wired in series with the ignition switch and the engine unit, which is an oil pressure switch.

The oil pressure switch contains a diaphragm and a set of contacts. When the ignition switch is turned on, the warning light circuit is energized and the circuit is completed through the closed contacts in the pressure switch. When the engine is started, build-up of oil pressure compresses the diaphragm, opening the contacts, thereby breaking the circuit and putting out the light.

TROUBLESHOOTING

On some models, the oil pressure indicator light also serves as the electric choke defect indicator. If Oil or engine indicator light does not light, check to ensure electric choke is not disconnected at carburetor. Also check for defect in electric choke heater, blown gauge fuse or defect in lamp or wiring circuit. If indicator light stays on with engine running possible causes are: oil pressure is low, switch to indicator light wiring has an open circuit, oil pressure switch wire connector has disconnected or on some models, gauge or radio fuse has blown.

The oil pressure warning light should go on when the ignition is turned on. If it does not light, disconnect the wire from the engine unit and ground the wire to the frame or cylinder block. Then if the warning light still does not go on with the ignition switch on, replace the bulb.

If the warning light goes on when the wire is grounded to the frame or cylinder block, the engine unit should be checked for being loose or poorly grounded. If the unit is found to be tight and properly grounded, it should be removed and a new one installed. The presence of sealing compound on the threads of the engine unit will cause a poor ground.

If the warning light remains lit when it normally should be out, replace the engine unit before proceeding to determine the cause for a low pressure indication.

The warning light sometimes will light up or will flicker when the engine is idling, even though the oil pressure is adequate. However, the light should go out when the engine speed is increased. There is no cause for alarm in such cases; it simply means that the pressure switch is not calibrated precisely correct.

TEMPERATURE INDICATOR LAMP
TROUBLESHOOTING

If the red light is not lit when the engine is being cranked, check for a burned out bulb, an open in the light circuit, or a defective ignition switch.

If the red light is lit when the engine is running, check the wiring between light and switch for a ground, temperature switch defective, or overheated cooling system. **As a test circuit to check whether the red bulb is functioning properly, a wire which is connected to the ground terminal of the ignition switch is tapped into its circuit. When the ignition is in the start engine cranking position, the ground terminal is grounded inside the switch and the red bulb will be lit. When the engine is started and the ignition switch is in the on position, the test circuit is opened and the bulb is then controlled by the temperature switch.**

SPEEDOMETERS

The following information covers only that service on speedometers which can be performed by the average service man. Repairs on the units themselves are not included as they require special equipment and extreme care when making repairs and adjustments and only an experienced speedometer mechanic should attempt such servicing.

The speedometer has two main parts: the indicator head and the speedometer drive cable. When the speedometer fails to indicate speed or mileage, the cable or housing is probably broken.

SPEEDOMETER CABLE

Most cables are broken due to lack of lubrication or a sharp bend or kink in the housing.

Cable can break because the speedometer head mechanism binds. If such is the case, the speedometer head should be repaired or replaced before a new cable or housing is installed.

A jumpy pointer condition, together with a sort of scraping noise, is due, in most instances, to a dry or kinked speedometer cable. The kinked cable rubs on the housing and winds up, slowing down the pointer. The cable then unwinds and the pointer jumps.

To check for kinks, remove the cable, lay it on a flat surface and twist one end with the fingers. If it turns over smoothly the cable is not kinked. But if part of the cable flops over as it is twisted, the cable is kinked and should be replaced.

Lubrication

The speedometer cable should be lubricated with special cable lubricant every 10,000 miles.

Fill the ferrule on the upper end of the housing with the cable lubricant. Insert the cable in the housing, starting at the upper end. Turn the cable around carefully while feeding it into the housing. Repeat filling the ferrule except for the last six inches of cable. Too much lubricant at this point may cause the lubricant to work into the indicating hand.

Installation

During installation, if the cable sticks when inserted in the housing and will not go through, the housing is damaged inside or kinked. Be sure to check the housing from one end to the other. Straighten any sharp bends by relocating clamps or elbows. Replace housing if it is badly kinked or broken. Position the cable and housing so that they lead into the head as straight as possible.

Check the new cable for kinks before installing it. Use wide, sweeping, gradual curves when the cable comes out of the transmission and connects to the head so the cable will not be damaged during its installation.

If inspection indicates that the cable and housing are in good condition, yet pointer action is erratic, check the speedometer head for possible binding.

The speedometer drive pinion should also be checked. If the pinion is dry or its teeth are stripped, the speedometer may not register properly.

The transmission mainshaft nut must be tight or the speedometer drive gear may slip on the mainshaft and cause slow speed readings.

WARNING SYSTEMS

FIBER OPTIC MONITORING SYSTEM

Fiber optics are non-electric light conductors made up of coated strands which, when exposed to a light source at one end, will reflect the light through their entire length, thereby illuminating a monitoring lens on the instrument panel or fender without the use of a bulb when the exterior lights are turned on.

LOW FUEL WARNING SYSTEM

The switch type consists of an indicator light and a low fuel warning switch located on the instrument panel.

The warning switch contacts are closed by the difference in voltage potential between the fuel gauge terminals. This voltage differential will activate the warning switch when the fuel tank is less than 1/4 full and, in turn, cause the indicator to light.

TROUBLESHOOTING

This system incorporates an indicator light. With ignition switch turned to on, the indicator should light. If not, check bulb and all electrical connections. Replace warning switch if bulb and connections prove satisfactory.

LOW WASHER FLUID INDICATOR

There are two types of low washer fluid indicating systems. They are the mechanical type and electrically controlled type. The mechanical type consists of a float and rod assembly, sending unit and a fiber optic. The electrically controlled type consists of a float, magnet, contact points and a resistor.

On the mechanical type, the upper end of the rod extends into the sending unit and has colored red and green portions. When the windshield wipers are activated, a lamp bulb in the sending unit lights either the red or green sections of the rod. The colored light is then picked up by the fiber optic and is transmitted through it to the telltale lens. The lens will show red or green depending upon washer fluid level.

The electrically controlled indicator is activated when the windshield wipers are engaged. A slight amount of current flows from the wiper motor to the washer bottle float unit. This current will either pass through the contact points or the resistor which is in parallel with the points. When the washer fluid level is high, the magnet holds the contact points open. The current will now flow through the resistor where it is reduced so the indicator will not light. When the washer fluid level is low, the float drops and the magnet will separate from the cap assembly allowing the current to pass through the contact points and activate the indicator light.

TROUBLESHOOTING

On the mechanical indicating system, if the telltale lens fails to glow when the windshield wipers are activated, check lamp bulb in sending unit and see that fiber optic is not broken.

On the electrically controlled system, the first item to check is the indicator bulb. With the windshield wipers On, connect a jumper wire between the two terminals on the washer bottle cap. The indicator should then light. If not, replace bulb. If the bulb is found to be satisfactory, remove cap and float assembly from washer bottle. Float should be able to move to the bottom of the stem and the magnet should separate from the cap. If not, replace float and cap assembly.

LOW COOLANT LEVEL INDICATOR

Some vehicles use a buzzer or indicator lamp to indicate a low coolant level condition. The buzzer or lamp is activated by a sensor, located in the radiator, when the coolant level becomes one quart or more low.

UPSHIFT INDICATOR

DESCRIPTION

This lamp is used on most models equipped with manual transmission. The Upshift lamp is illuminated to inform the driver of ideal shift points, with improved fuel economy as the specific objective. When the light is illuminated, the transmission should be shifted to the next highest gear, if driving conditions permit such an action.

TROUBLESHOOTING

If Upshift indicator is not working properly, perform the following test. It is necessary to refer to wiring diagrams located in MOTOR's "Vacuum & Wiring Diagram

Manual" for the specific year and model being serviced.

1. Disconnect ECM connector C1.
2. Place ignition switch in run.
3. Measure voltage at terminal A2 of ECM connector.
4. If battery voltage is present, further ECM diagnosis is necessary.
5. If battery voltage is not present, repair open circuit in brown/black wire, circuit 456.

DRIVER REMINDER PACKAGE

CUTLASS, TORONADO, 88 & 98

The driver reminder package incorporates several warning and reminder features into one system. The system uses

If engine coolant level is three quarts or more low, a red LOW COOLANT warning light will illuminate and a fast pulsed tone will be heard. The light will remain lit and the tone will be heard until coolant is added to the cooling system. The light will also illuminate during engine starting as a bulb check.

When the headlight switch is in the On position and the ignition is off, a red LIGHTS ON warning light will illuminate and a fast-pulsed tone will be heard. Turning the headlight switch to the right will dim the instrument panel lights and shutoff the tone.

When there is less than approximately three gallons of fuel in the tank, an amber LOW FUEL warning light will illuminate and a steady five second tone will be heard, however the lamp may not light until

fuel level is diminished to as low as a 1/2 gallon. The light will remain lit until fuel is added to the tank. This warning light will also illuminate during engine starting as a bulb check.

The amber LOW WASH FLUID reminder light will illuminate while the windshield wipers are operated if the washer fluid reservoir is less than approximately 1/3 full. This light will remain lit during wiper operation until fluid is added.

Additional tones used to warn operator of potential problems are: engine overheating, fast pulsed tone; malfunction in the charging system; fast-pulsed tone; seat belt reminder, slow pulsed tone; key reminder, steady tone.

three distinct sounds, and warning and reminder lights on the center instrument cluster.

STARTER MOTORS

TABLE OF CONTENTS

Starter Motor Applications

Year	Engine	VIN①	Ident. No.	Model
Buick Roadmaster, Cadillac Brougham/Fleetwood RWD, Chevrolet Caprice & Oldsmobile Custom Cruiser				
1991	5.0L/V8-305	E	10455012	Delco Remy
	5.7L/V8-350	7	1998579	Delco Remy
1992	5.0L/V8-305	E	10455012	Delco Remy
	5.7L/V8-350	7	10455301	Delco Remy
1993	4.3L/V6-262	Z	10455012	Delco Remy
	5.0L/V8-305	E	10455012	Delco Remy
	5.7L/V8-350	7	10455301	Delco Remy
Chevrolet Camaro & Pontiac Firebird				
1991	3.1L/V6-191	T	10455011	Delco Remy
	5.0L/V8-305	E & F④	1998548	Delco Remy
	5.0L/V8-305	E⑤	1998591	Delco Remy
	5.0L/V8-305	F⑤	1998580	Delco Remy
	5.7L/V8-350	8	1998591	Delco Remy
1992	3.1L/V6-191	T	10455011	Delco Remy
	5.0L/V8-305	E	10455012	Delco Remy
	5.0L/V8-305	F	10455011	Delco Remy
	5.7L/V8-350	8	10455300	Delco Remy
1993	3.4L/V6-204	S	10455054	Delco Remy
	5.7L/V8-350	P	10465143	Delco Remy
Chevrolet Corvette				
1991	5.7L/V8-350	8	10455702	Delco Remy
	5.7L/V8-350	J	10455704	Nippondenso

Continued

Year	Engine	VIN ①	Ident. No.	Model
Chevrolet Corvette-Continued				
1992-93	5.7L/V8-350	P	10455703	Delco Remy
	5.7L/V8-350	J	10455704	Nippondenso
Buick Century, Oldsmobile Cutlass Ciera & Cutlass Cruiser & Pontiac 6000				
1991	2.5L/4-151	R	⑧	Delco Remy
	3.1L/V6-189	T	10455019	Delco Remy
	3.3L/V6-204	N	10455006	Delco Remy
1992	2.5L/4-151	R	10455017	Delco Remy
	3.3L/V6-204	N	10455024	Delco Remy
1993	2.2L/4-134	4	10455055	Delco Remy
	3.3L/V6-204	N	10455024	Delco Remy
Buick Electra, LeSabre & Park Ave., Cadillac DeVille & Fleetwood FWD, Oldsmobile 88, 98 & Pontiac Bonneville				
1991	3800/V6-231	C	10455024	Delco Remy
	3800/V6-231	L	10455024	Delco Remy
	3800/V6-231	L	10455706	Delco Remy
	4.5L/V8-273	8	10455045	Delco Remy
	4.9L/V8-300	B	10455045	Delco Remy
1992	3800/V6-231	L	10455024	Delco Remy
	3800/V6-231	1	10455706	Delco Remy
	4.9L/V8-300	B	10455046	Delco Remy
1993	3800/V6-231	L	10455024	Delco Remy
	3800/V6-231	1	10455706	Delco Remy
	4.9L/V8-300	B	10455046	Delco Remy
Buick Reatta & Riviera, Cadillac Eldorado & Seville, Oldsmobile Toronado/Trofeo				
1991	3.8L/V6-231	C	10455024	Delco Remy
	4.5L/V8-273	8	10455046	Delco Remy
	4.9L/V8-300	B	10455046	Delco Remy
1992-93	3.8L/V6-231	L	10455024	Delco Remy
	4.9L/V8-300	B	10455046	Delco Remy
Chevrolet Beretta & Corsica				
1991	2.2L/4-134	G	10455010	Delco Remy
	2.3L/4-138	A	10455049	Delco Remy
	3.1L/V6-192	T	10455025	Delco Remy
1992	2.2L/4-134	4	10455048	Delco Remy
	2.3L/4-138	A	10455049	Delco Remy
	3.1L/V6-192	T	10455048	Delco Remy
1993	2.2L/4-134	4	10455055	Delco Remy
	2.3L/4-138	A	10455049	Delco Remy
	3.1L/V6-192	T	10455053	Delco Remy
Chevrolet Cavalier & Pontiac Sunbird				
1991	2.0L/4-121	K⑦	10455021	Delco Remy
	2.2L/4-134	G⑥	10455010	Delco Remy
	3.1L/V6-192	T	10455025	Delco Remy
1992-93	2.0L/4-121	H⑦	10455021	Delco Remy
	2.2L/4-134	4⑥	10455048	Delco Remy
	3.1L/V6-192	T	10455048	Delco Remy

Year	Engine	VIN ①	Ident. No.	Model
Buick Skylark, Oldsmobile Achieva, Cutlass Calais & Pontiac Grand Am				
1991	2.3L/4-138	D	10455049	Delco Remy
	2.3L/4-138 H.O.	A	10455049	Delco Remy
	2.5L/4-151	U	10455022	Delco Remy
	3.3L/V6-204	N	10455024	Delco Remy
1992-93	2.3L/4-138	D	10455049	Delco Remy
	2.3L/4-138 H.O.	A	10455049	Delco Remy
	2.3L/4-138	3	10455049	Delco Remy
	3.3L/V6-204	N	10455024	Delco Remy
Buick Regal, Chevrolet Lumina, Oldsmobile Cutlass Supreme & Pontiac Grand Prix				
1991	2.5L/4-151	R	10455019	Delco Remy
	3.1L/V6-192	T	10455025	Delco Remy
	3.4L/V6-204	X	10455047	Delco Remy
	3800/V6-231	L	10455023	Delco Remy
1992	2.5L/4-151	R	10455026	Delco Remy
	3.1L/V6-192	T	10455048	Delco Remy
	3.4L/V6-204	X	10455047	Delco Remy
	3800/V6-231	L	10455023	Delco Remy
1993	2.2L/4-134	4	10455053	Delco Remy
	3.1L/V6-192	T	10455053	Delco Remy
	3.4L/V6-204	X	10455051	Delco Remy
	3800/V6-231	L	10455023	Delco Remy
Geo Prizm				
1991-92	1.6L/4-97	5	—	Nippondenso
	1.6L/4-97	6	—	Nippondenso
1993	1.6L/4-97	6	94854717	Nippondenso
	1.8L/4-107.5	8	94854717	Nippondenso
Geo Metro				
1991-93	1.0L/3-61 ⑤	6	96060305	Nippondenso
	1.0L/3-61 ④	6	96051950	Nippondenso
Geo Storm				
1991	1.6L/4-97 ②	6	128000-7120	Nippondenso
	1.6L/4-97 ③	5	128000-7000	Nippondenso
	1.6L/4-97 ④	5 & 6	128000-7400	Nippondenso
1992	1.6L/4-97 ④	6	128000-7400	Nippondenso
	1.6L/4-97 ⑤	6	128000-7120	Nippondenso
	1.8L/4-110 ④	8	128000-6990	Nippondenso
	1.8L/4-110 ⑤	8	128000-7002	Nippondenso
1993	1.6L/4-97	6	—	Nippondenso
	1.8L/4-110 ④	8	—	Nippondenso
Pontiac LeMans				
1991-92	1.6L/4-98	6	1998525	Delco Remy
1993	1.6L/4-98	6	10465022	Delco Remy

① —The eighth digit of VIN denotes engine code.
② —3 speed auto. trans.
③ —4 speed auto. trans.
④ —Man. trans.
⑤ —Auto. trans.
⑥ —Overhead valve engine.
⑦ —Overhead cam engine.
⑧ —Buick models, 10455004; Pontiac models, 10455017.

General Information

INDEX

STARTER TROUBLESHOOTING

SLOW OR NOT CRANKING

When trouble develops in the starter motor circuit, and the starter cranks the engine slowly or not at all, several preliminary checks can be made to determine whether the trouble lies in the battery, in the starter, in the wiring between them, or elsewhere. Many conditions besides defects in the starter itself can result in poor cranking performance.

To make a quick check of the starter system, turn on the headlights. They should burn with normal brilliance. If they do not, the battery may be run down.

If the battery is in a charged condition so that lights burn brightly, operate the starter motor. Any one of three things will happen to the lights: (1) They will go out, (2) dim considerably or (3) stay bright without any cranking action taking place.

If Lights Go Out

If the lights go out as the starter switch is closed, it indicates that there is a poor connection between the battery and starter motor. This poor connection will most often be found at the battery terminals. Correction is made by removing the cable clamps from the terminals, cleaning the terminals and clamps, replacing the clamps and tightening them securely. A coating of corrosion inhibitor (petroleum jelly will do) may be applied to the clamps and terminals to retard the formation of corrosion.

If Lights Dim

If the lights dim considerably as the starter switch is closed and the starter operates slowly or not at all, the battery may be run down, or there may be some mechanical condition in the engine or starter motor that is throwing a heavy burden on the starter motor. This imposes a high discharge rate on the battery which causes noticeable dimming of the lights.

Check the battery state of charge. If it is charged, the trouble probably lies in either the engine or starter motor itself. In the engine, tight bearings or pistons or heavy oil place an added burden on the starter motor. Low temperatures also hamper starter motor performance since it thickens engine oil and makes the engine considerably harder to crank and start. Also, a battery is less efficient at low temperatures.

In the starter motor, a bent armature, loose pole shoe screws or worn bearings, any of which may allow the armature to drag, will reduce cranking performance and increase current draw.

In addition, more serious internal damage is sometimes found. Thrown armature windings or commutator bars, which sometimes occur on over-running clutch drive starter motors, are usually caused by excessive overrunning after starter. This is the result of such conditions as the driver keeping the starter switch closed too long after the engine has started, the driver opening the throttle too wide in starting, or improper carburetor fast idle adjustment. Any of these subject the over-running clutch to extra strain so it tends to seize, spinning the armature at high speed with resulting armature damage.

Another cause may be engine backfire during cranking which may result, among other things, from ignition timing being too far advanced.

To avoid such failures, the driver should pause a few seconds after a false start to make sure the engine has come completely to rest before another start is attempted. In addition, the ignition timing should be checked if engine backfiring has caused the trouble.

Lights Stay Bright; No Cranking Action

This condition indicates an open circuit at some point, either in the starter itself, the starter switch or control circuit. The solenoid control circuit can be eliminated momentarily by placing a heavy jumper lead across the solenoid main terminals to see if the starter will operate. This connects the starter directly to the battery and, if it operates, it indicates that the control circuit is not functioning normally. The wiring and control units must be checked to locate the trouble.

If the starter does not operate with the jumper attached, it will probably have to be removed from the engine so it can be examined in detail.

STARTER DRIVE TROUBLES

Starter drive troubles are easy to diagnose and they usually cannot be confused with ordinary starter difficulties. If the starter does not turn over at all or if it drags, look for trouble in the starter or electrical supply system. Concentrate on the starter drive or ring gear if the starter is noisy, if it turns but does not engage the engine, or if the starter won't disengage after the engine is started. After the starter is removed, the trouble can usually be located quickly.

Worn or chipped ring gear or starter pinion are the usual causes of noisy operation. Before replacing either or both of these parts try to find out what caused the damage. With the Bendix type drive, incomplete engagement of the pinion with the ring gear is a common cause of tooth damage. The wrong pinion clearance on starter drives of the over-running clutch type leads to poor meshing of the pinion and ring gear and too rapid tooth wear.

A less common cause of noise with either type of drive is a bent starter armature shaft. When this shaft is bent, the pinion gear alternately binds and then only partly meshes with the ring gear. Most manufacturers specify a maximum of .003 inch radial runout on the armature shaft.

Drive Clutch Failure

The over-running clutch type drive seldom becomes so worn that it fails to engage since it is directly activated by a fork and lever. The only thing that is likely to happen is that, once engaged, it will not turn the engine because the clutch itself is worn out. A much more frequent difficulty and one that rapidly wears ring gear and teeth is partial engagement. Proper meshing of the pinion is controlled by the end clearance between the pinion gear and the starter housing or pinion stop, if used.

On some starters, the solenoids are completely enclosed in the starter housing and the pinion clearance is not adjustable. If the clearance is not correct, the starter must be disassembled and checked for excessive wear of solenoid linkage, shift lever mechanism, or improper assembly of parts.

Failure of the over-running clutch drive to disengage is usually caused by binding between the armature shaft and the drive. If the drive, particularly the clutch, shows signs of overheating it indicates that it is not disengaging immediately after the engine starts. If the clutch is forced to over-run too long, it overheats and turns a bluish color. For the cause of the binding, look for rust or gum between the armature shaft and the drive, or for burred splines. Excess oil on the drive will lead to gumming, and inadequate air circulation in the flywheel housing will cause rust.

Over-running clutch drives cannot be overhauled in the field so they must be replaced. In cleaning, never soak them in a solvent because the solvent may enter the clutch and dissolve the sealed-in lubricant. Wipe them off lightly with kerosene and lubricate them sparingly with SAE 10 or 10W oil.

Bendix Drive Failure

When a Bendix type drive doesn't engage the cause usually is one of three things: either the drive spring is broken, one of the drive spring bolts has sheared off, or the screw shaft threads won't allow the pinion to travel toward the flywheel. In the first two cases, remove the drive by unscrewing the setscrew under the last coil of the drive spring and replace the broken parts. Gummed or rusty screw shaft threads are fairly common causes of Bendix drive failure and are easily cleaned with a little kerosene or steel wool, depending on the trouble. Here again, as in the case of over-running clutch drives, use light oil sparingly, and be sure the flywheel housing has adequate ventilation. There is usually a breather hole in the bottom of the flywheel housing which should be open.

The failure of a Bendix drive to disengage or to mesh properly is most often caused by gummed or rusty screw shaft threads. When this is not true, look for mechanical failure within the drive itself.

CHECKING CIRCUIT WITH VOLTMETER

Excessive resistance in the circuit between the battery and starter will reduce cranking performance. The resistance can be checked by using a voltmeter to measure voltage drop in the circuits while the starter is operated. There are three checks to be made:

1. Voltage drop between car frame and grounded battery terminal post.
2. Voltage drop between car frame and starter motor field frame.
3. Voltage drop between insulated battery terminal post and starter motor terminal stud, or the battery terminal stud of the solenoid.

Each of these should show no more than one-tenth (0.1) volt drop when the starter motor is cranking the engine. Do not use the starter for more than 30 sec-

onds at a time to avoid overheating it.

If excessive voltage drop is found in any of these circuits, make correction by disconnecting the cables, cleaning the connections carefully, and then reconnecting the cables firmly in place. A coating of petroleum jelly on the battery cables and terminal clamps will retard corrosion.

On some cars, extra long battery cables may be required due to the location of the battery and starter. This may result in somewhat higher voltage drop than the above recommended 0.1 volt. The only means of determining the normal voltage drop in such cases is to check several of these vehicles. Then when the voltage drop is well above the normal figure for all cars checked, abnormal resistance will be indicated and correction can be made as already explained.

SOLENOID SWITCHES

The solenoid switch on a cranking motor not only closes the circuit between the battery and the cranking motor but also shifts the drive pinion into mesh with the engine flywheel ring gear. This is done by means of a linkage between the solenoid switch plunger and the shift lever on the cranking motor.

There are two windings in the solenoid; a pull-in winding and a hold-in winding. Both windings are energized when the external control switch is closed. They produce a magnetic field which pulls the plunger in so that the drive pinion is shifted into mesh, and the main contacts in the solenoid switch are closed to connect the battery directly to the cranking motor. Closing the main switch contacts shorts out the pull-in winding since this winding is

connected across the main contacts. The magnetism produced by the hold-in winding is sufficient to hold the plunger in, and shorting out the pull-in winding reduces drain on the battery. When the control switch is opened, it disconnects the hold-in winding from the battery. When the hold-in winding is disconnected from the battery, the shift lever spring withdraws the plunger from the solenoid, opening the solenoid switch contacts and at the same time withdrawing the drive pinion from mesh. Proper operation of the switch depends on maintaining a definite balance between the magnetic strength of the pull-in and hold-in windings.

This balance is established in the design by the size of the wire and the number of turns specified. An open circuit in the hold-in winding or attempts to crank with a discharged battery will cause the switch to chatter.

STARTER MOTOR SERVICE

To obtain full performance data on a starter motor or to determine the cause of abnormal operation, the starter motor should be submitted to a no-load and torque test. These tests are best performed on a starter bench tester with the starter mounted on it.

From a practical standpoint, however, a simple torque test may be made quickly with the starter in the car. Make sure the battery is fully charged and that the starter circuit wires and terminals are in good condition. Then operate the starter to see if the engine turns over normally. If it does not, the torque developed is below standard and the starter should be removed for further checking.

Delco-Remy Starters

INDEX

DESCRIPTION

The Delco-Remy starter, **Fig. 1,** has the solenoid shift lever mechanism and the solenoid plunger enclosed in the drive housing to protect them from exposure to road dirt, icing conditions and splash. They have an extruded field frame and an overrunning clutch type drive. The overrunning clutch is operated by a solenoid switch mounted to a flange on the drive housing.

The solenoid is attached to the drive end housing by two screws. The cover can be removed to inspect the contacts and contact disc, but the switch is serviced as assembly only.

Most motors of this type have graphite and oil impregnated bronze bearings

which ordinarily require no added lubrication except at time of overhaul when a few drops of light engine oil should be placed on each bearing before reassembly.

DIAGNOSIS & TESTING

When diagnosing Delco-Remy starters, refer to **Fig. 2.**

FREE SPEED TEST

With the circuit connected as shown in **Fig. 3,** use a tachometer to measure armature revolutions per minute. Failure of the motor to perform to specifications may be due to tight or dry bearings, or high resistance connections.

PINION CLEARANCE

There is no provision for adjusting pinion clearance on this type motor. When the shift lever mechanism is correctly assembled, the pinion clearance should fall within the limits of .010 to .140 inch. When the clearance is not within these limits, it may indicate excessive wear of the solenoid linkage or shift lever yoke buttons.

Pinion clearance should be checked after the motor has been disassembled and reassembled. To check, disconnect motor field coil connector from solenoid terminal and insulate end. Connect one battery lead to solenoid switch terminal and the other lead to the solenoid frame, **Fig. 4.** Using a jumper lead connected to the solenoid mo-

Fig. 1   Delco-Remy starter motor

Fig. 2   Delco-Remy starter motor diagnosis (Part 1 of 2)

Fig. 3 Starter free speed test connections

SLOW CRANKING, SOLENOID CLICKS OR CHATTERS

CHECK:
BATTERY FOR GREEN INDICATOR.
VISUAL CONDITION OF BATTERY CABLES AND CONNECTIONS.
IF BATTERY NEEDS CHARGING, MAKE GENERATOR AND BATTERY DRAIN CHECK, CHARGE BATTERY AND RECHECK CRANKING. IF TROUBLE HAS NOT BEEN FOUND, PROCEED.

REMOVE BATTERY LEAD FROM DISTRIBUTOR ON HEI. MAKE ALL VOLTMETER READINGS WITH KEY IN START POSITION.

MEASURE CRANKING VOLTAGE AT BATTERY TERMINAL POSTS.

9.6 VOLTS OR MORE — LESS THAN 9.6 VOLTS

MEASURE VOLTAGE FROM BATTERY NEGATIVE TERMINAL TO ENGINE BLOCK. (POS. LEAD ON BLOCK.)

CHECK BATTERY CONDITION AND CAPACITY

.5 VOLT OR MORE — LESS THAN .5 VOLT

OK — DEFECTIVE

REPAIR GROUND CABLE AND CONNECTIONS

MEASURE VOLTAGE AT SOLENOID "B" TERMINAL, CLEAN AND TIGHTEN CONNECTIONS AT STARTER.

REPAIR STARTER

REPLACE BATTERY

9 VOLTS OR MORE — LESS THAN 9 VOLTS

REPAIR STARTER

CLEAN AND TIGHTEN POSITIVE CABLE CONNECTIONS. IF OK, REPLACE CABLE.

NOTE: THIS PROCEDURE IS DESIGNED FOR USE ON ENGINES AND BATTERIES AT ROOM OR NORMAL OPERATING TEMPERATURES. IT ALSO ASSUMES THERE ARE NO ENGINE DEFECTS WHICH WOULD CAUSE CRANKING PROBLEMS. TO USE IT UNDER OTHER CONDITIONS MIGHT RESULT IN MISDIAGNOSIS.

Fig. 2 Delco-Remy starter motor diagnosis (Part 2 of 2)

Fig. 4 Starter pinion clearance test connections

Fig. 5 Checking pinion clearance

tor terminal, momentarily flash the lead to the solenoid frame. This will shift the pinion into the cranking position until the battery is disconnected.

After energizing the solenoid with the clutch shifted toward the pinion stop retainer, push the pinion back toward the commutator end as far as possible to take up any slack movement; then check the clearance with feeler gauge, **Fig. 5.**

Nippondenso Starter

INDEX

1 COVER	10 HOLD-IN COIL	19 BUSHING
2 BUSHING	11 PULL-IN COIL	20 BRUSH
3 DRIVE HOUSING ASSEMBLY	12 COMMUTATOR END HOUSING ASSEMBLY	21 FRAME AND FIELD ASSEMBLY
4 SNAP RING	13 BRUSH SPRING	
5 PINION STOP RING	14 BRUSH HOLDER ASSEMBLY	22 ARMATURE
6 OVERRUNNING CLUTCH ASSEMBLY	15 END CAP GASKET	23 HOUSING BOLT
7 SHIFT LEVER	16 ARMATURE BRAKE SPRING	
8 BOOT	17 ARMATURE PLATE	
9 STARTER SOLENOID	18 COMMUTATOR END CAP	

Fig. 1   Exploded view of starter motor. Conventional w/manual trans

DESCRIPTION

Nippondenso starters, **Figs. 1 and 2**, are either a conventional type or reduction gear types. The conventional type used on manual transmissions consists of a frame and field assembly, an armature assembly, an overruning clutch assembly, a starter solenoid assembly, a commutator end housing, a brush holder and a shift lever. The reduction gear type starters used on automatic transmissions which use all of the above components along with a reduction gear and shock absorber assembly.

When the ignition switch is turned to start and the clutch start/neutral safety switch is closed, the solenoid windings are energized, resulting in plunger and shift lever movement. This causes the pinion to engage the engine flywheel ring gear and the starter solenoid contacts to close. With the contacts closed, the starter solenoid provides a closed circuit between the battery positive terminal and the starter motor. The starter motor is grounded to the engine block, therefore the circuit is complete and engine cranking may occur.

Once the engine starts, the pinion is designed to overrun and protect the armature from excessive speeds until the ignition switch is released from the start position. When the ignition switch is released, a return spring in the solenoid assembly opens the starter solenoid contacts, breaking the circuit and disengaging the pinion.

DIAGNOSIS & TESTING

Refer to **Fig. 3** when troubleshooting these starter motors.

Fig. 3 Diagnosis chart (Part 1 of 6)

Fig. 2 Exploded view of starter motor. Reduction w/automatic trans

A APPLY GREASE
B DO NOT WASH OR LUBRICATE
    SPARE PARTS HAVE BEEN LUBRICATED
1 NEEDLE BEARING
2 SNAP RING
3 PINION STOP RING
4 PLANETARY CARRIER SHAFT
5 DRIVE HOUSING ASSEMBLY
6 OVERRUNNING CLUTCH ASSEMBLY
7 SHIFT LEVER
8 C-CLIP
9 WASHER
10 WASHER
11 INTERNAL GEAR
12 PLANETARY GEAR
13 BOOT
14 STARTER SOLENOID
15 O-RING
16 PLATE
17 ARMATURE
18 BRUSH SPRING
19 BRUSH
20 BRUSH HOLDER ASSEMBLY
21 BUSHING
22 COMMUTATOR END HOUSING ASSEMBLY
23 FRAME AND FIELD ASSEMBLY
24 CENTER BEARING AND SHOCK
    ABSORBER ASSEMBLY
25 WASHER
26 BUSHING
27 BUSHING
28 HOUSING BOLT
29 SCREW WITH O-RING

Fig. 3   Diagnosis chart (Part 2 of 6)

Fig. 3   Diagnosis chart (Part 3 of 6)

Fig. 3   Diagnosis chart (Part 4 of 6)

Fig. 3   Diagnosis chart (Part 6 of 6)

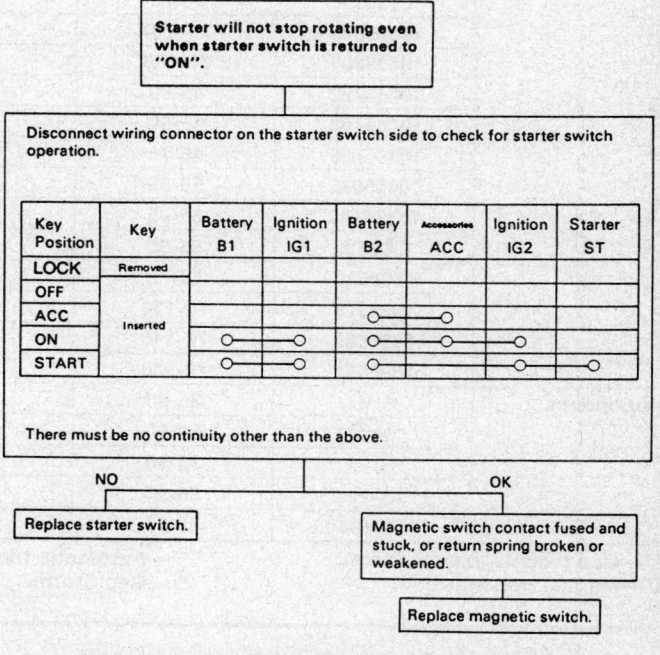

Fig. 3   Diagnosis chart (Part 5 of 6)

Starter Motor Specifications

Starter Make	Starter Ident. No	Free Speed Test			Solenoid	
		Amps	Volts	RPM	Hold-In Windings, amps	Pull-In Windings, amps
Delco-Remy	10455004	50-75	10	6000-11900	—	—
	10455006	45-74	10	6000-11900	13-19	23-30
	10455010	50-75	10	6000-11900	12-15	30-36
	10455011	50-75	10	6500-11000	—	—
	10455012	45-75	10	6500-11000	—	—
	10455017	50-75	10	6000-11900	—	—
	10455019	50-75	10	6000-11900	—	—
	10455021	55-85	10	6000-12000	—	—
	10455022	55-85	10	6000-12000	—	—
	10455023	45-75	10	8600-13000	—	—
	10455024	45-74	10	6000-11900	13-19	23-30
	10455025	50-75	10	6000-12000	—	—
	10455026	50-75	10	6000-11900	—	—
	10455045	50-62	10	8500-12700	13-19	64-76
	10455046	50-62	10	8500-12700	13-19	23-30
	10455047	50-75	10	7000-11000	—	—
	10455048	50-75	10	6000-11900	—	—
	10455049	52-76	10	6000-12000	—	—
	10455051	45-75	10	6000-11000	—	—
	10455053	45-75	10	6000-11000	—	—
	10455054	45-75	10	6000-11000	—	—
	10455055	50-75	10	6000-12000	—	—
	10455300	70-110	10	6500-10700	—	—
	10455301	70-100	10	6500-10700	10-20	60-80
	10455702	45-90	10	3300-5000	—	—
	10455703	45-90	10	2800-5000	—	—
	10455706	45-75	10	8600-12900	—	—
	10465022	55-85	10	6000-12000	—	—
	10465143	65-95	10	2750-3250	—	—
	1998525	55-85	10	6000-12000	13-19	23-30
	1998548	50-75	10	6000-11900	—	—
	1998579	70-110	10	6500-10700	—	—
	1998580	70-110	10	6500-10700	13-19	23-30
	1998591	70-110	10	6500-10700	13-19	23-30
Nippondenso	①②	35-50	11	1200-2380	—	—
	①③	60-90	11.5	3000-5950	—	—
	④②	35-90	11.5	1200-3000	—	—
	④③	60-90	11.5	3000-5950	—	—
	10455704⑤	45-90	10	3500-5000	—	—

① —Geo models except Storm.   ③ —Automatic transmission.   ⑤ —Corvette ZR-1.
② —Manual transmission.   ④ —Geo Storm.

ALTERNATOR SYSTEMS

TABLE OF CONTENTS

General Information

INDEX

INTRODUCTION

Alternators are composed of the same functional parts as the conventional D.C. generator but they operate differently. The field is called a rotor and is the turning portion of the unit. The generating part, called a stator, is the stationary member, comparable to the armature in a D.C. generator. The regulator, similar to those used in a D.C. system, regulates the output of the alternator-rectifier system.

The power source of the system is the alternator. Current is transmitted from the field terminal of the regulator through a slip ring to the field coil and back to ground through another slip ring. The strength of the field regulates the output of the alternating current. This alternating current is then transmitted from the alternator to the rectifier where it is converted to direct current.

These alternators employ a three-phase stator winding in which the phase windings are electrically 120° apart. The rotor consists of a field coil encased between interleaved sections producing. When the rotor is energized, a magnetic field with alternate north and south poles is created. By rotating the rotor inside the stator the alternating current is induced in the stator windings. This alternating current is rectified (changed to D.C.) by silicon diodes and brought out to the output terminal of the alternator.

DIODE RECTIFIERS

Six silicon diode rectifiers are used and act as electrical one-way valves. Three of the diodes have ground polarity and are pressed or screwed into a heat sink which is grounded. The other three diodes (ungrounded) are pressed or screwed into and insulated from the end head; these diodes are connected to the alternator output terminal.

Since the diodes have a high resistance to the flow of current in one direction and a low resistance in the opposite direction, they may be connected in a manner which allows current to flow from the alternator to the battery in the low resistance direction. The high resistance in the opposite direction prevents the flow of current from the battery to the alternator. Because of this feature no circuit breaker is required between the alternator and battery.

SERVICE PRECAUTIONS

1. Be certain that battery polarity is correct when servicing units. Reversed battery polarity will damage rectifiers and regulators.
2. If booster battery is used for starting, be sure to use correct polarity in hook up.
3. When a fast charger is used to charge a vehicle battery, the vehicle battery cables should be disconnected unless the fast charger is equipped with a special Alternator Protector, in which case the vehicle battery cables need not be disconnected. Also the fast charger should never be used to start a vehicle as damage to rectifiers will result.
4. Unless the system includes a load relay or field relay, grounding the alternator output terminal will damage the alternator and/or circuits. This is true even when the system is not in operation since no circuit breaker is used and the battery is applied to the alternator output terminal at all times. The field or load relay acts as a circuit breaker in that it is controlled by the ignition switch.
5. Before making any on vehicle tests of the alternator or regulator, the battery should be checked and the circuit inspected for faulty wiring or insulation. loose or corroded connections and poor ground circuits.
6. Check alternator belt tension to be sure the belt is tight enough to prevent slipping under load.
7. The ignition switch should be off and the battery ground cable disconnected before making any test connections to prevent damage to the system.
8. The vehicle battery must be fully charged or a fully charged battery may be installed for test purposes.

Nippondenso Alternator

INDEX

DESCRIPTION

This alternator has an IC integral solid state regulator. **Fig. 1.** All regulator components are enclosed into a solid mold and are attached to the slip ring end frame along with the brush holder assembly. The alternator voltage setting cannot be adjusted.

The alternator rotor bearing contain enough grease to eliminate the need for periodic lubrication. Two brushes carry current through the two slip rings to the field coil mounted on the rotor.

The stator windings are assembled on the inside of a laminated core that form part of the alternator frame. The rectifier bridge contains six diodes which electrically change stator A.C. voltage into D.C. voltage. The neutral diodes serve to convert the voltage fluctuation at the neutral point to direct current for increasing generator output.

F	FIELD COIL TERMINAL	**3**	ROTOR FAN
D	DUMMY TERMINAL	**4**	FIELD COIL
L	LAMP TERMINAL	**5**	STATOR CORE
B	GENERATOR OUTPUT (BATTERY TERMINAL)	**6**	STATOR COIL
IG	IGNITION TERMINAL	**7**	REGULATOR
E	GROUND	**8**	BRUSH
1	PULLEY NUT	**9**	REAR END FRAME
2	PULLEY	**10**	DRIVE END FRAME

Fig. 1   Nippondenso alternator

DIAGNOSIS & TESTING

SYSTEM TEST

1. Connect an ammeter and voltmeter as follows:
   a. Disconnect wire from B terminal of alternator, then connect ammeter negative probe to the wire.
   b. Connect ammeter positive probe to B terminal of alternator.
   c. Connect voltmeter positive probe to B terminal of alternator and the negative probe to ground.
2. Start engine and allow to run at 2,000 RPM, then check reading of ammeter and voltmeter. Ammeter should read less than 10 amps. Voltmeter should read 13.9-15.1 volts at 77°F.
3. If voltage reading is greater than specified voltage, replace IC regulator. If voltage reading is less than specified voltage, check the IC regulator and alternator as follows:
   a. With engine running and F terminal grounded, check voltage reading at B terminal.
   b. If voltage reading is greater than specified voltage, replace IC regulator. If voltage reading is less than specified voltage, check alternator.
4. With engine running at 2,000 RPM, turn on high beam headlights and place heater fan control switch in the HI position.
5. Check ammeter reading. If reading is less than 30 amps, repair alternator.

REGULATOR TEST

1. Connect a voltmeter and fast charger to battery.
2. Turn ignition switch On and slowly increase charge rate. Indicator lamp in vehicle will begin to dim when voltage setting is reached.
3. Observe voltmeter, light should dim at 13.5 -16.0 volts.
4. If no voltage is present, replace voltage regulator.

Delcotron Type CS Charging System

INDEX

DESCRIPTION

The CS alternator is available in three sizes: CS121, CS130 and CS144. The numerals denote the outer diameter of the stator laminations and the letters CS stand for charging system. The CS144 can be serviced. The CS121 and CS130 are serviced as an assembly only.

The CS alternators uses a new type regulator and a diode trio is not used. A delta stator, rectifier bridge, and rotor with slip rings and brushes are electrically similar to earlier alternators. A conventional fan mounted next to the pulley pulls air through the assembly for cooling. An internal fan mounted on the rotor pulls air through the slip ring end frame to cool rec-

Fig. 1 CS charging system wiring diagram

1—CARBON PILE
2—VOLTMETER
3—RESISTOR
4—TESTAMMETER
5—GENERATOR
6—BATTERY
7—CONNECT RESISTOR TO "L" TERMINAL

Fig. 2 CS alternator bench check

tifier, bridge and regulator. Air is expelled through openings in the end frame. No periodic maintenance is required.

SYSTEM OPERATION

CS130 and CS144 alternators may be used with only two connections. The battery positive BAT terminal must be connected to a battery during operation. The second required connection is through the indicator light, or a suitable external resistor to L terminal of the regulator which serves to turn unit On at start up. Three other regulator terminals are available for optional use in vehicle systems. The P terminal is connected to the stator, and may be connected to a tachometer or other device. The F terminal is connected internally to field positive, and may be used as a fault indicator. The S terminal may be connected externally to a voltage, such as battery voltage, to sense voltage to be controlled.

The regulator voltage setting varies with temperature, and limits system voltage by controlling rotor field current. Unlike others regulators, this regulator switches field current On and Off at a fixed frequency about 400 cycles per second. By varying On-Off time, correct average field current is obtained to provide proper system voltage. At high speeds, the On time may be 10% and Off time 90%. At low speeds with high electrical loads, On-Off time may be 90% and 10% respectively.

Alternator systems on some applications are controlled by a Body Control Module (BCM). If cause of a system malfunction cannot be determined using the following test procedure, a problem in the electronic control system is indicated. For complete system diagnosis, refer to MOTOR's Auto Engine Tune Up and Electronics Manual.

DIAGNOSIS & TESTING
CHARGING SYSTEM

When the charging system is operating normally, the indicator lamp will come On when ignition switch is turned On and will go out when the engine starts. If the lamp operates abnormally, or if an undercharge or overcharge battery condition occurs, the following may be used to diagnose the charging system.

1. An undercharged battery if often caused by accessories being left On extended periods of time, or if an accessory lamp stays On.
2. Noise from an alternator may be caused by a loose drive pulley, loose mounting bolts, worn or dirty bearings, defective diodes or a defective stator.
3. To avoid damage to electrical equipment, refer to charging circuit wiring diagram, **Fig. 1** and proceed as follows:
   a. Do not reverse connections to the alternator.
   b. Do not short across or ground any of the terminals in charging system.
   c. Never disconnect output terminal while alternator is running.
4. Trouble in the charging system will appear as follows:
   a. Faulty indicator lamp operation.
   b. Undercharge battery, as evidenced by slow cranking or dark hydrometer.
   c. Overcharge battery, as evidenced by spewing of electrolyte from the vents.

IN-VEHICLE TESTING

1. Visually check belt and wiring and make any necessary repairs.
2. **On models without charge indicator light,** proceed to step 5.
3. **On models with charge indicator light,** turn ignition switch to On position (engine stopped), lamp should be on. If not, disconnect harness from alternator, and ground L terminal.
   a. If lamp lights, replace alternator.
   b. If lamp does not light, locate open circuit between grounding lead and ignition switch and check for defective indicator light bulb.
4. With ignition switch on and engine running at a moderate speed, lamp should be off. If not, disconnect wiring harness from alternator.
   a. If lamp goes off, replace alternator.
   b. If lamp stays on, check for grounded L terminal in wiring harness.
5. Battery undercharged or overcharged.
   a. Disconnect wiring harness connector from alternator.
   b. With ignition switch on and engine not running, connect voltmeter from ground to L terminal.
   c. Zero reading indicates open circuit between terminal and battery. Correct as required.
   d. Reconnect harness connector to alternator.

e. Measure voltage across battery terminals with engine running at approximately 2000 RPM. If voltage is above 16 volts, replace alternator.

f. Turn on accessories and load battery with carbon pile to obtain maximum amperage. Maintain voltage at 13 volts or less. If alternator is within 15 amps of rated output, it is acceptable.

ON-VEHICLE OUTPUT TEST

1. Connect ammeter in series at alternator output BAT terminal, then connect voltmeter and carbon pile across battery terminal. Ensure battery is fully charged.

2. Operate engine at moderate speed. With carbon pile turned Off, check voltage across battery terminals.

3. If voltmeter reads above 16 volts, repair (CS-144) only or replace alternator.

4. If voltmeter reads below 16 volts, proceed as follows:
   a. With engine still running at moderate speed turn accessories On and load battery with carbon pile to obtain maximum amperage output. Maintain voltage above 13 volts.
   b. If output is within 15 amps of rated output, alternator is satisfactory.
   c. If output is not within 15 amps of rated output, alternator is defective and requires repair (CS-144 only) or replace alternator.

BENCH TESTING

1. Make connections as shown in **Fig. 2**, however leave the carbon pile disconnected. The ground polarity of the alternator and battery must be the same. The battery must be fully charged. Use a 30-500 ohm resistor between battery and L terminal.

2. Slowly increase alternator speed and observe voltage.

3. If voltage is uncontrolled and increases above 16 volts, the rotor field is shorted, the regulator is defective or both. A shorted rotor field can cause the regulator to become defective. **Battery must be fully charged when making this test.**

4. If voltage is below 16 volts, increase speed and adjust carbon pile obtain maximum amperage output. Maintain voltage above 13 volts.

5. If output is within 15 amps of rated output, alternator is satisfactory.

6. If output is not within 15 amps of rated output, alternator is defective and requires repair.

Bosch Charging System

INDEX

DESCRIPTION

Bosch generators are similar in output to Delco-Remy generators. They share a common mounting configuration and both use internal voltage regulators. The Bosch generator uses a single blade harness connector and does not require periodic maintenance.

Some models are equipped with a Generator Inverting Buffer (GIB) Module. The GIB module is located near the fuse box below the drivers side instrument panel housed in a aqua green box. The GIB module is connected in parallel to the charge indicator lamp. The basic purpose of the GIB module is to defeat the operation of the air conditioning and the rear window defogger if generator output drops below a certain level.

DIAGNOSIS & TESTING

CHARGING SYSTEM

When the charging system is operating normally, the indicator lamp will come On when ignition switch is turned On and will go out when the engine starts. If the lamp operates abnormally, or if an undercharge or overcharge battery condition occurs, the following may be used to diagnose the charging system.

1. An undercharged battery if often caused by accessories being left On extended periods of time, or if an accessory lamp stays On.

2. Noise from an alternator may be caused by a loose drive pulley, loose mounting bolts, worn or dirty bearings, defective diodes or a defective stator.

3. To avoid damage to electrical equipment, refer to charging circuit wiring diagram, **Fig. 1** and proceed as follows:
   a. Do not reverse connections to the alternator.
   b. Do not short across or ground any of the terminals in charging system.
   c. Never disconnect output terminal while alternator is running.

4. Trouble in the charging system will appear as follows:
   a. Faulty indicator lamp operation.
   b. Undercharge battery, as evidenced by slow cranking or dark hydrometer.
   c. Overcharge battery, as evidenced by spewing of electrolyte from the vents.

IN-VEHICLE TESTING

1. Visually check belt and wiring and make necessary repairs.

2. With ignition switch in RUN position and engine stopped, the charge indicator lamp should be on. If it is not on, disconnect harness at generator and ground negative terminal in harness with a fused jumper lead. If lamp lights, replace generator. If lamp does not light, locate open in circuit between ignition switch and harness connector and check for burned out indicator lamp.

3. With ignition switch in RUN position and engine running at a moderate speed, the charge indicator lamp should be off. If it is not off, disconnect harness at generator. If lamp goes off, replace generator. If lamp stays on, check for a short to ground in harness between connector and indicator lamp.

4. Check battery for an overcharged or undercharged condition as follows:
   a. Attach a suitable voltmeter, ammeter and carbon pile to vehicle.
   b. With ignition switch in OFF position, check and record battery voltage.
   c. Remove harness connector from generator.
   d. Turn ignition switch to Run position and check voltage at the brown wire in harness. Battery voltage should be present. If battery voltage is not present, check charge indicator circuits for open or grounded circuits causing voltage loss and repair as necessary.
   e. Reconnect generator harness connector.
   f. Run engine at a moderate idle and measure voltage across battery terminals. Voltage should read more than recorded in step B and less than 16 volts. If reading is not as specified, replace generator.

Fig. 1 Bosch charging system wiring diagram

g. Run engine at a moderate idle and check generator amperage output. Adjust carbon pile load to obtain maximum amperage while maintaining battery voltage above 13 volts. If amperage reading is within 15 amps of generators rating, generator is functioning properly. If amperage is not within 15 amps, replace generator.

h. With generator operating at maximum output, measure voltage between generator housing and battery negative terminal. Voltage drop should be .5 volt or less. If more than .5 volt, check ground path from generator housing to battery negative and determine cause of voltage drop. Repair loose or corroded ground connections as necessary.

Alternator Specifications

Year	Model	Rated Hot Output Amps
Buick Estate Wagon & Roadmaster, Cadillac Brougham, Fleetwood RWD, Chevrolet Caprice & Oldsmobile Custom Cruiser		
1991	1101599	100
	1101454	120
1992	10479906	100
1993	CS-130	100
	CS-144	124
Chevrolet Camaro & Pontiac Firebird		
1991—92	1101593	100
	1101600	105
	1101645	100
1993	CS-130	105
	CS-144	124

Year	Model	Rated Hot Output Amps
Chevrolet Corvette		
1991	1101597	124
	1101601	105
1992	10479904	124
	1102634	124
1993	CS-144	124
Buick Century, Chevrolet Celebrity, Oldsmobile Cutlass Ciera & Cutlass Cruiser & Pontiac 6000		
1991	1101142	85
	1101475	105
	1101603	105
	1101810	85
1992	10479902	100
	10479898	100

ALTERNATOR SPECIFICATIONS—Continued

Buick Century, Chevrolet Celebrity, Oldsmobile Cutlass Ciera & Cutlass Cruiser & Pontiac 6000 -Continued

Year	Model	Rated Hot Output Amps
1993	CS-130	⑫

Buick Electra, LeSabre & Park Ave., Cadillac DeVille, Fleetwood FWD, Oldsmobile 88, 98 & Pontiac Bonneville

Year	Model	Rated Hot Output Amps
1991	1101577	105
	1101580	140
1992	10479954	105
	1102607	105
	1102607	105
	1102625	140
	10480010	140
	10479966	140
1993	CS-130	105
	CS-144 Generation II	140

Buick Reatta & Riviera, Cadillac Eldorado & Seville, Oldsmobile Toronado/ Trofeo

Year	Model	Rated Hot Output Amps
1991-93	CS 144 Generation II	140

Chevrolet Cavalier & Pontiac Sunbird

Year	Model	Rated Hot Output Amps
1991	1101319②	74
	1102614②	80
	1102615②	80
	1105694①	100
1992	1101823②	74
	10479815②	80
	1101832①	100
1993	CS-121	80
	CS-130	100

Chevrolet Beretta & Corsica

Year	Model	Rated Hot Output Amps
1991	1105697③	74
	1101605④	100
	1101612⑤	85
	1101846⑥	100
	1101231⑦	100
1992	1101832	100
	10479909	100
	10479963	105
1993	CS-130	⑩

Buick Skylark, Oldsmobile Achieva, Cutlass Calais & Pontiac Grand Am

Year	Model	Rated Hot Output Amps
1991	1101124①	100
	1101277①	85
	1101278①	100
	1101320②	74
	1101483②	74

Buick Skylark, Oldsmobile Achieva, Cutlass Calais & Pontiac Grand Am -Continued

Year	Model	Rated Hot Output Amps
1992	10479909	100
	10479814	105
	1101642	100
1993	CS-130	100

Buick Regal, Chevrolet Lumina, Oldsmobile Cutlass Supreme & Pontiac Grand Prix

Year	Model	Rated Hot Output Amps
1991	1101143	100
	1101466	100
	1101583	105
1992	10479911	100
	10479897	100
	10480037	105
	10479998	105
1993	CS-130	100
	CS-130	105

Geo Prizm

Year	Model	Rated Hot Output Amps
1991-92	Delco⑧	60
	Nippondenso⑨	60
1993	Delco	⑪
	Nippondenso	70

Geo Metro

Year	Model	Rated Hot Output Amps
1991-93	Nippondenso	50

Geo Storm

Year	Model	Rated Hot Output Amps
1991	100211-7950	75
1992	Nippondenso	75
	Nippondenso	85
1993	Nippondenso	55

Pontiac LeMans

Year	Model	Rated Hot Output Amps
1991-93	1101531	72
	1101563	72
	1101564	60
	1101565	72
	90244847	55
	90244848	65

①—CS130.
②—CS121.
③—VIN G-KGO.
④—VIN G w/A/C-K60.
⑤—VIN T-K99.
⑥—VIN T w/A/C-K60.
⑦—VIN A.
⑧—Base & LSi models.
⑨—GSi models.
⑩—With 2.2L engine, 105 amps; w/2.3L & 3.1 engines, 100 amps.
⑪—Models w/1.8L/4-107.5 engine and automatic transmission, 77 amps. All other models, 70 amps.
⑫—With 2.2L engine, 105 amps; w/3.3L engine, 100 amps.

DISC BRAKES

NOTE: Refer To "Applications" To Determine Which Type Brakes Are Used On Vehicle Being Serviced.

TABLE OF CONTENTS

Applications

Model	Year	Front/Rear Brakes	Application
BUICK			
Century	1991-93	Front	Delco-Moraine Single Piston Type 2
LeSabre	1991-93	Front	Delco-Moraine Single Piston Type 2
Park Avenue	1991-93	Front	Delco-Moraine Single Piston Type 2
Reatta	1991	Front	Delco-Moraine Single Piston Type 3
		Rear	Delco-Moraine Single Piston Type 4
Regal	1991-93	Front	Delco-Moraine Dual Piston
		Rear	Delco-Moraine Single Piston Type 1
Riviera	1991	Front	Delco-Moraine Single Piston Type 3
	1992-93	Front	Delco-Moraine Single Piston Type 2
	1991	Rear	Delco-Moraine Single Piston Type 4

Model	Year	Front/Rear Brakes	Application
BUICK -Continued			
	1992-93	Rear	Delco-Moraine Single Piston Type 2
Roadmaster	1991-93	Front	Delco-Moraine Single Piston Type 1
Skylark	1991-93	Front	Delco-Moraine Single Piston Type 2
CADILLAC			
Brougham	1991-92	Front	Delco-Moraine Single Piston Type 1
DeVille	1991-93	Front	Delco-Moraine Single Piston Type 2
Eldorado	1991	Front	Delco-Moraine Single Piston Type 3
	1992-93	Front	Delco-Moraine Single Piston Type 2
	1991	Rear	Delco-Moraine Single Piston Type 4
	1992-93	Rear	Delco-Moraine Single Piston Type 2

APPLICATIONS—Continued

Model	Year	Front/Rear Brakes	Application
CADILLAC -Continued			
Fleetwood FWD	1991-92	Front	Delco-Moraine Single Piston Type 2
Fleetwood RWD	1993	Front	Delco-Moraine Single Piston Type 1
Seville	1991	Front	Delco-Moraine Single Piston Type 3
	1992-93	Front	Delco-Moraine Single Piston Type 2
	1991	Rear	Delco-Moraine Single Piston Type 4
	1992-93	Rear	Delco-Moraine Single Piston Type 2
CHEVROLET			
Beretta	1991-93	Front	Delco-Moraine Single Piston Type 2
Camaro	1991-92	Front (Standard)	Delco-Moraine Single Piston Type 1
	1991-92	Front (Optional)	PBR Dual Piston
	1993	Front	Delco-Moraine Single Piston Type 2
	1991-93	Rear	PBR Single Piston
Caprice	1991-93	Front	Delco-Moraine Single Piston Type 1
Cavalier	1991-93	Front	Delco-Moraine Single Piston Type 2
Corsica	1991-93	Front	Delco-Moraine Single Piston Type 2
Corvette	1991-93	Front	PBR Dual Piston
	1991-93	Rear	PBR Single Piston
Lumina	1991-93	Front	Delco-Moraine Dual Piston
	1991-93	Rear	Delco-Moraine Single Piston Type 3
GEO			
Metro Except Convertible	1991-93	Front	Aisin Seiki Type 2
Metro Convertible	1991-93	Front	Aisin Seiki Type 1
Prizm	1991-93	Front	Toyota/GM
Storm	1991-93	Front	Aisin Seiki Type 1
OLDSMOBILE			
Achieva	1992-93	Front	Delco-Moraine Single Piston Type 2

Model	Year	Front/Rear Brakes	Application
OLDSMOBILE -Continued			
Custom Cruiser	1991-92	Front	Delco-Moraine Single Piston Type 1
Cutlass Calais	1991	Front	Delco-Moraine Single Piston Type 2
Cutlass Ciera	1991-93	Front	Delco-Moraine Single Piston Type 2
Cutlass Cruiser	1991-93	Front	Delco-Moraine Single Piston Type 2
Cutlass Supreme	1991-93	Front	Delco-Moraine Dual Piston
	1991-93	Rear	Delco-Moraine Single Piston Type 3
Eighty-Eight	1991-93	Front	Delco-Moraine Single Piston Type 2
Ninety-Eight	1991-93	Front	Delco-Moraine Single Piston Type 2
Toronado	1991-92	Front	Delco-Moraine Single Piston Type 3
		Rear	Delco-Moraine Single Piston Type 4
Trofeo	1991-92	Front	Delco-Moraine Single Piston Type 3
		Rear	Delco-Moraine Single Piston Type 4
PONTIAC			
Bonneville	1991-93	Front	Delco-Moraine Single Piston Type 2
Firebird	1991-92	Front (Standard)	Delco-Moraine Single Piston Type 1
	1991-92	Front (Optional)	PBR Dual Piston
	1993	Front	Delco-Moraine Single Piston Type 2
	1991-93	Rear	PBR Single Piston
Grand Am	1991-93	Front	Delco-Moraine Single Piston Type 2
Grand Prix	1991-93	Front	Delco-Moraine Dual Piston
	1991-93	Rear	Delco-Moraine Single Piston Type 3
LeMans	1991-93	Front	DAEWOO Single Piston
Sunbird	1991-93	Front	Delco-Moraine Single Piston Type 2
6000	1991	Front	Delco-Moraine Single Piston Type 2

General Information

INDEX

TROUBLESHOOTING

When troubleshooting brake system, refer to **Fig. 1.**

BRAKE SHOES, LININGS & CALIPERS

Remove wheels and inspect brake disc, caliper and linings. The wheel bearings should be inspected at this time and repacked if necessary. Do not get any grease on the linings.

Do not replace individual pads or replace pads on one wheel of an axle set alone, as braking performance will be adversely affected.

If a visual inspection does not adequately determine the condition of the linings, the brake shoe and lining assemblies should be removed and inspected. If shoes do not require replacement, reinstall them in their original positions. Brake shoes and linings should also be replaced if cracked or damaged.

If the caliper is cracked or fluid leakage through the casting is evident, it must be replaced as a unit.

BRAKE ROUGHNESS

The most common cause of brake chatter on disc brakes is a variation in thickness of the disc. If roughness or vibration is encountered during highway operation or if pedal pulsation is experienced at low speeds, the disc may have excessive thickness variation. To check for this condition, measure the disc at 12 points with a micrometer at a radius approximately one inch from edge of disc. If thickness measurements vary by more than .0005 inch, the disc should be replaced with a new one.

Excessive lateral runout of braking disc may cause a "knocking back" of the pistons, possibly creating increased pedal travel and vibration when brakes are applied.

Before checking the runout, wheel bearings should be adjusted. The readjustment is very important and will be required at the completion of the test to prevent bearing failure. Be sure to make the adjustment according to the recommendations given under "Front Wheel Bearings, Adjust" in the car chapters.

BRAKE DISC SERVICE

Servicing of disc brakes is extremely critical due to the close tolerances required in machining the brake disc to insure proper brake operation.

The maintenance of these close controls of the shape of the rubbing surfaces is necessary to prevent brake roughness. In addition, the surface finish must be non-directional and maintained at a micro inch finish. This close control of the rubbing surface finish is necessary to avoid pulls and erratic performance, and to promote long lining life and equal lining wear of both left and right brakes.

In light of the foregoing remarks, refinishing of the rubbing surfaces should not be attempted unless precision equipment, capable of measuring in micro inches (millionths of an inch) is available.

To check lateral runout of a disc, mount a dial indicator on a convenient part (steering knuckle, tie rod, disc brake caliper housing) so that the plunger of the dial indicator contacts the disc at a point one inch from the outer edge, **Fig. 2.** If the total indicated runout exceeds specifications, install a new disc.

To check parallelism (thickness variation), mount dial indicators, **Fig. 3,** so the plunger contacts rotor approximately 1 inch from outer edge. If parallelism exceeds specifications, replace rotor.

GENERAL PRECAUTIONS

1. Grease or any other foreign material must be kept off the brake linings, caliper, surfaces of the disc and external surfaces of the hub, during service procedures. Handling the brake disc and caliper should be done in a way to avoid deformation of the disc and nicking or scratching brake linings.
2. If inspection reveals rubber piston seals are worn or damaged, they should be replaced immediately.
3. During removal and installation of a wheel assembly, exercise care so as not to interfere with or damage the caliper splash shield, or bleeder screw.
4. Front wheel bearings preload should be adjusted to specifications .
5. Be sure vehicle is centered on hoist before servicing any of the front end components to avoid bending or damaging the disc splash shield on full right or left wheel turns.
6. Before the vehicle is moved after any brake service work, be sure to obtain a firm brake pedal.
7. The assembly bolts of two piece caliper housings should not be disturbed unless the caliper requires service.

INSPECTION OF CALIPER

Should it become necessary to remove the caliper for installation of new parts, clean all parts in alcohol, wipe dry using lint free cloths, using an air hose to blow out drilled passages and bores. Check dust boots for punctures or tears. If punctures or tears are evident, new boots should be installed upon reassembly.

Inspect piston bores for scoring or pitting. Bores that show light scratches or corrosion can usually be cleaned with crocus cloth. However, bores that have deep scratches or scoring may be honed, provided the diameter of the bore is not increased more than .002 inches. If the bore does not clean up within this specification, a new caliper housing should be installed (black stains on the bore walls are caused by piston seals and will do no harm).

When using a hone, **Fig. 4,** be sure to install the hone baffle before honing bore. The baffle is used to protect the hone stones from damage. Use extreme care in cleaning the caliper after honing. Remove all dust and grit by flushing the caliper with alcohol. Wipe dry with clean lint free cloth and then clean a second time in the same manner.

BLEEDING DISC BRAKES

Pressure bleeding is recommended for all hydraulic disc brake systems.

The disc brake hydraulic system can be bled manually or with pressure bleeding equipment. **On vehicles with disc brakes** the brake pedal will require more pumping and frequent checking of fluid level in master cylinder during bleeding operation.

Never use brake fluid that has been drained from hydraulic system when bleeding the brakes. Be sure the disc brake pistons are returned to their normal positions and that the shoe and lining assemblies are properly seated. Before driving the vehicle, check brake operation to be sure that a firm pedal has been obtained.

PROPORTIONING VALVE

The proportioning valve (when used), **Fig. 5,** provides balanced braking action between front and rear brakes under a wide range of braking conditions. The valve regulates the hydraulic pressure applied to the rear wheel cylinders, thus limiting rear braking action when high pressures are required at the front brakes. In

CAUSE \\ SYMPTOM	Excessive Brake Pedal Travel	Brake Pedal Travel Gradually Increases	Excessive Brake Pedal Effort	Excessive Braking Action	Brakes Slow To Respond	Brakes Slow To Release	Brakes Drag	Uneven Braking Action (Side To Side)	Uneven Braking Action (Front To Rear)	Scraping Noise From Brakes	*Brakes Squeak During Application	Brakes Squeak During Stop	*Brakes Pulsate (Roughness)	**Brakes Groan At End of Stop	"BRAKE" Warning Lamp Glows
Leaking Brake Line or Connection	X	XX						X							XX
Leaking Wheel Cylinder or Piston Seal	X	XX		X				X							XX
Leaking Master Cylinder	X	XX													XX
Air in Brake System	XX							X							X
Contaminated or Improper Brake Fluid					X	X	X								X
Leaking Vacuum System			XX		X										
Restricted Air Passage in Power Head			X		XX	X									
Damaged Power Head			X	X	X	X	X								
Improperly Assembled Power Head Valving			X	X	X	X		XX							
Worn Out Brake Lining - Replace			X	X				X	X	X	X	X		X	
Uneven Brake Lining Wear - Replace and Correct	X			X				X	X	X	X	X		X	X
Incorrect Lining Material-Replace			X	X				X	X			X		X	
Contaminated Brake Lining - Replace				XX				XX	X	X	X	X		X	
Linings Damaged by Abusive Use-Replace			X	XX				X	X	X	X	X		X	
Heat Spotted or Scored Brake Drums or Rotors				X				X	X		X	X	X	X	
Out-of-Round Brake Drums													X		
Improper Rotor Thickness Variation													XX		
Excessive Lateral Runout	X											X	X		
Faulty Automatic Adjusters	X						X	X	X						X
Incorrect Wheel Cylinder Sizes	X		X	X				X	X						
Weak or Incorrect Brake Shoe Retention Springs				X		X	XX	X	X	XX	X	XX			
Brake Assembly Attachments - Missing or Loose	X						X	X	X		X	X	X		
Insufficient Brake Shoe Guide Lubricant						X	X	X	X	XX	XX				
Restricted Brake Fluid Passage or Sticking Wheel Cylinder Piston		X	X			X	X	X	X						
Incorrect Stoplamp Switch Adjustment		X		X			X								
Brake Pedal Linkage Interference or Binding			X		X	XX	XX								X
Improperly Adjusted Parking Brake							X								X
Parking Brake Cable Siezed						X	X		X						X
Drums Tapered or Threaded										XX					
Incorrect Front End Alignment								XX							
Incorrect Wheel Bearing Runout	X												X		
Loose Front Suspension Attachments								X			XX			X	
Operator Riding Brake Pedal	X	X	X				X		X			X		X	
Improper Booster Pushrod Length	X					X	XX								
Sticking Wheel Cylinder or Caliper Pistons			X			X	X	X	X						
Caliper Not Sliding Freely	X						X					X	XX		
Faulty Proportioning Valve			X	X	X	X	X								

XX — Indicates more probable cause(s)
X — Indicates other causes
*May be a normal condition.
**Can usually be corrected by servicing front brakes.

Fig. 1 Troubleshooting brake system chart

Fig. 2   Checking rotor for lateral runout

Fig. 3   Checking rotor parallelism (thickness variation)

Fig. 4   Honing caliper piston bore

Fig. 5   Gauge hook-up for testing proportioning valve (typical)

this manner, premature rear wheel skid is prevented.

TESTING PROPORTIONING VALVE

When a premature rear wheel slide is obtained on a brake application, it usually is an indication that the fluid pressure to the rear wheels is above the 50% reduction ratio for the rear line pressure and that malfunction has occurred within the proportioning valve.

To test the valve, install gauge set shown in **Fig. 5** in brake line between master cylinder and proportioning valve, and at output end of proportioning valve and brake line as shown. Be sure all joints are fluid tight.

Have a helper exert pressure on brake pedal (holding pressure). Obtain a reading on master cylinder output of approximately 700 psi. While pressure is being held as above, reading on valve outlet should be 550-610 psi. If the pressure readings do not meet these specifications, the valve should be removed and a new valve installed.

Aisin-Seiki Single Piston Front Disc Brake (Type 1)

INDEX

DESCRIPTION

This single piston sliding caliper assembly, **Figs. 1 and 2**, is mounted to a support bracket by two slide pins. The caliper assembly slides on the two mounting pins. Upon brake application, fluid pressure against the piston forces the inboard shoe and lining assembly against the inboard side of the disc. This action causes the caliper assembly to slide until the outboard lining comes into contact with the disc.

BRAKE PAD SERVICE

1. Remove approximately 2/3 of brake fluid from master cylinder.
2. Raise and support vehicle.
3. Mark relationship between front wheel and axle, then remove wheel and tire assembly.
4. Remove 2 caliper slide pins from bracket.
5. Unfasten caliper, and support with a length of wire, leaving hydraulic lines connected.
6. Remove brake pads, shims, wear indicators and retainers, **Fig. 1 and 2.**
7. Reverse procedure to install.

CALIPER SERVICE
CALIPER REMOVAL

1. Disconnect negative battery cable.
2. Remove approximately 2/3 of brake fluid from master cylinder.
3. Raise and support vehicle.
4. Mark relationship between front

AISIN-SEIKI SINGLE PISTON FRONT DISC BRAKE (TYPE 1)

1	SLIDE PIN BOLT
2	CALIPER BODY
3	WEAR INDICATOR
4	RETAINER
5	PAD
6	SLIDE PIN BUSHING
7	BRACKET
8	BOLT
9	RETAINER
10	PISTON BOOT
11	PISTON SEAL
12	PISTON
13	BLEEDER SCREW
14	CAP

Fig. 1 Exploded view of disc brake caliper assembly. Metro except convertible

1	CARRIER
2	PAD CLIPS
3	CALIPER PIN BOOT
4	CALIPER PIN
5	BLEEDER SCREW
6	CALIPER RETAINING SCREWS
7	CALIPER ASSEMBLY
8	PADS
9	INSULATOR

Fig. 2 Exploded view of disc brake caliper assembly. Metro convertible

Fig. 3 Removing caliper piston

5. Remove bleeder valve.
6. Inspect piston for scoring, nicks, corrosion, and wear and replace as needed.
7. Inspect caliper housing and seal groove for corrosion, nicks, scoring and excessive wear, and use crocus cloth to polish away corrosion from housing bore. Replace caliper housing if corrosion in and around seal groove will not clean up with crocus cloth.
8. Clean all parts with denatured alcohol. Dry with unlubricated compressed air. Blow out all passages in housing and bleeder valve.

CALIPER ASSEMBLY

1. Apply suitable grease to piston seal and cylinder wall, then install the seal. Check to ensure piston seal is not twisted.
2. Apply suitable grease to sliding portion of piston and install dust boot.
3. Insert edge of dust boot into boot groove, then slowly force piston fully into cylinder.
4. Install bleeder valve.

CALIPER INSTALLATION

1. Apply suitable grease to inner face of slide pin boot.
2. Install slide pin boot to bracket.
3. Install bracket and attaching bolts.
4. Install shoe and lining assembly, ensure wear indicators are located on trailing edge of shoe assemblies during forward wheel rotation.
5. Install caliper assembly to bracket. Tighten attaching bolts to specifications.
6. Attach hose to caliper.
7. Install wheel and tire assembly, then lower vehicle.
8. Fill master cylinder to proper level and bleed brakes. **Before moving vehicle, pump brake pedal several times to be sure it is firm. Do not move vehicle until a firm pedal is obtained.**

wheel and axle, then remove wheel and tire assembly.
5. If caliper assembly is to be serviced, remove inlet fitting attaching bolt, copper washer, and inlet fitting from caliper housing. Plug opening in inlet fitting to prevent fluid loss and contamination. **Do not crimp brake hose, as this may damage internal structure of hose. If only shoe and lining assemblies are to be replaced, do not disconnect brake line fitting from caliper.**
6. Remove caliper slide pins and the caliper. If only shoe and lining assemblies are to be replaced, suspend caliper from chassis using suitable hanger. **Do not allow caliper to hang by brake hose.**
7. Remove shoe and lining assembly.
8. Remove bracket attaching bolts and the bracket.

9. Remove slide pin boot from bracket.

CALIPER DISASSEMBLY

1. Remove caliper assembly as outlined previously, then drain brake fluid from caliper.
2. Use clean shop towels to pad interior of caliper assembly, then remove piston by directing compressed air into caliper brake hose inlet hole, **Fig. 3.** **Use just enough air pressure to ease piston out of bore. Do not place fingers in front of piston for any reason when applying compressed air. This could result in serious personal injury.**
3. Remove dust boot from piston.
4. Using a small piece of wood or plastic, remove piston seal from bore. **Do not use a metal tool of any kind to remove seal as it may damage bore.**

Aisin-Seiki Single Piston Front Disc Brake (Type 2)

INDEX

Fig. 1   Exploded view of brake caliper

1 Caliper bolt	8 Anti rattle inner spring
2 Dust boot support	9 Piston seal
3 Boot	10 Disc brake piston
4 Cylinder slide bushing	11 Cylinder boot
5 Bleeder plug cap	12 Set ring
6 Bleeder plug	13 Disc brake inner pad
7 Disc brake caliper	14 Disc brake outer pad
(Disc brake cylinder)	15 Anti rattle outer spring

1. Caliper
2. Mounting bolts
3. Disc

Fig. 2   Caliper mounting bolts removal

1. Pad clips
2. Knuckle
3. Outside pad

Fig. 3   Outside pad installation

DESCRIPTION

This single piston sliding caliper assembly, **Fig. 1,** is mounted to a support bracket by two slide pins. The caliper assembly slides on the two mounting pins. Upon brake application, fluid pressure against the piston forces the inboard shoe and lining assembly against the inboard side of the disc. This action causes the caliper assembly to slide until the outboard lining comes into contact with the disc.

BRAKE PAD SERVICE

1. Raise and support vehicle and remove wheel.
2. Remove caliper mounting bolts, **Fig. 2.**
3. Remove caliper from knuckle, taking care not to drop inside pad. If only shoe and lining assemblies are to be replaced, suspend caliper from chassis using suitable hanger. **Do not allow caliper to hang by brake hose.**
4. Remove outside pad.
5. Install pad clips, No. 1 & 2, then outside pad to knuckle, **Fig. 3.**
6. Install caliper and inside pad to knuckle, **Fig. 4.** Position outer springs over caliper as shown.
7. Tighten caliper bolts to specifications.
8. Install front wheel.
9. Lower vehicle and perform brake test.

CALIPER SERVICE
CALIPER REMOVAL

1. Remove approximately 2/3 of brake fluid from master cylinder.
2. Raise and support vehicle.
3. Mark relationship between front wheel and axle, then remove wheel and tire assembly.
4. If caliper assembly is to be serviced, remove inlet fitting attaching bolt, copper washer, and inlet fitting from caliper housing. Plug opening in inlet fitting to prevent fluid loss and contamination. **Do not crimp brake hose, as this may damage internal structure of hose. If only shoe and lining assemblies are to be replaced, do not disconnect brake line fitting from caliper.**
5. Remove caliper mounting bolts.
6. Remove caliper from knuckle. **Be careful not to drop inside pad which will come off with caliper.**

CALIPER DISASSEMBLY

1. Remove caliper assembly as outlined previously, then drain brake fluid from caliper.
2. Remove cylinder boot set ring and boot from cylinder groove, **Fig. 1.**
3. Use clean shop towels to pad interior of caliper assembly, then remove piston by directing compressed air into caliper brake hose inlet hole. **Use just enough air pressure to ease piston out of bore. Do not place fingers in front of piston for any reason when applying compressed air. This could result in serious personal injury.**
4. Using a small piece of wood or plastic, remove piston seal from bore. **Do not use a metal tool of any kind to remove seal as it may damage bore.**
5. Remove bleeder valve.
6. Inspect piston for scoring, nicks, corrosion, and wear and replace as needed.
7. Inspect caliper housing and seal groove for corrosion, nicks, scoring and excessive wear, and use crocus cloth to polish away corrosion from housing bore. Replace caliper housing if corrosion in and around seal

1. Caliper
2. Inside pad
3. Outer springs

Fig. 4   Inside pad & caliper installation

groove will not clean up with crocus cloth.

8. Clean all parts with denatured alcohol. Dry with unlubricated compressed air. Blow out all passages in housing and bleeder valve.

CALIPER ASSEMBLY & INSTALLATION

1. Apply suitable grease to piston seal and cylinder wall, then install the seal. Check to ensure piston seal is not twisted.

2. Install new boot on piston so side with 2 grooves faces in toward cylinder and side with 3 grooves faces out, **Fig. 5.**
3. Install piston in caliper so it projects about .4 inch to ease installation of boot on caliper housing. Install boot on caliper housing, then install set ring.
4. Install bleeder valve.
5. Check that caliper slide bushings are lubricated with rubber grease. Check that slide bushing in each carrier hole can be moved smoothly in each direction.
6. Install caliper and inside pad on knuckle.
7. Tighten caliper bolts.
8. Connect brake hose, then bleed hydraulic system.
9. Install wheel.
10. Lower vehicle and test brakes. **Before moving vehicle, pump brake pedal several times to be sure it is firm. Do not move vehicle until a firm pedal is obtained.**

TRIPLE GROOVED SIDE TOWARD OUTSIDE

DOUBLE GROOVED SIDE TOWARD INSIDE

507	BOOT RETAINING RING
508	PISTON BOOT
509	PISTON SEAL
510	PISTON
513	CALIPER MOUNTING BOLT
514	CALIPER
516	BLEEDER VALVE

Fig. 5   Caliper boot installation

Daewoo Single Piston Front Disc Brake

INDEX

DESCRIPTION

This caliper has a single bore, **Fig. 1**, and is mounted to the steering knuckle with two mounting bolts. Upon brake application, hydraulic pressure is converted by the caliper to stopping force. This force acts equally against the piston and the bottom of the caliper bore to move the piston outward and to slide the caliper inward resulting in a clamping action on the rotor. This clamping action forces the lining against the rotor, creating friction to stop the vehicle.

BRAKE PAD SERVICE

Caliper removal is not required to replace shoe and linings.
1. Remove approximately ⅔ of brake fluid from master cylinder.
2. Raise and support vehicle.
3. Mark relationship between front wheel and hub, then remove wheel and tire assembly.
4. Carefully drive pad retaining pins from inside out, **Fig. 2.**
5. Bottom piston into caliper bore using

suitable pliers, then remove brake pads.
6. Reverse procedure to install, noting the following:
   a. Install brake pads with wear sensor to the piston side.
   b. Ensure pads can be moved back and forth slightly when installed.
   c. Install retaining pins from outside in, ensuring openings align.
   d. Upon completion of installation, lower vehicle and pump brake pedal several times to properly position brake pads.

CALIPER SERVICE
CALIPER, REPLACE

1. Remove approximately ⅔ of brake fluid from master cylinder.
2. Raise and support vehicle.
3. Mark relationship between front wheel and hub, then remove wheel and hub assembly.
4. Bottom piston into caliper bore using suitable pliers to provide clearance between brake pads and rotor.
5. Disconnect brake hose from caliper.

Plug openings in brake hose and caliper to prevent leakage and contamination. **Do not crimp brake hose, as this may damage internal structure of hose.**
6. Remove outer protective caps from caliper housing seats.
7. Remove caliper attaching bolts, and the caliper.
8. Reverse procedure to install, noting the following:
   a. Original equipment caliper attaching bolts are micro-encapsulated. After removal of these bolts, threads in steering knuckle must be re-cut using a M12 X 1.5 thread tap.
   b. Install new caliper attaching bolts not micro-encapsulated and tighten to specification.
   c. Install brake hose inlet fitting attaching bolt.
   d. Install new outer protective caps. Ensure caps seat evenly on caliper.
   e. Upon completion of installation, bleed hydraulic system, then lower vehicle. **Before moving vehicle, pump brake pedal several times**

Fig. 2 Brake pad retaining pin removal

1 RETAINING PINS
2 EXPANDING SPRINGS

1	SPRINGS-EXPANDING	13	ROTOR
2	SHOE-INBOARD	14	PIN-COTTER
3	SHOE-OUTBOARD	15	NUT-WHEEL HUB
4	HOUSING-CALIPER	16	WASHER-WHEEL HUB
5	CAP-BLEEDER VALVE	17	SCREW-DETENT
6	VALVE-BLEEDER	18	SCREW-SHIELD
7	BOOT-PISTON	19	WASHER-SHIELD
8	SEAL-PISTON	20	PLUG-BLEEDER VALVE
9	PISTON-CALIPER	21	WASHER-BLEEDER VALVE
10	PINS-RETAINING	22	SPACER-CALIPER HOUSING
11	SHIELD	23	BOLT-CALIPER HOUSING
12	HUB-WHEEL	24	RETAINING FRAME

Fig. 1 Exploded view of brake caliper assembly

to be sure it is firm. Do not move vehicle until a firm pedal is obtained.

CALIPER DISASSEMBLY

1. Remove caliper and brake pads as previously described.
2. Remove inner protective caps for sliding sleeves.
3. Remove piston boot from housing.
4. Move sliding sleeve slightly toward protective cap and remove cap from groove in sleeve.
5. Remove boot from piston and housing.
6. Press sliding sleeves out of housing, **Fig. 3**, then remove seals using a suitable wood or plastic tool.
7. Clean outside of caliper, then drain brake fluid from caliper.
8. Use clean shop towels to pad interior of caliper assembly, then remove piston by directing compressed air into caliper brake hose inlet hole, **Use just enough air pressure to ease piston out of bore. Do not place fingers in front of piston for any reason when applying compressed air. This could result in serious personal injury.**
9. Secure caliper assembly in a suitable

vise, then remove caliper retaining frame attaching bolts and the frame.
10. Remove piston seal from groove in caliper bore using a suitable wood or plastic tool. **Do not use a metal tool of any kind to remove seal as it may damage bore.**
11. Remove bleeder valve from caliper.
12. Inspect piston for scoring, nicks, corrosion, and wear and replace as needed.
13. Inspect caliper housing and seal groove for corrosion, nicks, scoring and excessive wear, and use crocus cloth to polish away corrosion from housing bore. Replace caliper housing if corrosion in and around seal groove will not clean up with crocus cloth.
14. Clean all parts with denatured alcohol. Dry with unlubricated compressed air. Blow out all passages in housing and bleeder valve.

CALIPER ASSEMBLY

1. Lubricate, then install new piston seal into caliper bore. Ensure seal is not twisted.
2. Install lubricated piston into caliper bore, ensuring piston does not jam and piston seal is properly seated. **Leave piston exposed enough to**

1 SLIDING SLEEVE
2 SEAL

Fig. 3 Caliper sliding sleeve removal

permit installation of boot in groove.
3. Position boot in piston groove and press onto caliper housing. Seat boot using dust boot seal installer tool No. J36538 or equivalent.
4. Install caliper retaining frame, tighten attaching bolts to specifications.
5. Apply suitable grease to sliding sleeves, then install seals in center groove of sliding sleeves.
6. Position sliding sleeves in caliper with inner protective cap groove facing piston. **Leave sleeves exposed enough to permit installation of protective caps.**
7. Install new protective caps into sliding sleeve grooves and press onto caliper housing collar. Seat caps using sliding sleeve dust boot installer tool No. J36647 or equivalent.
8. Push sliding sleeves into housing, then install bleeder valve.
9. Install brake pads and caliper as previously described. Bleed hydraulic system, **Before moving vehicle, pump brake pedal several times to be sure it is firm. Do not move vehicle until a firm pedal is obtained.**

Delco-Moraine Single Piston Front Disc Brake (Type 1)

INDEX

Fig. 1 Typical Delco-Moraine 3000/3075/3100 series caliper exploded view

Fig. 2 Compressing piston and shoes w/C-clamp

DESCRIPTION

This single piston sliding caliper assembly, **Fig. 1**, incorporates a one piece housing with the inboard side of the housing bored for the piston. A seal within the housing bore provides a hydraulic seal between the piston and housing wall.

A spring steel scraper (wear sensor) is incorporated on each inboard shoe. When the shoe lining has worn to within .030 inch of the shoe, the sensor scrapes the rotor and emits an audible high frequency sound indicating that the linings should be replaced.

The caliper assembly slides on the mounting bolts. Upon brake application, fluid pressure against the piston forces the inboard shoe and lining assembly against the inboard side of the disc. This action causes the caliper assembly to slide until the outboard lining comes into contact with the disc. As pressure builds up, the linings are pressed against the disc with increased force.

CALIPER SERVICE

CALIPER REMOVAL

1. Siphon enough brake fluid out of the master cylinder to bring fluid level to 1/3 full to avoid fluid overflow when the caliper piston is pushed back into its bore.
2. Raise vehicle and remove front wheels.
3. Using a C-clamp, as illustrated in **Fig. 2**, push piston back into its bore.
4. If caliper assembly is to be serviced, remove inlet fitting attaching bolt, copper washer, and inlet fitting from caliper housing. Plug opening in inlet fitting to prevent fluid loss and contamination. **Do not crimp brake hose, as this may damage internal structure of hose. If only shoe and lining assemblies are to be replaced, do not disconnect brake line fitting from caliper.**
5. Remove two mounting bolts, **Fig. 3**,

and lift caliper away from disc. If only shoe and lining assemblies are to be replaced, suspend caliper from chassis using suitable hanger. **Do not allow caliper to hang by brake hose.**

CALIPER DISASSEMBLY

1. Remove caliper as outlined above.
2. Clean outside of caliper, then drain brake fluid from caliper.
3. Use clean shop towels to pad interior of caliper assembly, then remove piston by directing compressed air into caliper brake hose inlet hole, **Fig. 4. Use just enough air pressure to ease piston out of bore. Do not place fingers in front of piston for any reason when applying compressed air. This could result in serious personal injury.**
4. Carefully pry dust boot out of bore.
5. Using a small piece of wood or plastic, remove piston seal from bore. **Do not use a metal tool of any kind to remove seal as it may damage bore.**
6. Remove bleeder valve.
7. Inspect piston for scoring, nicks, corrosion, and wear and replace as needed.
8. Inspect caliper housing and seal groove for corrosion, nicks, scoring and excessive wear, and use crocus cloth to polish away corrosion from housing bore. Replace caliper hous-

Fig. 3 Caliper & mounting bolts

Fig. 4 Piston from caliper removal

Fig. 5 Boot to piston installation

Fig. 6 Boot to caliper installation

5. Install the brake hose in the caliper using a new copper gasket.
6. Install shoes and reinstall caliper assembly.

CALIPER INSTALLATION

1. Position caliper over disc, lining up holes in caliper with holes in mounting bracket. If brake hose was not disconnected during removal, be sure not to kink it during installation.
2. Start mounting bolts through sleeves in inboard caliper ears and the mounting bracket, making sure ends of bolts pass under ears on inboard shoe. **Right and left calipers must not be interchanged.**
3. Push mounting bolts through to engage holes in the outboard ears. Then thread mounting bolts into bracket.
4. Tighten mounting bolts to specifications.
5. Check the dimensions between each caliper stop and caliper, **Fig. 7.**
6. If brake hose was removed, reconnect it and bleed the calipers.
7. Replace front wheels, lower vehicle and add brake fluid to master cylinder to bring level to 1/4 inch from top. **Before moving vehicle, pump brake pedal several times to be sure it is firm. Do not move vehicle until a firm pedal is obtained. On some models with low drag calipers,** apply approximately 175 pounds of pressure to the brake pedal three times to properly seat the caliper and related components.

BRAKE PAD SERVICE
REMOVAL

1. Remove caliper assembly as outlined above.
2. Remove inboard shoe. Dislodge outboard shoe and position caliper on the front suspension so the brake hose will not support the weight of the caliper.
3. Remove shoe support spring from piston.
4. Remove two sleeves from inboard ears of the caliper.
5. Remove four rubber bushings from the grooves in each of the caliper ears.

INSTALLATION

1. Lubricate new sleeves, rubber bush-

THE DIMENSION BETWEEN EACH CALIPER STOP AND THE CALIPER SHOULD BE .005"—.012"

FILE TO OBTAIN CLEARANCE

Fig. 7 Checking clearance between caliper & stops

ings, bushing grooves and mounting bolt ends with Delco Silicone Lube or its equivalent.
2. Install new bushings and sleeves in caliper ears. **Position the sleeve so that the end toward the shoe is flush with the machined surface of the ear.**
3. Install shoe support spring by positioning single tang end of spring into notch cut at top of inboard shoe. Press remaining end of spring over bottom edge of shoe until shoe is engaged securely.
4. Position inboard shoe with spring attached into caliper with ear end facing downward and bottom end facing upward with spring resting on inside diameter of piston. Press downward on both ends of shoe until shoe contacts piston and support spring contacts piston inside diameter. **Some inboard replacement brake pads incorporate wear sensors and have a specific left and righthand assembly. Properly installed, the wear sensor will face toward the rear of caliper.**
5. Position outboard shoe in caliper with shoe ears over caliper ears and tab at

ing if corrosion in and around seal groove will not clean up with crocus cloth.
9. Clean all parts with denatured alcohol. Dry with unlubricated compressed air. Blow out all passages in housing and bleeder valve.

CALIPER ASSEMBLY

1. Lubricate caliper piston bore and new piston seal with clean brake fluid. Position seal in bore groove. **Ensure seal is not twisted.**
2. Lubricate piston with clean brake fluid and assemble a new boot into the groove in the piston so the fold faces the open end of the piston, **Fig. 5.**
3. Using care not to unseat the seal, insert piston into bore and force the piston to the bottom of the bore.
4. Position dust boot in caliper counterbore and install, using suitable seal installer, **Fig. 6.** Check the boot installation to be sure the retaining ring molded into the boot is not bent and that the boot is installed below the caliper face and evenly all around. If the boot is not fully installed, dirt and moisture may enter the bore and cause corrosion.

bottom of shoe engaged in caliper cutout.

6. With shoes installed, lift caliper and rest bottom edge of outboard lining on outer edge of brake disc to be sure there is no clearance between outboard shoe tab and caliper abutment.
7. Install caliper and tighten mounting bolts to specifications.
8. Clinch upper ears of outboard shoe by positioning pliers with one jaw on top of upper ear and one jaw in notch on bottom shoe opposite ear, **Fig. 8.** Ears

Fig. 8 Clinching loop eared brake shoe

are to be flat against caliper housing with no radial clearance. If clearance exists, repeat clinching procedure. **Before moving vehicle, pump brake pedal several times to be sure it is firm. Do not move vehicle until a firm pedal is obtained. On some models with low drag calipers,** apply approximately 175 pounds of pressure to the brake pedal three times to properly seat the caliper and related components.

Delco-Moraine Single Piston Front Disc Brake (Type 2)

INDEX

DESCRIPTION

The caliper has a single piston and is mounted to the support bracket by two mounting bolts, **Figs. 1 through 4.** The caliper assembly slides on the two mounting bolts. Upon brake application, fluid pressure against the piston forces the inboard shoe and lining assembly against the inboard side of the disc. This action causes the caliper assembly to slide until the outboard lining comes into contact with the disc. As pressure builds up the linings are pressed against the disc with increased force.

BRAKE PAD SERVICE

REMOVAL

1. Remove caliper assembly as outline above.
2. Remove shoe and lining assemblies from caliper, **Figs. 1 through 4,** noting the following:
   a. **On models with tab mount outer shoe (all except series 3264),** straighten bent over shoe tabs with suitable pliers.
   b. **On models with spring mount outer shoe (series 3264),** insert screwdriver between shoe and caliper and disengage buttons on shoe from holes in caliper.
3. Remove sleeves and bushings from grooves in caliper mounting bolt holes, **Figs. 1 through 4.**

1	MOUNTING BOLT AND SLEEVE	7	PISTON
2	BUSHING	8	BOOT
3	BLEEDER VALVE CAP	9	INBOARD SHOE AND LINING
4	BLEEDER VALVE	10	OUTBOARD SHOE AND LINING
5	CALIPER HOUSING	11	WEAR SENSOR
6	PISTON SEAL		

Fig. 1 Exploded view of Delco-Moraine 3200 series caliper

INSTALLATION

1. Lubricate new bushings with suitable grease, install bushings in caliper grooves, then insert sleeves through bushings.
2. Install retaining spring onto inboard shoe and lining assembly, **Fig. 5,** if equipped, then install inboard shoe into caliper housing.
3. Install outboard shoe and lining assembly into caliper housing ensuring wear sensor is properly positioned. **On models with spring mount shoe (series 3264),** ensure buttons on

shoe are properly engaged in holes in caliper.
4. Install caliper assembly as outlined.
5. **On models with tab mount outer shoe (except series 3264),** clinch outboard shoe to brake caliper as follows:
   a. Apply brakes several times to ensure caliper piston is extended and shoes are fully seated.
   b. Wedge a large flat blade screwdriver between outboard shoe flange and hat section of rotor, **Fig. 6.**
   c. Hold outer pad against caliper with

1. MOUNTING BOLT
2. SLEEVE
3. BUSHING
4. OUTBOARD SHOE & LINING
5. INBOARD SHOE & LINING
6. WEAR SENSOR
7. SHOE RETAINER SPRING
8. BOOT
9. PISTON
10. PISTON SEAL
11. BLEEDER VALVE
12. CALIPER HOUSING
22. BOOT

Fig. 2   Exploded view of Generation I Delco-Moraine 3257 series caliper

1. BOLT BOOT
2. MOUNTING BOLT
3. BUSHING
4. SLEEVE
5. OUTBOARD SHOE & LINING
6. WEAR SENSOR
7. INBOARD SHOE & LINING
8. BOOT
9. PISTON
10. PISTON SEAL
11. BLEEDER VALVE
12. CALIPER HOUSING

Fig. 3   Exploded view of Generation I Delco-Moraine 3264 series caliper

suitable clamp or by applying moderate pressure on brake pedal.

d. Position a ball peen hammer on outboard shoe tab, **Fig. 7**, then using a larger brass hammer, lightly tap the ball peen hammer to bend the outboard shoe tab. Tabs must be bent around casting to approximately 45°.

e. After both tabs have been bent pressure should be released and outboard shoe should be locked into position. If shoe is loose, repeat steps a. through d. **If an out-**board shoe is removed from the caliper, or the tabs unclinched for any reason, then it will be necessary to replace the shoe and lining assemblies. Do not re-clinch outboard shoe locking tabs after having removed shoe from caliper.

CALIPER SERVICE
CALIPER REMOVAL

1. Remove approximately ²/₃ of brake fluid from master cylinder.
2. Raise and support front of vehicle, then remove wheel and tire assembly.
3. Position suitable pliers over inboard pad and housing as shown in **Fig. 8**, and squeeze pliers to compress caliper piston.
4. If caliper assembly is being removed for service, remove inlet fitting attaching bolt, copper washer, and inlet fitting from caliper housing. Plug opening in inlet fitting to prevent fluid loss and contamination. **Do not crimp brake hose, as this may damage internal structure of hose. If only shoe and lining assemblies are to be replaced, do not disconnect brake line fitting from caliper.**
5. Remove Allen head caliper mounting bolts, **Fig. 9**. If bolts show signs of corrosion, use new bolts when installing caliper assembly.
6. Remove caliper assembly from disc. If only shoe and lining assemblies are to be replaced, using a length of wire suspend caliper from spring coil. Never allow caliper to hang from brake hose.

CALIPER DISASSEMBLY

1. Clean outside of caliper, then drain brake fluid from caliper.
2. Use clean shop towels to pad interior of caliper assembly, then remove piston by directing compressed air into caliper brake hose inlet hole, **Fig. 10**. **Use just enough air pressure to ease piston out of bore. Do not place fingers in front of piston for any reason when applying compressed air. This could result in serious personal injury.**
3. Using a screwdriver, remove dust boot from caliper bore, **Fig. 11**.
4. Using a small piece of wood or plastic, remove piston seal from bore. **Do not use a metal tool of any kind to remove seal as it may damage bore.**
5. Remove bleeder valve.
6. Inspect piston for scoring, nicks, corrosion, and wear and replace as needed.
7. Inspect caliper housing and seal groove for corrosion, nicks, scoring and excessive wear, and use crocus cloth to polish away corrosion from housing bore. Replace caliper housing if corrosion in and around seal groove will not clean up with crocus cloth.
8. Clean all parts with denatured alcohol. Dry with unlubricated compressed air. Blow out all passages in housing and bleeder valve.

CALIPER ASSEMBLY

1. Lubricate piston seal with clean brake fluid, then install piston seal into caliper bore groove. Check to ensure piston seal is not twisted.
2. Lubricate caliper bore with clean brake fluid.
3. Insert piston into caliper bore, then force piston down until piston bottoms in bore.

A WEAR SENSOR
2 BOLT/SCREW WITH SLEEVE, FRONT BRAKE CALIPER
3 BUSHING, FRONT BRAKE CALIPER BOLT
5 PAD ASSEMBLY, FRONT DISC BRAKE OUTER
7 PAD ASSEMBLY, FRONT DISC BRAKE INNER
8 BOOT, FRONT BRAKE CALIPER PISTON
9 PISTON, FRONT BRAKE CALIPER
10 SEAL, FRONT BRAKE CALIPER PISTON
11 VALVE, FRONT BRAKE CALIPER BLEEDER

12 HOUSING, FRONT BRAKE CALIPER
20 CAP, FRONT BRAKE CALIPER BLEEDER VALVE

Fig. 4   Exploded view of Generation II Delco-Moraine 3257 & 3264 series caliper

Fig. 10   Applying compressed air to caliper line port

Fig. 5   Retainer spring installation on inboard shoe

Fig. 11   Dust boot removal

Fig. 6   Positioning screwdriver between outboard shoe flange & hat section of rotor

12. CALIPER
14. PLIERS

Fig. 8   Compressing caliper piston w/pliers

TOOL NO. J-29077

Fig. 12   Seating dust boot in caliper

Fig. 7   Positioning hammer to clinch brake pad tabs

Fig. 9   Caliper mounting bolts removal

12. CALIPER
16. BRACKET

CLEARANCE BETWEEN CALIPER AND BRACKET STOPS SHALL BE 0.13-0.30 MM (0.005-0.012 IN.) TWO PLACES

Fig. 13   Checking clearance between caliper & stops

DELCO-MORAINE SINGLE PISTON FRONT DISC BRAKE (TYPE 2)

4. Position outer diameter of dust boot in caliper housing counterbore, then seat boot as shown in **Fig. 12.**
5. Install bleeder screw on caliper housing.

CALIPER INSTALLATION

1. Position caliper assembly over disc and align mounting bolt holes. If brake hoses were not disconnected during removal, use care not to kink hoses during installation.
2. Install mounting bolts and tighten to specifications, **Fig. 9.**
3. Check the dimensions between each caliper stop and caliper, **Fig. 13.** If necessary remove caliper and file ends of bracket to provide proper clearance.
4. If brake hose fitting was disconnected during removal, install brake hose fitting.
5. Fill master cylinder. Bleed brake system if brake line was disconnected and recheck master cylinder fluid level.
6. Install wheel and tire assembly on vehicle, then lower vehicle and check brake system operation. **Before moving vehicle, pump brake pedal several times to be sure it is firm. Do not move vehicle until a firm pedal is obtained.**

Delco-Moraine Single Piston Front Disc Brake (Type 3)

INDEX

1 MOUNTING BOLT	**9** PISTON
2 OUTBOARD SHOE & LINING	**10** PISTON SEAL
3 INBOARD SHOE & LINING	**11** CAP
5 BOLT BOOT	**12** BLEEDER VALVE
6 BUSHING	**13** CALIPER HOUSING
7 SUPPORT BUSHING	**14** BRACKET
8 CALIPER PISTON BOOT	**15** WEAR SENSOR

Fig. 1   Exploded view of Delco-Moraine series 3264M front disc brake caliper

DESCRIPTION

This caliper, **Fig. 1,** has a single bore and is mounted to the support bracket with two mounting bolts. Hydraulic pressure, created by applying force to the brake pedal, is converted by the caliper into friction. The hydraulic pressure is applied equally against the piston and the bottom of the caliper bore moving the piston outward and the housing inward, resulting in a clamping action on the brake rotor.

CALIPER SERVICE

CALIPER REMOVAL

1. Drain approximately 2/3 of brake fluid from master cylinder assembly.
2. Raise and support vehicle, then mark position of wheel and remove tire and wheel assembly.
3. If caliper is to be serviced or replaced, remove bolt securing inlet fitting, then disconnect brake hose, and plug end to prevent loss of fluid and contamination. **Do not crimp brake hose, as this may damage internal structure of hose. If only shoe and lining assemblies are being replaced, do not disconnect brake hose from caliper.**
4. Remove caliper to support mounting bolts, then lift caliper off support. If only shoe and lining assemblies are to be replaced, suspend caliper from chassis using suitable hanger. **Do not allow caliper to hang by brake hose.**
5. Remove insulators (4) from caliper support if equipped, **Fig. 1.**

CALIPER DISASSEMBLY

1. Drain brake fluid from caliper and clean thoroughly.
2. Use clean shop towels to pad inside of caliper, then remove piston by applying compressed air to fluid inlet port. Use only enough air pressure to ease piston from bore. **Keep fingers away from piston to avoid injury as piston is forced out.**
3. Pry dust boot from caliper, taking care not to damage housing bore.
4. With a small wood or plastic tool remove piston seal from caliper bore. **Do not use metal tool since this may damage caliper bore or seal groove.**
5. Inspect piston for scoring nicks, corrosion, wear and damage and replace as needed.
6. Inspect caliper housing and seal groove for corrosion, nicks, scoring and excessive wear. Use crocus cloth to polish away corrosion from housing bore. Replace caliper housing if corrosion in and around seal groove will not clean up with crocus cloth.
7. Remove bleeder screw from caliper housing, **Fig. 1.**
8. Clean components with denatured alcohol and dry with unlubricated compressed air. Blow out all passages in housing and bleeder valve.

MOUNTING BRACKET SERVICE
Removal

1. Remove caliper as outlined previously.
2. Remove mounting bracket attaching bolts, then mounting bracket.

Bushing & Boot Replacement

1. Remove mounting bracket from vehicle.
2. Remove bolt boots from support bushings, **Fig. 1.**
3. Clamp bracket in a suitable vise, then pry support bushings from inner bushings in bracket ears with small screwdriver.
4. Using a paper clip, pull inner bushings from mounting bracket ears.
5. Lubricate inner bushings with silicone based grease, then install bushings flush with bracket ears.
6. Position .080-.090 inch thick shim stock on bracket ear face, then tap support bushings, with plastic mallet, into inner bushings, **Fig. 2.** When properly installed, bushing should protrude .080-.090 inch above bracket ear face.
7. Snap new bolt boots over support bushing lip.

Installation

1. Coat mounting bracket attaching bolt threads with Loctite sealant or equivalent. **Failure to use sealant on mounting bolts may result in loosening of caliper to knuckle attachment.**
2. Align mounting bracket holes, then install mounting bracket and tighten attaching bolts to specifications.

CALIPER ASSEMBLY

1. Install bleeder screw.
2. Lubricate piston seal, piston, caliper bore and dust boot with new brake fluid.

7. SUPPORT BUSHING
20. SHIM STOCK

Fig. 2   Support bushing installation

3. Roll piston seal into seal groove in caliper bore, ensuring seal is fully seated and not twisted.
4. Install dust boot over piston, ensuring lip of boot engages piston groove.
5. Install piston in caliper bore, press piston to bottom of bore, then seat boot in caliper counterbore with suitable installer.

CALIPER INSTALLATION

1. If first design shoe and lining assemblies are being installed, mount insulators (4), **Fig. 1,** on caliper bracket.
2. Position caliper on mounting bracket, ensuring insulators, first design, and mounting bolt boots remain in place.
3. Apply thin coating of silicone grease to caliper mounting bolts, install bolts and tighten to specifications.
4. Install brake hose, if removed.
5. Install wheels and lower vehicle.
6. Fill master cylinder and bleed brakes as needed. **Do not attempt to move vehicle until brake pedal has been pumped several times and a firm brake pedal has been obtained.**

BRAKE PAD SERVICE
REMOVAL

1. Remove caliper assembly as outlined.
2. Remove outboard shoe and lining assembly, using screwdriver to disengage shoe springs from holes in caliper housing.
3. Remove inboard shoe and lining assembly, unsnapping shoe retainer spring from caliper piston bore.
4. If new shoe and lining assemblies are to be installed, compress piston into housing with suitable clamp or pliers, taking care not to damage piston.

INSTALLATION

1. If new shoe and lining assemblies are being installed, compress piston into caliper bore, taking care not to damage piston.
2. Install inboard shoe, snapping shoe retainer spring into piston bore, and ensure shoe is flat against piston.
3. Install outboard shoe assembly, snapping shoe springs into holes in caliper, and ensure shoe is flat against caliper housing.

Delco-Moraine Dual Piston Front Disc Brake

INDEX

1. MOUNTING BOLT
2. OUTBOARD SHOE & LINING
3. INBOARD SHOE & LINING
4. BOLT BOOT
5. BUSHING
6. SUPPORT BUSHING
7. CALIPER BOOT
8. PISTON
9. PISTON SEAL
10. CAP
11. BLEEDER VALVE
12. CALIPER HOUSING
13. BRACKET
14. WEAR SENSOR

Fig. 1 Exploded view of Delco-Moraine 3242 series dual piston caliper

DESCRIPTION

This dual piston sliding caliper, **Fig. 1,** is comprised of two interconnected bores and is attached to a mounting bracket with two mounting bolts. Hydraulic pressure acting on the bottom of the caliper bores forces the pistons outward, enabling the caliper to slide inward, thereby clamping the brake shoes against the rotor.

CALIPER SERVICE

CALIPER REMOVAL

1. Siphon enough brake fluid out of the master cylinder to bring fluid level to 1/3 full to avoid fluid overflow when the caliper pistons are pushed back into bores.
2. Raise vehicle and remove front wheels.
3. Mark relationship between wheel to hub and bearing assembly. Remove tire and wheel assembly.

4. Using a suitable C-clamp and block of wood, push pistons back together into caliper bores.
5. If caliper assembly is to be serviced, remove inlet fitting attaching bolt, copper washer, and inlet fitting from caliper housing. Plug opening in inlet fitting to prevent fluid loss and contamination. **Do not crimp brake hose, as this may damage internal structure of hose. If only shoe and lining assemblies are to be replaced, do not disconnect brake line fitting from caliper.**
6. Remove two mounting bolts, then remove caliper. If only shoe and lining assemblies are to be replaced, suspend caliper from chassis using suitable hanger. **Do not allow caliper to hang by brake hose.**

CALIPER DISASSEMBLY

1. Remove caliper assembly as outlined previously, then drain brake fluid from caliper.
2. Position shop towel in interior part of caliper, then slowly apply compressed air to inlet port and remove pistons. **It is imperative that one piston be**

partially installed to facilitate removal of second piston from bore. **A pad or wooden spacer may be used to prevent complete removal of first piston.**
3. Remove piston boots from caliper bores, then using suitable wooden or plastic tool, pry piston seals from caliper bore grooves. **Do not use a metal tool of any kind to remove seal as it may damage bore.**
4. Remove bleeder valve from caliper.
5. Inspect piston for scoring, nicks, corrosion, and wear and replace as needed.
6. Inspect caliper housing and seal grooves for corrosion, nicks, scoring and excessive wear, and use crocus cloth to polish away corrosion from housing bore. Replace caliper housing if corrosion in and around seal grooves will not clean up with crocus cloth.
7. Clean all parts with denatured alcohol. Dry with unlubricated compressed air. Blow out all passages in housing and bleeder valve.

MOUNTING BRACKET SERVICE

Removal

1. Remove caliper as outlined previously.
2. Using suitable Torx bit, remove mounting bracket attaching bolts and the mounting bracket.

Bushing & Boot Replacement

1. Remove mounting bracket from vehicle.
2. Remove bolt boots from support bushings, **Fig. 1.**
3. Clamp bracket in a suitable vise, then pry support bushings from inner bushings in bracket ears with small screwdriver.
4. Using a paper clip, pull inner bushings from mounting bracket ears.
5. Lubricate inner bushings with silicone based grease, then install bushings flush with bracket ears.

6. Position .080-.090 inch thick shim stock on bracket ear face, then drive support bushings into inner bushings, **Fig. 2**. When properly installed, bushing should protrude .080-.090 inch above bracket ear face.
7. Snap new bolt boots over support bushing lip.

Installation

1. Coat mounting bracket attaching bolt threads with Loctite sealant or equivalent.
2. Align mounting bracket holes, then install mounting bracket and tighten attaching bolts to specifications.

CALIPER ASSEMBLY

1. Install bleeder valve.
2. Lubricate piston seals with clean brake fluid, then carefully install seals into caliper bore grooves. **Ensure seals are not twisted.**
3. Lubricate boots and install onto pistons, then push pistons fully into caliper bores.
4. Seat boots into caliper bores using boot seal installer tool No. J-36349 or equivalent.

CALIPER INSTALLATION

1. Position caliper over rotor and onto

6. SUPPORT BUSHING
23. SHIM STOCK

Fig. 2   Support bushing installation

mounting bracket.
2. Lubricate entire length of mounting bolts with silicone based grease, then install bolts and tighten to specifications.
3. If inlet fitting was removed, install fitting using new copper washer.
4. Install front wheels, fill master cylinder

to proper level, then bleed brake system as required. **Before moving vehicle, pump brake pedal several times to be sure it is firm. Do not move vehicle until a firm pedal is obtained.**

BRAKE PAD SERVICE

REMOVAL

1. Remove caliper as outlined previously.
2. Lift upward on outward shoe retaining spring of outboard shoe until it clears center lug, then remove shoe from caliper.
3. Pull inboard shoe outward to disengage retainer springs from pistons, then remove inboard shoe from caliper.

INSTALLATION

1. Install inboard shoe into caliper, ensuring retainer spring tangs are fully positioned into pistons.
2. Snap outboard shoe retaining spring over housing center lug, then install outboard shoe into caliper.
3. Install brake caliper as outlined further on.

PBR Dual Piston Front Disc Brake

INDEX

DESCRIPTION

This front caliper, **Fig. 1**, consists of dual pistons and an aluminum housing which is suspended on the shoe and lining assemblies. Hydraulic pressure, created by applying force to the brake pedal, acts equally against the pistons and the bottom of the caliper bores to move the pistons outward. This action slides the caliper inward, resulting in a clamping action on the brake rotor. This clamping action forces the linings against the rotor, creating the friction necessary to stop the vehicle.

CALIPER SERVICE

CALIPER REMOVAL

1. Remove 2/3 of the total brake fluid capacity from master cylinder reservoir.
2. Raise and support vehicle, then remove tire and wheel assembly.
3. Install two wheel retaining nuts to retain rotor in position.

1 BLEEDER VALVE CAP
2 BLEEDER VALVE
3 CALIPER HOUSING
4 SEAL
5 CALIPER PISTON
6 BOOT
7 RETAINER PIN
8 INBOARD SHOE AND LINING ASSEMBLY
9 OUTBOARD SHOE AND LINING ASSEMBLY
10 BRACKET
11 CIRCLIP
12 BIAS SPRING

Fig. 1   Exploded view of PBR dual piston front caliper

4. If caliper requires overhaul, remove inlet fitting attaching bolt, then disconnect inlet fitting from caliper housing. Discard the two gaskets, then plug openings in inlet fitting and caliper to prevent loss or contamination of fluid. **Do not crimp brake hose, as this may damage internal structure of hose.**

5. Remove circlip (11) and retaining pin (7), **Fig. 1**, then pull caliper off rotor and mounting bracket. If only shoe and linings require replacement, suspend caliper from upper control arm to prevent damage to brake hose.

CALIPER DISASSEMBLY

1. Remove shoe and lining assemblies as previously described.
2. Pad interior of caliper housing with shop towels to prevent damage to pistons during removal.
3. Position shop towel in interior part of caliper, then slowly apply compressed air to inlet port and remove pistons. **It is imperative that one piston be partially installed to facilitate removal of second piston from bore. A pad or wooden spacer may be used to prevent complete removal of first piston.**
4. Remove dust boots from pistons.
5. Using a small piece of wood or plastic, remove piston seal from bore. **Do not use a metal tool of any kind to remove seal as it may damage bore.**
6. Remove bleeder valve cap and bleeder valve.
7. Inspect piston for scoring, nicks, corrosion, and wear and replace as needed.
8. Inspect caliper housing and seal groove for corrosion, nicks, scoring and excessive wear, and use crocus cloth to polish away corrosion from housing bore. Replace caliper housing if corrosion in and around seal groove will not clean up with crocus cloth.

3 CALIPER HOUSING
8 INBOARD SHOE AND LINING

Fig. 2 Bottoming pistons in caliper bore

9. Clean all parts with denatured alcohol. Dry with unlubricated compressed air. Blow out all passages in housing and bleeder valve.

CALIPER ASSEMBLY

1. Install cap onto bleeder valve, then install bleeder valve into caliper.
2. Using clean brake fluid, lubricate piston seals, then install seals into caliper bore grooves. Ensure seals are not twisted during installation.
3. Using clean brake fluid, lubricate caliper bores and piston assemblies.
4. Install boot over end of piston. Place piston into caliper bore, then push downward until fully bottomed in bore. Ensure boot is properly seated into groove around piston and into groove in caliper bore.
5. Repeat step 4 for remaining piston.
6. Install shoes and linings as outlined

further on, then bleed brake system.

CALIPER INSTALLATION

1. Ensure guiding surfaces on shoe and lining assemblies and mounting bracket are seated correctly, then position caliper over rotor and onto mounting bracket.
2. Press caliper housing downward to compress bias springs (12), **Fig. 1**, then install new retainer pin and circlip. **Two sets of retainer pins are available for service, one for base calipers and one for heavy duty. Since the circlip grooves are cut in different positions, ensure the correct retainer pin is used.**
3. If caliper was overhauled, reconnect inlet fitting using new gaskets, then bleed brake system as required.
4. Reinstall wheel and tire assembly, then lower vehicle.
5. Fill master cylinder to proper level, then pump brake pedal firmly and slowly three times to bring pads into contact with brake rotor.

BRAKE PAD SERVICE

REMOVAL

1. Remove brake caliper as outlined previously.
2. Position suitable pliers over caliper and center of inboard shoe and lining as shown, **Fig. 2**, then squeeze pliers to bottom pistons in caliper bores.
3. Remove shoe and lining assemblies.

INSTALLATION

1. Install inboard shoe and lining, ensuring tangs on shoe fully engage pistons. When properly installed, shoe should be flush with piston.
2. Install outboard shoe and lining into caliper housing, ensuring insulators are fully seated into holes in outboard side of housing.
3. Install caliper as outlined further on.

Delco-Moraine Single Piston Rear Disc Brake (Type 1)

INDEX

DESCRIPTION

Upon application of the brakes, **Figs. 1 and 2**, the cone and piston move out as one part. The nut remains stationary on the high lead screw and a gap develops between the cone and nut. When lining wear occurs, the cone and piston do not return to their original position, thereby leaving a small gap equal to the lining wear between the nut and cone. The adjusting spring causes the nut to rotate on the high lead screw to close the gap and adjust the caliper.

Upon application of parking brake, the lever rotation causes the high lead screw to turn and the nut to move down the screw, thereby loading through the cone and the cone-clutch interface of the piston, resulting in a clamp load on the linings.

When the parking brake is released, the cone rotates on the clutch interface to adjust the caliper. The clutch interface prevents the cone from turning when the parking brake is applied.

CALIPER SERVICE

CALIPER REMOVAL

Do not mix power steering fluid with

brake fluid. If brake seals contact steering fluid or steering seals contact brake fluid, damage will result.

1. Remove two thirds of the total brake fluid capacity from the master cylinder front reservoir, to prevent overflow of brake fluid.
2. Support vehicle on a hoist and remove tire and wheel assembly.
3. Install one nut with flat side facing rotor to prevent rotor from falling out when caliper is removed.
4. Loosen parking brake cable tension at equalizer, then remove cable from parking brake lever and remove return spring, locknut, lever, lever seal and anti-friction washer. **Lever must be held in place while removing nut.**
5. Clean surface in area of lever seal, then using a 7 inch (or larger) C-clamp, with the solid end on lever stop and screw end on back of outboard lining, turn clamp until piston is bottomed in caliper. **Do not position C-clamp on actuator screw.**
6. Before removing clamp, lubricate housing surface under lever seal with silicone lubricant.
7. Install anti-friction washer, a new lever seal and lever. **Install lever on hex with arm pointing downward.**
8. Rotate lever toward front of vehicle and while holding in this position, install nut and **torque** to 25 ft. lbs. and rotate lever back to stop.
9. Disconnect brake line from caliper and plug openings to prevent loss of fluid and contamination. **Do not crimp brake hose, as this may damage internal structure of hose.**
10. Remove the brass bolt from block, if applicable. **If brake line nut is seized, brass bolt and block can be removed with brake line attached by removing bolt. Plug openings to prevent loss of fluid and entry of dirt.**
11. Remove caliper mounting bolts and remove caliper.
12. Reverse procedure to install and **torque** caliper mounting bolts to 30 ft. lbs. **When installing brass bolt and block, use two new copper gaskets. Torque** bolt or connector to 30 ft. lbs.

CALIPER DISASSEMBLY

1. Clamp caliper in a vise and remove the two mounting sleeves and four bushings, **Fig. 2.**
2. Remove shoe dampening spring from end of piston.
3. If installed, remove locknut, lever, lever seal, and anti-friction washer.
4. Rotate parking brake lever in parking brake apply direction to remove piston from housing, **Fig. 3.** If piston will not move, Use a 9/16 inch wrench, rotate actuator screw clockwise on right-hand caliper or counterclockwise on lefthand caliper until the piston moves from housing. **Pad caliper with shop cloths when removing piston.**
5. Remove balance spring, then remove actuator screw by pressing on thread end.

1. NUT
2. LEVER
6. LEVER SEAL
6A. ANTIFRICTION WASHER
8. OUTBOARD SHOE & LINING
9. INBOARD SHOE & LINING
10. SHOE RETAINER
11. BOLT BOOT
12. SLEEVE
13. CALIPER BOOT
14. PLUG
15. PISTON ASSEMBLY
16. RETAINER
17. PISTON LOCATOR
18. PISTON SEAL
19. ACTUATOR SCREW
20. BALANCE SPRING & RETAINER
21. THRUST WASHER
22. SHAFT SEAL
25. CALIPER HOUSING

Fig. 1   Cross-sectional view of typical Delco-Moraine rear disc brake

1. NUT
2. LEVER
3. RETURN SPRING
4. BOLT
5. BRACKET
6. LEVER SEAL
6A. ANTIFRICTION WASHER
8. OUTBOARD SHOE & LINING
9. INBOARD SHOE & LINING
10. SHOE RETAINER
11. BOLT BOOT
12. SLEEVE
13. CALIPER BOOT
14. PLUG
15. PISTON ASSEMBLY
16. RETAINER
17. PISTON LOCATOR
18. PISTON SEAL
19. ACTUATOR SCREW
20. BALANCE SPRING & RETAINER
21. THRUST WASHER
22. SHAFT SEAL
23. CAP
24. BLEEDER VALVE
25. CALIPER HOUSING
26. WEAR SENSOR
27. MOUNTING BOLT

Fig. 2   Exploded view of rear disc brake caliper

6. Remove shaft seal, and thrust washer from actuator screw.
7. Remove dust boot. **Take care not to scratch caliper housing or bore.**
8. Using a small piece of wood or plastic, remove piston seal from bore. **Do not use a metal tool of any kind to remove seal as it may damage bore.**
9. Remove bleeder screw, fitting, copper washers, and bolt. Remove bracket only if damaged.
10. Inspect piston for scoring, nicks, corrosion, and wear and replace as needed.

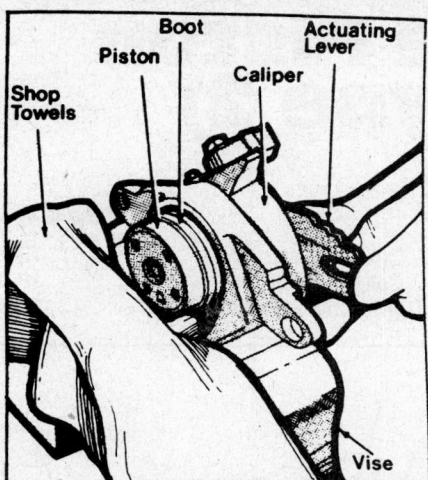

Fig. 3 Piston removal from bore

Fig. 6 Boot installation into caliper

Fig. 4 Piston positioning in caliper

Fig. 7 Piston check valve removal

Fig. 5 Piston installation into caliper

Fig. 8 Piston rotation in boot

11. Inspect caliper housing and seal groove for corrosion, nicks, scoring and excessive wear, and use crocus cloth to polish away corrosion from housing bore. Replace caliper housing if corrosion in and around seal groove will not clean up with crocus cloth.
12. Clean all parts with denatured alcohol. Dry with unlubricated compressed air. Blow out all passages in housing and bleeder valve.

CALIPER ASSEMBLY

1. Install bleeder screw and **torque** to 116 inch lbs., then install bracket, if removed, and **torque** to 31 ft. lbs.
2. Install fitting and bolt, if equipped, using new copper washer and **torque** to 24 ft. lbs.
3. Lubricate and install new piston seal. **Make sure is not twisted.**
4. Install new boot onto piston assembly with lip of boot located in piston groove and boot fold toward end of piston that contact inboard brake shoe.
5. Install new thrust washer on actuator screw, with copper side of washer towards the piston assembly.
6. Install lubricated shaft seal on actuator screw, then install actuator screw in piston.

7. Coat piston seal with clean brake fluid. Install balance spring into piston and install assembly into caliper housing, **Fig. 4.**
8. With piston installer tool No. J-23072 or equivalent push piston fully into caliper housing, **Fig. 5. The piston must be pushed straight into caliper to prevent damage to the actuator screw seal as it passes through hole in rear of piston bore.**
9. Before removing piston installer tool No. J-23072, install lubricated anti-friction washer, new lever seal, lever and locknut. Position lever away from stop, rotate forward and hold lever in position, then **torque** nut to 35 ft. lbs.
10. Remove piston installer tool No. J-23072, rotate lever back to stop and install return spring.
11. With dust boot installer tool No. J-26296 or equivalent, drive boot until seal bottoms in caliper housing, **Fig. 6.**
12. Install dampening spring in groove in end of piston.

BRAKE PAD SERVICE

1. Remove caliper as described previously and remove shoe and lining.
2. Remove and discard the two caliper mounting sleeves and the four bushings. Using silicone lubricant, install new bushings and seals. **Sleeves are installed in inner bushings.**
3. Remove and discard piston two-way check valve and install a new one, **Fig. 7. If leakage is noted from end of piston after check valve is re-**

moved caliper must be overhauled.
4. Position new inboard shoe assembly on piston. The D-shaped tab must fit into indentation in piston. If piston requires rotation, use spanner wrench to rotate piston, **Fig. 8. Install new spring retainers as applicable.**
5. Install new outboard shoe assembly onto caliper. Install caliper and **torque** mounting bolts to 30 ft. lbs.
6. Position channel lock pliers over brake shoe ears, if equipped, and bottom edge of caliper. While holding moderate force on brake pedal, clinch outboard shoe.

ADJUSTMENTS

PARKING BRAKE, ADJUST

1. Lubricate parking brake cables at underbody rub points and at equalizer hooks and ensure free movement of all cables.
2. With parking brake fully released, jack up both rear wheels.
3. Remove slack from cable by holding brake cable stud and tightening equalizer nut. **After tightening nut, check that caliper levers are against stops on caliper housing. If not, loosen cable until levers return to stops.**
4. Actuate parking brake several times to check adjustment.

Delco-Moraine Single Piston Rear Disc Brake (Type 2)

INDEX

1. SLEEVE BOLT
2. OUTBOARD SHOE & LINING
3. INBOARD SHOE & LINING
4. PAD CLIP
5. CABLE SPRING CLIP
6. PIN BOOT
7. BOLT BOOT
8. SLEEVE BOOT
9. BOLT SLEEVE
10. PIN BOLT
11. PIN SLEEVE
12. BOOT RING
13. PISTON BOOT
14. PISTON ASSEMBLY
15. PISTON SEAL
16. BLEEDER VALVE CAP
17. BLEEDER VALVE
18. LEVER RETURN SPRING
19. BOLT AND WASHER
20. CABLE SUPPORT BRACKET
21. CALIPER BODY ASSEMBLY
22. CALIPER SUPPORT
23. WEAR SENSOR

Fig. 1   Disassembled view of Delco Moraine single piston rear disc brake caliper. Type 2

1. SLEEVE BOLT
5. CABLE SPRING CLIP
19. BOLT AND WASHER
20. CABLE SUPPORT BRACKET
21. CALIPER BODY ASSEMBLY
22. CALIPER SUPPORT
24. PARKING BRAKE CABLE
25. PARKING BRAKE LEVER
26. BRAKE HOSE

Fig. 2   Caliper installation

DESCRIPTION

The caliper assembly, **Fig. 1,** has a single bore and is mounted to the support bracket with two mounting bolt and sleeve assemblies. Hydraulic pressure created by applying the brake pedal, is converted by the caliper to a stopping force. This force acts equally against the piston and the bottom of the piston bore to move the piston outward and to slide the caliper inward resulting in a clamping action. This clamping action presses the linings against the rotor, creating friction to stop the vehicle.

When the parking brake is applied, the external caliper parking brake lever moves and rotates a spindle within the caliper housing. As the spindle rotates, a connecting rod is pushed against an internal adjusting screw which is threaded into a sleeve nut in the piston assembly. This causes the piston assembly to move outward bringing the inboard shoe and lining assembly against the rotor. As the inboard shoe and lining contacts the rotor, a reaction force causes the caliper housing to

slide inward pressing the outboard shoe and lining against the rotor.

The piston assembly contains a self adjusting mechanism to keep the parking brake in proper adjustment. As the linings are worn, the piston moves through the seal to maintain proper lining to rotor clearance. The park brake adjusts to proper clearances through an internal sleeve nut that rotates and moves as one unit with the piston.

CALIPER SERVICE

CALIPER, REPLACE

1. Raise and support vehicle.
2. Mark relationship of wheel to axle flange, then remove wheel and tire assembly.
3. Remove brake hose from caliper, **Fig. 2.** Plug openings in caliper and brake hose to prevent fluid loss and contamination.
4. Lift up on end of cable spring to free end of cable from lever, then disconnect parking brake cable from lever.

5. Remove bolt and washer attaching cable support bracket to caliper body assembly.
6. Remove sleeve bolt and caliper body assembly.
7. Reverse procedure to install noting the following:
   a. **Torque** sleeve bolt to 20 ft. lbs.
   b. **Torque** cable support bracket to 32 ft. lbs.
   c. Bleed brakes.

CALIPER DISASSEMBLY

1. Remove caliper from vehicle as described under "Caliper Replace."
2. Pad interior of caliper assembly with a clean shop towel, then remove piston assembly using low pressure compressed air into caliper inlet hole, **Fig. 3. Do not place fingers in front of piston in an attempt to catch or protect piston when applying compressed air. This could result in serious injury.**
3. Using a small screwdriver, pry up one end of boot ring, **Fig. 4.** Work boot ring out of caliper groove.
4. Using a small wooden or plastic tool, remove piston seal from caliper bore groove.
5. Remove bleeder valve and bleeder valve cap.

Fig. 3   Removing piston

2. OUTBOARD SHOE & LINING
3. INBOARD SHOE & LINING
4. PAD CLIP
21. CALIPER BODY ASSEMBLY
22. CALIPER SUPPORT
23. WEAR SENSOR

Fig. 6   Shoe & lining installation

6. If lever return spring replacement is required, remove by using a screwdriver to disengage return spring from parking brake lever, then unhook spring from stopper pin, **Fig. 5**.
7. Remove pin boot, pin bolt, bolt sleeve and sleeve bolt from caliper body.
8. Remove pin bolt and pin sleeve from caliper support.
9. Clean all parts in clean denatured alcohol, then dry with unlubricated low pressure compressed air. Blow out all passages in caliper body and bleeder valve.
10. Inspect piston assembly for nicks, cracks, wear or corrosion. Replace piston if any damage is found.
11. Inspect piston bore for scoring, nicks, wear or corrosion. Use crocus cloth to polish out light corrosion. Replace caliper if any heavy corrosion is found. **Do not hone caliper bore.**
12. Inspect seal groove for nicks or burrs. If found, replace caliper.
13. Inspect boots for cuts, tears or deterioration. If damaged, replace boots.

12. BOOT RING
13. PISTON BOOT
14. PISTON ASSEMBLY
21. CALIPER BODY ASSEMBLY

Fig. 4   Removing boot ring

14. Inspect bolt sleeve and pin sleeve for corrosion or damage. Replace corroded or damaged sleeves. **Do not attempt to polish away corrosion.**

CALIPER ASSEMBLY

1. Lubricate pin sleeve with silicone grease, then install pin bolts and pin sleeve to caliper support. **Torque** bolts to 20 ft. lbs.
2. Lubricate sleeve boot with silicone grease, then compress lip on sleeve boot and push it all the way through caliper body assembly until lip emerges and seals on inboard face of caliper ear.
3. Lubricate push bolt sleeve with silicone grease, then push it in through lip end of boot until boot seats in sleeve groove at other end.
4. Install bolt boot onto caliper body.
5. Install small end of pin boot over pin sleeve until boot seats in pin groove.
6. If removed, position new lever return spring with hook end around stopper pin, then pry other end of spring over lever.
7. Install bleeder valve and bleeder valve cap. **Torque** bleeder valve to 8 ft. lbs.
8. Lubricate new piston seal with clean brake fluid and install in groove in caliper bore ensuring it is not twisted.
9. Install piston boot onto piston assembly.
10. Lubricate piston assembly with clean brake fluid.
11. Start piston assembly in by hand, then thread into bottom of caliper bore using spanner type tool in slots in end of piston assembly.
12. Ensure outside edge of piston boot is smoothly seated in counterbore of caliper body assembly.
13. Work boot ring into groove near open end of caliper bore using care not to pinch piston boot between boot ring and caliper body.
14. After installing ring, lift inner edge of boot next to piston assembly and press out any trapped air. Boot must lay flat.
15. Install caliper on vehicle as described under "Caliper Replace."

18. LEVER RETURN SPRING
21. CALIPER BODY ASSEMBLY
25. PARKING BRAKE LEVER
27. STOPPER PIN

Fig. 5   Removing lever return spring

PISTON SLOTS MUST BE ALIGNED AS SHOWN BEFORE INSTALLING CALIPER OVER SHOE & LININGS

13. PISTON BOOT
14. PISTON ASSEMBLY
21. CALIPER BODY ASSEMBLY

Fig. 7   Positioning piston slots

BRAKE PAD SERVICE

1. Remove 2/3 of brake fluid from master cylinder reservoir.
2. Raise and support vehicle.
3. Mark relationship of wheel to axle flange, then remove wheel and tire assembly.
4. Remove bolt and washer attaching cable support bracket to caliper body, **Fig. 2**.
5. Remove sleeve bolt and pivot caliper assembly up, **Fig. 6**. **Do not completely remove caliper assembly body.**
6. Remove outboard and inboard shoe and linings and two pad clips from caliper support.
7. Using a suitable spanner type tool in piston slots to turn piston assembly and thread it into caliper body assembly.
8. After bottoming piston, lift inner edge of boot next to piston assembly and press out any trapped air.
9. Ensure slots in end of piston are positioned as shown in **Fig. 7** before pivoting caliper body assembly down over shoe and linings in caliper support. Use suitable spanner type tool to turn piston as necessary.

10. Install pad clips and outboard and inboard shoe and linings in caliper support. **Ensure wear sensor is on outboard shoe positioned downward at leading edge of rotor during forward wheel rotation.**

11. Pivot caliper body assembly down over shoe and lining assemblies being careful not to damage piston boot on inboard shoe.

12. After caliper body is in position, recheck installation of pad clips. If necessary, use a small screwdriver to reseat or center pad clips on support abutments.

13. Install sleeve bolt and **torque** to 20 ft. lbs.

14. Install cable support bracket and **torque** bolt to 32 ft. lbs.

15. Install wheels and tires aligning previous marks, then lower vehicle.

16. Apply approximately 175 lbs. of force to brake pedal three times to seat shoe and linings against rotor.

ADJUSTMENTS

PARKING BRAKE, ADJUST

1. Cycle brake system as follows:
   a. Apply service brake with a pedal force of 150 lbs. and release.
   b. Fully apply parking brake using approximately 125 lbs. of force on final stroke, and release.
   c. Apply and release parking brake two additional times as described above.

2. Check parking brake pedal assembly for full release by turning ignition on and inspecting brake warning light. Light should be off. If brake warning light is on and parking brake appears to be fully released, operate the manual pedal release lever and pull downward on front park brake cable to remove slack from pedal assembly.

3. Raise and support vehicle.

4. Check parking brake levers on rear calipers. Levers should be against the stops on caliper housing. If levers are not against stops, check for binding in rear brake cables and position levers against stops.

5. Tighten parking brake cable at adjuster until either left or right lever begins to move off of stop.

6. Loosen adjuster until lever which moved off of stop in step four is again resting on stop. **Both levers should be resting on caliper stops after completing this step.**

7. Operate parking brake several times to check adjustment. A firm pedal feel should be obtained by pumping pedal less than one stroke.

8. Inspect left and right caliper levers. Both levers must be resting on stops after adjustment of parking brake.

9. Check operation of parking brake. If possible, place vehicle on a grade and check parking brake holding ability.

Delco-Moraine Single Piston Rear Disc Brake (Type 3)

INDEX

DESCRIPTION

This rear caliper, **Fig. 1,** has a single bore and is mounted to the support bracket with two mounting bolts. Hydraulic pressure, created by applying force to the brake pedal, is converted by the caliper into friction. The hydraulic pressure is applied equally against the piston and the bottom of the caliper bore moving the piston outward and the caliper housing inward, resulting in a clamping action on the brake rotor.

The caliper includes an integral parking brake mechanism. When the parking brake is applied, the lever turns an actuator screw which is threaded into a nut in the caliper piston. As the actuator screw turns, the piston is forced out, applying force on the rotor. The piston contains a self-adjusting mechanism to keep the parking brake in proper adjustment and to ensure proper clearance when the parking brake is released.

CALIPER SERVICE
CALIPER REMOVAL

1. Drain approximately 2/3 of brake fluid from master cylinder assembly.

2. Raise and support vehicle, then remove tire and wheel assembly.

1 NUT	15 PISTON ASSEMBLY
2 LEVER	16 RETAINER
3 RETURN SPRING	17 PISTON LOCATOR
4 BOLT	18 PISTON SEAL
5 BRACKET	19 ACTUATOR SCREW
6 LEVER SEAL	20 BALANCE SPRING & RETAINER
7 OUTBOARD SHOE & LINING	21 THRUST WASHER
8 OUTBOARD SHOE & LINING	22 SHAFT SEAL
9 INBOARD SHOE & LINING	23 CAP
10 SHOE RETAINER	24 BLEEDER VALVE
11 BOLT BOOT	25 CALIPER HOUSING
12 SLEEVE	26 WEAR SENSOR
13 CALIPER BOOT	27 MOUNTING BOLT
14 TWO WAY CHECK VALVE	

Fig. 1   Exploded view of Delco-Moraine 7735 series rear caliper

3. Loosen tension on parking brake cable at equalizer, then disconnect cable and remove return spring from parking brake lever, **Fig. 1.**

4. Hold parking brake lever in position, loosen retaining nut, then remove nut, lever and seal.

5. Position two adjustable pliers over inboard shoe tabs and flanges on caliper housing as shown, **Fig. 2,** then

Fig. 2 Bottoming piston in caliper bore

25. CALIPER HOUSING
29. SHOE TAB

bottom piston in caliper bore.
6. Reinstall lever seal, lever and retaining nut.
7. If caliper assembly is to be serviced, remove inlet fitting attaching bolt, copper washer, and inlet fitting from caliper housing. Plug opening in inlet fitting to prevent fluid loss and contamination. **Do not crimp brake hose, as this may damage internal structure of hose.** If only shoe and lining assemblies are to be replaced, do not disconnect brake line fitting from caliper.
8. Remove caliper mounting bolts, then lift caliper from mounting bracket. If only shoe and lining assemblies are being replaced, suspend caliper from chassis with suitable hanger. **Do not allow caliper to hang from brake hose.**

CALIPER DISASSEMBLY

1. Remove caliper assembly as outlined previously.
2. Secure caliper assembly in vise and drive out sleeves and bolt boots. Insulate interior of caliper with shop towels.
3. Rotate shoe retainer until tabs are aligned with notches in piston, then remove shoe retainer, **Fig. 1.**
4. Remove locknut, lever, and lever seal, if installed.
5. Remove piston by rotating actuator screw in parking brake apply direction to work piston from caliper bore **Fig. 3.**
6. Remove balance spring (20), then remove actuator screw by pressing on threaded end, **Fig. 1.**
7. Remove seal and thrust washer from actuator screw.
8. Pry dust boot from caliper taking care not to damage caliper bore.
9. Remove piston locator retainer, then the locator.
10. Using a small piece of wood or plastic,

23. ACTUATOR SCREW

Fig. 3 Piston removal from caliper

remove piston seal from bore. **Do not use a metal tool of any kind to remove seal as it may damage bore.**
11. Remove bleeder screw. Remove bracket (5) and bolt (4), **Fig. 1,** if damaged.
12. Inspect piston for scoring, nicks, corrosion, and wear and replace as needed.
13. Inspect caliper housing and seal groove for corrosion, nicks, scoring and excessive wear, and use crocus cloth to polish away corrosion from housing bore. Replace caliper housing if corrosion in and around seal groove will not clean up with crocus cloth.
14. Clean all parts with denatured alcohol. Dry with unlubricated compressed air. Blow out all passages in housing and bleeder valve.

CALIPER ASSEMBLY

1. Install bleeder screw.
2. If removed, install bracket (5) and bolt (4), **Fig. 1,** then tighten bolt to specifications.
3. Lubricate piston seals and bore grooves with new brake fluid, then roll piston seal into seal groove in bore, ensuring seal is fully seated and not twisted.
4. Lubricate piston locator with new brake fluid, then position locator on piston using piston locator installer tool No. J-36627 or equivalent.
5. Install thrust washer on actuator screw, with grayish side towards caliper housing, then install lubricated shaft seal onto actuator screw.
6. Install actuator screw into piston assembly.
7. Install balance spring in piston recess in housing.
8. Install piston assembly, pressing piston in until locator is past retainer groove, turn actuator screw as necessary to allow piston assembly to move toward bottom of caliper bore, then install retainer ring.
9. Install lubricated dust boot over piston with inside lip in groove in piston and boot fold toward end of piston that contacts brake shoe, then bottom piston in caliper bore.
10. Install lubricated lever seal over end of actuator screw, ensuring seal bead is against caliper housing.
11. Install parking brake lever over actuator screw, rotate lever away from stop,

11. SLEEVE BOOT
12. SLEEVE
25. CALIPER HOUSING

Fig. 4 Bolt boot & sleeve installation

then hold lever and **torque** retaining nut to 32 ft. lbs. After tightening retaining nut, rotate lever back to stop.
12. Seat dust boot in caliper counterbore using suitable driver.
13. Install shoe retainer in groove on end of piston, ensuring retainer tabs are properly aligned with piston notches.
14. Install sleeves and bolt boots into caliper housing as follows:
   a. Lubricate sleeves, bolt boots and caliper mounting bolt holes with silicone based grease.
   b. Install one bolt boot into groove in mounting bolt hole of caliper housing.
   c. Push sleeve into mounting bolt hole, past inner diameter of bolt boot, and position as shown in view A of **Fig. 4.**
   d. Install second bolt boot in groove at other end of mounting bolt hole as shown in view B of **Fig. 4.**
   e. Push sleeve in opposite direction until grooves of sleeve seat in inner diameter of both bolt boots as shown in view C of **Fig. 4.**
   f. Repeat steps b through e to install remaining bolt boots and sleeve.
15. Install caliper as outlined further on.

CALIPER INSTALLATION

1. Push sleeves inward, away from inboard brake shoe.
2. Reconnect brake hose bracket to suspension, then position caliper over rotor and onto mounting bracket.
3. Install mounting bolts and tighten to specifications.
4. Reinstall bracket (5) and bolt (4), **Fig. 1,** tighten bolt to specifications, then

reconnect brake line to caliper using new copper washers.

5. Remove retaining nut, parking brake lever and lever seal, then clean area around seal and actuator screw.
6. Lubricate, then install lever seal. Ensure seal is fully seated against caliper.
7. Install parking brake lever onto actuator screw hex, ensuring lever faces downward, then install retaining nut.
8. While holding lever against stop on caliper, **torque** retaining nut to 35 ft. lbs.
9. Install lever return spring, then reconnect parking brake cable.
10. Install wheels and lower vehicle, then fill master cylinder and bleed brakes as needed. **Before moving vehicle, pump brake pedal several times to be sure it is firm. Do not move vehicle until a firm pedal is obtained.**
11. After installation is completed, adjust parking brake as follows:
    a. Depress brake pedal several times to seat linings.
    b. Fully apply and release parking brake approximately three times. Each full application may require two full pedal strokes.
    c. Raise and support vehicle, then remove rear wheels. Reinstall two wheel nuts to retain rotor.
    d. Turn ignition switch on, and observe brake warning light. Light should be Off. If light remains on, operate manual brake release and pull downward on front parking brake cable to remove slack from pedal assembly.
    e. Check that parking brake levers on both calipers are against caliper stops. If not, check for binding at rear cables. If cables are not binding proceed to next step.
    f. Loosen adjustment at equalizer until both parking brake levers are against caliper stops.
    g. Tighten cable at equalizer until ei-

ther parking brake lever moves off caliper stop, then loosen cable until lever just contacts stop. With cable properly adjusted, a firm pedal should be obtained by pumping parking brake two full strokes. Rear wheels should be fully locked.
    h. After adjustment is completed, install wheels and lower vehicle.

BRAKE PAD SERVICE
REMOVAL

1. Remove caliper as outlined previously.
2. Remove outboard shoe assembly, disengaging buttons on shoe from holes in caliper.
3. Remove inboard shoe assembly, pressing in on edge of shoe from open side of caliper and tilting shoe outward to release it from retainer.
4. Remove two-way check valve from end of piston with screwdriver. **If leakage is noted from piston hole after removing check valve, caliper must be overhauled.**

INSTALLATION

1. Lubricate, then install two-way check valve into piston.
2. Install inboard shoe assembly as follows:
    a. Engage inboard shoe edge in retainer tabs closest to caliper bridge, then press down and snap shoe tabs at open side of caliper. Ensure shoe lays flat against piston.
    b. Ensure buttons on back of shoe engage D-shaped notches in piston. Rotate piston as needed with spanner wrench tool No. J-7624 or equivalent. Piston is properly aligned when one of the D-shaped notches is nearest caliper bridge.
    c. Wear sensor should be at the lead-

ing edge of shoe during forward wheel rotation.
3. Install outboard shoe assembly, snapping shoe springs into holes in caliper. Ensure pad lays flat against caliper.

ADJUSTMENTS
PARKING BRAKE, ADJUST

1. Apply service brake pedal three times with a force of approximately 175 lbs.
2. Fully apply and release parking brake three times. Full application may require two pedal strokes.
3. Raise and support vehicle, then mark relationship between wheel and axle flange.
4. Check parking brake pedal assembly for full release as follows:
    a. Turn ignition switch to On position.
    b. If "Brake" lamp is illuminated, operate manual brake release and pull downward on front parking brake cable to remove slack from pedal assembly.
5. Remove rear wheel and tire assemblies, then install two lug nuts to retain each rotor assembly.
6. If two parking brake levers on both calipers are not against lever stops on caliper housings, check for binding in rear cables and/or loosen cables at adjuster until both left and right levers are against their stops.
7. Tighten parking brake cable at adjuster until either the left or right lever begins to move off the stop, then loosen adjustment until lever moves back barely touching stop.
8. Operate parking brake several times to check adjustments. A firm pedal feel should be obtained by pumping pedal two full strokes and rear wheels should not rotate forward when parking brake is fully applied.
9. Install wheel and tire assemblies, aligning marks made in step 3.

Delco-Moraine Single Piston Rear Disc Brake (Type 4)

INDEX

DESCRIPTION

This caliper, Fig. 1, has a single bore and is mounted to the support bracket with two mounting bolts. Hydraulic pressure, created by applying force to the brake pedal, is converted by the caliper into friction.

The hydraulic pressure is applied equally against the piston and the bottom of the caliper bore moving the piston outward and the housing inward, resulting in a clamping action on the brake rotor.

Rear disc brake calipers include an integral parking brake mechanism. When the

parking brake is applied, the lever turns an actuator screw which is threaded into a nut in the caliper piston. As the actuator screw turns, the piston is forced out, applying force to the rotor. The piston contains a self adjusting mechanism to keep the parking brake in proper adjustment and to

Fig. 1 Exploded view of Delco-Moraine series 3738M rear disc brake caliper

1	NUT	12	SHOE RETAINER	23	ACTUATOR SCREW
2	PARK BRAKE LEVER	14	BOLT BOOT	24	BALANCE SPRING & RETAINER
3	RETURN SPRING	15	SUPPORT BUSHING	25	THRUST WASHER
4	DAMPER	16	BUSHING	26	SHAFT SEAL
5	BOLT	17	CALIPER PISTON BOOT	27	CAP
6	BRACKET	18	TWO-WAY CHECK VALVE	28	BLEEDER VALVE
7	LEVER SEAL	19	PISTON ASSEMBLY	29	CALIPER HOUSING
8	ANTI-FRICTION WASHER	20	RETAINER	30	BRACKET
9	MOUNTING BOLT	21	PISTON LOCATOR	31	WEAR SENSOR
10	OUTBOARD SHOE & LINING	22	PISTON SEAL	40	RETAINING CLIP
11	INBOARD SHOE & LINING				

Fig. 2 Inboard shoe installation

ensure proper clearance when the parking brake is released.

BRAKE PAD SERVICE

REMOVAL

1. Remove caliper assembly as outlined.
2. Remove outboard shoe assembly, unsnapping springs from holes in caliper.
3. Remove inboard shoe assembly, pressing in on edge of shoe from open side of caliper and tilting shoe outward to release it from retainer.
4. Remove bushings from caliper mounting bracket holes, **Fig. 1**, and remove two-way check valve from end of piston with screwdriver. **If leakage is noted from piston hole after removing check valve, replace actuator and overhaul caliper.**

INSTALLATION

1. Install lubricated bushings into bolt holes in caliper bracket.
2. Bottom piston in caliper bore using suitable pliers, protecting piston to prevent damage. **Do not allow pliers to contact actuator screw.**
3. Lubricate new two-way check valve, then insert valve into piston.
4. Install inboard shoe assembly as follows:
   a. Engage inboard shoe edge in straight tabs of retainer, then press

12	SHOE RETAINER
19	PISTON ASSEMBLY
29	CALIPER HOUSING

Fig. 3 Positioning caliper piston and pad retainer

down and snap shoe under S-shaped tabs, **Fig. 2**.
   b. Ensure shoe lays flat against piston and that retainer and piston are properly aligned. Note that tab on retainer are different, **Fig. 3**, and rotate retainer as needed.
   c. Ensure buttons on back of shoe engage D-shaped notches in piston. Rotate piston as needed with spanner wrench tool No. J-7624 or equivalent. Piston is properly aligned when D-shaped notches

are aligned with caliper mounting bolt holes, **Fig. 3**.
5. Install outboard shoe assembly, snap shoe springs into holes in caliper and ensure pad lays flat against caliper. **Wear sensor should be at trailing edge of shoe during forward wheel rotation.**

CALIPER SERVICE

CALIPER REMOVAL

1. Drain approximately 2/3 of brake fluid from master cylinder assembly.
2. Raise and support vehicle, then remove tire and wheel assembly.
3. Loosen tension on parking brake cable at equalizer.
4. Remove retaining clip from parking brake lever, if equipped, disconnect cable, then remove spring and damper, **Fig. 1**.
5. Hold parking brake lever, remove locknut.
6. Remove lever, lever seal, and anti-friction washer.
7. Bottom piston into caliper bore to provide clearance between linings and rotor.
8. Reinstall anti-friction washer, lever seal (sealing bead against housing), lever, and locknut.
9. If caliper is to be serviced, remove inlet fitting attaching bolt, then disconnect and plug inlet fitting. **Do not crimp brake hose, as this may damage internal structure of hose. If only shoe and lining assemblies are to be replaced, do not disconnect brake line.**
10. Remove caliper mounting bolts, then lift caliper from bracket. If only shoe and lining assemblies are being replaced, suspend caliper from chassis with suitable hanger. **Do not allow caliper to hang from brake hose.**

23. ACTUATOR SCREW

Fig. 4   Piston removal from caliper

11. Remove insulators from caliper bracket, if equipped.

CALIPER DISASSEMBLY

1. Remove caliper assembly as outlined.
2. Rotate shoe retainer until tabs are aligned with recesses in piston, then remove shoe retainer, **Fig. 1.**
3. If installed remove locknut, lever, lever seal, and anti-friction washer.
4. Secure caliper assembly in vise and insulate interior of caliper with shop towels.
5. Remove piston by rotating actuator screw in parking brake apply direction to work piston from caliper bore **Fig. 4.**
6. Remove balance spring (24), then remove actuator screw by pressing on threaded end, **Fig. 1.**
7. Remove shaft seal and thrust washer from actuator screw.
8. Pry dust boot from caliper taking care not to damage caliper.
9. Remove retainer snap ring, then the locator.
10. Using wooden or plastic tool remove piston seal from caliper bore. **Do not use metal tool since this may damage caliper bore or seal groove.**
11. Inspect piston for scoring, nicks, corrosion, and wear and replace as needed.
12. Inspect caliper housing and seal groove for corrosion, nicks, scoring and excessive wear, and use crocus cloth to polish away corrosion from housing bore. Replace caliper housing if corrosion in and around seal groove will not clean up with crocus cloth.
13. Remove bleeder screw. Remove bracket only is damaged.
14. Clean components with denatured alcohol and dry with unlubricated compressed air. Blow out all passages in housing and bleeder valve.

MOUNTING BRACKET SERVICE
Removal

1. Remove caliper as outlined previously.
2. Remove mounting bracket attaching bolts, then mounting bracket.

Bushing & Boot Replacement

1. Remove mounting bracket from vehicle.
2. Remove bolt boots from support bushings, **Fig. 1.**
3. Clamp bracket in a suitable vise, then pry support bushings from inner bushings in bracket ears with small screwdriver.
4. Using a paper clip, pull inner bushings from mounting bracket ears.
5. Lubricate inner bushings with silicone based grease, then install bushings flush with bracket ears.
6. Position .080-.090 inch thick shim stock on bracket ear face, then tap support bushings, with plastic mallet, into inner bushings, **Fig. 5.** When properly installed, bushing should protrude .080-.090 inch above bracket ear face.
7. Snap new bolt boots over support bushing lip.

Installation

1. Coat mounting bracket attaching bolt threads with Loctite sealant or equivalent. **Failure to use sealant on mounting bolts may result in loosening of caliper to knuckle attachment.**
2. Align mounting bracket holes, then install mounting bracket and tighten attaching bolts to specifications.

CALIPER ASSEMBLY

1. Install bleeder valve.
2. Install bracket, if removed.
3. Lubricate piston seal, piston, caliper bore and dust boot with new brake fluid.
4. Roll piston seal into seal groove in caliper bore, ensuring seal is fully seated and not twisted.
5. Lubricate piston locator with new brake fluid, then position locator on piston using piston locating tools No. J135588-1 and No. J135588-2 or equivalents.
6. Install thrust washer, grayish side towards caliper housing, on actuator screw.
7. Install lubricated shaft seal on actuator screw, then install actuator screw assembly into caliper housing.
8. Install balance spring in piston recess.
9. Install piston assembly, pressing piston in until locator is past snap ring groove, turn actuator screw as necessary to allow piston assembly to move toward bottom of caliper bore, then install snap ring.
10. Install lubricated dust boot over piston with inside lip in groove in piston and boot fold toward end of piston that contacts brake shoe, then bottom piston in caliper bore.
11. Install anti-friction washer and seal over end of actuator screw, ensuring seal bead is against caliper housing.

14. BOLT BOOT
15. SUPPORT BUSHING
30. BRACKET

Fig. 5   Support bushing installation

12. Install parking brake lever over actuator screw, rotate lever away from stop, hold lever and **torque** retaining nut to 35 ft. lbs., then rotate lever back to stop.
13. Seat dust boot in caliper counterbore using suitable driver.
14. Install shoe retainer on end of piston, ensuring piston and retainer are positioned as shown in **Fig. 3.**

CALIPER INSTALLATION

1. Lubricate sliding surfaces and mount insulators, if equipped, on caliper bracket.
2. Position caliper on mounting bracket ensuring insulators and retaining bolt boots remain in position.
3. Coat mounting bolts with thin film of silicone grease, install bolts and tighten bolts to specifications.
4. Install brake hose using new sealing washers.
5. Install parking brake lever as follows:
   a. Lubricate lever seal and anti-friction washer.
   b. Install washer, seal and parking brake lever. **Seal should be against caliper housing. Parking brake lever should be pointing downward.**
   c. Move lever off stop, hold lever and **torque** retaining nut to 35 ft. lbs., then rotate lever against stop.
6. Install spring and damper, connect parking brake cable, then secure assembly with retaining clip, if used.
7. Tighten brake cable at equalizer until parking brake lever moves off stop, then loosen cable until lever just contacts stop.
8. Install wheels and lower vehicle, fill master cylinder, and bleed brakes as needed. **Do not attempt to move vehicle until brake pedal has been moved several times a firm brake pedal is obtained.**

ADJUSTMENTS
PARKING BRAKE, ADJUST

1. Apply and release service brakes three times with a force of approxi-

mately 175 lbs.

2. Fully apply parking brake (may require up to 4 pedal strokes) using approximately 125 lbs. force on last stroke, then release. Repeat procedure two more times.

3. Inspect parking brake pedal assembly for full release by observing brake warning lamp.

4. If lamp is on and parking brake appears to be fully released, operate manual pedal release lever and pull down on front cable to remove slack from pedal assembly.

5. Raise and support vehicle and inspect parking brake levers on rear calipers.

6. If levers are not against stops, inspect rear cables for binding and position levers against stops.

7. Tighten brake cable at equalizer until either lever begins to move off stop.

8. Loosen cable until lever returns to stop. Both levers must be resting on stops after adjustment.

9. Operate parking brake several times, ensuring firm pedal can be obtained by pumping pedal less than 3 1/2 strokes.

10. Release parking brake and ensure both caliper levers are against stops.

PBR Single Piston Rear Disc Brake

INDEX

1. SEAL
2. SPRAG CLIP
3. PIVOT PIN
4. SPRING
5. LEVER
6. BLEEDER VALVE
7. BLEEDER VALVE CAP
8. BRACKET
9. BOLT/SCREW
10. BOLT/SCREW
11. ADJUSTER SCREW
12. NUT
13. BOLT/SCREW
14. CALIPER HOUSING
15. GUIDE PIN
16. BOOT
17. BRACKET
18. SEAL
19. PISTON
20. BOOT
21. RETAINER
22. PUSHROD
23. PRELOAD SPRING
24. ACTUATING COLLAR
25. BOCT
26. RETURN SPRING
27. BUSHING
28. CLAMP ROD
29. INBOARD SHOE AND LINING ASSEMBLY
30. OUTBOARD SHOE AND LINING ASSEMBLY
31. RETAINER

Fig. 1   Exploded view of PBR single piston rear caliper

DESCRIPTION

This rear caliper, **Fig. 1,** consists of a single piston and an aluminum housing which is suspended in a mounting bracket through two slide pins. Hydraulic pressure, created by applying force to the brake pedal, acts equally against the piston and the bottom of the caliper bore to move the piston outward. This action slides the caliper inward, resulting in a clamping action on the brake rotor. This clamping action forces the linings against the rotor, creating the friction necessary to stop the vehicle.

The parking brake mechanism on this caliper is completely independent of the hydraulic brake system. When the parking brake is applied, the lever on the caliper causes the pushrod, actuating collar and clamp rod assembly to move outward. This causes the caliper to move inward, mechanically forcing the linings against the rotor.

BRAKE PAD SERVICE

REMOVAL

1. Remove 2/3 of the total brake fluid capacity from master cylinder reservoir.

2. Raise and support vehicle, then remove tire and wheel assembly.

3. Install two wheel retaining nuts to retain rotor in position.

4. Position one end of a suitable C-clamp against inlet fitting bolt, and the other end against outboard shoe and lining, then tighten clamp as shown, **Fig. 2,** until piston fully bottoms in caliper bore.

5. Remove upper guide pin bolt and discard.

6. Loosen lower guide pin bolt, then pivot caliper downward on the lower guide pin bolt to expose the shoe & lining assemblies. Use care to avoid damaging brake hose.

7. Remove shoes and linings from mounting bracket.

14. CALIPER HOUSING
17. BRACKET

Fig. 2   Bottoming piston in caliper bore

INSTALLATION

1. Install outboard shoe and lining onto mounting bracket, ensuring insulator on shoe is positioned toward caliper housing.
2. Install inboard shoe and lining. Ensure wear sensor is positioned nearest caliper piston. When properly installed, sensor should be in trailing position when wheel is rotated in forward direction.
3. Pivot caliper into position over shoes and linings. Ensure springs on outboard shoe do not protrude through inspection hole in housing. If protrusion is evident, lift caliper housing and readjust position of outboard shoe and lining.
4. Install new upper guide pin bolt and **torque** to 26 ft. lbs., then **torque** lower bolt to 16 ft. lbs.
5. Fill master cylinder to proper level, then pump brake pedal firmly and slowly three times to bring pads into contact with brake rotor.

CALIPER SERVICE

CALIPER REMOVAL

1. Disable parking brake automatic adjuster as follows:
   a. Working from inside vehicle, remove driver seat cushion, then the parking brake lever cover screws and cover.
   b. Using .080 inch gauge wire, fabricate a tool to disengage drive pawl from sector, **Fig. 3.**
   c. Using tool mentioned above, disengage drive pawl from sector, then insert a nail through anchor plate to keep drive pawl in disengaged position.
   d. Pull up on lever until it aligns with pawl, then depress button until lever is fully downward.
   e. Visually inspect that anchor plate is fully against stud. If not, repeat procedure as needed.
   f. Pull front parking brake cable rearward to slacken cable at caliper assembly.
2. Raise and support vehicle, then remove tire and wheel assembly.
3. Install two wheel retaining nuts to retain rotor in position.

1	ANCHOR PLATE	5	LEVER
2	NAIL	6	SCREW
3	DRIVE PAWL	7	COVER
4	DRIVE SECTOR		

Fig. 3   Disabling parking brake automatic adjuster mechanism

4. If caliper requires overhaul, remove inlet fitting attaching bolt, then disconnect inlet fitting from caliper housing. Discard the two gaskets, then plug openings in inlet fitting and caliper to prevent loss or contamination of fluid.
5. Remove caliper lever return spring. Discard spring if coils are open.
6. Disconnect parking brake cable from lever (5) and caliper bracket (8), **Fig. 1.**
7. Remove upper and lower guide pin bolts, then remove caliper from rotor and mounting bracket. If caliper does not require overhaul, suspend it from suspension to prevent damage to brake line.

CALIPER DISASSEMBLY

1. Remove caliper as previously outlined.
2. Remove the two return springs from actuating collar, then pull collar out of caliper housing and remove clamp rod (28) and bushing (27), **Fig. 1.** Discard bushing.
3. Bend back boot retainer tabs, then remove retainers (21, 31), boots (20, 25) and pushrod (22) from actuating collar. Remove preload spring (23) from retainer (31), then discard retainers and boots.
4. Use clean shop towels to pad interior of caliper assembly, then remove piston by directing compressed air into caliper brake hose inlet hole, **Use just enough air pressure to ease piston out of bore. Do not place fingers in front of piston for any reason when applying compressed air. This could result in serious personal injury.**
5. Using a small piece of wood or plastic, remove piston seal from bore. **Do not use a metal tool of any kind to remove seal as it may damage bore.**
6. Remove bleeder valve cap and bleeder valve.
7. Remove seal (1), sprag clip (2) and lever (5) from pivot pin (3). Discard sprag clip.
8. Clean all metal components with suitable solvent, then dry with compressed air.
9. Inspect parking brake lever components, piston, caliper bore and mounting bracket for scoring, excessive wear or corrosion. Replace parts as necessary.

CALIPER ASSEMBLY

1. Using clean brake fluid, lubricate piston seal, then install seal into caliper bore groove. Ensure seal is not twisted during installation.
2. Using clean brake fluid, lubricate caliper bore and piston.
3. Place piston into caliper bore, then push downward until fully bottomed in bore.
4. Apply lubricant provided in repair kit to actuating collar (24), then install pushrod (22), new boots (20, 25) and new retainers (21, 31) onto collar, **Fig. 1.** Clamp retainers firmly against collar, then bend tabs on retainer (21) to hold assembly together.
5. Reconnect preload spring (23) onto retainer (31).
6. Apply lubricant provided in repair kit to clamp rod (28), then slide rod through holes in boot (25) and actuating collar (24). Ensure boot is firmly positioned against reaction plate on clamp rod.
7. Lubricate new compliance bushing (27), then install bushing onto clamp rod (28).
8. Lubricate grooved bead of inner boot (20), boot groove in caliper housing and actuating collar with lubricant provided in repair kit.
9. Push clamp rod to bottom of piston mating hole, then pull actuating collar (24) and seat inner boot (20) into boot groove in caliper housing.
10. Ensure pushrod (22) is positioned in hole in caliper housing, then install bleeder cap and valve.
11. If removed, install pivot pin (3) and new nut (12) onto caliper, **torque** nut

A. APPLY PRESSURE HERE
B. MEASURE HERE
5. LEVER
11. ADJUSTER SCREW
14. CALIPER HOUSING

Fig. 4   Parking brake free travel adjustment

to 16 ft. lbs., then lubricate parking brake lever (5) and pivot pin.

12. Install pivot pin seal (1), parking brake lever and new sprag clip (2), ensuring teeth of sprag clip face away from lever, then snap seal cap over pivot pin.
13. Install the two collar return springs (26) onto retainer (31). Ensure retainer enters springs at end of second coil.
14. Install adjustment screw (11) into caliper housing until actuating collar is parallel to piston bore face of housing.
15. Lubricate guide pins with suitable grease, then slide boots onto pins.
16. Fill boots with grease, then install into mounting bracket. Ensure boots are properly positioned in grooves in pins and mounting bracket.
17. Install caliper and bleed brake system, then adjust parking brake free travel as outlined under "Caliper Installation."

CALIPER INSTALLATION

1. Install shoe and lining assemblies, if removed, as outlined previously.

2. Position caliper over rotor and onto mounting bracket, then install upper and lower guide pin bolts. **Torque** upper bolt to 26 ft. lbs. and lower bolt to 16 ft. lbs.
3. Attach parking brake cable to caliper bracket and lever, then install lever return spring.
4. If removed, install inlet fitting using new gaskets, then bleed brake system.
5. If caliper was overhauled, adjust parking brake free travel as follows:
   a. Have an assistant apply a light load to brake pedal until rotor can no longer be turned by hand.
   b. Apply pressure to caliper lever in direction shown in **Fig. 4.**
   c. Measure free travel between caliper lever and housing. Free travel should be .024-.028 inch. If free travel is not as specified, proceed to next step.
   d. Remove adjustment screw, then clean thread adhesive from threads.
   e. Coat threads with new adhesive,

reinstall adjustment screw, then turn as required until specified free travel is obtained. **Turning screw clockwise increases free travel, while counterclockwise rotation decreases travel.**
   f. Release brake pedal, then firmly apply brake pedal three times and recheck free travel. Repeat adjustment procedure as necessary.
6. Remove nail from anchor plate installed during caliper removal procedure.
7. Apply and release parking brake three times, then lift lever upward and ensure parking brake fully engages at 7-9 clicks.
8. Release parking brake. No brake drag should exist and no gap between caliper housings and parking levers should be evident.
9. Install parking brake lever cover, screws and driver's cushion.
10. Reinstall tire and wheel assembly, then check and refill master cylinder as required.
11. Start engine and pump brake pedal several times to seat brake linings.

ADJUSTMENTS

PARKING BRAKE, ADJUST

1. Release parking brake lever, then raise and support vehicle.
2. Remove rear wheels then install lug nuts on two opposite wheel studs to hold brake rotor in position.
3. Back caliper pistons into bores.
4. Loosen parking brake cable adjusting nut until there is no tension on parking brake shoes.
5. Turn each brake rotor until parking brake shoe star adjuster is visible through hole in rotor.
6. Adjusting one side at a time, tighten adjuster until rotor cannot be turned by hand, then back star wheel off 5 to 7 notches. **Adjust parking brake shoes by inserting a suitable tool through hole in rotor. On drivers side, tighten adjuster by moving handle of tool upwards. On passenger side, tighten adjuster by moving handle of tool downward.**
7. Install rear wheels and pull parking lever up two notches.
8. Tighten cable adjusting nut at equalizer until there is drag on wheels.
9. Release parking brake lever and check adjustment. No drag should be felt when rotating wheels.

Toyota/GM Single Piston Caliper

INDEX

Fig. 2   Front caliper support installation

1 MOUNTING BOLT	6. PISTON	10. CAP	14. PAD
2. DUST BOOT	7. PISTON SEAL	11. BLEEDER SCREW	15. PAD SUPPORT PLATE
3. COLLAR	8. BOOT	12. ANTI-RATTLE SPRING	16. PAD WEAR INDICATOR PLATE
4 SLIDE BUSHING	9. SET RING	13. ANTI-SQUEAL SHIM	17. MOUNTING BRACKET
5 CALIPER HOUSING			

Fig. 1   Exploded view of Toyota/GM front brake caliper

DESCRIPTION

The caliper is a single bore design and is mounted to a carrier assembly. Hydraulic pressure, created by applying brake pedal, is converted by caliper to a stopping force. This force acts equally against the piston and bottom of caliper bore to move the piston outward and to slide caliper inward resulting in a clamping action on the rotor. The clamping action forces linings against the rotor, creating friction necessary to stop the vehicle.

COMPONENT REPLACEMENT

FRONT CALIPER

REMOVAL

1. Siphon 2/3 of the brake fluid from master cylinder, raise and support vehicle, and remove wheels.
2. Reinstall 2 wheel nuts to retain rotor, then remove caliper mounting bolts, **Fig. 1.**
3. Remove union nut securing brake hose to caliper and drain fluid into suitable container. **If caliper is only being removed for brake pad replacement, do not disconnect brake hose.**
4. Compress piston as needed, then remove caliper. If brake hose remains connected, secure caliper aside to prevent hose from being stretched.

INSTALLATION

1. Seat piston in caliper bore, taking care not to damage piston.
2. Ensure support plates, **Fig. 2,** and anti-rattle springs are properly positioned, then mount caliper over rotor onto mounting bracket.
3. Install caliper mounting bolts and **torque** bolts to 18 ft. lbs.
4. Install brake hose and mounting bolts, using new copper gaskets, then **torque** bolt to 17 ft. lbs.
5. Refill master cylinder and bleed brake system.

REAR CALIPER

REMOVAL

1. Siphon 2/3 of the brake fluid from master cylinder, raise and support vehicle, and remove wheels.
2. Reinstall 2 wheel nuts to retain rotor.
3. Remove union nut securing brake hose to caliper and drain fluid into suitable container.
4. Remove clip from parking brake and disconnect parking brake cable.
5. Remove caliper mounting bolt, lift caliper, then remove parking brake pin clip.
6. While pushing parking brake crank, **Fig. 3,** remove pin.
7. Lift caliper and remove from vehicle.

INSTALLATION

1. Position caliper over mounting bracket, then install mounting bolt and **torque** to 14 ft. lbs.
2. Install parking brake clip.
3. Install brake hose and union bolt, using new copper gaskets, then **torque** bolt to 22 ft. lbs.
4. Refill master cylinder and bleed brake system.
5. Adjust parking brake as follows:
   a. Pull upward on parking brake lever several times, then fully release lever.
   b. Depress brake pedal several times to automatically adjust brake.
   c. When properly adjusted, parking brake crank should just contact stopper pin.

1. ANTI-RATTLE SPRINGS	4. ANTI-SQUEAL SHIMS
2. BRAKE PADS	5. SUPPORT PLATES
3. WEAR INDICATOR	

Fig. 4 Front brake pad assembly

ILL NO.	DESCRIPTION	ILL NO.	DESCRIPTION
201	BLEEDER SCREW	218	PISTON
202	BRAKE HOSE	219	ADJUSTING BOLT SPRING RETAINER
203	UNION BOLT	220	ADJUSTING BOLT STOPPER
204	GASKET	221	O-RING
205	MAIN PIN BOOT	222	DUST BOOT
206	MOUNTING BRACKET BOLT	223	SLIDE BUSHING
207	MAIN PIN	224	STOPPER PIN
208	SLIDING BUSHING	225	SPRING
209	MOUNTING BRACKET	226	PARKING BRAKE CRANK
210	PARKING BRAKE STRUT	227	CALIPER HOUSING
211	ADJUSTING BOLT	228	MOUNTING BOLT
212	ADJUSTING BOLT SPRING PLATE	229	CABLE SUPPORT BRACKET
213	SPRING	230	CABLE SUPPORT BRACKET BOLT
214	SNAP RING	231	ANTI-SQUEAL SHIM
215	PISTON SEAL	232	ANTI-RATTLE SPRING
216	SET RING	233	PAD SUPPORT PLATE
217	BOOT	234	PAD

Fig. 3 Exploded view of Toyota/GM rear brake caliper

Fig. 5 Pressing piston into caliper bore

BRAKE PAD SERVICE
FRONT

Replace brake pads on one wheel at a time to prevent opposite side caliper piston from being forced out of bore.

REMOVAL

1. Remove caliper as outlined, leaving brake hose connected, and secure caliper aside.
2. Remove 2 anti-rattle clips, then the brake brake pads, **Fig. 4.**
3. Remove pad wear indicator plates and anti-squeal shims.
4. Remove support plates.

INSTALLATION

1. Install new support plates on caliper mounting bracket, **Fig. 2.**
2. Install new wear indicators and anti-squeal shims on each pad, **Fig. 4,** then position pads in caliper mounting bracket. **Ensure arrow on wear indicator is pointing in rotating direction of rotor.**

3. Install anti-rattle springs.
4. Seat piston in caliper bore, then install caliper and mounting bolts, and **torque** bolts to 18. ft lbs.
5. Refill master cylinder and bleed brakes as needed.

REAR

Replace brake pads on one wheel at a time to prevent opposite side caliper piston from being forced out of bore.

REMOVAL

1. Siphon 2/3 of the brake fluid from master cylinder, raise and support vehicle, and remove wheels.
2. Reinstall 2 wheel nuts to retain rotor.
3. Remove caliper mounting bolt, then swing caliper upward to expose brake compone nts. **Do not remove main pin from caliper.**
4. Remove brake pads, anti-squeal shims, anti-rattle springs and the two support plates, **Fig. 3.**

INSTALLATION

1. Install new pad support plates to lower part of mounting bracket.
2. Install new anti-rattle springs to upper side of mounting bracket.
3. Position new anti-squeal shims to backside of each brake pad, then install pads onto mounting bracket. Ensure pads are positioned so wear indicators are on top side.
4. Using brake piston driver tool No. J-37149 or equivalent, **Fig. 5,** slowly turn piston clockwise and press into caliper bore until it locks in position at bottom of bore.
5. With pad protrusion fitted into piston stopper groove, swing caliper downward and install mounting bolt. **Torque** bolt to 14 ft. lbs.
6. Fill master cylinder to proper level, then depress brake pedal several times to seat linings and to actuate parking brake automatic adjuster.

CALIPER SERVICE
FRONT CALIPER OVERHAUL
DISASSEMBLY

1. Remove 2 caliper slide bushings, 4 dust boots and spacer collars, **Fig. 1.**
2. Pry out caliper dust boot retaining ring and remove dust boot.
3. Place clean shop towels in caliper web to protect piston, then apply com-

Fig. 6   Lubrication points for front caliper assembly

Fig. 7   Lubrication points for rear caliper assembly

25 mm
(0.98 in.)

Fig. 8   Stopper pin installation

pressed air to caliper fluid inlet to force piston from bore. **Keep fingers clear of caliper web when removing piston. Use only enough air pressure to ease piston out of bore, or piston may be damaged.**
4. Remove piston seal from caliper bore, taking care not to mar machined surface of caliper.
5. Remove bleeder valve.
6. Clean components with alcohol and wipe dry with clean, lint free shop towels. Blow out caliper body and fluid passages with clean, filtered compressed air.
7. Inspect caliper and piston for damage, distortion, excessive wear and pitting, and replace as needed.
8. Replace mounting bolts, collars and caliper slides if they are damaged or worn.

ASSEMBLY

1. Apply lithium soap base glycol grease to components shown in **Fig. 6.**
2. Install piston seal in caliper, ensuring seal is squarely seated in groove.
3. Press piston into bore, ensuring piston enters bore straight.
4. Seat piston dust boot in caliper groove, then install retaining ring.
5. Install 2 collars and 4 slide bushing dust boots, **Fig. 1,** rotating boots as they are pressed in to ensure they are fully seated.
6. Install slide bushings through dust boots, ensuring boots remain seated in caliper grooves.

REAR CALIPER OVERHAUL
DISASSEMBLY

1. Remove sliding bushing and the four dust boots, **Fig. 3.**
2. Using a suitable screwdriver, remove caliper set ring and boot.
3. Using brake piston driver tool No. J-37149 or equivalent, rotate piston out of caliper bore.
4. Pry piston seal from caliper bore.
5. Position adjusting bolt guide nut tool No. J-37150 or equivalent over adjusting bolt, tighten tool, then remove snap ring from caliper bore and pull out adjusting bolt and components.
6. Remove parking brake strut and cable

support bracket, then the parking brake crank torsion spring.
7. Remove parking brake crank, then the crank boot by tapping on metal portion of boot with screwdriver or similar tool. **Do not remove crank boot unless boot is damaged or excessively worn.**
8. Using a suitable punch, drive stopper pin from caliper.
9. Inspect all components for damage, wear or corrosion, and replace as necessary.

ASSEMBLY

1. Clean all parts not included in repair kit and dry with compressed air.
2. Lubricate all components indicated in **Fig. 7** with lithium based grease.
3. Install stopper pin into caliper until pin protrudes .98 inch outward as shown in **Fig. 8.**
4. If removed during disassembly, tap parking brake crank boot into position in caliper using a 24mm socket.
5. Install parking brake crank. Ensure crank boot aligns with groove of crank seal.
6. Install cable support bracket, then press surface of bracket flush against caliper and **torque** bolt to 34 ft. lbs. When properly installed, clearance between parking brake crank and support bracket should be .236 inch.
7. Install torsion spring, then check that

parking brake crank subassembly touches stopper pin.
8. Install parking brake strut. **Before adjusting strut, ensure needle bearing rollers do not catch on caliper bore.**
9. Position new O-ring onto adjusting bolt, then assemble stopper, plate, spring and spring retainer onto bolt. Hand tighten assembly using adjusting bolt guide nut tool No. J-37150 or equivalent. When properly assembled, inscribed surface of stopper should face upward and notches of spring retainer should align with notches of stopper.
10. Position adjusting bolt subassembly into caliper, then install snap ring, ensuring opening faces toward bleeder side of caliper. Pull upward on adjusting bolt and ensure bolt does not move.
11. Check operation of parking brake by moving crank by hand. Adjusting bolt should move smoothly, with no evidence of binding.
12. Install piston seal into caliper bore, then using brake piston driver tool No. J-37149 or equivalent, install piston and bottom in bore by turning tool clockwise.
13. Align center of piston stopper groove with protrusion of caliper bore.
14. Install boot and set ring into caliper.
15. Using a 21mm socket and suitable vise, press new main pin boot into caliper housing.
16. Install sliding bushing and bolt, then install caliper as outlined previously.

ADJUSTMENTS
PARKING BRAKE, ADJUST

1. Check that parking brake lever travel is correct by pulling parking brake lever all the way up and counting the number of clicks.
2. Parking brake lever travel should be 4 to 7 clicks. If not, remove console, loosen locknut and turn adjusting nut until travel is correct.

Disc Brake Caliper Specifications

Year	Model	Caliper Bore Dia. Inch
BUICK		
1991	Reatta	④
1991-93	Century	②
	LeSabre	2.52
	Park Ave.	2.52
	Regal	⑤
	Riviera	④
	Skylark	2.24
	Roadmaster	2.94
CADILLAC		
1991-92	Brougham	2.94
	Fleetwood FWD	2.52
1991-93	DeVille	2.52
	Eldorado	④
	Seville	④
1993	Fleetwood RWD	2.94
CHEVROLET		
1991-93	Beretta	2.25
	Camaro	③
	Caprice	2.94
	Cavalier	2.24
	Corsica	2.25
	Corvette	①
	Lumina	⑤

Year	Model	Caliper Bore Dia. Inch
OLDSMOBILE		
1991	Cutlass Calais	2.24
1991-92	Custom Cruiser	2.94
	Toronado	④
	Trofeo	④
1991-93	Cutlass Ciera	②
	Cutlass Cruiser	②
	Cutlass Supreme	⑤
	Eighty-Eight	2.52
	Ninety-Eight	2.52
1992-93	Achieva	2.24
PONTIAC		
1991	6000	②
1991-93	Bonneville	2.52
	Firebird	③
	Grand Am	2.24
	Grand Prix	⑤
	Sunbird	2.24

① —Front, 1.5 inches; rear, 1.6 inches.
② —Except heavy duty, 2.24 inches; heavy duty, 2.50 inches.
③ —Front standard, 2.5 inches; front heavy duty, 1.5 inches; rear, 1.6 inches.
④ —Front, 2.5 inches; rear, 1.5 inches.
⑤ —Front, 1.65 inches each; rear, 1.38 inches.

Disc Brake Rotor Specifications

Car	Year	Nominal Thickness	Minimum Refinish Thickness ①	Thickness Variation (Parallelism)	Lateral Runout (T.I.R.)
BUICK					
Century	1991-93 ⑥	.885	.830	.0005	.004
	1991-93 ⑦	1.043	.972	.0005	.004
LeSabre	1991-93	1.043	.972	.0005	.004
Park Ave.	1991-93	1.043	.972	.0005	.004
Reatta ②	1991	1.035	.971	.0005	.004
Reatta ③	1991	.494	.444	.0005	.003
Regal ②	1991-93	1.040	.984	.0005	.004
Regal ③	1991-93	.492	.441	.0005	.004
Riviera ②	1991-93	1.035	.971	.0005	.004
Riviera ③	1991-93	.494	.444	.0005	.003
Roadmaster	1991-93	1.043	.980	.0005	.005
Skylark	1991-93	.806	.786	.0005	.004
CADILLAC					
Brougham	1991-92	1.031	.972	.0005	.004
DeVille	1991-93	1.276	1.226	.0005	.004
Eldorado ②	1991	1.035	.971	.0005	.004
	1992-93	1.260	1.250	.0005	.002
Eldorado ③	1991	.494	.444	.0005	.003
	1992-93	.433	.423	.0005	.002

Car	Year	Nominal Thickness	Minimum Refinish Thickness ①	Thickness Variation (Parallelism)	Lateral Runout (T.I.R.)
CADILLAC–Continued					
Fleetwood FWD	1991-92	1.276	1.226	.0005	.004
Fleetwood RWD	1993	1.031	.972	.0005	.004
Seville ②	1991	1.035	.971	.0005	.004
	1992-93	1.260	1.250	.0005	.002
Seville ③	1991	.494	.444	.0005	.003
	1992-93	.433	.423	.0005	.002
CHEVROLET					
Beretta	1991-93	.885	.830	.0005	.004
Camaro	1991-92 ②	1.043	.980	.0005	.004
	1993 ②	1.260	1.250	.0005	.005
	1991-92 ③	.795	.744	—	.005
	1993 ③	.787	.733	.0005	.006
Caprice	1991-93	1.043	.980	.0005	.004
Cavalier	1991-93	.885	.830	.0005	.004
Corsica	1991-93	.885	.830	.0005	.004
Corvette	1991-93 ④	.795	.744	.0005	.006
	1991-93 ⑤	1.110	1.059	.0005	.006
Lumina ②	1991-93	1.040	.984	.0005	.004
Lumina ③	1991-93	.492	.441	.0005	.004
GEO					
Metro	1991-93	.394	.315	—	.003
Prizm	1991-93 ②	.709	.669	.0005	.0035
Prizm GSi	1991-93 ③	.354	.315	—	—
Storm	1991-93	.866	.811	.0005	.005
OLDSMOBILE					
Achieva	1992-93	.806	.786	.0005	.004
Custom Cruiser	1991-92	1.043	.980	.0005	.004
Cutlass Calais	1991	.885	.830	.0005	.004
Cutlass Ciera ②	1991-93 ⑥	.885	.830	.0005	.004
	1991-93 ⑦	1.043	.972	.0005	.004
Cutlass Cruiser ②	1991-93 ⑥	.885	.830	.0005	.004
	1991-93 ⑦	1.043	.972	.0005	.004
Cutlass Supreme ②	1991-93	1.040	.984	.0005	.004
Cutlass Supreme ③	1991-93	.492	.441	.0005	.004
Eighty-Eight	1991-93	1.043	.972	.0005	.004
Ninety-Eight	1991-93	1.276	1.226	.0005	.004
Toronado ②	1991-92	1.035	.971	.0005	.004
Toronado ③	1991-92	.494	.444	.0005	.003
Trofeo ②	1991-92	1.035	.971	.0005	.004
Trofeo ③	1991-92	.494	.444	.0005	.003
PONTIAC					
Bonneville	1991-93	1.043	.972	.0005	.004
Firebird	1991-92 ②	1.043	.980	.0005	.004
	1993 ②	1.260	1.250	.0005	.005
	1991-92 ③	.795	.744	.0005	.005
	1993 ③	.787	.733	.0005	.006
Grand Am	1991-93	.806	.786	.0005	.004
Grand Prix ②	1991-93	1.040	.984	.0005	.004
Grand Prix ③	1991-93	.492	.441	.0005	.004
LeMans	1991-93	.500	.420	.0004	.004
Sunbird	1991-93	.885	.830	.0005	.004
6000 ②	1991 ⑥	.885	.830	.0005	.004
	1991 ⑦	1.043	.972	.0005	.004

① —All brake rotors have a discard dimension cast into them. This is a wear dimension, not a refinish dimension. Any rotor that does not meet specifications should be discarded.
② —Front.
③ —Rear.
④ —Except heavy duty front rotors.
⑤ —Heavy duty front rotors.
⑥ —Light duty.
⑦ —Medium and heavy duty.

DRUM BRAKES

NOTE: Refer To "Applications" To Determine Which Type Brakes Are Used On Vehicle Being Serviced.

TABLE OF CONTENTS

Applications

Model	Year	Application
BUICK		
Century	1991-92	Type 4
	1993	Type 9
LeSabre	1991-93	Type 9
Park Avenue	1991-92	Type 5
	1993	Type 9
Roadmaster	1991-93	Type 1
Skylark	1991-93	Type 4
CADILLAC		
Brougham	1991-92	Type 1
DeVille	1991	Type 5
Fleetwood FWD	1991	Type 5
	1992	Type 9
Fleetwood RWD	1993	Type 1
CHEVROLET		
Beretta	1991-92	Type 5
	1993	Type 4
Camaro	1991-93	Type 2
Caprice	1991-93	Type 1
Cavalier	1991-93	Type 4
Corsica	1991-92	Type 5
	1993	Type 4

Model	Year	Application
GEO		
Metro	1991-93	Type 8
Prizm	1991-93	Type 6
Storm	1991-93	Type 7
OLDSMOBILE		
Achieva	1992-93	Type 4
Custom Cruiser	1991-92	Type 1
Cutlass Calais	1991	Type 4
Cutlass Ciera	1991-92	Type 4
	1993	Type 9
Cutlass Cruiser	1991-92	Type 4
	1993	Type 9
Eighty-Eight	1991-93	Type 9
Ninety-Eight	1991-92	Type 5
	1993	Type 9
PONTIAC		
Bonneville	1991-93	Type 9
Firebird	1991-93	Type 2
Grand Am	1991-93	Type 4
LeMans	1991-93	Type 3
Sunbird	1991-93	Type 4
6000	1991	Type 4

General Information

INDEX

SERVICE PRECAUTIONS

When working on or around brake assemblies, care must be taken to prevent breathing asbestos dust, as many manufacturers incorporate asbestos fibers in the production of brake linings. During routine service operations the amount of asbestos dust from brake lining wear is at a low level due to a chemical breakdown during use, and a few precautions will minimize exposure.

1. Do not sand or grind brake linings unless suitable local exhaust ventilation equipment is used to prevent excessive asbestos exposure.
2. Wear a suitable respirator approved for asbestos dust use during all repair procedures.
3. When cleaning brake dust from brake parts, use a vacuum cleaner with a highly efficient filter system. If a suitable vacuum cleaner is not available, use a water soaked rag. **Do not use compressed air or dry brush to clean brake parts.**
4. Keep work area clean using same equipment as for cleaning brake parts.
5. Properly dispose of rags and vacuum cleaner bags by placing them in plastic bags.
6. Do not smoke or eat while working on brake systems. **Never use gasoline, kerosene, alcohol, motor oil, transmission fluid, or any fluid containing mineral oil to clean brake system components. These fluids will damage the rubber caps and seals. If system contamination is suspected, check brake fluid in the reservoir for dirt, discoloration, or separation (breakdown) of the brake fluid into distinct layers. Drain and flush the hydraulic sys-** tem with clean brake fluid if contamination is suspected.

GENERAL INSPECTION

BRAKE DRUMS

Any time the brake drums are removed for brake service, the braking surface diameter should be checked with a suitable brake drum micrometer at several points to determine if they are within the safe oversize limit stamped on the brake drum outer surface. If the braking surface diameter exceeds specifications, the drum must be replaced. If the braking surface diameter is within specifications, drums should be cleaned and inspected for cracks, scores, deep grooves, taper, out of round and heat spotting. If drums are cracked or heat spotted, they must be replaced. Minor scores should be removed with sandpaper. Grooves and large scores can only be removed by machining with special equipment, as long as the braking surface is within specifications stamped on brake drum outer surface. Any brake drum sufficiently out of round to cause vehicle vibration or noise while braking or showing taper should also be machined, removing only enough stock to true up the brake drum.

After a brake drum is machined, wipe the braking surface diameter with a denatured alcohol soaked cloth. If one brake drum is machined, the other should also be machined to the same diameter to maintain equal braking forces.

BRAKE LININGS & SPRINGS

Inspect brake linings for excessive wear, damage, oil, grease or brake fluid contamination. If any of the above conditions exists, brake linings should be replaced. Do not attempt to replace only one set of brake shoes; they should be replaced as an axle set only to maintain equal braking forces. Examine brake shoe webbing, hold-down and return springs for signs of overheating indicated by a slight blue color. If any component exhibits overheating signs, replace hold-down and return springs with new ones. Overheated springs lose their pull and could cause brake linings to wear out prematurely. Inspect all springs for sags, bends and external damage and replace as necessary.

Inspect hold-down retainers and pins for bends, rust and corrosion. If any of the above is found, replace as required.

BACKING PLATE

Inspect backing plate shoe contact surface for grooves that may restrict shoe movement and cannot be removed by lightly sanding with emery cloth or other suitable abrasive. If backing plate exhibits above condition, it should be replaced. Also inspect for signs of cracks, warpage and excessive rust, indicating need for replacement.

ADJUSTER MECHANISM

Inspect all components for rust, corrosion, bends and fatigue. Replace as necessary. **On adjuster mechanism equipped with adjuster cable, inspect cable for kinks, fraying or elongation of eyelet and replace as necessary.**

PARKING BRAKE CABLE

Inspect parking brake cable end for kinks, fraying and elongation and replace as necessary. Use a small hose clamp to compress clamp where it enters backing plate to remove.

Types 1 & 2

INDEX

1	RETURN SPRING	11	PRIMARY SHOE AND LINING	21	BOLT
2	RETURN SPRING	12	SECONDARY SHOE AND LINING	22	BOOT
3	HOLD-DOWN SPRING	13	ADJUSTING SCREW SPRING	23	PISTON
4	BEARING SLEEVE	14	SOCKET	24	SEAL
5	HOLD-DOWN PIN	15	PIVOT NUT	25	SPRING ASSEMBLY
6	ACTUATOR LINK	16	ADJUSTING SCREW	26	WHEEL CYLINDER
7	ACTUATOR LEVER	17	RETAINING RING	27	BACKING PLATE
8	LEVER RETURN SPRING	18	PIN	30	SHOE RETAINER
9	PARKING BRAKE STRUT	19	PARKING BRAKE LEVER	32	ANCHOR PIN
10	STRUT SPRING	20	BLEEDER VALVE	33	SHOE PADS (6 PLACES)

Fig. 1   Drum brake assembly. Type 1 typical

1	RETURN SPRING
2	RETURN SPRING
3	HOLD-DOWN SPRING
4	LEVER PIVOT
5	HOLD-DOWN PIN
6	ACTUATOR LINK
7	ACTUATOR LEVER
8	LEVER RETURN SPRING
9	SHOE GUIDE
10	PARKING BRAKE STRUT
11	STRUT SPRING
12	PRIMARY SHOE AND LINING
13	SECONDARY SHOE AND LINING
14	ADJUSTING SCREW SPRING
18	PARKING BRAKE LEVER
26	BACKING PLATE
27	ANCHOR PIN
29	ADJUSTING SCREW ASSEMBLY
33	SHOE PAD

Fig. 2   Drum brake assembly. Type 2

INSPECTION

1. Inspect components for damage and unusual wear. Replace as necessary.
2. Inspect wheel cylinders. Boots which are torn, cut or heat damaged indicate need for wheel cylinder replacement. **On type 1 brakes,** remove wheel cylinder links. Fluid spill from boot center hole indicates cup leakage and need for wheel cylinder replacement. **On type 2 brakes,** use a small screwdriver to pry center hole of boot away from piston. If fluid spills from center hole, cup leakage is indicated and wheel cylinder should be replaced. **On all types,** light fluid coatings on piston within cylinder is considered normal.
3. Inspect backing plate for evidence of axle seal leakage. If leakage exists, refer to individual car chapters for axle seal replacement procedures.
4. Inspect backing plate attaching bolts, and ensure they are tight.
5. Using fine emery cloth or other suitable abrasive, clean rust and dirt from shoe contact surface on backing plate.

BRAKE SERVICE

REMOVAL

1. Raise and support rear of vehicle, then remove tire and wheel assembly.
2. Remove brake drum. If brake lining is dragging on brake drum, back off brake adjustment by rotating adjustment screw. Refer to individual car chapter for procedure. **If brake drum is rusted or corroded to axle flange and cannot be removed, lightly tap axle flange to drum mounting surface with a suitable hammer.**
3. Using brake spring pliers or equivalent, unhook primary and secondary return springs, **Figs. 1 and 2.** Observe location of brake parts being removed to aid during installation.

4. Remove brake hold-down springs with suitable tool.
5. Lift actuating lever, then unhook actuating link from anchor pin and remove.
6. Remove actuating lever(s) and return spring.
7. Spread shoes apart and remove parking brake strut and spring.
8. Disconnect parking brake cable from lever, then remove brake shoes from backing plate.
9. Separate brake shoes by removing adjusting screw and spring, then unhook parking brake lever from shoe assembly.
10. Clean dirt from brake drum, backing plate and all other components. **Do not use compressed air or dry brush to clean brake parts. Many brake parts contain asbestos fibers which, if inhaled, can cause serious injury. Clean brake parts with a water soaked rag or a suitable vacuum cleaner to minimize airborne dust.**

INSTALLATION

1. Lubricate parking brake lever fulcrum with suitable brake lube, then attach lever to brake shoe. Ensure lever operates smoothly.
2. Connect brake shoes with adjusting screw spring, then position adjusting screw. **Ensure adjusting screw star wheel does not contact adjusting screw spring after installation and**

Fig. 3 Brake shoe gauge measuring inside diameter of brake drum

Fig. 4 Brake shoe gauge measuring outside diameter of brake shoes

Fig. 5 Backing off brake shoe adjustment

also ensure righthand thread adjusting screw is installed on left side of vehicle and lefthand thread adjusting screw is installed on right side of vehicle. **When brake shoe installation is completed, ensure starwheel lines up with adjusting hole in backing plate.**

3. Lightly lubricate backing plate shoe contact surfaces with suitable brake lube, then the area where parking brake cable contacts backing plate.

4. Install brake shoes on backing plate while engaging wheel cylinder links (if equipped) with shoe webbing. Connect parking brake cable to parking brake lever. **The primary shoe (short lining) faces towards front of vehicle.**

5. Install actuating levers, actuating link and return spring, **Figs. 1 and 2.**

6. Install hold-down springs with suitable tool.

7. Install primary and secondary shoe return springs using brake spring pliers or equivalent.

8. Using suitable brake drum to shoe gauge, measure brake drum inside diameter. Adjust brake shoes to dimension obtained on outside portion of gauge.

9. Install brake drum, wheel and tire assembly.

10. If any hydraulic connections have been opened, bleed brake system.

11. Adjust parking brake. Refer to individual car chapters for procedures.

12. Inspect all hydraulic lines and connections for leakage and repair as necessary.

13. Check master cylinder fluid level and replenish as necessary.

14. Check brake pedal for proper feel and return.

15. Lower vehicle and road test. **Do not severely apply brakes immediately after installation of new brake linings or permanent damage may occur to linings, and/or brake drums may become scored. Brakes must be used moderately during first several hundred miles of operation to ensure proper burnishing of linings.**

ADJUSTMENTS

These brakes have self-adjusting shoe mechanisms that assure correct lining-to-drum clearances at all times. The automatic adjusters operate only when the brakes are applied as the car is moving rearward.

Although the brakes are self-adjusting, an initial adjustment is necessary after the brake shoes have been relined or replaced, or when the length of the adjusting screw has been changed during some other service operation.

Frequent usage of an automatic transmission forward range to halt reverse vehicle motion may prevent the automatic adjusters from functioning, thereby inducing low pedal heights. Should low pedal heights be encountered, it is recommended that numerous forward and reverse stops be made until satisfactory pedal height is obtained. **If a low pedal condition cannot be corrected by making numerous reverse stops (provided the hydraulic system is free of air) it indicates that the self-adjusting mechanism is not functioning. Therefore, it will be necessary to remove the brake drum, clean, free up and lubricate the adjusting mechanism. Then adjust the brakes as follows, being sure the parking brake is fully released.**

SERVICE BRAKE ADJUSTMENT
Type 1

In as much as there is no way to adjust these brakes with the drums installed, the following procedure is mandatory after new linings are installed, or it becomes necessary to change the length of the brake shoe adjusting screw.

1. With brake drums removed, position the caliper shown in **Fig. 3,** to the inside diameter of the drum, then tighten the clamp screw.

2. Next position brake shoe end of the caliper tool over the brake shoes as shown in **Fig. 4.**

3. Rotate the gauge slightly around the shoes to ensure that the gauge contacts the linings at the largest diameter.

4. Adjust brake shoes until the gauge is a snug fit on the linings at the point of largest lining diameter. **If it is necessary to back off the brake shoe adjustment, it will be necessary to hold the adjuster lever away from the adjuster screw, Fig. 5.**

Type 2
1. Using a suitable punch, knock out lanced area in backing plate or drum. If drum is installed on vehicle when this is done, remove drum and clean brake compartment of all metal. **When adjustment is completed, a new hole cover must be installed in the backing plate.**

2. Using brake adjusting tool No. J-6166 or equivalent, turn brake adjusting screw to expand brake shoes at each wheel until wheel can just be turned by hand. Drag should be equal on all wheels.

3. **On all except Camaro,** back off adjusting screw at each wheel 30 notches.

4. **On Camaro,** back off screw 12 notches.

5. **On all models,** if shoe still drags slightly on drum, back off adjusting screw an additional one or two notches.

6. When adjusting screw has been backed off approximately 12 notches, brakes should be free of drag. Heavy drag at this point indicates tight parking brake cables.

7. Install adjusting hole cover in brake backing plate.

8. Check parking brake for proper adjustment.

PARKING BRAKE ADJUSTMENT
1. Jack up both rear wheels.
2. Apply parking brake three notches.
3. **Type 1,** tighten adjusting nut until right rear wheel can just be rotated rearward but is locked when forward rotation is attempted.
4. **Type 2,** tighten adjusting nut until left rear wheel can just be rotated rearward but is locked when forward rotation is attempted.
5. Release parking brake and check to ensure rear wheels rotate freely in either direction with no brake drag.

Type 3

INDEX

1 ACCESS HOLE PLUG
2 BOLT
3 HOLD-DOWN PIN
4 BACKING PLATE
5 WHEEL CYLINDER ASSEMBLY
6 SHOE & LINING
7 HOLD-DOWN SPRING
8 HOLD-DOWN WASHER
9 BRAKE DRUM
10 DETENT SCREW
11 UPPER RETURN SPRING
12 LOWER RETURN SPRING
13 SPRING CONNECTING LINK
14 ADJUSTER ASSEMBLY
15 ACTUATOR SPRING
16 ADJUSTER ACTUATOR
17 ADJUSTER SHOE & LINING

Fig. 1   Drum brake assembly. Type 3

Fig. 2   Backing plate lubrication points

INSPECTION

1. If any parts are of doubtful strength or quality due to heat discoloration, or are worn, replace them.
2. Inspect wheel cylinder dust boots for signs of excessive wear or damage.
3. Inspect adjusting screw for smooth operation over full length.
4. Clean adjusting screw components in denatured alcohol.
5. Apply suitable lubricant to adjuster screw threads, inside diameter of socket and socket face. Adequate lubrication is achieved when a continuous bead of lubricant is at open end of adjuster nut and socket when threads are fully engaged.
6. Clean dirt and/or rust from brake drum, backing plate and all other components. **Do not use compressed air or dry brush to clean brake parts. Many brake parts contain asbestos fibers which, if inhaled, can cause serious injury. Clean brake parts with a water soaked rag or a suitable vacuum cleaner to minimize airborne dust.**

7. Ensure adjuster nut turns freely on adjuster screw.

BRAKE SERVICE

REMOVAL

1. Raise and support vehicle.
2. Mark relationship between rear wheel and hub, then remove wheel and tire assembly.
3. Remove brake drum detent screw, then the brake drum. If drum is difficult to remove, proceed as follows:
   a. Ensure parking brake cable is released.
   b. Loosen parking brake cable.
   c. Remove access hole plug from backing plate, then move parking brake lever until lever stop rests on brake shoe.
4. Remove upper and lower return springs, then the adjuster actuator and actuator spring, **Fig. 1.**
5. Press brake shoes outward slightly and remove adjuster assembly.
6. Remove hold-down springs, washers and pins using a suitable tool.

7. Remove brake shoes from backing plate and parking brake cable.

INSTALLATION

1. Lubricate backing plate at points shown, **Fig. 2.**
2. Connect parking brake lever to parking brake cable.
3. Ensure parking brake cable is properly routed, then install shoes and lining to backing plate with hold-down spring, washer and pin.
4. Position adjuster shoe and lining and lower return spring against backing plate. Ensure spring is properly positioned under anchor plate.
5. Install hold-down spring, washer and pin.
6. Turn adjuster in to stop, then install adjuster assembly, **Fig. 3.** Ensure spring clip is positioned toward backing plate.
7. Install adjuster actuator onto pin and actuator spring.
8. Install spring connecting link to pin and press into brake hole.
9. Connect upper spring from connecting link to brake shoe.
10. Install brake drum and detent screw, then the wheel and tire assembly.
11. Adjust service and parking brakes as necessary.

ADJUSTMENTS
SERVICE BRAKE ADJUSTMENT

1. Raise and support vehicle.
2. Mark relationship between rear wheels and hubs, then remove wheel and tire assemblies.
3. Remove brake drum setscrew, then the brake drum. If drum is difficult to remove, proceed as follows:

a. Ensure parking brake cable releases.
b. Loosen parking brake cable.
c. Remove access hole plug from backing plate, then move parking brake lever until lever stop rests on brake shoe.
4. Turn adjuster assembly in as far as possible, **Fig. 3.**
5. Ensure parking brake lever stops make contact with edge of shoe web. If contact is not evident, loosen parking brake cable at equalizer as necessary.
6. Install brake drums and wheels. then lower vehicle.
7. Depress brake pedal at least ten times until clicking of adjustment actuator is no longer heard.
8. Adjust parking brake as necessary.

PARKING BRAKE ADJUSTMENT

1. Adjust service brakes as previously described.
2. Ensure parking brakes are fully released.
3. Raise and support vehicle.
4. Ensure parking brake cable moves freely, then turn self-locking nut until rear wheels are difficult to turn.
5. Back off self-locking nut until rear wheels are just free to turn.

1. ACTUATOR SPRING
2. UPPER RETURN SPRING
3. ADJUSTER ACTUATOR
4. ADJUSTER SHOE & LINING
5. SHOE & LINING
6. SPRING CLIP
7. ADJUSTER NUT
8. ADJUSTER SCREW
9. PARK BRAKE LEVER

SECTION A-A   SECTION B-B   SECTION C-C

Fig. 3   Cross-sectional view of drum brake assembly

Type 4

INDEX

INSPECTION

1. Inspect brake components for damage and/or wear. Replace as necessary.
2. Inspect wheel cylinders. Excessive fluid indicates cup leakage and need for wheel cylinder replacement.
3. Inspect backing plate for evidence of axle seal leakage.
4. Inspect backing plate attaching bolts. Ensure bolts are tight.
5. Check adjuster operation. If adjusters are worn, frozen or loose, replace adjuster and backing plate assembly as required.
6. Using fine emery cloth or other suitable abrasive, clean rust and/or dirt from shoe contact surface on backing plate.

BRAKE SERVICE

REMOVAL

1. Raise and support rear of vehicle, then remove tire and wheel assembly.
2. Remove brake drum. If brake lining is dragging on brake drum, back off brake adjustment by rotating adjusting screw. Refer to individual car chapter for procedure. **If brake drum is rusted or corroded to axle flange and cannot be removed, lightly tap axle flange to drum mounting surface with a suitable hammer.**
3. Using brake spring pliers or equivalent, remove brake return springs, **Fig. 1.**
4. Using suitable pliers, remove hold-down springs and lever pivot.
5. While lifting up on actuator lever, disconnect actuating link.
6. Remove actuator lever and return spring.

7. Remove parking brake strut and spring.
8. Disconnect parking brake cable, then remove brake shoe and lining assembly.
9. Remove adjusting screw assembly and spring as follows:
   a. Note position of adjusting spring.
   b. Remove retaining ring, pin, and parking brake lever from secondary shoe.
   c. Remove adjusting screw and spring. **Do not interchange adjusting screws from right and left brake assemblies.**

INSTALLATION

1. Install parking brake lever, pin and retaining ring onto secondary shoe.
2. Apply silicone brake lubricant onto adjuster screw threads, inside diameter of socket and socket face. Adequate lubrication is achieved when a continuous bead of lubricant is at open end of pivot nut and socket

*LUBRICATE WITH THIN COATING OF 5450032 LUBRICANT (OR EQUIVALENT)

6. ACTUATOR LINK	12. SECONDARY SHOE & LINING
7. ACTUATOR LEVER	13. ADJUSTING SCREW SPRING
8. LEVER RETURN SPRING	17. RETAINING RING
9. PARKING BRAKE STRUT	18. PIN
10. STRUT SPRING	19. PARKING BRAKE LEVER
11. PRIMARY SHOE & LINING	27. BACKING PLATE

1. RETURN SPRING
2. RETURN SPRING
3. HOLD-DOWN SPRING
4. LEVER PIVOT
5. HOLD-DOWN PIN

29. ADJUSTING SCREW ASSEMBLY
30. SHOE RETAINER
32. ANCHOR PIN
33. SHOE PADS (6 PLACES)

Fig. 1 Drum brake assembly. Type 4

Fig. 2 Measuring brake drum inside diameter

Fig. 3 Brake shoe clearance adjustment

when adjuster threads are completely engaged.

3. Install adjusting screw assembly and spring. **Spring coils must not overlap star wheel. Do not interchange right and lefthand springs.**
4. Connect parking brake cable, then install shoe and lining assembly.
5. Using a suitable tool, spread brake shoes apart, then install parking brake strut and spring. **Ensure parking brake strut is properly positioned. Ensure strut end without spring engages parking brake lever. Ensure strut end with spring engages primary brake shoe.**
6. Install actuator lever and return spring.
7. Install actuator link onto anchor pin.
8. While holding up on actuator lever, install link onto lever.
9. Install hold-down pins, lever pivot and hold-down springs.
10. Install shoe return springs.
11. Install brake drum, tire and wheel assembly.
12. If any hydraulic connections have been opened, bleed brake system.
13. Adjust brakes. Refer to individual car chapters for procedure.

ADJUSTMENTS

The rear drum brakes have self-adjusting shoe mechanisms that assure correct lining-to-drum clearances at all times. The automatic adjusters operate only when the service brakes are applied.

Although the brakes are self-adjusting, an initial adjustment is necessary after the brake shoes have been replaced, or when the length of the star wheel adjuster has been changed during some other service operation.

SERVICE BRAKE ADJUSTMENT

1. Raise and support vehicle, then remove rear wheels and brake drums.
2. Check to make sure parking brake cable linkage and levers on secondary brake shoe are in "free" position.
3. Using brake shoe measuring tool No. J-21177 or equivalent, measure drum inside diameter, **Fig. 2.**
4. Turn brake adjusting screw to expand shoes to .050 inch less than diameter obtained on outside caliper portion of brake shoe measuring tool No. J-21177, **Fig. 3.**
5. Adjust parking brake. **Whenever rear drum brakes are serviced, the parking brake linkage cable at the equalizer must always be readjusted to prevent possible damage to brake shoes.**
6. Install brake drums, wheels and tires and lower vehicle to ground.
7. Drive vehicle and apply and release service brake 30-35 times with normal pedal force. Allow about one second between brake applications until satisfactory pedal height is obtained.

PARKING BRAKE ADJUSTMENT

1. Jack up both rear wheels.
2. **On hand operated parking brakes,** apply parking brake three to five notches. **On foot operated brakes,** apply parking brake two notches.
3. Tighten adjusting nut until right rear wheel can just be rotated rearward but is locked when forward rotation is attempted.
5. Release parking brake and check to ensure rear wheels rotate freely in either direction with no brake drag.

Type 5

INDEX

INSPECTION

1. If any parts are of doubtful strength or quality due to heat discoloration, or are worn, replace them.
2. Inspect wheel cylinder dust boots for signs of excessive wear or damage.
3. Inspect adjusting screw for smooth operation over full length.
4. Clean adjusting screw components in denatured alcohol. **Ensure spring clip is installed in correct position, Fig. 1.**
5. Apply suitable lubricant to adjuster screw threads, inside diameter of socket and socket face. Adequate lubrication is achieved when a continuous bead of lubricant is at open end of adjuster nut and socket when threads are fully engaged.
6. Clean dirt and/or rust from brake drum, backing plate and all other components. **Do not use compressed air or dry brush to clean brake parts. Many brake parts contain asbestos fibers which, if inhaled, can cause serious injury. Clean brake parts with a water soaked rag or a suitable vacuum cleaner to minimize airborne dust.**
7. Ensure adjuster nut turns freely on adjuster screw.

BRAKE SERVICE

REMOVAL

1. Raise and support vehicle.
2. Mark relationship of wheel to axle flange, then remove wheel and tire assembly.
3. Mark relationship of brake drum to axle flange, then remove drum. **If brake drum is difficult to remove, back off parking brake cable adjustment, remove inspection hole plug from backing plate, insert screwdriver through hole and press in to push parking brake lever off stop.**
4. Using suitable tool, remove actuator spring, then upper return spring, **Fig. 1.**
5. Remove spring connecting link, adjuster actuator, and spring washer.
6. Remove hold-down springs and pins.
7. Disconnect parking brake cable, then remove shoe and lining assembly together with lower return spring.
8. Remove adjusting screw assembly, and lower return spring.

1. ACTUATOR SPRING
2. UPPER RETURN SPRING
3. SPRING CONNECTING LINK
4. ADJUSTER ACTUATOR
5. SPRING WASHER
6. LOWER RETURN SPRING
7. HOLD-DOWN SPRING ASSEMBLY
8. HOLD-DOWN PIN
9. ADJUSTER SHOE & LINING
10. SHOE & LINING
11. ADJUSTER SOCKET
12. SPRING CLIP
13. ADJUSTER NUT
14. ADJUSTER SCREW
15. RETAINING RING
16. PIN
17. SPRING WASHER
18. PARK BRAKE LEVER
19. SCREW & LOCKWASHER
20. BOOT
21. PISTON
22. SEAL
23. SPRING ASSEMBLY
24. BLEEDER VALVE
25. WHEEL CYLINDER
26. BLEEDER VALVE CAP
27. BACKING PLATE ASSEMBLY
32. ACCESS HOLE PLUG
33. ADJUSTER PIN

Fig. 1   Drum brake assembly. Type 5

9. Remove retaining ring, pin, spring washer and parking brake lever from shoe and lining assembly.

INSTALLATION

1. Press adjuster pin and spring washer into shoe and lining so that pin projects .275–.283 inch from the side on which the adjuster actuator is installed.
2. Install adjuster shoe and lining, to front of vehicle on left side or to rear of vehicle on right side.
3. Install parking brake lever on shoe and lining with spring washer, pin and retaining ring. Install spring washer with concave side against parking brake lever.
4. Attach adjuster shoe and lining to remaining shoe with lower return spring.
5. Install both shoes on backing plate, securing with hold-down pins and springs.
6. Install adjuster actuator, spring connecting link and actuator spring onto adjuster shoe and lining.

7. Install adjusting screw assembly, ensuring adjuster screw engages notch in adjuster shoe. Ensure adjuster screw spring clip is properly positioned and the adjuster actuator is properly engaged in notch in adjuster screw. **Do not over extend upper return spring. The spring will be damaged if extended length exceeds 5.49 inches.**
8. Install upper return spring by inserting angled hook end of spring through parking brake lever and shoe lining, using suitable tool to pull spring straight across and then down to hook into crook in spring connecting link.
9. Back off parking brake adjustment until parking brake lever rests on brake shoe.
10. Install brake drum and tire and wheel assembly, then lower vehicle.
11. Apply and release service brake at least 25 times, then continue to pump brake pedal until clicking noise at drum brake self adjusters stops on both sides.

Fig. 2   Measuring brake drum inside diameter

12. Adjust parking brake. Refer to individual car chapters for procedure.

ADJUSTMENTS

The rear drum brakes have self-adjusting shoe mechanisms that assure correct lining-to-drum clearances at all times. The automatic adjusters operate only when the brakes are applied as the vehicle is moving rearward.

Although the brakes are self-adjusting, an initial adjustment is necessary after the brake shoes have been replaced, or when the length of the star wheel adjuster has been changed during some other service operation.

SERVICE BRAKE ADJUSTMENT

1. Raise and support vehicle, then remove rear wheels and brake drums.
2. Check to make sure parking brake cable linkage and levers on secondary brake shoe are in "free" position.

Fig. 3   Brake shoe clearance adjustment

3. Using brake shoe measuring tool No. J-21177 or equivalent, measure drum inside diameter, **Fig. 2**.
4. Turn brake adjusting screw to expand shoes to .050 inch less than diameter obtained on outside caliper portion of brake shoe measuring tool No. J-21177, **Fig. 3**.
5. Install brake drums, wheels and tires and lower vehicle to ground.
6. Drive vehicle and apply and release service brake 30-35 times with normal pedal force. Allow about one second between brake applications until satisfactory pedal height is obtained.

PARKING BRAKE ADJUSTMENT

1. Apply and release parking brake 5 times to 10 clicks.

11	PARK BRAKE SHOE AND LINING
12	PARK BRAKE LEVER
20	1/8 INCH DRILL

Fig. 4   Park brake adjustment

2. Ensure that pedal is fully released by turning ignition switch "On" the brake warning light should be "Off."
3. If brake warning lamp is "On," operate pedal release lever and pull downward on parking brake cable.
4. Apply parking brake to four clicks.
5. Raise and support vehicle, then remove access hole plug.
6. Adjust cable until and 1/8 inch drill bit can be inserted through access hole into space between shoe web and park lever, **Fig. 4**. Proper adjustment is when a 1/8 inch drill bit will fit in the space and a 1/4 inch drill bit will not fit.
7. Release brake, then check that wheels rotate freely.
8. Replace access hole plug, then lower vehicle.

Type 6
INDEX

INSPECTION

1. Check brake drum, shoes, strut, auto adjuster lever, springs and backing plate for wear, distortion, cracks or other abnormal conditions.
2. If any parts are of doubtful strength or quality due to damage, heat discoloration, stress or wear, replace them.
3. Measure brake drum inside diameter and the brake shoe lining thickness.
4. Inspect lining and drum for proper contact.

BRAKE SERVICE
REMOVAL

1. Raise and support vehicle.
2. Mark relationship of wheel to axle, then remove wheel and tire assembly.
3. Remove brake drum. If drum is difficult to remove, insert screwdriver through hole in backing plate and hold automatic adjusting lever away from adjusting bolt, then, using a second screwdriver, reduce brake shoe adjustment.
4. Remove return spring, **Fig. 1**

5. Remove hold-down spring, retainers and pin retaining front shoe.
6. Disconnect anchor spring from front shoe, then remove front shoe.
7. Remove anchor spring.
8. Remove hold-down spring, retainers and pin retaining rear shoe.
9. Using screwdriver, disconnect parking brake cable from anchor plate.
10. Using pliers, disconnect parking brake cable from lever and remove rear shoe together with strut.
11. Remove adjusting lever spring, then the strut together with return spring.
12. Remove parking brake lever and au-

SHIM THICKNESS	
THICKNESS	THICKNESS
0.2 MM (0.008 IN.)	0.5 MM (0.020 IN.)
0.3 MM (0.012 IN.)	0.6 MM (0.024 IN.)
0.4 MM (0.016 IN.)	0.9 MM (0.035 IN.)

Fig. 2   Checking lever to shoe clearance

1. HOLD-DOWN PIN
2. PLUG
3. INSPECTION HOLE PLUG
4. BACKING PLATE
5. BOLT
6. WHEEL CYLINDER
7. PARKING BRAKE CABLE
8. RETURN SPRING
9. FRONT SHOE
10. REAR SHOE
11. STRUT
12. ANCHOR SPRING
13. ADJUSTING LEVER SPRING
14. RETAINER
15. HOLD-DOWN SPRING
16. C-WASHER
17. AUTOMATIC ADJUSTING LEVER
18. PARKING BRAKE LEVER
19. SHIM

Fig. 1   Drum brake assembly. Type 6

tomatic adjusting lever from rear shoe by prying out "C" washer and removing shims and levers.

13. Clean dirt from brake drum, backing plate and all other components. **Do not use compressed air or dry brush to clean brake parts. Many brake parts contain asbestos fibers which, if inhaled, can cause serious injury. Clean brake parts with a water soaked rag or a suitable vacuum cleaner to minimize airborne dust.**

INSTALLATION

1. Apply suitable lubricant to backing plate brake shoe contact points, anchor plate brake shoe contact points, strut and adjusting bolt contact points and the strut and brake shoe contact points.
2. Install parking brake lever and automatic adjusting lever to rear shoe as follows:
   a. Temporarily install levers and shim with a new "C" washer.
   b. Using feeler gauge, measure clearance between shoe and lever, **Fig. 2.**

c. If clearance is not 0-.0138 inch, adjust by installing replacement shim.
d. Using pliers, stake "C" washer.

3. Set strut and return spring in place on rear shoe and install adjusting lever spring.
4. Install rear shoe as follows:
   a. Using pliers, connect parking brake cable to lever.
   b. Pass parking brake cable through notch in anchor plate.
   c. Set rear shoe in place with end of shoe inserted in wheel cylinder and other end in anchor plate.
   d. Install hold-down spring, retainers and pin.
5. Install front shoe as follows:
   a. Install anchor spring between front and rear shoes.
   b. Set front shoe in place with end of shoe inserted in wheel cylinder and the strut in place.
   c. Install hold-down spring, retainers and pin.
   d. Connect return spring.
6. Check operation of automatic adjuster mechanism as follows:
   a. Move parking brake lever of rear shoe back and forth and check whether adjusting bolt turns. If bolt

does not turn, check brakes for incorrect installation.
   b. Adjust strut length to shortest possible distance.
   c. Install brake drum.
   d. Pull parking brake lever all the way up until a clicking sound can no longer be heard.
7. Check clearance between brake shoes and drum. Remove drum and measure brake drum inside diameter and diameter of brake shoes.
8. If clearance is not .024 inch, check parking brake system.
9. Install brake drum and the wheel and tire assembly.
10. Fill master cylinder as necessary and bleed brake system.
11. Check for fluid leakage.

ADJUSTMENTS

SERVICE BRAKE ADJUSTMENT

Adjustment is accomplished automatically by pulling the parking brake lever all the way up until a clicking sound can no longer be heard.

PARKING BRAKE ADJUSTMENT

1. Check that parking brake lever travel is correct by pulling parking brake lever all the way up and counting the number of clicks.
2. Parking brake lever travel should be 4-7 clicks. If not, remove console, loosen locknut and turn adjusting nut until travel is correct.

Type 7
INDEX

1	BOLT	9	SHOE HOLDING SPRING
2	BACKING PLATE	10	SHOE HOLDING SEAT
3	SHOE HOLDING PIN	11	AUTO ADJUSTER LEVER
4	GASKET	12	AUTO ADJUSTER SPRING
5	RETAINER	13	BRAKE ADJUSTER
6	WASHER	14	RETURN SPRING
7	PARKING BRAKE LEVER	15	LEADING SHOE
8	TRAILING SHOE	16	WHEEL CYLINDER

Fig. 1   Rear drum brake assembly. Type 7

INSPECTION

1. If any parts are of doubtful strength or quality due to heat discoloration, or are worn, replace them.
2. Inspect wheel cylinder dust boots for signs of excessive wear or damage.
3. Inspect auto adjuster gear for smooth operation over full length.
4. Clean adjusting gear components in denatured alcohol.
5. Apply suitable lubricant to adjuster screw threads, inside diameter of socket and socket face. Adequate lubrication is achieved when a continuous bead of lubricant is at open end of adjuster nut and socket when threads are fully engaged.
6. Clean dirt and/or rust from brake drum, backing plate and all other components. **Do not use compressed air or dry brush to clean brake parts. Many brake parts contain asbestos fibers which, if inhaled, can cause serious injury. Clean brake parts with a water soaked rag or a suitable vacuum cleaner to minimize airborne dust.**
7. Ensure adjuster gear turns freely on adjuster screw.

Fig. 3   Brake pedal height adjustment

BRAKE SERVICE
REMOVAL

1. Raise and support rear of vehicle.

Clearance	0.3 mm (.012 in.)

Fig. 2   Drum brake adjustment

2. Remove wheels, then brake hubs and drums.
3. Remove return spring and auto adjuster spring.
4. Remove leading shoe hold-down spring and pin, **Fig. 1.**
5. Remove leading shoe and auto adjuster.
6. Remove trailing shoe hold-down spring and pin, then shoe.
7. Disconnect parking brake cable from lever, then remove trailing shoe.
8. Remove parking brake lever from trailing shoe.

INSTALLATION

1. Apply suitable lubricant to backing plate and cylinder piston brake shoe contact points, adjuster and parking lever pin contact points.
2. Install parking brake lever to trailing shoe, then connect parking brake cable to lever.
3. Install trailing shoe to backing plate with hold-down pin and spring, then install brake adjuster.
4. Install leading shoe to backing plate with hold-down pin and spring.
5. Install auto adjuster lever and auto adjuster spring, then install return spring.
6. Install brake drum, then adjust brakes. Refer to individual car chapters for procedure.

7. Adjust bearing preload. Refer to individual car chapters for procedure.
8. If hydraulic connections have been opened, bleed system.

ADJUSTMENTS

SERVICE BRAKE ADJUSTMENT

1. Measure brake drum inside diameter and brake shoe diameter, **Fig. 2.**
2. Ensure clearance between diameters is as specified, **Fig. 2.**

PARKING BRAKE ADJUSTMENT

Parking brake stroke should measure 7 to 9 notches with approximately 14 lbs. pressure applied. Lever stroke is automatically adjusted when rear brakes are adjusted. If stroke is not within specifications after adjusting rear brakes, it may be adjusted by rotating the cable turnbuckle.

BRAKE PEDAL HEIGHT ADJUSTMENT

1. Ensure pedal is fully returned by pedal return spring, then measure brake pedal height, **Fig. 3.**
2. If measurement does not meet specifications, perform adjustment as follows:
   a. Loosen stop light switch and the locknut on pushrod.
   b. Adjust pushrod until brake pedal extends approximately 6.07 inches from floorboard.
   c. Position tip of stop lamp switch to rest lightly on pedal arm rubber stop.
   d. Carefully rotate stop lamp switch until freeplay between pedal arm and pushrod is eliminated from brake pedal.
   e. Tighten locknut.

Type 8

INDEX

INSPECTION

1. If any parts are of doubtful strength or quality due to heat discoloration, or are worn, replace them.
2. Inspect wheel cylinder dust boots for signs of excessive wear or damage. If any leakage is apparent replace or rebuild wheel cylinder.
3. Clean dirt and/or rust from brake drum, backing plate and all other components. **Do not use compressed air or dry brush to clean brake parts. Many brake parts contain asbestos fibers which, if inhaled, can cause serious injury. Clean brake parts with a water soaked rag or a suitable vacuum cleaner to minimize airborne dust.**

BRAKE SERVICE

REMOVAL

1. Raise and support vehicle.
2. Remove spindle cap by hammering lightly at 3 points around cap.
3. Remove cotter pin or unfasten staked portion of nut, then remove castle nut and washer.
4. Loosen parking brake cable adjusting nuts.
5. Remove backing plate plug, **Fig. 1.**
6. Insert screwdriver into plug hole until it contacts shoe hold-down spring and push in direction shown. **Fig. 1.** This pushes hold-down spring up and releases parking brake shoe lever from hold-down spring, resulting in added clearance between shoe and drum.

1. BACK PLATE PLUG

PUSH

Fig. 1   Backing plate plug removal

1 | RETURN SPRING
2 | RETURN SPRING
3 | ANTIRATTLE SPRING
4 | STRUT
5 | PARKING BRAKE SHOE LEVER
6 | RETAINER

Fig. 2   Brake shoe return spring identification

Fig. 4   Brake lining installation

1. Parking brake lever
2. Brake cable
3. Nuts

FRONT

Fig. 5   Parking brake adjustment

11. Disconnect return spring 3 from shoe.
12. Disconnect parking brake shoe lever from shoe.

INSTALLATION

1. Assemble brake shoes, levers and springs as shown in **Fig. 3**.
2. Push shoe hold-down springs down into place. Turn hold-down pins to engage springs.
3. To minimize dimension 'A-A,' **Fig. 4**, push strut towards backplate while pushing out on shoe as shown.
4. Position tab of spring clip behind parking lever.
5. Install brake drum and **torque** castle nut to 58-86.5 ft. lbs. Install cotter pin.
6. Install spindle cap.
7. Install wheel.
8. Depress brake pedal several times to obtain proper drum to shoe clearance and adjust parking brake.
9. Check that brake drum does not drag.
10. Lower vehicle and test brake operation.

ADJUSTMENTS

SERVICE BRAKE ADJUSTMENT

Adjustment is accomplished automatically by applying brake pedal 3 to 5 times with 66 lbs. of pressure. Brake pedal should be cycled 3 to 5 times when replacement components are installed to assure proper adjustment.

PARKING BRAKE ADJUSTMENT

Parking brake lever should be adjusted so lever comes up 4 to 9 notches with 44 to 55 lbs. of pull applied.
Adjust travel by loosening adjustment nuts, **Fig. 5**.

1. Brake back plate
2. Brake shoe
3. Parking brake shoe lever
4. Brake strut
5. Quadrant spring
6. Shoe return spring
7. Antirattle spring
8. Shoe hold down spring
9. Shoe hold down pin
10. Packing
11. Parking level retainer
12. Wheel cylinder
13. Bleeder plug cap
14. Rubber plug
15. Rubber plug

Fig. 3   Assembling rear brake unit. Type 8

7. Using slide hammer tool No. J-2619-01 and brake drum remover tool No. J-34866 or equivalents, pull off brake drum.
8. Remove brake shoe hold-down springs by turning hold-down pins.
9. Disconnect parking brake cable from parking brake shoe lever and remove brake shoes.
10. Remove spring 1 in **Fig. 2**, pull primary shoe in direction of arrow and disengage strut 4 and return spring 2.

Type 9

INDEX

1	ADJUSTER SOCKET	9	ACCESS HOLE PLUG
2	ADJUSTER SCREW	10	BACKING PLATE ASSEMBLY
3	PIVOT NUT	11	PARK BRAKE SHOE AND LINING
4	RETRACTOR SPRING	12	PARK BRAKE LEVER
5	ADJUSTER SHOE AND LINING	13	ACTUATOR SPRING
6	WHEEL CYLINDER ASSEMBLY	14	ADJUSTER ACTUATOR
7	BLEEDER VALVE	15	ADJUSTING SCREW ASSEMBLY
8	BOLT		

10	BACKING PLATE ASSEMBLY
21	SPLASH SHIELD HOLE

Fig. 2   Loosening drum through splash shield

Fig. 1   Brake drum assembly. Type 9

DESCRIPTION

This brake assembly is of an advanced design. It operates with fewer parts, but is equal to other drum brake systems in performance. In this assembly, a single spring holds both shoe and lining to the backing plate, and acts as a retractor spring for the shoe and lining assemblies, **Fig. 1.**

INSPECTION

1. If any parts are of doubtful strength or quality due to heat discoloration, or are worn, replace them.
2. Inspect wheel cylinder dust boots for signs of excessive wear or damage. If any leakage is apparent replace wheel cylinder.
3. Clean dirt and/or rust from brake drum, backing plate and all other components. **Do not use compressed air or dry brush to clean brake parts. Many brake parts contain asbestos fibers which, if inhaled, can cause serious injury. Clean brake parts with a water soaked rag or a suitable vacuum cleaner to minimize airborne dust.**

BRAKE SERVICE

REMOVAL

1. Raise and support vehicle.
2. Mark relationship of wheel to axle, then remove wheel and tire assembly.
3. Remove brake drum. If drum is difficult to remove, proceed as follows:
   a. Ensure parking brake is released.
   b. Back off parking brake cable adjustment.
   c. Remove access hole plug from backing plate, insert screwdriver through hole and push parking brake lever off its stop.
   d. Insert punch through hole in splash shield **Fig. 2,** tap on punch to loosen drum. Then remove drum.
4. Remove actuator spring using special brake tool J 38400 or equivalent to pry loop end of spring from adjuster actuator, **Fig. 3. When removing the retractor spring do not over stretch the spring, this will reduce its effectiveness.**
5. Remove end of retractor spring from

adjuster shoe and lining assembly using special brake tool J 38400 or equivalent, **Fig. 4. Keep finger away from retractor spring to prevent fingers from being pinched.**
6. Remove adjuster shoe and lining assembly, adjuster actuator, then adjusting screw assembly.
7. Remove park brake lever from shoe assembly, do not remove parking brake cable from lever unless parking brake lever is being replaced.
8. Remove retractor spring from park brake shoe and lining.
9. Pry end of retractor spring toward axle using special brake tool J 38400 or equivalent, until it snap off shoe web onto backing plate. Remove park brake shoe.

INSTALLATION

1. Lubricate raised shoe pads on backing plate, anchor surfaces on backing plate, and adjuster screw threads using brake lubricant No. 1052196 or equivalent.
2. Install retractor spring if removed by hooking center spring section under tab on anchor.
3. Install park shoe and lining assembly as follows:
   a. Place shoe on backing plate.
   b. Using special brake tool J 38400 or equivalent, pull end of retractor

13 ACTUATOR SPRING
14 ADJUSTER ACTUATOR

Fig. 3   Actuator spring removal

4 RETRACTOR SPRING
5 ADJUSTER SHOE LINING

Fig. 4   Disengaging retractor spring

4 RETRACTOR SPRING
11 PARK BRAKE SHOE AND LINING

Fig. 5   Spring end installation onto shoe web

4 RETRACTOR SPRING
11 PARK BRAKE SHOE AND LINING

Fig. 6   Spring end installation into shoe slot

spring up to rest on web of brake shoe, **Fig. 5**.
   c. Using special brake tool J 38400 or equivalent, pull end of retractor spring over until if locks into slot of brake shoe, **Fig. 6**.
4. Install park brake lever.
5. Install adjuster screw and adjuster shoe as follows:
   a. Place shoe on backing plate.
   b. Using special brake tool J 38400 or equivalent, pull end of retractor spring up to rest on web of brake shoe.
   c. Using special brake tool J 38400 or equivalent, pull end of retractor spring over until if locks into slot of brake shoe.
6. Install adjuster actuator by spreading shoes using special brake tool J 38400 or equivalent, **Fig. 7**. Then install adjuster actuator.
7. Install actuator spring.
8. Adjust brakes using suitable adjustment tool. Lining diameter should be 0.050 inches less than inside diameter of each drum.
9. Install drums, wheels and tires, aligning marks made during removal.

14 ADJUSTER ACTUATOR

Fig. 7   Spreading shoes to install adjuster actuator

ADJUSTMENTS
SERVICE BRAKE ADJUSTMENT

1. Raise and support vehicle.
2. Mark relationship of wheel to axle, then remove wheel and tire assembly.
3. Remove brake drum. If drum is difficult to remove, proceed as follows:
   a. Ensure parking brake is released.
   b. Back off parking brake cable adjustment.
   c. Remove access hole plug from backing plate, insert screwdriver through hole and push parking brake lever off its stop.

11 PARK BRAKE SHOE AND LINING
12 PARK BRAKE LEVER
20 1/8 INCH DRILL

Fig. 8   Parking brake adjustment

   d. Insert punch through hole in splash shield **Fig. 2**, tap on punch to loosen drum. Then remove drum.
4. Measure inside diameter of drum using special tool J 21177-A or J22364-01 or equivalent.
5. Adjust by turning star wheel adjuster. Lining diameter should be 0.050 inches less than inside diameter of each drum.
6. Install drums, wheels and tires.
7. Lower vehicle, then torque wheel lug nuts to specifications.

PARKING BRAKE ADJUSTMENT

1. Adjust brakes as outlined in "Service Brake Adjustment."
2. Apply and release parking brake 5 times to 10 clicks.
3. Ensure that pedal is fully released by turning ignition switch "On" the brake warning light should be "Off."
4. If brake warning lamp is "On," operate

pedal release lever and pull downward on parking brake cable.
5. Apply parking brake to four clicks.
6. Raise and support vehicle, then remove access hole plug.

7. Adjust cable until and 1/8 inch drill bit can be inserted through access hole into space between shoe web and park lever, **Fig. 8.** Proper adjustment is when a 1/8 inch drill bit will fit in the space and a 1/4 inch drill bit will not fit.
8. Release brake, then check that wheels rotate freely.
9. Replace access hole plug, then lower vehicle.

Drum Brake Specifications

Year	Model	Brake Drum Inside Dia. Inch
BUICK		
1991-93	Century	8.86
	LeSabre	8.86
	Park Ave	8.86
	Roadmaster	①
	Skylark	7.87
CADILLAC		
1991	DeVille	8.86
1991-92	Brougham	11
	Fleetwood FWD	8.86
1993	Fleetwood RWD	11
CHEVROLET		
1991-93	Beretta	7.87
	Camaro	①
	Caprice	①
	Cavalier	7.87
	Corsica	7.87
GEO		
1991-93	Metro	7.09

Year	Model	Brake Drum Inside Dia. Inch
GEO-Continued		
1991-93 —Cont'd	Prizm	7.87
	Storm	7.87
OLDSMOBILE		
1991	Cutlass Calais	7.87
1991-92	Custom Cruiser	①
1991-93	Cutlass Ciera	8.86
	Cutlass Cruiser	8.86
	Eighty-Eight	8.86
	Ninety-Eight	8.86
1992-93	Achieva	7.87
PONTIAC		
1991	6000	8.86
1991-93	Bonneville	8.86
	Firebird	①
	Grand Am	7.87
	LeMans	7.87
	Sunbird	7.87

①—With 4¾ inch bolt circle, 9.5 inches;
w/5 inch bolt circle, 11 inches.

Tightening Specifications

Component	Torque/Ft. Lbs.
BUICK ROADMASTER/CADILLAC BROUGHAM/, CHEVROLET. CAPRICE & OLDSMOBILE CUSTOM CRUISER	
Brake Hose To Caliper	33
Caliper Bleeder Screw	115①
Caliper Mounting Bolts	38
Master Cylinder To Booster	20
Wheel Cylinder Bleeder Screw	62①
Wheel Cylinder Line Fitting	18
Wheel Cylinder To Backing Plate	13
Wheel Lug Nuts	100
CHEVROLET CAMARO & PONTIAC FIREBIRD	
Base, Front Caliper Mounting Bolts	37
Brake Hose To Caliper	30
Caliper Bleeder Screw	115① ②
Heavy Duty Front Caliper Bracket	137
Heavy Duty Caliper Adapter Bracket	85

Component	Torque/Ft. Lbs.
CHEVROLET CAMARO & PONTIAC FIREBIRD -Continued	
Master Cylinder To Booster	24
Pivot Pin Nut	16
Rear Caliper Bracket	70
Rear Caliper Guide Pin (Hex Head)	26
Rear Caliper Guide Pin (Allen Head)	16
Wheel Cylinder Bleeder Screw	53①
Wheel Cylinder Line Fitting	11
Backing Plate To Axle Housing Nut	43
Wheel Lug Nuts	81
CHEVROLET BERETTA, CAVALIER, CORSICA & PONTIAC SUNBIRD	
Brake Hose To Caliper	32
Caliper Bleeder Screw	115①
Caliper Mounting Bolts	38

Continued

TIGHTENING SPECIFICATIONS—Continued

Component	Torque/Ft. Lbs.
CHEVROLET BERETTA, CAVALIER, CORSICA & PONTIAC SUNBIRD-Continued	
Master Cylinder To Booster	20
Wheel Cylinder Bleeder Screw	62①
Wheel Cylinder Line Fitting	11
Wheel Cylinder To Backing Plate	15
Wheel Lug Nuts	100
BUICK REGAL/CHEVROLET LUMINA/ OLDSMOBILE CUTLASS SUPREME & PONTIAC GRAND PRIX	
Accumulator④	24
Brake Hose To Caliper	30
Caliper Bleeder Screw	62③
Front Caliper Mounting Bolts	79
Front Caliper Mounting Bracket To Knuckle	148
Master Cylinder To Booster	28
Pressure Switch	18
Pump Motor Assembly Attaching Bolts④	80①
Rear Caliper Mounting Bolts	92
Wheel Speed Sensor Retaining Bolt④	59
Wheel Lug Nuts	100
CORVETTE	
Brake Hose To Caliper	30
Caliper Bleeder Screw	80①
Front Caliper Mounting Bracket	166
Master Cylinder To Booster	13
Rear Bracket Mounting Bolt	70
Rear Lower Guide Pin Bolt	16
Rear Pivot Pin Nut	16
Rear Upper Guide Pin Bolt	26
Wheel Lug Nuts	100
BUICK CENTURY/OLDSMOBILE CUTLASS CIERA & CRUISER: PONTIAC. 6000	
Brake Hose To Caliper	33
Booster Mounting Nut	25
Caliper Bleeder Screw	116①
Caliper Mounting Bolts	38
Master Cylinder To Booster	20
Wheel Cylinder Bleeder Screw	62①
Wheel Cylinder Line Fitting	12
Wheel Cylinder To Backing Plate	15
Wheel Lug Nuts	100
BUICK LESABRE/OLDSMOBILE EIGHTY-EIGHT & PONTIAC BONNEVILLE	
Brake Hose To Caliper	33

Component	Torque/Ft. Lbs.
BUICK LESABRE/OLDSMOBILE EIGHTY-EIGHT & PONTIAC BONNEVILLE-Continued	
Caliper Bleeder Screw	115①
Caliper Mounting Bolts	38
Master Cylinder To Booster	22
Wheel Cylinder Bleeder Screw	48①
Wheel Cylinder Line Fitting	11
Wheel Cylinder To Backing Plate	106①
Wheel Lug Nuts	100
BUICK PARK AVENUE/CADILLAC DEVILLE, FLEETWOOD & OLDSMOBILE NINETY-EIGHT	
Brake Hose To Caliper	33
Caliper Bleeder Screw	115①
Caliper Mounting Bolts	38
Master Cylinder To Booster	20
Wheel Cylinder Bleeder Screw	53①
Wheel Cylinder Line Fitting	133①
Wheel Cylinder To Backing Plate	106①
Wheel Lug Nuts	100
BUICK SKYLARK/OLDSMOBILE ACHIEVA & CUTLASS CALAIS & PONTIAC GRAND AM	
Brake Hose To Caliper	32
Caliper Bleeder Screw	115①
Caliper Mounting Bolts	38
Master Cylinder To Booster	20
Wheel Cylinder Bleeder Screw	62
Wheel Cylinder To Backing Plate	15
Wheel Lug Nuts	100
BUICK REATTA & RIVIERA/CADILLAC ELDORADO, SEVILLE & OLDS TORONADO/ TROFEO	
Brake Hose To Caliper	32
Caliper Bleeder Screw	9
Caliper Bracket Mounting Bolts	83
Caliper Mounting Bolts	63
Master Cylinder To Booster	22
Wheel Speed Sensor Mounting Bolt	9
Wheel Lug Nuts	100
GEO; METRO, PRIZM & STORM	
Brake Hose To Caliper	⑤
Caliper Bracket Mounts	⑥
Caliper Carrier Mounting Bolts	65⑦
Caliper Mounting Bolts	⑧
Caliper Slide Pins	36⑨
Master Cylinder Retaining Nut	⑩
Wheel Lug Nuts	⑪

TIGHTENING SPECIFICATIONS—Continued

Component	Torque/Ft. Lbs.
PONTIAC LEMANS	
Anchor Plate To Rear Axle	21
Booster To Support Bracket	13
Brake Hose To Caliper	29
Brake Drum To wheel Hub	35 ①
Caliper Bleeder Screw	80 ①
Caliper To Steering Knuckle	70
Master Cylinder To Booster	13
Rotor To Front Wheel Hub	35 ①
Wheel Cylinder Bleeder Screw	80 ①
Wheel Cylinder To Backing Plate	80 ①
Wheel Lug Nuts	66

① —Inch lbs.
② —Heavy duty front & rear caliper bleeder screw, 80 inch lbs.
③ —Lumina, 116 inch lbs.
④ —Anti-lock brakes
⑤ —Metro, 17 ft. lbs.; Prizm, 11 ft. lbs.; Storm, 113 inch lbs.;
⑥ —Storm, 76 ft. lbs.
⑦ —Prizm.
⑧ —Prizm, 19 ft. lbs.; Metro, 22 ft. lbs.
⑨ —Storm.
⑩ —Storm & Prizm, 115 inch lbs.; Metro, 10 ft. lbs.
⑪ —Storm, 87 ft. lbs.; Prizm, 76 ft. lbs.; Metro, 44 ft. lbs.

AUTOMATIC TRANSMISSIONS/TRANSAXLES

TABLE OF CONTENTS

Aisin Warner A131L Automatic Transaxle

INDEX

IDENTIFICATION

The transaxle identification number is stamped at top of transaxle rear cover at rear of transaxle, **Fig. 1.**

DESCRIPTION

The A131L 3 speed automatic transaxle is used on Geo Prizm. The torque converter is equipped with an integral lock-up clutch. For higher performance, greater fuel economy and quietness, a high efficiency torque converter, wider gear ratio, compact high-precision valve body, high efficiency oil pump and a light weight durable integral transaxle case are used.

TROUBLESHOOTING

FLUID DISCOLORED OR SMELLS BURNED

1. Contaminated fluid.
2. Faulty torque converter.
3. Faulty transaxle.

VEHICLE DOES NOT MOVE IN ANY DRIVE GEAR

1. Improperly adjusted transaxle control cable.
2. Faulty valve body or primary regulator.
3. Faulty transaxle.

VEHICLE DOES NOT MOVE IN ANY RANGE

1. Faulty park lock pawl.
2. Faulty valve body or primary regulator.
3. Faulty torque converter.
4. Broken converter driveplate.
5. Blocked oil pump intake strainer.
6. Faulty transaxle.

INCORRECT SHIFT LEVER POSITION

1. Improperly adjusted transaxle control cable.
2. Faulty manual valve and lever.
3. Faulty transaxle.

Fig. 1   Transaxle identification number plate location

Fig. 2   Manual shift linkage adjustment

1. ADJUSTING NUTS
2. RUBBER BOOT
3. CABLE STOP
4. 0-1 MM (0-0.04 IN.)

Fig. 3   Throttle cable adjustment

HARSH ENGAGEMENT INTO ANY DRIVE RANGE

1. Improperly adjusted transaxle control cable.
2. Faulty valve body or primary regulator.
3. Faulty accumulator pistons.
4. Faulty transaxle.

DELAYED UPSHIFTS & DOWNSHIFTS

1. Improperly adjusted throttle cable.
2. Faulty governors.
3. Faulty valve body.

SLIPS ON UPSHIFTS OR SHUDDERS ON TAKE-OFF

1. Improperly adjusted transaxle control cable.
2. Improperly adjusted throttle cable.
3. Faulty valve body.
4. Faulty transaxle.

DRAG OR BINDING ON UPSHIFT

1. Improperly adjusted transaxle control cable.

2. Faulty valve body.
3. Faulty transaxle.

HARSH DOWNSHIFT

1. Improperly adjusted throttle cable.
2. Faulty accumulator pistons.
3. Faulty valve body.
4. Faulty transaxle.

NO DOWNSHIFT WHEN COASTING

1. Faulty governor.
2. Faulty valve body.

INCORRECT DOWNSHIFT

1. Improperly adjusted throttle cable.
2. Faulty governor.
3. Faulty valve body.
4. Faulty transaxle.

NO KICKDOWN

1. Improperly adjusted throttle cable.
2. Faulty governor.
3. Faulty valve body.

NO ENGINE BRAKING

1. Faulty valve body.
2. Faulty transaxle.

NO HOLD IN PARK

1. Improperly adjusted transaxle control cable.
2. Faulty parking lock pawl and rod.

MAINTENANCE
CHANGING FLUID

1. Raise and support vehicle, then place a suitable container under transaxle drain plug.
2. Remove drain plug and drain fluid, then reinstall and **torque** drain plug to 29 ft. lbs..
3. With engine off, add 2.4 quarts of Dexron II type transmission fluid.
4. Start engine, then move selector lever through all ranges and end in "Park."
5. With engine idling, check fluid level, then if necessary, add fluid as necessary to bring fluid to "Cool" level on dipstick.

ADJUSTMENTS
MANUAL SHIFT LINKAGE, ADJUST

1. Loosen swivel nut on lever, then push manual lever fully toward right side of vehicle, **Fig. 2.**
2. Return lever two notches to Neutral position, then place selector lever in Neutral position.
3. Shift manual shift lever to N range, then tighten swivel nut.

THROTTLE CABLE, ADJUST

1. Hold accelerator pedal in fully depressed position, then loosen cable adjusting nuts. **Fig. 3.**

Fig. 4   Valve body bolt identification

Fig. 5   Manual valve body bolt identification

Fig. 7   Second brake servo plunger installation

Fig. 6   Positioning throttle cable for stopper installation

2. Adjust cable to obtain .04 inch between end of boot and stopper on cable, then tighten adjusting nut.
3. Fully depress accelerator pedal and recheck adjustment, then road test vehicle.

NEUTRAL SAFETY SWITCH, ADJUST

1. Loosen neutral start switch attaching bolts, then place selector lever in Neutral position.
2. Disconnect electrical connector, then connect a suitable ohmmeter between terminals.
3. Rotate switch until meter indicates continuity, then **torque** switch retaining bolts to 69 inch lbs. to secure adjustment.
4. Reconnect electrical connector to switch then ensure engine starts with selector lever in Neutral and Park only.

IN-VEHICLE REPAIRS

VALVE BODY, REPLACE
Removal

1. Disconnect negative battery cable.
2. Raise and support vehicle.
3. Clean area around pan, then drain transmission fluid.
4. Remove oil pan and gasket, then the oil strainer.
5. Remove oil apply tube bracket attaching bolts, then the apply tube.
6. Remove oil tubes using a suitable screwdriver, then the manual detent spring.
7. Remove manual valve attaching bolts, then the manual valve assembly.
8. Remove valve body to cable bracket attaching bolt, then disconnect throttle cable.
9. Remove valve body attaching bolts, then valve body, governor, apply gasket and governor oil gasket.

Installation

1. Install governor oil gasket, then the governor and governor apply gasket.
2. Hold valve body in place, then manually retain cam in downward position and slip cable end into slot.

3. Position valve body into place, then insert and finger tighten 14 attaching bolts. **Torque** bolts to 89 inch lbs. **Attaching bolt lengths (mm) are indicated in Fig. 4.**
4. Align manual valve with pin on manual valve lever, then install manual valve body.
5. Insert and finger tighten attaching bolts, then **torque** to 89 inch lbs. **Attaching bolt lengths (mm) are indicated in Fig. 5.**
6. Install detent spring, then insert and finger tighten attaching bolts. **Torque** attaching bolts to 89 inch lbs.
7. Ensure manual lever is in contact with center of roller at tip of detent spring, then install oil tubes.
8. Install apply tube bracket, then the oil strainer.
9. Insert magnet into pan, then install oil pan with new gasket.
10. Insert oil pan attaching bolts, then **torque** to 44 inch lbs.
11. Install drain plug with new gasket, then **torque** to 29 ft. lbs.
12. Fill transaxle to specifications, then ensure proper fluid level.

THROTTLE CABLE, REPLACE
Removal

1. Disconnect negative battery cable.
2. Loosen throttle valve cable jamb nuts.
3. Disconnect throttle cable from bracket and throttle plate.
4. Remove neutral start and back-up switch.

5. Remove valve body as previously described, then throttle cable end from throttle pressure valve cam.
6. Pull cable from transaxle case.

Installation

1. Insert cable into transaxle case, then install retaining plate and bolt.
2. Install valve body as previously described, then position cable stop for adjustment reference as follows. **Cable stop is not staked in place on replacement cable.**
   a. Bend cable to a radius of approximately 7.87 inches as shown, **Fig. 6.**
   b. Lightly pull inner cable from housing until a slight resistance is felt, then hold in position.
   c. Stake stopper onto inner cable so that .031-.059 inch clearance exists between stop and cable housing.
3. Connect throttle cable to throttle linkage, then adjust cable as previously described.
4. Install neutral safety switch, then the manual shift lever. Adjust switch as previously described.
5. Ensure transaxle fluid level is to specifications, then road test vehicle.

GOVERNOR VALVE, REPLACE
Removal

1. Raise and support vehicle.
2. Remove transaxle cover, then the left-hand driveshaft.
3. Remove governor cover, then the O-ring.
4. Remove governor body with thrust washer.
5. Remove washer, then the governor body adapter.

Installation

1. Install governor body adapter, then the governor body with thrust washer.
2. Install governor cover with O-ring, then the lefthand driveshaft.
3. Install transaxle dust cover, then ensure transaxle fluid level is to specifications.
4. Road test vehicle.

SECOND BRAKE SERVO ASSEMBLY, REPLACE
Removal

1. Disconnect negative battery cable.

2. Raise and support vehicle, then drain fluid from transaxle.
3. Remove shift cable bracket at transaxle.
4. Install second brake servo compressor tool No. J-35549-A or equivalent and compress second brake servo.
5. Remove second brake servo snap ring and second brake servo compressor.
6. Remove cover.
7. Remove piston, then the outer spring.

Installation

1. Insert piston, less outer spring, then install snap ring.
2. Install brake apply rod tool No. J-35679, then observe groove on plunger of tool.
3. Push button on tool, **Fig. 7**. This allows tool to push brake apply rod into case. If groove is visible, piston stroke is correct (.059-.118 inch). If stroke is greater than specified, replace piston rod with 2.870 inch or 2.811 inch rod as needed.
4. Remove snap ring, then install piston and outer spring.
5. Install spring compressor tool No. J-35549 to compress spring, then insert snap ring.
6. Install cover, then the shift cable bracket.
7. Lower vehicle.

TRANSAXLE REPLACE

1. Install engine support fixture No. J-28467-A or equivalent.
2. Remove battery hold-down, battery and battery tray.
3. Remove air cleaner assembly and neutral start switch connector.
4. Disconnect ground cable at transaxle and throttle cable from throttle body.
5. Disconnect transmission cooling lines and plug them to prevent excess leakage.
6. Remove shift cable retainer and end clip, then disconnect shift cable from brackets and lay aside.
7. Disconnect upper shift cable bracket from transaxle.
8. Remove left transaxle mount brace and through bolt.
9. Remove two upper transaxle to engine bolts, upper starter bolts and speedometer cable.
10. Raise and support vehicle.
11. Remove right and left lower stone shields and drain transaxle oil.
12. Disconnect starter electrical connectors and remove bottom starter bolt and starter.
13. Remove front drive axles as described in "Front Drive Axles section."
14. Remove three center crossmember to radiator support bolts and front and center mount bolt shields.
15. Remove two front mount bolts, two center mount bolts, two rear mount nuts and two center crossmember to main crossmember bolts.
16. Remove three exhaust hanger bracket nuts and exhaust hanger, eight main crossmember to underbody bolts and two lower A-frame bracket to underbody bolts, then remove main crossmember.
17. Remove front mount through bolt and mount, front mount bracket and center mount from transaxle.
18. Remove torque converter bolt shield and torque converter to flywheel bolts.
19. Remove two lower transaxle bracket to mount bolts, then lower vehicle.
20. Remove remaining transaxle mount to bracket bolt, then lower transaxle with engine support fixture to gain necessary clearance to remove transaxle.
21. Raise and support vehicle.
22. Support transaxle with a suitable transmission jack, then remove front and rear lower transaxle to engine bolts.
23. Remove transaxle from vehicle.
24. Reverse procedure to install, referring to "Tightening Specifications" chart for proper bolt and nut torques.

TIGHTENING SPECIFICATIONS

Component	Torque/Ft. Lbs.
Cable End Bolt	15
Center Crossmember To Main Crossmember Bolts	45
Center Crossmember To Radiator Support Bolts	45
Center Mount Mounting Nuts	45
Center Mount To Transaxle Bolts	45
Differential Check Fill Plug	29
Differential Fill And Drain Plug	29
Exhaust Hanger Bracket Nuts	115①
Fill Tube To Case Bolt	97①
Front, Center And Rear Mount Bolts	45
Front Mount Bracket Bolts	13
Front Mount Bolts	45
Front Mount Through Bolt	64
Governor Cover Bolts	97①
Left Mount Brace Bolts	13
Left Mount Through Bolt	66
Lower A-Frame To Underbody Bolts	94
Lower Mount To Bracket Bolts	45
Lower Starter Motor Bolt	29
Lower Transaxle Mount Bolts	45
Main Crossmember To Underbody Bolts	152
Manual Lever Cap Nut	89①

Component	Torque/Ft. Lbs.
Manual Valve and Manual Detent Spring Bolts	89①
Mount Cover And Brace Bolts	13
Neutral Start Switch Bolts	69①
Oil Apply Tube Retainer Bolts	44①
Oil Cooler Line Nuts	20
Oil Cooler Pipe Fittings	15
Oil Filter Bolts	89①
Oil Pan Drain Plug Bolt	29
Oil Pan Bolts	44①
Oil Pump Bolts	16
Rear Mount Through Bolt	64
Shift Control Assembly Bolts	15
Shift Control Bolts	15
Side Case Cover Bolts	44①
Throttle Valve Cable Housing Locknuts	89①
Torque Converter Bolts	31
Transaxle Fluid Drain Plug	29
Transaxle To Engine Bolts	34
Upper Mount To Bracket Bolts	45
Upper Starter Bolt	29
Upper Transaxle Mount Bracket Bolt	45
Valve Body Bolts	89①
Wheel Lug Nuts	76

①—Inch lbs.

Aisin Warner A240E Automatic Transaxle

INDEX

Fig. 1 Transaxle identification number plate location

TRANSAXLE IDENTIFICATION

The transaxle identification number is stamped on top of the transaxle rear cover at the rear of the transaxle, **Fig. 1.**

DESCRIPTION

The A240E 4 speed automatic transaxle is used on the 1991-92 Geo prizm. The torque converter is equipped with an Electronic lock-up clutch and is computer controlled.

TROUBLESHOOTING

FLUID DISCOLORED OR SMELLS BURNED

1. Contaminated fluid.
2. Faulty torque converter.
3. Faulty transaxle.

VEHICLE DOES NOT MOVE IN ANY RANGE

1. Faulty control cable.
2. Faulty valve body or primary regulator.
3. Faulty parking pawl.
4. Faulty torque converter.
5. Blocked oil pump strainer.
6. Faulty transaxle.

INCORRECT SHIFT LEVER POSITION

1. Improperly adjusted transaxle linkage.
2. Faulty manual valve or lever.
3. Faulty transaxle.

HARSH ENGAGEMENT INTO ANY DRIVE RANGE

1. Improperly adjusted throttle cable.
2. Faulty valve body or primary regulator.
3. Faulty transaxle.

DELAYED UPSHIFTS & DOWNSHIFTS

1. Improperly adjusted throttle cable.
2. Faulty valve body.
3. Faulty solenoid valve.
4. Faulty governor.

SLIPS ON UPSHIFTS OR SHUDDERS ON TAKE-OFF

1. Improperly adjusted transaxle control cable.
2. Improperly adjusted throttle cable.

Fig. 2 Manual shift linkage adjustment

1. ADJUSTING NUTS
2. RUBBER BOOT
3. CABLE STOP
4. 0-1 MM (0-0.04 IN.)

Fig. 3 Throttle cable adjustment

A | 0.8-1.5 mm (0.031-0.059'')
1 | THROTTLE CABLE
2 | CABLE STOPPER

Fig. 5 Positioning throttle cable for stopper installation

A   NEUTRAL BASIC LINE
B   BOLT
C   GROOVE
13 NEUTRAL START SWITCH

Fig. 4 Neutral safety switch adjustment

3. Faulty valve body.
4. Faulty solenoid valve.
5. Faulty transaxle.

NO HOLD IN PARK

1. Improperly adjusted transaxle control linkage.
2. Faulty parking pawl.

DRAG OR BINDING ON UPSHIFTS

1. Improperly adjusted transaxle control cable.
2. Faulty valve body.
3. Faulty transaxle.

NO LOCK-UP IN 2ND, 3RD OR OVERDRIVE

1. Faulty electronic control.
2. Faulty valve body.
3. Faulty solenoid valve.
4. Faulty transaxle.

HARSH DOWNSHIFT

1. Improperly adjusted throttle cable.
2. Faulty valve body.
3. Faulty transaxle.

NO DOWNSHIFT WHEN COASTING

1. Faulty governor.
2. Faulty valve body.
3. Faulty solenoid valve.
4. Faulty electronic control.

INCORRECT DOWNSHIFT

1. Improperly adjusted throttle cable.
2. Faulty governor.
3. Faulty valve body.
4. Faulty transaxle.
5. Faulty solenoid valve.
6. Faulty electronic control.

NO KICKDOWN

1. Improperly adjusted throttle cable.
2. Faulty governor.
3. Faulty solenoid valve.
4. Faulty electronic control.
5. Faulty valve body.

NO ENGINE BRAKING IN 2 OR L RANGE

1. Faulty solenoid valve.
2. Faulty electronic control.
3. Faulty valve body.
4. Faulty transaxle.

MAINTENANCE
CHANGING FLUID

1. Raise and support vehicle, then position suitable drain pan under transaxle oil pan.
2. Remove transaxle drain plug and allow fluid to drain, then re-install drain plug and **torque** to 13 ft. lbs.
3. Add 2.4 qts. of Dexron Type II transmission fluid to transaxle.
4. Start engine and move selector lever through all selector lever positions, then return to Park.
5. With engine idling, check fluid level and add fluid as necessary.

ADJUSTMENTS
MANUAL LINKAGE, ADJUST

1. Loosen swivel nut on lever, then push manual lever fully forward toward the right side of the vehicle, **Fig. 2.**
2. Return lever two notches to the Neutral position, then place selector lever in Neutral position.
3. Shift manual shift lever to N range, then tighten swivel nut.

THROTTLE CABLE, ADJUST

1. Hold accelerator pedal in the fully de-

pressed position, the loosen cable adjusting nuts, **Fig. 3.**
2. Adjust cable to obtain .04 inch clearance between end of boot and stopper on cable, then tighten adjusting nut.
3. Fully depress accelerator pedal and recheck adjustment, then road test vehicle.

NEUTRAL SAFETY SWITCH, ADJUST

1. Loosen neutral safety switch attaching bolts.
2. Place selector lever in the Neutral position.
3. Disconnect electrical connector.
4. Align groove with neutral basic line, **Fig. 4.**
5. **Torque** switch attaching bolts to 44 inch lbs.
6. Connect electrical connector and check to ensure engine starts on when selector lever is Neutral or Park.

IN-VEHICLE REPAIRS
VALVE BODY, REPLACE
Removal

1. Raise and support vehicle.
2. Drain fluid from transaxle and remove oil pan.
3. Remove oil strainer, oil tube bracket and five oil tubes.
4. Remove manual valve detent spring and three solenoid electrical connectors.
5. Remove 12 valve body bolts and lower valve body slightly to unhook throttle valve cable end from throttle valve cam.
6. Disconnect manual valve connecting rod, then remove valve body, valve body gasket and intermediate clutch apply passage O-ring seal.

Installation

1. Install a new intermediate clutch apply passage O-ring seal.
2. Install a new valve body gasket on valve body.
3. Install valve body to transaxle attaching manual valve and throttle cable valve.
4. Install 12 valve body bolts and **torque** to 84 inch lbs.
5. Connect three solenoid electrical connectors and install manual valve detent spring. **Torque** manual valve detent spring retaining bolts to 84 inch lbs.
6. Install five oil tubes and oil tube clamp bolt and bracket. **Torque** oil tube clamp bolt to 84 inch lbs.
7. Install oil strainer and new gasket.
8. Install oil pan and fill transaxle to proper level.

THROTTLE VALVE CABLE, REPLACE
Removal

1. Disconnect throttle valve cable from engine throttle body and retaining clamps.
2. Raise and support vehicle.
3. Drain fluid from transaxle, then remove oil pan and neutral safety switch.
4. Disconnect throttle cable retaining plate from transaxle.
5. Pull throttle cable out of transaxle case and remove from vehicle.

Installation

1. Install throttle cable into transaxle.
2. Connect throttle cable retaining plate to transaxle and **torque** bolts to 53 inch lbs.
3. Stake stopper to inner cable as follows:
   a. Bend cable until there is a 7.87 inch radius, **Fig. 5.**
   b. Pull lightly on inner cable until a slight resistance is felt.
   c. Stake the stopper .031-.059 inch from end of outer cable while holding inner cable.
4. Install transaxle oil pan and neutral safety switch.
5. Lower vehicle, then install throttle valve cable to engine throttle body and retaining clamps and adjust as described under "Throttle Cable Adjust."
6. Fill transaxle to proper level.

SHIFT LOCK MODULE, SOLENOID & SWITCH, REPLACE
Removal

1. Disconnect battery ground cable.
2. Remove five retaining screws from rear center console and rear center console.
3. Remove two retaining screws from shift selector cover and shift selector cover.
4. Disconnect shift lock control module electrical connectors.
5. Remove shift lock control module retaining screw and shift lock control module.
6. Disconnect shift lock solenoid and shift lock switch electrical connectors.
7. Remove two shift lock solenoid retaining screws and shift lock solenoid.
8. Remove two shift lock control switch retaining screws and shift lock control switch.

Installation

1. Install shift lock control switch and two retaining screws.
2. Install shift lock solenoid and two retaining screws.
3. Connect shift lock solenoid and shift lock switch electrical connectors.
4. Install shift lock control module and retaining screw.
5. Connect shift lock control electrical connectors.
6. Install shift selector cover and two retaining screws.
7. Install rear center console and five retaining screws.
8. Connect battery ground cable.

TRANSAXLE REPLACE

1. Disconnect battery ground cable.
2. Remove air cleaner assembly.
3. Disconnect transaxle solenoids, neutral safety switch and speed sensor electrical connectors.
4. Disconnect speedometer cable.
5. Disconnect throttle cable from engine throttle body and retaining clamps.
6. Remove thermostat housing to transaxle case retaining bolt and nut.
7. Remove two top transaxle to engine bolts.
8. Disconnect battery ground cable from transaxle case.
9. Install engine support fixture tool No. J-28467-A or equivalent.
10. Raise and support vehicle, then drain fluid from transaxle.
11. Remove dust covers from crossmember.
12. Remove front wheel and tire assemblies.
13. Remove front drive axles as described in "Front Drive Axles section."
14. Remove front and rear mount retaining bolts, control cable clamp bolts and center crossmember.
15. Disconnect and cap oil cooler lines.
16. Disconnect front exhaust pipe from exhaust manifold.
17. Remove shifter control cable to shift lever clip.
18. Remove shifter control cable bracket retaining bolts and set cable aside.
19. Remove starter and engine to transaxle support bracket.
20. Remove flywheel inspection cover and six torque converter bolts.
21. Remove left engine mount.
22. Place suitable transmission jack under transaxle and remove front and rear engine block to transaxle bolts, then remove transaxle.
23. Reverse procedure to install, referring to "Tightening specifications" chart for proper bolt and nut torques.

TIGHTENING SPECIFICATIONS

Component	Torque/Ft. Lbs.
Battery Negative Cable To Transaxle Case Bolt	20
Center Crossmember Bolts	29
Control Cable Bracket Bolts	20
Engine to Transaxle Bolts	47
Engine to Transaxle Support Bracket Nut And Bolt	38
Flywheel Inspection Cover Bolts	20
Front and Rear Engine Mount Bolts	29
Left Engine Mount Bolts	38
Manual Shift Lever Nut	22①
Manual Shift Shaft Nut	62①
Manual Valve Detent Spring Bolts	84①
Neutral Safety Switch Bolts	44①

Component	Torque/Ft. Lbs.
Oil Pan Bolts	44①
Oil Pan Drain Plug	13
Oil Tube Clamp Bolts	84①
Pressure Detection Plug	80①
Shifter Control Cable Clamp Bolts	10
Shifter Control Bolts	20
Strainer Screen Bolts	84①
Thermostat Housing To Transaxle Case Nut	20
Throttle Cable Retaining Plate Bolt	53①
Torque Converter Bolts	20
Valve Body Bolts	84①
Wheel Lug Nuts	76

①—Inch lbs.

Aisin Warner A245E Automatic Transaxle

INDEX

IDENTIFICATION

The A245E 4-speed automatic transaxle identification number is located on top of the transaxle case in front of the vent tube, **Fig. 1.**

DESCRIPTION

The A245E is used on the 1993 Geo Prizm. The A245E transaxle is an improved version of the A240E transaxle. It is equipped with an integral lock-up mechanism and fuel consumption has been reduced and power output increased by more precise shift control and monitoring of the throttle opening angle.

TROUBLESHOOTING

FLUID DISCOLORED OR BURNED

1. Contaminated fluid.
2. Faulty torque converter.
3. Faulty transaxle.

VEHICLE DOES NOT MOVE IN ANY DRIVE GEAR

1. Incorrectly adjusted transaxle control cable.
2. Faulty valve body or primary regulator.
3. Faulty transaxle.

VEHICLE DOES NOT MOVE IN ANY RANGE

1. Faulty park lock pawl.
2. Faulty valve body or Primary regulator.
3. Faulty torque converter.
4. Broken converter driveplate.
5. Blocked oil pump intake strainer.
6. Faulty transaxle.

701

701 TRANSAXLE IDENTIFICATION NUMBER LOCATION

Fig. 1 Transaxle identification number location.

INCORRECT SHIFT LEVER POSITION

1. Incorrectly adjusted transaxle control cable.
2. Faulty manual valve and lever.
3. Faulty transaxle.

HARSH ENGAGEMENT INTO ANY DRIVE RANGE

1. Incorrectly adjusted throttle cable.
2. Incorrectly adjusted transaxle control cable.
3. Faulty valve body or primary regulator.
4. Faulty accumulator pistons.
5. Faulty transaxle.

DELAYED UPSHIFTS & DOWNSHIFTS

1. Incorrectly adjusted throttle cable.
2. Faulty governors.
3. Faulty valve body.
4. Faulty solenoid valve.

SLIPS ON UPSHIFTS OR SHUDDERS ON TAKEOFFS

1. Incorrectly adjusted transaxle control cable.
2. Incorrectly adjusted throttle cable.
3. Faulty valve body.
4. Faulty transaxle.
5. Faulty solenoid valve.

DRAG OR BINDING ON UPSHIFTS

1. Incorrectly adjusted transaxle control cable.
2. Faulty valve body.
3. Faulty transaxle.

HARSH DOWNSHIFT

1. Incorrectly adjusted throttle cable.
2. Faulty accumulator pistons.
3. Faulty valve body.
4. Faulty transaxle.

NO DOWNSHIFT WHEN COASTING

1. Faulty governor.
2. Faulty valve body.
3. Faulty solenoid valve.
4. Faulty electronic controls.

INCORRECT DOWNSHIFT

1. Incorrectly adjusted throttle cable.
2. Faulty governor.
3. Faulty valve body.
4. Faulty transaxle.
5. Faulty solenoid valve.
6. Faulty electronic control.

7095 SHIFT SOLENOID NO. 1 ELECTRICAL CONNECTOR
7096 SHIFT SOLENOID NO. 2 ELECTRICAL CONNECTOR
7097 TORQUE CONVERTER CLUTCH (TCC) SOLENOID ELECTRICAL CONNECTOR

Fig. 2   Solenoid electrical connectors.

FLUID DRAIN & REFILL

1. **On all units, except A131L,** drain transaxle fluid.
2. **On A131L units,** using tool No. 09043-38100 or equivalent, remove drain plug and drain fluid.
3. **On all models,** install drain plug and new gasket.
4. Add fluid through filler tube. **Do not overfill.**
5. Refer to "Lubricant Data" for capacities.
6. Start engine, ensure smooth shift operation in all positions.
7. With engine at idle, check fluid COOL level, fill as required.
8. Allow vehicle to reach normal operating temperatures, then recheck level.

752 VALVE BODY ASSEMBLY BOLTS
790 VALVE BODY ASSEMBLY

Fig. 3   Valve body bolt location.

NO LOCK-UP IN 2, 3 OR O/D

1. Faulty valve body.
2. Faulty transaxle.
3. Faulty solenoid valve.
4. Faulty electronic control.
5. Faulty torque converter.

NO KICKDOWN

1. Incorrectly adjusted throttle cable.
2. Faulty governor.
3. Faulty valve body.
4. Faulty solenoid valve.
5. Faulty electronic control.

NO ENGINE BRAKING IN 2

1. Faulty valve body.
2. Faulty transaxle.
3. Faulty solenoid valve.
4. Faulty electronic control.

NO HOLD IN P

1. Incorrectly adjusted transaxle control cable.
2. Faulty parking lock pawl and rod.

NO CENTER DIFFERENTIAL CONTROL

1. Faulty electronic controls.
2. Faulty valve body.
3. Faulty transfer.
4. Faulty C/D clutch.

MAINTENANCE

FLUID LEVEL CHECK

1. Start engine, allow transaxle fluid to reach 158-176°F.
2. Position vehicle on level surface, then set parking brake.
3. With engine idling, brake pedal depressed, move shift lever through all positions.
4. Remove transaxle dipstick, wipe clean, then replace.
5. Remove dipstick again, check fluid at HOT level.
6. Refer to "Lubricant Data" for capacities.

IN-VEHICLE REPAIRS

VALVE BODY & ACCUMULATOR, REPLACE

1. Disconnect battery ground cable, then raise and support vehicle.
2. Remove six bolts and left splash shield from vehicle.
3. Place a drain pan or suitable container under transaxle fluid pan, then remove drain plug, drain transaxle fluid and remove transaxle fluid pan. **When removing transaxle fluid pan, use caution to not damage mating surfaces. Use a rubber mallet and wooden block if pan is frozen to transaxle; do not use metal objects (crow bar, screwdriver, etc.) to free pan.**
4. Remove filter and screen from valve body, then disconnect solenoid electrical connectors from shift solenoid Nos. 1 and 2 and TCC solenoid, **Fig. 2.**
5. Remove bolt and solenoid wire harness clip from valve body, then detent spring.
6. Remove TV cable from throttle valve cam. **The B2 accumulator, check ball and spring may drop from transaxle during valve body removal. The B2 accumulator is under intense spring pressure and may push valve body down after valve body bolts are loosened.**
7. Remove seventeen bolts **Fig. 3** and valve body from transaxle while simultaneously disconnecting manual valve link from manual lever.
8. Remove check ball and spring from transaxle, then B2 accumulator piston and spring. When using compressed air to remove components from transaxle case, air pressure should never exceed 14 psi.
9. Remove C2, C1 and C3 accumulator pistons and springs from transaxle case by slowly applying low pressure compressed air into accumulator apply passages, **Fig. 4 through 6.**

10. Reverse procedure to install. Prior to installation, inspect transaxle case for nicks or scars, accumulator seals for cuts or damage and accumulator pistons for cracks or porosity.

TV CABLE, REPLACE

1. Disconnect battery ground cable, then loosen TV cable locknut and adjust nut, **Fig. 7.**
2. Disconnect TV cable from throttle valve linkage and TV cable bracket, then from cable guide bracket at top of transaxle.
3. Raise and support vehicle and remove left splash shield.
4. Disconnect Park/Neutral Switch from transaxle, then place a drain pan or suitable container under transaxle fluid pan.
5. Drain transaxle fluid, then remove transaxle pan.
6. Disconnect TV cable from throttle valve cam at valve body, then remove cable retaining bolt and cable.
7. Inspect TV cable for fraying, kinks, excessive wear or damage.
8. **New TV cables do not have a staked TV cable stopper. A new stopper must be staked if using a new cable.** To stake cable stopper, bend cable to a radius of approximately 7.87 inches as shown, **Fig. 8.** Lightly pull inner cable from housing until a slight resistance is felt, then hold in position. Stake stopper onto inner cable so that .031–.059 inch clearance exists between stop and cable housing.
9. Reverse procedure to install.

TRANSAXLE REPLACE

1. Remove battery, holddown bracket and tray.
2. Disconnect intake air temperature (IAT) connector from IAT sensor.
3. Remove air cleaner cover and air cleaner, then disconnect Park/Neutral Position switch connector.

7057 C2 ACCUMULATOR PISTON
7101 C2 ACCUMULATOR APPLY PASSAGE

Fig. 4   C2 accumulator piston & spring removal.

7054 C1 ACCUMULATOR PISTON
7102 C1 ACCUMULATOR APPLY PASSAGE

Fig. 5   C1 accumulator piston & spring removal.

7103 C3 ACCUMULATOR PISTON
7104 C3 ACCUMULATOR APPLY PASSAGE

Fig. 6   C3 accumulator piston & spring removal.

712 THROTTLE VALVE LINKAGE
713 OUTER CABLE BOOT
714 TV CABLE ADJUST NUT
715 TV CABLE LOCKNUT
716 TV CABLE BRACKET

Fig. 7   TV cable locknut & adjust nut location.

4. Disconnect solenoid wire harness electrical connector from solenoid wire harness.
5. Remove ground strap from transaxle case and loosen TV cable locknut and adjust nut. Disconnect TV cable from throttle linkage and TV cable bracket.
6. Disconnect vehicle speed sensor (VSS) electrical connector.
7. Remove shift select cable from manual lever and shift select cable bracket.
8. Remove cable guise bracket from transaxle case, then remove two up-

per transaxle-to-engine bolts.
9. Remove upper starter motor retaining bolt from starter motor, then left transaxle mounting bracket reinforcement bolts and bracket from transaxle.
10. Remove one bolt from left transaxle mounting bracket, then raise and support vehicle and place a drain pan or suitable container under transaxle fluid pan. Drain transaxle fluid.
11. Remove starter positive terminal nut, positive battery cable and electrical connector from starter, then lower starter retaining bolt and starter.
12. Remove both splash shields, then plug fluid cooler pipes to prevent transaxle fluid cooler leakage.
13. Remove inner and outer cooler hoses and pipes at transaxle.
14. Remove two bolts from left transaxle mounting bracket, then both front wheel assemblies.
15. Remove both drive axles as outlined under -Front Wheel Drive Axles.-
16. Remove exhaust pipe support bolts and center crossmember.
17. **On Federal models,** remove front exhaust pipe-to-three way catalytic converter mating flange bolts.
18. **On California models,** remove front exhaust pipe-to-warm up three way catalytic converter mating flange nuts and front exhaust pipe.
19. **On all models,** remove front exhaust pipe-to-exhaust manifold mating flange nuts and front exhaust pipe.
20. Remove enter crossmember plastic access cover from center crossmember, then bolts and nuts from front transaxle mount.
21. Remove front suspension crossmem-

A   200 mm (7.87") RADIUS
717 TV CABLE
718 TV CABLE STOPPER

Fig. 8   Bending TV cable for stopper staking.

ber and center crossmember, then support transaxle with a suitable jack.
22. Remove flywheel access cover from engine rear end plate, then six flywheel-to-torque converter bolts from flywheel. Remove drain pan from underneath transaxle.
23. Remove two lower transaxle-to-engine bolts from transaxle. Disconnect transaxle from engine by carefully moving transaxle away from engine toward left side of engine compartment and very slowly lowering hydraulic jack ensuring no obstructions exist.
24. Reverse procedure to install.

TIGHTENING SPECIFICATIONS

Component	Torque/Ft. Lbs.
Air Cleaner Bolts	44①
Battery Ground Cable	11
Battery Holddown Bracket Bolt	44①
Battery Holddown Bracket Nut	71①
Center Crossmember Rear Bolt And Nuts	45
Detent Spring Bolts	89①
Fluid Filter Screen Bolts	89①
Flywheel To Torque Converter Bolts	14
Front Exhaust Pipe Support Nuts And Bolts	14
Front Exhaust Pipe To Exhaust Manifold Nuts	46
Front Exhaust Pipe To Three Way Catalytic Converter Mating Flange Bolts	32
Front Exhaust Pipe To Warm Up Three Way Catalytic Converter Mating Flange Nuts	46
Front Exhaust Pipe Support Bolts	14
Front Suspension Crossmember Bolts	152
Front Transaxle Mount Bolts	35
Front Transaxle Mount Through Bolt And Nut	64
Ground Strap Bolt	115①

Component	Torque/Ft. Lbs.
Left Transaxle Mount Through Bolt	64
Left Transaxle Mounting Bracket Bolts	35
Left Transaxle Mounting Bracket Reinforcement Bolts	15
Lower Engine Reinforcement Brace Bolts	47
Rear Transaxle Mount Nuts	42
Rear Transaxle Mount Through Bolt	64
Solenoid Wire Harness Clip Bolt	53①
Solenoid Wire Harness Retaining Bolt	53①
Splash Shield Bolts	44①
Starter Motor Positive Terminal Nut	44①
Starter Motor Retaining Bolts	29
Transaxle Fluid Drain Plug	13
Transaxle Fluid Pan Bolts	43①
Transaxle To Engine Bolts	47
TV Cable Guide Bracket Bolt	71①
TV Cable Locknut	71①
TV Cable Retaining Bolt	71①

①—Inch lbs.

Turbo Hydra-Matic 3T40 (125C) Automatic Transaxle

INDEX

IDENTIFICATION

This transaxle may be identified by a model tag attached to the case exterior, **Fig. 1.**

DESCRIPTION

This automatic transaxle consists primarily of a 3 element torque converter, **Fig. 2**, compound planetary gear set and dual sprockets, drive link assembly and a pressure plate and damper assembly. A differential and final drive gear set is also incorporated in the transaxle case. Three multiple disc clutches, a roller clutch and a band provide the friction elements required to obtain the desired functions of the planetary gear set. Hydraulic pressure required to operate the friction elements and automatic control is provided by a vane type pump.

TROUBLESHOOTING

Always check for the following conditions when troubleshooting any type of transaxle malfunction:
1. Incorrect oil level.
2. Improperly adjusted, disconnected, bound or broken TV cable.
3. Manual linkage improperly adjusted.
4. Incorrect oil pressure.

CHATTERS OR SLIPS IN FIRST GEAR

1. Low oil level
2. Restricted feed to forward clutch.
3. Burned clutch plates.
4. Drive sprocket support.
5. Incorrect case cover gasket.

NO REVERSE OR SLIPS IN REVERSE

1. Forward clutch:

a. Burned clutch plates.
b. Seal ring off piston.
c. Exhaust check ball sticking.
2. Lo and reverse clutch:
  a. Housing cup plug assembly restricted or not fully seated.
  b. Leaking seals.
3. Low and reverse pipe O-ring seal damaged or missing.
4. Incorrect, damaged or leaking case to cover gasket.
5. Burned direct clutch plates.
6. Burned low and reverse clutch plates.
7. Low line pressure.

NO UPSHIFTS, DELAYED UPSHIFTS OR FULL THROTTLE SHIFTS

1. Governor or speed sensor:
  a. Cover worn.
  b. Thrust washer missing.
  c. Governor seal worn or cut.
  d. Governor spring not seated.
  e. Governor weights binding on pin.
  f. Ball missing.
  g. Governor driven gear stripped.
2. Intermediate servo:
  a. Wrong or sticking apply pin.
  b. Seals cut, damaged or missing.
  c. Porosity in case servo bore.
3. Control valve assembly:
  a. Valves sticking.
  b. Spacer plate gaskets leaking or incorrectly installed.
4. Valve body spacer:
  a. Governor feed orifice to 1-2 and 2-3 shift valve plugged.
  b. Drive to governor orifice plugged.
5. Burned or worn intermediate band.
6. Case cover:
  a. Porosity.
  b. Undrilled holes.
  c. Missing cup plugs.
  d. Second oil passage leaking.
7. Leaks in governor passage and/or pipe.

SLIPPING OR ROUGH 1-2 SHIFT

1. Intermediate servo:
  a. Seals cut, damaged or leaking.
  b. Piston damaged.
  c. Servo bore in case damaged.
  d. Apply pin too long or too short.
  e. Servo orifice bleed cup plug missing.
  f. Leak between servo apply pin and case.
2. Binding intermediate servo band apply pin.
3. Incorrect TV link or bent TV link.
4. Control valve assembly:
  a. TV plunger binding.
  b. Shift TV linkage binding.
  c. 1-2 accumulator valve binding.
5. 1-2 accumulator:
  a. Binding piston.
  b. Broken spring.
  c. Piston seal or groove damaged.
  d. Bore damaged.
6. Incorrect spacer plate or gasket, or gasket incorrectly installed.
7. Second oil passage leaking.

Copyrighted Material Reprinted with Permission from Hydra-Matic Div., GM Corp.

Fig. 1 Transaxle identification tag location

Copyrighted Material Reprinted with Permission from Hydra-Matic Div., GM Corp.

Fig. 2 Exploded view of torque converter clutch

2-3 SHIFT ROUGH OR DELAYED

1. Plugged accumulator exhaust port.
2. Direct clutch exhaust No. 1 check ball mispositioned or missing.
3. Control valve assembly:
  a. Binding plunger and throttle valve.
  b. Binding shift TV valve.

2-3 SHIFT SOFT, SLIPS OR EARLY

1. Intermediate servo:
  a. Piston to case oil seal damaged.
  b. Servo piston damaged.
  c. Servo bore in case damaged.
2. Accumulator exhaust check valve not seating in case.
3. Spacer plate:
  a. Plugged or restricted direct clutch feed orifice.
  b. Incorrect case cover gaskets.
  c. Drive sprocket support passages interconnected, leaking or restricted.
  d. Sleeve loose or out of position.
4. Direct clutch:
  a. Check ball leaking.
  b. Check ball capsule damaged.
  c. Damaged or missing seals.
  d. Cracked or damaged housing or piston.
  e. Missing or incorrect apply ring.

f. Wrong number of clutch plates.

NO 2-3 SHIFT OR 2-3 SHIFT DELAYED

1. Governor or speed sensor:
  a. Cover worn.
  b. Thrust washer missing.
  c. Governor seal worn or cut.
  d. Governor weights binding on pin.
  e. Governor spring not seated.
  f. Ball missing.
  g. Governor driven gear stripped.
2. Intermediate servo:
  a. Piston to case oil seal damaged.
  b. Servo piston damaged.
  c. Servo bore damaged.
  d. Servo orifice bleed cup plug missing in case.
3. Accumulator exhaust check valve is not seating in case.
4. Case:
  a. Direct clutch accumulator cup plug (third oil) leaking or missing.
  b. Case to governor shaft sleeve missing or damaged.
  c. Center gasket leaking.
5. Case cover:
  a. Case cover bolts loose.
  b. Drive sprocket support passages interconnected, leaking or restricted.
  c. Drive sprocket support oil seal rings damaged or missing.

d. Sleeve loose or out of position.
6. Throttle lever and bracket assembly binding.
7. TV link incorrect, disconnected or binding.
8. Control valve assembly:
   a. 2-3 shift valve, 2-3 TV valve sticking.
   b. Shift TV valve sticking.
   c. Governor feed to 2-3 shift valve restricted.
   d. Direct clutch feed orifice restricted.
   e. No. 5 check ball missing or mislocated.
9. Spacer place or gaskets leaking, damaged or incorrectly installed.
10. Case to governor shaft sleeve damaged or missing.
11. Direct clutch:
    a. Check ball leaking.
    b. Check ball capsule damaged.
    c. Seals damaged or missing.
    d. Cracked or damaged housing or piston.
    e. Backing plate snap ring out of groove.
    f. Clutch plates damaged or missing.

DELAY IN DRIVE AND REVERSE

1. Converter, drive sprocket and support bushings.
2. Turbine shaft:
   a. Scarf seals damaged or leaking.

NO DRIVE IN DRIVE OR INTERMEDIATE RANGE

1. Lo roller clutch springs missing, rollers galled or missing.

NO DRIVE IN ANY FORWARD RANGE

1. Manual linkage not moving manual valve.
2. Drive sprocket support:
   a. Drive oil passage blocked in driven sprocket support.
   b. Sleeve loose or mislocated.
3. Case cover drive oil passage leak.
4. Forward clutch plates burned or damaged.
5. Control valve assembly body pipe leaking or missing.

NO DRIVE IN ALL RANGES

1. Oil pressure:
   a. Pressure regulator valve sticking in bushing.
   b. Worn pump seals.
   c. Oil pump shaft broken.
2. Differential damaged or broken.
3. Drive link broken or interference between drive link and sprocket.
4. Manual valve retainer clip missing.
5. Input shaft loose or broken away from forward clutch drum.
6. Reaction carrier broken at Lo roller clutch cam.

NO DRIVE IN DRIVE RANGE

1. Forward clutch feed in input shaft re-

stricted with cold engine at fast idle.
2. Case cover:
   a. Leak between case cover and driven sprocket passages.
   b. Incorrect gaskets between case cover and driven sprocket support passages.

SECOND SPEED START

1. Governor springs distorted or out of position.
2. Governor weights binding on pin.
3. Control valve:
   a. 1-2 sift valve sticking in upshifted position.
   b. 1-2 throttle valve sticking in upshifted position.

SHIFTS 1-3, MISSES SECOND

1. Intermediate servo:
   a. Wrong or sticking apply pin.
   b. Seals cut, damaged or missing.
2. Accumulator exhaust valve sticking or not seating.
3. Control valve assembly 1-2 shift valve sticking.
4. Spacer plate:
   a. Gaskets incorrectly installed.
   b. Governor feed to 1-2 shift valve blocked.
   c. Intermediate band apply feed orifice blocked.
   d. Wrong spacer plate.
5. Intermediate servo apply passage blocked.
6. Intermediate band improperly installed, burned or broken.

SHIFTS 3-1 AT HIGH SPEEDS FOR PASSING GEAR

1. Governor or speed sensor:
   a. Cover worn.
   b. Thrust washer missing.
   c. Governor seal worn or cut.
   d. Governor spring not seated.
   e. Governor weights binding on pin.
   f. Ball missing.
   g. Governor driven gear stripped.
2. Intermediate servo sticking.
3. Restriction in direct clutch orifice controlled by No. 2 check ball.
4. 1-2 accumulator piston missing or seal leaking.

NO FULL THROTTLE DOWNSHIFT

1. Throttle cable assembly not opening sufficiently.
2. Control valve assembly shift TV valve binding.
3. Spacer plate holes plugged, gasket not positioned correctly or damaged.

NO OVERRUN BRAKING IN LO

1. Manual linkage improperly adjusted.
2. LO and Reverse clutch pipe leaking.
3. Control valve assembly LO blow off valve damaged.

NO INTERMEDIATE RANGE

1. Intermediate servo oil seal ring missing or damaged.
2. Intermediate band mispositioned, broken or burned.
3. 1-2 accumulator piston or pin missing or damaged.

BINDS IN THIRD GEAR

1. Direct clutch center seal missing.

NOISE IN ALL RANGES

Refer to **Fig. 3**, for noise troubleshooting procedures.

MAINTENANCE

To check fluid, drive vehicle for at least 15 minutes to bring fluid to operating temperature (200°F). With vehicle on a level surface and engine idling in Park and parking brake applied, the level on the dipstick should be at the "Full" mark. To bring the fluid level from the ADD mark to the FULL mark requires one pint of fluid. If vehicle cannot be driven sufficiently to bring fluid to operating temperature, the level on the dipstick should be between the two dimples on the dipstick with fluid temperature at 70°F. Note that the two dimples are located above the FULL mark.

If additional fluid is required, use only Dexron II automatic transmission fluid.

An early change to a darker color from the usual red color and or a strong odor that is usually associated with overheated fluid is normal and should not be considered as a positive sign of required maintenance or unit failure.

When adding fluid, do not overfill, as foaming and loss of fluid through the vent may occur as the fluid heats up. Also, if fluid level is too low, complete loss of drive may occur especially when cold, which can cause transaxle failure.

Every 100,000 miles, the oil should be drained, the oil pan removed, the screen cleaned and fresh fluid added. For vehicles subjected to more severe use such as heavy city traffic especially in hot weather, prolonged periods of idling or towing, this maintenance should be performed every 15,000 miles.

CHANGING FLUID

1. Raise and support vehicle, then position drain pan under oil pan.
2. Remove front and side oil pan attaching bolts, then loosen rear pan attaching bolts.
3. Carefully pry oil pan loose from transaxle case and allow fluid to drain.
4. Remove remaining attaching bolt, oil pan and gasket. Thoroughly clean pan before reinstalling.
5. Remove and discard screen and O-ring seal.
6. Install replacement screen and O-ring seal, locating screen against dipstick stop.
7. Install gasket on oil pan, then install pan and **torque** attaching bolts to 8 ft. lbs.
8. Lower vehicle and add approximately

CONDITION	INSPECT COMPONENT	FOR CAUSE
NOISE IN ALL RANGES OR (A Whine Which May Be RPM Or Load Sensitive Or Ceases When The TCC Engages)	• Torque Converter	– Verify noise internal to torque converter by placing left foot on brake with the gear selector in Drive and momentarily stall engine. Torque converter noise increases under load.
(A High Pitch Whine Which Will Intensify With Engine RPM Or Is Oil Pressure Sensitive)	• Oil Pump System	– Verify noise internal to oil pump during preliminary oil pressure check. An increase in line pressure will vary an oil pump noise.
(A "Popping" Noise Similar To Popcorn Popping)		– Pump cavitation—indicated by bubbles on fluid level indicator. – Transmission fluid strainer for filter seam leak. – Transmission fluid strainer seal for proper positioning or cut seal.
(A Buzz Or High Frequency Rattle Sound)	• Trace Cooler Pipes And Check For Binding Or Contact At The Radiator Other Than The Cooler Pipe Connectors	– Verify pressure buzz by watching for a needle vibration on the pressure gage. (Road test may be necessary.)
(A Whine Or Growl That Increases And Fades With Vehicle Speed And Is Most Noticeable Under Light Throttle)	• Drive Link Assembly System Verify noise from sprockets and/or drive link assembly (chain) by placing left foot on brake and moving gear selector from Park or Neutral to Drive or Reverse. If noise stops, check items below:	
	• Drive Link (Chain) Assembly	– Stretched.
	• Drive Sprocket And Driven Sprocket	– Teeth broken or sheared. – Bearing surfaces nicked or scored.
	• Drive And Driven Sprocket Support Bearing Assemblies	– Bearing race or roller bearing surfaces rough or pitted.
	• Drive Sprocket Support And Driven Sprocket Support	– Bearing outer race support rough or nicked.

CONDITION	INSPECT COMPONENT	FOR CAUSE
NOISE IN 1ST OR REVERSE (A Gear Noise, Or Whine Is Most Noticeable In First Or Reverse And Is Related To Vehicle Speed. Whine May Diminish Or Go Away After An Upshift To Second Gear.)	• Input Gear Set • Input Internal Gear • Input Carrier Assembly • Input Sun Gear	– Gears worn or pitted. – Thrust washer mating surfaces rough or pitted.
NOISE IN SECOND	• Reaction Gear Set • Reaction Internal Gear • Reaction Carrier Assembly • Reaction Sun Gear • Reaction Sun Gear To Reaction Internal Gear Thrust Bearing	– Gears worn or pitted. – Thrust washer or thrust bearing mating surfaces rough or pitted. – Thrust bearing races or roller bearing surfaces rough or pitted.
(A Final Drive Noise, Or Hum, Is Most Noticeable Under Light Throttle Acceleration And/Or Turns) (Noise In First, Second, Or Third)	• Final Drive Gear Set • Final Drive Internal Gear • Differential Carrier • Final Drive Sun Gear • Differential Pinions • Differential Side Gears • Final Drive Sun Gear To Final Drive Internal Gear Thrust Bearing • Final Drive Sun Gear To Differential Carrier Thrust Bearing • Differential Carrier To Case Thrust Bearing	– Gears worn or pitted. – Thrust washer or thrust bearing mating surfaces rough or pitted. – Thrust bearing races or roller bearing surfaces rough or pitted.
(A Light Metallic Rattle Noise Most Noticeable In Second Or Third Between 25 MPH And 40 MPH Under Coast Or Drive Operation)	• Lo And Reverse Clutch Pack • Case	– Steel plates not flat. – Clutch pack clearance. – Parallel grooved fiber plates. – Excess plate-to-case clearance due to case machining.

Fig. 3   Noise troubleshooting (Part 1 Of 2)   **Fig. 3   Noise troubleshooting (Part 2 Of 2)**

4 qts. of fluid.

9. With selector in park, parking brake applied and engine at idle speed and operating temperature, check fluid level and add fluid as necessary. **Do not race engine. Move shift lever through ranges, then back to "Park" position.**

ADJUSTMENTS

MANUAL LINKAGE, ADJUST

ACHIEVA, BERETTA, CAVALIER, CORSICA, & SUNBIRD

1. Position shift lever to Neutral.
2. Install cable to bracket and to column or floorshift lever.
3. Snap cable onto transaxle shift lever, then tighten nut with lever held out of Park.

EXCEPT ACHIEVA, BERETTA, CAVALIER, CORSICA & SUNBIRD

1. Lift shift cable locking button up.
2. Position transaxle shift lever to Neutral by rotating selector shaft clockwise from Park through Reverse to Neutral.
3. Position shift control assembly to Neutral.

4. Lock shift cable by pressing locking button down.

DETENT/T.V. CABLE, ADJUST

MODELS w/LOCK TAB ADJUSTING CABLE

1. Depress and hold re-adjust tab, **Fig. 4.**
2. Move slider back through fitting in direction away from throttle idler lever until slider stops against fitting, then release re-adjust tab.
3. **On all except Cutlass Calais, Grand Am and Skylark models with 2.5L/4-151 engine**, rotate throttle idler lever to full travel stop position, then release throttle lever.
4. **On Cutlass Calais, Grand Am and Skylark models with 2.5L/4-151 engine,** press accelerator pedal to full travel, then release accelerator pedal.

MODELS LESS LOCK TAB ADJUSTING CABLE

Except 3.3L/V6-204

1. Ensure cable is in "Non-Adjusted" position as shown, **Fig. 5.**
2. Using a suitable torque wrench, rotate idler pulley counterclockwise to 65 inch lbs. on all except Cutlass Calais, Grand Am and Skylark models, or 75 inch lbs. on Cutlass Calais, Grand Am and Skylark models.

3. Ensure cable moves freely, then test drive vehicle.

3.3L/V6-204

1. Ensure TV cable and throttle cable are properly installed in throttle lever and TV cable slider is in full non-adjusted position. **Fig. 6.**
2. Rotate throttle lever to full travel position, applying no more torque than necessary to reach throttle body stop.
3. Depress and hold adjustment button.
4. Pull cable conduit out until slider contacts against adjustment.
5. Release button. Repeat procedure to ensure proper adjustment.

IN-VEHICLE REPAIRS

AUXILIARY VALVE BODY, VALVE BODY & OIL PUMP ASSEMBLY, REPLACE

1. Disconnect battery ground cable, then the TV cable.
2. Raise and support vehicle.
3. Remove left front wheel and tire assembly.
4. Remove valve body cover retaining bolts and the cover.
5. Remove TCC solenoid retaining bolt and the solenoid. Disconnect TCC solenoid and 3rd gear pressure switch electrical connectors.

Copyrighted Material Reprinted with Permission from Hydra-Matic Div., GM Corp.

Fig. 4   Detent/TV cable adjuster. Models w/lock tab adjusting cable

A BOLT
B AUXILIARY VALVE BODY
C VALVE BODY

Copyrighted Material Reprinted with Permission from Hydra-Matic Div., GM Corp.

Fig. 7   Valve body bolt location

6. Remove remove bolt securing linkage/bracket to valve body, then remove TV linkage.
7. Remove remaining valve body retaining bolts, then the valve body and six check balls. Do not remove the bolts marked "A" **Fig. 7**, at this time.
8. Remove bolt "A" and separate auxiliary valve body from the valve body.
9. Remove oil pump drive rod, auxiliary valve body and cover.
10. Remove oil pump assembly.
11. Reverse procedure to install noting the following:
    a. Tighten bolts in a clockwise pattern, starting from center.
    b. Refer to **Fig. 8** for check ball location.
    c. Adjust TV cable and fluid level.

INTERMEDIATE SERVO & ACCUMULATOR CHECK VALVE, REPLACE

1. Raise and support vehicle.
2. Remove transaxle oil pan and gasket, then remove screen and O-ring.
3. Remove reverse oil pipe retaining brackets, intermediate servo cover and gasket.
4. Remove accumulator valve and spring.
5. Remove intermediate servo assembly.
6. Reverse procedure to install

Copyrighted Material Reprinted with Permission from Hydra-Matic Div., GM Corp.

Fig. 5   Detent/TV cable adjustment. Except 3.3L/V6-204

1–5 CHECK BALL

REAR OF VALVE BODY

Copyrighted Material Reprinted with Permission from Hydra-Matic Div., GM Corp.

Fig. 8   Check ball locations

GOVERNOR, REPLACE

Century, Cutlass Ciera, Cutlass Cruiser, Cutlass Supreme, Grand Prix, Lumina & 6000

Refer to **Fig. 9** for following procedure.
1. Remove screws, speed sensor housing and oil seal.
2. Remove bearing and rotor.
3. Remove governor assembly.
4. Remove fluid seal ring.
5. Reverse procedure to install.

Achieva, Beretta, Cavalier, Corsica, Cutlass Calais, Grand Am, Skylark & Sunbird

1. Raise and support vehicle.
2. Remove engine to transaxle brace attaching bolts, then the heat shield if equipped.
3. Remove speedometer cable or wire connector from transaxle.
4. Remove speedometer driven gear and sleeve assembly or speed sensor if equipped.
5. Remove governor cover and O-ring.
6. Remove speedometer drive gear thrust washer and gear, then the governor assembly, **Fig. 10**.
7. Reverse procedure to install.

NON-ADJUSTED POSITION

ADJUSTED POSITION

SLIDER DIRECTION OF ADJSUTMENT

MEASUREABLE AMOUNT OF ADJUSTMENT (EITHER LOCATION)

1. READJUSTMENT BUTTON   4. CONDUIT
2. FITTING   5. SLIDER
3. SLIDER AGAINST FITTING   6. TO THROTTLE LEVER
   IN FULL NON-ADJUSTED
   POSITION

Copyrighted Material Reprinted with Permission from Hydra-Matic Div., GM Corp.

Fig. 6   Detent/TV cable adjustment. 3.3L/V6-204

TRANSAXLE
REPLACE
LEMANS

1. Disconnect battery ground cable, then remove air cleaner assembly.
2. Disconnect throttle valve cable from throttle and transaxle.
3. Disconnect selector cable from transaxle lever.
4. Remove selector cable bracket, leaving cable attached to bracket.
5. Disconnect electrical connectors from speed sensor, torque converter clutch and neutral safety switch.
6. Disconnect vent hose at top of transaxle.
7. Remove starter support bolts and starter from transaxle.
8. Disconnect speedometer drive cable from transaxle.
9. Remove top three engine to transaxle attaching bolts.
10. Install engine support fixture No. J28467-A with adapter No. J228467-70 or equivalent.
11. Raise and support vehicle.
12. Remove both front wheel and tire assemblies.
13. Remove lower ball joint retaining clips and stud nuts, then separate ball joints from steering knuckles using ball joint tool No. J36226 or equivalent. **Disregard "This Side Towards Wheel" marking on tool. Tool must be turned to opposite position when used on these vehicles.**
14. Remove both axle shafts from transaxle.
15. Disconnect oil cooler lines from transaxle.
16. Remove converter cover attaching bolts and the cover.
17. Mark relationship between flywheel and torque converter for installation reference, then remove torque converter-to-flywheel attaching bolts.

3. FLUID SEAL RING
4. COMPLETE GOVERNOR ASM.
6. GEAR/COVER THRUST BEARING ASM.
7. "O" RING SEAL
8. GOVERNOR COVER TO CASE COVER
15. CASE ASM.
37. GOV. SHAFT SLEEVE & SCREEN ASM.
39. GOVERNOR COVER BEARING ASM.
687. SPEED SENSOR ROTOR
688. SPEED SENSOR HOUSING
689. COIL ASM.
690. WASHER
691. MAGNET
692. "O" RING SEAL
693. WAVE SPRING WASHER
694. COVER GASKET
695. HOUSING COVER
696. BOLT

Copyrighted Material Reprinted with Permission from Hydra-Matic Div., GM Corp.

Fig. 9   Governor replacement

18. Remove left transaxle mount attaching bolts and the mount.
19. Support transaxle with a suitable jack, then remove rear transaxle mount attaching bolts and the mount.
20. Remove right transaxle mount attaching bolts and the mount.
21. Remove remaining transaxle to engine attaching bolts, then carefully lower transaxle from vehicle.
22. Reverse procedure to install referring to "Tightening Specifications" chart.

CENTURY, CUTLASS CIERA & 6000

1991

1. Disconnect battery ground cable from transaxle.
2. Install engine support tool No. J 28467-A or equivalent.
3. Remove air cleaner assembly and TV cable routing clips and straps.
4. Remove bolt securing TV cable to transaxle, then remove shift cable.
5. Remove strut bracket bolts from transaxle, then disconnect electrical connector from neutral switch.
6. Remove torque converter clutch and speedometer speed sensor.
7. Disconnect and plug oil cooler lines from transaxle bracket. Remove

3. RING OIL SEAL
4. GOVERNOR ASSEMBLY
5. GEAR, SPEEDOMETER DRIVE
6. THRUST BEARING ASM. GEAR/COVER
7. SEAL, 'O' RING
8. SCREW, GOVERNOR COVER TO CASE
9. COVER, GOVERNOR
10. SPEEDO DRIVEN GEAR
11. SEAL, 'O' RING
12. SLEEVE, SPEEDO DRIVEN GEAR
13. RETAINER, SPEEDO GEAR
14. BOLT, SPEEDO GEAR RETAINING

Copyrighted Material Reprinted with Permission from Hydra-Matic Div., GM Corp.

Fig. 10   Governor assembly

transaxle to engine bolts, leaving one bolt loosely installed, near starter motor.
8. Remove shift linkage bracket and bolts.
9. Disconnect oil cooler lines from transaxle.
10. Raise and support vehicle. Remove front and left frame sections as follows:
   a. Install engine support fixture tool No. J-28467 or equivalent and tighten fasteners when properly positioned.
   b. Position support hook into lifting bracket and tighten coupling nut only enough to remove slack from hook. **Engine support fixture must be located in center of cowl for 4 cylinder engines and on strut towers for 6 cylinder engines. Support fixture is not designed to support entire weight of engine and transaxle. Improper use may result in vehicle damage and/or personal injury.**
   c. Remove intermediate shaft to steering gear stub shaft attaching bolt, then raise and support vehicle.
   d. Support engine with suitable jack, then remove left front wheel/tire assembly.
   e. Remove power steering line brackets and steering gear mounting bolts.
   f. Disconnect drive line vibration absorber, if equipped.
   g. Disconnect left lower ball joint at steering knuckle, then remove both front stabilizer bar reinforcements and bushings.
   h. Using a 1/2 inch drill bit, drill through spot weld located between rear holes of left stabilizer bar mounting, **Fig. 11.**
   i. Disconnect engine and transaxle mounts from cradle, then remove side crossmember bolts.
   j. Remove left side body mount bolts, then the left and front frame assembly.
11. **Failure to disconnect intermediate shaft from rack and pinion steering gear stub shaft can result in damage to steering gear and/or inter-**

Copyrighted Material Reprinted with Permission from Hydra-Matic Div., GM Corp.

Fig. 11   Frame spot weld location

mediate shaft. **This damage may cause loss of steering control.**

12. Install drive axle seal protector tool No. J 34754 or equivalent, on drive axle seal. Remove drive axle. Rotate strut assembly until axle is clear.
13. Remove starter and converter shields.
14. Remove three flywheel to converter bolts.
15. Remove two extension bolts from engine to transaxle bracket.
16. Remove rear transaxle mounting bracket assembly. It may be necessary to slightly raise transaxle.
17. Position transaxle jack below transaxle case, then remove two braces on right end of transaxle bolts.
18. Remove remaining transaxle to engine bolt, located near starter.
19. Remove transaxle by sliding towards driver's side of vehicle, away from engine.
20. Reverse procedure to install, noting the following:
   a. Refer to "Tightening Specifications" chart.
   b. Adjust shift linkage, TV cable and fluid level.
   c. Check front wheel alignment.

1992–93

1. Disconnect battery ground cable from transaxle, then remove air cleaner and air duct assembly.
2. Remove bolt securing TV cable to transaxle, then remove shift cable.
3. Disconnect neutral switch electrical connector, then remove torque convertor clutch and speedometer speed sensor.
4. Disconnect and plug transaxle oil cooler lines from transaxle and bracket.
5. Remove transaxle to engine bolts. Leave one bolt near starter loosely installed.
6. Install engine support fixture tool No. J-28467-A or equivalent, and engine

support adapter leg tool No. J-36462 or equivalent.

7. Raise and support vehicle. Remove left front wheel and splash shield.

8. Disconnect left lower ball joint from control arm.

9. Remove intermediate shaft to steering gear stub shaft retaining bolt. **Failure to disconnect intermediate shaft from rack and pinion tube shaft will result in damage to steering gear and/or intermediate shaft. This damage could result in loss of steering control.**

10. Disconnect stabilizer bar from left control arm. Remove left and right stabilizer mount bolts from frame.

11. Center punch two spot welds at frame crossmember near left stabilizer bar to frame mount. Drill out spot welds enough to separate frame and crossmember.

12. Remove left steering gear to frame bolt, then remove left to right frame section retaining bolts.

13. Support frame with suitable jack stand and remove left frame to body bolts.

14. Remove transaxle mounting nuts from frame, then carefully remove jack stand and the frame assembly.

15. Remove starter and converter shields.

16. Remove three flywheel to converter bolts, the remove two transaxle extension bolts from engine to transaxle bracket.

17. Remove rear transaxle mount bracket assembly. It may be necessary to raise transaxle.

18. Position transaxle jack to transaxle case, then remove two bolts from braces to right end of transaxle.

19. Remove left drive axle, then the remaining engine to transaxle bolt, located near starter.

20. Carefully remove transaxle along with right drive axle, as an assembly.

21. Reverse procedure to install, noting the following:
    a. Align and insert right axle shaft while transaxle is being lifted into position.
    b. Ensure intermediate shaft is seated prior to pinch bolt installation. **If pinch bolt is inserted into coupling before shaft installation, two mating shafts may disengage.**
    c. Refer to "Tightening Specifications" chart.
    d. Adjust shift linkage, TV cable and fluid level.

3.1L/V6-189

1. Disconnect battery ground cable.

2. Remove air cleaner, mounting bracket, MAF sensor and air tube as an assembly.

3. Remove exhaust crossover bolts at RH manifold, then LH manifold bolts at cylinder head. **If necessary, raise and support manifold/crossover assembly.**

4. Disconnect TV cable from throttle lever and transaxle, then transaxle to vent pipe rubber hose.

5. Disconnect shift cable from transaxle.

6. Disconnect neutral start switch and TCC electrical connectors.

7. Remove fluid level indicator and fill tube.

8. Install engine support fixture tool No. J-28467 and adapter No. J-35953 or equivalent.

9. Remove nut attaching wiring harness from transaxle.

10. Remove transaxle mount through bolt, then mount bracket and mount from transaxle.

11. Remove upper transaxle to engine attaching bolts, then raise and support vehicle.

12. Remove both front wheels, then LH splash shield.

13. Remove transaxle converter cover, then scribe alignment marks on flexplate and torque converter for reassembly.

14. Remove torque converter to flexplate attaching bolts.

15. Remove torsional strut and lateral strut from transaxle, then transaxle bracket bolts.

16. Disconnect speedometer connector from transaxle, then shift cable bracket.

17. Install drive axle boot seal protectors No. J-34754 or equivalent on inner seals. **Failure to install seal protectors can result in seal damage and possible joint failure.**

18. Remove both drive axles.

19. Remove left stabilizer bar link pin bolt, left stabilizer bar frame bushing attaching nuts, then the left frame support assembly.

20. Remove transaxle cooler lines. **Plug lines to prevent leakage or dirt from entering system.**

21. Position a suitable jack under transaxle, then remove remaining transaxle to engine attaching bolts.

22. Remove transaxle assembly from vehicle.

23. Reverse procedure to install, noting the following:
    a. Refer to "Tightening Specifications" chart.
    b. Adjust shift linkage, TV cable and fluid level.
    c. Check front suspension alignment after transaxle installation.

BERETTA & CORSICA

1. Disconnect battery ground cable and remove TV cable from throttle lever and transaxle.

2. **On models with 3.1L/V6-189 engines,** remove battery.

3. **On all models,** remove fluid level indicator and filler tube.

4. Remove bolt securing wiring harness to transaxle, then disconnect electrical connectors from TCC and park/neutral switch.

5. Remove upper shift control cable bracket and disconnect cable form shift lever at transaxle.

6. Remove rubber hose from vent pipe to transaxle.

7. **On models with 3.2L/V6-189 engines,** remove exhaust crossover pipe.

8. **On all models,** install engine support tools No. J28467 and J35943 or equivalents.

9. Remove top two transaxle to engine mounting bolts and transaxle mounting bracket bolts, then the mounting bracket.

10. Remove remaining upper transaxle to engine bolts. Raise and support vehicle.

11. Remove front wheels and left front engine splash shield.

12. Install axle boot protector tool No. J34754 to protect boot from damage. **Failure to protect boot may result in boot damage and joint failure.**

13. Remove left and right drive axles as follows:
    a. Place a screwdriver through caliper, into rotor, to prevent from turning.
    b. Remove drive axle nut and washer.
    c. Remove ball joint cotter pin and nut. Separate ball joint from control arm with removal tool No. J29330 or equivalent.
    d. Disengage axle from hub and bearing using removal tool No. J28733-A or equivalent.
    e. Separate hub and bearing assembly from drive axle and move strut and knuckle assembly rearward.
    f. Remove inner joints from transaxle using inner joint removal tools No. J28468 and J29794 or equivalents.

14. Remove both stabilizer links and left stabilizer bar clamp nuts.

15. Remove left suspension supports and bolts.

16. Remove transaxle strut bolts from transaxle, then disconnect vehicle speed sensor electrical connector from transaxle.

17. Remove converter cover, then the flywheel to converter bolts. Mark relationship of flywheel to converter to ease installation.

18. Disconnect and plug transaxle cooler lines. Remove shift cable from lower cable bracket.

19. Remove transaxle to engine brace bolts.

20. Position suitable transaxle jack below assembly. Remove remaining engine to transaxle mounting bolts.

21. Carefully lower transaxle from vehicle.

22. Reverse procedure to install, noting the following:
    a. Refer to "Tightening Specifications" chart.
    b. Adjust TV cable, shift linkage and fluid level. Check for leaks.

ACHIEVA, CAVALIER, CUTLASS CALAIS, GRAND AM, SKYLARK & SUNBIRD
Except 2.3L/4-143

1. Disconnect battery ground cable, then remove air cleaner assembly.

2. Drain cooling system, then disconnect heater core hoses using clamp tool No. J-37097 or equivalent.

3. Disconnect TV cable from throttle lever and transaxle.
4. Remove fluid level indicator and fill tube.
5. Install engine support fixture tool No. J-28467-A, or equivalent.
6. Remove wire harness to transaxle attaching nut, then disconnect electrical connectors from speed sensor, TCC connector, park/neutral and back-up lamp switch.
7. Disconnect shift linkage from transaxle. Remove two top transaxle to engine attaching bolts, then the left upper transaxle mount and bracket assembly.
8. Remove transaxle to vent pipe rubber hose, then the remaining upper engine to transaxle attaching bolts.
9. Raise and support vehicle, then remove both front wheels.
10. Drain transaxle fluid, then remove shift linkage and bracket assembly.
11. Install drive axle boot seal protectors No. J-34754 or equivalent on inner seals, then disconnect both ball joints from control arms. Failure to install seal protectors can result in seal damage and possible joint failure.
12. Remove both drive axles.
13. Remove transaxle mounting strut, then left stabilizer bar link pin bolt.
14. Remove left stabilizer bar frame bushing clamp attaching nuts, then the left frame support assembly.
15. **On models equipped with 4 cylinder engines,** disconnect exhaust pipe from manifold.
16. **On models equipped with V6 cylinder engines,** remove front exhaust manifold and pipe.
17. **On all models,** disconnect speedometer connector from transaxle, then remove starter motor, if necessary.
18. Remove transaxle converter cover, then disconnect and plug transaxle cooler lines.
19. Mark relationship of flywheel and torque converter to ease installation, then remove converter to flywheel bolts.
20. Remove transaxle to engine support bracket, then position a suitable jack below transaxle.
21. Remove remaining transaxle to engine attaching bolts, then lower transaxle from vehicle.
22. Reverse procedure to install, noting the following:
    a. Refer to "Tightening Specifications" chart.
    b. Check and adjust fluid level, shift linkage and TV cable.
    c. Check front suspension alignment following transaxle installation.

2.3L/4-143
1. Disconnect battery ground cable and remove intake air duct.
2. Drain cooling system and disconnect heater hoses at heater core.
3. Remove cable control cover and disconnect throttle and TV cables.
4. Remove shift cable and bracket from transaxle.
5. Remove throttle cable from throttle body, then disconnect vacuum lines and electrical connectors.
6. Remove power steering pump and fluid filler tube.
7. Install engine support tool No. J28467-A or equivalent.
8. Remove top engine to transaxle bolts, then raise and support vehicle.
9. Remove front wheels and left inner engine splash shield. Disconnect lower ball joints from control arms.
10. Remove stabilizer shaft links.
11. Remove front air deflector and left suspension support assembly.
12. Install drive axle seal protector tools No. J34754 or equivalent.
13. Remove both drive axles.
14. Remove flywheel cover, then the flywheel to converter bolts. Mark relationship of flywheel and converter to ease in installation.
15. Disconnect and plug transaxle cooler lines.
16. Remove bolt securing ground wires from engine and transaxle.
17. Remove cooler pipe brace and exhaust brace.
18. Remove bolts from engine to transaxle mount.
19. Support transaxle with suitable jack, remove remaining engine to transaxle bolts.
20. Carefully remove transaxle from vehicle.
21. Reverse procedure to install, noting the following:
    a. Ensure torque converter is properly seated in oil pump.
    b. Install transaxle assembly into position with jack, while installing right drive axle.
    c. Refer to "Tightening Specifications" chart.
    d. Adjust TV cable, shift linkage and fluid level.

CUTLASS SUPREME, GRAND PRIX & LUMINA
1. Disconnect battery ground cable.
2. **On Cutlass Supreme and Grand Prix models,** remove coolant recovery reservoir.
3. **On all models,** disconnect shift control and TV cable from transaxle.
4. Remove throttle cable bracket, then disconnect brake booster hose if equipped.
5. Remove both torque struts from engine.
6. Remove left torque strut bracket, then disconnect and plug oil cooler lines from transaxle.
7. Install engine support fixture No. J28467-A with adapter tools No. J28467-90 and J36462 or equivalents.
8. Raise and support vehicle, then remove front wheels.
9. Remove calipers, rotors and lower engine splash shields.
10. Remove nuts and washers from driveshafts, then separate hub/bearing assemblies from axle splines using hub spindle removal tool No. J28733 or equivalent.
11. Remove hub/bearing assembly to knuckle attaching bolts. If equipped, remove ABS sensor attaching bolts and position sensors aside.
12. Remove hub/bearing assemblies from vehicle.
13. Using axle shaft removal tool No. J33008, extension tool No. J29794 and slide hammer tool No. J2619-01 or equivalents, separate right and left axles from transaxle.
14. Remove axle assemblies from knuckles, then disconnect tie rod ends and ball joints from steering knuckle.
15. **On Lumina models,** drain oil and remove oil filter, then remove and support A/C compressor. **Do not disconnect refrigerant lines.**
16. **On all models,** remove heat shield from rack and pinion, then disconnect electrical connector.
17. Remove main engine wiring harness to transaxle case retaining bolts.
18. Secure rack and pinion unit to exhaust system, then remove rack and pinion to frame attaching bolts.
19. Remove power steering line to frame retaining bolts.
20. Remove engine and transaxle mounts from frame.
21. Support frame with jackstands, then remove frame bolts. Remove frame and jackstands from vehicle.
22. Remove flywheel access cover, then the torque converter bolts.
23. Remove starter retaining bolts, then support starter with wire. **Do not allow starter to hang from electrical wires.**
24. Disconnect battery ground cable from transaxle and remove transaxle fill tube bolt.
25. Remove transaxle mount bracket, then lower vehicle.
26. Disconnect transaxle electrical connector and remove fill tube.
27. Using engine support, lower left side of engine approximately four inches.
28. Raise and support vehicle.
29. **On Cutlass Supreme and Grand Prix models,** remove fuel line bracket from transaxle.
30. **On all models,** position a jack under transaxle, remove transaxle to engine retaining bolts and lower transaxle from vehicle.
31. Reverse procedure to install noting the following:
    a. Refer to "Tightening Specifications" chart.
    b. Adjust shift linkage, TV cable and fluid level.
    c. Check front suspension alignment.

TIGHTENING SPECIFICATIONS

Component	Torque/Ft. Lbs.
Century, Cutlass Ciera, Cutlass Cruiser & 6000	
Bracket To Transaxle Bolt	41
Channel Plate Attaching Bolts	41
Console Shift Control Assembly Nut	18
Fill Tube Bolt	18
Flywheel Cover Bolts	89①
Governor Housing Bolts	98①
Mount To Bracket Nut	35
Oil Pan Bolts	98①
Park/Neutral Switch Bolts	21
Shift Control Bracket	18
Shift Control Lever	15
TCC Solenoid Screws	125①
Torque Converter Bolts	46
Transaxle Case Side Cover	125①
Transaxle Cooler Pipe Clip Bolt	35
Transaxle Cooler Pipe To Radiator	13
Valve Body Bolts	125①
Wheel Lug Nuts	100
Cutlass Calais, Grand Am, Skylark, Somerset Regal & Sunbird	
Cooler Lines At Radiator	20
Cooler Lines At Transaxle	16
Flywheel Cover	115①
Governor Cover	133①
Neutral Start Switch	22
Oil Pan Bolts	133①
Shift Cable To Shift Lever	90①
Starter Bolts	32
Throttle Cable To Case	90①
Torque Converter Bolts	46
Transaxle Mount Bolts	22
Transaxle To Engine Bolts	55
Wheel Lug Nuts	100
Corsica & Beretta	
Case Cover Bolts	18
Clutch Switches	97①
Cooler Lines At Radiator	20
Cooler Lines At Transaxle	16
Filler Tube Mounting Bolt②	20
Filler Tube Mounting Bolt③	32
Floor Shift Control	17
Flywheel Cover	115①
Governor Cover	97①
Neutral Start Switch	20
Oil Pan Bolts	97①
Shift Control Cable Grommet	17①
Shift Lever	15
TCC Solenoid	97①
Throttle Cable Bolt	89①
Torque Converter Bolts	46
Transaxle Brace	37
Transaxle Mount Bracket To Transaxle	40

Component	Torque/Ft. Lbs.
Corsica & Beretta-Continued	
Transaxle To Engine Bolts	55
Transaxle Strut Bolts	40
Upper Shift Cable Bracket Nut & Bolt	18
Valve Body Cover Bolts	97①
Wheel Lug Nuts	100
Cavalier & Beretta	
Cooler Lines At Radiator	20
Cooler Lines At Transaxle	16
Flywheel Cover	115①
Governor Cover	133①
Neutral Start Switch	22
Oil Pan Bolts	133①
Starter Bolts	32
Shift Cable To Shift Lever Nut	90①
Throttle Cable To Transaxle	90①
Torque Converter Bolts	46
Transaxle Mount Bolts	22
Transaxle To Engine Bolts	55
Wheel Lug Nuts	100
Cutlass Supreme, Grand Prix & Lumina	
Auxiliary Oil Cooler Bolt	18
Auxiliary Oil Cooler Nut	89①
Bracket To Transaxle Front Bolts	35
Bracket To Transaxle Top Stud	40
Bracket To Transaxle Rear Bolt	61
Console Shift Control Nut	18
Engine To Transaxle Brace Bolt	35
Fill Tube Bolt	18
Flywheel Cover Bolt	89①
Governor Housing Bolts	98①
Mount To Bracket Nut	22
Neutral Start Switch	18
Oil Cooler Line Clip Bolt	35
Oil Cooler Line To Radiator	13
Oil Pan Bolts	98①
Shift Control Bracket	18
Shift Control Lever	15
TCC Solenoid Screws	125①
Throttle Cable Bolt	89①
Torque Converter Bolt	44
Transaxle Case Side Cover	125①
Transaxle To Engine Bolts	55
Valve Body Bolts	125①
Wheel Lug Nuts	100
LeMans	
Brake Band Booster Cover	8
Cooler Lines At Radiator	16
Cooler Lines At Transaxle	28
Cooler Line Bracket At Transaxle	18
Drive Chain Sprocket Carrier	18
Governor Cover To Case	8

Continued

TURBO HYDRA-MATIC 3T40 (125C) AUTOMATIC TRANSAXLE

TIGHTENING SPECIFICATIONS—Continued

Component	Torque/Ft. Lbs.
LeMans-Continued	
Intermediate Servo Cover	8
Left Transaxle Mount At Transaxle	16
Oil Pan Bolts w/Coated Cork Gasket	10
Oil Pan Bolts Without Less Cork Gasket	7.5
Oil Pressure Tap Port	8
Parking Pawl Bracket	18
Right Transaxle Mount At Engine	30
Selector Lever Shaft Nut	20

Component	Torque/Ft. Lbs.
LeMans-Continued	
Torque Converter Bolts	44
Transaxle To Engine Bolts	55
Throttle Cable At Transaxle	7.5
Transaxle Housing Cover Retaining Spring	28
Wheel Lug Nuts	66

① —Inch lbs.
② —4 cylinder engine
③ —6 cylinder engine

Turbo Hydra-Matic 4T60 (440-T4) & 4T60E Automatic Transaxle

INDEX

IDENTIFICATION

This transaxle may be identified by codes stamped into the horizontal cast rib on the right rear side of the transaxle housing, **Fig. 1.**

DESCRIPTION

The 4T60 and 4T60E transaxles are fully automatic units which provides four forward speeds including an overdrive top gear. The transmission unit includes a three element hydraulic torque converter and lock-up clutching element, four multiple disc clutch, two bands and a compound reaction planetary gear set, **Fig. 2.** Power transmitted to the drive wheels from the planetary gear through a final drive gear set and differential assembly.

The converter is designed to provide torque multiplication during acceleration and at slow vehicle speed, and lock-up during normal operation for increase operating economy. Operation of the converter lock-up is controlled automatically by the engine fuel system electronic control module. In addition, the converter drives the vane type oil pump by means of a shaft splined to the converter cover.

The torque converter hydraulically couples the engine to the planetary gears through a turbine and shaft assembly which drives the transmission output shaft by means of a drive link chain and sprockets.

TROUBLESHOOTING

OIL LEAK

1. Side cover distorted.
2. Oil pan attaching bolts loose.
3. Oil pan gaskets damaged.
4. T.V. cable, fill tube and/or electrical connector seal damaged.
5. Manual shaft seal assembly damaged.
6. Governor cover and/or servo covers O-rings damaged.
7. Cooler fittings and/or pressure taps insufficiently tightened, or threads stripped.
8. Converter seal damaged, or garter spring missing.
9. Axle seals damaged, or garter spring missing.
10. Modulator O-ring damaged.
11. Parking plunger guide O-ring damaged.
12. Speedometer O-ring damaged.

OIL FORCED OUT VENT OR FOAMING OIL

1. High fluid level.
2. Overheated or contaminated oil.
3. Damaged filter or filter seal.

SRTA TAG LOCATION

TRANSAXLE I.D. NAMEPLATE LOCATION

TRANSAXLE VEHICLE IDENTIFICATION NUMBER

Copyrighted Material Reprinted with Permission from Hydra-Matic Div., GM Corp.

Fig. 1 Transaxle identification number locations

4. Leaking accumulator cover pipe or drive socket support lubrication pipes.
5. Thermo element not closing properly.
6. Thermo element improperly installed or incorrect pin height.
7. Defective or improperly installed modulator port gasket.
8. Plugged drive sprocket support drain back holes.

OIL PRESSURE HIGH OR LOW

1. Incorrect fluid level.
2. Contaminated fluid or engine overheating.
3. Vacuum line leaking.
4. Modulator leaking or modulator diaphragm damaged.
5. Nicked, scored or stuck modulator valve.
6. Pressure regulator valve or spring damaged.
7. Pressure relief valve spring damaged or ball missing.
8. Oil pump damaged or restricted.
9. Aspirator "T" blocked or incorrectly installed.

DELAYED ENGAGEMENT

1. Low oil level.
2. Cooler check ball not seating.
3. Damaged or defective reverse servo seal.
4. Damaged or defective 1-2 servo seal.
5. Leaking 1-2 servo oil pipes.

NO DRIVE IN D RANGE

1. Low fluid level.
2. Low oil pressure.
3. Manual linkage improperly adjusted or disconnected.
4. Torque converter stator roller clutch sluggish or converter not properly attached to flex plate.
5. Drive axles disengaged.
6. Damaged or broken drive link chain, sprockets or bearings.
7. Damaged 1-2 servo or incorrect apply pin.
8. 1-2 servo oil pipes or pipe seals leaking.
9. Damaged oil pump or pump driveshaft.
10. Input clutch reverse check ball out of position.
11. Burned input clutch plates, damaged clutch seals or damaged piston.
12. Leaking input housing check ball.
13. Damaged input shaft seals or blocked input shaft passages.
14. Defective input sprag or improper sprag and input sun gear assembly. **When servicing transaxle for intermittent or complete loss of drive, the input sprag assembly should always be replaced. A sprag causing intermittent loss of drive may appear in satisfactory condition while still being susceptible to "pop-out" during operation.**
15. Third roller clutch burned due to lack of lubrication.
16. Damaged input carrier and/or reaction carrier.
17. Damaged or improperly installed output shaft.
18. Burned or improperly installed 1-2 band.
19. Damaged final drive assembly and/or final drive sun gear shaft.
20. Broken parking pawl spring.

SLIPS IN DRIVE

1. Incorrect oil level.
2. Cut or damaged vacuum line to modulator or defective modulator.
3. Low oil pressure.
4. Damaged 1-2 servo or servo piston seal.
5. Plugged filter screen.
6. Leaking servo oil pipes or pipe seals.
7. Defective converter stator clutch.
8. Defective input clutch accumulator or damaged input shaft seals.
9. Damaged or defective input clutch or leaks at ball capsule.

NO 1-2 UPSHIFT, 1ST SPEED ONLY

1. Governor weights binding.
2. Governor springs or gear damaged.
3. Leaking governor oil pipes.
4. Leaking governor retainer or blocked governor screen.
5. Leaking accumulator cover, retainer or oil pipes.
6. 1-2 shift valve sticking or binding.
7. Valve body spacer plate or gaskets damaged or improperly positioned.
8. Damaged driven sprocket support oil rings.
9. Damaged or improperly assembled second clutch.
10. Clutch housing check ball damaged.
11. Damaged reverse reaction drum splines or missing drum plate.

HARSH OR SOFT 1-2 SHIFT

1. Incorrect oil pressure.
2. Accumulator cover bolts improperly tightened.
3. Accumulator pistons, seals or springs damaged.
4. Control valve assembly accumulator valve binding.
5. Check ball No. 8 missing or improperly installed.

INCORRECT SHIFT SPEED 4T60

1. T.V. cable disconnected or improperly adjusted.
2. T.V. link, lever or bracket damaged.
3. T.V. valve and plunger binding.
4. Governor pressure incorrect.

NO 2-3 UPSHIFT, 1ST & 2ND SPEEDS ONLY

1. Governor damaged.
2. Accumulator cover oil hole blocked.
3. Leaking drive sprocket support oil pipe.
4. 2-3 shift valve binding or sticking.
5. Control valve assembly bolts improperly torqued.
6. Leaking or improperly positioned check balls.
7. Sticking 2-3 accumulator valve.
8. Leaking 1-2 servo release oil pipe.
9. Improperly installed channel plate gasket.
10. Blocked oil passage to driven sprocket support.
11. Damaged input housing and shaft seals or blocked oil passages.
12. Damaged third clutch assembly.
13. Damaged third clutch piston check ball.

Copyrighted Material Reprinted with Permission from Hydra-Matic Div., GM Corp.

Fig. 2 Turbo Hydra-Matic 4T60 (440-T4) automatic transaxle

14. Damaged third roller clutch assembly.
15. Third roller clutch improperly assembled on input sun gear shaft.

HARSH OR SOFT 2-3 SHIFT

4T60

1. Incorrect oil pressure.
2. Leaking 1-2 servo check ball and capsule assembly.
3. Leaking 1-2 servo release oil pipe or pipe seals.
4. Improperly located 1-2 servo feed passage check ball.

4T60E

1. Incorrect oil pressure.
2. Number 4 checkball mislocated causing a soft shift.
3. Number 9 checkball mislocated causing a harsh shift.
4. Missing or damaged seals or springs on 2-3 accumulator piston.

NO 3-4 UPSHIFT

4T60

1. Incorrect throttle valve adjustment.

2. Defective governor.
3. Leaking governor feed or return oil pipes.
4. 3-4 shift valve binding or stuck.
5. Damaged fourth clutch shift spline.
6. Damaged or improperly assembled fourth clutch.

4T60E

1. 3-4 shift valve binding or stuck.
2. 4-3 manual shift valve binding or stuck.
3. Spline damage on fourth clutch shaft.
4. Damaged fourth clutch shift spline.
5. Damaged or improperly assembled fourth clutch.

HARSH OR SOFT 3-4 SHIFT

4T60

1. Incorrect oil pressure.
2. Accumulator cover and pistons seal damaged or cover bolts improperly tightened.
3. Check ball No. 1 improperly located.

4T60E

1. Incorrect oil pressure.
2. Accumulator cover and pistons seal damaged or springs missing.
3. Check ball No. 10 improperly located.
4. 3-4 accumulator valve stuck.

NO CONVERTER CLUTCH OPERATION

4T60

1. ECM malfunction.
2. Damaged, loose or corroded connectors.
3. Pinched wires.
4. Third clutch switch inoperative.
5. Inoperative solenoid.
6. Solenoid screen blocked.
7. Solenoid seal leaking.
8. Converter clutch shift valve and/or apply valve sticking.
9. Damaged or defective torque converter.

10. Damaged turbine shaft seals.
11. Damaged pump shaft seals.
12. Converter clutch blow-off check ball not properly seated in channel plate.

4T60E

1. Verify proper P.C.M. operation or wiring.
2. Pinched wires or damaged connectors.
3. Stuck converter clutch valve.
4. Stuck converter clutch regulator valve.
5. TCC solenoid O-ring leaking.
6. Solenoid screen blocked.
7. Damaged torque converter.
8. Damaged turbine shaft seals.
9. Damaged oil pump driveshaft seal.
10. Improperly seated or damaged converter clutch blow-off check ball.
11. Number 1 check ball missing.

CONVERTER CLUTCH DOES NOT RELEASE

1. No ECM signal to solenoid or defective solenoid, if equipped.
2. Sticking converter clutch apply piston.
3. Missing TCC orificed screen.

ROUGH CONVERTER CLUTCH OPERATION

4T60

1. Sticking converter clutch regulator valve.
2. Turbine shaft seals damaged or missing.
3. Converter clutch blow-off valve check ball damaged.
4. Damaged converter clutch accumulator piston or seal.
5. Damaged or incorrect TCC blow-off spring.

4T60E

1. Sticking converter clutch regulator valve.
2. Turbine shaft seals damaged or missing.
3. Converter clutch blow-off valve check ball damaged.
4. Drive sprocket support bushing worn.
5. Worn or glazed fiber material in torque converter.

HARSH 4-3 DOWNSHIFT

4T60

1. Control valve assembly check ball No. 1 missing.

4T60E

1. Control valve assembly check ball No. 10 missing.
2. 3-4 accumulator seal cut or damaged.
3. 3-4 accumulator valve stuck.

HARSH 3-2 DOWNSHIFT

4T60

1. Improper vacuum signal or defective modulator.
2. Sticking 1-2 servo control valve.
3. No. 12 check ball missing.

4. Sticking 3-2 control valve.
5. No. 4 check ball missing.
6. Sticking 3-2 coast valve.
7. No. 2 check ball missing or improperly positioned.

4T60E

1. Control valve assembly No. 9 check ball missing.
2. 2-3 accumulator seal cut or damaged.
3. 2-3 accumulator valve stuck.

HARSH 2-1 DOWNSHIFT

4T60

1. Control valve assembly check ball No. 8 missing.
2. No. 2 check ball missing or improperly positioned.

4T60E

1. Wrong spacer plate installed.
2. 1-2 accumulator seal cut or damaged.
3. 1-2 accumulator valve stuck.

NO REVERSE IN R RANGE

1. Incorrect oil pressure.
2. Damaged reverse servo piston or seal.
3. Reverse servo improperly assembled or improper apply pin installed.
4. Damaged or defective oil pump.
5. Damaged input clutch accumulator piston seal.
6. Damaged drive link assembly.
7. Burned, damaged or improperly installed reverse band.
8. Damaged or defective input clutch.
9. Defective input sprag.
10. Reverse reaction drum splines, input carrier and/or reaction carrier damaged.

SLIPS IN REVERSE

1. Incorrect oil pressure.
2. Damaged reverse servo seal.
3. Damaged reverse reaction carrier splines.
4. Refer to "Slips In Drive" comments.

WILL NOT HOLD IN PARK

1. Damaged or disconnect manual linkage.
2. Damaged parking pawl spring, pawl and/or parking gear.
3. Damaged actuator assembly or actuator spring.

HARSH N-D OR D-N SHIFT

4T60

1. Improper vacuum signal to modulator or defective modulator.
2. Aspirator T-fitting improperly installed or plugged.
3. No. 9 check ball missing from control valve (harsh into reverse).
4. No. 12 check ball missing from control valve (harsh into drive).
5. Thermal element does not close when hot.

4T60E

1. Improper vacuum signal to modulator or defective modulator.

2. Broken reverse servo cushion spring.
3. No. 5 check ball missing from control valve (harsh into reverse).
4. No. 6 check ball missing from control valve (harsh into drive).
5. Broken forward servo cushion spring.
6. Thermal element does not close when hot.

2ND GEAR STARTS

4T60

1. Incorrect oil pressure.
2. 1-2 shift valve stuck.
3. Governor weights stuck.
4. 1-2 throttle valve bushing retainer installed too deep.

4T60E

1. 1-2 shift valve stuck.

HARSH ENGAGEMENT OR SHUDDER IN REVERSE

4T60

1. 2ND clutch housing drum assembly surface scored or hot spots caused by band slippage.
2. Burned fiber material on reverse band assembly.
3. Reverse servo apply pin too short.

4T60E

1. 2ND clutch housing drum assembly surface scored or hot spots caused by band slippage.
2. Burned fiber material on reverse band assembly.
3. Number 5 checkball missing or mislocated.
4. Damaged servo cushion spring.

MAINTENANCE

To check fluid, drive vehicle for at least 15 minutes to bring fluid to operating temperature (200°F). With vehicle on a level surface and engine idling in Park and parking brake applied, the level on the dipstick should be at the FULL mark. To bring the fluid level from the ADD mark to the FULL mark requires one pint of fluid. If vehicle cannot be driven sufficiently to bring fluid to operating temperature, the level on the dipstick should be between the two dimples on the dipstick with fluid temperature at 70°F. Note that the two dimples are located above the FULL mark.

If additional fluid is required, use only Dexron II automatic transmission fluid.

An early change to a darker color from the usual red color and/or a strong odor that is usually associated with overheated fluid is normal and should not be considered as a positive sign of required maintenance or unit failure.

When adding fluid, do not overfill, as foaming and loss of fluid through the vent may occur as the fluid heats up. Also, if fluid level is too low, complete loss of drive may occur especially when cold, which can cause transaxle failure.

Every 100,000 miles, the oil should be drained, the oil pan removed, the screen cleaned and fresh fluid added. For vehicles

Fig. 3   Manual linkage adjustment

Fig. 4   T.V. cable adjustment. Except Cutlass Supreme, Grand Prix Lumina, Regal & 6000

1. READJUSTMENT BUTTON
2. FITTING
3. SLIDER AGAINST FITTING IN FULL NON-ADJUSTED POSITION
4. CONDUIT
5. SLIDER
6. TO THROTTLE LEVER

Fig. 5   T.V. cable adjustment. Cutlass Supreme, Grand Prix, Lumina, Regal & 6000

subjected to more severe use such as heavy city traffic especially in hot weather, prolonged periods of idling or towing, this maintenance should be performed every 15,000 miles.

CHANGING FLUID

Step 7 of this procedure has been modified by service bulletin 91-7440-2.

1. Raise and support vehicle, then position drain pan under oil pan.
2. Remove front and side oil pan attaching bolts, then loosen rear pan attaching bolts.
3. Carefully pry oil pan loose from transaxle case and allow fluid to drain.
4. Remove remaining attaching bolt, oil pan and gasket. Thoroughly clean pan before reinstalling.
5. Remove and discard screen and O-ring seal.
6. Install replacement screen and O-ring seal, locating screen against dipstick stop.
7. Install gasket on oil pan, then apply Loctite 242 or equivalent to oil pan bolts to prevent leakage.
8. **Torque** oil pan bolts to 12-13 ft. lbs.
8. Lower vehicle and add approximately 6 qts. of fluid.
9. With selector in park, parking brake applied and engine at idle speed and operating temperature, check fluid level and add fluid as necessary. **Do not race engine or move shift lever through ranges.**

ADJUSTMENTS

MANUAL LINKAGE, ADJUST

1. Lift up on cable lock button, located near transaxle cable bracket.
2. Place transaxle manual control lever in Neutral position. Neutral position

can be obtained by rotating the manual lever counterclockwise to Park position, then rotate lever clockwise from Park, through Reverse to Neutral.

3. Place transaxle selector lever in the Neutral position.
4. Push down on cable lock button **Fig. 3.**

T.V. CABLE, ADJUST

Except Cutlass Supreme, Grand Prix, Lumina, Regal & 6000

1. Ensure ignition is in the Off position.
2. Depress and hold metal adjustment

tab at engine end of T.V. cable, **Fig. 4.**
3. Move slider until it contacts fitting, then release tab.
4. Check cable for sticking or binding and road test vehicle. **Recheck cable after engine has reached normal operating temperature, as cable may appear to operate properly with engine cold.**

Cutlass Supreme, Grand Prix, Lumina, Regal & 6000

1. Depress and hold adjustment button, **Fig. 5.**
2. Pull cable conduit out until slider hits against adjustment.
3. Release button.
4. Repeat adjustment.

IN-VEHICLE REPAIRS

VALVE BODY, REPLACE

Lumina, Cutlass Supreme, Grand Prix & Regal Except 3.4L/V6-204 Engine

1. Disconnect negative battery cable and remove air cleaner assembly.
2. Install engine support fixture tool No. J-28467-A, engine support fixture adapter tool No. J-28467-90 and engine support adapter leg tool No. J-36462 or equivalents.
3. Disconnect torque struts at engine mounts.
4. Remove exhaust crossover pipe and two bolts at top of transaxle mount bracket.
5. Raise and support vehicle, then remove left front tire and wheel assembly.
6. Remove left front brake caliper and bracket.
7. Remove four bolts at hub and bearing assembly, then remove front drive axle.
8. Disconnect left lower ball joint, then remove left inner splash shield.
9. Remove pinch bolt at intermediate steering shaft.
10. Support left and right sides of frame with jack stands.
11. Remove frame to body bolts, then adjust left jackstand to lower left side of frame.
12. Remove transaxle mount and mount support.
13. Lower left side of engine/transaxle using engine support fixture.
14. Remove two clamps holding wiring harness to transaxle mount bracket.
15. Remove transaxle mount bracket & case side cover pan.
16. Disconnect electrical connectors from pressure switches.
17. Remove pump to valve body bolts. **Do not remove the three Torx screws that hold the pump assembly together.**
18. Remove 1-2 servo pipe clip and bolt from valve body.
19. Remove valve body to channel plate bolts.
20. Remove valve body, keeping spacer plate with transaxle.
21. Reverse procedure to install.

Lumina, Cutlass Supreme & Grand Prix w/3.4L/V6-204 Engine

1. Disconnect negative battery cable and remove air cleaner assembly.
2. Remove exhaust crossover pipe and bolt at top of transaxle mount bracket.
3. Install engine support fixture tool No. J-28467-A, engine support fixture adapter tool No. J-28467-90 and engine support adapter leg tool No. J-36462 or equivalents.
4. Raise and support vehicle, then remove left front tire and wheel assembly.
5. Remove left inner splash shield.
6. Remove transaxle mount and loosen

engine mount nuts at frame.
7. Remove pinch bolt at intermediate steering shaft.
8. Disconnect ball joints at steering knuckle.
9. Support left and right sides of frame with jack stands.
10. Remove left side frame to body bolts, then loosen right side frame to body bolts.
11. Remove left side steering rack bolt and left side drive axle.
12. Remove transaxle mount bracket and case side cover pan.
13. Disconnect electrical connectors from pressure switches.
14. Remove pump to valve body bolts. **Do not remove the three screws that hold the pump assembly together.**
15. Remove valve body to channel plate bolts.
16. Remove valve body, keeping spacer plate with transaxle.
17. Reverse procedure to install.

Century, Cutlass Ciera, Cutlass Cruiser & 6000

1. Disconnect battery ground cable and remove air cleaner assembly.
2. **Remove air cleaner housing and intake tube.**
3. **Remove torque struts at engine mounts.**
4. **Disconnect crossover pipe-to-left manifold clamp.**
5. **Loosen crossover pipe-to-right manifold clamp.**
6. **Remove two (2) bolts at top of transaxle mount bracket. Pry crossover pipe to allow removal of front bolt. DO NOT pry on crossover pipe heat shield. If shield is bent, heat damage to other components may occur.**
7. Install engine support assembly J-28467 or equivalent.
8. Rotate steering wheel until bolt securing intermediate shaft to steering gear is facing up, remove bolt, then disconnect intermediate shaft from steering gear stub shaft.
9. Remove upper case side cover retaining bolts.
10. Raise and support vehicle, position jack and block of wood under engine to act as support during cradle removal, then remove left front wheel.
11. Disconnect brake line support clip from underbody.
12. Remove power steering line brackets, steering gear brackets and driveline vibration damper as needed.
13. Remove pinch bolt from left steering knuckle and disconnect lower ball joint.
14. Disconnect stabilizer bar from left control arm, then remove both front stabilizer bar reinforcements and bushings from left and right side members.
15. Disconnect engine and transaxle mounts from cradle.
16. Remove side member to crossmember bolts.
17. Remove bolts securing left side body mounts.

18. Remove left side member and front crossmember assembly. **It may be necessary to pull or gently pry crossmember loose.**
19. Disconnect and remove AIR pipe, if equipped.
20. Remove jack and lower vehicle, then lower transaxle by adjusting engine support fixture.
21. Remove remaining bolts securing transaxle side cover pan.
22. Disconnect drive axle and remove nuts surrounding flange at channel plate. **Do not pry against case side cover to remove axle. Insert pry bar behind axle and use suitable block of wood as fulcrum when removing axle.**
23. Remove case side cover pan and gaskets.
24. Remove valve body retaining bolts, valve body and oil pump as an assembly, **Fig. 6. Do not remove three pump cover to valve body retaining bolts.**
25. Reverse procedure to install.

Bonneville, Electra, LeSabre, Park Avenue, Reatta, Riviera, Toronado, 88 & 98

1. Disconnect battery ground cable.
2. Disconnect vacuum hoses from cruise control servo unit, if equipped.
3. Disconnect electrical connector from neutral/back-up lamp switch.
4. Raise and support vehicle, then remove left front wheel.
5. Remove inner splash shield.
6. Disconnect left tie rod from steering knuckle using suitable puller.
7. Disconnect stabilizer link from left control arm.
8. Install drive axle boot seal protectors, as needed. **Models using silicone (gray) boots on drive axle joints require the use of seal protectors J-33162 or equivalent. Models using thermoplastic boots (black) do not require use of seal protectors.**
9. Disconnect ball joint from left steering knuckle.
10. Disconnect left drive axle from transaxle, using suitable puller, and secure drive axle aside, taking care not to extend drive axle joints.
11. Remove pinch bolt securing intermediate shaft to steering gear and disconnect intermediate shaft from gear.
12. Position suitable jack under transaxle oil pan and raise jack until weight of transaxle is supported.
13. Remove 3 bolts securing frame to body on left side.
14. Lower transaxle just enough to gain access to side cover pan bolts.
15. Disconnect cooler lines from transaxle and plug lines and open fittings.
16. Remove side cover bolts, side cover and gaskets.
17. Remove valve body retaining bolts, valve body, oil pump and gaskets as an assembly, **Fig. 6. Do not remove three No. 40 Torx bolts securing oil pump together.**
18. Reverse procedure to install.

30 GASKET, SPACER PLATE/CHANNEL PLATE
31 PLATE, VALVE BODY SPACER
32 GASKET, SPACER PLATE/VALVE BODY
34 BALL, CHECK VALVE (8)
35 VALVE ASSEMBLY, CONTROL
44 PUMP ASSEMBLY
45 BOLT, PUMP BODY TO CASE (2)
46 BOLT, PUMP COVER TO CHANNEL PLATE (10)

47 BOLT, PUMP COVER TO VALVE BODY (1)
48 HARNESS, WIRING
49 LINK, THROTTLE LEVER TO CABLE
50 LEVER & BRACKET ASSEMBLY, THROTTLE
51 PAN, CASE SIDE COVER
52 SCREW, SPECIAL M8X1.25X16.0
53 NUT, FLANGED HEX (M6X1.0)
61 CLIP, TWO WIRE
62 CLIP, TWO WIRE
64 GASKET, SIDE COVER PAN
65 GASKET, SIDE COVER TO CHANNEL PLATE

Fig. 6 Valve body assembly

DeVille & Fleetwood

1. Disconnect battery ground cable and remove air cleaner.
2. Install engine support fixture J-28467 or equivalent.
3. Remove upper side cover retaining bolts and the fuel pipe bracket.
4. Raise and support vehicle, and remove left front wheel.
5. Disconnect stabilizer shaft from left control arm, noting position of bushings and spacers.
6. Support control arm using suitable jack, then disconnect ball joint from left steering knuckle using suitable puller.
7. Remove left engine splash shield.
8. Remove vacuum pump mounting bolts and secure pump aside, leaving hoses connected.
9. Install drive boot seal protectors J-34754 or equivalent.
10. Disconnect left drive axle from transaxle and secure aside, taking care not to extend drive axle joints.
11. Support transaxle using suitable jack and remove left front transaxle mount.
12. Remove right front engine mount as follows: **Vehicle should be supported at each front frame horn to prevent vehicle from tipping on hoist.**
    a. Disconnect brace between engine bracket and engine.
    b. Remove two nuts securing mount to frame.
    c. Remove two nuts securing transaxle bracket to mount.
    d. Remove two nuts securing transaxle mount to frame bracket.
    e. Raise engine using support fixture, then remove stud and two bolts securing mount bracket to block.
    f. Remove mount and bracket by pulling forward.
13. Loosen left and right rear transaxle mounts.
14. Remove left cradle mounts, separate left cradle and remove from vehicle, **Figs. 7 and 8.**
15. Loosen but do not remove right cradle mounts 2 and 3.
16. Remove jacks ensuring vehicle remains stable, then lower vehicle.
17. Note position of engine support fixture support rods and lower engine/transaxle assembly as follows. **In order to obtain maximum clearance for side cover removal it is necessary to tilt front of engine downwards.**
    a. Move left (driver's side) rear support rod until it extends approximately six inches above "T" nut.
    b. Lower left front support rod until top is flush with top of "T" nut.
18. Raise and support vehicle.
19. Disconnect transaxle cooler lines from bracket and secure aside.
20. Remove remaining side cover retaining bolts and nuts securing axle opening cover.
21. Remove side cover pan and gaskets.
22. Remove wiring harness and VCC solenoid, disconnecting harness from pressure switches and case connector.
23. Remove TV lever, bracket and link assembly.
24. Remove oil pump retaining bolts and the pump assembly. **Do not remove three bolts (A), Fig. 6, securing pump cover to valve body.**

Copyrighted Material Reprinted with Permission from Hydra-Matic Div., GM Corp.

Fig. 7   Support cradle mounting. Cadillac

Copyrighted Material Reprinted with Permission from Hydra-Matic Div., GM Corp.

Fig. 8   Separating support cradle. Cadillac

25. Remove valve body retaining bolts and the valve body, noting position of four control valve to spacer plate check balls.
26. Remove oil pump driveshaft.
27. Remove spacer plate and gaskets, noting position of eight spacer to channel plate check balls.
28. Reverse procedure to install.

Eldorado & Seville

1. Disconnect battery ground cable and remove air cleaner assembly.
2. Remove inner engine cooling fan assembly.
3. Disconnect vacuum hoses from cruise control servo and vacuum modulator (if equipped).
4. Disconnect electrical connectors from cruise control servo, distributor, oil pressure sending unit and transaxle.
5. Disconnect TV cable from throttle lever and bracket, and from transaxle.
6. Remove vacuum modulator (if equipped).
7. Install engine support fixture J-28467 or equivalent and note position of left side support hooks.
8. Raise and support vehicle, then remove left wheel assembly.
9. Remove right and left wheel housing lower splash shields.
10. Remove left stabilizer bar link and support left control arm with suitable jack.
11. Remove left ball joint cotter pin and nut, then disconnect ball joint using suitable puller.
12. Remove four nuts securing transaxle to cradle and bracket.
13. Remove A/C compressor splash shield, No. 1 cradle mount insulator cover, **Fig. 7**, and the left side engine mount and damper fasteners.
14. Remove six right front cradle joining bolts, **Fig. 8**.
15. Remove left stabilizer mount retaining bolts.
16. Remove two left rear cradle joining bolts, **Fig. 8**.
17. Disconnect wire loom and vacuum

hoses from retainers on cradle and transaxle.
18. Disconnect hoses from AIR pipe and disconnect pipe retainer from rear of cradle.
19. Lower vehicle.
20. Raise engine/transaxle assembly two inches using support fixture hooks at flywheel end of engine.
21. Raise and support vehicle.
22. Remove No. 1 insulator bolt and separate right front corner of cradle assembly, **Fig. 8**, then remove left cradle section.
23. Disconnect AIR valve from transaxle and position aside.
24. Remove stud bolts securing transaxle bracket to bellhousing, noting position of bolts for installation.
25. Lower vehicle, the lower engine/transaxle assembly to position noted in step 7.
26. Remove transaxle mount bracket upper stud bolts and the bracket, rotating bracket clockwise to air removal.
27. Lower left side of transaxle to limit allowed by support hooks.
28. Raise vehicle and install suitable drive axle boot seal protectors.
29. Disconnect drive axle and secure toward rear of vehicle, taking care not to overextend drive axle joints.
30. Remove case side cover pan bolts, pan and gaskets.
31. Remove wiring harness and VCC solenoid from pressure switches and case connector.
32. Remove TV lever, bracket and link assembly.
33. Remove oil pump retaining bolts and the pump assembly. **Do not remove three bolts (A), Fig. 6, securing pump cover to valve body.**
34. Remove valve body retaining bolts and the valve body, noting position of four control valve to spacer plate check balls.
35. Remove oil pump driveshaft.
36. Remove spacer plate and gaskets, noting position of eight spacer to

channel plate check balls.
37. Reverse procedure to install.

GOVERNOR, REPLACE
4T60 (440-T4)

1. Raise and support vehicle.
2. Remove speed sensor assembly.
3. Remove governor cover attaching bolts, then the cover and seal.
4. Remove governor complete with sleeve and speedometer drive gear, **Fig. 9**.
5. Reverse procedure to install.

ACCUMULATOR, REPLACE

1. Raise and support vehicle.
2. Drain transaxle fluid into a suitable container, then remove oil pan.
3. Remove oil filter and seal, then the accumulator cover attaching bolts and cover.
4. Remove accumulator piston, oil seal and spring.
5. Reverse procedure to install.

1-2 & REVERSE SERVO, REPLACE
4T60 (440-T4)

1. Disconnect exhaust crossover pipe.
2. Depress servo cover, then remove snap ring and servo cover.
3. Remove servo piston, sealing ring, apply pin and servo spring, **Fig. 10**.
4. Reverse procedure to install.

REVERSE SERVO, REPLACE
4T60E

1. Remove air cleaner assembly and exhaust crossover pipe.
2. Raise drivers side of car so it is higher than differential side. This will ensure that the reverse band will be in the proper location.
3. Depress servo cover, then remove

4 RING, OIL SEAL (GOVERNOR SHAFT)
5 GOVERNOR ASSEMBLY
6 GEAR, SPEEDOMETER DRIVE
7 BEARING ASM., THRUST (SPEEDO GEAR)
8 SEAL, "O" RING (GOVERNOR COVER)
9 COVER, GOVERNOR
10 SCREW, GOVERNOR COVER·CASE

4 RING, OIL SEAL (GOVERNOR SHAFT)
5 GOVERNOR ASSEMBLY
7 BEARING ASM., THRUST (SPEEDO GEAR)
8 SEAL, "O" RING (GOVERNOR COVER)
10 SCREW, GOVERNOR COVER CASE
74 ROTOR, SPEED SENSOR
75 HOUSING, SPEED SENSOR
76 COIL ASSEMBLY
77 WASHER
78 MAGNET
79 SEAL, "O" RING
80 WASHER, WAVE SPRING
81 GASKET, COVER
82 COVER, HOUSING
83 BOLT

Copyrighted Material Reprinted with Permission from Hydra-Matic Div., GM Corp.

Fig. 9   Governor assembly

6 TRANSAXLE EXTENSION CASE
12 BOLT
13 COVER, FORWARD SERVO
14 O–RING
16 FORWARD SERVO PISTON ASM
17 RETAINER
22 SPRING, SERVO RETURN
39 RING, SERVO COVER RETAINING
40 COVER, REVERSE SERVO
41 O–RING
44 REVERSE SERVO PISTON ASM
49 SPRING, SERVO RETURN

543 RING, SERVO COVER RETAINING
544 COVER, SERVO (REVERSE)
545 SEAL, "O" RING (COVER TO CASE)
546 RING, SNAP (BAND APPLY PIN)
547 RING, OIL SEAL PISTON
548 PISTON, REVERSE SERVO
549 SPRING, REVERSE SERVO CUSHION
550 RETAINER, SERVO CUSHION SPRING
551 PIN, REVERSE APPLY
552 SPRING, SERVO RETURN
553 RING, SERVO COVER RETAINING
554 COVER, SERVO (1-2)
555 SEAL, "O" RING (COVER TO CASE)
556 RING, SNAP (BAND APPLY PIN)
557 RING, OIL SEAL PISTON
558 PISTON, 1-2 SERVO
559 SPRING, 1-2 SERVO CUSHION
560 RETAINER, SERVO CUSHION SPRING
561 PIN, 1-2 BAND APPLY
562 SPRING, SERVO RETURN
563 SPRING, REVERSE SERVO CURVED
568 RETAINER, SERVO SPRING

Copyrighted Material Reprinted with Permission from Hydra-Matic Div., GM Corp.

Fig. 10   1-2 & reverse servo assembly

Copyrighted Material Reprinted with Permission from Hydra-Matic Div., GM Corp.

Fig. 11   Reverse & forward servo. 4T60E

snap ring, servo cover, servo piston, sealing ring, apply pin and servo spring, **Fig. 11.**

4. Reverse procedure to install.

FORWARD SERVO, REPLACE

4T60E

1. Install engine support fixture tool No. J-28467-A, engine support fixture adapter tool No. J-28467-90 and engine support adapter leg tool No. J-36462 or equivalents.
2. Raise and support vehicle.
3. Remove power steering rack and pinion heat shield.
4. Remove power steering rack and pinion mounting bolts and hang steering rack from exhaust pipe flange.
5. Disconnect transaxle and engine mounts.

6. Support rear of frame with jackstand, then loosen front frame bolts and remove rear frame bolts.
7. Lower frame from jackstand, then disconnect power steering lines from right side of frame.
8. Remove servo cover bolts, servo cover, servo piston, sealing ring, apply pin, servo spring retainer and servo spring, **Fig 11.**
9. Reverse procedure to install.

TRANSAXLE REPLACE

1991 CENTURY, CUTLASS CIERA, CUTLASS CRUISER & 6000

1. Disconnect battery ground cable.
2. Remove air cleaner assembly, then

disconnect T.V. cable (if equipped) at both ends.
3. Disconnect shift linkage from transaxle.
4. Install engine support fixture, then disconnect converter clutch electrical connector.
5. Remove 3 transaxle-to-engine attaching bolts.
6. Disconnect vacuum line from modulator (if equipped).
7. Raise and support vehicle.
8. Remove left front wheel, then the lower ball joint pinch nut.
9. Remove brake line bracket from strut, then disconnect drive axles from transaxle.
10. Remove cradle-to-stabilizer attaching bolts.
11. Remove stabilizer-to-control arm attaching bolts, then the left front cradle assembly.
12. Disconnect speedometer cable from transaxle, then remove extension

FRT
POSITION #4
POSITION #5
POSITION #6
POSITION #3
POSITION #2
POSITION #1
153
152

| 152 | BOLT (75 N·m/55 FT. LBS.) |
| 153 | STUD (75 N·m/55 FT. LBS.) |

Copyrighted Material Reprinted with Permission from Hydra-Matic Div., GM Corp.

Fig. 12   Bellhousing bolt removal. Cadillac

housing-to-engine block support bracket.
13. Disconnect cooler lines from transaxle, then remove right and left insulator attaching bolts.
14. Remove flywheel splash shield.
15. Mark relationship of flywheel to converter, then remove flywheel attaching bolts.
16. Remove all remaining transaxle-to-engine attaching bolts except one.
17. Support transaxle with a suitable jack, then remove remaining bolt and carefully lower transaxle from vehicle.
18. Reverse procedure to install.

1992–93 CENTURY, CUTLASS CIERA & CUTLASS CRUISER

1. Disconnect battery ground cable, then remove air cleaner and duct assembly.
2. Disconnect the following electrical connectors: TCC switch, A/C low pressure switch and Park/Neutral Position switch.
3. Disconnect TV cable from throttle body and transaxle, then shift control cable from transaxle mounting bracket and lever.
4. Disconnect vacuum modulator line from modulator, then remove three upper transaxle bolts from engine and ground wires.
5. Remove steering shaft pinch bolt, then install engine support fixture.
6. Raise and support vehicle, then remove front wheel assemblies and splash shields.
7. Remove pinch bolts from control arms, then stabilizer shaft bolts and reinforcement plates from frame.
8. Remove stabilizer shaft nuts and bracket from control arm, then separate shaft from arm. Using a 7/16 inch drill bit, drill two spot welds located between front and rear holes of left

front stabilizer shaft mounting.
9. Remove front and rear transaxle nuts, then power steering cooler line bolts.
10. Remove right frame to left frame retaining bolt, then position jack stand under frame for support.
11. Loosen two right frame mounts and discard bolts, then two left frame bolts and left frame assembly.
12. Remove transaxle mount retaining bolts from transaxle case, then mount.
13. Remove transaxle converter covers and torque converter bolts.
14. Remove drive axles from transaxle as outlined under "Front Wheel Drive Axles."
15. Remove transaxle support bracket bolts from transaxle, then disconnect vehicle speed sensor electrical connector rom transaxle.
16. Disconnect transaxle cooler lines, then install transaxle jack.
17. Remove rear transaxle bolts from engine, remaining transaxle bolts, then transaxle.
18. Reverse procedure to install.

1991 BONNEVILLE, ELECTRA, LESABRE, 88 & 98

1. Disconnect battery ground cable.
2. Disconnect electrical connector from mass air flow sensor.
3. Loosen two hose clamps at air intake duct, then remove intake duct and mass air flow sensor as an assembly.
4. Disconnect T.V. cable (if equipped) at both ends.
5. **On models equipped with cruise control,** disconnect cable from throttle body and the vacuum hoses from servo, then remove servo assembly.
6. **On all models,** disconnect shift control linkage from transaxle.
7. Disconnect electrical connectors from park/neutral switch, torque converter clutch and vehicle speed sensor.
8. Disconnect vacuum modulator hose

from modulator (if equipped).
9. Remove 3 upper transaxle-to-engine attaching bolts, then install suitable engine support fixture.
10. Turn steering wheel to the full left position, then remove both front wheels.
11. Remove right front ball joint nut and separate control arm from steering knuckle.
12. Remove right drive axle from case, using care to avoid damaging the seal.
13. Remove left drive axle, using a suitable pry bar with axle boot seal protectors installed.
14. Disconnect electrical connector from aspirator, then remove left front transaxle mount.
15. Remove right front transaxle mount attaching nuts.
16. Remove left rear transaxle mount-to-transaxle attaching bolts, then the right rear transaxle mount.
17. Remove engine support bracket-to-transaxle case attaching bolts.
18. Remove stabilizer link-to-control arm bolt.
19. Remove flywheel cover attaching bolts and the cover.
20. Mark relationship of flywheel to converter, then remove flywheel attaching bolts.
21. Remove rear cradle-to-front cradle attaching bolts.
22. Install suitable transaxle support fixture, then cradle assembly by swinging to one side and supporting with a suitable stand.
23. Disconnect cooler lines from transaxle, then remove remaining lower transaxle-to-engine attaching bolts.
24. Carefully lower transaxle from vehicle.
25. Reverse procedure to install.

1992–93 BONNEVILLE, LESABRE, PARK AVENUE, RIVIERA, TORONADO, 88 & 98

1. Disconnect battery ground cable.
2. Disconnect cross brace from struts towers as follows:
   a. Loosen bar assembly through-bolts.
   b. Remove inboard strut nuts.
   c. Remove brace assembly.
   d. Install inboard strut nuts.
3. Remove air intake duct.
4. Remove cruise control cable at throttle body, vacuum hoses at servo, then servo assembly.
5. Remove shift control linkage mounting bracket at transaxle, then lever at manual shaft.
6. Disconnect wiring connectors at: transaxle Park/Neutral Position switch and back up lamp switch, transaxle electrical connector and vehicle speed sensor.
7. Remove fuel pipe retainers, then disconnect vacuum modulator hose at modulator.
8. Remove top three transaxle-to-engine bolts, then install

engine support fixture. -Load- the **support fixture by tightening the wingnuts several turns to relieve tension on frame and mounts.**

9. Raise and support vehicle, then remove front wheel and ball joint assemblies.

10. Separate control arms from steering knuckles. **Drive axle seal protector J 34754 should be modified and installed on any drive axle prior to service. Failure to observe this can result in damage and possible joint failure.**

11. Remove right drive axle from transaxle **only; do not remove from hub/knuckle assembly.**

12. Remove left drive axle from transaxle **and** hub/knuckle assembly.

13. Support transaxle with jackstand, then remove left front transaxle mount.

14. Remove torque strut bracket from transaxle, then left rear transaxle mount-to-transaxle bolts.

15. Remove transaxle brace from engine bracket, then stabilizer shaft link-to-control arm bolt.

16. Remove flywheel cover bolts, flywheel cover and flywheel-to-converter bolts. Mark flywheel to converter relationship to ensure proper installation.

17. Remove bolts attaching rear frame member to front frame dog leg.

18. Remove front left frame-to-body bolts, then front left frame dog leg-to-right frame member bolts.

19. Remove frame assembly by swinging aside and supporting with suitable stand, then disconnect cooler pipes at transaxle.

20. Remove remaining transaxle-to-engine bolts. **One bolt is located between transaxle case and engine block and is installed in opposite direction.**

21. Lower transaxle away from vehicle.

22. Reverse procedure to install.

DEVILLE & FLEETWOOD

1. Disconnect battery ground cable and remove air cleaner assembly.

2. Remove T.V. cable (if equipped) and cable-to-cooler line bracket.

3. Remove exhaust crossover pipe.

4. Disconnect shift cable bracket and manual lever from transaxle, then secure cable, bracket and lever aside.

5. Disconnect electrical connectors from transaxle, cruise control servo and neutral/back-up lamp switch.

6. Remove upper bolts and studs securing bellhousing to engine block (positions 2, 3, 4 and 5), **Fig. 12.**

7. Disconnect vacuum line from modulator (if equipped).

8. Install engine support fixture J-28467 or equivalent, noting the following:
   a. Ensure fixture is installed in extreme forward position across both strut towers.
   b. The two-piece, link-type hook should be used at passenger side rear engine hook, and both drivers side hooks should be positioned vertically.

   c. Hooks should be tightened to remove all looseness and slack, but it is not necessary to actually raise engine.

9. Raise and support vehicle, then remove front wheels.

10. Support lower control arms using suitable jacks, then disconnect both ball joints from steering knuckles using suitable puller.

11. Install suitable drive axle boot seal protectors, separate drive axles from transaxle, then secure drive axles aside. **Care must be taken not to overextend driveshaft pot joints, as joint will be damaged.**

12. Remove left stabilizer link and mounting clamp bolts, then clamp, bushings and spacers, noting position for installation.

13. Remove A/C compressor and left engine splash shields, left No. 1 mount cover and wiring harness cover.

14. Remove vacuum pump from left cradle and secure aside, then disconnect electrical connector from vehicle speed sensor.

15. Remove fasteners securing right and left front engine/transaxle mounts to cradle.

16. Remove left No. 1 mount bolts, then separate and remove left cradle assembly.

17. Disconnect and plug cooler lines, then unfasten cooler line bracket.

18. Remove transaxle-to-engine support bracket.

19. Remove right rear mount-to-transaxle bracket and fasteners securing left rear mount to transaxle.

20. Remove flexplate dust cover and colts securing flexplate to torque converter.

21. Support transaxle with suitable jack, then remove bellhousing-to-engine bolts at positions No. 1 and 6, **Fig. 12. To remove bolt No. 6, it is necessary to use a suitable extension and access bolt through right wheel house opening.**

22. Separate and remove transaxle assembly.

23. Reverse procedure to install.

ELDORADO & SEVILLE

1. Disconnect battery ground cable and remove air cleaner assembly.

2. Disconnect and remove T.V. cable (if equipped).

3. Remove cruise control servo.

4. Disconnect electrical connectors from distributor, oil pressure sending unit and transaxle.

5. Remove engine oil cooler line bracket.

6. Disconnect shift cable bracket and manual lever from transaxle, then secure cable, bracket and lever aside.

7. Remove fuel line bracket and disconnect neutral safety switch electrical connector.

8. Remove vacuum modulator (if equipped).

9. Remove T.V. cable support bracket (if equipped) and remaining engine oil cooler line bracket.

10. Remove bellhousing bolts No. 2, 3, 4

and 6, **Fig. 12.**

11. Disconnect AIR crossover pipe fitting and reposition pipe.

12. Remove radiator hose bracket and fasteners securing transaxle mount to bracket.

13. Install engine support bracket J-28467 or equivalent, and note position of support hooks.

14. Raise and support vehicle and remove front wheels.

15. Remove left and right stabilizer link bolts, ball joint cotter pins and ball joint retaining nuts.

16. Support control arms using suitable jacks, then disconnect left and right ball joints using suitable puller.

17. Remove A/C compressor splash shield and No. 1 cradle mount cover.

18. Disconnect AIR pipe end hose connections and rear mounting clip.

19. Disconnect vacuum hoses and wire loom from front of cradle.

20. Remove fasteners securing engine mount, damper and transaxle mount to cradle and wire loom to transaxle bracket.

21. Lower vehicle, then raise transaxle 2 inches from position noted in step 13 using left support hooks of engine support fixture.

22. Raise and support vehicle.

23. Remove left side stabilizer mounting bolts and bolts joining cradle at right front and left rear corners.

24. Remove No. 1 cradle mount bolts. Separate cradle at right front corner, then remove left cradle section.

25. Disconnect AIR management valve bracket from transaxle mounting bracket and secure valve and bracket assembly to transaxle stud bolt.

26. Lower vehicle, then lower engine/transaxle assembly to position noted in step 13.

27. Remove transaxle mounting bracket.

28. Raise and support vehicle.

29. Remove bracket from right transaxle mount to transaxle and bolts securing engine/transaxle brace to transaxle.

30. Disconnect electrical connector from vehicle speed sensor.

31. Remove flexplate dust covers and bolts securing flexplate to torque converter.

32. Support transaxle with suitable jack, then remove bellhousing bolts No. 1 and 6, **Fig. 12. To remove bolt No. 6, use suitable extension to gain access through right front wheel house opening.**

33. Disconnect cooler lines from transaxle, then plug lines and open fittings.

34. Install suitable drive axle boot seal protectors, separate drive axles from transaxle and secure axles aside. **Care must be taken not to overextend drive axle pot joints, as joint will be damaged.**

35. Separate and remove transaxle assembly.

36. Reverse procedure to install.

REATTA, RIVIERA, TORONADO & TROFEO

1. Disconnect battery ground cable and

install engine support fixture J-28467 or equivalent.

2. Disconnect vacuum hose from modulator (if equipped) and electrical connectors from transaxle.
3. Disconnect T.V. cable (if equipped) from throttle body and transaxle.
4. Remove cruise control servo, if equipped.
5. Disconnect selector cable bracket and manual selector lever from transaxle, then secure cable, bracket and lever assembly aside.
6. Remove neutral start/back-up lamp switch assembly.
7. Remove top 3 bellhousing bolts, bolts securing wiring harness and the driveline damper bracket.
8. Raise and support vehicle.
9. Disconnect cooler lines from transaxle, then plug lines and open fittings.
10. Remove flexplate dust cover and bolts securing flexplate to torque converter.
11. Remove engine mount nuts and left transaxle mounting bolts.
12. Remove sway bar links from lower control arms.
13. Ensure control arm is properly supported, then remove cotter pin and nut and disconnect left ball joint.
14. Disconnect left drive axle from transaxle, taking care not to overextend drive axle pot joints. **Use drive axle boot seal protector J-33162 or equivalent on models with silicone (gray) drive axle boots. Models with thermoplastic (black) boots do not require the use of protectors.**
15. Remove left side frame (cradle) as follows:
    a. Remove bolt securing lower control arm assembly to frame and the strut rod nut, then rotate control arm aside.
    b. Remove engine splash shield.
    c. Disconnect wiring harness from front crossmember.
    d. Remove lower nut securing driveline vibration damper and 2 nuts securing front engine mount to frame.
    e. Disconnect left transaxle mount from frame.
    f. Remove 3 bolts from rear left side of rail and 4 bolts from right end of front crossmember.
    g. Remove left front frame mount cover and mounting bolt.
    h. Separate and remove left frame section.
16. Support transaxle with suitable jack, then remove 2 remaining bellhousing bolts.
17. Remove engine-to-transaxle brace.
18. Disconnect right drive axle and secure aside, taking care not to overextend drive axle pot joints.
19. Separate and remove transaxle.
20. Reverse procedure to install.

CUTLASS SUPREME, GRAND PRIX & REGAL

1. Remove air cleaner assembly and intake air tube.
2. Remove exhaust crossover pipe to left-hand exhaust manifold attaching bolts.
3. Disconnect shift control cable at transaxle, then remove cable from mounting bracket.
4. Disconnect electrical connection at transaxle.
5. Disconnect vacuum line from vacuum modulator (if equipped).
6. Install engine support fixture J 28477-1, adapter 28467-90 and leg J36462.
7. Raise and support vehicle, then remove both wheel and tire assemblies.
8. Remove left wheel housing splash shield.
9. Disconnect power steering rack and pinion and support it to body.
10. Disconnect right and left ball joints at steering knuckle. Use ball joint remover tool No. J35917 or equivalent to separate ball joints at steering knuckle.
11. Disconnect power steering cooler lines from frame.
12. Remove engine mount nuts, then loosen splash shield. Support frame with jackstand, then disconnect frame from vehicle.
13. Remove support.
14. **On models equipped with 3.4L engine,** remove generator splash shield.
15. **On all models,** remove torque converter cover and converter-to-flywheel bolts/screws.
16. Disconnect wiring harness at transaxle.
17. Disconnect drive axles from transaxle.
18. Install jackstand to transaxle, then disconnect ground wires at transaxle.
19. Remove lower transaxle oil cooler lines at transaxle, then disconnect engine wiring harness.
20. Lower transaxle side using engine support fixture.
21. Transaxle oil cooler lines should be flushed whenever transaxle has ben removed for overhaul or replacement of torque converter, pump or case.
22. Reverse procedure to install

TIGHTENING SPECIFICATIONS

Component	Torque/Ft. Lbs.
Bonneville, Electra, LeSabre, 88 & 98	
Flywheel Cover	136①
Governor Cover	132①
Left Front And Right Rear Mount To Transaxle	40
Left Rear Mount To Transaxle	30
Neutral Start And Back-up Switch	20
Oil Cooler Lines At Radiator	20
Oil Cooler Lines At Transaxle	16
Starter Bolts	32
Throttle Cable To Transaxle	75①
Transaxle Mount To Frame Nuts	30
Transaxle To Engine Bolts	55
Torque Converter Bolts	46
Wheel Lug Nuts	100
Century, Cutlass Ciera, Cutlass Cruiser & 6000	
Bracket To Transaxle Bolt	41
Channel Plate Attaching Bolts	41
Console Shift Control Assembly Nut	18

Component	Torque/Ft. Lbs.
Century, Cutlass Ciera, Cutlass Cruiser & 6000-Continued	
Fill Tube Bolt	18
Flywheel Cover Bolts	89①
Governor Housing Bolts	98①
Modulator retaining bolt	20
Mount To Bracket Nut	35
Oil Pan Bolts	12
Park/Neutral Switch Bolts	21
Shift Control Bracket	18
Shift Control Lever	15
TCC Solenoid Screws	125①
Torque Converter Bolts	46
Transaxle Case Side Cover	125①
Transaxle Cooler Pipe Clip Bolt	35
Transaxle Cooler Pipe To Radiator	13
Valve Body Bolts	125①
Wheel Lug Nuts	100

Continued

TIGHTENING SPECIFICATIONS—Continued

Component	Torque/Ft. Lbs.
Cutlass Supreme, Grand Prix & Regal	
Auxiliary Oil Cooler Bolt	18
Auxiliary Oil Cooler Nut	89 ①
Bracket To Transaxle Front Bolts	35
Bracket To Transaxle Top Bolt	61
Console Shift Control Nut	18
Engine To Transaxle Brace Bolt	35
Fill Tube Bolt	18
Flywheel Cover Bolt	89 ①
Governor Housing Bolts	98 ①
Modulator Retaining Bolt	18
Mount To Support Nut	35
Neutral Start Switch	18
Oil Cooler Line Clip Bolt	35
Oil Cooler Line To Radiator	13
Oil Pan Bolts ②	12
Oil Pan Bolts ③	13
Oil Scoop Retaining Bolt ②	116 ①
Oil Scoop Retaining Bolt ③	71 ①
Shift Control Bracket	18
Shift Control Lever	15
Support Frame Bolt	38
Support Frame Nut	32
TCC Solenoid Screws	125 ①
Throttle Cable Bolt	89 ①
Torque Converter Bolt	44
Transaxle Case Side Cover	125 ①
Transaxle To Engine Bolts	55
Valve Body Bolts	125 ①
Wheel Lug Nuts	100
DeVille, Eldorado, Fleetwood & Seville	
Accumulator Assembly Bolt	20
Case Side Cover Bolts	7–10
Extension Cover Bolts	22–30
Filler Tube Bracket Bolt	15
Flywheel Cover Bolts	10
Frame To Body Bolts	83
Modular Retainer Bolt	15–20
Oil Cooler Line And Tube Nut	24–33
Oil Cooler Line Ballcheck Fitting At Transaxle	34–43

Component	Torque/Ft. Lbs.
DeVille, Eldorado, Fleetwood & Seville-Continued	
Oil Pan Bolt	12–13
Oil Scoop Retaining Bolt	4–8
Shift Control Cable Bracket To Transaxle	18
Speed Sensor To Transaxle Extension Bolt	8
Torque Converter Bolts	46
Wheel Lug Nuts	100
Reatta, Riviera, Toronado & Trofeo	
Accumulator Assembly Attaching Bolt	20
Auxiliary Oil Cooler Mounting Bolt	15
Auxiliary Oil Cooler Pipe Fitting	20
Brace To Engine Bracket Bolt	37
Brace To Transaxle Bolt	33
Bracket To Case Extension Bolt	50
Bracket To Transaxle Mount Nut	30
Case Extension Bolt	27
Case Side Cover Bolt	7–10
Engine Bracket To Engine Bolt	70
Extension Cover Bolt	22–30
Filler Tube Bracket Bolt	15
Flywheel Cover Bolt	115 ①
Frame Nut	30
Frame To Body Bolt	83
Front Side Of Bracket To Transaxle Bolt/Stud	47
Front Top Of Bracket To Transaxle/Engine Bolt	55
Modulator Bolt	15–20
Neutral Start Switch Shift Lever Nut	15
Neutral Start Switch Bolt	20
Oil Cooler Line Ballcheck Fitting At Transaxle	34–43
Oil Cooler Line To Radiator	20
Oil Cooler Line To Transaxle	24–33
Oil Pan Bolt	12–13
Oil Scoop Bolt	44–97 ①
Rear Top Of Bracket To Transaxle Bolt	43
Shift Control Cable Bracket To Transaxle	18
Shift Lever To Neutral Start Switch	15
Speed Sensor To Case Extension Bolt	97 ①
Starter Bolts	32
Torque Converter Bolts	46
Wheel Lug Nuts	100

① —Inch lbs.
② —4T60.
③ —4T60E.

Turbo Hydra-Matic 200-4R Automatic Transmission

INDEX

IDENTIFICATION

The transmission identification number tag is located on the case exterior of the transmission, **Fig. 1.**

DESCRIPTION

This transmission is a fully automatic unit consisting primarily of a three-element hydraulic torque converter with a converter clutch, a compound planetary gear set and an overdrive unit, **Fig. 2.** Five multiple-disc clutches and a band provide the friction elements required to obtain the desired function of the compound planetary gear set and the overdrive unit.

The torque converter couples the engine to the overdrive unit and planetary gears through oil and provides torque multiplication. The combination of the compound planetary gear set and the overdrive unit provides four forward ratios and one reverse. Fully automatic changing of the gear ratios is determined by vehicle speed and engine torque.

The hydraulic system in this transmission is pressurized by a variable capacity vane type pump to provide the working pressure required to operate the friction elements and automatic controls.

TROUBLESHOOTING

OIL LEAK

1. Inspect oil pan for the following:
   a. Bolts incorrectly torqued.
   b. Improperly installed or damaged pan gasket.
2. Inspect filler pipe for damaged or missing multi-lip seal.
3. Ensure filler pipe bracket is positioned correctly.
4. Inspect throttle valve cable for dam-

TRANSMISSION I.D. NAMEPLATE LOCATION

Copyrighted Material Reprinted with Permission from Hydra-Matic Div., GM Corp.

Fig. 1 Transmission identification nameplate location

aged, missing or improperly installed lip seal.
5. Check for damaged or improperly installed rear seal assembly.
6. Check for damaged speedometer driven gear O-ring seal.
7. Inspect manual shaft for damaged or improperly installed lip seal.
8. Inspect case for the following:
   a. leaking line pressure tap plug.
   b. Leaking 4th clutch pressure tap plug.
   c. Porosity.
9. Check for damaged intermediate servo O-rings.
10. Inspect oil pump for the following:
    a. Leaking front pump seal.
    b. Loose front pump attaching bolts or damaged or missing bolt seal.
    c. Damaged or cut front pump housing O-ring.
    d. Porous casting.
    e. Converter weld area.
    f. Foreign matter between pump and case or between pump cover and body.
    g. Pump to case gasket improperly positioned.
    h. Pump shy of stock on mounting faces.

i. Breather hole plugged in pump cover.
11. Inspect vent pipe for signs of the following:
    a. Transmission overfilled.
    b. Water in oil.
    c. vent pipe plugged.
12. Check for incorrect fluid level indicator.

NO DRIVE IN DRIVE RANGE

1. Check for correct oil level and/or external leaks.
2. Inspect manual linkage for proper adjustment.
3. Check for the following possible causes of incorrect oil pressure:
   a. Plugged or restricted oil filter.
   b. Cut or missing oil filter seals.
   c. Pump assembly pressure regulator stuck.
   d. Pump rotor tangs damaged by converter.
   e. Porosity in oil filter to pump intake bore.
4. Inspect overdrive unit for the following:
   a. Springs missing in roller clutch.
   b. Rollers galled or missing.
5. Inspect forward clutch for the following:
   a. Piston cracked and/or seals missing or damaged.
   b. Clutch plates burned.
   c. Snap ring out of groove.
   d. Missing or damaged turbine shaft oil seal rings.
   e. Leak in feed circuits.
   f. Pump to case gasket improperly positioned or damaged.
   g. Leaking or missing cup plug in rear of forward clutch shaft clutch apply passage.
6. Inspect lo and reverse roller clutch for the following:

STATOR SHAFT
VANE TYPE PUMP ASSEMBLY
FOURTH CLUTCH
OVERDRIVE PLANETARY GEAR SET
CENTER SUPPORT
OVERRUN CLUTCH
INPUT PLANETARY GEAR SET
LO AND REVERSE CLUTCH HOUSING
OVERDRIVE ROLLER CLUTCH
FORWARD CLUTCH
LO AND REVERSE CLUTCH
LO ROLLER CLUTCH ASSEMBLY
STATOR ROLLER CLUTCH
DIRECT CLUTCH
REACTION PLANETARY GEAR SET
OUTPUT SHAFT
STATOR
SPEEDOMETER DRIVEN GEAR ASSEMBLY
CONVERTER COVER
GOVERNOR ASSEMBLY
PARKING LOCK ACTUATOR ASSEMBLY
OIL FILTER ASSEMBLY
LO AND REVERSE SEAL ASSEMBLY
PRESSURE PLATE
TURBINE
TURBINE SHAFT
CONTROL VALVE ASSEMBLY
DRIVE-2 OIL PIPE
CONVERTER PUMP
INSIDE DETENT LEVER
INTERMEDIATE BAND

Copyrighted Material Reprinted with Permission from Hydra-Matic Div., GM Corp.

Fig. 2   THM 200-4R cross-sectional view

a. Springs missing and/or rollers galled or missing.

HIGH OR LOW OIL PRESSURE

1. Check for binding, disconnected, broken, or improperly adjusted throttle valve cable.
2. Inspect throttle valve assembly for the following:
   a. Damaged or leaking throttle valve assembly.
   b. Throttle lever and bracket assembly binding, disconnected, or improperly positioned.
   c. Throttle valve or plunger valve binding.
3. Check pressure regulator valve for binding.
4. Check throttle valve boost valve for binding.
5. Check for incorrect throttle valve boost valve, causing low oil pressure only.
6. Check reverse boost valve for binding.
7. Check for disconnected or improperly positioned manual valve.
8. Check pressure relief valve for missing ball or damaged spring.
9. Check oil pump for the following:
   a. Slide stuck and/or slide seal damaged or missing.
   b. Decrease air bleed orifice missing

or damaged, causing high oil pressure.
   c. Decrease air bleed orifice plugged, causing low oil pressure.
10. Check throttle valve limit valve for binding.
11. Check line bias valve for binding in open position, causing high oil pressure or binding in closed position, causing low oil pressure.
12. Check for incorrect orifices or passages in control valve assembly spacer plate and case.

1-2 SHIFT ONLY AT FULL THROTTLE ONLY

1. Check for binding, disconnected, broken, or improperly adjusted throttle valve cable.
2. Check for binding or disconnected throttle lever and bracket assembly.
3. Check for binding, improperly positioned, or disconnected throttle valve exhaust ball or No. 5 ball, allowing No. 5 ball to seal, causing full throttle valve pressure regardless of throttle valve position.
4. Check for binding throttle valve and plunger.
5. Check for leaking, damaged, or incorrectly installed valve body gaskets on control valve assembly.
6. Check for case porosity.

NO 1-2 SHIFT

1. Inspect governor and/or governor

feed passages for the following:
   a. Plugged governor oil feed orifice in spacer plate.
   b. Missing ball(s) in governor assembly.
   c. Leaking or missing inner governor cover rubber O-ring seal.
   d. Missing or damaged governor shaft seal.
   e. Governor driven gear stripped.
   f. Governor weights binding on pin.
   g. Governor driven gear not engaged with governor shaft.
2. Inspect control valve assembly for the following:
   a. 1-2 shift, Lo 1st/detent or 1-2 throttle valve stuck in downshift position.
   b. Improperly positioned spacer plate gaskets.
3. Inspect case for the following:
   a. Porosity in case channels or undrilled 2nd oil feed hole.
   b. Excessive leakage between case bore and intermediate band apply rings.
   c. Intermediate band anchor pin missing or disconnected from band.
   d. Broken or missing band.
4. Inspect intermediate servo assembly for the following:
   a. Missing servo cover oil seal ring.
   b. Porosity in servo cover, inner or outer piston.
   c. Incorrect intermediate band apply

pin.
d. Incorrect usage of cover and piston.
5. Inspect 1-2 accumulator for the following:
a. Loose housing bolts.
b. Damaged housing face.
c. Missing or damaged accumulator plate.

NO 2-3 SHIFT

1. Inspect control valve assembly and spacer plate for the following:
a. 2-3 shift valve or 2-3 throttle valve stuck in the downshift position.
b. Leaking, damaged or incorrectly installed valve body gaskets.
c. Reverse/3rd check ball not seating, damaged or missing.
2. Inspect case channels for porosity.
3. Inspect center support for the following:
a. Direct clutch feed passage in center support plugged or not drilled through.
b. Damaged steel oil seal rings on center support.
4. Inspect direct clutch for the following:
a. Inner oil seal ring on piston damaged or missing.
b. Center oil seal ring on direct clutch hub damaged or missing.
c. Check ball and/or retainer damaged or missing from direct clutch piston.
d. Damaged or missing direct clutch piston or housing.
e. Damaged or missing direct clutch plates.
f. Direct clutch backing plate snap ring not in groove.
g. Release spring guide improperly located, preventing piston check ball from seating in retainer.
5. Inspect intermediate servo assembly (third clutch accumulator oil passages) for the following:
a. Broken or missing servo to case oil seal ring on intermediate servo piston.
b. Intermediate servo and/or capsule missing or damaged.
c. Exhaust hole in case between servo piston seal rings plugged, or not drilled through.
d. Bleed orifice cup plug missing from intermediate servo pocket in case.

NO REVERSE OR SLIPS IN REVERSE

1. Check for binding or improperly adjusted throttle valve cable.
2. Check for improperly adjusted manual linkage.
3. Check for binding throttle valve.
4. Check for binding throttle valve limit valve.
5. Check for binding line bias valve.
6. Inspect reverse boost valve for binding in pressure regulator bore.
7. Check for missing reverse/3rd or Lo/reverse check ball, or damaged seat in spacer plate.
8. Inspect reverse clutch for the following:

a. Cracked piston or missing inner or outer seals.
b. Clutch plates burned.
c. Missing or damaged reverse oil seal in case.
d. Missing clutch or wave plate.
9. Inspect center support for the following:
a. Loose or missing attaching bolts.
b. Passages blocked or not drilled through.
c. Porosity.
10. Inspect direct clutch for the following:
a. Cracked housing or piston.
b. Missing or damaged inner or outer piston seal.
c. Missing or damaged check ball in housing or piston.
d. Plates burned.
11. Check spacer plate for plugged Lo/Reverse overrun clutch orifice.

DRIVE IN NEUTRAL

1. Check for improperly adjusted or disconnected manual linkage.
2. Inspect forward clutch for the following:
a. Clutch does not release.
b. Plates burned together.
3. Inspect case for cross leakage to forward clutch passage.

SLIPPING 1-2 SHIFT

1. Check for low oil level.
2. Check spacer plate and gaskets for damaged or incorrectly installed gaskets.
3. Inspect accumulator valve for the following:
a. Valve sticking in valve body causing low 1-2 accumulator pressure.
b. Weak or missing spring.
4. Inspect 1-2 accumulator piston for the following:
a. Leaking seal, spring broken or missing.
b. Leak between piston and pin.
c. Binding piston.
d. Damaged piston bore.
5. Inspect intermediate band apply pin for the following:
a. Incorrect selection of apply pin.
b. Excessive leakage between apply pin and case.
c. Apply pin feed hole not completely drilled.
6. Inspect intermediate servo assembly for the following:
a. Porosity in piston.
b. Damaged or missing cover to servo oil seal ring.
c. Leak between servo apply pin and case.
7. Check for improperly adjusted throttle valve cable.
8. Check for binding throttle valve, causing low throttle valve pressure.
9. Check for binding throttle valve limit valve.
10. Check for sticking line bias valve, causing low line pressure.

11. Check for worn or burned intermediate band.
12. Inspect case for porosity in 2nd clutch passage.

ROUGH 1-2 SHIFT

1. Check for binding or improperly adjusted throttle cable.
2. Check for binding throttle valve or throttle valve plunger.
3. Check for binding throttle valve limit valve.
4. Check for binding accumulator valve.
5. Check for binding line bias valve.
6. Inspect intermediate servo assembly for the following:
a. Incorrect apply pin selection.
b. Damaged or missing servo piston to case oil seal ring.
c. Bleed cup plug missing in case.
7. Inspect 1-2 accumulator for the following:
a. Oil ring damaged.
b. Piston stuck.
c. Broken or missing spring.
d. Damaged bore.
8. Check for missing or sticking 1-2 shift check ball No. 8.

SLIPPING 2-3 SHIFT

1. Check for low oil level.
2. Check for improperly adjusted throttle valve cable.
3. Check for binding throttle valve.
4. Inspect spacer plate and gaskets for the following:
a. Direct clutch orifice partially blocked in spacer plate.
b. Gaskets improperly positioned or damaged.
5. Inspect intermediate servo assembly for the following:
a. Damaged or missing servo to case oil seal ring.
b. Damaged piston or servo bore.
c. Intermediate servo orifice bleed cup plug in case missing.
d. Case porous in servo bore area.
6. Inspect direct clutch for the following:
a. Circuit feed channels in case porous.
b. Loose case to support bolts causing leakage.
c. Cracked direct clutch piston or housing.
d. Cut or missing piston seals.
e. Burned clutch plates.
f. Check ball in piston and/or housing missing, damaged, or leaking.
g. Check ball capsule damaged.
h. Release spring guide improperly located preventing check ball from seating in piston.
7. Inspect center support for the following:
a. Channels cross feeding, leaking, or restricted.
b. Damaged or missing oil seal rings.

ROUGH 2-3 SHIFT

1. Check for missing or improperly positioned throttle valve cable.

2. Check for throttle valve or throttle valve plunger binding.
3. Check for throttle valve limit valve binding.
4. Check for intermediate servo assembly exhaust hole not drilled out, or plugged between intermediate servo piston seals, preventing intermediate servo piston from completing its stroke.
5. Check for missing or improperly positioned 3-2 exhaust check ball No. 4.
6. Check for missing or improperly positioned 3rd accumulator check ball No. 2.

SLIPPING 3-4 SHIFT

1. Check for low oil level.
2. Inspect control valve assembly and spacer plate for the following:
   a. Spacer plate or gaskets damaged or incorrectly installed.
   b. Accumulator valve sticking, causing low 3-4 accumulator pressure.
   c. Weak or missing accumulator valve spring.
3. Inspect 3-4 accumulator for the following:
   a. Piston stuck.
   b. Damaged bore or oil ring.
4. Inspect Center support for the following:
   a. Porosity.
   b. Loose attaching bolts.
5. Check fourth clutch piston surface or seals for damage.
6. Check for improper fourth clutch plate usage.
7. Check for burned fourth clutch plates.
8. Inspect case for the following:
   a. Porosity.
   b. 1-2 accumulator housing bolts loose.
   c. 3-4 accumulator piston seal damaged.
   d. 3-4 accumulator leaking between piston and pin.
   e. 3-4 accumulator bore damaged.

ROUGH 3-4 SHIFT

1. Check for improperly positioned or missing throttle valve cable.
2. Inspect throttle valve and plunger for binding.
3. Inspect throttle valve limit valve for binding.
4. Check for 3-4 accumulator piston stuck or bore damage.
5. Check for fourth clutch piston binding.

NO CONVERTER CLUTCH APPLICATION

1. Check for the following electrical problems:
   a. 12 volts not being supplied to solenoid.
   b. Defective solenoid.
   c. Damaged electrical connector.
   d. Defective pressure switch.
   e. Wire grounded.
   f. Also, refer to "Computer Controlled Converter Clutch Diagnosis" section for electrical diagnosis.

2. Check control valve assembly and spacer plate for a sticking converter clutch shift valve or throttle valve.
3. Inspect pump assembly for the following:
   a. Plugged converter signal oil orifice in pump.
   b. Damaged or missing solenoid O-ring.
   c. Orifice cup plug missing in oil cooler passage in pump.
   d. Damaged or improperly positioned pump to case gasket.
   e. Converter clutch apply valve stuck.
   f. Cup plug missing from apply passage.

ROUGH CONVERTER CLUTCH APPLICATION

1. Check for damaged converter clutch pressure plate.
2. Check for damaged or missing check ball in end of turbine shaft.

NO CONVERTER CLUTCH RELEASE

1. Check for converter clutch apply valve stuck.
2. Check for damaged converter.
3. Check for missing cup plug in pump release passage.
4. Check for missing or damaged turbine shaft end seal.
5. Check for hole not drilled through on turbine shaft.

NO 3-4 SHIFT

1. Inspect control valve assembly and spacer plate for the following:
   a. 3-4 shift valve or 3-4 throttle valve stuck.
   b. Plugged spacer plate orifice.
2. Inspect center support for the following:
   a. Oil passages plugged, or not drilled through.
   b. Loose or missing attaching bolts.
3. Check for cracked or damaged fourth clutch piston.
4. Check for damaged, missing or improperly assembled fourth clutch piston seals.
5. Check for improper fourth clutch plate usage.
6. Check for burned fourth clutch plates.
7. Check overrun clutch plates for binding.
8. Inspect Case for the following:
   a. Porosity.
   b. Orifice cup plug missing in 3-4 accumulator passage.
   c. Leakage between accumulator piston and pin.
   d. 3-4 accumulator bore damaged.

NO MANUAL 3RD OR 2ND

1. Inspect turbine shaft and overrun clutch for the following:
   a. D-3 oil passage not drilled or plugged in turbine shaft.
   b. D-3 oil passage not drilled through in overrun clutch hub.

c. Oil seals missing or damaged in overrun clutch piston.
d. Overrun clutches burned.
e. Overrun clutch backing plate snap ring out of groove.

NO ENGINE BRAKING IN MANUAL LO/1ST GEAR

1. Check for improperly adjusted manual linkage.
2. Inspect control valve assembly and spacer plate for the following:
   a. D-3 orifice in spacer plate plugged.
   b. Valve body gaskets leaking, damaged or incorrectly installed.
   c. D-2 oil pipe leaking or out of position.
   d. Lo overrun clutch valve binding in valve body.
   e. Lo/Reverse check ball No. 10 improperly positioned or missing.
   f. Lo/Detent check ball No. 9 improperly positioned or missing.
   g. PT/D-3 check ball No. 3 improperly positioned or missing.
3. Inspect turbine shaft and overrun clutch for the following:
   a. D-3 oil passage in turbine shaft plugged or not drilled through.
   b. D-3 oil passage not drilled through in overrun clutch hub.
   c. Missing or damaged oil seals in the overrun clutch piston.
   d. Burned overrun clutches.
   e. Overrun clutch backing plate snap ring out of groove.
4. Inspect case for porosity.
5. Inspect Lo/Reverse clutch assembly for the following:
   a. Broken or missing piston seals.
   b. Clutch housing snap ring out of case.
   c. Cracked or porous piston or housing.
   d. Missing or damaged cup plug or rubber seal between case and Lo/Reverse clutch housing.

NO ENGINE BRAKING IN MANUAL 2ND/2ND GEAR

1. Check for improperly adjusted manual linkage.
2. Inspect control valve assembly and spacer plate for the following:
   a. Valve body gaskets leaking, damaged or improperly installed.
   b. D-2 oil pipe leaking or out of position.
   c. Plugged D-3 orifice in spacer plate.
   d. PT/D-3 check ball No. 3 improperly positioned or missing.
3. Inspect case for porosity.
4. Inspect intermediate servo assembly for missing or damaged servo cover to case oil seal ring.
5. Check for intermediate band off anchor pin.
6. Check for broken or burned intermediate band.
7. Inspect turbine shaft and overrun clutch for the following:
   a. D-3 oil passage in turbine shaft plugged or not drilled through.

b. D-3 oil passage not drilled through in overrun clutch hub.

c. Missing or damaged oil seals in the overrun clutch piston.

d. Burned overrun clutches.

e. Overrun clutch backing plate snap ring out of groove.

NO ENGINE BRAKING IN MANUAL 3RD/3RD GEAR

1. Check for improperly adjusted manual linkage.
2. Inspect control valve assembly and spacer plate for the following:
   a. Valve body gaskets leaking, damaged or improperly installed.
   b. Plugged D-3 orifice in spacer plate.
   c. PT/D-3 check ball No. 3 improperly positioned or missing.
3. Inspect turbine shaft and overrun clutch for the following:
   a. D-3 oil passage in turbine shaft plugged or not drilled through.
   b. D-3 oil passage not drilled through in overrun clutch hub.
   c. Missing or damaged oil seals in the overrun clutch piston.
   d. Burned overrun clutches.
   e. Overrun clutch backing plate snap ring out of groove.

WILL NOT HOLD IN PARK

1. Check for improperly adjusted manual linkage.
2. Inspect internal linkage for the following:
   a. Parking pawl binding in case.
   b. Damaged actuator rod, spring or plunger.
   c. Broken parking pawl.
   d. Loose or damaged parking bracket.
   e. Missing or improperly positioned manual shaft to case pin.
3. Inspect inside detent lever and pin assembly for loose nut or worn or damaged hole in lever.
4. Inspect manual detent roller and spring assembly for the following:
   a. Roller assembly to valve body bolt loose.
   b. Pin or roller damaged, improperly positioned or missing.

NO PART THROTTLE DOWNSHIFTS

1. Check for binding throttle valve.
2. Check for throttle valve limit valve binding.
3. Check for spacer plate hole plugged or not drilled through.
4. Check for improperly positioned or damaged valve body gaskets.
5. Check for throttle valve modulator downshift valve stuck.
6. Check for improperly set throttle valve cable.

NO PART THROTTLE 4-3 DOWNSHIFT

On selected models with a part throttle passage in the throttle plunger bushing.

1. Check for throttle plunger bushing passages not open.
2. Check for 3-4 throttle valve bushing passages not open.
3. Check for PT/D-3 check ball No. 3 incorrectly positioned or missing.
4. Check for improperly positioned or damaged valve body gaskets.
5. Check for improperly set throttle valve cable.
6. Check for throttle valve limit valve binding.

LOW OR HIGH SHIFT POINTS

1. Check for binding or improperly adjusted throttle valve cable.
2. Check for throttle valve limit valve binding.
3. Check for throttle valve binding.
4. Check for throttle valve modulator upshift valve binding.
5. Check for throttle valve modulator downshift valve binding.
6. Check for improperly positioned, leaking or damaged valve body gaskets.
7. Check for throttle valve plunger binding.
8. Check for 1-2, 2-3 or 3-4 throttle valves binding in bushings.
9. Check for pressure regulator valve binding.
10. Check for throttle valve exhaust ball No. 5 and lifter improperly positioned, disconnected, or missing.
11. Inspect throttle lever and bracket assembly for the following:
    a. Binding, disconnected or loose at mounting valve body bolt.
    b. Not positioned at throttle valve plunger bushing pin locator.
12. Check for broken or missing governor shaft to cover seal ring.
13. Check for broken or missing governor cover gasket.
14. Inspect case for porosity.

MAINTENANCE

To check fluid, drive vehicle for at least 15 minutes to bring fluid to operating temperature (200°F). With vehicle on a level surface and engine idling in Park and parking brake applied, the level on the dipstick should be at the "F" mark. To bring the fluid level from the ADD mark to the FULL mark requires 1 pint of fluid. If vehicle cannot be driven sufficiently to bring fluid to operating temperature, the level on the dipstick should be between the two dimples on the dipstick with fluid temperature at 70°F.

If additional fluid is required, use only Dexron II automatic transmission fluid.

An early change to a darker color from the usual red color and or a strong odor that is usually associated with overheated fluid is normal and should not be considered as a positive sign of required maintenance of unit failure.

When adding fluid, do not overfill, as foaming and loss of fluid through the vent may occur as the fluid heats up. Also, if fluid level is too low, complete loss of drive may occur especially when cold, which can cause transmission failure.

Every 100,000 miles, the oil should be drained, the oil pan removed, the screen cleaned and fresh fluid added. For vehicles subjected to more severe use such as heavy city traffic especially in hot weather, prolonged periods of idling or towing, this maintenance should be performed every 15,000 miles.

DRAINING BOTTOM PAN

1. Remove front and side oil pan attaching bolts, then loosen the rear oil pan attaching bolts.
2. Carefully pry oil pan loose and allow fluid to drain into a suitable container.
3. Remove the oil pan and gasket, then remove the screen attaching bolts and remove screen.
4. Thoroughly clean oil screen and oil pan with solvent.
5. Install oil screen using a new gasket, then install oil pan using a new gasket and **torque** attaching bolts to 97 inch lbs.
6. Add approximately 3 quarts of fluid, then with engine idling and parking brake applied, move selector lever through each range and return selector lever to PARK.
7. Check fluid level and add fluid as required to bring level between the two dimples on the dipstick.

ADJUSTMENTS

THROTTLE VALVE CABLE, ADJUST

1. With engine Off, depress and hold down locking tab, then move slider until it stops against fitting, **Fig. 1.**
2. Release locking tab, then rotate throttle lever to its full travel position. **Slider must ratchet toward lever when lever is rotated to its full travel position.**
3. Check cable for sticking or binding, then road test vehicle and ensure proper operation.

MANUAL LINKAGE, ADJUST

Column Mounted

1. Position transmission shift lever in Neutral.
2. Position transmission manual valve lever in Neutral detent.
3. With clamp spring washer and screw assembled onto equalizer lever and control rod, hold clamp against equalizer lever, then snug tighten clamp screw against control rod, **Fig. 3.**

Console Mounted

1. Position console shift lever in Park position.
2. Position transmission manual valve lever in Park detent.
3. Position pin, **Fig. 4,** until pin fits loosely in transmission lever, then tighten attaching nut.

TURBO HYDRA-MATIC 200-4R AUTOMATIC TRANSMISSION

Fig. 3   Column mounted shift linkage adjustment

IN-VEHICLE REPAIRS

INTERMEDIATE SERVO, REPLACE

1. Raise and support vehicle.
2. Remove four catalytic converter heat shield screws, then position heat shield aside.
3. Install servo cover depressor tool No. J-29714 or equivalent, using two oil pan screws.
4. Depress servo cover, then remove retaining ring.
5. Remove servo cover, then the O-ring. O-ring may be located in the case.
6. Remove the servo assembly.
7. Reverse procedure to install.

SPEEDOMETER DRIVEN GEAR, REPLACE

1. Disconnect speedometer cable.
2. Remove bolt, retainer, speedometer driven gear and the O-ring seal.
3. Reverse procedure to install.

REAR OIL SEAL, REPLACE

1. Remove propeller shaft.
2. Pry seal from extension housing with a suitable tool.
3. Drive new oil seal into extension housing, using a suitable tool.
4. Install propeller shaft.

VALVE BODY, REPLACE

1. Remove transmission oil pan and filter.
2. Remove screw and washer securing T.V. cable to the transmission.
3. Disconnect electrical connectors.

4. Remove bolts securing the electrical connector clips.
5. Remove bolts securing the solenoid assembly, then solenoid with O-ring.
6. Disconnect case electrical connector, then remove O-ring seal.
7. If equipped, remove temperature switch and attaching bolt.
8. Remove pressure switch, then the T.V. lever and bracket assembly, from cable link.
9. Remove T.V. lever bracket assembly, then manual detent roller and spring assembly.
10. Remove the signal oil pipe retainer and signal pipe.
11. Support the control valve assembly, then remove the remaining valve body bolts and control valve assembly. **Care must be taken when removing the control valve assembly to prevent loss of three check balls located in the assembly. Do Not carry assembly by attached pipe.**
12. Remove the check balls.
13. Lay control valve assembly down with the sensor plate side up. Do not damage the switches.
14. Reverse procedure to install. **Torque** valve body bolts to 11 ft. lbs.

1-2 & 3-4 ACCUMULATOR, REPLACE

1. Remove transmission pan attaching bolts, then the pan.
2. Remove housing to valve body bolts.
3. Remove housing and pin assembly.
4. Remove 1-2 accumulator piston from housing pin and assembly. Apply low air pressure, 3 psi, to orifice housing.
5. Remove the accumulator piston seal ring from the 1-2 accumulator piston.
6. Remove the spacer plate and gaskets.
7. Remove the 3-4 accumulator piston, spring and pin.
8. Remove piston seal ring from piston.
9. Reverse procedure to install.

GOVERNOR, REPLACE

1. Drain transmission oil pan.
2. Remove oil pan and filter.
3. Remove governor attaching bolts, cover and gasket. The governor may come out with the cover. Also, it may be necessary to rotate output shaft counterclockwise while removing governor.
4. Reverse procedure to install.

TRANSMISSION REPLACE

1. Disconnect battery ground cable and remove air cleaner.

Fig. 4   Console mounted shift linkage adjustment

2. Disconnect throttle valve cable from carburetor.
3. Remove transmission oil level dipstick. Remove upper bolt on dipstick tube.
4. Raise and support vehicle.
5. Mark driveshaft and companion flange for reference during installation, then remove driveshaft.
6. Disconnect speedometer cable and manual shift linkage from transmission.
7. Disconnect torque converter clutch solenoid electrical connector.
8. Remove flywheel undercover. Mark flywheel and converter for reference during installation. Remove three flywheel to converter attaching bolts.
9. Remove catalytic converter support bracket bolts and the tunnel strap.
10. Remove transmission crossmember to transmission mount bolts. Remove transmission crossmember to frame bolts.
11. Support transmission with a jack, then move crossmember rearward.
12. Lower transmission slightly and disconnect throttle valve cable and oil cooler lines.
13. Support engine with a jack, then remove engine to transmission mounting bolts.
14. Lower jack and remove transmission from vehicle. Use caution not to drop torque converter as transmission is removed. Install a converter holding tool to secure converter.
15. Reverse procedure to install.

TIGHTENING SPECIFICATIONS

Component	Torque/Ft. Lbs.
Accumulator 1-2 Housing Bolts	8
Catalytic Converter Bracket	15
Center Support Bolts	18

Component	Torque/Ft. Lbs.
Converter Cover Housing Bolts	7
Converter To Flex Plate Bolts	46
Cooler Connector	28

Continued

Component	Torque/Ft. Lbs.
Direct Clutch Pressure Take-Off	7
Equalizer Lever To Control Rod	21
Filler Tube To Transmission Bolt	35
Floor Pan Reinforcement	20
Fluid Level Indicator Tube Brace To Transmission	7
Governor Cover To Case	18
Line Pressure Take-Off	7
Low Gear Block Out To Transmission Oil Pan Screw	13
Manual Shaft Hex Nut	23
Mount To Transmission Support Nut	35
Oil Cooler Lines To Transmission	28
Oil Cooler Pipes To Radiator Connector	20
Oil Pan Bolts	97 ①

Component	Torque/Ft. Lbs.
Oil Pump Cover To Pump Body	18
Oil Pump To Case	18
Parking Pawl Lock Bracket Bolt	18
Pressure Switch	10
Propeller Shaft Strap Bolts	16
Solenoid To Case	10
Speedometer Retainer To Case	10
Stator Shaft To Pump Cover	10
Starter Bolts	30
Transmission Support To Frame	25
Transmission To Engine Bolts	35
T.V. Cable To Case	7
Valve Body Bolts	11

① —Inch lbs.

Turbo Hydra-Matic 4L60 (700-R4) Automatic Transmission

INDEX

IDENTIFICATION

The 700-R4 transmission has a metal identification nameplate attached to the case exterior or a stamped identification number on the pan rail, **Fig. 1.**

DESCRIPTION

The model 700-R4, **Fig. 2,** is a fully automatic transmission consisting of a 3-element hydraulic torque converter with the addition of a converter clutch.

Also two planetary gear sets, five multiple-disc type clutches, two roller or one-way clutches and a band are used which provide the friction elements to produce four forward speeds, the last of which is overdrive.

The torque converter, through oil, couples the engine power to the gear sets and

TRANSMISSION I.D. NAMEPLATE LOCATION

Copyrighted Material Reprinted with Permission from Hydra-Matic Div., GM Corp.

Fig. 1   Transmission identification number location

hydraulically provides additional torque multiplication when required. Also, through the converter clutch, the converter drive and driven members operate as one unit

when applied, providing mechanical drive from the engine through the transmission.

The gear ratio changes are fully automatic in relation to the vehicle speed and engine torque. Vehicle speed and engine torque are directed to the transmission providing the proper gear ratio for maximum efficiency and performance at all throttle openings.

A hydraulic system pressurized by a variable capacity vane-type pump, provides the operating pressure required for the operation of the friction elements and automatic controls.

TROUBLESHOOTING
OIL PRESSURE HIGH OR LOW

1. Oil pump assembly pressure regulator valve stuck.

STATOR SHAFT — REVERE INPUT CLUTCH — OVERRUN CLUTCH — FORWARD ROLLER CLUTCH ASSEMBLY — INPUT PLANETARY GEAR SET — LO AND REVERSE CLUTCH

VANE TYPE PUMP ASSEMBLY — INPUT CLUTCH HOUSING — FORWARD CLUTCH — 3-4 CLUTCH — LO AND REVERSE CLUTCH SUPPORT — LO ROLLER CLUTCH ASSEMBLY

STATOR — REACTION PLANETARY GEAR SET

STATOR ROLLER CLUTCH

CONVERTER COVER — OUTPUT SHAFT

PRESSURE PLATE

CONVERTER TURBINE — TURBINE SHAFT — 2-4 BAND — REACTION SUN SHELL — GOVERNOR DRIVEN GEAR — SPEEDOMETER DRIVEN GEAR ASSEMBLY

CONVERTER PUMP — INSIDE DETENT LEVER — OIL FILTER ASSEMBLY — CONTROL VALVE ASSEMBLY

Copyrighted Material Reprinted with Permission from Hydra-Matic Div., GM Corp.

Fig. 2   700-R4 automatic transmission

2. Oil pump assembly pressure regulator valve spring damaged.
3. Oil pump rotor guide missing or incorrectly installed.
4. Oil pump rotor cracked or damaged.
5. T.V. valve and reverse boost valve or bushing stuck, damaged or incorrectly installed.
6. Orifice hole in pressure regulator valve plugged.
7. Oil pump assembly slide sticking or excessive rotor clearance.
8. Oil pump pressure relief ball not sealed or damaged.
9. Oil pump cover or body porous.
10. Incorrect pump cover or defective pump faces.
11. Oil filter intake pipe and filter body restricted or cracked.
12. Oil filter O-ring seal missing, cut or damaged.
13. T.V. exhaust ball stuck or damaged.
14. Throttle lever and bracket assembly or throttle link binding, damaged or incorrectly installed.
15. Valve body manual valve scored or damaged.
16. Valve body spacer plate or gaskets incorrect, damaged or incorrectly installed.
17. Valve body throttle valve sticking, sleeve rotated in bore or retaining pin not seated.
18. T.V. limit valve, line bias valve, modulated downshift valve or 2-3 shift valve stuck.
19. Valve body check balls missing or incorrectly installed.

HIGH OR LOW SHIFT POINTS

1. T.V. cable binding or incorrectly adjusted.
2. T.V. exhaust ball stuck or damaged.
3. Throttle lever and bracket assembly binding, damaged or incorrectly installed.
4. Sticking oil pump slide, pressure regulator valve or T.V. boost valve.
5. Valve body modulated T.V. up or down valves sticking.
6. T.V. limit valve, throttle valve or plunger sticking.
7. Valve body spacer plate or gaskets damaged or incorrect.

FIRST SPEED ONLY—NO UPSHIFT

1. Governor valve sticking.
2. Governor driven gear loose or damaged.
3. Governor driven gear retaining pin missing.
4. Nicks or burrs on output shaft, governor sleeve or case bore.
5. Governor support pin in case too long or short.
6. Governor weights or springs missing, binding or damaged.
7. 1-2 shift valve sticking.
8. Valve body spacer plate or gaskets damaged or incorrectly installed.
9. Case to valve body face not flat or damaged.
10. Governor screen restricted or damaged.

11. Restricted or blocked 2-4 servo assembly apply passages.
12. Nicks or burrs on 2-4 servo assembly pin or pin bore in case.
13. Missing or damaged 2-4 servo assembly piston or pin seals.
14. Fourth servo piston installed backwards.
15. 2-4 band assembly worn or damaged.
16. 2-4 band assembly anchor pin not engaged.

SLIPS IN FIRST GEAR

1. Forward clutch assembly plates worn.
2. Porosity or damage in forward clutch piston.
3. Forward clutch piston inner and outer seals missing, cut or damaged.
4. Input housing to forward clutch housing O-ring seal missing, cut or damaged.
5. Forward clutch housing damaged.
6. Forward clutch housing retainer and ball assembly not sealing or damaged.
7. Turbine shaft seals missing, cut or damaged.
8. Valve body accumulator valve stuck.
9. Valve body face not flat, damaged lands or interconnected passages.
10. Valve body spacer plate or gaskets incorrect, damaged or incorrectly installed.
11. T.V. cable binding or broken.
12. Damaged ring grooves on 1-2 accumulator piston.
13. 1-2 accumulator piston seal missing, cut or damaged.

14. 1-2 accumulator cover gasket missing or damaged.
15. Leak between 1-2 accumulator piston and pin.
16. Broken 1-2 accumulator spring.
17. Fourth servo piston installed backwards.
18. Incorrect oil pressure. Refer to "High Or Low Oil Pressure."

1-2 SHIFT SPEED HIGH OR LOW

1. T.V. cable binding, broken or incorrectly adjusted.
2. Faulty governor assembly. Refer to "First Speed Only — No Upshift."
3. Throttle lever and bracket assembly damaged, binding or incorrectly installed.
4. T.V. link missing, binding or damaged.
5. T.V. exhaust check ball and T.V. plunger sticking.
6. Valve body or oil pump assembly face not flat.

1-2 SHIFT SLIPPING OR ROUGH

1. Throttle lever and bracket assembly incorrectly installed or damaged.
2. T.V. cable damaged.
3. Throttle valve sticking.
4. T.V. bushing turned in its bore.
5. 1-2 shift valve train stuck.
6. Valve body assembly gaskets or spacer plate incorrect, damaged or incorrectly installed.
7. T.V. limit valve, line bias valve or accumulator valve stuck.
8. Valve body face not flat.
9. 2-4 servo assembly apply pin too long or short.
10. 2-4 servo seals or O-ring seals missing, cut or damaged.
11. 2-4 servo assembly bore damaged.
12. Restricted or missing 2-4 servo assembly oil passages.
13. Porosity in 1-2 accumulator housing or piston.
14. Second accumulator piston seal or groove damaged.
15. Nicks or burrs in 1-2 accumulator housing.
16. 2-4 band worn or incorrectly installed.
17. Oil pump assembly faces not flat.

NO 2-3 SHIFT OR 2-3 SHIFT SLIPPING, ROUGH OR HUNTING

1. Internal converter damage.
2. Governor valve stuck.
3. Governor assembly drive gear retaining pin missing or loose.
4. Governor weights binding.
5. Governor drive gear damaged.
6. Governor support pin in case too long or short.
7. Oil pump stator shaft sleeve scored or improperly installed.
8. Accumulator valve, throttle valve, T.V. limit valve or 2-3 valve train stuck.
9. Valve body spacer plate or gaskets incorrect, damaged or incorrectly installed.

10. Forward or 3-4 clutch plates worn.
11. Excessive clutch plate travel.
12. Cut or damaged piston seals in input housing assembly.
13. Porosity in 3-4 clutch housing or piston.
14. 3-4 piston check ball stuck, damaged or incorrectly sealing.
15. Restricted input housing assembly apply passages.
16. Forward clutch piston retainer and ball assembly not seating.
17. Input housing assembly sealing balls loose or missing.
18. Third accumulator retainer and ball assembly not seating.
19. Second apply piston seals missing, cut or damaged.
20. 2-4 servo pin seals missing, cut or damaged.

NO 3-4 SHIFT OR ROUGH 3-4 SHIFT

1. Governor weights bonding.
2. Governor valve stuck.
3. Governor drive gear retaining pin missing or loose.
4. Governor drive gear damaged.
5. Governor support pin in case too long or short.
6. Oil pump assembly faces not flat.
7. Pump cover retainer and ball assembly missing or damaged.
8. Accumulator valve, throttle valve, T.V. limit valve, 3-2 control valve, 1-2 shift valve train or 2-3 shift valve train stuck.
9. Manual valve link bent or damaged.
10. Valve body assembly spacer plates or gaskets incorrect, damaged or incorrectly installed.
11. Incorrect 2-4 servo assembly band apply pin.
12. Missing or damaged 2-4 servo seals.
13. Porosity in 2-4 servo pistons, cover and case.
14. Damaged 2-4 servo piston seal grooves.
15. Plugged or missing orifice cup plug in 2-4 servo assembly.
16. Third accumulator retainer and ball assembly leaking.
17. Porosity in 3-4 accumulator piston or bore.
18. 3-4 accumulator piston seal or seal grooves damaged.
19. Plugged or missing orifice cup plug.
20. Restricted case oil passage.
21. Faulty input housing assembly. Refer to" No 2-3 Shift Or 2-3 Shift Slipping, Rough Or Hunting."
22. 2-4 band assembly worn or incorrectly installed.

NO REVERSE OR SLIPS IN REVERSE

1. 3-4 apply ring stuck in applied position.
2. Forward clutch not releasing.
3. Turbine shaft seals missing, cut or damaged.
4. Manual linkage incorrectly adjusted.
5. Oil pump retainer and ball assembly missing or damaged.
6. Oil pump stator shaft sleeve scored or damaged.

7. Reverse boost valve stuck, damaged or incorrectly installed.
8. Oil pump cup plug missing.
9. Oil pump converter clutch apply valve stuck.
10. Oil pump face not flat or restricted oil passage.
11. 2-3 shift valve stuck.
12. Valve body spacer plate and gaskets incorrect, damaged or incorrectly installed.
13. Reverse input clutch plate worn.
14. Reverse input housing and drum assembly cracked at weld.
15. Reverse input clutch plate retaining ring out of groove.
16. Reverse input clutch return spring assembly retaining ring out of groove.
17. Reverse input clutch seals cut or damaged.
18. Reverse input clutch retainer and ball assembly not sealing.
19. Restricted oil apply passage in reverse input clutch.
20. Lo and reverse clutch plates worn.
21. Lo and reverse clutch plate retaining ring incorrectly installed.
22. Porosity in low and reverse clutch piston.
23. Low and reverse clutch seals damaged or oil apply passage restricted.
24. Case cover plate gasket missing, damaged or incorrectly torqued.

NO PART THROTTLE OR DELAYED DOWNSHIFTS

1. Throttle linkage incorrectly adjusted.
2. 2-4 servo assembly apply pin cut or damaged.
3. 2-4 servo cover retaining ring missing or incorrectly installed.
4. Fourth apply piston damaged or incorrectly installed.
5. 2-4 servo inner housing damaged or incorrectly installed.
6. Governor weights binding.
7. Governor valve stuck.
8. Throttle valve, 3-2 control valve or T.V. modulated downshift valve stuck.
9. T.V. sleeve turned in bore.
10. 4-3 sequence valve body channel blocked.
11. Number 5 check ball missing from valve body.

NO OVERRUN BRAKING — MANUAL 3-2-1

1. Throttle linkage incorrectly adjusted.
2. Throttle valve or 4-3 sequence valve stuck.
3. Number 3 check ball incorrectly installed.
4. Valve body spacer plate and gaskets incorrect, damaged or incorrectly installed.
5. Turbine shaft oil passages plugged or not drilled.
6. Turbine shaft seal rings damaged.
7. Turbine shaft sealing balls loose or missing.
8. Porosity in forward or overrun clutch piston.
9. Overrun piston seals cut or damaged.
10. Overrun piston check ball not seating.

TURBO HYDRA-MATIC 4L60 (700-R4) AUTOMATIC TRANSMISSION

NO CONVERTER CLUTCH APPLY

1. 12 volts not being applied to the transmission.
2. Defective outside electrical connector.
3. Defective inside electrical connector, wiring harness or solenoid.
4. Solenoid shorted or incorrectly grounded.
5. Incorrect or damaged pressure switches.
6. Internal converter damage.
7. Oil pump converter clutch apply valve stuck or incorrectly installed.
8. Oil pump converter clutch apply valve retaining ring incorrectly installed.
9. Oil pump to case gasket incorrectly installed.
10. Oil pump orifice cup plug clogged.
11. Oil pump solenoid O-ring seal cut or damaged.
12. Oil pump orifice cup plug missing from cooler in passage.
13. High or uneven oil pump body to cover bolt torque.
14. Converter clutch shift valve or throttle valve stuck.
15. Turbine shaft O-ring seal cut or damaged.
16. Turbine shaft retainer and ball assembly plugged.

CONVERTER SHUDDER

1. Internal torque converter damage.
2. Converter clutch shift valve stuck.
3. Oil pump converter clutch apply valve stuck.
4. Restricted oil pump oil passage.
5. Crack in oil filter body or restriction in filter neck.
6. Oil filter O-ring seal cut or damaged.
7. Low oil pressure or engine not properly tuned.
8. Turbine shaft O-ring cut or damaged.
9. Turbine shaft retainer and ball assembly damaged.

NO CONVERTER CLUTCH RELEASE

1. Oil pump converter clutch apply valve stuck.
2. Internal torque converter damage.
3. Solenoid grounded.

DRIVES IN NEUTRAL

1. Forward clutch burned or not releasing.
2. Manual linkage disconnected or incorrectly adjusted.
3. Internal leakage in case or case face not flat.

SECOND GEAR START IN DRIVE RANGE

1. Governor valve stuck.
2. Governor support pin too long or missing.
3. Forward sprag clutch assembly installed backwards.

NO PARK

1. Parking linkage actuator rod assembly bent or damaged.

2. Parking linkage actuator rod spring binding or improperly crimped.
3. Parking linkage actuator rod not attached to inside detent lever.
4. Parking linkage bracket damaged or not torqued properly.
5. Inside detent lever not torqued properly.
6. Detent roller improperly installed.
7. Parking pawl binding or damaged.

RATCHETING NOISE

1. Parking pawl return spring weak, damaged or incorrectly installed.

OIL OUT OF THE VENT

1. Chamfer in oil pump body rotor pocket too large.
2. T.V. limit valve stuck.

VIBRATION IN REVERSE & WHINING NOISE IN PARK

1. Broken vane rings in oil pump.

NO DRIVE IN DRIVE RANGE

1. Stator roller clutch not holding.
2. Torque converter not bolted to flex plate.

DELAY IN DRIVE & REVERSE

1. Torque converter drain back.

MAINTENANCE

Fluid level should be checked at every engine oil change. Frequency of change for transmission fluid is dependent on the type of driving conditions in which the vehicle is used. If the transmission is subjected to severe service such as: use in heavy city traffic when the outside temperature regularly reaches 90°F, use in very hilly or mountainous areas, commercial use such as taxi or delivery service, the fluid should be changed every 15,000 miles. Otherwise, change the fluid every 100,000 miles, using Dexron II or equivalent automatic transmission fluid. To check fluid at operating temperature (190°-200°F), which is obtained only after 15 miles of highway-type driving:
1. Apply parking brake and block wheels.
2. Place selector lever in park then start, but do not race, engine. Move selector lever through each range pausing three seconds in each.
3. Check fluid immediately with selector lever in park, engine running at slow idle, and vehicle on level surface. Fluid level should be at full hot mark.

CHANGING FLUID

1. Raise and support vehicle.
2. Place drain pan under transmission oil pan, loosen pan bolts on front of pan, pry carefully with screwdriver to loosen oil pan, and allow fluid to drain.
3. Remove remaining oil pan bolts, oil pan, and gasket.
4. Drain fluid from pan, then clean pan and dry thoroughly with compressed air.

5. Remove oil filter to valve body bolt, then remove filter and gasket, replace with new filter and gasket and install filter attaching bolt.
6. Install new gasket on oil pan, then install oil pan and **torque** bolts to 12 ft. lbs.
7. Lower vehicle and add five quarts of automatic transmission fluid through filler tube.
8. With selector lever in park and parking brake applied, start engine and let idle. Do not race engine.
9. Move selector lever through each range, return to park position, check fluid, and add additional fluid to bring level between dimples on dipstick.

ADDING FLUID TO FILL DRY TRANSMISSION & CONVERTER

1. Add fluid through filler tube until oil level is between add and hot marks on dipstick.
2. Place selector lever in park, depress accelerator to place carburetor on fast idle cam, and move selector lever through each range. Do not race engine.
3. With selector lever in park, engine running at idle (1-3 minutes), and vehicle on level surface, check fluid level and add additional fluid to bring level between dimples on dipstick.

ADJUSTMENTS
MANUAL LINKAGE OR SHIFT CONTROL CABLE, ADJUST
Camaro & Firebird

1. Place transmission control lever in neutral position.
2. Loosen cable attachment nut(s) or bolt(s) at shift lever.
3. Rotate shift lever "clockwise" to park detent and then back to neutral position.
4. **Torque** cable attaching nuts or bolts to 11 ft. lbs. **Control lever must be held out of "Park" position when tightening nut.**
5. Check cable adjustment by rotating transmission control lever through each detent position.

Brougham, Caprice, Custom Cruiser & Roadmaster

1. Loosen swivel clamp screw.
2. Position shift lever in neutral gate.
3. Position transmission lever in neutral detent.
4. While holding swivel clamp flush against equalizer lever, tighten swivel clamp screw, **Fig. 3. Do not exert force in either direction on rod or equalizer lever while tightening swivel clamp screw.**

Corvette

1. Disconnect battery ground cable.
2. Place transmission control lever in neutral position.
3. Loosen cable attachment at shift lever.

Copyrighted Material Reprinted with Permission from Hydra-Matic Div., GM Corp.

Fig. 3   Shift linkage adjustment. Brougham, Caprice, Custom Cruiser & Roadmaster

Copyrighted Material Reprinted with Permission from Hydra-Matic Div., GM Corp.

Fig. 4   T.V. cable & linkage

A	SLIDER AGAINST FITTING (ZERO OR READJUST POSITION)	826 CABLE
B	READJUSTING DIRECTION	832 READJUSTMENT TAB
C	DIRECTION OF CABLE ACTUATING LEVER	833 FITTING
		834 SLIDER

Copyrighted Material Reprinted with Permission from Hydra-Matic Div., GM Corp.

Fig. 6   T.V. cable adjustment

Copyrighted Material Reprinted with Permission from Hydra-Matic Div., GM Corp.

Fig. 5   Throttle lever & bracket assembly

4. Rotate shift lever "clockwise" to park detent and then back to neutral position.
5. **Torque** cable attachment to 15 ft. lbs. **Lever must be held out of park when tightening the nut.**
6. Check cable adjustment by rotating control lever through the detents, reconnect battery ground cable.

THROTTLE VALVE CABLE, ADJUST

The TV cable should not be thought of as an automatic downshift cable. It controls line pressures, shift points, shift feel, part throttle downshifts, and detent downshifts. The function of the cable is similar to the combined functions of a vacuum modulator and detent downshift cable. The TV cable operates throttle lever and bracket assembly, **Figs. 4 and 5.**
1. Stop engine.
2. Depress and hold down readjust tab, **Fig. 6**, move slider through fitting, away from lever assembly, until slider stops against fitting.
3. Release readjust tab, then open throttle lever to its full throttle position to automatically adjust cable.
4. Release throttle lever and check cable for sticking or binding. **The cable may appear to function properly with engine stopped and cold. Recheck cable with engine at normal operating temperature.**
5. Road test vehicle.

IN-VEHICLE REPAIRS
SERVO ASSEMBLY, REPLACE
1991–92 Brougham, Caprice, Custom Cruiser & Roadmaster

1. Raise and support vehicle.
2. Remove floor pan reinforcement, then the catalytic converter heat shield.
3. Remove transmission mount to transmission support attaching nut.
4. Remove transmission support to frame attaching bolts.
5. Using a transmission jack, support, then raise transmission slightly.
6. Remove transmission support, then lower transmission to gain access to servo cover.
7. Remove two oil pan bolts from below servo cover.

8. Install servo cover compressor tool No. J-29714 or equivalent on oil pan flange and depress servo cover.
9. Remove servo cover retaining ring.
10. Remove servo cover and seal ring.
11. Remove servo piston and bore-apply pin assembly.
12. Reverse procedure to install. **Whenever any servo parts are replaced, apply-pin length must be checked.**

Camaro & Firebird

1. Raise and support vehicle.
2. **On 1991-92 models,** remove rear suspension torque arm to transmission attaching bolts.
3. **On 1993 models, remove crossover pipe assembly and catalytic converter hanger assembly.**
4. **On 1991-92 models,** remove propeller shaft as follows:
   a. Using a center punch or suitable equivalent, mark propeller shaft and rear axle yoke for installation reference.
   b. Remove propeller shaft strap bolts and retaining straps.
   c. Slide propeller shaft slip yoke out of the transmission.
5. **On 1993 models, remove propeller shaft as follows:**
   a. Using a center punch or suitable equivalent, mark propeller shaft and pinion gear yoke for installation reference.

A	WASHER, WIRE RETAINING
33	CONNECTOR, ELECTRICAL
96	TUBE, AUXILIARY ACCUMULATOR VALVE
97	CLAMP
374	BOLT, SPECIAL HEX HEAD (M6 X 1 X 16)
375	BOLT, HEX HEAD (M6 X 1 X 35)
376	BOLT, HEX HEAD (M6 X 1 X 45)
377	AUXILIARY ACCUM. VALVE BODY ASM.
710	BRACKET, PARKING LOCK
715	BOLT, PARKING LOCK BRACKET

Copyrighted Material Reprinted with Permission from Hydra-Matic Div., GM Corp.

Fig. 7   Auxiliary valve body replacement

b. If removing a two-piece shaft, remove bolts/screws from center support bearing, then center support bearing and washers from torque arm.
c. Remove four bolts and two retainers.
d. Slide propeller shaft slip yoke out of the transmission.
6. **On 1991-92 models,** remove exhaust hanger and support transmission with suitable lifting device.
7. **On 1993 models,** remove rear axle torque arm, then support transmission with suitable stand.
8. **On all models,** remove transmission upper support and mount.
9. **On 1993 models,** remove catalytic converter heat shield.
10. **On all models,** lower transmission, then remove two oil pan bolts from below servo cover.
11. Install servo cover compressor tool No. J-29714 or equivalent on oil pan flange and depress servo cover.
12. Remove servo cover retaining ring.
13. Remove servo cover and seal ring.
14. Remove servo piston and bore-apply pin assembly.
15. Reverse procedure to install. **Whenever any servo parts are replaced, apply-pin length must be checked.**

Corvette

1. Disconnect battery ground cable.
2. Raise and support vehicle.
3. Remove upper and lower body braces, if equipped.
4. Remove exhaust system.
5. Remove oil pan retaining bolt directly below servo cover.
6. Install servo cover compressor tool No. J29714-A or equivalent, then de-

---

press servo cover and remove retaining ring.
7. Remove cover, seal ring, servo piston and bore apply pin assembly.
8. Reverse procedure to install. **Whenever any servo parts are replaced, apply-pin length must be checked.**

SPEEDOMETER DRIVEN GEAR, REPLACE

Except 1993 Camaro & Firebird

1. Disconnect speedometer cable or P.M. generator electrical connector from transmission.
2. Remove retainer bolt, retainer, P.M. generator (if equipped), speedometer driven gear and O-ring seal.
3. Reverse procedure to install, using new O-ring and adjusting fluid level.

1993 Camaro & Firebird

1. Raise and support vehicle.
2. Remove propeller shaft assembly as follows:
   a. Using a center punch or suitable equivalent, mark propeller shaft and pinion gear yoke for installation reference.
   b. If removing a two-piece shaft, remove bolts/screws from center support bearing, then center support bearing and washers from torque arm.
   c. Remove four bolts and two retainers.
   d. Slide propeller shaft slip yoke out of the transmission.
3. Remove rear axle torque arm assembly.
4. Remove catalytic converter hanger assembly.
5. Remove vehicle speed sensor and speedometer driven gear.
6. Remove extension with seal. Discard and replace seal.
7. Remove sleeve, seal (if necessary), drive gear and clip.
8. Reverse procedure to install.

REAR OIL SEAL, REPLACE

1. Remove driveshaft, and tunnel strap, if equipped.
2. Using suitable tool, pry out lip oil seal.
3. Coat outer casting of new oil seal with suitable sealer and drive into place with seal installer tool No. J-21426.
4. Install tunnel strap if used, then install driveshaft.

GOVERNOR, REPLACE

Except 1993 Camaro and Firebird

1. Raise and support vehicle
2. **On Corvette models,** remove upper and lower body braces, then the complete exhaust system.
3. **On 1991-92 Caprice, Custom Cruiser and Roadmaster models,** proceed as follows:
   a. Remove transmission mount to support nut.
   b. Remove support to frame attaching bolts.
   c. Using a transmission jack, support and raise transmission slightly.

55A	BALL, #2 CHECK (3RD CLUTCH ACCUMULATOR)
55B	BALL, #12 CHECK (FORWARD CLUTCH)
55C	BALL, #6 CHECK (DRIVE 3)
91	BALL, #10 CHECK (TV EXHAUST) (COPPER FLASH)
359	CUP PLUG, ORIFICE
377	BODY, AUXILIARY VALVE

Copyrighted Material Reprinted with Permission from Hydra-Matic Div., GM Corp.

Fig. 8   Control valve body replacement. 1993 Camaro & Firebird

d. Remove transmission support, then lower transmission to gain access to governor cover.
4. **On all models,** remove governor cover from case using extreme care not to damage cover. If cover is damaged, it should be replaced.
5. Remove governor.
6. Reverse procedure to install and check fluid level.

1993 Camaro & Firebird

1. Raise and support vehicle.
2. Remove propeller shaft assembly as follows:
   a. Using a center punch or suitable equivalent, mark propeller shaft and pinion gear yoke for installation reference.
   b. If removing a two-piece shaft, remove bolts/screws from center support bearing, then center support bearing and washers from torque arm.
   c. Remove four bolts and two retainers.
   d. Slide propeller shaft slip yoke out of the transmission.
3. Remove rear axle torque arm assembly.
4. Remove catalytic converter hanger assembly.
5. Support transmission with a suitable stand, then remove transmission support member assembly.
6. lower transmission slightly to access governor.
7. Remove cover, then tap around cover flange with punch to remove.
8. Remove governor assembly. Reverse procedure to install.

AUXILIARY VALVE BODY, REPLACE

1. Raise and support vehicle, then drain transmission fluid.
2. Remove transmission oil pan and filter.
3. Remove two bolts that attach auxilia-

---

ry accumulator valve tube to control valve assembly and accumulator valve body assembly, **Fig. 7.**

4. Remove two tube clamps, gently pry tube loose from oil pump assembly and auxiliary accumulator valve body assembly.
5. Remove three auxiliary accumulator valve body to transmission case attaching bolts.
6. Remove auxiliary valve body and check ball.
7. Reverse procedure to install.

CONTROL VALVE ASSEMBLY, REPLACE

Except 1993 Camaro & Firebird

1. Disconnect battery ground cable.
2. Disconnect TV cable at throttle lever, then raise and support vehicle.
3. Drain transmission fluid, then remove transmission oil pan, filter and gasket.
4. Remove two bolts that attach auxiliary accumulator valve tube to control valve assembly and accumulator valve body assembly, **Fig. 7.**
5. Remove two tube clamps, gently pry tube loose from oil pump assembly, then the auxiliary accumulator valve body assembly.
6. Disconnect electrical connectors at valve body.
7. Remove detent spring and roller assembly from valve body and remove valve body-to-case bolts.
8. Remove valve body assembly while disconnecting manual control valve link from range selector inner lever and removing throttle lever bracket from TV link.
9. Reverse procedure to install.

1993 Camaro & Firebird

1. Disconnect battery ground cable.
2. Disconnect TV cable at throttle lever, then raise and support vehicle.
3. Drain transmission fluid, then remove transmission oil pan, filter and gasket.
4. Remove two bolts that attach auxiliary accumulator valve tube to control valve assembly and auxiliary valve body assembly.
5. Remove two retainers, then accumulator tube.
6. Remove attaching clip and solenoid wire from harness connectors from pressure switch and temperature switch.
7. Remove temperature switch to control valve assembly bolt/screw, then temperature switch.
8. Loosen bolt/screw attaching wire retainer washer to control valve assembly.
9. Disconnect solenoid wire harness connector from transmission wiring electrical connector assembly by prying back lock tabs. Allow harness to be suspended from solenoid valve assembly.
10. Remove bolt/screw and manual shift detent assembly, then TV lever to control valve attaching bolt/screws.
11. Loosen remaining bolt/screws completely. Bolt/screws should remain in

control valve assembly to aid in reassembly.
12. Remove manual valve link assembly. Pick up control valve assembly while holding manual valve link assembly and rotate control valve assembly to disconnect manual link assembly from manual valve.
13. Remove control valve assembly and check balls 2, 6, and 10, **Fig. 8.**
14. Reverse procedure to install.

TRANSMISSION REPLACE

1991–92 CAMARO & FIREBIRD

1. Disconnect battery ground cable.
2. Remove air cleaner assembly and disconnect TV cable at upper end.
3. Remove fluid level indicator and oil dipstick tube.
4. Raise and support vehicle. **Do not use a twin post type hoist.**
5. Support rear axle with an adjustable jackstand.
6. Remove track bar mounting bolt at axle assembly, then loosen track bar bolt at body brace.
7. Remove rear brake hose clip at underbody to allow for additional axle drop.
8. Remove lower mounting bolts from right and left side shock absorbers.
9. Carefully lower rear axle and remove coil springs.
10. Remove torque arm to rear axle attaching bolts.
11. Remove torque arm clamp from transmission, then the torque arm from the vehicle.
12. Remove propeller shaft, then disconnect shift linkage at the transmission.
13. Disconnect any electrical leads at transmission, then remove any clips that hold leads to transmission case.
14. Remove flywheel cover, then mark relationship between flywheel and converter for installation reference.
15. Remove torque converter attaching bolts.
16. Remove catalytic converter support bracket, then the transmission mount to support attaching nut.
17. Remove transmission support to frame bolts, then any insulators, if used.
18. Using a transmission jack, support and raise transmission slightly.
19. Slide transmission support rearward, then lower transmission to gain access to oil cooler pipes and TV cable attachments.
20. Disconnect oil cooler pipes from transmission, cap all openings.
21. Disconnect speedometer cable or P.M. generator, then the TV cable from transmission.
22. Support engine assembly, then remove transmission to engine attaching bolts.
23. Install torque converter holding fixture tool, No. J-21366 or equivalent, then carefully lower transmission from vehicle.
24. Reverse procedure to install.

1993 CAMARO & FIREBIRD

1. Disconnect battery ground cable, then TV cable at throttle lever.
2. Raise and support vehicle, then mark position of propeller shaft to pinion yoke.
3. Remove propeller shaft as follows:
   a. Using a center punch or suitable equivalent, mark propeller shaft and pinion gear yoke for installation reference.
   b. If removing a two-piece shaft, remove bolts/screws from center support bearing, then center support bearing and washers from torque arm.
   c. Remove four bolts and two retainers.
   d. Slide propeller shaft slip yoke out of the transmission.
4. Support transmission, then remove washer and nut from support and transmission.
5. Remove bolt/screws from support and rail, then remove support from transmission and rail.
6. Remove rear axle torque arm and catalytic converter hanger assembly.
7. Remove bolt/screws from torque converter cover, then cover from transmission.
8. Remove bolt/screws from converter, then flywheel from converter.
9. Move catalytic converter heat shield if necessary.
10. Remove range selector lever cable and transmission cooler pipes from pipe clips.
11. Disconnect electrical connectors at transmission, then remove transmission fluid level indicator bolts/screws and indicator.
12. Separate transmission from engine, then disconnect TV cable at transmission.
13. Disconnect transmission oil cooler lines, then lower transmission from vehicle.
14. Reverse procedure to install.

CAPRICE, CUSTOM CRUISER & ROADMASTER

1. Disconnect battery ground cable.
2. Remove air cleaner assembly, if necessary, then disconnect TV cable at its upper end.
3. Remove transmission oil dipstick.
4. Raise and support vehicle, then remove the propeller shaft.
5. Disconnect speedometer cable, shift linkage, then all the electrical leads at transmission and any clips that retain the leads to the transmission case.
6. Remove flywheel cover, mark flywheel and torque converter for installation reference.
7. Remove torque converter to flywheel bolts.
8. Remove catalytic converter support bracket.
9. Remove floor pan reinforcement if it interferes with removal or installation of propeller shaft.

10. Remove transmission support to transmission mount bolt and transmission support to frame bolts and insulators, if used.
11. Using a suitable jack transmission, support and raise transmission slightly, then slide transmission support rearward.
12. Lower transmission to gain access to oil cooler lines and TV cable attachments, then disconnect oil cooler lines and TV cable, cap all openings.
13. Support engine with suitable tool, remove transmission to engine attaching bolts.
14. Install torque converter holding fixture tool, No. J-21366 or equivalent, then carefully lower transmission assembly from vehicle.
15. Reverse procedure to install.

CORVETTE
1. Disconnect battery ground cable.
2. Disconnect TV cable at upper end, then remove dipstick.
3. Raise and support vehicle.
4. Remove upper and lower underbody braces, if equipped.
5. Remove complete exhaust system, then support transmission with a suitable transmission jack.
6. Remove driveline support beam.

7. Mark propeller shaft trunnion and axle yoke for installation reference, then remove propeller shaft.
8. Disconnect speedometer cable or P.M. generator electrical connector, shift linkage, and all electrical leads at transmission as well as any clips that retain the leads to transmission case.
9. Remove flywheel cover, then mark flywheel and torque converter to maintain original balance. Remove torque converter to flywheel bolts.
10. Lower transmission to gain access to the oil cooler lines and TV cable attachments, then disconnect oil cooler lines and TV cable, cap all openings.
11. Support engine using suitable jack, then remove transmission to engine attaching bolts.
12. Separate transmission assembly from engine, install torque converter holding fixture tool, No. J-21366, then lower transmission from vehicle.
13. Reverse procedure to install.

BROUGHAM
1. Disconnect battery ground cable.
2. Remove air cleaner assembly, then disconnect TV cable at upper end.
3. Remove transmission oil dipstick, dipstick tube retaining bolt and dipstick tube.

4. Raise and support vehicle.
5. Remove propeller shaft. If necessary remove floor pan reinforcement.
6. Disconnect speedometer cable, shift linkage and all electrical connectors.
7. Remove flexplate cover, then mark flexplate and torque converter to maintain original balance. Remove torque converter-to-flexplate attaching nuts and/or bolts.
8. Remove catalytic converter support bracket.
9. Remove transmission support to transmission mount bolt, then transmission support to frame bolts and insulator if used.
10. Position a suitable jack under transmission, then raise transmission slightly and slide transmission support rearward.
11. Lower transmission slightly, then disconnect oil cooler lines and TV cable.
12. Support engine, then remove transmission-to-engine bolts and disconnect transmission assembly. **Use caution not to damage cables, lines or linkage.**
13. Using torque converter holding fixture tool No. J-21366 or equivalent remove transmission assembly from vehicle.
14. Reverse procedure to install.

TIGHTENING SPECIFICATIONS

Component	Torque/Ft. Lbs.
Camaro & Firebird	
Auxiliary Valve Body Bolt	97①
Case Extension Bolt	26
Filler Tube To Transmission Case②	35
Filler Tube To Transmission Case③	55
Floorshift Control Bolt	44①
Flywheel Cover	89①
Manual Shift Detent Assembly	16
Neutral Safety/Back-up Lamp Switch	18①
Oil Cooler Connector At Transmission	28
Oil Cooler Connector At Radiator	20
Oil Pan Bolts	12
Shift Cable Nut	11
Torque Converter Bolts	46
Transmission Case Extension To Transmission	26
Transmission To Engine Bolt⑤	35
Transmission To Engine Bolts	70②
Transmission Support To Frame Bolt	40
Transmission Mount To Transmission Bolt	40
Transmission Mount To Transmission Support Nut	35
T.V. Cable To Transmission Bolt	89①
Valve Body Bolts	11
Wheel Lug Nuts	81
Caprice, Custom Cruiser & Roadmaster	
Equalizer Lever To Control Rod	21
Flywheel Cover Bolts	89①
Mount To Transmission Bolts④	30
Oil Cooler Lines To Radiator	20

Component	Torque/Ft. Lbs.
Caprice, Custom Cruiser & Roadmaster-Continued	
Oil Pan Bolts	12
Torque Converter Bolts	46
Transmission Support To Frame Bolt	25
Transmission To Engine Bolts	35
Transmission To Mount Bolt	35
Valve Body Bolts	11
Wheel Lug Nuts	100
Corvette	
Filler Tube To Transmission Bolt	35
Floorshift Control Bolt	89①
Flywheel Cover Bolt	89①
Neutral Safety/Back-Up Lamp Switch	27①
Oil Cooler Line Fitting At Radiator	20
Oil Cooler Line Fitting At Transmission	11
Oil Cooler Line Retaining Clip Bolt	107①
Oil Pan Bolt	12
Shift Control Cable Attachment	15
Throttle Valve Link To Transmission Case	89①
Torque Converter Bolts	46
Transmission To Engine Bolts	35
Underbody Brace Stud Nut	20
Underbody Brace To Frame Bolt	47
Valve Body Bolts	11
Wheel Lug Nuts	100

①—Inch lbs.
②—V-8 engine.
③—V-6 engine.
④—1991-92 models.
⑤—1991-92 models & 1993 V6 models.

Geo Metro Automatic Transaxle

INDEX

Fig. 1 Transaxle identification number location

Fig. 2 Transaxle troubleshooting chart. Gear change failure

Fig. 3 Transaxle troubleshooting chart. No starting or slipping in any drive range

IDENTIFICATION

The transaxle identification number is located on the top center of the transaxle assembly, **Fig. 1.**

TROUBLESHOOTING

In conjunction with the prerequisites noted below, refer to charts, **Figs. 2 through 4,** when troubleshooting the transaxle:

1. Engine coolant is at normal operating temperature.
2. Engine idle speed is 800~900 RPM.
3. Transaxle fluid level is correct and at normal operating temperature.
4. Accelerator cable, oil pressure control cable and selector cable are properly adjusted.
5. Gear shift control system wiring is in good condition.
6. Vacuum switch hose is properly connected.

MAINTENANCE

CHECKING FLUID LEVEL

1. Drive vehicle for approximately 15 minutes to bring fluid up to normal operating temperature.
2. With vehicle on level surface, apply parking brake and block drive wheels.

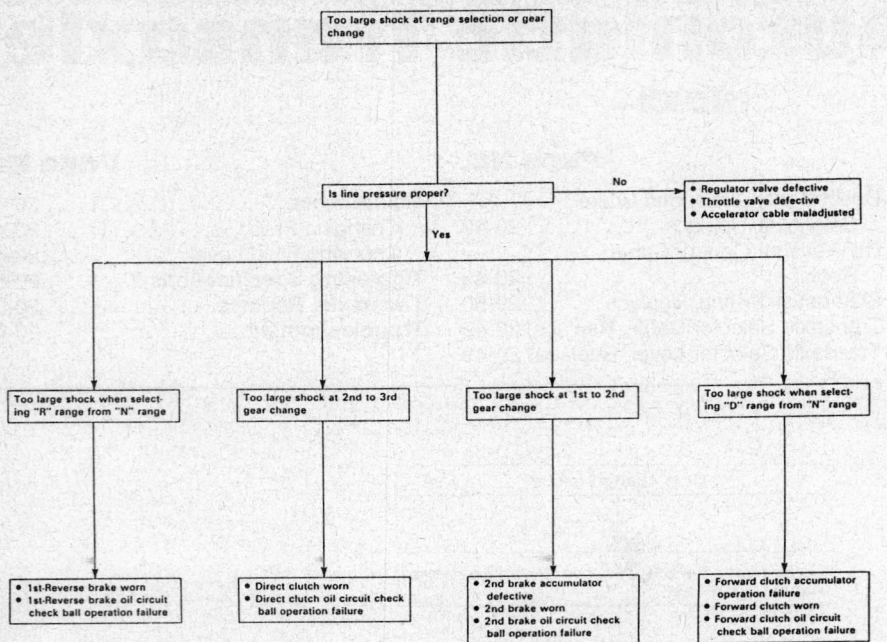

Fig. 4 Transaxle troubleshooting chart. Too large shock at range selection of gear change

PAN BOLTS
4-6 N·m
(3-4 LB. FT.)

1. CROSS GROOVED BOLTS
2. SEALANT

Fig. 5 Oil pan installation

1	SHIFT LOCK SOLENOID	5	DETENT PIN
2	LOCK PLATE	6	SELECTOR LEVER
3	GUIDE PLATE	7	KEY RELEASE PLATE
4	"NO CLEARANCE"	8	INTERLOCK CABLE

Fig. 7 Interlock solenoid lock plate clearance

WHEN SHIFT LOCK SOLENOID IS NOT OPERATED:

WHEN SHIFT LOCK SOLENOID IS OPERATED:

1	SHIFT LOCK SOLENOID
2	DETENT PIN
3	LOCK PLATE
4	DETENT PLATE
A	MORE THAN 1.0 MM (0.040 IN)
B	APPLY GREASE HERE

Fig. 6 Interlock solenoid adjustment

1. Raise and support front of vehicle.
2. Remove drain plug and drain fluid from oil pan.
3. Remove oil pan attaching bolts and the oil pan.
4. Remove oil strainer-to-valve body attaching bolts, then the oil strainer.
5. Clean strainer and oil pan in solvent. Engine magnet in oil pan is positioned directly below oil strainer.
6. Install oil strainer and attaching bolts. **Torque** bolts to 53 inch lbs.
7. Install oil pan using new gasket. **Torque** attaching bolts to 53 inch lbs. **Two of the oil pan attaching bolts have crossed grooves on the bolt head. When installing these two bolts, coat threads with sealant and install in positions shown in Fig. 5.**
8. Lower vehicle and refill oil pan with approximately 1.5 quarts of Dexron II type transaxle fluid or equivalent.
9. Check fluid level as previously described and adjust as necessary.

ADJUSTMENTS

INTERLOCK DRIVE SOLENOID, ADJUST

1. Shift selector lever to Park.
2. Adjust solenoid position so that solenoid operates as follows:
   a. When ignition switch is turned Off (solenoid is not operated) and On (solenoid is operated), lock plate should be positioned as shown in **Fig. 6.**
   b. There should be no clearance between lock plate and guide plate as shown in **Fig. 7.**
3. After adjusting solenoid position, tighten solenoid screws.

4. After tightening solenoid screws, check the following:
   a. When ignition switch is turned Off, selector lever is locked in Park range and cannot be shifted into any other range.
   b. When ignition switch is turned On, selector lever can be shifted into any other range.
   c. If manual release knob is pulled with ignition switch Off, selector lever can be shifted into any other range.

INTERLOCK CABLE, ADJUST

1. Shift selector lever to Park.
2. Loosen nuts (A) and (B) as shown in **Fig. 8**
3. With outer wire pulled forward so that there is no deflection on inner wire, tighten nut (A), then nut (B) hand-tight.
4. Tighten nuts (A) and (B) again, then check the following:
   a. With selector lever in Park, ensure ignition key can be turned from "ACC" to "LOCK" position and removed from ignition switch.
   b. With selector lever shifted in any drive range other than Park, ignition key cannot be turned from Acc to Lock position.

3. With selector lever in Park, start engine, then move selector lever through each range and return to Park.
4. Remove dipstick and check fluid level.
5. Fluid level should be between the two "HOT" marks on dipstick.
6. Add fluid as required to bring fluid to specified level. When adding fluid use only Dexron II type transaxle fluid or equivalent.

CHANGING FLUID

Under normal driving conditions, fluid should be changed and oil strainer cleaned every 100,000 miles. Under harsh driving conditions fluid should be changed every 15,000 miles. To service, proceed as follows:

1. INTERLOCK CABLE (OUTER WIRE)
2. INNER WIRE
3. NUT A
4. NUT B
5. SHIFT LOCK SOLENOID
6. MANUAL RELEASE KNOB
7. SELECTOR LEVER
8. KEY RELEASE PLATE

Fig. 8 Interlock cable adjustment

1. OIL PRESSURE CONTROL CABLE
2. ACCELERATOR CABLE
3. BOOT
4. INNER CABLE STOPPER
5. CLEARANCE (0-0.5 MM, 0-0.02 IN.)
6. ADJUSTING NUTS Ⓐ
7. ADJUSTING NUTS Ⓑ

Fig. 9 Oil pressure control cable adjustment

1. COUPLERS
2. DIRECT CLUTCH SOLENOID
3. 2ND BRAKE SOLENOID

Fig. 10 Direct clutch & second brake solenoid replacement

1. OIL PRESSURE CONTROL CABLE
2. ACCELERATOR CABLE
3. CABLE COVER

Fig. 11 Oil pressure control cable replacement

OIL PRESSURE CONTROL CABLE, ADJUST

1. Check and, if necessary, adjust accelerator cable.
2. Start engine and allow to reach normal operating temperature.
3. Remove control cable cover and check that boot to inner cable stopper clearance is 0-.020 inch as shown, **Fig. 9.**
4. If clearance is not as specified, loosen, then tighten adjusting nuts (A) until specified clearance is obtained. If clearance is still not within specifications, turn adjusting nuts (B) and repeat procedure outlined above.

IN-VEHICLE REPAIRS
DIRECT CLUTCH & SECOND BRAKE SOLENOIDS, REPLACE

1. Disconnect battery ground cable.
2. Drain transaxle fluid and remove oil pan.
3. Disconnect electrical connectors from direct clutch and second brake solenoids, then remove the solenoids, **Fig. 10.**
4. Remove solenoid wire harness with grommet from upper side.
5. Reverse procedure to install.

OIL PRESSURE CONTROL CABLE, REPLACE

1. Remove cable cover, then disconnect oil pressure control cable from accelerator cable, **Fig. 11.**
2. Drain transaxle fluid and remove oil pan.
3. Disconnect oil pressure control cable from throttle valve cam, then remove the cable from transaxle case.
4. Reverse procedure to install, then adjust cable as previously described.

TRANSAXLE SELECTOR LEVER, REPLACE

1. Disconnect battery ground cable.
2. Remove selector lever knob, then the console assembly.
3. Remove selector indicator assembly, then disconnect cable from selector lever.
4. Disconnect back drive cable and the back drive solenoid electrical connector.
5. Raise and support vehicle.
6. Remove four housing attaching nuts, then the housing seat and housing with selector lever.
7. Reverse procedure to install.

TRANSAXLE SELECTOR CABLE, REPLACE
Removal

1. Remove console assembly, then the selector indicator assembly.
2. Disconnect selector cable from selector lever, floor and transaxle.
3. Raise and support vehicle.
4. Remove selector cable from front panel.

Installation

1. Raise and support vehicle.
2. Position selector cable in front panel, then lower vehicle.
3. Apply grease to selector cable pin, then connect cable to lever.
4. Install selector indicator, then the console assembly.

1. NUT Ⓐ
2. MANUAL SELECT CABLE JOINT
3. NUT Ⓑ

Fig. 12 Transaxle selector cable installation

1. SHIFT LEVER SWITCH
2. SHIFT LEVER SWITCH JOINT

Fig. 13 Shift lever switch installation

1. SHIFT LEVER SWITCH
2. BOLT

Fig. 14 Shift lever switch adjustment

1. DRIVE PLATE
2. DRIVE PLATE BOLT
3. NOTCH
4. STANDARD SCREWDRIVER
5. ENGINE OIL PAN

Fig. 15 Driveplate bolt removal

1. SNAP RING
2. DIFFERENTIAL SIDE GEAR
3. DIFFERENTIAL SIDE JOINT
4. TIRE LEVER
5. TRANSAXLE

Fig. 16 Differential side gear snap ring removal

1. TORQUE CONVERTER
2. TRANSAXLE CASE HOUSING
3. FLANGE NUT
4. CUP
5. "APPLY GREASE HERE"
A: MORE THAN 21.4 mm (0.85 IN.)

Fig. 17 Torque converter installation

5. Connect cable to bracket on transaxle, then slide cable into manual select joint hole and position manual shift lever in Neutral range.
6. Turn nut (A), **Fig. 12**, by hand until it contacts manual select cable joint, then tighten nut (B) with wrench.
7. After tightening cable nuts, check the following:
   a. With selector lever in Park, vehicle can not move when pushed.
   b. With selector lever in Neutral, vehicle cannot be driven.
   c. With selector in Drive, Second or Low ranges, vehicle can be driven.
   d. With selector lever in Reverse, vehicle can be backed up.

SHIFT LEVER SWITCH, REPLACE

Removal

1. Disconnect battery ground cable.
2. Disconnect electrical connectors from shift lever switch.
3. Remove shift lever switch from manual shift shaft.

Installation

1. Shift manual shift lever to Manual range.
2. Using a screwdriver, turn shift lever switch to the position shown in **Fig. 13** and ensure a click is heard from joint at this position.
3. Install switch to manual shift shaft, then move the shaft in direction of arrow, **Fig. 14**, until a click is heard. Stop at this position and **torque** attaching

bolts to 9.5–16.5 ft. lbs.
4. Connect electrical connectors to switch, then install clamp.
5. Apply parking brake and block wheels, then check the following:
   a. With selector lever in Park and ignition switch On, starter motor operates.
   b. With selector lever in Neutral and ignition switch On, starter motor operates.
   c. After moving selector lever from Neutral to Low, then back to Neutral, starter motor operates with ignition switch On.
   d. With selector lever in Park and ignition switch On, starter motor operates.
   e. In any range other than Park or Neutral, starter motor cannot be operated.
   f. With selector lever in Reverse and ignition switch On (engine not running), back-up lamps light.

TRANSAXLE REPLACE

1. Disconnect battery ground cable.
2. Remove air suction guide from air cleaner.
3. Disconnect battery cables and remove battery and tray.
4. Remove ground cable from transaxle.
5. Disconnect solenoid and shift lever connectors.
6. Remove wire harness and speedometer cable from transaxle.
7. Remove oil pressure control cable

from accelerator cable, then the accelerator cable from transaxle.
8. Disconnect select cable from transaxle, then remove starter.
9. Drain transaxle fluid.
10. Disconnect oil outlet and inlet hoses from oil pipes. Plug all openings.
11. Raise and support vehicle.
12. Remove exhaust system components as necessary, then the clutch housing lower plate.
13. Remove driveplate attaching bolts using a screwdriver in notch provided to hold driveplate, **Fig. 15**.
14. Remove LH front drive axle as follows:
   a. Remove wheel center cap, then the cotter pin and driveshaft nut.
   b. Remove wheel nuts, then the wheel and tire assembly.
   c. Remove snap ring from spline of differential side joint using a screwdriver, **Fig. 16**.
   d. Remove stabilizer bar bracket bolts and ball stud bolt.
   e. Disconnect ball stud from steering knuckle by pulling down on stabilizer bar.
   f. Disconnect inboard joint from differential side gear and wheel side joint from steering knuckle, then remove the drive axle assembly.
15. Disconnect inboard joint of RH drive axle from differential.
16. Remove RH side transaxle mounting member bolts, then secure transaxle using a jack.
17. Remove LH side transaxle mounting bolts.

18. Remove engine-to-transaxle attaching bolts.
19. Remove transaxle from engine by sliding toward left side and carefully lowering jack.
20. Reverse procedure to install, noting the following:
    a. Apply suitable grease around the cup at center of torque converter.

b. Measure distance A, **Fig. 17.** Distance should measure more than .85 inch. If distance is less than specified, converter installation is improper and must be corrected.
c. Guide right drive axle into differential side gear as transaxle is being raised.
d. After installing inboard joints into

differential side gear, push inboard joints into side gears until snap rings on drive axles engage side gears.
e. Adjust oil pressure control cable if necessary.
f. Fill transaxle with fluid.
g. Refer to "Tightening Specifications" chart for bolt torques.

TIGHTENING SPECIFICATIONS

Component	Torque/ Ft. Lbs.	Component	Torque/ Ft. Lbs.
Automatic Transaxle Controller Retaining Bolts	11	**Rear Engine Torque Rod Assembly Bolts**	40
Ball Stud Nuts & Bolts	44	**Second Brake Solenoid Retaining Bolt**	35①
Direct Clutch Solenoid Retaining Bolt	35①	**Selector Lever Assembly Housing Seat Nuts**	25
Engine Wiring Harness Bracket Bolts	12	**Shift Lever Backup & Neutral Safety Switch Mounting Bolt**	17
Filler Tube Bracket Bolt	53①	**Shift Select Cable Bulkhead Grommet Bolts**	15
Fluid Filter Screen Bolts	53①		
Flywheel Cover Bolts	89①	**Solenoid Wiring Harness Retaining Bracket Bolt**	15
Flywheel To Torque Converter Bolts	14	**Solenoid Wiring Harness Retaining Plate Nut**	15
Inlet & Outlet Union Bolts	20	**Speedometer Driven Gear Case Bolt**	11
Left Transaxle Mount Bracket Bolts	40	**Starter Motor Bolts**	17
Left Transaxle Mount Retaining Nuts	40	**Stoplamp Switch Adjustment Locknut**	11
Lower Valve Body Cover Bolts	35①	**Transaxle Cooler Pipe Retaining Bracket Bolt**	20
Lower Engine To Transaxle Retaining Bolt	40	**Transaxle Drain Plug**	17
Lower Rear Engine Mount To Bulkhead Bolt	40	**Transaxle Fluid Pan Bolts**	53①
Lower Valve Body Bolts	106①	**Upper Rear Transaxle Mount To Bulkhead Bolt**	40
Negative Battery Cable To Negative Battery Terminal Retainer	11	**Upper Transaxle To Engine Retaining Bolts**	40
Negative Battery Cable To Transaxle Case Bolt	11	**Upper Valve Body Bolts**	53①
Rear Engine Mount Bracket Bolts & Nuts	40	**Vehicle Speed Sensor Retaining Bolt**	17
		①—Inch lbs.	

KF 400 & JF403E Automatic Transaxles (Storm)

INDEX

IDENTIFICATION

The transaxle identification number for the JF403E is located on top of the transaxle near the transaxle VIN plate and on the KF 400, the identification number is located at the front left side of the transaxle near the engine, **Fig. 1.**

DESCRIPTION

KF 400

The KF 400 is a 3-speed automatic transaxle. Power is transferred from the

output gear through the ring gear to the idler gear.

The output gear, idler gear and differential gear case are supported by tapered roller bearings. The preload on the roller bearings can be adjusted by using shims.

The final drive gear is a helical type design.

JF403E

The JF403E is a 4-speed automatic transaxle. This transaxle utilizes a microcomputer as a control unit to evaluate driving conditions including throttle opening and vehicle speed.

This transaxle also incorporates a shift mode change control. The economy mode (ECON switch ON) is suitable for economical driving. The normal mode (ECON switch OFF) is suitable for hill climbing and/or acceleration.

MAINTENANCE

Check transaxle fluid level every 7,500 miles, adding Dexron II automatic transmission fluid as necessary.

Change transaxle fluid and filter every 30,000 miles under normal driving conditions, or every 15,000 miles if vehicle is op-

1. TRANSAXLE NUMBER (4 SPEED AUTOMATIC)
2. TRANSAXLE NUMBER (3 SPEED AUTOMATIC AND MANUAL)
3. ENGINE IDENTIFICATION NUMBER

Fig. 1   Transaxle identification number location

erated under severe conditions such as city driving during hot weather or driving over hilly or mountainous terrain.

CHECKING FLUID LEVEL

1. Park vehicle on level ground.
2. Start engine and operate for 15 minutes to allow fluid to reach operating temperature.
3. Move gear selector through all gear positions, then to park.
4. Remove and check fluid level on dipstick, add Dexron II as necessary. **Do not over fill.**

CHANGING FLUID

1. Raise and support vehicle.
2. Remove drain plug at bottom of differential and drain fluid.
3. Remove oil pan and discard pan gasket.
4. Clean drain pan, then using a new gasket, install gasket and pan to transaxle. Torque pan bolts to specifications.
5. Install drain plug and **torque** to 20 ft. lbs., then fill transaxle through oil filler tube with Dexron II automatic transmission fluid.

ADJUSTMENTS
MANUAL LINKAGE, ADJUST

Shift Control Cable, Adjust

1. Place the ignition key in the LOCK position.
2. Set the gear selector lever in the Park position.
3. Loosen the adjuster nuts at the transaxle **Fig. 2.**
4. Ensure shift lever at the transaxle is in the "PARK" position.
5. Pull the cable forward and tighten forward adjuster nut until it contacts shift lever.

6. Tighten rear adjuster nut until it contacts shift lever, then tighten both adjuster nuts.

Back Drive Cable, Adjust

1. Place shift lever in Park position.
2. Place ignition switch to the LOCK position.
3. Pull cable forward at shift lever bracket, then tighten forward adjuster nut until contact is made against the bracket.
4. Tighten rear nut until it makes contact with shift lever bracket, then tighten both adjuster nuts.

IN-VEHICLE REPAIRS
SHIFTER CONTROL, REPLACE

1. Disconnect battery ground cable.
2. Remove ashtray, shift trim bezel, heater control knobs, then radio bezel.
3. Remove lower console, then shift knob from lever.
4. Disconnect back drive cable for shift control.
5. Disconnect shift lock out module from shift control, then electrical connections.
6. Disconnect shift control cable from shift control.
7. Remove shift control retaining bolts, then shift control.
8. Remove solenoid and switch assembly from shift control.
9. Reverse procedure to install.

SPEEDOMETER DRIVEN GEAR, REPLACE

1. Disconnect battery ground cable.
2. Remove air breather tube, then air intake duct from air cleaner assembly.
3. Disconnect speedometer cable at transaxle.
4. Remove speedometer driven gear retaining bolt, then gear and O-ring seal.

Fig. 2   Shift cable adjustment

5. Reverse procedure to install, noting the following:
   a. Replace speedometer O-ring seal.
   b. Torque speedometer driven gear retaining bolt to specifications.

CONTROL VALVE ASSEMBLY, REPLACE
KF 400

1. Disconnect negative battery cable.
2. Raise and support vehicle.
3. Remove left and right undercovers.
4. Drain transaxle fluid.
5. Remove oil pan attaching bolts, then oil pan.
6. Remove control valve assembly bolts, then control valve assembly.
7. Reverse procedure to install, noting the following:
   a. Torque control valve assembly bolts specifications.
   b. Torque oil pan bolts to specifications.
   c. Refill transaxle fluid as described under "Changing Fluid."

JF403E

1. Disconnect negative battery cable, then the terminal assembly connector.
2. Remove the terminal assembly clip.
3. Raise and support vehicle.
4. Remove left and right undercovers, then drain the transaxle.
5. Remove oil pan protector and oil pan.
6. Remove the fifteen control valve assembly bolts.
7. Remove control valve and terminal assemblies from transaxle.
8. Remove terminal valve assembly from control valve assembly.
9. Reverse procedure to install. **Torque** Control valve assembly bolts and oil pan bolts to specifications.

TRANSAXLE REPLACE

1. Disconnect negative battery cable.
2. Remove battery and battery tray.
3. Remove air duct, then air breather tube from air cleaner assembly.
4. **On KF 400 models,** disconnect vacuum diaphragm at vacuum hose.
5. **On all models,** disconnect electrical connectors from transaxle, then shift cable from lever.
6. Disconnect shift cable bracket from transaxle case.
7. remove breather hose from transaxle, then the speedometer cable.
8. Install engine support fixture tool No.

J 28467-A or equivalent to engine.

9. Remove left transaxle mount through bolt, then four transaxle to engine mounting bolts.
10. Raise and support vehicle.
11. Remove left and right undercovers, then front wheel and tire assemblies
12. Disconnect left control arm from steering knuckle.
13. Drain transaxle fluid.
14. Disconnect drive axles from transaxle.
15. Remove front transaxle mount

through bolt, then dampener from rear mount through bolt.
16. Remove rear transaxle mount through bolt, then two front center crossmember mounting bolts.
17. Disconnect front pipe to exhaust manifold.
18. Remove two rear crossmember mounting bolts.
19. Remove center crossmember bolts from vehicle, place suitable transaxle jack under transaxle.
20. Remove rear mount to transaxle case

bolt, then front mount retaining bolt.
21. Remove front mount bracket from the engine, then the flywheel cover.
22. Remove flywheel to torque converter bolts.
23. Disconnect oil cooler lines from transaxle.
24. Remove two rear mount transaxle bolts, then carefully lower transaxle from vehicle.
25. Reverse procedure to install. Refer to "Tightening Specifications" chart for bolt torques.

TIGHTENING SPECIFICATIONS

Component	Torque/ Ft. Lbs.
Automatic Transaxle Control Module Bolts	11
Backup/Neutral Switch	15
Center Crossmember Bolts	45
Center Crossmember Strut Nut & Bolt	37
Dampner Nut	18
Drive Axle Nuts	137
Fluid Temperature Sensor Bolt ③	71①
Fluid Filler Tube Bracket Bolts ③	44①
Fluid Filler Tube Retaining Bolt	44①
Fluid Filter Screen Bolts ②	53①
Fluid Filter Screen Bolts ③	71①
Flywheel Cover Bolts ②	89①
Flywheel To Torque Converter Bolts	31
Front Engine Mounting Strut Bracket Bolts	45
Front Engine Mounting Strut Stud Nut	45
Front Engine Mounting Strut Through Bolt & Nut	64
Front Exhaust Pipe Bracket Bolts	32
Front Exhaust Pipe To Catalytic Converter Bolts	32
Front Exhaust Pipe To Exhaust Manifold Nuts	46
Governor Bolts ②	71①
Inhibitor Switch Mounting Bolts	26①
Inlet Fluid Cooler Pipe Bracket Bolt ②	15
Inlet Fluid Cooler Union Bolt	11
Interlock Cable Adjustment Nuts	35①
Kickdown Switch Locknuts ②	44①
Left Transaxle Mount Bolts	29
Left Transaxle Mount Through Bolt	64
Lower Valve Body Bolts	71①
Lower Valve Body To Upper Valve Body Bolts ②	26①
Manual Selector Mounting Bolts	20
Manual Shift Shaft Nut	20
Negative Battery Cable To Negative Battery Terminal Retainer	11
Oil Pan Bolts ②	62①
Oil Pan Bolts ③	71①
Outlet Fluid Cooler Union Bolt	11
Positive Battery Cable To Positive Battery Terminal Retainer	11

Continued

TIGHTENING SPECIFICATIONS—Continued

Component	Torque/Ft. Lbs.
Rear Engine Mounting Bracket Nut & Bolts	45
Rear Transaxle Mount Bolts	29
Rear Transaxle Mount Through Bolt	64
Shift Select Cable Adjustment Nut	42
Shift Select Cable Cover Bolts	89 ①
Shift Select Cable Retaining Nuts	20
Speedometer Driven Gear Case Bolt	44 ①
Stoplamp Switch Locknut ②	11
Sub Body Bolts & Nut ②	26 ①
Suction Bolts ③	71 ①
Support Plate Bolts ③	71 ①
Transaxle Solenoid Bolts ③	71
Upper Transaxle To Engine Bolts	31
Upper Valve Body Side Plate Bolts ②	26 ①
Valve Body Locating Bolts ②	53 ①
Valve Body Locating Bolts ③	71 ①
Valve Body Mounting Bolts ②	89 ①
Valve Body Mounting Bolts ③	71 ①
Vehicle Speed Sensor Bolt ③	53 ①

① —Inch lbs.
② —KF400
③ —JF403E

FRONT WHEEL DRIVE AXLES

INDEX

Fig. 1 Front wheel drive components & axle shaft removal. Except Geo & LeMans

TROUBLESHOOTING

CLICKING NOISE IN TURNS

Worn or damaged outboard joint.

CLUNK WHEN ACCELERATING FROM COAST TO DRIVE

Worn or damaged constant velocity joint.

SHUDDER OR VIBRATION DURING ACCELERATION

1. Excessive C.V. joint angle.
2. Incorrect toe in or out.
3. Incorrect trim height.
4. Worn or damaged inboard or outboard C.V. joints.
5. Sticking tri-pot joint spider assembly.

VIBRATION AT HIGHWAY SPEEDS

1. Out-of-balance front tires or wheels.
2. Out-of-round front tires.
3. Worn C.V. joint.
4. Binding or tight C.V. joint.

DRIVE AXLE REPLACE

DESCRIPTION

The front wheel drive system, **Figs. 1 and 2**, consists of left and righthand output shafts and drive axles. Each drive axle consists of an axle shaft, with a ball type constant velocity joint at the outboard end and a tri-pot joint at the inboard end.

On all except Geo models and LeMans, a ball type constant velocity joint is used at the outboard end, while a tri-pot type joint is used at the inboard end, **Fig. 3**. Snap rings are used to lock the male splines of the axle shafts into the transaxle gears, except for the left side inboard joint

used with the automatic transaxles. The left side inboard joint used on automatic transaxle models utilizes a female spline which installs over a transaxle stub shaft.

On some manual transmissions, a constant velocity joint is used on the inboard end of the drive axle, **Fig. 4**.

On Storm, a ball type constant velocity joint is used at the outboard end, while a tri-pot type joint is used at the inboard end.

On Metro, a constant velocity ball joint is used on the outboard side of the drive axle and a constant velocity tripod joint on the inboard side, **Fig. 5**.

On models equipped with tri-pot joints on inboard axles, care must be taken not to overextend joints. When either or both ends are disconnected, overextending the tri-pot joint could result in internal joint separation.

On vehicles equipped with ball type constant velocity inboard joints, install inner drive joint seal protector J-34754, on

1	HUB NUT
2	WASHER
3	KNUCKLE & HUB ASSEMBLY
4	DRIVE AXLE-OUTER JOINT
5	DRIVE AXLE-INNER JOINT

Fig. 2 Front wheel drive components & axle shaft installation. Except Metro & Storm (Typical)

Key No.	Part Name
1 –	RACE, C.V. JOINT OUTER
2 –	CAGE, C.V. JOINT
3 –	RACE, C.V. JOINT INNER
4 –	RING, SHAFT RETAINING
5 –	BALL (6)
6 –	PROTECTOR, CLAMP (2)
7 –	SEAL, C.V. JOINT
8 –	CLAMP, SEAL RETAINING
9 –	SHAFT, AXLE (LH)
10 –	SEAL, TRI-POT JOINT
11 –	SPIDER, TRI-POT JOINT
12 –	ROLLER, NEEDLE
13 –	BALL, TRI-POT JOINT (3)
14 –	RETAINER, BALL & NEEDLE (3)
15 –	HOUSING ASM, TRI-POT
16 –	HOUSING ASM, DAMPER & TRI-POT (RH)
17 –	SHAFT, AXLE (RH)
18 –	RING, SPACER
19 –	RING, RACE RETAINING
20 –	CLAMP, SEAL RETAINING
21 –	RETAINER, NEEDLE
22 –	RING, NEEDLE RETAINER
23 –	RING, JOINT RETAINING
24 –	HOUSING, TRI-POT (RH)
25 –	SHAFT ASM, DAMPER &
26 –	RING, DEFLECTOR
27 –	BUSHING, TRILOBAL TRI-POT

DESIGN TYPE A

DESIGN TYPE B

DESIGN TYPE B

DESIGN TYPE A

Fig. 3 Exploded view of drive axle with tri-pot inboard joint. Except Geo & LeMans

1. RING, DEFLECTOR
2. RACE, C V JOINT OUTER
3. CAGE, C V JOINT
4. RACE, C V JOINT INNER
5. BALL, CHROME ALLOY
6. RING, RACE RETAINING
7. CLAMP, SEAL RETAINING
8. SEAL, DRIVE AXLE OUTBOARD
9. CLAMP, SEAL RETAINING
10. SHAFT, AXLE
11. SEAL, DRIVE AXLE INBOARD
12. RING, BALL RETAINING
13. RACE, C/G JOINT INNER
14. CAGE, C/G JOINT
15. RACE, C/G JOINT OUTER
16. RING, JOINT RETAINING

(LH AUTO ONLY)
(EQUAL LENGTH, RH MAN ONLY)

Fig. 4   Exploded view of cross-groove design drive axle. w/manual transmission except Geo & LeMans

1. SNAP RING
2. DIFFERENTIAL-SIDE JOINT ASSEMBLY (CONSTANT VELOCITY TRIPOD JOINT)
3. SNAP RING
4. DIFFERENTIAL-SIDE BOOT BAND
5. DIFFERENTIAL-SIDE BOOT
6. BOOT BAND
7. GREASE IN BOOT SET (YELLOW 90 GRAM 3.2 OZ.)
8. GREASE IN BOOT SET (YELOW 70 GRAM 2.5 OZ.)
9. WHEEL-SIDE BOOT
10. WHEEL-SIDE BOOT BAND
11. WHEEL-SIDE JOINT ASSEMBLY (CONTANT VELOCITY BALL JOINT)
12. BEARING OIL SEAL
13. WASHER
14. DRIVESHAFT NUT

Fig. 5   Exploded view of drive axle. Metro

1. DRIFT PUNCH
2. 6 POINT DEEP WELL SOCKET

Fig. 6   Removing & installing axle shaft nut

inboard seal and install axle boot protector J-28712 on outboard seal if necessary. On vehicles equipped with tri-pot inboard joints, install axle boot seal protector J-28712 on outboard seal and J-33162 on inboard seal, if necessary.

ELDORADO, REATTA, RIVIERA, SEVILLE, TORONADO/TROFEO
Removal

1. Remove hub nut, then raise and support vehicle and remove wheel and tire assembly.
2. Remove brake caliper and rotor assembly.
3. Remove stabilizer link or stabilizer bar from control arm.
4. Remove tie rod end at steering knuckle, then remove lower ball joint stud at steering knuckle.
5. Remove axle from transaxle using a prybar or screwdriver and a wood block as a fulcrum to protect case cover.
6. Drive axle from hub and bearing assembly using drive axle spindle remover tool No. J-28733.
7. Remove axle from vehicle.

Installation

1. Install drive axle at steering knuckle.
2. Install lower ball joint stud at steering knuckle.
3. Install stabilizer link or stabilizer bar to lower control arm.
4. Install tie rod end at steering knuckle.
5. Install brake caliper, rotor and new caliper mounting bolts.
6. Install new torque prevailing nut and washer.
7. Insert a screwdriver or drift into caliper and rotor to prevent rotor from turning, then install hub nut and **torque** to 183 ft. lbs. **Fig. 6.**
8. Seat the drive axle into the transaxle by placing a screwdriver into the groove on the joint housing and tapping until seated, then grasp the inner housing and pull outward. If the snap ring is properly seated, the axle will remain in place, **Fig. 2.**
9. Install the front wheel and tire assembly and lower vehicle.

BONNEVILLE, CAVALIER, CENTURY, CUTLASS CALAIS, CUTLASS CIERA, CUTLASS CRUISER, ELECTRA, 1991 GRAND AM, LESABRE, PARK AVENUE, SKYLARK & SUNBIRD, 88 & 98

Removal

1. Raise and support vehicle, then remove tire and wheel assembly.
2. Install a brass drift or a screwdriver to prevent the rotor from turning, **Fig. 6.**
3. Remove shaft nut and washer using shaft nut socket tool No. J-34826.
4. Remove brake caliper from steering knuckle and suspend caliper assembly.
5. Remove rotor from hub and bearing assembly, then stabilizer shaft or link from control arm.
6. Remove ball joint from steering knuckle.
7. Remove drive axle from transaxle using axle shaft remover tool No. J-33008, axle shaft remover tool No. J-29794 and slide hammer tool No. J-2619-01 if necessary, **Fig. 1.**
8. Remove drive axle from hub and bearing assembly using front hub spindle remover tool No. J-28733-A, **Fig. 7.**

Installation

1. Install drive axle into hub and bearing assembly and transaxle.
2. Install lower ball joint to steering knuckle.
3. Install stabilizer shaft or link to control arm.
4. Install rotor to hub and bearing assembly.
5. Insert a screwdriver or drift into caliper and rotor to prevent rotor from turning, **Fig. 6.**
6. Install a new hub nut and washer, **torque** to 185 ft. lbs. On Cavalier, Celebrity, Century, Cutlass, Grand Am, LeSabre, Skylark and Sunbird. On Bonneville, 88 and 98, Electra, LeSabre and Park Avenue **torque** to 192 ft. lbs.
7. Seat the drive axle into the transaxle by placing a screwdriver into the groove on the joint housing and tapping until seated.
8. Ensure drive axle is seated by pulling outward on the housing. Do not pull on the drive axle.
9. Install tire and wheel assembly and lower vehicle.

CUTLASS SUPREME, GRAND PRIX, LUMINA & REGAL

Removal

1. Raise and support vehicle, then remove tire and wheel assembly.

1. J-28733
2. TURN FORCING SCREW UNTIL AXLE SPLINES ARE JUST LOOSE

Fig. 7 Removing drive axle from hub & bearing assembly

2. Remove brake caliper and bracket assembly, then the rotor.
3. Remove the four bolts holding the hub/bearing assembly to the knuckle.
4. **On vehicles equipped with Anti-Lock Brake System (ABS),** remove the ABS sensor mounting bolt, then position the sensor aside to avoid damage.
5. **On vehicles equipped with 125C and HM-282 transaxles and right shaft of vehicles with 440-T4 transaxles,** separate the drive axle from the transaxle using axle shaft remover tool No. J-3308, extension tool No. J-29794 and puller tool No. J-2619-01, **Fig. 1. On the left shaft of vehicles equipped with 440-T4 transmissions,** using the frame for leverage, separate the drive axle from the transaxle with a screwdriver or prybar in the groove provided on the inner joint, **Fig. 2.**
6. **On all transmissions,** remove the axle/bearing assembly through the knuckle.

Installation

1. **On all transmissions,** install the axle/bearing assembly through the knuckle and into the transaxle. **If equipped with ABS,** install the ABS assembly.
2. Loosely secure the bearing to knuckle bolts.
3. Seat the drive axle into the transaxle by placing a screwdriver into the groove on the joint housing and tapping until seated, then grasp the inner housing and pull outward. If the snap ring is properly seated, the axle will remain in place, **Fig. 2.**
4. Using a new nut and washer, install the hub and bearing assembly to axle, **torque** hub and bearing assembly to knuckle attaching bolts to 52 ft. lbs.
5. Install rotor and brake assembly.
6. Install tire and wheel assembly.
7. **Torque** drive axle nut to 184 ft. lbs, then lower vehicle.

DEVILLE & FLEETWOOD

Removal

1. Raise and support vehicle, then remove tire and wheel assembly.
2. Install a brass drift or a screwdriver to

prevent the rotor from turning, **Fig. 6.**
3. Remove shaft nut and washer.
4. Remove lower ball joint cotter and nut, then loosen ball joint using ball joint separator tool No. J-29330. **If removing right axle,** turn wheel to left, **if removing left axle,** turn wheel to the right.
5. Separate the joint by using a pry bar between the suspension support and lower control arm.
6. Pull out on lower knuckle area and with a plastic or rubber mallet strike the end of the axle shaft to disengage axle from hub and bearing.
7. Separate hub and bearing assembly from drive axle and move strut and knuckle assembly rearward.
8. Remove inner joint from transaxle using axle shaft remover tool No. J-28468 or J-33008 if equipped with intermediate shaft, **Fig. 1.**

Installation

1. Seat the drive axle into the transaxle by placing a screwdriver into the groove on the joint housing and tapping until seated, then grasp the inner housing and pull outward. If the snap ring is properly seated, the axle will remain in place, **Fig. 2.**
2. Drive axle into hub and bearing assembly.
3. Install lower ball joint to knuckle, **torque** to 41-50 ft. lbs., then install cotter pin.
4. Install washer and new shaft nut.
5. Insert a screwdriver or drift into caliper and rotor to prevent rotor from turning. **Fig. 6.**
6. Install hub nut, **torque** to 192 ft. lbs.
7. Install tire and wheel assembly and lower vehicle.

METRO

1. Remove wheel center cap.
2. Remove caulking, driveshaft nut and washer.
3. Raise and support vehicle.
4. Remove wheel and tire assembly.
5. Drain transaxle fluid.
6. Pry inboard driveshaft from transaxle using a large screwdriver or equivalent.
7. Remove lower ball joint retaining nut, then separate suspension arm from steering knuckle.
8. Remove drive axle assembly from transaxle, then from steering knuckle.
9. Reverse procedure to install, noting the following:
   a. Clean front wheel bearing seal, then apply grease to seal.
   b. Check seal for breakage or deterioration, replace if necessary.
   c. Apply sealant to drain plug for manual transaxle.
   d. Install the wheel side joint to the steering knuckle, then the differential-side joint to the transaxle. Push drive axle into transaxle by hand until snap ring is seated in spline. **Torque** hub nut to 129 ft. lbs. and ball joint stud bolt to 44 ft. lbs.

PRIZM

1. Disconnect battery ground cable.
2. Raise and support vehicle.
3. Drain transaxle fluid.
4. Remove hub nut cap, then cotter pin, hub nut and washer.
5. Remove tie rod end from steering knuckle.
6. Remove brake caliper from steering knuckle.
7. Disconnect control arm from steering knuckle.
8. Remove brake rotor.
9. Remove drive axle from hub assembly using a plastic hammer. **If shaft is difficult to remove, use crankshaft gear puller (Tool No. J 25287) or equivalent.**
10. Remove drive axle assembly from transaxle using slide hammer (Tool No. J 6125-1B) and axle shaft puller (Tool No. J 35762).
11. Reverse procedure to install, noting the following:
    a. Install drive axle in transaxle first, then hub assembly.
    b. **Torque** lower control arm bolts to 105 ft. lbs.
    c. **Torque** tie rod end nut to 36 ft. lbs.
    d. **Torque** brake caliper mounting bolts to 65 ft. lbs.
    e. **Torque** drive axle hub nut to 137 ft.lbs.

STORM

1. Disconnect battery ground cable.
2. Raise and support vehicle.
3. Drain transaxle fluid.
4. Remove wheel assembly.
5. Unstake hub nut, then remove nut.
6. Remove tie rod end from steering knuckle.
7. Disconnect lower control arm from steering knuckle.
8. Remove drive axle from hub assembly, using a plastic hammer.
9. Remove drive axle assembly from transaxle, using slide hammer (Tool No. J 2619-01) and axle shaft puller (Tool No. J 35762).
10. Remove drive axle from vehicle.
11. Reverse procedure to install, noting the following:
    a. **Torque** lower control arm bolts to 115 ft. lbs.
    b. **Torque** tie rod end to 40 ft. lbs.
    c. **Torque** hub nut to 137 ft. lbs., then stake nut.

LEMANS
Removal

1. Loosen both upper strut mount attaching bolts.
2. Remove wheel cover, then loosen wheel lug nuts and remove cotter pin and drive axle shaft-to-hub nut and washer.
3. Raise and support vehicle.
4. Remove wheel and tire assembly.
5. Remove ball joint retaining clip and stud nut, then separate ball joint from steering knuckle using ball joint separator tool No. J-36226 or equivalent. **Disregard "This Side Towards Wheel" marking on tool. Tool must be turned to opposite position when used on these vehicles.**
6. Remove tie rod nut, then separate tie rod from steering knuckle using tie rod separator tool No. J-24319-01 or equivalent.
7. Separate drive axle shaft from wheel hub using axle shaft to hub separator tool No. J-37105 or equivalent.
8. Position a drain pan under transaxle, then remove drive axle from transaxle using axle shaft to transaxle separator tool No. J-36639 and slide hammer tool No. J-23907 or equivalents.

Installation

1. Install drive axle into transaxle, using care to avoid damaging seal. Pull on outer joint race to ensure it will not come out of transaxle.
2. Install drive axle into knuckle hub bearing.
3. Install steering knuckle onto lower ball joint, then connect tie rod to the knuckle. **Torque** tie rod nut to 45 ft. lbs. and ball joint stud nut to 50 ft. lbs., then tie rod nut cotter pin and stud nut retaining clip.
4. Install drive axle shaft-to-wheel hub washer and nut.
5. Install wheel and tire assembly, then lower vehicle.
6. With weight of vehicle on wheels, **torque** new drive axle-to-hub nut to 74 ft. lbs., then back off nut and **retorque** to 15 ft. lbs. Tighten nut an additional 1/4 turn, then install cotter pin. If necessary, loosen nut slightly to align cotter pin holes.
7. **Torque** upper strut mount attaching nuts to 22 ft. lbs.
8. Check transaxle fluid and replenish as needed.

6000
Removal

1. Raise and support vehicle, then remove tire and wheel assembly.
2. Insert drift or screwdriver into caliper to prevent rotor from turning, **Fig. 6.**
3. Remove hub nut and washer using hub nut socket tool No. J-34826 and discard the shaft nut, **Fig. 6.**
4. Remove brake caliper from steering knuckle and suspend caliper assembly.
5. Remove rotor from hub and bearing assembly.
6. Remove stabilizer shaft from control arm.
7. Remove ball joint from steering knuckle.
8. Install drive axle seal protector J-34754 or equivalent on drive axle.
9. Using axle shaft remover tool No. J-33008 with extension J-29794 on slide hammer, remove drive axle from transaxle, then vehicle, **Fig. 1.**
10. Remove drive axle from hub and bearing assembly using puller No. J-28733, **Fig. 7.**

Installation

1. Install drive axle into hub and bearing assembly, then the transmission.
2. Install the lower ball joint to the steering knuckle and **torque** ball joint pinch bolt to 33 ft. lbs.
3. Install the stabilizer shaft to the control arm.
4. Install caliper to steering knuckle, then install washer and a new torque prevailing shaft nut.
5. Insert a screwdriver or drift into caliper and rotor to prevent rotor from turning, **Fig. 6.**
6. Install hub nut, **torque** to 185 ft. lbs.
7. Seat the drive axle into the transaxle by placing a screwdriver into the groove on the joint housing and tapping until seated, then grasp the inner housing and pull outward. If snap ring is properly seated, the axle will remain in place, **Fig. 2.**
8. Install tire and wheel assembly and lower vehicle.

BERETTA & CORSICA
Removal

1. Disconnect battery ground cable.
2. Raise and support vehicle, then remove wheel and tire assembly.
3. Install drive axle seal protector J-34754 on outer joint.
4. Insert a screwdriver or drift into caliper and rotor to prevent rotor from turning and remove hub nut and washer, **Fig. 6.**
5. Remove lower ball joint cotter pin and nut, then loosen joint using tool No. J-29330. If right axle is being removed, turn wheel to left, if left axle is being removed, turn wheel to right.
6. Insert a prybar between suspension support and lower control arm and separate joint.
7. Disengage axle from hub and bearing using tool No. J-28733-A.
8. **On all models,** separate hub and bearing assembly from drive axle and move strut and knuckle assembly rearward.
9. Remove inner joint from transaxle or intermediate shaft (if equipped) using tool No. J-28468 or J-33008 attached to J-29794 and J-2619-01.
10. Remove drive axle from vehicle.

Installation

1. Install seal protector No. J-37292-B into transaxle.
2. Install drive axle into the transaxle by placing a screwdriver into the groove on the joint housing and tapping until seated, then grasp the inner housing and pull outward. If the snap ring is properly seated, the axle will remain in place, **Fig. 2.**
3. Lubricate inside diameter of seal lips and completely fill cavity between hub and bearing assembly and seal with chassis grease.
4. Install drive axle into hub and bearing assembly and lower ball joint to knuckle.
5. **Torque** ball joint to steering knuckle

nut to 26 ft. lbs. plus 60° rotation, then install cotter pin.

6. Insert a screwdriver or drift into caliper and rotor to prevent rotor from turning and install hub nut and washer, **Fig. 6.**
7. **Torque** hub nut to 192 ft. lbs.
8. Remove both seal protectors and install wheel and tire assembly.
9. Lower vehicle and connect battery ground cable.

ACHIEVA, 1992-93 GRAND AM & SKYLARK
Removal

1. Disconnect battery ground cable.
2. Raise and support vehicle, then remove wheel and tire assembly.
3. Install drive axle seal protector J-34754 on outer joint.
4. Insert a screwdriver or drift into caliper and rotor to prevent rotor from turning and remove hub nut and washer, **Fig. 6.**
5. Remove lower ball joint cotter pin and nut, then loosen joint using tool No. J-29330. If right axle is being removed, turn wheel to left, if left axle is being removed, turn wheel to right.
6. Insert a prybar between suspension support and lower control arm and separate joint.
7. Disengage axle from hub and bearing using tool No. J-28733-A.
8. Separate hub and bearing assembly from drive axle and move strut and knuckle assembly rearward.
9. Remove inner joint from transaxle or intermediate shaft (if equipped) using tool No. J-28468 or J-33008 attached to J-29794 and J-2619-01.
10. Remove drive axle from vehicle.

Installation

1. Install seal protector No. J-37292-B into transaxle.
2. Install drive axle into the transaxle by placing a screwdriver into the groove on the joint housing and tapping until seated, then grasp the inner housing and pull outward. If the snap ring is properly seated, the axle will remain in place, **Fig. 2.**
3. Lubricate inside diameter of seal lips and completely fill cavity between hub and bearing assembly and seal with chassis grease.
4. Install drive axle into hub and bearing assembly and lower ball joint to knuckle.
5. **Torque** ball joint to steering knuckle nut to 41-50 ft. lbs.
6. Insert a screwdriver or drift into caliper and rotor to prevent rotor from turning and install hub nut and washer, **Fig. 6.**
7. **Torque** hub nut to 185 ft. lbs.
8. Remove both seal protectors and install wheel and tire assembly.
9. Lower vehicle and connect battery ground cable.

1	RING JOINT RETAINING
2	RACE JOINT OUTER
3	RING RACE RETAINING
4	CLAMP SEAL RETAINING
5	SEAL JOINT INNER
6	CLAMP SEAL RETAINING
7	SHAFT DRIVE AXLE
8	CLAMP SEAL RETAINING
9	SEAL JOINT OUTER
10	CLAMP SEAL RETAINING
11	RING RACE RETAINING
12	BALLS BEARING
13	RACE INNER
14	CAGE BEARING
15	RACE JOINT OUTER

Fig. 8   Exploded view of front drive axle assembly. LeMans

INTERMEDIATE SHAFT REPLACE

EXCEPT CUTLASS SUPREME, GRAND PRIX & LUMINA

1. Install engine support fixture No. J-28467-A or equivalent, then raise and support vehicle.
2. Remove right tire assembly. Using shop towels, protect outer joint front any sharp edges.
3. Remove stabilizer shaft from right control arm, then disconnect right ball joint from knuckle.
4. Remove rear engine mount through bolt, then separate drive axle from intermediate shaft.
5. Remove intermediate shaft support bracket to engine bolts.
6. Disengage intermediate shaft from transaxle, then remove intermediate shaft from vehicle.
7. Reverse procedure to install, noting the following:
   a. **Torque** intermediate shaft support bracket bolts to 37 ft. lbs.
   b. **Torque** rear engine mount through bolt to 55 ft. lbs.

1991-92 CUTLASS SUPREME, GRAND PRIX & LUMINA

1. Raise and support vehicle, then remove right wheel assembly.
2. Drain transaxle fluid, then remove right drive axle.
3. Remove intermediate shaft housing to bracket bolts, then the bracket.
4. Remove housing to transaxle bolts.
5. Disengage intermediate axle shaft from transaxle, then remove intermediate shaft assembly from vehicle.

6. Reverse procedure to install, noting the following:
   a. **Torque** housing to transaxle bolts to 18 ft. lbs.
   b. **Torque** bracket to engine case to 37 ft. lbs.
   c. **Torque** housing to bracket bolts to 37 ft. lbs.
   d. Coat splines of intermediate axle shaft with chassis grease.

1993 GRAND PRIX & LUMINA

1. Remove transaxle from vehicle.
2. Remove intermediate shaft to transaxle bolts, then the intermediate shaft from transaxle.
3. Reverse procedure to install, noting the following:
   a. **Torque** intermediate shaft to transaxle bolts to 18 ft. lbs.
   b. Lubricate splines of intermediate shaft with chassis grease.

AXLE SHAFT SERVICE
DISASSEMBLY
LEMANS

1. Secure axle shaft in a soft-jawed vise.
2. Cut off seal clamps and remove seals, then spread bearing retaining rings, **Fig. 8.**
3. Mark relationship between shaft and joints for assembly reference, then tap joints off shaft using a plastic mallet.
4. Inspect all components for excessive wear or damage and replace as necessary.

METRO

Do not disassemble outboard joint or differential side ball joint. If any malfunction is detected in these components, replace as an assembly.

1. Remove tripod joint boot band, **Fig. 5.**
2. Remove tripod joint housing.

MANUAL TRANSAXLE

AUTOMATIC TRANSAXLE

1 DEFLECTOR RING	11 BALL GUIDE
2 CONSTANT VELOCITY JOINT HOUSING	12 BALLS
3 AXLE SHAFT SNAP RING	13 BALL RETAINER
4 LARGE BOOT CLAMP	14 DOUBLE OFFSET JOINT-OUTER RACE
5 OUTER BOOT	15 AXLE SHAFT RETAINING CLIP
6 SMALL BOOT CLAMP	16 AXLE SHAFT SNAP RING
7 LEFT-HAND DRIVE AXLE SHAFT	17 TRI-POT JOINT HOUSING
8 DRIVE AXLE DAMPENER	18 TRI-POT JOINT BALL
9 INNER BOOT	19 TRI-POT JOINT BALL AND BEARING RETAINER
10 CIRCULAR CLIP	20 TRI-POT JOINT NEEDLE BEARINGS
	21 TRI-POT JOINT SPIDER

Fig. 9 Exploded view of front drive axle assembly. Storm

3. Using snap ring pliers, remove snap ring from shaft.
4. Remove tripod joint spider from shaft.
5. Remove boot band from inner driveshaft joint, then boot.
6. Release boot bands from outer boot, then remove boot.

STORM

Double Offset Joint

1. Secure axle assembly in a soft-jawed vise.
2. Remove boot band from differential side joint.
3. Move boot slightly and remove circular clip.
4. Separate case from shaft and remove 6 balls using a suitable screwdriver.
5. Turn ball guide on an angle and move it to center shaft side.
6. Remove snap ring from shaft **Fig. 9**, then slide out ball guide and retainer.
7. Remove boot from shaft, and if necessary, tap damper off shaft with brass hammer.

Tripod Joint

1. Secure axle assembly in a soft-jawed vise.
2. Using a screwdriver, remove boot band from differential side joint.
3. Place alignment marks on both housing and shaft, then remove housing from shaft.
4. Remove snap ring from shaft, then make alignment marks on both shaft and tripod.
5. Using a hammer and brass drift, remove tripod from shaft. **Ensure care is taken not to hit roller.**
6. Remove boot from shaft, and if necessary, tap damper off shaft with brass hammer.

PRIZM

1. Secure axle assembly in a soft-jawed vise.
2. Remove boot retaining clamps, **Fig. 10**.
3. Remove race retaining ring using

snap ring pliers.
4. Disconnect inner race from drive axle shaft.
5. Remove boot from axle shaft.
6. Tilt cage, then remove ball bearings.
7. Tilt cage and inner race 90°, then pull from outer race.

ASSEMBLY
METRO

Thoroughly inspect parts for wear prior to assembly. Replace any excessively worn parts. Ensure wheel-side joint assembly and tripod joint housing are washed and air dried, and that the boots are cleaned with a cloth.

1. Apply joint grease liberally to wheel-side joint, **Fig. 11.**
2. Install wheel-side boot on shaft, then fill inside of boot with joint grease, approximately 80 grams.
3. Install boot bands.
4. Install transaxle-side boot clamp, then boot onto shaft.
5. Apply yellow grease liberally to transaxle-side joint.
6. Install spider joint on shaft with beveled side facing wheel-side joint.
7. Install spider joint snap ring.
8. Fill inside of transaxle-side boot with joint grease, approximately 130 grams.
9. Install spider joint housing, then boot band.
10. Check boots for distortion or dents, correct as necessary.

STORM

1. Install boot clamp on shaft, then boot.
2. Install ball guide and ball retainer on shaft, then snap ring.
3. Move ball guide into place, then install six balls into ball guide.
4. Install circular clip in outer race.
5. Pack one half of joint with GM grease (Part No.7845393).
6. Remove drive axle from vise.

PRIZM

1. Apply GM grease (Part No. 7845393) to tri-pot housing and spider joint.
2. Install boot clamp on drive axle shaft, then boot.
3. Install spider joint assembly on drive axle using a brass drift and hammer.
4. Install outboard snap ring.
5. Install spider assembly in tri-pot housing.
6. Connect boot and boot clamp to tri-pot housing.
7. Remove driveshaft assembly from vise.

LEMANS

1. Pack joints with suitable grease, then tap joint assemblies into shaft splines until retaining rings are properly seated.
2. Install inner joint on long side of shaft and outer joint on short side of shaft.
3. Install joint seals and with new clamps. Secure clamps using seal clamp installer tool No. J-22610 or equivalent.

1	DEFLECTOR RING	12	TRI-POT JOINT HOUSING
2	CONSTANT VELOCITY JOINT OUTER RACE	13	AXLE SHAFT RETAINING PINS
3	CASE	14	DRIVE AXLE DUST COVER
4	CONSTANT VELOCITY JOINT INNER RACE	15	AXLE SHAFT SNAP RING
5	BALLS	16	LARGE BOOT CLAMPS
6	AXLE SNAFT SHAP RING	17	LEFT HAND DRIVE AXLE SHAFT
7	OUTBOARD BOOT	18	TRI-POT JOINT BALL
8	SMALL BOOT CLAMP	19	TRI-POT JOINT BALL AND BEARING RETAINER
9	RIGHT HAND DRIVE AXLE SHAFT	20	TRI-POT JOINT NEEDLE BEARINGS
10	TRI-POT BOOT	21	TRI-POT JOINT SPIDER
11	AXLE SHAFT RETAINING RING	22	DRIVE AXLE DAMPENER

Fig. 10   Exploded view of front drive axle assembly. Prizm

A	BLACK GREASE (70 GRAM 2.5 OZ.)		
B	YELLOW GREASE (90 GRAM 3.2 OZ.)		
C	CHAMFER		
1	WHEEL-SIDE JOINT ASSEMBLY		
2	WHEEL-SIDE BOOT BAND		
3	WHEEL-SIDE BOOT		
4	BOOT BAND	7	TRIPOD JOINT SPIDER
5	DIFFERENTIAL-SIDE BOOT BAND	8	SNAP RING
6	DIFFERENTIAL-SIDE BOOT BAND	9	TRIPOD JOINT HOUSING
		10	SNAP RING

Fig. 11   Assembling drive axle assembly. Metro

1 RETAINING RING
2 LIP SEAL
3 OUTER SLINGER
4 SUPPORT
5 BEARING
6 RETAINER
7 SCREW
8 INNER SLINGER
9 SHAFT

Fig. 12 Exploded view of intermediate shaft. Except Cutlass Supreme, Grand Prix & Lumina

1. "O" RING SEAL
2. HOUSING
3. ROLLER BEARING
4. SPACER
5. WASHER
6. SNAP RING
7. LIP SEAL

Fig. 13 Exploded view of intermediate shaft. Cutlass Supreme, Grand Prix & Lumina

INTERMEDIATE SHAFT SERVICE

DISASSEMBLY

Except Cutlass Supreme, Grand Prix & Lumina

1. Remove retaining ring and lip seal, **Fig. 12.**
2. Using split plate No. J-22912-1 or equivalent behind inner slinger, press shaft from bearing.
3. Remove retainer from support screws.
4. Using replacer No. J-23694 or equivalent, press bearing from support.

Fig. 14 Outer constant velocity joint seal removal & installation

Cutlass Supreme, Grand Prix & Lumina

1. Remove intermediate shaft from vehicle.
2. Remove lip seal, snap ring and washer from housing, **Fig. 13.**
3. Using handle No. J-8592 and bearing remover No. J-8810 or equivalents, press spacer and bearing from housing.

ASSEMBLY

Except Cutlass Supreme, Grand Prix & Lumina

1. Press bearing into support using press arbor plate across bearing.
2. Using split plate No. J-22912-1 or equivalent, press inner slinger on shaft.
3. Install retainer over shaft.
4. Place support with bearing on press arbor plate and press shaft into bear-

Fig. 15 Outer constant velocity joint disassembly & assembly

ing until bearing inner race contacts chamfer on shaft. **Do not press bearing beyond where chamfer begins on shaft.**
5. Using split plate, press outer slinger on shaft.
6. Apply sealer to outer slinger and shaft joint, then install lip seal using seal installer No. J-34115 or equivalent.
7. Install retaining ring.
8. Install retainer to support. **Torque screws to 89 inch lbs.**

Cutlass Supreme, Grand Prix & Lumina

1. Using bearing installer No. J-36379 or equivalent, press bearing into housing support.
2. Install spacer, washer and snap ring into housing, **Fig. 13.**
3. Using seal installer No. J-23771 or equivalent, install lip seal.
4. Install intermediate shaft assembly in vehicle.

Fig. 16 Inner tri-pot seal removal & installation. Less bearing blocks

Fig. 17 Inner tri-pot seal removal & installation (Part 1 of 2). w/bearing blocks

OUTER CONSTANT VELOCITY JOINT & SEAL REPLACE

EXCEPT GEO & LEMANS

For removal and installation procedures refer to **Figs. 14 and 15.**

GEO & LEMANS

For replacement procedure, refer to "Axle Shaft Disassembly."

INNER TRI-POT SEAL REPLACE

EXCEPT GEO & LEMANS

For removal and installation procedures, refer to **Figs. 16 and 17.**

GEO & LEMANS

For replacement procedure, refer to "Axle Shaft Disassembly."

INNER CONSTANT VELOCITY JOINT & SEAL REPLACE

CROSS GROOVE DESIGN FRONT AXLE

For removal and installation procedures refer to **Fig. 18.**

DEFLECTOR RING REPLACE

EXCEPT GEO & LEMANS

For removal and installation procedures, refer to **Fig. 19.**

GEO & LEMANS

1. Disconnect battery ground cable.
2. Raise and support vehicle.
3. Remove drive axle assembly.
4. Remove deflector ring using shaft removal fork (Part No. J-37780).
5. Reverse procedure to install.

REMOVE AND INSTALL INNER TRI-POT SEAL

REMOVE
1. Cut seal retaining clamps with side cutters
2. Remove parts as shown

INSTALL
1. Flush grease from housing and repack housing with approximately half of grease furnished with new seal
2. Put remainder of grease in seal
3. Install parts as shown Insert bearing blocks in housing grooves and remove metal plate Use tool J-35910 or J-35566 to secure seal retaining clamp Torque to specifications

Fig. 17 Inner tri-pot seal removal & installation (Part 2 of 2). w/bearing blocks

REMOVE AND INSTALL INNER JOINT SEAL

REMOVE
1. Cut seal retaining clamps
2. Remove parts as shown

INSTALL
1. Flush grease from joint Repack joint with approx half of grease provided
2. Put remainder of grease in seal
3. Install parts as shown Use tool J-35910 to secure seal retaining clamp Torque to specifications

CLEAN AND FLUSH INNER JOINT

1. Push inner race and cage to bottom of housing to displace grease
2. Thoroughly wipe all excess grease from joint
3. Repack joint with recommended grease

NOTICE: The cross-groove joint design uses precision grinding and selected dimensional component fits for proper assembly and operation Due to its complexity it is not recommended that the joint be disassembled for service

Fig. 18 Cross groove inner joint seal removal & installation. w/cross groove inner joint

REMOVE AND INSTALL DEFLECTOR RING

REMOVE
1. For damaged deflector ring remove parts as shown

INSTALL
1. Install part as shown

Fig. 19 Deflector ring removal & installation. Except Geo & LeMans

TIGHTENING SPECIFICATIONS

Component	Model	Torque/ Ft. Lbs.
Caliper Bolts	Prizm & Storm	65
Hub Nut	Metro	129
	Prizm & Storm	137
	LeMans	③
	④	185
	⑤	192
	⑥	184
	Cutlass Supreme, Grand Prix, Lumina & Regal	183
Lower Ball Joint	Metro	44
	LeMans	50

TIGHTENING SPECIFICATIONS—Continued

Component	Model	Torque/Ft. Lbs.
Lower Ball Joint-Cont'd	Beretta & Corsica	③
	Achieva, Deville, Fleetwood; 1992-93 Grand Am & Skylark	41–50
Lower Ball Joint Pinch Bolt	6000	33
Lower Control Arm Bolts	Prizm & Storm	105①
Tie Rod Nut	Prizm & Storm	36②
	LeMans	45
Upper Strut Mount Nut	LeMans	22
Wheel Hub To Knuckle Bolts	Cutlass Supreme, Grand Prix, Lumina & Regal	52
Wheel Lug Nuts	Prizm	76
	Storm	87
	Metro	44
	LeMans	66
	⑨	100

① —Storm, 115 ft. lbs.
② —Storm, 40 ft. lbs.
③ —See text.
④ —Achieva, Cavalier, Century, Cutlass, Grand Am, Skylark, Sunbird, 6000.
⑤ —Bonneville, 88 & 98, Electra, LeSabre, Park Avenue; Beretta, Corsica, Deville & Fleetwood.
⑥ —Eldorado, Reatta, Riviera, Seville & Toronado.
⑦ —Except Prizm, Storm, Metro & LeMans.

HYDRAULIC BRAKE SYSTEM

INDEX

Fig. 1   Front & rear split brake system

1 TO RIGHT FRONT WHEEL
2 TO LEFT FRONT WHEEL
3 TO RIGHT REAR WHEEL
4 TO LEFT REAR WHEEL
5 MASTER CYLINDER
6 CLIP
7 HEAT SHIELD
8 RETAINER

Fig. 2   Diagonally split brake system

DESCRIPTION

SYSTEM OPERATION

Front & Rear Split System

When the brake pedal is depressed, both the primary (front brake) and the secondary (rear brake) master cylinder pistons are moved simultaneously to exert hydraulic fluid pressure on their respective systems, **Fig. 1**.

If the rear (secondary) brake system fails, initial brake pedal movement will cause the unrestricted secondary piston to bottom in the master cylinder bore. Primary piston movement will displace hydraulic fluid in the primary section of the master cylinder to actuate the front brake system.

If the front (primary) brake system fails, initial brake pedal movement will cause the unrestricted primary piston to bottom out against the secondary piston. Continued downward movement of the brake pedal moves the secondary piston to displace hydraulic fluid in the rear brake system to actuate the rear brakes.

Diagonally Split System

This system operates on the same principle as conventional front and rear split systems, using primary and secondary master cylinders which move simultaneously to exert hydraulic pressure on their respective systems. The hydraulic brake lines on this system, however, have been diagonally split front to rear (left front to right rear and right front to left rear) in place of separate lines to the front and rear wheels, **Fig. 2**.

In the event of a system failure, the remaining non-failed system will do all the braking on one front wheel and one rear wheel, thus maintaining 50% of the total braking force.

COMPONENT DESCRIPTION

BRAKE WARNING LAMP SWITCHES

There are four basic types of brake warning lamp switches as shown, **Figs. 3 through 6**. When a pressure differential occurs between the front and rear brake systems, the valves will shuttle toward the side with the low pressure.

In the switch shown in **Fig. 3**, movement of the differential valve forces the switch plunger upward over the tapered shoulder of the valve to close the switch contacts and light the dual brake warning lamp, signaling a brake system failure.

In **Fig. 4**, the valve assembly consists of two valves in a common bore that are spring loaded toward the centered position. The spring-loaded switch contact plunger rests on top of the valves in the centered position (right view). When a pressure differential occurs between the front and rear brake systems, the valves will shuttle toward the side with the low

Fig. 3 Pressure differential valve & brake warning lamp switch

Fig. 5 Pressure differential valve & brake warning lamp switch

Fig. 4 Pressure differential valve & brake warning lamp switch

Fig. 6 Dual master cylinder with built in warning lamp switch

pressure. The spring-loaded switch plunger is "triggered" and the ground circuit for the warning lamp is completed, lighting the lamp (left view).

In **Fig. 5**, as pressure falls in one system, the other system's normal pressure forces the piston to the inoperative side, contacting the switch terminal, causing the warning lamp on the instrument panel to glow.

Fig. 6 shows the switch mounted directly in the master cylinder assembly. Whenever there is a specified differential pressure, the switch piston will activate the brake failure warning switch and cause the brake warning lamp to glow.

Testing Warning Lamp Operation

The warning lamp should illuminate when the ignition switch is in the start position, and turn off when the switch returns to run. If the brake lamp remains on after the ignition returns to run, check fluid level in master cylinder reservoir and inspect parking brake. If the warning lamp does not turn on during cranking, check for defective bulb or blown fuse.

COMBINATION VALVE

The combination valve, **Fig. 7** is a metering valve, failure warning switch, and a proportioner in one assembly and is used

Fig. 7 Combination valve

on disc brake applications. The metering valve delays front disc braking until the rear drum brake shoes contact the drum. The failure warning switch is actuated in event of front or rear brake system failure, in turn activating a dash warning lamp. The proportioner balances front to rear braking action during rapid deceleration.

Metering Valve

When the brakes are not applied, the metering valve permits the brake fluid to flow through the valve, thus allowing the fluid to expand and contract with temperature changes.

When the brakes are initially applied, the

Fig. 8 Metering valve. Initial braking

Fig. 9 Metering valve. continued braking

Fig. 10 Failure warning switch. Rear system failure

Fig. 11 Proportioner. Rapid deceleration

Fig. 12 Proportioner. Normal braking

Fig. 13 Proportioners installed in master cylinder

metering valve stem moves to the left, preventing fluid to flow through the valve to the front disc brakes. This is accomplished by the smooth end of the metering valve stem contacting the metering valve seal lip at 4 to 30 psi, **Fig. 8.** The metering valve spring holds the retainer against the seal until a predetermined pressure is produced at the valve inlet port which overcomes the spring pressure and permits hydraulic pressure to actuate the front disc brakes, **Fig. 9.** The increased pressure into the valve is metered through the valve seal, to the front disc brakes, producing an increased force on the diaphragm. The diaphragm then pulls the pin, in turn pulling the retainer and reduces the spring pressure on the metering valve seal. Eventually, the pressure reaches a point at which the spring is pulled away by the diaphragm pin and retainer, leaving the metering valve unrestricted, permitting full pressure to pass through the metering valve.

Failure Warning Switch

If the rear brake system fails, the front system pressure forces the switch piston to the right, **Fig. 10.** The switch pin is then forced up into the switch, completing the electrical circuit and activates the dash warning lamp.

When repairs are made and pressure returns to the system, the piston moves to the left, resetting the switch. The detent on the piston requires approximately 100 to 450 psi to permit full reset of the piston. In event of front brake system failure, the piston moves to the left and the same sequence of events is followed as for rear

system failure except the piston resets to the right.

Fluid Level Sensor

This sensor mounted on the master cylinder will activate the Brake Warning lamp if a low brake fluid level is detected. The lamp will turn off once the fluid level is corrected.

Proportioning Or Pressure Control Valve

During rapid deceleration, a portion of vehicle weight is transferred to the front wheels. This resultant loss of weight at rear wheels must be compensated for to avoid early rear wheel skid. The proportioner or pressure control valve reduces rear brake system pressure, delaying rear wheel skid. When the proportioner or pressure control valve is incorporated in the combination valve assembly, pressure developed within the valve acts against the large end of the piston, overcoming the spring pressure, moving the piston left, **Fig. 11.** The piston then contacts the stem seat and restricts line pressure through the valve.

During normal braking operation, the proportioner or pressure control valve is not functional. Brake fluid flows into the proportioner or pressure control valve between the piston center hole and the valve stem, through the stop plate and to the rear brakes. Spring pressure loads the piston during normal braking, causing it to rest against the stop plate, **Fig. 12.**

On diagonally split brake systems, two proportioners or pressure control valves

are used. One controls the left rear brake, the other the right rear brake. The proportioners or pressure control valves are installed in the master cylinder rear brake outlet ports, **Fig. 13.**

BRAKE DISTRIBUTION VALVE & SWITCH

This switch assembly, **Fig. 14,** is used on some diagonally split brake systems and Corvette four wheel disc brake systems. It is connected to the outlet ports of the master cylinder and to the brake warning lamp and warns the driver if either the primary or secondary brake system has failed.

When hydraulic pressure is equal in both primary and secondary brake systems, the switch remains centered, **Fig. 15.** If pressure fails in one of the systems, the piston moves toward the inoperative side, **Fig. 16.** The shoulder of the piston contacts the switch terminal, providing a ground and lighting the warning lamp.

TROUBLESHOOTING

When troubleshooting the hydraulic brake system, perform the following checks and inspections as outlined below. If problem still exists within system, refer to **Fig. 17** first, then to **Fig. 18** as necessary.

Fig. 14 Distribution switch. Diagonally split brake systems

Fig. 15 Brake distribution switch. Normal

Fig. 16 Brake distribution switch. Failed

ROAD TESTING

When testing brakes, ensure the road is level and dry. Test brakes at both light and heavy pedal pressure. Do not lock up brakes or slide tires during a brake test.

Check the tires on the vehicle before performing a brake test. Tires should be equally inflated, identical in size and with equal tread pattern. Excessive camber and caster will cause the brakes to pull. An overloaded vehicle will also brake erratically.

CHECKING FOR FLUID LEAKAGE

Start engine and depress the brake pedal. If the pedal gradually falls under constant pressure, the hydraulic system may be leaking. Raise the vehicle on a lift and check all tubing lines and backing plates for signs of leakage. It may be necessary to lift or remove the carpeting or floor mats to check for booster or master cylinder leakage.

BRAKE BLEEDING
MANUAL BLEEDING

Pressure bleeding is recommended for all hydraulic systems. However, if a pressure bleeder is unavailable, use the following procedure. **Brake fluid damages painted surfaces. Immediately clean any spilled fluid.**

1. Remove vacuum reserve by pumping brakes several times with engine off.
2. Fill master cylinder reservoir with clean brake fluid. Check fluid level often during bleeding procedure; do not let reservoir fall below half full.
3. If necessary, bleed master cylinder as follows:
   a. Disconnect master cylinder forward brake line connection until fluid flows from reservoir. Reconnect and tighten brake line.
   b. Instruct an assistant to slowly depress brake pedal one time and hold.
   c. Crack open front brake line connection again, purging air from cylinder.
   d. Retighten connection and slowly release brake pedal.
   e. Wait 15 seconds, then repeat until all air is purged.
   f. Bleed the rearward (nearest the cowl) brake line connection by repeating steps a through e.

4. Loosen, then slightly retighten bleeder valves at all four wheels. Repair any broken, stripped or frozen valves at this time.
5. Proceed to appropriate wheel first and follow set sequence according to "Wheel Bleeding Sequence."
6. Place transparent tube over bleeder valve, then allow tube to hang down into transparent container, **Fig. 19.**

CAUSE	Excessive Brake Pedal Travel	Brake Pedal Travel Gradually Increases	Excessive Brake Pedal Effort	Excessive Braking Action	Brakes Slow To Respond	Brakes Slow To Release	Brakes Drag	Uneven Braking Action (Side To Side)	Uneven Braking Action (Front To Rear)	Scraping Noise From Brakes	Brakes Squeak During Application*	Brakes Squeak During Stop*	Brakes Chatter (Roughness)	Brakes Groan At End Of Stop*	Brake Warning Lamp Glows During Stop
Leaking Brake Line or Connection	X	XX								X					XX
Leaking Wheel Cylinder or Piston Seal	X	XX	X					X							X
Leaking Master Cylinder	X	XX													X
Air in Brake System	XX									X					XX
Contaminated or Improper Brake Fluid					X	X	X								X
Leaking Vacuum System			XX		X										
Restricted Air Passage in Power Head			X		XX	X									
Damaged Power Head			X	X	X	X	X								
Improperly Assembled Power Head Valving			X	X	X	XX									
Worn Out Brake Lining-Replace			X	X				X	X	X	X	X		X	
Uneven Brake Lining Wear-Replace and Correct	X			X				X	X	X	X	XX		X	X
Glazed Brake Lining			XX		X			X	X		X		X		
Incorrect Lining Material-Replace			X	X				X	X					X	
Contaminated Brake Lining-Replace				XX				XX	XX	X	X		X		
Linings Damaged by Abusive Use-Replace			X	XX				X	X	X	X		X	X	
Excessive Brake Lining Dust			X	XX				XX	XX		X		XX		
Heat Spotted or Scored Brake Drums or Rotors				X				X	X		X	X	XX	XX	
Out-of-Round or Vibrating Brake Drums												X	XX		
Improper Thickness Variation on Brake Rotors													XX		
Excessive Lateral Run-Out													X		
Faulty Automatic Adjusters	X					X	X	X							X
Incorrect Wheel Cylinder Sizes		X	X					X	X						
Weak or Incorrect Brake Shoe Retention Springs			X			X	XX	X	X	XX	X	XX			
Brake Assembly Attachments-Missing or Loose	X					X	X	X	X		X	X	X	X	
Insufficient Brake Shoe Guide Lubricant					X	X	X	X	XX	XX					
Restricted Brake Fluid Passage or Sticking Wheel Cylinder Piston		X	X		X	X	X	X							
Faulty Metering Valve	X		X	X	X	X	X								X
Brake Pedal Linkage Interference or Binding			X		X	XX	XX								
Improperly Adjusted Parking Brake							X								
Drums Tapered or Threaded													XX		
Incorrect Front End Alignment								XX							
Incorrect Tire Pressure								X	X						
Incorrect Wheel Bearing Adjustment	X										X		X		
Loose Front Suspension Attachments								X			X	XX	X	X	
Out-of-Balance Wheel Assemblies													XX		
Operator Riding Brake Pedal	X	X	X				X		X		X			X	
Improperly Adjusted Booster Pushrod	X					X	XX								X
Sticking Wheel Cylinder or Caliper Pistons			X			X	X	X	X						
Faulty Proportioning Valve		X				X		X	X						

XX — Indicates more probable cause(s)   X — Indicates other causes   *May be a normal condition.

Fig. 17 Brake diagnosis chart (Part 1 of 2). Front disc/rear drum system

CAUSE	Excessive Brake Pedal Travel	Brake Pedal Travel Gradually Increases	Excessive Brake Pedal Effort	Excessive Braking Action	Brakes Slow To Respond	Brakes Slow To Release	Brakes Drag	Uneven Braking Action (Side To Side)	Uneven Braking Action (Front To Rear)	Scraping Noise From Brakes	Brakes Squeak During Application*	Brakes Squeak During Stop*	Brakes Chatter (Roughness)	Brakes Groan At End Of Stop*	Brake Warning Lamp Glows
Leaking Brake Line or Connection	X	XX	X						X						XX
Leaking Piston Seal	X	XX	X	X				X	X						X
Leaking Master Cylinder	X	XX	X						X						X
Air in Brake System	XX		X						X						XX
Contaminated or Improper Brake Fluid	X			X	X	X	X	X							X
Leaking Vacuum System			XX		X										
Restricted Air Passage in Power Head		X	X		XX	X									
Damaged Power Head		X	X	X	X	XX									
Worn Out Brake Lining			X	X				X	X	X	X	X		X	
Uneven Brake Lining Wear-Replace	X		X					X	X	X	X	XX		X	X
Glazed Brake Lining			XX		X			X	X		X			X	
Incorrect Lining Material-Replace			X	X		X		X			X			X	
Contaminated Brake Lining-Replace				XX		X		XX	XX		X			X	
Linings Damaged by Abusive Use-Replace				X		X		X	X	X	X	X		X	
Heat Spotted or Scored Discs				X							X	X	XX	X	
Improper Thickness Variation	X												XX		
Excessive Lateral Run-Out	X												X		
Automatic Adjuster Problem	X	X						X	X	X					X
Brake Assembly Attachments-Missing or Loose	X							X	X	X	X	X	X		
Restricted Brake Fluid Passage		X	X		X	X	X	X	X						X
Improperly Adjusted Stoplamp Switch Or Cruise Control Vacuum Dump							X								
Metering Valve Problem	X	X	X	X	X	X			X						X
Proportioning Valve Problem	X	X	X	X	X	X			X						X
Brake Pedal Linkage Interference or Binding		X		X	X	XX	XX								
Improperly Adjusted Parking Brake							X		X						
Improper Length Booster Pushrod	X			X		X	X	XX	X						
Incorrect Front End Alignment								XX							
Incorrect Tire Pressure								X	X						
Incorrect Wheel Bearing Adjustment	X										X		X		
Loose Front Suspension Attachments								X	X		XX		X	X	
Out-of-Balance Wheel Assemblies													XX		
Operator Riding Brake Pedal		X					X		X					X	
Sticking Caliper or Wheel Cylinder Pistons					X	X	XX	X	X						
Park Brake Switch Circuit Grounded															XX
Park Brake Not Releasing						X									XX

XX — Indicates more probable cause(s)
X — Indicates other causes
*May be a normal condition.

Fig. 17 Brake diagnosis chart (Part 2 of 2). Four wheel disc system

Ensure end of tube is submerged in clean brake fluid.
7. Instruct an assistant to slowly depress brake pedal one time and hold.
8. Crack open bleeder valve, purging air from cylinder. Retighten bleeder screw and slowly release pedal.
9. Wait 15 seconds, then repeat steps 7 and 8. Repeat these steps until all air is bled from system.

PRESSURE BLEEDING

1. Loosen, then slightly retighten bleeder valves at all four wheels. Repair any broken, stripped or frozen valves at this time.
2. Using a diaphragm type pressure bleeder, install suitable bleeder adapter to master cylinder, **Fig. 20.**
3. Charge bleeder ball to 20-25 psi.
4. Connect pressure bleeder line to adapter.

5. Open line valve on pressure bleeder, then depress bleed-off valve on adapter until a small amount of brake fluid is released.
6. Raise and support vehicle.
7. Proceed to appropriate wheel first and follow set sequence according to "Wheel Bleeding Sequence."
8. Place transparent tube over bleeder valve, then allow tube to hang down into transparent container, **Fig. 19.** Ensure end of tube is submerged in clean brake fluid.
9. Open bleeder valve 1/2 to 3/4 turn and allow fluid to flow into container until all air is purged from line.

WHEEL BLEEDING SEQUENCE

Rear wheel drive models except 1991 Corvette: if manual bleeding, RR-LR-RF-LF; if pressure bleeding, bleed front brakes together and rear brakes together.

Front wheel drive models: RR-LF-LR-RF
1991 Corvette: RR-RR-LR-LF

FLUSHING HYDRAULIC SYSTEM

If brake fluid is old, rusty or contaminated, or whenever new parts are installed in hydraulic system, the system must be flushed. Bleed brakes, allowing at least one quart of clean brake fluid to pass through system. Any rubber parts in hydraulic system which were exposed to contaminated fluid must be replaced.

COMPONENT REPLACEMENT

MASTER CYLINDER, REPLACE

1. Disconnect wire connector from brake warning pressure switch.
2. Disconnect brake lines from master cylinder.
3. Remove two master cylinder mounting nuts, then the master cylinder.
4. Reverse procedure to install.

COMPONENT SERVICE

MASTER CYLINDER OVERHAUL

EXCEPT CORVETTE
Disassembly

Refer to **Figs. 21 and 22** when performing the following procedures.
1. Remove master cylinder from vehicle as follows:
   a. Disconnect and plug hydraulic lines.
   b. Remove two master cylinder attaching nuts, then the master cylinder.
2. Remove reservoir cover and diaphragm. Discard old brake fluid in reservoir.
3. Inspect cover and diaphragm. Replace if cut, cracked or deformed.
4. Remove fluid level switch, if equipped.
5. **On models with compact master cylinder,** remove proportioner valve assembly, **Fig. 22.**
6. Depress primary piston and remove lock ring.
7. Plug primary fluid outlet (outlet nearest to cowl when master cylinder is installed), then apply compressed air into secondary fluid outlet to remove primary and secondary pistons.
8. Remove spring retainer and seals from secondary piston.
9. Clamp master cylinder in a vise as shown in **Fig. 23**, then remove reservoir using a pry bar. Remove reservoir grommets.
10. Inspect master cylinder bore for corrosion. **Do not use abrasive material on master cylinder bore.** Replace if bore is corroded.

The same types of brake trouble are encountered with power brakes as with standard brakes. Before checking power brake system for source of trouble, refer to the brake system diagnosis charts. After these possible causes have been eliminated, check for cause as outlined below:

HARD PEDAL

CAUSE	CORRECTION
Broken or damaged hydraulic brake pipes.	Inspect and replace as necessary.
Vacuum failure.	Check for:
	Faulty vacuum check valve or grommet. Replace.
	Collapsed or damaged vacuum hose. Replace.
	Plugged or loose vacuum fitting. Repair.
	Faulty air valve seal or support plate seal. Replace.
	Damaged floating control valve. Replace.
	Bad stud welds on front or rear housing or power head. Replace unless easily repaired.
Faulty diaphragm.	Replace.
Restricted air filter element.	Replace.
Worn or distorted reaction plate or levers.	Replace plate or levers.
Cracked or broken power pistons or retainer.	Replace power pistons and piston rod retainer.

GRABBY BRAKES
(Apparent Off-On Condition)

CAUSE	CORRECTION
Broken or damaged hydraulic brake pipes.	Inspect and replace as necessary.
Insufficient fluid in master cylinder.	Fill reservoirs with approved brake fluid. Check for leaks.
Faulty master cylinder seals.	Repair or replace as necessary.
Cracked master cylinder casting.	Replace.
Leaks in pipes or connections at disc brake calipers or wheel cylinders.	Inspect and repair as necessary.
Air in hydraulic system.	Bleed system.

BRAKES FAIL TO RELEASE

CAUSE	CORRECTION
Blocked passage in power piston.	Inspect and repair or replace as necessary.
Air valve sticking shut.	Check for proper lubrication of air valve "O" ring.
Broken piston return spring.	Replace.
Broken air valve spring.	Replace.
Tight pedal linkage.	Repair or replace as necessary.

Fig. 18   Power brake diagnosis chart

TUBE MUST BE SUBMERGED IN BRAKE FLUID

1 BLEEDER WRENCH   3 CALIPER
2 TUBE

Fig. 19   Bleeding brakes

HOSE TO BLEEDER

BLEED OFF VALVE

BLEEDER ADAPTER

MASTER CYLINDER ASSEMBLY

Fig. 20   Installing pressure bleeder adapter

Assembly

Clean all parts not included in repair kit with brake fluid. **Do not dry with compressed air.** Lubricate all rubber parts with clean brake fluid prior to installation.
1. Lubricate new reservoir grommets with silicone brake lube, then press grommets into master cylinder body. Ensure grommets are properly seated.
2. Lay reservoir upside down on flat, hard surface. Press master cylinder body onto reservoir using rocking motion.
3. Install new seals on secondary piston, then the spring retainer.
4. Install spring and secondary piston assembly into cylinder.
5. Install primary piston. Depress primary piston into cylinder, then install lock ring.
6. Install fluid level switch, if equipped.

7. **On models with compact master cylinder,** install proportioner valve assembly, **Fig. 22.**
8. Fit diaphragm into reservoir cover, then install cover onto reservoir.
9. Install master cylinder and bleed brake system.

1991 CORVETTE
1. Disconnect warning switch assembly connector, then the brake tubing from Master cylinder. **Plug brake tubes to prevent contamination.**
2. Remove two master cylinder to power booster retaining nuts.
3. Position battery and cruise control cables aside, then remove master cylinder.
4. Remove reservoir caps and diaphragms and check for cracks or damage.
5. Remove retaining ring, then depress primary and secondary pistons, **Fig.**

24, using a brass or wooden dowel.
6. **Do not remove piston stop bolt unless both pistons are fully bottomed in bore.**
7. Remove piston stop bolt and dowel, **Fig. 25,** then tap open end of cylinder against a wooden block to dislodge the primary piston.
8. **Do not remove or disturb screw in secondary piston center valve.** It may effect valve performance, making it necessary to replace the valve.
9. Remove secondary valve and center valve by taping cylinder against the wooden block.
10. Using a small screwdriver to pry apart seal retainer legs, remove seal retainer **Fig. 26.**
11. Remove seals, recuperating guide and seals working over secondary piston lands **Fig. 27.**
12. Remove warning switch, keeping switch and probe together as an assembly.

Fig. 21   Dual master cylinder assembly. Composite type

1. FLUID LEVEL SENSOR
2. PROPORTIONER VALVE CAP ASSEMBLY
3. O-RING
4. SPRING
5. PROPORTIONER VALVE PISTON
6. PROPORTIONER VALVE SEAL
7. RESERVOIR CAP
8. DIAPHRAGM
9. SPRING PIN
10. RESERVOIR ASSEMBLY
11. O-RING
12. O-RING
13. RETAINER
14. PRIMARY PISTON ASSEMBLY
15. SECONDARY SEAL
16. SPRING RETAINER
17. PRIMARY SEAL
18. SECONDARY PISTON
19. SPRING
20. CYLINDER BODY

Fig. 22   Compact master cylinder assembly

Fig. 23   Removing master cylinder reservoir. Composite type

13. Remove end plug and O-ring.
14. Tape cylinder against wooden block and dislodge proportioning valve, then remove the valve.
15. **The proportioning valve and other cylinder parts are prelubricated with a special grease, do not use a cleaning solution to clean these parts. Clean all parts in denatured alcohol. Use filtered unlubricated compressed air to dry all parts and passages within the cylinder.**
16. Reverse procedure to assemble, ensuring that all seals and parts are lubricated with clean brake fluid. **Do not install piston stop bolt unless both pistons assemblies are bottomed in the bore.**

1992—93 CORVETTE

1. Remove reservoir cap and diaphragm from reservoir.
2. Drain fluid, then remove master cylinder prime pipe clamp and prime pipe.
3. Remove reservoir retaining screw and reservoir, **Fig. 28.**
4. Remove reservoir O-rings from reservoir wells.
5. Slightly depress piston and remove retaining ring with retaining ring pliers.
6. Invert cylinder so the reservoir wells face downward. Depress the primary and secondary pistons with a brass rod or wooden dowel until fully bottomed in bore. The secondary stop pin should fall freely from the cylinder.
7. Gently bump open end of cylinder body against a piece of wood to dislodge the primary piston, then remove primary piston.
8. Gently bump open end of cylinder body against a piece of wood to dislodge the secondary piston and center the valve assembly, then remove secondary piston. **Do not remove or disturb screw which retains primary spring to secondary piston. This has been set to a predetermined height and will severely affect cylinder performance if setting is changed.**
9. Remove secondary return spring from secondary piston assembly.
10. Remove spring retainer from secondary piston using a small screwdriver to lift crimp to allow retainer to slide off piston, **Fig. 29.**

1	CYLINDER BODY	8	SEAL	15	RETAINING RING
2	GROMMETS	9	SECONDARY PISTON	16	WARNING SWITCH
3	PISTON STOP BOLT	10	SEAL RETAINER	17	PROPORTIONING VALVE
4	RESERVOIRS	11	SEAL	18	GROUND SPRING
5	RESERVOIR DIAPHRAGMS	12	RECUPERATING GUIDE	19	O-RING SEAL
6	RESERVOIR CAPS	13	PRIMARY PISTON	20	END PLUG
7	CENTER VALVE	14	SEALS		

Fig. 24   Composite master cylinder. 1991 Corvette

A	BRASS ROD OR WOODEN DOWEL
1	PISTON STOP BOLT

Fig. 25   Removing stop bolt. 1991 Corvette

1	RETAINING RING
2	SEAL
3	PRIMARY PISTON
4	RECUPERATING GUIDE
5	SEAL
6	SEAL RETAINER

Fig. 26   Primary piston components. 1991 Corvette

1	SECONDARY SEAL
2	SECONDARY PISTON
3	PRIMARY SEAL

Fig. 27   Secondary piston assembly components. 1991 Corvette

11. Remove center valve plunger and spring from secondary piston.
12. Remove seal retainer using a sharp knife or razor blade to cut and remove plastic retaining cup retaining ring from primary piston, **Fig. 30.**
13. Remove recuperating guide.
14. Remove all rubber seals from both pistons, **Figs. 31 and 32. Take extreme care not to damage any surfaces on piston, particularly areas where seals seat.**
15. Remove pressure differential switch assembly. **Do not disassemble spring or probe from switch body.**
16. Remove end plug and O-ring. **Care must be taken not to lose small electrical bias spring located just inside end plug.**
17. Remove warning switch assembly from master cylinder assembly. **Keep warning switch and probe together as an assembly.**
18. Remove end plug, O-ring and electrical bias spring.

19. Gently tap cylinder body against a piece of wood to dislodge proportioning valve spool assembly then, remove proportioning valve spool assembly including O-ring and spacer. **Do not disassemble proportioning valve, it is serviced as an assembly only.**
20. **The proportioning valve is prelubricated with a special grease, do not use a cleaning solution to clean it or parts included in repair kit. Clean all other parts in denatured alcohol. Use filtered unlubricated compressed air to dry all parts and passages within the cylinder.**
21. Reverse procedure to assemble, ensuring that all seals and parts are lubricated with clean brake fluid.

WHEEL CYLINDER OVERHAUL

1. Raise and support vehicle.

2. Remove wheel, drum and brake shoes.
3. Disconnect hydraulic line at wheel cylinder. **Do not pull metal line away from cylinder, as this may kink or bend line.** Line will separate from cylinder when cylinder is moved away from brake backing plate.
4. Remove wheel cylinder-to-brake plate attaching screws, then the wheel cylinder.
5. Remove boots, pistons, springs and cups from cylinder, **Fig. 33.**
6. Clean all parts with brake fluid.
7. Inspect cylinder bore. A scored bore may be honed as long as the diameter is not increased by more than .005 inch. Replace worn or damaged parts as necessary.
8. Ensure hands are clean before proceeding with assembly. Lubricate cylinder wall and rubber cups with brake fluid, then install springs, cups, pistons and boots in housing.
9. Wipe end of hydraulic line to remove any foreign matter, then place wheel

Fig. 29 Lifting crimp on secondary spring retainer. 1992–93 Corvette

Fig. 30 Cutting seal retainer. 1992–93 Corvette

1 RESERVOIR CAP	14 RECUPERATING TYPE CUP SEAL
2 RESERVOIR CAP DIAPHRAGM	15 RECUPERATING GUIDE
3 RESERVOIR BODY	16 PRIMARY PISTON
4 RESERVOIR 'O' RING	17 RETAINING RING
5 SECONDARY PISTON STOP PIN	18 ENG PLUG
6 CYLINDER BODY	19 END PLUG 'O' RING
7 SECONDARY RETURN SPRING	20 ELECTRICAL BIAS SPRING
8 SECONDARY SPRING RETAINER	21 PROPORTIONING VALVE O-RING
9 CENTER VALVE SPRING	22 PROPORTIONING VALVE SPACER
10 CENTER VALVE PLUNGER	23 PROPORTIONING VALVE/PRESSURE DIFFERENTIAL ASSEMBLY
11 'L' TYPE CUP SEAL	24 PRESSURE DIFFERENTIAL WARNING SWITCH ASSEMBLY
12 SECONDARY PISTON ASSEMBLY	25 RESERVOIR RETAINER SCREW
13 PRIMARY CUP RETAINING RING	26 FLUID LEVEL SWITCH ASSEMBLY

Fig. 28 Composite master cylinder. 1992–93 Corvette

1 PRIMARY CUP RETAINING RING
2 RECUPERATING TYPE CUP SEAL
3 RECUPERATING GUIDE
4 PRIMARY PISTON
5 'L' TYPE CUP SEAL

Fig. 31 Primary piston components. 1992–93 Corvette

1 'L' TYPE CUP SEAL
2 SECONDARY PISTON ASSEMBLY

Fig. 32 Secondary piston components. 1992–93 Corvette

21 BOOT	24 SPRING ASSEMBLY
22 PISTON	25 BLEEDER VALVE
23 SEAL	26 CYLINDER BODY

Fig. 33 Exploded view of wheel cylinder

cylinder in position. Enter tubing into cylinder and start threads on fitting.
10. Secure cylinder to backing plate, then complete tightening of tubing fitting.

11. Install brake shoes, drum and wheel.
12. Bleed system as outlined previously, then adjust brakes.

HYDRAULIC BRAKE SPECIFICATIONS

Model	Year	Master Cylinder Bore Dia., Inch	Front Caliper Bore Dia., Inch	Rear Caliper Bore Dia., Inch	Wheel Cylinder Bore Dia., Inch
BUICK					
Century	1991-93	①	—	—	②
LeSabre	1991-93	1.000	2.52	—	.937
Park Avenue	1991-93	1.000	2.52	—	.937
Reatta	1991	1.000	2.52	1.50	—
Regal	1991-93	.945	1.65	1.378	—
Riviera	1991-93	1.000	2.52	1.50	—
Roadmaster	1991-93	1.125	2.952	—	③
Skylark	1991-93	.874	2.244	—	.689
CADILLAC					
Brougham	1991-92	⑦	2.952	—	1.00
DeVille	1991-93	1.00	2.52	—	.937
Eldorado	1991-93	1.00	2.52	1.50	—
Fleetwood (FWD)	1991-92	1.00	2.52	—	.937
Fleetwood (RWD)	1993	1.125	2.952	—	1.00
Seville	1991-93	1.000	2.52	—	.937
Sixty Special	1993	1.00	2.52	—	.937
CHEVROLET					
Beretta	1991-93	.875	2.25	—	⑤
Camaro	1991-92	⑧	⑨	1.60	.748
	1993	1.00	2.500	1.595	.810
Caprice	1991-92	1.125	2.952	—	.748 ⑩
	1993	1.125	2.952	—	④
Cavalier	1991-93	.874	2.244	—	.625
Corsica	1991-93	.875	2.25	—	⑤
Corvette	1991-93	.870	1.50	1.60	—
Lumina	1991-93	.945	1.65	1.378	—
GEO					
Metro	1991-93	.810	1.889	—	.620
Prizm	1991-93	.812	2.01	—	.690
Prizm GSI	1991-93	.874	2.13	1.19	—
Storm	1991-93	⑪	2.00	—	.600
OLDSMOBILE					
Achieva	1992-93	.874	2.244	—	.689
Calais	1991	.874	2.244	—	.689
Custom Cruiser	1991-92	1.125	2.952	—	.748
Cutlass Ciera	1991-93	.945	1.65	1.378	—
Cutlass Cruiser	1991-93	9.44	—	—	⑬
Cutlass Supreme	1991-93	.945	1.65	1.378	—
Toronado	1991-93	1.000	2.52	1.50	—
Trofeo	1991-93	1.000	2.52	1.50	—
88	1991-93	1.000	2.52	—	.937
98	1991-93	1.000	2.52	—	.937
PONTIAC					
Bonneville	1991-93	1.000	2.52	—	.937
Firebird	1991-92	⑧	2.5 ⑥	1.60	.748
	1993	1.00	2.500	1.595	.810
Grand Am	1991-93	.874	2.244	—	.689
Grand Prix	1991-93	.945	1.65	1.378	—

Continued

HYDRAULIC BRAKE SPECIFICATIONS –Continued

Model	Year	Master Cylinder Bore Dia., Inch	Front Caliper Bore Dia., Inch	Rear Caliper Bore Dia., Inch	Wheel Cylinder Bore Dia., Inch
PONTIAC-Continued					
LeMans	1991-93	.874	—	—	.678
Sunbird	1991-93	.874	2.244	—	.625
Trans Am	1991-92	⑧	2.5 ⑥	1.60	.748
6000	1991	.874 ⑫	2.244	1.92	⑬

① —Light duty, .874. Medium & heavy duty, .944.
② —Sedan/coupe, .689. Wagon: medium duty, .811, heavy duty, .748.
③ —1991–92, .748 inch; 1993, 1.00 inch.
④ —Standard duty, .874 inch; heavy duty, 1.00 inch.
⑤ —Anchor plate drum brakes, .625, Leading/Trailing drum brakes, .748.
⑥ —Heavy duty, 1.50.
⑦ —Main bore, 1.126. Quick Take Up bore, 1.574.
⑧ —Disc & drum system, .945. Four wheel disc system, 1.00.
⑨ —Standard, 2.52. Heavy duty, 1.50.
⑩ —Heavy duty, .937.
⑪ —Single overhead cam, .810. Dual overhead cam, .875.
⑫ —Heavy duty, .944.
⑬ —Coupe/sedan standard, .689. Coupe/sedan medium duty & wagon standard, .811. All heavy duty, .748.

POWER BRAKE UNITS

INDEX

APPLICATIONS

BUICK

Century	Tandem diaphragm
LeSabre	Tandem diaphragm
Park Avenue	Tandem diaphragm
Reatta	Tandem diaphragm
Regal	Tandem diaphragm
Riviera	Tandem diaphragm
Roadmaster	Tandem diaphragm
Skyhawk	Tandem diaphragm
Skylark	Tandem diaphragm

CADILLAC

Brougham	Tandem diaphragm
DeVille	Tandem diaphragm
Eldorado	Tandem diaphragm
Fleetwood (FWD)	Tandem diaphragm
Fleetwood (RWD)	Tandem diaphragm
Seville	Tandem diaphragm

CHEVROLET

Beretta	Tandem diaphragm
Camaro	Tandem diaphragm
Caprice	Tandem diaphragm
Cavalier	Tandem diaphragm
Corsica	Tandem diaphragm
Corvette	Single diaphragm
Lumina	Tandem diaphragm

GEO

Metro	Single diaphragm
Prizm	Single diaphragm
Storm	Single diaphragm

OLDSMOBILE

Achieva	Tandem diaphragm
Cutlass Calais	Tandem diaphragm
Custom Cruiser	Tandem diaphragm
Cutlass Ciera	Tandem diaphragm
Cutlass Cruiser	Tandem diaphragm
Cutlass Supreme	Tandem diaphragm
Toronado	Tandem diaphragm
Trofeo	Tandem diaphragm
88	Tandem diaphragm
98	Tandem diaphragm

PONTIAC

Bonneville	Tandem diaphragm
Firebird	Tandem diaphragm
Grand Am	Tandem diaphragm
Grand Prix	Tandem diaphragm
LeMans	Single diaphragm
Sunbird	Tandem diaphragm
Trans Am	Tandem diaphragm
6000	Tandem diaphragm

GENERAL SERVICE

Two basic types of power assist mechanisms are used: vacuum assist diaphragm assemblies, which use engine vacuum or, in some cases vacuum pressure developed by an external vacuum pump. The second type is a hydraulic pressure assist mechanism, which use pressure developed by an external pump (usually the power steering pump). Both systems act to increase the force exerted on the master cylinder piston by the operator. This in turn increases the hydraulic pressure delivered to the wheel cylinders, while decreasing driver effort necessary to obtain acceptable stopping performance.

Vacuum assist units are similar in operation and get their energy by opposing engine vacuum to atmospheric pressure. A piston and cylinder, flexible diaphragm (bellows) utilize this energy to provide brake assistance. The fundamental difference between these types of vacuum as-

Fig. 1 Master cylinder pushrod adjustment. Delco-Moraine type vacuum booster

10. PISTON ROD
24. GAGE J-22647

1. GASKET
2. MASTER CYLINDER
3. PISTON
4. PIN HEAD

Fig. 2 Master cylinder adjustment tool

SPECIAL TOOL (D)

CLEARANCE 0 MM (0 IN) BETWEEN SPECIAL TOOL AND PISTON ROD

1. BOOSTER BODY
2. PISTON ROD

Fig. 3 Booster piston rod adjustment

sist systems lies simply in how the diaphragm within the power unit is suspended when the brakes are not applied.

In order to properly diagnose vacuum assist system malfunctions it is important to know whether the diaphragm within a power unit is air suspended or vacuum suspended. Air-suspended units are under atmospheric pressure until the brakes are applied. Engine vacuum is then admitted, causing the piston or diaphragm to move (or the bellows to collapse). Vacuum-suspended types are balanced with engine vacuum until the brake pedal is depressed, allowing atmospheric pressure to unbalance the unit and apply force to the brake system.

Regardless of whether the brakes are vacuum or hydraulically assisted, certain general service procedures apply. Only specified, clean brake fluid should be used in brake system. On hydro boost systems, use of the specified hydraulic fluid in the boost circuit is essential to proper system operation. Care must be taken not to mix the fluids of the two separate operating circuits. Use of improper fluids, or contaminated fluid will cause damage to the seals and valves.

PRECAUTIONS

1. After disassembling a power brake unit, soak all metal parts in solvent.
2. Use only alcohol on parts containing rubber. After the parts have been thoroughly cleaned and rinsed in solvent, they should be rewashed in clean alcohol before assembly.
3. Use compressed air to blow dirt and cleaning fluid from the recesses and internal passages.
4. Always use all the parts furnished in the repair kit.
5. **Use extreme caution when disassembling power assist mechanisms, as suddenly releasing internal spring tension could cause damage or personal injury.**
6. **On models with hydro-boost assist systems,** do not disassemble the accumulator. If the accumulator is damaged or diagnosed as defective, it must be replaced as an assembly.

PUSHROD ADJUSTMENT

Proper adjustment of the master cylinder pushrod is necessary to ensure proper operation of the power brake system. A pushrod that is too long will cause the master cylinder piston to close off the compensating port, preventing hydraulic pressure from being released and resulting in brake drag. A pushrod that is too short will cause excessive brake pedal travel and cause groaning noises to come from the booster when the brakes are applied. A properly adjusted pushrod that remains assembled to the booster with which it was matched during production should not require service adjustment. However, if the booster, master cylinder or pushrod are serviced, the pushrod may require adjustment.

There are two methods that can be used to check for proper pushrod length and installation: the gauge method and air method. Usually, if the power unit pushrod requires adjustment, use the power unit repair kit gauge. The gauge measures from the end of the pushrod to the power unit shell.

GAUGE METHOD
Delco-Moraine Type

On these models, the master cylinder pushrod length is fixed and is usually only checked after the unit has been overhauled.

1. Assemble booster unit and install pushrod, ensuring pushrod is fully seated.
2. Position go/no go gauge furnished in repair kit over pushrod as shown in **Fig. 1**
3. If pushrod height is not within limits of gauge, install service adjustable pushrod and adjust rod to obtain correct height.
4. Install power unit and check adjustment, ensuring master cylinder compensating port is open with engine running and brake pedal released.

Single Diaphragm Type

This unit is used on late model GEO Metro. The length of the booster piston rod is adjusted to provide specified clearance between the piston rod end and master cylinder piston. Before making an adjustment, push piston rod several times to ensure reaction disc is in place. Ensure gasket is installed to master cylinder and keep inside of booster at atmospheric pressure.

1. Place booster pin rod gauge No. J-34873 or equivalent on master cylinder and push pin until it contacts piston, **Fig. 2**
2. Turn tool upside down and place it on booster. Adjust booster piston rod length until rod end contacts pin head.
3. Adjust clearance by turning adjusting bolt of piston rod, **Fig. 3**. If negative pressure is applied to booster with engine at idle, piston to piston rod clearance should measure 0.004–0.020 inch.

AIR METHOD

1. Be sure master cylinder attaching nuts are tight.
2. Remove master cylinder filler cap.
3. With brake released, force compressed air into the hydraulic outlet of the master cylinder. **Regulate air pressure to a value of approximately 5 psi, to prevent spraying brake fluid from master cylinder. Care must be taken not to allow brake fluid to contact painted surfaces of vehicle, skin or eyes, as damage or personal injury will result.**
4. If air passes through the compensating port, which is the smaller of the two holes in the bottom of the master cylinder reservoir, the adjustment is satisfactory.
5. If air does not flow through the compensating port, adjust the pushrod as required, either by means of the adjustment screw (if provided) or by adding shims between the master cylinder and power unit shell until the air flows freely.
6. Reconnect brake lines and bleed system.

POWER BOOSTER
REPLACE

1. Disconnect brake unit pushrod from brake pedal.
2. Remove two master cylinder to power brake unit mounting nuts.
3. Position master cylinder away from brake unit, leaving brake lines attached. **Do not bend, or kink brake lines.**

Fig. 4 Delco-Moraine tandem diaphragm booster exploded view

Fig. 5 Power head assembly exploded view. Delco-Moraine tandem diaphragm booster

4. Disconnect vacuum hose from vacuum check valve. cap all open hose ends and fittings to prevent contamination.
5. Remove power brake unit to dash panel attaching nuts, then the brake unit.
6. Reverse procedure to install.

DELCO-MORAINE TANDEM DIAPHRAGM TYPE

DESCRIPTION

This unit utilizes a vacuum power chamber, consisting of a front and rear shell, housing divider, front and rear diaphragm, plate assemblies, hydraulic pushrod and a diaphragm return spring, **Figs. 4 and 5.**

The unit operates in much the same manner as the single diaphragm unit described previously. The diaphragm and plate assemblies utilize the pressure differential between the engine intake manifold vacuum and atmospheric pressure to assist in braking.

TROUBLESHOOTING

Hard Pedal

1. Internal vacuum leak.
2. Faulty control valve.

Brakes Grab

1. Faulty control valve.

Slow Or No Release

1. Faulty pushrod adjustment.
2. Bind in linkage.

POWER BRAKE UNIT SERVICE

OVERHAUL

Disassembly

1. Remove pedal pushrod boot, silencer, check valve, vacuum switch and grommets, as equipped, then the front housing seal.
2. Scribe matching marks between front and rear housing sections, then mount booster assembly in suitable holding fixture with rear housing facing up.
3. Apply pressure to housing with holding fixture forcing screw and rotate rear housing counterclockwise to unlock housing halves.
4. Slowly release spring tension, then remove booster assembly from holding fixture. **Do not allow spring tension to release suddenly, as damage or personal injury may result.**
5. Lift off rear housing, then remove primary power piston bearing from housing.
6. Remove power piston group and return spring from front housing, **Fig. 4.**
7. Remove master cylinder piston rod

and reaction retainer from front of piston, then the silencer from the rear of the assembly, **Fig. 5.**

8. Hold piston assembly at edges of divider and strike pedal pushrod against work surface to dislodge diaphragm retainer.
9. Remove primary diaphragm and support plate, secondary power piston bearing and housing divider, then the secondary diaphragm and support plate from piston, noting installation position of components, **Fig. 6.**
10. Clean and inspect components as outlined in "General Service," then replace as needed. **Do not disassemble power piston. If service is required, power piston must be replaced as an assembly.**

Assembly

1. Position power piston assembly on work surface with pedal pushrod facing up.
2. Lubricate inner lip of secondary diaphragm, fit diaphragm over support plate, then install assembly onto power piston.
3. Install secondary power piston bearing into divider with flat surface of bearing on side of divider with 6 lugs, **Fig. 5.**
4. Install guide sleeve J-28458 or equivalent over power piston, lubricate inner diameter of secondary bearing, then install divider assembly with lugged side facing up.
5. Lubricate inner lip of primary diaphragm. Fit diaphragm over support plate, then install diaphragm assembly on power piston.
6. Ensure diaphragms and support plates are properly positioned, install new diaphragm retainer, then seat retainer on power piston using guide sleeve J-28458 or equivalent and hammer.
7. Install primary power piston bearing in rear housing, then lubricate inner diameter of bearing.
8. Mount front housing in holding fixture J-23456 or equivalent, then install diaphragm return spring, power piston group and the rear housing assembly, **Fig. 4.**
9. Ensure housing scribe marks are properly aligned, then press housing sections together with holding fixture forcing screw. **Assembly of housing can be facilitated by applying vacuum to front housing port. Block opening for vacuum switch, if equipped.**
10. Rotate rear housing clockwise to lock housing, then stake two tabs 180° apart to secure assembly. Do not stake tabs which have previously been used.
11. Lubricate grommets and front seal, install grommets, check valve and vacuum switch, as equipped, then the front housing seal.
12. Install silencer and pedal pushrod boot.

Fig. 6   Girlock brake booster exploded view

1	FRONT SHELL	7	VACUUM CHECK VALVE	12	VACUUM PISTON	17	RETURN SPRING
2	REAR SHELL	8	GROMMET*	13	DIAPHRAGM*	18	STOP PLATE*
3	TIE ROD UNIT	9	VALVE*	14	SPRING WASHER*	19	SPRAG RETAINER*
4	NUT	10	OUTPUT PUSH ROD	15	REACTION DISC*	20	GASKET
5	BOOT*	11	FRONT SEAL	16	TIE ROD BOOT*	21	STEEL WASHER*
6	REAR SEAL*						* REPAIR KIT

98.1-98.4 mm (3.86-3.87 in.) — Dimension must be measured across washer face of tie rod (3) and nut (4)

98.1-98.4 mm (3.86-3.87 in.)

J 35498

3	ROD, TIE
4	NUT

Fig. 7   Measuring booster shell assembly. Girlock booster

GIRLOCK SINGLE DIAPHRAGM TYPE

DESCRIPTION

This booster is a single diaphragm, vacuum suspended unit with a lightweight cast alloy housing, **Fig. 6.** Vacuum is applied to the front and rear housings. When the brake pedal is released, negative pressure is equalized on both sides of the diaphragm and power piston assembly. Spring tension holds the piston at the rest position. When the brakes are applied, the atmospheric port in the power piston is opened. Negative pressure in the front chamber pulls the diaphragm and vacuum piston assembly, reaction disc and output rod forward. Pressure on the master cylinder piston is increased. When the brakes are released, the atmospheric port in the valve assembly is closed. Negative pressure is equalized on both sides of the diaphragm and piston assembly. Spring tension forces the piston back to the rest position. When the atmospheric port is opened, air is drawn into the rear chamber through a filter in the valve assembly.

TROUBLESHOOTING
Brakes Grab

1. Contaminated, damaged or dirty linings.
2. Damaged booster.
3. Improperly assembled booster valve.

Excessive Pedal Effort

1. Leak in booster vacuum supply system.
2. Glazed linings.
3. Restricted filter or booster valve air passage.

1. CIRCULAR RING
2. BODY SEAL
3. FRONT BODY
4. DIAPHRAGM SPRING
5. PUSH ROD

6. REACTION DISC
7. STOPPER KEY
8. VALVE BODY
9. OPERATING ROD

10. BOOSTER PISTON
11. DIAPHRAGM
12. REAR BODY
13. BODY SEAL

14. SPONGE ELEMENT
15. FELT ELEMENT
16. BOOT
17. NUT

Fig. 8   Toyota/GM brake booster exploded view

Fig. 9   Brake booster lubrication points

4. Damaged booster or improperly assembled booster valve.

Brakes Slow To Respond

1. Restricted filter or booster valve air passage.
2. Contaminated brake fluid.
3. Leak in booster vacuum supply system.
4. Damaged booster or improperly assembled booster valve.

Brakes Slow To Release Or Drag

1. Damaged booster assembly.
2. Improperly assembled booster valve.
3. Pedal linkage damaged or improperly adjusted.

4. Restricted booster air passage.
5. Insufficient caliper guide lubrication; damaged or defective calipers.
6. Contaminated brake fluid.

POWER BRAKE UNIT SERVICE
OVERHAUL
Disassembly

1. Remove vacuum check valve from front housing.
2. Loosen tie rod nuts several turns (approximately 1/2 inch), but do not remove nuts.
3. Pry housing shells apart using a thin blade screw driver, taking care not to chip or mar housing shells, or cut diaphragm.

4. Clamp housing shells together with suitable holding fixtures, then remove tie rod nuts and spring washers. **Failure to secure housing shells prior to removing tie rod nuts may allow housing shells to separate due to spring tension, causing damage and/or personal injury.**
5. Slowly loosen clamp securing housing shells, then separate front shell and remove return spring, grommet and front seal from housing.
6. Remove pedal pushrod boot, gasket and tie rods from rear shell, **Fig. 6.**
7. Separate diaphragm bead from rear shell, tie rod boots from posts on shell, then remove vacuum piston assembly.
8. Remove diaphragm and tie rod boots from piston.
9. Remove rear seal from shell and washers from tie rod posts.
10. Remove output rod, retainer and reaction disc.
11. Remove stop plate from vacuum piston, pressing on open end while pulling on closed end of plate.
12. Remove valve assembly from vacuum piston. **Do not disassemble valve assembly. If service is required, entire valve assembly must be replaced.**

Assembly

Lubricate components where indicated with silicone grease.
1. Lubricate outer surface of valve assembly, then insert valve into vacuum piston and secure valve with stop plate, **Fig. 6.** Ensure plate is in fully locked position.
2. Lubricate reaction disc, then install disc in vacuum piston.
3. Install new tie rod boots in openings in vacuum piston, then liberally coat insides of boots with silicone grease.
4. Lubricate outer lip of diaphragm, then fit diaphragm into vacuum piston.
5. Press rear seal into shell, lubricate inner diameter of seal, then install washers over tie rod posts on rear shell.
6. Mount vacuum piston assembly in rear shell, pushing tie rod boots over posts. Ensure diaphragm bead is properly located around perimeter of shell.
7. Install tie rods through bores in rear shell.
8. Mount rear shell assembly in fixture J-23456-51A or equivalent, lubricate output rod, then install rod and new retainer in vacuum piston. **Do not alter adjustment of convex screw on output rod. Rod length is determined during manufacturing and should not be disturbed.**
9. Seat new front seal in front shell with metal face of seal toward outside.
10. Position return spring in vacuum piston, then install front housing. Ensure diaphragm bead remains properly positioned.
11. Press shell halves together by hand, then install spring washers and new

retaining nuts on tie rods. Ensure concave side of washers face shell. **Use only new replacement nuts furnished with repair kit when assembling booster shells.**

12. Tighten nuts evenly until shells are .20 inch apart, then ensure diaphragm bead is still properly positioned.
13. Continue tightening nuts evenly, approximately 1/2 turn at a time. Gauge housing assembly with tool J-35498, or equivalent as shown in **Fig. 7.**
14. Housing shells are properly assembled when distance between face of washer (3) and face of nut (4) is 3.87–4.86 inches, **Fig. 7.**
15. Reverse steps 1 and 2 of disassembly procedure to complete assembly.

TOYOTA/GM SINGLE DIAPHRAGM TYPE

ADJUSTMENTS

Brake Pedal

1. With engine running and brake pedal in rest position, measure distance between face of pedal and floor mat.
2. If distance is not 5.79–6.18 inches, adjust pedal height as follows:
   a. Remove left lower instrument panel trim section and air duct.
   b. Loosen stop lamp switch sufficiently to gain clearance for pedal adjustment.
   c. Loosen locknut and rotate pedal pushrod as needed to obtain specified pedal height, then tighten locknut.
   d. Adjust position of brake light switch so that plunger lightly contacts pedal stopper and brake lamps are off when pedal is released.
   e. Check pedal free travel.
3. With engine stopped, depress brake pedal several times to ensure there is no vacuum pressure in booster.
4. Release pedal, then press pedal down until the beginning of resistance is felt, measuring the pedal travel. **Pedal free travel is the amount that the brake booster air valve is moved by the pedal pushrod.**
5. If pedal travel is not .12–.24 inch, adjust pedal freeplay as follows:
   a. Adjust pedal free travel by loosening locknut and rotating pedal pushrod.
   b. Ensure brake lamp switch and pedal height are properly adjusted, then start engine and confirm that free travel still exists.
   c. Check pedal reserve distance.
6. Release parking brake, then start engine.
7. Depress brake pedal, then measure distance from face of pedal to floor mat. If pedal reserve distance is not more than 2.56 inch with an applied force of 110.2 lbs., check and repair brake system as needed.

Booster Pushrod

The following adjustment procedure is performed with the brake booster removed, using gauge J-34873-A or equivalent. This procedure should produce a clearance of .004–.020 inch between booster pushrod and master cylinder piston, with idling vacuum applied to booster.

1. Position gauge on rear of master cylinder, with gasket in place.
2. Lower gauge pin until lightly contacting master cylinder piston, then secure position of gauge pin.
3. Invert gauge and position gauge over pushrod on booster.
4. Adjust length of pushrod so that tip of pushrod lightly contacts head of gauge pin with gauge resting on booster shell.

TROUBLESHOOTING

Low Or Spongy Brake Pedal

1. Worn linings.
2. Air, or leaks in hydraulic system.
3. Defective master cylinder.
4. Defective wheel cylinder or calipers.
5. Improperly adjusted pedal linkage or booster pushrod.
6. Defective rear brake adjuster.

Brakes Drag

1. Improperly adjusted parking brake, or binding cables.
2. Improperly adjusted, or binding pedal linkage.
3. Improperly adjusted booster pushrod.
4. Defective booster return spring.
5. Sticking caliper or wheel cylinder piston.
6. Defective master cylinder.

Brakes Grab

1. Contaminated, worn, or defective brake linings.
2. Drum or brake rotor out of round.
3. Defective brake booster.

Hard Pedal/Brakes Inefficient

1. Contaminated, glazed, or defective brake linings.
2. Frozen caliper piston.
3. Defective vacuum pump, or leak in booster vacuum supply system.
4. Defective brake booster.

POWER BRAKE UNIT SERVICE

OVERHAUL

Disassembly

1. Attach holding fixture J-22805-01 or equivalent to front of booster, then mount fixture in vise. Mounting holes of holding fixture may have to be elongated toward inside in order to accommodate booster master cylinder studs.
2. Scribe matching marks between front and rear booster shells to aid assembly.
3. Remove nut from pedal pushrod and boot from rear shell, **Fig. 8.**
4. Attach lever J-9504-01 or equivalent to booster mounting studs.Rotate rear shell counterclockwise to unlock housing, separate booster shells, then remove holding fixtures. **Do not suddenly release spring tension when separating booster shells.**
5. Remove diaphragm spring and pushrod from front shell.
6. Remove diaphragm and piston assembly from rear shell.
7. Support rear shell inboard of mounting studs, then drive out rear seal using a spacer.
8. Rotate valve body clockwise, then separate valve body and diaphragm from booster piston.
9. Push pedal pushrod into valve body, supporting valve body on cushioned work surface, then remove stopper key from side of valve body.
10. Pull pushrod from valve body, then remove two felt and one sponge element, noting position for assembly.
11. Remove reaction disc from front of valve body.
12. Pry out retaining ring, then remove seal from front shell.

Assembly

Apply silicone grease to components indicated in **Fig. 9** prior to assembly.

1. Install new seal in front shell, then secure with new retaining ring.
2. Install holding fixture J-22805-01 or equivalent on front shell, then mount holding fixture in vise.
3. Support front of valve body on cushioned work surface, press pedal pushrod into valve body, then secure pushrod by inserting stopper key into side of valve body.
4. Pull up on pushrod to ensure key is properly seated. Install elements (2 felt and 1 sponge), in rear of valve body, then the reaction disc in front of valve body, **Fig. 8.**
5. Mount diaphragm on booster piston.
6. Insert valve body assembly into booster piston, then rotate valve body counterclockwise to lock in position.
7. Support rear shell from inside, inboard of mounting studs, and drive new rear seal into place using a spacer.
8. Install diaphragm assembly into rear shell, then the pushrod and return spring into front shell.
9. Position rear shell and diaphragm assembly over front shell, then re-install rotating lever J-9504-01 or equivalent, ensuring matching marks will be aligned when assembly is rotated to locked position.
10. Apply vacuum to inlet port in front shell, then rotate rear housing clockwise to the locked position. **If rear shell is too tight to be rotated when pressed into position, apply more silicone grease to lip of diaphragm contacting front shell.**
11. Remove rotating lever and holding fixture, then install rear boot and pedal pushrod nut.
12. Adjust pushrod as outlined.

ANTI-LOCK BRAKES
TABLE OF CONTENTS
Page No.

1991 Cutlass Supreme, Grand Prix & Regal (Delco-Moraine III Type)

NOTE: Wire Color Code Identification And Symbol Identification Located In The Front Of This Manual Can Be Used As An Aid When Using Wiring Circuits Found In This Section.

INDEX

PRECAUTIONS
OPERATING

Some of the following procedures require that hydraulic lines, hoses and fit-tings be disconnected for inspection of testing. This Delco-Moraine brake system uses a hydraulic boost-er/modulator called a Powermaster III, which, when completely charged, con-tains brake fluid under high pressure.

Before disconnecting any hydraulic lines, hoses or fittings, ensure the Powermaster III is completely depres-surized as described further on. Failure to depressurize the Powermaster III may result in personal injury and/or damage to painted surfaces and/or the vehicle.

COMPUTER SYSTEM SERVICE

The Delco-Moraine system is designed to withstand normal current draws associated with vehicle operation. During testing of opens or shorts, do not ground or apply voltage to any of the circuits unless instructed to do so by the appropriate diagnostic procedure.

DESCRIPTION

The Delco-Moraine anti-lock brake system (DM ABS-III), **Fig. 1,** is designed to reduce the tendency of a wheel to lose traction (lock), while braking. In most instances, the base power brake system operates. Anti-lock braking occurs only when a combination of wheel speed sensors and a microprocessor determine a wheel is about to loose traction during braking. The DM ABS-III then adjusts brake pressure to both front wheels and/or both rear wheels to reduce the tendency of the wheels to lock-up. This system helps the driver maintain steering during braking, over a variety of road surfaces.

SYSTEM COMPONENTS

The main components of the Delco-Moraine ABS-III, are the Powermaster III hydraulic booster/master cylinder, four wheel speed sensors, speed sensor rings, remote proportioner valve assembly and an anti-lock brake controller.

ANTI-LOCK BRAKE CONTROLLER

The anti-lock brake controller monitors the speed of each wheel to determine if a wheel is approaching lock-up. If this condition is detected, the controller pulses the appropriate solenoids in the Powermaster III, to adjust brake pressures. The controller also monitors the system for malfunctions, provides diagnostic information and shuts system down in case of a serious malfunction. The controller is located beneath the front passenger seat, in a protective plastic case. The controller is non-serviceable.

POWERMASTER III

The Powermaster III is a booster/modulator designed to provide base (normal) and anti-lock braking power. Fluid pressure is created and maintained by a combination of an electric motor/pump and accumulator. The accumulator is pre-charged to 1200 psi and the electric pump maintains system pressure at 2700 psi. During anti-lock braking, the fluid pressure is modulated by three solenoid assemblies. One assembly for each front wheel and one assembly for the rear brakes. Each solenoid assembly can apply, hold, or release pressure in the line it

controls. Each front wheel can be modulated separately (first one, then the other), but the rear brakes have to be modulated together. This system is commonly called a Select-Low 3-Channel System. The Powermaster III is located in the left rear corner of engine compartment.

FRONT WHEEL SPEED SENSORS & RINGS

Front speed sensors are bolted to the strut assemblies above the axle shafts. The speed sensor rings are located on the outer the constant velocity joints, directly beneath the wheel speed sensors. As a ring moves past a speed sensor, an oscillating voltage is sent to the controller. The frequency of this signal increases and decreases with wheel speed. No repair or gap adjustment to the wheel speed sensor is permitted.

REAR WHEEL SPEED SENSORS & RINGS

Rear wheel speed sensors and speed sensor rings are integral parts of the rear wheel hub and bearing assemblies. Each sensor and ring is self-contained sealed from the environment. If a sensor or ring is malfunctioning or damaged, the entire rear hub and bearing assembly must be replaced. No repair or gap adjustment to the wheel speed sensor is permitted.

REMOTE PROPORTIONER VALVE

The proportioner valve proportions brake pressure to the rear brakes. Proportioning occurs only after a preset input pressure has been reached. Beyond this preset pressure, the valve limits output pressure to the rear brakes at a set percentage of the total system output. The separate parts of the remote proportioner valve cannot be serviced. The valve must be replaced if it is malfunctioning.

BRAKE WARNING INDICATOR

The red brake warning lamp illuminates after engine is started to indicate one or all of the following; parking brake is applied, fluid level is low, or accumulator pressure is below 1800 psi. Any of these three conditions can damage brake system or greatly reduce braking action. If the red brake warning lamp is on, check above possible causes. The brake warning lamp can be tested for proper operation by when ignition switch is in the Start position. The indicator should be on in this position.

ANTI-LOCK WARNING INDICATOR

The anti-lock warning indicator illuminates after the engine is running to indicate the following conditions. Constant illumination indicates the anti-lock brake controller has detected a fault and disabled part or all of the anti-lock brake system. The base power brake system will not be disabled. A flashing light indicates the anti-lock brake controller has detected a fault, but still retaining ABS operation. Prolonged operation with a flashing indicator may further damage the ABS system. The anti-lock warning indicator can be tested for proper operation with ignition switch in the Start position. The indicator should illuminate in this position. The indicator should also illuminate for approximately three seconds after engine is started.

OPERATION

During ABS operation, the Delco-Moraine ABS-III system cycles (pulses), the brakes, adjusting line pressures, to obtain optimum stopping distance and vehicle control. During this cycling, the brake pedal will pulsate and clicking noises will be heard from the solenoids as they control the cycling. Clicking of the solenoids and pulsating of the brake pedal at this time and during a short period after vehicle starting is normal.

Fig. 1 Anti-lock brake system components

PRE-DIAGNOSIS INSPECTION		
ITEM	INSPECT FOR:	CORRECTIVE ACTION
BRAKE FLUID RESERVOIR, MASTER CYLINDER UNIT, BRAKE CALIPERS AND BRAKE HOSES AND LINES	— LOW FLUID LEVEL — EXTERNAL LEAKS — BLINDING OR STICKING CALIPERS	— FILL RESERVOIR — REPAIR LEAKS AS REQUIRED — REPAIR AS NEEDED
PARKING BRAKE	— FULL RELEASE	— RELEASE PARKING BRAKE — ADJUST CABLE IF REQUIRED
BATTERY	— ADEQUATE CHARGE ("GREEN EYE")	— CHARGE OR REPLACE BATTERY AS REQUIRED (SEE SECTION 6D) — SERVICE CHARGING SYSTEM AS REQUIRED
FUSES AND FUSIBLE ELEMENTS FUSE BLOCK • ABS 2 FUSE 12 10 AMP • STOP FUSE 10 20 AMP • INDIC FUSE 11 10 AMP ANTILOCK BRAKE POWER CENTER • CONTROLLER FUSE 10 AMP • ELECT BRAKE VALVE FUSE 15 AMP • FUSIBLE ELEMENT K PUMP MOTOR 30 AMP • FUSIBLE ELEMENT L ELECT BRAKE VALVE 30 AMP	— BLOWN FUSE OR FUSIBLE ELEMENT	— REPLACE FUSE OR FUSIBLE ELEMENT AND VERIFY OPERATION
CONNECTORS • ANTILOCK BRAKE CONTROLLER • PUMP MOTOR RELAY • PUMP MOTOR • ACCUMULATOR SWITCH • REAR ENABLE RELAY • FRONT ENABLE RELAY • RIGHT FRONT SOLENOID • LEFT FRONT SOLENOID • REAR SOLENOID • WHEEL SPEED SENSORS • LAMP DRIVER MODULE • ANTILOCK BRAKE DIODE	— PROPER ENGAGEMENT OF CONNECTOR — LOOSE WIRES IN CONNECTOR	— PROPERLY ENGAGE CONNECTORS — REPAIR LOOSE WIRES
GROUND G106	— CLEAN AND TIGHT CONNECTION	— TIGHTEN — REPAIR LOOSE WIRES
INDICATORS OPERATION DURING BULB TEST • ANTILOCK WARNING INDICATOR • BRAKE WARNING INDICATOR	— LIGHTS	— CHECK CONNECTIONS — REPLACE BULB AND VERIFY OPERATION

Fig. 2   Pre-diagnosis inspection procedure & corrective actions

During ABS braking, to optimize stopping distance, the ABS will pump the brake pedal. The driver should press steadily and firmly on the brake pedal. **The driver should never pump the brake pedal when ABS is activated.**

During ABS operation, some tire noise may be heard. This noise is normal and results from slippage of the tire on the road surface. The amount of tire slippage will depend upon road and tire conditions. A tire will also seem to lock momentarily. This is a result of rapid changes in wheel speed and is also normal. A wheel that locks and stays locked for more than one second is not normal and should be serviced immediately.

PRE-DIAGNOSIS INSPECTION

Refer to **Fig. 2,** for pre-diagnosis procedure and corrective actions.

DIAGNOSIS & TESTING

A bi-directional scan tool connected to the assembly line diagnostic link (ALDL), is needed to access fault codes in the Delco-Moraine anti-lock braking system.

Follow manufacturers directions for accessing fault codes. Refer to **Figs. 3 and 4,** for system wiring circuits and **Figs. 5 through 62** for trouble code diagnosis.

The ABS controller, when accessed with a bi-directional scan tool, identifies faults as specifically as possible. This diagnosis will also determine whether or not the fault is intermittent. There are 58 diagnostic fault codes. The first five codes stored, are stored in order of occurrence, from least recent to most recent. Fault codes will not disappear when ignition is turned Off, or when the battery is disconnected. Fault codes can only be read and erased with a bi-directional scan tool. If no faults occur within 50 drive cycles, all fault codes will be cleared. A drive cycle is defined as turning the ignition switch to the On position and vehicle is driven at speeds over 10 mph.

if a fault is detected, which disables the front ABS, the rear anti-lock brakes will continue to operate. The front brakes will have use of the normal power brake system only. If a fault is detected, which disables the rear ABS, the entire ABS will shutdown, leaving normal power brake capability only.

Always turn ignition switch to the Off position prior to troubleshooting. This will ensure all diagnostic data is preserved. If ignition switch is not turned to the Off position, any information stored for a fault, in the last drive cycle, will be lost.

NOTE ON INTERMITTENTS

If an intermittent fault cannot be diagnosed using Indicator Lamp Sequence chart, the problem will most probably be caused by a defective electrical connection or wiring. When an intermittent problem is encountered, check questionable circuits and electrical connectors for the following:

1. Poor mating of connector halves or terminals not fully seated in connector body.
2. Improperly formed or damaged terminals. All connector terminals in the problem circuit should be carefully removed to increase contact tension.
3. Poor terminal wire connection.

If a visual check does not locate cause of problem, operate vehicle with EBCM connected and attempt to duplicate condition and use Indicator Lamp Sequence chart to isolate potential cause.

Continued on page 23-42

Fig. 3   Anti-Lock brake system wiring diagram (Part 1 of 2)

Fig. 3   Anti-Lock brake system wiring diagram (Part 2 of 2)

DIAGNOSTIC (TROUBLE CODE) CHART INDEX

Code	Description	Page No.	Fig. No.
—	Anti-Lock Brake System Diagnostics Cannot Be Entered	23-6	4
A001	Anti-Lock Warning Indicator Open Or Shorted To Ground	23-7	5
A002	Anti-Lock Warning Indicator Shorted To Battery Or Anti-Lock Brake Diode Shorted	23-7	6
A003	Anti-Lock Brake Diode Open Or Ground Open	23-8	7
A004	Enable Relay Or Solenoid Fault Detected (FR Fault)	23-8	8
A005	Front Enable Relay Coil Open, Contacts Open, Fuse Open	23-9	9
A006	Front Enable Relay Coil Shorted To Battery	23-10	10
A007	Rear Enable Relay Coil Open, Contacts Open, Fuse Open	23-10	11
A008	Rear Enable Relay Coil Shorted To Battery	23-11	12
A009	Right Front Hold Solenoid Open Or Shorted To Ground	23-11	13
A010	Left Front Hold Solenoid Open Or Shorted To Ground	23-12	14
A011	Rear Hold Solenoid Open Or Shorted To Ground	23-12	15
A012	Right Front Release Solenoid Open Or Shorted To Ground	23-13	16
A013	Left Front Release Solenoid Open Or Shorted To Ground	23-13	17
A014	Rear Release Solenoid Open Or Shorted To Ground	23-14	18
A015	One Or More Front Solenoids Shorted	23-14	19
A016	One Or Both Rear Solenoids Shorted	23-15	20
A017	Right Front Hold Solenoid Shorted	23-15	21
A018	Left Front Hold Solenoid Shorted	23-16	22
A019	Rear Hold Solenoid Shorted	23-16	23
A020	Right Front Release Solenoid Shorted	23-17	24
A021	Left Front Release Solenoid Shorted	23-17	25
A022	Rear Release Solenoid Shorted	23-18	26
A023	Right Front Release Solenoid Energized Too Long	23-18	27
A024	Left Front Release Solenoid Energized Too Long	23-19	28
A025	Rear Release Solenoid Energized Too Long	23-19	29
A026	Right Front Hold Solenoid Energized Too Long	23-20	30
A027	Left Front Hold Solenoid Energized Too Long	23-20	31
A028	Rear Hold Solenoid Energized Too Long	23-21	32
A030	Both Front, Or One Front And One Rear Wheel Speed Sensor Open Or Shorted To Ground	23-21	33
A031	Open Pump Motor Feedback Circuit	23-22	34
A032	Open Brake Switch Or Hydraulic Leak	23-22	35
A033	Brake Switch Is Open	23-23	36
A034	Brake Switch Shorted	23-23	37
A035	Pump Motor Running Too Long	23-24	38
A036	Pump Motor Will Not Run	23-24	39
A037	Front Enable Relay Coil Shorted To Ground	23-25	40
A038	Rear Enable Relay Coil Shorted To Ground	23-25	41
A039	Front Enable Relay Contacts Shorted To Battery	23-26	42
A040	Rear Enable Relay Contacts Shorted To Battery	23-26	43
A041	Brake Switch Circuit Open	23-27	44
A042	Low Brake Pressure Circuit Open	23-27	45
A043	System Voltage Is Low	23-28	46
A044	Right Front Wheel Speed At 0 MPH	23-28	47
A045	Left Front Wheel Speed At 0 MPH	23-29	48
A046	Right Rear Wheel Speed At 0 MPH	23-30	49
A047	Left Rear Wheel Speed At 0 MPH	23-32	50
A048	Excessive Right Front Wheel Acceleration	23-33	51
A049	Excessive Left Front Wheel Acceleration	23-34	52
A050	Excessive Right Rear Wheel Acceleration	23-35	53
A051	Excessive Left Rear Wheel Acceleration	23-37	54

Continued

DIAGNOSTIC (TROUBLE CODE) CHART INDEX-Continued

Code	Description	Page No.	Fig. No.
A052	Anti-Lock Brake Control Calibration Error	23-38	55
A054	Rear Enable Relay Coil Circuit Open	23-39	56
A055	Anti-Lock Brake Controller Internal Voltage Fault	23-39	57
A056	Open Brake Switch Or Hydraulic Leak	23-40	58
A059	Low Brake Pressure While In An ABS Stop	23-40	59
A060	Anti-Lock Brake Controller Internal Fault	23-41	60
A062	Low Accumulator Precharge	23-41	61
A063	Both Rear Wheel Speed Sensors Open	23-42	62

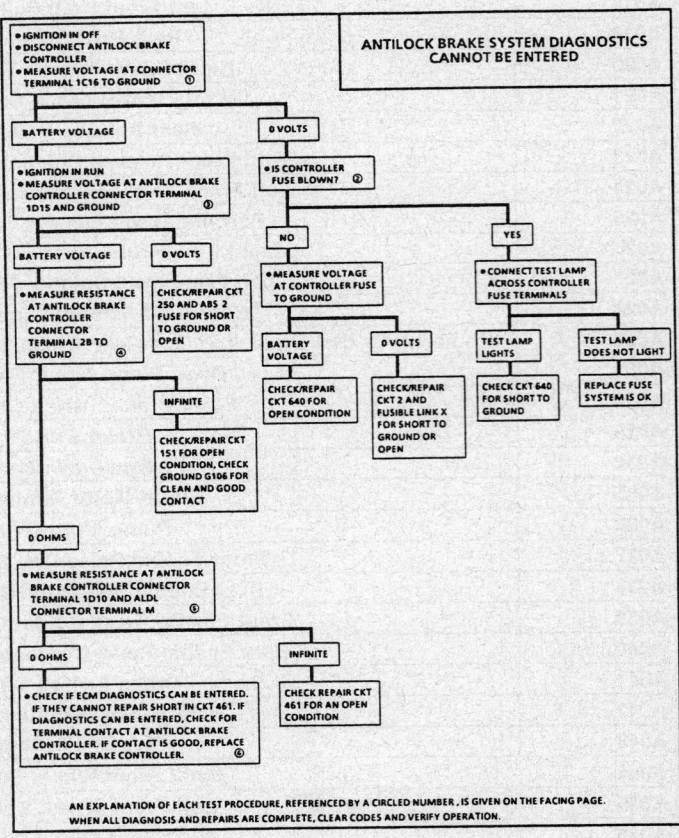

ANTILOCK BRAKE SYSTEM DIAGNOSTICS CANNOT BE ENTERED

The Antilock Brake System will be disabled and the Antilock Warning Indicator will be on if a loss of power or ground occurs at the Antilock Brake Controller. A loss of power or ground at the controller or a open or shorted serial data line will also prevent access to the Antilock Brake System's diagnostics.

TEST DESCRIPTION: The following provides an explanation of the procedures being followed in the facing trouble tree.

① Determines if voltage is being applied to the Antilock Brake Controller at Terminal 1C16.

② Indicates whether the fault is due to open condition or a possible short to ground in CKT 640.

③ Determines if voltage is being applied to Antilock Brake Controller at Terminal 1D15.

④ A measurement of infinite resistance indicates an open condition in the Antilock Brake Controller's ground circuit.

⑤ A measurement of infinite resistance indicates an open condition exists in the data line CKT 461. If an open condition exists in the data line the controller would be unable to communicate with a bi-directional scan tool.

⑥ If a short to ground existed in CKT 461, communication with the ECM would not be possible. If communication with the ECM is possible a poor terminal connection at the Antilock Brake Controller is indicated or the controller is defective.

Fig. 4 Anti-lock brake system diagnostics cannot be entered

CODE A001

Antilock Warning Indicator open or shorted to ground.

When the Front Enable Relay is energized, its contacts close. This opens the ground path from the Antilock Warning Indicator. Voltage from the INDIC Fuse should now be present at terminal 1D14.

CODE A001 will set when all of the following conditions exist:
- The Front Enable Relay is energized.
- The Antilock Warning Indicator Control is open.
- The Antilock Brake Controller senses no voltage at terminal 1D14.

TEST DESCRIPTION: The following provides an explanation of the procedures being followed in the facing trouble tree.

① If the Antilock Warning Indicator lights, the circuit from the Indicator to ground G106 must be good.

② By energizing the Front Enable Relay, one can determine if CKT 852 to Antilock Brake Controller is defective. In this mode, the Controller should ground the Indicator causing it to light.

③ Voltage at terminal 1D14 indicates that CKT 852 is OK. The fault must then be internal to the Controller.

④ This determines if the problem is an open or short to ground.

⑤ Isolates the Antilock Warning Indicator from its possible grounds and therefore determines whether a short to ground is present in CKT 852 or whether the Antilock Brake Controller is defective.

⑥ Checks for a short to ground in CKT 39.

⑦ Determines whether open is in CKT 852 or CKT 39.

Fig. 5 Code A001, anti-lock warning indicator open or shorted to ground

CODE A002

Antilock Warning Indicator shorted to Battery or Antilock Brake Diode shorted.

The Antilock Brake Diode prevents battery voltage from being applied to the Antilock Warning Indicator when the Front Enable Relay is energized. If the Antilock Brake Controller is inoperative, the Antilock Brake Diode allows the Antilock Warning Indicator to be grounded through the deenergized Front Enable Relay.

CODE A002 will set during system initialization when all of the following conditions exist:
- The Front Enable Relay is energized.
- The Antilock Warning Indicator Control is closed.
- The Antilock Brake Controller senses battery voltage at terminal 1D14.

TEST DESCRIPTION: The following provides an explanation of the procedures being followed in the facing trouble tree.

① Isolates the Antilock Warning Indicator circuit from it's power source and therefore determines whether another voltage source is shorted into the circuit or whether the Antilock Brake Controller is defective.

② Determines whether the Antilock Brake Diode is shorted or whether a short to battery exists in CKT 852.

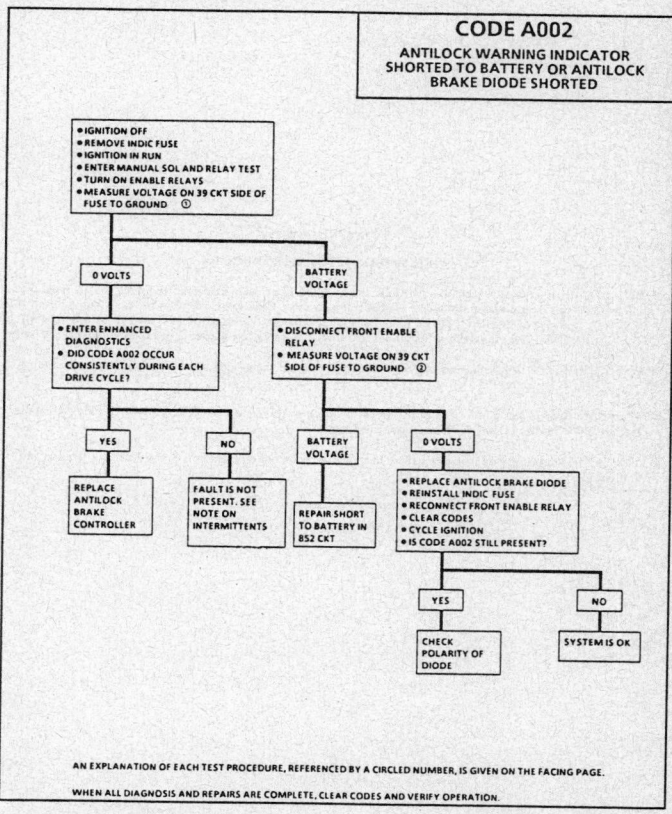

Fig. 6 Code A002, anti-lock warning indicator shorted to battery, or anti-lock brake diode shorted

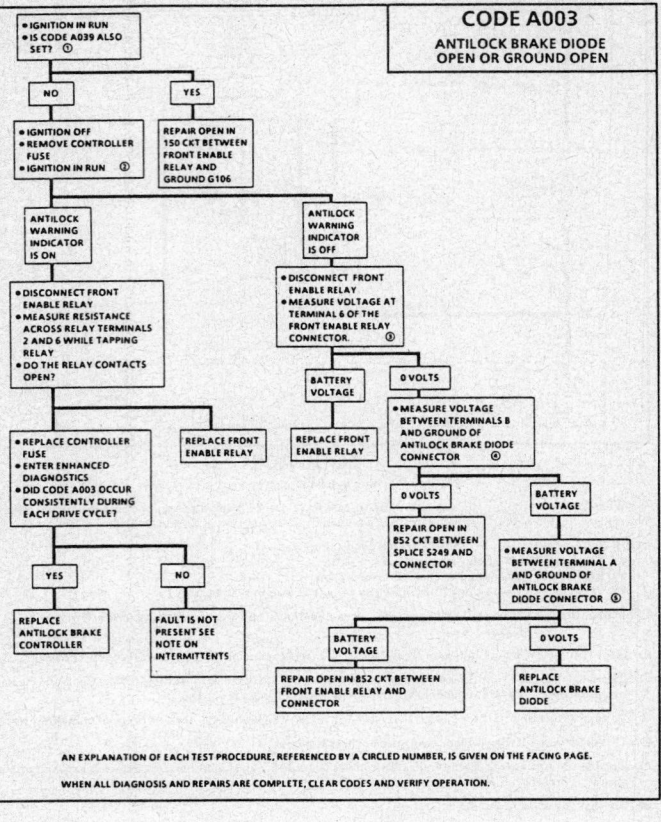

CODE A003
Antilock Brake Diode open or ground open

If the Antilock Brake Controller loses power or ground, the Antilock Warning Indicator is grounded through the 852 CKT, the Antilock Brake Diode, the open contacts of the Front Enable Relay, and CKT 150. The Antilock Brake Diode prevents Battery Voltage from being applied to the Antilock Warning Indicator when the Front Enable Relay is energized.

CODE A003 will set during system initialization when all of the following conditions exist:
- The Front Enable Relay is deenergized.
- The Antilock Warning Indicator Control is open.
- The Antilock Brake Controller senses battery voltage at terminal 1D14.

TEST DESCRIPTION: The following provides an explanation of the procedures being followed in the facing trouble tree.

① If code A039 is also set, the ground CKT 150 must be open.

② Determines if an open condition exists or if a possible intermittent condition exists.

③ Checks if the condition exists between splice S249 and the Front Enable Relay.

④ Indicates if an open condition exists in CKT 852 between splice S249 and the Antilock Brake Diode.

⑤ Determines if an open condition exists in CKT 852 to Front Enable Relay, or in Antilock Brake Diode.

Fig. 7   Code A003, anti-lock brake diode open or ground open

CODE A004
Enable Relay or Solenoid fault detected

CODE A004 is a pretest which the Antilock Brake Controller uses in order to detect that a malfunction has occurred in the solenoid or enable relay circuits. Once the Controller has set Code 4 it will initiate a series of tests in order to pinpoint the malfunction. Code A004 will always set along with another Code. The other code which is set will indicate the nature of the malfunction and where it occurred.

TEST DESCRIPTION: The following provides an explanation of the procedures being followed in the facing trouble tree.

① If another code is set a fault exists in the solenoid or enable relay circuits. The other code will indicate the nature of the malfunction and where it occurred.

② If Code A004 sets and no other codes have been set, an internal malfunction in the Antilock Brake Controller is indicated.

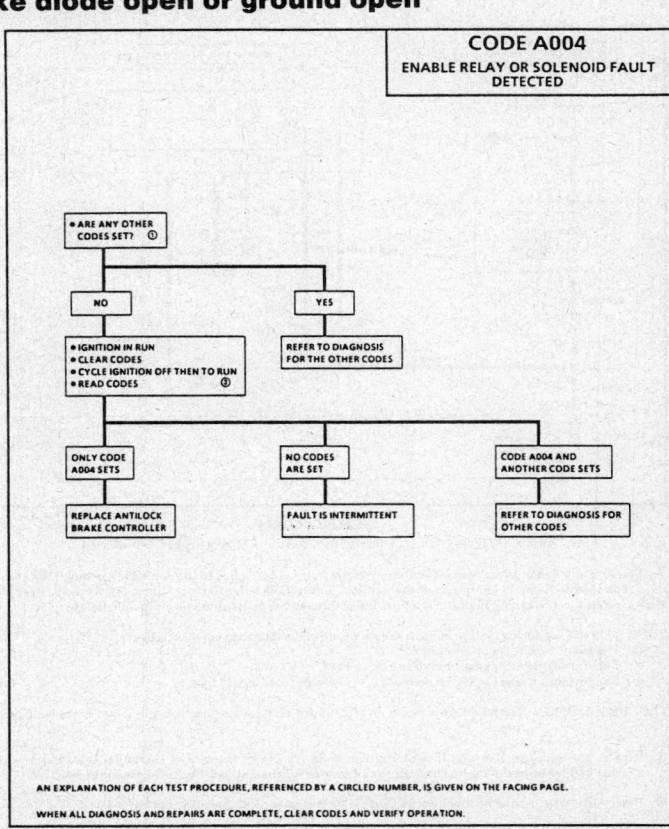

Fig. 8   Code A004, enable relay or solenoid fault detected (FR fault)

CODE A005
Front Enable Relay Coil open, contacts open, fuse open

If the Ignition is in RUN and the Antilock Brake Controller does not detect any faults, the Controller will close the Front Enable Relay Control. This grounds the Front Enable Relay Coil and the Relay becomes energized. The contacts close, and voltage is applied from Fusible Element L to the Left Front Solenoid and the Right Front Solenoid. If the Controller is not closing any of the Solenoid Controls, the Controller will sense battery voltage at terminals 1D1, 1C3, 1C6, and 1C9.

CODE A005 will set when all of the following conditions exist.
- The Front Enable Relay Control is closed (Front Enable Relay energized).
- The Antilock Brake Controller senses no voltage at terminals 1D1, 1C3, 1C6 and 1C9.

Fig. 9   Code A005, front enable relay coil open, contacts open, fuse open (1 of 2)

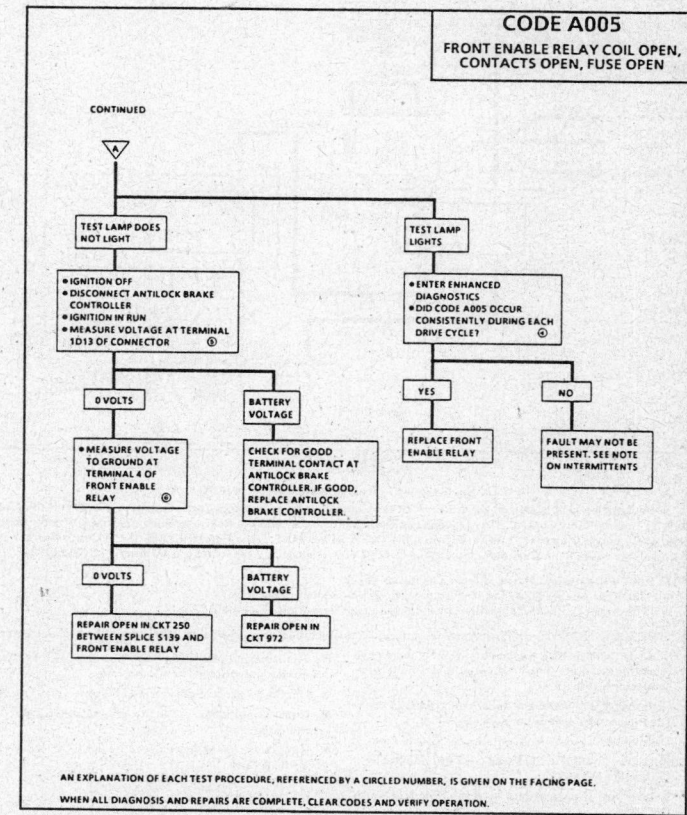

AN EXPLANATION OF EACH TEST PROCEDURE, REFERENCED BY A CIRCLED NUMBER, IS GIVEN ON THE FACING PAGE.

WHEN ALL DIAGNOSIS AND REPAIRS ARE COMPLETE, CLEAR CODES AND VERIFY OPERATION.

TEST DESCRIPTION: The following provides an explanation of the procedures being followed in the facing trouble tree.

① If voltage is present at Front Enable Relay, but not at terminal 1D13, an open in CKT 972 is indicated.

② If Code A007 is also set, none of the solenoids are receiving voltage. This indicates a problem with Connector C161.

③ If the test lamp lights, it shows that CKT 250, CKT 972, and the Antilock Brake Controller are good. This indicates that the fault is in the Front Enable Relay or connector, or the fault is intermittent.

CODE A005
Front Enable Relay Coil open, contacts open, fuse open

TEST DESCRIPTION: The following provides an explanation of the procedures being followed in the facing trouble tree.

④ This determines if Code A005 was set due to a hard failure or an intermittent condition.

⑤ If voltage is present at terminal 1D13, all external circuits must be good. this indicates an internal problem with the Controller.

⑥ If voltage is present at Front Enable Relay, but not at terminal 1D13, an open in CKT 972 is indicated.

CONTINUED

AN EXPLANATION OF EACH TEST PROCEDURE, REFERENCED BY A CIRCLED NUMBER, IS GIVEN ON THE FACING PAGE.

WHEN ALL DIAGNOSIS AND REPAIRS ARE COMPLETE, CLEAR CODES AND VERIFY OPERATION.

Fig. 9   Code A005, front enable relay coil open, contacts open, fuse open (2 of 2)

CODE A006
Front Enable Relay Coil shorted to Battery.

Battery Voltage is applied to the Front Enable Relay and CKT 972 whenever the Ignition is in RUN and the Front Enable Relay Control is open.
When the Front Enable Relay Control is closed, ground is applied to terminal 3 of the Front Enable Relay. CKT 972 is now grounded, so voltage is no longer present at terminal 1D13 of the Antilock Brake Controller.

CODE A006 will set when all of the following conditions exist:
- The Front Enable Relay control is closed (Front Enable Relay energized).
- The Antilock Brake Controller senses Battery voltage at Terminal 1D13.
- The Antilock Brake Controller senses no voltage at Terminals 1D1, 1C3, 1C6 and 1C9.

TEST DESCRIPTION: The following provides an explanation of the procedures being followed in the facing trouble tree.

① Code A008 will also be set if both Enable Relay Connectors are disconnected simultaneously.

② With the Front Enable Relay disconnected it can be determined whether a short to Battery exists in CKT 972 (Battery voltage present at Terminal 3 of Front Enable Relay connector).

③ Determines if a short exists internally in the Front Enable Relay.

④ It is possible for an open Relay Coil to set this Code. Code A005 will now set if this fault is present.

⑤ If Code A006 is a consistent failure, the Controller is faulty.

CODE A006
FRONT ENABLE RELAY COIL SHORTED TO BATTERY

(trouble tree flowchart)

AN EXPLANATION OF EACH TEST PROCEDURE, REFERENCED BY A CIRCLED NUMBER, IS GIVEN ON THE FACING PAGE.

WHEN ALL DIAGNOSIS AND REPAIRS ARE COMPLETE, CLEAR CODES AND VERIFY OPERATION.

Fig. 10   Code A006, front enable relay coil shorted to battery

CODE A007
Rear Enable Relay Coil open, contacts open, fuse open

If the Ignition is in RUN and the Antilock Brake Controller does not detect any faults, the Controller will close the Rear Enable Relay Control. This grounds the Rear Enable Relay and the Relay becomes energized. The contacts close, and voltage is applied from the ELECT BRAKE VALVE Fuse to the Rear Solenoid. If the Controller is not closing either of the Rear Solenoid Controls, the Controller will sense Battery voltage at terminals 1C14 and 1C15.

CODE A007 will set when all the following conditions exist:
- The Rear Enable Relay Control is closed (Rear Enable Relay energized).:
- The Antilock Brake Controller senses no voltage at Terminals 1C14 and 1C15.:

TEST DESCRIPTION: The following provides an explanation of the procedures being followed in the trouble tree.

① If Code A005 is also set, none of the Solenoids are receiving voltage. This indicates a problem with connector C161.

② Code A054 will set if the relay coil circuit is open. Diagnostics are covered under code A054.

③ Determines if power feed to Relay contacts is good.

④ If Battery voltage is measured CKT 961 and Rear Solenoid are good.

⑤ Determines if open exists in Rear Solenoid or in CKT 961.

⑥ This determines if Code A007 was set due to a hard failure or an intermittent condition.

⑦ Checks for short to ground in CKT 140.

⑧ If test lamp lights, a short to ground in CKT 961 is indicated.

⑨ Checks for good power feed to ELECT BRAKE VALVE Fuse.

CODE A007
REAR ENABLE RELAY COIL OPEN, CONTACTS OPEN, FUSE OPEN

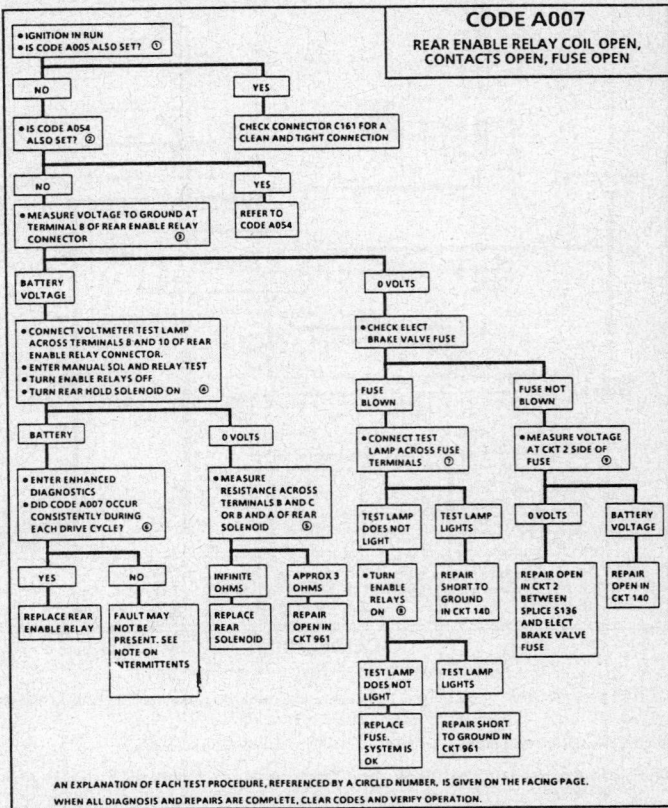

AN EXPLANATION OF EACH TEST PROCEDURE, REFERENCED BY A CIRCLED NUMBER, IS GIVEN ON THE FACING PAGE.

WHEN ALL DIAGNOSIS AND REPAIRS ARE COMPLETE, CLEAR CODES AND VERIFY OPERATION.

Fig. 11   Code A007, rear enable relay coil open, contacts open, fuse open

CODE A008
Rear Enable Relay Coil shorted to Battery

Battery voltage is applied to the Rear Enable Relay and CKT 971 whenever the Ignition is in RUN and the Rear Enable Relay Control is open. When the Rear Enable Relay Control is closed, ground is applied to terminal 7 of the Rear Enable Relay. CKT 971 is now grounded, so voltage is no longer present at terminal 1D12 of the Antilock Brake Controller.

CODE A008 will set when all the following conditions exist:
- The Rear Enable Relay Control is closed (Rear Enable Relay energized).
- The Antilock Brake Controller senses Battery voltage at Terminal 1D12.
- The Antilock Brake Controller senses no voltage at Terminals 1C14 and 1C15.

TEST DESCRIPTION: The following provides an explanation of the procedures being followed in the facing trouble tree.

① With the Rear Enable Relay disconnected it can be determined whether a short to Battery exists in the 971 CKT (Battery voltage present at Terminal 7 of Rear Enable Relay connector).

② Determines if a short exists internally in the Rear Enable Relay or whether the Antilock Brake Controller is defective.

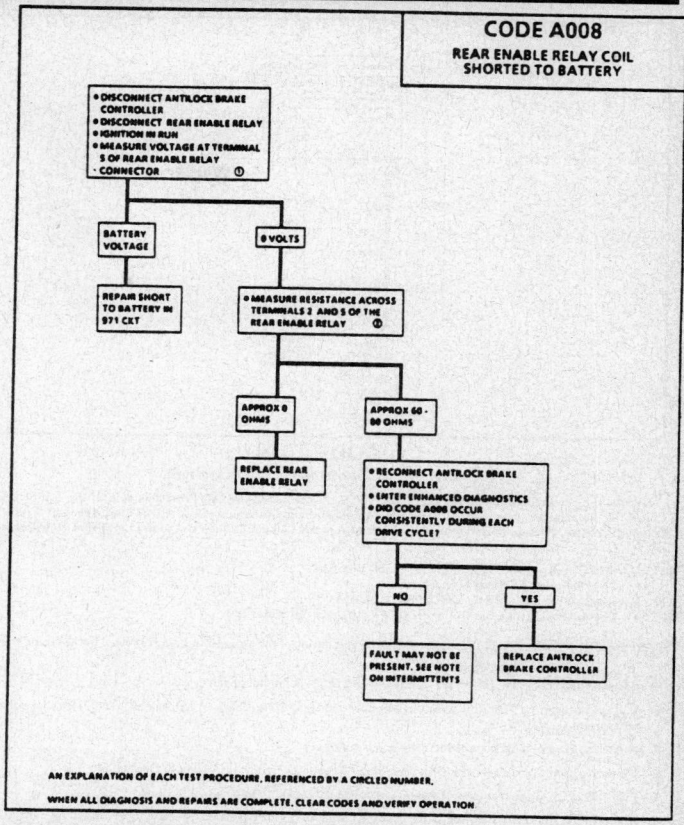

Fig. 12   Code A008, rear enable relay coil shorted to battery

CODE A009
Right Front Hold Solenoid open or shorted to ground

When the Front Enable Relay is energized, voltage is applied to the Right Front Solenoid. If the Antilock Brake Controller determines that the Right Front Hold Solenoid should be activated, it will close the Right Front Hold Solenoid Control. Ground is now applied at terminal A of the Right Front Solenoid, so the Right Front Hold Solenoid is on.

CODE A009 will set when all the following conditions exist:
- The Front Enable Relay is energized.
- The Right Front Hold Solenoid control is open.
- The Antilock Brake Controller senses no voltage at terminal 1C6.

TEST DESCRIPTION: The following provides an explanation of the procedures being followed in the facing trouble tree.

① If Code A012 is also set, the power feed to the Right Front Solenoid is open.

② Voltge at terminal 1C6 will cause the scan tool to display a HI feedback. A LO feedback indicates that voltage is not present.

③ A short to ground must be present if the test lamp lights.

④ If short to ground does not exist with Controller disconnected, short is internal to Controller.

⑤ CKT 962 is OK if the test lamp lights. Open must be internal to solenoid.

⑥ If continuity to ground through the Front Enable Relay contacts is present, open must be internal to Controller.

⑦ Determines if open is in Solenoid or 857 CKT.

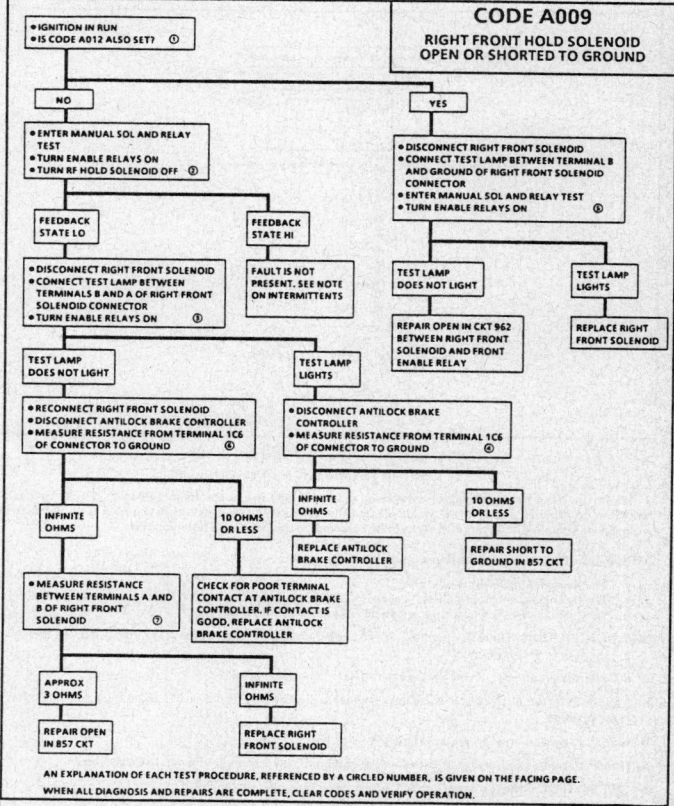

Fig. 13   Code A009, right front hold solenoid open or shorted to ground

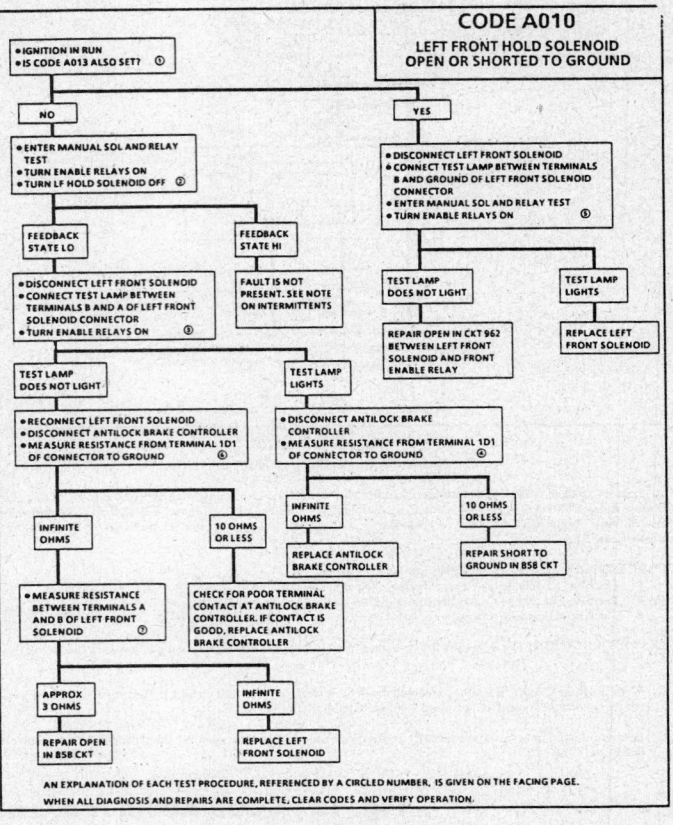

CODE A010

Left Front Hold Solenoid open or shorted to ground

When the Front Enable Relay is energized, voltage is applied to the Left Front Solenoid. If the Antilock Brake Controller determines that the Left Front Hold Solenoid should be activated, it will close the Left Front Hold Solenoid Control. Ground is now applied at terminal A of the Left Front Solenoid, so the Left Front Hold Solenoid is on.

CODE A010 will set when all the following conditions exist:
- The Front Enable Relay is energized.
- The Left Front Hold Solenoid Control is open.
- The Antilock Brake Controller senses no voltage at Terminal 1D1.

TEST DESCRIPTION: The following provides an explanation of the procedures being followed in the facing trouble tree.

① If Code A013 is also set, the power feed to the Left Front Solenoid is open.

② Voltage at terminal 1D1 will cause the scan tool to display HI feedback. A LO feedback indicates that voltage is not present.

③ A short to ground must be present if the test lamp lights.

④ If short to ground does not exist with controller disconnected, short is internal to Controller.

⑤ CKT 962 is OK if the test lamp lights. Open must be internal to solenoid.

⑥ If continuity to ground through the Front Enable Relay Contacts is present, open must be internal to Controller.

⑦ Determines if open is in solenoid or 858 CKT.

Fig. 14   Code A010, left front hold solenoid open or shorted to ground

CODE A011

Rear Hold Solenoid open or shorted to ground

When the Rear Enable Relay is energized, voltage is applied to the Rear Solenoid. If the Antilock Brake Controller determines that the Rear Hold Solenoid should be activated, it will close the Rear Hold Solenoid Control. Ground is now applied at terminal A of the Rear Solenoid, so the Rear Hold Solenoid is on.

CODE A011 will set when all the following conditions exist:
- The Rear Enable Relay is energized.
- The Rear Hold Solenoid Control is open.
- The Antilock Brake Controller senses no voltage at Terminal 1C14.

TEST DESCRIPTION: The following provides an explanation of the procedures being followed in the facing trouble tree.

① If Code A014 is also set, the power feed to the Rear Solenoid is open.

② Voltage at terminal 1C14 will cause the scan tool to display a HI feedback. A LO feedback indicates that voltage is not present.

③ A short to ground must be present if the test lamp lights.

④ If short to ground does not exist with Controller disconnected, short is internal to Controller.

⑤ CKT 961 is OK if the test lamp lights. Open must be internal to solenoid.

⑥ If test lamp lights, Rear Hold Solenoid and CKT 859 are good. Open must be internal to Controller.

⑦ Determines if open is in Solenoid or 859 CKT.

Fig. 15   Code A011, rear hold solenoid open or shorted to ground

CODE A012
Right Front Release Solenoid open or shorted to ground

When the Front Enable Relay is energized, voltage is applied to the Right Front Solenoid. If the Antilock Brake Controller determines that the Right Front Release Solenoid should be activated, it will close the Right Front Release Solenoid Control. Ground is now applied at terminal C of the Right Front Solenoid, so the Right Front Release Solenoid is on.

CODE A012 will set when all the following conditions exist:
- The Front Enable Relay is energized.
- The Right Front Release Solenoid Control is open.
- The Antilock Brake Controller senses no voltage at Terminal 1C9.

TEST DESCRIPTION: The following provides an explanation of the procedures being followed in the facing trouble tree.

① If Code A009 is also set, the power feed to the Right Front Solenoid is open.

② Voltage at terminal 1C9 will cause the scan tool to display a HI feedback. A LO feedback indicates that voltage is not present.

③ A short to ground must be present if the test lamp lights.

④ If short to ground does not exist with Controller disconnected, short is internal to Controller.

⑤ CKT 962 is OK, if the test lamp lights. Open must be internal to solenoid.

⑥ If continuity to ground through the Front Enable Relay is present, open must be internal to Controller.

⑦ Determines if open is in Solenoid or 861 CKT.

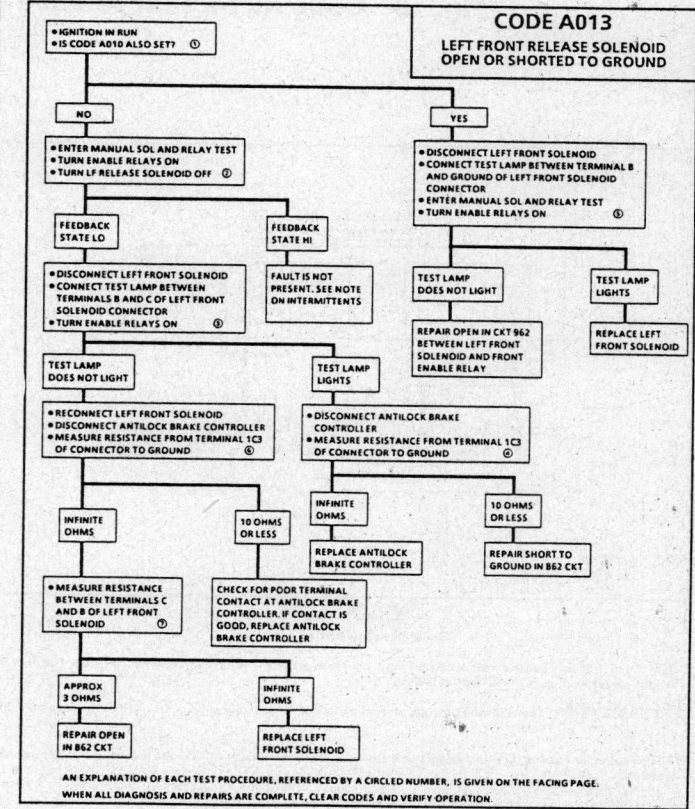

Fig. 16 Code A012, right front release solenoid open or shorted to ground

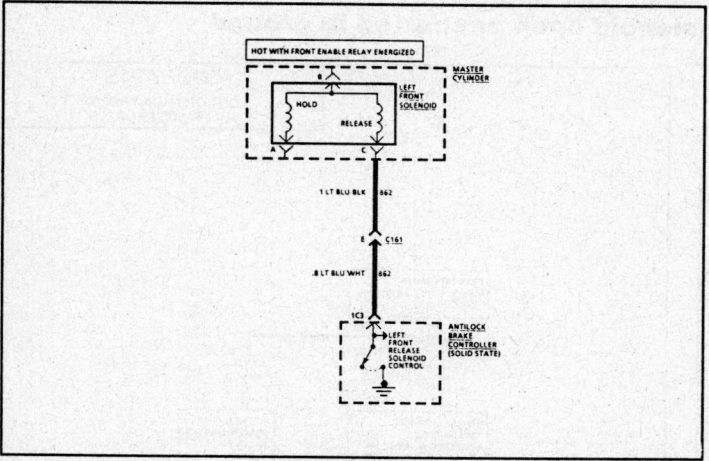

CODE A013
Left Front Release Solenoid open or shorted to ground

When the Front Enable Relay is energized, voltage is applied to the Left Front Solenoid. If the Antilock Brake Controller determines that the Left Front Release Solenoid should be activated, it will close the Left Front Release Solenoid Control. Ground is now applied at terminal C of the Left Front Solenoid, so the Left Front Release Solenoid is on.

CODE A013 will set when all the following conditions exist:
- The Front Enable Relay is energized.
- The Left Front Release Solenoid Control is open.
- The Antilock Brake Controller senses no voltage at Terminal 1C3.

TEST DESCRIPTION: The following provides an explanation of the procedures being followed in the facing trouble tree.

① If Code A010 is also set, the power feed to the Left Front Solenoid is open.

② Voltage at terminal 1C3 will cause the scan tool to display a HI feedback. A LO feedback indicates that voltage is not present.

③ A short to ground must be present if the test lamp lights.

④ If short to ground does not exist with controller disconnected, short is internal to controller.

⑤ CKT 962 is OK if the test lamp lights. Open must be internal to solenoid.

⑥ If continuity to ground through the Front Enable Relay is present, open must be internal to Controller.

⑦ Determines if open is in solenoid or 862 CKT.

Fig. 17 Code A013, left front release solenoid open or shorted to ground

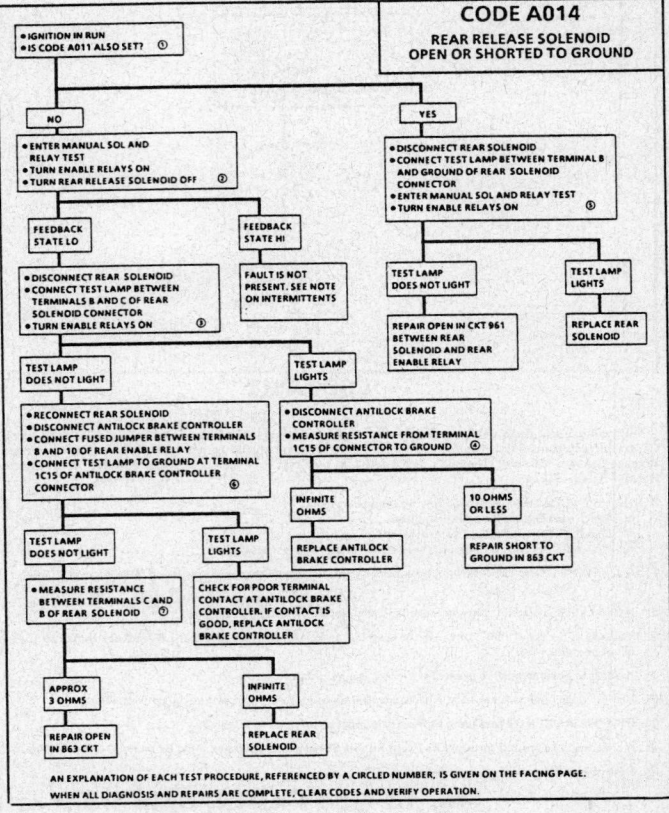

CODE A014

Rear Release Solenoid open or shorted to ground

When the Rear Enable Relay is energized, voltage is applied to the Rear Solenoid. If the Antilock Brake Controller determines that the Rear Release Solenoid should be activated, it will close the Rear Release Solenoid Control. Ground is now applied at terminal C of the Rear Solenoid, so the Rear Release Solenoid is on.

CODE A014 will set when all the following conditions exist:
- The Rear Enable Relay is energized.
- The Rear Release Solenoid Control is open.
- The Antilock Brake Controller senses no voltage at terminal 1C15.

TEST DESCRIPTION: The following provides an explanation of the procedures being followed in the facing trouble tree.

① If Code A011 is also set, the power feed to the Rear Solenoid is open.

② Voltage at terminal 1C15 will cause the scan tool to display a HI feedback. A LO feedback indicates that voltage is not present.

③ A short to ground must be present if the test lamp lights.

④ If short to ground does not exist with controller disconnected, short is internal to controller.

⑤ CKT 962 is OK if test lamp lights. Open must be internal to solenoid.

⑥ If test lamp lights, Rear Release Solenoid and CKT 863 are good. Open must be internal to controller.

⑦ Determines if open is in Solenoid or 863 CKT.

Fig. 18 Code A014, rear release solenoid open or shorted to ground

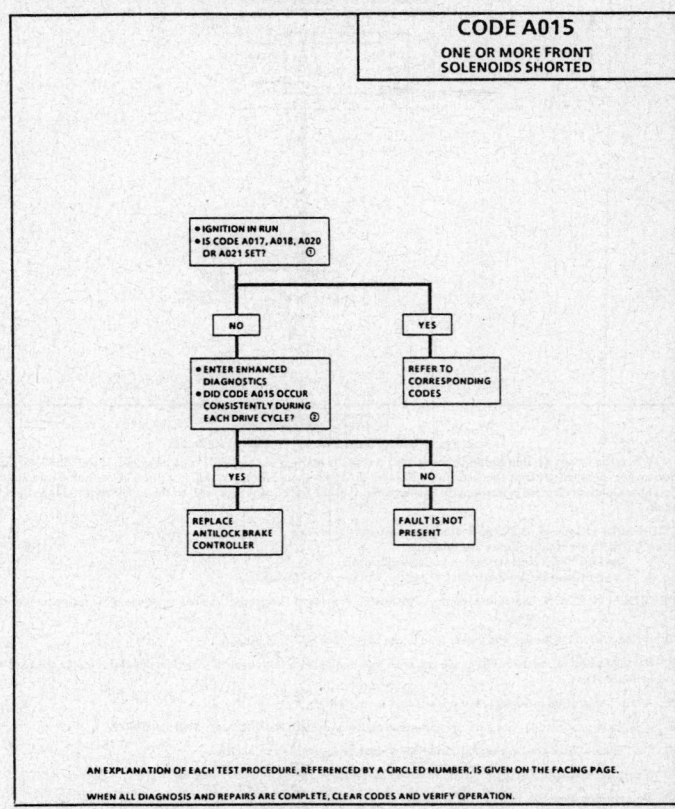

CODE A015

One or more Front Solenoids shorted

CODE A015 will set when the Antilock Brake Controller senses Battery voltage at Terminal 1D1, 1C3, 1C6 or 1C9 when the corresponding Solenoid Control is closed.

TEST DESCRIPTION: The following provides an explanation of the procedures being followed in the facing trouble tree.

① The reason for refering to these codes is that the fault that caused Code A015 to set will be linked to a specific circuit.

② If the failure is consistent, Antilock Brake Controller has an internal fault.

Fig. 19 Code A015, one or more front solenoids shorted

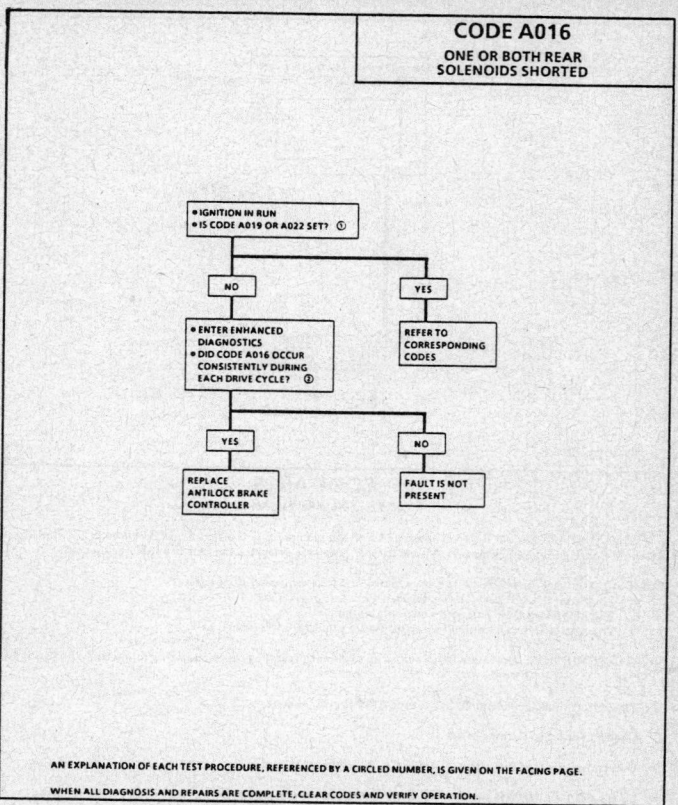

CODE A016
One or both Rear Solenoids shorted

CODE A016 will set when the Antilock Brake Controller senses Battery voltage at Terminal 1C14 or 1C15 when the corresponding Solenoid Control is closed.

TEST DESCRIPTION: The following provides an explanation of the procedures being followed in the facing trouble tree.

① The reason for refering to these codes is that the fault that caused Code A016 to set will be linked to a specific circuit.

② If the failure is consistent, Antilock Brake Controller has an internal fault.

Fig. 20 Code A016, one or both rear solenoids shorted

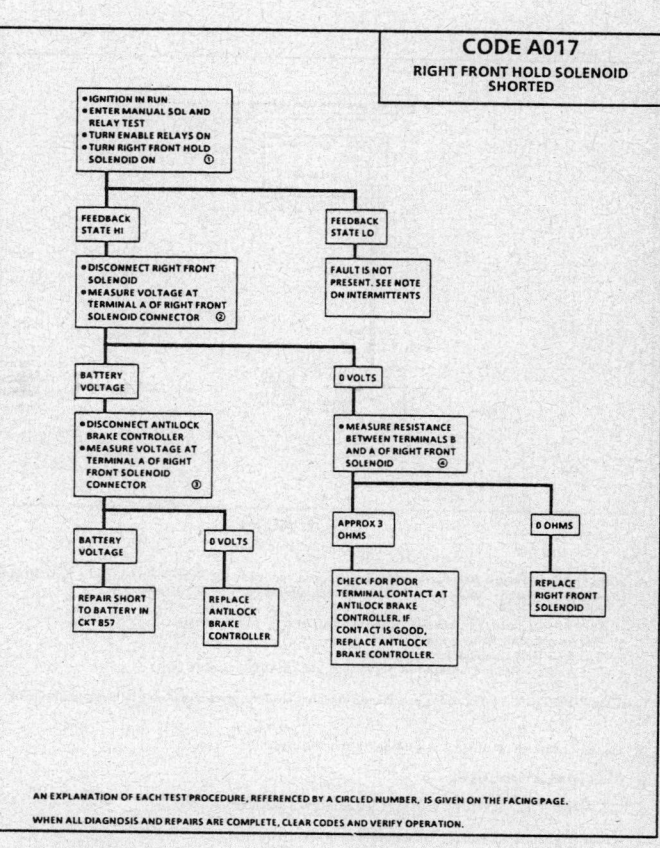

CODE A017
Right Front Hold Solenoid shorted

When the Front Enable Relay is energized, voltage is applied to the Right Front Solenoid. If the Right Front Hold Solenoid Control is closed, ground is applied to CKT 857. This activates the Right Front Hold Solenoid.

CODE A017 will set during initialization when all the following conditions exist:
- The Front Enable Relay is energized.
- The Right Front Hold Solenoid Control is closed.
- The Antilock Brake Controller senses Battery voltage at Terminal 1C6.

TEST DESCRIPTION: The following provides an explanation of the procedures being followed in the facing trouble tree.

① This determines if condition that set code A017 is still present.

② Determines if short to Battery exists.

③ Determines if short to Battery is in 857 CKT or internal to controller.

④ If Right Front Solenoid is not shorted, fault must be internal to controller.

Fig. 21 Code A017, right front hold solenoid shorted

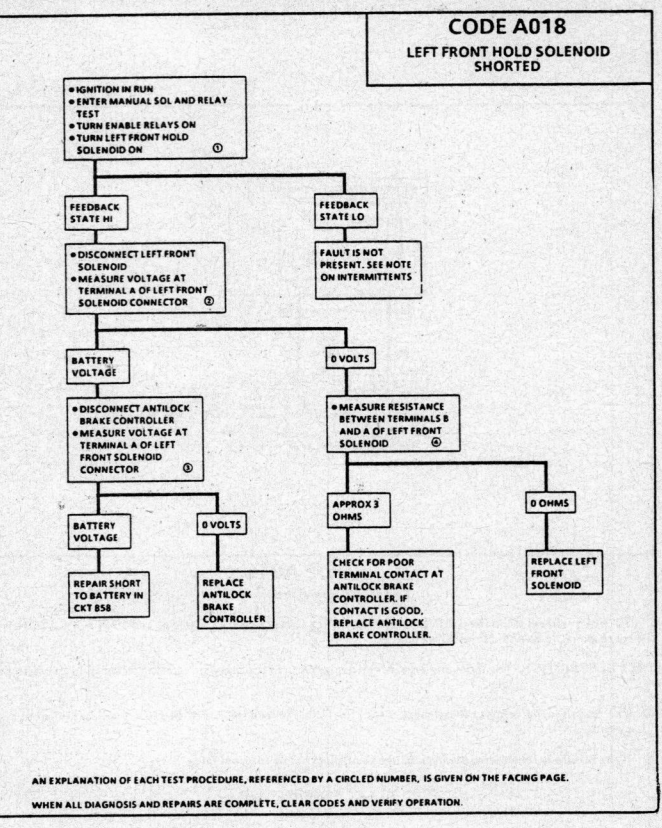

CODE A018

Left Front Hold Solenoid shorted

When the Front Enable Relay is energized, voltage is applied to the Left Front Solenoid. If the Left Front Hold Solenoid Control is closed, ground is applied to CKT 858. This activates the Left Front Hold Solenoid.

CODE A018 will set during initialization when all the following conditions exist:
- The Front Enable Relay is energized.
- The Left Front Hold Solenoid Control is closed.
- The Antilock Brake Controller senses Battery voltage at Terminal 1D1.

TEST DESCRIPTION: The following provides an explanation of the procedures being followed in the facing trouble tree.

① This determines if condition that set code A018 is still present.

② Checks if short to Battery exists.

③ Determines if short to Battery is in 858 CKT or internal to controller.

④ If Left Front Solenoid is not shorted, fault must be internal to controller.

Fig. 22   Code A018, left front hold solenoid shorted

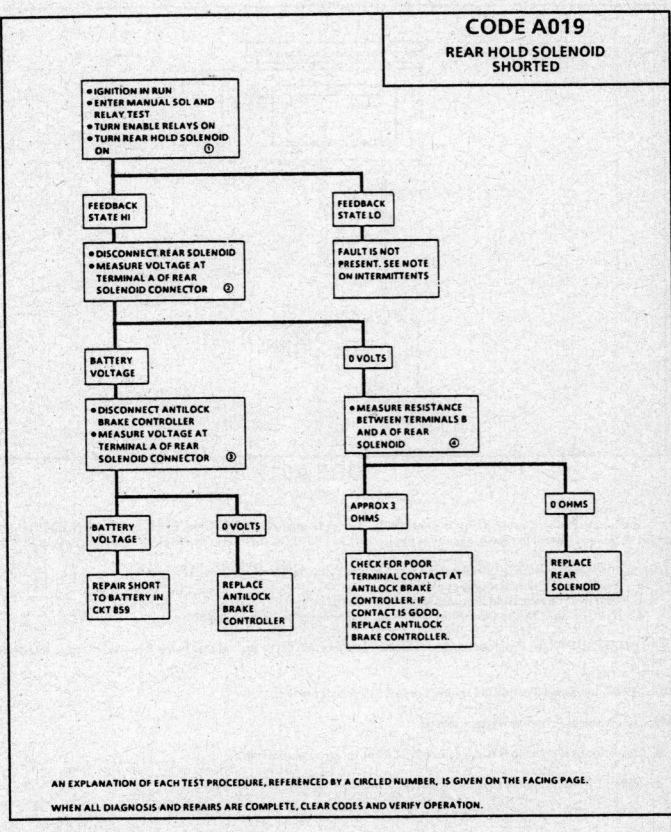

CODE A019

Rear Hold Solenoid shorted

When the Rear Enable Relay is energized, voltage is applied to the Rear Solenoid. If the Rear Hold Solenoid Control is closed, ground is applied to CKT 859. This activates the Rear Hold Solenoid.

CODE A019 will set during initialization when all the following conditions exist:
- The Rear Enable Relay is energized.
- The Rear Hold Solenoid Control is closed.
- The Antilock Brake Controller senses Battery voltage at Terminal 1C14.

TEST DESCRIPTION: The following provides an explanation of the procedures being followed in the facing trouble tree.

① This determines if condition that set code A019 is still present.

② Checks if short to Battery exists.

③ Determines if short to Battery is in 859 CKT or internal to controller.

④ If Rear Solenoid is not shorted, fault must be internal to controller.

Fig. 23   Code A019, rear hold solenoid shorted

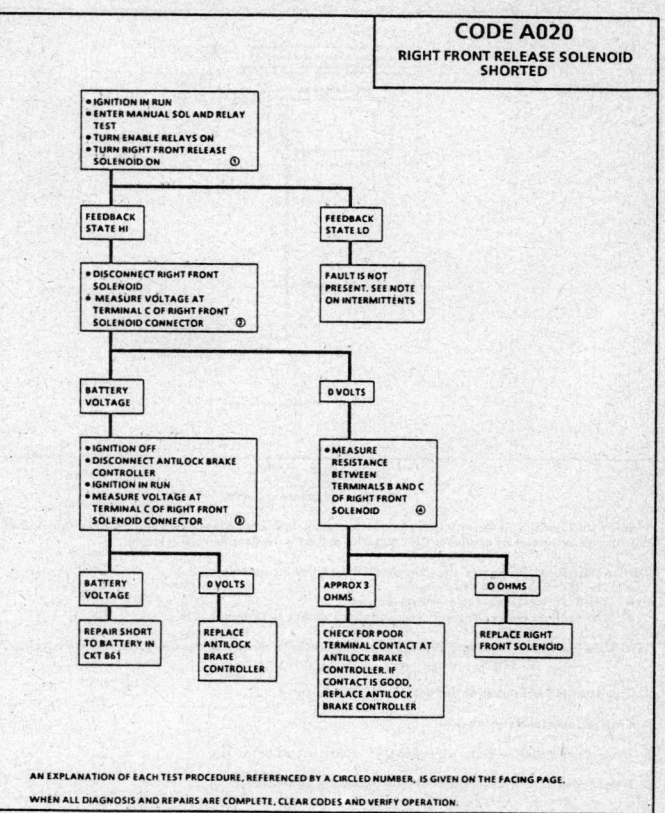

CODE A020
Right Front Release Solenoid shorted

When the Front Enable Relay is energized, voltage is applied to the Right Front Solenoid. If the Right Front Release Solenoid Control is closed, ground is applied to CKT 861. This activates the Right Front Release Solenoid.

CODE A020 will set during initialization when all the following conditions exist:
- The Front Enable Relay is energized.
- The Right Front Release Solenoid Control is closed.
- The Antilock Brake Controller senses Battery voltage at Terminal 1C9.

TEST DESCRIPTION: The following provides an explanation of the procedures being followed in the facing trouble tree.

① This determines if condition that set Code A020 is still present.

② Checks if short to Battery exists.

③ Determines if short to Battery is in 861 CKT or internal to Controller.

④ If Right Front Solenoid is not shorted, fault must be internal to Controller.

Fig. 24   Code A020, right front release solenoid shorted

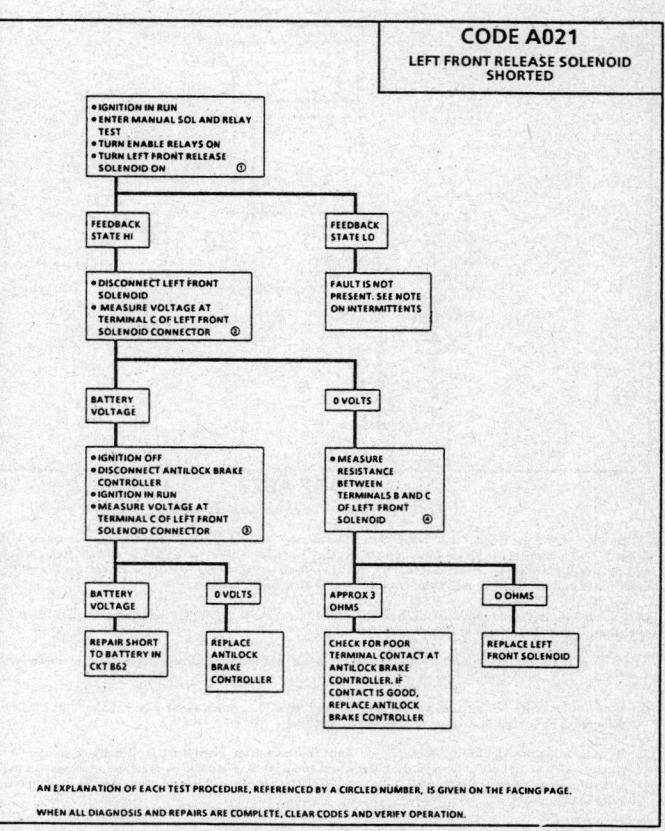

CODE A021
Left Front Release Solenoid shorted

When the Front Enable Relay is energized, voltage is applied to the Left Front Solenoid. If the Left Front Release Solenoid Control is closed, ground is applied to CKT 862. This activates the Left Front Release Solenoid.

CODE A021 will set during initialization when all the following conditions exist:
- The Front Enable Relay is energized.
- The Left Front Release Solenoid Control is closed.
- The Antilock Brake Controller senses Battery voltage at Terminal 1C3.

TEST DESCRIPTION: The following provides an explanation of the procedures being followed in the facing trouble tree.

① This determines if condition that set Code A021 is still present.

② Checks if short to Battery exists.

③ Determines if short to Battery is in 862 CKT or internal to Controller.

④ If Left Front Solenoid is not shorted, fault must be internal to Controller.

Fig. 25   Code A021, left front release solenoid shorted

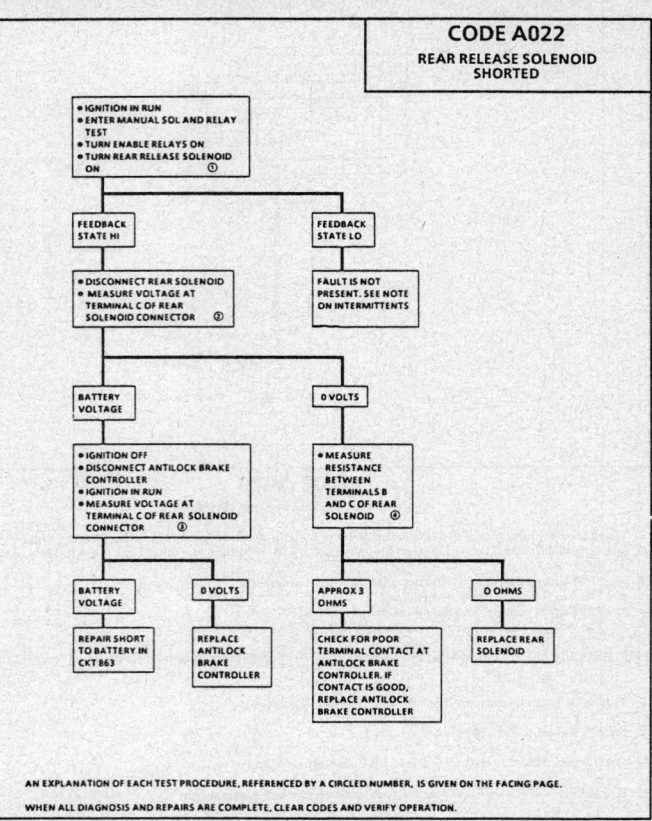

CODE A022

Rear Release Solenoid shorted

When the Rear Enable Relay is energized, voltage is applied to the Rear Solenoid. If the Rear Release Solenoid Control is closed, ground is applied to CKT 863. This activates the Rear Release Solenoid.

CODE A022 will set during initialization when all the following conditions exist:
- The Rear Enable Relay is energized.
- The Rear Release Solenoid Control is closed.
- The Antilock Brake Controller senses Battery voltage at Terminal 1C15.

TEST DESCRIPTION: The following provides an explanation of the procedures being followed in the facing trouble tree.

① This determines if condition that set Code A022 is still present.

② Checks if short to Battery exists.

③ Determines if short to Battery is in 863 CKT or internal to Controller.

④ If Rear Solenoid is not shorted, fault must be internal to Controller.

Fig. 26   Code A022, rear release solenoid shorted

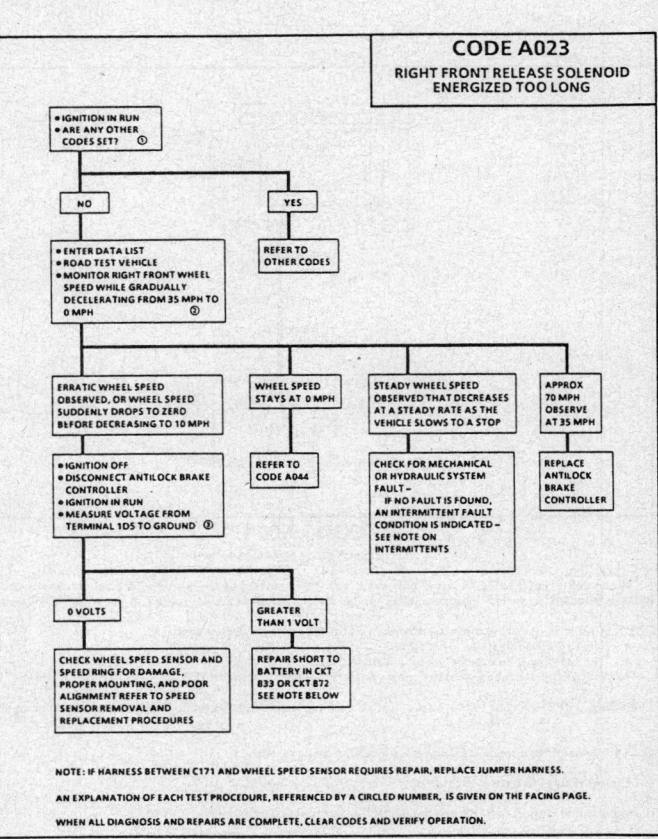

CODE A023

Right Front Release Solenoid energized too long

By monitoring the Right Front Wheel Speed Sensor, the Antilock Brake Controller can determine if the Right Front Wheel is locking up. If this condition occurs, the controller will activate the Right Front Release Solenoid by closing the Right Front Release Solenoid Control. The Solenoid Control will be closed until the Controller determines that the Right Front Wheel has increased to an acceptable speed.

CODE A023 will set when the Antilock Brake Controller senses that the Right Front Release Solenoid has been energized longer than proper operation requires.

TEST DESCRIPTION: The following provides an explanation of the procedures being followed in the facing trouble tree.

① If any other codes are set they should be addressed first. The reason for this is that the fault that caused the solenoid to be energized too long will be better identified.

② By examining the Right Front Wheel Speed input, it can be determined if the fault is due to erratic wheel speed inputs which occur only at low speeds. If the wheel speed input is found to be steady at a low speed a mechanical or hydraulic problem is indicated   A wheel speed that stays at 0 MPH indicates an open – refer to Code A044.

③ This checks for a possible short to voltage on CKT 833 and CKT 872.

Fig. 27   Code A023, right front release solenoid energized too long

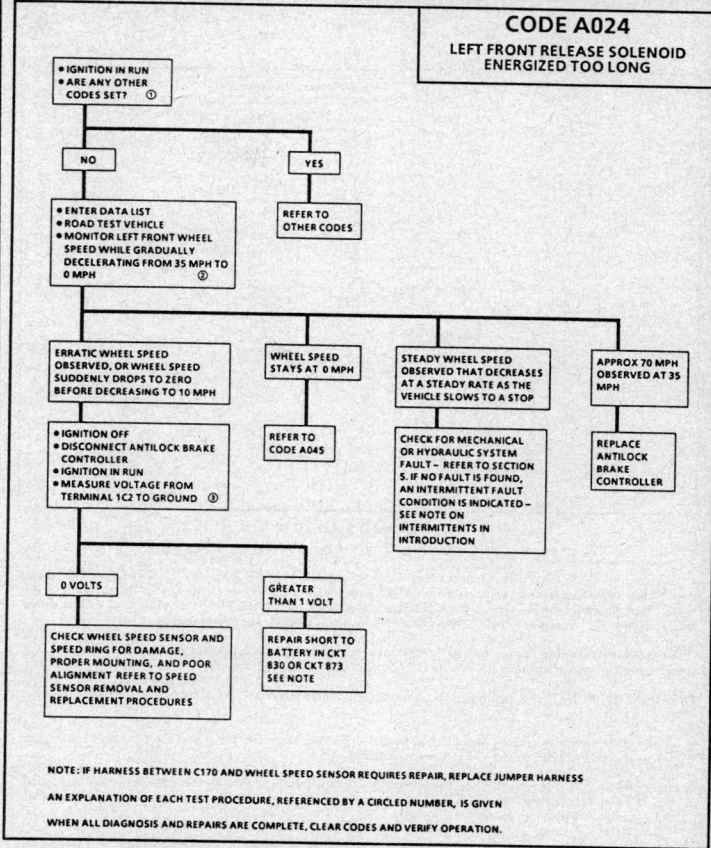

CODE A024
Left Front Release Solenoid energized too long

By monitoring the Left Front Wheel Speed Sensor, the Antilock Brake Controller can determine if the Left Front Wheel is locking up during an ABS stop. If this condition occurs, the Controller will activate the Left Front Release Solenoid by closing the Left Front Release Solenoid Control. The Solenoid Control will be closed until the Controller determines that the Left Front Wheel has increased to an acceptable speed.

CODE A024 will set when the Antilock Brake Controller senses that the Left Front Release Solenoid has been energized longer than proper operation requires.

TEST DESCRIPTION: The following provides an explanation of the procedures being followed in the facing trouble tree.

① If any other codes are set they should be addressed first. The reason for this is that the fault that caused the solenoid to be energized too long will be better identified.

② By examining the Left Front Wheel Speed input, it can be determined if the fault is due to erratic wheel speed inputs which occur only at low speeds. If the wheel speed input is found to be steady at a low speed a mechanical or hydraulic problem is indicated   A wheel speed that stays at 0 MPH indicates an open – refer to Code A045.

③ This checks for a possible short to voltage on CKT 830 and CKT 873.

Fig. 28   Code A024, left front release solenoid energized too long

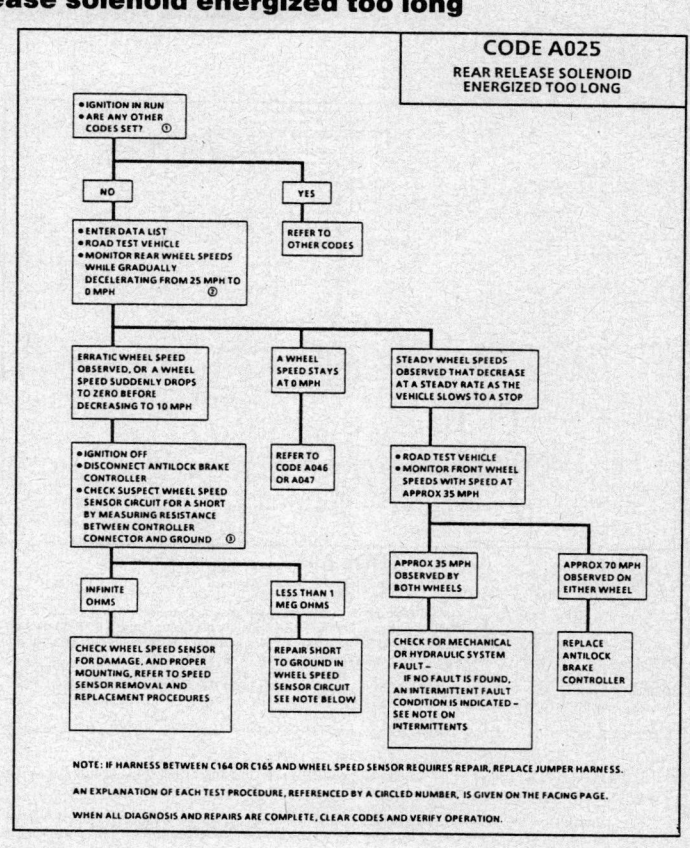

CODE A025
Rear Release Solenoid energized too long

By monitoring the Rear Wheel Speed Sensors, the Antilock Brake Controller can determine if a rear wheel is locking up during an ABS stop. If the condition occurs, the Controller will activate the Rear Release Solenoid by closing the Rear Release Solenoid Control. The Solenoid Control will be closed until the Controller determines that both rear wheels have increased to acceptable speeds.

CODE A025 will set when the Antilock Brake Controller senses that the Rear Release Solenoid has been energized longer than proper operation requires.

TEST DESCRIPTION: The following provides an explanation of the procedures being followed in the facing trouble tree.

① If any other codes are set they should be addressed first. The reason for this is that the fault that caused the solenoid to be energized too long will be better identified.

② By examining the rear wheel speed inputs, it can be determined if the fault is due to erratic wheel speed inputs which occur only at low speeds. If the wheel speed input is found to be steady at low speed, a mechanical or hydraulic problem is indicated   A wheel speed that stays at 0 MPH indicates an open – refer to Code A046 or A047.

③ This checks for a possible short to ground on the suspect Wheel Speed Sensor Circuit.

Fig. 29   Code A025, rear release solenoid energized too long

CODE A026
Right Front Hold Solenoid energized too long

By monitoring the Right Front Wheel Speed Sensor, the Antilock Brake Controller can determine if the Right Front Wheel is not decelerating properly during an ABS stop. If this condition occurs, the Controller will activate the Right Front Hold Solenoid by closing the Right Front Hold Solenoid Control. The Solenoid Control will be closed until the Controller determines that the Right Front Wheel has decreased to an acceptable speed.

CODE A026 will set when the Antilock Brake Controller senses that the Right Front Hold Solenoid has been energized longer than proper operation requires.

TEST DESCRIPTION: The following provides an explanation of the procedures being followed in the facing trouble tree.

① If any other codes are set they should be addressed first. The reason for this is that the fault that caused the solenoid to be energized too long will be better identified.

② By examining the Right Front Wheel Speed input, it can be determined if the fault is due to erratic wheel speed inputs which occur only at low speeds. If the wheel speed input is found to be steady at a low speed a mechanical or hydraulic problem is indicated

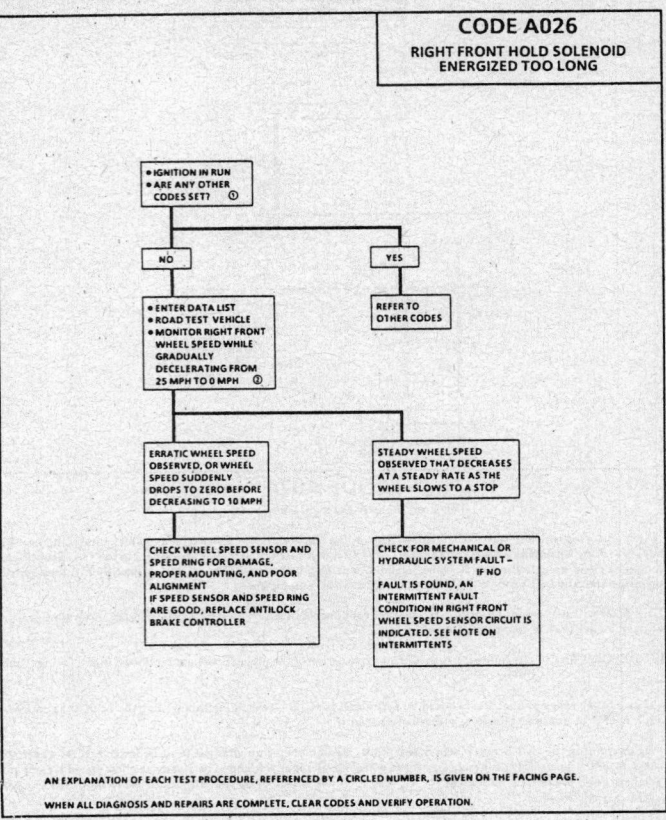

Fig. 30   Code A026, right front hold solenoid energized too long

CODE A027
Left Front Hold Solenoid energized too long

By monitoring the Left Front Wheel Speed Sensor, the Antilock Brake Controller can determine if the Left Front Wheel is not decelerating properly during an ABS stop. If this condition occurs, the Controller will activate the Left Front Hold Solenoid by closing the Left Front Hold Solenoid Control. The Solenoid Control will be closed until the Controller determines that the Left Front Wheel has decreased to an acceptable speed.

CODE A027 will set when the Antilock Brake Controller senses that the Left Front Hold Solenoid has been energized longer than proper operation requires.

TEST DESCRIPTION: The following provides an explanation of the procedures being followed in the facing trouble tree.

① If any other codes are set they should be addressed first. The reason for this is that the fault that caused the solenoid to be energized too long will be better identified.

② By examining the Left Front Wheel Speed input, it can be determined if the fault is due to erratic wheel speed inputs which occur only at low speeds. If the wheel speed input is found to be steady at a low speed a mechanical or hydraulic problem is indicated

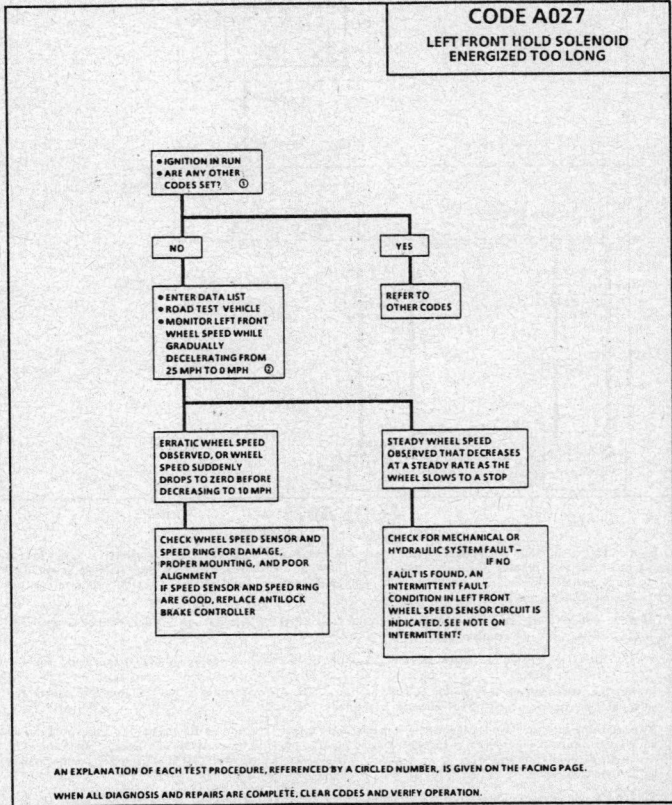

Fig. 31   Code A027, left front hold solenoid energized too long

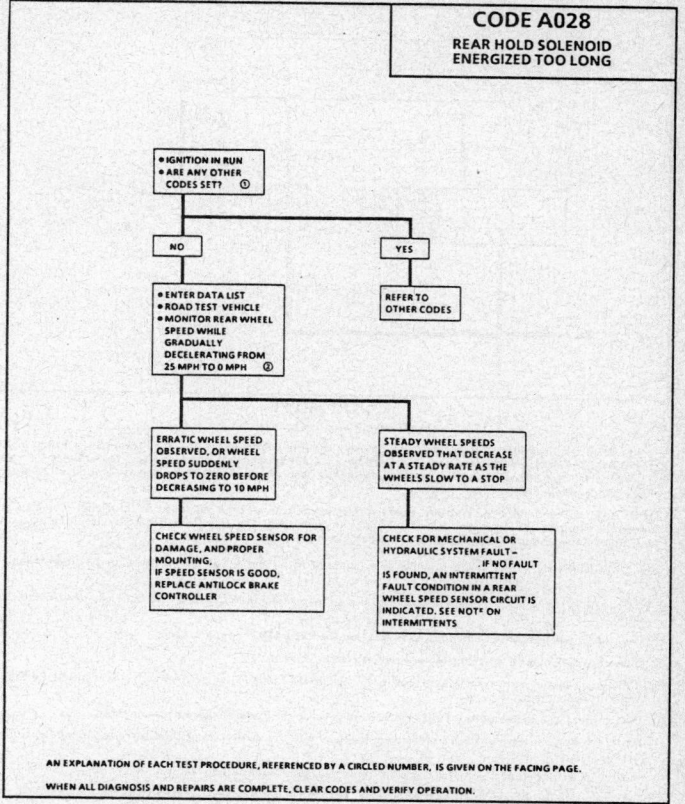

CODE A028

Rear Hold Solenoid energized too long

By monitoring the Rear Wheel Speed Sensors, the Antilock Brake Controller can determine if a Rear Wheel is not decelerating properly during an ABS stop. If this condition occurs, the Controller will activate the Rear Hold Solenoid by closing the Rear Hold Solenoid Control. The Solenoid Control will be closed until the Controller determines that the Rear Wheel has decreased to an acceptable speed.

CODE A028 will set when the Antilock Brake Controller senses that the Rear Hold Solenoid has been energized longer than proper operation requires.

TEST DESCRIPTION: The following provides an explanation of the procedures being followed in the facing trouble tree.

① If any other codes are set they should be addressed first. The reason for this is that the fault that caused the solenoid to be energized too long will be better identified.

② By examining the rear wheel speed inputs, it can be determined if the fault is due to erratic wheel speed inputs which occur only at low speeds. If the wheel speed input is found to be steady at low speed a mechanical or hydraulic problem is indicated

Fig. 32 Code A028, rear hold solenoid energized too long

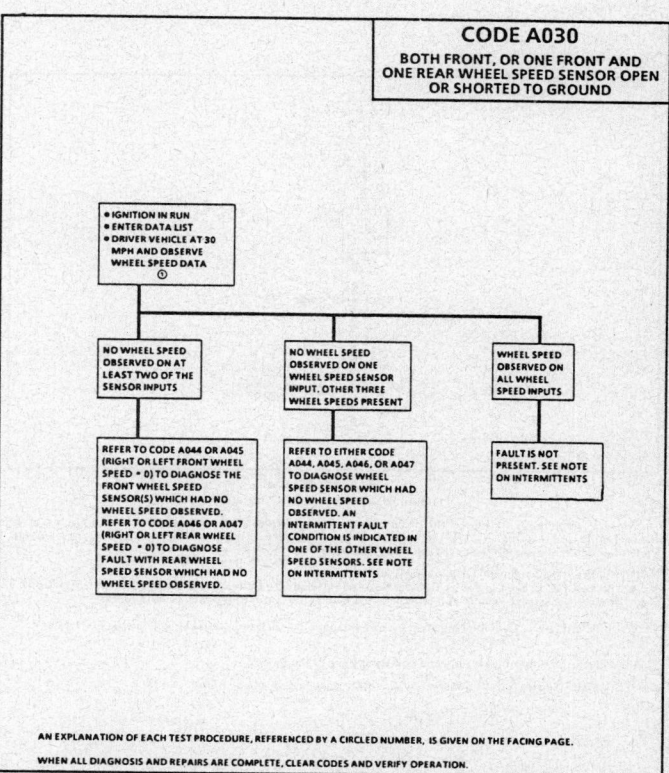

CODE A030

Both front, or one front and one rear wheel Speed Sensor open or shorted to ground

The Antilock Brake Controller monitors the Wheel Speed Sensors. If one or more wheel speed inputs are not receiving data from the Wheel Speed Sensor, the Controller can not detect wheel lockup. When only one speed input is not receiving data, Code A044, A045, A046 or A047 will be set. This Code (A030) is set when more than one speed input is faulty.

CODE A030 will set when the Antilock Brake Controller senses that either both Front Wheel Speed Sensors or both a Front and a Rear Wheel Speed Sensor input are 0 mph for greater than 20 seconds.

TEST DESCRIPTION: The following provides an explanation of the procedures being followed in the facing trouble tree.

① By observing all four Wheel Speed Sensor inputs (while driving vehicle), you can determine which Wheel Speed Sensor circuits are faulty (no wheel speed observed). Faults can be diagnosed by refering to Codes A044, A045, A046, and A047 (right front, left front, right rear or left rear wheel speed = 0).

Fig. 33 Code A030, both front, or one front and one rear wheel speed sensor open or shorted to ground

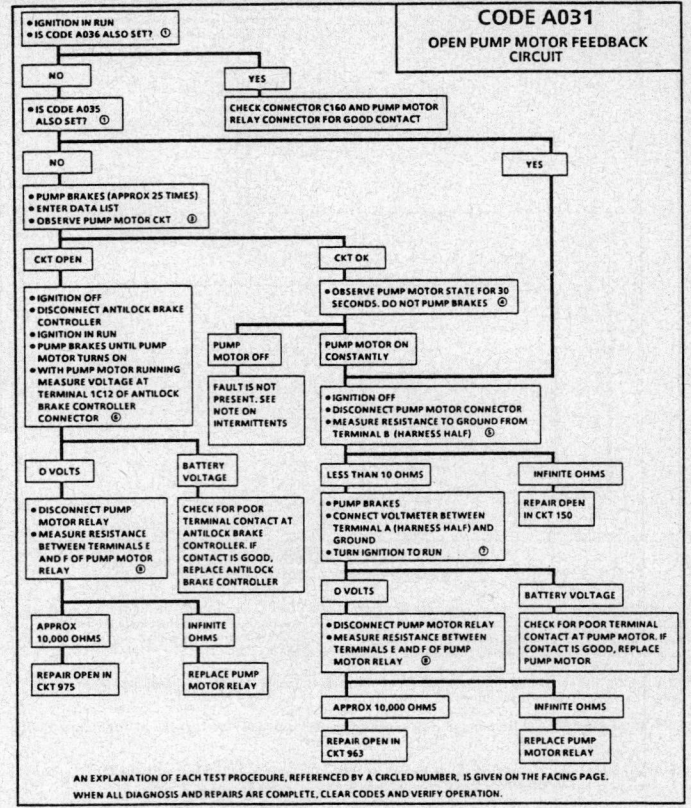

CODE A031
Open Pump Motor feedback circuit

Whenever the Pump Motor Relay contacts are open, the Pump On Input is grounded through the Pump Motor Relay and the Pump Motor. The Pump On Input will have voltage applied to it when the Pump Motor Relay contacts are closed (the Pump Motor also has voltage applied to it). If the Pump On Input does not sense ground or the proper voltage, the Controller will set Code A031.

CODE A031 will set when the Antilock Brake Controller detects an open condition in the Pump Motor circuit between the Pump Motor Relay and ground or detects an open condition in the Pump On Input circuit between the Pump Motor Relay and the Antilock Brake Controller.

TEST DESCRIPTION: The following provides an explanation of the procedures being followed in the facing trouble tree.

① If Code A036 is also set, the problem is isolated to poor connections at either the Pump Motor Relay or Connector C160.

② Code A035, when set with Code A031, indicates that the Pump Motor circuit is open.

③ This step determines if the Pump Motor Feedback circuit is open.

④ If the Pump Motor is always on, there must be an open in the Pump Motor circuit which is preventing the Pump Motor from operating.

⑤ Determines if the open condition exists in CKT 150 between the Pump Motor and ground G106.

⑥ Battery voltage at terminal 1C12 indicates a problem with the connection at the Controller or the Controller itself.

⑦ Detects if circuit to Pump Motor is good. This would indicate a faulty Pump Motor.

⑧ Determines that the open condition is internal to the Pump Motor Relay if the resistance across terminals E and F of the Pump Motor Relay is infinite.

Fig. 34   Code A031, open pump motor feedback circuit

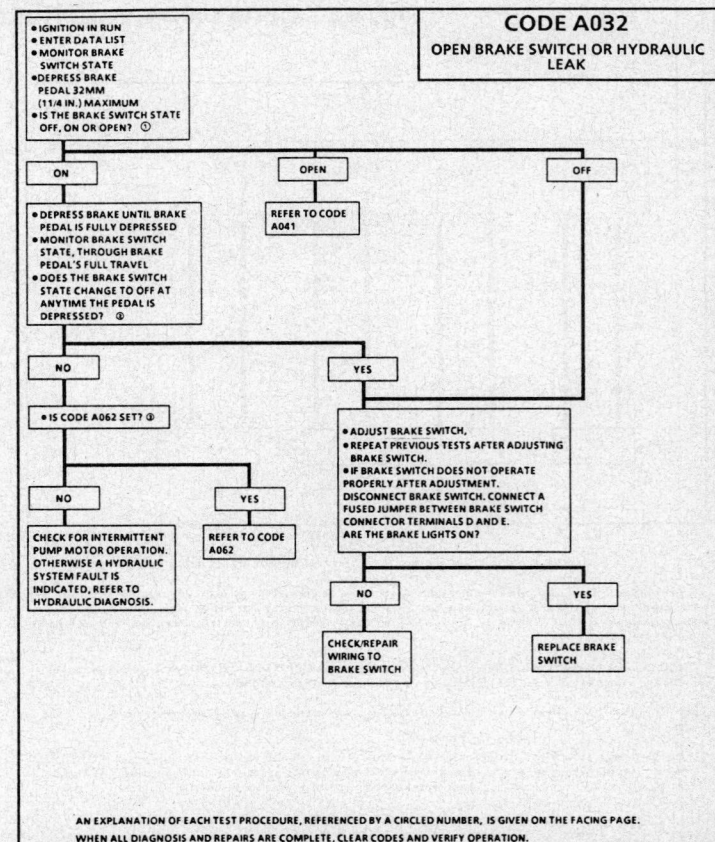

CODE A032
Open Brake Switch or Hydraulic Leak

Voltage is applied at all times to the Brake Switch. When the Brake Switch is closed, voltage is applied to the Brake Lights and terminal 1C11 of the Antilock Brake Controller. If the Brake Apply Input receives voltage, the Controller determines that the brakes are being applied.

CODE A032 will set when all the following conditions exist:
- The Antilock Brake Controller receives three pump on inputs without receiving a brake switch on input. This allows a brake switch fault to be detected without an Antilock Braking condition present.

TEST DESCRIPTION: The following provides an explanation of the procedures being following in the facing trouble tree.

① & ② Checks for a improperly adjusted or intermittent Brake Switch.

③ If Code A062 is also set, the pump motor was cycling too fast. See Code A062.

Fig. 35   Code A032, Open brake switch or hydraulic leak

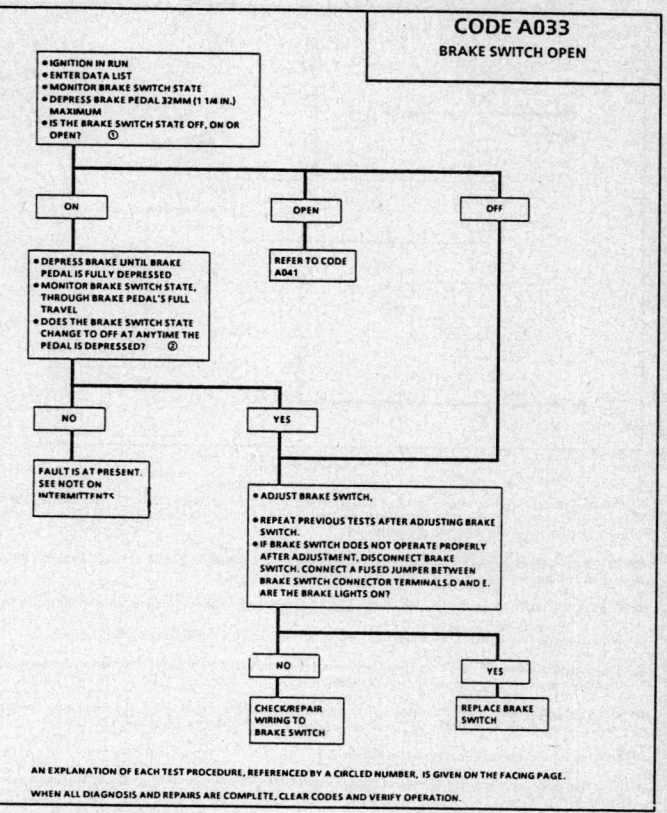

CODE A033
Brake Switch open

Voltage is applied at all times to the Brake Switch. When the Brake Switch is closed, voltage is applied to the Brake Lights and terminal 1C11 of the Antilock Brake Controller. If the Brake Apply Input receives voltage, the Controller determines that the brakes are being applied.

CODE A033 will set when all of the following conditions exist:
- The Antilock Brake Controller senses no voltage at terminal 1C11 (brake apply input is lo).
- The Antilock Brake Controller senses that two wheels (one of which is in the front) are decelerating at a rate greater than normally possible without using the brakes (vehicle is slowing down fast enough that the controller knows the brakes are being applied).

TEST DESCRIPTION: The following provides an explanation of the procedures being followed in the facing trouble tree.

① & ② Checks for improperly adjusted or intermittent Brake Switch.

Fig. 36   Code A033, brake switch is open

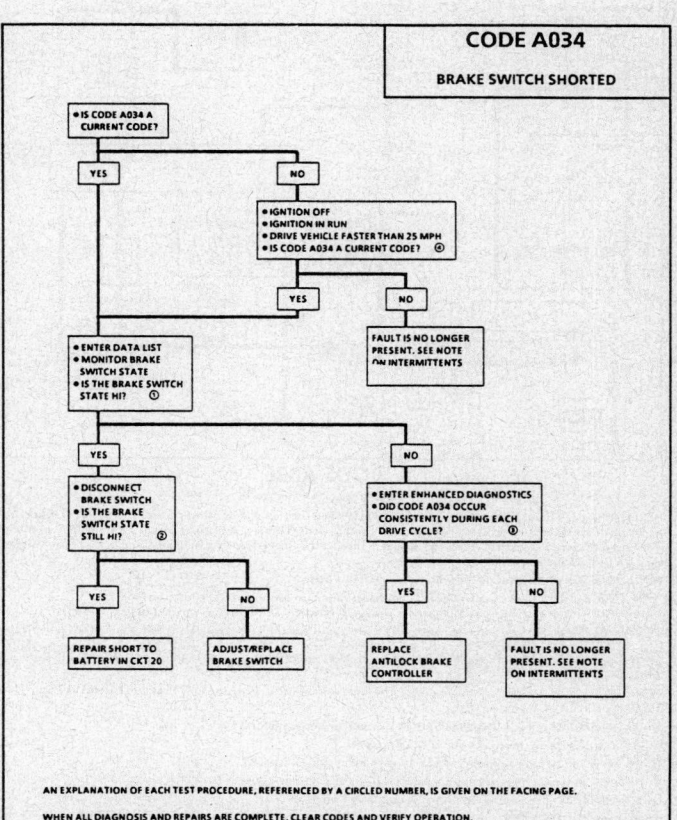

CODE A034
Brake Switch shorted

When the Brake Pedal is depressed, the Brake Switch closes. This applies voltage from the Stop Fuse to the Antilock Brake Controller and the brake lights. Before the Controller will initiate an Antilock Brake Stop, it must first sense voltage at the Brake Apply Input.

CODE A034 will set when all of the following conditions exist:
- The Antilock Brake Controller senses battery voltage at terminal 1C11 for a complete ignition cycle in which the vehicle speed surpasses 25 mph.
- The Antilock Brake Controller senses Battery voltage at terminal 1C11 during any following ignition cycle in which the vehicle speed surpasses 25 mph.

TEST DESCRIPTION: The following provides an explanation of the procedures being followed in the facing trouble tree.

① Confirms that a short exists in the circuit (brake lights on).

② Determines whether a short to Battery exists in the CKT 20; or whether the Brake Switch is shorted or maladjusted.

③ If Code A034 is a consistent failure, but CKTS and Brake Switch are good, the Antilock Brake Controller must have an internal fault.

④ This step verifies that the code is not about to become a current code by passing the second condition (see above).

Fig. 37   Code A034, brake switch shorted

CODE A035
Pump Motor running too long

The Accumulator Switch Motor Control closes when the pressure drops below 2200 PSI. This grounds the Pump Motor Relay Coil causing voltage to be applied to the Pump Motor and Pump On Input. Whenever the Pump Motor is on, the Pump On Input will have voltage applied to it.

CODE A035 will set when the Antilock Brake Controller senses voltage at Terminal 1C12 "Pump on input" for more than 3 minutes.

TEST DESCRIPTION: The following provides an explanation of the procedures being followed in the facing trouble tree.

① When Code A035 and A031 are both set, the problem is isolated to the Pump Motor Circuit.

② This step determines if the Pump Motor is running constantly (electrical fault), running longer than normal (hydraulic fault), or running too long intermittently.

③ It can be determined if the accumulator switch is causing the fault by disconnecting the accumulator switch and observing the Pump Motor State. OFF indicates a defective accumulator switch or hydraulic failure.

④ Determines if a short to ground exists in 973 wire.

⑤ This step detects if a short to Battery exists by isolating the 975 wire and Antilock Brake Controller from the Pump Motor Circuit.

⑥ Determines if a short to ground exists in the 963 wire, or whether the Pump Motor Relay is defective.

[Right flowchart - CODE A035 PUMP MOTOR RUNNING TOO LONG]

Fig. 38 Code A035, pump motor running too long

CODE A036
Pump Motor will not run

The Pump On Input will have voltage applied to it when the Pump Motor Relay contacts are closed. If the Brake Pressure drops below 1800 PSI, the Accumulator Switch opens. This removes ground from the Lamp Driver Module. The Lamp Driver Module then closes the switch to turn on the Brake Warning Indicator, and also applies voltage to the Low Brake Pressure Input of the Controller.

CODE A036 will set when all of the following conditions exist:
- The Antilock Brake Controller does not sense voltage at terminal 1C12 (Pump on input).
- The Antilock Brake Controller senses voltage at terminal 1C10 (Brake Warning Indicator is on).

TEST DESCRIPTION: The following provides an explanation of the procedures being followed in the facing trouble tree.

① If code A031 is also set, the problem is isolated to poor connections at either the Pump Motor Relay or Connector C160.

② By observing if the Pump Motor operates, the fault is isolated to either the Low Pressure Circuit or Pump Motor Relay Circuit.

③ Determines if fault is in Pump Motor Relay Circuit or Accumulator Switch Circuit.

④ This step checks if there is an actual fault present.

⑤ Battery voltage at terminal A indicates a good Relay Coil power feed.

⑥ If Pump Motor operates, the fault is either a hydraulic system failure or faulty Accumulator Switch.

⑦ Checks for an open ground circuit to Accumulator Switch.

⑧ Determines if 973 CKT is open.

⑨ At this point, a good Relay Contact power feed indicates a faulty Pump Motor Relay.

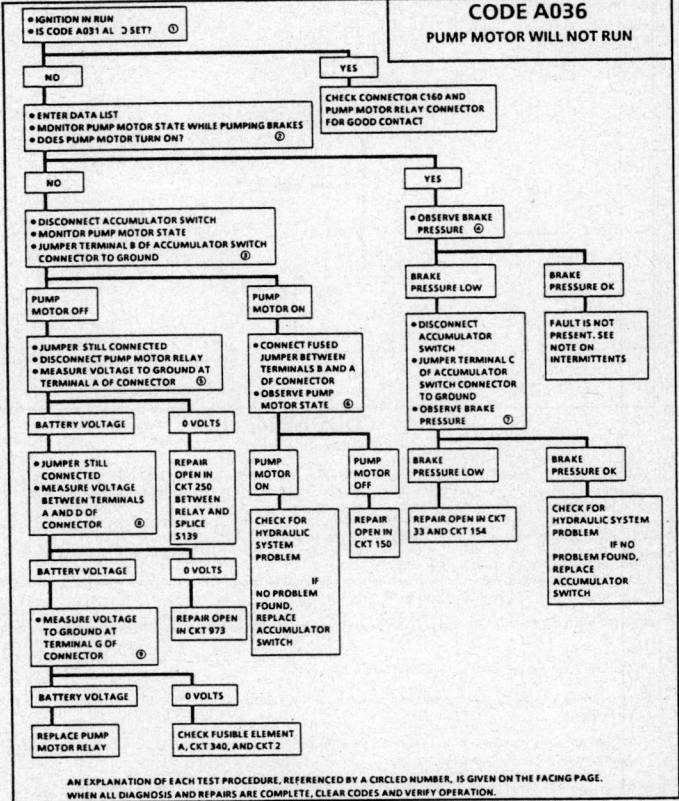

[Right flowchart - CODE A036 PUMP MOTOR WILL NOT RUN]

Fig. 39 Code A036, pump motor will not run

CODE A037
Front Enable Relay Coil shorted to ground

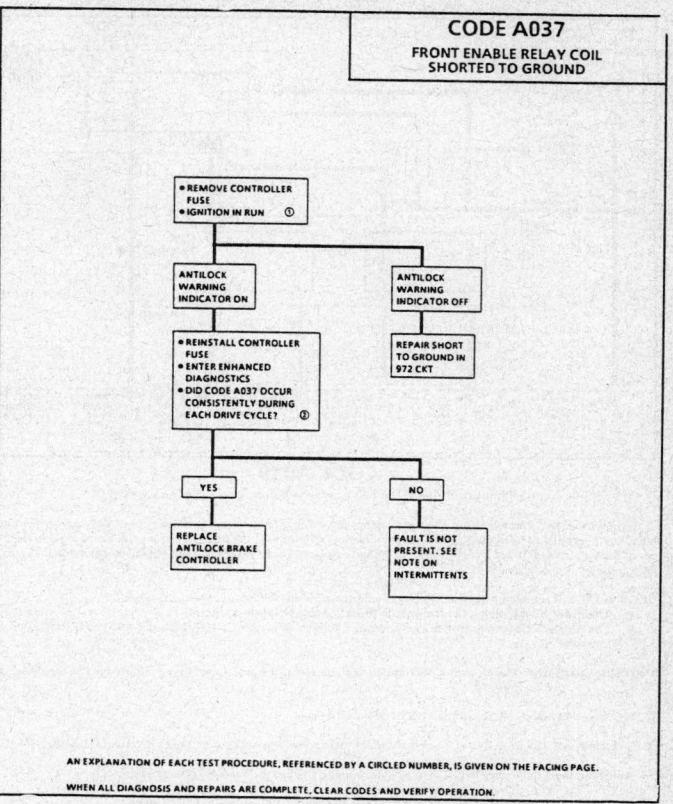

Fig. 40   Code A037, front enable relay coil shorted to ground

When the Front Enable Relay Control is open, the Front Enable Relay is deenergized. This prevents voltage from being applied to the Front Solenoids and Solenoid Controls. If the Front Enable Relay is deenergized and the Ignition is in RUN, voltage should be present at terminal 1D13.

CODE A037 will set during system initialization when all of the following conditions exist:
- The Front Enable Relay Control is open (Front Enable Relay deenergized).
- The Antilock Brake Controller senses no voltage at Terminal 1D13.
- The Antilock Brake Controller senses Battery voltage at Terminals 1D1, 1C3, 1C6 and 1C9.

TEST DESCRIPTION: The following provides an explanation of the procedures being followed in the facing trouble tree.

① By isolating the Front Enable Relay Coil from its ground and observing the Antilock Warning Indicator, it can be determined whether the Front Enable Relay has deenergized (Antilock Warning Indicator lights) which indicates a possible defective Antilock Brake Controller or whether the Front Enable Relay has remained energized (Antilock Warning Indicator does not light) which indicates a short to ground in the 972 wire.

② If Code A037 is a consistent failure, the Antilock Brake Controller has an internal fault.

CODE A038
Rear Enable Relay Coil shorted to Ground

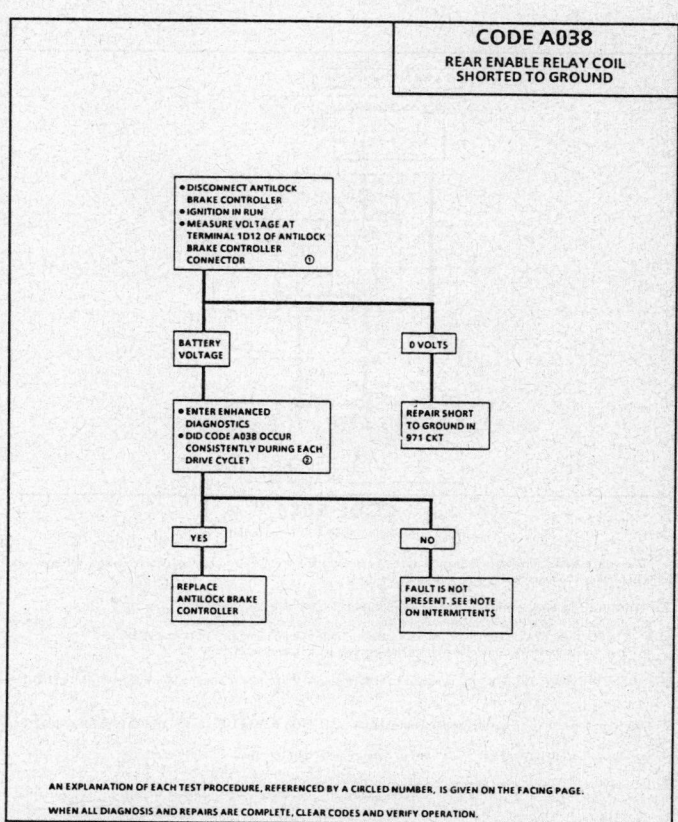

Fig. 41   Code A038, rear enable relay coil shorted to ground

When the Rear Enable Relay Control is open, the Rear Enable Relay is deenergized. This prevents voltage from being applied to the Rear Solenoid and Solenoid controls. If the Rear Enable Relay is deenergized and the Ignition is in RUN, voltage should be present at terminal 1D12.

CODE A038 will set during system initialization when all the following conditions exist:
- The Rear Enable Relay control is open (Rear Enable Relay deenergized).
- The Antilock Brake Controller senses no voltage at Terminal 1D12.
- Antilock Brake Controller senses Battery voltage at Terminal 1C14 and 1C15.

TEST DESCRIPTION: The following provides an explanation of the procedures being followed in the facing trouble tree.

① By isolating the Rear Enable Relay Control from its ground and measuring the voltage at Terminal 1D12 of the Antilock Brake Controller connector it can be determined whether the Rear Enable Relay has deenergized (Battery voltage at Terminal 1D12) which indicates a possible defective Antilock Brake Controller or whether the Rear Enable Relay has remained energized (0 volts at Terminal 1D12) which indicates a short to ground in the 971 circuit.

② If Code A038 is a consistent failure, the Antilock Brake Controller has an internal fault.

CODE A039

Front Enable Relay contacts shorted to Battery or relay ground open.

When the Front Enable Relay Control is open, the Front Enable Relay is deenergized. This prevents voltage from being applied to the Front Solenoids and Solenoid Controls. If the 150 CKT from the Front Enable Relay is open, Battery voltage from the Antilock Warning Indicator will be applied to the solenoids even when the Front Enable Relay is deenergized.

CODE A039 will set during system initialization when all of the following conditions exist:
- The Front Enable Relay Control is open (Front Enable Relay deenergized).
- The Antilock Brake Controller senses Battery voltage at Terminals 1D1, 1C3, 1C6 and 1C9 (Front Solenoid controls).

TEST DESCRIPTION: The following provides an explanation of the procedures being followed in the facing trouble tree.

② If Code A003 is also set, the ground CKT 150 must be open.

③ Determines if a short to Battery is present in the circuit or if the Antilock Brake Controller is possibly defective.

④ Isolates a short to Battery in CKT 962 or determines if the Front Enable relay is defective.

⑤ If Code A039 is a consistent failure, the Antilock Brake Controller has an internal fault.

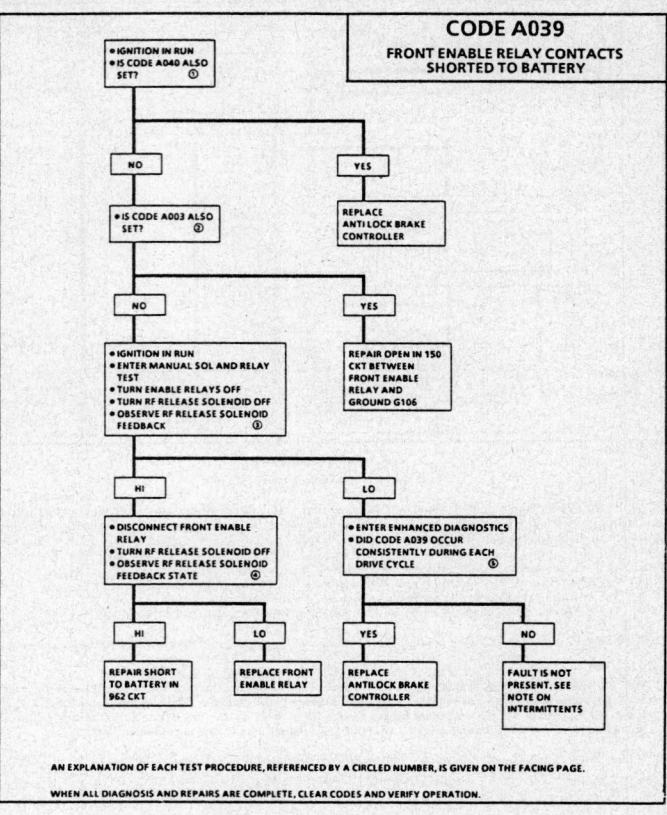

Fig. 42 Code A039, front enable relay contacts shorted to battery

CODE A040

Rear Enable Relay contacts shorted to Battery

When the Rear Enable Relay Control is open, the Rear Enable Relay is deenergized. This prevents voltage from being applied to the Rear Solenoid and Solenoid Controls.

CODE A040 will set during initialization when all the following conditions exist:
- The Rear Enable Relay Control is open (Rear Enable Relay deenergized).
- The Antilock Brake Controller senses Battery voltage at both terminals 1C14 and 1C15.
- The Antilock Brake Controller senses Battery voltage at terminal 1D12.

TEST DESCRIPTION: The following provides an explanation of the procedures being followed in the facing trouble tree.

② Determines if a short to Battery is present in the circuit or if the Antilock Brake Controller is possibly defective.

③ Isolates a short to Battery in the CKT 961 or determines if the Rear Enable Relay is defective.

④ If Code A040 is a consistent failure, the Antilock Brake controller has an internal fault.

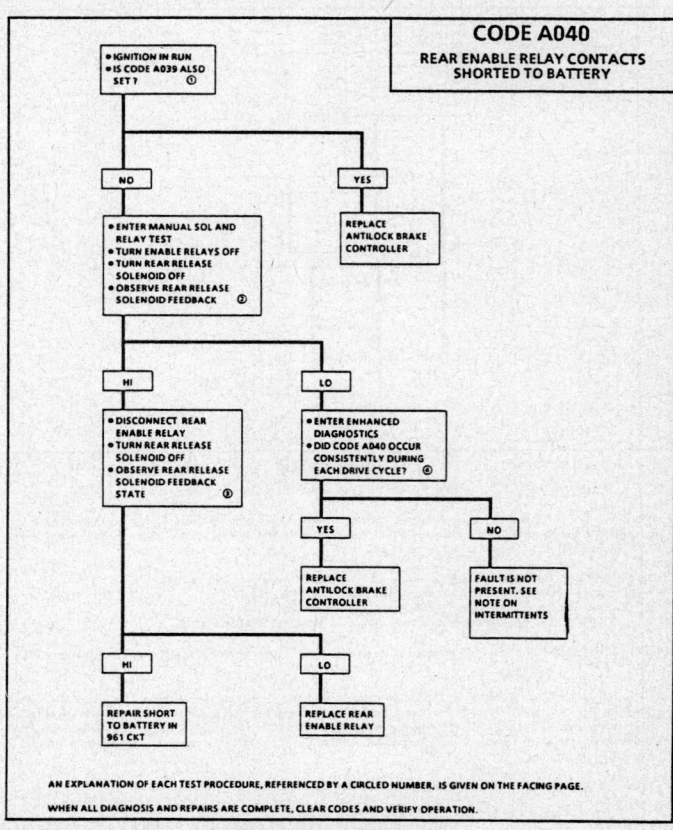

Fig. 43 Code A040, rear enable relay contacts shorted to battery

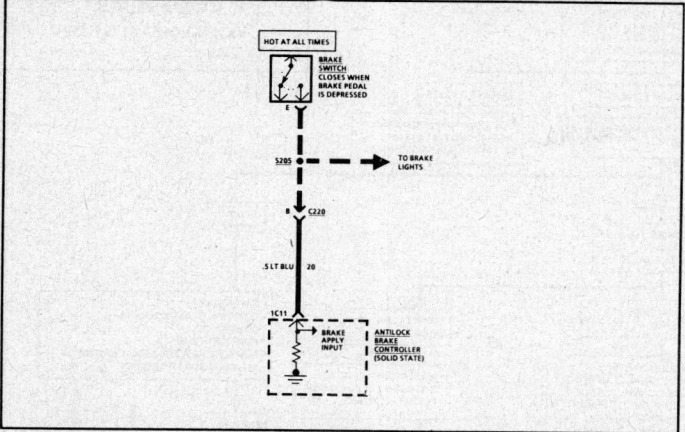

CODE A041
Brake Switch circuit open

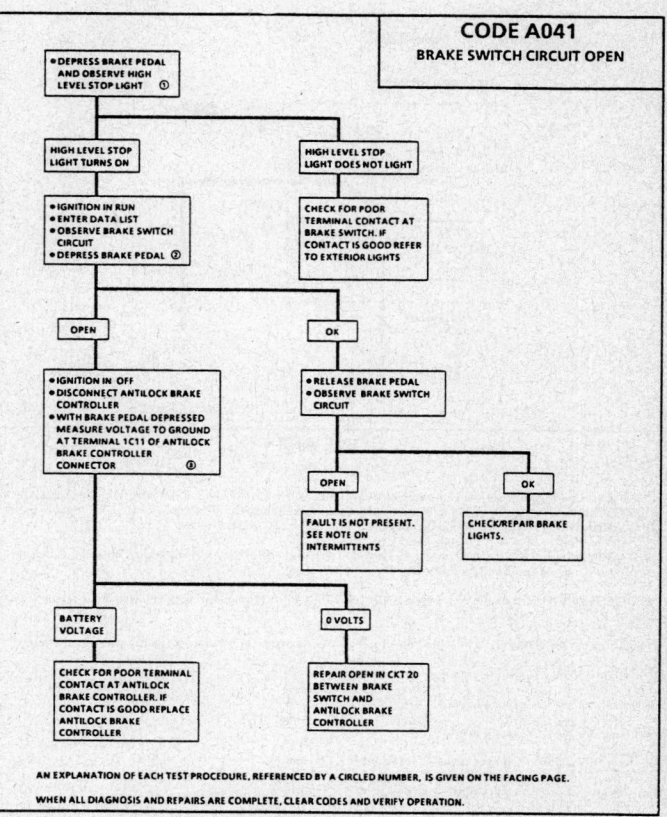

CODE A041
BRAKE SWITCH CIRCUIT OPEN

The Antilock Brake Controller determines that the Brake Pedal is pressed when battery voltage is sensed at the Brake Apply Input. If battery voltage is not present, the Controller should sense ground through CKT 20, CKT 17, and the Brake Lights. It should be noted that this code will set if the Hazard Lights are turned on and the High Level Stop Light is open or burned out.

CODE A041 will set when all the following conditions exist:
- Brake Switch is open (Battery voltage not sensed at Brake Apply Input)
- Antilock Brake Controller does not sense ground at Brake Apply Input (through CKT 20 and brake light bulbs)

TEST DESCRIPTION: The following provides an explanation of the procedures being followed in the facing trouble tree.

① Determines if the open condition exists in CKT 20 between the Brake Switch and the brake lights (High Level Stop Light did not light with brake pedal depressed) or if the open condition exists in CKT 20 between the Brake Switch and the Antilock Brake Controller (High Level Stop Light did light with Brake Pedal depressed).

② By observing the Brake Switch State when it is known that the Brake Switch is closed it can be determined if the Antilock Brake Controller is sensing the proper input (a proper input at this point would indicate an intermittent fault condition).

③ Isolates the open condition to CKT 20 between the Brake Switch and the Antilock Brake Controller if 0 volts was measured at Terminal 1C11 of Antilock Brake Controller. If Battery voltage was measured at Terminal 1C11 it indicates that the Antilock Brake Controller is defective.

AN EXPLANATION OF EACH TEST PROCEDURE, REFERENCED BY A CIRCLED NUMBER, IS GIVEN ON THE FACING PAGE.

WHEN ALL DIAGNOSIS AND REPAIRS ARE COMPLETE, CLEAR CODES AND VERIFY OPERATION.

Fig. 44   Code A041, brake switch circuit open

CODE A042
Low Brake Pressure Circuit open

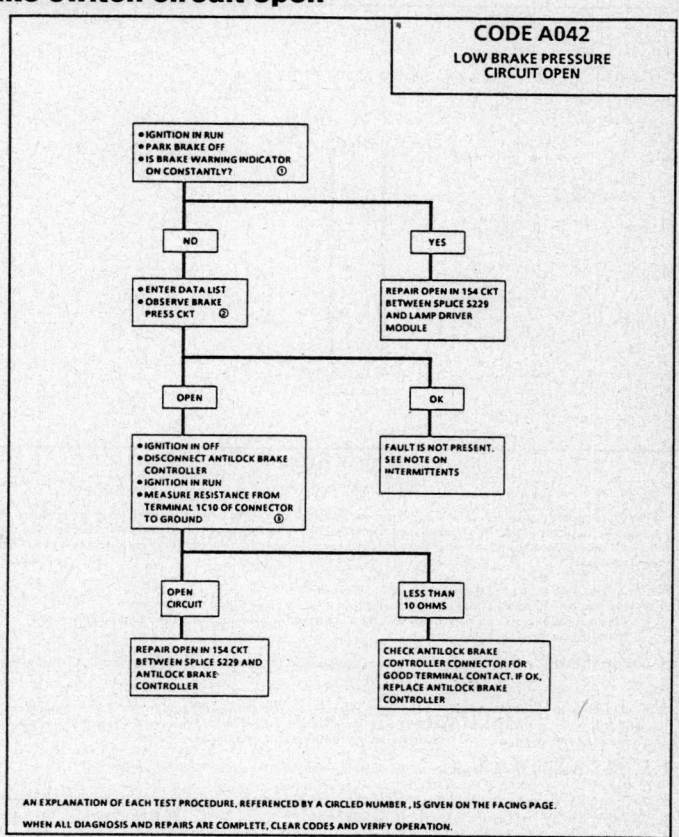

CODE A042
LOW BRAKE PRESSURE CIRCUIT OPEN

When the Low Pressure Switch in the Accumulator Switch is closed (pressure greater than approximately 1800 PSI), the Antilock Brake Controller senses ground at the Low Brake Pressure Input. If the Low Pressure Switch is open (pressure less than 1800 PSI) the Lamp Driver Module loses ground at terminal C. The Lamp Driver Module turns on the Brake Warning Indicator and applies voltage to the Low Brake Pressure Input. If the Controller does not sense ground or battery voltage at the Low Brake Pressure Input, it will set Code A042.

CODE A042 will set when the Antilock Brake Controller senses that an open condition exists in the 154 CKT between the Controller and the Lamp Driver Module.

TEST DESCRIPTION: The following provides an explanation of the procedures being followed in the facing trouble tree.

① If the Brake Warning Indicator lights constantly, there must be an open in the 154 CKT between the Lamp Driver Module and Splice S245.

② Determines if open condition is currently present.

③ Isolates the open condition to CKT 154 between splice S245 and the Antilock Brake Controller or determines a defective Antilock Brake Controller.

AN EXPLANATION OF EACH TEST PROCEDURE, REFERENCED BY A CIRCLED NUMBER, IS GIVEN ON THE FACING PAGE.

WHEN ALL DIAGNOSIS AND REPAIRS ARE COMPLETE, CLEAR CODES AND VERIFY OPERATION.

Fig. 45   Code A042, low brake pressure circuit open

CODE A043

System voltage is low

Voltage from Fusible Element L is applied at all times to the Front Enable Relay terminal 1 and the Antilock Brake Controller Battery Sense Input. Since the Antilock Brake Controller needs greater than 9.7 volts to properly operate, Code A043 is set when the applied voltage is less than9.7 volts.

CODE A034 will set when the voltage being supplied to terminal 1D8 of the Antilock Brake Controller is below 9.7 volts and vehicle speed has exceeded 10 mph.

TEST DESCRIPTION: The following provides an explanation of the procedures being followed in the facing trouble tree.

① Determines if the Battery or charging system is faulty, or isolates the problem to the Antilock Brake system.

② If Code A005 is not set, the problem is in the 990 CKT.

③ Checks for short to ground in 962 CKTS.

④ Checks for short to ground in 962 CKTS.

⑤ Determines if open is present before or after Fusible Element L.

⑥ Indicates if open is in 990 CKT or possibly internal to Controller.

⑦ Determines if fault is a constant failure internal to Controller or an intermittent.

CODE A043

SYSTEM VOLTAGE IS LOW

- IGNITION IN RUN
- MEASURE VOLTAGE ACROSS BATTERY TERMINALS ①

ABOVE 9.7 VOLTS → **IS CODE A005 ALSO SET** ①

BELOW 9.7 VOLTS → CHECK FOR PORPER GENERATOR OUTPUT AND TEST BATTERY AS NECESSARY (SEE SECTION 6D)

YES
- CHECK FUSIBLE ELEMENT ELECT BRAKE VALVE

FUSIBLE ELEMENT BLOWN
- IGNITION OFF
- DISCONNECT ANTILOCK BRAKE CONTROLLER
- CONNECT TEST LAMP ACROSS FUSIBLE ELEMENT L TERMINALS ③

TEST LAMP DOES NOT LIGHT
- RECONNECT ANTILOCK BRAKE CONTROLLER
- IGNITION IN RUN
- ENTER MANUAL SOL AND RELAY TEST
- TURN ENEABLE RELAY ON ④

TEST LAMP DOES NOT LIGHT

REPLACE FUSIBLE ELEMENT L, SYSTEM IS OK

FUSIBLE ELEMENT GOOD
- MEASURE VOLTAGE TO GROUND AT CKT 2 SIDE OF FUSIBLE ELEMENT L ⑤

TEST LAMP LIGHT
REPAIR SHORT TO GROUND IN CKT 240 OR CKT 990

0 VOLTS
REPAIR OPEN IN CKT 2 OR FUSIBLE LINKY

BATTERY VOLTAGE
REPAIR OPEN IN CKT 240

NO
- IGNITION OFF
- DISCONNECT ANTILOCK BRAKE CONTROLLER
- IGNITION IN RUN
- MEASURE VOLTAGE FROM CONNECTOR TERMINAL 1D8 TO GROUND ⑥

BATTERY VOLTAGE
- IGNITION IN RUN
- ENTER DATA LIST
- READ BATTERY VOLTAGE STATE ⑦

0 VOLTS
REPAIR OPEN IN CKT 990

OK
FAULT IS NOT PRESENT. SEE NOTE ON INTERMITTENTS IN INTRODUCTION

LOW
CHECK FOR POOR TERMINAL CONTACT AT ANTILOCK BRAKE CONTROLLER, IF CONTACT IS GOOD REPALCE ANTILOCK BRAKE CONTROLLER

AN EXPLANATION OF EACH TEST PROCEDURE REFERENCED BY A CIRCLED NUMBER, IS GIVEN

WHEN ALL DIAGNOSIS AND REPAIRS ARE COMPLETE, CLEAR CODES AND VERIFY OPERATION.

Fig. 46   Code A043, system voltage is low

CODE A044

Right Front Wheel Speed = 0

The Wheel Speed Sensor generates a signal that indicates the speed of the wheel. Voltage pulses are produced as the magnetic teeth pass a coil. The frequency of this AC voltage is used by the Controller to determine how fast the wheel is turning. By comparing this wheel speed to the other wheel speeds, the Controller can detect if wheel lock-up is about to occur.

CODE A044 will set when all of the following conditions exist:
- The Antilock Brake Controller Senses the right front wheel speed to be 0 mph.
- The Antilock Brake Controller senses that the other three wheel speeds are greater than 5 mph and are operating correctly.

TEST DESCRIPTION: The following provides an explanation of the procedures being followed in the following trouble tree.

① By observing the Right Front Wheel speed input, you can verify what type of input the controller is sensing. An unsteady or erratic wheel speed input indicates that a fault is present in the Wheel Speed Sensor or its related circuitry. If a steady wheel speed is observed, an intermittent fault condition is indicated.

② Indicates a defective Wheel Speed Sensor by isolating a short to ground internal to the sensor.

③ If resistance measured across the Wheel Speed Sensor is infinite, the fault is due to an open condition internal to the Speed Sensor.

④ Determines a short to Battery is present in CKT 833 if Battery voltage is measured at Terminal A of the harness side of the Wheel Speed Sensor Connector

⑤ Determines a short to Battery is present in CKT 872 if Battery voltage is measured at Terminal B of the harness side of the Wheel Speed Sensor Connector.

⑥ With Terminal A of CKT 833 connected to ground, the resistance from Terminal 1D5 to ground should be zero. If infinite resistance is measured, an open condition is indicated in CKT 833.

⑦ With Terminal B of CKT 872 connected to ground, the resistance from Terminal 1D4 to ground should be zero. If infinite resistance is measured, an open condition is indicated in CKT 872.

⑧ At this point, all the connecting circuitry has tested good. The fault may be due to a poorly mated connector at the Wheel Speed Sensor or the Antilock Brake Controller. Other possible causes could be due to damage to the Speed Sensor or Speed Ring. Check for proper mounting, or poor alignment.   If everything above tests good, replace the Antilock Brake Controller.

Fig. 47   Code A044, right front wheel speed at 0 mph (Part 1 of 2)

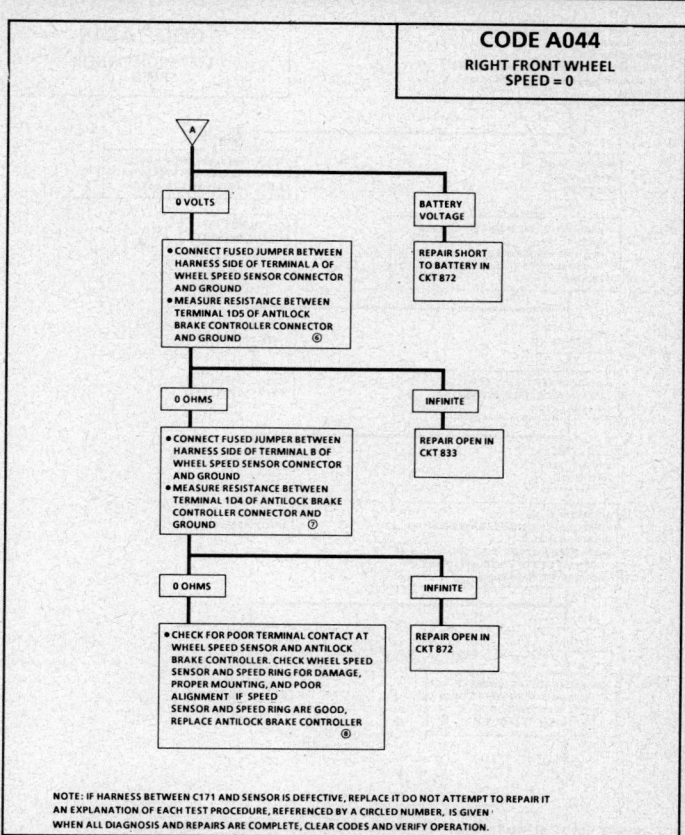

Fig. 47   Code A044, right front wheel speed at 0 mph (Part 2 of 2)

CODE A045
Left Front Wheel Speed = 0

The Wheel Speed Sensor generates a signal that indicates the speed of the wheel. Voltage pulses are produced as the magnetic teeth pass a coil. The frequency of this AC voltage is used by the Controller to determine how fast the wheel is turning. By comparing this wheel speed to the other wheel speeds, the Controller can detect if wheel lock-up is about to occur.

CODE A045 will set when all of the following conditions exist:
- The Antilock Brake Controller Senses the left front wheel speed to be 0 mph.
- The Antilock Brake Controller senses that the other three wheel speeds are greater than 5 mph and are operating correctly.

TEST DESCRIPTION: The following provides an explanation of the procedures being followed in the following trouble tree.

① By observing the Left Front Wheel speed input, you can verify what type of input the controller is sensing. An unsteady or erratic wheel speed input indicates that a fault is present in the Wheel Speed Sensor or its related circuitry. If a steady wheel speed is observed, an intermittent fault condition is indicated.

② Indicates a defective Wheel Speed Sensor by isolating a short to ground internal to the sensor.

③ If resistance measured across the Wheel Speed Sensor is infinite, the fault is due to an open condition internal to the Speed Sensor.

④ Determines a short to Battery is present in CKT 830 if Battery voltage is measured at Terminal A of the harness side of the Wheel Speed Sensor Connector.

⑤ Determines a short to battery is present in CKT 873 if Battery voltage is measured at Terminal B of the harness side of the Wheel Speed Sensor Connector.

⑥ With Terminal A of CKT 830 connected to ground, the resistance from Terminal 1C2 to ground should be zero. If infinite resistance is measured, an open condition is indicated in CKT 830.

⑦ With Terminal B of CKT 873 connected to ground, the resistance from Terminal 1C1 to ground should be zero. If infinite resistance is measured, an open condition is indicated in CKT 873.

⑧ At this point, all the connecting circuitry has tested good. The fault may be due to a poorly mated connector at the Wheel Speed Sensor or the Antilock Brake Controller. Other possible causes could be due to damage to the Speed Sensor or Speed Ring. Check for proper mounting or poor alignment. If everything above tests good, replace the Antilock Brake Controller.

Fig. 48   Code A045, left front wheel speed at 0 mph (Part 1 of 2)

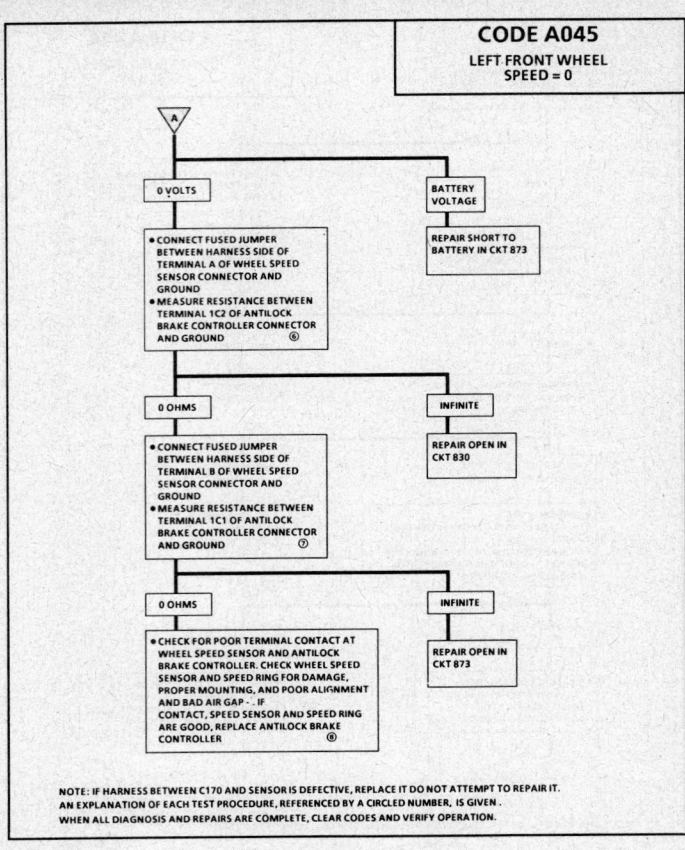

Fig. 48   Code A045, left front wheel speed at 0 mph (Part 2 of 2)

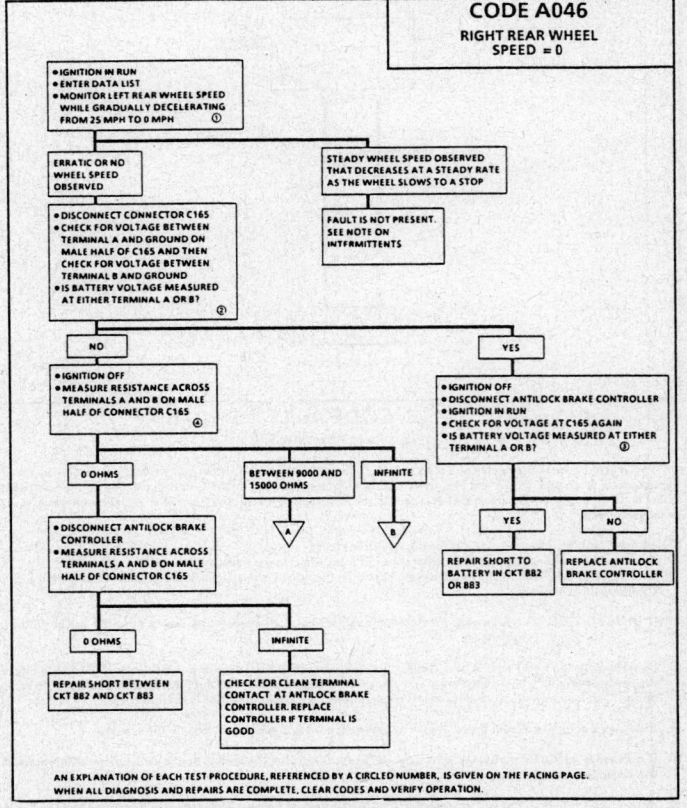

Fig. 49   Code A046, right rear wheel speed at 0 mph (Part 1 of 3)

CODE A046
Right Rear Wheel Speed = 0

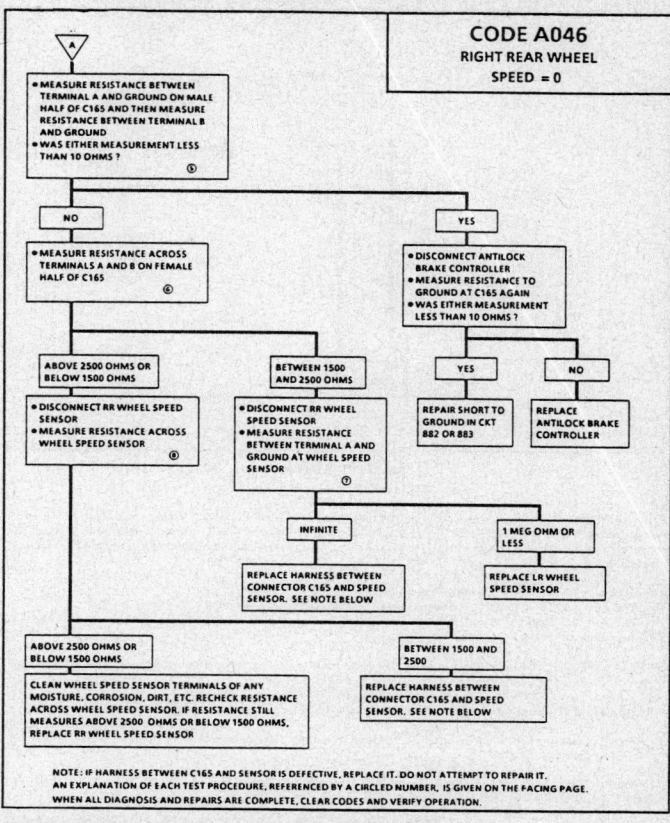

Fig. 49   Code A046, right rear wheel speed at 0 mph (Part 2 of 3)

TEST DESCRIPTION: The following provides an explanation of the procedures being followed in the following trouble tree.

⑤ If more than 10 ohms is measured the circuits between the controller and C165 are ok. This isolates the fault to be between the Wheel Speed Sensor and C165. Since this area of circuit is exposed to the elements and road debris, it should be carefully inspected for damage.

⑥ This procedure isolate is its fault to a short to ground (1500 to 2500 ohms) or open (above 2500 ohms) or a shorted sensor circuit (below 1500 ohms)

⑦ & ⑧ Determines if the fault is in the harness or the Wheel Speed Sensor. If the harness between C165 and the sensor is defective, replace it. Do not attempt to repair the harness.

CODE A046
Right Rear Wheel Speed = 0

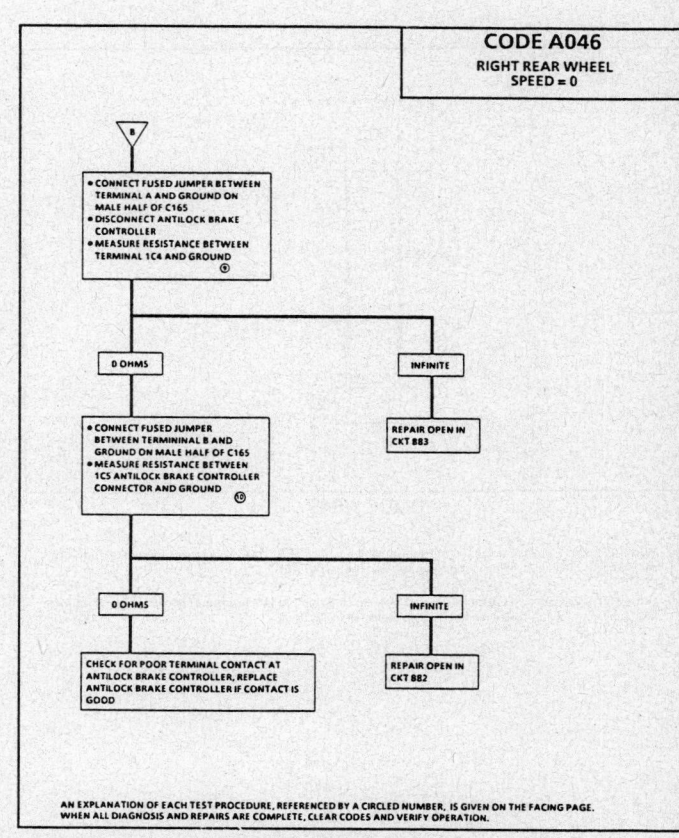

⑩ With CKT 883 connected to ground, the resistance from Terminal 1C4 to ground should be zero. If infinite resistance is measured, an open condition is indicated in CKT 883.

⑪ With CKT 882 connected to ground, the resistance from Terminal 1C5 to ground should be zero. If infinite resistance is measured, an open condition is indicated in CKT 882.

Fig. 49   Code A046, right rear wheel speed at 0 mph (Part 3 of 3)

CODE A047
Left Rear Wheel Speed = 0

CODE A047
Left Rear Wheel Speed = 0

The Wheel Speed Sensor generates a signal that indicates the speed of the wheel. Voltage pulses are produced as the magnetic teeth pass the coil. The frequency of this AC voltage is used by the Controller to determine how fast the wheel is turning. By comparing this wheel speed to the other wheel speeds, the Controller can detect if wheel lock-up is about to occur.

CODE A047 will set when all of the following conditions exist:
- The Antilock Brake Controller Senses the left rear wheel speed to be 0 mph.
- The Antilock Brake Controller senses that the other three wheel speeds are greater than 5 mph and are operating correctly.

TEST DESCRIPTION: The following provides an explanation of the procedures being followed in the following trouble tree.

① Observation of erratic or no wheel speed input indicates the fault is present and is not intermittent.

② & ③ Step 2 determines if a short to battery is the fault. If battery voltage is measured, step 3 isolates the short to the harness or controller.

④ If 9000 to 15000 ohms was measured, the possibility of an open or short in the circuit between the Antilock Brake Controller and Connector C164 has been eliminated.

TEST DESCRIPTION: The following provides an explanation of the procedures being followed in the following trouble tree.

⑤ If more than 10 ohms is measured the circuit between the controller and C164 are ok. This isolates the fault to be between the Wheel Speed Sensor and C165. Since this area of circuit is exposed to the elements and road debris, it should be carefully inspected for damage.

⑥ This procedure isolates the fault to a short to ground (1500 to 2500 ohms) or open (above 2500 ohms) or a shorted sensor circuit (below 1500 ohms).

⑦ & ⑧ Determines if the fault is in the harness or the Wheel Speed Sensor. If the harness between C164 and the sensor is defective, replace it, do not attempt to repair the harness.

Fig. 50   Code A047, left rear wheel speed at 0 mph (Part 1 of 3)

CODE A047
Left Rear Wheel Speed = 0

⑩ With CKT 884 connected to ground, the resistance from Terminal 1D2 to ground should be zero. If infinite resistance is measured, an open condition is indicated in CKT 884.

⑪ With CKT 885 connected to ground, the resistance from Terminal 1D3 to ground should be zero. If infinite resistance is measured, an open condition is indicated in CKT 885.

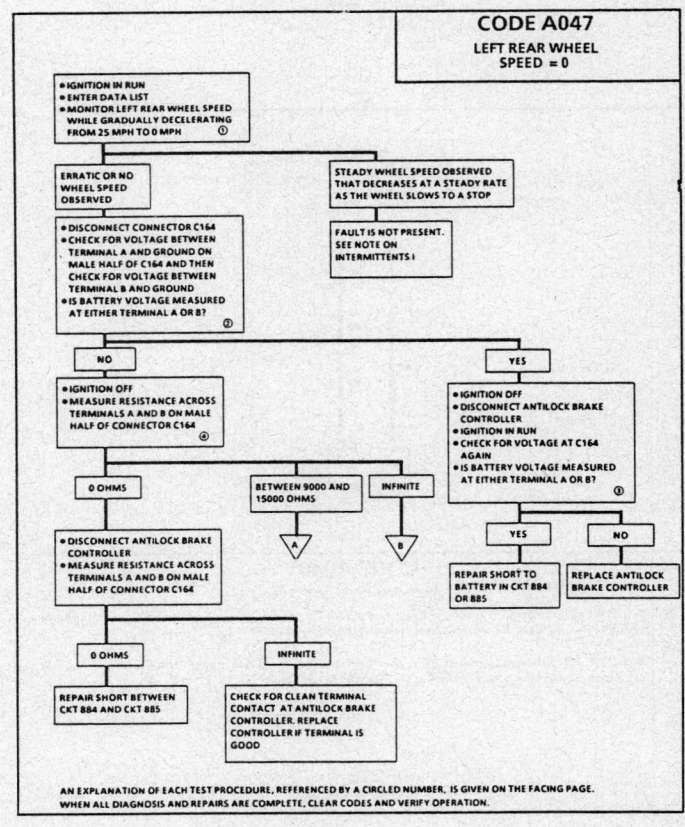

Fig. 50   Code A047, left rear wheel speed at 0 mph (Part 2 of 3)

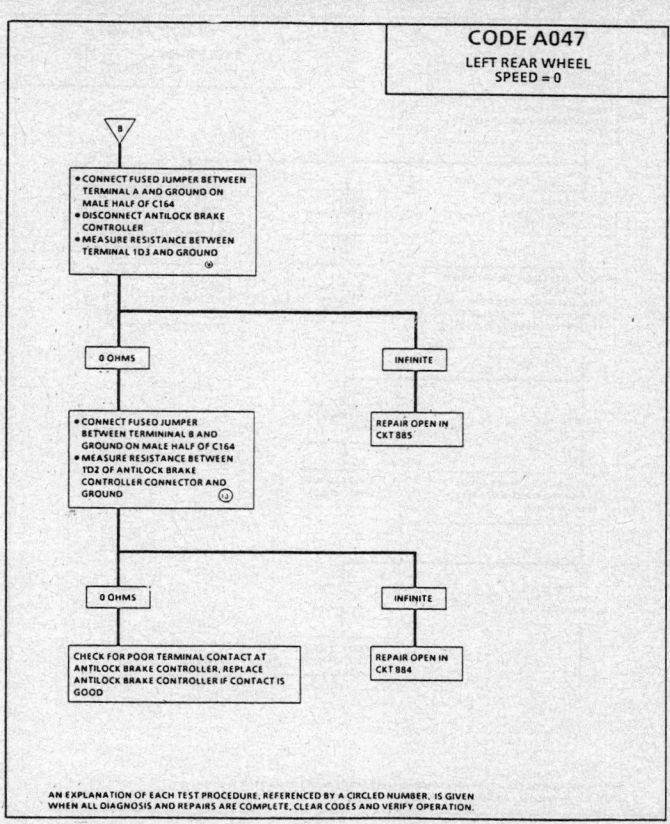

Fig. 50   Code A047, left rear wheel speed at 0 mph (Part 3 of 3)

CODE A048
Excessive Right Front Wheel Acceleration

The Antilock Brake Controller uses the signal from the Wheel Speed Sensor to detect if wheel lock-up is impending. If the frequency of the AC voltage produced by the wheel speed sensor indicates that the wheel is accelerating or decelerating faster than physically possible, the Controller determines the signal is faulty and sets the code.

CODE A048 will set when all of the following conditions exist:
- The Brakes are not being applied (Brake Switch is off).
- The Antilock Brake Controller senses that the Right Front Wheel has accelerated or decelerated greater than physically possible.

TEST DESCRIPTION: The following provides an explanation of the procedures being followed in the facing trouble tree.

① By observing the Right Front Wheel speed input, you can verify what type of input the controller is sensing. An unsteady or erratic wheel speed input indicates that a fault is present in the Wheel Speed Sensor or its related circuitry. If a steady wheel speed is observed, an intermittent fault condition is indicated.

② Indicates a defective Wheel Speed Sensor by isolating a short to ground internal to the sensor.

③ If resistance measured across the Wheel Speed Sensor is infinite, the fault is due to an open condition internal to the Speed Sensor.

CODE A048
Excessive Right Front Wheel Acceleration

TEST DESCRIPTION: The following provides an explanation of the procedures being followed in the facing trouble tree

② With Terminal A of CKT 833 connected to ground, the resistance from Terminal 1D5 to ground should be zero. If infinite resistance is measured, an open condition is indicated in CKT 833.

② With Terminal B of CKT 872 connected to ground, the resistance from Terminal 1D4 to ground should be zero. If infinite resistance is measured, an open condition is indicated in CKT 872.

③ At this point, all the connecting circuitry has tested good. The fault may be due to a poorly mated connector at the Wheel Speed Sensor or the Antilock Brake Controller. Other possible causes could be due to damage to the Speed Sensor or Speed Ring. Check for proper mounting or poor alignment.   If everything above tests good, replace the Antilock Brake Controller.

Fig. 51   Code A048, excessive right front wheel acceleration (Part 1 of 2)

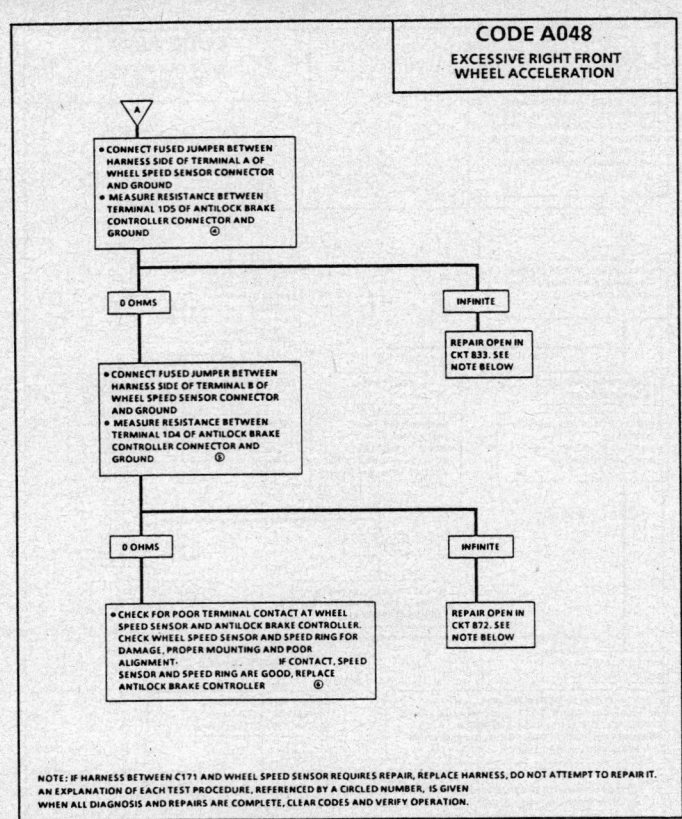

Fig. 51   Code A048, excessive right front wheel acceleration (Part 2 of 2)

CODE A049
Excessive Left Front Wheel Acceleration

CODE A049
Excessive Left Front Wheel Acceleration

The Antilock Brake Controller uses the signal from the Wheel Speed Sensor to detect if wheel lock-up is impending. If the frequency of the AC voltage produced by the wheel speed sensor indicates that the wheel is accelerating or decelerating faster than physically possible, the Controller determines the signal is faulty and sets the code.

CODE A049 will set when all of the following conditions exist:
- The Brakes are not being applied (Brake Switch is off).
- The Antilock Brake Controller senses that the Left Front Wheel has accelerated or decelerated greater than physically possible.

TEST DESCRIPTION: The following provides an explanation of the procedures being followed in the facing trouble tree.

① By observing the Left Front Wheel speed input, you can verify what type of input the controller is sensing. An unsteady or erratic wheel speed input indicates that a fault is present in the Wheel Speed Sensor or its related circuitry. If a steady wheel speed is observed, an intermittent fault condition is indicated.

② Indicates a defective Wheel Speed Sensor by isolating a short to ground internal to the sensor.

③ If resistance measured across the Wheel Speed Sensor is infinite, the fault is due to an open condition internal to the Speed Sensor.

TEST DESCRIPTION: The following provides an explanation of the procedures being followed in the facing trouble tree

① With Terminal A of CKT 830 connected to ground, the resistance from Terminal 1C2 to ground should be zero. If infinite resistance is measured, an open condition is indicated in CKT 830.

② With Terminal B of CKT 873 connected to ground, the resistance from Terminal 1C1 to ground should be zero. If infinite resistance is measured, an open condition is indicated in CKT 873.

③ At this point, all the connecting circuitry has tested good. The fault may be due to a poorly mated connector at the Wheel Speed Sensor or the Antilock Brake Controller. Other possible causes could be due to damage to the Speed Sensor or Speed Ring. Check for proper mounting or poor alignment.   If everything above tests good, replace the Antilock Brake Controller.

Fig. 52   Code A049, excessive left front wheel acceleration (Part 1 of 2)

Fig. 52 Code A049, excessive left front wheel acceleration (Part 2 of 2)

CODE A050
Excessive Right Rear Wheel Acceleration

The Antilock Brake Controller uses the signal from the wheel speed sensor to detect if wheel lock-up is impending. If the frequency of the AC voltage produced by the wheel speed sensor indicates that the wheel is accelerating or decelerating faster than physically possible, the Controller determines the signal is faulty and sets the code.

CODE A050 will set when all of the following conditions exist:
- The Brakes are not being applied (Brake Switch is off).
- The Antilock Brake Controller senses that the Right Rear Wheel has accelerated or decelerated greater than physically possible.

TEST DESCRIPTION: The following provides an explanation of the procedures being followed in the following trouble tree.

① Observation of erratic or no wheel speed input indicates the fault is present and is not intermittent.

②& ③ Step 2 determines if a short to battery is the fault. If battery voltage is measured, step 3 isolates the short to the harness or controller.

④ If 9000 to 15000 ohms is measured, the possibility of an open or short in the circuit between the Antilock Brake Controller and Connector C165 is eliminated.

Fig. 53 Code A050, excessive right rear wheel acceleration (Part 1 of 3)

CODE A050

Excessive Right Rear Wheel Speed Acceleration

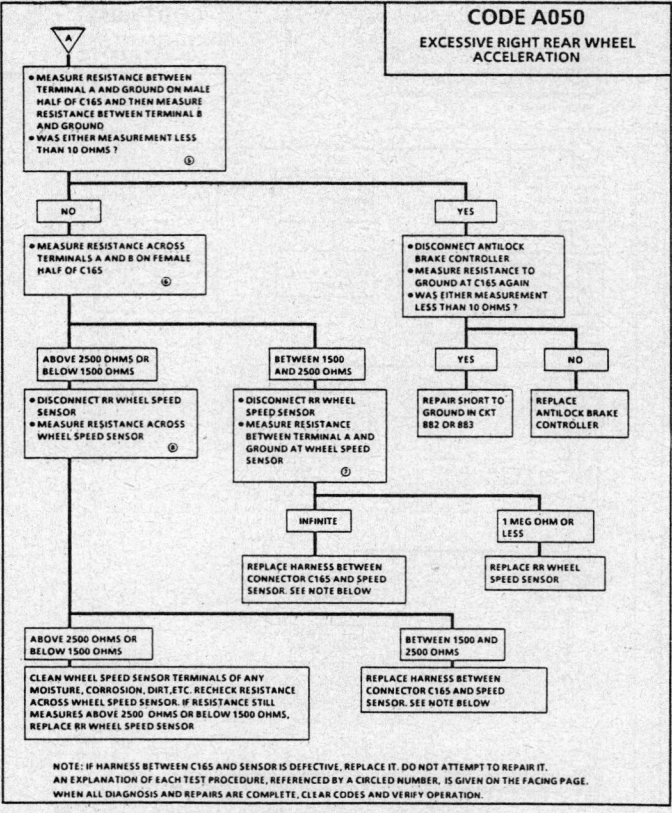

TEST DESCRIPTION: The following provides an explanation of the procedures being followed in the following trouble tree.

⑤ If more than 10 ohms is measured, the circuit between the Controller and C165 are ok. This isolates the fault to be between the Wheel Speed Sensor and C165. Since this area of the circuit is exposed to the elements and road debris it should be carefully inspected for damage.

⑥ This procedure isolates the fault to a short to ground (1500 to 2500 ohms) or open (above 2500 ohms) or a shorted sensor circuit (below 1500 ohms)

⑦ & ⑧ Determine if the fault is in the harness or the Wheel Speed Sensor. If the harness between C165 and the sensor is defective, replace it. Do not attempt to repair the harness.

Fig. 53   Code A050, excessive right rear wheel acceleration (Part 2 of 3)

CODE A050

Excessive Right Rear Wheel Speed Acceleration

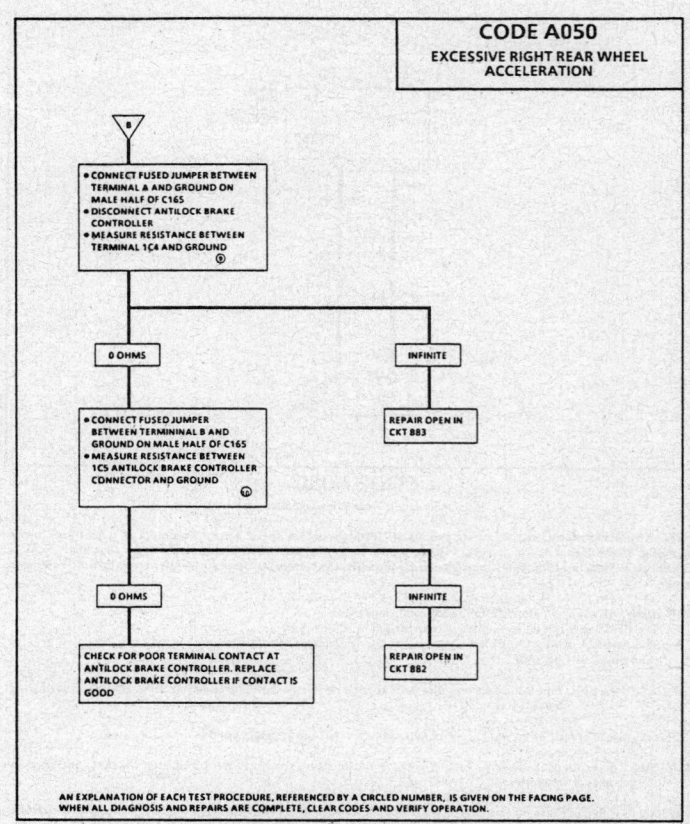

⑩ With CKT 883 connector to ground, the resistance from Terminal 1C4 to ground should be zero. If infinite resistance is measured, an open condition is indicated in CKT 883.

⑪ With CKT 882 connector to ground, the resistance from Terminal 1C5 to ground should be zero. If infinite resistance is measured, an open condition is indicated in CKT 882.

Fig. 53   Code A050, excessive right rear wheel acceleration (Part 3 of 3)

CODE A051

Excessive Left Rear Wheel Acceleration

The Antilock Brake Controller uses the signal from the wheel speed sensor to detect if wheel speed lock-up is impending. If the frequency of the AC voltage produced by the wheel speed sensor indicates that the wheel is accelerating or decelerating faster than physically possible, the Controller determines the signal is faulty and sets the code.

CODE A051 will set when all of the following conditions exist:
- The Brakes are not being applied (Brake Switch is off).
- The Antilock Brake Controller senses that the Left Rear Wheel has accelerated or decelerated greater than physically possible.

TEST DESCRIPTION: The following provides an explanation of the procedures being followed in the following trouble tree.

① Observation of erratic or no wheel speed input indicates the fault is present and is not intermittent.

②&③ Step 2 determines is if a short to Battery is the fault. If Battery voltage is measured, step 3 isolates the short to the harness or controller.

④ If 9000 to 15000 ohms were measured, the possibility of an open or short in the circuit between the Antilock Brakes Controller and Connector C164 has been eliminated.

Fig. 54   Code A051, excessive left rear wheel acceleration (Part 1 of 3)

CODE A051

Excessive Left Rear Wheel Acceleration

TEST DESCRIPTION: The following provides an explanation of the procedures being followed in the following trouble tree

⑤ If more than 10 ohms is measured, the circuits between the controller and C164 are OK. This isolates the fault between the Wheel Speed Sensor and C164. Since this area of the circuit is exposed to the elements and road debris, it should be carefully inspected for damage.

⑥ This procedure isolates the fault to a short to ground(1500 to 2500 ohms) or open (above 2500 ohms) or a shorted sensor circuit (below 1500 ohms).

⑦&⑧ Determines if the fault is in the harness or the Wheel Speed Sensor. If the harness between C164 and the sensor is defective, replace it, do not attempt to repair the harness.

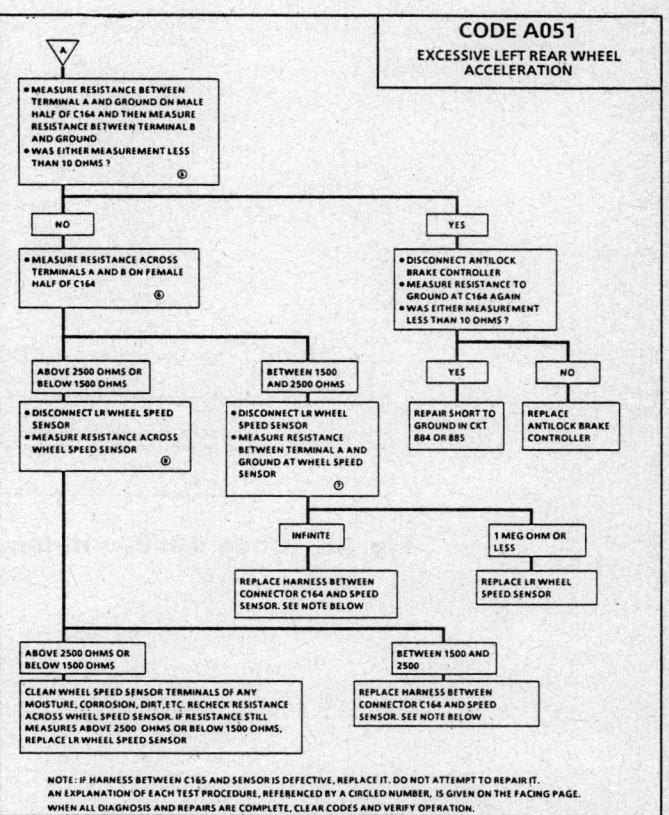

Fig. 54   Code A051, excessive left rear wheel acceleration (Part 2 of 3)

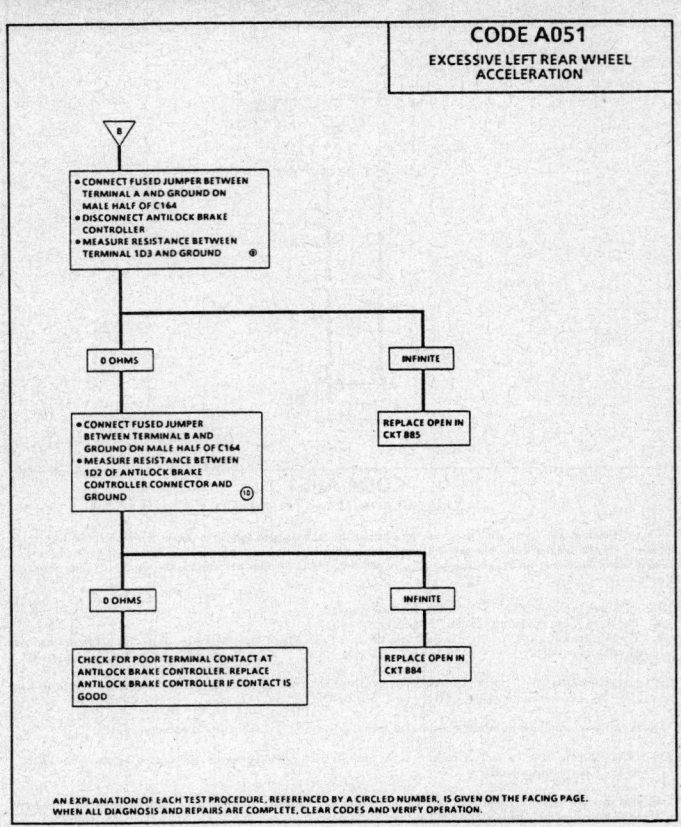

CODE A051

EXCESSIVE LEFT REAR WHEEL ACCELERATION

AN EXPLANATION OF EACH TEST PROCEDURE, REFERENCED BY A CIRCLED NUMBER, IS GIVEN ON THE FACING PAGE. WHEN ALL DIAGNOSIS AND REPAIRS ARE COMPLETE, CLEAR CODES AND VERIFY OPERATION.

CODE A051

Excessive Left Rear Wheel Speed Acceleration

⑩ With CKT 884 connector to ground, the resistance from Terminal 1D2 to ground should be zero. If infinite resistance is measured, an open condition is indicated in CKT 884.

⑪ With CKT 885 connector to ground, the resistance from Terminal 1D3 to ground should be zero. If infinite resistance is measured, an open condition is indicated in CKT 885.

Fig. 54   Code A051, excessive left rear wheel acceleration (Part 3 of 3)

CODE A052

Antilock Brake Controller Calibration Error

CODE A052 will set when the Antilock Brake Controller detects a malfunction internal to itself. If this code is set, replace the Antilock Brake Controller.

Fig. 55   Code A052, anti-lock brake control calibration error

CODE A054

Rear Enable Relay Coil circuit open

When the ignition is in RUN, voltage is applied from the ABS 2 Fuse to the Rear Enable Relay Coil. As long as the Rear Enable Relay Control is open, this voltage should also be present at terminal 1D12 of the Controller.

CODE A054 will set when all the following conditions exist:
- The Rear Enable Relay Control is open (Rear Enable Relay deenergized).
- The Antilock Brake Controller senses no voltage at Terminal 1D12.
- The Antilock Brake Controller senses no voltage at Terminals 1C14 and 1C15.
- Codes A004 and A007 are current failures.

TEST DESCRIPTION: The following provides an explanation of the procedures being followed in the facing trouble tree.

① By monitoring the test lamp with the enable relays on, it can be determined if the power and ground circuits, as well as the Controller, are good.

② If the test lamp does not light, the open must be between the Rear Enable Relay and Splice S139.

③ Voltage at terminal 1D12 indicates a problem with the connection to the Controller or the Controller itself.

④ Determines if the Code was set due to a hard failure. At this point the hard failure must be in the Rear Enable Relay.

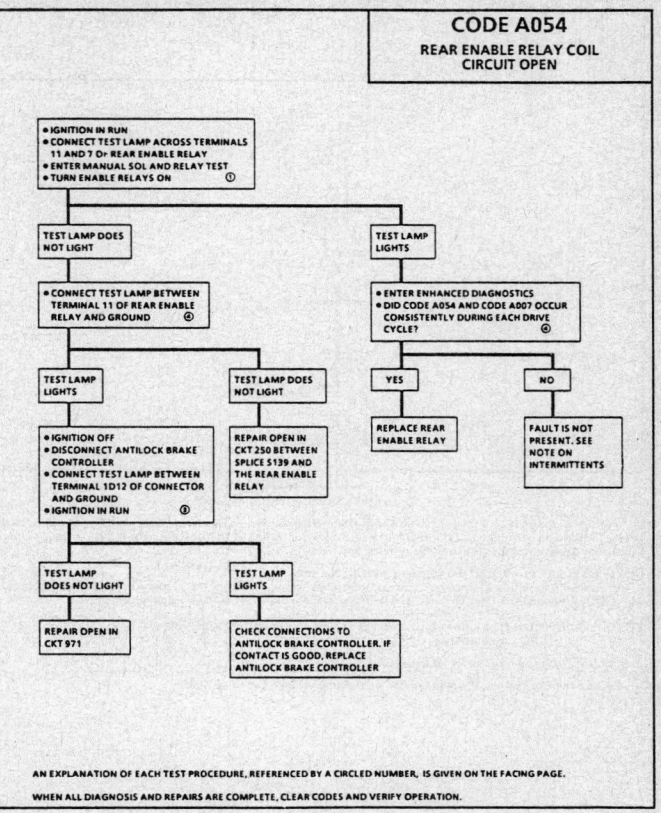

Fig. 56   Code A054, rear enable relay coil circuit open

CODE A055

Antilock Brake Controller internal voltage fault

CODE A055 will set when the Antilock Brake Controller detects a malfunction internal to itself. If this code is set, replace the Antilock Brake Controller.

Fig. 57   Code A055, anti-lock brake controller internal voltage fault

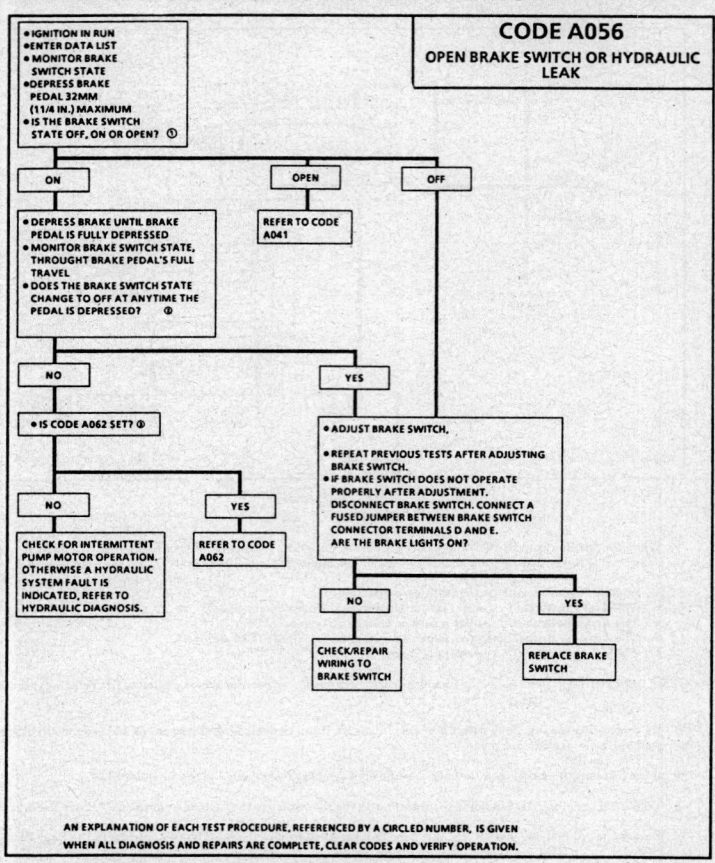

CODE A056
Open Brake Switch or Hydraulic Leak

Voltage is applied at all times to the Brake Switch. When the Brake Switch is closed, voltage is applied to the Brake Lights and terminal 1C11 of the Antilock Brake Controller. If the Brake Apply Input receives voltage, the Controller determines that the brakes are being applied.

CODE A056 will set when all the following conditions exsist:
- The Antilock Brake Controller receives three pump on inputs without receiving a brake switch on input. This allows a brake switch fault to be detected without an Antilock Braking condition present.

TEST DESCRIPTION: The following provides an explanation of the procedures being following in the facing trouble tree.

① & ② Checks for an improperly adjusted Brake Switch.

② If Code A062 is also set, the pump motor was cycling too fast. See Code A062.

Fig. 58   Code A056, open brake switch or hydraulic leak

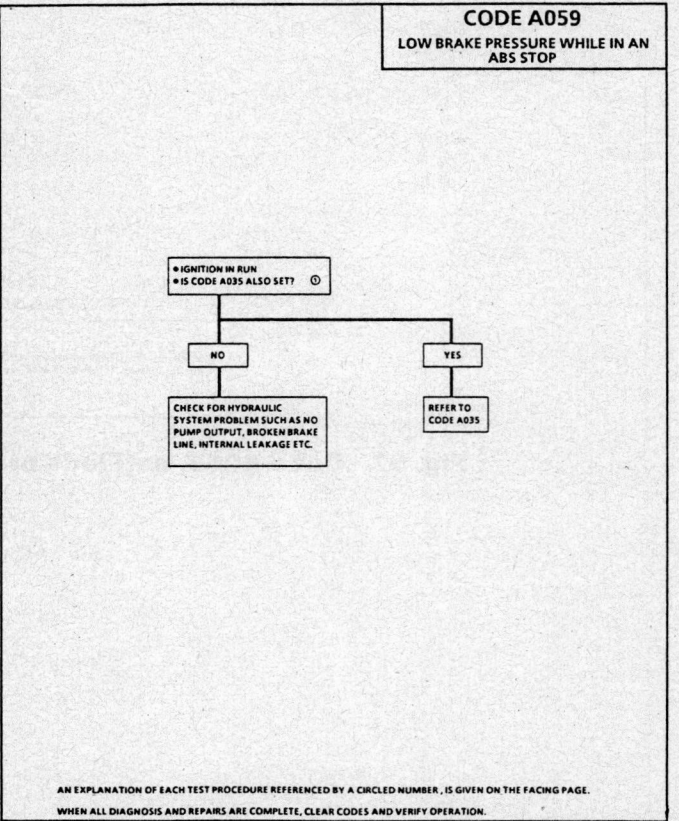

CODE A059
Low Brake Pressure while in an ABS stop

CODE A059 will set when all of the following conditions exist:
- The car is in an Antilock Brake stop.
- The Pump On Input senses voltage (pump running).
- The Antilock Brake Controller senses voltage at the Low Brake Pressure Input for greater than 10 seconds during and after the Antilock Brake stop.

TEST DESCRIPTION: The following provides an explanation of the procedures being followed in the facing trouble tree.

① If Code A035 is also set, the fault is due to an electrical problem which can be diagnosed by refering to Code A035. If Code A059 has not set along with any other codes, a hydraulic system fault is indicated and can be diagnosed   Possible causes are no pump output, broken brake line, internal leakage, etc.

Fig. 59   Code A059, low brake pressure while in an ABS stop

CODE A060

Antilock Brake Controller internal fault

CODE A060 will set when the Antilock Brake Controller detects a malfunction internal to itself. If this code is set, replace the Antilock Brake Controller.

Fig. 60 Code A060, anti-lock brake controller internal fault

CODE A062

Low Accumulator Pre-charge

The Accumulator is precharged to approximately 1200 PSI with nitrogen gas. The Pump Motor maintains system pressure between 2200 PSI and approximately 2700 PSI. The Accumulator Switch Motor Control closes when the pressure drops below 2200 PSI. This grounds the Pump Motor Relay Coil causing voltage to be applied to the Pump Motor and Pump On Input. Whenever the Pump Motor is on, the Pump On Input will have voltage applied to it. The Pump Motor will run until system pressure is restored to approximately 2700 PSI.

CODE A062 will set when the Antilock Brake Controller detects short pump run times of less than 1.4 seconds in duration.

TEST DESCRIPTION: The following provides an explanation of the procedures being followed in the facing trouble tree.

① If the pump run time from "OK pressure" to "pump off time" is less than six seconds a low accumulator precharge or poor accumulator switch point condition is indicated.

② If normal pump run cycle is less than 1.7 seconds a miscalibrated accumulator switch or low accumulator precharge is indicated. Section 5F contains tests with a pressure gage to check switch calibrations.

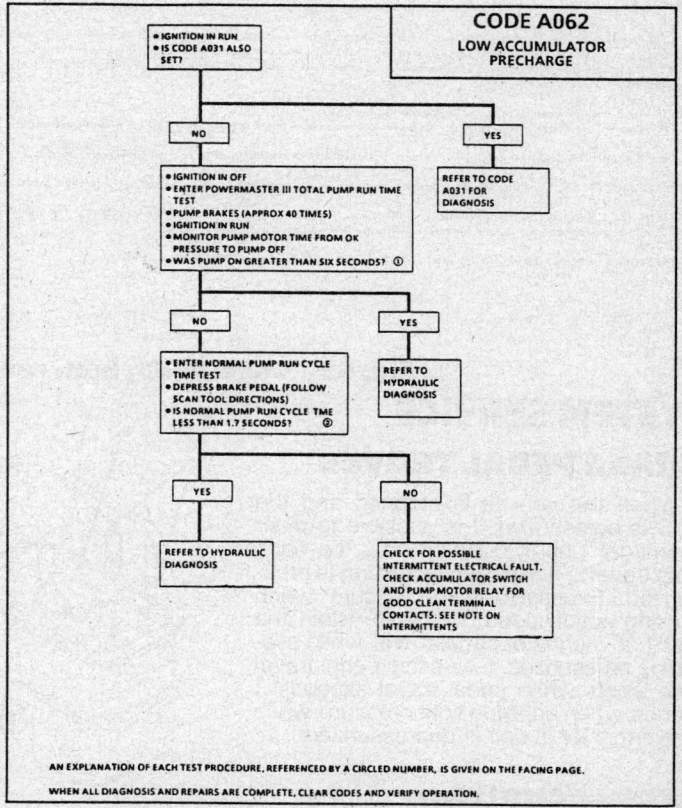

AN EXPLANATION OF EACH TEST PROCEDURE, REFERENCED BY A CIRCLED NUMBER, IS GIVEN ON THE FACING PAGE.

WHEN ALL DIAGNOSIS AND REPAIRS ARE COMPLETE, CLEAR CODES AND VERIFY OPERATION.

Fig. 61 Code A062, low accumulator precharge

CODE A063
Both Rear Wheel Speed Sensors open

The Antilock Brake Controller monitors the Wheel Speed Sensors. If one or both rear wheel speeds are zero, the Controller cannot accurately detect wheel lock-up. Since three good wheel speeds are needed to set Codes A046 or A047, these Codes cannot determine if both wheel speed sensors are faulty. Code A063 can detect if both Rear Wheel Speed Sensors are malfunctioning.

CODE A063 will set when all of the following conditions exist:
- The Antilock Brake Controller senses both front wheel speeds are greater than 10 mph and are operating correctly.
- The Antilock Brake Controller senses both rear wheel speeds are 0 mph for more than 20 seconds.

TEST DESCRIPTION: The following provides an explanation of the procedures being followed in the facing trouble tree.

① If the front wheel were spinning while the vehicle was being serviced on a lift code, A063 would set. The code should be cleared and the vehicle road tested to insure this was the reason code A063 set.

② Determines whether the fault is due to a hard failure or a possible intermittent failure.

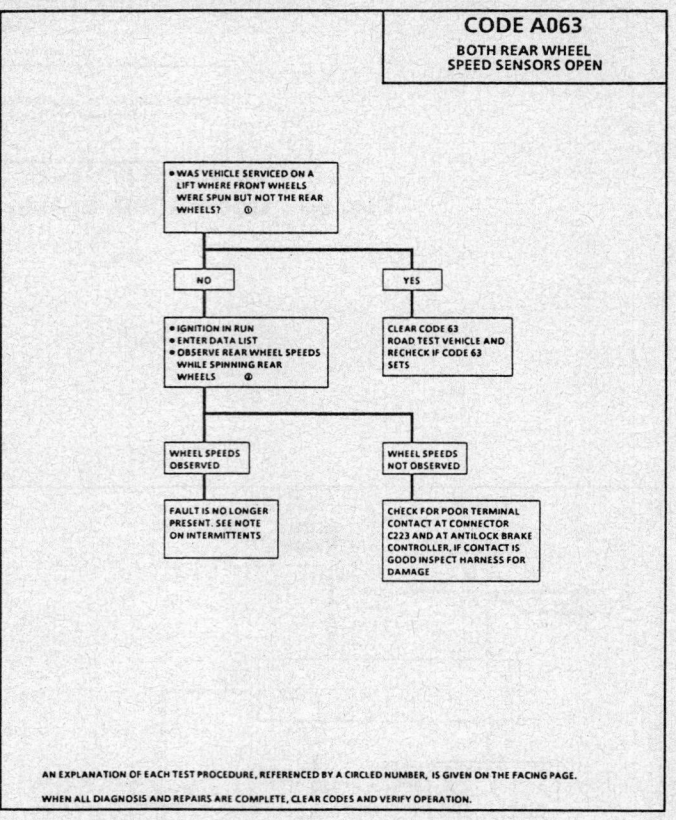

CODE A063
BOTH REAR WHEEL SPEED SENSORS OPEN

AN EXPLANATION OF EACH TEST PROCEDURE, REFERENCED BY A CIRCLED NUMBER, IS GIVEN ON THE FACING PAGE.

WHEN ALL DIAGNOSIS AND REPAIRS ARE COMPLETE, CLEAR CODES AND VERIFY OPERATION.

Fig. 62   Code A063, both rear wheel speed sensors open

SYSTEM SERVICE

BRAKE PEDAL TRAVEL

When the vehicle is stopped and the ABS is pressurized, it is possible to push the pedal, until it bottoms near the floor. This travel is normal while system is pressurized. Excessive travel occurs when braking action does not begin within the first 1.25 inches of pedal travel, while system is pressurized. Excessive pedal travel also exists when pedal travel exceeds 3 inches, when applying light pressure, while Powermaster III unit is depressurized.

DEPRESSURIZING POWERMASTER III

The Powermaster III must be depressurized prior to performing any service operations.
1. Turn ignition switch to the Off position, or disconnect negative battery cable.
2. Firmly apply, then release the brake pedal a minimum of 40 times. A noticeable change in pedal feel (from soft to hard), will occur when accumulator is completely discharged.
3. Do not turn ignition switch to the On or Start position after depressurizing Powermaster III, unless instructed by service procedure, or until service operations have been completed.

CHECKING FLUID LEVEL
1. Park vehicle on a level surface, then

49. FLUID LEVEL MARKS
50. FRONT CHAMBER
51. REAR CHAMBER

Fig. 63   Fluid level fill marks

depressurize Powermaster III, see "Depressurizing Powermaster III."
2. Clean reservoir cover, then remove cover and diaphragm assembly from the Powermaster III. Note fluid level in reservoir chambers.
3. If any chamber is underfilled, **Fig. 63**, check for signs of leakage. Make repairs as necessary. **Fill chambers with clean DOT 3 fluid only.**
4. If chamber is overfilled, adjust fluid level. **Do not contaminate fluid in**

brake system with dirt, dust, lubricants, oils, or other substance.
5. Replace diaphragm assembly and cover.
6. Turn ignition switch to the On position. Allow system to pressurize.
7. Depressurize Powermaster III, then check fluid level.
8. If reservoir chamber is again overfilled, repair or replace components as necessary.

POWERMASTER III BLEEDING

Pressure Bleeding

If a Powermaster III unit has been replaced, or air is suspected in the brake lines, the entire braking system must be bled.

If only a hydraulic portion of the Powermaster III unit has been replaced, without allowing air into the brake lines, it may only be necessary to manually bleed the Powermaster III unit.

Pressure bleeding must be done with diaphragm type bleeding equipment. Use only DOT 3 type brake fluid from a sealed container.
1. Turn ignition switch to the Off position, then depressurize the Powermaster III unit, see "Depressurizing Powermaster III."
2. Clean reservoir cover and diaphragm assembly, then remove assembly.
3. Check fluid in both reservoir sections, then fill to proper level, using clean DOT 3 brake fluid, if necessary.

4. Install bleeder adapter tool No. J-37115 or equivalent and secure with attachment cable. Ensure cable does not interfere with bleeder valve access.

5. Attach bleeder adapter to pressure bleed equipment, charge to 5-10 psi. for approximately 30 seconds, then slowly increase pressure to 30-35 psi.

6. Bleed adapter tool No. J-37115 or equivalent by connecting a clear plastic hose to adapter bleeder screw and submerging opposite end in a clean container partially filled with brake fluid.

7. Slowly open bleeder valve, allowing fluid to flow until no more air is seen in fluid, then close valve.

8. Raise and support vehicle, then bleed brakes in sequence: right rear, left rear, right front, then left front, as described below.

9. Attach bleeder hose to bleeder valve, then submerge opposite end in a clean container partially filled with brake fluid.

10. Slowly open bleeder valve and allow fluid to flow for 20-30 seconds. To aid in releasing entrapped air, lightly tap on caliper castings with a rubber mallet.

11. Close valve when fluid begins to run with no bubbles. **Repeat steps 9-11 for each wheel, following wheel sequence in step 8.**

12. Lower vehicle, then attach bleeder hose to bleeder valve on inboard side of Powermaster III unit and submerge opposite end of hose in a clean container partially filled with brake fluid.

13. Slowly open bleeder valve and allow fluid to flow for 20-30 seconds.

14. Close valve when fluid begins to run with no bubbles.

15. Repeat steps 13-15 for outboard side bleeder valve.

16. Remove bleeder adapter tool No. J-37115 or equivalent from Powermaster III unit, then check fluid level in both reservoirs. Fill if necessary.

17. Snap reservoir cover into place, then apply moderate to heavy force to the brake pedal.

18. With the pedal applied, turn ignition switch to the On position for 5 seconds, then turn ignition switch to the Off position. Do this 10 times in succession to cycle solenoids. **Do not start engine, or place ignition switch in the Start position.**

19. Depressurize Powermaster III unit, then wait two minutes for air to clear from reservoir.

20. Attach bleeder hose to bleeder valve on inboard side of Powermaster III unit and submerge opposite end in a clean container partially filled with brake fluid.

21. With the ignition switch in the On position, apply light force to the brake pedal, then slowly open bleeder valve and allow fluid to flow until no air is seen.

22. Close valve when no air is seen in fluid.

23. Repeat steps 21-23, on outboard side

bleeder valve.

24. Turn ignition switch to the Off position, then depressurize Powermaster III unit.

25. Remove reservoir cover and diaphragm assembly, then check fluid level in reservoirs. Use clean DOT 3 fluid to fill if necessary.

26. Snap reservoir cover onto reservoir, then turn ignition switch to the On position. Allow pump to run.

27. Turn ignition switch to the Off position if pump runs longer than 60 seconds, inspect pump for malfunction.

28. Apply brake pedal and note travel and feel. If pedal feels firm and smooth, without excessive travel, system is properly bled.

29. If pedal feels soft, spongy, or has excessive travel, see "Excessive Pedal Travel."

30. If a bump is noted upon initial pedal apply, or pedal apply does not feel smooth and uniform, see "Non-Uniform Pedal Apply."

31. Road test vehicle. If any of the above symptoms appear, refer to appropriate procedure.

Manual Bleeding

1. Turn ignition switch to the Off position, then depressurize Powermaster III unit.

2. Clean reservoir and diaphragm assembly, then remove reservoir cover assembly.

3. Fill reservoir to proper level wit DOT 3 brake fluid, then reinstall cover assembly.

4. Raise and support vehicle, then attach a clear bleeder hose to right front bleeder valve and submerge opposite end in clean container partially filled with brake fluid.

5. Open bleeder valve, then slowly depress bleeder valve. To aid in releasing trapped air, lightly tap on caliper castings with a rubber mallet.

6. Close bleeder valve, then release brake valve.

7. Check, then add brake fluid if necessary.

8. Repeat steps 4-7 until pedal feels firm and no air is observed bleeder hose.

9. Repeat steps 4-8 for left front brake.

10. Turn ignition switch to the On position, allowing pump to run. If pump runs longer than 60 seconds, inspect pump for malfunctions.

11. Attach clear bleeder hose to right rear bleeder valve and submerge opposite end in a clean container partially filled with brake fluid.

12. Turn ignition switch to the On position, open bleeder valve, then slowly depress brake pedal part-way, until fluid begins to flow from hose. **Do not depress brake pedal fully.**

13. Hold pedal for 15 seconds. To aid in freeing entrapped air, tap lightly on caliper casting with a rubber mallet.

14. Close bleeder valve, then release brake pedal.

15. Repeat steps 12-14, until no air is observed in the fluid.

16. Turn ignition switch to the Off position, depressurize Powermaster III unit, then check brake fluid. Add fluid as needed.

17. Repeat steps 10-16 for left rear wheel.

18. Repeat steps 10-16 for inboard bleeder valve of Powermaster III unit.

19. Repeat steps 10-16 for outboard bleeder valve of Powermaster III unit.

20. Turn ignition switch to the Off position, then depressurize Powermaster III unit. Check brake fluid level and fill as needed.

21. Apply moderate to heavy force on brake pedal.

22. With pedal applied, turn ignition switch to the On position for 5 seconds, then turn ignition switch to the Off position. Repeat this step 10 times. **Do not turn ignition switch to the Start position, or start motor.**

23. Depressurize Powermaster III unit, then wait two minutes for air to clear from within reservoir.

24. Attach bleeder hose to bleeder valve on inboard side of Powermaster III unit and submerge opposite end in clean container partially filled with brake fluid.

25. Turn ignition switch to the On position, then apply light force to brake pedal.

26. With pedal applied, slowly open bleeder valve and allow fluid to flow until no air is seen in fluid.

27. Close valve when no air is seen in fluid.

28. Repeat steps 24-27, for outboard bleeder valve.

29. Turn ignition switch to the Off position, then depressurize Powermaster III unit.

30. Remove reservoir cover and diaphragm assembly, check and fill reservoirs with DOT 3 brake fluid as needed.

31. Install reservoir cover, then turn ignition switch to the On position. Allow pump to run. If pump runs for longer than 60 seconds, inspect pump for malfunctions.

32. Apply brake pedal, noting feel and travel.

33. If pedal feels firm and smooth, without excessive travel, system is properly bled.

34. If pedal feels soft, spongy, or has excessive travel, see "Excessive Pedal Travel."

35. If a bump is noted upon initial pedal apply, or pedal apply does not feel smooth and uniform, see "Non-Uniform Pedal Apply."

36. Road test vehicle. If any of the above symptoms appear, refer to appropriate procedure.

EXCESSIVE PEDAL TRAVEL

Excessive pedal travel exists when braking action does not start within the first 1.25 inches of pedal travel, while the Powermaster III unit is pressurized. When the Powermaster III unit is not pressurized, excessive pedal travel exists when brake

Fig. 64   CPA locking pins

Fig. 65   Exploded view of Powermaster III

1. 2-PIN ELECTRICAL CONNECTOR
   (BODY HARNESS)
2. FLUID LEVEL SENSOR SWITCH
3. RESERVOIR ASSEMBLY
4. BLEEDER VALVE
5. RESERVOIR COVER ASSEMBLY
6. HOSE CLAMP
7. RESERVOIR HOSE
8. SCREWS (3)
9. RELIEF VALVE
10. POWERMASTER-III
11. RESERVOIR SEAL
13. SCREWS (2 PER SOLENOID)
14. SOLENOID ASSEMBLY
26. PRESSURE SWITCH
27. O-RING
28. ACCUMULATOR
29. O-RING
33. MOTOR RELAY
34. POWERMASTER-III WIRING HARNESS
35. TUBE AND NUT ASSEMBLY
36. NUTS (3)
37. FLAT RUBBER WASHERS (3)
38. CUPPED WASHERS (3)
39. PUMP AND MOTOR ASSEMBLY
40. MOUNTING BRACKET
41. END COVER ASSEMBLY
42. MOUNTING GROMMETS (3)
43. BOLTS (2)
44. BOLTS (4)
48. FLAT STEEL WASHERS (3)
57. SOLENOID SEALS
    (ONE PER SOLENOID)

pedal moves more than 3 inches while applying light pedal pressure.

1. Apply moderate to heavy force on brake pedal, turn ignition switch to the On position for 5 seconds, then turn ignition switch to the Off position. **Do not turn ignition switch to the Start position, or start motor.**
2. Release brake pedal, then repeat step 1, twice.
3. Bleed front brakes, as described in "Pressure Bleeding."
4. If excessive pedal travel exists, check brake fluid level, then for leaks in braking system.

NON-UNIFORM PEDAL APPLY

1. Raise rear of vehicle until Powermaster III unit is level with ground, or sloping downward slightly.
2. Depressurize Powermaster III unit.
3. Wait two minutes, then turn ignition switch to the On position. Allow pump to pressurize unit. **Do not turn ignition switch to the Start position or start engine.**

4. If condition still exists, raise rear of vehicle, as described in step 1, then bleed rear brakes. See "Pressure Bleeding," or "Manual Bleeding."

PUMP RUNS CONTINUOUSLY

Only perform this procedure if pump runs for more than 60 seconds. **Do not allow brake fluid to come into contact with painted surfaces.**

1. Turn ignition switch to the Off position, then depressurize Powermaster III unit.
2. Loosen, but do not remove tube nuts from both front master cylinder chambers.
3. Apply brake pedal as far as possible. Check that brake fluid runs from around tube nuts.
4. With pedal still applied, tighten tube nuts.
5. Quickly release brake pedal, then reapply with a sharp, rapid motion with full force.

6. Continue from step 25, of "Pressure Bleeding."

DELCO-MORAINE POWERMASTER III ELECTRICAL CONNECTORS

The Powermaster III unit is equipped with electrical connectors which utilize a connector position assurance locking pin. This locking pin assures proper alignment and engagement of the connector, **Fig. 64.**

Always remove the locking pin prior to disconnecting electrical connector. Use extreme caution as to not damage locking pin during removal or installation. Note position of rubber seals when disconnecting connectors for installation purposes. Always reinstall locking pins after reconnecting connector.

32. 5-PIN CONNECTOR
33. MOTOR RELAY
45. RELAY BRACKET
47. RELAY BRACKET RELEASE TAB

Fig. 66   Motor relay location

10. POWERMASTER-III
12. 3-PIN ELECTRICAL CONNECTOR
13. SCREWS (2 PER SOLENOID)
14. SOLENOID ASSEMBLY
57. SOLENOID SEALS (ONE PER SOLENOID)

Fig. 67   Solenoid assemblies

1. 2-PIN ELECTRICAL CONNECTOR (BODY HARNESS)
10. POWERMASTER-III
15. VEHICLE 7-PIN CONNECTOR
16. 7-PIN WIRING HARNESS CONNECTOR
17. VEHICLE 10-PIN CONNECTOR
18. 10-PIN WIRING HARNESS CONNECTOR
19. BRAKE PIPE
20. NUTS (2)
21. COWL BRACKET STUD
22. PUSHROD
24. MOUNTING BRACKET

Fig. 68   Powermaster III brake tube

COMPONENT REPLACEMENT

FLUID LEVEL SENSOR SWITCH, REPLACE

1. Disconnect 2-pin connector (1), from fluid level sensor switch (2), **Fig. 65.**
2. Remove fluid level sensor switch from reservoir.
3. Depress locking tabs at inboard end of switch, under reservoir on opposite end of 2-pin connector.
4. Reverse procedure to install. Ensure sensor switch locking tabs snap into place.

BLEEDER VALVES, REPLACE

1. Depressurize Powermaster III, see "Depressurizing Powermaster III."
2. Remove bleeder valves (4), **Fig. 65.** Clean valves in denatured alcohol, then dry with compressed air. **Do not use lubricated compressed air.**
3. Reverse procedure to install, noting the following:
   a. **Torque** bleeder valve to 40-90 inch lbs.
   b. Bleed Powermaster III as described in "Powermaster III Bleeding."

ACCUMULATOR, REPLACE

The accumulator is nitrogen-charged and holds brake fluid under high pressure. It cannot be serviced and must be replaced as an assembly.
1. Depressurize the Powermaster III, see "Depressurizing Powermaster III."
2. Remove the accumulator (28), by turning hex nut on the end of accumulator with a 17 mm socket, **Fig. 65.**
3. Remove from vehicle by sliding out from underneath Powermaster III, toward left front wheelwell.
4. Remove O-ring (29), from accumulator.
5. Reverse procedure to install, noting the following:

a. Lightly lubricate, then install a new O-ring on accumulator.
b. **Torque** accumulator to 23-36 ft. lbs.
c. Bleed Powermaster III as described in "Powermaster III Bleeding."

TUBE & NUT ASSEMBLY (HIGH PRESSURE SIDE), REPLACE

1. Depressurize the Powermaster III, see "Depressurizing Powermaster III."
2. Remove air cleaner, duct and stud.
3. Remove tube and nut assembly (35), from Powermaster III unit (10). Plug all openings to prevent fluid loss and contamination, **Fig. 65.**
4. Inspect tube and nut assembly for crack, deformation and scratches or nicks on sealing surfaces. Replace tube and nut assembly if any of the above conditions are found.
5. Reverse procedure to install, noting the following:
   a. **Torque** tube and nut assembly to Powermaster III unit to 10-15 ft. lbs.
   b. Bleed Powermaster III unit, see "Powermaster III Bleeding."

MOTOR RELAY, REPLACE

1. Push relay bracket tab (47), with a small screwdriver, to clear button on motor relay (33), **Fig. 66.**
2. Pull motor relay from relay bracket (45).
3. Disconnect 5-pin connector (32), from motor relay.
4. Reverse procedure to install.

RESERVOIR COVER, HOSE & RESERVOIR ASSEMBLY, REPLACE

Clean reservoir cover assembly (5) and surrounding area before removing, **Fig. 65.**
1. Depressurize Powermaster III, see "Depressurizing Powermaster III."
2. Unsnap reservoir cover assembly, then remove from reservoir (3).

3. Inspect reservoir cover assembly for cuts, cracks, nicks and deformation. Replace any damaged parts.
4. Remove fluid level sensor switch, as described in "Fluid Level Sensor Switch, Replace."
5. To gain access, loosen but do not remove cowl bracket attaching nuts, then pull Powermaster III forward slightly.
6. Use a clean syringe to remove as much brake fluid from reservoir as possible. **Brake fluid will cause damage to all painted surfaces.**
7. Cover electrical connectors and engine/body parts with clean shop towels to catch any brake fluid dripped from reservoir. Use a suitable container to catch brake fluid when upper end reservoir hose is disconnected from reservoir.
8. Remove upper hose clamp, then disconnect hose from reservoir. **Discard all used brake fluid. Never reuse brake fluid.**
9. Remove reservoir assembly from Powermaster III unit, then lift rear of reservoir assembly up and carefully pull away from under secondary dash. Use caution as to not damage solenoids or solenoid seals when removing reservoir.
10. Remove reservoir seal. This seal may remain attached to reservoir assembly.
11. Remove lower hose clamp, hose, reservoir seal and solenoid if necessary.
12. Inspect reservoir assembly, hose, seal and solenoid for any type of damage or wear. Replace any damaged or worn parts.

13. Reverse procedure to install, noting the following:
   a. **Torque** cowl bracket attaching nuts to 15-25 ft. lbs.
   b. Bleed Powermaster III, see "Powermaster III Bleeding."

SOLENOID ASSEMBLIES, REPLACE

Clean reservoir cover assembly (5) and surrounding area before removing, **Fig. 65.**
1. Depressurize Powermaster III, see "Depressurizing Powermaster III."
2. Clean surrounding area, then remove reservoir cover and assembly.
3. Disconnect 3-pin connector (12), from solenoid assembly (14), **Fig. 67.**
4. Remove solenoid attaching screws (13), then the solenoid assembly. Ensure lower solenoid O-rings are in place and in good condition.
5. Reverse procedure to install, noting the following:
   a. **Torque** solenoid assembly attaching screws to 33-45 ft. lbs.
   b. Bleed Powermaster III, see "Powermaster III Bleeding."

PRESSURE SWITCH, REPLACE

1. Depressurize Powermaster III, see "Depressurizing Powermaster III."
2. Disconnect 3-pin electrical connector from pressure switch (26), **Fig. 65.**
3. Loosen, but do not completely remove cowl bracket attaching nuts (20), then pull Powermaster III unit slightly forward.
4. Raise and support vehicle. Using switch socket tool No. J-37117 or equivalent, swivel joint and extensions, remove switch through bottom of engine compartment.
5. Remove O-ring (27), from pressure switch, then discard O-ring.
6. Reverse procedure to install, noting the following:
   a. **Torque** pressure switch to 15-20 ft. lbs.

b. **Torque** cowl bracket attaching nuts to 15-25 ft. lbs.
c. Bleed Powermaster III unit, see "Powermaster III Bleeding."

POWERMASTER III UNIT, REPLACE

Do not use wiring harness to aid in lifting or supporting of Powermaster III unit.
1. Depressurize Powermaster III, see "Depressurizing Powermaster III."
2. Disconnect 7-pin connector (15), from Powermaster III harness connector (16), **Fig. 68.**
3. Disconnect 10-pin connector (17), from Powermaster III wiring harness connector (18).
4. Disconnect 2-pin connector (1), from fluid level sensor switch (2).
5. Remove three brake pipes (19), from Powermaster III unit. Plug open lines and fittings to prevent fluid loss and contamination.
6. Remove hair pin clip (located inside vehicle), and pushrod (22), from brake pedal.
7. Remove two attaching nuts (20), from cowl bracket studs, then remove Powermaster III unit.
8. Reverse procedure to install, noting the following:
   a. **Torque** two cowl bracket attaching nuts to 15-25 ft. lbs.
   b. **Torque** tube-to-Powermaster III unit nuts to 10-15 ft. lbs.
   c. Bleed Powermaster III unit, see "Powermaster III Bleeding."

ANTI-LOCK BRAKE CONTROLLER, REPLACE

The anti-lock brake controller can be removed from vehicle without removing front seat.
1. Turn ignition switch to the Off position, slide passenger seat forward, then tip seat forward.

2. Remove bolts securing case cover, then remove anti-lock controller. It is not necessary to remove the harness connectors to slide controller out of the case.
3. Remove connectors from controller.
4. Reverse procedure to install, tightening case cover bolts hand tight.

PROPORTIONER VALVE ASSEMBLY, REPLACE

The proportioner valve is not repairable and must be serviced as a complete assembly. The use of rubber hoses or hydraulic lines other than those specified may lead to functional problems and major repairs.
1. Depressurize Powermaster III, see "Depressurizing Powermaster III."
2. Remove input brake line, then two output brake lines, from proportioner valve assembly. Input brake line has a 12 mm threaded nut and output brake lines have 10 mm threaded nuts. Plug open lines and fittings to prevent fluid loss and contamination.
3. Remove proportioner valve assembly.
4. Reverse procedure to install, noting the following:
   a. **Torque** tube nuts to 10-15 ft. lbs.
   b. Bleed system, see "Manual Bleeding," or "Pressure Bleeding."

FRONT WHEEL SPEED SENSORS, REPLACE

1. Raise and support vehicle, then remove sensor connector from wiring harness.
2. Remove two front wheel speed sensor bolts, then one bracket connector bolt.
3. Remove front speed sensor.
4. Reverse procedure to install, noting the following:
   a. **Torque** 15 mm bolts to 52-65 ft. lbs.
   b. **Torque** 10 mm bolts to 6-9 ft. lbs.

NOTE: Wire Code Identification And Symbol Identification Located In The Front Of This Manual Can Be Used As An Aid When Using Wiring Circuits Found In This Section.

INDEX

1	HYDRAULIC UNIT
2	ELECTRONIC CONTROLLER
3	FRONT WHEEL SPEED SENSOR
4	REAR WHEEL SPEED SENSOR
5	RELAYS
6	PROPORTIONER VALVE
7	SENSOR CONNECTION TO HARNESS (TRUNK AREA)

Fig. 1   Bosch anti-lock brake (ABS II) system. 1991

PRECAUTIONS
AIRBAG SYSTEM DISARMING

The diagnostic energy reserve module (DERM) can maintain voltage to cause a system deployment for up to ten minutes after the ignition switch is turned off and the battery is disconnected. Servicing the SIR system during this period may result in accidental deployment and personal injury.

1. Ensure front wheels are pointed straight ahead.
2. Turn ignition switch to LOCK position and remove SIR or AIRBAG fuse.
3. Remove left sound insulator. **Remove courtesy lamp from sound insulator, if necessary.**
4. Remove Connector Position Assurance (CPA), then disconnect yellow two-way SIR electrical connector at base of steering column.

AIRBAG SYSTEM ARMING

The diagnostic energy reserve module (DERM) can maintain voltage to cause a system deployment for up to ten minutes after the ignition switch is turned off and the battery is disconnected. Servicing the SIR system during this period may result in accidental deployment and personal injury.
1. Turn ignition switch to OFF position, then remove I/P fuse 7 from fuse block.
2. Disconnect yellow two-way SIR electrical connector at base of steering column.

DESCRIPTION
1991 SYSTEM

The Bosch anti-lock brake II system (ABS II), **Fig. 1**, maintains vehicle steerability, directional stability, and maximum deceleration under severe braking conditions. The ABS II performs this function by monitoring rotational speed and controlling line pressure of each vehicle wheel during a braking maneuver, to prevent the braked wheels from locking.

1992-93 SYSTEM

The anti-lock brake system (ABS) with an integrated acceleration slip regulation (ASR) system, **Fig. 2**, maintains vehicle maneuverability under severe braking conditions on most road surfaces. The ABS/ASR systems monitors each wheel speed during braking. The Electronic

1	SCREW	3	PUMP MOTOR RELAY
2	RETAINER	4	SOLENOID RELAY

Fig. 3   Modulator valve

RIGHT FRONT SENSOR   RIGHT REAR SENSOR

RIGHT SIDES SHOWN-LEFT SIDES MIRROR IMAGE

Fig. 4   Wheel speed sensor

1	ADJUSTER ASSEMBLY SPLASH COVER	7	MODULATOR VALVE
2	ADJUSTER ASSEMBLY	8	ELECTRONIC BRAKE CONTROL MODULE (EBCM)
3	LATERAL ACCELEROMETER	9	BRAKE FLUID LEVEL ISOLATION DIODE
4	I/P CARRIER	10	BATTERY
5	TPS MODULE	11	CRUISE CONTROL CUT-OFF RELAY
6	BLOWER MOTOR		

Fig. 2   Bosch ABS/ASR brake system. 1992–93

Brake & Traction Control Module (EBTCM) uses this information to produce signals to prevent the braking wheels from locking.

The modulator valve regulates brake fluid pressure based on road conditions as interpreted by the , regardless of master cylinder output pressure. The modulator valve can maintain, reduce and increase brake fluid pressure to the calipers under ABS conditions, but it can not increase pressure above that applied from the master cylinder. However, during ASR operation, the modulator can apply pressure to the rear calipers if the requires that a wheel be slowed or regulated.

The ASR traction system uses engine spark retard, throttle close down and rear brake intervention to provide better acceleration and vehicle stability. The ASR system can function up to maximum vehicle speed. The system enhances the directional control, traction and maneuverability. The ASR system uses input information from wheel speed, vehicle speed, to allow traction priority to low speeds and directional control at high speeds, vehicle acceleration and throttle position, during low vehicle acceleration the controls are more sensitive and brake application input.

The ABS/ASR common components are four wheel speed sensors and sensor rings, master cylinder reservoir which supplies the ABS/ASR modulator valve, the EBTCM and wire harness. The ABS/ASR components that are specific to the ASR system are the adjuster assembly - throttle and cruise control cables, prime pipe from master cylinder to modulator valve, ASR Off switch, spark retard table added to the ECM, throttle position sensor (TPS) module, cruise control cutoff relay, ASR lamps and lateral accelerometer.

SYSTEM COMPONENTS
MODULATOR VALVE
1991

The modulator valve, **Fig. 3,** consists of three rapidly switching solenoid valves, two accumulator chambers (one for each brake circuit) and a return pump. One solenoid valve is assigned to each front wheel brake, the third is assigned to the rear wheel brakes. This system is known as a "Three-channel system."

The modulator valve receives its instructions from control module. The modulator valve regulates brake fluid pressure based upon road conditions as interpreted by the control module, regardless of master cylinder output pressure. **The modulator valve can maintain or reduce brake fluid pressure to the wheel calipers. However, the modulator valve can not increase the pressure above that sent by the master cylinder. The modulator valve alone can not apply the brakes.**

Two relays are mounted on top of modulator valve. These are the only replaceable parts of the modulator valve. The pump motor relay controls the return pump and the solenoid relay controls power supply to solenoid valves. Modulator valve is mounted in rear storage compartment located behind drivers seat. The modulator valve itself cannot be repaired and must be replaced as an assembly.

1992–93

The modulator valve assembly, located in the rear compartment behind the left-hand seat, contains a recirculation pump with separate circuits for the front and rear brakes. During the ABS pressure reduction function the modulator valve transfers fluid from the brake calipers back to the master cylinder. During the ASR brake intervention function, the valve transfers fluid from the master cylinder reservoir to the rear brake calipers.

The ASR portions of the hydraulics circuit to the ABS hydraulic include and additional three way valve added to the rear brakes. These valves control each rear brake individually and use an additional rear brake pipe. The load valve is used to isolate the master cylinder prime pipe from the pump during brake application and ABS control, the valve is spring loaded to the open position. The two way pilot valve is electronically operated to isolate the master cylinder from the pump during ASR operation. When the pilot valve is closed, the pump can direct fluid to the rear brake circuit, with excess fluid passing through the pressure limiting valve. The master cylinder positive center valve is designed to open when the secondary piston returns to the rest position. This happens when the center valve pintle contacts a cross shaft at the rest position, ensuring pressure relief if excess fluid is pumped into the master cylinder.

CONTROL MODULE

1991

The control module consists of two printed circuit board plates. Resistors, diodes, transistors and large integrated circuits are mounted on one side of plates and both sides have conductor paths. These integrated circuits (IC), contain thousands of transistors, resistors and diodes mounted on a single silicon chip. Plates are housed in control module and surrounded by light alloy casting.

Wheel acceleration, deceleration and slip values are calculated from electric signals, transmitted from wheel speed sensors, which are proportional to wheel speed. Electrical signals from this module produce commands for the hydraulic modulator valves.

The control module is located in rear storage compartment behind drivers seat. If control module is defective, it must be replaced as an assembly. **No attempt should be made to repair this module.**

ELECTRONIC BRAKE & TRACTION CONTROL MODULE (EBTCM)

1992–93

The EBTCM is located in the rear compartment behind the lefthand seat. The EBTCM receives information from the ECM, wheel speed sensor and the TPS module. The information is output to the ECM, modulator valve assembly and the adjuster assembly. The EBTCM determines when the ASR system should be actuated through timing retard, throttle

close down and brake intervention. The ignition retard signal is based on engine RPM. Engine RPM information is received from the tach filter circuit on models equipped with VIN P engine or from the direct ignition module on models equipped with VIN J engine. The EBTCM controls the amount of adjuster assembly output and throttle rate. As required, the EBTCM controls the modulator valve assembly pressure. The EBTCM will disable the ASR system when the ignition switch is On but the engine is not running.

The EBTCM must reset its idle position detection capabilities whenever a new throttle position sensor or throttle body is installed.

LATERAL ACCELERATION SWITCH (ACCELEROMETER)

The lateral acceleration switch is made up of two mercury switches connected in series. They are used to detect if the vehicle is cornering faster than a predetermined curve speed. When this speed is exceeded, one of two switches opens up and sends a signal to control module.

The lateral acceleration switch is located under the A/C control head on the floor pan. This switch is not serviceable and should be replaced as an assembly.

WHEEL SPEED SENSORS

Rotational speed of each wheel is detected separately by an inductive wheel speed sensor, **Fig. 4.** Electrical signal sensed from the speed sensors are transmitted to control module.

In this system, front wheels are controlled individually and rear wheels together. Control of rear wheels works on the "Select Low" principle. "Select Low" means wheel with the greatest tendency to lock-up (lower tire to road friction co-efficient), determines level of control.

Wheel speed sensors are installed in knuckles. Toothed rings are pressed onto front hub and bearing assemblies and rear driveshaft spindles. **The wheel speed sensors do not require adjustment.**

THROTTLE POSITION SENSOR (TPS) MODULE

1992–93

The TPS module is located in the engine compartment near the RH side of the blower case. The module is used to allow the EBTCM to read the TPS signal. The TPS module scales the TPS signal, indicates the ground difference between the ECM and the EBTCM and buffers the signal so the TPS signal to the ECM is not affected by the EBTCM. The EBTCM uses the information for determining potential adjuster assembly requirements for engine torque management.

OPERATION

When ignition switch is turned to On position, amber ANTI-LOCK warning lamp in the instrument panel illuminates. When engine is started, it goes out. If ABS warning light does not go out or comes on permanently while driving, it indicates a fault in ABS system.

When starting vehicle, the control module performs a functional check of electrical circuitry. The test cycle checks components of the monitoring circuit as well as the logic section. Test sample signals are sent to the control module, which checks whether or not the correct output signals are available.

Since the ABS system may not be used every day, there is an additional test which actually runs the modulator valve. Whenever ignition switch is turned to On position and vehicle reaches 4 mph, the test starts. Operation of the modular valve can be heard and felt, if the driver's foot is on the brake pedal. This test is performed once, each time the vehicle is started.

This system continuously monitors the following components: modulator valve, control module, lateral acceleration switch, wheel speed sensors, wiring harness and relays.

The control module constantly monitors its own supply voltage. If supply voltage drops below a predetermined value, ABS will be switched Off and the amber ANTI-LOCK lamp will come on. When supplied voltage returns to or exceeds the predetermined value, ANTI-LOCK lamp will go off. If a fault occurs in ABS, the ANTI-LOCK warning lamp comes on and ABS will be switched off. The system will remain off until vehicle is restarted at which time the functional check is repeated.

DIAGNOSIS & TESTING

Prior to service, disarm airbag as outlined under "Airbag System Disarming." Once service is complete rearm airbag system as outlined under "Airbag System Arming."

INTERMITTENT FAILURES

1991

If an ABS fault occurs, the -SERVICE ABS- indicator will be On during the ignition cycle in which the fault was detected. If an intermittent problem which seems to have corrected itself (-SERVICE ABS- indicator On), a history trouble code will be stored. Also stored will be the history data of the code at the time the fault occurred. -Flash Code- diagnostics may be used to identify the stored history code but the Tech 1 must be used to read ABS history data.

Record all current codes and code history information. Also, if available, record any descriptive driving circumstances during which the failure occurred. This information can help duplicate the condition.

Use the Tech 1 Snapshot mode (Mode F3) while test driving the vehicle and trying to duplicate the driving condition. If an intermittent condition is still undetected, or is not related to the wheel speed circuitry, go to the appropriate chart or code chart. Follow the chart while moving the wiring and connectors around and looking for intermittent type failures in the circuitry.

Most intermittent problems are caused by faulty electrical connections or wiring.

When an intermittent failure is encountered, check suspect wiring for the following:

1. Poor mating of connector halves or terminals not fully seated (backed out).
2. Improperly formed or damaged terminals.
3. Poor terminal-to-wire connection. This requires removing the terminal from the connector body to inspect.

INTERMITTENTS & POOR CONNECTIONS
1992–93

Most intermittents are caused by faulty electrical connections or wiring, although a sticking or faulty relay or solenoid can be a problem. Check for the following items:

1. Poor mating of connector halves, or terminal not fully seated in the connector body (backed out).
2. Dirt or corrosion on the terminals. The terminals must be clean and free of foreign material which may impede proper terminal contact.
3. Damaged connector body, exposing the terminals to moisture or dirt, as well as not maintaining proper terminal orientation with the component or mating surface.
4. Improperly formed or damaged terminals. All connector terminals in problem circuits should be checked carefully to ensure full contact tension. Use corresponding mating terminal to check for proper tension.
5. The J 35616-A Connector Test Adapter Kit must be used whenever a diagnostic procedure requests checking or probing a terminal. Using the adapter will ensure no damage to the terminal will occur, as well as giving an idea of whether contact tension is sufficient.
6. Poor terminal-to-wire connection. Some conditions which fall under this description are poor crimps, poor solder joints, crimping over wire insulation rather than the wire itself, corrosion in the wire-to-terminal contact area, etc.
7. Wire insulation which has rubbed through, causing an intermittent short as the bare area touches other wiring or parts of the vehicle.
8. Wiring broken inside the insulation. This condition could cause a continuity check to show a good circuit, but if only one or two strands of a multi-strand type wire are intact, resistance would be far too high.

1991 Models
DESCRIPTION

The Electronic Brake & Traction Control

Module (EBTCM)q monitors its own performance and certain input and output signals to determine if a system malfunction has occurred. Most ABS self-diagnostics are performed by the controller after the vehicle reaches 1.7 mph. For this reason, the vehicle must be road tested to check for malfunctions that will set fault codes.

The Built-In Test Equipment (BITE) test is performed once during each ignition cycle when the vehicle reaches 3-11 mph. The BITE test cycles each solenoid valve and the pump motor to test component operation. The EBTCM also checks its own logic section and circuitry. If faults are detected during this test, the EBTCM will set a code. The BITE test occurs once each ignition cycle as follows:

1. After receiving an Ignition On input, the EBTCM grounds and activates the solenoid relay.
2. When the vehicle reaches 3-11 mph, the EBTCM tests the solenoid valves and pump in the hydraulic modulator.
3. If the pump or solenoid valves fail to operate, the ABS will be disabled, a fault code will set and the SERVICE ABS indicator will illuminate.
4. When the EBTCM receives a signal from any of the wheel speed sensors, it checks wheel speed sensor output. If any wheel speed sensor signal is missing, the ABS will be disabled, a fault code will set and the SERVICE ABS indicator will illuminate.

Once the vehicle is moving, the EBTCM continuously monitors itself and the following components:

1. Modulator valves.
2. Wheel speed sensors.
3. Wiring harness and relays.
4. Battery voltage.

If battery voltage drops below approximately 9 volts, the ABS is disabled and the SERVICE ABS indicator will illuminate.

Each malfunction has an associated fault code, which is a two-digit number flashed over the SERVICE ABS lamp in the Driver Information Center (DIC). The system can store up to three fault code at once (in addition to Code 12). These codes may be either three separate fault codes, or three of the same codes if an intermittent condition occurs three times.

Some fault codes involving the solenoid valves and pump motor prevent the SERVICE ABS lamp from flashing. If one of these codes is present, the SERVICE ABS lamp will remain On and the system will be unable to enter the diagnostic display (flash codes) mode. In this case, the Tech 1 Diagnostic Computer tool No. 94-00101-A or equivalent must be used.

REQUIRED TEST EQUIPMENT

The following test equipment may be required during diagnostic procedures:

1. High Impedance Digital Multimeter tool No. J 34029-A or equivalent.
2. Pinout box tool No. J 35592 or equivalent.
3. Tech 1 Diagnostic Computer (with Bosch ABS ALDL Adapter) tool No. 94-00101-A or equivalent.

PRELIMINARY INSPECTION

Refer to ABS wiring circuits **Fig. 5** when performing diagnostic procedures.

If a malfunction in the ABS system occurs, check the following before using the code diagnostic charts:

1. Check the STOP/HAZ, BRAKE, SIR and CLUSTER fuses.
2. Check fusible link J.
3. Ensure that all ABS connectors are securely connected.
4. Ensure control module connector is securely connected.
5. Check ABS system grounds.

ACCESSING CODES
Diagnostic Display Mode

To enable the diagnostic display mode, ground pin H of the ALDL connector, then turn the ignition On. The diagnostic display mode will remain enabled as long as pin H is grounded, serial data link communication has not been initiated and vehicle speed is less than 5 mph.

Approximately three seconds after ALDL pin H is grounded, the EBTCM will begin the flash code sequence. The flash sequence will begin with Code 12 to signal the beginning of the fault code display. Each stored code will then be displayed three times. After all codes have been displayed, the sequence will repeat, starting with Code 12.

Some fault codes involving the solenoid valves and pump motor prevent the SERVICE ABS lamp from flashing. If one of these codes is present, the SERVICE ABS lamp will remain On and the system will be unable to enter the diagnostic display (flash codes) mode. In this case, the Tech 1 Diagnostic Computer must be used. Refer to procedure outlined under "Tech 1 Diagnostics."

CODE INTERPRETATION

Refer to **Figs. 6 and 7** for code identification and ABS functional test. **Some codes can only be read through the ALDL connector using the Tech 1 Diagnostic Computer.**

CODE DIAGNOSIS
1991

Refer to **Figs. 8 through 28,** for diagnostic procedures and brake warning system wiring diagram.

CLEARING CODES

Fault codes stored in the EBTCM's memory can be erased in one of the three following ways:

1. Diagnostic Enable Line Procedure.
2. Tech 1 "Clear Codes" selection.
3. Ignition Cycle Default.

Whichever method is used, ensure to verify proper system operation and absence of fault codes when clearing procedure is completed.

**Fig. 5   ABS system wiring circuit (Part 1 of 3).
1991**

**Fig. 5   ABS system wiring circuit (Part 2 of 3).
1991**

The EBTCM will not allow codes to be cleared until all codes have been displayed. Codes cannot be cleared by disconnecting the EBTCM, disconnecting battery cables or turning the ignition Off.

Diagnostic Enable Line Procedure

Clear codes using ALDL enable line (pin H) as follows:
1. Turn ignition Off.

2. Ground ALDL pin H.
3. Turn ignition On.
4. Wait for codes to begin flashing.
5. Unground pin H for at least one second, then ground pin H. This must be done three times within ten seconds.
6. Wait at least 15 seconds. Before turning ignition Off, verify that Code 12 is the only code being flashed. If not, codes have not been properly cleared. Repeat above procedure.

Tech 1 "Clear Codes" Procedure

Following tool manufacturer's instructions, select the appropriate menu, then select the "Clear Codes" function. Verify that codes are cleared by using Tech 1 to read codes. Refer to "Tech 1 Diagnostics" for procedure. If any codes other than Code 12 are present, codes were not cleared or a fault is still present.

Ignition Cycle Default

If the ignition is cycled 100 times without a particular fault reappearing, that particular fault code will be erased and the ignition cycle counter will be reset to zero.

TECH 1 DIAGNOSTICS

The Tech 1 has five test modes for diagnosing the ABS. The test modes are as follows:
1. Mode F0 - Data List: In this test mode, the Tech 1 continuously monitors wheel speed data and brake switch status.
2. Mode F1 - History Data: In this test mode, fault code history data is displayed. This data includes the number of ignition cycles since the fault code occurred and other information. Up to three fault codes are included in the ABS history data.
3. Mode F2 - Trouble Codes: In this test mode, trouble (fault) codes stored by the EBTCM may be displayed or cleared.
4. Mode F3 - ABS Snapshot: In this test mode, the Tech 1 captures and records ABS data before and after a fault occurs.
5. Mode F4 - ABS Tests: In this test mode, the Tech 1 performs hydraulic modulator functional tests to assist in problem isolation during diagnosis.

Mode F0: ABS Data List

The DATA LIST mode allows continuous monitoring of wheel speed data and brake switch status. When monitoring wheel speed data, the signals being sent from the wheel speed sensors to the EBTCM are displayed. In this test mode, the vehicle can be driven while wheel speed data is displayed. The readings can be compared with vehicle speed to check for proper operation. Wheel speed signals can also be compared with each other to determine whether they are within specification.

If one wheel speed signal differs greatly from the other signals, improper operation of that sensor may be indicated. Intermittent wheel speed signals can be located in the DATA LIST mode by looking for signals that vary for no reason during vehicle operation.

In the DATA LIST mode, brake switch operation is displayed. With the brake pedal depressed, the Tech 1 screen reads ON, when the pedal is released, the screen reads OFF.

Mode F1: History Data

In the HISTORY DATA test mode, fault code history data is displayed. This data includes the number of ignition cycles since the fault occurred, brake switch status and ABS state when the fault occurred. Up to three codes are included in the ABS history data.

Mode F2: Trouble Codes

In the TROUBLE CODES test mode, ABS trouble (fault) codes stored by the EBTCM are displayed. The EBTCM can store up to three different codes. The Tech 1 can also clear stored codes when it is used in this test mode.

In addition to storing three trouble codes, the EBTCM records when each code was set and ABS status when each code was set. Each code is accompanied by a brief description of what the code number represents.

After displaying the codes, the Tech 1 can be ordered to clear the codes. It will respond to the clear codes command by displaying one of the following screens:
1. ABS CODES CLEARED.
2. CODE CLEAR FAIL.

In addition to storing fault codes, the EBTCM stores other information about the codes that may aid in diagnosis. This function is called ENHANCED DIAGNOSTIC DATA. The Tech 1 can be ordered to display the following ENHANCED DIAGNOSTIC DATA:
1. Brake Light Switch Status: Indicates whether the brake light switch was On or Off when the code set.
2. ABS State: Indicates whether or not the anti-lock mode was engaged when the code set.
3. Vehicle Speed: Indicates vehicle speed when the code set.
4. Ignition Cycles: Indicates how many ignition cycles have occurred since the code set.

Mode F3: ABS Snapshot

The ABS SNAPSHOT mode mode will help isolate intermittent problems by capturing data before and after a trigger condition. This data can then be analyzed to determine the cause of the complaint. Three different trigger conditions can activate the ABS SNAPSHOT mode:
1. Automatic Trigger: When the snapshot mode is used with the automatic trigger, the Tech 1 captures data which deviates from normal operation without setting a code.
2. ABS Code Set Trigger: Snapshot data can be captured by specifying an ABS code. When the Tech 1 is used with the code set trigger, it captures data immediately before and after the code setting.

Fig. 5   ABS system wiring circuit (Part 3 of 3). 1991

3. Snapshot On Command: Snapshot data can be captured on command by pressing the Tech 1 ENTER key. When used with the command trigger, the Tech 1 continuously monitors data and waits for the ENTER command to begin storing data.

The snapshot can be set to capture data at the beginning, center or end of the data stream. Approximately 15 seconds of data are captured before the Tech 1 data buffer is full. If "Beginning" is selected, data occurring approximately 15 seconds before and up to the trigger point is captured. If "Center" is selected, data occurring approximately 8 seconds before through 8 seconds after the trigger point is captured. If "End" is selected, data occurring approximately 15 seconds after the trigger point is captured.

Mode F4: ABS Tests

The ABS TESTS mode performs functional tests on the ABS which help verify proper operation. In this mode, error conditions can be further identified by testing and observing the test results. In the ABS

TESTS mode the following tests can be performed:
1. Solenoid Valve-Pressure Reduction: This test indicates whether specific solenoid valves in the hydraulic modulator release pressure to assigned wheel circuits.
2. Solenoid Valve-Pressure Hold: This test indicates whether specific solenoid valves in the hydraulic modulator hold pressure in assigned wheel circuits.
3. Static "BITE" Test: This test cycles each solenoid valve and operates the pump motor briefly. The EBTCM will store a fault code if the test conditions fail.

The PRESSURE REDUCE test activates a selected hydraulic wheel circuit valve, placing it in the pressure reduce position. Valve action can then be verified by checking the appropriate wheel for proper brake action. The Tech 1 will indicate whether the valve action was commanded properly. This test is used in conjunction with the PRESSURE HOLD test to completely check each solenoid valve. With an

Code	Definition
12	Diagnostic System Operational
21	RF Wheel Speed Sensor Fault
22	RF Toothed Wheel Frequency Error
25	LF Wheel Speed Sensor Fault
26	LF Toothed Wheel Frequency Error
31	RR Wheel Speed Sensor Fault
32	RF Toothed Wheel Frequency Error
35	LR Wheel Speed Sensor Fault
36	LR Toothed Wheel Frequency Error
41①	RF Solenoid Valve Fault
45①	LF Solenoid Valve Fault
55①	Rear Solenoid Valve Fault
61①	Pump Motor Or Motor Relay Fault
63①	Solenoid Valve Relay Fault
71	EBTCM Fault
72	Serial Data Link Fault
75	Lateral Accelerometer Fault (Short To B+ Or Ground Or Open Circuit)
76	Lateral Accelerometer Fault (Signal Out Of Range Or Incorrect)

① —Requires Tech 1 Diagnostic Computer.

Fig. 6   Trouble code identification. 1991

assistant, the pressure reduce test can be verified as follows:
1. Have an assistant apply the brakes.
2. Use Tech 1 to command the PRESSURE REDUCE mode.
3. Try to spin wheel being tested. It should spin due to the reduce command.

The PRESSURE HOLD test activates a selected hydraulic wheel circuit valve, placing it in the pressure hold position. Valve action can then be verified by checking the appropriate wheel for proper brake action. The Tech 1 will indicate whether the valve action was commanded properly. This test is used in conjunction with the PRESSURE REDUCE test to completely check each solenoid valve. With an assistant, the pressure reduce test can be verified as follows:
1. Spin wheel freely.
2. Use Tech 1 to command the PRESSURE HOLD mode.
3. Have an assistant apply the brakes.
4. Try to spin wheel being tested. It should spin due to the hold command, even if the brakes are applied.

The STATIC "BITE" test is performed automatically by the EBTCM once during each ignition cycle when the vehicle speed reaches 3-11 mph. The Tech 1 will perform this test automatically the ABS TESTS mode. The BITE test cycles each solenoid valve and the pump motor to check component operation. If any error is detected during this test, the EBTCM will set a code.

1992–93 Models
DESCRIPTION

When the vehicle is started, the EBTCM performs a functional test of the electrical circuits. The test cycle inspects the monitoring system components and system logic; the cycle is completed in about six seconds. An additional AUTO test operates the modulator valve assembly when the vehicle is started and vehicle speed reaches 4 mph in forward or reverse. The modulator valve assembly, EBTCM, lateral accelerometer, wheel speed sensors and wiring harness and relays are continuously monitored.

The EBTCM monitors its own voltage supply, if the supply drops below a specified minimum value, the ABS/ASR lamp will not be illuminated and the Service ABS lamp will be illuminated. When voltage exceeds the specified minimum value the Service ABS lamp will go out. If a fault occurs in the ABS system the warning lamp will be illuminated, the ABS system will be turned Off until the ignition switch is cycled Off then On, then the functional inspection will be repeated. The standard brake system will remain fully operational. Under normal driving conditions the ABS functions the same as a standard power assisted brake system.

Brake pedal pulsation and occasional tire noise are normal during ABS operation on dry pavement. During light braking in a turn, the rear brake pressure may be mod-ulated to enhance vehicle stability under certain conditions. A slight brake pedal vibration may be experienced during light braking during lateral acceleration speeds above 30 mph.

PRELIMINARY INSPECTION

Refer to ABS wiring circuits **Fig. 29 and 31** when performing diagnostic procedures and **Figs. 30 and 32** for ABS functional tests.

If a malfunction in the ABS system occurs, check the following before using the code diagnostic charts:
1. Inspect fusible link.
2. Ensure ABS connectors are properly connected.
3. Ensure control module connectors is properly connected.
4. Inspect ABS system grounds.

ACCESSING CODES
TECH 1

Refer to "Tech 1 Diagnostics" for accessing trouble code procedure.

CENTRAL CONTROL MODULE (CCM)
Automatic Mode

1. Ground ALDL pin G, then turn ignition switch to On position. If A/C fuse is blown CCM will not receive IGN 3 power and will not enter diagnostic mode and code 16 will be indicated.
2. CCM will display codes and module for which they apply in an automatic code display sequence. ABS/ASR EBTCM is module 9.
3. Each code is displayed for three seconds followed by a one second pause before the next code is displayed. There will be a three second pause between code display sequence for each module.
4. Each module code list end will be indicated by an "- - -."
5. If a communication problem between ECM or EBTCM and CCM is indicated the speedometer will display Err.

Manual Mode

The manual mode may be entered after the automatic mode sequence has been completed. When manual mode is entered the speedometer will be blank and the trip monitor will display 1.0 indicating module 1 (CCM). Driver Information Center (DIC) buttons control manual diagnostic functions. Fuel info indicates previous value, gauges is previous test, fuel reset is previous module, eng met is next value, trip odo is next test and trip reset is next module. The speedometer will indicate "- - -" if the end or the beginning of a list of codes is reached using the DIC buttons or no codes are indicated for the module being tested. To display ABS/ASR codes trip monitor must indicate 9.1 to clear ABS/ASR codes 9.7 must be indicated.

CODE INTERPRETATION

Refer to **Fig. 33**, for trouble code identification.

CODE DIAGNOSIS

Refer to **Figs. 34 through 78**, for code diagnostic procedures and brake warning system wiring diagrams.

CLEARING CODES

Tech 1 Method

1. Ensure ignition switch is Off, then connect Tech 1 scan tool with suitable brake cartridge.
2. Select ABS/ASR system features.
3. Select F2 Trouble Codes.
4. Select Clear Codes.
5. Remove Tech 1 tool, then test drive vehicle.

CCM Method

1. Turn ignition switch to Off position.
2. Connect suitable jumper wire between ALDL terminals A and G.
3. Turn ignition switch On.
4. Depress DIC trip reset button repeatedly to display 9.0 in trip monitor.
5. Depress DIC trip odo twice to change display to 9.7.
6. Hold eng/met button until "- - -" appears in speedometer area.
7. Remove jumper from ALDL.

Ignition Cycle Default

If the ignition is cycled 50 times without a particular fault reappearing, that particular fault code will be erased and the ignition cycle counter will be reset to zero.

TECH 1 DIAGNOSTICS

When using the Tech 1 scan tool for ABS/ASR system diagnostics, the ABS and ASR systems are disabled and the Service ABS and Service ASR indicator lamps will be illuminated. Normal power assisted braking is still applicable. After completion of all diagnostic procedures, turn the ignition switch Off for at least 10 seconds and disconnect Tech 1 tool, then the system will return to normal operation. The valve solenoid relay is turned Off by the EBTCM when a code is set. When monitoring the data list with the Tech 1, the valve solenoid relay will be noted as Off, this is normal and should not be considered a system problem. Also when monitoring the data list, the throttle angle readings may stop updating. This is normal and should not be considered as system problem.

The Tech 1 has five test modes for diagnosis and testing of the ABS/ASR system as follows:

1. Mode F0 - Data List: Tech 1 monitors wheel speed data and brake switch status.
2. Mode F1 - Code History: In this mode, fault code history is displayed and includes the number of ignition cycles since the codes was set and other system information. Up to three codes

are included in the ABS history data.

3. Mode F2 - Trouble Codes: In this test, trouble codes stored by the EBTCM may be displayed or cleared.
4. Mode F3 - Snapshot: In this test, displays data before and after a snapshot triggering condition which may not set a code.
5. Mode F4 - Miscellaneous Tests: In this mode, the Tech 1 performs modulator valve assembly functional tests, lamp output tests, pilot valve tests and ASR tests to assist in problem isolation during diagnostics.
6. Mode F5 - TPS Learn: If the TPS or throttle body has been replaced, the EBTCM must learn the TPS idle position voltage. This is required to ensure effective engine torque reduction during ASR operation.

MODE F3: SNAPSHOT

Conditions that will trigger the Tech 1 snapshot feature are as follows:

1. Loss of serial data.
2. Valve solenoid relay less then 11 volts (low voltage.)
3. Valve solenoid relay Off, less then two volts (relay will be Off if codes are set).
4. One wheel speed sensor ±8 mph of others (intermittent wheel speed).
5. Three wheel speed sensor ±3 mph of each other and one ±5 mph of the others (wheel speed out of range).
6. Low brake fluid.
7. Lateral accelerometer greater then 4.35 or less then 1.05 volts (out of range).
8. System voltage more then 17 volts (high voltage).
9. Sudden engine RPM change greater then 1100 RPM (intermittent engine RPM).
10. Brake switch state change of On-Off-On in less then 200 milliseconds (intermittent brake switch).

MODE F4: ABS TESTS

AUTO Test

The auto test cycles each valve solenoid, pump motor and relays to inspect component operation. This test is the same as the auto test the system performs when vehicle speed reaches 4 mph in forward or reverse. Stored codes will be indicated upon completion of the test.

1. With ignition switch in Off position.
2. Connect Tech 1 scan tool with appropriate brake cartridge.
3. Turn ignition switch to On position.
4. Select F4, Misc Tests.
5. Select F1, Auto Test.
6. Depress enter key to run auto test.
7. Record any stored codes.

Valve Solenoid–Pressure Hold

The pressure hold test activates the hydraulic wheel circuit valve in the pressure hold position. In that position the valve will not allow master cylinder pressure to be delivered to the wheel circuit. In this test, the tech 1 tool operates the valve to the pressure position which will allow wheel movement with brake pedal application.

1. With ignition switch in Off position.
2. Connect Tech 1 scan tool with appropriate brake cartridge.
3. Turn ignition switch to On position.
4. Raise and support vehicle with wheels about six inches from floor.
5. Select valve solenoid test, then depress Tech 1 tool HOLD PRESSURE.
6. Depress brake pedal.
7. Attempt to turn rear wheel, movement should be indicated.

Valve Solenoid–Pressure Reduction

The pressure reduction test activates the hydraulic wheel circuit valve, placing it

Fig. 7   ABS functional check. 1991

in the pressure reduce position. In that position, the valve allows caliper pressure to return to the master cylinder. During this test the wheel should be moveable with brake pressure applied.

1. With ignition switch in Off position.
2. Connect Tech 1 scan tool with appropriate brake cartridge.
3. Turn ignition switch to On position.
4. Raise and support vehicle with wheels about six inches from floor.
5. Have an assistant depress brake pedal.
6. Select valve solenoid test, then depress Tech 1 tool RELEASE PRESSURE.
7. Depress brake pedal, turn rear wheel, movement should be indicated.

Lamp Test

The lamp test is used to inspect the Service ABS, Service ASR, ABS Active, ASR Active and ASR Off lamp operation.

1. With ignition switch in Off position.
2. Connect Tech 1 scan tool with appropriate brake cartridge.
3. Turn ignition switch to On position.
4. Select F4, Misc Tests.
5. Select F2, Lamp Test.
6. Select lamp to be tested.
7. Depress up arrow to turn lamp On and down arrow to turn lamp Off.

Pilot Valve Test

The test indicates whether the pilot valve in the modulator valve assembly moves to the position which blocks pressure to the master cylinder. The pilot valve blocks pressure to the master cylinder before pump motor activation and fluid pressure application to the rear wheel circuits during ASR activation.

1. With ignition switch in Off position.
2. Connect Tech 1 scan tool with appropriate brake cartridge.
3. Turn ignition switch to On position.
4. Raise and support vehicle with wheels about six inches from floor.
5. Select F4, Misc Tests.
6. Select F3, Pilot Vlv Test.
7. Have assistant depress Tech 1 up arrow, then depress and hold brake pedal.
8. Attempt to move rear wheel by hand, no movement should be indicated.

ASR Test

The ASR test runs the pump motor to apply fluid pressure to the rear wheel circuits. The "Pilot Valve Test" as outlined previously must be run prior to the ASR test.

1. With ignition switch in Off position.
2. Connect Tech 1 scan tool with appropriate brake cartridge.
3. Turn ignition switch to On position.
4. Raise and support vehicle with wheels about six inches from floor.
5. Select F4, Misc Tests.
6. Select F4, ASR Test.
7. Perform pilot valve test to confirm valve operation.
8. Depress up arrow to begin ASR test.
9. Attempt to move rear wheel by hand, no movement should be indicated.

MODE 5: TPS LEARN

When a throttle position sensor or throttle body assembly are replaced the TPS must relearn the TPS idle position voltage.

1. Place ignition switch in Off position.
2. Connect Tech 1 scan tool with appropriate brake system cartridge.
3. Turn ignition switch On.
4. Follow menus to reach ABS/ASR feature.
5. Select F5, TPS LEARN.
6. Depress up arrow to begin learn procedure.
7. Wait for Tech 1 tool to indicate COMPLETE.
8. Disconnect Tech 1 scan tool.

Continued on page 23-110

DIAGNOSTIC (TROUBLE CODE) CHART INDEX

Chart	Description	Page No.	Fig. No.
1991 Models			
Chart A	"Service ABS" Indicator ON No Codes Set	23-57	8
Chart B	"Service ABS" Indicator Inoperative	23-58	9
Chart C	"ABS Active" Indicator Inoperative	23-58	10
Code 21	RF Wheel Speed Sensor (Sensor Fault)	23-59	11
Code 22	RF Toothed Wheel (Frequency Error)	23-60	12
Code 25	LF Wheel Speed Sensor (Sensor Fault)	23-60	13
Code 26	RF Toothed Wheel (Frequency Error)	23-61	14
Code 31	RR Wheel Speed Sensor (Sensor Fault)	23-61	15
Code 32	RR Toothed Wheel (Frequency Error)	23-62	16
Code 35	LR Wheel Speed Sensor (Sensor Fault)	23-62	17
Code 36	LR Toothed Wheel (Frequency Error)	23-63	18
Code 41	RF Solenoid Valve (Valve Fault)	23-63	19
Code 45	LF Solenoid Valve (Valve Fault)	23-64	20
Code 55	Rear Solenoid Valve (Valve Fault)	23-64	21
Code 61	Pump Motor/Relay (Motor Or Relay Fault)	23-65	22
Code 63	Solenoid Valve Relay (Relay Fault)	23-66	23
Code 71	Electronic Brake & Traction Control Module (Control Module Fault)	23-67	24
Code 72	Electronic Brake & Traction Control Module (Serial Data Link Fault)	23-68	25
Code 75	Lateral Accelerometer (Short To B+ Or Ground, Or Open Circuit)	23-68	26
Code 76	Lateral Accelerometer (Signal Out Of Range Or Incorrect)	23-69	27
1992–93 Models			
Chart A ①	Service ABS Indicator On w/No Codes Set	23-76	34
Chart A ②	Service ABS Indicator On w/No Codes Set	23-76	35
Chart B	Service ABS Indicator Inoperative Or Flickers w/Ignition On	23-77	36
Chart C	Service ASR Indicator On w/No Codes Set	23-77	37
Chart D	Service ASR Indicator Inoperative	23-78	38
Chart E	ABS Active Indicator Always On	23-79	39

Continued

Chart	Description	Page No.	Fig. No.
1992–93 Models-Continued			
Chart F	ABS Active Indicator Inoperative	23-80	40
Chart G	ASR Active Indicator On w/No Codes Set	23-80	41
Chart H	ASR Active Indicator Inoperative w/No Codes Set	23-81	42
Chart I	ASR Off Indicator Always On	23-82	43
Chart J	ASR Off Indicator Inoperative	23-83	44
Code 21	RF Wheel Speed Sensor Fault	23-84	45
Code 23	RF Wheel Speed Sensor Continuity Fault	23-84	46
Code 25	LF Wheel Speed Sensor Fault	23-85	47
Code 27	LF Wheel Speed Sensor Continuity Fault	23-85	48
Code 28	Wheel Speed Sensor Frequency Error	23-86	49
Code 31	RR Wheel Speed Sensor Fault	23-86	50
Code 33	RR Wheel Speed Sensor Continuity Fault	23-87	51
Code 35	LR Wheel Speed Sensor Fault	23-87	52
Code 37	LR Wheel Speed Sensor Continuity Fault	23-88	53
Code 41	RF Solenoid Valve Fault	23-88	54
Code 44	Pilot Valve Solenoid Fault	23-89	55
Code 45	LF Solenoid Valve Fault	23-90	56
Code 51	RR Solenoid Valve Fault	23-90	57
Code 55	LR Solenoid Valve Fault	23-91	58
Code 57	Cruise Control Output Monitoring Fault	23-92	59
Code 58	EBTCM Internal Adjuster Assembly Fault	23-93	60
Code 61	Pump Motor Or Motor Relay Fault	23-93	61
Code 62	Tach Pulses Fault	23-95	62
Code 63	Valve Solenoid Relay Fault	23-95	63
Code 64	Throttle Position Signal Fault (LT1)	23-97	64
Code 64	Throttle Position Signal Fault (LT5)	23-98	65
Code 65 ①	Adjuster Assembly Fault	23-100	66
Code 65 ②	Adjuster Assembly Fault	23-101	67
Code 66	Adjuster Assembly Control Fault	23-102	68
Code 71	EBTCM Fault	23-102	69
Code 72	Serial Data Link Fault	23-103	70
Code 73	Spark Retard Monitoring Fault	23-103	71
Code 74 ①	Low Voltage	23-104	72
Code 74 ②	Low Voltage	23-104	73
Code 75	Lateral Accelerometer Wiring Fault	23-105	74
Code 76	Lateral Accelerometer Signal Out Of Range	23-106	75
Code 83	Brake Fluid Level Low	23-108	76

① —1992
② —1993

CHART A
(1 of 2)
"SERVICE ABS" INDICATOR "ON"
WITH NO CODES SET

Circuit Description:

The "SERVICE ABS" indicator is located in the Driver Information Center (DIC) display. Battery voltage is applied with the ignition in the "Run" or "Start" positions through the CLSTR fuse and CKT 139. The indicator is grounded through CKT 852 and is controlled by the EBCM at pin 29 when the EBCM is active, or by the ABS Diode through CKT 1077 to the Hydraulic Modulator Assembly pin 4 and the Solenoid Valve relay when the EBCM is inactive. The EBCM will supply ground to the indicator for approximately 2 seconds when the ignition is first turned "ON." During the first 2 seconds, if no faults are detected, the EBCM will allow the Solenoid Valve relay coil to energize. With the relay energized, the ground circuit through the ABS Diode, CKT 1077, and the relay, will be opened. This allows the indicator to be activated only when the EBCM indicator control line at pin 29 supplies ground to the indicator.

When the ignition is in the "Run" or "Start" positions, the EBCM relay coil is energized through the AIRBAG fuse and CKT 439. When energized, the EBCM relay closes the normally open contacts, supplying power from the BRAKE fuse through CKT 740 and CKT 850 to the EBCM at pin 1, the Ignition "ON" input. If a high system voltage (above approximately 16 volts) occurs, the EBCM relay will short CKT 740 to ground through CKT 801, causing the BRAKE fuse to blow in order to prevent damage to the EBCM.

Test Description: Number(s) below refer to circled number(s) on the diagnostic chart.
1. This test checks for proper system voltage.
2. This test checks for blown fuses which could cause the indicator to remain "ON."
3. This test checks for an open in CKT 801.
4. This test checks for an open in CKT 850.
5. This test checks for proper supply voltage to the EBCM relay contacts.
6. This test checks for proper supply voltage to the EBCM relay coil.
7. This test checks for proper operation of the EBCM relay.

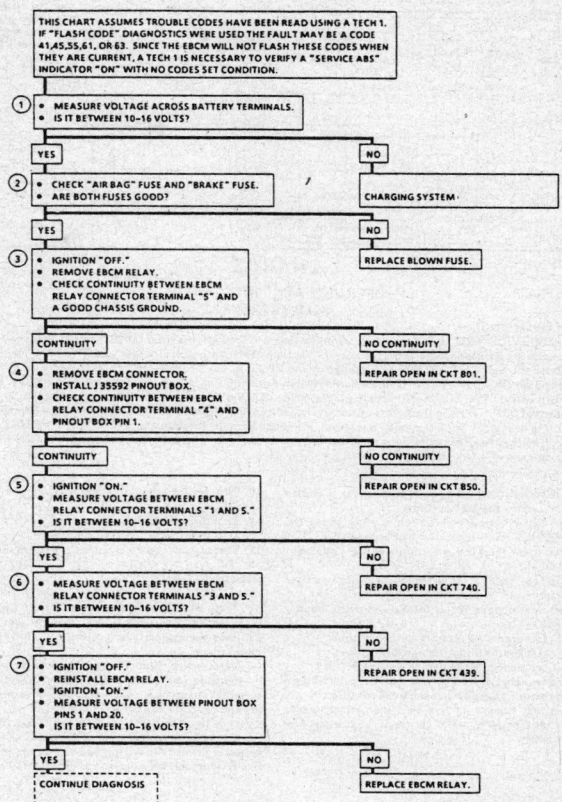

Fig. 8   Chart A, Service ABS indicator on no codes set (Part 1 of 2). 1991

CHART A
(2 of 2)
"SERVICE ABS" INDICATOR "ON"
WITH NO CODES SET

Circuit Description:

The "SERVICE ABS" indicator is located in the Driver Information Center (DIC) display. Battery voltage is applied with the ignition in the "Run," or "Start" positions through the CLSTR fuse and CKT 139. The indicator is grounded through CKT 852 and is controlled by the EBCM at pin 29 when the EBCM is active, or by the ABS Diode through CKT 1077 to the Hydraulic Modulator Assembly pin 4 and the Solenoid Valve relay when the EBCM is inactive. The EBCM will supply ground to the indicator for approximately 2 seconds when the ignition is first turned "ON." During the first 2 seconds, if no faults are detected, the EBCM will allow the Solenoid Valve relay coil to energize. With the relay energized, the ground circuit through the ABS Diode, CKT 1077, and the relay, will be opened. This allows the indicator to be activated only when the EBCM indicator control line at pin 29 supplies ground to the indicator.

When the ignition is in the "Run," or "Start" positions, the EBCM relay coil is energized through the AIRBAG fuse and CKT 437. When energized, the EBCM relay closes the normally open contacts, supplying power from the BRAKE fuse through CKT 740 and CKT 850 to the EBCM at pin 1, the Ignition "ON" input. If a high system voltage (above approximately 16 volts) occurs, the EBCM relay will short CKT 740 to ground through CKT 801, causing the BRAKE fuse to blow in order to prevent damage to the EBCM.

Test Description: Number(s) below refer to circled number(s) on the diagnostic chart.
8. This test checks for a short to ground in CKT 852.
9. This test checks for connector or wiring problems which could cause an intermittent condition.

Diagnostic Aids:

It is important that a thorough inspection of the wiring and connectors is performed. Failure to properly inspect the wiring and connectors may result in a misdiagnosis of a faulty EBCM.

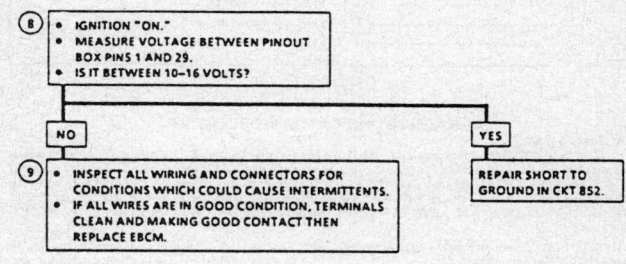

Fig. 8   Chart A, Service ABS indicator on no codes set (Part 2 of 2). 1991

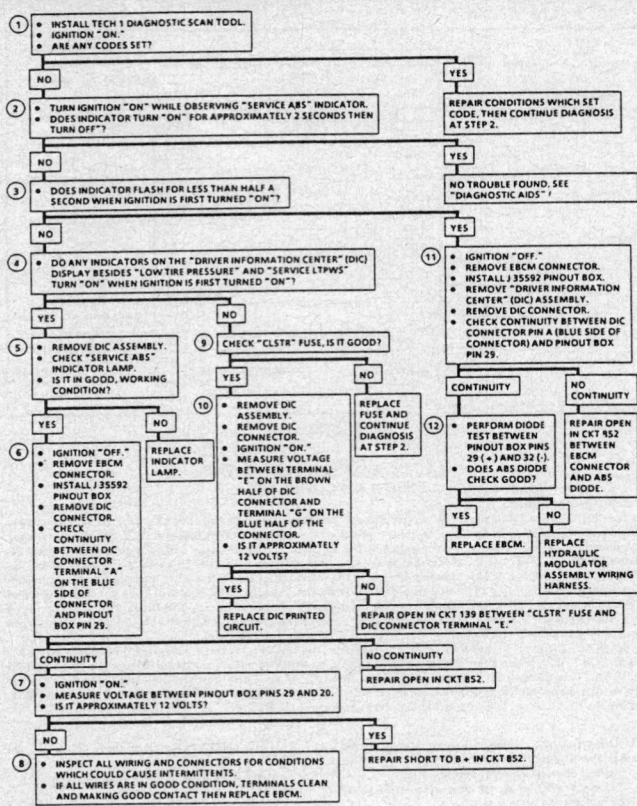

CHART B
"SERVICE ABS" INDICATOR INOPERATIVE

Circuit Description:

The "SERVICE ABS" indicator is located in the Driver Information Center (DIC) display. Battery voltage is applied with the ignition in the "Run," or "Start" positions through the CLSTR fuse and CKT 139. The indicator is grounded through CKT 852 and is controlled by the EBCM at pin 29 when the EBCM is active, or by the ABS Diode through CKT 1077 to the Hydraulic Modulator Assembly pin 4 and the Solenoid Valve relay when the EBCM is inactive. The EBCM will supply ground to the indicator for approximately 2 seconds when the ignition is first turned "ON." During the first 2 seconds, if no faults are detected, the EBCM will allow the Solenoid Valve relay coil to energize. With the relay energized, the ground circuit through the ABS Diode, CKT 1077, and the relay, will be opened. This allows the indicator to be activated only when the EBCM indicator control line at pin 29 supplies ground to the indicator.

Test Description: Number(s) below refer to circled number(s) on the diagnostic chart.
1. This test checks for codes which may cause the "SERVICE ABS" indicator to be inoperative.
2. This test verifies an inoperative indicator condition.
3. This test checks for a faulty indicator control circuit.
4. This test checks for a faulty indicator supply circuit.
5. This test checks for a faulty indicator lamp.
6. This test checks for an open in CKT 852.
7. This test checks for a short to B + in CKT 852.
8. This test checks for connector or wiring problems which could cause an intermittent condition.
9. This test checks for a blown fuse which would prevent supply voltage from reaching the indicators.

10. This test checks for supply voltage at the DIC display.
11. This test checks for an open in CKT 852 between EBCM connector and the ABS Diode.
12. This test checks the integrity of the ABS Diode.

Diagnostic Aids:

Tests which require a connection at Pinout Box terminal "20" are using this terminal as ground. This assumes the integrity of ground CKT 801 has been maintained.

Tests which require a connection to terminal "G" on the Blue half of the DIC connector are using this terminal as ground. This assumes the integrity of ground CKT 150 has been maintained.

It is important that a thorough inspection of the wiring and connectors is performed. Failure to properly inspect the wiring and connectors may result in a misdiagnosis of a defective EBCM.

Fig. 9   Chart B, Service ABS indicator inoperative. 1991

CHART C
1 of 2
"ABS ACTIVE" INDICATOR INOPERATIVE

Circuit Description:

The "ABS ACTIVE" indicator is located in the Drive Information Center (DIC) display. Battery voltage is applied with the ignition in the "Run," or "Start" positions through the CLSTR fuse and CKT 139. The indicator is grounded through CKT 1537 through the "ABS ACTIVE" indicator relay contacts to CKT 150 only when the EBCM is active and receiving a Pump "ON" Input signal from the Pump Motor Relay contacts through CKT 2 and Fusible Link "J." The "ABS ACTIVE" indicator will illuminate only while the Return Pump Motor is receiving power.

Test Description: Number(s) below refer to circled number(s) on the diagnostic chart.
1. This test checks for codes which may cause the "ABS ACTIVE" indicator to be inoperative.
2. This test verifies an inoperative indicator condition.
3. This test checks for a faulty indicator supply circuit.
4. This test checks for a faulty indicator lamp.
5. This test checks the integrity of the "ABS ACTIVE" indicator relay coil.
6. This test determines whether the "ABS ACTIVE" indicator relay contacts are stuck open.
7. This test checks for an open in CKT 1537.
8. This test checks for a blown fuse which would prevent supply voltage from reaching the indicators.
9. This test checks for supply voltage at the DIC display.

10. This test determines whether the problem revealed in Step 3 is due to a faulty indicator lamp or faulty circuitry internal to the DIC display.

Diagnostic Aids:

All tests which require a connection to Pinout Box pin 20 are using this pin as ground. This assumes that the integrity of ground CKT 801 has been maintained.

All tests which require a connection to terminal "G" on the Blue half of the DIC connector are using this terminal as ground. This assumes that the integrity of ground CKT 150 has been maintained.

It is important that a thorough inspection of the wiring and connectors is performed. Failure to properly inspect the wiring and connectors could result in a misdiagnosis of a faulty EBCM.

Fig. 10   Chart C, ABS active indicator inoperative (Part 1 of 2). 1991

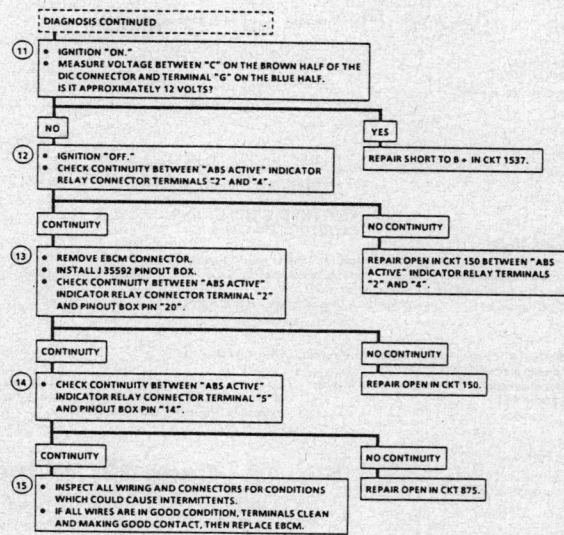

CHART C

2 of 2
"ABS ACTIVE" INDICATOR
INOPERATIVE

Circuit Description:

The "ABS ACTIVE" indicator is located in the Driver Information Center (DIC) display. Battery voltage is applied with the ignition in the "Run," or "Start" positions through the CLSTR fuse and CKT 139. The indicator is grounded through CKT 1537 through the "ABS ACTIVE" indicator relay contacts to CKT 150 only when the EBCM is active and receiving a Pump "ON" input signal from the Pump Motor Relay contacts through CKT 2 and Fusible Link "J". The "ABS ACTIVE" indicator will illuminate only while the Return Pump Motor is receiving power.

Test Description: Number(s) below refer to circled number(s) on the diagnostic chart.

11. This test checks for a short to B+ in CKT 1537.
12. This test checks for an open in CKT 150 at the "ABS ACTIVE" indicator relay contacts.
13. This test checks for an open in CKT 150 at the "ABS ACTIVE" indicator relay coil.
14. This test checks for an open in CKT 875.
15. This test checks for connector or wiring problems which may cause an intermittent condition.

Diagnostic Aids:

All tests which require a connection to Pinout Box pin 20 are using this pin as ground. This assumes that the integrity of ground CKT 801 has been maintained.

All tests which require a connection to terminal "G" on the Blue half of the DIC connector are using this terminal as ground. This assumes that the integrity of ground CKT 150 has been maintained.

It is important that a thorough inspection of the wiring and connectors is performed. Failure to properly inspect wiring and connectors could result in a misdiagnosis of a faulty EBCM.

Fig. 10   Chart C, ABS active indicator inoperative (Part 2 of 2). 1991

CODE 21

RF WHEEL SPEED SENSOR
(SENSOR FAULT)

Circuit Description:

The toothed wheel generates a voltage pulse as it moves past the sensor; each tooth-gap-tooth on the wheel generates these pulses. The frequency of these pulses is used by the EBCM to determine wheel speed. The amount of voltage generated in each pulse depends on the air gap between the sensor and the toothed wheel, and on wheel speed.

Code 21 is set if there is a loss of continuity in CKT 872 or 833 while the ignition is "ON," or if no signal is being produced by the wheel speed sensor at vehicle speeds of approximately 19 MPH or more.

Test Description: Number(s) refer to circled number(s) on the diagnostic chart.

1. This test checks for a correct resistance reading of the sensor itself.
2. This test checks for a short between the wires for the RF wheel speed sensor.
3. This test checks for an open in the wires between the speed sensor and the EBCM.
4. This test checks for a short to ground or B+ in CKT 872.
5. This test checks for an intermittent in the RF wheel speed sensor circuitry. If no intermittent is found in the wiring, it may be in the sensor itself.

Diagnostic Aids:

Be sure speed sensor wiring is properly routed; this will help prevent false signals.

It is important that a thorough inspection of the wiring and connectors be performed prior to road testing the vehicle. This code can only be set when the vehicle is in motion. Failure to properly inspect wiring and connectors may result in a misdiagnosis of a faulty Hydraulic Modulator Assembly or EBCM.

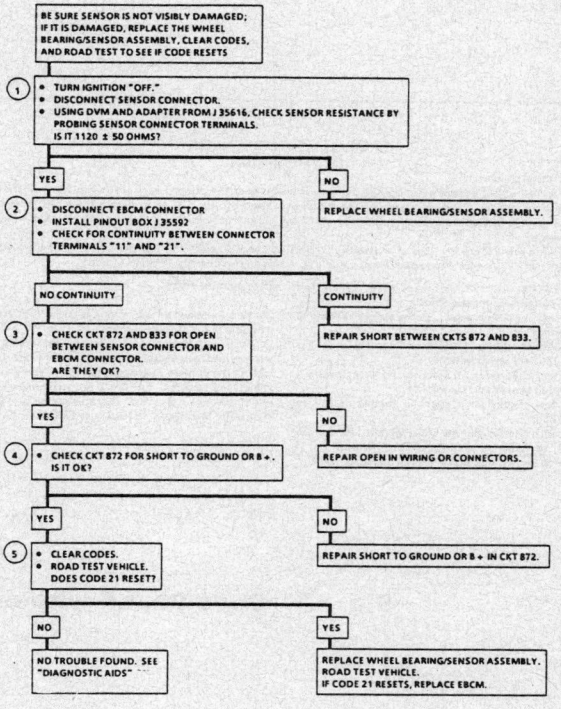

Fig. 11   Code 21, RF wheel speed sensor (Sensor fault). 1991

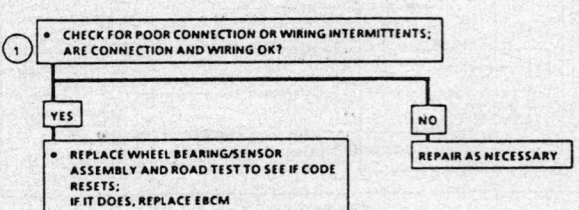

CODE 22
RF TOOTHED WHEEL
(FREQUENCY ERROR)

Circuit Description:
The toothed wheel generates a voltage pulse as it moves past the sensor; each tooth-gap-tooth on the wheel generates these pulses. The frequency of these pulses is used by the EBCM to determine wheel speed, and is determined by the number of teeth on the toothed wheel.
Code 22 will set if an incorrect number of teeth or damaged teeth are present on the toothed wheel.

Test Description: Number(s) refer to circled number(s) on the diagnostic chart.
1. This test checks for a physical problem with the wiring or connector.

Diagnostic Aids:
A worn hub/bearing assembly may cause this fault in extreme cases; the bearing play allows the sensor-to-toothed ring gap to change excessively.

Fig. 12   Code 22, RF toothed wheel (Frequency error). 1991

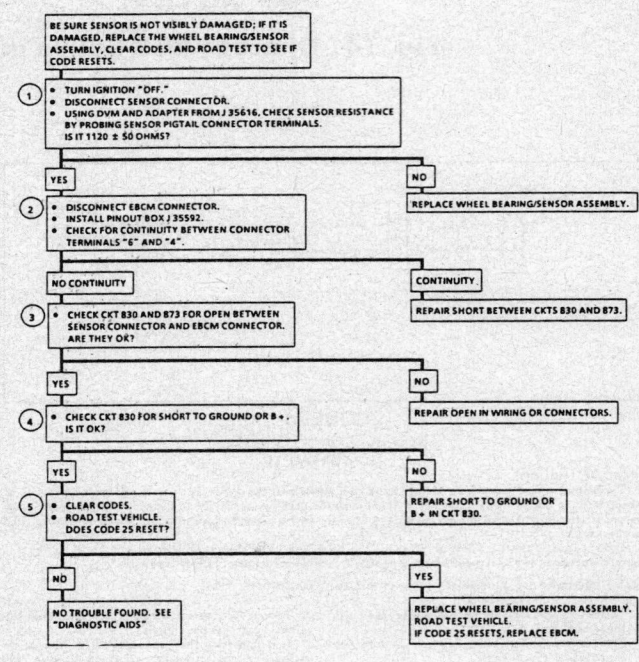

CODE 25
LF WHEEL SPEED SENSOR
(SENSOR FAULT)

Circuit Description:
The toothed wheel generates a voltage pulse as it moves past the sensor; each tooth-gap-tooth on the wheel generates these pulses. The frequency of these pulses is used by the EBCM to determine wheel speed. The amount of voltage generated in each pulse depends on the air gap between the sensor and the toothed wheel, and on wheel speed.
Code 25 is set if there is a loss of continuity in CKT 830 or 873 while the ignition is "ON," or if no signal is being produced by the wheel speed sensor at vehicle speeds of approximately 19 MPH or more.

Test Description: Number(s) refer to circled number(s) on the diagnostic chart.
1. This test checks for a correct resistance reading of the sensor itself.
2. This test checks for a short between the wires for the LF wheel speed sensor.
3. This test checks for an open in the wires between the speed sensor and the EBCM.
4. This test checks for a short to ground or B+ in CKT 830.
5. This test checks for an intermittent in the LF wheel speed sensor circuitry. If no intermittent is found in the wiring, it may be in the sensor itself.

Diagnostic Aids:
Be sure speed sensor wiring is properly routed; this will help prevent false signals.
It is important that a thorough inspection of the wiring and connectors be performed prior to road testing the vehicle. This code can only be set when the vehicle is in motion. Failure to properly inspect wiring and connectors may result in a misdiagnosis of a faulty Hydraulic Modulator Assembly or EBCM.

Fig. 13   Code 25, LF wheel speed sensor (Sensor fault). 1991

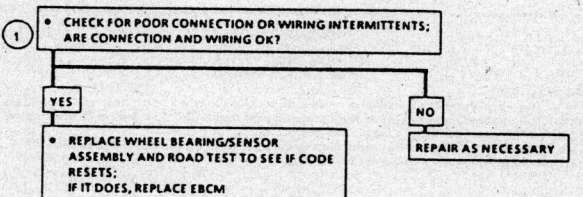

CODE 26
LF TOOTHED WHEEL
(FREQUENCY ERROR)

Circuit Description:

The toothed wheel generates a voltage pulse as it moves past the sensor; each tooth-gap-tooth on the wheel generates these pulses. The frequency of these pulses is used by the EBCM to determine wheel speed, and is determined by the number of teeth on the toothed wheel.

Code 26 will set if an incorrect number of teeth or damaged teeth are present on the toothed wheel.

Test Description: Number(s) refer to circled number(s) on the diagnostic chart.
1. This test checks for a physical problem with the wiring or connector.

Diagnostic Aids:

A worn hub/bearing assembly may cause this fault in extreme cases; the bearing play allows the sensor-to-toothed ring gap to change excessively.

Fig. 14   Code 26, LF toothed wheel (Frequency error). 1991

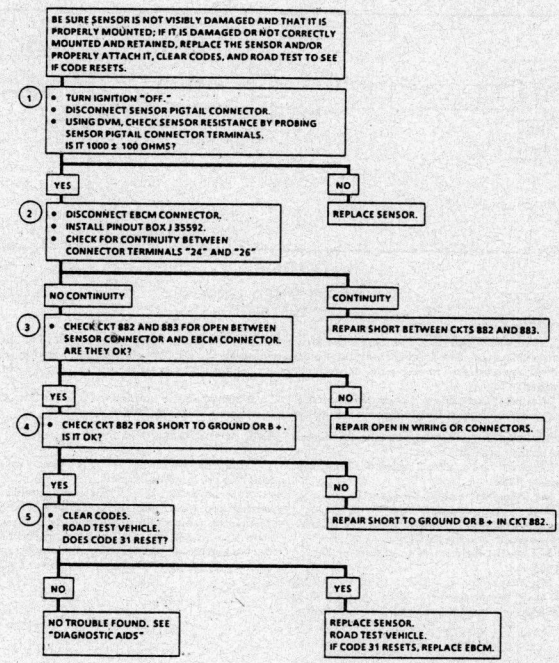

CODE 31
RR WHEEL SPEED SENSOR
(SENSOR FAULT)

Circuit Description:

The toothed wheel generates a voltage pulse as it moves past the sensor; each tooth-gap-tooth on the wheel generates these pulses. The frequency of these pulses is used by the EBCM to determine wheel speed. The amount of voltage generated in each pulse depends on the air gap between the sensor and the toothed wheel, and on wheel speed.

Code 31 is set if there is a loss of continuity in CKT 882 or 883 while the ignition is "ON," or if no signal is being produced by the wheel speed sensor at vehicle speeds of approximately 19 MPH or more.

Test Description: Number(s) refer to circled number(s) on the diagnostic chart.
1. This test checks for a correct resistance reading of the sensor itself.
2. This test checks for a short between the wires for the RR wheel speed sensor.
3. This test checks for an open in the wires between the speed sensor and the EBCM.
4. This test checks for a short to ground or B+ in CKT 882.
5. This test checks for an intermittent in the RR wheel speed sensor circuitry. If no intermittent is found in the wiring, it may be in the sensor itself.

Diagnostic Aids:

Be sure speed sensor wiring is properly routed; this will help prevent false signals.

It is important that a thorough inspection of the wiring and connectors be performed prior to road testing the vehicle. This code can only be set when the vehicle is in motion. Failure to properly inspect wiring and connectors may result in a misdiagnosis a faulty Hydraulic Modulator Assembly or EBCM.

Fig. 15   Code 31, RR wheel speed sensor (Sensor fault). 1991

CODE 32
RR TOOTHED WHEEL
(FREQUENCY ERROR)

Circuit Description:

The toothed wheel generates a voltage pulse as it moves past the sensor; each tooth-gap-tooth on the wheel generates these pulses. The frequency of these pulses is used by the EBCM to determine wheel speed, and is determined by the number of teeth on the toothed wheel.

Code 32 will set if an incorrect number of teeth or damaged teeth are present on the toothed wheel. It may also be set if the sensor-to-toothed-wheel air gap is incorrect.

Test Description: Number(s) refer to circled number(s) on the diagnostic chart.
1. This test checks for a physical problem with the toothed wheel.
2. This test checks for proper mounting, which includes O-ring quality and position, and mounting torque.

Diagnostic Aids:

A worn hub/bearing assembly may cause this fault in extreme cases; the bearing play allows the sensor-to-toothed ring gap to change excessively.

Check for a buildup of foreign material in the gaps between teeth on the toothed wheel; this material may cause this error.

Also check the toothed wheel for any large grooves, gouges, marks, etc. that might influence the tooth's signal at the wheel speed sensor.

Fig. 16   Code 32, RR toothed wheel (Frequency error). 1991

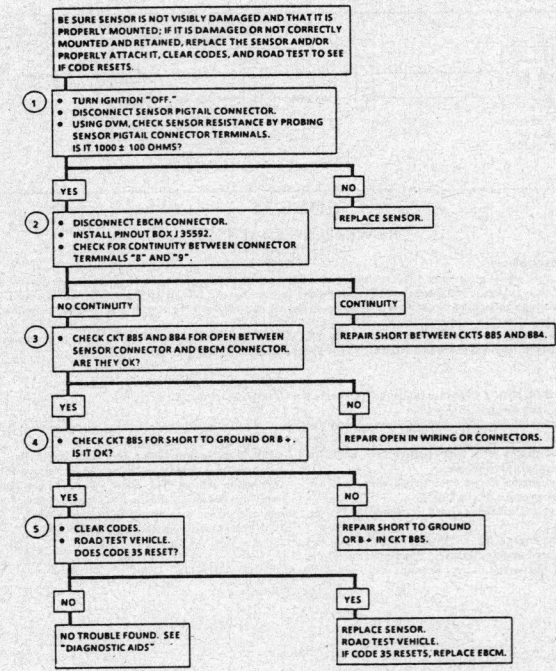

CODE 35
LR WHEEL SPEED SENSOR
(SENSOR FAULT)

Circuit Description:

The toothed wheel generates a voltage pulse as it moves past the sensor; each tooth-gap-tooth on the wheel generates these pulses. The frequency of these pulses is used by the EBCM to determine wheel speed. The amount of voltage generated in each pulse depends on the air gap between the sensor and the toothed wheel, and on wheel speed.

Code 35 is set if there is a loss of continuity in CKT 885 or 884 while the ignition is "ON," or if no signal is being produced by the wheel speed sensor at vehicle speeds of approximately 19 MPH or more.

Test Description: Number(s) refer to circled number(s) on the diagnostic chart.
1. This test checks for a correct resistance reading of the sensor itself.
2. This test checks for a short between the wires for the LR wheel speed sensor.
3. This test checks for an open in the wires between the speed sensor and the EBCM.
4. This test checks for a short to ground or B+ in CKT 885.
5. This test checks for an intermittent in the LR wheel speed sensor circuitry. If no intermittent is found in the wiring, it may be in the sensor itself.

Diagnostic Aids:

Be sure speed sensor wiring is properly routed; this will help prevent false signals.

It is important that a thorough inspection of the wiring and connectors be performed prior to road testing the vehicle. This code can only be set when the vehicle is in motion. Failure to properly inspection wiring and connectors may result in a misdiagnosis of a faulty Hydraulic Modulator Assembly or EBCM.

Fig. 17   Code 35, LR wheel speed sensor (Sensor fault). 1991

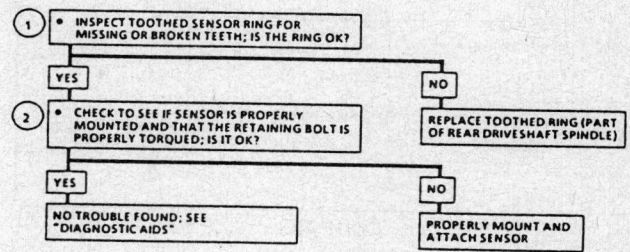

CODE 36
LR TOOTHED WHEEL
(FREQUENCY ERROR)

Circuit Description:

The toothed wheel generates a voltage pulse as it moves past the sensor; each tooth-gap-tooth on the wheel generates these pulses. The frequency of these pulses is used by the EBCM to determine wheel speed, and is determined by the number of teeth on the toothed wheel.

Code 36 will set if an incorrect number of teeth or damaged teeth are present on the toothed wheel. It may also set if the sensor-to-toothed-wheel air gap is incorrect.

Test Description: Number(s) refer to circled number(s) on the diagnostic chart.
1. This test checks for a physical problem with the toothed wheel.
2. This test checks for proper mounting, which includes O-ring quality and position, and mounting torque.

Diagnostic Aids:

A worn hub/bearing assembly may cause this fault in extreme cases; the bearing play allows the sensor-to-toothed ring gap to change excessively.

Check for a buildup of foreign material in the gaps between teeth on the toothed wheel; this material may cause this error.

Also check the toothed wheel for any large grooves, gouges, marks, etc. that might influence the tooth's signal at the wheel speed sensor.

Fig. 18   Code 36, LR toothed wheel (Frequency error). 1991

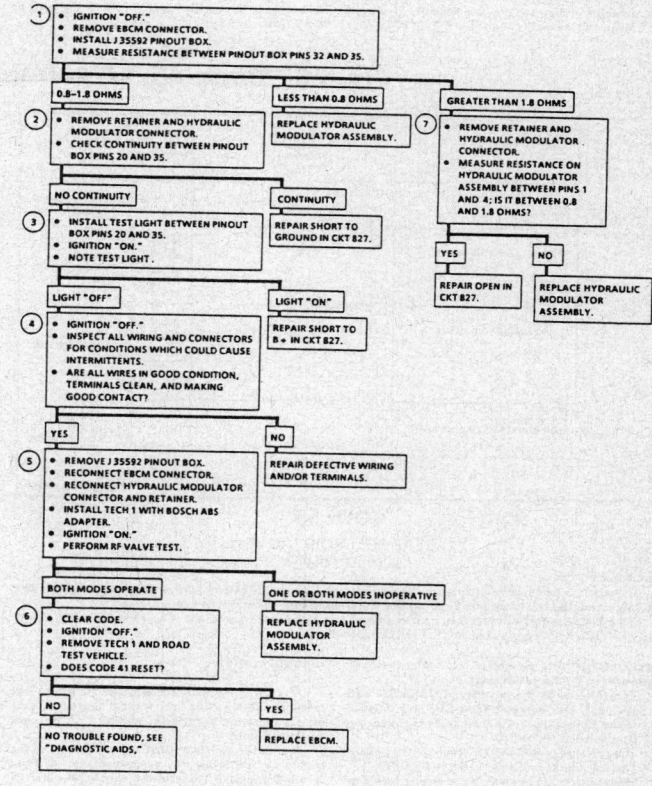

CODE 41
RF SOLENOID VALVE
(VALVE FAULT)

Circuit Description:

The wheel solenoid valve circuits are supplied with power from the battery when the ignition is "ON." The EBCM controls the valve functions by permitting one of three levels of current flow (0, 2.5, 5 amps).

If the EBCM senses a discrepancy such as an open or ground in the circuit, the valve relay will turn "OFF," the "SERVICE ABS" light will come "ON," and Code 41 will set.

Test Description: Number(s) below refer to circled number(s) on the diagnostic chart.
1. This test checks the integrity of CKTs 827 and 1077, the RF Solenoid Valve Circuitry internal to the Hydraulic Modulator Assembly, and the RF Solenoid Valve Coil.
2. This test checks for a short to ground in CKT 827.
3. This test checks for a short to B+ in CKT 827.
4. This test checks for connector or wiring problems which may cause an intermittent condition.
5. This test uses the Tech 1 to check for proper Solenoid Valve operation.
6. This test determines whether the code was set by an intermittent condition or an EBCM fault.
7. This test determines whether the problem revealed in Step 1 is due to a defective Hydraulic Modulator Assembly or an open in CKT 827.

Diagnostic Aids:

All tests which require a connection to Pinout Box terminal "20" are using this terminal as ground. This assumes that the integrity of ground CKT 801 has been maintained.

It is important that a thorough inspection of the wiring and connectors be performed prior to road testing the vehicle. This code can only be set when the vehicle is in motion. Failure to properly inspect wiring and connectors may result in a misdiagnosis of a faulty Hydraulic Modulator Assembly or EBCM.

If Codes 41 and 45 are both set the fault is likely to be a short to B+ on CKT 827.

If Codes 41 and 55 are both set the fault is likely to be a short to B+ on CKT 829.

Fig. 19   Code 41, RF solenoid valve (Valve fault). 1991

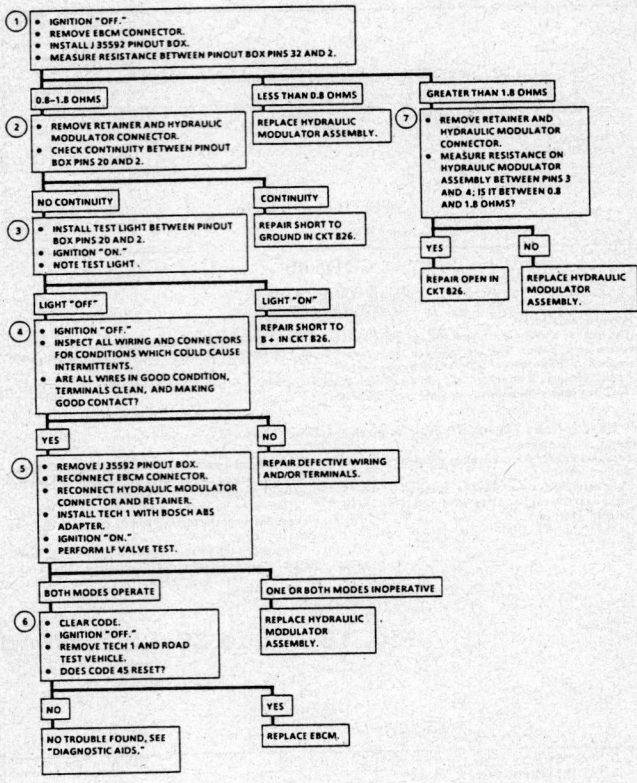

CODE 45
LF SOLENOID VALVE
(VALVE FAULT)

Circuit Description:

The wheel solenoid valve circuits are supplied with power from the battery when the ignition is "ON." The EBCM controls the valve functions by permitting one of three levels of current flow (0, 2.5, 5 amps).

If the EBCM senses a discrepancy such as an open or ground in the circuit, the valve relay will turn "OFF," the "SERVICE ABS" light will come "ON" and Code 45 will set.

Test Description: Number(s) below refer to circled number(s) on the diagnostic chart.

1. This test checks the integrity of CKTs 826 and 1077, the LF Solenoid Valve Circuitry internal to the Hydraulic Modulator Assembly, and the LF Solenoid Valve Coil.
2. This test checks for a short to ground in CKT 826.
3. This test checks for a short to B+ in CKT 826.
4. This test checks for connector or wiring problems which may cause an intermittent condition.
5. This test uses the Tech 1 to check for proper Solenoid Valve operation.
6. This test determines whether the code was set by an intermittent condition or an EBCM fault.
7. This test determines whether the problem revealed in Step 1 is due to a defective Hydraulic Modulator Assembly or an open in CKT 826.

Diagnostic Aids:

All tests which require a connection to Pinout Box terminal "20" are using this terminal as ground. This assumes that the integrity of ground CKT 801 has been maintained.

It is important that a thorough inspection of the wiring and connectors be performed prior to road testing the vehicle. This code can only be set when the vehicle is in motion. Failure to properly inspect wiring and connectors may result in a misdiagnosis of a faulty Hydraulic Modulator Assembly or EBCM.

If Codes 41 and 45 are both set the fault is likely to be a short to B+ on CKT 827.

If Codes 45 and 55 are both set the fault is likely to be a short to B+ on CKT 826 or a short to ground on CKT 1079.

Fig. 20 Code 45, LF solenoid valve (Valve fault). 1991

CODE 55
REAR SOLENOID VALVE
(VALVE FAULT)

Circuit Description:

The wheel solenoid valve circuits are supplied with power from the battery when the ignition is "ON." The EBCM controls the valve functions by permitting one of three levels of current flow (0, 2.5, 5 amps).

If the EBCM senses a discrepancy such as an open or ground in the circuit, the valve relay will turn "OFF," the "SERVICE ABS" light will come "ON" and Code 55 will set.

Test Description: Number(s) below refer to circled number(s) on the diagnostic chart.

1. This test checks the integrity of CKTs 829 and 1077, the Rear Solenoid Valve Circuitry internal to the Hydraulic Modulator Assembly, and the Rear Solenoid Valve Coil.
2. This test checks for a short to ground in CKT 829.
3. This test checks for a short to B+ in CKT 829.
4. This test checks for connector or wiring problems which may cause an intermittent condition.
5. This test uses the Tech 1 to check for proper Solenoid Valve operation.
6. This test determines whether the code was set by an intermittent condition or an EBCM fault.
7. This test determines whether the problem revealed in Step 1 is due to a defective Hydraulic Modulator Assembly or an open in CKT 829.

Diagnostic Aids:

All tests which require a connection to Pinout Box terminal "20" are using this terminal as ground. This assumes that the integrity of ground CKT 801 has been maintained.

It is important that a thorough inspection of the wiring and connectors be performed prior to road testing the vehicle. This code can only be set when the vehicle is in motion. Failure to properly inspect wiring and connectors may result in a misdiagnosis of a faulty Hydraulic Modulator Assembly or EBCM.

If Codes 41 and 55 are both set the fault is likely to be a short to B+ on CKT 829.

If Codes 45 and 55 are both set the fault is likely to be a short to B+ on CKT 826 or a short to ground on CKT 1079.

Fig. 21 Code 55, Rear solenoid valve (Valve fault). 1991

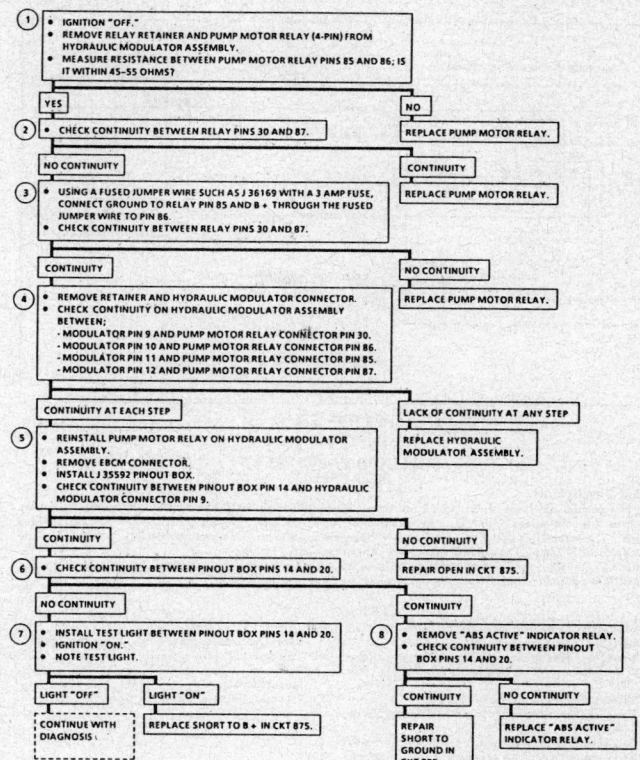

CODE 61

PUMP MOTOR/RELAY
(MOTOR OR RELAY FAULT)

Circuit Description:

When the pump motor relay is grounded by the EBCM, it provides B+ to operate the pump. Once the motor circuit is energized, a "Pump ON" signal is sent back to the EBCM to verify operation.

Code 61 will set if 12 volts is present at the pump motor without motor relay activation, or if 12 volts is NOT present at the pump motor within 60 milliseconds after the motor relay is activated.

Test Description: Number(s) below refer to circled number(s) on the diagnostic chart.
1. This test checks the integrity of the Pump Motor Relay coil.
2. This test determines whether the Pump Motor Relay contacts are stuck closed.
3. This test determines whether the Pump Motor Relay contacts are stuck open.
4. This test checks the integrity of the Pump Motor Relay circuitry internal to the Hydraulic Modulator Assembly.

5. This test checks for an open in CKT 875.
6. This test checks for a short to ground in CKT 875.
7. This test checks for a short to B+ in CKT 875.
8. This test determines whether the problem revealed in Step 6 is due to a shorted coil in the "ABS ACTIVE" indicator relay or in CKT 875's wiring.

Fig. 22   Code 61, Pump motor/relay (Motor or relay fault, Part 1 of 2). 1991

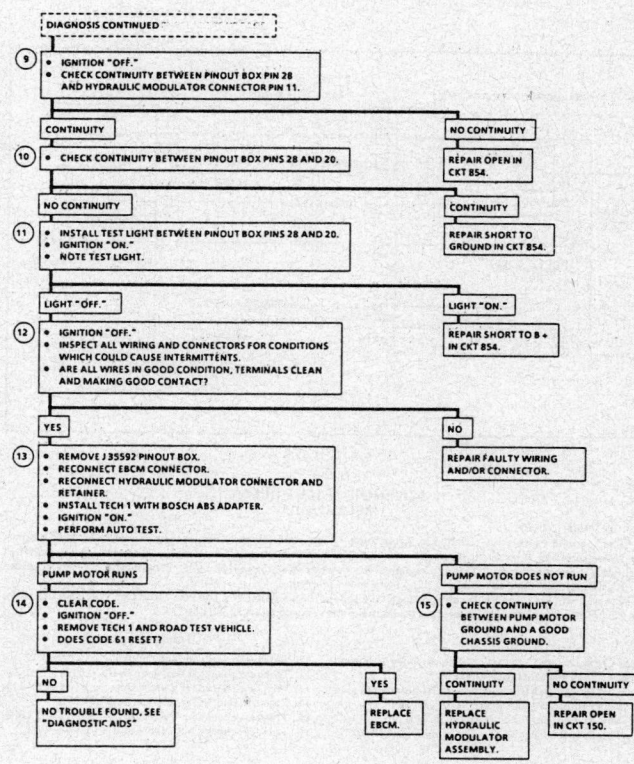

CODE 61

PUMP MOTOR/RELAY
(MOTOR OR RELAY FAULT)

Circuit Description:

When the pump motor relay is grounded by the EBCM, it provides B+ to operate the pump. Once the motor circuit is energized, a "Pump ON" signal is sent back to the EBCM to verify operation.

Code 61 will set if 12 volts is present at the pump motor without motor relay activation, or if 12 volts is NOT present at the pump motor within 60 milliseconds after the motor relay is activated.

Test Description: Number(s) below refer to circled number(s) on the diagnostic chart.
9. This test checks for an open in CKT 854.
10. This test checks for a short to ground in CKT 854.
11. This test checks for a short to B+ in CKT 854.
12. This test checks for connector or wiring problems which could cause an intermittent condition.
13. This test uses the Tech 1 to check for proper operation of the Pump Motor and associated circuitry.
14. This test determines whether the code was set by an intermittent condition or an EBCM fault.
15. This test determines whether the problem revealed in Step 13 is due to a defective Pump Motor or a problem with CKT 150's wiring.

Diagnostic Aids:

All tests which require a connection to Pinout Box terminal "20" are using this terminal as ground. This assumes the integrity of ground CKT 801 has been maintained.

It is important that a thorough inspection of the wiring and connectors is performed prior to road testing the vehicle. This code can only be set when the vehicle is in motion. Failure to properly inspect wiring and connectors may result in a misdiagnosis of a defective Hydraulic Modulator Assembly or EBCM.

Fig. 22   Code 61, Pump motor/relay (Motor or relay fault, Part 2 of 2). 1991

CODE 63

SOLENOID VALVE RELAY
(RELAY FAULT)

Circuit Description:

The solenoid valve relay circuit has 2 functions. When ABS is active, the relay provides voltage to actuate the three solenoid valves. However, the solenoid valves do not use this voltage unless the EBCM provides grounds. The second function of the solenoid valve relay circuit is to provide a ground path for illumination of the "SERVICE ABS" lamp if the solenoid relay loses power or ground.

Code 63 will set if the valve relay voltage falls to less than 5 volts, or if the relay feed line is at 12 volts when the EBCM is not requesting it to be; this would make the relay constantly "ON."

Test Description: Number(s) below refer to circled number(s) on the diagnostic chart.
1. This test checks the availability of Battery voltage to the Solenoid Valve Relay through Fusible Link "J".
2. This test checks for an open in CKT 2.
3. This test checks the integrity of the Solenoid Valve Relay Coil.
4. This test determines whether the Solenoid Valve Relay contacts for the ground circuit are stuck open.

5. This test determines whether the Solenoid Valve Relay Contacts for the B+ circuit are stuck open.
6. This test checks the integrity of the Solenoid Valve Relay circuitry internal to the Hydraulic Modulator Assembly.
7. This test checks for a short to ground in CKT 2.

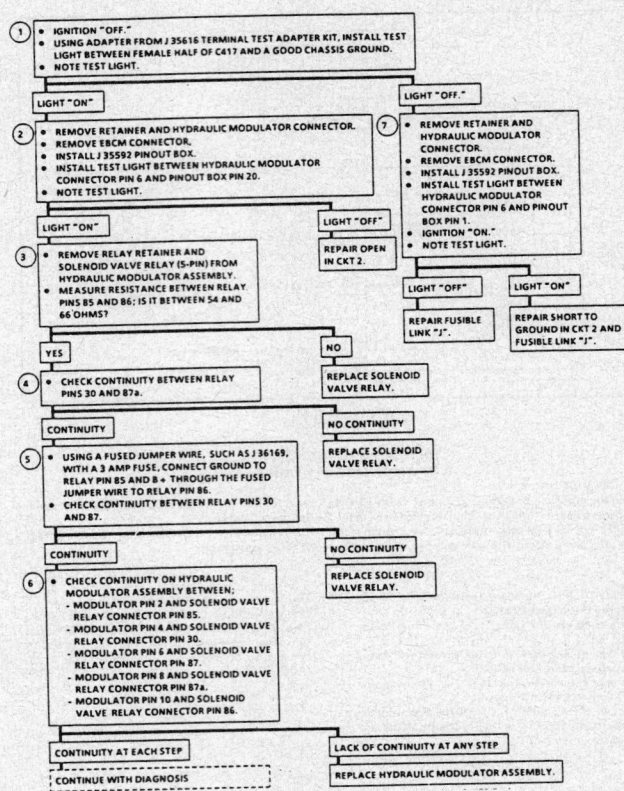

Fig. 23   Code 63, Solenoid valve relay (Relay fault, Part 1 of 3). 1991

CODE 63

SOLENOID VALVE RELAY
(RELAY FAULT)

Circuit Description:

The solenoid valve relay circuit has 2 functions. When ABS is active, the relay provides voltage to actuate the three solenoid valves. However, the solenoid valves do not use this voltage unless the EBCM provides grounds. The second function of the solenoid valve relay circuit is to provide a ground path for illumination of the "SERVICE ABS" lamp if the solenoid relay loses power or ground.

Code 63 will set if the valve relay voltage falls to less than 5 volts, or if the relay feed line is at 12 volts when the EBCM is not requesting it to be; this would make the relay constantly "ON."

Test Description: Number(s) below refer to circled number(s) on the diagnostic chart.
8. This test checks the integrity of the Solenoid Valve Relay contacts ground circuit (CKT 150).
9. This test checks for an open in CKT 1077.
10. This test checks for a short to ground in CKT 1077.

11. This test checks for a short to B+ in CKT 1077.
12. This test checks for an open in CKT 1079.
13. This test checks for a short to ground in CKT 1079.
14. This test checks for an open in CKT 1078.
15. This test checks for a short to ground in CKT 1078.
16. This test checks for a short to B+ in CKT 1078.

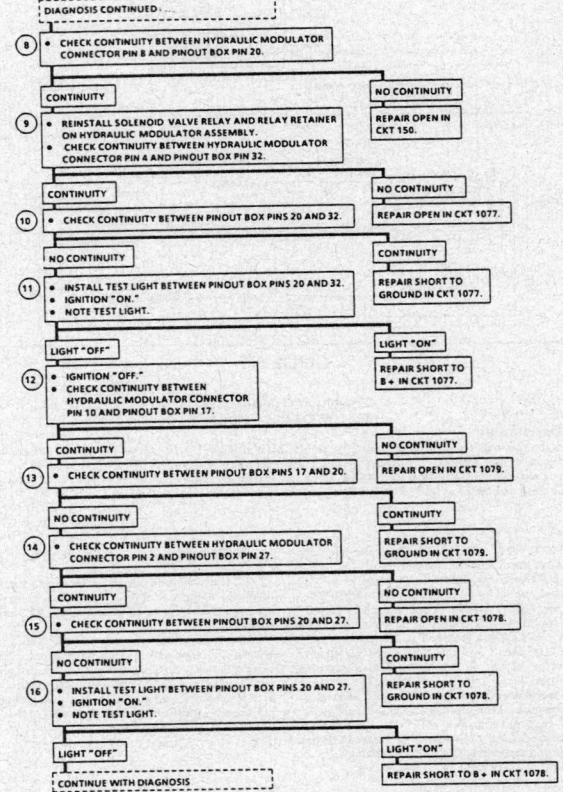

Fig. 23   Code 63, Solenoid valve relay (Relay fault, Part 2 of 3). 1991

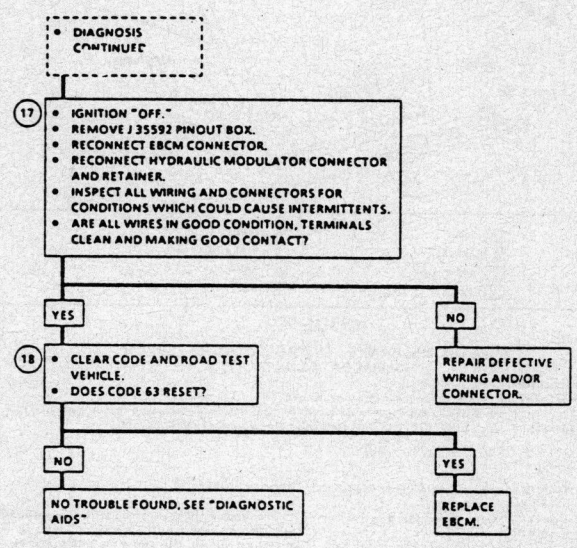

CODE 63

SOLENOID VALVE RELAY
(RELAY FAULT)

Circuit Description:

The solenoid valve relay circuit has 2 functions. When ABS is active, the relay provides voltage to actuate the three solenoid valves. However, the solenoid valves do not use this voltage unless the EBCM provides grounds. The second function of the solenoid valve relay circuit is to provide a ground path for illumination of the "SERVICE ABS" lamp if the solenoid relay loses power or ground.

Code 63 will set if the valve relay voltage falls to less than 5 volts, or if the relay feed line is at 12 volts when the EBCM is not requesting it to be; this would make the relay constantly "ON."

Test Description: Number(s) below refer to circled number(s) on the diagnostic chart.

17. This test checks for connector or wiring problems which could cause an intermittent condition.

18. This test determines whether the code was set by an intermittent condition or an EBCM fault.

Diagnostic Aids:

All tests which require a connection to Pinout Box terminal "20" are using this terminal as ground. This assumes the integrity of ground CKT 801 has been maintained.

It is important that a thorough inspection of the wiring and connectors be performed prior to road testing the vehicle. This code can only be set when the vehicle is in motion. Failure to properly inspect wiring and connectors may result in a misdiagnosis of a defective EBCM.

A disconnected or improperly seated Hydraulic Modulator connector may set this code.

Fig. 23   Code 63, Solenoid valve relay (Relay fault, Part 3 of 3). 1991

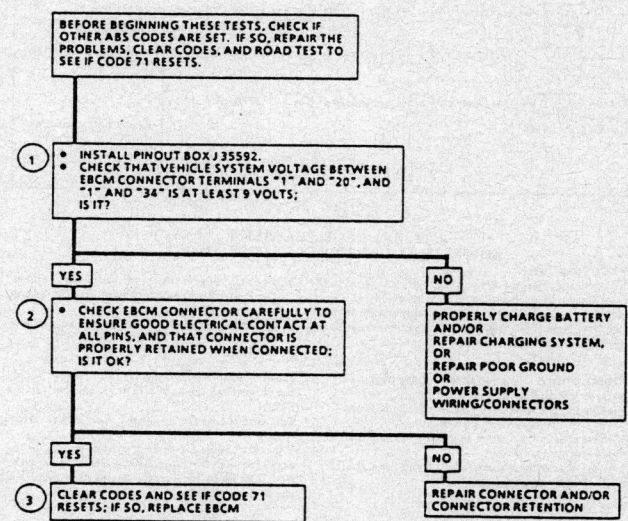

1	RIVET	5	U-NUT
2	BRACKET	6	REAR FLOOR PANEL
3	EBCM RELAY	7	EBCM
4	BRACKET	8	BOLT 2.5 N·m (22 lb. in.)

CODE 71

ELECTRONIC BRAKE CONTROL MODULE (EBCM)
(CONTROL MODULE FAULT)

Circuit Description:

The EBCM performs various diagnostic checks on itself. If it finds a problem, Code 71 will set.

Test Description: Number(s) refer to circled number(s) on the diagnostic chart.

1. This test checks to see if the minimum voltage for proper EBCM operation is available to the EBCM.

2. This test checks for good connections from the harness to the EBCM itself.

3. This test checks to see if the fault was false; if not, replace the EBCM.

Fig. 24   Code 71, Electronic Brake & Traction Control Module (Control module fault). 1991

CORVETTE (BOSCH TYPE)

1 RIVET
2 BRACKET
3 EBCM RELAY
4 BRACKET
5 U-NUT
6 REAR FLOOR PANEL
7 EBCM
8 BOLT 2.5 N·m (22 lb. in.)

CODE 72
ELECTRONIC BRAKE CONTROL MODULE (EBCM)
(SERIAL DATA LINK FAULT)

Circuit Description:
The Serial Data Link is an asynchronous link operating at 8192 bits per second.
Code 72 will set if the EBCM detects three consecutive serial data link messages that are ignored due to errors in transmission. *The "SERVICE ABS" indicator will not be illuminated for this fault.*

Test Description: Number(s) below refer to circled number(s) on the diagnostic chart.
1. This test checks to see if the off-board device can communicate with the EBCM.
2. This test checks for a short to battery in the ABS serial data circuit.
3. This test checks for a short to ground in the ABS serial data circuit.
4. This test checks for an open in the ABS serial data circuit.
5. This test checks to see if the off-board device can communicate with the EBCM.
6. If the connections at the EBCM and ALDL connector are OK, replace the EBCM.

Diagnostic Aids:

The problem may be intermittent. Try performing the tests shown while "wiggling" wiring and connectors; this can often cause the fault to appear.

Fig. 25 Code 72, Electronic Brake & Traction Control Module (Serial data link fault). 1991

CODE 75
LATERAL ACCELEROMETER
(SHORT TO B + OR GROUND, OR OPEN CIRCUIT)

Circuit Description:
The lateral accelerometer circuit provides a signal to the EBCM which reflects the severity of a vehicle turn. This information is used by the EBCM to modify the control of the rear wheel brakes to help prevent loss of control in a turn due to light brake pedal application at speeds above 50 km/h (30 mph).
Code 75 will set if the EBCM senses the lateral accelerometer voltage to be out of its permissible range due to an electrical wiring fault.

Test Description: Number(s) below refer to circled number(s) on the diagnostic chart.
1. This test checks to ensure good connections at the lateral accelerometer and the EBCM.
2. This test checks for a short to ground in the power supply and signal circuits.
3. This test checks for a short to battery in the signal and ground circuits.
4. This test checks for continuity in the power supply circuit through the accelerometer, and back to the EBCM.
5. This test checks for an open in the signal circuit wiring.
6. This test checks for correct voltage supply to the accelerometer from the EBCM. If it is OK, the EBCM must be incorrectly setting this code, and should be replaced.

Fig. 26 Code 75, Lateral accelerometer (Short to B+ or ground, or open circuit). 1991

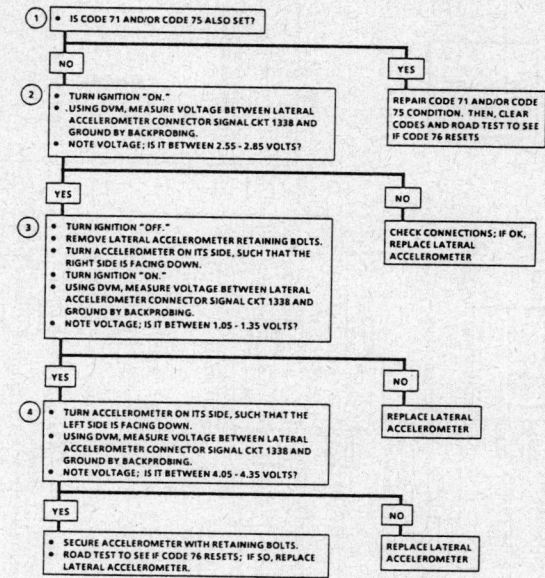

CODE 76
LATERAL ACCELEROMETER
(SIGNAL OUT OF RANGE OR INCORRECT)

Circuit Description:
The lateral accelerometer circuit provides a signal to the EBCM which reflects the severity of a vehicle turn. This information is used by the EBCM to modify the control of the rear wheel brakes to help prevent loss of control in a turn due light brake pedal application at speeds above 50 km/h (30 mph).

Code 76 will be set when the accelerometer signal is greater than 0.6g for 120 seconds or more.

Test Description: Number(s) below refer to circled number(s) on the diagnostic chart.
1. This test checks if another ABS system problem may be causing the Code 76.
2. This test checks for the appropriate accelerometer signal voltage at a 0g (no-turn) condition.
3. This test checks for the appropriate accelerometer signal voltage at a full-scale left hand turn. The full-scale left turn is simulated by the right side of the accelerometer being exposed to the 1g force of gravity.

4. This test checks for the appropriate accelerometer signal voltage at a full-scale right hand turn. The full-scale right turn is simulated by the left side of the accelerometer being exposed to the 1g force of gravity.

Fig. 27   Code 76, Lateral accelerometer (Signal out of range or incorrect). 1991

Fig. 28   Brake warning system wiring diagram.
1991

Fig. 29 ABS system wiring circuit (Part 2 of 5). 1992

Fig. 29 ABS system wiring circuit (Part 1 of 5). 1992

Fig. 29 ABS system wiring circuit (Part 4 of 5). 1992

Fig. 29 ABS system wiring circuit (Part 3 of 5). 1992

Fig. 29   ABS system wiring circuit (Part 5 of 5). 1992

Anti-Lock Brakes–GENERAL MOTORS

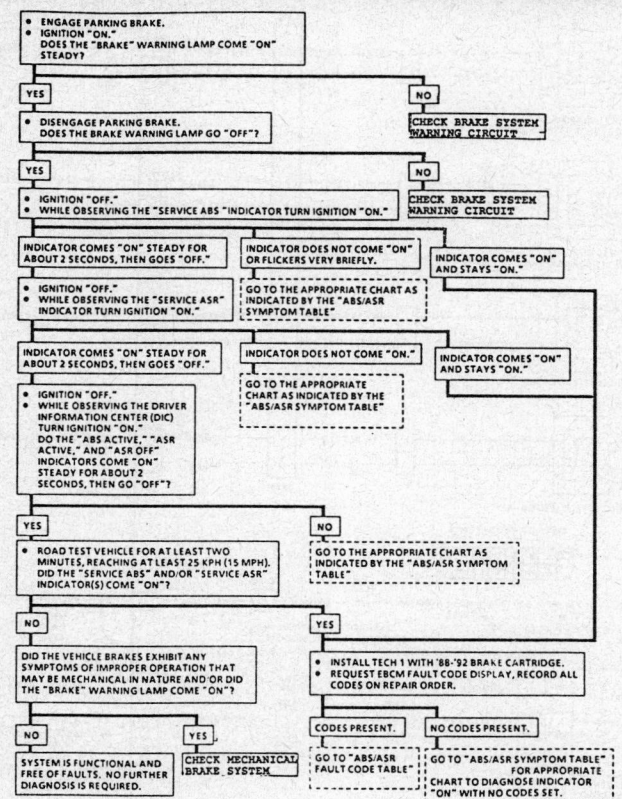

Fig. 30 ABS/ASR functional test. 1992

Fig. 31 ABS system wiring circuit (Part 1 of 6). 1993

Fig. 31 ABS system wiring circuit (Part 2 of 6). 1993

Fig. 31 ABS system wiring circuit (Part 3 of 6). 1993

Fig. 31   ABS system wiring circuit (Part 4 of 6). 1993

Fig. 31   ABS system wiring circuit (Part 5 of 6). 1993

Fig. 31   ABS system wiring circuit (Part 6 of 6). 1993

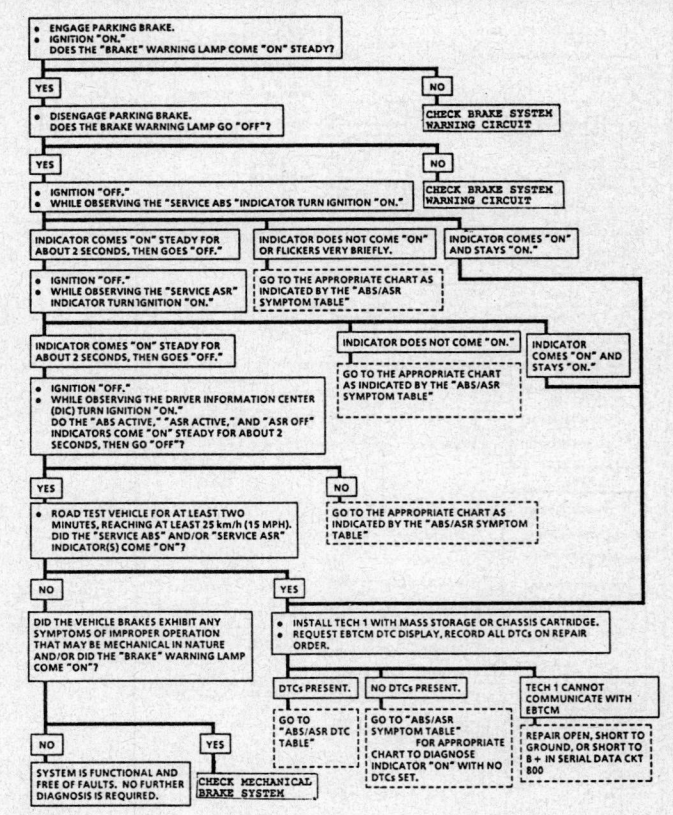

Fig. 32   ABS/ASR functional test. 1993

Code	Definition
21	RF Wheel Speed Sensor Fault
23	RF Wheel Speed Sensor Continuity Fault
25	LF Wheel Speed Sensor Fault
27	LF Wheel Speed Sensor Continuity Fault
28	Wheel Speed Sensor Frequency Error
31	RR Wheel Speed Sensor Fault
33	RR Wheel Speed Sensor Continuity Fault
35	LR Wheel Speed Sensor Fault
37	LR Wheel Speed Sensor Continuity Fault
41	RF Solenoid Valve Fault
44	Pilot Valve Solenoid Fault
45	LF Solenoid Valve Fault
51	RR Solenoid Valve Fault
55	LR Solenoid Valve Fault
57	Cruise Control Output Monitoring Fault
58	EBTCM Internal Adjuster Assembly Fault
61	Pump Motor Or Motor Relay Fault
62	Tach Pulses Fault
63	Valve Solenoid Relay Fault
64	Throttle Position Signal Fault
65	Adjuster Assembly Fault
66	Adjuster Assembly Control Fault
71	EBTCM Fault
72	Serial Data Link Fault
73	Spark Retard Monitoring Fault
74	Low Voltage
75	Lateral Accelerometer Wiring Fault
76	Lateral Accelerometer Signal Out Of Range
83	Brake Fluid Level Low

Fig. 33   Trouble code identification. 1992–93

CHART A
"SERVICE ABS" INDICATOR "ON" WITH NO CODES SET

Test Description: Number(s) below refer to circled number(s) on the diagnostic chart.
1. This test confirms that a fault condition exists.
2. This test determines whether the fault is due to a fault code setting condition, an indicator low side circuit fault, or an EBCM supply power fault.
3. This test determines whether the supply power fault is in the power feed to the EBCM or the ground feed to the EBCM.
4. This test checks whether the power feed fault is due to an open fuse.
5. This test checks for an open power feed circuit.
6. This test checks for an open in the ground feed to the EBCM.
7. This test checks whether the fuse failure is due to a short to ground.

Fig. 34   Chart A, Service ABS indicator on w/no codes set.1992

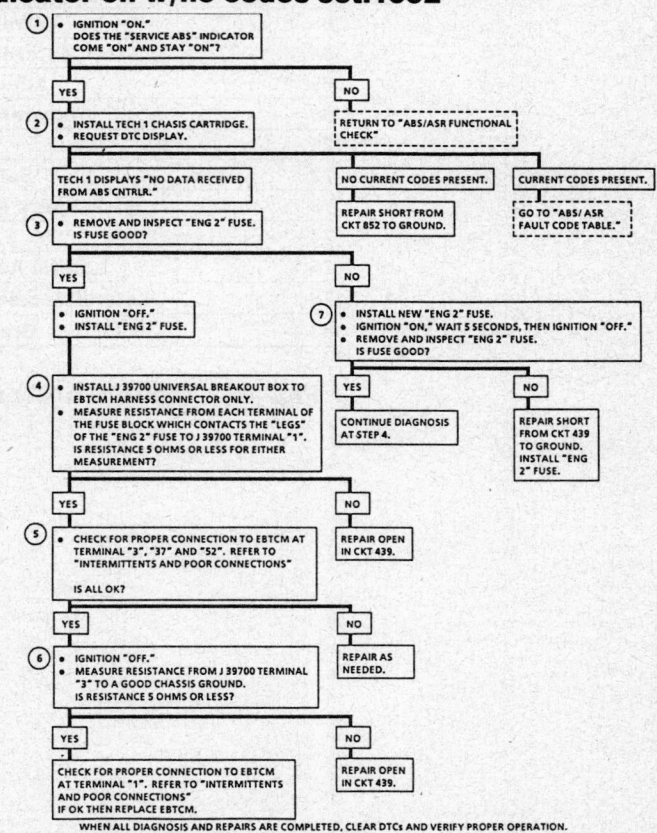

CHART A
"SERVICE ABS" INDICATOR "ON" WITH NO DTCs SET

Test Description: Number(s) below refer to circled number(s) on the diagnostic chart.
1. This test confirms that a malfunction condition exists.
2. This test determines whether the malfunction is due to a DTC setting condition, an indicator low side circuit malfunction, or an EBTCM supply power malfunction.
3. Checks whether the power feed fuse is blown.
4. Checks for an open power feed circuit.
5. Checks for a poor connection of power from harness to EBTCM.
6. Checks for an open in the ground feed to the EBTCM.
7. Checks whether the fuse problem is due to a short to ground.

Fig. 35   Chart A, Service ABS indicator on w/no codes set. 1993

CHART B

"SERVICE ABS" INDICATOR INOPERATIVE OR FLICKERS BRIEFLY AT IGNITION "ON"

Test Description: Number(s) below refer to circled number(s) on the diagnostic chart.
1. This test confirms that a fault condition exists.
2. This test checks the integrity of the indicator bulb.
3. This test checks for an indicator low side circuit open.
4. This test checks for an indicator low side circuit short to B+.
5. This test determines whether the fault is due to an EBCM circuit fault or an open in the DIC printed circuit.

1992

CHART B

"SERVICE ABS" INDICATOR INOPERATIVE OR FLICKERS BRIEFLY AT IGNITION "ON"

Test Description: Number(s) below refer to circled number(s) on the diagnostic chart.
1. This test confirms that a malfunction condition exists.
2. This test checks the integrity of the indicator bulb.
3. This test checks for an indicator low side circuit open.
4. This test checks for an indicator low side circuit short to B+.
5. This test determines whether the malfunction is due to an EBTCM circuit malfunction or an open in the DIC printed circuit.

1993

Fig. 36   Chart B, Service ABS indicator inoperative or flickers w/ignition on (Part 1 of 2)

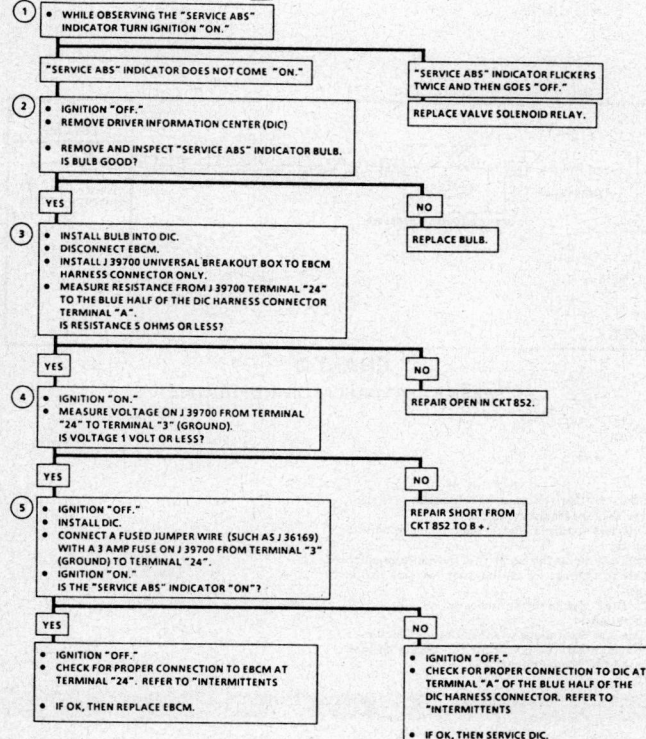

Fig. 36   Chart B, Service ABS indicator inoperative or flickers w/ignition on (Part 2 of 2)

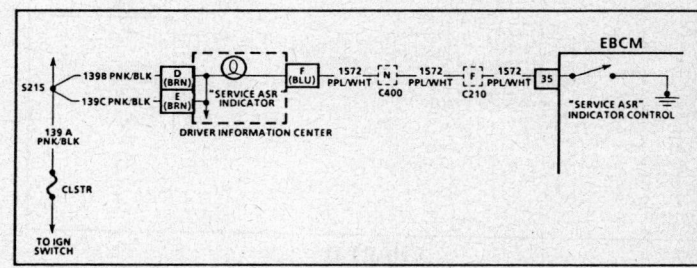

CHART C

"SERVICE ASR" INDICATOR "ON" WITH NO CODES SET

Test Description: Number(s) below refer to circled number(s) on the diagnostic chart.
1. This test confirms that a fault condition exists.
2. This test checks if the fault is due to a fault code setting condition.
3. This test checks whether the fault is due to an indicator low side circuit short to ground or an EBCM circuit fault.

1992

Fig. 37   Chart C, Service ASR indicator on w/no codes set (Part 1 of 2)

CHART C

"SERVICE ASR" INDICATOR "ON" WITH NO DTCs SET

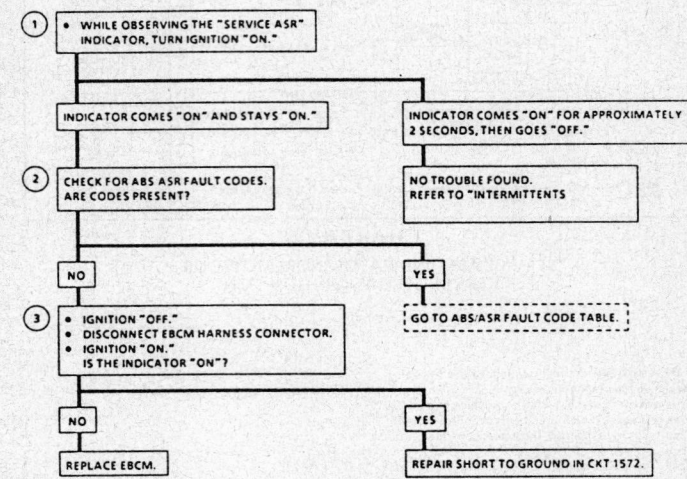

Test Description: Number(s) below refer to circled number(s) on the diagnostic chart.
1. This test confirms that a malfunction condition exists.
2. This test checks if the malfunction is due to a DTC setting condition.
3. This test checks whether the malfunction is due to an indicator low side circuit short to ground or an EBTCM circuit malfunction.

1993

**Fig. 37   Chart C, Service ASR indicator on
w/no codes set (Part 2 of 2)**

CHART D

"SERVICE ASR" INDICATOR INOPERATIVE

Test Description: Number(s) below refer to circled number(s) on the diagnostic chart.
1. This test confirms that a fault condition exists.
2. This test checks the integrity of the indicator bulb.
3. This test checks for an indicator low side circuit open.
4. This test checks for an indicator low side circuit short to B+.
5. This test determines whether the fault is due to an EBCM circuit fault or an open in the DIC printed circuit.

1992

CHART D

"SERVICE ASR" INDICATOR INOPERATIVE

Test Description: Number(s) below refer to circled number(s) on the diagnostic chart.
1. This test confirms that a malfunction condition exists.
2. This test checks the integrity of the indicator bulb.
3. This test checks for an indicator low side circuit open.
4. This test checks for an indicator low side circuit short to B+.
5. This test determines whether the malfunction is due to an EBTCM circuit malfunction or an open in the DIC printed circuit.

1993

**Fig. 38   Chart D, Service ASR indicator
inoperative (Part 1 of 2)**

Fig. 38   Chart D, Service ASR indicator inoperative (Part 2 of 2)

CHART E
"ABS ACTIVE" INDICATOR ALWAYS "ON"

Test Description: Number(s) below refer to circled number(s) on the diagnostic chart.
1. This test confirms that a fault condition exists.
2. This test checks if the fault is due to a fault code setting condition.
3. This test checks whether the fault is due to an indicator low side circuit short to ground or an EBCM circuit fault.

1992

Fig. 39   Chart E, ABS active indicator always on (Part 1 of 2)

CHART E
"ABS ACTIVE" INDICATOR ALWAYS "ON"

Test Description: Number(s) below refer to circled number(s) on the diagnostic chart.
1. This test confirms that a malfunction condition exists.
2. This test checks if the malfunction is due to a DTC setting condition.
3. This test checks whether the malfunction is due to an indicator low side circuit short to ground or an EBTCM circuit malfunction.

1993

Fig. 39   Chart E, ABS active indicator always on (Part 2 of 2)

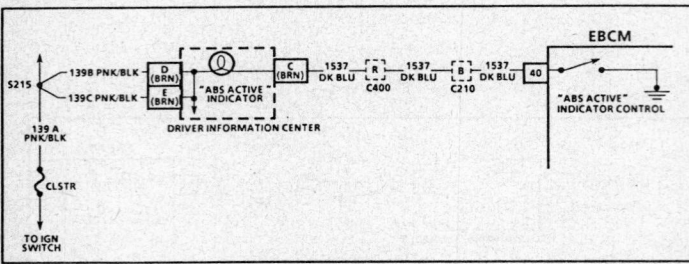

CHART F

"ABS ACTIVE" INDICATOR INOPERATIVE

Test Description: Number(s) below refer to circled number(s) on the diagnostic chart.
1. This test confirms that a fault condition exists.
2. This test checks the integrity of the indicator bulb.
3. This test checks for an indicator low side circuit open.
4. This test checks for an indicator low side circuit short to B+.
5. This test determines whether the fault is due to an EBCM circuit fault or an open in the DIC printed circuit.

1992

CHART F

"ABS ACTIVE" INDICATOR INOPERATIVE

Test Description: Number(s) below refer to circled number(s) on the diagnostic chart.
1. This test confirms that a malfunction condition exists.
2. This test checks the integrity of the indicator bulb.
3. This test checks for an indicator low side circuit open.
4. This test checks for an indicator low side circuit short to B+.
5. This test determines whether the malfunction is due to an EBTCM circuit malfunction or an open in the DIC printed circuit.

1993

Fig. 40   Chart F, ABS active indicator inoperative (Part 1 of 2)

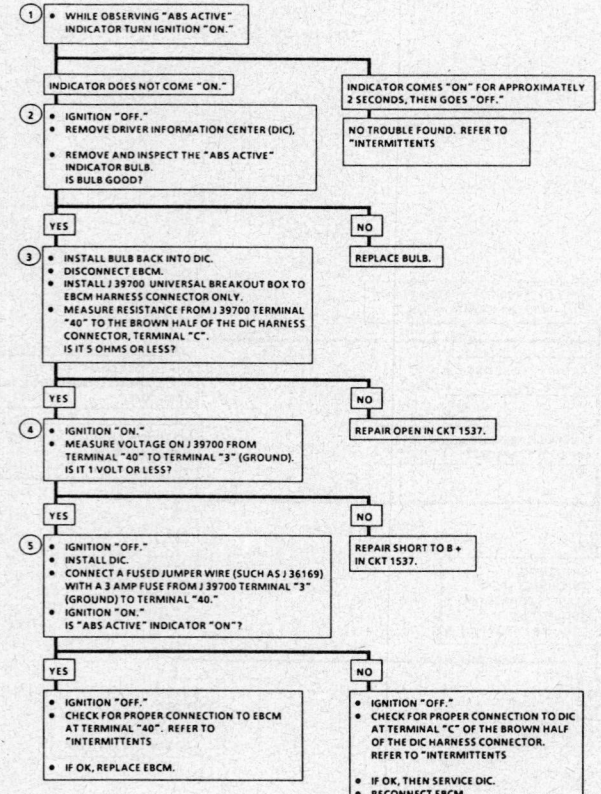

Fig. 40   Chart F, ABS active indicator inoperative (Part 2 of 2)

CHART G

"ASR ACTIVE" INDICATOR "ON" WITH NO CODES SET

Test Description: Number(s) below refer to circled number(s) on the diagnostic chart.
1. This test confirms that a fault condition exists.
2. This test checks whether the fault is due to a fault code setting condition, specifically Code 57.
3. This test determines whether the fault is due to an indicator low side circuit short to ground or stuck contacts in the Cruise Control Cutoff Relay.

1992

Fig. 41   Chart G, ASR active indicator on w/no codes set (Part 1 of 2)

CHART G
"ASR ACTIVE" INDICATOR "ON" WITH NO DTCs SET

Test Description: Number(s) below refer to circled number(s) on the diagnostic chart.
1. This test confirms that a malfunction condition exists.
2. This test checks whether the malfunction is due to a DTC setting condition, specifically DTC 57.
3. This test determines whether the malfunction is due to an indicator low side circuit short to ground or stuck contacts in the cruise control cutoff relay.

1993

Fig. 41 Chart G, ASR active indicator on w/no codes set (Part 2 of 2)

CHART H
"ASR ACTIVE" INDICATOR INOPERATIVE WITH NO CODES SET

Test Description: Number(s) below refer to circled number(s) on the diagnostic chart.
1. This test confirms that a fault condition exists.
2. This test checks whether the fault is due to a fault code setting condition, specifically Code 57.
3. This determines whether the fault is due to stuck contacts in the Cruise Control Cutoff Relay or a fault in the indicator low side circuit.
4. This test checks whether the indicator low side circuit fault is a short to B+.
5. This test checks the integrity of the indicator bulb.
6. This test determines whether the fault is an open in the indicator low side circuit or an open in the DIC printed circuit.

1992

CHART H
"ASR ACTIVE" INDICATOR INOPERATIVE WITH NO DTCs SET

Test Description: Number(s) below refer to circled number(s) on the diagnostic chart.
1. This test confirms that a malfunction condition exists.
2. This test checks whether the malfunction is due to a DTC setting condition, specifically DTC 57.
3. This test determines whether the malfunction is due to stuck contacts in the cruise control cutoff relay or a malfunction in the indicator low side circuit.
4. This test checks whether the indicator low side circuit malfunction is a short to B+.
5. This test checks the integrity of the indicator bulb.
6. This test determines whether the malfunction is an open in the indicator low side circuit or an open in the DIC printed circuit.

1993

Fig. 42 Chart H, ASR active indicator inoperative w/no codes set (Part 1 of 2)

Fig. 42   Chart H, ASR active indicator inoperative w/no codes set (Part 2 of 2)

CHART I
"ASR OFF" INDICATOR ALWAYS "ON"

Test Description: Number(s) below refer to circled number(s) on the diagnostic chart.

1. This test confirms that a fault condition exists.
2. This test checks whether the fault is due to a fault code setting condition.
3. This test determines whether the fault is due to an indicator low side circuit short to ground or an EBCM circuit fault.
4. This test determines whether the extended "ON" time of the indicator is due to an "ASR OFF" input to the EBCM or an EBCM circuit fault.

1992

Fig. 43   Chart I, ASR Off indicator always on (Part 1 of 2)

Fig. 43   Chart I, ASR Off indicator always on (Part 2 of 2)

CHART J
"ASR OFF" INDICATOR INOPERATIVE

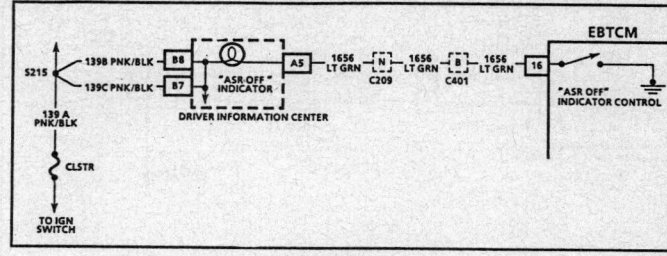

CHART J
"ASR OFF" INDICATOR INOPERATIVE

Test Description: Number(s) below refer to circled number(s) on the diagnostic chart.
1. This test confirms that a fault condition exists.
2. This test checks the integrity of the indicator bulb.
3. This test checks for an indicator low side circuit open.
4. This test checks for an indicator low side circuit short to B+.
5. This test determines whether the fault is due to an EBCM circuit fault or an open in the DIC printed circuit.

Test Description: Number(s) below refer to circled number(s) on the diagnostic chart.
1. This test confirms that a malfunction condition exists.
2. This test checks the integrity of the indicator bulb.
3. This test checks for an indicator low side circuit open.
4. This test checks for an indicator low side circuit short to B+.
5. This test determines whether the malfunction is due to an EBTCM circuit malfunction or an open in the DIC printed circuit.

1992

1993

Fig. 44   Chart J, ASR Off indicator inoperative
(Part 1 of 2)

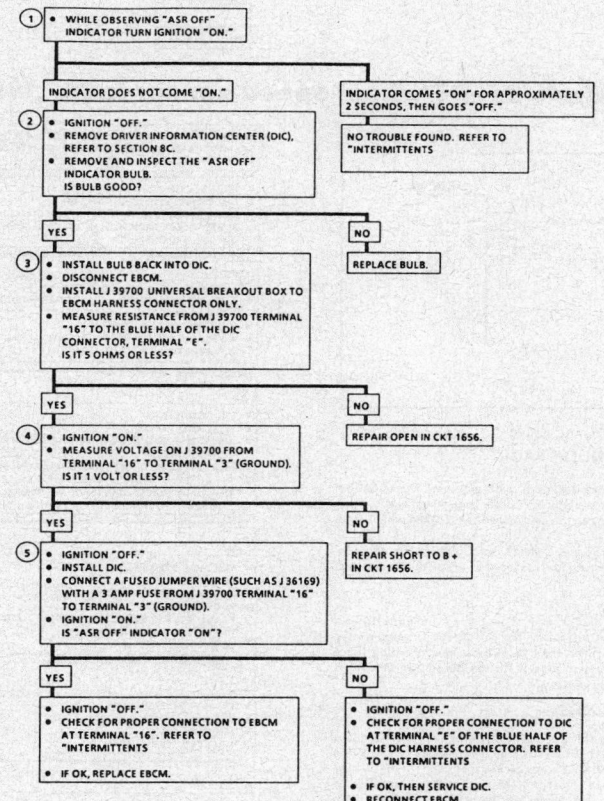

Fig. 44   Chart J, ASR Off indicator inoperative
(Part 2 of 2)

CODE 21
RF WHEEL SPEED SENSOR FAULT

Circuit Description:

The toothed wheel generates a voltage pulse as it moves past the sensor; each tooth-gap-tooth series on the wheel generates these pulses. The frequency of these pulses is used by the EBCM to determine wheel speed. The amount of voltage generated in each pulse depends on the air gap between the sensor and the toothed wheel, and on wheel speed.

The "SERVICE ABS" and "SERVICE ASR" indicators will be "ON" and Code 21 is set if there is a short to voltage or ground in CKT 872 or 833, or a faulty speed sensor. The testing for this fault occurs when the vehicle is in motion; it will not set with the ignition "ON" and the vehicle at rest.

Test Description: Number(s) below refer to circled number(s) on the diagnostic chart.
1. Checks for proper resistance in the sensor itself.
2. Checks for a short to battery in either of the Speed Sensor circuit wires.
3. Checks for a short between the Speed Sensor circuit wires.
4. Checks for a short to ground in the Speed Sensor input circuit wire. The ground may be either a "hard" short to ground, or a resistive (partial) short. A short with a resistance less than 2 megohms, though not a hard short, can still cause Code 21 to set.
5. Checks if the code resets during a road test. If so, since Tests 1-4 have validated that the circuitry and components are good, intermittent problems are suspected.
6. Checks wiring and connectors for intermittents.
7. Replace the Wheel Bearing/Speed Sensor Assembly, as it is likely the cause of a code reset experienced during the road test, since other portions of the circuit have checked out OK. If the code resets after sensor replacement, the EBCM must be concluding there is a problem present in the Speed Sensor circuit when there is not.

Diagnostic Aids:

Be sure the speed sensor wiring is properly routed and retained. This will help prevent false signals due to electrical noise being picked up by the wiring.

It is very important that a thorough inspection of the wiring and connectors be performed. Failure to carefully and fully inspect wiring and connectors may result in misdiagnosis, causing part replacement with reappearance of the fault.

The Tech 1 can also be used to monitor the wheel speeds during a road test. Watch the wheel speeds being displayed on the Tech 1 to see if any of the readings are unusual, such as one sensor varying in speed from the other three, a signal going intermittently high or low, etc. If this does not identify the intermittent, wet the speed sensor harness on the underside of the vehicle and road test monitoring wheel speeds with the Tech 1.

Fig. 45   Code 21, RF wheel speed sensor fault. 1992–93

CODE 23
RF WHEEL SPEED SENSOR CONTINUITY FAULT

Circuit Description:

The toothed wheel generates a voltage pulse as it moves past the sensor; each tooth-gap-tooth series on the wheel generates these pulses. The frequency of these pulses is used by the EBCM to determine wheel speed. The amount of voltage generated in each pulse depends on the air gap between the sensor and the toothed wheel, and on wheel speed.

The "SERVICE ABS" and "SERVICE ASR" indicators will be "ON" and Code 23 is set if there is a short to voltage or an open in CKT 872 or 833, or a faulty speed sensor. The testing for this fault occurs with the ignition "ON" and the vehicle at rest.

Test Description: Number(s) below refer to circled number(s) on the diagnostic chart.
1. Checks for proper resistance in the sensor itself.
2. Checks for a short to battery in either of the Speed Sensor circuit wires.
3. Checks for an open in both the Speed Sensor circuit wires.
4. Manipulates wiring and connectors, trying to induce a intermittent fault not currently present.
5. This test checks if the code resets on key-up. If so, since Tests 1-4 have validated that the circuitry and components are good, the Wheel Bearing/Speed Sensor assembly may be causing the fault.
6. Checks if Code 21 sets during a road test.
7. Code 23 sets when the vehicle is at rest. Code 21 sets with a problem in the Speed Sensor circuitry with the vehicle in motion. If problems are still present, Code 21 would set during the road test, not a 23. If the Code 21 sets at this point, the Code 21 diagnostics should be used.

8. The wheel speed sensor may be causing an intermittent fault. If Code 23 resets after sensor replacement, the EBCM must be concluding there is a problem present in the Speed Sensor circuit when there is not.

Diagnostic Aids:

Be sure the speed sensor wiring is properly routed and retained. This will help prevent false signals due to electrical noise being picked up by the wiring.

It is very important that a thorough inspection of the wiring and connectors be performed. Failure to carefully and fully inspect wiring and connectors may result in misdiagnosis, causing part replacement with reappearance of the fault.

Fig. 46   Code 23, RF wheel speed sensor continuity fault. 1992–93

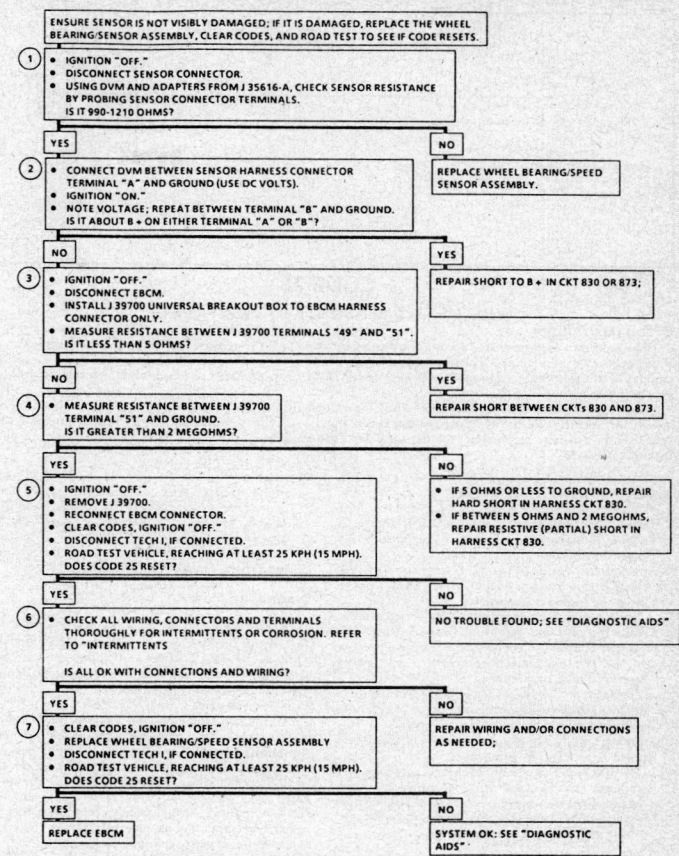

CODE 25
LF WHEEL SPEED SENSOR FAULT

Circuit Description:

The toothed wheel generates a voltage pulse as it moves past the sensor; each tooth-gap-tooth series on the wheel generates these pulses. The frequency of these pulses is used by the EBCM to determine wheel speed. The amount of voltage generated in each pulse depends on the air gap between the sensor and the toothed wheel, and on wheel speed.

The "SERVICE ABS" and "SERVICE ASR" indicators will be "ON" and Code 25 is set if there is a short to voltage or ground in CKT 830 or 873, or a faulty speed sensor. The testing for this fault occurs when the vehicle is in motion; it will not set with the ignition "ON" and the vehicle at rest.

Test Description: Number(s) below refer to circled number(s) on the diagnostic chart.

1. Checks for proper resistance in the sensor itself.
2. Checks for a short to battery in either of the Speed Sensor circuit wires.
3. Checks for a short between the Speed Sensor circuit wires.
4. Checks for a short to ground in the Speed Sensor input circuit wire. The ground may be either a "hard" short to ground, or a resistive (partial) short. A short with a resistance less than 2 megohms, though not a hard short, can still cause Code 25 to set.
5. Checks if the code resets during a road test. If so, since Tests 1-4 have validated that the circuitry and components are good, intermittent problems are suspected.
6. Checks wiring and connectors for intermittents.
7. Replace the Wheel Bearing/Speed Sensor Assembly, as it is likely the cause of a code reset experienced during the road test, since other portions of the circuit have checked out OK. If the code resets after sensor replacement, the EBCM must be concluding there is a problem present in the Speed Sensor circuit when there is not.

Diagnostic Aids:

Be sure the speed sensor wiring is properly routed and retained. This will help prevent false signals due to electrical noise being picked up by the wiring.

It is very important that a thorough inspection of the wiring and connectors be performed. Failure to carefully and fully inspect wiring and connectors may result in misdiagnosis, causing part replacement with reappearance of the fault.

The Tech 1 can also be used to monitor the wheel speeds during a road test. Watch the wheel speeds being displayed on the Tech 1 to see if any of the readings are unusual, such as one sensor varying in speed from the other three, a signal going intermittently high or low, etc. If this does not identify the intermittent, wet the speed sensor harness on the underside of the vehicle and road test monitoring wheel speeds with the Tech 1.

Fig. 47   Code 25, LF wheel speed sensor fault. 1992–93

CODE 27
LF WHEEL SPEED SENSOR CONTINUITY FAULT

Circuit Description:

The toothed wheel generates a voltage pulse as it moves past the sensor; each tooth-gap-tooth series on the wheel generates these pulses. The frequency of these pulses is used by the EBCM to determine wheel speed. The amount of voltage generated in each pulse depends on the air gap between the sensor and the toothed wheel, and on wheel speed.

The "SERVICE ABS" and "SERVICE ASR" indicators will be "ON" and Code 27 is set if there is a short to voltage or an open in CKT 830 or 873, or a faulty speed sensor. The testing for this fault occurs with the ignition "ON" and the vehicle at rest.

Test Description: Number(s) below refer to circled number(s) on the diagnostic chart.

1. Checks for proper resistance in the sensor itself.
2. Checks for a short to battery in either of the Speed Sensor circuit wires.
3. Checks for an open in both the Speed Sensor circuit wires.
4. Manipulates wiring and connectors, trying to induce a intermittent fault not currently present.
5. This test checks if the code resets on key-up. If so, since Tests 1-4 have validated that the circuitry and components are good, the Wheel Bearing/Speed Sensor assembly may be causing the fault.
6. Checks if Code 25 sets during a road test.
7. Code 27 sets when the vehicle is at rest; Code 25 sets with a problem in the Speed Sensor circuitry with the vehicle in motion. If problems are still present, Code 25 would set during the road test, not a 27. If the Code 25 sets at this point, the Code 25 diagnostics should be used.

8. The wheel speed sensor may be causing an intermittent fault. If Code 27 resets after sensor replacement, the EBCM must be concluding there is a problem present in the Speed Sensor circuit when there is not.

Diagnostic Aids:

Be sure the speed sensor wiring is properly routed and retained. This will help prevent false signals due to electrical noise being picked up by the wiring.

It is very important that a thorough inspection of the wiring and connectors be performed. Failure to carefully and fully inspect wiring and connectors may result in misdiagnosis, causing part replacement with reappearance of the fault.

Fig. 48   Code 27, LF wheel speed sensor continuity fault. 1992–93

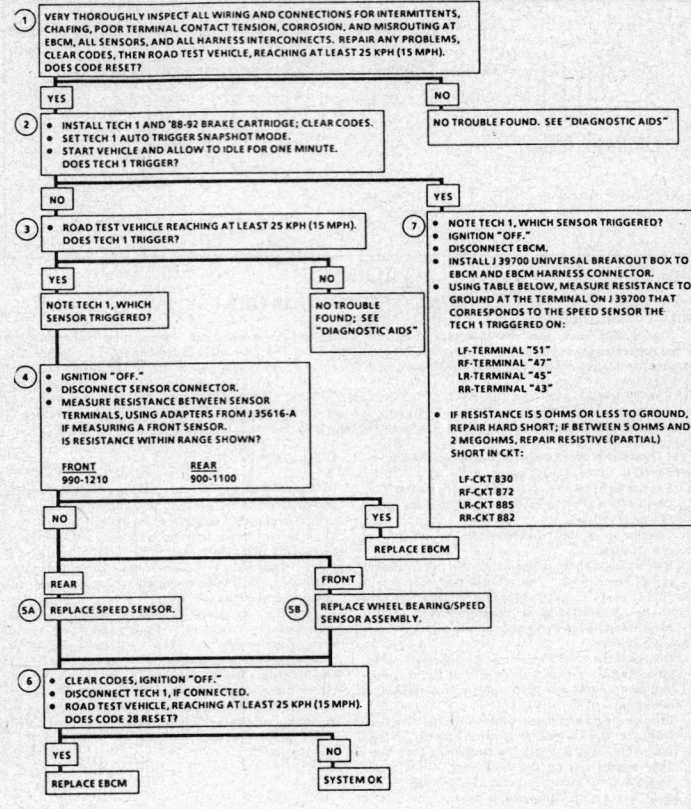

CODE 28
WHEEL SPEED SENSOR FREQUENCY ERROR

Circuit Description:

The toothed wheel generates a voltage pulse as it moves past the sensor; each tooth-gap-tooth series on the wheel generates these pulses. The frequency of these pulses is used by the EBCM to determine wheel speed. The amount of voltage generated in each pulse depends on the air gap between the sensor and the toothed wheel, and on wheel speed.

The "SERVICE ABS" and "SERVICE ASR" indicators will be "ON" and Code 28 is set if the EBCM cannot specifically identify which wheel speed sensor is causing the frequency error problem. If it can define the specific speed sensor causing the problem, the Sensor Fault code associated with the sensor (21, 25, 31, 35) will be set instead of Code 28.

Test Description: Number(s) below refer to circled number(s) on the diagnostic chart.
1. Checks wiring and connections for problems. It is critical that this step is performed thoroughly, as wiring/connector problems are the most likely cause for this code.
2. Uses the Tech 1 to monitor for vehicle electrical/electronic system "noise" being picked up by the speed sensor circuits.
3. Uses the Tech 1 to monitor the wheel speed sensors while the vehicle is operating. If the Tech 1 Auto-Trigger Snapshot mode triggers, the speed sensor or the wiring and/or connectors are going intermittent during the road test.
4. Checks for proper resistance in the sensor itself.
5a. Replace rear wheel speed sensor as the likely cause of the triggering intermittent.
5b. Replace front wheel speed sensor as the likely cause of the triggering intermittent.
6. Uses the Tech 1 to monitor the wheel speed sensors while the vehicle is operating. If the Tech 1 Auto-Trigger Snapshot mode triggers, the EBCM must be concluding there is a problem with wheel speed sensor frequencies when there is not.

7. Checks for a short to ground in the seed sensor input circuit wires. The circuit to be tested depends on which speed sensor triggered the Tech 1. The ground may be either a "hard" short to ground, or a resistive (partial) short. A short with a resistance less than 2 megohms, though not a hard short, can still cause Code 28 to set.

Diagnostic Aids:

Code 28 may be set by running the Tech 1 Auto Test if the throttle angle readings are not updating while in the Data List mode. If this is the case, clear codes, disconnect Tech 1, and road test to at least 25 kph (15 mph) to see if code resets.

Rear Speed Sensors Only:

Check the toothed wheel for any large grooves, gouges, marks, etc. that may influence the tooth's signal at the wheel speed sensor. Also check for a buildup of foreign material in the gaps between teeth in the toothed wheel; this material may cause this fault.

A worn hub/bearing assembly may cause this fault in extreme cases; the bearing play allows the sensor-to-toothed-ring gap to change excessively.

Fig. 49   Code 28, wheel speed sensor frequency error. 1992–93

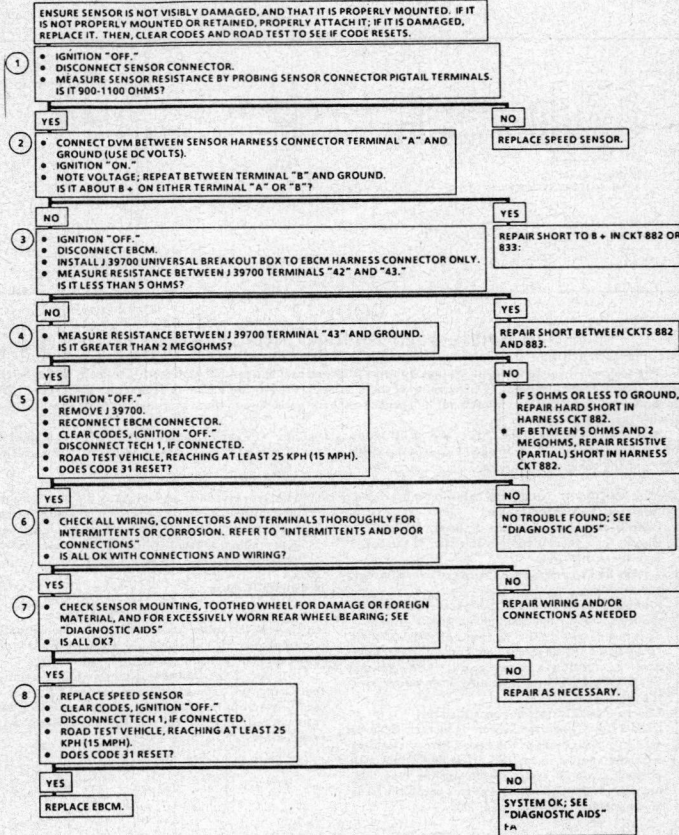

CODE 31
RR WHEEL SPEED SENSOR FAULT

Circuit Description:

The toothed wheel generates a voltage pulse as it moves past the sensor; each tooth-gap-tooth series on the wheel generates these pulses. The frequency of these pulses is used by the EBCM to determine wheel speed. The amount of voltage generated in each pulse depends on the air gap between the sensor and the toothed wheel, and on wheel speed.

The "SERVICE ABS" and "SERVICE ASR" indicators will be "ON" and Code 31 is set if there is a short to voltage or ground in CKT 882 or 883, or a faulty speed sensor. The testing for this fault occurs when the vehicle is in motion; it will not set with the ignition "ON" and the vehicle at rest.

Test Description: Number(s) below refer to circled number(s) on the diagnostic chart.
1. Checks for proper resistance in the sensor itself.
2. Checks for a short to battery in either of the Speed Sensor circuit wires.
3. Checks for a short between the Speed Sensor circuit wires.
4. Checks for a short to ground in the Speed Sensor input circuit wire. The ground may be either a "hard" short to ground, or a resistive (partial) short. A short with a resistance less than 2 megohms, though not a hard short, can still cause Code 31 to set.
5. Checks if the code resets during a road test. If so, since Tests 1-4 have validated that all of the circuitry and components are good, intermittent problems are suspected.
6. Checks wiring and connectors for intermittents.
7. Checks for sensor mounting, toothed wheel, and rear wheel bearing problems which may be causing the problem. Check the toothed wheel for any large grooves, gouges, marks, etc. that might influence the tooth's signal at the wheel speed sensor. Also check for a buildup of foreign material in the gaps between teeth in the toothed wheel; this material may cause this fault.

8. Replace the Speed Sensor Assembly, as it is likely the cause of a code reset experienced during the road test, since other portions of the circuit have checked out OK.

Diagnostic Aids:

A worn hub-bearing assembly may cause this fault in extreme cases; the bearing play allows the sensor-to-toothed-ring gap to change excessively.

Be sure the speed sensor wiring is properly routed and retained. This will help prevent false signals due to electrical noise being picked up by the wiring.

It is very important that a thorough inspection of the wiring and connectors be performed. Failure to carefully and fully inspect wiring and connectors may result in misdiagnosis, causing part replacement with reappearance of the fault.

The Tech 1 can also be used to monitor the wheel speeds during a road test. Watch the wheel speeds being displayed on the Tech 1 to see if any of the readings are unusual, such as one sensor varying in speed from the other three, a signal going intermittently high or low, etc. If this does not identify the intermittent, wet the speed sensor harness on the underside of the vehicle and road test monitoring wheel speeds with the Tech 1.

Fig. 50   Code 31, RR wheel speed sensor fault. 1992–93

CODE 33

RR WHEEL SPEED SENSOR CONTINUITY FAULT

Circuit Description:

The toothed wheel generates a voltage pulse as it moves past the sensor; each tooth-gap-tooth series on the wheel generates these pulses. The frequency of these pulses is used by the EBCM to determine wheel speed. The amount of voltage generated in each pulse depends on the air gap between the sensor and the toothed wheel, and on wheel speed.

The "SERVICE ABS" and "SERVICE ASR" indicators will be "ON" and Code 33 is set if there is a short to voltage or an open in CKT 882 or 883, or a faulty speed sensor. The testing for this fault occurs with the ignition "ON" and the vehicle at rest.

Test Description: Number(s) below refer to circled number(s) on the diagnostic chart.
1. Checks for proper resistance in the sensor itself.
2. Checks for a short to battery in either of the Speed Sensor circuit wires.
3. Checks for an open in both the Speed Sensor circuit wires.
4. Manipulates wiring and connectors, trying to induce a intermittent fault not currently present.
5. This test checks if the code resets on key-up. If so, since Tests 1-4 have validated that the circuitry and components are good, the Speed Sensor may be causing the fault.
6. Checks if Code 31 sets during a road test.
7. Code 31 sets when the vehicle is at rest; Code 33 sets with a problem in the Speed Sensor circuitry with the vehicle in motion. If problems are still present, Code 31 would set during the road test, not a 33. If the Code 33 sets at this point, the Code 31 diagnostics should be used.

8. The wheel speed sensor may be causing an intermittent fault. If Code 33 resets after sensor replacement, the EBCM must be concluding there is a problem present in the Speed Sensor circuit when there is not.

Diagnostic Aids:

Be sure the speed sensor wiring is properly routed and retained. This will help prevent false signals due to electrical noise being picked up by the wiring.

It is very important that a thorough inspection of the wiring and connectors be performed. Failure to carefully and fully inspect wiring and connectors may result in misdiagnosis, causing part replacement with reappearance of the fault.

Fig. 51   Code 33, RR wheel speed sensor continuity fault. 1992–93

CODE 35

LR WHEEL SPEED SENSOR FAULT

Circuit Description:

The toothed wheel generates a voltage pulse as it moves past the sensor; each tooth-gap-tooth series on the wheel generates these pulses. The frequency of these pulses is used by the EBCM to determine wheel speed. The amount of voltage generated in each pulse depends on the air gap between the sensor and the toothed wheel, and on wheel speed.

The "SERVICE ABS" and "SERVICE ASR" indicators will be "ON" and Code 35 is set if there is a short to voltage or ground in CKT 885 or 884, or a faulty speed sensor. The testing for this fault occurs when the vehicle is in motion; it will not set with the ignition "ON" and the vehicle at rest.

Test Description: Number(s) below refer to circled number(s) on the diagnostic chart.
1. Checks for proper resistance in the sensor itself.
2. Checks for a short to battery in either of the Speed Sensor circuit wires.
3. Checks for a short between the Speed Sensor circuit wires.
4. Checks for a short to ground in the Speed Sensor input circuit wire. The ground may be either a "hard" short to ground, or a resistive (partial) short. A short with a resistance less than 2 megohms, though not a hard short, can still cause Code 35 to set.
5. Checks if the code resets during a road test. If so, since Tests 1-4 have validated that all of the circuitry and components are good, intermittent problems are suspected.
6. Checks wiring and connectors for intermittents.
7. Checks for sensor mounting, toothed wheel, and rear wheel bearing problems which may be causing the problem. Check the toothed wheel for any large grooves, gouges, marks, etc. that might influence the tooth's signal at the wheel speed sensor. Also check for a buildup of foreign material in the gaps between teeth in the toothed wheel; this material may cause this fault.

8. Replace the Speed Sensor Assembly, as it is likely the cause of a code reset experienced during the road test, since other portions of the circuit have checked out OK.

Diagnostic Aids:

A worn hub-bearing assembly may cause this fault in extreme cases; the bearing play allows the sensor-to-toothed-ring gap to change excessively.

Be sure the speed sensor wiring is properly routed and retained. This will help prevent false signals due to electrical noise being picked up by the wiring.

It is very important that a thorough inspection of the wiring and connectors be performed. Failure to carefully and fully inspect wiring and connectors may result in misdiagnosis, causing part replacement with reappearance of the fault.

The Tech 1 can also be used to monitor the wheel speeds during a road test. Watch the wheel speeds being displayed on the Tech 1 to see if any of the readings are unusual, such as one sensor varying in speed from the other three, a signal going intermittently high or low, etc. If this does not identify the intermittent, wet the speed sensor harness on the underside of the vehicle and road test monitoring wheel speeds with the Tech 1.

Fig. 52   Code 35, LR wheel speed sensor fault. 1992–93

CODE 37
LR WHEEL SPEED SENSOR CONTINUITY FAULT

Circuit Description:

The toothed wheel generates a voltage pulse as it moves past the sensor; each tooth-gap-tooth series on the wheel generates these pulses. The frequency of these pulses is used by the EBCM to determine wheel speed. The amount of voltage generated in each pulse depends on the air gap between the sensor and the toothed wheel, and on wheel speed.

The "SERVICE ABS" and "SERVICE ASR" indicators will be "ON" and Code 37 is set if there is a short to voltage or an open in CKT 885 or 884, or a faulty speed sensor. The testing for this fault occurs with the ignition "ON" and the vehicle at rest.

Test Description: Number(s) below refer to circled number(s) on the diagnostic chart.

1. Checks for proper resistance in the sensor itself.
2. Checks for a short to battery in either of the Speed Sensor circuit wires.
3. Checks for an open in both the Speed Sensor circuit wires.
4. Manipulates wiring and connectors, trying to induce an intermittent fault not currently present.
5. This test checks if the code resets on key-up. If so, since Tests 1-4 have validated that the circuitry and components are good, the Speed Sensor may be causing the fault.
6. Checks if Code 35 sets during a road test.
7. Code 37 sets when the vehicle is at rest; Code 35 sets with a problem in the Speed Sensor circuitry with the vehicle in motion. If problems are still present, Code 35 would set during the road test, not a 37. If the Code 35 sets at this point, the Code 35 diagnostics should be used.

8. The wheel speed sensor may be causing an intermittent fault. If Code 37 resets after sensor replacement, the EBCM must be concluding there is a problem present in the Speed Sensor circuit when there is not.

Diagnostic Aids:

Be sure the speed sensor wiring is properly routed and retained. This will help prevent false signals due to electrical noise being picked up by the wiring.

It is very important that a thorough inspection of the wiring and connectors be performed. Failure to carefully and fully inspect wiring and connectors may result in misdiagnosis, causing part replacement with reappearance of the fault.

Fig. 53 Code 37, LR wheel speed sensor continuity fault. 1992–93

CODE 41
RF VALVE SOLENOID FAULT

Circuit Description:

The wheel valve solenoid circuits are supplied with battery power when the ignition is "ON." The EBCM controls the valve functions by permitting one of three levels of current flow (0, 2.5, 5 amps) to the solenoid.

If the EBCM senses a discrepancy such as an open or ground in the circuit, the Valve Solenoid Relay will turn "OFF," the "SERVICE ABS" and "SERVICE ASR" lights will come "ON," and Code 41 will set.

Test Description: Number(s) below refer to circled number(s) on the diagnostic chart.

1. Checks the integrity of CKTs 1682 and 1077, the RF Valve Solenoid circuitry internal to the Modulator Valve Solenoid Assembly, and the RF Valve Solenoid coil.
2. Checks for a short to battery in CKT 1682, using EBCM terminal 3 as ground.
3. Checks for a short to ground in CKT 1682, using EBCM terminal 3 as ground.
4. Checks wiring and connectors for intermittents.
5. Uses the Tech 1 to exercise the RF Valve Solenoid and check it for proper operation.
6. Determines whether the code was set by an intermittent condition or an EBCM fault.

7. Determines whether a problem found in Step 1 is due to an open in CKT 1682 or a faulty Modulator Valve Assembly.

Diagnostic Aids:

All tests using J 39700 Universal Breakout Box terminal 3 are using the terminal as ground. These tests, of course, assume that the ground CKT 801 at terminal 3 is good.

If Codes 41 and 45 are both set the fault is likely to be a short to B+ on CKT 1682.

If Codes 41 and 55 are both set the fault is likely to be a short to B+ on CKT 829.

1992

DTC 41
RF VALVE SOLENOID MALFUNCTION

Circuit Description:

The wheel valve solenoid circuits are supplied with battery power when the ignition is "ON." The EBTCM controls the valve functions by permitting one of three levels of current flow (0, 2.5, 5 amps) to the solenoid.

If the EBTCM senses a discrepancy such as an open or ground in the circuit, the valve solenoid relay will turn "OFF," the "SERVICE ABS" and "SERVICE ASR" lights will come "ON," and DTC 41 will set.

Test Description: Number(s) below refer to circled number(s) on the diagnostic chart.

1. Checks the integrity of CKTs 1682 and 1077, the RF valve solenoid circuitry internal to the modulator valve solenoid assembly, and the RF valve solenoid coil.
2. Checks for a short to battery in CKT 1682, using EBTCM terminal "3" as ground.
3. Checks for a short to ground in CKT 1682, using EBTCM terminal "3" as ground.
4. Checks wiring and connectors for intermittents.
5. Uses the Tech 1 to exercise the RF valve solenoid and check it for proper operation.
6. Determines whether the DTC was set by an intermittent condition or an EBTCM malfunction.

7. Determines whether a problem found in Step 1 is due to an open in CKT 1682 or a malfunctioning modulator valve assembly.

Diagnostic Aids:

All tests using J 39700 Universal Breakout Box terminal "3" are using the terminal as ground. These tests, of course, assume that the ground CKT 801 at terminal "3" is good.

If DTCs 41 and 45 are both set the malfunction is likely to be a short to B+ on CKT 1682.

If DTCs 41 and 55 are both set the malfunction is likely to be a short to B+ on CKT 829.

1993

Fig. 54 Code 41, RF solenoid valve fault (Part 1 of 2)

Circuit Description:
The Pilot Valve Solenoid circuit is supplied with battery power when the ignition is "ON." The EBCM controls the valve by grounding the circuit when necessary.

If the EBCM senses a discrepancy such as an open or ground in the circuit, the Valve Solenoid Relay will turn "OFF," the "SERVICE ABS" and "SERVICE ASR" lights will come "ON," and Code 44 will set.

Test Description: Number(s) below refer to circled number(s) on the diagnostic chart.
1. Checks the integrity of CKTs 1683 and 1077, the Pilot Valve Solenoid circuitry internal to the Modulator Valve Assembly, and the Pilot Valve Solenoid coil.
2. Checks for a short to battery in CKT 1683, using EBCM terminal 3 as ground.
3. Checks for a short to ground in CKT 1683, using EBCM terminal 3 as ground.
4. Checks for connector or wiring problems which could cause intermittents.
5. Uses the Tech 1 to exercise the Pilot Valve Solenoid and check it for proper operation.
6. Determines whether the code was set by an intermittent condition or an EBCM fault.
7. Determines whether a problem found in Step 1 is due to an open in CKT 1683 or a faulty Modulator Valve Assembly.

Diagnostic Aids:
All tests using J 39700 Universal Breakout Box terminal 3 are using the terminal as ground. These tests, of course, assume that the ground CKT 801 at terminal 3 is good.

1992

Fig. 55   Code 44, Pilot valve solenoid fault (Part 1 of 2)

Fig. 54   Code 41, RF solenoid valve fault (Part 2 of 2)

Circuit Description:
The pilot valve solenoid circuit is supplied with battery power when the ignition is "ON." The EBTCM controls the valve by grounding the circuit when necessary.

If the EBTCM senses a discrepancy such as an open or ground in the circuit, the valve solenoid relay will turn "OFF," the "SERVICE ABS" and "SERVICE ASR" lights will come "ON," and DTC 44 will set.

Test Description: Number(s) refer to circled number(s) on the diagnostic chart.
1. Checks the integrity of CKTs 1683 and 1077, the pilot valve solenoid circuitry internal to the modulator valve assembly, and the pilot valve solenoid coil.
2. Checks for a short to battery in CKT 1683, using EBTCM terminal "3" as ground.
3. Checks for a short to ground in CKT 1683, using EBTCM terminal "3" as ground.
4. Checks for connector or wiring problems which could cause intermittents.
5. Uses the Tech 1 to exercise the pilot valve solenoid and check it for proper operation.
6. Determines whether the DTC was set by an intermittent condition or an EBTCM malfunction.
7. Determines whether a problem found in Step 1 is due to an open in CKT 1683 or a malfunctioning modulator valve assembly.

Diagnostic Aids:
All tests using J 39700 Universal Breakout Box terminal "3" are using the terminal as ground. These tests, of course, assume that the ground CKT 801 at terminal "3" is good.

1993

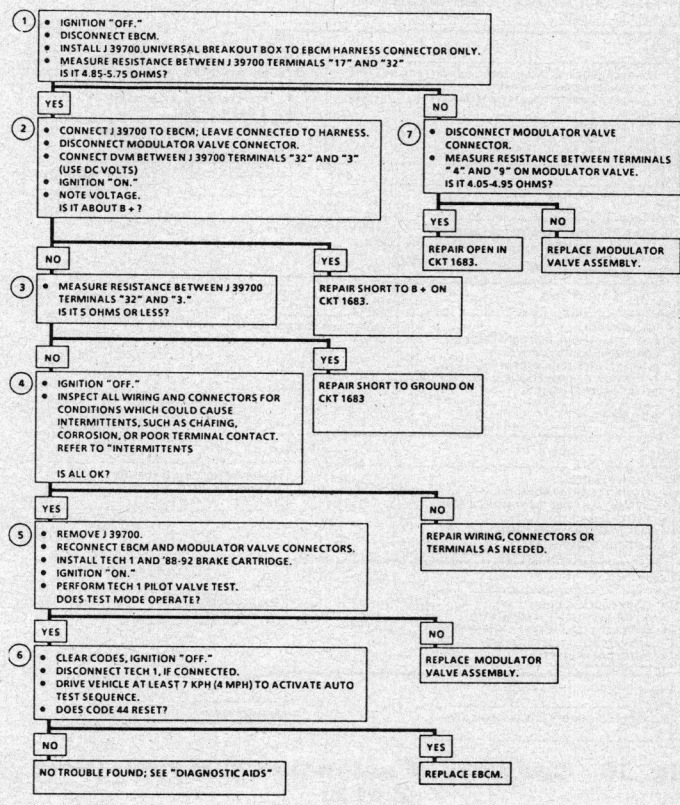

Fig. 55   Code 44, Pilot valve solenoid fault (Part 2 of 2)

CODE 45
LF VALVE SOLENOID FAULT

Circuit Description:
The wheel valve solenoid circuits are supplied with battery power when the ignition is "ON." The EBCM controls the valve functions by permitting one of three levels of current flow (0, 2.5, 5 amps) to the solenoid.

If the EBCM senses a discrepancy such as an open or ground in the circuit, the Valve Solenoid Relay will turn "OFF," the "SERVICE ABS" and "SERVICE ASR" lights will come "ON," and Code 45 will set.

Test Description: Number(s) below refer to circled number(s) on the diagnostic chart.
1. Checks the integrity of CKTs 826 and 1077, the LF Valve Solenoid circuitry internal to the Modulator Valve Assembly, and the LF Valve Solenoid coil.
2. Checks for a short to battery in CKT 826, using EBCM terminal 3 as ground.
3. Checks for a short to ground in CKT 826, using EBCM terminal 3 as ground.
4. Checks wiring and connectors for intermittents.
5. Uses the Tech 1 to exercise the LF Valve Solenoid and check it for proper operation.
6. Determines whether the code was set by an intermittent condition or an EBCM fault.

7. Determines whether a problem found in Step 1 is due to an open in CKT 826 or a faulty Modulator Valve Assembly.

Diagnostic Aids:

All tests using J 39700 Universal Breakout Box terminal 3 are using the terminal as ground. These tests, of course, assume that the ground CKT 801 at terminal 3 is good.
If Codes 41 and 45 are both set the fault is likely to be a short to B + on CKT 826.

Fig. 56   Code 45, LF solenoid valve fault (Part 1 of 2)

DTC 45
LF VALVE SOLENOID MALFUNCTION

Circuit Description:
The wheel valve solenoid circuits are supplied with battery power when the ignition is "ON." The EBTCM controls the valve functions by permitting one of three levels of current flow (0, 2.5, 5 amps) to the solenoid.

If the EBTCM senses a discrepancy such as an open or ground in the circuit, the valve solenoid relay will turn "OFF," the "SERVICE ABS" and "SERVICE ASR" lights will come "ON," and DTC 45 will set.

Test Description: Number(s) below refer to circled number(s) on the diagnostic chart.
1. Checks the integrity of CKTs 826 and 1077, the LF valve solenoid circuitry internal to the modulator valve assembly, and the LF valve solenoid coil.
2. Checks for a short to battery in CKT 826, using EBTCM terminal "3" as ground.
3. Checks for a short to ground in CKT 826, using EBTCM terminal "3" as ground.
4. Checks wiring and connectors for intermittents.
5. Uses the Tech 1 to exercise the LF valve solenoid and check it for proper operation.
6. Determines whether the DTC was set by an intermittent condition or an EBTCM malfunction.

7. Determines whether a problem found in Step 1 is due to an open in CKT 826 or a malfunctioning modulator valve assembly.

Diagnostic Aids:

All tests using J 39700 Universal Breakout Box terminal "3" are using the terminal as ground. These tests, of course, assume that the ground CKT 801 at terminal "3" is good.
If DTCs 41 and 45 are both set the malfunction is likely to be a short to B + on CKT 826.

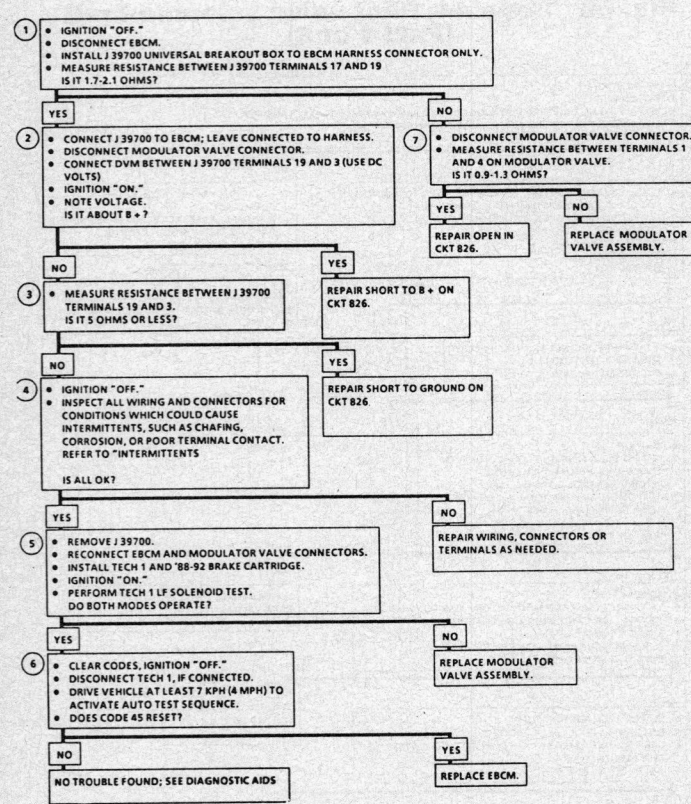

Fig. 56   Code 45, LF solenoid valve fault (Part 2 of 2)

CODE 51
RR VALVE SOLENOID FAULT

Circuit Description:
The wheel valve solenoid circuits are supplied with battery power when the ignition is "ON." The EBCM controls the valve functions by permitting one of three levels of current flow (0, 2.5, 5 amps) to the solenoid.

If the EBCM senses a discrepancy such as an open or ground in the circuit, the Valve Solenoid Relay will turn "OFF," the "SERVICE ABS" and "SERVICE ASR" lights will come "ON," and Code 51 will set.

Test Description: Number(s) below refer to circled number(s) on the diagnostic chart.
1. Checks the integrity of CKTs 827 and 1077, the RR Valve Solenoid circuitry internal to the Modulator Valve Assembly, and the RR Valve Solenoid coil.
2. Checks for a short to battery in CKT 827, using EBCM terminal 3 as ground.
3. Checks for a short to ground in CKT 827, using EBCM terminal 3 as ground.
4. Checks wiring and connectors for intermittents.
5. Uses the Tech 1 to exercise the RR Valve Solenoid and check it for proper operation.

6. Determines whether the code was set by an intermittent condition or an EBCM fault.
7. Determines whether a problem found in Step 1 is due to an open in CKT 827 or a faulty Modulator Valve Assembly.

Diagnostic Aids:

All tests using J 39700 Universal Breakout Box terminal 3 are using the terminal as ground. These tests, of course, assume that the ground CKT 801 at terminal 3 is good.

1992

Fig. 57   Code 51, RR solenoid valve fault (Part 1 of 2)

DTC 51
RR VALVE SOLENOID MALFUNCTION

Circuit Description:

The wheel valve solenoid circuits are supplied with battery power when the ignition is "ON." The EBTCM controls the valve functions by permitting one of three levels of current flow (0, 2.5, 5 amps) to the solenoid.

If the EBTCM senses a discrepancy such as an open or ground in the circuit, the valve solenoid relay will turn "OFF," the "SERVICE ABS" and "SERVICE ASR" lights will come "ON," and DTC 51 will set.

Test Description: Number(s) below refer to circled number(s) on the diagnostic chart.

1. Checks the integrity of CKTs 827 and 1077, the RR valve solenoid circuitry internal to the modulator valve assembly, and the RR valve solenoid coil.
2. Checks for a short to battery in CKT 827, using EBTCM terminal "3" as ground.
3. Checks for a short to ground in CKT 827, using EBTCM terminal "3" as ground.
4. Checks wiring and connectors for intermittents.
5. Uses the Tech 1 to exercise the RR valve solenoid and check it for proper operation.
6. Determines whether the DTC was set by an intermittent condition or an EBTCM chart.
7. Determines whether a problem found in Step 1 is due to an open in CKT 827 or a malfunctioning modulator valve assembly.

Diagnostic Aids:

All tests using J 39700 Universal Breakout Box terminal "3" are using the terminal as ground. These tests, of course, assume that the ground CKT 801 at terminal "3" is good.

1993

Fig. 57 Code 51, RR solenoid valve fault (Part 2 of 2)

CODE 55
LR VALVE SOLENOID FAULT

Circuit Description:

The wheel valve solenoid circuits are supplied with battery power when the ignition is "ON." The EBCM controls the valve functions by permitting one of three levels of current flow (0, 2.5, 5 amps) to the solenoid.

If the EBCM senses a discrepancy such as an open or ground in the circuit, the Valve Solenoid Relay will turn "OFF," the "SERVICE ABS" and "SERVICE ASR" lights will come "ON," and Code 55 will set.

Test Description: Number(s) below refer to circled number(s) on the diagnostic chart.

1. Checks the integrity of CKTs 829 and 1077, the LR Valve Solenoid circuitry internal to the Modulator Valve Assembly, and the LR Valve Solenoid coil.
2. Checks for a short to battery in CKT 829, using EBCM terminal 3 as ground.
3. Checks for a short to ground in CKT 829, using EBCM terminal 3 as ground.
4. Checks wiring and connectors for intermittents.
5. Uses the Tech 1 to exercise the LR Valve Solenoid and check it for proper operation.
6. Determines whether the code was set by an intermittent condition or an EBCM fault.
7. Determines whether a problem found in Step 1 is due to an open in CKT 829 or a faulty Modulator Valve Assembly.

Diagnostic Aids:

All tests using J 39700 Universal Breakout Box terminal 3 are using the terminal as ground. These tests, of course, assume that the ground CKT 801 at terminal 3 is good.

If Codes 41 and 55 are both set the fault is likely to be a short to B + on CKT 829.

1992

DTC 55
LR VALVE SOLENOID MALFUNCTION

Circuit Description:

The wheel valve solenoid circuits are supplied with battery power when the ignition is "ON." The EBTCM controls the valve functions by permitting one of three levels of current flow (0, 2.5, 5 amps) to the solenoid.

If the EBTCM senses a discrepancy such as an open or ground in the circuit, the valve solenoid relay will turn "OFF," the "SERVICE ABS" and "SERVICE ASR" lights will come "ON," and DTC 55 will set.

Test Description: Number(s) below refer to circled number(s) on the diagnostic chart.

1. Checks the integrity of CKTs 829 and 1077, the LR valve solenoid circuitry internal to the modulator valve assembly, and the LR valve solenoid coil.
2. Checks for a short to battery in CKT 829, using EBTCM terminal "3" as ground.
3. Checks for a short to ground in CKT 829, using EBTCM terminal "3" as ground.
4. Checks wiring and connectors for intermittents.
5. Uses the Tech 1 to exercise the LR valve solenoid and check it for proper operation.
6. Determines whether the DTC was set by an intermittent condition or an EBTCM malfunction.
7. Determines whether a problem found in Step 1 is due to an open in CKT 829 or a malfunctioning modulator valve assembly.

Diagnostic Aids:

All tests using J 39700 Universal Breakout Box terminal "3" are using the terminal as ground. These tests, of course, assume that the ground CKT 801 at terminal "3" is good.

If DTCs 41 and 55 are both set the malfunction is likely to be a short to B + on CKT 829.

1993

Fig. 58 Code 55, LR solenoid valve fault (Part 1 of 2)

Fig. 58   Code 55, LR solenoid valve fault (Part 2 of 2)

DTC 57

CRUISE CONTROL OUTPUT MONITORING MALFUNCTION

Circuit Description:
The cruise control output monitoring circuit is used to determine the state of CKT 1679. The cruise control cutoff relay completes the cruise control engage circuit through terminals C2 and A1 when the cruise is requested to be "ON," the brake pedal is not depressed, and there is not an ASR event taking place. Whenever the cruise control cutoff relay is activated by the EBTCM supplying B+ to CKT 1679, the cruise control circuit is opened by the relay switch moving off relay terminal A1.
The "SERVICE ASR" light will come "ON" and DTC 57 will set if CKT 1679 is always high when the EBTCM requests energization of the relay coil, which should take the circuit low.

Test Description: Number(s) below refer to circled number(s) on the diagnostic chart.
1. Checks the relay coil for proper resistance.
2. Checks the integrity of CKT 150 to ground.
3. Checks for an open in CKT 1679.
4. Checks for a short to B+ in CKT 1679, which would keep CKT 1679 high at all times.
5. Checks for an EBTCM-switched short to B+.
6. Checks for recurrence of DTC 57 after checks on other system components and wiring have been made. If the DTC comes back, the EBTCM must be concluding there is a problem present in CKT 1679 when there is not.
7. Checks for proper system operation after malfunctioning relay diagnosed in Step 1 has been replaced.

8. Checks for additional DTC-setting problems other than malfunctioning relay diagnosed in Step 1 and replace in Step 7.

Diagnostic Aids:

All tests using J 39700 Universal Breakout Box terminal "3" are using the terminal as ground. These tests, of course, assume that the ground CKT 801 at terminal "3" is good.
If the "ASR ACTIVE" lamp is always "ON" and cruise control will not engage, the malfunction is likely a short to B+ on CKT 1679.

1993

1992

Fig. 59   Code 57, Cruise control output monitoring fault (Part 1 of 2)

Circuit Description:
The Cruise Control Output Monitoring circuit is used to determine the state of CKT 1679. The Cruise Control Cutoff Relay completes the cruise control engage circuit through terminals C2 and A1 when the cruise is requested to be "ON", the brake pedal is not depressed, and there is not an ASR event taking place. Whenever the Cruise Control Cutoff Relay is activated by the EBCM supplying B+ to CKT 1679, the cruise control circuit is opened by the relay switch moving off relay terminal A1.
The "SERVICE ASR" light will come "ON" and Code 57 will set if CKT 1679 is always high when the EBCM requests energization of the relay coil, which should take the circuit low.

Test Description: Number(s) below refer to circled number(s) on the diagnostic chart.
1. Checks the relay coil for proper resistance.
2. Checks the integrity of CKT 150 to ground.
3. Checks for an open in CKT 1679.
4. Checks for a short to B+ in CKT 1679, which would keep CKT 1679 high at all times.
5. Checks for an EBCM-switched short to B+.
6. Checks for recurrence of Code 57 after checks on other system components and wiring have been made. If the code comes back, the EBCM must be concluding there is a problem present in CKT 1679 when there is not.
7. Checks for proper system operation after faulty relay diagnosed in Step 1 has been replaced.

8. Checks for additional code-setting problems other than faulty relay diagnosed in Step 1 and replace in Step 7.

Diagnostic Aids:

All tests using J 39700 Universal Breakout Box terminal 3 are using the terminal as ground. These tests, of course, assume that the ground CKT 801 at terminal 3 is good.
If the "ASR ACTIVE" lamp is always "ON" and cruise control will not engage, the fault is likely a short to B+ on CKT 1679.

Fig. 59   Code 57, Cruise control output monitoring fault (Part 2 of 2)

CODE 58
EBCM INTERNAL ADJUSTER ASSEMBLY FAULT

Circuit Description:

The EBCM contains a microprocessor for ABS/ASR calculations and functions, as well as a microprocessor for Adjuster Assembly calculations and functions. If the two microprocessors cannot communicate with each other properly, Code 58 will set.

Test Description: Number(s) below refer to circled number(s) on the diagnostic chart.
1. Clears codes and checks for Code 58 reset. If the code resets, the microprocessor communication problem does exist within the EBCM.

Fig. 60   Code 58, EBTCM internal adjuster assembly fault. 1992–93

CODE 61
(1 of 2)
PUMP MOTOR OR PUMP MOTOR RELAY FAULT

Circuit Description:

When the pump motor relay is grounded by the EBCM, it closes and provides B+ to operate the pump. Once the motor circuit is energized, a "Pump ON" signal is sensed by the EBCM through CKT 875 to verify pump operation.

The "SERVICE ABS" and "SERVICE ASR" indicators will be "ON" and Code 61 will set if B+ is present at the pump motor without pump motor relay activation from the EBCM, or if B+ is NOT present at the pump motor within 60 milliseconds after the EBCM requests pump motor relay activation.

Test Description: Number(s) below refer to circled number(s) on the diagnostic chart.
1. Checks the Pump Motor Relay coil for proper resistance.
2. Checks for an open in power feed CKT 2C.
3. Determines if the Pump Motor Relay contacts are stuck closed.
4. Determines if the Pump Motor Relay contacts are stuck open.
5. Checks the integrity of the Pump Motor and Pump Motor Relay circuitry internal to the Modulator Valve Assembly.
6. Checks for an open in CKT 875.
7. Checks for a short to ground in CKT 875.
8. Checks for a short to B+ in CKT 875.

Diagnostic Aids:

All tests using J 39700 Universal Breakout Box terminal 3 are using that terminal as ground. These tests, of course, assume that the ground CKT 801 at terminal 3 is good.

It is very important that a thorough inspection of the wiring and connectors be performed. Failure to carefully and fully inspect wiring and connectors may result in misdiagnosis, causing part replacement with reappearance of the fault.

1992

DTC 61
1 of 2
PUMP MOTOR OR PUMP MOTOR RELAY MALFUNCTION

Circuit Description:

When the pump motor relay is grounded by the EBTCM, it closes and provides B+ to operate the pump. Once the motor circuit is energized, a "Pump ON" signal is sensed by the EBTCM through CKT 875 to verify pump operation.

The "SERVICE ABS" and "SERVICE ASR" indicators will be "ON" and DTC 61 will set if B+ is present at the pump motor without pump motor relay activation from the EBTCM, or if B+ is NOT present at the pump motor within 60 milliseconds after the EBTCM requests pump motor relay activation.

Test Description: Number(s) below refer to circled number(s) on the diagnostic chart.
1. Checks the pump motor relay coil for proper resistance.
2. Checks for an open in power feed CKT 2C.
3. Determines if the pump motor relay contacts are stuck closed.
4. Determines if the pump motor relay contacts are stuck open.
5. Checks the integrity of the pump motor and pump motor relay circuitry internal to the modulator valve assembly.
6. Checks for an open in CKT 875.
7. Checks for a short to ground in CKT 875.
8. Checks for a short to B+ in CKT 875.

Diagnostic Aids:

All tests using J 39700 Universal Breakout Box terminal "3" are using that terminal as ground. These tests, of course, assume that the ground CKT 801 at terminal "3" is good.

It is very important that a thorough inspection of the wiring and connectors be performed. Failure to carefully and fully inspect wiring and connectors may result in misdiagnosis, causing part replacement with reappearance of the malfunction.

1993

Fig. 61   Code 61, Pump motor or motor relay fault (Part 1 of 3)

CODE 61
(2 of 2)
PUMP MOTOR OR PUMP MOTOR RELAY FAULT

Circuit Description:

When the pump motor relay is grounded by the EBCM, it closes and provides B+ to operate the pump. Once the motor circuit is energized, a "Pump ON" signal is sensed by the EBCM through CKT 875 to verify pump operation.

The "SERVICE ABS" and "SERVICE ASR" indicators will be "ON" and Code 61 will set if B+ is present at the pump motor without pump motor relay activation from the EBCM, or if B+ is NOT present at the pump motor within 60 milliseconds after the EBCM requests pump motor relay activation.

Test Description: Number(s) below refer to circled number(s) on the diagnostic chart.
9. Checks for an open in CKT 854.
10. Checks for a short to ground in CKT 854.
11. Checks for a short to B+ in CKT 854.
12. Checks wiring and connectors for intermittents.
13. Uses the Tech 1 to check for proper operation of the Pump Motor and associated circuitry.
14. Determines whether the problem found in Step 13 was due to a faulty EBCM or an open in Pump Motor ground CKT 150.

Diagnostic Aids:

All tests using J 39700 Universal Breakout Box terminal 3 are using that terminal as ground. These tests, of course, assume that the ground CKT 801 at terminal 3 is good.

It is very important that a thorough inspection of the wiring and connectors be performed. Failure to carefully and fully inspect wiring and connectors may result in misdiagnosis, causing part replacement with reappearance of the fault.

1992

Fig. 61   Code 61, Pump motor or motor relay fault (Part 2 of 3)

DTC 61
2 of 2
PUMP MOTOR OR PUMP MOTOR RELAY MALFUNCTION

Circuit Description:

When the pump motor relay is grounded by the EBTCM, it closes and provides B+ to operate the pump. Once the motor circuit is energized, a "Pump ON" signal is sensed by the EBTCM through CKT 875 to verify pump operation.

The "SERVICE ABS" and "SERVICE ASR" indicators will be "ON" and DTC 61 will set if B+ is present at the pump motor without pump motor relay activation from the EBTCM, or if B+ is NOT present at the pump motor within 60 milliseconds after the EBTCM requests pump motor relay activation.

Test Description: Number(s) below refer to circled number(s) on the diagnostic chart.
9. Checks for an open in CKT 854.
10. Checks for a short to ground in CKT 854.
11. Checks for a short to B+ in CKT 854.
12. Checks wiring and connectors for intermittents.
13. Uses the Tech 1 to check for proper operation of the pump motor and associated circuitry.
14. Determines whether the problem found in Step 13 was due to a malfunctioning EBTCM or an open in pump motor ground CKT 150.

Diagnostic Aids:

All tests using J 39700 Universal Breakout Box terminal "3" are using that terminal as ground. These tests, of course, assume that the ground CKT 801 at terminal 3 is good.

It is very important that a thorough inspection of the wiring and connectors be performed. Failure to carefully and fully inspect wiring and connectors may result in misdiagnosis, causing part replacement with reappearance of the malfunction.

1993

```
DIAGNOSIS CONTINUED

9   • IGNITION "OFF."
    • MEASURE RESISTANCE BETWEEN J 39700 TERMINAL 5 AND
      MODULATOR VALVE CONNECTOR TERMINAL 14.
      IS IT 5 OHMS OR LESS?

YES                                          NO

10  • MEASURE RESISTANCE BETWEEN J 39700 TERMINALS 5 AND 3.     REPAIR OPEN IN CKT 854.
      IS IT 5 OHMS OR LESS?

NO                                           YES

11  • CONNECT DVM BETWEEN J 39700 TERMINALS 5 AND 3 (USE DC VOLTS).   REPAIR SHORT TO GROUND IN CKT 854.
    • IGNITION "ON."
    • NOTE VOLTAGE.
      IS IT ABOUT B + ?

NO                                           YES

12  • IGNITION "OFF."                                            REPAIR SHORT TO B + IN CKT 854.
    • INSPECT ALL WIRING AND CONNECTORS FOR CONDITIONS WHICH
      COULD CAUSE INTERMITTENTS, SUCH AS CHAFING, CORROSION, OR
      POOR TERMINAL CONTACT. REFER TO "INTERMITTENTS"

      IS ALL OK?

YES                                          NO

13  • REMOVE J 39700.                                            REPAIR WIRING CONNECTORS, OR TERMINALS
    • RECONNECT EBCM AND MODULATOR VALVE CONNECTORS.             AS NEEDED.
    • INSTALL TECH 1 AND '88-92 BRAKE CARTRIDGE.
    • IGNITION "ON."
    • PERFORM TECH 1 AUTO TEST.
      DOES PUMP MOTOR RUN?

YES                                          NO

NO TROUBLE FOUND; SEE DIAGNOSTIC          14  • IGNITION "OFF."
AIDS                                          • MEASURE RESISTANCE BETWEEN PUMP
                                                MOTOR GROUND STUD AND A GOOD
                                                CHASSIS GROUND.
                                                IS IT 5 OHMS OR LESS?

                                          YES              NO

                                          REPLACE EBCM     REPAIR OPEN
                                                           IN CKT 150.
```

Fig. 61   Code 61, Pump motor or motor relay fault (Part 3 of 3)

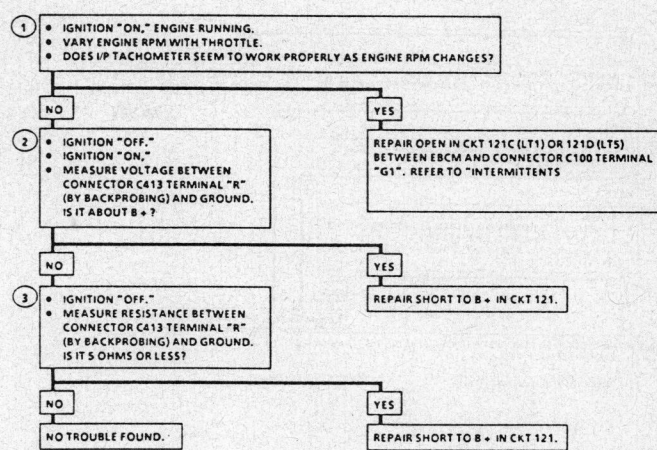

CODE 62
TACH PULSES FAULT

Circuit Description:

The Tach Pulses Circuit provides the EBCM with an indication of engine rpm to help determine ASR control methods and rates when as ASR event takes place.

The "SERVICE ASR" indicator will be "ON" and Code 62 will set if there is a short to ground, short to B+, or an open in CKT 121.

Test Description: Number(s) below refer to circled number(s) on the diagnostic chart.

1. Checks if the instrument panel tachometer works properly. If so, there is likely an open between the common connection point of the I/P tach wiring and the CKT 121 wiring at bulkhead connector C100 terminal "G1".
2. Checks for a short to B+ in CKT 121.
3. Checks for a short to ground in CKT 121.

Diagnostic Aids:

A short to ground in CKT 121 with the LT1 (VIN P) engine may cause driveability problems. If the ground is on the ignition system side of the tach filter, there may be a no-start or extremely poor driveability condition. However, these symptoms do not apply to the LT5 (VIN J) engine.

Fig. 62   Code 62, Tach pulses fault. 1992–93

CODE 63
(1 of 2)
VALVE SOLENOID RELAY FAULT

Circuit Description:

The Valve Solenoid Relay has two functions. When the ignition is "ON" and the EBCM is operating, the relay provides voltage to actuate the Valve Solenoids. However, the Valve Solenoids do not use this voltage unless the EBCM provides the ground. The second function of the Valve Solenoid Relay is to provide a ground path for illumination of the "SERVICE ABS" lamp if the relay loses power or ground.

The "SERVICE ABS" and "SERVICE ASR" indicators will be "ON" and Code 63 will set if the Valve Solenoid Relay voltage falls to less than 5 volts.

Test Description: Number(s) below refer to circled number(s) on the diagnostic chart.

1. Checks for the availability of battery voltage to the Valve Solenoid Relay through Fusible Link J and CKT 2.
2. Checks the Valve Solenoid Relay coil for proper resistance.
3. Checks for the Valve Solenoid Relay contacts being internally open when in the relay-unenergized position.
4. Checks for the Valve Solenoid Relay contacts being stuck open when in the relay-energized position.
5. Checks the integrity of the Valve Solenoid Relay circuitry internal to the Modulator Valve Assembly.
6. Checks for an open in ground CKT 150.
7. Checks for an open in CKT 1077.

Diagnostic Aids:

All tests using J 39700 Universal Breakout Box terminal 3 are using that terminal as ground. These tests, of course, assume that the ground CKT 801 at terminal 3 is good.

It is very important that a thorough inspection of the wiring and connectors be performed. Failure to carefully and fully inspect wiring and connectors may result in misdiagnosis, causing part replacement with reappearance of the fault.

DTC 63
1 of 2
VALVE SOLENOID RELAY MALFUNCTION

Circuit Description:

The valve solenoid relay has two functions. When the ignition is "ON" and the EBTCM is operating, the relay provides voltage to actuate the valve solenoids. However, the valve solenoids do not use this voltage unless the EBTCM provides the ground. The second function of the valve solenoid relay is to provide a ground path for illumination of the "SERVICE ABS" lamp if the relay loses power or ground.

The "SERVICE ABS" and "SERVICE ASR" indicators will be "ON" and DTC 63 will set if the valve solenoid relay voltage falls to less than 5 volts.

Test Description: Number(s) below refer to circled number(s) on the diagnostic chart.

1. Checks for the availability of battery voltage to the valve solenoid relay through the BRAKE HYDRAULICS fuse and CKT 1470.
2. Checks the valve solenoid relay coil for proper resistance.
3. Checks for the valve solenoid relay contacts being internally open when in the relay-unenergized position.
4. Checks for the valve solenoid relay contacts being stuck open when in the relay-energized position.
5. Checks the integrity of the valve solenoid relay circuitry internal to the modulator valve assembly.
6. Checks for an open in ground CKT 150.
7. Checks for an open in CKT 1077.

Diagnostic Aids:

All tests using J 39700 Universal Breakout Box terminal "3" are using that terminal as ground. These tests, of course, assume that the ground CKT 801 at terminal "3" is good.

It is very important that a thorough inspection of the wiring and connectors be performed. Failure to carefully and fully inspect wiring and connectors may result in misdiagnosis, causing part replacement with reappearance of the malfunction.

1992

1993

Fig. 63   Code 63, Valve solenoid relay fault
(Part 1 of 3)

CODE 63
(2 of 2)
VALVE SOLENOID RELAY FAULT

Circuit Description:

The Valve Solenoid Relay has two functions. When the ignition is "ON" and the EBCM is operating, the relay provides voltage to actuate the Valve Solenoids. However, the Valve Solenoids do not use this voltage unless the EBCM provides the ground. The second function of the Valve Solenoid Relay is to provide a ground path for illumination of the "SERVICE ABS" lamp if the relay loses power or ground.

The "SERVICE ABS" and "SERVICE ASR" indicators will be "ON" and Code 63 will set if the Valve Solenoid Relay voltage falls to less than 5 volts.

Test Description: Number(s) below refer to circled number(s) on the diagnostic chart.

8. Checks for a short to ground in CKT 1077.
9. Checks for a short to B+ in CKT 1077.
10. Checks for an open in CKT 1079.
11. Checks for a short to ground in CKT 1079.
12. Checks for an open in CKT 1078.
13. Checks for a short to ground in CKT 1078.
14. Checks wiring and connectors for intermittents.
15. Determines whether the code was set due to an intermittent condition or an EBCM fault.

Diagnostic Aids:

All tests using J 39700 Universal Breakout Box terminal 3 are using that terminal as ground. These tests, of course, assume that the ground CKT 801 at terminal 3 is good.

It is very important that a thorough inspection of the wiring and connectors be performed. Failure to carefully and fully inspect wiring and connectors may result in misdiagnosis, causing part replacement with reappearance of the fault.

1992

Fig. 63   Code 63, Valve solenoid relay fault
(Part 2 of 3)

DTC 63
2 of 2
VALVE SOLENOID RELAY MALFUNCTION

Circuit Description:

The valve solenoid relay has two functions. When the ignition is "ON" and the EBTCM is operating, the relay provides voltage to actuate the valve solenoids. However, the valve solenoids do not use this voltage unless the EBTCM provides the ground. The second function of the valve solenoid relay is to provide a ground path for illumination of the "SERVICE ABS" lamp if the relay loses power or ground.

The "SERVICE ABS" and "SERVICE ASR" indicators will be "ON" and DTC 63 will set if the valve solenoid relay voltage falls to less than 5 volts.

Test Description: Number(s) below refer to circled number(s) on the diagnostic chart.

8. Checks for a short to ground in CKT 1077.
9. Checks for a short to B+ in CKT 1077.
10. Checks for an open in CKT 1079.
11. Checks for a short to ground in CKT 1079.
12. Checks for an open in CKT 1078.
13. Checks for a short to ground in CKT 1078.
14. Checks wiring and connectors for intermittents.
15. Determines whether the DTC was set due to an intermittent condition or an EBTCM malfunction.

Diagnostic Aids:

All tests using J 39700 Universal Breakout Box terminal "3" are using that terminal as ground. These tests, of course, assume that the ground CKT 801 at terminal "3" is good.

It is very important that a thorough inspection of the wiring and connectors be performed. Failure to carefully and fully inspect wiring and connectors may result in misdiagnosis, causing part replacement with reappearance of the malfunction.

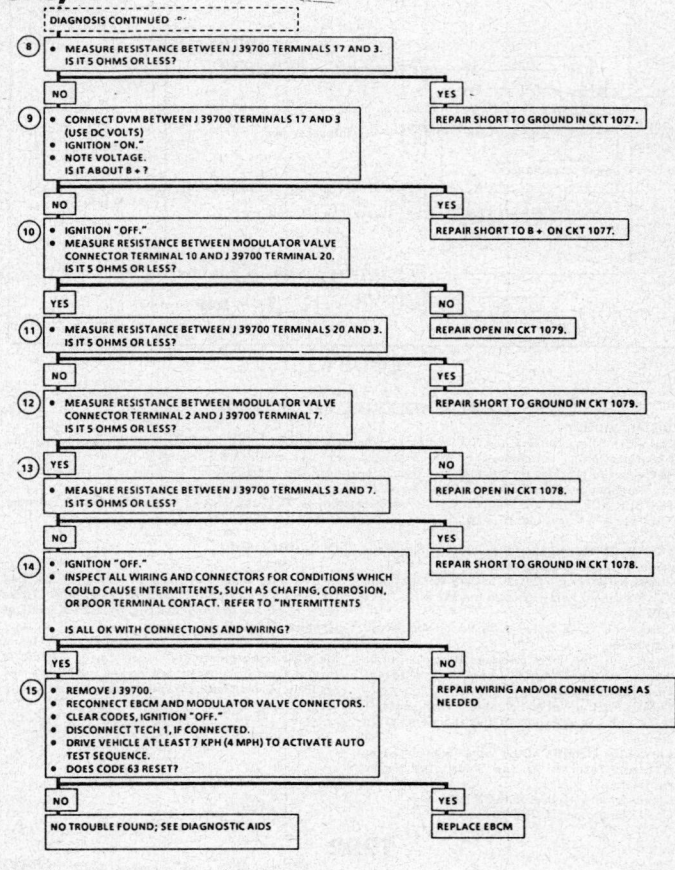

1993

Fig. 63   Code 63, Valve solenoid relay fault
(Part 3 of 3)

CODE 64
(1 of 2)
THROTTLE POSITION SIGNAL FAULT
LT1 ONLY

Circuit Description:

The Throttle Position Signal circuit is used by the EBCM to monitor the actual throttle position versus desired throttle position to monitor and control engine torque during an ASR event. The Throttle Position Sensor Module is used to allow EBCM monitoring of the TPS signal without affecting the TPS signal to the ECM.

Code 64 will set if the EBCM is not receiving reference voltage or a TPS signal from the Throttle Position Sensor Module.

Test Description: Number(s) below refer to circled number(s) on the diagnostic chart.
1. Checks for TPS-related ECM trouble codes. Many of the same conditions which could cause an ASR Code 64 will also cause ECM codes. The ECM codes should be repaired first to eliminate those problems from affecting the ASR Code 64 condition.
2. Checks for a Lateral Accelerometer Code 75. Since the Lateral Accelerometer and the TPS Module share the same ground, a Code 75 likely indicates an open in CKT 1339.
3. Checks for a short to ground in CKT 1689.
4. Checks for a short to ground in CKT 1688.
5. Checks for proper voltage in CKT 1688 at the EBCM connection. (This voltage measurement is only appropriate when the EBCM is disconnected from the circuit.)
6. Checks for proper voltage in CKT 1689 at the EBCM connection. (This voltage measurement is only appropriate when the EBCM is disconnected from the circuit.)
7. Checks for an additional Code 64 problem after ground CKT 1339 is repaired.
8. Determines if a problem found in Step 5 is due to a fuse, CKT 339J, or CKT 1688.
9. Determines if a problem found in Steps 5 and 13 is due to an open in CKT 1688 or a faulty TPS Module.

1992

DTC 64
1 of 2
THROTTLE POSITION SIGNAL MALFUNCTION
LT1 ONLY

Circuit Description:

The throttle position signal circuit is used by the EBTCM to monitor the actual throttle position versus desired throttle position to monitor and control engine torque during an ASR event. The throttle position sensor interface module is used to allow EBTCM monitoring of the TP sensor signal without affecting the TP sensor signal to the ECM.

DTC 64 will set if the EBTCM is not receiving reference voltage or a TP sensor signal from the throttle position sensor interface module.

Test Description: Number(s) below refer to circled number(s) on the diagnostic chart.
1. Checks for TP sensor-related ECM DTCs. Many of the same conditions which could cause an ASR DTC 64 will also cause ECM DTCs. The ECM DTCs should be repaired first to eliminate those problems from affecting the ASR DTC 64 condition.
2. Checks for a lateral accelerometer DTC 75. Since the lateral accelerometer and the TP sensor interface module share the same ground, a DTC 75 likely indicates an open in CKT 1339.
3. Checks for a short to ground in CKT 1689.
4. Checks for a short to ground in CKT 1688.
5. Checks for proper voltage in CKT 1688 at the EBTCM connection. (This voltage measurement is only appropriate when the EBTCM is disconnected from the circuit.)
6. Checks for proper voltage in CKT 1689 at the EBTCM connection. (This voltage measurement is only appropriate when the EBTCM is disconnected from the circuit.)
7. Checks for an additional DTC 64 problem after ground CKT 1339 is repaired.
8. Determines if a problem found in Step 5 is due to a fuse, CKT 339J, or CKT 1688.
9. Determines if a problem found in Steps 5 and 13 is due to an open in CKT 1688 or a malfunctioning TP sensor interface module.

1993

Fig. 64 Code 64, Throttle position signal fault
(Part 1 of 3). LT1

CODE 64
(2 of 2)
THROTTLE POSITION SIGNAL FAULT
LT1 ONLY

Circuit Description:

The Throttle Position Signal circuit is used by the EBCM to monitor the actual throttle position versus desired throttle position to monitor and control engine torque during an ASR event. The Throttle Position Sensor Module is used to allow EBCM monitoring of the TPS signal without affecting the TPS signal to the ECM.

Code 64 will set if the EBCM is not receiving reference voltage or a TPS signal from the Throttle Position Sensor Module.

Test Description: Number(s) below refer to circled number(s) on the diagnostic chart.
10. Checks for an open in CKT 1689.
11. Checks for TPS reference voltage from the ECM at the TPS Module connector.
12. Checks for TPS signal voltage on CKT 808F at the TPS Module connector.
13. Checks for an open in TPS signal ground CKT 474A to the TPS Module connector.
14. Checks for an open in signal ground CKT 1339 to the TPS Module connector.
15. Checks for Code 64 reset after most system components have checked OK.
16. Replaces TPS Module as likely cause of Code reset in Step 15. If the code resets again, the EBCM must be concluding there is a problem present when there is not.

Diagnostic Aids:

It is very important that a thorough inspection of the wiring and connectors be performed. Failure to carefully and fully inspect wiring and connectors may result in misdiagnosis, causing part replacement with reappearance of the fault.

1992

Fig. 64 Code 64, Throttle position signal fault
(Part 2 of 3). LT1

FOR LT1 ONLY

DIAGNOSIS CONTINUED

10
- IGNITION "OFF."
- DISCONNECT TPS MODULE.
- MEASURE RESISTANCE BETWEEN J 39700 TERMINAL "8" AND TPS MODULE CONNECTOR TERMINAL "B", USING ADAPTER FROM J 35616-A.
  IS IT 5 OHMS OR LESS?

YES → **11** | NO → REPAIR OPEN IN CKT 1689.

11
- CONNECT DVM BETWEEN TPS MODULE CONNECTOR TERMINAL "E", USING ADAPTER FROM J 35616-A, AND J 39700 TERMINAL "3" (USE DC VOLTS)
- IGNITION "ON."
- NOTE VOLTAGE.
  IS IT ABOUT 5 VOLTS?

YES → **12** | NO → REPAIR OPEN IN CKT 417A.

12
- CONNECT DVM BETWEEN MODULE CONNECTOR TERMINAL "C" AND J 39700 TERMINAL "3".
- NOTE VOLTAGE.
  IS IT ABOUT 0.5 VOLTS?

YES → **13** | NO → REPAIR OPEN IN CKT 808F.

13
- IGNITION "OFF."
- CONNECT DVM BETWEEN TPS MODULE CONNECTOR TERMINALS "E" AND "C".
- IGNITION "ON."
- NOTE VOLTAGE.
  IS IT ABOUT 0.5 VOLTS?

YES → **14** | NO → REPAIR OPEN IN CKT 474A.

14
- IGNITION "OFF."
- MEASURE RESISTANCE BETWEEN J 39700 TERMINAL "3" AND TPS MODULE CONNECTOR TERMINAL "K".
  IS IT 5 OHMS OR LESS?

YES → **15** | NO → REPAIR OPEN IN CKT 1339 TO SPLICE.

15
- IGNITION "OFF."
- REMOVE J 39700; RECONNECT TPS MODULE.
- CLEAR CODES, IGNITION "OFF."
- DISCONNECT TECH 1, IF CONNECTED.
- IGNITION "ON."
- DOES CODE 64 RESET?

YES → **16** | NO → NO TROUBLE FOUND; SEE "DIAGNOSTIC AIDS"

16
- IGNITION "OFF."
- REPLACE TPS MODULE.
- CLEAR CODES, IGNITION "OFF."
- DISCONNECT TECH 1, IF CONNECTED.
- IGNITION "ON."
- DOES CODE 64 RESET?

YES → REPLACE EBCM | NO → SYSTEM OK

1993

DTC 64
2 of 2
THROTTLE POSITION SIGNAL MALFUNCTION
LT1 ONLY

Circuit Description:
The throttle position signal circuit is used by the EBTCM to monitor the actual throttle position versus desired throttle position to monitor and control engine torque during an ASR event. The throttle position sensor module is used to allow EBTCM monitoring of the TP sensor signal without affecting the TP sensor signal to the ECM.
DTC 64 will set if the EBTCM is not receiving reference voltage or a TP sensor signal from the throttle position sensor interface module.

Test Description: Number(s) below refer to circled number(s) on the diagnostic chart.
10. Checks for an open in CKT 1689.
11. Checks for TP sensor reference voltage from the ECM at the TP sensor interface module connector.
12. Checks for TP sensor signal voltage on CKT 808F at the TP sensor interface module connector.
13. Checks for an open in TP sensor signal ground CKT 474A to the TP sensor interface module connector.
14. Checks for an open in signal ground CKT 1339 to the TP sensor interface module connector.
15. Checks for DTC 64 reset after most system components have checked OK.
16. Replaces TP sensor interface module as likely cause of DTC reset in Step 15. If the DTC resets again, the EBTCM must be concluding there is a problem present when there is not.

Diagnostic Aids:
It is very important that a thorough inspection of the wiring and connectors be performed. Failure to carefully and fully inspect wiring and connectors may result in misdiagnosis, causing part replacement with reappearance of the malfunction.

Fig. 64 Code 64, Throttle position signal fault (Part 3 of 3). LT1

FOR LT5 ONLY

CODE 64
(1 of 2)
THROTTLE POSITION SIGNAL FAULT
LT5 ONLY

Circuit Description:
The Throttle Position Signal circuit is used by the EBCM to monitor the actual throttle position versus desired throttle position to monitor and control engine torque during an ASR event. The Throttle Position Sensor Module is used to allow EBCM monitoring of the TPS signal without affecting the TPS signal to the ECM.
Code 64 will set if the EBCM is not receiving reference voltage or a TPS signal from the Throttle Position Sensor Module.

Test Description: Number(s) below refer to circled number(s) on the diagnostic chart.
1. Checks for TPS-related ECM trouble codes. Many of the same conditions which could cause an ASR Code 64 will also cause ECM codes. The ECM codes should be repaired first to eliminate those problems from affecting the ASR Code 64 condition.
2. Checks for a Lateral Accelerometer Code 75. Since the Lateral Accelerometer and the TPS Module share the same ground, a Code 75 likely indicates an open in CKT 1339.
3. Checks for a short to ground in CKT 1689.
4. Checks for a short to ground in CKT 1688.
5. Checks for proper voltage in CKT 1688 at the EBCM connection. (This voltage measurement is only appropriate when the EBCM is disconnected from the circuit.)
6. Checks for proper voltage in CKT 1689 at the EBCM connection. (This voltage measurement is only appropriate when the EBCM is disconnected from the circuit.)
7. Checks for an additional Code 64 problem after ground CKT 1339 is repaired.
8. Determines if a problem found in Step 5 is due to a fuse, CKT 339J, or CKT 1688.
9. Determines if a problem found in Steps 5 and 13 is due to an open in CKT 1688 or a faulty TPS Module.

1992

FOR LT5 ONLY

DTC 64
1 of 2
THROTTLE POSITION SIGNAL MALFUNCTION
LT5 ONLY

Circuit Description:
The throttle position signal circuit is used by the EBTCM to monitor the actual throttle position versus desired throttle position to monitor and control engine torque during an ASR event. The throttle position sensor module is used to allow EBTCM monitoring of the TP sensor signal without affecting the TP sensor signal to the ECM.
DTC 64 will set if the EBTCM is not receiving reference voltage or a TP sensor signal from the throttle position sensor interface module.

Test Description: Number(s) below refer to circled number(s) on the diagnostic chart.
1. Checks for TP sensor-related ECM DTCs. Many of the same conditions which could cause an ASR DTC 64 will also cause ECM DTCs. The ECM DTCs should be repaired first to eliminate those problems from affecting the ASR DTC 64 condition.
2. Checks for an lateral accelerometer DTC 75. Since the lateral accelerometer and the TP sensor interface module share the same ground, a DTC 75 likely indicates an open in CKT 1339.
3. Checks for a short to ground in CKT 1689.
4. Checks for a short to ground in CKT 1688.
5. Checks for proper voltage in CKT 1688 at the EBTCM connection. (This voltage measurement is only appropriate when the EBTCM is disconnected from the circuit.)
6. Checks for proper voltage in CKT 1689 at the EBTCM connection. (This voltage measurement is only appropriate when the EBTCM is disconnected from the circuit.)
7. Checks for an additional DTC 64 problem after ground CKT 1339 is repaired.
8. Determines if a problem found in Step 5 is due to a fuse, CKT 339J, or CKT 1688.
9. Determines if a problem found in Steps 5 and 13 is due to an open in CKT 1688 or a malfunctioning TP sensor interface module.

1993

Fig. 65 Code 64, Throttle position signal fault (Part 1 of 3). LT5

① IF ECM TPS CODES 21 OR 22 ARE SET, USE THE ECM DIAGNOSTIC CHARTS TO REPAIR THOSE CODES. THEN, CLEAR ECM AND ASR CODES. TURN IGNITION "OFF." DISCONNECT TECH 1, IF CONNECTED. TURN IGNITION "ON." IF ASR CODE 64 RESETS, CONTINUE WITH THIS DIAGNOSTIC CHART.

② IS CODE 75 ALSO SET?

③ • IGNITION "OFF."
• DISCONNECT EBCM.
• INSTALL J 39700 UNIVERSAL BREAKOUT BOX TO EBCM HARNESS CONNECTOR ONLY.
• MEASURE RESISTANCE BETWEEN J 39700 TERMINALS "8" AND "3".
IS IT 5 OHMS OR LESS?

④ • MEASURE RESISTANCE BETWEEN J 39700 TERMINALS "41" AND "3".
IS IT 5 OHMS OR LESS?

⑤ • CONNECT DVM BETWEEN J 39700 TERMINALS "41" AND "3" (USE DC VOLTS).
• IGNITION "ON."
• NOTE VOLTAGE.
IS IT ABOUT 10 VOLTS?

⑥ • CONNECT DVM BETWEEN J 39700 TERMINALS "8" AND "3".
• NOTE VOLTAGE.
IS IT ABOUT 9.5 VOLTS?

⑦ • REPAIR OPEN IN CKT 1339.
• CLEAR CODES, IGNITION "OFF."
• DISCONNECT TECH 1, IF CONNECTED.
• IGNITION "ON."
DOES CODE 64 RESET?

REPAIR SHORT TO GROUND IN CKT 1689.

CONTINUE DIAGNOSTICS AT STEP 3.

SYSTEM OK

REPAIR SHORT TO GROUND IN CKT 1688.

CONTINUE DIAGNOSIS

NO TROUBLE FOUND; SEE "DIAGNOSTIC AIDS"

⑧ • IGNITION "OFF."
• DISCONNECT TPS MODULE.
• CONNECT DVM BETWEEN TPS MODULE CONNECTOR TERMINAL "A" AND J 39700 TERMINAL "3".
• IGNITION "ON."
• NOTE VOLTAGE.
IS IT ABOUT 8 + ?

⑨ • IGNITION "OFF."
• MEASURE RESISTANCE BETWEEN J 39700 TERMINAL "41" AND TPS MODULE CONNECTOR TERMINAL "F".
IS IT 5 OHMS OR LESS?

REPLACE FUSE OR REPAIR OPEN IN CKT 339J.

REPLACE TPS MODULE

REPAIR OPEN IN CKT 1688.

Circuit Description:

The Throttle Position Signal circuit is used by the EBCM to monitor the actual throttle position versus desired throttle position to monitor and control engine torque during an ASR event. The Throttle Position Sensor Module is used to allow EBCM monitoring of the TPS signal without affecting the TPS signal to the ECM.

Code 64 will set if the EBCM is not receiving reference voltage or a TPS signal from the Throttle Position Sensor Module.

Test Description: Number(s) below refer to circled number(s) on the diagnostic chart.
10. Checks for an open in CKT 1689.
11. Checks for TPS reference voltage from the ECM at the TPS Module connector.
12. Checks for TPS signal voltage on CKT 808F at the TPS Module connector.
13. Checks for an open in TPS signal ground CKT 416A to the TPS Module connector.
14. Checks for an open in signal ground CKT 1339 to the TPS Module connector.
15. Checks for Code 64 reset after most system components have checked OK.
16. Replaces TPS Module as likely cause of Code reset in Step 15. If the code resets again, the EBCM must be concluding there is a problem present when there is not.

Diagnostic Aids:

It is very important that a thorough inspection of the wiring and connectors be performed. Failure to carefully and fully inspect wiring and connectors may result in misdiagnosis, causing part replacement with reappearance of the fault.

1992

Fig. 65 Code 64, Throttle position signal fault (Part 2 of 3). LT5

DTC 64

2 of 2

THROTTLE POSITION SIGNAL MALFUNCTION
LT5 ONLY

Circuit Description:

The throttle position signal circuit is used by the EBTCM to monitor the actual throttle position versus desired throttle position to monitor and control engine torque during an ASR event. The throttle position sensor interface module is used to allow EBTCM monitoring of the TP sensor signal without affecting the TP sensor signal to the ECM.

DTC 64 will set if the EBTCM is not receiving reference voltage or a TP sensor signal from the throttle position sensor interface module.

Test Description: Number(s) below refer to circled number(s) on the diagnostic chart.
10. Checks for an open in CKT 1689.
11. Checks for TP sensor reference voltage from the ECM at the TP sensor interface module connector.
12. Checks for TP sensor signal voltage on CKT 808F at the TP sensor interface module connector.
13. Checks for an open in TP sensor signal ground CKT 416A to the TP sensor interface module connector.
14. Checks for an open in signal ground CKT 1339 to the TP sensor interface module connector.
15. Checks for DTC 64 reset after most system components have checked OK.

16. Replaces TP sensor interface module as likely cause of DTC reset in Step 15. If the DTC resets again, the EBTCM must be concluding there is a problem present when there is not.

Diagnostic Aids:

It is very important that a thorough inspection of the wiring and connectors be performed. Failure to carefully and fully inspect wiring and connectors may result in misdiagnosis, causing part replacement with reappearance of the malfunction.

1993

DIAGNOSIS CONTINUED

⑩ • IGNITION "OFF."
• DISCONNECT TPS MODULE.
• MEASURE RESISTANCE BETWEEN J 39700 TERMINAL "8" AND TPS MODULE CONNECTOR TERMINAL "B", USING ADAPTER FROM J 35616-A.
IS IT 5 OHMS OR LESS?

REPAIR OPEN IN CKT 1689.

⑪ • CONNECT DVM BETWEEN TPS MODULE CONNECTOR TERMINAL "E", USING ADAPTER FROM J 35616-A, AND J 39700 TERMINAL "3" (USE DC VOLTS).
• IGNITION "ON."
• NOTE VOLTAGE.
IS IT ABOUT 5 VOLTS?

REPAIR OPEN IN CKT 1689.

⑫ • CONNECT DVM BETWEEN MODULE CONNECTOR TERMINAL "C" AND J 39700 TERMINAL "3".
• NOTE VOLTAGE.
IS IT ABOUT 0.5 VOLTS?

REPAIR OPEN IN CKT 417A.

⑬ • IGNITION "OFF."
• CONNECT DVM BETWEEN TPS MODULE CONNECTOR TERMINALS "E" AND "C".
• IGNITION "ON."
• NOTE VOLTAGE.
IS IT ABOUT 0.5 VOLTS?

REPAIR OPEN IN CKT 808F.

⑭ • IGNITION "OFF."
• MEASURE RESISTANCE BETWEEN J 39700 TERMINAL "3" AND TPS MODULE CONNECTOR TERMINAL "K".
IS IT 5 OHMS OR LESS?

REPAIR OPEN IN CKT 416A.

⑮ • IGNITION "OFF."
• REMOVE J 39700; RECONNECT TPS MODULE.
• CLEAR CODES, IGNITION "OFF."
• DISCONNECT TECH 1, IF CONNECTED.
• IGNITION "ON."
DOES CODE 64 RESET?

REPAIR OPEN IN CKT 1339 TO SPLICE.

⑯ • IGNITION "OFF."
• REPLACE TPS MODULE.
• CLEAR CODES, IGNITION "OFF."
• DISCONNECT TECH 1, IF CONNECTED.
• IGNITION "ON."
DOES CODE 64 RESET?

NO TROUBLE FOUND; SEE "DIAGNOSTIC AIDS"

REPLACE EBCM.

SYSTEM OK.

Fig. 65 Code 64, Throttle position signal fault (Part 3 of 3). LT5

CODE 65

ADJUSTER ASSEMBLY FAULT

Circuit Description:

The Adjuster Assembly circuit provides both power and ground to the Adjuster Assembly to help control engine torque during an ASR event.

Code 65 will set if CKT 1685 or CKT 1686 are shorted to ground, shorted to B+, shorted to each other, or both open at the same time. The ASR system will be disabled for the remainder of the ignition cycle and the "SERVICE ASR" lamp will illuminate.

Test Description: Number(s) below refer to circled number(s) on the diagnostic chart.

1. Checks for proper Adjuster Assembly motor winding resistance.
2. Checks for open(s) in CKT 1685B and/or 1685C.
3. Checks for open(s) in CKT 1686B and/or 1686C.
4. Checks for a short between CKTs 1685 and 1686.
5. Checks for short(s) to B+ in CKT 1685B and/or 1685C.
6. Checks wiring and connectors for intermittents and/or shorts. Information given under "Intermittents and Poor Connections" in SECTION 8A-4 details conditions which can cause intermittents and how to identify them. The Adjuster Assembly requires special wiring repair procedures. Use only the instructions as shown under "Adjuster Assembly Wiring Repair" in this section if wiring repairs on the Adjuster Assembly are needed.

Diagnostic Aids:

It is very important that a thorough inspection of the wiring and connectors be performed. Failure to carefully and fully inspect wiring and connectors may result in misdiagnosis, causing part replacement with reappearance of the fault.

Fig. 66 Code 65, Adjuster assembly fault (Part 1 of 2). 1992

CODE 65

ADJUSTER ASSEMBLY FAULT

Circuit Description:

The Adjuster Assembly circuit provides both power and ground to the Adjuster Assembly to help control engine torque during an ASR event.

Code 65 will set if CKT 1685 or CKT 1686 are shorted to ground, shorted to B+, shorted to each other, or both open at the same time. The ASR system will be disabled for the remainder of the ignition cycle and the "SERVICE ASR" lamp will illuminate.

Test Description: Number(s) below refer to circled number(s) on the diagnostic chart.

7. Checks for short(s) to B+ in CKT 1686B and/or 1686C.
8. Checks for short(s) to ground in CKT 1685B and/or 1685C.
9. Checks for short(s) to ground in CKT 1686B and/or 1686C.
10. Checks for continued code setting after wiring and Adjuster Assembly inspections.
11. Sets throttle to a position which enables one of the EBCM's special monitoring systems of the Adjuster Assembly circuits, checking for a code reset. If the code resets, the EBCM is likely at fault.

12. Checks for shorts to B+ or ground that are EBCM-switched. If you have reached Step 12 for a second time after performing checks for EBCM-switched faults, the EBCM is likely at fault for the code reset.

Diagnostic Aids:

It is very important that a thorough inspection of the wiring and connectors be performed. Failure to carefully and fully inspect wiring and connectors may result in misdiagnosis, causing part replacement with reappearance of the fault.

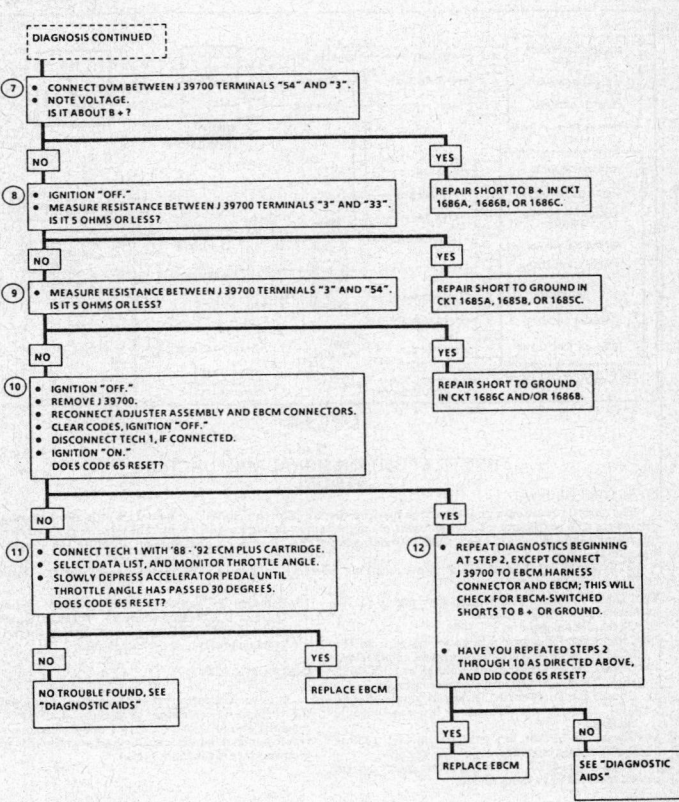

Fig. 66 Code 65, Adjuster assembly fault (Part 2 of 2). 1992

DTC 65
1 of 2
ADJUSTER ASSEMBLY MALFUNCTION

Circuit Description:

The adjuster assembly circuit provides both power and ground to the adjuster assembly to help control engine torque during an ASR event.

DTC 65 will set if CKT 1685 or CKT 1686 are shorted to ground, shorted to B+, shorted to each other, or both open at the same time. The ASR system will be disabled for the remainder of the ignition cycle and the "SERVICE ASR" lamp will illuminate.

Test Description: Number(s) below refer to circled number(s) on the diagnostic chart.

1. Checks for proper adjuster assembly motor winding resistance. It is very important to do the "rotate & release" procedure before measuring to allow the motor to reach the "home" position.
2. Checks for open(s) in CKT 1685B and/or 1685C.
3. Checks for open(s) in CKT 1686B and/or 1686C.
4. Checks for a short between CKTs 1685 and 1686.
5. Checks for short(s) to B+ in CKT 1685B and/or 1685C.
6. Repeats "rotate & release" procedure from Step 1. The adjuster assembly resistance should be 0.5-10 ohms at least once after the "rotate and release" procedure.
7. Sets throttle to a position which enables one of the EBCMs special monitoring systems of the adjuster assembly circuits, checking for a code reset.
8. Checks wiring and connectors for intermittents and/or shorts. Information given under "Intermittents and Poor Connections" conditions which can cause intermittents and how to identify them. The adjuster assembly requires special wiring repair procedures. Use only the instructions as shown "Adjuster Assembly Wiring Repair" section if wiring repairs on the adjuster assembly are needed.

Diagnostic Aids:

It is very important that a thorough inspection of the wiring and connectors be performed. Failure to carefully and fully inspect wiring and connectors may result in misdiagnosis, causing part replacement with reappearance of the fault.

If the "SERVICE ABS," "SERVICE ASR," "ABS ACTIVE," "ASR ACTIVE," and "ASR OFF" indicators all come "ON" when the ignition is turned "ON" but do not turn "OFF" after a few seconds (bulb check). Check for a poor connection or an open in ground CKT 801, especially at the connection point to the engine.

Fig. 67 Code 65, Adjuster assembly fault (Part 1 of 2). 1993

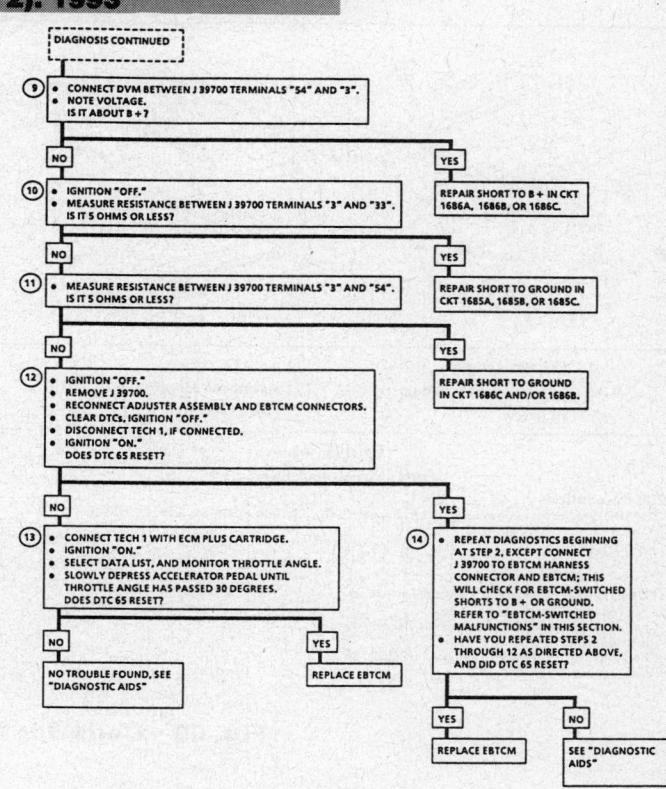

DTC 65
2 of 2
ADJUSTER ASSEMBLY MALFUNCTION

Circuit Description:

The adjuster assembly circuit provides both power and ground to the adjuster assembly to help control engine torque during an ASR event.

DTC 65 will set if CKT 1685 or CKT 1686 are shorted to ground, shorted to B+, shorted to each other, or both open at the same time. The ASR system will be disabled for the remainder of the ignition cycle and the "SERVICE ASR" lamp will illuminate.

Test Description: Number(s) below refer to circled number(s) on the diagnostic chart.

9. Checks for short(s) to B+ in CKT 1686B and/or 1686C.
10. Checks for short(s) to ground in CKT 1685B and/or 1685C.
11. Checks for short(s) to ground in CKT 1686B and/or 1686C.
12. Checks for continued code setting after wiring and adjuster assembly inspections.
13. Sets throttle to a position which enables one of the EBCMs special monitoring systems of the adjuster assembly circuits, checking for a code reset. If the code resets, the EBCM is likely at fault.
14. Checks for shorts to B+ or ground that are EBCM-switched. If you have reached Step 14 for a second time after performing checks for EBCM-switched faults, the EBCM is likely at fault for the code reset.

Diagnostic Aids:

It is very important that a thorough inspection of the wiring and connectors be performed. Failure to carefully and fully inspect wiring and connectors may result in misdiagnosis, causing part replacement with reappearance of the fault.

If the "SERVICE ABS," "SERVICE ASR," "ABS ACTIVE," "ASR ACTIVE," and "ASR OFF" indicators all come "ON" when the ignition is turned "ON" but do not turn "OFF" after a few seconds (bulb check). Check for a poor connection or an open in ground CKT 801, especially at the connection point to the engine.

Fig. 67 Code 65, Adjuster assembly fault (Part 2 of 2). 1993

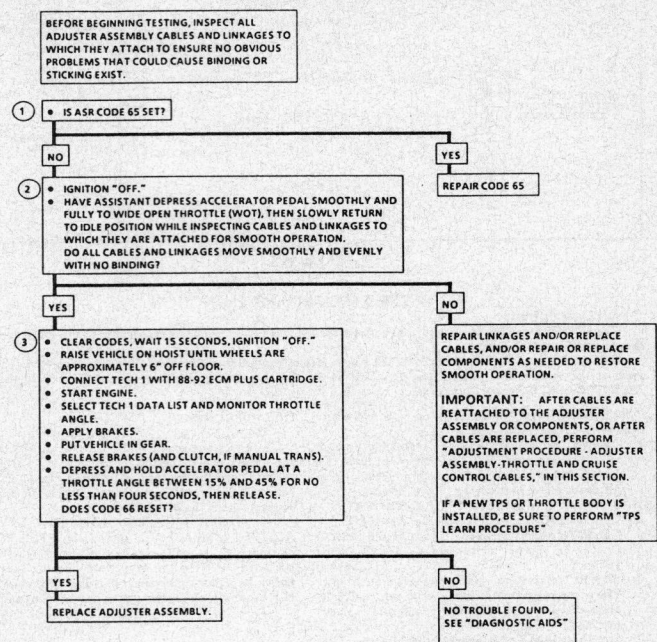

CODE 66
ADJUSTER ASSEMBLY CONTROL FAULT

Circuit Description:

The Adjuster Assembly circuit provides both power and ground to the Adjuster Assembly to help control engine torque during an ASR event.

Code 66 will set if, during an ASR event, the EBCM delivers current greater than 16 amps to the Adjuster Assembly for more than three seconds without the Adjuster Assembly reaching its desired position.

Test Description: Number(s) below refer to circled number(s) on the diagnostic chart.

1. Checks to see if ASR Code 65 is set, since Code 65 conditions might affect Code 66.
2. Checks for any mechanical binding of the Adjuster Assembly, attached cables, and components to which the cables are attached, which could cause excessive load on the Adjuster Assembly.
3. Since Code 66 only sets during an ASR event, this check raises the vehicle on a hoist such that the rear wheels will spin while the fronts do not, inducing the system into attempting ASR control. The throttle angle must be greater than 15%, and less than 50%, and the system must attempt ASR control for greater than 3 seconds to ensure that the code-setting throttle and timing parameters are met when checking for a Code 66 reset.

Diagnostic Aids:

It may be helpful to disconnect all cables from the adjuster assembly and move them manually throughout their entire operating range. Also check the components to which the cables are attached for binding.

💡 Important
- After cables are reconnected to the Adjuster Assembly, perform "Adjustment Procedure-Adjuster Assembly - Accelerator and Cruise Control Cables"

Fig. 68   Code 66, Adjuster assembly control fault. 1992–93

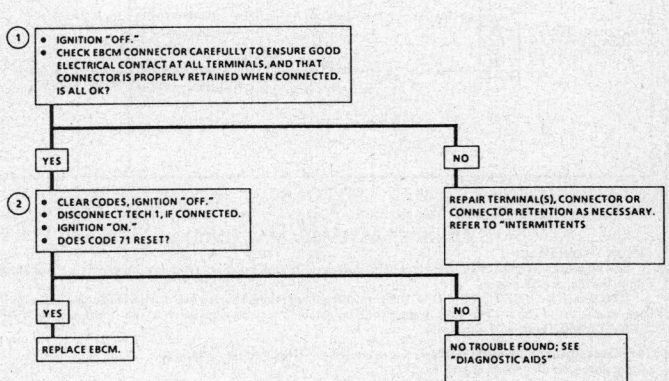

1	MODULATOR VALVE ASSEMBLY
2	ABS/ASR WIRING HARNESS
3	EBCM
4	NUT 10 N·m (89 lb. in.)
5	REAR STORAGE COMPARTMENT - LH
6	EBCM SUPPORT

CODE 71
EBCM INTERNAL FAULT

Circuit Description:

The EBCM performs various diagnostic checks on itself. If it finds a problem, Code 71 will set.

Test Description: Number(s) below refer to circled number(s) on the diagnostic chart.

1. Checks for good connections from the harness to the EBCM itself.
2. Checks to see if the fault was false. If Code 71 resets, replace the EBCM.

Fig. 69   Code 71, EBTCM fault. 1992–93

CODE 72
SERIAL DATA LINK FAULT

Circuit Description:

The Serial Data Link is an asynchronous link operating at 8192 bits per second.

Code 72 will set and the "SERVICE ASR" indicator will illuminate if the EBCM detects three consecutive serial data link messages that are ignored due to errors in transmission.

Test Description: Number(s) below refer to circled number(s) on the diagnostic chart.

1. This test checks to see if the off-board device can communicate with the EBCM. CCM code display mode can also be used to communicate the the EBCM. Refer to "Display ABS/ASR Fault Codes" in SECTION 8D for details. If the CCM cannot communicate with the EBCM, it will display "Err" when the EBCM is selected for code display.
2. This test checks for a short to battery in the ABS/ASR serial data circuit.
3. This test checks for a short to ground in the ABS/ASR serial data circuit.
4. This test checks for an open in the ABS/ASR serial data circuit.
5. This test checks to see if the off-board device can communicate with the EBCM.
6. If the connections at the EBCM and ALDL connector are OK, replace the EBCM.

Diagnostic Aids:

The problem may be intermittent. Try performing the tests shown while "wiggling" wiring and connectors; this can often cause the fault to appear.

CCM Code 41 will likely be set along with this code if the problem is a short to ground or B+ on the Serial Data circuit.

If ABS/ASR Code 72 is set and CCM Code 41 is not, the fault is likely to be an open between the EBCM and the CCM.

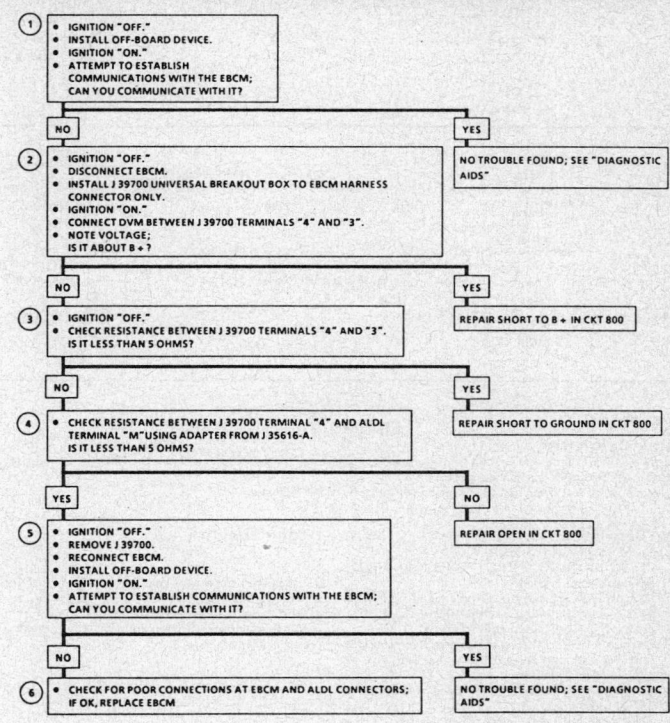

Fig. 70   Code 72, Serial data link fault. 1992–93

CODE 73
SPARK RETARD MONITORING FAULT

Circuit Description:

The EBCM, upon sensing the need for ASR intervention, requests spark retard from the ECM by supplying B+ to CKT 1687.

Code 73 will set if the EBCM senses an open, short to B+, or short to ground on CKT 1687.

Test Description: Number(s) below refer to circled number(s) on the diagnostic chart.

1. Checks for a short to B+ on CKT 1687.
2. Checks for a short to ground on CKT 1687.
3. Checks CKT 1687 and internal ECM circuitry for proper resistance.
4. Checks for code reset after the rest of the system has checked OK.
5. Checks if a problem found in Step 3 is due to an open in CKT 1687 or an internally-faulty ECM.

Diagnostic Aids:

It is very important that a thorough inspection of the wiring and connectors be performed. Failure to carefully and fully inspect wiring and connectors may result in misdiagnosis, causing part replacement with reappearance of the fault.

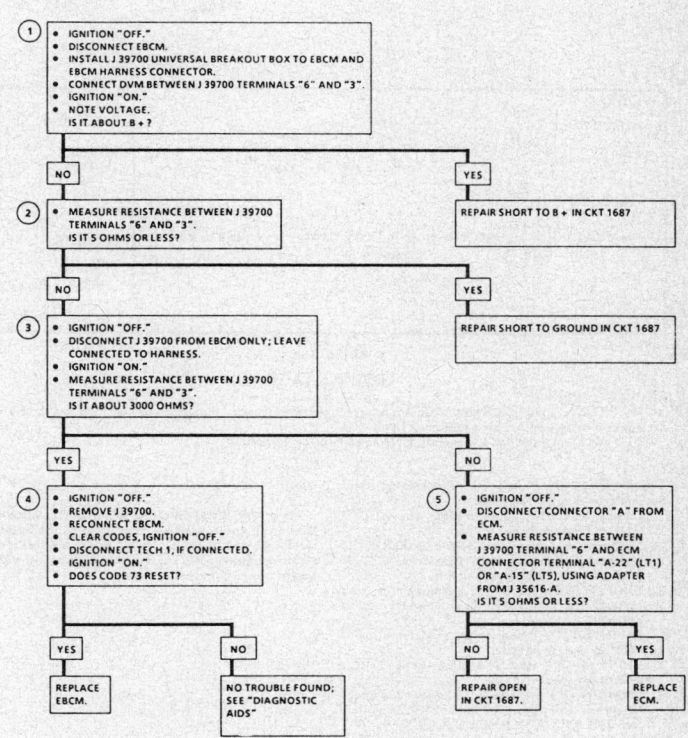

Fig. 71   Code 73, Spark retard monitoring fault. 1992–93

CODE 74
LOW VOLTAGE

Circuit Description:

The EBCM, requires a certain minimum voltage to operate properly. It monitors the ignition feed circuit to determine if voltage fails below a minimum level.

Code 74 will set if the EBCM operating voltage falls below 9.0 volts.

Test Description: Number(s) below refer to circled number(s) on the diagnostic chart.

1. Checks that AIRBAG fuse feeding the EBCM ignition circuit is good.
2. Measures for appropriate voltage from the EBCM ignition circuit, using each of the three EBCM ground lines to complete the circuit.
3. Checks EBCM connector terminals for good contact, i.e. not spread open, backed out of connector, corroded, etc.
4. Checks EBCM connector for good retention to EBCM when installed.
5. Checks for code reset after other portions of the system have tested as OK.
6. Determines if a problem found in Step 2 is due to an open or poor connection in the EBCM Ignition Feed CKT 439, or poor ground(s) in CKT 801.

Diagnostic Aids:

It is very important that a thorough inspection of the wiring and connectors be performed. Failure to carefully and fully inspect wiring and connectors may result in misdiagnosis, causing part replacement with reappearance of the fault.

Fig. 72   Code 74, Low voltage. 1992

DTC 74
LOW VOLTAGE

Circuit Description:

The EBTCM, requires a certain minimum voltage to operate properly. It monitors the ignition feed circuit to determine if voltage fails below a minimum level.

DTC 74 will set if the EBTCM operating voltage falls below 9.0 volts.

Test Description: Number(s) below refer to the circled number(s) on the diagnostic chart.

1. Checks that ENG2 fuse feeding the EBTCM ignition circuit is good.
2. Measures for appropriate voltage from the EBTCM ignition circuit, using each of the three EBTCM ground lines to complete the circuit.
3. Checks EBTCM connector terminals for good contact, i.e. not spread open, backed out of connector, corroded, etc.
4. Checks EBTCM connector for good retention to EBTCM when installed.
5. Checks for DTC reset after other portions of the system have tested as OK.
6. Determines if a problem found in Step 2 is due to an open or poor connection in the EBTCM ignition feed CKT 439, or poor ground(s) in CKT 801.

Diagnostic Aids:

It is very important that a thorough inspection of the wiring and connectors be performed. Failure to carefully and fully inspect wiring and connectors may result in misdiagnosis, causing part replacement with reappearance of the malfunction.

Fig. 73   Code 74, Low voltage. 1993

CODE 75
(1 of 2)
LATERAL ACCELEROMETER WIRING FAULT

Circuit Description:

The Lateral Accelerometer circuitry provides a signal to the EBCM which reflects the severity of a vehicle turn, i.e. the "yaw" forces on the vehicle. The EBCM uses this information to modify the control of the rear wheel brakes, to help prevent loss of control in a turn due to light brake pedal application at speeds above 50 km/h (30 mph).

Code 75 will set if the EBCM senses the Lateral Accelerometer voltage to be out of its permissible range due to an electrical wiring fault.

Test Description: Number(s) below refer to circled number(s) on the diagnostic chart.
1. Checks for an ASR Code 64, which, along with a Code 75, likely indicates an open in CKT 1339.
2. Checks for short to B+ on CKT 1338. The Lateral Accelerometer should also be replaced if this condition is found, since it will be damaged by the fault.
3. Checks for short to B+ on CKT 1337. The Lateral Accelerometer should also be replaced if this condition is found, since it will be damaged by the fault.
4. Checks for a short to ground in CKT 1338.
5. Checks for a short to ground in CKT 1337.
6. Checks for an appropriate supply voltage to the accelerometer from the EBCM, using the EBCM supply and ground terminals. If either is faulty, the supply voltage will not be present; the EBCM should be replaced.
7. Checks for a Code 75 reset after Code 64 conditions are repaired.

Diagnostic Aids:

It is very important that a thorough inspection of the wiring and connectors be performed. Failure to carefully and fully inspect wiring and connectors may result in misdiagnosis, causing part replacement with reappearance of the fault.

All tests using J 39700 Universal Breakout Box terminal 3 are using that terminal as ground. These tests, of course, assume that the ground CKT 801 at terminal 3 is good.

1992

DTC 75
1 of 2
LATERAL ACCELEROMETER WIRING MALFUNCTION

Circuit Description:

The lateral accelerometer circuitry provides a signal to the EBTCM which reflects the severity of a vehicle turn, i.e. the "yaw" forces on the vehicle. The EBTCM uses this information to modify the control of the rear wheel brakes, to help prevent loss of control in a turn due to light brake pedal application at speeds above 50 km/h (30 mph).

DTC 75 will set if the EBTCM senses the lateral accelerometer voltage to be out of its permissible range due to an electrical wiring malfunction.

Test Description: Number(s) below refer to circled number(s) on the diagnostic chart.
1. Checks for an ASR DTC 64, which, along with a DTC 75, likely indicates an open in CKT 1339.
2. Checks for short to B+ on CKT 1338. The lateral accelerometer should also be replaced if this condition is found, since it will be damaged by the malfunction.
3. Checks for short to B+ on CKT 1337. The lateral accelerometer should also be replaced if this condition is found, since it will be damaged by the malfunction.
4. Checks for a short to ground in CKT 1338.
5. Checks for a short to ground in CKT 1337.
6. Checks for an appropriate supply voltage to the accelerometer from the EBTCM, using the EBTCM supply and ground terminals. If either is malfunctioning, the supply voltage will not be present; the EBTCM should be replaced.
7. Checks for a DTC 75 reset after DTC 64 conditions are repaired.

Diagnostic Aids:

It is very important that a thorough inspection of the wiring and connectors be performed. Failure to carefully and fully inspect wiring and connectors may result in misdiagnosis, causing part replacement with reappearance of the malfunction.

All tests using J 39700 Universal Breakout Box terminal "3" are using that terminal as ground. These tests, of course, assume that the ground CKT 801 at terminal "3" is good.

1993

Fig. 74 Code 75, Lateral accelerometer wiring fault (Part 1 of 3)

CODE 75
(2 of 2)
LATERAL ACCELEROMETER WIRING FAULT

Circuit Description:

The Lateral Accelerometer circuitry provides a signal to the EBCM which reflects the severity of a vehicle turn, i.e. the "yaw" forces on the vehicle. The EBCM uses this information to modify the control of the rear wheel brakes, to help prevent loss of control in a turn due to light brake pedal application at speeds above 50 km/h (30 mph).

Code 75 will set if the EBCM senses the Lateral Accelerometer voltage to be out of its permissible range due to an electrical wiring fault.

Test Description: Number(s) below refer to circled number(s) on the diagnostic chart.
8. Checks for short to B+ on CKT 1339.
9. Checks for correct vehicle-stationary (no yaw) signal from the lateral accelerometer.
10. Checks for code reset after most other portions of the system have checked as OK.
11. Replaces Lateral Accelerometer first as likely cause of code reset in Step 8. If Code 75 resets after Lateral Accelerometer replacement, the EBCM must be interpreting a fault condition when none exists.
12. Checks for an appropriate supply voltage to the accelerometer from the EBCM through CKTs 1337 and 1339.
13. Determines if a problem found in Step 11 is due to an open in CKT 1337 or an open in CKT 1339 from the Lateral Accelerometer harness connector up to the CKT 1339 splice to the Throttle Position Sensor Module.
14. Determines if a problem found in Step 11 is due to an open in CKT 1338 or a faulty Lateral Accelerometer.

Diagnostic Aids:

It is very important that a thorough inspection of the wiring and connectors be performed. Failure to carefully and fully inspect wiring and connectors may result in misdiagnosis, causing part replacement with reappearance of the fault.

All tests using J 39700 Universal Breakout Box terminal 3 are using that terminal as ground. These tests, of course, assume that the ground CKT 801 at terminal "3" is good.

1992

Fig. 74 Code 75, Lateral accelerometer wiring fault (Part 2 of 3)

DTC 75
2 of 2
LATERAL ACCELEROMETER WIRING MALFUNCTION

Circuit Description:

The lateral accelerometer circuitry provides a signal to the EBTCM which reflects the severity of a vehicle turn, i.e. the "yaw" forces on the vehicle. The EBTCM uses this information to modify the control of the rear wheel brakes, to help prevent loss of control in a turn due to light brake pedal application at speeds above 50 km/h (30 mph).

DTC 75 will set if the EBTCM senses the lateral accelerometer voltage to be out of its permissible range due to an electrical wiring malfunction.

Test Description: Number(s) below refer to circled number(s) on the diagnostic chart.

8. Checks for short to B + on CKT 1339.
9. Checks for correct vehicle-stationary (no yaw) signal from the lateral accelerometer.
10. Checks for DTC reset after most other portions of the system have checked as OK.
11. Replaces lateral accelerometer first as likely cause of DTC reset in Step 8. If DTC 75 resets after lateral accelerometer replacement, the EBTCM must be interpreting a malfaction condition when none exists.
12. Checks for an appropriate supply voltage to the accelerometer from the EBTCM through CKTs 1337 and 1339.
13. Determines if a problem found in Step 11 is due to an open in CKT 1337 or an open in CKT 1339 from the lateral accelerometer harness connector up to the CKT 1339 splice to the throttle position sensor interface module.
14. Determines if a problem found in Step 11 is due to an open in CKT 1338 or a malfunctioning lateral accelerometer.

Diagnostic Aids:

It is very important that a thorough inspection of the wiring and connectors be performed. Failure to carefully and fully inspect wiring and connectors may result in misdiagnosis, causing part replacement with reappearance of the malfunction.

All tests using J 39700 Universal Breakout Box terminal "3" are using that terminal as ground. These tests, of course, assume that the ground CKT 801 at terminal "3" is good.

1993

Fig. 74   Code 75, Lateral accelerometer wiring fault (Part 3 of 3)

CODE 76
(1 of 2)
LATERAL ACCELEROMETER SIGNAL OUT OF RANGE

Circuit Description:

The Lateral Accelerometer circuitry provides a signal to the EBCM which reflects the severity of a vehicle turn, i.e. the "yaw" forces on the vehicle. The EBCM uses this information to modify the control of the rear wheel brakes, to help prevent loss of control in a turn due to light brake pedal application at speeds above 50 km/h (30 mph).

Code 76 will set when the Lateral Accelerometer signal is out of range for 7.5 minutes or more.

Test Description: Number(s) below refer to circled number(s) on the diagnostic chart.

1. Checks if another ABS/ASR system code may be causing the Code 76 to set.
2. Checks for appropriate signal voltage at a 0g (no-turn, stationary) condition.
3. Checks for appropriate signal voltage for a full-scale left-hand turn. The full-scale left turn is simulated by the right side of the Lateral Accelerometer being exposed to the 1g force of gravity.
4. Repairs other ABS/ASR code problems that may affect Code 76, then checks for Code 76 reset.
5. Checks wiring and connectors for intermittents and/or shorts.
6. Checks for Code 76 reset after Lateral Accelerometer is replaced; Lateral Accelerometer is causing problem noted in Step 2, since Code 75 would identify other problems that could cause Step 2 to measure incorrectly, and the existence of Code 75 was eliminated in Step 1. If Code 76 resets after Lateral Accelerometer replacement, the EBCM is interpreting a problem when it should not be.

Diagnostic Aids:

It is very important that a thorough inspection of the wiring and connectors be performed. Failure to carefully and fully inspect wiring and connectors may result in misdiagnosis, causing part replacement with reappearance of the fault.

It is possible that the customer may complain of pedal pulsation during normal straight-line braking if the Lateral Accelerometer has failed.

1992

DTC 76
1 of 2
LATERAL ACCELEROMETER SIGNAL OUT OF RANGE

Circuit Description:

The lateral accelerometer circuitry provides a signal to the EBTCM which reflects the severity of a vehicle turn, i.e. the "yaw" forces on the vehicle. The EBTCM uses this information to modify the control of the rear wheel brakes, to help prevent loss of control in a turn due to light brake pedal application at speeds above 50 km/h (30 mph).

DTC 76 will set when the lateral accelerometer signal is out of range for 7.5 minutes or more.

Test Description: Number(s) below refer to circled number(s) on the diagnostic chart.

1. Checks if another ABS/ASR system DTC may be causing the DTC 76 to set.
2. Checks for appropriate signal voltage at a 0g (no-turn, stationary) condition.
3. Checks for appropriate signal voltage for a full-scale left-hand turn. The full-scale left turn is simulated by the right side of the lateral accelerometer being exposed to the 1g force of gravity.
4. Repairs other ABS/ASR code problems that may affect DTC 76, then checks for DTC 76 reset.
5. Checks wiring and connectors for intermittents and/or shorts.
6. Checks for DTC 76 reset after lateral accelerometer is replaced; lateral accelerometer is causing problem noted in Step 2, since DTC 75 would identify other problems that could cause Step 2 to measure incorrectly, and the existence of DTC 75 was eliminated in Step 1. If DTC 76 resets after lateral accelerometer replacement, the EBTCM is interpreting a problem when it should not be.

Diagnostic Aids:

It is very important that a thorough inspection of the wiring and connectors be performed. Failure to carefully and fully inspect wiring and connectors may result in misdiagnosis, causing part replacement with reappearance of the malfunction.

It is possible that the customer may complain of pedal pulsation during normal straight-line braking if the lateral accelerometer has failed.

1993

Fig. 75   Code 76, Lateral accelerometer signal out of range (Part 1 of 3)

Circuit Description:

The Lateral Accelerometer circuitry provides a signal to the EBCM which reflects the severity of a vehicle turn, i.e. the "yaw" forces on the vehicle. The EBCM uses this information to modify the control of the rear wheel brakes, to help prevent loss of control in a turn due to light brake pedal application at speeds above 50 km/h (30 mph).

Code 76 will set when the Lateral Accelerometer signal is out of range for 7.5 minutes or more.

Test Description: Number(s) below refer to circled number(s) on the diagnostic chart.

7. Checks for appropriate signal voltage for a full-scale right-hand turn. The full-scale right turn is simulated by the left side of the Lateral Accelerometer being exposed to the 1g force of gravity.
8. Checks for code reset after most other portions of the system have checked as OK.
9. Checks for the Lateral Accelerometer causing the Step 5 code reset, using the Tech 1 snapshot feature. In Snapshot Mode, the Tech 1 will trigger if the Lateral Accelerometer suddenly changes signal greater than high and low calibrated parameters. It is important when road-testing not to make any SEVERE directional changes that might incorrectly cause the Tech 1 to trigger by "spiking" the Lateral Accelerometer signal.
10. Checks if Lateral Accelerometer was replaced in Step 6. If so, the EBCM is at fault. If not, the Lateral Accelerometer may be faulty and should be replaced before continuing with diagnosis.
11. Road tests to check for continuing Code 76 reset. If Code 76 resets, the EBCM is interpreting a problem when it should not be.

Diagnostic Aids:

It is very important that a thorough inspection of the wiring and connectors be performed. Failure to carefully and fully inspect wiring and connectors may result in misdiagnosis, causing part replacement with reappearance of the fault.

It is possible that the customer may complain of pedal pulsation during normal light straight-line braking if the Lateral Accelerometer has failed.

1992

Fig. 75   Code 76, Lateral accelerometer signal out of range (Part 2 of 3)

DTC 76
2 of 2
LATERAL ACCELEROMETER SIGNAL OUT OF RANGE

Circuit Description:

The lateral accelerometer circuitry provides a signal to the EBTCM which reflects the severity of a vehicle turn, i.e. the "yaw" forces on the vehicle. The EBTCM uses this information to modify the control of the rear wheel brakes, to help prevent loss of control in a turn due to light brake pedal application at speeds above 50 km/h (30 mph).

DTC 76 will set when the lateral accelerometer signal is out of range for 7.5 minutes or more.

Test Description: Number(s) below refer to circled number(s) on the diagnostic chart.

7. Checks for appropriate signal voltage for a full-scale right-hand turn. The full-scale right turn is simulated by the left side of the lateral accelerometer being exposed to the 1g force of gravity.
8. Checks for DTC reset after most other portions of the system have checked as OK.
9. Checks for the lateral accelerometer causing the Step 5 DTC reset, using the Tech 1 snapshot feature. In snapshot mode, the Tech 1 will trigger if the lateral accelerometer suddenly changes signal greater than high and low calibrated parameters. It is important when road-testing not to make any SEVERE directional changes that might incorrectly cause the Tech 1 to trigger by "spiking" the lateral accelerometer signal.
10. Checks if lateral accelerometer was replaced in Step 6. If so, the EBTCM is at fault. If not, the lateral accelerometer may be faulty and should be replaced before continuing with diagnosis.
11. Road tests to check for continuing DTC 76 reset. If DTC 76 resets, the EBTCM is interpreting a problem when it should not be.

Diagnostic Aids:

It is very important that a thorough inspection of the wiring and connectors be performed. Failure to carefully and fully inspect wiring and connectors may result in misdiagnosis, causing part replacement with reappearance of the malfunction.

It is possible that the customer may complain of pedal pulsation during normal light straight-line braking if the lateral accelerometer has failed.

1993

Fig. 75   Code 76, Lateral accelerometer signal out of range (Part 3 of 3)

CODE 83
(1 of 2)
BRAKE FLUID LEVEL LOW

Circuit Description:

The Brake Fluid Level circuit monitors the fluid level in the master cylinder reservoir. If the fluid level becomes low, as indicated by the Brake Fluid Level Switch, the ABS/ASR system is disabled. This is done to prevent introduction of air into the brake system. The Fluid Level Isolation Diode is used to prevent disabling ABS/ASR if illumination of the red "BRAKE" warning lamp occurs for reasons of brake pressure differential or application of the parking brake.

Code 83 will set and the "SERVICE ABS" and "SERVICE ASR" lamps will illuminate if CKT 1684 is low (grounded). For some 1992 vehicles, the engine must be running for this code to set.

Test Description: Number(s) below refer to circled number(s) on the diagnostic chart.

1. Checks for proper brake fluid level in the master cylinder reservoir.
2. Checks for illumination of the red "BRAKE" warning lamp for reasons other than parking brake engagement.
3. Checks for Brake Fluid Level Switch stuck closed.
4. Checks for short from CKT 1684 to ground CKT 801B.
5. Checks for short from CKT 1684 to chassis ground.
6. Adds fluid, noted to be low in Step 1, then checks for code reset.

Diagnostic Aids:

For some 1992 vehicles, the engine must be running for this code to set.

It is very important that a thorough inspection of the wiring and connectors be performed. Failure to carefully and fully inspect wiring and connectors may result in misdiagnosis, causing part replacement with reappearance of the fault.

1992

Circuit Description:

The Brake fluid level circuit monitors the fluid level in the master cylinder reservoir. If the fluid level becomes low, as indicated by the brake fluid level switch, the ABS/ASR system is disabled. This is done to prevent introduction of air into the brake system. The fluid level isolation diode is used to prevent disabling ABS/ASR if illumination of the red "BRAKE" warning lamp occurs for reasons of brake pressure differential or application of the parking brake.

DTC 83 will set and the "SERVICE ABS" and "SERVICE ASR" lamps will illuminate if the engine is running and CKT 1684 is low (grounded).

Test Description: Number(s) below refer to circled number(s) on the diagnostic chart.

1. Checks for proper brake fluid level in the master cylinder reservoir.
2. Checks for illumination of the red "BRAKE" warning lamp for reasons other than parking brake engagement.
3. Checks for brake fluid level switch stuck closed.
4. Checks for short from CKT 1684 to ground CKT 801B.
5. Checks for short from CKT 1684 to chassis ground.
6. Adds fluid, noted to be low in Step 1, then checks for DTC reset.

Diagnostic Aids:

The engine must be running for this DTC to set.

It is very important that a thorough inspection of the wiring and connectors be performed. Failure to carefully and fully inspect wiring and connectors may result in misdiagnosis, causing part replacement with reappearance of the malfunction.

1993

Fig. 76   Code 83, Brake fluid level low (Part 1 of 3)

CODE 83
(2 of 2)
BRAKE FLUID LEVEL LOW

Circuit Description:

The Brake Fluid Level circuit monitors the fluid level in the master cylinder reservoir. If the fluid level becomes low, as indicated by the Brake Fluid Level Switch, the ABS/ASR system is disabled. This is done to prevent introduction of air into the brake system. The Fluid Level Isolation Diode is used to prevent disabling ABS/ASR if illumination of the red "BRAKE" warning lamp occurs for reasons of brake pressure differential or application of the parking brake.

Code 83 will set and the "SERVICE ABS" and "SERVICE ASR" lamps will illuminate if CKT 1684 is low (grounded). For some 1992 vehicles, the engine must be running for this code to set.

Test Description: Number(s) below refer to circled number(s) on the diagnostic chart.

7. Checks for continuing code reset after checks in Steps 1-5.
8. Checks for code reset when parking brake is engaged, likely due to a faulty diode.
9. Checks for parking brake switch stuck closed.
10. Checks for short to ground in parking brake switch CKT 33.
11. Replaces faulty diode found in Step 7 or Step 10, then checks for code reset. If code resets, the EBCM is determining there is a problem in CKT 1684 and related circuitry when there is not.

Diagnostic Aids:

For some 1992 vehicles, the engine must be running for this code to set.

It is very important that a thorough inspection of the wiring and connectors be performed. Failure to carefully and fully inspect wiring and connectors may result in misdiagnosis, causing part replacement with reappearance of the fault.

1992

Fig. 76   Code 83, Brake fluid level low (Part 2 of 3)

Circuit Description:

The brake fluid level circuit monitors the fluid level in the master cylinder reservoir. If the fluid level becomes low, as indicated by the brake fluid level switch, the ABS/ASR system is disabled. This is done to prevent introduction of air into the brake system. The fluid level isolation diode is used to prevent disabling ABS/ASR if illumination of the red "BRAKE" warning lamp occurs for reasons of brake pressure differential or application of the parking brake.

DTC 83 will set and the "SERVICE ABS" and "SERVICE ASR" lamps will illuminate if the engine is running and CKT 1684 is low (grounded).

Test Description: Number(s) below refer to circled number(s) on the diagnostic chart.
7. Checks for continuing DTC reset after checks in Steps 1-5.
8. Checks for DTC reset when parking brake is engaged, likely due to a malfunctioning diode.
9. Checks for parking brake switch stuck closed.
10. Checks for short to ground in parking brake switch CKT 33.
11. Replaces malfunctioning diode found in Step 7 or Step 10, then checks for DTC reset. If DTC resets, the EBTCM is determining there is a problem in CKT 1684 and related circuitry when there is not.

Diagnostic Aids:

The engine must be running for this DTC to set.
It is very important that a thorough inspection of the wiring and connectors be performed. Failure to carefully and fully inspect wiring and connectors may result in misdiagnosis, causing part replacement with reappearance of the malfunction.

1993

Fig. 76   Code 83, Brake fluid level low (Part 3 of 3)

Fig. 77   Brake warning system wiring diagram. 1992

Fig. 78   Brake warning system wiring diagram. 1993

Fig. 79 Modulator valve location. 1991

Fig. 80 Modulator valve location. 1992-93

SYSTEM SERVICE

Before performing any service procedure on the ABS system, the following precautions should be followed:

1. Disarm air airbag system as outlined under "Airbag System Disarming."
2. The control module must be disconnected before performing any electric welding on these vehicles.
3. **On 1991 models,** use caution not to subject control module to a maximum heat of 203°F for brief periods, or a maximum of 184°F for longer than 2 hours.
4. **On 1992-93 models,** use caution not to subject control module to a maximum heat of 185°F for longer than 2 hours.
5. After replacement of any ABS component, the entire ABS system should be tested.
6. Ensure inlet and outlet brake lines are properly routed.
7. Do not use a fast charger for starting engine.
8. Never disconnect battery from vehicle when engine is running.
9. Do not connect or disconnect control module electrical connector with ignition switch in On position. Ensure all harness connectors are securely connected.
10. No screws on the modulator valve should be loosened. If screws are loosened, it is no longer possible to get brake circuit leak-tight.
11. When replacing modulator valve, it should be removed through access panel in rear storage compartment. Ensure vehicle interior and exterior are protected to avoid damage from brake fluid spillage. Do not remove bottom of storage compartment to replace modulator valve.
12. Ensure rear storage compartment is wiped clean after replacing modulator valve.
13. Do not support suspension components by wheel speed sensor wires.
14. Wheel speed sensors are a tight fit into knuckle, but should be pushed in by hand. Do not hammer sensors into position.
15. Each replacement wheel speed sensor is identified with a white tag, located approximately 3/4 inch from neck of sensor, labeled L (left), or R (right).
16. Tire and wheel assemblies should be removed when replacing wheel speed sensors.
17. **On 1991 models,** wheel speed sensors should be given an anti-corrosion coating, No. 9981128 or equivalent, before installation to prevent corrosion. Do not use grease.
18. **On 1992 models,** wheel speed sensors should be given an anti-corrosion coating, use sealant No. 12345489 or equivalent, prior to installation. Do not use grease.
19. Ensure proper routing, position, mounting and location of all components, wiring, connectors, clips, bracket and brake pipes, when performing ABS/ASR service.
20. Use caution not to use silicone type brake fluid.
21. Rearm airbag system as outlined under "Airbag System Arming."

ON-VEHICLE SERVICE

When a diagnostic chart refers to removing, replacing or checking a component for proper mounting, refer to "Component Replacement."

After all diagnosis and repairs are completed, road test the vehicle to ensure proper ABS operation and that the SERVICE ABS light does not illuminate. If the Tech 1 was used for diagnosis, disconnect it from the ALDL connector and turn the ignition Off before road testing the vehicle. This is required to reset the EBTCM, it is disabled during Tech 1 diagnostics and does not reset until serial data communication is stopped and ignition power is lost.

COMPONENT REPLACEMENT
MODULATOR VALVE
1991

Replace modulator valve through access panel in rear storage compartment.

1. Disarm air airbag system as outlined under "Airbag System Disarming,"
   then disconnect battery ground cable.
2. Remove storage tray and insulation.
3. Disconnect and remove entire ABS wiring harness from storage compartment.
4. Disconnect modulator valve ground from body wiring harness.
5. Disconnect five brake pipes from modulator valve, noting location for reassembly.
6. Remove three modulator valve to bracket attaching nuts, then the modulator valve, **Fig. 79.**
7. Reverse procedure to install, noting the following:
   a. **Torque** modulator valve to bracket attaching nuts to 7 ft. lbs.
   b. Remove shipping caps from modulator valve if necessary, then connect brake pipes. **Torque** brake pipes to 13 ft. lbs.
   c. Bleed brakes as necessary.
   d. Rearm airbag system as outlined under "Airbag System Arming."

1992-93

Do not remove rear storage compartment panel opening cover to replace modulator valve.

1. Disarm airbag system as outlined under "Airbag System Disarming."
2. Disconnect battery ground cable.
3. Remove rear storage compartment door and frame assembly.
4. Remove sound insulator pad.
5. **On models equipped with selective ride control,** disconnect wiring harness with selective ride control module.
6. **On all models,** disconnect brake pipes from modulator valve, noting pipe position.
7. Raise and support vehicle.
8. Remove modulator valve bracket to underbody cover attaching bolts, **Fig. 80.**
9. Lower vehicle.
10. Disconnect ground wire from modulator valve.
11. Remove valve from bracket.
12. Remove pump motor and solenoid valve relays.
13. Reverse procedure to install, noting the following:

Fig. 81   Control module location. 1991

Fig. 82   Control module location. 1992–93

1	CONTROL MODULE
2	BOLT/SCREW
3	BRACKET
4	RIVET
5	NUT
6	LR STORAGE COMPARTMENT
7	MODULE RELAY

1	EBCM MOUNTING STUDS
2	EBCM RETAINING NUTS
3	LEFT HAND REAR FLOOR PANEL
4	EBCM SUPPORT BRACKET
5	EBCM
6	INSULATION

1	SCREW
2	ACCELEROMETER, LATERAL
3	CONNECTOR, ELECTRICAL
4	CARRIER ASSEMBLY, INSTRUMENT PANEL

Fig. 83   Lateral acceleration switch (accelerometer). 1991

a. **Torque** modulator valve attaching nuts and valve bracket to underbody cover attaching bolts to 86 inch lbs.

b. Ensure brake pipes are correctly connected to valve. If brake pipes are switched, wheel lockup will occur and personal injury may result.

c. **Torque** valve brake pipes to 13 ft. lbs.

d. Use only DOT 3 brake fluid, do not use silicone brake fluid or system damage will result.

e. Ensure sound insulator pad covers valve or excessive system noise may result.

f. Rearm airbag system as outlined under "Airbag System Arming."

CONTROL MODULE
1991

1. Disarm air airbag system as outlined

under "Airbag System Disarming," then disconnect battery ground cable.

2. Remove storage tray and insulation.

3. Disconnect control module electrical connector, then depress spring clip located under neck of compressor to remove module relay from control module bracket.

4. Remove two control module attaching bolts, then the control module, **Fig. 81.**

5. Reverse procedure to install. **Torque** control module mounting bolts to 22 inch lbs. Perform ABS system check.

6. Rearm airbag system as outlined under "Airbag System Arming."

1992–93

1. Disarm airbag system as outlined under "Airbag System Disarming."

2. Disconnect battery ground cable.

3. **On Coupe models,** open left rear storage compartment cover.

4. **On convertible models,** remove storage compartment frame and covers.

5. **On all models,** remove sound insulator pad.

6. Pull EBTCM electrical connector retaining clip to release front of connector, then slide connector toward front of vehicle to release rear of connector.

7. Remove EBTCM attaching nut, then remove EBTCM, **Fig. 82.**

8. Reverse procedure to install, noting the following:

   a. **Torque** EBTCM attaching nut to 8 ft. lbs.

   b. Ensure wiring harness connector is tight and fully seated.

   c. Ensure sound insulator pad covers valve or excessive system noise may result.

   d. Rearm airbag system as outlined under "Airbag System Arming."

LATERAL ACCELERATION SWITCH (ACCELEROMETER)
1991

1. Disarm air airbag system as outlined under "Airbag System Disarming," then disconnect battery ground cable.

2. Remove console trim plate attaching screws, then the console trim plate.

3. Remove radio assembly.

4. Remove lateral acceleration switch attaching screws, **Fig. 83.**

5. Disconnect lateral acceleration switch electrical connector, then remove switch.

6. Reverse procedure to install. **Torque** lateral acceleration mounting bolts to 15 inch lbs. Rearm airbag system as outlined under "Airbag System Arming."

1992–93

1. Disarm airbag system as outlined under "Airbag System Disarming."

2. Disconnect battery ground cable.

3. Remove console trim plate.

4. Remove accessory trim plate.

5. Remove radio control assembly.

6. Depress ABS/ASR harness to lateral accelerometer electrical connector to release, **Fig. 84.**

7. Remove accelerometer to I/P carrier attaching bolts.

Fig. 84   Lateral acceleration switch (accelerometer). 1992–93

1 FRONT SENSOR	5 REAR SENSOR
2 FRONT KNUCKLE	6 REAR DRIVE SHAFT SPINDLE
3 TOOTHED RING (PART OF 4 & 6)	7 REAR KNUCKLE
4 FRONT HUB & BEARING ASSEMBLY	8 REAR DRIVE SHAFT

LEFT SIDES SHOWN RIGHT SIDES TYPICAL

Fig. 85   Wheel speed sensors

8. Remove lateral accelerometer from I/P carrier.
9. Reverse procedure to install, noting the following:
   a. Ensure accelerometer electrical connector is tight and fully seated.
   b. **Torque** accelerometer attaching bolts to 29 inch lbs.
   c. Rearm airbag system as outlined under "Airbag System Arming."

WHEEL SPEED SENSOR
Front

The front wheel speed sensor is part of the wheel hub assembly and must be serviced as an assembly.

Rear

1. Disarm air airbag system as outlined under "Airbag System Disarming," then disconnect battery ground cable.
2. Raise and support vehicle, then remove tire and wheel assembly.
3. Remove sensor electrical connector from bracket, then disconnect sensor connector.
4. Remove sensor wire grommets from brackets, noting sensor wire routing for reassembly.
5. Remove sensor to knuckle attaching bolts, then the sensor, **Fig. 85.**
6. Reverse procedure to install, noting the following:
   a. **On 1991 models,** coat new wheel speed sensor with anti-corrosion compound No. 9981128, or equivalent prior to installation.
   b. **On 1992 models,** coat new wheel speed sensor with anti-corrosion compound No. 12345489, or equivalent prior to installation.
   c. **On all models,** do not use hammer to install sensor.
   d. **On 1991 models,** torque sensor attaching bolt to 89 inch lbs.
   e. **On 1992 models, torque** sensor attaching bolt to 86 inch. lbs.
   f. **On all models,** rearm airbag system as outlined under "Airbag System Arming."

WIRING HARNESS & MODULE RELAY
1991

1. Disarm air airbag system as outlined under "Airbag System Disarming," then disconnect battery ground cable.
2. Remove storage tray and insulation.
3. Disconnect control module harness connector by depressing spring clip located under neck of connector, **Figs. 86 and 87.**

A	DO NOT CONNECT OR DISCONNECT ABS MODULE CONNECTOR UNTIL THE IGNITION IS TURNED "OFF."
1	HARNESS, BODY
2	HARNESS, ABS
3	HARNESS, GROUND
4	RELAY, MODULE
5	COMPARTMENT, LEFT REAR STORAGE
6	MODULE, SELECTIVE RIDE CONTROL
7	VALVE, MODULATOR
8	WIRING, WHEEL SPEED SENSOR
9	RELAY, SOLENOID (PART OF 7)
10	RELAY, PUMP MOTOR (PART OF 7)
11	MODULE, CONTROL
12	JUMPER, SELECTIVE RIDE CONTROL

Fig. 86   Wiring harness & relays. 1991 w/selective ride control

4. Remove two screws from modulator valve harness retainer clip, then disconnect harness connector.
5. Disconnect battery feed (red), wire harness connector.
6. Disconnect wheel speed sensor connectors from wiring harness connector.
7. Remove module relay from control module bracket, then disconnect modular relay harness connector.
8. Remove wiring harness, noting routing for installation.
9. Reverse procedure to install. Ensure all connectors are securely connected. Rearm airbag system as outlined under "Airbag System Arming."

A DO NOT CONNECT OR DISCONNECT ABS MODULE CONNECTOR UNTIL THE IGNITION IS TURNED "OFF."

1 HARNESS, BODY
2 HARNESS, ABS
3 HARNESS, GROUND
4 RELAY, MODULE
5 COMPARTMENT, LEFT REAR STORAGE
6 VALVE, MODULATOR
7 WIRING, WHEEL SPEED SENSOR
8 RELAY, SOLENOID (PART OF 6)
9 RELAY, PUMP MOTOR (PART OF 6)
10 MODULE, CONTROL

Fig. 87 Wiring harness & relays. 1991 less selective ride control

1 THROTTLE POSITION SENSOR MODULE
2 SCREWS
3 WIRE HARNESS

Fig. 88 TPS module. 1992

WIRING HARNESS
1992–93

1. Disarm airbag system as outlined under "Airbag System Disarming."
2. Disconnect battery ground cable.
3. Remove left rear storage compartment cover.
4. **On Coupe models,** disconnect EBTCM wiring harness electrical connector.
5. **On Convertible models,** proceed as follows:
   a. Remove EBTCM attaching nut.
   b. Pull connector retaining clip to release front of connector.
   c. Push retaining clip back down without relocking front of connector.
   d. Push EBTCM toward front of vehicle as possible.
   e. Lift front front of connector to release connector rear.
6. **On models equipped with Selective Ride Control,** disconnect selective ride control module electrical connector.
7. **On all models,** disconnect wheel speed sensor electrical connectors.
8. **On models equipped with Selective Ride Control,** disconnect selective ride control actuator electrical connector.
9. **On all models,** disconnect body harness connector.
10. Remove modulator valve cover.
11. Disconnect modulator valve electrical connector.
12. Remove wiring harness, noting harness routing.

13. Reverse procedure to install, noting the following:
    a. Ensure all connectors are tight and fully seated.
    b. Ensure EBTCM connector retaining clip is locked.
    c. Rearm airbag system as outlined under "Airbag System Arming."

THROTTLE POSITION SENSOR MODULE
1992

1. Disarm airbag system as outlined under "Airbag System Disarming."
2. Disconnect battery ground cable.
3. Disconnect TPS module electric connector, **Fig. 88.**
4. Remove module attaching screws, then remove module.
5. Reverse procedure to install, noting the following:
   a. **Torque** TPS module attaching screws to 13 inch lbs.
   b. Rearm airbag system as outlined under "Airbag System Arming."

1991 Reatta, 1991–92 Brougham, Toronado & Trofeo & 1991–93 Caprice, Custom Cruiser, Eldorado, Riviera, Roadmaster, Seville (Bosch 2 U Type)

NOTE: Wire Code Identification And Symbol Identification Located In The Front Of This Manual Can Be Used As An Aid When Using Wiring Circuits Found In This Section.

INDEX

PRECAUTIONS
AIRBAG SYSTEM
DISARMING
ELDORADO, FLEETWOOD (RWD), REATTA, RIVIERA, SEVILLE & TORONADO/TROFEO

The diagnostic energy reserve module (DERM) can maintain voltage to cause a system deployment for up to ten minutes after the ignition switch is turned off and the battery is disconnected. Servicing the SIR system during this period may result in accidental deployment and personal injury.

1. Ensure front wheels are pointed straight ahead.
2. Turn ignition switch to LOCK position and remove SIR or AIRBAG fuse.
3. Remove left sound insulator. **Remove courtesy lamp from sound insulator, if necessary.**
4. Remove Connector Position Assurance (CPA), then disconnect yellow two-way SIR electrical connector at base of steering column.

CAPRICE, CUSTOM CRUISER & ROADMASTER

The diagnostic energy reserve module (DERM) can maintain voltage to cause a system deployment for up to ten minutes after the ignition switch is turned off and the battery is disconnected. Servicing the SIR system during this period may result in accidental deployment and personal injury.

1. Ensure front wheels are pointed straight ahead.
2. Turn ignition switch to LOCK position and remove SIR fuse from fuse block.
3. Remove Connector Position Assurance (CPA), then disconnect yellow two-way SIR electrical connector at base of steering column.

AIRBAG SYSTEM ARMING

ELDORADO, FLEETWOOD (RWD), REATTA, RIVIERA, SEVILLE & TORONADO/TROFEO

1. Connect yellow two-way SIR electrical connector, then install Connector Position Assurance (CPA).
2. Install left sound insulator. **Install courtesy lamp to sound insulator, if applicable.**
3. Install SIR fuse to fuse block, turn ignition switch to RUN position and ensure that "Inflatable Restraint" lamp flashes 7 to 9 times, then turns off.

CAPRICE, CUSTOM CRUISER & ROADMASTER

1. Connect yellow two-way SIR electrical connector at base of column, then install Connector Position Assurance (CPA).
2. Install SIR fuse into fuse block, turn ignition switch to RUN position and ensure that "Inflatable Restraint" lamp flashes 7 to 9 times and then turns off.

DESCRIPTION

SYSTEM

The function of the Anti-Lock Brake System (ABS) is to minimize wheel lockup during heavy braking on most road surfaces. The system performs this function by monitoring wheel speed and controlling the brake fluid pressure to each front wheel and both rear wheels during braking. This allows the driver to retain directional stability and better steering capability.

1993 Eldorado and Seville models with the 4.6L Northstar engine are also equipped with a real-time traction control system (TCS). The purpose of the traction control system is to prevent excessive wheel spin during acceleration or when turning a corner at high speed. The TCS also prevents wheel slip on slippery surfaces such as ice-covered roads; this allows for improved acceleration and improved stability while driving. The ABS and TCS are both part of the same hydraulic and electrical system.

TORQUE MANAGEMENT

1993 Eldorado & Seville w/4.6L Northstar Engine

Traction control is simultaneously controlled by the PCM in the event that applying the brakes does not provide necessary traction. The PCM receives a torque request via a Pulse Width Modulated (PWM) signal from the EBTCM/EBCM requesting the desired torque level for proper traction control system operation. Torque reduction will be indicated if the duty cycle of the PWM signal is between 10% (100% torque reduction) and 90% (no torque reduction) and at least one (up to five) cylinder is requested to be disabled (the outside limits are used for diagnostic

purposes and open or shorted PWM circuit). The percent duty cycle will indicate the percent torque required. The PCM will selectively disable fuel to certain cylinders to achieve this reduction. The timing of this action will be controlled by the EBTCM/EBCM with the following constraints:

1. The PCM will not allow traction control fuel shutoff if: engine coolant temperature is less than -40°C, greater than or equal to 131°C or low coolant level is detected.
2. Cylinders will be disabled under the following circumstance: engine speed is greater than or equal to 600 RPM.

PCM OVERRIDE

1993 Eldorado & Seville w/4.6L Northstar Engine

Traction control enable, PS24 may be used to temporarily disable traction control. When PS24 is selected, the display will alternate between -- -- for one second and the current state of traction control disable (99 for override active and 00 for override not active). Pressing the WARMER button will disable traction control for the next eleven cycles and display 99. The TRACTION DISABLED message will be displayed for the duration of this override. No TCS diagnostic trouble codes will be set. Pressing the COOLER button will allow normal program control of traction control and display 00.

SYSTEM COMPONENTS

ELECTRONIC BRAKE CONTROL MODULE (EBCM)

Except 1993 Eldorado & Seville

The EBCM is a small control computer located under the trim panel on the left-hand side of passenger compartment on wagon models, and on the lefthand side of the luggage compartment on sedan models. This computer monitors the speed of each wheel and the electrical status of the hydraulic modulator. The primary functions of EBCM are to detect wheel locking, control the brake function while in anti-lock mode and monitor system for correct electrical operation. The EBCM also controls the display of the ABS diagnostic codes. If the EBCM detects a fault, it can disable the ABS system and activate the ABS warning lamp.

1993 Eldorado & Seville

The EBTCM or EBCM (if not equipped with traction control), is a small control computer located in the trunk in the center of the electronics bay, which monitors the speed of each wheel as well as several other functions internal to the BPM (brake pressure modulator) valve. The EBTCM/EBCM's main functions are to detect wheel locking or wheel slip tendencies, control the brake system while in antilock mode or traction control mode and monitor the system for proper operation.

On vehicles equipped with the 4.6L Northstar engine, the EBTCM/EBCM communicates torque requests (PWM sig-

nals) and receives delivered torque (PWM signals) from the PCM. The EBTCM/EBCM also communicates with the ABS/TCS diagnostic trouble codes (DTC) while in diagnostic mode to the IPC via serial data.

ACCELERATOR & CRUISE CONTROL CABLE ADJUSTER ASSEMBLY

1993 Fleetwood (RWD)

The adjuster is mounted in the engine compartment and is used as a cable extender. It moves the throttle lever cam on the throttle body toward the closed throttle position when the traction control system requests it to reduce engine power to control wheel spin. The EBCM provides control logic. ACCELERATOR PEDAL ASSEMBLY

1993 Fleetwood (RWD)

To prevent overstressing of the adjuster assembly and transmission TV cable assembly due to over travel of the accelerator pedal, a spring loaded cable adjuster has been added. Refer to Speed Control section for replacement or adjustment.

OVERVOLTAGE PROTECTION RELAY (OVP)

This relay located on the EBCM mounting bracket, protects the EBCM from possible spike voltage, due to a faulty alternator regulator.

WHEEL SPEED SENSORS

The wheel speed sensors are located at each front wheel and on the rear axle differential on Caprice, Custom Cruiser and Roadmaster models. On Eldorado, Reatta, Riviera, Seville, Toronado and Trofeo models, wheel speed sensors are located at each wheel. These sensors transmit wheel speed information to the EBCM using a small amount of AC voltage.

HYDRAULIC MODULATOR VALVE

The hydraulic modulator (also known as brake pressure modulator (BPM)) is located on the front lefthand side of the engine compartment, provides brake fluid modulation for each individual wheel circuit as required during anti-lock braking. During anti-lock braking, the modulator can maintain or reduce brake fluid pressure independent of the pressure generated in the master cylinder.

SOLENOID VALVES

The solenoid valves are located inside the hydraulic modulator are not serviceable. The solenoid valves increase, decrease or maintain the brake fluid pressure to the wheel circuits. During anti-lock braking the valves are controlled by signals received by the EBCM. During normal braking, the valves are positioned in a pressure increase or open position.

PUMP MOTOR

The pump motor located in the modulator circulates brake fluid back to the master cylinder circuit during anti-lock braking.

ABS VALVE RELAY & PUMP RELAY

Eldorado, Reatta, Riviera, Seville, Toronado & Trofeo

These two relays are the only parts of the hydraulic modulator that can be serviced. The valve relay provides power to the three solenoid valves in the modulator. The pump relay provides power to the pump motor during anti-lock braking.

ABS/TCS SYSTEM OPERATION

The BPM valve regulates brake fluid pressure based on road conditions as interpreted by the EBTCM/EBCM, regardless of master cylinder output pressure. The BPM valve can maintain, reduce or increase brake fluid pressure to the brake calipers under ABS conditions, but it cannot increase pressure above that applied from the master cylinder. However, during TCS operation, the BPM valve can apply to the front brake calipers if the EBTCM/EBCM requires that a wheel be slowed or regulated.

TCS PILOT VALVES (VEHICLE EQUIPPED W/TCS)

There are two pilot valves within the BPM valve. These valves isolate the master cylinder so the pump motor can build brake fluid pressure to the front brakes during traction control. Unlike the ABS solenoid, the pilot valves do not modulate. They are normally open and then closed during traction control operation.

TCS PRIME PIPE & NOZZLE (VEHICLE EQUIPPED W/TCS)

On the side of the BPM valve there is the TCS prime pipe nozzle. The pump draws fluid during traction control through the 6mm prime pipe. This prime pipe is a rubber hose which runs up to the master cylinder reservoir to provide the BPM valve with brake fluid when necessary for traction control operation. It is a low pressure line.

TCS PRIME PIPE BLEED SCREW (VEHICLE EQUIPPED W/TCS)

On the side of the BPM valve, near the TCS prime pipe nozzle, is the TCS prime pipe bleed screw. This allows bleeding of the TCS prime pipe. The prime pipe must be bled anytime the master cylinder, the reservoir or BPM valve is replaced or if the reservoir fluid level becomes too low due to a leak in the system or brake system service.

DIAGNOSIS & TESTING

When a malfunction occurs in the ABS system, the EBCM will activate the amber Anti-Lock Warning Lamp. Before performing diagnosis on the ABS system when the warning lamp comes on, check that the EBCM connector and all other system electrical connectors are secure and that fuses are satisfactory. Refer to **Figs. 1 through 8** for ABS system functional check(s). Sometimes use of the compact spare will activate a wheel sensor fault code and deactivate the ABS system, if this occurs, recycle the ignition switch to reset the system.

There are trouble codes that may be set by the EBCM, **Figs. 9 through 14.** All codes except 72 will cause the EBCM to disable the ABS system, allowing power assisted braking only.

The EBCM performs an automatic (AUTO) test once each ignition cycle when vehicle reaches approximately 4 mph. The AUTO test cycles each solenoid valve and pump motor to check component operation. If any error is detected during this test the EBCM will set a trouble code. This test may be heard and felt while it is taking place and should be considered normal mode of operation.

The EBCM can display codes only when the "Diagnostic Service Mode" has been entered. There are two ways to enter the diagnostic service mode, either using a TECH 1 diagnostic computer, or by grounding pin "H" of the ALDL connector and using "Flash Code Diagnosis." The use of a TECH 1 computer is recommended for diagnosing the ABS system.

INTERMITTENTS & POOR CONNECTIONS

Intermittent failures in the anti-lock brake system may be difficult to accurately diagnose. The ABS trouble codes which may be stored by the EBCM are not designated as current or history codes. These codes can be helpful in diagnosing intermittent conditions.

If an intermittent condition is being diagnosed, the ABS system can be used in the following manner to help isolate the suspected circuit.

1. Display, then clear any ABS trouble codes present in the EBCM.
2. Test drive vehicle, attempting to repeat failure condition. A description of driving conditions under which the last failure occurred can be helpful.
3. After duplicating condition, stop the vehicle, then display any trouble codes stored.
4. If no codes were stored, proceed to "Symptom Diagnosis."
5. If a code was stored, check electrical connections and wiring for the following:
   a. Poor mating of connector halves.
   b. Terminals not fully seated in connector halves.
   c. Improperly formed, or damaged terminals. All connector terminals in a problem circuit should be carefully reformed to increase contact tension.
   d. Poor terminal to wire connection. In most cases, this will require removing wire from connector body.

6. If a complaint of intermittent warning lamp operation is encountered, the following circuits to the EBCM should be checked:
   a. Low system voltage. If low voltage is detected at the EBCM, the Anti-lock lamp will illuminate until normal operating voltage is detected.
   b. Low brake fluid. This condition in the Pressure Modulator Valve (PMV) reservoir will cause the Brake and Anti-lock lamps to illuminate. When an acceptable fluid level is registered, the lamps will no longer be illuminated.
7. Any condition which results in interruption of power to the EBCM or hydraulic unit may cause the warning lamps to turn on intermittently. These circuits include the main relay, pump motor relay, fuses and related wiring.

EBTCM/EBCM SWITCHED FAULTS

The J 39700 Universal Breakout Box is connected both to the ABS/TCS wiring harness and the EBTCM/EBCM. The EBTCM/EBCM provides power or ground on many circuits only when it is powered up and operational. If a diagnostic test indicates a short to the system voltage or ground, turn ignition Off and disconnect J 39700 from the EBTCM/EBCM. Leave it connected to the harness, then repeat the test which indicated the short (turn ignition On if the test directs to do so). If the short is now not present, it is likely that the short is to circuit from the EBTCM/EBCM when the EBTCM/EBCM is operating. Inspect the wiring harness and connectors to determine the location of the problem, then repair the short condition as needed. Examples of switched power and ground circuits are as follows: Power: 854, Ground: 833; Power: 1715, Ground: 595; Power: 851, Grounds: 886, 883, 884, 856, 874, 594 and 1676.

If the above process does not show fault as EBTCM/EBCM—switched, the short is likely located in other circuits than those mentioned. If continued diagnostics are necessary after this process, always turn ignition Off and reconnect J 39700 to the EBTCM/EBCM before continuing the chart, unless specified to do otherwise.

THROTTLE POSITION SENSOR LEARN

1993 FLEETWOOD (RWD)

If a new throttle position sensor or throttle body is installed, the EBTCM must -learn- the throttle position sensor idle position voltage with the new component(s) installed. This is necessary to ensure effective engine torque reduction during TCS events. The procedure required TECH 1 or T-100 (CAMS) unit; the following procedure is descried as using a TECH 1 unit.

1. Turn ignition Off, then connect Chassis or Mass Storage Cartridge.

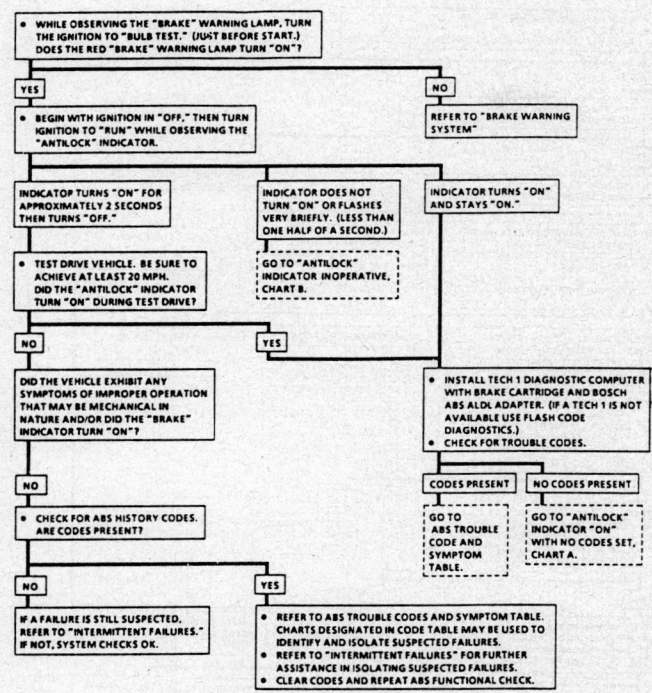

Fig. 1   ABS functional check. Caprice, Custom Cruiser & Roadmaster

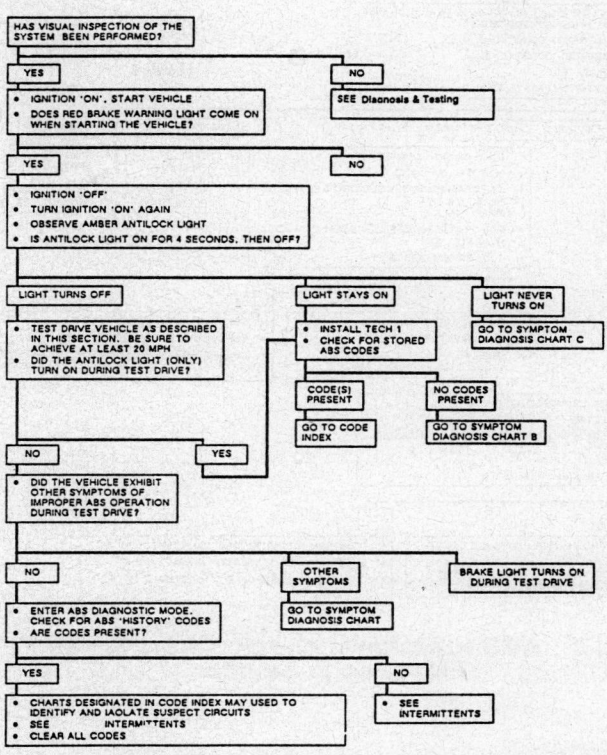

Fig. 2   ABS functional check. Reatta, Riviera, 1991—92 Brougham, Eldorado, Seville, Toronado & Trofeo

Fig. 3   ABS functional check, Chart 1. 1993 Eldorado & Seville

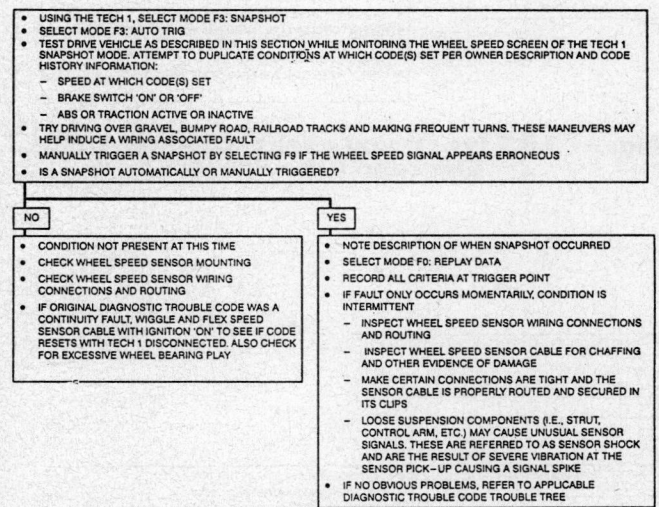

Fig. 4   ABS functional check, Chart 2. 1993 Eldorado & Seville

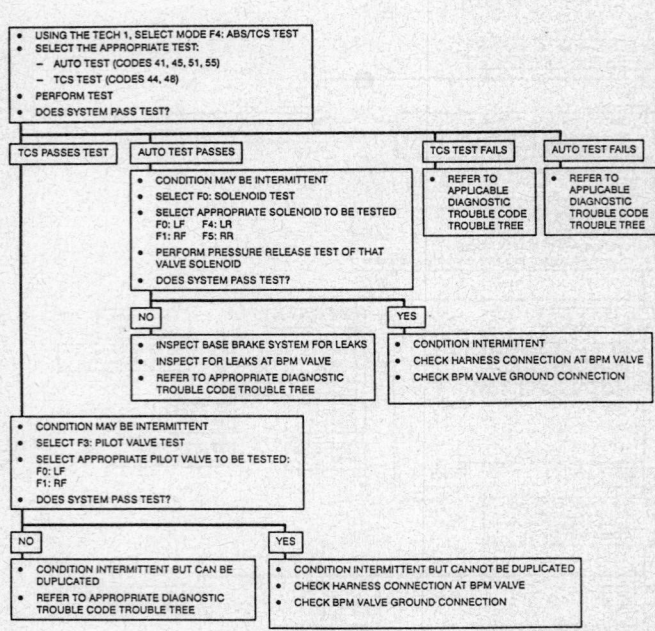

Fig. 5   ABS functional check, Chart 3. 1993 Eldorado & Seville

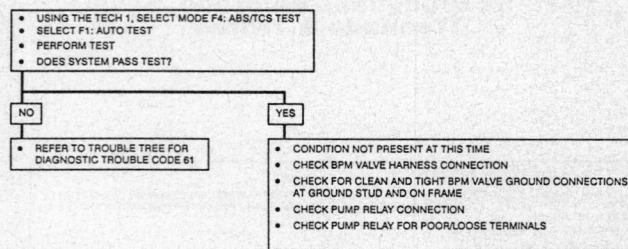

Fig. 6   ABS functional check, Chart 4. 1993 Eldorado & Seville

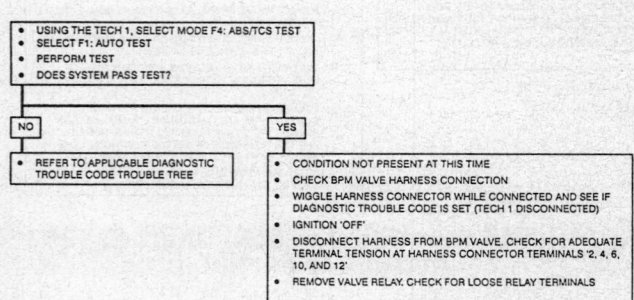

Fig. 7   ABS functional check, Chart 5. 1993 Eldorado & Seville

Fig. 8   ABS functional check. 1993 Fleetwood (RWD)

TROUBLE CODE	DESCRIPTION
21	RIGHT FRONT WHEEL SPEED SENSOR FAULT
22	RIGHT FRONT TOOTHED WHEEL FREQUENCY ERROR
25	LEFT FRONT WHEEL SPEED SENSOR FAULT
26	LEFT FRONT TOOTHED WHEEL FREQUENCY ERROR
35	REAR AXLE SPEED SENSOR FAULT
36	REAR AXLE TOOTHED WHEEL FREQUENCY ERROR
41	RIGHT FRONT SOLENOID VALVE FAULT
45	LEFT FRONT SOLENOID VALVE FAULT
55	REAR WHEELS SOLENOID VALVE FAULT
61	PUMP MOTOR OR MOTOR RELAY FAULT
63	SOLENOID VALVE RELAY FAULT
71	ELECTRONIC BRAKE CONTROL MODULE FAULT
72	SERIAL DATA LINE FAULT

CHART	SYMPTOM
A	"ANTILOCK" INDICATOR "ON" WITH NO CODES SET OR WITH TECH 1 UNABLE TO RECEIVE DATA
B	"ANTILOCK" INDICATOR INOPERATIVE OR INDICATOR FLASHES VERY BRIEFLY AT IGNITION "ON" (LESS THAN ONE HALF OF A SECOND)
Refer to Trouble Code Chart 72	WHEN ATTEMPTING TO COMMUNICATE WITH THE EBCM USING THE TECH 1, THE EBCM ENTERS FLASH CODE DIAGNOSTICS. (FLASHING THE "ANTILOCK" INDICATOR)

Fig. 9   ABS trouble code chart. Caprice, Custom Cruiser & Roadmaster

ABS CODE	SYSTEM
21	RIGHT FRONT WHEEL SPEED SENSOR FAULT
22	RIGHT FRONT TOOTHED WHEEL FREQUENCY ERROR
25	LEFT FRONT WHEEL SPEED SENSOR FAULT
26	LEFT FRONT TOOTHED WHEEL FREQUENCY ERROR
31	RIGHT REAR WHEEL SPEED SENSOR FAULT
32	RIGHT REAR TOOTHED WHEEL FREQUENCY ERROR
35	LEFT REAR SPEED SENSOR FAULT
36	LEFT REAR TOOTHED WHEEL FREQUENCY ERROR
41	RIGHT FRONT SOLENOID VALVE FAULT
45	LEFT FRONT SOLENOID VALVE FAULT
55	REAR SOLENOID VALVE FAULT
61	MOTOR PUMP CIRCUIT FAULT
63	SOLENOID VALVE RELAY FAULT
71	ELECTRONIC BRAKE CONTROL MODULE FAULT
72	SERIAL DATA LINK FAULT (TECH 1 ERROR)

GO TO CHART	SYMPTOM
A	NO SYSTEM POWER
B	ANTILOCK LIGHT ON, NO CODES SET
C	ANTILOCK LIGHT INOPERATIVE AT KEY-ON
D	VALVE CYCLING (CHATTER) DURING NORMAL STOPS.

Fig. 10   ABS trouble code chart. Reatta, Riviera, 1991–92 Brougham, Eldorado, Seville, Toronado & Trofeo

ABS/TCS DTC TABLE

DIAGNOSTIC TROUBLE CODE	DESCRIPTION
21	RF WHEEL SPEED SENSOR MALFUNCTION
23	RF WHEEL SPEED SENSOR CONTINUITY MALFUNCTION
25	LF WHEEL SPEED SENSOR MALFUNCTION
27	LF WHEEL SPEED SENSOR CONTINUITY MALFUNCTION
28	WHEEL SPEED SENSOR FREQUENCY ERROR
31	RR WHEEL SPEED SENSOR MALFUNCTION
33	RR WHEEL SPEED SENSOR CONTINUITY MALFUNCTION
35	LR WHEEL SPEED SENSOR MALFUNCTION
37	LR WHEEL SPEED SENSOR CONTINUITY MALFUNCTION
41	RF VALVE SOLENOID MALFUNCTION
44	PILOT VALVE SOLENOID MALFUNCTION
45	LF VALVE SOLENOID MALFUNCTION
51	RR VALVE SOLENOID MALFUNCTION
55	LR VALVE SOLENOID MALFUNCTION
57	TCC DISABLE RELAY OUTPUT MALFUNCTION
58	EBTCM INTERNAL ADJUSTER ASSEMBLY MALFUNCTION
61	PUMP MOTOR OR PUMP MOTOR RELAY MALFUNCTION
62	RPM SIGNAL MALFUNCTION
63	VALVE SOLENOID RELAY CIRCUIT MALFUNCTION
64	THROTTLE POSITION SIGNAL MALFUNCTION
65	ADJUSTER ASSEMBLY MALFUNCTION
66	ADJUSTER ASSEMBLY CONTROL MALFUNCTION
71	EBTCM INTERNAL MALFUNCTION
72	SERIAL DATA LINK MALFUNCTION
83	BRAKE DIFFERENTIAL PRESSURE MALFUNCTION

Fig. 12   ABS trouble code chart. 1993 Fleetwood (RWD)

ABS/TCS FAULT CODE TABLE

FAULT CODE	DESCRIPTION
21	RF WHEEL SPEED SENSOR FAULT
22	RF WHEEL SPEED SENSOR FREQUENCY ERROR
23	RF WHEEL SPEED SENSOR CONTINUITY FAULT
25	LF WHEEL SPEED SENSOR FAULT
26	LF WHEEL SPEED SENSOR FREQUENCY ERROR
27	LF WHEEL SPEED SENSOR CONTINUITY FAULT
28	WHEEL SPEED SENSOR FREQUENCY ERROR
31	RR WHEEL SPEED SENSOR FAULT
32	RR WHEEL SPEED SENSOR FREQUENCY ERROR
33	RR WHEEL SPEED SENSOR CONTINUITY FAULT
35	LR WHEEL SPEED SENSOR FAULT
36	LR WHEEL SPEED SENSOR FREQUENCY ERROR
37	LR WHEEL SPEED SENSOR CONTINUITY FAULT
41	RF ABS VALVE SOLENOID FAULT
44	RF TCS PILOT VALVE FAULT
45	LF ABS VALVE SOLENOID FAULT
48	LF TCS PILOT VALVE FAULT
51	RR ABS VALVE SOLENOID FAULT
55	LR VALVE SOLENOID FAULT (TCS)
55	REAR VALVE SOLENOID FAULT (NON-TCS)
61	PUMP MOTOR OR PUMP MOTOR RELAY FAULT
63	VALVE RELAY CIRCUIT FAULT
67	BRAKE LIGHT SWITCH FAULT
71	EBTCM/EBCM INTERNAL FAULT
72	SERIAL DATA LINK FAULT
73	PCM–EBTCM/EBCM PWM SIGNAL FAULT (4.6L)
83	BRAKE FLUID LEVEL LOW

Fig. 11   ABS trouble code chart. 1993 Eldorado & Seville

ABS/TCS SYMPTOM TABLE

CHART	DESCRIPTION
A	'ANTILOCK' INDICATOR AND 'TRACTION DISABLED' MESSAGE 'ON' – NO TCS CODES SET / NO TCS DATA
B	'ANTILOCK' INDICATOR 'ON'
C	VALVE CYCLING DURING NORMAL STOPS (UNWANTED ABS MODULATION)
D	TRACTION CONTROL OPERATION CHECK
•	'ANTILOCK' INDICATOR INOPERATIVE

Fig. 13   ABS symptom table. 1993 Eldorado & Seville

ABS/TCS SYMPTOM TABLE

CHART	SYMPTOM
A	"ANTI-LOCK" INDICATOR "ON" WITH NO DTCs SET
B	"ANTI-LOCK" INDICATOR INOPERATIVE OR FLICKERS BRIEFLY AT IGNITION "ON"
C	"TRACTION CONTROL" INDICATOR "ON" WITH NO DTCs SET
D	"TRACTION CONTROL" INDICATOR INOPERATIVE
E	"TRACTION ENGAGED" INDICATOR "ON" WITH NO DTCs SET
F	"TRACTION ENGAGED" INDICATOR INOPERATIVE WITH NO DTCs SET

Fig. 14   ABS symptom table. 1993 Fleetwood (RWD)

Fig. 15   ABS flash code diagnosis

Fig. 16   ABS wiring circuit (Part 1 of 2). 1991 Caprice, Custom Cruiser & Roadmaster

Fig. 16   ABS wiring circuit (Part 2 of 2). 1991 Caprice, Custom Cruiser & Roadmaster

2. Turn ignition On, then follow menus to reach ABS/TCS features.
3. Select F5:TP SENSOR LEARN, then press UP arrow to begin learn procedure.
4. Wait for TECH 1 to indicate COMPLETE, then turn ignition Off and disconnect TECH 1.

FLASH CODE DIAGNOSIS

Flash code diagnosis can only be used to identify codes in the EBCM history. The flash code diagnostic mode cannot be initiated if the Anti-Lock warning lamp is on steady.

To initiate flash code diagnostics, ground pin "H" of the diagnostic connector, then turn ignition on. Flash Code Diagnostics will remain on as long as pin "H" is grounded, serial data line communication

has not been initiated, and vehicle speed is less than 4 mph.

Approximately three seconds after ALDL has been grounded, the EBCM will begin flashing the Anti-Lock Indicator Lamp in flash code sequence. The flash code sequence **Fig. 15** will begin with Code 12 flashing three times to signal the beginning of the trouble code display. Each stored code will than be flashed three times. After all codes have been displayed, the sequence will repeat, starting with Code 12.

Current Codes 41, 45, 55, 61 and 63 can only be read using the TECH 1 diagnostic computer. If these codes are present as history codes only, they can be read through flash code diagnosis.

When performing diagnosis on Caprice, Custom Cruiser and Roadmaster models refer to wiring circuits **Figs. 16 and 17**, code charts **Figs. 18 through 37**, A charts

Figs. 38 and 39 and B charts **Figs. 40 and 41.**

When performing diagnosis on Brougham models refer to wiring circuits **Fig. 42**, code charts **Figs. 43 through 55**, A chart **Fig. 56**, B chart **Fig. 57**, C chart **Fig. 58**, and D chart **Fig. 59.**

When performing diagnosis on 1991 Eldorado, Reatta, Riviera, Seville, Toronado and Trofeo models refer to wiring circuits **Fig. 60**, code charts **Figs. 61 through 75**, A chart **Fig. 76**, B chart **Fig. 77**, C chart **Fig. 78**, and D chart **Fig. 79.**

When performing diagnosis on 1992 Eldorado, Riviera, Seville, Toronado and Trofeo models refer to wiring circuits **Figs. 80 and 81**, code charts **Figs. 82 through 97**, A chart **Fig. 98**, B chart **Fig. 99**, C chart **Fig. 100**, and D chart **Fig. 101.**

When performing diagnosis on 1993 Eldorado and Seville models, refer to wiring circuits **Figs. 102 and 103**, code charts **Figs. 104 through 129**, A chart **Fig. 130**, B chart **Fig. 131**, C chart **Fig. 132**, and D chart **Fig. 133.**

**Fig. 17   ABS wiring circuit (Part 1 of 2).
1992–93 Caprice, Custom Cruiser &
Roadmaster**

**Fig. 17   ABS wiring circuit (Part 2 of 2).
1992–93 Caprice, Custom Cruiser &
Roadmaster**

When performing diagnosis on 1993 Fleetwood RWD models refer, to wiring circuit **Figs. 134**, code charts **Figs. 135 through 159, A chart Fig. 160, B chart Fig. 161, C chart Fig. 162, D chart Fig. 163, E chart Fig. 164**, and **F chart Fig. 165.**

TECH 1 DIAGNOSTICS

When using the TECH 1 for ABS system diagnosis, the ABS system is disabled when communication with the TECH 1. The Anti-Lock indicator lamp will be lit, indicating only power assisted braking is possible. A Bosch ABS adapter is required when connecting the TECH 1 to the ALDL connector.

When performing diagnosis on Caprice, Custom Cruiser and Roadmaster models refer to wiring circuits **Figs. 16 and 17**, code charts **Figs. 18 through 37**, A charts **Figs. 38 and 39** and B charts **Figs. 40 and 41.**

When performing diagnosis on Brougham models refer to wiring circuits **Fig. 42**, code charts **Figs. 43 through 55**, A chart **Fig. 56**, B chart **Fig. 57**, C chart **Fig. 58**, and D chart **Fig. 59.**

When performing diagnosis on 1991 Eldorado, Reatta, Riviera, Seville, Toronado and Trofeo models refer to wiring circuits **Figs. 60**, code charts **Figs. 61 through 75**, A chart **Fig. 76**, B chart **Fig. 77**, C chart **Fig. 78**, and D chart **Fig. 79.**

When performing diagnosis on 1992 Eldorado, Riviera, Seville, Toronado and Trofeo models refer to wiring circuits **Figs. 80 and 81**, code charts **Figs. 82 through 97**, A chart **Fig. 98**, B chart **Fig. 99**, C chart **Fig. 100**, and D chart **Fig. 101.**

When performing diagnosis on 1993 Eldorado and Seville models, refer to wiring circuits **Figs. 102 and 103**, code charts **Figs. 104 through 129, A chart Fig. 130, B chart Fig. 131, C chart Fig. 132**, and D chart **Fig. 133.**

When performing diagnosis on 1993 Fleetwood RWD models refer, to wiring circuit **Figs. 134**, code charts **Figs. 135 through 159, A chart Fig. 160, B chart Fig. 161, C chart Fig. 162, D chart Fig. 163, E chart Fig. 164**, and **F chart Fig. 165.**

TECH 1 TEST MODES

Mode F0: Data List

In this mode, TECH 1 continuously monitors wheel speed data and brake switch status. When monitoring speed data, the TECH 1 screen displays signals being sent from wheel speed sensors to the EBCM. In this mode, vehicle can be driven while TECH 1 displays speed data. These reading can be compared with actual vehicle speed to check proper operation. Speed signals can also can be compared with each other to determine whether they are within specification.

If one speed signal differs greatly from another signal, improper operation of that sensor may be indicated. Intermittent speed signals can be located in the DATA LIST mode by checking for signals that vary for no reason.

In DATA LIST mode, the TECH 1 screen displays brake switch operation. When brake pedal is depressed, screen reads ON; when pedal is released, screen reads OFF.

Mode F1: Code History

In this mode, trouble code history is displayed. This data include how many ignition cycles since the trouble code first occurred, brake switch status, vehicle speed and ABS state when fault occurred. Up to three codes are included in the ABS history data.

Mode F2: Trouble Codes

In this mode, the TECH 1 displays trouble codes stored in the EBCM. The EBCM can store up to three different trouble codes. The TECH 1 can also clear codes when in this mode.

When this mode is accessed, trouble codes are displayed, with a three second interval between each code displayed. When each code is displayed, it will be accompanied by a brief description of what that code represents.

After displaying trouble codes, the TECH

1 can be ordered to clear any trouble codes stored in th EBCM. The TECH 1 will respond to a clear codes command by displaying either an "ABS CODES CLEARED" or "CODES CLEAR FAIL" on the screen.

The EBCM stores other information about trouble codes which may prove useful in diagnosis procedure. This function is called "ENHANCED DIAGNOSTIC DATA." The TECH 1 can be ordered to display any of the following ENHANCED DIAGNOSTIC DATA:

1. **Brake Switch Status,** indicates whether brake light switch was ON or OFF when code was set.
2. **ABS State,** indicates whether or not anti-lock mode ws engaged when code was set.
3. **Vehicle Speed,** indicates vehicle speed when code was set.
4. **Ignition Cycles,** indicates how many ignition cycles have occurred since code was set.

Mode F3: ABS Snapshot

The ABS snapshot will help to isolate problems caused by the speed sensor signals which may cause intermittent operation of the ABS system. The ABS SNAPSHOT mode captures data before and after a trigger condition.

If "MANUAL TRIGGER" is selected, the TECH 1 will wait for "ENTER" to be pressed before storing speed sensor information. When TECH 1 is waiting for "ENTER" or "F9" to be pressed, a "W" will be displayed in the lower righthand corner of the display. While the TECH 1 is waiting for the trigger, it continuously stores ABS speed sensor data. The TECH 1 can store up to 81 samples of ABS data before the trigger, and 81 samples after the trigger. If more than 81 samples occur before the trigger, the oldest data will be discarded. It takes approximately eight seconds for the TECH 1 to store 81 samples.

As soon as "ENTER" or "F9" is pressed, the TECH 1 will begin to store speed sensor data, this is indicated by an "I" displayed on the screen. When data storage is full, the data point when the "ENTER" button was pressed will be displayed indicated by ")" on the display.

To view the speed information that was stored, use the UP ARROW and DOWN ARROW keys. The numbers on the display indicate the sample number relative to the trigger. An "+1" on the display indicates the first sample after the "ENTER" button was pressed. An "-1" on the display indicates the sample proceeding the time when "ENTER" was pressed. By selecting the up and down arrow keys, all of the stored data can be displayed and examined for conditions which might indicate a problem. While displaying data, select F7 to convert English to Metric or select "ENTER" to convert number in the righthand lower corner of the screen to time in seconds.

If "AUTOMATIC TRIGGER" is selected, the TECH 1 will store data which may deviate from normal operating conditions but may not set a code. For example, when driving over bumpy roads or railroad tracks, the wheel speed signal may change rapidly or drop out. This condition may be caused by loose connections or intermittent wiring problems. Using the "AUTOMATIC TRIGGER," data will be stored when the TECH 1 recognizes that a wheel speed signal has deviated from it normal operating range. While the TECH 1 is waiting for a trigger, the "ENTER" or "F9" button may be used to force a trigger. While displaying the information, the cause of the trigger can be displayed by selecting F3.

Mode F4: ABS Tests

This mode performs functional tests on the ABS system which help verify proper system operation. Error conditions can be further identified by testing and observing test results. In the "ABS TESTS" mode the following test can be performed:

1. **Solenoid Valve-Pressure Reduction:** This test indicates whether specific solenoid valves in the hydraulic modulator release pressure to assigned hydraulic wheel circuits.
2. **Solenoid Valve-Hold Pressure:** This test indicates whether specific solenoid valves in the hydraulic modulator hold pressure in assigned hydraulic wheel circuits.
3. **AUTO Test:** This test cycles each solenoid valve and operates the pump motor briefly. The EBCM will store an error code if test conditions fail.

The "PRESSURE REDUCE" test activates a selected hydraulic wheel circuit valve, placing it in the pressure reduce position. Valve action can then be verified by checking the appropriate wheel for proper brake action. The TECH 1 will indicate whether the valve action was commanded properly. This test used in conjunction with the "PRESSURE HOLD" test, completely checks each solenoid valve. With the aid of an assistant, perform the following procedure.

1. Have assistant press brake pedal.
2. Set TECH 1 to command "PRESSURE REDUCE" mode.
3. Try to spin wheel being tested, wheel should spin due to reduce command.

The "PRESSURE HOLD" test activates a selected hydraulic wheel circuit valve, placing it in the pressure hold position. Valve action can then be verified by checking the appropriate wheel for proper brake action. The TECH 1 will indicate whether the valve action was commanded properly. This test used in conjunction with the "PRESSURE REDUCE" test, completely checks each solenoid valve. With the aid of an assistant, perform the following procedure.

1. Spin wheel freely, then set TECH 1 to command "PRESSURE HOLD."
2. Have assistant press brake pedal.
3. Try to spin wheel being tested, wheel should spin due to hold command, even though brake is applied.

CLEARING CODES

The trouble codes in the EBCM memory are erased in one of three ways, diagnostic request line procedure, TECH 1 "CLEAR CODES" selection and ignition cycle default.

Whichever method is used, ensure to verify proper system operation and absence of codes when clearing procedure is completed.

The EBCM will not allow codes to be cleared until all codes have been displayed. Codes cannot be cleared by unplugging the EBCM, disconnecting the battery cables, or turning off the ignition.

Diagnostic Line Procedure

1. Turn ignition switch off, then attach a jumper to ALDL connector terminal "H."
2. Attach a jumper wire to ALDL connector terminal "A," then connect both jumper wires to each other.
3. Turn ignition switch to the "RUN" position.
4. Disconnect jumpers for approximately one second then reconnect jumpers for no less than one second intervals taking them apart briefly between intervals. Repeat this action four times within 10 seconds, leaving jumpers connected upon completion of the fourth interval. Check ANTI-LOCK indicator. Only Code 12 should be present. If not, trouble codes have not been properly cleared. Begin clearing procedures again at step 1. If codes are cleared, wait at least 15 seconds before turning ignition off.

TECH 1 Procedure

Before clearing codes, check and note history code data, as this information will also be cleared.

Select appropriate menu, and select the clear codes function. Verify that codes are cleared by using the TECH 1 to read codes. If any code other than Code 12 is present, either codes were not cleared, or an ABS fault still exists.

Ignition Cycle Default

If vehicle power is cycled 100 times without a particular fault reappearing, that particular fault code will be erased from the EBCM memory, and ignition cycle counter will be reset to zero.

Continued on page 23-231

DIAGNOSTIC (TROUBLE CODE) CHART INDEX

Chart	Description	Year	Page No.	Fig. No.
Brougham				
Code 21	RF Wheel Speed Sensor Fault	1991–92	23-146	43
Code 22	RF Toothed Wheel Frequency Error	1991–92	23-147	44
Code 25	LF Wheel Speed Sensor Fault	1991–92	23-147	45
Code 26	LF Toothed Wheel Frequency Error	1991–92	23-148	46
Code 35	LR Wheel Speed Sensor Fault	1991–92	23-149	47
Code 36	Rear Axle Toothed Wheel Frequency Error	1991–92	23-150	48
Code 41	RF Solenoid Valve Fault	1991–92	23-150	49
Code 45	LF Solenoid Valve Fault	1991–92	23-151	50
Code 55	Rear Axle Solenoid Valve Fault	1991–92	23-151	51
Code 61	Pump Motor Circuit Failure	1991–92	23-152	52
Code 63	Solenoid Valve Relay Fault	1991–92	23-153	53
Code 71	EBCM Fault	1991–92	23-154	54
Code 72	Serial Data Link Error	1991–92	23-154	55
Chart A	No System Power	1991–92	23-154	56
Chart B	ABS Indicator On w/No Codes Set	1991–92	23-155	57
Chart C	ABS Indicator Inoperative w/Key On	1991–92	23-155	58
Chart D	Valve Cycling During Normal Stops	1991–92	23-156	59
Caprice, Custom Cruiser & Roadmaster				
Code 21	RF Wheel Speed Sensor (Sensor Fault)	1991-93	23-126	18
Code 22	RF Toothed Wheel (Frequency Fault)	1991-93	23-127	19
Code 25	LF Wheel Speed Sensor (Sensor Fault)	1991-93	23-128	20
Code 26	LF Toothed Wheel (Frequency Fault)	1991-93	23-129	21
Code 35	Rear Axle Speed Sensor (Sensor Fault)	1991-93	23-130	22
Code 36	Rear Axle Toothed Wheel (Frequency Fault)	1991-92	23-131	23
Code 36	Rear Axle Toothed Wheel (Frequency Fault)	1993	23-132	24
Code 41	RF Solenoid Valve (Valve Fault)	1991	23-132	25
Code 41	RF Solenoid Valve (Valve Fault)	1992-93	23-133	26
Code 45	LF Solenoid Valve (Valve Fault)	1991	23-134	27
Code 45	LF Solenoid Valve (Valve Fault)	1992-93	23-134	28
Code 55	Rear Wheels Solenoid Valve (Valve Fault)	1991	23-135	29
Code 55	Rear Wheels Solenoid Valve (Valve Fault)	1992-93	23-135	30
Code 61	Pump Motor Or Relay Fault	1991	23-136	31
Code 61	Pump Motor Or Relay Fault	1992-93	23-137	32
Code 63	Solenoid Valve Relay Fault	1991	23-138	33
Code 63	Solenoid Valve Relay Fault	1992-93	23-140	34
Code 71	Electronic Brake Control Module (EBCM Fault)	1991	23-141	35
Code 71	Electronic Brake Control Module (EBCM Fault)	1992-93	23-141	36
Code 72	Electronic Brake Control Module (Serial Line Data Fault)	1991-93	23-142	37
Chart A	Anti-Lock Indicator On w/No Codes Set	1991	23-143	38
Chart A	Anti-Lock Indicator On w/No Codes Set	1992-93	23-144	39
Chart B	Anti-Lock Indicator Inoperative	1991	23-144	40
Chart B	Anti-Lock Indicator Inoperative	1992-93	23-145	41
Fleetwood (RWD)				
Code 21	RF Wheel Speed Sensor Malfunction	1993	23-213	135
Code 23	RF Wheel Speed Sensor Continuity Malfunction	1993	23-213	136
Code 25	LF Wheel Speed Sensor Malfunction	1993	23-214	137
Code 27	LF Wheel Speed Continuity Malfunction	1993	23-214	138
Code 28	Wheel Speed Sensor Frequency Error	1993	23-215	139
Code 31	RR Wheel Speed Sensor Malfunction	1993	23-215	140

Continued

Chart	Description	Year	Page No.	Fig. No.
Fleetwood (RWD)-Continued				
Code 33	RR Wheel Speed Sensor Continuity Malfunction	1993	23-216	141
Code 35	LR Wheel Speed Sensor Malfunction	1993	23-216	142
Code 37	LR Wheel Speed Continuity Malfunction	1993	23-217	143
Code 41	RF Solenoid Valve Malfunction	1993	23-217	144
Code 44	Pilot Valve Solenoid Malfunction	1993	23-218	145
Code 45	LF Solenoid Valve Malfunction	1993	23-218	146
Code 51	RR Valve Solenoid Malfunction	1993	23-219	147
Code 55	LR Valve Solenoid Malfunction	1993	23-219	148
Code 57	TCC Disable Relay Output Malfunction	1993	23-220	149
Code 58	EBTCM Internal Adjuster Assembly Malfunction	1993	23-220	150
Code 61	Pump Motor Or Pump Motor Relay Malfunction	1993	23-221	151
Code 62	RPM Signal Malfunction	1993	23-222	152
Code 63	Valve Solenoid Relay Circuit Malfunction	1993	23-222	153
Code 64	Throttle Position Signal Malfunction	1993	23-223	154
Code 65	Adjuster Assembly Malfunction	1993	23-224	155
Code 66	Adjuster Assembly Control Malfunction	1993	23-225	156
Code 71	EBTCM Internal Malfunction	1993	23-226	157
Code 72	Serial Data Link Malfunction	1993	23-226	158
Code 83	Brake Differential Pressure Malfunction	1993	23-227	159
Chart A	Anti-Lock Indicator On w/No Codes Set	1993	23-228	160
Chart B	Anti-Lock Indicator Inoperative Or Flickers Briefly At Ignition ON	1993	23-228	161
Chart C	Traction Control Indicator ON w/No Codes Set	1993	23-229	162
Chart D	Traction Control Indicator Inoperative	1993	23-229	163
Chart E	Traction Engaged Indicator ON w/No Codes Set	1993	23-230	164
Chart F	Traction Engaged Indicator Inoperative w/No Codes Set	1993	23-230	165
1991 Eldorado, Reatta, Riviera, Seville, Toronado & Trofeo				
Code 21	RF Wheel Speed Sensor Fault	1991	23-157	61
Code 22	RF Toothed Wheel Frequency Error	1991	23-159	62
Code 25	LF Wheel Speed Sensor Fault	1991	23-160	63
Code 26	LF Toothed Wheel Frequency Error	1991	23-161	64
Code 31	RR Wheel Speed Sensor Fault	1991	23-162	65
Code 32	RR Toothed Wheel Frequency Error	1991	23-163	66
Code 35	LR Wheel Speed Sensor Fault	1991	23-164	67
Code 36	LR Toothed Wheel Frequency Error	1991	23-165	68
Code 41	RF Solenoid Valve Fault	1991	23-166	69
Code 45	LF Solenoid Valve Fault	1991	23-166	70
Code 55	Rear Solenoid Valve Fault	1991	23-167	71
Code 61	Pump Motor Circuit Fault	1991	23-168	72
Code 63	Solenoid Valve Relay Fault	1991	23-169	73
Code 71	EBCM Fault	1991	23-170	74
Code 72	Serial Line Data Fault	1991	23-170	75
Chart A	No System Power	1991	23-171	76
Chart B	ABS Indicator On w/No Codes Set	1991	23-172	77
Chart C	ABS Indicator Inoperative At Key On	1991	23-173	78
Chart D	Valve Cycling During Normal Stops	1991	23-174	79
1992 Eldorado, Riviera, Seville, Toronado & Trofeo				
Code 21	RF Wheel Speed Sensor Fault	1992	23-176	82
Code 22	RF Toothed Wheel Frequency Error	1992	23-177	83
Code 25	LF Wheel Speed Sensor Fault	1992	23-177	84
Code 26	LF Toothed Wheel Frequency Error	1992	23-178	85
Code 31	RR Wheel Speed Sensor Fault	1992	23-179	86
Code 32	RR Toothed Wheel Frequency Error	1992	23-180	87

Continued

Chart	Description	Year	Page No.	Fig. No.
1992 Eldorado, Riviera, Seville, Toronado & Trofeo-Continued				
Code 35	LR Wheel Speed Sensor Fault	1992	23-180	88
Code 36	LR Toothed Wheel Frequency Error	1992	23-181	89
Code 41	RF Solenoid Valve Fault	1992	23-182	90
Code 45	LF Solenoid Valve Fault	1992	23-182	91
Code 55	Rear Solenoid Valve Fault	1992	23-183	92
Code 61	Pump Motor Circuit Fault (Eldorado & Seville)	1992	23-183	93
Code 61	Pump Motor Circuit Fault (Riviera, Toronado & Trofeo)	1992	23-184	94
Code 63	Solenoid Valve Relay Fault	1992	23-185	95
Code 71	EBCM Fault	1992	23-186	96
Code 72	Serial Line Data Fault	1992	23-186	97
Chart A	No System Power	1992	23-1873	98
Chart B	ABS Indicator On w/No Codes Set	1992	23-187	99
Chart C	ABS Indicator Inoperative At Key On	1992	23-188	100
Chart D	Valve Cycling During Normal Stops	1992	23-188	101
1993 Eldorado & Seville				
Code 21	RF Wheel Speed Sensor Fault	1993	23-191	104
Code 22	RF Speed Wheel Frequency Error	1993	23-191	105
Code 23	RF Speed Wheel Continuity Error	1993	23-191	106
Code 25	LF Wheel Speed Sensor Fault	1993	23-192	107
Code 26	LF Speed Wheel Frequency Error	1993	23-193	108
Code 27	LF Speed Wheel Continuity Error	1993	23-193	109
Code 28	Wheel Speed Sensor Frequency Error	1993	23-194	110
Code 31	RR Wheel Speed Sensor Fault	1993	23-194	111
Code 32	RR Toothed Wheel Frequency Error	1993	23-195	112
Code 33	RR Toothed Wheel Continuity Error	1993	23-196	113
Code 35	LR Wheel Speed Sensor Fault	1993	23-196	114
Code 36	LR Toothed Wheel Frequency Error	1993	23-197	115
Code 37	LR Toothed Wheel Continuity Error	1993	23-198	116
Code 41	RF ABS Valve Solenoid Fault	1993	23-198	117
Code 44	RF TCS Pilot Valve Fault	1993	23-199	118
Code 45	LF ABS Valve Solenoid Fault	1993	23-200	119
Code 48	LF TCS Pilot Valve Fault	1993	23-201	120
Code 51	RR ABS Valve Solenoid Fault (TCS)	1993	23-202	121
Code 55	Rear Valve Solenoid Fault (Non-TCS)	1993	23-203	122
Code 61	Pump Motor Or Pump Motor Relay Fault	1993	23-204	123
Code 63	Valve Relay Circuit Fault	1993	23-206	124
Code 67	Brake Light Switch Fault	1993	23-207	125
Code 71	EBTCM/EBCM Fault	1993	23-208	126
Code 72	Serial Data Link Fault	1993	23-208	127
Code 73	PCM-EBTCM/EBCM PWM Signal Fault (4.6L)	1993	23-209	128
Code 83	Brake Fluid Level Low	1993	23-209	129
Chart A	Antilock & Traction Disabled Message ON w/No TCS Codes Set/ No TCS Data	1993	23-210	130
Chart B	ABS Indicator ON	1993	23-210	131
Chart C	Valve Cycling During Normal Stops (Unwanted ABS Modulation)	1993	23-211	132
Chart D	Traction Control Operation Check	1993	23-211	133

1991

1992–93

Circuit Description:

As each wheel turns, the wheel speed sensor for that wheel creates a low current AC voltage as the toothed sensor ring rotates by the stationary sensor. The sensor consists of a permanent magnet and coil that generates voltage by magnetic induction. The frequency and voltage of the induced signal is proportional to wheel speed.

The EBCM uses the wheel speed sensor signal to calculate vehicle reference speeds and individual speed, acceleration and slip values for each wheel. These values are used to determine when antilock control is required.

Failure Conditions:

The EBCM performs two basic types of checks on the wheel speed sensors to check sensor continuity and sensor output. Any condition which would result in lack of continuity or output on the right front wheel speed sensor circuit could result in setting Code 21. These conditions include an open, short to ground or short to B + in CKT 872, an open in CKT 833 or an open across the sensor coil.

Code 21 will also set if low output from the wheel speed sensor is detected by the EBCM. These conditions include a shorted sensor coil or an improperly installed sensor.

Action Taken:

If a failure is detected which causes a speed sensor Code 21 to set, antilock braking is disabled and the EBCM turns "ON" the "Antilock" indicator for the remainder of the ignition cycle. If the failure is intermittent, the EBCM will enable the system at the next ignition cycle and a history Code 21 will be present.

❓ Important

• The RF wheel speed sensor is located in the RF steering knuckle. In order to prevent electromagnetic interference from disturbing the wheel speed sensor signal, the sensor wires are twisted together 9 times for every foot of wire.

Test Description: Number(s) below refer to circled number(s) on the diagnostic chart.

1. Checks for a correct resistance reading of the sensor itself.
2. Checks for a short between the wires for the RF wheel speed sensor.
3. Checks for an open, high resistance or short to voltage in the wires between the speed sensor and the EBCM.
4. Checks for a short to ground in CKT 872.
5. Checks for an "Intermittent" in the RF wheel speed sensor circuitry. If no "Intermittent" is found in the wiring, it may be in the sensor itself. Replace the sensor and road test the vehicle. If the code returns, replace the EBCM.

Diagnostic Aids:

Intermittent setting of speed sensor error codes may be caused by improperly mounted sensors or improper wire routing. Verify that the sensor is mounted correctly and the sensor face does not contain an accumulation of metallic particles, dirt or grease. Verify that sensor wires are properly routed and secure. To aid in troubleshooting intermittent conditions, the Tech 1 can be used while test driving the vehicle.

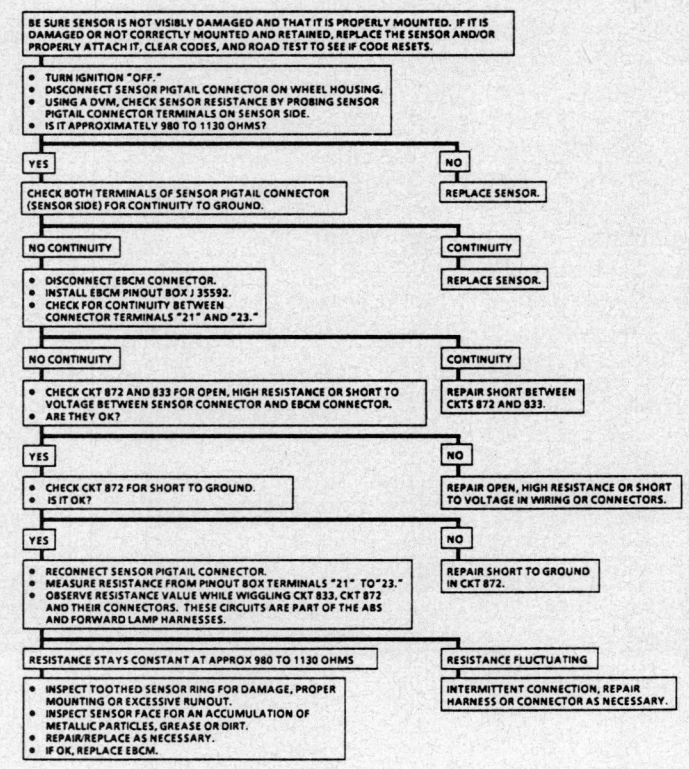

Fig. 18 Code 21, RF wheel speed sensor fault. Caprice, Custom Cruiser & Roadmaster

1991

1992—93

Circuit Description:

As each wheel turns, the wheel speed sensor for that wheel creates a low current AC voltage as the toothed sensor ring rotates by the stationary sensor. The sensor consists of a permanent magnet and coil that generates voltage by magnetic induction. The frequency and voltage of the induced signal is proportional to wheel speed.

The EBCM uses the wheel speed sensor signal to calculate vehicle reference speeds and individual speed, acceleration and slip values for each wheel. These values are used to determine when antilock control is required.

Failure Conditions:

Code 22 will set if improper speed signals are being generated by the toothed wheel. Causes of improper speed signals include; an incorrect number of teeth or damaged teeth present on the toothed wheel, toothed wheel or sensor face covered with dirt, grease or metallic particles that may impair magnetic induction.

Code 22 may also set if the mini-spare tire has previously been used or the size of the tires on the vehicle differ. In addition to Code 22, Codes 26 and 36 may also set if the mini-spare tire has been used. If it is known that the spare tire was used, clear codes and test drive the vehicle again. Verify that codes do not set.

Action Taken:

If a failure is detected which causes a speed sensor Code 22 to set, antilock braking is disabled and the EBCM turns "ON" the "Antilock" indicator for the remainder of the ignition cycle. If the failure is intermittent, the EBCM will enable the system at the next ignition cycle and a history Code 22 will be present.

Test Description: Number(s) below refer to circled number(s) on the diagnostic chart.
1. Checks for properly mounted sensor and mounting torque.
2. Checks for a physical problem with the toothed wheel.
3. Checks for an improper sensor ring.

Diagnostic Aids:

A worn hub/bearing assembly may cause this fault in extreme cases; the bearing play allows the sensor-to-toothed ring gap to change excessively.

Check for a buildup of foreign material in the gaps between teeth on the toothed wheel; this material may cause this error.

Also, check the toothed wheel for any large grooves, gouges, marks, etc., that might influence the tooth's signal at the wheel speed sensor.

Remove and inspect wheel speed sensor for damage or contamination. If OK, and Code 22 is still present, refer to Code 21 Chart.

Fig. 19   Code 22, RF toothed wheel frequency error. Caprice, Custom Cruiser & Roadmaster

1991

1992-93

Circuit Description:

As each wheel turns, the wheel speed sensor for that wheel creates a low current AC voltage as the toothed sensor ring rotates by the stationary sensor. The sensor consists of a permanent magnet and coil that generates voltage by magnetic induction. The frequency and voltage of the induced signal is proportional to wheel speed.

The EBCM uses the wheel speed sensor signal to calculate vehicle reference speeds and individual speed, acceleration and slip values for each wheel. These values are used to determine when antilock control is required.

Failure Conditions:

The EBCM performs two basic types of checks on the wheel speed sensors to check sensor continuity and sensor output. Any condition which would result in lack of continuity or output on the left front wheel speed sensor circuit could result in setting Code 25. These conditions include an open, short to ground or short to B+ in CKT 830, an open in CKT 873 or an open across the sensor coil.

Code 25 will also set if low output from the wheel speed sensor is detected by the EBCM. These conditions include a shorted sensor coil or an improperly installed sensor.

Action Taken:

If a failure is detected which causes a speed sensor Code 25 to set, antilock braking is disabled and the EBCM turns "ON" the "Antilock" indicator for the remainder of the ignition cycle. If the failure is intermittent, the EBCM will enable the system at the next ignition cycle and a history Code 25 will be present.

💡 **Important**
- The LF wheel speed sensor is located in the LF steering knuckle. In order to prevent electromagnetic interference from disturbing the wheel speed sensor signal, the sensor wires are twisted together 9 times for every foot of wire.

Test Description: Number(s) below refer to circled number(s) on the diagnostic chart.

1. Checks for a correct resistance reading of the sensor itself.
2. Checks for a short between the wires for the LF wheel speed sensor.
3. Checks for an open, high resistance or short to voltage in the wires between the speed sensor and the EBCM.
4. Checks for a short to ground in CKT 830.
5. Checks for an "Intermittent" in the LF wheel speed sensor circuitry. If no "Intermittent" is found in the wiring, it may be in the sensor itself. Replace the sensor and road test the vehicle. If the code returns, replace the EBCM.

Diagnostic Aids:

Intermittent setting of speed sensor error codes may be caused by improperly mounted sensors or improper wire routing. Verify that the sensor is mounted correctly and the sensor face does not contain an accumulation of metallic particles, dirt or grease. Verify that sensor wires are properly routed and secure. To aid in troubleshooting intermittent conditions, the Tech 1 can be used while test driving the vehicle.

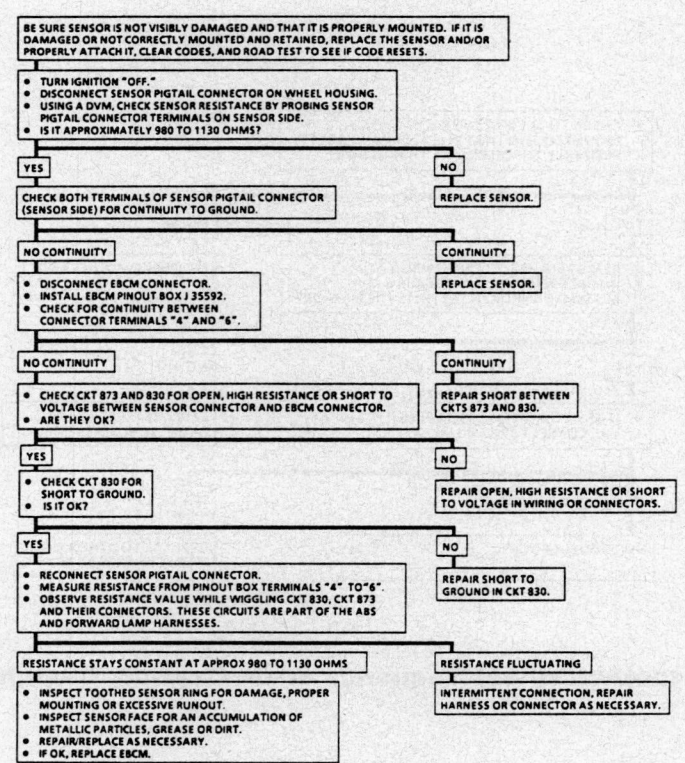

Fig. 20   Code 25, LF wheel speed sensor fault. Caprice, Custom Cruiser & Roadmaster

1991

1992–93

Circuit Description:
As each wheel turns, the wheel speed sensor for that wheel creates a low current AC voltage as the toothed sensor ring rotates by the stationary sensor. The sensor consists of a permanent magnet and coil that generates voltage by magnetic induction. The frequency and voltage of the induced signal is proportional to wheel speed.
The EBCM uses the wheel speed sensor signal to calculate vehicle reference speeds and individual speed, acceleration and slip values for each wheel. These values are used to determine when antilock control is required.

Failure Conditions:
Code 26 will set if improper speed signals are being generated by the toothed wheel. Causes of improper speed signals include: an incorrect number of teeth or damaged teeth present on the toothed wheel, toothed wheel or sensor face covered with dirt, grease or metallic particles that may impair magnetic induction.
Code 26 may also set if the mini-spare tire has previously been used or the size of the tires on the vehicle differ. In addition to Code 26, Codes 22 and 36 may also set if the mini-spare tire has been used. If it is known that the spare tire was used, clear codes and test drive the vehicle again. Verify that codes do not set.

Action Taken:
If a failure is detected which causes a speed sensor Code 26 to set, antilock braking is disabled and the EBCM turns "ON" the "Antilock" indicator for the remainder of the ignition cycle. If the failure is intermittent, the EBCM will enable the system at the next ignition cycle and a history Code 26 will be present.

Test Description: Number(s) below refer to circled number(s) on the diagnostic chart.
1. Checks for properly mounted sensor and mounting torque.
2. Checks for a physical problem with the toothed wheel.
3. Checks for an improper sensor ring.

Diagnostic Aids:
A worn hub/bearing assembly may cause this fault in extreme cases; the bearing play allows the sensor-to-toothed ring gap to change excessively.
Check for a buildup of foreign material in the gaps between teeth on the toothed wheel; this material may cause this error.
Also, check the toothed wheel for any large grooves, gouges, marks, etc., that might influence the tooth's signal at the wheel speed sensor.
Remove and inspect wheel speed sensor for damage or contamination. If OK, and Code 26 is still present refer to Code 25 Chart.

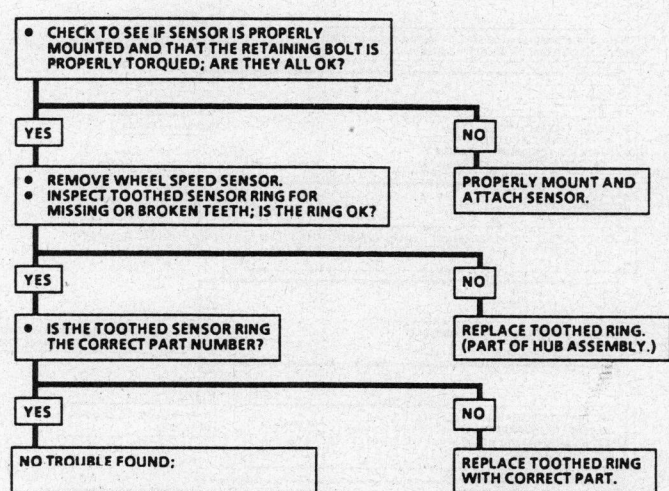

Fig. 21 Code 26, LF toothed wheel frequency error. Caprice, Custom Cruiser & Roadmaster

1991

1992-93

Circuit Description:

As the differential pinion gear turns, the rear axle speed sensor creates a low current AC voltage as the toothed sensor ring (mounted to the differential pinion gear) rotates by the stationary sensor. The sensor consists of a permanent magnet and coil that generates voltage by magnetic induction. The frequency and voltage of the induced signal is proportional to rear axle speed.

The EBCM uses the rear axle speed sensor signal to calculate vehicle reference speeds and individual speed, acceleration and slip values for each wheel. These values are used to determine when antilock control is required.

Failure Conditions:

The EBCM performs two basic types of checks on the rear axle speed sensor to check sensor continuity and sensor output. Any condition which would result in lack of continuity or output on the rear axle speed sensor circuit could result in setting Code 35. These conditions include an open, short to ground or short to B+ in CKT 882, an open in CKT 883 or an open across the sensor coil.

Code 35 will also set if low output from the rear axle speed sensor is detected by the EBCM. These conditions include a shorted sensor coil or an improperly installed sensor.

Action Taken:

If a failure is detected which causes a speed sensor Code 35 to set, antilock braking is disabled and the EBCM turns "ON" the "Antilock" indicator for the remainder of the ignition cycle. If the failure is intermittent, the EBCM will enable the system at the next ignition cycle and a history Code 35 will be present.

Important

- The rear axle speed sensor is located in the rear axle housing. In order to prevent electromagnetic interference from disturbing the rear axle speed sensor signal, the sensor wires are twisted together 9 times for every foot of wire.

Test Description: Number(s) below refer to circled number(s) on the diagnostic chart.

1. Checks for a correct resistance reading of the sensor itself.
2. Checks for a short between the wires for the rear axle speed sensor.
3. Checks for an open, high resistance or short to voltage in the wires between the speed sensor and the EBCM.
4. Checks for a short to ground in CKT 882.
5. Checks for an "Intermittent" in the rear axle speed sensor circuitry. If no intermittent is found in the wiring, it may be in the sensor itself. Replace the sensor and road test the vehicle. If the code returns, replace the EBCM.

Diagnostic Aids:

Intermittent setting of speed sensor error codes may be caused by improperly mounted sensors or improper wire routing. Verify that the sensor is mounted correctly and the sensor face does not contain an accumulation of metallic particles, dirt or grease. Verify that sensor wires are properly routed and secure. To aid in troubleshooting intermittent conditions, the Tech 1 can be used while test driving the vehicle.

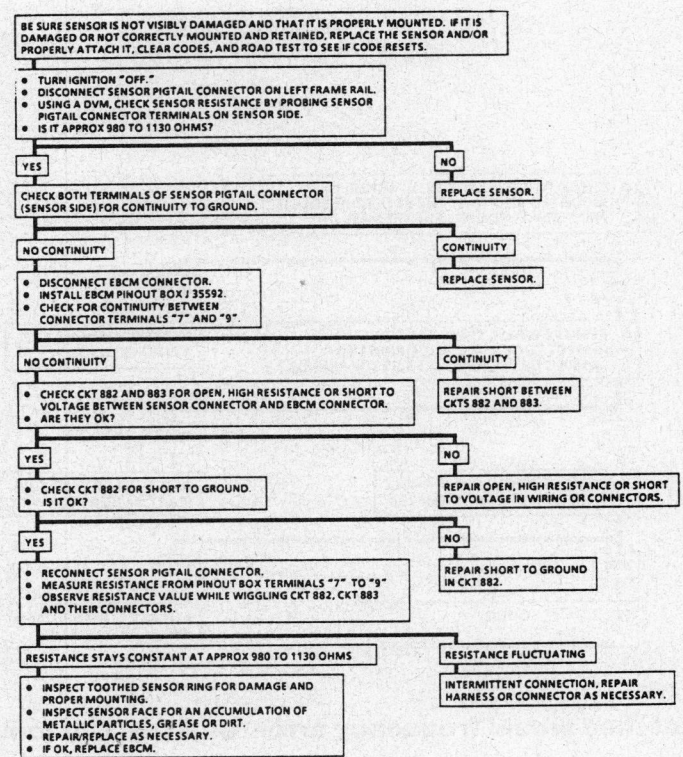

Fig. 22 Code 35, rear axle speed sensor fault. Caprice, Custom Cruiser & Roadmaster

1991

1992

Circuit Description:

As the differential pinion gear turns, the rear axle speed sensor creates a low current AC voltage as the toothed sensor ring (mounted to the differential pinion gear) rotates by the stationary sensor. The sensor consists of a permanent magnet and coil that generates voltage by magnetic induction. The frequency and voltage of the induced signal is proportional to rear axle speed.

The EBCM uses the rear axle speed sensor signal to calculate vehicle reference speeds and individual speed, acceleration and slip values for each wheel. These values are used to determine when antilock control is required.

Failure Conditions:

Code 36 will set if improper speed signals are being generated by the toothed wheel. Causes of improper speed signals include; an incorrect number of teeth or damaged teeth present on the toothed wheel, toothed wheel or sensor face covered with dirt, grease or metallic particles that may impair magnetic induction.

Code 36 may also set if the mini-spare tire has previously been used or the size of the tires on the vehicle differ. In addition to Code 36, Codes 22 and 26 may also set if the mini-spare tire has been used. If it is known that the spare tire was used, clear codes and test drive the vehicle again. Verify that codes do not set.

Action Taken:

If a failure is detected which causes a speed sensor Code 36 to set, antilock braking is disabled and the EBCM turns "ON" the "Antilock" indicator for the remainder of the ignition cycle. If the failure is intermittent, the EBCM will enable the system at the next ignition cycle and a history Code 36 will be present.

Test Description: Number(s) below refer to circled number(s) on the diagnostic chart.

1. Checks for properly mounted sensor and mounting torque.
2. Checks for a physical problem with the toothed wheel.
3. Checks for an improper sensor ring.

Diagnostic Aids:

Check for a buildup of foreign material in the gaps between teeth on the toothed wheel; this material may cause this error.

Also, check the toothed wheel for any large grooves, gouges, marks, etc., that might influence the tooth's signal at the speed sensor.

Inspect speed sensor for damage or contamination. If OK, and Code 36 is still present, refer to Code 35 Chart.

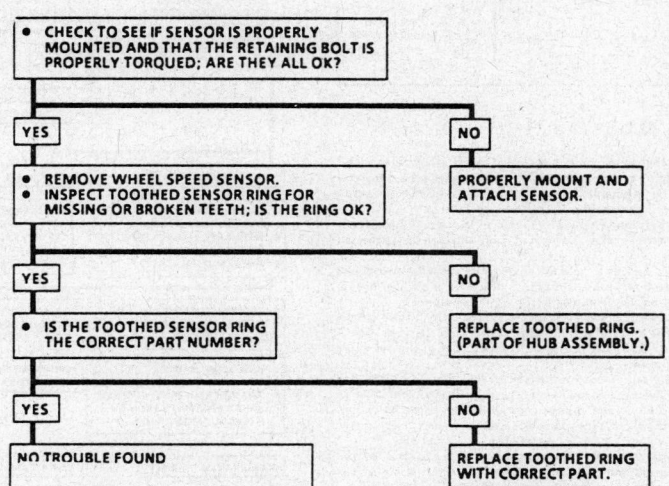

Fig. 23 Code 36, rear axle toothed wheel frequency error. 1991–92 Caprice, Custom Cruiser & Roadmaster

GENERAL MOTORS—Anti-Lock Brakes

DTC 36
REAR AXLE TOOTHED RING
(FREQUENCY ERROR)

Circuit Description:
As the differential pinion gear turns, the speed sensor creates an AC voltage as the toothed ring (mounted to the differential pinion gear) rotates by the stationary sensor. The sensor consists of a permanent magnet and coil generating voltage by magnetic induction. The frequency and voltage of the induced signal is proportional to rear axle speed.

The EBCM uses the speed sensor signal to calculate vehicle reference speed, individual speed, acceleration and slip values for the rear wheels which determine when antilock control is required.

Failure Conditions:
DTC 36 will set if improper speed signals are being generated by the toothed ring. Causes of improper speed signals include; an incorrect number of teeth or damaged teeth present on the toothed ring, toothed ring or sensor face covered with dirt, grease or metallic particles that may impair magnetic induction.

DTC 36 may also set if the mini-spare tire has previously been used or the size of the tires on the vehicle differ. In addition to DTC 36, DTCs 22 and 26 may also set if the mini-spare tire has been used. If it is known that the spare tire was used, clear DTCs and test drive the vehicle again. Verify that DTCs do not set.

Action Taken:
If a failure is detected which causes a speed sensor DTC 36 to set, antilock braking is disabled and the EBCM turns "ON" the "ANTILOCK" indicator for the remainder of the ignition cycle. If the failure is intermittent, the EBCM will enable the system at the next ignition cycle and a history DTC 36 will be present.

Test Description: Number(s) below refer to circled number(s) on the diagnostic chart.
1. Checks for properly mounted sensor and mounting torque.
2. Checks for a physical problem with the toothed ring.
3. Checks for contamination on sensor face or toothed ring.

Diagnostic Aids:
Check for a buildup of foreign material in the gaps between teeth on the toothed ring; this material may cause this error.

Also, check the toothed ring for any large grooves, gouges, marks, etc., that might influence the tooth's signal at the speed sensor.

Inspect speed sensor for damage or contamination. If OK, and DTC 36 is still present, refer to DTC 35 chart.

Fig. 24   Code 36, rear axle toothed wheel frequency error. 1993 Caprice, Custom Cruiser & Roadmaster

CODE 41
RF SOLENOID VALVE (VALVE FAULT)

Circuit Description:
With the ignition in Run, Bulb Test or Start the EBCM applies voltage to the Coil of the solenoid valve relay. The EBCM will complete an internal self-check before providing ground to the coil. Once energized the relay will provide B + to the solenoid valves. The solenoid valve can be commanded to three different positions depending upon the amount of current the EBCM allows to flow through the solenoid valve coil.

Pressure Increase position is the normal operating position of the valves for braking. Brake fluid flows through the modulator from the master cylinder to the wheel brake. No current flows through the valve coil during pressure increase.

Pressure Hold position is commanded when the EBCM desires to hold the pressure in the wheel hydraulic circuit constant. The modulator will not allow pressure flow from the master cylinder to the wheel brake. The pressure hold position is commanded by passing approximately 2.0 amps through the valve coil.

Pressure Reduction position is used to decrease hydraulic pressure in a specific wheel hydraulic circuit without decreasing pressure in the rest of the system. The modulator takes brake fluid from the wheel brake and injects it into the master cylinder hydraulic circuit. This fully energized position of the solenoid valve occurs when approximately 5 amps are passed through the valve coil.

Failure Conditions: The solenoid valves are continuously monitored by the EBCM through CKT 1077 and through each individual valve line. Code 41 will set when the expected position of the right front solenoid valve does not match the commanded position from the EBCM (if valve line voltage does not match expected value). Conditions which could cause Code 41 to set are damage to the right front solenoid, an open or short to ground or battery voltage on CKT 827.

Action Taken: If a failure is detected which causes a valve Code 41 to set, antilock braking is disabled and the EBCM turns "ON" the "Antilock" indicator for the remainder of the ignition cycle. If the failure is intermittent, the EBCM will enable the system at the next ignition cycle and a history Code 41 will be present.

Important:
- The Auto test (as described under "ABS Self Diagnostics") is performed once during each ignition cycle when the vehicle reaches approximately 4 mph. This Test may be heard and felt while it is taking place and should be considered a normal mode of operation. This test can also be performed by using the Tech 1 in "ABS Tests" mode F4.

Test Description: Number(s) below refer to circled number(s) on the diagnostic chart.
1. Checks the resistance in the RF Solenoid Valve circuitry.
2. Checks for a short to ground in CKT 827
3. This test uses the Tech 1 Diagnostic Computer to check for proper RF Solenoid Valve operation.
4. This test determines if a problem found in Step 3 is due to the EBCM or the Hydraulic Modulator

5. Checks for a short in CKT 827 to CKT 1077.
6. This test determines if a problem found in Step 1 is due to the Hydraulic Modulator or a problem in CKT 827.
7. This test determines if a problem found in Step 3 is due to an intermittent in the wiring and/or connectors, or a fault with the EBCM.

Fig. 25   Code 41, RF solenoid valve fault. 1991 Caprice, Custom Cruiser & Roadmaster

CODE 41
RF SOLENOID VALVE
(VALVE FAULT)

Circuit Description:

With the ignition in "Run," "Bulb Test" or "Start," the EBCM applies voltage to the coil of the solenoid valve relay. The EBCM will complete an internal self-check before providing ground to the coil. Once energized, the relay will provide B+ to the solenoid valves.

Failure Conditions: Code 41 will set when the expected position of the right front solenoid valve does not match the commanded position from the EBCM (if valve line voltage does not match expected value). Conditions which could cause Code 41 to set are damage to the right front solenoid, an open or short to ground or battery voltage on CKT 827.

Action Taken: If a failure is detected which causes a valve Code 41 to set, antilock braking is disabled and the EBCM turns "ON" the "Antilock" indicator for the remainder of the ignition cycle. If the failure is intermittent, the EBCM will enable the system at the next ignition cycle and a history Code 41 will be present.

> **Important**
> • The Auto test (as described under "ABS Self Diagnostics") is performed once during each ignition cycle when the vehicle reaches approximately 4 mph. This test may be heard and felt while it is taking place and should be considered a normal mode of operation. This test can also be performed by using the Tech 1 in "ABS Tests" mode F4.

Test Description: Number(s) below refer to circled number(s) on the diagnostic chart.

1. This test checks the integrity of CKTs 827 and 1077, the RF Solenoid Valve Circuitry internal to the Brake Pressure Modulator and the RF Solenoid Valve Coil.
2. This test checks for a short to ground in CKT 827.
3. This test checks for a short to B+ in CKT 827.
4. This test checks for connector or wiring problems which may cause an intermittent condition.
5. This test uses the Tech 1 to check for proper Solenoid Valve operation.
6. This test determines whether the code was set by an intermittent condition or an EBCM fault.
7. This test determines whether the problem revealed in Step 1 is due to a faulty Brake Pressure Modulator or a wiring problem.
8. This test determines whether the problem is an open CKT 827 or a short from CKT 827 to CKT 1077.

Diagnostic Aids:

All tests which require a connection to Pinout Box terminal "20" are using this terminal as ground. This assumes that the integrity of ground CKT 151 has been maintained.

It is important that a thorough inspection of the wiring and connectors be performed prior to road testing the vehicle. This code can only be set when the vehicle is in motion. Failure to properly inspect wiring and connectors may result in a misdiagnosis of a faulty Brake Pressure Modulator or EBCM.

If Codes 41 and 45 are both set the fault is likely to be a short to B+ on CKT 827.

If Codes 41 and 55 are both set the fault is likely to be a short to B+ on CKT 829.

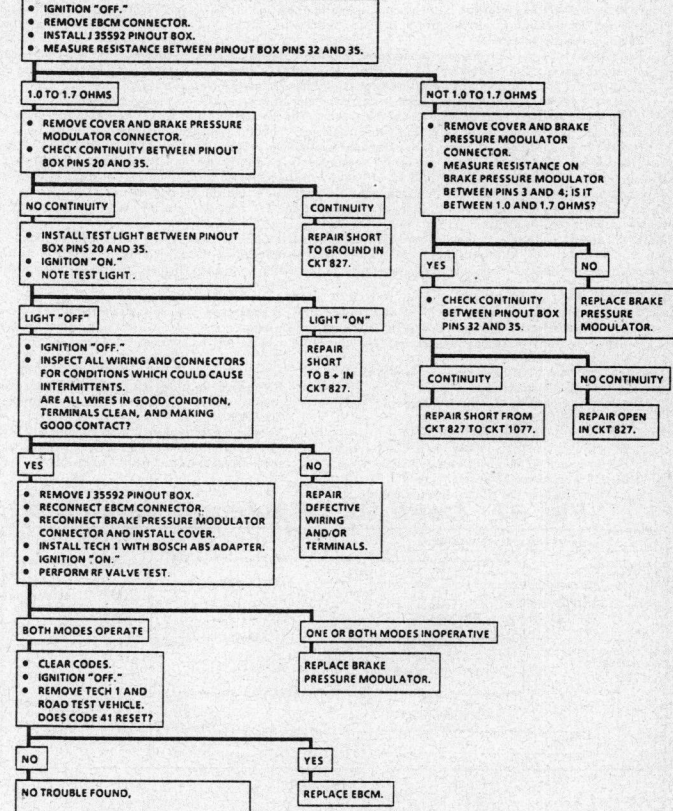

Fig. 26   Code 41, RF solenoid valve fault. 1992–93 Caprice, Custom Cruiser & Roadmaster

CODE 45
LF SOLENOID VALVE (VALVE FAULT)

Circuit Description:

With the ignition in Run, Bulb Test or Start the EBCM applies voltage to the Coil of the solenoid valve relay. The EBCM will complete an internal self-check before providing ground to the coil. Once energized the relay will provide B+ to the solenoid valves. The solenoid valve can be commanded to three different positions depending upon the amount of current the EBCM allows to flow through the solenoid valve coil.

Pressure Increase position is the normal operating position of the valves for braking. Brake fluid flows through the modulator from the master cylinder to the wheel brake. No current flows through the valve coil during pressure increase.

Pressure Hold position is commanded when the EBCM desires to hold the pressure in the wheel hydraulic circuit constant. The modulator will not allow pressure flow from the master cylinder to the wheel brake. The pressure hold position is commanded by passing approximately 2.0 amps through the valve coil.

Pressure Reduction position is used to decrease hydraulic pressure in a specific wheel hydraulic circuit without decreasing pressure in the rest of the system. The modulator takes brake fluid from the wheel brake and injects it into the master cylinder hydraulic circuit. This fully energized position of the solenoid valve occurs when approximately 5 amps are passed through the valve coil.

Failure Conditions: The solenoid valves are continuously monitored by the EBCM through CKT 1077 and through each individual valve line. Code 45 will set when the expected position of the left front solenoid valve does not match the commanded position from the EBCM (if valve line voltage does not match expected value). Conditions which could cause Code 45 to set are damage to the left front solenoid, an open or short to ground or battery voltage on CKT 826.

Action Taken: If a failure is detected which causes a valve Code 45 to set, antilock braking is disabled and the EBCM turns "ON" the "Antilock" indicator for the remainder of the ignition cycle. If the failure is intermittent, the EBCM will enable the system at the next ignition cycle and a history Code 45 will be present.

⚡ Important:

- The Auto test (as described under "ABS Self Diagnostics") is performed once during each ignition cycle when the vehicle reaches approximately 4 mph. This Test may be heard and felt while it is taking place and should be considered a normal mode of operation. This test can also be performed by using the Tech 1 in "ABS Tests" mode F4.

Test Description: Number(s) below refer to circled number(s) on the diagnostic chart.

1. Checks the resistance in the LF Solenoid Valve circuitry.
2. Checks for a short to ground in CKT 826.
3. This test uses the Tech 1 Diagnostic Computer to check for proper LF Solenoid Valve operation.
4. This test determines if a problem found in Step 3 is due to the EBCM or the Hydraulic Modulator.
5. Checks for a short in CKT 826 to CKT 1077.
6. This test determines if a problem found in Step 1 is due to the Hydraulic Modulator or a problem in CKT 826.
7. This test determines if a problem found in Step 3 is due to an intermittent in the wiring and/or connectors, or a fault with the EBCM.

Fig. 27 Code 45, LF solenoid valve fault. 1991 Caprice, Custom Cruiser & Roadmaster

CODE 45
LF SOLENOID VALVE (VALVE FAULT)

Circuit Description:

With the ignition in "Run," "Bulb Test" or "Start," the EBCM applies voltage to the coil of the solenoid valve relay. The EBCM will complete an internal self-check before providing ground to the coil. Once energized, the relay will provide B+ to the solenoid valves.

Failure Conditions: Code 45 will set when the expected position of the right front solenoid valve does not match the commanded position from the EBCM (if valve line voltage does not match expected value). Conditions which could cause Code 45 to set are damage to the left front solenoid, an open or short to ground or battery voltage on CKT 826.

Action Taken: If a failure is detected which causes a valve Code 45 to set, antilock braking is disabled and the EBCM turns "ON" the "Antilock" indicator for the remainder of the ignition cycle. If the failure is intermittent, the EBCM will enable the system at the next ignition cycle and a history Code 45 will be present.

⚡ Important

- The Auto test (as described under "ABS Self Diagnostics") is performed once during each ignition cycle when the vehicle reaches approximately 4 mph. This test may be heard and felt while it is taking place and should be considered a normal mode of operation. This test can also be performed by using the Tech 1 in "ABS Tests" mode F4.

Test Description: Number(s) below refer to circled number(s) on the diagnostic chart.

1. This test checks the integrity of CKTs 826 and 1077, the LF Solenoid Valve Circuitry internal to the Brake Pressure Modulator and the LF Solenoid Valve Coil.
2. This test checks for a short to ground in CKT 826.
3. This test checks for a short to B+ in CKT 826.
4. This test checks for inspect connector or wiring problems which may cause an intermittent condition.
5. This test uses the Tech 1 to check for proper Solenoid Valve operation.
6. This test determines whether the code was set by an intermittent condition or an EBCM fault.
7. This test determines whether the problem revealed in Step 1 is due to a faulty Brake Pressure Modulator or a wiring problem.
8. This test determines whether the problem is an open CKT 826 or a short from CKT 826 to CKT 1077.

Diagnostic Aids:

All tests which require a connection to Pinout Box terminal "20" are using this terminal as ground. This assumes that the integrity of ground CKT 151 has been maintained.

It is important that a thorough inspection of the wiring and connectors be performed prior to road testing the vehicle. This code can only be set when the vehicle is in motion. Failure to properly inspect wiring and connectors may result in a misdiagnosis of a faulty Brake Pressure Modulator or EBCM.

If Codes 45 and 45 are both set the fault is likely to be a short to B+ on CKT 827.

If Codes 41 and 55 are both set the fault is likely to be a short to B+ on CKT 826 or a short to ground on CKT 1079.

Fig. 28 Code 45, LF solenoid valve fault. 1992–93 Caprice, Custom Cruiser & Roadmaster

CODE 55
REAR WHEELS SOLENOID VALVE (VALVE FAULT)

Circuit Description:
With the ignition in Run, Bulb Test or Start the EBCM applies voltage to the Coil of the solenoid valve relay. The EBCM will complete an internal self-check before providing ground to the coil. Once energized the relay will provide B + to the solenoid valves. The solenoid valve can be commanded to three different positions depending upon the amount of current the EBCM allows to flow through the solenoid valve coil.

Pressure Increase position is the normal operating position of the valves for braking. Brake fluid flows through the modulator from the master cylinder to the wheel brake. No current flows through the valve coil during pressure increase.

Pressure Hold position is commanded when the EBCM desires to hold the pressure in the wheel hydraulic circuit constant. The modulator will not allow pressure flow from the master cylinder to the wheel brake. The pressure hold position is commanded by passing approximately 2.0 amps through the valve coil.

Pressure Reduction position is used to decrease hydraulic pressure in a specific wheel hydraulic circuit without decreasing pressure in the rest of the system. The modulator takes brake fluid from the wheel brake and injects it into the master cylinder hydraulic circuit. This fully energized position of the solenoid valve occurs when approximately 5 amps are passed through the valve coil.

Failure Conditions: The solenoid valves are continuously monitored by the EBCM through CKT 1077 and through each individual valve line. Code 55 will set when the expected position of the rear wheels solenoid valve does not match the commanded position from the EBCM (if valve line voltage does not match expected value). Conditions which could cause Code 55 to set are damage to the rear wheels solenoid, an open or short to ground or battery voltage on CKT 829.

Action Taken: If a failure is detected which causes a valve Code 55 to set, antilock braking is disabled and the EBCM turns "ON" the "Antilock" indicator for the remainder of the ignition cycle. If the failure is intermittent, the EBCM will enable the system at the next ignition cycle and a history Code 55 will be present.

Important
- The Auto test (as described under "ABS Self Diagnostics") is performed once during each ignition cycle when the vehicle reaches approximately 4 mph. This Test may be heard and felt while it is taking place and should be considered a normal mode of operation. This test can also be performed by using the Tech 1 in "ABS Tests" mode F4.

Test Description: Number(s) below refer to circled number(s) on the diagnostic chart.
1. Checks the resistance in the rear wheels Solenoid Valve circuitry.
2. Checks for a short to ground in CKT 829.
3. This test uses the Tech 1 Diagnostic Computer to check for proper rear wheels Solenoid Valve operation.
4. This test determines if a problem found in Step 3 is due to the EBCM or the Hydraulic Modulator.
5. Checks for a short in CKT 829 to CKT 1077.
6. This test determines if a problem found in Step 1 is due to the Hydraulic Modulator or a problem in CKT 829.
7. This test determines if a problem found in Step 3 is due to an intermittent in the wiring and/or

Fig. 29   Code 55, rear wheels solenoid valve fault. 1991 Caprice, Custom Cruiser & Roadmaster

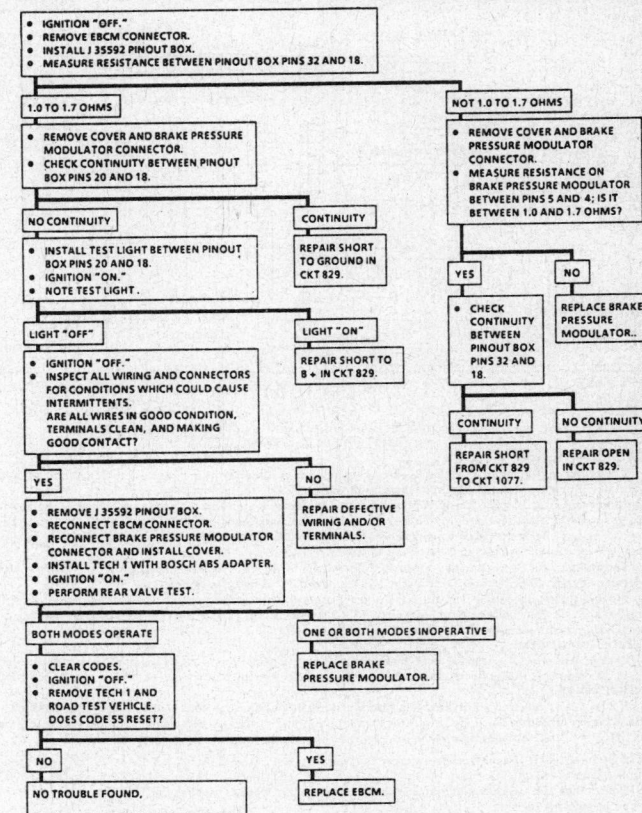

CODE 55
REAR WHEELS SOLENOID VALVE
(VALVE FAULT)

Circuit Description:
With the ignition in "Run," "Bulb Test" or "Start," the EBCM applies voltage to the coil of the solenoid valve relay. The EBCM will complete an internal self-check before providing ground to the coil. Once energized, the relay will provide B + to the solenoid valves.

Failure Conditions: Code 55 will set when the expected position of the right front solenoid valve does not match the commanded position from the EBCM (if valve line voltage does not match expected value). Conditions which could cause Code 55 to set are damage to the left front solenoid, an open or short to ground or battery voltage on CKT 829.

Action Taken: If a failure is detected which causes a valve Code 55 to set, antilock braking is disabled and the EBCM turns "ON" the "Antilock" indicator for the remainder of the ignition cycle. If the failure is intermittent, the EBCM will enable the system at the next ignition cycle and a history Code 55 will be present.

Important
- The Auto test (as described under "ABS Self Diagnostics") is performed once during each ignition cycle when the vehicle reaches approximately 4 mph. This test may be heard and felt while it is taking place and should be considered a normal mode of operation. This test can also be performed by using the Tech 1 in "ABS Tests" mode F4.

Test Description: Number(s) below refer to circled number(s) on the diagnostic chart.
1. This test checks the integrity of CKTs 829 and 1077, the Rear Solenoid Valve Circuitry internal to the Brake Pressure Modulator and the Rear Solenoid Valve Coil.
2. This test checks for a short to ground in CKT 829.
3. This test checks for a short to B + in CKT 829.
4. This test checks for connector or wiring problems which may cause an intermittent condition.
5. This test uses the Tech 1 to check for proper Solenoid Valve operation.
6. This test determines whether the code was set by an intermittent condition or an EBCM fault.
7. This test determines whether the problem revealed in Step 1 is due to a faulty Brake Pressure Modulator or a wiring problem.
8. This test determines whether the problem is an open CKT 829 or a short from CKT 829 to CKT 1077.

Diagnostic Aids:
All tests which require a connection to Pinout Box terminal "20" are using this terminal as ground. This assumes that the integrity of ground CKT 151 has been maintained.

It is important that a thorough inspection of the wiring and connectors be performed prior to road testing the vehicle. This code can only be set when the vehicle is in motion. Failure to properly inspect wiring and connectors may result in a misdiagnosis of a faulty Brake Pressure Modulator or EBCM.

If Codes 41 and 45 are both set the fault is likely to be a short to B + on CKT 829.

If Codes 45 and 55 are both set the fault is likely to be a short to B + on CKT 826 or a short to ground on CKT 1079.

Fig. 30   Code 55, rear wheels solenoid valve fault. 1992–93 Caprice, Custom Cruiser & Roadmaster

1991 REATTA, 1991-92 BROUGHAM, TORONADO & TROFEO & 1991-93 CAPRICE, CUSTOM CRUISER, ELDORADO, RIVIERA, **23-135**
ROADMASTER, SEVILLE (BOSCH 2 U TYPE)

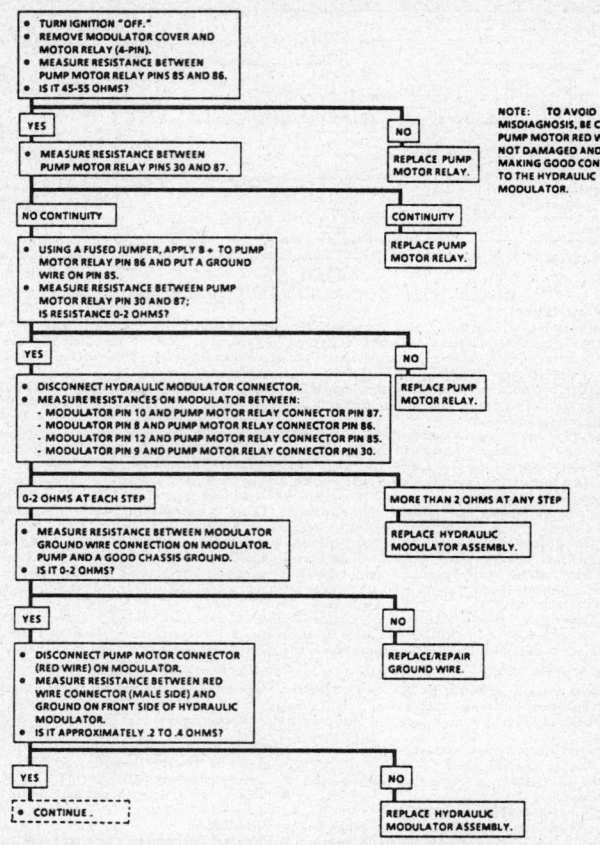

CODE 61
(Page 1 of 3)
PUMP MOTOR/RELAY
(MOTOR OR RELAY FAULT)

Circuit Description:
The pump motor returns brake fluid to the master cylinder brake hydraulic circuit at the hydraulic modulator, during antilock braking. During normal braking, the pump does not operate. When the vehicle begins to move after start-up, the EBCM will turn on the pump motor and perform a self-check of the pump motor and pump motor electrical circuit. This check may be felt and heard by the driver when the vehicle begins to move. The self-check should be considered normal operation. The pump motor is an integral component of the hydraulic modulator and cannot be serviced separately.

The pump motor relay provides power to the pump motor in the hydraulic modulator. The pump motor relay is located on the hydraulic modulator and may be replaced if it is found to be defective.

When antilock operation is required, the motor relay is grounded through CKT 854 (EBCM pin 28). The pump motor relay has voltage supplied from CKT 1079 (EBCM pin 17). When the relay toggles, battery power is provided to the pump motor.

Failure Conditions:
Code 61 will set if B + is present at the pump motor without the pump motor being requested to activate, or if B + is not present at the pump motor within 60 milliseconds after the pump motor has been requested to activate.

Action Taken:
If a failure is detected which causes a pump motor/relay Code 61 to set antilock braking is disabled and the EBCM turns "ON" the "Antilock" indicator for the remainder of the ignition cycle. If the failure is intermittent, the EBCM will enable the system at the next ignition cycle and a History Code 61 will be present.

Test Description: Number(s) below refer to circled number(s) on the diagnostic chart.
1. Checks the relay for correct resistance.
2. Checks if relay is stuck closed.
3. Checks for proper switching action in pump motor relay.
4. Checks for an open in the Hydraulic Modulator Circuitry.
5. Checks for a good ground.
6. Checks the pump motor for correct resistance.

Fig. 31 Code 61, pump motor or relay fault (Part 1 of 3). 1991 Caprice, Custom Cruiser & Roadmaster

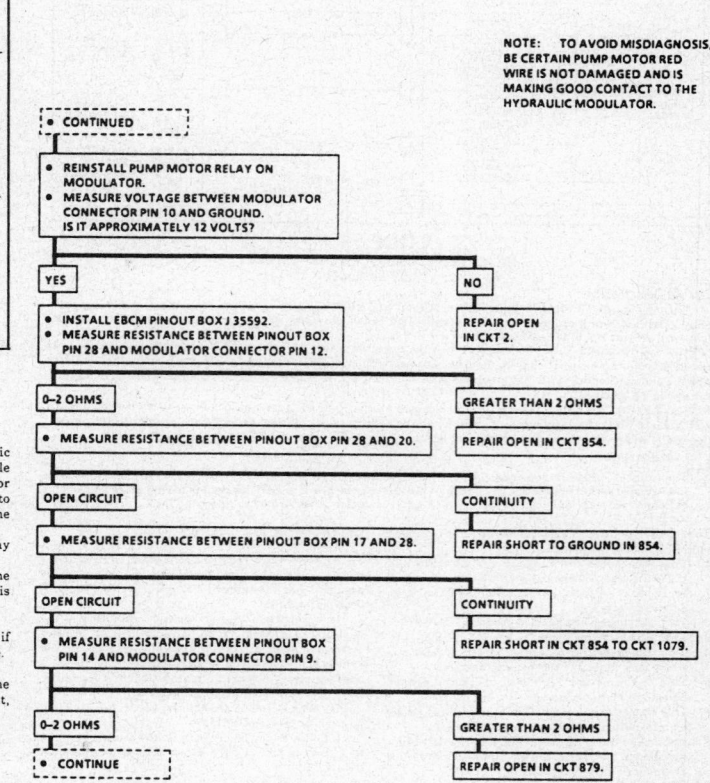

CODE 61
(Page 2 of 3)
PUMP MOTOR/RELAY
(MOTOR OR RELAY FAULT)

Circuit Description:
The pump motor returns brake fluid to the master cylinder brake hydraulic circuit at the hydraulic modulator, during antilock braking. During normal braking, the pump does not operate. When the vehicle begins to move after start-up, the EBCM will turn on the pump motor and perform a self-check of the pump motor and pump motor electrical circuit. This check may be felt and heard by the driver when the vehicle begins to move. The self-check should be considered normal operation. The pump motor is an integral component of the hydraulic modulator and cannot be serviced separately.

The pump motor relay provides power to the pump motor in the hydraulic modulator. The pump motor relay is located on the hydraulic modulator and may be replaced if it is found to be defective.

When antilock operation is required, the motor relay is grounded through CKT 854 (EBCM pin 28). The pump motor relay has voltage supplied from CKT 1079 (EBCM pin 17). When the relay toggles, battery power is provided to the pump motor.

Failure Conditions:
Code 61 will set if B + is present at the pump motor without the pump motor being requested to activate, or if B + is not present at the pump motor within 60 milliseconds after the pump motor has been requested to activate.

Action Taken:
If a failure is detected which causes a pump motor/relay Code 61 to set antilock braking is disabled and the EBCM turns "ON" the "Antilock" indicator for the remainder of the ignition cycle. If the failure is intermittent, the EBCM will enable the system at the next ignition cycle and a History Code 61 will be present.

Test Description: Number(s) below refer to circled number(s) on the diagnostic chart.
7. Determines if battery voltage is available to the pump motor relay.
8. Checks for open in CKT 854.
9. Determines if CKT 854 is shorted to ground.
10. Checks for a short in CKT 854 to CKT 1079.
11. Checks for open in CKT 879.

Fig. 31 Code 61, pump motor or relay fault (Part 2 of 3). 1991 Caprice, Custom Cruiser & Roadmaster

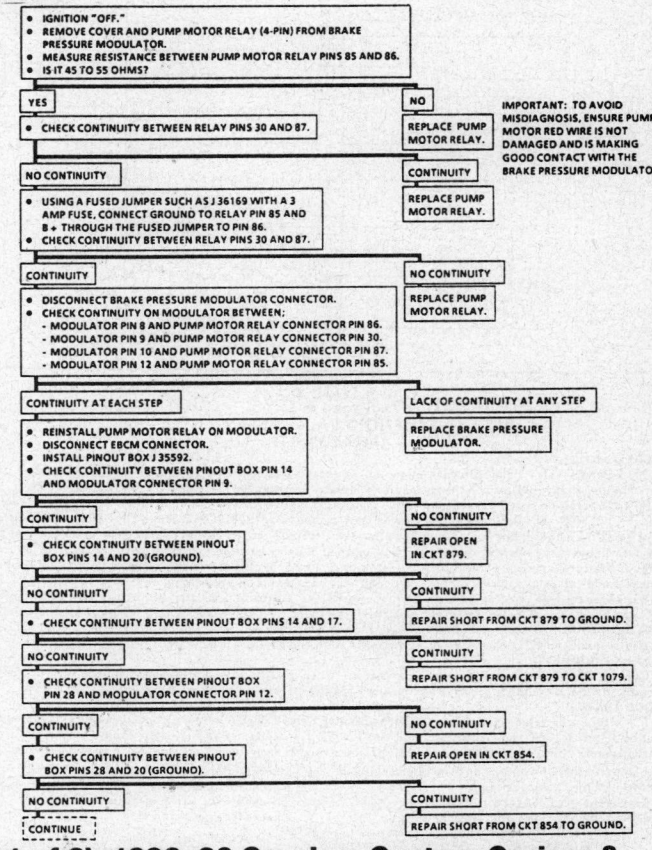

NOTE: TO AVOID MISDIAGNOSIS, BE CERTAIN PUMP MOTOR RED WIRE IS NOT DAMAGED AND IS MAKING GOOD CONTACT TO THE HYDRAULIC MODULATOR.

CODE 61
(Page 3 of 3)
PUMP MOTOR/RELAY
(MOTOR OR RELAY FAULT)

Circuit Description:

The pump motor returns brake fluid to the master cylinder brake hydraulic circuit at the hydraulic modulator, during antilock braking. During normal braking, the pump does not operate. When the vehicle begins to move after start-up, the EBCM will turn on the pump motor and perform a self-check of the pump motor and pump motor electrical circuit. This check may be felt and heard by the driver when the vehicle begins to move. The self-check should be considered normal operation. The pump motor is an integral component of the hydraulic modulator and cannot be serviced separately.

The pump motor relay provides power to the pump motor in the hydraulic modulator. The pump motor relay is located on the hydraulic modulator and may be replaced if it is found to be defective.

When antilock operation is required, the motor relay is grounded through CKT 854 (EBCM pin 28). The pump motor relay has voltage supplied from CKT 1079 (EBCM pin 17). When the relay toggles, battery power is provided to the pump motor.

Failure Conditions:

Code 61 will set if B+ is present at the pump motor without the pump motor being requested to activate, or if B+ is not present at the pump motor within 60 milliseconds after the pump motor has been requested to activate.

Action Taken:

If a failure is detected which causes a pump motor/relay Code 61 to set antilock braking is disabled and the EBCM turns "ON" the "Antilock" indicator for the remainder of the ignition cycle. If the failure is intermittent, the EBCM will enable the system at the next ignition cycle and a History Code 61 will be present.

Test Description: Number(s) below refer to circled number(s) on the diagnostic chart.

12. Determines if CKT 879 is shorted to ground.
13. Checks for a short to ground in CKT 879 to 1079.
14. Checks for a short to voltage on CKT 854 or CKT 879.
15. Checks for an internal short to ground within the hydraulic modulator.

Fig. 31   Code 61, pump motor or relay fault (Part 3 of 3). 1991 Caprice, Custom Cruiser & Roadmaster

CODE 61
(Page 1 of 2)
PUMP MOTOR/RELAY
(MOTOR OR RELAY FAULT)

Circuit Description:

The pump motor returns brake fluid to the master cylinder brake hydraulic circuit at the hydraulic modulator, during antilock braking. During normal braking, the pump does not operate. When the vehicle begins to move after start-up, the EBCM will turn "ON" the pump motor and perform a self-check of the pump motor and pump motor electrical circuit. This check may be felt and heard by the driver when the vehicle begins to move. The self-check should be considered normal operation. The pump motor is an integral component of the hydraulic modulator and cannot be serviced separately.

The pump motor relay provides power to the pump motor in the hydraulic modulator. The pump motor relay is located on the hydraulic modulator and may be replaced if it is found to be defective.

Failure Conditions:

Code 61 will set if B+ is present at the pump motor without the pump motor being requested to activate, or if B+ is not present at the pump motor within 60 milliseconds after the pump motor has been requested to activate.

Action Taken:

If a failure is detected which causes a pump motor/relay Code 61 to set antilock braking is disabled and the EBCM turns "ON" the "Antilock" indicator for the remainder of the ignition cycle. If the failure is intermittent, the EBCM will enable the system at the next ignition cycle and a History Code 61 will be present.

Test Description: Number(s) below refer to circled number(s) on the diagnostic chart.

1. Checks for proper resistance of the relay coil.
2. Checks for relay contacts stuck closed.
3. Checks for relay contacts stuck open.
4. Checks the integrity of the circuits internal to the modulator.
5. Checks for an open in the pump "ON" input circuit.
6. Checks for a short to ground in the pump "ON" input circuit.
7. Checks for a short from the pump "ON" input circuit to the relay feed circuit.
8. Checks for an open in the pump motor relay coil switched ground circuit.
9. Checks for a short to ground in the pump motor relay coil switched ground circuit.

Fig. 32   Code 61, pump motor or relay fault (Part 1 of 2). 1992–93 Caprice, Custom Cruiser & Roadmaster

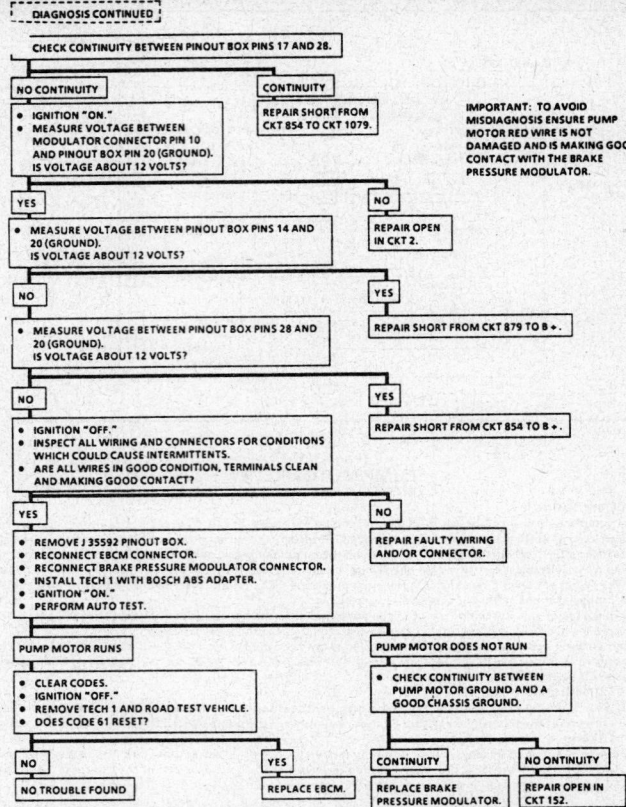

CODE 61
PUMP MOTOR/RELAY
(MOTOR OR RELAY FAULT)

Circuit Description:

The pump motor returns brake fluid to the master cylinder brake hydraulic circuit at the hydraulic modulator, during antilock braking. During normal braking, the pump does not operate. When the vehicle begins to move after start-up, the EBCM will turn "ON" the pump motor and perform a self-check of the pump motor and pump motor electrical circuit. This check may be felt and heard by the driver when the vehicle begins to move. The self-check should be considered normal operation. The pump motor is an integral component of the hydraulic modulator and cannot be serviced separately.

The pump motor relay provides power to the pump motor in the hydraulic modulator. The pump motor relay is located on the hydraulic modulator and may be replaced if it is found to be defective.

Failure Conditions:

Code 61 will set if B+ is present at the pump motor without the pump motor being requested to activate, or if B+ is not present at the pump motor within 60 milliseconds after the pump motor has been requested to activate.

Action Taken:

If a failure is detected which causes a pump motor/relay Code 61 to set antilock braking is disabled and the EBCM turns "ON" the "Antilock" indicator for the remainder of the ignition cycle. If the failure is intermittent, the EBCM will enable the system at the next ignition cycle and a History Code 61 will be present.

Test Description: Number(s) below refer to circled number(s) on the diagnostic chart.

10. Checks for a short from the pump motor relay coil switched ground circuit to the relay feed circuit.
11. Checks for an open in the modulator battery feed circuit.
12. Checks for a short to B+ in the pump "ON" input circuit.
13. Checks for a short to B+ in the pump motor relay coil switched ground circuit.
14. Checks for improper connections which may have set the code.
15. Checks that the pump motor is operational.
16. Checks for a code which set falsely.
17. Checks for a good pump motor ground circuit.

Fig. 32 Code 61, pump motor or relay fault (Part 2 of 2). 1992–93 Caprice, Custom Cruiser & Roadmaster

CODE 63
(Page 1 of 3)
SOLENOID VALVE RELAY
(RELAY FAULT)

Circuit Description:

The Solenoid Valve Relay provides power to the three solenoid valves in the Hydraulic Modulator. The Solenoid Valve Relay is located on the Hydraulic Modulator and may be replaced if it is found to be defective.

When the ignition switch is turned to "Run" the EBCM applies voltage to the coil of the Solenoid Valve Relay through CKT 1079. The Solenoid Valve Relay is then grounded by the EBCM through CKT 1078. The Solenoid Valve Relay is energized and provides voltage through CKT 1077 to the EBCM (Valve Relay Monitor) and also provides voltage to the solenoid valves. The Solenoid Valve Relay remains energized until the ignition is turned "OFF" or a failure is detected. If antilock operation is required the EBCM varies the amount of current supplied to the solenoid valves and the valves are positioned to provide for optimum braking.

Whenever the Solenoid Valve Relay is not energized, the "Antilock" indicator will turn "ON." With ignition "ON" and the Solenoid Valve Relay not energized, the indicator CKT 875 is pulled low through the Solenoid Valve Relay to the hydraulic modulator ground, illuminating the "Antilock" indicator. The "antilock" indicator can also be commanded "ON" by the EBCM through CKT 875 if a failure is detected.

Failure Conditions:

Code 63 will set if the valve relay monitor is at B+ when the EBCM is not requesting it to be, or if the EBCM is requesting the Solenoid Valve Relay be energized and the valve relay monitor voltage is less than 5 volts.

Action Taken:

If a failure is detected which causes a Solenoid Valve Relay Code 63 to set, antilock braking is disabled and the EBCM turns "ON" the "Antilock" indicator for the remainder of the ignition cycle. If the failure is intermittent, the EBCM will enable the system at the next ignition cycle and a History Code 63 will be present.

Test Description: Number(s) below refer to circled number(s) on the diagnostic chart.

1. Checks the relay coil for correct resistance.
2. Checks the relay for a poor internal contact.
3. Checks the relay for a stuck internal contact.
4. Checks for proper switching action in Relay.
5. Checks for faulty diode in Solenoid Valve Relay.
6. Checks circuitry in Hydraulic Modulator.
7. Checks for a good ground.

Fig. 33 Code 63, solenoid valve relay fault (Part 1 of 3). 1991 Caprice, Custom Cruiser & Roadmaster

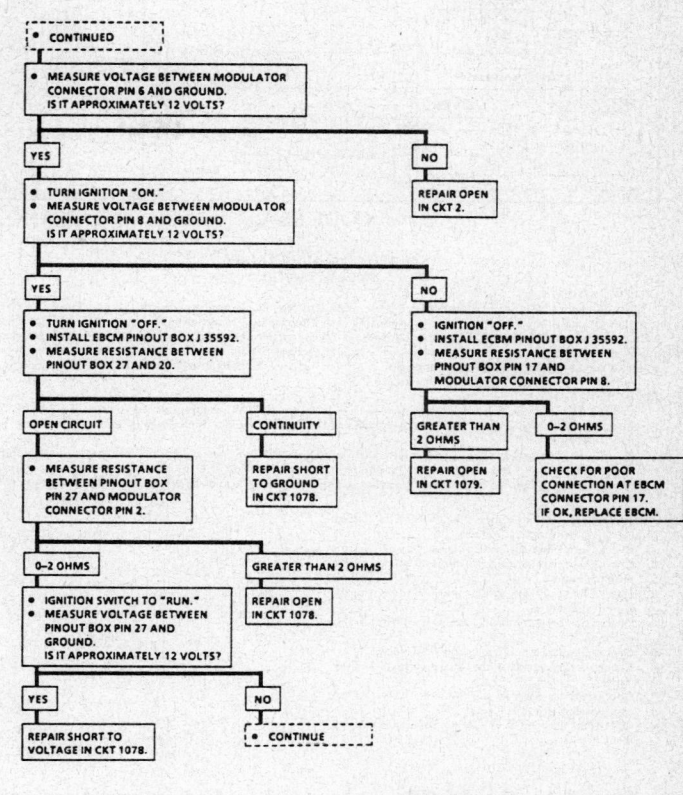

CODE 63
(Page 2 of 3)
SOLENOID VALVE RELAY
(RELAY FAULT)

Circuit Description:

The Solenoid Valve Relay provides power to the three solenoid valves in the Hydraulic Modulator. The Solenoid Valve Relay is located on the Hydraulic Modulator and may be replaced if it is found to be defective.

When the ignition switch is turned to "Run" the EBCM applies voltage to the coil of the Solenoid Valve Relay through CKT 1079. The Solenoid Valve Relay is then grounded by the EBCM through CKT 1078. The Solenoid Valve Relay is energized and provides voltage through CKT 1077 to the EBCM (Valve Relay Monitor) and also provides voltage to the solenoid valves. The Solenoid Valve Relay remains energized until the ignition is turned "OFF" or a failure is detected. If antilock operation is required the EBCM varies the amount of current supplied to the solenoid valves and the valves are positioned to provide for optimum braking.

Whenever the Solenoid Valve Relay is not energized, the "Antilock" indicator will turn "ON." With ignition "ON" and the Solenoid Valve Relay not energized, the indicator CKT 875 is pulled low through the Solenoid Valve Relay to the hydraulic modulator ground, illuminating the "Antilock" indicator. The "antilock" indicator can also be commanded "ON" by the EBCM through CKT 875 if a failure is detected.

Failure Conditions:

Code 63 will set if the valve relay monitor is at B + when the EBCM is not requesting it to be, or if the EBCM is requesting the Solenoid Valve Relay be energized and the valve relay monitor voltage is less than 5 volts.

Action Taken:

If a failure is detected which causes a Solenoid Valve Relay Code 63 to set, antilock braking is disabled and the EBCM turns "ON" the "Antilock" indicator for the remainder of the ignition cycle. If the failure is intermittent, the EBCM will enable the system at the next ignition cycle and a History Code 63 will be present.

Test Description: Number(s) below refer to the circled number(s) on the diagnostic chart.

8. Checks power feed to solenoid valve relay.
9. Checks for a potential open or short to ground in CKT 1079.
10. Checks for a short to ground in CKT 1078.
11. Checks for an open in CKT 1078.
12. Checks for a short to B + in CKT 1078.
13. Determines if fault is in CKT 1079 or in EBCM.

Fig. 33   Code 63, solenoid valve relay fault (Part 2 of 3). 1991 Caprice, Custom Cruiser & Roadmaster

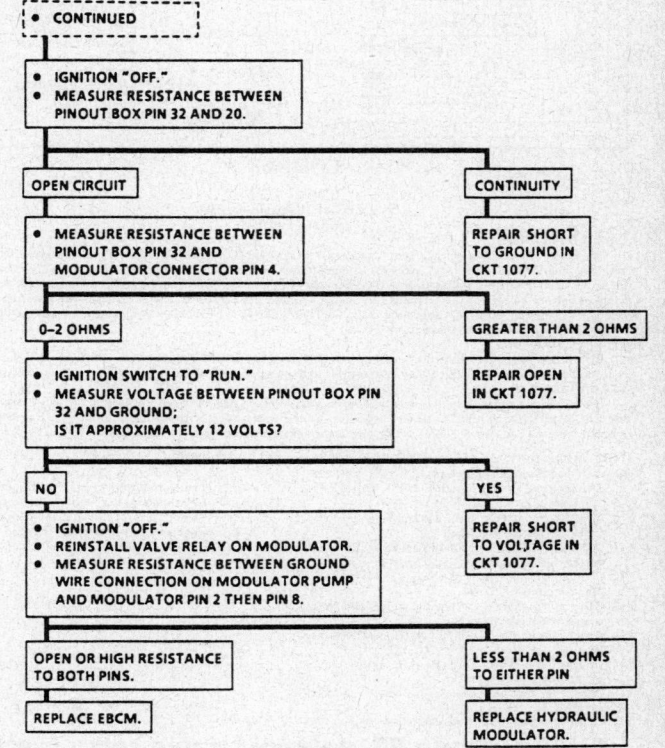

CODE 63
(Page 3 of 3)
SOLENOID VALVE RELAY
(RELAY FAULT)

Circuit Description:

The Solenoid Valve Relay provides power to the three solenoid valves in the Hydraulic Modulator. The Solenoid Valve Relay is located on the Hydraulic Modulator and may be replaced if it is found to be defective.

When the ignition switch is turned to "Run" the EBCM applies voltage to the coil of the Solenoid Valve Relay through CKT 1079. The Solenoid Valve Relay is then grounded by the EBCM through CKT 1078. The Solenoid Valve Relay is energized and provides voltage through CKT 1077 to the EBCM (Valve Relay Monitor) and also provides voltage to the solenoid valves. The Solenoid Valve Relay remains energized until the ignition is turned "OFF" or a failure is detected. If antilock operation is required the EBCM varies the amount of current supplied to the solenoid valves and the valves are positioned to provide for optimum braking.

Whenever the Solenoid Valve Relay is not energized, the "Antilock" indicator will turn "ON." With ignition "ON" and the Solenoid Valve Relay not energized, the indicator CKT 875 is pulled low through the Solenoid Valve Relay to the hydraulic modulator ground, illuminating the "Antilock" indicator. The "anti-lock" indicator can also be commanded "ON" by the EBCM through CKT 875 if a failure is detected.

Failure Conditions:

Code 63 will set if the valve relay monitor is at B + when the EBCM is not requesting it to be, or if the EBCM is requesting the Solenoid Valve Relay be energized and the valve relay monitor voltage is less than 5 volts.

Action Taken:

If a failure is detected which causes a Solenoid Valve Relay Code 63 to set, antilock braking is disabled and the EBCM turns "ON" the "Antilock" indicator for the remainder of the ignition cycle. If the failure is intermittent, the EBCM will enable the system at the next ignition cycle and a History Code 63 will be present.

Test Description: Number(s) below refer to the circled number(s) on the diagnostic chart.

14. Checks for a short to ground in CKT 1077.
16. Checks for a short to B + in CKT 1077.
17. Determines if fault is in hydraulic modulator or EBCM.

Fig. 33   Code 63, solenoid valve relay fault (Part 3 of 3). 1991 Caprice, Custom Cruiser & Roadmaster

CODE 63

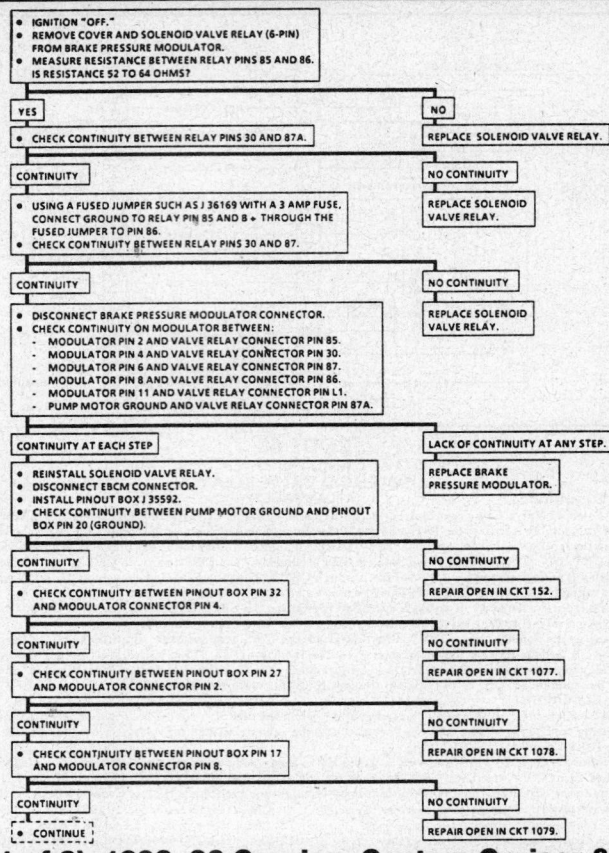

SOLENOID VALVE RELAY
(RELAY FAULT)

Circuit Description:

The Solenoid Valve Relay has a dual function. With ignition "ON" and the relay coil not energized, the relay provides ground to the "Antilock" indicator causing it to illuminate. This allows illumination of the "Antilock" indicator when the EBCM is disconnected or disabled. With ignition "ON" and the relay coil energized, the relay supplies battery voltage to the solenoid valves. This allows the EBCM to control actuation and position of the solenoid valves by controlling the ground path. CKT 1077 allows the EBCM to monitor the state of the Solenoid Valve Relay to compare with the requested state.

Failure Conditions:

Code 63 will set if the valve relay monitor is at B+ when the EBCM is not requesting it to be, or if the EBCM is requesting the Solenoid Valve Relay be energized and the valve relay monitor voltage is less than 5 volts.

Action Taken:

If a failure is detected which causes a Solenoid Valve Relay Code 63 to set, antilock braking is disabled and the EBCM turns "ON" the "Antilock" indicator for the remainder of the ignition cycle. If the failure is intermittent, the EBCM will enable the system at the next ignition cycle and a History Code 63 will be present.

Test Description: Number(s) below refer to circled number(s) on the diagnostic chart.

1. Checks for proper resistance of the relay coil.
2. Checks for the relay contacts stuck in the normally open position.
3. Checks for the relay contacts stuck in the normally closed position.
4. Checks for integrity of the circuitry internal to the modulator.
5. Checks for a good pump motor ground circuit.
6. Checks for an open in the Valve Relay Monitor circuit.
7. Checks for an open in the Solenoid Valve Relay coil switched ground circuit.
8. Checks for an open in the Relay Feed (coil battery feed) circuit.

Fig. 34   Code 63, solenoid valve relay fault (Part 1 of 2). 1992–93 Caprice, Custom Cruiser & Roadmaster

CODE 63
(Page 2 of 2)
SOLENOID VALVE RELAY
(RELAY FAULT)

Circuit Description:

The Solenoid Valve Relay has a dual function. With ignition "ON" and the relay coil not energized, the relay provides ground to the "Antilock" indicator causing it to illuminate. This allows illumination of the "Antilock" indicator when the EBCM is disconnected or disabled. With ignition "ON" and the relay coil energized, the relay supplies battery voltage to the solenoid valves. This allows the EBCM to control actuation and position of the solenoid valves by controlling the ground path. CKT 1077 allows the EBCM to monitor the state of the Solenoid Valve Relay to compare with the requested state.

Failure Conditions:

Code 63 will set if the valve relay monitor is at B+ when the EBCM is not requesting it to be, or if the EBCM is requesting the Solenoid Valve Relay be energized and the valve relay monitor voltage is less than 5 volts.

Action Taken:

If a failure is detected which causes a Solenoid Valve Relay Code 63 to set, antilock braking is disabled and the EBCM turns "ON" the "Antilock" indicator for the remainder of the ignition cycle. If the failure is intermittent, the EBCM will enable the system at the next ignition cycle and a History Code 63 will be present.

Test Description: Number(s) below refer to circled number(s) on the diagnostic chart.

9. Checks for a short to ground in the Valve Relay Monitor circuit.
10. Checks for a short to ground in the Solenoid Valve Relay coil switch ground circuit.
11. Checks for a short to ground in the Relay Feed (coil battery feed) circuit.
12. Checks for a short to B+ in the Valve Relay Monitor circuit.
13. Checks for a short B+ in the Solenoid Valve Relay coil switched ground circuit.
14. Checks for an open in the modulator battery feed circuit.
15. Checks for a short to ground internal to the modulator.
16. Checks for improper connections which may have set the code.
17. Checks for a code which may have set falsely.

Diagnostic Aids:

All tests which require a connection to pinout box Pin 20 are using this pin as ground. This assumes the integrity of ground CKT 151 has been maintained.

A disconnected or improperly seated Brake Pressure Modulator connector may set this code.

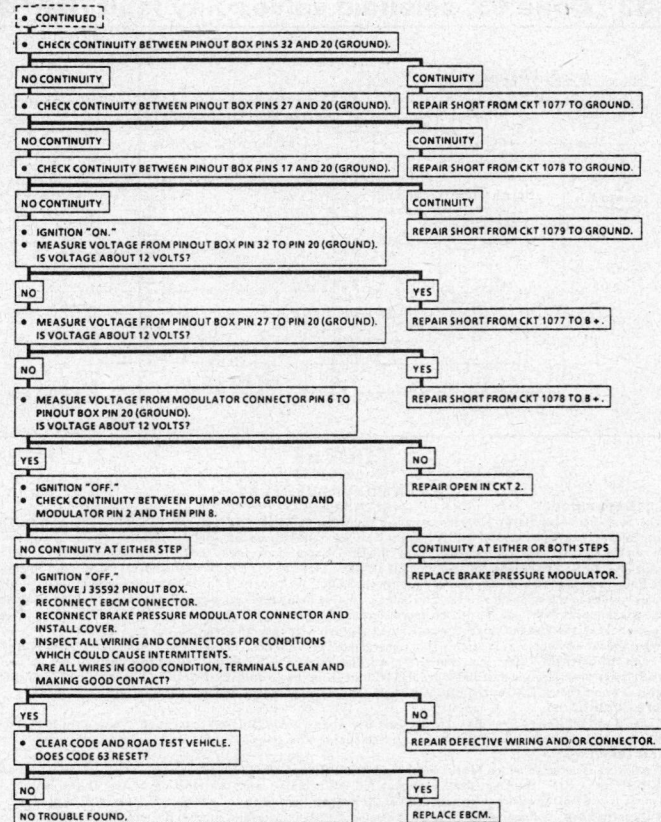

Fig. 34   Code 63, solenoid valve relay fault (Part 2 of 2). 1992–93 Caprice, Custom Cruiser & Roadmaster

1991 REATTA, 1991-92 BROUGHAM, TORONADO & TROFEO & 1991-93 CAPRICE, CUSTOM CRUISER, ELDORADO, RIVIERA, ROADMASTER, SEVILLE (BOSCH 2 U TYPE)

CODE 71
ELECTRONIC BRAKE CONTROL MODULE (EBCM)
(EBCM FAULT)

Circuit Description:
The EBCM has self diagnostics that can detect an internal failure within the module.
If a failure is detected which causes a EBCM Code 71 to set, antilock braking is disabled and the EBCM turns "ON" the "Antilock" indicator for the remainder of the ignition cycle. If the failure is "Intermittent'" the EBCM will enable the system at the next ignition cycle and a History Code 71 will be present.

Fig. 35   Code 71, EBCM fault. 1991 Caprice, Custom Cruiser & Roadmaster

CODE 71
ELECTRONIC BRAKE CONTROL MODULE (EBCM)
(EBCM FAULT)

Circuit Description:
The EBCM has self diagnostics that can detect an internal failure within the module. The EBCM also monitors its supply voltage and the integrity of the EBCM harness connection. When a fault is detected for any of these conditions Code 71 is set.

Action Taken:
If a failure is detected which causes a EBCM Code 71 to set, antilock braking is disabled and the EBCM turns "ON" the "Antilock" indicator for the remainder of the ignition cycle. If the failure is intermittent, the EBCM will enable the system at the next ignition cycle and a History Code 71 will be present.

Test Description: Number(s) below refer to circled number(s) on the diagnostic chart.
1. Checks for additional faults which may be causing Code 71 to set.
2. Checks the integrity of the EBCM ground circuit.
3. Checks for the minimum supply voltage necessary for proper ABS operation.
4. Checks for intermittent connections of the EBCM harness connector and terminals to the EBCM.

Fig. 36   Code 71, EBCM fault. 1992–93 Caprice, Custom Cruiser & Roadmaster

1991 REATTA, 1991-92 BROUGHAM, TORONADO & TROFEO & 1991-93 CAPRICE, CUSTOM CRUISER, ELDORADO, RIVIERA, ROADMASTER, SEVILLE (Bosch 2 U TYPE)

Circuit Description:
The Serial Data Line is an asynchronous line operating at 8192 bits per second.
Code 72 will set if the EBCM detects three consecutive serial data line messages that are ignored due to errors in transmission. *The "Antilock" indicator will not be illuminated and the system will remain operational with this fault.*

Test Description: Number(s) below refer to circled number(s) on the diagnostic chart.
1. Checks to see if the Tech 1 can communicate with the EBCM.
2. Determines if the serial data circuit is open.
3. Checks for a short to battery in the ABS serial data circuit.
4. Checks for a short to ground in the ABS serial data circuit.
5. Checks to see if the Tech 1 can communicate with the EBCM.

Diagnostic Aids:

The problem may be intermittent. Try performing the tests shown while "wiggling" wiring and connectors; this can often cause the fault to appear.

1991

1992

NOTE: THIS CODE WILL SET ONLY WHEN AN OFF-BOARD SERIAL DATA DEVICE, SUCH AS THE TECH 1 (T-1) IS ATTEMPTING TO COMMUNICATE WITH THE EBCM. SINCE, BY DEFINITION, THIS CODE MEANS YOU CANNOT COMMUNICATE WITH THE EBCM USING AN OFF-BOARD SERIAL DATA DEVICE, YOU MUST READ AND CLEAR THE CODE USING ALDL FLASH CODE AND CODE CLEARING TECHNIQUES.

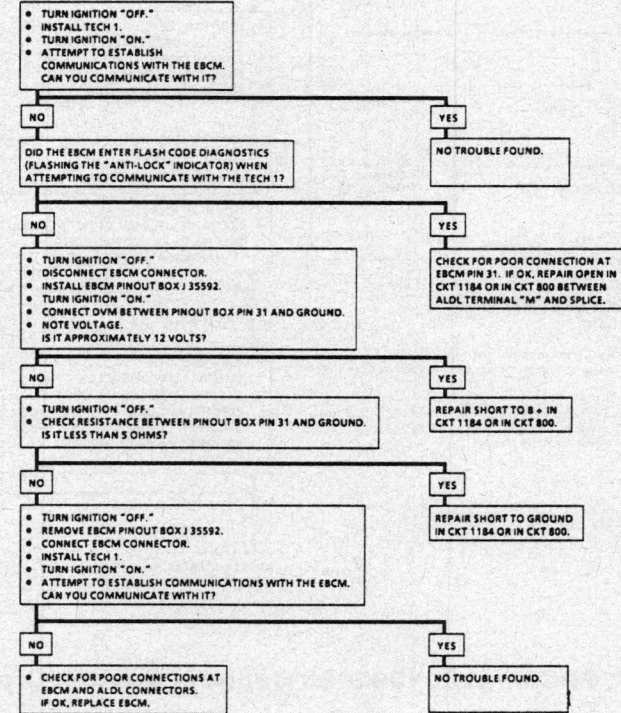

Fig. 37 Code 72, EBCM serial line data fault. Caprice, Custom Cruiser & Roadmaster

1991 REATTA, 1991-92 BROUGHAM, TORONADO & TROFEO & 1991-93 CAPRICE, CUSTOM CRUISER, ELDORADO, RIVIERA, ROADMASTER, SEVILLE (BOSCH 2 U TYPE)

CHART A
(Page 1 of 2)
"ANTILOCK" INDICATOR "ON" WITH NO CODES SET OR
WITH TECH 1 UNABLE TO RECEIVE DATA

Circuit Description:

The "Antilock" Indicator is located on the right side of the instrument panel. Battery voltage is applied with ignition in "Run, Bulb Test or Start" through fuse 17 and CKT 39. The indicator is grounded through CKT 875 and is controlled by the EBCM at pin 29 and the Hydraulic Modulator at pin 11 through the Solenoid Valve Relay. The EBCM will supply ground to the indicator for approximately 2 seconds when ignition is first turned "ON." During the first 2 seconds, if no faults are detected, the EBCM will energize the Solenoid Valve Relay. With the relay energized, the ground CKT 875 through the relay will be opened. This allows the indicator to go "OFF" when the EBCM indicator control line at pin 29 is opened.

When the ignition is turned to "Run," the Over Voltage Protection (OVP) relay coil is energized by Fuse 17. When energized the OVP closes its normally open contacts, supplying power from fuse 3 through CKT 880 and CKT 850 to the EBCM at pin 1. If high system voltages occur (at or above approx. 16 volts) the OVP relay will short CKT 880 to ground causing fuse 3 to blow in order to prevent damage to the antilock brake system.

NOTICE: Do not use a quick charger for engine starting or for battery charging if the battery is still connected to the vehicle's electrical system. Always disconnect the negative battery cable when charging a battery. Failure to do so may cause fuse 3 to blow or cause serious damage to other electronic components.

Test Description: Number(s) below refer to circled number(s) on the diagnostic chart.
1. Determines if EBCM has proper supply voltage.
2. Determines if fault is in charging system or power feed to OVP relay (Fuse 3).
3. Checks for open or high resistance in ckt 850.
4. Determines if OVP relay is faulty.
5. Determines whether open is in CKT 150 or CKT 39.

Fig. 38   Chart A, ABS indicator On w/no codes set or TECH 1 unable to receive data (Part 1 of 2). 1991 Caprice, Custom Cruiser & Roadmaster

CHART A
(Page 2 of 2)
"ANTILOCK" INDICATOR "ON" WITH NO CODES SET OR
WITH TECH 1 UNABLE TO RECEIVE DATA

Circuit Description:

The "Antilock" Indicator is located on the right side of the instrument panel. Battery voltage is applied with ignition in "Run, Bulb Test or Start" through fuse 17 and CKT 39. The indicator is grounded through CKT 875 and is controlled by the EBCM at pin 29 and the Hydraulic Modulator at pin 11 through the Solenoid Valve Relay. The EBCM will supply ground to the indicator for approximately 2 seconds when ignition is first turned "ON." During the first 2 seconds, if no faults are detected, the EBCM will energize the Solenoid Valve Relay. With the relay energized, the ground CKT 875 through the relay will be opened. This allows the indicator to go "OFF" when the EBCM indicator control line at pin 29 is opened.

When the ignition is turned to "Run," the Over Voltage Protection (OVP) relay coil is energized by Fuse 17. When energized the OVP closes its normally open contacts, supplying power from fuse 3 through CKT 880 and CKT 850 to the EBCM at pin 1. If high system voltages occur (at or above approx. 16 volts) the OVP relay will short CKT 880 to ground causing fuse 3 to blow in order to prevent damage to the antilock brake system.

NOTICE: Do not use a quick charger for engine starting or for battery charging if the battery is still connected to the vehicle's electrical system. Always disconnect the negative battery cable when charging a battery. Failure to do so may cause fuse 3 to blow or cause serious damage to other electronic components.

Test Description: Number(s) below refer to circled number(s) on the diagnostic chart.
6. Checks for possible fault in Solenoid Valve Relay or EBCM.
7. Determines whether Solenoid Valve Relay or EBCM is faulty.
8. Determines whether fault is in hydraulic modulator or short to ground in CKT 875.

Fig. 38   Chart A, ABS indicator On w/no codes set or TECH 1 unable to receive data (Part 2 of 2). 1991 Caprice, Custom Cruiser & Roadmaster

1991 REATTA, 1991-92 BROUGHAM, TORONADO & TROFEO & 1991-93 CAPRICE, CUSTOM CRUISER, ELDORADO, RIVIERA, ROADMASTER, SEVILLE (BOSCH 2 U TYPE)

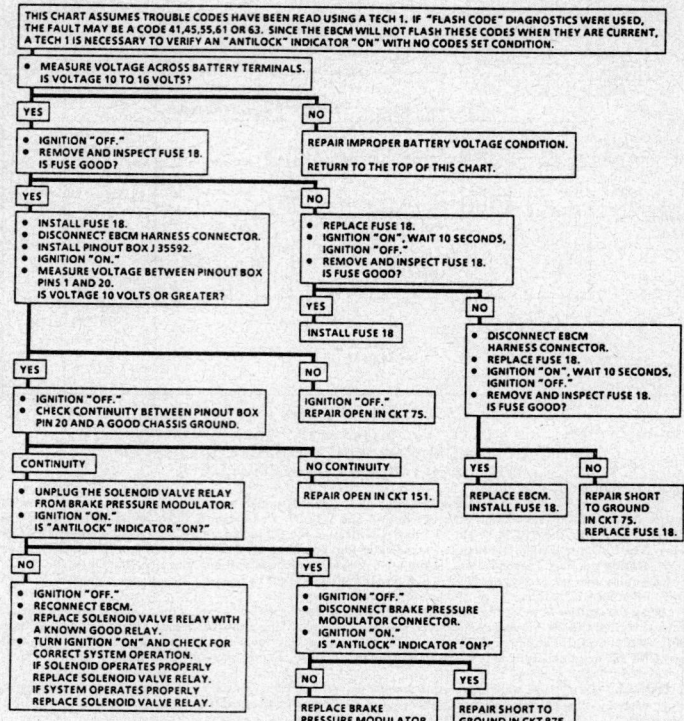

THIS CHART ASSUMES TROUBLE CODES HAVE BEEN READ USING A TECH 1. IF "FLASH CODE" DIAGNOSTICS WERE USED, THE FAULT MAY BE A CODE 41,45,55,61 OR 63. SINCE THE EBCM WILL NOT FLASH THESE CODES WHEN THEY ARE CURRENT, A TECH 1 IS NECESSARY TO VERIFY AN "ANTILOCK" INDICATOR "ON" WITH NO CODES SET CONDITION.

CHART A

"ANTILOCK" INDICATOR "ON" WITH NO CODES SET OR WITH TECH 1 UNABLE TO RECEIVE DATA

Circuit Description:

The "Antilock" Indicator is located on the right side of the instrument panel. Battery voltage is applied with ignition in "Run, Bulb Test or Start" through Fuse 17 and CKT 39. The indicator is grounded through CKT 875 and is controlled by the EBCM at Pin "29" and the Modulator at Pin "11" through the Solenoid Valve Relay. The EBCM will supply ground to the indicator for approximately 2 seconds when ignition is first turned "ON." During the first 2 seconds, if no faults are detected, the EBCM will energize the Solenoid Valve Relay. With the relay energized, the ground CKT 875 through the relay will be opened. This allows the indicator to go "OFF" when the EBCM indicator control line at Pin "29" is opened.

Test Description: Number(s) below refer to circled number(s) on the diagnostic chart.
1. Checks for proper battery and/or charging system operation.
2. Checks for an open fuse in the EBCM power feed circuit.
3. Checks for an open in the EBCM power feed circuit.
4. Checks for an open in the EBCM ground circuit.
5. Checks for a possible fault in the Solenoid Valve Relay.
6. Determines whether the fault is in the Solenoid Valve Relay or the EBCM.
7. Checks for a short to ground in the EBCM or the EBCM power feed circuit.
8. Determines whether the short to ground is in the EBCM or the EBCM power feed circuit.
9. Determines whether the short to ground is in the Brake Pressure Modulator or the indicator control circuit.

Fig. 39   Chart A, ABS indicator On w/no codes set or TECH 1 unable to receive data. 1992–93 Caprice, Custom Cruiser & Roadmaster

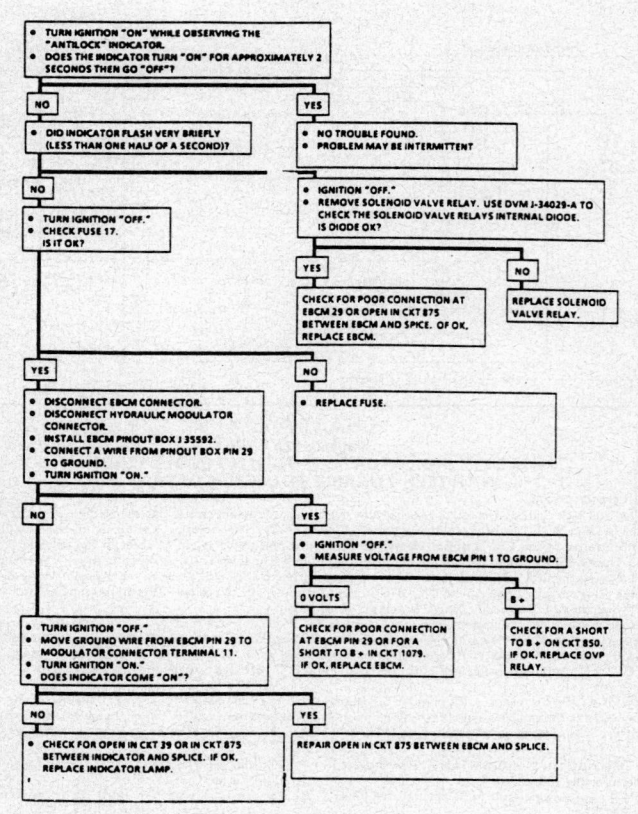

CHART B

"ANTILOCK" INDICATOR INOPERATIVE OR INDICATOR FLASHES VERY BRIEFLY AT IGNITION "ON"

Circuit Description:

The "Antilock" Indicator is located on the right side of the instrument panel. Battery voltage is applied with ignition in "Run, Bulb Test or Start" through fuse 17 and CKT 39. The indicator is grounded through CKT 875 and is controlled by the EBCM at pin 29 and the Hydraulic Modulator at pin 11 through the Solenoid Valve Relay. The EBCM will supply ground to the indicator for approximately 2 seconds when ignition is first turned "ON." During the first 2 seconds, if no faults are detected, the EBCM will energize the Solenoid Valve Relay. With the relay energized, the ground CKT 875 through the relay will be opened. This allows the indicator to go "OFF" when the EBCM indicator control line at pin 29 is opened.

Test Description: Number(s) below refer to circled number(s) on the diagnostic chart.
1. Verifies an inoperative indicator.
2. Checks for a faulty EBCM indicator control.
3. Checks Fuse 17.
4. Checks Diode within Solenoid Valve Relay.
5. Checks for a faulty EBCM or connection at EBCM pin 29. (This test will detect a bad EBCM even if the Solenoid Valve Relay energized before the indicator had a chance to flash in Step 2.)
6. This test will detect a short to B + in CKT 850 or a faulty OVP relay. Either failure would appear as an inoperative indicator during bulb test.
7. A short to B + in CKT 1079 would back feed through the EBCM appearing as ignition "ON," causing the indicator not to illuminate.
8. Checks for open in CKT 875 between EBCM and splice.
9. Checks for open in CKT 39 or CKT 875. At this point if replacing the lamp does not correct the problem, either CKT 39 or CKT 875 is open.

Diagnostic Aids:

If indicator failure is intermittent, install the Tech 1 diagnostic tool and select any ABS test mode so the "Antilock" indicator will be turned "ON." While observing the indicator, go through the indicators power and ground circuits wiggling the wiring and connectors. Watch for flickering or failure of the indicator to pin point problem area.

Fig. 40   Chart B, ABS indicator inoperative or indicator flashes very briefly at ignition On. 1991 Caprice, Custom Cruiser & Roadmaster

CHART B

"ANTILOCK" INDICATOR INOPERATIVE OR INDICATOR FLASHES VERY BRIEFLY AT IGNITION "ON"
(LESS THAN ONE HALF OF A SECOND)

Circuit Description:

The "Antilock" Indicator is located on the right side of the instrument panel. Battery voltage is applied with ignition in "Run, Bulb Test or Start" through Fuse 17 and CKT 39. The indicator is grounded through CKT 875 and is controlled by the EBCM at Pin "29" and the Hydraulic Modulator at Pin "11" through the Solenoid Valve Relay. The EBCM will supply ground to the indicator for approximately 2 seconds when ignition is first turned "ON." During the first 2 seconds, if no faults are detected, the EBCM will energize the Solenoid Valve Relay. With the relay energized, the ground CKT 875 through the relay will be opened. This allows the indicator to go "OFF" when the EBCM indicator control line at Pin "29" is opened.

Test Description: Number(s) below refer to circled number(s) on the diagnostic chart.

1. Verifies an improperly operating indicator.
2. Determines whether the fault is an inoperative indicator or an improperly operating indicator.
3. Checks for an inoperative Instrument Cluster.
4. Determines whether the fault is in the Instrument Cluster portion of the circuitry or in the ABS portion.
5. Checks for a bad bulb.
6. Determines whether the fault is in the wiring, connections, or in the Instrument Cluster printed circuits. (For LTZ only the Instrument Cluster will have different terminals for the "Antilock" indicator.)
7. Determines whether the fault is in the wiring, connections, or Solenoid Valve Relay.
8. Determines whether the fault is in the wiring or connections.

Diagnostic Aids:

If indicator failure in "Intermittent," install the Tech 1 diagnostic tool and select any "ABS test mode so the "Antilock" indicator will be turned "ON." While observing the indicator, go through the indicators power and ground circuits wiggling the wiring and connectors. Watch for flickering or failure of the indicator to pin point roblem area. Instrument Cluster terminals are different for the LTZ.

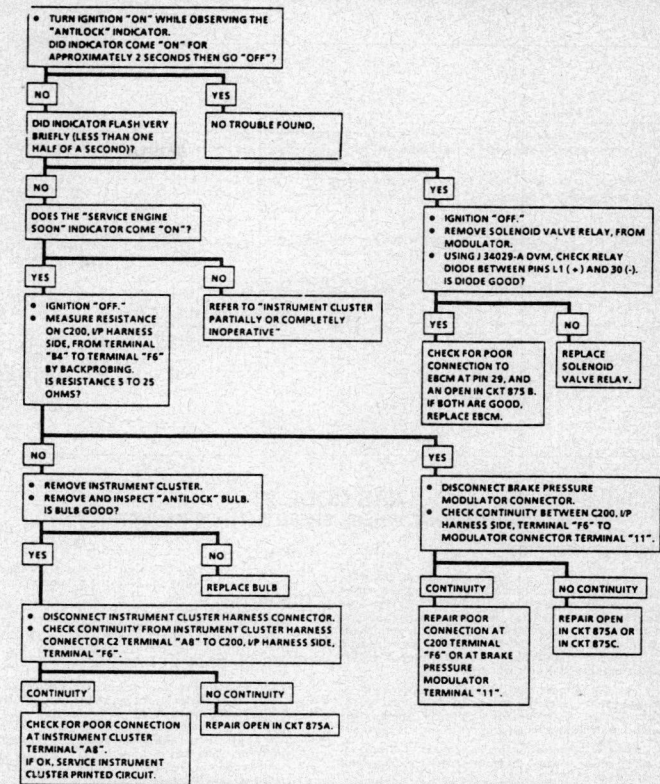

Fig. 41   Chart B, ABS indicator inoperative or indicator flashes very briefly at ignition On. 1992–93 Caprice, Custom Cruiser & Roadmaster

Fig. 42   ABS wiring circuit (Part 1 of 2). Brougham

Fig. 42   ABS wiring circuit (Part 2 of 2). Brougham

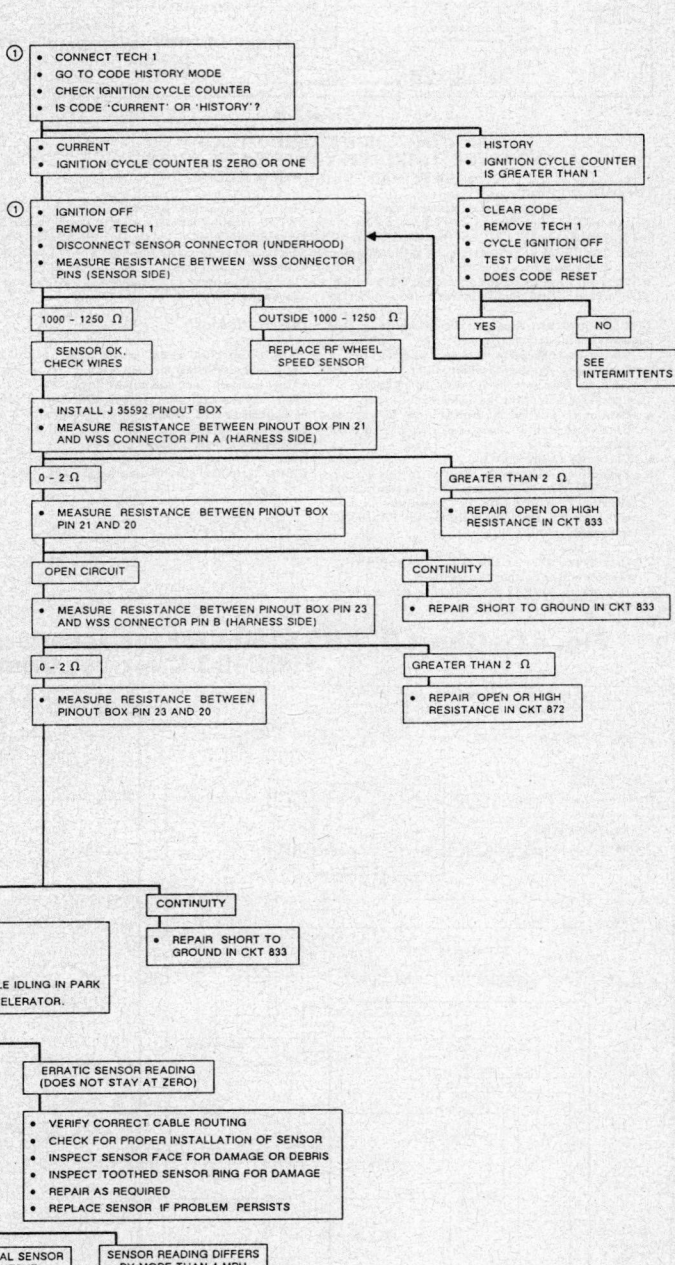

ABS CODE 21
RIGHT FRONT WHEEL SPEED SENSOR FAULT

CIRCUIT DESCRIPTION

As each wheel turns, the wheel speed sensor for that wheel creates a small AC voltage as a toothed sensor ring, mounted on the brake rotor (in the front) or differential pinion shaft (in the rear), is passed by the stationary sensor. The sensor consists of a permanent magnet and coil and generates voltage by magnetic induction. The frequency of the wheel speed sensor signal is proportional to wheel speed.

The EBCM uses the wheel speed sensor signal to calculate vehicle reference speeds and individual speed, acceleration and slip values for each wheel. These values are used to determine when antilock control is required.

The EBCM performs two basic types of checks on the wheel speed sensors, these are sensor continuity and sensor output.

TEST CONDITIONS

1. Tested continuously.

FAILURE CONDITIONS

Sensor Output:

1. Drive-away: Speed signal is not detected when vehicle reaches 12 kph or 7.5 mph
– or –

2. While Driving: Speed signal is lost while vehicle speed is greater than 40 kph or 25 mph
– or –

Continuity:

3. While Standing: Open circuit is seen while the vehicle is standing still with the ignition on.

ACTION TAKEN

1. Code set
2. ABS switched 'OFF'

NOTES ON CODE 21 CHART

1. This section of the fault tree determines if the code stored is due to a current fault condition. 'Current' wheel speed sensor faults will be detected when the vehicle is driven and reaches a speed of 4 mph (6 kph). If the ABS light turns on, the fault is current. The TECH 1 will indicate ignition cycle since code was set. If the ignition cycle counter is at zero or one the code is current.

2. This section of the fault tree checks for an open or short in the wheel speed sensor wiring or sensor coil.

3. This section of the fault tree checks for conditions which may cause intermittent code setting. Some causes of intermittent wheel speed sensor codes to set are: improper routing or sensor cables next to spark plug wires, cables not retained in brackets, loose fitting or improperly mounted sensors, damaged sensors or toothed rings, poor terminal engagement of connectors, or intermittent shorts or opens in wiring.

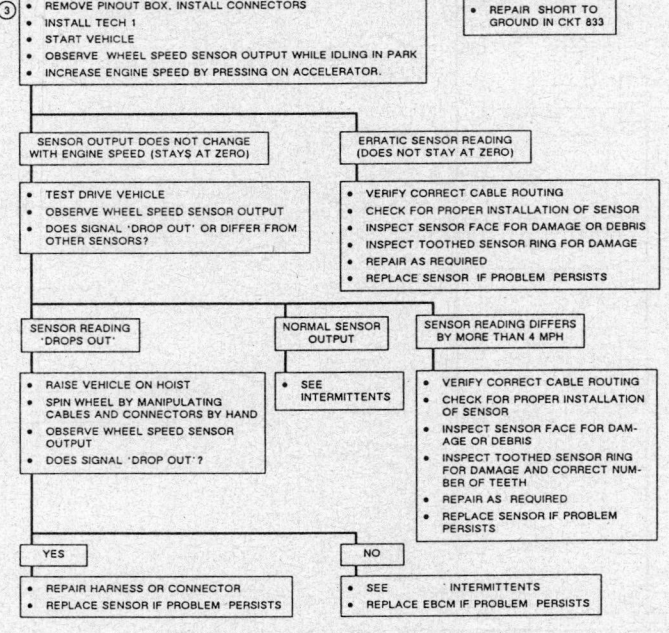

Fig. 43 Code 21, RF wheel speed sensor fault. Brougham

ABS CODE 22

RIGHT FRONT TOOTHED WHEEL FREQUENCY ERROR

CIRCUIT DESCRIPTION

As each wheel turns, the wheel speed sensor for that wheel creates a small AC voltage as a toothed sensor ring, mounted on the brake rotor (in the front) or differential pinion shaft (in the rear), is passed by the stationary sensor. The sensor consists of a permanent magnet and coil and generates voltage by magnetic induction. The frequency of the wheel speed sensor signal is proportional to wheel speed.

The EBCM uses the wheel speed sensor signal to calculate vehicle reference speeds and individual speed, acceleration and slip values for each wheel. These values are used to determine when antilock control is required.

TEST CONDITIONS

1. Tested continuously.

FAILURE CONDITIONS

1. While Driving: One wheel is detected at least 30 kph or 19 mph faster than the remaining wheels for an extended period of time.

— or —

One wheel is at least 6 kph or 4 mph less than or greater than the remaining wheels for an extended period of time.

ACTION TAKEN

1. Code set.

2. ABS switched 'OFF'.

Code 22 will set from improper speed signals generated by the toothed ring sensor. Causes of improper speed signal may be caused by incorrect number of teeth on sensor ring, sensor rings which are covered with dirt, grease or metallic particles, or damaged toothed sensor ring.

Code 22 may also set if the mini-spare tire has been previously used or the size of the tires on the vehicle differ from each other. In addition to Code 22, Codes 26 and 36 may also set if the mini-spare tire has been used. If it is known that the spare tire was used, clear codes and test drive the vehicle again, verify that no codes set.

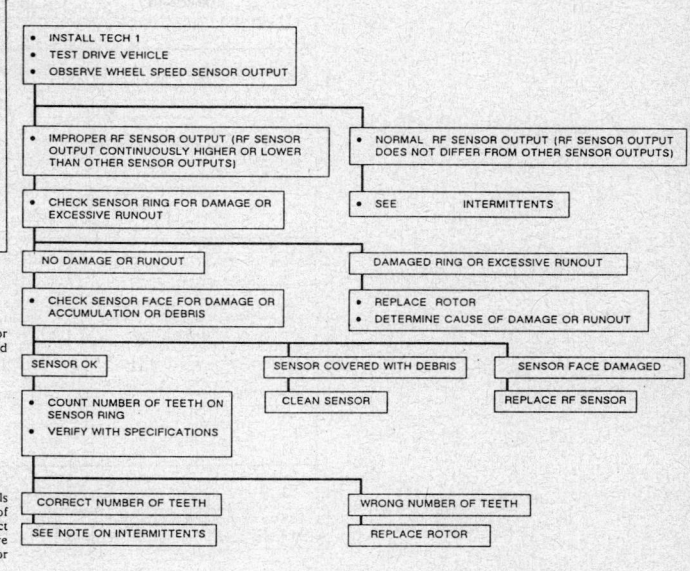

Fig. 44   Code 22, RF toothed wheel frequency error. Brougham

ABS CODE 25

LEFT FRONT WHEEL SPEED FAULT

CIRCUIT DESCRIPTION

As each wheel turns, the wheel speed sensor for that wheel creates a small AC voltage as a toothed sensor ring, mounted on the brake rotor (in the front) or differential pinion shaft (in the rear), is passed by the stationary sensor. The sensor consists of a permanent magnet and coil and generates voltage by magnetic induction. The frequency of the wheel speed sensor signal is proportional to wheel speed.

The EBCM uses the wheel speed sensor signal to calculate vehicle reference speeds and individual speed, acceleration and slip values for each wheel. These values are used to determine when antilock control is required.

The EBCM performs two basic types of checks on the wheel speed sensors, these are sensor continuity and sensor output.

TEST CONDITIONS

1. Tested continuously.

FAILURE CONDITIONS

Sensor Output:

1. Drive-away: Speed signal is not detected when vehicle reaches 12 kph or 7.5 mph
   — or —
2. While Driving: Speed signal is lost while vehicle speed is greater than 40 kph or 25 mph
   — or —

Continuity:

3. While Standing: Open circuit is seen while the vehicle is standing still with the ignition on.

ACTION TAKEN

1. Code set
2. ABS switched 'OFF'

NOTES ON CODE 25 CHART

1. This section of the fault tree determines if the code stored is due to a current fault condition. 'Current' wheel speed sensor faults will be detected when the vehicle is driven and reaches a speed of 4 mph (6 kph). If the ABS light turns on, the fault is current. The TECH 1 will indicate ignition cycle since code was set. If the ignition cycle counter is at zero or one the code is current.

2. This section of the fault tree checks for an open or short in the wheel speed sensor wiring or sensor coil.

3. This section of the fault tree checks for conditions which may cause intermittent code setting. Some causes of intermittent wheel speed sensor codes to set are: improper routing or sensor cables next to spark plug wires, cables not retained in brackets, loose fitting or improperly mounted sensors, damaged sensors or toothed rings, poor terminal engagement of connectors, or intermittent shorts or opens in wiring.

Fig. 45   Code 25, LF wheel speed sensor fault (Part 1 of 2). Brougham

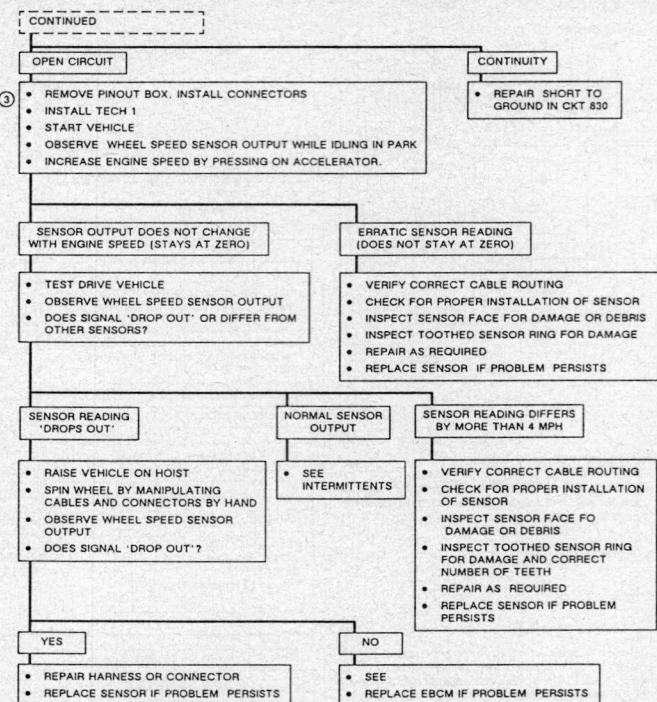

Fig. 45   Code 25, LF wheel speed sensor fault (Part 2 of 2). Brougham

ABS CODE 26

LEFT FRONT TOOTHED WHEEL FREQUENCY ERROR

CIRCUIT DESCRIPTION

As each wheel turns, the wheel speed sensor for that wheel creates a small AC voltage as a toothed sensor ring, mounted on the brake rotor (in the front) or differential pinion shaft (in the rear), is passed by the stationary sensor. The sensor consists of a permanent magnet and coil and generates voltage by magnetic induction. The frequency of the wheel speed sensor signal is proportional to wheel speed.

The EBCM uses the wheel speed sensor signal to calculate vehicle reference speeds and individual speed, acceleration and slip values for each wheel. These values are used to determine when antilock control is required.

TEST CONDITIONS

1. Tested continuously.

FAILURE CONDITIONS

1. While Driving: One wheel is detected at least 30 kph or 19 mph faster than the remaining wheels for an extended period of time.

  – or –

One wheel is at least 6 kph or 4 mph less than or greater than the remaining wheels for an extended period of time.

ACTION TAKEN

1. Code set.

2. ABS switched 'OFF'.

Code 26 will set from improper speed signals generated by the toothed ring sensor. Causes of improper speed signal may be caused by incorrect number of teeth on sensor ring, sensor rings which are covered with dirt, grease or metallic particles, or damaged toothed sensor ring.

Code 26 may also be set if the mini-spare tire has been previously used or the size of the tires on the vehicle differ from each other. In addition to Code 26, Codes 22 and 36 may also set if the mini-spare tire has been used. If it is known that the spare tire was used, clear codes and test drive the vehicle again, verify that no codes set.

Fig. 46   Code 26, LF toothed wheel frequency error. Brougham

ABS CODE 35

REAR AXLE SPEED SENSOR FAULT

CIRCUIT DESCRIPTION

As each wheel turns, the wheel speed sensor for that wheel creates a small AC voltage as a toothed sensor ring, mounted on the brake rotor (in the front) or differential pinion shaft (in the rear), is passed by the stationary sensor. The sensor consists of a permanent magnet and coil and generates voltage by magnetic induction. The frequency of the wheel speed sensor signal is proportional to wheel speed.

The EBCM uses the wheel speed sensor signal to calculate vehicle reference speeds and individual speed, acceleration and slip values for each wheel. These values are used to determine when antilock control is required.

The EBCM performs two basic types of checks on the wheel speed sensors, these are sensor continuity and sensor output.

TEST CONDITIONS

1. Tested continuously.

FAILURE CONDITIONS

Sensor Output:

1. Drive-away: Speed signal is not detected when vehicle reaches 12 kph or 7.5 mph
   – or –
2. While Driving: Speed signal is lost while vehicle speed is greater than 40 kph or 25 mph
   – or –

Continuity:

3. While Standing: Open circuit is seen while the vehicle is standing still with the ignition on.

ACTION TAKEN

1. Code set
2. ABS switched 'OFF'

NOTES ON CODE 35 CHART

1. This section of the fault tree determines if the code stored is due to a current fault condition. 'Current' wheel speed sensor faults will be detected when the vehicle is driven and reaches a speed of 4 mph (6 kph). If the ABS light turns on, the fault is current. The TECH 1 will indicate ignition cycle since code was set. If the ignition cycle counter is at zero or one the code is current.

2. This section of the fault tree checks for an open or short in the wheel speed sensor wiring or sensor coil.

3. This section of the fault tree checks for conditions which may cause intermittent code setting. Some causes of intermittent wheel speed sensor codes to set are: improper routing or sensor cables next to spark plug wires, cables not retained in brackets, loose fitting or improperly mounted sensors, damaged sensors or toothed rings, poor terminal engagement of connectors, or intermittent shorts or opens in wiring.

Fig. 47 Code 35, LR wheel speed sensor fault. Brougham

ABS CODES 36

REAR AXLE TOOTHED WHEEL FREQUENCY ERROR

CIRCUIT DESCRIPTION

As each wheel turns, the wheel speed sensor for that wheel creates a small AC voltage as a toothed sensor ring, mounted on the brake rotor (in the front) or differential pinion shaft (in the rear), is passed by the stationary sensor. The sensor consists of a permanent magnet and coil and generates voltage by magnetic induction. The frequency of the wheel speed sensor signal is proportional to wheel speed.

The EBCM uses the wheel speed sensor signal to calculate vehicle reference speeds and individual speed, acceleration and slip values for each wheel. These values are used to determine when antilock control is required.

TEST CONDITIONS

1. Tested continuously.

FAILURE CONDITIONS

1. While Driving: One wheel is detected at least 30 kph or 19 mph faster than the remaining wheels for an extended period of time.

  – or –

One wheel is at least 6 kph or 4 mph less than or greater than the remaining wheels for an extended period of time.

ACTION TAKEN

1. Code set.

2. ABS switched 'OFF'.

Code 36 will set from improper speed signals generated by the toothed ring sensor. Causes of improper speed signal may be caused by incorrect number of teeth on sensor ring, sensor rings which are covered with dirt, grease or metallic particles, or damaged toothed sensor ring.

Code 36 may also set if the mini-spare tire has been previously used or the size of the tires on the vehicle differ from each other. In addition to Code 36, Codes 22 and 26 may also set if the mini-spare tire has been used. If it is known that the spare tire was used, clear codes and test drive the vehicle again, verify that no codes set.

Fig. 48   Code 36, rear axle toothed wheel frequency error. Brougham

ABS CODE 41

RIGHT FRONT SOLENOID VALVE FAULT

CIRCUIT DESCRIPTION

The right front solenoid valve in the hydraulic modulator may be commanded to three different positions by the EBCM. Valve position is determined by the amount of current which is allowed to flow through the solenoid valve coil.

The solenoid valve circuits receive power through the valve relay on the hydraulic modulator. The valve relay is engaged at key-on and remains engaged throughout the ignition cycle. Solenoid valve lines should have battery voltage available at all times.

When the key is turned to RUN, power is supplied to the EBCM. The EBCM will complete an internal self-check before providing ground to the valve relay. When the valve relay is energized, battery power is supplied to the solenoid valves.

Code 41 will set when the expected position of the right front solenoid valve does not match the commanded position from the EBCM. Conditions which could cause Code 41 to set are damage to the right front solenoid, an open circuit or a short circuit to ground or battery on CKT 827.

TEST CONDITIONS

1. Tested continuously.

FAILURE CONDITIONS

While Standing Or Driving:

1. Valve cannot be activated.

  – or –

2. Valve activated in a defective way.

ACTION TAKEN

1. Code Set.

2. ABS switched 'OFF'.

Fig. 49   Code 41, RF solenoid valve fault. Brougham

ABS CODE 45

LEFT FRONT SOLENOID VALVE FAULT

CIRCUIT DESCRIPTION

The left front solenoid valve in the hydraulic modulator may be commanded to three different positions by the EBCM. Valve position is determined by the amount of current which is allowed to flow through the solenoid valve coil.

The solenoid valve circuits receive power through the valve relay on the hydraulic modulator. The valve relay is engaged at key-on and remains engaged throughout the ignition cycle. Solenoid valve lines should have battery voltage available at all times.

When the key is turned to RUN, power is supplied to the EBCM. The EBCM will complete an internal self-check before providing ground to the valve relay. When the valve relay is energized, battery power is supplied to the solenoid valves.

Code 45 will set when the expected position of the left front solenoid valve does not match the commanded position from the EBCM. Conditions which could cause Code 45 to set are damage to the left front solenoid, an open circuit or a short circuit to ground or battery on CKT 826.

TEST CONDITIONS

1. Tested continuously.

FAILURE CONDITIONS

While Standing Or Driving:
1. Valve cannot be activated.
   – or –
2. Valve activated in a defective way.

ACTION TAKEN

1. Code Set.
2. ABS switched 'OFF'.

Fig. 50   Code 45, LF solenoid valve fault. Brougham

ABS CODE 55

REAR AXLE SOLENOID VALVE FAULT

CIRCUIT DESCRIPTION

The rear axle solenoid valve in the hydraulic modulator may be commanded to three different positions by the EBCM. The rear axle solenoid valve modulates hydraulic brake pressure to both rear wheel circuits. Valve position is determined by the amount of current which is allowed to flow through the solenoid valve coil.

The solenoid valve circuits receive power through the valve relay on the hydraulic modulator. The valve relay is engaged at key-on and remains engaged throughout the ignition cycle. Solenoid valve lines should have battery voltage available at all times.

When the key is turned to RUN, power is supplied to the EBCM. The EBCM will complete an internal self-check before providing ground to the valve relay. When the valve relay is energized, battery power is supplied to the solenoid valves.

Code 55 will set when the expected position of the rear axle solenoid valve does not match the commanded position from the EBCM. Conditions which could cause Code 55 to set are damage to the rear axle solenoid, an open circuit or a short circuit to ground or battery on CKT 828.

TEST CONDITIONS

1. Tested continuously.

FAILURE CONDITIONS

While Standing Or Driving:
1. Valve cannot be activated.
   – or –
2. Valve activated in a defective way.

ACTION TAKEN

1. Code Set.
2. ABS switched 'OFF'.

Fig. 51   Code 55, rear axle solenoid valve fault. Brougham

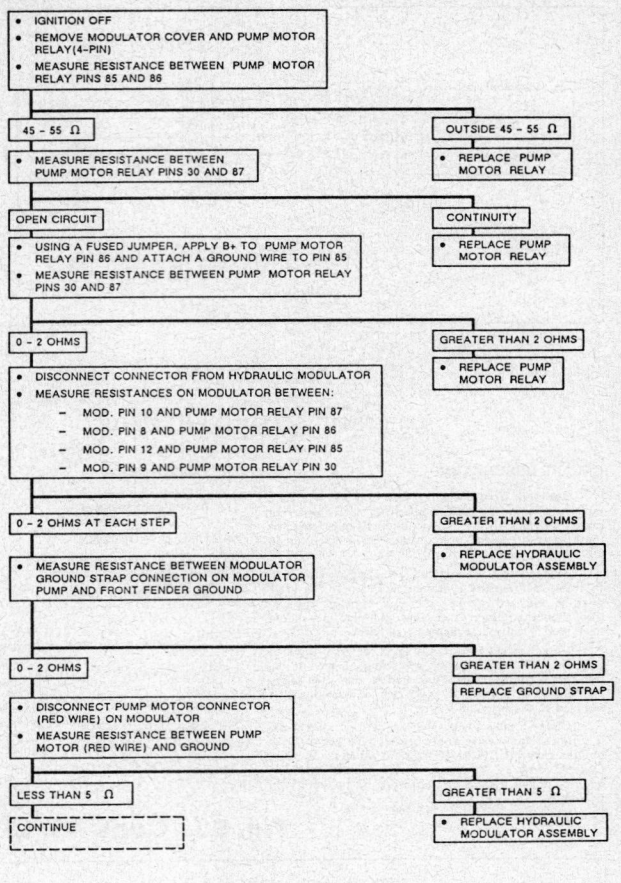

ABS CODE 61

PUMP MOTOR CIRCUIT FAULT

CIRCUIT DESCRIPTION

The pump motor returns brake fluid to the master cylinder brake circuit at the hydraulic modulator during antilock braking. During normal braking, the pump does not operate. When the vehicle begins to move after start-up, the EBCM will turn on the pump motor and perform a self-check of the pump motor and pump motor circuit. This check may be felt and heard by the driver when the vehicle begins to move. The self-check should be considered normal operation. The pump motor is an integral component of the hydraulic modulator and cannot be serviced separately.

The pump motor relay provides power to the pump motor in the hydraulic modulator. The pump motor relay is located on the hydraulic modulator an may be replaced if it is found to be defective.

TEST CONDITIONS

1. Tested continuously.

FAILURE CONDITIONS

1. **Drive Away:** Motor voltage is not detected during first drive away after engine start.

2. **While driving:** Motor relay is energized and motor voltage is not detected.

– or –

3. Voltage at EBCM pin 14 below system voltage

– or –

4. Pump runs continuously

When the pump motor relay is engaged, the motor monitor line should be at battery voltage. With the pump motor relay disengaged, the monitoring line should be at ground. If the commanded position of the pump motor relay and motor monitor line do not agree, Code 61 will set. Some conditions which will cause Code 61 to set are:

- An open circuit on CKTs 854 or 1078
- A short to voltage on CKTs 854 or 1078
- A short to ground on CKTs 854 or 1078
- A defective pump motor relay or pump motor

Fig. 52 Code 61, pump motor circuit failure. Brougham

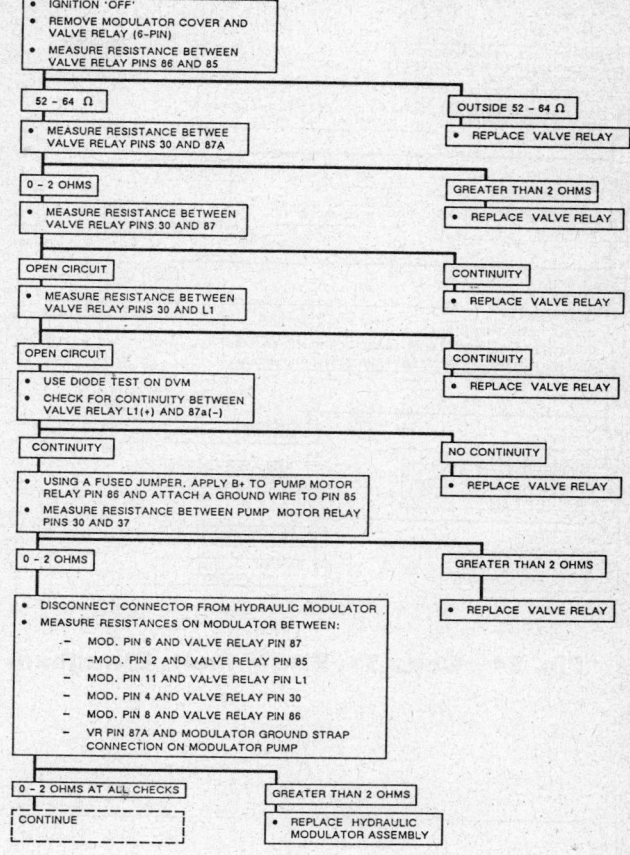

ABS CODE 63
SOLENOID VALVE RELAY FAULT

CIRCUIT DESCRIPTION

The solenoid valve relay provides power to the three solenoid valves in the hydraulic modulator. The solenoid valve relay is located on the hydraulic modulator and may be replaced if it is found to be defective.

The valve relay is engaged during normal system operation. When the ignition is switched to RUN, the EBCM commands the solenoid valve relay on by grounding the valve relay actuation line on CKT 879 (EBCM pin 27). When this ground is provided, the valve relay is energized from the voltage supply line on CKT 1079 (EBCM pin 17). The valve relay switches and battery voltage is provided to the three solenoid valves and the solenoid valve relay feedback line on CKT 851 (EBCM pin 32). The valve relay remains engaged until the ignition is turned off or a failure is detected.

Whenever the solenoid valve relay is not engaged, the ANTILOCK light will turn on. With the ignition on and the solenoid valve relay not engaged, a path to ground exists from the GA/TRANS fuse (20 amps) thru the ANTILOCK light on CKT 39 which turns on the warning light. The ANTILOCK light can also be commanded on by the EBCM on CKT 852 (EBCM pin 29). The EBCM will provide ground on this line and turn on the warning light when a failure is detected.

The pump motor relay is not engaged during normal system operation. When antilock operation is required, the motor relay actuation line on CKT 854 (EBCM pin 28) is pulled to ground. The pump motor relay is engaged by the relay supply voltage line on CKT 1079 (EBCM pin 17). When the relay switches, battery power is provided to the pump motor.

ANTILOCK OPERATION

With the solenoid valve relay engaged, battery power is provided to the three solenoid valves. If antilock operation is required, the EBCM varies the amount of current supplied to the solenoid valves (EBCM pins 2, 18, 35) and the valve is positioned to provide for optimum braking.

TEST CONDITIONS
1. Tested continuously.

FAILURE CONDITIONS
1. While Standing Or Driving: Open circuit is detected
   - or -
2. Relay sticks during initial ignition

ACTION TAKEN
1. Code set.
2. ABS switched 'OFF'.

When the valve relay is engaged, the valve relay feedback line should be at battery voltage. With the valve relay disengaged the feedback line is at ground. If the commanded position of the valve relay and valve relay position indicated by the feedback line do not agree, Code 63 will set. Some conditions which will cause Code 63 to set are:
- An open circuit on CKTs 851 or 879.
- A short to voltage on CKTs 851 or 879.
- A short to ground on CKTs 851 or 879.
- A defective solenoid valve relay.
- Open circuit on CKT 1079.

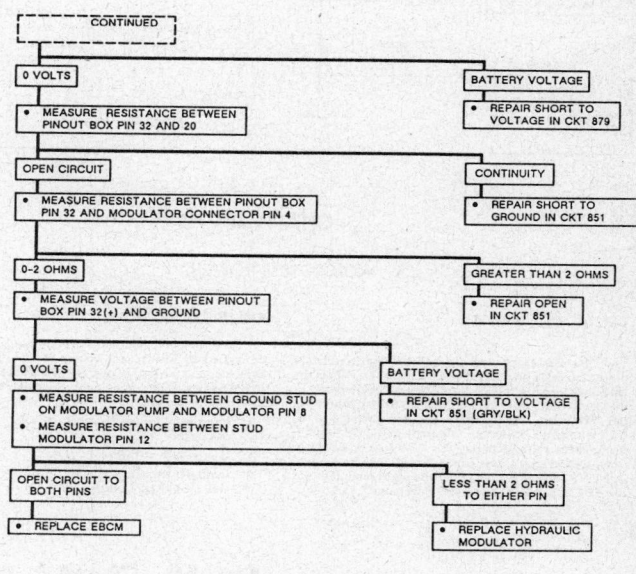

Fig. 53   Code 63, solenoid valve relay fault. Brougham

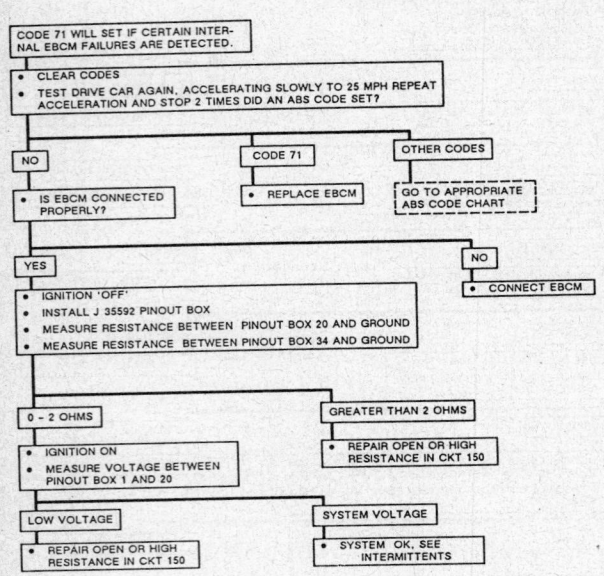

Fig. 54   Code 71, EBCM fault. Brougham

ABS CODE 72

SERIAL DATA LINK ERROR (TECH 1 ERROR)

CIRCUIT DESCRIPTION

An ABS Code 72 may set when there is a momentary serial data communications error between the EBCM and the TECH 1. This code may set when power to the EBCM is interrupted while the ignition remains powered; such as when the ignition is cycled while the Tech-1 is hooked-up. When this occurs, simply cycle power to the Tech-1 and allow it to reset.

Although it is not an indication of a serious condition this code should be cleared prior to completion of diagnosis.

TEST CONDITIONS

Tested continuously in Diagnostics Mode. (TECH- 1 CONNECTED)

FAILURE CONDITIONS

EBCM receives 3 consecutive invalid messages during diagnostics.

ACTION TAKEN

1.   Code set.
2.   Transmission from and to TECH- 1 is impossible.

Fig. 55   Code 72, serial data link error. Brougham

CHART A

NO SYSTEM POWER

CIRCUIT DESCRIPTION

The EBCM receives power from the overvoltage protection relay on CKT 850 (EBCM Pin 1). When the ignition is turned to RUN, the OVP relay is energized by the GA/TRANS fuse; the normally open relay contacts of the OVP relay close. Battery voltage is supplied to the EBCM thru the ABS fuse (10 amp) and CKT 640. If high system voltages occur, the ABS fuse will blow in order to prevent damage to the Antilock Brake System. The OVP relay is located under the dash, mounted near the EBCM bracket behind the glovebox.

FAILURE CONDITIONS

Intermittent operation of the ANTILOCK light may be caused by intermittent voltage levels which do not correspond to the proper operating range of the Antilock Brake System. Some conditions which may cause a lack of system power are:

*   Improper electrical contact of the EBCM connector.
*   Low system voltage.
*   Improper electrical contact of the vehicle power and ground connections.

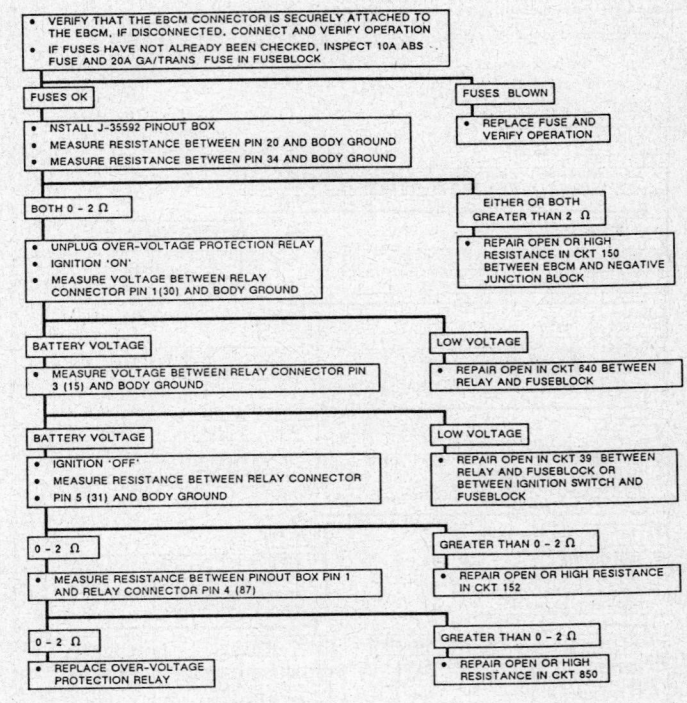

Fig. 56   Chart A, no system power. Brougham

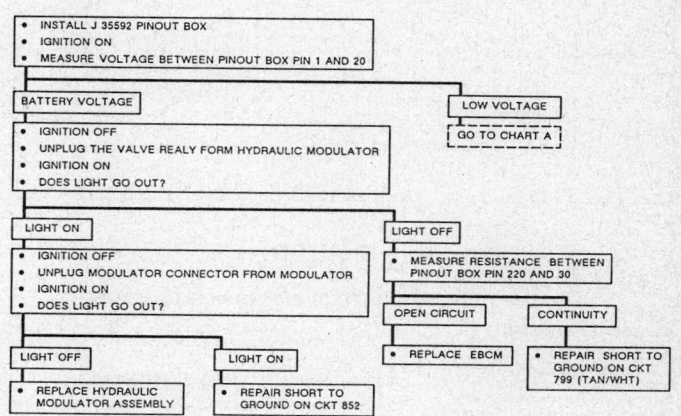

CHART B

ABS LIGHT ON, NO CODES SET

CIRCUIT DESCRIPTION

The amber ANTILOCK light is located in the top of the instrument panel. It may be illuminated by the EBCM or a path to ground in the valve relay on the hydraulic modulator.

The ANTILOCK light is powered by the Ignition 1 feed and receives power anytime the ignition switch is turned to RUN or START. Power is provided on CKT 39 through the 20 amp GA/TRANS fuse located in the fuseblock.

Light Operation – Valve Relay Ground

The ANTILOCK light is illuminated anytime the valve relay is not enabled. When the relay is not enabled, the light is grounded through CKT 852 and the valve relay to the modulator ground on the left front fender. During normal operation (no fault conditions found), the valve will switch and the ground will be removed, and the ANTILOCK light will turn off.

Light Operation – EBCM Ground

If the EBCM detects a fault in the ABS, the EBCM can turn on the ANTILOCK light by grounding pin 29. A ground path exists for the light through CKT 852. The EBCM will disable the valve relay when CKT 852 is grounded at pin 29.

FAILURE CONDITIONS

The chart on the next page addresses conditions which result in continuous operation of the ANTILOCK light. If the ANTILOCK light is on and no codes can be extracted from the EBCM, the EBCM connector should be checked for proper connection and system power should be checked.

Fig. 57   Chart B, ABS indicator On w/no codes set. Brougham

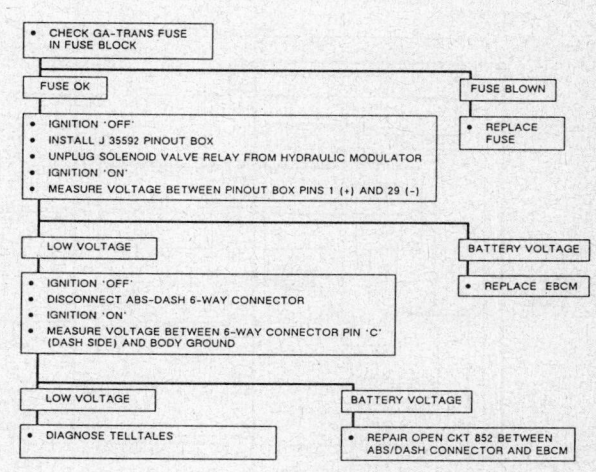

CHART C

ANTILOCK LIGHT INOPERATIVE AT KEY-ON

CIRCUIT DESCRIPTION

The amber ANTILOCK light is located in the top of the instrument panel. It may be illuminated by the EBCM or a path to ground in the valve relay on the hydraulic modulator.

The ANTILOCK light is powered by the Ignition 1 feed and receives power anytime the ignition switch is turned to RUN or START. Power is provided on CKT 39 through the 20 amp GA/TRANS fuse located in the fuseblock.

Light Operation – Valve Relay Ground

The ANTILOCK light is illuminated anytime the valve relay is not enabled. When the relay is not enabled, the light is grounded through CKT 852 and the valve relay to the modulator ground on the left front fender. During normal operation (no fault conditions found), the valve will switch and the ground will be removed, and the ANTILOCK light will turn off.

Light Operation – EBCM Ground

Whether the valve relay is engaged or not, the EBCM can turn on the ANTILOCK light by grounding pin 29. A ground path exists for the light through CKT 852.

FAILURE CONDITIONS

The chart on the next page addresses conditions which result in no ANTILOCK light operation. As described at the beginning of this section, the ANTILOCK light should illuminate for a minimum of four seconds when the key is moved from OFF to RUN. This chart addresses conditions such as lack of power to the ANTILOCK light which would prevent the light from turning on. This condition could prevent the EBCM from turning on the light in the event of an antilock failure.

Fig. 58   Chart C, ABS indicator inoperative w/key On. Brougham

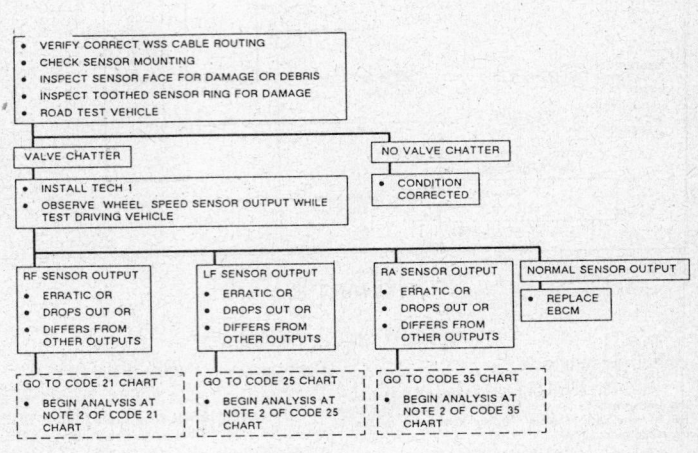

CHART D

VALVE CYCLING (CHATTER) DURING NORMAL STOPS

CIRCUIT DESCRIPTION

As each wheel turns, the wheel speed sensor for that wheel creates a small AC voltage as a toothed sensor ring, mounted on the brake rotor (in the front) or differential pinion shaft (in the rear), is passed by the stationary sensor. The sensor consists of a permanent magnet and coil and generates voltage by magnetic induction. The frequency of the wheel speed sensor signal is proportional to wheel speed.

The EBCM uses the wheel speed sensor signal to calculate vehicle reference speeds and individual speed, acceleration and slip values for each wheel. These values are used to determine when antilock control is required.

The EBCM performs two basic types of checks on the wheel speed sensors, these are sensor continuity and sensor output.

WHEEL SPEED SENSOR CABLES

In order to prevent electromagnetic interference from disturbing the wheel speed sensor signal, the sensor cables are protected with grounded shielding (indicated by dashed lines in the above schematic). This shield surrounds the two individual sensor wires. A black conduit surrounds the wires and shield. When servicing the sensor cables, the sensor wires are accessible by separating the shielding. If the shielding is disturbed, repair as required.

Fig. 59   Chart D, valve cycling during normal stops. Brougham

Fig. 60   ABS wiring circuit (Part 1 of 2). 1991 Eldorado, Reatta, Riviera, Seville, Toronado & Trofeo

Fig. 60   ABS wiring circuit (Part 2 of 2). 1991 Eldorado, Reatta, Riviera, Seville, Toronado & Trofeo

Eldorado & Seville

Reatta, Riviera, Toronado & Trofeo

CIRCUIT DESCRIPTION

As each wheel turns, the wheel speed sensor for that wheel creates a small AC voltage as a toothed sensor ring, mounted on the front suspension knuckle or in the rear integral hub–bearing assembly, is passed by the stationary sensor. The sensor consists of a permanent magnet and coil and generates voltage by magnetic induction. The frequency of the wheel speed sensor signal is proportional to wheel speed.

The EBCM uses the wheel speed sensor signal to calculate vehicle reference speeds and individual speed, acceleration and slip values for each wheel. These values are used to determine when anti-lock control is required.

The EBCM performs two basic types of checks on the wheel speed sensors, these are sensor continuity and sensor output.

WHEEL SPEED SENSOR CABLES

In order to prevent electromagnetic interference from disturbing the wheel speed sensor signal, the sensor cables are protected with grounded shielding (indicated by dashed lines in the above schematic). This shield surrounds the two individual sensor wires. A black conduit surrounds the wires and shield. When servicing the sensor cables, the sensor wires are accessible by separating the shielding. If the shielding is disturbed, repair as required.

NOTES ON CODE 21 CHART

1. This section of the fault tree determines if the code stored is due to a current fault condition. 'Current' wheel speed sensor faults will be detected when the vehicle is driven and reaches a speed of 4 mph (6 kph). If the ABS light turns on, the fault is current. The TECH 1 will indicate ignition cycle since code was set. If the ignition cycle counter is at zero, the code is current.

2. This section of the fault tree checks for an open or short in the wheel speed sensor wiring or sensor coil.

3. This section of the fault tree checks for conditions which may cause intermittent code setting. Some causes of intermittent wheel speed sensor codes to set are: improper routing or sensor cables next to spark plug wires, cables not retained in brackets, loose fitting or improperly mounted sensors, damaged sensors or toothed rings, poor terminal engagement of connectors, or intermittent shorts or opens in wiring.

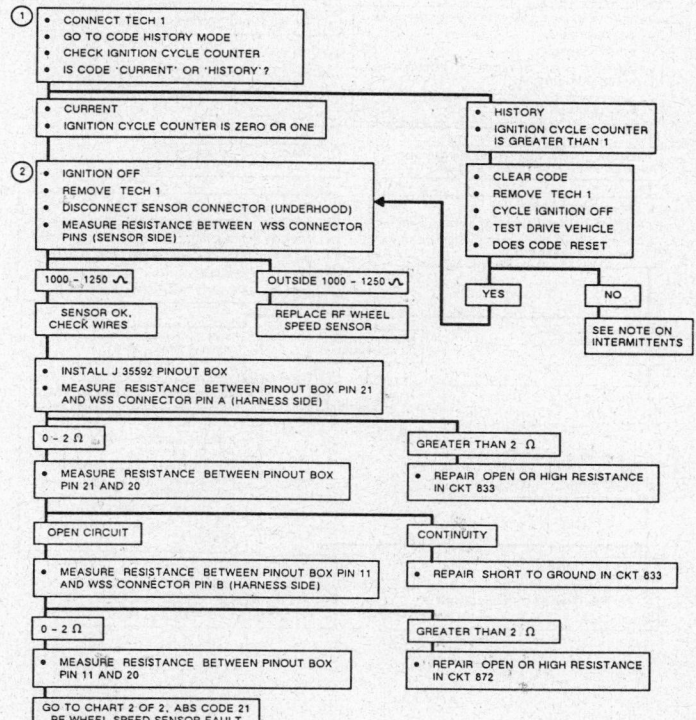

Fig. 61   Code 21, RF wheel speed sensor fault (Part 1 of 2). 1991 Eldorado, Reatta, Riviera, Seville, Toronado & Trofeo

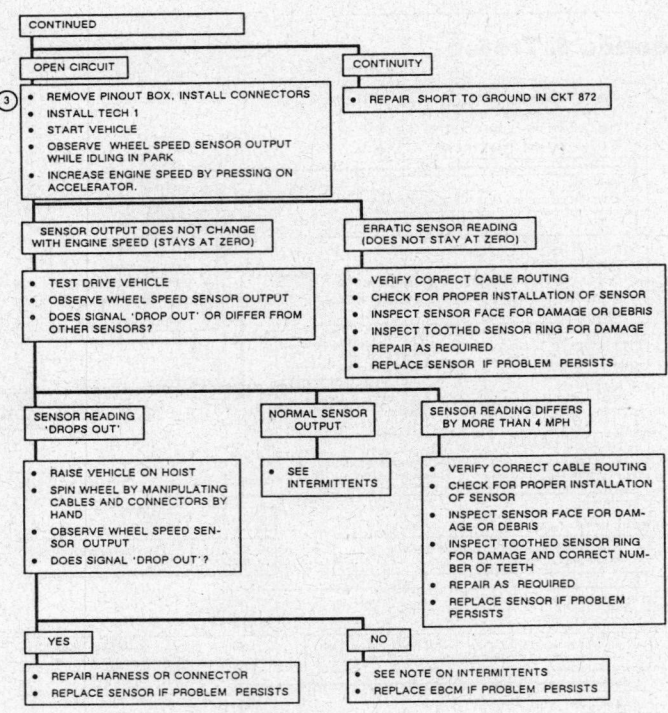

Fig. 61   Code 21, RF wheel speed sensor fault (Part 2 of 2). 1991 Eldorado, Reatta, Riviera, Seville, Toronado & Trofeo

Reatta, Riviera, Toronado & Trofeo

Eldorado & Seville

CIRCUIT DESCRIPTION

As each wheel turns, the wheel speed sensor for that wheel creates a small AC voltage as a toothed sensor ring, mounted on the front suspension knuckle or in the rear integral hub-bearing assembly, is passed by the stationary sensor. The sensor consists of a permanent magnet and coil and generates voltage by magnetic induction. The frequency of the wheel speed sensor signal is proportional to wheel speed.

The EBCM uses the wheel speed sensor signal to calculate vehicle reference speeds and individual speed, acceleration and slip values for each wheel. These values are used to determine when anti-lock control is required.

FAILURE CONDITIONS

Code 22 will set from improper speed signals generated by the toothed ring sensor lasting longer than 20 seconds. Causes of improper speed signal may be caused by incorrect number of teeth on sensor ring, sensor rings which are covered with dirt, grease or metallic particles, or damaged toothed sensor ring.

Fig. 62 Code 22, RF toothed wheel frequency error. 1991 Eldorado, Reatta, Riviera, Seville, Toronado & Trofeo

Eldorado & Seville

Reatta, Riviera, Toronado & Trofeo

CIRCUIT DESCRIPTION

As each wheel turns, the wheel speed sensor for that wheel creates a small AC voltage as a toothed sensor ring, mounted on the front suspension knuckle or in the rear integral hub–bearing assembly, is passed by the stationary sensor. The sensor consists of a permanent magnet and coil and generates voltage by magnetic induction. The frequency of the wheel speed sensor signal is proportional to wheel speed.

The EBCM uses the wheel speed sensor signal to calculate vehicle reference speeds and individual speed, acceleration and slip values for each wheel. These values are used to determine when anti-lock control is required.

The EBCM performs two basic types of checks on the wheel speed sensors, these are sensor continuity and sensor output.

WHEEL SPEED SENSOR CABLES

In order to prevent electromagnetic interference from disturbing the wheel speed sensor signal, the sensor cables are protected with grounded shielding (indicated by dashed lines in the above schematic). This shield surrounds the two individual sensor wires. A black conduit surrounds the wires and shield. When servicing the sensor cables, the sensor wires are accessible by separating the shielding. If the shielding is disturbed, repair as required.

NOTES ON CODE 25 CHART

1. This section of the fault tree determines if the code stored is due to a current fault condition. 'Current' wheel speed sensor faults will be detected when the vehicle is driven and reaches a speed of 4 mph (6 kph). If the ABS light turns on, the fault is current. The TECH 1 will indicate ignition cycle since code was set. If the ignition cycle counter is at zero, the code is current.

2. This section of the fault tree checks for an open or short in the wheel speed sensor wiring or sensor coil.

3. This section of the fault tree checks for conditions which may cause intermittent code setting. Some causes of intermittent wheel speed sensor codes to set are: improper routing or sensor cables next to spark plug wires, cables not retained in brackets, loose fitting or improperly mounted sensors, damaged sensors or toothed rings, poor terminal engagement of connectors, or intermittent shorts or opens in wiring.

Fig. 63   Code 25, LF wheel speed sensor fault. 1991 Eldorado, Reatta, Riviera, Seville, Toronado & Trofeo

Eldorado & Seville

CIRCUIT DESCRIPTION

As each wheel turns, the wheel speed sensor for that wheel creates a small AC voltage as a toothed sensor ring, mounted on the front suspension knuckle or in the rear integral hub–bearing assembly, is passed by the stationary sensor. The sensor consists of a permanent magnet and coil and generates voltage by magnetic induction. The frequency of the wheel speed sensor signal is proportional to wheel speed.

The EBCM uses the wheel speed sensor signal to calculate vehicle reference speeds and individual speed, acceleration and slip values for each wheel. These values are used to determine when anti–lock control is required.

FAILURE CONDITIONS

Code 26 will set from improper speed signals generated by the toothed ring sensor lasting longer than 20 seconds. Causes of improper speed signal may be caused by incorrect number of teeth on sensor ring, sensor rings which are covered with dirt, grease or metallic particles, or damaged toothed sensor ring.

Reatta, Riviera, Toronado & Trofeo

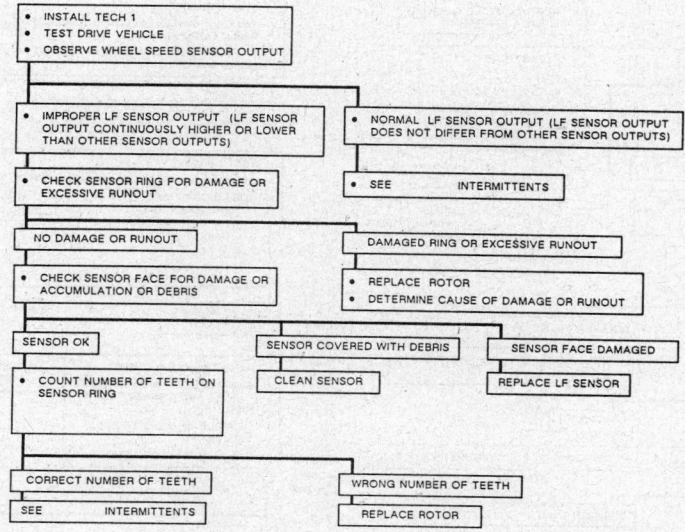

Fig. 64   Code 26, LF toothed wheel frequency error. 1991 Eldorado, Reatta, Riviera, Seville, Toronado & Trofeo

Eldorado & Seville

Reatta, Riviera, Toronado & Trofeo

CIRCUIT DESCRIPTION

As each wheel turns, the wheel speed sensor for that wheel creates a small AC voltage as a toothed sensor ring, mounted on the front suspension knuckle or in the rear integral hub—bearing assembly, is passed by the stationary sensor. The sensor consists of a permanent magnet and coil and generates voltage by magnetic induction. The frequency of the wheel speed sensor signal is proportional to wheel speed.

The EBCM uses the wheel speed sensor signal to calculate vehicle reference speeds and individual speed, acceleration and slip values for each wheel. These values are used to determine when anti-lock control is required.

The EBCM performs two basic types of checks on the wheel speed sensors, these are sensor continuity and sensor output.

WHEEL SPEED SENSOR CABLES

In order to prevent electromagnetic interference from disturbing the wheel speed sensor signal, the sensor cables are protected with grounded shielding (indicated by dashed lines in the above schematic). This shield surrounds the two individual sensor wires. A black conduit surrounds the wires and shield. When servicing the sensor cables, the sensor wires are accessible by separating the shielding. If the shielding is disturbed, repair as required.

NOTES ON CODE 31 CHART

1. This section of the fault tree determines if the code stored is due to a current fault condition. 'Current' wheel speed sensor faults will be detected when the vehicle is driven and reaches a speed of 4 mph (6 kph). If the ABS light turns on, the fault is current. The TECH 1 will indicate ignition cycle since code was set. If the ignition cycle counter is at zero, the code is current.

2. This section of the fault tree checks for an open or short in the wheel speed sensor wiring or sensor coil.

3. This section of the fault tree checks for conditions which may cause intermittent code setting. Some causes of intermittent wheel speed sensor codes to set are: improper routing or sensor cables next to spark plug wires, cables not retained in brackets, loose fitting or improperly mounted sensors, damaged sensors or toothed rings, poor terminal engagement of connectors, or intermittent shorts or opens in wiring.

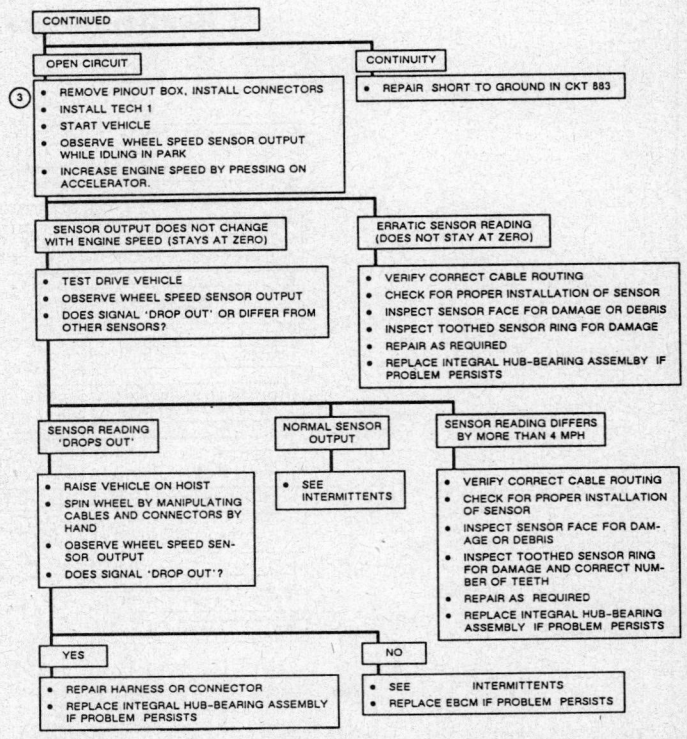

Fig. 65   Code 31, RR wheel speed sensor fault. 1991 Eldorado, Reatta, Riviera, Seville, Toronado & Trofeo

Eldorado & Seville

Reatta, Riviera, Toronado & Trofeo

CIRCUIT DESCRIPTION

As each wheel turns, the wheel speed sensor for that wheel creates a small AC voltage as a toothed sensor ring, mounted on the front suspension knuckle or in the rear integral hub-bearing assembly, is passed by the stationary sensor. The sensor consists of a permanent magnet and coil and generates voltage by magnetic induction. The frequency of the wheel speed sensor signal is proportional to wheel speed.

The EBCM uses the wheel speed sensor signal to calculate vehicle reference speeds and individual speed, acceleration and slip values for each wheel. These values are used to determine when anti-lock control is required.

FAILURE CONDITIONS

Code 32 will set from improper speed signals generated by the toothed ring sensor lasting longer than 20 seconds. Causes of improper speed signal may be caused by incorrect number of teeth on sensor ring, sensor rings which are covered with dirt, grease or metallic particles, or damaged toothed sensor ring.

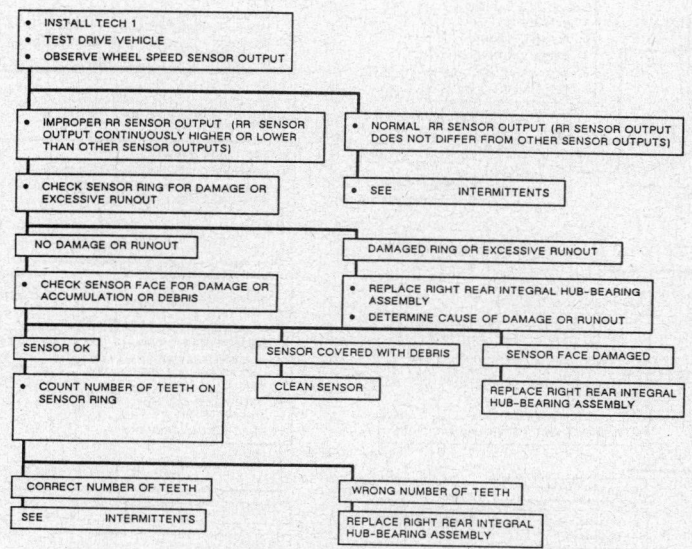

Fig. 66 Code 32, RR toothed wheel frequency error. 1991 Eldorado, Reatta, Riviera, Seville, Toronado & Trofeo

Eldorado & Seville

Reatta, Riviera, Toronado & Trofeo

CIRCUIT DESCRIPTION

As each wheel turns, the wheel speed sensor for that wheel creates a small AC voltage as a toothed sensor ring, mounted on the front suspension knuckle or in the rear integral hub–bearing assembly, is passed by the stationary sensor. The sensor consists of a permanent magnet and coil and generates voltage by magnetic induction. The frequency of the wheel speed sensor signal is proportional to wheel speed.

The EBCM uses the wheel speed sensor signal to calculate vehicle reference speeds and individual speed, acceleration and slip values for each wheel. These values are used to determine when anti-lock control is required.

The EBCM performs two basic types of checks on the wheel speed sensors, these are sensor continuity and sensor output.

WHEEL SPEED SENSOR CABLES

In order to prevent electromagnetic interference from disturbing the wheel speed sensor signal, the sensor cables are protected with grounded shielding (indicated by dashed lines in the above schematic). This shield surrounds the two individual sensor wires. A black conduit surrounds the wires and shield. When servicing the sensor cables, the sensor wires are accessible by separating the shielding. If the shielding is disturbed, repair as required.

NOTES ON CODE 35 CHART

1. This section of the fault tree determines if the code stored is due to a current fault condition. 'Current' wheel speed sensor faults will be detected when the vehicle is driven and reaches a speed of 4 mph (6 kph). If the ABS light turns on, the fault is current. The TECH 1 will indicate ignition cycle since code was set. If the ignition cycle counter is at zero, the code is current.

2. This section of the fault tree checks for an open or short in the wheel speed sensor wiring or sensor coil.

3. This section of the fault tree checks for conditions which may cause intermittent code setting. Some causes of intermittent wheel speed sensor codes to set are: improper routing or sensor cables next to spark plug wires, cables not retained in brackets, loose fitting or improperly mounted sensors, damaged sensors or toothed rings, poor terminal engagement of connectors, or intermittent shorts or opens in wiring.

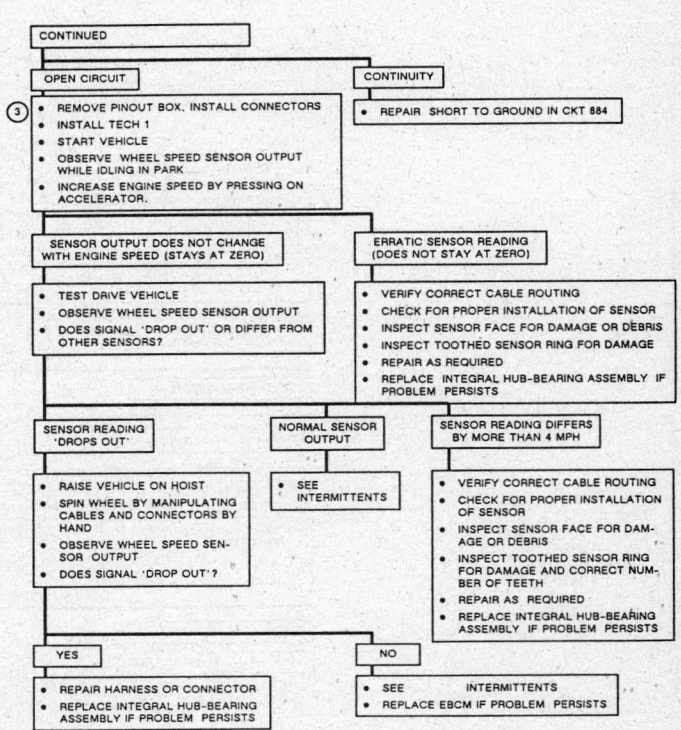

Fig. 67   Code 35, LR wheel speed sensor fault. 1991 Eldorado, Reatta, Riviera, Seville, Toronado & Trofeo

CIRCUIT DESCRIPTION

As each wheel turns, the wheel speed sensor for that wheel creates a small AC voltage as a toothed sensor ring, mounted on the front suspension knuckle or in the rear integral hub-bearing assembly, is passed by the stationary sensor. The sensor consists of a permanent magnet and coil and generates voltage by magnetic induction. The frequency of the wheel speed sensor signal is proportional to wheel speed.

The EBCM uses the wheel speed sensor signal to calculate vehicle reference speeds and individual speed, acceleration and slip values for each wheel. These values are used to determine when anti-lock control is required.

FAILURE CONDITIONS

Code 36 will set from improper speed signals generated by the toothed ring sensor. Causes of improper speed signal may be caused by incorrect number of teeth on sensor ring, sensor rings which are covered with dirt, grease or metallic particles, or damaged toothed sensor ring.

Fig. 68   Code 36, LR toothed wheel frequency error (Part 1 of 2). 1991 Eldorado, Reatta, Riviera, Seville, Toronado & Trofeo

Fig. 68   Code 36, LR toothed wheel frequency error (Part 2 of 2). 1991 Eldorado, Reatta, Riviera, Seville, Toronado & Trofeo

ABS CODE 41

RIGHT FRONT SOLENOID VALVE FAULT

CIRCUIT DESCRIPTION

The right front solenoid valve in the hydraulic modulator may be commanded to three different positions by the EBCM. Valve position is determined by the amount of current which is allowed to flow through the solenoid valve coil.

The solenoid valve circuits receive power through the valve relay on the hydraulic modulator. The valve relay is engaged at key-on and remains engaged throughout the ignition cycle. Solenoid valve lines should have battery voltage available at all times.

When the key is turned to RUN, power is supplied to the EBCM. The EBCM will complete an internal self-check before providing ground to the valve relay. When the valve relay is energized, battery power is supplied to the solenoid valves.

VALVE OPERATION

The valves are continuously monitored by the EBCM (CKT 851) and each individual solenoid valve line. If valve line voltage does not match expected values, an ABS code will set. When the vehicle reaches approximately 4 mph after key-on, the EBCM cycles each valve and checks for a proper response. This check may be heard and felt while it is taking place and should be considered a normal mode of operation.

Pressure Increase

The pressure increase position is the normal operating position of the valves for braking. Brake fluid flows thru the modulator from the master cylinder to the wheel brake. No current is supplied to the valve coil during pressure increase.

Pressure Hold

The pressure hold position is commanded when the EBCM desires to hold the pressure in the wheel circuit constant. The modulator will not allow pressure flow from the master cylinder to the wheel brake. The pressure hold position is commanded by passing approximately 2.0 amps to the valve coil.

Pressure Reduction

The pressure reduction position is used to decrease hydraulic pressure in a specific wheel circuit without decreasing pressure in the rest of the system. The modulator takes brake fluid from the wheel brake and injects it into the master cylinder circuit. This fully energized position of the solenoid valve occurs when approximately 5 amps are passed to the valve coil.

FAILURE CONDITIONS

Code 41 will set when the expected position of the right front solenoid valve does not match the commanded position from the EBCM. Conditions which could cause Code 41 to set are damage to the right front solenoid, an open circuit or a short circuit to ground or battery on CKT 827.

Fig. 69 Code 41, RF solenoid valve fault. 1991 Eldorado, Reatta, Riviera, Seville, Toronado & Trofeo

ABS CODE 45

LEFT FRONT SOLENOID VALVE FAULT

CIRCUIT DESCRIPTION

The left front solenoid valve in the hydraulic modulator may be commanded to three different positions by the EBCM. Valve position is determined by the amount of current which is allowed to flow through the solenoid valve coil.

The solenoid valve circuits receive power through the valve relay on the hydraulic modulator. The valve relay is engaged at key-on and remains engaged throughout the ignition cycle. Solenoid valve lines should have battery voltage available at all times.

When the key is turned to RUN, power is supplied to the EBCM. The EBCM will complete an internal self-check before providing ground to the valve relay. When the valve relay is energized, battery power is supplied to the solenoid valves.

VALVE OPERATION

The valves are continuously monitored by the EBCM (CKT 851) and each individual solenoid valve line. If valve line voltage does not match expected values, an ABS code will set. When the vehicle reaches approximately 4 mph after key-on, the EBCM cycles each valve and checks for a proper response. This check may be heard and felt while it is taking place and should be considered a normal mode of operation.

Pressure Increase

The pressure increase position is the normal operating position of the valves for braking. Brake fluid flows thru the modulator from the master cylinder to the wheel brake. No current is supplied to the valve coil during pressure increase.

Pressure Hold

The pressure hold position is commanded when the EBCM desires to hold the pressure in the wheel circuit constant. The modulator will not allow pressure flow from the master cylinder to the wheel brake. The pressure hold position is commanded by passing approximately 2.0 amps to the valve coil.

Pressure Reduction

The pressure reduction position is used to decrease hydraulic pressure in a specific wheel circuit without decreasing pressure in the rest of the system. The modulator takes brake fluid from the wheel brake and injects it into the master cylinder circuit. This fully energized position of the solenoid valve occurs when approximately 5 amps are passed to the valve coil.

FAILURE CONDITIONS

Code 45 will set when the expected position of the left front solenoid valve does not match the commanded position from the EBCM. Conditions which could cause Code 45 to set are damage to the left front solenoid, an open circuit or a short circuit to ground or battery on CKT 826.

Fig. 70 Code 45, LF solenoid valve fault. 1991 Eldorado, Reatta, Riviera, Seville, Toronado & Trofeo

ABS CODE 55
REAR WHEEL SOLENOID VALVE FAULT

CIRCUIT DESCRIPTION

The rear axle solenoid valve in the hydraulic modulator may be commanded to three different positions by the EBCM. The rear axle solenoid valve modulates hydraulic brake pressure to both rear wheel circuits. Valve position is determined by the amount of current which is allowed to flow through the solenoid valve coil.

The solenoid valve circuits receive power through the valve relay on the hydraulic modulator. The valve relay is engaged at key-on and remains engaged throughout the ignition cycle. Solenoid valve lines should have battery voltage available at all times.

When the key is turned to RUN, power is supplied to the EBCM. The EBCM will complete an internal self-check before providing ground to the valve relay. When the valve relay is energized, battery power is supplied to the solenoid valves.

VALVE OPERATION

The valves are continuously monitored by the EBCM (CKT 851) and each individual solenoid valve line. If valve line voltage does not match expected values, an ABS code will set. When the vehicle reaches approximately 4 mph after key-on, the EBCM cycles each valve and checks for a proper response. This check may be heard and felt while it is taking place and should be considered a normal mode of operation.

Pressure Increase

The pressure increase position is the normal operating position of the valves for braking. Brake fluid flows thru the modulator from the master cylinder to the wheel brake. No current is supplied to the valve coil during pressure increase.

Pressure Hold

The pressure hold position is commanded when the EBCM desires to hold the pressure in the wheel circuit constant. The modulator will not allow pressure flow from the master cylinder to the wheel brake. The pressure hold position is commanded by passing approximately 2.0 amps to the valve coil.

Pressure Reduction

The pressure reduction position is used to decrease hydraulic pressure in a specific wheel circuit without decreasing pressure in the rest of the system. The modulator takes brake fluid from the wheel brake and injects it into the master cylinder circuit. This fully energized position of the solenoid valve occurs when approximately 5 amps are passed to the valve coil.

FAILURE CONDITIONS

Code 55 will set when the expected position of the rear axle solenoid valve does not match the commanded position from the EBCM. Conditions which could cause Code 55 to set are damage to the rear axle solenoid, an open circuit or a short circuit to ground or battery on CKT 829.

Fig. 71   Code 55, rear solenoid valve fault. 1991 Eldorado, Reatta, Riviera, Seville, Toronado & Trofeo

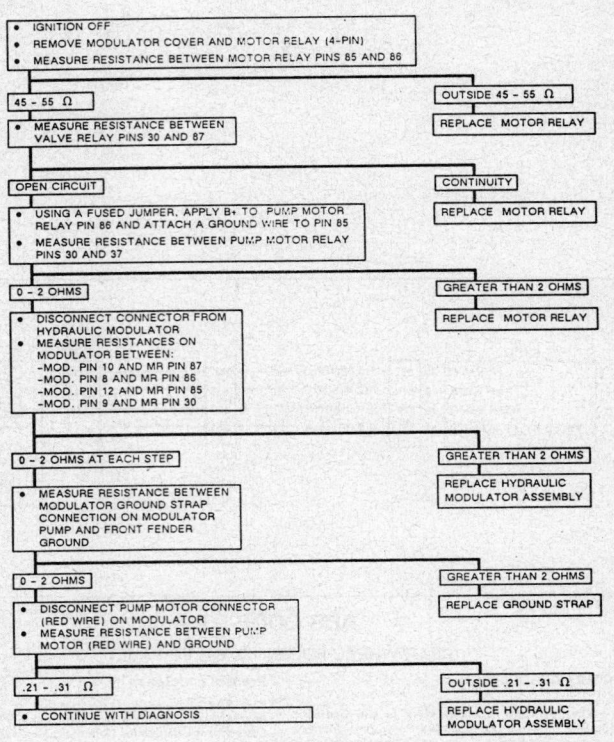

ABS CODE 61
PUMP MOTOR CIRCUIT FAULT

CIRCUIT DESCRIPTION

The pump motor returns brake fluid to the master cylinder brake circuit at the hydraulic modulator during anti-lock braking. During normal braking, the pump does not operate. When the vehicle begins to move after start-up, the EBCM will turn on the pump motor and perform a self-check of the pump motor and pump motor circuit. This check may be felt and heard by the driver when the vehicle begins to move. The self-check should be considered normal operation. The pump motor is an integral component of the hydraulic modulator and cannot be serviced separately.

The pump motor relay provides power to the pump motor in the hydraulic modulator. The pump motor relay is located on the hydraulic modulator an may be replaced if it is found to be defective.

The pump motor relay is not engaged during normal system operation. When anti-lock operation is

required, the motor relay actuation line on CKT 874 (EBCM pin 28) is pulled to ground. The pump motor relay is engaged by the relay supply voltage line on CKT 854 (EBCM pin 17). When the relay switches, battery power is provided to the pump motor.

FAILURE CONDITIONS

When the pump motor relay is engaged, the motor monitor line should be at battery voltage. With the pump motor relay disengaged, the monitoring line should be at ground. If the commanded position of the pump motor relay and motor monitor line do not agree, Code 61 will set. Some conditions which will cause Code 61 to set are:
- An open circuit on CKTs 874 or 1292
- A short to voltage on CKTs 874 or 1292
- A short to ground on CKTs 874 or 1292
- A defective pump motor relay or pump motor

Fig. 72   Code 61, pump motor circuit fault (Part 1 of 2). 1991 Eldorado, Reatta, Riviera, Seville, Toronado & Trofeo

Fig. 72   Code 61, pump motor circuit fault (Part 2 of 2). 1991 Eldorado, Reatta, Riviera, Seville, Toronado & Trofeo

Eldorado & Seville

Reatta, Riviera, Toronado & Trofeo

CIRCUIT DESCRIPTION

The solenoid valve relay provides power to the three solenoid valves in the hydraulic modulator. The solenoid valve relay is located on the hydraulic modulator and may be replaced if it is found to be defective.

The valve relay is engaged during normal system operation. When the ignition is switched to RUN, the EBCM commands the solenoid valve relay on by grounding the valve relay actuation line on CKT 879 (EBCM pin 27). When this ground is provided, the valve relay is energized from the voltage supply line on CKT 854 (EBCM pin 17). The valve relay switches and battery voltage is provided to the three solenoid valves and the solenoid valve relay feedback line on CKT 851 (EBCM pin 32). The valve relay remains engaged until the ignition is turned off or a failure is detected.

Whenever the solenoid valve relay is not engaged, the ANTI-LOCK light will turn on. With the ignition on and the solenoid valve relay not engaged, a path to ground exists from the BODY IGNITION fuse 14 (15 amps) thru the ANTI-LOCK light on CKT 39 which turns on the warning light. The ANTI-LOCK light can also be commanded on by the EBCM on CKT 852 (EBCM pin 29). The EBCM will provide ground on this line and turn on the warning light when a failure is detected.

ANTI-LOCK OPERATION

With the solenoid valve relay engaged, battery power is provided to the three solenoid valves. If anti-lock operation is required, the EBCM varies the amount of current supplied to the solenoid valves (EBCM pins 2, 18, 35) and the valve is positioned to provide for optimum braking.

FAILURE CONDITIONS

When the valve relay is engaged, the valve relay feedback line should be at battery voltage. With the valve relay disengaged the feedback line is at ground. If the commanded position of the valve relay and the position indicated by the feedback line do not agree, Code 63 will set. Some conditions which will cause Code 63 to set are:

- An open circuit on CKTs 851 or 879
- A short to voltage on CKTs 851 or 879
- A short to ground on CKTs 851 or 879
- A defective solenoid valve relay
- Open circuit on CKT 854.

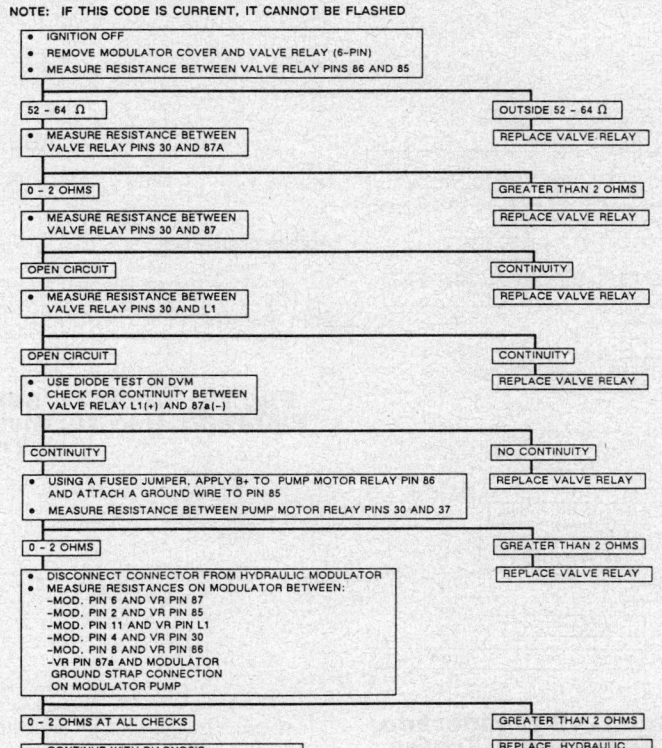

Fig. 73   Code 63, solenoid valve relay fault (Part 1 of 2). 1991 Eldorado, Reatta, Riviera, Seville, Toronado & Trofeo

Fig. 73   Code 63, solenoid valve relay fault (Part 2 of 2). 1991 Eldorado, Reatta, Riviera, Seville, Toronado & Trofeo

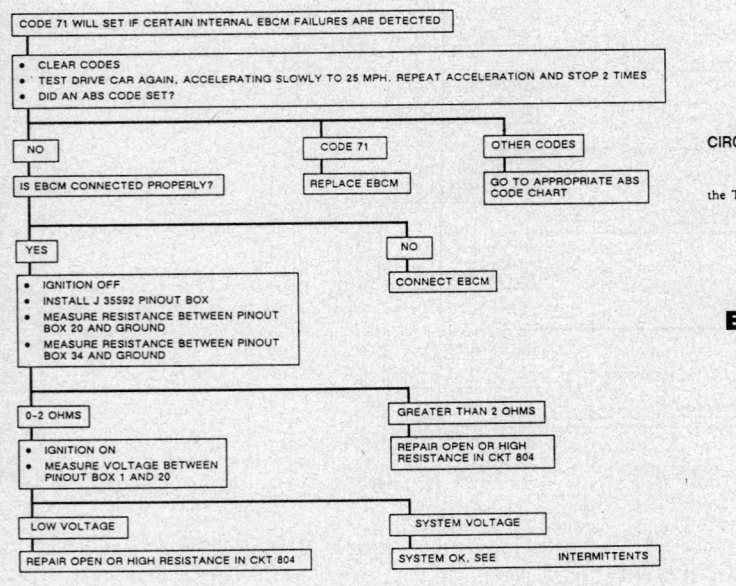

Fig. 74   Code 71, EBCM fault. 1991 Eldorado, Reatta, Riviera, Seville, Toronado & Trofeo

ABS CODE 72

SERIAL DATA LINK ERROR (TECH 1 ERROR)

CIRCUIT DESCRIPTION

An ABS Code 72 may set when there is a momentary serial data communications error between the EBCM and the TECH 1.

Although it is not an indication of a serious condition, this code should be cleared prior to completion of diagnosis.

Fig. 75   Code 72, serial line data fault. 1991 Eldorado, Reatta, Riviera, Seville, Toronado & Trofeo

Eldorado & Seville

Reatta, Riviera, Toronado & Trofeo

CIRCUIT DESCRIPTION

The EBCM receives power from CRUISE/BRAKE Fuse 18, (located in the interior relay center) on CKT 1176. If high system voltages occur, the EBCM is internally protected by a network of diodes which directs excess voltage to ground.

FAILURE CONDITIONS

Intermittent operation of the ANTI-LOCK light may be caused by intermittent voltage levels which do not correspond to the proper operating range of the Anti-Lock Brake System. Some conditions which may cause a lack of system power are:

- Improper electrical contact of the EBCM connector.
- Low system voltage.
- Improper electrical contact of the vehicle power and ground connections.

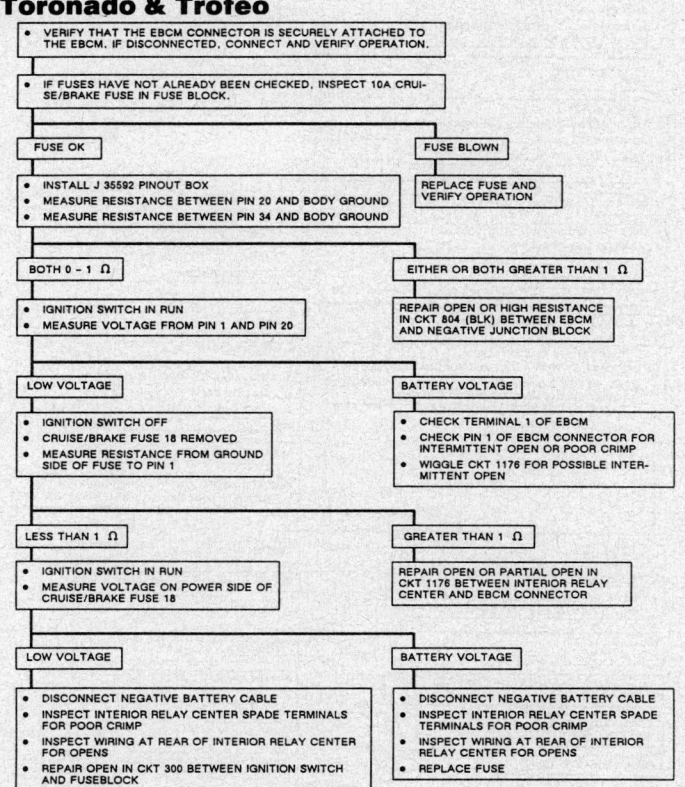

Fig. 76   Chart A, no system power. 1991 Eldorado, Reatta, Riviera, Seville, Toronado & Trofeo

Eldorado & Seville

Reatta, Riviera, Toronado & Trofeo

CIRCUIT DESCRIPTION

The amber ANTI-LOCK light is located below the instrument panel cluster. It may be illuminated by the EBCM or a path to ground in the valve relay on the hydraulic modulator.

The ANTI-LOCK light is powered by the Ignition 1 feed and receives power anytime the ignition switch is turned to RUN or START. Power is provided on CKT 39 through the 15 amp BODY IGNITION fuse 14 located in the center.

LIGHT OPERATION – VALVE RELAY GROUND

The ANTI-LOCK light is illuminated anytime the valve relay is not enabled. When the relay is not enabled, the light is grounded through CKT 852 and the valve relay to the modulator ground. During normal operation (no fault conditions found), the valve will switch and the ground will be removed, and the ANTI-LOCK light will turn off. The ABS light is on whenever the EBCM is disconnected.

LIGHT OPERATION – EBCM GROUND

If the EBCM detects a fault in the ABS, the EBCM can turn on the ANTI-LOCK light by grounding pin 29. A ground path exists for the light through CKT 852. The EBCM will disable the valve relay when CKT 852 is grounded at pin 29.

NOTE: It is best to check for codes using a TECH-1. It is possible that a valve (Code 41, 45, 55 and 63) may have set. It is NOT possible to flash codes when a valve code is present.

FAILURE CONDITIONS

The chart on the next page addresses conditions which result in continuous operation of the ANTI-LOCK light. If the ANTI-LOCK light is on and no codes can be extracted from the EBCM, the EBCM connector should be checked for proper connection and system power should be checked.

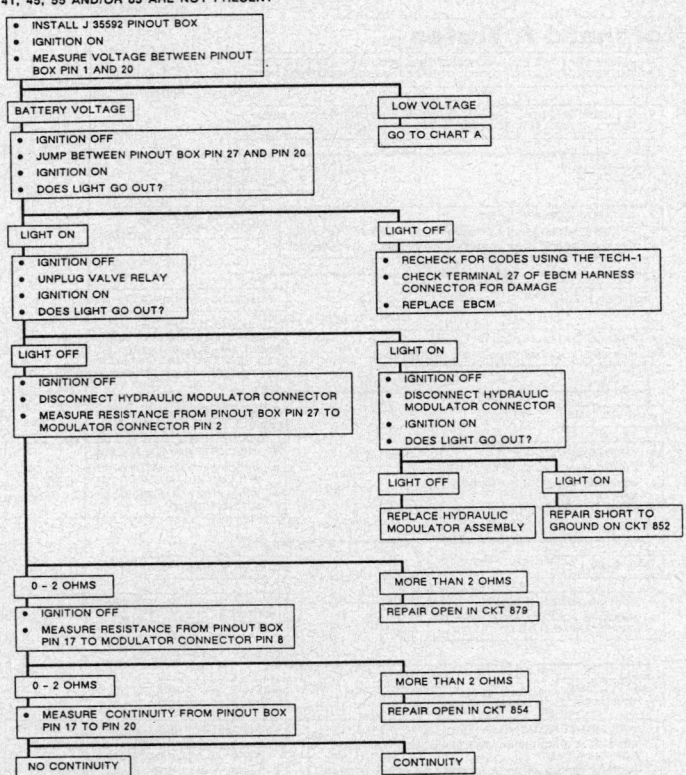

Fig. 77   Chart B, ABS indicator On w/no codes set. 1991 Eldorado, Reatta, Riviera, Seville, Toronado & Trofeo

Eldorado & Seville

Reatta, Riviera, Toronado & Trofeo

CIRCUIT DESCRIPTION

The amber ANTI-LOCK light is located below the instrument panel cluster. It may be illuminated by the EBCM or a path to ground in the valve relay on the hydraulic modulator.

The ANTI-LOCK light is powered by the Ignition 1 feed and receives power anytime the ignition switch is turned to RUN or START. Power is provided on CKT 39 through the 15 amp BODY IGNITION fuse 14.

LIGHT OPERATION – VALVE RELAY GROUND

The ANTI-LOCK light is illuminated anytime the valve relay is not enabled. When the relay is not enabled, the light is grounded through CKT 852 and the valve relay to the modulator ground. During normal operation (no fault conditions found), the valve will switch and the ground will be removed, and the ANTI-LOCK light will turn off.

LIGHT OPERATION – EBCM GROUND

Whether the valve relay is engaged or not, the EBCM can turn on the ANTI-LOCK light by grounding pin 29. A ground path exists for the light through CKT 852.

FAILURE CONDITIONS

The chart on the next page addresses conditions which result in no ANTI-LOCK light operation; the ABS operates properly. As described at the beginning of this section, the ANTI-LOCK light should illuminate for a minimum of four seconds when the key is moved from OFF to RUN. This chart addresses conditions such as lack of power to the ANTI-LOCK light which would prevent the light from turning on. This condition could prevent the EBCM from turning on the light in the event of an anti-lock failure.

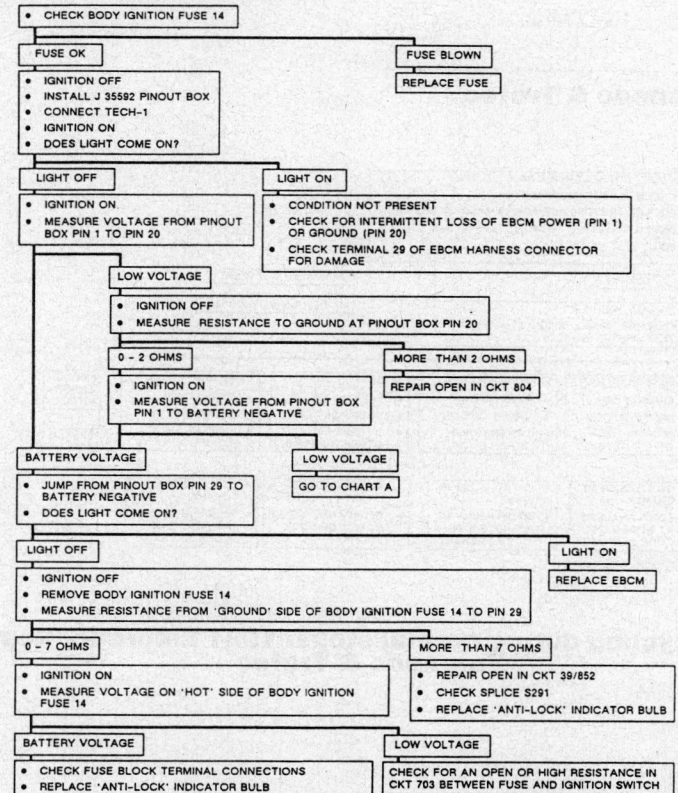

Fig. 78   Chart C, ABS indicator inoperative at key On. 1991 Eldorado, Reatta, Riviera, Seville, Toronado & Trofeo

Eldorado & Seville

Reatta, Riviera, Toronado & Trofeo

CIRCUIT DESCRIPTION

As each wheel turns, the wheel speed sensor for that wheel creates a small AC voltage as a toothed sensor ring, mounted on the front suspension knuckle or in the rear integral hub-bearing assembly, is passed by the stationary sensor. The sensor consists of a permanent magnet and coil and generates voltage by magnetic induction. The frequency of the wheel speed sensor signal is proportional to wheel speed.

The EBCM uses the wheel speed sensor signal to calculate vehicle reference speeds and individual speed, acceleration and slip values for each wheel. These values are used to determine when anti-lock control is required.

The EBCM performs two basic types of checks on the wheel speed sensors, these are sensor continuity and sensor output.

WHEEL SPEED SENSOR CABLES

In order to prevent electromagnetic interference from disturbing the wheel speed sensor signal, the sensor cables are protected with grounded shielding (indicated by dashed lines in the above schematic). This shield surrounds the two individual sensor wires. A black conduit surrounds the wires and shield. When servicing the sensor cables, the sensor wires are accessible by separating the shielding. If the shielding is disturbed, repair as required.

Notes On Chart D:

1. The wheel speed sensor output should gradually increase with vehicle speed. There should be no skips or jumps. All four wheel speed sensor outputs should be identical. On a slow down, one of the signals may drop off faster than the others, indicating a lock-up condition or a problem with the speed sensor air gap, wiring, or sensor itself.

Fig. 79 Chart D, valve cycling during normal stops. 1991 Eldorado, Reatta, Riviera, Seville, Toronado & Trofeo

Fig. 80   ABS wiring circuit (Part 1 of 2). 1992 Eldorado & Seville

Fig. 80   ABS wiring circuit (Part 2 of 2). 1992 Eldorado & Seville

Fig. 81   ABS wiring circuit (Part 1 of 2). 1992 Riviera, Toronado & Trofeo

Fig. 81   ABS wiring circuit (Part 2 of 2). 1992 Riviera, Toronado & Trofeo

1991 REATTA, 1991-92 BROUGHAM, TORONADO & TROFEO & 1991-93 CAPRICE, CUSTOM CRUISER, ELDORADO, RIVIERA, ROADMASTER, SEVILLE (BOSCH 2 U TYPE)

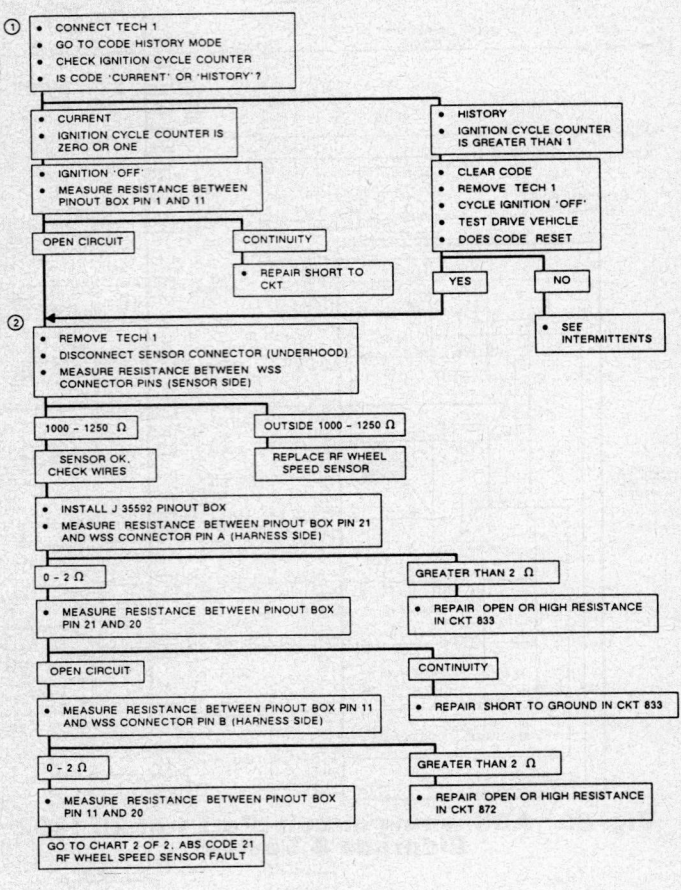

ABS CODE 21
RIGHT FRONT WHEEL SPEED SENSOR FAULT

CIRCUIT DESCRIPTION

As each wheel turns, the wheel speed sensor for that wheel creates a small AC voltage as a toothed sensor ring, mounted in the front integral hub/bearing assembly, is passed by the stationary sensor. The sensor consists of a permanent magnet and coil and generates voltage by magnetic induction. The frequency of the wheel speed sensor signal is proportional to wheel speed.

The EBCM uses the wheel speed sensor signal to calculate vehicle reference speeds and individual speed, acceleration and slip values for each wheel. These values are used to determine when antilock control is required.

The EBCM performs two basic types of checks on the wheel speed sensors, these are sensor continuity and sensor output.

The EBCM will only set one wheel speed sensor fault code at a time, even if multiple faults exist. Detection is prioritized accordingly: LF, RR, LR, RF. Always check for additional stored codes after making repairs.

TEST CONDITIONS

1. Tested continuously.

FAILURE CONDITIONS

Sensor Output:

1. Drive away: speed signal is not detected when vehicle reaches 12 kph or 7.5 mph.

2. While Driving: speed signal is lost while vehicle speed is greater than 40 kph or 25 mph.

Continuity:

1. While Standing: open circuit is seen while the vehicle is standing still with the ignition on.

ACTION TAKEN

1. Code set.
2. ABS switched 'OFF'.

NOTES ON CODE 21 CHART

1. This section of the fault tree determines if the code stored is due to a current fault condition. 'Current' wheel speed sensor faults may be detected even at vehicle standstill. If the ABS light turns on, the fault is current. The TECH 1 will indicate ignition cycle since code was set. If the ignition cycle counter is at zero, the code is current.

2. This section of the fault tree checks for an open or short in the wheel speed sensor wiring or sensor coil.

3. This section of the fault tree checks for conditions which may cause intermittent code setting. Some causes of intermittent wheel speed sensor codes to set are: improper routing or sensor cables next to spark plug wires, cables not retained in brackets, loose fitting or improperly mounted sensors, damaged sensors or toothed rings, poor terminal engagement of connectors, or intermittent shorts or opens in wiring.

Fig. 82   Code 21, RF wheel speed sensor fault. 1992 Eldorado, Riviera, Seville, Toronado & Trofeo

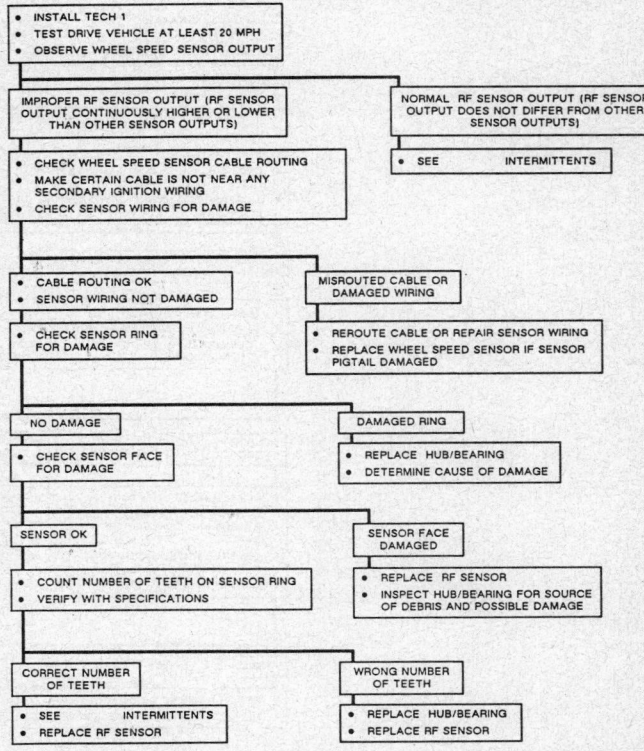

ABS CODE 22
RIGHT FRONT TOOTHED WHEEL FREQUENCY ERROR

CIRCUIT DESCRIPTION

As each wheel turns, the wheel speed sensor for that wheel creates a small AC voltage as a toothed sensor ring, mounted in the front integral hub/bearing assembly, is passed by the stationary sensor. The sensor consists of a permanent magnet and coil and generates voltage by magnetic induction. The frequency of the wheel speed sensor signal is proportional to wheel speed.

The EBCM uses the wheel speed sensor signal to calculate vehicle reference speeds and individual speed, acceleration and slip values for each wheel. These values are used to determine when antilock control is required.

TEST CONDITIONS

1. Tested continuously.

FAILURE CONDITIONS

1. While Driving: one wheel is detected at least 30 kph or 19 mph faster than the remaining wheels for an extended period of time.
   or
   One wheel is at least 6 kph or 4 mph less than or greater than the remaining wheels for an extended period of time.

ACTION TAKEN

1. Code set.
2. ABS switched 'OFF'.
   Causes of improper speed signal may be caused by incorrect number of teeth on sensor ring, sensor rings which are covered with dirt, grease or metallic particles, or damaged toothed sensor ring.

Fig. 83 Code 22, RF toothed wheel frequency error. 1992 Eldorado, Riviera, Seville, Toronado & Trofeo

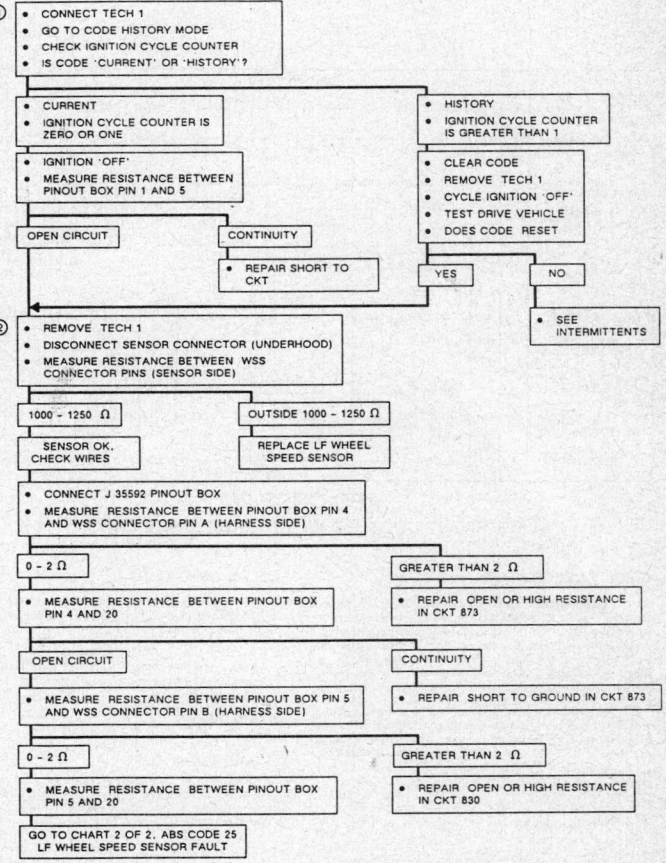

ABS CODE 25
LEFT FRONT WHEEL SPEED SENSOR FAULT

CIRCUIT DESCRIPTION

As each wheel turns, the wheel speed sensor for that wheel creates a small AC voltage as a toothed sensor ring, mounted in the front integral hub/bearing assembly, is passed by the stationary sensor. The sensor consists of a permanent magnet and coil and generates voltage by magnetic induction. The frequency of the wheel speed sensor signal is proportional to wheel speed.

The EBCM uses the wheel speed sensor signal to calculate vehicle reference speeds and individual speed, acceleration and slip values for each wheel. These values are used to determine when antilock control is required.

The EBCM performs two basic types of checks on the wheel speed sensors, these are sensor continuity and sensor output.

The EBCM will only set one wheel speed sensor fault code at a time, even if multiple faults exist. Detection is prioritized accordingly: LF, RR, LR, RF. Always check for additional stored codes after making repairs.

TEST CONDITIONS

1. Tested continuously.

FAILURE CONDITIONS

Sensor Output:

1. Drive away: speed signal is not detected when vehicle reaches 12 kph or 7.5 mph.

2. While Driving: speed signal is lost while vehicle speed is greater than 40 kph or 25 mph.

Continuity:

1. While Standing: open circuit is seen while the vehicle is standing still with the ignition on.

ACTION TAKEN

1. Code set.
2. ABS switched 'OFF'.

NOTES ON CODE 25 CHART

1. This section of the fault tree determines if the code stored is due to a current fault condition. 'Current' wheel speed sensor faults may be detected even at vehicle standstill. If the ABS light turns on, the fault is current. The TECH 1 will indicate ignition cycle since code was set. If the ignition cycle counter is at zero, the code is current.

2. This section of the fault tree checks for an open or short in the wheel speed sensor wiring or sensor coil.

3. This section of the fault tree checks for conditions which may cause intermittent code setting. Some causes of intermittent wheel speed sensor codes to set are: improper routing or sensor cables next to spark plug wires, cables not retained in brackets, loose fitting or improperly mounted sensors, damaged sensors or toothed rings, poor terminal engagement of connectors, or intermittent shorts or opens in wiring.

Fig. 84 Code 25, LF wheel speed sensor fault (Part 1 of 2). 1992 Eldorado, Riviera, Seville, Toronado & Trofeo

Fig. 84   Code 25, LF wheel speed sensor fault (Part 2 of 2). 1992 Eldorado, Riviera, Seville, Toronado & Trofeo

ABS CODE 26
LEFT FRONT TOOTHED WHEEL FREQUENCY ERROR

CIRCUIT DESCRIPTION

As each wheel turns, the wheel speed sensor for that wheel creates a small AC voltage as a toothed sensor ring, mounted in the front integral hub/bearing assembly, is passed by the stationary sensor. The sensor consists of a permanent magnet and coil and generates voltage by magnetic induction. The frequency of the wheel speed sensor signal is proportional to wheel speed.

The EBCM uses the wheel speed sensor signal to calculate vehicle reference speeds and individual speed, acceleration and slip values for each wheel. These values are used to determine when antilock control is required.

TEST CONDITIONS

1. Tested continuously.

FAILURE CONDITIONS

1. While Driving: one wheel is detected at least 30 kph or 19 mph faster than the remaining wheels for an extended period of time.
   or
   One wheel is at least 6 kph or 4 mph less than or greater than the remaining wheels for an extended period of time.

ACTION TAKEN

1. Code set.
2. ABS switched 'OFF'.

Causes of improper speed signal may be caused by incorrect number of teeth on sensor ring, sensor rings which are covered with dirt, grease or metallic particles, or damaged toothed sensor ring.

Fig. 85   Code 26, LF toothed wheel frequency error. 1992 Eldorado, Riviera, Seville, Toronado & Trofeo

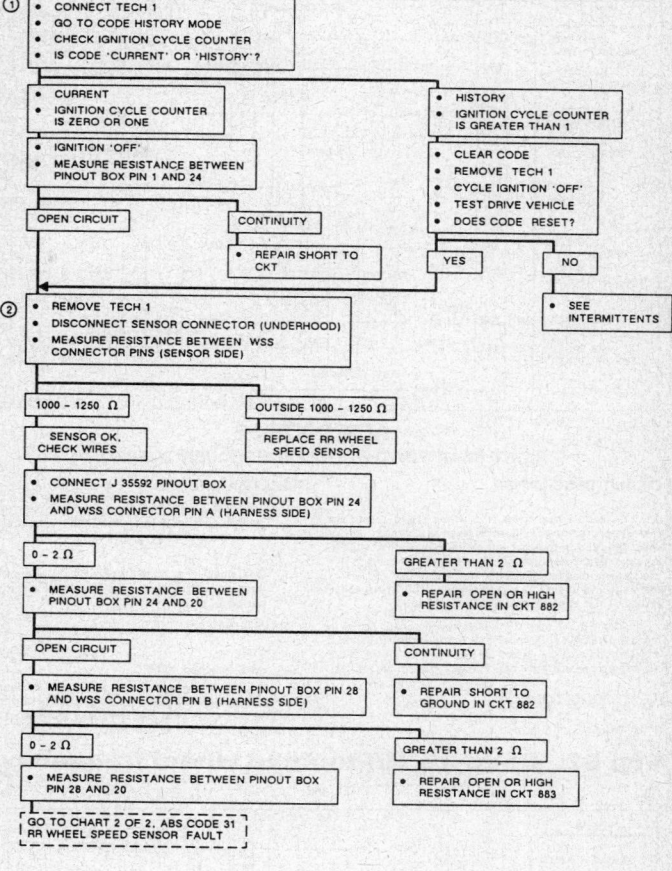

ABS CODE 31
RIGHT REAR WHEEL SPEED SENSOR FAULT

CIRCUIT DESCRIPTION

As each wheel turns, the wheel speed sensor for that wheel creates a small AC voltage as a toothed sensor ring, mounted in the rear integral hub/bearing assembly, is passed by the stationary sensor. The sensor consists of a permanent magnet and coil and generates voltage by magnetic induction. The frequency of the wheel speed sensor signal is proportional to wheel speed.

The EBCM uses the wheel speed sensor signal to calculate vehicle reference speeds and individual speed, acceleration and slip values for each wheel. These values are used to determine when antilock control is required.

The EBCM performs two basic types of checks on the wheel speed sensors, these are sensor continuity and sensor output.

The EBCM will only set one wheel speed sensor fault code at a time, even if multiple faults exist. Detection is prioritized accordingly: LF, RR, LR, RF. Always check for additional stored codes after making repairs.

TEST CONDITIONS
1. Tested continuously.

FAILURE CONDITIONS

Sensor Output:
1. Drive away: speed signal is not detected when vehicle reaches 12 kph or 7.5 mph.

2. While Driving: speed signal is lost while vehicle speed is greater than 40 kph or 25 mph.

Continuity:
1. While Standing: open circuit is seen while the vehicle is standing still with the ignition on.

ACTION TAKEN
1. Code set.
2. ABS switched 'OFF'.

NOTES ON CODE 31 CHART

1. This section of the fault tree determines if the code stored is due to a current fault condition. 'Current' wheel speed sensor faults may be detected even at vehicle standstill. If the ABS light turns on, the fault is current. The TECH 1 will indicate ignition cycle since code was set. If the ignition cycle counter is at zero, the code is current.

2. This section of the fault tree checks for an open or short in the wheel speed sensor wiring or sensor coil.

3. This section of the fault tree checks for conditions which may cause intermittent code setting. Some causes of intermittent wheel speed sensor codes to set are: improper routing or sensor cables next to spark plug wires, cables not retained in brackets, loose fitting or improperly mounted sensors, damaged sensors or toothed rings, poor terminal engagement of connectors, or intermittent shorts or opens in wiring.

Fig. 86 Code 31, RR wheel speed sensor fault. 1992 Eldorado, Riviera, Seville, Toronado & Trofeo

1991 REATTA, 1991-92 BROUGHAM, TORONADO & TROFEO & 1991-93 CAPRICE, CUSTOM CRUISER, ELDORADO, RIVIERA, ROADMASTER, SEVILLE (BOSCH 2 U TYPE)   **23-179**

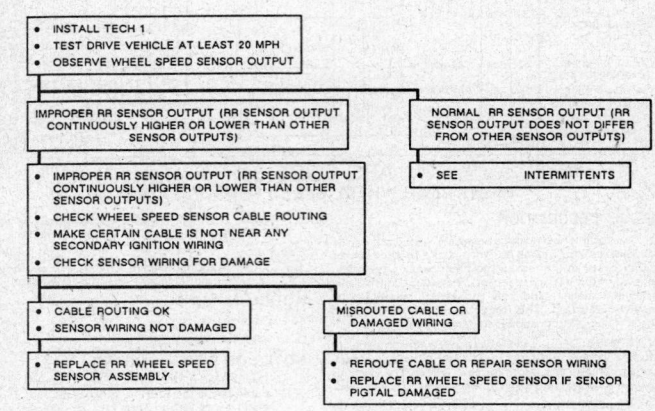

ABS CODE 32
RIGHT REAR TOOTHED WHEEL FREQUENCY ERROR

CIRCUIT DESCRIPTION

As each wheel turns, the wheel speed sensor for that wheel creates a small AC voltage as a toothed sensor ring, mounted in the rear integral hub/bearing assembly, is passed by the stationary sensor. The sensor consists of a permanent magnet and coil and generates voltage by magnetic induction. The frequency of the wheel speed sensor signal is proportional to wheel speed.

The EBCM uses the wheel speed sensor signal to calculate vehicle reference speeds and individual speed, acceleration and slip values for each wheel. These values are used to determine when antilock control is required.

TEST CONDITIONS

1. Tested continuously.

FAILURE CONDITIONS

1. While Driving: one wheel is detected at least 30 kph or 19 mph faster than the remaining wheels for an extended period of time.

    or

    One wheel is at least 6 kph or 4 mph less than or greater than the remaining wheels for an extended period of time.

ACTION TAKEN

1. Code set.
2. ABS switched 'OFF'.

    Causes of improper speed signal may be caused by incorrect number of teeth on sensor ring, sensor rings which are covered with dirt, grease or metallic particles, or damaged toothed sensor ring.

Fig. 87   Code 32, RR toothed wheel frequency error. 1992 Eldorado, Riviera, Seville, Toronado & Trofeo

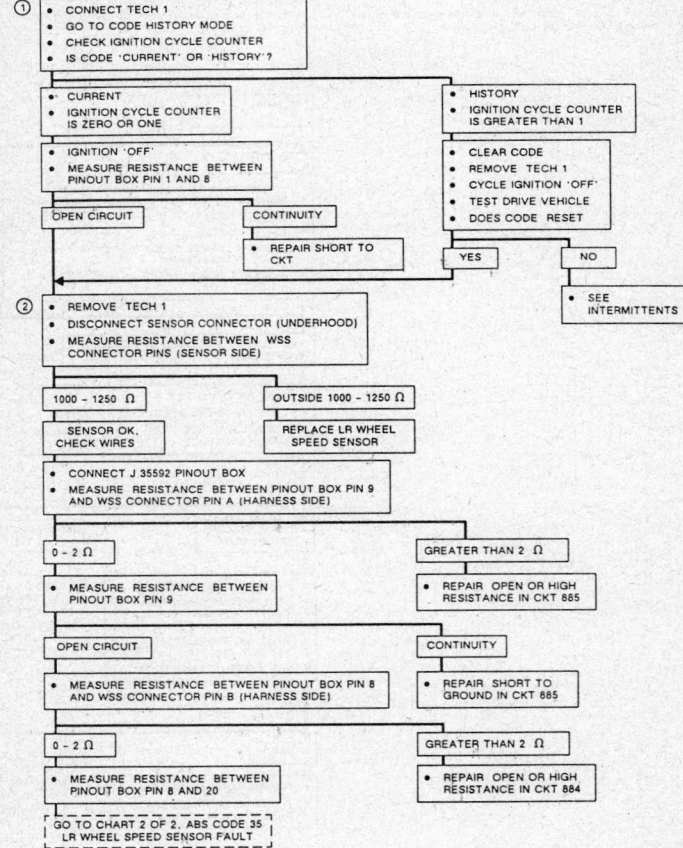

ABS CODE 35
LEFT REAR WHEEL SPEED SENSOR FAULT

CIRCUIT DESCRIPTION

As each wheel turns, the wheel speed sensor for that wheel creates a small AC voltage as a toothed sensor ring, mounted in the rear integral hub/bearing assembly, is passed by the stationary sensor. The sensor consists of a permanent magnet and coil and generates voltage by magnetic induction. The frequency of the wheel speed sensor signal is proportional to wheel speed.

The EBCM uses the wheel speed sensor signal to calculate vehicle reference speeds and individual speed, acceleration and slip values for each wheel. These values are used to determine when antilock control is required.

The EBCM performs two basic types of checks on the wheel speed sensors, these are sensor continuity and sensor output.e

The EBCM will only set one wheel speed sensor fault code at a time, even if multiple faults exist. Detection is prioritized accordingly: LF, RR, LR, RF. Always check for additional stored codes after making repairs.

TEST CONDITIONS

1. Tested continuously.

FAILURE CONDITIONS

Sensor Output:

1. Drive away: speed signal is not detected when vehicle reaches 12 kph or 7.5 mph.

2. While Driving: speed signal is lost while vehicle speed is greater than 40 kph or 25 mph.

Continuity:

1. While Standing: open circuit is seen while the vehicle is standing still with the ignition on.

ACTION TAKEN

1. Code set.
2. ABS switched 'OFF'.

NOTES ON CODE 35 CHART

1. This section of the fault tree determines if the code stored is due to a current fault condition. 'Current' wheel speed sensor faults may be detected even at vehicle standstill. If the ABS light turns on, the fault is current. The TECH 1 will indicate ignition cycle since code was set. If the ignition cycle counter is at zero, the code is current.

2. This section of the fault tree checks for an open or short in the wheel speed sensor wiring or sensor coil.

3. This section of the fault tree checks for conditions which may cause intermittent code setting. Some causes of intermittent wheel speed sensor codes to set are: improper routing or sensor cables next to spark plug wires, cables not retained in brackets, loose fitting or improperly mounted sensors, damaged sensors or toothed rings, poor terminal engagement of connectors, or intermittent shorts or opens in wiring.

Fig. 88   Code 35, LR wheel speed sensor fault (Part 1 of 2). 1992 Eldorado, Riviera, Seville, Toronado & Trofeo

Fig. 88   Code 35, LR wheel speed sensor fault (Part 2 of 2). 1992 Eldorado, Riviera, Seville, Toronado & Trofeo

ABS CODE 36

LEFT REAR TOOTHED WHEEL FREQUENCY ERROR

CIRCUIT DESCRIPTION

As each wheel turns, the wheel speed sensor for that wheel creates a small AC voltage as a toothed sensor ring, mounted in the rear integral hub/bearing assembly, is passed by the stationary sensor. The sensor consists of a permanent magnet and coil and generates voltage by magnetic induction. The frequency of the wheel speed sensor signal is proportional to wheel speed.

The EBCM uses the wheel speed sensor signal to calculate vehicle reference speeds and individual speed, acceleration and slip values for each wheel. These values are used to determine when antilock control is required.

TEST CONDITIONS

1. Tested continuously.

1. While Driving: one wheel is detected at least 30 kph or 19 mph faster than the remaining wheels for an extended period of time.
    or
    One wheel is at least 6 kph or 4 mph less than or greater than the remaining wheels for an extended period of time.

FAILURE CONDITIONS

ACTION TAKEN

1. Code set.
2. ABS switched 'OFF'.
    Causes of improper speed signal may be caused by incorrect number of teeth on sensor ring, sensor rings which are covered with dirt, grease or metallic particles, or damaged toothed sensor ring.

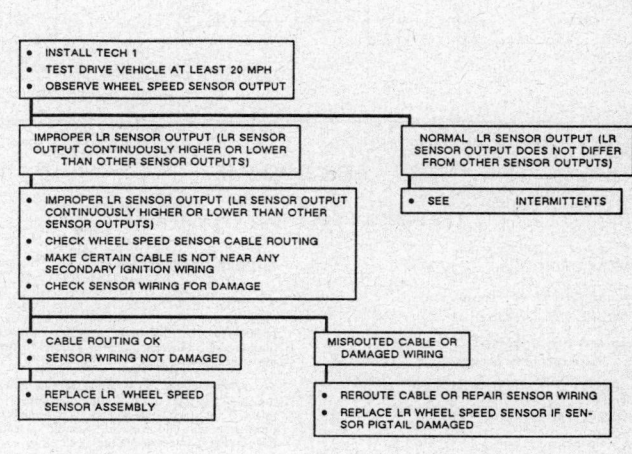

Fig. 89   Code 36, LR toothed wheel frequency error. 1992 Eldorado, Riviera, Seville, Toronado & Trofeo

NOTE: IF THIS CODE IS CURRENT, IT CANNOT BE FLASHED

ABS CODE 41

RIGHT FRONT SOLENOID VALVE FAULT

TEST CONDITIONS

1. Tested continuously.

FAILURE CONDITIONS

While standing or driving:

1. Valve cannot be activated

   or

2. Valve is activated in a defective way

ACTION TAKEN

1. Code Set.
2. ABS switched 'OFF'.

   Code 41 will set when the expected position of the right front solenoid valve does not match the commanded position from the EBCM. Conditions which could cause Code 41 to set are damage to the right front solenoid, an open circuit or a short circuit to ground or battery on CKT 827.

CIRCUIT DESCRIPTION

The right front solenoid valve in the hydraulic modulator may be commanded to three different positions by the EBCM. Valve position is determined by the amount of current which is allowed to flow through the solenoid valve coil.

The solenoid valve circuits receive power through the valve relay on the hydraulic modulator. The valve relay is engaged at key-on and remains engaged throughout the ignition cycle. Solenoid valve lines should have battery voltage available at all times.

When the key is turned to RUN, power is supplied to the EBCM. The EBCM will complete an internal self-check before providing ground to the valve relay. When the valve relay is energized, battery power is supplied to the solenoid valves.

Fig. 90   Code 41, RF solenoid valve fault. 1992 Eldorado, Riviera, Seville, Toronado & Trofeo

NOTE: IF THIS CODE IS CURRENT, IT CANNOT BE FLASHED

ABS CODE 45

LEFT FRONT SOLENOID VALVE FAULT

TEST CONDITIONS

1. Tested continuously.

FAILURE CONDITIONS

While standing or driving:

1. Valve cannot be activated

   or

2. Valve is activated in a defective way.

ACTION TAKEN

1. Code Set.
2. ABS switched 'OFF'.

   Code 45 will set when the expected position of the left front solenoid valve does not match the commanded position from the EBCM. Conditions which could cause Code 45 to set are damage to the left front solenoid, an open circuit or a short circuit to ground or battery on CKT 826.

CIRCUIT DESCRIPTION

The left front solenoid valve in the hydraulic modulator may be commanded to three different positions by the EBCM. Valve position is determined by the amount of current which is allowed to flow through the solenoid valve coil.

The solenoid valve circuits receive power through the valve relay on the hydraulic modulator. The valve relay is engaged at key-on and remains engaged throughout the ignition cycle. Solenoid valve lines should have battery voltage available at all times.

When the key is turned to RUN, power is supplied to the EBCM. The EBCM will complete an internal self-check before providing ground to the valve relay. When the valve relay is energized, battery power is supplied to the solenoid valves.

Fig. 91   Code 45, LF solenoid valve fault. 1992 Eldorado, Riviera, Seville, Toronado & Trofeo

ABS CODE 55

REAR WHEEL SOLENOID VALVE FAULT

TEST CONDITIONS

1. Tested continuously.

FAILURE CONDITIONS

While standing or driving:

1. Valve cannot be activated

   or

2. Valve is activated in a defective way

ACTION TAKEN

1. Code Set.

2. ABS switched 'OFF'.

Code 55 will set when the expected position of the rear solenoid valve does not match the commanded position from the EBCM. Conditions which could cause Code 55 to set are damage to the rear solenoid, an open circuit or a short circuit to ground or battery on CKT 829.

CIRCUIT DESCRIPTION

The rear wheels share the same solenoid valve and are connected by a hydraulic plunger internal to the modulator. There are two separate hydraulic lines from the modulator to each rear wheel.

The rear solenoid valve in the hydraulic modulator may be commanded to three different positions by the EBCM. The rear solenoid valve modulates hydraulic brake pressure to both rear wheel circuits. Valve position is determined by the amount of current which is allowed to flow through the solenoid valve coil.

The solenoid valve circuits receive power through the valve relay on the hydraulic modulator. The valve relay is engaged at key-on and remains engaged throughout the ignition cycle. Solenoid valve lines should have battery voltage available at all times.

When the key is turned to RUN, power is supplied to the EBCM. The EBCM will complete an internal self-check before providing ground to the valve relay. When the valve relay is energized, battery power is supplied to the solenoid valves.

Fig. 92   Code 55, rear solenoid valve fault. 1992 Eldorado, Riviera, Seville, Toronado & Trofeo

ABS CODE 61

PUMP MOTOR CIRCUIT FAULT

CIRCUIT DESCRIPTION:

The pump motor returns brake fluid to the master cylinder brake circuit at the hydraulic modulator during anti-lock braking. When normal braking, the pump does not operate. When the vehicle begins to move after start-up, the EBCM will turn on the pump motor and perform a self-check of the pump motor and pump motor circuit. This check may be felt and heard by the driver when the vehicle begins to move. The self-check should be considered normal operation. The pump motor is an integral component of the hydraulic modulator and cannot be serviced separately.

The pump motor relay provides power to the pump motor in the hydraulic modulator. The pump motor relay is located on the hydraulic modulator an may be replaced if it is found to be defective.

The pump motor relay is not engaged during normal system operation. When antilock operation is required, the motor relay actuation line on CKT 874 (EBCM pin 28) is pulled to ground. The pump motor relay is engaged by the relay supply voltage line on CKT 854 (EBCM pin 17). When the relay switches, battery power is provided to the pump motor.

TEST CONDITION(S):

1. Tested continuously.

FAILURE CONDITION(S):

1. Drive Away: Motor voltage is not detected during first drive away after engine start.

2. While Driving: Motor relay is energized and motor voltage is not detected.

3. Voltage at EBCM pin 14 below 9 volts.

   OR

4. Pump runs continuously.

ACTION TAKEN:

1. Code set.

2. ABS switched 'OFF'.

When the pump motor relay is engaged, the motor monitor line should be at battery voltage. With the pump motor relay disengaged, the monitoring line should be at ground. If the commanded position of the pump motor relay and motor monitor line do not agree, Code 61 will set. Some conditions which will cause Code 61 to set are:

- An open circuit on CKTs 874 or 1292
- A short to voltage on CKTs 874 or 1292
- A short to ground on CKTs 874 or 1292
- A defective pump motor relay or pump motor

Fig. 93   Code 61, pump motor circuit fault (Part 1 of 2). 1992 Eldorado & Seville

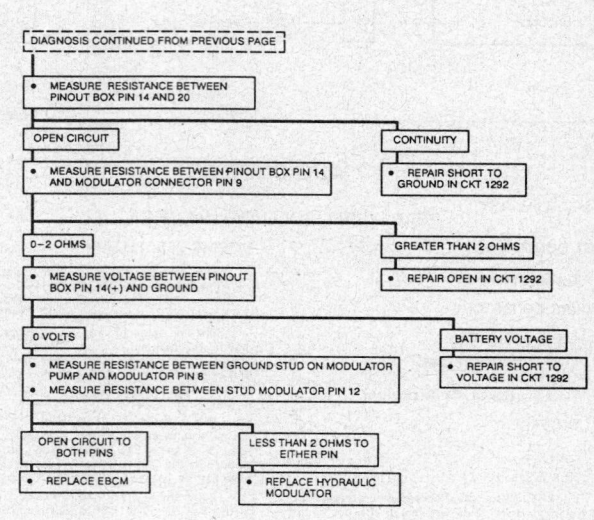

Fig. 93   Code 61, pump motor circuit fault (Part 2 of 2). 1992 Eldorado & Seville

ABS CODE 61

PUMP MOTOR CIRCUIT FAULT

TEST CONDITIONS

1. Tested continuously.

FAILURE CONDITIONS

1. Drive Away: motor voltage is not detected during first drive away after engine start.
2. While Driving: motor relay is energized and motor voltage is not detected.
   or
3. Voltage at EBCM pin 14 below 9 volts.
   or
4. Pump runs continuously.

ACTION TAKEN

1. Code set.
2. ABS switched 'OFF'.

When the pump motor relay is engaged, the motor monitor line should be at battery voltage. With the pump motor relay disengaged, the monitoring line should be at ground. If the commanded position of the pump motor relay and motor monitor line do not agree, Code 61 will set. Some conditions which will cause Code 61 to set are:

- An open circuit on CKTs 874 or 1292
- A short to voltage on CKTs 874 or 1292

- A short to ground on CKTs 874 or 1292
- A defective pump motor relay or pump motor

CIRCUIT DESCRIPTION

The pump motor returns brake fluid to the master cylinder brake circuit at the hydraulic modulator during antilock braking. During normal braking, the pump does not operate. When the vehicle begins to move after start-up, the EBCM will turn on the pump motor and perform a self-check of the pump motor and pump motor circuit. This check may be felt and heard by the driver when the vehicle begins to move. The self-check should be considered normal operation. The pump motor is an integral component of the hydraulic modulator and cannot be serviced separately.

The pump motor relay provides power to the pump motor in the hydraulic modulator. The pump motor relay is located on the hydraulic modulator an may be replaced if it is found to be defective.

The pump motor relay is not engaged during normal system operation. When antilock operation is required, the motor relay actuation line on CKT 874 (EBCM pin 28) is pulled to ground. The pump motor relay is engaged by the relay supply voltage line on CKT 854 (EBCM pin 17). When the relay switches, battery power is provided to the pump motor.

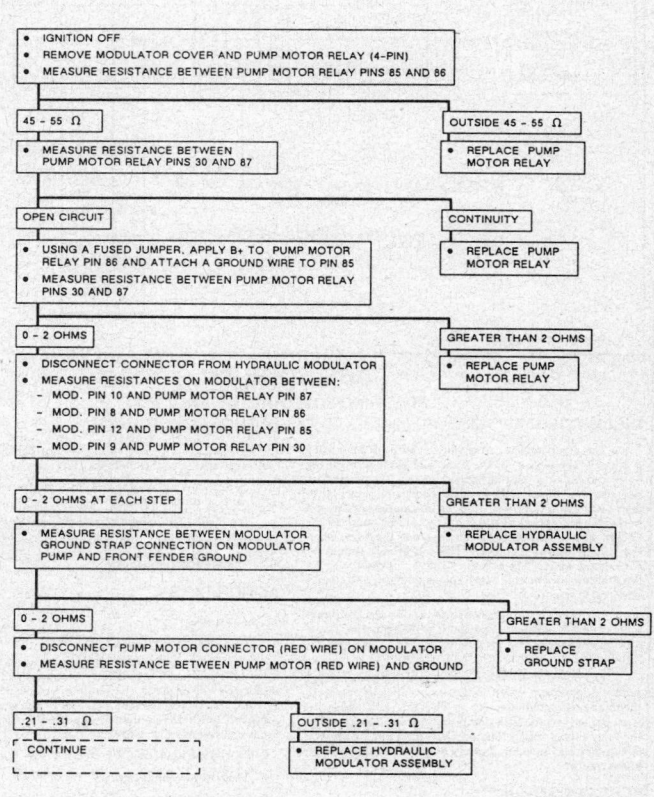

Fig. 94   Code 61, pump motor circuit fault (Part 1 of 2). 1992 Riviera, Toronado & Trofeo

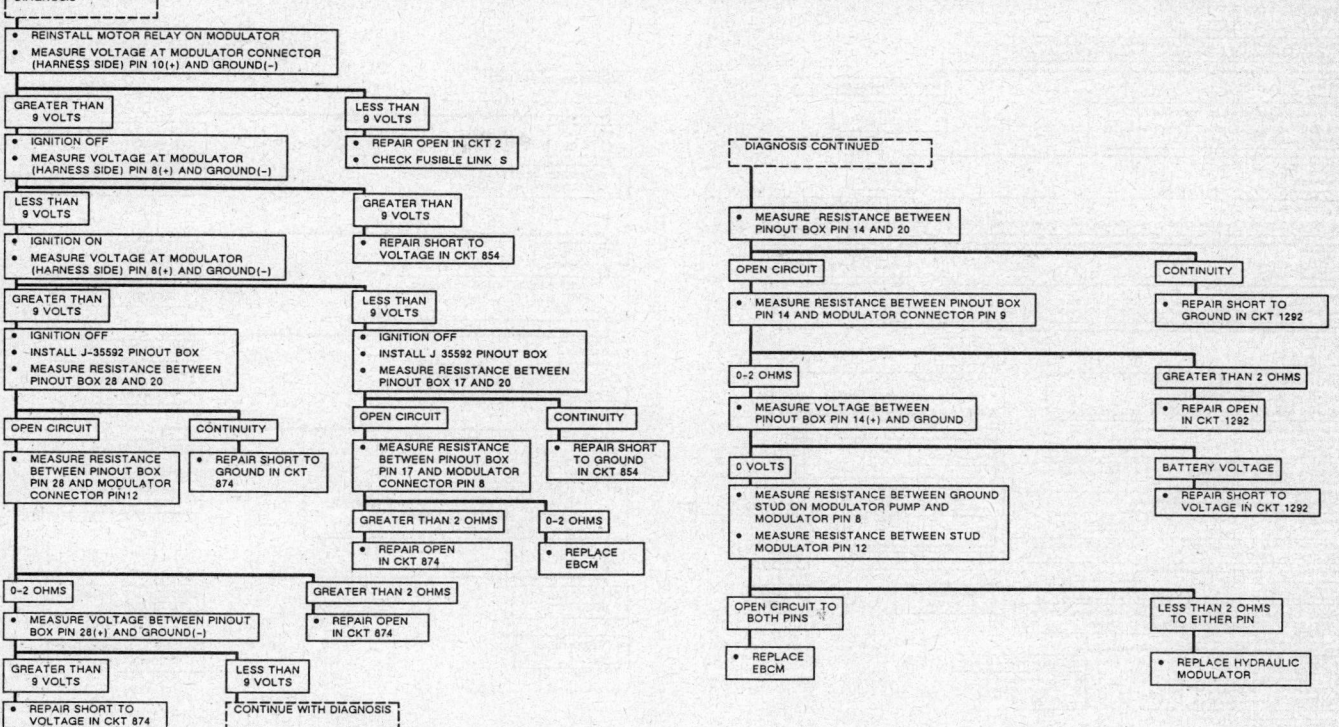

Fig. 94   Code 61, pump motor circuit fault (Part 2 of 2). 1992 Riviera, Toronado & Trofeo

ABS CODE 63
SOLENOID VALVE RELAY FAULT

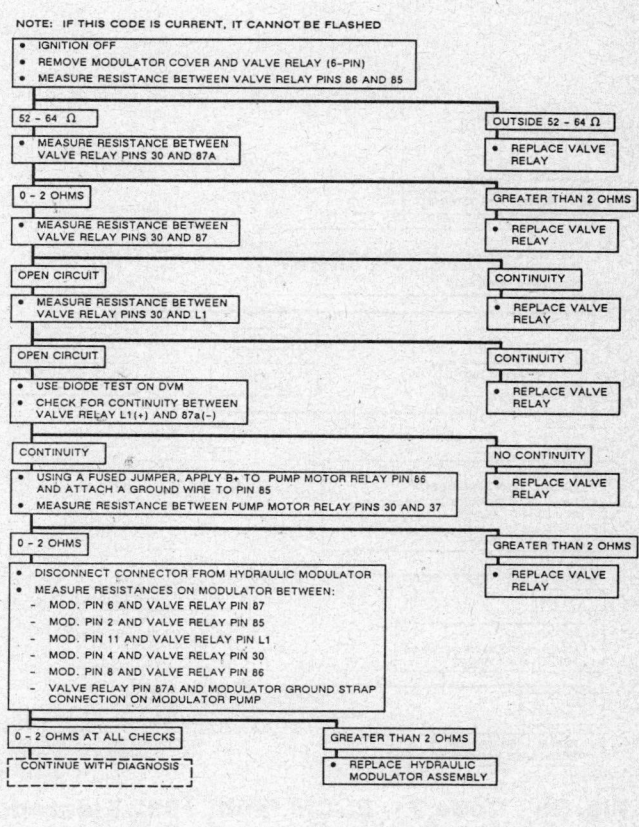

CIRCUIT DESCRIPTION

The solenoid valve relay provides power to the three solenoid valves in the hydraulic modulator. The solenoid valve relay is located on the hydraulic modulator and may be replaced if it is found to be defective.

The valve relay is engaged during normal system operation. When the ignition is switched to RUN, the EBCM commands the solenoid valve relay on by grounding the valve relay actuation line on CKT 879 (EBCM pin 27). When this ground is provided, the valve relay is energized from the voltage supply line on CKT 854 (EBCM pin 17). The valve relay switches and battery voltage is provided to the three solenoid valves and the solenoid valve relay feedback line on CKT 851 (EBCM pin 32). The valve relay remains engaged until the ignition is turned off or a failure is detected.

Whenever the solenoid valve relay is not engaged, the ANTILOCK light will turn on. With the ignition on and the solenoid valve relay not engaged, a path to ground exists from the IGN1-ISO fuse (10 amps) thru the ANTILOCK light on CKT 139 which turns on the warning light. The ANTILOCK light can also be commanded on by the EBCM on CKT 852 (EBCM pin 29). The EBCM will provide ground on this line and turn on the warning light when a failure is detected.

TEST CONDITIONS

1. Tested continuously.

FAILURE CONDITIONS

1. Less than 5 volts at EBCM pin 32, valve relay monitor
   or
2. Voltage at EBCM pin 32, valve relay monitor, remains high, although voltage a EBCM pin 27, valve relay control, is low (valve relay sticks).

ACTION TAKEN

1. ABS switched 'OFF'.
2. Code Set.
   When the valve relay is engaged, the valve relay feedback line should be at battery voltage. With the valve relay disengaged the feedback line is at ground. If the commanded position of the valve relay and the position indicated by the feedback line do not agree, Code 63 will set. Some conditions which will cause Code 63 to set are:
   - An open circuit on CKTs 851 or 879
   - A short to voltage on CKTs 851 or 879
   - A short to ground on CKTs 851 or 879
   - A defective solenoid valve relay
   - Open circuit on CKT 854.

ANTILOCK OPERATION

With the solenoid valve relay engaged, battery power is provided to the three solenoid valves. If antilock operation is required, a path to ground is required and the amount of current supplied to the solenoid valves (EBCM pins 2, 18, 35) and the valve is positioned to provide for optimum braking.

Fig. 95   Code 63, solenoid valve relay fault (Part 1 of 2). 1992 Eldorado, Riviera, Seville, Toronado & Trofeo

Fig. 95   Code 63, solenoid valve relay fault (Part 2 of 2). 1992 Eldorado, Riviera, Seville, Toronado & Trofeo

Fig. 96   Code 71, EBCM fault. 1992 Eldorado, Riviera, Seville, Toronado & Trofeo

TEST CONDITIONS

Tested continuously in Diagnostics Mode.   (TECH- 1 CONNECTED)

FAILURE CONDITIONS

EBCM receives 3 consecutive invalid message during diagnostics.

ACTION TAKEN

1. Code set.
2. Transmission from and to scan tool is impossible.

CIRCUIT DESCRIPTION

An ABS Code 72 may set when there is a momentary serial data communications error between the EBCM and the TECH 1. This code may set when power to the EBCM is interrupted while the Tech-1 remains powered; such as when the ignition is cycled while the Tech-1 is hooked-up. When this occurs, simply cycle power to the Tech-1 and allow it to reset.

Although it is not an indication of a serious condition, this code should be cleared prior to completion of diagnosis.

Fig. 97   Code 72, serial line data fault. 1992 Eldorado, Riviera, Seville, Toronado & Trofeo

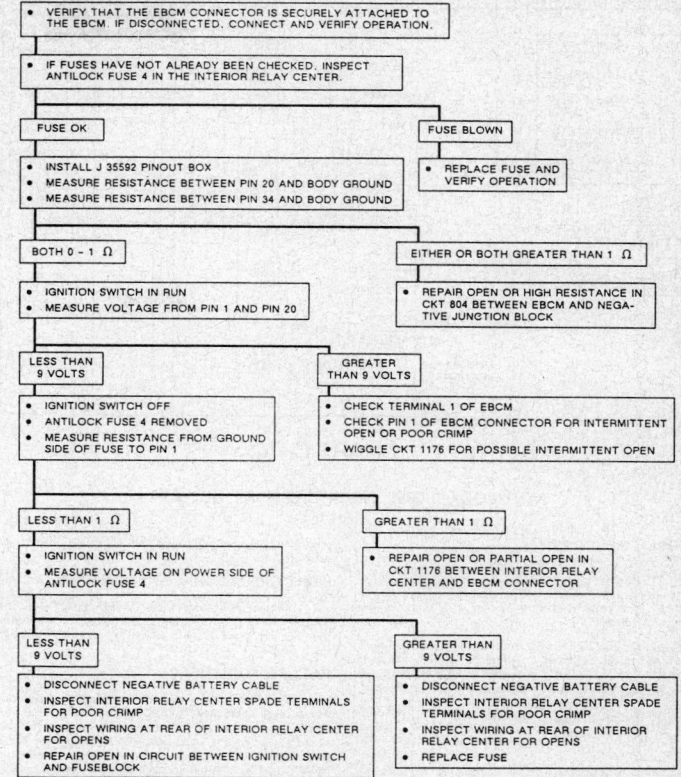

CHART A

NO SYSTEM POWER

CIRCUIT DESCRIPTION

The EBCM receives power from ABS/CCR/HW fuse 7, (located in the interior relay center) on CKT 1176. If high system voltages occur, the EBCM is internally protected by a network of diodes which directs excess voltage to ground.

FAILURE CONDITIONS

Intermittent operation of the ANTILOCK light may be caused by intermittent voltage levels which do not correspond to the proper operating range of the Antilock Brake System. Some conditions which may cause a lack of system power are:

- Improper electrical contact of the EBCM connector.
- Low system voltage.
- Improper electrical contact of the vehicle power and ground connections.

Fig. 98   Chart A, no system power. 1992 Eldorado, Riviera, Seville, Toronado & Trofeo

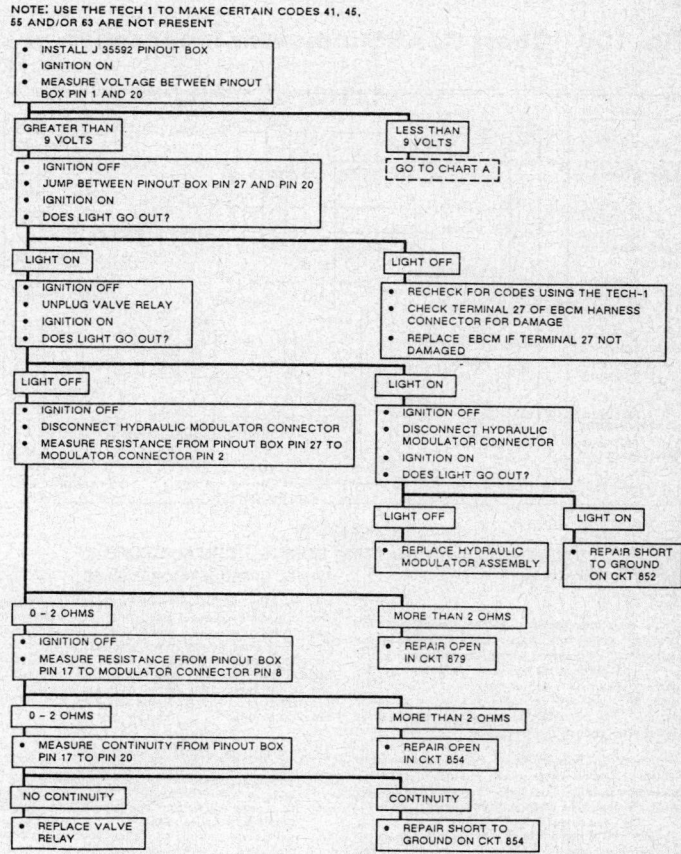

CHART B

ABS LIGHT ON, NO CODES SET

CIRCUIT DESCRIPTION

The amber ANTILOCK light is located below the instrument panel cluster. It may be illuminated by the EBCM or a path to ground in the valve relay on the hydraulic modulator.

The ANTILOCK light is powered by the Ignition 1 feed and receives power anytime the ignition switch is turned to RUN. Power is provided on CKT 750 through the 10 amp HVAC fuse 9 located in the fuse block.

LIGHT OPERATION – VALVE RELAY GROUND

The ANTILOCK light is illuminated anytime the valve relay is not enabled. When the relay is not enabled, the light is grounded through CKT 852 and the valve relay to the modulator ground. During normal operation (no fault conditions found), the valve will switch and the ground will be removed, and the ANTILOCK light will turn off. The ABS light is on whenever the EBCM is disconnected.

LIGHT OPERATION – EBCM GROUND

If the EBCM detects a fault in the ABS, the EBCM can turn on the ANTILOCK light by grounding pin 29. A ground path exists for the light through CKT 852. The EBCM will disable the valve relay when CKT 852 is grounded at pin 29.

NOTE: It is best to check for codes using a TECH-1. It is possible that a valve (Code 41, 45, 55 and 63) may have set. It is **NOT** possible to flash codes when a valve code is present.

FAILURE CONDITIONS

The chart   addresses conditions which result in continuous operation of the ANTILOCK light. If the ANTILOCK light is on and no codes can be extracted from the EBCM, the EBCM connector should be checked for proper connection and system power should be checked.

Fig. 99   Chart B, ABS indicator On w/no codes set. 1992 Eldorado, Riviera, Seville, Toronado & Trofeo

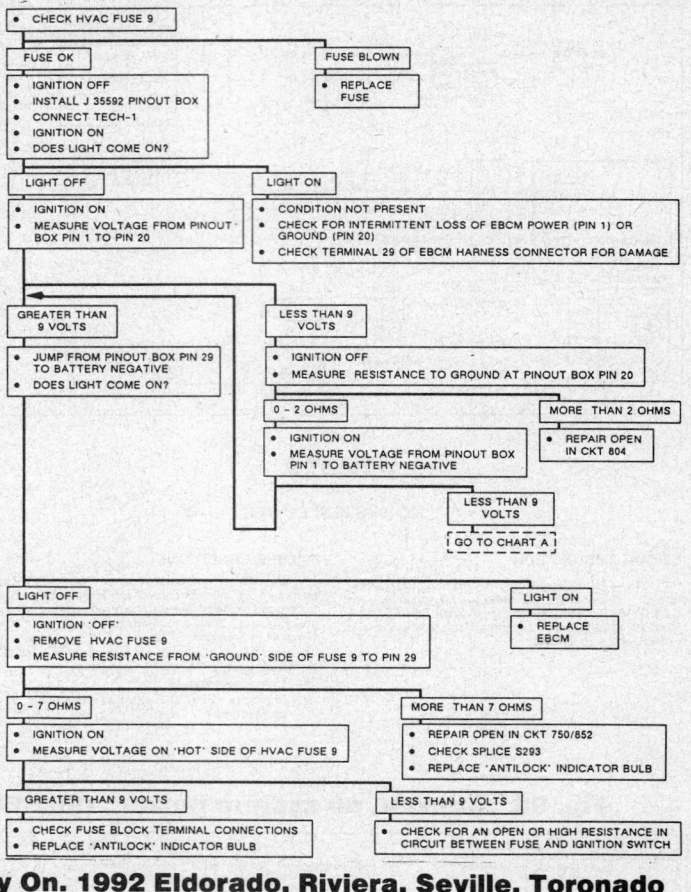

CHART C

ANTILOCK LIGHT INOPERATIVE AT KEY–ON

CIRCUIT DESCRIPTION

The amber ANTILOCK light is located below the instrument panel cluster. It may be illuminated by the EBCM or a path to ground in the valve relay on the hydraulic modulator.

The ANTILOCK light is powered by the Ignition 1 feed and receives power anytime the ignition switch is turned to RUN. Power is provided on CKT 750 through the 10 amp HVAC fuse 9 located in the fuse block.

LIGHT OPERATION – VALVE RELAY GROUND

The ANTILOCK light is illuminated anytime the valve relay is not enabled. When the relay is not enabled, the light is grounded through CKT 852 and the valve relay to the modulator ground. During normal operation (no fault conditions found), the valve will switch and the

ground will be removed, and the ANTILOCK light will turn off.

LIGHT OPERATION – EBCM GROUND

Whether the valve relay is engaged or not, the EBCM can turn on the ANTILOCK light by grounding pin 29. A ground path exists for the light through CKT 852.

FAILURE CONDITIONS

The chart on the next page addresses conditions which result in no ANTILOCK light operation; the ABS operates properly. As described at the beginning of this section, the ANTILOCK light should illuminate for a minimum of four seconds when the key is moved from 'OFF' to RUN. This chart addresses conditions such as lack of power to the ANTILOCK light which would prevent the light from turning on. This condition could prevent the EBCM from turning on the light in the event of an antilock failure.

Fig. 100 Chart C, ABS indicator inoperative at key On. 1992 Eldorado, Riviera, Seville, Toronado & Trofeo

CHART D

VALVE CYCLING (CHATTER) DURING NORMAL STOPS

CIRCUIT DESCRIPTION

As each wheel turns, the wheel speed sensor for that wheel creates a small AC voltage as a toothed sensor ring, mounted on the front suspension knuckle or in the rear integral hub/bearing assembly, is passed by the stationary sensor. The sensor consists of a permanent magnet and coil and generates voltage by magnetic induction. The frequency of the wheel speed sensor signal is proportional to wheel speed.

The EBCM uses the wheel speed sensor signal to calculate vehicle reference speeds and individual speed, acceleration and slip values for each wheel. These values are used to determine when antilock braking is required.

The EBCM performs two basic types of checks on the wheel speed sensors, these are sensor continuity and sensor output.

WHEEL SPEED SENSOR CABLES

In order to prevent electromagnetic interference from disturbing the wheel speed sensor signal, the sensor cables are protected with grounded shielding (indicated by dashed lines in the above schematic). This shield surrounds the two individual sensor wires. A black conduit surrounds the sensor cables. When servicing the sensor cables, the sensor wires are accessible by separating the shielding and shield. If the shielding is disturbed, repair as required.

NOTES ON CHART D

1. The wheel speed sensor output should gradually increase with vehicle speed. There should be no skips or jumps. All four wheel speed sensor outputs should be identical. On a slow down, one of the signals may drop off faster than the others, indicating a lock-up condition or a problem with the speed sensor air gap, wiring, or sensor itself.

Fig. 101 Chart D, valve cycling during normal stops. 1992 Eldorado, Riviera, Seville, Toronado & Trofeo

Fig. 102 ABS & Traction Control System (TCS) wiring circuit (Part 1 of 3). 1993 Eldorado & Seville w/4.6L Northstar engine

Fig. 102 ABS & Traction Control System (TCS) wiring circuit (Part 2 of 3). 1993 Eldorado & Seville w/4.6L Northstar engine

Fig. 102 ABS & Traction Control System (TCS) wiring circuit (Part 3 of 3). 1993 Eldorado & Seville w/4.6L Northstar engine

Fig. 103 ABS & Traction Control System (TCS) wiring circuit (Part 1 of 2). 1993 Eldorado & Seville w/4.9L engine

1991 REATTA, 1991-92 BROUGHAM, TORONADO & TROFEO & 1991-93 CAPRICE, CUSTOM CRUISER, ELDORADO, RIVIERA, ROADMASTER, SEVILLE (BOSCH 2 U TYPE)

23-189

Fig. 103   ABS & Traction Control System (TCS) wiring circuit (Part 2 of 2). 1993 Eldorado & Seville w/4.9L engine

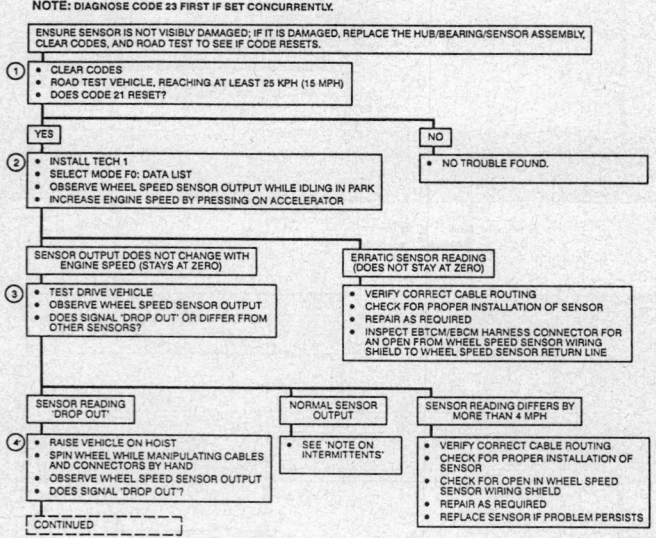

Fig. 104   DTC 21, Right front wheel speed sensor fault (Part 2 of 4). 1993 Eldorado & Seville

DIAGNOSTIC TROUBLE CODE 21
RIGHT FRONT WHEEL SPEED SENSOR FAULT
1 of 4

CIRCUIT DESCRIPTION:

As each wheel turns, the wheel speed sensor for that wheel creates a small AC voltage as a toothed sensor ring, mounted in the front integral hub/bearing assembly, is passed by the stationary sensor. The sensor consists of a permanent magnet and coil and generates voltage by magnetic induction. The frequency of the wheel speed sensor signal is proportional to wheel speed.

The EBTCM/EBCM uses the wheel speed sensor signal to calculate vehicle reference speeds and individual speed, acceleration and slip values for each wheel. These values are used to determine when antilock control is required.

The EBTCM/EBCM will only set one wheel speed sensor fault code at a time, even if multiple faults exist. Detection is prioritized accordingly: LF, RR, LR, RF. Always check for additional stored codes after making repairs.

TEST CONDITION(S):
1. Tested continuously.

FAILURE CONDITION(S):

Sensor Output
1. Drive–away: Speed signal is not detected when vehicle reaches 12 kph or 7.5 mph.
2. While Driving: Speed signal is lost while vehicle speed is greater than 40 kph or 25 mph.

ACTION TAKEN:
1. Code set.
2. ABS/TCS switched 'OFF'.
3. 'ANTILOCK' indicator 'ON'.
4. 'TRACTION DISABLED' message displayed.

Code 31 is set if there is a short to voltage or ground in CKT 882 or 883, or faulty speed sensor. The testing for this fault occurs when the vehicle is in motion, it will not set with the ignition 'ON' and the vehicle at rest.

NOTICE: A Code 21 may set if CKT 872 or 833 lose continuity and the WSS signal is lost while driving. A Code 23 should accompany this code on the subsequent ignition cycle. If both Code 21 and Code 23 are set concurrently, diagnose Code 23 first.

TEST DESCRIPTION: Test numbers refer to circled numbers on the diagnostic chart.
1. Checks if the code resets during a road test.
2. Use the TECH 1 to check for sources of induced electrical noise. Some sources of induced electrical noise which may cause intermittent wheel speed sensor codes to set are: improper routing or sensor cables next to spark plug wires; cables not retained in brackets; loose fitting or improperly mounted sensors; damaged sensors or toothed rings; poor terminal engagement of connectors; or intermittent shorts or opens in wiring; or a loss of sensor circuit shield.
3. Checks for damaged wheel speed sensor circuit shield. The shield is a foil insulator that is wrapped around the wheel speed sensor circuits. Inside the EBTCM/EBCM harness connecter there is an uninsulated drain wire that is attached to the shield and jumped to the wheel speed sensor return line and taken to ground through the EBTCM/EBCM. A shield which has lost its ground through the EBTCM/EBCM leaves the sensor signal circuit susceptible to noise. It may be necessary to disassemble the EBTCM/EBCM connector to check if the drain wire has a poor connection with the wheel speed sensor return connector terminal. The shield can be repaired by redetermining the sensor return line circuit, including the drain wire.
4. Checks for intermittent opens/shorts in wheel speed sensor circuits and cables.

Fig. 104   DTC 21, Right front wheel speed sensor fault (Part 1 of 4). 1993 Eldorado & Seville

DIAGNOSTIC TROUBLE CODE 21
RIGHT FRONT WHEEL SPEED SENSOR FAULT
4 of 4

CIRCUIT DESCRIPTION:

As each wheel turns, the wheel speed sensor for that wheel creates a small AC voltage as a toothed sensor ring, mounted in the front integral hub/bearing assembly, is passed by the stationary sensor. The sensor consists of a permanent magnet and coil and generates voltage by magnetic induction. The frequency of the wheel speed sensor signal is proportional to wheel speed.

The EBTCM/EBCM uses the wheel speed sensor signal to calculate vehicle reference speeds and individual speed, acceleration and slip values for each wheel. These values are used to determine when antilock control is required.

The EBTCM/EBCM will only set one wheel speed sensor fault code at a time, even if multiple faults exist. Detection is prioritized accordingly: LF, RR, LR, RF. Always check for additional stored codes after making repairs.

TEST DESCRIPTION: Test numbers refer to circled numbers on the diagnostic chart.
5. Checks for proper resistance in the sensor itself.
6. Checks for a short to battery in either of the speed sensor circuit wires.
7. Checks for a short between the speed sensor circuit wires.
8. Checks for a short to ground in the speed sensor input circuit wire. The ground may be either a 'hard' short to ground, or a resistive short. A short with a resistance less than 2 megaohms, though not a hard short, can still cause Code 21 to set.
9. Checks wiring and connectors for intermittents.

Fig. 104   DTC 21, Right front wheel speed sensor fault (Part 3 of 4). 1993 Eldorado & Seville

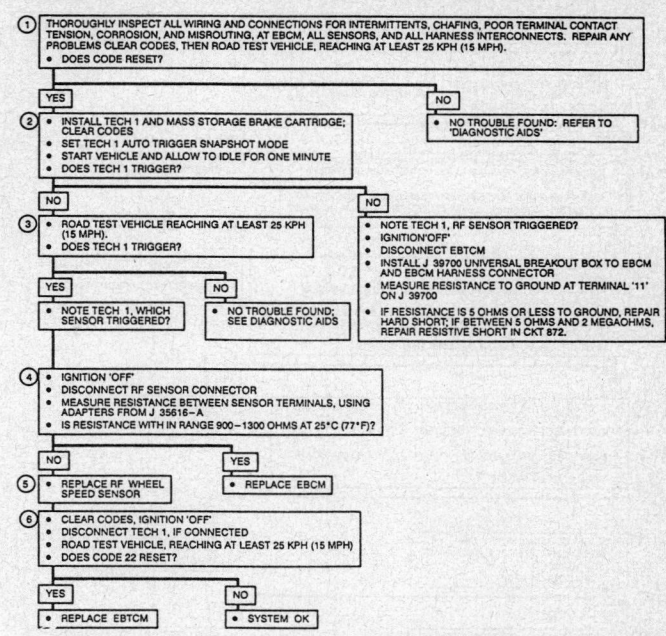

Fig. 105 DTC 22, Right front wheel speed sensor frequency error (Part 2 of 2). 1993 Eldorado & Seville

TEST CONDITION(S):
1. Tested continuously.

FAILURE CONDITION(S):
1. While Driving: The RF wheel is detected at least 30 kph or 19 mph faster than the remaining wheels for an extended period of time.
   OR
   The RF wheel is at least 6 kph or 4 mph less than or greater than the remaining wheels for an extended period of time.

ACTION TAKEN:
1. Code set.
2. ABS/TCS switched 'OFF'.
3. 'ANTILOCK' indicator 'ON'.

TEST DESCRIPTION: Test numbers refer to circled numbers on the diagnostic chart.

DIAGNOSTIC AIDS:

Be sure the speed sensor wiring is properly routed and retained.

Fig. 105 DTC 22, Right front wheel speed sensor frequency error (Part 1 of 2). 1993 Eldorado & Seville

CIRCUIT DESCRIPTION:

As each wheel turns, the wheel speed sensor creates a small AC voltage.

TEST CONDITION(S):
1. Tested continuously.

FAILURE CONDITION(S):
Continuity
1. While standing: Open circuit is seen while the vehicle is standing still with the ignition 'ON'.

ACTION TAKEN:
1. Code set.
2. ABS/TCS switched 'OFF'.
3. 'ANTILOCK' indicator 'ON'.
4. 'TRACTION DISABLED' message displayed (vehicles with TCS).

DIAGNOSTIC AIDS:

Be sure the speed sensor wiring is properly routed and retained.

Fig. 106 DTC 23, Right front wheel speed sensor continuity fault (Part 1 of 2). 1993 Eldorado & Seville

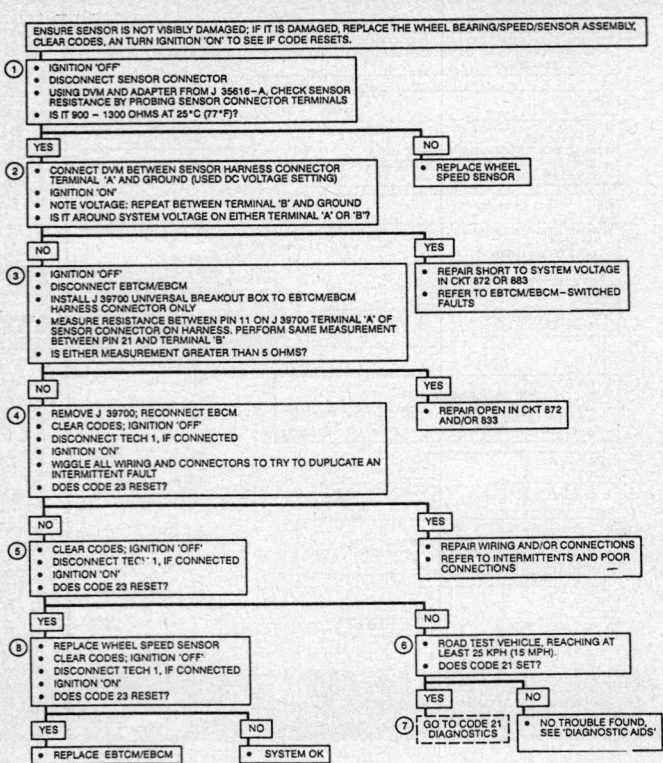

ENSURE SENSOR IS NOT VISIBLY DAMAGED; IF IT IS DAMAGED, REPLACE THE WHEEL BEARING/SPEED/SENSOR ASSEMBLY, CLEAR CODES, AN TURN IGNITION 'ON' TO SEE IF CODE RESETS.

① • IGNITION 'OFF'
• DISCONNECT SENSOR CONNECTOR
• USING DVM AND ADAPTER FROM J 35616–A, CHECK SENSOR RESISTANCE BY PROBING SENSOR CONNECTOR TERMINALS
• IS IT 900 – 1300 OHMS AT 25°C (77°F)?

YES → NO → • REPLACE WHEEL SPEED SENSOR

② • CONNECT DVM BETWEEN SENSOR HARNESS CONNECTOR TERMINAL 'A' AND GROUND (USED DC VOLTAGE SETTING)
• IGNITION 'ON'
• NOTE VOLTAGE: REPEAT BETWEEN TERMINAL 'B' AND GROUND
• IS IT AROUND SYSTEM VOLTAGE ON EITHER TERMINAL 'A' OR 'B'?

NO → YES → • REPAIR SHORT TO SYSTEM VOLTAGE IN CKT 872 OR 883
• REFER TO EBTCM/EBCM – SWITCHED FAULTS

③ • IGNITION 'OFF'
• DISCONNECT EBTCM/EBCM
• INSTALL J 39700 UNIVERSAL BREAKOUT BOX TO EBTCM/EBCM HARNESS CONNECTOR ONLY
• MEASURE RESISTANCE BETWEEN PIN 11 ON J 39700 TERMINAL 'A' OF SENSOR CONNECTOR ON HARNESS. PERFORM SAME MEASUREMENT BETWEEN PIN 21 AND TERMINAL 'B'
• IS EITHER MEASUREMENT GREATER THAN 5 OHMS?

NO → YES → • REPAIR OPEN IN CKT 872 AND/OR 833

④ • REMOVE J 39700; RECONNECT EBCM
• CLEAR CODES; IGNITION 'OFF'
• DISCONNECT TECH 1, IF CONNECTED
• IGNITION 'ON'
• WIGGLE ALL WIRING AND CONNECTORS TO TRY TO DUPLICATE AN INTERMITTENT FAULT
• DOES CODE 23 RESET?

NO → YES →

⑤ • CLEAR CODES; IGNITION 'OFF'
• DISCONNECT TECH 1, IF CONNECTED
• IGNITION 'ON'
• DOES CODE 23 RESET?

→ • REPAIR WIRING AND/OR CONNECTIONS
• REFER TO INTERMITTENTS AND POOR CONNECTIONS

⑧ • REPLACE WHEEL SPEED SENSOR
• CLEAR CODES; IGNITION 'OFF'
• DISCONNECT TECH 1, IF CONNECTED
• IGNITION 'ON'
• DOES CODE 23 RESET?

⑥ • ROAD TEST VEHICLE, REACHING AT LEAST 25 KPH (15 MPH).
• DOES CODE 21 SET?

YES → NO →

YES → NO

⑦ GO TO CODE 21 DIAGNOSTICS | • NO TROUBLE FOUND, SEE 'DIAGNOSTIC AIDS'

YES → NO

• REPLACE EBTCM/EBCM | • SYSTEM OK

Fig. 106 DTC 23, Right front wheel speed sensor continuity fault (Part 2 of 2). 1993 Eldorado & Seville

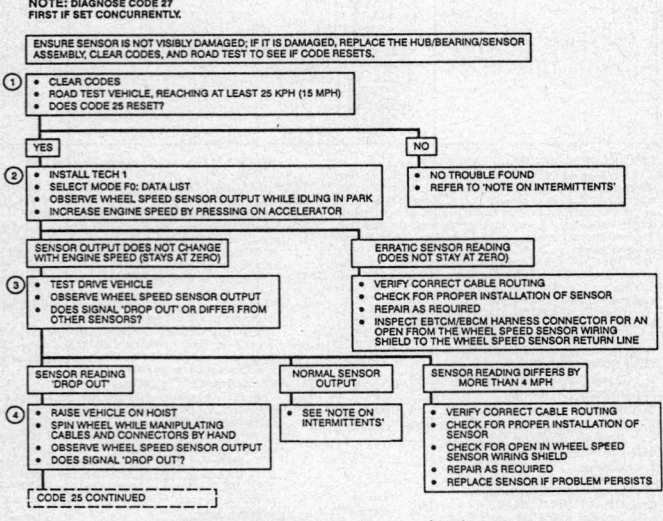

NOTE: DIAGNOSE CODE 27 FIRST IF SET CONCURRENTLY.

ENSURE SENSOR IS NOT VISIBLY DAMAGED; IF IT IS DAMAGED, REPLACE THE HUB/BEARING/SENSOR ASSEMBLY, CLEAR CODES, AND ROAD TEST TO SEE IF CODE RESETS.

① • CLEAR CODES
• ROAD TEST VEHICLE, REACHING AT LEAST 25 KPH (15 MPH)
• DOES CODE 25 RESET?

YES → NO →

② • INSTALL TECH 1
• SELECT MODE F0: DATA LIST
• OBSERVE WHEEL SPEED SENSOR OUTPUT WHILE IDLING IN PARK
• INCREASE ENGINE SPEED BY PRESSING ON ACCELERATOR

→ • NO TROUBLE FOUND
• REFER TO 'NOTE ON INTERMITTENTS'

SENSOR OUTPUT DOES NOT CHANGE WITH ENGINE SPEED (STAYS AT ZERO) | ERRATIC SENSOR READING (DOES NOT STAY AT ZERO)

③ • TEST DRIVE VEHICLE
• OBSERVE WHEEL SPEED SENSOR OUTPUT
• DOES SIGNAL 'DROP OUT' OR DIFFER FROM OTHER SENSORS?

• VERIFY CORRECT CABLE ROUTING
• CHECK FOR PROPER INSTALLATION OF SENSOR
• REPAIR AS REQUIRED
• INSPECT EBTCM/EBCM HARNESS CONNECTOR FOR AN OPEN FROM THE WHEEL SPEED SENSOR WIRING SHIELD TO THE WHEEL SPEED SENSOR RETURN LINE

SENSOR READING 'DROP OUT' | NORMAL SENSOR OUTPUT | SENSOR READING DIFFERS BY MORE THAN 4 MPH

④ • RAISE VEHICLE ON HOIST
• SPIN WHEEL WHILE MANIPULATING CABLES AND CONNECTORS BY HAND
• OBSERVE WHEEL SPEED SENSOR OUTPUT
• DOES SIGNAL 'DROP OUT'?

• SEE 'NOTE ON INTERMITTENTS'

• VERIFY CORRECT CABLE ROUTING
• CHECK FOR PROPER INSTALLATION OF SENSOR
• CHECK FOR OPEN IN WHEEL SPEED SENSOR WIRING SHIELD
• REPAIR AS REQUIRED
• REPLACE SENSOR IF PROBLEM PERSISTS

CODE 25 CONTINUED

Fig. 107 DTC 25, Left front wheel speed sensor fault (Part 2 of 4). 1993 Eldorado & Seville

CIRCUIT DESCRIPTION:

As each wheel turns, the wheel speed sensor for that wheel creates a small AC voltage as a toothed sensor ring, mounted in the front integral hub/bearing assembly, is passed by the stationary sensor. The sensor consists of a permanent magnet and coil and generates voltage by magnetic induction. The frequency of the wheel speed sensor signal is proportional to wheel speed.

The EBTCM/EBCM uses the wheel speed sensor signal to calculate vehicle reference speeds and individual speed, acceleration and slip values for each wheel. These values are used to determine when antilock control is required.

The EBTCM/EBCM will only set one wheel speed sensor fault code at a time, even if multiple faults exist. Detection is prioritized accordingly: LF, RR, LR, RF. Always check for additional stored codes after making repairs.

TEST CONDITION(S):
1. Tested continuously.

FAILURE CONDITION(S):
Sensor Output
1. Drive–away: Speed signal is not detected when vehicle reaches 12 kph or 7.5 mph.
   OR
2. While Driving: Speed signal is lost while vehicle speed is greater than 40 kph or 25 mph

ACTION TAKEN:
1. Code set.
2. ABS/TCS switched 'OFF'.
3. 'ANTILOCK' indicator 'ON'.
4. 'TRACTION DISABLED' message displayed. (vehicles with TCS)
   Code 25 is set if there is a short to voltage or ground in CKT 830 or 873, or faulty speed sensor. The testing for this fault occurs when vehicle is in motion; it will not set with the ignition 'ON' and the vehicle at rest.

NOTICE: A Code 25 may set if CKT 830 or 873 lose continuity and the WSS signal is lost while driving. Some sources of induced electrical noise which may cause intermittent wheel speed sensor codes to set are: improper routing or sensor cables next to spark plug wires; loose fitting or improperly mounted sensors; damaged sensors or toothed rings; poor terminal engagement of connectors; or intermittent shorts or opens in wiring; or a loss of sensor circuit shield.

A Code 27 should accompany this code on the subsequent ignition cycle. If both Code 25 and Code 27 are set concurrently, diagnose Code 27 first.

TEST DESCRIPTION:
Test numbers refer to circled numbers on the diagnostic chart.
1. Checks if the code resets during a road test.
2. Use the TECH 1 to check for sources of induced electrical noise. Some sources of induced electrical noise which may cause intermittent wheel speed sensor codes to set are: improper routing or sensor cables next to spark plug wires; cables not retained in brackets; loose fitting or improperly mounted sensors; damaged sensors or toothed rings; poor terminal engagement of connectors; or intermittent shorts or opens in wiring; or a loss of sensor circuit shield.
3. Checks for damaged wheel speed sensor circuit shield. The shield is a foil insulator that is wrapped around the wheel speed sensor circuits. Inside the EBTCM/EBCM harness connector there is an uninsulated drain wire that is attached to the shield and jumped to the wheel speed sensor return line and taken to ground through the EBTCM/EBCM. A shield which has lost its ground through the EBTCM/EBCM leaves the sensor signal circuit susceptible to noise. It may be necessary to disassemble the EBTCM/EBCM connector to check if the drain wire has a poor connection with the wheel speed sensor return connector terminal. The shield can be repaired by reterminating the sensor return line circuit, including the drain wire.
4. Checks for intermittent opens/shorts in wheel speed sensor circuits and cables.

Fig. 107 DTC 25, Left front wheel speed sensor fault (Part 1 of 4). 1993 Eldorado & Seville

DIAGNOSTIC TROUBLE CODE 25
LEFT FRONT WHEEL SPEED SENSOR FAULT

3 of 4

CIRCUIT DESCRIPTION:

As each wheel turns, the wheel speed sensor for that wheel creates a small AC voltage as a toothed sensor ring, mounted in the front integral hub/bearing assembly, is passed by the stationary sensor. The sensor consists of a permanent magnet and coil and generates voltage by magnetic induction. The frequency of the wheel speed sensor signal is proportional to wheel speed.

The EBTCM/EBCM uses the wheel speed sensor signal to calculate vehicle reference speeds and individual speed, acceleration and slip values for each wheel. These values are used to determine when antilock control is required.

The EBTCM/EBCM will only set one wheel speed sensor fault code at a time, even if multiple faults exist. Detection is prioritized accordingly: LF, RR, LR, RF. Always check for additional stored codes after making repairs.

TEST DESCRIPTION:
Test numbers refer to circled numbers on the diagnostic chart.
5. Checks for proper resistance in the sensor itself.
6. Checks for a short to battery in either of the speed sensor circuit wires.
7. Checks for a short between the speed sensor circuit wires.
8. Checks for a short to ground in the speed sensor input circuit wire. The ground may be either a 'hard' short to ground, or a resistive short. A short with a resistance less than 2 megaohms, though not a hard short, can still cause Code 21 to set.
9. Checks wiring and connectors for intermittents.

Fig. 107 DTC 25, Left front wheel speed sensor fault (Part 3 of 4). 1993 Eldorado & Seville

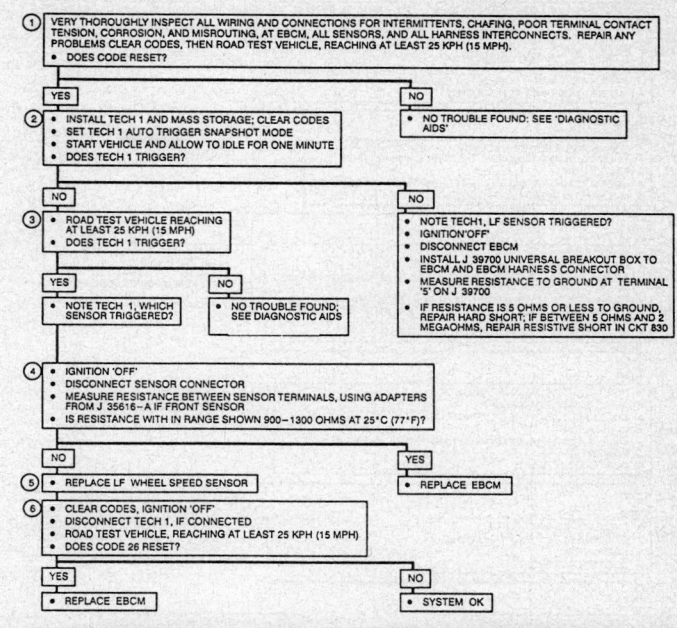

CONTINUED FROM CODE 25

Fig. 108 DTC 26, Left front wheel speed sensor frequency error (Part 2 of 2). 1993 Eldorado & Seville

Fig. 107 DTC 25, Left front wheel speed sensor fault (Part 4 of 4). 1993 Eldorado & Seville

TEST CONDITION(S):
1. Tested continuously.

FAILURE CONDITION(S):
1. While Driving: The LF wheel is detected at least 30 kph or 19 mph faster than the remaining wheels for an extended period of time.

   OR

   The LF wheel is at least 6 kph or 4 mph less than or greater than the remaining wheels for an extended period of time.

ACTION TAKEN:
1. Code set.
2. ABS switched 'OFF'.
3. 'ANTILOCK' indicator 'ON'.

TEST DESCRIPTION: Test numbers refer to circled numbers on the diagnostic chart.

1. Checks wiring and connections for problems. It is critical that this step is performed thoroughly, as wiring/connector problems are the most likely cause for this code.
2. Use the TECH 1 to monitor for vehicle electrical/electronic system 'noise' being picked up by the speed sensor circuits.
3. Use the TECH 1 to monitor the wheel speed sensors while the vehicle is operating. If the TECH 1 Auto–Trigger Snapshot mode triggers, the speed sensor or the wiring and/or connectors are going intermittent during the road test.
4. Checks for proper resistance in the sensor itself.

5. Replaces front wheel speed sensor as the likely cause of the triggering intermittent.
6. Use the TECH 1 to monitor the wheel speed sensors while the vehicle is operating. If the TECH 1 Auto–Snapshot mode triggers, the EBCM must be concluding there is a problem with wheel speed sensor frequencies when there is not.
7. Checks for a short to ground in the speed sensor input circuit wires. The circuit to be tested depends on which speed sensor triggered the TECH 1. The ground may be either a 'hard' short to ground, or a resistive short. A short with a resistance less that 2 megaohms, though not a hard short, can still cause Code 26 to set.

DIAGNOSTIC AIDS:

Be sure the speed sensor wiring is properly routed and retained. This will help prevent false signals due to electrical noise being picked up by the wiring.

It is very important that a thorough inspection of the wiring and connectors be performed. Failure to carefully and fully inspect wiring and connectors may result in misdiagnosis, causing part replacement with reappearance of the fault.

Check the toothed wheel for any large grooves, gouges, marks, etc. that might influence the tooth's signal at the wheel speed sensor. Also check for a buildup of foreign material in the gaps between teeth in the toothed wheel; this material may cause this fault.

A worn hub/bearing assembly may cause this fault in extreme cases; the bearing play allows the sensor–to–toothed–ring gap to change excessively. Never reuse a wheel speed sensor once it has been separated from the front hub/bearing assembly.

Fig. 108 DTC 26, Left front wheel speed sensor frequency error (Part 1 of 2). 1993 Eldorado & Seville

CIRCUIT DESCRIPTION:
As each wheel turns, the wheel speed sensor for that wheel creates a small AC voltage as a toothed speed ring, mounted in the front integral hub/bearing assembly, is passed by the stationary sensor. The sensor consists of a permanent magnet and coil and generates voltage by magnetic induction. The frequency of the wheel speed sensor signal is proportional to wheel speed.

The EBTCM/EBCM uses the wheel speed sensor signal to calculate vehicle reference speeds and individual speed, acceleration and slip values for each wheel. These values are used to determine when antilock control is required.

The EBTCM/EBCM will only set one wheel speed sensor fault code at a time, even if multiple faults exist. Detection is prioritized accordingly: LF, RR, LR, RF. Always check for additional stored codes after making repairs.

TEST CONDITION(S):
1. Tested continuously.

FAILURE CONDITION(S):
Continuity
1. While Standing: Open circuit is seen while the vehicle is standing still with the ignition 'ON'.

ACTION TAKEN:
1. Code set.
2. ABS/TCS switched 'OFF'.
3. 'ANTILOCK' indicator 'ON'.
4. 'TRACTION DISABLED' message displayed. (vehicles with TCS)

Code 27 is set if there is a short to voltage or an open in CKT 830 or 873, or faulty speed sensor. The testing for this fault occurs with the ignition 'ON' and the vehicle at rest.

NOTICE: A Code 25 may set CKT 830 or 873 lose continuity and the WSS signal is lost while driving. A Code 27 should accompany this code on the subsequent ignition cycle. If both Code 25

and Code 27 are set concurrently, diagnose Code 27 first.

TEST DESCRIPTION: Test numbers refer to circled numbers on the diagnostic chart.

1. Checks for proper resistance in the sensor itself.
2. Checks for a short to battery in either of the speed sensor circuit wires. There should be 5V on CKT 830. If there is, CKT 830 has no hard opens or shorts. The condition may be intermittent.
3. Checks for an open in both the speed sensor circuit wires.
4. Manipulates wiring and connectors, trying to induce an intermittent fault not currently present.
5. This test checks if the code resets on key–up. If so, since Tests 1–4 have validated that the circuitry and components are good, the Wheel Bearing/Speed Sensor assembly may be causing the fault.
6. Checks if Code 25 sets during a road test.
7. Code 27 sets when the vehicle is at rest: Code 25 sets with a problem in the speed sensor circuitry with the vehicle in motion. If problems are still present, Code 25 would set during the road test, not a 27. If Code 25 sets at this point, Code 25 diagnostics should be used.
8. The wheel speed sensor may be causing an intermittent fault. If Code 27 resets after sensor replacement, the EBTCM/EBCM must be concluding there is a problem present in the speed sensor circuit when there is not.

DIAGNOSTIC AIDS:

Be sure the speed sensor wiring is properly routed and retained. This will help prevent false signals due to electrical noise being picked up by the wiring.

It is very important that a thorough inspection of the wiring and connectors be performed. Failure to carefully and fully inspect wiring and connectors may result in misdiagnosis, causing part replacement with reappearance of the fault.

Fig. 109 DTC 27, Left front wheel speed sensor continuity fault (Part 1 of 2). 1993 Eldorado & Seville

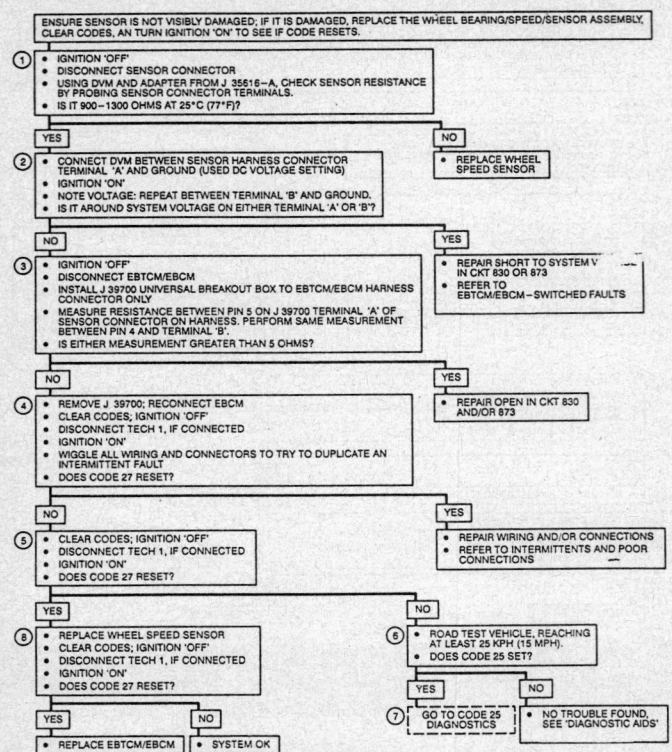

Fig. 109   DTC 27, Left front wheel speed sensor continuity fault (Part 2 of 2). 1993 Eldorado & Seville

Fig. 110   DTC 28, Wheel speed sensor frequency error (Part 1 of 2). 1993 Eldorado & Seville

TEST CONDITION(S):
1.   Tested continuously.
FAILURE CONDITION(S):
1.   While Driving: One wheel is detected at least 30 kph or 19 mph faster than the remaining wheels for an extended period of time.
     OR
     One wheel is at least 6 kph or 4 mph less than or greater than the remaining wheels for an extended period of time.
ACTION TAKEN:
1.   Code set.
2.   ABS/TCS switched 'OFF'.
3.   'ANTILOCK' indicator 'ON'.
4.   'TRACTION DISABLED' message displayed.
     Code 28 is set if the EBTCM cannot specifically identify which wheel speed sensor is causing the frequency error problem. If it can define the specific speed sensor causing the problem, the Sensor Fault code associated with the sensor (21, 25, 31, 35) will be set instead of Code 28.
TEST DESCRIPTION: Test numbers refer to circled numbers on the diagnostic chart.
1.   Checks wiring and connections for problems. It is critical that this step is performed thoroughly, as wiring/connector problems are the most likely cause for this code.
2.   Use the TECH 1 to monitor for vehicle electrical/electronic system 'noise' being picked up by the speed sensor circuits.
3.   Use the TECH 1 to monitor the wheel speed sensors while the vehicle is operating. If the TECH 1 Auto–Trigger Snapshot mode triggers, the speed sensor or the wiring and/or connectors are going intermittent during the road test.
4.   Checks for proper resistance in the sensor itself.

5a. Replace rear wheel speed sensor as the likely cause of the triggering intermittent.
5b. Replaces front wheel speed sensor as the likely cause of the triggering intermittent.
6.   Use the TECH 1 to monitor the wheel speed sensors while the vehicle is operating. If the TECH 1 Auto–Snapshot mode triggers, the EBTCM must be concluding there is a problem with wheel speed sensor frequencies when there is not.
7.   Checks for a short to ground in the speed sensor input circuit wires. The circuit to be tested depends on which speed sensor triggered the TECH 1. The ground may be either a 'hard' short to ground, or a resistive short. A short with a resistance less that 2 megaohms, though not a hard short, can still cause Code 28 to set.
DIAGNOSTIC AIDS: —
     Be sure the speed sensor wiring is properly routed and retained. This will help prevent false signals due to electrical noise being picked up by the wiring.
     It is very important that a thorough inspection of the wiring and connectors be performed. Failure to carefully and fully inspect wiring and connectors may result in misdiagnosis, causing part replacement with reappearance of the fault.
Front Speed Sensors Only:
     Check the toothed wheel for any large grooves, gouges, marks, etc. that might influence the tooth's signal at the wheel speed sensor. Also check for a buildup of foreign material in the gaps between teeth in the toothed wheel; this material may cause this fault.
     A worn hub/bearing assembly may cause this fault in extreme cases; the bearing play allows the sensor–to–toothed–ring gap to change excessively. Never reuse a wheel speed sensor once it has been separated from the front hub/bearing assembly.

Fig. 110   DTC 28, Wheel speed sensor frequency error (Part 2 of 2). 1993 Eldorado & Seville

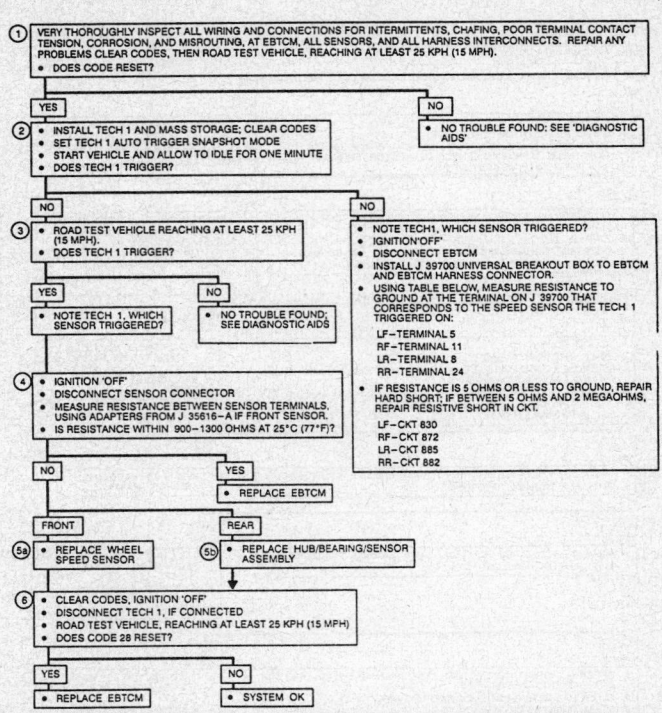

Fig. 110   DTC 28, Wheel speed sensor frequency error (Part 2 of 2). 1993 Eldorado & Seville

CIRCUIT DESCRIPTION:
     As each wheel turns, the wheel speed sensor for that wheel creates a small AC voltage as a toothed sensor ring, mounted in the front integral hub/bearing assembly, is passed by the stationary sensor. The sensor consists of a permanent magnet and coil and generates voltage by magnetic induction. The frequency of the wheel speed sensor signal is proportional to wheel speed.
     The EBTCM/EBCM uses the wheel speed sensor signal to calculate vehicle reference speeds and individual speed, acceleration and slip values for each wheel. These values are used to determine when antilock control is required.
     The EBTCM/EBCM will only set one wheel speed sensor fault code at a time, even if multiple faults exist. Detection is prioritized according: LF, RR, LR, RF. Always check for additional stored codes after making repairs.
TEST CONDITION(S):
1.   Tested continuously.
FAILURE CONDITION(S):
Sensor Output
1.   Drive–away: Speed signal is not detected when vehicle reaches 12 kph or 7.5 mph.
2.   While Driving: Speed signal is lost while vehicle speed is greater than 40 kph or 25 mph
ACTION TAKEN:
1.   Code set.
2.   ABS/TCS switched 'OFF'.
3.   'ANTILOCK' indicator 'ON'.
4.   'TRACTION DISABLED' message displayed. (vehicles with TCS)
     Code 21 is set if there is a short to voltage or ground in CKT 882 or 883, or faulty speed sensor. The testing for this fault occurs when the vehicle is in motion, it will not set with the ignition 'ON' and the vehicle at rest.

NOTICE: A Code 31 may set if CKT 882 or 883 lose continuity while driving. A Code 33 should accompany this code on the subsequent ignition cycle. If both Code 31 and Code 33 are set concurrently, diagnose Code 33 first.

TEST DESCRIPTION: Test numbers refer to circled numbers on the diagnostic chart.
1.   Checks if the code resets during a road test.
2.   Use the TECH 1 to check for sources of induced electrical noise. Some sources of induced electrical noise which may cause intermittent wheel speed sensor codes to set are: improper routing or sensor cables next to spark plug wires; cables not retained in brackets; loose fitting or improperly mounted sensors; damaged sensors or toothed rings; poor terminal engagement of connectors; or intermittent shorts or opens in wiring; or a loss of sensor circuit shield.
3.   Checks for damaged wheel speed sensor circuit shield. The shield is a foil insulator that is wrapped around the wheel speed sensor circuits. Inside the EBTCM/EBCM harness connector there is an uninsulated drain wire that is attached to the shield and jumped to the wheel speed sensor return line and taken to ground through the EBTCM/EBCM. A shield which has lost its ground through the EBTCM/EBCM leaves the sensor signal circuit susceptible to noise. It may be necessary to disassemble the EBTCM/EBCM connector to check if the drain wire has a poor connection with the wheel speed sensor return connector terminal. The shield can be repaired by reterminating the sensor return line circuit, including the drain wire.
4.   Checks for intermittent opens/shorts in wheel speed sensor circuits and connectors.

Fig. 111   DTC 31, Right rear wheel speed sensor fault (Part 1 of 4). 1993 Eldorado & Seville

CIRCUIT DESCRIPTION:

As each wheel turns, the wheel speed sensor for that wheel creates a small AC voltage as a toothed sensor ring, mounted in the front integral hub/bearing assembly, is passed by the stationary sensor. The sensor consists of a permanent magnet and coil and generates voltage by magnetic induction. The frequency of the wheel speed sensor signal is proportional to wheel speed.

The EBTCM/EBCM uses the wheel speed sensor signal to calculate vehicle reference speeds and individual speed, acceleration and slip values for each wheel. These values are used to determine when antilock control is required.

The EBTCM/EBCM will only set one wheel speed sensor fault code at a time, even if multiple faults exist. Detection is prioritized accordingly: LF, RR, LR, RF. Always check for additional stored codes after making repairs.

TEST DESCRIPTION: Test numbers refer to circled numbers on the diagnostic chart.

5. Checks for proper resistance in the sensor itself.

6. Checks for a short to battery in either of the speed sensor circuit wires.

7. Checks for a short between the speed sensor circuit wires.

8. Checks for a short to ground in the speed sensor input circuit wire. The ground may be either a 'hard' short to ground, or a resistive short. A short with a resistance less than 2 megaohms, through not a hard short, can still cause Code 21 to set.

9. Checks wiring and connectors for intermittents.

Fig. 111   DTC 31, Right rear wheel speed sensor fault (Part 3 of 4). 1993 Eldorado & Seville

NOTE: DIAGNOSE CODE 33 FIRST IF SET CONCURRENTLY.

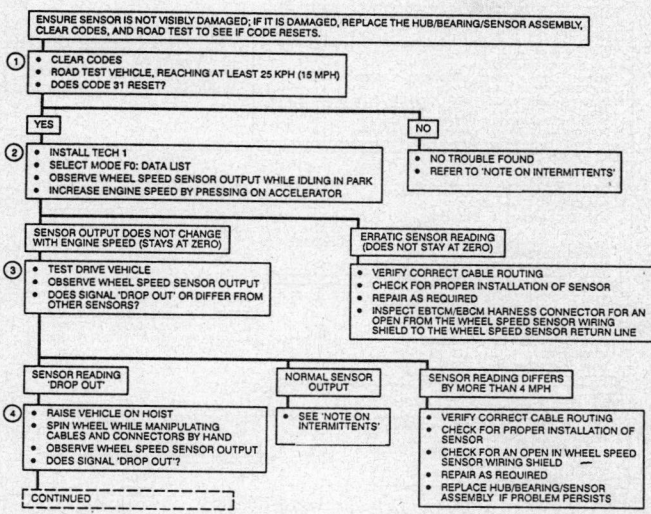

Fig. 111   DTC 31, Right rear wheel speed sensor fault (Part 2 of 4). 1993 Eldorado & Seville

DIAGNOSTIC TROUBLE CODE 32
RIGHT REAR WHEEL SPEED SENSOR FREQUENCY ERROR

TEST CONDITION(S):

1. Tested continuously.

FAILURE CONDITION(S):

1. While Driving: One wheel is detected at least 30 kph or 19 mph faster than the remaining wheels for an extended period of time.

   OR

   One wheel is at least 6 kph or 4 mph less than or greater than the remaining wheels for an extended period of time.

ACTION TAKEN:

1. Code set.
2. ABS switched 'OFF'.
3. 'ANTILOCK' indicator 'ON'.

TEST DESCRIPTION: Test numbers refer to circled numbers on the diagnostic chart.

1. Checks wiring and connections for problems. It is critical that this step is performed thoroughly, as wiring/connector problems are the most likely cause for this code.

2. Use the TECH 1 to monitor for vehicle electrical/electronic system 'noise' being picked up by the speed sensor circuits.

3. Use the TECH 1 to monitor the wheel speed sensors while the vehicle is operating. If the TECH 1 Auto–Trigger Snapshot mode triggers, the speed sensor or the wiring and/or connectors are going intermittent during the road test.

4. Checks for proper resistance in the sensor itself.

5. Replace rear wheel speed sensor as the likely cause of the triggering intermittent.

6. Use the TECH 1 to monitor the wheel speed sensors while the vehicle is operating. If the TECH 1 Auto–Snapshot mode triggers, the EBTCM/EBCM must be concluding there is a problem with wheel speed sensor frequencies when there is not.

7. Checks for a short to ground in the speed sensor input circuit wires. The circuit to be tested depends on which speed sensor triggered the TECH 1. The ground may be either a 'hard' short to ground, or a resistive short. A short with a resistance less that 2 megaohms, though not a hard short, can still cause Code 32 to set.

DIAGNOSTIC AIDS:

Be sure the speed sensor wiring is properly routed and retained. This will help prevent false signals due to electrical noise being picked up by the wiring.

It is very important that a thorough inspection of the wiring and connectors be performed. Failure to carefully and fully inspect wiring and connectors may result in misdiagnosis, causing part replacement with reappearance of the fault.

Fig. 112   DTC 32, Right rear wheel speed sensor frequency error (Part 1 of 2). 1993 Eldorado & Seville

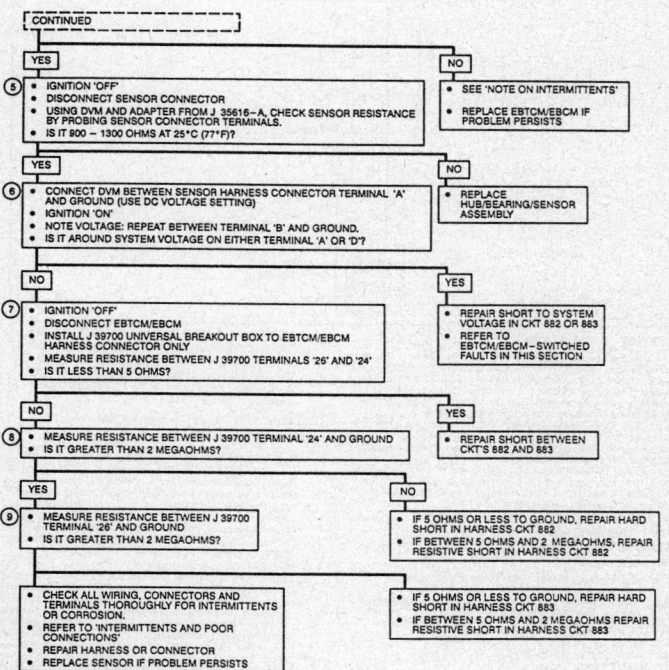

Fig. 111   DTC 31, Right rear wheel speed sensor fault (Part 4 of 4). 1993 Eldorado & Seville

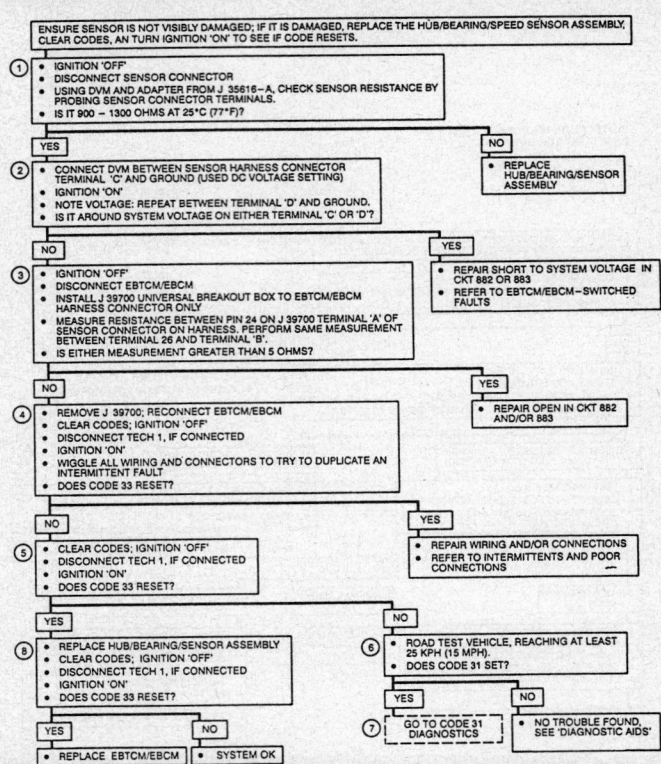

Fig. 112 DTC 32, Right rear wheel speed sensor frequency error (Part 2 of 2). 1993 Eldorado & Seville

Fig. 113 DTC 33, Right rear wheel speed sensor continuity fault (Part 2 of 2). 1993 Eldorado & Seville

CIRCUIT DESCRIPTION:

As each wheel turns, the wheel speed sensor for that wheel creates a small AC voltage as a toothed sensor ring, mounted in the front integral hub/bearing assembly, is passed by the stationary sensor. The sensor consists of a permanent magnet and coil and generates voltage by magnetic induction. The frequency of the wheel speed sensor signal is proportional to wheel speed.

The EBTCM/EBCM uses the wheel speed sensor signal to calculate vehicle reference speeds and individual speed, acceleration and slip values for each wheel. These values are used to determine when antilock control is required.

The EBTCM/EBCM will only set one wheel speed sensor fault code at a time, even if multiple faults exist. Detection is prioritized accordingly: LF,RR,LR,RF. Always check for additional stored codes after making repairs.

TEST CONDITION(S):
1. Tested continuously.

FAILURE CONDITION(S):

Continuity
1. While standing: Open circuit is seen while the vehicle is standing still with the ignition 'ON'.

ACTION TAKEN:
1. Code set.
2. ABS/TCS switched 'OFF'.
3. 'ANTILOCK' indicator 'ON'.
4. 'TRACTION DISABLED' message displayed. (vehicles with TCS)

Code 33 is set if there is a short to voltage or an open in CKT 882 or 883, or faulty speed sensor. The testing for this fault occurs with the ignition 'ON' and the vehicle at rest.

NOTICE: A Code 31 may set if CKT 882 or 883 lose continuity and the WSS signal is lost while driving. A Code 33 should accompany this code on the subsequent ignition cycle. If both Code 31 and Code 33 are set concurrently, diagnose Code 33 first.

TEST DESCRIPTION: Test numbers refer to circled numbers on the diagnostic chart.
1. Checks for proper resistance in the sensor itself.
2. Checks for a short to battery in either of the speed sensor circuit wires. There should be 5 V on CKT 882. If there is, CKT 882 has no hard opens or shorts. The condition may be intermittent.
3. Checks for an open in both the speed sensor circuit wires.
4. Manipulates wiring and connectors, trying to induce an intermittent fault not currently present.
5. This test checks if the code resets on key-up. If so, since Tests 1–4 have validated that the circuitry and components are good, the speed sensor may be causing the fault.
6. Checks if the Code 31 sets during a road test.
7. Code 33 sets when the vehicle is at rest: Code 31 sets with a problem in the speed sensor circuitry with the vehicle in motion. If problems are still present, Code 31 would set during the road test, not a 33. If Code 33 sets at this point, Code 31 diagnostics should be used.
8. The wheel speed sensor may be causing an intermittent fault. If Code 33 resets after sensor replacement, the EBTCM/EBCM must be concluding there is a problem present in the speed sensor circuit when there is not.

DIAGNOSTIC AIDS:

Be sure the speed sensor wiring is properly routed and retained. This will help prevent false signals due to electrical noise being picked up by the wiring.

It is very important that a thorough inspection of the wiring and connectors be performed. Failure to carefully and fully inspect wiring and connectors may result in misdiagnosis, causing part replacement with reappearance of the fault.

Fig. 113 DTC 33, Right rear wheel speed sensor continuity fault (Part 1 of 2). 1993 Eldorado & Seville

CIRCUIT DESCRIPTION:

As each wheel turns, the wheel speed sensor for that wheel creates a small AC voltage as a toothed sensor ring, mounted in the front integral hub/bearing assembly, is passed by the stationary sensor. The sensor consists of a permanent magnet and coil and generates voltage by magnetic induction. The frequency of the wheel speed sensor signal is proportional to wheel speed.

The EBTCM/EBCM uses the wheel speed sensor signal to calculate vehicle reference speeds and individual speed, acceleration and slip values for each wheel. These values are used to determine when antilock control is required.

The EBTCM/EBCM will only set one wheel speed sensor fault code at a time, even if multiple faults exist. Detection is prioritized accordingly: LF,RR,LR,RF. Always check for additional stored codes after making repairs.

TEST CONDITION(S):
1. Tested continuously.

FAILURE CONDITION(S):

Sensor Output
1. Drive–away: Speed signal is not detected when vehicle reaches 12 kph or 7.5 mph.
2. While Driving: Speed signal is lost when vehicle speed is greater than 40 kph or 25 mph.

ACTION TAKEN:
1. Code set.
2. ABS/TCS switched 'OFF'.
3. 'ANTILOCK' indicator 'ON'.
4. 'TRACTION DISABLED' message displayed. (vehicles with TCS)

Code 35 is set if there is a short to voltage or ground in CKT 885 or 884, or faulty speed sensor. The testing for this fault occurs when the vehicle is in motion, it will not set with the ignition 'ON' and the vehicle at rest.

NOTICE: A Code 35 may set if CKT 884 or 885 lose continuity and the WSS signal is lost while driving. A Code 37 should accompany this code on the subsequent ignition cycle. If both Code 35 and Code 37 are set concurrently, diagnose Code 37 first.

TEST DESCRIPTION: Test numbers refer to circled numbers on the diagnostic chart.
1. Checks if the code resets during a road test.
2. Use the TECH 1 to check for sources of induced electrical noise. Some sources of induced electrical noise which may cause intermittent wheel speed sensor codes to set are: improper routing or sensor cables next to spark plug wires; cables not retained in brackets; loose fitting or improperly mounted sensors; damaged sensors or toothed rings; poor terminal engagement of connectors; or intermittent shorts or opens in wiring; or a loss of sensor circuit shield.
3. Checks for damaged wheel speed sensor circuit shield. The shield is a foil insulator that is wrapped around the wheel speed sensor circuits. Inside the EBTCM/EBCM harness connector there is an uninsulated drain wire that is attached to the shield and jumped to the wheel speed sensor return line and taken to ground through the EBTCM/EBCM. A shield which has lost its ground through the EBTCM/EBCM leaves the sensor signal circuit susceptible to noise. It may be necessary to disassemble the EBTCM/EBCM connector to check if the drain wire has a poor connection with the wheel speed sensor return connector terminal. The shield can be repaired by reterminating the sensor return line circuit, including the drain wire.
4. Checks for intermittent opens/shorts in wheel speed sensor circuits and cables.

Fig. 114 DTC 35, Left rear wheel speed sensor fault (Part 1 of 4). 1993 Eldorado & Seville

Fig. 119   DTC 45, Left front ABS valve solenoid fault (Part 2 of 4). 1993 Eldorado & Seville

CIRCUIT DESCRIPTION:

The left front valve solenoid in the BPM Valve may be commanded to three different positions by the EBTCM/EBCM. Valve position is determined by the amount of current which is allowed to flow through the solenoid valve coil.

The valve solenoid circuits receive power through the valve relay on the BPM Valve. The valve relay is engaged at KEY—ON and remains engaged throughout the ignition cycle. Valve solenoid circuits should have battery voltage available at all times.

When the key is turned to RUN, power is supplied to the EBTCM/EBCM. The EBTCM/EBCM will complete an internal self—check before providing ground to the valve relay. When the valve relay is energized, battery power is supplied to the valve solenoids.

TEST DESCRIPTION: Test numbers refer to circled numbers on the diagnostic chart.

7. Checks for a short to battery in CKT 886 using

EBTCM/EBCM terminal '20' as ground.
8. Checks for a short to battery in CKT 886 using EBTCM/EBCM terminal '20' as ground.
9. Checks for a short to ground in CKT 886 using EBTCM/EBCM terminal '20' as ground.
10. Checks for a short to ground in CKT 858 using EBTCM/EBCM terminal '20' as ground.
11. Checks wiring and connectors for intermittents.
12. Uses the TECH 1 to exercise the LF ABS valve solenoid and check it for proper operation.
13. Determines whether the code was set by an intermittent condition or an EBTCM/EBCM fault.

DIAGNOSTIC AIDS:

All tests using J 39700 Universal Breakout Box terminal '20' are using the terminal as ground. These tests, of course, assume that the ground CKT 1250 terminal '20' is good.

If Codes 41 and 45 are both set, the fault is likely to be an open or high resistance on CKT 886.

Fig. 119   DTC 45, Left front ABS valve solenoid fault (Part 3 of 4). 1993 Eldorado & Seville

Fig. 119   DTC 45, Left front ABS valve solenoid fault (Part 4 of 4). 1993 Eldorado & Seville

CIRCUIT DESCRIPTION:

The left front TCS pilot valve in the BPM Valve may be commanded to close, isolating the master cylinder.

The pilot valve circuits receive power through the valve relay on the BPM Valve. The valve relay is engaged at KEY—ON and remains engaged throughout the ignition cycle. Pilot valve circuits should have battery voltage available at all times.

When the key is turned to RUN, power is supplied to the EBTCM. The EBTCM will complete an internal self—check before providing ground to the valve relay. When the valve relay is energized, battery power is supplied to the pilot valves.

TEST CONDITION(S):
1. Tested continuously.

FAILURE CONDITION(S):
While standing or driving:
1. Valve cannot be activated.

    OR

2. Valve is activated in a defective way.

ACTION TAKEN:
1. Code set.
2. ABS/TCS switched 'OFF'.
3. 'ANTILOCK' indicator 'ON'.
4. 'TRACTION DISABLED' message displayed.

Code 48 will set when the expected position of the right front TCS pilot valve does not match the commanded position from the EBTCM. Conditions which could cause Code 48 to set are: damage to the right front TCS pilot valve; an open circuit; or a short circuit to ground or battery on CKT 1657.

TEST DESCRIPTION: Test numbers refer to circled numbers on the diagnostic chart.

1. Damage to CKT 886 may result in multiple valve solenoid codes setting.
2. Checks CKT 886 for opens or high resistance from EBTCM/EBCM terminal '23' to '32'.
3. Checks which branch of CKT 886 has an open or high resistance.
4. Checks the integrity of CKTs 1657 and 886, the TCS Pilot Valve circuitry internal to the BPM Valve, and the TCS Pilot Valve Solenoid coil.
5. Determines whether a problem found in Step 4 is due to an open in CKTs 886, 1657 or a faulty BPM Modulator Valve.
6. Determines whether the problem found in Step 4 is due to an open in CKT 886 or 1657.

DIAGNOSTIC AIDS:

All tests using J 39700 Universal Breakout Box terminal '20' are using the terminal as ground. These tests, of course, assume that the ground CKT 1250 terminal '20' is good.

If Codes 44 and 48 are both set, the fault is likely to be an open or short in CKT 886.

Fig. 120   DTC 48, Left front TCS pilot valve fault (Part 1 of 4). 1993 Eldorado & Seville

1991 REATTA, 1991-92 BROUGHAM, TORONADO & TROFEO & 1991-93 CAPRICE, CUSTOM CRUISER, ELDORADO, RIVIERA, ROADMASTER, SEVILLE (BOSCH 2 U TYPE)

23-201

CIRCUIT DESCRIPTION:

The left front TCS pilot valve in the BPM VALVE may be commanded to close, isolating the master cylinder.

The pilot valve circuits receive power through the valve relay on the BPM VALVE. The valve relay is engaged at KEY–ON and remains engaged throughout the ignition cycle. Pilot valve circuits should have battery voltage available at all times.

When the key is turned to RUN, power is supplied to the EBTCM. The EBTCM will complete an internal self–check before providing ground to the valve relay. When the valve relay is energized, battery power is supplied to the pilot valves.

TEST DESCRIPTION: Test numbers refer to circled numbers on the diagnostic chart.

7. Checks for a short to battery in CKT 886 using EBTCM/EBCM terminal '20' as ground.

8. Checks for a short to battery in CKT 1657, using EBTCM terminal '20' as ground.

9. Checks for a short to ground in CKT 886 using EBTCM terminal '20' as ground.

10. Checks for a short to ground in CKT 1657, using EBTCM terminal '20' as ground.

11. Checks for connector or wiring problems which could cause intermittents.

12. Uses the TECH 1 to exercise the TCS pilot valve solenoid and check it for proper operation.

13. Determines whether the code was set by an intermittent conditions or an EBTCM fault.

DIAGNOSTIC AIDS:

All tests using J 39700 Universal Breakout Box terminal '20' are using the terminal as ground. These tests, of course, assume that the ground CKT 1250 terminal '20' is good.

If Codes 44 and 48 are both set, the fault is likely to be an open or short in CKT 886.

Fig. 120   DTC 48, Left front TCS pilot valve fault (Part 2 of 4). 1993 Eldorado & Seville

Fig. 120   DTC 48, Left front TCS pilot valve fault (Part 3 of 4). 1993 Eldorado & Seville

CIRCUIT DESCRIPTION:

The right rear valve solenoid in the BPM Valve may be commanded to three different positions by the EBTCM/EBCM. Valve position is determined by the amount of current which is allowed to flow through the valve solenoid coil.

The valve solenoid circuits receive power through the valve relay on the BPM Valve. The valve relay is engaged at KEY–ON and remains engaged throughout the ignition cycle. Valve solenoid circuits should have battery voltage available at all times.

When the key is turned to RUN, power is supplied to the EBTCM/EBCM. The EBTCM/EBCM will complete an internal self–check before providing ground to the valve relay. When the valve relay is energized, battery power is supplied to the valve solenoids.

TEST CONDITION(S):
1. Tested continuously.

FAILURE CONDITION(S):
While standing or driving:
1. Valve solenoid cannot be activated.
OR
2. Valve solenoid is activated in a defective way.

ACTION TAKEN:
1. Code set.
2. ABS/TCS switched 'OFF'.
3. 'ANTILOCK' indicator 'ON'.

4. 'TRACTION DISABLED' message displayed. (vehicles with TCS)

Code 51 will set when the expected position of the right rear valve solenoid does not match the commanded position from the EBTCM/EBCM. Conditions which could cause Code 51 to set are: damage to the right rear valve solenoid; and open circuit; or a short circuit to ground or battery on CKT 859.

TEST DESCRIPTION: Test numbers refer to circled numbers on the diagnostic chart.

1. Damage to CKT 886 may result in multiple valve solenoid codes setting.

2. Checks CKT 886 for opens or high resistance from EBTCM/EBCM terminal '23' to '32'.

3. Determines which branch of CKT 886 has an open or high resistance.

4. Checks the integrity of CKTs 859 and 886, the RR ABS Valve Solenoid circuitry internal to the BPM Valve, and the RR ABS Valve Solenoid coil.

5. Determines whether a problem found in Step 4 is due to an open in CKT 859, 886, or a faulty BPM Valve.

6. Determines whether the problem found in Step 4 is due to an open in CKT 859 or 886.

DIAGNOSTIC AIDS:

All tests using J 39700 Universal Breakout Box terminal '20' are using the terminal as ground. These tests, of course, assume that the ground CKT 1250 terminal '20' is good.

Fig. 120   DTC 48, Left front TCS pilot valve fault (Part 4 of 4). 1993 Eldorado & Seville

Fig. 121   DTC 51, Right rear ABS valve solenoid fault (Part 1 of 4). 1993 Eldorado & Seville

Fig. 121 DTC 51, Right rear ABS valve solenoid fault (Part 2 of 4). 1993 Eldorado & Seville

CIRCUIT DESCRIPTION:

The right rear valve solenoid in the BPM Valve may be commanded to three different positions by the EBTCM/EBCM. Valve position is determined by the amount of current which is allowed to flow through the valve solenoid coil.

The valve solenoid circuits receive power through the valve relay on the BPM Valve. The valve relay is engaged at KEY—ON and remains engaged throughout the ignition cycle. Valve solenoid circuits should have battery voltage available at all times.

When the key is turned to RUN, power is supplied to the EBTCM/EBCM. The EBTCM/EBCM will complete an internal self—check before providing ground to the valve relay. When the valve relay is energized, battery power is supplied to the valve solenoids.

TEST DESCRIPTION: Test numbers refer to circled numbers on the diagnostic chart.

7. Checks for a short to battery in CKT 886 using EBTCM/EBCM terminal '20' as ground.
8. Checks for a short to battery in CKT 859, using EBTCM/EBCM terminal '20' as ground.
9. Checks for a short to ground in CKT 886 using EBTCM/EBCM terminal '20' as ground.
10. Checks for a short to ground in CKT 859, using EBTCM/EBCM terminal '20' as ground.
11. Checks wiring and connectors for intermittents.
12. Uses the TECH 1 to exercise the RR ABS valve solenoid and check it for proper operation.
13. Determines whether the code was set by an intermittent conditions or an EBTCM/EBCM fault.

DIAGNOSTIC AIDS:

All tests using J 39700 Universal Breakout Box terminal '20' are using the terminal as ground. These tests, of course, assume that the ground CKT 1250 terminal '20' is good.

Fig. 121 DTC 51, Right rear ABS valve solenoid fault (Part 3 of 4). 1993 Eldorado & Seville

CIRCUIT DESCRIPTION:

The left rear valve solenoid (TCS) or rear valve solenoid (non–TCS) in the BPM Valve may be commanded to three different positions by the EBTCM/EBCM. Valve position is determined by the amount of current which is allowed to flow through the valve solenoid coil.

The valve solenoid circuits receive power through the valve relay on the BPM Valve. The valve relay is engaged at KEY–ON and remains engaged throughout the ignition cycle. Valve solenoid circuits should have battery voltage available at all times.

When the key is turned to RUN, power is supplied to the EBTCM/EBCM. The EBTCM/EBCM will complete an internal self–check before providing ground to the valve relay. When the valve relay is energized, battery power is supplied to the valve solenoids.

TEST CONDITION(S):
1. Tested continuously.

FAILURE CONDITION(S):
While standing or driving:
1. Valve solenoid cannot be activated.
    OR
2. Valve solenoid is activated in a defective way.

ACTION TAKEN:
1. Code set.
2. ABS/TCS switched 'OFF'.
3. 'ANTILOCK' indicator 'ON'.
4. 'TRACTION DISABLED' message displayed (vehicles with TCS)

Code 55 will set when the expected position of the right rear valve solenoid does not match the commanded position from the EBTCM/EBCM. Conditions which could cause Code 55 to set are: damage to the left rear/rear valve solenoid; an open circuit; or a short circuit to ground or battery on CKT 1290.

TEST DESCRIPTION: Test numbers refer to circled numbers on the diagnostic chart.

1. Damage to CKT 886 may result in multiple valve solenoid codes setting.
2. Checks CKT 886 for opens or high resistance from EBTCM/EBCM terminal '23' to '32'.
3. Determines which branch of CKT 886 has an open or high resistance.
4. Checks the integrity of CKTs 1290 and 886, the LR/Rear ABS Valve Solenoid circuitry internal to the BPM Valve, and the LR/Rear ABS Valve Solenoid coil.
5. Determines whether a problem found in Step 4 is due to an open in CKT 1290, 886, or a faulty BPM Valve.
6. Determines whether the problem found in Step 4 is due to an open in CKT 1290 or 886.

DIAGNOSTIC AIDS:

All tests using J 39700 Universal Breakout Box terminal '20' are using the terminal as ground. These tests, of course, assume that the ground CKT 1250 terminal '20' is good.

If Codes 41 and 55 are both set, the fault is likely to be a short to B+ on 1290.

Fig. 121 DTC 51, Right rear ABS valve solenoid fault (Part 4 of 4). 1993 Eldorado & Seville

Fig. 122 DTC 55, Left rear valve solenoid valve (vehicles equipped w/TCS; rear valve solenoid valve fault for vehicles not equipped w/TCS) (Part 1 of 4). 1993 Eldorado & Seville

1991 REATTA, 1991-92 BROUGHAM, TORONADO & TROFEO & 1991-93 CAPRICE, CUSTOM CRUISER, ELDORADO, RIVIERA, ROADMASTER, SEVILLE (BOSCH 2 U TYPE)

23-203

CIRCUIT DESCRIPTION:

The left rear valve solenoid (TCS) or rear valve solenoid (non–TCS) in the BPM Valve may be commanded to three different positions by the EBTCM/EBCM. Valve position is determined by the amount of current which is allowed to flow through the valve solenoid coil.

The valve solenoid circuits receive power through the valve relay on the BPM valve. The valve relay is engaged at KEY–ON and remains engaged throughout the ignition cycle. Valve solenoid circuits should have battery voltage available at all times.

When the key is turned to RUN, power is supplied to the EBTCM/EBCM. The EBTCM/EBCM will complete an internal self–check before providing ground to the valve relay. When the valve relay is energized, battery power is supplied to the valve solenoids.

TEST DESCRIPTION: Test numbers refer to circled numbers on the diagnostic chart.

7. Checks for a short to battery in CKT 886 using EBTCM/EBCM terminal '20' as ground.

8. Checks for a short to battery in CKT 1290, using EBTCM/EBCM terminal '20' as ground.
9. Checks for a short to ground in CKT 886 using EBTCM/EBCM terminal '20' as ground.
10. Checks for a short to ground in CKT 1290, using EBTCM/EBCM terminal '20' as ground.
11. Checks wiring and connectors for intermittents.
12. Uses the TECH 1 to exercise the LR (TCS) or rear (non–TCS) ABS valve solenoid and check it for proper operation.
13. Determines whether the code was set by an intermittent conditions or an EBTCM/EBCM fault.

DIAGNOSTIC AIDS:

All tests using J 39700 Universal Breakout Box terminal '20' are using the terminal as ground. These tests, of course, assume that the ground CKT 1250 terminal '20' is good.

If Codes 41 and 55 are both set, the fault is likely to be a short to B+ on CKT 1290.

Fig. 122 DTC 55, Left rear valve solenoid valve (vehicles equipped w/TCS; rear valve solenoid valve fault for vehicles not equipped w/TCS) (Part 3 of 4). 1993 Eldorado & Seville

Fig. 122 DTC 55, Left rear valve solenoid valve (vehicles equipped w/TCS; rear valve solenoid valve fault for vehicles not equipped w/TCS) (Part 2 of 4). 1993 Eldorado & Seville

CIRCUIT DESCRIPTION:

The pump motor returns brake fluid to the master cylinder brake circuit at the BPM Valve during antilock braking and provides brake fluid pressure to the front wheels during traction control. During normal braking, the pump does not operate. When the vehicle begins to move after start–up, the EBTCM/EBCM will turn on the pump motor and perform a self–check of the pump motor and pump motor circuit. This check may be felt and heard by the driver when the vehicle begins to move. The self–check should be considered normal operation. The pump motor is an integral component of the BPM Valve and cannot be serviced separately.

The pump motor relay provides power to the pump motor in the BPM Valve. The pump motor relay is located on the BPM Valve and may be replaced if it is found to be defective.

The pump motor relay is not engaged during normal system operation. When antilock or traction control operation is required, the motor relay actuation line on CKT 874 (EBTCM/EBCM pin '28') is pulled to ground. The pump motor relay is engaged by the relay supply voltage line on CKT 854 (EBTCM/EBCM pin '17'). When the relay switches, battery power is provided to the pump motor.

TEST CONDITION(S):
1. Tested continuously.

FAILURE CONDITION(S):
1. Drive Away: Motor relay voltage is not detected during first drive away after engine start.
2. While Driving: Motor relay is energized and motor voltage is not detected.
3. Voltage at EBTCM/EBCM pin '14' below 9 volts.
4. Pump runs continuously.

ACTION TAKEN:
1. Code set.
2. ABS/TCS switched 'OFF'.
3. 'ANTILOCK' indicator 'ON'.
4. 'TRACTION DISABLED' message displayed. (vehicles with TCS)

When the pump motor relay is engaged, the motor monitor line should be at battery voltage. With the pump motor relay disengaged, the monitoring line should be at ground. If the commanded position of the pump motor relay and motor monitor line do not agree, Code 61 will set. Some conditions which will cause Code 61 to set are:
• An open circuit on CKTs 874 or 1292
• A short to voltage on CKTs 874 or 1292
• A short to ground on CKTs 874 or 1292
• A defective pump motor relay or pump motor

TEST DESCRIPTION: Test numbers refer to circled numbers on the diagnostic chart.
1. Checks the pump motor relay coil for proper resistance.
2. Determines if the pump motor relay contacts are stuck closed.
3. Determines if the pump motor relay contacts are stuck open.

DIAGNOSTIC AIDS:

All tests using J 39700 Universal Breakout Box terminal '20' are using the terminal as ground. These tests, of course, assume that the ground CKT 1250 at terminal '20' is good.

It is very important that a thorough inspection of the wiring and connectors be performed. Failure to carefully and fully inspect wiring and connectors may result in misdiagnosis, causing part replacement with reappearance of the fault.

Fig. 122 DTC 55, Left rear valve solenoid valve (vehicles equipped w/TCS; rear valve solenoid valve fault for vehicles not equipped w/TCS) (Part 4 of 4). 1993 Eldorado & Seville

Fig. 123 DTC 61, Pump motor or pump motor relay fault (Part 1 of 6). 1993 Eldorado & Seville

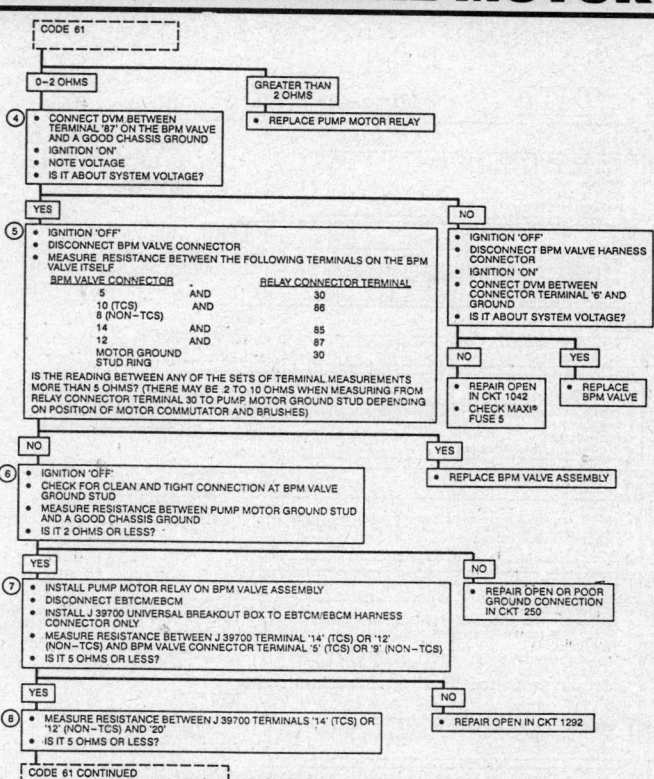

CODE 61

0–2 OHMS | GREATER THAN 2 OHMS
→ REPLACE PUMP MOTOR RELAY

④
- CONNECT DVM BETWEEN TERMINAL '87' ON THE BPM VALVE AND A GOOD CHASSIS GROUND
- IGNITION 'ON'
- NOTE VOLTAGE
- IS IT ABOUT SYSTEM VOLTAGE?

YES / NO

⑤
- IGNITION 'OFF'
- DISCONNECT BPM VALVE CONNECTOR
- MEASURE RESISTANCE BETWEEN THE FOLLOWING TERMINALS ON THE BPM VALVE ITSELF

BPM VALVE CONNECTOR		RELAY CONNECTOR TERMINAL
5	AND	30
10 (TCS)	AND	86
8 (NON–TCS)		
14	AND	85
12	AND	87
MOTOR GROUND STUD RING	AND	30

IS THE READING BETWEEN ANY OF THE SETS OF TERMINAL MEASUREMENTS MORE THAN 5 OHMS? (THERE MAY BE .2 TO 10 OHMS WHEN MEASURING FROM RELAY CONNECTOR TERMINAL 30 TO PUMP MOTOR GROUND STUD DEPENDING ON POSITION OF MOTOR COMMUTATOR AND BRUSHES.)

(right branch of ⑤)
- IGNITION 'OFF'
- DISCONNECT BPM VALVE HARNESS CONNECTOR
- IGNITION 'ON'
- CONNECT DVM BETWEEN CONNECTOR TERMINAL '6' AND GROUND
- IS IT ABOUT SYSTEM VOLTAGE?

NO → REPAIR OPEN IN CKT 1042 • CHECK MAXI® FUSE 5

YES → REPLACE BPM VALVE

NO / YES → REPLACE BPM VALVE ASSEMBLY

⑥
- IGNITION 'OFF'
- CHECK FOR CLEAN AND TIGHT CONNECTION AT BPM VALVE GROUND STUD
- MEASURE RESISTANCE BETWEEN PUMP MOTOR GROUND STUD AND A GOOD CHASSIS GROUND
- IS IT 2 OHMS OR LESS?

YES / NO → REPAIR OPEN OR POOR GROUND CONNECTION IN CKT 250

⑦
- INSTALL PUMP MOTOR RELAY ON BPM VALVE ASSEMBLY
- DISCONNECT EBTCM/EBCM
- INSTALL J 39700 UNIVERSAL BREAKOUT BOX TO EBTCM/EBCM HARNESS CONNECTOR ONLY
- MEASURE RESISTANCE BETWEEN J 39700 TERMINAL '14' (TCS) OR '12' (NON–TCS) AND BPM VALVE CONNECTOR TERMINAL '5' (TCS) OR '9' (NON–TCS)
- IS IT 5 OHMS OR LESS?

YES / NO → REPAIR OPEN IN CKT 1292

⑧
- MEASURE RESISTANCE BETWEEN J 39700 TERMINALS '14' (TCS) OR '12' (NON–TCS) AND '20'
- IS IT 5 OHMS OR LESS?

CODE 61 CONTINUED

Fig. 123   DTC 61, Pump motor or pump motor relay fault (Part 3 of 6). 1993 Eldorado & Seville

①
- IGNITION 'OFF'
- REMOVE BPM COVER AND PUMP MOTOR RELAY (4–PIN)
- MEASURE RESISTANCE BETWEEN PUMP MOTOR RELAY PINS 85 AND 86

45–55 Ω | OUTSIDE 45–55 Ω

②
- MEASURE RESISTANCE BETWEEN PUMP MOTOR RELAY PINS 30 AND 87 → REPLACE PUMP MOTOR RELAY

OPEN CIRCUIT | CONTINUITY

③
- USING A FUSED JUMPER, APPLY SYSTEM VOLTAGE TO PUMP MOTOR RELAY PIN 86 AND ATTACH A GROUND WIRE TO PIN 85
- MEASURE RESISTANCE BETWEEN PUMP MOTOR RELAY PINS 30 AND 87 → REPLACE PUMP MOTOR RELAY

CODE 61 CONTINUED

Fig. 123   DTC 61, Pump motor or pump motor relay fault (Part 2 of 6). 1993 Eldorado & Seville

CIRCUIT DESCRIPTION:

The pump motor returns brake fluid to the master cylinder brake circuit at the BPM valve during antilock braking and provides brake fluid pressure to the front wheels during traction control. During normal braking, the pump does not operate. When the vehicle begins to move after start–up, the EBTCM/EBCM will turn on the pump motor and perform a self–check of the pump motor and pump motor circuit. This check may be felt and heard by the driver when the vehicle begins to move. The self–check should be considered normal operation. The pump motor is an integral component of the BPM valve and cannot be serviced separately.

The pump motor relay provides power to the pump motor in the BPM valve. The pump motor relay is located on the BPM valve and may be replaced if it is found to be defective.

The pump motor relay is not engaged during normal system operation. When antilock or traction control operation is required, the motor relay actuation line on CKT 874 (EBTCM/EBCM pin '28') is pulled to ground. The pump motor relay is engaged by the relay supply voltage line on CKT 854 (EBTCM/EBCM pin '17'). When the relay switches, battery power is provided to the pump motor.

TEST DESCRIPTION: Test numbers refer to circled numbers on the diagnostic chart.

4. Checks for an open in power feed CKT 1042.
5. Checks the integrity of the pump motor and pump motor relay circuitry internal to the BPM valve.
6. Checks for a good ground to the BPM valve (CKT 250).
7. Checks for an open in CKT 1292.
8. Checks for a short to ground in CKT 1292.

DIAGNOSTIC AIDS:

All tests using J 39700 Universal Breakout Box terminal '20' are using the terminal as ground. These tests, of course, assume that the ground CKT 1250 at terminal '20' is good.

It is very important that a thorough inspection of the wiring and connectors be performed. Failure to carefully and fully inspect wiring and connectors may result in misdiagnosis, causing part replacement with reappearance of the fault.

Fig. 123   DTC 61, Pump motor or pump motor relay fault (Part 4 of 6). 1993 Eldorado & Seville

CIRCUIT DESCRIPTION:

The pump motor returns brake fluid to the master cylinder brake circuit at the BPM valve during antilock braking and provides brake fluid pressure to the front wheels during traction control. During normal braking, the pump does not operate. When the vehicle begins to move after start–up, the EBTCM/EBCM will turn on the pump motor and perform a self–check of the pump motor and pump motor circuit. This check may be felt and heard by the driver when the vehicle begins to move. The self–check should be considered normal operation. The pump motor is an integral component of the BPM valve and cannot be serviced separately.

The pump motor relay provides power to the pump motor in the BPM valve. The pump motor relay is located on the BPM valve and may be replaced if it is found to be defective.

The pump motor relay is not engaged during normal system operation. When antilock or traction control operation is required, the motor relay actuation line on CKT 874 (EBTCM/EBCM pin '28') is pulled to ground. The pump motor relay is engaged by the relay supply voltage line on CKT 854 (EBTCM/EBCM pin '17'). When the relay switches, battery power is provided to the pump motor.

TEST DESCRIPTION: Test numbers refer to circled numbers on the diagnostic chart.

9. Checks for a short to system voltage in CKT 1292.
10. Checks for an open in CKT 874.
11. Checks for a short to ground on CKT 874.
12. Checks for a short to B+ in CKT 874.
13. Checks wiring and connectors for intermittents.
14. Uses the TECH 1 to check for proper operation of the pump motor and associated circuitry.
15. Determines whether the problem found in Step 13 was due to a faulty EBTCM/EBCM or BPM valve.

DIAGNOSTIC AIDS:

All tests using J 39700 Universal Breakout Box terminal '20' are using the terminal as ground. These tests, of course, assume that the ground CKT 1250 at terminal '20' is good.

It is very important that a thorough inspection of the wiring and connectors be performed. Failure to carefully and fully inspect wiring and connectors may result in misdiagnosis, causing part replacement with reappearance of the fault.

Fig. 123   DTC 61, Pump motor or pump motor relay fault (Part 5 of 6). 1993 Eldorado & Seville

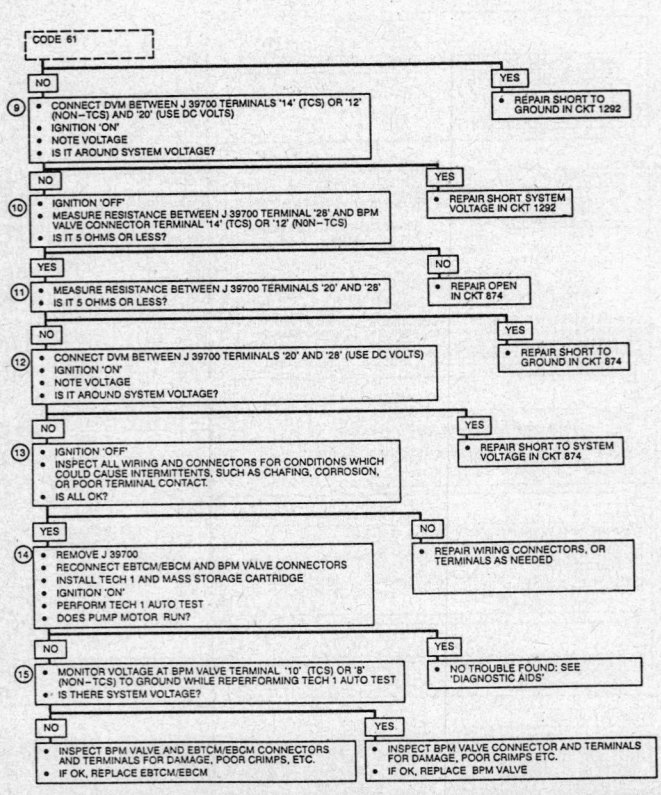

Fig. 123   DTC 61, Pump motor or pump motor relay fault (Part 6 of 6). 1993 Eldorado & Seville

CIRCUIT DESCRIPTION:

The valve relay provides power to the four ABS valve solenoids and two TCS Pilot Valves (if applicable) in the BPM valve. The valve relay is located on the BPM valve an may be replaced if it is found to be defective.

The valve relay is engaged during normal system operation. When the ignition is switched to RUN, the EBTCM/EBCM commands the valve relay ON by grounding the valve relay actuation line on CKT 856 (EBTCM/EBCM pin '27'). When this ground is provided, the valve relay is energized from the voltage supply line on CKT 854 (EBTCM/EBCM pin '17'). The valve relay switches and battery voltage is provided to the four valve solenoids, the pilot valves and the valve relay voltage sense line on CKT 886 (EBTCM/EBCM pin '23'). The valve relay remains engaged until the ignition is turned OFF or a failure is detected.

The valve relay voltage feedback (EBTCM/EBCM pin '32') provides suppression of voltage spikes created during operation of both front ABS valve solenoids during antilock and traction control.

TEST CONDITION(S):
1. Tested continuously.

FAILURE CONDITION(S):
1. Less than 5 volts at EBTCM/EBCM pin '23', valve relay sense;

   OR
2. Voltage at EBTCM/EBCM pin '23', valve relay sense remains high, although voltage at EBTCM/EBCM pin '27', valve relay control, is low (valve relay sticks).

ACTION TAKEN:
1. Code set.
2. ABS/TCS switched 'OFF'.
3. 'ANTILOCK' indicator 'ON'.
4. 'TRACTION DISABLED' message displayed.

When the valve relay is engaged, the valve relay sense line should be at battery voltage. With the valve relay disengaged, the sense line should be at ground. If the commanded position of the valve relay and the position indicated by the sense line do not agree, Code 63 will set. Some conditions which will cause Code 63 to set are:
- An open circuit on CKT 886 or 856.
- A short to voltage on CKT 886 or 856.
- A short to ground on CKT 886 or 856.
- A defective solenoid valve relay.
- Open circuit on CKT 854.
- Loss of voltage to BPM valve terminals '6' and '12' during pump run.

TEST DESCRIPTION: Test numbers refer to circled numbers on the diagnostic chart.
1. Checks for availability of battery voltage to the Valve Relay through Maxi® fuse 5 and CKT 1042.
2. Checks for possible loss of voltage current when system is under load. At Key–ON, system performs the power on Reset Test and cycles the valve relay, checking the current draw of valves.
3. Checks the Valve Relay coil for proper resistance.
4. Checks for the Valve Relay contacts being internally open when in the relay unenergized position.
5. Checks for the Valve Relay contacts being stuck open when in the relay–energized position.

DIAGNOSTIC AIDS:

All tests using J 39700 Universal Breakout Box terminal '20' are using the terminal as ground. These tests, of course, assume that the ground CKT 1250 at terminal '20' is good.

It is very important that a thorough inspection of the wiring and connectors be performed. Failure to carefully and fully inspect wiring and connectors may result in misdiagnosis, causing part replacement with reappearance of the fault.

Fig. 124   DTC 63, Valve relay fault (Part 1 of 6). 1993 Eldorado & Seville

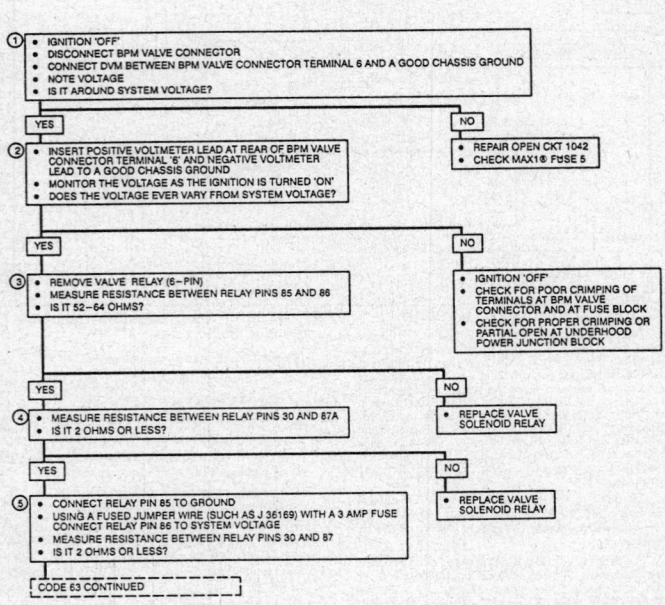

Fig. 124   DTC 63, Valve relay fault (Part 2 of 6). 1993 Eldorado & Seville

CIRCUIT DESCRIPTION:

The valve relay provides power to the four ABS valve solenoids and two TCS Pilot Valves (if applicable) in the BPM valve. The valve relay is located on the BPM valve an may be replaced if it is found to be defective.

The valve relay is engaged during normal system operation. When the ignition is switched to RUN, the EBTCM/EBCM commands the valve relay ON by grounding the valve relay actuation line on CKT 856 (EBTCM/EBCM pin '27'). When this ground is provided, the valve relay is energized from the voltage supply line on CKT 854 (EBTCM/EBCM pin '17'). The valve relay switches and battery voltage is provided to the four valve solenoids, the pilot valves and the valve relay voltage sense line on CKT 886 (EBTCM/EBCM pin '23'). The valve relay remains engaged until the ignition is turned 'OFF' or a failure is detected.

The valve relay voltage feedback (EBTCM/EBCM pin '32') provides suppression of voltage spikes created during operation of both front ABS valve solenoids during antilock and traction control.

TEST DESCRIPTION: Test numbers refer to circled numbers on the diagnostic chart.
5. Checks the integrity of the Valve Relay circuitry internal to the BPM valve.
6. Checks for an open in CKT 250.
7. Checks for an open in CKT 886.
8. Checks for an open between splice S140 and EBTCM/EBCM terminal '23'.
9. Checks for a short to ground in CKT 886.
10. Checks for a short to system voltage in CKT 886.
11. Checks for an open in CKT 854.
12. Checks for a short to ground in CKT 854.

DIAGNOSTIC AIDS:

All tests using J 39700 Universal Breakout Box terminal '20' are using the terminal as ground. These tests, of course, assume that the ground CKT 1250 at terminal '20' is good.

It is very important that a thorough inspection of the wiring and connectors be performed. Failure to carefully and fully inspect wiring and connectors may result in misdiagnosis, causing part replacement with reappearance of the fault.

Fig. 124   DTC 63, Valve relay fault (Part 3 of 6). 1993 Eldorado & Seville

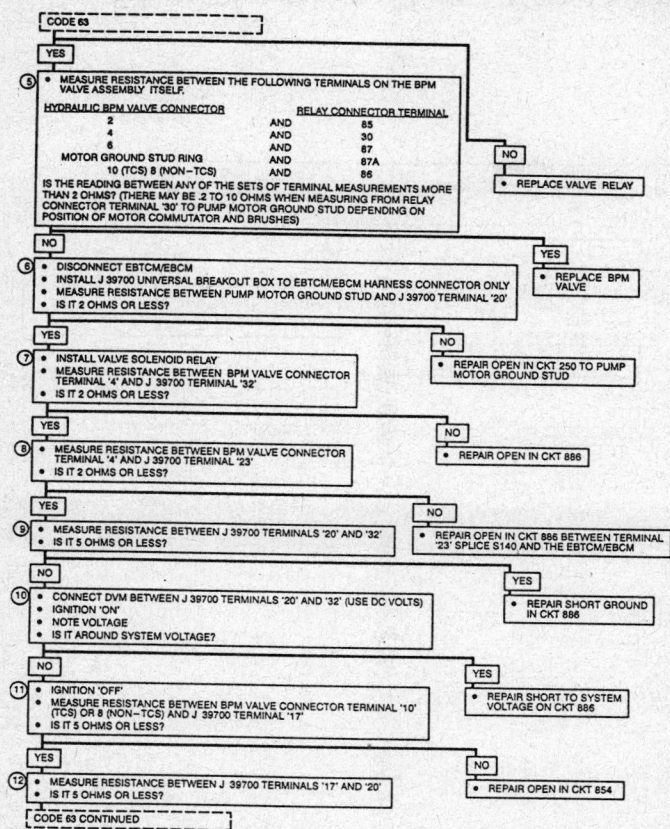

CODE 63

5
- MEASURE RESISTANCE BETWEEN THE FOLLOWING TERMINALS ON THE BPM VALVE ASSEMBLY ITSELF.

HYDRAULIC BPM VALVE CONNECTOR		RELAY CONNECTOR TERMINAL
2	AND	85
4	AND	30
6	AND	87
MOTOR GROUND STUD RING	AND	87A
10 (TCS) 8 (NON-TCS)	AND	86

IS THE READING BETWEEN ANY OF THE SETS OF TERMINAL MEASUREMENTS MORE THAN 2 OHMS? (THERE MAY BE .2 TO 10 OHMS WHEN MEASURING FROM RELAY CONNECTOR TERMINAL '30' TO PUMP MOTOR GROUND STUD DEPENDING ON POSITION OF MOTOR COMMUTATOR AND BRUSHES)

- NO → **REPLACE VALVE RELAY**

6
- DISCONNECT EBTCM/EBCM
- INSTALL J 39700 UNIVERSAL BREAKOUT BOX TO EBTCM/EBCM HARNESS CONNECTOR ONLY
- MEASURE RESISTANCE BETWEEN PUMP MOTOR GROUND STUD AND J 39700 TERMINAL '20'
- IS IT 2 OHMS OR LESS?

- YES → **REPLACE BPM VALVE**

7
- INSTALL VALVE SOLENOID RELAY
- MEASURE RESISTANCE BETWEEN BPM VALVE CONNECTOR TERMINAL '4' AND J 39700 TERMINAL '32'
- IS IT 2 OHMS OR LESS?

- NO → **REPAIR OPEN IN CKT 250 TO PUMP MOTOR GROUND STUD**

8
- MEASURE RESISTANCE BETWEEN BPM VALVE CONNECTOR TERMINAL '4' AND J 39700 TERMINAL '23'
- IS IT 2 OHMS OR LESS?

- NO → **REPAIR OPEN IN CKT 886**

9
- MEASURE RESISTANCE BETWEEN J 39700 TERMINALS '20' AND '32'
- IS IT 5 OHMS OR LESS?

- NO → **REPAIR OPEN IN CKT 886 BETWEEN TERMINAL '23' SPLICE S140 AND THE EBTCM/EBCM**

10
- CONNECT DVM BETWEEN J 39700 TERMINALS '20' AND '32' (USE DC VOLTS)
- IGNITION 'ON'
- NOTE VOLTAGE
- IS IT AROUND SYSTEM VOLTAGE?

- YES → **REPAIR SHORT GROUND IN CKT 886**

11
- IGNITION 'OFF'
- MEASURE RESISTANCE BETWEEN BPM VALVE CONNECTOR TERMINAL '10' (TCS) OR 8 (NON-TCS) AND J 39700 TERMINAL '17'
- IS IT 5 OHMS OR LESS?

- NO → **REPAIR SHORT TO SYSTEM VOLTAGE ON CKT 886**

12
- MEASURE RESISTANCE BETWEEN J 39700 TERMINALS '17' AND '20'
- IS IT 5 OHMS OR LESS?

- NO → **REPAIR OPEN IN CKT 854**

CODE 63 CONTINUED

Fig. 124 DTC 63, Valve relay fault (Part 4 of 6). 1993 Eldorado & Seville

DIAGNOSTIC TROUBLE CODE 63

VALVE RELAY FAULT
5 of 6

CIRCUIT DESCRIPTION:

The valve relay provides power to the four ABS solenoids and two TCS Pilot Valves (if applicable) in the BPM valve. The valve relay is located on the BPM valve and may be replaced if it is found to be defective.

The valve relay is engaged during normal system operation. When the ignition is switched to RUN, the EBTCM/EBCM commands the valve relay ON by grounding the valve relay actuation line on CKT 856 (EBTCM/EBCM pin '27'). When this ground is provided, the valve relay is energized from the voltage supply line on CKT 854 (EBTCM/EBCM pin '17'). The valve relay switches and battery voltage is provided to the four valve solenoids, the pilot valves and the valve relay voltage sense line on CKT 886 (EBTCM/EBCM pin '23'). The valve relay remains engaged until the ignition is turned 'OFF' or a failure is detected.

The valve relay voltage feedback (EBTCM/EBCM pin '32') provides suppression of voltage spikes created during operation of both front ABS valve solenoids during antilock and traction control.

TEST DESCRIPTION: Test numbers refer to circled numbers on the diagnostic chart.

13. Checks for a short to system voltage in CKT 854.
14. Checks for an open in CKT 856.
15. Checks for a short to ground in CKT 856.
16. Checks for a short to system voltage in CKT 856.
17. Checks wiring and connectors for intermittents.
18. Determines whether the code was set due to an intermittent condition or an EBTCM/EBCM fault.
19. Checks if problem found in step 13 is due to a short to system voltage in CKT 874, 856, or 854.

DIAGNOSTIC AIDS:

All tests using J 39700 Universal Breakout Box terminal '20' are using the terminal as ground. These tests, of course, assume that the ground CKT 1250 at terminal '20' is good.

It is very important that a thorough inspection of the wiring and connectors be performed. Failure to carefully and fully inspect wiring and connectors may result in misdiagnosis, causing part replacement with reappearance of the fault.

Fig. 124 DTC 63, Valve relay fault (Part 5 of 6). 1993 Eldorado & Seville

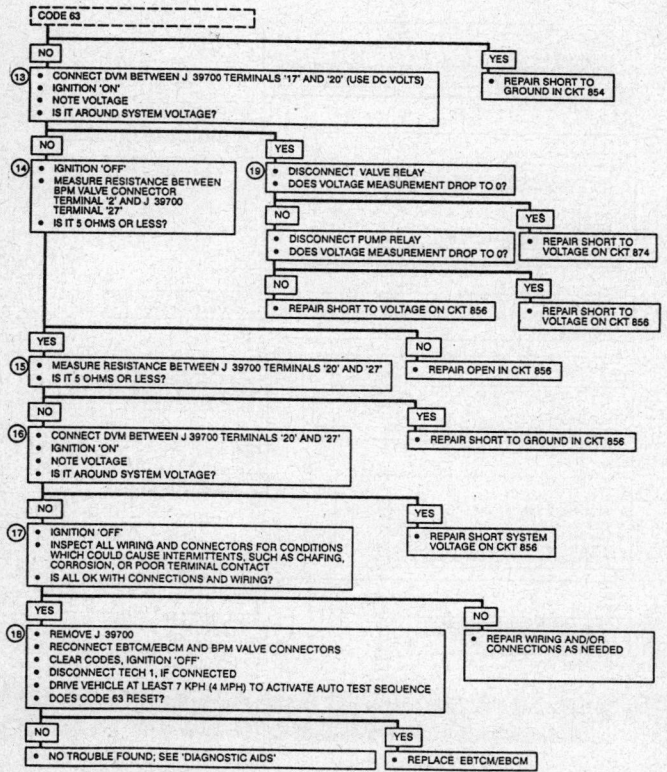

CODE 63

13
- CONNECT DVM BETWEEN J 39700 TERMINALS '17' AND '20' (USE DC VOLTS)
- IGNITION 'ON'
- NOTE VOLTAGE
- IS IT AROUND SYSTEM VOLTAGE?

- YES → **REPAIR SHORT TO GROUND IN CKT 854**

14
- IGNITION 'OFF'
- MEASURE RESISTANCE BETWEEN BPM VALVE CONNECTOR TERMINAL '2' AND J 39700 TERMINAL '27'
- IS IT 5 OHMS OR LESS?

- YES → **19**
  - DISCONNECT VALVE RELAY
  - DOES VOLTAGE MEASUREMENT DROP TO 0?

  - NO → DISCONNECT PUMP RELAY
    - DOES VOLTAGE MEASUREMENT DROP TO 0?

    - YES → **REPAIR SHORT TO VOLTAGE ON CKT 874**
    - NO → **REPAIR SHORT TO VOLTAGE ON CKT 856**

  - YES → **REPAIR SHORT TO VOLTAGE ON CKT 856**

15
- MEASURE RESISTANCE BETWEEN J 39700 TERMINALS '20' AND '27'
- IS IT 5 OHMS OR LESS?

- NO → **REPAIR OPEN IN CKT 856**

16
- CONNECT DVM BETWEEN J 39700 TERMINALS '20' AND '27'
- IGNITION 'ON'
- NOTE VOLTAGE
- IS IT AROUND SYSTEM VOLTAGE?

- YES → **REPAIR SHORT TO GROUND IN CKT 856**

17
- IGNITION 'OFF'
- INSPECT ALL WIRING AND CONNECTORS FOR CONDITIONS WHICH COULD CAUSE INTERMITTENTS, SUCH AS CHAFING, CORROSION, OR POOR TERMINAL CONTACT
- IS ALL OK WITH CONNECTIONS AND WIRING?

- YES → **REPAIR SHORT SYSTEM VOLTAGE ON CKT 856**

18
- REMOVE J 39700
- RECONNECT EBTCM/EBCM AND BPM VALVE CONNECTORS
- CLEAR CODES, WITH TECH 1
- DISCONNECT TECH 1, IF CONNECTED
- DRIVE VEHICLE AT LEAST 7 KPH (4 MPH) TO ACTIVATE AUTO TEST SEQUENCE
- DOES CODE 63 RESET?

- NO → **REPAIR WIRING AND/OR CONNECTIONS AS NEEDED**

- NO → **NO TROUBLE FOUND; SEE 'DIAGNOSTIC AIDS'**
- YES → **REPLACE EBTCM/EBCM**

Fig. 124 DTC 63, Valve relay fault (Part 6 of 6). 1993 Eldorado & Seville

DIAGNOSTIC TROUBLE CODE 67

BRAKE LIGHT SWITCH FAULT

(TRACTION CONTROL EQUIPPED VEHICLES ONLY)

CIRCUIT DESCRIPTION:

The electronic brake control module receives Brake Light Switch status from the PCM via serial data. If fault Code 67 sets, it may be indicative of a loss of switch input to the PCM, check for PCM fault Code PO90 (STOP/BITSI/CRUISE BRAKE SWITCH FAULT CODE) or P106 (BRAKE LIGHT SWITCH FAULT CODE).

TEST CONDITION(S):

1. Tested continuously.

FAILURE CONDITION(S):

1. EBTCM receives failure status of Brake Light Switch from PCM.

ACTION TAKEN:

1. Code set.
2. TCS disabled.
3. 'TRACTION DISABLED' message ON.

Fig. 125 DTC 67, Brake light switch fault. 1993 Eldorado & Seville w/TCS

1991 REATTA, 1991-92 BROUGHAM, TORONADO & TROFEO & 1991-93 CAPRICE, CUSTOM CRUISER, ELDORADO, RIVIERA, ROADMASTER, SEVILLE (BOSCH 2 U TYPE)

23-207

ELECTRONIC BRAKE AND TRACTION CONTROL (EBTCM/EBCM) INTERNAL FAULT

CIRCUIT DESCRIPTION:

The EBTCM/EBCM performs various diagnostic checks on itself. If it finds a problem, Code 71 will set.

TEST CONDITION(S):

1. Tested continuously.

FAILURE CONDITION(S):

1. While Standing or Driving: EBTCM/EBCM internal error is detected.

ACTION TAKEN:

1. Code set.
2. ABS and TCS switched 'OFF'.
3. 'ANTILOCK' indicator ON.
4. 'TRACTION DISABLED' message ON. (vehicles with TCS)

TEST DESCRIPTION: Test numbers refer to circled numbers on the diagnostic chart.

1. Checks for good connections from the harness to the EBTCM/EBCM itself.
2. Checks to see if the fault was false. If Code 71 resets, replace the EBTCM/EBCM.

Fig. 126 DTC 71, EBTCM/EBCM internal fault (Part 1 of 2). 1993 Eldorado & Seville

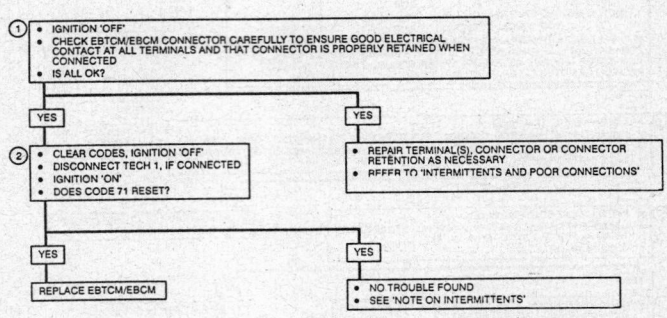

Fig. 126 DTC 71, EBTCM/EBCM internal fault (Part 2 of 2). 1993 Eldorado & Seville

DIAGNOSTIC TROUBLE CODE 72

SERIAL DATA LINK FAULT

CIRCUIT DESCRIPTION:

The Serial Data Link is an asynchronous link operating at 8192 bits per second.

Code 72 will set and the 'ANTILOCK' indicator will illuminate if the EBTCM/EBCM does not get polled by the IPC for information, or if it does not see PCM information on the data link.

TEST CONDITION(S):

1. Tested continuously.

FAILURE CONDITION(S):

1. While Standing or Driving: Serial Data communications are lost.

ACTION TAKEN:

1. Code set.
2. ABS and TCS switched 'OFF'.
3. 'ANTILOCK' indicator ON.
4. 'TRACTION DISABLED' message ON (vehicles with TCS).

TEST DESCRIPTION: Test numbers refer to circled numbers on the diagnostic chart.

1. This test checks to see if the off–board device can communicate with the EBTCM/EBCM.
2. This test checks for a short to battery in the serial data circuit.
3. This test checks for a short to ground in the serial data circuit.
4. This test checks for an open in the serial data circuit.
5. This test checks to see if the off–board device can communicate with the EBTCM/EBCM.
6. If the connections at the EBTCM/EBCM and DLC connector are OK, replace the EBTCM/EBCM.

DIAGNOSTIC AIDS:

The problem may be intermittent. Try performing the tests shown while 'wiggling' wiring and connectors; this can often cause the fault to appear.

NOTICE: Diagnostic Trouble Code 72 will never be displayed while serial data fault is current. A current Code 72 will result in a 'NO TCS DATA', and 'TRACTION DISABLED' messages as well as IPC Diagnostic Trouble Code B332 and PCM Code P133.

Fig. 127 DTC 72, Serial data link fault (Part 1 of 2). 1993 Eldorado & Seville

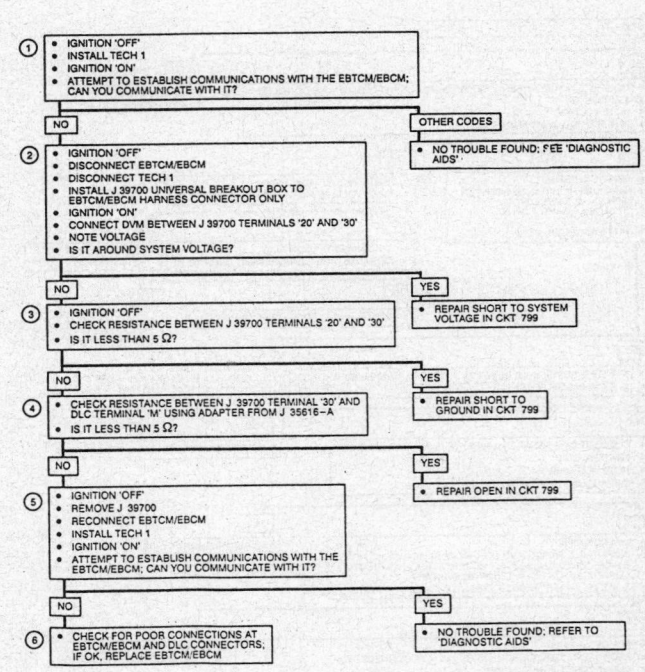

Fig. 127 DTC 72, Serial data link fault (Part 2 of 2). 1993 Eldorado & Seville

CIRCUIT DESCRIPTION:

Traction control is simultaneously controlled by the EBTCM on the vehicles equipped with the 4.6L Northstar, and the PCM. The PCM receives a 'DESIRED TORQUE' request via a Pulse Width Modulated (PWM) signal from the EBTCM (CKT 594) requesting the desired torque level for proper traction control system operation. Torque reduction will be indicated if the duty cycle of the PWM signal is between 10% (100 % torque reduction) and 90% (no torque reduction) and at least one (up to five) cylinder is requested to be disabled. The percent duty cycle will indicate the percent torque required. The PCM will selectively disable fuel to certain cylinders to achieve this reduction and communicate the actual torque output back to the EBTCM (CKT 595).

TEST CONDITION(S):
1. Tested continuously.

FAILURE CONDITION(S):
1. While Standing or Driving: PWM interface between EBTCM/EBCM and PCM is lost.

ACTION TAKEN:
1. Code set.
2. 'TRACTION DISABLED' message 'ON'.

A Code 73 may set if either CKT 594 or 595 is open, shorted to ground or shorted to voltage.

If CKT 595, Delivered Torque, is damaged and the EBTCM loses this input, a TCS Diagnostic Code 73 will be set. The PCM monitors the serial data line to see if the traction control has been disabled. If it has, the PCM will not set Code 93.

If CKT 594, Desired Torque is damaged and the PCM loses this input, the PCM monitors the serial data line to see if the traction control has been disabled. If not, the PCM sets a Code 93 and then tells the EBTCM/EBCM, via serial data, that there is a PWM circuit problem and the EBTCM/EBCM sets a Code 73.

TEST DESCRIPTION: Test numbers refer to circled numbers on the diagnostic chart.
1. Checks if the PCM Diagnostic Trouble Code 93 is set. If it is, there is likely a problem with CKT 594.
2. Checks for an open or high resistance in CKT 595.
3. Checks for a short to ground in CKT 595.
4. Checks for a short to voltage in CKT 595.
5. If no problem is found up until this point, CKT 594 should be checked.
6. Checks for an open or high resistance in CKT 594.
7. Checks for a short to ground in CKT 594.
8. Checks for a short to voltage in CKT 594.
9. If CKT 595 has not been checked, proceed to the left hand side of the trouble tree. If it has, continue downward. Problem is intermittent or in one of the controllers.
10. Checks if Code 73 and/or 93 are intermittent. If not, trouble is in either PCM or EBTCM.

DIAGNOSTIC AIDS:
- It is theoretically impossible for only a PCM Code 93 to set. If only a PCM Code 93 is present, either the TCS Code 73 has been cleared or there is a problem with the PCM.
- A Code 73 may set by itself if the PCM PROM has been improperly installed.

Fig. 128 DTC 73, PCM-EBTCM/EBCM PWM signal fault (Part 1 of 2). 1993 Eldorado & Seville w/4.6L Northstar engine

Fig. 128 DTC 73, PCM-EBTCM/EBCM PWM signal fault (Part 2 of 2). 1993 Eldorado & Seville w/4.6L Northstar engine

CIRCUIT DESCRIPTION:

The IPC outputs 5 volts on CKT 209 to the brake fluid level sensor. The IPC determines the level of brake fluid by the voltage drop it detects across the sensor circuit. This information is delivered to the EBTCM via the serial data line.

TEST CONDITION(S):
1. Tested continuously.

FAILURE CONDITION(S):
1. While Standing or Driving: Brake fluid falls below acceptable level.
2. Brake fluid level sensor disconnected.
3. Open, short to ground or short to battery on CKT 209.

ACTION TAKEN:
1. Code set.
2. ABS and TCS switched 'OFF'.
3. Red BRAKE warning lamp and 'ANTILOCK' indicator ON.
4. 'TRACTION DISABLED' message ON.

TEST DESCRIPTION: Test numbers refer to circled numbers on the diagnostic chart.
1. Check the brake fluid level in master cylinder reservoir.
2. Check brake fluid level as detected by IPC.
3. Brake fluid level not acceptable. Fill and recheck.
4. Brake fluid level as detected by IPC. See 'DIAGNOSTIC AIDS'.
5. Checks IPC input parameter ID80 with sensor disconnected for a short to ground in CKT 209, or bad sensor.
6. Checks IPC input parameter ID80 with sensor disconnected and connector shorted.
7. IPC detects acceptable brake fluid level. Problem not present.
8. Checks sensor resistor and checks for a short between CKTs 901 and 51.
9. Checks for open in CKTs 209 and 51.

DIAGNOSTIC AIDS:
IPC data parameter ID80 will display the following:
- 3.6–5V — open in sensor circuit.
- 1.5–3.5V — circuit OK. Problem not present.
- 0–1.4V — short between CKTs 209 and 51.

Fig. 129 DTC 83, Low brake fluid level (Part 1 of 2). 1993 Eldorado & Seville w/TCS

Fig. 129 DTC 83, Low brake fluid level (Part 2 of 2). 1993 Eldorado & Seville w/TCS

CHART A

'ANTILOCK' INDICATOR AND 'TRACTION DISABLED' MESSAGE 'ON', (IF APPLICABLE) NO CODES SET / NO TCS DATA

TEST DESCRIPTION: Test numbers refer to circled numbers on the diagnostic chart.

1. Checks if condition is due to a poor connection at the EBTCM/EBCM. Make sure the connecter is not 'cocked' on module.
2. Verifies that fuse A1 is intact.
3. Checks EBTCM/EBCM ground resistances. Should be less than 5 ohms.
4. Checks EBTCM/EBCM ignition voltage.
5. This step checks for possible open or high resistance in CKT 141 if there is insufficient voltage measured in Step 4. It is assumed a short to ground on CKT 141 would have blown fuse 'A1'.
6. Checks for possible insufficient voltage on power side of fuse 'A1'. This may be due to Maxi® fuse 6 being

damaged or an intermittent connection in the ignition switch.
7. Checks for EBTCM/EBCM terminal '1' having a poor solder joint or for being partially backed out.
8. Checks if a loss of serial data communication between EBTCM/EBCM and BCM is due to a damaged CKT 799.
9. If there is no voltage measured in Step 8, there is a possible short to ground on CKT 799. If not, regulated 5V supply from EBTCM/EBCM is lost and EBTCM/EBCM should be replaced.

DIAGNOSTIC AIDS:

BCM Diagnostic Trouble Code B332 and PCM Code P137 should be present. If all of the IPC data line codes are present, refer to Section 8C1 'SYSTEM CHECK'.

Fig. 130 Chart A, ANTILOCK indicator & TRACTION DISABLED message ON (if applicable) w/no codes set or no TCS data (Part 1 of 2). 1993 Eldorado & Seville

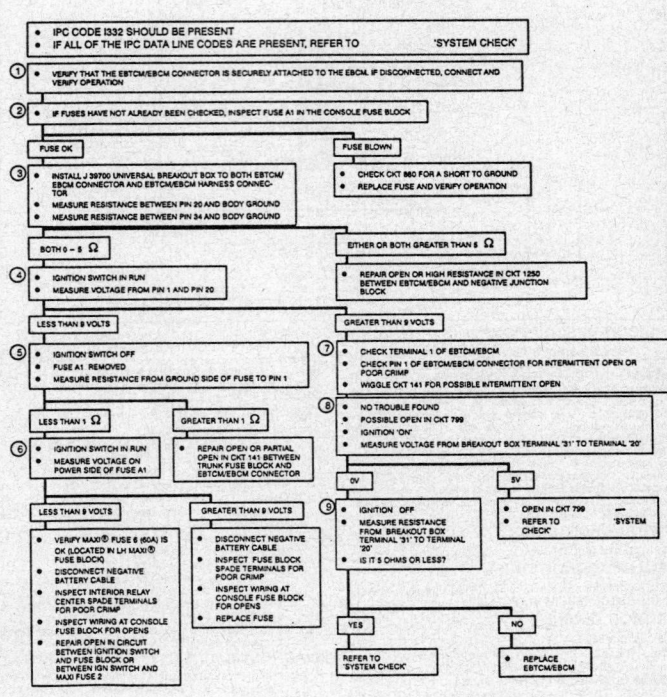

Fig. 130 Chart A, ANTILOCK indicator & TRACTION DISABLED message ON (if applicable) w/no codes set or no TCS data (Part 2 of 2). 1993 Eldorado & Seville

CHART B

'ANTILOCK' INDICATOR 'ON', NO CODES SET

TEST DESCRIPTION: Test numbers refer to circled numbers on the diagnostic chart.

1. Checks if 'ANTILOCK' indicator is ON due to a loss of communication between the IPC and EBTCM/EBCM.
2. Checks for a short to ground in CKT 852.
3. Final check for diagnostic trouble codes.

DIAGNOSTIC AIDS:

The EBTCM/EBCM controls the 'ANTILOCK' indicator only in instances where serial data communication with the IPC is lost. In all other instances the IPC controls this lamp.

Fig. 131 Chart B, ANTILOCK indicator ON w/no codes set (Part 1 of 2). 1993 Eldorado & Seville

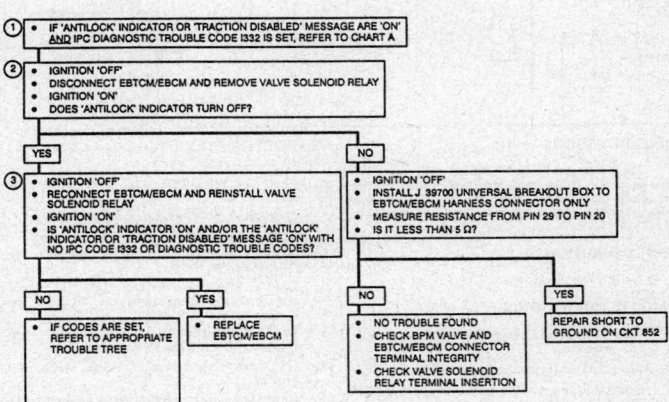

Fig. 131 Chart B, ANTILOCK indicator ON w/no codes set (Part 2 of 2). 1993 Eldorado & Seville

CHART C

VALVE CYCLING (CHATTER) DURING NORMAL STOPS (UNWANTED ABS MODULATION)

TEST DESCRIPTION: Test numbers refer to circled numbers on the diagnostic chart.

1. Checks if valve activation due to erroneous electrical 'noise' induced onto wheel speed sensor circuits.
2. The wheel speed sensor output should gradually increase with vehicle speed. There should be no skips or jumps. All four wheel speed sensor outputs should be identical. On a slow down, one of the signals may drop off faster than the others, indicating a lock–up condition or a problem with the speed sensor or wiring (corrosion etc.).

Fig. 132 Chart C, Valve cycling (chatter) during normal stops (unwanted ABS modulation) (Part 1 of 2). 1993 Eldorado & Seville

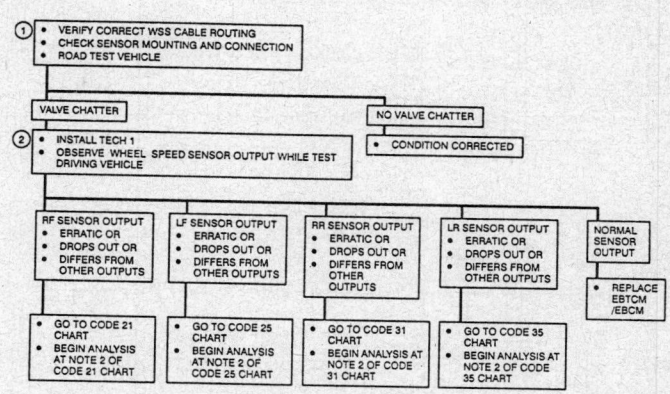

Fig. 132 Chart C, Valve cycling (chatter) during normal stops (unwanted ABS modulation) (Part 2 of 2). 1993 Eldorado & Seville

CHART D

TRACTION CONTROL OPERATION CHECK (NO DIAGNOSTIC TROUBLE CODES SET)

TEST DESCRIPTION: Test numbers refer to circled numbers on the diagnostic chart.

1. Traction control system should interpret the elevated front wheels as an icy or free spin condition. At ½ throttle a properly operating system will allow both front wheels to spin up quickly to about 20–25 MPH and then slow down (but not stop) to about 5–10 MPH and have a jerky appearance. The traction control 'ACTIVE' message should display on the DIC. The pump motor should also be heard.
2. System is building up pressure to the front brake and operating correctly.
3. System is not building up pressure to the front brakes. Possible air or dirt in the system.
4. No dirt in reservoir and the fluid level is OK. Air may still be trapped in system. The TCS hydraulic circuit should be bled using TECH 1 TCS test and bleed procedure outlined in Section 5. One of the front caliper bleed screws must be open to allow air to escape.
5. Fluid level OK. Air may still be trapped in the system. The TCS hydraulic circuit should be bled using TECH 1 TCS test and bleed procedure outlined in Section 5. One of the front caliper bleed screws must be open to allow air to escape.
6. Reservoir TCS prime pipe may be contaminated. Flush pipe and reservoir to remove any debris. Air may still be trapped in system. The TCS hydraulic circuit should be bled using TECH 1 TCS test and bleed procedure outlined in Section 5. One of the front caliper bleed screws must be open to allow air to escape.

DIAGNOSTIC AIDS:
- The Brake Light Switch must be properly adjusted to prevent an erroneous brake application input to the EBTCM/EBCM. Misadjustment may prevent brake intervention during traction control operation. Also, the EBTCM/EBCM receives TCC switch status over serial data from the PCM. If serial data is lost or the switch remains engaged, brake intervention during traction control may be lost. Monitor PCM TCC switch input PI71 while cycling brake switch. The input should cycle 'HI' and 'LO'.
- The PCM shall not allow traction control fuel shutoff if:
  – Engine Coolant Temperature less than −40°C
  – Engine Coolant Temperature greater than or equal to 131°C
  – Low Coolant Level Detected
- Cylinders shall be disabled if the engine speed greater than or equal to 600 RPM.
- The PCM can disable traction control for up to 11 ignition cycles if override PS24, Traction Control Disable, is activated. When PS24 is selected, the display will alternate between '– –' for one second and the current state of Traction Control Disable override ('99' for override active and '00' for override not active). Pressing the WARMER button will disable traction control for the next eleven ignition cycles and display '99'. The 'TRACTION DISABLED' message will be displayed for the duration of this override and no TCS diagnostic trouble codes will be set. Pressing the COOLER button will allow normal program control of traction control and display '00'.

Fig. 133 Chart D, Traction control operation check (no DTCs set) (Part 1 of 2). 1993 Eldorado & Seville

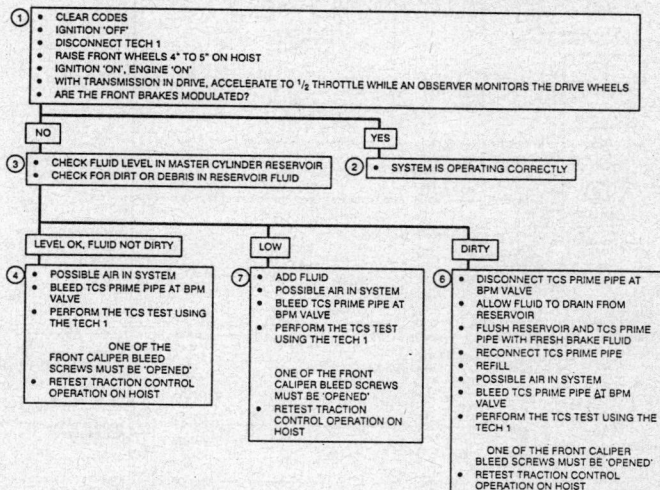

Fig. 133 Chart D, Traction control operation check (no DTCs set) (Part 2 of 2). 1993 Eldorado & Seville

Fig. 134   ABS & Traction Control System (TCS) wiring circuit (Part 1 of 4). 1993 Fleetwood (RWD)

Fig. 134   ABS & Traction Control System (TCS) wiring circuit (Part 2 of 4). 1993 Fleetwood (RWD)

Fig. 134   ABS & Traction Control System (TCS) wiring circuit (Part 3 of 4). 1993 Fleetwood (RWD)

Fig. 134   ABS & Traction Control System (TCS) wiring circuit (Part 4 of 4). 1993 Fleetwood (RWD)

DTC 21
RF WHEEL SPEED SENSOR MALFUNCTION

Circuit Description:

The toothed wheel generates a voltage pulse as it moves past the sensor; each tooth-gap-tooth series on the wheel generates these pulses. The frequency of these pulses is used by the EBTCM to determine wheel speed. The amount of voltage generated in each pulse depends on the air gap between the sensor and the toothed wheel, and on wheel speed.

The "ANTI-LOCK" and "TRACTION CONTROL" indicators will be "ON" and DTC 21 is set if there is a short to voltage or ground in CKT 872 or 833, or a malfunctioning speed sensor. The testing for this malfunction occurs when the vehicle is in motion; it will not set with the ignition "ON" and the vehicle at rest.

Test Description: Number(s) below refer to circled number(s) on the diagnostic chart.

1. Checks for proper resistance in the sensor itself.
2. Checks for a short to battery in either of the speed sensor circuit wires.
3. Checks for a short between the speed sensor circuit wires.
4. Checks for a short to ground in the speed sensor input circuit wire. The ground may be either a "hard" short to ground, or a resistive (partial) short. A short with a resistance less than 2 megohms, though not a hard short, can still cause DTC 21 to set.
5. Checks if the DTC resets during a road test. If so, since Tests 1-4 have validated that the circuitry and components are good, intermittent problems are suspected.
6. Checks wiring and connectors for intermittents.
7. Replace the wheel speed sensor, as it is likely the cause of a DTC reset experienced during the road test, since other portions of the circuit have checked out OK. If the DTC resets after sensor replacement, the EBTCM must be concluding there is a problem present in the speed sensor circuit when there is not.

Diagnostic Aids:

Be sure the speed sensor wiring is properly routed and retained. This will help prevent false signals due to electrical noise being picked up by the wiring.

It is very important that a thorough inspection of the wiring and connectors be performed. Failure to carefully and fully inspect wiring and connectors may result in misdiagnosis, causing part replacement with reappearance of the malfunction.

The Tech 1 can also be used to monitor the wheel speeds during a road test. Watch the wheel speeds being displayed on the Tech 1 to see if any of the readings are unusual, such as one sensor varying in speed from the other three, a signal going intermittently high or low, etc. If this does not identify the intermittent, wet the-speed sensor harness on the underside of the vehicle and road test monitoring wheel speeds with the Tech 1.

Fig. 135   DTC 21, Right front wheel speed sensor malfunction (Part 1 of 2). 1993 Fleetwood (RWD)

Fig. 135   DTC 21, Right front wheel speed sensor malfunction (Part 2 of 2). 1993 Fleetwood (RWD)

DTC 23
RF WHEEL SPEED SENSOR CONTINUITY MALFUNCTION

Circuit Description:

The toothed wheel generates a voltage pulse as it moves past the sensor; each tooth-gap-tooth series on the wheel generates these pulses. The frequency of these pulses is used by the EBTCM to determine wheel speed. The amount of voltage generated in each pulse depends on the air gap between the sensor and the toothed wheel, and on wheel speed.

The "ANTI-LOCK" and "TRACTION CONTROL" indicators will be "ON" and DTC 23 is set if there is a short to voltage or an open in CKT 872 or 833, or a malfunctioning speed sensor. The testing for this malfunction occurs with the ignition "ON" and the vehicle at rest.

Test Description: Number(s) below refer to circled number(s) on the diagnostic chart.

1. Checks for proper resistance in the sensor itself.
2. Checks for a short to battery in either of the speed sensor circuit wires.
3. Checks for an open in both the speed sensor circuit wires.
4. Manipulates wiring and connectors, trying to induce an intermittent malfunction not currently present.
5. This test checks if the DTC resets on key-up. If so, since Tests 1-4 have validated that the circuitry and components are good, the wheel speed sensor may be causing the malfunction.
6. Checks if DTC 21 sets during a road test.
7. DTC 23 sets when the vehicle is at rest; DTC 21 sets with a problem in the speed sensor circuitry with the vehicle in motion. If problems are still present, DTC 21 would not set during the road test, not a 23. If the DTC 21 sets at this point, the DTC 21 diagnostics should be used.

8. The wheel speed sensor may be causing an intermittent fault. If DTC 23 resets after sensor replacement, the EBTCM must be concluding there is a problem present in the speed sensor circuit when there is not.

Diagnostic Aids:

Be sure the speed sensor wiring is properly routed and retained. This will help prevent false signals due to electrical noise being picked up by the wiring.

It is very important that a thorough inspection of the wiring and connectors be performed. Failure to carefully and fully inspect wiring and connectors may result in misdiagnosis, causing part replacement with reappearance of the malfunction..

Fig. 136   DTC 23, Right front wheel speed sensor continuity malfunction (Part 1 of 2). 1993 Fleetwood (RWD)

Fig. 136   DTC 23, Right front wheel speed sensor continuity malfunction (Part 2 of 2). 1993 Fleetwood (RWD)

DTC 25
LF WHEEL SPEED SENSOR MALFUNCTION

Circuit Description:

The toothed wheel generates a voltage pulse as it moves past the sensor; each tooth-gap-tooth series on the wheel generates these pulses. The frequency of these pulses is used by the EBTCM to determine wheel speed. The amount of voltage generated in each pulse depends on the air gap between the sensor and the toothed wheel, and on wheel speed.

The "ANTI-LOCK" and "TRACTION CONTROL" indicators will be "ON" and DTC 25 is set if there is a short to voltage or ground in CKT 830 or 873, or a malfunctioning speed sensor. The testing for this malfunction occurs when the vehicle is in motion; it will not set with the ignition "ON" and the vehicle at rest.

Test Description: Number(s) below refer to circled number(s) on the diagnostic chart.
1. Checks for proper resistance in the sensor itself.
2. Checks for a short to battery in either of the speed sensor circuit wires.
3. Checks for a short between the speed sensor circuit wires.
4. Checks for a short to ground in the speed sensor input circuit wire. The ground may be either a "hard" short to ground, or a resistive (partial) short. A short with a resistance less than 2 megohms, though not a hard short, can still cause DTC 25 to set.
5. Checks if the DTC resets during a road test. If so, since Tests 1-4 have validated that the circuitry and components are good, intermittent problems are suspected.
6. Checks wiring and connectors for intermittents.
7. Replace the wheel speed sensor, as it is likely the cause of a DTC reset experienced during the road test, since other portions of the circuit have checked out OK. If the DTC resets after sensor replacement, the EBTCM must be concluding there is a problem present in the speed sensor circuit when there is not.

Diagnostic Aids:

Be sure the speed sensor wiring is properly routed and retained. This will help prevent false signals due to electrical noise being picked up by the wiring.

It is very important that a thorough inspection of the wiring and connectors be performed. Failure to carefully and fully inspect wiring and connectors may result in misdiagnosis, causing part replacement with reappearance of the malfunction.

The Tech 1 can also be used to monitor the wheel speeds during a road test. Watch the wheel speeds being displayed on the Tech 1 to see if any of the readings are unusual, such as one sensor varying in speed from the other three, a signal going intermittently high or low, etc. If this does not identify the intermittent, wet the speed sensor harness on the underside of the vehicle and road test monitoring wheel speeds with the Tech 1.

Fig. 137 DTC 25, Left front wheel speed sensor malfunction (Part 1 of 2). 1993 Fleetwood (RWD)

Fig. 137 DTC 25, Left front wheel speed sensor malfunction (Part 2 of 2). 1993 Fleetwood (RWD)

DTC 27
LF WHEEL SPEED SENSOR CONTINUITY MALFUNCTION

Circuit Description:

The toothed wheel generates a voltage pulse as it moves past the sensor; each tooth-gap-tooth series on the wheel generates these pulses. The frequency of these pulses is used by the EBTCM to determine wheel speed. The amount of voltage generated in each pulse depends on the air gap between the sensor and the toothed wheel, and on wheel speed.

The "ANTI-LOCK" and "TRACTION CONTROL" indicators will be "ON" and DTC 27 is set if there is a short to voltage or an open in CKT 830 or 873, or a malfunctioning speed sensor. The testing for this malfunction occurs with the ignition "ON" and the vehicle at rest.

Test Description: Number(s) below refer to circled number(s) on the diagnostic chart.
1. Checks for proper resistance in the sensor itself.
2. Checks for a short to battery in either of the speed sensor circuit wires.
3. Checks for an open in both the speed sensor circuit wires.
4. Manipulates wiring and connectors, trying to induce an intermittent malfunction not currently present.
5. This test checks if the DTC resets on key-up. If so, since Tests 1-4 have validated that the circuitry and components are good, the wheel speed sensor may be causing the malfunction.
6. Checks if DTC 25 sets during a road test.
7. DTC 27 sets when the vehicle is at rest; DTC 25 sets with a problem in the speed sensor circuitry with the vehicle in motion. If problems are still present, DTC 25 would set during the road test, not a 27. If the DTC 25 sets at this point, the DTC 25 diagnostics should be used.

8. The wheel speed sensor may be causing an intermittent malfunction. If DTC 27 resets after sensor replacement, the EBTCM must be concluding there is a problem present in the speed sensor circuit when there is not.

Diagnostic Aids:

Be sure the speed sensor wiring is properly routed and retained. This will help prevent false signals due to electrical noise being picked up by the wiring.

It is very important that a thorough inspection of the wiring and connectors be performed. Failure to carefully and fully inspect wiring and connectors may result in misdiagnosis, causing part replacement with reappearance of the malfunction.

Fig. 138 DTC 26, Left front wheel speed sensor continuity malfunction (Part 1 of 2). 1993 Fleetwood (RWD)

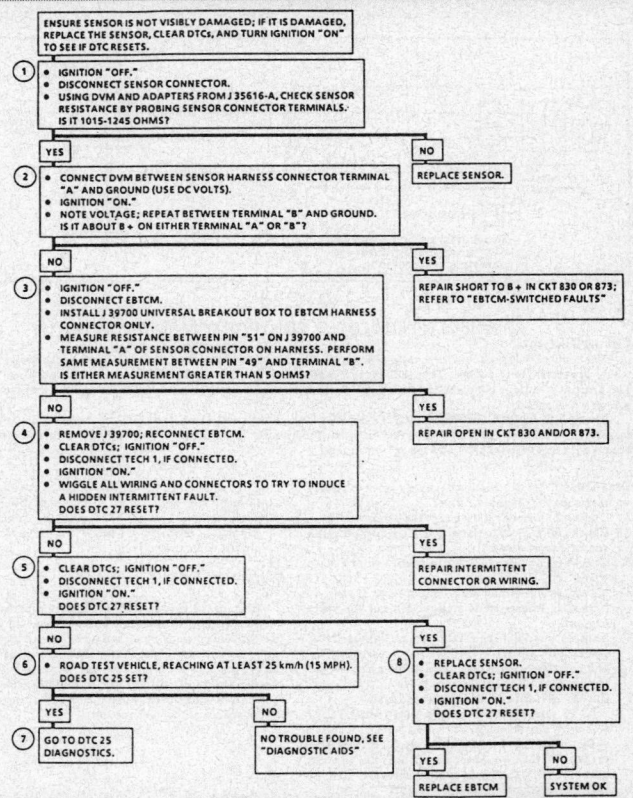

Fig. 138 DTC 26, Left front wheel speed sensor continuity malfunction (Part 2 of 2). 1993 Fleetwood (RWD)

DTC 28
WHEEL SPEED SENSOR FREQUENCY ERROR

Circuit Description:

The toothed wheel generates a voltage pulse as it moves past the sensor; each tooth-gap-tooth series on the wheel generates these pulses. The frequency of these pulses is used by the EBTCM to determine wheel speed. The amount of voltage generated in each pulse depends on the air gap between the sensor and the toothed wheel, and on wheel speed.

The "ANTI-LOCK" and "TRACTION CONTROL" indicators will be "ON" and DTC 28 is set if the EBTCM cannot specifically identify which wheel speed sensor is causing the frequency error problem. If it can define the specific speed sensor causing the problem, the sensor DTC associated with the sensor (21, 25, 31, 35) will be set instead of DTC 28.

Test Description: Number(s) below refer to circled number(s) on the diagnostic chart.

1. Checks wiring and connections for problems. It is critical that this step is performed thoroughly, as wiring/connector problems are the most likely cause for this DTC being set.
2. Uses the Tech 1 to monitor for vehicle electrical/electronic system "noise" being picked up by the speed sensor circuits.
3. Uses the Tech 1 to monitor the wheel speed sensors while the vehicle is operating. If the Tech 1 auto-trigger snapshot mode triggers, the speed sensor or the wiring and/or connectors are going intermittent during the road test.
4. Checks for proper resistance in the sensor itself.
5. Replaces wheel speed sensor as the likely cause of the triggering intermittent. If DTC resets, replace EBTCM.
6. Checks for a short to ground in the speed sensor input circuit wires. The circuit to be tested depends on which speed sensor triggered the Tech 1. The ground may be either a "hard" short to ground, or a resistive (partial) short. A short with a resistance less than 2 megohms, though not a hard short, can still cause DTC 28 to set.

Diagnostic Aids:

DTC 28 may be set by running the Tech 1 "Auto Test" if the throttle angle readings are not updating while in the data list mode. If this is the case, clear DTCs, disconnect Tech 1, and road test to at least 25 km/h (15 mph) to see if DTC resets.

Rear Speed Sensors Only:

Check the toothed wheel for any large grooves, gouges, marks, etc. that might influence the tooth's signal at the wheel speed sensor. Also check for a buildup of foreign material in the gaps between teeth in the toothed wheel; this material may cause this malfunction.

A worn hub/bearing assembly may cause this fault in extreme cases; the bearing play allows the sensor-to-toothed-ring gap to change excessively.

Fig. 139   DTC 28, Wheel speed sensor frequency error (Part 1 of 2). 1993 Fleetwood (RWD)

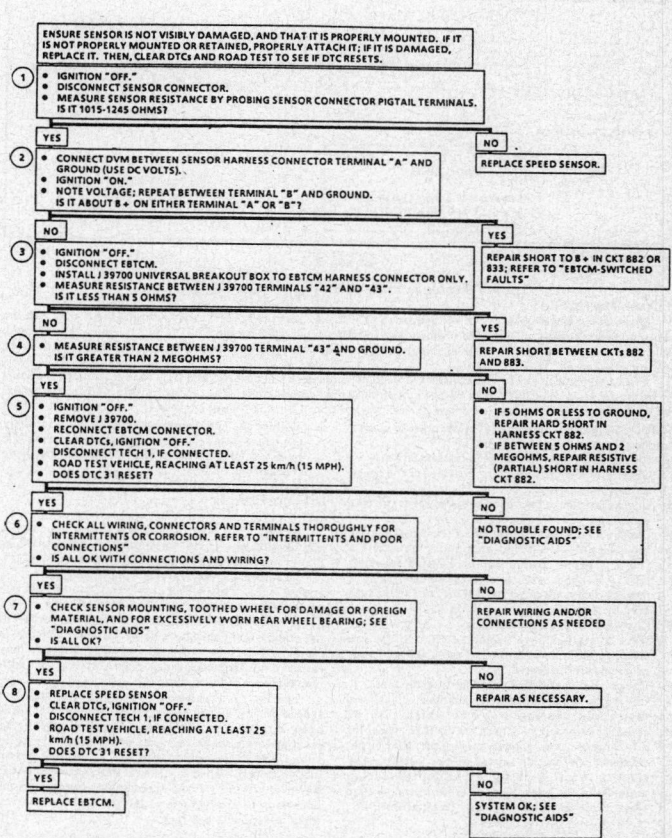

Fig. 139   DTC 28, Wheel speed sensor frequency error (Part 2 of 2). 1993 Fleetwood (RWD)

DTC 31
RR WHEEL SPEED SENSOR MALFUNCTION

Circuit Description:

The toothed wheel generates a voltage pulse as it moves past the sensor; each tooth-gap-tooth series on the wheel generates these pulses. The frequency of these pulses is used by the EBTCM to determine wheel speed. The amount of voltage generated in each pulse depends on the air gap between the sensor and the toothed wheel, and on wheel speed.

The "ANTI-LOCK" and "TRACTION CONTROL" indicators will be "ON" and DTC 31 is set if there is a short to voltage or ground in CKT 882 or 883, or a malfunctioning speed sensor. The testing for this malfunction occurs when the vehicle is in motion; it will not set with the ignition "ON" and the vehicle at rest.

Test Description: Number(s) below refer to circled number(s) on the diagnostic chart.

1. Checks for proper resistance in the sensor itself.
2. Checks for a short to battery in either of the speed sensor circuit wires.
3. Checks for a short between the speed sensor circuit wires.
4. Checks for a short to ground in the speed sensor input circuit wire. The ground may be either a "hard" short to ground, or a resistive (partial) short. A short with a resistance less than 2 megohms, though not a hard short, can still cause DTC 31 to set.
5. Checks if the DTC resets during a road test. If so, since Tests 1-4 have validated that all of the circuitry and components are good, intermittent problems are suspected.
6. Checks wiring and connectors for intermittents.
7. Checks for sensor mounting, toothed wheel, and rear wheel bearing problems which may be causing the problem. Check the toothed wheel for any large grooves, gouges, marks, etc. that might influence the tooth's signal at the wheel speed sensor. Also check for a buildup of foreign material in the gaps between teeth in the toothed wheel; this material may cause this malfunction.

8. Replace the speed sensor assembly, as it is likely the cause of a DTC reset experienced during the road test, since other portions of the circuit have checked out OK.

Diagnostic Aids:

A worn hub-bearing assembly may cause this malfunction in extreme cases; the bearing play allows the sensor-to-toothed-ring gap to change excessively.

Be sure the speed sensor wiring is properly routed and retained. This will help prevent false signals due to electrical noise being picked up by the wiring.

It is very important that a thorough inspection of the wiring and connectors be performed. Failure to carefully and fully inspect wiring and connectors may result in misdiagnosis, causing part replacement with reappearance of the malfunction.

The Tech 1 can also be used to monitor the wheel speeds during a road test. Watch the wheel speeds being displayed on the Tech 1 to see if any of the readings are unusual, such as one sensor varying in speed from the other three, a signal going intermittently high or low, etc. If this does not identify the intermittent, wet the speed sensor harness on the underside of the vehicle and road test monitoring wheel speeds with the Tech 1.

Fig. 140   DTC 31, Right rear wheel speed sensor malfunction (Part 1 of 2). 1993 Fleetwood (RWD)

Fig. 140   DTC 31, Right rear wheel speed sensor malfunction (Part 2 of 2). 1993 Fleetwood (RWD)

DTC 33

RR WHEEL SPEED SENSOR CONTINUITY MALFUNCTION

Circuit Description:

The toothed wheel generates a voltage pulse as it moves past the sensor; each tooth-gap-tooth series on the wheel generates these pulses. The frequency of these pulses is used by the EBTCM to determine wheel speed. The amount of voltage generated in each pulse depends on the air gap between the sensor and the toothed wheel, and on wheel speed.

The "ANTI-LOCK" and "TRACTION CONTROL" indicators will be "ON" and DTC 33 is set if there is a short to voltage or an open in CKT 882 or 883, or a malfunctioning speed sensor. The testing for this malfunction occurs with the ignition "ON" and the vehicle at rest.

Test Description: Number(s) below refer to circled number(s) on the diagnostic chart.

1. Checks for proper resistance in the sensor itself.
2. Checks for a short to battery in either of the speed sensor circuit wires.
3. Checks for an open in both the speed sensor circuit wires.
4. Manipulates wiring and connectors, trying to induce an intermittent malfunction not currently present.
5. This test checks if the DTC resets on key-up. If so, since Tests 1-4 have validated that the circuitry and components are good, the speed sensor may be causing the malfunction.
6. Checks if DTC 31 sets during a road test.
7. DTC 33 sets when the vehicle is at rest; DTC 31 sets with a problem in the speed sensor circuitry with the vehicle in motion. If problems are still present, DTC 31 would set during the road test, not a 33. If the DTC 33 sets at this point, the DTC 31 diagnostics should be used.

8. The wheel speed sensor may be causing an intermittent malfunction. If DTC 33 resets after sensor replacement, the EBTCM must be concluding there is a problem present in the speed sensor circuit when there is not.

Diagnostic Aids:

Be sure the speed sensor wiring is properly routed and retained. This will help prevent false signals due to electrical noise being picked up by the wiring.

It is very important that a thorough inspection of the wiring and connectors be performed. Failure to carefully and fully inspect wiring and connectors may result in misdiagnosis, causing part replacement with reappearance of the malfunction.

Fig. 141 DTC 33, Right rear wheel speed sensor continuity malfunction (Part 1 of 2). 1993 Fleetwood (RWD)

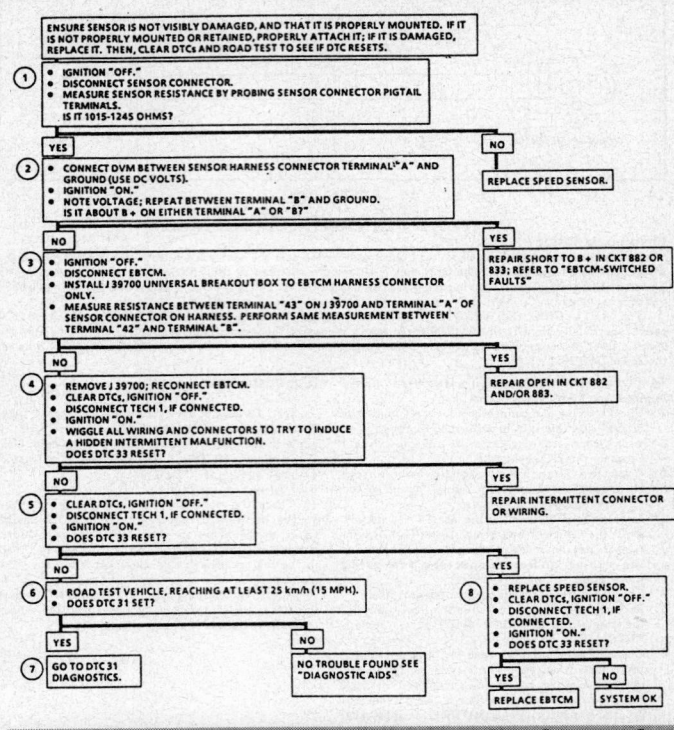

Fig. 141 DTC 33, Right rear wheel speed sensor continuity malfunction (Part 2 of 2). 1993 Fleetwood (RWD)

DTC 35

LR WHEEL SPEED SENSOR MALFUNCTION

Circuit Description:

The toothed wheel generates a voltage pulse as it moves past the sensor; each tooth-gap-tooth series on the wheel generates these pulses. The frequency of these pulses is used by the EBTCM to determine wheel speed. The amount of voltage generated in each pulse depends on the air gap between the sensor and the toothed wheel, and on wheel speed.

The "ANTI-LOCK" and "TRACTION CONTROL" indicators will be "ON" and DTC 35 is set if there is a short to voltage or ground in CKT 885 or 884, or a malfunctioning speed sensor. The testing for this malfunction occurs when the vehicle is in motion; it will not set with the ignition "ON" and the vehicle at rest.

Test Description: Number(s) below refer to circled number(s) on the diagnostic chart.

1. Checks for proper resistance in the sensor itself.
2. Checks for a short to battery in either of the speed sensor circuit wires.
3. Checks for a short between the speed sensor circuit wires.
4. Checks for a short to ground in the speed sensor input circuit wire. The ground may be either a "hard" short to ground, or a resistive (partial) short. A short with a resistance less than 2 megohms, though not a hard short, can still cause DTC 35 to set.
5. Checks if the DTC resets during a road test. If so, since Tests 1-4 have validated that all of the circuitry and components are good, intermittent problems are suspected.
6. Checks wiring and connectors for intermittents.
7. Checks for sensor mounting, toothed wheel, and rear wheel bearing problems which may be causing the problem. Check the toothed wheel for any large grooves, gouges, marks, etc. that might influence the tooth's signal at the wheel speed sensor. Also check for a buildup of foreign material in the gaps between teeth in the toothed wheel; this material may cause this malfunction.

8. Replace the speed sensor assembly, as it is likely the cause of a DTC reset experienced during the road test, since other portions of the circuit have checked out OK.

Diagnostic Aids:

A worn hub-bearing assembly may cause this malfunction in extreme cases; the bearing play allows the sensor-to-toothed-ring gap to change excessively.

Be sure the speed sensor wiring is properly routed and retained. This will help prevent false signals due to electrical noise being picked up by the wiring.

It is very important that a thorough inspection of the wiring and connectors be performed. Failure to carefully and fully inspect wiring and connectors may result in misdiagnosis, causing part replacement with reappearance of the malfunction.

The Tech 1 can also be used to monitor the wheel speeds during a road test. Watch the wheel speeds being displayed on the Tech 1 to see if any of the readings are unusual, such as one sensor varying in speed from the other three, a signal going intermittently high or low, etc. If this does not identify the intermittent, wet the speed sensor harness on the underside of the vehicle and road test monitoring wheel speeds with the Tech 1.

Fig. 142 DTC 35, Left rear wheel speed sensor malfunction (Part 1 of 2). 1993 Fleetwood (RWD)

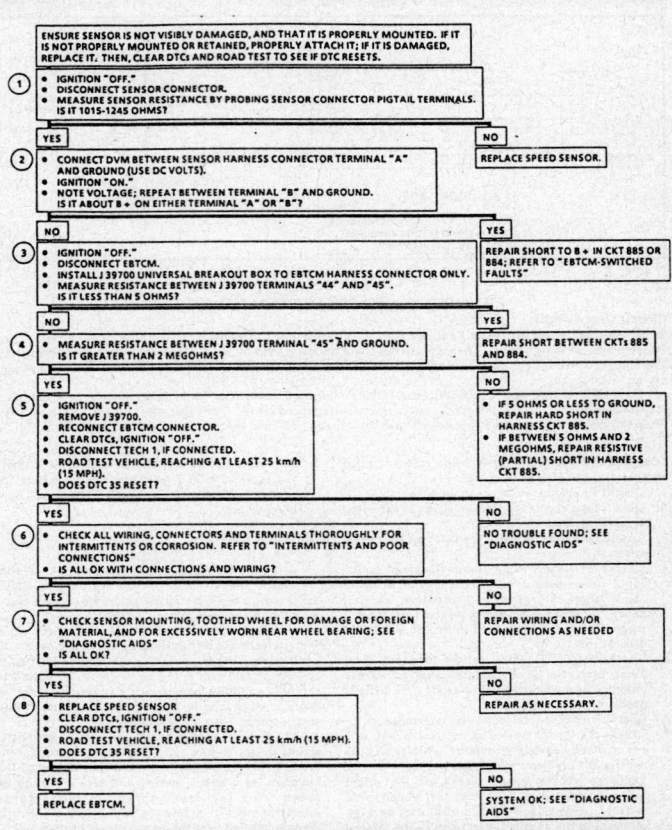

Fig. 142 DTC 35, Left rear wheel speed sensor malfunction (Part 2 of 2). 1993 Fleetwood (RWD)

DTC 37
LR WHEEL SPEED SENSOR CONTINUITY MALFUNCTION

Circuit Description:

The toothed wheel generates a voltage pulse as it moves past the sensor; each tooth-gap-tooth series on the wheel generates these pulses. The frequency of these pulses is used by the EBTCM to determine wheel speed. The amount of voltage generated in each pulse depends on the air gap between the sensor and the toothed wheel, and on wheel speed.

The "ANTI-LOCK" and "TRACTION CONTROL" indicators will be "ON" and DTC 37 is set if there is a short to voltage or an open in CKT 885 or 884, or a malfunctioning speed sensor. The testing for this malfunction occurs with the ignition "ON" and the vehicle at rest.

Test Description: Number(s) below refer to circled number(s) on the diagnostic chart.
1. Checks for proper resistance in the sensor itself.
2. Checks for a short to battery in either of the speed sensor circuit wires.
3. Checks for an open in both the speed sensor circuit wires.
4. Manipulates wiring and connectors, trying to induce an intermittent malfunction not currently present.
5. This test checks if the DTC resets on key-up. If so, since Tests 1-4 have validated that the circuitry and components are good, the speed sensor may be causing the malfunction.
6. Checks if DTC 35 sets during a road test.
7. DTC 37 sets when the vehicle is at rest; DTC 35 sets with a problem in the speed sensor circuitry with the vehicle in motion. If problems are still present, DTC 35 would set during the road test, not a 37. If the DTC 35 sets at this point, the DTC 35 diagnostics should be used.

8. The wheel speed sensor may be causing an intermittent malfunction. If DTC 37 resets after sensor replacement, the EBTCM must be concluding there is a problem present in the speed sensor circuit when there is not.

Diagnostic Aids:

Be sure the speed sensor wiring is properly routed and retained. This will help prevent false signals due to electrical noise being picked up by the wiring.

It is very important that a thorough inspection of the wiring and connectors be performed. Failure to carefully and fully inspect wiring and connectors may result in misdiagnosis, causing part replacement with reappearance of the malfunction.

Fig. 143 DTC 36, Left rear wheel speed sensor continuity malfunction (Part 1 of 2). 1993 Fleetwood (RWD)

Fig. 143 DTC 36, Left rear wheel speed sensor continuity malfunction (Part 2 of 2). 1993 Fleetwood (RWD)

DTC 41
RF VALVE SOLENOID MALFUNCTION

Circuit Description:

The wheel valve solenoid circuits are supplied with battery power when the ignition is "ON." The EBTCM controls the valve functions by permitting one of three levels of current flow (0, 2.5, 5 amps) to the solenoid.

If the EBTCM senses a discrepancy such as an open or ground in the circuit, the valve solenoid relay will turn "OFF," the "ANTI-LOCK" and "TRACTION CONTROL" lights will come "ON," and DTC 41 will set.

Test Description: Number(s) below refer to circled number(s) on the diagnostic chart.
1. Checks the integrity of CKTs 827 and 856, the RF valve solenoid circuitry internal to the modulator valve assembly, and the RF valve solenoid coil.
2. Checks for a short to battery in CKT 827, using EBTCM terminal "3" as ground.
3. Checks for a short to ground in CKT 827, using EBTCM terminal "3" as ground.
4. Checks wiring and connectors for intermittents.
5. Uses the Tech 1 to exercise the RF valve solenoid and check it for proper operation.
6. Determines whether the DTC was set by an intermittent condition or an EBTCM malfunction.

7. Determines whether a problem found in Step 1 is due to an open in CKT 827 or a malfunctioning modulator valve assembly.

Diagnostic Aids:

All tests using J 39700 Universal Breakout Box terminal "3" are using the terminal as ground. These tests, of course, assume that the ground at terminal "3" is good.

If DTCs 41 and 45 are both set the malfunction is likely to be a short to B+ on CKT 827.

If DTCs 41 and 55 are both set the malfunction is likely to be a short to B+ on CKT 828.

Fig. 144 DTC 41, Right front valve solenoid malfunction (Part 1 of 2). 1993 Fleetwood (RWD)

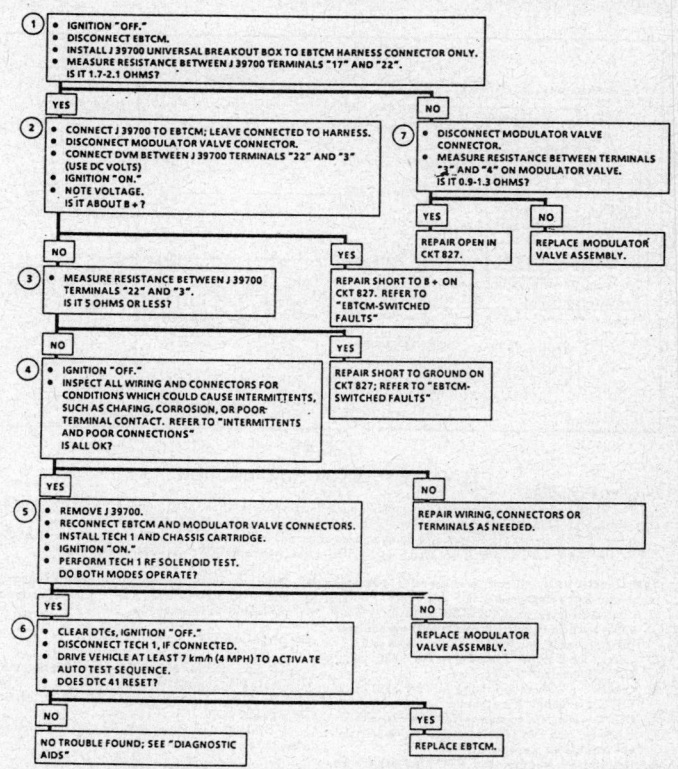

Fig. 144 DTC 41, Right front valve solenoid malfunction (Part 2 of 2). 1993 Fleetwood (RWD)

DTC 44
PILOT VALVE SOLENOID MALFUNCTION

Circuit Description:

The pilot valve solenoid circuit is supplied with battery power when the ignition is "ON." The EBTCM controls the valve by grounding the circuit when necessary.

If the EBTCM senses a discrepancy such as an open or ground in the circuit, the valve solenoid relay will turn "OFF," the "ANTI-LOCK" and "TRACTION CONTROL" lights will come "ON," and DTC 44 will set.

Test Description: Number(s) below refer to circled number(s) on the diagnostic chart.

1. Checks the integrity of CKTs 1683 and 1077, the pilot valve solenoid circuitry internal to the modulator valve assembly, and the pilot valve solenoid coil.
2. Checks for a short to battery in CKT 1683, using EBTCM terminal "3" as ground.
3. Checks for a short to ground in CKT 1683, using EBTCM terminal "3" as ground.
4. Checks for connector or wiring problems which could cause intermittents.
5. Uses the Tech 1 to exercise the pilot valve solenoid and check it for proper operation.

6. Determines whether the DTC was set by an intermittent condition or an EBTCM malfunction.
7. Determines whether a problem found in Step 1 is due to an open in CKT 1683 or a malfunctioning modulator valve assembly.

Diagnostic Aids:

All tests using J 39700 Universal Breakout Box terminal "3" are using the terminal as ground. These tests, of course, assume that the ground at terminal "3" is good.

Fig. 145   DTC 44, Pilot valve solenoid malfunction (Part 1 of 2). 1993 Fleetwood (RWD)

DTC 45
LF VALVE SOLENOID MALFUNCTION

Circuit Description:

The wheel valve solenoid circuits are supplied with battery power when the ignition is "ON." The EBTCM controls the valve functions by permitting one of three levels of current flow (0, 2.5, 5 amps) to the solenoid.

If the EBTCM senses a discrepancy such as an open or ground in the circuit, the valve solenoid relay will turn "OFF," the "ANTI-LOCK" and "TRACTION CONTROL" lights will come "ON," and DTC 45 will set.

Test Description: Number(s) below refer to circled number(s) on the diagnostic chart.

1. Checks the integrity of CKTs 826 and 1077, the LF valve solenoid circuitry internal to the modulator valve assembly, and the LF valve solenoid coil.
2. Checks for a short to battery in CKT 826, using EBTCM terminal "3" as ground.
3. Checks for a short to ground in CKT 826, using EBTCM terminal "3" as ground.
4. Checks wiring and connectors for intermittents.
5. Uses the Tech 1 to exercise the LF valve solenoid and check it for proper operation.
6. Determines whether the DTC was set by an intermittent condition or an EBTCM malfunction.

7. Determines whether a problem found in Step 1 is due to an open in CKT 826 or a malfunctioning modulator valve assembly.

Diagnostic Aids:

All tests using J 39700 Universal Breakout Box terminal "3" are using the terminal as ground. These tests, of course, assume that the ground at terminal "3" is good.

If DTCs 41 and 45 are both set, the malfunction is likely to be a short to B + on CKT 826.

Fig. 146   DTC 45, Left front valve solenoid malfunction (Part 1 of 2). 1993 Fleetwood (RWD)

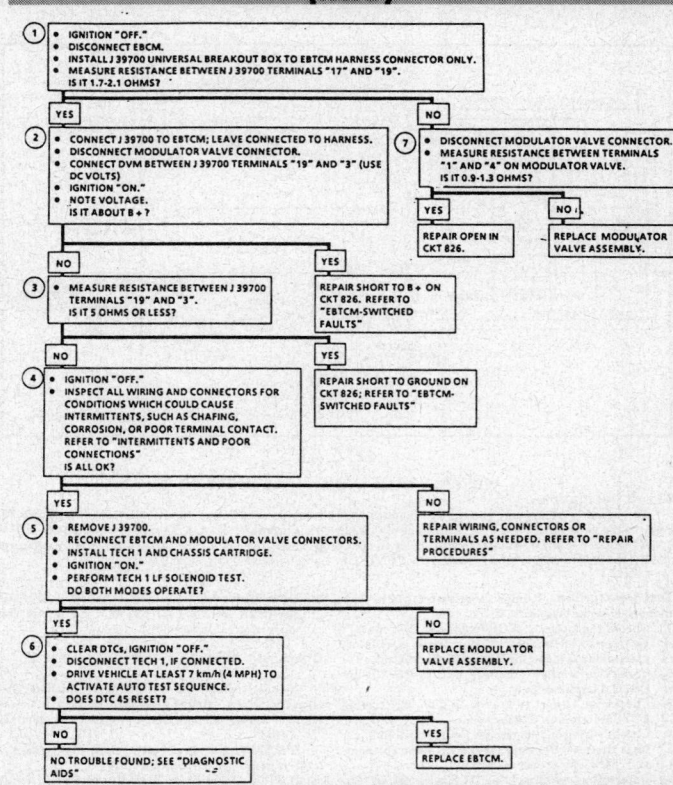

Fig. 145   DTC 44, Pilot valve solenoid malfunction (Part 2 of 2). 1993 Fleetwood (RWD)

Fig. 146   DTC 45, Left front valve solenoid malfunction (Part 2 of 2). 1993 Fleetwood (RWD)

DTC 51
RR VALVE SOLENOID MALFUNCTION

Circuit Description:

The wheel valve solenoid circuits are supplied with battery power when the ignition is "ON." The EBTCM controls the valve functions by permitting one of three levels of current flow (0, 2.5, 5 amps) to the solenoid.

If the EBTCM senses a discrepancy such as an open or ground in the circuit, the valve solenoid relay will turn "OFF;" the "ANTI-LOCK" and "TRACTION CONTROL" lights will come "ON," and DTC 51 will set.

Test Description: Number(s) below refer to circled number(s) on the diagnostic chart.

1. Checks the integrity of CKTs 829 and 856, the RR valve solenoid circuitry internal to the modulator valve assembly, and the RR valve solenoid coil.
2. Checks for a short to battery in CKT 829, using EBTCM terminal "3" as ground.
3. Checks for a short to ground in CKT 829, using EBTCM terminal "3" as ground.
4. Checks wiring and connectors for intermittents.
5. Uses the Tech 1 to exercise the RR valve solenoid and check it for proper operation.

6. Determines whether the DTC was set by an intermittent condition or an EBTCM malfunction.
7. Determines whether a problem found in Step 1 is due to an open in CKT 829 or a malfunctioning modulator valve assembly.

Diagnostic Aids:

All tests using J 39700 Universal Breakout Box terminal "3" are using the terminal as ground. These tests, of course, assume that the ground at terminal "3" is good.

Fig. 147   DTC 51, Right front valve solenoid malfunction (Part 1 of 2). 1993 Fleetwood (RWD)

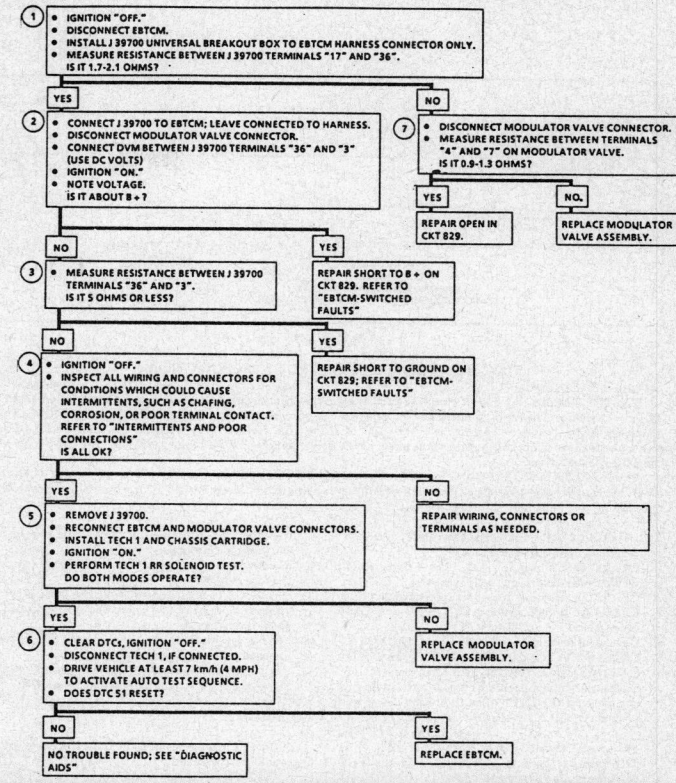

Fig. 147   DTC 51, Right front valve solenoid malfunction (Part 2 of 2). 1993 Fleetwood (RWD)

DTC 55
LR VALVE SOLENOID MALFUNCTION

Circuit Description:

The wheel valve solenoid circuits are supplied with battery power when the ignition is "ON." The EBTCM controls the valve functions by permitting one of three levels of current flow (0, 2.5, 5 amps) to the solenoid.

If the EBTCM senses a discrepancy such as an open or ground in the circuit, the valve solenoid relay will turn "OFF," the "ANTI-LOCK" and "TRACTION CONTROL" lights will come "ON," and DTC 55 will set.

Test Description: Number(s) below refer to circled number(s) on the diagnostic chart.

1. Checks the integrity of CKTs 828 and 856, the LR valve solenoid circuitry internal to the modulator valve assembly, and the LR valve solenoid coil.
2. Checks for a short to battery in CKT 828, using EBTCM terminal "3" as ground.
3. Checks for a short to ground in CKT 828, using EBTCM terminal "3" as ground.
4. Checks wiring and connectors for intermittents.
5. Uses the Tech 1 to exercise the LR valve solenoid and check it for proper operation.

6. Determines whether the DTC was set by an intermittent condition or an EBTCM malfunction.
7. Determines whether a problem found in Step 1 is due to an open in CKT 828 or a malfunctioning modulator valve assembly.

Diagnostic Aids:

All tests using J 39700 Universal Breakout Box terminal "3" are using the terminal as ground. These tests, of course, assume that the ground at terminal "3" is good.

If DTCs 41 and 55 are both set the malfunction is likely to be a short to B + on CKT 828.

Fig. 148   DTC 55, Left rear valve solenoid malfunction (Part 1 of 2). 1993 Fleetwood (RWD)

Fig. 148   DTC 55, Left rear valve solenoid malfunction (Part 2 of 2). 1993 Fleetwood (RWD)

DTC 57
TCC DISABLE RELAY OUTPUT MALFUNCTION

Circuit Description:
The TCC disable relay output circuit is used to open the TCC circuit to the automatic transmission when a TCS event occurs. The EBTCM energizes the relay coil by grounding CKT 1679 at EBTCM terminal "14". This opens the switch between contacts "D3" and "D4" of of the TCC disable relay, opening the TCC circuit to the automatic transmission; this has the same effect as the driver depressing the brake pedal, opening the circuit via the TCC release switch.

The "TRACTION CONTROL" lamp will come "ON" and DTC 57 will set if CKT 1679 remains high when the EBTCM requests energization of the relay coil (by grounding EBTCM terminal "14"), which should take the circuit low.

Test Description: Number(s) below refer to circled number(s) on the diagnostic chart.
1. Checks for a blown I/P #13, Chime fuse, which would cause the relay to be inoperative.
2. Checks the relay coil for proper resistance.
3. Checks for a good ground CKT 1500 and G201 connection.
4. Checks for an open in CKT 639, since fuse is OK.
5. Checks for an open in CKT 1679 to ensure relay coil can receive EBTCM ground when needed.
6. Checks for intermittents and poor connections as the cause of the DTC, since the relay, power and ground circuits all check OK. If wiring checks out the EBTCM is either malfunctioning on terminal "14", or is determining there is a problem with the TCC disable output when there is not.

7. Replaces bad fuse found in Step 1 and checks for the fuse blowing again.
8. Checks for a short to ground in CKT 639 causing the fuse to blow.
9. Checks CKTs 1680 and 420 together for a short to ground, since they are connected until the brake pedal is depressed.
10. Checks for internal shorting in the relay itself between power and ground points.
11. Checks for an intermittent short to ground as the cause of the DTC, since all else checks out OK.

Diagnostic Aids:
If the TCC never engages, the fault is likely a short to ground in CKT 1679.

Fig. 149   DTC 57, TCC disable relay output malfunction (Part 1 of 2). 1993 Fleetwood (RWD)

Fig. 149   DTC 57, TCC disable relay output malfunction (Part 2 of 2). 1993 Fleetwood (RWD)

19 NUT, INFLATABLE RESTRAINT DIAGNOSTIC ENERGY RESERVE MODULE, 1.9 N·m (17 lb. in.)
20 MODULE ASSEMBLY, INFLATABLE RESTRAINT DIAGNOSTIC ENERGY RESERVE
21 BOLT/SCREW, INFLATABLE RESTRAINT DIAGNOSTIC ENERGY RESERVE MODULE BRACKET, 2.8 N·m (25 lb. in.)
22 BRACKET, INFLATABLE RESTRAINT DIAGNOSTIC ENERGY RESERVE MODULE
23 MODULE ASSEMBLY, ELECTRONIC BRAKE AND TRACTION CONTROL
24 BOLT/SCREW, ELECTRONIC BRAKE AND TRACTION CONTROL BRACKET, 6 N·m (53 lb. in.)
25 BRACKET ASSEMBLY, ELECTRONIC BRAKE AND TRACTION CONTROL MODULE
26 NUT, ELECTRONIC BRAKE AND TRACTION CONTROL MODULE, 1.9 N·m (17 lb. in.)
27 RETAINER, INFLATABLE RESTRAINT DIAGNOSTIC ENERGY RESERVE MODULE, 1.9 N·m (17 lb. in.)
37 RELAY, RETAINED ACCESSORY POWER

DTC 58
EBTCM INTERNAL ADJUSTER ASSEMBLY MALFUNCTION

Circuit Description:
The EBTCM contains a microprocessor for ABS/TCS calculations and functions, as well as a microprocessor for adjuster assembly calculations and functions. If the two microprocessors cannot communicate with each other properly, DTC 58 will set.

Test Description: Number(s) below refer to circled number(s) on the diagnostic chart.
1. Clears DTCs and checks for DTC 58 reset. If the DTC resets, the microprocessor communication problem does exist within the EBTCM.

Fig. 150   DTC 58, EBTCM internal adjuster assembly malfunction (Part 1 of 2). 1993 Fleetwood (RWD)

Fig. 150   DTC 58, EBTCM internal adjuster assembly malfunction (Part 2 of 2). 1993 Fleetwood (RWD)

DTC 61
1 of 2
PUMP MOTOR OR PUMP MOTOR RELAY MALFUNCTION

Circuit Description:

When the pump motor relay is grounded by the EBTCM, it closes and provides B+ to operate the pump. Once the motor circuit is energized, a "Pump ON" signal is sensed by the EBTCM through CKT 875 to verify pump operation.

The "ANTI-LOCK" and "TRACTION CONTROL" indicators will be "ON" and DTC 61 will set if B+ is present at the pump motor without pump motor relay activation from the EBTCM, or if B+ is NOT present at the pump motor within 60 milliseconds after the EBTCM requests pump motor relay activation.

Test Description: Number(s) below refer to circled number(s) on the diagnostic chart.
1. Checks the pump motor relay coil for proper resistance.
2. Checks for an open in power feed CKT 1447B.
3. Determines if the pump motor relay contacts are stuck closed.
4. Determines if the pump motor relay contacts are stuck open.
5. Checks the integrity of the pump motor and pump motor relay circuitry internal to the modulator valve assembly.
6. Checks for an open in CKT 879.
7. Checks for a short to ground in CKT 879.
8. Checks for a short to B+ in CKT 879.

Diagnostic Aids:

All tests using J 39700 Universal Breakout Box terminal "3" are using that terminal as ground. These tests, of course, assume that the ground at terminal "3" is good.

It is very important that a thorough inspection of the wiring and connectors be performed. Failure to carefully and fully inspect wiring and connectors may result in misdiagnosis, causing part replacement with reappearance of the malfunction.

Fig. 151 DTC 61, Pump motor or pump motor relay malfunction (Part 1 of 4). 1993 Fleetwood (RWD)

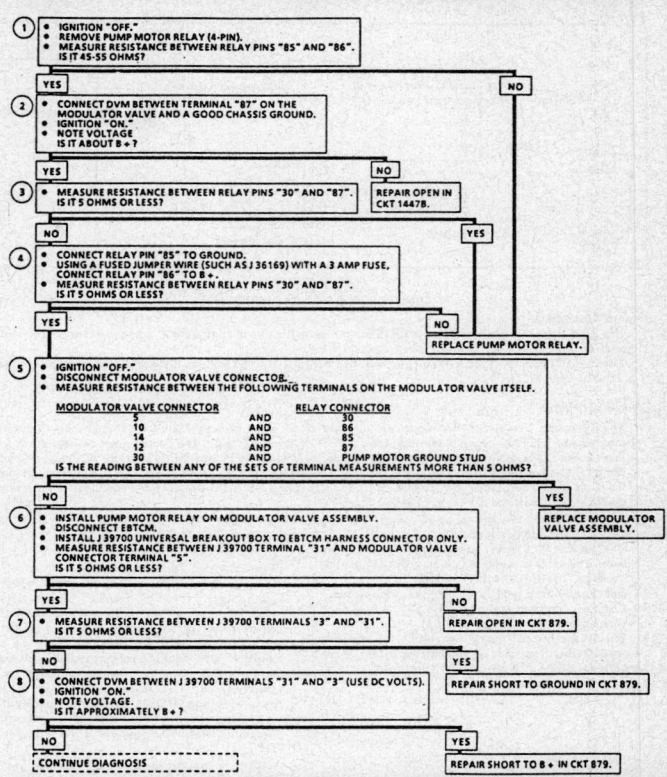

Fig. 151 DTC 61, Pump motor or pump motor relay malfunction (Part 2 of 4). 1993 Fleetwood (RWD)

DTC 61
2 of 2
PUMP MOTOR OR PUMP MOTOR RELAY MALFUNCTION

Circuit Description:

When the pump motor relay is grounded by the EBTCM, it closes and provides B+ to operate the pump. Once the motor circuit is energized, a "Pump ON" signal is sensed by the EBTCM through CKT 875 to verify pump operation.

The "ANTI-LOCK" and "TRACTION CONTROL" indicators will be "ON" and DTC 61 will set if B+ is present at the pump motor without pump motor relay activation from the EBTCM, or if B+ is NOT present at the pump motor within 60 milliseconds after the EBTCM requests pump motor relay activation.

Test Description: Number(s) below refer to circled number(s) on the diagnostic chart.
9. Checks for an open in CKT 854.
10. Checks for a short to ground in CKT 854.
11. Checks for a short to B+ in CKT 854.
12. Checks wiring and connectors for intermittents.
13. Uses the Tech 1 to check for proper operation of the pump motor and associated circuitry.
14. Determines whether the problem found in Step 13 was due to a malfunctioning EBTCM or an open in pump motor ground CKT 150.

Diagnostic Aids:

All tests using J 39700 Universal Breakout Box terminal "3" are using that terminal as ground. These tests, of course, assume that the ground at terminal "3" is good.

It is very important that a thorough inspection of the wiring and connectors be performed. Failure to carefully and fully inspect wiring and connectors may result in misdiagnosis, causing part replacement with reappearance of the malfunction.

Fig. 151 DTC 61, Pump motor or pump motor relay malfunction (Part 3 of 4). 1993 Fleetwood (RWD)

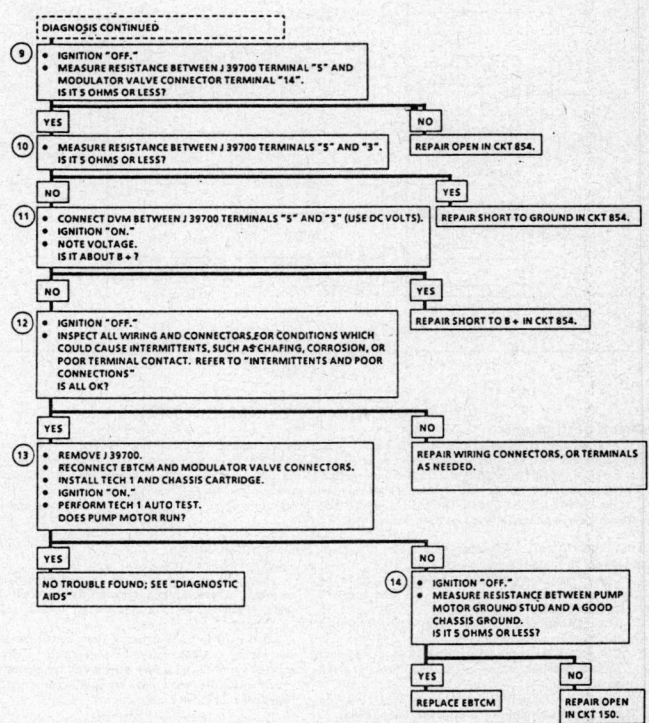

Fig. 151 DTC 61, Pump motor or pump motor relay malfunction (Part 4 of 4). 1993 Fleetwood (RWD)

DTC 62
RPM SIGNAL MALFUNCTION

Circuit Description:

The RPM signal circuit provides the EBTCM with an indication of engine RPM to help determine TCS control methods and rates when a TCS event takes place.

The "TRACTION CONTROL" indicator will be "ON" and DTC 62 will be set if there is a short to ground, short to B+, or an open in CKT 121.

Important
- The "Traction Disable" switch also can set this DTC, since it disables TCS by purposely inducing a momentary "short to ground" malfunction at EBTCM terminal "53". The switch must be held down for at least 2 seconds to do so. Be sure to clear DTCs, turn ignition "OFF," then turn ignition "ON" again to verify the DTC was not set by the owner using the traction disable switch. Review Tech 1 DTC History information for clues as to when the DTC set and how frequently it has set. Also, speak to the customer to determine if traction disable switch use is the cause for this DTC.

Test Description: Number(s) below refer to circled number(s) on the diagnostic chart.
1. Checks for DTC reset after clearing DTCs to ensure a problem really exists, not that the owner used the "Traction Disable" switch.
2. Checks for "Traction Disable" switch stuck closed.
3. Checks for short to ground in CKT 627.
4. Checks for short to B+ in CKT 627.
5. Checks for normal operating voltage of about 5 volts from output side of tachometer filter. If no voltage, CKT 627 is open.

Diagnostic Aids:

Important
- The "Traction Disable" switch also can set this DTC, since it disables TCS by purposely inducing a momentary "short to ground" malfunction at EBTCM terminal "53". The switch must be held down for at least 2 seconds to do so. Be sure to clear DTCs, turn ignition "OFF," then turn ignition "ON" again to verify the DTC was not set by the owner using the "Traction Disable" switch. Review Tech 1 DTC History information for clues as to when the DTC set and how frequently it has set. Also, speak to the customer to determine if "Traction Disable" switch use is the cause for this DTC.

A short to ground in CKT 121 on the ignition system side of the tach filter may cause a no-start or extremely poor driveability condition.

Fig. 152   DTC 62, RPM signal malfunction (Part 1 of 2). 1993 Fleetwood (RWD)

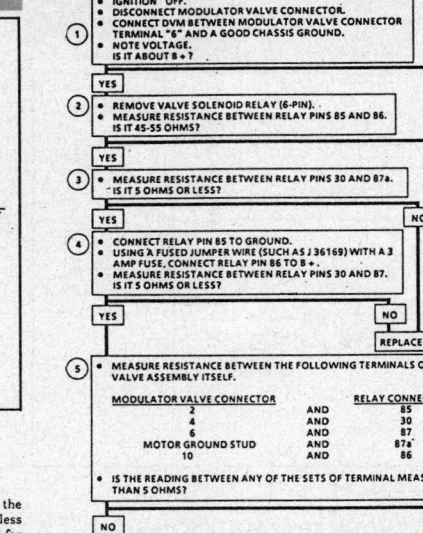

Fig. 152   DTC 62, RPM signal malfunction (Part 2 of 2). 1993 Fleetwood (RWD)

DTC 63
1 of 2
VALVE SOLENOID RELAY MALFUNCTION

Circuit Description:

The valve solenoid relay has two functions. When the ignition is "ON" and the EBTCM is operating, the relay provides voltage to actuate the valve solenoids. However, the valve solenoids do not use this voltage unless the EBTCM provides the ground. The second function of the valve solenoid relay is to provide a ground path for illumination of the "ANTI-LOCK" lamp if the relay loses power or ground.

The "ANTI-LOCK" and "TRACTION CONTROL" indicators will be "ON" and DTC 63 will set if the valve solenoid relay voltage falls to less than 5 volts.

Test Description: Number(s) below refer to circled number(s) on the diagnostic chart.
1. Checks for the availability of battery voltage to the valve solenoid relay through ABS maxifuse #5 and CKT 1447.
2. Checks the valve solenoid relay coil for proper resistance.
3. Checks for the valve solenoid relay contacts being internally open when in the relay-unenergized position.
4. Checks for the valve solenoid relay contacts being stuck open when in the relay-energized position.
5. Checks the integrity of the valve solenoid relay circuitry internal to the modulator valve assembly.
6. Checks for an open in ground CKT 150.
7. Checks for an open in CKT 856.

Diagnostic Aids:

All tests using J 39700 Universal Breakout Box terminal "3" are using that terminal as ground. These tests, of course, assume that the ground at terminal "3" is good.

It is very important that a thorough inspection of the wiring and connectors be performed. Failure to carefully and fully inspect wiring and connectors may result in misdiagnosis, causing part replacement with reappearance of the malfunction.

Fig. 153   DTC 63, Valve solenoid relay malfunction (Part 2 of 4). 1993 Fleetwood (RWD)

Fig. 153   DTC 63, Valve solenoid relay malfunction (Part 1 of 4). 1993 Fleetwood (RWD)

DTC 63
2 of 2
VALVE SOLENOID RELAY MALFUNCTION

Circuit Description:
The valve solenoid relay has two functions. When the ignition is "ON" and the EBTCM is operating, the relay provides voltage to actuate the valve solenoids. However, the valve solenoids do not use this voltage unless the EBTCM provides the ground. The second function of the valve solenoid relay is to provide a ground path for illumination of the "ANTI-LOCK" lamp if the relay loses power or ground.
The "ANTI-LOCK" and "TRACTION CONTROL" indicators will be "ON" and DTC 63 will set if the valve solenoid relay voltage falls to less than 5 volts.

Test Description: Number(s) below refer to circled number(s) on the diagnostic chart.
8. Checks for a short to ground in CKT 856.
9. Checks for a short to B+ in CKT 856.
10. Checks for an open in CKT 1079.
11. Checks for a short to ground in CKT 1079.
12. Checks for an open in CKT 1077.
13. Checks for a short to ground in CKT 1077.
14. Checks wiring and connectors for intermittents.
15. Determines whether the DTC was set due to an intermittent condition or an EBTCM malfunction.

Diagnostic Aids:
All tests using J 39700 Universal Breakout Box terminal "3" are using that terminal as ground. These tests, of course, assume that the ground at terminal "3" is good.
It is very important that a thorough inspection of the wiring and connectors be performed. Failure to carefully and fully inspect wiring and connectors may result in misdiagnosis, causing part replacement with reappearance of the malfunction.

Fig. 153   DTC 63, Valve solenoid relay malfunction (Part 3 of 4). 1993 Fleetwood (RWD)

DTC 64
1 of 2
THROTTLE POSITION SIGNAL MALFUNCTION

Circuit Description:
The throttle position signal circuit is used by the EBTCM to monitor the actual throttle position versus desired throttle position to monitor and control engine torque during a TCS event. The throttle position sensor interface module is used to allow EBTCM monitoring of the TP sensor signal without affecting the TP sensor signal to the ECM.
DTC 64 will set if the EBTCM is not receiving reference voltage or a TP sensor signal from the throttle position interface module.

Test Description: Number(s) below refer to circled number(s) on the diagnostic chart.
1. Checks for TP sensor-related ECM DTCs. Many of the same conditions which could cause a TCS DTC 64 will also cause ECM DTCs. The ECM DTCs should be repaired first to eliminate those problems from affecting the TCS DTC 64 condition.
2. Checks for a short to ground in CKT 1689.
3. Checks for an open in CKT 1915.
4. Checks for a short to ground in CKT 1688.
5. Checks for proper voltage in CKT 1688 at the EBTCM connection. (This voltage measurement is only appropriate when the EBTCM is disconnected from the circuit).
6. Checks for proper voltage in CKT 1689 at the EBTCM connection. (This voltage measurement is only appropriate when the EBTCM is disconnected from the circuit).
7. Checks for an additional DTC 64 problem after ground CKT 1915 is repaired.
8. Determines if a problem found in Step 5 is due to a fuse, CKT 839, or CKT 1688.
9. Determines if a problem found in Steps 5 and 13 is due to an open in CKT 1688 or a malfunctioning TP sensor interface module.

Fig. 154   DTC 64, Throttle position signal malfunction (Part 1 of 4). 1993 Fleetwood (RWD)

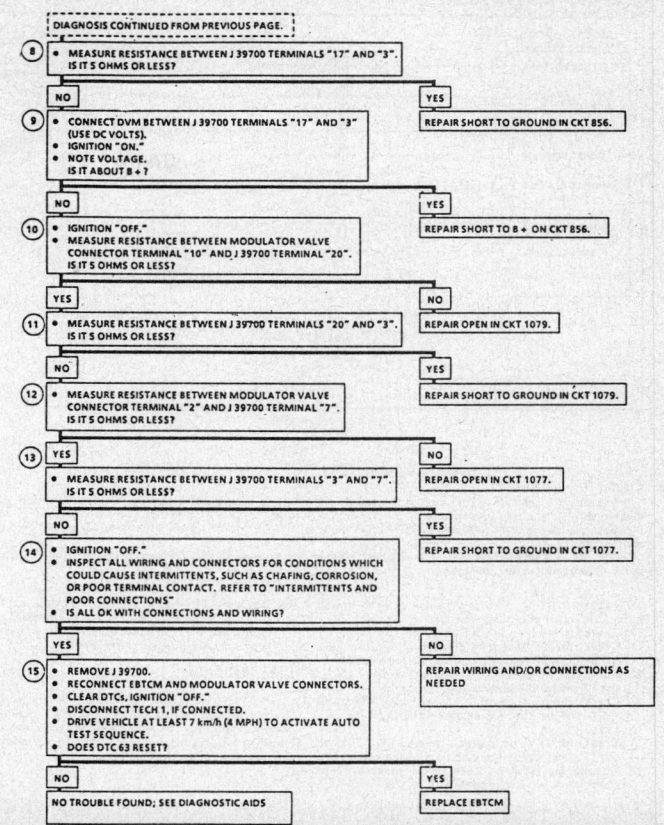

Fig. 153   DTC 63, Valve solenoid relay malfunction (Part 4 of 4). 1993 Fleetwood (RWD)

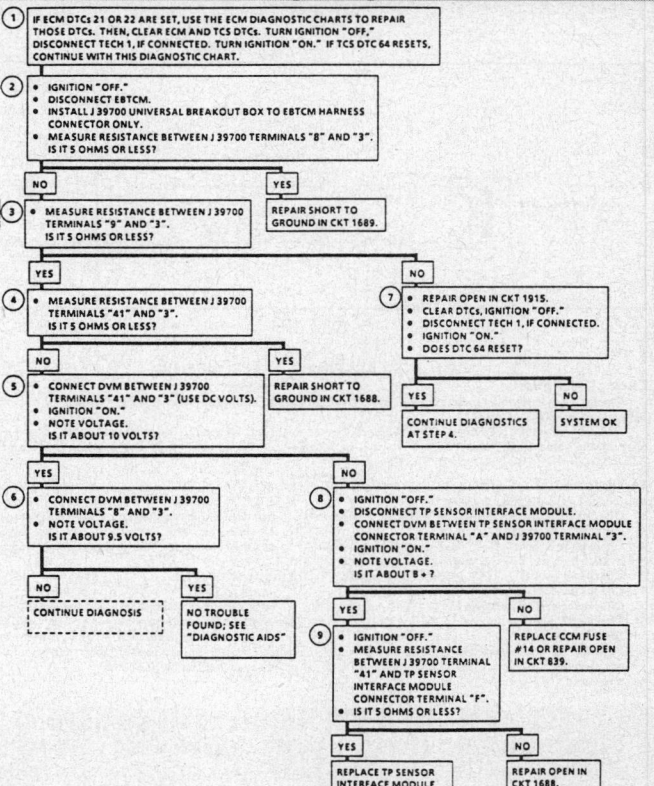

Fig. 154   DTC 64, Throttle position signal malfunction (Part 2 of 4). 1993 Fleetwood (RWD)

DTC 64

2 of 2

THROTTLE POSITION SIGNAL MALFUNCTION

Circuit Description:

The throttle position signal circuit is used by the EBTCM to monitor the actual throttle position versus desired throttle position to monitor and control engine torque during a TCS event. The throttle position sensor interface module is used to allow EBTCM monitoring of the TP sensor signal without affecting the TP sensor signal to the ECM.

DTC 64 will set if the EBTCM is not receiving reference voltage or a TP sensor signal from the throttle position sensor interface module.

Test Description: Number(s) below refer to circled number(s) on the diagnostic chart.

10. Checks for an open in CKT 1689.
11. Checks for TP sensor reference voltage from the ECM at the TP sensor interface module connector.
12. Checks for TP sensor signal voltage on CKT 452 at the TP sensor interface module connector.
13. Checks for an open in TP sensor signal ground CKT 416 to the TP sensor interface module connector.
14. Checks for an open in signal ground CKT 1917 to the TP sensor interface module connector.
15. Checks for DTC 64 reset after most system components have checked OK.

16. Replaces TP sensor interface module as likely cause of DTC reset in Step 15. If the DTC resets again, the EBTCM must be concluding there is a problem present when there is not.

Diagnostic Aids:

It is very important that a thorough inspection of the wiring and connectors be performed. Failure to carefully and fully inspect wiring and connectors may result in misdiagnosis, causing part replacement with reappearance of the malfunction.

Fig. 154   DTC 64, Throttle position signal malfunction (Part 3 of 4). 1993 Fleetwood (RWD)

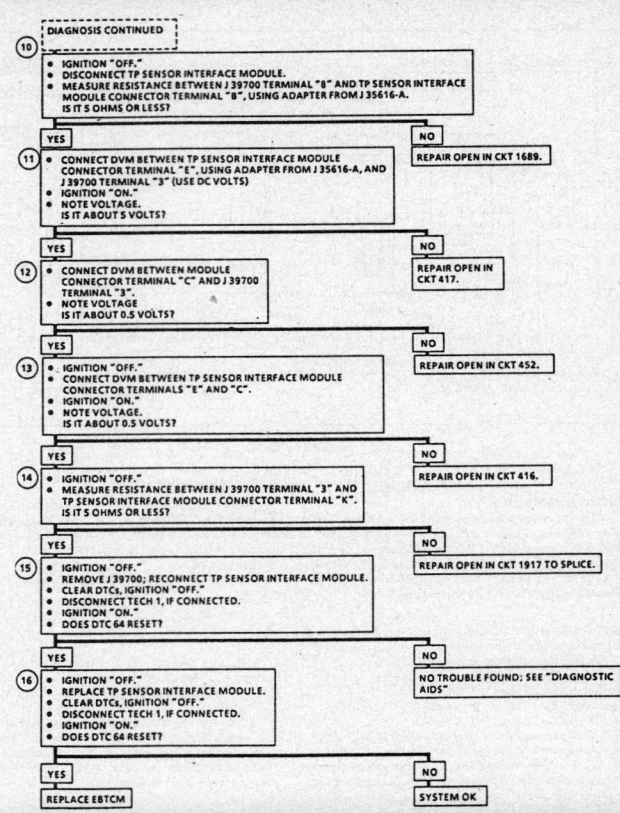

Fig. 154   DTC 64, Throttle position signal malfunction (Part 4 of 4). 1993 Fleetwood (RWD)

DTC 65

1 of 2

ADJUSTER ASSEMBLY MALFUNCTION

Circuit Description:

The adjuster assembly circuit provides both power and ground to the adjuster assembly to help control engine torque during a TCS event.

DTC 65 will set if CKT 1685 or CKT 1686 are shorted to ground, shorted to B+, shorted to each other, or both open at the same time. The TCS system will be disabled for the remainder of the ignition cycle and the "TRACTION CONTROL" lamp will illuminate.

Test Description: Number(s) below refer to circled number(s) on the diagnostic chart.

1. Checks for proper adjuster assembly motor winding resistance.
2. Checks for a poor power feed condition in CKT 2140, which the EBTCM might sense as an open.
3. Checks for open(s) in CKT 1685A and/or 1685B.
4. Checks for open(s) in CKT 1686A and/or 1686B.
5. Checks for a short between CKTs 1685 and 1686.
6. Checks for short(s) to B+ in CKT 1685A and/or 1685B.
7. Repeat Step 1 tests to ensure motor is in "home" position and a correct resistance value can be measured.

8. Sets throttle to a position which enables a special EBTCM monitor. If DTC 65 resets, there is a problem which requires continuing diagnosis.
9. Determines whether wiring or the adjuster assembly are at fault for problems found in Step 7.

Diagnostic Aids:

It is very important that a thorough inspection of the wiring and connectors be performed. Failure to carefully and fully inspect wiring and connectors may result in misdiagnosis, causing part replacement with reappearance of the malfunction.

Fig. 155   DTC 65, Adjuster assembly malfunction (Part 1 of 4). 1993 Fleetwood (RWD)

Fig. 155   DTC 65, Adjuster assembly malfunction (Part 2 of 4). 1993 Fleetwood (RWD)

DTC 65
2 of 2
ADJUSTER ASSEMBLY MALFUNCTION

Circuit Description:
The adjuster assembly circuit provides both power and ground to the adjuster assembly to help control engine torque during a TCS event.

DTC 65 will set if CKT 1685 or CKT 1686 are shorted to ground, shorted to B+, shorted to each other, or both open at the same time. The TCS system will be disabled for the remainder of the ignition cycle and the "TRACTION CONTROL" lamp will illuminate.

Test Description: Number(s) below refer to circled number(s) on the diagnostic chart.
10. Checks for short(s) to B+ in CKT 1686B and/or 1686C.
11. Checks for short(s) to ground in CKT 1685B and/or 1685C.
12. Checks for short(s) to ground in CKT 1686B and/or 1686C.
13. Checks for continued DTC setting after wiring and adjuster assembly inspections.
14. Sets throttle to a position which enables one of the EBTCM's special monitoring systems of the adjuster assembly circuits, checking for a DTC reset. If the DTC resets, the EBTCM is likely malfunctioning.

15. Checks for shorts to B+ or ground that are EBTCM-switched. If you have reached Step 13 for a second time after performing checks for EBTCM-switched malfunctions, the EBTCM is likely malfunctioning for the DTC reset.

Diagnostic Aids:

It is very important that a thorough inspection of the wiring and connectors be performed. Failure to carefully and fully inspect wiring and connectors may result in misdiagnosis, causing part replacement with reappearance of the malfunction.

Fig. 155   DTC 65, Adjuster assembly malfunction (Part 3 of 4). 1993 Fleetwood (RWD)

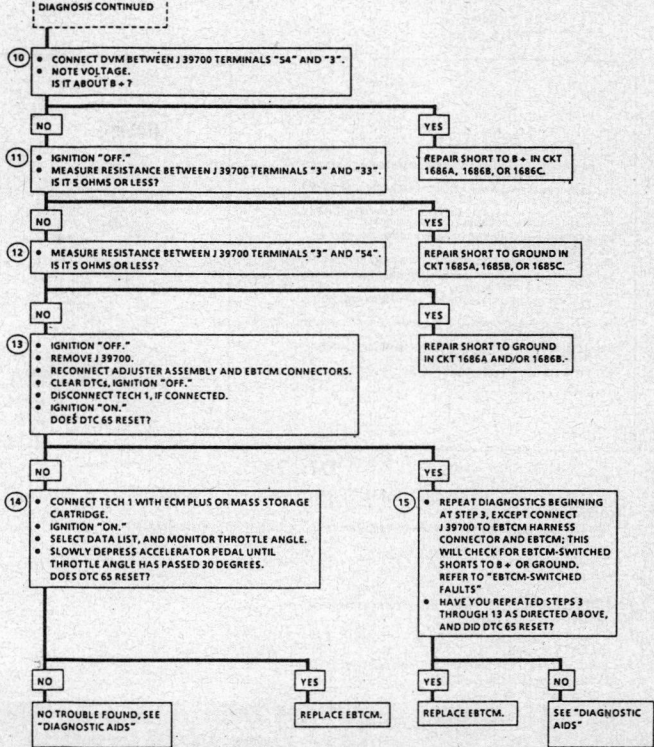

Fig. 155   DTC 65, Adjuster assembly malfunction (Part 4 of 4). 1993 Fleetwood (RWD)

DTC 66
ADJUSTER ASSEMBLY CONTROL MALFUNCTION

Circuit Description:
The adjuster assembly circuit provides both power and ground to the adjuster assembly to help control engine torque during a TCS event.

DTC 66 will set if, during a TCS event, the EBTCM delivers current greater than 16 amps to the adjuster assembly for more than three seconds without the adjuster assembly reaching its desired position.

Test Description: Number(s) below refer to circled number(s) on the diagnostic chart.
1. Checks to see if TCS DTC 65 is set, since DTC 65 conditions might affect DTC 66.
2. Checks for any mechanical binding of the adjuster assembly, attached cables, and components to which the cables are attached, which could cause excessive load on the adjuster assembly.
3. Since DTC 66 only sets during a TCS event, this check raises the vehicle on a hoist such that the rear wheels will spin while the fronts do not, inducing the system into attempting TCS control. The throttle angle must be greater than 15%, and less than 50%, and the system must attempt TCS control for greater than 3 seconds to ensure that the DTC-setting throttle and timing parameters are met when checking for a DTC 66 reset.

Diagnostic Aids:

It may be helpful to disconnect all cables from the adjuster assembly and move them manually throughout their entire operating range. Also check the components to which the cables are attached for binding.

💡 **Important**
• After cables are reconnected to the adjuster assembly, perform "Adjustment Procedure-Adjuster Assembly - Accelerator and Cruise Control Cables"

Fig. 156   DTC 66, Adjuster assembly control malfunction (Part 1 of 2). 1993 Fleetwood (RWD)

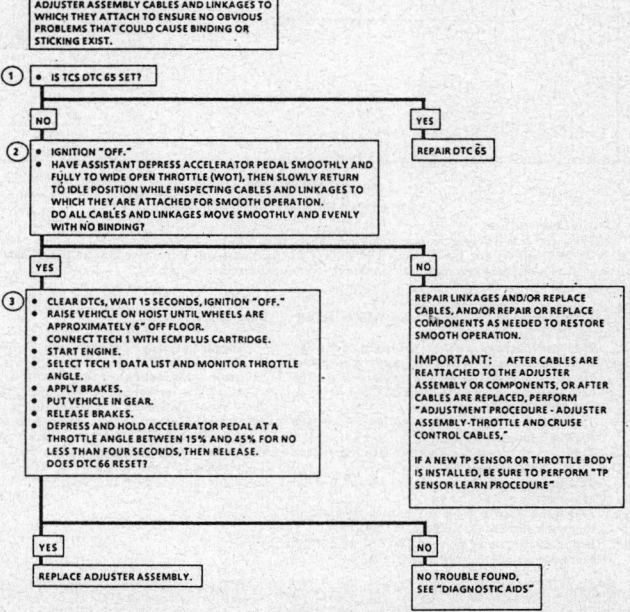

Fig. 156   DTC 66, Adjuster assembly control malfunction (Part 2 of 2). 1993 Fleetwood (RWD)

19 NUT, INFLATABLE RESTRAINT DIAGNOSTIC ENERGY RESERVE MODULE, 1.9 N·m (17 lb. in.)
20 MODULE ASSEMBLY, INFLATABLE RESTRAINT DIAGNOSTIC ENERGY RESERVE
21 BOLT/SCREW, INFLATABLE RESTRAINT DIAGNOSTIC ENERGY RESERVE MODULE BRACKET, 2.8 N·m (25 lb. in.)
22 BRACKET, INFLATABLE RESTRAINT DIAGNOSTIC ENERGY RESERVE MODULE
23 MODULE ASSEMBLY, ELECTRONIC BRAKE AND TRACTION CONTROL
24 BOLT/SCREW, ELECTRONIC BRAKE AND TRACTION CONTROL BRACKET, 6 N·m (53 lb. in.)
25 BRACKET ASSEMBLY, ELECTRONIC BRAKE AND TRACTION CONTROL MODULE
26 NUT, ELECTRONIC BRAKE AND TRACTION CONTROL MODULE, 1.9 N·m (17 lb. in.)
27 RETAINER, INFLATABLE RESTRAINT DIAGNOSTIC ENERGY RESERVE MODULE, 1.9 N·m (17 lb. in.)
37 RELAY, RETAINED ACCESSORY POWER

DTC 71
EBTCM INTERNAL MALFUNCTION

Circuit Description:
The EBTCM performs various diagnostic checks on itself. If it finds a problem, DTC 71 will set.

Test Description: Number(s) below refer to circled number(s) on the diagnostic chart.
1. Checks for good connections from the harness to the EBTCM itself.
2. Checks to see if the malfunction was false. If DTC 71 resets, replace the EBTCM.

Fig. 157   DTC 71, EBTCM internal malfunction (Part 1 of 2). 1993 Fleetwood (RWD)

Fig. 157   DTC 71, EBTCM internal malfunction (Part 2 of 2). 1993 Fleetwood (RWD)

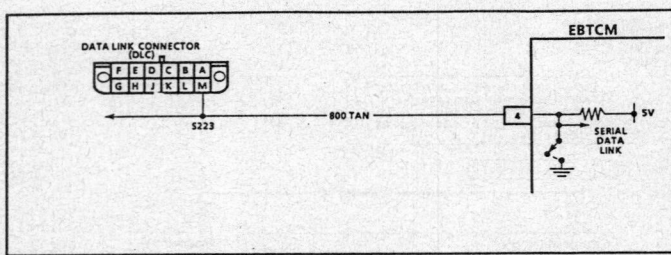

DTC 72
SERIAL DATA LINK MALFUNCTION

Circuit Description:
The serial data link is an asynchronous link operating at 8192 bits per second.
DTC 72 will set and the "TRACTION CONTROL" indicator will illuminate if the EBTCM detects three consecutive serial data link messages that are ignored due to errors in transmission.

Test Description: Number(s) below refer to circled number(s) on the diagnostic chart.
1. This test checks to see if the off-board device can communicate with the EBTCM. Automatic control air conditioning DTC display mode can also be used to communicate the the EBTCM. Refer to SECTION 1C for details.
2. This test checks for a short to battery in the ABS/TCS serial data circuit.
3. This test checks for a short to ground in the ABS/TCS serial data circuit.
4. This test checks for an open in the ABS/TCS serial data circuit.
5. This test checks to see if the off-board device can communicate with the EBTCM.
6. If the connections at the EBTCM and DLC connector are OK, replace the EBTCM.

Diagnostic Aids:

The problem may be intermittent. Try performing the tests shown while "wiggling" wiring and connectors; this can often cause the fault to appear.
Automatic control air conditioning DTC 32 will likely be set along with this DTC if the problem is a, short to ground or B+ on the serial data circuit.
If ABS/TCS DTC 72 is set and automatic control air conditioning DTC 41 is not, the malfunction is likely to be an open between the EBTCM and the automatic control air conditioning.

Fig. 158   DTC 72, Serial data link malfunction (Part 1 of 2). 1993 Fleetwood (RWD)

Fig. 158   DTC 72, Serial data link malfunction (Part 2 of 2). 1993 Fleetwood (RWD)

DTC 83
1 of 2
BRAKE FLUID DIFFERENTIAL PRESSURE MALFUNCTION

Circuit Description:
The brake fluid differential pressure circuit monitors the pressure in the brake system. If the pressure becomes significantly different between the two brake hydraulic circuits, as indicated by the brake differential pressure switch, the ABS/TCS system is disabled. This is done to prevent introduction of air into the brake system. The diode is used to prevent disabling ABS/TCS if illumination of the red "BRAKE" warning lamp occurs because of application of the parking brake.
DTC 83 will set and the "ANTI-LOCK" and "TRACTION CONTROL" lamps will illuminate if CKT 1684 is low (grounded).

Test Description: Number(s) below refer to circled number(s) on the diagnostic chart.
1. Checks for proper brake fluid level in the master cylinder reservoir.
2. Checks for illumination of the red "BRAKE" warning lamp for reasons other than parking brake engagement. Refer to "Warning/Indicator Lamp Operation"
3. Checks for brake pressure switch stuck closed.
4. Checks for short from CKT 1684 to chassis ground.
5. Adds fluid, noted to be low in Step 1, then checks for DTC reset.

Diagnostic Aids:
It is very important that a thorough inspection of the wiring and connectors be performed. Failure to carefully and fully inspect wiring and connectors may result in misdiagnosis, causing part replacement with reappearance of the malfunction.

Fig. 159   DTC 83, Brake fluid differential pressure malfunction (Part 1 of 4). 1993 Fleetwood (RWD)

DTC 83
2 of 2
BRAKE FLUID DIFFERENTIAL PRESSURE MALFUNCTION

Circuit Description:
The brake fluid differential pressure circuit monitors the pressure in the brake system. If the pressure becomes significantly different between the two brake hydraulic circuits, as indicated by the brake differential pressure switch, the ABS/TCS system is disabled. This is done to prevent introduction of air into the brake system. The diode is used to prevent disabling ABS/TCS if illumination of the red "BRAKE" warning lamp occurs because of application of the parking brake.
DTC 83 will set and the "ANTI-LOCK" and "TRACTION CONTROL" lamps will illuminate if CKT 1684 is low (grounded).

Test Description: Number(s) refer to circled number(s) on the diagnostic chart.
6. Checks for continuing DTC reset after checks in Steps 1-4.
7. Checks for DTC reset when parking brake is engaged, likely due to a malfunctioning diode.
8. Checks for parking brake switch stuck closed.
9. Checks for short to ground in parking brake switch CKT 33.
10. Replaces malfunctioning diode found in Step 7 or Step 10, then checks for DTC reset. If DTC resets, the EBTCM is determining there is a problem in CKT 1684 and related circuitry when there is not

Diagnostic Aids:
It is very important that a thorough inspection of the wiring and connectors be performed. Failure to carefully and fully inspect wiring and connectors may result in misdiagnosis, causing part replacement with reappearance of the malfunction.

Fig. 159   DTC 83, Brake fluid differential pressure malfunction (Part 3 of 4). 1993 Fleetwood (RWD)

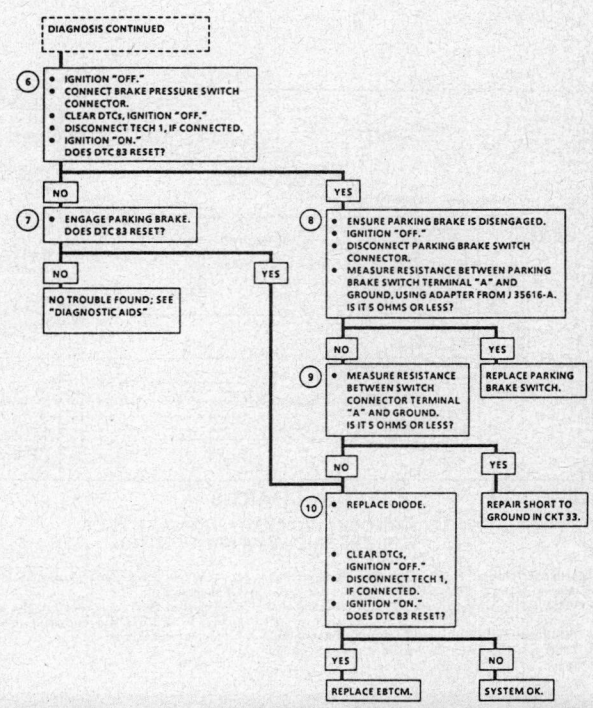

Fig. 159   DTC 83, Brake fluid differential pressure malfunction (Part 2 of 4). 1993 Fleetwood (RWD)

Fig. 159   DTC 83, Brake fluid differential pressure malfunction (Part 4 of 4). 1993 Fleetwood (RWD)

CHART A

"ANTI-LOCK" INDICATOR "ON" WITH NO DTCs SET

Test Description: Number(s) below refer to circled number(s) on the diagnostic chart.

1. This test confirms that a malfunction condition exists.
2. This test determines whether the malfunction is due to a DTC setting condition, an indicator low side circuit malfunction, or an EBTCM supply power malfunction.
3. This test checks whether the malfunction is due to an open fuse.
4. This test checks for an open in the ground feed to the EBTCM.
5. This test checks for an open power feed circuit.
6. This test checks whether the fuse failure is due to a short to ground.

Fig. 160 Chart A, ANTILOCK indicator ON w/no codes set (Part 1 of 2). 1993 Fleetwood (RWD)

Fig. 160 Chart A, ANTILOCK indicator ON w/no codes set (Part 2 of 2). 1993 Fleetwood (RWD)

CHART B

"ANTI-LOCK" INDICATOR INOPERATIVE OR FLICKERS BRIEFLY AT IGNITION "ON"

Test Description: Number(s) below refer to circled number(s) on the diagnostic chart.

1. This test confirms that a malfunction condition exists.
2. This test checks the integrity of the indicator bulb.
3. This test checks for an indicator low side circuit open.
4. This test checks for an indicator low side circuit short to B+.
5. This test determines whether the malfunction is due to an EBTCM circuit fault or an open in the instrument cluster.

Fig. 161 Chart B, ANTILOCK indicator inoperative or flickers briefly at ignition ON (Part 1 of 2). 1993 Fleetwood (RWD)

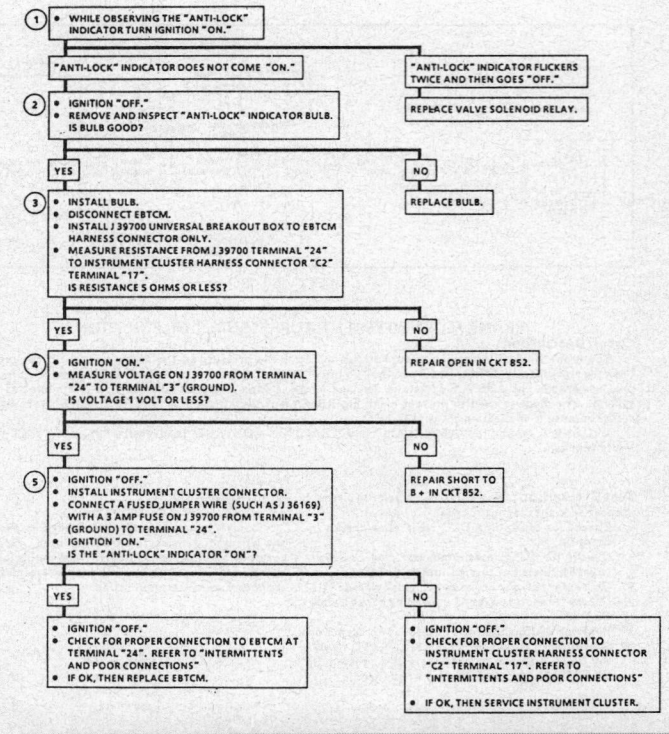

Fig. 161 Chart B, ANTILOCK indicator inoperative or flickers briefly at ignition ON (Part 2 of 2). 1993 Fleetwood (RWD)

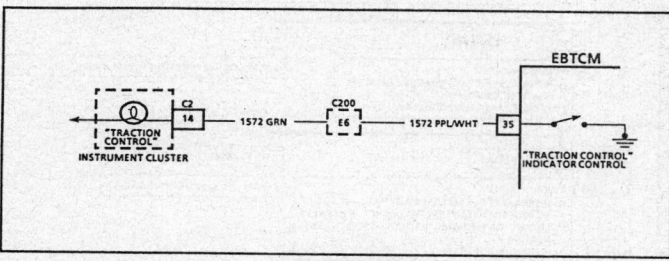

CHART C

"TRACTION CONTROL" INDICATOR "ON" WITH NO DTCs SET

Test Description: Number(s) below refer to circled number(s) on the diagnostic chart.
1. This test confirms that a malfunction condition exists.
2. This test checks if the malfunction is due to a DTC-setting condition.
3. This test checks whether the malfunction is due to an indicator low side circuit short to ground or an EBTCM circuit fault.

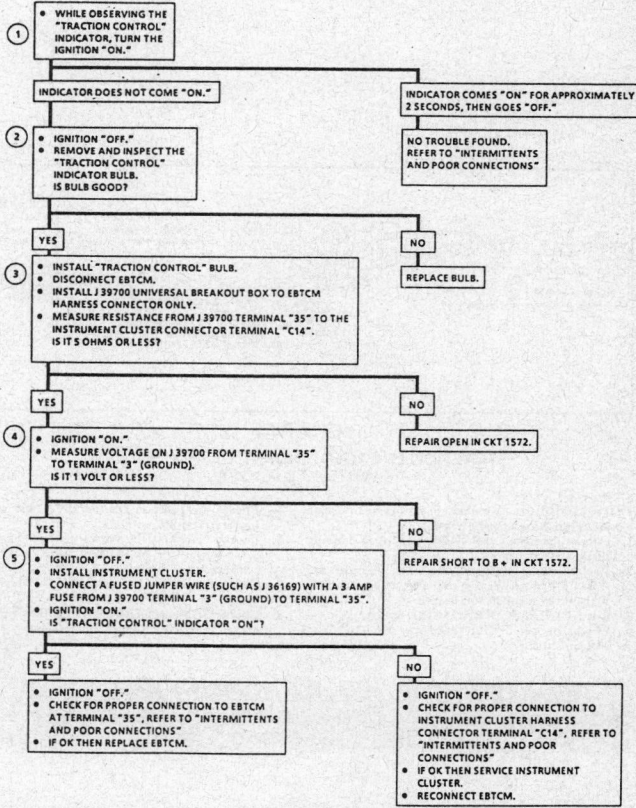

Fig. 162   Chart C, TRACTION CONTROL indicator ON w/no codes set (Part 1 of 2). 1993 Fleetwood (RWD)

Fig. 162   Chart C, TRACTION CONTROL indicator ON w/no codes set (Part 2 of 2). 1993 Fleetwood (RWD)

CHART D

"TRACTION CONTROL" INDICATOR INOPERATIVE

Test Description: Number(s) below refer to circled number(s) on the diagnostic chart.
1. This test confirms that a malfunction condition exists.
2. This test checks the integrity of the indicator bulb.
3. This test checks for an indicator low side circuit open.
4. This test checks for an indicator low side circuit short to B+.
5. This test determines whether the malfunction is due to an EBTCM circuit malfunction or an open in the instrument cluster.

Fig. 163   Chart D, TRACTION CONTROL indicator inoperative (Part 1 of 2). 1993 Fleetwood (RWD)

Fig. 163   Chart D, TRACTION CONTROL indicator inoperative (Part 2 of 2). 1993 Fleetwood (RWD)

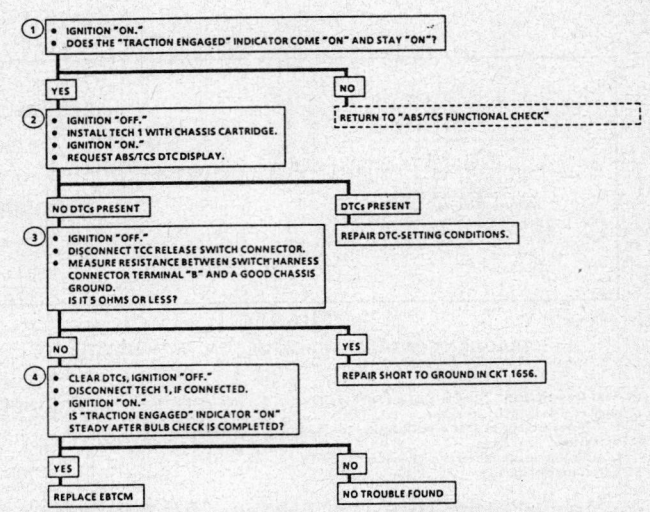

CHART E

"TRACTION ENGAGED" INDICATOR "ON" WITH NO DTCs SET

Test Description: Number(s) below refer to circled number(s) on the diagnostic chart.
1. This test confirms that a malfunction condition exists.
2. This test checks whether the malfunction is due to a DTC-setting condition.
3. This test determines if the malfunction is due to an indicator low side circuit short to ground.
4. Checks for the indicator remaining "ON" after the bulb check is complete. Since all other portions of the circuit are OK, the EBTCM must be incorrectly commanding the indicator "ON" when it should not.

Fig. 164   Chart E, TRACTION ENGAGED indicator ON w/no codes set (Part 1 of 2). 1993 Fleetwood (RWD)

Fig. 164   Chart E, TRACTION ENGAGED indicator ON w/no codes set (Part 2 of 2). 1993 Fleetwood (RWD)

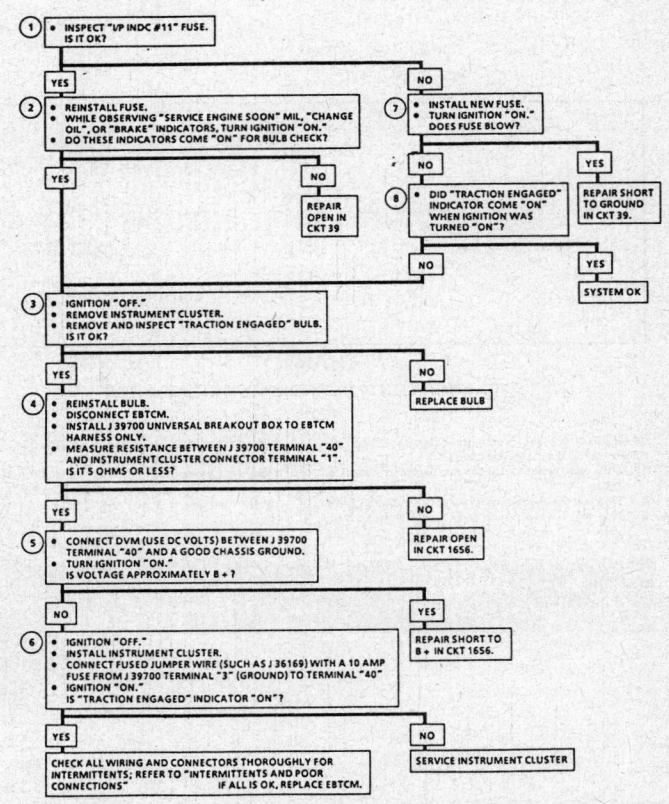

CHART F

"TRACTION ENGAGED" INDICATOR INOPERATIVE WITH NO DTCs SET

Test Description: Number(s) below refer to circled number(s) on the diagnostic chart.
1. Checks for blown "I/P INDC #11" fuse causing inoperative indicator.
2. Replaces fuse, then checks for other indicators fed from CKT 39 as working properly. If not, CKT 39 to the instrument cluster is open.
3. Checks "TRACTION ENGAGED" bulb itself.
4. Checks for open in CKT 1656 between EBTCM and instrument cluster.
5. Checks for short to B+ on CKT 1656 causing inoperative bulb.
6. Checks if problem is within instrument cluster circuitry, due to intermittent wiring or connections, or due to a malfunctioning EBTCM.
7. Checks for short to ground in CKT 39 which blows fuses.
8. Checks for proper "TRACTION ENGAGED" lamp operation after blown fuse replacement.

Fig. 165   Chart F, TRACTION ENGAGED indicator inoperative w/no codes set (Part 1 of 2). 1993 Fleetwood (RWD)

Fig. 165   Chart F, TRACTION ENGAGED indicator inoperative w/no codes set (Part 2 of 2). 1993 Fleetwood (RWD)

SYSTEM SERVICE

SERVICE PRECAUTIONS

Before performing any repairs on the ABS system, note the following precautions:

a. If any welding work is to be done on the vehicle using and arc welder, the EBCM and hydraulic modulator connectors should be disconnected.

b. Hydraulic modulator and EBCM connectors should never be disconnected when the ignition switch is on.

c. Do not use a fast charger to charge battery when battery is connected. Always disconnect battery from system before using a fast charger. **Never disconnect battery from system with engine running.**

d. Always note routing, position and mounting of electrical components, wiring and connectors of the ABS system.

e. Many components of the ABS system are non-serviceable and must be replaced as assemblies. **Do not disassemble any component which is designated non-serviceable.**

f. After any component of the ABS system has been replaced it will be necessary to check the system. Refer to "Diagnosis & Testing."

HYDRAULIC MODULATOR VALVE, REPLACE

CAPRICE, CUSTOM CRUISER, ROADMASTER & 1993 FLEETWOOD (RWD)

1. Disconnect battery ground cable.
2. Disconnect and remove air intake duct and resonator, then position upper coolant hose aside.
3. Disconnect canister purge line at canister and position aside.
4. Remove modulator valve cover attaching screw and cover.
5. Disconnect modulator valve electrical connector and ground wire.
6. Disconnect all hydraulic lines to modulator valve, then plug pipes to prevent loss of fluid and fluid contamination. **Note location of pipes for installation reference.**
7. Remove three modulator valve to bracket attaching nuts, then the modulator valve from vehicle.
8. Reverse procedure to install, perform ABS system check as described in "Diagnosis & Testing." **Ensure brake hydraulic pipes are installed correctly. Pipes that are crossed during installation could cause wheel lockup.**

REATTA, RIVIERA, TORONADO & TROFEO & 1991–92 ELDORADO & SEVILLE

1. Disconnect battery ground cable.
2. Drain brake fluid from master cylinder

and remove left front radiator brace.
3. Remove air cleaner air intake hose, then the modulator relay cover.
4. Disconnect modulator 12-way connector and ground strap.
5. Disconnect all brake line connections to the modulator.
6. Remove modulator mounting nuts, then the modulator from mounting bracket. **When removing modulator, do not allow and fluid to leak from the modulator onto the vehicle's painted surface.**
7. Remove modulator insulators from modulator.
8. Reverse procedure to install, noting the following:
   a. **Torque** modulator to mounting bracket nuts to 8 ft. lbs.
   b. **Torque** brake lines to modulator fittings to 9 ft. lbs.
   c. Bleed brake system as described in "Hydraulic Brakes."

1993 ELDORADO & SEVILLE

1. Disconnect battery ground cable, then raise and support vehicle and remove left front wheel.
2. Support front of cradle with screw jack, then disconnect Y-pipe from catalytic converter.
3. Remove left front wheel housing splash shields, then disconnect brake lines from BPM valve.
4. Remove brake line bundle from left hand frame rail.
5. Remove bolts from Nos. 1 and 2 body mounts, then loosen No. 3 body mount, then using a a screw jack, slowly lower front cradle about 4–5 inches.
6. Remove BPM valve cover (No. 2 Torx), then TCS prime pipe (if equipped).
7. Remove BPM valve ground straps, mounting nuts then BPM valve through wheel housing.
8. Reverse procedure to install noting the following:
   a. Tighten BPM valve mounting nuts to 86 inch lbs.
   b. **When installing ABS/TCS harness, ensure ignition is Off and all connectors are connected.**
   c. **Ensure brake pipes are correctly installed to BPM valve (inlet vs. outlet). If pipes are switched, brake lockup will occur and personal injury may result.**
   d. Tighten BPM valve brake pipes to 13 ft. lbs.
   e. Tighten body mount bolts to 50 ft. lbs.
   f. Tighten exhaust manifold front pipe to catalytic converter bolts to 9 ft. lbs.
   g. Tighten left front wheel nuts to 100 ft. lbs.

ACCELERATOR PEDAL ASSEMBLY

1993 FLEETWOOD (RWD)

1. Remove left hand sound insulator panel.
2. Disconnect cable from accelerator

pedal.
3. Remove bolts/screws and stud attaching pedal to dash panel, then pedal assembly.
4. Reverse procedure to install noting the following:
   a. **Mounting surface between accelerator plate and dash panel must be free of insulation. The floor carpet in pedal area must be positioned to lay flat and be free o wrinkles and bunches.**
   b. Tighten bolts/screws to 25 inch lbs.
   c. **Cable assembly must not be kinked or damaged in nay way during assembly. Throttle must operate smoothly without bind between full and closed throttle.**

ELECTRONIC BRAKE CONTROL MODULE (EBCM), REPLACE

1. Disconnect battery ground cable.
2. **On wagon models,** remove rear quarter trim panel as follows:
   a. Pull top edge of lefthand side rear quarter trim panel from groove in quarter window garnish molding.
   b. Pull tabs on quarter trim panel from slots in back body pillar and lock pillar trim panel.
   c. Remove bottom edge of quarter trim panel from groove on load floor, then remove panel.
3. **On all models,** disconnect EBCM electrical connector.
4. Remove two EBCM to bracket attaching nuts, then the EBCM from the vehicle.
5. Reverse procedure to install, perform ABS system check as described in "Diagnosis & Testing."

OVERVOLTAGE PROTECTION RELAY (OVP), REPLACE

CAPRICE, CUSTOM CRUISER & ROADMASTER

1. Disconnect battery ground cable.
2. **On wagon models,** remove left quarter trim panel as described in "Electronic Brake Control Module (EBCM), Replace."
3. **On all models,** disconnect OVP relay from EBCM bracket.
4. Disconnect OVP relay electrical connector, then remove OVP relay from the vehicle.
5. Reverse procedure to install, perform ABS system check as described in "Diagnosis & Testing."

SOLENOID VALVE RELAY & PUMP MOTOR RELAY, REPLACE

1. Disconnect battery ground cable.
2. **On 1993 Fleetwood RWD models,** remove air intake duct and resonator assembly, then disconnect radiator upper coolant hose and position out of way.

1991 REATTA, 1991-92 BROUGHAM, TORONADO & TROFEO & 1991-93 CAPRICE, CUSTOM CRUISER, ELDORADO, RIVIERA, ROADMASTER, SEVILLE (BOSCH 2 U TYPE)

23-231

3. Remove ABS modulator protective cover.
4. Remove relay from modulator.
5. Reverse procedure to install.

LEFT FRONT WHEEL SPEED SENSOR, REPLACE

1. Raise and support vehicle.
2. Disconnect wheel speed sensor harness connector and sensor assembly connector from clip.
3. Disconnect speed sensor connector from harness connector.
4. Remove sensor bracket attaching bolt from frame rail.
5. Disconnect wheel speed sensor assembly harness with grommets from brackets and combination valve brake pipe clip. **Note position of grommets and harness for installation reference.**
6. Remove speed sensor retaining bolt, then the speed sensor from steering knuckle.
7. Reverse procedure to install. **The wheel speed sensors are a tight fit into the knuckle and are to be pushed in by hand. Do not hammer sensor into position. Proper installation of sensor assembly wire into the bracket is critical. Failure to install wire on bracket could cause wire to come in contact with moving parts, causing circuit damage.**

RIGHT FRONT WHEEL SPEED SENSOR, REPLACE

1. Disconnect forward lamp harness wheel speed sensor connector and wheel speed sensor assembly connector from clip.
2. Disconnect forward lamp harness connector from wheel speed sensor connector.
3. Raise and support vehicle.
4. Remove sensor bracket attaching bolt from frame rail.
5. Remove sensor assembly harness with grommets from brackets. **Note position of grommets and harness for assembly reference.**
6. Remove sensor retaining bolt, then the sensor from vehicle.
7. Reverse procedure to install. **The wheel speed sensors are a tight fit into the knuckle and are to be pushed in by hand. Do not hammer sensor into position. Proper installation of sensor assembly wire into the bracket is critical. Failure to install wire on bracket could cause wire to come in contact with moving parts, causing circuit damage.**

REAR AXLE SPEED SENSOR, REPLACE
CAPRICE, CUSTOM CRUISER, 1993 FLEETWOOD RWD & ROADMASTER

1. Raise and support vehicle.

2. Unclip sensor assembly connector and differential sensor connector, then separate the connectors.
3. Disconnect speed sensor harness assembly wiring harness with grommets from sensor bracket. **Note position of grommets and harness for installation reference.**
4. Remove sensor attaching bolt, then the sensor from the vehicle.
5. Reverse procedure to install. **The wheel speed sensors are a tight fit into the axle housing and are to be pushed in by hand. Do not hammer sensor into position. Proper installation of sensor assembly wire into the bracket is critical. Failure to install wire on bracket could cause wire to come in contact with moving parts, causing circuit damage.**

REAR WHEEL SPEED SENOR, REPLACE
ELDORADO, REATTA, RIVIERA, SEVILLE, TORONADO & TROFEO

The rear wheel speed sensor is an integral part of the rear bearing assembly. Refer to "Rear Wheel Bearing, Replace" in "Rear Suspension" for replacement procedure. **Do not attempt to remove sensor from bearing assembly.**

Bonneville, DeVille, Eighty Eight, LeSabre, Ninety Eight, Park Avenue & 1991–92 Fleetwood (FWD) (Teves Type)

NOTE: Wire Code Identification And Symbol Identification Located In The Front Of This Manual Can Be Used As An Aid When Using Wiring Circuits Found In This Section.

INDEX

PRECAUTIONS
AIRBAG SYSTEM DISARMING
1991 PARK AVENUE

When carrying a live inflator module, ensure bag and trim cover are pointed away from you. Never carry inflator module by the wires or connector on underside of module.

The diagnostic energy reserve module (DERM) can maintain voltage to cause a system deployment for up to ten minutes after the ignition switch is turned off and the battery is disconnected. Servicing the SIR system during this period may result in accidental deployment and personal injury.

1. Turn ignition switch to OFF position, then disconnect and tape battery ground cable terminal.
2. Remove Connector Position Assurance (CPA), then disconnect yellow two-way SIR electrical connector at base of steering column.
3. Remove screws and/or nuts from back of steering wheel, then the inflator module from steering wheel.
4. Remove Connector Position Assurance (CPA), then disconnect coil assembly connector and horn lead.
5. Place inflator module on a bench or other surface with bag and trim cover facing Up.

1991 88 & 98

The diagnostic energy reserve module (DERM) can maintain voltage to cause a system deployment for up to ten minutes after the ignition switch is turned off and the battery is disconnected. Servicing the SIR system during this period may result in accidental deployment and personal injury.

1. Turn ignition switch to OFF position, then remove I/P fuse 7 from fuse block.
2. Disconnect yellow two-way SIR electrical connector at base of steering column.

BONNEVILLE w/SINGLE AIRBAG, DEVILLE, FLEETWOOD (FWD), LESABRE & 1992-93 PARK AVENUE, 88 & 98

The diagnostic energy reserve module (DERM) can maintain voltage to cause a system deployment for up to ten minutes after the ignition switch is turned off and the battery is disconnected. Servicing the SIR system during this period may result in accidental deployment and personal injury.

1. Ensure front wheels are pointed straight ahead.
2. Turn ignition switch to LOCK position and remove SIR or AIRBAG fuse.
3. Remove left sound insulator. **Remove courtesy lamp from sound insulator, if necessary.**
4. Remove Connector Position Assurance (CPA), then disconnect yellow two-way SIR electrical connector at base of steering column.

BONNEVILLE w/DUAL AIRBAGS

The diagnostic energy reserve module (DERM) can maintain voltage to cause a system deployment for up to ten minutes after the ignition switch is turned off and the battery is disconnected. Servicing the SIR system during this period may result in accidental deployment and personal injury.

1. Ensure front wheels are pointed straight ahead.
2. Turn ignition switch to OFF position and remove SIR fuse from fuse panel.
3. Remove left and right sound insulators.
4. Remove Connector Position Assurance (CPA), then disconnect yellow two-way SIR electrical connector at base of steering column.
5. Remove Connector Position Assurance (CPA), then disconnect yellow two-way passenger inflator module connector at base of right side instrument panel, clipped to knee bolster.

AIRBAG SYSTEM ARMING
1991 PARK AVENUE

1. Turn ignition switch to OFF position, connect horn lead and coil assembly connector, then install Connector Position Assurance (CPA).
2. Install inflator module and secure to steering wheel using new screws and/or nuts.
3. **Torque** screws and/or nuts to 25 inch lbs.
4. Connect yellow two-way SIR electrical connector at base of steering column, then install Connector Position Assurance (CPA).
5. Install left sound insulator, then the SIR fuse into fuse block.
6. Turn ignition switch to RUN position and ensure that "Inflatable Restraint" indicator flashes 7 to 9 times, then turns off.

1991 88 & 98

1. Connect yellow two-way SIR electrical connector at base of steering column.
2. Install I/P fuse 7 into fuse block, turn ignition switch to RUN position and ensure that "Inflatable Restraint" indicator flashes 7 to 9 times, then turns off.

BONNEVILLE w/SINGLE AIRBAG, DEVILLE, FLEETWOOD (FWD), LESABRE & 1992-93 PARK AVENUE, 88 & 98

1. Connect yellow two-way SIR electrical connector, then install Connector Position Assurance (CPA).
2. Install left sound insulator. **Install courtesy lamp to sound insulator, if applicable.**
3. Install SIR fuse to fuse block, turn ignition switch to RUN position and ensure that "Inflatable Restraint" lamp flashes 7 to 9 times, then turns off.

BONNEVILLE w/DUAL AIRBAGS

1. Connect yellow two-way passenger inflator module connector at base of right side instrument panel, clipped to knee bolster, then install Connector Position Assurance (CPA).
2. Connect yellow two-way SIR electrical connector at base of steering column, then install Connector Position Assurance (CPA).
3. Install left and right sound insulators, then the SIR fuse into fuse panel.
4. Turn ignition switch to RUN position and ensure that "Inflatable Restraint" lamp flashes 7 to 9 times, then turns off.

DESCRIPTION

Refer to **Fig. 1,** for overview of anti-lock brake system.

The purpose of the anti-lock brake system is tho prevent wheel lock-up under heavy braking conditions, on virtually any road surface. When a wheel locking condition exists, the pressure modulator valve (PMV) assembly isolates each wheel hydraulic circuit, then begins modulation of fluid pressure to each wheel according to wheel speed input to the EBCM. The PMV is controlled by the Electronic Brake Control Module (EBCM).

Modulation occurs by means of three ABS modes: pressure hold, pressure reduce and pressure increase. The PMV assembly has two valves per individual hydraulic circuit. These valves work in pairs to achieve the three ABS modes. The ABS system isolates, monitors and controls all wheels simultaneously.

BRAKE WARNING LAMP

The red brake warning lamp is located in the instrument panel. This lamp illuminates to warn driver of conditions which could reduce braking efficiency. Specific conditions causing illumination are the parking brake not fully released, low brake fluid and Bulb Test or Start positions of the ignition switch.

ELECTRONIC BRAKE CONTROL MODULE (EBCM)

The Electronic Brake Control Module (EBCM), is mounted in the passenger compartment and monitors the speed of each wheel and the electrical status of the Pressure Modulator Valve (PMV) assembly. The primary functions of the EBCM are to monitor wheel locking/slipping, control of braking within the anti-lock/traction mode and to monitor the system for proper electrical operation. The EBCM also controls the display of ABS diagnostic codes within the diagnostic mode.

WHEEL SPEED SENSORS

Wheel speed sensors are located at each wheel. The sensor transmits wheel speed information to the EBCM my means of a small AC voltage. This voltage is generated when the toothed sensor ring rotates past a stationary sensor.

1 FRONT WHEEL SPEED SENSOR

2 ELECTRONIC BRAKE CONTROL MODULE (EBCM)

3 ABS RELAY

4 REAR WHEEL SPEED SENSOR

5 PROPORTIONER VALVES

6 BRAKE PIPE HARNESS FROM PMV ASSEMBLY

7 PRESSURE MODULATOR VALVE (PMV) ASSEMBLY

Fig. 1   Anti-lock brake system overview

DIAGNOSIS & TESTING
DESCRIPTION
Anti-Lock Warning Lamp

The amber Anti-lock warning lamp is located in the instrument panel cluster. This lamp will illuminate when the EBCM detects a malfunction in the anti-lock brake system. The warning lamp is intended only to warn the driver that a condition has been detected which results in partial or total reduction of the anti-lock brake system. Under this condition full operation of the standard hydraulic braking system is available. If both the red Brake and the amber Anti-Lock brake lights are illuminated, there may be something wrong with the hydraulic brake system, limiting all braking functions.

ABS System Self-Diagnosis Description

In the process of controlling the anti-lock brake system, the Electronic Brake Control Module (EBCM) continually monitors operating conditions for possible malfunctions. By comparing system conditions against standard operating limits, certain circuit and component malfunctions can be detected. A four-digit numerical trouble code is stored in computer memory when a problem is detected by this self-diagnostic system. The trouble codes can later be accessed with a bi-directional scan tool.

To access trouble codes, connect a bi-directional scan tool to the Assembly Line Diagnostic Link (ALDL) connector, then follow manufacturer's instruction for use of the tool. After code have been read, proceed to "Code Diagnosis," if the ABS Functional Test has been performed. After repairs have been made, clear all codes, using the scan tool.

History & Current ABS Codes

The ABS trouble codes which may be stored by the EBCM are not specifically designated as Current or History codes. The Anti-lock lamp may be used to differentiate between Current and History codes.

If the Anti-lock lamp is illuminated prior to entering the ABS diagnostic mode, at least one of the stored codes is current. If the Anti-lock lamp is not illuminated prior to entering the ABS diagnostic mode, none of the stored codes are current.

If more than one code is stored and the Anti-lock lamp was illuminated prior to entering the diagnostic mode, it is impossible to determine which code is Current or History.

Note On Intermittents

Intermittent failures in the anti-lock brake system may be difficult to accurately diagnose. The ABS trouble codes which may be stored by the EBCM are not designated as Current or History codes. These codes can be helpful in diagnosing intermittent conditions.

If an intermittent condition is being diagnosed, the ABS system can be used in the following manner to help isolate the suspected circuit.

1. Display, then clear any ABS trouble codes present in the EBCM.
2. Test Drive Vehicle, attempting to repeat failure condition. A description of driving conditions under which the last failure occurred can be helpful.
3. After duplicating condition, stop the vehicle, then display any trouble codes stored.
4. If no codes were stored, proceed to "Symptom Diagnosis."

5. If a code was stored, check electrical connections and wiring for the following:
   a. Poor mating of connector halves.
   b. Terminals not fully seated in connector halves.
   c. Improperly formed, or damaged terminals. All connector terminals in a problem circuit should be carefully reformed to increase contact tension.
   d. Poor terminal to wire connection. In most cases, this will require removing wire from connector body.
6. If a complaint of intermittent warning lamp operation is encountered, the following circuits to the EBCM should be checked:
   a. Low system voltage. If low voltage is detected at the EBCM, the Anti-lock lamp will illuminate until normal operating voltage is detected.
   b. Low brake fluid. This condition in the Pressure Modulator Valve (PMV) reservoir will cause the Brake and Anti-lock lamps to illuminate. When an acceptable fluid level is registered, the lamps will no longer be illuminated.
7. Any condition which results in interruption of power to the EBCM or hydraulic unit may cause the warning lamps to turn on intermittently. These circuits include the main relay, pump motor relay, fuses and related wiring.

DIAGNOSTIC PROCEDURES

Prior to service disarm airbag as outlined under "Airbag System Disarming." Once service is complete rearm airbag system as outlined under "Airbag System Arming."

Refer to **Figs. 2 through 64,** for ABS system diagnostic procedures and charts. Refer to **Figs. 65 through 72,** for system wiring diagrams. *Continued on page 23-290*

Fig. 2 Visual inspection

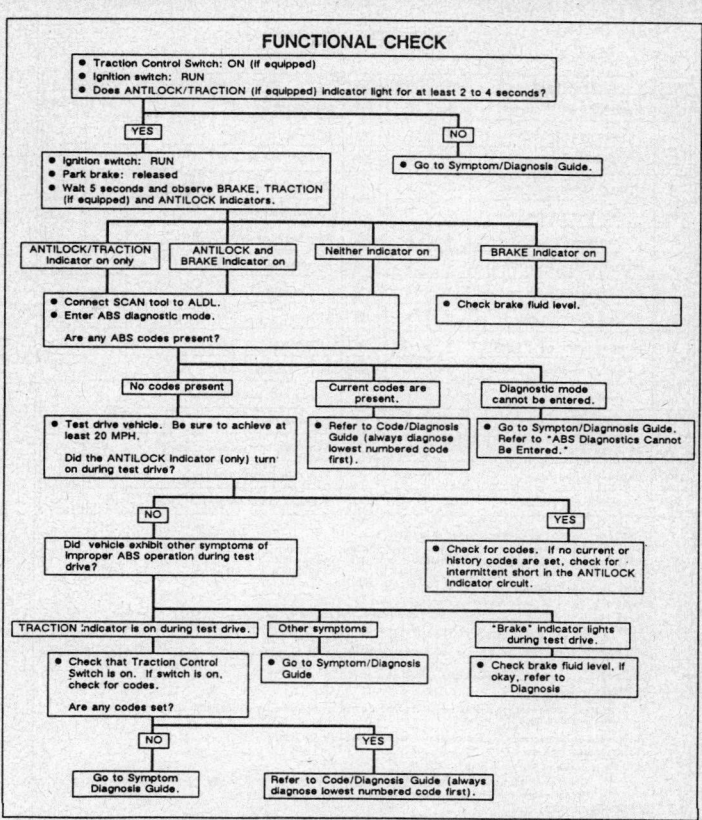

Fig. 3 Functional check. 1991 98 & Park Ave.

Fig. 4 Functional check. 1991 Bonneville, 88 & LeSabre

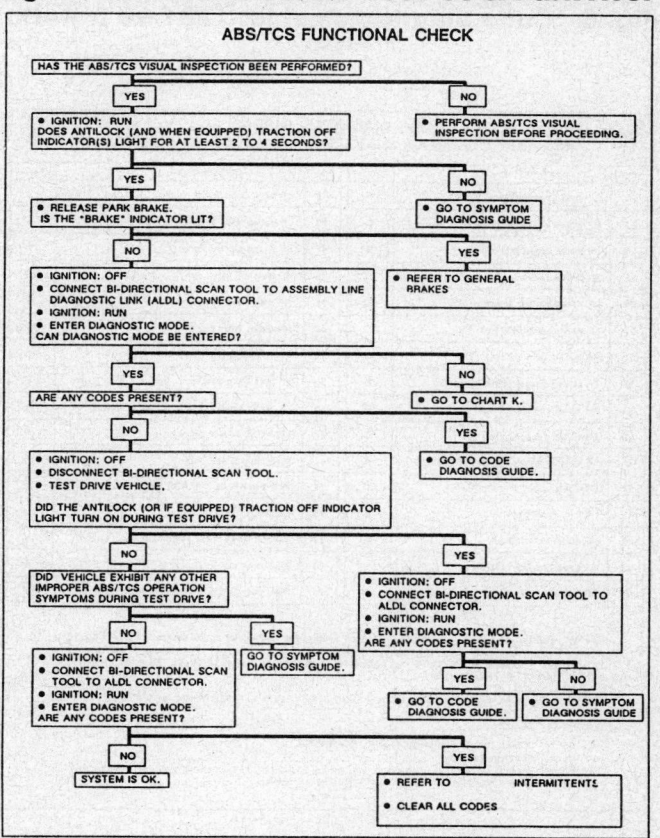

Fig. 5 Functional check. 1991–92 DeVille/Fleetwood (FWD) & all 1992–93 models

CODE DIAGNOSIS GUIDE

PERFORM THE FUNCTIONAL CHECK BEFORE PROCEEDING WITH ANY DIAGNOSIS.

CODE	DESCRIPTION	CAUSE	CHART	CODE	DESCRIPTION	CAUSE	CHART
21	RF speed sensor circuit open	B	B	45	LF inlet valve circuit	A	A
22	RF speed sensor signal erratic	C	D	46	LF outlet valve circuit	A	A
23	RF wheel speed is 0 mph	D	B	47	LF speed sensor noisy	I	D
25	LF speed sensor circuit open	B	B	48	RF isolation valve circuit malfunction	A	O
26	LF speed sensor signal erratic	C	D	51	RR inlet valve circuit	A	A
27	LF wheel speed is 0 mph	D	B	52	RR outlet valve circuit	A	A
31	RR speed sensor circuit open	B	C	53	RR speed sensor noisy	I	D
32	RR speed sensor signal is erratic	C	D	55	LR inlet valve circuit	A	A
33	RR wheel speed is 0 mph	D	C	56	LR outlet valve circuit	A	A
35	LR speed sensor circuit open	B	C	57	LR speed sensor noisy	I	D
36	LR speed sensor signal erratic	C	D	61	Pump motor test fault	G	F
37	LR wheel speed is 0 mph	D	C	62	Pump motor fault in ABS stop	H	I
41	RF inlet valve circuit	A	A	71	EBCM problem	J	J
42	RF outlet valve circuit	A	A	72	VCC/antilock brake switch sircuit	F	G
43	RF speed sensor noisy	I	D	73	Fluid level switch circuit	E	H
44	LF isolation valve circuit	A	O	74	Pressure switch circuit malfunction	K	P

CAUSE "A" • Circuit open or shorted to ground.
CAUSE "B" • Wheel speed sensor circuit open or shorted.
CAUSE "C" • Wheel speed sensor circuit open or shorted intermittently.
CAUSE "D" • Wheel speed sensor signal missing.
CAUSE "E" • Fluid level switch circuit.
CAUSE "F" • VCC/antilock brake switch circuit open.
CAUSE "G" • Malfunctioning pump motor, electrical or mechanical failure.
CAUSE "H" • Pump pressure is too low, defective pump motor or pump motor run sensor circuit, or air in hydraulic system.
CAUSE "I" • Electrical noise or excessive vibration detected in wheel speed sensor circuit above 40 km/h (25 mph).
CAUSE "J" • Internal electronic brake control module (EBCM) fault.

HISTORY CODES:

"History" codes indicate intermittent problems. Do not use trouble code diagnosis for intermittent problems until you have done the following:

- Check all connectors for good contact. Repair/replace as necessary.
- Test drive vehicle.
  The purpose of test drive is to:
  1) Observe an abnormal condition that does not cause ANTILOCK and BRAKE indicators to light; and
  2) To determine exact conditions which cause one of the indicators to light.

CLEARING CODES:

- To clear codes use a scan tool.
- After codes have been cleared, test drive vehicle (refer to TEST DRIVE) to assure all problems have been repaired.

Fig. 6   Code diagnosis guide. 1991 98 & Park Ave.

ABS CODE DIAGNOSIS GUIDE

PERFORM THE ABS FUNCTIONAL CHECK BEFORE PROCEEDING WITH ANY DIAGNOSIS.

CODE	DESCRIPTION	CAUSE	CHART	CODE	DESCRIPTION	CAUSE	CHART
21	RF speed sensor circuit open	B	B	45	LF inlet valve circuit	A	A
22	RF speed sensor signal erratic	C	D	46	LF outlet valve circuit	A	A
23	RF wheel speed is 0 mph	D	B	47	LF speed sensor noisy	I	D
25	LF speed sensor circuit open	B	B	51	RR inlet valve circuit	A	A
26	LF speed sensor signal erratic	C	D	52	RR outlet valve circuit	A	A
27	LF wheel speed is 0 mph	D	B	53	RR speed sensor noisy	I	D
31	RR speed sensor circuit open	B	C	55	LR inlet valve circuit	A	A
32	RR speed sensor signal is erratic	C	D	56	LR outlet valve circuit	A	A
33	RR wheel speed is 0 mph	D	C	57	LR speed sensor noisy	I	D
35	LR speed sensor circuit open	B	C	61	Pump motor test fault	G	F
36	LR speed sensor signal erratic	C	D	62	Pump motor fault in ABS stop	H	I
37	LR wheel speed is 0 mph	D	C	71	EBCM problem	J	J
41	RF inlet valve circuit	A	A	72	VCC/antilock brake switch sircuit	F	G
42	RF outlet valve circuit	A	A	73	Fluid level switch circuit	E	H
43	RF speed sensor noisy	I	D				

CAUSE "A" • Inlet or outlet valve circuit open or shorted to ground.
CAUSE "B" • Wheel speed sensor circuit open or shorted.
CAUSE "C" • Wheel speed sensor circuit open or shorted intermittently.
CAUSE "D" • Wheel speed sensor signal missing.
CAUSE "E" • Fluid level switch circuit.
CAUSE "F" • VCC/antilock brake switch circuit open or shorted.
CAUSE "G" • Malfunctioning pump motor, electrical or mechanical failure.
CAUSE "H" • Pump pressure is too low, defective pump motor or pump motor run sensor circuit, or air in hydraulic system.
CAUSE "I" • Electrical noise or excessive vibration detected in wheel speed sensor circuit above 40 km/h (25 mph).
CAUSE "J" • Internal electronic brake control module (EBCM) fault.

HISTORY CODES:

"History" codes indicate intermittent problems. Do not use trouble code diagnosis for intermittent problems until you have done the following:

- Check all connectors for good contact. Repair/replace as necessary.
- Test drive vehicle.
  The purpose of test drive is to:
  1) Observe an abnormal condition that does not cause ANTILOCK and BRAKE indicators to light; and
  2) To determine exact conditions which cause one of the indicators to light.

CLEARING CODES:

- To clear codes use a scan tool.
- After codes have been cleared, test drive vehicle to assure all problems have been repaired.

Fig. 7   Code diagnosis guide. 1991 Bonneville, 88 & LeSabre

CODE DIAGNOSIS GUIDE

PERFORM THE ABS/TCS FUNCTIONAL CHECK BEFORE PROCEEDING WITH ANY DIAGNOSIS.

CODE	DESCRIPTION	CHART	CODE	DESCRIPTION	CHART
21	RF speed sensor circuit open	B	45	LF inlet valve circuit	A
22	RF speed sensor signal erratic	D	46	LF outlet valve circuit	E
23	RF wheel speed is 0 mph	D	47	LF speed sensor noisy	D
25	LF speed sensor circuit open	B	48	RF isolation valve circuit	O
26	LF speed sensor signal erratic	D	51	RR inlet valve circuit	E
27	LF wheel speed is 0 mph	D	52	RR outlet valve circuit	E
31	RR speed sensor circuit open	C	53	RR speed sensor noisy	D
32	RR speed sensor signal is erratic	D	55	LR inlet valve circuit	E
33	RR wheel speed is 0 mph	D	56	LR outlet valve circuit	E
35	LR speed sensor circuit open	C	57	LR speed sensor noisy	D
36	LR speed sensor signal erratic	D	61	Pump motor test fault	F
37	LR wheel speed is 0 mph	D	62	Pump motor fault in ABS stop	I
41	RF inlet valve circuit	E	71	EBCM problem	J
42	RF outlet valve circuit	E	72	TCC/antilock brake switch circuit	G
43	RF speed sensor noisy	D	73	Fluid level switch circuit	H
44	LF isolation valve circuit	O	74	PMV pressure switch circuit	P

INTERMITTENT "HISTORY" CODES: (Refer to "System Self-Diagnosis" in this section for clarification.)
STORED CODES THAT DO NOT LIGHT THE AMBER "ANTILOCK" INDICATOR ARE INTERMITTENT PROBLEMS. DO NOT USE TROUBLE CODE DIAGNOSIS FOR INTERMITTENT PROBLEMS UNTIL REFERRING TO "NOTE ON INTERMITTENTS" IN THIS SECTION.

MULTIPLE CODES: DIAGNOSE FIRST CODE THAT APPEARS ON BI-DIRECTIONAL SCAN TOOL SCREEN.

CLEARING CODES:

- CLEAR CODES USING A BI-DIRECTIONAL SCAN TOOL.
- CYCLE IGNITION SWITCH.
- AFTER CODES HAVE BEEN CLEARED, REFER TO "ABS/TCS FUNCTIONAL CHECK" CHART IN THIS SECTION TO ASSURE ALL PROBLEMS HAVE BEEN REPAIRED.

Fig. 8   Code diagnosis guide. 1991–92 DeVille/Fleetwood (FWD) & all 1992 models

PERFORM ABS/TCS FUNCTIONAL CHECK BEFORE PROCEEDING WITH ANY DIAGNOSIS.

INTERMITTENT "HISTORY" DIAGNOSTIC TROUBLE CODES:

STORED DIAGNOSTIC TROUBLE CODES THAT DO NOT LIGHT THE AMBER "ANTILOCK" INDICATOR ARE INTERMITTENT PROBLEMS OR HISTORY CODES THAT WERE NOT CLEARED DURING PRIOR SERVICE. DO NOT USE DIAGNOSTIC TROUBLE CODE DIAGNOSIS FOR INTERMITTENT PROBLEMS UNTIL REFERRING TO "INTERMITTENTS AND POOR CONNECTIONS"

MULTIPLE DIAGNOSTIC TROUBLE CODES: DIAGNOSE FIRST DIAGNOSTIC TROUBLE CODE THAT APPEARS ON BI-DIRECTIONAL SCAN TOOL SCREEN.

CLEARING DIAGNOSTIC TROUBLE CODES:

- CLEAR DIAGNOSTIC TROUBLE CODES USING A BI-DIRECTIONAL SCAN TOOL.
- CYCLE IGNITION SWITCH.
- AFTER DIAGNOSTIC TROUBLE CODES HAVE BEEN CLEARED, REFER TO "ABS/TCS FUNCTIONAL CHECK" CHART TO ASSURE ALL PROBLEMS HAVE BEEN REPAIRED.

DTC	DESCRIPTION	CHART	DTC	DESCRIPTION	CHART
21	RF speed sensor circuit open	B	44	LF isolation valve circuit	O
22	RF speed sensor signal erratic	D	45	LF inlet valve circuit	A
23	RF wheel speed is 0 mph	D	46	LF outlet valve circuit	E
25	LF speed sensor circuit open	B	48	RF isolation valve circuit	O
26	LF speed sensor signal erratic	D	51	RR inlet valve circuit	E
27	LF wheel speed is 0 mph	D	52	RR outlet valve circuit	E
31	RR speed sensor circuit open	C	55	LR inlet valve circuit	E
32	RR speed sensor signal is erratic	D	56	LR outlet valve circuit	E
33	RR wheel speed is 0 mph	D	61	Pump motor test fault	F
35	LR speed sensor circuit open	C	62	Pump motor fault in ABS stop	I
36	LR speed sensor signal erratic	D	71	EBCM problem	J
37	LR wheel speed is 0 mph	D	72	TCC/antilock brake switch circuit	G
41	RF inlet valve circuit	E	73	Fluid level switch circuit	H
42	RF outlet valve circuit	E	74	PMV pressure switch circuit	P

Fig. 9   Code diagnosis guide. 1993 models

SYMPTOM	FOR DIAGNOSIS GO TO CHART
ABS diagnosis cannot be entered.	Chart K
ANTILOCK indicator is on all the time and no codes are set.	Chart K
ANTILOCK indicator does not light.	Chart N
Poor vehicle tracking during ABS stop (ABS engaged).	Chart L
Brake pedal rises or drops excessively during an ABS stop (ABS engaged).	Chart G
Pressure modulator valve (PMV) assembly pump motor runs continuously.	Chart M
Traction indicator does not light during bulb test or when system is turned off.	Chart Q
Traction indicator is on all the time and no codes are set.	Chart R
Traction control engaged message does not operate.	Chart S

Fig. 10   Symptom diagnosis guide. 1991 98 & Park Ave.

SYMPTOM	FOR DIAGNOSIS GO TO CHART
ABS diagnosis cannot be entered.	Chart K
ANTILOCK indicator is on all the time and no codes are set.	Chart K
ANTILOCK indicator does not light.	Chart N
Poor vehicle tracking during ABS stop (ABS engaged).	Chart L
Brake pedal rises or drops excessively during an ABS stop (ABS engaged)	Chart G
Pressure modulator valve (PMV) assembly pump motor runs continuously.	Chart M

Fig. 11   Symptom diagnosis guide. 1991 Bonneville, 88 & LeSabre

SYMPTOM	FOR DIAGNOSIS GO TO CHART
Diagnostic mode cannot be entered.	Chart K
ANTILOCK indicator is on all the time and no codes are set.	Chart K
ANTILOCK indicator does not light.	Chart N
Poor vehicle tracking during ABS stop (ABS engaged).	Chart L
Brake pedal rises or drops excessively during an ABS stop (ABS engaged).	Chart I
Pressure modulator valve (PMV) assembly pump motor runs continuously.	Chart M
Only TRACTION OFF Indicator does not light.	Chart Q
Only TRACTION OFF Indicator is on all the time and no codes are set.	Chart R
Traction control engaged message/bulb does not operate properly	Chart S

Fig. 12   Symptom diagnosis guide. 1991–92 DeVille/Fleetwood (FWD) & 1992 Bonneville, LeSabre, Park Ave., 88 & 98

PERFORM ABS/TCS FUNCTIONAL CHECK BEFORE PROCEEDING WITH ANY DIAGNOSIS.

SYMPTOM	FOR DIAGNOSIS GO TO CHART
Diagnostic mode cannot be entered.	Chart K
ANTILOCK indicator is on all the time and no diagnostic trouble codes are set.	Chart K
ANTILOCK indicator does not light.	Chart N
Poor vehicle tracking during ABS stop (ABS engaged).	Chart L
Brake pedal rises or drops excessively during an ABS stop (ABS engaged).	Chart I
Pressure modulator valve (PMV) assembly pump motor runs continuously.	Chart M
Only TRACTION OFF Indicator does not light.	Chart Q
Only TRACTION OFF Indicator is on all the time and no diagnostic trouble codes are set.	Chart R
Traction control switch illumination bulb does not operate properly.	Chart S
Brake pedal vibrates (fluctuates) during slow speed (under 16 km/h [10 mph]) braking.	Chart D

Fig. 13   Symptom diagnosis guide. 1993 Bonneville, 88 & 98

- Perform "ABS/TCS Functional Check" before beginning diagnosis.

INTERMITTENT "HISTORY" DIAGNOSTIC TROUBLE CODES:
Stored diagnostic trouble codes that do not light the amber ANTILOCK indicator are intermittent problems or history codes that were not cleared during prior service. Do not use diagnostic trouble code diagnosis for intermittent problems until referring to "intermittents and poor connections"

MULTIPLE DIAGNOSTIC TROUBLE CODES: Diagnose first diagnostic trouble code that appears on bi-directional scan tool screen.

CLEARING DIAGNOSTIC TROUBLE CODES:
- Repair problem.
- Use a bi-directional scan tool to clear codes.
- Cycle ignition switch.
- After clearing diagnostic trouble code, repeat "ABS/TCS Functional Check" to assure all problems have been repaired.

DIAGNOSTIC TROUBLE CODE (DTC) GUIDE

DTC	DIAGNOSIS:
DTC 21, DTC 25, DTC 31, DTC 35	Test F: Wheel Speed Sensor Continuity Test
DTC 23, DTC 27, DTC 33, DTC 37	Test I: Wheel Speed Signal Erratic Or Noisy Test
DTC 22, DTC 26, DTC 32, DTC 36	
DTC 45	Test A: Main Relay Power Test
DTC 41, DTC 42, DTC 46, DTC 51, DTC 52, DTC 55, DTC 56	Test D: Pressure Modulator Valve (PMV) Assembly Continuity Test
DTC 44, DTC 48	Test Z: Isolation Valve Continuity Test
DTC 61	Test J: Pump Motor Circuit Test
DTC 62	Test M: Brake Hydraulic Test
DTC 71	Test Y: EBCM/EBTCM Problem Test
DTC 72	Test O: EBCM/EBTCM Grounded Switch Input Test
	Note: When DTC 72 and DTC 73 are both set, check wiring (CKT 848) for a short to ground
DTC 73	
DTC 74	Test P: EBCM/EBTCM Open Switch Input Test
	Note: When DTC 73 and DTC 74 are both set, check wiring (CKT 1659) for a short to ground

DIAGNOSTIC SYMPTOM GUIDE

SYMPTOM	DIAGNOSIS		
	Do 1st	Do 2nd	Do 3rd
Diagnostics cannot be entered.	Data Line Test Q.		
ANTILOCK indicator does not light.	Do Antilock Indicator "OFF" Fault Test S.		
ANTILOCK indicator is on all the time and no diagnostic trouble codes are set.	Check PMV reservoir brake fluid level.	Do Antilock Indicator "ON" Fault Test R.	
Brake pedal rises or drops excessively during an ABS stop (ABS engaged).	Do TCC/Antilock Brake Switch Test L.		
Brake pedal vibrates (fluctuates) during slow speed (under 16 km/h [10 mph]) braking.	Do Wheel Speed Signal Erratic or Noisy Test I.		
Poor vehicle tracking during an ABS stop (ABS engaged).	Do Inlet/Outlet Valve Hydraulic Test BB.		
Pump motor runs continuously.	Do Pump Motor Short Test K.		

Fig. 14   Symptom diagnosis guide (Part 1 of 2). 1993 LeSabre & Park Avenue

DIAGNOSTIC SYMPTOM GUIDE (continued)

SYMPTOM	DIAGNOSIS		
	Do 1st	Do 2nd	Do 3rd
BRAKE indicator is on all the time.	CHECK MECHANICAL BRAKE SYSTEM	Do Brake Warning Short Circuit Test U.	Replace instrument cluster (U23) or Information center (UB3), see ⑥ or ⑬, respectively.
BRAKE indicator does not light.	Check BRAKE indicator bulb and wiring (CKT 33) for an open.	Replace instrument cluster (U23) or information center (UB3), see ⑥ or ⑬, respectively.	
BRAKE indicator does not light with park brake applied.	Do Park Brake Switch Test W.		
BRAKE indicator does not light with low brake fluid or during bulb test.	Do Brake Fluid Level Switch Test V.		
Brake pedal is spongy.	CHECK MECHANICAL BRAKE SYSTEM		
BRAKE indicator lights properly, but chime does not sound with park brake applied.	Check wiring (CKT 33) to MFC module for an open.		
Only TRACTION OFF Indicator does not light.	Check TRACTION OFF indicator and wiring (CKT 1572) for an open.	Replace information center, see ⑬.	Check EBTCM connector for proper terminal contact; if OK, replace EBTCM. see ③.
Only TRACTION OFF Indicator is on all the time and no diagnostic trouble codes are set.	Wait 20 minutes. If indicator is now off, system OK. If indicator is still on, continue diagnosis.	Do Transaxle Temperature Switch Test X.	Check wiring (CKT 1572) for a short to ground; if OK, replace EBTCM, see ③.

🖐 **Important**
- Customers may comment that they hear the PMV assembly run at slow speeds (11 km/h [7 mph]). This is simply the ABS system running through its self-test. It is also possible to feel the PMV assembly running through the brake pedal, when it is barely applied, and to hear brake fluid return to the master cylinder. Also, the vehicle may slowly decrease in speed while the PMV modulator valves increase fluid pressure to the wheel cylinders during this test. In both these instances, the driver must be traveling at a very low speed (11 km/h [7 mph]) and have one foot touching the brake pedal (as some two-footed drivers may) to feel the PMV assembly running. These are normal conditions and in no way signify a problem with the ABS system.

- When vehicle is equipped with traction control, any symptom which lights the ANTILOCK indicator also lights the TRACTION OFF indicator. Therefore, when both indicators are lit, follow ANTILOCK indicator diagnosis when no diagnostic trouble codes are set.

- Vehicles with traction control contain a preventive system to avoid brake overheating. During heavy braking conditions, if a traction control mode is entered and the EBTCM determines the brakes are too hot, the EBTCM disables the traction control system and lights only the TRACTION OFF indicator. After a sufficient cooling time, approximately 15-20 minutes, the EBTCM enables traction control system and turns off the indicator. This condition is normal and should not be mistaken as an intermittent system malfunction.

Fig. 14   Symptom diagnosis guide (Part 1 of 2). 1993 LeSabre & Park Avenue

Chart	Description	Page No.	Fig. No.
1991 Except DeVille & Fleetwood			
Chart A	Inlet/Outlet Valve Circuit Test	23-240	15
Chart B	Front Wheel Speed Sensor Circuit Test	23-241	16
Chart C	Rear Wheel Speed Sensor Circuit Test	23-241	17
Chart D	Wheel Speed Signal Erratic Or Noisy	23-242	18
Chart F	Pump Motor Circuit Test	23-242	19
Chart G	VCC/Anti-Lock Brake Switch Test	23-243	20
Chart H	Fluid Level Switch Circuit Test	23-244	21
Chart I	Pump Motor Fault During ABS Stop	23-244	22
Chart J	EBCM Problem	23-244	23
Chart K	Anti-Lock Indicator Is On & No Codes Set	23-245	24
Chart L	Inlet/Outlet Valve Hydraulic Test	23-246	25
Chart M	Pump Motor Runs Continuously	23-246	26
Chart N	Anti-Lock Indicator Does Not Light	23-248	27
Chart O	Isolation Valve Circuit Failure	23-248	28
Chart P	Pressure Switch Circuit Failure	23-249	30
Chart Q	Traction Indicator Does Not Light	23-250	32
Chart R	Traction Indicator Is On All The Time	23-251	34
Chart S	Traction Control Engaged, Does Not Operate	23-252	36
1991–92 DeVille/Fleetwood (FWD), 1992 LeSabre & Park Avenue & 1992–93 Bonneville, Eighty Eight & Ninety Eight			
Chart A	Inlet/Outlet Valve Voltage Test	23-253	38
Chart B	Front Wheel Speed Sensor Circuit Test	23-254	39
Chart C	Rear Wheel Speed Sensor Circuit Test	23-255	40
Chart D	Wheel Speed Signal Erratic Or Noisy (1992)	23-255	41
Chart D	Wheel Speed Signal Erratic Or Noisy (1993)	23-256	42
Chart E	Inlet/Outlet Valve Circuit Test	23-257	43
Chart F	Pump Motor Circuit Test (1991–92 DeVille & Fleetwood (FWD))	23-258	44
Chart F	Pump Motor Circuit Test (1992 Models Except DeVille & Fleetwood (FWD))	23-259	45
Chart G	VCC/Anti-Lock Brake Switch Test	23-261	46
Chart H	Fluid Level Switch Circuit Test (1991–92 DeVille & Fleetwood (FWD))	23-261	47
Chart H	Fluid Level Switch Circuit Test (1992 Models Except DeVille & Fleetwood (FWD))	23-262	48
Chart I	Pump Motor Fault During ABS Stop	23-262	49
Chart J	EBCM Problem	23-263	50
Chart K	Anti-Lock Indicator Is On & No Codes Set	23-264	51
Chart L	Inlet/Outlet Valve Hydraulic Test	23-265	52
Chart M	Pump Motor Runs Continuously	23-265	53
Chart N	Anti-Lock Indicator Does Not Light	23-266	54
Chart O	Isolation Valve Circuit Failure	23-248	29
Chart P	Pressure Switch Circuit Failure	23-249	31
Chart Q	Traction Indicator Does Not Light	23-250	33
Chart R	Traction Indicator Is On All The Time	23-252	35
Chart S	Traction Control Engaged, Does Not Operate	23-253	37
1993 LeSabre & Park Avenue			
	System Diagnosis, Test 1	23-267	55
	System Diagnosis, Test 2	23-267	56
	System Diagnosis, Test 3	23-268	57
	System Diagnosis, Test 4	23-269	58
	System Diagnosis, Test 5	23-270	59
	System Diagnosis, Test 6	23-271	60
	System Diagnosis, Test 7	23-271	61
	System Diagnosis, Test 8	23-272	62
	System Diagnosis, Test 9	23-272	63
	System Diagnosis, Test 10	23-273	64

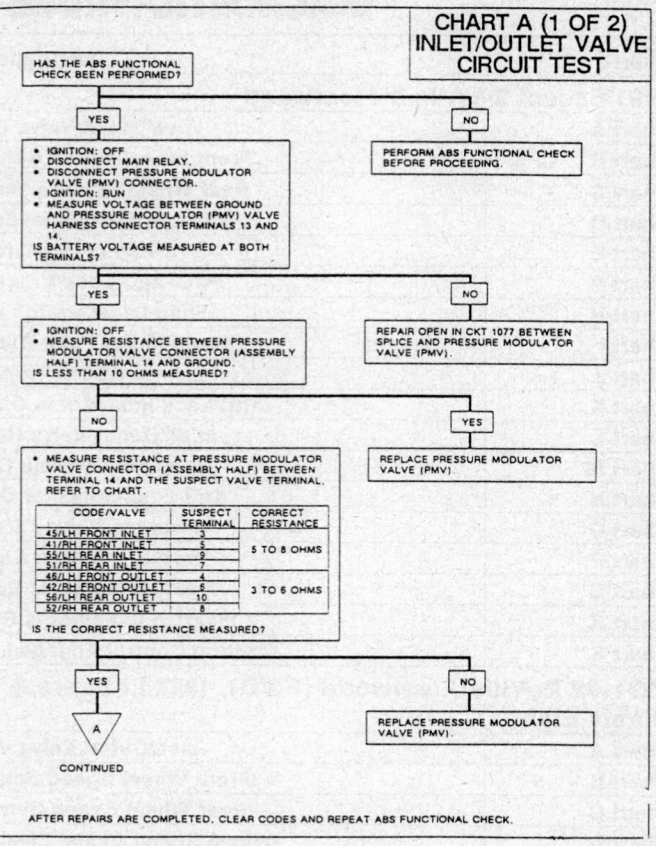

CHART A
INLET/OUTLET VALVE TEST

CIRCUIT OPERATION

Inlet Valves

Voltage is applied to the normally open inlet valves whenever the main relay is energized. The inlet valves will close when the electronic brake control module (EBCM) supplies a ground path at the respective inlet valve control terminal. The EBCM closes the inlet valves for short periods to maintain (hold) or reduce pressure at a particular wheel during an ABS stop.

Outlet Valves

The normally closed outlet valve's operation is similar to the inlet valve's except that when the EBCM grounds the outlet valve, the outlet valve opens instead of closing. The EBCM open the outlet valve for short periods to reduce pressure at a particular wheel during an ABS stop.

VALVE MODES

Pressure Increase

The pressure increase position is the normal operating position of the valves for braking without antilock control. Neither valve is energized when the valves are in this mode.

Pressure Hold

The pressure hold position is commanded when the EBCM desire to hold the pressure in the wheel circuit constant. The inlet valve is closed by the EBCM when the pressure hold mode is desired.

Pressure Reduce

The pressure reduce position is used to decrease hydraulic pressure in a specific wheel circuit without decreasing pressure in the rest of the system. Both the inlet and outlet valve are energized in the pressure reduce mode.

Failure Conditions

Codes 41, 42, 45, 46, 51, 52, 55, or 56 will set if the electronic brake control module (EBCM) detects an open or short to ground in the respective inlet or outlet valve circuit.

Fig. 15   Chart A (Part 1 of 2). 1991 Except DeVille & Fleetwood (FWD)

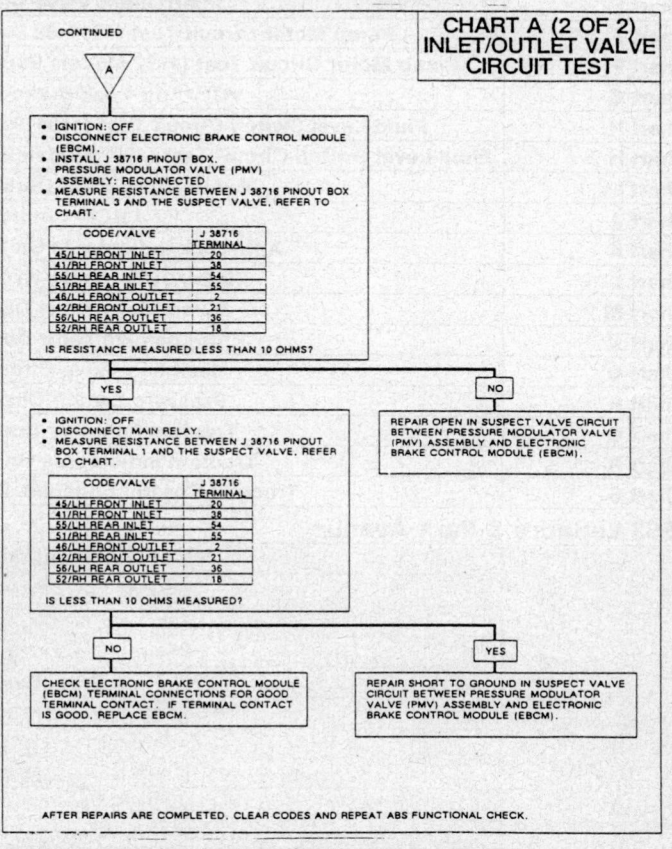

CHART A
INLET/OUTLET VALVE TEST

CIRCUIT OPERATION

Inlet Valves

Voltage is applied to the normally open inlet valves whenever the main relay is energized. The inlet valves will close when the electronic brake control module (EBCM) supplies a ground path at the respective inlet valve control terminal. The EBCM closes the inlet valves for short periods to maintain (hold) or reduce pressure at a particular wheel during an ABS stop.

Outlet Valves

The normally closed outlet valve's operation is similar to the inlet valve's except that when the EBCM grounds the outlet valve, the outlet valve opens instead of closing. The EBCM open the outlet valve for short periods to reduce pressure at a particular wheel during an ABS stop.

VALVE MODES

Pressure Increase

The pressure increase position is the normal operating position of the valves for braking without antilock control. Neither valve is energized when the valves are in this mode.

Pressure Hold

The pressure hold position is commanded when the EBCM desire to hold the pressure in the wheel circuit constant. The inlet valve is closed by the EBCM when the pressure hold mode is desired.

Pressure Reduce

The pressure reduce position is used to decrease hydraulic pressure in a specific wheel circuit without decreasing pressure in the rest of the system. Both the inlet and outlet valve are energized in the pressure reduce mode.

Failure Conditions

Codes 41, 42, 45, 46, 51, 52, 55, or 56 will set if the electronic brake control module (EBCM) detects an open or short to ground in the respective inlet or outlet valve circuit.

Fig. 15   Chart A (Part 2 of 2). 1991 Except DeVille & Fleetwood (FWD)

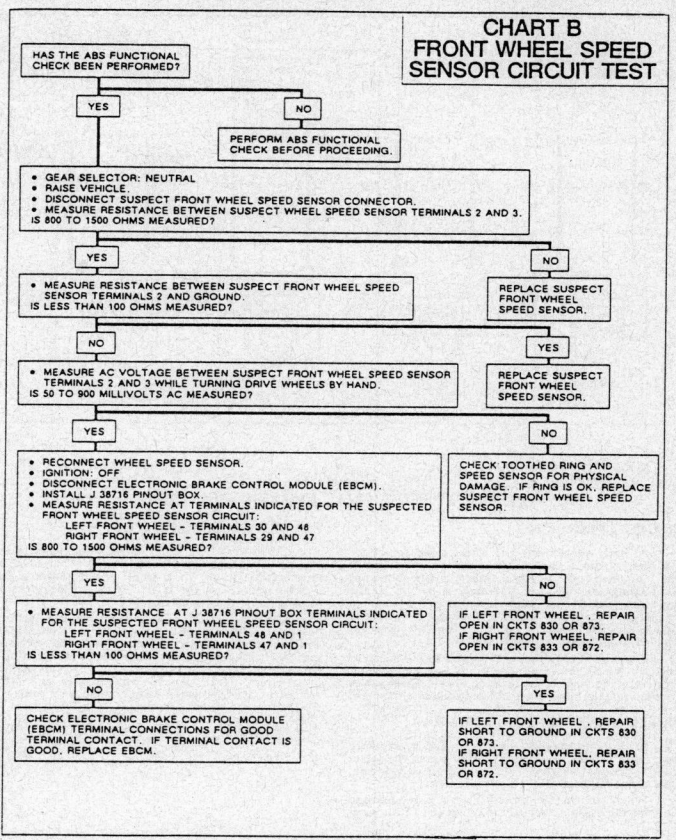

CHART B
FRONT WHEEL SPEED SENSOR CIRCUIT TEST

CIRCUIT OPERATION

As each wheel turns, the wheel speed sensor for that wheel creates a small AC voltage as a toothed sensor ring, mounted on the drive axle, passes the stationary sensor pickup coil.

The sensor consists of a permanent magnet (toothed ring) and coil (stationary pickup) which generates voltage by magnetic induction. The frequency of the wheel speed sensor signal is proportional to wheel speed.

The EBCM uses the wheel speed sensor signal to calculate vehicle reference speeds and individual speed, acceleration and slip values for each wheel. These values are used to determine when antilock control is required.

WHEEL SPEED SENSOR CABLES

In order to prevent electromagnetic interference from disturbing the wheel speed sensor signal, the cables from the EBCM to each wheel speed sensor are twisted in pairs a minimum of 6 to 9 turns per foot.

When servicing the sensor cables it is important to maintain the original twists of the cables (6 to 9 turns per foot).

FAILURE CONDITIONS

The EBCM performs two basic types of checks on the wheel speed sensors, including sensor continuity (checking that the sensor is installed) and sensor output (checking that the sensor is producing a readable signal).

Sensor Continuity Check

Any condition which would result in lack of continuity on the front wheel speed sensor circuit could result in an ABS code being set. These conditions include an open in the wiring harness between the speed sensor and EBCM or an open across the speed sensor coil.

Sensor Output Check

Conditions which result in low wheel speed sensor output can also cause an ABS code to set. These conditions include a short to ground in the wiring harness, a shorted wheel speed sensor coil, or an improperly installed sensor.

Fig. 16   Chart B. 1991 Except DeVille & Fleetwood (FWD)

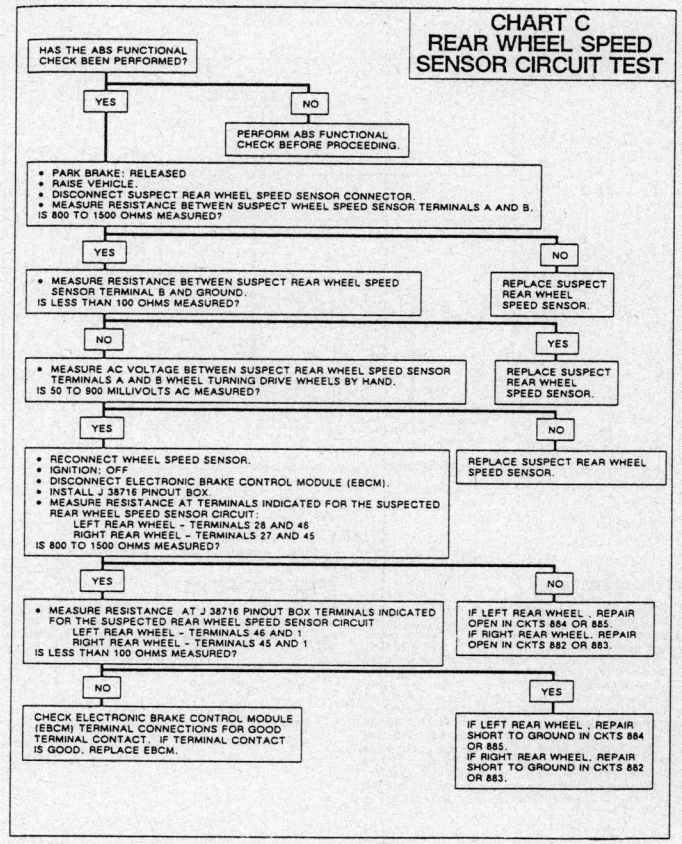

CHART C
REAR WHEEL SPEED SENSOR CIRCUIT TEST

CIRCUIT OPERATION

As each wheel turns, the wheel speed sensor for that wheel creates a small AC voltage as a toothed sensor ring passes the stationary sensor pickup coil. Both the ring and the stationary coil are part of the hub and bearing assembly.

The sensor consists of a permanent magnet (toothed ring) and coil (stationary pickup) which generates voltage by magnetic induction. The frequency of the wheel speed sensor signal is proportional to wheel speed.

The EBCM uses the wheel speed sensor signal to calculate vehicle reference speeds and individual speed, acceleration and slip values for each wheel. Theses values are used to determine when antilock control is required.

WHEEL SPEED SENSOR CABLES

In order to prevent electromagnetic interference from disturbing the wheel speed sensor signal, the cables from the EBCM to each wheel speed sensor are twisted in pairs a minimum of 6 to 9 turns per foot.

When servicing the sensor cables it is important to maintain the original twists of the cables (6 to 9 per foot).

FAILURE CONDITIONS

The EBCM performs two basic types of checks on the wheel speed sensors, including sensor continuity (checking that the sensor is installed) and sensor output (checking that the sensor is producing a readable signal).

Sensor Continuity Check

Any condition which would result in lack of continuity on the rear wheel speed sensor circuit could result in an ABS code being set. These conditions include an open in the wiring harness between the speed sensor and EBCM or an open across the speed sensor coil.

Sensor Output Check

Conditions which result in low wheel speed sensor output can also cause an ABS code to set. These conditions include a short to ground in the wiring harness, a shorted wheel speed sensor coil, or an improperly installed sensor.

Fig. 17   Chart C. 1991 Except DeVille & Fleetwood (FWD)

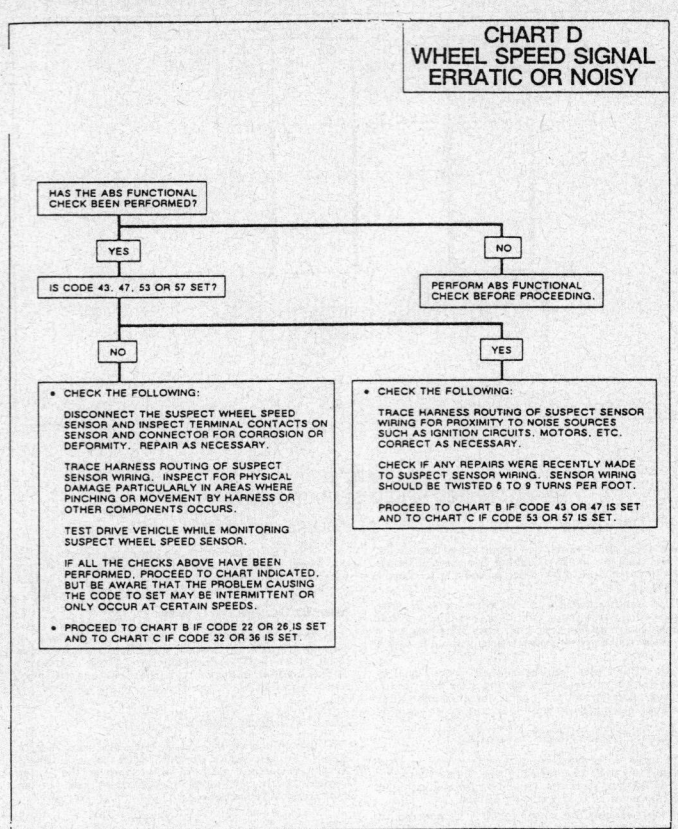

CHART D
WHEEL SPEED SIGNAL ERRATIC OR NOISY

CIRCUIT OPERATION

As each wheel turns, the wheel speed sensor for that wheel creates a small AC voltage as a toothed sensor ring, mounted on the drive axle (in the front) or hub/bearing assembly (in the rear), is passed by the stationary sensor. The sensor consists of a permanent magnet and coil, and generates voltage by magnetic induction. The frequency of the wheel speed sensor signal is proportional to wheel speed.

The EBCM uses the wheel speed sensor signal to calculate vehicle reference speeds and individual speed, acceleration and slip values for each wheel. These values are used to determine when antilock control is required.

WHEEL SPEED SENSOR CABLES

In order to prevent electromagnetic interference from disturbing the wheel speed sensor signal, the cables from the EBCM to each wheel speed sensor are twisted in pairs a minimum of 6 to 9 turns per foot.

When servicing the sensor cables it is important to maintain the original twists of the cables (6 to 9 turns per foot).

FAILURE CONDITIONS

Codes 43, 47, 53, or 57 will set when the electronic brake control module (EBCM) detects electromagnetic interference (noise) in a wheel speed sensor signal. Possible sources of the interference include accessory motors, wiper motors and ignition circuits.

Codes 22, 26, 32, or 36 will set when the electronic brake control module (EBCM) determines a wheel speed signal is erratic and can occur at any speed. A wheel speed signal that indicates that a wheel is accelerating or decelerating faster than physically possible is an example of an erratic signal. An intermittent open or short to ground in a wheel speed sensor could also cause the EBCM to set a code.

Fig. 18 Chart D. 1991 Except DeVille & Fleetwood (FWD)

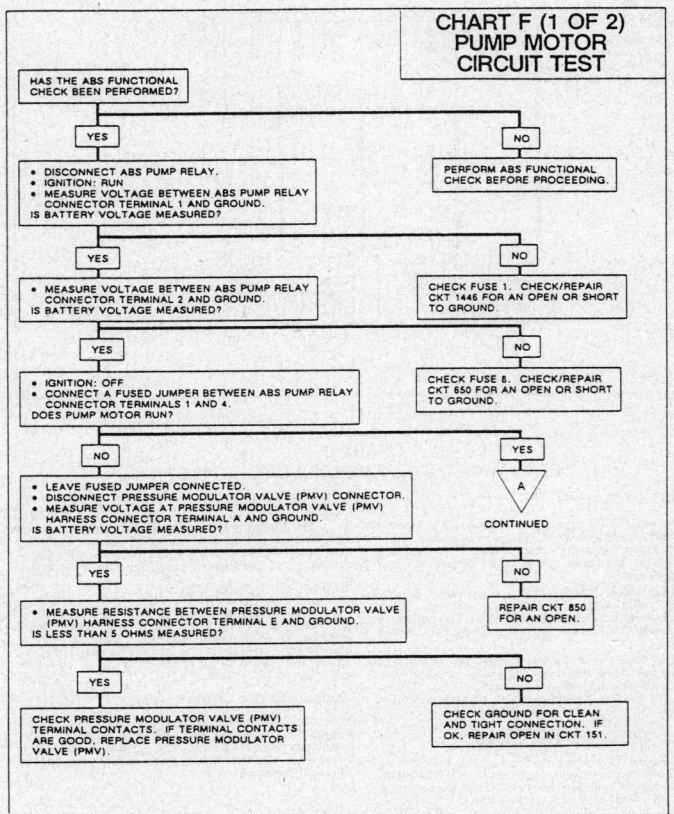

CHART F
PUMP MOTOR CIRCUIT TEST

CIRCUIT OPERATION

When the electronic brake control module (EBCM) grounds the ABS pump relay coil, the pump relay contacts close applying voltage to the pump motor which is part of the pressure modulator valve (PMV) assembly. The EBCM turns on the pump motor when the VCC/antilock brake switch opens indicating brake pedal travel has exceeded a preset level. When the pump motor runs, the PMV assembly reservoir is replenished and fluid pressure is applied to the master cylinder causing the brake pedal to rise gradually. The EBCM will keep on until the brake pedal rises to close the VCC/antilock brake switch. Generally the pump is on whenever the ABS is activated. The EBCM monitors pump motor operation via the pump motor run sensor. When the pump is operating, voltage is induced into the sensor's coil and the EBCM monitors this voltage at terminals 49 and 31.

FAILURE CONDITIONS

Code 61 will set when the electronic brake control module (EBCM) determines the pump motor is not running (voltage at EBCM terminals 31 and 49) when the EBCM grounds the ABS pump motor relay.

Fig. 19 Chart F (Part 1 of 2). 1991 Except DeVille & Fleetwood (FWD)

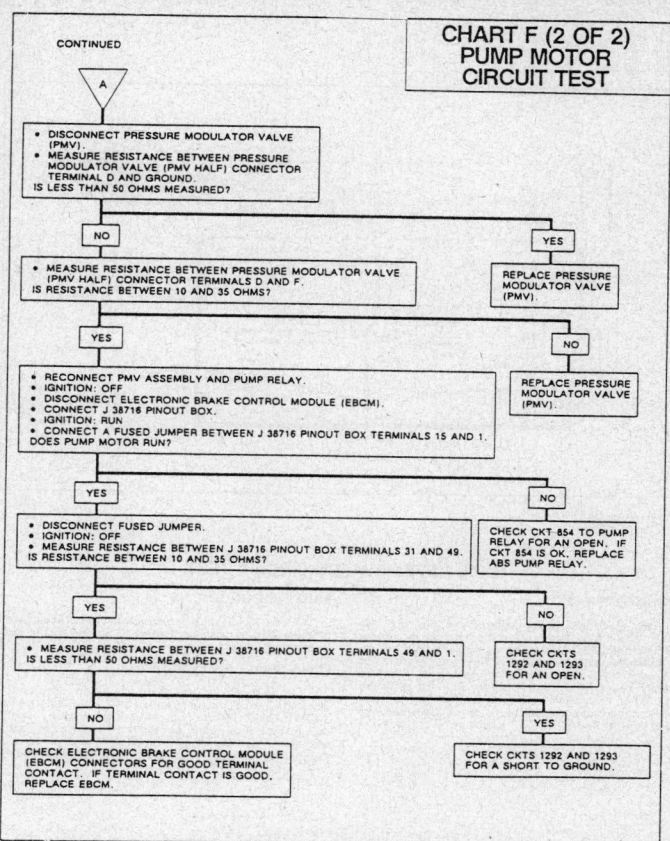

CHART F
PUMP MOTOR CIRCUIT TEST

CIRCUIT OPERATION

When the electronic brake control module (EBCM) grounds the ABS pump relay coil, the pump relay contacts close applying voltage to the pump motor which is part of the pressure modulator valve (PMV) assembly. The EBCM turns on the pump motor when the VCC/antilock brake switch opens indicating brake pedal travel has exceeded a preset level. When the pump motor runs, the PMV assembly reservoir is replenished and fluid pressure is applied to the master cylinder causing the brake pedal to rise gradually. The EBCM will keep on until the brake pedal rises to close the VCC/antilock brake switch. Generally the pump is on whenever the ABS is activated. The EBCM monitors pump motor operation via the pump motor run sensor. When the pump is operating, voltage is induced into the sensor's coil and the EBCM monitors this voltage at terminals 49 and 31.

FAILURE CONDITIONS

Code 61 will set when the electronic brake control module (EBCM) determines the pump motor is not running (voltage at EBCM terminals 31 and 49) when the EBCM grounds the ABS pump motor relay.

Fig. 19   Chart F (Part 2 of 2). 1991 Except DeVille & Fleetwood (FWD)

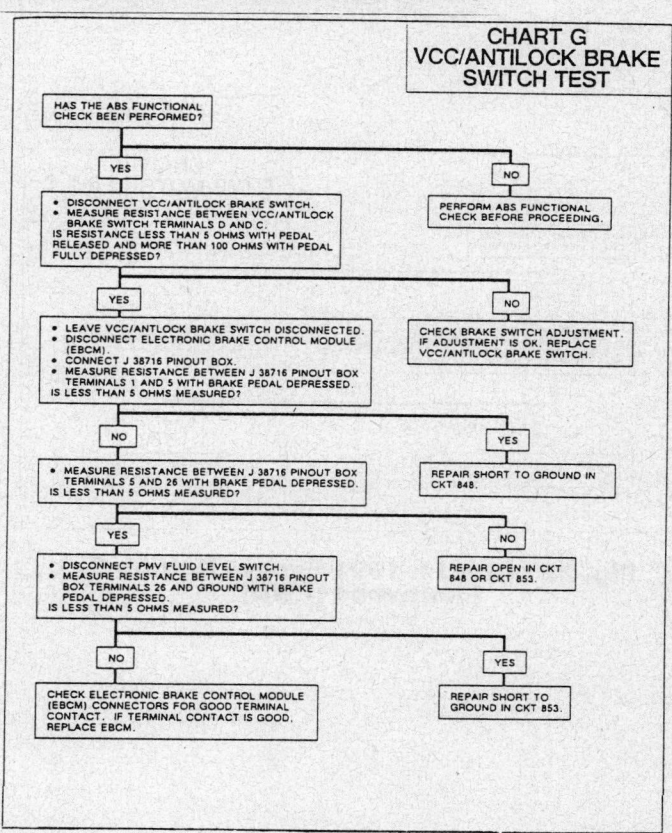

CHART G
VCC/ANTILOCK BRAKE SWITCH TEST

CIRCUIT OPERATION

The electronic brake control module (EBCM) monitors the brake pedal position by monitoring the VCC/antilock brake switch position. The VCC/antilock switch is normally closed. When the brake pedal is depressed approximately 40% down, the switch opens. If the ABS system is active when the VCC/antilock switch opens the EBCM will turn on the pump motor by energizing the ABS pump relay. The EBCM will turn off the pump motor when pedal height rises sufficiently to close the VCC/antilock brake switch.

FAILURE CONDITIONS

Code 72 will set when the electronic brake control module (EBCM) detects the VCC/antilock brake switch is open or shorted to ground.

Fig. 20   Chart G. 1991 Except DeVille & Fleetwood (FWD)

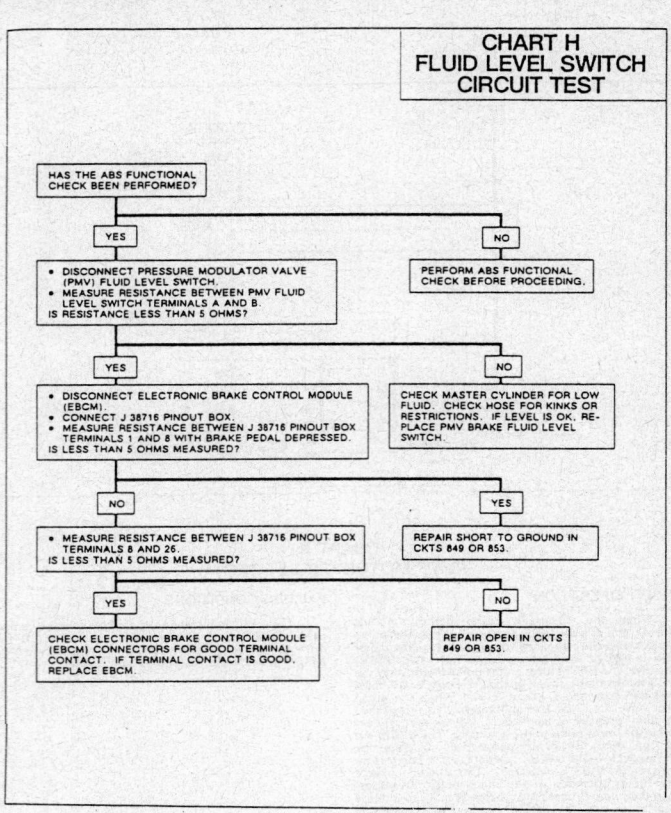

CHART H
FLUID LEVEL SWITCH CIRCUIT TEST

CIRCUIT OPERATION

The electronic brake control module (EBCM) monitors the brake fluid level in the pressure modulator valve assembly (PMV) reservoir via the fluid level switch. The fluid level switch is located in the pressure modulator valve assembly's reservoir. The fluid level switch is normally closed when the reservoir contains sufficient fluid. When the switch opens the fluid level is low and the electronic brake control module (EBCM) reacts by turning on the "ANTILOCK" indicator.

FAILURE CONDITIONS

Code 73 will set when the electronic brake control module (EBCM) detects a short to ground in the fluid level switch circuit.

Open Fluid Level Circuit

If an open or low fluid condition occurs, the electronic brake control module (EBCM) will turn on the "ANTILOCK" indictor but will not set a code. In the case of a low fluid condition, the red "BRAKE" indicator will also most likely light since the master cylinder supplies the pressure modulator valve assembly (PMV).

Fig. 21   Chart H. 1991 Except DeVille & Fleetwood (FWD)

Fig. 22   Chart I. 1991 Except DeVille & Fleetwood (FWD)

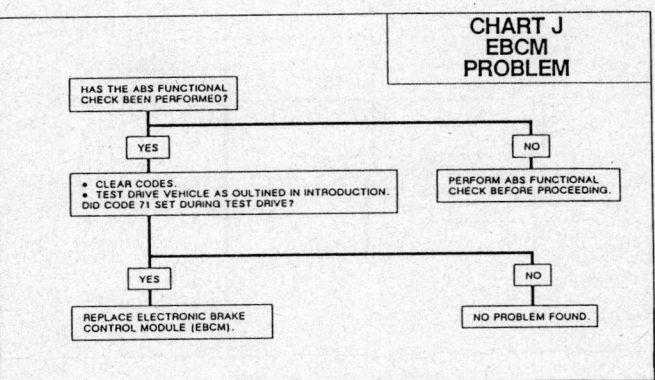

Fig. 23   Chart J. 1991 Except DeVille & Fleetwood (FWD)

CHART K
"ANTILOCK" INDICATOR IS ON AND NO CODES ARE SET

CIRCUIT OPERATION

When the ignition is first turn to "RUN," the EBCM goes through a self test. During this test the EBCM grounds the "ANTILOCK" indicator at terminal 52 causing the indicator to light for several seconds. This acts as a bulb test for the indicator. During normal operation the main relay applies voltage to the EBCM and PMV assembly. If the EBCM should detect a fault, the main relay will de-energized causing the "ANTILOCK" indicator to light since it is grounded through the main relay contacts.

FAILURE CONDITIONS

Possible Causes
- Open or short to ground in CKT 852.
- Open in CKT 151, 650, 800, 803, or 1077.
- Open main relay coil.
- Brake fluid level low or open fluid level switch.

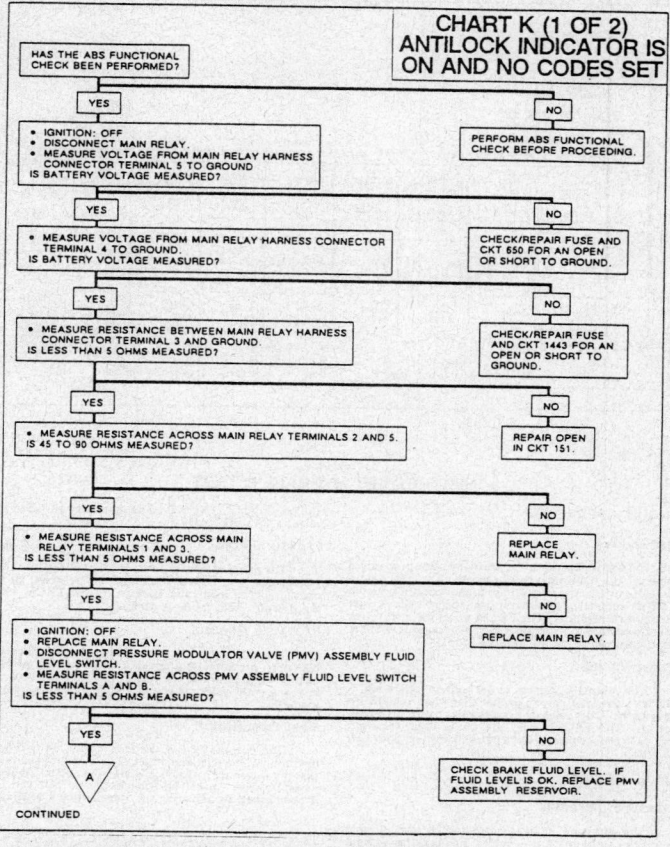

Fig. 24 Chart K (Part 1 of 2). 1991 Except DeVille & Fleetwood (FWD)

CHART K
"ANTILOCK" INDICATOR IS ON AND NO CODES ARE SET/
DIAGNOSTIC MODE CANNOT BE ENTERED

CIRCUIT OPERATION

When the ignition is first turned to "RUN," the electronic brake control module (EBCM) goes through a self-test lasting 2–4 seconds. During this test, the EBCM grounds terminal 52 causing the amber "ANTILOCK" indicator to light. This serves as an indicator bulb test.

When a low fluid condition exists, the EBCM turns on the amber "ANTILOCK" indicator but does not set a code. A low fluid level condition usually lights the red "BRAKE" indicator since the master cylinder supplies the PMV reservoir. However, restrictions or air in the hose could cause a low fluid condition in the PMV reservoir without lighting the red "BRAKE" indicator.

FAILURE CONDITIONS

Possible Causes
- Open in CKT 650, 800, 803, 849 or 853.
- Low brake fluid level or open PMV fluid level switch.
- Short to ground in CKT 650, 800 or 852.

Fig. 24 Chart K (Part 2 of 2). 1991 Except DeVille & Fleetwood (FWD)

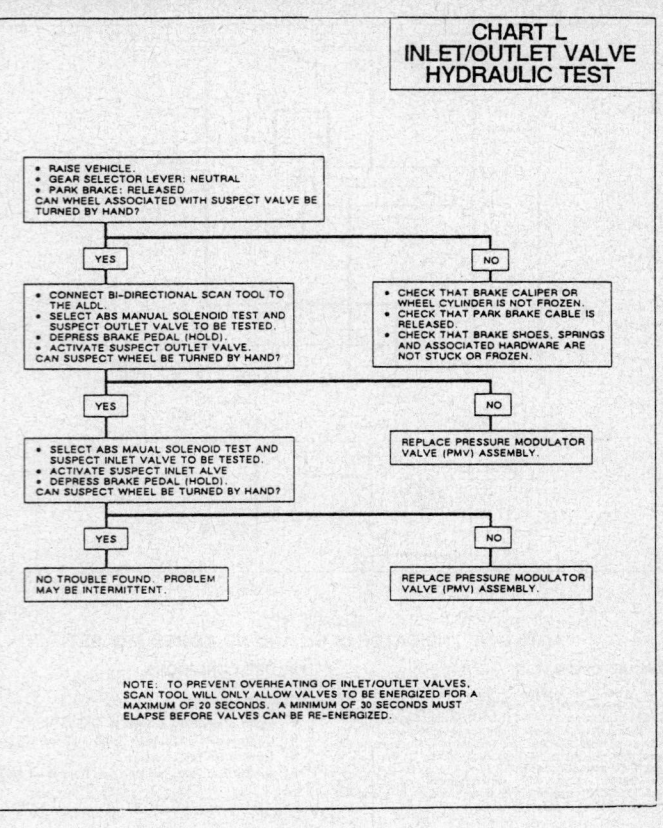

CHART L
INLET/OUTLET VALVE
HYDRAULIC TEST

CHART L
INLET/OUTLET HYDRAULIC TEST

CIRCUIT OPERATION

Inlet Valves

Voltage is applied to the normally open inlet valves whenever the main relay is energized. The inlet valves will close when the electronic brake control module (EBCM) supplies a ground path at the respective inlet valve control terminal. The EBCM closes the inlet valves for short periods to maintain (hold) or reduce pressure at a particular wheel during an ABS stop.

Outlet Valves

The normally closed outlet valve's operation is similar to the inlet valve's except that when the EBCM grounds the outlet valve, the outlet valve opens instead of closing. The EBCM opens the outlet valve for short periods to reduce pressure at a particular wheel during an ABS stop.

VALVE MODES

Pressure Increase

The pressure increase position is the normal operating position of the valves for braking without antilock control. Neither valve is energized when the valves are in this mode.

Pressure Hold

The pressure hold position is commended when the EBCM desire to hold the pressure in the wheel circuit constant. The inlet valve is closed by the EBCM when the pressure hold mode is desired.

Pressure Reduce

The pressure reduce position is used to decrease hydraulic pressure in a specific wheel circuit without decreasing pressure in the rest of the system. Both the inlet and outlet valve are energized in the pressure reduce mode.

Test Description

The purpose of this test is to verify the hydraulic operation of the inlet and outlet valves. In order to verify that the valves are hydraulically effective, behavior of the wheel brakes must be checked. This can be accomplished by actuating the valves using a scan tool.

NOTE: TO PREVENT OVERHEATING OF INLET/OUTLET VALVES, SCAN TOOL WILL ONLY ALLOW VALVES TO BE ENERGIZED FOR A MAXIMUM OF 20 SECONDS. A MINIMUM OF 30 SECONDS MUST ELAPSE BEFORE VALVES CAN BE RE-ENERGIZED.

Fig. 25   Chart L. 1991 Except DeVille & Fleetwood (FWD)

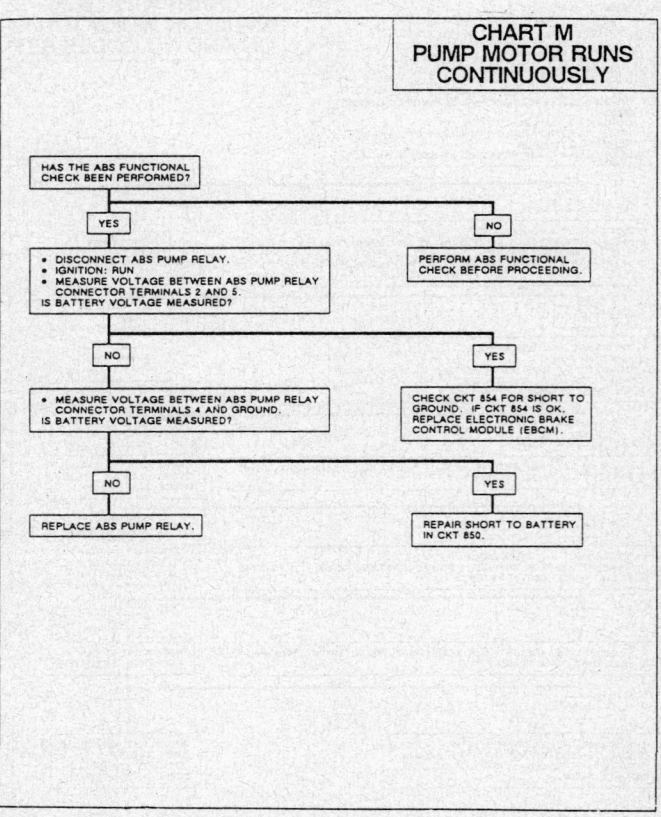

CHART M
PUMP MOTOR RUNS CONTINUOUSLY

CIRCUIT OPERATION

When the electronic brake control module (EBCM) grounds the ABS pump relay coil, the pump relay contacts close applying voltage to the pump motor which is part of the pressure modulator valve (PMV) assembly. The EBCM turns on the pump motor when the VCC/antilock brake switch opens indicating brake pedal travel has exceeded a preset level. When the pump motor runs, the PMV assembly reservoir is replenished and fluid pressure is applied to the master cylinder causing the brake pedal to rise gradually. The EBCM will keep on until the brake pedal rises to close the VCC/antilock brake switch. Generally the pump is on whenever the ABS is activated. The EBCM monitors pump motor operation via the pump motor run sensor. When the pump is operating, voltage is induced into the sensor's coil and the EBCM monitors this voltage at terminals 49 and 31.

TEST DESCRIPTION

A continuously running pump motor will occur if the pump relay coil is shorted to ground, the relay contacts are shorted, closed, or CKT 850 is shorted to a battery source.

Fig. 26   Chart M. 1991 Except DeVille & Fleetwood (FWD)

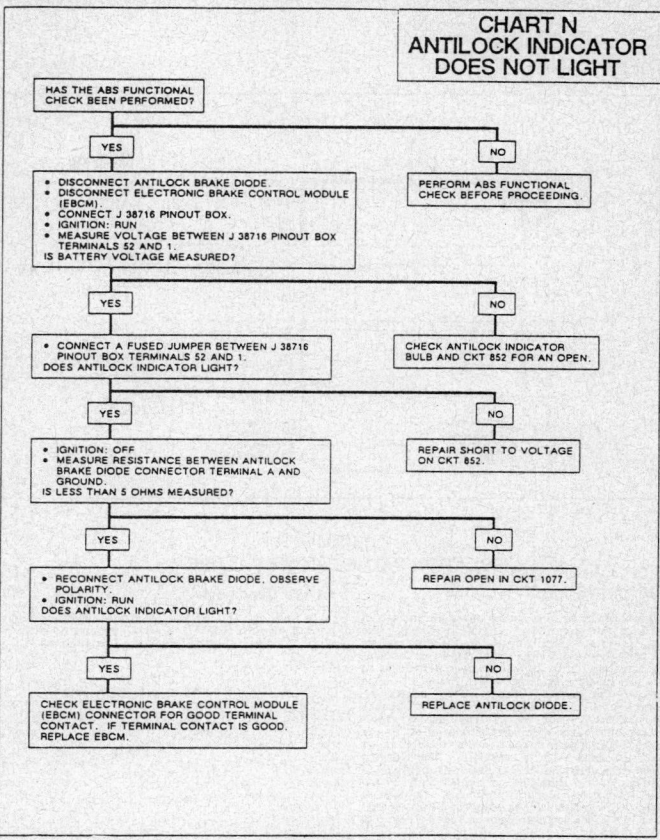

CHART N
"ANTILOCK" INDICATOR DOES NOT LIGHT

CIRCUIT OPERATION

When the ignition is first turned to "RUN," the EBCM goes through a self test. During this test the EBCM grounds the "ANTILOCK" indicator at terminal 52 causing the indicator to light for several seconds. This acts as a bulb test for the indicator. During normal operation the main relay applies voltage to the EBCM and PMV assembly. If the EBCM should detect a fault, the main relay will be de-energized causing the "ANTILOCK" indicator to light since it is grounded through the main relay contacts.

FAILURE CONDITIONS

Possible Causes

- Open bulb.
- Open in CKT 852.
- Short to voltage in CKT 852.
- Open or shorted antilock diode.
- Open in CKT 1077
- Faulty EBCM.

Fig. 27   Chart N. 1991 Except DeVille & Fleetwood (FWD)

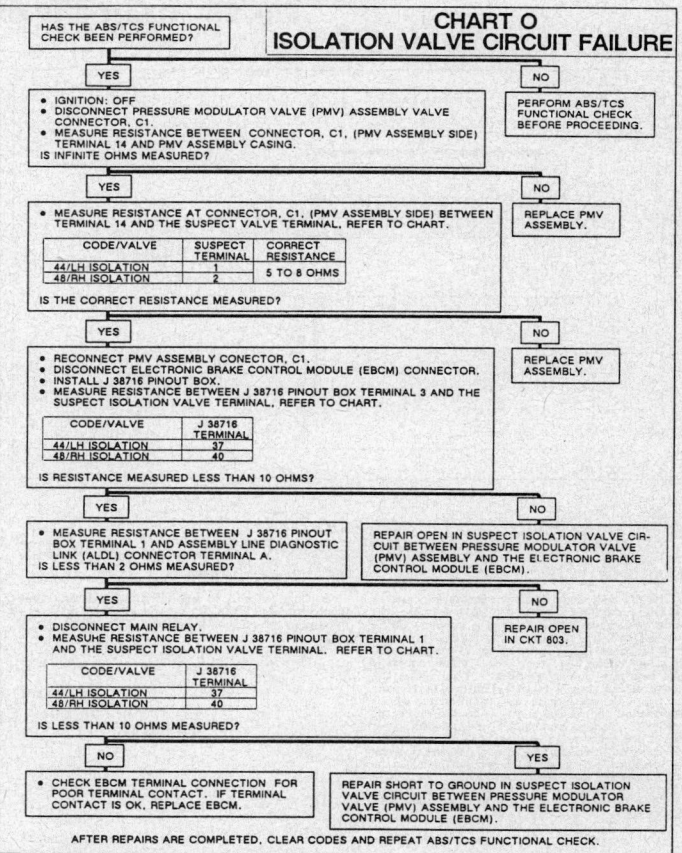

CHART O
ISOLATION VALVE CIRCUIT FAILURE

CIRCUIT OPERATION

Voltage is applied to the normally open isolation valves whenever the main relay is energized. An isolation valve closes when the electronic brake control module (EBCM) supplies a ground path at the isolation valve control terminal. The EBCM closes an isolation valve when the EBCM detects wheel slip in a drive wheel and vehicle speed is below 40 km/h (25 mph).

The isolation valves are closed only during traction control operations, and are not used during any antilock or normal braking conditions. The isolation valves separate (isolate) the front brake hydraulic circuits from the master cylinder and rear brake hydraulic circuits. Once the front brake hydraulic circuits are isolated, pressure can be applied to the front wheels without affecting any other brake hydraulic circuit.

FAILURE CONDITIONS

Code 44 or 48 sets when the electronic brake control module (EBCM) detects an open or short to ground in the respective isolation valve circuit.

Fig. 28   Chart O. 1991 98 & Park Ave.

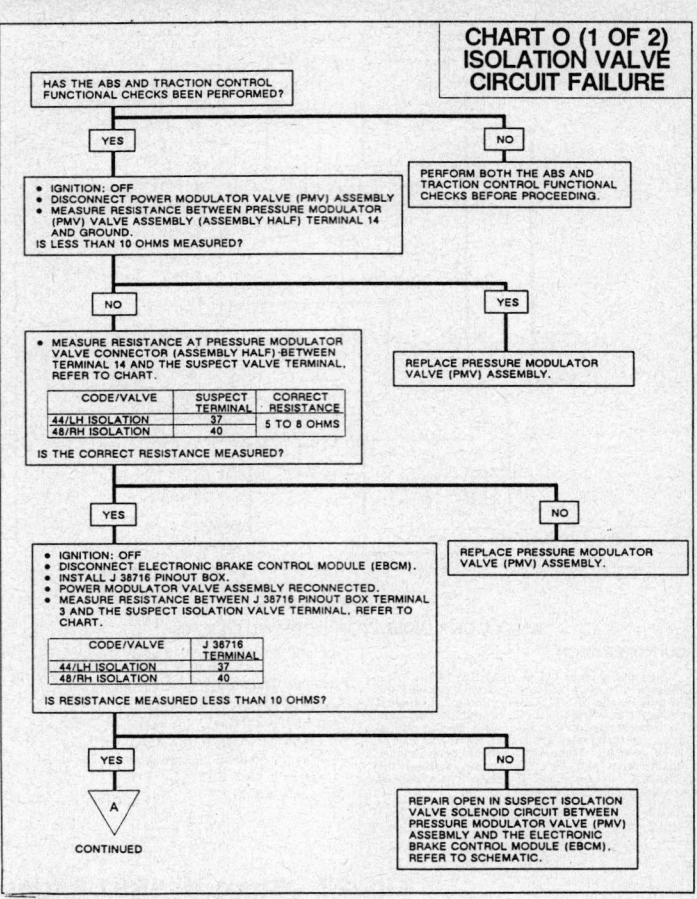

**CHART O (1 OF 2)
ISOLATION VALVE
CIRCUIT FAILURE**

CHART O
ISOLATION VALVE CIRCUIT FAILURE

CIRCUIT OPERATION

The normally open isolation valves are located in the pressure modulator valve (PMV) assembly. the isolation valves are used only during traction control operations, the valves are not used during any antilock or braking functions. The isolation valves purpose is to separate or isolate the front wheel brake hydraulic circuits and the master cylinder. This allows the electronic brake control module (EBCM) to regulate brake hydraulic pressure to the front driven wheels during traction control operations without effect on the rear wheels. Voltage is applied to the isolation valves whenever the main relay is energized. The isolation valves will close when the EBCM energizes the isolation valve solenoids by supplying a ground path at the EBCM's isolation valve control terminals. The EBCM will energize the isolation valves when the EBCM detects wheel slip in a driven wheel and vehicle speed is below 20 km/h (12 mph).

Failure Conditions

Code 44 and 48 will set if the electronic brake control module (EBCM) detects an open or short to ground in the respective isolation valve circuits.

Fig. 29   Chart O (Part 1 of 2). 1992 models

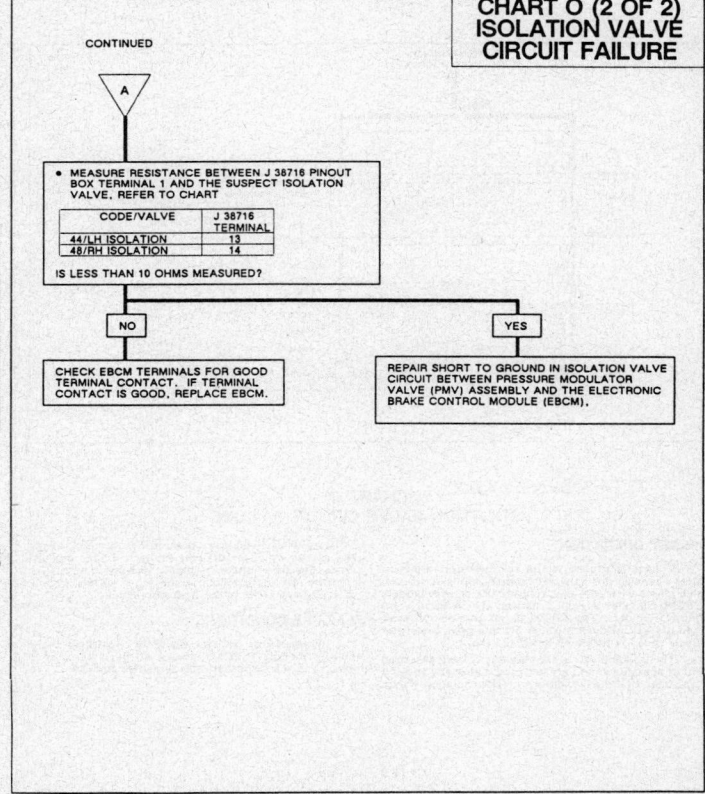

**CHART O (2 OF 2)
ISOLATION VALVE
CIRCUIT FAILURE**

CHART O
ISOLATION VALVE CIRCUIT FAILURE

CIRCUIT OPERATION

The normally open isolation valves are located in the pressure modulator valve (PMV) assembly. the isolation valves are used only during traction control operations, the valves are not used during any antilock or braking functions. The isolation valves purpose is to separate or isolate the front wheel brake hydraulic circuits and the master cylinder. This allows the electronic brake control module (EBCM) to regulate brake hydraulic pressure to the front driven wheels during traction control operations without effect on the rear wheels. Voltage is applied to the isolation valves whenever the main relay is energized. The isolation valves will close when the EBCM energizes the isolation valve solenoids by supplying a ground path at the EBCM's isolation valve control terminals. The EBCM will energize the isolation valves when the EBCM detects wheel slip in a driven wheel and vehicle speed is below 20 km/h (12 mph).

FAILURE CONDITIONS

Code 44 and 48 will set if the electronic brake control module (EBCM) detects an open or short to ground in the respective isolation valve circuit.

Fig. 29   Chart O (Part 2 of 2). 1992 models

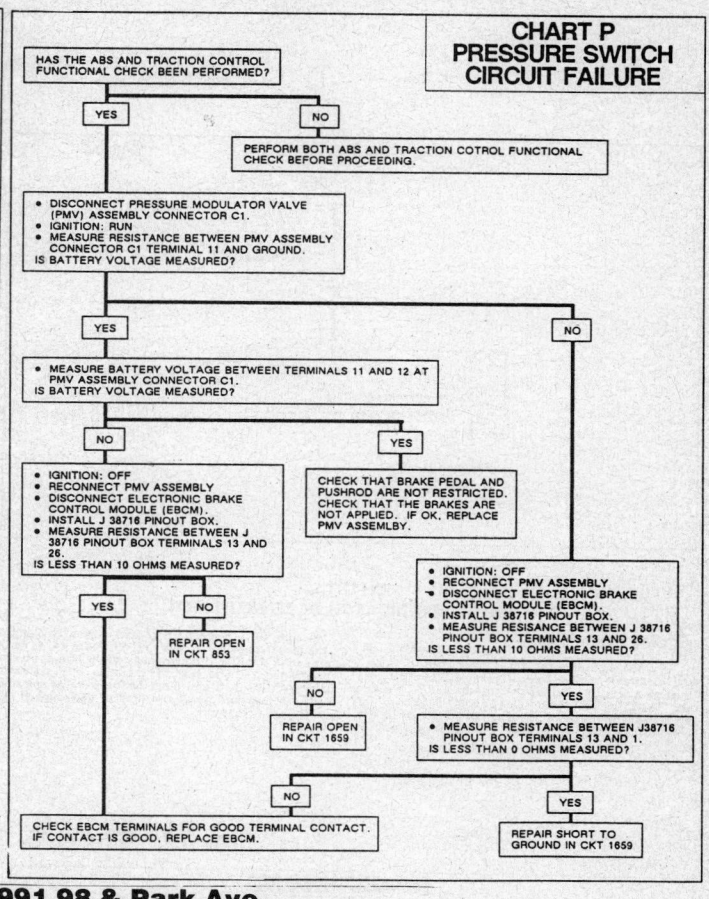

CHART P
PRESSURE SWITCH CIRCUIT FAILURE

CIRCUIT OPERATION

The normally open pressure switch opens when brake pressure exceeds 696 kPa (101 psi). An open pressure switch indicates that the brakes are being applied by the driver, this signals the electronic brake control module (EBCM) to disable traction control. The pressure switch is part of the pressure modulator Valve (PMV) assembly and is not serviceable. The pressure switch is located in the hydraulic circuit so that the isolation valves will not effect its operation.

FAILURE CONDITIONS

Code 74 will set if the electronic bake control module (EBCM) detects an open or short to ground in the pressure switch circuit.

Fig. 30   Chart P. 1991 98 & Park Ave.

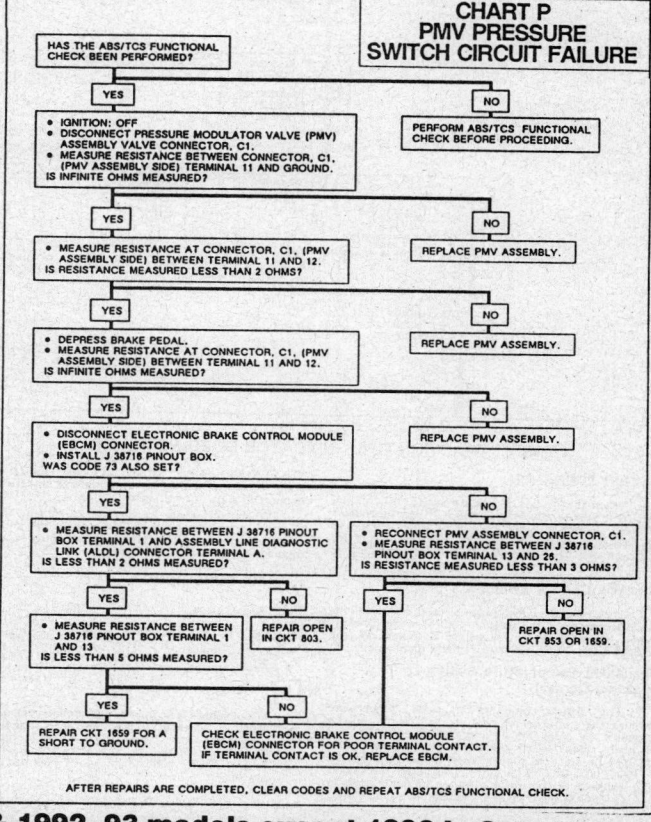

CHART P
PMV PRESSURE SWITCH CIRCUIT FAILURE

CHART P
PRESSURE SWITCH CIRCUIT FAILURE

CIRCUIT OPERATION

The pressure switch monitors primary brake system pressure. The normally closed switch opens when the brakes are applied (pressure exceeds 700 kPa [101 psi]). If the brakes are manually applied during traction control mode, the PMV pressure switch input, along with the brake switch input, signal the electronic brake control module (EBCM) to disable traction control and allow manual braking. The pressure switch is part of the pressure modulator valve (PMV) assembly and is not serviceable.

FAILURE CONDITIONS

Code 74 sets when the electronic brake control module (EBCM) detects an open or short to ground in the PMV pressure switch circuitry.

Possible Causes

- Open in CKT 853 or 1659.
- Short to ground in CKT 1659 with the brakes applied.
- Failed PMV pressure switch.

Fig. 31   Chart P. 1991 DeVille & Fleetwood (FWD) & 1992–93 models except 1993 LeSabre & Park Avenue

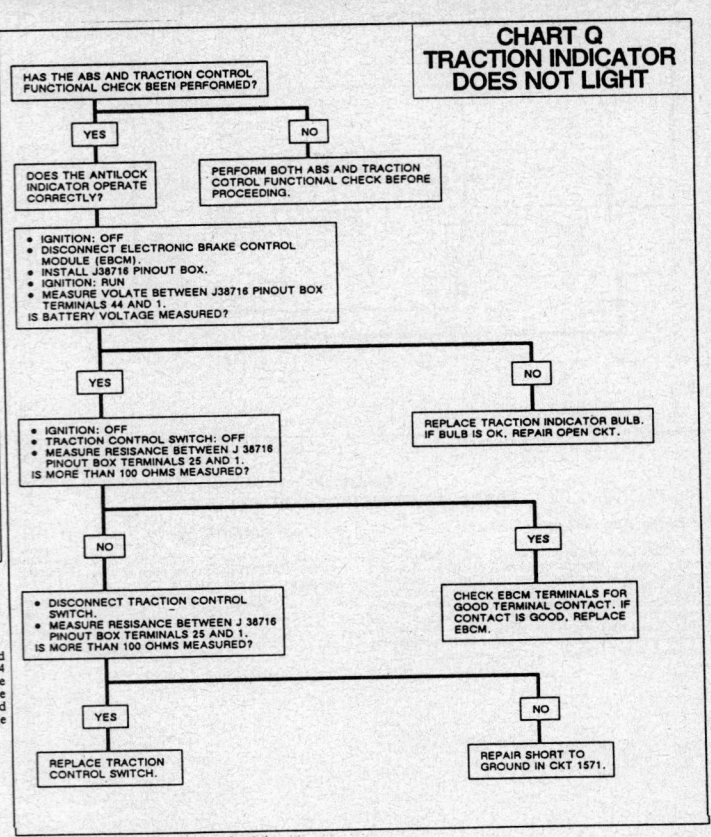

CHART Q
TRACTION INDICATOR DOES NOT LIGHT

CHART Q
TRACTION INDICATOR DOES NOT LIGHT

CIRCUIT OPERATION

When the ignition switch is first turned to "RUN" the electronic brake control module (EBCM) goes through a self test. During this test the EBCM grounds the "ANTILOCK" and "TRACTION" indicators for approximately 4 seconds. This acts as a bulb test for the indicators. The "TRACTION" indicator will stay lit indicating that the traction control system is disabled when the traction control switch is off, codes 44, 48 or 74 are set, or the EBCM determines that the brakes may be overheating. The EBCM monitors the transaxle temperature switch and other factors such as solenoid valve on time and pump run time to determine if the brakes are overheating.

Fig. 32   Chart Q. 1991 98 & Park Ave

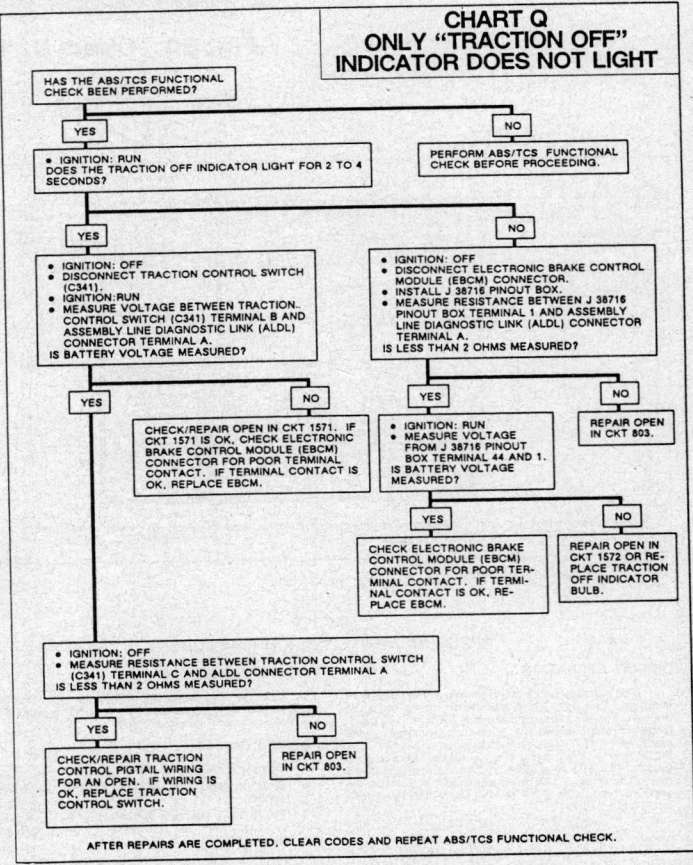

CHART Q
ONLY "TRACTION OFF" INDICATOR DOES NOT LIGHT

CHART Q
ONLY "TRACTION OFF" INDICATOR DOES NOT LIGHT

CIRCUIT OPERATION

When the ignition is first turned to "RUN," the electronic brake control module (EBCM) goes through a self-test. During this test, the EBCM grounds both the "ANTILOCK" and "TRACTION OFF" indicators for approximately 2 to 4 seconds. This acts as a bulb test for the indicators.

Traction Control Switch

Located in the console trim plate, the switch allows the driver to select the traction control mode (on/off). When the traction control system is turned off, the "TRACTION OFF" indicator remains illuminated.

Transaxle Temperature Switch (with Traction Control)

The EBCM monitors transaxle temperature through the transaxle temperature switch. When the transaxle becomes hot, about 160°C (320°F), the normally closed switch opens signaling the EBCM to disable the traction control system and turn on the "TRACTION OFF" indicator. This allows the brakes and transaxle to cool down. As the transaxle cools to 149°C (300°F) the transaxle temperature switch closes.

The EBCM keeps the "TRACTION OFF" indicator on and the system disabled for an additional three to five minutes to allow for sufficient cooling.

When performing tests on this system, if the transaxle temperature switch is disconnected, and the ignition is turned to "RUN" the traction control system is disabled for three to five minutes.

FAILURE CONDITIONS

Possible Causes

- Open in CKT 803, 1571 or 1572.
- Open bulb.
- Faulty traction control switch.

Important

- When vehicle is equipped with traction control, any symptom which lights the "ANTILOCK" indicator also lights the "TRACTION OFF" indicator. Therefore, when both indicators are lit, follow "ANTILOCK" indicator diagnosis when no codes are set.

Fig. 33   Chart Q. 1991 DeVille & Fleetwood (FWD) & 1992–93 models except 1993 LeSabre & Park Avenue

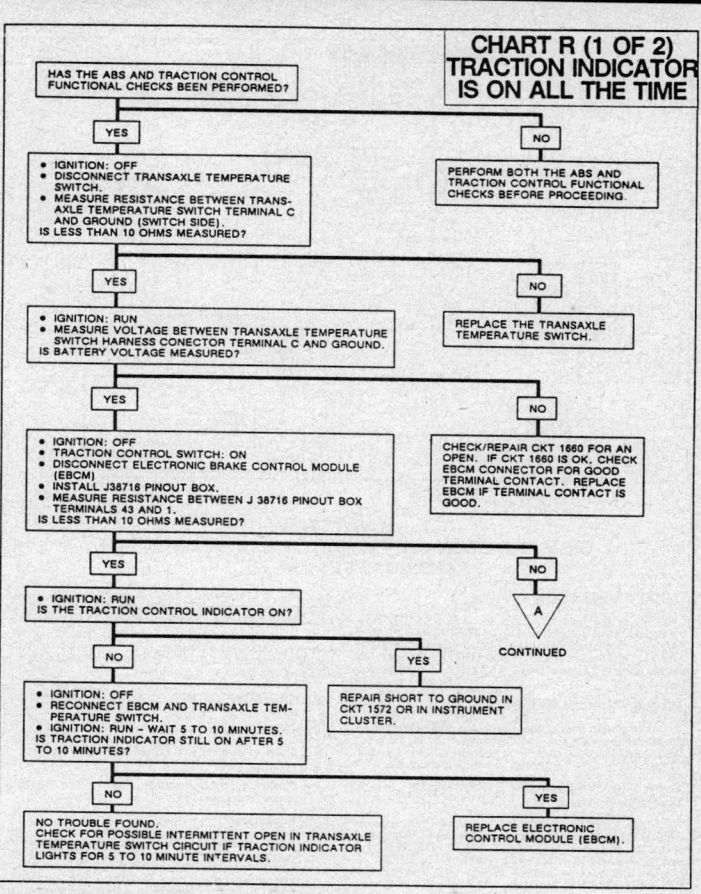

CHART R
TRACTION INDICATOR IS ON ALL THE TIME
AND NO CODES ARE SET

When the ignition switch is first turned to "RUN" the electronic brake control module (EBCM) goes through a self test. During this test the EBCM grounds the "ANTILOCK" and "TRACTION" indicators for approximately 4 seconds. This acts as a bulb test for the indicators. The "TRACTION" indicator will stay lit indicating that the traction control system is disabled when the traction control switch is off, codes 44, 48 or 74 are set, or the EBCM determines that the brakes may be overheating. The EBCM monitors the transaxle temperature switch and other factors such as solenoid valve on time and pump run time to determine if the brakes are overheating.

When the EBCM detects an overheat condition the EBCM will disable traction control and turn on the "TRACTION" indicator. Once the transaxle temperature switch opens, the EBCM will leave the indicator and the system on for an additional five minutes to allow the brakes to cool.

Fig. 34   Chart R (Part 1 of 2). 1991 98 & Park Ave.

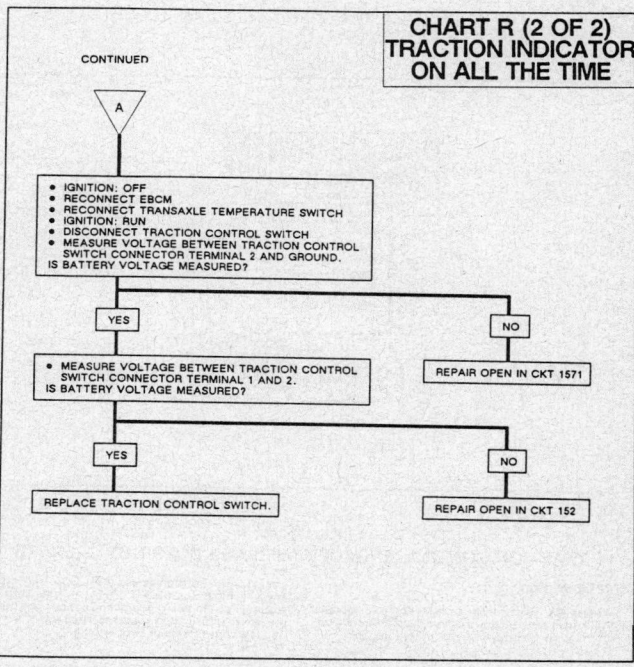

CHART R
TRACTION INDICATOR IS ON ALL THE TIME
AND NO CODES ARE SET

When the ignition switch is first turned to "RUN" the electronic brake control module (EBCM) goes through a self test. During this test the EBCM grounds the "ANTILOCK" and "TRACTION" indicators for approximately 4 seconds. This acts as a bulb test for the indicators. The "TRACTION" indicator will stay lit indicating that the traction control system is disabled when the traction control switch is off, codes 44, 48 or 74 are set, or the EBCM determines that the brakes may be overheating. The EBCM monitors the transaxle temperature switch and other factors such as solenoid valve on time and pump run time to determine if the brakes are overheating.

When the EBCM detects an overheat condition the EBCM will disable traction control and turn on the "TRACTION" indicator. Once the transaxle temperature switch opens, the EBCM will leave the indicator and the system on for an additional five minutes to allow the brakes to cool.

Fig. 34   Chart R (Part 2 of 2). 1991 98 & Park Ave.

CHART R
ONLY "TRACTION OFF" INDICATOR IS ON ALL THE TIME AND NO CODES ARE SET

CIRCUIT OPERATION

When the ignition is first turned to "RUN," the electronic brake control module (EBCM) goes through a self-test. During this test, the EBCM grounds both the "ANTILOCK" and "TRACTION OFF" indicators for approximately 2 to 4 seconds. This acts as a bulb test for the indicators.

Traction Control Switch

Located in the console trim plate, the switch allows the driver to select the traction control mode (on/off). When the traction control system is turned off, the "TRACTION OFF" indicator remains illuminated.

Transaxle Temperature Switch (with Traction Control)

The EBCM monitors transaxle temperature through the transaxle temperature switch. When the transaxle becomes hot, about 160°C (320°F), the normally closed switch opens signaling the EBCM to disable the traction control system and turn on the "TRACTION OFF" indicator. This allows the brakes and transaxle to cool down. As the transaxle cools to 149°C (300°F) the transaxle temperature switch closes.

The EBCM keeps the "TRACTION OFF" indicator on and the system disabled for an additional three to five minutes to allow for sufficient cooling.

When performing tests on this system, if the transaxle temperature switch is disconnected, and the ignition is turned to "RUN" the traction control system is disabled for three to five minutes.

FAILURE CONDITIONS

Possible Causes

- Short to ground in CKT 1571 and 1572.
- Open in CKT 1660.
- Faulty traction control switch to transaxle temperature switch.

Important

- When vehicle is equipped with traction control, any symptom which lights the "ANTILOCK" indicator also lights the "TRACTION OFF" indicator. Therefore, when both indicators are lit, follow "ANTILOCK" indicator diagnosis when no codes are set.

Fig. 35   Chart R. 1991 DeVille & Fleetwood (FWD) & 1992–93 models except 1993 LeSabre & Park Avenue

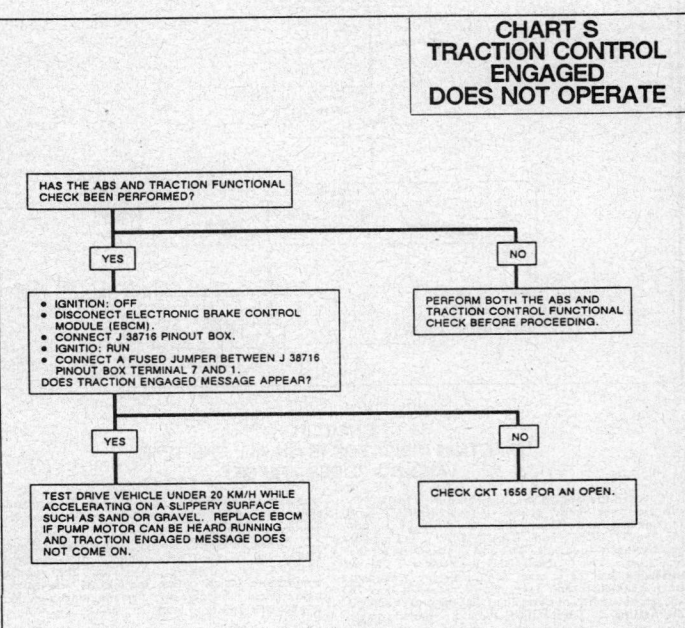

CHART S
TRACTION CONTROL ENGAGED MESSAGE DOES NOT OPERATE

Circuit Operation

When the electronic brake control module (EBCM) is operating in the traction control mode, the EBCM's traction control engaged output (terminal 7) grounds the instrument cluster's DIC traction control engaged input (terminal C1/B14). When this input is grounded, a chime will sound and a message will appear on the driver information center alerting the driver that the traction control system is operating.

Fig. 36   Chart S. 1991 98 & Park Ave.

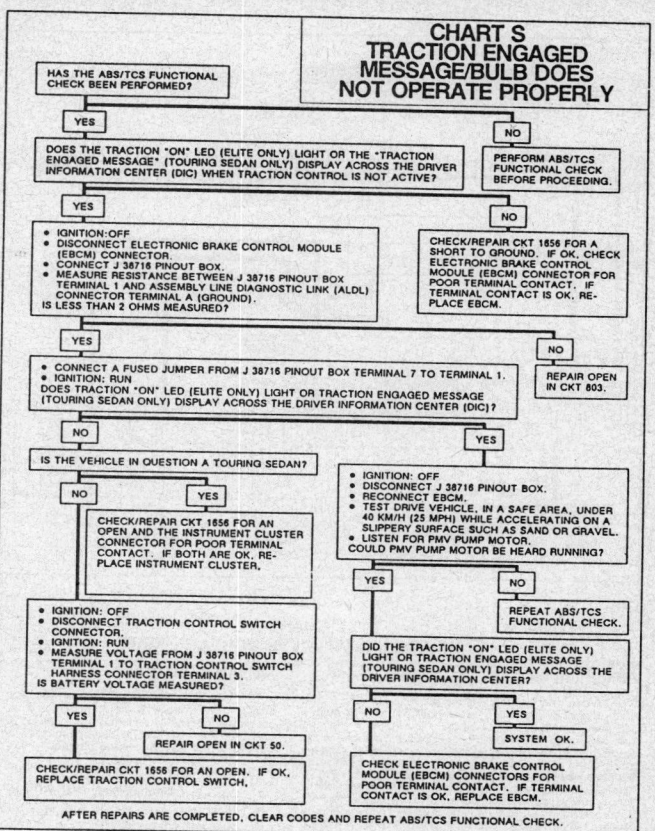

CHART S
TRACTION ENGAGED MESSAGE/BULB DOES NOT OPERATE PROPERLY

CIRCUIT OPERATION

When the electronic brake control module (EBCM) is operating in the traction control mode, the EBCM's traction control engaged output (terminal 7) closes, grounding either the instrument cluster's DIC traction control engaged input (Touring Sedan) or the traction control switch LED (Elite). The EBCM grounds this terminal to alert the driver that the traction control system (TCS) is operating.

Fig. 37   Chart S. 1992 98 & Park Ave.

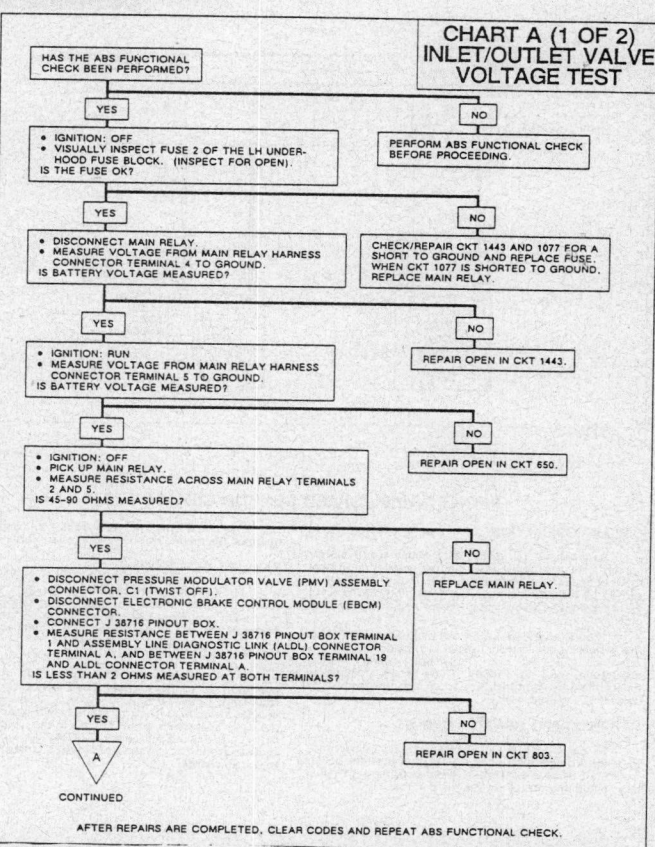

CHART A (1 OF 2)
INLET/OUTLET VALVE VOLTAGE TEST

CHART A
INLET/OUTLET VALVE VOLTAGE TEST

CIRCUIT OPERATION

When the ignition is first turned to "RUN," the electronic brake control module (EBCM) goes through a self-check lasting 2–4 seconds. During this test the EBCM grounds terminal 34, energizing the main relay. Once the self-check is completed the main relay remains energized. This delivers battery voltage to both the EBCM and the pressure modulator valve (PMV) assembly during vehicle operation. The constant voltage supply allows the vehicle to enter ABS mode without delay. The main relay is de-energized whenever the amber "ANTILOCK" indicator lights due to a system fault, causing the ABS system to shut down.

FAILURE CONDITIONS

Code 45 sets when the ignition switch is at "RUN" and battery voltage is neither detected at the PMV assembly nor EBCM terminal 20, 3 and/or 33. Code 45 also sets when the EBCM detects an open or a short to ground in the LH inlet valve circuit.

Possible Causes

- Open in CKT 650, 855, 858, 1077 or 1443.
- Short to ground in CKT 858, 1077 or 1443.
- Main relay fails "open."

Fig. 38   Chart A (Part 1 of 2). 1991–92 DeVille/Fleetwood (FWD) & 1992–93 models except 1993 LeSabre & Park Avenue

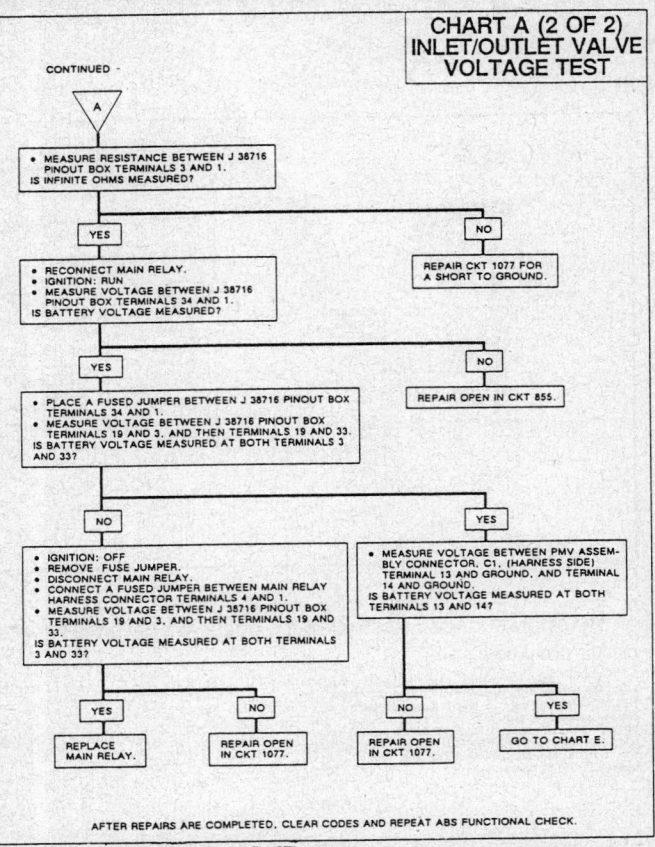

CHART A
INLET/OUTLET VALVE VOLTAGE TEST

CIRCUIT OPERATION

When the ignition is first turned to "RUN," the electronic brake control module (EBCM) goes through a self-check lasting 2–4 seconds. During this test the EBCM grounds terminal 34, energizing the main relay. Once the self-check is completed the main relay remains energized. This delivers battery voltage to both the EBCM and the pressure modulator valve (PMV) assembly during vehicle operation. The constant voltage supply allows the vehicle to enter ABS mode without delay. The main relay is de-energized whenever the amber "ANTILOCK" indicator lights due to a system fault, causing the ABS system to shut down.

FAILURE CONDITIONS

Code 45 sets when the ignition switch is at "RUN" and battery voltage is neither detected at the PMV assembly nor EBCM terminal 20, 3 and/or 33. Code 45 also sets when the EBCM detects an open or a short to ground in the LH inlet valve circuit.

Possible Causes

- Open in CKT 650, 855, 858, 1077 or 1443.
- Short to ground in CKT 858, 1077 or 1443.
- Main relay fails "open."

Fig. 38   Chart A (Part 2 of 2). 1991–92 DeVille/Fleetwood (FWD) & 1992–93 models except 1993 LeSabre & Park Avenue

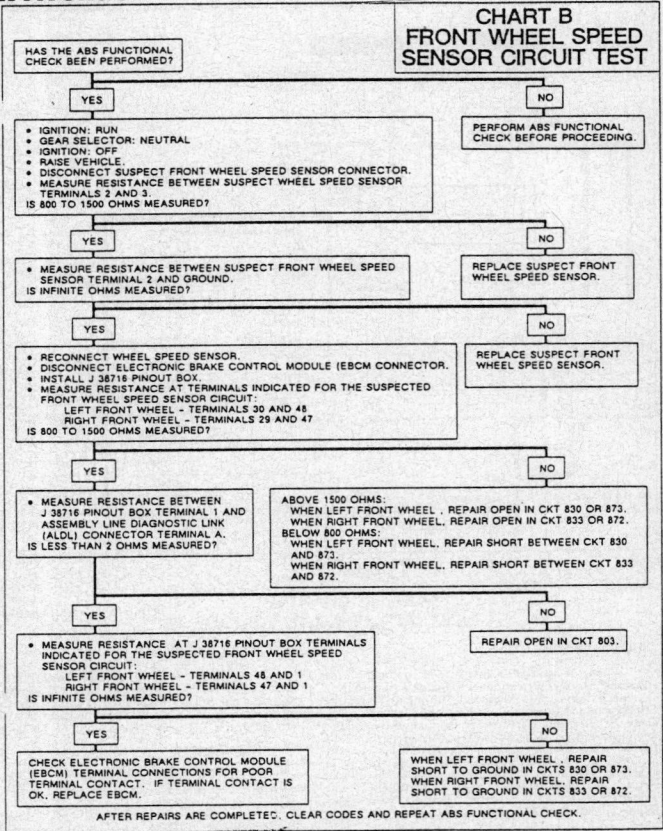

CHART B
FRONT WHEEL SPEED SENSOR CIRCUIT TEST

CIRCUIT OPERATION

As each wheel turns, the wheel speed sensor creates a small AC voltage with a frequency proportional to wheel speed. This magnetically induced voltage is caused by a toothed sensor ring (mounted on the drive axle) passing the wheel speed sensor's stationary pickup coil.

The electronic brake control module (EBCM) uses the wheel speed sensor signal to calculate vehicle reference speeds and individual wheel speed, acceleration and slip values. These values are used to determine when antilock (or when equipped) traction control is required.

WHEEL SPEED SENSOR CABLES

In order to prevent electromagnetic interference from disturbing the wheel speed sensor signal, the cables from the EBCM to each wheel speed sensor are twisted in pairs a minimum of 6 to 9 turns per foot.

When servicing the sensor cables it is important to maintain the original cables' twists (6 to 9 turns per foot).

FAILURE CONDITIONS

The EBCM performs two basic checks on the wheel speed sensors: sensor continuity and sensor output. When the ignition is first turned to "RUN," the EBCM performs the wheel speed sensor continuity check.

Sensor Continuity Check

Any condition which would result in lack of continuity in the front wheel speed sensor circuit could result in a Code 21 or 25 being set. These conditions include an open, a short to ground, or a short between the two wheel sensor circuits in the wiring harness between the speed sensor and EBCM. Also an open or short to ground across the wheel speed sensor coil could trigger this code.

Fig. 39   Chart B. 1991–92 DeVille/Fleetwood (FWD) & 1992–93 models except 1993 LeSabre & Park Avenue

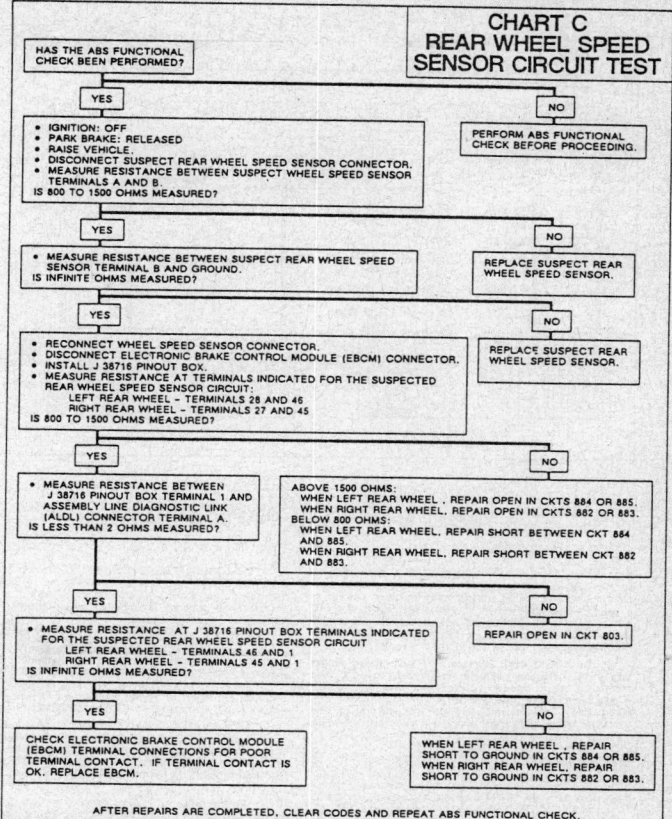

CHART C
REAR WHEEL SPEED SENSOR CIRCUIT TEST

CIRCUIT OPERATION

When each wheel turns, the wheel speed sensor creates a small AC voltage with a frequency proportional to wheel speed. This magnetically induced voltage is caused by a toothed sensor ring passing the wheel speed sensor's stationary pickup coil. Both sensors are part of the hub and bearing assembly.

The electronic brake control module (EBCM) uses the wheel speed sensor signal to calculate vehicle reference speeds and individual wheel speed, acceleration and slip values. These values are used to determine when antilock control is required.

WHEEL SPEED SENSOR CABLES

In order to prevent electromagnetic interference from disturbing the wheel speed sensor signal, the cables from the EBCM to each wheel speed sensor are twisted in pairs a minimum of 6 to 9 turns per foot.

When servicing the sensor cables it is important to maintain the original cables' twists (6 to 9 per foot).

FAILURE CONDITIONS

The EBCM performs two basic checks on the wheel speed sensors: sensor continuity and sensor output. When the ignition is first turned to "RUN," the EBCM performs the wheel speed sensor continuity check.

Sensor Continuity Check

Any condition which would result in lack of continuity in the rear wheel speed sensor circuit could result in a Code 31 or 35 being set. These conditions include an open, a short to ground, or a short between the two wheel speed sensor circuits in the wiring harness between the speed sensor and EBCM. Also an open or short to ground across the wheel speed sensor coil could trigger this code.

Fig. 40   Chart C. 1991–92 DeVille/Fleetwood (FWD) & 1992–93 models except 1993 LeSabre & Park Avenue

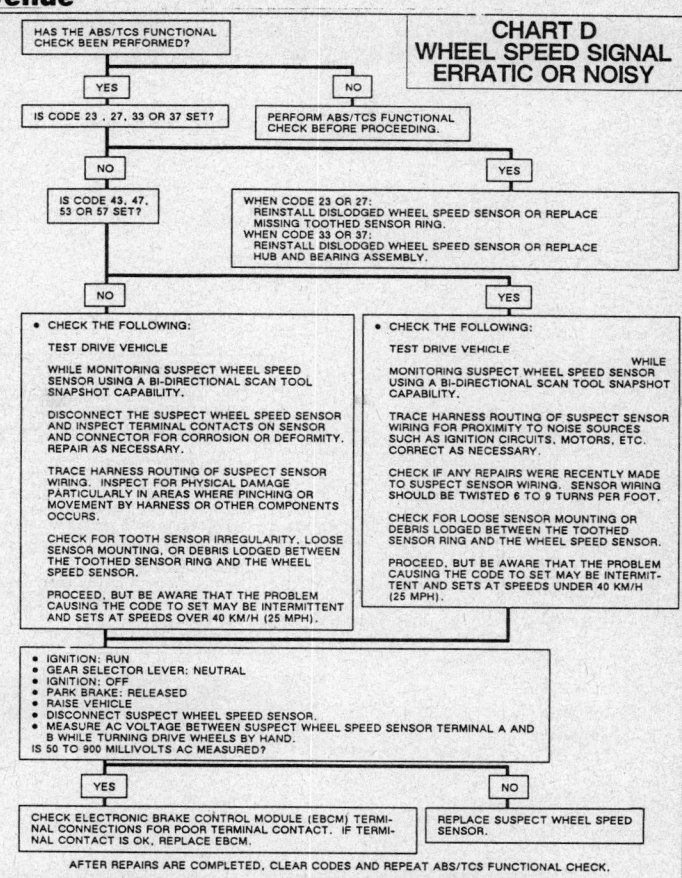

CHART D
WHEEL SPEED SIGNAL ERRATIC OR NOISY

CIRCUIT OPERATION

When each wheel turns, the wheel speed sensor creates a small AC voltage with a frequency proportional to wheel speed. This magnetically induced voltage is caused by a toothed sensor ring passing the wheel speed sensor's stationary pickup coil. The toothed ring sensor is mounted on the drive axle in the front, and in the hub/bearing assembly in the rear.

The electronic brake control module (EBCM) uses the wheel speed sensor signal to calculate vehicle reference speeds, and individual wheel speed, acceleration and slip values. These values are used to determine when antilock control is required. Vehicles equipped with traction control also use front wheel speed sensor signals to determine when traction control is required.

WHEEL SPEED SENSOR CABLES

In order to prevent electromagnetic interference from disturbing the wheel speed sensor signal, the cables from the EBCM to each wheel speed sensor are twisted in pairs a minimum of 6 to 9 turns per foot.

When servicing the sensor cables it is important to maintain the original cables' twists (6 to 9 per foot).

FAILURE CONDITIONS

Code 43, 47, 53 or 57 sets when the EBCM detects electromagnetic interference (noise) in a wheel speed sensor signal. Possible interference sources include accessory motors, wiper motors and ignition circuits.

Code 22, 26, 32 or 36 sets when the EBCM determines a wheel speed signal is erratic. A wheel speed signal indicating that a wheel is accelerating or decelerating faster than physically possible is an example of an erratic signal. An intermittent open or short to ground in a wheel speed sensor could also cause the EBCM to set a code.

Code 23, 27, 33 or 37 sets when the EBCM does not see any wheel speed sensor signal, but determines continuity exists in the circuit. This is caused by a dislodged wheel speed sensor, missing toothed sensor ring (front) or defective hub and bearing assembly (rear).

Fig. 41   Chart D. 1991–92 DeVille/Fleetwood (FWD) & 1992–93 models except 1993 LeSabre & Park Avenue

CHART D
WHEEL SPEED SIGNAL ERRATIC OR NOISY

CIRCUIT OPERATION

When each wheel turns, the wheel speed sensor creates a small AC voltage with a frequency proportional to wheel speed. This magnetically induced voltage is caused by a toothed sensor ring passing the wheel speed sensor's stationary pickup coil. The toothed ring sensor is mounted on the drive axle in the front, and in the hub/bearing assembly in the rear.

The EBCM/EBTCM uses the wheel speed sensor signal to calculate vehicle reference speeds, and individual wheel speed, acceleration and slip values. These values are used to determine when antilock control is required. Vehicles equipped with traction control also use front wheel speed sensor signals to determine when traction control is required.

WHEEL SPEED SENSOR CABLES

In order to prevent electromagnetic interference from disturbing the wheel speed sensor signal, the cables from the EBCM/EBTCM to each wheel speed sensor are twisted in pairs a minimum of 6 to 9 turns per foot.

When servicing the sensor cables it is important to maintain the original cables' twists (6 to 9 turns per foot).

FAILURE CONDITIONS

DTC 22, DTC 26, DTC 33 or DTC 36 sets when the EBCM/EBTCM detects electromagnetic interference (noise) in a wheel speed sensor signal. Possible interference sources include accessory motors, wiper motors and ignition circuits.

DTC 22, DTC 26, DTC 32 or DTC 36 also sets when the EBCM/EBTCM determines a wheel speed signal is erratic. A wheel speed signal indicating that a wheel is accelerating or decelerating faster than physically possible is an example of an erratic signal. An intermittent open or short to ground in a wheel speed sensor could also cause the EBCM/EBTCM to set a DTC.

DTC 23, DTC 27, DTC 33 or DTC 37 sets when the EBCM/EBTCM does not see any wheel speed sensor signal, but determines continuity exists in the circuit. This is caused by a dislodged wheel speed sensor, missing toothed sensor ring (front) or defective hub and bearing assembly (rear).

An intermittent open or short to ground in a wheel speed sensor (or its circuitry) could cause the pump motor to run inadvertently without setting a DTC. This condition is usually noticed at slow speed driving (under 16 km/h [10 mph]).

Fig. 42   Chart D (Part 1 of 3). 1993 models except LeSabre & Park Avenue

---

HAS ABS/TCS FUNCTIONAL CHECK BEEN PERFORMED?
- YES → **IS DTC 23 , DTC 27, DTC 33 OR DTC 37 SET?**
  - NO → **IS DTC 22, DTC 26, DTC 32 OR DTC 36 SET?**
    - YES ↓
  - YES →
- NO → **PERFORM ABS/TCS FUNCTIONAL CHECK BEFORE PROCEEDING.**
  - YES → **WHEN DTC 23 OR DTC 27: REINSTALL DISLODGED WHEEL SPEED SENSOR OR REPLACE MISSING TOOTHED SENSOR RING. WHEN DTC 33 OR DTC 37: REINSTALL DISLODGED WHEEL SPEED SENSOR OR REPLACE HUB AND BEARING ASSEMBLY.**
    - NO → **A** CONTINUED

- **PERFORM FOLLOWING AND REPAIR/REPLACE AS NECESSARY:**
  TEST DRIVE VEHICLE
  WHILE MONITORING SUSPECT WHEEL SPEED SENSOR USING BI-DIRECTIONAL SCAN TOOL SNAPSHOT CAPABILITY.
  DISCONNECT SUSPECT WHEEL SPEED SENSOR CONNECTOR AND APPLICABLE IN-LINE CONNECTOR. INSPECT TERMINAL CONTACTS ON SENSOR AND CONNECTORS FOR CORROSION OR DEFORMITY. CHECK CONNECTORS FOR PROPER TERMINAL CONTACT.
  TRACE HARNESS ROUTING OF SUSPECT SENSOR WIRING. INSPECT FOR PHYSICAL DAMAGE PARTICULARLY IN AREAS WHERE PINCHING OR MOVEMENT BY HARNESS OR OTHER COMPONENTS OCCURS.
  TRACE HARNESS ROUTING OF SUSPECT SENSOR WIRING FOR PROXIMITY TO NOISE SOURCES SUCH AS IGNITION CIRCUITS, MOTORS, ETC.
  CHECK IF ANY REPAIRS WERE RECENTLY MADE TO SUSPECT SENSOR WIRING. SENSOR WIRING SHOULD BE TWISTED 6 TO 9 TURNS PER FOOT.
  CHECK FOR TOOTH SENSOR IRREGULARITY, LOOSE SENSOR MOUNTING, OR DEBRIS LODGED BETWEEN TOOTHED SENSOR RING AND WHEEL SPEED SENSOR.
- IF ALL ABOVE CHECKS ARE OK, PROCEED, BUT BE AWARE THAT PROBLEM CAUSING DIAGNOSTIC TROUBLE CODE TO SET MAY BE INTERMITTENT AND IS USUALLY NOT CAUSED BY A DEFECTIVE EBCM/EBTCM.

- IGNITION: RUN
- GEAR SELECTOR LEVER: NEUTRAL
- IGNITION: OFF
- PARK BRAKE: RELEASED
- RAISE VEHICLE
- DISCONNECT SUSPECT WHEEL SPEED SENSOR.
- MEASURE AC VOLTAGE BETWEEN SUSPECT WHEEL SPEED SENSOR TERMINAL A AND B WHILE TURNING DRIVE WHEELS BY HAND.
IS 50 TO 900 MILLIVOLTS AC MEASURED?
- YES → **CHECK EBCM/EBTCM CONNECTOR FOR PROPER TERMINAL CONTACT. IF TERMINAL CONTACT IS OK, REPLACE EBCM/EBTCM.**
- NO → **REPLACE SUSPECT WHEEL SPEED SENSOR.**

AFTER REPAIRS ARE COMPLETED, CLEAR DTC AND REPEAT ABS/TCS FUNCTIONAL CHECK.

Fig. 42   Chart D (Part 2 of 3). 1993 models except LeSabre & Park Avenue

---

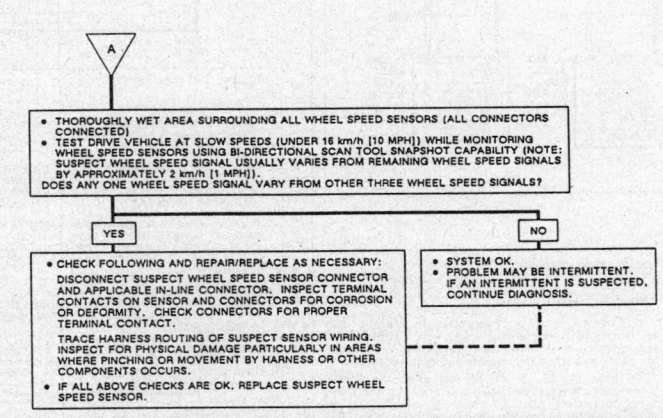

Fig. 64   System diagnosis, test 10 (Part 2 of 3). 1993 LeSabre Park Avenue

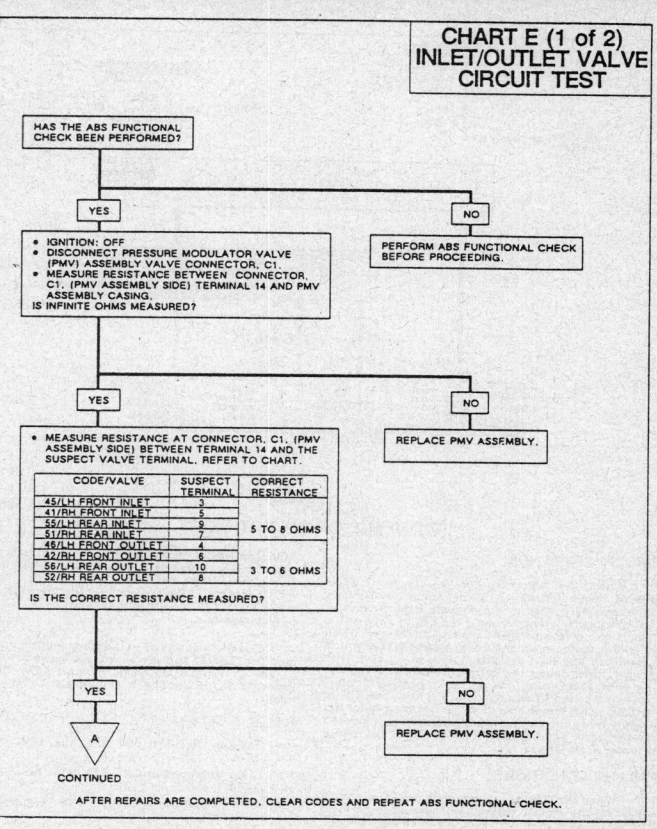

CHART E
INLET/OUTLET VALVE CIRCUIT TEST

CIRCUIT OPERATION

Inlet Valves

Voltage is applied to the normally open inlet valves whenever the main relay is energized. An inlet valve closes when the electronic brake control module (EBCM) supplies a ground path at the inlet valve control terminal. The EBCM closes an inlet valve for short periods to maintain (hold) or reduce pressure at a particular wheel.

Outlet Valves

The normally closed outlet valves operate similarly to the inlet valves, except that when the EBCM grounds an outlet valve, the valve opens instead of closes. The EBCM opens an outlet valve for short periods to reduce pressure at a particular wheel.

VALVE MODES

Pressure Increase

The pressure increase position is the operating valve position for normal (non-ABS) braking and traction control mode (when equipped). The EBCM does not energize either valve, leaving the inlet valve open and the outlet valve closed.

Pressure Hold

The pressure hold position occurs when the EBCM first notices an abnormal hydraulic pressure increase. This signifies an impending wheel lockup condition. The EBCM closes the corresponding inlet valve in an attempt to avoid any additional hydraulic pressure increase (avoiding an ABS braking condition).

Pressure Reduce

During a wheel lockup condition, the EBCM close the inlet valve while pulsing open the outlet valve. This decreases hydraulic pressure at a specific wheel without decreasing overall system pressure. The reduced hydraulic pressure allows greater wheel spin, eliminating the wheel lockup condition.

Test Description

This test checks for proper inlet and outlet valve operation. The wheel brake behavior must be checked to verify the valves hydraulic effectiveness. This is accomplished using the TECH 1 to actuate the valves.

Failure Conditions

Code 41, 42, 45, 46, 51, 52, 55, or 56 sets when the electronic brake control module (EBCM) detects an open or short to ground in the respective inlet or outlet valve circuit.

Fig. 43 Chart E (Part 1 of 2). 1991–92 DeVille/Fleetwood (FWD) & 1992–93 models except 1993 LeSabre & Park Avenue

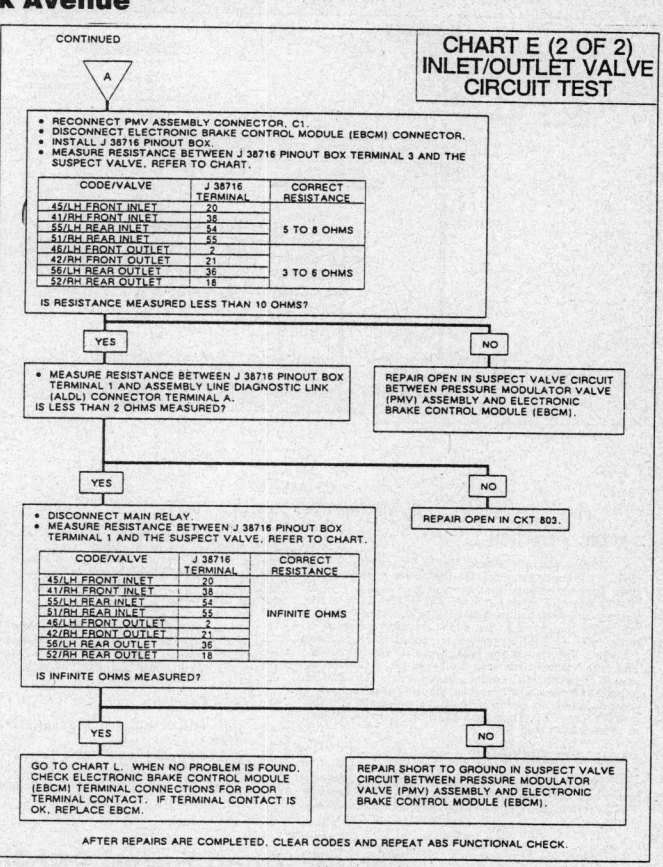

CHART E
INLET/OUTLET VALVE CIRCUIT TEST

CIRCUIT OPERATION

Inlet Valves

Voltage is applied to the normally open inlet valves whenever the main relay is energized. An inlet valve closes when the electronic brake control module (EBCM) supplies a ground path at the inlet valve control terminal. The EBCM closes an inlet valve for short periods to maintain (hold) or reduce pressure at a particular wheel.

Outlet Valves

The normally closed outlet valves operate similarly to the inlet valves, except that when the EBCM grounds an outlet valve, the valve opens instead of closes. The EBCM opens an outlet valve for short periods to reduce pressure at a particular wheel.

VALVE MODES

Pressure Increase

The pressure increase position is the operating valve position for normal (non-ABS) braking and traction control mode (when equipped). The EBCM does not energize either valve, leaving the inlet valve open and the outlet valve closed.

Pressure Hold

The pressure hold position occurs when the EBCM first notices an abnormal hydraulic pressure increase. This signifies an impending wheel lockup condition. The EBCM closes the corresponding inlet valve in an attempt to avoid any additional hydraulic pressure increase (avoiding an ABS braking condition).

Pressure Reduce

During a wheel lockup condition, the EBCM close the inlet valve while pulsing open the outlet valve. This decreases hydraulic pressure at a specific wheel without decreasing overall system pressure. The reduced hydraulic pressure allows greater wheel spin, eliminating the wheel lockup condition.

Test Description

This test checks for proper inlet and outlet valve operation. The wheel brake behavior must be checked to verify the valves hydraulic effectiveness. This is accomplished using the TECH 1 to actuate the valves.

Failure Conditions

Code 41, 42, 45, 46, 51, 52, 55, or 56 sets when the electronic brake control module (EBCM) detects an open or short to ground in the respective inlet or outlet valve circuit.

Fig. 43 Chart E (Part 2 of 2). 1991–92 DeVille/Fleetwood (FWD) & 1992–93 models except 1993 LeSabre & Park Avenue

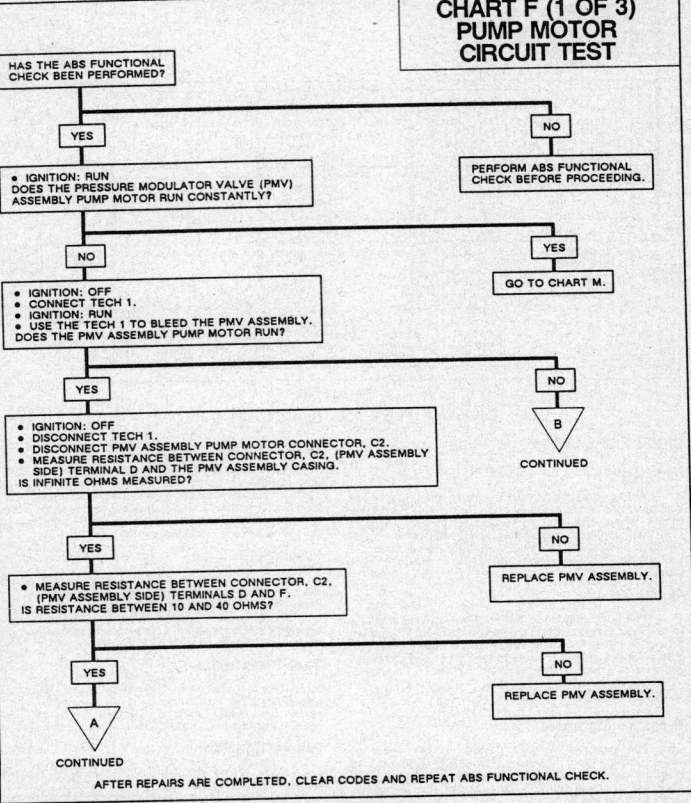

CHART F (1 OF 3)
PUMP MOTOR
CIRCUIT TEST

CHART F
PUMP MOTOR CIRCUIT TEST

CIRCUIT OPERATION

When the electronic brake control module (EBCM) grounds terminal 15, the pump relay contacts close applying voltage to the pressure modulator valve (PMV) assembly's pump motor. The EBCM turns on the pump motor during most ABS braking conditions. When the pump motor runs, the PMV assembly reservoir is replenished and fluid pressure is applied to the master cylinder. This causes the brake pedal to rise gradually. The pump motor runs until the brake pedal sufficiently rises to close the VCC/antilock brake switch. The EBCM monitors pump motor operation via the pump motor run sensor. When the pump is operating, voltage is induced into the sensor's coil and the EBCM monitors this voltage at terminals 49 and 31.

FAILURE CONDITIONS

When the EBCM grounds terminal 15, Code 61 sets when the EBCM determines the voltage between EBCM terminals 31 and 49 is not between 500–800 mV

AC. The EBCM recognizes this condition only during ABS braking requiring pump motor operation, and during the EBCM self-check which occurs when the vehicle reaches 11 km/h (7 mph). Therefore, be sure to test drive vehicle, clearing the code to assure correct diagnosis.

Code 61 also sets when the pump motor runs all the time (i.e. EBCM sees proper voltage between terminals 31 and 49 without grounding terminal 15). Refer to Chart M for diagnosing a continuous running pump motor.

Possible Causes

- Open in CKT 151, 650, 850, 854, 1292, 1293 or 1446.
- Short to ground in CKT 850, 854, 1292, 1293 or 1446.
- ABS pump relay fails "open" or "engaged."

Fig. 44   Chart F (Part 1 of 3). 1991–92 DeVille/Fleetwood (FWD)

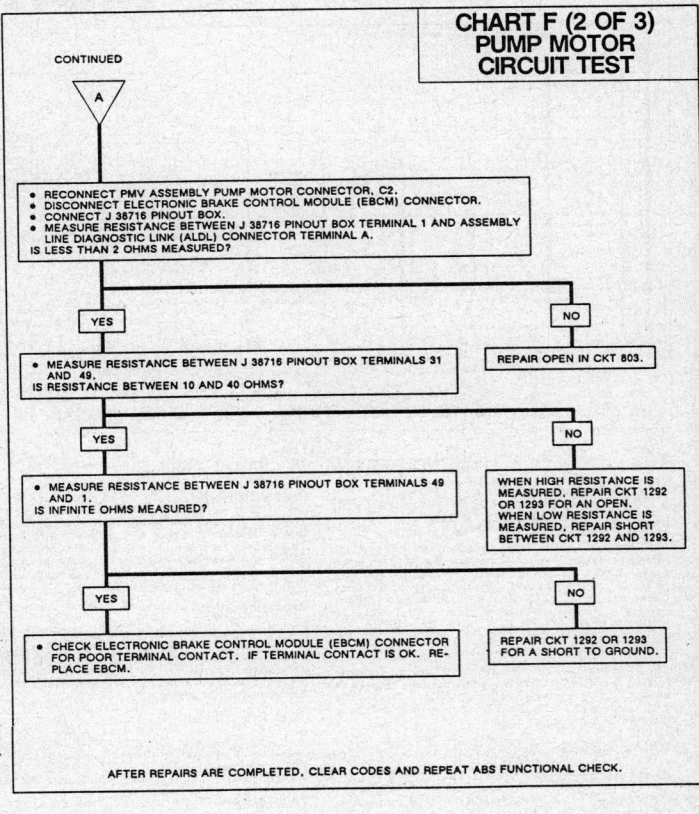

CHART F (2 OF 3)
PUMP MOTOR
CIRCUIT TEST

CHART F
PUMP MOTOR CIRCUIT TEST

CIRCUIT OPERATION

When the electronic brake control module (EBCM) grounds terminal 15, the pump relay contacts close applying voltage to the pressure modulator valve (PMV) assembly's pump motor. The EBCM turns on the pump motor during most ABS braking conditions. When the pump motor runs, the PMV assembly reservoir is replenished and fluid pressure is applied to the master cylinder. This causes the brake pedal to rise gradually. The pump motor runs until the brake pedal sufficiently rises to close the VCC/antilock brake switch. The EBCM monitors pump motor operation via the pump motor run sensor. When the pump is operating, voltage is induced into the sensor's coil and the EBCM monitors this voltage at terminals 49 and 31.

FAILURE CONDITIONS

When the EBCM grounds terminal 15, Code 61 sets when the EBCM determines the voltage between EBCM terminals 31 and 49 is not between 500–800 mV

AC. The EBCM recognizes this condition only during ABS braking requiring pump motor operation, and during the EBCM self-check which occurs when the vehicle reaches 11 km/h (7 mph). Therefore, be sure to test drive vehicle,   after clearing the code to assure correct diagnosis.

Code 61 also sets when the pump motor runs all the time (i.e. EBCM sees proper voltage between terminals 31 and 49 without grounding terminal 15). Refer to Chart M for diagnosing a continuous running pump motor.

Possible Causes

- Open in CKT 151, 650, 850, 854, 1292, 1293 or 1446.
- Short to ground in CKT 850, 854, 1292, 1293 or 1446.
- ABS pump relay fails "open" or "engaged."

Fig. 44   Chart F (Part 2 of 3). 1991–92 DeVille/Fleetwood (FWD)

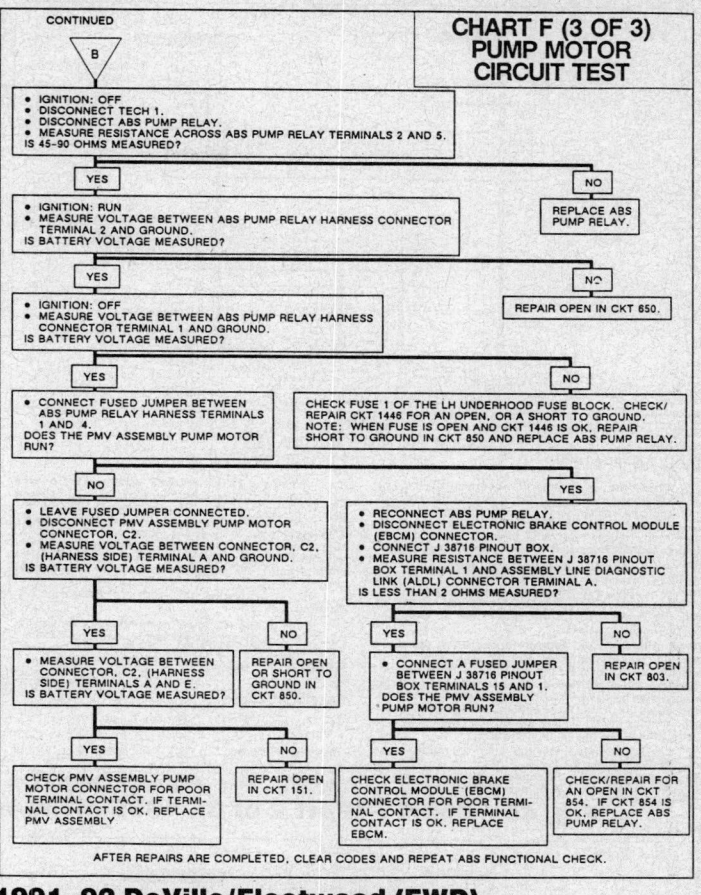

CHART F (3 OF 3) PUMP MOTOR CIRCUIT TEST

CHART F PUMP MOTOR CIRCUIT TEST

CIRCUIT OPERATION

When the electronic brake control module (EBCM) grounds terminal 15, the pump relay contacts close applying voltage to the pressure modulator valve (PMV) assembly's pump motor. The EBCM turns on the pump motor during most ABS braking conditions. When the pump motor runs, the PMV assembly reservoir is replenished and fluid pressure is applied to the master cylinder. This causes the brake pedal to rise gradually. The pump motor runs until the brake pedal sufficiently rises to close the VCC/antilock brake switch. The EBCM monitors pump motor operation via the pump motor run sensor. When the pump is operating, voltage is induced into the sensor's coil and the EBCM monitors this voltage at terminals 49 and 31.

FAILURE CONDITIONS

When the EBCM grounds terminal 15, Code 61 sets when the EBCM determines the voltage between EBCM terminals 31 and 49 is not between 500-800 mV

AC. The EBCM recognizes this condition only during ABS braking requiring pump motor operation, and during the EBCM self-check which occurs when the vehicle reaches 11 km/h (7 mph). Therefore, be sure to test drive vehicle, after clearing the code to assure correct diagnosis.

Code 61 also sets when the pump motor runs all the time (i.e. EBCM sees proper voltage between terminals 31 and 49 without grounding terminal 15). Refer to Chart M for diagnosing a continuous running pump motor.

Possible Causes

- Open in CKT 151, 650, 850, 854, 1292, 1293 or 1446.
- Short to ground in CKT 850, 854, 1292, 1293 or 1446.
- ABS pump relay fails "open" or "engaged."

Fig. 44   Chart F (Part 3 of 3). 1991–92 DeVille/Fleetwood (FWD)

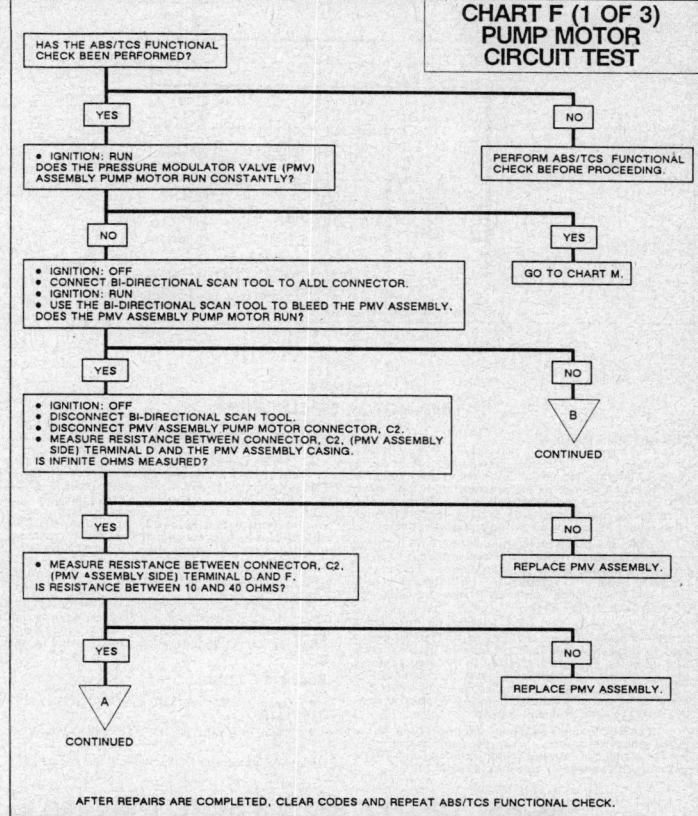

CHART F (1 OF 3) PUMP MOTOR CIRCUIT TEST

CHART F PUMP MOTOR CIRCUIT TEST

CIRCUIT OPERATION

When the electronic brake control module (EBCM) grounds terminal 15, the pump relay contacts close applying voltage to the pressure modulator valve (PMV) assembly's pump motor. The EBCM turns on the pump motor during most ABS braking conditions (and when equipped) during all traction control conditions.

When the pump motor runs during ABS braking, the PMV assembly reservoir is replenished and fluid pressure is applied to the master cylinder. This causes the brake pedal to rise gradually. The pump motor runs until the brake pedal sufficiently rises to close the TCC/antilock brake switch.

During traction control mode, after the front hydraulic brake circuits are isolated, the pump motor runs to increase brake fluid pressure in these circuits. The increased pressure is directed through the PMV assembly's front inlet and outlet valves. This causes the brakes to be applied, reducing wheel spin at the slipping wheel. Traction control is disabled as soon as the brakes are manually applied.

The EBCM monitors pump motor operation via the pump motor run sensor. When the pump is operating, voltage is induced into the sensor's coil and the EBCM monitors this voltage at terminals 49 and 31.

FAILURE CONDITIONS

When the EBCM grounds terminal 15, Code 61 sets when the EBCM determines the voltage between EBCM terminals 31 and 49 is not between 500-800 mV AC. The EBCM recognizes this condition only during ABS braking requiring pump motor operation, traction control mode (when equipped), and during the EBCM self-check which occurs when the vehicle reaches 11 km/h (7 mph). Therefore, be sure to test drive vehicle, clearing the code to assure correct diagnosis.

Code 61 also sets when the pump motor runs all the time (i.e. EBCM sees proper voltage between terminals 31 and 49 without grounding terminal 15). Refer to Chart M for diagnosing a continuous running pump motor.

Possible Causes

- Open in CKT 151, 850, 854, 1077, 1292, 1293 or 1446.
- Short to ground in CKT 850, 854, 1292, 1293 or 1446.
- ABS pump relay fails "open" or "engaged."

Fig. 45   Chart F (Part 1 of 3). 1992–93 models except 1993 LeSabre & Park Avenue

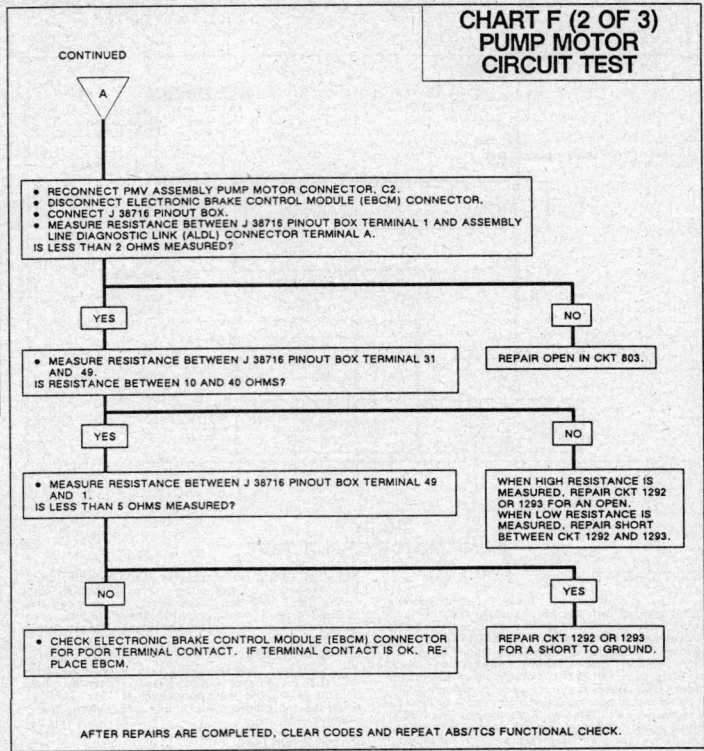

CHART F
PUMP MOTOR CIRCUIT TEST

CIRCUIT OPERATION

When the electronic brake control module (EBCM) grounds terminal 15, the pump relay contacts close applying voltage to the pressure modulator valve (PMV) assembly's pump motor. The EBCM turns on the pump motor during most ABS braking conditions (and when equipped) during all traction control conditions.

When the pump motor runs during ABS braking, the PMV assembly reservoir is replenished and fluid pressure is applied to the master cylinder. This causes the brake pedal to rise gradually. The pump motor runs until the brake pedal sufficiently rises to close the TCC/antilock brake switch.

During traction control mode, after the front hydraulic brake circuits are isolated, the pump motor runs to increase brake fluid pressure in these circuits. The increased pressure is directed to the slipping wheel through the PMV assembly's front inlet and outlet valves. This causes the brakes to be applied, reducing wheel spin at the slipping wheel. Traction control is disabled as soon as the brakes are manually applied.

The EBCM monitors pump motor operation via the pump motor run sensor. When the pump is operating, voltage is induced into the sensor's coil and the EBCM monitors this voltage at terminals 49 and 31.

FAILURE CONDITIONS

When the EBCM grounds terminal 15, Code 61 sets when the EBCM determines the voltage between EBCM terminals 31 and 49 is not between 500–800 mV AC. The EBCM recognizes this condition only during ABS braking requiring pump motor operation, traction control mode (when equipped), and during the EBCM self-check which occurs when the vehicle reaches 11 km/h (7 mph). Therefore, be sure to test drive vehicle, clearing the code to assure correct diagnosis.

Code 61 also sets when the pump motor runs all the time (i.e. EBCM sees proper voltage between terminals 31 and 49 without grounding terminal 15). Refer to Chart M for diagnosing a continuous running pump motor.

Possible Causes

- Open in CKT 151, 850, 854, 1077, 1292, 1293 or 1446.
- Short to ground in CKT 850, 854, 1292, 1293 or 1446.
- ABS pump relay fails "open" or "engaged."

Fig. 45 Chart F (Part 2 of 3). 1992–93 models except 1993 LeSabre & Park Avenue

CHART F
PUMP MOTOR CIRCUIT TEST

CIRCUIT OPERATION

When the electronic brake control module (EBCM) grounds terminal 15, the pump relay contacts close applying voltage to the pressure modulator valve (PMV) assembly's pump motor. The EBCM turns on the pump motor during most ABS braking conditions (and when equipped) during all traction control conditions.

When the pump motor runs during ABS braking, the PMV assembly reservoir is replenished and fluid pressure is applied to the master cylinder. This causes the brake pedal to rise gradually. The pump motor runs until the brake pedal sufficiently rises to close the TCC/antilock brake switch.

During traction control mode, after the front hydraulic brake circuits are isolated, the pump motor runs to increase brake fluid pressure in these circuits. The increased pressure is directed to the slipping wheel through the PMV assembly's front inlet and outlet valves. This causes the brakes to be applied, reducing wheel spin at the slipping wheel. Traction control is disabled as soon as the brakes are manually applied.

The EBCM monitors pump motor operation via the pump motor run sensor. When the pump is operating, voltage is induced into the sensor's coil and the EBCM monitors this voltage at terminals 49 and 31.

FAILURE CONDITIONS

When the EBCM grounds terminal 15, Code 61 sets when the EBCM determines the voltage between EBCM terminals 31 and 49 is not between 500–800 mV AC. The EBCM recognizes this condition only during ABS braking requiring pump motor operation, traction control mode (when equipped), and during the EBCM self-check which occurs when the vehicle reaches 11 km/h (7 mph). Therefore, be sure to test drive vehicle.

Code 61 also sets when the pump motor runs all the time (i.e. EBCM sees proper voltage between terminals 31 and 49 without grounding terminal 15). Refer to Chart M for diagnosing a continuous running pump motor.

Possible Causes

- Open in CKT 151, 850, 854, 1077, 1292, 1293 or 1446.
- Short to ground in CKT 850, 854, 1292, 1293 or 1446.
- ABS pump relay fails "open" or "engaged."

Fig. 45 Chart F (Part 3 of 3). 1992–93 models except 1993 LeSabre & Park Avenue

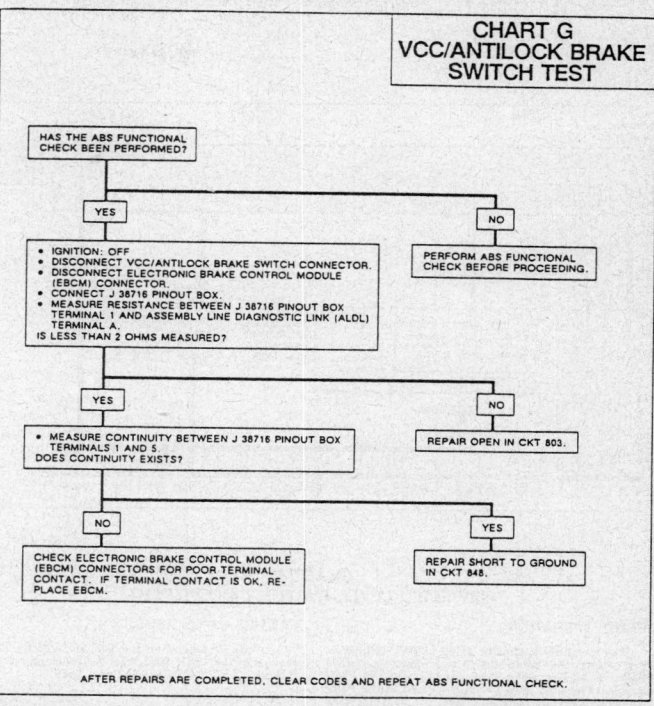

CHART G
TCC/ANTILOCK BRAKE SWITCH TEST

CIRCUIT OPERATION

The electronic brake control module (EBCM) monitors brake pedal position using the TCC/antilock brake switch. The switch is normally closed. It opens when the brake pedal is depressed approximately 40% down. During most ABS braking conditions the EBCM turns on the pump motor, replenishing the PMV assembly reservoir and applying fluid pressure to the master cylinder. This causes the brake pedal to gradually rise. The EBCM turns off the pump motor when brake pedal height sufficiently rises to close the TCC/antilock brake switch.

FAILURE CONDITIONS

Code 72 sets when the EBCM detects the TCC/antilock brake switch CKT 848 is shorted to ground.

Fig. 46   Chart G. 1991–92 DeVille/Fleetwood (FWD) & 1992–93 except LeSabre & Park Avenue

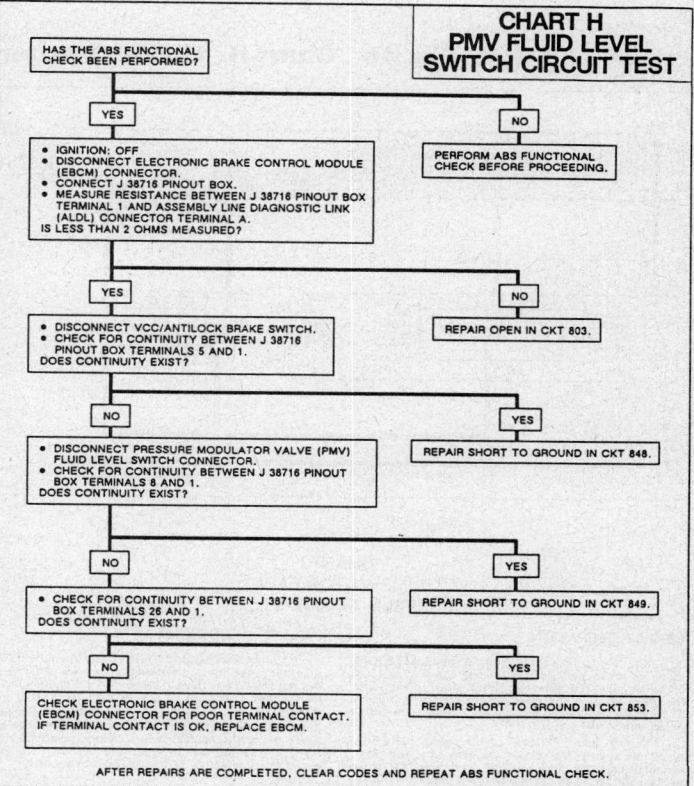

CHART H
PMV FLUID LEVEL SWITCH CIRCUIT TEST

CIRCUIT OPERATION

The pressure modulator valve (PMV) fluid level switch alerts the electronic brake control module (EBCM) to a low brake fluid condition in the PMV reservoir. The fluid level switch is located in the PMV assembly's reservoir. The fluid level switch is normally closed when the reservoir contains sufficient fluid. When fluid level is low, the switch opens, causing the EBCM to turn on the "ANTILOCK" indicator.

FAILURE CONDITIONS

Code 73 will set when the EBCM detects a short to ground in the PMV fluid level switch circuitry. These include: CKT 848, 849, and 853.

Fig. 47   Chart H. 1991–92 DeVille/Fleetwood (FWD)

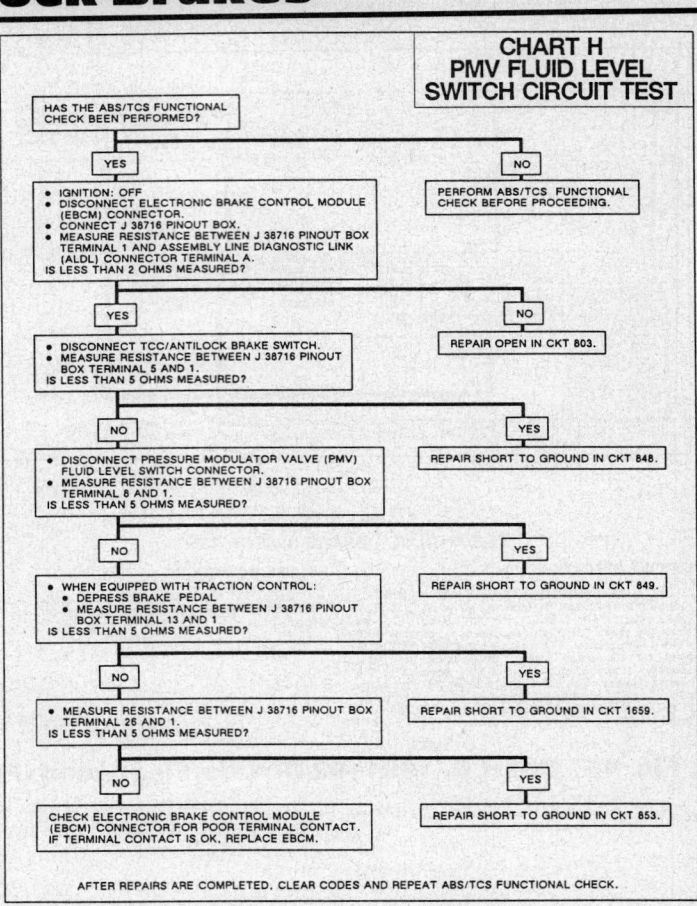

CHART H
PMV FLUID LEVEL SWITCH CIRCUIT TEST

CIRCUIT OPERATION

The pressure modulator valve (PMV) fluid level switch alerts the electronic brake control module (EBCM) to a low brake fluid condition in the PMV reservoir. The fluid level switch is located in the PMV assembly's reservoir. The fluid level switch is normally closed when the reservoir contains sufficient fluid. When fluid level is low, the switch opens, causing the EBCM to turn on the "ANTILOCK" indicator.

FAILURE CONDITIONS

Code 73 sets when the EBCM detects a short to ground in the PMV fluid level switch circuitry. These include: CKT 848, 849, 853 and 1659.

Fig. 48   Chart H. 1992–93 except 1993 LeSabre & Park Avenue

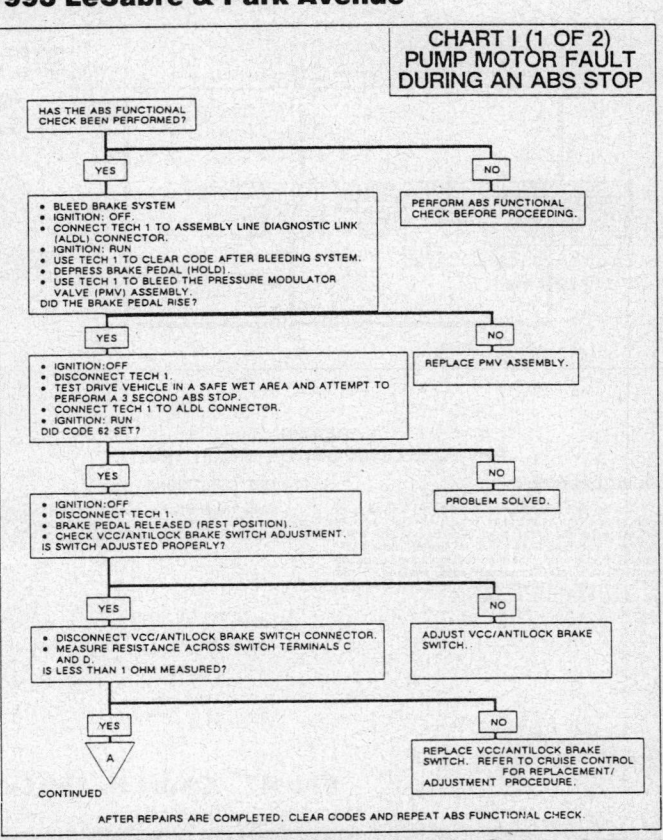

CHART I
PUMP MOTOR FAULT DURING AN ABS STOP

CIRCUIT OPERATION

The electronic brake control module (EBCM) monitors brake pedal position using the TCC/antilock brake switch. The normally closed switch opens when the brake pedal is depressed approximately 40% down. The EBCM also monitors pump motor operation using a pump motor run sensor.

During most ABS braking conditions the EBCM turns on the pump motor, replenishing the PMV assembly reservoir and applying fluid pressure to the master cylinder. This causes the brake pedal to gradually rise. The EBCM turns off the pump motor when brake pedal height sufficiently rises to close the TCC/antilock brake switch.

FAILURE CONDITIONS

During ABS braking, Code 62 sets when the EBCM determines the pump is working, and brake pedal height has not sufficiently risen to close the TCC/antilock brake switch after 3 seconds.

This code usually indicates a hydraulic problem. Some possible causes include air in the brake lines or a pump motor mechanical failure. Non-hydraulic causes for Code 62 include an open 848 or 853 CKT or a misadjusted/defective TCC/antilock brake switch.

Fig. 49   Chart I (Part 1 of 2). 1991–92 DeVille/Fleetwood (FWD) & 1992–93 except LeSabre & Park Avenue

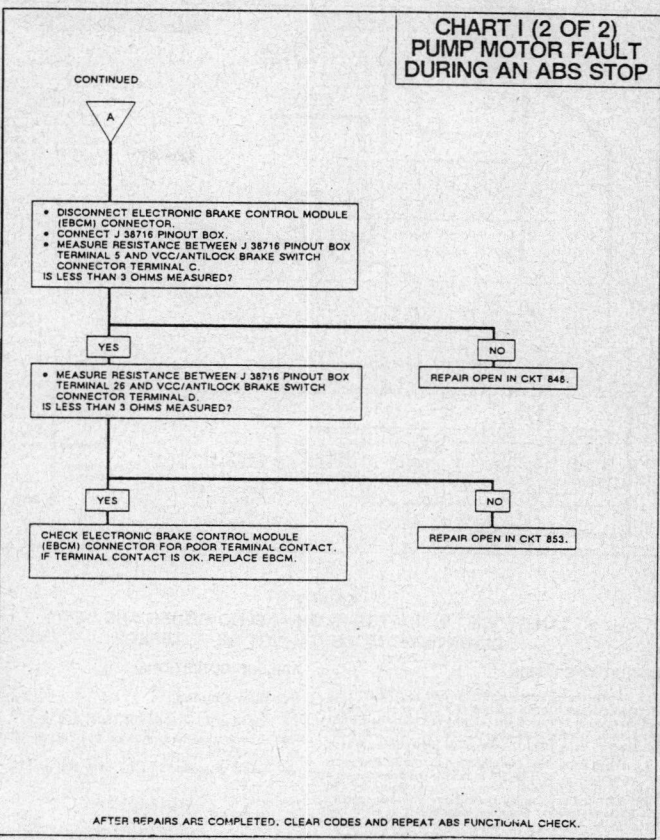

CHART I (2 OF 2) PUMP MOTOR FAULT DURING AN ABS STOP

CHART I
PUMP MOTOR FAULT
DURING AN ABS STOP

CIRCUIT OPERATION

The electronic brake control module (EBCM) monitors brake pedal position using the TCC/antilock brake switch. The normally closed switch opens when the brake pedal is depressed approximately 40% down. The EBCM also monitors pump motor operation using a pump motor run sensor.

During most ABS braking conditions the EBCM turns on the pump motor, replenishing the PMV assembly reservoir and applying fluid pressure to the master cylinder. This causes the brake pedal to gradually rise. The EBCM turns off the pump motor when brake pedal height sufficiently rises to close the TCC/antilock brake switch.

FAILURE CONDITIONS

During ABS braking, Code 62 sets when the EBCM determines the pump is working, and brake pedal height has not sufficiently risen to close the TCC/antilock brake switch after 3 seconds.

This code usually indicates a hydraulic problem. Some possible causes include air in the brake lines or a pump motor mechanical failure. Non-hydraulic causes for Code 62 include an open 848 or 853 CKT or a misadjusted/defective TCC/antilock brake switch.

Fig. 49   Chart I (Part 2 of 2). 1991–92 DeVille/Fleetwood (FWD) & 1992–93 except LeSabre & Park Avenue

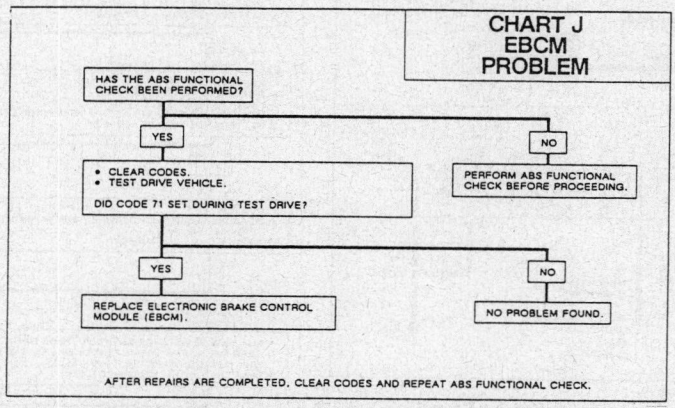

CHART J
EBCM
PROBLEM

Fig. 50   Chart J. 1991–92 DeVille/Fleetwood (FWD) & 1992–93 models except 1993 LeSabre & Park Avenue

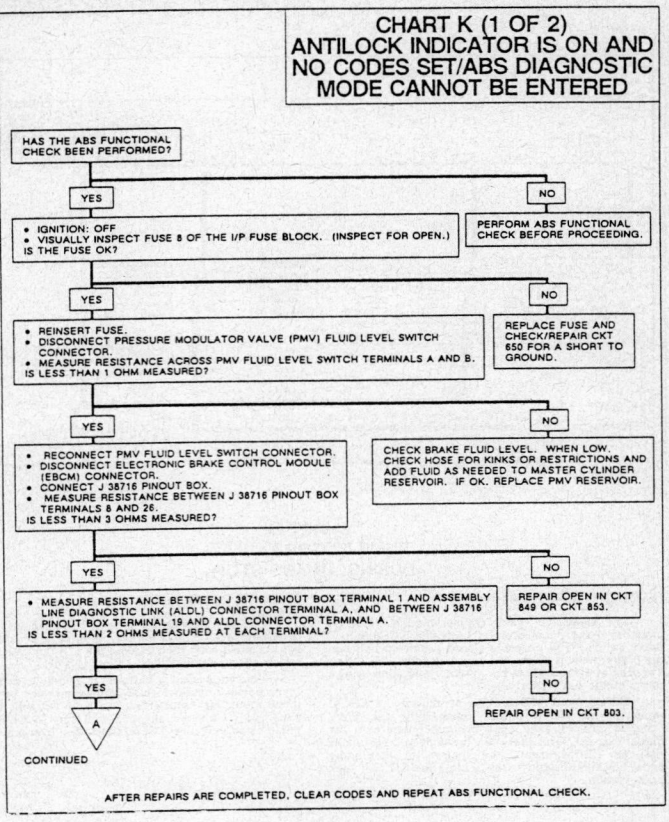

**CHART K (1 OF 2)
ANTILOCK INDICATOR IS ON AND
NO CODES SET/ABS DIAGNOSTIC
MODE CANNOT BE ENTERED**

CHART K
"ANTILOCK" INDICATOR IS ON AND NO CODES ARE SET/ DIAGNOSTIC MODE CANNOT BE ENTERED

CIRCUIT OPERATION

When the ignition is first turned to "RUN," the electronic brake control module (EBCM) goes through a self-test lasting 2–4 seconds. During this test, the EBCM grounds terminal 52 causing the amber "ANTILOCK" indicator to light. This serves as an indicator bulb test.

When a low fluid condition exists, the EBCM turns on the amber "ANTILOCK" indicator but does not set a code. A low fluid level condition usually lights the red "BRAKE" indicator since the master cylinder supplies the PMV reservoir. However, restrictions or air in the hose could cause a low fluid condition in the PMV reservoir without lighting the red "BRAKE" indicator.

FAILURE CONDITIONS

Possible Causes

- Open in CKT 650, 800, 803, 849 or 853.
- Low brake fluid level or open PMV fluid level switch.
- Short to ground in CKT 650, 800 or 852.

Fig. 51   Chart K (Part 1 of 2). 1991–92 DeVille/Fleetwood (FWD) & 1992–93 except 1993 LeSabre & Park Avenue

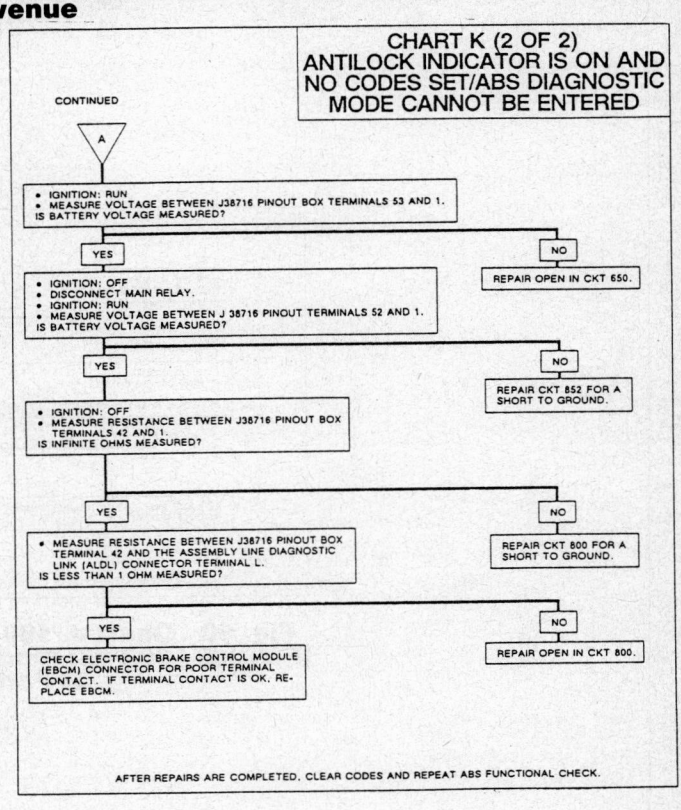

**CHART K (2 OF 2)
ANTILOCK INDICATOR IS ON AND
NO CODES SET/ABS DIAGNOSTIC
MODE CANNOT BE ENTERED**

CHART K
"ANTILOCK" INDICATOR IS ON AND NO CODES ARE SET/ DIAGNOSTIC MODE CANNOT BE ENTERED

CIRCUIT OPERATION

When the ignition is first turned to "RUN," the electronic brake control module (EBCM) goes through a self-test lasting 2–4 seconds. During this test, the EBCM grounds terminal 52 causing the amber "ANTILOCK" indicator to light. This serves as an indicator bulb test.

When a low fluid condition exists, the EBCM turns on the amber "ANTILOCK" indicator but does not set a code. A low fluid level condition usually lights the red "BRAKE" indicator since the master cylinder supplies the PMV reservoir. However, restrictions or air in the hose could cause a low fluid condition in the PMV reservoir without lighting the red "BRAKE" indicator.

FAILURE CONDITIONS

Possible Causes

- Open in CKT 650, 800, 803, 849 or 853.
- Low brake fluid level or open PMV fluid level switch.
- Short to ground in CKT 650, 800 or 852.

Fig. 51   Chart K (Part 2 of 2). 1991–92 DeVille/Fleetwood (FWD) & 1992–93 except 1993 LeSabre & Park Avenue

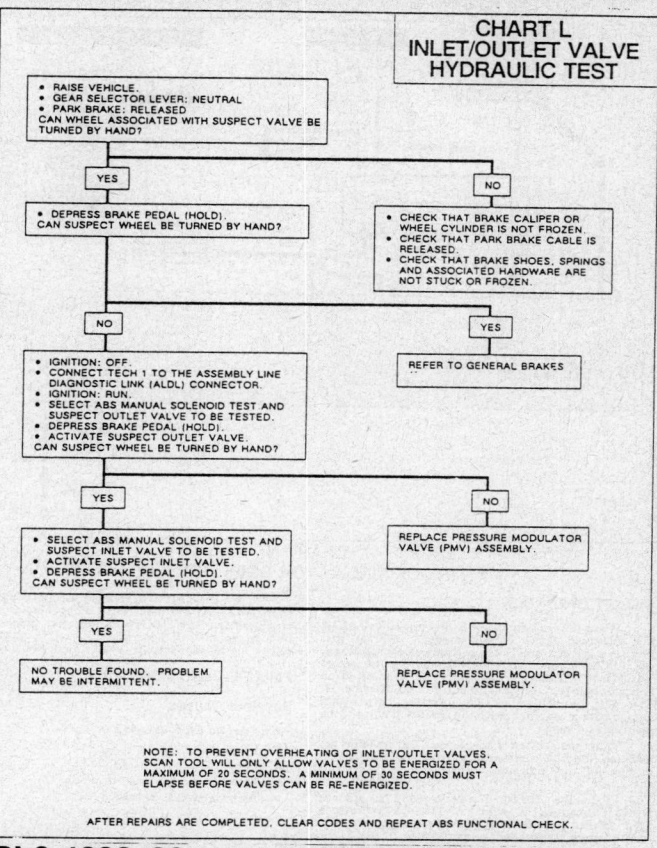

CHART L
INLET/OUTLET VALVE
HYDRAULIC TEST

CHART L
INLET/OUTLET VALVE HYDRAULIC TEST

CIRCUIT OPERATION

Inlet Valves

Voltage is applied to the normally open inlet valves whenever the main relay is energized. An inlet valve closes when the electronic brake control module (EBCM) supplies a ground path at the inlet valve control terminal. The EBCM closes an inlet valve for short periods to maintain (hold) or reduce pressure at a particular wheel.

Outlet Valves

The normally closed outlet valves operate similarly to the inlet valves, except that when the EBCM grounds an outlet valve, the valve opens instead of closes. The EBCM opens an outlet valve for short periods to reduce pressure at a particular wheel.

VALVE MODES

Pressure Increase

The pressure increase position is the operating valve position for normal (non-ABS) braking and traction control mode (when equipped). The EBCM does not energize either valve, leaving the inlet valve open and the outlet valve closed.

Pressure Hold

The pressure hold position occurs when the EBCM first notices an abnormal hydraulic pressure increase. This signifies an impending wheel lockup condition. The EBCM closes the corresponding inlet valve in an attempt to avoid any additional hydraulic pressure increase (avoiding an ABS braking condition).

Pressure Reduce

During a wheel lockup condition, the EBCM close the inlet valve while pulsing open the outlet valve. This decreases hydraulic pressure at a specific wheel without decreasing overall system pressure. The reduced hydraulic pressure allows greater wheel spin, eliminating the wheel lockup condition.

Test Description

This test checks for proper inlet and outlet valve operation. The wheel brake behavior must be checked to verify the valves hydraulic effectiveness. This is accomplished using the TECH 1 to actuate the valves.

Fig. 52   Chart L. 1991–92 DeVille/Fleetwood (FWD) & 1992–93 except 1993 LeSabre & Park Avenue

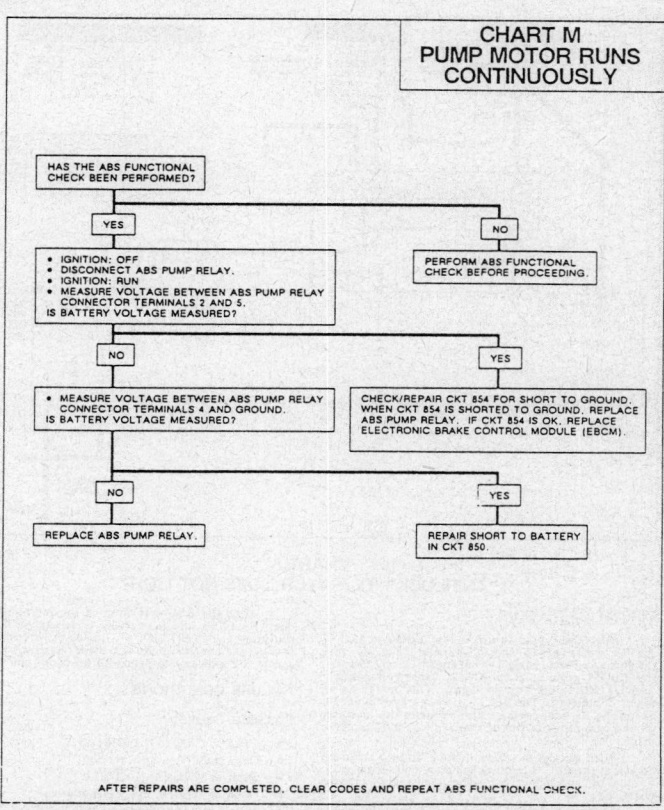

CHART M
PUMP MOTOR RUNS
CONTINUOUSLY

CHART M
PUMP MOTOR RUNS CONTINUOUSLY

CIRCUIT OPERATION

When the electronic brake control module (EBCM) grounds terminal 15, the ABS pump relay is energized. The pump relay contacts close, applying voltage to the pressure modulator valve (PMV) assembly's pump motor.

During most ABS braking conditions, the EBCM turns on the pump motor while monitoring the TCC/antilock switch to determine brake pedal position. The switch opens when the brake pedal is depressed approximately 40% down. The motor restores the master cylinder's fluid pressure, causing the brake pedal to gradually rise. The pump motor continues to run until the brake pedal sufficiently rises to close the TCC/antilock brake switch.

During traction control mode (when equipped), after the front hydraulic brake circuits are isolated, the pump motor runs to increase brake fluid pressure in these circuits. The increased pressure is directed to the slipping wheel through the PMV assembly's front inlet and outlet valves. This causes the brakes to be applied, reducing wheel spin at the slipping wheel. Traction control is disabled as soon as the brakes are manually applied.

The EBCM monitors pump motor operation via the pump motor run sensor. When the pump is operating, voltage is induced into the sensor's coil and the EBCM monitors this voltage at terminals 49 and 31.

FAILURE CONDITIONS

A continuously running pump motor occurs when CKT 854 is shorted to ground, the pump relay fails "engaged," or CKT 850 is shorted to a battery source. This condition illuminates the amber "ANTILOCK" indicator and sets Code 61.

Fig. 53   Chart M. 1991–92 DeVille/Fleetwood (FWD) & 1992–93 except 1993 LeSabre & Park Avenue

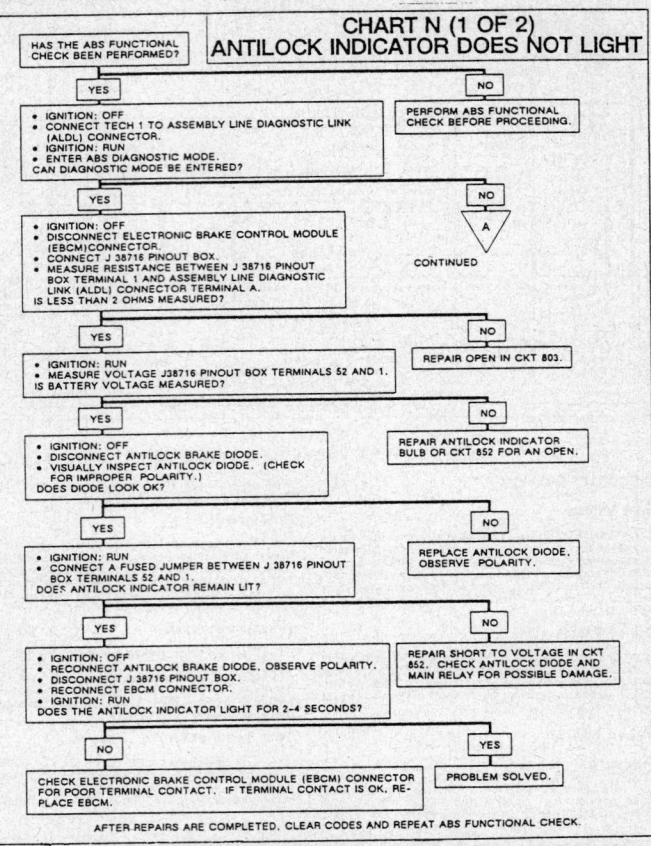

CHART N (1 OF 2)
ANTILOCK INDICATOR DOES NOT LIGHT

CHART N
"ANTILOCK" INDICATOR DOES NOT LIGHT

CIRCUIT OPERATION

When the ignition switch is first turned to "RUN" the electronic brake control module (EBCM) goes through a self-test lasting 2–4 seconds. During this test, the EBCM grounds terminal 52, causing the amber "ANTILOCK" indicator to light. This serves as an indicator bulb test. The EBCM also grounds terminal 34, energizing the main relay. This removes the indicator ground path provided through the antilock diode and the main relay contacts.

When the self-test is completed (and no faults are detected) the EBCM removes the ground at terminal 52, turning off the indicator. The main relay remains energized.

When the EBCM detects a fault, it grounds terminal 52 causing the amber "ANTILOCK" indicator to light. (Note: The EBCM will also de-energize the main relay creating a redundant ground path.)

When the EBCM is disabled for any reason (i.e. open Fuse 19), the main relay is de-energized. This provides an "ANTILOCK" indicator ground path through the antilock diode and main relay contacts, and causes the indicator to light with no codes being set.

FAILURE CONDITIONS

Possible Causes

- Open in CKT 151, 852 or 1077.
- Open bulb.
- Short to voltage in CKT 852.
- Open or shorted anilock diode.
- Main relay fails "engaged."
- Short to ground in CKT 855.

Fig. 54 Chart N (Part 1 of 2). 1991–92 DeVille/Fleetwood (FWD) & 1992–93 except 1993 LeSabre & Park Avenue

---

CHART N (2 OF 2)
ANTILOCK INDICATOR DOES NOT LIGHT

CHART N
"ANTILOCK" INDICATOR DOES NOT LIGHT

CIRCUIT OPERATION

When the ignition switch is first turned to "RUN" the electronic brake control module (EBCM) goes through a self-test lasting 2–4 seconds. During this test, the EBCM grounds terminal 52, causing the amber "ANTILOCK" indicator to light. This serves as an indicator bulb test. The EBCM also grounds terminal 34, energizing the main relay. This removes the indicator ground path provided through the antilock diode and the main relay contacts.

When the self-test is completed (and no faults are detected) the EBCM removes the ground at terminal 52, turning off the indicator. The main relay remains energized.

When the EBCM detects a fault, it grounds terminal 52 causing the amber "ANTILOCK" indicator to light. (Note: The EBCM will also de-energize the main relay creating a redundant ground path.)

When the EBCM is disabled for any reason (i.e. open Fuse 19), the main relay is de-energized. This provides an "ANTILOCK" indicator ground path through the antilock diode and main relay contacts, and causes the indicator to light with no codes being set.

FAILURE CONDITIONS

Possible Causes

- Open in CKT 151, 852 or 1077.
- Open bulb.
- Short to voltage in CKT 852.
- Open or shorted antilock diode.
- Main relay fails "engaged."
- Short to ground in CKT 855.

Fig. 54 Chart N (Part 2 of 2). 1991–92 DeVille/Fleetwood (FWD) & 1992–93 except 1993 LeSabre & Park Avenue

OPERATION:

When the ignition switch is first turned to RUN, EBCM/EBTCM goes through a self-check lasting 2-4 seconds. During this test, the EBCM/EBTCM grounds terminal 34, energizing the main relay. Once the self-check is completed, the main relay remains energized and delivers battery voltage to both the EBCM/EBTCM and the pressure modulator valve (PMV) assembly during vehicle operation. The constant voltage supply allows the vehicle to enter ABS mode without delay. The main relay is de-energized whenever the amber ANTILOCK indicator lights due to a system fault, causing the ABS system to shut down.

DTC 45 sets when the ignition switch is at run and battery voltage is detected at neither the PMV assembly nor EBCM/EBTCM terminals 20, 3 and/or 33. DTC 45 also sets when the EBCM/EBTCM detects an open or a short to ground in the LH inlet valve circuit.

POSSIBLE CAUSES:
— Open CKT 650, 855, 858, 1077 or 1443.
— Short to ground in CKT 858, 1077 or 1443.
— Main relay fails "open."

Fig. 55   System diagnosis, test 1 (Part 1 of 3). 1993 LeSabre & Park Avenue

A: MAIN RELAY POWER TEST

- Make sure "ABS/TCS Functional Check" is performed before proceeding.
- Ignition switch: OFF
- Main relay: disconnected

1 Battery voltage. If not: check LH underhood fuse block fuse 2; check wiring (CKTS 1077 and 1443) for an open or short to ground. NOTE: When CKT 1077 is found shorted to ground, replace main relay after wiring is repaired.

Ignition switch: RUN

2 Battery voltage. If not: check 650 wire for an open.

3 45-90 ohms. If not: replace main relay.

- If all measurements are correct: go to EBCM/EBTCM Power/Ground Test B.
- After repairs are completed, clear diagnostic trouble codes and repeat "ABS/TCS Functional Check."

B: EBCM/EBTCM POWER/GROUND TEST

- Ignition switch: OFF
- Electronic brake and traction control module (EBCM/EBTCM) connector: disconnected
- Connect J 38716 Pinout Box

1 Less than 5 ohms. If not: check wiring for an open.

2 (Traction control only) Battery voltage. If not: check wiring for an open.

- If all measurements are correct: go to EBCM/EBTCM Power/Ground Test B1.

Fig. 55   System diagnosis, test 1 (Part 2 of 3). 1993 LeSabre & Park Avenue

B1: EBCM/EBTCM POWER/GROUND TEST

- Ignition switch: OFF
- Electronic brake and traction control module (EBCM/EBTCM) connector: disconnected
- Connect J 38716 Pinout Box
- Pressure modulator valve (PMV) assembly connector C1: disconnected (twist off)
- Main relay: disconnected

1 Greater than 5 ohms. If not: check wiring for a short to ground.

- Main relay: connected
- Ignition switch: RUN

4 Battery voltage at both terminals 3 and 33. If not: check wiring for an open. If OK: replace main relay.

2 Battery voltage. If not, check wiring for an open.

3 Connect fused jumper as shown.

- If all measurements are correct: go to Pressure Modulator Valve (PMV) Assembly Voltage Test C.
- After repairs are completed, clear diagnostic trouble codes and repeat "ABS/TCS Functional Check."

C: PRESSURE MODULATOR VALVE (PMV) ASSEMBLY VOLTAGE TEST

- Pressure modulator valve (PMV) assembly connector C1: disconnected
- Electronic brake and traction control module (EBCM/EBTCM) connector: disconnected
- Connect J 38716 Pinout Box
- Fused jumper: connected (from EBCM/EBTCM Power/Ground Test B1, step 3)
- Ignition switch: RUN

Battery voltage. If not: check wiring for an open.

Battery voltage. If not: check wiring for an open.

- If both measurements are correct: remove fused jumper and go to Pressure Modulator Valve (PMV) Assembly Continuity Test D.
- After repairs are completed, clear diagnostic trouble codes and repeat "ABS/TCS Functional Check."

Fig. 55   System diagnosis, test 1 (Part 3 of 3). 1993 LeSabre & Park Avenue

OPERATION:
INLET/OUTLET VALVES

- Voltage is applied to the normally open inlet valves whenever the main relay is energized. An inlet valve closes when the EBCM/EBTCM supplies a ground path at the inlet valve control terminal. The EBCM/EBTCM closes an inlet valve for short periods to maintain (hold) or reduce pressure at a particular wheel.
- The normally closed outlet valves operate similarly to the inlet valves, except that when the EBCM/EBTCM grounds an outlet valve, the valve opens instead of closes. The EBCM/EBTCM opens an outlet valve for short periods to reduce pressure at a particular wheel.

VALVE MODES
- The pressure increase position is the operating valve position for normal (non-ABS) braking and traction control mode (when equipped). The EBCM/EBTCM does not energize either valve, leaving the inlet valve open and the outlet valve closed.
- The pressure hold position occurs when the EBCM/EBTCM first notices an abnormal hydraulic pressure increase. This signifies an impending wheel lockup condition. The EBCM/EBTCM closes the corresponding inlet valve to avoid any additional hydraulic pressure increase (avoiding an ABS braking condition).

- During a wheel lockup condition, the EBCM/EBTCM closes the inlet valve while pulsing open the outlet valve. This decreases hydraulic pressure at a specific wheel without decreasing overall system pressure. The reduced hydraulic pressure allows greater wheel spin, eliminating the wheel lockup condition.
- DTC 41, 42, 45, 46, 51, 52, 55, or 56 sets when the (EBCM/EBTCM) detects an open or short to ground in the respective inlet or outlet valve circuit.

POSSIBLE CAUSES:
— Open in CKT 857, 858, 859, 861, 862, 863, 1290 or 1291.
— Short to ground in CKT 857, 858, 859, 861, 862, 863, 1290 or 1291.

Fig. 56   System diagnosis, test 2 (Part 1 of 2). 1993 LeSabre & Park Avenue

D: PRESSURE MODULATOR VALVE (PMV) ASSEMBLY CONTINUITY TEST

- Make sure "ABS/TCS Functional Check" is performed before proceeding.
- Ignition switch: OFF
- Pressure modulator valve (PMV) assembly connector C1: disconnected

[1] Infinite ohms between pressure modulator valve (PMV) assembly casing. If not: replace PMV assembly, see ⑦.

[2] Measure resistance across suspect solenoid valve terminal(s). When a measurement is incorrect: replace PMV assembly, see ⑦.

VALVE	SUSPECT TERMINAL	CORRECT RESISTANCE
LH front inlet	3	
RH front inlet	5	
LH rear inlet	9	5 to 8 ohms
RH rear inlet	7	
LH front outlet	4	
RH front outlet	6	
LH rear outlet	10	3 to 6 ohms
RH rear outlet	8	

PRESSURE MODULATOR VALVE (PMV) ASSEMBLY CONNECTOR C1 (PMV Assembly side)

- If all measurements are correct: go to Valve Control Test E.
- After repairs are completed, clear diagnostic trouble codes and repeat "ABS/TCS Functional Check."

E: VALVE CONTROL TEST

- Ignition switch: OFF
- Pressure modulator valve (PMV) assembly connector C1: connected
- (EBCM/EBTCM) connector: disconnected
- Connect J 38716 Pinout Box
- Main relay: disconnected

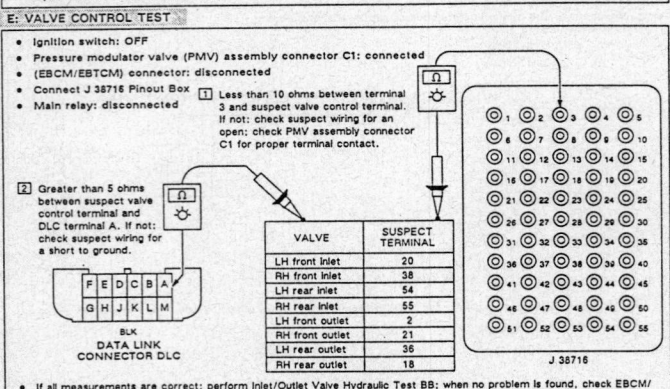

[1] Less than 10 ohms between terminal 3 and suspect valve control terminal. If not: check suspect wiring for an open; check PMV assembly connector C1 for proper terminal contact.

[2] Greater than 5 ohms between suspect valve control terminal and DLC terminal A. If not: check suspect wiring for a short to ground.

VALVE	SUSPECT TERMINAL
LH front inlet	20
RH front inlet	38
LH rear inlet	54
RH rear inlet	55
LH front outlet	2
RH front outlet	21
LH rear outlet	36
RH rear outlet	18

DATA LINK CONNECTOR DLC

- If all measurements are correct: perform Inlet/Outlet Valve Hydraulic Test BB; when no problem is found, check EBCM/EBTCM connector for proper terminal contacts; if OK, replace EBCM/EBTCM, see ③.
- After repairs are completed, clear diagnostic trouble codes and repeat "ABS/TCS Functional Check."

Fig. 56   System diagnosis, test 2 (Part 2 of 2). 1993 LeSabre & Park Avenue

F: WHEEL SPEED SENSOR CONTINUITY TEST

- Make sure "ABS/TCS Functional Check" is performed before proceeding.
- Raise vehicle
- Ignition switch: RUN
- Gear selector lever: NEUTRAL
- Ignition switch: OFF
- Park brake: released
- Make measurements at suspect wheel speed sensor (connector disconnected).

[1] 800-1500 ohms. If not: replace suspect wheel speed sensor.
  - Rear wheel speed sensor, see ⑫.
  - Front wheel speed sensor, see ⑩.

[2] Greater than 5 ohms. If not: replace suspect wheel speed sensor.
  - Rear wheel speed sensor, see ⑫.
  - Front wheel speed sensor, see ⑩.

WHEEL SPEED SENSOR

- If all measurements are correct: go to EBCM/EBTCM/Wheel Speed Circuit Input Test H.
- After repairs are completed, clear diagnostic trouble codes and repeat "ABS/TCS Functional Check."

G: WHEEL SPEED SENSOR OUTPUT TEST

- Raise vehicle
- Ignition switch: RUN
- Gear selector lever: NEUTRAL
- Ignition switch: OFF
- Park brake: released
- Make measurements at suspect wheel speed sensor (connector disconnected).

[1] 50-900 mVAC while turning wheel by hand. If measurement is incorrect: replace suspect wheel speed sensor.
  - Rear wheel speed sensors, see ⑫.
  - Front wheel speed sensors, see ⑩.

WHEEL SPEED SENSOR

- If all measurements are correct: check EBCM/EBTCM connector for proper terminal contact; if OK, replace EBCM/EBTCM, see ③.
- After repairs are completed, clear diagnostic trouble codes and repeat "ABS/TCS Functional Check."

Fig. 57   System diagnosis, test 3 (Part 2 of 4). 1993 LeSabre & Park Avenue

ELECTRONIC BRAKE AND TRACTION CONTROL MODULE (EBCM/EBTCM)

OPERATION:

- When each wheel turns, the wheel speed sensor creates a small AC voltage with a frequency proportional to wheel speed. This magnetically induced voltage is caused by a toothed sensor ring passing the wheel speed sensor's stationary pickup coil. The toothed sensor ring is mounted on the drive axle in the front, and the hub/bearing assembly in the rear.
- The EBCM/EBTCM uses the wheel speed sensor signal to calculate vehicle reference speeds, and individual wheel speed, acceleration and slip values. These values are used to determine when antilock control is required. Vehicles equipped with traction control also use front wheel speed sensor signals to determine when traction control is required.
- To prevent electromagnetic interference from disturbing the wheel speed sensor signal, the cables from the EBCM/EBTCM to each wheel speed sensor are twisted a minimum of 6 to 9 turns per foot. When servicing the sensor cables, it is important to maintain the original cables' twists (6 to 9 turns per foot).
- DTC 22, 26, 32, or 36 sets when the EBCM/EBTCM determines that a wheel speed signal is erratic. A wheel speed signal indicating that a wheel is accelerating or decelerating faster than physically possible is an example of an erratic signal. An intermittent open or short to ground in a wheel speed sensor could also cause the EBCM/EBTCM to set a diagnostic trouble code. DTC 22, 26, 32 or 36 also sets when the EBCM/EBTCM detects electromagnetic in-

terference (noise) in a wheel speed sensor signal. Possible interference sources include accessory motors, wiper motors and ignition circuits.
- DTC 23, 27, 33 or 37 sets when the EBCM/EBTCM does not see any wheel speed sensor signal, but determines that continuity exists in the circuit. This is caused by a dislodged wheel speed sensor, missing toothed sensor ring (front) or defective hub and bearing assembly (rear).
- Any condition which would result in lack of continuity in a wheel speed sensor circuit could result in DTC 21 or 25 (front) or 31 or 35 (rear) being set. These conditions include an open, a short to ground, or a short between the two wheel speed sensor circuits in the wiring harness between the speed sensor and EBCM/EBTCM. Also, an open or short to ground across the wheel speed sensor coil could trigger this diagnostic trouble code.

POSSIBLE CAUSES:

- Faulty or dislodged wheel speed sensor.
- Missing or irregular toothed sensor ring.
- Open or short to ground in wheel speed sensor circuit.
- Short between wheel speed sensor circuits.
- Erratic wheel speed signal.
- Defective hub and bearing assembly.
- Intermittent open or short to ground in wheel speed sensor circuit.
- Noise interference in wheel speed sensor signal.
- Improperly twisted sensor cable.

Fig. 57   System diagnosis, test 3 (Part 1 of 4). 1993 LeSabre & Park Avenue

H: EBCM/EBTCM/WHEEL SPEED CIRCUIT INPUT TEST

- Ignition switch: OFF
- Suspect wheel speed sensor connector: connected
- EBCM/EBTCM connector: disconnected
- Connect J 38716 Pinout Box
- Do steps [1] and [2] at suspect wheel speed sensor terminals
- Example shown is for LH rear wheel speed circuit; other wheels similar.

LH REAR WHEEL SPEED

[1] 800 to 1500 ohms. If greater than 1500 ohms: check suspect wiring for an open; check in-line connector and wheel speed sensor connector for proper terminal contact. If less than 800 ohms: check for a short between suspect wheel speed sensor wiring.

RH REAR WHEEL SPEED
RH FRONT WHEEL SPEED
LH FRONT WHEEL SPEED

[2] Greater than 5 ohms. If not: check suspect wiring for a short to ground.

DATA LINK CONNECTOR DLC

- If all measurements are correct: check EBCM/EBTCM connector for proper terminal contact; if OK, replace EBCM/EBTCM, see ③.
- After repairs are completed, clear diagnostic trouble codes and repeat "ABS/TCS Functional Check."

Fig. 57   System diagnosis, test 3 (Part 3 of 4). 1993 LeSabre & Park Avenue

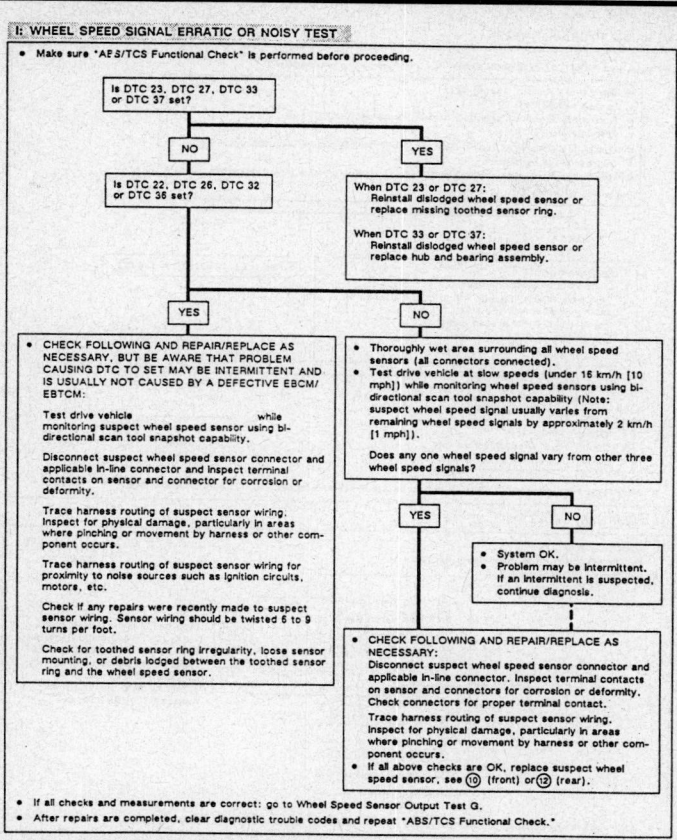

I: WHEEL SPEED SIGNAL ERRATIC OR NOISY TEST

- Make sure "ABS/TCS Functional Check" is performed before proceeding.

Is DTC 23, DTC 27, DTC 33 or DTC 37 set?

NO → **Is DTC 22, DTC 26, DTC 32 or DTC 36 set?**

YES → When DTC 23 or DTC 27:
Reinstall dislodged wheel speed sensor or replace missing toothed sensor ring.

When DTC 33 or DTC 37:
Reinstall dislodged wheel speed sensor or replace hub and bearing assembly.

Is DTC 22, DTC 26, DTC 32 or DTC 36 set?

YES →
- CHECK FOLLOWING AND REPAIR/REPLACE AS NECESSARY, BUT BE AWARE THAT PROBLEM CAUSING DTC TO SET MAY BE INTERMITTENT AND IS USUALLY NOT CAUSED BY A DEFECTIVE EBCM/EBTCM.

Test drive vehicle while monitoring suspect wheel speed sensor using bi-directional scan tool snapshot capability.

Disconnect suspect wheel speed sensor connector and applicable in-line connector and inspect terminal contacts on sensor and connector for corrosion or deformity.

Trace harness routing of suspect sensor wiring. Inspect for physical damage, particularly in areas where pinching or movement by harness or other component occurs.

Trace harness routing of suspect sensor wiring for proximity to noise sources such as ignition circuits, motors, etc.

Check if any repairs were recently made to suspect sensor wiring. Sensor wiring should be twisted 6 to 9 turns per foot.

Check for toothed sensor ring irregularity, loose sensor mounting, or debris lodged between the toothed sensor ring and the wheel speed sensor.

NO →
- Thoroughly wet area surrounding all wheel speed sensors (all connectors connected).
- Test drive vehicle at slow speeds (under 16 km/h [10 mph]) while monitoring wheel speed sensors using bi-directional scan tool snapshot capability (Note: suspect wheel speed signal usually varies from remaining wheel speed signals by approximately 2 km/h [1 mph]).

Does any one wheel speed signal vary from other three wheel speed signals?

YES →
- CHECK FOLLOWING AND REPAIR/REPLACE AS NECESSARY:
Disconnect suspect wheel speed sensor connector and applicable in-line connector. Inspect terminal contacts on sensor and connectors for corrosion or deformity. Check connectors for proper terminal contact.

Trace harness routing of suspect sensor wiring. Inspect for physical damage, particularly in areas where pinching or movement by harness or other component occurs.

If all above checks are OK, replace suspect wheel speed sensor, see (10) (front) or (12) (rear).

NO →
- System OK.
- Problem may be intermittent. If an intermittent is suspected, continue diagnosis.

- If all checks and measurements are correct: go to Wheel Speed Sensor Output Test G.
- After repairs are completed, clear diagnostic trouble codes and repeat "ABS/TCS Functional Check."

Fig. 57 System diagnosis, test 3 (Part 4 of 4). 1993 LeSabre & Park Avenue

OPERATION:
- When EBCM/EBTCM grounds terminal 15, the ABS pump relay is energized. The pump relay contacts close, applying voltage to the pressure modulator valve (PMV) assembly's pump motor. The EBCM/EBTCM turns on the pump motor during most ABS braking conditions and, when equipped, during all traction control conditions.
- During most ABS braking conditions, the EBCM/EBTCM turns on the pump motor while monitoring the TCC/antilock brake switch to determine brake pedal position. The switch opens when the brake pedal is depressed approximately 40%. The motor restores the master cylinder's fluid pressure, causing the brake pedal to gradually rise. The pump motor continues to run until the brake pedal sufficiently rises to close the TCC/antilock brake switch.
- During traction control mode (when equipped), after the front hydraulic brake circuits are isolated, the pump motor runs to increase brake fluid pressure in these circuits. The increased pressure is directed to the slipping wheel through the PMV assembly's front inlet and outlet valves. This causes the brakes to be applied, reducing wheel spin at the slipping wheel. Traction control is disabled as soon as the brakes are manually applied.

- When the EBCM/EBTCM grounds terminal 15, DTC 61 sets when the EBCM/EBTCM determines that the voltage between EBCM/EBTCM terminals 31 and 49 is not between 500-800 mVAC. The EBCM/EBTCM recognizes this condition only during ABS braking requiring pump motor operation, traction control mode (when equipped), and during the EBCM/EBTCM self-check which occurs when the vehicle reaches 11 km/h (7 mph). Therefore, be sure to test drive vehicle; after clearing the diagnostic trouble code to assure correct diagnosis.
- DTC 61 also sets when the pump motor runs all the time (i.e., EBCM/EBTCM sees proper voltage between terminals 31 and 49 without grounding terminal 15).

POSSIBLE CAUSES:
- Open in CKT 151, 850, 854, 1077, 1292, 1293 or 1446.
- Short to ground in CKT 850, 854, 1292, 1293 or 1446.
- ABS pump relay fails "open" or "engaged."

Fig. 58 System diagnosis, test 4 (Part 1 of 3). 1993 LeSabre & Park Avenue

J: PUMP MOTOR CIRCUIT TEST

- Make sure "ABS/TCS Functional/Check" is performed before proceeding.
- Ignition switch: OFF
- Connect bi-directional scan tool to data link connector DLC.
- Ignition switch: RUN
- Command bi-directional scan tool to bleed pressure modulator valve (PMV) assembly.
  - If pump motor runs: turn ignition switch OFF, disconnect bi-directional scan tool and go to step (6).
  - If pump motor does not run: clear diagnostic trouble codes, turn ignition switch OFF, disconnect bi-directional scan tool and go to step (1).

- Ignition switch: OFF
- ABS pump relay connector: disconnected
- Ignition switch: RUN

(1) Battery voltage. If not: check wiring for an open.

(2) Battery voltage. If not: check LH underhood fuse block fuse 1; check wiring (CKTS 850 and 1446) for an open or short to ground. NOTE: When CKT 850 is found shorted to ground, replace ABS pump relay after wiring is repaired.

(3) Pump motor runs. If motor does not run: go to step (4). If motor runs: reconnect ABS pump relay and go to Pump Motor Circuit Test J1.

- Ignition switch: OFF
- Pressure modulator valve (PMV) assembly connector C2: disconnected

(5) Battery voltage. If not: check wiring for an open. If measurement is correct: check PMV connector C2 for proper terminal contact; if OK, replace pressure modulator valve (PMV) assembly, see (7).

(4) Battery voltage with jumper still in place from step (3). If not: check wiring for an open or short to ground.

(6) Infinite ohms between pressure modulator valve (PMV) assembly casing. If not: replace PMV assembly, see (7).

(7) 10 to 40 ohms. If not: replace pressure modulator valve (PMV) assembly, see (7). If measurement is correct: reconnect PMV assembly connector C2, and go to Pump Motor Circuit Test J1.

Fig. 58 System diagnosis, test 4 (Part 2 of 3). 1993 LeSabre & Park Avenue

J1: PUMP MOTOR CIRCUIT TEST

- Ignition switch: OFF
- EBCM/EBTCM connector: disconnected
- Connect J 38716 Pinout Box
- Disconnect fused jumper.
- Ignition switch: OFF

(1) Less than 5 ohms. If not: check wiring for an open.

(3) Greater than 5 ohms. If not: check wiring CKTS 1292 and 1293 for a short to ground.

(4) 10 to 40 ohms. If high resistance is measured: check wiring (CKTS 1292 and 1293) for an open; check PMV assembly connector C2 for proper terminal contact. If low resistance is measured: check for a short between wiring.

(2) Pump motor runs. If not: check wiring (CKT 854) for an open; if OK, replace ABS pump relay.

- Connect fused jumpers as shown
- Ignition switch: RUN

- If all measurements are correct: check EBCM/EBTCM connector for proper terminal contact; if OK, replace EBCM/EBTCM, see (3).
- After repairs are completed, clear diagnostic trouble codes and repeat "ABS/TCS Functional Check."

K: PUMP MOTOR SHORT TEST

- Make sure "ABS/TCS Functional Check" is performed before proceeding.
- Ignition switch: OFF
- ABS pump relay connector: disconnected
- Ignition switch: RUN

(1) 0 volts. If not: check wiring (CKT 854) for a short to ground. If wiring is shorted to ground, replace ABS pump relay; if wiring is OK, check EBCM/EBTCM connector for proper terminal contact; if OK, replace EBCM/EBTCM, see (3).

(2) 0 volts. If not: check wiring for a short to battery.

- If all measurements are correct: replace ABS pump relay.
- After repairs are completed, clear diagnostic trouble codes and repeat "ABS/TCS Functional Check."

Fig. 58 System diagnosis, test 4 (Part 3 of 3). 1993 LeSabre & Park Avenue

M: BRAKE HYDRAULIC TEST

- Make sure "ABS/TCS Functional Check" is performed before proceeding.
  - Bleed brake system, see ① or ② .
  - Ignition switch: OFF
  - Connect bi-directional scan tool to data link connector DLC.
  - Ignition switch: RUN
  - Use bi-directional scan tool to clear diagnostic trouble code after bleeding system.
  - Depress brake pedal (hold).
  - Use bi-directional scan tool to bleed pressure modulator valve (PMV) assembly.
  - Did brake pedal rise?

  YES →
  - Ignition switch: OFF
  - Disconnect bi-directional scan tool.
  - Test drive vehicle in a safe wet area and attempt to perform a 3 second ABS stop.
  - Connect bi-directional scan tool to DLC.
  - Ignition switch: RUN
  - Did DTC 62 set?

  NO → Replace PMV assembly, see ⑦ .

  YES →
  - Ignition switch: OFF
  - Disconnect bi-directional scan tool.
  - Go to TCC/Antilock Brake Switch Test L.

  NO → Problem solved.

- After repairs are completed, clear diagnostic trouble codes and repeat "ABS/TCS Functional Check."

OPERATION:

- The EBCM/EBTCM monitors brake pedal position using the TCC/antilock brake switch. The normally closed switch opens when the brake pedal is depressed approximately 40%. The EBCM/EBTCM also monitors pump motor operation using a pump motor run sensor.
- During most ABS braking conditions the EBCM/EBTCM turns on the pump motor, replenishing the PMV assembly reservoir and applying fluid pressure to the master cylinder. This causes the brake pedal to gradually rise. The EBCM/EBTCM turns off the pump motor when brake pedal

height rises sufficiently to close the TCC/antilock brake switch.
- During ABS braking, DTC 62 sets when the EBCM/EBTCM determines the pump is working, and brake pedal height has not risen sufficiently to close the TCC/antilock brake switch after 3 seconds.

POSSIBLE CAUSES:
- Air in the brake lines.
- Pump motor mechanical failure.
- Open in CKT 848 or 853.
- Misadjusted/defective TCC/antilock brake switch.

L: TCC/ANTILOCK BRAKE SWITCH TEST

- Ignition switch: OFF
- Brake pedal: released (rest position)
- TCC/antilock brake switch connector: disconnected

  ① Less than 1 ohm. If not, check switch adjustment; replace if necessary, see ④ .

  ② Brake pedal: fully depressed
  - Infinite ohms. If not: check switch adjustment; replace if necessary, see ④ .

- If both measurements are correct and DTC 62 is set: reconnect TCC/antilock brake switch connector and go to Pump On Request Circuit Test N.
- After repairs are completed, clear diagnostic trouble codes and repeat "ABS/TCS Functional Check."

N: PUMP ON REQUEST CIRCUIT TEST

- Ignition switch: OFF
- EBCM/EBTCM connector: disconnected
- Connect J 38716 Pinout Box

J 38716

Less than 3 ohms. If not, check wiring (CKTS 848 and 853) for an open. If OK, check TCC/antilock brake switch connector and EBCM/EBTCM connector for proper terminal contact. If OK, replace EBCM/EBTCM, see ③ .

- After repairs are completed, clear diagnostic trouble codes and repeat "ABS/TCS Functional Check."

Fig. 59 System diagnosis, test 5 (Part 1 of 4). 1993 LeSabre & Park Avenue

Fig. 59 System diagnosis, test 5 (Part 2 of 4). 1993 LeSabre & Park Avenue

O: EBCM/EBTCM GROUNDED SWITCH INPUT TEST

- Make sure "ABS/TCS Functional Check" is performed before proceeding.
- Ignition switch: OFF
- EBCM/EBTCM connector: disconnected
- Connect J 38716 Pinout Box
- TCC/antilock brake switch connector: disconnected
- Pressure modulator valve (PMV) fluid level switch: disconnected
- PMV assembly connector, C1: disconnected (traction control [NW9] only)

  ① Less than 5 ohms between data link connector DLC terminal A. If not: check wiring for an open.

  ② Greater than 5 ohms. If not: check wiring (see schematic) for a short to ground.

  ③ Greater than 5 ohms. If not: check wiring for a short to ground.

J 38716

- If all measurements are correct: check EBCM/EBTCM connector for proper terminal contact. If OK: replace EBCM/EBTCM, see ③ .
- After repairs are completed, clear diagnostic trouble codes and repeat "ABS/TCS Functional Check."

P: EBCM/EBTCM OPEN SWITCH INPUT TEST

- Make sure "ABS/TCS Functional Check" is performed before proceeding.
- Ignition switch: OFF
- EBCM/EBTCM connector: disconnected
- Connect J 38716 Pinout Box
- Brake pedal: fully depressed

  ① Less than 3 ohms. If not: check wiring (CKTS 853 and 1659) and PMV pressure switch for an open: check PMV assembly connector C1 for proper terminal contact; check PMV assembly pigtail wiring for a short to PMV casing; if switch or PMV assembly pigtail wiring is defective, replace PMV assembly, see ⑦ .

  ② Infinite ohms. If not: check for a short between (CKTS 853 and 1659). If OK, replace PMV assembly, see ⑦ .

J 38716

OPERATION:

- The EBCM/EBTCM monitors brake pedal position using the TCC/antilock brake switch. The normally closed switch opens when the brake pedal is depressed approximately 40%. The EBCM/EBTCM also monitors pump motor operation using a pump motor run sensor.
- During most ABS braking condition, the EBCM/EBTCM turns on the pump motor, replenishing the PMV assembly reservoir and applying fluid pressure to the master cylinder. This causes the brake pedal to gradually rise. The EBCM/EBTCM turns off the pump motor when brake pedal height rises sufficiently to close the TCC/antilock brake switch.
- The pressure modulator valve (PMV) fluid level switch alerts the EBCM/EBTCM to a low brake fluid condition in the PMV reservoir. The fluid level switch is located in the PMV assembly's reservoir. The fluid level switch is normally closed when the reservoir contains sufficient fluid. When fluid level is low, the switch opens, causing the EBCM/EBTCM to turn on the ANTILOCK indicator.
- The pressure switch monitors primary brake system pressure. The normally closed switch opens when the brakes

are applied (pressure exceeds 700 kPa [101 psi]). If the brakes are manually applied during traction control mode, the PMV pressure switch input, along with the brake switch input, signal EBCM/EBTCM to disable traction control and allow manual braking. The pressure switch is part of the pressure modulator valve (PMV) assembly and is not serviceable.
- DTC 72 sets when the EBCM/EBTCM detects that the TCC/antilock brake switch CKT 848 is shorted to ground.
- DTC 73 sets when the EBCM detects a short to ground in the PMV fluid level switch circuitry. These include CKTS 848, 849, 853 and 1659.
- DTC 74 sets when the EBCM/EBTCM detects an open or short to ground in the PMV pressure switch circuitry.

POSSIBLE CAUSES:
- Short to ground in CKT 848 with TCC/antilock brake switch open.
- Short to ground in CKT 848, 849, 853 or 1659.
- Open in CKT 853 or 1659.
- Short to ground in CKT 1659 with brake pedal depressed.
- Failed PMV pressure switch.

- If all measurements are correct, check EBCM/EBTCM connector for proper terminal contact. If OK, replace EBCM/EBTCM, see ③ .
- After repairs are completed, clear diagnostic trouble codes and repeat "ABS/TCS Functional Check."

Fig. 59 System diagnosis, test 5 (Part 3 of 4). 1993 LeSabre & Park Avenue

Fig. 59 System diagnosis, test 5 (Part 4 of 4). 1993 LeSabre & Park Avenue

OPERATION:
- When the ignition switch is first turned to RUN, the EBCM/EBTCM goes through a self-test lasting 2-4 seconds. During this test, the EBCM/EBTCM grounds terminal 52, causing the amber ANTILOCK indicator to light. This serves as an indicator bulb test.
- When a low fluid condition exists, the EBCM/EBTCM turns on the amber ANTILOCK indicator but does not set a code. A low fluid level condition usually lights the red

BRAKE indicator since the master cylinder supplies the PMV reservoir. However, restrictions or air in the hose could cause a low fluid condition in the PMV reservoir without lighting the red BRAKE indicator.

POSSIBLE CAUSES:
- Open in CKT 650, 800, 803, 849 or 853.
- Low brake fluid level or open PMV fluid level switch.
- Short to ground in CKT 650, 800 or 852.

Fig. 60   System diagnosis, test 6 (Part 1 of 2). 1993 LeSabre & Park Avenue

---

Q: DATA LINE TEST
- Make sure "ABS/TCS Functional Check" is performed before proceeding.
- Ignition switch: OFF
- EBCM/EBTCM connector: disconnected
- Connect J 38716 Pinout Box

1 Less than 2 ohms between data link connector DLC terminal A. If not: repair open in wiring (CKT 803).

- Ignition switch: RUN
2 5 volts. If not: check wiring (CKT 800) and components for an open or short to ground. See Data Line for complete circuit details.

J 38716

- If both measurements are correct, check EBCM/EBTCM connector for proper terminal contact. If OK: replace EBCM/EBTCM, see ③.

R: ANTILOCK INDICATOR "ON" FAULT TEST
- Make sure "ABS/TCS Functional Check" is performed before proceeding.
- Ignition switch: OFF
- EBCM/EBTCM connector: disconnected
- Connect J 38716 Pinout Box

1 Less than 5 ohms between data link connector DLC terminal A. If not: check wiring (CKT 803) for an open.

2 Less than 5 ohms between data link connector DLC terminal A. If not: check wiring (CKT 803) for an open.

3 Less than 3 ohms. If not: check wiring (CKTS 849 and 853) and PMV fluid level switch for an open. If switch is open, check PMV fluid level switch connector for proper terminal contact. If OK, replace PMV assembly reservoir, see ⑨.
- Ignition switch: RUN
- Main relay: disconnected
- Ignition switch: RUN
5 Battery voltage. If not: check wiring (CKT 852) for a short to ground.

4 Ignition switch: RUN
Battery voltage. If not: check wiring (CKT 650) for an open or short to ground. When necessary, replace I/P fuse block fuse 19.

J 38716

- If all measurements are correct: check EBCM/EBTCM connector for proper terminal contact. If OK: replace EBCM/EBTCM, see ③.
- After repairs are completed, clear diagnostic trouble codes and repeat "ABS/TCS Functional Check."

Fig. 60   System diagnosis, test 6 (Part 2 of 2). 1993 LeSabre & Park Avenue

---

OPERATION:
- When the ignition switch is first turned to RUN, the EBCM/EBTCM goes through a self-test lasting 2-4 seconds. During this test, the EBCM/EBTCM grounds terminal 52, causing the ANTILOCK indicator to light. This serves as an indicator bulb test. The EBCM/EBTCM also grounds terminal 34, energizing the main relay. This removes the indicator ground path through the antilock diode and the main relay contacts.
- When the self-test is completed (and no faults are detected), the EBCM/EBTCM removes the ground at terminal 52, turning off the indicator. The main relay remains energized.
- When the EBCM/EBTCM detects a fault, it grounds terminal 52, causing the amber ANTILOCK indicator to light.

(Note: The EBCM/EBTCM also de-energizes the main relay, creating a redundant ground path.)
- When the EBCM/EBTCM is disabled for any reason (i.e., open fuse 19), the main relay is de-energized. This provides an alternate ground path through the antilock diode and main relay contacts, and causes the indicator to light with no codes being set.

POSSIBLE CAUSES:
- Open in CKT 803, 852 or 1077.
- Open bulb.
- Short to voltage in CKT 852.
- Open or shorted antilock diode.
- Main relay falls "engaged."
- Short to ground in CKT 855.

Fig. 61   System diagnosis, test 7 (Part 1 of 2). 1993 LeSabre & Park Avenue

---

S: ANTILOCK INDICATOR "OFF" FAULT TEST
- Make sure "ABS/TCS Functional Check" is performed before proceeding.
- Ignition switch: OFF
- Connect bi-directional scan tool to data link connector DLC.
- Ignition switch: RUN
- Enter scan tool Diagnostic Mode.
- If Diagnostic Mode cannot be entered: disconnect scan tool, do Data Line Test Q, then do Main Relay Ground Test T.
- If Diagnostic Mode can be entered: disconnect scan tool and continue to step 1.

4 Ignition switch: RUN
ANTILOCK indicator remains lit. If not: check wiring (CKT 852) for a short to voltage. NOTE: When a short to voltage is found, inspect antilock diode and main relay for possible damage.

- If all measurements are correct: check EBCM/EBTCM connector for proper terminal contact. If OK, replace EBCM/EBTCM, see ③.
- After repairs are completed, clear diagnostic trouble codes and repeat "ABS/TCS Functional Check."

1 - Ignition switch: OFF
- EBCM/EBTCM connector: disconnected
- Connect J 38716 Pinout Box

Less than 5 ohms between data link connector DLC terminal A. If not: check wiring (CKT 803) for an open.

2 - Main relay: disconnected
- Ignition switch: RUN
Battery voltage. If not: check ANTILOCK indicator bulb and wiring (CKT 852) for an open. If both OK: replace information center (UB3 only), see ⑬ or instrument cluster (U23 only), see ⑤.

3 - Ignition switch: OFF
Disconnect antilock diode and inspect for damage; replace as necessary, observe diode polarity.

J 38716

T: MAIN RELAY GROUND TEST
- Ignition switch: OFF
- Main relay: disconnected
- I/P fuse block fuse 19: removed
- Ignition switch: RUN

1 Battery voltage. If not: check antilock diode and wiring (CKTS 852 and 1077) for an open.

2 Battery voltage. If not: check wiring (CKT 803) for an open.

3 - Ignition switch: OFF
Greater than 5 ohms. If not: check wiring (CKT 855) for a short to ground. If OK: check EBCM/EBTCM connector for proper terminal contact. If OK: replace EBCM/EBTCM, see ③.

4 Less than 3 ohms. If not: replace main relay.

BLK
MAIN RELAY CONNECTOR   MAIN RELAY

- After repairs are completed, clear diagnostic trouble codes and repeat "ABS/TCS Functional Check."

Fig. 61   System diagnosis, test 7 (Part 2 of 2). 1993 LeSabre & Park Avenue

Fig. 62   System diagnosis, test 8 (Part 1 of 2). 1993 LeSabre & Park Avenue

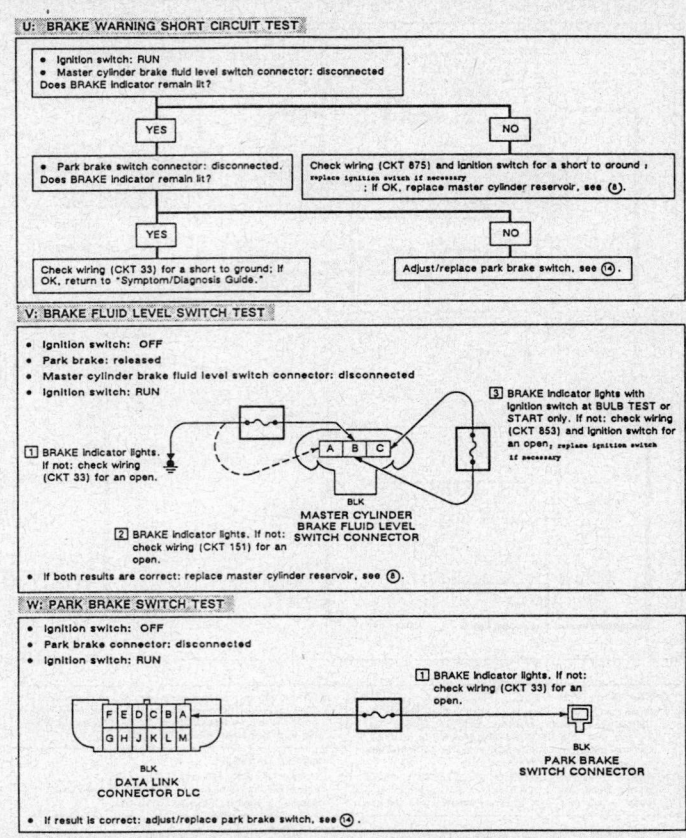

Fig. 62   System diagnosis, test 8 (Part 2 of 2). 1993 LeSabre & Park Avenue

Fig. 63   System diagnosis, test 9 (Part 1 of 2). 1993 LeSabre & Park Avenue

Fig. 63   System diagnosis, test 9 (Part 2 of 2). 1993 LeSabre & Park Avenue

OPERATION:

- Voltage is applied to the normally open isolation valves whenever the main relay is energized. An isolation valve closes when the EBTCM supplies a ground path at the isolation valve control terminal. The EBTCM closes an isolation valve when the EBTCM detects wheel slip in a drive wheel and vehicle speed is below 40 km/h (25 mph).
- The isolation valves are closed only during traction control operations, and are not used during any antilock or normal braking conditions. The isolation valves separate (isolate) the front brake hydraulic circuits from the master cylinder and rear brake hydraulic circuits. Once the front brake hydraulic circuits are isolated, pressure can be applied to the front wheels without affecting any other brake hydraulic circuit.
- DTC 44 or 48 sets when the EBTCM detects an open or short to ground in the respective isolation valve circuit.

POSSIBLE CAUSES:
— Open in CKT 1077, 1657 or 1658.
— Short to ground in CKT 1657 or 1658.
— Faulty pressure modulator valve (PMV) assembly.

Fig. 64   System diagnosis, test 10 (Part 1 of 3). 1993 LeSabre & Park Avenue

Fig. 64   System diagnosis, test 10 (Part 2 of 3). 1993 LeSabre & Park Avenue

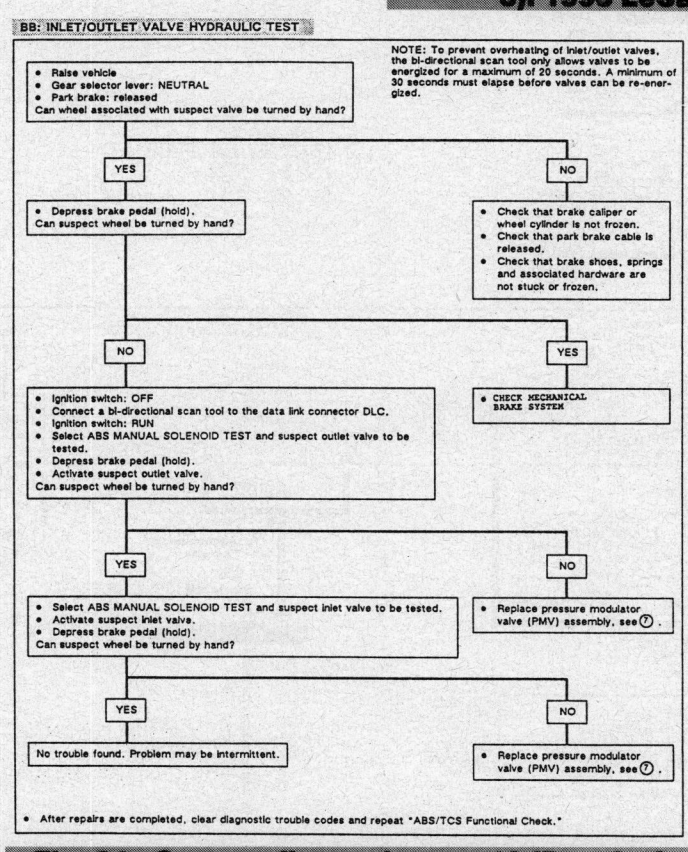

Fig. 64   System diagnosis, test 10 (Part 3 of 3). 1993 LeSabre & Park Avenue

Fig. 65   ABS wiring circuit (Part 1 of 3). 1991 Bonneville, 88 & LeSabre

Fig. 65   ABS wiring circuit (Part 2 of 3). 1991 Bonneville, 88 & LeSabre

Fig. 65   ABS wiring circuit (Part 3 of 3). 1991 Bonneville, 88 & LeSabre

Fig. 66   ABS wiring circuit (Part 1 of 4). 1991 98 & Park Ave.

Fig. 66   ABS wiring circuit (Part 2 of 4). 1991 98 & Park Ave.

Fig. 66   ABS wiring circuit (Part 3 of 4). 1991 98 & Park Ave.

Fig. 66   ABS wiring circuit (Part 4 of 4). 1991 98 & Park Ave.

Fig. 67   ABS wiring circuit (Part 1 of 3). 1991 DeVille/Fleetwood (FWD)

Fig. 67   ABS wiring circuit (Part 2 of 3). 1991 DeVille/Fleetwood (FWD)

Fig. 67   ABS wiring circuit (Part 3 of 3). 1991 DeVille/Fleetwood (FWD)

Fig. 68   ABS wiring circuit (Part 1 of 5). 1992–93 Bonneville, 88 & LeSabre

Fig. 68   ABS wiring circuit (Part 2 of 5). 1992–93 Bonneville, 88 & LeSabre

BONNEVILLE, DEVILLE, EIGHTY EIGHT, LESABRE, NINETY EIGHT, PARK AVENUE & 1991-92 FLEETWOOD (FWD) (TEVES TYPE)   **23-279**

Fig. 68   ABS wiring circuit (Part 3 of 5). 1992–93 Bonneville, 88 & LeSabre

Fig. 68   ABS wiring circuit (Part 4 of 5). 1992–93 Bonneville, 88 & LeSabre

Fig. 68 ABS wiring circuit (Part 5 of 5). 1992—93 Bonneville, 88 & LeSabre

Fig. 69 ABS wiring circuit (Part 1 of 3). 1992 98 & Park Ave.

Fig. 69   ABS wiring circuit (Part 2 of 3). 1992 98 & Park Ave.

Fig. 69   ABS wiring circuit (Part 3 of 3). 1992 98 & Park Ave.

Fig. 70   ABS wiring circuit (Part 1 of 5). 1992 DeVille/Fleetwood (FWD)

Fig. 70   ABS wiring circuit (Part 3 of 5). 1992 DeVille/Fleetwood (FWD)

Fig. 70   ABS wiring circuit (Part 2 of 5). 1992 DeVille/Fleetwood (FWD)

Fig. 70   ABS wiring circuit (Part 4 of 5). 1992 DeVille/Fleetwood (FWD)

Fig. 70   ABS wiring circuit (Part 5 of 5). 1992 DeVille/Fleetwood (FWD)

Fig. 71 ABS wiring circuit (Part 1 of 6). 1993 LeSabre & Park Avenue

Fig. 71 ABS wiring circuit (Part 2 of 6). 1993 LeSabre & Park Avenue

Fig. 71 ABS wiring circuit (Part 3 of 6). 1993 LeSabre & Park Avenue

Fig. 71 ABS wiring circuit (Part 4 of 6). 1993 LeSabre & Park Avenue

Fig. 71   ABS wiring circuit (Part 6 of 6). 1993 LeSabre & Park Avenue

Fig. 71   ABS wiring circuit (Part 5 of 6). 1993 LeSabre & Park Avenue

Fig. 72   ABS wiring circuit (Part 1 of 7). 1993 88 & 98

Fig. 72   ABS wiring circuit (Part 2 of 7). 1993 88 & 98

Fig. 72   ABS wiring circuit (Part 3 of 7). 1993 88 & 98

Fig. 72   ABS wiring circuit (Part 4 of 7). 1993 88 & 98

Fig. 72   ABS wiring circuit (Part 5 of 7). 1993 98 Elite Series w/TCS

Fig. 72 ABS wiring circuit (Part 6 of 7). 1993 88 w/TCS

Fig. 72 ABS wiring circuit (Part 7 of 7). 1993 Touring Sedan w/TCS

① FILLING AND MANUAL BLEEDING PROCEDURE

NOTICE:
- The reservoir must be properly filled to insure correct operating conditions. However, brake fluid addition is not usually necessary unless there is a leak, indicated by the BRAKE warning indicator, or the system is being serviced.
- Use only Delco Supreme 11 Brake Fluid or equivalent DOT 3 brake fluid from a clean, sealed container.
- Thoroughly clean master cylinder reservoir cover before removal to avoid getting dirt in reservoir.
1. Fill master cylinder reservoir to proper level with brake fluid and keep at least one-half full of fluid during bleeding operation.
- Have an assistant press brake pedal during bleeding operation.
- IMPORTANT: Master cylinder reservoir cap must be installed before pressing on brake pedal during bleeding operation. This prevents the reservoir from spraying brake fluid.
- If master cylinder is known or suspected to have air in the bore, continue to step 2; otherwise go to step 9.
2. Loosen forward (secondary) brake pipe connection at master cylinder.
3. Allow brake fluid to flow from connector port. Maintain reservoir fluid level.
4. Tighten forward brake pipe connection at master cylinder.
5. Depress brake pedal slowly one time and hold. Loosen forward brake pipe connection at master cylinder to purge air from bore. Tighten connection and then release brake pedal slowly. Wait 15 seconds. Repeat sequence, including 15 second wait, until all air is removed from bore.
6. Tighten forward brake pipe connection to 15 N·M (11 LB-FT).

7. After all air has been removed at forward connection, repeat steps 2 through 6 to bleed master cylinder at rear primary connection.
8. If it is known that calipers and wheel cylinders do not contain any air, then it is not necessary to bleed them; otherwise, continue to step 9.
9. If all the wheel circuits must be bled, use the following sequence: RH rear, LH rear, RH front, LH front.
10. Raise vehicle and suitable support.
11. Remove bleeder valve cap and place proper size box-end wrench, J 28434, or J 21472 over caliper/cylinder bleeder valve. Attach a transparent tube to bleeder valve and allow tube to hang submerged in a transparent container, partially filled with clean brake fluid.
12. Depress brake pedal slowly one time and hold. Loosen bleeder valve to purge air from caliper/cylinder. Tighten bleeder valve and slowly release pedal. Wait 15 seconds. Repeat sequence, including 15 second wait until all air is removed. It may be necessay to repeat sequence 10 or more times to remove all air. Rapid pedal pumping pushes master cylinder secondary piston down the bore in a manner that makes it difficult to bleed system.
13. Tighten wheel cylinder bleeder valves to 7 N·M (62 LB-IN).
- Tighten caliper bleeder valve to 13 N·M (10 LB-FT).
14. Install bleeder valve caps.
15. Lower vehicle.
16. Fill master cylinder to proper level.
17. Check brake pedal for "sponginess."
- Repeat entire bleeding procedure to correct "sponginess."

② FILLING AND PRESSURE BLEEDING PROCEDURE

NOTICE:
- The reservoir must be properly filled to insure correct operating conditions. However, brake fluid addition is not usually necessary unless there is a leak, indicated by the BRAKE indicator, or the system is being serviced.
- Use only Delco Supreme 11 Brake Fluid or equivalent DOT 3 brake fluid from a clean, sealed container.
- Thoroughly clean master cylinder reservoir cover before removal to avoid getting dirt in reservoir.
NOTICE: Pressure bleeding equipment must be of the diaphragm type. It must have a rubber diaphragm between the air supply and the brake fluid to prevent air, moisture, oil and other contaminants from entering the hydraulic system.
Important: The correct master cylinder bleeder adapter must be used to avoid possible damage to the master cylinder reservoirs.
1. Fill master cylinder reservoir to proper level with brake fluid.
2. Install J 35589 to master cylinder.
3. Charge J 29532 to 140-172 kPa (20-25 psi).
4. Connect J 29532 hose to adapter and open the line valve.

5. Raise vehicle and suitably support.
6. If all the wheel circuits must be bled, use the following sequence: RH rear, LH rear, RH front, LH front.
7. Remove bleeder valve cap and place proper size box-end wrench, J 28434, or J 21472 over caliper/cylinder bleeder valve. Attach a transparent tube to bleeder valve and allow tube to hang submerged in a transparent container, partially filled with clean brake fluid.
8. Loosen bleeder valve at least ¾ turn, and allow fluid to flow until no air is seen in fluid.
9. Tighten wheel cylinder bleeder valves to 7 N·M (62 LB-FT).
- Tighten caliper bleeder valve to 13 N·M (10 LB-FT).
10. Repeat steps 7 through 9 until all calipers/cylinders have been bled. Then install bleeder valve caps.
11. Lower vehicle.
12. Check brake pedal for "sponginess."
- Repeat entire bleeding procedure to correct "sponginess."
13. Remove J 29532 and J 35589.
14. Fill master cylinder to proper level.

Fig. 73   Procedures 1 & 2, bleeding brakes & filling & pressure bleeding brakes. 1993 models

③ ELECTRONIC BRAKE AND TRACTION CONTROL MODULE (EBCM/EBTCM), REPLACE

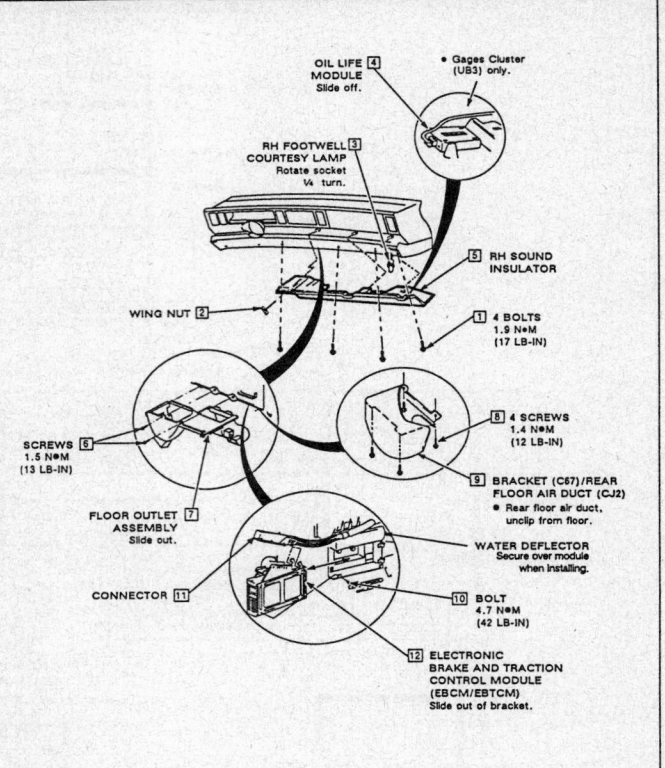

Fig. 74   Procedure 3. 1993 LeSabre & Park Avenue

SYSTEM SERVICE
BLEEDING BRAKES
Refer to **Fig. 73** for procedure.

FILLING & PRESSURE BLEEDING
Refer to **Fig. 73** for procedure.

COMPONENT REPLACEMENT
1993 LeSabre & Park Avenue
Refer to **Figs. 74 through 81** for replacement and adjustment procedures as outlined under -Diagnosis & Testing.-

Except 1993 LeSabre & Park Avenue
ELECTRONIC BRAKE CONTROL MODULE (EBCM)
Ignition switch must be in the Off position prior to disconnecting or connecting the EBCM.
1. Disarm air airbag system as outlined under "Airbag System Disarming," then remove right and left sound insulators.
2. Disconnect floor outlet, then remove bolt retaining EBCM, **Fig 82.**

3. Slide EBCM toward accelerator pedal just far enough to expose connector.
4. Disconnect EBCM harness connector, then remove EBCM.
5. Reverse procedure to install. **Torque** EBCM retaining bolt to 19 inch lbs. Rearm airbag system as outlined under "Airbag System Arming."

WHEEL SPEED SENSORS
Front
Wheel speed sensor is non-adjustable. Left and right speed sensors are not interchangeable.
Proper installation of speed sensor cables is critical. Failure to route cables properly could cause system malfunction due to over-stressing or abrasion. Refer to **Fig. 83**, for proper routing of cables.
1. Disarm air airbag system as outlined under "Airbag System Disarming," then open hood, then disconnect wheel speed sensor connector, **Fig. 83.**
2. Cut strap retaining sensor lead, then raise and support vehicle.
3. Remove sensor lead from brackets, sensor retaining bolt, then the sensor.
4. Inspect sensor face for build up of metallic particles, dirt, grease, or other contaminants. Clean as needed.
5. Inspect sensor face for damage. Replace sensor if damage causes improper operation.
6. If sensor is removed or replaced, coat sensor body with anti-corrosion compound where the sensor contacts knuckle.

7. Reverse procedure to install. **Torque** sensor retaining bolt to 7 ft. lbs. Rearm airbag system as outlined under "Airbag System Arming."

Rear
Refer to **Figs. 84 and 85**, during removal and installation procedure.
1. Disarm air airbag system as outlined under "Airbag System Disarming," then remove hub and bearing assembly.
2. Clean area surrounding sensor housing/interface area.
3. Remove Torx type screws securing sensor, then the sensor. **Do not allow dirt or other contaminants to enter sensor housing.**
4. **Do not add lubricant to bearing through sensor housing opening.** This bearing is lubricated for life of vehicle.
5. **Do not clean grease from toothed sensor ring.** Grease does not effect operation of sensor.
6. Reverse procedure to install. Ensure O-ring is not torn or missing. **Torque** Torx screws to 33 inch lbs. Rearm airbag system as outlined under "Airbag System Arming."

WHEEL SPEED SENSOR RINGS
Front
For front wheel speed sensor ring replacement procedure, refer to "Front Drive Axle, Replace."

④ TCC/ANTILOCK AND CRUISE/SHIFT INTERLOCK/BRAKE SWITCH, ADJUST/REPLACE

CAUTION: THIS VEHICLE IS EQUIPPED WITH SUPPLEMENTAL INFLATABLE RESTRAINT (SIR).

FAILURE TO FOLLOW CAUTIONS COULD RESULT IN POSSIBLE AIR BAG DEPLOYMENT, PERSONAL INJURY, OR OTHERWISE UNNEEDED SIR SYSTEM REPAIRS.

[1] Disable/Enable SIR System, see [13].

MOUNTING BRACKET

Note: Push mounting clip flush against body of brake switch assembly before installation.

Adjustment Procedure
Fully depress brake pedal. Insert brake switch assemblies into modular brake pedal mounting bracket. Press assembly firmly until clicks can no longer be heard and retainer locking tabs engage in mounting bracket. Pull brake pedal rearward until clicks can no longer be heard. Verify adjustment; depress brake pedal. Pull brake pedal rearward to assure no clicks remain.

BRAKE SWITCH [4] ASSEMBLIES
Replace and adjust.

[2] VACUUM HOSE

[3] CONNECTORS

⑤ INSTRUMENT CLUSTER, REPLACE

CAUTION: THIS VEHICLE IS EQUIPPED WITH SUPPLEMENTAL INFLATABLE RESTRAINT (SIR).

FAILURE TO FOLLOW CAUTIONS COULD RESULT IN POSSIBLE AIR BAG DEPLOYMENT, PERSONAL INJURY, OR OTHERWISE UNNEEDED SIR SYSTEM REPAIRS.

[1] Disable/Enable SIR System, see [13].
[2] Remove RH sound insulator, see [3].
[3] Remove I/P lower trim pad, see [6].

STEERING COLUMN

[3] CLIP
Slide on/off with gear selector at NEUTRAL. Note cable routing.

[5] 4 BOLTS
1.5 N•M
(14 LB-IN)

[6] INSTRUMENT CLUSTER
Pull straight out to remove.

Fig. 75   Procedures 4 & 5. 1993 LeSabre & Park Avenue

⑥ I/P LOWER TRIM PAD, REPLACE

[7] PARK BRAKE CABLE

[11] I/P LOWER TRIM PAD

[10] CONNECTOR

[9] SCREW
1.9 N•M
(17 LB-IN)

[8] 7 SCREWS
10 N•M
(89 LB-IN)

I/P ACCESSORY TRIM PLATE [6]

10 BOLTS [5]
1.9 N•M
(17 LB-IN)

[4] I/P COMPARTMENT

I/P LOWER TRIM PLATE [1]
Pry out carefully.

4 AIR VENT [2] DEFLECTORS

[3] 6 BOLTS
1.9 N•M
(17 LB-IN)

Fig. 76   Procedure 6. 1993 LeSabre & Park Avenue

⑦ PRESSURE MODULATOR VALVE (PMV) ASSEMBLY, REPLACE

• See [1] or [2] Filling And Bleeding Procedure after installation.

[1] Remove air cleaner assembly.

MASTER CYLINDER [2] RESERVOIR HOSE
Plug hose to prevent escape of brake fluid.

[8] BOLTS
27 N•M
(20 LB-FT)

[11] BRACKET
Remove bracket for transfer to new assembly.

3 CONNECTORS [3]

[10] 3 NUTS
20 N•M
(15 LB-FT)

[9] PRESSURE MODULATOR VALVE (PMV) ASSEMBLY

[5] 4 BRAKE PIPES
Use a back up wrench.
15 N•M (11 LB-FT)

[7] BOLT
27 N•M
(20 LB-FT)

[6] Remove LH splash shield.

[4] 2 BRAKE PIPES
Use a back up wrench.
15 N•M (11 LB-FT)

Fig. 77   Procedure 7. 1993 LeSabre & Park Avenue

⑧ MASTER CYLINDER RESERVOIR, REPLACE

• Before installing reservoir, clean with denatured alcohol.

[3] CLAMP

[5] BRAKE MASTER CYLINDER RESERVOIR (brake fluid level switch inside and is serviced as part of reservoir). Tap back spring slotted pins until clear of reservoir to remove.

[4] HOSE

[2] CONNECTOR

BRAKE MASTER CYLINDER

• Plug hose with 15.5 MM (5/8 In.) plug to prevent escape of brake fluid.
• Recover brake fluid from reservoir.

RETAINER [1]

[6] 2 SEALS
Lubricate new seals with brake fluid when installing.

• See [1] or [2] Filling and Bleeding Procedure after installation.

⑨ PRESSURE MODULATOR VALVE (PMV) ASSEMBLY RESERVOIR, REPLACE

MASTER CYLINDER [3] RESERVOIR HOSE
Plug hose with 15.5 MM (5/8 In.) plug to prevent escape of brake fluid.

[5] Before installing, clean reservoir and ports with denatured alcohol.

• See [1] or [2] Filling and Bleeding Procedure after installation.

[2] CLAMP

CONNECTOR [1]

BRAKE HYDRAULIC UNIT RESERVOIR [4]
(fluid level switch inside and is serviced as part of reservoir).

[5] 3 SEALS
Lubricate new seals with clean brake fluid when installing.

Fig. 78   Procedures 8 & 9. 1993 LeSabre & Park Avenue

10 FRONT WHEEL SPEED SENSOR, REPLACE

1 Raise vehicle

1 CONNECTOR

3 Remove hub and bearing assembly.
- Clean all dirt and debris from sensor housing/interface area.

Wheel Speed Sensor Slinger

Screwdriver

Wheel Speed Sensor

Hub and Bearing Assembly

Screwdriver

4 FRONT WHEEL SPEED SENSOR

IMPORTANT:
- Do not allow debris to enter bearing when sensor is removed.
- Do not add lubricant to bearing through sensor housing opening. The bearing is lubricated for the life of the vehicle.
- Do not clean grease from toothed sensor ring. Grease does not affect sensor operation.

- Removal:
- Carefully pry off wheel speed sensor slinger using a screwdriver.
- Carefully pry up wheel speed sensor using a screwdriver.
- Clean sealant from outer diameter of bearing hub using only a lint free cloth.

- Installation:
- Place hub and bearing assembly on J 38764-4 (or equivalent) when using press to prevent possible damage to assembly's studs.
- Apply liquid o-ring to outer diameter of bearing hub per instructions in the service kit.
- Use J 38764-1 along with a press to install hub.

Fig. 79 Procedure 10. 1993 LeSabre & Park Avenue

---

11 DISABLING/ENABLING SIR SYSTEM

1 Turn ignition switch to OFF.

DATA LINK CONNECTOR DLC 11

2 RETAINERS 10

LH FOOTWELL COURTESY LAMP 9
Rotate socket 1/4 turn.

LH SOUND INSULATOR 8

I/P FUSE BLOCK Lower. 2

WING NUT 7

3 AIR BAG FUSE 7 Remove.

4 BOLTS 1.9 N•M (17 LB-IN)

5 RETAINER Pull out.

6 YELLOW TWO-WAY SIR HARNESS CONNECTOR
Unclip from sound insulator and separate.

12 REAR WHEEL SPEED SENSOR, REPLACE

1 Raise vehicle

2 CONNECTOR

3 Remove hub and bearing assembly.

4 Clean all dirt and debris from sensor housing/sensor interface area.

5 3 SCREWS 3.7 N•M (33 LB-IN)

6 REAR WHEEL SPEED SENSOR

HUB AND BEARING ASSEMBLY

NOTE:
- Do not allow debris to enter sensor housing when sensor is removed.
- Do not add lubricant to bearing through sensor housing opening. The bearing is lubricated for the life of the vehicle.
- Do not clean grease from toothed sensor ring. Grease does not affect sensor operation.

Fig. 80 Procedures 11 & 12. 1993 LeSabre & Park Avenue

---

13 Information Center, Replace

CONNECTOR 6

INFORMATION CENTER 5

2 BOLTS 2
1.5 N•M (14 LB-IN)

1 2 REVEAL COVERS
Pull forward, pry up carefully.

3 I/P UPPER TRIM PLATE
Pull forward.

3 BOLTS 4
1.5 N•M (14 LB-IN)

14 PARK BRAKE SWITCH, REPLACE

CAUTION: THIS VEHICLE IS EQUIPPED WITH SUPPLEMENTAL INFLATABLE RESTRAINT (SIR).

FAILURE TO FOLLOW CAUTIONS COULD RESULT IN POSSIBLE AIR BAG DEPLOYMENT, PERSONAL INJURY, OR OTHERWISE UNNEEDED SIR SYSTEM REPAIRS.

1 Disable/Enable Sir System, see 11.

2 CONNECTOR

3 BOLT 1.9 N•M (17 LB-IN)

4 PARK BRAKE SWITCH

Fig. 81 Procedures 13 & 14. 1993 LeSabre & Park Avenue

Fig. 83 Front wheel speed sensor replace

1	CONNECTOR, RIGHT WHEEL SPEED SENSOR
2	BRACKET
3	RIVET
4	WHEEL SPEED SENSOR LEAD
5	RIGHT WHEEL SPEED SENSOR
6	BOLT
7	SCREW
8	SHIELD
9	STRAP
10	BRAKE PIPE
11	FRAME RAIL
12	CONNECTOR, LEFT WHEEL SPEED SENSOR
13	LEFT WHEEL SPEED SENSOR

Fig. 82 EBCM mounting bolt locations

1	EBCM
2	STUD
3	EBCM MOUNTING BRACKET
4	NUT
5	SCREW
6	EBCM HARNESS
7	HVAC MODULE
8	EBCM CONNECTOR
9	RETAINER LOCKING ROTATION

Fig. 84   Rear wheel speed sensor replace

1	WHEEL SPEED SENSOR CONNECTOR
2	RIGHT REAR WHEEL SPEED SENSOR LEAD
3	LEFT REAR WHEEL SPEED SENSOR LEAD
4	WHEEL SPEED SENSOR

1	SCREW
2	WHEEL SPEED SENSOR
3	HUB

Fig. 85   Rear wheel sensor alignment

1	PRESSURE MODULATOR VALVE RESERVOIR
2	SEAL
3	PRESSURE MODULATOR VALVE BRACKET
4	NUT: 20 N·M (15 LB. FT.)
5	STUD
6	INSULATOR
7	BOLT: 8 N·M (71 LB. IN.)
8	PRESSURE MODULATOR VALVE (PVM) ASSEMBLY
9	BRAKE PIPE ADAPTER (SECONDARY) 17 N·M (13 LB. FT.)
10	BRAKE PIPE ADAPTER (PRIMARY) 17 N·M (13 LB. FT.)

Fig. 86   Pressure Modulator Valve (PMV) replace

Rear

For rear wheel speed sensor ring replacement procedure, refer to "Hub & Bearing, Replace."

PRESSURE MODULATOR VALVE (PMV)

1. Disarm air airbag system as outlined under "Airbag System Disarming," then disconnect battery ground cable and the air cleaner assembly.
2. Disconnect fluid level switch, pump motor and valve block electrical connectors from the PMV.
3. Clamp PMV reservoir hose, disconnect reservoir hose, then plug using a 5/8 inch plug.
4. Remove primary and secondary hoses, then the brake pipes from PMV assembly, **Fig. 86.**
5. Raise and support vehicle, then remove lower PMV assembly bolt.
6. Lower vehicle, remove upper PMV assembly bolts, then the PMV assembly.
7. Reverse procedure to install, noting the following:
   a. **Torque** upper and lower PMV assembly bolts to 20 ft. lbs.
   b. **Torque** brake pipes to 11 ft. lbs.

c. **Torque** battery cable to 13 ft. lbs.
d. Rearm airbag system as outlined under "Airbag System Arming."

PROPORTIONER VALVE

1. Disarm air airbag system as outlined under "Airbag System Disarming," then raise and support vehicle, then clean proportioner valve and brake pipe connections to avoid system contamination.
2. Remove lines from proportioner valve.
3. Remove proportioner valve.
4. Reverse procedure to install. **Torque** proportioner valve fittings to 11 ft. lbs. Rearm airbag system as outlined under "Airbag System Arming."

1991 Calais & 1991-92 Grand Am, Skylark & 1992 Achieva, Beretta, Cavalier, Corsica, Cutlass Supreme, Grand Prix, Lumina, Regal & Sunbird (Delco-Moraine VI Type)

NOTE: Wire Code Identification And Symbol Identification Located In The Front Of This Manual Can Be Used As An Aid When Using Wiring Circuits Found In This Section.

INDEX

PRECAUTIONS

AIRBAG SYSTEM DISARMING

BERETTA & CORSICA

The diagnostic energy reserve module (DERM) can maintain voltage to cause a system deployment for up to ten minutes after the ignition switch is turned off and the battery is disconnected. Servicing the SIR system during this period may result in accidental deployment and personal injury.

1. Ensure front wheels are pointed straight ahead.
2. Turn ignition switch to Lock position and remove SIR or AIRBAG fuse.
3. Remove left sound insulator. **Remove** courtesy lamp from sound insulator, if necessary.
4. Remove Connector Position Assurance (CPA), then disconnect yellow two-way SIR electrical connector at base of steering column.

AIRBAG SYSTEM ARMING

BERETTA & CORSICA

1. Connect yellow two-way SIR electrical connector, then install Connector Position Assurance (CPA).
2. Install left sound insulator. **Install** courtesy lamp to sound insulator, if applicable.
3. Install SIR fuse to fuse block, turn ignition switch to Run position and ensure that "Inflatable Restraint" lamp flashes 7 to 9 times, then shuts off.

DESCRIPTION

SYSTEM

The function of the Anti-Lock Brake System (ABS) is to minimize wheel lockup during heavy braking on most road surfaces. The system performs this function by monitoring wheel speed and controlling the brake fluid pressure to each front wheel and both rear wheels during braking. This allows the driver to retain directional stability and better steering capability.

SYSTEM COMPONENTS

Refer to **Fig. 1** for system component locations.

ELECTRONIC CONTROL UNIT (ECU)

The ECU located on the rear righthand side of the engine compartment uses various inputs to control ABS operation and provide information to the ALDL connector for system diagnosis. Inputs to the ECU include four wheel speed sensors, the brake switch, ignition switch and unswitched battery voltage. ECU outputs include three bidirectional motor controls, two Electromagnetic Brakes (EMB), two solenoids, system enable relay and serial data link.

The ECU using signals from the wheel sensors, monitors the speed of each wheel. If any wheel begins to approach a lock-up condition and the brake switch is "ON," the ECU will control the motors, EMB's and solenoids to reduce brake hydraulic pressure to that wheel. Once the wheel regains traction, brake pressure is increased until the wheel begins to lock-up again. This cycle will repeat until the vehicle stops, the brake is released, or no wheels approach a lock-up condition.

The ECU monitors itself, each input and each output for proper operation. If any system fault is detected, the ECU will store a fault code.

WHEEL SPEED SENSORS

These sensors located on the front steering knuckles and under the wheel bearing dust caps on the rear wheels, send a low voltage signal to the ECU. This signal is produced by rotating a toothed ring around the sensor pole piece, which produces a magnetic field that increases and decreases in magnitude.

HYDRAULIC MODULATOR

The hydraulic modulator located on the front lefthand side of the engine compartment controls hydraulic brake pressure during ABS operation. The modulator contains three motors, two solenoids and two Electromagnetic Brakes EMB's. The modulator acts on signals it receives from the ECU.

ABS WARNING LIGHT (AMBER)

The ABS warning light operates on a signal it receives from the ECU. If the ECU detects a fault that does not interfere immediately with ABS operation, the ABS warning lamp will flash. However, ABS operation will continue. If the ECU detects a fault that does interfere with ABS operation, the ABS warning lamp will stay lit and ABS operation will be suspended until the fault is repaired. In any case, the warning lamp is indicating that the system be serviced as soon as possible.

BRAKE WARNING LAMP (RED)

This warning lamp can be activated by a low brake fluid condition, a closed parking brake switch, a bulb test switch section of the ignition switch is closed or under the control of the ECU when certain ABS codes are set.

1 RIGHT FRONT WHEEL SPEED SENSOR	**8** LEFT REAR WHEEL SPEED SENSOR
2 ECU	**9** I/P HARNESS
3 ECM HARD SHELL CONNECTOR	**10** ENGINE HARNESS
4 BODY EXTENSION HARNESS	**11** SENSOR HARNESS
5 REAR BODY PASS THROUGH	**12** LEFT FRONT WHEEL SPEED SENSOR
6 RIGHT REAR WHEEL SPEED SENSOR	**13** ABS HYDRAULIC MODULATOR ASSEMBLY
7 REAR AXLE HARNESS	**14** ABS SOLENOIDS

Fig. 1 ABS system components

DIAGNOSIS & TESTING
System Testing

On Beretta and Corsica models, prior to service disarm airbag as outlined under "Airbag System Disarming." Once service is complete rearm airbag system as outlined under "Airbag System Arming."

This system contains a sophisticated onboard diagnostics that can be accessed with a bidirectional "SCAN" tool. **To properly diagnose the ABS system a GM TECH 1 bidirectional scan tool or suitable equivalent is necessary.** The scan tool can be used to identify system faults as specifically as possible including whether or not the fault is intermittent. The scan tool can also be used to monitor the input and output signals of the ABS Module, manually control system components and perform automated functional tests. Using the scan tool, allows for accurate fault confirmation and repair verification.

DIAGNOSTIC PROCEDURE

When performing diagnostic procedures on these systems refer to **Figs. 2 through 9** for ABS system wiring and **Figs. 6 through 17** for ECU connector terminal identification.

In order to properly diagnose and repair this system the following steps should be followed in order. Failure to follow the procedure in order could result in loss of diagnostic data.

1. Connect GM TECH 1 or suitable equivalent to ALDL connector, then read all current and history diagnostic codes. Refer to **Fig. 18** for scan tool operation. **Be sure to note which codes are current code failures. Do not clear codes unless directed to do so.**
2. Read "CODE HISTORY" data, note diagnostic codes stored and their frequency of failure. Ensure to note the last failure code entered and the conditions present when the failure occurred. This last failure code should be the starting point for diagnosis and repair.
3. Before beginning service on this system, perform the following preliminary inspection:
   a. Check master cylinder for proper brake fluid level.
   b. Inspect hydraulic modulator for any leaks or wiring damage.
   c. Inspect brakes at all four wheels to ensure that no drag exists and that brakes are operating normally.
   d. Check wheel bearings for any excessive wear or damage.
   e. Inspect wheel speed sensors for correct air gap, solid sensor attachment, damaged toothed ring or damaged wiring. Refer to "Wheel Sensors, Replace."
   f. Check CV joint for proper operation and alignment.
4. When plugged into the ALDL connector the TECH 1 scan tool can display ABS data, display and clear ABS trouble codes, control ABS components, perform diagnostic testing for intermittent conditions. The TECH 1 uses five different test modes to aid in diagnosis. Use the following TECH 1 diagnostic modes when servicing this system:

a. **MODE F0: DATA LIST:** In this mode the SCAN tool continuously monitors wheel speed data, brake switch status and other inputs and outputs.

b. **MODE F1: CODE HISTORY:** In this mode, fault code history data is displayed. This includes how many ignition cycles since the fault code occurred and other ABS information.

c. **MODE F2: TROUBLE CODES:** In this mode both current and history codes can be displayed or cleared.

d. **MODE F3: ABS SNAPSHOT:** In this mode, SCAN tool captures ABS data before and after a fault occurrence or a forced manual trigger.

e. **MODE F4: ABS TESTS:** In this mode, SCAN tool performs hydraulic modulator functional tests to assist in problem isolation during troubleshooting.

5. Refer to **Figs. 19 through 24** for diagnostic circuit check and warning lamp diagnosis. Refer to **Figs. 26 through 197** for ABS system code diagnosis and repair.

6. If no codes are present, or mechanical component failure codes are present, perform automated modulator test using the SCAN tool to isolate the cause of the problem. If the failure is intermittent and not reproducible, test drive vehicle while using the automatic snapshot feature of the SCAN tool. Perform normal acceleration, stopping and turning maneuvers. If this does not reproduce the fault, perform an ABS stop from approximately 30-50 mph while triggering an ABS code. If failure still will not reproduce, use enhanced diagnostic information found in CODE HISTORY to determine whether or not this failure should be further diagnosed.

7. Once all failures have been corrected, clear ABS codes.

Component Testing

Prior to service, disarm airbag as outlined under "Airbag System Disarming." Once service is complete rearm airbag system as outlined under "Airbag System Arming."

Component testing can only be accomplished by using a TECH 1 scan tool or suitable equivalent.

AUTOMATED SELF-DIAGNOSING MODULATOR

If a mechanical modulator fault is suspected, rough ABS performance is indicated, or if any modulator service has been performed, this test should be run to verify the repair has corrected the problem and the displacement pistons are returned to their top most position. The scan tool will prompt for replies to changes in brake pedal position. These pedal changes are a result of modular component control in a specific order that allows component faults to be determined. It is important, when testing the rear channel, that each reply to the scan tool questions be carefully considered. During rear channel testing, pedal movement will be felt as as bump, which is much different than the movement felt in the front channels.

ABS AUTOMATED MOTOR PACK

This test should be performed to identify a potential problem in the motor pack assembly. If a problem exists, the results of the motor pack test will be indicated by the scan tool. If the motor is found to be defective, the motor pack is not serviceable and must be replaced as an assembly.

HYDRAULIC FUNCTIONAL CONTROL

This test is used to verify, ABS hold and ABS release functions. Raise and support the vehicle, then allow scan tool to perform the entire test.

MOTOR PACK FUNCTIONAL

The motor pack must be separated from the modulator to perform this test. Refer to "Motor Assembly" in "Component Replacement." The scan tool will rotate the motors first in one direction, then the other. If any motor does not rotate in both directions, the motor pack is defective and must be replaced. If all three motors rotate, try to rotate each gear on the modulator assembly, refer to "No Gear Movement Test."

GEAR TENSION RELIEF SEQUENCE

When the displacement cylinder pistons are in their top most position, each motor has prevailing torque due to the force necessary to hold each piston at the top of its travel. This torque results in gear tension or force on each gear that makes motor pack separation difficult. To avoid injury or damaging the aluminum gears, this sequence will briefly reverse each motor to eliminate the prevailing torque.

ENABLE RELAY

This test monitors the voltage at the EBCM while turning the enable relay on and off. When the relay is commanded "ON," the voltage should be equal to battery voltage. When relay is commanded "OFF," the voltage should drop below five volts. Voltage will not drop to zero when relay contacts are open due to capacitors within the EBCM. If voltage drops below five volts, the relay is working properly.

VOLTAGE (BATTERY) LOAD

This ABS system can draw a significant amount of voltage when in operation. This test turns on many of the ABS system components to load test the vehicle electrical system. If low voltage faults or intermittent EBCM operation are occurring while this test is being performed. This test will allow monitoring of two separate power circuits for ABS (ignition and battery). If only one of these inputs drops below 10 volts during testing, a high resistance may be present in that power feed circuit.

ABS & RED BRAKE WARNING LAMP CONTROL

This test allows a functional test of the ABS warning light circuit, lamp driver module and brake warning light circuit.

ABS VERSION

This selection allows the display of the EEPROM identification, date code, sequence number and calibration identification.

MOTOR

In this test the motor can be turned on manually for up to five seconds at a current of 10 amps forward or 6 amps reverse. To verify correct front motor operation, the test must be done with engine off and all vacuum reverse depleted. Depress brake pedal as you would during a normal stop. "Release" one of the motors. Brake pedal should move smoothly towards the floor. Rough or jumpy brake pedal movement indicates an intermittent electrical connections within the motor. As the pedal drops, the feedback current should momentarily drop to only a few amps (indicating motor movement), and then become equal to the command current (6 amps), this indicates the motor is no longer moving since the displacement cylinder has bottomed out. With foot still on brake, "Apply" the same motor. Brake pedal should smoothly rise back up to the top of its travel. The feedback current should momentarily drop to a few amps then quickly increase to the command current (10 amps) as the displacement cylinder reaches the top of its travel and the motor stops moving. The rear motor is tested in the same manner, except there will only be a slight pedal drop and slight pedal rise.

If the brake pedal does not move in both directions and no trouble codes are set indicating an electrical problem, monitor the feedback current. If the feedback current is always only a few amps, the motor is free spinning. In either case, the motor pack must be separated from the hydraulic modulator to identify an ESB, motor, gear or ball screw problem.

SOLENOIDS

To functionally test the solenoids, select one front channel at a time. "Release" the motor for the channel and solenoid that is being tested. With foot off the brake pedal, turn "ON" the solenoid. Depress the brake, pedal should be very high and firm. If the pedal goes nearly to the floor, the solenoid is not closing or the check valve is leaking. Leaving brake pedal depressed, turn off the solenoid. The brake pedal should drop as the solenoid is being turned off. If the brake pedal does not drop and the motor is running, the solenoid is stuck on or off. To verify whether the solenoid is stuck on

Fig. 2 ABS system wiring circuit (Part 1 of 2). 1991–92 Achieva, Calais, Grand Am & Skylark

Fig. 2 ABS system wiring circuit (Part 2 of 2). 1991–92 Achieva, Calais, Grand Am & Skylark

Fig. 3 ABS system wiring circuit (Part 1 of 2). 1993 Achieva, Grand Am & Skylark

Fig. 3 ABS system wiring circuit (Part 2 of 2). 1993 Achieva, Grand Am & Skylark

Fig. 4   ABS system wiring circuit (Part 1 of 2). 1992 Beretta & Corsica

Fig. 4   ABS system wiring circuit (Part 2 of 2). 1992 Beretta & Corsica

Fig. 5   ABS system wiring circuit (Part 1 of 2). 1993 Beretta & Corsica

Fig. 5   ABS system wiring circuit (Part 2 of 2). 1993 Beretta & Corsica

Fig. 6 ABS system wiring circuit (Part 1 of 2). 1992 Cavalier & Sunbird

Fig. 6 ABS system wiring circuit (Part 2 of 2). 1992 Cavalier & Sunbird

Fig. 7 ABS system wiring circuit (Part 1 of 2). 1993 Cavalier

Fig. 7 ABS system wiring circuit (Part 2 of 2). 1993 Cavalier

Fig. 8 ABS system wiring circuit (Part 1 of 2). 1993 Sunbird

Fig. 8 ABS system wiring circuit (Part 2 of 2). 1993 Sunbird

Fig. 9 ABS system wiring circuit (Part 1 of 2). 1992–93 Cutlass Supreme, Grand Prix, Lumina & Regal

Fig. 9 ABS system wiring circuit (Part 2 of 2). 1992–93 Cutlass Supreme, Grand Prix, Lumina & Regal

EBCM 24 PIN WORLD CONNECTOR

PIN	CIRCUIT NO.	COLOR	CIRCUIT
1	799	TAN/WHT	NOT USED
2	461	ORN	SERIAL DATA LINE
3	OPEN		NOT USED
4	1289	LT BLU/BLK	R/F ABS SOLENOID
5	830	LT BLU	L/F WHEEL SIGNAL HIGH
6	873	YEL	L/F WHEEL SIGNAL LOW
7	882	BRN	R/R WHEEL SIGNAL HIGH
8	883	WHT	R/R WHEEL SIGNAL LOW
9	872	DK GRN	R/F WHEEL SIGNAL HIGH
10	833	TAN	R/F WHEEL SIGNAL LOW
11	885	RED	L/R WHEEL SIGNAL LOW
12	884	BLK	L/R WHEEL SIGNAL HIGH
13	20	LT BLU	BRAKE SWITCH INPUT
14	50	BRN	SWITCH IGNITION
15	2	RED	B + FEED
16	OPEN		NOT USED
17	OPEN		NOT USED
18	VENT TUBE	BLK	VENT TUBE
19	1286	LT GRN	L/F EMB
20	1287	GRY	R/F EMB
21	33	TAN/WHT	BRAKE TELLTALE
22	879	PPL/WHT	ENABLE RELAY CONTROL
23	852	WHT	ABS WARNING LIGHT CONTROL
24	1288	DK GRN/YEL	L/F ABS SOLENOID

Fig. 10   ECU 24-pin connector. 1991–92 Achieva, Calais, Grand Am & Skylark

EBCM 24 PIN WORLD CONNECTOR

PIN	CIRCUIT NO.	COLOR	CIRCUIT
1	OPEN		NOT USED
2	461	ORN	SERIAL DATA LINE
3	OPEN		NOT USED
4	1289	LT BLU/BLK	R/F ABS SOLENOID
5	830	LT BLU	L/F WHEEL SIGNAL HIGH
6	873	YEL	L/F WHEEL SIGNAL LOW
7	882	BRN	R/R WHEEL SIGNAL HIGH
8	883	WHT	R/R WHEEL SIGNAL LOW
9	872	DK GRN	R/F WHEEL SIGNAL HIGH
10	833	TAN	R/F WHEEL SIGNAL LOW
11	885	RED	L/R WHEEL SIGNAL LOW
12	884	BLK	L/R WHEEL SIGNAL HIGH
13	20	LT BLU	BRAKE SWITCH INPUT
14	50	BRN	SWITCH IGNITION
15	1733	ORN/BLK	B + FEED
16	OPEN		NOT USED
17	OPEN		NOT USED
18	VENT TUBE	BLK	VENT TUBE
19	1286	LT GRN	L/F EMB
20	1287	GRY	R/F EMB
21	33	TAN/WHT	BRAKE WARNING LAMP CONTROL
22	879	PPL/WHT	ENABLE RELAY CONTROL
23	852	WHT	ABS INDICATOR LAMP CONTROL
24	1288	DK GRN/YEL	L/F ABS SOLENOID

Fig. 11   ECU 24-pin connector. 1993 Achieva, Grand Am & Skylark

or off, depress the brake pedal and "apply" the motor for the channel that is being tested. If the brake pedal rises, the solenoid is stuck open or the check valve is leaking. If the pedal drops suddenly, the solenoid is stuck closed.

If when depressing the brake pedal, the pedal slowly sinks to the floor or the pedal rose during the "apply," swap the two solenoids. Be sure to install the electrical connectors so that the left and right front channels are correct. Repeat the test for the other channel (different check valve but the same solenoid). If the solenoid does not check out (pedal also sank or rose during the second test), the solenoid is leaking and should be replaced. If the solenoid does check out, retest the first channel. If the brake pedal should rise or fall, indicating a leaking check valve, the ABS hydraulic modulator would have to be replaced.

NO GEAR MOVEMENT

If all three motors release, the motor pack appears to be satisfactory. Rotate each gear on the ABS hydraulic modulator assembly by hand. The front gears (non-center) should be able to rotate approximately 12 1/4 turns from lock to lock and the rear gear should turn approximately 7 1/4 turns. If the front gear will not freely turn at least 12 turns or the rear gear will not freely turn at least 7 turns, replace hydraulic modulator assembly.

Continued on page 23-454

EBCM 24 PIN WORLD CONNECTOR

PIN	CIRCUIT NO.	COLOR	CIRCUIT
1	799	TAN/WHT	NOT USED
2	461	ORN	SERIAL DATA LINE
3	OPEN		NOT USED
4	1289	LT BLU/BLK	R/F ABS SOLENOID
5	830	LT BLU	L/F WHEEL SIGNAL HIGH
6	873	YEL	L/F WHEEL SIGNAL LOW
7	882	BRN	R/R WHEEL SIGNAL HIGH
8	883	WHT	R/R WHEEL SIGNAL LOW
9	872	DK GRN	R/F WHEEL SIGNAL HIGH
10	833	TAN	R/F WHEEL SIGNAL LOW
11	885	RED	L/R WHEEL SIGNAL LOW
12	884	BLK	L/R WHEEL SIGNAL HIGH
13	20	LT BLU	BRAKE SWITCH INPUT
14	250	BRN	SWITCH IGNITION
15	340	ORN	B + FEED
16	OPEN		NOT USED
17	OPEN		NOT USED
18	VENT TUBE	BLK	VENT TUBE
19	1286	LT GRN	L/F EMB
20	1287	GRY	R/F EMB
21	33	TAN/WHT	BRAKE TELLTALE
22	879	PPL/WHT	ENABLE RELAY CONTROL
23	1290	DK BLU	ABS WARNING LIGHT CONTROL
24	1288	DK GRN/YEL	L/F ABS SOLENOID

Fig. 12   ECU 24-pin connector. 1992 Beretta & Corsica

EBCM 24 PIN WORLD CONNECTOR

PIN	CIRCUIT NO.	COLOR	CIRCUIT
1	OPEN		NOT USED
2	461	ORN	SERIAL DATA LINE
3	OPEN		NOT USED
4	1289	LT BLU/BLK	R/F ABS SOLENOID
5	830	LT BLU	L/F WHEEL SIGNAL HIGH
6	873	YEL	L/F WHEEL SIGNAL LOW
7	882	BRN	R/R WHEEL SIGNAL HIGH
8	883	WHT	R/R WHEEL SIGNAL LOW
9	872	DK GRN	R/F WHEEL SIGNAL HIGH
10	833	TAN	R/F WHEEL SIGNAL LOW
11	885	RED	L/R WHEEL SIGNAL LOW
12	884	BLK	L/R WHEEL SIGNAL HIGH
13	20	LT BLU	BRAKE SWITCH INPUT
14	250	BRN	SWITCHED IGNITION
15	340	ORN	B + FEED
16	OPEN		NOT USED
17	OPEN		NOT USED
18	VENT TUBE	BLK	VENT TUBE
19	1286	LT GRN	L/F EMB
20	1287	GRY	R/F EMB
21	33	TAN/WHT	BRAKE WARNING LAMP CONTROL
22	879	PPL/WHT	ENABLE RELAY CONTROL
23	1290	DK BLU	ABS INDICATOR LAMP CONTROL
24	1288	DK GRN/YEL	L/F ABS SOLENOID

Fig. 13   ECU 24-pin connector. 1993 Beretta & Corsica

EBCM 24 PIN WORLD CONNECTOR

PIN	CIRCUIT NO.	COLOR	CIRCUIT
1	OPEN		NOT USED
2	461	ORN	SERIAL DATA LINE
3	OPEN		NOT USED
4	1289	LT BLU/BLK	R/F ABS SOLENOID
5	830	LT BLU	L/F WHEEL SIGNAL HIGH
6	873	YEL	L/F WHEEL SIGNAL LOW
7	882	BRN	R/R WHEEL SIGNAL HIGH
8	883	WHT	R/R WHEEL SIGNAL LOW
9	872	DK GRN	R/F WHEEL SIGNAL HIGH
10	833	TAN	R/F WHEEL SIGNAL LOW
11	885	RED	L/R WHEEL SIGNAL LOW
12	884	BLK	L/R WHEEL SIGNAL HIGH
13	820	YEL	BRAKE SWITCH INPUT
14	650	BRN/WHT	SWITCH IGNITION
15	2	RED	B + FEED
16	OPEN		NOT USED
17	OPEN		NOT USED
18	VENT TUBE	BLK	VENT TUBE
19	1286	LT GRN	L/F EMB
20	1287	GRY	R/F EMB
21	33	TAN/WHT	BRAKE WARNING LAMP CONTROL
22	879	PPL/WHT	ENABLE RELAY CONTROL
23	852	WHT	ABS WARNING LAMP CONTROL
24	1288	DK GRN/YEL	L/F ABS SOLENOID

Fig. 14   ECU 24-pin connector. 1992–93 Cavalier & Sunbird

EBCM 24 PIN WORLD CONNECTOR

PIN	CIRCUIT NO.	COLOR	CIRCUIT
1	PLUGGED		NOT USED
2	461	ORN	SERIAL DATA LINE
3	PLUGGED		NOT USED
4	1289	LT BLU/BLK	R/F ABS SOLENOID
5	830	LT BLU	L/F WHEEL SIGNAL HIGH
6	873	YEL	L/F WHEEL SIGNAL LOW
7	882	BRN	R/R WHEEL SIGNAL HIGH
8	883	WHT	R/R WHEEL SIGNAL LOW
9	872	DK GRN	R/F WHEEL SIGNAL HIGH
10	833	TAN	R/F WHEEL SIGNAL LOW
11	885	RED	L/R WHEEL SIGNAL LOW
12	884	BLK	L/R WHEEL SIGNAL HIGH
13	20	LT BLU	BRAKE SWITCH INPUT
14	350	PNK/WHT	SWITCH IGNITION
15	140	ORN	B + FEED
16	PLUGGED		NOT USED
17	PLUGGED		NOT USED
18	VENT TUBE	BLK	VENT TUBE
19	PLUGGED		NOT USED
20	PLUGGED		NOT USED
21	33	TAN/WHT	BRAKE TELLTALE
22	879	PPL/WHT	ENABLE RELAY CONTROL
23	852	WHT	ABS WARNING LIGHT CONTROL
24	1288	DK GRN/YEL	L/F ABS SOLENOID

Fig. 15   ECU 24-pin connector. 1992–93 Cutlass Supreme, Grand Prix, Lumina & Regal

6 WAY EBCM CONNECTOR

PIN	CIRCUIT NO.	COLOR	CIRCUIT
C	1284	DK GRN/WHT	REAR MOTOR HIGH
D	1285	ORN/BLK	REAR MOTOR LOW
E	1281	PNK	L/F MOTOR LOW
F	1280	BLK/WHT	L/F MOTOR HIGH
G	1283	BLK/PNK	R/F MOTOR LOW
H	1282	PPL	R/F MOTOR HIGH

Fig. 16   ECU 6-pin connector

2 WAY EBCM CONNECTOR

PIN	CIRCUIT NO.	COLOR	CIRCUIT
A	850	RED/WHT	SWITCHED BATTERY INPUT
B	150	BLK	GROUND

Fig. 17   ECU 2-pin connector

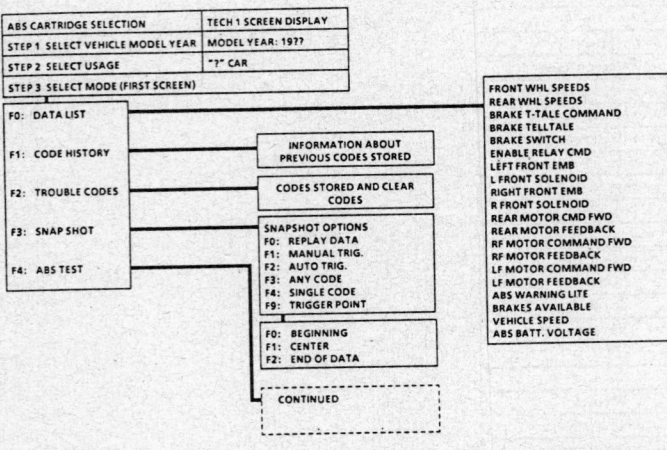

Fig. 18   TECH 1 scan tool operation (Part 1 of 3)

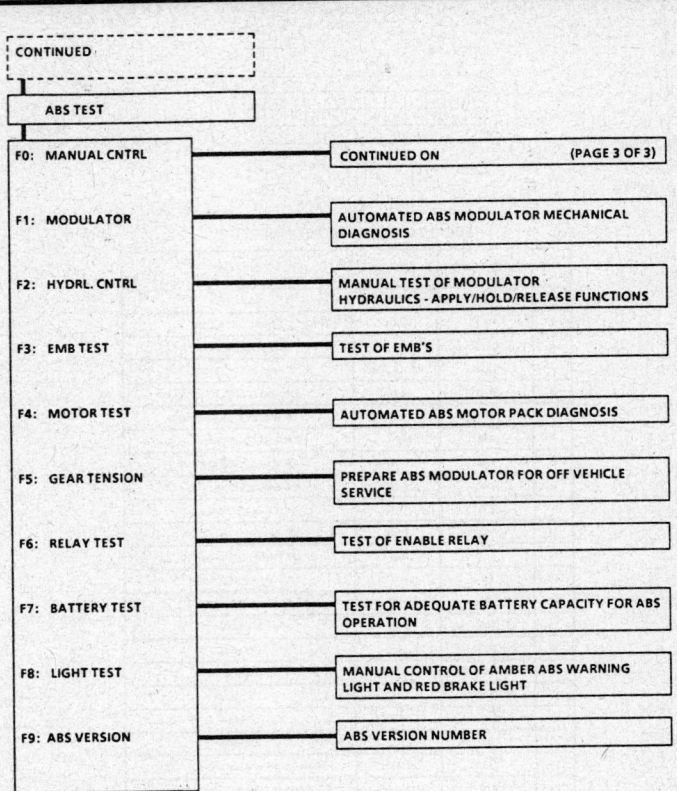

Fig. 18   TECH 1 scan tool operation (Part 2 of 3)

Fig. 18   TECH 1 scan tool operation (Part 3 of 3)

DIAGNOSTIC (TROUBLE CODE) CHART INDEX

Code	Description	Page No.	Fig. No.
—	Diagnostic Circuit Check ①	23-309	19
—	Diagnostic Circuit Check ②	23-309	20
—	Diagnostic Circuit Check ③	23-309	21
—	ABS Warning Lamp On Constantly, No Codes Stored	23-310	22
—	ABS Warning Lamp On Intermittently, No Codes Stored	23-310	23
—	ABS Warning Lamp Off Constantly w/No Codes Stored	23-310	24
—	Tech 1 Displays Undefined DTCs	23-310	25
A011 ④	ABS Warning Light Open Or Shorted To Ground	23-311	26
A011 ⑥	ABS Warning Light Open Or Shorted To Ground	23-373	91
A011 ③	ABS Warning Light Open Or Shorted To Ground	23-374	92
A013 ④	ABS Warning Light Circuit Shorted To Battery	23-312	27
A013 ⑤	ABS Warning Light Circuit Shorted To Battery	23-375	93
A014 ④	Enable Relay Contacts Open, Fuse Open	23-313	28
A014 ⑦	Enable Relay Contacts Open, Fuse Open	23-376	94
A014 ⑧	Enable Relay Contacts Open, Fuse Open	23-376	95
A014 ②	Enable Relay Contacts Open, Fuse Open	23-377	96
A014 ③	Enable Relay Contacts Open, Fuse Open	23-377	97
A015 ④	Enable Relay Contacts Shorted To Battery	23-314	29
A015 ⑥	Enable Relay Contacts Shorted To Battery	23-378	98
A015 ③	Enable Relay Contacts Shorted To Battery	23-379	99
A016 ④	Enable Relay Coil Circuit Open	23-315	30
A016 ⑥	Enable Relay Coil Circuit Open	23-380	100
A016 ③	Enable Relay Coil Circuit Open	23-381	101
A017 ④	Enable Relay Coil Circuit Shorted To Ground	23-316	31
A017 ⑥	Enable Relay Coil Circuit Shorted To Ground	23-382	102
A017 ③	Enable Relay Coil Circuit Shorted To Ground	23-383	103
A018 ④	Enable Relay Coil Circuit Shorted To Battery Positive, Or Coil Has Zero Ohms	23-317	32
A018 ⑥	Enable Relay Coil Circuit Shorted To Battery Positive, Or Coil Has Zero Ohms	23-384	104
A018 ③	Enable Relay Coil Circuit Shorted To Battery Positive, Or Coil Has Zero Ohms	23-385	105
A021 ④	Left Front Wheel Speed = 0	23-318	33
A021 ⑥	Left Front Wheel Speed = 0	23-386	106
A021 ③	Left Front Wheel Speed = 0	23-388	107
A022 ④	Right Front Wheel Speed = 0	23-320	34
A022 ⑥	Right Front Wheel Speed = 0	23-389	108
A022 ③	Right Front Wheel Speed = 0	23-390	109
A023 ④	Left Rear Wheel Speed = 0	23-322	35
A023 ⑥	Left Rear Wheel Speed = 0	23-391	110
A023 ③	Left Rear Wheel Speed = 0°	23-393	111
A024 ④	Right Rear Wheel Speed = 0	23-324	36
A024 ⑥	Right Rear Wheel Speed = 0	23-394	112
A024 ③	Right Rear Wheel Speed = 0	23-395	113
A025 ④	Excessive Left Front Wheel Acceleration	23-326	37
A025 ⑥	Excessive Left Front Wheel Acceleration	23-396	114
A025 ③	Excessive Left Front Wheel Acceleration	23-398	115
A026 ④	Excessive Right Front Wheel Acceleration	23-328	38
A026 ⑥	Excessive Right Front Wheel Acceleration	23-399	116
A026 ③	Excessive Right Front Wheel Acceleration	23-400	117
A027 ④	Excessive Left Rear Wheel Acceleration	23-330	39
A027 ⑥	Excessive Left Rear Wheel Acceleration	23-401	118
A027 ③	Excessive Left Rear Wheel Acceleration	23-403	119
A028 ④	Excessive Right Rear Wheel Acceleration	23-332	40
A028 ⑥	Excessive Right Rear Wheel Acceleration	23-404	120
A028 ③	Excessive Right Rear Wheel Acceleration	23-405	121
A031 ④	Two Wheel Speed Sensors Open. Less Tubular Rear Axle	23-334	41

Continued

DIAGNOSTIC (TROUBLE CODE) CHART INDEX—Continued

Code	Description	Page No.	Fig. No.
A031 [4]	Two Wheel Speed Sensors Open. With Tubular Rear Axle	23-336	42
A031 [3]	Two Wheel Speed Sensors=0	23-406	122
A032 [9]	LH Front Wheel Speed Sensor Shorted To Battery Or Ground	23-337	43
A032 [3]	LH Front Wheel Speed Sensor Shorted To Battery Or Ground	23-407	123
A033 [9]	RH Front Wheel Speed Sensor Shorted To Battery Or Ground	23-337	44
A033 [9]	RH Front Wheel Speed Sensor Shorted To Battery Or Ground	23-408	124
A034 [9]	LH Rear Wheel Speed Sensor Shorted To Battery Or Ground	23-338	45
A034 [3]	LH Rear Wheel Speed Sensor Shorted To Battery Or Ground	23-408	125
A035 [9]	RH Rear Wheel Speed Sensor Shorted To Battery Or Ground	23-338	46
A035 [3]	RH Rear Wheel Speed Sensor Shorted To Battery Or Ground	23-409	126
A036 [4]	System Voltage Is Low	23-339	47
A036 [6]	System Voltage Is Low	23-409	127
A036 [3]	System Voltage Is Low	23-410	128
A037 [4]	System Voltage Is High	23-340	48
A037 [5]	System Voltage Is High	23-411	129
A038 [4]	Left Front EMB Will Not Hold Motor	23-341	49
A038 [6]	Left Front EMB Will Not Hold Motor	23-412	130
A038 [3]	Left Front ESB Will Not Hold Motor	23-412	131
A041 [4]	Right Front EMB Will Not Hold Motor	23-342	50
A041 [6]	Right Front EMB Will Not Hold Motor	23-413	132
A041 [3]	Right Front ESB Will Not Hold Motor	23-413	133
A042 [4]	Rear Axle ESB Will Not Hold Motor	23-343	51
A042 [6]	Rear Axle ESB Will Not Hold Motor	23-414	134
A042 [3]	Rear Axle ESB Will Not Hold Motor	23-415	135
A044 [10]	Left Front EMB Will Not Release Motor, Gears Frozen	23-344	52
A044 [6]	Left Front EMB Will Not Release Motor, Gears Frozen	23-415	136
A044 [9]	Left Front EMB Will Not Release Motor, Gears Frozen	23-344	53
A044 [3]	Left Front EMB Will Not Release Motor, Gears Frozen	23-416	137
A045 [10]	Right Front EMB Will Not Release Motor, Gears Frozen	23-345	54
A045 [6]	Right Front EMB Will Not Release Motor, Gears Frozen	23-417	138
A045 [9]	Right Front EMB Will Not Release Motor, Gears Frozen	23-345	55
A045 [3]	Right Front EMB Will Not Release Motor, Gears Frozen	23-418	139
A046 [4]	Rear Axle ESB Will Not Release Motor, Gears Frozen	23-346	56
A046 [5]	Rear Axle ESB Will Not Release Motor, Gears Frozen	23-418	140
A047 [4]	Left Front Nut Failure, Motor Free Spins	23-346	57
A047 [6]	Left Front Nut Failure, Motor Free Spins	23-419	141
A047 [3]	Left Front Nut Failure, Motor Free Spins	23-419	142
A048 [4]	Right Front Nut Failure, Motor Free Spins	23-347	58
A048 [6]	Right Front Nut Failure, Motor Free Spins	23-420	143
A048 [3]	Right Front Nut Failure, Motor Free Spins	23-420	144
A051 [4]	Rear Axle Nut Failure, Motor Free Spins	23-348	59
A051 [6]	Rear Axle Nut Failure, Motor Free Spins	23-421	145
A051 [3]	Rear Axle Nut Failure, Motor Free Spins	23-422	146
A052 [4]	Left Front Channel In Release Too Long	23-349	60
A052 [5]	Left Front Channel In Release Too Long	23-422	147
A053 [4]	Right Front Channel In Release Too Long	23-349	61
A053 [5]	Right Front Channel In Release Too Long	23-423	148

Continued

DIAGNOSTIC (TROUBLE CODE) CHART INDEX—Continued

Code	Description	Page No.	Fig. No.
A054 [4]	Rear Axle In Release Too Long	23-350	62
A054 [5]	Rear Axle In Release Too Long	23-423	149
A055 [4]	Motor Driver Interface MDI Fault Detected	23-351	63
A055 [6]	Motor Driver Interface MDI Fault Detected	23-424	150
A055 [3]	Motor Driver Interface MDI Fault Detected	23-424	151
A056 [4]	Left Front Motor Circuit Open	23-352	64
A056 [6]	Left Front Motor Circuit Open	23-425	152
A056 [3]	Left Front Motor Circuit Open	23-425	153
A057 [4]	Left Front Motor Circuit Shorted To Ground	23-352	65
A057 [6]	Left Front Motor Circuit Shorted To Ground	23-426	154
A057 [3]	Left Front Motor Circuit Shorted To Ground	23-426	155
A058 [4]	Left Front Motor Circuit Shorted To Battery	23-353	66
A058 [6]	Left Front Motor Circuit Shorted To Battery	23-427	156
A058 [3]	Left Front Motor Circuit Shorted To Battery	23-427	157
A061 [4]	Right Front Motor Circuit Open	23-353	67
A061 [6]	Right Front Motor Circuit Open	23-428	158
A061 [3]	Right Front Motor Circuit Open	23-428	159
A062 [4]	Right Front Motor Circuit Shorted To Ground	23-354	68
A062 [6]	Right Front Motor Circuit Shorted To Ground	23-429	160
A062 [3]	Right Front Motor Circuit Shorted To Ground	23-429	161
A063 [4]	Right Front Motor Circuit Shorted To Battery	23-354	69
A063 [6]	Right Front Motor Circuit Shorted To Battery	23-430	162
A063 [3]	Right Front Motor Circuit Shorted To Battery	23-430	163
A064 [4]	Rear Axle Motor Circuit Open	23-355	70
A064 [6]	Rear Axle Motor Circuit Open	23-431	164
A064 [3]	Rear Axle Motor Circuit Open	23-431	165
A065 [4]	Rear Axle Motor Circuit Shorted To Ground	23-355	71
A065 [6]	Rear Axle Motor Circuit Shorted To Ground	23-432	166
A065 [3]	Rear Axle Motor Circuit Shorted To Ground	23-432	167
A066 [4]	Rear Axle Motor Circuit Shorted To Battery	23-356	72
A066 [6]	Rear Axle Motor Circuit Shorted To Battery	23-433	168
A066 [3]	Rear Axle Motor Circuit Shorted To Battery	23-433	169
A067 [10]	Left Front EMB Release Circuit Open Or Shorted To Ground	23-356	73
A067 [6]	Left Front EMB Release Circuit Open Or Shorted To Ground	23-434	170
A068 [10]	Left Front EMB Release Circuit Shorted To Battery Or Driver Open	23-357	74
A068 [6]	Left Front EMB Release Circuit Shorted To Battery Or Driver Open	23-434	171
A071 [10]	Right Front EMB Release Circuit Open Or Shorted To Ground	23-357	75
A071 [6]	Right Front EMB Release Circuit Open Or Shorted To Ground	23-435	172
A072 [10]	Right Front EMB Release Circuit Shorted To Battery Or Driver Open	23-358	76
A072 [6]	Right Front EMB Release Circuit Shorted To Battery Or Driver Open	23-436	173
A076 [4]	Left Front Solenoid Circuit Open Or Shorted To Battery	23-359	77
A076 [6]	Left Front Solenoid Circuit Open Or Shorted To Battery	23-437	174
A076 [3]	Left Front Solenoid Circuit Open Or Shorted To Battery	23-438	175
A077 [4]	Left Front Solenoid Shorted To Ground Or Driver Open	23-360	78
A077 [6]	Left Front Solenoid Shorted To Ground Or Driver Open	23-438	176
A077 [3]	Left Front Solenoid Shorted To Ground Or Driver Open	23-439	177
A078 [4]	Right Front Solenoid Circuit Open Or Shorted To Battery	23-361	79
A078 [6]	Right Front Solenoid Circuit Open Or Shorted To Battery	23-439	178

Continued

Code	Description	Page No.	Fig. No.
A078③	Right Front Solenoid Circuit Open Or Shorted To Battery	23-440	179
A081④	Right Front Solenoid Shorted To Ground Or Driver Open	23-362	80
A081⑥	Right Front Solenoid Shorted To Ground Or Driver Open	23-440	180
A081③	Right Front Solenoid Shorted To Ground Or Driver Open	23-441	181
A082④	Calibration Memory Failure	23-363	81
A082⑤	Calibration Memory Failure	23-441	182
A086④	ABS Enable Red Brake Telltale	23-364	82
A086⑤	ABS Enable Red Brake Telltale	23-442	183
A087④	Red Brake Telltale Circuit Open	23-365	83
A087⑥	Red Brake Telltale Circuit Open	23-443	184
A087③	Red Brake Telltale Circuit Open	23-444	185
A088④	Red Brake Telltale Circuit Shorted To Battery Or Driver Open	23-366	84
A088⑥	Red Brake Telltale Circuit Shorted To Battery Or Driver Open	23-444	186
A088③	Red Brake Telltale Circuit Shorted To Battery Or Driver Open	23-445	187
A091④	Open Brake Switch Contacts, Decel Detection	23-367	85
A091⑥	Open Brake Switch Contacts, Decel Detection	23-446	188
A091③	Open Brake Switch Contacts, Decel Detection	23-447	189
A092④	Open Brake Switch Contacts	23-368	86
A092⑥	Open Brake Switch Contacts	23-447	190
A092③	Open Brake Switch Contacts	23-448	191
A093④	Test 91 Or 92 Failed Last Or Current Ignition Cycle	23-369	87
A093⑤	Test 91 Or 92 Failed Last Or Current Ignition Cycle	23-449	192
A094④	Brake Switch Contacts Or Brake Switch Input Shorted To Battery	23-370	88
A094⑥	Brake Switch Contacts Or Brake Switch Input Shorted To Battery	23-450	193
A094③	Brake Switch Contacts Or Brake Switch Input Shorted To Battery	23-451	194
A095④	Brake Switch Circuit Open	23-371	89
A095⑥	Brake Switch Circuit Open	23-451	195
A095③	Brake Switch Circuit Open	23-452	196
A096④	Brake Lights Open, Brake Light Grounds Open, CHMSL Open During 4-Way Flasher Operation	23-372	90
A096⑤	Brake Lights Open, Brake Light Grounds Open, CHMSL Open During 4-Way Flasher Operation	23-453	197

①—1992 models & 1993 except Achieva, Cutlass Supreme, Grand Am, Grand Prix, Lumina, Regal & Skylark
②—Achieva, Grand Am & Skylark
③—1993 Cutlass Supreme, Grand Prix, Lumina & Regal
④—1991-92 models
⑤—1993 models
⑥—1993 except Cutlass Supreme, Grand Prix, Lumina & Regal
⑦—Cavalier & Sunbird
⑧—Beretta & Corsica
⑨—1991-92 Cutlass Supreme, Grand Prix, Lumina & Regal
⑩—1991-92 except Cutlass Supreme, Grand Prix, Lumina & Regal

DIAGNOSTIC CIRCUIT CHECK

The Diagnostic Circuit Check is an organized approach to identifying a problem created by an Antilock Brake System (ABS) malfunction. It must be the starting point for any ABS complaint diagnosis, because it directs the Service Technician to the next logical step in diagnosing the complaint.

The "Scan" Data listed in the table may be used after completing the Diagnostic Circuit Check and finding the on-board diagnostics functioning properly and no trouble codes displayed.

A "SCAN" TOOL THAT DISPLAYS FAULTY DATA SHOULD NOT BE USED, AND THE PROBLEM SHOULD BE REPORTED TO THE MANUFACTURER. THE USE OF A FAULTY "SCAN" TOOL CAN RESULT IN MISDIAGNOSIS AND UNNECESSARY PARTS REPLACEMENT.

Only the parameters listed below are used in this manual for diagnosing. If a "Scan" reads other parameters, the values are not recommended by General Motors for use in diagnosing.

"SCAN" DATA

"SCAN" Position	Units Displayed
Front WHL Speeds	MPH/KPH
Rear WHL Speeds	MPH/KPH
Brake T-TALE CMD	ON/OFF
Brake Tell-TALE	ON/OFF/CIRCUIT OPEN
Brake Switch	ON/OFF/CIRCUIT OPEN
Enable Relay CMD	ON/OFF
R Front Solenoid	ON/OFF
Right Front EMB	RELEASE/HOLD
L Front Solenoid	ON/OFF
Left Front EMB	RELEASE/HOLD
Rear Motor CMD FWD/REV	AMPS
Rear Motor FDBK	AMPS
RF Motor Command FWD/REV	AMPS
RF Motor Feedbac	AMPS
LF Motor Command FWD/REV	AMPS
LF Motor Feedbac	AMPS
ABS Warning Lite	ON/OFF/FLASHING
Brakes Available	ANTILOCK/BASE BRAKES
Vehicle Speed	MPH/KPH
ABS BATT Voltage	VOLTS

Fig. 19   Diagnostic circuit check. 1992 models & 1993 Beretta, Cavalier, Corsica & Sunbird

Fig. 20   Diagnostic circuit check. 1993 Achieva, Grand Am & Skylark

Fig. 21   Diagnostic circuit check. 1993 Cutlass Supreme, Grand Prix, Lumina & Regal

NOTICE: DIAGNOSTIC CIRCUIT CHECK MUST BE COMPLETED FIRST BEFORE USING THIS CHART.

Fig. 22 ABS warning lamp diagnosis, ABS warning lamp on constantly w/no codes stored. 1992

- USING TECH 1, COMMAND (AMBER) WARNING LIGHT "OFF."
- WARNING LAMP SHOULD BE "OFF." IS IT?

NO →
DISCONNECT LAMP DRIVER MODULE FROM HARNESS. WARNING LAMP SHOULD BE "OFF." IS IT?

YES →
FAULT IS NOT PRESENT AT THIS TIME.

NO →
REPAIR SHORT TO GROUND IN CKT 875.

YES →
REPLACE LAMP DRIVER MODULE ASSEMBLY.

Fig. 23 ABS warning lamp diagnosis, ABS warning lamp on intermittently w/no codes stored. 1992

- IGNITION "OFF."
- DISCONNECT 24 WAY WORLD CONNECTOR.
- CONNECT A TEST LIGHT TO GROUND AND PROBE TERMINAL "15" OF THE WORLD HARNESS CONNECTOR.
- OBSERVE TEST LIGHT WHEN MOVING WIRE HARNESS AND CONNECTORS. TEST LIGHT SHOULD STAY ON STEADY. DOES IT?

YES →
- CONNECT TEST LIGHT BETWEEN GROUND AND 24 WAY WORLD CONNECTOR HARNESS TERMINAL "14."
- TURN IGNITION "ON" AND OBSERVE TEST LIGHT WHEN MOVING WIRE HARNESS AND CONNECTORS. TEST LIGHT SHOULD STAY ON STEADY. DOES IT?

NO →
REPAIR INTERMITTENT CONNECTION IN CKT 2.

YES →
PROBLEM IS NOT PRESENT AT THIS TIME. INTERMITTENTS COULD BE CAUSED BY INCORRECT WIRING HARNESS ROUTING OR LOOSE GROUND CONNECTIONS.

NO →
REPAIR INTERMITTENT CONNECTION IN CKT 50.

NOTICE: DIAGNOSTIC CIRCUIT CHECK MUST BE COMPLETED BEFORE USING THIS CHART.

- IGNITION "ON," ENGINE "OFF."
- USING TECH 1, SELECT LAMP TEST AND COMMAND THE ABS INDICATOR LAMP "ON." IS ABS INDICATOR LAMP "ON"?

NO →
- IGNITION "OFF."
- DISCONNECT LAMP DRIVER MODULE (LDM) FROM HARNESS CONNECTOR.
- IGNITION "ON."
- WITH A FUSED JUMPER, SUCH AS J 36169 WITH A 3 AMP FUSE, CONNECT TERMINAL "E" OF THE LDM HARNESS CONNECTOR TO GROUND. IS ABS INDICATOR LAMP "ON"?

YES →
MALFUNCTION IS NOT PRESENT AT THIS TIME.

NO →
- IGNITION "OFF."
- REMOVE CLUSTER.
- USING J 39200, MEASURE RESISTANCE BETWEEN TERMINAL "E" OF THE LDM HARNESS CONNECTOR AND TERMINAL * OF THE CLUSTER HARNESS CONNECTOR. IS RESISTANCE 2 OHMS OR LESS?

YES →
- IGNITION "OFF."
- CONNECT TEST LIGHT BETWEEN B + AND TERMINAL "D" OF THE LDM HARNESS CONNECTOR. IS TEST LIGHT "ON"?

YES →
INSPECT ABS INDICATOR BULB. IS BULB BLOWN?

NO →
REPAIR OPEN IN CKT B75.

YES →
REPLACE LAMP DRIVER MODULE.

NO →
REPAIR OPEN IN CKT 150.

NO →
- IGNITION "ON."
- CONNECT TEST LIGHT BETWEEN GROUND AND TERMINAL "E" OF THE LDM HARNESS CONNECTOR. IS TEST LIGHT "ON"?

YES →
REPLACE BULB.

NO →
DIAGNOSE I/P CLUSTER

YES →
REPAIR SHORT TO B + IN CKT 875 AND REPLACE LAMP DRIVER MODULE.

* A (UB3)
J (U39 OR UH7)

Fig. 24 ABS warning lamp diagnosis, ABS warning lamp off constantly w/no codes stored. 1993

NOTE: USE THIS CHART IF ANY OF THE FOLLOWING UNDEFINED DTCs ARE SET: A012, A031, A032, A033, A034, A035, A043, A073, A074, A075, A083, A084, A085, A097, A098.

- IGNITION "ON."
- USING TECH 1, CLEAR DTCs. DOES UNDEFINED DTC RESET?

YES →
REPLACE EBCM.

NO →
MALFUNCTION IS NOT PRESENT AT THIS TIME.

Fig. 25 Tech 1 displays undefined DTCs. 1993

Cavalier & Sunbird

Beretta & Corsica

Achieva, Calais & Grand Am

Cutlass Supreme, Grand Prix, Lumina & Regal

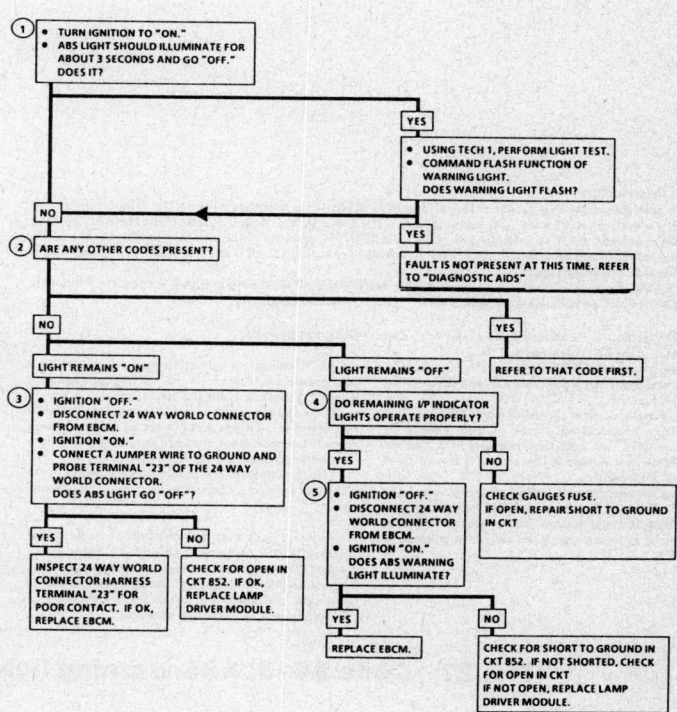

Circuit Description:

This code checks the state of the ABS warning light to identify a situation in which the driver could not be warned of a system fault by the ABS warning light, or the warning light is always "ON." The Lamp Driver Module (LDM) turns the ABS warning light "ON," unless the EBCM provides ground to turn it "OFF." Because of the circuitry in the LDM, only external faults can be detected. As a result, the ABS warning light itself is not diagnosable, only the control line to the EBCM can be diagnosed. In the event of an open CKT 852, the ABS warning light will be on at all times, due to the loss of ground at the LDM input. If the control line is shorted to ground, the ABS warning light is kept "OFF," due to the LDM input being grounded.

Test Description: Number(s) below refer to circled number(s) on the diagnostic chart.

1. Checks to see if ABS light functions properly. Normal operation would indicate that the problem is not present.
2. This step determines if any other codes are present.
3. This step insures that the circuitry from the EBCM to the lamp driver module is complete.
4. This step insures that the ignition circuit to the lamp driver module is functional. An open gauge fuse or open CKT 3, 39 or 875 would result in inoperative indicator lights.
5. Isolates the cause of the ABS lamp remaining "OFF," by disconnecting the 24 way world connector, CKT 852 should be open and cause the ABS lamp to be "ON."

Diagnostic Aids:

An "Intermittent" problem may be caused by a poor connection, rubbed through wire insulation, or a wire that is broken inside the insulation.

The light test function of the "Scan" tool may be used to command the light "ON" while looking for an intermittent problem in the warning light circuitry.

The frequency of the problem can be checked by using the enhanced diagnostic function of the "Scan" tool.

Any circuitry that is suspected as causing the intermittent complaint should be thoroughly checked for backed out terminals, improper mating, broken locks, improperly formed or damaged terminals, poor terminal to wiring connections or physical damage to the wiring harness.

Fig. 26   Code A011, ABS warning light open or shorted to ground. 1991–92

Cavalier & Sunbird

Beretta & Corsica

Achieva, Calais & Grand Am

Cutlass Supreme, Grand Prix, Lumina & Regal

Circuit Description:

This code checks the state of the ABS warning light to identify a situation in which the driver could not be warned of a system fault by the ABS warning light. The Lamp Driver Module (LDM) turns the ABS warning light "ON," unless the EBCM provides ground to turn it "OFF." Because of the circuitry internal to the LDM, only external faults can be detected. As a result, the ABS warning light itself is not diagnosable, only the control line to the EBCM can be diagnosed.

If the ABS warning light control line is shorted to battery or the EBCM control circuit is open, the Electronic Brake Control Module (EBCM) is not able to turn "OFF" the ABS warning light.

Test Description: Number(s) below refer to circled number(s) on the diagnostic chart.

1. Checks to see if ABS light functions properly. Normal operation would indicate that the problem is not present.
2. After the ignition is turned to the "OFF" position, voltage to the lamp driver module should be interrupted. A light that remains "ON" would indicate that voltage to this circuit is from a point other than ignition.
3. After removing the 10 amp gauges fuse, voltage on CKT 852 will be eliminated. If voltage is still present, it would indicate that a short to voltage is present between the lamp driver module and EBCM.

Diagnostic Aids:

An "Intermittent" problem may be caused by a poor connection, rubbed through wire insulation or a wire that is broken inside the insulation.

Code A013 must be currently set before it should be addressed. If Code A013 is set as a history code, proceed to those codes that are currently set before attempting to repair a Code A013 fault.

The frequency of the problem can be checked by using the enhanced diagnostic function of the "Scan" tool.

Any circuitry that is suspected as causing the "Intermittent" complaint should be thoroughly checked for backed out terminals, improper mating, broken locks, improperly formed or damaged terminals, poor terminal to wiring connections or physical damage to the wiring harness.

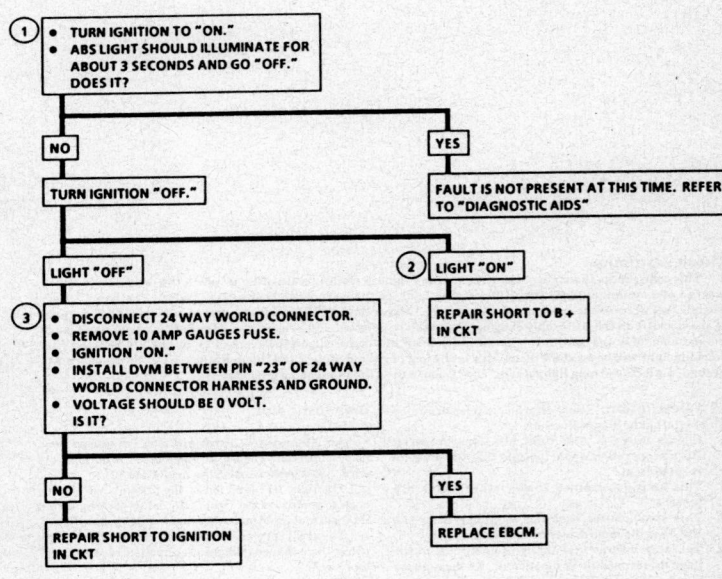

Fig. 27   Code A013, ABS warning light circuit shorted to battery. 1991–92

Cavalier & Sunbird

Beretta & Corsica

Achieva, Calais & Grand Am

Cutlass Supreme, Grand Prix, Lumina & Regal

Circuit Description:

Ignition voltage is supplied through terminal "5" of the ABS enable relay. The EBCM then is able to energize the pull-in coil by completing the ground circuit at Pin "22" of the EBCM. The magnetic field created closes the enable contacts and allows battery voltage and current to be supplied to the EMB's and EBCM, which supplies power to the motors and solenoids.

This code monitors the availability of current/voltage to the motors, solenoids and EMB's. This fault indicates voltage is not available and would therefore not allow ABS operation if required.

Test Description:
Number(s) below refer to circled number(s) on the diagnostic chart.

1. This step would indicate that the EBCM is sensing battery voltage present through the relay contacts at terminal "A." This shows that the relay and circuitry is functional.
2. This insures that battery voltage is available to terminals "1" and "5" of the relay.
3. This step checks to make sure that the pull-in coil of the enable relay has continuity.
4. This checks the ability of the EBCM to energize the enable relay. An open circuit in the EBCM or CKT 879 would not allow the enable relay to be energized.
5. This step checks for an open CKT 850 between the enable relay and EBCM.

Diagnostic Aids:

An "Intermittent" problem may be caused by a poor connection, rubbed through wire insulation, or a wire that is broken inside the insulation.

The frequency of the problem can be checked by using the enhanced diagnostic function of the "Scan" tool

Any circuitry that is suspected as causing the "Intermittent" complaint should be thoroughly checked for backed out terminals, improper mating, broken locks, improperly formed or damaged terminals, poor terminal to wiring connections or physical damage to the wiring harness.

VIBRATION, TEMPERATURE EFFECTS:

Check for vibration effects by performing the relay test function of the "Scan" tool. With the relay test commanded "ON," lightly tap the top and sides of the relay while monitoring relay voltage. If the relay voltage changes significantly, replace the relay.

If Code A014 only fails when the vehicle is initially started in cold ambient conditions (temperature less than 32°F - 0°C), replace the relay.

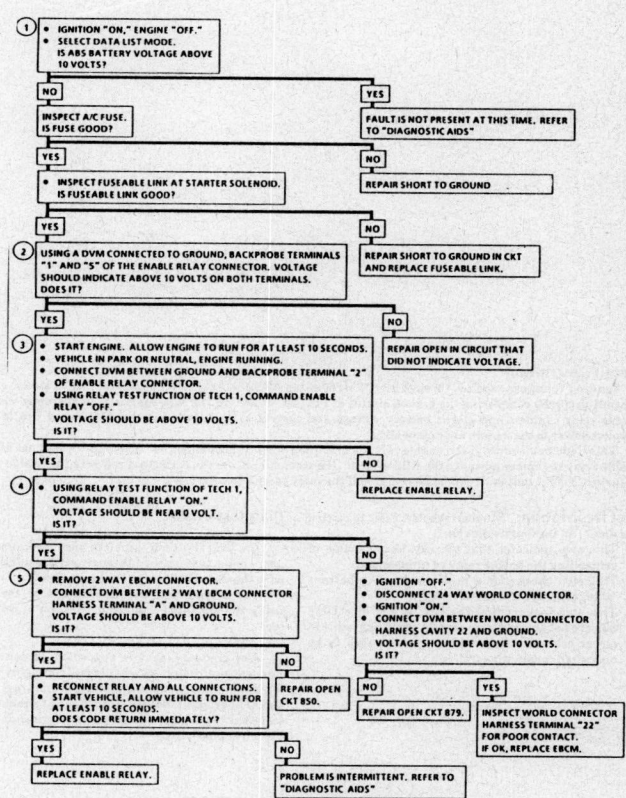

Fig. 28   Code A014, enable relay contacts open or fuse open. 1991—92

Cavalier & Sunbird

Beretta & Corsica

Achieva, Calais & Grand Am

Cutlass Supreme, Grand Prix, Lumina & Regal

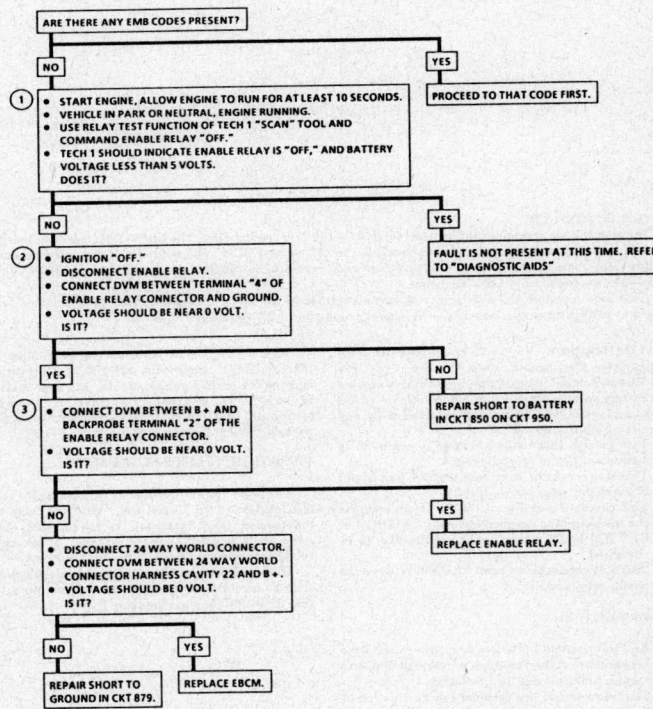

Circuit Description:

Ignition voltage is supplied through terminal "5" of the ABS enable relay. The EBCM then is able to energize the pull-in coil by completing the ground circuit at Pin "22" of the EBCM. The magnetic field created closes the enable relay contacts and allows battery voltage and current to be supplied to the EMB's and EBCM, which supplies power to the motors and solenoids.

This Code determines if the enable relay is energized when it should not be. This fault would not allow the enable relay to remove power to the ABS system. If a second fault were to occur that requires the enable relay to be turned "OFF," that fault cannot be removed if the relay cannot be controlled.

Test Description: Number(s) below refer to circled number(s) on the diagnostic chart.

1. This step indicates that the EBCM is capable of controlling the enable relay as commanded.
2. This step checks for a possible short to battery voltage in CKT 850 or CKT 950.
3. This step insures that the EBCM and also CKT 879 are not shorted to ground. A short to ground in either case would cause the enable relay to be energized constantly.

Diagnostic Aids:

An "Intermittent" problem may be caused by a poor connection, rubbed through wire insulation, or a wire that is broken inside the insulation.

The frequency of the problem can be checked by using the enhanced diagnostic function of the "Scan" tool.

Any circuitry, that is suspected as causing the intermittent complaint, should be thoroughly checked for backed out terminals, improper mating, broken locks, improperly formed or damaged terminals, poor terminal to wiring connections or physical damage to the wiring harness.

Fig. 29   Code A015, enable relay contacts shorted to battery. 1991–92

Cavalier & Sunbird

Beretta & Corsica

Achieva, Calais & Grand Am

Cutlass Supreme, Grand Prix, Lumina & Regal

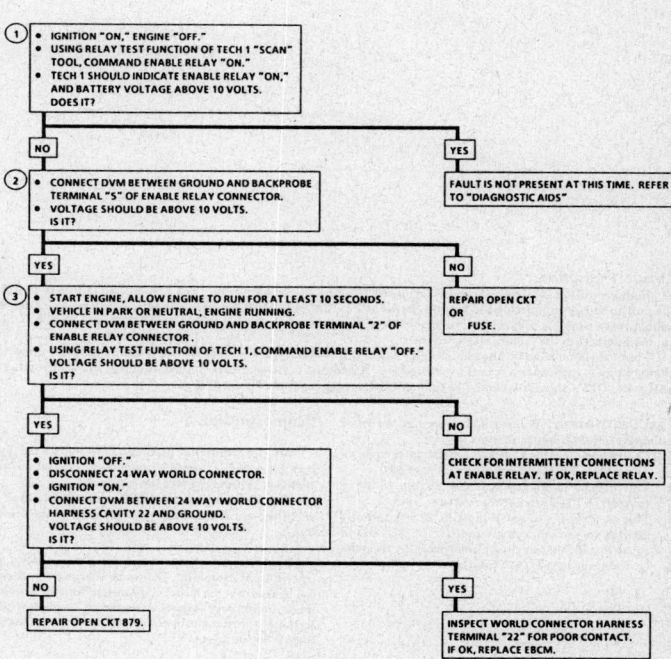

Circuit Description:

Ignition voltage is supplied through terminal "5" of the ABS enable relay. The EBCM then is able to energize the pull-in coil by completing the ground circuit at Pin "22" of the EBCM. The magnetic field created closes the enable relay contacts and allows battery voltage and current to be supplied to the EMB's and EBCM, which supplies power to the motors and solenoids.

This code detects opens in the enable relay coil circuit. An open in this circuit will not allow the enable relay to be energized, thus preventing voltage/current to the motors, EMB's and solenoids.

Test Description: Number(s) below refer to circled number(s) on the diagnostic chart.

1. This step indicates the EBCM is capable of controlling the enable relay as commanded.
2. This step checks to insure that voltage is available to the pull-in coil of the enable relay.
3. This step insures that there is continuity through the pull-in coil of the enable relay.

Diagnostic Aids:

An "Intermittent" problem may be caused by a poor connection, rubbed through wire insulation, or a wire that is broken inside the insulation.

The frequency of the problem can be checked by using the enhanced diagnostic function of the "Scan" tool

If the frequency of the problem is high, but is currently intermittent, check for high coil resistance by measuring between relay terminals 5 and 2 using a DVM. If resistance shows greater than 100 ohms, replace the relay.

Any circuitry, that is suspected as causing the intermittent complaint, should be thoroughly checked for backed out terminals, improper mating, broken locks, improperly formed or damaged terminals, poor terminal to wiring connections or physical damage to the wiring harness.

Fig. 30   Code A016, enable relay coil circuit open. 1991–92

Cavalier & Sunbird

Beretta & Corsica

Achieva, Calais & Grand Am

Cutlass Supreme, Grand Prix, Lumina & Regal

Circuit Description:
Ignition voltage is supplied through terminal "5" of the ABS enable relay. The EBCM then is able to energize the pull-in coil by completing the ground circuit at Pin "22" of the EBCM. The magnetic field created closes the enable relay contacts and allows battery voltage and current to be supplied to the EMB's and EBCM, which supplies voltage to the motors and solenoids.

This code determines if the enable relay is energized when it should not be. This fault would not allow the enable relay to remove power to the ABS system. If a second fault were to occur that requires the enable relay to be turned "OFF," that fault cannot be removed if the relay cannot be controlled.

Test Description: Number(s) below refer to circled number(s) on the diagnostic chart.
1. This step indicates that the EBCM is capable of controlling the enable relay as commanded.
2. This checks to insure that the enable relay or control CKT 879 are not shorted to ground.
3. This step checks to see if the EBCM is internally shorted to ground. A grounded Pin "22" would cause the enable relay to be energized any time the ignition was in the "ON" position.

Diagnostic Aids:
An "Intermittent" problem may be caused by a poor connection, rubbed through wire insulation, or a wire that is broken inside the insulation.

The frequency of the problem can be checked by using the enhanced diagnostic function of the "Scan" tool.

Any circuitry, that is suspected as causing the intermittent complaint, should be thoroughly checked for backed out terminals, improper mating, broken locks, improperly formed or damaged terminals, poor terminal to wiring connections or physical damage to the wiring harness.

Fig. 31 Code A017, enable relay coil circuit shorted to ground. 1991–92

Except Cutlass Supreme, Grand Prix, Lumina & Regal

Cutlass Supreme, Grand Prix, Lumina & Regal

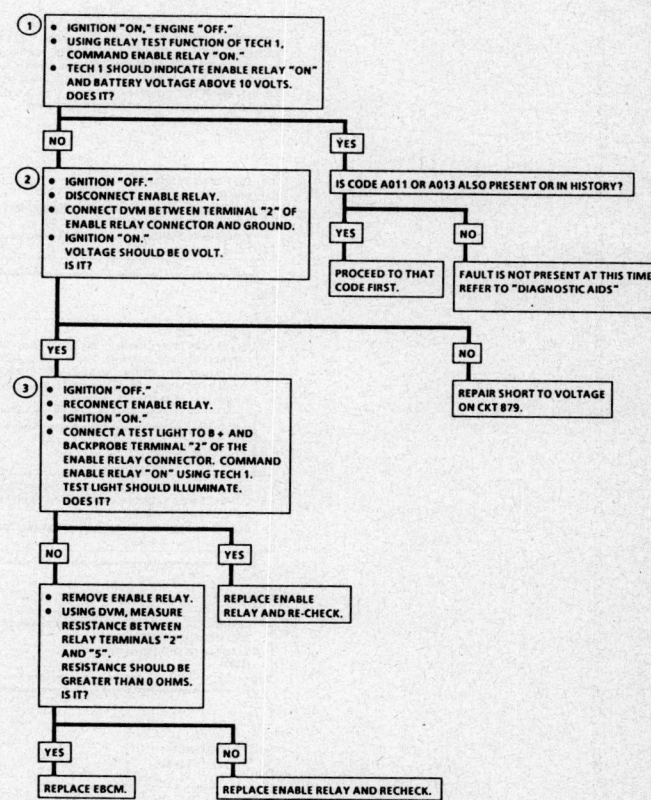

Circuit Description:

Ignition voltage is supplied through terminal "5" of the ABS enable relay. The EBCM then is able to energize the pull-in coil by completing the ground circuit at Pin "22" of the EBCM. The magnetic field created closes the enable relay contacts and allows battery voltage and current to be supplied to the EMB's and EBCM, which supplies voltage to the motors and solenoids.

This code monitors the availability of current/voltage to the motors, solenoids and EMB's. A fault of the type specified above would not allow voltage to be available to the motors, solenoids and EMB's and would, therefore, not allow ABS operation if required.

Test Description: Number(s) below refer to circled number(s) on the diagnostic chart.

1. This step indicates that the EBCM is capable of controlling the enable relay as commanded.
2. With the enable relay removed, voltage should not be available at cavity 2. Any voltage at this point would indicate that CKT 879 was shorted to a voltage source.
3. This step checks for an open Quad-Driver in the EBCM.

Diagnostic Aids:

An "Intermittent" problem may be caused by a poor connection, rubbed through wire insulation, or a wire that is broken inside the insulation.

The frequency of the problem can be checked by using the enhanced diagnostic function of the "Scan" tool

Any circuitry, that is suspected as causing the intermittent complaint, should be thoroughly checked for backed out terminals, improper mating, broken locks, improperly formed or damaged terminals, poor terminal to wiring connections or physical damage to the wiring harness.

Fig. 32   Code A018, enable relay coil circuit shorted to battery positive or coil has zero ohms. 1991–92

Except Cutlass Supreme, Grand Prix, Lumina & Regal

Cutlass Supreme, Grand Prix, Lumina & Regal

Circuit Description:

As a toothed ring passes by the wheel speed sensor, changes in the electromagnetic field cause the wheel speed sensor to produce a sinusoidal (AC) voltage signal whose frequency is proportional to wheel speed. The magnitude of this signal is directly related to wheel speed and the proximity of the wheel speed sensor to the toothed ring, often referred to as the air gap.

The code detects opens, shorts to ground, and shorts to battery that cause a wheel speed of 0 mph to be calculated by the ABS EBCM. The conditions present to fail this test are: (1) Three (3) wheels are rotating at least 5 mph, and (2) The fourth wheel is 0 mph.

Test Description: Number(s) below refer to circled number(s) on the diagnostic chart.
1. This test verifies whether the fault is currently present.
2. This step is designed to identify a wheel speed sensor or circuitry that is damaged and visibly apparent.
3. This test checks to see that the wheel speed sensor is within proper resistance values.
4. This insures that the wheel speed sensor is not shorted to ground.

Diagnostic Aids:

An "Intermittent" problem may be caused by a poor connection, rubbed through wire insulation, or a wire that is broken inside the insulation.

The frequency of the problem can be checked by using the enhanced diagnostic function of the "Scan" tool.

If the customers comments reflect that the ABS Amber warning light is "ON" only during moist environmental changes, (rain, snow, vehicle wash) all wheel speed sensor circuitry should be thoroughly inspected for signs of water intrusion. Use the following procedure. Spray down the suspected area with 5% salt water solution (two teaspoons of salt to 12 oz. of water). Start vehicle, allow vehicle to run for 10 seconds. If code returns immediately, replace suspected harness.

Any circuitry, that is suspected as causing the intermittent complaint, should be thoroughly checked for backed out terminals, improper mating, broken locks, improperly formed or damaged terminals, poor terminal to wiring connections or physical damage to the wiring harness.

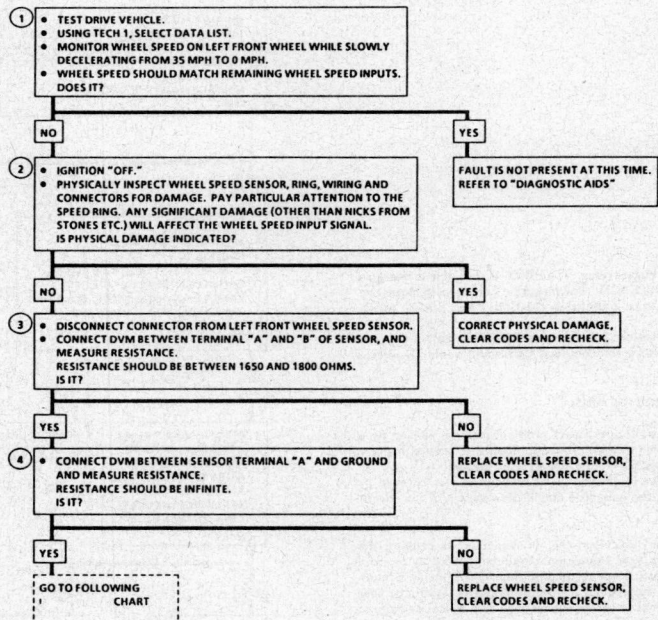

IMPORTANT: WHEEL SPEED SENSOR INTERMITTENT PROBLEMS MAY BE DIFFICULT TO LOCATE. CARE SHOULD BE TAKEN NOT TO DISTURB ANY ELECTRICAL CONNECTIONS PRIOR TO AN INDICATED STEP OF THIS CHART. THIS WILL INSURE THAT AN INTERMITTENT CONNECTION WILL NOT BE CORRECTED BEFORE THE SOURCE OF THE PROBLEM IS FOUND.

Fig. 33   Code A021, left front wheel speed = 0 (Part 1 of 2). 1991-92

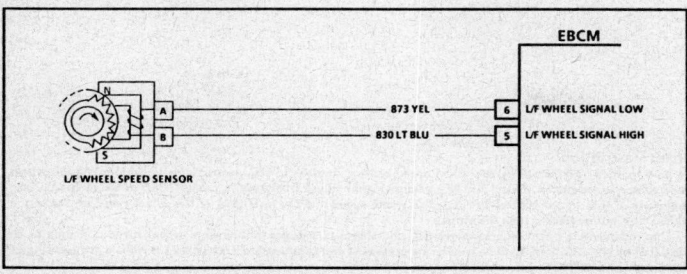

Except Cutlass Supreme, Grand Prix, Lumina & Regal

Cutlass Supreme, Grand Prix, Lumina & Regal

Circuit Description:

As a toothed ring passes by the wheel speed sensor, changes in the electromagnetic field cause the wheel speed sensor to produce a sinusoidal (AC) voltage signal whose frequency is proportional to wheel speed. The magnitude of this signal is directly related to wheel speed and the proximity of the wheel speed sensor to the toothed ring often referred to as the air gap.

This code detects opens, shorts to ground, and shorts to battery that cause a wheel speed of 0 mph to be calculated by the ABS EBCM. The conditions present to fail this test are: (1) Three (3) wheels are rotating at least 5 mph, and (2) The fourth wheel is 0 mph.

Test Description: Number(s) below refer to circled number(s) on the diagnostic chart.

5. This step checks to see if the wheel speed sensor circuitry is shorted to voltage.
6. This step insures that the wheel speed sensor circuitry resistance is within the proper value.
7. This checks for an open in the wheel signal low circuit.
8. This checks for an open in the wheel signal high circuit.
9. This step insures that Code A021 was not set due to a poor connection between the world connector and EBCM.

Diagnostic Aids:

An "Intermittent" problem may be caused by a poor connection, rubbed through wire insulation, or a wire that is broken inside the insulation.

The frequency of the problem can be checked by using the enhanced diagnostic function of the "Scan" tool

If the customers comments reflect that the ABS Amber warning light is "ON" only during moist environmental changes, (rain, snow, vehicle wash) all wheel speed sensor circuitry should be thoroughly inspected for signs of water intrusion. Use the following procedure. Spray down the suspected area with 5% salt water solution (two teaspoons of salt to 12 oz. of water). Start vehicle, allow vehicle to run for 10 seconds. If code returns immediately, replace suspected harness.

Any circuitry, that is suspected as causing the intermittent complaint, should be thoroughly checked for backed out terminals, improper mating, broken locks, improperly formed or damaged terminals, poor terminal to wiring connections or physical damage to the wiring harness.

Fig. 33 Code A021, left front wheel speed = 0 (Part 2 of 2). 1991-92

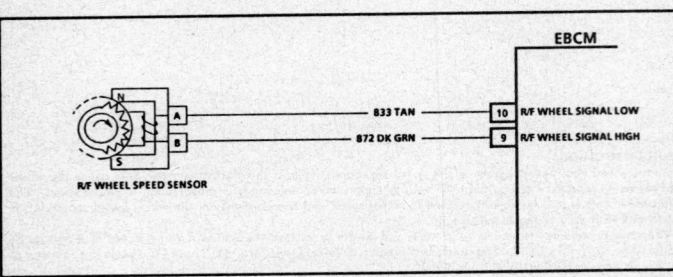

Except Cutlass Supreme, Grand Prix, Lumina & Regal

Circuit Description:

As a toothed ring passes by the wheel speed sensor, changes in the electromagnetic field cause the wheel speed sensor to produce a sinusoidal (AC) voltage signal whose frequency is proportional to wheel speed. The magnitude of this signal is directly related to wheel speed and the proximity of the wheel speed sensor to the toothed ring, often referred to as the air gap.

This code detects opens, shorts to ground, and shorts to battery that cause a wheel speed of 0 mph to be calculated by the ABS EBCM. The conditions present to fail this test are: (1) Three (3) wheels are rotating at least 5 mph, and (2) The fourth wheel is 0 mph.

Test Description: Number(s) below refer to circled number(s) on the diagnostic chart.

1. This test verifies whether the fault is currently present.
2. This step is designed to identify a wheel speed sensor or circuitry that is damaged and visibly apparent.
3. This test checks to see that the wheel speed sensor is within proper resistance values.
4. This insures that the wheel speed sensor is not shorted to ground.

Diagnostic Aids:

An "Intermittent" problem may be caused by a poor connection, rubbed through wire insulation, or a wire that is broken inside the insulation.

The frequency of the problem can be checked by using the enhanced diagnostic function of the "Scan" tool

If the customers comments reflect that the ABS Amber warning light is on only during moist environmental changes, (rain, snow, vehicle wash) all wheel speed sensor circuitry should be thoroughly inspected for signs of water intrusion. Use the following procedure. Spray down the suspected area with 5% salt water solution (two teaspoons of salt to 12 oz. of water). Start vehicle, allow vehicle to run for 10 seconds. If code returns immediately, replace suspected harness.

Any circuitry, that is suspected as causing the intermittent complaint, should be thoroughly checked for backed out terminals, improper mating, broken locks, improperly formed or damaged terminals, poor terminal to wiring connections or physical damage to the wiring harness.

Cutlass Supreme, Grand Prix, Lumina & Regal

IMPORTANT: WHEEL SPEED SENSOR INTERMITTENT PROBLEMS MAY BE DIFFICULT TO LOCATE. CARE SHOULD BE TAKEN NOT TO DISTURB ANY ELECTRICAL CONNECTIONS PRIOR TO AN INDICATED STEP OF THIS CHART. THIS WILL INSURE THAT AN INTERMITTENT CONNECTION WILL NOT BE CORRECTED BEFORE THE SOURCE OF THE PROBLEM IS FOUND.

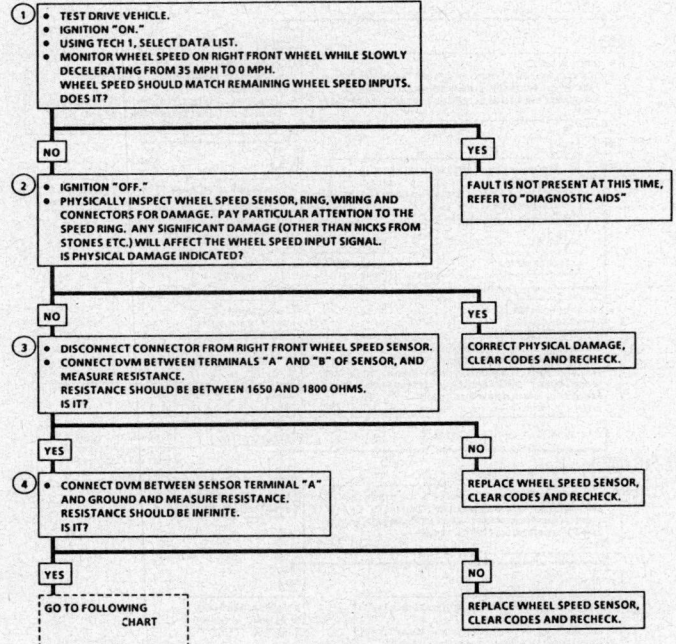

Fig. 34   Code A022, right front wheel speed = 0 (Part 1 of 2). 1991–92

Circuit Description:

As a toothed ring passes by the wheel speed sensor, changes in the electromagnetic field cause the wheel speed sensor to produce a sinusoidal (AC) voltage signal whose frequency is proportional to wheel speed. The magnitude of this signal is directly related to wheel speed and the proximity of the wheel speed sensor to the toothed ring, often referred to as the air gap.

This code detects opens, shorts to ground, and shorts to battery that cause a wheel speed of 0 mph to be calculated by the ABS EBCM. The conditions present to fail this test are: (1) Three (3) wheels are rotating at least 5 mph, and (2) The fourth wheel is 0 mph.

Test Description: Number(s) below refer to circled number(s) on the diagnostic chart.

5. This step checks to see if the wheel speed sensor circuitry is shorted to voltage.
6. This step insures that the wheel speed sensor circuitry resistance is within the proper value.
7. This checks for an open in the wheel signal low circuit.
8. This checks for an open in the wheel signal high circuit.
9. This step insures that Code A022 was not set due to a poor connection between the world connector and EBCM:

Diagnostic Aids:

An "Intermittent" problem may be caused by a poor connection, rubbed through wire insulation, or a wire that is broken inside the insulation.

The frequency of the problem can be checked by using the enhanced diagnostic function of the "Scan" tool

If the customers comments reflect that the ABS Amber warning light is "ON" only during moist environmental changes, (rain, snow, vehicle wash) all wheel speed sensor circuitry should be thoroughly inspected for signs of water intrusion. Use the following procedure. Spray down the suspected area with 5% salt water solution (two teaspoons of salt to 12 oz. of water). Start vehicle, allow vehicle to run for 10 seconds. If code returns immediately, replace suspected harness.

Any circuitry, that is suspected as causing the intermittent complaint, should be thoroughly checked for backed out terminals, improper mating, broken locks, improperly formed or damaged terminals, poor terminal to wiring connections or physical damage to the wiring harness.

Fig. 34   Code A022, right front wheel speed = 0 (Part 2 of 2). 1991–92

Cavalier & Sunbird

Beretta & Corsica

Achieva, Calais & Grand Am

Cutlass Supreme, Grand Prix, Lumina & Regal

Circuit Description:

As a toothed ring passes by the wheel speed sensor, changes in the electromagnetic field cause the wheel speed sensor to produce a sinusoidal (AC) voltage signal whose frequency is proportional to wheel speed. The magnitude of this signal is directly related to wheel speed and the proximity of the wheel speed sensor to the toothed ring, often referred to as the air gap.

This code detects opens, shorts to ground, and shorts to battery that cause a wheel speed of 0 mph to be calculated by the ABS EBCM. The conditions present to fail this test are: (1) Three (3) wheels are rotating at least 5 mph, (2) The fourth wheel is 0 mph.

Test Description: Number(s) below refer to circled number(s) on the diagnostic chart.

1. This test verifies whether the fault is currently present.
2. This step is designed to identify a wheel speed sensor or circuitry that is damaged and visibly apparent.
3. This test checks to see that the wheel speed sensor is within proper resistance values.
4. This insures that the wheel speed sensor is not shorted to ground.

Diagnostic Aids:

An "Intermittent" problem may be caused by a poor connection, rubbed through wire insulation, or a wire that is broken inside the insulation.

The frequency of the problem can be checked by using the enhanced diagnostic function of the "Scan" tool.

If the customers comments reflect that the ABS Amber warning light is "ON" only during moist environmental changes, (rain, snow, vehicle wash) all wheel speed senor circuitry should be thoroughly inspected for signs of water intrusion. Use the following procedure. Spray down the suspected area with 5% salt water solution (two teaspoons of salt to 12 oz. of water). Start vehicle, allow vehicle to run for 10 seconds. If code returns immediately, replace suspected harness.

Any circuitry, that is suspected as causing the intermittent complaint, should be thoroughly checked for backed out terminals, improper mating, broken locks, improperly formed or damaged terminals, poor terminal to wiring connections or physical damage to the wiring harness.

Fig. 35   Code A023, left rear wheel speed = 0 (Part 1 of 2). 1991–92

Cavalier & Sunbird

Beretta & Corsica

Achieva, Calais & Grand Am

Cutlass Supreme, Grand Prix, Lumina & Regal

Circuit Description:

As a toothed ring passes by the wheel speed sensor, changes in the electromagnetic field cause the wheel speed sensor to produce a sinusoidal (AC) voltage signal whose frequency is proportional to wheel speed. The magnitude of this signal is directly related to wheel speed and the proximity of the wheel speed sensor to the toothed ring, often referred to as the air gap.

This code detects opens, shorts to ground, and shorts to battery that cause a wheel speed of 0 mph to be calculated by the ABS EBCM. The conditions present to fail this test are: (1) Three (3) wheels are rotating at least 5 mph, and (2) The fourth wheel is 0 mph.

Test Description:
Number(s) below refer to circled number(s) on the diagnostic chart.

5. This step checks to see if the wheel speed sensor circuitry is shorted to voltage.
6. This step insures that the wheel speed sensor circuitry resistance is within the proper value.
7. This checks for an open in the wheel signal high circuit.
8. This checks for an open in the wheel signal low circuit.
9. This step insures that Code A023 was not set due to a poor connection between the world connector and EBCM.

Diagnostic Aids:

An "Intermittent" problem may be caused by a poor connection, rubbed through wire insulation, or a wire that is broken inside the insulation.

The frequency of the problem can be checked by using the enhanced diagnostic function of the "Scan" tool

If the customers comments reflect that the ABS Amber warning light is "ON" only during moist environmental changes, (rain, snow, vehicle wash) all wheel speed sensor circuitry should be thoroughly inspected for signs of water intrusion. Use the following procedure. Spray down the suspected area with 5% salt water solution (two teaspoons of salt to 12 oz. of water). Start vehicle, allow vehicle to run for 10 seconds. If code returns immediately, replace suspected harness.

Any circuitry, that is suspected as causing the intermittent complaint, should be thoroughly checked for backed out terminals, improper mating, broken locks, improperly formed or damaged terminals, poor terminal to wiring connections or physical damage to the wiring harness.

Fig. 35 Code A023, left rear wheel speed = 0 (Part 2 of 2). 1991–92

Cavalier & Sunbird

Beretta & Corsica

Achieva, Calais & Grand Am

Cutlass Supreme, Grand Prix, Lumina & Regal

Circuit Description:

As a toothed ring passes by the wheel speed sensor, changes in the electromagnetic field cause the wheel speed sensor to produce a sinusoidal (AC) voltage signal whose frequency is proportional to wheel speed. The magnitude of this signal is directly related to wheel speed and the proximity of the wheel speed sensor to the toothed ring, often referred to as the air gap.

This code detects opens, shorts to ground, and shorts to battery that cause a wheel speed of 0 mph to be calculated by the ABS EBCM. The conditions present to fail this test are: (1) Three (3) wheels are rotating at least 5 mph, and (2) The fourth wheel is 0 mph.

Test Description:
Number(s) below refer to circled number(s) on the diagnostic chart.

1. This test verifies whether the fault is currently present.
2. This step is designed to identify a wheel speed sensor or circuitry that is damaged and visibly apparent.
3. This test checks to see that the wheel speed sensor is within proper resistance values.
4. This insures that the wheel speed sensor is not shorted to ground.

Diagnostic Aids:

An "Intermittent" problem may be caused by a poor connection, rubbed through wire insulation, or a wire that is broken inside the insulation.

The frequency of the problem can be checked by using the enhanced diagnostic function of the "Scan" tool

If the customers comments reflect that the ABS Amber warning light is on only during moist environmental changes, (rain, snow, vehicle wash) all wheel speed sensor circuitry should be thoroughly inspected for water intrusion. Use the following procedure. Spray down the suspected area with 5% salt water solution (two teaspoons of salt to 12 oz. of water). Start vehicle, allow vehicle to run for 10 seconds. If code returns immediately, replace suspected harness.

Any circuitry, that is suspected as causing the intermittent complaint, should be thoroughly checked for backed out terminals, improper mating, broken locks, improperly formed or damaged terminals, poor terminal to wiring connections or physical damage to the wiring harness.

Fig. 36   Code A024, right rear wheel speed = 0 (Part 1 of 2). 1991–92

Cavalier & Sunbird

Beretta & Corsica

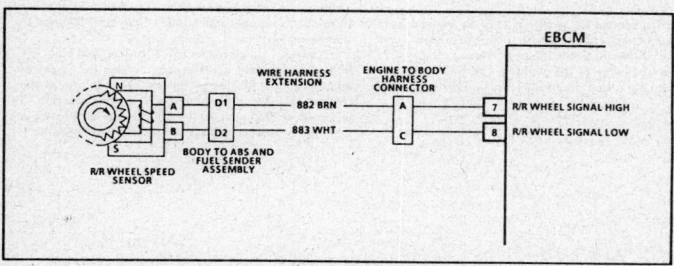

Achieva, Calais & Grand Am

Cutlass Supreme, Grand Prix, Lumina & Regal

Circuit Description:

As a toothed ring passes by the wheel speed sensor, changes in the electromagnetic field cause the wheel speed sensor to produce a sinusoidal (AC) voltage signal whose frequency is proportional to wheel speed. The magnitude of this signal is directly related to wheel speed and the proximity of the wheel speed sensor to the toothed ring, often referred to as the air gap.

This code detects opens, shorts to ground, and shorts to battery that cause a wheel speed of 0 mph to be calculated by the ABS EBCM. The conditions present to fail this test are: (1) Three (3) wheels are rotating at least 5 mph, and (2) The fourth wheel is 0 mph.

Test Description: Number(s) below refer to circled number(s) on the diagnostic chart.
5. This step checks to see if the wheel speed sensor circuitry is shorted to voltage.
6. This step insures that the wheel speed sensor circuitry resistance is within the proper value.
7. This checks for an open in the wheel signal high circuit.
8. This checks for an open in the wheel signal low circuit.
9. This step insures that Code A024 was not set due to a poor connection between the world connector and EBCM.

Diagnostic Aids:

An "Intermittent" problem may be caused by a poor connection, rubbed through wire insulation, or a wire that is broken inside the insulation.

The frequency of the problem can be checked by using the enhanced diagnostic function of the "Scan" tool

If the customers comments reflect that the ABS Amber warning light is on only during moist environmental changes, (rain, snow, vehicle wash) all wheel speed sensor circuitry should be thoroughly inspected for water intrusion. Use the following procedure. Spray down the suspected area with 5% salt water solution (two teaspoons of salt to 12 oz. of water). Start vehicle, allow vehicle to run for 10 seconds. If code returns immediately, replace suspected harness.

Any circuitry, that is suspected as causing the intermittent complaint, should be thoroughly checked for backed out terminals, improper mating, broken locks, improperly formed or damaged terminals, poor terminal to wiring connections or physical damage to the wiring harness.

Fig. 36   Code A024, right rear wheel speed = 0 (Part 2 of 2). 1991–92

Except Cutlass Supreme, Grand Prix, Lumina & Regal

Cutlass Supreme, Grand Prix, Lumina & Regal

Circuit Description:

As a toothed ring passes by the wheel speed sensor, changes in the electromagnetic field cause the wheel speed sensor to produce a sinusoidal (AC) voltage signal whose frequency is proportional to wheel speed. The magnitude of this signal is directly related to wheel speed and the proximity of the wheel speed sensor to the toothed ring, often referred to as the air gap.

This code detects opens, shorts to ground, and shorts to battery that cause intermittent wheel speed operation. Also detected is any sudden change in wheel speed determined to the unreasonable.

Test Description: Number(s) below refer to circled number(s) on the diagnostic chart.
1. This test verifies whether the fault is currently present.
2. This step is designed to identify a wheel speed sensor or circuitry that is damaged and visibly apparent.
3. This test checks to see that the wheel speed sensor circuitry is within proper resistance value.
4. This insure that the wheel speed sensor is not shorted to ground.

Diagnostic Aids:

An "Intermittent" problem may be caused by a poor connection, rubbed through wire insulation, or a wire that is broken inside the insulation.

The frequency of the problem can be checked by using the enhanced diagnostic function of the "Scan" tool

If the customer's comments reflect that the ABS Amber warning light is on only during moist environmental changes, (rain, snow, vehicle wash) all wheel speed sensor circuitry should be thoroughly inspected for water intrusion. Use the following procedure. Spray down the suspected area with 5% salt water solution (two teaspoons of salt to 12 oz. of water). Start vehicle, allow vehicle to run for 10 seconds. If code returns immediately, replace suspected harness.

Any circuitry, that is suspected as causing the intermittent complaint, should be thoroughly checked for backed out terminals, improper mating, broken locks, improperly formed or damaged terminals, poor terminal to wiring connections or physical damage to the wiring harness.

A careful visual inspection of the toothed ring, CV joint, bearing and wheel speed sensor for physical damage should also be performed. If code sets at the same mph every time and wheel speed variation is noted above this mph on the Tech 1, the speed ring is most likely damaged. This can occur at any speed.

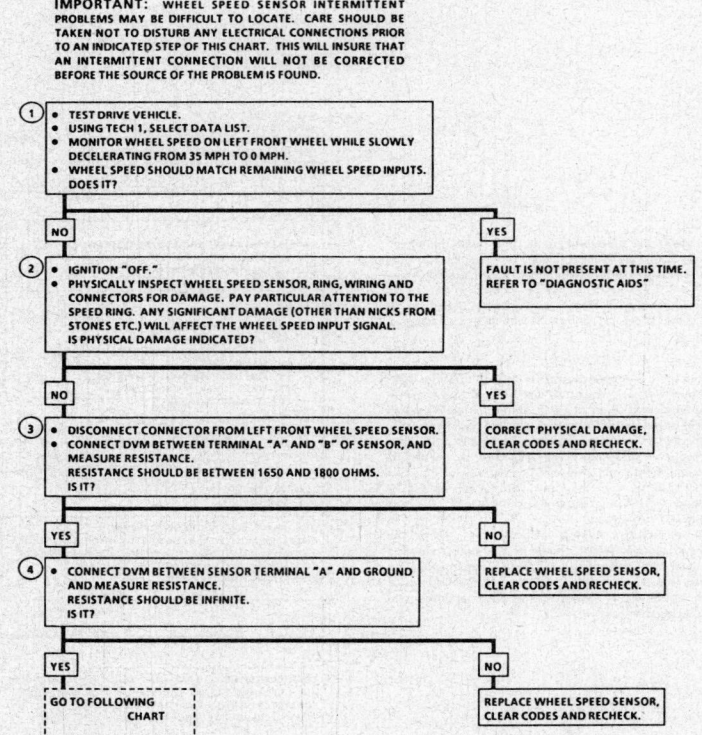

Fig. 37   Code A025, excessive left front wheel acceleration (Part 1 of 2). 1991–92

Except Cutlass Supreme, Grand Prix, Lumina & Regal

Cutlass Supreme, Grand Prix, Lumina & Regal

Circuit Description:

As a toothed ring passes by the wheel speed sensor, changes in the electromagnetic field cause the wheel speed sensor to produce a sinusoidal (AC) voltage signal whose frequency is proportional to wheel speed. The magnitude of this signal is directly related to wheel speed and the proximity of the wheel speed sensor to the toothed ring, often referred to as the air gap.

This code detects opens, shorts to ground, and shorts to battery that cause intermittent wheel speed operational. Also detected is any sudden change in wheel speed determined to be unreasonable.

Test Description:
Number(s) below refer to circled number(s) on the diagnostic chart.
5. This step checks to see if the wheel speed sensor circuitry is shorted to voltage.
6. This step insures that the wheel speed sensor circuitry resistance is within the proper value.
7. This checks for an open in the wheel signal low circuit.
8. This checks for an open in the wheel signal high circuit.
9. This step insures that Code A025 was not set due to a poor connection between the world connector and EBCM.

Diagnostic Aids:

An "Intermittent" problem may be caused by a poor connection, rubbed through wire insulation, or a wire that is broken inside the insulation.

The frequency of the problem can be checked by using the enhanced diagnostic function of the Tech 1 "Scan" tool

If the customers comments reflect that the ABS Amber warning light is on only during moist environmental changes, (rain, snow, vehicle wash) all wheel speed sensor circuitry should be thoroughly inspected for water intrusion. Use the following procedure. Spray down the suspected area with 5% salt water solution (two teaspoons of salt to 12 oz. of water). Start vehicle, allow vehicle to run for 10 seconds. If code returns immediately, replace suspected harness.

Any circuitry, that is suspected as causing the intermittent complaint, should be thoroughly checked for backed out terminals, improper mating, broken locks, improperly formed or damaged terminals, poor terminal to wiring connections or physical damage to the wiring harness.

A careful visual inspection of the toothed ring, CV joint, bearing and wheel speed sensor for physical damage should also be performed. If code sets at the same mph every time and wheel speed variation is noted above this mph on the Tech 1, the speed ring is most likely damaged. This can occur at any speed.

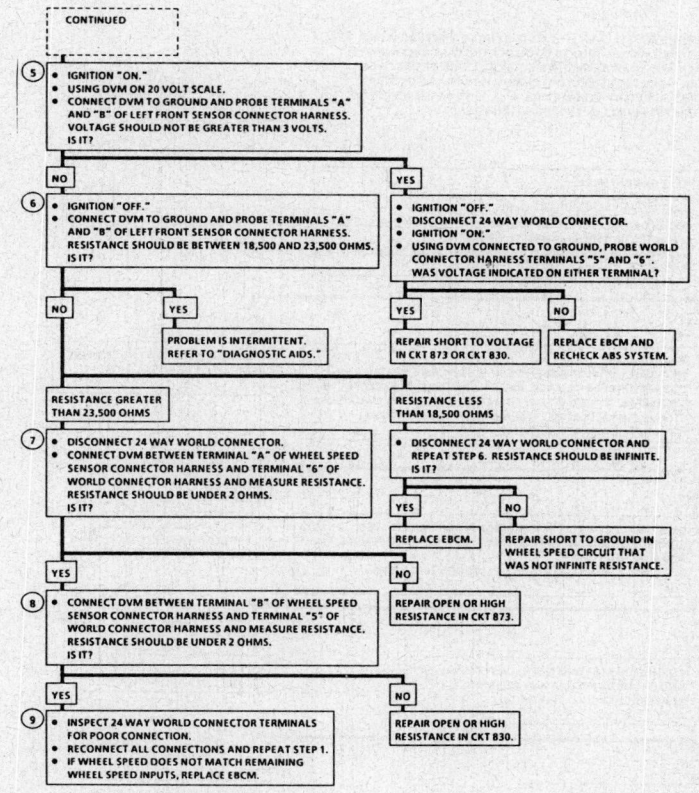

Fig. 37 Code A025, excessive left front wheel acceleration (Part 2 of 2). 1991-92

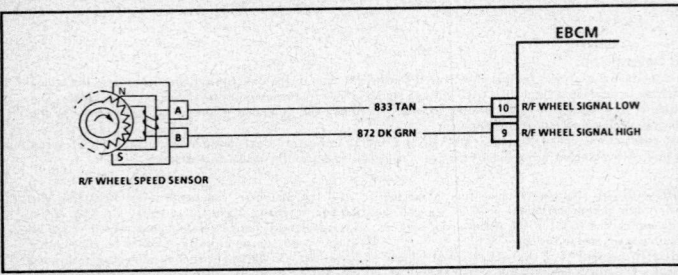

Except Cutlass Supreme, Grand Prix, Lumina & Regal

Cutlass Supreme, Grand Prix, Lumina & Regal

Circuit Description:

As a toothed ring passes by the wheel speed sensor, changes in the electromagnetic field cause the wheel speed sensor to produce a sinusoidal (AC) voltage signal whose frequency is proportional to wheel speed. The magnitude of this signal is directly related to wheel speed and the proximity of the wheel speed sensor to the toothed ring, often referred to as the air gap.

This code detects opens, shorts to ground, and shorts to battery that cause intermittent wheel speed operation. Also detected is any sudden change in wheel speed determined to be unreasonable.

Test Description: Number(s) below refer to circled number(s) on the diagnostic chart.

1. This test verifies whether the fault is currently present.
2. This step is designed to identify a wheel speed sensor or circuitry that is damaged and visibly apparent.
3. This test checks to see that the wheel speed sensor circuitry is within proper resistance value.
4. This insures that the wheel speed sensor is not shorted to ground.

Diagnostic Aids:

An "Intermittent" problem may be caused by a poor connection, rubbed through wire insulation, or a wire that is broken inside the insulation.

The frequency of the problem can be checked by using the enhanced diagnostic function of the "Scan" tool

If the customers comments reflect that the ABS Amber warning light is on only during moist environmental changes, (rain, snow, vehicle wash) all wheel speed sensor circuitry should be thoroughly inspected for water intrusion. Use the following procedure. Spray down the suspected area with 5% salt water solution (two teaspoons of salt to 12 oz. of water). Start vehicle, allow vehicle to run for 10 seconds. If code returns immediately, replace suspected harness.

Any circuitry, that is suspected as causing the intermittent complaint, should be thoroughly checked for backed out terminals, improper mating, broken locks, improperly formed or damaged terminals, poor terminal to wiring connections or physical damage to the wiring harness.

A careful visual inspection of the toothed ring, CV joint, bearing and wheel speed sensor for physical damage should also be performed. If code sets at the same mph every time and wheel speed variation is noted above this mph on the Tech 1, the speed ring is most likely damaged. This can occur at any speed.

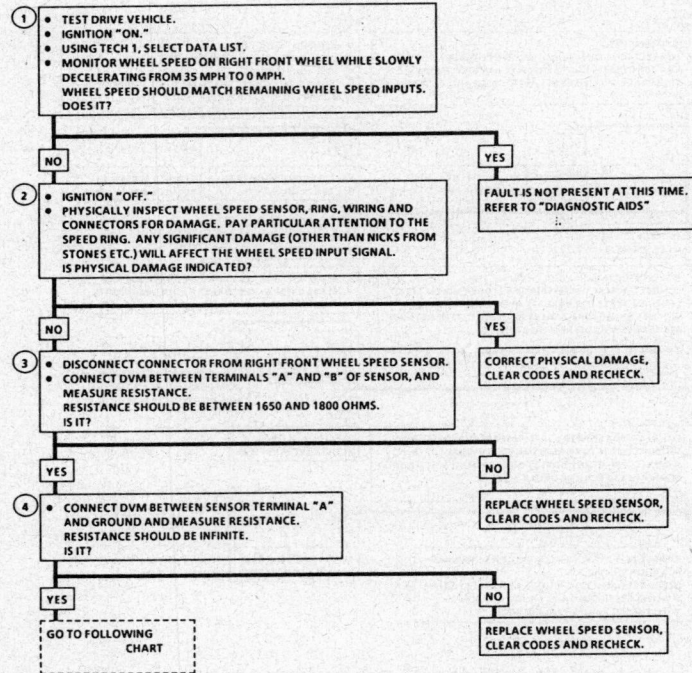

Fig. 38   Code A026, excessive right front wheel acceleration (Part 1 of 2). 1991–92

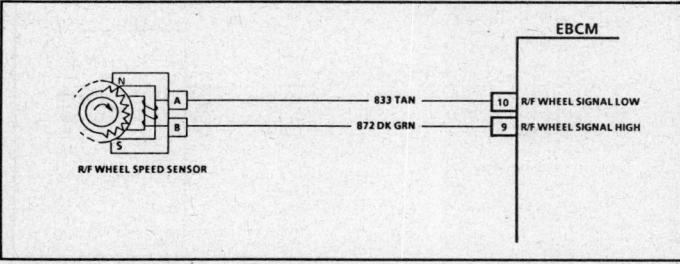

Except Cutlass Supreme, Grand Prix, Lumina & Regal

Cutlass Supreme, Grand Prix, Lumina & Regal

Circuit Description:

As a toothed ring passes by the wheel speed sensor, changes in the electromagnetic field cause the wheel speed sensor to produce a sinusoidal (AC) voltage signal whose frequency is proportional to wheel speed. The magnitude of this signal is directly related to wheel speed and the proximity of the wheel speed sensor to the toothed ring, often referred to as the air gap.

This code detects opens, shorts to ground, and shorts to battery that cause intermittent wheel speed operation. Also detected is any sudden change in wheel speed determined to be unreasonable.

Test Description: Number(s) below refer to circled number(s) on the diagnostic chart.

5. This step checks to see if the wheel speed sensor circuitry is shorted to voltage.
6. This step insures that the wheel speed sensor circuitry resistance is within the proper value.
7. This checks for an open in the wheel signal low circuit.
8. This checks for an open in the wheel signal high circuit.
9. This step insures that Code A026 was not set due to a poor connection between the world connector and EBCM.

Diagnostic Aids:

An "Intermittent" problem may be caused by a poor connection, rubbed through wire insulation, or a wire that is broken inside the insulation.

The frequency of the problem can be checked by using the enhanced diagnostic function of the "Scan" tool

If the customers comments reflect that the ABS Amber warning light is on only during moist environmental changes, (rain, snow, vehicle wash) all wheel speed sensor circuitry should be thoroughly inspected for water intrusion. Use the following procedure. Spray down the suspected area with 5% salt water solution (two teaspoons of salt to 12 oz. of water). Start vehicle, allow vehicle to run for 10 seconds. If code returns immediately, replace suspected harness.

Any circuitry, that is suspected as causing the intermittent complaint, should be thoroughly checked for backed out terminals, improper mating, broken locks, improperly formed or damaged terminals, poor terminal to wiring connections or physical damage to the wiring harness.

A careful visual inspection of the toothed ring, CV joint, bearing and wheel speed sensor for physical damage should also be performed. If code sets at the same mph every time and wheel speed variation is noted above this mph on the Tech 1, the speed ring is most likely damaged. This can occur at any speed.

Fig. 38   Code A026, excessive right front wheel acceleration (Part 2 of 2). 1991–92

Cavalier & Sunbird

Beretta & Corsica

Achieva, Calais & Grand Am

Cutlass Supreme, Grand Prix, Lumina & Regal

Circuit Description:

As a toothed ring passes by the wheel speed sensor, changes in the electromagnetic field cause the wheel speed sensor to produce a sinusoidal (AC) voltage signal whose frequency is proportional to wheel speed. The magnitude of this signal is directly related to wheel speed and the proximity of the wheel speed sensor to the toothed ring, often referred to as the air gap.

This code detects opens, shorts to ground, and shorts to battery that cause intermittent wheel speed operation. Also detected is any sudden change in wheel speed determined to be unreasonable.

Test Description: Number(s) below refer to circled number(s) on the diagnostic chart.

1. This test verifies whether the fault is currently present.
2. This step is designed to identify a wheel speed sensor or circuitry that is damaged and visibly apparent.
3. This test checks to see that the wheel speed sensor circuitry is within proper resistance value.
4. This insures that the wheel speed sensor is not shorted to ground.

Diagnostic Aids:

An "Intermittent" problem may be caused by a poor connection, rubbed through wire insulation, or a wire that is broken inside the insulation.

The frequency of the problem can be checked by using the enhanced diagnostic function of the "Scan" tool

If the customers comments reflect that the ABS Amber warning light is on only during moist environmental changes, (rain, snow, vehicle wash) all wheel speed sensor circuitry should be thoroughly inspected for water intrusion. Use the following procedure. Spray down the suspected area with 5% salt water solution (two teaspoons of salt to 12 oz. of water). Start vehicle, allow vehicle to run for 10 seconds. If code returns immediately, replace suspected harness.

Any circuitry, that is suspected as causing the intermittent complaint, should be thoroughly checked for backed out terminals, improper mating, broken locks, improperly formed or damaged terminals, poor terminal to wiring connections or physical damage to the wiring harness.

Excessive end play can cause this code to set. Check integral bearing for excessive axial end play,

Fig. 39   Code A027, excessive left rear wheel acceleration (Part 1 of 2). 1991–92

Cavalier & Sunbird

Beretta & Corsica

Achieva, Calais & Grand Am

Cutlass Supreme, Grand Prix, Lumina & Regal

Circuit Description:

As a toothed ring passes by the wheel speed sensor, changes in the electromagnetic field cause the wheel speed sensor to produce a sinusoidal (AC) voltage signal whose frequency is proportional to wheel speed. The magnitude of this signal is directly related to wheel speed and the proximity of the wheel speed sensor to the toothed ring, often referred to as the air gap.

This code detects opens, shorts to ground, and shorts to battery that cause intermittent wheel speed operation. Also detected is any sudden change in wheel speed determined to be unreasonable.

Test Description:
Number(s) below refer to circled number(s) on the diagnostic chart.

5. This step checks to see if the wheel speed sensor circuitry is shorted to voltage.
6. This step insures that the wheel speed sensor circuitry resistance is within the proper value.
7. This checks for an open in the wheel signal high circuit.
8. This checks for an open in the wheel signal low circuit.
9. This step insures that Code A027 was not set due to a poor connection between the world connector and EBCM.

Diagnostic Aids:

An "Intermittent" problem may be caused by a poor connection, rubbed through wire insulation, or a wire that is broken inside the insulation.

The frequency of the problem can be checked by using the enhanced diagnostic function of the "Scan" tool

If the customers comments reflect that the ABS Amber warning light is on only during moist environmental changes, (rain, snow, vehicle wash) all wheel speed sensor circuitry should be thoroughly inspected for water intrusion. Use the following procedure. Spray down the suspected area with 5% salt water solution (two teaspoons of salt to 12 oz. of water). Start vehicle, allow vehicle to run for 10 seconds. If code returns immediately, replace suspected harness.

Any circuitry, that is suspected as causing the intermittent complaint, should be thoroughly checked for backed out terminals, improper mating, broken locks, improperly formed or damaged terminals, poor terminal to wiring connections or physical damage to the wiring harness.

Excessive end play can cause this code to set. Check integral bearing for excessive axial end play,

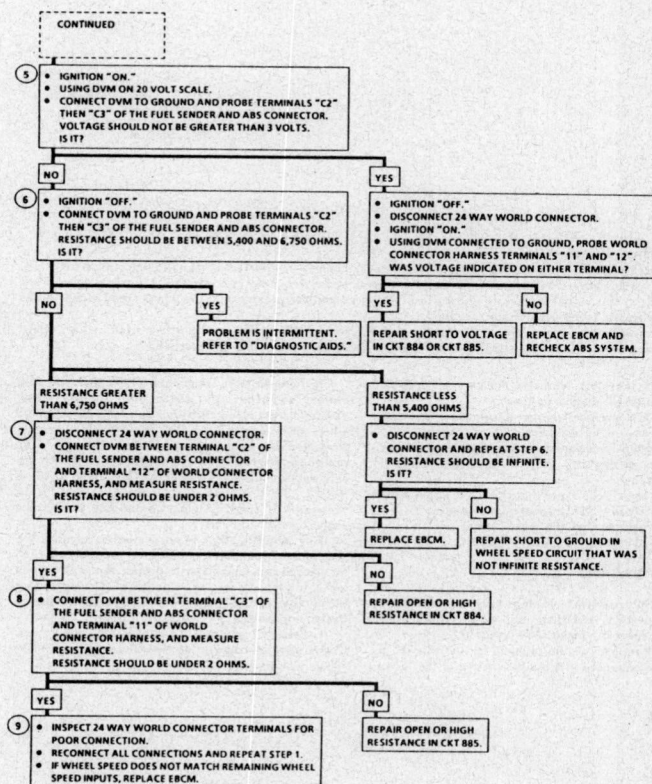

Fig. 39 Code A027, excessive left rear wheel acceleration (Part 2 of 2). 1991–92

Cavalier & Sunbird

Beretta & Corsica

Achieva, Calais & Grand Am

Cutlass Supreme, Grand Prix, Lumina & Regal

Circuit Description:

As a toothed ring passes by the wheel speed sensor, changes in the electromagnetic field cause the wheel speed sensor to produce a sinusoidal (AC) voltage signal whose frequency is proportional to wheel speed. The magnitude of this signal is directly related to wheel speed and the proximity of the wheel speed sensor to the toothed ring, often referred to as the air gap.

This code detects opens, shorts to ground, and shorts to battery that cause intermittent wheel speed operation. Also detected is any sudden change in wheel speed determined to be unreasonable.

Test Description: Number(s) below refer to circled number(s) on the diagnostic chart.

1. This test verifies whether the fault is currently present.
2. This step is designed to identify a wheel speed sensor or circuitry that is damaged and visibly apparent.
3. This test checks to see that the wheel speed sensor circuitry is within proper resistance value.
4. This insures that the wheel speed sensor is not shorted to ground.

Diagnostic Aids:

An "Intermittent" problem may be caused by a poor connection, rubbed through wire insulation, or a wire that is broken inside the insulation.

The frequency of the problem can be checked by using the enhanced diagnostic function of the "Scan" tool

If the customers comments reflect that the ABS Amber warning light is on only during moist environmental changes, (rain, snow, vehicle wash) all wheel speed sensor circuitry should be thoroughly inspected for water intrusion. Use the following procedure. Spray down the suspected area with 5% salt water solution (two teaspoons of salt to 12 oz. of water). Start vehicle, allow vehicle to run for 10 seconds. If code returns immediately, replace suspected harness.

Any circuitry, that is suspected as causing the intermittent complaint, should be thoroughly checked for backed out terminals, improper mating, broken locks, improperly formed or damaged terminals, poor terminal to wiring connections or physical damage to the wiring harness.

Excessive end play can cause this code to set. Check integral bearing for excessive axial end play,

Fig. 40   Code A028, excessive right rear wheel acceleration (Part 1 of 2). 1991–92

Cavalier & Sunbird

Beretta & Corsica

Achieva, Calais & Grand Am

Cutlass Supreme, Grand Prix, Lumina & Regal

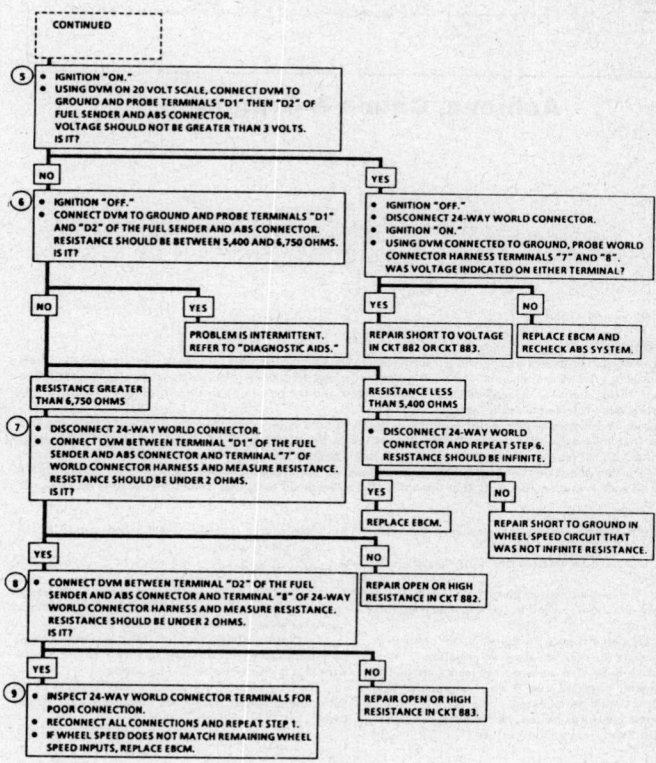

Circuit Description:

As a toothed ring passes by the wheel speed sensor, changes in the electromagnetic field cause the wheel speed sensor to produce a sinusoidal (AC) voltage signal whose frequency is proportional to wheel speed. The magnitude of this signal is directly related to wheel speed and the proximity of the wheel speed sensor to the toothed ring, often referred to as the air gap.

This code detects opens, shorts to ground, and shorts to battery that cause intermittent wheel speed operation. Also detected is any sudden change in wheel speed determined to be unreasonable.

Test Description:
Number(s) below refer to circled number(s) on the diagnostic chart.

5. This step checks to see if the wheel speed sensor circuitry is shorted to voltage.
6. This step insures that the wheel speed sensor circuitry resistance is within proper value.
7. This checks for an open in the wheel signal high circuit.
8. This checks for an open in the wheel signal low circuit.
9. This step insures that Code A028 was not set due to a poor connection between the world connector and EBCM.

Diagnostic Aids:

An "Intermittent" problem may be caused by a poor connection, rubbed through wire insulation, or a wire that is broken inside the insulation.

The frequency of the problem can be checked by using the enhanced diagnostic function of the "Scan" tool

If the customers comments reflect that the ABS Amber warning light is on only during moist environmental changes, (rain, snow, vehicle wash) all wheel speed sensor circuitry should be thoroughly inspected for water intrusion. Use the following procedure. Spray down the suspected area with 5% salt water solution (two teaspoons of salt to 12 oz. of water). Start vehicle, allow vehicle to run for 10 seconds. If code returns immediately, replace suspected harness.

Any circuitry, that is suspected as causing the intermittent complaint, should be thoroughly checked for backed out terminals, improper mating, broken locks, improperly formed or damaged terminals, poor terminal to wiring connections or physical damage to the wiring harness.

Excessive end play can cause this code to set. Check integral bearing for excessive axial end play.

Fig. 40   Code A028, excessive right rear wheel acceleration (Part 2 of 2). 1991–92

Cavalier & Sunbird

Beretta & Corsica

Achieva, Calais & Grand Am

Cutlass Supreme, Grand Prix, Lumina & Regal

Circuit Description:

As a toothed ring passes by the wheel speed sensor, changes in the electromagnetic field cause the wheel speed sensor to produce a sinusoidal (AC) voltage signal whose frequency is proportional to wheel speed. The magnitude of this signal is directly related to wheel speed and the proximity of the wheel speed sensor to the toothed ring, often referred to as the air gap.

This code is designed to detect two open wheel speed sensors in any combination. This test exists due to a condition that may exist that does not allow the driver to be informed by the ABS warning light of non-functioning ABS. If one wheel speed sensor is open, the driver is informed. If a second fails, the driver is no longer informed without this test and ABS is not available. By requiring the two operating wheels to be within 7 mph, a false code is prevented during spin-ups while still allowing for detection when the stowaway spare tire is used.

Test Description: Number(s) below refer to circled number(s) on the diagnostic chart.

1. This test verifies whether the fault is currently present.
2. This step is designed to identify a wheel speed sensor or circuitry that is damaged and visibly apparent.
3. This step identifies if the cause of the problem is common to the rear wheel sensor circuitry.
4. Because both rear sensors are common to the extension harness, the 4 way connectors and harness should be inspected.
5. This test checks to see that the wheel speed sensor is within proper resistance values.

6. This insures that the wheel speed sensor is not shorted to ground.

Diagnostic Aids:

A false Code A031 may be set as a result of vehicle operation while on a hoist or a lifted condition or stuck in mud or snow, when the vehicle is in gear.

An "Intermittent" problem may be caused by a poor connection, rubbed through wire insulation, or a wire that is broken inside the insulation.

The frequency of the problem can be checked by using the enhanced diagnostic function of the "Scan" tool

IMPORTANT: WHEEL SPEED SENSOR INTERMITTENT PROBLEMS MAY BE DIFFICULT TO LOCATE. CARE SHOULD BE TAKEN NOT TO DISTURB ANY ELECTRICAL CONNECTIONS PRIOR TO AN INDICATED STEP OF THIS CHART. THIS WILL INSURE THAT AN INTERMITTENT CONNECTION WILL NOT BE CORRECTED BEFORE THE SOURCE OF THE PROBLEM IS FOUND.

SENSOR	CODE
L/F SENSOR	A021
R/F SENSOR	A022
L/R SENSOR	A023
R/R SENSOR	A024

Fig. 41 Code A031, two wheel speed sensors open (Part 1 of 2). Less tubular rear axle. 1991—92

Cavalier & Sunbird

Beretta & Corsica

Achieva, Calais & Grand Am

Cutlass Supreme, Grand Prix, Lumina & Regal

Circuit Description:

As a toothed ring passes by the wheel speed sensor, changes in the electromagnetic field cause the wheel speed sensor to produce a sinusoidal (AC) voltage signal whose frequency is proportional to wheel speed. The magnitude of this signal is directly related to wheel speed and the proximity of the wheel speed sensor to the toothed ring, often referred to as the air gap.

This code is designed to detect two open wheel speed sensors in any combination. This test exists due to a condition that may exist that does not allow the driver to be informed by the ABS warning light of non-functioning ABS. If one wheel speed sensor is open, the driver is informed. If a second fails, the driver is no longer informed without this test and ABS is not available. By requiring the two operating wheels to be within 7 mph, a false code is prevented during spin-ups while still allowing for detection when the stowaway spare tire is used.

Test Description: Number(s) below refer to circled number(s) on the diagnostic chart.

7. This step checks for an open in the wheel speed sensor circuitry of one side of the sensor.
8. This step checks for an open on the other side of the sensor in question.
9. This step checks for a short to ground in the wheel speed sensor circuitry.
10. This insures that the circuitry is not shorted to voltage.

Diagnostic Aids:

A false Code A031 may be set as a result of vehicle operation while on a hoist or a lifted condition, or stuck in mud or snow while the vehicle is in gear.

An "Intermittent" problem may be caused by a poor connection, rubbed through wire insulation, or a wire that is broken inside the insulation.

The frequency of the problem can be checked by using the enhanced diagnostic function of the "Scan" tool.

SENSOR TERMINAL	24 WAY WORLD CONNECTOR	CIRCUIT NUMBER
L/R WHEEL A	PIN 12	884
L/R WHEEL B	PIN 11	885
R/R WHEEL A	PIN 7	882
R/R WHEEL B	PIN 8	883

Fig. 41 Code A031, two wheel speed sensors open (Part 2 of 2). Less tubular rear axle. 1991–92

CODE A031
(Page 1 of 2)
TWO WHEEL SPEEDS = 0
(TUBULAR REAR AXLE)

Circuit Description:

As a toothed ring passes by the wheel speed sensor, changes in the electromagnetic field cause the wheel speed sensor to produce a sinusoidal (AC) voltage signal whose frequency is proportional to wheel speed. The magnitude of this signal is directly related to wheel speed and the proximity of the wheel speed sensor to the toothed ring, often referred to as the air gap.

This code is designed to detect two open wheel speed sensors in any combination. This test exists due to a condition that may exist that does not allow the driver to be informed by the ABS warning light of non-functioning ABS. If one wheel speed sensor is open, the driver is informed. If a second fails, the driver is no longer informed without this test and ABS is not available. By requiring the two operating wheels to be within 7 mph, a false code is prevented during spin-ups while still allowing for detection when the stowaway spare tire is used.

Test Description: Number(s) below refer to circled number(s) on the diagnostic chart.
1. This test verifies whether the fault is currently present.
2. This step is designed to identify a wheel speed sensor or circuitry that is damaged and visibly apparent.
3. This step identifies if the cause of the problem is common to the rear wheel sensor circuitry.
4. Because both rear sensors are common to the extension harness, the 4 way connectors and harness should be inspected.
5. This test checks to see that the wheel speed sensor is within proper resistance values.

6. This insures that the wheel speed sensor is not shorted to ground.

Diagnostic Aids:

A false Code A031 may be set as a result of vehicle operation while on a hoist or a lifted condition or stuck in mud or snow, when the vehicle is in gear.

An "Intermittent" problem may be caused by a poor connection, rubbed through wire insulation, or a wire that is broken inside the insulation.

The frequency of the problem can be checked by using the enhanced diagnostic function of the "Scan" tool, as described in the "General Information."

Fig. 42   Code A031, two wheel speed sensors open (Part 1 of 2). With tubular rear axle. 1991–92

CODE A031
(Page 2 of 2)
TWO WHEEL SPEEDS = 0
(TUBULAR REAR AXLE)

Circuit Description:

As a toothed ring passes by the wheel speed sensor, changes in the electromagnetic field cause the wheel speed sensor to produce a sinusoidal (AC) voltage signal whose frequency is proportional to wheel speed. The magnitude of this signal is directly related to wheel speed and the proximity of the wheel speed sensor to the toothed ring, often referred to as the air gap.

This code is designed to detect two open wheel speed sensors in any combination. This test exists due to a condition that may exist that does not allow the driver to be informed by the ABS warning light of non-functioning ABS. If one wheel speed sensor is open, the driver is informed. If a second fails, the driver is no longer informed without this test and ABS is not available. By requiring the two operating wheels to be within 7 mph, a false code is prevented during spin-ups while still allowing for detection when the stowaway spare tire is used.

Test Description: Number(s) below refer to circled number(s) on the diagnostic chart.
7. This step checks for an open in the wheel speed sensor circuitry of one side of the sensor.
8. This step checks for an open on the other side of the sensor in question.
9. This step checks for a short to ground in the wheel speed sensor circuitry.
10. This insures that the circuitry is not shorted to voltage.

Diagnostic Aids:

A false Code A031 may be set as a result of vehicle operation while on a hoist or a lifted condition, or stuck in mud or snow when the vehicle is in gear.

An "Intermittent" problem may be caused by a poor connection, rubbed through wire insulation, or a wire that is broken inside the insulation.

The frequency of the problem can be checked by using the enhanced diagnostic function of the "Scan" tool,

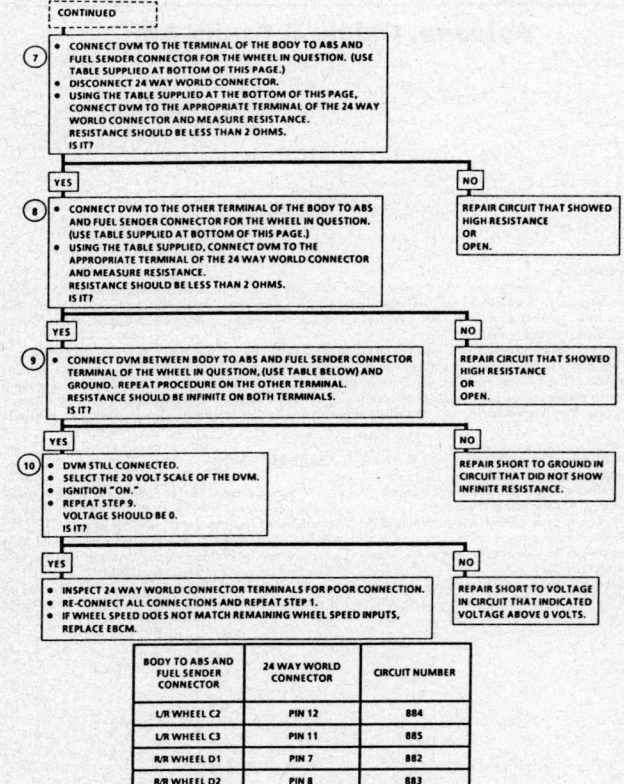

Fig. 42   Code A031, two wheel speed sensors open (Part 2 of 2). With tubular rear axle. 1991–92

1991 CALAIS & 1991–92 GRAND AM, SKYLARK & 1992 ACHIEVA, BERETTA, CAVALIER, CORSICA, CUTLASS SUPREME, GRAND PRIX, LUMINA, REGAL & SUNBIRD (DELCO-MORAINE VI TYPE)

IMPORTANT: WHEEL SPEED SENSOR INTERMITTENT PROBLEMS MAY BE DIFFICULT TO LOCATE. CARE SHOULD BE TAKEN NOT TO DISTURB ANY ELECTRICAL CONNECTIONS PRIOR TO AN INDICATED STEP OF THIS CHART. THIS WILL INSURE THAT AN INTERMITTENT CONNECTION WILL NOT BE CORRECTED BEFORE THE SOURCE OF THE PROBLEM IS FOUND.

CODE A032

LEFT FRONT WHEEL SENSOR SHORTED TO BATTERY OR GROUND

Circuit Description:

As a toothed ring passes by the wheel speed sensor, changes in the electromagnetic field cause the wheel speed sensor to produce a sinusoidal (AC) voltage signal whose frequency is proportional to wheel speed. The magnitude of this signal is directly related to wheel speed and the proximity of the wheel speed sensor to the toothed ring often referred to as the air gap.

This code detects shorts to ground, and shorts to battery in the wheel speed circuitry sensed by ABS EBCM.

Test Description: Number(s) below refer to circled number(s) on the diagnostic chart.

1. This test helps to identify whether the code is due to a short to battery or short to ground.
2. This insures that the wheel speed sensor is not shorted to ground.
3. This step checks to see if wheel speed sensor circuitry is shorted to voltage.
4. This insures that the wheel speed sensor circuitry has good continuity.
5. This checks for short to ground in wheel speed sensor wiring.
6. This checks for short to voltage in wheel speed sensor wiring.

Diagnostic Aids:

An "Intermittent" problem may be caused by a poor connection, rubbed through wire insulation, or a wire that is broken inside the insulation.

The frequency of the problem can be checked by using the enhanced diagnostic function of the "Scan" tool.

If the customers comments reflect that the ABS Amber warning lamp is "ON" only during moist environmental changes, (rain, snow, vehicle wash) all wheel speed sensor circuitry should be thoroughly inspected for signs of water intrusion. If code is not current clear codes and simulate the effects of water intrusion. Use the following procedure. Spray down the suspected area with a 5% salt water solution (two teaspoons of salt to 12 oz. of water). Start vehicle, allow vehicle to run for 10 seconds. If code returns immediately, replace suspected harness.

Any circuitry, that is suspected as causing the intermittent complaint, should be thoroughly checked for backed out terminals, improper mating, broken locks, improperly formed or damaged terminals, poor terminal to wiring connections or physical damage to the wiring harness.

Fig. 43   Code A032, LH front wheel speed sensor shorted to battery or ground. Cutlass Supreme, Grand Prix, Lumina & Regal. 1991–92

IMPORTANT: WHEEL SPEED SENSOR INTERMITTENT PROBLEMS MAY BE DIFFICULT TO LOCATE. CARE SHOULD BE TAKEN NOT TO DISTURB ANY ELECTRICAL CONNECTIONS PRIOR TO AN INDICATED STEP OF THIS CHART. THIS WILL INSURE THAT AN INTERMITTENT CONNECTION WILL NOT BE CORRECTED BEFORE THE SOURCE OF THE PROBLEM IS FOUND.

CODE A033

RIGHT FRONT WHEEL SENSOR SHORTED TO BATTERY OR GROUND

Circuit Description:

As a toothed ring passes by the wheel speed sensor, changes in the electromagnetic field cause the wheel speed sensor to produce a sinusoidal (AC) voltage signal whose frequency is proportional to wheel speed. The magnitude of this signal is directly related to wheel speed and the proximity of the wheel speed sensor to the toothed ring, often referred to as the air gap.

This code detects shorts to ground, and shorts to battery in the wheel speed circuitry sensed by the ABS EBCM.

Test Description: Number(s) below refer to circled number(s) on the diagnostic chart.

1. This test helps identify whether the code is due to a short to battery or short to ground.
2. This insures that the wheel speed sensor is not shorted to ground.
3. This step checks to see if wheel speed sensor circuitry is shorted to voltage.
4. This insures that the wheel speed sensor circuitry has good continuity.
5. This checks for short to ground in wheel speed sensor wiring.
6. This checks for short to voltage in wheel speed sensor wiring.

Diagnostic Aids:

An "Intermittent" problem may be caused by a poor connection, rubbed through wire insulation, or a wire that is broken inside the insulation.

The frequency of the problem can be checked by using the enhanced diagnostic function of the "Scan" tool.

If the customers comments reflect that the ABS Amber warning lamp is "ON" only during moist environmental changes, (rain, snow, vehicle wash) all wheel speed sensor circuitry should be thoroughly inspected for signs of water intrusion. If code is not current clear codes and simulate the effects of water intrusion. Use the following procedure. Spray down the suspected area with a 5% salt water solution (two teaspoons of salt to 12 oz. of water). Start vehicle, allow vehicle to run for 10 seconds. If code returns immediately, replace suspected harness.

Any circuitry, that is suspected as causing the intermittent complaint, should be thoroughly checked for backed out terminals, improper mating, broken locks, improperly formed or damaged terminals, poor terminal to wiring connections or physical damage to the wiring harness.

Fig. 44   Code A033, RH front wheel speed sensor shorted to battery or ground. Cutlass Supreme, Grand Prix, Lumina & Regal. 1991–92

CODE A034

LEFT REAR WHEEL SENSOR SHORTED TO BATTERY OR GROUND

Circuit Description:

As a toothed ring passes by the wheel speed sensor, changes in the electromagnetic field cause the wheel speed sensor to produce a sinusoidal (AC) voltage signal whose frequency is proportional to wheel speed. The magnitude of this signal is directly related to wheel speed and the proximity of the wheel speed sensor to the toothed ring, often referred to as the air gap.

This code detects opens, shorts to ground, and shorts to battery in the wheel speed circuitry sensed by the ABS EBCM.

Test Description: Number(s) below refer to circled number(s) on the diagnostic chart.

1. This test helps to identify whether the code is due to a short to battery or short to ground.
2. This insures that the wheel speed sensor is not shorted to ground.
3. This step checks to see if wheel speed sensor circuitry is shorted to voltage.
4. This insures that the wheel speed sensor circuitry has good continuity.
5. This checks for short to ground in wheel speed sensor wiring.
6. This checks for short to voltage in wheel speed sensor wiring.

Diagnostic Aids:

An "Intermittent" problem may be caused by a poor connection, rubbed through wire insulation, or a wire that is broken inside the insulation.

The frequency of the problem can be checked by using the enhanced diagnostic function of the "Scan" tool.

If the customers comments reflect that the ABS Amber warning lamp is "ON" only during moist environmental changes, (rain, snow, vehicle wash) all wheel speed sensor circuitry should be thoroughly inspected for signs of water intrusion. If code is not current clear codes and simulate the effects of water intrusion. Use the following procedure. Spray down the suspected area with a 5% salt water solution (two teaspoons of salt to 12 oz. of water). Start vehicle, allow vehicle to run for 10 seconds. If code returns immediately, replace suspected harness.

Any circuitry, that is suspected as causing the intermittent complaint, should be thoroughly checked for backed out terminals, improper mating, broken locks, improperly formed or damaged terminals, poor terminal to wiring connections or physical damage to the wiring harness.

Fig. 45   Code A034, LH rear wheel speed sensor shorted to battery or ground. Cutlass Supreme, Grand Prix, Lumina & Regal. 1991–92

CODE A035

RIGHT REAR WHEEL SENSOR SHORTED TO BATTERY OR GROUND

Circuit Description:

As a toothed ring passes by the wheel speed sensor, changes in the electromagnetic field cause the wheel speed sensor to produce a sinusoidal (AC) voltage signal whose frequency is proportional to wheel speed. The magnitude of this signal is directly related to wheel speed and the proximity of the wheel speed sensor to the toothed ring, often referred to as the air gap.

This code detects opens, shorts to ground, and shorts to battery in the wheel speed circuitry sensed by the ABS EBCM.

Test Description: Number(s) below refer to circled number(s) on the diagnostic chart.

1. This helps to identify whether the code is due to a short to battery or short to ground.
2. This insures that the wheel speed sensor is not shorted to ground.
3. This step checks to see if wheel speed sensor circuitry is shorted to voltage.
4. This insures that the wheel speed sensor circuitry has good continuity.
5. This checks for short to ground in wheel speed sensor wiring.
6. This checks for short to voltage in wheel speed sensor wiring.

Diagnostic Aids:

An "Intermittent" problem may be caused by a poor connection, rubbed through wire insulation, or a wire that is broken inside the insulation.

The frequency of the problem can be checked by using the enhanced diagnostic function of the "Scan" tool.

If the customers comments reflect that the ABS Amber warning lamp is "ON" only during moist environmental changes, (rain, snow, vehicle wash) all wheel speed sensor circuitry should be thoroughly inspected for signs of water intrusion. If code is not current clear codes and simulate the effects of water intrusion. Use the following procedure. Spray down the suspected area with a 5% salt water solution (two teaspoons of salt to 12 oz. of water). Start vehicle, allow vehicle to run for 10 seconds. If code returns immediately, replace suspected harness.

Any circuitry, that is suspected as causing the intermittent complaint, should be thoroughly checked for backed out terminals, improper mating, broken locks, improperly formed or damaged terminals, poor terminal to wiring connections or physical damage to the wiring harness.

Fig. 46   Code A035, RH rear wheel speed sensor shorted to battery or ground. Cutlass Supreme, Grand Prix, Lumina & Regal. 1991–92

Cavalier & Sunbird

Beretta & Corsica

Achieva, Calais & Grand Am

Cutlass Supreme, Grand Prix, Lumina & Regal

Circuit Description:

This code is used to monitor the voltage level available to the ABS EBCM. If the voltage drops below 11 volts, full performance of the ABS system cannot be guaranteed. During ABS operation, there are several current requirements that will cause battery voltage to drop. Because of this, voltage is monitored prior to ABS to indicate good charging system condition and also during ABS when voltage may drop significantly. If voltage falls below a level that will provide adequate ABS performance, Code A036 will result.

Test Description: Number(s) below refer to circled number(s) on the diagnostic chart.

1. This test checks to see what voltage is readily available at terminal "A" of the EBCM. If voltage is representative of good charging system condition, a fault is not present.
2. This step isolates the EBCM to check the condition of the circuitry and charging system.
3. This step isolates the low voltage condition to high circuit resistance, or improper charging system operation.

Diagnostic Aids

An "Intermittent" problem may be caused by a poor connection, rubbed through wire insulation, or a wire that is broken inside the insulation.

The frequency of the problem can be checked by using the enhanced diagnostic function of the "Scan" tool.

Any circuitry, that is suspected as causing the intermittent complaint, should be thoroughly checked for backed out terminals, improper mating, broken locks, improperly formed or damaged terminals, poor terminal to wiring connections or physical damage to the wiring harness.

While performing a voltage load test, if it is noted that <u>only</u> ignition voltage drops below acceptable voltage levels, CKT 650 should be checked for high resistance or an open condition.

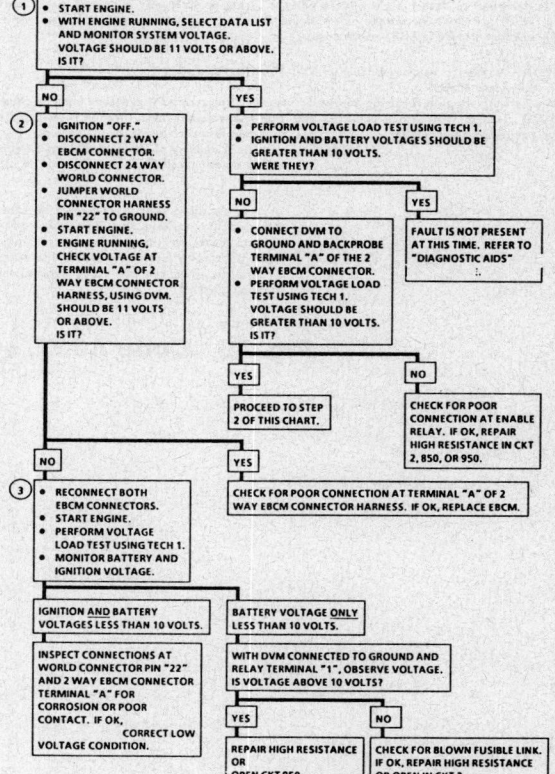

Fig. 47 Code A036, system voltage is low. 1991–92

Cavalier & Sunbird

Beretta & Corsica

Achieva, Calais & Grand Am

Cutlass Supreme, Grand Prix, Lumina & Regal

Circuit Description:

This code is designed to detect high vehicle voltage levels prior to any required motor movement (initialization or ABS). If excessive voltage exists, demagnetization of the motor magnets may occur, which would eventually affect or eliminate ABS performance.

Test Description: Number(s) below refer to circled number(s) on the diagnostic chart.

1. This step checks the voltage level being received by the EBCM. If high voltage is present, a charging system problem is indicated.

Diagnostic Aids:

An "Intermittent" problem may be caused by a poor connection, rubbed through wire insulation, or a wire that is broken inside the insulation.

The frequency of the problem can be checked by using the enhanced diagnostic function of the "Scan" tool

Any circuitry, that is suspected as causing the intermittent complaint, should be thoroughly checked for backed out terminals, improper mating, broken locks, improperly formed or damaged terminals, poor terminal to wiring connections or physical damage to the wiring harness.

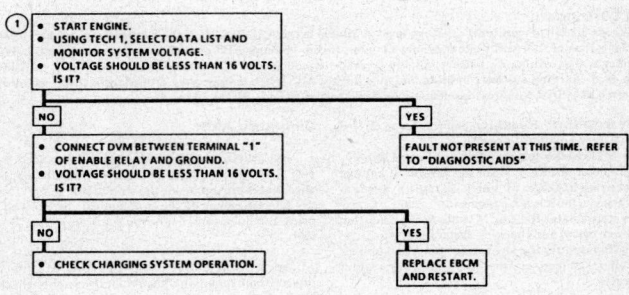

Fig. 48   Code A037, system voltage is high. 1991–92

Except Cutlass Supreme, Grand Prix, Lumina & Regal

Cutlass Supreme, Grand Prix, Lumina & Regal

Circuit Description:

Current is supplied to the EMB's through terminal "B" of the three way motor pack connector. When a release of the EMB is commanded, the EBCM grounds the EMB input and allows the EMB to be energized to release the motor.

This code is designed to detect slipping EMB's during initialization. When the release is commanded during initialization, the EMB is not energized and should hold the motor, resulting in sensed current of the motor being equal to commanded current (motor is at stall). If the motor is moving, sensed current will be less than stall current.

Test Description: Number(s) below refer to circled number(s) on the diagnostic chart.

1. This functionally checks the ability of the EMB to hold the motor. If the brake pedal moves during this test, it would indicate the EMB is slipping.
2. This step is used to release the tension of the motor pack prior to removal.

Diagnostic Aids:

An "Intermittent" fault in this code may result from a mechanical part of the system that sticks, binds, or slips.

The frequency of the problem can be checked by using the enhanced diagnostic function of the "Scan tool"

Depending on the frequency of the failure, a physical inspection of the mechanical parts suspected may be necessary.

The static modulator test function of the Tech 1 or T-100 may be used to locate an intermittent problem associated with the EMB.

NOTICE: This test may fail if low voltage (10 volts or less) was present when initialization occurred. Ensure battery/charging system is functioning properly.

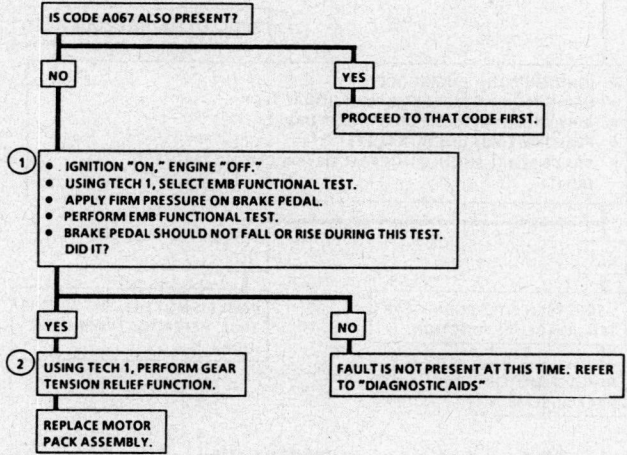

Fig. 49   Code A038, left front EMB will not hold motor. 1991–92

Except Cutlass Supreme, Grand Prix, Lumina & Regal

Cutlass Supreme, Grand Prix, Lumina & Regal

Circuit Description:

Current is supplied to the EMB's through terminal "B" of the three way motor pack connector. When a release of the EMB is commanded, the EBCM grounds the EMB input and allows the EMB to be energized to release the motor.

This code is designed to detect slipping EMB's during initialization. When the release is commanded during initialization, the EMB is not energized and should hold the motor, resulting in sensed current of the motor being equal to commanded current (motor is at stall). If the motor is moving, sensed current will be less than stall current.

Test Description: Number(s) below refer to circled number(s) on the diagnostic chart.

1. This functionally checks the ability of the EMB to hold the motor. If the brake pedal moves during this test, it would indicate the EMB is slipping.
2. This step is used to release the tension of the motor pack prior to removal.

Diagnostic Aids:

An "Intermittent" fault in this code may result from a mechanical part of the system that sticks, binds, or slips.

The frequency of the problem can be checked by using the enhanced diagnostic function of the "Scan" tool.

Depending on the frequency of the failure, a physical inspection of the mechanical parts suspected may be necessary.

The static modulator test function of the Tech 1 or T-100 may be used to locate an intermittent problem associated with the EMB.

NOTICE: This code may fail if low voltage (10 volts or less) was present when initialization occurred. Ensure battery/charging system is functioning properly.

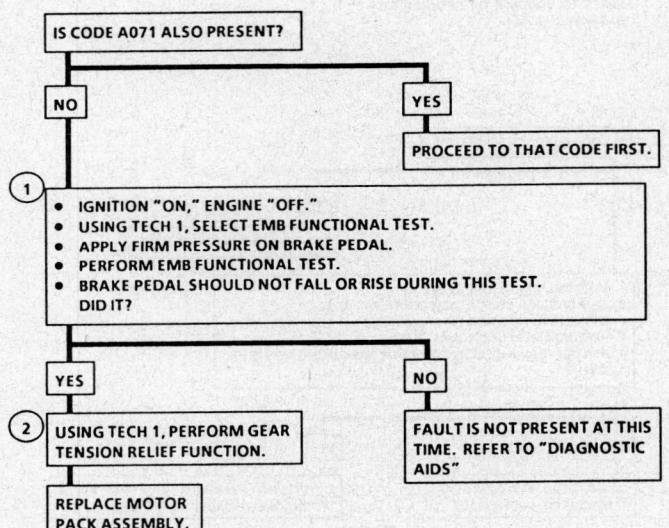

Fig. 50   Code A041, right front EMB will not hold motor. 1991—92

Except Cutlass Supreme, Grand Prix, Lumina & Regal

Cutlass Supreme, Grand Prix, Lumina & Regal

Circuit Description:

This code is designed to detect a slipping rear axle ESB. During initialization and braking, the rear motor is re-homed. If the ESB slips, the motor/piston will move. During the next key on initialization, a re-home of the motor verifies the motor/piston remained at the home position. If motor movement is detected, the ESB must be slipping.

Test Description: Number(s) below refer to circled number(s) on the diagnostic chart.

1. This step checks the rear axle ESB. A broken or defective ESB would result in the rear piston being back driven by hydraulic pressure, and wheel movement would result.
2. This step is used to release the tension of the motor pack prior to removal.

Diagnostic Aids:

An "Intermittent" fault in this code may result from a mechanical part of the system that sticks, binds, or slips.

The frequency of the problem can be checked by using the enhanced diagnostic function of the "Scan" tool

Depending on the frequency of the failure, a physical inspection of the mechanical parts suspected may be necessary.

The static modulator test function of the Tech 1 or T-100 may be used to locate an intermittent problem associated with the ESB.

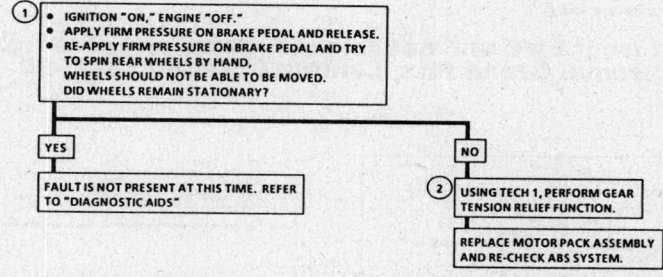

Fig. 51   Code A042, rear axle ESB will not hold motor. 1991–92

CODE A044
LEFT FRONT CHANNEL WILL NOT MOVE

Circuit Description:

Current is supplied to the EMB through terminal "B" of the three way motor pack connector. When a release of the EMB is commanded, the EBCM grounds the EMB input and allows the EMB to be energized to release the motor.

This code is designed to detect non-actuating EMB, stuck motor or a seized hydraulic modulator. When the release is commanded during initialization, the EMB should release the motor, resulting in sensed current being less than commanded current (motor is spinning freely). If the motor is not moving, sensed current will be equal to stall current.

Test Description: Number(s) below refer to circled number(s) on the diagnostic chart.

1. This step checks for motor movement while also positioning the brake pedal at the top of its travel.
2. This procedure functionally checks to see if the EMB is capable of releasing.
3. This step identifies a short to voltage in the EMB control circuitry.
4. This step is used to release the tension of the motor pack prior to removal.
5. This step serves to isolate the fault to either the motor pack assembly or ABS hydraulic modulator.

Diagnostic Aids:

An "Intermittent" fault in this code may result from a mechanical part of the system that sticks, binds, or slips.

The frequency of the problem can be checked by using the enhanced diagnostic function of the "Scan" tool

Code A044 may set after modulator disassembly if the modulator pistons are positioned at the bottom of their bore.

Any circuitry, that is suspected as causing the intermittent complaint, should be thoroughly checked for backed out terminals, improper mating, broken locks, improperly formed or damaged terminals, poor terminal to wiring connections or physical damage to the wiring harness.

NOTICE: This code may fail if low voltage (10 volts or less) was present when initialization occurred. Ensure battery/charging system is functioning properly.

Fig. 52 Code A044, left front EMB will not release motor or gears frozen. Except Cutlass Supreme, Grand Prix, Lumina & Regal. 1991–92

CODE A044
LEFT FRONT CHANNEL WILL NOT MOVE

Circuit Description:

This code is designed to detect bound-up ESB, a stuck motor, or a seized hydraulic modulator. When the release is commanded during initialization, the ESB should release the motor, resulting in sensed current being less than commanded current (motor is spinning freely). If the motor is not moving, sensed current will be equal to stall current.

Test Description: Number(s) below refer to circled number(s) on the diagnostic chart.

1. This step checks for motor movement.
2. This step is used to release the tension of the motor pack prior to removal.
3. This step serves to isolate the fault to either the motor pack assembly or ABS hydraulic modulator.

Diagnostic Aids:

An "Intermittent" fault in this code may result from a mechanical part of the system that sticks, binds, or slips.

The frequency of the problem can be checked by using the enhanced diagnostic function of the "Scan" tool

Code A044 may set after modulator disassembly if the modulator pistons are positioned at the bottom of their bore.

Any circuitry, that is suspected as causing the intermittent complaint, should be thoroughly checked for backed out terminals, improper mating, broken locks, improperly formed or damaged terminals, poor terminal to wiring connections or physical damage to the wiring harness.

Fig. 53 Code A044, left front EMB will not release motor or gears frozen. Cutlass Supreme, Grand Prix, Lumina & Regal. 1991–92

CODE A045
RIGHT FRONT CHANNEL WILL NOT MOVE

Circuit Description:

Current is supplied to the EMB through terminal "B" of the three way motor pack connector. When a release of the EMB is commanded, the EBCM grounds the EMB input and allows the EMB to be energized to release the motor.

This code is designed to detect non-actuating EMB, stuck motor or a seized hydraulic modulator. When the release is commanded during initialization, the EMB should release the motor, resulting in sensed current being less than commanded current (motor is spinning freely). If the motor is not moving, sensed current will be equal to stall current.

Test Description: Number(s) below refer to circled number(s) on the diagnostic chart.
1. This step checks for motor movement while also positioning the brake pedal at the top of its travel.
2. This procedure functionally checks to see if the EMB is capable of releasing.
3. This step is used to release the tension of the motor pack prior to removal.
4. This step serves to isolate the fault to either the motor pack assembly or ABS hydraulic modulator.

Diagnostic Aids:

An "Intermittent" fault in this code may result from a mechanical part of the system that sticks, binds, or slips.

The frequency of the problem can be checked by using the enhanced diagnostic function of the "Scan" tool

Code A045 may set after modulator disassembly if the modulator pistons are positioned at the bottom of their bore.

Any circuitry, that is suspected as causing the intermittent complaint, should be thoroughly checked for backed out terminals, improper mating, broken locks, improperly formed or damaged terminals, poor terminal to wiring connections or physical damage to the wiring harness.

NOTICE: This code may fail if low voltage (10 volts or less) was present when initialization occurred. Ensure battery/charging system is functioning properly.

Fig. 54 Code A045, right front EMB will not release motor or gears frozen. Except Cutlass Supreme, Grand Prix, Lumina & Regal. 1991–92

CODE A045
RIGHT FRONT CHANNEL WILL NOT MOVE

Circuit Description:

This code is designed to detect bound-up ESB, a stuck motor, or a seized hydraulic modulator. When the release is commanded during initialization, the ESB should release the motor, resulting in sensed current being less than commanded current (motor is spinning freely). If the motor is not moving, sensed current will be equal to stall current.

Test Description: Number(s) below refer to circled number(s) on the diagnostic chart.
1. This step checks for motor movement.
2. This step is used to release the tension of the motor pack prior to removal.
3. This step serves to isolate the fault to either the motor pack assembly or ABS hydraulic modulator.

Diagnostic Aids:

An "Intermittent" fault in this code may result from a mechanical part of the system that sticks, binds, or slips.

The frequency of the problem can be checked by using the enhanced diagnostic function of the "Scan" tool

Code A045 may set after modulator disassembly if the modulator pistons are positioned at the bottom of their bore.

Any circuitry, that is suspected as causing the intermittent complaint, should be thoroughly checked for backed out terminals, improper mating, broken locks, improperly formed or damaged terminals, poor terminal to wiring connections or physical damage to the wiring harness.

Fig. 55 Code A045, right front EMB will not release motor or gears frozen. Cutlass Supreme, Grand Prix, Lumina & Regal. 1991–92

CODE A046
REAR AXLE CHANNEL WILL NOT MOVE

Circuit Description:

This code is designed to detect a bound-up ESB's, stuck motor or a seized hydraulic modulator. When the release is commanded during initialization, the ESB should release the motor, resulting in sensed current being less than commanded current (motor is spinning freely). If the motor is not moving, sensed current will be equal to stall current.

Test Description: Number(s) below refer to circled number(s) on the diagnostic chart.

1. This checks the ability of the motor to move, applying hydraulic pressure to the wheel cylinders. A frozen piston or gear would result in no apply of rear brakes and a wheel that freely spins.
2. This step checks to see that the motor can also move to the release position. If a motor were not able to release hydraulic pressure, the wheel would not spin.
3. This step is used to release the tension of the motor pack prior to removal.
4. Isolation of the faulty component is identified in this step.

Diagnostic Aids:

An "Intermittent" fault in this code may result from a mechanical part of the system that sticks or binds.

The frequency of the problem can be checked by using the enhanced diagnostic function of the Tech 1 "Scan" tool)

Code A046 may set after modulator disassembly if the modulator pistons are positioned at the bottom of their bore.

Depending on the frequency of the failure, a physical inspection of the mechanical parts suspected may be necessary.

Any circuitry, that is suspected as causing the intermittent complaint, should be thoroughly checked for backed out terminals, improper mating, broken locks, improperly formed or damaged terminals, poor terminal to wiring connections or physical damage to the wiring harness.

Fig. 56   Code A046, rear axle ESB will not release motor or gears frozen. 1991–92

CODE A047
LEFT FRONT MOTOR FREE SPINS

Circuit Description:

This code is designed to detect a stripped nut or gear assembly during initialization. During the homing sequence, the piston should reach the top of the bore resulting in a stalled motor. If this does not occur, the motor must be spinning with little or no resistance, indicating a nut/screw or gear failure.

Test Description: Number(s) below refer to circled number(s) on the diagnostic chart.

1. This step positions the motor at the bottom of its travel.
2. This checks to see if the nut or gear is stripped. If either were stripped, the hydraulic pressure applied from the master cylinder would not be able to be overcome by the hydraulic ball screw, resulting in a brake pedal that would not rise.
3. During a full apply, once the ball screw reaches the top of its travel, the motor should stall. If the motor continues to run, an indication of a stripped nut or gear is present.
4. This step is used to release the tension of the motor pack prior to removal.

Diagnostic Aids:

An "Intermittent" fault in this code may result from a mechanical part of the system that sticks, binds, or slips.

The frequency of the problem can be checked by using the enhanced diagnostic function of the "Scan" tool

If code only fails once and Code A056 also fails see Code A056. If intermittent and enhanced diagnostics shows this code fails during ABS, see Code A056.

Depending on the frequency of the failure, a physical inspection of the mechanical parts suspected may be necessary.

Fig. 57   Code A047, left front nut failure, motor free spins. 1991–92

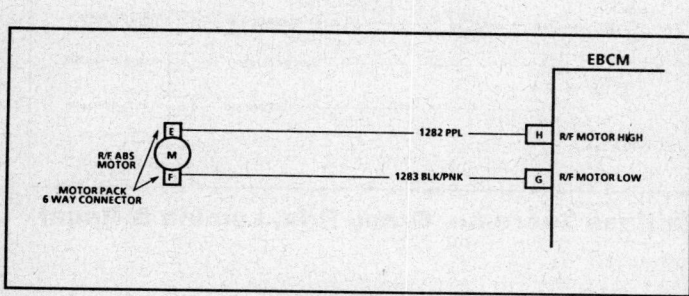

CODE A048
RIGHT FRONT MOTOR FREE SPINS

Circuit Description:

This code is designed to detect a stripped nut or gear assembly during initialization. During the homing sequence, the piston should reach the top of the bore resulting in a stalled motor. If this does not occur, the motor must be spinning with little or no resistance, indicating a nut/screw or gear failure.

Test Description: Number(s) below refer to circled number(s) on the diagnostic chart.

1. This step positions the motor at the bottom of its travel.
2. This checks to see if the nut or gear is stripped. If either were stripped, the hydraulic pressure applied from the master cylinder would not be able to be overcome by the hydraulic ball screw, resulting in a bake pedal that would not rise.
3. During a full apply, once the ball screw reaches the top of its travel, the motor should stall. If the motor continues to run, an indication of a stripped nut or gear is present.
4. This step is used to release the tension of the motor pack prior to removal.

Diagnostic Aids:

An "Intermittent" fault in this code may result from a mechanical part of the system that sticks, binds, or slips.

The frequency of the problem can be checked by using the enhanced diagnostic function of the "Scan" tool

If code only fails once and Code A061 also fails see Code A061. If intermittent and enhanced diagnostics shows this code fails during ABS, see Code A061.

Depending on the frequency of the failure, a physical inspection of the mechanical parts suspected may be necessary.

Fig. 58   Code A048, right front nut failure, motor free spins. 1991–92

Cavalier & Sunbird

Beretta & Corsica

Achieva, Calais & Grand Am

Cutlass Supreme, Grand Prix, Lumina & Regal

Circuit Description:

This code is designed to detect a stripped nut or gear assembly during initialization. During the homing sequence, the piston should reach the top of the bore resulting in a stalled motor. If this does not occur, the motor must be spinning with little or no resistance, indicating a nut/screw or gear failure.

Test Description: Number(s) below refer to circled number(s) on the diagnostic chart.

1. This step checks for a slipping nut or gear. if either were to slip, it would result in a lack of hydraulic pressure being applied at the rear wheels, causing the wheels to be able to be moved.
2. During a full apply, once the ball screw reaches the top of its travel, the motor should stall. If the motor continues to run, an indication of a stripped nut or gear is present.
3. This step is used to release the tension of the motor pack prior to removal.

Diagnostic Aids:

An "Intermittent" fault in this code may result from a mechanical part of the system that sticks, binds, or slips.

The frequency of the problem can be checked by using the enhanced diagnostic function of the "Scan" tool

If code only fails once and Code A064 also fails, see Code A064. If intermittent and enhanced diagnostics show this code fails during ABS, see Code A064.

Depending on the frequency of the failure, a physical inspection of the mechanical parts suspected may be necessary.

Fig. 59   Code A051, rear axle nut failure, motor free spins. 1991–92

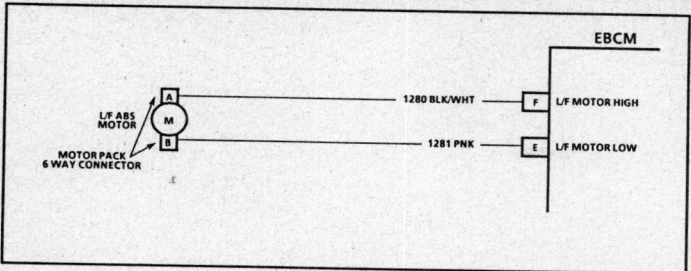

CODE A052
LEFT FRONT CHANNEL IN RELEASE TOO LONG

Circuit Description:

This code will diagnose a motor that is energized longer than expected. This could occur if a wheel speed sensor is faulty, the motor does not turn, the left front solenoid mechanically fails open, or the motor wires are crossed.

Test Description: Number(s) below refer to circled number(s) on the diagnostic chart.

1. This step identifies a problem in a wheel speed sensor that may cause the system to be in release too long.
2. This step identifies a motor fault as being failed or wired incorrectly.
3. This step checks for a solenoid that may have mechanically failed open.
4. If Step 3 has failed, this serves to isolate the cause of the hydraulic problem, to either the solenoid or the ABS hydraulic modulator assembly.
5. This step is used to release the tension of the motor pack.

Diagnostic Aids:

An "Intermittent" problem may be caused by a mechanical part of the system that sticks or binds.

The frequency of the problem can be checked by using the enhanced diagnostic function of the "Scan" tool

Code A052 may fail if on ice and steering wheel is turned to lock during braking. Using "scan" tool perform Hydraulic test to ensure total brake system is functional.

Any circuitry, that is suspected as causing the intermittent complaint, should be thoroughly checked for backed out terminals, improper mating, broken locks, improperly formed or damaged terminals, poor terminal to wiring connections or physical damage to the wiring harness.

Fig. 60   Code A052, left front channel in release too long. 1991–92

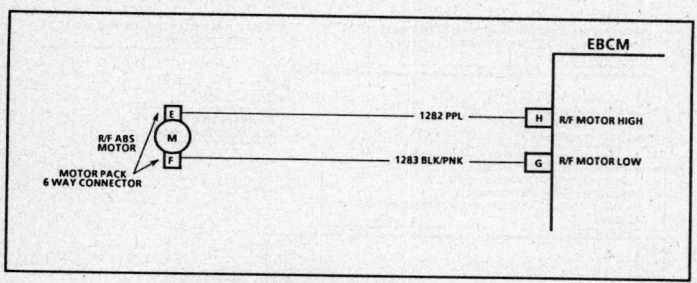

CODE A053
RIGHT FRONT CHANNEL IN RELEASE TOO LONG

Circuit Description:

This code will diagnose a motor that is energized longer than expected. This could occur if a wheel speed sensor is faulty, the motor does not turn, the right front solenoid mechanically fails open, or the motor wires are crossed.

Test Description: Number(s) below refer to circled number(s) on the diagnostic chart.

1. This step identifies a problem in a wheel speed sensor that may cause the system to be in release too long.
2. This step identifies a motor fault as being failed or wired incorrectly.
3. This step checks for a solenoid that may have mechanically failed open.
4. If Step 3 has failed, this serves to isolate the cause of the hydraulic problem, to either the solenoid or the ABS hydraulic modulator assembly.
5. This step is used to release the tension of the motor pack prior to removal.

Diagnostic Aids:

An "Intermittent" problem may be caused by a mechanical part of the system that sticks or binds.

The frequency of the problem can be checked by using the enhanced diagnostic function of the "Scan" tool,

Code A053 may fail on ice if steering wheel is turned to lock during braking. Using "Scan" tool perform Hydraulic test to ensure total brake system is functional.

Any circuitry, that is suspected as causing the intermittent complaint, should be thoroughly checked for backed out terminals, improper mating, broken locks, improperly formed or damaged terminals, poor terminal to wiring connections or physical damage to the wiring harness.

Fig. 61   Code A053, right front channel in release too long. 1991–92

CODE A054
REAR AXLE IN RELEASE TOO LONG

Circuit Description:

This code will diagnose a motor that is energized longer than expected. This could occur if a wheel speed sensor is faulty, the motor does not turn, or the motor wires are crossed.

Test Description: Numbers below refer to circled numbers on the diagnostic chart.

1. This step identifies a problem in a wheel speed sensor that may cause the system to be in release too long.
2. This checks for a wheel that may stick or bind because of a mechanical fault.
3. This checks to see if the motor is capable of moving and applying the hydraulic piston for the rear wheels.
4. This step insures that the motor wiring is not crossed.
5. This step is used to release the tension of the motor pack prior to removal.
6. This isolates the fault of a "no-apply" situation to either the motor pack or ABS hydraulic modulator assembly.

Diagnostic Aids:

An "Intermittent" problem may be caused by a mechanical part of the system that sticks or binds.

The frequency of the problem can be checked by using the enhanced diagnostic function of the "Scan" tool

Using "Scan" tool perform hydraulic test to ensure total brake system is functional.

Any circuitry, that is suspected as causing the intermittent complaint, should be thoroughly checked for backed out terminals, improper mating, broken locks, improperly formed or damaged terminals, poor terminal to wiring connections or physical damage to the wiring harness.

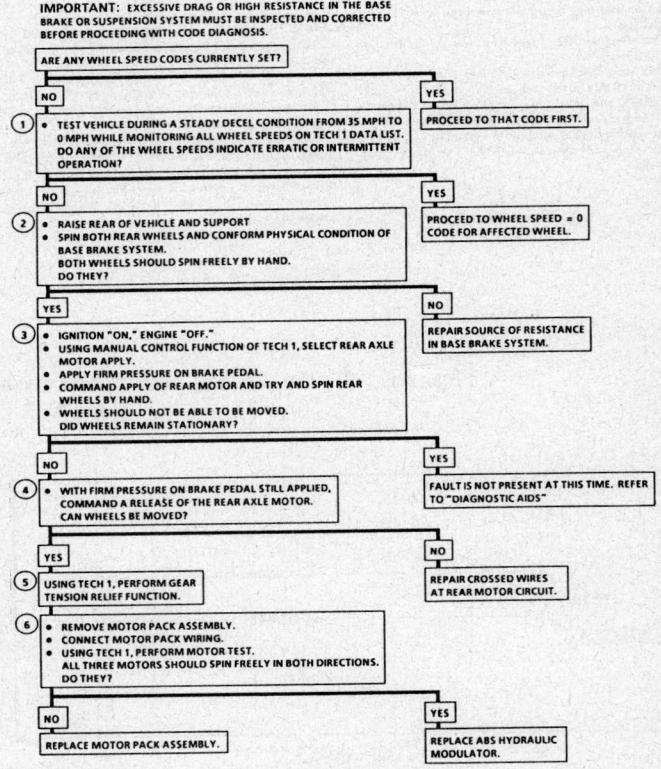

Fig. 62   Code A054, rear axle in release too long. 1991—92

Except Cutlass Supreme, Grand Prix, Lumina & Regal

Cutlass Supreme, Grand Prix, Lumina & Regal

Circuit Description:

This code identifies a fault detected by the MDI custom IC. It also ensures the cause of the fault is not a result of a problem with the enable relay under a Code A055 failure. The MDI fault tests will be run to identify which circuit has failed, and may also cause additional codes to set to pinpoint the problem circuit.

Test Description: Number(s) below refer to circled number(s) on the diagnostic chart.
1. This insures that the Code A055 fault was not set due to a motor or EMB fault.
2. This checks to see if the fault is still present.
3. This step insures that Code A055 was not due to poor terminal contact at the motor pack connector.

Diagnostic Aids:

An "Intermittent" problem may be caused by a poor connection, rubbed through wire insulation, or a wire that is broken inside the insulation.

The frequency of the problem can be checked by using the enhanced diagnostic function of the "Scan" tool

Any circuitry, that is suspected as causing the intermittent complaint, should be thoroughly checked for backed out terminals, improper mating, broken locks, improperly formed or damaged terminals, poor terminal to wiring connections or physical damage to the wiring harness.

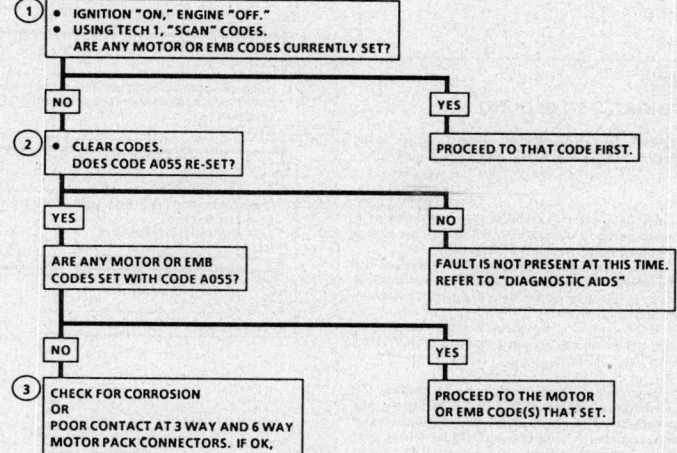

Fig. 63   Code A055, motor Driver Interface MDI fault detected. 1991–92

CODE A056
LEFT FRONT MOTOR CIRCUIT OPEN

Circuit Description:

This code identifies a motor that cannot be energized due to an open in its circuitry. This fault will not allow proper front ABS operation.

Test Description: Number(s) below refer to circled number(s) on the diagnostic chart.
1. This step checks for proper resistance of the motor.
2. This step is used to release the tension of the motor pack prior to removal.
3. This step checks for an open in the motor "high" circuitry.
4. This step checks for an open in the motor "low" circuitry.

Diagnostic Aids:

Using Tech 1, select manual control function, and exercise motor movement of affected channel in both directions while applying light pressure on the brake pedal.

If erratic or "jumpy" brake pedal movement is detected while performing an "apply" or "release" function of the motor, an intermittent fault may be indicated.

An "Intermittent" problem may be caused by a poor connection, rubbed through wire insulation, or a wire that is broken inside the insulation.

If the fault is not current, wiggle the wires of the affected channel and check if the code resets. This will help to pinpoint an intermittent problem in the motor circuitry or connections.

The frequency of the problem can be checked by using the enhanced diagnostic function of the "Scan" tool

Any circuitry, that is suspected as causing the intermittent complaint, should be thoroughly checked for backed out terminals, improper mating, broken locks, improperly formed or damaged terminals, poor terminal to wiring connections or physical damage to the wiring harness.

Fig. 64   Code A056, left front motor circuit open. 1991–92

CODE A057
LEFT FRONT MOTOR CIRCUIT SHORTED TO GROUND

Circuit Description:

This code identifies a motor circuit that is shorted to ground. This fault will not allow the motor to be controlled at the commanded current rate or will cause the driver circuit to allow current directly to ground.

Test Description: Number(s) below refer to circled number(s) on the diagnostic chart.
1. This step checks for a short to ground in the motor "high" circuitry.
2. This step checks for a short to ground in the motor "low" circuitry.
3. This step checks for a motor that is internally shorted to ground.
4. This step is used to release the tension of the motor pack prior to removal.

Diagnostic Aids:

Using Tech 1, select manual control function, and exercise motor movement of affected channel in both directions while applying light pressure on the brake pedal.

If erratic or "jumpy" brake pedal movement is detected while performing an "apply" or "release" function of the motor, an intermittent fault may be indicated.

An "Intermittent" problem may be caused by a poor connection, rubbed through wire insulation, or a wire that is broken inside the insulation.

If the fault is not current, wiggle the wires of the affected channel and check if the code resets. This will help to pinpoint an intermittent problem in the motor circuitry or connections.

The frequency of the problem can be checked by using the enhanced diagnostic function of the Tech 1 "Scan" tool

Any circuitry, that is suspected as causing the intermittent complaint, should be thoroughly checked for backed out terminals, improper mating, broken locks, improperly formed or damaged terminals, poor terminal to wiring connections or physical damage to the wiring harness.

Fig. 65   Code A057, left front motor circuit shorted to ground1

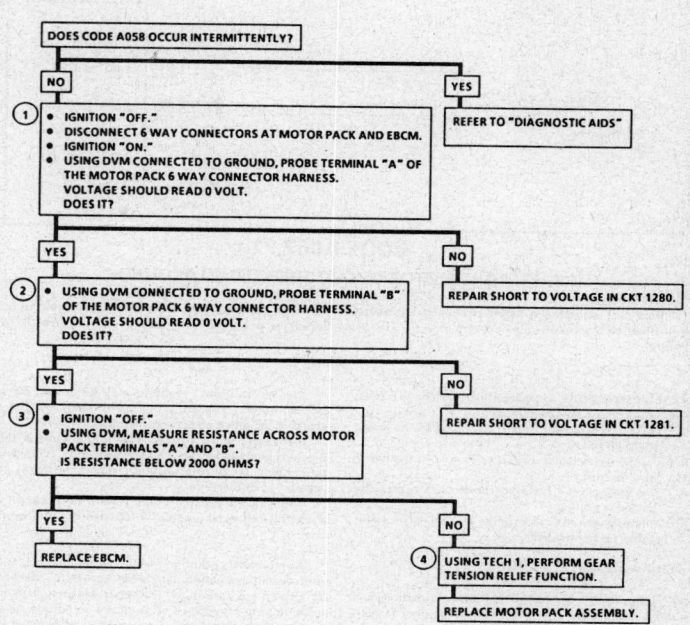

CODE A058

LEFT FRONT MOTOR CIRCUIT SHORTED TO BATTERY OR MOTOR SHORTED

Circuit Description:

This code identifies a motor circuit that is shorted to battery or a motor that has low or no resistance. This fault will not allow the motor to be controlled at the commanded current rate or will cause the motor to turn in the opposite direction, or not at all.

Test Description: Number(s) below refer to circled number(s) on the diagnostic chart.

1. This step checks for a short to voltage in the motor "high" circuitry.
2. This step checks for a short to voltage in the motor "low" circuitry.
3. This step checks for a motor that is internally shorted.
4. This step is used to release the tension of the motor pack prior to removal.

Diagnostic Aids:

Using Tech 1, select manual control function, and exercise motor movement of affected channel in both directions while applying light pressure on the brake pedal.

If erratic or "jumpy" brake pedal movement is detected while performing an "apply" or "release" function of the motor, an intermittent fault may be indicated.

An "Intermittent" problem may be caused by a poor connection, rubbed through wire insulation, or a wire that is broken inside the insulation.

If the fault is not current, wiggle the wires of the affected channel and check if the code resets. This will help to pinpoint an intermittent problem in the motor circuitry or connections.

The frequency of the problem can be checked by using the enhanced diagnostic function of the "Scan" tool

Code A038 sets as a current code and A058 is an infrequent history code, see Code A038 diagnostics.

Any circuitry, that is suspected as causing the intermittent complaint, should be thoroughly checked for backed out terminals, improper mating, broken locks, improperly formed or damaged terminals, poor terminal to wiring connections or physical damage to the wiring harness.

Fig. 66   Code A058, left front motor circuit shorted to battery. 1991–92

CODE A061

RIGHT FRONT MOTOR CIRCUIT OPEN

Circuit Description:

This code identifies a motor that cannot be energized due to an open in its circuitry. This fault will not allow proper front ABS operation.

Test Description: Number(s) below refer to circled number(s) on the diagnostic chart.

1. This step checks for proper resistance of the motor.
2. This step is used to release the tension of the motor pack prior to removal.
3. This step checks for an open in the motor "high" circuitry.
4. This step checks for an open in the motor "low" circuitry.

Diagnostic Aids:

Using Tech 1, select manual control function, and exercise motor movement of affected channel in both directions while applying light pressure on the brake pedal.

If erratic or "jumpy" brake pedal movement is detected while performing an "apply" or "release" function of the motor, an intermittent fault may be indicated.

An "Intermittent" problem may be caused by a poor connection, rubbed through wire insulation, or a wire that is broken inside the insulation.

If the fault is not current, wiggle the wires of the affected channel and check if the code resets. This will help to pinpoint an intermittent problem in the motor circuitry or connections.

The frequency of the problem can be checked by using the enhanced diagnostic function of the "Scan" tool

Any circuitry, that is suspected as causing the intermittent complaint, should be thoroughly checked for backed out terminals, improper mating, broken locks, improperly formed or damaged terminals, poor terminal to wiring connections or physical damage to the wiring harness.

Fig. 67   Code A061, right front motor circuit open. 1991–92

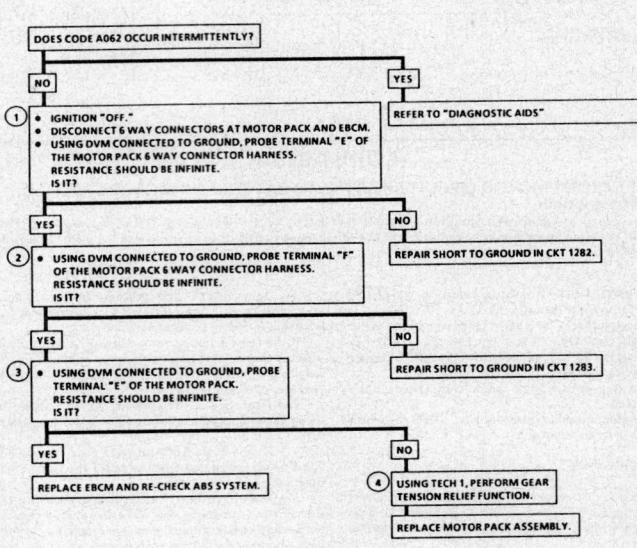

CODE A062

RIGHT FRONT MOTOR CIRCUIT SHORTED TO GROUND

Circuit Description:

This code identifies a motor circuit that is shorted to ground. This fault will not allow the motor to be controlled at the commanded current rate or will cause the motor driver circuit to allow current directly to ground.

Test Description: Number(s) below refer to circled number(s) on the diagnostic chart.

1. This step checks for a short to ground in the motor "high" circuitry.
2. This step checks for a short to ground in the motor "low" circuitry.
3. This step checks for a motor that is internally shorted to ground.
4. This step is used to release the tension of the motor pack prior to removal.

Diagnostic Aids:

Using Tech 1, select manual control function, and exercise motor movement of affected channel in both directions while applying light pressure on the brake pedal.

If erratic or "jumpy" brake pedal movement is detected while performing an "apply" or "release" function of the motor, an intermittent fault may be indicated.

An "Intermittent" problem may be caused by a poor connection, rubbed through wire insulation, or a wire that is broken inside the insulation.

If the fault is not current, wiggle the wires of the affected channel and check if the code resets. This will help to pinpoint an intermittent problem in the motor circuitry or connections.

The frequency of the problem can be checked by using the enhanced diagnostic function of the "Scan" tool.

Any circuitry, that is suspected as causing the intermittent complaint, should be thoroughly checked for backed out terminals, improper mating, broken locks, improperly formed or damaged terminals, poor terminal to wiring connections or physical damage to the wiring harness.

Fig. 68   Code A062, right front motor circuit shorted to ground. 1991–92

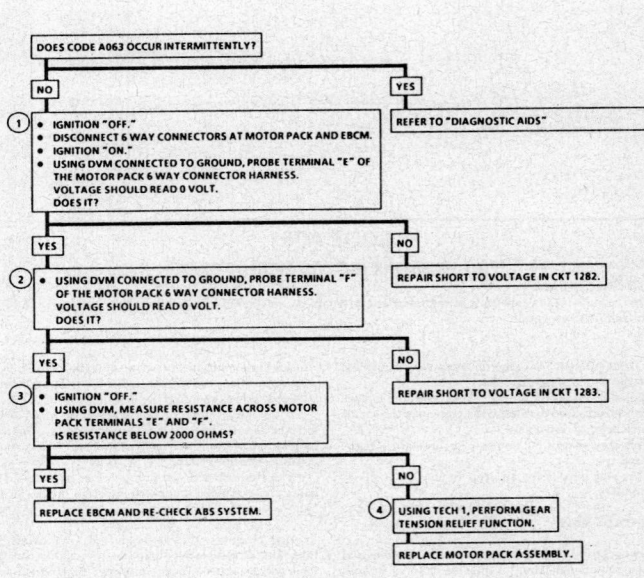

CODE A063

RIGHT FRONT MOTOR CIRCUIT SHORTED TO BATTERY OR MOTOR SHORTED

Circuit Description:

This code identifies a motor circuit that is shorted to battery or a motor that has low or no resistance. This fault will not allow the motor to be controlled at the commanded current rate or will cause the motor to turn in the opposite direction or not at all.

Test Description: Number(s) below refer to circled number(s) on the diagnostic chart.

1. This step checks for a short to voltage in the motor "high" circuitry.
2. This step checks for a short to voltage in the motor "low" circuitry.
3. This step checks for a motor that is internally shorted.
4. This test is used to release the tension of the motor pack prior to removal.

Diagnostic Aids:

Using Tech 1, select manual control function, and exercise motor movement of affected channel in both directions while applying light pressure on the brake pedal.

If erratic or "jumpy" brake pedal movement is detected while performing an "apply" or "release" function of the motor, an intermittent fault may be indicated.

An "Intermittent" problem may be caused by a poor connection, rubbed through wire insulation, or a wire that is broken inside the insulation.

If the fault is not current, wiggle the wires of the affected channel and check if the code resets. This will help to pinpoint an intermittent problem in the motor circuitry or connections.

The frequency of the problem can be checked by using the enhanced diagnostic function of the Tech 1 "Scan" tool.

If Code A041 sets as a current code and A063 is infrequent history code, see Code A041 for diagnosis.

Any circuitry, that is suspected as causing the intermittent complaint, should be thoroughly checked for backed out terminals, improper mating, broken locks, improperly formed or damaged terminals, poor terminal to wiring connections or physical damage to the wiring harness.

Fig. 69   Code A063, right front motor circuit shorted to battery. 1991–92

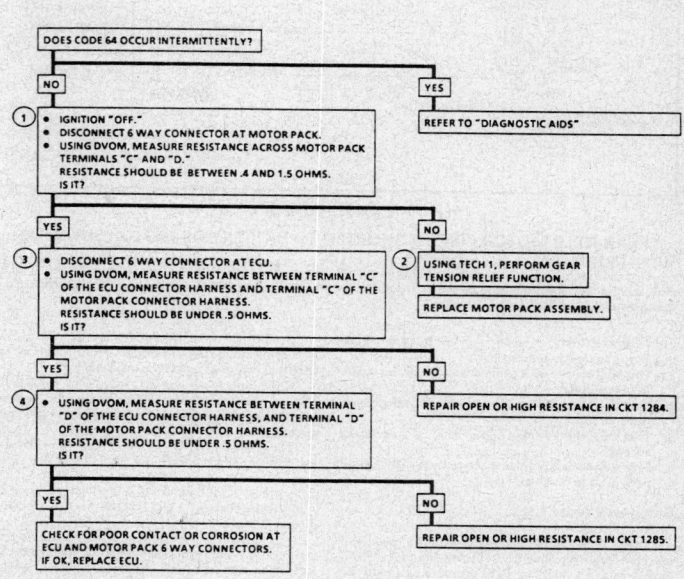

CODE A064

REAR AXLE MOTOR CIRCUIT OPEN

Circuit Description:

This code identifies a motor that cannot be energized due to an open in its circuitry. This fault will not allow proper rear ABS operation.

Test Description: Number(s) below refer to circled number(s) on the diagnostic chart.
1. This checks for an open circuit in the motor.
2. This step is used to release the tension of the motor pack prior to removal.
3. This step checks for an open in the motor "high" circuitry.
4. This step checks for an open in the motor "low" circuitry.

Diagnostic Aids:

Using Tech 1, select manual control function, and exercise motor movement of affected channel in both directions while applying light pressure on the brake pedal.

If erratic or "jumpy" brake pedal movement is detected while performing an "apply" or "release" function of the motor, an intermittent fault may be indicated.

An "Intermittent" problem may be caused by a poor connection, rubbed through wire insulation, or a wire that is broken inside the insulation.

If the fault is not current, wiggle the wires of the affected channel and check if the code resets. This will help to pinpoint an intermittent problem in the motor circuitry or connections.

The frequency of the problem can be checked by using the enhanced diagnostic function of the "Scan" tool.

Any circuitry, that is suspected as causing the intermittent complaint, should be thoroughly checked for backed out terminals, improper mating, broken locks, improperly formed or damaged terminals, poor terminal to wiring connections or physical damage to the wiring harness.

Fig. 70   Code A064, rear axle motor circuit open. 1991–92

CODE A065

REAR AXLE MOTOR CIRCUIT SHORTED TO GROUND

Circuit Description:

This test identifies a motor circuit that is shorted to ground. This fault will not allow the motor to be controlled at the commanded current rate or will cause the driver circuit to allow current directly to ground.

Test Description: Number(s) below refer to circled number(s) on the diagnostic chart.
1. This step checks for a short to ground in the motor "high" circuitry.
2. This step checks for a short to ground in the motor "low" circuitry.
3. This step checks for a motor that is internally shorted to ground.
4. This step is used to release the tension of the motor pack prior to removal.

Diagnostic Aids:

Using Tech 1, select manual control function, and exercise motor movement of affected channel in both directions while applying light pressure on the brake pedal.

If erratic or "jumpy" brake pedal movement is detected while performing an "apply" or "release" function of the motor, an intermittent fault may be indicated.

An "Intermittent" problem may be caused by a poor connection, rubbed through wire insulation, or a wire that is broken inside the insulation.

If the fault is not current, wiggle the wires of the affected channel and check if the code resets. This will help to pinpoint an intermittent problem in the motor circuitry or connections.

The frequency of the problem can be checked by using the enhanced diagnostic function of the "Scan" tool,

Any circuitry, that is suspected as causing the intermittent complaint, should be thoroughly checked for backed out terminals, improper mating, broken locks, improperly formed or damaged terminals, poor terminal to wiring connections or physical damage to the wiring harness.

Fig. 71   Code A065, rear axle motor circuit shorted to ground. 1991–92

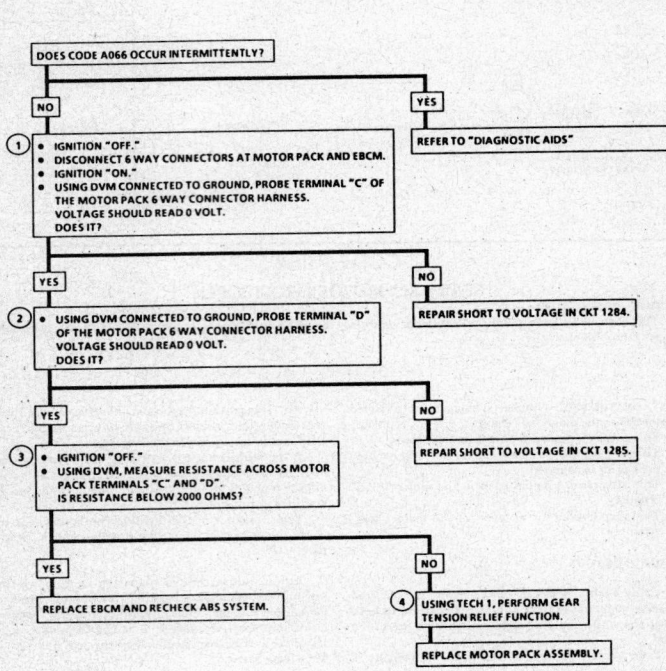

CODE A066

REAR AXLE MOTOR CIRCUIT SHORTED TO BATTERY OR MOTOR SHORTED

Circuit Description:

This code identifies a motor circuit that is shorted to battery or a motor that has low or zero resistance. This fault will not allow the motor to be controlled at the commanded current rate or will cause the motor to turn in the opposite direction or not turn at all.

Test Description: Number(s) below refer to circled number(s) on the diagnostic chart.

1. This step checks for a short to voltage in the motor "high" circuitry.
2. This step checks for a short to voltage in the motor "low" circuitry.
3. This step checks for a motor that is internally shorted.
4. This step is used to release the tension of the motor pack prior to removal.

Diagnostic Aids:

Using Tech 1, select manual control function, and exercise motor movement of affected channel in both directions while applying light pressure on the brake pedal.

If erratic or "jumpy" brake pedal movement is detected while performing an "apply" or "release" function of the motor, an intermittent fault may be indicated.

An "Intermittent" problem may be caused by a poor connection, rubbed through wire insulation, or a wire that is broken inside the insulation.

If the fault is not current, wiggle the wires of the affected channel and check if the code resets. This will help to pinpoint an intermittent problem in the motor circuitry or connections.

The frequency of the problem can be checked by using the enhanced diagnostic function of the "Scan" tool

If Code A042 sets as current code and A066 is infrequent history code, see Code A042 diagnostics.

Any circuitry, that is suspected as causing the intermittent complaint, should be thoroughly checked for backed out terminals, improper mating, broken locks, improperly formed or damaged terminals, poor terminal to wiring connections or physical damage to the wiring harness.

Fig. 72   Code A066, rear axle motor circuit shorted to battery. 1991–92

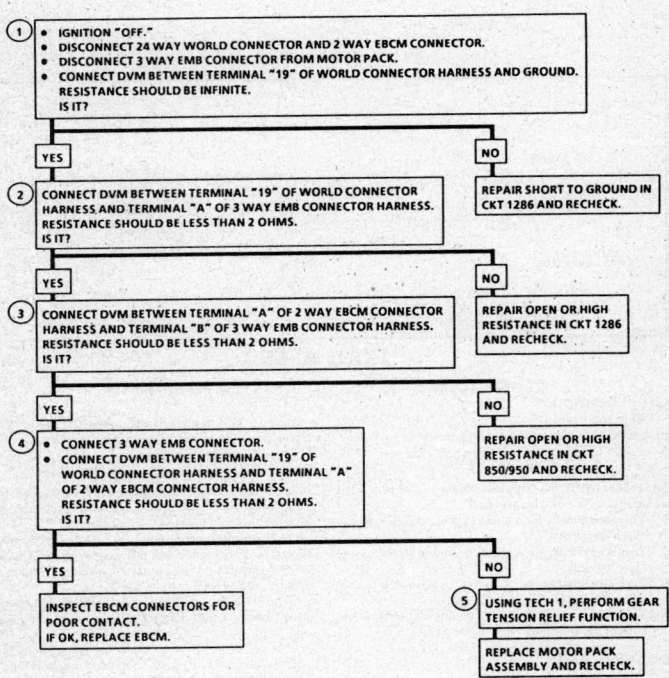

CODE A067

LEFT FRONT EMB RELEASE CIRCUIT OPEN OR SHORTED TO GROUND

Circuit Description:

This code is designed to detect shorts to ground and opens in the EMB release circuit.

A short to ground between the EMB and the ABS EBCM will cause the EMB to be energized indefinitely at an uncontrolled current, causing the EMB to damage itself. To remove the effects of the fault, the enable relay must be turned "OFF," eliminating power to the EMB as well as the ABS system.

Test Description: Number(s) below refer to circled number(s) on the diagnostic chart.

1. This step checks for a short to ground in the EMB control circuitry.
2. This step insures that the EMB is not internally shorted or open.
3. This step checks to see if CKT 850/950 has continuity to the EMB connector.
4. This step looks for an open in the EMB control circuitry.
5. This step is used to release the tension of the motor pack prior to removal.

Diagnostic Aids:

An "Intermittent" problem may be caused by a poor connection, rubbed through wire insulation, or a wire that is broken inside the insulation.

The frequency of the problem can be checked by using the enhanced diagnostic function of the "Scan" tool

Any circuitry, that is suspected as causing the intermittent complaint, should be thoroughly checked for backed out terminals, improper mating, broken locks, improperly formed or damaged terminals, poor terminal to wiring connections or physical damage to the wiring harness.

Fig. 73   Code A067, left front EMB release circuit open or shorted to ground. Except Cutlass Supreme, Grand Prix, Lumina & Regal. 1991–92

CODE A068
LEFT FRONT EMB CIRCUIT SHORTED TO BATTERY OR EMB SHORTED

Circuit Description:
This code is designed to detect shorts to battery and shorts in the EMB release circuit. These faults will not allow the EMB to be energized when needed.

Test Description: Number(s) below refer to the circled number(s) on the diagnostic chart.
1. This step checks to see if the fault is currently present.
2. This step identifies a short to voltage in the EMB control circuitry.
3. This step checks for an EMB that has lower than normal resistance.
4. This step is used to release the tension of the motor pack prior to removal.

Diagnostic Aids:
An "Intermittent" problem may be caused by a poor connection, rubbed through wire insulation, or a wire that is broken inside the insulation.

The frequency of the problem can be checked by using the enhanced diagnostic function of the "Scan" tool

Any circuitry, that is suspected as causing the intermittent complaint, should be thoroughly checked for backed out terminals, improper mating, broken locks, improperly formed or damaged terminals, poor terminal to wiring connections or physical damage to the wiring harness.

Fig. 74   Code A068, left front EMB release circuit shorted to battery or driver open. Except Cutlass Supreme, Grand Prix, Lumina & Regal. 1991–92

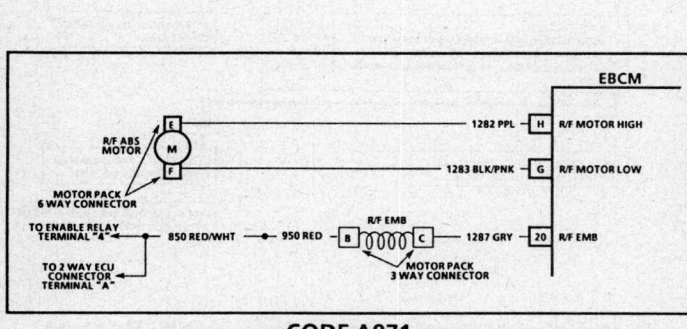

CODE A071
RIGHT FRONT EMB CIRCUIT OPEN OR SHORTED TO GROUND

Circuit Description:
This code is designed to detect shorts to ground and opens in the EMB release circuit.
A short to ground between the EMB and the ABS EBCM will cause the EMB to be energized indefinitely at an uncontrolled current causing the EMB to damage itself.

Test Description: Number(s) below refer to the circled number(s) on the diagnostic chart.
1. This step checks for a short to ground in the EMB control circuitry.
2. This step insures that the EMB is not internally shorted or open.
3. This step checks to see if CKT 850/950 has continuity to the EMB connector.
4. This step looks for an open in the EMB control circuitry.
5. This step is used to release the tension of the motor pack prior to removal.

Diagnostic Aids:
An "Intermittent" problem may be caused by a poor connection, rubbed through wire insulation, or a wire that is broken inside the insulation.
The frequency of the problem can be checked by using the enhanced diagnostic function of the "Scan" tool

Any circuitry, that is suspected as causing the intermittent complaint, should be thoroughly checked for backed out terminals, improper mating, broken locks, improperly formed or damaged terminals, poor terminal to wiring connections or physical damage to the wiring harness.

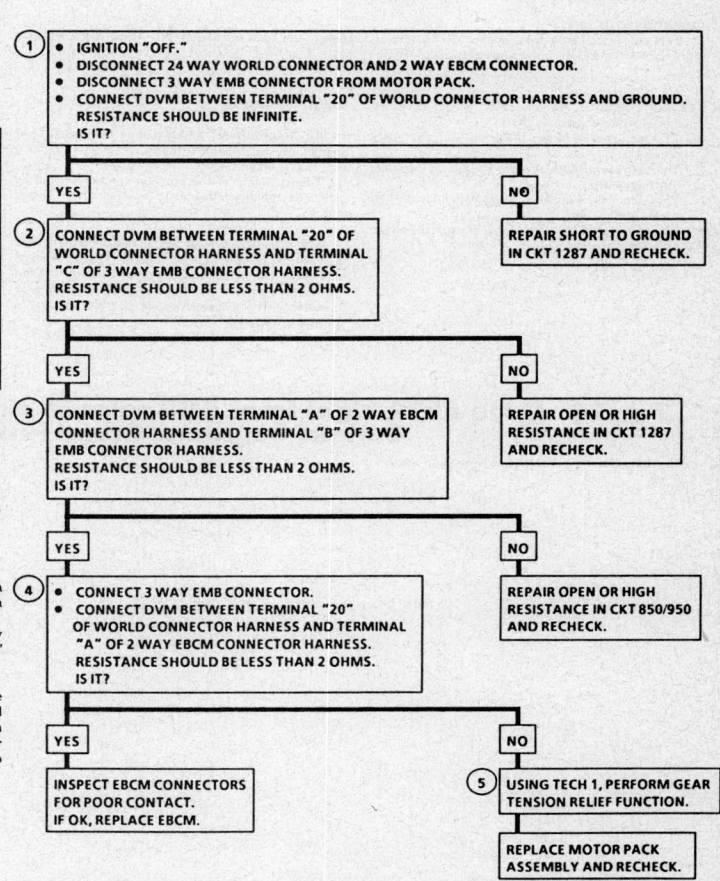

Fig. 75   Code A071, right front EMB release circuit open or shorted to ground. Except Cutlass Supreme, Grand Prix, Lumina & Regal. 1991–92

CODE A072

RIGHT FRONT EMB CIRCUIT SHORTED TO BATTERY OR EMB SHORTED

Circuit Description:

This code is designed to detect shorts to battery and shorts in the EMB release circuit. These faults will not allow the EMB to be energized when needed.

Test Description: Number(s) below refer to circled number(s) on the diagnostic chart.

1. This step checks to see if the fault is currently present.
2. This step identifies a short to voltage in the EMB control circuitry.
3. This step checks for an EMB that has lower than normal resistance.
4. This step is used to release the tension of the motor pack prior to removal.

Diagnostic Aids:

An "Intermittent" problem may be caused by a poor connection, rubbed through wire insulation, or a wire that is broken inside the insulation.

The frequency of the problem can be checked by using the enhanced diagnostic function of the "Scan" tool

Any circuitry, that is suspected as causing the intermittent complaint, should be thoroughly checked for backed out terminals, improper mating, broken locks, improperly formed or damaged terminals, poor terminal to wiring connections or physical damage to the wiring harness.

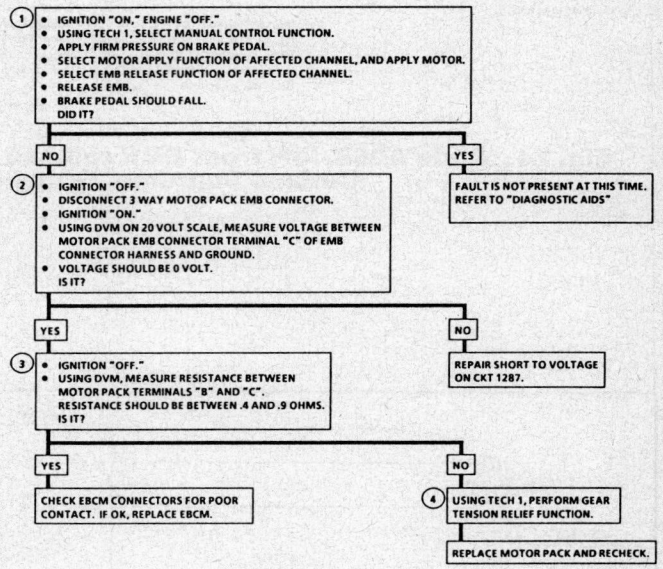

Fig. 76 Code A072, right front EMB release circuit shorted to battery or driver open. Except Cutlass Supreme, Grand Prix, Lumina & Regal. 1991–92

Cavalier & Sunbird

Except Cavalier & Sunbird

Circuit Description:

This code identifies a solenoid that cannot be energized due to an open in its circuitry, or a solenoid that is always energized due to a short to battery in its circuitry between the driver and the solenoid. An open will not allow proper ABS operation, but the short to battery simply turns "ON" the solenoid. A path for base brakes is still allowed once the motor re-homes and the check valve is lifted off its seat during key on initialization.

Test Description: Number(s) below refer to circled number(s) on the diagnostic chart.
1. This checks for a short to voltage in the control circuitry of the solenoid.
2. This checks for an open in the control circuit of the solenoid.
3. This step identifies an open in the solenoid or ground circuit.
4. This step checks for a possible intermittent problem in the solenoid circuitry due to poor terminal contact.

Diagnostic Aids:

An "Intermittent" problem may be caused by a poor connection, rubbed through wire insulation, or a wire that is broken inside the insulation.

The frequency of the problem can be checked by using the enhanced diagnostic function of the "Scan" tool.

Any circuitry, that is suspected as causing the intermittent complaint, should be thoroughly checked for backed out terminals, improper mating, broken locks, improperly formed or damaged terminals, poor terminal to wiring connections or physical damage to the wiring harness.

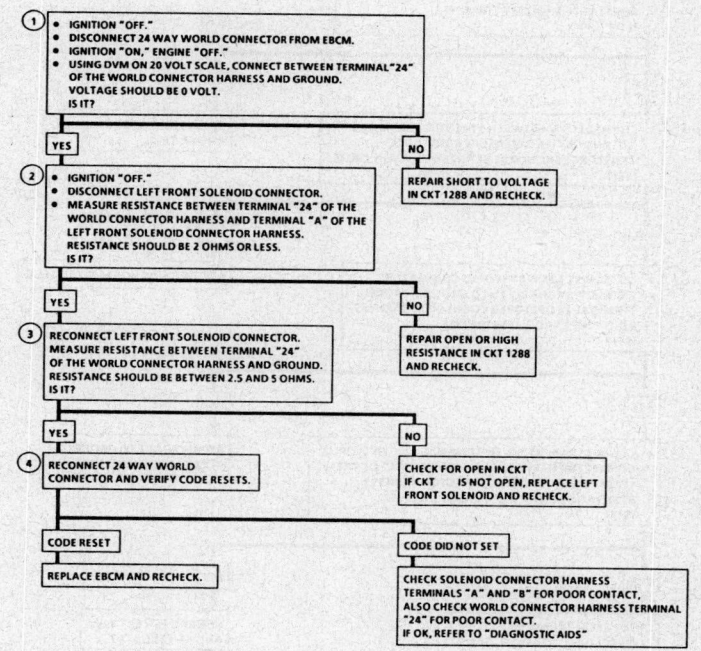

Fig. 77   Code A076, left front solenoid circuit open or shorted to battery. 1991–92

Cavalier & Sunbird

Except Cavalier & Sunbird

Circuit Description:

This code identifies a solenoid that cannot be energized due to an open in its driver circuitry, or a short to ground between the solenoid driver and the solenoid. These faults can affect ABS operation since the flow of brake fluid to the wheel cylinder cannot be stopped, making ABS operation for that channel impossible.

Test Description: Number(s) below refer to circled number(s) on the diagnostic chart.

1. This step checks for a solenoid that is internally shorted to ground.
2. This step checks for a solenoid that is not within proper resistance values.
3. This step indicates if a short to ground exists in the solenoid circuitry.
4. This checks for an open control circuit to the EBCM.

Diagnostic Aids:

An "Intermittent" problem may be caused by a poor connection, rubbed through wire insulation, or a wire that is broken inside the insulation.

The frequency of the problem can be checked by using the enhanced diagnostic function of the Tech 1 "Scan" tool.

Any circuitry, that is suspected as causing the intermittent complaint, should be thoroughly checked for backed out terminals, improper mating, broken locks, improperly formed or damaged terminals, poor terminal to wiring connections or physical damage to the wiring harness.

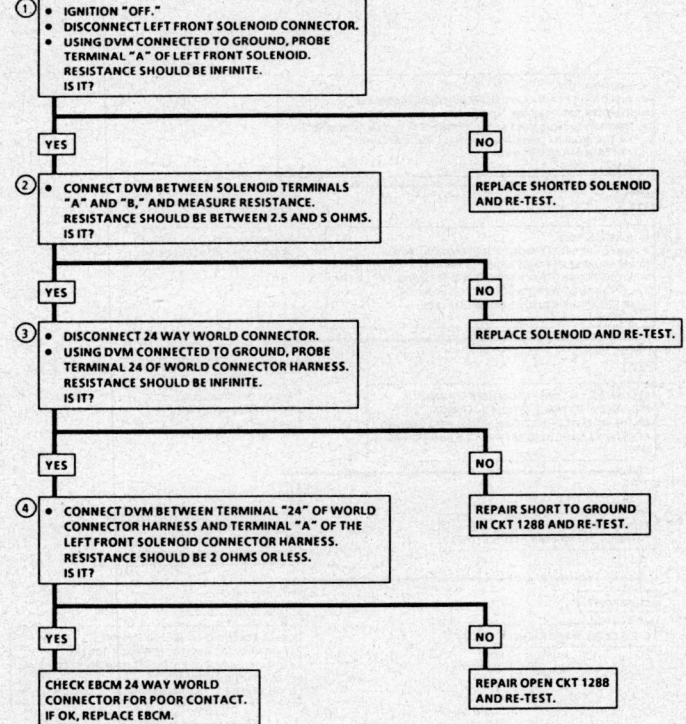

Fig. 78   Code A077, left front solenoid shorted to ground or driver open. 1991–92

Cavalier & Sunbird

Except Cavalier & Sunbird

Circuit Description:

This code identifies a solenoid that cannot be energized due to an open in its circuitry, or a solenoid that is always energized due to a short to battery in its circuitry between the driver and the solenoid. An open will not allow proper ABS operation, but the short to battery simply turns "ON" the solenoid. A path for base brakes is still allowed once the motor re-homes and the check valve is lifted off its seat during key on initialization.

Test Description: Number(s) below refer to circled number(s) on the diagnostic chart.
1. This checks for a short to voltage in the control circuitry of the solenoid.
2. This checks for an open in the control circuit of the solenoid.
3. This step identifies an open in the solenoid or ground circuit.
4. This step checks for a possible intermittent problem in the solenoid circuitry due to poor terminal contact.

Diagnostic Aids:

An "Intermittent" problem may be caused by a poor connection, rubbed through wire insulation, or a wire that is broken inside the insulation.

The frequency of the problem can be checked by using the enhanced diagnostic function of the "Scan" tool.

Any circuitry, that is suspected as causing the intermittent complaint, should be thoroughly checked for backed out terminals, improper mating, broken locks, improperly formed or damaged terminals, poor terminal to wiring connections or physical damage to the wiring harness.

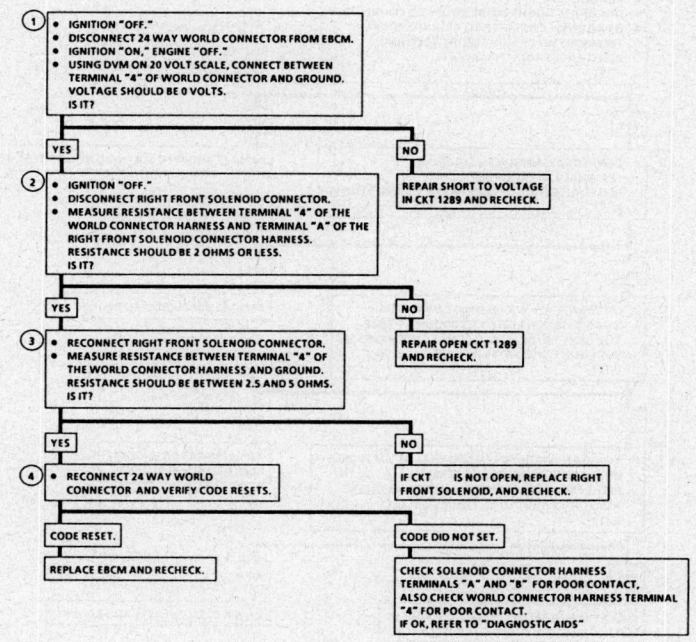

Fig. 79   Code A078, right front solenoid circuit open or shorted to battery. 1991–92

Cavalier & Sunbird

Except Cavalier & Sunbird

Circuit Description:

This code identifies a solenoid that cannot be energized due to an open in its driver circuitry, or a short to ground between the solenoid driver and the solenoid. These faults can affect ABS operation since the flow of brake fluid to the wheel cylinder cannot be stopped, making ABS operation for that channel impossible.

Test Description: Number(s) below refer to circled number(s) on the diagnostic chart.

1. This step checks for a solenoid that is internally shorted to ground.
2. This step checks for a solenoid that is not within proper resistance values.
3. This step indicates if a short to ground exists in the solenoid circuitry.
4. This checks for an open control circuit to the EBCM.

Diagnostic Aids:

An "Intermittent" problem may be caused by a poor connection, rubbed through wire insulation, or a wire that is broken inside the insulation.

The frequency of the problem can be checked by using the enhanced diagnostic function of the "Scan" tool.

Any circuitry, that is suspected as causing the intermittent complaint, should be thoroughly checked for backed out terminals, improper mating, broken locks, improperly formed or damaged terminals, poor terminal to wiring connections or physical damage to the wiring harness.

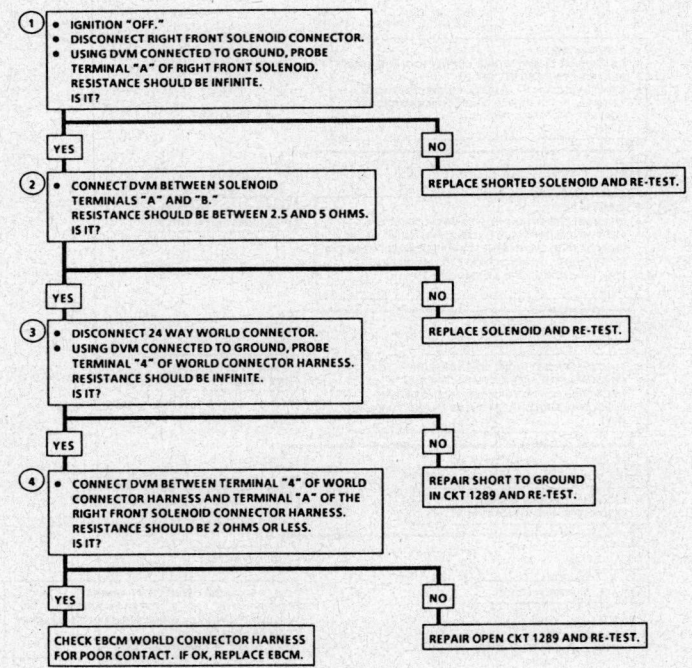

Fig. 80   Code A081, right front solenoid shorted to ground or driver open. 1991–92

CODE A082
CALIBRATION MEMORY FAILURE

Circuit Description:
This code allows the EBCM to check for a calibration failure by comparing the calibration value to a known value stored in the EEPROM.

This test is also used as a security measure to prevent improper use of calibrations or changes to these calibrations that may alter the designed function of ABS.

Test Description: Number(s) below refer to circled number(s) on the diagnostic chart.
1. This step checks to see if the fault is present during diagnosis. If present, the EBCM is not functioning correctly and must be replaced.

IMPORTANT: At the time of printing, 1992 vehicles with ABS-VI were not being field reprogrammed to correct this failure. A service bulletin will be issued when EEPROM reprogramming is authorized.

Diagnostic Aids:

An intermittent Code A082 may be caused by a bad cell in the EEPROM that is sensitive to temperature changes. If Code A082 failed more than once, but is intermittent, replace EBCM.

The frequency of the problem can be checked by using the enhanced diagnostic function of the "Scan" tool

Fig. 81   Code A082, calibration memory failure. 1991–92

Cavalier & Sunbird

Beretta & Corsica

Achieva, Calais & Grand Am

Cutlass Supreme, Grand Prix, Lumina & Regal

Circuit Description:

This code is provided as an information only test, and reflects the status of the command issued by the ABS EBCM to illuminate the red brake warning light. If another diagnostic code issues a command to illuminate the red brake warning light, Code A086 will be stored in EEPROM as a history code at the conclusion of the ignition cycle.

Test Description: Number(s) below refer to circled number(s) on the diagnostic chart.

1. This step serves to identify if a code other than Code A086 commanded the red brake warning light "ON."

Diagnostic Aids:

Any ABS mechanical code that issues a command to illuminate the red brake warning light will also result in Code A086 being stored in EEPROM during shut down. These codes are: A038, A041, A042, A045, A046, A047, A048 and A051. If the motors are not in their home position, certain electrical codes will also command the red brake warning light "ON." These codes are: A014; A018, A055, A056, A057, A0587, A061, A062, A063, A064, A065, A066, A067, A068, A071 and A072.

If any of these codes are indicated along with Code A086, they must be corrected prior to addressing a Code A086 fault.

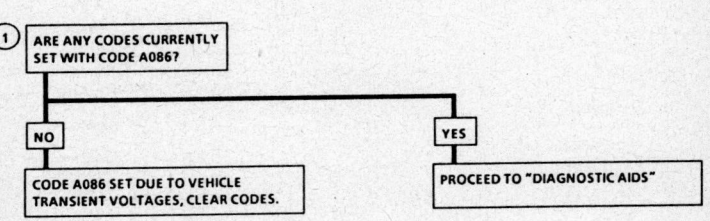

Fig. 82 Code A086, ABS enable red brake telltale. 1991–92

Cavalier & Sunbird

Beretta & Corsica

Achieva, Calais & Grand Am

Cutlass Supreme, Grand Prix, Lumina & Regal

Circuit Description:
This code is used to verify the EBCM has continuity to the brake warning light in case the EBCM must turn it "ON." This will only occur if an ABS fault is detected that may degrade base brake operation.

Because ABS is not the only device controlling the brake warning light (parking brake and low fluid sensor may also turn "ON" the light) a short to ground in this circuit cannot be detected.

Test Description: Number(s) below refer to circled number(s) on the diagnostic chart.
1. This step identifies if the fault is currently present.
2. This step indicates if the EBCM and circuitry has the ability to complete the ground to the brake warning light and illuminate it.
3. Because the brake warning light has current supplied to it through the 10 amp gauge fuse, this step would indicate if the ignition circuit is complete to the I/P cluster.
4. This step isolates if the open circuit is due to a EBCM failure or open circuitry to the brake warning light.

Diagnostic Aids:

An "Intermittent" problem may be caused by a poor connection, rubbed through wire insulation, or a wire that is broken inside the insulation.

The frequency of the problem can be checked by using the enhanced diagnostic function of the Tech 1 "Scan" tool

If a Tech 1 or T-100 are not available the parking brake handle may be lifted to verify proper light operation and continuity of CKTs 3 and 39.

Any circuitry, that is suspected as causing the intermittent complaint, should be thoroughly checked for backed out terminals, improper mating, broken locks, improperly formed or damaged terminals, poor terminal to wiring connections or physical damage to the wiring harness.

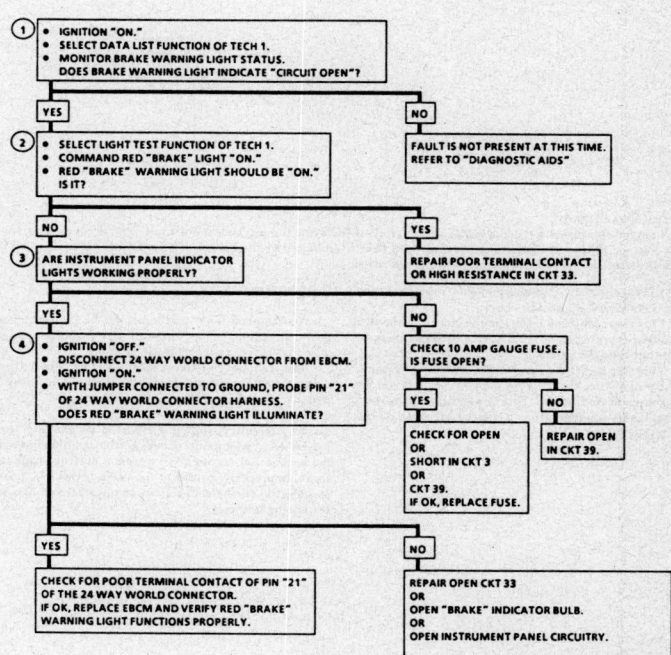

Fig. 83   Code A087, red brake telltale circuit open. 1991—92

Cavalier & Sunbird

Beretta & Corsica

Achieva, Calais & Grand Am

Cutlass Supreme, Grand Prix, Lumina & Regal

Circuit Description:
This code identifies a short to battery between the EBCM and the RED brake warning light, or an open driver that does not allow the RED brake warning light to be illuminated by the EBCM. This will only occur if an ABS fault is detected that may degrade base brake operation.

Test Description: Number(s) below refer to circled number(s) on the diagnostic chart.
1. This step identifies if the ground circuit to the Red brake warning light is being completed by a source other than the EBCM.
2. This step identifies if the fault is currently present.
3. By removing the 10 amp gauge fuse, the voltage source is eliminated. This test indicates if voltage is being supplied from a source other than the gauge fuse.

Diagnostic Aids:

An "Intermittent" problem may be caused by a poor connection, rubbed through wire insulation, or a wire that is broken inside the insulation.
The frequency of the problem can be checked by using the enhanced diagnostic function of the "Scan" tool.

Any circuitry, that is suspected as causing the intermittent complaint, should be thoroughly checked for backed out terminals, improper mating, broken locks, improperly formed or damaged terminals, poor terminal to wiring connections or physical damage to the wiring harness.

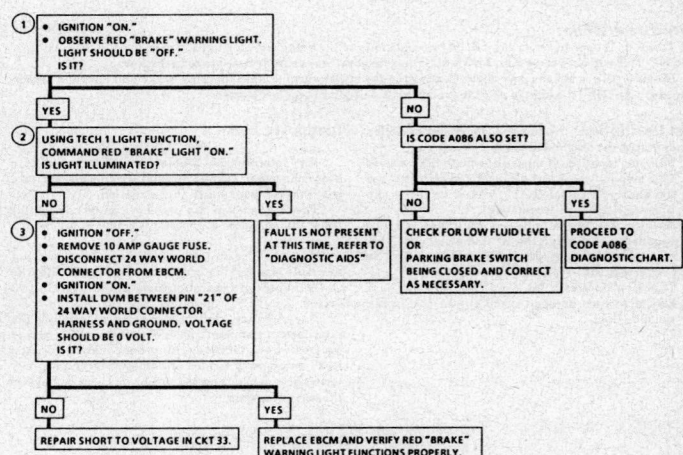

Fig. 84 Code A088, red brake telltale circuit shorted to battery or driver open. 1991–92

Cavalier & Sunbird

Beretta & Corsica

Achieva, Calais & Grand Am

Cutlass Supreme, Grand Prix, Lumina & Regal

Circuit Description:
This code is used to detect an open brake switch in the non-ABS mode. The EBCM looks for decel rates that would indicate braking action and verifies this assumption by requiring several repeats of this detection method. In each case, ABS will not be available since no brake switch is seen.

Test Description: Number(s) below refer to circled number(s) on the diagnostic chart.

1. This step indicates if the brake switch signal is being received by the EBCM.
2. This step indicates if an open circuit exists in the brake switch or brake lamp circuitry.
3. This step isolates the open circuit to either the brake switch input circuitry, or the EBCM.

Diagnostic Aids:

An "Intermittent" problem may be caused by a poor connection, rubbed through wire insulation, or a wire that is broken inside the insulation.
The frequency of the problem can be checked by using the enhanced diagnostic function of the "Scan" tool.

Any circuitry, that is suspected as causing the intermittent complaint, should be thoroughly checked for backed out terminals, improper mating, broken locks, improperly formed or damaged terminals, poor terminal to wiring connections or physical damage to the wiring harness.

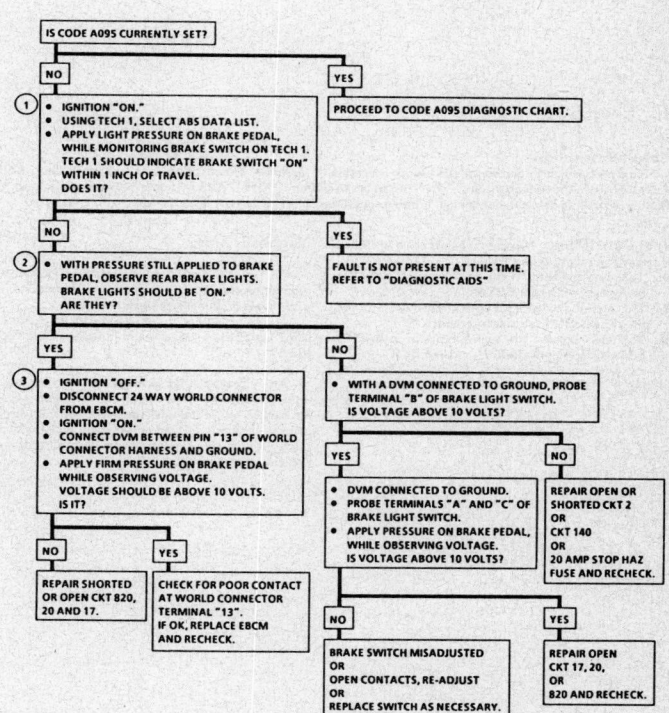

Fig. 85 Code A091, open brake switch contacts, decel detection. 1991–92

Cavalier & Sunbird

Beretta & Corsica

Achieva, Calais & Grand Am

Cutlass Supreme, Grand Prix, Lumina & Regal

Circuit Description:
This code is run to determine the proper operation of the brake switch. This is important because ABS is activated when the brake switch is "ON." If the brake switch is "OFF," ABS will never be activated. Since this fault is difficult to detect under normal braking conditions, this fault is only detected when ABS is required.

Test Description: Number(s) below refer to circled number(s) on the diagnostic chart.
1. This step indicates if the brake switch signal is being received by the EBCM.
2. This step indicates if an open circuit exists in the brake switch or brake lamp circuitry.
3. This step isolates the open circuit to either the brake switch input circuitry, or the EBCM.

Diagnostic Aids:
An "Intermittent" problem may be caused by a poor connection, rubbed through wire insulation, or a wire that is broken inside the insulation.
The frequency of the problem can be checked by using the enhanced diagnostic function of the "Scan" tool

Any circuitry, that is suspected as causing the intermittent complaint, should be thoroughly checked for backed out terminals, improper mating, broken locks, improperly formed or damaged terminals, poor terminal to wiring connections or physical damage to the wiring harness.

Fig. 86   Code A092, open brake switch contacts. 1991–92

Cavalier & Sunbird

Beretta & Corsica

Achieva, Calais & Grand Am

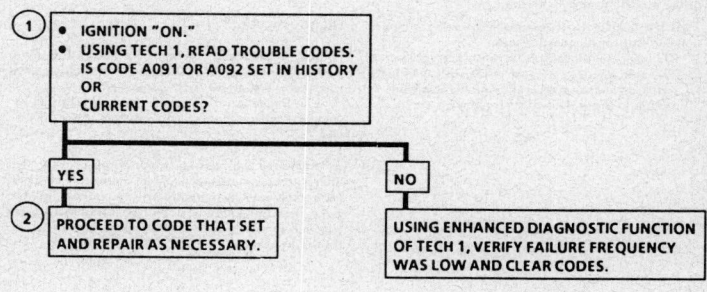

Cutlass Supreme, Grand Prix, Lumina & Regal

Circuit Description:

This code is the second portion of Codes A091 and A092. If Codes A091 or A092 failed during the last ignition cycle, Code A093 becomes a current failure during the next ignition cycle, keeping ABS disabled until a brake switch "ON" state is seen. When a change is seen during an ignition cycle in which Code A093 is a current failure, Code A091 or A092 will clear itself at the end of the current ignition cycle, and ABS will enable itself at the start of the next ignition cycle. Code A093 alone indicates Codes A091 or A092 failed previously, but is intermittent, or has been corrected.

Test Description: Number(s) below refer to circled number(s) on the diagnostic chart.

1. This step indicates which code (either A091 or A092) caused Code A093 to set.
2. This insures that the code that set is repaired so that Code A093 can be cleared.

Diagnostic Aids:

An "Intermittent" problem may be caused by a poor connection, rubbed through wire insulation, or a wire that is broken inside the insulation.

The frequency of the problem can be checked by using the enhanced diagnostic function of the "Scan" tool

Any circuitry, that is suspected as causing the intermittent complaint, should be thoroughly checked for backed out terminals, improper mating, broken locks, improperly formed or damaged terminals, poor terminal to wiring connections or physical damage to the wiring harness.

Also, verify proper brake switch operation using the data list of the "Scan" tool. As the brake is applied, the data list should display the brake switch "ON" within 1 inch of travel.

① • IGNITION "ON."
   • USING TECH 1, READ TROUBLE CODES.
     IS CODE A091 OR A092 SET IN HISTORY
     OR
     CURRENT CODES?

YES

② PROCEED TO CODE THAT SET AND REPAIR AS NECESSARY.

NO

USING ENHANCED DIAGNOSTIC FUNCTION OF TECH 1, VERIFY FAILURE FREQUENCY WAS LOW AND CLEAR CODES.

Fig. 87   Code A093, test 91 or 92 failed last or current ignition cycle. 1991–92

Cavalier & Sunbird

Beretta & Corsica

Achieva, Calais & Grand Am

Cutlass Supreme, Grand Prix, Lumina & Regal

Circuit Description:

This code is run to determine the proper operation of the brake switch. This is important because ABS is activated when the brake switch is "ON" and turned "OFF" when the brake is "OFF." If the brake switch is always "ON," ABS operation will always be requested resulting in potential modulator cycling on rough roads. Additionally, this failure will most likely result in a dead battery (due to the brake lights staying "ON") if the driver is not informed of this fault.

Test Description: Number(s) below refer to circled number(s) on the diagnostic chart.

1. This checks if the fault is currently present.
2. This step isolates the cause of the fault to either a faulty or misadjusted brake switch, or a short to voltage in the brake switch circuitry.

Diagnostic Aids:

An "Intermittent" problem may be caused by a poor connection, rubbed through wire insulation, or a wire that is broken inside the insulation.

The frequency of the problem can be checked by using the enhanced diagnostic function of the "Scan" tool

Any circuitry, that is suspected as causing the intermittent complaint, should be thoroughly checked for backed out terminals, improper mating, broken locks, improperly formed or damaged terminals, poor terminal to wiring connections or physical damage to the wiring harness.

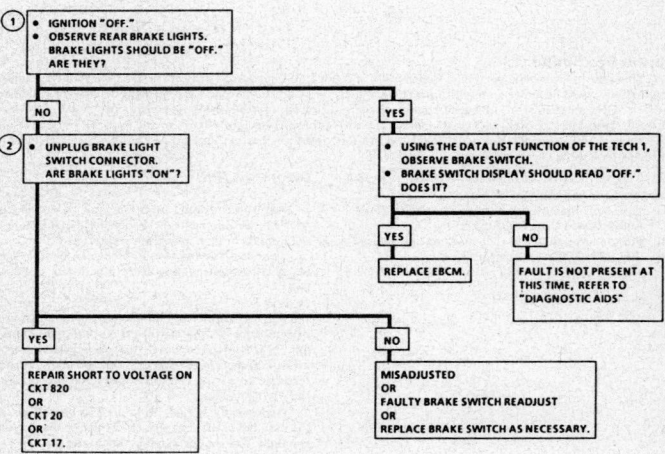

Fig. 88 Code A094, brake switch contacts or brake switch input shorted to battery. 1991–92

Cavalier & Sunbird

Beretta & Corsica

Achieva, Calais & Grand Am

Cutlass Supreme, Grand Prix, Lumina & Regal

Circuit Description:

This code is used to identify open brake switch circuitry that prevents the brake switch input to the EBCM from changing states when the brake is applied. This code is used in conjunction with Codes A091 and A092 to determine the cause of an open brake switch fault.

Test Description: Number(s) below refer to circled number(s) on the diagnostic chart.
1. This step is used to confirm that an open in the brake switch circuitry currently exists.
2. This step indicates if the brake switch signal is being received by the EBCM.
3. This step indicates if an open circuit exists in the brake switch or brake light circuitry.
4. This step isolates the open circuit to either the brake switch input circuitry, or the EBCM.

Diagnostic Aids:

An "Intermittent" problem may be caused by a poor connection, rubbed through wire insulation, or a wire that is broken inside the insulation.

The frequency of the problem can be checked by using the enhanced diagnostic function of the "Scan" tool.

Any circuitry, that is suspected as causing the intermittent complaint, should be thoroughly checked for backed out terminals, improper mating, broken locks, improperly formed or damaged terminals, poor terminal to wiring connections or physical damage to the wiring harness.

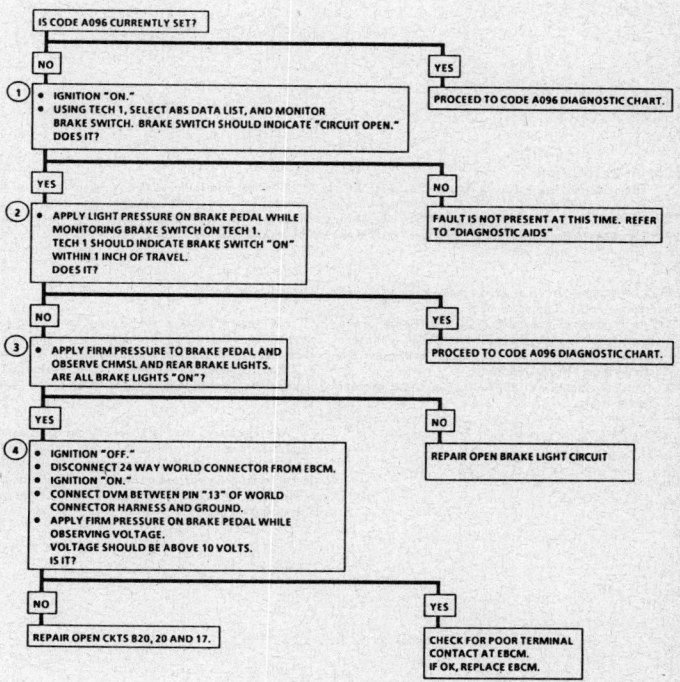

Fig. 89 Code A095, brake switch circuit open. 1991–92

Cavalier & Sunbird

Beretta & Corsica

Achieva, Calais & Grand Am

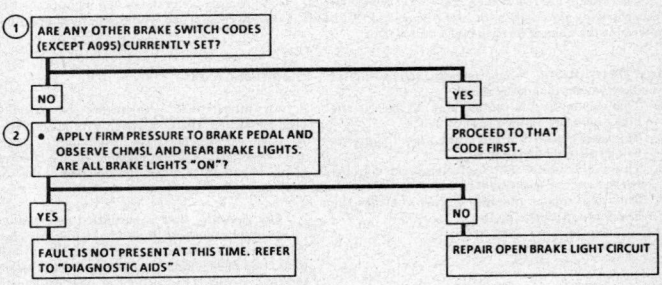

Cutlass Supreme, Grand Prix, Lumina & Regal

Circuit Description:

This code is designed to isolate the cause of a Code A095 failure and indicate to the driver ABS is still available. If Code A095 fails with Code A096, the brake lights are open, the brake light grounds are open, or the Center High Mounted Stop Light (CHMSL) circuit is open during 4 way flasher use. The presence of battery voltage at the brake switch input indicates a valid brake switch input is still available.

Test Description: Number(s) below refer to circled number(s) on the diagnostic chart.

1. As a result of a failure of an additional brake switch circuit code, this code may be set. To insure proper diagnosis, any additional brake switch codes must be repaired first.
2. This step identifies if the fault is currently present in the brake circuit.

Diagnostic Aids:

An "Intermittent" problem may be caused by a poor connection, rubbed through wire insulation, or a wire that is broken inside the insulation.

The frequency of the problem can be checked by using the enhanced diagnostic function of the "Scan" tool

Any circuitry, that is suspected as causing the intermittent complaint, should be thoroughly checked for backed out terminals, improper mating, broken locks, improperly formed or damaged terminals, poor terminal to wiring connections or physical damage to the wiring harness.

① ARE ANY OTHER BRAKE SWITCH CODES (EXCEPT A095) CURRENTLY SET?

NO → **② • APPLY FIRM PRESSURE TO BRAKE PEDAL AND OBSERVE CHMSL AND REAR BRAKE LIGHTS. ARE ALL BRAKE LIGHTS "ON"?**

YES → **PROCEED TO THAT CODE FIRST.**

YES → **FAULT IS NOT PRESENT AT THIS TIME. REFER TO "DIAGNOSTIC AIDS"**

NO → **REPAIR OPEN BRAKE LIGHT CIRCUIT**

Fig. 90 Code A096, brake lights open, brake light grounds open, CHMSL open during 4-way flasher operation. 1991–92

Cavalier

Sunbird

Beretta & Corsica

Achieva, Grand Am & Skylark

DTC A011

ABS INDICATOR LAMP CIRCUIT OPEN OR SHORTED TO GROUND

Circuit Description:

This test checks the state of the ABS indicator lamp to identify a situation in which the driver could not be warned of a system malfunction by the ABS indicator lamp, or the indicator lamp is always "ON." The Lamp Driver Module (LDM) turns the ABS indicator lamp "ON," unless the EBCM provides ground to turn it "OFF." Because of the circuitry in the LDM, only external malfunctions can be detected. As a result, the ABS indicator lamp itself is not diagnosable, only the control line to the EBCM can be diagnosed. In the event of an open CKT 1290, the ABS indicator lamp will be "ON" at all times, due to the loss of ground at the LDM input. If the control line is shorted to ground, the ABS indicator lamp is kept "OFF," due to the LDM input being grounded.

Failure Condition:

DTC A011 can be set only during the three second bulb check or when the ABS indicator lamp is commanded "ON." If the EBCM can not control the ABS indicator lamp for two seconds, a malfunction exists.

Action Taken:

A malfunction DTC is stored; however, ABS is not disabled.

Test Description: Number(s) below refer to circled number(s) on the diagnostic chart.

1. Checks to see if ABS indicator lamp functions properly. Normal operation would indicate that the malfunction is not present.

2. This step ensures that the circuitry from the EBCM to the lamp driver module is complete.

3. This step ensures that the ignition circuit to the lamp driver module is functional. An open gauge fuse or open CKT 3 or 39 would result in inoperative indicator lamps.

4. Isolates the cause of the ABS lamp remaining "OFF," by disconnecting the 24-way world connector, CKT 1290 should be open and cause the ABS lamp to be "ON."

Diagnostic Aids:

An "Intermittent" malfunction may be caused by a poor connection, rubbed through wire insulation, or a wire that is broken inside the insulation.

The lamp test function of the Tech I may be used to command the lamp "ON" while looking for an intermittent malfunction in the indicator lamp circuitry.

The frequency of the malfunction can be checked by using the enhanced diagnostic function of the Tech I

Any circuitry that is suspected as causing the intermittent complaint should be thoroughly checked for backed out terminals, improper mating, broken locks, improperly formed or damaged terminals, poor terminal to wiring connections or physical damage to the wiring harness.

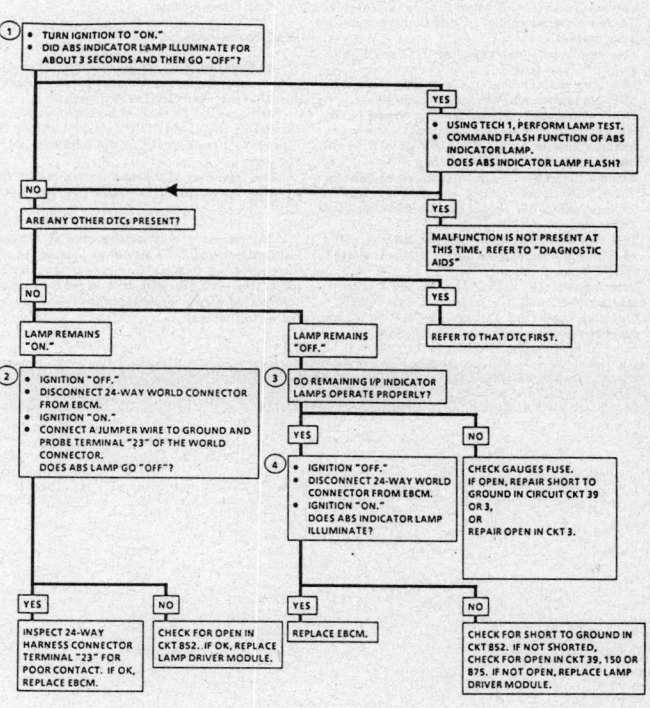

THIS CHART ASSUMES THAT A CURRENT DTC IS STORED INDICATING THAT THIS MALFUNCTION IS PRESENT.

Fig. 91   Code A011, ABS warning light open or shorted to ground. 1993 except Cutlass Supreme, Grand Prix, Lumina & Regal

1991 CALAIS & 1991-92 GRAND AM, SKYLARK & 1992 ACHIEVA, BERETTA, CAVALIER, CORSICA, CUTLASS SUPREME, GRAND **23-373**
PRIX, LUMINA, REGAL & SUNBIRD (DELCO-MORAINE VI TYPE)

DTC A011

ABS INDICATOR LAMP CIRCUIT OPEN OR SHORTED TO GROUND

Circuit Description:

This DTC checks the state of the ABS indicator lamp to identify a situation in which the driver could not be warned of a system malfunction by the ABS indicator lamp, or the indicator lamp is always "ON." The Lamp Driver Module (LDM) turns the ABS indicator lamp "ON," unless the EBCM provides ground to turn it "OFF." Because of the circuitry in the LDM, only external malfunctions can be detected. As a result, the ABS indicator lamp itself is not diagnosable, only the control line to the EBCM can be diagnosed. In the event of an open CKT 852, the ABS indicator lamp will be "ON" at all times, due to the loss of ground at the LDM input. If the control line is shorted to ground, the ABS indicator lamp is kept "OFF," due to the LDM input being grounded.

Failure Condition:

DTC A011 can be set only during the three second bulb check or when the ABS indicator lamp is commanded "ON." If the EBCM cannot control the ABS indicator lamp for two seconds, a malfunction exists.

Action Taken:

A malfunction DTC is stored; however, ABS is not disabled.

Test Description: Number(s) below refer to circled number(s) on the diagnostic chart.

1. Checks to see if ABS lamp functions properly. Normal operation would indicate that the problem is not present.
2. This step determines if any other DTCs are present or if A018 is set falsely.
3. This step insures that the circuitry from the EBCM to the lamp driver module is complete.
4. This step insures that the ignition circuit to the lamp driver module is functional. An open indicator fuse or open CKT 3, 39, or 875 would result in inoperative indicator lamp.
5. Isolates the cause of the ABS lamp remaining "OFF," by disconnecting the 24-way EBCM connector, CKT 852 should be open and cause the ABS lamp to be "ON."
6. This step determines whether the lamp remains "ON" due to a lamp driver malfunction or an open in CKT 852.
7. Determines if the "INDIC" fuse or CKT 3 is open, causing the I/P indicator lamps to remain "OFF."
8. This step checks for an open in CKT 39 which supplies voltage to the lamp driver module.

9. Isolates the cause of the lamp remaining "OFF" to a short to ground in CKT 852 or a malfunctioning lamp driver module.

Diagnostic Aids:

An "Intermittent" malfunction may be caused by a poor connection, rubbed through wire insulation, or a wire that is broken inside the insulation.

The lamp test function of the Tech 1 may be used to command the lamp "ON" while looking for an intermittent malfunction in the ABS indicator lamp circuitry.

The frequency of the malfunction can be checked by using the enhanced diagnostic function of the Tech 1.

Any circuitry that is suspected as causing the intermittent complaint should be thoroughly checked for backed out terminals, improper mating, broken locks, improperly formed or damaged terminals, poor terminal to wiring connections or physical damage to the wiring harness.

THIS CHART ASSUMES THAT A CURRENT DTC IS STORED INDICATING THAT THIS MALFUNCTION IS PRESENT.

Fig. 92   Code A011, ABS warning light open or shorted to ground. 1993 Cutlass Supreme, Grand Prix, Lumina & Regal

Cavalier

Sunbird

Beretta & Corsica

Achieva, Grand Am & Skylark

Cutlass Supreme, Grand Prix, Lumina & Regal

DTC A013
ABS INDICATOR LAMP CIRCUIT SHORTED TO BATTERY

Circuit Description:

This test checks the state of the ABS indicator lamp to identify a situation in which the driver could not be warned of a system malfunction by the ABS indicator lamp. The Lamp Driver Module (LDM) turns the ABS indicator lamp "ON," unless the EBCM provides ground to turn it "OFF." Because of the circuitry internal to the LDM, only external malfunctions can be detected. As a result, the ABS indicator lamp itself is not diagnosable, only the control line to the EBCM can be diagnosed.

If the ABS indicator lamp control line is shorted to battery or the EBCM control circuit is open, the Electronic Brake Control Module (EBCM) is not able to turn "OFF" the ABS indicator lamp.

Failure Condition:

DTC A013 can be set anytime the EBCM commands the ABS indicator lamp "OFF." If the EBCM can not control the ABS indicator lamp for two seconds, a malfunction exists.

Action Taken:

A malfunction DTC is stored; however, ABS is not disabled.

Test Description: Number(s) below refer to circled number(s) on the diagnostic chart.

1. Checks to see if ABS lamp functions properly. Normal operation would indicate that the problem is not present.
2. After removing the 10 amp gauge fuse, voltage on CKT 852 will be eliminated. If voltage is still present, it would indicate that a short to voltage is present between the lamp driver module and EBCM.

Diagnostic Aids:

An "Intermittent" malfunction may be caused by a poor connection, rubbed through wire insulation or a wire that is broken inside the insulation.

DTC 13 must be currently set before it should be addressed. If DTC 13 is set as a history DTC, proceed to those DTCs that are currently set before attempting to repair a DTC 13 malfunction.

The frequency of the malfunction can be checked by using the enhanced diagnostic function of the Tech 1

Any circuitry that is suspected as causing the "Intermittent" complaint should be thoroughly checked for backed out terminals, improper mating, broken locks, improperly formed or damaged terminals, poor terminal to wiring connections or physical damage to the wiring harness.

Fig. 93   Code A013, ABS warning light circuit shorted to battery. 1993

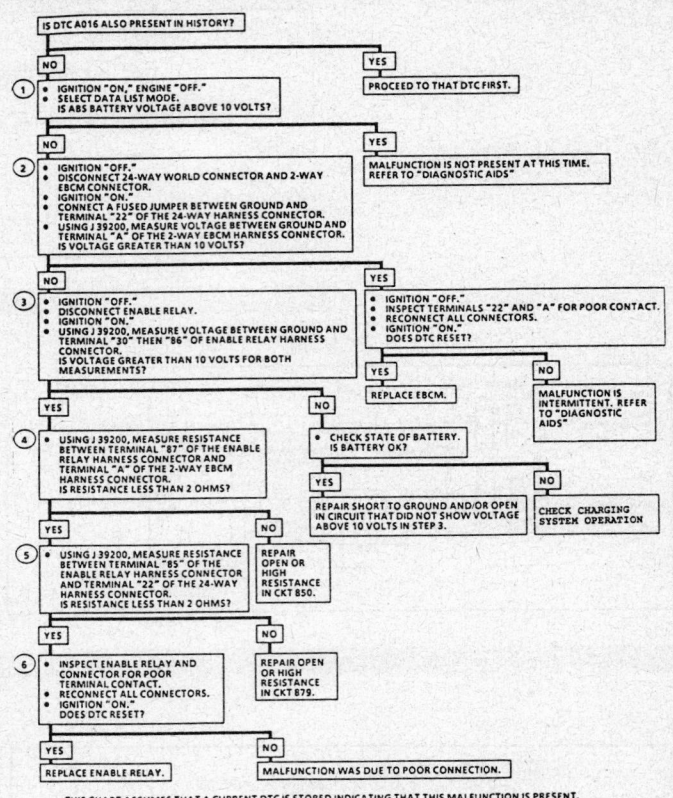

DTC A014

Circuit Description: ENABLE RELAY CONTACTS OR FUSE OPEN

Ignition voltage is supplied through terminal "86" of the ABS enable relay. The EBCM then is able to energize the pull-in coil by completing the ground circuit at Pin "22" of the EBCM. The magnetic field created closes the enable relay contacts and allows battery voltage and current to be supplied to the EMBs and EBCM, which supplies power to the motors and solenoids.

Failure Condition:

DTC A014 can be set anytime after the EBCM commands the enable relay "ON" (the relay is first commanded "ON" during the three second bulb check). This test monitors the availability of current/voltage to the motors, solenoids and EMBs. This malfunction indicates voltage is not available and would therefore not allow ABS operation if required.

Action Taken:

A malfunction DTC is stored, ABS is disabled and the ABS indicator lamp is turned "ON."

Test Description: Number(s) below refer to circled number(s) on the diagnostic chart.

1. This step would indicate that the EBCM is sensing battery voltage present through the relay contacts at terminal "A." This shows that the relay and circuitry is functional.
2. This step ensures the enable relay and related circuitry are operating properly.
3. This ensures that battery voltage is available to terminals "30" and "86" of the relay.
4. This step checks for an open in CKT 850 between the enable relay and EBCM.
5. This step checks for an open in CKT 879 between enable relay and EBCM.
6. This test ensures malfunction was not due to poor harness connections.

Diagnostic Aids:

An "Intermittent" malfunction may be caused by a poor connection, rubbed through wire insulation, or a wire that is broken inside the insulation.

The frequency of the malfunction can be checked by using the enhanced diagnostic function of the Tech 1

Any circuitry that is suspected as causing the "Intermittent" complaint should be thoroughly checked for backed out terminals, improper mating, broken locks, improperly formed or damaged terminals, poor terminal to wiring connections or physical damage to the wiring harness.

VIBRATION, TEMPERATURE EFFECTS:

Check for vibration effects by performing the relay test function of the Tech 1. With the relay commanded "ON," lightly tap the top and sides of the relay while monitoring relay voltage. If the relay voltage changes significantly, replace the relay.

If test 14 only fails when the vehicle is initially started in cold ambient conditions (temperature less than 32°F - 0°C), replace the relay.

Fig. 94   Code A014, Enable relay contacts or fuse open. 1993 Cavalier & Sunbird

DTC A014

ENABLE RELAY CONTACTS OR FUSE OPEN

Circuit Description:

Ignition voltage is supplied through terminal "86" of the ABS enable relay. The EBCM then is able to energize the pull-in coil by completing the ground circuit at Pin "22" of the EBCM. The magnetic field created closes the enable relay contacts and allows battery voltage and current to be supplied to the EMBs and EBCM, which supplies power to the motors and solenoids.

Failure Condition:

DTC A014 can be set anytime after the EBCM commands the enable relay "ON" (the relay is first commanded "ON" during the three second bulb check). This test monitors the availability of current/voltage to the motors, solenoids and EMBs. This malfunction indicates voltage is not available and would therefore not allow ABS operation if required.

Action Taken:

A malfunction DTC is stored, ABS is disabled and the ABS indicator lamp is turned "ON."

Test Description: Number(s) below refer to circled number(s) on the diagnostic chart.

1. This step would indicate that the EBCM is sensing battery voltage present through the relay contacts at terminal "A." This shows that the relay and circuitry is functional.
2. This step ensures voltage is available at terminal "A."
3. This ensures that battery voltage is available to terminals "30" and "86" of the relay.
4. This step checks for an open in CKT 850 between the enable relay and EBCM.
5. This step checks for an open in CKT 879 between enable relay and EBCM.
6. This test ensures malfunction was not due to poor harness connections.
7. This step checks for high resistance in the switched battery input circuitry.
8. This step checks for an intermittent malfunction.

Diagnostic Aids:

An "Intermittent" malfunction may be caused by a poor connection, rubbed through wire insulation, or a wire that is broken inside the insulation.

The frequency of the malfunction can be checked by using the enhanced diagnostic function of the Tech 1

Any circuitry that is suspected as causing the "Intermittent" complaint should be thoroughly checked for backed out terminals, improper mating, broken locks, improperly formed or damaged terminals, poor terminal to wiring connections or physical damage to the wiring harness.

VIBRATION, TEMPERATURE EFFECTS:

Check for vibration effects by performing the relay test function of the Tech 1. With the relay commanded "ON," lightly tap the top and sides of the relay while monitoring relay voltage. If the relay voltage changes significantly, replace the relay.

If test 14 only fails when the vehicle is initially started in cold ambient conditions (temperature less than 32°F - 0°C), replace the relay.

Fig. 95   Code A014, Enable relay contacts or fuse open. 1993 Beretta & Corsica

DTC A014
ENABLE RELAY CONTACTS OR FUSE OPEN

Circuit Description:

Ignition voltage is supplied through terminal "5" of the ABS enable relay. The EBCM then is able to energize the pull-in coil by completing the ground circuit at Pin "22" of the EBCM. The magnetic field created closes the enable relay contacts and allows battery voltage and current to be supplied to the EMBs and EBCM, which supplies power to the motors and solenoids.

Failure Condition:

DTC A014 can be set anytime after the EBCM commands the enable relay "ON" (the relay is first commanded "ON" during the three second bulb check). This test monitors the availability of current/voltage to the motors, solenoids and EMBs. This malfunction indicates voltage is not available and would therefore not allow ABS operation if required.

Action Taken:

A malfunction DTC is stored, ABS is disabled and the ABS indicator lamp is turned "ON."

Test Description: Number(s) below refer to circled number(s) on the diagnostic chart.
1. This step would indicate that the EBCM is sensing battery voltage present through the relay contacts at terminal "A." This shows that the relay and circuitry is functional.
2. This step ensures the enable relay and related circuitry are operating properly.
3. This ensures that battery voltage is available to terminals "1" and "5" of the relay.
4. This step checks for an open in CKT 850 between the enable relay and EBCM.
5. This step checks for an open in CKT 879 between the enable relay and EBCM.
6. This test ensures malfunction was not due to poor harness connections.

Diagnostic Aids:

An "Intermittent" malfunction may be caused by a poor connection, rubbed through wire insulation, or a wire that is broken inside the insulation.

The frequency of the malfunction can be checked by using the enhanced diagnostic function of the Tech 1 as described in "Enhanced Diagnostics," found in this section.

Any circuitry that is suspected as causing the "Intermittent" complaint should be thoroughly checked for backed out terminals, improper mating, broken locks, improperly formed or damaged terminals, poor terminal to wiring connections or physical damage to the wiring harness.

VIBRATION, TEMPERATURE EFFECTS:

Check for vibration effects by performing the relay test function of the Tech 1. With the relay commanded "ON," lightly tap the top and sides of the relay while monitoring relay voltage. If the relay voltage changes significantly, replace the relay.

If test 14 only fails when the vehicle is initially started in cold ambient conditions (temperature less than 32°F - 0°C), replace the relay.

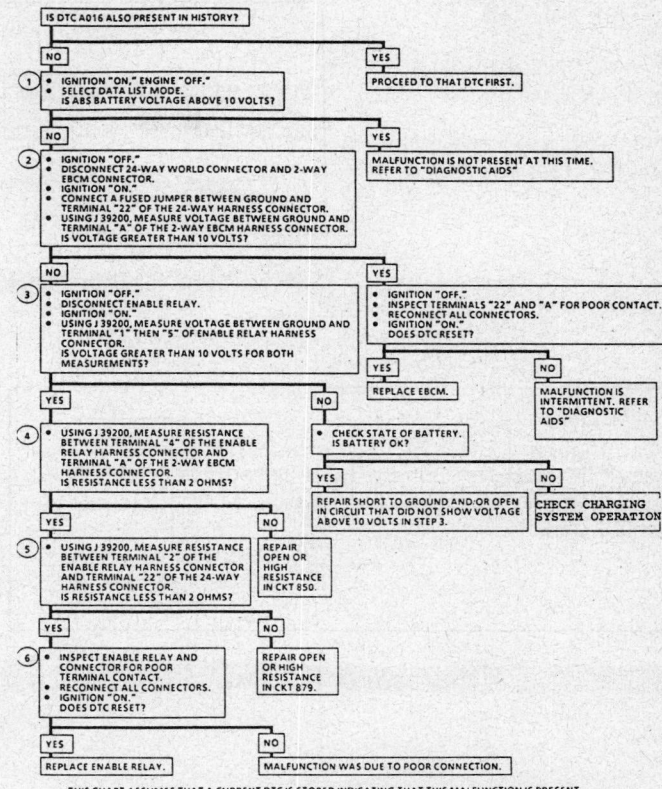

THIS CHART ASSUMES THAT A CURRENT DTC IS STORED INDICATING THAT THIS MALFUNCTION IS PRESENT.

Fig. 96   Code A014, Enable relay contacts or fuse open. 1993 Achieva, Grand Am & Skylark

---

DTC A014
ENABLE RELAY CONTACTS OR FUSE OPEN

Circuit Description:

Ignition voltage is supplied through terminal "A2" of the ABS enable relay. The EBCM then is able to energize the pull-in coil by completing the ground circuit at terminal "22" of the EBCM. The magnetic field created closes the enable relay contacts and allows battery voltage and current to be supplied to the EBCM, which supplies power to the motors and solenoids.

Failure Condition:

DTC A014 can be set anytime after the EBCM commands the enable relay "ON" (the relay is first commanded "ON" during the three second bulb check). This test monitors the availability of current/voltage to the motors and solenoids. This malfunction indicates voltage is not available and would therefore not allow ABS operation if required.

Action Taken:

A malfunction DTC is stored, ABS is disabled and the ABS indicator lamp is turned "ON."

Test Description: Number(s) below refer to circled number(s) on the diagnostic chart.
1. This step checks to see if DTC A016 is also set as current or history. If DTC A016 is also set, proceed to that chart first.
2. This step verifies that the malfunction is currently present.
3. This step verifies that voltage is available at the relay coil and at the relay switch.
4. This step checks to see if a malfunctioning EBCM is the cause of DTC A014 being set.
5. This step checks for an open in the switched battery input circuit.
6. This step checks for an open in the relay control circuit.
7. This step determines whether the malfunction is intermittent or caused by a malfunctioning relay.
8. This step determines if the low voltage condition was caused by an open in the voltage feed circuits to the relay or by a vehicle charging system malfunction.
9. This step checks for a possible intermittent malfunction.

Diagnostic Aids:

An "Intermittent" problem may be caused by a poor connection, rubbed through wire insulation, or a wire that is broken inside the insulation.

The frequency of the problem can be checked by using the enhanced diagnostic function of the Tech 1

Any circuitry that is suspected as causing the "Intermittent" complaint should be thoroughly checked for backed out terminals, improper mating, broken locks, improperly formed or damaged terminals, poor terminal to wiring connections or physical damage to the wiring harness.

VIBRATION, TEMPERATURE EFFECTS:

Check for vibration effects by performing the relay test function of the Tech 1. With the relay test commanded "ON," lightly tap the top and sides of the relay while monitoring relay voltage. If the relay voltage changes significantly, replace the relay.

If DTC A014 only sets when the vehicle is initially started in cold ambient conditions (temperature less than 32°F-0°C), replace the relay.

THIS CHART ASSUMES THAT A CURRENT DTC IS STORED INDICATING THAT THIS MALFUNCTION IS PRESENT.

Fig. 97   Code A014, Enable relay contacts or fuse open. 1993 Cutlass Supreme, Grand Prix, Lumina & Regal

Cavalier & Sunbird

Beretta & Corsica

Achieva, Grand Am & Skylark

DTC A015
ENABLE RELAY CONTACTS SHORTED TO BATTERY

Circuit Description:

Ignition voltage is supplied through terminal "86" of the ABS enable relay. The EBCM then is able to energize the pull-in coil by completing the ground circuit at Pin "22" of the EBCM. The magnetic field created closes the enable relay contacts and allows battery voltage and current to be supplied to the EMBs and EBCM, which supplies power to the motors and solenoids.

Failure Condition:

DTC A015 can be set only before the EBCM commands the relay "ON." This test determines if the enable relay is energized when it should not be. This malfunction would not allow the enable relay to remove power to the ABS system. If a second malfunction were to occur that requires the enable relay to be turned "OFF," that malfunction can not be removed if the relay can not be controlled. The malfunction must be present for three consecutive drive cycles before the DTC is set.

Action Taken:

A malfunction DTC is stored. ABS is not disabled; however, the ABS indicator lamp will flash to indicate a malfunction exists.

Test Description: Number(s) below refer to circled number(s) on the diagnostic chart.
1. This step indicates that the EBCM is capable of controlling the enable relay as commanded.
2. This step checks for voltage at terminal "A" of the 2-way EBCM harness connector. If voltage is present, the malfunction exists in the enable relay and/or its circuitry.
3. This test checks for a short to ground in the enable relay control circuit.
4. This step checks for a short to voltage in CKT 850.
5. This step identifies if the EBCM is malfunctioning.

Diagnostic Aids:

An "Intermittent" malfunction may be caused by a poor connection, rubbed through wire insulation, or a wire that is broken inside the insulation.

The frequency of the malfunction can be checked by using the enhanced diagnostic function of the Tech 1

Any circuitry, that is suspected as causing the intermittent complaint, should be thoroughly checked for backed out terminals, improper mating, broken locks, improperly formed or damaged terminals, poor terminal to wiring connections or physical damage to the wiring harness.

THIS CHART ASSUMES THAT A CURRENT DTC IS STORED INDICATING THAT THIS MALFUNCTION IS PRESENT.

Fig. 98   Code A015, Enable relay contacts shorted to battery. 1993 except Cutlass Supreme, Grand Prix, Lumina & Regal

DTC A015
ENABLE RELAY CONTACTS SHORTED TO BATTERY

Circuit Description:
Ignition voltage is supplied through terminal "A2" of the ABS enable relay. The EBCM then is able to energize the pull-in coil by completing the ground circuit at terminal "22" of the EBCM. The magnetic field created closes the enable relay contacts and allows battery voltage and current to be supplied to the EBCM, which supplies power to the motors and solenoids.

Failure Condition:
DTC A015 can be set only before the EBCM commands the relay "ON." This test determines if the enable relay is energized when it should not be. This malfunction would not allow the enable relay to remove power to the ABS system. If a second malfunction were to occur that requires the enable relay to be turned "OFF," that malfunction cannot be removed if the relay cannot be controlled. The malfunction must be present for three consecutive drive cycles before the DTC is set.

Action Taken:
A malfunction DTC is stored. ABS is not disabled; however, the ABS indicator lamp will flash to indicate a malfunction exists.

Test Description: Number(s) below refer to circled number(s) on the diagnostic chart.
1. This step indicates that the EBCM is capable of controlling the enable relay as commanded.
2. This step checks for a possible short to battery voltage in CKT 850.
3. This step checks for a possible short to ground in CKT 879.
4. This step determines whether the short to B+ is in CKT 850 or internal to the EBCM.
5. This step checks for a possible intermittent in wiring or connectors.

Diagnostic Aids:

An "Intermittent" malfunction may be caused by a poor connection, rubbed through wire insulation, or a wire that is broken inside the insulation.

The frequency of the malfunction can be checked by using the enhanced diagnostic function of the Tech 1

Any circuitry, that is suspected as causing the intermittent complaint, should be thoroughly checked for backed out terminals, improper mating, broken locks, improperly formed or damaged terminals, poor terminal to wiring connections or physical damage to the wiring harness.

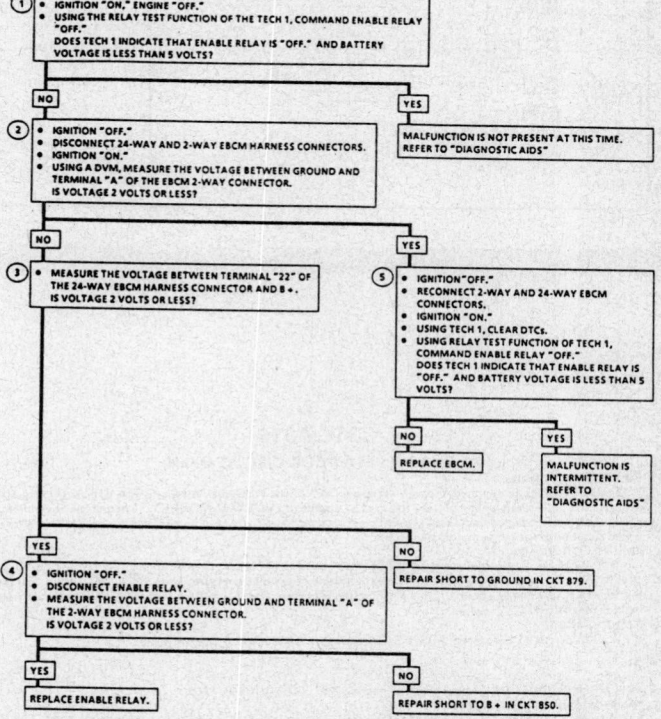

Fig. 99   Code A015, Enable relay contacts shorted to battery. 1993 Cutlass Supreme, Grand Prix, Lumina & Regal

Cavalier & Sunbird

Beretta & Corsica

Achieva, Grand Am & Skylark

DTC A016
ENABLE RELAY COIL CIRCUIT OPEN

Circuit Description:
Ignition voltage is supplied through terminal "86" of the ABS enable relay. The EBCM then is able to energize the pull-in coil by completing the ground circuit at Pin "22" of the EBCM. The magnetic field created closes the enable relay contacts and allows battery voltage and current to be supplied to the EMBs and EBCM, which supplies power to the motors and solenoids.

Failure Condition:
DTC A016 can be set only after DTC A014 has been set. This test detects an open in the enable relay coil circuit. An open in this circuit will not allow the enable relay to be energized thus preventing voltage/current to the motors, EMBs and solenoids. If this malfunction is present and the ignition is turned "OFF" before 5 km/h (3 mph) is reached, DTC A014 is set alone.

Action Taken:
A malfunction DTC is stored, ABS is disabled and the ABS indicator lamp is turned "ON."

Test Description: Number(s) below refer to circled number(s) on the diagnostic chart.
1. This step indicates if the EBCM is capable of controlling the enable relay as commanded.
2. This step ensures that there is continuity through the pull-in coil of the enable relay.
3. This step checks to ensure that voltage is available to the pull-in coil of the enable relay.
4. This step checks continuity in CKT 879.
5. This step ensures DTC was not set due to a poor connection.

Diagnostic Aids:

An "Intermittent" malfunction may be caused by a poor connection, rubbed through wire insulation, or a wire that is broken inside the insulation.
The frequency of the malfunction can be checked by using the enhanced diagnostic function of the Tech 1

If the frequency of the malfunction is high, but is currently intermittent, check for high coil resistance by measuring resistance between relay terminals "86" and "85". If resistance is greater than 100 ohms, replace the relay.
Any circuitry, that is suspected as causing the intermittent complaint, should be thoroughly checked for backed out terminals, improper mating, broken locks, improperly formed or damaged terminals, poor terminal to wiring connections or physical damage to the wiring harness.

AFTER DIAGNOSIS IS COMPLETE, CLEAR DTCs AND TEST DRIVE VEHICLE FOR THREE (3) DRIVE CYCLES TO VERIFY DTC DOES NOT RESET. A DRIVE CYCLE CONSISTS OF STARTING THE VEHICLE, DRIVING OVER 16 km/h (10 MPH) AND THEN KEYING DOWN.

Fig. 100 Code A016, Enable relay coil circuit open. 1993 except Cutlass Supreme, Grand Prix, Lumina & Regal

DTC A016
ENABLE RELAY COIL CIRCUIT OPEN

Circuit Description:

Ignition voltage is supplied through terminal "A2" of the ABS enable relay. The EBCM then is able to energize the pull-in coil by completing the ground circuit at terminal "22" of the EBCM. The magnetic field created closes the enable relay contacts and allows battery voltage and current to be supplied to the EBCM, which supplies power to the motors and solenoids.

Failure Condition:

DTC A016 can be set only after DTC A014 has been set. This test detects an open in the enable relay coil circuit. An open in this circuit will not allow the enable relay to be energized thus preventing voltage/current to the motors and solenoids. If this malfunction is present and the ignition is turned "OFF" before 5 km/h (3 mph) is reached, DTC A014 is set alone.

Action Taken:

A malfunction DTC is stored, ABS is disabled and the ABS indicator lamp is turned "ON."

Test Description: Number(s) below refer to circled number(s) on the diagnostic chart.

1. This step indicates the EBCM is capable of controlling the enable relay as commanded.
2. This step checks to insure that voltage is available to the pull-in coil of the enable relay.
3. This step insures that there is continuity through the pull-in coil of the enable relay.
4. This step verifies the integrity of the relay control circuit.
5. This step checks for a possible intermittent in the wiring or connectors.

Diagnostic Aids:

An "Intermittent" malfunction may be caused by a poor connection, rubbed through wire insulation, or a wire that is broken inside the insulation.

The frequency of the malfunction can be checked by using the enhanced diagnostic function of the Tech 1

If the frequency of the malfunction is high, but is currently intermittent, check for high coil resistance by measuring between relay terminals "A1" and "A2" using a DVM. If resistance shows greater than 100 ohms, replace the relay.

Any circuitry, that is suspected as causing the intermittent complaint, should be thoroughly checked for backed out terminals, improper mating, broken locks, improperly formed or damaged terminals, poor terminal to wiring connections or physical damage to the wiring harness.

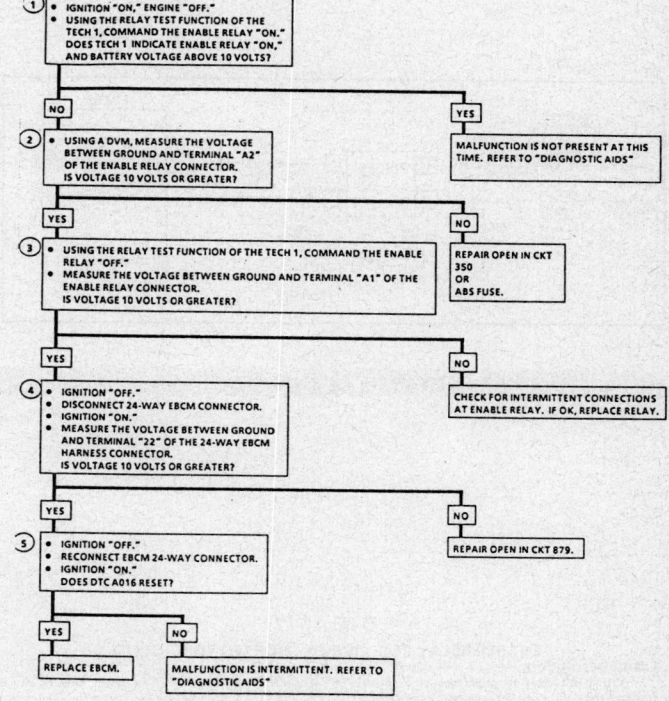

* AFTER ALL DIAGNOSIS IS COMPLETE, CLEAR DTCs AND TEST DRIVE VEHICLE FOR THREE (3) DRIVE CYCLES TO VERIFY THAT DTC DOES NOT RESET. A DRIVE CYCLE CONSISTS OF STARTING THE VEHICLE, DRIVING OVER 16 km/h (10 MPH), AND THEN KEYING DOWN.

THIS CHART ASSUMES THAT A CURRENT DTC IS STORED INDICATING THAT THIS MALFUNCTION IS PRESENT.

Fig. 101   Code A015, Enable relay coil circuit open. 1993 Cutlass Supreme, Grand Prix, Lumina & Regal

Cavalier & Sunbird

Beretta & Corsica

Achieva, Grand Am & Skylark

DTC A017
ENABLE RELAY COIL CIRCUIT SHORTED TO GROUND

Circuit Description:
Ignition voltage is supplied through terminal "86" of the ABS enable relay. The EBCM then is able to energize the pull-in coil by completing the ground circuit at Pin "22" of the EBCM. The magnetic field created closes the enable relay contacts and allows battery voltage and current to be supplied to the EMBs and EBCM, which supplies voltage to the motors and solenoids.

Failure Condition:
DTC A017 can be set before the EBCM commands the enable relay "ON." This test determines if the enable relay is energized when it should not be. This malfunction would not allow the enable relay to remove power to the ABS system. If a second malfunction were to occur that requires the enable relay to be turned "OFF," that malfunction can not be removed if the relay can not be controlled.

Action Taken:
A malfunction DTC is stored. ABS is not disabled; however the ABS indicator lamp flashes to indicate a malfunction exists.

Test Description: Number(s) below refer to circled number(s) on the diagnostic chart.
1. This step indicates if the EBCM is capable of controlling the enable relay as commanded.
2. This checks to ensure the enable relay or control CKT 879 are not shorted to ground.
3. This step ensures DTC was not set due to a poor connection.

Diagnostic Aids:

An "Intermittent" malfunction may be caused by a poor connection, rubbed through wire insulation, or a wire that is broken inside the insulation.

The frequency of the malfunction can be checked by using the enhanced diagnostic function of the Tech 1

Any circuitry, that is suspected as causing the intermittent complaint, should be thoroughly checked for backed out terminals, improper mating, broken locks, improperly formed or damaged terminals, poor terminal to wiring connections or physical damage to the wiring harness.

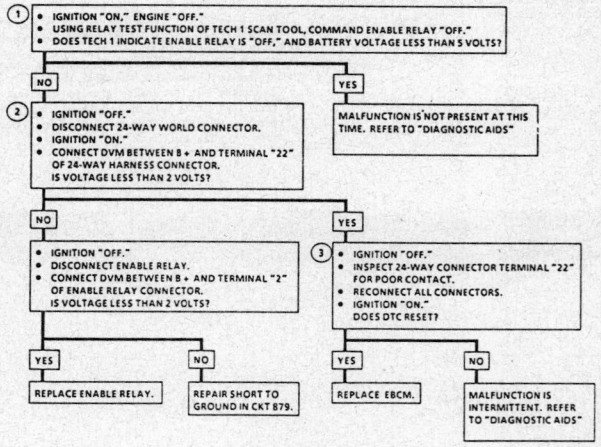

Fig. 102   Code A017, Enable relay coil circuit shorted to ground. 1993 except Cutlass Supreme, Grand Prix, Lumina & Regal

DTC A017
ENABLE RELAY COIL CIRCUIT SHORTED TO GROUND

Circuit Description:

Ignition voltage is supplied through terminal "A2" of the ABS enable relay. The EBCM then is able to energize the pull-in coil by completing the ground circuit at terminal "22" of the EBCM. The magnetic field created closes the enable relay contacts and allows battery voltage and current to be supplied to the EBCM, which supplies voltage to the motors and solenoids.

Failure Condition:

DTC A017 can be set before the EBCM commands the enable relay "ON." This test determines if the enable relay is energized when it should not be. This malfunction would not allow the enable relay to remove power to the ABS system. If a second malfunction were to occur that requires the enable relay to be turned "OFF," that malfunction cannot be removed if the relay cannot be controlled.

Action Taken:

A malfunction DTC is stored. ABS is not disabled; however the ABS indicator lamp is flashed to indicate a malfunction exists.

Test Description: Number(s) below refer to circled number(s) on the diagnostic chart.
1. This step indicates that the EBCM is capable of controlling the enable relay as commanded.
2. This checks to insure that the enable relay or control CKT 879 are not shorted to ground.
3. This step checks to see if the EBCM is internally shorted to ground. A grounded terminal "22" would cause the enable relay to be energized any time the ignition was in the "ON" position.
4. This step checks for a short to ground in control CKT 879 or a defective relay.

Diagnostic Aids:

An "Intermittent" malfunction may be caused by a poor connection, rubbed through wire insulation, or a wire that is broken inside the insulation.

The frequency of the malfunction can be checked by using the enhanced diagnostic function of the Tech 1

Any circuitry, that is suspected as causing the intermittent complaint, should be thoroughly checked for backed out terminals, improper mating, broken locks, improperly formed or damaged terminals, poor terminal to wiring connections or physical damage to the wiring harness.

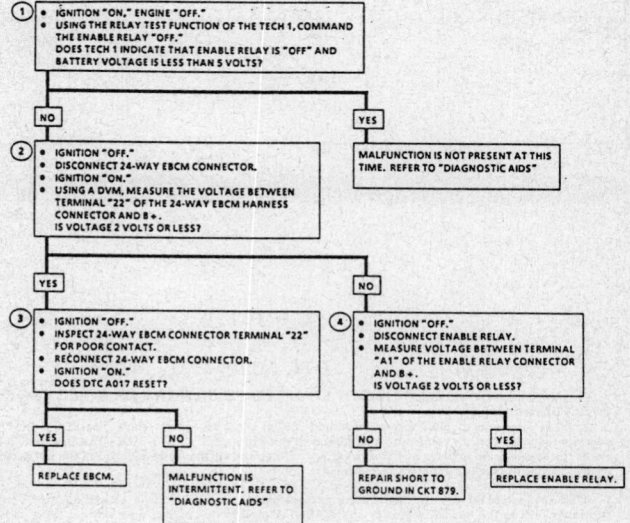

AFTER ALL DIAGNOSIS IS COMPLETE, CLEAR DTCs AND TEST DRIVE VEHICLE FOR THREE (3) DRIVE CYCLES TO VERIFY THAT DTC DOES NOT RESET. A DRIVE CYCLE CONSISTS OF STARTING THE VEHICLE, DRIVING OVER 16 km/h (10 MPH), AND THEN KEYING DOWN.

Fig. 103   Code A017, Enable relay coil circuit shorted to ground. 1993 Cutlass Supreme, Grand Prix, Lumina & Regal

Cavalier & Sunbird

Beretta & Corsica

Achieva, Grand Am & Skylark

DTC A018

ENABLE RELAY COIL CIRCUIT SHORTED TO BATTERY OR COIL SHORTED

Circuit Description:

Ignition voltage is supplied through terminal "86" of the ABS enable relay. The EBCM then is able to energize the pull-in coil by completing the ground circuit at Pin "22" of the EBCM. The magnetic field created closes the enable relay contacts and allows battery voltage and current to be supplied to the EMBs and EBCM, which supplies voltage to the motors and solenoids.

Failure Condition:

DTC A018 can be set after the EBCM commands the enable relay "ON." This test monitors the availability of current/voltage to the motors, solenoids and EMBs. A malfunction of this type will not allow voltage to be available to the motors, solenoids and EMBs; therefore, ABS operation would not be allowed if required.

Action Taken:

A malfunction DTC is stored, ABS is disabled and the ABS indicator lamp is turned "ON."

Test Description: Number(s) below refer to circled number(s) on the diagnostic chart.

1. This step indicates if the EBCM is capable of controlling the enable relay as commanded.
2. With the enable relay removed, voltage should not be available at terminal "85". Any voltage at this point would indicate that CKT 879 was shorted to a voltage source.
3. This step checks for a shorted coil.
4. This ensures malfunction was not due to a poor connection.

Diagnostic Aids:

An "Intermittent" malfunction may be caused by a poor connection, rubbed through wire insulation, or a wire that is broken inside the insulation.

The frequency of the malfunction can be checked by using the enhanced diagnostic function of the Tech 1.

Any circuitry, that is suspected as causing the intermittent complaint, should be thoroughly checked for backed out terminals, improper mating, broken locks, improperly formed or damaged terminals, poor terminal to wiring connections or physical damage to the wiring harness.

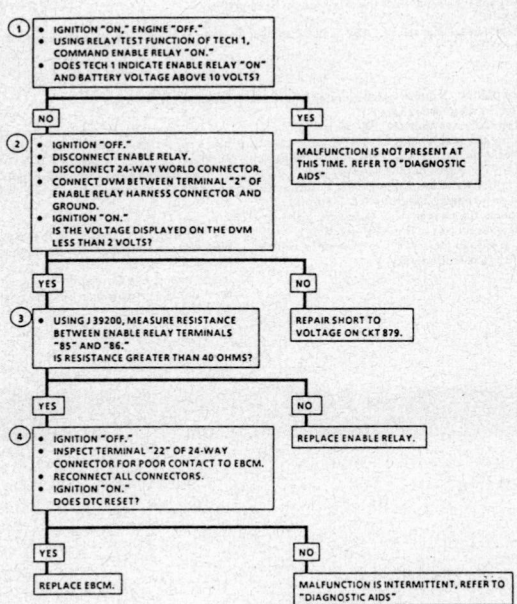

Fig. 104 Code A018, Enable relay coil circuit shorted to battery or coil shorted. 1993 except Cutlass Supreme, Grand Prix, Lumina & Regal

23-384 *1991 CALAIS & 1991-92 GRAND AM, SKYLARK & 1992 ACHIEVA, BERETTA, CAVALIER, CORSICA, CUTLASS SUPREME, GRAND PRIX, LUMINA, REGAL & SUNBIRD (DELCO-MORAINE VI TYPE)*

DTC A018

ENABLE RELAY COIL CIRCUIT SHORTED TO B + OR COIL SHORTED

Circuit Description:

Ignition voltage is supplied through terminal "A2" of the ABS enable relay. The EBCM then is able to energize the pull-in coil by completing the ground circuit at terminal "22" of the EBCM. The magnetic field created closes the enable relay contacts and allows battery voltage and current to be supplied to the EBCM, which supplies voltage to the motors and solenoids.

Failure Condition:

DTC A018 can be set after the EBCM commands the enable relay "ON." This test monitors the availability of current/voltage to the motors and solenoids. A malfunction of this type will not allow voltage to be available to the motors and solenoids; therefore, ABS operation would not be allowed if required.

Action Taken:

A malfunction DTC is stored, ABS is disabled and the ABS indicator lamp is turned "ON."

Test Description: Number(s) below refer to circled number(s) on the diagnostic chart.

1. This step indicates that the EBCM is capable of controlling the enable relay as commanded.
2. This step checks for a short to B+ on the relay control circuit.
3. This step verifies that the relay coil has the appropriate resistance.
4. This step checks for possible poor terminal contact at the EBCM.
5. This step checks for additional DTCs present.

Diagnostic Aids:

An "Intermittent" malfunction may be caused by a poor connection, rubbed through wire insulation, or a wire that is broken inside the insulation.

The frequency of the malfunction can be checked by using the enhanced diagnostic function of the Tech 1

Any circuitry, that is suspected as causing the intermittent complaint, should be thoroughly checked for backed out terminals, improper mating, broken locks, improperly formed or damaged terminals, poor terminal to wiring connections or physical damage to the wiring harness.

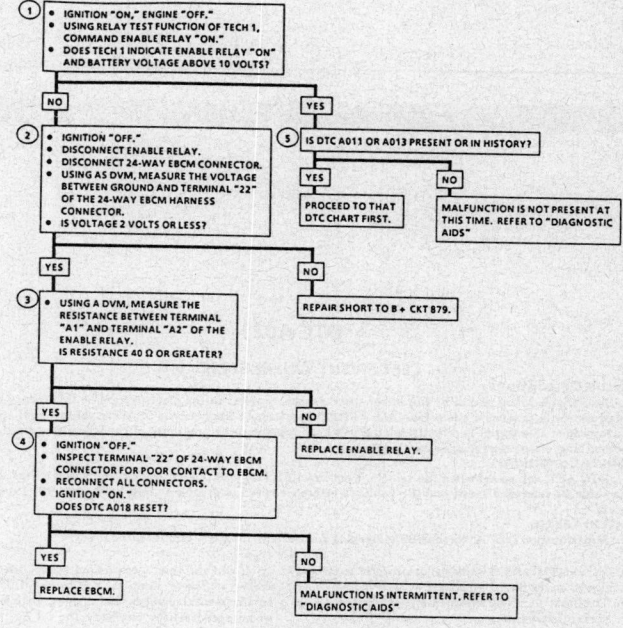

* AFTER ALL DIAGNOSIS IS COMPLETE, CLEAR DTCs AND TEST DRIVE VEHICLE FOR THREE (3) DRIVE CYCLES TO VERIFY THAT DTC DOES NOT RESET A DRIVE CYCLE CONSISTS OF STARTING THE VEHICLE, DRIVING OVER 16 km/h (10 MPH), AND THEN KEYING DOWN.

Fig. 105   Code A018, Enable relay coil circuit shorted to battery or coil shorted. 1993 Cutlass Supreme, Grand Prix, Lumina & Regal

Cavalier & Sunbird

Achieva, Beretta, Corsica, Grand Am & Skylark

DTC A021

LEFT FRONT WHEEL SPEED = 0

Circuit Description:
As a toothed ring passes by the wheel speed sensor, changes in the electromagnetic field cause the wheel speed sensor to produce a sinusoidal (AC) voltage signal whose frequency is proportional to wheel speed. The magnitude of this signal is directly related to wheel speed and the proximity of the wheel speed sensor to the toothed ring, often referred to as the air gap.

Failure Condition:
DTC A021 can be set when the vehicle is not in an ABS stop. If the left front wheel speed is less than 1/2 of the vehicle's reference speed and the vehicle's reference speed is greater than 8 km/h (5 mph), a malfunction exists.

Action Taken:
A malfunction DTC is stored, ABS is disabled and the ABS indicator lamp is turned "ON."

Test Description: Number(s) below refer to circled number(s) on the diagnostic chart.
1. This test verifies whether the malfunction is currently present.
2. This step will identify a wheel speed sensor or circuitry that is damaged and visibly apparent.
3. This test checks wheel speed sensor for proper resistance values.
4. This test ensures the wheel speed sensor and sensor ring generate the proper voltage.
5. This step ensures the wheel speed sensor is not shorted to ground.

Diagnostic Aids:

An "Intermittent" malfunction may be caused by a poor connection, rubbed through wire insulation, or a wire that is broken inside the insulation.

The frequency of the malfunction can be checked by using the enhanced diagnostic function of the Tech 1

If the customer's comments reflect that the ABS amber indicator lamp is "ON" only during moist environmental changes, (rain, snow, vehicle wash) all wheel speed sensor circuitry should be thoroughly inspected for signs of water intrusion. Use the following procedure. Spray down the suspected area with 5% salt water solution (two teaspoons of salt to 12 oz. of water). Start vehicle, allow vehicle to run for 10 seconds. If DTC returns immediately, replace suspected harness.

Any circuitry, that is suspected as causing the intermittent complaint, should be thoroughly checked for backed out terminals, improper mating, broken locks, improperly formed or damaged terminals, poor terminal to wiring connections or physical damage to the wiring harness.

When measuring wheel speed sensor resistance, ensure vehicle is at room temperature. Wheel speed sensor resistance will vary with temperature.

When replacing a wheel speed sensor, inspect the sensor terminals and harness connector for corrosion and/or water intrusion. If evidence of corrosion or water intrusion exists, replace wheel speed sensor harness.

IMPORTANT: WHEEL SPEED SENSOR INTERMITTENT MALFUNCTIONS MAY BE DIFFICULT TO LOCATE. CARE SHOULD BE TAKEN NOT TO DISTURB ANY ELECTRICAL CONNECTIONS PRIOR TO AN INDICATED STEP OF THIS CHART. THIS WILL INSURE THAT AN INTERMITTENT CONNECTION WILL NOT BE CORRECTED BEFORE THE SOURCE OF THE MALFUNCTION IS FOUND.

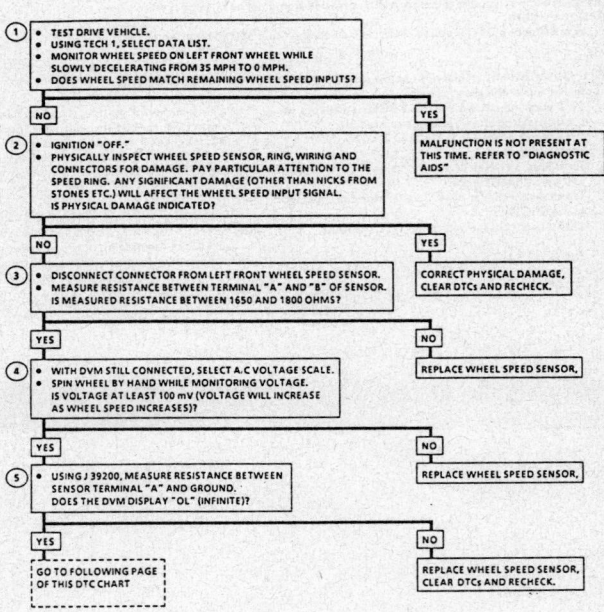

Fig. 106   Code A021, Left front wheel speed–0. 1993 except Cutlass Supreme, Grand Prix, Lumina & Regal (Part 1 of 2)

23-386 *1991 CALAIS & 1991-92 GRAND AM, SKYLARK & 1992 ACHIEVA, BERETTA, CAVALIER, CORSICA, CUTLASS SUPREME, GRAND PRIX, LUMINA, REGAL & SUNBIRD (DELCO-MORAINE VI TYPE)*

DTC A021

LEFT FRONT WHEEL SPEED = 0

Circuit Description:

As a toothed ring passes by the wheel speed sensor, changes in the electromagnetic field cause the wheel speed sensor to produce a sinusoidal (AC) voltage signal whose frequency is proportional to wheel speed. The magnitude of this signal is directly related to wheel speed and the proximity of the wheel speed sensor to the toothed ring often referred to as the air gap.

Failure Condition:

DTC A021 can be set when the vehicle is not in an ABS stop. If the left front wheel speed is less than 1/2 of the vehicle's reference speed and the vehicle's reference speed is greater than 8 km/h (5 mph), a malfunction exists.

Action Taken:

A malfunction DTC is stored, ABS is disabled and the ABS indicator lamp is turned "ON."

Test Description: Number(s) below refer to circled number(s) on the diagnostic chart.

6. This step checks for proper voltages at speed sensor harness connector.
7. This test ensures that the wheel speed sensor circuitry is not internally shorted.
8. This checks for an open in the wheel signal low circuit.
9. This checks for an open in the wheel signal high circuit.
10. This test checks for a short to ground in both high and low wheel signal circuits.
11. This step ensures that DTC A021 was not set due to a poor connection between the world connector and EBCM.

Diagnostic Aids:

An "Intermittent" malfunction may be caused by a poor connection, rubbed through wire insulation, or a wire that is broken inside the insulation.

The frequency of the malfunction can be checked by using the enhanced diagnostic function of the Tech 1

If the customer's comments reflect that the ABS amber indicator lamp is "ON" only during moist environmental changes, (rain, snow, vehicle wash) all wheel speed sensor circuitry should be thoroughly inspected for signs of water intrusion. Use the following procedure. Spray down the suspected area with 5% salt water solution (two teaspoons of salt to 12 oz. of water). Start vehicle, allow vehicle to run for 10 seconds. If DTC returns immediately, replace suspected harness.

Any circuitry, that is suspected as causing the intermittent complaint, should be thoroughly checked for backed out terminals, improper mating, broken locks, improperly formed or damaged terminals, poor terminal to wiring connections or physical damage to the wiring harness.

When measuring wheel speed sensor resistance, ensure vehicle is at room temperature. Wheel speed sensor resistance will vary with temperature.

When replacing a wheel speed sensor, inspect the sensor terminals and harness connector for corrosion and/or water intrusion. If evidence of corrosion or water intrusion exists, replace wheel speed sensor harness.

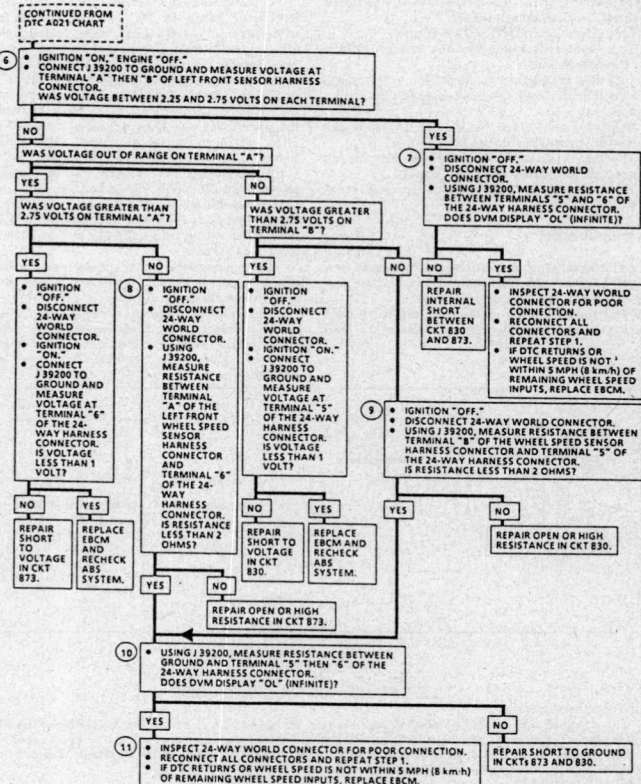

Fig. 106   Code A021, Left front wheel speed=0. 1993 except Cutlass Supreme, Grand Prix, Lumina & Regal (Part 2 of 2)

DTC A021
LEFT FRONT WHEEL SPEED = 0

Circuit Description:

As a toothed ring passes by the wheel speed sensor, changes in the electromagnetic field cause the wheel speed sensor to produce a sinusoidal (AC) voltage signal whose frequency is proportional to wheel speed. The magnitude of this signal is directly related to wheel speed and the proximity of the wheel speed sensor to the toothed ring, often referred to as the air gap.

Failure Condition:

DTC A021 can be set when the vehicle is not in an ABS stop. If the left front wheel speed = 0 and the vehicle's reference speed is greater than 8 km/h (5 mph), a malfunction exists.

Action Taken:

A malfunction DTC is stored, ABS is disabled and the ABS indicator lamp is turned "ON."

Test Description: Number(s) below refer to circled number(s) on the diagnostic chart.

1. This determines if DTC A032 is present.
2. This test verifies whether the malfunction is currently present.
3. This step is designed to identify a wheel speed sensor or circuitry that is damaged and visibly apparent.
4. This test checks to see that the wheel speed sensor is within proper resistance values.
5. This step verifies that the wheel speed sensor can generate an appropriate output signal.
6. This test checks for proper output voltage from the EBCM.

Diagnostic Aids:

An "Intermittent" malfunction may be caused by a poor connection, rubbed through wire insulation, or a wire that is broken inside the insulation.

The frequency of the malfunction can be checked by using the enhanced diagnostic function of the Tech 1.

If the customers comments reflect that the ABS indicator lamp is "ON" only during moist environmental changes (rain, snow, vehicle wash), all wheel speed sensor circuitry should be thoroughly inspected for signs of water intrusion. If DTC is not current, clear DTCs and simulate the effects of water intrusion. Use the following procedure. Spray down the suspected area with a 5% salt water solution (two teaspoons of salt to 12 oz. of water). Start vehicle, allow vehicle to run for 10 seconds. If DTC returns immediately, replace suspected harness.

Any circuitry, that is suspected as causing the intermittent complaint, should be thoroughly checked for backed out terminals, improper mating, broken locks, improperly formed or damaged terminals, poor terminal to wiring connections or physical damage to the wiring harness.

When measuring wheel speed sensor resistance, insure vehicle is at room temperature. Wheel speed sensor resistance will vary with temperature.

When replacing a wheel speed sensor, inspect the sensor terminals and harness connector for corrosion and/or water intrusion. If evidence of corrosion or water intrusion exists, replace wheel speed sensor harness.

IMPORTANT: WHEEL SPEED SENSOR INTERMITTENT PROBLEMS MAY BE DIFFICULT TO LOCATE. CARE SHOULD BE TAKEN NOT TO DISTURB ANY ELECTRICAL CONNECTIONS PRIOR TO AN INDICATED STEP OF THIS CHART. THIS WILL INSURE THAT AN INTERMITTENT CONNECTION WILL NOT BE CORRECTED BEFORE THE SOURCE OF THE PROBLEM IS FOUND.

DTC A021
LEFT FRONT WHEEL SPEED = 0

Circuit Description:

As a toothed ring passes by the wheel speed sensor, changes in the electromagnetic field cause the wheel speed sensor to produce a sinusoidal (AC) voltage signal whose frequency is proportional to wheel speed. The magnitude of this signal is directly related to wheel speed and the proximity of the wheel speed sensor to the toothed ring often referred to as the air gap.

Failure Condition:

DTC A021 can be set when the vehicle is not in an ABS stop. If the left front wheel speed = 0 and the vehicle's reference speed is greater than 8 km/h (5 mph), a malfunction exists.

Action Taken:

A malfunction DTC is stored, ABS is disabled and the ABS indicator lamp is turned "ON."

Test Description: Number(s) below refer to circled number(s) on the diagnostic chart.

7. This checks for an open in the wheel signal high circuit.
8. This step insures that DTC A021 was not set due to a poor connection between the 24-way EBCM connector and the EBCM.
9. This step insures that wheel speed sensor circuitry is not internally shorted.
10. This checks for an open in the wheel signal low circuit.

Diagnostic Aids:

An "Intermittent" malfunction may be caused by a poor connection, rubbed through wire insulation, or a wire that is broken inside the insulation.

The frequency of the malfunction can be checked by using the enhanced diagnostic function of the Tech 1

If the customers comments reflect that the ABS indicator lamp is "ON" only during moist environmental changes (rain, snow, vehicle wash), all wheel speed sensor circuitry should be thoroughly inspected for signs of water intrusion. If DTC is not current, clear DTCs and simulate the effects of water intrusion. Use the following procedure. Spray down the suspected area with a 5% salt water solution (two teaspoons of salt to 12 oz. of water). Start vehicle, allow vehicle to run for 10 seconds. If DTC returns immediately, replace suspected harness.

Any circuitry, that is suspected as causing the intermittent complaint, should be thoroughly checked for backed out terminals, improper mating, broken locks, improperly formed or damaged terminals, poor terminal to wiring connections or physical damage to the wiring harness.

When measuring wheel speed sensor resistance, insure vehicle is at room temperature. Wheel speed sensor resistance will vary with temperature.

When replacing a wheel speed sensor, inspect the sensor terminals and harness connector for corrosion and/or water intrusion. If evidence of corrosion or water intrusion exists, replace wheel speed sensor harness.

Fig. 107   Code A021, Left front wheel speed=0. 1993 Cutlass Supreme, Grand Prix, Lumina & Regal

Cavalier & Sunbird

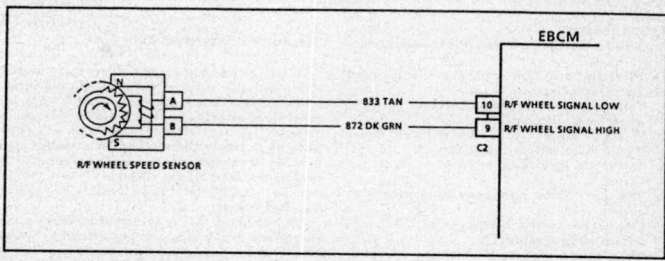

Achieva, Beretta, Corsica, Grand Am & Skylark

DTC A022

RIGHT FRONT WHEEL SPEED = 0

Circuit Description:
As a toothed ring passes by the wheel speed sensor, changes in the electromagnetic field cause the wheel speed sensor to produce a sinusoidal (AC) voltage signal whose frequency is proportional to wheel speed. The magnitude of this signal is directly related to wheel speed and the proximity of the wheel speed sensor to the toothed ring, often referred to as the air gap.

Failure Condition:
DTC A022 can be set when the vehicle is not in an ABS stop. If the right front wheel speed is less than 1/2 of the vehicle's reference speed and the vehicle's reference speed is greater than 8 km/h (5 mph), a malfunction exists.

Action Taken:
A malfunction DTC is stored, ABS is disabled and the ABS indicator lamp is turned "ON."

Test Description: Number(s) below refer to circled number(s) on the diagnostic chart.
1. This test verifies whether the malfunction is currently present.
2. This step will identify a wheel speed sensor or circuitry that is damaged and visibly apparent.
3. This test checks wheel speed sensor for proper resistance values.
4. This test ensures the wheel speed sensor and sensor ring generate the proper voltage.
5. This step ensures the wheel speed sensor is not shorted to ground.

Diagnostic Aids:

An "Intermittent" malfunction may be caused by a poor connection, rubbed through wire insulation, or a wire that is broken inside the insulation.

The frequency of the malfunction can be checked by using the enhanced diagnostic function of the Tech 1

If the customer's comments reflect that the ABS amber indicator lamp is "ON" only during moist environmental changes, (rain, snow, vehicle wash) all wheel speed sensor circuitry should be thoroughly inspected for signs of water intrusion. Use the following procedure. Spray down the suspected area with 5% salt water solution (two teaspoons of salt to 12 oz. of water). Start vehicle, allow vehicle to run for 10 seconds. If DTC returns immediately, replace suspected harness.

Any circuitry, that is suspected as causing the intermittent complaint, should be thoroughly checked for backed out terminals, improper mating, broken locks, improperly formed or damaged terminals, poor terminal to wiring connections or physical damage to the wiring harness.

When measuring wheel speed sensor resistance, ensure vehicle is at room temperature. Wheel speed sensor resistance will vary with temperature.

When replacing a wheel speed sensor, inspect the sensor terminals and harness connector for corrosion and/or water intrusion. If evidence of corrosion or water intrusion exists, replace wheel speed sensor harness.

IMPORTANT: WHEEL SPEED SENSOR INTERMITTENT MALFUNCTIONS MAY BE DIFFICULT TO LOCATE. CARE SHOULD BE TAKEN NOT TO DISTURB ANY ELECTRICAL CONNECTIONS PRIOR TO AN INDICATED STEP OF THIS CHART. THIS WILL INSURE THAT AN INTERMITTENT CONNECTION WILL NOT BE CORRECTED BEFORE THE SOURCE OF THE MALFUNCTION IS FOUND.

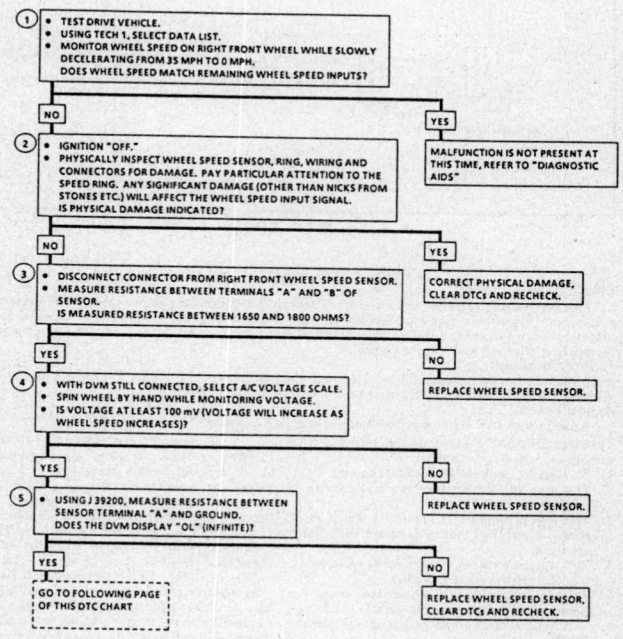

Fig. 108   Code A022, Right front wheel speed=0 (Part 1 of 2). 1993 except Cutlass Supreme, Grand Prix, Lumina & Regal

DTC A022

RIGHT FRONT WHEEL SPEED = 0

Circuit Description:
As a toothed ring passes by the wheel speed sensor, changes in the electromagnetic field cause the wheel speed sensor to produce a sinusoidal (AC) voltage signal whose frequency is proportional to wheel speed. The magnitude of this signal is directly related to wheel speed and the proximity of the wheel speed sensor to the toothed ring, often referred to as the air gap.

Failure Condition:
DTC A022 can be set when the vehicle is not in an ABS stop. If the right front wheel speed is less than 1/2 of the vehicle's reference speed and the vehicle's reference speed is greater than 8 km/h (5 mph), a malfunction exists.

Action Taken:
A malfunction DTC is stored, ABS is disabled and the ABS indicator lamp is turned "ON."

Test Description: Number(s) below refer to circled number(s) on the diagnostic chart.
6. This step checks for proper voltages at speed sensor harness connector.
7. This test ensures that the wheel and speed sensor circuitry is not internally shorted.
8. This checks for an open in the wheel signal low circuit.
9. This checks for an open in the wheel signal high circuit.
10. This test checks for a short to ground in both high and low wheel signal circuits.
11. This step ensures that DTC A022 was not set due to a poor connection between the world connector and EBCM.

Diagnostic Aids:

An "Intermittent" malfunction may be caused by a poor connection, rubbed through wire insulation, or a wire that is broken inside the insulation.
The frequency of the malfunction can be checked by using the enhanced diagnostic function of the Tech 1

If the customer's comments reflect that the ABS amber indicator lamp is "ON" only during moist environmental changes, (rain, snow, vehicle wash) all wheel speed sensor circuitry should be thoroughly inspected for signs of water intrusion. Use the following procedure. Spray down the suspected area with 5% salt water solution (two teaspoons of salt to 12 oz. of water). Start vehicle, allow vehicle to run for 10 seconds. If DTC returns immediately, replace suspected harness.

Any circuitry, that is suspected as causing the intermittent complaint, should be thoroughly checked for backed out terminals, improper mating, broken locks, improperly formed or damaged terminals, poor terminal to wiring connections or physical damage to the wiring harness.

When measuring wheel speed sensor resistance, ensure vehicle is at room temperature. Wheel speed sensor resistance will vary with temperature.

When replacing a wheel speed sensor, inspect the sensor terminals and harness connector for corrosion and/or water intrusion. If evidence of corrosion or water intrusion exists, replace wheel speed sensor harness.

Fig. 108   Code A022, Right front wheel speed—0 (Part 2 of 2). 1993 except Cutlass Supreme, Grand Prix, Lumina & Regal

DTC A022

RIGHT FRONT WHEEL SPEED = 0

Circuit Description:
As a toothed ring passes by the wheel speed sensor, changes in the electromagnetic field cause the wheel speed sensor to produce a sinusoidal (AC) voltage signal whose frequency is proportional to wheel speed. The magnitude of this signal is directly related to wheel speed and the proximity of the wheel speed sensor to the toothed ring, often referred to as the air gap.

Failure Condition:
DTC A022 can be set when the vehicle is not in an ABS stop. If the right front wheel speed=0 and the vehicle's reference speed is greater than 8 km/h (5 mph), a malfunction exists.

Action Taken:
A malfunction DTC is stored, ABS is disabled and the ABS indicator lamp is turned "ON."

Test Description: Number(s) below refer to circled number(s) on the diagnostic chart.
1. This test determines if DTC A033 is present.
2. This step verifies whether the malfunction is currently present.
3. This step is designed to identify a wheel speed sensor or circuitry that is damaged and visibly apparent.
4. This test checks to see that the wheel speed sensor is within proper resistance values.
5. This step verifies that the wheel speed sensor can generate an appropriate output signal.
6. This test checks for proper output voltage from the EBCM.

Diagnostic Aids:

An "Intermittent" malfunction may be caused by a poor connection, rubbed through wire insulation, or a wire that is broken inside the insulation.
The frequency of the malfunction can be checked by using the enhanced diagnostic function of the Tech 1

If the customers comments reflect that the ABS indicator lamp is "ON" only during moist environmental changes (rain, snow, vehicle wash), all wheel speed sensor circuitry should be thoroughly inspected for signs of water intrusion. If DTC is not current, clear DTCs and simulate the effects of water intrusion. Use the following procedure. Spray down the suspected area with a 5% salt water solution (two teaspoons of salt to 12 oz. of water). Start vehicle, allow vehicle to run for 10 seconds. If DTC returns immediately, replace suspected harness.

Any circuitry, that is suspected as causing the intermittent complaint, should be thoroughly checked for backed out terminals, improper mating, broken locks, improperly formed or damaged terminals, poor terminal to wiring connections or physical damage to the wiring harness.

When measuring wheel speed sensor resistance, insure vehicle is at room temperature. Wheel speed sensor resistance will vary with temperature.

When replacing a wheel speed sensor, inspect the sensor terminals and harness connector for corrosion and/or water intrusion. If evidence of corrosion or water intrusion exists, replace wheel speed sensor harness.

Fig. 109   Code A022, Right front wheel speed—0 (Part 1 of 2). 1993 Cutlass Supreme, Grand Prix, Lumina & Regal

DTC A022

RIGHT FRONT WHEEL SPEED = 0

Circuit Description:

As a toothed ring passes by the wheel speed sensor, changes in the electromagnetic field cause the wheel speed sensor to produce a sinusoidal (AC) voltage signal whose frequency is proportional to wheel speed. The magnitude of this signal is directly related to wheel speed and the proximity of the wheel speed sensor to the toothed ring, often referred to as the air gap.

Failure Condition:

DTC A022 can be set when the vehicle is not in an ABS stop. If the right front wheel speed=0 and the vehicle's reference speed is greater than 8 km/h (5 mph), a malfunction exists.

Action Taken:

A malfunction DTC is stored, ABS is disabled and the ABS indicator lamp is turned "ON".

Test Description: Number(s) below refer to circled number(s) on the diagnostic chart.

7. This checks for an open in the wheel signal low circuit.
8. This step insures that DTC A022 was not set due to a poor connection between the 24-way EBCM connector and the EBCM.
9. This test insures that wheel speed sensor circuitry is not internally shorted.
10. This checks for an open in the wheel signal high circuit.

Diagnostic Aids:

An "Intermittent" malfunction may be caused by a poor connection, rubbed through wire insulation, or a wire that is broken inside the insulation.

The frequency of the malfunction can be checked by using the enhanced diagnostic function of the Tech 1

If the customers comments reflect that the ABS indicator lamp is "ON" only during moist environmental changes (rain, snow, vehicle wash), all wheel speed sensor circuitry should be thoroughly inspected for signs of water intrusion. If DTC is not current, clear DTCs and simulate the effects of water intrusion. Use the following procedure. Spray down the suspected area with a 5% salt water solution (two teaspoons of salt to 12 oz. of water). Start vehicle, allow vehicle to run for 10 seconds. If DTC returns immediately, replace suspected harness.

Any circuitry, that is suspected as causing the intermittent complaint, should be thoroughly checked for backed out terminals, improper mating, broken locks, improperly formed or damaged terminals, poor terminal to wiring connections or physical damage to the wiring harness.

When measuring wheel speed sensor resistance, insure vehicle is at room temperature. Wheel speed sensor resistance will vary with temperature.

When replacing a wheel speed sensor, inspect the sensor terminals and harness connector for corrosion and/or water intrusion. If evidence of corrosion or water intrusion exists, replace wheel speed sensor harness.

Fig. 109   Code A022, Right front wheel speed=0 (Part 2 of 2). 1993 Cutlass Supreme, Grand Prix, Lumina & Regal

Cavalier & Sunbird

DTC A023

LEFT REAR WHEEL SPEED = 0

Circuit Description:

As a toothed ring passes by the wheel speed sensor, changes in the electromagnetic field cause the wheel speed sensor to produce a sinusoidal (AC) voltage signal whose frequency is proportional to wheel speed. The magnitude of this signal is directly related to wheel speed and the proximity of the wheel speed sensor to the toothed ring, often referred to as the air gap.

Failure Condition:

DTC A023 can be set when the vehicle is not in an ABS stop. If the left rear wheel speed=0 and the vehicle's reference speed is greater than 8 km/h (5 mph), a malfunction exists.

Action Taken:

A malfunction DTC is stored, ABS is disabled and the ABS indicator lamp is turned "ON".

Test Description: Number(s) below refer to circled number(s) on the diagnostic chart.

1. This determines if DTC A034 is present.
2. This test verifies whether the malfunction is currently present.
3. This step is designed to identify a wheel speed sensor or circuitry that is damaged and visibly apparent.
4. This test checks to see that the wheel speed sensor is within proper resistance values.
5. This step verifies that the wheel speed sensor can generate an appropriate output signal.
6. This test checks for proper output voltage from the EBCM.

Diagnostic Aids:

An "Intermittent" malfunction may be caused by a poor connection, rubbed through wire insulation, or a wire that is broken inside the insulation.

The frequency of the malfunction can be checked by using the enhanced diagnostic function of the Tech 1,

If the customers comments reflect that the ABS indicator lamp is "ON" only during moist environmental changes (rain, snow, vehicle wash), all wheel speed senor circuitry should be thoroughly inspected for signs of water intrusion. If DTC is not current, clear DTCs and simulate the effects of water intrusion. Use the following procedure. Spray down the suspected area with a 5% salt water solution (two teaspoons of salt to 12 oz. of water). Start vehicle, allow vehicle to run for 10 seconds. If DTC returns immediately, replace suspected harness.

Any circuitry, that is suspected as causing the intermittent complaint, should be thoroughly checked for backed out terminals, improper mating, broken locks, improperly formed or damaged terminals, poor terminal to wiring connections or physical damage to the wiring harness.

When measuring wheel speed sensor resistance, insure vehicle is at room temperature. Wheel speed sensor resistance will vary with temperature.

When replacing a wheel speed sensor, inspect the sensor terminals and harness connector for corrosion and/or water intrusion. If evidence of corrosion or water intrusion exists, replace wheel speed sensor harness.

Achieva, Beretta, Corsica, Grand Am & Skylark

Fig. 110   Code A023, Left rear wheel speed=0 (Part 1 of 2). 1993 except Cutlass Supreme, Grand Prix, Lumina & Regal

IMPORTANT: WHEEL SPEED SENSOR INTERMITTENT MALFUNCTIONS MAY BE DIFFICULT TO LOCATE. CARE SHOULD BE TAKEN NOT TO DISTURB ANY ELECTRICAL CONNECTIONS PRIOR TO AN INDICATED STEP OF THIS CHART. THIS WILL INSURE THAT AN INTERMITTENT CONNECTION WILL NOT BE CORRECTED BEFORE THE SOURCE OF THE MALFUNCTION IS FOUND.

DTC A023

LEFT REAR WHEEL SPEED = 0

Circuit Description:

As a toothed ring passes by the wheel speed sensor, changes in the electromagnetic field cause the wheel speed sensor to produce a sinusoidal (AC) voltage signal whose frequency is proportional to wheel speed. The magnitude of this signal is directly related to wheel speed and the proximity of the wheel speed sensor to the toothed ring, often referred to as the air gap.

Failure Condition:

DTC A023 can be set when the vehicle is not in an ABS stop. If the left rear wheel speed is less than 1/2 of the vehicle's reference speed and the vehicle's reference speed is greater than 8 km/h (5 mph), a malfunction exists.

Action Taken:

A malfunction DTC is stored, ABS is disabled and the ABS indicator lamp is turned "ON."

Test Description: Number(s) below refer to circled number(s) on the diagnostic chart.

6. This step checks for proper voltages at body to ABS and fuel sender harness connector.
7. This test ensures that the wheel speed sensor circuitry is not internally shorted.
8. This checks for an open in the wheel signal high circuit.
9. This checks for an open in the wheel signal low circuit.
10. This test checks for a short to ground in both high and low wheel signal circuits.
11. This step ensures that DTC A023 was not set due to a poor connection between the world connector and EBCM.

Diagnostic Aids:

An "Intermittent" malfunction may be caused by a poor connection, rubbed through wire insulation, or a wire that is broken inside the insulation.

The frequency of the malfunction can be checked by using the enhanced diagnostic function of the Tech 1

If the customer's comments reflect that the ABS amber indicator lamp is "ON" only during moist environmental changes, (rain, snow, vehicle wash) all wheel speed sensor circuitry should be thoroughly inspected for signs of water intrusion. Use the following procedure. Spray down the suspected area with 5% salt water solution (two teaspoons of salt to 12 oz. of water). Start vehicle, allow vehicle to run for 10 seconds. If DTC returns immediately, replace suspected harness.

Any circuitry, that is suspected as causing the intermittent complaint, should be thoroughly checked for backed out terminals, improper mating, broken locks, improperly formed or damaged terminals, poor terminal to wiring connections or physical damage to the wiring harness.

When measuring wheel speed sensor resistance, ensure vehicle is at room temperature. Wheel speed sensor resistance will vary with temperature.

When replacing a wheel speed sensor, inspect the sensor terminals and harness connector for corrosion and/or water intrusion. If evidence of corrosion or water intrusion exists, replace wheel speed sensor harness.

Fig. 110   Code A023, Left rear wheel speed-0 (Part 2 of 2). 1993 except Cutlass Supreme, Grand Prix, Lumina & Regal

DTC A023

LEFT REAR WHEEL SPEED = 0

Circuit Description:

As a toothed ring passes by the wheel speed sensor, changes in the electromagnetic field cause the wheel speed sensor to produce a sinusoidal (AC) voltage signal whose frequency is proportional to wheel speed. The magnitude of this signal is directly related to wheel speed and the proximity of the wheel speed sensor to the toothed ring, often referred to as the air gap.

Failure Condition:

DTC A023 can be set when the vehicle is not in an ABS stop. If the left rear wheel speed = 0 and the vehicle's reference speed is greater than 8 km/h (5 mph), a malfunction exists.

Action Taken:

A malfunction DTC is stored, ABS is disabled and the ABS indicator lamp is turned "ON."

Test Description: Number(s) below refer to circled number(s) on the diagnostic chart.

1. This determines if DTC A034 is present.
2. This test verifies whether the malfunction is currently present.
3. This step is designed to identify a wheel speed sensor or circuitry that is damaged and visibly apparent.
4. This test checks to see that the wheel speed sensor is within proper resistance values.
5. This step verifies that the wheel speed sensor can generate an appropriate output signal.
6. This test checks for proper output voltage from the EBCM.

Diagnostic Aids:

An "Intermittent" malfunction may be caused by a poor connection, rubbed through wire insulation, or a wire that is broken inside the insulation.

The frequency of the malfunction can be checked by using the enhanced diagnostic function of the Tech 1

If the customers comments reflect that the ABS indicator lamp is "ON" only during moist environmental changes (rain, snow, vehicle wash), all wheel speed senor circuitry should be thoroughly inspected for signs of water intrusion. If DTC is not current, clear DTCs and simulate the effects of water intrusion. Use the following procedure. Spray down the suspected area with a 5% salt water solution (two teaspoons of salt to 12 oz. of water). Start vehicle, allow vehicle to run for 10 seconds. If DTC returns immediately, replace suspected harness.

Any circuitry, that is suspected as causing the intermittent complaint, should be thoroughly checked for backed out terminals, improper mating, broken locks, improperly formed or damaged terminals, poor terminal to wiring connections or physical damage to the wiring harness.

When measuring wheel speed sensor resistance, insure vehicle is at room temperature. Wheel speed sensor resistance will vary with temperature.

When replacing a wheel speed sensor, inspect the sensor terminals and harness connector for corrosion and/or water intrusion. If evidence of corrosion or water intrusion exists, replace wheel speed sensor harness.

DTC A023

LEFT REAR WHEEL SPEED = 0

Circuit Description:

As a toothed ring passes by the wheel speed sensor, changes in the electromagnetic field cause the wheel speed sensor to produce a sinusoidal (AC) voltage signal whose frequency is proportional to wheel speed. The magnitude of this signal is directly related to wheel speed and the proximity of the wheel speed sensor to the toothed ring, often referred to as the air gap.

Failure Condition:

DTC A023 can be set when the vehicle is not in an ABS stop. If the left rear wheel speed = 0 and the vehicle's reference speed is greater than 8 km/h (5 mph), a malfunction exists.

Action Taken:

A malfunction DTC is stored, ABS is disabled and the ABS indicator lamp is turned "ON."

Test Description: Number(s) below refer to circled number(s) on the diagnostic chart.

7. This checks for an open in the wheel signal low circuit.
8. This step insures that DTC A023 was not set due to a poor connection between the 24-way EBCM connector and the EBCM.
9. This test insures that wheel speed sensor circuitry is not internally shorted.
10. This checks for an open in the wheel signal high circuit.

Diagnostic Aids:

An "Intermittent" malfunction may be caused by a poor connection, rubbed through wire insulation, or a wire that is broken inside the insulation.

The frequency of the malfunction can be checked by using the enhanced diagnostic function of the Tech 1

If the customers comments reflect that the ABS indicator lamp is "ON" only during moist environmental changes (rain, snow, vehicle wash), all wheel speed sensor circuitry should be thoroughly inspected for signs of water intrusion. If DTC is not current, clear DTCs and simulate the effects of water intrusion. Use the following procedure. Spray down the suspected area with a 5% salt water solution (two teaspoons of salt to 12 oz. of water). Start vehicle, allow vehicle to run for 10 seconds. If DTC returns immediately, replace suspected harness.

Any circuitry, that is suspected as causing the intermittent complaint, should be thoroughly checked for backed out terminals, improper mating, broken locks, improperly formed or damaged terminals, poor terminal to wiring connections or physical damage to the wiring harness.

When measuring wheel speed sensor resistance, insure vehicle is at room temperature. Wheel speed sensor resistance will vary with temperature.

When replacing a wheel speed sensor, inspect the sensor terminals and harness connector for corrosion and/or water intrusion. If evidence of corrosion or water intrusion exists, replace wheel speed sensor harness.

Fig. 111   Code A023, Left rear wheel speed=0. 1993 Cutlass Supreme, Grand Prix, Lumina & Regal

Cavalier & Sunbird

Achieva, Beretta, Corsica, Grand Am & Skylark

DTC A024

RIGHT REAR WHEEL SPEED = 0

Circuit Description:

As a toothed ring passes by the wheel speed sensor, changes in the electromagnetic field cause the wheel speed sensor to produce a sinusoidal (AC) voltage signal whose frequency is proportional to wheel speed. The magnitude of this signal is directly related to wheel speed and the proximity of the wheel speed sensor to the toothed ring, often referred to as the air gap.

Failure Condition:

DTC A024 can be set when the vehicle is not in an ABS stop. If the right rear wheel speed is less than 1/2 of the vehicle's reference speed and the vehicle's reference speed is greater than 8 km/h (5 mph), a malfunction exists.

Action Taken:

A malfunction DTC is stored, ABS is disabled and the ABS indicator lamp is turned "ON."

Test Description: Number(s) below refer to circled number(s) on the diagnostic chart.
1. This test verifies whether the malfunction is currently present.
2. This step will identify a wheel speed sensor or circuitry that is damaged and visibly apparent.
3. This test checks wheel speed sensor for proper resistance values.
4. This test ensures the wheel speed sensor and sensor ring generate the proper voltage.
5. This step ensures the wheel speed sensor is not shorted to ground.

Diagnostic Aids:

An "Intermittent" malfunction may be caused by a poor connection, rubbed through wire insulation, or a wire that is broken inside the insulation.

The frequency of the malfunction can be checked by using the enhanced diagnostic function of the Tech 1

If the customer's comments reflect that the ABS amber indicator lamp is "ON" only during moist environmental changes, (rain, snow, vehicle wash) all wheel speed sensor circuitry should be thoroughly inspected for water intrusion. Use the following procedure. Spray down the suspected area with 5% salt water solution (two teaspoons of salt to 12 oz. of water). Start vehicle, allow vehicle to run for 10 seconds. If DTC returns immediately, replace suspected harness.

Any circuitry, that is suspected as causing the intermittent complaint, should be thoroughly checked for backed out terminals, improper mating, broken locks, improperly formed or damaged terminals, poor terminal to wiring connections or physical damage to the wiring harness.

When measuring wheel speed sensor resistance, ensure vehicle is at room temperature. Wheel speed sensor resistance will vary with temperature.

When replacing a wheel speed sensor, inspect the sensor terminals and harness connector for corrosion and/or water intrusion. If evidence of corrosion or water intrusion exists, replace wheel speed sensor harness.

Fig. 112 Code A024, Right rear wheel speed—0 (Part 1 of 2). 1993 except Cutlass Supreme, Grand Prix, Lumina & Regal

DTC A024

RIGHT REAR WHEEL SPEED = 0

Circuit Description:
As a toothed ring passes by the wheel speed sensor, changes in the electromagnetic field cause the wheel speed sensor to produce a sinusoidal (AC) voltage signal whose frequency is proportional to wheel speed. The magnitude of this signal is directly related to wheel speed and the proximity of the wheel speed sensor to the toothed ring, often referred to as the air gap.

Failure Condition:
DTC A024 can be set when the vehicle is not in an ABS stop. If the right rear wheel speed is less than 1/2 of the vehicle's reference speed and the vehicle's reference speed is greater than 8 km/h (5 mph), a malfunction exists.

Action Taken:
A malfunction DTC is stored, ABS is disabled and the ABS indicator lamp is turned "ON."

Test Description: Number(s) below refer to circled number(s) on the diagnostic chart.
6. This step checks for proper voltages at body to ABS and fuel sender harness connector.
7. This test ensures that the wheel speed sensor circuitry is not internally shorted.
8. This checks for an open in the wheel signal high circuit.
9. This checks for an open in the wheel signal low circuit.
10. This test checks for a short to ground in both high and low wheel signal circuits.
11. This step ensures that DTC A024 was not set due to a poor connection between the world connector and EBCM.

Diagnostic Aids:
An "Intermittent" malfunction may be caused by a poor connection, rubbed through wire insulation, or a wire that is broken inside the insulation.
The frequency of the malfunction can be checked by using the enhanced diagnostic function of the Tech 1

If the customer's comments reflect that the ABS amber indicator lamp is "ON" only during moist environmental changes, (rain, snow, vehicle wash) all wheel speed sensor circuitry should be thoroughly inspected for water intrusion. Use the following procedure. Spray down the suspected area with 5% salt water solution (two teaspoons of salt to 12 oz. of water). Start vehicle, allow vehicle to run for 10 seconds. If DTC returns immediately, replace suspected harness.

Any circuitry, that is suspected as causing the intermittent complaint, should be thoroughly checked for backed out terminals, improper mating, broken locks, improperly formed or damaged terminals, poor terminal to wiring connections or physical damage to the wiring harness.

When measuring wheel speed sensor resistance, ensure vehicle is at room temperature. Wheel speed sensor resistance will vary with temperature.

When replacing a wheel speed sensor, inspect the sensor terminals and harness connector for corrosion and/or water intrusion. If evidence of corrosion or water intrusion exists, replace wheel speed sensor harness.

Fig. 112 Code A024, Right rear wheel speed=0 (Part 2 of 2). 1993 except Cutlass Supreme, Grand Prix, Lumina & Regal

DTC A024

RIGHT REAR WHEEL SPEED = 0

Circuit Description:
As a toothed ring passes by the wheel speed sensor, changes in the electromagnetic field cause the wheel speed sensor to produce a sinusoidal (AC) voltage signal whose frequency is proportional to wheel speed. The magnitude of this signal is directly related to wheel speed and the proximity of the wheel speed sensor to the toothed ring, often referred to as the air gap.

Failure Condition:
DTC A024 can be set when the vehicle is not in an ABS stop. If the right rear wheel speed=0 and the vehicle's reference speed is greater than 8 km/h (5 mph), a malfunction exists.

Action Taken:
A malfunction DTC is stored, ABS is disabled and the ABS indicator lamp is turned "ON."

Test Description: Number(s) below refer to circled number(s) on the diagnostic chart.
1. This test determines if DTC A035 is present.
2. This test verifies whether the malfunction is currently present.
3. This step is designed to identify a wheel speed sensor or circuitry that is damaged and visibly apparent.
4. This test checks to see that the wheel speed sensor is within proper resistance values.
5. This step verifies that the wheel speed sensor can generate an appropriate output signal.
6. This test checks for proper output voltage from the EBCM.

Diagnostic Aids:
An "Intermittent" malfunction may be caused by a poor connection, rubbed through wire insulation, or a wire that is broken inside the insulation.
The frequency of the malfunction can be checked by using the enhanced diagnostic function of the Tech 1

If the customers comments reflect that the ABS indicator lamp is "ON" only during moist environmental changes (rain, snow, vehicle wash), all wheel speed sensor circuitry should be thoroughly inspected for signs of water intrusion. If DTC is not current, clear DTCs and simulate the effects of water intrusion. Use the following procedure. Spray down the suspected area with a 5% salt water solution (two teaspoons of salt to 12 oz. of water). Start vehicle, allow vehicle to run for 10 seconds. If DTC returns immediately, replace suspected harness.

Any circuitry, that is suspected as causing the intermittent complaint, should be thoroughly checked for backed out terminals, improper mating, broken locks, improperly formed or damaged terminals, poor terminal to wiring connections or physical damage to the wiring harness.

When measuring wheel speed sensor resistance, insure vehicle is at room temperature. Wheel speed sensor resistance will vary with temperature.

When replacing a wheel speed sensor, inspect the sensor terminals and harness connector for corrosion and/or water intrusion. If evidence of corrosion or water intrusion exists, replace wheel speed sensor harness.

IMPORTANT: WHEEL SPEED SENSOR INTERMITTENT PROBLEMS MAY BE DIFFICULT TO LOCATE. CARE SHOULD BE TAKEN NOT TO DISTURB ANY ELECTRICAL CONNECTIONS PRIOR TO AN INDICATED STEP OF THIS CHART. THIS WILL INSURE THAT AN INTERMITTENT CONNECTION WILL NOT BE CORRECTED BEFORE THE SOURCE OF THE PROBLEM IS FOUND.

Fig. 113 Code A024, Right rear wheel speed=0 (Part 1 of 2). 1993 Cutlass Supreme, Grand Prix, Lumina & Regal

DTC A024

RIGHT REAR WHEEL SPEED = 0

Circuit Description:

As a toothed ring passes by the wheel speed sensor, changes in the electromagnetic field cause the wheel speed sensor to produce a sinusoidal (AC) voltage signal whose frequency is proportional to wheel speed. The magnitude of this signal is directly related to wheel speed and the proximity of the wheel speed sensor to the toothed ring, often referred to as the air gap.

Failure Condition:

DTC A024 can be set when the vehicle is not in an ABS stop. If the right rear wheel speed = 0 and the vehicle's reference speed is greater than 8 km/h (5 mph), a malfunction exists.

Action Taken:

A malfunction DTC is stored, ABS is disabled and the ABS indicator lamp is turned "ON."

Test Description: Number(s) below refer to circled number(s) on the diagnostic chart.

7. This checks for an open in the wheel signal low circuit.
8. This step insures that DTC A024 was not set due to a poor connection between the 24-way EBCM connector and the EBCM.
9. This test insures that wheel speed sensor circuitry is not internally shorted.
10. This checks for an open in the wheel signal high circuit.

Diagnostic Aids:

An "Intermittent" malfunction may be caused by a poor connection, rubbed through wire insulation, or a wire that is broken inside the insulation.

The frequency of the malfunction can be checked by using the enhanced diagnostic function of the Tech 1

If the customers comments reflect that the ABS indicator lamp is "ON" only during moist environmental changes (rain, snow, vehicle wash), all wheel speed sensor circuitry should be thoroughly inspected for signs of water intrusion. If DTC is not

current, clear DTCs and simulate the effects of water intrusion. Use the following procedure. Spray down the suspected area with a 5% salt water solution (two teaspoons of salt to 12 oz. of water). Start vehicle, allow vehicle to run for 10 seconds. If DTC returns immediately, replace suspected harness.

Any circuitry, that is suspected as causing the intermittent complaint, should be thoroughly checked for backed out terminals, improper mating, broken locks, improperly formed or damaged terminals, poor terminal to wiring connections or physical damage to the wiring harness.

When measuring wheel speed sensor resistance, insure vehicle is at room temperature. Wheel speed sensor resistance will vary with temperature.

When replacing a wheel speed sensor, inspect the sensor terminals and harness connector for corrosion and/or water intrusion. If evidence of corrosion or water intrusion exists, replace wheel speed sensor harness.

Fig. 113   Code A024, Right rear wheel speed = 0 (Part 2 of 2). 1993 Cutlass Supreme, Grand Prix, Lumina & Regal

Cavalier & Sunbird

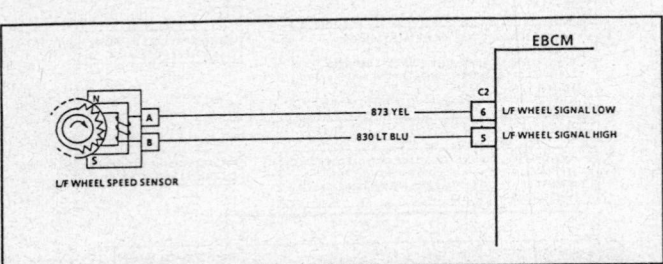

Achieva, Beretta, Corsica, Grand Am & Skylark

DTC A025

LEFT FRONT EXCESSIVE WHEEL SPEED VARIATION

Circuit Description:

As a toothed ring passes by the wheel speed sensor, changes in the electromagnetic field cause the wheel speed sensor to produce a sinusoidal (AC) voltage signal whose frequency is proportional to wheel speed. The magnitude of this signal is directly related to wheel speed and the proximity of the wheel speed sensor to the toothed ring, often referred to as the air gap.

Failure Condition:

DTC A025 can be set when the brake is "OFF." The purpose of this test is to detect a situation in which the left front wheel acceleration or deceleration is beyond specified limits.

Action Taken:

A malfunction DTC is stored, ABS is disabled and the ABS indicator lamp is turned "ON."

Test Description: Number(s) below refer to circled number(s) on the diagnostic chart.

1. This test verifies whether the malfunction is currently present.
2. This step will identify a wheel speed sensor or circuitry that is damaged and visibly apparent.
3. This test checks wheel speed sensor for proper resistance values.
4. This test ensures the wheel speed sensor and sensor ring generate the proper voltage.
5. This step ensures the wheel speed sensor is not shorted to ground.

Diagnostic Aids:

An "Intermittent" malfunction may be caused by a poor connection, rubbed through wire insulation, or a wire that is broken inside the insulation.

The frequency of the malfunction can be checked by using the enhanced diagnostic function of the Tech 1

If the customer's comments reflect that the ABS amber indicator lamp is "ON" only during moist environmental changes, (rain, snow, vehicle wash) all wheel speed sensor circuitry should be thoroughly

inspected for water intrusion. Use the following procedure. Spray down the suspected area with 5% salt water solution (two teaspoons of salt to 12 oz. of water). Start vehicle, allow vehicle to run for 10 seconds. If DTC returns immediately, replace suspected harness.

Any circuitry, that is suspected as causing the intermittent complaint, should be thoroughly checked for backed out terminals, improper mating, broken locks, improperly formed or damaged terminals, poor terminal to wiring connections or physical damage to the wiring harness.

A careful visual inspection of the toothed ring, CV joint, bearing and wheel speed sensor for physical damage should also be performed. If DTC sets at the same mph every time and wheel speed variation is noted above this mph on the Tech 1, the speed ring is most likely damaged. This can occur at any speed.

When measuring wheel speed sensor resistance, ensure vehicle is at room temperature. Wheel speed sensor resistance will vary with temperature.

When replacing a wheel speed sensor, inspect the sensor terminals and harness connector for corrosion and/or water intrusion. If evidence of corrosion or water instrusion exists, replace wheel speed sensor harness.

Fig. 114   Code A025, Left front excessive wheel speed variation (Part 1 Of 2). 1993 except Cutlass Supreme, Grand Prix, Lumina & Regal

IMPORTANT: WHEEL SPEED SENSOR INTERMITTENT MALFUNCTIONS MAY BE DIFFICULT TO LOCATE. CARE SHOULD BE TAKEN NOT TO DISTURB ANY ELECTRICAL CONNECTIONS PRIOR TO AN INDICATED STEP OF THIS CHART. THIS WILL INSURE THAT AN INTERMITTENT CONNECTION WILL NOT BE CORRECTED BEFORE THE SOURCE OF THE MALFUNCTION IS FOUND.

DTC A025

LEFT FRONT EXCESSIVE WHEEL SPEED VARIATION

Circuit Description:

As a toothed ring passes by the wheel speed sensor, changes in the electromagnetic field cause the wheel speed sensor to produce a sinusoidal (AC) voltage signal whose frequency is proportional to wheel speed. The magnitude of this signal is directly related to wheel speed and the proximity of the wheel speed sensor to the toothed ring, often referred to as the air gap.

Failure Condition:

DTC A025 can be set when the brake is "OFF." The purpose of this test is to detect a situation in which the left front wheel acceleration or deceleration is beyond specified limits.

Action Taken:

A malfunction DTC is stored, ABS is disabled and the ABS indicator lamp is turned "ON."

Test Description: Number(s) below refer to circled number(s) on the diagnostic chart.

6. This step checks for proper voltages at speed sensor harness connector.
7. This test ensures that the wheel speed sensor circuitry is not internally shorted.
8. This checks for an open in the wheel signal low circuit.
9. This checks for an open in the wheel signal high circuit.
10. This test checks for a short to ground in both high and low wheel signal circuits.
11. This step ensures that DTC A025 was not set due to a poor connection between the world connector and EBCM.

Diagnostic Aids:

An "Intermittent" malfunction may be caused by a poor connection, rubbed through wire insulation, or a wire that is broken inside the insulation.

The frequency of the malfunction can be checked by using the enhanced diagnostic function of the Tech 1

If the customer's comments reflect that the ABS amber indicator lamp is "ON" only during moist environmental changes, (rain, snow, vehicle wash) all wheel speed sensor circuitry should be thoroughly inspected for water intrusion. Use the following procedure. Spray down the suspected area with 5% salt water solution (two teaspoons of salt to 12 oz. of water). Start vehicle, allow vehicle to run for 10 seconds. If DTC returns immediately, replace suspected harness.

Any circuitry, that is suspected as causing the intermittent complaint, should be thoroughly checked for backed out terminals, improper mating, broken locks, improperly formed or damaged terminals, poor terminal to wiring connections or physical damage to the wiring harness.

A careful visual inspection of the toothed ring, CV joint, bearing and wheel speed sensor for physical damage should also be performed. If DTC sets at the same mph every time and wheel speed variation is noted above this mph on the Tech 1, the speed ring is most likely damaged. This can occur at any speed.

When measuring wheel speed sensor resistance, ensure vehicle is at room temperature. Wheel speed sensor resistance will vary with temperature.

When replacing a wheel speed sensor, inspect the sensor terminals and harness connector for corrosion and/or water intrusion. If evidence of corrosion or water intrusion exists, replace wheel speed sensor harness.

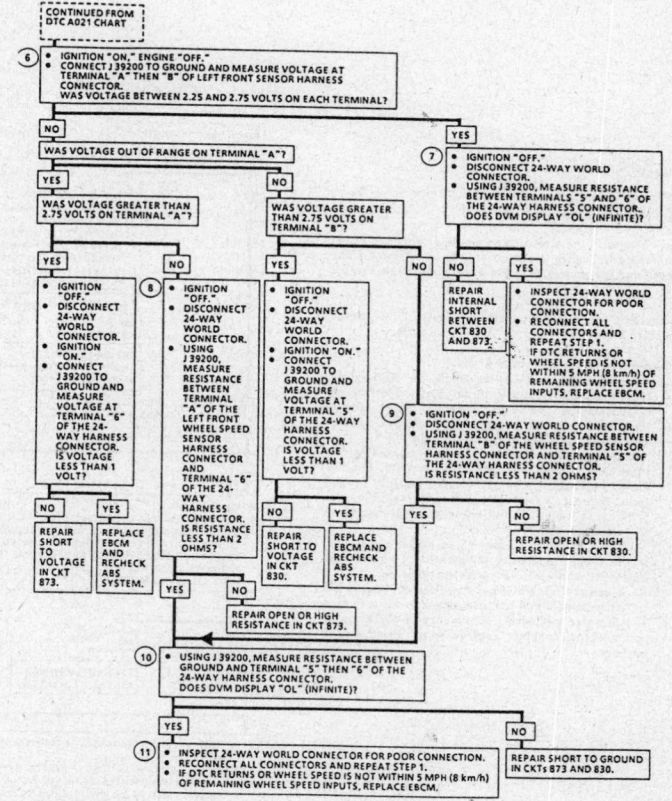

Fig. 114   Code A025, Left front excessive wheel speed variation (Part 2 Of 2). 1993 except Cutlass Supreme, Grand Prix, Lumina & Regal

DTC A025

LEFT FRONT EXCESSIVE WHEEL SPEED VARIATION

Circuit Description:

As a toothed ring passes by the wheel speed sensor, changes in the electromagnetic field cause the wheel speed sensor to produce a sinusoidal (AC) voltage signal whose frequency is proportional to wheel speed. The magnitude of this signal is directly related to wheel speed and the proximity of the wheel speed sensor to the toothed ring, often referred to as the air gap.

Failure Condition:

DTC A025 can be set when the brake is "OFF." The purpose of this test is to detect a situation in which the left front wheel acceleration or deceleration is beyond specified limits.

Action Taken:

A malfunction DTC is stored, ABS is disabled and the ABS indicator lamp is turned "ON."

Test Description: Number(s) below refer to circled number(s) on the diagnostic chart.

1. This test determines if DTC A032 is also set.
2. This test verifies whether the malfunction is currently present.
3. This step is designed to identify a wheel speed sensor or circuitry that is damaged and visibly apparent.
4. This test checks to see that the wheel speed sensor is within proper resistance values.
5. This step verifies that the wheel speed sensor can generate an appropriate output signal.
6. This test checks for proper output voltage from the EBCM.

Diagnostic Aids:

An "Intermittent" malfunction may be caused by a poor connection, rubbed through wire insulation, or a wire that is broken inside the insulation.

The frequency of the malfunction can be checked by using the enhanced diagnostic function of the Tech 1

If the customers comments reflect that the ABS indicator lamp is "ON" only during moist environmental changes (rain, snow, vehicle wash), all wheel speed sensor circuitry should be thoroughly

inspected for signs of water intrusion. If DTC is not current, clear DTCs and simulate the effects of water intrusion. Use the following procedure. Spray down the suspected area with a 5% salt water solution (two teaspoons of salt to 12 oz. of water). Start vehicle, allow vehicle to run for 10 seconds. If DTC returns immediately, replace suspected harness.

Any circuitry, that is suspected as causing the intermittent complaint, should be thoroughly checked for backed out terminals, improper mating, broken locks, improperly formed or damaged terminals, poor terminal to wiring connections or physical damage to the wiring harness.

When measuring wheel speed sensor resistance, insure vehicle is at room temperature. Wheel speed sensor resistance will vary with temperature.

When replacing a wheel speed sensor, inspect the sensor terminals and harness connector for corrosion and/or water intrusion. If evidence of corrosion or water intrusion exists, replace wheel speed sensor harness.

DTC A025

LEFT FRONT EXCESSIVE WHEEL SPEED VARIATION

Circuit Description:

As a toothed ring passes by the wheel speed sensor, changes in the electromagnetic field cause the wheel speed sensor to produce a sinusoidal (AC) voltage signal whose frequency is proportional to wheel speed. The magnitude of this signal is directly related to wheel speed and the proximity of the wheel speed sensor to the toothed ring, often referred to as the air gap.

Failure Condition:

DTC A025 can be set when the brake is "OFF." The purpose of this test is to detect a situation in which the left front wheel acceleration or deceleration is beyond specified limits.

Action Taken:

A malfunction DTC is stored, ABS is disabled and the ABS indicator lamp is turned "ON."

Test Description: Number(s) below refer to circled number(s) on the diagnostic chart.

7. This checks for an open in the wheel signal high circuit.
8. This step insures that DTC A025 was not set due to a poor connection between the 24-way EBCM connector and the EBCM.
9. This step insures that wheel speed sensor circuitry is not internally shorted.
10. This checks for an open in the wheel signal low circuit.

Diagnostic Aids:

An "Intermittent" malfunction may be caused by a poor connection, rubbed through wire insulation, or a wire that is broken inside the insulation.

The frequency of the malfunction can be checked by using the enhanced diagnostic function of the Tech 1

If the customers comments reflect that the ABS indicator lamp is "ON" only during moist environmental changes (rain, snow, vehicle wash), all wheel speed sensor circuitry should be thoroughly inspected for signs of water intrusion. If DTC is not current, clear DTCs and simulate the effects of water

intrusion. Use the following procedure. Spray down the suspected area with a 5% salt water solution (two teaspoons of salt to 12 oz. of water). Start vehicle, allow vehicle to run for 10 seconds. If DTC returns immediately, replace suspected harness.

Any circuitry, that is suspected as causing the intermittent complaint, should be thoroughly checked for backed out terminals, improper mating, broken locks, improperly formed or damaged terminals, poor terminal to wiring connections or physical damage to the wiring harness.

When measuring wheel speed sensor resistance, insure vehicle is at room temperature. Wheel speed sensor resistance will vary with temperature.

When replacing a wheel speed sensor, inspect the sensor terminals and harness connector for corrosion and/or water intrusion. If evidence of corrosion or water intrusion exists, replace wheel speed sensor harness.

Fig. 115 Code A025, Left front excessive wheel speed variation. 1993 Cutlass Supreme, Grand Prix, Lumina & Regal

Cavalier & Sunbird

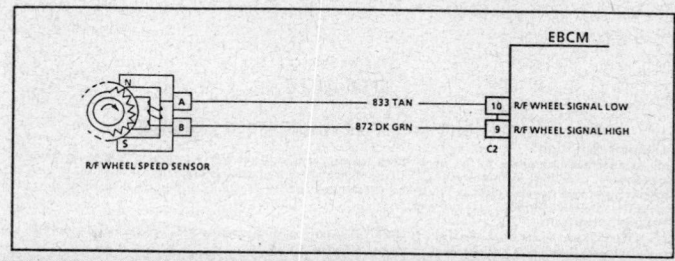

Achieva, Beretta, Corsica, Grand Am & Skylark

DTC A026

RIGHT FRONT EXCESSIVE WHEEL SPEED VARIATION

Circuit Description:

As a toothed ring passes by the wheel speed sensor, changes in the electromagnetic field cause the wheel speed sensor to produce a sinusoidal (AC) voltage signal whose frequency is proportional to wheel speed. The magnitude of this signal is directly related to wheel speed and the proximity of the wheel speed sensor to the toothed ring, often referred to as the air gap.

Failure Condition:

DTC A026 can be set when the brake is "OFF." The purpose of this test is to detect a situation in which the right front wheel acceleration or deceleration is beyond specified limits.

Action Taken:

A malfunction DTC is stored, ABS is disabled and the ABS indicator lamp is turned "ON."

Test Description: Number(s) below refer to circled number(s) on the diagnostic chart.

1. This test verifies whether the malfunction is currently present.
2. This step will identify a wheel speed sensor or circuitry that is damaged and visibly apparent.
3. This test checks wheel speed sensor for proper resistance values.
4. This test ensures the wheel speed sensor and sensor ring generate the proper voltage.
5. This step ensures the wheel speed sensor is not shorted to ground.

Diagnostic Aids:

An "Intermittent" malfunction may be caused by a poor connection, rubbed through wire insulation, or a wire that is broken inside the insulation.

The frequency of the malfunction can be checked by using the enhanced diagnostic function of the Tech 1

If the customer's comments reflect that the ABS amber indicator lamp is "ON" only during moist environmental changes, (rain, snow, vehicle wash) all wheel speed sensor circuitry should be thoroughly inspected for water intrusion. Use the following procedure. Spray down the suspected area with 5% salt water solution (two teaspoons of salt to 12 oz. of water). Start vehicle, allow vehicle to run for 10 seconds. If DTC returns immediately, replace suspected harness.

Any circuitry, that is suspected as causing the intermittent complaint, should be thoroughly checked for backed out terminals, improper mating, broken locks, improperly formed or damaged terminals, poor terminal to wiring connections or physical damage to the wiring harness.

A careful visual inspection of the toothed ring, CV joint, bearing and wheel speed sensor for physical damage should also be performed. If DTC sets at the same mph every time and wheel speed variation is noted above this mph on the Tech 1, the speed ring is most likely damaged. This can occur at any speed.

When measuring wheel speed sensor resistance, ensure vehicle is at room temperature. Wheel speed sensor resistance will vary with temperature.

When replacing a wheel speed sensor, inspect the sensor terminals and harness connector for corrosion and/or water intrusion. If evidence of corrosion or water intrusion exists, replace wheel speed sensor harness.

IMPORTANT: WHEEL SPEED SENSOR INTERMITTENT MALFUNCTIONS MAY BE DIFFICULT TO LOCATE. CARE SHOULD BE TAKEN NOT TO DISTURB ANY ELECTRICAL CONNECTIONS PRIOR TO AN INDICATED STEP OF THIS CHART. THIS WILL INSURE THAT AN INTERMITTENT CONNECTION WILL NOT BE CORRECTED BEFORE THE SOURCE OF THE MALFUNCTION IS FOUND.

Fig. 116   Code A026, Right front excessive wheel speed variation (Part 1 of 2). 1993 except Cutlass Supreme, Grand Prix, Lumina & Regal

DTC A026

RIGHT FRONT EXCESSIVE WHEEL SPEED VARIATION

Circuit Description:

As a toothed ring passes by the wheel speed sensor, changes in the electromagnetic field cause the wheel speed sensor to produce a sinusoidal (AC) voltage signal whose frequency is proportional to wheel speed. The magnitude of this signal is directly related to wheel speed and the proximity of the wheel speed sensor to the toothed ring, often referred to as the air gap.

Failure Condition:

DTC A026 can be set when the brake is "OFF." The purpose of this test is to detect a situation in which the right front wheel acceleration or deceleration is beyond specified limits.

Action Taken:

A malfunction DTC is stored, ABS is disabled and the ABS indicator lamp is turned "ON."

Test Description: Number(s) below refer to circled number(s) on the diagnostic chart.

6. This step checks for proper voltages at speed sensor harness connector.
7. This test ensures that the wheel speed sensor circuitry is not internally shorted.
8. This checks for an open in the wheel signal low circuit.
9. This checks for an open in the wheel signal high circuit.
10. This test checks for a short to ground in both high and low wheel signal circuits.
11. This step ensures that DTC A026 was not set due to a poor connection between the world connector and EBCM.

Diagnostic Aids:

An "Intermittent" malfunction may be caused by a poor connection, rubbed through wire insulation, or a wire that is broken inside the insulation.

The frequency of the malfunction can be checked by using the enhanced diagnostic function of the Tech 1

If the customer's comments reflect that the ABS amber indicator lamp is "ON" only during moist environmental changes, (rain, snow, vehicle wash) all

wheel speed sensor circuitry should be thoroughly inspected for water intrusion. Use the following procedure. Spray down the suspected area with 5% salt water solution (two teaspoons of salt to 12 oz. of water). Start vehicle, allow vehicle to run for 10 seconds. If DTC returns immediately, replace suspected harness.

Any circuitry, that is suspected as causing the intermittent complaint, should be thoroughly checked for backed out terminals, improper mating, broken locks, improperly formed or damaged terminals, poor terminal to wiring connections or physical damage to the wiring harness.

A careful visual inspection of the toothed ring, CV joint, bearing and wheel speed sensor for physical damage should also be performed. If DTC sets at the same mph every time and wheel speed variation is noted above this mph, the speed ring is most likely damaged. This can occur at any speed.

When measuring wheel speed sensor resistance, ensure vehicle is at room temperature. Wheel speed sensor resistance will vary with temperature.

When replacing a wheel speed sensor, inspect the sensor terminals and harness connector for corrosion and/or water intrusion. If evidence or corrosion or water intrusion exists, replace wheel speed sensor harness.

Fig. 116   Code A026, Right front excessive wheel speed variation (Part 2 of 2). 1993 except Cutlass Supreme, Grand Prix, Lumina & Regal

DTC A026

RIGHT FRONT EXCESSIVE WHEEL SPEED VARIATION

Circuit Description:

As a toothed ring passes by the wheel speed sensor, changes in the electromagnetic field cause the wheel speed sensor to produce a sinusoidal (AC) voltage signal whose frequency is proportional to wheel speed. The magnitude of this signal is directly related to wheel speed and the proximity of the wheel speed sensor to the toothed ring, often referred to as the air gap.

Failure Condition:

DTC A026 can be set when the brake is "OFF." The purpose of this test is to detect a situation in which the right front wheel acceleration or deceleration is beyond specified limits.

Action Taken:

A malfunction DTC is stored, ABS is disabled and the ABS indicator lamp is turned "ON."

Test Description: Number(s) below refer to circled number(s) on the diagnostic chart.

1. This determines if DTC A033 is present.
2. This step verifies whether the malfunction is currently present.
3. This test is designed to identify a wheel speed sensor or circuitry that is damaged and visibly apparent.
4. This test checks to see that the wheel speed sensor is within proper resistance values.
5. This step verifies that the wheel speed sensor can generate an appropriate output signal.
6. This test checks for proper output voltage from the EBCM.

Diagnostic Aids:

An "Intermittent" malfunction may be caused by a poor connection, rubbed through wire insulation, or a wire that is broken inside the insulation.

The frequency of the malfunction can be checked by using the enhanced diagnostic function of the Tech 1

If the customers comments reflect that the ABS indicator lamp is "ON" only during moist environmental changes, (rain, snow, vehicle wash), all wheel speed sensor circuitry should be thoroughly

inspected for signs of water intrusion. If DTC is not current, clear DTCs and simulate the effects of water intrusion. Use the following procedure. Spray down the suspected area with a 5% salt water solution (two teaspoons of salt to 12 oz. of water). Start vehicle, allow vehicle to run for 10 seconds. If DTC returns immediately, replace suspected harness.

Any circuitry, that is suspected as causing the intermittent complaint, should be thoroughly checked for backed out terminals, improper mating, broken locks, improperly formed or damaged terminals, poor terminal to wiring connections or physical damage to the wiring harness.

When measuring wheel speed sensor resistance, insure vehicle is at room temperature. Wheel speed sensor resistance will vary with temperature.

When replacing a wheel speed sensor, inspect the sensor terminals and harness connector for corrosion and/or water intrusion. If evidence of corrosion or water intrusion exists, replace wheel speed sensor harness.

Fig. 117   Code A026, Right front excessive wheel speed variation (Part 1 of 2). 1993 Cutlass Supreme, Grand Prix, Lumina & Regal

DTC A026

RIGHT FRONT EXCESSIVE WHEEL SPEED VARIATION

Circuit Description:

As a toothed ring passes by the wheel speed sensor, changes in the electromagnetic field cause the wheel speed sensor to produce a sinusoidal (AC) voltage signal whose frequency is proportional to wheel speed. The magnitude of this signal is directly related to wheel speed and the proximity of the wheel speed sensor to the toothed ring, often referred to as the air gap.

Failure Condition:

DTC A026 can be set when the brake is "OFF." The purpose of this test is to detect a situation in which the right front wheel acceleration or deceleration is beyond specified limits.

Action Taken:

A malfunction DTC is stored, ABS is disabled and the ABS indicator lamp is turned "ON."

Test Description: Number(s) below refer to circled number(s) on the diagnostic chart.

7. This checks for an open in the wheel signal low circuit.
8. This step insures that DTC A026 was not set due to a poor connection between the 24-way EBCM connector and the EBCM.
9. This test insures that wheel speed sensor circuitry is not internally shorted.
10. This checks for an open in the wheel signal high circuit.

Diagnostic Aids:

An "Intermittent" malfunction may be caused by a poor connection, rubbed through wire insulation, or a wire that is broken inside the insulation.

The frequency of the malfunction can be checked by using the enhanced diagnostic function of the Tech 1

If the customers comments reflect that the ABS indicator lamp is "ON" only during moist environmental changes (rain, snow, vehicle wash), all wheel speed sensor circuitry should be thoroughly inspected for signs of water intrusion. If DTC is not current, clear DTCs and simulate the effects of water intrusion. Use the following procedure. Spray down the suspected area with a 5% salt water solution (two teaspoons of salt to 12 oz. of water). Start vehicle, allow vehicle to run for 10 seconds. If DTC returns immediately, replace suspected harness.

Any circuitry, that is suspected as causing the intermittent complaint, should be thoroughly checked for backed out terminals, improper mating, broken locks, improperly formed or damaged terminals, poor terminal to wiring connections or physical damage to the wiring harness.

When measuring wheel speed sensor resistance, insure vehicle is at room temperature. Wheel speed sensor resistance will vary with temperature.

When replacing a wheel speed sensor, inspect the sensor terminals and harness connector for corrosion and/or water intrusion. If evidence of corrosion or water intrusion exists, replace wheel speed sensor harness.

Fig. 117   Code A026, Right front excessive wheel speed variation (Part 2 of 2). 1993 Cutlass Supreme, Grand Prix, Lumina & Regal

Cavalier & Sunbird

Achieva, Beretta, Corsica, Grand Am & Skylark

DTC A027

LEFT REAR EXCESSIVE WHEEL SPEED VARIATION

Circuit Description:

As a toothed ring passes by the wheel speed sensor, changes in the electromagnetic field cause the wheel speed sensor to produce a sinusoidal (AC) voltage signal whose frequency is proportional to wheel speed. The magnitude of this signal is directly related to wheel speed and the proximity of the wheel speed sensor to the toothed ring, often referred to as the air gap.

Failure Condition:

DTC A027 can be set when the brake is "OFF." The purpose of this test is to detect a situation in which the left rear wheel acceleration or deceleration is beyond specified limits.

Action Taken:

A malfunction DTC is stored, ABS is disabled and the ABS indicator lamp is turned "ON."

Test Description: Number(s) below refer to circled number(s) on the diagnostic chart.

1. This test verifies whether the malfunction is currently present.
2. This step will identify a wheel speed sensor or circuitry that is damaged and visibly apparent.
3. This test checks wheel speed sensor for proper resistance values.
4. This test ensures the wheel speed sensor and sensor ring generate the proper voltage.
5. This step ensures the wheel speed sensor is not shorted to ground.

Diagnostic Aids:

An "Intermittent" malfunction may be caused by a poor connection, rubbed through wire insulation, or a wire that is broken inside the insulation.

The frequency of the malfunction can be checked by using the enhanced diagnostic function of the Tech 1

If the customer's comments reflect that the ABS amber indicator lamp is "ON" only during moist environmental changes, (rain, snow, vehicle wash) all wheel speed sensor circuitry should be thoroughly inspected for water intrusion. Use the following procedure. Spray down the suspected area with 5% salt water solution (two teaspoons of salt to 12 oz. of water). Start vehicle, allow vehicle to run for 10 seconds. If DTC returns immediately, replace suspected harness.

Any circuitry, that is suspected as causing the intermittent complaint, should be thoroughly checked for backed out terminals, improper mating, broken locks, improperly formed or damaged terminals, poor terminal to wiring connections or physical damage to the wiring harness.

Excessive end play can cause this DTC to set. Check integral bearing for excessive axial end play

When measuring wheel speed sensor resistance, ensure vehicle is at room temperature. Wheel speed sensor resistance will vary with temperature.

When replacing a wheel speed sensor, inspect the sensor terminals and harness connector for corrosion and/or water intrusion. If evidence of corrosion or water intrusion exists, replace wheel speed sensor harness.

Fig. 118   Code A027, Left rear excessive wheel speed variation (Part 1 of 2). 1993 except Cutlass Supreme, Grand Prix, Lumina & Regal

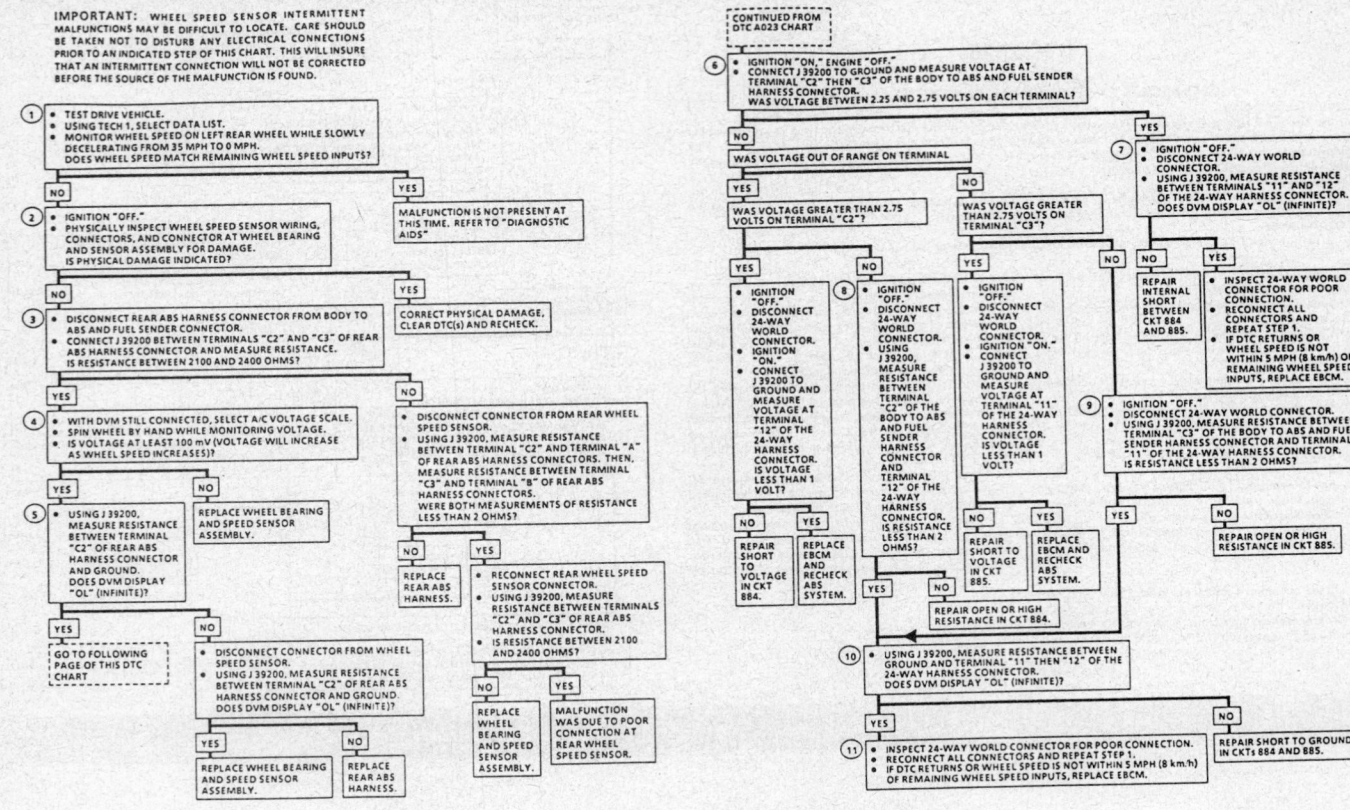

DTC A027

LEFT REAR EXCESSIVE WHEEL SPEED VARIATION

Circuit Description:

As a toothed ring passes by the wheel speed sensor, changes in the electromagnetic field cause the wheel speed sensor to produce a sinusoidal (AC) voltage signal whose frequency is proportional to wheel speed. The magnitude of this signal is directly related to wheel speed and the proximity of the wheel speed sensor to the toothed ring, often referred to as the air gap.

Failure Condition:

DTC A027 can be set when the brake is "OFF." The purpose of this test is to detect a situation in which the left rear wheel acceleration or deceleration is beyond specified limits.

Action Taken:

A malfunction DTC is stored, ABS is disabled and the ABS indicator lamp is turned "ON."

Test Description: Number(s) below refer to circled number(s) on the diagnostic chart.

6. This step checks for proper voltages at body to ABS and fuel sender harness connector.
7. This test ensures that the wheel speed sensor circuitry is not internally shorted.
8. This checks for an open in the wheel signal high circuit.
9. This checks for an open in the wheel signal low circuit.
10. This test checks for a short to ground in both high and low wheel signal circuits.
11. This step ensures that DTC A027 was not set due to a poor connection between the world connector and EBCM.

Diagnostic Aids:

An "Intermittent" malfunction may be caused by a poor connection, rubbed through wire insulation, or a wire that is broken inside the insulation.

The frequency of the malfunction can be checked by using the enhanced diagnostic function of the Tech 1

If the customer's comments reflect that the ABS amber indicator lamp is "ON" only during moist environmental changes, (rain, snow, vehicle wash) all wheel speed sensor circuitry should be thoroughly inspected for water intrusion. Use the following procedure. Spray down the suspected area with 5% salt water solution (two teaspoons of salt to 12 oz. of water). Start vehicle, allow vehicle to run for 10 seconds. If DTC returns immediately, replace suspected harness.

Any circuitry, that is suspected as causing the intermittent complaint, should be thoroughly checked for backed out terminals, improper mating, broken locks, improperly formed or damaged terminals, poor terminal to wiring connections or physical damage to the wiring harness.

Excessive end play can cause this DTC to set. Check integral bearing for excessive axial end play

When measuring wheel speed sensor resistance, ensure vehicle is at room temperature. Wheel speed sensor resistance will vary with temperature.

When replacing a wheel speed sensor, inspect the sensor terminals and harness connector for corrosion and/or water intrusion. If evidence of corrosion or water intrusion exists, replace wheel speed sensor harness.

Fig. 118   Code A027, Left rear excessive wheel speed variation (Part 2 of 2). 1993 except Cutlass Supreme, Grand Prix, Lumina & Regal

DTC A027

LEFT REAR EXCESSIVE WHEEL SPEED VARIATION

Circuit Description:

As a toothed ring passes by the wheel speed sensor, changes in the electromagnetic field cause the wheel speed sensor to produce a sinusoidal (AC) voltage signal whose frequency is proportional to wheel speed. The magnitude of this signal is directly related to wheel speed and the proximity of the wheel speed sensor to the toothed ring, often referred to as the air gap.

Failure Condition:

DTC A027 can be set when the brake is "OFF." The purpose of this test is to detect a situation in which the left rear wheel acceleration or deceleration is beyond specified limits.

Action Taken:

A malfunction DTC is stored, ABS is disabled and the ABS indicator lamp is turned "ON."

Test Description: Number(s) below refer to circled number(s) on the diagnostic chart.

1. This determines if DTC A034 is present.
2. This test verifies whether the malfunction is currently present.
3. This step is designed to identify a wheel speed sensor or circuitry that is damaged and visibly apparent.
4. This test checks to see that the wheel speed sensor is within proper resistance values.
5. This step verifies that the wheel speed sensor can generate an appropriate output signal.
6. This test checks for proper output voltage from the EBCM.

Diagnostic Aids:

An "Intermittent" malfunction may be caused by a poor connection, rubbed through wire insulation, or a wire that is broken inside the insulation.

The frequency of the malfunction can be checked by using the enhanced diagnostic function of the Tech 1.

If the customers comments reflect that the ABS indicator lamp is "ON" only during moist environmental changes (rain, snow, vehicle wash), all

wheel speed sensor circuitry should be thoroughly inspected for signs of water intrusion. If DTC is not current clear DTCs and simulate the effects of water intrusion. Use the following procedure. Spray down the suspected area with a 5% salt water solution (two teaspoons of salt to 12 oz. of water). Start vehicle, allow vehicle to run for 10 seconds. If DTC returns immediately, replace suspected harness.

Any circuitry, that is suspected as causing the intermittent complaint, should be thoroughly checked for backed out terminals, improper mating, broken locks, improperly formed or damaged terminals, poor terminal to wiring connections or physical damage to the wiring harness.

When measuring wheel speed sensor resistance, insure vehicle is at room temperature. Wheel speed sensor resistance will vary with temperature.

When replacing a wheel speed sensor, inspect the sensor terminals and harness connector for corrosion and/or water intrusion. If evidence of corrosion or water intrusion exists, replace wheel speed sensor harness

DTC A027

LEFT REAR EXCESSIVE WHEEL SPEED VARIATION

Circuit Description:

As a toothed ring passes by the wheel speed sensor, changes in the electromagnetic field cause the wheel speed sensor to produce a sinusoidal (AC) voltage signal whose frequency is proportional to wheel speed. The magnitude of this signal is directly related to wheel speed and the proximity of the wheel speed sensor to the toothed ring, often referred to as the air gap.

Failure Condition:

DTC A027 can be set when the brake is "OFF." The purpose of this test is to detect a situation in which the left rear wheel acceleration or deceleration is beyond specified limits.

Action Taken:

A malfunction DTC is stored, ABS is disabled and the ABS indicator lamp is turned "ON."

Test Description: Number(s) below refer to circled number(s) on the diagnostic chart.

7. This checks for an open in the wheel signal low circuit.
8. This step insures that DTC A027 was not set due to a poor connection between the 24-way EBCM connector and the EBCM.
9. This test insures that wheel speed sensor circuitry is not internally shorted.
10. This checks for an open in the wheel signal high circuit.

Diagnostic Aids:

An "Intermittent" malfunction may be caused by a poor connection, rubbed through wire insulation, or a wire that is broken inside the insulation.

The frequency of the malfunction can be checked by using the enhanced diagnostic function of the Tech 1

If the customers comments reflect that the ABS indicator lamp is "ON" only during moist environmental changes (rain, snow, vehicle wash), all wheel speed sensor circuitry should be thoroughly

inspected for signs of water intrusion. If DTC is not current, clear DTCs and simulate the effects of water intrusion. Use the following procedure. Spray down the suspected area with a 5% salt water solution (two teaspoons of salt to 12 oz. of water). Start vehicle, allow vehicle to run for 10 seconds. If DTC returns immediately, replace suspected harness.

Any circuitry, that is suspected as causing the intermittent complaint, should be thoroughly checked for backed out terminals, improper mating, broken locks, improperly formed or damaged terminals, poor terminal to wiring connections or physical damage to the wiring harness.

When measuring wheel speed sensor resistance, insure vehicle is at room temperature. Wheel speed sensor resistance will vary with temperature.

When replacing a wheel speed sensor, inspect the sensor terminals and harness connector for corrosion and/or water intrusion. If evidence of corrosion or water intrusion exists, replace wheel speed sensor harness.

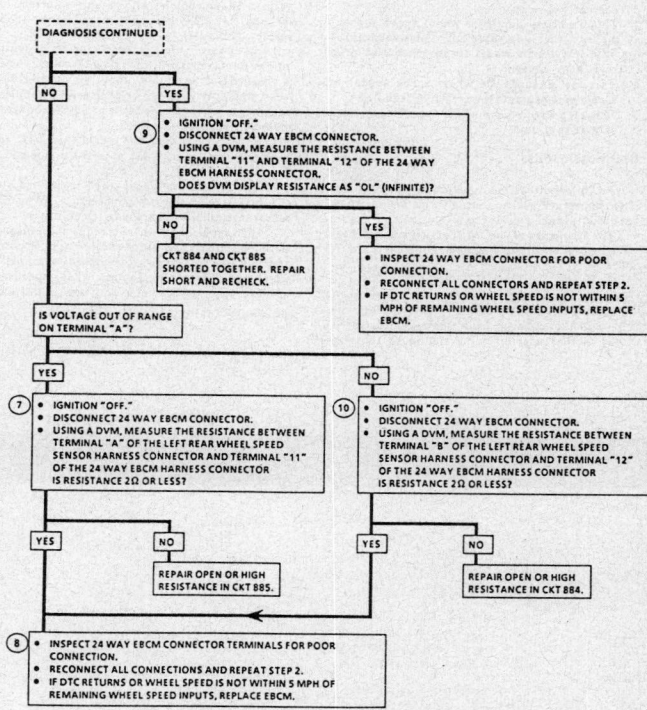

Fig. 119   Code A027, Left rear excessive wheel speed variation. 1993 Cutlass Supreme, Grand Prix, Lumina & Regal

Cavalier & Sunbird

Achieva, Beretta, Corsica, Grand Am & Skylark

DTC A028

RIGHT REAR EXCESSIVE WHEEL SPEED VARIATION

Circuit Description:

As a toothed ring passes by the wheel speed sensor, changes in the electromagnetic field cause the wheel speed sensor to produce a sinusoidal (AC) voltage signal whose frequency is proportional to wheel speed. The magnitude of this signal is directly related to wheel speed and the proximity of the wheel speed sensor to the toothed ring, often referred to as the air gap.

Failure Condition:

DTC A028 can be set when the brake is "OFF." The purpose of this test is to detect a situation in which the right rear wheel acceleration or deceleration is beyond specified limits.

Action Taken:

A malfunction DTC is stored, ABS is disabled and the ABS indicator lamp is turned "ON."

Test Description: Number(s) below refer to circled number(s) on the diagnostic chart.

1. This test verifies whether the malfunction is currently present.
2. This step will identify a wheel speed sensor or circuitry that is damaged and visibly apparent.
3. This test checks wheel speed sensor for proper resistance values.
4. This test ensures the wheel speed sensor and sensor ring generate the proper voltage.
5. This step ensures the wheel speed sensor is not shorted to ground.

Diagnostic Aids:

An "Intermittent" malfunction may be caused by a poor connection, rubbed through wire insulation, or a wire that is broken inside the insulation.

The frequency of the malfunction can be checked by using the enhanced diagnostic function of the Tech 1

If the customer's comments reflect that the ABS amber indicator lamp is "ON" only during moist environmental changes, (rain, snow, vehicle wash) all wheel speed sensor circuitry should be thoroughly inspected for water intrusion. Use the following procedure. Spray down the suspected area with 5% salt water solution (two teaspoons of salt to 12 oz. of water). Start vehicle, allow vehicle to run for 10 seconds. If DTC returns immediately, replace suspected harness.

Any circuitry, that is suspected as causing the intermittent complaint, should be thoroughly checked for backed out terminals, improper mating, broken locks, improperly formed or damaged terminals, poor terminal to wiring connections or physical damage to the wiring harness.

Excessive end play can cause this DTC to set. Check integral bearing for excessive axial end play

When measuring wheel speed sensor resistance, ensure vehicle is at room temperature. Wheel speed sensor resistance will vary with temperature.

When replacing a wheel speed sensor, inspect the sensor terminals and harness connector for corrosion and/or water intrusion. If evidence of corrosion or water intrusion exists, replace wheel speed sensor harness. Refer to "On-Vehicle Service" in this section.

IMPORTANT: WHEEL SPEED SENSOR INTERMITTENT MALFUNCTIONS MAY BE DIFFICULT TO LOCATE. CARE SHOULD BE TAKEN NOT TO DISTURB ANY ELECTRICAL CONNECTIONS PRIOR TO AN INDICATED STEP OF THIS CHART. THIS WILL INSURE THAT AN INTERMITTENT CONNECTION WILL NOT BE CORRECTED BEFORE THE SOURCE OF THE MALFUNCTION IS FOUND.

Fig. 120 Code A028, Right rear excessive wheel speed variation (Part 1 of 2). 1993 except Cutlass Supreme, Grand Prix, Lumina & Regal

DTC A028

RIGHT REAR EXCESSIVE WHEEL SPEED VARIATION

Circuit Description:

As a toothed ring passes by the wheel speed sensor, changes in the electromagnetic field cause the wheel speed sensor to produce a sinusoidal (AC) voltage signal whose frequency is proportional to wheel speed. The magnitude of this signal is directly related to wheel speed and the proximity of the wheel speed sensor to the toothed ring, often referred to as the air gap.

Failure Condition:

DTC A028 can be set when the brake is "OFF." The purpose of this test is to detect a situation in which the right rear wheel acceleration or deceleration is beyond specified limits.

Action Taken:

A malfunction DTC is stored, ABS is disabled and the ABS indicator lamp is turned "ON."

Test Description: Number(s) below refer to circled number(s) on the diagnostic chart.

6. This step checks for proper voltages at body to ABS and fuel sender harness connector.
7. This test ensures that the wheel speed sensor circuitry is not internally shorted.
8. This checks for an open in the wheel signal high circuit.
9. This checks for an open in the wheel signal low circuit.
10. This test checks for a short to ground in both high and low wheel signal circuits.
11. This step ensures that DTC A028 was not set due to a poor connection between the world connector and EBCM.

Diagnostic Aids:

An "Intermittent" malfunction may be caused by a poor connection, rubbed through wire insulation, or a wire that is broken inside the insulation.

The frequency of the malfunction can be checked by using the enhanced diagnostic function of the Tech 1

If the customer's comments reflect that the ABS amber indicator lamp is "ON" only during moist environmental changes, (rain, snow, vehicle wash) all

wheel speed sensor circuitry should be thoroughly inspected for water intrusion. Use the following procedure. Spray down the suspected area with 5% salt water solution (two teaspoons of salt to 12 oz. of water). Start vehicle, allow vehicle to run for 10 seconds. If DTC returns immediately, replace suspected harness.

Any circuitry, that is suspected as causing the intermittent complaint, should be thoroughly checked for backed out terminals, improper mating, broken locks, improperly formed or damaged terminals, poor terminal to wiring connections or physical damage to the wiring harness.

Excessive end play can cause this DTC to set. Check integral bearing for excessive axial end play

When measuring wheel speed sensor resistance, ensure vehicle is at room temperature. Wheel speed sensor resistance will vary with temperature.

When replacing a wheel speed sensor, inspect the sensor terminals and harness connector for corrosion and/or water intrusion. If evidence of corrosion or water intrusion exists, replace wheel speed sensor harness.

Fig. 120   Code A028, Right rear excessive wheel speed variation (Part 2 of 2). 1993 except Cutlass Supreme, Grand Prix, Lumina & Regal

DTC A028

RIGHT REAR EXCESSIVE WHEEL SPEED VARIATION

Circuit Description:

As a toothed ring passes by the wheel speed sensor, changes in the electromagnetic field cause the wheel speed sensor to produce a sinusoidal (AC) voltage signal whose frequency is proportional to wheel speed. The magnitude of this signal is directly related to wheel speed and the proximity of the wheel speed sensor to the toothed ring, often referred to as the air gap.

Failure Condition:

DTC A028 can be set when the brake is "OFF." The purpose of this test is to detect a situation in which the right rear wheel acceleration or deceleration is beyond specified limits.

Action Taken:

A malfunction DTC is stored, ABS is disabled and the ABS indicator lamp is turned "ON."

Test Description: Number(s) below refer to circled number(s) on the diagnostic chart.

1. This determines if DTC A035 is present.
2. This test verifies whether the malfunction is currently present.
3. This step is designed to identify a wheel speed sensor or circuitry that is damaged and visibly apparent.
4. This test checks to see that the wheel speed sensor is within proper resistance values.
5. This step verifies that the wheel speed sensor can generate an appropriate output signal.
6. This test checks for proper output voltage from the EBCM.

Diagnostic Aids:

An "Intermittent" malfunction may be caused by a poor connection, rubbed through wire insulation, or a wire that is broken inside the insulation.

The frequency of the malfunction can be checked by using the enhanced diagnostic function of the Tech 1

If the customers comments reflect that the ABS indicator lamp is "ON" only during moist environmental changes, (rain, snow, vehicle wash), all

wheel speed sensor circuitry should be thoroughly inspected for signs of water intrusion. If DTC is not current, clear DTCs and simulate the effects of water intrusion. Use the following procedure. Spray down the suspected area with a 5% salt water solution (two teaspoons of salt to 12 oz. of water). Start vehicle, allow vehicle to run for 10 seconds. If DTC returns immediately, replace suspected harness.

Any circuitry, that is suspected as causing the intermittent complaint, should be thoroughly checked for backed out terminals, improper mating, broken locks, improperly formed or damaged terminals, poor terminal to wiring connections or physical damage to the wiring harness.

When measuring wheel speed sensor resistance, insure vehicle is at room temperature. Wheel speed sensor resistance will vary with temperature.

When replacing a wheel speed sensor, inspect the sensor terminals and harness connector for corrosion and/or water intrusion. If evidence of corrosion or water intrusion exists, replace wheel speed sensor harness.

IMPORTANT: WHEEL SPEED SENSOR INTERMITTENT PROBLEMS MAY BE DIFFICULT TO LOCATE. CARE SHOULD BE TAKEN NOT TO DISTURB ANY ELECTRICAL CONNECTIONS PRIOR TO AN INDICATED STEP OF THIS CHART. THIS WILL INSURE THAT AN INTERMITTENT CONNECTION WILL NOT BE CORRECTED BEFORE THE SOURCE OF THE PROBLEM IS FOUND.

Fig. 121   Code A028, Right rear excessive wheel speed variation (Part 1 of 2). 1993 Cutlass Supreme, Grand Prix, Lumina & Regal

DTC A028

RIGHT REAR EXCESSIVE WHEEL SPEED VARIATION

Circuit Description:

As a toothed ring passes by the wheel speed sensor, changes in the electromagnetic field cause the wheel speed sensor to produce a sinusoidal (AC) voltage signal whose frequency is proportional to wheel speed. The magnitude of this signal is directly related to wheel speed and the proximity of the wheel speed sensor to the toothed ring, often referred to as the air gap.

Failure Condition:

DTC A028 can be set when the brake is "OFF." The purpose of this test is to detect a situation in which the right rear wheel acceleration or deceleration is beyond specified limits.

Action Taken:

A malfunction DTC is stored, ABS is disabled and the ABS indicator lamp is turned "ON."

Test Description: Number(s) below refer to circled number(s) on the diagnostic chart.

7. This checks for an open in the wheel signal low circuit.
8. This step insures that DTC A028 was not set due to a poor connection between the 24-way EBCM connector and the EBCM.
9. This test insures that wheel speed sensor circuitry is not internally shorted.
10. This checks for an open in the wheel signal high circuit.

Diagnostic Aids:

An "Intermittent" malfunction may be caused by a poor connection, rubbed through wire insulation, or a wire that is broken inside the insulation.

The frequency of the malfunction can be checked by using the enhanced diagnostic function of the Tech 1

If the customers comments reflect that the ABS indicator lamp is "ON" only during moist environmental changes (rain, snow, vehicle wash), all wheel speed sensor circuitry should be thoroughly inspected for signs of water intrusion. If DTC is not current clear DTCs and simulate the effects of water intrusion. Use the following procedure. Spray down the suspected area with a 5% salt water solution (two teaspoons of salt to 12 oz. of water). Start vehicle, allow vehicle to run for 10 seconds. If DTC returns immediately, replace suspected harness.

Any circuitry, that is suspected as causing the intermittent complaint, should be thoroughly checked for backed out terminals, improper mating, broken locks, improperly formed or damaged terminals, poor terminal to wiring connections or physical damage to the wiring harness.

When measuring wheel speed sensor resistance, insure vehicle is at room temperature. Wheel speed sensor resistance will vary with temperature.

When replacing a wheel speed sensor, inspect the sensor terminals and harness connector for corrosion and/or water intrusion. If evidence of corrosion or water intrusion exists, replace wheel speed sensor harness.

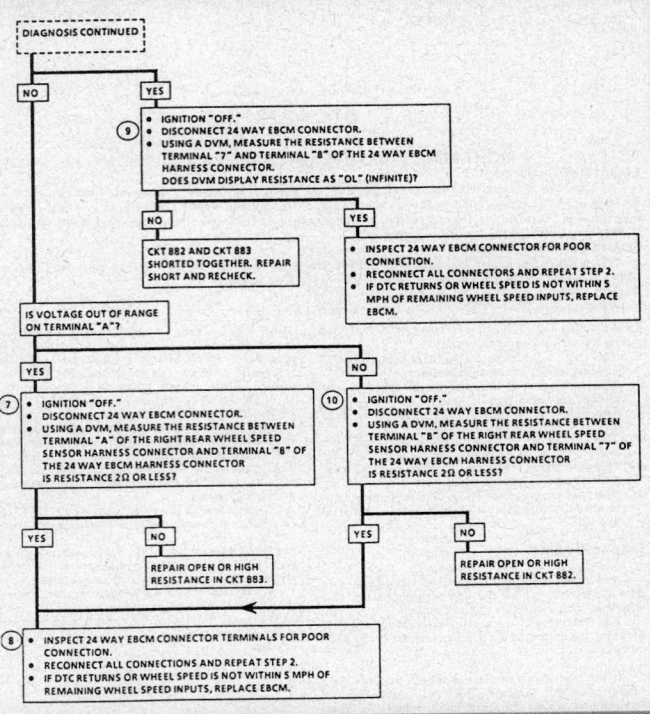

Fig. 121 Code A028, Right rear excessive wheel speed variation (Part 2 of 2). 1993 Cutlass Supreme, Grand Prix, Lumina & Regal

DTC A031

TWO WHEEL SPEEDS = 0

Circuit Description:

As a toothed ring passes by the wheel speed sensor, changes in the electromagnetic field cause the wheel speed sensor to produce a sinusoidal (AC) voltage signal whose frequency is proportional to wheel speed. The magnitude of this signal is directly related to wheel speed and the proximity of the wheel speed sensor to the toothed ring, often referred to as the air gap.

This DTC is designed to detect two wheel speed sensors in any combination. This DTC exists due to a condition that may exist that does not allow the driver to be informed by the ABS indicator lamp of non-functioning ABS. If one wheel speed sensor is open, the driver is informed. If a second fails, the driver is no longer informed without this DTC and ABS is not available. By requiring the two operating wheels to be within 7 mph, a false DTC is prevented during spin-ups while still allowing for detection when the stowaway spare tire is used.

Test Description: Number(s) below refer to circled number(s) on the diagnostic chart.

1. This test verifies whether the malfunction is currently present.
2. This step is designed to identify a wheel speed sensor or circuitry that is damaged and visibly apparent.
3. This step identifies if the cause of the malfunction is common to the rear wheel sensor circuitry.
4. This test checks to see if connectors at pass thru are connected properly.
5. This test checks to see that the wheel speed sensor is within proper resistance values.

Diagnostic Aids:

A false DTC A031 may be set as a result of vehicle operation while on a hoist or a lifted condition or stuck in mud or snow, when the vehicle is in gear.

An "Intermittent" malfunction may be caused by a poor connection, rubbed through wire insulation, or a wire that is broken inside the insulation.

The frequency of the malfunction can be checked by using the enhanced diagnostic function of the Tech 1

SENSOR	DTC
L/F SENSOR	A021
R/F SENSOR	A022
L/R SENSOR	A023
R/R SENSOR	A024

Fig. 122 Code A031, Two wheel speeds–0 (Part 1 of 2). 1993 Cutlass Supreme, Grand Prix, Lumina & Regal

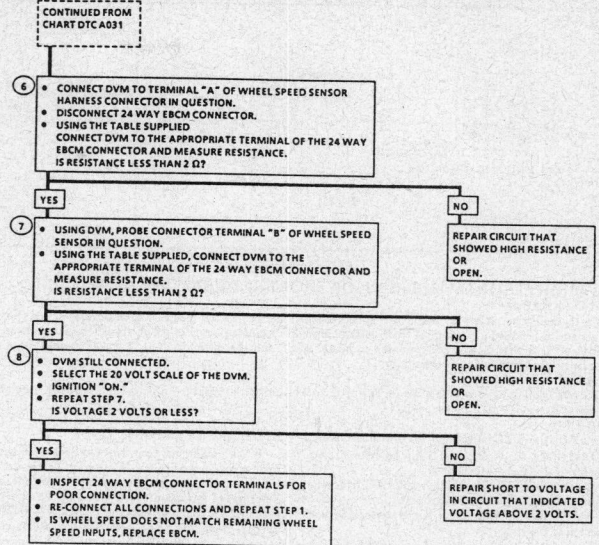

DTC A031

TWO WHEEL SPEEDS = 0

Circuit Description:

As a toothed ring passes by the wheel speed sensor, changes in the electromagnetic field cause the wheel speed sensor to produce a sinusoidal (AC) voltage signal whose frequency is proportional to wheel speed. The magnitude of this signal is directly related to wheel speed and the proximity of the wheel speed sensor to the toothed ring, often referred to as the air gap.

This DTC is designed to detect two open wheel speed sensors in any combination. This DTC exists due to a condition that may exist that does not allow the driver to be informed by the ABS indicator lamp of non-functioning ABS. If one wheel speed sensor is open, the driver is informed. If a second fails, the driver is no longer informed without this DTC and ABS is not available. By requiring the two operating wheels to be within 7 mph, a false DTC is prevented during spin-ups while still allowing for detection when the stowaway spare tire is used.

Test Description: Number(s) below refer to circled number(s) on the diagnostic chart.
6. This step checks for an open in the wheel speed sensor circuitry of one side of the sensor.
7. This step checks for an open on the other side of the sensor in question.
8. This insures that the circuitry is not shorted to voltage.

Diagnostic Aids:

A false DTC A031 may be set as a result of vehicle operation while on a hoist or a lifted condition, or stuck in mud or snow when the vehicle is in gear.

An "Intermittent" malfunction may be caused by a poor connection, rubbed through wire insulation, or a wire that is broken inside the insulation.

The frequency of the malfunction can be checked by using the enhanced diagnostic function of the Tech 1

SENSOR TERMINAL	24 WAY EBCM CONNECTOR TERMINAL	CIRCUIT NUMBER
L/R WHEEL B	12	884
L/R WHEEL A	11	885
R/R WHEEL B	7	882
R/R WHEEL A	8	883

Fig. 122   Code A031, Two wheel speeds–0 (Part 2 of 2). 1993 Cutlass Supreme, Grand Prix, Lumina & Regal

DTC A032

LEFT FRONT WHEEL SENSOR SHORTED TO BATTERY OR GROUND

Circuit Description:

As a toothed ring passes by the wheel speed sensor, changes in the electromagnetic field cause the wheel speed sensor to produce a sinusoidal (AC) voltage signal whose frequency is proportional to wheel speed. The magnitude of this signal is directly related to wheel speed and the proximity of the wheel speed sensor to the toothed ring often referred to as the air gap.

Failure Condition:

DTC A032 can be set anytime after initialization. If either of the left front wheel speed circuits are shorted to voltage or ground, a malfunction exists.

Action Taken:

A malfunction DTC is stored, ABS is disabled and the ABS indicator lamp is turned "ON."

Test Description: Number(s) below refer to circled number(s) on the diagnostic chart.
1. This test helps to identify whether the DTC is due to a short to battery or short to ground.
2. This insures that the wheel speed sensor is not shorted to ground.
3. This step checks to see if wheel speed sensor circuitry is shorted to voltage.
4. This insures that the wheel speed sensor circuitry has good continuity.
5. This checks for short to ground in wheel speed sensor wiring.
6. This checks for short to voltage in wheel speed sensor wiring.
7. This step checks for a possible intermittent malfunction.

Diagnostic Aids:

An "Intermittent" malfunction may be caused by a poor connection, rubbed through wire insulation, or a wire that is broken inside the insulation.

The frequency of the malfunction can be checked by using the enhanced diagnostic function of the Tech 1

If the customers comments reflect that the ABS indicator lamp is "ON" only during moist environmental changes (rain, snow, vehicle wash), all wheel speed sensor circuitry should be thoroughly inspected for signs of water intrusion. If DTC is not current, clear DTCs and simulate the effects of water intrusion. Use the following procedure. Spray down the suspected area with a 5% salt water solution (two teaspoons of salt to 12 oz. of water). Start vehicle, allow vehicle to run for 10 seconds. If DTC returns immediately, replace suspected harness.

Any circuitry, that is suspected as causing the intermittent complaint, should be thoroughly checked for backed out terminals, improper mating, broken locks, improperly formed or damaged terminals, poor terminal to wiring connections or physical damage to the wiring harness.

When replacing a wheel speed sensor, inspect the sensor terminals and harness connector for corrosion and/or water intrusion. If evidence of corrosion or water intrusion exists, replace wheel speed sensor harness.

IMPORTANT: WHEEL SPEED SENSOR INTERMITTENT PROBLEMS MAY BE DIFFICULT TO LOCATE. CARE SHOULD BE TAKEN NOT TO DISTURB ANY ELECTRICAL CONNECTIONS PRIOR TO AN INDICATED STEP OF THIS CHART. THIS WILL INSURE THAT AN INTERMITTENT CONNECTION WILL NOT BE CORRECTED BEFORE THE SOURCE OF THE PROBLEM IS FOUND.

Fig. 123   Code A032, Left front wheel sensor shorted to battery or ground. 1993 Cutlass Supreme, Grand Prix, Lumina & Regal

DTC A033
RIGHT FRONT WHEEL SENSOR SHORTED TO BATTERY OR GROUND

Circuit Description:

As a toothed ring passes by the wheel speed sensor, changes in the electromagnetic field cause the wheel speed sensor to produce a sinusoidal (AC) voltage signal whose frequency is proportional to wheel speed. The magnitude of this signal is directly related to wheel speed and the proximity of the wheel speed sensor to the toothed ring, often referred to as the air gap.

Failure Condition:

DTC A033 can be set anytime after initialization. If either of the right front wheel speed circuits are shorted to voltage or ground, a malfunction exists.

Action Taken:

A malfunction DTC is stored, ABS is disabled and the ABS indicator lamp is turned "ON."

Test Description: Number(s) below refer to circled number(s) on the diagnostic chart.

1. This test helps identify whether the DTC is due to a short to battery or short to ground.
2. This insures that the wheel speed sensor is not shorted to ground.
3. This step checks to see if wheel speed sensor circuitry is shorted to voltage.
4. This insures that the wheel speed sensor circuitry has good continuity.
5. This checks for short to ground in wheel speed sensor wiring.
6. This checks for short to voltage in wheel speed sensor wiring.
7. This step checks for a possible intermittent malfunction.

Diagnostic Aids:

An "Intermittent" malfunction may be caused by a poor connection, rubbed through wire insulation, or a wire that is broken inside the insulation.

The frequency of the malfunction can be checked by using the enhanced diagnostic function of the Tech 1

If the customers comments reflect that the ABS indicator lamp is "ON" only during moist environmental changes (rain, snow, vehicle wash), all wheel speed sensor circuitry should be thoroughly inspected for signs of water intrusion. If DTC is not current, clear DTCs and simulate the effects of water intrusion. Use the following procedure. Spray down the suspected area with a 5% salt water solution (two teaspoons of salt to 12 oz. of water). Start vehicle, allow vehicle to run for 10 seconds. If DTC returns immediately, replace suspected harness.

Any circuitry, that is suspected as causing the intermittent complaint, should be thoroughly checked for backed out terminals, improper mating, broken locks, improperly formed or damaged terminals, poor terminal to wiring connections or physical damage to the wiring harness.

When replacing a wheel speed sensor, inspect the sensor terminals and harness connector for corrosion and/or water intrusion. If evidence of corrosion or water intrusion exists, replace wheel speed sensor harness.

Fig. 124   Code A033, Right front wheel sensor shorted to battery or ground. 1993 Cutlass Supreme, Grand Prix, Lumina & Regal

DTC A034
LEFT REAR WHEEL SENSOR SHORTED TO BATTERY OR GROUND

Circuit Description:

As a toothed ring passes by the wheel speed sensor, changes in the electromagnetic field cause the wheel speed sensor to produce a sinusoidal (AC) voltage signal whose frequency is proportional to wheel speed. The magnitude of this signal is directly related to wheel speed and the proximity of the wheel speed sensor to the toothed ring, often referred to as the air gap.

Failure Condition:

DTC A034 can be set anytime after initialization. If either of the left rear wheel speed circuits are shorted to voltage or ground, a malfunction exists.

Action Taken:

A malfunction DTC is stored, ABS is disabled and the ABS indicator lamp is turned "ON."

Test Description: Number(s) below refer to circled number(s) on the diagnostic chart.

1. This test helps to identify whether the DTC is due to a short to battery or short to ground.
2. This insures that the wheel speed sensor is not shorted to ground.
3. This step checks to see if wheel speed sensor circuitry is shorted to voltage.
4. This insures that the wheel speed sensor circuitry has good continuity.
5. This checks for short to ground in wheel speed sensor wiring.
6. This checks for short to voltage in wheel speed sensor wiring.
7. This step checks for a possible intermittent malfunction.

Diagnostic Aids:

An "Intermittent" malfunction may be caused by a poor connection, rubbed through wire insulation, or a wire that is broken inside the insulation.

The frequency of the malfunction can be checked by using the enhanced diagnostic function of the Tech 1

If the customers comments reflect that the ABS indicator lamp is "ON" only during moist environmental changes (rain, snow, vehicle wash), all wheel speed sensor circuitry should be thoroughly inspected for signs of water intrusion. If DTC is not current, clear DTCs and simulate the effects of water intrusion. Use the following procedure. Spray down the suspected area with a 5% salt water solution (two teaspoons of salt to 12 oz. of water). Start vehicle, allow vehicle to run for 10 seconds. If DTC returns immediately, replace suspected harness.

Any circuitry, that is suspected as causing the intermittent complaint, should be thoroughly checked for backed out terminals, improper mating, broken locks, improperly formed or damaged terminals, poor terminal to wiring connections or physical damage to the wiring harness.

When replacing a wheel speed sensor, inspect the sensor terminals and harness connector for corrosion and/or water intrusion. If evidence of corrosion or water intrusion exists, replace wheel speed sensor harness.

Fig. 125   Code A034, Left rear wheel sensor shorted to battery or ground. 1993 Cutlass Supreme, Grand Prix, Lumina & Regal

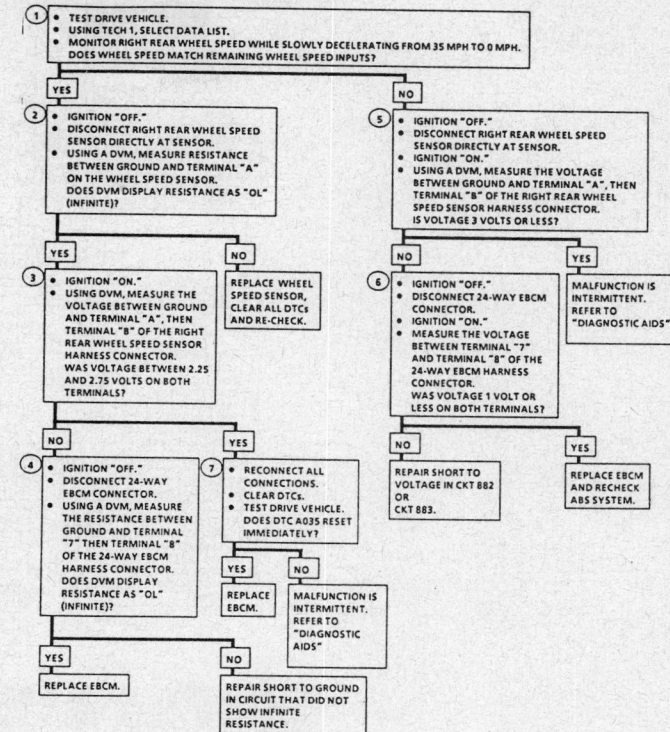

DTC A035

RIGHT REAR WHEEL SENSOR SHORTED TO BATTERY OR GROUND

Circuit Description:

As a toothed ring passes by the wheel speed sensor, changes in the electromagnetic field cause the wheel speed sensor to produce a sinusoidal (AC) voltage signal whose frequency is proportional to wheel speed. The magnitude of this signal is directly related to wheel speed and the proximity of the wheel speed sensor to the toothed ring, often referred to as the air gap.

Failure Condition:

DTC A035 can be set anytime after initialization. If either of the right rear wheel speed circuits are shorted to voltage or ground, a malfunction exists.

Action Taken:

A malfunction DTC is stored, ABS is disabled and the ABS indicator lamp is turned "ON."

Test Description: Number(s) below refer to circled number(s) on the diagnostic chart.

1. This helps to identify whether the DTC is due to a short to battery or short to ground.
2. This insures that the wheel speed sensor is not shorted to ground.
3. This step checks to see if wheel speed sensor circuitry is shorted to voltage.
4. This insures that the wheel speed sensor circuitry has good continuity.
5. This checks for short to ground in wheel speed sensor wiring.
6. This checks for short to voltage in wheel speed sensor wiring.
7. This step checks for a possible intermittent malfunction.

Diagnostic Aids:

An "Intermittent" malfunction may be caused by a poor connection, rubbed through wire insulation, or a wire that is broken inside the insulation.

The frequency of the malfunction can be checked by using the enhanced diagnostic function of the Tech 1,

If the customers comments reflect that the ABS indicator lamp is "ON" only during moist environmental changes (rain, snow, vehicle wash), all wheel speed sensor circuitry should be thoroughly inspected for signs of water intrusion. If DTC is not current, clear DTCs and simulate the effects of water intrusion. Use the following procedure. Spray down the suspected area with a 5% salt water solution (two teaspoons of salt to 12 oz. of water). Start vehicle, allow vehicle to run for 10 seconds. If DTC returns immediately, replace suspected harness.

Any circuitry, that is suspected as causing the intermittent complaint, should be thoroughly checked for backed out terminals, improper mating, broken locks, improperly formed or damaged terminals, poor terminal to wiring connections or physical damage to the wiring harness.

When replacing a wheel speed sensor, inspect the sensor terminals and harness connector for corrosion and/or water intrusion. If evidence of corrosion or water intrusion exists, replace wheel speed sensor harness.

Fig. 126   Code A035, Right rear wheel sensor shorted to battery or ground. 1993 Cutlass Supreme, Grand Prix, Lumina & Regal

Cavalier & Sunbird

Achieva, Beretta, Corsica, Grand Am & Skylark

DTC A036

LOW SYSTEM VOLTAGE

Circuit Description:

This DTC is used to monitor the voltage level available to the ABS EBCM. If the voltage drops below 11 volts, full performance of the ABS system cannot be guaranteed. During ABS operation, there are several current requirements that will cause battery voltage to drop. Because of this, voltage is monitored prior to ABS to indicate good charging system condition and also during ABS when voltage may drop significantly.

Failure Condition:

DTC A036 can only be set if the vehicle's speed is greater than 5 km/h (3 mph). If the switched battery voltage is less than 11.2 volts non-ABS or less than 9.6 volts ABS, a malfunction exists.

Action Taken:

A malfunction DTC is stored, ABS is disabled and the ABS indicator lamp is turned "ON."

Test Description: Number(s) below refer to circled number(s) on the diagnostic chart.

1. This test checks to see what voltage is readily available at terminal "A" of the EBCM. If voltage is representative of good charging system condition, a malfunction is not present.
2. This step isolates the EBCM to check the condition of the circuitry and charging system.
3. This step isolates the low voltage condition to high circuit resistance, or improper charging system operation.

Diagnostic Aids:

An "Intermittent" malfunction may be caused by a poor connection, rubbed through wire insulation, or a wire that is broken inside the insulation.

The frequency of the malfunction can be checked by using the enhanced diagnostic function of the Tech 1

Any circuitry, that is suspected as causing the intermittent complaint, should be thoroughly checked for backed out terminals, improper mating, broken locks, improperly formed or damaged terminals, poor terminal to wiring connections or physical damage to the wiring harness.

While performing a voltage load test, if it is noted that only ignition voltage drops below acceptable voltage levels, CKT 650 should be checked for high resistance or an open condition.

Fig. 127   Code A036, Low system voltage (Part 1 of 2). 1993 except Cutlass Supreme, Grand Prix, Lumina & Regal

Fig. 127 Code A036, Low system voltage (Part 2 of 2). 1993 except Cutlass Supreme, Grand Prix, Lumina & Regal

DTC A036
LOW SYSTEM VOLTAGE

Circuit Description:
This DTC is used to monitor the voltage level available to the EBCM controller. If the voltage drops below 11 volts, full performance of the ABS system cannot be guaranteed. During ABS operation, there are several current requirements that will cause battery voltage to drop. Because of this, voltage is monitored prior to ABS to indicate good charging system condition and also during ABS when voltage may drop significantly.

Failure Condition:
DTC A036 can only be set if the vehicle's speed is greater than 5 km/h (3 mph). If the switched battery voltage is less than 11.2 volts non-ABS or less than 9.6 volts ABS, a malfunction exists.

Action Taken:
A malfunction DTC is stored, ABS is disabled and the ABS indicator lamp is turned "ON."

Test Description: Number(s) below refer to circled number(s) on the diagnostic chart.
1. This test checks to see what voltage is readily available at terminal "A" on the EBCM. If voltage is representative of good charging system condition, a malfunction is not present.
2. This step isolates the EBCM to check the condition of the circuitry and charging system.
3. This step isolates the low voltage condition to high circuit resistance, or improper charging system operation.
4. This step checks for a possible intermittent malfunction.
5. This step checks for adequate voltage at the EBCM when a load is applied to the system.
6. This step isolates which circuit is the source of the low voltage condition.

Diagnostic Aids:

An "Intermittent" malfunction may be caused by a poor connection, rubbed through wire insulation, or a wire that is broken inside the insulation.
The frequency of the malfunction can be checked by using the enhanced diagnostic function of the Tech 1

Any circuitry, that is suspected as causing the intermittent complaint, should be thoroughly checked for backed out terminals, improper mating, broken locks, improperly formed or damaged terminals, poor terminal to wiring connections or physical damage to the wiring harness.
While performing a voltage load test, if it is noted that only ignition voltage drops below acceptable voltage levels, CKT 350 should be checked for high resistance or an open condition.

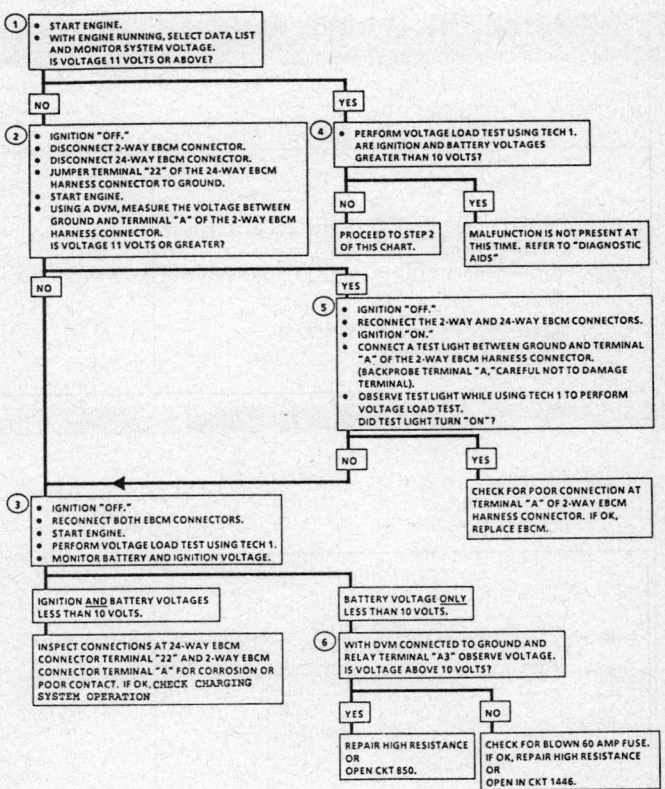

Fig. 128 Code A036, Low system voltage. 1993 Cutlass Supreme, Grand Prix, Lumina & Regal

Cavalier & Sunbird

Achieva, Beretta, Corsica, Grand Am & Skylark

Cutlass Supreme, Grand Prix, Lumina & Regal

DTC A037
HIGH SYSTEM VOLTAGE

Circuit Description:
This DTC is designed to detect high vehicle voltage levels prior to any required motor movement (initialization or ABS). If excessive voltage exists, demagnetization of the motor magnets may occur, which would eventually affect or eliminate ABS performance.

Failure Condition:
DTC A037 can only be set if the vehicle's speed is greater than 5 km/h (3 mph). If the switched battery voltage is greater than 17 volts, a malfunction exists.

Action Taken:
A malfunction DTC is stored, ABS is disabled and the ABS indicator lamp is turned "ON."

Test Description: Number(s) below refer to circled number(s) on the diagnostic chart.
1. This step checks the voltage level being received by the EBCM. If high voltage is present, a charging system problem is indicated.

Diagnostic Aids:
An "Intermittent" malfunction may be caused by a poor connection, rubbed through wire insulation, or a wire that is broken inside the insulation.

The frequency of the malfunction can be checked by using the enhanced diagnostic function of the Tech 1 tool

Any circuitry, that is suspected as causing the intermittent complaint, should be thoroughly checked for backed out terminals, improper mating, broken locks, improperly formed or damaged terminals, poor terminal to wiring connections or physical damage to the wiring harness.

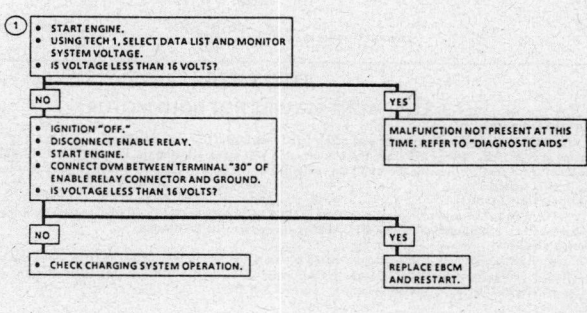

Fig. 129   Code A037, High system voltage. 1993

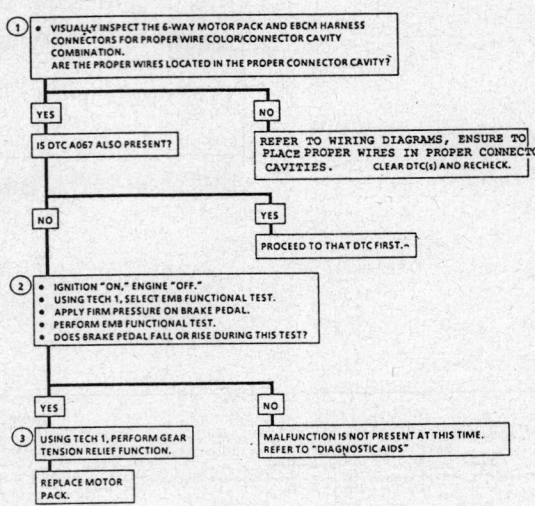

DTC A038
LEFT FRONT EMB WILL NOT HOLD MOTOR

Circuit Description:

Current is supplied to the EMBs through terminal "B" of the three way motor pack connector. When a release of the EMB is commanded, the EBCM grounds the EMB input and allows the EMB to be energized to release the motor.

This DTC is designed to detect slipping EMBs during initialization. When the release is commanded during initialization, the EMB is not energized and should hold the motor, resulting in sensed current of the motor being equal to commanded current (motor is at stall). If the motor is moving, sensed current will be less than stall current.

Failure Condition:

DTC A038 can be set during initialization. DTC A086 is always set with A038.

Action Taken:

If an EMB can not hold a motor in the home position, the motor may be backdriven when the brake pedal is applied causing the brake pedal to drop. A malfunction DTC is stored, ABS is disabled and the ABS indicator lamp is turned "ON."

Test Description: Number(s) below refer to circled number(s) on the diagnostic chart.
1. This step ensures motor circuits are in the proper connector cavity.
2. This functionally checks the ability of the EMB to hold the motor. If the brake pedal moves during this test, it would indicate the EMB is slipping.
3. This step is used to release the tension of the motor pack prior to removal.

Diagnostic Aids:

An "Intermittent" malfunction in this DTC may result from a mechanical part of the system that sticks, binds, or slips. The frequency of the malfunction can be checked by using the enhanced diagnostic function of the Tech 1

The static modulator test function of the Tech 1 may be used to locate an intermittent malfunction associated with the EMB.

NOTICE: This test may fail if low voltage (10 volts or less) was present when initialization occurred. Ensure battery/charging system is functioning properly.

Fig. 130   Code A038, Left front EMB will not hold motor. 1993 except Cutlass Supreme, Grand Prix, Lumina & Regal

DTC A038
LEFT FRONT ESB WILL NOT HOLD MOTOR

Circuit Description:

This DTC is designed to detect a slipping left front ESB. During initialization and braking, the left front motor is re-homed. If the ESB slips, the motor/piston will move. During the next key "ON" initialization, a re-home of the motor verifies the motor/piston remained at the home position. If motor movement is detected, the ESB must be slipping.

Failure Condition:

DTC A038 can be set during initialization. If the EBCM detects that the ESB could not hold the piston in the home position, a malfunction exists. DTC A086 is always set with DTC A038.

Action Taken:

If an ESB cannot hold a piston in the home position, the piston may be backdriven when the brake pedal is applied, causing the brake pedal to drop. A malfunction DTC is stored, ABS is disabled, and the ABS indicator lamp and the red "BRAKE" warning lamp are turned "ON."

Test Description: Number(s) below refer to circled number(s) on the diagnostic chart.
1. This step insures that the proper motor circuits are located in the proper connector cavities.
2. This step checks the left front ESB. A broken or defective ESB would result in the left front piston being backdriven by hydraulic pressure and pedal movement would result.

Diagnostic Aids:

An "Intermittent" malfunction in this DTC may result from a mechanical part of the system that sticks, binds, or slips. The frequency of the malfunction can be checked by using the enhanced diagnostic function of the Tech 1

The static modulator test function of the Tech 1 or T-100 may be used to locate an intermittent malfunction associated with the ESB.

Fig. 131   Code A038, Left front ESB will not hold motor. 1993 Cutlass Supreme, Grand Prix, Lumina & Regal

DTC A041
RIGHT FRONT EMB WILL NOT HOLD MOTOR

Circuit Description:

Current is supplied to the EMBs through terminal "B" of the three way motor pack connector. When a release of the EMB is commanded, the EBCM grounds the EMB input and allows the EMB to be energized to release the motor.

This DTC is designed to detect slipping EMBs during initialization. When the release is commanded during initialization, the EMB is not energized and should hold the motor, resulting in sensed current of the motor being equal to commanded current (motor is at stall). If the motor is moving, sensed current will be less than stall current.

Failure Condition:

DTC A041 can be set during initialization. DTC A086 is always set with DTC A041.

Action Taken:

If an EMB can not hold a motor in the home position, the motor may be backdriven when the brake pedal is applied causing the brake pedal to fall. A malfunction DTC is stored, ABS is disabled and the ABS indicator lamp is turned "ON."

Test Description: Number(s) below refer to circled number(s) on the diagnostic chart.
1. This step ensures motor circuits are in the proper connector cavity.
2. This functionally checks the ability of the EMB to hold the motor. If the brake pedal moves during this test, it would indicate the EMB is slipping.
3. This step is used to release the tension of the motor pack prior to removal.

Diagnostic Aids:

An "Intermittent" malfunction in this DTC may result from a mechanical part of the system that sticks, binds, or slips.

The frequency of the malfunction can be checked by using the enhanced diagnostic function of the Tech 1 tool.

The static modulator test function of the Tech 1 may be used to locate an intermittent malfunction associated with the EMB.

NOTICE: This DTC may fail if low voltage (10 volts or less) was present when initialization occurred. Ensure battery/charging system is functioning properly.

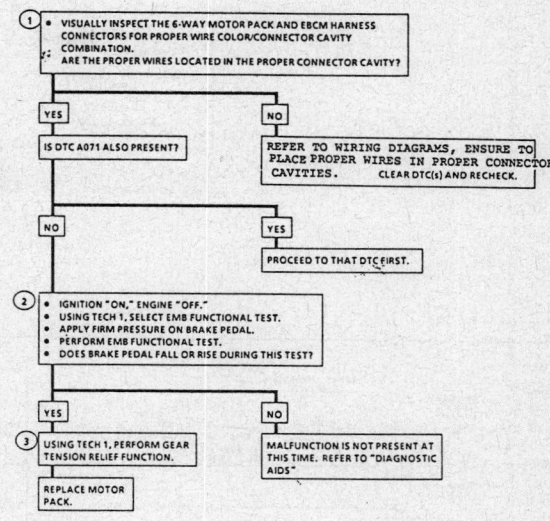

Fig. 132   Code A041, Right front EMB will not hold motor. 1993 except Cutlass Supreme, Grand Prix, Lumina & Regal

---

DTC A041
RIGHT FRONT ESB WILL NOT HOLD MOTOR

Circuit Description:

This DTC is designed to detect a slipping right front ESB. During initialization and braking, the right front motor is re-homed. If the ESB slips, the motor/piston will move. During the next key "ON" initialization, a re-home of the motor verifies the motor/piston remained at the home position. If motor movement is detected, the ESB must be slipping.

Failure Condition:

DTC A041 can be set during initialization. If the EBCM detects that the ESB could not hold the piston in the home position, a malfunction exists. DTC A086 is always set with DTC A041.

Action Taken:

If an ESB cannot hold a piston in the home position, the piston may be backdriven when the brake pedal is applied, causing the brake pedal to drop. A malfunction DTC is stored, ABS is disabled, and the ABS indicator lamp and the red "BRAKE" warning lamp are turned "ON."

Test Description: Number(s) below refer to circled number(s) on the diagnostic chart.
1. This step insures that the proper motor circuits are located in the proper connector cavities.
2. This step checks the right front ESB. A broken or defective ESB would result in the right front piston being backdriven by hydraulic pressure, and pedal movement would result.

Diagnostic Aids:

An "Intermittent" malfunction in this DTC may result from a mechanical part of the system that sticks, binds, or slips.

The frequency of the malfunction can be checked by using the enhanced diagnostic function of the Tech 1

The static modulator test function of the Tech 1 or T-100 may be used to locate an intermittent malfunction associated with the ESB.

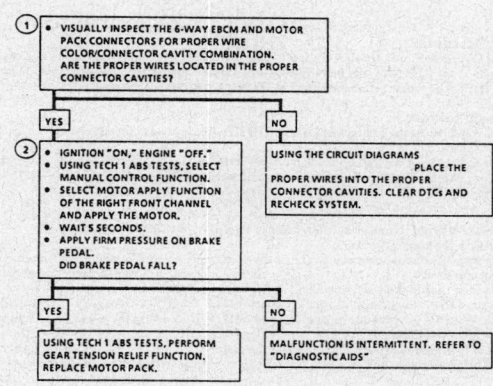

Fig. 133   Code A041, Right front ESB will not hold motor. 1993 Cutlass Supreme, Grand Prix, Lumina & Regal

---

Cavalier & Sunbird

Beretta & Corsica

Achieva, Grand Am & Skylark

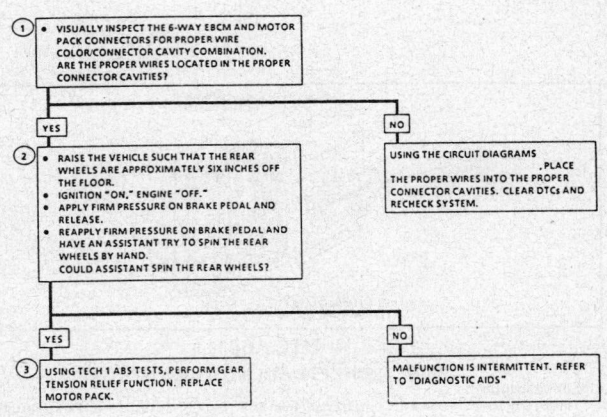

DTC A042
REAR AXLE ESB WILL NOT HOLD MOTOR

Circuit Description:
This DTC is designed to detect a slipping rear axle ESB. During initialization and braking, the rear motor is re-homed. If the ESB slips, the motor/piston will move. During the next key on initialization, a re-home of the motor verifies the motor/piston remained at the home position. If motor movement is detected, the ESB must be slipping.

Failure Condition:
DTC A042 can be set during initialization. DTC A086 is always set with A042.

Action Taken:
If an ESB can not hold a motor in the home position, the motor may be backdriven when the brake pedal is applied causing the brake pedal to drop. A malfunction DTC is stored, ABS is disabled and the ABS indicator lamp is turned "ON."

Test Description: Number(s) below refer to circled number(s) on the diagnostic chart.
1. This step ensures motor circuits are in the proper connector cavity.
2. This step checks the rear axle ESB. A broken or defective ESB would result in the rear piston being back driven by hydraulic pressure, and wheel movement would result.
3. This step is used to release the tension of the motor pack prior to removal.

Diagnostic Aids:

An "Intermittent" malfunction in this DTC may result from a mechanical part of the system that sticks, binds, or slips.

The frequency of the malfunction can be checked by using the enhanced diagnostic function of the Tech 1

The static modulator test function of the Tech 1 may be used to locate an intermittent malfunction associated with the ESB.

AFTER DIAGNOSIS IS COMPLETE, CLEAR DTCs AND TEST DRIVE VEHICLE FOR THREE (3) DRIVE CYCLES TO VERIFY DTC DOES NOT RESET. A DRIVE CYCLE CONSISTS OF STARTING THE VEHICLE, DRIVING OVER 16 km/h (10 MPH) AND THEN KEYING DOWN.

Fig. 134   Code A042, Rear axle ESB will not hold motor. 1993 except Cutlass Supreme, Grand Prix, Lumina & Regal

DTC A042
REAR AXLE ESB WILL NOT HOLD MOTOR

Circuit Description:
This DTC is designed to detect a slipping rear axle ESB. During initialization and braking, the rear motor is re-homed. If the ESB slips, the motor/piston will move. During the next key "ON" initialization, a re-home of the motor verifies the motor/piston remained at the home position. If motor movement is detected, the ESB must be slipping.

Failure Condition:
DTC A042 cannot be set during initialization. If the EBCM detects that the ESB could not hold the piston in the home position, a malfunction exists. DTC A086 is always set with DTC A042.

Action Taken:
If an ESB cannot hold a piston in the home position, the piston may be backdriven when the brake pedal is applied, causing the brake pedal to drop. A malfunction DTC is stored, ABS is disabled, and the ABS indicator lamp and the red "BRAKE" warning lamp are turned "ON."

Test Description: Number(s) below refer to circled number(s) on the diagnostic chart.
1. This step insures that the proper motor circuits are located in the proper connector cavities.
2. This step checks the rear axle ESB. A broken or defective ESB would result in the rear piston being backdriven by hydraulic pressure, and wheel movement would result.
3. This step performs the gear tension relief function to prepare the hydraulic modulator/motor pack assembly for separation.

Diagnostic Aids:
An "Intermittent" malfunction in this DTC may result from a mechanical part of the system that sticks, binds, or slips.
The frequency of the malfunction can be checked by using the enhanced diagnostic function of the Tech 1

The static modulator test function of the Tech 1 or T-100 may be used to locate an intermittent malfunction associated with the ESB.

AFTER DIAGNOSIS IS COMPLETE, CLEAR DTCs AND TEST DRIVE VEHICLE FOR THREE (3) DRIVE CYCLES TO VERIFY DTC DOES NOT RESET. A DRIVE CYCLE CONSISTS OF STARTING THE VEHICLE, DRIVING OVER 16 km/h (10 MPH) AND THEN KEYING DOWN.

Fig. 135   Code A042, Right front ESB will not hold motor. 1993 Cutlass Supreme, Grand Prix, Lumina & Regal

Cavalier & Sunbird

Achieva, Beretta, Corsica, Grand Am & Skylark

DTC A044
LEFT FRONT CHANNEL WILL NOT MOVE

Circuit Description:
Current is supplied to the EMB through terminal "B" of the three way motor pack connector. When a release of the EMB is commanded, the EBCM grounds the EMB input and allows the EMB to be energized to release the motor.
This DTC is designed to detect non-actuating EMB, stuck motor or a seized hydraulic modulator. When the release is commanded during initialization, the EMB should release the motor, resulting in sensed current being less than commanded current (i.e. the motor is spinning freely). If the motor is not moving, sensed current will be equal to stall current.

Failure Condition:
DTC A044 can be set at 5 km/h (3 mph). If the EBCM detects a condition in which it cannot move the motor in either direction, a malfunction exists.

Action Taken:
This malfunction indicates the channel can not be moved properly. A malfunction DTC is stored, ABS is disabled and the ABS indicator lamp is turned "ON."

Test Description: Number(s) below refer to circled number(s) on the diagnostic chart.
1. This step ensures motor circuits are in the proper connector cavity.
2. This step checks for motor movement during release.
3. This procedure compares feedback current to command current during apply.
4. This step checks to see if hydraulic modulator is functioning properly.
5. This step checks if motor can apply properly under load.
6. This step serves to isolate the malfunction to either the EBCM or a short between CKTs 1280 and 1281.

Diagnostic Aids:
An "Intermittent" malfunction in this DTC may result from a mechanical part of the system that sticks, binds, or slips.
The frequency of the malfunction can be checked by using the enhanced diagnostic function of the Tech 1

DTC A044 may set after modulator disassembly if the modulator pistons are positioned at the bottom of their bore.
Any circuitry, that is suspected as causing the intermittent complaint, should be thoroughly checked for backed out terminals, improper mating, broken locks, improperly formed or damaged terminals, poor terminal to wiring connections or physical damage to the wiring harness.

NOTICE: This DTC may fail if low voltage (10 volts or less) was present when initialization occurred. Ensure battery/charging system is functioning properly.

Fig. 136   Code A044, Left front channel will not move (Part 1 of 2). 1993 except Cutlass Supreme, Grand Prix, Lumina & Regal

Fig. 136   Code A044, Left front channel will not move (Part 2 of 2). 1993 except Cutlass Supreme, Grand Prix, Lumina & Regal

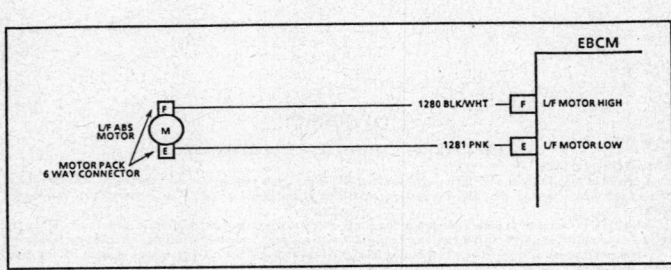

DTC A044
LEFT FRONT CHANNEL WILL NOT MOVE

Circuit Description:

This DTC is designed to detect bound-up ESB, a stuck motor, or a seized hydraulic modulator. When the release is commanded during initialization, the ESB should release the motor, resulting in sensed current being less than commanded current (motor is spinning freely). If the motor is not moving, sensed current will be equal to stall current.

Failure Condition:

DTC A044 can be set during normal operation. If the EBCM detects a condition in which it cannot move the motor in either direction, a malfunction exists.

Action Taken:

This malfunction indicates the channel cannot be moved properly. A malfunction DTC is stored, ABS is disabled and the ABS indicator lamp is turned "ON."

Test Description: Number(s) below refer to circled number(s) on the diagnostic chart.

1. This step insures that proper motor circuits are located in the proper connector cavities.
2. This step checks for proper motor movement during apply and release commands from the Tech 1.
3. This step compares EBCM command current to motor feedback current.
4. This step checks for proper hydraulic modulator gear and piston movement.
5. This step verifies that the motor can actually apply when commanded.
6. This test determines if the malfunction is caused by a defective EBCM or by a short circuit.

Diagnostic Aids:

An "Intermittent" malfunction in this DTC may result from a mechanical part of the system that sticks, binds, or slips.

The frequency of the malfunction can be checked by using the enhanced diagnostic function of the Tech 1.

DTC A044 may set after modulator disassembly if the modulator pistons are positioned at the bottom of their bore.

Any circuitry, that is suspected as causing the intermittent complaint, should be thoroughly checked for backed out terminals, improper mating, broken locks, improperly formed or damaged terminals, poor terminal to wiring connections or physical damage to the wiring harness.

Fig. 137   Code A044, Left front channel will not move. 1993 Cutlass Supreme, Grand Prix, Lumina & Regal

Cavalier & Sunbird

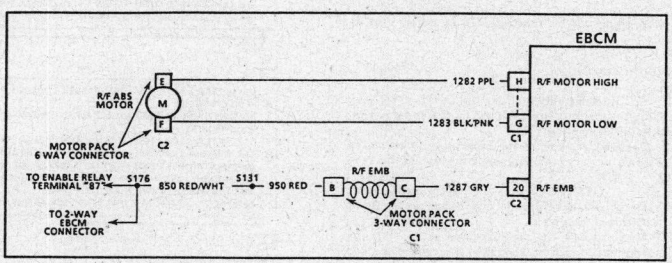

Achieva, Beretta, Corsica, Grand Am & Skylark

DTC A045
RIGHT FRONT CHANNEL WILL NOT MOVE

Circuit Description:
Current is supplied to the EMB through terminal "B" of the three way motor pack connector. When a release of the EMB is commanded, the EBCM grounds the EMB input and allows the EMB to be energized to release the motor.

This DTC is designed to detect non-actuating EMB, stuck motor or a seized hydraulic modulator. When the release is commanded during initialization, the EMB should release the motor, resulting in sensed current being less than commanded current (motor is spinning freely). If the motor is not moving, sensed current will be equal to stall current.

Failure Condition:
DTC A045 can be set at 5 km/h (3 mph). If the EBCM detects a condition in which it cannot move the motor in either direction, a malfunction exists.

Action Taken:
This malfunction indicates the channel can not be moved properly. A malfunction DTC is stored, ABS is disabled and the ABS indicator lamp is turned "ON."

Test Description: Number(s) below refer to circled number(s) on the diagnostic chart.
1. This step ensures motor circuits are in the proper connector cavity.
2. This step checks for the motor movement during release.
3. This procedure compares feedback current to command current during apply.
4. This step checks to see if hydraulic modulator is functioning properly.
5. This step checks if motor can apply properly under load.
6. This step serves to isolate the malfunction to either the EBCM or a short between CKTs 1282 and 1283.

Diagnostic Aids:

An "Intermittent" malfunction in this DTC may result from a mechanical part of the system that sticks, binds, or slips.

The frequency of the malfunction can be checked by using the enhanced diagnostic function of the Tech 1

DTC A045 may set after modulator disassembly if the modulator pistons are positioned at the bottom of their bore.

Any circuitry, that is suspected as causing the intermittent complaint, should be thoroughly checked for backed out terminals, improper mating, broken locks, improperly formed or damaged terminals, poor terminal to wiring connections or physical damage to the wiring harness.

NOTICE: This DTC may fail if low voltage (10 volts or less) was present when initialization occurred. Ensure battery/charging system is functioning properly.

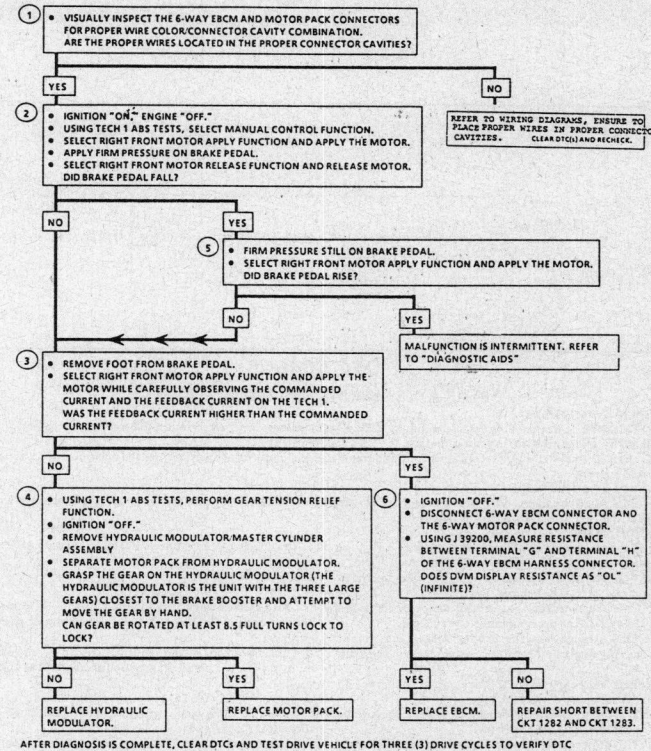

Fig. 138 Code A045, Right front channel will not move. 1993 except Cutlass Supreme, Grand Prix, Lumina & Regal

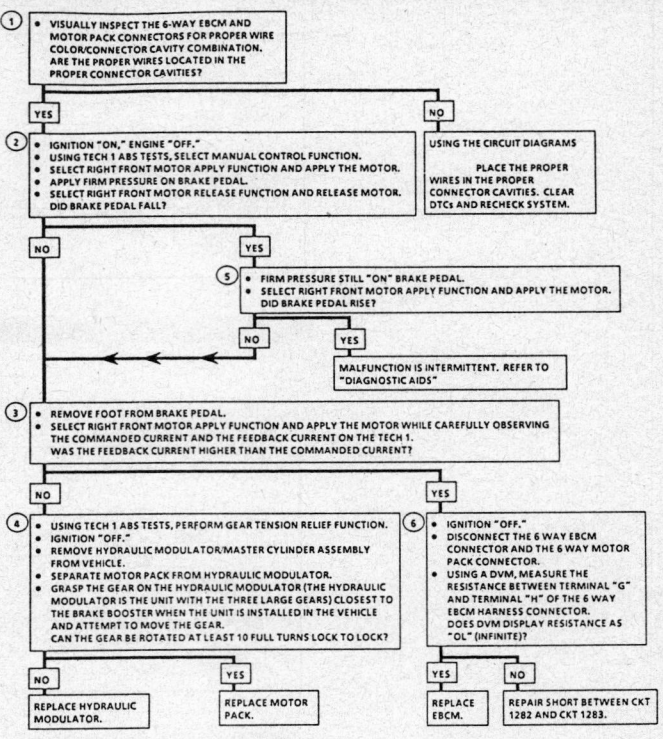

DTC A045
RIGHT FRONT CHANNEL WILL NOT MOVE

Circuit Description:
This DTC is designed to detect bound-up ESB, a stuck motor, or a seized hydraulic modulator. When the release is commanded during initialization, the ESB should release the motor, resulting in sensed current being less than commanded current (motor is spinning freely). If the motor is not moving, sensed current will be equal to stall current.

Failure Condition:
DTC A045 can be set during normal operation. If the EBCM detects a condition in which it cannot move the motor in either direction, a malfunction exists.

Action Taken:
This malfunction indicates the channel cannot be moved properly. A malfunction DTC is stored, ABS is disabled and the ABS indicator lamp is turned "ON."

Test Description: Number(s) below refer to circled number(s) on the diagnostic chart.
1. This step insures that proper motor circuits are located in the proper connector cavities.
2. This step checks for proper motor movement during apply and release commands from the Tech 1.
3. This step compares EBCM command current to motor feedback current.
4. This step checks for proper hydraulic modulator gear and piston movement.
5. This step verifies that the motor can actually apply when commanded.
6. This test determines if the malfunction is caused by a defective EBCM or by a short circuit.

Diagnostic Aids:

An "Intermittent" malfunction in this DTC may result from a mechanical part of the system that sticks, binds, or slips.

The frequency of the malfunction can be checked by using the enhanced diagnostic function of the Tech 1

DTC A045 may set after modulator disassembly if the modulator pistons are positioned at the bottom of their bore.

Any circuitry, that is suspected as causing the intermittent complaint, should be thoroughly checked for backed out terminals, improper mating, broken locks, improperly formed or damaged terminals, poor terminal to wiring connections or physical damage to the wiring harness.

Fig. 139   Code A045, Right front channel will not move. 1993 Cutlass Supreme, Grand Prix, Lumina & Regal

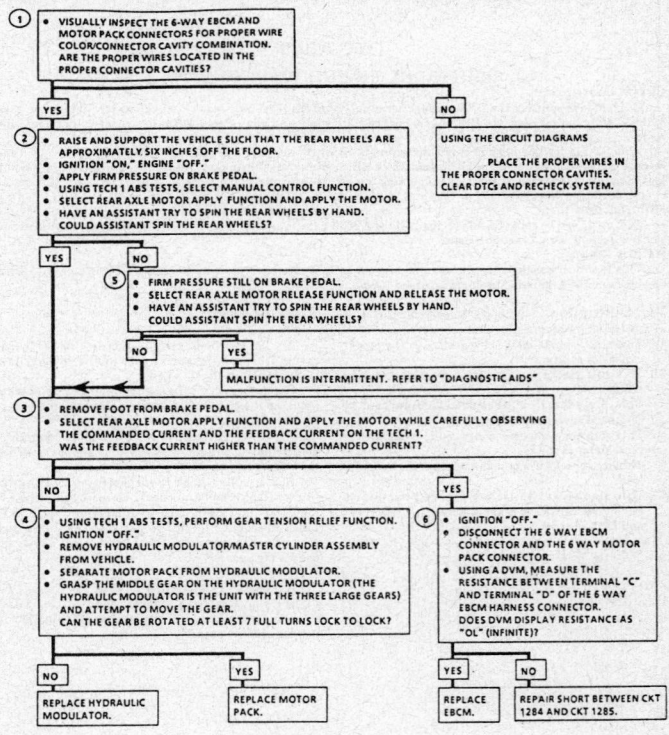

DTC A046
REAR AXLE CHANNEL WILL NOT MOVE

Circuit Description:
This DTC is designed to detect bound-up ESB, a stuck motor, or a seized hydraulic modulator. When the release is commanded during initialization, the ESB should release the motor, resulting in sensed current being less than commanded current (motor is spinning freely). If the motor is not moving, sensed current will be equal to stall current.

Failure Condition:
DTC A046 can be set during normal operation. If the EBCM detects a condition in which it cannot move the motor in either direction, a malfunction exists.

Action Taken:
This malfunction indicates the channel cannot be moved properly. A malfunction DTC is stored, ABS is disabled and the ABS indicator lamp is turned "ON."

Test Description: Number(s) below refer to circled number(s) on the diagnostic chart.
1. This step insures that proper motor circuits are located in the proper connector cavities.
2. This step checks for proper motor movement during apply and release commands from the Tech 1.
3. This step compares EBCM command current to motor feedback current.
4. This step checks for proper hydraulic modulator gear and piston movement.
5. This step verifies that the motor can actually apply when commanded.
6. This test determines if the malfunction is caused by a defective EBCM or by a short circuit.

Diagnostic Aids:

An "Intermittent" malfunction in this DTC may result from a mechanical part of the system that sticks or binds.

The frequency of the malfunction can be checked by using the enhanced diagnostic function of the Tech 1

DTC A046 may set after modulator disassembly if the modulator pistons are positioned at the bottom of their bore.

Depending on the frequency of the malfunction, a physical inspection of the mechanical parts suspected may be necessary.

Any circuitry, that is suspected as causing the intermittent complaint, should be thoroughly checked for backed out terminals, improper mating, broken locks, improperly formed or damaged terminals, poor terminal to wiring connections or physical damage to the wiring harness.

Fig. 140   Code A046, Rear axle channel will not move. 1993

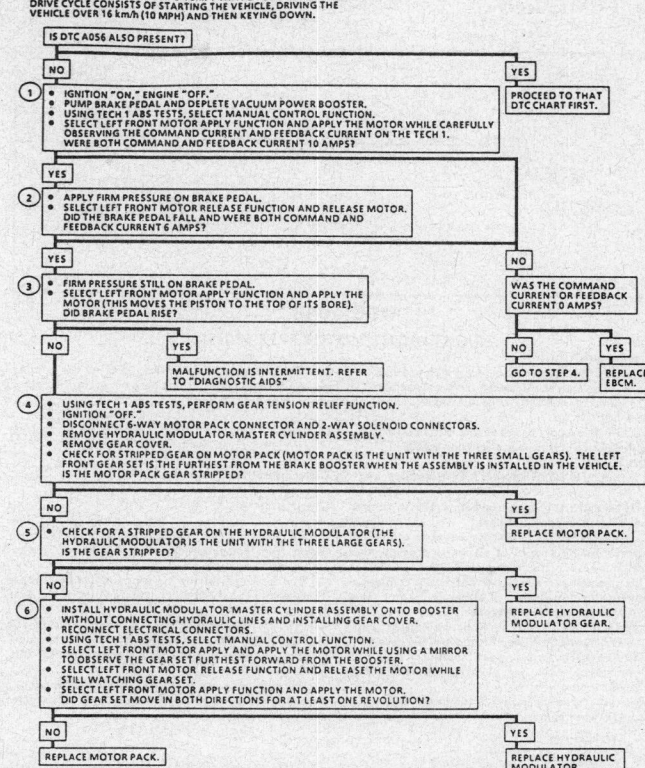

DTC A047
LEFT FRONT MOTOR FREE SPINS

Circuit Description:
This DTC is designed to detect a stripped nut or gear assembly during initialization. During the homing sequence, the piston should reach the top of the bore resulting in a stalled motor. If this does not occur, the motor must be spinning with little or no resistance, indicating a nut/screw or gear failure.

Failure Condition:
DTC A047 can only be set during initialization. If the feedback current is less than the command current for a specified period to time, a malfunction exists.

Action Taken:
A malfunction DTC is stored, ABS is disabled, and the ABS indicator lamp is turned "ON."

Test Description: Number(s) below refer to circled number(s) on the diagnostic chart.
1. This step compares feedback current to command current during apply. If either is 0 amps, the EBCM is not functioning properly.
2. This step compares feedback current to command current during release. If either is 0 amps, the EBCM is not functioning properly.
3. Steps 1, 2 and 3 verify malfunction exists. This step also moves the position to the top of the bore.
4. This step checks for a stripped motor pack gear.
5. This step checks for a stripped hydraulic modulator gear.
6. This test checks the ability of the motor to operate properly when commanded.

Diagnostic Aids:
An "Intermittent" malfunction in this DTC may result from a mechanical part of the system that sticks, binds, or slips.
The frequency of the malfunction can be checked by using the enhanced diagnostic function of the Tech 1
If DTC only fails once and DTC A056 also fails see DTC A056. If intermittent and enhanced diagnostics shows this DTC fails during ABS, see DTC A056.
Depending on the frequency of the malfunction, a physical inspection of the mechanical parts suspected may be necessary.

Fig. 141   Code A047, Left front motor free spins. 1993 except Cutlass Supreme, Grand Prix, Lumina & Regal

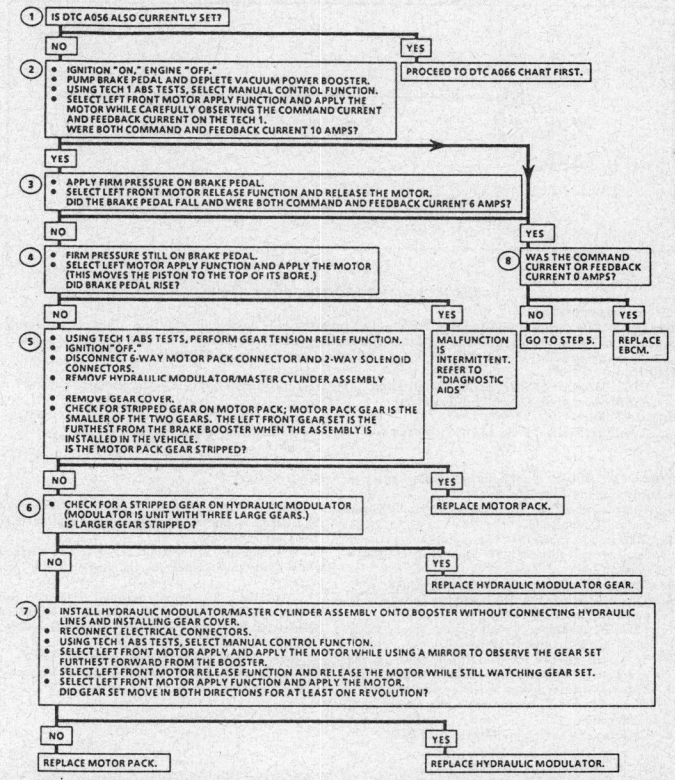

DTC A047
LEFT FRONT MOTOR FREE SPINS

Circuit Description:
This DTC is designed to detect a stripped nut or gear assembly during initialization. During the homing sequence, the piston should reach the top of the bore resulting in a stalled motor. If this does not occur, the motor must be spinning with little or no resistance, indicating a nut/screw or gear malfunction.

Failure Condition:
DTC A047 can only be set during initialization. If the feedback current is less than the command current for a specified period of time, a malfunction exists.

Action Taken:
A malfunction DTC is stored, ABS is disabled, and the ABS indicator lamp is turned "ON."

Test Description: Number(s) below refer to circled number(s) on the diagnostic chart.
1. This step checks to see if the corresponding open motor DTC is also set.
2. This step verifies that the motor was actually applied as command by observing feedback current.
3. This step verifies that the motor can release.
4. This step verifies that the motor can be applied by observing pedal movement.
5. This step checks for a stripped gear on the motor pack (unit with three small gears).
6. This step checks for a stripped gear on the hydraulic modulator (unit with three large gears).
7. This step determines whether the hydraulic modulator or the motor pack has an internal malfunction.
8. This step checks for a malfunctioning EBCM.

Diagnostic Aids:
An "Intermittent" malfunction in this DTC may result from a mechanical part of the system that sticks, binds, or slips.
The frequency of the malfunction can be checked by using the enhanced diagnostic function of the Tech 1
If the DTC only fails once and DTC A056 also fails, refer to DTC A056. If intermittent and enhanced diagnostics shows this DTC fails during ABS, refer to DTC A056.
Depending on the frequency of the malfunction, a physical inspection of the mechanical parts suspected may be necessary.

Fig. 142   Code A047, Left front motor free spins. 1993 Cutlass Supreme, Grand Prix, Lumina & Regal

DTC A048
RIGHT FRONT MOTOR FREE SPINS

Circuit Description:
This DTC is designed to detect a stripped nut or gear assembly during initialization. During the homing sequence, the piston should reach the top of the bore resulting in a stalled motor. If this does not occur, the motor must be spinning with little or no resistance, indicating a nut/screw or gear failure.

Failure Condition:
DTC A048 can only be set during initialization. If the feedback current is less than the command current for a specified period of time, a malfunction exists.

Action Taken:
A malfunction DTC is stored, ABS is disabled, and the ABS indicator lamp is turned "ON."

Test Description: Number(s) below refer to circled number(s) on the diagnostic chart.
1. This step compares feedback current to command current during apply. If either is 0 amps, the EBCM is not functioning properly.
2. This step compares feedback current to command current during release. If either is 0 amps, the EBCM is not functioning properly.
3. Steps 1, 2 and 3 verify malfunction exists. This step also moves the piston to the top of the bore.
4. This step checks for a stripped motor pack gear.
5. This step checks for a stripped hydraulic modulator gear.
6. This test checks the ability of the motor to operate properly when commanded.

Diagnostic Aids:
An "Intermittent" malfunction in this DTC may result from a mechanical part of the system that sticks, binds, or slips.
The frequency of the malfunction can be checked by using the enhanced diagnostic function of the Tech 1
If the DTC only fails once and DTC A061 also fails see DTC A061. If intermittent and enhanced diagnostics shows this DTC fails during ABS, see DTC A061.
Depending on the frequency of the malfunction, a physical inspection of the mechanical parts suspected may be necessary.

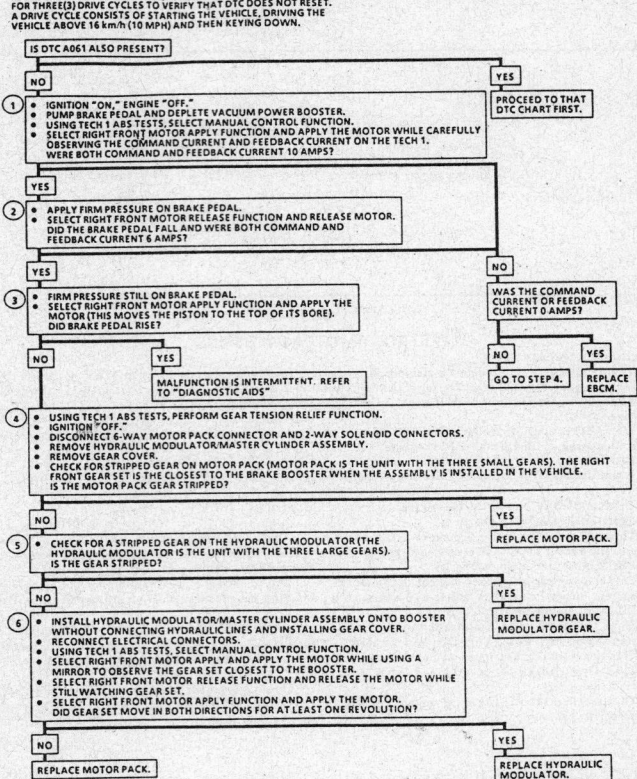

Fig. 143   Code A048, Right front motor free spins. 1993 except Cutlass Supreme, Grand Prix, Lumina & Regal

DTC A048
RIGHT FRONT MOTOR FREE SPINS

Circuit Description:
This DTC is designed to detect a stripped nut or gear assembly during initialization. During the homing sequence, the piston should reach the top of the bore resulting in a stalled motor. If this does not occur, the motor must be spinning with little or no resistance, indicating a nut/screw or gear malfunction.

Failure Condition:
DTC A048 can only be set during initialization. If the feedback current is less than the command current for a specified period of time, a malfunction exists.

Action Taken:
A malfunction DTC is stored, ABS is disabled, and the ABS indicator lamp is turned "ON."

Test Description: Number(s) below refer to circled number(s) on the diagnostic chart.
1. This step checks to see if the corresponding open motor DTC is also set.
2. This step verifies that the motor was actually applied as command by observing feedback current.
3. This step verifies that the motor can release.
4. This step verifies that the motor can be applied by observing pedal movement.
5. This step checks for a stripped gear on the motor pack (unit with three small gears).
6. This step checks for a stripped gear on the hydraulic modulator (unit with three large gears).
7. This step determines whether the hydraulic modulator or the motor pack has an internal malfunction.
8. This step checks for a malfunctioning EBCM.

Diagnostic Aids:
An "Intermittent" malfunction in this DTC may result from a mechanical part of the system that sticks, binds, or slips.
The frequency of the malfunction can be checked by using the enhanced diagnostic function of the Tech 1
If the DTC only fails once and DTC A061 also fails, refer to DTC A061. If intermittent and enhanced diagnostics shows this DTC fails during ABS, refer to DTC A061.
Depending on the frequency of the malfunction, a physical inspection of the mechanical parts suspected may be necessary.

Fig. 144   Code A048, Right front motor free spins. 1993 Cutlass Supreme, Grand Prix, Lumina & Regal

Cavalier & Sunbird

Achieva, Beretta, Corsica, Grand Am & Skylark

DTC A051
REAR AXLE MOTOR FREE SPINS

Circuit Description:

This DTC is designed to detect a stripped nut or gear assembly during initialization. During the homing sequence, the piston should reach the top of the bore resulting in a stalled motor. If this does not occur, the motor must be spinning with little or no resistance, indicating a nut/screw or gear failure.

Failure Condition:

DTC A051 can be set during initialization. If the feedback current is less than the command current for a specified period of time, a malfunction exists.

Action Taken:

A malfunction DTC is stored, ABS is disabled, and the ABS indicator lamp is turned "ON."

Test Description: Number(s) below refer to circled number(s) on the diagnostic chart.

1. This step compares feedback current to command current during apply. If either is 0 amps, the EBCM is not functioning properly.
2. This step compares feedback current to command current during release. If either is 0 amps, the EBCM is not functioning properly.
3. Steps 1, 2 and 3 verify malfunction exists. This step also moves the piston to the top of the bore.
4. This step checks for a stripped motor pack gear.
5. This step checks for a stripped hydraulic modulator gear.
6. This test checks the ability of the motor to operator properly when commanded.

Diagnostic Aids:

An "Intermittent" malfunction in this DTC may result from a mechanical part of the system that sticks, binds, or slips.

The frequency of the malfunction can be checked by using the enhanced diagnostic function of the Tech 1

If DTC only fails once and DTC A064 also fails, see DTC A064. If intermittent and enhanced diagnostics show this DTC fails during ABS, see DTC A064.

Depending on the frequency of the failure, a physical inspection of the mechanical parts suspected may be necessary.

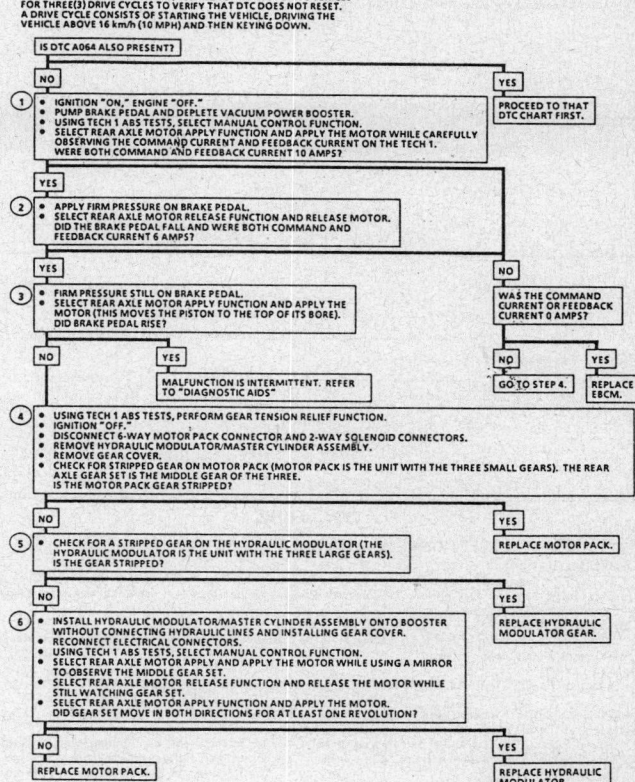

Fig. 145 Code A051, Rear axle motor free spins. 1993 except Cutlass Supreme, Grand Prix, Lumina & Regal

AFTER ALL DIAGNOSIS IS COMPLETE, CLEAR DTCs AND TEST DRIVE VEHICLE FOR THREE (3) DRIVE CYCLES TO VERIFY THAT DTC DOES NOT RESET. A DRIVE CYCLE CONSISTS OF STARTING THE VEHICLE DRIVING OVER 16 km/h (10 MPH), AND THEN KEYING DOWN.

DTC A051
REAR AXLE MOTOR FREE SPINS

Circuit Description:
This DTC is designed to detect a stripped nut or gear assembly during initialization. During the homing sequence, the piston should reach the top of the bore resulting in a stalled motor. If this does not occur, the motor must be spinning with little or no resistance, indicating a nut/screw or gear malfunction.

Failure Condition:
DTC A051 can be set during initialization. If the feedback current is less than the command current for a specified period of time, a malfunction exists.

Action Taken:
A malfunction DTC is stored, ABS is disabled, and the ABS indicator lamp is turned "ON."

Test Description: Number(s) below refer to circled number(s) on the diagnostic chart.
1. This step checks to see if the corresponding open motor DTC is also set.
2. This step verifies that the motor was actually applied as command by observing feedback current.
3. This step verifies that the motor can release.
4. This step verifies that the motor can be applied by observing pedal movement.
5. This step checks for a stripped gear on the motor pack (unit with three small gears).
6. This step checks for a stripped gear on the hydraulic modulator (unit with three large gears).
7. This step determines whether the hydraulic modulator or the motor pack has an internal malfunction.
8. This step checks for a malfunctioning EBCM.

Diagnostic Aids:
An "Intermittent" malfunction in this DTC may result from a mechanical part of the system that sticks, binds, or slips.
The frequency of the malfunction can be checked by using the enhanced diagnostic function of the Tech 1
If the DTC only fails once and DTC A064 also fails, refer to DTC A064. If intermittent and enhanced diagnostics show this DTC fails during ABS, refer to DTC A064.
Depending on the frequency of the malfunction, a physical inspection of the mechanical parts suspected may be necessary.

Fig. 146   Code A051, Rear axle motor free spins. 1993 Cutlass Supreme, Grand Prix, Lumina & Regal

IMPORTANT: EXCESSIVE DRAG OR HIGH RESISTANCE IN THE BASE BRAKE OR SUSPENSION SYSTEM MUST BE INSPECTED AND CORRECTED BEFORE PROCEEDING WITH DTC DIAGNOSIS.

DTC A052
LEFT FRONT CHANNEL IN RELEASE TOO LONG

Circuit Description:
This DTC will diagnose a motor that is energized longer than expected. This could occur if a wheel speed sensor is faulty, the motor does not turn, the left front solenoid mechanically fails open, the brakes are dragging, or the motor wires are crossed.

Failure Condition:
DTC A052 can be set only during an ABS stop. If the EBCM commands the left front channel in release for three seconds, a malfunction exists.

Action Taken:
A malfunction DTC is stored, ABS is disabled, and the ABS indicator lamp is turned "ON."

Test Description: Number(s) below refer to circled number(s) on the diagnostic chart.
1. This step identifies a malfunction in a wheel speed sensor that may cause the system to be in release too long.
2. This step identifies a motor fault as being failed or wired incorrectly.
3. This step checks for a solenoid that may have mechanically failed open.
4. If Step 3 has failed, this serves to isolate the cause of the hydraulic problem, to either the solenoid or the ABS hydraulic modulator.
5. This step is used to release the tension of the motor pack.
6. This step checks for proper operation of hydraulic modulator.

Diagnostic Aids:
An "Intermittent" malfunction may be caused by a mechanical part of the system that sticks or binds.
The frequency of the malfunction can be checked by using the enhanced diagnostic function of the "Tech 1
DTC A052 may fail if on ice and steering wheel is turned to lock during braking. Using Tech 1 perform Hydraulic test to ensure total brake system is functional.
Any circuitry, that is suspected as causing the intermittent complaint, should be thoroughly checked for backed out terminals, improper mating, broken locks, improperly formed or damaged terminals, poor terminal to wiring connections or physical damage to the wiring harness.

AFTER DIAGNOSIS IS COMPLETE, CLEAR DTCs AND TEST DRIVE VEHICLE FOR THREE (3) DRIVE CYCLES TO VERIFY DTC DOES NOT RESET. A DRIVE CYCLE CONSISTS OF STARTING THE VEHICLE, DRIVING OVER 16 km/h (10 MPH) AND THEN KEYING DOWN.

Fig. 147   Code A052, Left front channel release too long. 1993

DTC A053
RIGHT FRONT CHANNEL IN RELEASE TOO LONG

Circuit Description:
This DTC will diagnose a motor that is energized longer than expected. This could occur if a wheel speed sensor is faulty, the motor does not turn, the right front solenoid mechanically fails open, the brakes are dragging, or the motor wires are crossed.

Failure Condition:
DTC A053 can be set only during an ABS stop. If the EBCM commands the right front channel in release for three seconds, a malfunction exists.

Action Taken:
A malfunction DTC is stored, ABS is disabled, and the ABS indicator lamp is turned "ON."

Test Description: Number(s) below refer to circled number(s) on the diagnostic chart.
1. This step identifies a malfunction in a wheel speed sensor that may cause the system to be in release too long.
2. This step identifies a motor fault as being failed or wired incorrectly.
3. This step checks for a solenoid that may have mechanically failed open.
4. If Step 3 has failed, this serves to isolate the cause of the hydraulic problem, to either the solenoid or the ABS hydraulic modulator.
5. This step is used to release the tension of the motor pack prior to removal.
6. This step checks for proper operation of hydraulic modulator.

Diagnostic Aids:

An "Intermittent" malfunction may be caused by a mechanical part of the system that sticks or binds.

The frequency of the malfunction can be checked by using the enhanced diagnostic function of the Tech 1

DTC A053 may fail on ice if steering wheel is turned to lock during braking. Using Tech 1 perform Hydraulic test to ensure total brake system is functional.

Any circuitry, that is suspected as causing the intermittent complaint, should be thoroughly checked for backed out terminals, improper mating, broken locks, improperly formed or damaged terminals, poor terminal to wiring connections or physical damage to the wiring harness.

Fig. 148   Code A053, Right front channel release too long. 1993

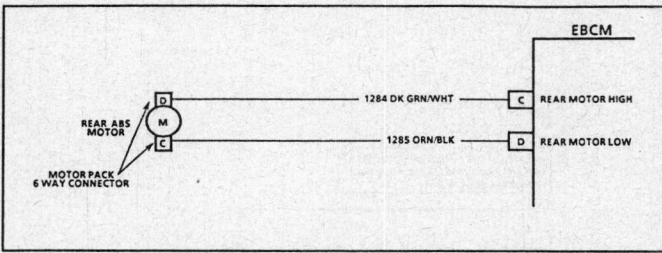

DTC A054
REAR AXLE CHANNEL IN RELEASE TOO LONG

Circuit Description:
This DTC will diagnose a motor that is energized longer than expected. This could occur if a wheel speed sensor is malfunctioning, the motor does not turn, or the motor wires are crossed.

Failure Condition:
DTC A054 can be set only during an ABS stop. If the EBCM commands the rear axle channel in release for three seconds, a malfunction exists.

Action Taken:
A malfunction DTC is stored, ABS is disabled and the ABS indicator lamp is turned "ON."

Test Description: Number(s) below refer to circled number(s) on the diagnostic chart.
1. This step identifies a problem in a wheel speed sensor that may cause the system to be in release too long.
2. This checks for a wheel that may stick or bind because of a mechanical fault.
3. This checks to see if the motor is capable of moving and applying the hydraulic piston for the rear wheels.
4. This step insures that the motor wiring is not crossed.
5. This isolates the fault of a "no-apply" situation to either the motor pack or ABS hydraulic modulator assembly.

Diagnostic Aids:

An "Intermittent" malfunction may be caused by a mechanical part of the system that sticks or binds.

The frequency of the malfunction can be checked by using the enhanced diagnostic function of the Tech 1

Using the Tech 1, perform hydraulic test to ensure total brake system is functional.

Any circuitry, that is suspected as causing the intermittent complaint, should be thoroughly checked for backed out terminals, improper mating, broken locks, improperly formed or damaged terminals, poor terminal to wiring connections or physical damage to the wiring harness.

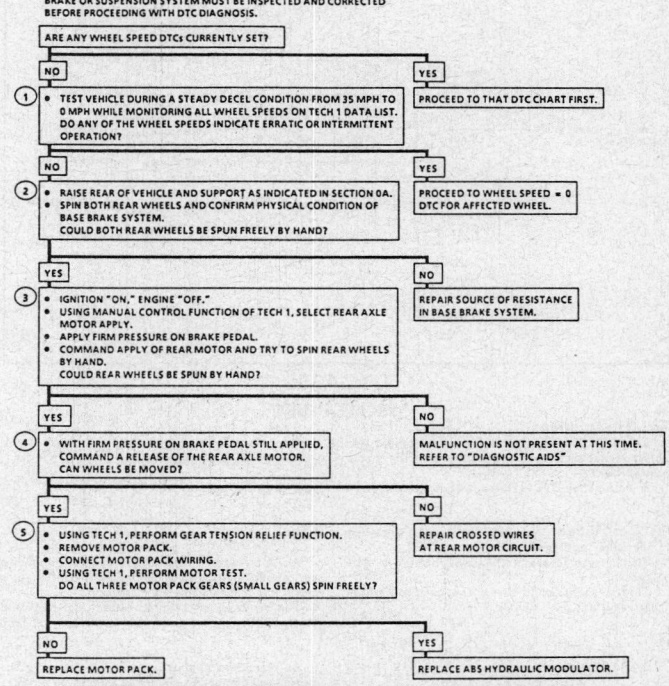

Fig. 149   Code A054, Right front channel release too long. 1993

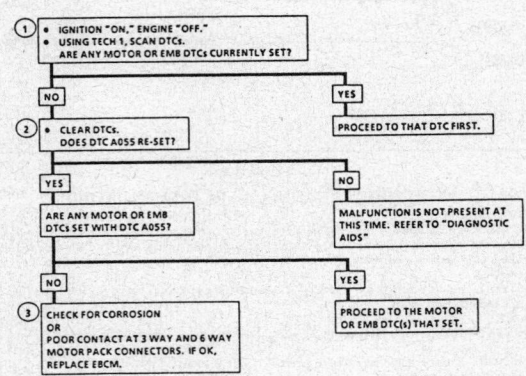

DTC A055
MOTOR DRIVER FAULT DETECTED

Circuit Description:
This DTC identifies a malfunction detected by the MDI custom IC. It also ensures the cause of the malfunction is not a result of a malfunction with the enable relay under a DTC A055 failure. The MDI malfunction tests will be run to identify which circuit has failed and may also cause additional DTCs to set to pinpoint the malfunctioning circuit.

Failed Condition:
DTC A055 is set simultaneously with one or more of DTCs A056 through A072.

Action Taken:
A malfunction DTC is stored, ABS is disabled and the ABS indicator lamp is turned "ON."

Test Description: Number(s) below refer to circled number(s) on the diagnostic chart.
1. This insures the DTC A055 malfunction was not set due to a motor or EMB malfunction.
2. This checks to see if the malfunction is still present.
3. This step insures that DTC A055 was not due to poor terminal contact at the motor pack connector.

Diagnostic Aids:

An "Intermittent" malfunction may be caused by a poor connection, rubbed through wire insulation, or a wire that is broken inside the insulation.
The frequency of the malfunction can be checked by using the enhanced diagnostic function of the Tech 1

Any circuitry, that is suspected as causing the intermittent complaint, should be thoroughly checked for backed out terminals, improper mating, broken locks, improperly formed or damaged terminals, poor terminal to wiring connections or physical damage to the wiring harness.

AFTER DIAGNOSIS IS COMPLETE, CLEAR DTCs AND TEST DRIVE VEHICLE FOR THREE (3) DRIVE CYCLES TO VERIFY DTC DOES NOT RESET. A DRIVE CYCLE CONSISTS OF STARTING THE VEHICLE, DRIVING OVER 16 km/h (10 MPH) AND THEN KEYING DOWN.

Fig. 150   Code A055, EBCM failure. 1993 except Cutlass Supreme, Grand Prix, Lumina & Regal

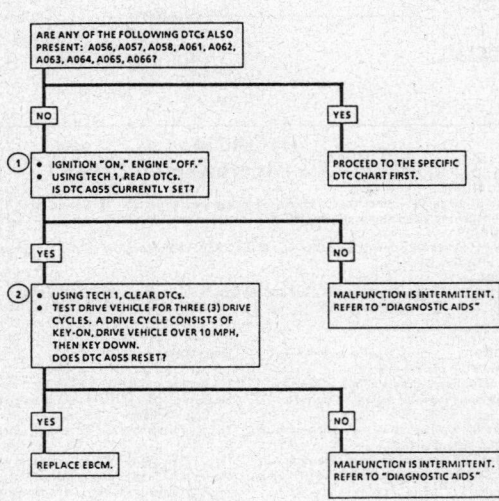

DTC A055
EBCM FAILURE

Circuit Description:
This DTC identifies a malfunction detected by the MDI custom IC. It also insures the cause of the malfunction is not a result of a problem with the enable relay under a DTC A055 malfunction.

Action Taken:
A malfunction DTC is stored, ABS is disabled and the ABS indicator lamp is turned "ON."

Test Description: Number(s) below refer to circled number(s) on the diagnostic chart.
1. This checks to see if the malfunction is still present.
2. This step checks to see if the malfunction is intermittent.

Diagnostic Aids:

An "Intermittent" malfunction may be caused by a poor connection, rubbed through wire insulation, or a wire that is broken inside the insulation.
The frequency of the malfunction can be checked by using the enhanced diagnostic function of the Tech 1

Any circuitry, that is suspected as causing the intermittent complaint, should be thoroughly checked for backed out terminals, improper mating, broken locks, improperly formed or damaged terminals, poor terminal to wiring connections or physical damage to the wiring harness.

Fig. 151   Code A055, EBCM failure. 1993 Cutlass Supreme, Grand Prix, Lumina & Regal

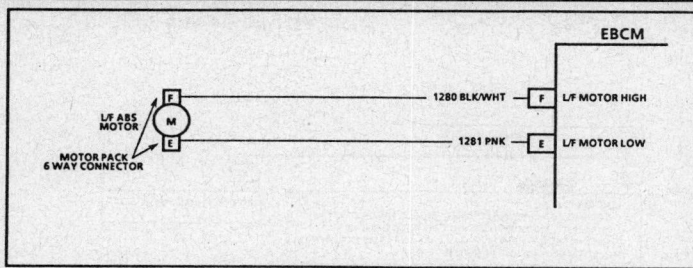

DTC A056
LEFT FRONT MOTOR CIRCUIT OPEN

Circuit Description:
This DTC identifies a motor that cannot be energized due to an open in its circuitry.

Failure Condition:
DTC A056 can be set only when the motor is commanded "OFF." If the EBCM detects an out of range voltage on either of the left front motor circuits indicating an open circuit, a malfunction exists.

Action Taken:
An open motor will not activate when requested. A malfunction DTC is stored, ABS is disabled and the ABS indicator lamp is turned "ON."

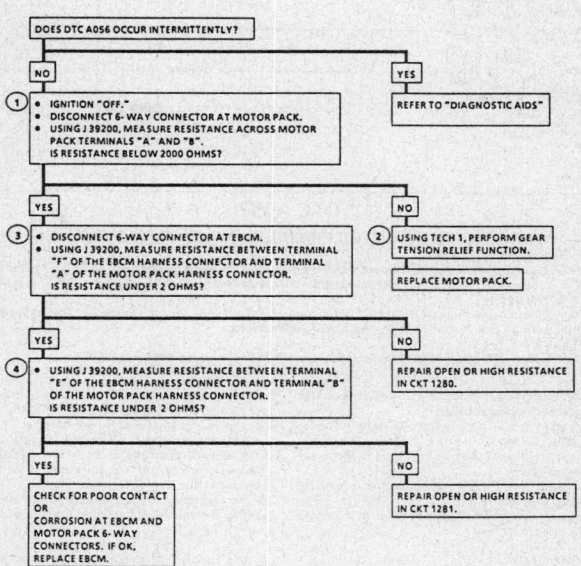

Test Description: Number(s) below refer to circled number(s) on the diagnostic chart.
1. This step checks for proper resistance of the motor.
2. This step checks for an open in the motor "high" circuitry.
3. This step checks for an open in the motor "low" circuitry.

Diagnostic Aids:

Using Tech 1, select manual control function, and exercise motor movement of affected channel in both directions while applying light pressure on the brake pedal.

If erratic or "jumpy" brake pedal movement is detected while performing an "apply" or "release" function of the motor, an intermittent malfunction may be indicated.

An "Intermittent" malfunction may be caused by a poor connection, rubbed through wire insulation, or a wire that is broken inside the insulation.

If the malfunction is not current, wiggle the wires of the affected channel and check if the DTC resets. This will help to pinpoint an intermittent malfunction in the motor circuitry or connections.

The frequency of the malfunction can be checked by using the enhanced diagnostic function of the Tech 1,

Any circuitry, that is suspected as causing the intermittent complaint, should be thoroughly checked for backed out terminals, improper mating, broken locks, improperly formed or damaged terminals, poor terminal to wiring connections or physical damage to the wiring harness.

Fig. 152   Code A056, Left front motor circuit open. 1993 except Cutlass Supreme, Grand Prix, Lumina & Regal

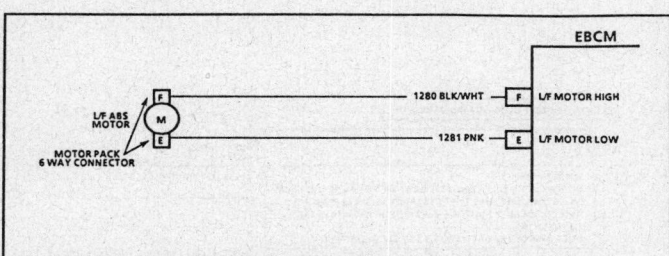

DTC A056
LEFT FRONT MOTOR CIRCUIT OPEN

Circuit Description:
This DTC identifies a motor that cannot be energized due to an open in its circuitry.

Failure Condition:
DTC A056 can be set only when the motor is commanded "OFF." If the EBCM detects an out of range voltage on either of the left front motor circuits indicating an open circuit, a malfunction exists.

Action Taken:
An open motor will not activate when requested. A malfunction DTC is stored, ABS is disabled and the ABS indicator lamp is turned "ON."

Test Description: Number(s) below refer to circled number(s) on the diagnostic chart.
1. This step checks for proper resistance of the motor.
2. This step checks for an open in the motor "high" circuitry.
3. This step checks for an open in the motor "low" circuitry.

Diagnostic Aids:

Using Tech 1, select manual control function, and exercise motor movement of affected channel in both directions while applying light pressure on the brake pedal.

If erratic or "jumpy" brake pedal movement is detected while performing an "apply" or "release" function of the motor, an intermittent malfunction may be indicated.

An "Intermittent" malfunction may be caused by a poor connection, rubbed through wire insulation, or a wire that is broken inside the insulation.

If the malfunction is not current, wiggle the wires of the affected channel and check if the DTC resets. This will help to pinpoint an intermittent malfunction in the motor circuitry or connections.

The frequency of the malfunction can be checked by using the enhanced diagnostic function of the Tech 1

Any circuitry, that is suspected as causing the intermittent complaint, should be thoroughly checked for backed out terminals, improper mating, broken locks, improperly formed or damaged terminals, poor terminal to wiring connections or physical damage to the wiring harness.

Fig. 153   Code A056, Left front motor circuit open. 1993 Cutlass Supreme, Grand Prix, Lumina & Regal

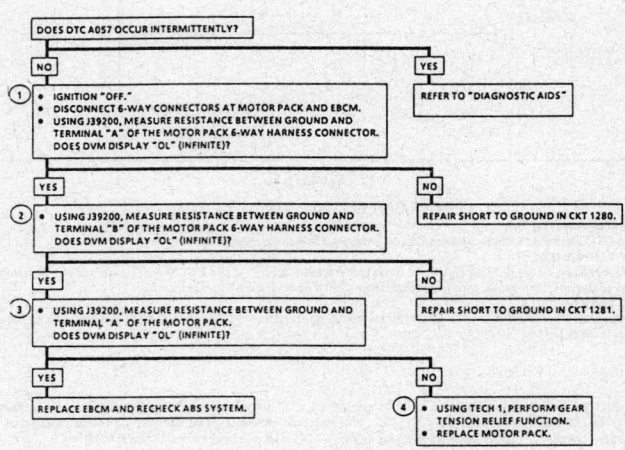

DTC A057
LEFT FRONT MOTOR CIRCUIT SHORTED TO GROUND

Circuit Description:
This DTC identifies a motor circuit that is shorted to ground. This malfunction will not allow the motor to be controlled at the commanded current rate or will cause the driver circuit to allow current directly to ground.

Failure Condition:
DTC A057 can be set anytime. If the EBCM detects an out of range voltage in either of the left front motor circuits indicating a circuit shorted to ground, a malfunction exists.

Action Taken:
A malfunction DTC is stored, ABS is disabled and the ABS indicator lamp is turned "ON."

Test Description: Number(s) below refer to circled number(s) on the diagnostic chart.
1. This step checks for a short to ground in the motor "high" circuitry.
2. This step checks for a short to ground in the motor "low" circuitry.
3. This step checks for a motor that is internally shorted to ground.
4. This step is used to release the tension of the motor pack prior to removal.

Diagnostic Aids:

Using Tech 1, select manual control function, and exercise motor movement of affected channel in both directions while applying light pressure on the brake pedal.

If erratic or "jumpy" brake pedal movement is detected while performing an "apply" or "release" function of the motor, an intermittent malfunction may be indicated.

An "Intermittent" malfunction may be caused by a poor connection, rubbed through wire insulation, or a wire that is broken inside the insulation.

If the malfunction is not current, wiggle the wires of the affected channel and check if the DTC resets. This will help to pinpoint an intermittent malfunction in the motor circuitry or connections.

The frequency of the malfunction can be checked by using the enhanced diagnostic function of the Tech 1

Any circuitry, that is suspected as causing the intermittent complaint, should be thoroughly checked for backed out terminals, improper mating, broken locks, improperly formed or damaged terminals, poor terminal to wiring connections or physical damage to the wiring harness.

AFTER DIAGNOSIS IS COMPLETE, CLEAR DTCs AND TEST DRIVE VEHICLE FOR THREE (3) DRIVE CYCLES TO VERIFY DTC DOES NOT RESET. A DRIVE CYCLE CONSISTS OF STARTING THE VEHICLE, DRIVING OVER 16 km/h (10 MPH) AND THEN KEYING DOWN.

Fig. 154   Code A057, Left front motor circuit shorted to ground. 1993 except Cutlass Supreme, Grand Prix, Lumina & Regal

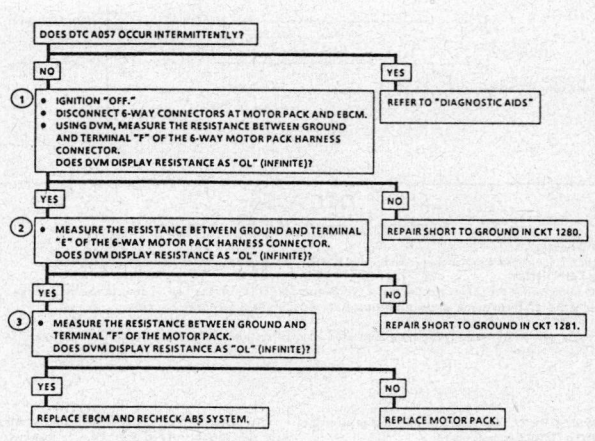

DTC A057
LEFT FRONT MOTOR CIRCUIT SHORTED TO GROUND

Circuit Description:
This DTC identifies a motor circuit that is shorted to ground. This malfunction will not allow the motor to be controlled at the commanded current rate or will cause the driver circuit to allow current directly to ground.

Failure Condition:
DTC A057 can be set anytime. If the EBCM detects an out of range voltage on either of the left front motor circuits indicating a circuit shorted to ground, a malfunction exists.

Action Taken:
A malfunction DTC is stored, ABS is disabled and the ABS indicator lamp is turned "ON."

Test Description: Number(s) below refer to circled number(s) on the diagnostic chart.
1. This step checks for a short to ground in the motor "high" circuitry.
2. This step checks for a short to ground in the motor "low" circuitry.
3. This step checks for a motor that is internally shorted to ground.

Diagnostic Aids:

Using Tech 1, select manual control function, and exercise motor movement of affected channel in both directions while applying light pressure on the brake pedal.

If erratic or "jumpy" brake pedal movement is detected while performing an "apply" or "release" function of the motor, an intermittent malfunction may be indicated.

An "Intermittent" malfunction may be caused by a poor connection, rubbed through wire insulation, or a wire that is broken inside the insulation.

If the malfunction is not current, wiggle the wires of the affected channel and check if the DTC resets. This will help to pinpoint an intermittent malfunction in the motor circuitry or connections.

The frequency of the malfunction can be checked by using the enhanced diagnostic function of the Tech 1

Any circuitry, that is suspected as causing the intermittent complaint, should be thoroughly checked for backed out terminals, improper mating, broken locks, improperly formed or damaged terminals, poor terminal to wiring connections or physical damage to the wiring harness.

* AFTER ALL DIAGNOSIS IS COMPLETE, CLEAR DTCs AND TEST DRIVE VEHICLE FOR THREE (3) DRIVE CYCLES TO VERIFY THAT DTC DOES NOT RESET. A DRIVE CYCLE CONSISTS OF STARTING THE VEHICLE, DRIVING OVER 16 km/h (10 MPH), AND THEN KEYING DOWN.

Fig. 155   Code A057, Left front motor circuit shorted to ground. 1993 Cutlass Supreme, Grand Prix, Lumina & Regal

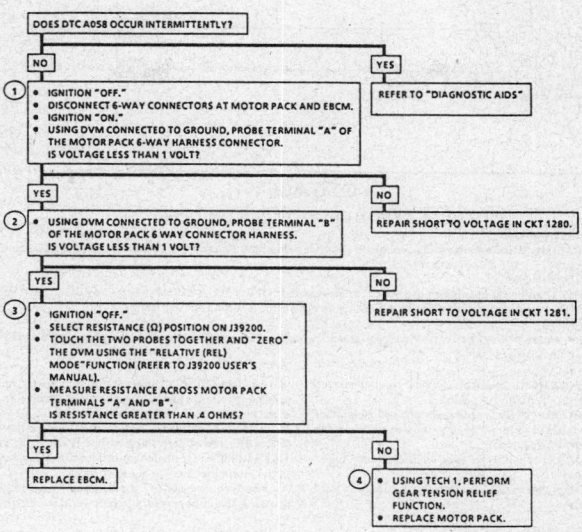

DTC A058

LEFT FRONT MOTOR CIRCUIT SHORTED TO BATTERY OR MOTOR SHORTED

Circuit Description:

This DTC identifies a motor circuit that is shorted to battery or a motor that has low or no resistance. This malfunction will not allow the motor to be controlled at the commanded current rate or will cause the motor to turn in the opposite direction, or not at all.

Failure Condition:

DTC A058 can be set anytime. If the EBCM detects an out of range voltage in either of the left front motor circuits indicating a circuit shorted to battery or a motor shorted, a malfunction exists.

Action Taken:

A malfunction DTC is stored, ABS is disabled and the ABS indicator lamp is turned "ON."

Test Description: Number(s) below refer to circled number(s) on the diagnostic chart.

1. This step checks for a short to voltage in the motor "high" circuitry.
2. This step checks for a short to voltage in the motor "low" circuitry.
3. This step checks for a motor that is internally shorted.
4. This step is used to release the tension of the motor pack prior to removal.

Diagnostic Aids:

Using Tech 1, select manual control function, and exercise motor movement of affected channel in both directions while applying light pressure on the brake pedal.

If erratic or "jumpy" brake pedal movement is detected while performing an "apply" or "release" function of the motor, an intermittent malfunction may be indicated.

An "Intermittent" malfunction may be caused by a poor connection, rubbed through wire insulation, or a wire that is broken inside the insulation.

If the malfunction is not current, wiggle the wires of the affected channel and check if the DTC resets. This will help to pinpoint an intermittent malfunction in the motor circuitry or connections.

The frequency of the malfunction can be checked by using the enhanced diagnostic function of the Tech 1

If DTC A038 sets as a current DTC and A058 is an infrequent history DTC, see DTC A038 diagnostics.

Any circuitry, that is suspected as causing the intermittent complaint, should be thoroughly checked for backed out terminals, improper mating, broken locks, improperly formed or damaged terminals, poor terminal to wiring connections or physical damage to the wiring harness.

Fig. 156 Code A058, Left front motor circuit shorted to battery or motor shorted. 1993 except Cutlass Supreme, Grand Prix, Lumina & Regal

---

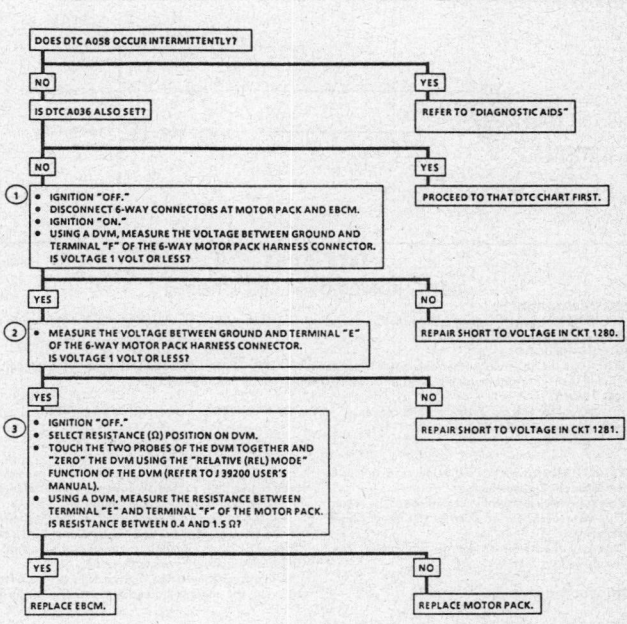

DTC A058

LEFT FRONT MOTOR CIRCUIT SHORTED TO BATTERY OR MOTOR SHORTED

Circuit Description:

This DTC identifies a motor circuit that is shorted to battery or a motor that has low or no resistance. This malfunction will not allow the motor to be controlled at the commanded current rate or will cause the motor to turn in the opposite direction, or not at all.

Failure Condition:

DTC A058 can be set only when the motor is commanded "OFF." If the EBCM detects an out of range voltage on either of the left front motor circuits indicating a circuit shorted to battery or a motor shorted, a malfunction exists.

Action Taken:

A malfunction DTC is stored, ABS is disabled and the ABS indicator lamp is turned "ON."

Test Description: Number(s) below refer to circled number(s) on the diagnostic chart.

1. This step checks for a short to voltage in the motor "high" circuitry.
2. This step checks for a short to voltage in the motor "low" circuitry.
3. This step checks for a motor that is internally shorted.

Diagnostic Aids:

Using Tech 1, select manual control function, and exercise motor movement of affected channel in both directions while applying light pressure on the brake pedal.

If erratic or "jumpy" brake pedal movement is detected while performing an "apply" or "release" function of the motor, an intermittent malfunction may be indicated.

An "Intermittent" malfunction may be caused by a poor connection, rubbed through wire insulation, or a wire that is broken inside the insulation.

If the malfunction is not current, wiggle the wires of the affected channel and check if the DTC resets. This will help to pinpoint an intermittent malfunction in the motor circuitry or connections.

The frequency of the malfunction can be checked by using the enhanced diagnostic function of the Tech 1

Any circuitry, that is suspected as causing the intermittent complaint, should be thoroughly checked for backed out terminals, improper mating, broken locks, improperly formed or damaged terminals, poor terminal to wiring connections or physical damage to the wiring harness.

Fig. 157 Code A058, Left front motor circuit shorted to battery or motor shorted. 1993 Cutlass Supreme, Grand Prix, Lumina & Regal

---

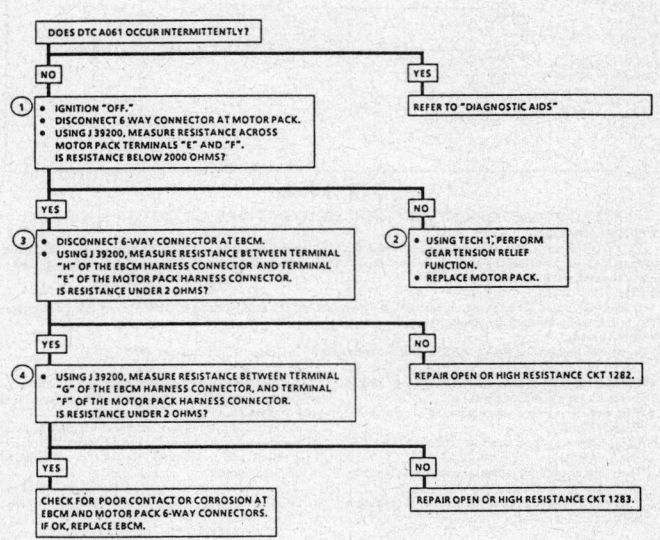

DTC A061
RIGHT FRONT MOTOR CIRCUIT OPEN

Circuit Description:
This DTC identifies a motor that cannot be energized due to an open in its circuitry. This malfunction will not allow proper front ABS operation.

Failure Condition:
DTC A061 can be set only when the motor is commanded "OFF." If the EBCM detects an out of range voltage in either of the right front motor circuits indicating an open circuit, a malfunction exists.

Action Taken:
An open motor will not activate when requested. A malfunction DTC is stored, ABS is disabled and the ABS indicator lamp is turned "ON."

Test Description: Number(s) below refer to circled number(s) on the diagnostic chart.
1. This step checks for proper resistance of the motor.
2. This step is used to release the tension of the motor pack prior to removal.
3. This step checks for an open in the motor "high" circuitry.
4. This step checks for an open in the motor "low" circuitry.

Diagnostic Aids:

Using Tech 1, select manual control function, and exercise motor movement of affected channel in both directions while applying light pressure on the brake pedal.

If erratic or "jumpy" brake pedal movement is detected while performing an "apply" or "release" function of the motor, an intermittent malfunction may be indicated.

An "Intermittent" malfunction may be caused by a poor connection, rubbed through wire insulation, or a wire that is broken inside the insulation.

If the malfunction is not current, wiggle the wires of the affected channel and check if the DTC resets. This will help to pinpoint an intermittent malfunction in the motor circuitry or connections.

The frequency of the malfunction can be checked by using the enhanced diagnostic function of the Tech 1

Any circuitry, that is suspected as causing the intermittent complaint, should be thoroughly checked for backed out terminals; improper mating, broken locks, improperly formed or damaged terminals, poor terminal to wiring connections or physical damage to the wiring harness.

Fig. 158   Code A061, Right front motor circuit open. 1993 except Cutlass Supreme, Grand Prix, Lumina & Regal

---

DTC A061
RIGHT FRONT MOTOR CIRCUIT OPEN

Circuit Description:
This DTC identifies a motor that cannot be energized due to an open in its circuitry. This malfunction will not allow proper front ABS operation.

Failure Condition:
DTC A061 can be set only when the motor is commanded "OFF." If the EBCM detects an out of range voltage on either of the right front motor circuits indicating an open circuit, a malfunction exists.

Action Taken:
An open motor will not activate when requested. A malfunction DTC is stored, ABS is disabled and the ABS indicator lamp is turned "ON."

Test Description: Number(s) below refer to circled number(s) on the diagnostic chart.
1. This step checks for proper resistance of the motor.
2. This step checks for an open in the motor "high" circuitry.
3. This step checks for an open in the motor "low" circuitry.

Diagnostic Aids:

Using Tech 1, select manual control function, and exercise motor movement of affected channel in both directions while applying light pressure on the brake pedal.

If erratic or "jumpy" brake pedal movement is detected while performing an "apply" or "release" function of the motor, an intermittent malfunction may be indicated.

An "Intermittent" malfunction may be caused by a poor connection, rubbed through wire insulation, or a wire that is broken inside the insulation.

If the malfunction is not current, wiggle the wires of the affected channel and check if the DTC resets. This will help to pinpoint an intermittent malfunction in the motor circuitry or connections.

The frequency of the malfunction can be checked by using the enhanced diagnostic function of the Tech 1

Any circuitry, that is suspected as causing the intermittent complaint, should be thoroughly checked for backed out terminals, improper mating, broken locks, improperly formed or damaged terminals, poor terminal to wiring connections or physical damage to the wiring harness.

Fig. 159   Code A061, Right front motor circuit open. 1993 Cutlass Supreme, Grand Prix, Lumina & Regal

---

DTC A062
RIGHT FRONT MOTOR CIRCUIT SHORTED TO GROUND

Circuit Description:

This DTC identifies a motor circuit that is shorted to ground. This malfunction will not allow the motor to be controlled at the commanded current rate or will cause the motor driver circuit to allow current directly to ground.

Failure Condition:

DTC A062 can be set anytime. If the EBCM detects an out of range voltage in either of the right front motor circuits indicating a circuit shorted to ground, a malfunction exists.

Action Taken:

A malfunction DTC is stored, ABS is disabled and the ABS indicator lamp is turned "ON."

Test Description: Number(s) below refer to circled number(s) on the diagnostic chart.
1. This step checks for a short to ground in the motor "high" circuitry.
2. This step checks for a short to ground in the motor "low" circuitry.
3. This step checks for a motor that is internally shorted to ground.
4. This step is used to release the tension of the motor pack prior to removal.

Diagnostic Aids:

Using Tech 1, select manual control function, and exercise motor movement of affected channel in both directions while applying light pressure on the brake pedal.

If erratic or "jumpy" brake pedal movement is detected while performing an "apply" or "release" function of the motor, an intermittent malfunction may be indicated.

An "Intermittent" malfunction may be caused by a poor connection, rubbed through wire insulation, or a wire that is broken inside the insulation.

If the malfunction is not current, wiggle the wires of the affected channel and check if the DTC resets. This will help to pinpoint an intermittent malfunction in the motor circuitry or connections.

The frequency of the malfunction can be checked by using the enhanced diagnostic function of the Tech 1

Any circuitry, that is suspected as causing the intermittent complaint, should be thoroughly checked for backed out terminals, improper mating, broken locks, improperly formed or damaged terminals, poor terminal to wiring connections or physical damage to the wiring harness.

AFTER DIAGNOSIS IS COMPLETE, CLEAR DTCs AND TEST DRIVE VEHICLE FOR THREE (3) DRIVE CYCLES TO VERIFY DTC DOES NOT RESET. A DRIVE CYCLE CONSISTS OF STARTING THE VEHICLE, DRIVING OVER 16 km/h (10 MPH) AND THEN KEYING DOWN.

Fig. 160   Code A062, Right front motor circuit shorted to ground. 1993 except Cutlass Supreme, Grand Prix, Lumina & Regal

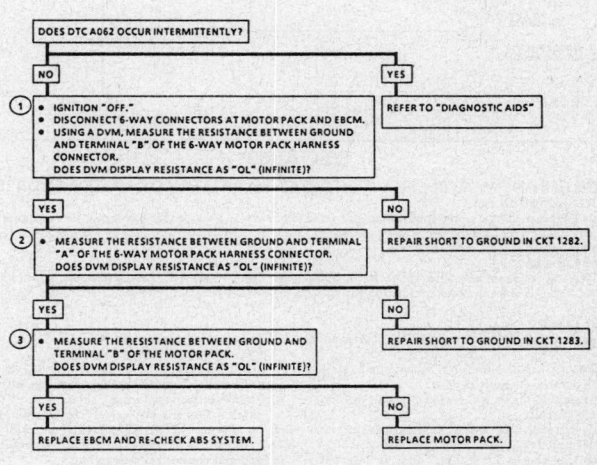

DTC A062
RIGHT FRONT MOTOR CIRCUIT SHORTED TO GROUND

Circuit Description:

This DTC identifies a motor circuit that is shorted to ground. This malfunction will not allow the motor to be controlled at the commanded current rate or will cause the motor driver circuit to allow current directly to ground.

Failure Condition:

DTC A062 can be set anytime. If the EBCM detects an out of range voltage on either of the right front motor circuits indicating a circuit shorted to ground, a malfunction exists.

Action Taken:

A malfunction DTC is stored, ABS is disabled and the ABS indicator lamp is turned "ON."

Test Description: Number(s) below refer to circled number(s) on the diagnostic chart.
1. This step checks for a short to ground in the motor "high" circuitry.
2. This step checks for a short to ground in the motor "low" circuitry.
3. This step checks for a motor that is internally shorted to ground.

Diagnostic Aids:

Using Tech 1, select manual control function, and exercise motor movement of affected channel in both directions while applying light pressure on the brake pedal.

If erratic or "jumpy" brake pedal movement is detected while performing an "apply" or "release" function of the motor, an intermittent malfunction may be indicated.

An "Intermittent" malfunction may be caused by a poor connection, rubbed through wire insulation, or a wire that is broken inside the insulation.

If the malfunction is not current, wiggle the wires of the affected channel and check if the DTC resets. This will help to pinpoint an intermittent malfunction in the motor circuitry or connections.

The frequency of the malfunction can be checked by using the enhanced diagnostic function of the Tech 1

Any circuitry, that is suspected as causing the intermittent complaint, should be thoroughly checked for backed out terminals, improper mating, broken locks, improperly formed or damaged terminals, poor terminal to wiring connections or physical damage to the wiring harness.

* AFTER ALL DIAGNOSIS IS COMPLETE, CLEAR DTCs AND TEST DRIVE VEHICLE FOR THREE (3) DRIVE CYCLES TO VERIFY THAT DTC DOES NOT RESET. A DRIVE CYCLE CONSISTS OF STARTING THE VEHICLE, DRIVING OVER 16 km/h (10 MPH), AND THEN KEYING DOWN.

Fig. 161   Code A062, Right front motor circuit shorted to ground. 1993 Cutlass Supreme, Grand Prix, Lumina & Regal

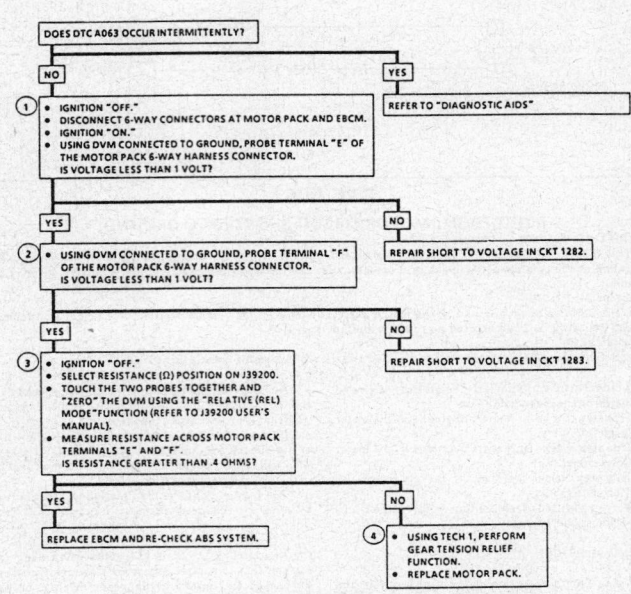

DTC A063

RIGHT FRONT MOTOR CIRCUIT SHORTED TO BATTERY OR MOTOR SHORTED

Circuit Description:
This DTC identifies a motor circuit that is shorted to battery or a motor that has low or no resistance. This malfunction will not allow the motor to be controlled at the commanded current rate or will cause the motor to turn in the opposite direction or not at all.

Failure Condition:
DTC A063 can be set anytime. If the EBCM detects an out of range voltage in either of the right front motor circuits indicating a circuit shorted to battery or a motor shorted, a malfunction exists.

Action Taken:
A malfunction DTC is stored, ABS is disabled and the ABS indicator lamp is turned "ON."

Test Description: Number(s) below refer to circled number(s) on the diagnostic chart.
1. This step checks for a short to voltage in the motor "high" circuitry.
2. This step checks for a short to voltage in the motor "low" circuitry.
3. This step checks for a motor that is internally shorted.
4. This test is used to release the tension of the motor pack prior to removal.

Diagnostic Aids:

Using Tech 1, select manual control function, and exercise motor movement of affected channel in both directions while applying light pressure on the brake pedal.

If erratic or "jumpy" brake pedal movement is detected while performing an "apply" or "release" function of the motor, an intermittent malfunction may be indicated.

An "Intermittent" malfunction may be caused by a poor connection, rubbed through wire insulation, or a wire that is broken inside the insulation.

If the malfunction is not current, wiggle the wires of the affected channel and check if the DTC resets. This will help to pinpoint an intermittent malfunction in the motor circuitry or connections.

The frequency of the malfunction can be checked by using the enhanced diagnostic function of the Tech 1

If DTC A041 sets as a current DTC and A063 is infrequent history DTC, see DTC A041 for diagnosis.

Any circuitry, that is suspected as causing the intermittent complaint, should be thoroughly checked for backed out terminals, improper mating, broken locks, improperly formed or damaged terminals, poor terminal to wiring connections or physical damage to the wiring harness.

Fig. 162   Code A063, Right front motor circuit shorted to battery or motor shorted. 1993 except Cutlass Supreme, Grand Prix, Lumina & Regal

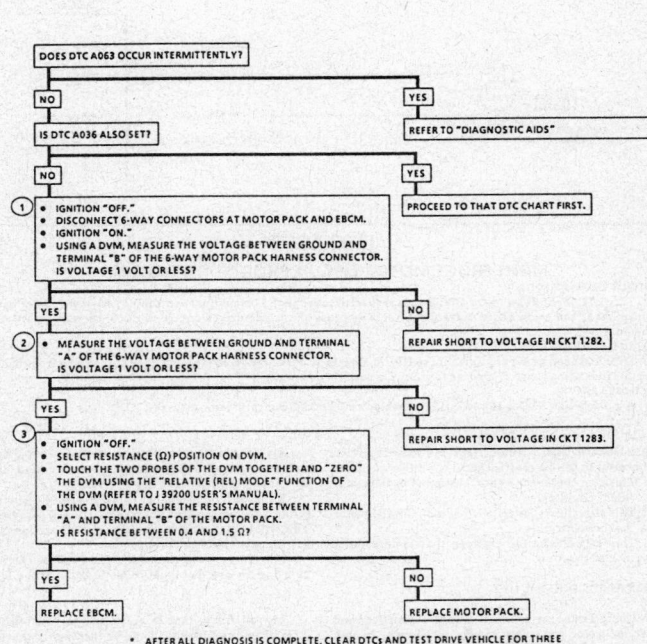

DTC A063

RIGHT FRONT MOTOR CIRCUIT SHORTED TO BATTERY OR MOTOR SHORTED

Circuit Description:
This DTC identifies a motor circuit that is shorted to battery or a motor that has low or no resistance. This malfunction will not allow the motor to be controlled at the commanded current rate or will cause the motor to turn in the opposite direction or not at all.

Failure Condition:
DTC A063 can be set only when the motor is commanded "OFF." If the EBCM detects an out of range voltage on either of the right front motor circuits indicating a circuit shorted to battery or a motor shorted, a malfunction exists.

Action Taken:
A malfunction DTC is stored, ABS is disabled and the ABS indicator lamp is turned "ON."

Test Description: Number(s) below refer to circled number(s) on the diagnostic chart.
1. This step checks for a short to voltage in the motor "high" circuitry.
2. This step checks for a short to voltage in the motor "low" circuitry.
3. This step checks for a motor that is internally shorted.

Diagnostic Aids:

Using Tech 1, select manual control function, and exercise motor movement of affected channel in both directions while applying light pressure on the brake pedal.

If erratic or "jumpy" brake pedal movement is detected while performing an "apply" or "release" function of the motor, an intermittent malfunction may be indicated.

An "Intermittent" malfunction may be caused by a poor connection, rubbed through wire insulation, or a wire that is broken inside the insulation.

If the malfunction is not current, wiggle the wires of the affected channel and check if the DTC resets. This will help to pinpoint an intermittent malfunction in the motor circuitry or connections.

The frequency of the malfunction can be checked by using the enhanced diagnostic function of the Tech 1

Any circuitry, that is suspected as causing the intermittent complaint, should be thoroughly checked for backed out terminals, improper mating, broken locks, improperly formed or damaged terminals, poor terminal to wiring connections or physical damage to the wiring harness.

Fig. 163   Code A063, Right front motor circuit shorted to battery or motor shorted. 1993 Cutlass Supreme, Grand Prix, Lumina & Regal

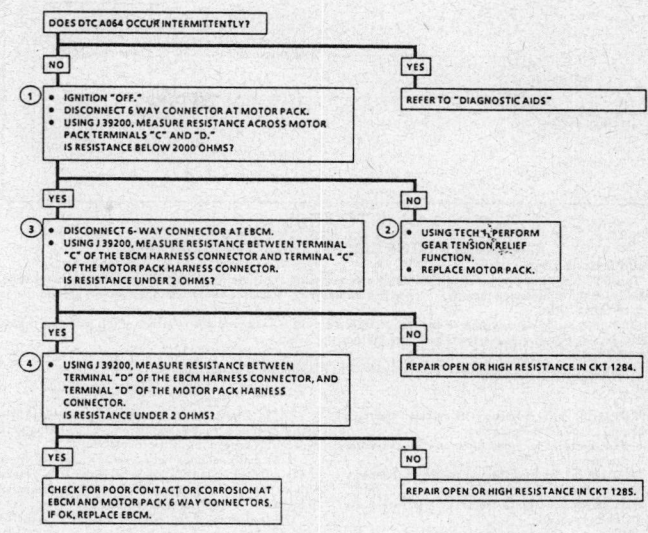

DTC A064
REAR AXLE MOTOR CIRCUIT OPEN

Circuit Description:
This DTC identifies a motor that cannot be energized due to an open in its circuitry. This malfunction will not allow proper rear ABS operation.

Failure Condition:
DTC A064 can be set only when the motor is commanded "OFF." If the EBCM detects an out of range voltage in either of the rear axle motor circuits indicating an open circuit, a malfunction exists.

Action Taken:
An open motor will not activate when requested. A malfunction DTC is stored, ABS is disabled and the ABS indicator lamp is turned "ON."

Test Description: Number(s) below refer to circled number(s) on the diagnostic chart.
1. This checks for an open circuit in the motor.
2. This step is used to release the tension of the motor pack prior to removal.
3. This step checks for an open in the motor "high" circuitry.
4. This step checks for an open in the motor "low" circuitry.

Diagnostic Aids:

Using Tech 1, select manual control function, and exercise motor movement of affected channel in both directions while applying light pressure on the brake pedal.

If erratic or "jumpy" brake pedal movement is detected while performing an "apply" or "release" function of the motor, an intermittent malfunction may be indicated.

An "Intermittent" malfunction may be caused by a poor connection, rubbed through wire insulation, or a wire that is broken inside the insulation.

If the malfunction is not current, wiggle the wires of the affected channel and check if the DTC resets. This will help to pinpoint an intermittent malfunction in the motor circuitry or connections.

The frequency of the malfunction can be checked by using the enhanced diagnostic function of the Tech 1

Any circuitry, that is suspected as causing the intermittent complaint, should be thoroughly checked for backed out terminals, improper mating, broken locks, improperly formed or damaged terminals, poor terminal to wiring connections or physical damage to the wiring harness.

Fig. 164   Code A064, Rear axle motor circuit open. 1993 except Cutlass Supreme, Grand Prix, Lumina & Regal

DTC A064
REAR AXLE MOTOR CIRCUIT OPEN

Circuit Description:
This DTC identifies a motor that cannot be energized due to an open in its circuitry. This malfunction will not allow proper rear ABS operation.

Failure Condition:
DTC A064 can be set only when the motor is commanded "OFF." If the EBCM detects an out of range voltage on either of the rear axle motor circuits indicating an open circuit, a malfunction exists.

Action Taken:
An open motor will not activate when requested. A malfunction DTC is stored, ABS is disabled and the ABS indicator lamp is turned "ON."

Test Description: Number(s) below refer to circled number(s) on the diagnostic chart.
1. This checks for proper resistance of the motor.
2. This step checks for an open in the motor "high" circuitry.
3. This step checks for an open in the motor "low" circuitry.

Diagnostic Aids:

Using Tech 1, select manual control function, and exercise motor movement of affected channel in both directions while applying light pressure on the brake pedal.

If erratic or "jumpy" brake pedal movement is detected while performing an "apply" or "release" function of the motor, an intermittent malfunction may be indicated.

An "Intermittent" malfunction may be caused by a poor connection, rubbed through wire insulation, or a wire that is broken inside the insulation.

If the malfunction is not current, wiggle the wires of the affected channel and check if the DTC resets. This will help to pinpoint an intermittent malfunction in the motor circuitry or connections.

The frequency of the malfunction can be checked by using the enhanced diagnostic function of the Tech 1

Any circuitry, that is suspected as causing the intermittent complaint, should be thoroughly checked for backed out terminals, improper mating, broken locks, improperly formed or damaged terminals, poor terminal to wiring connections or physical damage to the wiring harness.

Fig. 165   Code A064, Rear axle motor circuit open. 1993 Cutlass Supreme, Grand Prix, Lumina & Regal

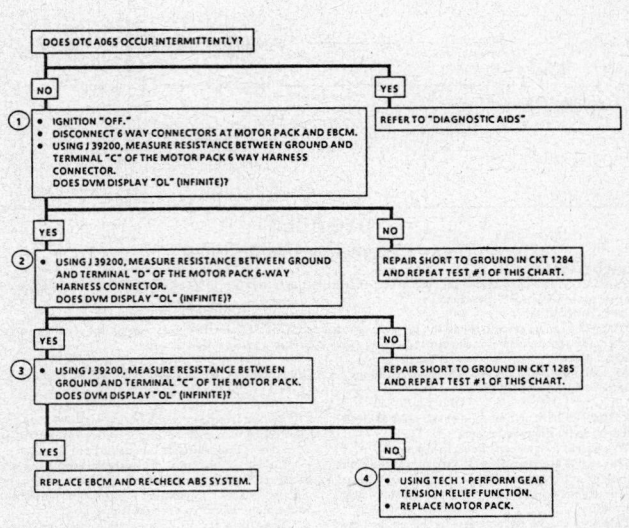

DTC A065
REAR AXLE MOTOR CIRCUIT SHORTED TO GROUND

Circuit Description:

This DTC identifies a motor circuit that is shorted to ground. This malfunction will not allow the motor to be controlled at the commanded current rate or will cause the driver circuit to allow current directly to ground.

Failure Condition:

DTC A065 can be set anytime. If the EBCM detects an out of range voltage in either of the rear axle motor circuits indicating a circuit shorted to ground, a malfunction exists.

Action Taken:

A malfunction DTC is stored, ABS is disabled and the ABS indicator lamp is turned "ON."

Test Description: Number(s) below refer to circled number(s) on the diagnostic chart.
1. This step checks for a short to ground in the motor "high" circuitry.
2. This step checks for a short to ground in the motor "low" circuitry.
3. This step checks for a motor that is internally shorted to ground.
4. This step is used to release the tension of the motor pack prior to removal.

Diagnostic Aids:

Using Tech 1, select manual control function, and exercise motor movement of affected channel in both directions while applying light pressure on the brake pedal.

If erratic or "jumpy" brake pedal movement is detected while performing an "apply" or "release" function of the motor, an intermittent malfunction may be indicated.

An "Intermittent" malfunction may be caused by a poor connection, rubbed through wire insulation, or a wire that is broken inside the insulation.

If the malfunction is not current, wiggle the wires of the affected channel and check if the DTC resets. This will help to pinpoint an intermittent malfunction in the motor circuitry or connections.

The frequency of the problem can be checked by using the enhanced diagnostic function of the Tech 1

Any circuitry, that is suspected as causing the intermittent complaint, should be thoroughly checked for backed out terminals, improper mating, broken locks, improperly formed or damaged terminals, poor terminal to wiring connections or physical damage to the wiring harness.

Fig. 166   Code A065, Rear axle motor circuit shorted to ground. 1993 except Cutlass Supreme, Grand Prix, Lumina & Regal

---

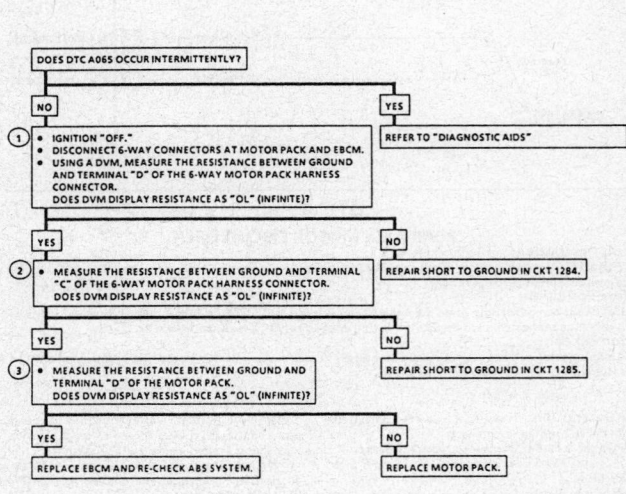

DTC A065
REAR AXLE MOTOR CIRCUIT SHORTED TO GROUND

Circuit Description:

This DTC identifies a motor circuit that is shorted to ground. This malfunction will not allow the motor to be controlled at the commanded current rate or will cause the driver circuit to allow current directly to ground.

Failure Condition:

DTC A065 can be set anytime. If the EBCM detects an out of range voltage on either of the rear axle motor circuits indicating a circuit shorted to ground, a malfunction exists.

Action Taken:

A malfunction DTC is stored, ABS is disabled and the ABS indicator lamp is turned "ON."

Test Description: Number(s) below refer to circled number(s) on the diagnostic chart.
1. This step checks for a short to ground in the motor "high" circuitry.
2. This step checks for a short to ground in the motor "low" circuitry.
3. This step checks for a motor that is internally shorted to ground.

Diagnostic Aids:

Using Tech 1, select manual control function, and exercise motor movement of affected channel in both directions while applying light pressure on the brake pedal.

If erratic or "jumpy" brake pedal movement is detected while performing an "apply" or "release" function of the motor, an intermittent malfunction may be indicated.

An "Intermittent" malfunction may be caused by a poor connection, rubbed through wire insulation, or a wire that is broken inside the insulation.

If the malfunction is not current, wiggle the wires of the affected channel and check if the DTC resets. This will help to pinpoint an intermittent malfunction in the motor circuitry or connections.

The frequency of the malfunction can be checked by using the enhanced diagnostic function of the Tech 1

Any circuitry, that is suspected as causing the intermittent complaint, should be thoroughly checked for backed out terminals, improper mating, broken locks, improperly formed or damaged terminals, poor terminal to wiring connections or physical damage to the wiring harness.

Fig. 167   Code A065, Rear axle motor circuit shorted to ground. 1993 Cutlass Supreme, Grand Prix, Lumina & Regal

---

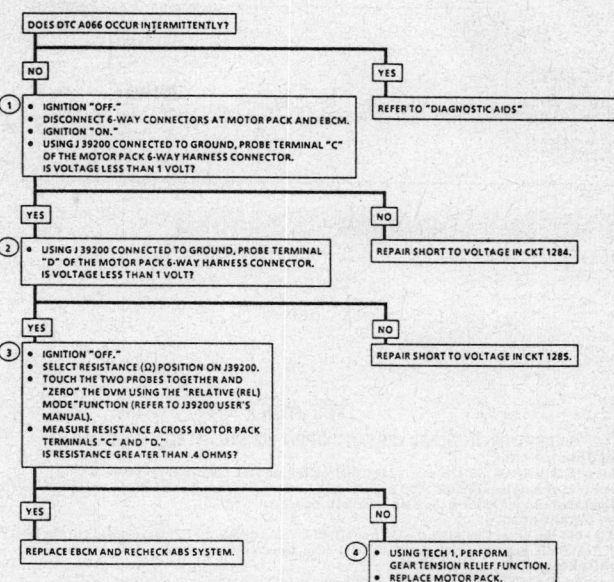

DTC A066

REAR AXLE MOTOR CIRCUIT SHORTED TO BATTERY OR MOTOR SHORTED

Circuit Description:

This DTC identifies a motor circuit that is shorted to battery or a motor that has low or zero resistance. This malfunction will not allow the motor to be controlled at the commanded current rate or will cause the motor to turn in the opposite direction or not turn at all.

Failure Condition:

DTC A066 can be set anytime. If the EBCM detects an out of range voltage in either of the rear axle motor circuits indicating a circuit shorted to battery or a motor shorted, a malfunction exists.

Action Taken:

A malfunction DTC is stored, ABS is disabled and the ABS indicator lamp is turned "ON."

Test Description: Number(s) below refer to circled number(s) on the diagnostic chart.
1. This step checks for a short to voltage in the motor "high" circuitry.
2. This step checks for a short to voltage in the motor "low" circuitry.
3. This step checks for a motor that is internally shorted.
4. This step is used to release the tension of the motor pack prior to removal.

Diagnostic Aids:

Using Tech 1, select manual control function, and exercise motor movement of affected channel in both directions while applying light pressure on the brake pedal.

If erratic or "jumpy" brake pedal movement is detected while performing an "apply" or "release" function of the motor, an intermittent malfunction may be indicated.

An "Intermittent" malfunction may be caused by a poor connection, rubbed through wire insulation, or a wire that is broken inside the insulation.

If the malfunction is not current, wiggle the wires of the affected channel and check if the DTC resets. This will help to pinpoint an intermittent malfunction in the motor circuitry or connections.

The frequency of the malfunction can be checked by using the enhanced diagnostic function of the Tech 1

If DTC A042 sets as current DTC and A066 is infrequent history DTC, see DTC A042 diagnostics.

Any circuitry, that is suspected as causing the intermittent complaint, should be thoroughly checked for backed out terminals, improper mating, broken locks, improperly formed or damaged terminals, poor terminal to wiring connections or physical damage to the wiring harness.

Fig. 168   Code A066, Rear axle motor circuit shorted to battery or motor shorted. 1993 except Cutlass Supreme, Grand Prix, Lumina & Regal

---

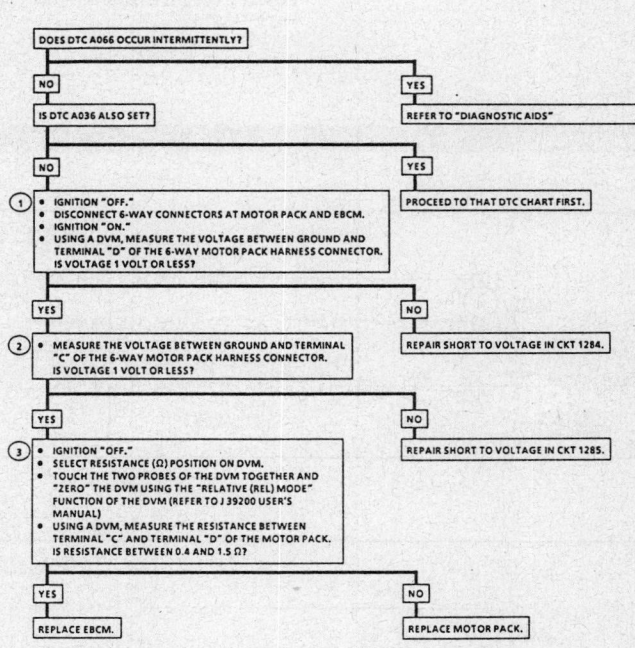

DTC A066

REAR AXLE MOTOR CIRCUIT SHORTED TO BATTERY OR MOTOR SHORTED

Circuit Description:

This DTC identifies a motor circuit that is shorted to battery or a motor that has low or zero resistance. This malfunction will not allow the motor to be controlled at the commanded current rate or will cause the motor to turn in the opposite direction or not turn at all.

Failure Condition:

DTC A066 can be set only when the motor is commanded "OFF." If the EBCM detects an out of range voltage on either of the rear axle motor circuits indicating a circuit shorted to battery or a motor shorted, a malfunction exists.

Action Taken:

A malfunction DTC is stored, ABS is disabled and the ABS indicator lamp is turned "ON."

Test Description: Number(s) below refer to circled number(s) on the diagnostic chart.
1. This step checks for a short to voltage in the motor "high" circuitry.
2. This step checks for a short to voltage in the motor "low" circuitry.
3. This step checks for a motor that is internally shorted.

Diagnostic Aids:

Using Tech 1, select manual control function, and exercise motor movement of affected channel in both directions while applying light pressure on the brake pedal.

If erratic or "jumpy" brake pedal movement is detected while performing an "apply" or "release" function of the motor, an intermittent malfunction may be indicated.

An "Intermittent" malfunction may be caused by a poor connection, rubbed through wire insulation, or a wire that is broken inside the insulation.

If the malfunction is not current, wiggle the wires of the affected channel and check if the DTC resets. This will help to pinpoint an intermittent malfunction in the motor circuitry or connections.

The frequency of the malfunction can be checked by using the enhanced diagnostic function of the Tech 1

Any circuitry, that is suspected as causing the intermittent complaint, should be thoroughly checked for backed out terminals, improper mating, broken locks, improperly formed or damaged terminals, poor terminal to wiring connections or physical damage to the wiring harness.

Fig. 169   Code A066, Rear axle motor circuit shorted to battery or motor shorted. 1993 Cutlass Supreme, Grand Prix, Lumina & Regal

---

GENERAL MOTORS—Anti-Lock Brakes

Cavalier & Sunbird

Achieva, Beretta, Corsica, Grand Am & Skylark

AFTER DIAGNOSIS IS COMPLETE, CLEAR DTCs AND TEST DRIVE VEHICLE FOR THREE (3) DRIVE CYCLES TO VERIFY DTC DOES NOT RESET. A DRIVE CYCLE CONSISTS OF STARTING THE VEHICLE, DRIVING OVER 16 km/h (10 MPH) AND THEN KEYING DOWN.

DTC A067
LEFT FRONT EMB CIRCUIT OPEN OR SHORTED TO GROUND

Circuit Description:

This DTC is designed to detect shorts to ground and opens in the EMB release circuit.

A short to ground between the EMB and the ABS EBCM will cause the EMB to be energized indefinitely at an uncontrolled current, causing the EMB to be destroyed.

Failure Condition:

DTC A067 can be set only when the left front EMB is commanded "OFF" (not released). If the EBCM detects the left front EMB control circuit is constantly at ground, a malfunction exists.

Action Taken:

A malfunction DTC is stored, ABS is disabled and the ABS indicator lamp is turned "ON."

Test Description: Number(s) below refer to circled number(s) on the diagnostic chart.
1. This step checks for a short to ground in the EMB control circuitry.
2. This step looks for an open in the EMB control circuitry.
3. This step checks to see if CKT 850 has continuity to the EMB connector.
4. This step ensures the EMB is not internally open.
5. This step is used to release the tension of the motor pack prior to removal.

Diagnostic Aids:

An "Intermittent" malfunction may be caused by a poor connection, rubbed through wire insulation, or a wire that is broken inside the insulation.

The frequency of the malfunction can be checked by using the enhanced diagnostic function of the Tech 1

Any circuitry, that is suspected as causing the intermittent complaint, should be thoroughly checked for backed out terminals, improper mating, broken locks, improperly formed or damaged terminals, poor terminal to wiring connections or physical damage to the wiring harness.

Fig. 170   Code A067, Left front EMB circuit open or shorted to ground. 1993

Achieva, Beretta, Corsica, Grand Am & Skylark

DTC A068
LEFT FRONT EMB CIRCUIT SHORTED TO BATTERY OR DRIVER OPEN

Circuit Description:

This DTC is designed to detect shorts to battery, shorts in the EMB release circuit, or an open EMB driver. These malfunctions will not allow the EMB to be energized (released) when needed.

Failure Condition:

DTC A068 can be set only when the left front EMB is commanded "ON" (released). If an excessive voltage drop is across the motor driver for the left front EMB, a malfunction exists.

Action Taken:

A malfunction DTC is stored, ABS is disabled and the ABS indicator lamp is turned "ON."

Test Description: Number(s) below refer to circled number(s) on the diagnostic chart.
1. This step checks to see if the malfunction is currently present.
2. This step identifies a short to voltage in the EMB control circuitry.
3. This step checks for an EMB that has lower than normal resistance.
4. This step is used to release the tension of the motor pack prior to removal.

Diagnostic Aids:

An "Intermittent" malfunction may be caused by a poor connection, rubbed through wire insulation, or a wire that is broken inside the insulation.

The frequency of the malfunction can be checked by using the enhanced diagnostic function of the Tech 1

Any circuitry, that is suspected as causing the intermittent complaint, should be thoroughly checked for backed out terminals, improper mating, broken locks, improperly formed or damaged terminals, poor terminal to wiring connections or physical damage to the wiring harness.

Fig. 171   Code A068, Left front EMB circuit shorted to battery or driver open (Part 1 of 2). 1993

Fig. 171   Code A068, Left front EMB circuit shorted to battery or driver open (Part 2 of 2). 1993

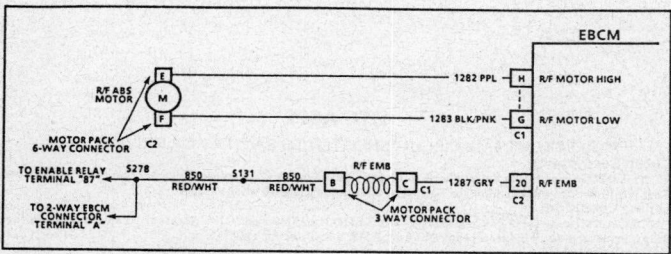

Cavalier & Sunbird

DTC A071
RIGHT FRONT EMB CIRCUIT OPEN OR SHORTED TO GROUND

Circuit Description:

This DTC is designed to detect shorts to ground and opens in the EMB release circuit.

A short to ground between the EMB and the ABS EBCM will cause the EMB to be energized indefinitely at an uncontrolled current causing the EMB to be destroyed.

Failure Condition:

DTC A071 can be set only when the right front EMB is commanded "OFF" (not released). If the EBCM detects the right front EMB control circuit is constantly at ground, a malfunction exists.

Action Taken:

A malfunction DTC is stored, ABS is disabled and the ABS indicator lamp is turned "ON."

Test Description: Number(s) below refer to circled number(s) on the diagnostic chart.
1. This step checks for a short to ground in the EMB control circuitry.
2. This step looks for an open in the EMB control circuitry.
3. This step checks to see if CKT 850 has continuity to the EMB connector.
4. This step ensures the EMB is not internally open.
5. This step is used to release the tension of the motor pack prior to removal.

Diagnostic Aids:

An "Intermittent" malfunction may be caused by a poor connection, rubbed through wire insulation, or a wire that is broken inside the insulation.

The frequency of the malfunction can be checked by using the enhanced diagnostic function of the Tech 1

Any circuitry, that is suspected as causing the intermittent complaint, should be thoroughly checked for backed out terminals, improper mating, broken locks, improperly formed or damaged terminals, poor terminal to wiring connections or physical damage to the wiring harness.

Achieva, Beretta, Corsica, Grand Am & Skylark

Fig. 172   Code A071, Right front EMB circuit open or shorted to ground (Part 1 of 2). 1993

Fig. 172 Code A071, Right front EMB circuit open or shorted to ground (Part 2 of 2). 1993

Cavalier & Sunbird

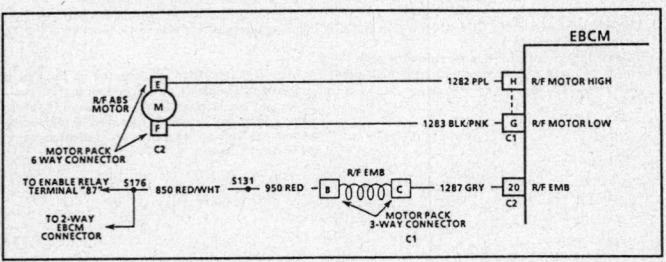

Achieva, Beretta, Corsica, Grand Am & Skylark

DTC A072

RIGHT FRONT EMB CIRCUIT SHORTED TO BATTERY OR DRIVER OPEN

Circuit Description:
This DTC is designed to detect shorts to battery, shorts in the EMB release circuit, or an open EMB driver. These malfunctions will not allow the EMB to be energized (released) when needed.

Failure Condition:
DTC A072 can be set only when the right front EMB is commanded "ON" (released). If an excessive voltage drop is across the motor driver for the right front EMB, a malfunction exists.

Action Taken:
A malfunction DTC is stored, ABS is disabled and the ABS indicator lamp is turned "ON."

Test Description: Number(s) below refer to circled number(s) on the diagnostic chart.
1. This step checks to see if the malfunction is currently present.
2. This step identifies a short to voltage in the EMB control circuitry.
3. This step checks for an EMB that has lower than normal resistance.
4. This step is used to release the tension of the motor pack prior to removal.

Diagnostic Aids:

An "Intermittent" malfunction may be caused by a poor connection, rubbed through wire insulation, or a wire that is broken inside the insulation.

The frequency of the malfunction can be checked by using the enhanced diagnostic function of the Tech 1

Any circuitry, that is suspected as causing the intermittent complaint, should be thoroughly checked for backed out terminals, improper mating, broken locks, improperly formed or damaged terminals, poor terminal to wiring connections or physical damage to the wiring harness.

Fig. 173 Code A072, Right front EMB circuit shorted to battery or driver open (Part 1 of 2). 1993

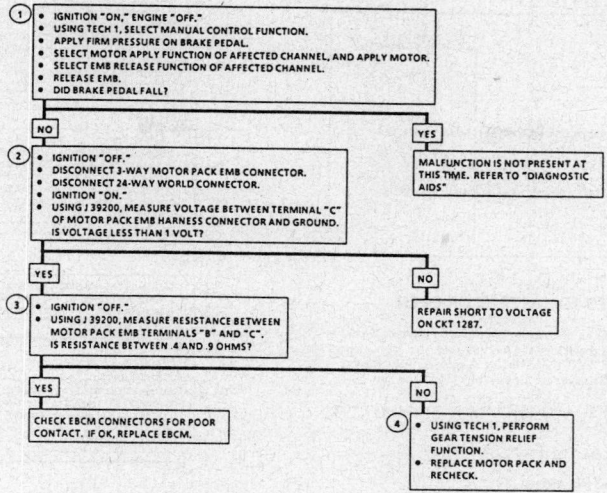

Fig. 173   Code A072, Right front EMB circuit shorted to battery or driver open (Part 2 of 2). 1993

DTC A076

LEFT FRONT SOLENOID CIRCUIT OPEN OR SHORTED TO BATTERY

Circuit Description:

This DTC identifies a solenoid that cannot be energized due to an open in its circuitry, or a solenoid that is always energized due to a short to battery in its circuitry between the driver and the solenoid. An open will not allow proper ABS operation. The short to battery energizes the solenoid indefinitely causing it to be destroyed. A path for base brakes is still allowed once the motor re-homes and the check valve is lifted off its seat during key on initialization.

Failure Condition:

DTC A076 can be set only when the solenoid is commanded "OFF." If the EBCM detects an excessive voltage in the left front solenoid control circuit, a malfunction exists.

Action Taken:

A malfunction DTC is stored, ABS is disabled and the ABS indicator lamp is turned "ON."

Test Description: Number(s) below refer to circled number(s) on the diagnostic chart.

1. This checks for a short to voltage in the control circuitry of the solenoid.
2. This checks for an open in the control circuit of the solenoid.
3. This step identifies an open in the solenoid or ground circuit.
4. This step checks for a possible intermittent malfunction in the solenoid circuitry due to poor terminal contact.

Diagnostic Aids:

An "Intermittent" malfunction may be caused by a poor connection, rubbed through wire insulation, or a wire that is broken inside the insulation.

The frequency of the malfunction can be checked by using the enhanced diagnostic function of the Tech 1

Any circuitry, that is suspected as causing the intermittent complaint, should be thoroughly checked for backed out terminals, improper mating, broken locks, improperly formed or damaged terminals, poor terminal to wiring connections or physical damage to the wiring harness.

Fig. 174   Code A076, Left front solenoid circuit open or shorted to battery. 1993 except Cutlass Supreme, Grand Prix, Lumina & Regal

DTC A076

LEFT FRONT SOLENOID CIRCUIT SHORTED TO BATTERY OR OPEN

Circuit Description:

This DTC identifies a solenoid that cannot be energized due to an open in its circuitry, or a solenoid that is always energized due to a short to battery in its circuitry between the driver and the solenoid. An open will not allow proper ABS operation, but the short to battery simply turns "ON" for base brakes is still allowed once the motor re-homes and the check ball is lifted off its seat during key "ON" initialization.

Failure Condition:

DTC A076 can be set only when the solenoid is commanded "OFF." If the EBCM detects an excessive voltage in the left front solenoid control circuit, a malfunction exists.

Action Taken:

A malfunction DTC is stored, ABS is disabled and the ABS indicator lamp is turned "ON."

Test Description: Number(s) below refer to circled number(s) on the diagnostic chart.

1. This checks for a short to voltage in the control circuitry of the solenoid.
2. This checks for an open in the control circuit of the solenoid.
3. This step checks the solenoid coil for proper resistance.
4. This step checks for an open in the solenoid ground circuit.
5. This step checks for a possible intermittent malfunction in the solenoid circuitry due to poor terminal contact.

Diagnostic Aids:

An "Intermittent" malfunction may be caused by a poor connection, rubbed through wire insulation, or a wire that is broken inside the insulation.

The frequency of the malfunction can be checked by using the enhanced diagnostic function of the Tech 1

Any circuitry, that is suspected as causing the intermittent complaint, should be thoroughly checked for backed out terminals, improper mating, broken locks, improperly formed or damaged terminals, poor terminal to wiring connections or physical damage to the wiring harness.

Fig. 175 Code A076, Left front solenoid circuit open or shorted to battery. 1993 Cutlass Supreme, Grand Prix, Lumina & Regal

DTC A077

LEFT FRONT SOLENOID CIRCUIT SHORTED TO GROUND OR DRIVER OPEN

Circuit Description:

This DTC identifies a solenoid that cannot be energized due to an open in its driver circuitry, or a short to ground between the solenoid driver and the solenoid. These malfunctions can affect ABS operation since the flow of brake fluid to the wheel cylinder cannot be stopped, making ABS operation for that channel impossible.

Failure Condition:

DTC A077 can be set only when the solenoid is commanded "ON." If the EBCM detects the left front solenoid control circuit voltage is out of specification, a malfunction exists.

Action Taken:

A malfunction DTC is stored, ABS is disabled and the ABS indicator lamp is turned "ON."

Test Description: Number(s) below refer to circled number(s) on the diagnostic chart.

1. This step checks for a solenoid that is internally shorted to ground.
2. This step checks for a solenoid that is not within proper resistance values.
3. This step indicates if a short to ground exists in the solenoid control circuitry.
4. This checks for an open control circuit to the EBCM.

Diagnostic Aids:

An "Intermittent" malfunction may be caused by a poor connection, rubbed through wire insulation, or a wire that is broken inside the insulation.

The frequency of the malfunction can be checked by using the enhanced diagnostic function of the Tech 1

Any circuitry, that is suspected as causing the intermittent complaint, should be thoroughly checked for backed out terminals, improper mating, broken locks, improperly formed or damaged terminals, poor terminal to wiring connections or physical damage to the wiring harness.

Fig. 176 Code A077, Left front solenoid circuit shorted to ground or driver open. 1993 except Cutlass Supreme, Grand Prix, Lumina & Regal

DTC A077

LEFT FRONT SOLENOID CIRCUIT SHORTED TO GROUND OR DRIVER OPEN

Circuit Description:

This DTC identifies a solenoid that cannot be energized due to an open in its driver circuitry, or a short to ground between the solenoid driver and the solenoid. These malfunctions can affect ABS operation since the flow of brake fluid to the wheel cylinder cannot be stopped, making ABS operation for that channel impossible.

Failure Condition:

DTC A077 can be set only when the solenoid is commanded "ON." If the EBCM detects the left front solenoid control circuit voltage is out of specification, a malfunction exists.

Action Taken:

A malfunction DTC is stored, ABS is disabled and the ABS indicator lamp is turned "ON."

Test Description: Number(s) below refer to circled number(s) on the diagnostic chart.

1. This step checks for a solenoid that is internally shorted to ground.
2. This step checks for a solenoid that is not within proper resistance values.
3. This step indicates if a short to ground exists in the solenoid circuitry.
4. This checks for an open control circuit to the EBCM.
5. This step checks for a possible intermittent malfunction in the solenoid circuitry due to poor terminal contact.

Diagnostic Aids:

An "Intermittent" malfunction may be caused by a poor connection, rubbed through wire insulation, or a wire that is broken inside the insulation.

The frequency of the malfunction can be checked by using the enhanced diagnostic function of the Tech 1

Any circuitry, that is suspected as causing the intermittent complaint, should be thoroughly checked for backed out terminals, improper mating, broken locks, improperly formed or damaged terminals, poor terminal to wiring connections or physical damage to the wiring harness.

Fig. 177   Code A077, Left front solenoid circuit shorted to ground or driver open. 1993 Cutlass Supreme, Grand Prix, Lumina & Regal

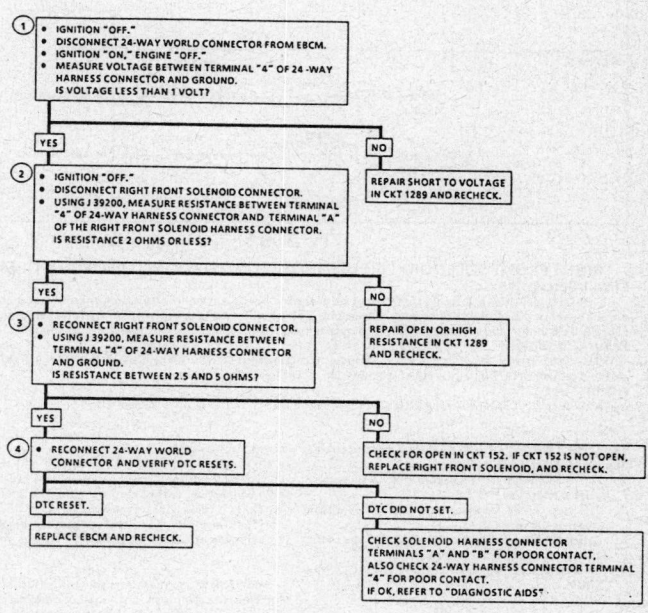

DTC A078

RIGHT FRONT SOLENOID CIRCUIT OPEN OR SHORTED TO BATTERY

Circuit Description:

This DTC identifies a solenoid that cannot be energized due to an open in its circuitry, or a solenoid that is always energized due to a short to battery in its circuitry between the driver and the solenoid. An open will not allow proper ABS operation, but the short to battery simply turns "ON" the solenoid. A path for base brakes is still allowed once the motor re-homes and the check valve is lifted off its seat during key on initialization.

Failure Condition:

DTC A078 can be set only when the solenoid is commanded "OFF." If the EBCM detects an excessive voltage in the right front solenoid control circuit, a malfunction exists.

Action Taken:

A malfunction DTC is stored, ABS is disabled and the ABS indicator lamp is turned "ON."

Test Description: Number(s) below refer to circled number(s) on the diagnostic chart.

1. This checks for a short to voltage in the control circuitry of the solenoid.
2. This checks for an open in the control circuit of the solenoid.
3. This step identifies an open in the solenoid or ground circuit.
4. This step checks for a possible intermittent malfunction in the solenoid circuitry due to poor terminal contact.

Diagnostic Aids:

An "Intermittent" malfunction may be caused by a poor connection, rubbed through wire insulation, or a wire that is broken inside the insulation.

The frequency of the malfunction can be checked by using the enhanced diagnostic function of the Tech 1

Any circuitry, that is suspected as causing the intermittent complaint, should be thoroughly checked for backed out terminals, improper mating, broken locks, improperly formed or damaged terminals, poor terminal to wiring connections or physical damage to the wiring harness.

Fig. 178   Code A078, Right front solenoid circuit open or shorted to battery. 1993 except Cutlass Supreme, Grand Prix, Lumina & Regal

DTC A078

RIGHT FRONT SOLENOID CIRCUIT SHORTED TO BATTERY OR OPEN

Circuit Description:

This DTC identifies a solenoid that cannot be energized due to an open in its circuitry, or a solenoid that is always energized due to a short to battery in its circuitry between the driver and the solenoid. An open will not allow proper ABS operation, but the short to battery simply turns "ON" the solenoid. A path for base brakes is still allowed once the motor re-homes and the check ball is lifted off its seat during key "ON" initialization.

Failure Condition:

DTC A078 can be set only when the solenoid is commanded "OFF." If the EBCM detects an excessive voltage in the right front solenoid control circuit, a malfunction exists.

Action Taken:

A malfunction DTC is stored, ABS is disabled and the ABS indicator lamp is turned "ON."

Test Description: Number(s) below refer to circled number(s) on the diagnostic chart.

1. This checks for a short to voltage in the control circuitry of the solenoid.
2. This checks for an open in the control circuit of the solenoid.
3. This step checks the solenoid coil for proper resistance.
4. This step checks for an open in the solenoid ground circuit.
5. This step checks for a possible intermittent malfunction in the solenoid circuitry due to poor terminal contact.

Diagnostic Aids:

An "Intermittent" malfunction may be caused by a poor connection, rubbed through wire insulation, or a wire that is broken inside the insulation.

The frequency of the malfunction can be checked by using the enhanced diagnostic function of the Tech 1

Any circuitry, that is suspected as causing the intermittent complaint, should be thoroughly checked for backed out terminals, improper mating, broken locks, improperly formed or damaged terminals, poor terminal to wiring connections or physical damage to the wiring harness.

Fig. 179   Code A078, Right front solenoid circuit open or shorted to battery. 1993 Cutlass Supreme, Grand Prix, Lumina & Regal

DTC A081

RIGHT FRONT SOLENOID CIRCUIT SHORTED TO GROUND OR DRIVER OPEN

Circuit Description:

This DTC identifies a solenoid that cannot be energized due to an open in its driver circuitry, or a short to ground between the solenoid driver and the solenoid. These malfunctions can affect ABS operation since the flow of brake fluid to the wheel cylinder cannot be stopped, making ABS operation for that channel impossible.

Failure Condition:

DTC A081 can be set only when the solenoid is commanded "ON." If the EBCM detects the right front solenoid control circuit voltage is out of specification, a malfunction exists.

Action Taken:

A malfunction DTC is stored, ABS is disabled and the ABS indicator lamp is turned "ON."

Test Description: Number(s) below refer to circled number(s) on the diagnostic chart.

1. This step checks for a solenoid that is internally shorted to ground.
2. This step checks for a solenoid that is not within proper resistance values.
3. This step indicates if a short to ground exists in the solenoid control circuitry.
4. This checks for an open control circuit to the EBCM.

Diagnostic Aids:

An "Intermittent" malfunction may be caused by a poor connection, rubbed through wire insulation, or a wire that is broken inside the insulation.

The frequency of the malfunction can be checked by using the enhanced diagnostic function of the Tech 1

Any circuitry, that is suspected as causing the intermittent complaint, should be thoroughly checked for backed out terminals, improper mating, broken locks, improperly formed or damaged terminals, poor terminal to wiring connections or physical damage to the wiring harness.

Fig. 180   Code A081, Right front solenoid circuit open or shorted to ground or driver open. 1993 except Cutlass Supreme, Grand Prix, Lumina & Regal

DTC A081

RIGHT FRONT SOLENOID CIRCUIT SHORTED TO GROUND OR DRIVER OPEN

Circuit Description:

This DTC identifies a solenoid that cannot be energized due to an open in its driver circuitry, or a short to ground between the solenoid driver and the solenoid. These malfunctions can affect ABS operation since the flow of brake fluid to the wheel cylinder cannot be stopped, making ABS operation for that channel impossible.

Failure Condition:

DTC A081 can be set only when the solenoid is commanded "ON." If the EBCM detects the right front solenoid control circuit voltage is out of specification, a malfunction exists.

Action Taken:

A malfunction DTC is stored, ABS is disabled and the ABS indicator lamp is turned "ON."

Test Description: Number(s) below refer to circled number(s) on the diagnostic chart.

1. This step checks for a solenoid that is internally shorted to ground.
2. This step checks for a solenoid that is not within proper resistance values.
3. This step indicates if a short to ground exists in the solenoid circuitry.
4. This checks for an open control circuit to the EBCM.
5. This step checks for a possible intermittent malfunction in the solenoid circuitry due to poor terminal contact.

Diagnostic Aids:

An "Intermittent" malfunction may be caused by a poor connection, rubbed through wire insulation, or a wire that is broken inside the insulation.

The frequency of the malfunction can be checked by using the enhanced diagnostic function of the Tech 1

Any circuitry, that is suspected as causing the intermittent complaint, should be thoroughly checked for backed out terminals, improper mating, broken locks, improperly formed or damaged terminals, poor terminal to wiring connections or physical damage to the wiring harness.

Fig. 181   Code A081, Right front solenoid circuit open or shorted to ground or driver open. 1993 Cutlass Supreme, Grand Prix, Lumina & Regal

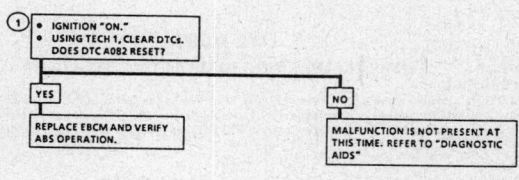

DTC A082

CALIBRATION MEMORY FAILURE

Circuit Description:

This DTC allows the EBCM to check for a calibration malfunction by comparing the calibration value to a known value stored in the EEPROM.

This DTC is also used as a security measure to prevent improper use of calibrations or changes to these calibrations that may alter the designed function of ABS.

Failure Condition:

DTC A082 can be set at key-up. If the program identifier is incorrect or the memory checksum is incorrect, a malfunction exists.

Action Taken:

A malfunction DTC is stored, ABS is disabled and the ABS indicator lamp is turned "ON."

Test Description: Number(s) below refer to circled number(s) on the diagnostic chart.

1. This step checks to see if the malfunction is present during diagnosis. If present, the EBCM is not functioning correctly and must be replaced.

Important

- At the time of printing, 1993 vehicles with ABS-VI were not being field reprogrammed to correct this failure. A service bulletin will be issued when EEPROM reprogramming is authorized.

Diagnostic Aids:

An intermittent DTC A082 may be caused by a bad cell in the EEPROM that is sensitive to temperature changes. If DTC A082 failed more than once, but is intermittent, replace EBCM.

The frequency of the malfunction can be checked by using the enhanced diagnostic function of the Tech 1

Fig. 182   Code A082, Calibration memory failure. 1993

Cavalier & Sunbird

Beretta & Corsica

Achieva, Grand Am & Skylark

Cutlass Supreme, Grand Prix, Lumina & Regal

DTC A086
RED BRAKE WARNING LAMP ACTIVATED BY ABS

Circuit Description:
This DTC is provided as an information only test, and reflects the status of the command issued by the ABS EBCM to illuminate the red brake warning lamp. If another diagnostic DTC issues a command to illuminate the red brake warning lamp, DTC A086 will be stored in EEPROM as a history DTC at the conclusion of the ignition cycle.

Test Description: Number(s) below refer to circled number(s) on the diagnostic chart.
1. This step serves to identify if a DTC other than DTC A086 commanded the red brake warning lamp "ON."

Diagnostic Aids:
Any ABS mechanical DTC that issues a command to illuminate the red brake warning lamp will also result in DTC A086 being stored in EEPROM during shut down. These DTCs are: A038, A041, A042, A045, A046, A047, A048 and A051. If the motors are not in their home position, certain electrical DTCs will also command the red brake warning lamp "ON." These DTCs are: A014, A018, A055, A056, A057, A0587, A061, A062, A063, A064, A065, A066, A067, A068, A071 and A072.

If any of these DTCs are indicated along with DTC A086, they must be corrected prior to addressing a DTC A086 malfunction.

Fig. 183   Code A086, Red brake warning lamp activated by ABS. 1993

Cavalier & Sunbird

Beretta & Corsica

Achieva, Grand Am & Skylark

DTC A088

RED BRAKE WARNING LAMP CIRCUIT SHORTED TO BATTERY

Circuit Description:
This DTC identifies a short to battery between the EBCM and the RED brake warning lamp, or an open driver that does not allow the RED brake warning lamp to be illuminated by the EBCM. This will only occur if an ABS malfunction is detected that may degrade base brake operation.

Failure Condition:
DTC A088 can be set only at the beginning of the three second bulb check. If the EBCM detects battery voltage on the red brake warning lamp control circuit, a malfunction exists.

Action Taken:
A malfunction DTC is stored. ABS is not disabled; however, the ABS indicator lamp will flash to indicate a malfunction exists.

Test Description: Number(s) below refer to circled number(s) on the diagnostic chart.

1. This step identifies if the ground circuit to the red brake warning lamp is being completed by a source other than the EBCM.
2. This step identifies if the malfunction is currently present.
3. By removing the 10 amp gauge fuse, the voltage source is eliminated. This test indicates if voltage is being supplied from a source other than the gauge fuse.

Diagnostic Aids:

An "Intermittent" malfunction may be caused by a poor connection, rubbed through wire insulation, or a wire that is broken inside the insulation.

The frequency of the malfunction can be checked by using the enhanced diagnostic function of the Tech 1

Any circuitry, that is suspected as causing the intermittent complaint, should be thoroughly checked for backed out terminals, improper mating, broken locks, improperly formed or damaged terminals, poor terminal to wiring connections or physical damage to the wiring harness.

Fig. 184   Code A087, Red brake warning lamp circuit open. 1993 except Cutlass Supreme, Grand Prix, Lumina & Regal

DTC A087
RED BRAKE WARNING LAMP CIRCUIT OPEN

Circuit Description:
This DTC is used to verify the EBCM has continuity to the red brake warning lamp in case the EBCM must turn it "ON." This will only occur if an ABS malfunction is detected that may degrade base brake operation.

Because ABS is not the only device controlling the red brake warning lamp (parking brake and low fluid sensor may also turn "ON" the lamp) a short to ground in this circuit cannot be detected.

Failure Condition:
DTC A087 can be set after initialization is completed. If the red brake warning lamp circuit voltage is out of specification indicating an open circuit, a malfunction exists.

Action Taken:
A malfunction DTC is stored, ABS is not disabled; however, the ABS indicator lamp will flash to indicate a malfunction exists.

Test Description: Number(s) below refer to circled number(s) on the diagnostic chart.

1. This step identifies if the malfunction is currently present.
2. This step indicates if the EBCM and circuitry has the ability to complete the ground to the brake telltale lamp and illuminate it.
3. Because the red brake warning lamp has current supplied to it through the 10 amp INDIC fuse, this step would indicate if the ignition circuit is complete to the I/P cluster.
4. This step isolates if the open circuit is due to a EBCM failure or open circuitry to the brake telltale.
5. This step checks for an open in the park brake circuitry.
6. This step determines if the malfunction is intermittent.
7. This step verifies the condition of the INDIC fuse.

Diagnostic Aids:
An "Intermittent" malfunction may be caused by a poor connection, rubbed through wire insulation, or a wire that is broken inside the insulation.

The frequency of the malfunction can be checked by using the enhanced diagnostic function of the Tech 1

If a Tech 1 or T-100 are not available, the parking brake handle may be lifted to verify proper lamp operation and continuity of CKTs 3 and 39.

Any circuitry, that is suspected as causing the intermittent complaint, should be thoroughly checked for backed out terminals, improper mating, broken locks, improperly formed or damaged terminals, poor terminal to wiring connections or physical damage to the wiring harness.

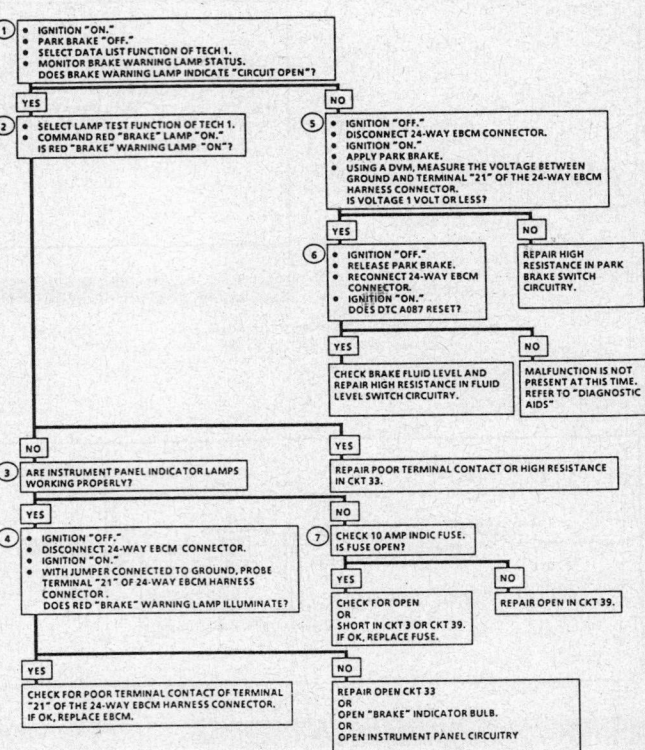

Fig. 185   Code A087, Red brake warning lamp circuit open. 1993 Cutlass Supreme, Grand Prix, Lumina & Regal

Cavalier & Sunbird

Achieva, Grand Am & Skylark

Beretta & Corsica

Fig. 186   Code A088, Red brake warning lamp circuit shorted to battery (Part 1 of 2). 1993 except Cutlass Supreme, Grand Prix, Lumina & Regal

DTC A088
RED BRAKE WARNING LAMP CIRCUIT SHORTED TO BATTERY

Circuit Description:

This DTC identifies a short to battery between the EBCM and the RED brake warning lamp, or an open driver that does not allow the RED brake warning lamp to be illuminated by the EBCM. This will only occur if an ABS malfunction is detected that may degrade base brake operation.

Failure Condition:

DTC A088 can be set only at the beginning of the three second bulb check. If the EBCM detects battery voltage on the red brake warning lamp control circuit, a malfunction exists.

Action Taken:

A malfunction DTC is stored. ABS is not disabled; however, the ABS indicator lamp will flash to indicate a malfunction exists.

Test Description: Number(s) below refer to circled number(s) on the diagnostic chart.
1. This step identifies if the ground circuit to the red brake warning lamp is being completed by a source other than the EBCM.
2. This step identifies if the malfunction is currently present.
3. By removing the 10 amp gauge fuse, the voltage source is eliminated. This test indicates if voltage is being supplied from a source other than the gauge fuse.

Diagnostic Aids:

An "Intermittent" malfunction may be caused by a poor connection, rubbed through wire insulation, or a wire that is broken inside the insulation.

The frequency of the malfunction can be checked by using the enhanced diagnostic function of the Tech 1

Any circuitry, that is suspected as causing the intermittent complaint, should be thoroughly checked for backed out terminals, improper mating, broken locks, improperly formed or damaged terminals, poor terminal to wiring connections or physical damage to the wiring harness.

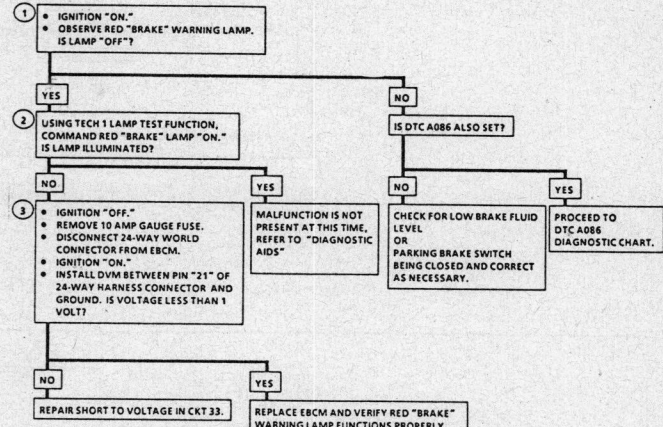

Fig. 186   Code A088, Red brake warning lamp circuit shorted to battery (Part 2 of 2). 1993 except Cutlass Supreme, Grand Prix, Lumina & Regal

DTC A088
RED BRAKE WARNING LAMP CIRCUIT SHORTED TO BATTERY

Circuit Description:

This DTC identifies a short to battery between the EBCM and the red brake warning lamp, or an open driver that does not allow the red brake warning lamp to be illuminated by the EBCM. This will only occur if an ABS fault is detected that may degrade base brake operation.

Failure Condition:

DTC A088 can be set only at the beginning of the three second bulb check. If the EBCM detects battery voltage on the red brake warning lamp control circuit, a malfunction exists.

Action Taken:

A malfunction DTC is stored. ABS is not disabled; however, the ABS indicator lamp will flash to indicate a malfunction exists.

Test Description: Number(s) below refer to circled number(s) on the diagnostic chart.
1. This step identifies if the ground circuit to the red brake warning lamp is being completed by a source other than the EBCM.
2. This step identifies if the malfunction is currently present.
3. By removing the 10 amp INDIC fuse, the voltage source is eliminated. This test indicates if voltage is being supplied from a source other than the gauge fuse.
4. This step checks for DTC A086 also being set.

Diagnostic Aids:

An "Intermittent" malfunction may be caused by a poor connection, rubbed through wire insulation, or a wire that is broken inside the insulation.

The frequency of the malfunction can be checked by using the enhanced diagnostic function of the Tech 1

Any circuitry, that is suspected as causing the intermittent complaint, should be thoroughly checked for backed out terminals, improper mating, broken locks, improperly formed or damaged terminals, poor terminal to wiring connections or physical damage to the wiring harness.

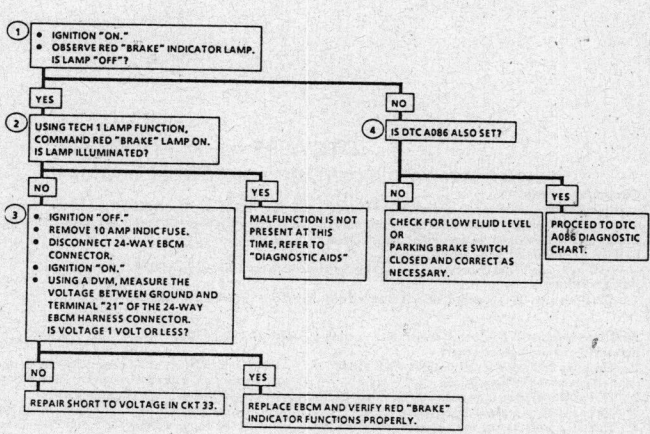

Fig. 187   Code A088, Red brake warning lamp circuit shorted to battery. 1993 Cutlass Supreme, Grand Prix, Lumina & Regal

Cavalier & Sunbird

Achieva, Grand Am & Skylark

Beretta & Corsica

DTC A091
OPEN BRAKE SWITCH CONTACTS DURING DECELERATION

Circuit Description:
This DTC is used to detect an open brake switch in the non-ABS mode. The EBCM looks for decel rates that would indicate braking action and verifies this assumption by requiring several repeats of this detection method. In each case, ABS will not be available since no brake switch is seen.

Failure Condition:
DTC A091 can be set if three deceleration cycles occur with the brake switch "OFF."

Action Taken:
A malfunction DTC is stored, ABS is disabled and the ABS indicator lamp is turned "ON."

Test Description: Number(s) below refer to circled number(s) on the diagnostic chart.
1. This step indicates if the brake switch signal is being received by the EBCM.
2. This step indicates if an open circuit exists in the brake switch or brake lamp circuitry.
3. This step isolates the open circuit to either the brake switch input circuitry, or the EBCM.

Diagnostic Aids:

An "Intermittent" malfunction may be caused by a poor connection, rubbed through wire insulation, or a wire that is broken inside the insulation.

The frequency of the malfunction can be checked by using the enhanced diagnostic function of the Tech 1

Any circuitry, that is suspected as causing the intermittent complaint, should be thoroughly checked for backed out terminals, improper mating, broken locks, improperly formed or damaged terminals, poor terminal to wiring connections or physical damage to the wiring harness.

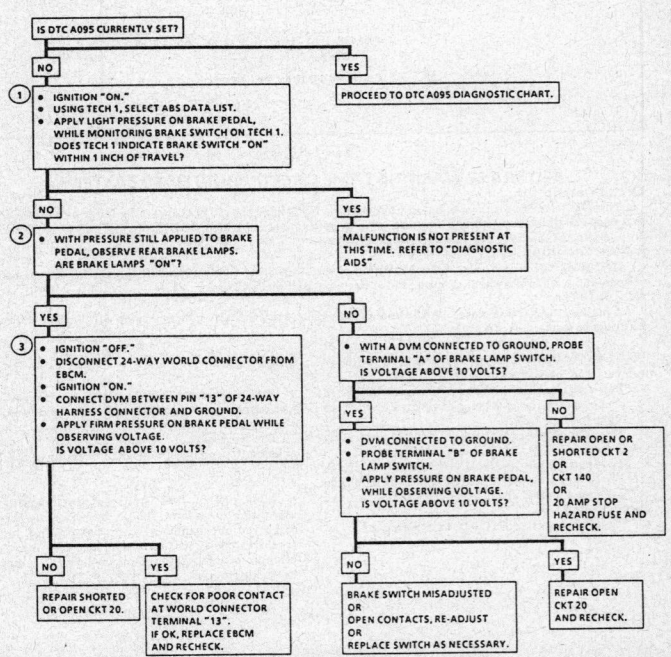

Fig. 188 Code A091, Open brake switch contacts during acceleration. 1993 except Cutlass Supreme, Grand Prix, Lumina & Regal

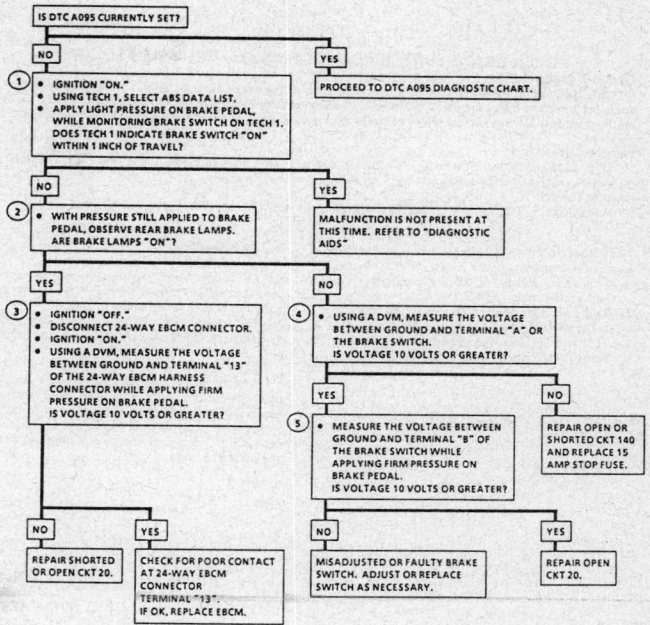

DTC A091
OPEN BRAKE SWITCH CONTACTS DURING DECELERATION

Circuit Description:
This DTC is used to detect an open brake switch in the non-ABS mode. The EBCM looks for deceleration rates that would indicate braking action and verifies this assumption by requiring several repeats of this detection method. In each case, ABS will not be available since no brake switch is seen.

Failure Condition:
DTC A091 can be set if three deceleration cycles occur with the brake switch "OFF."

Action Taken:
A malfunction DTC is stored, ABS is disabled and the ABS indicator lamp is turned "ON."

Test Description: Number(s) below refer to circled number(s) on the diagnostic chart.
1. This step indicates if the brake switch signal is being received by the EBCM.
2. This step indicates if an open circuit exists in the brake switch or brake lamp circuitry.
3. This step isolates the open circuit to either the brake switch input circuitry, or the EBCM.
4. This step verifies that voltage is available at the brake switch.
5. This step verifies that the brake switch is functioning properly.

Diagnostic Aids:
An "Intermittent" malfunction may be caused by a poor connection, rubbed through wire insulation, or a wire that is broken inside the insulation.
The frequency of the malfunction can be checked by using the enhanced diagnostic function of the Tech 1.
Any circuitry, that is suspected as causing the intermittent complaint, should be thoroughly checked for backed out terminals, improper mating, broken locks, improperly formed or damaged terminals, poor terminal to wiring connections or physical damage to the wiring harness.

Fig. 189   Code A091, Open brake switch contacts during acceleration. 1993 Cutlass Supreme, Grand Prix, Lumina & Regal

Cavalier & Sunbird

Achieva, Grand Am & Skylark

Beretta & Corsica

Fig. 190   Code A092, Open brake switch contacts when ABS required (Part 1 of 2). 1993 except Cutlass Supreme, Grand Prix, Lumina & Regal

DTC A092

OPEN BRAKE SWITCH CONTACTS WHEN ABS WAS REQUIRED

Circuit Description:
This DTC is run to determine the proper operation of the brake switch. This is important because ABS is activated when the brake switch is "ON." If the brake switch is "OFF," ABS will never be activated. Since this malfunction is difficult to detect under normal braking conditions, this malfunction is only detected when ABS is required.

Failure Condition:
DTC A092 can be set if the vehicle's speed is greater than 8 km/h (5 mph). If the brake was not "ON" and a release was required on two channels for .7 seconds, a malfunction exists.

Action Taken:
A malfunction DTC is stored, ABS is disabled and the ABS indicator lamp is turned "ON."

Test Description: Number(s) below refer to circled number(s) on the diagnostic chart.
1. This step indicates if the brake switch signal is being received by the EBCM.
2. This step indicates if an open circuit exists in the brake switch or brake lamp circuitry.
3. This step isolates the open circuit to either the brake switch input circuitry, or the EBCM.

Diagnostic Aids:

An "Intermittent" malfunction may be caused by a poor connection, rubbed through wire insulation, or a wire that is broken inside the insulation.

The frequency of the malfunction can be checked by using the enhanced diagnostic function of the Tech 1

Any circuitry, that is suspected as causing the intermittent complaint, should be thoroughly checked for backed out terminals, improper mating, broken locks, improperly formed or damaged terminals, poor terminal to wiring connections or physical damage to the wiring harness.

Fig. 190 Code A092, Open brake switch contacts when ABS required (Part 2 of 2). 1993 except Cutlass Supreme, Grand Prix, Lumina & Regal

DTC A092

OPEN BRAKE SWITCH CONTACTS WHEN ABS WAS REQUIRED

Circuit Description:
This DTC is run to determine the proper operation of the brake switch. This is important because ABS is activated when the brake switch is "ON." If the brake switch is "OFF," ABS will never be activated. Since this malfunction is difficult to detect under normal braking conditions, this malfunction is only detected when ABS is required.

Failure Condition:
DTC A092 can be set if the vehicle's speed is greater than 8 km/h (5 mph). If the brake was not "ON" and a release was required on two channels for 0.5 seconds, a malfunction exists.

Action Taken:
A malfunction DTC is stored, ABS is disabled and the ABS indicator lamp is turned "ON."

Test Description: Number(s) below refer to circled number(s) on the diagnostic chart.
1. This step indicates if the brake switch signal is being received by the EBCM.
2. This step indicates if an open circuit exists in the brake switch or brake lamp circuitry.
3. This step isolates the open circuit to either the brake switch input circuitry, or the EBCM.
4. This step verifies the voltage is available at the brake switch.
5. This step verifies that the brake switch is functioning properly.

Diagnostic Aids:

An "Intermittent" malfunction may be caused by a poor connection, rubbed through wire insulation, or a wire that is broken inside the insulation.

The frequency of the malfunction can be checked by using the enhanced diagnostic function of the Tech 1

Any circuitry, that is suspected as causing the intermittent complaint, should be thoroughly checked for backed out terminals, improper mating, broken locks, improperly formed or damaged terminals, poor terminal to wiring connections or physical damage to the wiring harness.

Fig. 191 Code A092, Open brake switch contacts when ABS required. 1993 Cutlass Supreme, Grand Prix, Lumina & Regal

Cavalier & Sunbird

Achieva, Grand Am & Skylark

Beretta & Corsica

Cutlass Supreme, Grand Prix, Lumina & Regal

DTC A093
DTCs A091 OR A092 SET IN CURRENT OR PREVIOUS IGNITION CYCLE

Circuit Description:

This DTC is the second portion of DTCs A091 and A092. If DTCs A091 or A092 failed during the last ignition cycle, DTC A093 becomes a current failure during the next ignition cycle, keeping ABS disabled until a brake switch "ON" state is seen. When a change is seen during an ignition cycle in which DTC A093 is a current failure, DTC A091 or A092 will clear itself at the end of the current ignition cycle, and ABS will enable itself at the start of the next ignition cycle. DTC A093 alone indicates DTCs A091 or A092 failed previously, but is intermittent, or has been corrected.

Test Description: Number(s) below refer to circled number(s) on the diagnostic chart.
1. This step indicates which DTC (either A091 or A092) caused DTC A093 to set.
2. This insures that the DTC that set is repaired so that DTC A093 can be cleared.

Diagnostic Aids:

An "Intermittent" malfunction may be caused by a poor connection, rubbed through wire insulation, or a wire that is broken inside the insulation.

The frequency of the malfunction can be checked by using the enhanced diagnostic function of the Tech 1

Any circuitry, that is suspected as causing the intermittent complaint, should be thoroughly checked for backed out terminals, improper mating, broken locks, improperly formed or damaged terminals, poor terminal to wiring connections or physical damage to the wiring harness.

Also, verify proper brake switch operation using the data list of the Tech 1. As the brake is applied, the data list should display the brake switch "ON" within 1 inch of travel.

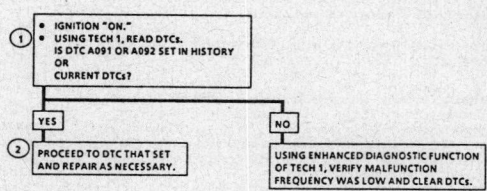

Fig. 192   Code A093, DTCs A091 or A092 set in current or previous ignition cycle. 1993

Cavalier & Sunbird

Beretta & Corsica

Achieva, Grand Am & Skylark

DTC A094
BRAKE SWITCH CONTACTS ALWAYS CLOSED

Circuit Description:

This DTC is run to determine the proper operation of the brake switch. This is important because ABS is activated when the brake switch is "ON" and turned "OFF" when the brake is "OFF." If the brake switch is always "ON," ABS operation will always be requested resulting in potential modulator cycling on rough roads. Additionally, this malfunction will most likely result in a dead battery (due to the brake lamps staying "ON") if the driver is not informed of this malfunction.

Failure Condition:

DTC A094 can be set if the vehicle speed reaches at least 40 km/h (25 mph). If the brake was never "OFF" during two consecutive drive cycles, a malfunction exists.

Action Taken:

A malfunction DTC is stored. ABS is not disabled; however, the ABS indicator will flash to indicate a malfunction exists.

Test Description: Number(s) below refer to circled number(s) on the diagnostic chart.
1. This step checks to see if brake lamps are "ON."
2. This step isolates the cause of the malfunction to either a faulty or misadjusted brake switch, or a short to voltage in the brake switch circuitry.
3. This step checks for a resistive short to voltage in the brake switch circuitry.
4. This step ensures malfunction was not due to a poor connection.

Diagnostic Aids:

An "Intermittent" malfunction may be caused by a poor connection, rubbed through wire insulation, or a wire that is broken inside the insulation.

The frequency of the malfunction can be checked by using the enhanced diagnostic function of the Tech 1

Any circuitry, that is suspected as causing the intermittent complaint, should be thoroughly checked for backed out terminals, improper mating, broken locks, improperly formed or damaged terminals, poor terminal to wiring connections or physical damage to the wiring harness.

Fig. 193   Code A094, Brake switch contacts always closed. 1993 except Cutlass Supreme, Grand Prix, Lumina & Regal

DTC A094
BRAKE SWITCH CONTACTS ALWAYS CLOSED

Circuit Description:
This DTC is run to determine the proper operation of the brake switch. This is important because ABS is activated when the brake switch is "ON" and turned "OFF" when the brake is "OFF." If the brake switch is always "ON," ABS operation will always be requested resulting in potential modulator cycling on rough roads. Additionally, this malfunction will most likely result in a dead battery (due to the brake lights staying "ON") if the driver is not informed of this malfunction.

Failure Condition:
DTC A094 can be set when the vehicle reaches at least 40 km/h (25 mph). If the brake was never "OFF" during two consecutive drive cycles, a malfunction exists.

Action Taken:
A malfunction DTC is stored. ABS is not disabled; however, the ABS indicator will flash to indicate a malfunction exists.

Test Description: Number(s) below refer to circled number(s) on the diagnostic chart.
1. This checks if the malfunction is currently present.
2. This step isolates the cause of the malfunction to either a malfunctioning or misadjusted brake switch, or a short to voltage in the brake switch circuitry.
3. This step checks for unwanted voltage on the brake switch input circuit.
4. This step checks for a possible intermittent malfunction.

Diagnostic Aids:

An "Intermittent" malfunction may be caused by a poor connection, rubbed through wire insulation, or a wire that is broken inside the insulation. The frequency of the malfunction can be checked by using the enhanced diagnostic function of the Tech 1

Any circuitry, that is suspected as causing the intermittent complaint, should be thoroughly checked for backed out terminals, improper mating, broken locks, improperly formed or damaged terminals, poor terminal to wiring connections or physical damage to the wiring harness.

Fig. 194   Code A094, Brake switch contacts always closed. 1993 Cutlass Supreme, Grand Prix, Lumina & Regal

Cavalier & Sunbird

Beretta & Corsica

Achieva, Grand Am & Skylark

Fig. 195   Code A095, Brake switch circuit open (Part 1 of 2). 1993 except Cutlass Supreme, Grand Prix, Lumina & Regal

DTC A095
BRAKE SWITCH CIRCUIT OPEN

Circuit Description:
This DTC is used to identify open brake switch circuitry that prevents the brake switch input to the EBCM from changing states when the brake is applied. This DTC is used in conjunction with DTCs A091 and A092 to determine the cause of an open brake switch malfunction.

Failure Condition:
DTC A095 can be set after initialization is completed. If the brake switch input voltage is out of specification for one second indicating an open circuit, a malfunction exists.

Action Taken:
A malfunction DTC is stored, ABS is disabled and the ABS indicator lamp is turned "ON."

Test Description: Number(s) below refer to circled number(s) on the diagnostic chart.
1. This step is used to confirm that an open in the brake switch circuitry currently exists.
2. This step indicates if the brake switch signal is being received by the EBCM.
3. This step indicates if an open circuit exists in the brake switch or brake lamp circuitry.
4. This step isolates the open circuit to either the brake switch input circuitry, or the EBCM.

Diagnostic Aids:
An "Intermittent" malfunction may be caused by a poor connection, rubbed through wire insulation, or a wire that is broken inside the insulation.

The frequency of the malfunction can be checked by using the enhanced diagnostic function of the Tech 1

Any circuitry, that is suspected as causing the intermittent complaint, should be thoroughly checked for backed out terminals, improper mating, broken locks, improperly formed or damaged terminals, poor terminal to wiring connections or physical damage to the wiring harness.

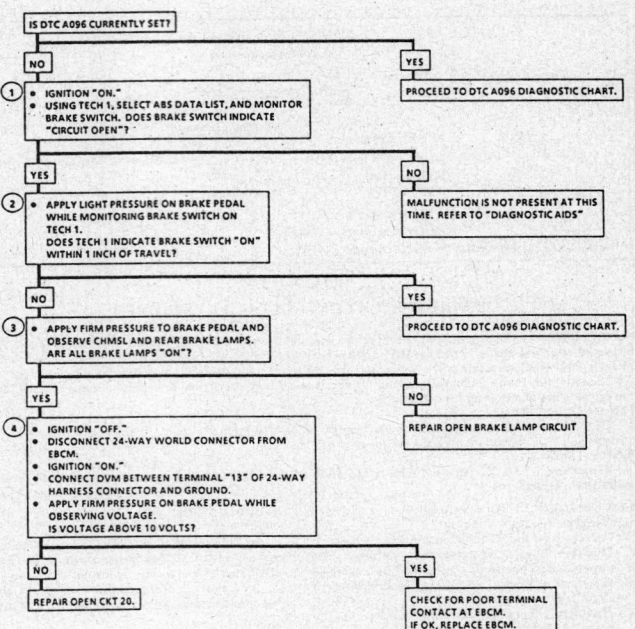

Fig. 195   Code A095, Brake switch circuit open (Part 2 of 2). 1993 except Cutlass Supreme, Grand Prix, Lumina & Regal

DTC A095
BRAKE SWITCH CIRCUIT OPEN

Circuit Description:
This DTC is used to identify open brake switch circuitry that prevents the brake switch input to the EBCM from changing states when the brake is applied. This DTC is used in conjunction with DTCs A091 and A092 to determine the cause of an open brake switch malfunction.

Failure Condition:
DTC A095 can be set after initialization is completed. If the brake switch input voltage is out of specification for one second indicating an open circuit, a malfunction exists.

Action Taken:
A malfunction DTC is stored, ABS is disabled and the ABS indicator lamp is turned "ON."

Test Description: Number(s) below refer to circled number(s) on the diagnostic chart.
1. This step is used to confirm that an open in the brake switch circuitry currently exists.
2. This step indicates if the brake switch signal is being received by the EBCM.
3. This step indicates if an open circuit exists in the brake switch or brake lamp circuitry.
4. This step isolates the open circuit to either the brake switch input circuitry, or the EBCM.

Diagnostic Aids:
An "Intermittent" malfunction may be caused by a poor connection, rubbed through wire insulation, or a wire that is broken inside the insulation.

The frequency of the malfunction can be checked by using the enhanced diagnostic function of the Tech 1

Any circuitry, that is suspected as causing the intermittent complaint, should be thoroughly checked for backed out terminals, improper mating, broken locks, improperly formed or damaged terminals, poor terminal to wiring connections or physical damage to the wiring harness.

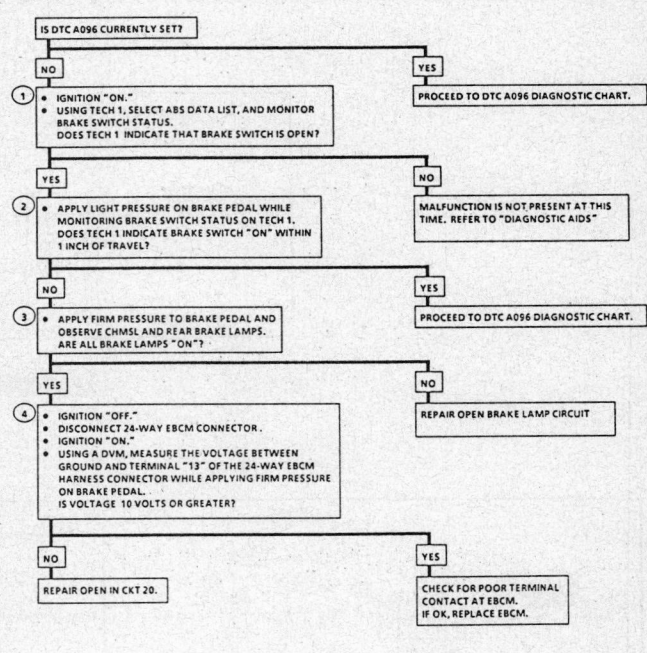

Fig. 196   Code A095, Brake switch circuit open. 1993 Cutlass Supreme, Grand Prix, Lumina & Regal

Cavalier & Sunbird

Beretta & Corsica

Achieva, Grand Am & Skylark

Cutlass Supreme, Grand Prix, Lumina & Regal

DTC A096
BRAKE LAMPS CIRCUIT OPEN

Circuit Description:

This DTC is designed to isolate the cause of a DTC A095 failure and indicate to the driver ABS is still available. If DTC A095 fails with DTC A096, the brake lamps are open, the brake lamp grounds are open, or the Center High Mounted Stop Lamp (CHMSL) circuit is open during 4 way flasher use. The presence of battery voltage at the brake switch input indicates a valid brake switch input is still available.

Failure Condition:

DTC A096 can be set only after DTC A095 has been set. If the EBCM detects battery voltage on the brake switch input circuit for one second, a malfunction exists.

Action Taken:

A malfunction DTC is stored. ABS is not disabled; however, the ABS indicator lamp will flash indicating a malfunction exists.

Test Description: Number(s) below refer to circled number(s) on the diagnostic chart.

1. As a result of a failure of an additional brake switch circuit DTC, this DTC may be set. To insure proper diagnosis, any additional brake switch DTCs must be repaired first.
2. This step identifies if the malfunction is currently present in the brake circuit.

Diagnostic Aids:

An "Intermittent" malfunction may be caused by a poor connection, rubbed through wire insulation, or a wire that is broken inside the insulation.

The frequency of the malfunction can be checked by using the enhanced diagnostic function of the Tech 1

Any circuitry, that is suspected as causing the intermittent complaint, should be thoroughly checked for backed out terminals, improper mating, broken locks, improperly formed or damaged terminals, poor terminal to wiring connections or physical damage to the wiring harness.

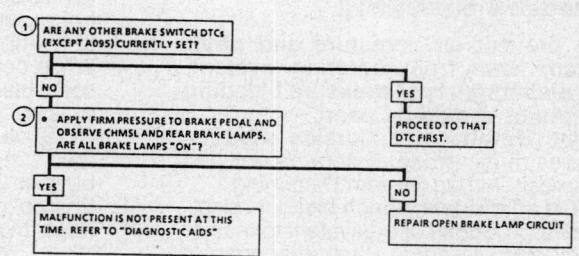

Fig. 197   Code A096, Brake lamps circuit open. 1993

1   SOLENOID ELECTRICAL CONNECTOR

2   TORX* HEAD BOLTS

3   SOLENOID ASSEMBLY

4   ABS HYDRAULIC MODULATOR

Fig. 198 Brake control solenoid removal

SYSTEM SERVICE

BRAKE SYSTEM BLEEDING

Before bleeding the rear brakes, the rear displacement cylinder pistons must be returned to their top most position. Using a TECH 1 scan tool or suitable equivalent, enter the manual control function and "APPLY" the rear motor. Ensure the enable relay is "ON." If a scan tool is not available, bleed the front brakes to ensure that a firm brake pedal exists, then carefully drive vehicle over 4 mph to cause the ABS to initialize itself. This will return the rear displacement cylinder to the top position. The entire brake system should now be rebled.

Pressure Bleeding

To prevent air, moisture and other contaminants from entering system, only diaphragm type pressure bleeding equipment should be used.

1. **On Beretta and Corsica models,** disarm air airbag system as outlined under "Airbag System Disarming."
2. **On all models,** attach bleeder adapter tool J35589 or equivalent to master cylinder reservoir, then the adapter tool to the pressure bleeder.
3. Connect a clear plastic hose to the front bleeder valve on the control assembly, then put opposite end of the hose into a clean container partially filled with brake fluid.
4. Set pressure bleeder to 5-10 psi and wait for approximately 30 seconds to insure there is no leakage.
5. Set pressure bleed equipment to 30-35 psi.
6. Slowly open bleeder valve and allow fluid to flow into container until no air bubbles are seen in fluid, then close the bleeder valve and **torque** to 65 inch. lbs.
7. Attach bleeder hose to rear bleeder valve of the control assembly and repeat step 5.
8. Position a cloth under hydraulic brake pipe connections.
9. Working from front of the control assembly to the rear, slowly turn each pipe nut and check for air in escaping fluid.
10. When air flow ceases, **torque** pipe nut to 13 ft. lbs.
11. Raise and support vehicle, then bleed wheel cylinders and calipers using the following sequence:
    a. Right rear.
    b. Left rear.
    c. Right front.
    d. Left front.
12. Lower vehicle and remove bleeder adapter tool from master cylinder.
13. Check fluid level in reservoir, fill as necessary.
14. Turn on ignition and note pedal travel and feel as follows:
    a. If pedal feels firm and constant, start the engine and recheck pedal travel, if pedal still feels firm and constant, proceed to step 14.
    b. If pedal feels soft or has excessive travel either initially or after engine is started, repeat bleeding procedure.
15. Road test vehicle, make several normal stops from a moderate speed, then make one or two ABS stops at approximately 50 mph.
16. Ensure pedal is still firm and constant.
17. Rearm airbag system as outlined under "Airbag System Arming."

Manual Bleeding

1. **On Beretta and Corsica models,** disarm air airbag system as outlined under "Airbag System Disarming."
2. **On all models,** remove master cylinder reservoir cover, then fill reservoir as necessary.
3. Attach one end of a clear plastic hose to rear bleeder valve of the brake control assembly, then put opposite end of the hose into a clean container.
4. While depressing brake pedal, slowly open bleeder valve, until fluid begins to flow.
5. Close valve and release brake pedal, then repeat procedure for front bleeder valve.
6. Ensure master cylinder is full, then raise and support vehicle.
7. Bleed wheel cylinders and calipers using the following sequence:
    a. Right rear.
    b. Left rear.
    c. Right front.
    d. Left front.
8. Lower vehicle and check fluid level in reservoir, fill as necessary.
9. Turn on ignition and note pedal travel and feel as follows:
    a. If pedal feels firm and constant, start the engine and recheck pedal travel, if pedal still feels firm and

1   EBCM ELECTRICAL CONNECTORS

2   HEX HEAD SCREWS

3   EBCM

Fig. 199 EBCM assembly removal. Except Cutlass Supreme, Grand Prix, Lumina & Regal

constant, proceed to step 14.
    b. If pedal feels soft or has excessive travel either initially or after engine is started, repeat bleeding procedure.
10. Road test vehicle, make several normal stops from a moderate speed, then make one or two ABS stops at approximately 50 mph.
11. Ensure pedal is still firm and constant.
12. Rearm airbag system as outlined under "Airbag System Arming."

COMPONENT REPLACEMENT

BRAKE CONTROL SOLENOID ASSEMBLY

1. **On Beretta and Corsica models,** disarm air airbag system as outlined under "Airbag System Disarming."
2. **On all models,** disconnect battery ground cable.
3. Disconnect solenoid electrical connector, **Fig. 198.**
4. Remove solenoid assembly retaining bolt, then the solenoid from the modulator.
5. Reverse procedure to install, **torque** retaining bolt to 39 inch lbs. and bleed ABS brake control assembly as described under "Brake System Bleeding." Rearm airbag system as outlined under "Airbag System Arming."

1. EBCM MOUNTING BRACKET
2. EBCM
3. ELECTROMAGNETIC COMPATIBILITY (EMC) SHEILD

Fig. 200 EBCM assembly removal. Cutlass Supreme, Grand Prix, Lumina & Regal

1. FRONT SENSOR ELECTRICAL CONNECTOR
2. FRONT SENSOR ATTACHING BOLT
3. FRONT SENSOR
4. KNUCKLE

Fig. 201 Front wheel speed sensor removal

1. REAR SENSOR ELECTRICAL CONNECTOR
2. SENSOR RETAINING BOLTS (4)
3. SENSOR RETAINING NUTS (4)
4. BOLT REMOVAL ACCESS HOLE
5. DRUM BRAKE ASSEMBLY
6. REAR BEARING/SENSOR ASSEMBLY

Fig. 202 Rear wheel bearing & speed sensor removal

ELECTRONIC BRAKE CONTROL MODULE (EBCM)

Except Cutlass Supreme, Grand Prix, Lumina & Regal

1. **On Beretta and Corsica models,** disarm air airbag system as outlined under "Airbag System Disarming."
2. **On all models,** disconnect battery ground cable.
3. Disconnect EBCM electrical connectors, **Fig. 199.**
4. Remove ECU to dash panel attaching screws, then the ECU from dash panel.
5. Reverse procedure to install, ensure all four plastic grommets are located properly and **torque** screws to 14 inch lbs. Rearm airbag system as outlined under "Airbag System Arming."

Cutlass Supreme, Grand Prix, Lumina & Regal

1. Disconnect battery ground cable.
2. Raise and support vehicle, then remove left front tire and wheel assembly.
3. Remove inner fender retaining screws.
4. Remove screw retaining Electromagnetic Compatibility (EMC) shield, **Fig. 200.**
5. Slide shield back on harness, then remove EBCM retaining screws.
6. Disconnect EBCM electrical connectors and remove EBCM.
7. Reverse procedure to install.

FRONT WHEEL SPEED SENSOR

1. **On Beretta and Corsica models,** disarm air airbag system as outlined under "Airbag System Disarming."
2. **On all models,** disconnect battery ground cable.
3. Raise and support vehicle.
4. Disconnect wheel sensor electrical connector, **Fig. 201.**
5. Remove sensor attaching bolt, then the sensor from the mounting bracket.
6. Reverse procedure to install, ensure sensor is properly aligned and lays flat against bracket bosses, **torque** attaching bolt to 9 ft. lbs. Rearm airbag system as outlined under "Airbag System Arming."

REAR WHEEL BEARING & SPEED SENSOR

Except Cutlass Supreme, Grand Prix, Lumina & Regal

1. **On Beretta and Corsica models,** disarm air airbag system as outlined under "Airbag System Disarming."
2. **On all models,** disconnect battery ground cable.
3. Raise and support vehicle, then remove rear wheel and tire assembly.
4. Remove rear brake drum, then disconnect sensor electrical connector, **Fig. 202.**
5. Remove wheel bearing and sensor attaching nuts and bolts, then then bearing and sensor assembly. **After bolts are removed, the rear brake assembly will be held in place by the hydraulic pipe. Use care not to bump or exert any force on the brake assembly to prevent any damage to the hydraulic pipe.**
6. Reverse procedure to install, noting the following:
   a. Align bolt holes in wheel bearing and speed sensor assembly, drum brake assembly and rear suspension bracket.
   b. When installing bolts, rotate axle flange to align large hole with each bolt location, then install bolt while

holding nut.

c. **Torque** bolts to 37 ft. lbs.

d. **On Beretta and Corsica models,** rearm airbag system as outlined under "Airbag System Arming."

Cutlass Supreme, Grand Prix, Lumina & Regal

The rear speed sensors and rings on these models are an integral part of the hub and bearing assembly. If speed sensors or rings are defective, the entire assembly must be replaced as a unit.

1. Disconnect battery ground cable.
2. Raise and support vehicle, then remove tire and wheel assembly.
3. Remove brake hose bracket, caliper and rotor.
4. Disconnect ABS electrical harness, then remove hub and bearing assembly mounting bolts.
5. Remove hub and bearing assembly.
6. Reverse procedure top install, **torque** bearing assembly mounting bolts to 52 ft. lbs.

ABS HYDRAULIC MODULATOR ASSEMBLY

To avoid personal injury, due to a retained load on the modulator assembly, the "Gear Tension Relief" function of the TECH 1 scan tool must be performed prior to removal of the brake control and motor assembly. Refer to "Component Testing" for procedure.

1. **On Beretta and Corsica models,** disarm air airbag system as outlined under "Airbag System Disarming."
2. **On all models,** disconnect battery ground cable.
3. Disconnect two solenoid electrical connectors, **Fig. 203.**
4. Disconnect fluid level sensor connec-

1	SOLENOID ELECTRICAL CONNECTORS	5	MASTER CYLINDER ATTACHING NUTS (2)
2	FLUID LEVEL SENSOR CONNECTOR	6	HYDRAULIC MODULATOR AND MASTER CYLINDER ASSEMBLY
3	MOTOR PACK CONNECTORS	7	VACUUM BOOSTER
4	HYDRAULIC BRAKE PIPES (4)		

Fig. 203   ABS hydraulic modulator assembly removal

tor, then the 6-pin and 3-pin motor pack electrical connectors.

5. Place a shop cloth on top of motor pack to catch any dripping hydraulic fluid, then disconnect four hydraulic pipes from modulator assembly. **Plug open lines to prevent any fluid loss.**

6. Remove two modulator assembly to brake booster attaching nuts. It may be necessary to remove vacuum check valve from the booster to gain access to nut closest to check valve.

7. Remove modulator assembly from vehicle.

7. Reverse procedure to install, noting the following:

a. Torque modulator assembly to booster attaching nuts to 20 ft. lbs.

b. **Torque** hydraulic pipe nuts to 13 ft. lbs.

c. Bleed hydraulic system as described in "Hydraulic Brakes."

d. **On Beretta and Corsica models,** rearm airbag system as outlined under "Airbag System Arming."

REAR DRIVE AXLES
TABLE OF CONTENTS

Drive Axle Identification

Axle identification numbers can be found on either the code tag or sticker attached to the axle housing cover or stamped on the right front section of the axle shaft housing and on Corvette, the axle I.D. is underneath the differential.

Model	Axle Code Standard	Axle Code Limited Slip	Gear Ratio
1991			
Camaro	8HP①	8HT/8RC①	2.73
	8HK①	8HB/8HF①	3.08
	—	2PM/2PN①	3.23
	—	9EQ②	3.27
	8HL①	—	3.42
	—	9ER②	3.45
Caprice & Roadmaster Sedan	4GM①	—	2.56
	4LG①	4NC①	3.08
	4ZK①⑤	4ZJ①⑤	3.42
Caprice Wagon, Custom Cruiser & Roadmaster Wagon	4YL①	—	2.73
	4YE①	4YM①	3.23
Corvette	—	CQT③	2.59
	—	CQU③	2.73
	—	CQW③	3.07
	—	CQR④	3.45
	—	CQX④	3.54
Firebird	8HP	8HE/8HT①	2.73
	—	4ET②	2.77
	8HK①	8HB/8HF①	3.08
	8HJ①	2PM①	3.23
	—	8EV/9EQ②	3.27
	8HL①	2PM①	3.42
	—	8EW②	3.45
Brougham	4MF	—	3.08
	4ML	—	3.73
	—	4MM	3.73
1992			
Camaro	6HJ	6HK/6HM	2.73
	6HG	6HH/6HL	3.08
	6HF	6PC	3.23
	6HE	6PD	3.42
Caprice & Roadmaster Sedan	4GM①	—	2.56
	4LG①	4NC①	3.08
	4ZK①⑤	4ZJ①⑤	3.42

Model	Axle Code Standard	Axle Code Limited Slip	Gear Ratio
1992-Continued			
Caprice Wagon, Custom Cruiser & Roadmaster Wagon	4YL①	—	2.73
	4YE①	4YM①	3.23
Corvette	—	CQT③	2.59
	—	CQU③	2.73
	—	CQW③	3.07
	—	CQR④	3.45
	—	CQX④	3.54
Firebird	6HJ	6HK/6HM	2.73
	6HG	6HH/6HL	3.08
	6HF	6PC	3.23
	6HE	6PD	3.42
Brougham	4MF	—	3.08
	4ML	—	3.73
	—	4MM	3.73
1993			
Camaro	—	—	2.73
	—	—	3.23
Caprice & Roadmaster Sedan	4GM①	—	2.56
	4LL⑥	—	2.56
	4LM⑥	4NQ	3.08
	4LG①	4NC①	3.08
	4ZK①⑤	4ZJ①⑤	3.42
Caprice Wagon, Custom Cruiser & Roadmaster Wagon	4YL①	—	2.73
	4YE①	4YM①	3.23
Corvette	—	CQT③	2.59
	—	CQU③	2.73
	—	CQW③	3.07
	—	CQR④	3.45
	—	CQX④	3.54
Fleetwood (RWD)	4MM⑦	—	3.73
Firebird	—	—	2.73
	—	—	3.23

①—General Motors
②—Borg-Warner
③—Corvette w/Automatic Transmission
④—Corvette w/Manual Transmission
⑤—Police Option
⑥—Roadmaster Sedan
⑦—Locking differential

Troubleshooting

INDEX

PRELIMINARY CHECKS

Before the rear axle is to be serviced, ensure the source of the problem is the rear axle itself and not from other sources such as noise from the tires, road surface, engine, transmission, wheel bearings, muffler or body parts. Perform the following procedures to check for other sources that could be mistaken for axle noise:

1. Ensure rear axle lubricant is at the correct level and type, then select a level asphalt road to reduce tire and body noise.
2. After vehicle has been driven far enough to warm lubricant, note at which speed the noise occurs then stop vehicle. With vehicle in neutral run engine slowly through the RPM range that the noise occurred to check if noise was caused by the exhaust or power train.
3. Check for tire noise by temporarily inflating all tires to approximately 50 psi for test purposes only. Drive vehicle on a level asphalt road and note if a change in noise occurs compared to noise while tires are inflated at normal pressure. After test is completed ensure tires are inflated to manufacturer's specification.
4. Check the front and rear wheel bearings by lightly applying the brakes while keeping vehicle speed steady. If the noise diminishes, inspect front and rear wheel bearings by jacking up the front wheels, then spinning or shaking them to determine if bearings are loose. Replace if necessary.
5. With vehicle jacked up, check for metal to metal contact between the spring and the spring opening in the frame, upper and lower control arm bushings and frame and axle housing brackets. Ensure there is no metal to metal contact between the floor of the body and the frame. Replace bushings or rubber insulators if necessary.

REAR AXLE NOISES

After noise has been determined to be in the axle and not from other sources, check for the specific type of axle noise as follows:

ROUGH GROWL OR GRATING

1. Faulty pinion or rear axle case side bearing.

CHATTER ON TURNS

1. Wrong lubricant in axle.
2. Clutch cones worn.

KNOCK AT LOW SPEEDS

1. Worn universal joint.
2. Side gear hub counterbore in the differential case worn oversize.

CLUNK WHILE ACCELERATING OR DECELERATING

1. Worn differential case.
2. Excessive clearance between the axle shaft and side gear splines.
3. Excessive clearance between side gear hub and counterbore in case.
4. Excessive drive pinion and ring gear backlash.
5. Worn pinion and side gear teeth.
6. Worn thrust washers.

CONSTANT SCRAPING NOISE AT LOW SPEEDS

1. Defective or worn pinion bearing.

CONSTANT WHINE WHILE DRIVING

1. Defective or worn ring and pinion gear.

GROAN IN FORWARD OR REVERSE

1. Wrong lubricant in axle.

WHINE LOUDER WHILE TURNING

1. Defective or worn axle side gear and/or pinion.

LIMITED SLIP AXLE OPERATION

On all models, improper operation is often indicated by clutch slipping or grabbing which produces a whirring or chattering noise. These noises do not always indicate an axle failure but could be from lack of proper lubrication or normal noise when axle clutches are engaged during certain road conditions. Since the operational life of the limited slip unit is dependent on equal rotation of the wheels while driving straight ahead, it is important that there is no major difference in rear wheel tire size, air pressure or wear pattern, otherwise the vehicle may swerve during acceleration. If improper limited slip differential problems are not caused by the above, check for proper operation as follows:

AUBURN CONE TYPE DIFFERENTIAL

1. With parking brake released and automatic transmission in park or manual transmission in gear, raise both tires off the floor.
2. Remove hubcap or wheel disc and apply torque wrench and axle shaft puller tool No. J-21579 to either wheel. Measure torque required to rotate one wheel. **Torque** should be between 125 and 225 ft. lbs.
3. Place transmission in neutral position, then lower one rear tire to the ground.
4. Measure torque required to rotate the raised wheel. **On full size wagons and sedans, torque** should be between 45 and 110 ft. lbs. **On Camaro and Firebird models, torque** should be between 44 and 66 ft. lbs.
5. The differential case must be replaced as a unit if proper specifications are not obtained.

BORG WARNER 4 PINION DIFFERENTIAL

1. With automatic transmission in park and manual transmission in gear, raise rear of vehicle until one rear tire is off the ground.
2. Remove the rear tire and wheel assembly, then attach side hammer assembly tool No. J-2619-01 and axle shaft remover tool No. J-21579 to axle shaft flange and then a 1/2 inch-13 bolt into adapter.
3. Raise the other tire off the ground and attach torque wrench to side hammer assembly tool No. J-2619-01, then measure torque required to rotate axle shaft. If **torque** reading is less than 48 ft. lbs., remove and repair the differential unit.

Except Borg Warner Four Pinion Differential

INDEX

Fig. 1 Exploded view of rear axle assembly. Except Corvette

REMOVAL

DIFFERENTIAL ASSEMBLY

Except Corvette & 1993 Camaro & Firebird

1. Raise and support rear of vehicle, then loosen axle housing cover bolts and allow lubricant to drain into suitable container, **Fig. 1.**
2. Remove axle housing cover, then proceed as follows:
   a. Wipe excess lubricant from inside axle housing, then visually inspect parts for wear and/or damage.
   b. Rotate gears and check for roughness, indicating damaged bearings or gears.
   c. Install dial indicator on axle housing cover flange, then check and record ring gear to drive pinion backlash.
3. Remove rear axles and propeller shaft. Refer to "Rear Axle, Propeller Shaft & Brakes" for procedures.
4. If not previously marked, scribe reference marks on differential bearing bearing caps to be used during reassembly, then loosen bearing cap bolts.
5. Using suitable tool, pry differential case, bearing races and shims out of housing until loose in the bearing caps. Remove bearing races, then the differential assembly. Mark side cups and shims for reference during reassembly.

Corvette

1. Remove rear axle assembly. Refer to "Rear Axle, Propeller Shaft & Brakes" for procedure.
2. Remove axle housing cover and allow lubricant to drain.
3. Mount carrier assembly in a holding fixture, then remove snap rings retaining yoke shafts and the yoke shafts. Tag snap rings indicating which side they were removed from.
4. Remove bearing cap bolts, then the bearing caps. **When removing bearing caps, note matched letters stamped on caps and carrier. During reassembly, the caps must be installed in the exact position they were removed from.**
5. Install spreader tool, J-24385-01, adapter, J-24385 and a dial indicator set, **Fig. 2.** Zero indicator and ensure indicator stylus contacts one side of housing opening.
6. While observing micrometer, spread housing with tool. Do not spread housing more than 0.010 inch or distortion could result.
7. Using two pry bars, pry differential assembly upwards to remove. **Tag bearing cups and shims to indicate which side removed from.**
8. Remove spreader tool to prevent housing from taking a set.

1993 Camaro & Firebird w/Drum Brakes

1. Remove rear axle assembly. Refer to "Rear Axle, Propeller Shaft & Brakes" for procedure.
2. Remove rear brake pipe assemblies from rear brake cylinders, then disconnect center hose assembly from junction block.
3. Remove rear brake assemblies from housing, then rear axle shaft bearings and seals.
4. Remove rear backing plates, then differential case and differential drive pinion gear.

1993 Camaro & Firebird w/Disc Brakes

A shim may be installed between the rear brake caliper mounting plate and axle shaft tube flange on housing. This shim centers the rear brake caliper and pads over the brake rotor, ensuring even brake pad assembly pressure during braking. This shim may have to be changed when the housing is replaced.

SPREADER
J-24385-01
ADAPTERS
J-24385-20

Fig. 2 Spreader tool installation. Corvette

1. Remove rear axle assembly. Refer to "Rear Axle, Propeller Shaft & Brakes" for procedure.
2. Remove rear brake pipe assemblies from rear brake hose junction block, then junction block from housing.
3. Remove rear brake pipe and hose assemblies from housing.
4. Remove brake shaft bearing assemblies and seals, then caliper anchor brackets and mounting plates.
5. Remove shim, if installed.
6. Remove differential case, then differential drive pinion gear.

DRIVE PINION

1. Scribe reference mark between drive pinion and driveshaft yoke, then hold yoke with suitable tool and remove pinion nut and yoke. **If yoke shows wear in the seal-to-flange contacting surface, the yoke should be replaced.**
2. Install original pinion nut a few turns on pinion shaft, then using hammer and drift, tap pinion shaft out of pinion housing. **Hold gear end of pinion shaft when removing to prevent it from falling from axle housing. On Corvette models, the pinion preload shims may stick to the pinion housing or the rear bearing during removal. These shims must be collected and kept together for use during reassembly.**
3. Remove and discard pinion nut and collapsible spacer.
4. If being replaced, remove front and rear bearing races from pinion housing using drift positioned in race slots and hammer.
5. If rear pinion bearing is being replaced, remove using arbor press and adapters. Measure and record thickness of shim which is found under rear bearing.

DIFFERENTIAL CASE OVERHAUL

STANDARD DIFFERENTIAL

1. If side carrier bearings are to be replaced, remove bearings using a bearing puller.
2. Remove differential pinion shaft lock

1. CARRIER	15. VENT	29. CLUTCH PACK PLATES
2. RING AND PINION GEARS	16. BUSHING	30. CLUTCH PACK DISCS
3. INNER PINION BEARING AND CUP	17. SIDE BEARING BOLT	31. BELLEVILLE SPRING SPACER
4. PINION DEPTH SHIMS	18. SIDE BEARING CAP	32. CLUTCH PACK RETAINER CLIP
5. PINION BEARING PRELOAD SHIMS	19. SIDE BEARING AND CUP	33. YOKE (AXLE) SHAFT
6. OUTER PINION BEARING AND CUP	20. SIDE BEARING SHIMS	34. YOKE (AXLE) SEAL DUST SHIELD
7. OIL SLINGER	21. RING GEAR BOLT	35. YOKE (AXLE) SEAL
8. PINION YOKE SEAL	22. CASE	36. YOKE (AXLE) BEARING
9. PINION YOKE SEAL DUST SHIELD	23. PINION SHAFT	37. LUBRICANT FILLER PLUG
10. PINION YOKE	24. PINION SHAFT RETAINER	38. LUBRICANT IDENTIFICATION TAG
11. WASHER	25. THRUST WASHER	
12. PINION NUT	26. PINION GEAR	
13. CARRIER COVER BEAM	27. YOKE (AXLE)SHAFT SNAP RING RETAINER	
14. COVER BEAM BOLT	28. SIDE GEAR	

Fig. 3 Exploded view of Dana Trac-Lok limited slip differential. Corvette

bolt and the pinion shaft, **Fig. 1.**
3. Remove differential pinions and thrust washers, side gears and side gear thrust washers, noting installation position for assembly. Keep thrust washers with respective gears.
4. Remove ring gear bolts, then the ring gear, driving ring gear from case using drift and hammer. **Ring gear bolts have left hand threads. Do not pry between ring gear and case, as mating surfaces will be damaged.**
5. Inspect components as outlined in "Cleaning and Inspection" and replace as needed.
6. Install thrust washers on side gears and mount side gears in case. **Lubricate all components with specified gear lubricant prior to assembly.**
7. Position one differential pinion (less thrust washer) between side gears and rotate gears until pinion is directly opposite case loading opening.
8. Install other pinion with pinion shaft holes aligned, then rotate side gears and ensure pinions align with shaft

openings in case.
9. When pinions are properly aligned, rotate pinions toward loading opening just enough to allow thrust washer installation and install washers.
10. Align pinions with shaft opening in case, insert pinion shaft through case, install new lock bolt. It is not necessary to torque lock bolt at this time.
11. Ensure ring gear and case mating surfaces are clean and free from burrs, mount gear on case, install 2 new retaining bolts at opposite sides of gear and alternately tighten bolts to draw gear on case.
12. Install remaining ring gear bolts hand tight and ensure gear is squarely seated on case. **Always use new bolts of proper type when installing ring gear. Do not reuse old bolts.**
13. Alternately **torque** ring gear bolts to 89 ft. lbs.
14. Press side bearings onto case. If old bearings are reused, ensure bearings are installed in their original position.

Fig. 4 Installing special tools

Fig. 5 Clutch plate arrangement. Dana Trac-Lok

Fig. 6 Tool & pinion installation

2 PINION CONE TYPE (AUBURN) DIFFERENTIAL
Except Corvette

1. Remove case side bearings using tool J-22888.
2. Remove all but two opposite ring gear attaching bolts, then loosen the two remaining bolts.
3. Loosen ring gear by tapping on bolts, then remove ring gear from differential.
4. This limited slip rear axle case is not serviceable. If differential case is not satisfactory, replace complete assembly.

DANA TRAC-LOK LIMITED SLIP DIFFERENTIAL
Corvette

For side gear removal, refer to "Standard Differential."

1. Remove ring gear bolts, then using a brass drift tap gear from case, **Fig. 3.**
2. Remove cross pin retainers, then using punch and hammer, tap cross pin from case.
3. Assemble adapter plate from tool J-34174 into bottom side gear, then install threaded adapter plate into top side gear. Thread forcing screw into threaded adapter, and tighten until snug. This will force dished spacers to collapse and allow a loose condition in the case, **Fig. 4.**
4. Using a .020 inch feeler gauge, push out both pinion gear spherical washers, then back off forcing screw.
5. Using suitable tools, rotate case assembly until pinion gears can be removed. Remove pinion and differential gears, then the top side gear and clutch pack. **Keep stack of plates and discs in order they were removed from case.**
6. Remove retaining clips from plate tangs then separate plates and discs. **Note position of plates and discs before disassembling.**
7. Lubricate, then install dished spacer, discs and plates on side gear splines, **Fig. 5. When lubricating parts during assembly always use special limited slip differential lubricant.**
8. Install retaining clips on plate tangs, ensuring clips are completely seated on tangs.

4.32mm (.170") SERVICE SPACER

TOTAL THICKNESS OF BOTH PROD. SHIMS REMOVED	TOTAL THICKNESS OF SERVICE SHIMS TO BE USED AS A STARTING POINT
10.57mm .420"	1.52mm .060"
10.92mm .430"	1.78mm .070"
11.18mm .440"	2.03mm .080"
11.43mm .450"	2.29mm .090"
11.68mm .460"	2.54mm .100"
11.94mm .470"	2.79mm .110"
12.19mm .480"	3.05mm .120"
12.45mm .490"	3.30mm .130"
12.70mm .500"	3.56mm .140"
12.95mm .510"	3.81mm .150"
13.21mm .520"	4.06mm .160"
13.46mm .530"	4.32mm .170"
13.97mm .550"	4.83mm .190"

Fig. 7 Service shim thickness chart

9. Install side gear and clutch packs in case, ensuring retaining clips are properly seated in case recesses. Assemble adapter plate from tool J-34174 onto side gear, **Fig. 6.**
10. Install plates and discs on other differential gear and install in same manner.
11. Install threaded adapter plate into side gear. Thread forcing screw into threaded adapter, and tighten until snug. This will hold clutch packs in position.
12. Position pinion gears in case. Rotate differential case with suitable tool until pinion gear holes align with case bores.
13. Lubricate and install spherical washers, using a screwdriver. **Ensure pinion gear and spherical washer holes are aligned with case bores.**
14. Remove tools, then lubricate and install cross pin shaft and install retainers.
15. Do not install ring gear at this time. The ring gear will be installed during Final Assembly & Backlash Adjustment.

CLEANING & INSPECTION

1. Clean components in solvent and blow dry with compressed air, noting the following:
   a. Do not use brush when cleaning bearings.
   b. Do not spin dry bearings, as bearings will be damaged.
   c. Lightly lubricate components after cleaning to retard corrosion.
   d. Keep all components in order to ensure proper assembly.
2. Inspect gears for cracks, chipped teeth, wear and scoring, and damaged bearing or mounting surfaces. Replace gears that are damaged or excessively worn. **Ring gear and pinion must be replaced as an assembly.**
3. Inspect differential case for cracks, damage, worn side gear bores and scored bearing surfaces and replace as needed.
4. Inspect housing for scored bearing mount surfaces, cracks and distortion, and replace as needed.
5. Inspect bearing rollers and races for pitting, scoring, overheating and damage.
6. Mate bearing with race and check operation.
7. Replace any bearing that is damaged, excessively worn or that fails to operate smoothly.
8. Mount differential case along with side bearings and ring gear in housing, and check run-out with side bearings adjusted for zero preload and a dial indicator positioned against machined edge of ring gear.
9. If run-out exceeds .003 inch, and gear cannot be positioned to eliminate run-out, ring gear and/or case should be replaced.

DIFFERENTIAL SIDE BEARING PRELOAD ADJUSTMENT

EXCEPT CORVETTE

On these models, side bearing preload should be set before pinion is installed. If pinion is installed, remove ring gear.

1. Ensure bearing bores in housing and bearing caps are clean and free from burrs.
2. Measure production shims or service spacer and shim packs removed during disassembly to determine approximate thickness of shims needed for installation. **Do not reuse cast iron production shims as they may break during installation. If service spacers and shims were previously installed, they can be reused.**
3. In addition to .170 inch service spacers for each side, refer to chart, **Fig. 7,** and select service shim thickness required based on measurements made in step 2.

Fig. 8 Pinion gauge plate installation

4. Place outer races over side bearings, mount differential assembly in housing and insert service spacer between each bearing race and housing with chamfered edge against housing.
5. Install left bearing cap to retain case assembly and tighten bolts hand tight so that case can be moved while checking adjustments. **A bearing cap bolt can be installed in lower right bearing cap hole to prevent case from dropping while performing shim adjustments.**
6. Select one or two shims totaling thickness calculated in step 3 and insert shims between right bearing cap and service spacer.
7. Insert progressively larger feeler gauges between shim and service spacer until noticeable increase in drag can be felt, pushing gauge down until it contacts housing bore to obtain proper reading. **Rotate case while inserting gauges to ensure even readings.**
8. The gauge used just before additional drag is felt is correct thickness to obtain "zero preload." By starting with a thin gauge a sense of feel can be obtained for the original light drag caused by the weight of the case, allowing the drag caused by the beginning of preload to be recognized. **It will be necessary to work case in and out and to the left in order to insert feeler gauges.**
9. When the proper gauge thickness has been determined to obtain zero preload, remove bearing cap, case assembly service spacers and shim pack.
10. Select 2 service shims of approximate equal thickness whose total thickness is equal to the thickness of the shims installed in step 6 plus the thickness of the feeler gauge used to obtain zero preload.
11. Shims selected during this procedure allow differential assembly to be installed at zero preload, the equivalent of a "slip-fit" in case, during backlash adjustment. Final preload is not added until backlash has been adjusted.

CORVETTE

This procedure is performed before the drive pinion or ring gear is installed. If yoke seals and bearings were removed, install then at this time.

Fig. 9 Checking pinion depth

1. Ensure bearing bores and caps are clean and free of burrs.
2. Install master differential bearings J-34170 on 7.874 inch axles or J-35505 on 8.5 inch axles.
3. Assemble case assembly into carrier. Mount dial indicator with plunger travel of at least .200 inch to supporting fixture with plunger on the flange face.
4. Force case assembly as far as possible in dial indicator direction. With force still applied to case, zero dial indicator.
5. While observing dial indicator movement, force differential case in opposite direction. Repeat this step until the same reading is obtained.
6. Record dial indicator reading. The reading will be used during "Final Assembly And Backlash Adjustment."
7. Remove differential case assembly from carrier.

DRIVE PINION INSTALLATION & ADJUSTMENT

EXCEPT CORVETTE
Pinion Depth Adjustment

1. Install pinion bearing races in housing using a suitable driver.
2. Lubricate pinion bearings and install bearings in races.
3. Mount depth gauging jig in housing, **Fig. 8**, noting the following:
   a. Assemble gauge plate onto preload stud.
   b. Hold pinion bearings in position, insert stud through rear bearing and pilot and front bearing and pilot, then install retaining nut and tighten nut until snug.
   c. Rotate tool to ensure bearings are properly seated.
   d. Hold preload stud and tighten nut until 20 inch lbs. of **torque** which is required to rotate stud. To prevent

damage to bearing, **tighten nut in small increments, checking rotating torque after each adjustment.**
   e. Mount side bearing discs on arbor, using step for disc that corresponds to base of housing.
   f. Mount arbor and plunger assembly in housing, ensuring side bearing discs are properly seated, install bearing caps and tighten cap bolts to prevent bearing discs from moving, **Fig. 9.**
4. Mount dial indicator on arbor stud with indicator contact button bearing against top of arbor plunger.
5. Preload indicator ³/₄ revolution and secure to arbor mounting stud in this position.
6. Place arbor plunger on gauge plate, rotating plate as needed so that plunger rests directly on button corresponding to ring gear size.
7. Slowly rock plunger rod back and forth across button while observing dial indicator.
8. At point on button where indicator registers greatest deflection, zero dial indicator. **Perform steps 7 and 8 several times to ensure correct setting.**
9. Once verified zero reading is obtained, swing plunger aside until it is clear of gauge plate button and record dial indicator reading. **Indicator will now read required pinion depth shim thickness for a "nominal" pinion.**
10. Inspect rear face of drive pinion to be installed for a pinion code number. This number indicates in thousandths of an inch necessary modification of pinion shim thickness obtained in step 9.
11. Select pinion depth adjusting shim as follows:
   a. If pinion is stamped with a plus (+) number, add that number of thousandths to dimension obtained in step 9.

Fig. 10 Pinion depth gauge tool installation. Corvette

b. If pinion is stamped with a minus (−) number, subtract that many thousandths from dimension obtained in step 9.

c. If pinion is not stamped with plus or minus number, dimension obtained in step 9 is correct shim thickness.

12. Remove gauging tools and pinion bearings from housing, noting installation position of bearings.

Pinion Installation

1. Install selected shim onto pinion shaft, lubricate rear pinion bearing with specified axle lubricant, then press rear bearing onto pinion using suitable spacers.
2. Install new collapsible spacer onto pinion shaft, then insert pinion assembly into housing.
3. Lubricate front pinion bearing, install bearing into housing and tap bearing over pinion shaft with a drift while assistant holds pinion in place. **Old pinion nut and a large washer can be used to seat front bearing on pinion, but care must be taken not to collapse spacer if this method is used.**
4. Install new pinion seal in housing, coat seal lips with grease, then mount driveshaft yoke on pinion shaft, lightly tapping yoke until several pinion shaft threads protrude from yoke.
5. Coat rear of pinion washer with suitable sealer, then install washer and new pinion nut.
6. Hold driveshaft yoke with suitable tool, then alternately tighten pinion nut and rotate pinion until endplay is reduced to zero.
7. When endplay is reduced to zero, check pinion bearing preload using a torque wrench.
8. **On models except 1993 Camaro & Firebird,** continue tightening pinion nut in small increments until 35-40

inch lbs. of bearing preload is obtained with new bearings or 20-25 inch lbs. of bearing preload is obtained with used bearings, rotating pinion and checking preload after each adjustment. **Exceeding preload specification will compress collapsible spacer too far, requiring replacement of spacer. If preload specification is exceeded, spacer must be replaced and adjustment procedure must be repeated. Do not loosen pinion nut to reduce preload.**

9. **On 1993 Camaro & Firebird models,** nut should be further tightened only slightly and preload should be checked after each tightening. Exceeding preload specifications will compress the collapsible spacer too far and require installation of a new spacer. Set preload at 15-30 inch lbs. on new inner and outer bearing assemblies or 10-15 inch lbs. on used inner and outer bearing assemblies. Rotate drive pinion several times to ensure that inner and outer baring assemblies have been seated, then check preload again. If preload has been reduced by rotating drive pinion gear, reset preload to specifications.

CORVETTE

Pinion Depth Adjustment

The standard setting for the drive pinion is 2.565 inches on 7.874 ring gear axles or 2.625 inches on 8.5 inch ring gear axles.

1. Install pinion bearing races in housing using suitable driver.
2. Lubricate pinion bearings and install bearings in races.
3. Mount depth gauging jig in housing, **Fig. 10,** noting the following:
   a. Assemble gauge plate onto preload stud.
   b. Hold pinion bearings in position, insert stud through rear bearing and pilot and front bearing and pilot, then install retaining nut and tighten nut until snug.
   c. Rotate tool to ensure bearings are properly seated.
   d. Hold preload stud and tighten nut until 10 inch lbs. of **torque** which is required to rotate stud. To prevent damage to bearing, **tighten nut in small increments, checking rotating torque after each adjustment.**
   e. Mount proper side bearing discs on arbor.
   f. Mount arbor and plunger assembly in housing, ensuring side bearing discs are properly seated, install bearing caps and tighten cap bolts until a slight resistance is felt while rotating arbor.
4. Mount a dial indicator on arbor stud with indicator contact button bearing against top of arbor plunger.
5. Preload indicator ¾ revolution and secure to arbor mounting stud in this position.
6. Place arbor plunger on gauge plate,

Fig. 11 Checking ring gear & pinion backlash

rotating plate as needed so that plunger rests directly on button corresponding to ring gear size.

7. Slowly rock plunger rod back and forth across button while observing dial indicator.
8. At point on button where indicator registers greatest deflection, zero dial indicator. **Perform steps 7 and 8 several times to ensure correct setting.**
9. Once verified zero reading is obtained, swing plunger aside until it is clear of gauge plate button and record dial indicator reading. **Indicator will now read required pinion depth shim thickness for a "nominal" pinion.**
10. Inspect rear face of drive pinion to be installed for a pinion code number. This number indicates in thousandths of an inch necessary modification of pinion shim thickness obtained in step 9.
11. Select pinion depth adjusting shim as follows:
    a. If pinion is stamped with a plus (+) number, add that number of thousandths to dimension obtained in step 9.
    b. If pinion is stamped with a minus (−) number, subtract that many thousandths from dimension obtained in step 9.
    c. If pinion is not stamped with plus or minus number, dimension obtained in step 9 is correct shim thickness.
12. Remove gauging tools and pinion bearings from housing, noting installation position of bearings.

Pinion Installation

1. Install correct pinion depth shim in axle housing bearing cup bore, then install inner bearing cup using a bearing installer.
2. Apply appropriate axle lubricant to inner and outer pinion bearings. Apply oil to pinion seal, then install with seal installer.
3. Assemble new pinion preload shim stack with thickness being the same as was removed, then place preload stack on pinion and install pinion, oil slinger and end yoke in axle housing. Use a wooden hammer to tap end

yoke onto pinion splines.

4. Install pinion nut and washer. While holding end yoke, **torque** pinion nut to 200 ft. lbs.
5. Using an inch lbs. torque wrench, check rotating torque of pinion shaft. Pinion rotating **torque** should be 25 inch lbs on 7.875 axles or 30 inch lbs. on 8.5 axles with new bearings. To increase preload, remove shims. To decrease preload, add shims.

FINAL ASSEMBLY & BACKLASH ADJUSTMENT

EXCEPT CORVETTE

1. Ensure pinion depth and bearing preload are properly adjusted.
2. Install differential case assembly and selected side bearing shims as outlined in "Differential Side Bearing Preload, Adjust."
3. Install bearing caps in proper position and **torque** cap bolts to 55 ft. lbs.
4. Rotate assembly to ensure bearings are properly seated.
5. Mount dial indicator on housing with plunger bearing against tooth on ring gear, **Fig. 11.** Use small contact button on indicator plunger so that contact can be made at heel end of tooth and position dial indicator with plunger inline with gear rotation and perpendicular to gear tooth.
6. Hold pinion stationary and rock ring gear back and forth while reading backlash on indicator.
7. Check backlash at 3 evenly spaced positions around ring gear and record readings. **If backlash varies by more than .002 inch at any position, check ring gear installation and run-out, and correct as needed.**
8. If backlash is not within specifications, remove differential case assembly and bearing shims keeping shims in order.
9. Backlash is adjusted by increasing thickness of one shim while decreasing thickness of opposite side shim by the same amount in order to maintain proper side bearing preload. Select shims to adjust backlash as follows:
   a. If backlash is excessive, increase thickness of shim on gear tooth side and decrease thickness of shim on opposite side by the same amount.
   b. If backlash is less than specified, decrease thickness of shim on gear tooth side while increasing thickness of opposite shim by the same amount. **Each .002 inch change in shim thickness alters backlash by .001 inch.**
10. Reinstall differential assembly, shims and bearing caps, **torque** bearing cap bolts to 55 ft. lbs., then recheck backlash and adjust as needed.
11. If side bearing preload was set to zero during side bearing preload adjustment, proceed as follows:
    a. Remove both bearing caps and shim packs, keeping shim packs in

respective left or right positions.
   b. Select left side differential preload shim from specifications chart and insert shim between left bearing race and spacer, then install left bearing cap with bolts hand tight.
   c. Select right side differential preload shim from specifications chart and insert shim between right bearing race and spacer using a soft faced hammer.
   d. Install right bearing cap and **torque** all cap bolts to 55 ft. lbs.
12. Ensure ring gear teeth are clean and free from oil, then coat both drive and coast side of each tooth with marking compound.
13. Apply braking force to "load" ring gear, then rotate driveshaft yoke with wrench so that ring gear rotates one full revolution in each direction. **Test made without "loading" gears will not yield satisfactory pattern, and excessive rotating of gears is not recommended.**
14. Compare gear tooth pattern with **Fig. 12,** and correct assembly adjustments as needed.
15. When proper gear tooth contact pattern has been obtained, clean marking compound from gears.
16. Install axles and driveshaft. Refer to "Rear Axle, Propeller Shaft & Brakes" for procedure.
17. Install rear cover using RTV or new gasket and **torque** cover bolts to 20 ft. lbs., then fill rear axle with appropriate lubricant. On models equipped with limited slip differential, add additive No. 1050428 or equivalent to rear axle lubricant.

CORVETTE

1. Ensure differential case flange is free of nicks and burrs, then install ring gear on case using new bolts. **Torque** attaching bolts to 80 ft. lbs. **Tighten bolts evenly so that ring gear will be properly seated on case.**
2. Install master differential bearings J-34170 on 7.874 inch axles or J-35505 on 8.5 inch axles.
3. Assemble case assembly into carrier and install bearing caps with retaining bolts finger tight, then mount dial indicator to supporting fixture.
4. Force differential case away from pinion gear until completely seated against carrier cross bore face. With force still applied to case, place dial indicator plunger on a flat machined surface of differential case, if available, or on the head of a ring gear screw. Zero dial indicator.
5. Force ring gear to mesh with drive pinion. Rock gear slightly to ensure gear teeth are meshed and note dial indicator reading. Repeat procedure several times to ensure the reading is accurate. Ensure dial indicator reads zero each time the case is seated against cross bore face. The reading, .006 inch for preload and backlash adjustment will be the size of the shim pack between differential case and differential bearing on ring gear side.
6. Remove dial indicator, differential case and master bearings.
7. Assemble shim pack as determined in step 5 to ring gear side hub, then install bearing cone.

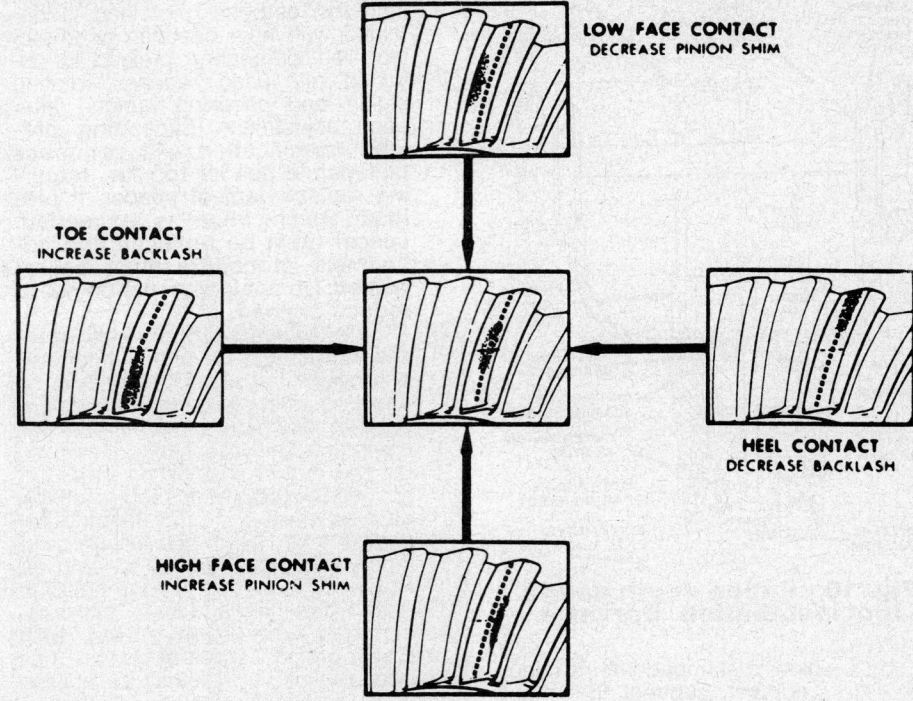

Fig. 12   Gear tooth contact pattern check

LOW FACE CONTACT
DECREASE PINION SHIM

TOE CONTACT
INCREASE BACKLASH

HEEL CONTACT
DECREASE BACKLASH

HIGH FACE CONTACT
INCREASE PINION SHIM

8. Take measurement obtained during differential side bearing preload adjustment and subtract shim pack dimension determined in step 5. The resulting dimension should be .015-.020 inch on models with 7.874 inch axle or .008-.012 inch on models with 8.5 inch rear axle.
9. Assemble shim pack as determined in step 8 to hub opposite ring gear, then install bearing cone.
10. Install spreader tool, J-24385-01, adapter, J-24385 and dial indicator set, **Fig. 2.** Zero indicator and ensure indicator stylus contacts one side of housing opening.
11. While observing micrometer, spread housing with tool. Do not spread housing more than 0.010 inch or distortion could result.
12. Assemble differential bearing cups on case, then install case in rear housing. If necessary, use a soft faced hammer to seat case in carrier cross bore.
13. Install bearing caps and bolts. Ensure letters stamped on caps correspond in position and direction with letters stamped in carrier. **Torque** bolts to 45 ft. lbs. on models with 7.874 inch rear axle or 63 ft. lbs. on models with 8.5 inch rear axle.
14. Check ring gear and pinion backlash at three equally spaced points with dial indicator. Backlash tolerance is .006-.009. Backlash cannot vary between points checked more than .001-.0015.
15. If backlash is excessive, move shims from side opposite ring gear to ring gear side, but do not change the combined total thickness of both shim packs.
16. If backlash is too small, move shims from ring gear side to side opposite ring gear, but do not change the combined total thickness of both shim packs.
17. Install inner yoke shafts into carrier, then the shaft snap rings. Check axle shaft endplay. If endplay is not within .0005-.0085 inch, install thicker or narrower axle shaft snap ring as necessary.
18. Install axle housing cover with RTV or gasket to rear housing and install bolts.
19. Install rear axle assembly. Refer to "Rear Axle, Propeller Shaft & Brakes" for procedure.
20. Add four ounces of limited slip additive No. 1052358 or equivalent to rear axle, then top off with rear axle lubricant No. 1052271 or equivalent.

Borg Warner Four Pinion Differential

INDEX

REMOVAL

DIFFERENTIAL ASSEMBLY

1. Raise and support rear of vehicle, then loosen axle housing cover bolts and allow lubricant to drain into a container.
2. Remove axle housing cover, then proceed as follows:
   a. Wipe excess lubricant from inside axle housing, then visually inspect parts for wear and/or damage.
   b. Rotate gears and check for roughness, indicating damaged bearings or gears.
   c. Install dial indicator on axle housing cover flange, then check and record ring gear to drive pinion backlash.
3. Remove rear axles and propeller shaft. Refer to "Rear Axle, Propeller Shaft & Brakes" section for procedures.
4. If not previously marked, scribe reference marks on differential bearing caps to be used during reassembly, then remove bearing cap attaching bolts and caps.
5. Remove differential assembly from carrier by putting a box wrench on ring gear bolt and rotating companion flange with suitable tool. When differential assembly is removed from carrier, shims will also come out. Mark shims for reference during reassembly.

DRIVE PINION & BEARINGS

1. Remove pinion nut and companion flange using tool J-8614-01 or equivalent.
2. Remove drive pinion gear through rear of carrier using a hammer.
3. Pry front seal out of carrier assembly, then remove bearing cone.
4. Remove rear pinion bearing using tool J-33868 or equivalent and press.
5. Remove rear bearing cone from carrier using a punch.
6. Remove selective spacer washer.

DIFFERENTIAL CASE OVERHAUL

4 PINION STANDARD DIFFERENTIAL ASSEMBLY

1. Remove ring gear attaching bolts, then the ring gear from differential housing.
2. Drive out three differential pinion cross shaft retaining pins, **Fig. 1,** using a punch.
3. Drive three differential pinion shafts from housing using a punch. Remove long pinion shaft first.
4. Scribe alignment marks on differential case halves, then separate differential case halves by holding one side and tapping against other side with a soft hammer.
5. Remove four differential pinions, side gears and thrust washers from housing.
6. Remove differential case bearings using puller tool J-22888-20 or equivalent.
7. Inspect components as outlined in "Cleaning & Inspection" and replace as required.
8. Lubricate all gears and thrust washers with appropriate lubricant.
9. Install side gear thrust washers in differential case. Hold washers in position with grease.
10. Install side gear in large half of differential case.
11. Install thrust block in case, then drive long pinion cross shaft through case, pinion and thrust block bores. Align retainer pin hole with hole in case. **Use caution not to damage differential pinion thrust washers.**

1–DIFF. CASE
2–SIDE GEAR (2)
3–THRUST WASHER (S. G.) (2)
4–DIFF. CASE
5–PINION CROSS SHAFT (1)
6–RETAINER PINS (3)
7–PINION SHAFT (SHORT) (2)
8–THRUST WASHERS (DIFF PINION) (4)
9–DIFF. PINIONS (4)
10–THRUST BLOCK (1)
11–SIDE CASE BEARINGS

Fig. 1   Exploded view of Borg Warner 4 pinion standard differential

1–DIFF. CASE–FLANGE HALF
2–BRAKE CONES (2)
3–SPRING PLATES (2)
4–SIDE GEARS (2)
5–SHIMS (SIDE GEAR) (IF REQUIRED)
6–DIFF. CASE–CAP HALF
7–COMPRESSION SPRINGS
8–DIFF. PINIONS (4)
9–PINION SHAFT
10–THRUST WASHERS (DIFF. PINION) (4)
11–MOUNTING SCREWS (8)

Fig. 2   Exploded view of Borg Warner 4 pinion limited slip differential

12. Install two remaining pinions and thrust washers in large half of differential case. Drive two short pinion cross shafts through case, pinions and into thrust block bores. Align retainer pin hole with hole in case.
13. Install three cross shaft retaining pins through case and shafts. Ensure long cross shaft retaining pin extends 6 mm from case.
14. Install remaining side gear and thrust washer in small case half.
15. Install side gear through case bore, then align case halves on retaining pin. Rotate side gear to ensure gears are meshing.
16. Install ring gear and ring gear attaching bolts onto housing. **Torque** ring gear attaching bolts to 101 ft. lbs.
17. Press differential bearings on housing journals using tool J-21784 or equivalent.

4 PINION LIMITED SLIP DIFFERENTIAL ASSEMBLY

1. Remove ring gear attaching bolts, then the ring gear from differential housing.
2. Scribe alignment marks on differential case halves, then remove differential housing half attaching bolts and separate halves.
3. Scribe alignment marks on brake cones and shims, then remove pinion shaft, four differential pinions, thrust washer side gears, side gear shims if required, spring plates, compression springs and brake cones from housing, **Fig. 2**. Discard used compression springs.

4. Remove differential bearing using puller tool J-22888-20 or equivalent.
5. Inspect components as outlined in "Cleaning & Inspection" and replace as required.
6. Install brake cones in case, then select correct side gear positioning shim as follows:
   a. With brake cones fully seated, measure distance from case mating surface to flat surface on brake cone.
   b. If distance is 1.155-1.162 inches, no shims are required. If distance is 1.163-1.167 inches, .005 inch shim is required. If distance is 1.168-1.172 inches, .010 inch shim is required.
   c. Remove brake cones.
7. Apply suitable lubricant to both sides of pinion thrust washers, pinion bores and differential pinion shafts.

Fig. 3 Installing shims

J-25588

Fig. 4 Gear tooth contact pattern check

TOE CONTACT (INCREASE BACKLASH)

LOW FLANK CONTACT (DECREASE PINION SHIM)

HEEL CONTACT (DECREASE BACKLASH)

HIGH FACE CONTACT (INCREASE PINION SHIM)

A— FRONT PINION BEARING AND RACE
B— SPACER J-35118-5
C— SIDE DISCS J-21777-45
D— THRU BOLT J-21777-43

E— SPACER J-21777-42
F— REAR PINION BEARING
G— ARBOR J-23597-1
H— GAGE PLATE 35118-2

Fig. 5 Drive pinion & bearing shim adjustment

8. Install four pinions and spherical thrust washers.
9. Install brake cones, shims (if required) and side gear in cap half of differential case, then apply suitable lubricant to face of side gear. If cone or case is defective, they should be replaced as an assembly.
10. Install spring plate on side gear with convex side towards flange half.
11. Install differential pinion shaft, pinions and spherical thrust washers into cap half of differential case with pinions meshing with side gear.
12. Install three new concentric thrust washer springs through center of pinion shaft spider, then assemble second spring plate and spring with convex side toward springs.
13. Apply suitable lubricant to other side gear face, then install side gear shim, if required.

14. Install brake cone on spring plate.
15. Install flange half of case on top of assembly. Ensure oil channels are aligned.
16. Install two case attaching bolts 180° apart and tighten finger tight.
17. Align side gear and brake cone splines with axle shafts. Install clamp on one axle shaft so 3 inches extends beyond clamp.
18. Install differential housing on axle shaft splines, flanged half first.
19. Install remaining axle shaft through cap side of differential case, aligning side gear and cone splines.
20. Install remaining case attaching bolts. **Torque** bolts to 29 ft. lbs.
21. Install ring gear and ring gear attaching bolts. **Torque** attaching bolts to 101 ft. lbs.
22. Install differential bearings using tool J-21784 or equivalent.

CLEANING & INSPECTION

1. Clean components in solvent and blow dry with compressed air, noting the following:
   a. Do not use brush when cleaning bearings.
   b. Do not "spin dry" bearings, as bearings will be damaged.
   c. Lightly lubricate components after cleaning to retard corrosion.
   d. Keep all components in order to ensure proper assembly.
2. Inspect gears for cracks, chipped teeth, wear and scoring, and damaged bearing or mounting surfaces. Replace gears that are damaged or excessively worn.
3. Inspect differential case for cracks, damage, worn side gear bores and

scored bearing surfaces and replace as needed.
4. Inspect housing for scored bearing mount surfaces, cracks and distortion, and replace as needed.
5. Inspect bearing rollers and races for pitting, scoring, overheating and damage.
6. Mate bearing with race and check operation.
7. Replace any bearing that is damaged, excessively worn or that fails to operate smoothly.

ASSEMBLY
DIFFERENTIAL BEARING PRELOAD ADJUSTMENT

To adjust differential side bearing preload, change thickness of right and left shims equally so original backlash is not disturbed.
1. Ensure side bearing surfaces are clean and free of burrs.
2. Apply suitable lubricant to side bearings. **If original bearings are to be reused, original outer races should also be used.**
3. Install differential case in carrier, with bearing outer races in position.
4. Install left bearing cap and cap attaching bolts loosely so case may be moved during adjustment.
5. Measure original spacers and subtract .004 inch from each reading. Use caution not to interchange right and left spacers.
6. Select a service spacer for each side equal to thickness of original shim minus .004 inch, then install shim as shown in **Fig. 3**. Ensure flat edge of spacer faces against housing.
7. At this point, bearings should have no play and no drag (zero preload). If zero preload is not present, shims should be added or removed equally from both sides as necessary.
8. Check case for zero endplay using a dial indicator. **If shim installation causes excessive pinion to ring gear clearance, select thinner left shim and add difference to right side. Keep total shim thickness at a value equal to that obtained in step 6.**
9. Install both bearing caps and cap attaching bolts. **Torque** bolts 40 ft. lbs.
10. If pinion was not removed, check backlash and tooth pattern as follows:
   a. Apply marking compound on ring gear teeth.
   b. Rotate drive pinion one revolution and check gear tooth contact pattern as shown on **Fig. 4**. Add or remove shims as required.
   c. After backlash and tooth pattern operation has been completed, remove shim packs using caution not to mix them.
   d. Select new shims for each side .004 inch thicker than those removed, then install each shim on its proper side. This additional thickness will ensure proper bearing preload.
   e. Check total rotational torque. Total **torque** with differential case pre-

loaded and pinion installed should be 16-29 inch lbs. if new bearings are installed or 10-16 inch lbs. if original bearings are installed.
   f. If total rotational torque is not as specified, repeat steps 4 through 10.
11. If drive pinion was removed, remove differential case and shims, then proceed to "Drive Pinion & Bearing Shim Adjustment" procedure.

DRIVE PINION & BEARING SHIM ADJUSTMENT

1. Install front pinion bearing cup in carrier using tool J-7817 or equivalent.
2. Install spacer (E) into carrier bore, **Fig. 5.**
3. Slide rear pinion bearing and cap (F) onto thru bolt (D) and rear bearing into axle housing.
4. Install thru bolt (D), rear bearing and cap (F) into axle housing.
5. Assemble front bearing cone (A) and spacer (B) onto thru bolt.
6. Rotate nut and shaft while increasing torque on nut until a rotational **torque** of 15-22 inch lbs. is obtained. Rotate thru bolt back and forth when tightening nut to properly seat bearing.
7. Install discs on thru bolt assembly as shown in **Fig. 5**. Position carrier so dial indicator contact rod is directly over gauging area of gauge plate J-35118-2. **Discs must be fully seated in side bearing bores.**
8. Install bearing caps over gauge shaft discs, then the cap attaching bolts. **torque** attaching bolts to 40 ft. lbs.
9. With dial indicator rod contacting gauging area of J-35118-2, rock gauge shaft back and forth until dial indicator measures the greatest deflection. then zero dial indicator.
10. Rotate gauge shaft until shaft does not contact gauge plate, then note measurement.
11. Select correct pinion shim as follows:
   a. If reusing production pinion, and pinion is marked with a "+," correct shim will have a thickness equal to gauge reading minus amount specified on pinion.
   b. If reusing production pinion, and pinion is marked with a "−," correct shim will have a thickness equal to gauge reading plus amount specified on pinion.
   c. If using a production or service pinion which has no marking, correct shim will have a thickness equal to gauge reading.
12. Install selected pinion shim into carrier, then press rear pinion bearing cup into carrier using tool J-5590 or equivalent.
13. Press rear pinion bearing onto pinion using a bearing installation tool, then install pinion in carrier.
14. Install collapsible spacer and front bearing onto pinion while supporting pinion under head.
15. Install oil seal, companion flange and new nut on pinion, then tighten pinion

nut until a rotating **torque** of 10-25 inch lbs. with new bearings or 5-12 inch lbs. with original bearings is obtained while rotating pinion forwards to seat bearings.
16. If preload is excessive after tightening pinion nut, replace collapsible spacer and repeat steps 14 and 15.

FINAL ASSEMBLY & BACKLASH ADJUSTMENT

1. Ensure pinion depth and bearing preload are properly adjusted.
2. Install differential case assembly and selected side bearing shims as outlined in "Differential Bearing Preload Adjustment" procedure.
3. Rotate assembly to ensure bearings are properly seated.
4. Mount dial indicator on housing with indicator stem against tooth on ring gear. Use small contact button on indicator stem so that contact can be made at heel end of tooth and position dial indicator with stem inline with gear rotation and perpendicular to gear tooth.
5. Hold pinion stationary and rock ring gear back and forth while reading backlash on indicator.
6. Check backlash at 3 evenly spaced positions around ring gear and record readings. **If backlash varies by more than .002 inch at any position, check ring gear installation and run-out, and correct as needed.**
7. If backlash is not within .004-.007 inch, remove differential case assembly and bearing shims keeping shims in order.
8. Backlash is adjusted by increasing thickness of one shim while decreasing thickness of opposite side shim by the same amount in order to maintain proper side bearing preload. Select shims to adjust backlash as follows:
   a. If backlash is excessive, increase thickness of shim on gear tooth side and decrease thickness of shim on opposite side by the same amount.
   b. If backlash is less than specified, decrease thickness of shim on gear tooth side while increasing thickness of opposite side by the same amount. **Each .002 inch change in shim thickness alters backlash by .001 inch.**
9. Reinstall differential assembly, shims and bearing caps, **torque** bearing cap bolts to 40 ft. lbs., then recheck backlash and adjust as needed.
10. Ensure ring gear teeth are clean and free from oil, then coat both drive and coast side of each tooth with marking compound.
11. Apply braking force to "load" ring gear, then rotate driveshaft yoke with wrench so that ring gear rotates one full revolution in each direction. **Test made without "loading" gears will not yield satisfactory pattern, and excessive rotating of gears is not recommended.**

12. Compare gear tooth pattern with **Fig. 4**, and correct assembly adjustments as needed.
13. When proper gear tooth contact pattern has been obtained, clean marking compound from gears.
14. Install axles and driveshaft. Refer to "Rear Axle, Propeller Shaft & Brakes" section for procedure.
15. Install rear cover using new gasket, then fill rear axle with appropriate lubricant.

Rear Axle Specifications

CAMARO & FIREBIRD

Year	Axle Model	Ring Gear Diameter, Inch	Ring Gear Backlash, Inch	Pinion Bearing Preload, Inch Lbs.		Total Assembly Preload, Inch Lbs.		Side Bearing Preload, Inch Lbs.		Differential Bearings, Inch Lbs.	
				New	Used	New	Used	New	Used	Used	New
1991	GM ①	7.62	.005–.009	24–32	9–12	35–40	20–25	—	—	—	—
	Borg Warner ②	7.75	.004–.007	12–25	5–12	—	—	10–25	5–12	10–25	5–12
1992	GM	7.62	.005–.009	15–30	9–12	32–55	16–28	—	—	—	—
1993	GM	7.62	.005–.009	15–30	10–15	32–55	16–28	—	—	—	—

①—Models with rear drum brakes.
②—Models with rear disc brakes.

BROUGHAM, CAPRICE, CAPRICE WAGON, CUSTOM CRUISER, FLEETWOOD (RWD), ROADMASTER & ROADMASTER WAGON

Year	Model	Ring Gear Back Lash, Inch	Pinion Bearing Preload, Inch Lbs. ①		Differential Assembly Preload, Inch Lbs. ①	
			New Bearings	Used Bearings	New Bearings	Used Bearings
1991–93	All	.005–.009	②	10–15	35–40	20–25

①—Rotating torque with new seal.
②—7½ ring gear, 15 to 30 inch lbs., 8½ ring gear 18 to 36 inch lbs.

CORVETTE

Year	Axle Model	Carrier Type	Ring Gear Backlash		Pinion Bearing Preload		Side Gear Preload	
			Method	Adjustment, Inch	Method	New Bearings Inch Lbs.	Method	Adjustment, Inch
1991–93	Dana Model 36 ①	Integral	Shims	.006–.009	Shims	15–35	Shims	.015–.020
	Dana Model 44 ②	Integral	Shims	.006–.009	Shims	20–40	Shims	.008–.012

① —Models with automatic transmission.
② —Models with manual transmission.

MANUAL STEERING GEARS

TABLE OF CONTENTS

Applications

CAVALIER, LEMANS & SUNBIRD

Saginaw Rack & Pinion

PRIZM

Toyota Rack & Pinion

METRO

Suzuki Rack & Pinion

Saginaw Rack & Pinion

INDEX

DESCRIPTION

The rack and pinion steering system consists of two main components, the rack and the pinion. The motion of turning the steering wheel is transferred to the pinion. The rotary motion of the pinion is then transferred through the pinion teeth which mesh with teeth on the rack, which gives the rack linear motion. The linear motion is then transmitted through the inner and outer tie rods to the steering knuckles which turn the wheels.

STEERING GEAR SERVICE

Refer to **Figs. 1 and 2** for service procedures on this Saginaw rack and pinion steering gear.

Refer to the rear of this section for tightening specifications.

1. REMOVE AND INSTALL OUTER TIE ROD

REMOVE

1. Loosen pinch bolts.
2. Remove tie rod from steering knuckle, using Tool J-24319-01 or BT7101.

INSTALL

1. Install parts as shown.
2. Make toe-in adjustment by turning tie rod adjuster.
3. Torque pinch bolts to 55 N·m (41 Ft. Lbs)

2. REMOVE AND INSTALL INNER TIE ROD AND INNER PIVOT BUSHING

REMOVE

1. Pry-off lock plate and dispose
2. Loosen inner tie rod bolt and remove.
3. Inner tie rod can now be removed by sliding out between bolt support plate and rack and pinion boot.

If both inner tie rods are to be removed, after removing the first tie rod reinstall inner tie rod bolt to keep rack and pinion boot and other parts properly aligned.

INSTALL

1. Be sure center housing cover washers are fitted into rack and pinion boot.
2. Install parts as shown.
3. Torque inner tie rod to specifications
4. Install new lock plate with notches in proper position, refer below

3. REMOVE AND INSTALL RACK AND PINION BOOT, RACK GUIDE, BEARING GUIDE, MOUNTING GROMMET OR HOUSING END COVER

REMOVE

1. Separate right-hand mounting grommet and remove. Left-hand mounting grommet need not be removed unless replacement is required.
2. Cut both boot clamps and discard.
3. Using constant pressure, slide rack and pinion boot over boot retaining bushing and off housing.
4. The boot retaining bushing on housing end need not be removed unless damaged.
5. Remove housing end cover only if damaged.

INSTALL

1. Remove boot retaining bushing from pinion end of boot.
2. Slide new boot clamp on boot. Install bushing into boot.
3. Install new boot retaining bushing on housing if necessary.
4. Install rack guide on rack.
5. Coat inner lip of boot retaining bushing lightly with grease for ease of assembly.
6. Install boot on housing.
7. Be sure center housing washers are in place on boot.
8. For ease of assembly, install inner tie rod bolts through cover washers and boot screw onto rack lightly. This will keep rack, rack guide and boot in proper alignment.
9. Slide boot and boot retaining bushing until seated in bushing groove at pinion end of housing. Crimp new boot clamp.
10. Slide other end of boot onto boot retaining bushing in housing at tube end. Crimp new boot clamp

Fig. 2 Saginaw rack & pinion steering gear service procedures. (Part 1 of 3)

Fig. 1 Exploded view of Saginaw rack & pinion steering gear

1 SNAP RING	12 PLUNGER SPRING
2 STEERING RACK BUSHING	13 PLUNGER
3 STEERING RACK HOUSING AND GEAR CASE	14 WIRE BOOT CLAMP
4 PINION NEEDLE BEARING	15 BOOT
5 GEAR CASE SEAL	16 OUTER BOOT CLAMP
6 UPPER CASE PACKING	17 TIE ROD END LOCKNUT
7 GEAR CASE OIL SEAL	18 TIE ROD END
8 PINION BEARING PLUG	19 TIE ROD
9 PINION	20 LOCK WASHER
10 RACK DAMPER SCREW CAP	21 STEERING RACK MOUNT
11 RACK DAMPER SCREW	22 STEERING RACK

9. REMOVE AND INSTALL RACK

REMOVE

1. Thread inner tie rod bolt into rack. Use rack as slide hammer until housing end cover separates from housing.
2. Unthread bolt. Remove rack from housing.

INSTALL

1. Slide rack into housing.
2. Seat housing end cover in housing.

HOUSING END COVER — Slide rack back and forth to remove end cover.

INNER TIE ROD BOLT

Remove rack from housing

RACK AND PINION HOUSING ASSEMBLY

HOUSING END COVER

RACK — Coat rack teeth with lithium based grease

10. REMOVE AND INSTALL ROLLER BEARING ASSEMBLY

REMOVE

1. Remove parts as shown.

INSTALL

1. Install bearing assembly as shown.

ROLLER BEARING ASSEMBLY

HOUSING

Tool J-26269

ROLLER BEARING ASSEMBLY

Arbor press

NOTICE: Be sure bearing is fully bottomed.

Install roller bearing

Arbor press

Drift

Remove roller bearing

Fig. 2 Saginaw rack & pinion steering gear service procedures. (Part 3 of 3)

---

7. REMOVE AND INSTALL VISCOUS STEERING DAMPER ASSEMBLY

REMOVE

1. Using a three-fingered wheel puller on flange of viscous damper, remove damper.
2. Replace dust seal if necessary.

NOTICE: Three finger puller must be used or damage to damper will occur.

INSTALL

1. Remove retaining shield from damper.
2. Be sure dust seal is installed on damper.
3. Line up flat on damper with adjuster plug.
4. Using a press, press on inner hub of damper with suitable pipe. Be sure tabs on damper line up with slots in housing. Press until seated on pinion shaft.
5. Using suitable pipe, press on outer housing of damper until fully seated in rack and pinion housing.
6. Reinstall retaining shield.

Remove Damper

RETAINING SHIELD

DAMPER ASSEMBLY

DUST SEAL

VISCOUS DAMPER

Press — Suitable pipe

Install damper

Press — Suitable pipe

8. REMOVE AND INSTALL PINION SHAFT ASSEMBLY

REMOVE

1. Turn pinion shaft until rack guide is equal distance from both sides of housing opening.
2. Mark location of stub shaft flat on housing.
3. Remove pinion.

INSTALL

1. Measure rack guide so it is equal distance on both sides of housing opening.
2. Install pinion assembly so when fully seated pinion shaft flat and mark on housing line up and rack guide is centered in housing opening.

RETAINING RING — Remove using pliers J-4245.

PINION ASSEMBLY

Center of flat

Start approx. 1.30

Finished 3.00

Center of flat

HOUSING OPENING

Tap on housing to separate pinion assembly from housing

Soft jaw vise

Remove pinion assembly

RACK GUIDE

Equal distance

Equal distance

Install pinion assembly

Fig. 2 Saginaw rack & pinion steering gear service procedures. (Part 2 of 3)

---

4. REMOVE AND INSTALL FLANGE AND STEERING COUPLING ASSEMBLY

REMOVE

1. Loosen and remove pinch bolt.
2. Remove coupling.

INSTALL

1. Install flange and steering coupling assembly on pinion shaft.
2. Install bolt and torque to specifications.

PINCH BOLT Torque to 40 N·m (29 Ft. Lbs.)

FLANGE AND STEERING COUPLING ASSEMBLY

5. REMOVE AND INSTALL DASH SEAL

REMOVE

1. Remove dash seal from viscous steering damper assembly.

INSTALL

1. Line up flat on seal and damper assembly and install seal.

DASH SEAL

VISCOUS STEERING DAMPER ASSEMBLY

Flat on seal

Flat on damper

Install dash seal

6. REMOVE AND INSTALL RACK BEARING

ON CAR ADJUSTMENT

If only the rack bearing requires adjustment, refer to INSTALL Step 2 below. Make adjustment with front wheels raised and steering wheel centered. WHEN ADJUSTING ON CAR, checking pinion torque is not required. Be sure to check returnability of the steering wheel to center after adjustment.

REMOVE

1. Remove parts as shown.

INSTALL

1. Install parts as shown.
2. With rack centered, turn adjuster plug clockwise until it bottoms, then back off 50° to 70°. Check torque on pinion.
3. Assemble lock nut and tighten while holding adjuster plug stationary. Coat with lithium base grease before adjustment.

NOTICE: Due to tolerances, some sockets will require a wrapping of card stock around the pinion serrations to make a tight enough fit.

Pinion torque — 0.9 to 2.3 N·m (8 In. Lbs. to 20 In. Lbs.)

9/16" socket

ADJUSTER PLUG LOCK NUT

ADJUSTER PLUG

RACK BEARING

O-RING SEAL

SPRING

ADJUSTER PLUG

Check pinion torque

LOCK NUT — Tighten to 70 N·m (50 Ft. Lbs.)

Fig. 2 Saginaw rack & pinion steering gear service procedures. (Part 2 of 3)

Suzuki Rack & Pinion

INDEX

1. PINION
2. PLASTIC HAMMER

Fig. 2 Separating pinion from housing

1. STEERING GEAR CASE PACKING
2. STEERING GEAR CASE OIL SEAL
3. PINION BEARING PLUG
4. STEERING PINION
5. STEERING PINION NEEDLE BEARING
6. RACK DAMPER SCREW CAP
7. RACK DAMPER SCREW
8. RACK PLUNGER SPRING
9. STEERING RACK PLUNGER
10. STEERING RACK HOUSING AND GEAR CASE
11. TIE-ROD END
12. TIE-ROD END LOCK NUT
13. RACK BOOT CLIP
14. BOOT
15. WIRE
16. STEERING TIE-ROD
17. TIE-ROD LOCK WASHER
18. STEERING RACK BUSHING
19. STEERING RACK SIDE MOUNT
20. STEERING RACK
21. STEERING PINION SIDE MOUNT
22. GEAR CASE SEAL
23. SNAP RING

Fig. 1 Exploded view of manual rack & pinion steering assembly

TORQUE WRENCH

J-34871

Fig. 3 Checking pinion torque

DESCRIPTION

The rack and pinion steering system consists of two main components, the rack and the pinion. The motion of turning the steering wheel is transferred to the pinion. The rotary motion of the pinion is then transferred through the pinion teeth which mesh with teeth on the rack, which gives the rack linear motion. The linear motion is then transmitted through the inner and outer tie rods to the steering knuckles which turn the wheels.

STEERING GEAR SERVICE

Refer to Fig. 1 when servicing steering gear assembly.

STEERING PINION
Removal

1. Remove rack damper screw cap and damper screw.
2. Remove rack plunger spring and rack plunger.
3. Remove steering gear case packing.
4. Using a 43 mm socket, remove pinion bearing plug with oil seal.
5. Tap on position shown in **Fig. 2** with a plastic hammer to separate pinion assembly from housing.

Inspection

1. Inspect pinion teeth for wear or damage.
2. Inspect oil seal for wear or damage.
3. Inspect plunger spring for deterioration and screw cap, screw and plunger for wear or damage.
4. Inspect gear case packing for damage. Replace all seals and any parts found defective.

Assembly

1. Apply grease to pinion teeth and gear case oil seal lip.
2. Install pinion assembly.
3. Install pinion case seal and bearing plug. **Torque** plug to 70. ft. lbs.
4. Install oil seal and gear case packing.
5. Install rack plunger, plunger spring and damper screw.
6. After tightening damper screw, back it off 90° and check rotational torque of pinion. Pinion **torque** should be 9.6 inch lbs., **Fig. 3**.

STEERING RACK
Removal

1. Remove boot wires and clips. Slide boots toward tie rod end.
2. Unbend tie rod lock washers and remove tie rods. Mark left and right tie rods.
3. Remove rack plunger and pinion assembly as described under Steering Pinion.
4. Remove rack from gear case as shown in **Fig. 4.**

Inspection

1. Inspect steering rack for deflection and rack teeth for wear or damage. Rack deflection should not exceed .016 inch.

Assembly

1. Apply a suitable lithium based grease to rack teeth surface.
2. Install rack into steering gear case, in opposite direction of removal.
3. Install pinion assembly and plunger assembly as described under "Steering Rack" Removal.
4. Install boot to steering rack housing, ensuring that rack side mount is posi-

Fig. 4 Rack removal from gear case

BUSH REMOVER
J34869

Fig. 7 Rack bushing removal

tioned as shown in **Fig. 5**.
5. Install tie rods as described under "Steering Rack."

PINION BEARING
Removal
1. Remove rack from steering gear case as described under "Steering Rack Removal."
2. Remove pinion bearing using tools Nos. J-34839 and J-6125-1B, as shown in **Fig. 6**.

Inspection
Check pinion bearing for wear or damages. Replace if found defective.

1. STEERING RACK HOUSING
2. RACK SIDE MOUNT

1.0 — 2.0 mm (0.04 — 0.08 in.)

Fig. 5 Ensuring rack side mount is positioned

BUSHING INSTALLER
J34868

1.0 — 2.0 mm (0.04 — 0.08 in.)

Fig. 8 Rack bushing installation

Assembly
1. Apply a suitable lithium based grease to pinion bearing rollers.
2. Press fit pinion bearing into gear case using bearing installer tool No. J-34840 or equivalent.
3. After bearing has been installed, ensure that rollers are installed properly.
4. Refer to "Steering Rack Assembly" for steering rack installation.

BEARING REMOVER
J-34839

PINION BEARING

SLIDING SHAFT
J-6125-1B

Fig. 6 Pinion bearing removal

RACK BUSHING
Removal
1. Remove rack from steering gear case as described under "Steering Rack Removal."
2. Remove snap ring. **When removing bushing, be careful not to pull bushing while holding gear case in vise as the housing may come off gear case.**
3. Remove bushing from rack housing using tool J-34869 or equivalent, **Fig. 7.**

Inspection
Inspect bushing for wear or damage and replace if necessary.

Assembly
1. Apply a suitable lithium based grease to inner surface of bushing.
2. Using bushing installer tool No.J-34868 or equivalent, install bushing into rack housing, ensuring bushing to housing clearance is as shown, **Fig. 8.**
3. Install snap ring.
4. Install steering rack assembly as described under Steering Rack Assembly.

Toyota Rack & Pinion

DESCRIPTION

This steering system converts rotary motion to linear motion as follows; when the steering wheel is turned, rotary motion is transferred to the steering shaft, shaft joint and rack pinion. The pinion teeth mesh with teeth on the rack and the rotary motion is transferred to the rack and changed to linear motion. The linear force is then transmitted through the tie rods and to the steering knuckles which steer the front wheels.

STEERING GEAR SERVICE

DISASSEMBLY

1. Clamp steering gear housing in a suitable vise, **Fig. 1.**
2. Remove tie rod ends as follows:
   a. Place match marks on tie rod ends and tie rods.
   b. Loosen and remove locknuts and tie rod ends.
3. Remove rack boots.
4. Remove tie rods and locking washers as follows:
   a. Push back bent section of locking washer.
   b. Using tie rod housing wrench tool No. J-35414 and steering rack end wrench tool No. J-35418 or equivalents, remove tie rod.
5. Remove steering gear case upper oil seal as follows:
   a. Remove dust cover.
   b. Remove snap ring with suitable snap ring pliers.
   c. Remove oil seal.

1	BOOT CLIP
2	STEERING GEAR RACK BOOT
3	BOOT CLAMP
4	RACK BUSHING
5	STEERING GEAR RACK HOUSING
6	PINION DUST COVER
7	LOCKING NUT
8	UPPER PINION SEAL
9	PINION BEARING ADJUSTING SCREW
10	PINION UPPER BEARING
11	STEERING PINION
12	PINION LOWER BEARING
13	RACK GUIDE
14	RACK GUIDE SPRING
15	RACK GUIDE SPRING CAP
16	RACK GUIDE LOCKING NUT
17	INNER TIE ROD
18	LOCKING WASHER
19	STEERING RACK
20	OUTER TIE ROD
21	TIE ROD LOCKING NUT

Fig. 1   Exploded view of Toyota rack & pinion steering gear

ASSEMBLY

1. Coat new upper oil seal with manual steering gear lube No. 1052182 or equivalent, then install seal followed by snap ring and dust cover.
2. Install tie rods and locking washers as follows:
   a. Install new locking washer.
   b. Using tie rod housing wrench tool No. J-35414 and steering rack end wrench tool No. J-35418 or equivalents, install tie rods and **torque** to 53 ft. lbs.
   c. Stake locking claw washer with a brass bar and hammer.
3. Install rubber rack boots being careful not to twist or damage them.
4. Install tie rod ends as follows:
   a. Screw locknuts and tie rod ends onto tie rods until match marks are aligned.
   b. **Torque** tie rod end locknuts to 41 ft. lbs.

Tightening Specifications

NOTE: All Specifications In Ft. Lbs. Unless Noted.

Year & Model	Adjuster Plug Locknut	Flange & Coupling Pinch Bolt	Coupling To Column Pinch Bolt	Inner Tie Rod Pinch Bolts	Outer Tie Rod Pinch Bolts	Inner Tie Rod Bolt	Pinion Preload ① ②	Inner Tie Rod Housing To Rack	Outer Tie Rod Jam Nut
1991–92									
LeMans	52	18	18	16	16	66	14 max.	—	44
Metro	70	18	18	—	33③	—	7 max.	63	32
Prizm	—	26	26	—	41③	53	—	—	41

① —Inch lbs.
② —Effort required to sustain input shaft rotation with gear filled with lubricant.
③ —Locknut

POWER STEERING

NOTE: Automatic Transmission Fluid Should Not Be Used In These Power Steering Systems. ATF Is Not Compatible With The Seals And Hoses Used In This System And Will Eventually Cause Damage. Also, Power Steering Fluid Must Withstand Very High Pressure (About 1400 psi), Whereas Transmission Fluid Does Not Have The Need To Operate At These Pressures. If ATF Has Been Added To A Power Steering System As In An Emergency Situation, The System Should Be Drained, Flushed And Refilled With Power Steering Fluid As Soon As Possible To Avoid Damage.

TABLE OF CONTENTS

Applications

FRONT WHEEL DRIVE VEHICLES

EXCEPT PRIZM & STORM

Saginaw Rack & Pinion
Toyota Rack & Pinion

PRIZM

Toyota Rack & Pinion

STORM

Jidosha Kiki Rack & Pinion

REAR WHEEL DRIVE VEHICLES

EXCEPT CORVETTE

Saginaw Rotary Valve

CORVETTE

Saginaw Rack & Pinion

Power Steering Pressure Specifications

Model	Year	Engine	Maximum Pressure Reading, Gauge Valve Open	Minimum Pressure Reading, Gauge Valve Closed
Achieva	1992–93	2.3L & 3.3L	150	1000②
Beretta	1991–93	2.2L, 2.3L & 3.1L	150	1000②
Bonneville	1991	3800	200	1000①
	1992–93	3800	150	1000②
Brougham	1991–92	5.0L & 5.7L	200	1250
Camaro	1991–92	3.1L, 5.0L & 5.7L	200	1000
	1993	3.4L & 5.7L	150	1000②
Caprice	1991–92	5.0L & 5.7L	200	1000
	1993	4.3L, 5.0L & 5.7L	150	1000②
Cavalier	1991	2.2L & 3.1L	200	1250
	1992–93	2.2L & 3.1L	150	1000②
Century	1991–92	2.5L & 3.3L	150	1250
	1993	2.2L & 3.3L	150	②
Corsica	1991–93	2.2L, 2.3L & 3.1L	150	1000
Corvette	1991–93	5.7L	150	1250
Custom Cruiser	1991–92	5.0L & 5.7L	200	1000
Cutlass Calais	1991	2.3L, 2.5L & 3.3L	200	1250
Cutlass Ciera	1991–92	2.5L & 3.3L	150	1250
	1993	2.2L & 3.3L	150	②
Cutlass Cruiser	1991–92	2.5L & 3.3L	150	1250
	1993	2.2L & 3.3L	150	②
Cutlass Supreme	1991	2.3L & 3.1L	150	1250
	1991	3.4L	181	1250
	1992–93	3.1L	150	②
	1992–93	3.4L	181	②
DeVille	1991–92	4.5L & 4.9L	200	1250
	1993	4.9L	150	1000②
Eldorado	1991–92	4.5L & 4.9L	200	1250
	1993	4.6L & 4.9L	200	1500②
Firebird	1991–92	3.1L	200	1000
	1991–92	5.0L & 5.7L	200	1000
	1993	3.4L & 5.7L	150	1000②
Fleetwood	1991–92	4.5L & 4.9L	200	1250
	1993	4.9L	150	1000②
Grand Am	1991	2.3L & 2.5L	200	—
	1992–93	2.3L & 3.3L	150	1000②
Grand Prix	1991	3.1L	150	1250
	1991	2.3L	150	1250
	1992–93	3.1L	150	②
	1992–93	3.4L	181	②
LeMans	1991	1.6L & 2.0L	200	1000①
	1992–93	1.6L	200	②
LeSabre	1991–92	3800	200	1250
	1993	3800	150	1000②

Continued

POWER STEERING PRESSURE SPECIFICATIONS—Continued

Model	Year	Engine	Maximum Pressure Reading, Gauge Valve Open	Minimum Pressure Reading, Gauge Valve Closed
Lumina	1991	2.5L	200	1250
	1991	3.1L	150	1250
	1991	3.4L	181	1250
	1992	2.5L	200	②
	1992–93	3.1L	150	②
	1992–93	3.4L	181	②
	1993	2.2L	200	②
Park Avenue	1991–92	3800	200	1250
	1993	3800	150	1000 ②
Prizm	1991–93	1.6L	—	924
Reatta	1991	3800	200	1250
Regal	1991–92	3.1L	150	1250
	1992	3800	200	1250
	1993	3.1L	150	②
	1993	3800	200	②
Riviera	1991–93	3800	200	1250
Roadmaster	1991	5.0L & 5.7L	200	1000
	1992–93	5.7L	150	1000 ②
Seville	1993	4.6L & 4.9L	200	1500 ②
Skylark	1991	2.3L, 2.5L & 3.3L	200	—
	1992–93	2.3L & 3.3L	150	1000 ②
Storm	1991	1.6L	—	924
	1992–93	1.6L & 1.8L	—	924
Sunbird	1991	2.0L & 3.1L	200	—
	1992–93	2.0L & 3.1L	150	1000 ②
Toronado/Trofeo	1991–92	3800	200	1250
88	1991–92	3800	200	1000 ①
	1993	3800	150	1000 ②
98	1991–92	3800	200	1000 ①
	1993	3800	150	1000 ②
6000	1991	2.5L & 3.1L	200	1000

① —1250 psi w/TC style pump.
② — Fully close and reopen valve three times. Record highest pressure readings each time valve is closed. Do not leave valve fully closed for more than five seconds. Each reading should be at least 1000 psi; readings should be within 50 psi of each other.

Power Steering Pumps

INDEX

DIAGNOSIS & TESTING
System Pressure Test

When performing system test procedures, power steering pressures can easily exceed 1000 psi. Extreme caution must be exercised when performing these tests to prevent personal injury.

CUTLASS SUPREME, GRAND PRIX, LUMINA & REGAL
Models w/2.3L, 3.1L, 3.4L & 3800 ENGINES

This procedure has been modified by Chevrolet service bulletin No. 90-45-3B and Buick service bulletin No. 89-3-21A.

1. **On models with 3.4L and 3800 engines,** remove ECM cover/coolant reservoir and lay aside.
2. **On models with 3.1L engines,** remove fuse block shield and A.I.R. belt, if equipped.
3. **On models with 3.1L and 3800 engines,** partially remove serpentine belt.
4. **On all models,** open retaining clip from high pressure pipe.
5. Remove high pressure pipe from pump. **Catch any fluid that may drain to avoid fluid seepage into engine and keep high pressure pipe away from belt.**
6. **On models with 3.1L and 3800 engines,** install serpentine belt.
7. **On all models,** install power steering pressure gauge tool No. J-5176-D or equivalent as shown in **Fig. 1.**
8. Open valve on pressure gauge.
9. Start engine and allow system to reach operating temperature. Stop engine and check fluid level, add if necessary.
10. Start engine and check pressure.
11. **On models with 3.4L engine,** pressure reading should be under 181 psi. If pressure is above 181 psi, check hoses for restrictions.
12. **On models with 2.3L and 3.1L engines,** pressure reading should be under 150 psi. If pressure is above 150 psi, check hoses for restrictions.
13. **On models with 3800 engine,** pressure reading should be under 200 psi. If pressure is above 200 psi, check

NOTE: Tighten adapter fittings to prevent leakage at gauge and power steering line connections.

J 38049-2   J 5176-D   J 38049-3   J 5176-30   J 38049-1

To Pump   To Steering Gear

Fig. 1 Power steering pressure gauge connections. Cutlass Supreme, Grand Prix, Lumina & Regal w/2.3L, 3.1L, 3.4L & 3800 Engines

hoses for restrictions.
14. **On all models,** with engine running, close valve fully three times for not more than five seconds each time. Each reading should show at least 1250 psi.
15. If pressures recorded are high enough and within 50 psi of each other, the pump is operating normally.
16. If pressures recorded are high enough but not within 50 psi of each other, the control valve in the pump is sticking. Remove but do not disassemble control valve and clean it with crocus cloth or a fine hone to remove any burrs.
17. If pressures recorded are less than 1250 psi, replace control valve and recheck. If pressures are still low, inspect pump rotor and vanes.
18. Shutoff engine and remove pressure gauge.
19. **On models with 3.1L and 3800 engines,** partially remove serpentine belt.
20. **On all models,** install high pressure pipe to pump and close retaining clip to pipe.
21. **On models with 3.1L and 3800 engines,** install serpentine belt, fuse block shield and A.I.R. belt, if equipped.
22. **On models with 3.4L engine,** install

ECM cover/coolant reservoir.
23. **On all models,** bleed system and check fluid level.

Lumina w/2.2L & 2.5L Engines

This procedure has been modified by Chevrolet service bulletin No. 90-45-3B.
1. Raise and support vehicle.
2. Remove high pressure pipe from pump. Catch any fluid that may drain out.
3. Install hoses J-38049-25 and J-5176-30 or equivalents to pump.
4. Lower vehicle and install pressure gauge J-5176-D or equivalent as shown in **Fig. 2.**
5. Open valve on pressure gauge.
6. Start engine and allow system to reach operating temperature. Stop engine and check fluid level, add if necessary.
7. Start engine and check pressure.
8. Pressure reading should be 80–125 psi. If pressure is above 200 psi, check hoses for restrictions and poppet valve for proper assembly.
9. With engine running, close valve fully three times for not more than five seconds each time. Each reading should show at least 1250 psi.
10. If pressures recorded are high enough and within 50 psi of each other, the

NOTE: Tighten adapter fittings to prevent leakage at gauge and power steering line connections.

Fig. 2   Power steering pressure gauge connections. Lumina w/2.5L Engine

Fig. 3   Power steering pressure gauge connections. Geo models

pump is operating normally.

11. If pressures recorded are high enough but not within 50 psi of each other, the control valve in the pump is sticking. Remove but do not disassemble control valve and clean it with crocus cloth or a fine hone to remove any burrs.

12. If pressures recorded are less than 1250 psi, replace flow control valve and recheck. If pressures are still low, inspect rotor and vanes.

13. Shutoff engine and remove pressure gauge.

14. Raise and support vehicle and install high pressure pipe to pump.

15. Lower vehicle and check fluid level.

GEO MODELS

1. Disconnect pressure line from gear housing.
2. Connect pressure gauge J-5176 and gauge adapter J-35465 to power steering system as shown in **Fig. 3.**
3. Bleed system, then start engine and turn steering wheel from right and left stops two or three times.
4. Shutoff engine and ensure fluid temperature is at least 176°F and that fluid is full.
5. Start engine and run at idle speed. Check fluid pressure with valve on pressure gauge closed. If pressure is below 924 psi, power steering pump is defective and must be repaired or replaced as necessary. **Do not keep valve closed for more than 10 seconds. This could cause damage to the power steering system.**
6. Open valve on power steering gear and record pressure reading at 1000 RPM and at 3000 RPM. If there is more than 71 psi difference between 1000 and 3000 RPM checks, repair or replace steering gear valve.

A — LINE TO STEERING GEAR
B — LINE TO POWER STEERING PUMP

Fig. 4   Power steering pressure gauge connections. Except Cavalier, Cutlass Calais, Cutlass Supreme, Geo, Grand Am, Grand Prix, Lumina, Regal, Skylark, Sunbird & 1991–92 Beretta/Corsica

EXCEPT BERETTA, CAVALIER, CORSICA, CUTLASS CALAIS, CUTLASS SUPREME, GEO MODELS, GRAND AM, GRAND PRIX, LUMINA, REGAL, SKYLARK, SUNBIRD & 1992 ACHIEVA

1. **On models except 1993 Camaro and Firebird with 5.7L engine,** disconnect pressure hose from pump.
2. **On 1993 Camaro and Firebird models with 5.7L engine,** disconnect pressure hose from remote reservoir assembly.
3. **On 1993 Camaro and Firebird models,** place drain pan under pump assembly (3.4L engine) or remote reservoir assembly (5.7L engine).
4. Connect a spare pressure hose to

pump, then connect pressure gauge J-5176-D or equivalent between both hoses, **Fig. 4.**

5. Open valve on gauge, then start engine and allow it to reach operating temperature. Check fluid level and add if necessary.

6. Pressure reading should be 80-125 psi. Refer to chart for proper pressure readings; if pressure is more than specified, check hoses for restrictions and poppet valve on steering gear for proper assembly.

7. Close valve fully three times for not more than five seconds each time. Refer to chart for pressure readings (models without T/C style pump).

8. If pressures recorded are high enough and within 50 psi of each other, the pump is operating normally.

9. If pressures recorded are high enough but are not within 50 psi of each other, the control valve in the pump is sticking. Remove but do not disassemble control valve and clean it with crocus cloth or a fine hone to remove any burrs. Flush system if fluid appears to be dirty.

10. If pressures recorded are less than specification in step 5, replace control valve and recheck. If pressures are still low, inspect pump rotor and vanes.

11. If pump pressure meets specifications, leave valve open and turn steering wheel to both stops. Record highest pressures and compare with maximum pump pressure recorded. If pressure is not the same (at both stops) as maximum pressure, steering gear is leaking internally and must be disassembled and repaired.

12. Turn off engine and remove pressure gauge and spare hose, then reconnect pressure hose and restore fluid level to full level.

BERETTA, CAVALIER, CORSICA, CUTLASS CALAIS, GRAND AM, SKYLARK, SUNBIRD & 1992 ACHIEVA

1. Disconnect high pressure line at pow-

1-TUBE, RETURN
2-HOUSING ASM, HYD PUMP
3-SEAL, DRIVE SHAFT
4-SPRING, FLOW CONTROL
5-VALVE ASM, CONTROL
6-SEAL, O-RING
7-FITTING, O-RING UNION
8-SHAFT, DRIVE
9-PIN, PUMP RING DOWEL (2)
10-PLATE, THRUST
11-RING, PUMP
12-VANE (10)
13-ROTOR, PUMP
14-RING, SHAFT RETAINING
15-PLATE, PRESSURE
16-SEAL, O-RING
17-SPRING, PRESSURE PLATE
18-SEAL, O-RING
19-COVER, END
20-RING, RETAINING

Fig. 5 Exploded view of CB series power steering pump

Fig. 6 Removing return tube. CB series power steering pump

er steering pump.
2. Connect power steering analyzer J-25323-B to power steering pressure line at power steering pump.
3. Shift vehicle to park or neutral and set parking brake.
4. Open valve on analyzer, then start engine and allow system to reach operating temperature. Check fluid level and add if necessary.
5. Check and note pressure and flow readings at idle speed. **Do not move steering wheel while engine is running, this will give inaccurate pressure readings.** Pressure readings should be less than 200 psi. If pressure is above 200 psi, check hoses for restrictions.
6. Partially close valve to build 700 psi and record flow. Subtract flow from flow reading taken in step 5. Flow should not drop more than 1 gallon per minute (GPM). If flow drops more than 1 GPM, replace ring, rotor and vanes in pump. Check if pressure plate and thrust plates are worn or damaged.
7. Close valve fully three times for not more than five seconds each time. All three readings should be within 50 psi of each other. If reading are not within 50 psi or the same, replace flow control valve ensuring it is free to move in its bore.
8. Increase engine speed to 1500 RPM and read flow. Subtract flow from flow reading taken in step 5. Flow should not vary more than 1 GPM. If flow varies more than 1 GPM, remove flow control valve and clean. **Do not disassemble flow control valve.**
9. Turn steering wheel all the way left and right. Record flow at each stop. Flow should drop below 1 GPM at 1500 RPM at each stop. If flow is OK, check steering gear for leakage.
10. After completing any repairs, remove analyzer and reconnect high pressure line to pump, then bleed system and fill fluid to full level.

PUMP OVERHAUL
CB SERIES PUMP
Disassembly

1. Disconnect battery ground cable, then remove power steering pump from vehicle. Refer to individual car chapters for procedures.
2. Remove union fitting with O-ring and

Fig. 7 Rotor and/or pump ring installation. CB series power steering pump

the O-ring seal, **Fig. 5**.
3. Remove control valve assembly and flow control spring.
4. Protect driveshaft with shim stock and remove driveshaft seal by cutting with small chisel. Discard seal.
5. Remove return tube using tap, nut and washers, **Fig. 6**, as follows. **Plug return tube to prevent chips from entering pump.**
   a. Stack five 5/8 inch washers onto return tube.
   b. Run one 9/16 inch-12 nut midway up a 9/16 inch 12 tap.
   c. Install threaded end of tap into return tube until nut is positioned against washers.
   d. Using wrench, hold top stationary while turning nut clockwise.
6. Remove end cover retaining ring by inserting punch in access hole.

6 - PIN, PUMP RING DOWEL
7 - SHAFT, DRIVE
10 - HOUSING ASM, BUSHING &
11 - SEAL, DRIVE SHAFT
12 - SPRING, FLOW CONTROL
13 - VALVE ASM, CONTROL
15 - SEAL, O-RING
16 - FITTING, O-RING UNION
25 - PLATE, THRUST

26 - RING, PUMP
27 - VANE, PUMP
28 - ROTOR, PUMP
30 - RING, SHAFT RETAINING
31 - PLATE, PRESSURE
32 - SEAL, O-RING
33 - SPRING, PRESSURE PLATE
35 - SEAL, O-RING
36 - COVER, END
37 - RING, RETAINING

Fig. 8   Power steering pump assembly overhaul. Reverse rotation

7. Gently push on driveshaft to assist in removing end cover, O-ring, pressure plate spring, pump ring, pump vanes and the driveshaft subassembly, consisting of pump rotor, thrust plate, driveshaft and shaft retaining ring.
8. Remove O-ring from housing.
9. Remove dowel pins, then the driveshaft seal if not previously removed.
10. Remove pressure plate, pressure plate spring and O-ring from end cover.
11. Remove shaft retaining ring from driveshaft, then the pump rotor and thrust plate.

Inspection

1. Clean all parts in power steering fluid, then dry thoroughly.
2. Inspect pump ring, vanes, thrust plate, pressure plate and driveshaft for scoring, pitting or chatter marks, replacing parts as necessary.

Assembly

1. Lubricate new driveshaft seal with power steering fluid and, using seal installer, tool No. J 7728 or equivalent, press driveshaft seal into pump housing.
2. Install pump ring dowel pins into housing.
3. Install thrust plate and pump rotor onto driveshaft, **Fig. 7.**
4. Install new shaft retaining ring onto driveshaft.
5. Install driveshaft subassembly into housing.
6. Install pump ring, with holes positioned correctly onto dowel pins, **Fig. 7,** in housing.
7. Install vanes into pump rotor.
8. Lubricate new O-ring (large) with power steering fluid and install O-ring into end cover.
9. Install pressure plate and pressure plate spring.
10. Lubricate new O-ring (small) and install O-ring into end cover.
11. Lubricate outer edge of end cover with power steering fluid and press end cover into housing.
12. Insert retaining ring into groove in housing, with ring opening near access hole opening.
13. Remove plug and any chips, then coat end of new return tube with Loctite

solvent 75559 and Loctite 290 adhesive, or equivalents, and press return tube into housing until bottomed.

REVERSE ROTATION
Disassembly

1. Disconnect battery ground cable, then remove power steering pump from vehicle. Refer to individual car chapters for procedures.
2. Remove retaining ring using punch in access hole, **Fig. 8.**
3. Remove internal components from pump assembly by gently pushing on driveshaft. Components should include pressure plate sub-assembly consisting of the following parts: end cover, O-ring seal, pressure plate spring and pressure plate. Driveshaft sub-assembly consists of pump rotor, thrust plate, driveshaft and shaft retaining ring.
4. Remove O-ring from pump housing.
5. Remove dowel pins and driveshaft seal.
6. Remove end cover, pressure plate spring and O-ring from pressure plate.
7. Remove pump ring and vanes from driveshaft sub-assembly, then shaft retaining rings from driveshaft.
8. Remove thrust plate and pump rotor from driveshaft.

Inspection

1. Clean all parts in power steering fluid, then dry thoroughly.
2. Inspect pump ring, vanes, thrust plate, pressure plate, rotor and driveshaft for scoring, pitting or chatter marks, replacing parts as necessary.

Assembly

1. Lubricate new driveshaft seal with power steering fluid and, using seal installer, tool No. J 7728 or equivalent, press driveshaft seal into pump housing.
2. Install pump ring dowel pins into housing.
3. Install thrust plate and pump rotor onto driveshaft.
4. Install new shaft retaining ring onto driveshaft.
5. Install driveshaft sub-assembly into housing.
6. Install vanes into pump rotor.
7. Install pump ring, with holes positioned correctly onto dowel pins in housing.
8. Lubricate new O-ring with power steering fluid and install O-ring into groove in pump housing.
9. Install pressure plate and pressure plate spring.
10. Lubricate new O-ring and install O-ring into end cover.
11. Lubricate outer edge of end cover with power steering fluid and press end cover into housing.
12. Insert retaining ring into groove in housing, with ring opening near access hole opening.
13. Remove plug and any chips, then coat end of new return tube with Loctite solvent 75559 and Loctite 290 adhesive, or equivalents, and press return tube into housing until bottomed.

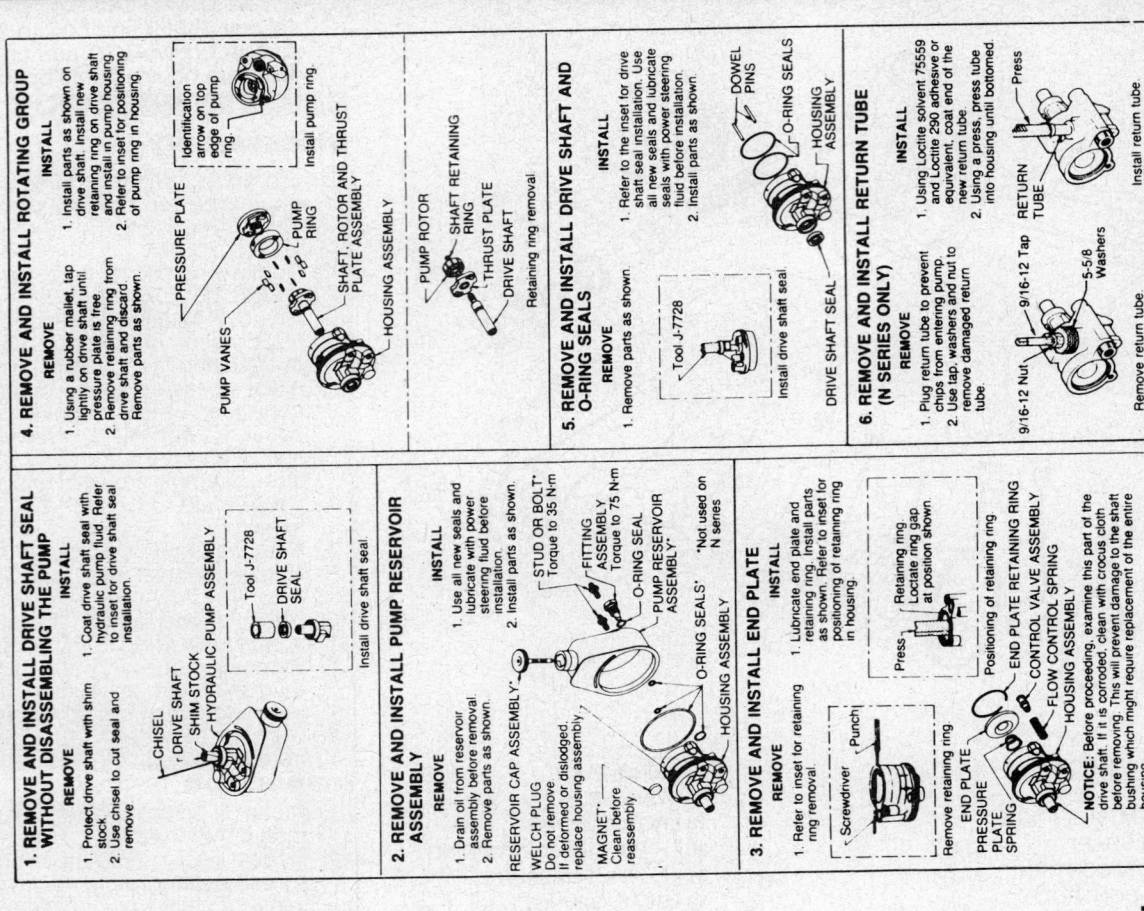

1. REMOVE AND INSTALL DRIVE SHAFT SEAL WITHOUT DISASSEMBLING THE PUMP

REMOVE
1. Protect drive shaft with shim stock.
2. Use chisel to cut seal and remove.

INSTALL
1. Coat drive shaft seal with hydraulic pump fluid. Refer to inset for drive shaft seal installation.

Install drive shaft seal.

2. REMOVE AND INSTALL PUMP RESERVOIR ASSEMBLY

REMOVE
1. Drain oil from reservoir assembly before removal.
2. Remove reservoir as shown.

WELCH PLUG
Do not remove.
If deformed or dislodged, replace housing assembly.

MAGNET—
Clean before reassembly.

INSTALL
1. Use all new seals and lubricate with power steering fluid before installation.
2. Install parts as shown.

STUD OR BOLT—
Torque to 35 N·m

FITTING ASSEMBLY—
Torque to 75 N·m.

O-RING SEAL

PUMP RESERVOIR ASSEMBLY

O-RING SEALS*   *Not used on N series

HOUSING ASSEMBLY

3. REMOVE AND INSTALL END PLATE

REMOVE
1. Refer to inset for retaining ring removal.

Screwdriver   Punch

Remove retaining ring

END PLATE
PRESSURE PLATE
SPRING

INSTALL
1. Lubricate end plate and retaining ring. Install parts as shown. Refer to inset for positioning of retaining ring in housing.

Press   Retaining ring
Locate ring gap at position shown.

Positioning of retaining ring

END PLATE RETAINING RING
CONTROL VALVE ASSEMBLY
FLOW CONTROL SPRING
HOUSING ASSEMBLY

NOTICE: Before proceeding, examine this part of the drive shaft. If it is corroded, clean with crocus cloth before removing. This will prevent damage to the shaft bushing which might require replacement of the entire housing.

4. REMOVE AND INSTALL ROTATING GROUP

REMOVE
1. Using a rubber mallet, tap lightly on drive shaft until pressure plate is free.
2. Remove retaining ring from drive shaft and discard. Remove parts as shown.

PRESSURE PLATE
PUMP RING
PUMP VANES
SHAFT, ROTOR AND THRUST PLATE ASSEMBLY
HOUSING ASSEMBLY

INSTALL
1. Install parts as shown on drive shaft. Install new retaining ring on drive shaft and install in pump housing. Refer to inset for positioning of pump ring in housing.

Identification arrow on top edge of pump ring.

Install pump ring.

PUMP ROTOR
SHAFT RETAINING RING
THRUST PLATE
DRIVE SHAFT

Retaining ring removal.

5. REMOVE AND INSTALL DRIVE SHAFT AND O-RING SEALS

REMOVE
1. Remove parts as shown.

Tool J-7728

Install drive shaft seal.

DRIVE SHAFT SEAL

INSTALL
1. Refer to the inset for drive shaft seal installation. Use all new seals and lubricate seals with power steering fluid before installation.
2. Install parts as shown.

DOWEL PINS
O-RING SEALS
HOUSING ASSEMBLY

6. REMOVE AND INSTALL RETURN TUBE (N SERIES ONLY)

REMOVE
1. Plug return tube to prevent chips from entering pump.
2. Remove damaged return tube.

9/16-12 Nut   9/16-12 Tap
5-5/8 Washers

Remove return tube

INSTALL
1. Using Loctite solvent 75559 and Loctite 290 adhesive or equivalent, coat end of the new return tube.
2. Using a press, press tube into housing until bottomed.

RETURN TUBE   Press

Install return tube

Fig. 9 Power steering pump assembly overhaul (Part 2 of 2). N & P series

---

POWER STEERING PUMP ASSEMBLY
(N SERIES–REMOTE RESERVOIR)
(P SERIES–SUBMERGED)

1–SHAFT, DRIVE
2–SEAL, DRIVE SHAFT
3–SEAL, O-RING (HOUSING)
4–HOUSING ASM., PUMP
5–SPRING, FLOW CONTROL
6–VALVE ASM., FLOW CONTROL
7–SEAL, O-RING (HOUSING)
8–SEAL, O-RING (PRESSURE & END PLATE)
9–PIN, DOWEL
10–PLATE, THRUST
11–ROTOR, PUMP
12–RING, SHAFT RETAINING

13–VANE, PUMP
14–RING, PUMP
15–PLATE, PRESSURE
16–SPRING, PRESSURE PLATE
17–PLATE, END
18–RING, END PLATE RETAINING
19–SEAL, O-RING (HOUSING TO STUD)
20–RESERVOIR ASM.
21–CAP ASM., RESERVOIR
22–STUD OR BOLT, PUMP MOUNTING
23–SEAL, O-RING (FITTING ASM.)
24–FITTING ASM. (CONNECTOR &)
25–MAGNET
26–RESERVOIR ASM.
27–HOUSING ASM., PUMP
28–TUBE, RETURN

3,4,7,19, 20, 21,22,23,26
not used with the housing

27,28 not used with this housing

P SERIES

N SERIES

20&21 not used with this reservoir

BENCH REPAIR INDEX (N&P SERIES PUMP)

TO REMOVE	EXPLODED VIEW NO.	PERFORM STEPS
Drive Shaft Seal	2	1
Pump Reservoir	20 or 26	2
Control Valve Asm.	6	2-3
End Plate	17	3
Rotating Group	1-10-11-12-13-14-15	2-3-4
O-Ring Seals (Rotating Group) & Drive Shaft	2-8	2-3-4-5
Return Tube	28	6

Fig. 9 Power steering pump assembly overhaul (Part 1 of 2). N & P series

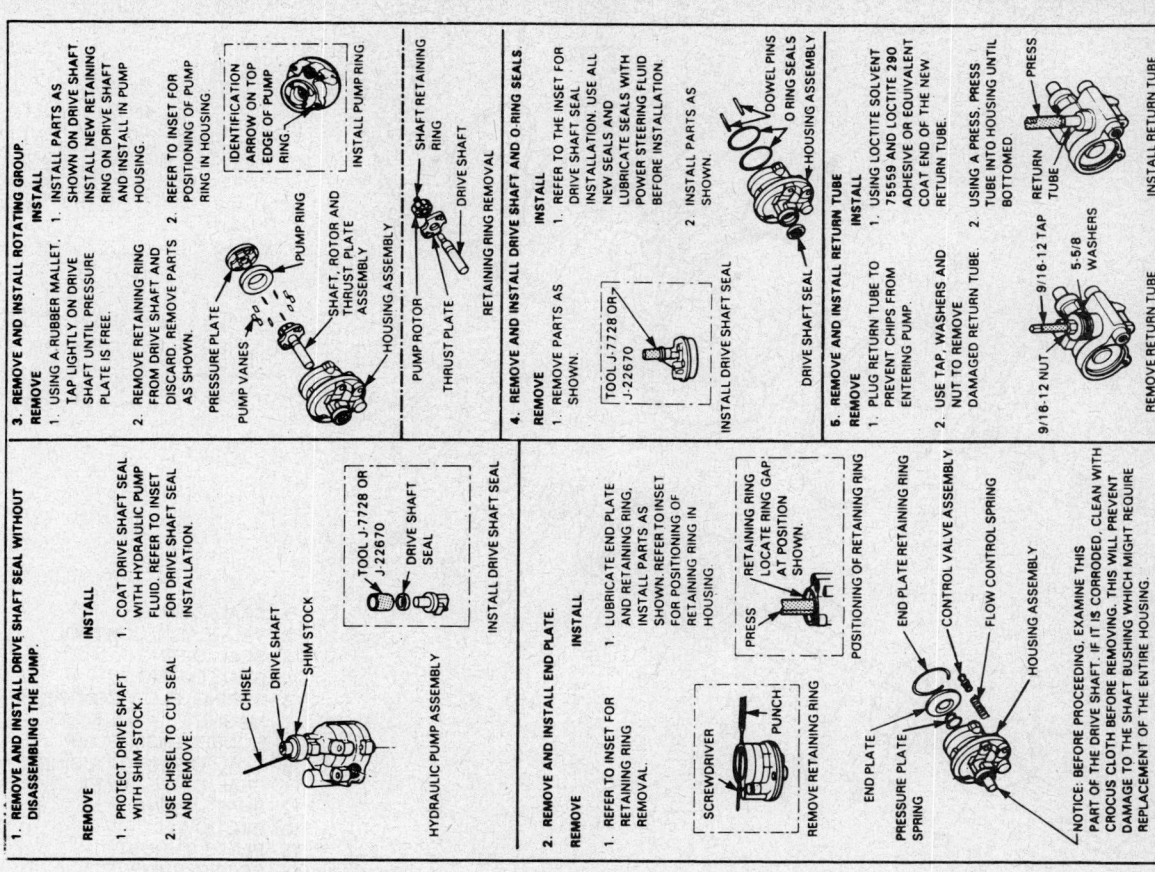

1. **REMOVE AND INSTALL DRIVE SHAFT SEAL WITHOUT DISASSEMBLING THE PUMP.**

REMOVE

1. PROTECT DRIVE SHAFT WITH SHIM STOCK.
2. USE CHISEL TO CUT SEAL AND REMOVE.

INSTALL

1. COAT DRIVE SHAFT SEAL WITH HYDRAULIC PUMP FLUID. REFER TO INSET FOR DRIVE SHAFT SEAL INSTALLATION.

3. **REMOVE AND INSTALL ROTATING GROUP.**

REMOVE

1. USING A RUBBER MALLET, TAP LIGHTLY ON DRIVE SHAFT UNTIL PRESSURE PLATE IS FREE.
2. REMOVE RETAINING RING FROM DRIVE SHAFT AND DISCARD. REMOVE PARTS AS SHOWN.

INSTALL

1. INSTALL PARTS AS SHOWN ON DRIVE SHAFT INSTALL NEW RETAINING RING ON DRIVE SHAFT AND INSTALL IN PUMP HOUSING.
2. REFER TO INSET FOR POSITIONING OF PUMP RING IN HOUSING.

IDENTIFICATION ARROW ON TOP EDGE OF PUMP RING

INSTALL PUMP RING

4. **REMOVE AND INSTALL DRIVE SHAFT AND O-RING SEALS**

REMOVE

1. REMOVE PARTS AS SHOWN.

INSTALL

1. REFER TO THE INSET FOR DRIVE SHAFT SEAL INSTALLATION. USE ALL NEW SEALS AND LUBRICATE SEALS WITH POWER STEERING FLUID BEFORE INSTALLATION.
2. INSTALL PARTS AS SHOWN.

5. **REMOVE AND INSTALL RETURN TUBE**

REMOVE

1. PLUG RETURN TUBE TO PREVENT CHIPS FROM ENTERING PUMP.
2. USE TAP, WASHERS AND NUT TO REMOVE DAMAGED RETURN TUBE.

INSTALL

1. USING LOCTITE SOLVENT 75559 AND LOCTITE 290 ADHESIVE OR EQUIVALENT COAT END OF THE NEW RETURN TUBE.
2. USING A PRESS, PRESS TUBE INTO HOUSING UNTIL BOTTOMED.

2. **REMOVE AND INSTALL END PLATE.**

REMOVE

1. REFER TO INSET FOR RETAINING RING REMOVAL.

INSTALL

1. LUBRICATE END PLATE AND RETAINING RING, INSTALL PARTS AS SHOWN. REFER TO INSET FOR POSITIONING OF RETAINING RING IN HOUSING

NOTICE: BEFORE PROCEEDING, EXAMINE THIS PART OF THE DRIVE SHAFT. IF IT IS CORRODED, CLEAN WITH CROCUS CLOTH BEFORE INSTALLING PUMP. THIS WILL PREVENT DAMAGE TO THE SHAFT BUSHING WHICH MIGHT REQUIRE REPLACEMENT OF THE ENTIRE HOUSING.

Fig. 10 Power steering pump assembly overhaul (Part 2 of 2). P series, L/reservoir except 1993 Camaro & Firebird

1-SHAFT, DRIVE
2-SEAL, DRIVE SHAFT
3-SPRING, FLOW CONTROL
4-VALVE ASM., CONTROL
5-SEAL, O-RING (PRESSURE & END PLATE)
6-PIN, DOWEL
7-PLATE, THRUST
8-ROTOR PUMP
9-RING, SHAFT RETAINING
10-VANE, PUMP
11-RING, PUMP
12-PLATE, PRESSURE
13-SPRING, PRESSURE PLATE
14-PLATE, END
15-RING, END PLATE RETAINING
16-SEAL, O-RING (FITTING ASM.)
17-FITTING ASM. (CONNECTOR &)
18-HOUSING ASM., PUMP
19-TUBE, RETURN

REMOVE POWER STEERING PUMP PULLEY

INSTALL POWER STEERING PUMP PULLEY

Fig. 10 Power steering pump assembly overhaul (Part 1 of 2). P series, L/reservoir, except 1993 Camaro & Firebird

1 - SEAL, O-RING
2 - VALVE ASM, CONTROL
3 - SEAL, O-RING
5 - SEAL, O-RING
6 - SPRING, FLOW CONTROL
7 - MAGNET
8 - HOUSING ASM, PUMP
10 - SEAL, O-RING (HOUSING)
11 - SEAL, DRIVE SHAFT
12 - SHAFT, DRIVE
13 - PIN, DOWEL
15 - PLATE, THRUST
16 - ROTOR, PUMP
17 - RING, SHAFT RETAINING
18 - VANE, PUMP
20 - RING, PUMP
21 - PLATE, PRESSURE
22 - SPRING, PRESSURE PLATE
23 - PLATE, END
25 - RING, END PLATE RETAINING
33 - FITTING ASM (CONNECTOR &)
35 - SEAL, O-RING
36 - BOLT, PUMP MOUNTING
37 - RESERVOIR ASM
38 - CAP ASM, RESERVOIR
40 - SEAL, O-RING (HOUSING TO STUD)

Fig. 11   Power steering pump assembly overhaul. P series, 1993 Camaro & Firebird

JIDOSHA KIKI

This pump is only serviced as an assembly, except for relief valve and pulley.

N & P SERIES PUMP

Refer to **Fig. 9** for service procedures on this power steering pump.

P SERIES L/RESERVOIR PUMP

Refer to **Fig. 10 and 11** for service procedures on this power steering pump.

TC SERIES PUMP

Refer to **Fig. 12** for service procedures on this power steering pump.

3. REMOVE AND INSTALL DRIVE SHAFT AND OR BALL BEARING ASSEMBLY

REMOVE
1. Remove retaining ring with suitable snap ring pliers.
2. Remove drive shaft and bearing assembly from housing.
3. Refer to inset for bearing removal.

INSTALL
1. See inset for installation of bearing on drive shaft.
2. Slide assembly into housing while rotating drive shaft so shaft serrations engage with rotor.
3. Bottom bearing in housing.
4. Install retaining ring with beveled side outward.

Note position of large lug to be sure beveled side of ring is properly located

4. REMOVE AND INSTALL DRIVE SHAFT SEAL

REMOVE
1. Using a screwdriver, pry seal from housing.

INSTALL
1. Using suitable socket, press seal into housing until bottomed.

1. REMOVE AND INSTALL RESERVOIR ASSEMBLY

REMOVE
1. Remove reservoir cap stick, drain hydraulic oil from reservoir.
2. Pry tab on reservoir retaining clip.
3. Slide retaining clips off pump assembly.
4. Remove reservoir assembly.
5. Remove O-Ring seal and dispose.

INSTALL
1. Lubricate O-Ring seal and install as shown.
2. Fit reservoir on pump assembly.
3. Install both (RH) and (LH) reservoir retaining clips.
NOTE: Be sure tabs are engaged on pump fully.

2. REMOVE AND INSTALL CONTROL VALVE ASSEMBLY

REMOVE
1. Remove parts as shown.

INSTALL
1. Install parts as shown.
2. Tighten to specifications.

FITTING Tighten to 75 Nm

Fig. 12 Power steering pump assembly overhaul (Part 2 of 4). TC series

POWER STEERING PUMP ASSEMBLY (TC SERIES)

USED ON SOME MODELS

NOTE: Return tube (15) used in place of Reservoir Assembly (24) and related parts (25 thru 28).

1 - HOUSING ASM. HYD. PUMP
2 - SLEEVE ASM
3 - PIN, DOWEL
4 - SEAL, O-RING
5 - SPRING, PRESSURE PLATE
6 - SEAL, O-RING
7 - PLATE, PRESSURE
8 - PIN, PUMP RING DOWEL (2)
9 - VANE (10)
10 - ROTOR, PUMP
11 - RING, PUMP
12 - SEAL, O-RING
13 - PLATE ASM, THRUST
14 - RING, THRUST PLATE RETAINING
15 - TUBE, RETURN
16 - SEAL, DRIVE SHAFT
17 - SHAFT, DRIVE
18 - BEARING ASM, BALL
19 - RING, RETAINING
20 - SPRING, FLOW CONTROL
21 - VALVE ASM, CONTROL
22 - SEAL, O-RING
23 - FITTING, O-RING UNION
24 - RESERVOIR ASM, HYD. PUMP
25 - SEAL, O-RING
26 - CLIP, RESERVOIR RETAINING (LH)
27 - CLIP, RESERVOIR RETAINING (RH)
28 - CAPSTICK ASM, RESERVOIR
29 - BAFFLE, PUMP ASM.

BENCH REPAIR INDEX (TC SERIES)

TO REMOVE	EXPLODED VIEW NO.	PERFORM STEPS
Return Tube	15	7
Control Valve Asm.	21	2
Drive Shaft	17	3
Ball Bearing (Drive Shaft)	18	3
Drive Shaft Seal	16	3-4
Rotating Group	7-9-10-11-12-13	3&5
Sleeve Asm.	2	3-5-6
Hydraulic Pump Reservoir Asm.	24	1

Fig. 12 Power steering pump assembly overhaul (Part 1 of 4). TC series

7. REMOVE AND INSTALL RETURN TUBE

REMOVE

1. Plug return tube to prevent chips from entering pump.
2. Use tap, washers and nut to remove damaged return tube.

Remove return tube

INSTALL

1. Using Loctite Solvent 75559 and Loctite 290 Adhesive, or equivalent, coat end of the new return tube.
2. Using a press, press tube into housing until bottomed.

Install return tube

6. REMOVE AND INSTALL SLEEVE ASSEMBLY

REMOVE

1. From the drive shaft side of housing, remove sleeve assembly using a punch.

INSTALL

1. Using a suitable socket, press sleeve assembly into housing from pressure plate side.
2. Be sure sleeve assembly is fully sealed in housing.

GENERAL SPECIFICATIONS

Power Steering Fluid No. 1050017 or Equivalent

Capacity	LITERS	PINTS
Complete System – Diesel	75	1-5/8
Complete System – Gas	70	1-1/2
Pump Only – Gas	50	1.0

Lubricant

POWER STEERING PUMP SPECIAL TOOLS

1.	BT-7185	PULLEY REMOVER
2.	BT-7005-A	PULLEY INSTALLER
3.	J-22670	SEAL DRIVER
4.	J-25033-B	PULLEY INSTALLER
5.	J-29785-A	PULLEY REMOVER
6.	J-23600-B	BELT TENSION GAGE
7.	BT-33-73F	BELT TENSION GAGE

Fig. 12 Power steering pump assembly overhaul (Part 4 of 4). TC series

5. REMOVE AND INSTALL ROTATING GROUP

REMOVE

1. Using a small punch in the access hole, remove the retaining ring.
2. Using a 5/8" piece of bar stock or suitable brass drift, press on pressure plate hub from drive shaft side of housing until thrust plate can be removed.
3. The O-ring seal in housing must be removed next. It is now not possible to remove the remaining parts of the rotating group from housing. It may still be necessary to use a press to remove the pressure plate.
4. Remove O-ring seal from the sleeve assembly and dispose.

INSTALL

1. Lubricate new O-ring seal and install into sleeve assembly.
2. Insert dowel pin in housing.
3. Install spring over sleeve assembly in housing.
4. Lubricate O-ring seal on pressure plate.
5. Mark top of pressure plate directly over dowel pin hole in plate. This will help line up hole with dowel pin.
6. Install pressure plate in housing. Be sure dowel pin and hole in pressure plate engage properly.
7. Install two (2) pump ring dowel pins in holes in pressure plate. Slide pump ring over these two pins. Be sure identification marks on pump ring are facing upward.
8. Install rotor with counter bore side toward drive shaft end of housing. Add ten vanes.
9. Lubricate O-ring seal and install in housing.
10. Install thrust plate in housing, making sure that dimples in thrust plate line up with bolt holes in housing and that thrust plate engages pump ring dowel pins.
11. Using a press, press on thrust plate far enough to install retaining ring.
12. Install retaining ring with opening of ring centered with bolt hole in housing nearest to access hole.

Install rotor

Retaining ring removal

Thrust plate removal

Install spring

Install seal and thrust plate.

Install pressure plate

Install retaining ring

Fig. 12 Power steering pump assembly overhaul (Part 3 of 4). TC series

Jidosha Kiki Rack & Pinion Power Steering Gear (Storm)

INDEX

1 INNER TIE ROD
2 LOCKING WASHER

Fig. 1   Unstaking lock washer

Fig. 2   Inner tie rod assembly removal

1 PLUNGER
2 SPRING
3 ADJUSTING PLUG
4 LOCK NUT

Fig. 3   Adjusting plug, spring & plunger assembly

1 NOTCH ON SHAFT
2 DIMENSION "A"
3 RACK HOUSING

Fig. 4   Pinion shaft measurement location

1 RACK HOUSING
2 VALVE PLUG

Fig. 5   Valve plug removal

1 PINION HOUSING
2 RACK HOUSING

Fig. 6   Pinion fixing nut removal

DESCRIPTION

This steering system converts rotary motion to linear motion as follows; when the steering wheel is turned, rotary motion is transferred to the steering shaft, shaft joint and rack pinion. The pinion teeth mesh with teeth on the rack and the rotary motion is transferred to the rack and changed to linear motion. The linear force is then transmitted through the tie rods and to the steering knuckles which steer the front wheels.

STEERING GEAR SERVICE

DISASSEMBLY

1. Remove retaining ring and dust boot from rack.
2. Clamp steering gear in suitable vise.

1 RACK HOUSING
2 PINION HOUSING
3 PINION RETAINING RING

Fig. 7   Retaining snap ring removal

3. Remove clamps from tie rod boots, then separate boots from rack and slide down tie rods.
4. Unstake locking washers between inner tie rods and rack, **Fig. 1.**

5. Remove right tie rod, then left tie rod assembly from rack, **Fig. 2.**
6. Loosen adjusting plug nut, then remove spring and rack plunger, **Fig. 3.**
7. Center rack and mark position of pinion valve. Rotate pinion gear until notch is parallel to rack, then carefully measure and record dimension "A," **Fig. 4.** This measurement **must** be used upon reassembly.
8. Remove valve plug, **Fig. 5.**
9. Remove pinion fixing nut, **Fig. 6.**
10. Remove pinion retaining snap ring, **Fig. 7.**
11. Remove rack from housing.
12. Remove inner rack seal and shock damper using inner rack seal remover tool No. 38304-5, **Fig. 8.**
13. Remove lower pinion bearing from rack housing.
14. Remove bearing and seal from valve housing using lower pinion valve housing seal and bearing remover tool No. 38304-1, **Fig. 9.**

[1] PINION VALVE HOUSING

Fig. 8 Inner rack seal & shock damper removal

[1] PINION VALVE HOUSING

Fig. 9 Pinion bearing removal

J 38304-4

[1] PINION VALVE HOUSING

Fig. 10 Pinion valve bearing & seal installation

[1] RACK HOUSING
[2] RACK GEAR

Fig. 11 Inner rack seal installation

[1] RACK HOUSING
[2] RACK GEAR

Fig. 12 Seating inner rack seal

[1] PINION VALVE ASSEMBLY

Fig. 13 Pinion valve assembly installation

ASSEMBLY

1. Install inner rack seal onto rack seal ring installer, tool No. J 33997-3 using rack seal ring expander, tool No. J 33997-2.
2. Install upper bearing and seal into pinion valve housing using lower pinion valve housing seal and bearing installer tool No. J 38304-4, **Fig. 10.**
3. Install rack into housing and seat inner rack seal using pack piston ring installer tool No. J 38304-7 and inner

rack seal installer tool No. J 38304-6, **Figs. 11 and 12.**

4. Install seal holder on to housing, then retaining ring on seal holder.
5. Install pinion valve assembly into housing using pinion ring compressor tool No. 38304-8, **Fig. 13.**
6. Install lower bearing on pinion valve.
7. Install pinion fixing nut and **torque** to 29 ft. lbs.
8. Install pinion valve housing cap, then rack plunger and plunger plug. **Torque** rack plunger adjusting plug to

44 inch lbs. Back off plug, then **torque** to 44 inch lbs. Back off plug 26° then, tighten locknut.
9. Install upper pinion valve seal, then retaining ring on upper pinion valve seal.
10. Install left tie rod assembly, then **torque** inner tie rod to 65 ft. lbs. and peen over stake washer. Install left tie rod boot.
11. Install right tie rod assembly, then **torque** inner tie rod to 65 ft. lbs. and peen over stake washer. Install right tie rod boot.

Saginaw Rack & Pinion Power Steering Gear

INDEX

DESCRIPTION

This power steering gear assembly, incorporates an integral tube and housing, containing a pinion shaft and steering rack. The tube and housing are joined by a plastic injection-bonding process. The pinion

shaft is supported in the housing by thrust bearings and bushings. A bushing and bulkhead assembly supports the steering in the tube.

OPERATION

A rotary-type valve body is used to con-

trol the hydraulic steering assist. Fluid under pressure is directed to the gear housing and into the valve body. The valve body then directs fluid to the power cylinder.

A spool valve, connected to the stub shaft by a locating pin, rotates within the valve body. Fluid directional passages, machined into the spool valve, are aligned with fluid passages in the valve body as the spool valve rotates. Fluid is directed through these passages, into either side of the power cylinder through the externally mounted oil lines.

STEERING GEAR SERVICE

FRONT WHEEL DRIVE EXCEPT ACHIEVA, BERETTA, CAVALIER, CORSICA, CUTLASS CALAIS, GRAND AM, LEMANS, SKYLARK & SUNBIRD

To prevent damage to the rack and pinion boot seal when removing it, the following should be noted. Slide the small end of the boot towards the rack until the groove is exposed. Place a small rubber band in the groove then, slide the small end of the boot over the rubber band and off the threaded end of the tie rod. This will prevent boot damage.

OUTER TIE ROD

1. Remove cotter pin, then hex slotted nut from outer tie rod assembly, **Figs. 1 and 2.**
2. Loosen jam nut, then remove outer tie rod from steering knuckle using steering linkage remover tool No. J 24319-01.
3. Remove outer tie rod from inner tie rod.
4. Reverse procedure to install, noting the following:
   a. **Torque** hex slotted nut to 35 ft. lbs. with a maximum of 45 ft. lbs. to install cotter pin.
   b. **Adjust** toe by turning inner tie rod.
   c. **Torque** jam nut against outer tie rod to 50 ft. lbs.

RACK & PINION BOOT & BREATHER TUBE

Removal

1. Remove outer tie rod.
2. Remove hex jam nut from inner tie rod assembly.
3. Remove tie rod end clamp, **Fig. 3,** then boot clamp with side cutters and discard.
4. Mark location of breather tube on housing before removing tube, then remove boot and breather tube.

Installation

1. Install new boot clamp onto boot.
2. Apply grease to inner tie rod or housing as shown in **Fig. 4.**
3. Align and install breather tube.
4. Install boot onto housing until seated in housing groove tang.
5. Position boot clamp on boot and crimp.
6. Position tie rod end clamp with pliers on boot.

1 - HOUSING ASM, R & P
2 - BUSHING, UPPER PINION
3 - SEAL, RACK & PINION
4 - VALVE ASM, PINION &
5 - RING, VALVE BODY
6 - RING, RETAINING
7 - ANNULUS, STUB SHAFT BEARING
8 - BEARING ASM, NEEDLE
9 - SEAL, STUB SHAFT
10 - SEAL, STUB SHAFT DUST
11 - RING, RETAINING
12 - ADAPTER, SEAL
13 - BEARING, RACK
14 - SPRING, ADJUSTER
15 - PLUG, ADJUSTER
16 - NUT, ADJUSTER PLUG LOCK

17 - RING, SHOCK DAMPENER
18 - ROD ASM, INNER TIE (LT)
19 - CLAMP, BOOT
20 - BOOT, RACK & PINION
21 - NUT, HEX JAM
22 - ROD ASM, OUTER TIE (LT)
23 - FITTING, LUBRICATION
24 - SEAL, TIE ROD
25 - NUT, HEXAGON SLOTTED
26 - PIN, COTTER
27 - BEARING ASM, BALL
28 - RING, RETAINING
29 - NUT, HEX LOCK
30 - COVER, DUST
31 - CLAMP, TIE ROD END
32 - GROMMET, MOUNTING
33 - BRACKET ASM, MOUNTING

34 - TUBE, BREATHER
35 - SEAL, O-RING
36 - THIS NUMBER NOT USED
37 - LINE ASM, CYLINDER (LT)
38 - LINE ASM, CYLINDER (RT)
39 - THIS NUMBER NOT USED
40 - SEAL, INNER RACK
41 - RACK ASM, PISTON & STEERING
42 - RING PISTON
43 - BULKHEAD, CYLINDER INNER
44 - SEAL, RACK & PINION (BULKHEAD)
45 - SEAL, O-RING
46 - BULKHEAD, CYLINDER OUTER
47 - RING, BULKHEAD RETAINING
48 - ROD ASM, INNER TIE (RT)
49 - ROD ASM, OUTER TIE (RT)
50 - PLUG ASM, O-RING

Fig. 1 Exploded view, power rack & pinion assembly. Front wheel drive except Achieva, Beretta, Cavalier, Corsica, Cutlass Calais, Grand Am, LeMans, Skylark & Sunbird

18-ROD ASM, INNER TIE (LT)
21-NUT, HEX JAM
22-ROD ASM, OUTER TIE (LT)
25-NUT, HEXAGON SLOTTED

Fig. 2 Outer tie rod replacement

19-CLAMP, BOOT
20-BOOT, RACK & PINION
21-NUT, HEX JAM
31-CLAMP, TIE ROD END
34-TUBE, BREATHER

Fig. 3 Boot replacement

APPLY GREASE TO THESE AREAS

1-HOUSING ASM, R & P
18-ROD ASM, INNER TIE (LT)
20-BOOT, RACK & PINION

Fig. 4   Boot seal application

STAKE BOTH SIDES OF HOUSING

SUPPORT HOUSING WHILE STAKING

.25mm (0.10 IN.) FEELER GAGE MUST NOT PASS BETWEEN RACK AND HOUSING STAKE (CHECK BOTH SIDES)

17-RING, SHOCK DAMPENER
18-ROD ASM, INNER TIE (LT)
41-RACK ASM, PISTON & STEERING

Fig. 7   Inner tie rod staking procedure

INNER TIE ROD
Removal

1. Remove rack and pinion steering assembly from vehicle.
2. Remove outer tie rod from inner tie rod assembly, then rack and pinion boot.
3. Place wrench on flat of rack assembly and place wrench on flats of inner tie rod housing **Fig. 5.**
4. Rotate housing counterclockwise until inner tie rod separates from rack.

Installation

Rack must be held during inner tie rod installation to prevent internal gear damage.

1. Install inner tie rod on rack and **torque** to 70 ft. lbs., **Fig. 6.**
2. Support rack and housing of inner tie rod assembly, then stake **both** sides of inner tie rod housing to flats on rack, **Fig. 7.**
3. Check both stakes by inserting a .010 inch feeler gauge between rack and housing stake.
4. Slide shock damper over housing until it engages.
5. Install boot and rack outer tie rod, then rack and pinion assembly to vehicle.

INNER TIE ROD HOUSING

1-HOUSING ASM, R & P
17-RING, SHOCK DAMPENER
18-ROD ASM, INNER TIE (LT)
41-RACK ASM, PISTON & STEERING

Fig. 5   Inner tie rod removal

1-HOUSING ASM, R & P
13-BEARING, RACK
14-SPRING, ADJUSTER
15-PLUG, ADJUSTER
16-NUT, ADJUSTER PLUG LOCK

Fig. 8   Rack bearing removal

WITH RACK CENTERED MARK LOCATION OF STUB SHAFT NOTCH ON HOUSING

NOTCH LOCATION MAY VARY WITH VEHICLE MODEL

1-HOUSING ASM, R & P
4-VALVE ASM, PINION &

"A" MEASURE DISTANCE

Fig. 10   Housing reference mark

RACK BEARING PRELOAD

Make adjustment with front wheels raised and steering wheel centered. Ensure to check returnability of steering wheel to center after adjustment.

1. Loosen locknut, then turn adjuster plug clockwise until it bottoms in housing, then back off 50° to 70°.
2. **Torque** locknut to 50 ft lbs while holding adjuster plug.

PINION & VALVE ASSEMBLY
Removal

1. Remove rack and pinion steering assembly from vehicle.
2. Remove adjuster plug locknut from

TORQUE 95 N•m (70 FT. LBS.)

MAKE SURE TIE ROD ROCKS FREELY IN HOUSING BEFORE STAKING

INNER TIE ROD HOUSING

1-HOUSING ASM, R & P
17-RING, SHOCK DAMPENER
18-ROD ASM, INNER TIE (LT)
41-RACK ASM, PISTON & STEERING

Fig. 6   Inner tie rod installation

1-HOUSING ASSEMBLY, R & P
11-RING, RETAINING
29-NUT, HEX LOCK
30-COVER, DUST

Fig. 9   Retaining ring & locknut removal

adjuster plug, **Fig. 8.**
3. Remove adjuster plug from housing, then adjuster spring and rack bearing.
4. Remove retaining ring from valve bore of housing, then dust cover, **Fig. 9.**
5. Holding stub shaft, remove hex locknut from pinion and valve assembly. **Stub shaft must be held to prevent damage to pinion teeth.**
6. With rack centered, mark location of stub shaft notch on housing, then measure distance "A," as shown in **Fig. 10.**
7. Using a suitable press, press threaded end of pinion until the pinion and valve assembly is almost removed. Mark a second location of stub shaft notch on housing. The second mark is used to position notch prior to reassemble.
8. Remove stub shaft dust seal, stub shaft seal, stub shaft bearing annulus assembly and pinion and valve assembly with retaining ring and valve body rings attached.
9. If necessary, remove valve body rings from pinion and valve assembly, then clean ring grooves. Inspect pinion and valve assembly for broken drive pin. If found, replace gear assembly.

Installation

1. If valve body rings are to be replaced, apply grease to ring grooves and rings. Install new rings, ensure split tabs are engaged and staggered, **Fig. 1.**
2. Place pinion and valve assembly into clear pinion and valve assembly ring

1. HOUSING, RACK AND PINION
10. RING, RETAINING
11. SEAL, DASH
12. COUPLING ASM., FLANGE AND STEERING
13. BOLT PINCH
18. NUT ADJUSTER PLUG LOCK
24. COVER, DUST
26. PLATE, BOLT SUPPORT
27. INNER TIE ROD ASSEMBLY
28. BUSHING, INNER PIVOT
29. INNER TIE ROD ASSEMBLY
32. PLATE, LOCK
33. BOLT, PINCH
34. ADJUSTER, TIE ROD
35. OUTER TIE ROD
36. OUTER TIE ROD
39. NUT
40. COTTER PIN
51. CLAMP, BOOT
52. CLAMP, BOOT
53. BOOT
54. BUSHING, BOOT RETAINING
56. GROMMET, MOUNTING
57. LINE, CYLINDER
58. LINE, CYLINDER
59. O-RING

Fig. 11 Exploded view, power rack & pinion assembly. Front wheel drive Achieva, Beretta, Cavalier, Corsica, Cutlass Calais, Grand Am, LeMans, Skylark & Sunbird

29 - INNER TIE ROD
33 - PINCH BOLT
34 - TIE ROD ADJUSTER
35 or 36 - OUTER TIE ROD
39 - HEX LOCK NUT
40 - COTTER PIN

Fig. 12 Outer tie rod assembly

INSTALL WITH LOCATION NOTCHES IN THIS POSITION

26 - CENTER COVER HSG WASHER
27 OR 29 - INNER TIE ROD ASSEMBLY
31 - INNER TIE ROD BOLTS
32 - LOCK PLATE
53 - RACK & PINION BOOT

Fig. 13 Inner tie rod assembly

16. With rack centered in housing, turn adjuster plug clockwise until it bottoms in housing, then back off 50° to 70°. Check torque on pinion. Maximum pinion preload torque is 16 inch lbs.
17. Install adjuster plug locknut to adjuster plug, then tighten firmly against housing while holding adjuster plug stationary.
18. Install rack and pinion assembly, then flush power steering system.

ACHIEVA, BERETTA, CAVALIER, CORSICA, CUTLASS CALAIS, GRAND AM, LEMANS, SKYLARK & SUNBIRD

OUTER TIE ROD

1. Remove cotter pin, then hex slotted nut from outer tie rod ball stud, **Fig. 11 and 12.**
2. Loosen outer tie rod pinch bolts, then separate outer tie rod from steering knuckle using steering linkage puller, tool No. J 24319-01 or equivalent.
3. Remove outer tie rod from tie rod adjuster.
4. Reverse procedure to install, noting the following:
   a. **On all models except LeMans, torque** hex slotted nut to 35 ft. lbs., with a maximum of 50 ft. lbs. to install cotter pin. **On LeMans models, torque** nut to 44 ft. lbs., with a

---

protector tool No. 37090. Allow to set for at least three minutes.
3. Center rack in housing, refer to measurement "A" taken during disassembly.
4. Wipe housing bore clean and apply grease to valve housing bore. Inspect stub shaft bearing annulus for damage and ensure bearing is flush with annulus.
5. Align notch on valve stub shaft with second mark on housing made during disassembly.
6. Install pinion and valve assembly with spool shaft retaining ring and valve body rings installed into housing using clear pinion and valve assembly ring protector tool No. 37090 to prevent ring damage.
7. Install pinion and valve assembly onto rack using clear pinion and valve assembly ring protector tool No. J 37090 and pinion seal installer tool No. J 29822. **Do not hammer or use excessive force.**

8. Ensure notch in stub shaft and first mark on housing are lined up while rack is centered in housing. Refer to measurement "A" taken during disassembly.
9. Hold valve stub shaft and thread hex locknut into pinion, then **torque** to 26 ft lbs. **If stub shaft is not held, damage to pinion teeth will result.**
10. Install dust cover onto housing.
11. Install stub shaft bearing annulus assembly onto valve stub shaft.
12. Place seal protector, tool No. J 29810 onto valve stub shaft, then apply a small quantity of grease between stub shaft seals.
13. Install stub shaft seal and stub shaft dust seal over protector and into housing.
14. Install retaining ring into groove in housing.
15. Lubricate stub shaft and dust seal area, then coat rack bearing, adjuster spring and adjuster plug with lithium grease and install in housing.

27 OR 29 – INNER TIE ROD
28 – PIVOT BUSHING

Fig. 14   Inner pivot bushing removal

27 OR 29 – INNER TIE ROD ASSEMBLY
28 – PIVOT BUSHING

Fig. 15   Inner pivot bushing installation

12 – FLANGE & COUPLING ASSEMBLY
13 – PINCH BOLT

Fig. 16   Flange & steering coupling assembly

RACK GUIDE ASSEMBLY.
FLATTENED CYLINDRICAL CORNERS DO
NOT INDICATE THAT THE PART SHOULD BE
REPLACED.

25 – INSERT & RACK GUIDE ASM
26 – CENTER HSG COVER WASHER
51 – BOOT CLAMP
52 – BOOT RETAINING BUSHING
53 – RACK & PINION BOOT
55 – BOOT CLAMP
56 – MOUNTING GROMMET

Fig. 17   Boot & rack guide assembly

POSITION BRIDGE
OF BOOT CLAMP
OVER SPLIT IN
BUSHING

SPLIT IN BOOT
RETAINING BUSHING

53 - RACK AND PINION BOOT
54 - BOOT RETAINING BUSHING
55 - BOOT CLAMP

Fig. 18   Boot clamp position

COAT WITH LITHIUM BASE
GREASE BEFORE ASSEMBLY.

1 – HOUSING ASSEMBLY
14 – RACK BEARING
15 – O-RING SEAL
16 – ADJUSTER SPRING
17 – ADJUSTER PLUG
18 – ADJUSTER PLUG LOCK NUT

Fig. 19   Rack bearing assembly

maximum of 55 ft. lbs. to install cotter pin.

b. Adjust toe by turning tie rod adjuster.

c. **Torque** pinch bolts to 15 ft. lbs. on LeMans models and 41 ft. lbs. on all models except LeMans.

INNER TIE ROD

1. Remove and dispose of lock plate from inner tie rod bolts, **Fig. 13.**
2. Remove inner tie rod bolt.
3. Slide out and remove inner tie rod between bolt support plate and rack and pinion boot. **If both inner tie rods are to be removed, after removing the first tie rod, reinstall bolt to keep rack and pinion and other parts aligned.**
4. Reverse procedure to install. Ensure center housing cover washers are fitted into rack and pinion boot. **Torque** inner tie rod bolts to 65 ft. lbs. and install new lock plate with notches in proper position over flats of inner tie rod bolts.

INNER PIVOT BUSHINGS

Refer to **Figs. 14 and 15,** for replacement procedure.

FLANGE & STEERING COUPLING ASSEMBLY

1. Remove rack and pinion assembly from vehicle.
2. Remove pinch bolt from flange and steering coupling assembly, then coupling, **Fig. 16.**
3. Reverse procedure to install. **Torque** pinch bolt to 29 ft. lbs.

HYDRAULIC CYLINDER LINES

Refer to **Fig. 11,** for replacement procedure. Ensure new O-rings are installed. **Torque** line fittings at valve end to 14 ft. lbs. and at cylinder end to 20 ft. lbs.

RACK GUIDE
Removal

1. Remove rack and pinion steering assembly from vehicle.
2. Remove and dispose lock plate from inner tie rod bolts, **Figs. 11 and 17.**
3. Remove inner tie rod bolts, bolt support plate, cylinder lines and inner tie rod assemblies.
4. Cut and remove mounting grommet and boot clamp.
5. Slide boot retaining bushing from rack and pinion boot, then boot assembly from rack and pinion housing.
6. Insert rack guide assembly from rod and rack assembly if necessary.

Installation

1. Slide boot retaining bushing from rack and pinion housing.
2. Slide new boot clamp on rack and pin-

ion boot and install boot retaining bushing into rack and pinion boot.

3. Install rack guide on rack.
4. Coat inner lip of boot retaining bushing lightly with grease, then install boot on housing. Ensure that center housing cover washers are in place on boot.
5. Install inner tie rod bolts bolts through cover washers and rack and pinion boot. Screw into rack lightly.
6. Slide boot and boot retaining bushing until seated in bushing groove in housing. Crimp new boot clamp.
7. Slide other end of boot into boot groove on cylinder end of housing.
8. Slide other end of boot into boot groove on cylinder end of housing and crimp new boot clamp. **Bridge of boot clamp must be crimped over split in boot retaining bushing to ensure proper sealing, Fig. 18.**
9. Install new lock plate with notches in proper position over flats of inner tie rod bolts.

RACK BEARINGS
Removal

1. Remove rack and pinion assembly from vehicle.
2. Remove adjuster plug nut from adjuster plug, then adjuster plug from

9/16 CROWFOOT 14 mm

17 – ADJUSTER PLUG
18 – ADJUSTER PLUG LOCK NUT

Fig. 20   Rack bearing adjustment

LONG PUNCH

21 – PINION BEARING ASSEMBLY
22 – RETAINING RING

Fig. 23   Pinion bearing assembly removal

housing, **Fig. 19.**
3. Remove adjuster spring and rack bearing with O-ring seal attached.

Installation

1. Coat parts with lithium grease, then install rack bearing with O-ring seal adjuster spring and adjuster plug into housing.
2. With rack centered in housing, turn adjuster plug clockwise until it bottoms in housing, then back off 35° to 45° and check torque on pinion. Maximum pinion preload torque is 16 inch lbs.
3. Install locknut to adjuster plug and tighten to 50 ft. lbs. while holding adjuster plug stationary, **Fig. 20.**

STUB SHAFT SEALS & UPPER BEARING

Removal

1. Remove rack and pinion assembly from vehicle.
2. Remove retaining ring, then dust cover, **Fig. 21.**
3. While holding stub shaft, remove locknut from pinion. **If stub shaft is not held, damage to the pinion teeth will occur.**
4. Using a suitable press, press on

BEARING AND ANNULUS ARE PRESSED TOGETHER. DISASSEMBLE ONLY IF BEARING REPLACEMENT IS REQUIRED.

J 29810

7 – STUB SHAFT ANNULUS & BEARING
8 – STUB SHAFT SEAL
9 – STUB SHAFT DUST SEAL
10 – RETAINING RING
23 – HEX LOCK NUT
24 – DUST COVER

Fig. 21   Stub shaft seals & upper bearing assembly

threaded end of pinion until flush with ball bearing assembly. Complete removal of valve and pinion assembly is not required.
5. Remove stub shaft dust seal, stub shaft seal and stub shaft bearing annulus assembly from valve end of housing.

Installation

1. Install annulus assembly into gear.
2. Place seal protector, tool No. J 29810 onto stub shaft and install stub shaft seal and stub shaft dust seal over protector and into housing.
3. While holding the stub shaft firmly, seat the locknut, **torque** to 26 ft. lbs.

PINION & VALVE ASSEMBLY

Removal

1. Turn stub shaft until rack guide is equal distance from both sides of housing opening, then mark location of stub shaft notch on housing, **Fig. 22.**
2. Using a suitable press, press on threaded end of pinion until it is possible to remove valve and pinion assembly from housing.
3. Replace valve body rings if necessary.

Installation

1. Install rack so it is centered in housing.
2. Using valve body ring protector, tool No. J 33057 to prevent damaging valve body rings, install valve and pinion assembly.
3. When pinion and valve assembly is fully seated, ensure notch in stub shaft and mark on housing line up, and the rack is centered in housing.

RACK BEARING PRELOAD

On Vehicle Adjustment

Make adjustment with front wheels

---

4 – PINION & VALVE ASSEMBLY
5 – SPOOL SHAFT RETAINING RING
6 – VALVE BODY RINGS

J 37090

Fig. 22   Pinion & valve assembly

J 29822

2 – UPPER PINION BUSHING
3 – PINION SHAFT SEAL

Fig. 24   Pinion shaft seal & bushing removal

raised and steering wheel centered. Be sure to check returnability of steering wheel to center after adjustment.
1. Loosen locknut, then turn adjuster plug clockwise until it bottoms in housing, then back off 35° to 45°.
2. **Torque** locknut to adjuster plug to 50 ft. lbs. while holding adjuster plug.

PINION BEARING ASSEMBLY

1. Remove bearing retainer ring, **Fig. 23.**
2. Using a drift or punch, gently tap on bearing until removed.
3. To install, use a suitable socket and press on outer race of bearing until firmly seated.
4. Install retaining ring.

UPPER PINION BUSHING AND PINION SHAFT SEAL

1. Remove upper pinion bushing and seal with a hearty punch, and install new bushing, **Fig. 24.**
2. Using pinion seal installer, tool No. J 29822 seat new seal in housing with seal tip facing up.

BOOT OR RACK GUIDE

1. Cut off RH mounting grommet and boot clamps, **Fig. 11.**
2. Slide boot retaining bushing bushing from rack and pinion boot.
3. Slide boot assembly, consisting of rack and pinion boot, boot retaining bushing and center housing cover washers, captured in the rack and pinion boot, from rack and pinion housing.
4. Remove insert and rack guide assem-

---

1 – HOUSING ASM, R&P
2 – BUSHING, UPPER PINION
3 – SEAL, RACK & PINION
4 – VALVE ASM, PINION &
5 – RING, VALVE BODY (4)
6 – RING, RETAINING
7 – ANNULUS, STUB SHAFT BEARING
8 – BEARING ASM, NEEDLE
9 – SEAL, STUB SHAFT
10 – SEAL, STUB SHAFT DUST
11 – RING, RETAINING
12 – SLEEVE ASM, BUSHING &
13 – BEARING, RACK
14 – SPRING, ADJUSTER
15 – PLUG, ADJUSTER
16 – NUT, ADJUSTER PLUG LOCK
17 – RING, SHOCK DAMPENER
18 – ROD ASM, INNER TIE (LT)
19 – CLAMP, BOOT
20 – BOOT, RACK & PINION
21 – NUT, HEX JAM
22 – ROD ASM, OUTER TIE (LT)
23 – FITTING, LUBRICATION
24 – SEAL, TIE ROD
25 – NUT, HEXAGON SLOTTED

26 – PIN, COTTER
27 – BEARING ASM, BALL
28 – RING, RETAINING
29 – NUT, HEX LOCK
30 – COVER, DUST
31 – GROMMET, MOUNTING
32 – THIS NUMBER NOT USED
33 – THIS NUMBER NOT USED
34 – THIS NUMBER NOT USED
35 – SEAL, O-RING
36 – THIS NUMBER NOT USED
37 – LINE ASM, CYLINDER (LT)
38 – LINE ASM, CYLINDER (RT)
39 – THIS NUMBER NOT USED
40 – SEAL, INNER RACK
41 – RACK ASM, PISTON & STEERING
42 – RING, PISTON
43 – BULKHEAD, CYLINDER INNER
44 – SEAL, RACK & PINION (BULKHEAD)

45 – SEAL, O-RING
46 – BULKHEAD, CYLINDER OUTER
47 – RING, BULKHEAD RETAINING
48 – ROD ASM, INNER TIE (RT)
49 – ROD ASM, OUTER TIE (RT)

VIEW AA

Fig. 25   Exploded view, power rack & pinion assembly. Corvette

bly as necessary.

5. Slide boot retaining bushing from rack and pinion boot.
6. Slide new boot clamp onto rack and pinion boot.
7. Insert boot retaining bushing into rack and pinion boot.
8. Coat inner lip of boot retaining bushing lightly with suitable grease to facilitate assembly, then slide assembly onto housing assembly.
9. Ensure center housing cover washers are in place on rack and pinion boot.
10. For ease of assembly, insert inner tie rod bolt through center housing cover washers, insert and rack guide and lightly thread bolt into rod and rack assembly to keep components in proper alignment.
11. Place boot retaining bushing onto cylinder tube of rack and pinion assembly, then slide into end of rack and pinion boot.
12. Slide boot clamp over cylinder end of housing and position on rack and pinion boot.
13. Slide rack and pinion boot and boot retaining bushing until seated in bushing groove in housing.
14. Position boot clamp on rack and pinion boot and crimp clamp.
15. Position bridge of boot clamp over split in boot retaining bushing and crimp clamp. **Bridge of boot clamp must be crimped over split in boot retaining bushing to ensure proper sealing.**

ROD & RACK & CYLINDER TUBE ASSEMBLY

1. Remove dust cover from housing, **Fig. 11.**
2. While holding stub shaft, remove locknut from pinion.
3. With gear centered, mark location of stub shaft notch on housing to aid in proper installation of the pinion and valve assembly. **Using a press, press on threaded end of pinion until it is possible to remove the pinion and valve assembly from the housing.**
4. Remove stub shaft dust seal, stub shaft seal, stub shaft bearing annulus assembly, then the pinion and valve assembly with spool shaft retaining ring and valve body rings attached.
5. Using wrench, tool No. J 36343 or equivalent, remove cylinder tube assembly from housing. **Mark location of fittings on housing before removal.**
6. Remove piston rod guide rack from housing and disassemble as follows:
   a. Remove hex nut from rod and rack assembly.
   b. Remove rack piston, containing O-ring seal, and piston ring, piston rod guide assembly, consisting of piston rod guide, O-ring seal, piston rod seal and seal backup washer for rod and rack assembly.
   c. Remove O-ring seal and piston rod

seal from from piston rod guide.
7. Remove retaining ring from housing.
8. Remove pinion bearing assembly from housing.
9. Remove pinion shaft seal and upper pinion bushing from housing.
10. Coat all seals with power steering fluid.
11. Install upper pinion bushing into valve bore in housing.
12. Using seal installer, tool No. J 29822 or equivalent, seat pinion shaft seal into housing.
13. Using suitable press, install pinion bearing assembly into housing.
14. Install retaining ring in groove in housing, positioning properly.
15. Assemble piston rod seal and O-ring seal to piston rod guide.
16. Assemble O-ring seal and piston ring to rack piston.
17. Slide seal backup washer, piston rod guide assembly and rack piston onto rod and rack assembly.
18. Install hex nut on rod and rack assembly, **on all models except LeMans torque** to 30 ft. lbs., **on LeMans models, torque** to 22 ft. lbs.
19. Slide piston rod guide assembly into housing.
20. Apply one small drop of Loctite 242 or equivalent in three equally spaced locations around the threaded portion of housing. **Be sure to use the Loctite 242 sparingly to ensure ease of removal of cylinder tube assembly if future repairs are necessary.**

6. REMOVE AND INSTALL VALVE AND PINION ASM

REMOVE

1. Turn stub plug until rack is equal distance on both sides of housing, with pinion fully engaged.
2. Mark location of stub shaft pinch bolt notch on housing.
3. **USING A PRESS,** press on threaded end, pinion until it is possible to remove valve and pinion assy.
4. Remove valve body rings if replacement is necessary.

Valve Body Ring Protector Tool J-33057

Pinch Bolt Notch

Before installing valve and pinion assy both ends of the rack should be equal in the housing.

INSTALL

1. Install new valve body rings if required.
2. Care should be taken not to cut rings at installation.
3. Measure rack so that it's equal on both sides.
4. Use valve body ring protector, Tool J-33057 to prevent damaging valve body rings while installing valve and pinion assembly.
5. Install valve and pinion assembly so when fully seated, stub shaft pinch bolt notch and mark on housing line up.

RETAINING RING
VALVE BODY RINGS
VALVE AND PINION ASM

7. REMOVE AND INSTALL BULKHEAD

REMOVE

1. Use punch in access hole to remove bulkhead retaining ring.
2. If only the bulkhead, bulkhead O-ring seal or rack seal (bulkhead) are to be replaced. Loosen (LT) fitting and remove cylinder line.
3. Plug (LT) cylinder line hole at cylinder using a finger or plastic cap set at 7/16 x 20 internal threads over hole to prevent oil leaking from cylinder.
4. Using a 9/16 crowfoot turn stub shaft. Move rack to the right forcing the bulkhead out of the housing. Use drain pan to catch hydraulic oil from assy.
5. If inner rack seal or piston ring are to be replaced, use rack to remove bulkhead instead of compressed oil method.

INSTALL

1. Using crocus cloth remove burrs or sharp edges from retaining ring groove in housing. This must be done to insure that the new O-ring is not damaged at assembly.
2. Install parts as shown.
3. Coat all seals with power steering fluid.
4. Slip bullet seal protector over end of rack and install bulkhead.
5. Make sure open end of retaining ring is approximately 13 millimeters (.50 inch) from access hole.
6. Retaining ring must be fully seated.

(Install Seal (Bulkhead) Installer J-28527)

Rack Seal (Bulkhead) Removal

Pliers

Retaining ring access hole

Tool J-28478-A Bullet Seal Protector
CYLINDER INNER BULKHEAD
O-RING SEAL
CYLINDER OUTER BULKHEAD
BULKHEAD RETAINING RING
SHOCK DAMPENER

RACK SEAL (BULKHEAD)
CYLINDER OUTER BULKHEAD
RACK SEAL (BULKHEAD)

4. REMOVE AND INSTALL RACK BEARING

REMOVE

1. Loosen adjuster plug lock nut.
2. Turn adjuster plug counterclockwise until it separates from housing.
3. Remove parts as shown:

INSTALL

1. Install parts as shown.
2. Turn adjuster plug clockwise until it bottoms, then back off 50° to 70°. Check torque on pinion.
3. Assemble lock nut and tighten while holding adjuster plug stationary.

ADJUSTER PLUG
LOCK NUT
ADJUSTER PLUG
SPRING
RACK BEARING

Coat with lithium base grease before assembly.

LOCK NUT –
Tighten to 70 Newton Metres (50 Ft. Lbs.)

ADJUSTER PLUG

9/16" Crowfoot

Pinion preload torque 2.2 Newton Metres (19 in lbs)

5. REMOVE AND INSTALL STUB SHAFT SEALS

REMOVE

1. Remove retaining ring.
2. Remove dust cover.
3. While holding the stub shaft remove lock nut from pinion.

NOTICE: If stub shaft is not held, damage to the pinion teeth will occur.

4. **USING A PRESS,** press on threaded end of pinion until flush with ball bearing assy.
5. Complete removal of valve and pinion assy is not necessary

INSTALL

1. Install annulus assembly in gear.
2. Place seal protector Tool J-29810 on stub shaft and install stub shaft seals and snapring.
3. While holding stub shaft firmly seat the lock nut, torque to specifications.

Bearing and annulus are pressed together. Disassemble only if bearing replacement is required.

RETAINING RING
STUB SHAFT SEAL
STUB SHAFT DUST SEAL
STUB SHAFT SEAL
NEEDLE BEARING
STUB SHAFT BEARING ANNULUS
Seal Protector Tool J-29810
DUST COVER

LOCK NUT – Torque nut to 35 Newton metres (26 Ft. Lbs.) after lock nut has been firmly seated.

Fig. 26 Service procedures, power rack & pinion assembly (Part 2 of 3). Corvette

THE FOLLOWING STEPS MUST BE PERFORMED WITH RACK & PINION ASSEMBLY REMOVED FROM CAR

3. REMOVE AND INSTALL INNER TIE ROD

REMOVE

1. Remove shock dampener ring from inner tie rod housing and slide back on rack.
2. Put wrench on rack to prevent rack damage when removing the rod.
3. Put wrench on tie rod pivot housing flats.
4. Turn housing counterclockwise until tie rod assy separates from rack.

INSTALL

1. Bottom inner tie rod assy on rack.
2. Torque housing. (Use wrench on rack to avoid internal gear damage.)
3. Support rack and housing and stake tie rod housing to rack flat. (Stake both sides.)
4. Inspect stake, a .25 millimetres (.010 inch) feeler gage must not pass between rack and housing stake on both sides.
5. Slide shock dampener over inner tie rod housing until it engages.

RACK
SHOCK DAMPENER
INNER TIE ROD HOUSING

A. Torque inner tie rod.

Crowfoot Tool J-34028
Torque 95 Newton metres (70 Ft. Lbs.)
Make sure tie rod rocks freely in housing before staking.

INNER TIE ROD

B. Stake housing to rack (both sides).
Stake both sides of housing.
Support housing while staking.

.25 Millimetres (.010 inch) feeler gage must not pass between rack and housing stake. (Check both sides.)

Fig. 26 Service procedures, power rack & pinion assembly (Part 1 of 3). Corvette

1. REMOVE AND INSTALL OUTER TIE ROD

REMOVE

1. Loosen jam nut.
2. Remove tie rod from steering knuckle, using Tool J-24319-01 or BT 7101.
3. Remove outer tie rod.

INSTALL

1. Install parts as shown.
2. Do not tighten jam nut.
3. Make toe-in adjustment by turning inner tie rod.
4. Be sure boot is not twisted.

NOTICE: Torque jam nut to 70 Newton metres (50 Ft. Lbs.)

INNER TIE ROD
JAM NUT
STEERING KNUCKLE
OUTER TIE ROD

2. REMOVE AND INSTALL BOOT SEAL

REMOVE

1. Remove jam nut.
2. Cut boot clamp and discard.
3. See insert for proper boot seal removal.

INSTALL

1. Install new clamp on boot before installing boot.
2. See insert for proper installation of boot seal.
3. Engage boot onto housing.
4. Secure boot clamp.

JAM NUT
GROOVE
BOOT SEAL
BOOT CLAMP

A. Cut boot clamp.
J-22610
B. Secure boot clamp.
BOOT CLAMP

REPLACE

1. Remove rubber band.
2. Slide boot on tie rod until boot snaps into groove.

BOOT GROOVE

REMOVE
Side cutters

To prevent boot damage, slide the rod end of boot toward center of gear enough to expose boot groove on the tie rod. Place a rubber band in groove. This fills the groove and allows removal of boot from gear without damage.

Fig. 26 Service procedures, power rack & pinion assembly (Part 1 of 3). Corvette

10 Torque fitting to 27 N•M (20 FT. LBS.). If leakage persists, replace "O" ring seal. If leakage is due to damaged threads, repair fitting nut or replace line as required. If housing threads are badly damaged, replace housing.

11 Replace dust and stub shaft seals.

12 If leakage is observed between torsion bar and stub shaft, replace the valve assembly.

13 If leakage is observed at driver side and is not affected by the direction of turn, replace pinion shaft seal.

14 If leakage is observed at the housing end and spurts when bottomed in left turn, replace inner rack seal.

15 Replace inner rack seal.

16 If leakage is observed at passenger side, it is necessary to remove bulkhead and replace both "O" ring seals and lip seal.

Fig. 27 Power rack & pinion steering gear leak diagnosis. Front wheel drive except Achieva, Beretta, Cavalier, Corsica, Cutlass Calais, Grand Am, LeMans, Skylark & Sunbird

8. REMOVE AND INSTALL INNER RACK SEAL, RACK AND PISTON RING

REMOVE
1. Remove rack from housing.
2. Remove piston ring and dispose.
3. Fit tool J-29738 into housing. Using rod approx. 12" long, gently tap on rod until seal is removed.
4. Dispose of old seal.

INSTALL
1. Install new piston ring on rack.
2. Care should be taken not to cut ring at installation.
3. Wrap card stock around end of rack and rack teeth.
4. Coat seal lip with power steering fluid, slide seal with seal lip facing piston on to card stock, slide card and seal over rack teeth.
5. Remove card stock and bottom seal on rack piston.
6. Coat lip of seal insert with power steering fluid and slide on rack with lip facing seal. Be sure insert is fully engaged with seal before installing seal in housing.
7. Coat seal completely with power steering fluid, slide rack and seal in housing. Using rubber mallet tap on rack in housing.

NOTICE: Seal must be fully seated in housing.

Tool J-29738

PISTON RING
RACK AND PISTON ASM

INNER RACK SEAL
INSERT
INNER RACK SEAL

RACK

RACK PISTON
Tool J-29708-A
Rack Seal Installer

INNER RACK SEAL

9. REMOVE AND INSTALL BALL BEARING ASM

REMOVE
1. Remove bearing retaining ring.
2. Use drift or punch on bearing and gently tap on bearing until bearing is removed.

INSTALL
1. Install new ball bearing assy. Using a suitable socket, press on outer race. Be careful not to cock bearing in housing.
2. Install retaining ring.

Note position of large lug to be sure beveled side of ring is properly located.

INNER
RACK SEAL
HOUSING
ASSEMBLY

Long Punch

BALL BEARING ASM
RETAINING RING

10. REMOVE AND INSTALL UPPER PINION BEARING & SEAL

REMOVE
1. Remove upper pinion bushing and seal with a punch.
2. Dispose of bushing and seal.

INSTALL
1. Install new bushing as shown.
2. Install new seal. Using installer, seat seal in housing with seal lip facing up.

Seal installer tool J-29822

PINION SEAL
UPPER PINION BUSHING

Long Punch

UPPER PINION BUSHING
PINION SEAL

11. REMOVE AND INSTALL CYLINDER LINE

REMOVE
1. Using flare wrench loosen fittings and remove cylinder line.

INSTALL
1. Place new O-ring seal on cylinder line.
2. Be sure O-ring is also removed and disposed of.
2. Assemble both ends to housing finger tight to assure proper alignment.
3. Tighten to specifications.

NOTICE: Care should be taken not to strip aluminum housing.

O-RINGS

FITTINGS – Torque 27 Newton metres
(20 Ft. Lbs.) 2 places

FITTINGS – Torque 16 Newton metres
(12 Ft. Lbs.) 2 places

12. REMOVE AND INSTALL GROMMET OR BUSHING ASM

REMOVE
1. Slide mounting grommet from cylinder end of housing.
2. If the bushing and sleeve assemblies require replacement a press will be required to remove them from the housing.

INSTALL
1. Install mounting grommet onto cylinder end of housing.
2. Press new bushing & sleeve assemblies into housing.

BUSHING & SLEEVE
ASM

BUSHING & SLEEVE
ASM

MOUNTING
GROMMET

Fig. 26 Service procedures, power rack & pinion assembly (Part 3 of 3). Corvette

C TORQUE CYLINDER LINE FITTING TO 18 N·m (13 FT. LBS.). IF LEAKAGE PERSISTS, REPLACE BOTH "O" RINGS.

A IF SEEPAGE IS OBSERVED BETWEEN TORSION BAR AND STUB SHAFT, REPLACE THE VALVE ASSEMBLY.

B TORQUE HOSE FITTING TO 27 N·m (20 FT. LBS.). IF LEAKAGE PERSISTS, REPLACE "O" RING.

D IF SEEPAGE LEAK IS OBSERVED AT DRIVER SIDE OF HOUSING OPENING, REPLACE PINION SHAFT SEAL.

E IF LEAKAGE IS OBSERVED AT CYLINDER END AND SPURTS WHEN BOTTOMED IN LEFT TURN, REPLACE THE PISTON ROD GUIDE SEAL AND "O" RING SEAL.

Fig. 28 Power rack & pinion steering gear leak diagnosis. Front wheel drive Achieva, Beretta, Cavalier, Corsica, Cutlass Calais, Grand Am, LeMans, Skylark & Sunbird

1. IF LEAKAGE IS OBSERVED AT (A), APPLY LOCTITE SAFETY SOLVENT AND LOCTITE 290 OR EQUIVALENT TO TUBE/ HOUSING CONNECTION. IF LEAKAGE IS FROM (B), REPLACE RETURN TUBE. IF LEAKAGE IS FROM (C), REPLACE HOSE OR CLAMP.

2. TORQUE FITTING TO 27 N·m (20 FT. LBS.). IF LEAKAGE PERSISTS, REPLACE "O" RING SEAL.

3. TORQUE FITTING TO 75 N·m (55 FT. LBS.). IF LEAKAGE PERSISTS, REPLACE "O" RING SEAL.

4. SEAT BALL IN HOUSING WITH BLUNT PUNCH. APPLY LOCTITE SAFETY SOLVENT AND LOCTITE 290 OR EQUIVALENT TO AREA.

5. REPLACE DRIVE SHAFT SEAL. MAKE CERTAIN THAT DRIVE SHAFT IS CLEAN AND FREE OF PITTING IN SEAL AREA.

6. SEAT PLUG IN HOUSING. APPLY LOCTITE SAFETY SOLVENT AND LOCTITE 290 OR EQUIVALENT TO AREA.

7. REPLACE "O" RING SEAL.

8. REPLACE RESERVOIR IF CRACKED OR DENTED

9. IF CAP LEAKS WITH CORRECT FLUID LEVEL, REPLACE CAP.

Fig. 29 Power steering pump leak diagnosis. Front wheel drive models w/rack & pinion steering

21. Slide cylinder tube assembly over rack piston ring to housing, then, using torque wrench or equivalent, torque to 82 ft. lbs. **Be sure to align fittings on cylinder tube with mark on housing before tightening to ensure cylinder line installation.**

22. Assemble insert and rack guide assembly to rod and rack assembly in housing.

23. Center rack guide assembly in housing window opening.

24. Using protector tool, No. J 33057 or equivalent, install pinion and valve assembly, together with new valve body rings, and spool shaft retaining ring into housing. **When pinion and valve assembly is fully seated in housing, notch in stub shaft and mark on housing line up and insert and rack guide assembly is centered in window housing.**

25. While holding stub shaft, tighten locknut to 26 ft. lbs.

26. Install dust cover on housing.

27. Install stub shaft bearing annulus assembly onto stub shaft and slide into housing.

28. Place seal protector, tool No. J 29810 or equivalent onto stub shaft, then slide stub shaft seal and stub shaft dust seal over protector and into housing.

29. Install retaining ring into groove in housing.

30. Coat rack bearing, with O-ring seal attached, adjuster spring and the adjuster plug with lithium base grease and install in housing.

31. With rack centered in window in housing, turn adjuster plug clockwise until it bottoms in housing, then back off 50-70°. Check pinion preload torque, which should not exceed 16 inch lbs.

32. Install locknut on adjuster plug and **torque** to 50 ft. lbs. while holding adjuster plug stationary.

CORVETTE

For service procedures on this power rack and pinion steering gear assembly, refer to **Figs. 25 and 26.**

DIAGNOSIS & TESTING

EXTERNAL LEAK CHECK

1. With engine off, wipe dry the entire power steering system.
2. Ensure fluid level is correct.
3. Start engine, then turn steering wheel from stop to stop a few times. Do not hold at stop for a long period.
4. Find the exact area of leak and repair as necessary, **Figs. 27 through 29.**

Saginaw Rotary Valve Type Power Steering Gear

INDEX

DESCRIPTION

The Saginaw rotary valve steering gear incorporates a recirculating ball system in which steel balls act as a rolling thread between a steering worm shaft and the rack piston.

STEERING GEAR SERVICE

Whenever a part which forms a sealing surface for an O-ring is removed, the O-ring seal should also be removed and replaced with a new seal. Whenever one of the Pitman shaft or stub shaft seals are removed, all adjacent seals should be removed and replaced with new seals. Lubricate all new seals with power steering fluid to facilitate assembly.

For service procedures on this power steering gear assembly, refer to **Figs. 1 and 2.**

ADJUSTMENT SPECIFICATIONS

Adjustment of steering gear in the vehicle is not recommended because of the difficulty encountered in adjusting the worm thrust bearing preload and confirming the effects of the hydraulic fluid in the gear. Since a gear adjustment is made only as a correction and not a periodic adjustment, it is better to take the extra time and make the adjustment correctly the first time.

Since a handling stability complaint can be caused by improperly adjusted worm thrust bearings as well as an improper gear over-center adjustment, it is necessary that the steering gear assembly be removed from vehicle and both thrust bearing and over-center preload be checked and corrected as necessary. An in-vehicle check of steering gear will not show a thrust bearing adjustment error.

Valve assembly and seal drag should be 1-4 inch lbs. Thrust bearing preload should be 3-4 inch lbs. in excess of valve assembly and seal drag.

OVER CENTER ADJUSTMENT

Brougham

Refer to **Fig. 2,** part 4 of 4 for proper procedure. Over-center adjustment should be 5-11 inch lbs. (new gear) or 4-5 inch lbs.

1	HOUSING, STEERING GEAR	
2	RACE, THRUST BEARING (WORM)	
3	BEARING ASSY, ROLLER THRUST (WORM)	
4	RACE, THRUST BEARING (WORM)	
5	WORM, STEERING	
6	SEAL, "O" RING (STUB SHAFT)	
7	SHAFT, STUB	
8	SPOOL, VALVE	
9	SEAL, "O" RING (SPOOL)	
10	BODY, VALVE	
11	RING, VALVE BODY (3)	
12	SEAL, "O" RING (VALVE BODY) (3)	
13	RETAINER, BEARING (ADJUSTER)	
14	SPACER, THRUST BEARING	
15	RACE, UPPER THRUST BEARING (SMALL)	
16	BEARING, UPPER THRUST	
17	RACE, UPPER THRUST BEARING (LARGE)	
18	SEAL, "O" RING (ADJUSTER)	
19	PLUG, ADJUSTER	
20	BEARING, NEEDLE	
21	SEAL, STUB SHAFT	
22	SEAL, STUB SHAFT DUST	
23	RING, RETAINING	
24	NUT, ADJUSTER PLUG LOCK	
25	BEARING ASSY, NEEDLE (PITMAN SHAFT)	
26	SEAL, PITMAN SHAFT (SINGLE LIP)	
27	WASHER, SEAL BACK-UP (PITMAN SHAFT)	
28	SEAL, PITMAN SHAFT (DOUBLE LIP)	
29	WASHER, SEAL BACK-UP (PITMAN SHAFT)	
30	RING, RETAINING (PITMAN SHAFT SEAL	
31	WASHER, PITMAN SHAFT LOCK	
32	NUT, PITMAN SHAFT	
33	NUT, RACK PISTON	
34	BALL	
35	GUIDE, BALL RETURN (2)	
36	CLAMP, BALL RETURN GUIDE	
37	SCREW ASSY, LOCKWASHER & (2)	
38	PLUG, RACK PISTON	
39	SEAL, "O" RING (RACK PISTON)	
40	RING, RACK PISTON	
41	SEAL, "O" RING (HOUSING END PLUG)	
42	PLUG, HOUSING END	
43	RING, RETAINING (HOUSING END PLUG)	
44	GEAR ASSY, PITMAN SHAFT	
45	SEAL ASSY, GASKET	
46	COVER ASSY, HOUSING SIDE	
47	BOLT, HEX HEAD (SIDE COVER) (4)	
48	NUT, LASH ADJUSTER	
49	SPRING, CHECK VALVE	
50	POPPET, CHECK VALVE	
51	CONNECTOR, INVERTED FLARE	
52	CONNECTOR, INVERTED FLARE	

Fig. 1   Exploded view of Saginaw rotary valve type power steering gear

(used gear) in excess of combined thrust bearing preload.

Except Brougham

1. Rotate stub shaft back and forth to drain fluid.
2. Turn pitman shaft adjuster screw counterclockwise until fully extended, then turn back one full turn, **Fig. 3.**
3. Rotate stub shaft from stop to stop and count the turns.
4. Starting at either stop, turn the stub shaft back one-half the total number of turns.
5. When the gear is centered, the flat on stub shaft should face upward and be parallel with side cover and master spline on pitman shaft should be in-line with adjuster screw, **Fig. 4.**
6. Rotate stub shaft 45° each side of center using a torque wrench with handle in vertical position, **Fig. 5,** record the highest drag torque measured on or near center.
7. Adjust over-center drag torque by loosening adjuster locknut and turning the pitman shaft adjuster screw clockwise until correct drag torque is obtained. On new steering gears (under 400 miles) add 5-11 inch lbs. to previously measured worm bearing preload. Do not exceed total preload of 18 inch lbs. On used steering gears (400 miles or more) add 4-5 inch lbs. to previously measured worm bearing preload. Do not exceed total gear preload of 13 inch lbs.
8. Hold adjuster screw and **torque** adjuster locknut to 20 ft. lbs. on 1991-92 models and 22 ft. lbs. on 1993 models.

7. REMOVE AND INSTALL BEARING, WORM, AND VALVE ASSEMBLY.

REMOVE
1. Grasp stub shaft and remove valve and worm assembly as a unit.

SEPARATE THE VALVE FROM THE WORM. NOTE HOW THE PIN IN THE WORM FITS THE SLOT IN THE VALVE.

WHEN REASSEMBLING GEAR, MAKE SURE ANGLE OF THRUST RACES ARE AS SHOWN.

INSTALL
1. Install parts as shown.

VALVE ASSEMBLY

WORM ASSEMBLY

THRUST BEARING AND RACES

8. DISASSEMBLE AND ASSEMBLE VALVE.

DISASSEMBLE
1. Disassemble parts as shown.

ASSEMBLE
1. Assemble parts as shown.

SHAFT CAP

VALVE BODY

VALVE SPOOL

STUB SHAFT

VALVE BODY RING (TEFLON)

SPOOL TO BODY "O" RING

VALVE BODY TO BODY "O" RING

* TO EASE ASSEMBLY, SOAK TEFLON RINGS IN WARM WATER.

A. LOOSEN SHAFT CAP.

B. REMOVE AND INSTALL STUB SHAFT.

PULL CAP OUT APPROX. 6 mm (¼") (DISENGAGE TO REMOVE)

TAP LIGHTLY ON WOOD BLOCK.

C. REMOVE AND INSTALL VALVE SPOOL.

ROTATE WHILE REMOVING OR INSTALLING.

LUBRICATE SPOOL AND BODY WITH POWER STEERING FLUID.

PIN ON SHAFT AND HOLE IN SPOOL (DISENGAGE TO REMOVE)

D. ENGAGE STUB SHAFT.

NOTCH MUST FULLY ENGAGE PIN AND CAP MUST SEAT AGAINST SHOULDER.

5. REMOVE AND INSTALL ADJUSTER PLUG ASSEMBLY.

REMOVE
1. Loosen lock nut. Use punch against edge of slots.
2. Remove adjuster plug using spanner wrench J-7624.

INSTALL
1. Install parts as shown.

WHEN INSTALLING ADJUSTER PLUG, CARE SHOULD BE TAKEN NOT TO CUT SEALS.

LOCK NUT

ADJUSTER PLUG

6. DISASSEMBLE AND ASSEMBLE ADJUSTER PLUG ASSEMBLY.

DISASSEMBLE
1. Disassemble parts as shown.

ASSEMBLE
1. Assemble parts as shown.

RETAINING RING

ADJUSTER PLUG

NEEDLE BEARING

UPPER BEARING RACE (LARGE)

UPPER BEARING RACE (SMALL)

UPPER THRUST BEARING

THRUST BEARING SPACER

BEARING RETAINER

*STUB SHAFT SEAL

STUB SHAFT DUST SEAL

"O" RING SEAL

RETAINER

SCREWDRIVER

* USE STUB SHAFT SEAL PROTECTOR J-29810 ON STUB SHAFT WHEN INSTALLING STUB SHAFT SEAL.

PRY BEARING RETAINER AT RAISED AREA.

USE SUITABLE SIZE ARBOR TO PRESS BEARING IN PLACE.

BEARING TO BE PRESSED 16mm (⅝ INCH) INTO ADJUSTER WITH STAMPED I.D. END UP AND FROM DIRECTION OF ARROW.

16 mm (⅝ INCH)

INSTALL BEARING

Fig. 2 Service procedures, Saginaw power steering gear (Part 2 of 4)

3. REMOVE AND INSTALL HOUSING END PLUG.

REMOVE
1. Remove parts as shown.

INSTALL
1. Install parts as shown. OPEN END OF RETAINING RING TO BE APPROX. 25mm (1 INCH) FROM ACCESS HOLE.

HOUSING ASSEMBLY

HOUSING END PLUG

HOUSING END PLUG "O" RING SEAL

RETAINING RING

RETAINING RING ACCESS HOLE (USE PUNCH)

4. REMOVE AND INSTALL RACK PISTON.

REMOVE
1. Remove parts as shown.

INSTALL
1. Install parts as shown.

WHEN INSTALLING RACK, CARE SHOULD BE TAKEN NOT TO CUT TEFLON SEAL. RACK PISTON SEAL COMPRESSOR J-7576 OR J-8947 MAY BE USED TO COMPRESS SEAL.

INSERT BALL RETAINER J-21552. HOLD TOOL TIGHTLY AGAINST WORM WHILE TURNING STUB SHAFT COUNTER-CLOCKWISE. THE RACK-PISTON WILL BE FORCED ONTO THE TOOL, THE RACK PISTON WILL REMOVE THE BALL RETAINER FROM AND BALL RETAINER FROM THE GEAR HOUSING TOGETHER.

RACK PISTON PLUG MUST BE REMOVED BEFORE REMOVING RACK.

1. REMOVE AND INSTALL PITMAN SHAFT SEALS IN CAR.

REMOVE
1. Clean exposed end of pitman shaft and end of housing after removing pitman arm.
2. Remove retaining ring with snap ring pliers J-4245.
3. Start engine and turn wheels fully to the left to force seals and washer out.
4. Turn off engine.
5. Inspect housing and shaft.

INSTALL
1. Install parts as shown.

INSPECT FOR BURRS

SEAL (SINGLE LIP)

WASHER

SEAL (DOUBLE LIP)

WASHER

RETAINING RING

PITMAN ARM

LOCK WASHER

NUT — TORQUE TO 250 N·m (184 FT. LBS.)

PITMAN SHAFT—INSPECT SEAL SURFACE FOR ROUGHNESS AND PITTING

INSTALLER J-6219

INSTALL SEALS

PULLER J-6632 E, K J-9172 C, D

REMOVE PITMAN ARM

2. REMOVE AND INSTALL PITMAN SHAFT AND SIDE COVER.

REMOVE
1. If pitman shaft and side cover are to be separated, remove preload adjuster nut.
2. Rotate stub shaft to center gear, then remove parts as shown.

INSTALL
1. If removed, install gasket by bending tabs around cover edges.
2. Install parts as shown.

SIDE COVER BOLTS TORQUE TO 60 N·m (44 FT LBS.)

PRELOAD ADJUSTER NUT

SIDE COVER

GASKET SEAL

PITMAN SHAFT GEAR

STUB SHAFT

HOUSING ASSEMBLY

SEPARATE PITMAN SHAFT AND GASKET SEAL FROM SIDE COVER IF REQUIRED.

Fig. 2 Service procedures, Saginaw power steering gear (Part 1 of 4)

13. PITMAN SHAFT "OVER-CENTER" SECTOR ADJUSTMENT.

A.

WHEN GEAR IS ON CENTER FLAT ON STUB SHAFT IS NORMALLY ON SAME SIDE AS, AND PARALLEL WITH, SIDE COVER.

THE BLOCK TOOTH ON THE PITMAN SHAFT IS IN LINE WITH THE OVER-CENTER PRELOAD ADJUSTER.

B. BACK OFF PRELOAD ADJUSTER UNTIL IT STOPS, THEN TURN IT IN ONE FULL TURN.

WITH GEAR AT CENTER OF TRAVEL CHECK TORQUE TO TURN STUB SHAFT (READING #1).

C. TURN ADJUSTER IN UNTIL TORQUE TO TURN STUB SHAFT IS 0.6 TO 1.2 N·m (6 TO 11 IN. LBS.) MORE THAN READING #1.

TORQUE ADJUSTER LOCK NUT TO 27 N·m (20 FT. LBS.)

PREVENT ADJUSTER SCREW FROM TURNING WHILE TORQUING LOCK NUT.

Fig. 2 Service procedures, Saginaw power steering gear (Part 4 of 4)

---

11. REMOVE AND INSTALL CHECK VALVE.

REMOVE
1. REMOVE PARTS AS SHOWN.

WITH SMALL SCREWDRIVER, PRY CHECK VALVE FROM HOUSING.

CARE SHOULD BE TAKEN NOT TO DAMAGE THREADS WHEN PRYING ON EDGE OF HOUSING.

REMOVE CHECK VALVE.

INSTALL
1. INSTALL PARTS AS SHOWN.

USING A PIECE OF 3/8 TUBING, 4 INCHES LONG, CAREFULLY DRIVE THE CHECK VALVE INTO THE HOUSING.

INSTALL CHECK VALVE.

12. ADJUST THRUST BEARING PRELOAD.

A. USING SPANNER WRENCH J-7624, TIGHTEN ADJUSTER PLUG UNTIL THRUST BEARING IS FIRMLY BOTTOMED, 27 N·m (20 FT. LBS.)

B. MEASURE BACK COUNTERCLOCKWISE 3mm (1/8") AND PLACE A SECOND MARK ON HOUSING.

MARK HOUSING AND FACE OF ADJUSTER PLUG.

C. TURN ADJUSTER COUNTERCLOCKWISE UNTIL MARK ON FACE OF ADJUSTER LINES UP WITH SECOND MARK ON HOUSING.

D. USING PUNCH IN NOTCH TIGHTEN LOCK NUT SECURELY, HOLD ADJUSTER PLUG TO MAINTAIN ALIGNMENT OF THE MARKS.

Fig. 2 Service procedures, Saginaw power steering gear (Part 3 of 4)

---

10. REMOVE AND INSTALL PITMAN SHAFT SEALS AND BEARING.

REMOVE
1. CLEAN END OF HOUSING THOROUGHLY TO PREVENT DIRT FROM ENTERING AND BE EXTREMELY CAREFUL NOT TO SCORE THE HOUSING BORE.
2. REMOVE RETAINING RING WITH SNAP RING PLIERS J-4245.
3. USING SCREWDRIVER, PRY SEALS AND WASHERS FROM BORE.

INSTALL
1. COAT SEAL LIP AND WASHER FACE WITH ANHYDROUS CALCIUM GREASE.
2. INSTALL PARTS AS SHOWN.

NEEDLE BEARING REMOVE ONLY IF IT NEEDS REPLACING.

HOUSING ASSEMBLY INSPECT FOR BURRS.

PITMAN SHAFT SEAL (SINGLE LIP)

SEAL BACK UP WASHER

PITMAN SHAFT SEAL (DOUBLE LIP)

RETAINING RING

BEARING REMOVER J-6278

REMOVING BEARING

INSTALLER J-6219

INSTALL PITMAN SHAFT SEALS.

INSTALLER J-6278

WHEN TOOL BOTTOMS ON HOUSING BEARING IS FULLY INSTALLED.

INSTALL PITMAN SHAFT BEARING.

9. DISASSEMBLE AND ASSEMBLE RACK PISTON.

DISASSEMBLE
1. DISASSEMBLE PARTS AS SHOWN.
2. CLEAN AND INSPECT ALL PARTS FOR EXCESSIVE WEAR.

ASSEMBLE
1. ASSEMBLE PARTS AS SHOWN.

THE BLACK BALLS ARE SMALLER THAN THE SILVER BALLS AND THE BLACK AND SILVER BALLS MUST BE INSTALLED ALTERNATELY INTO THE RACK-PISTON AND RETURN GUIDE TO MAINTAIN RACK PISTON TO WORM GEAR PRELOAD.

TEFLON SEAL AND 'O' RING — IF REPLACED LUBRICATE NEW SEAL AND 'O' RING WITH POWER STEERING FLUID.

BEFORE ASSEMBLING RACK IN HOUSING, BALL RETAINER J-21552 MUST BE INSERTED INTO RACK TO ALLOW REMOVAL OF WORM.

WORM — SLIDE ALL THE WAY INTO THE RACK-PISTON.

TURN WORM UNTIL WORM GROOVE IS ALIGNED WITH LOWER BALL RETURN GUIDE HOLE.

LUBRICATE BALLS WITH POWER STEERING FLUID. INSTALL BALLS, THROUGH BALL RETURN GUIDE HOLE, WHILE ROTATING WORM COUNTERCLOCKWISE.

GUIDE — ALTERNATELY INSTALL REMAINDER OF BALLS AND RETAIN WITH GREASE AT EACH END OF GUIDE.

CLAMP

SCREW — TIGHTEN TO 5 N·m (44 IN. LBS.)

Fig. 2 Service procedures, Saginaw power steering gear (Part 3 of 4)

51 SIDE COVER
60 STUB SHAFT

Fig. 3 Aligning stub shaft. Except Brougham

A MASTER SPLINE ON THE PITMAN SHAFT
80 ADJUSTER SCREW

Fig. 4 Aligning pitman shaft master spline. Except Brougham

A CENTER LINE

Fig. 5 Checking over center rotational torque. Except Brougham

Toyota (Prizm) Rack & Pinion Power Steering Gear

INDEX

1 MOUNTING BRACKET
2 COTTER PIN
3 PRESSURE AND RETURN LINES
4 COLUMN HOLE COVER
5 UNIVERSAL JOINT
6 INTERMEDIATE SHAFT
7 GEAR HOUSING ASSEMBLY
8 RUBBER BOOT
9 TIE ROD
10 TIE ROD END
11 ENGINE MOUNT
12 GROMMET

Fig. 1 Toyota (Prizm) power rack & pinion steering gear assembly. 1991–92

DESCRIPTION

This steering system converts rotary motion to linear motion as follows; when the steering wheel is turned, rotary motion is transferred to the steering shaft, shaft joint and rack pinion. The pinion teeth mesh with teeth on the rack and the rotary motion is transferred to the rack and changed to linear motion. The linear force is then transmitted through the tie rods and to the steering knuckles which steer the front wheels.

Fig. 3 Tie rod ends removal. 1991—92

Fig. 4 Tie rod removal. 1991—92

Fig. 5 Lower valve nut removal. 1991—92

1	RIGHT TURN OIL PRESSURE PIPE	13	RACK GUIDE CAP LOCKING NUT
2	LEFT TURN OIL PRESSURE PIPE	14	RACK GUIDE SPRING CAP
3	UNION SEAT (AIR)	15	RACK GUIDE SPRING
4	OIL SEAL (6.5 mm THICK)	16	RACK GUIDE
5	RACK HOUSING BUSHING	17	RACK GUIDE SEAT
6	UPPER BEARING	18	SCREW
7	RACK HOUSING SEAL (7.8 mm THICK)	19	BOOT CLAMP
8	SNAP RING	20	RACK BOOT
9	DUST COVER	21	HOSE CLAMP
10	CONTROL VALVE	22	END STOPPER SNAP RING
11	CONTROL VALVE SNAP RING (TEFLON)	23	RACK HOUSING STOPPER
12	UNION SEAT (PRESSURE FEED TUBE)	24	SPACER (6 mm THICK)

25	OUTER OIL SEAL
26	RACK END
27	CLAW WASHER
28	TEFLON O-RING
29	STEERING RACK
30	OUTER O-RING
31	RACK HOUSING CAP
32	CONTROL VALVE LOCKING NUT
33	LOWER BEARING
34	CONTROL VALVE SPACER
35	STEERING RACK HOUSING
36	SPACER (2 mm THICK)
37	INNER OIL SEAL

Fig. 2 Exploded view of Toyota (Prizm) power rack & pinion steering gear assembly. 1991—92

STEERING GEAR SERVICE

REMOVAL

The power steering gear is non-serviceable and therefore must be replaced as a unit. To remove the power steering gear proceed as follows:
1. Remove steering unit from vehicle and place in suitable vise, **Fig. 1.**
2. Remove power steering lines.
3. Scribe alignment mark on tie rod end and tie rod, then remove tie rod ends.
4. Remove rack boots, then bend back locking washer using appropriate punch or chisel and remove.
5. Using tie rod housing wrench, tool No. J 35414 and steering rack end wrench, tool No. J 35418, remove tie rod.

6. Remove dust cover, snap ring then, oil seal.

DISASSEMBLY

1991—92

1. Remove steering unit from vehicle and place in suitable vise, **Fig. 2.**
2. Remove right and left turn pressure pipes between valve housing and cylinder using injection line wrench tool No. J-29698-A or equivalent.
3. Place match marks on tie rod ends and tie rods, then remove tie rod ends, **Fig. 3.**
4. Remove both rack boots.
5. Unstake claw washers retaining both tie rods to steering rack, then remove using tie rod housing wrench tool No. J-35414 and steering rack end wrench tool No. J-35418 or equivalents, **Fig. 4.**

6. Remove steering rack guide cap nut, cap, spring, rack guide and seat using rack guide spring cap wrench tool No. J-35423 and spring cap locknut wrench tool No. J-35692 or equivalents.
7. Remove rack housing dust cover, housing snap ring and housing cap.
8. Remove lower valve nut, lower bearing and spacer using pinion preload socket tool No. J-35428 or equivalent, **Fig. 5.**
9. Remove pinion valve using steering gear bushing remover tool No. J-35420 or equivalent, **Fig. 6.**
10. Remove cylinder end stopper snap ring, cylinder end stopper and spacer.

Fig. 6 Pinion valve removal. 1991–92

Fig. 7 Cylinder inner oil seal removal. 1991–92

Fig. 8 Measuring steering rack bar runout. 1991–92

J 35420

1	INNER BUSHING
2	INNER OIL SEAL
3	CONTROL VALVE HOUSING

Fig. 9 Inner pinion valve bushing removal. 1991–92

A	69.5 mm (2.736″)
1	INNER BUSHING
2	INNER OIL SEAL
3	CONTROL VALVE

Fig. 10 Proper inner bushing installation. 1991–92

1	OUTER OIL SEAL
2	OUTER CYLINDER SPACER
3	SNAP RING
4	RACK HOUSING STOPPER

Fig. 11 Seating rack housing stopper. 1991–92

1	GASKET

Fig. 12 Pressure testing cylinder seals. 1991–92

11. Lightly tap rack end with a brass bar and hammer to free rack from housing, then remove rack and oil seal from housing.
12. Remove cylinder oil seal and spacer using rack cylinder seal remover tool No. J-35434 or equivalent, **Fig. 7.**
13. Clean all disassembled parts. **Do not use a wire brush.**
14. Inspect rack bar for corrosion, pits, scratches, dents, teeth wear or damage.
15. Measure steering rack runout using a suitable dial indicator. If runout is

greater than .012 inch, replace rack bar, **Fig. 8.**
16. Remove inner (teflon) and outer O-ring seal.
17. Measure control valve shaft outer diameter using a suitable micrometer. Maximum shaft outside diameter should not exceed 1.0925 inches. If measurement exceeds specified limit, replace control valve shaft.
18. Measure control valve bushing inner diameter using vernier caliper tool No. J-26900-5 or equivalent. Maximum bushing inside diameter should not exceed 1.1102 inches. If measurement exceeds specified limit, replace control valve bushing.
19. Remove inner bushing from valve housing using steering gear bushing remover tool No. J-35420 or equivalent, **Fig. 9.**
20. Remove housing oil seal using a brass bar.
21. Remove four control valve (teflon) rings.
22. Inspect housing union seat for damage, corrosion or excessive wear. If necessary, remove using a screw extractor and replace seat.

ASSEMBLY

1. Install new inner (teflon) and outer O-ring seals as follows:

1	SPACER
2	LOWER BEARING
3	LOCKNUT

Fig. 13 Pinion shaft locknut installation. 1991–92

  a. Expand teflon ring slightly with fingers.
  b. Install teflon ring to steering rack piston.
  c. Coat teflon ring with suitable power steering fluid and snug it down with fingers.
2. Install new pinion valve (teflon) rings.
3. Coat new housing oil seal with suitable power steering fluid and install.
4. Install inner bushing to valve housing with inner pinion bushing installer tool No. J-35695 and driver handle tool No. J-8092 or equivalents, **Fig. 10. Bushing must be installed to a depth of 2.736 inches.**
5. Coat pinion valve with suitable power steering fluid, then install and inspect for proper operation. Remove valve after inspection.
6. Clean rack teeth, then cover teeth with electrical tape. Tape both ends of rack bar, especially over air bleed

Fig. 14 Rack guide spring cap preload adjustment. 1991–92

holes to prevent damage to oil seal lips.

7. Coat cylinder bore and new inner oil seal with suitable power steering fluid, then install inner oil seal onto rack, lip end first.

8. Install a .079 inch cylinder spacer.

9. Cover rack teeth with electrical tape, then coat cylinder outer seal with suitable power steering fluid and install on to rack, lip end first.

10. Coat cylinder bore with suitable power steering fluid, then carefully install steering rack into cylinder. Push inner oil seal, piston seal ring and outer oil seal into bore being careful not to damage components on cylinder bore end or snap ring groove.

11. Install a .236 inch cylinder spacer with shallow side facing out.

12. Coat rack housing stopper with suitable power steering fluid, then install rack housing stopper onto rack and push into cylinder bore.

13. Install rack into cylinder. Tap end of rack with with a fiber hammer to seat inner seal and spacer.

14. Seat rack housing stopper using power rack pinion bearing and seal installer tool No. J-35425 or equivalent. Stopper should be in far enough to expose snap ring groove, **Fig. 11.**

15. Install snap ring to cylinder end stopper.

16. Test inner and outer seals as follows:
   a. Install valve stem seal tester tool No. J-23728 and cylinder pressure tester tool No. J-35376 or equivalents, **Fig. 12.**
   b. Apply 15 inches Hg.
   c. If vacuum does not hold for a minimum of 30 seconds, replace faulty seals.

17. Install pinion valve into housing.

18. Install rack housing upper bearing using power rack pinion bearing and seal installer tool No. J-35425 or equivalent.

19. Coat rack housing oil seal and snap ring with suitable power steering fluid, then install rack housing oil seal, snap ring and dust cover.

20. Install spacer and lower bearing on pinion valve shaft.

21. Install new self-locking nut on pinion

309	LEFT TURN FLUID PRESSURE PIPE
310	RIGHT TURN FLUID PRESSURE PIPE
311	CONTROL VALVE HOUSING
312	CONTROL VALVE HOUSING GASKET
313	CONTROL VALVE UPPER FLUID SEAL
314	CONTROL VALVE UPPER BEARING
315	CONTROL VALVE
316	CONTROL VALVE TEFLON SEAL RINGS
317	STEERING RACK HOUSING UPPER BEARING
318	CONTROL VALVE LOWER FLUID SEAL
319	RACK GUIDE SPRING CAP LOCKNUT
320	RACK GUIDE SPRING CAP
321	RACK GUIDE SPRING
322	RACK GUIDE
323	RACK GUIDE SEAT
324	LEFT TIE ROD
325	RIGHT TIE ROD
326	CONTROL VALVE LOWER BEARING
327	CONTROL VALVE LOCKNUT
328	RACK HOUSING CAP
329	RACK HOUSING
330	CLAW WASHER
331	STEERING RACK
332	STEERING RACK TEFLON SEAL RING
333	STEERING RACK INNER FLUID SEAL
334	STEERING RACK INNER SPACER
335	STEERING RACK OUTER FLUID SEAL
336	STEERING RACK OUTER SPACER
337	STEERING RACK OUTER SPACER O-RING
338	CYLINDER END STOPPER
339	CYLINDER END STOPPER WIRE
340	TIE ROD BOOT
341	OUTER BOOT CLAMP
342	INNER BOOT CLAMP

Fig. 15 Exploded view of Toyota (Prizm) power rack & pinion steering gear assembly. 1993

shaft using pinion preload socket tool No. J-35428 or equivalent, **Fig. 13.** **Torque** pinion shaft locknut to 43 ft. lbs.

22. Coat threads of new rack housing cap with suitable power steering fluid, then install new rack housing cap and **torque** to 51 ft. lbs. Stake housing using a hammer and chisel.

23. Install rack guide seat, rack guide and rack guide spring.

24. Coat threads of rack guide spring cap with thread sealer No. 1052080 or equivalent, then install using rack guide spring cap wrench tool No. J-35423 or equivalent. **Torque** rack guide spring cap to 18 ft. lbs.

25. Adjust total preload as follows:
   a. Turn rack guide spring cap 12 degrees counterclockwise.
   b. Turn pinion valve shaft right and left 3 to 4 times.
   c. Using a torque wrench and pinion preload socket tool No. J-35428 or equivalent, adjust pinion valve to 7-11 inch lbs., then install rack guide spring cap locking nut and **torque** to 33 ft. lbs., **Fig. 14.**
   d. Recheck preload of pinion valve. If preload is not 7-11 inch lbs., readjust preload.

26. Install tie rods and new claw washers. **Torque** tie rods to 61 ft. lbs., then using a brass bar and hammer, stake

321 RACK GUIDE SPRING
322 RACK GUIDE
323 RACK GUIDE SEAT

Fig. 16   Rack guide spring, rack guide and rack guide seat removal. 1993

311 CONTROL VALVE HOUSING
329 STEERING RACK HOUSING

Fig. 17   Control valve housing removal. 1993

1993

1. Remove steering unit, **Fig. 15.** from vehicle and place in suitable vise.
2. Remove right and left turn pressure pipes between valve housing and cylinder using injection line wrench tool No. J-29698-A or equivalent.
3. Place match marks on tie rod ends and tie rods, then remove tie rod ends.
4. Remove both rack boots.
5. Unstake claw washers retaining both tie rods to steering rack, then remove using tie rod housing wrench tool No. J-35414 and steering rack end wrench tool No. J-35418 or equivalents.
6. Remove steering rack guide cap nut, cap, spring, rack guide and seat using rack guide spring cap wrench tool No. J-35309-2 and spring cap locknut wrench tool No. J-35692 or equivalents, **Fig. 16.**
7. Remove control valve locknut from control using pinion preload socket J-35428 or equivalent to hold control valve stationary.
8. Remove dust cover from top of pinion gear, then two bolts, control valve housing and gasket from steering rack housing, **Fig. 17.**
9. Turn cylinder end stopper using cylinder end stopper end wrench or equivalent until both ends of cylinder end stopper wire appear in slot on top of steering rack housing.
10. Turn cylinder end stopper using cylinder end stopper end wrench or equivalent so that loose end of cylinder end stopper wire is fed out of slot on top of steering rack housing.
11. Remove cylinder end stopper wire and cylinder end stopper from steering rack housing, **Fig. 18.**. Install a rack seal protector J-36595 or equivalent onto toothed portion os steering rack to protect inner steering rack fluid seal.

339 CYLINDER END STOPPER WIRE

Fig. 18   Cylinder end stopper wire removal. 1993

1 GASKET

Fig. 20   Steering rack fluid seal integrity testing. 1993

12. Remove steering rack and steering rack outer spacer from steering rack housing.
13. Remove steering rack outer fluid seal from outer spacer.
14. Remove O-ring from steering outer spacer.
15. Remove steering rack inner fluid seal and spacer from steering rack housing using rack cylinder seal remover J-35434-1 with drive handle J-35343-2 or equivalents.
16. Remove steering rack housing lower bearing from steering rack housing using a brass drift punch and hammer.
17. Remove steering rack upper bearing using a control valve bearing remover J-39902 with drive handle J-35343-2 or equivalents.
18. Clean all disassembled parts. **Do not use a wire brush.**
19. Inspect rack bar for corrosion, pits, scratches, dents, teeth wear or damage.
20. Measure steering rack runout using a suitable dial indicator. If runout is greater than .006 inch, replace steering rack.

INSTALLATION
1991–92

1. Install a new upper oil seal, then install snap ring and dust cover.
2. Install a new claw washer, then using tie rod housing wrench, tool No. J 351414 and steering rack end wrench, tool No. J 35418 install tie rods and **torque** tie rods to 53 ft. lbs.

311 CONTROL VALVE HOUSING
318 CONTROL VALVE LOWER FLUID SEAL

Fig. 19   Steering rack housing upper bearing installation. 1993

claw washers.
27. Ensure air bleed hole is clear of grease and contaminants, then coat inside of steering rack boots small end with suitable power steering fluid.
28. install steering rack boots to steering rack being careful not to damage or twist boots during installation.
29. Install clips securing boots to steering rack with open ends of clips facing outward.
30. Install locknuts and tie rod ends on to tie rods until matchmarks are aligned. **Torque** tie rod locknuts to 41 ft. lbs.
31. Install left and right turn pressure pipes using injection line wrench tool No. J-29698-A or equivalent. **Torque** pipe fittings to 32 ft. lbs.

3. Install rubber rack boot, then screw locknuts and tie rod ends onto the tie rods until match marks are aligned, **torque** locknut to 41 ft. lbs.
4. Adjust toe-in, then **torque** locknut to 41 ft. lbs.
5. Install power steering lines, **torque** nuts to 8 ft. lbs.
6. Install steering assembly into vehicle.

1993

1. Install steering rack housing upper bearing into steering rack housing using control valve bearing stopper J-39903 and driver handle J-7079-2 or equivalents, **Fig. 19**.
2. Install steering rack inner fluid seal and spacer into steering rack housing using rack seal protector J-36595 or equivalent and steering rack. Place rack seal protector J-36595 or equivalent over toothed portion of steering rack and slide fluid seal and spacer over rack seal protector J-36595 or equivalent and onto steering rack. Install steering rack into steering rack housing and tap gently with plastic mallet until inner fluid seal and spacer have been seated.
3. Remove rack seal protector J-36595 or equivalent from steering rack.
4. Install new O-ring onto steering rack outer spacer.
5. Install new steering rack outer fluid seal into steering rack outer spacer.
6. Install cylinder end stopper into steering rack housing as follows:
   a. Turn cylinder end stopper using cylinder end stopper wrench J-39901 until wire end hole appears in slot on top of steering rack housing.
   b. Place hooked end of cylinder end stopper wire into wire end of hole of cylinder end stopper and turn cylinder end stopper using cylinder end stopper wrench J-39901 while feeding cylinder end stopper wire into slot on top of steering rack housing.

321 RACK GUIDE SPRING
322 RACK GUIDE
323 RACK GUIDE SEAT

Fig. 21 Rack guide spring, rack guide and rack guide seat installation. 1993

   c. Continue to turn cylinder end stopper until both ends of cylinder end stopper wire are no longer visible.
7. Inspect steering rack fluid seal integrity using cylinder pressure tester J-35376 and suitable vacuum pipe, **Fig. 20**. Apply 15 inch Hg. of vacuum to steering rack housing and observe vacuum pump. If pressure tester indicates a loss of vacuum, inspect steering rack inner and outer fluid seals.
8. Install new control valve housing gasket and control valve housing onto steering rack housing, then tighten two bolts to 13 ft. lbs.
9. Install dust cover onto top of pinion gear.
10. Install steering rack housing lower bearing and new control valve locknut onto control valve using pinion preload socket J-35428 or equivalent to hold control valve stationary.
11. Apply Loctite pipe sealant or equivalent to threaded portion of rack housing cap.
12. Install housing cap into steering rack housing and tighten cap to 51 ft. lbs., **Fig. 21**. Apply Loctite pipe sealant or equivalent to threaded portion of rack guide spring cap.
13. Install rack guide spring cap into

steering rack housing using locknut wrench J-35309-2 or equivalent and tighten to 18 ft. lbs.
14. Adjust total pinion preload as follows:
   a. Loosen rack guide spring cap 15° (1/24 of a turn) using locknut wrench J-35309-2 or equivalent.
   b. Turn pinion shaft to right and left one rotation each.
   c. Loosen rack guide spring cap using locknut wrench J-35309-2 or equivalent until all tension on rack guide spring is released.
   d. Tighten rack guide spring cap using locknut wrench J-35309-2 or equivalent gradually until pinion preload is within specifications. Measure total pinion preload (starting torque) using pinion preload socket J-35428 or equivalent and a torque wrench. Standard pinion preload should be 6.9-11.3 ft. lbs.
15. Install rack guide spring cap locknut onto rack guide spring cap using locknut wrench J-35309-2 or equivalent while holding rack guide spring cap stationary using locknut wrench J-35309-2 or equivalent. Tighten rack guide spring cap locknut to 33 ft. lbs.
16. Install tie rods onto steering rack using tie rod housing wrench J-35414 and steering rack end wrench J-35418, then tighten tie rods to 61 ft. lbs.
17. Stake both claw washers, then slide both tie rod boots toward steering rack housing.
18. Install inner and outer boot clamps to both boots.
19. Inspect right and left turn fluid pressure pipe O-rings for cuts or other damage, replacing as necessary.
20. Install right and left turn fluid pressure pipes to power steering gear, then tighten four fluid pressure pipe flare nuts to 18 ft. lbs.
21. Remove power steering gear from vise.

Tightening Specifications

NOTE: All Specifications In Ft. Lbs. Unless Noted.

ACHIEVA, BERETTA, CAVALIER, CORSICA, CUTLASS CALAIS, GRAND AM, LEMANS, SKYLARK & SUNBIRD

Year	Adjuster Plug Locknut	Coupling To Stub Shaft	Coupling To Steering Column	Inner Tie Rod Bolts	Pinion Locknut	Pinion Preload	Power Steering Line Fittings	Rack & Pinion Mounting Clamp Nuts	Rod & Piston Assembly To Rack	Tie Rod End To Steering Knuckle Nut	Tie Rod Pinch Bolts
1991-93	50	③	⑥	65	26	16①	②	22	65	④	⑤

①—Inch lbs.
②—Valve end, 14 ft. lbs.; cylinder end, 20 ft. lbs.
③—Except LeMans, 37 ft. lbs.; LeMans, 18 ft. lbs.
④—Except LeMans, 35 ft. lbs.; LeMans, 44 ft. lbs.
⑤—Except LeMans, 41 ft. lbs.; LeMans, 15 ft. lbs.
⑥—Except LeMans, 34 ft. lbs.; LeMans, 18 ft. lbs.

MODELS w/SAGINAW RACK & PINION POWER STEERING EXCEPT ACHIEVA, BERETTA, CAVALIER, CORSICA, CUTLASS CALAIS, GRAND AM, LEMANS, SKYLARK & SUNBIRD

Year	Adjuster Plug Locknut	Inner Tie Rod Housing To Rack	Intermediate Shaft Pinch Bolts	Outer Tie Rod Jam Nut	Pinion Locknut	Pinion Preload①	Power Steering Line Fittings	Tie Rod Pinch Bolts
1991-93	50	70	35	30	26	16①	②	41

①—Inch lbs.
②—Valve end, 12 ft. lbs.; cylinder end, 20 ft. lbs.

PRIZM & STORM

Model	Inner Tie Rod Pinch Bolts	Pinion Preload①	Power Steering Line Fittings	Inner Tie Rod Housing To Rack	Outer Tie Rod Jam Nut
1991-93					
Prizm	26	—	7-11	32	41
Storm	—	65	44①	20	41

①—Inch lbs.

Technical Service Bulletins

INDEX

IDENTIFYING RACK & PINION STEERING NOISES

When removing or installing any rack and pinion steering gear for service, be sure to inspect the intermediate steering shaft or steering coupling seal for cuts or tears which would allow noises to be transmitted into the passenger area.

All models are susceptible to having the power steering pump lines lay against other components which could transmit steering system noises into the car. Hoses should be inspected to ensure they are not touching any other components and creating the noise.

When diagnosing a growl, ground out, or rattle noise, there is a possibility that one of the cylinder lines of the gear could be grounding out on the heater case on the right side of the cowl. If this condition exists, bend pipe away from the contact area.

Check upper portion of steering coupling seal to be sure it is seated over the bushing or a noise path could be created. On 6000 and Bonneville models, check seal to be sure it is securely fastened to the cowl and lower column.

The center-take-off gears, also use a dash seal which must be properly indexed on the housing before the gear is installed. If the dash seal is improperly installed another noise path can be created. A mispositioned dash seal could also cause a condition of stiff steering.

POWER STEERING HOSE LINE CONNECTION FITTING LEAKS

Fitting **torque** specification is 20 ft. lbs. If a leak is experienced at the fitting area when properly tightened, this condition may be caused by a damaged fitting O-ring. Inspect the O-ring for damage, pipe end for cracks, fitting threads for damage, replace as necessary.

Do not exceed fitting torque specification. Additional torque will not increase O-ring sealing ability and may result in cracking the connection boss on aluminum gear housings. If a leak is experienced at the connection area with a new undamaged O-ring under correct torque, inspect housing boss for casting defects. A casting defect will require housing or short gear replacement.

DASH PANEL SERVICE

INDEX

PRECAUTIONS

AIRBAG SYSTEM DISARMING

1991 PARK AVENUE

When carrying a live inflator module, ensure bag and trim cover are pointed away from you. Never carry inflator module by the wires or connector on underside of module.

The diagnostic energy reserve module (DERM) can maintain voltage to cause a system deployment for up to ten minutes after the ignition switch is turned off and the battery is disconnected. Servicing the SIR system during this period may result in accidental deployment and personal injury.

1. Turn ignition switch to Off position, then disconnect and tape battery ground cable terminal.
2. **On except 88 and 98 models,** remove SIR fuse from fuse block, then the left sound insulator.
3. Remove Connector Position Assurance (CPA), then disconnect yellow two-way SIR electrical connector at base of steering column.
4. **On Corvette models,** install Load Tool J 37808 or equivalent by connecting "Base of Column" lead of tool.
5. **On all models,** remove screws and/or nuts from back of steering wheel, then the inflator module from steering wheel.
6. Remove Connector Position Assurance (CPA), then disconnect coil assembly connector and horn lead.
7. Place inflator module on a bench or other surface with bag and trim cover facing UP.

BERETTA, CAMARO, CENTURY, CORSICA, CORVETTE, DEVILLE, ELDORADO, FIREBIRD, FLEETWOOD, LESABRE, RIVIERA, SEVILLE, TORONADO, TROFEO, 88 & 98, 1991 REATTA, 1992 BONNEVILLE w/SINGLE AIRBAG & 1992–93 PARK AVENUE

The diagnostic energy reserve module (DERM) can maintain voltage to cause a system deployment for up to ten minutes after the ignition switch is turned off and the battery is disconnected. Servicing the SIR system during this period may result in accidental deployment and personal injury.

1. Ensure front wheels are pointed straight ahead.
2. Turn ignition switch to Lock position and remove SIR or AIRBAG fuse.
3. Remove left sound insulator. **Remove courtesy lamp from sound insulator, if necessary.**
4. Remove Connector Position Assurance (CPA), then disconnect yellow two-way SIR electrical connector at base of steering column.
5. **On 1993 Camaro and Firebird models,** remove instrument panel door assembly, then Connector Position Assurance (CPA) and yellow 24-way DERM harness connector.

1991 88 & 98

The diagnostic energy reserve module (DERM) can maintain voltage to cause a system deployment for up to ten minutes after the ignition switch is

turned off and the battery is disconnected. Servicing the SIR system during this period may result in accidental deployment and personal injury.

1. Turn ignition switch to Off position, then remove I/P fuse 7 from fuse block.
2. Disconnect yellow two-way SIR electrical connector at base of steering column.

CAPRICE, CUSTOM CRUISER & ROADMASTER

The diagnostic energy reserve module (DERM) can maintain voltage to cause a system deployment for up to ten minutes after the ignition switch is turned off and the battery is disconnected. Servicing the SIR system during this period may result in accidental deployment and personal injury.

1. Ensure front wheels are pointed straight ahead.
2. Turn ignition switch to Lock position and remove SIR or AIR BAG fuse from fuse block.
3. Remove Connector Position Assurance (CPA), then disconnect yellow two-way SIR electrical connector at base of steering column.

1992–93 BONNEVILLE W/DUAL AIRBAGS

The diagnostic energy reserve module (DERM) can maintain voltage to cause a system deployment for up to ten minutes after the ignition switch is turned off and the battery is disconnected. Servicing the SIR system during this period may result in accidental deployment and personal injury.

1. Ensure front wheels are pointed straight ahead.

2. Turn ignition switch to OFF position and remove SIR fuse from fuse panel.
3. Remove left and right sond insulators.
4. Remove Connector Position Assurance (CPA), then disconnect yellow two-way SIR electrical connector at base of steering column.
5. Remove Connector Position Assurance (CPA), then disconnect yellow two-way passenger inflator module connector at base of right side instrument panel, clipped to knee bolster.

METRO

The diagnostic energy reserve module (DERM) can maintain voltage to cause a system deployment for up to ten minutes after the ignition switch is turned off and the battery is disconnected. Servicing the SIR system during this period may result in accidental deployment and personal injury.

1. Place steering wheel so that wheels are pointing straight ahead, then turn ignition switch to LOCK position.
2. Remove SIR IG fuse from SIR fuse block.
3. Remove rear plastic access cover from inflator module housing.
4. Remove Connector Position Assurance (CPA), then disconnect yellow two-way SIR electrical connector inside inflator module housing.

STORM

1991

The diagnostic energy reserve module (DERM) can maintain voltage to cause a system deployment for up to ten minutes after the ignition switch is turned off and the battery is disconnected. Servicing the SIR system during this period may result in accidental deployment and personal injury.

1. Turn ignition switch to Off position, then disconnect battery ground cable.
2. Remove fuses C-22 and C-23 from fuse box, then disconnect orange three-way connector at the base of the steering column.

1992—93

The diagnostic energy reserve module (DERM) can maintain voltage to cause a system deployment for up to ten minutes after the ignition switch is turned off and the battery is disconnected. Servicing the SIR system during this period may result in accidental deployment and personal injury.

1. Place steering wheel so that wheels are pointing straight ahead, then turn ignition switch to LOCK position.
2. Remove fuses C-22 and C-23 from fuse block.
3. Remove switch bezel from instrument panel, then disconnect electrical connector from switches.
4. Remove cigar lighter bezel from instrument panel, then disconnect cigar lighter electrical connectors.
5. Remove two screws and hood latch release handle from knee bolster, then the three screws, three bolts and two nuts retaining knee bolster.

6. Disconnect lap cooler air duct from knee bolster, then remove knee bolster from vehicle.
7. Remove Connector Position Assurance (CPA), then disconnect orange three-way connector at the base of the steering column.

AIRBAG SYSTEM ARMING
1991 PARK AVENUE

1. Turn ignition switch to Off position, connect horn lead and coil assembly connector, then install Connector Position Assurance (CPA).
2. Install inflator module and secure to steering wheel with NEW screws and/or nuts.
3. **Torque** screws and/or nuts to 25 inch lbs.
4. Connect yellow two-way SIR electrical connector at base of steering column, then install Connector Position Assurance (CPA).
5. Install left sound insulator, then the SIR fuse into fuse block.
6. Connect battery ground cable.
7. Turn ignition switch to RUN position and ensure that "Inflatable Restraint" indicator flashes 7 to 9 times, then shuts Off.

BERETTA, CAMARO, CENTURY, CORSICA, CORVETTE, DEVILLE, ELDORADO, FIREBIRD, FLEETWOOD, LESABRE, RIVIERA, SEVILLE, TORONADO, TROFEO, 88 & 98, 1991 REATTA, 1992 BONNEVILLE w/SINGLE AIRBAG & 1992—93 PARK AVENUE

1. **On 1993 Camaro and Firebird models,** install instrument panel door assembly, then Connector Position Assurance (CPA) and yellow 24-way DERM harness connector.
2. Connect yellow two-way SIR electrical connector, then install Connector Position Assurance (CPA).
3. Install left sound insulator. **Install courtesy lamp to sound insulator, if applicable.**
4. Install SIR fuse to fuse block, turn ignition switch to Run position and ensure that "Inflatable Restraint" lamp flashes 7 to 9 times, then shuts off.

1991 88 & 98

1. Connect yellow two-way SIR electrical connector at base of steering column.
2. Install I/P fuse 7 into fuse block, turn ignition switch to RUN position and ensure that "Inflatable Restraint" indicator flashes 7 to 9 times, then shuts Off.

CAPRICE, CUSTOM CRUISER & ROADMASTER

1. Connect yellow two-way SIR electrical connector at base of column, then install Connector Position Assurance (CPA).

2. Install SIR fuse into fuse block, turn ignition switch to RUN position and ensure that "Inflatable Restraint" lamp flashes 7 to 9 times and then shuts off.

1992—93 BONNEVILLE w/DUAL AIRBAGS

1. Connect yellow two-way passenger inflator module connector at base of right side instrument panel, clipped to knee bolster, then install Connector Position Assurance (CPA).
2. Connect yellow two-way SIR electrical connector at base of steering column, then install Connector Position Assurance (CPA).
3. Install left and right sound insulators, then the SIR fuse into fuse panel.
4. Turn ignition switch to Run position and ensure that "Inflatable Restraint" lamp flashes 7 to 9 times, then shuts off.

METRO

1. Turn ignition switch to LOCK position.
2. **On all models,** connect yellow two-way SIR electrical connector inside inflator module housing, then install Connector Position Assurance (CPA).
3. Install SIR IG fuse into SIR fuse block, then the rear plastic access cover onto inflator module housing.
4. Turn ignition switch to Run position and ensure that "Inflatable Restraint" lamp flashes 7 to 9 times and then shuts Off.

STORM
1991

1. Turn ignition switch to Off position, then connect orange three-way connector at the base of the steering column.
2. Install fuses C-22 and C-23 into fuse box, then connect battery ground cable.

1992—93

1. Turn ignition switch to Off position, then connect orange three-way connector at the base of the steering column.
2. Connect lap cooler air duct to knee bolster, then install knee bolster.
3. **Torque** knee bolster bolts and nuts to 89 inch lbs.
4. Install hood latch release handle to knee bolster.
5. Connect cigar lighter electrical connector, then snap cigar lighter bezel into place on instrument panel.
6. Connect switch bezel electrical connectors, then snap switch bezel into place on instrument panel.

DASH PANEL
REPLACE

BROUGHAM

1. Disable airbag system as described under "Airbag System Disarming."

INSULATOR AS VIEWED FROM BELOW

1 BRAKE PEDAL
2 LEFT-SIDE SOUND INSULATOR

Fig. 1 Left side sound insulator. Brougham

1 GLOVE BOX LINER
2 LINER BRACKET

Fig. 4 Glove box liner removal. Brougham

1 RIGHT-SIDE SOUND INSULATOR   2 INSTRUMENT PANEL   VIEW A

Fig. 2 Right side sound insulator. Brougham

1 DIGITAL INSTRUMENT CLUSTER
2 MOUNTING BOLT (1 OF 4)

Fig. 3 Instrument cluster removal. Brougham

2. Disconnect battery ground cable.
3. Remove sound insulators, **Figs. 1 and 2.**
4. Remove screw securing left side A/C outlet duct extension and remove duct.
5. Remove two steering column cover retaining screws and lower cover.
6. Remove A/C left side outlet duct extension retaining screw, then the duct.
7. Remove instrument panel retaining screws at each end of instrument panel.
8. Remove top cover attaching screw through access hole located in top of glove box liner.
9. Remove four top cover to cowl retaining screws located in the defroster grilles.
10. Remove top cover by pulling panel up and out of retaining clips.
11. Using a 1/16 inch Allen wrench, loosen key on bottom of each center outlet grille directional knob, then remove knobs.
12. Remove four center trim panel retaining screws, then the trim panel.
13. Remove remaining grille directional knob.
14. Remove six trim panel retaining screws, then the trim panel.
15. Remove four instrument cluster retaining screws, **Fig. 3.**

16. Remove upper steering column mounting bolts and set column on front seat.
17. Remove two windshield wiper switch retaining screws.
18. Remove three headlamp switch to instrument panel retaining screws.
19. **On models equipped with cruise control,** remove two cruise control switch retaining screws, then slide switch forward.
20. Disconnect switch two piece electrical connector.
21. Remove twilight Sentinel wiring if equipped.
22. **On all models,** remove headlamp switch retaining nut, then the switch from housing.
23. Remove two 10mm mounting bolts and ground strap from chime mounting bracket.
24. Remove 10mm retaining nut from stud on bottom of radio chassis.
25. Pull chime module, bracket and chime wiring downward, then position aside.
26. Disconnect antenna lead.
27. Pull radio chassis down and pivot towards front of car until connector end of chassis is horizontal with floorpan.
28. Disconnect (2) electrical connectors from side opposite coax cable.
29. Pull chassis out from behind instrument panel and disconnect three electrical connectors.
30. Remove two ECC head retaining screws.
31. Disconnect electrical connector from ECC head, then the EEC.
32. Remove right side mirror remote control retaining screws, then the remote control.

33. Remove three glove box liner retaining screws, **Fig. 4.**
34. Remove four glove box door retaining screws, then remove accessory relay bracket and position aside.
35. Remove four upper instrument panel retaining screws and two lower instrument panel retaining bolts.
36. Disconnect instrument panel electrical connectors.
37. Remove instrument panel.
38. Reverse procedure to install.
39. Reactivate airbag system as described under "Airbag System Disarming."

1991 CORVETTE
REMOVAL

Refer to **Fig. 5** when performing this procedure.
1. Disable airbag system as described under "Airbag System Disarming."
2. Remove right hand side window outlet defogger duct, assembly screw and retainer.
3. Remove center outlet air deflector.
4. Remove fuse box by drilling out rivet heads.
5. Disconnect alarm module connector and low tire pressure module connector.
6. Remove inside air temperature sensor screws from instrument panel.
7. Remove lateral accelerometer screws and upper instrument reinforcement screws.
8. Remove driver and passenger knee bolster outer bracket nuts.

#		#	
1	SIDE WINDOW DEFOG OUTLET DUCT - LH	18	CENTRAL CONTROL MODULE
2	AIR DISTRIBUTOR DUCT	19	DERM/ARMING SENSOR BRACKET
3	LAP AIR OUTLET DUCT - RH	20	DIAGNOSTIC ENERGY RESERVE MODULE (DERM)
4	FLOOR AIR OUTLET DUCT	21	DERM BRACKET - LH
5	CRUISE CONTROL MODULE	22	CENTRAL CONTROL MODULE BRACKET
6	MULTI USE RELAY BRACKET	23	KNEE BOLSTER INNER BRACKET - LH
7	RADIO RECEIVER	24	WIRING HARNESS
8	PLASTIC 7" ADJUSTABLE STRAP RETAINER	25	KNEE BOLSTER, DRIVERS SIDE
9	SIDE WINDOW DEFOG OUTLET DUCT - RH	26	KNEE BOLSTER OUTER BRACKET - LH
10	LOWER TRIM PANEL SUPPORT	27	INSTRUMENT PANEL
11	WIRING HARNESS FUSE BLOCK BRACKET	28	LAP AIR OUTLET DUCT - LH
12	KNEE BOLSTER OUTER BRACKET - RH	29	MULTI USE RELAY BRACKET
13	ACCELEROMETER	30	ALARM MODULE
14	CARRIER	31	ALARM MODULE BRACKET
15	KNEE BOLSTER INNER BRACKET BRACE	32	HEADLAMP AUTO CONTROL MODULE - (CAN ONLY)
16	KNEE BOLSTER INNER BRACKET - RH	33	LOW TIRE PRESSURE INDICATOR MODULE
17	DERM BRACKET - RH		

Fig. 5 I/P removal. 1991 Corvette

#		#	
1	AIR DISTRIBUTOR DUCT	15	DERM BRACKET - RH
2	ALARM MODULE	16	CENTRAL CONTROL MODULE
3	PKE MODULE	17	DERM/ARMING SENSOR BRACKET
4	MULTI USE RELAY BRACKET	18	DIAGNOSTIC ENERGY RESERVE MODULE (DERM)
5	CRUISE MODULE	19	DERM BRACKET - LH
6	PLASTIC 7" ADJUSTABLE STRAP RETAINER	20	KNEE BOLSTER INNER BRACKET - LH
7	SIDE WINDOW DEFOG OUTLET DUCT - RH	21	I/P WIRING HARNESS
8	LOWER TRIM PANEL SUPPORT	22	CENTRAL CONTROL MODULE BRACKET
9	WIRING HARNESS FUSE BLOCK BRACKET	23	KNEE BOLSTER, DRIVERS SIDE
10	KNEE BOLSTER OUTER BRACKET - RH	24	KNEE BOLSTER OUTER BRACKET - LH
11	LOWER CENTER SUPPORT	25	INSTRUMENT PANEL
12	CARRIER	26	SIDE WINDOW DEFOG OUTLET DUCT - LH
13	KNEE BOLSTER INNER BRACKET BRACE	27	MULTI USE RELAY BRACKET - LH
14	KNEE BOLSTER INNER BRACKET - RH	28	LOW TIRE PRESSURE INDICATOR MODULE

Fig. 6 I/P removal. 1992–93 Corvette

9. Remove driver and passenger knee bolster inner bracket nuts on bulkhead and bolts on console bracket.
10. Remove right hand lap air outlet duct.
11. Remove left hand side window outlet defogger duct and assembly screws.
12. Remove two wiring harness retainers from rear of instrument panel (cluster area).
13. Remove three multi-use relay bracket nuts from instrument panel and bolts for each cluster mounted bracket nuts for passenger side bracket.
14. Remove air distributor duct from instrument panel and screws.
15. Disconnect instrument panel harness connectors from alarm assembly, daytime running lamp module and low tire pressure module, CCM and SIR.
16. Remove instrument panel from vehicle.

INSTALLATION

1. Position instrument panel in vehicle, then mount left and right hand inner knee bolster brackets to console bolts.
2. Install left and right hand outer knee bolster brackets nuts to studs on bulkhead. Tighten inner bolster bracket to bulkhead studs 116 ft. lbs., outer knee bolster to bulkhead 116 ft. lbs. and inner knee bolster bracket to brace to 116 ft. lbs.

3. Install four rivets and washers attaching fuse box to instrument panel carrier.
4. Install all multi-use relay brackets.
5. Connect two wiring harness retainers to inside left multi-use bracket.
6. Install left hand side window defogger outlet duct, then left hand lap air outlet duct.
7. Install accelerometer assembly.
8. Install inside air temperature sensor to carrier.
9. Connect low tire pressure connector and alarm module electrical connector.
10. Install center air outlet deflector.
11. Install right hand side window defogger outlet duct, then air distributor duct to instrument panel.
12. Install upper instrument panel reinforcement brace.
13. Connect instrument panel connectors to alarm assembly module, daytime running lamp module, low tire pressure module, CCM and SIR.
14. Reactivate airbag system as described under "Airbag System Disarming."

1992–93 CORVETTE

Refer to **Fig. 6** when performing this procedure.
1. Disable airbag system as described under "Airbag System Disarming."

2. Remove driver knee bolster, then right hand lower trim panel and support.
3. Remove console and accessory trim plates.
4. Remove console to instrument panel bolt and screws, then console side trim plates.
5. Remove instrument panel to knee bolster brackets bolts and screws.
6. Remove stack bracket bolts.
7. Remove Driver Information Center (DIC) and Heater/Vent/Air Conditioning (HVAC) control and radio control.
8. Remove lateral accelerometer.
9. Remove upper trim pad, then cluster and headlamp switch.
10. Disconnect wire harness retainers from instrument panel.
11. Remove side window defogger outlet ducts.
12. Remove inside air temperature sensor.
13. Remove upper instrument panel brace, then upper and lower outer instrument panel to dash nuts from studs.
14. Remove fuse box by drilling out rivet heads.
15. Remove multi-use relay brackets.
16. Remove air distribution duct from instrument panel.
17. Disconnect harness connectors from instrument panel mounted modules.

Fig. 7 Left side trim plate removal. 1991 Caprice

3	LOCATOR PIN
4	SCREW
5	TRIM PLATE

Fig. 8 Left side trim plate removal. 1991 Custom Cruiser & Roadmaster

A	LOCATOR PIN
4	TRIM PLATE
5	SCREW

Fig. 9 Upper trim pad removal. 1991 Caprice

7	SCREW
8	CLIP
9	PAD

Fig. 10 Upper trim pad removal. 1991 Custom Cruiser & Roadmaster

A	CLIP
7	SCREW
8	PAD

Fig. 11 Knee Deflector & bolster. 1991 Caprice, Custom Cruiser & Roadmaster

A	TIE BAR
13	DEFLECTOR
14	BOLT
15	BOLSTER
16	BOLT

18. Remove instrument panel from vehicle.
19. Reverse procedure to install.
20. Reactivate airbag system as described under "Airbag System Disarming."

1991 CAPRICE, CUSTOM CRUISER & ROADMASTER

1. Disable airbag system as described under "Airbag System Disarming."
2. Disconnect battery ground cable.
3. Remove righthand sound insulator attaching screws, then the sound insulator from under instrument panel.
4. Remove two steering column opening filler attaching screws.
5. Loosen but do not remove steering column support bracket attaching nuts, then lower steering column.
6. **On Caprice models,** remove six lefthand trim plate retaining screws, then carefully unsnap and pull trim plate away from instrument panel, **Fig. 7.**
7. **On Custom Cruiser and Roadmaster models,** remove eight lefthand trim plate retaining screws, then

carefully unsnap and pull trim plate away from instrument panel, **Fig. 8.**
8. **On all models,** remove windshield defroster nozzle grille from upper trim pad. Remove in-car temperature sensor by twisting clockwise.
9. **On Caprice models,** remove eight upper trim pad attaching screws, then unsnap pad and pull away from windshield frame, **Fig. 9.**
10. **On Custom Cruiser and Roadmaster models,** remove seven upper trim pad attaching screws, then unsnap pad and pull away from windshield frame, **Fig. 10.**
11. **On all models,** remove two righthand trim pad attaching screws, then pull pad up from bottom of plate to unsnap.
12. Remove air deflector by unsnapping from plate.
13. Remove four instrument panel compartment door attaching screws.
14. Remove four ashtray assembly attaching screws, then disconnect lamp connector and lighter from assembly.
15. Remove four lefthand side knee deflector attaching screws, then the bolster bolts and bolster, **Fig. 11.**

16. Remove four deflector attaching bolts and deflector.
17. Remove four instrument cluster retaining screws, then disconnect shift indicator cable from steering column.
18. Gently pull instrument cluster from adapters.
19. Remove stop lamp switch, then loosen capsule nuts and lower steering column.
20. Remove two steering column guide brackets bolts and steering column guide bracket.
21. Remove headlamp switch, accessory switch, parking brake release handle, multi-function alarm module and heater/air conditioning control assembly.
22. Remove radio, instrument panel compartment lamp switch, courtesy lamps, low oil module and ALDL link.
23. Remove lefthand and righthand shroud covers.
24. Remove four instrument panel carrier attaching bolts at windshield frame, one bolt at each door pillar and one bolt attaching lower reinforcement to instrument panel carrier, **Fig. 12.**
25. Remove instrument panel carrier from windshield lower frame flange, then unsnap and pull away.
26. Remove three outer reinforcement attaching screws, air distributor and inside air temperature sensor duct.
27. Disconnect wiring harness from back of carrier.
28. Reverse procedures to install.
29. Reactivate airbag system as described under "Airbag System Arming."

CENTURY

1. Disconnect battery ground cable.

72	WINDSHIELD LOWER FRAME FLANGE
73	BOLT
74	BOLT
75	CARRIER
76	LOWER REINFORCEMENT

77	BOLT
78	NUT
79	OUTER REINFORCEMENT
80	LOCATOR PIN
81	SCREW

Fig. 12 Instrument panel carrier mounting. 1991 Caprice, Custom Cruiser & Roadmaster

Fig. 13 LH side I/P sound insulator removal. Century

Fig. 14 RH side I/P sound insulator removal. Century

Fig. 15 I/P filler panel removal. Century

2. Remove two screws from front of left side instrument panel sound insulator, **Fig. 13.**
3. Remove one bolt from rear left side and one nut from accelerator pedal bracket, then pull left sound insulator straight forward to remove.
4. Remove three screws from front of right side sound insulator, **Fig. 14.**
5. Remove nut from right back side, then pull right side sound insulator straight forward to remove.
6. Remove two screws from instrument panel filler panel, **Fig. 15.**
7. Gently pull forward on left side trim cover to release hooks on front of lower instrument panel filler panel.
8. Disconnect lap vent hose and ALDL connector, then remove instrument panel filler.

9. Remove two screws from steering column opening filler, **Fig. 16.**
10. Lower steering column by removing shift indicator clip, then the three retaining bolts and one nut.
11. Disconnect electrical connectors at steering column and disconnect parking brake cable.
12. Disconnect instrument panel harness connectors to body connectors at junction block.
13. Disconnect speaker connectors, A/C vacuum harness and temperature door cable.
14. Disconnect emission harness connectors, antenna cable and side window defroster hoses.
15. **On 1991-92 models,** disconnect speedometer cable from engine compartment split if a two piece cable is used, or from the transmission for slack.
16. **On all models,** split bulk head connector by removing 1/4 inch bolt, then slide instrument panel side of connector out of clip.
17. Disconnect electrical connectors from windshield wiper motor, master brake cylinder and hood light.
18. Disconnect harness cowl connector, then feed harness through cowl.
19. Remove two screws, then pull speaker-defroster grille straight out.
20. Remove two nuts on both inner sides of steering column opening.
21. Remove three bolts on bottom side of instrument panel, then remove six screws in defroster area at top of instrument panel, **Fig. 17.**
22. **On 1991-92 models,** pull instrument

Fig. 16 Steering column opening filler removal. Century

panel forward and disconnect speedometer cable.
23. **On all models,** remove panel. **On vehicles equipped with digital instrument cluster,** the Vehicle Speed Sensor (VSS) buffer must be disconnected.
24. Reverse procedure to install.

6000

1. Disconnect battery ground cable.
2. Remove steering column filler and four screws to instrument panel pad, **Fig. 18.**
3. Remove right side trim plate, then one screw inside glove compartment.
4. Using a small flat blade tool remove clips that hold right plate to pad.

Fig. 17 I/P removal. Century

1–STEERING COLUMN
 FILLER PANEL

2–IP TRIM L.H.

**Fig. 18 Steering column filler
panel removal. 6000**

1–SWITCH ASM.
2–I/P TRIM PLATE ASM.
3–INST. PANEL WIRING HARN.
4–INSTRUMENT PANEL RETAINER

**Fig. 19 Disconnecting fog
lamp switch. 6000**

5. Remove clips that hold left plate to
   pad.
6. Disconnect memory seat switch and
   fog light switch electrical connections,
   Figs. 19 and 20
7. Remove two screws from right side
   cluster pad air outlet, and one screw
   from left side air outlet.
8. **On models with column shift,** disconnect shift indicator light, then rotate and pull out of indicator, **Fig. 21.**
9. **On all models,** remove cluster trim
   pad.
10. Remove A/C lower distributor duct or
    vent duct on vehicles without A/C,
    Fig. 22.
11. Remove distributor duct.
12. Remove eight screws that hold the in-
    strument cluster to the instrument
    panel.
13. Pull cluster assembly carefully to the
    rear and disengage electrical connec-
    tors.
14. Using a small flat blade, carefully pry
    out speaker grilles.
15. Remove defroster grilles, then the
    glove box lamp and deck release
    switches, **Fig. 23.**

1 – 2 N·m (18 LB.IN.)

2 – SWITCH

3 – IP TRIM PLATE

**Fig. 20 Disconnecting
memory seat switch. 6000**

16. Remove sound insulation, then dis-
    connect fuse block and convenience
    center, **Fig. 24.**
17. Remove four bolts holding ECM to
    bracket, then disconnect electrical
    connector and remove ECM, **Fig. 25.**
18. Remove radio attaching bolts, then
    disconnect electrical connectors and
    remove radio.
19. Remove headlight switch, heater nd
    A/C control and multi-function switch.
20. Remove ashtray and lighter, then the
    two bolts at lower right and left hinge
    pillar brackets.
21. Remove four bolts in the speaker and
    defroster duct openings.
22. Remove one bolt at center brace.
23. Remove side window defroster ducts,
    then park brake release cable.
24. Remove non A/C vent cables.
25. Remove wire harness clips, then re-
    move instrument panel pad, **Fig. 26.**
26. Reverse procedure to install.

CUTLASS CIERA &
CUTLASS CRUISER

1. Disconnect battery ground cable.
2. Remove left and right sound insulators, **Figs. 27 and 28.**

3. **On models with center console,**
   proceed as follows:
   a. Open armrest and remove cas-
      sette holder.
   b. Remove six screws, then lift com-
      partment straight up.
   c. Remove ashtray, then two screws
      in ashtray opening.
   d. **On models with column shifter,**
      open center compartment and re-
      move two screws at rear of center
      compartment.
   e. **On models with console shifter,**
      use a small screwdriver to pry off
      snap ring that holds shift knob in
      place. Remove shift knob and re-
      move two screws at rear of shifter
      plate.
4. **On all models,** remove center compartment or shifter plate, **Fig. 29.**
5. Pull console trim plate rearward, then
   disconnect the electrical connectors
   to DIS, ashtray light and lighter.
6. Remove console trim plate, then remove two screws from console trim
   plate opening.
7. Remove upper console, **Fig. 30.**
8. Remove steering column collar by
   carefully prying rearward to release
   the five clips.
9. Remove outer air deflectors by pulling
   rearward.
10. Remove one bolt and one screw from
    deflector openings, then one bolt and
    one screw from steering column
    opening.
11. **On models with center console,** re-
    move four bolts from ashtray trim cov-
    er. Remove ashtray trim cover and the
    two bolts holding accessory trim plate.
12. **On models less center console,**
    open ashtray and remove two bolts
    holding accessory trim plate.
13. **On models with column shift,** move
    shift lever to the 1 position.

1—CLUSTER PAD
2—SHIFT INDICATOR
3—PAD ASSY.
4—SHIFT INDICATOR
   LIGHT

VIEW A

Fig. 21   Cluster pad & shift indicator light removal. 6000

1 CLUSTER
2 INSTRUMENT PANEL PAD
4 A C LOWER DISTRIBUTION DUCT
5 VENT DUCT NON A/C
6 SEALS

Fig. 22   A/C & non A/C distribution ducts removal. 6000

1—PLUG
2—DECK LID RELEASE SWITCH
3—GLOVEBOX LAMP SWITCH

Fig. 23   Glove box lamp switch & deck lid release switch removal. 6000

FWD

1 — BRACKET

2 — 1.5 N·m (13 LB.IN.)

3 — FUSE BLOCK

4 — CONVENIENCE CENTER

Fig. 24   Fuse block & convenience center mounting. 6000

1 — MULTI-USE BRACKET

2 — 3 N·m (27 LB.IN.)

3 — ECM

4 — HARNESS ASSEMBLY

FWD

Fig. 25   Disconnecting & removing ECM. 6000

14. **On all models,** remove accessory trim panel by carefully pulling rearward to release clips, **Fig. 31.**
15. Remove Torx screws from bottom and top of cluster trim plate, then remove trim plate, **Fig. 32.**
16. **On models with column shifter,** remove shift indicator clip from steering column shift bowl.
17. **On all models,** remove four bolts holding instrument cluster, pull cluster rearward and disconnect speedometer.
18. Remove speaker grilles by prying carefully.
19. Remove ventilation control assembly.
20. Remove parking brake release handle, then side window defogger hoses from heater outlet.
21. Disconnect steering column wiring harness from the steering column.
22. Remove wiper motor to cowl attaching bolts, then disconnect bulkhead connector at cowl.
23. Remove lower instrument panel attaching bolts, then using a small screwdriver remove defroster grille by carefully prying upward.
24. Remove upper instrument panel attaching bolts, **Fig. 33,** then open engine compartment hood.
25. Remove clip in engine compartment holding instrument panel wiring harness to cowl.

26. Disconnect electrical connectors from wiring harness in engine compartment.
27. Pull wiring harness through cowl opening into passenger compartment.
28. Tilt instrument panel forward and disconnect remaining electrical connectors and remove instrument panel.
29. Reverse procedure to install.

DEVILLE & FLEETWOOD

Refer to **Fig. 34,** when performing this procedure.
1. Disable airbag system as described under "Airbag System Disarming."
2. Disconnect battery ground cable.
3. Remove right and left side sound insulators, **Fig. 35.**

4. Remove upper trim pad as shown in **Fig. 34.**
5. Remove lower steering column filler.
6. Remove steering column to support bracket attaching bolts, then lower steering column.
7. Remove lower instrument panel trim pad support.
8. Remove lower instrument panel brace retaining nut from accelerator pedal stud.
9. Disconnect electrical connectors between instrument panel and dash, then remove glove box switches.
10. Remove instrument panel to dash attaching screws, **Fig. 36.**
11. Remove trim pad assembly.
12. Reverse procedure to install.
13. Reactivate airbag system as described under "Airbag System Arming."

1 STEERING COLUMN
  FILLER PANEL
2 IP TRIM
3 IP TRIM
4 CENTER BRACE
5 INST. PAD ASSY.

VIEW A

Fig. 26 I/P & trim plate removal. 6000

1. PARKING BRAKE
2. I.P. PAD
3. NUT
4. INSULATOR
5. FULLY DRIVEN, SEATED AND NOT STRIPPED
6. STUD ON ACCELERATOR SUPPORT

**Fig. 27 Left side I/P sound
insulator removal. Cutlass
Ciera & Cutlass Cruiser**

1	PARKING BRAKE
2	I.P. PAD
3	NUT
4	INSULATOR
5	FULLY DRIVEN, SEATED AND NOT STRIPPED
6	STUD ON ACCELERATOR SUPPORT

**Fig. 28 Right side I/P sound
insulator removal. Cutlass
Ciera & Cutlass Cruiser**

1. CONSOLE BASE
2. COMPARTMENT DOOR
3. COMPARTMENT
4. CENTER COMPARTMENT
5. SHIFTER PLATE
6. TAPE STORAGE
7. ASHTRAY

**Fig. 29 Center console
assembly. Cutlass Ciera &
Cutlass Cruiser**

1. CONSOLE BASE
2. TRANSMISSION SHIFTER ASSEMBLY
3. 6 N·m (4 LBS. FT.)
4. PAD ASM.
5. COMPARTMENT ASM.
6. FULLY DRIVEN, SEATED AND NOT STRIPPED

**Fig. 30 Upper console
removal. Cutlass Ciera &
Cutlass Cruiser**

1991 LESABRE

1. Disable airbag system as described under "Airbag System Disarming."
2. Disconnect battery ground cable.
3. Refer to **Fig. 37** for dash panel service.
4. Reactivate airbag system as described under "Airbag System Disarming."

PARK AVENUE & 1992–93 LESABRE

1. Disable airbag system as described under "Airbag System Disarming."
2. Disconnect battery ground cable.
3. Refer to **Fig. 38** for dash panel service.
4. Reactivate airbag system as described under "Airbag System Disarming."

1991 88

1. Disable airbag system as described under "Airbag System Disarming."
2. Disconnect battery ground cable.
3. Remove center trim plate.
4. Remove lower trim plate.
5. Remove screws from left and right speaker grilles.

6. Remove speaker grilles and defroster duct screen.
7. Remove left and right sound insulators.
8. Disconnect parking brake release cable.
9. Remove two screws from dash wire electrical connectors between radio and steering column.
10. Remove four steering column support bolts, disconnect shift indicator cable.
11. Lower steering column, and rest it on driver's seat.
12. Remove two ALDL connector attaching screws.
13. Remove two clips from steering column and pull forward and down.
14. Remove three bolts on lower rail of instrument panel.
15. Remove two instrument panel attaching bolts from brace directly above steering column opening.

1. TRIM PLATE
2. I.P.
3. SPEAKER OPENING
4. DUCT
5. 1.5 N·m (13 LBS. IN.)

Fig. 31   Accessory trim plate removal. Cutlass Ciera & Cutlass Cruiser

1. CLUSTER TRIM PLATE
2. SPEAKER OPENING
3. CLUSTER
4. RADIO

Fig. 32   Cluster trim plate removal. Cutlass Ciera & Cutlass Cruiser

16. Remove two bolts in instrument panel bracket, behind instrument panel compartment opening.
17. Remove air sensor duct, lift upward on instrument panel and pull rearward. Disconnect two side window defogger hoses at distributor outlet.
18. Remove instrument panel assembly from vehicle.
19. Reverse procedure to install.
20. Reactivate airbag system as described under "Airbag System Arming."

98 & 1992–93 88

Refer to **Fig. 39** when performing this procedure.
1. Disable airbag system as described under "Airbag System Disarming."
2. Remove lower console if necessary.
3. Disconnect connectors from sensors (if equipped).
4. Remove instrument panel trim plates, **Fig. 40.**
5. Remove steering column filler screws from instrument panel, then steering column filler, **Fig. 41.**
6. Remove instrument panel compartment tray by pulling rearward.
7. Remove PRNDL cable and park brake release cable.
8. Remove bolts to instrument panel support brackets and center bracket, then lower steering column.
9. Remove bolts to dash nuts and instrument panel end support bracket, then pull assembly away from dash.
10. Disconnect electrical connectors.
11. Remove antenna coax cable.
12. Remove vacuum line.
13. Remove instrument panel assembly.
14. Reverse procedure to install.
15. Reactivate airbag system as described under "Airbag System Arming."

TORONADO & TROFEO

1. Disable airbag system as described under "Airbag System Disarming."
2. Disconnect battery ground cable.
3. Turn ignition to the Off position, then remove fuse No. 9 from fuse panel.
4. Remove four left side sound insulator retaining screws.
5. Disconnect courtesy lamp from panel and remove sound insulator from vehicle.
6. Remove four right side sound insula-

1. INSTRUMENT PANEL
2. CENTER SUPPORT
3. 8 N·m (70 LBS. IN.)
4. 9 N·m (80 LBS. IN.)

Fig. 33   I/P removal. Cutlass Ciera & Cutlass Cruiser

tor retaining screws, **Fig. 42.**
7. Disconnect courtesy lamp from panel and remove sound insulator from vehicle.
8. Remove two knee bolster retaining screws, then remove bolster from vehicle, **Fig. 43.**
9. Remove four steering column reinforcement plate retaining screws, then remove plate from vehicle.
10. Remove instrument panel cluster trim plate retaining screws, then remove plate from vehicle, **Fig. 44.**
11. Remove right and left side switch assembly retaining screws, then disconnect switch assemblies from electrical connectors and remove from vehicle.
12. Remove instrument panel cluster retaining screws, then pull cluster outward disengaging electrical connector.
13. Remove electronic climate control head retaining screws, if equipped.
14. **On models equipped with integral radio unit,** proceed as follows:
   a. Remove radio/ECC retaining screws.
   b. Remove radio bracket to radio retaining nuts.
   c. Disconnect radio electrical connectors and remove radio from vehicle.
15. **On models equipped with remote radio chassis,** proceed as follows:

a. Open console storage tray and remove CD, cassette holder or phone handset if equipped.
b. Remove four T-15 Torx screws.
c. Remove storage tray liner, then disconnect two seat control electrical connectors and handset connector if equipped.
d. Open ashtray and remove cigar lighter and ashtray bucket.
e. Pull console trim plate upward, then disconnect trim plate bulb and cigar lighter electrical connectors.
f. Remove console trim plate from vehicle.
g. Remove three 10mm chassis to CRTC bracket retaining nuts.
h. Disconnect six remote chassis and one coax lead electrical connectors.
16. **On all models,** remove four driver information display to mounting bracket retaining bolts.
17. Disconnect driver information display electrical connector and remove from vehicle.
18. Remove center A/C deflector, then unsnap and remove defroster grille.
19. Remove upper and lower left instrument panel retaining screws.
20. Remove hood release assembly, remaining instrument panel retaining screws and center instrument panel brace.

1 PAD ASSEMBLY, INSTRUMENT PANEL (I/P) UPPER TRIM PAD	12 BOX, GLOVE COMPARTMENT MODULE	25 TELLTALE, LEFT-HAND INFORMATION CENTER
2 GRILLE, FRONT SPEAKER	13 PANEL, GLOVE BOX DOOR INNER	26 TELLTALE, RIGHT-HAND INFORMATION CENTER
3 SPEAKER	14 PANEL, GLOVE BOX DOOR OUTER	27 SWITCH, CRUISE CONTROL ON-OFF
4 PLATE, I/P CLUSTER CENTER TRIM	15 NAMEPLATE, GLOVE BOX	28 TRAY, ASH RECEPTACLE
5 PLATE, I/P CLUSTER RIGHT-HAND TRIM	16 LATCH ASSEMBLY, GLOVE BOX	29 HOUSING, ASHTRAY
6 FILLER, STEERING COLUMN OPENING UPPER	17 LOCK CYLINDER, GLOVE BOX LATCH ASSEMBLY	30 ALARM, SEAT BELT WARNING, IGNITION KEY AND HEADLAMPS "ON" REMINDER
7 PLATE, I/P CLUSTER LEFT-HAND TRIM	18 PLATE, GLOVE BOX SWITCHES	31 PLATE, I/P SPEEDOMETER CLUSTER
8 FILLER, I/P STEERING COLUMN OPENING LOWER	19 SWITCH, FUEL FILLER DOOR RELEASE	32 PLATE, RADIO TRIM
9 COVER, FUSE PANEL ACCESS OPENING	20 SWITCH, GLOVE BOX LIGHT	33 INSULATOR, LEFT-HAND SOUND
10 BRACKET, I/P MOUNTING	21 SWITCH, REAR DECK LID RELEASE	34 INSULATOR, RIGHT-HAND SOUND
11 BRACKET, HEADLIGHT SWITCH	22 CLUSTER, SPEEDOMETER	
	23 DISPLAY, FUEL DATA CENTER	
	24 CONTROL, HEATER AND AIR CONDITIONER (A/C)	

Fig. 34   Exploded view of I/P. DeVille & Fleetwood

1. LEFT SOUND INSULATOR
2. RIGHT SOUND INSULATOR
3. SCREW; 1.9 N•M (17 LB-IN)
4. NUT
5. NUT; 9.5 N•M (84 LB-IN)

Fig. 35   Insulator sound panel removal. DeVille & Fleetwood

16 BRACKET	22 BRACKET
17 SCREW	90 SCREW
18 NUT	91 SCREW
19 SCREW	92 NUT
20 SCREW	93 TRIMPAD
21 NUT	

Fig. 36   I/P removal. DeVille & Fleetwood

1 DEFROST GRILLE — Pry out carefully.
4 10 BOLTS — 1.9 N•M (16 LB-IN)
8 I/P TRIM PAD
6 IN-VEHICLE TEMPERATURE SENSOR CONNECTOR (C68 only.)
5 ASPIRATOR TUBE (C68 only.)
19 INSTRUMENT CLUSTER — Pull straight out to unplug.
18 5 BOLTS — 1.4 N•M (12 LB-IN)
3 RETAINER — Push in, twist off.
2 TWILIGHT SENTINEL/ DAYTIME RUNNING LIGHTS PHOTOCELL — Pry out gently.
7 PANEL LIGHT — Unsnap.

13 RH PLATE
12 4 SCREWS — 1.4 N•M (12 LB-IN)
11 PLATE — Pull to remove.
16 FILLER
14 4 BOLTS — 1.4 N•M (12 LB-IN)
9 2 RETAINERS — Push/turn.
10 LH PLATE
FRT

15 RUBBER COLLAR — Slide up on steering column.
17 CLIP — Slide on/off with gear selector at N. Note cable routing.
STEERING COLUMN

Fig. 37 I/P removal & installation. 1991 LeSabre

Fig. 38 I/P removal & installation. Park Avenue & 1992–93 LeSabre

Fig. 39 Exploded view of I/P front. 98 & 1992–93 88

1	IP CLUSTER TRIM PLATE	9	RIGHT SOUND INSULATOR
2	CLUSTER ASSEMBLY	10	LEFT SOUND INSULATOR
3	HEATER AND A/C CONTROLS	11	INNER AIR OUTLET
4	RADIO BRACKET	12	CD PLAYER
5	RADIO ASSEMBLY	13	LEFT CENTER TRIM PLATE
6	CD PLAYER BRACKET	14	IP STEERING COLUMN FILLER
7	RIGHT CENTER TRIM PLATE	15	HEADLAMP SWITCH
8	OUTER AIR OUTLET	16	DRIVER INFORMATION DISPLAY SWITCH

1	SIDE WINDOW DEFOGGER OUTLET	4	SCREW
2	RIGHT CENTER TRIM PLATE	5	LEFT CENTER TRIM PLATE
3	AIR OUTLET DEFLECTOR		

Fig. 40 Center trim plate assembly. 98 & 1992–93 88

1	STEERING COLUMN FILLER
2	SCREW

Fig. 41 I/P steering column filler. 98 & 1992–93 88

21. Remove four inflator module retaining screws located on back of steering wheel assembly.
22. Remove position assurance (CPA) and coil assembly connector from inflator module.
23. Remove inflator module from vehicle. **When carrying a live inflator, ensure the bag and trim cover are pointed away in case of accidental deployment. Do not carry inflator module by wires of connector on the underside of the module. In case of accidental deployment, the bag will then deploy with minimal chance of injury. When placing a live inflator module on a bench or other surface, ensure the bag and** trim cover faces in a upward direction. **Never rest steering column assembly on the steering wheel with the inflator module face down and column vertical. This is necessary in case of accidental deployment. Otherwise, personal injury may result.**
24. Remove horn contact by pushing slightly and twisting counterclockwise.
25. Remove glove box door and glove box unit retaining screws.
26. Remove lower right instrument panel retaining bolt.
27. Remove fuse box retaining screws.
28. Remove console assembly to floor retaining screws and nuts.

29. Disconnect console electrical connectors and remove console from vehicle.
30. Disconnect instrument panel electrical connectors, then remove instrument panel.
31. Reverse procedure to install.
32. Reactivate airbag system as described under "Airbag System Arming."

REATTA & RIVIERA

1. Disable airbag system as described under "Airbag System Disarming."

Fig. 43   Knee bolster removal. Toronado/Trofeo

1	I/P PAD
2	I/P STEERING COLUMN REINFORCEMENT PLATE
3	KNEE BOLSTER

1	I/P PAD
2	I/P CLUSTER TRIM PLATE
3	I/P CLUSTER HOUSING (CLUSTER REMOVED)

Fig. 44   I/P cluster trim plate removal. Toronado/Trofeo

1	LOWER METAL STEERING COLUMN COVER
2	LEFT-SIDE SOUND INSULATOR
3	SCREWS
4	RIGHT-SIDE SOUND INSULATOR
5	WING NUTS

Fig. 42   Sound insulators removal. Toronado/Trofeo

1	LEFT-SIDE SOUND INSULATOR
2	SCREWS
3	RIGHT-SIDE SOUND INSULATOR
4	WING NUTS
5	KNEE BOLSTER

Fig. 45   I/P sound insulators removal. Reatta & Riviera

2. Disconnect battery ground cable.
3. Turn ignition to the Off position, then remove fuse No. 14 from fuse panel.
4. Remove left side sound insulator retaining screws and nuts, **Fig. 45.**
5. Disconnect courtesy lamp from insulator panel and remove from vehicle.
6. Remove instrument panel cluster trim plate retaining screws, then remove plate from vehicle, **Fig. 46.**
7. Remove center air duct assembly.
8. Remove 13 instrument panel cluster retaining screws, then pull cluster outward from instrument panel, **Fig. 47.**
9. Remove two headlamp switch to instrument panel retaining screws, then disconnect headlamp switch electrical connector and remove from vehicle.
10. Remove four electronic climate control head retaining screws, if equipped.
11. Remove climate control electrical connector then the climate control assembly.
12. **On models equipped with integral radio unit,** proceed as follows:

a. Remove radio/ECC retaining screws.
b. Remove radio bracket to radio retaining nuts.
c. Disconnect radio electrical connectors and remove radio from vehicle.
13. **On models equipped with cassette tape/compact disc,** remove holder from rear console storage compartment.
14. Remove two outer and three inner console trim plate retaining screws, then the trim plate.
15. **On models equipped with CD player,** proceed as follows:
a. Remove CD trim plate from instrument panel.
b. Disconnect two CD player electrical connectors accessed through ashtray.
c. Remove two T-15 Torx retaining screws to CD mounting bracket, then pull player and bracket forward.

d. Remove two 10mm bracket to CD retaining nuts.
16. **On all models,** remove two front storage compartment retaining screws, then the storage compartment.
17. Remove right side sound insulator retaining screws and nuts.
18. Disconnect courtesy lamp from panel and remove sound insulator from vehicle.

1. I/P CLUSTER HOUSING (CLUSTER REMOVED)
2. I/P CLUSTER TRIM PLATE
3. SCREW (4)

Fig. 46 I/P cluster trim plate removal. Reatta & Riviera

1. REAR RETAINING SCREW (11)
2. I/P (REMOVED FROM VEHICLE)
3. FRONT RETAINING SCREW (2)
4. I/P CLUSTER HOUSING

Fig. 47 I/P cluster housing removal. Reatta & Riviera

1. I/P UPPER TRIM PAD (DEFROSTER GRILLE REMOVED)
2. SCREW (3)
3. INSTRUMENT PANEL

Fig. 48 I/P trim pad assembly removal. Reatta & Riviera

1. FRONT COWL
2. UPPER MOUNTING SCREWS
3. INSTRUMENT PANEL
4. LOWER MOUNTING BOLTS

Fig. 49 I/P assembly removal. Reatta & Riviera

FRONT OF CAR

1. CENTER INSULATOR
2. LEFT INSULATOR
3. RIGHT INSULATOR
4. LEFT COURTESY LAMP
5. RIGHT COURTESY LAMP

Fig. 50 I/P sound insulators removal. 1991 Eldorado & Seville

19. Remove six knee bolster retaining screws, then remove bolster from vehicle.
20. Remove four steering column reinforcement plate retaining screws, then remove plate from vehicle.
21. Remove glove box door and glove box unit retaining screws.
22. Remove three upper trim pad retaining screws, then pull trim pad up and out of retaining clips to remove from vehicle, **Fig. 48.**
23. Remove lower left side instrument panel retaining bolt.
24. Remove hood release retaining screws.
25. Remove two instrument panel brace retaining screws, then the brace.
26. Remove four inflator module retaining screws located on back of steering wheel assembly.

27. Remove inflator module from vehicle. **When carrying a live inflator, ensure the bag and trim cover are pointed away in case of accidental deployment. Do not carry inflator module by wires of connector on underside of module. When placing a live inflator module on a bench or other surface, ensure the bag and trim cover faces in a upward direction. Never rest steering column assembly on the steering wheel with the inflator module face down and column vertical. This is necessary in case of accidental deployment. Otherwise, personal injury may result.**
28. Disconnect ignition wiring and multi-function switch electrical connectors.
29. Remove pinch bolt from intermediate

shaft.
30. Remove upper and lower steering column support brackets, then remove steering column from vehicle.
31. Remove lower right instrument panel retaining bolt and three upper instrument panel retaining screws.
32. Disconnect instrument panel electrical connectors, then remove instrument panel from vehicle, **Fig. 49.**
33. Reverse procedure to install.
34. Reactivate airbag system as described under "Airbag System Arming."

ELDORADO & SEVILLE
1991

1. Disable airbag system as described under "Airbag System Disarming."
2. Disconnect battery ground cable.
3. Remove lower instrument panel sound insulators, **Fig. 50.**
4. Remove instrument panel steering column cover, **Fig. 51.**
5. Remove four bolts attaching steering column to support bracket.
6. Remove climate control driver information center.
7. Remove dash to instrument panel interconnect.
8. Remove glove box module, **Fig. 52.**
9. Remove fuse panel from glove box, **Fig. 53.**

1 CENTER TRIM PLATE   2 INSTRUMENT PANEL STEERING COLUMN COVER   3 COLLAR

Fig. 51   Steering column cover removal. 1991 Eldorado & Seville

1 GLOVE BOX MODULE
2 SCREW
3 NUT
4 PLATE AND KNOB

Fig. 52   Glove box module removal. 1991 Eldorado & Seville

1 FUSE PULLER
2 GLOVE BOX MODULE
3 GLOVE BOX FUSE PANEL

Fig. 53   Fuse panel removal. 1991 Eldorado & Seville

1 INSTRUMENT PANEL ASSEMBLY
2 INSTRUMENT PANEL REINFORCEMENT BRACE

Fig. 54   I/P removal. 1991 Eldorado & Seville

10. Disconnect instrument panel compartment electrical connector.
11. Remove instrument panel reinforcement brace, **Fig. 54.**
12. Remove six instrument panel attaching screws, then remove instrument panel, **Fig. 54.**
13. Reverse procedure to install.
14. Reactivate airbag system as described under "Airbag System Arming."

1992–93

1. Disable airbag system as described under "Airbag System Disarming."
2. Remove instrument panel upper trim panel as follows:
   a. Pry defroster grill upward using a small flat bladed tool, then remove, **Fig. 55.**
   b. Disconnect sunload and auto control sensors from defroster grill.
   c. Remove screws retaining upper trim panel through defroster grill opening.
   d. Remove heat and A/C vents from front of instrument panel by gently prying on both sides and pulling out.

1 INSTRUMENT PANEL UPPER TRIM PANEL   4 SCREWS
2 INSTRUMENT PANEL CARRIER   5 WINDSHIELD DEFROSTER GRILLE
3 SCREWS

Fig. 55   Upper trim panel removal. 1992–93 Eldorado & Seville

   e. Remove screws retaining upper trim panel through vent openings, then the upper trim panel.
3. Remove instrument panel cluster as follows:
   a. Remove fuses A5 and B5 from rear compartment fuse panel and fuse A3 from engine compartment fuse panel.
   b. Disconnect two electrical connectors on top of instrument panel.
   c. Remove screws retaining cluster to instrument panel, **Fig. 56.**
   d. **On models with digital cluster,**

Fig. 56 I/P cluster removal. 1992–93 Eldorado & Seville

1	INSTRUMENT CLUSTER
2	SCREW
3	INSTRUMENT PANEL
4	PRNDL ASSEMBLY (COLUMN SHIFT ONLY)
5	PRNDL ASSEMBLY RETAINING SCREWS

Fig. 57 Sound insulators removal. 1992–93 Eldorado & Seville

1	INSTRUMENT PANEL
2	STEERING COLUMN OPENING BRACKET
3	STEERING COLUMN OPENING FILLER TRIM

Fig. 58 Steering column opening bracket & filler trim removal. 1992–93 Eldorado & Seville

| 1 | UPPER MOUNTING SCREW | 3 | INSTRUMENT PANEL | 4 | INNER MOUNTING SCREWS (THROUGH RADIO OPENING) |
| 2 | LOWER MOUNTING SCREW | | | | |

Fig. 59 I/P removal. 1992–93 Eldorado & Seville

raise cluster and remove two screws retaining PRNDL mechanism.
  e. **On all models,** remove cluster.
4. Remove right and left A/C vent trim panels.
5. Remove glove compartment as follows:
  a. Open glove compartment door and remove screws retaining glove compartment assembly to instrument panel.
  b. Pull glove compartment out slightly, then disconnect electrical connectors from glove compartment switches.
  c. Remove glove compartment.
6. Remove right and left sound insulators, **Fig. 57.**
7. Remove steering column opening filler trim and bracket, **Fig. 58.**
8. If equipped with full console, remove as follows:
  a. Remove storage compartment by pulling up and out.
  b. Remove shift handle retaining clip and handle, then the console upper trim plate.
  c. Disconnect cigar lighter electrical connector, then remove radio.
  d. Remove gear selector trim plate

1. INSTRUMENT PANEL
2. STEERING COLUMN FILLER
3. SCREW · 1.7 N.m (15 LBS. IN.)

Fig. 60 Steering column opening filler removal. Cavalier

and PRNDL illumination lamp socket.
  e. Remove shifter plate upper mounting bolts, then the nuts retaining shifter assembly to floor.
  f. Remove nuts retaining console to floor through storage compartment opening.
  g. Disconnect console blower air supply duct, then slide console up and disconnect electrical connectors.
  h. Slide console back to clear shifter, then remove from vehicle.
9. Remove headlamp switch module from instrument panel by pulling outward on switch knob. Disconnect electrical connector.

10. Remove two bolts and hood latch release, then place drivers seat in full rearward position.
11. Remove steering column as described in "Steering Columns" section.
12. Remove screws retaining instrument panel, then disconnect electrical connectors.
13. Remove instrument panel from vehicle, **Fig. 59.**
14. Reverse procedure to install.
15. Reactivate airbag system as described under "Airbag System Arming."

CAVALIER

1. Disconnect battery ground cable, then remove three screws from steering column opening filler, **Fig. 60,** and pull downward to disengage clips and remove.
2. Remove left and right sound insulators.
3. Remove instrument panel compartment housing as follows:
  a. Open instrument panel compartment door, **Fig. 61,** then remove screws attaching instrument panel housing to instrument panel.
  b. Pull out housing enough to disconnect rear compartment lid release switch and remove instrument panel compartment light and right courtesy lamp.
  c. Remove instrument panel compartment housing.

1. INSTRUMENT PANEL
2. INSULATOR
3. I.P. COMPARTMENT HOUSING
4. SCREW - 2 N.m (19 LBS. IN.)
5. I.P. COMPARTMENT DOOR

Fig. 61 I/P compartment housing removal. Cavalier

4. Remove console assembly, then the convenience center, **Fig. 62.**
5. Disconnect forward lamp and engine electrical harnesses from bulkhead connector.
6. Remove two corner instrument panel retaining screws, and one screw to instrument panel brace at left side of instrument panel opening, **Fig. 63.**
7. Remove defroster grilles, then the upper retaining screws located in defroster duct openings.
8. Remove steering column as described in "Steering Columns" section.
9. Pull instrument panel assembly out enough to disconnect all electrical connectors and vacuum lines.
10. Remove instrument panel assembly with electrical harness attached.
11. If necessary, remove electrical harness assembly.
12. Reverse procedure to install.

SUNBIRD

1. Disconnect battery ground cable, then remove left and right sound insulators.
2. Remove steering column opening filler by gently prying out.
3. Remove retaining screws and/or nut, then the right and left instrument panel trim plates. **It may be necessary to loosen righthand console housing bracket.**
4. Remove console housing as follows:
   a. Remove side panels by prying outward, then pull rearward to remove accessory trim plate.
   b. Remove console bracket to instrument panel nuts, housing to console bracket screws, then the housing assembly.

5. Remove instrument panel compartment/door as follows:
   a. Open instrument panel compartment door, then gently pull out compartment/door until retaining pins on door unsnap from their retainers.
   b. Unsnap instrument panel compartment strap from instrument panel center support, then remove instrument panel compartment/door.
6. Remove heater and A/C control, then the convenience center, **Fig. 64.**
7. Disconnect forward lamp and engine electrical harnesses from bulkhead connector.
8. Remove bulkhead from cowl, then the hood release handle.
9. Remove defroster grilles, then the upper instrument panel retaining screws located in defroster duct openings.
10. Remove two lower corner instrument panel retaining nuts, and one screw to instrument panel brace at left side of instrument panel opening, **Fig. 65.**
11. Remove two nuts securing electrical harness to neutral start switch, if necessary, then the three steering column retaining bolts and lower column.
12. Pull instrument panel assembly out enough to disconnect all electrical connectors and vacuum lines.
13. Remove instrument panel assembly with electrical harness attached.
14. If necessary, remove electrical harness assembly.
15. Reverse procedure to install.

BERETTA & CORSICA
1991

1. Disable airbag system as described under "Airbag System Disarming."
2. Disconnect battery ground cable.
3. Remove two sound insulator retaining nuts from under instrument panel, then the three bolts that attach insulator to instrument panel, **Fig. 65.**
4. Pulling insulator downward, remove courtesy lamp, then the insulator.
5. Remove two instrument cluster bezel screws from under panel, then pull bezel rearward to release clips.
6. Disconnect headlamp and windshield wiper switch electrical connectors.
7. Remove instrument cluster retaining screws, then pull cluster rearward and disconnect electrical connectors.
8. Using a flat tool, pry trim bezel from instrument panel, then remove A/C/heater control and radio.
9. Disconnect electrical connectors and vacuum lines from A/C controls, then the electrical connectors from radio.
10. Remove four knee bolster retaining screws, then the knee bolster.
11. Remove two steering column to upper support attaching bolts, then the two bolts on the lower support. Lower column, ensuring that the flange and coupling assembly is not under tension.
12. Remove two ALDL retaining screws, then lower the connector.
13. Remove convenience center retaining bolts.

VIEW A

VIEW B

1. SCREW - 2 N.m (19 LBS. IN.)
2. CONVENIENCE CENTER
3. RETAINER
4. I/P HARNESS
5. BRACKET
6. NUT
7. I/P HARNESS CONNECTOR
8. BOLT - 7 N.m (62 LBS. IN.)
9. FLASHER ASM. HAZARD
10. HORN RELAY
11. MULTI-FUNCTION ALARM

Fig. 62 Convenience center removal. Cavalier & Sunbird

14. Remove turn signal flasher and electrical connector from convenience center.
15. Remove lefthand side center brace bolts, then disconnect left side window defogger hose from heater module.
16. Remove instrument panel compartment, cruise control module and righthand side wire harness retaining screw.
17. Remove righthand side center brace bolts and nuts from instrument panel, then the left and right side pillar nuts.
18. Remove windshield defogger grille, then upper instrument panel attaching screws and knee bolster brace.
19. Remove center wire harness retaining screws and fuse block.
20. Remove righthand wiring harness retainer from side of steering column, then the instrument panel pad.

Fig. 63   I/P removal. Cavalier

1	DASH PANEL
2	NUT
3	SCREW - 2 N.m (19 LBS. IN.)
4	NUT
5	I.P. SUPPORT BRACKET
6	SCREW - 9 N.m (80 LBS. IN.)
7	INSTRUMENT PANEL
8	I.P TIE BAR
9	SCREW - 1.4 N.m (12 LBS. IN.)
	A. TIGHTEN 1ST
	B. TIGHTEN 2ND
	C. TIGHTEN 3RD
	D. TIGHTEN 4TH

1	"U" NUT
2	DASH PANEL
3	WELD NUTS
4	BOLT/SCREW — 10 N·m (8 LBS. FT.)
5	CENTER SUPPORT, INSTRUMENT PANEL
6	BOLT/SCREW — 7 N·m (5 LBS. FT.)
7	NUT — 10 N·m (8 LBS. FT.)
8	BOLT/SCREW — 1 N·m (8 LBS. IN.)

Fig. 64   I/P removal. Sunbird

1. Disable airbag system as described under "Airbag System Disarming."
2. Disconnect battery ground cable.
3. Remove sound insulators and left speaker panel.
4. Disconnect electrical connectors.
5. Remove knee bolster and bulkhead.
6. Disconnect electrical connectors to brake switches and clutch pedal switches.
7. Remove heater and A/C control, then radio.
8. Remove defroster grille, then screws to cowl through defroster duct.
9. Remove lower left nut, left support screw, the instrument panel compartment.
10. Disconnect electrical connectors: DERM, body harness and arming sensor.
11. Remove right support screw and lower right nut.
12. Lower steering column, then disconnect electrical connections.
13. Remove instrument panel from cowl.
14. Reverse procedure to install.

1991 SKYLARK

1. Disconnect battery ground cable.
2. Remove left and right sound insulators.
3. Remove steering column opening filler.
4. Remove center cluster trim plate.
5. Remove screws and then disconnect ALDL connector.
6. Open instrument panel compartment door to gain access to attaching screws, then remove compartment from panel.
7. Remove right side trim plate.
8. Remove lower center trim plate and radio, disconnecting electrical leads and antenna.
9. Remove two screws attaching instrument panel to console bracket.
10. Remove two nuts from instrument panel to cowl, **Fig. 67.**
11. Loosen ¼ inch screws and unplug connector under instrument panel.
12. Open hood and disconnect bulkhead connector.
13. Remove two nuts attaching steering column harness to cowl.
14. Remove three steering column sup-

1	DASH PANEL	10	COMPARTMENT	19	FUSE BOX COVER
2	CLUSTER	11	HEATER CONTROL	20	HEADLIGHT SWITCH
3	WIPER SWITCH	12	RADIO BRACKET	21	CENTER REINFORCEMENT
4	CLUSTER BEZEL	13	RADIO RECEIVER	22	RIGHT BOLSTER BRACE
5	DEFROSTER GRILLE	14	SOUND INSULATOR	23	CENTER BOLSTER BRACE
6	PANEL PAD	15	KNEE BOLSTER	24	KNEE BOLSTER BRACKET
7	SIDE DEFROSTER GRILLE	16	SUPPORT/COLUMN	25	BRACE
8	CUP HOLDER	17	BRACKET/COLUMN	26	LOWER REINFORCEMENT
9	TRIM BEZEL	18	BRACE	27	STEERING COLUMN SUPPORT

Fig. 65   Instrument panel assembly. 1991 Beretta & Corsica

21. Remove left and right side window defogger outlets, then the center air outlets
22. Remove bracket from righthand side of steering column opening, then the knee bolster reinforcement on the lefthand side of steering column opening.
23. Remove pillar studs.

24. Reverse procedure to install.
25. Reactivate airbag system as described under "Airbag System Arming."

1992–93

Refer to **Fig. 66** when performing this procedure.

15. Unplug high beam dimmer switch, ignition switch, turn signal, brake light, TCC, cruise and clutch start connectors.
16. Remove defroster grilles, then remove four screws located inside defroster grille opening attaching instrument panel to top of cowl.
17. Remove screw from instrument panel pad brace located by the instrument panel compartment.
18. Remove instrument panel pad, then remove antenna lead from pad.
19. Disconnect body electrical lead located on the right side of instrument panel.
20. Remove side window defroster hoses from heater and or A/C evaporator module.
21. Reverse procedure to install.

ACHIEVA & 1992–93 SKYLARK

1. Disconnect battery ground cable, then remove center instrument panel trim plate, radio and heater and A/C control.
2. Remove left instrument panel trim plate, then the instrument panel compartment.
3. Remove screw to brace in left side of instrument panel compartment, then disconnect 26 way body connector.
4. Remove left sound insulator, then the bulkhead.
5. Remove defroster grille, then the steering column filler.
6. Remove screw to left brace, lower instrument panel screws, then the console.
7. Remove steering column upper and lower covers, then disconnect electrical connectors on column.
8. Remove steering column bolts, then lower column and allow to rest on seat.
9. Disconnect electrical connectors to brake switches, then remove remaining screws through defroster duct.
10. Remove instrument panel from vehicle, **Figs. 68 and 69.**
11. Reverse procedure to install.

CUTLASS CALAIS

1. Disconnect battery ground cable.
2. Remove left and right sound insulators, **Figs. 70 and 71.**
3. Remove steering column opening filler and cluster trim plate.
4. Remove screws, and then disconnect ALDL connector.
5. Open instrument panel compartment door, remove compartment attaching screws and then compartment.
6. Remove right side trim plate by pulling rearward, **Fig. 72.**
7. Remove lower center trim plate.
8. Remove heater and A/C controls.
9. Pulling control head rearward, disconnect both illumination bulbs, blower switch connector, rotary switch connector, vacuum harness and temperature cable.

1	DASH PANEL	6	INSTRUMENT PANEL PAD	11	MOUNTING BOLT
2	CLAMP-ON NUT	7	RIGHT REINFORCEMENT	12	BOLT
3	BODY LOCK PILLAR	8	BOLT	13	NUT TO COLUMN
4	SUPPORT	9	BOLT TO I/P	14	LEFT CENTER BRACE
5	NUT	10	KNEE BOLSTER SUPPORT	15	KNEE BOLSTER BRACKET

Fig. 66   Instrument panel assembly. 1992–93 Beretta & Corsica

1	NUT
2	DASH PANEL
3	NUT - 9 N.m (80 LBS. IN.)
4	SUPPORT, CENTER
5	NUT
6	SCREW - 3 N.m (27 LBS. IN.)
7	SCREW - FULLY DRIVEN SEATED AND NOT STRIPPED
8	INSTRUMENT PANEL ASM.

Fig. 67   I/P pad removal. 1991 Skylark

10. Remove radio, disconnecting electrical and antenna connections.
11. Remove two screws from instrument panel to console bracket, then remove two nuts from instrument panel pad to cowl.
12. Loosen screw and unplug connector under instrument panel compartment.
13. Open engine compartment hood, then remove two nuts attaching bulkhead connector.
14. Using a ¼ inch socket loosen bolt of bulkhead connector, and disconnect bulkhead connector.
15. Remove two nuts attaching steering column harness to cowl, then remove three bolts from steering column support.
16. Unplug high beam dimmer switch, ignition switch, turn signal, brake light, TCC, cruise and clutch start connectors.
17. Remove defroster grilles, then remove four instrument panel to top of cowl attaching screws located in defroster grille opening.
18. Remove screw attaching instrument panel pad to brace located near instrument panel compartment, **Fig. 73.**
19. Pull instrument panel pad rearward

and disconnect antenna lead and body electrical lead located on right side of instrument panel.
20. Disconnect side window defroster hoses from heater and/or A/C module.
21. Reverse procedure to install.

GRAND AM
1991

1. Disconnect battery ground cable.
2. Remove left side hush panel, steering column filler panel and right side hush panel, **Fig. 74.**
3. Remove instrument cluster trim plate.
4. Remove three bolts from steering column mounting bracket.
5. Lower steering column, then remove instrument cluster as shown in **Fig. 75.**
7. Remove attaching screw from bottom of windshield wiper/washer switch, then remove switch.
8. Remove screw from bottom of headlight switch, then remove switch.
9. Remove two retaining screws from instrument panel pad above cluster.
10. Remove defroster grilles, then remove Torx screws from under each defroster grille.

1. INSTRUMENT PANEL
2. SCREWS (8) - 2 N·m (17 LBS. IN.)
3. BOLTS (2) - 9 N·m (70 LBS. IN.)
4. I/P CENTER SUPPORT

5. J-NUT
6. RETAINER
7. DEFROSTER GRILLE SCREWS

VIEW A

Fig. 68   I/P removal. Achieva

1. INSTRUMENT PANEL
2. DEFROSTER GRILLE
3. RETAINING CLIP
4. I/P CENTER SUPPORT

5. SCREWS (8) - 2 N·m (17 LBS. IN.)
6. BOLTS (2) - 9 N·m (70 LBS. IN.)
7. J-NUT

VIEW A

Fig. 69   I/P removal. 1992–93 Skylark

1. INSTRUMENT PANEL
2. SCREW – FULLY DRIVEN, SEATED AND NOT STRIPPED
3. INSULATOR ASM., RIGHT SIDE

Fig. 70   Right side I/P sound insulator removal. Cutlass Calais

1. L.H. SOUND INSULATOR
2. ACCELERATOR CABLE STUD
3. FULLY DRIVEN, SEATED AND NOT STRIPPED

Fig. 71   Left side I/P sound insulator removal. Cutlass Calais

1. L.H. TRIM PLATE
2. R.H. TRIM PLATE

Fig. 72   Trim plate removal. Cutlass Calais

control.

5. Remove defroster grille, then the upper instrument panel screw covers and screws.
6. Disconnect brake switches, then remove bulkhead.
7. Remove steering column upper and lower covers, steering column bolts, then lower column and allow to rest on seat.
8. Remove right center support screw at left of instrument panel compartment opening, then the right sound insulator.
9. Disconnect 23 way electrical connector.
10. Remove lower instrument panel screws, then the instrument panel from vehicle, **Fig. 77.**
11. Reverse procedure to install.

CAMARO & FIREBIRD

1991–92

1. Disable airbag system as described under "Airbag System Disarming."
2. Disconnect battery ground cable.
3. Remove shifter handle and seven shift gate trim plate attaching screws.
4. Remove radio and A/C heater controller trim plate.
5. Remove A/C heater controller attaching screws, then pull controller rearward and disconnect electrical connections, vacuum connections and remove heater control cable.
6. Remove four radio retaining screws, then pull radio rearward and disconnect the power, speaker and antenna connectors.
7. Disconnect all console electrical connectors.

1. I.P. PAD
2. 10 N·m (88 LBS. IN.)
3. FULLY DRIVEN, SEATED AND NOT STRIPPED

Fig. 73   Instrument pad removal. Cutlass Calais

11. Remove two screws from bottom of right side instrument panel trim pad above glove box, **Fig. 76.**
12. Remove right side instrument panel trim pad, then remove three screws below trim pad.
13. Remove two screws from bottom of right and left side air outlet grilles.
14. With center grille staying in place, remove right and left air outlet grilles.
15. Disconnect right and left speaker wires, then remove instrument panel.

16. Reverse procedure to install.

1992–93

1. Disconnect battery ground cable, then remove left sound insulator.
2. Remove steering column filler, drivers side air deflectors, then the instrument panel cover.
3. Remove left instrument panel trim plate, then the upper and lower instrument panel compartments.
4. Remove radio and heater and A/C

8. Remove six console hold-down and two console to instrument panel screws and remove console.
9. Remove instrument panel trim pad and hush panels, **Figs. 78 through 81.**
10. Remove right and left lower instrument panel covers and trim plates, **Figs. 82 and 83.**
11. Remove six instrument cluster attachment screws, then pull cluster back and disconnect speedometer cable and electrical connections.
12. Remove headlight switch assembly.
13. Lower the steering column, then remove five upper and six lower instrument panel carrier to cowl screws.
14. Disconnect instrument panel electrical harness at bulkhead connector and under dash.
15. Remove instrument panel carrier, **Fig. 84.**
16. Reverse procedure to install.
17. Reactivate airbag system as described under "Airbag System Arming."

1993

1. Remove both sound insulator assemblies.
2. Remove removable top assembly, then window rail trim panel assembly.
3. Remove knee bolster assembly and deflector.
4. Remove stop lamp switch before fully lowering the steering column assembly. **Failure to do so may cause the stop lamp switch to be damaged or thrown out of adjustment resulting in a malfunctioning stop lamp switch or premature brake failure.**
5. Fully, gently lower steering column.
6. Remove trim panel and trim plate assemblies.
7. Remove bezel and instrument cluster assemblies.
8. Remove radio and temperature control assemblies.
9. Remove left side duct assemblies.
10. Remove transmission gear shift knob, cover and console assemblies.
11. Remove fuse block, then disconnect assembly line data link connector (ALDL).
12. Remove hazard and chime assembly.
13. Remove upper bolts and screws, lower nuts and reposition carrier.
14. Remove air duct and audio alarm assemblies.
15. Disconnect wiring harness from carrier, then remove carrier.
16. Reverse procedure to install.

BONNEVILLE

1991

1. Disconnect battery ground cable.
2. If equipped with tilt wheel steering, move wheel to the lowest position.
3. Move shift lever to the 1 position.
4. Pry lightly around perimeter of instrument panel trim plate, and remove trim plate, **Fig. 85.**
5. Remove speaker, side defogger and defroster grilles by carefully prying around perimeter of grille.

Fig. 74 I/P hush & trim panels. Grand Am

1—STEERING COLUMN FILLER PANEL
2—FULLY DRIVEN, SEATED, NOT STRIPPED
3—RH HUSH PANEL
4—2 N•m (18 LBS. IN.)
5—LH HUSH PANEL
6—ACCELERATOR ROD

VIEW A

1. SCREW - 1 N.m (11 LBS. IN.)
2. TOP PAD, I.P.
3. SPEAKER ASM., RIGHT
4. SCREW - FULLY DRIVEN, SEATED AND NOT STRIPPED
5. CONNECTOR, RIGHT SPEAKER
6. SCREW - FULLY DRIVEN, SEATED AND NOT STRIPPED
7. SPEAKER ASM., LEFT
8. CONNECTOR, LEFT SPEAKER
9. CLUSTER
10. INSTRUMENT PANEL
11. DOOR , I.P. COMPARTMENT

Fig. 75 Instrument cluster removal. 1991 Grand Am

6. Remove speaker retaining screws, disconnect electrical connectors, then remove speakers.
7. Remove instrument panel pad attaching screws, then the pad, **Fig. 86.**
8. Remove instrument cluster attaching screws, then disconnect the PRNDL indicator cable from steering column bowl and remove cluster.
9. Remove steering column filler and reinforcement panels, **Fig. 87.**
10. Remove electronic brake control module.
11. Remove left and right side hush panels, **Fig. 88.**
12. Remove headlamp/twilight sentinel/instrument panel dimmer control.
13. Remove radio and HVAC control unit.
14. Remove glove box/door assembly.
15. Reaching through glove box opening, disconnect deck lid, fuel door and glove box lamp switch electrical connectors.
16. Disconnect electrical connector from instrument panel dimmer module.
17. Remove screws attaching ALDL connector to instrument panel.
18. Disconnect wires to cigarette lighter, then remove ashtray.
19. Remove screws attaching ashtray slide to instrument panel, unsnap ashtray lamp/socket assembly from slide and remove slide.
20. Disconnect parking brake release

1—INSULATOR
2—DASH PANEL
3—IP
4—1.5 N·m (13 LBS. IN.)
5—10 N·m (90 LBS. IN.)
6—SUPPORT

Fig. 76   I/P. Grand Am

1. SCREWS (8) - 2 N·m (17 LBS. IN.)
2. I/P SCREW COVER
3. INSTRUMENT PANEL
4. J-NUT
5. BOLTS (2) - 9 N·m (70 LBS. IN.)
6. I/P CENTER SUPPORT
7. DEFROSTER GRILLE

Fig. 77   I/P removal. 1992–93 Grand Am

1—PAD ASM.	4—BRACKET
2—4 N·m (36 LB. IN.)	5—TRIM PLATE
3—6 N·m (54 LB. IN.)	

Fig. 78   I/P lower trim pad removal. 1991–92 Camaro & Firebird

1—NUT

2—BOLT/SCREW

3—PAD ASM.

Fig. 79   I/P pad removal. 1991–92 Camaro & Firebird

handle cable from release mechanism on pedal assembly. Pop release cable grommet from parking brake pedal bracket.
21. Pushing up on lower fuse block release tab, push fuse panel behind instrument panel.
22. Remove screw attaching instrument panel to panel stiffener rod, located on the right side of steering column.
23. Remove instrument panel to instrument panel center support screw, **Fig. 89.**
24. Remove all other instrument panel at-

taching screws shown in **Fig. 89.**
25. Disengage cluster connectors from instrument panel by using a small screwdriver to push locking tangs from holes in instrument panel.
26. Slide wiring conduit just above steering column upward to disengage tabs from instrument panel, then push behind instrument panel.
27. Remove bolts holding steering column to column support.
28. Remove bolts holding metal instrument panel bracket to steering column support.

29. Disconnect side defogger hoses from instrument panel outlet connections.
30. Remove harness retaining clips from various points on metal instrument panel bracket.
31. Remove instrument panel from vehicle.
32. Reverse procedure to install.

1992–93

When servicing an instrument panel assembly containing a live inflator module, or when leaving an instrument panel assembly containing a live inflator module unattended on a bench or other surface, always face airbag module away from surface to allow airbag to expand in case of an accidental deployment.

1. Disable airbag system as described under "Airbag System Disarming."

Fig. 80 I/P hush panel removal (with A/C). 1991–92 Camaro & Firebird

VIEW A

1—INSTRUMENT PANEL
2—CLIP, STRG. COLUMN
3—BOLT/SCREW
4—CLIP
5—NUT
6—LH INSULATOR ASM.
7—ACCL. PEDAL BRKT.
8—REST ON EXISTING DASH STUD
9—RH INSULATOR ASM.
10—KICK PANEL TRIM

VIEW A
VIEW B

6—CLIP INTO STEERING COLUMN
7—NUT
8—ACCEL. PEDAL BRK'T.
9—REST ON EXISTING DASH STUD
10—RH INSULATOR ASM.

1—KICK PANEL TRIM
2—INSTRUMENT PANEL
3—LH VENT DUCT EXTENSION
4—LH INSULATOR ASM.
5—BOLT/SCREW

Fig. 81 I/P hush panel removal (less A/C). 1991–92 Camaro & Firebird

---

VIEW A

• WITH DIGITAL CLUSTER •
INSTALLATION PROCEDURE FOR LEFT & RIGHT HAND PLATE ASSEMBLIES

1— POSITION BOSS ON PLATE ASSEMBLY OVER LOCATING PIN.
2— ALIGN SCREW HOLES.
3— INSTALL SCREWS, BEGINNING WITH SCREW LOCATIONS ALONG THE LOWER EDGE OF EACH PLATE. SECURE SCREWS ALONG TOP EDGE OF EACH PLATE LAST.

1—TRIM PLATE (RH)   3—1.5 N·m (13 LB. IN.)
2—TRIM PLATE (LH)

STANDARD CLUSTER

WITH DIGITAL CLUSTER

VIEW A

Fig. 83 I/P trim plate removal. 1991–92 Camaro & Firebird

VIEW A

5—W/O A/C
6—IP LOWER REINFORCEMENT
7—BRACKET
8—CONVENIENCE CENTER MOUNTING BRACKET

1—RH COVER
2—RETAINER
3—PLATE
4—STEERING COLUMN FILLER PANEL

Fig. 82 Lower I/P cover removal. 1991–92 Camaro & Firebird

Fig. 85 I/P trim plate removal. 1991 Bonneville

5 — RETAINER: PUSH RETAINER THRU
REINFORCEMENT AND RECEP-
TACLE IN IP TIE BAR AND TWIST
TO FASTEN
6 — BOLT/SCREW: 1.4 N•M (12 LB-IN)
7 — RECEPTACLE: IP ASM

1 — LOCATOR PIN
2 — IP ASSEMBLY
3 — REINFORCEMENT, IP STRG COL
4 — STRG COL FILLER PANEL

**Fig. 87 Steering column filler & reinforcement panels removal.
1991 Bonneville**

Fig. 84 I/P removal. 1991–92 Camaro & Firebird

1 — IP PAD
2 — BOLT/SCREW: FULLY DRIVEN,
SEATED, NOT STRIPPED
3 — SIDE WINDOW DEFOGGER
OUTLET SEAL
4 — SEAL (RIGHT)
5 — SEAL (LEFT)

Fig. 86 I/P pad removal. 1991 Bonneville

VIEW A

1—SUPPORT
2—NUT
3—BOLT/SCREW
4—PANEL ASM.

2. Remove lower console, **Fig. 90**, automatic transmission control assembly and automatic transmission cable bracket.
3. Remove instrument panel trim plate, **Fig. 91**, then the steering column filler.
4. Remove steering column as described in "Steering Columns" section.
5. Remove instrument panel insert screws and insert, then the bolts to steering column support bracket brace.
6. Remove bolts to dash panel, instrument panel support bracket and steering column support.
7. Disconnect instrument panel wiring interconnect, then the vacuum harness connector.
8. Remove instrument panel assembly.
9. Reverse procedure to install.
10. Reactivate airbag system as described under "Airbag System Arming."

REGAL

Refer to **Fig. 92**, when performing this procedure.
1. Disable airbag system as described under "Airbag System Disarming."
2. Disconnect battery ground cable.
3. Remove speaker grilles by prying carefully at edge of grille.
4. Remove one instrument panel pad cover retaining screw from under each speaker grille.
5. Remove five screws under lower edge of instrument panel pad.
6. Remove pad by lifting front, pulling rearward to release, then lifting up and out.
7. Remove two speaker retaining bolts, then disconnect electrical connectors and remove speakers.
8. Remove one cluster trim plate retaining bolt on left side, then the trim plate.
9. Remove electrical connectors, then six cluster retaining bolts and the cluster.
10. With glove box open, remove gasket from around air outlet.
11. Remove two screws behind gasket, then open fuse block cover.
12. Remove two glove box retaining screws, located on the left side of glove box.
13. Disconnect electrical connector, then remove glove box.
14. Remove three bolts holding right side sound insulator.
15. Remove insulator by pushing towards front of car, then pulling down.
16. Remove four ventilation control assembly retaining bolts, then the control assembly and connectors.
17. Remove bolts securing radio, then the radio and connectors.
18. Remove bolts securing English/Metric switch, then the switch.
19. Remove bolts securing headlight switch, then the switch.
20. Remove four cassette player retaining bolts, then pulling unit rearward, disconnect electrical connectors.

1—LEFT HUSH PANEL
2—BOLT/SCREW; 18 LB.IN./2 N·m
3—MOUNTING TAB OF RIGHT HUSH PANEL
4—NUT; 90 LB.IN./10 N·m
5—PARKING BRAKE STUD
6—ACCELERATOR PEDAL BRACKET STUD

Fig. 88 I/P hush panels removal. 1991 Bonneville

1. DEFROSTER DUCT
2. IP CENTER SUPPORT BRACKET
3. 10 N·M (88 LB-IN)
4. 6 N·M (53 LB-IN)
5. 1.9 N·M (17 LB-IN)
6. 1.4 N·M (12 LB-IN)
7. 3 N·M (27 LB-IN)
8. IP ASSEMBLY
9. IP CENTER SUPPORT
10. BRACE
11. STUD
12. COWL SUPPORT
13. DIC MODULE BRACKET

Fig. 89 I/P removal. 1991 Bonneville

21. Remove ashtray and bracket.
22. Remove two ALDL connector retaining bolts, then lower ALDL connector.
23. Remove two parking brake retaining bolts, then lower lever and pull to the right.
24. Remove bolt holding right side courtesy light, then disconnect electrical connector.
25. Remove two radio receiver retaining bolts, then the receiver, electrical and antenna connectors.
26. Remove one nut and two screws holding left side sound insulator.
27. Remove four steering column trim cover retaining screws, then the cover.
28. Remove four steering column retaining bolts, lower steering column.
29. Remove seven instrument panel carrier assembly retaining bolts, five at top and two at bottom.
30. Remove two carrier assembly retaining bolts, located above steering column.

31. Remove five carrier assembly to air duct attaching bolts.
32. Remove three conduit retaining nuts, two above glove compartment and one through cassette compartment opening.
33. Remove nine clips holding wiring harness.
34. Remove instrument panel by pulling top out, then lifting panel up and out.
35. Reverse procedure to install.
36. Reactivate airbag system as described under "Airbag System Disarming."

CUTLASS SUPREME

Refer to **Fig. 93**, when performing this procedure.
1. Disconnect battery ground cable.
2. Open glove compartment door, then remove lower storage compartment by lifting it out.
3. Remove two screws inside glove compartment opening.

Fig. 90 Console removal. 1992–93 Bonneville

1	TRANS LEVER CONTROL HANDLE	
2	CONSOLE CENTER TRIM PLATE	
3	CONSOLE SEAT SWITCHES	
4	CONSOLE BEZEL/LATCH/CUP HOLDER ASSEMBLY	
5	ARMREST BIN LOWER TRIM PLATE	
6	ARMREST BIN REAR TRIM PLATE	
7	CONSOLE TO FLOOR STUD NUT	
8	ARMREST BIN LID	
9	CONSOLE CIGAR LIGHTER ASSEMBLY	
10	CONSOLE VENT ASSEMBLY	
11	LOWER CONSOLE	
12	CONSOLE FLOOR VENT TRIM PLATE	
13	CONSOLE DUCT ASSEMBLY	
14	AUTO TRANS CABLE BRACKET	
15	CONSOLE TO AUTO TRANS CABLE BRACKET	
16	CONSOLE TO TRANS LEVER BRACKET BOLT	
17	CONSOLE CENTER TRIM PLATE TO AUTO TRANS CABLE BRACKET BOLT	
18	ASH TRAY	
19	CONSOLE CENTER TRIM PLATE SWITCHES	
20	TRANS LEVER CONTROL HANDLE RETAINER	
21	NUTS	
22	BOLT	

Fig. 91 I/P removal. 1992–93 Bonneville

1	CLUSTER ASSEMBLY	7	RIGHT SOUND INSULATOR
2	HEATER AND A/C CONTROLS	8	LEFT SOUND INSULATOR
3	WINDSHIELD DEFROSTER GRILLE	9	IP TRIM PLATE ASSEMBLY
4	RADIO BRACKET	10	IP STEERING COLUMN FILLER
5	RADIO ASSEMBLY	11	HEADLAMP SWITCH ASSEMBLY
6	IP CLUSTER TRIM PLATE ASSEMBLY	12	SIDE WINDOW DEFOGGER OUTLET

1	CLUSTER
2	I.P. CARRIER
3	SPEAKER
4	HINGE ASM — COMPARTMENT DOOR
5	PLATE — I/P ACSRY TRIM
6	TRAY ASM-ASH

Fig. 92 Exploded view of I/P assembly. Regal

4. Remove defroster grille and deflector.
5. Remove two instrument panel upper pad retaining screws, located in defroster grille opening.
6. Remove five instrument panel cluster trim plate attaching screws.
7. Pull top of trim plate outward, then starting at one side of trim plate carefully pull bottom outward to release five spring clips.

8. Remove two screws at sides of instrument cluster opening.
9. Lift upper pad and disconnect electrical connector to glove compartment light, then remove upper pad.
10. Remove two screws attaching speakers to instrument panel.
11. Disconnect speaker electrical connectors, and remove speaker.
12. Remove radio assembly retaining screws, then pulling assembly rearward, disconnect antenna, speaker and electrical connectors.
13. Remove two screws holding left air outlet trim plate to instrument panel.
14. Carefully pull at bottom of trim plate to release spring clips.
15. Disconnect electrical connector for headlight switch, and remove air outlet trim plate.
16. **On vehicles equipped with sport pod,** remove sport pod as follows:
   a. Remove two screws on bottom of assembly.
   b. Remove three screws holding assembly to instrument panel.
   c. Pull assembly outward and disconnect electrical connector to lighter.
   d. Remove four screws holding filler to instrument panel.
17. **On vehicles not equipped with sport pod,** remove left center air outlet plate assembly as follows:
   a. Remove three screws holding left center air outlet assembly to instrument panel trim plate.

b. Remove air outlet trim plate by pulling carefully at bottom of plate to release spring clips.

18. **On all models,** remove left and right instrument panel sound insulators.
19. Remove two screws holding ALDL connector to instrument panel.
20. Remove four steering column trim plate attaching screws.
21. Pull trim cover rearward and disconnect trunk release electrical connector.
22. Remove two bolts at upper part of column and one bolt at lower part of column, then lower column.
23. Disconnect left and right courtesy light assemblies.
24. Remove two screws holding parking brake release handle to instrument panel.
25. Turn handle and remove it from instrument panel.
26. Remove three fuse block bracket to instrument panel attaching screws.
27. Remove seven screws holding main ventilation duct to the instrument panel.
28. Remove nut holding wiring harness clip to instrument panel.
29. Remove screw holding glove compartment light, then slide off bracket.
30. Remove two instrument panel attaching screws, located at lower left and right sides of panel.
31. Remove five instrument panel attaching screws at top of instrument panel.
32. Remove two instrument panel attaching screws at steering column support.
33. Remove instrument panel from vehicle.
34. Reverse procedure to install.

GRAND PRIX

Refer to **Fig. 94** when performing this procedure.
1. Disconnect battery ground cable.
2. Remove two instrument panel pad cover attaching screws at top of cluster trim plate.
3. Remove two screws securing glove compartment hinges to instrument panel.
4. Holding door at the bottom, open door, then lift door up and out to release.
5. Remove three glove compartment attaching screws, located at the top of glove compartment.
6. Remove two screws securing plastic clips under the compartment.
7. Slide glove compartment out of instrument panel and disconnect electrical connectors to light and trunk release switch.
8. Remove one instrument panel pad cover attaching screw above glove compartment opening.
9. Lift front of pad and pull rearward to release clips.
10. Remove light switch assembly retaining screw, then remove assembly by carefully pulling out to release two spring clips at the top.
11. Remove windshield wiper/washer switch assembly retaining screw, then

1- INSTRUMENT PANEL CARRIER
2- INSTRUMENT CLUSTER
3- SPEAKER COVERS
4- DEFROSTER GRILLE
5- SPEAKER
6- INSTRUMENT PANEL UPPER PAD
7- LOWER COMPARTMENT
8- COMPARTMENT DOOR (SPORT OPTION)
9- INSTRUMENT PANEL CARRIER TIE BAR
10- LEFT AIR OUTLET PLATE ASSEMBLY
11- LEFT CENTER AIR OUTLET PLATE ASSEMBLY
12- LEFT CENTER AIR OUTLET PLATE ASSEMBLY (SPORT OPTION)
13- SWITCH INSTRUMENT PANEL COMPARTMENT LIGHT
14- INSTRUMENT CLUSTER TRIM PLATE
15- STEERING COLUMN LOWER FILLER
16- RIGHT AND RIGHT CENTER AIR OUTLET HOUSINGS
17- RIGHT AND RIGHT CENTER AIR OUTLET GRILLES
18- LEFT AND LEFT CENTER AIR OUTLET GRILLES
19- ASH TRAY
20- ASH TRAY (SPORT OPTION)

Fig. 93 Exploded view of I/P. Cutlass Supreme

remove assembly by carefully pulling out to release two spring clips at the top.
12. Remove four cluster trim plate attaching screws, located inside switch openings.
13. Remove two cluster trim plate attaching screws from top of trim plate.
14. Remove two switch assembly connectors by sliding out of holders.
15. Remove two screws attaching clutch brake release lever, then disconnect linkage from brake assembly.
16. Remove two bolts securing ALDL connector, then lower connector.
17. Remove two left side sound insulator attaching screws, located on the rear edge of the insulator.
18. Remove one slide clip from front of insulator, then remove insulator.
19. Remove three attaching screws at the bottom of steering column cover.
20. Remove cover by carefully pulling rearward to release it from the three clips at the top.
21. Remove two bolts at upper part of steering column.
22. Remove two bolts at lower part of column, then lower column.
23. Disconnect electrical connectors at steering column.
24. Remove two screws securing right side sound insulator, then remove insulator.
25. Disconnect electrical connectors to fuse block.
26. Remove four bolts securing fuse block, and remove fuse block.
27. Disconnect electrical connector at HVAC assembly.
28. Remove two remote radio amplifier attaching screws, disconnect electrical connectors and remove amplifier.
29. Remove four radio trim plate attaching bolts, then trim plate.
30. Remove two ventilation control attaching screws.
31. Pull control rearward, disconnect electrical connectors.
32. Remove two radio control attaching bolts, disconnect electrical connectors and remove radio control assembly.
33. Remove two cassette player attaching bolts, disconnect electrical connectors and remove cassette player assembly.
34. Remove two radio receiver retaining nuts, disconnect electrical connectors and antenna connector, remove radio receiver.
35. Remove four cluster retaining screws, lift cluster and disconnect electrical connector, remove cluster.

Fig. 94 Exploded view of I/P. Grand Prix

1	SPEAKER GRILLE (RIGHT)
2	INSTRUMENT PANEL PAD
3	AIR DISTRIBUTOR
4	WIPER/WASHER SWITCH
5	SPEAKER
6	OUTLET (RIGHT)
7	LOCK
8	COMPARTMENT
9	INSTRUMENT PANEL ACCESSORY TRIM PLATE
10	COMPARTMENT
11	BUMPER
12	RETAINER
13	PLUG
14	SWITCH
15	DOOR
16	COVER
17	RADIO ASSEMBLY
18	SOUND INSULATOR (RIGHT)
19	RADIO BRACKET
20	ASH TRAY
21	SOUND INSULATOR (LEFT)
22	HEATER/AIR CONDITIONING CONTROL
23	AUDIO POWER BOOSTER
24	FILLER
25	OUTLET (CENTER)
26	OUTLET (LEFT)
27	INSTRUMENT PANEL PAD
28	CLUSTER
29	HEADLAMP SWITCH
30	CLUSTER TRIM PLATE
31	DUCT
32	SPEAKER GRILLE (LEFT)
33	DEFROSTER GRILLE

1. SCREW
2. SCREW (UNDER CAP)

Fig. 95 front center console removal. LeMans

1. SCREW
2. PULL REARWARD

Fig. 96 Center console removal. LeMans

36. Remove four radio speaker retaining screws, and remove both speaker assemblies.
37. Remove seven screws securing ventilation duct to instrument panel.
38. Remove three retaining nuts from wiring harness carrier.
39. Lift instrument panel carrier up and rearward then out through the passenger door.
40. Remove ventilation duct and wiring harness carrier as a unit.
41. Reverse procedure to install.

LEMANS

1. Disconnect battery ground cable.
2. Remove horn pad and disconnect horn lead.
3. Remove nut and retainer, mark shaft and wheel for assembly reference.
4. Using steering wheel puller tool No. J-3651 or equivalent, remove steering wheel.
5. If necessary remove contact ring from steering wheel.
6. Using a pointed plastic tool, pry package panel out of console.
7. Remove two screws from under ashtray.
8. **On models with automatic transmission,** pull gear selector lever off. Pull out indicator strap from cover, then remove retaining clips and cover.
9. **On models with manual transmission,** remove shift knob, trim plate and boot.
10. **On all models,** remove front center console, **Fig. 95.**
11. Remove two attaching screws, then pull center back and out, **Fig. 96.**

1. GLOVE BOX MOUNTING SCREW
2. RETAINER
3. PANEL

Fig. 97 Right side hush panel removal. LeMans

12. Remove right side hush panel, **Fig. 97.**
13. Open glove box door and pry off two retaining straps.
14. Remove two screws attaching glove box to instrument panel pad.
15. Remove A/C or heater control.
16. Turning steering wheel to gain access to turn signal switch housing attaching screws, remove turn signal switch housing.
17. Remove instrument panel trim plate, then remove dimmer switch from trim plate.
18. While pressing down on speedometer cable retainer spring, pull out speedometer cable.
19. Remove instrument cluster attaching screws, pull cluster rearward and disconnect electrical connectors.
20. Remove cluster from instrument panel.

21. Remove instrument panel center section.
22. Remove air nozzles and air vents from instrument panel.
23. Remove fuse box, disconnect wiring harness from all switches and lamps.
24. Disconnect wiring harness from instrument panel.
25. Remove six instrument panel screw on panel and remove instrument panel.
26. Reverse procedure to install.

METRO

1991

Refer to **Fig. 98** when performing the following procedure.

1. Disable airbag system as described under "Airbag System Disarming."
2. Disconnect battery ground cable.
3. If equipped with center console, remove four attaching screws from the console box, **Fig. 99.**
4. Shift gear selector to the LOW position and gently pull outward at bottom of console box to disengage the two retaining pins.
5. Remove four attaching screws from cluster switch panel.
6. Disconnect front windshield wiper/washer switch and light/hazard flasher switch electrical connectors and remove cluster bezel and switch panel as an assembly.
7. Remove six attaching screws from cluster bezel and bezel from the switch panel.

Fig. 99 Exploded view of console. 1991 Metro

1 PARKING BRAKE LEVER BEZEL ATTACHING SCREW
2 PARKING BRAKE LEVER BEZEL
3 SHIFT CONTROL LEVER CONSOLE ATTACHING SCREWS
4 SHIFT CONTROL LEVER CONSOLE
5 CONSOLE BOX ATTACHING SCREWS
6 CONSOLE BOX

Fig. 98 Exploded view of I/P. 1991 Metro

1 INSTRUMENT PANEL SUPPORT MEMBER MOUNTING SCREWS
2 INSTRUMENT PANEL SUPPORT MEMBER
3 ASHTRAY UPPER PLATE
4 ASHTRAY ASSEMBLY
5 ASHTRAY UPPER PLATE ATTACHING SCREW
6 HEATER CONTROL PANEL
7 HEATER CONTROL PANEL MOUNTING SCREW
8 INSTRUMENT PANEL BEZEL ATTACHING SCREW
9 INSTRUMENT PANEL BEZEL
10 GLOVE-BOX DOOR
11 GLOVE BOX UPPER PANEL
12 GLOVE BOX UPPER PANEL ATTACHING SCREW
13 GARNISH COVER PUSH PINS
14 (RH) FRONT SPEAKER GARNISH COVER
15 FRONT SPEAKER GARNISH COVER ATTACHING SCREWS
16 INSTRUMENT PANEL PAD
17 CLUSTER SWITCH PANEL
18 CLUSTER BEZEL
19 CLUSTER BEZEL ATTACHING SCREWS
20 CLUSTER SWITCH PANEL ATTACHING SCREWS
21 INSTRUMENT MAIN PANEL ACCESS PANEL
22 INSTRUMENT MAIN PANEL
23 (LH) FRONT SPEAKER GARNISH PANEL
24 HOOD LATCH RELEASE LEVER MOUNTING SCREW
25 HOOD LATCH RELEASE LEVER ASSEMBLY
26 LOWER STEERING COLUMN PANEL
27 LOWER STEERING COLUMN PANEL ATTACHING SCREW
28 GLOVEBOX LATCH ASSEMBLY
29 GLOVEBOX LATCH ASSEMBLY ATTACHING SCREW
30 GLOVEBOX DOOR MOUNTING SCREW
31 GLOVEBOX LATCH BUTTON
32 GLOVEBOX STRIKER
33 GLOVEBOX STRIKER MOUNTING SCREW

828 INSTRUMENT PANEL

Fig. 100   I/P removal. 1992–93 Metro

| 1 | TRIM PLATE |
| 2 | INSTRUMENT PANEL |

Fig. 101   Instrument panel pad removal. 1991–92 Lumina

8. Remove front wiper switch and light/hazard switch from the switch panel.
9. Remove four cluster housing mounting screws from the housing.
10. Disconnect two electrical connectors and speedometer cable from the rear of cluster housing.
11. Remove turn signal/dimmer switch.
12. Remove two mounting screws from heater control panel and disconnect blower switch electrical connector.
13. Remove hood latch release lever mounting screw and lever from instrument panel carrier assembly.
14. Remove two main instrument panel mounting screws from both the left and right sides of the main panel.
15. Remove four attaching screws from the instrument panel support member.
16. Remove two mounting screws from the heater control assembly.
17. Remove one attaching screw from rear of glove box upper panel.
18. Remove main instrument panel access cover and one attaching screw at each panel.
19. Remove both front speaker garnish covers, then remove one attaching screw at each speaker.
20. Remove two push pins from both left and right side kick panels and remove panels from vehicle.
21. Remove one attaching screw from instrument main panel behind each kick panel.
22. Disconnect both left and right side speaker connectors.
23. Disconnect all instrument panel switches; rheostat, rear wiper/washer, rear window defogger.
24. Disconnect instrument panel wiring harness from instrument panel carrier assembly.
25. Remove instrument panel carrier assembly from the vehicle.
26. Reverse procedure to install.
27. Reactivate airbag system as described under "Airbag System Arming."

1992–93

1. Disable airbag system as described under "Airbag System Disarming."
2. Disconnect battery ground cable.

3. **On convertible models,** remove inflator module from steering wheel as described in "Passive Restraints" section.
4. **On all models,** remove lower steering column trim panel.
5. Remove steering wheel as described in "Electrical" section of "Metro" section.
6. **On convertible models,** remove SIR coil/combination switch assembly as described in "Passive Restraints" section.
7. **On hardtop models,** remove combination switch as described in "Electrical" section of "Metro" section.
8. **On all models,** remove right and left kick panels, then the right and left speaker grilles from instrument panel.
9. **On convertible models,** remove plastic retaining clips securing instrument panel to door jambs.
10. **On all models,** if equipped, remove front speakers from instrument panel.
11. Remove glove box inner panel, then disconnect A/C switch electrical connector, if equipped.
12. Remove heater control lever knobs, then the heater control unit cover plate.
13. Remove heater control unit from instrument panel.
14. **On models with manual transmission,** remove gearshift control lever upper boot from console.
15. **On all models,** remove console, ashtray and center console trim bezel.
16. Remove instrument panel center trim bezel, then the radio, if equipped.
17. Remove instrument panel cluster trim bezel, then disconnect electrical connectors from cluster trim bezel mounted switches, if equipped.
18. Disconnect retaining clip and speedometer cable at transaxle, then remove cluster assembly from instrument panel.
19. Disconnect ashtray illumination lamp, cigar lighter and cigar lighter illumination lamp bulb socket electrical connectors.
20. Remove retaining ring from rear of cigar lighter, then the cigar lighter from instrument panel.
21. **On convertible models,** remove two retaining screws from cluster cavity.

22. **On all models,** remove upper and lower instrument panel retaining screws, **Fig. 100,** and screw retaining instrument panel to bracket to floor pan.
23. Disconnect illumination controller electrical connector, then pull instrument panel from support member.
24. Remove screw retaining hood latch release lever, then disconnect cable from lever.
25. Disconnect wiring harnesses from instrument panel.
26. Remove instrument panel from vehicle.
27. Reverse procedure to install.
28. Reactivate airbag system as described under "Airbag System Arming."

LUMINA
1991–92

1. Disable airbag system as described under "Airbag System Disarming."
2. Disconnect battery ground cable.
3. Remove instrument panel pad retaining screws under edge of instrument panel pad, **Fig. 101.**
4. Lift upward on front of pad assembly, then pull rearward to release.
5. Remove speaker retaining bolts, then lift speaker and disconnect speaker electrical connectors.
6. Disconnect instrument cluster assembly electrical connectors, then remove cluster retaining screws, **Fig. 102.**
7. Remove glove compartment door.
8. Remove glove compartment assembly retaining screws.
9. Disconnect glove compartment electrical connector.
10. Remove glove compartment assembly.
11. Remove right side sound insulator retaining screws.
12. Push insulator toward front of vehicle then pull downward to remove.
13. Remove ventilation system control retaining bolts.
14. Disconnect control assembly electrical connectors and remove from vehicle.
15. Remove radio retaining bolts, then disconnect electrical connectors and remove from vehicle.
16. Remove headlamp switch retaining screws, then disconnect switch elec-

1	SCREWS	4	PRNDL CABLE
2	CLUSTER	5	INSTRUMENT PANEL CARRIER
3	CONNECTOR		

Fig. 102   I/P cluster removal. 1991–92 Lumina

trical connector and remove from vehicle.
17. Remove ashtray, slide bracket retaining screws, then the bracket.
18. Remove ALDL cover.
19. Remove ALDL retaining screws then disconnect ALDL electrical connector.
20. Remove two parking brake release handle retaining screws then lower handle and pull to right to remove.
21. Disconnect fuse block electrical connectors.
22. Remove fuse block retaining screws, then the fuse block.
23. Remove left sound insulator and steering column trim panel.
24. Remove two upper and lower steering column support retaining bolts, then lower steering column.
25. Remove seven instrument panel carrier assembly retaining bolts, **Fig. 103.**
26. Remove carrier assembly from vehicle.
27. Reverse procedure to install.
28. Reactivate airbag system as described under "Airbag System Arming."

1993

1. Remove instrument panel pad and trim plates.
2. Remove sound insulators, then steering column trim panel.
3. Remove accessory trim plate.
4. Remove audio system, then headlamp switch.
5. Remove instrument cluster assembly as follows:
   a. Remove air cleaner assembly.
   b. Remove screws holding cluster, then disconnect electrical connectors.
   c. Remove automatic transaxle control indicator cable, if equipped.
6. Remove ventilation controls, then data link connector (DLC).
7. Remove parking brake release handle, then ashtray and bracket.

1	INSTRUMENT PANEL CARRIER
2	10 N·m (89 LB. IN.)

Fig. 103   I/P carrier assembly removal. 1991–92 Lumina

1	DEFROSTER GRILLE	12	INSTRUMENT CLUSTER	23	TRIM BEZEL
2	DEFROSTER DUCT	13	CLUSTER BEZEL	24	CENTER CONSOLE TRIM
3	CENTER VENTILATION DUCT	14	GLOVE BOX AND TRIM ASSEMBLY	25	HOOD RELEASE LEVER
4	RIGHT VENTILATION DUCT	15	CASSETTE BOX	26	LEFT LOWER DASH TRIM
5	BRACE	16	REAR CONSOLE	27	SCUFF PLATE
6	"A" PILLAR TRIM	17	SHIFT LEVER BOOT (M/T)	28	COWL SIDE TRIM
7	A/C DUCT	18	REAR CONSOLE	29	INSTRUMENT PANEL
8	LOWER A/C DEFLECTOR	19	FRONT CONSOLE	30	"A" PILLAR TRIM
9	RIGHT VENTILATION DEFLECTOR	20	ASHTRAY	31	LEFT WINDOW DEFLECTOR
10	RIGHT WINDOW DEFLECTOR	21	RETAINER	32	LEFT VENTILATION DUCT
11	COWL SIDE TRIM	22	CUP HOLDER		

Fig. 104   Exploded view of I/P. 1991–92 Prizm

1 LEFT LOWER DASH TRIM

Fig. 105 Lower left trim panel removal. 1991–92 Prizm

1 CLUSTER BEZEL

Fig. 106 I/P cluster removal. 1991–92 Prizm

1 GLOVE BOX AND TRIM ASSEMBLY

Fig. 107 Glove box assembly removal. 1991–92 Prizm

8. Remove lower compartment, fuse block, then lower the steering column.
9. Remove two bolts above steering column and bolts from ventilation duct.
10. Remove front door opening carpet retainer.
11. Remove instrument panel center support bolts, then center support.
12. Disconnect instrument panel wiring harness, then remove instrument panel bolts.
13. Remove instrument panel by pulling top out, then lifting panel up and out.
14. Reverse procedure to install.

PRIZM

1991–92

Refer to **Fig. 104**, when performing the following procedure.
1. Disconnect battery ground cable.
2. Remove two steering wheel pad retaining bolts from back of steering wheel.
3. Remove steering wheel pad.
4. Disconnect horn switch electrical connector.
5. Remove steering wheel shaft nut.
6. Using steering wheel puller tool No. 1859-03 or equivalent, remove steering wheel.
7. Remove two hood release attaching screws lever.
8. Remove four lower left trim panel retaining screws, **Fig. 105**.
9. Disconnect speaker electrical connector, then remove A/C duct from lower A/C register, if equipped.
10. Remove seven steering column cover retaining screws.
11. Remove two trim bezel retaining screws.
12. Disconnect control/defogger switch electrical connector.

13. Disconnect rear wiper/washer switch, if equipped.
14. Disconnect two electrical connectors and cigar lighter from trim bezel.
15. Remove trim bezel, then four cluster bezel retaining screws.
16. Disconnect hazard flasher and dimmer switch electrical connectors.
17. Remove four instrument cluster retaining screws, **Fig. 106**.
18. Disconnect speedometer cable and remaining electrical connectors from instrument cluster.
19. Remove instrument cluster.
20. Remove two cup holder retaining screws, then the cup holder.
21. Remove four radio retaining screws, then pull radio from console.
22. Disconnect two radio electrical connectors and antenna from radio.
23. Remove three glove box door scuff plate retaining screws.
24. Remove one side trim panel retaining screw.
25. Remove cowl side trim, then five glove box and trim assembly retaining screws, **Fig. 107**.
26. Pull glove box out of trim assembly, then disconnect speaker electrical connector.
27. Remove glove box and trim assembly.
28. Remove glove box retaining pins and glove box door from trim panel.
29. Remove four heater and A/C control unit retaining screws.
30. Remove remaining console retaining screws, then the console.
31. Remove five instrument panel retaining screws, **Fig. 108**.
32. Disconnect three instrument panel electrical connectors and one relay unit from left side of instrument panel.
33. Remove one electrical connector from right side of instrument panel, then disconnect defroster duct retainers and remove instrument panel.
34. Reverse procedure to install.

1993

1. Disable airbag system as described under "Airbag System Disarming."
2. Disconnect battery ground cable.
3. Remove A-pillar lower trim panel from both sides.
4. Remove steering wheel as follows:
   a. Place front wheel in straight ahead position.
   b. Remove inflator module.
   c. Remove horn electrical connector and cruise control electrical connector, if equipped.
   d. Remove steering wheel retaining nut, then place matchmarks on steering wheel and main shaft.
   e. Remove steering wheel using suitable puller.
5. Remove five screws and steering column upper and lower trim panels.
6. Remove center console.
7. Remove two screws and instrument cluster trim panel, disengaging two lower clips.
8. Remove four screws and instrument cluster assembly, disconnecting three electrical connectors.
9. Remove one screw and instrument panel left side ventilation duct. Unsnap and remove right side ventilation duct.
10. Disconnect left, center and right side electrical connectors and fuse blocks from under instrument panel.
11. Disconnect left and right ground wires.
12. Remove three heater control assembly screws and set heater control assembly aside.
13. **On models with cruise control,** remove cruise control module and disconnect electrical connector.
14. **On all models,** disconnect and remove ground wires from instrument panel support bracket.
15. Disconnect electrical connectors from heater evaporator case, then unclip and remove right and left lower B-pillar trim covers.
16. Disconnect rear door lock connectors, if equipped, then unclip and remove A-pillar trim covers and remote control mirror switch electrical connecter, if equipped.
17. Remove two bolts and two nuts and disconnect steering column from instrument panel.
18. Remove four mounting bolts from instrument panel.
19. Remove instrument panel from vehicle by lifting up and pulling rearward, disengaging five clips, **Fig. 109**
20. Reverse procedure to install.

STORM

1. Disable airbag system as described under "Airbag System Disarming."
2. Disconnect battery ground cable. **After disconnecting battery, wait 10 minutes before proceeding with removal procedure. The Energy Reserve Module in the DERM may maintain SIR system voltage for a**

Fig. 108 I/P assembly removal. 1991–92 Prizm

A   CLIP LOCATIONS
805   INSTRUMENT PANEL

Fig. 109 I/P assembly removal. 1993 Prizm

period after the battery is disconnected.
3. Pull out on switch bezel, **Fig. 110,** then disconnect electrical connectors and remove bezel.
4. Pull out on cigar lighter bezel, then disconnect cigar lighter electrical connector and remove bezel, **Fig. 111.**
5. Remove two hood release retaining screws, then disconnect hood release cable, **Fig. 112.**
6. Remove knee bezel retaining screws and nuts.
7. Remove two glove box hinge pins, then the glove box.
8. Remove front console mounting bracket.
9. Remove two meter hood hole covers, **Fig. 112.**
10. Remove four meter hood retaining screws.
11. Disconnect lighting and windshield wiper switch electrical connectors.
12. Remove meter hood and meter assembly.
13. Remove three defroster grille plastic retaining covers, **Fig. 113.**
14. Remove three bolts and two screws from defroster grille assembly, then the defroster grille.
15. Remove four bolts, two screws and one nut attaching instrument panel assembly.
16. Remove electrical harness to instrument panel retaining clips.
17. Remove instrument panel assembly.
18. Reverse procedure to install.
19. Reactivate airbag system as described under "Airbag System Arming."

1 METER HOOD
2 METER ASSEMBLY
3 FRONT COVER HOLE COVER
4 FRONT COVER
5 INSTRUMENT PANEL ASSEMBLY

6 GLOVE BOX
7 CIGAR LIGHTER BEZEL
8 SWITCH BEZEL
9 KNEE PAD ASSEMBLY

Fig. 110 I/P assembly. Storm

Fig. 111 Disconnecting hood release cable. Storm

Fig. 112 I/P hood retaining screws removal. Storm

Fig. 113 I/P front cover retaining screws removal. Storm

FLEETWOOD

1. Disable airbag system as described under "Airbag System Disarming."
2. Remove left and right molding assemblies.
3. Remove windshield washer nozzle grille from upper trim pad assembly as follows:
   a. Pry upward to unseat spring clips.
   b. Remove sunload sensor and light sensor assembly (photocell) from grille assembly by rotating counterclockwise.
4. Remove upper trim pad assembly, then left and right sound insulators.
5. Remove steering column opening filler assembly and knee bolster assembly.
6. Remove tilt wheel lever assembly and transmission shift indicator cable.
7. Remove cluster trim plate assembly, instrument cluster assembly and trim plate assembly, **Fig. 114.**
8. Remove heater and air conditioning control assembly, then radio assembly.
9. Disconnect and remove passenger inflator module as follows:
   a. Disconnect connector position assurance (CPA) and electrical connector.
   b. Disconnect fasteners from passenger inflator module.
   c. Remove passenger inflator module from vehicle.
10. Remove inside air temperature sensor assembly and duct.
11. Remove ashtray assembly.
12. Remove floor carpet retainer assemblies.
13. Remove instrument panel compartment, lamp and switch assemblies.
14. Remove rear compartment lid release switch assembly, then headlight switch assembly.
15. Remove steering column bracket nuts and lower steering column assembly.
16. Remove data link connector (DLC), **Fig. 115.**
17. Remove oil level module and coolant level sensor.
18. Remove instrument panel screws and nuts and lower tie bar bolt and screw.
19. Remove center lower brace bolt and screw attaching center lower brace to instrument panel assembly. Remove center lower brace and nut if necessary.

19 CLUSTER ASSEMBLY, INSTRUMENT
20 BOLT/SCREW, INSTRUMENT CLUSTER, 1.9 N·m
   (17 LB. IN.)
75 PANEL ASSEMBLY, INSTRUMENT

Fig. 114   Instrument cluster assembly removal. 1993 Fleetwood

A BRACKET, DATA LINK CONNECTOR
B CONNECTOR, DATA LINK
67 BOLT/SCREW, INSTRUMENT PANEL WIRING HARNESS
   ENGINE CONTROL MODULE DATA LINK
   CONNECTOR, 1.9 N·m (17 LB. IN.)

Fig. 115   Data link Connector (DLC) removal. 1993 Fleetwood

A PANEL ASSEMBLY, DASH
B RIBS, SUPPORT
C FLANGE, BODY HINGE PILLAR TIE BAR
D HARNESS ASSEMBLY, INSTRUMENT PANEL WIRING
E CONNECTOR, ELECTRICAL
73 BOLT/SCREW, INSTRUMENT PANEL, 10 N·m (89 LB. IN.)
74 BOLT/SCREW, INSTRUMENT PANEL, LOWER TIE BAR,
   10 N·m (89 LB. IN.)
75 PANEL ASSEMBLY, INSTRUMENT
76 BRACE, INSTRUMENT PANEL CENTER LOWER
77 NUT, INSTRUMENT PANEL
78 NUT, INSTRUMENT PANEL CENTER LOWER BRACE, 10 N·m
   (89 LB. IN.)
79 BOLT/SCREW, INSTRUMENT PANEL CENTER LOWER
   BRACE, 10 N·m (89 LB. IN.)
112 MODULE ASSEMBLY, HEATER AND AIR CONDITIONING
    EVAPORATOR

Fig. 116   Instrument panel mounting. 1993 Fleetwood

20. Remove instrument panel wiring harness assembly as follows:
    a. Disconnect harness assembly clips.
    b. Note harness assembly routing before removal.
21. Remove instrument panel, **Fig. 116.** Replace instrument panel nuts if necessary.

STEERING COLUMNS
INDEX

STEERING COLUMN EXPLODED VIEWS

Model	Year	Column Type		Fig. No.	Page No.
		Standard	Tilt		
Achieva	1992-93	X	—	46	27-23
	1992-93	—	X	49	27-25
Beretta & Corsica	1991-93	—	X	60	27-35
	1991-93	X	—	55	27-33
Bonneville	1991④	—	X	74	27-44
	1991-93④	X	—	72	27-42
	1992-93②⑤	—	X	87	27-57
	1992-93①⑤	—	X	89	27-59
Brougham	1991-92	—	X	77	27-45
Camaro & Firebird	1991-93	—	X	81	27-51
Caprice	1991-93④	X	—	72	27-42
	1991-93⑤	X	—	103	27-69
	1991-93⑤	—	X	104	27-70

STEERING COLUMN EXPLODED VIEWS-Continued

Model	Year	Column Type Standard	Column Type Tilt	Fig. No.	Page No.
Cavalier	1991-93	X	—	45	27-22
	1991-93	—	X	48	27-25
Century	1991-93	X	—	78	27-47
	1991-93	—	X	79	27-48
Corvette	1991-93	—	X	82	27-52
Custom Cruiser	1991-92 ④	X	—	72	27-42
	1991-92 ⑤	X	—	103	27-69
	1991-92 ⑤	—	X	104	27-70
Cutlass Calais	1991 ①	X	—	33	27-18
	1991 ②	X	—	32	27-18
Cutlass Ciera	1991-93	X	—	78	27-47
	1991-93	—	X	79	27-48
Cutlass Cruiser	1991-93	X	—	78	27-47
	1991-93	—	X	79	27-48
Cutlass Supreme	1991-93	X	—	66	27-38
	1991-93	—	X	71	27-40
DeVille	1991	—	X	80	27-50
	1992-93	—	X	87	27-57
Eldorado & Seville	1991-92	—	X	83	27-53
	1993 ②	—	X	96	27-63
	1993 ③	—	X	97	27-64
Fleetwood (FWD)	1991	—	X	80	27-50
	1992-93	—	X	87	27-57
Fleetwood (RWD)	1993	—	X	11	27-10
Grand Am	1991 ①	X	—	33	27-18
	1991 ②	X	—	32	27-18
	1992-93	X	—	46	27-23
	1992-93	—	X	49	27-25
Grand Prix	1991-93	X	—	66	27-38
	1991-93	—	X	71	27-40
LeMans	1991-93	X	—	112	27-76
	1991-93	—	X	113	27-76
LeSabre	1991 ④	—	X	74	27-44
	1991-93 ④	X	—	72	27-42
	1992-93 ⑤	—	X	87	27-57
Lumina	1991-93	X	—	66	27-38
	1991-93	—	Tilt	71	27-40
Metro	1991-93 ④	X	—	106	27-73
	1991-93 ⑤	X	—	23	27-16
Park Avenue	1991-93 ④	X	—	72	27-42
	1991 ④	—	X	74	27-44
	1991 ⑤	—	X	85	27-55
	1992-93 ⑤	—	X	87	27-57
Prizm	1991-92	X	X	114	27-77
	1991-92	—	X	115	27-78
	1993	X	X	119	27-80
Reatta & Riviera	1991-93	—	X	84	27-54
Regal	1991-93	X	—	66	27-38
	1991-93	—	X	71	27-40
Roadmaster	1991-93	X	—	103	27-69
	1991-93	—	X	104	27-70

Continued

STEERING COLUMN EXPLODED VIEWS-Continued

Model	Year	Column Type Standard	Column Type Tilt	Fig. No.	Page No.
Skylark	1991①	X	—	33	27-18
	1991②	X	—	32	27-18
	1992-93	X	—	47	27-23
	1992-93	—	X	50	27-26
Sunbird	1991①	X	—	33	27-18
	1991②	X	—	32	27-18
	1992-93	X	—	53	27-28
	1992-93	—	X	54	27-30
Toronado & Trofeo	1991	—	X	86	27-56
	1992	—	X	88	27-58
88 & 98	1991⑤	—	X	85	27-55
	1991④	—	X	74	27-44
	1991-93④	X	—	72	27-42
	1992-93①	—	X	89	27-59
	1992-93②	—	X	87	27-57
6000	1991	—	X	79	27-48
	1991	X	—	78	27-47

①—Floor shift.
②—Column shift.
③—Console shift.

④—Less airbag (Supplemental Inflatable Restraint (SIR)).

⑤—With airbag (Supplemental Inflatable Restraint (SIR)).

PRECAUTIONS

SERVICE

It is important that only the specified screws, bolts and nuts be used during the mandatory reassembly sequence and torqued to specifications to insure proper breakaway action of column under impact. Avoid using excessively long bolts as they may prevent a portion of the steering column from collapsing under impact.

When removing or installing, steering wheel, ignition switch or lock, turn signal switch, adjusting transmission linkage, or installing and adjusting neutral-start or back-up light switch, refer to appropriate car chapter.

If a shift tube shows a sheared plastic injection, a new shift tube must be installed. If a steering shaft shows a sheared plastic, but it is not bent, it can be repaired by using a Service Steering Shaft Repair Kit part number 7810077. The kit contains instructions and dimensions for all steering columns. On some models, the attaching brackets will shear under impact and must also be replaced.

STEERING COLUMN DAMAGE

When the steering column is removed from the vehicle, it is extremely susceptible to damage. Dropping the steering column assembly on its end could collapse the steering shaft assembly or loosen plastic injections that keep the steering column assembly rigid. Leaning on the steering column assembly could cause the jacket to bend or deform. Any of these conditions could impair the steering column assembly's collapsible design. If the steering wheel must be removed, use only the specified steering wheel puller and steering wheel puller bolts. Never hammer on the end of the shaft.

AIRBAG SYSTEM DISARMING

1991 Park Avenue

When carrying a live inflator module, ensure bag and trim cover are pointed away from you. Never carry inflator module by the wires or connector on underside of module.

The diagnostic energy reserve module (DERM) can maintain voltage to cause a system deployment for up to ten minutes after the ignition switch is turned off and the battery is disconnected. Servicing the SIR system during this period may result in accidental deployment and personal injury.

1. Turn ignition switch to OFF position, then disconnect and tape battery ground cable terminal.
2. Remove Connector Position Assurance (CPA), then disconnect yellow two-way SIR electrical connector at base of steering column.
3. Remove screws and/or nuts from back of steering wheel, then the inflator module from steering wheel.
4. Remove Connector Position Assurance (CPA), then disconnect coil assembly connector and horn lead.
5. Place inflator module on a bench or other surface with bag and trim cover facing up.

1991 88 & 98

The diagnostic energy reserve module (DERM) can maintain voltage to cause a system deployment for up to ten minutes after the ignition switch is turned off and the battery is disconnected. Servicing the SIR system during this period may result in accidental deployment and personal injury.

1. Turn ignition switch to OFF position, then remove I/P fuse 7 from fuse block.
2. Disconnect yellow two-way SIR electrical connector at base of steering column.

Beretta, Bonneville w/Single Airbag, Camaro, Corsica, Corvette, DeVille, Eldorado, Firebird, Fleetwood (FWD), Fleetwood (RWD), LeSabre, Reatta, Riviera, Seville & Toronado/Trofeo & 1992–93 Park Avenue, 88 & 98

The diagnostic energy reserve module (DERM) can maintain voltage to cause a system deployment for up to ten minutes after the ignition switch is turned off and the battery is disconnected. Servicing the SIR system during this period may result in accidental deployment and personal injury.

1. Ensure front wheels are pointed straight ahead.
2. Turn ignition switch to LOCK position and remove SIR or AIRBAG fuse.
3. Remove left sound insulator. Remove courtesy lamp from sound insulator, if necessary.
4. Remove Connector Position Assurance (CPA), then disconnect yellow two-way SIR electrical connector at base of steering column.

Caprice, Custom Cruiser & Roadmaster

The diagnostic energy reserve module (DERM) can maintain voltage to cause a system deployment for up to ten minutes after the ignition switch is turned off and the battery is disconnected. Servicing the SIR system during this period may result in accidental deployment and personal injury.
1. Ensure front wheels are pointed straight ahead.
2. Turn ignition switch to LOCK position and remove SIR fuse from fuse block.
3. Remove Connector Position Assurance (CPA), then disconnect yellow two-way SIR electrical connector at base of steering column.

Bonneville w/Dual Airbags

The diagnostic energy reserve module (DERM) can maintain voltage to cause a system deployment for up to ten minutes after the ignition switch is turned off and the battery is disconnected. Servicing the SIR system during this period may result in accidental deployment and personal injury.
1. Ensure front wheels are pointed straight ahead.
2. Turn ignition switch to OFF position and remove SIR fuse from fuse panel.
3. Remove left and right sound insulators.
4. Remove Connector Position Assurance (CPA), then disconnect yellow two-way SIR electrical connector at base of steering column.
5. Remove Connector Position Assurance (CPA), then disconnect yellow two-way passenger inflator module connector at base of right side instrument panel, clipped to knee bolster.

Metro

The diagnostic energy reserve module (DERM) can maintain voltage to cause a system deployment for up to ten minutes after the ignition switch is turned off and the battery is disconnected. Servicing the SIR system during this period may result in accidental deployment and personal injury.
1. **On 1992-93 models,** place steering wheel so that wheels are pointing straight ahead, then turn ignition switch to LOCK position.
2. **On 1991 models,** turn ignition switch to OFF position.
3. **On all models,** remove SIR IG fuse from SIR fuse block.
4. Remove rear plastic access cover from inflator module housing.
5. Remove Connector Position Assurance (CPA), then disconnect yellow two-way SIR electrical connector inside inflator module housing.

1991 Storm

The diagnostic energy reserve module (DERM) can maintain voltage to cause a system deployment for up to ten minutes after the ignition switch is turned off and the battery is disconnected. Servicing the SIR system dur-

ing this period may result in accidental deployment and personal injury.
1. Turn ignition switch to OFF position, then disconnect battery ground cable.
2. Remove fuses C-22 and C-23 from fuse box, then disconnect orange three-way connector at the base of the steering column.

1992–93 Storm

The diagnostic energy reserve module (DERM) can maintain voltage to cause a system deployment for up to ten minutes after the ignition switch is turned off and the battery is disconnected. Servicing the SIR system during this period may result in accidental deployment and personal injury.
1. Place steering wheel so that wheels are pointing straight ahead, then turn ignition switch to LOCK position.
2. Remove fuses C-22 and C-23 from fuse block.
3. Remove switch bezel from instrument panel, then disconnect electrical connector from switches.
4. Remove cigar lighter bezel from instrument panel, then disconnect cigar lighter electrical connectors.
5. Remove two screws and hood latch release handle from knee bolster, then the three screws, three bolts and two nuts retaining the knee bolster.
6. Disconnect lap cooler air duct from knee bolster, then remove knee bolster from vehicle.
7. Remove Connector Position Assurance (CPA), then disconnect orange three-way connector at the base of the steering column.

1993 Prizm

1. Ensure front wheels are pointed straight ahead, then turn ignition switch to LOCK position.
2. Remove IGN and CIG & RADIO fuse from junction block No. 1.
3. Remove Connector Position Assurance (CPA) and disconnect lower steering column (yellow two-cavity) connector at base of steering column.

AIRBAG SYSTEM ARMING
1991 Park Avenue

1. Turn ignition switch to OFF position, connect horn lead and coil assembly connector, then install Connector Position Assurance (CPA).
2. Install inflator module and secure to steering wheel using new screws and/or nuts.
3. **Torque** screws and/or nuts to 25 inch lbs.
4. Connect yellow two-way SIR electrical connector at base of steering column, then install Connector Position Assurance (CPA).
5. Install left sound insulator, then the SIR fuse into fuse block.
6. Turn ignition switch to RUN position and ensure that "Inflatable Restraint" indicator flashes 7 to 9 times, then turns off.

1991 88 & 98

1. Connect yellow two-way SIR electrical connector at base of steering column.
2. Install I/P fuse 7 into fuse block, turn ignition switch to RUN position and ensure that "Inflatable Restraint" indicator flashes 7 to 9 times, then turns off.

Beretta, Bonneville w/Single Airbag, Camaro, Corsica, Corvette, DeVille, Eldorado, Firebird, Fleetwood (FWD), Fleetwood (RWD), LeSabre, Reatta, Riviera, Seville, Toronado, Trofeo & 1992–93 Park Avenue, 88 & 98

1. Connect yellow two-way SIR electrical connector, then install Connector Position Assurance (CPA).
2. Install left sound insulator. **Install courtesy lamp to sound insulator, if applicable.**
3. Install SIR fuse to fuse block, turn ignition switch to RUN position and ensure that "Inflatable Restraint" lamp flashes 7 to 9 times, then turns off.

Caprice, Custom Cruiser & Roadmaster

1. Connect yellow two-way SIR electrical connector at base of column, then install Connector Position Assurance (CPA).
2. Install SIR fuse into fuse block, turn ignition switch to RUN position and ensure that "Inflatable Restraint" lamp flashes 7 to 9 times and then turns off.

Bonneville w/Dual Airbags

1. Connect yellow two-way passenger inflator module connector at base of right side instrument panel, clipped to knee bolster, then install Connector Position Assurance (CPA).
2. Connect yellow two-way SIR electrical connector at base of steering column, then install Connector Position Assurance (CPA).
3. Install left and right sound insulators, then the SIR fuse into fuse panel.
4. Turn ignition switch to RUN position and ensure that "Inflatable Restraint" lamp flashes 7 to 9 times, then turns off.

Metro

1. Turn ignition switch to LOCK position.
2. Connect yellow two-way SIR electrical connector inside inflator module housing, then install Connector Position Assurance (CPA).
3. Install SIR IG fuse into SIR fuse block, then the rear plastic access cover onto inflator module housing.
4. Turn ignition switch to RUN position and ensure that "Inflatable Restraint" lamp flashes 7 to 9 times and then turns off.

ALL COLUMNS (NO MARK)
TILT COLUMN ONLY*

LOCK SYSTEM

Will Not Unlock
1. Shear flange on sector shaft collapsed.
2. Lock bolt damaged.
3. Damaged lock cylinder.
4. Damaged housing.
5. Damaged sector.
6. Damaged rack.

Will Not Lock
1. Lock bolt spring broken or defective.
2. Damaged sector.
3. Damaged lock cylinder
4. Burr on lock bolt.
5. Damaged housing.
6. Transmission linkage adjustment incorrect.
7. Damaged rack.
8. Interference between bowl and rack coupling*.
9. Ignition switch stuck.
10. Actuator rod restricted.

High Lock Effort
1. Lock cylinder damaged.
2. Ignition switch damaged.
3. Rack preload spring broken or deformed.
4. Burrs on sector, rack, housing, support or actuator rod coupling.
5. Bent sector shaft.
6. Damaged rack.
7. Extreme misalignment of housing to cover.*
8. Distorted coupling slot in rack.*
9. Bent actuator rod.
10. Ignition switch mounting bracket bent.
11. Improper shift linkage adjustment.

Will Stick In "Start"
1. Actuator rod deformed.
2. Check items under "High Lock Effort".

Key Cannot Be Removed In "Off-Lock"
1. Ignition switch is not set correctly.
2. Damaged lock cylinder.

Lock Cylinder Can Be Removed
1. Lock cylinder retaining screw missing.

COLUMN

Noise In Column
1. Intermediate shaft pinch bolt not tightened.
2. Column not correctly aligned.
3. Horn contact ring not lubricated.
4. Lack of grease on bearings.
5. Loose sight shields.*
6. Lower or upper steering shaft bearing worn or broken.
7. Shaft lock snap ring not seated.
8. Plastic spherical joint not lubricated.*

High Steering Shaft Effort
1. Column assembly misaligned.
2. Improperly installed or deformed dust seal.
3. Damaged upper or lower bearing.
4. Flash on I.D. of shift tube from plastic joint.
5. Tight intermediate steering shaft universal joint.

High Shift Effort (Automatic)
1. Column not aligned correctly in car.
2. Wave washer with burrs.*
3. Improperly installed dust seal.
4. Lack of grease on seal or bearing.
5. Improper screws used for ignition switch.
6. Burr on upper or lower end of shift tube.

Improper Transmission Shifting (Automatic Transmission)
1. Sheared shift tube joint or lower shift lever weld.
2. Improper transmission linkage adjustment.
3. Improper gate plate.

Lash In Mounted Column Assembly
1. IP to column upper and lower bracket mounting bolts loose.
2. Broken weld nuts on jacket.
3. IP upper bracket capsule sheared.
4. Loose shoes in housing.*
5. Loose tilt head pivot pins.*
6. Loose shoe lock pin in support.*
7. Loose support screws.
8. Column upper and lower bracket to jacket bolts loose.

Fig. 1   Steering column troubleshooting

1991 Storm
1. Turn ignition switch to OFF position, then connect orange three-way connector at the base of the steering column.
2. Install fuses C-22 and C-23 into fuse box, then connect battery ground cable.

1992 Storm
1. Turn ignition switch to OFF position, then connect orange three-way connector at the base of the steering column.
2. Connect lap cooler air duct to knee bolster, then install knee bolster.
3. **Torque** knee bolster bolts and nuts to 89 inch lbs.
4. Install hood latch release handle to knee bolster.

5. Connect cigar lighter electrical connector, then snap cigar lighter bezel into place on instrument panel.
6. Connect switch bezel electrical connectors, then snap switch bezel into place on instrument panel.

1993 Prizm
1. Turn ignition switch to LOCK position.
2. Connect lower steering column yellow two-cavity connector.
3. Install IGN and CIG & RADIO fuses.
4. Turn ignition switch to ACC or ON positions and verify that the airbag indicator illuminates steady for approximately six seconds and then turns off.

TROUBLESHOOTING

Refer to **Figs. 1 and 2**, for steering column troubleshooting.

STEERING COLUMN REPLACE

CAPRICE, CUSTOM CRUISER & ROADMASTER

Removal

Wheels must be in a straight forward position and the key must be in the Lock position when removing or installing column to ensure proper alignment of components during installation.

Care must be taken when handling column with a live inflator module. Never point bag deploy surface toward you, and never stand column on steering wheel. Accidental deployment in these positions may cause injury. Always face bag deploy surface toward open space to allow for unrestricted expansion.

1. Disable airbag system as described under "Airbag System Disarming."
2. Disconnect battery ground cable, then remove stop lamp switch.
3. Remove nut and bolt from pot joint coupling, attaching upper intermediate shaft to the steering column, **Fig. 3.**
4. Disconnect shift linkage from steering column.
5. If steering column is to be replaced or serviced, remove steering wheel as described in the "Electrical" section of the appropriate vehicle section in the front of this manual.
6. Remove steering column opening filler, then driver side knee bolster and deflector.
7. Remove bolts attaching toe plate to cowl, then the shift indicator cable from steering column.
8. Disconnect electrical connectors from column, then remove capsule nuts attaching column support bracket to instrument panel carrier. If shims are used, retain for use in installation.
9. Remove steering column from vehicle.

Installation

If a service replacement column is being installed, do not remove anti-rotation pin until after steering column has been connected to steering gear. Removing pin before column is installed or connected will damage SIR coil assembly.

1. Carefully place column into position in vehicle.
2. Raise column and loosely install capsule nuts, Install shims, if equipped.
3. **Torque** capsule nuts to 20 ft. lbs.
4. Install nut and bolt to pot joint, attaching upper intermediate shaft to steering column shaft. **Torque** to 40 ft. lbs.
5. Connect shift linkage to steering column.
6. Install toe plate attaching bolts and **torque** to 58 inch lbs.
7. Connect electrical connectors to column.
8. If a service replacement steering column is being installed, remove anti-rotation pin.
9. Install shift indicator cable clip to steering column and adjust shift indicator if necessary.
10. Install driver knee bolster and deflector, then the steering column opening filler.
11. If a service replacement steering column is being installed, remove hexagon locking nut, then the coil assembly shipping cover and disengage connector from cover.
12. Replace steering wheel if removed.
13. Connect battery ground cable.
14. Install stop lamp switch, adjust if necessary.
15. Rearm airbag system as described under "Airbag System Arming."

Housing Scraping On Bowl
1. Bowl bent or not concentric with hub.*

Steering Wheel Loose
1. Excessive clearance between holes in support or housing and pivot pin diameters.*
2. Defective or missing anti-lash spring in spheres.*
3. Upper bearing not seated in housing.*
4. Upper bearing inner race seal missing.*
5. Loose support screws.
6. Bearing proload spring missing or broken.*

Steering Wheel Loose (Every Other Tilt Position)
1. Loose fit between shoe and shoe pivot pin.*
2. Shoe not free in slot.*

Steering Column Not Locking In Any Tilt Position
1. Shoe seized on its pivot pin.*
2. Shoe grooves may have burrs or dirt.*
3. Shoe lock spring weak or broken.*

Steering Wheel Fails To Return To Top Tilt Position
1. Pivot pins are bound up.*
2. Wheel tilt spring is defective.*
3. Turn signal switch wires too tight.*

Noise When Tilting Column
1. Upper tilt bumpers worn.*
2. Tilt spring rubbing in housing.*

Miscellaneous
1. Housing loose on jacket — will be noticed with ignition in "off-lock" and a torque applied to the steering wheel.

Fig. 2 Steering column troubleshooting

BONNEVILLE, DEVILLE, FLEETWOOD (FWD), LESABRE, PARK AVENUE, 88 & 98

MODELS w/SUPPLEMENTAL INFLATABLE RESTRAINT (SIR)

Removal

Wheels must be in a straight forward position and the key must be in the Lock position when removing or installing column to ensure proper alignment of components during installation.

Care must be taken when handling column with a live inflator module. Never point bag deploy surface toward you, and never stand column on steering wheel. Accidental deployment in these positions may cause injury. Always face bag deploy surface toward open space to allow for unrestricted expansion.

1. Disable airbag system as described under "Airbag System Disarming."
2. Remove the inflator module as follows:
   a. With the ignition switch in the Off position and the battery ground cable.
   b. Remove left side sound insulator.
   c. Remove the Torx screws from the back of the steering wheel, then remove the inflator module from steering wheel.
   d. Remove the horn contact by pushing lightly and twisting counterclockwise.
   e. Disconnect the coil assembly connector from inflator module.
3. Remove instrument panel steering column trim plate.
4. Remove two screws retaining filler, then four bolt/screws from column reinforcement plate and the reinforcement plate.
5. Disconnect any necessary electrical connectors.
6. Disconnect shift control cable at actuator, then remove four seal assembly mounting bolts, **Fig. 4.**
7. Remove bolt from upper knuckle of intermediate steering shaft, **Fig. 4.**
8. Remove nut and bolt holding lower brace assembly, then remove lower brace.
9. Remove remaining bracket bolts, then remove the lower support bracket.
10. Remove two column to upper support retaining bolts/screws, then the column.

9 UPPER INTERMEDIATE SHAFT
10 SEAL
11 COUPLING SHIELD
12 LOWER INTERMEDIATE SHAFT
13 FLEXIBLE COUPLING
14 BOLT
15 BOLT
16 LOWER STEERING SHAFT
17 TOE PLATE
18 BRACKET
19 SHIFT LEVER
20 LOCK CYLINDER SET
21 SCREW
22 HAZARD WARNING BUTTON
23 SPRING
24 HAZARD WARNING KNOB
25 RETAINING RING
26 NUT
57 LOWER BEARING ADAPTER CLIP
58 STEERING WHEEL ROTATION SENSOR
60 SCREW

1 INFLATOR MODULE
2 STEERING WHEEL
3 MULTIFUNCTION LEVER
4 TILT LEVER
5 STEERING COLUMN
6 BOLT
7 POT JOINT COUPLING
8 NUT

A HORN LEAD
B COIL HARNESS
C CONNECTOR POSITION ASSURANCE

Fig. 3 Steering column removal & installation. Caprice, Custom Cruiser & Roadmaster

1. UPPER SUPPORT
2. STEERING COLUMN
3. STEERING WHEEL
4. HORN WIRE LEAD
5. INFLATOR MODULE
6. LOCK NUT.
7. SIR COIL ASSEMBLY LEAD
8. CONNECTOR POSITION ASSURANCE (CPA)
9. BOLT/SCREW
10. BUTTON
11. SPRING
12. KNOB
13. MULTI-FUNCTION TURN SIGNAL LEVER
14. TILT LEVER
15. YELLOW TWO-WAY SIR HARNESS CONNECTOR
16. CONNECTOR POSITION ASSURANCE
17. LOWER SUPPORT BRACKET
18. INTERMEDIATE SHAFT ASSEMBLY
19 BRACE

Fig. 5 Steering column removal & installation. Bonneville, DeVille, Fleetwood (FWD), LeSabre, Park Avenue, 88 & 98 w/Supplemental Inflatable Restraint (SIR)

Installation

1. Install lower support bracket to steering column, **Fig. 5.** Do not tighten fasteners at this time.
2. Install two bolts into upper support as-

sembly, **Fig. 5.** Do not tighten completely.
3. Position steering column with lower support bracket slots over fasteners installed in step 2. Do not allow to hang freely and do not tighten fasten-

1. BOLT; 47 N·M (35 LB-FT)
2. STEERING COLUMN
3. SCREW (4); 2.4 N·M (21 LB-IN)
4. SEAL ASSEMBLY
5. INTERMEDIATE SHAFT ASSEMBLY

Fig. 4 Intermediate shaft & boot installation. Bonneville, DeVille, Fleetwood (FWD), LeSabre, Park, Avenue, 88 & 98 w/Supplemental Inflatable Restraint (SIR)

ers.

4. Install two bolts through steering column into upper support assembly, but do not tighten.
5. Install upper knuckle of intermediate steering shaft on upper steering shaft. **Torque** bolt to 35 ft. lbs.
6. Install seal assembly and **torque** four bolts to 21 inch lbs.
7. Remove left bolt from lower support bracket, then install lower brace assembly. **Torque** bolts to 84 inch lbs.
8. **Torque** remaining lower brace and bracket bolts to 84 inch lbs. and upper support assembly bolts to 20 ft. lbs.
9. **Torque** two lower support bracket through bolts to 20 ft. lbs., then connect shift control cable and electrical connections.
10. Install steering wheel inflator module as follows:
   a. With ignition off, install horn contact, then connect coil assembly connector to inflator module.
   b. Push coil assembly lead wires into channel in lower right portion of steering wheel, then install inflator module in steering wheel.
   c. **Torque** screws holding inflator module to steering wheel to 25 inch lbs.
   d. Install left side sound insulator.
   e. Connect battery ground cable.
11. Install reinforcement plate and **torque** bolts to 17 inch lbs.
12. Install instrument panel column filler and trim plate.
13. Rearm airbag system as described under "Airbag System Arming."

MODELS LESS SUPPLEMENTAL INFLATABLE RESTRAINT (SIR)
Removal

1. Disconnect battery ground cable.
2. Remove left instrument panel sound insulator, trim pad and column trim collar.
3. Remove steering shaft to intermediate shaft connection.

1. Steering Column
2. Steering Column Mounting Bolts 27 N·m (20 Lbs. Ft.)
3. Shift Cable
4. Shift Cable Bracket
5. Shift Cable Bracket Bolts 17 N·m (13 Lbs. Ft.)

Fig. 6   Steering column installation. Bonneville, DeVille, Fleetwood (FWD), LeSabre, Park Avenue, 88 & 98 less Supplemental Inflatable Restraint (SIR)

4. Remove column bracket support bolts and nut.
5. Remove shift indicator cable.
6. Disconnect steering column wiring connectors.
7. Remove shift cable at actuator and housing.
8. Remove steering column from vehicle.

Installation

1. Position steering column in vehicle and install shift cable and housing, **Fig. 6**.
2. Connect steering column wiring connectors.
3. Install shift indicator cable.
4. Install steering column mounting bolts and nut and **torque** bolts to 20 ft. lbs.
5. Install intermediate shaft and upper pinch bolt, **Fig. 7**, and **torque** bolt to 35 ft. lbs.
6. Install left instrument panel sound insulator, trim pad and column trim collar.
7. Connect battery ground cable.

ELDORADO, REATTA, RIVIERA, SEVILLE & TORONADO/TROFEO
Removal

Wheels must be in a straight forward position and the key must be in the Lock position when removing or installing column to ensure proper alignment of components during installation.

Care must be taken when handling column with a live inflator module.

1. INTERMEDIATE SHAFT
2. 47 N·m (35 LBS. FT.)
3. SEAL
4. STEERING GEAR
5. 2.0mm (5/64") MINIMUM CLEARANCE

VIEW A

Fig. 7   Intermediate shaft & boot installation. Bonneville, DeVille, Fleetwood (FWD), LeSabre, Park Avenue, 88 & 98 less Supplemental Inflatable Restraint (SIR)

FRONT OF DASH

2 mm (5/64") MINIMUM CLEARANCE
VIEW A

FRONT OF DASH

FRONT OF CAR

1	STEERING GEAR
2	INTERMEDIATE SHAFT ASM.
3	DASH SEAL
4	STEERING COLUMN
5	BOLTS
6	SEAL MOUNTING SCREWS

Fig. 8   Intermediate shaft & boot installation. Eldorado, Reatta, Riviera, Seville & Toronado/Trofeo

Never point bag deploy surface toward you, and never stand column on steering wheel. Accidental deployment in these positions may cause injury. Always face bag deploy surface toward open space to allow for unrestricted expansion.

1. Disable airbag system as described

1	I/P BRACKET
2	STEERING COLUMN
3	UPPER COLUMN BRACKET
4	MOUNTING BOLTS
5	MOUNTING NUT
6	LOWER COLUMN BRACKET
7	BRACKET SCREWS

Fig. 9   Steering column installation. Eldorado, Reatta, Riviera, Seville & Toronado/Trofeo

under "Airbag System Disarming."
2. Disconnect battery ground cable, then remove inflator module as follows:
   a. Remove screws from back of steering wheel, then the inflator module from steering wheel.
   b. Disconnect horn contact by pushing lightly and twisting counterclockwise.
   c. Disconnect coil assembly connector from inflator module.
3. Remove knee bolster and steering column reinforcement plate.
4. Disconnect electrical connectors from column.
5. Remove pinch bolt from intermediate shaft, **Fig. 8**.
6. Remove lower support bracket from vehicle.

A	STEERING COLUMN	3	SHAFT NUT
B	RETAINER	4	MOUNTING NUT
1	GUIDE BRACKET	5	TURN SIGNAL/CRUISE CONTROL LEVER
2	UPPER SUPPORT		

Fig. 10 Steering column installation. Brougham

7. Remove upper column support from instrument panel, then the column from vehicle.

Installation

1. Install column in vehicle and support at upper bracket with two bolts, **Fig. 9**, do not tighten at this time.
2. Install column lower support bracket in vehicle, do not tighten at this time.
3. Connect column intermediate shaft to steering rack, install pinch bolt and **torque** to 35 ft. lbs.
4. **Torque** upper and lower column support bolts to 20 ft. lbs. and lower bracket to column screws to 12 ft. lbs.
5. Connect electrical connectors to column.
6. Install knee bolster and column reinforcement plate.
7. Install steering wheel inflator module as follows:
   a. With ignition off, install horn contact, then connect coil assembly connector to inflator module.
   b. Install inflator module in steering wheel and **torque** screws to 27 inch lbs.
   c. Connect battery ground cable.
8. Rearm airbag system as described under "Airbag System Arming."

BROUGHAM
Removal

1. Disconnect battery ground cable.
2. Disconnect transmission linkage at lower shift lever.
3. Remove nut attaching intermediate shaft and column, then separate shaft from the column.
4. Remove column lower cover and lower fuse panel cover.
5. Remove lefthand A/C outlet duct.
6. Disconnect turn signal harness connector, park neutral switch, parking brake release hose and headlamp dimmer switch from column.
7. Remove clip retaining shift cable and loosen two upper support nuts.
8. Position carpet out of the way to gain access to the cowl insulator and seal fasteners.
9. Remove cowl insulator and cover seal.
10 Remove two upper column support nuts, then the column from vehicle.

Installation

1. Install column in vehicle and finger tighten upper mounting bracket nuts, **Fig. 10.**
2. Install nut securing column to the intermediate shaft and finger tighten.
3. Connect transmission linkage to lower shaft lever.
4. Connect shift cable and securing clip.
5. Install cowl seal and finger tighten nuts and bolts.
6. Connect turn signal harness, park neutral switch, parking brake release hose and headlamp dimmer switch connectors.
7. **Torque** upper column bracket nuts to 20 ft. lbs., cowl cover seal nuts and bolts to 35 inch lbs. and column to intermediate shaft bolt to 52 ft. lbs.
8. Install cowl seal insulator, lefthand A/C outlet duct, lower fuse panel cover and steering column lower cover.
9. Connect battery ground cable.

1993 FLEETWOOD (RWD)
Removal

Front wheels must be straight ahead and the ignition switch in the LOCK position before disconnecting the steering column assembly or the intermediate steering shaft assembly from the steering gear assembly. Failure to do so will cause the SIR coil assembly to become uncentered, which will case damage to the SIR coil assembly.

1. Disarm airbag system as described under "Airbag System Disarming."
2. Remove stop lamp switch assembly.
3. Remove instrument panel steering column opening filler assembly.
4. Remove instrument panel driver knee bolster assembly and deflector.
5. Disconnect steering wheel rotation sensor electrical connector.
6. Remove bolt and nut from pot joint coupling, attaching upper intermediate steering shaft assembly to steering column assembly, **Fig. 11.**
7. Remove nuts attaching steering column bracket to instrument panel carrier, then lower the steering column assembly.
8. Disconnect shift indicator cable from steering column assembly.

9. Disconnect all electrical connectors, then remove automatic transmission range selector rod assembly from steering column.
10. Remove bolts attaching jacket to cowl, then remove the steering wheel assembly, if required.
11. Remove steering column assembly from vehicle.

Installation

If a service replacement steering column assembly is being installed, do not remove the anti-rotation pin until the steering column assembly has been connected to the steering gear. **Removing the anti-rotation pin before steering column is connected to the steering gear assembly may damage the SIR coil assembly.**

1. Place steering column in vehicle and install bolts securing jacket to cowl. **Torque** bolts to 58 inch lbs.
2. Connect electrical connectors, then remove anti-rotation pin if service replacement steering column assembly is being installed.
3. Connect indicator cable to steering column assembly, then install nuts attaching steering column bracket. **Torque** nuts to 20 ft. lbs.
4. Install bolt and nut to coupling, attaching upper intermediate steering shaft assembly to steering column assembly. **Torque** nut to 40 ft. lbs.
5. Connect steering wheel rotation sensor electrical connector.
6. Install automatic transmission range selector rod assembly to steering column assembly.
7. Adjust shift linkage, then install stop lamp switch assembly.
8. Install instrument panel driver knee bolster assembly and deflector.
9. Install instrument panel steering column opening filler assembly.
10. Remove hexagon locking nut, if a service replacement steering column is being installed.
11. Install steering wheel, if removed.
12. Enable airbag system as described under "Airbag System Arming."

CAMARO & FIREBIRD
Removal

Wheels must be in a straight forward position and the key must be in the Lock position when removing or installing column to ensure proper alignment of components during installation.

Care must be taken when handling column with a live inflator module. Never point bag deploy surface toward you, and never stand column on steering wheel. Accidental deployment in these positions may cause injury. Always face bag deploy surface toward open space to allow for unrestricted expansion.

1. Disable airbag system as described under "Airbag System Disarming."
2. Remove the inflator module as follows:
   a. Remove the Torx screws from the

52-RETAINER, SPRING
55-SHAFT ASM, STEERING
56-SHAFT ASM, RACE & UPPER
57-SPHERE, CENTERING
58-SPRING, JOINT PRELOAD
59-SHAFT ASM, LOWER STEERING
61-SCREW, SUPPORT
62-SUPPORT ASM, STRG COL HSG
63-SUPPORT, STRG COL HSG
64-SCREW, OVL HD CROSS RECESS
65-GATE, SHIFT LEVER
66-RING, SHIFT TUBE RETAINING
67-WASHER, THRUST
68-PLATE, LOCK
69-WASHER, WAVE
70-SPRING, SHIFT LEVER
71-BOWL ASM, GEARSHIFT LEVER
72-SHROUD, GEARSHIFT BOWL
73-JACKET ASM, STRG COL
75-SCREW, WASH HD (#10-24x.25)
76-ROD, DIMMER SWITCH
77-SCREW, HEX WASH HD TAP
78-NUT, HEXAGON
79-SWITCH ASM, IGNITION
80-STUD, DIMR & IGN SWITCH MTG
81-SWITCH ASM, DIMMER
82-BRACKET, SOLENOID
83-SOLENOID ASM, INTERLOCK
84-SCREW, HEX WASH HD (10-24X.25)
85-SPRING, BALL JOINT
86-ACTUATOR ASM, IGN SWITCH
87-TUBE ASM, SHIFT
88-BUSHING ASM, STRG SHAFT
89-RETAINER, BEARING ADAPTER
90-SENSOR ASM, ATTACHMENT PLATE &
91-CLIP, LOWER BEARING ADAPTER

Service Kits

201-RACK SERV KIT, COL SECTOR &
 -INCLUDES: 14,31,33,44,47,48
202-SPRING SERV KIT, TILT COLUMN
 -INCLUDES: 13,14,39,50,51,52
203-COIL SERV KIT, INFL RESTRAINT
 -INCLUDES: 3,28
204-SPHERE SERV KIT, TILT COLUMN
 -INCLUDES: 57,58
205-GREASE SERV KIT, (SYNTHETIC)
206-GREASE SERV KIT, BTSI

1-NUT, HEX LOCKING (M14x1.5)
2-RING, RETAINING
3-COIL ASM, INFL RESTRAINT
4-WASHER, WAVE
5-RING, RETAINING
6-LOCK, SHAFT
7-CAM ASM, TURN SIG CANCEL
8-SPRING, UPPER BEARING
9-SCREW, BNDG HD CR RECESS
10-SCREW, FLAT HD TAP
11-ARM, SIGNAL SWITCH
12-SWITCH ASM, TURN SIGNAL
13-SEAT, UPPER BRG INNER RACE
14-RACE, INNER
15-SCREW, PAN HD SOC TAP
16-SWITCH ASM, BUZZER
18-SCREW, LOCK RETAINING
19-COVER ASM, LOCK HOUSING
20-LOCK CYLINDER SET, STRG COL
 PASS KEY
21-ACTUATOR, DIMMER SW ROD
22-PIN, SWITCH ACTUATOR PIVOT
23-SWITCH ASM, PIVOT & (PULSE)
24-BASE PLATE, COL HSG CVR END
25-CAP, COL HSG COVER END
26-PROTECTOR, WIRING
27-SCREW, C/S TAP (#8-18)
28-SHROUD, CONNECTOR
30-HOUSING ASM, STRG COLUMN
31-BEARING ASM
32-BOLT, LOCK
33-SPRING, LOCK BOLT
34-SHOE, STEERING WHEEL LOCK
35-SHOE, STEERING WHEEL LOCK
36-SHIELD, WIRE PROTECTOR
37-SHAFT, DRIVE
38-PIN, DOWEL
39-PIN, PIVOT
40-SPRING, SHOE
41-SPRING, RELEASE LEVER
42-PIN, RELEASE LEVER
43-LEVER, SHOE RELEASE
44-RACK, SWITCH ACTUATOR
45-SPRING, RACK PRELOAD
46-HOUSING, STRG COLUMN
47-SECTOR, SWITCH ACTUATOR
48-SCREW, HEX WASHER HEAD
50-GUIDE, SPRING
51-SPRING, WHEEL TILT

Fig. 11 Exploded view of tilt steering column (Part 2 of 2). 1993 Fleetwood (RWD)

Fig. 11 Exploded view of tilt steering column (Part 1 of 2). 1993 Fleetwood (RWD)

1	STEERING COLUMN BRACKET		4	LOWER SUPPORT PLATE NUT
2	STEERING COLUMN LOWER SUPPORT BRACKET		5	CABLE BACKDRIVE (AUTOMATIC ONLY)
3	STEERING COLUMN CAPSULE BOLT			

Fig. 13   Steering column installation. Corvette

A	HORN CONNECTOR					
B	COIL-TO-INFLATOR CONNECTOR	9	SPRING	19	SEAL
C	CONNECTOR POSITIVE ASSURANCE	10	HAZARD WARNING KNOB	20	COUPLING SHIELD
1	INFLATOR MODULE	11	MULTIFUNCTION LEVER	21	LOWER INTERMEDIATE SHAFT
2	LOCK NUT	12	TILT LEVER	22	FLEXIBLE COUPLING
3	SCREW	13	BOLT	23	BOLT
4	NUT	14	WASHER	24	STEERING COLUMN
5	RETAINING RING	15	TOE PLATE	25	COIL ASSEMBLY
6	STEERING WHEEL	16	BOLT	30	POT JOINT COUPLING
7	SCREW	17	NUT		
8	HAZARD WARNING BUTTON	18	UPPER INTERMEDIATE SHAFT		

Fig. 12   Steering column removal & installation. Camaro & Firebird

back of the steering wheel, then remove the inflator module from steering wheel.

b. Disconnect the coil assembly connector from inflator module.

3. Disconnect park lock cable from the ignition switch inhibitor, if applicable.
4. Remove bolt and nut from upper intermediate shaft clamp, **Fig. 12**.
5. Remove knee bolster and bracket and screws attaching toe pan cover to the cowl.
6. Disconnect electrical connectors and remove capsule nuts attaching column support bracket to the instrument panel.
7. Remove steering column from the vehicle.

Installation

1. Install steering column into the vehicle, then connect the park lock cable to the ignition switch inhibitor, if applicable.
2. Install the capsule nuts attaching the column support bracket to the instrument panel.
3. Install the bolt and nut to the clamp attaching the intermediate shaft to the steering column and **torque** to 44 ft. lbs.
4. Install screws attaching toe pan cover to the cowl and connect electrical connectors.
5. Install knee bolster and bracket and sound insulator panel.

6. Connect coil assembly to the inflator module, then install inflator module to the steering wheel and **torque** screws to 25 inch lbs.
7. Install left side sound insulator, then connect the battery ground cable.
8. Rearm airbag system as described under "Airbag System Arming."

CORVETTE

Wheels must be in a straight forward position and the key must be in the Lock position when removing or installing column to ensure proper alignment of components during installation.

Care must be taken when handling column with a live inflator module. Never point bag deploy surface toward you, and never stand column on steering wheel. Accidental deployment in these positions may cause injury. Always face bag deploy surface toward open space to allow for unrestricted expansion.

1. Remove the inflator module as follows:
   a. Turn the ignition switch to the Off position and disconnect battery ground cable.
   b. Remove left side sound insulator.
   c. Install Load Tool No. J 37808 or equivalent by connecting "base of column" lead of tool.
   d. Remove the Torx screws from the

back of the steering wheel, then remove the inflator module from steering wheel.

e. Disconnect the coil assembly connector from inflator module.

2. Remove steering wheel retaining nut, steering wheel and disconnect horn connector.
3. Remove intermediate shaft upper bolt.
4. Disconnect the (ALDL) Assembly Line Diagnostic Link connector and lamp from the sound insulator and remove sound insulator.
5. Remove column housing cover end cap by pulling toward front of vehicle.
6. Disconnect harness connector and grommet and remove multi-function lever by pulling toward driver side door.
7. Remove driver's side knee bolster and tilt lever.
8. Remove nuts from lower support plate and capsule bolts from reinforcement assembly.
9. Disconnect electrical connectors from column.
10. Remove sound insulator to column lower support bracket and nuts from the accelerator pedal bracket.
11. Remove steering column from vehicle.

Installation

1. Install steering column assembly in vehicle and insert lower steering shaft assembly into U-joint of intermediate shaft.
2. Install intermediate shaft upper bolt and loosely attach column and upper support plate to instrument panel reinforcement assembly with capsule bolts, **Fig. 13**.
3. Install cable backdrive on vehicles with automatic transmission, then loosely attach column nuts to support plate studs.
4. **Torque** intermediate shaft bolt to 26 ft. lbs., capsule bolts to 20 ft. lbs. and lower support plate nuts to 10 ft. lbs.
5. Connect electrical connectors to column and install driver's side knee bolster.
6. Install multi-function lever, harness and grommet, column housing cover end cap and tilt lever.

1. LOWER SUPPORT
2. INSTRUMENT PANEL
3. SHIFT INDICATOR CABLE
4. INTERMEDIATE SHAFT
5. 15 N·m (10 LBS. FT.)
6. 47 N·m (35 LBS. FT.)
7. 33 N·m (25 LBS. FT.)
8. 28 N·m (20 LBS. FT.)

Fig. 14 Steering column installation. Century, Cutlass Ciera, Cutlass Cruiser & 6000

1 UPPER PINCH BOLT

2 FLANGE AND STEERING COUPLING

3 RETAINERS

4 STEERING COLUMN

5 BOLT

6 BOLT

7 BOLT

8 STEERING COLUMN UPPER SUPPORT

9 SHIMS

VIEW A

Fig. 15 Steering column removal & installation. Beretta & Corsica

7. Align tilt lever tab into slot, with lever in Off position.
8. Install sound insulator bracket to column lower support and accelerator pedal bracket nuts. **Torque** accelerator pedal bracket nuts to 71 inch lbs.
9. Install steering wheel, retaining nut and connect horn connector.
10. Connect coil assembly to the inflator module, then install inflator module to the steering wheel, using new screws and **torque** screws to 87 inch lbs.
11. Remove Load Tool No. J 37808.
12. Install left side sound insulator, ALDL and lamp connectors.
13. Connect battery ground cable.
14. Rearm airbag as outlined in "Airbag System Arming."

CENTURY, CUTLASS CIERA, CUTLASS CRUISER & 6000

Removal

1. Disconnect battery ground cable.
2. Remove left instrument panel sound absorber, trim pad and column trim collar.
3. Remove bolt and disconnect column to intermediate shaft connection.
4. Remove column support bracket bolts and nut.
5. Disconnect shift indicator cable and electrical connectors.
6. Disconnect shift cable at actuator and housing holder, then remove column assembly from vehicle.

Installation

1. Install column assembly in vehicle, **Fig. 14.**
2. Connect shift cable at actuator and housing holder, then the electrical connectors.
3. Connect shift indicator cable and install column bracket support bolts and nut.
4. Install intermediate shaft to column upper shaft pinch bolt and **torque** to 35 ft. lbs.
5. **Torque** column bracket support bolts and nut to 20 ft. lbs.
6. Install column trim collar, left instrument panel trim pad and sound insulator, then connect battery ground cable.

BERETTA & CORSICA

Wheels must be in a straight forward position and the key must be in the Lock position when removing or installing column to ensure proper alignment of components during installation.

Care must be taken when handling column with a live inflator module. Never point bag deploy surface toward you, and never stand column on steering wheel. Accidental deployment in these positions may cause injury. Always face bag deploy surface toward open space to allow for unrestricted expansion.

1. Disable airbag system as described under "Airbag System Disarming."
2. Disconnect hazard and turn signal electrical connector, then cruise switch terminal connector.
3. Remove column support bracket bolts, then flange and coupling pinch bolt, **Fig. 15.**
4. Remove upper and lower steering column support bolts.
5. Disconnect ignition and dimmer switch electrical connections.
6. Remove park lock cable from ignition switch.
7. Remove column assembly.
8. Reverse procedure to install noting the following:
   a. **Torque** lower steering column support bolts to 21 ft. lbs.
   b. **Torque** steering column support bracket to steering column to 22 ft. lbs.
   c. **Torque** upper steering column support bolts to 21 ft. lbs.
   d. **Torque** flange and coupling pinch bolt to 30 ft. lbs.
   e. Rearm airbag system as described under "Airbag System Arming."

CAVALIER, CUTLASS CALAIS, GRAND AM, SKYLARK & SUNBIRD

Removal

1. Disconnect battery ground cable and remove left instrument panel sound insulator, lower trim panel or duct assembly, and steering column collar, as equipped.

1. UPPER PINCH BOLT
2. FLANGE AND STEERING COUPLING
3. RETAINERS
4. STEERING COLUMN
5. BOLT
6. BOLT
7. SHIMS

Fig. 16 Steering column installation. Achieva, Cavalier, Cutlass Calais, Grand Am, Skylark & Sunbird

2. If column is to be disassembled, remove horn contact pad and steering wheel.
3. Push back seal to expose flexible coupling, **Fig. 16**, then remove coupling pinch bolt.
4. Remove lower column support bracket bolt, then the upper bracket to instrument panel support bolts and lower column.
5. Disconnect column electrical connectors and shift indicator cable, if equipped.
6. Disconnect shift cable at actuator and housing holder, then remove steering column.

Installation

1. Insert steering shaft into flexible coupling.
2. Connect shift cable to actuator and housing holder.
3. Connect column electrical connectors and shift indicator cable.
4. Raise column into position, then install upper and lower bracket mounting bolts hand tight.
5. Install flexible coupling pinch bolt and **torque** bolt to 29 ft. lbs.
6. Ensure steering shaft is centered in mast jacket, repositioning column as needed, then **torque** mounting bolts to 20 ft. lbs.
7. Adjust shift cable and shift indicator as needed, then reverse remaining procedure to complete installation.

CUTLASS SUPREME, GRAND PRIX, LUMINA & REGAL

Removal

Steering wheel removal for vehicles with redundant steering wheel controls has been revised by service bulletin No. 90-110-9.
1. Remove air cleaner.
2. Disconnect battery ground cable, then remove steering wheel as necessary. **When removing steering wheel that is equipped with redundant steering wheel controls, insert wheel puller bolts only four to six threads deep to prevent bolts from going all the way through the hub.**
3. Remove left hand sound insulator and the trim panel below steering column.
4. Unlock steering column, then push top of intermediate shaft seal down for access to upper intermediate shaft coupling and upper coupling pinch bolt.
5. Rotate intermediate shaft as necessary to remove upper coupling pinch bolt.
6. Disconnect shift indicator cable end and casing from steering column and transaxle shift lever, or park lock cable if equipped with floor shift.
7. Disconnect transaxle shift cable from ball stud on transaxle shift lever, then remove transaxle shift cable casing from steering column bracket by depressing two tabs.

1. STEERING SHAFT-LOWER END
2. STEERING COLUMN ASSEMBLY
3. INTERMEDIATE SHAFT COUPLING-UPPER
4. PINCH BOLT-LOWER COUPLING
5. SCREW
6. STEERING GEAR
7. SEAL-INTERMEDIATE SHAFT
8. INTERMEDIATE SHAFT COUPLING-LOWER
9. INTERMEDIATE SHAFT
10. PINCH BOLT-UPPER COUPLING
11. BRACKET-BRAKE PEDAL
12. BOLT-LOWER STEERING COLUMN
13. BOLT-UPPER STEERING COLUMN

Fig. 17 Steering column removal & installation. Cutlass Supreme, Grand Prix, Lumina & Regal

8. Remove lower steering column attaching bolts, **Fig. 17**, then the upper steering column attaching bolts, and lower steering column to seat.
9. Disconnect electrical connector by loosening the screw and separating the two halves.
10. Withdraw lower end of steering shaft from upper intermediate shaft coupling and remove column. **It may be necessary to spread coupling clamp with a screwdriver to withdraw steering shaft.**

Installation

1. Install column back into vehicle and insert lower end of column shaft into upper intermediate shaft coupling.
2. Connect column electrical connector, tightening screw that draws the two halves together.
3. Connect transaxle shift cable and transaxle shift cable casing to column bracket and shift lever ball stud, or park lock cable if equipped with floor shift.

NOTICE:
Once the steering column is removed from the car, the column is extremely susceptible to damage. Dropping the column assembly on its end could collapse the steering shaft or loosen the plastic injections which maintain column length. Leaning on the column assembly could cause the jacket to bend or deform. Any of the above damage could impair the column's collapsible design. If it is necessary to remove the steering wheel, use standard wheel puller. Under no condition should the end of the shaft be hammered upon as hammering could loosen the plastic injections which maintain column length.

REMOVAL

1) Disconnect negative battery cable.
2) Remove steering wheel.

3) Remove turn signal/dimmer switch.

4) Disconnect lead wires from ignition and ignition key warning switch electrical connector at junction/fusebox.
5) Pull off floor mat at the foot of steering shaft and remove steering joint cover.

1 JOINT COVER

6) Remove steering shaft joint upper side bolt.

1 STEERING SHAFT JOINT UPPER SIDE BOLT

7) Remove steering column mount nuts.

1 STEERING COLUMN MOUNTING NUTS
2 STEERING COLUMN

8) Remove steering column assembly.

NOTICE: Do not disassemble steering column assembly into column and shaft. If steering column or shaft is found defective, replace as an assembly.

1 STEERING COLUMN ASSEMBLY

Fig. 18   Steering column removal. Metro

INSTALLATION

1) Align flat part "A" of lower joint shaft with bolt hole "B" of upper side joint as shown. Then insert upper side joint into lower joint shaft.

1 LOWER JOINT
2 UPPER JOINT

2) Install steering column assembly to lower and upper brackets. Torque steering column nuts to specifications as given below:
   • Tighten nuts (a) to 14 N·m (10 lb.ft.)
   • Tighten nuts (b) to 14 N·m (10 lb.ft.).

A 14 N·m (10 lb.ft.)
B 14 N·m (10 lb.ft.)
1 LOWER BRACKET
2 STEERING COLUMN
3 UPPER BRACKET

3) Install bolt to steering shaft upper joint and tighten it to specified torque.

NOTICE: After tightening column nuts, steering shaft joint upper side bolt should be tightened.

1 STEERING SHAFT JOINT UPPER SIDE BOLT 25 N·m (18 ft.lb.)

4) Install steering joint cover and put floor mat back as it was originally.
5) Connect lead wires from ignition switch and ignition key warning switch at connector.
6) Install turn signal/dimmer switch. Refer to steps 1 through 4 under TURN SIGNAL/DIMMER SWITCH INSTALLATION.
7) Install steering wheel and steering pad. Refer to STEERING WHEEL INSTALLATION.

Fig. 19   Steering column installation. Metro

4. Install transaxle shift indicator cable end and casing and connect cable to transaxle shift lever.
5. Loosely install upper and lower steering column attaching bolts, then **torque** to 18 ft. lbs.
6. Install upper coupling pinch bolt into upper intermediate shaft coupling and **torque** to 35 ft. lbs.
7. Ensure clearance between lower shaft coupling and steering gear is at least .08 inch, then pull up intermediate shaft seal over lower column until it locks in place.
8. Install trim panel below steering column and the left hand sound insulator.
9. In stall steering wheel, if removed, then connect battery ground cable and confirm proper operation of all steering column components and functions.
10. Install air cleaner.

LEMANS
Removal

1. Disconnect battery ground cable.
2. Remove the turn signal/wiper switch lever as follows:
   a. Remove lower instrument cluster trim.
   b. Remove screws from upper cover panel by turning wheel 90° right or left for access.
   c. Remove the three screws from the lower panel. Pull handle from the lock release lever and unscrew tilt lever, if so equipped.

   d. Unclip switch from housing by pushing in on tab on either side of switch.
3. Disconnect wire harness and park lock actuation cable, if equipped.
4. Adjust steering to the straight ahead position, then remove pinch bolt from steering shaft flange.
5. Remove column jacket assembly lower mounting bolt from the instrument panel.
6. Remove shear plates below instrument panel as follows:
   a. Center punch the lefthand shear bolt, then drill a hole using a 1/8 inch drill bit.
   b. Install Drive No. 1411 bolt extractor or equivalent into hole and unscrew shear bolt.
   c. Remove shear plates.
7. Guide column assembly out of shaft flange and remove from vehicle.

Installation

1. Guide steering shaft into steering shaft flange and provide support for column until shear bolts are fastened.
2. Loosely mount shear plates on instrument panel, then install column jacket assembly lower mounting bolt to instrument panel and pinch bolt in steering shaft flange.
3. **Torque** column jacket assembly lower mounting bolt to 12 ft. lbs. and shear bolt and self locking nut to 16 ft. lbs.
4. Draw steering shaft upwards until the stop reaches the steering shaft ball

bearing and **torque** pinch bolt to 18 ft. lbs.
5. Slide alignment bushing out of column allowing bushing to remain on steering shaft.
6. Connect wiring harness and park lock actuation cable, if equipped.
7. Connect electrical connectors to turn signal/wiper switch, then clip switch back into housing.
8. Install cover panels, lock release lever and tilt lever, if equipped.
9. Install lower cluster trim, then connect battery ground cable.
10. Inspect steering for straight ahead position.

METRO
Models Less Supplemental Inflatable Restraint (SIR)

Refer to **Figs. 18 through 21** for removal and installation procedures.

Models w/Supplemental Inflatable Restraint (SIR)

Wheels must be in a straight forward position and the key must be in the LOCK position when removing or installing column to ensure proper alignment of components during installation.

Care must be taken when handling column with a live inflator module. Never point bag deploy surface toward you, and never stand column on steering wheel. Accidental deployment in these positions may cause injury. Always face bag deploy surface toward open space to allow for unrestricted expansion.
1. Disable airbag system as described under "Airbag System Disarming."

REMOVAL

1) Disconnect negative battery cable.
2) Pull steering pad off and disconnect ground wire from inside of steering pad.
3) Remove steering wheel damper attaching screws and then steering wheel damper.
4) Remove steering wheel nut.
5) Scribe a line on the steering wheel and shaft to use as guide during reinstallation.
6) Remove steering wheel with special tool (A).

INSTALLATION

1) Install steering wheel onto shaft, using the alignment marks.
2) Install steering shaft nut and torque to 33 N·m (24.0 lb.ft.) as shown below.
3) Install steering wheel damper and damper attaching screws.

NOTICE: When installing steering wheel damper, be sure ground wire runs through center of damper and is not pinched underneath it.

4) Connect ground wire to inside of steering pad and press steering pad on.
5) Connect negative battery cable.

A	STEERING WHEEL REMOVER J1859-03
1	SCRIBE ALIGNMENT LINE
2	STEERING WHEEL

1	STEERING SHAFT	4	STEERING WHEEL BUMPER
2	STEERING WHEEL	5	STEERING PAD
3	BUMPER SCREW	6	STEERING SHAFT NUT TIGHTENING TORQUE 33 N·m (24.0 lb. ft.)

NOTICE: The horn switch is incorporated into the steering pad and is not serviceable. If the horn switch is found to be faulty, the steering pad must be replaced.

Fig. 20 Steering wheel removal & installation. Metro

REMOVAL

1) Disconnect negative battery cable.
2) Before removing this switch, remove steering wheel. Refer to STEERING WHEEL REMOVAL.
3) Remove column covers (under and lower).

INSTALLATION

1) Install turn signal/dimmer switch and three attaching screws to the steering column shaft.
2) Connect lead wire to turn signal/dimmer switch electrical connector.
3) Tighten wire bands.
4) Install column lower and under covers.
5) Install steering wheel and steering pad. Refer to STEERING WHEEL INSTALLATION.

1	UPPER COVER
2	LOWER COVER
3	UNDER COVER

NOTE: MARKED WITH * ARE STANDARD SCREWS. ALL OTHERS ARE TAPPING SCREWS.

4) Disconnect lead wire from turn signal/dimmer switch electrical connector.
5) Loosen wire bands.
6) Remove three turn signal/dimmer switch attaching screws and the switch from the steering column shaft.

1	STEERING COLUMN SHAFT
2	TURN SIGNAL/DIMMER SWITCH

Fig. 21 Turn signal/dimmer switch removal & installation. Metro

1	STEERING WHEEL
2	TWO 1/4 X 2-INCH THROUGH BOLTS AND NUTS

Fig. 22 Steering wheel removal. Metro w/airbag

2. Disconnect battery ground cable.
3. Remove steering wheel as follows:
  a. Remove four screw from rear of steering wheel, then remove inflator module from steering wheel.
  b. Remove steering attaching nut.
  c. Attach wheel puller J 8433-1 and J 8433-3 or equivalent **Fig. 22**, then remove steering wheel.
4. Remove steering shaft trim panel.
5. Remove lower column steering trim panel attaching screws, then trim panel.
6. Remove lower column reinforcement plate attaching screws, then plate.
7. Disconnect steering column electrical connectors.
8. **On models with automatic transmissions**, remove transaxle shift interlock cable from ignition switch.
9. **On all models**, remove column to steering shaft joint pinch bolt, **Fig. 23**.
10. Remove two upper and lower column attaching bolts, then column.
11. Measure column as shown in **Fig. 24**. If measurement is less than 20.96 inches, replace column.
12. Reverse procedure to install noting the following:
  a. **Torque** upper and lower steering column attaching bolts to 124 inch lbs.
  b. **Torque** steering column to steering shaft pinch bolt to 18 ft. lbs.
  c. Rearm airbag system as described under "Airbag System Arming."

1991-92 PRIZM
Removal

1. Disconnect battery ground cable.
2. Remove left side lower instrument finish panel, upper and lower column covers.
3. Disconnect multi-function and ignition switch harnesses.
4. Disconnect park lock cable from lock cylinder housing.
5. Remove air intake filter assembly to gain access to column yoke and disconnect yoke from steering gear.
6. Remove lower column bolts, then upper column bolts and remove steering column.

Installation

1. Install steering column securing with upper and lower column bolts. **Torque** bolts to 19 ft. lbs.
2. Connect shaft yoke to steering gear and **torque** bolt to 26 ft. lbs.
3. Install air intake filter assembly and connect multi-function and ignition switch harnesses.
4. Connect park lock cable to lock cylinder housing, then install upper and lower column covers.

5. Install left side lower instrument finish panel, then connect battery ground cable.

1993 PRIZM
Removal

Wheels must be in straight ahead position and the key must be in the LOCK position when removing or installing the steering column. Failure to do so may cause the airbag coil assembly to become uncentered and may result in unnecessary airbag system repairs.

1. Disarm airbag system (SIR) as described under "Airbag System Disarming."
2. Remove steering wheel.
3. Unclip left front carpet retainer, then loosen two screws and disconnect hood release lever from knee bolster.
4. Remove two trim caps, then the four bolts securing knee bolster to the instrument panel.
5. Pull out instrument panel left-side ventilation duct.
6. Loosen five screws and remove upper and lower steering column trim covers.
7. Disconnect steering column electrical connectors.

A | 532.5 mm (20.96 INCHES)
1 | STEERING COLUMN

Fig. 24 Steering column measurement. Metro w/airbag

1 | STEERING COLUMN
2 | STEERING COLUMN UPPER TRIM COVER
3 | SIR COIL AND TURN SIGNAL/DIMMER SWITCH ASSEMBLY
4 | STEERING WHEEL
5 | INFLATOR MODULE
6 | STEERING COLUMN LOWER TRIM COVER
7 | LOWER STEERING COLUMN TRIM PANEL
8 | STEERING COLUMN REINFORCEMENT PLATE
9 | IGNITION SWITCH
10 | STEERING SHAFT JOINT

Fig. 23 Exploded view of steering column. Metro w/airbag

8. Remove steering column pinch bolt.
9. Remove two bolts, two nuts and remove the steering column from the instrument panel.
10. Reverse procedure to install, noting the following:
    a. **Torque** steering column mounting bolts to 19 ft. lbs.
    b. **Torque** steering column pinch bolt to 26 ft. lbs.
    c. **Torque** knee bolster bolts to 89 inch lbs.
    d. Enable airbag system (SIR) as described under "Airbag System Arming."

STORM

Removal

Wheels must be in a straight forward position and the key must be in the Lock position when removing or installing column to ensure proper alignment of components during installation.

Care must be taken when handling column with a live inflator module. Never point bag deploy surface toward you, and never stand column on steering wheel. Accidental deployment in these positions may cause injury. Always face bag deploy surface toward open space to allow for unrestricted expansion.

1. Disable airbag system as described under "Airbag System Disarming."
2. Remove the inflator module as follows:
   a. With the ignition switch in the Off position, disconnect battery ground cable..
   b. Remove left side sound insulator.
   c. Remove the Torx screws from the back of the steering wheel, then remove the inflator module from steering wheel.
   d. Remove the horn contact by pushing lightly and twisting counterclockwise.
   e. Disconnect the coil assembly connector from inflator module.
3. Remove steering wheel retaining nut and wheel from column using No. J 1859-03 or equivalent steering wheel puller.
4. Remove lower switch panel and dash lighter panel.
5. Disconnect hood release cable and remove lap air deflector.
6. Remove left lower dash trim panel and upper column mounting bolts, then allow column to drop down.
7. Remove the two piece column cover and disconnect necessary electrical connectors.
8. Disconnect backdrive cable from ignition switch, then remove pinch bolt from column knuckle.
9. Remove the two nuts from the lower column mount, then the column from vehicle.

Installation

1. Install column assembly into vehicle and secure with retaining nuts on lower column mount. **Torque** retaining nuts to 18 ft. lbs.
2. Connect intermediate shaft to column and install pinch bolt. **Torque** pinch bolt to 30 ft. lbs.
3. Connect backdrive cable to ignition switch and necessary electrical connectors.
4. Install two piece column cover and upper column bolts. **Torque** bolts to 18 ft. lbs.
5. Install lower dash trim panel and lap air deflector.
6. Connect hood release cable, install lighter panel and lower switch panel.
7. Install steering wheel and retaining nut onto column and **torque** retaining nut to 25 ft. lbs.
8. Install steering wheel inflator module as follows:
   a. With ignition off, install horn contact, then connect coil assembly connector to inflator module.
   b. Push coil assembly lead wires into channel in lower right portion of steering wheel, then install inflator module in steering wheel.
   c. **Torque** screws holding inflator module to steering wheel to 25 inch lbs.
   d. Install left side sound insulator.
   e. Connect battery ground cable.
   f. Rearm airbag system as described under "Airbag System Arming."

STEERING COLUMN SERVICE

1991 Cutlass Calais, Grand Am, Skylark & Sunbird

STANDARD COLUMN

Refer to **Figs. 25 through 34** when servicing these steering columns.

TILT COLUMN

Refer to **Figs. 35 through 44** when servicing these steering columns.

Fig. 25 Servicing lock plate and/or cancelling cam. 1991 Cutlass Calais, Grand Am, Skylark & Sunbird

Fig. 26 Servicing turn signal switch. 1991 Cutlass Calais, Grand Am, Skylark & Sunbird

Fig. 27 Servicing ignition lock & key warning buzzer. 1991 Cutlass Calais, Grand Am, Skylark & Sunbird

Fig. 29 Servicing ignition & dimmer switch. 1991 Cutlass Calais, Grand Am, Skylark & Sunbird

Fig. 30 Servicing lower steering shaft assembly. 1991 Cutlass Calais, Grand Am, Skylark & Sunbird

Fig. 28 Servicing housing & wiper switch. 1991 Cutlass Calais, Grand Am, Skylark & Sunbird

Fig. 31 Servicing steering shaft & shift tube. 1991 Cutlass Calais, Grand Am, Skylark & Sunbird

REMOVE

1. Remove parts as shown.

INSTALL

1. Install parts as shown.
2. Position rod in slider hole and install ignition switch. Install lower stud and tighten to 4.0 N·m.
3. Install dimmer switch and depress switch slightly to insert 3/32" drill. Force switch up to remove lash, then tighten screw, and nut to 4.0 N·m.
4. Place shifter in neutral and install shift lever.

17 - HOUSING
25 - SPRING
26 - RACK
27 - ROD. IGNITION
31 - BOWL
32 - SCREW
33 - ROD, DIMMER
34 - SWITCH ASM, DIMMER
35 - NUT
36 - JACKET ASM
43 - BUSHING
44 - RING
45 - SHAFT ASM
46 - HOUSING ASM, IGN SWITCH
47 - SCREW
48 - STUD
49 - STUD
50 - SWITCH ASM, IGNITION

MOVE SWITCH SLIDER TO EXTREME LEFT POSITION AND THEN MOVE SLIDER ONE DETENT TO THE RIGHT (OFF LOCK)

INSTALL IGNITION SWITCH

DIMMER SWITCH ACTUATOR ROD

DIMMER SWITCH

3/32" Drill

ADJUST DIMMER SWITCH

Fig. 33 Exploded view of standard steering column. 1991 Cutlass Calais, Grand Am, Skylark & Sunbird w/floor shift automatic transmission

REMOVE

1. Remove parts as shown.

INSTALL

1. Install parts as shown.
2. Position rod in slider hole and install ignition switch. Install lower stud and tighten to 4.0 N·m.
3. Install dimmer switch and depress switch slightly to insert 3/32" drill. Force switch up to remove lash, then tighten screw, and nut to 4.0 N·m.
4. Place shifter in neutral and install shift lever.

25 - SPRING
26 - RACK ASM
27 - GATE
28 - SCREW
41 - BOWL
42 - SCREW
43 - ARM ASM
48 - SHROUD
49 - BUSHING
50 - BEARING
51 - SEAL
52 - WASHER
53 - RING
54 - SHAFT ASM
56 - ROD, DIMMER
57 - SCREW
58 - SWITCH, DIMMER
59 - NUT
60 - STUD
61 - SWITCH, IGNITION
62 - SCREW
63 - BRACKET

1. REMOVE COLUMN
2. BREAK OFF GEARSHIFT BOWL
3. REPLACE SHIFT LEVER ARM
4. SLIP NEW SHROUD ONTO COLUMN FROM LOWER END AND SNAP IN PLACE

REPLACE SHIFT LEVER ARM ASM

MOVE SWITCH SLIDER TO EXTREME LEFT POSITION AND THEN MOVE SLIDER TWO DETENTS TO THE RIGHT (OFF LOCK)

INSTALL IGNITION SWITCH

DIMMER SWITCH ACTUATOR ROD

DIMMER SWITCH

3 32" Drill

ADJUST DIMMER SWITCH

Fig. 32 Exploded view of standard steering column. 1991 Cutlass Calais, Grand Am, Skylark & Sunbird w/column shift automatic transmission

REMOVE
1. Remove parts as shown.

INSTALL
1. Install parts as shown.
2. Position rod in slider hole and install ignition switch. Install lower stud and tighten to 4.0 N·m.
3. Install dimmer switch and depress switch slightly to insert 3/32" drill. Force switch up to remove lash, then tighten screw, and nut to 4.0 N·m.
4. Place shifter in neutral and install shift lever.

17 - HOUSING
24 - BOLT ASM
25 - SPRING
26 - RACK
27 - ROD, IGNITION
28 - WASHER
34 - STUD
35 - SCREW
36 - SWITCH ASM, IGNITION
37 - BOWL
38 - SHROUD
39 - SCREW
40 - ROD, DIMMER
41 - SWITCH ASM, DIMMER
42 - NUT
43 - JACKET ASM
44 - RING
45 - SHAFT ASM
48 - BUSHING

Fig. 34 Servicing standard column steering shaft, ignition & dimmer switch assembly. 1991 Cutlass Calais, Grand Am, Skylark & Sunbird w/floor shift manual transmission

1. REMOVE AND INSTALL SHAFT LOCK AND/OR CANCELLING CAM

REMOVE
1. Remove parts as shown.

INSTALL
1. Install parts as shown.

Fig. 35 Servicing shaft lock and/or cancelling cam. 1991 Cutlass Calais, Grand Am, Skylark & Sunbird w/tilt column

2. REMOVE AND INSTALL TURN SIGNAL SWITCH

REMOVE
1. Remove parts as shown.

INSTALL
1. Install parts as shown.

Fig. 36 Servicing turn signal switch. 1991 Cutlass Calais, Grand Am, Skylark & Sunbird w/tilt column

3. REMOVE AND INSTALL IGNITION LOCK AND KEY WARNING BUZZER

REMOVE
1. Turn lock to "RUN" position and remove key warning buzzer.
2. Remove parts as shown.

INSTALL
1. Install lock cylinder.
2. Turn lock to "RUN" position and install key warning buzzer switch.

Fig. 37 Servicing ignition lock & key warning buzzer. 1991 Cutlass Calais, Grand Am, Skylark & Sunbird w/tilt column

4. REMOVE AND INSTALL COVER AND WIPER SWITCH

REMOVE
1. Remove parts as shown.

INSTALL
1. Install parts as shown.

Fig. 38 Servicing cover & wiper switch. 1991 Cutlass Calais, Grand Am, Skylark & Sunbird w/tilt column

Fig. 39 Servicing housing. 1991 Cutlass Calais, Grand Am, Skylark & Sunbird w/tilt column

Fig. 40 Servicing lower steering shaft assembly. 1991 Cutlass Calais, Grand Am, Skylark & Sunbird w/tilt column

Fig. 41 Servicing shift tube, ignition & dimmer switch assemblies. 1991 Cutlass Calais, Grand Am, Skylark & Sunbird w/tilt column

Cavalier & 1992-93 Achieva, Grand Am & Skylark

STANDARD COLUMN

Refer to **Figs. 45 through 47** when servicing these steering columns.

STEERING COLUMN COVERS

1. Remove steering wheel as described in the "Electrical" section of the appropriate vehicle chapter in the front of this manual.
2. Remove cover screws, then the upper steering column cover.
3. Remove lower steering column cover screws, then the lower steering column cover.
4. Reverse procedure to install. **Torque** mounting screws to 49 inch lbs.

TURN SIGNAL SWITCH

1. Remove steering wheel as described in the "Electrical" section of the appropriate vehicle section in the front of this manual.
2. Remove turn signal switch mounting screws, then the turn signal switch.
3. Disconnect electrical connectors from switch.
4. Reverse procedure to install. **Torque** mounting screws to 49 inch lbs.

WASH/WIPE SWITCH

1. Remove steering wheel as described in the "Electrical" section of the appropriate vehicle section in the front of this manual.
2. Remove wash/wipe switch mounting screws, then the wash/wipe switch.

3. Disconnect electrical connectors from switch.
4. Reverse procedure to install. **Torque** mounting screws to 49 inch lbs.

IGNITION SWITCH

Removal

1. Remove steering wheel as described in the "Electrical" section of the appropriate vehicle section in the front of this manual.
2. Place shifter lever in Park position, then the ignition key in OFF-LOCK position and remove key.
3. Remove ignition switch mounting screws, then the ignition switch.
4. Disconnect electrical connectors from switch.

Installation

1. Connect electrical connectors to switch.

2. Ensure shifter lever in Park position and ignition key is in OFF-LOCK position with key removed.
3. Ensure tab on lock cylinder housing assembly aligns with slotted opening on ignition switch, then install ignition switch assembly to lock cylinder housing assembly with two screws. **Torque** mounting screws to 49 inch lbs.
4. Install steering wheel as described in the "Electrical" section of the appropriate vehicle section in the front of this manual.

INTERLOCK SOLENOID ASSEMBLY

Column Shift

1. Remove steering wheel as described in the "Electrical" section of the appropriate vehicle section in the front of this manual.

INSTALL

1. Install parts as shown.
2. Position rod in slider hole and install ignition switch. Install lower stud and tighten to 4.0 N·m.
3. Install dimmer switch and depress switch slightly to insert 3/32" drill. Force switch up to remove lash, then tighten screw, and nut to 4.0 N·m.
4. Place shifter in neutral and install shift lever.

REMOVE

1. Remove parts as shown.

Key No.	Part Name
34 -	ACTUATOR ASM, IGN SWITCH
53 -	SCREW
54 -	PIN
54 -	SUPPORT
55 -	PLATE, LOCK
56 -	SHROUD
57 -	JACKET ASM
58 -	ROD, DIMMER
59 -	SWITCH ASM, DIMMER
60 -	NUT
67 -	BUSHING
68 -	SCREW
69 -	STUD
70 -	SWITCH ASM, IGNITION
71 -	SCREW
72 -	HOUSING ASM

MOVE SWITCH SLIDER TO EXTREME RIGHT POSITION AND THEN MOVE SLIDER ONE DETENT TO THE LEFT (OFF LOCK)

INSTALL IGNITION SWITCH ASSEMBLY

ADJUST DIMMER SWITCH ASSEMBLY

Fig. 43 Servicing tilt column support, ignition & dimmer switch assemblies. 1991 Cutlass Calais, Grand Am, Skylark & Sunbird w/tilt column & floor shift automatic transmission

INSTALL

1. Install parts as shown.
2. Position rod in slider hole and install ignition switch. Install lower stud and tighten to 4.0 N·m.
3. Install dimmer switch and depress switch slightly to insert 3/32" drill. Force switch up to remove lash, then tighten screw, and nut to 4.0 N·m.
4. Place shifter in neutral and install shift lever.

REMOVE

1. REMOVE COLUMN.
2. BREAK OFF GEARSHIFT BOWL SHROUD.
3. REPLACE SHIFT LEVER ARM.
4. SLIP NEW SHROUD ONTO COLUMN FROM LOWER END AND SNAP IN PLACE.

REPLACE SHIFT LEVER ARM ASM

Key No.	Part Name
34 -	ACTUATOR ASM
53 -	SCREW
54 -	SUPPORT
55 -	PIN
56 -	GATE
57 -	BOWL
63 -	BOWL
64 -	SCREW
65 -	ARM ASM
66 -	SHROUD
70 -	JACKET ASM
71 -	BUSHING
72 -	BEARING
73 -	SEAL
74 -	WASHER
75 -	ROD, DIMMER
76 -	SCREW
77 -	SWITCH, DIMMER
78 -	NUT
79 -	STUD
80 -	SWITCH, IGNITION
81 -	SCREW
82 -	BRACKET

MOVE SWITCH SLIDER TO EXTREME RIGHT POSITION AND THEN MOVE SLIDER TWO DETENTS TO THE LEFT (OFF LOCK)

INSTALL IGNITION SWITCH ASSEMBLY

ADJUST DIMMER SWITCH ASSEMBLY

Fig. 42 Servicing tilt column support, ignition & dimmer switch assemblies. 1991 Cutlass Calais, Grand Am, Skylark & Sunbird w/tilt column & column shift automatic transmission

1 - SWITCH, WASH/WIPE
2 - SCREW, SWITCH
3 - COVER, STRG COL. UPPER
4 - NUT, HEXAGON
5 - RING, RETAINING
6 - CAM, ORIENTATION PLATE
7 - CAM ASM, TURN SIGNAL CANCELLING
8 - SPRING, UPPER STRG SHAFT
9 - WASHER, THRUST
10 - SCREW, HEX HD TAPPING
11 - RING, RETAINING
12 - BEARING ASM
13 - BOLT, SHEAR

15 - HOUSING, STEERING COLUMN
16 - JACKET ASM, STEERING COLUMN
17 - BUSHING ASM, STRG COL JACKET
18 - SWITCH, TURN SIGNAL
19 - LOCK CYL. ASM, IGN SWITCH &
20 - SWITCH ASM, IGNITION
21 - SCREW, IGN SWITCH
22 - SCREW, PAN HEAD 6-LOBED
23 - NUT, SPRING (U-TYPE)
24 - COVER, STRG COL, LOWER
25 - SHAFT ASM, STEERING COLUMN
26 - SCREW, PAN HEAD 6-LOBED

Fig. 45 Exploded view of standard steering column. Cavalier w/floor shift

---

REMOVE

1. Remove parts as shown.

INSTALL

1. Install parts as shown.
2. Position rod in slider hole and install ignition switch. Install lower stud and tighten to 4.0 N·m.
3. Install dimmer switch and depress switch slightly to insert 3/32" drill. Force switch up to remove lash, then tighten screw, and nut to 4.0 N·m.
4. Place shifter in neutral and install shift lever.

Key No.	Part Name
35 -	ACTUATOR ASM, IGNITION SWITCH
36 -	RACK
37 -	SPRING
48 -	SWITCH ASM, IGNITION
49 -	STUD
50 -	SCREW
51 -	PLATE
52 -	SCREW
53 -	PIN
59 -	SCREW
60 -	SUPPORT
61 -	PLATE, LOCK
62 -	FINGER PAD
63 -	LEVER
64 -	SPRING
65 -	SHROUD
66 -	ROD, DIMMER
67 -	SWITCH ASM, DIMMER
68 -	NUT
69 -	JACKET ASM
70 -	BUSHING

DIMMER SWITCH ASSEMBLY

DIMMER SWITCH ROD

3/32" Drill

ADJUST DIMMER SWITCH ASSEMBLY

MOVE SWITCH SLIDER TO EXTREME RIGHT POSITION

INSTALL IGNITION SWITCH

KEY RELEASE LEVER

KEY RELEASE SPRING

KEY RELEASE LEVER

Fig. 44 Servicing tilt column support, ignition & dimmer switch assemblies. 1991 Cutlass Calais, Grand Am, Skylark & Sunbird w/tilt column & floor shift manual transmission

Fig. 47 Exploded view of standard steering column. 1992-93 Skylark w/column shift

Key No.	Part Name
1 -	SWITCH, WASH/WIPE
2 -	SCREW, SWITCH
3 -	NUT, HEXAGON JAM (M14X1.5)
4 -	RING, RETAINING
5 -	CAM, ORIENTATION PLATE
6 -	CAM ASM, TURN SIGNAL CANCEL
7 -	SPRING, UPPER BEARING
8 -	WASHER, THRUST
9 -	SCREW, PAN HD TAPPING
10 -	RETAINER, BEARING
11 -	BEARING ASM
12 -	BOLT, SHEAR (M6X1.0) WITH WASHER
14 -	HOUSING ASM, BRG & STRG
15 -	SWITCH, TURN SIGNAL
16 -	HOUSING ASM, LOCK CYL A/TRNS
17 -	SWITCH ASM, IGNITION

Key No.	Part Name
18 -	SWITCH, IGN SWITCH
19 -	SOLENOID ASM, INTERLOCK
20 -	SCREW, SOLENOID
21 -	CABLE, PARK LOCK
22 -	SPACER, CLEVIS
23 -	CLEVIS ASM, STUD &
24 -	SCREW, SHOULDER TAPPING
25 -	RETAINER, SPRING
26 -	SPRING, SHIFT LEVER
27 -	SCREW, BUTTON HEAD
28 -	BUSHING, SHIFT PIVOT
29 -	GATE ASM, FLAT HEAD
30 -	GATE ASM, SHIFT LEVER
31 -	JACKET ASM, STEERING COLUMN
32 -	BUSHING ASM, STRG COL JACKET
33 -	SHAFT ASM, STEERING COLUMN

Fig. 46 Exploded view of standard steering column. 1992-93 Achieva & Grand Am w/floor shift

Key No.	Part Name
1 -	SWITCH, WASH/WIPE
2 -	SCREW, SWITCH
3 -	NUT, HEXAGON JAM (M14X1.5)
4 -	RING, RETAINING
5 -	CAM, ORIENTATION PLATE
6 -	CAM ASM, TURN SIGNAL CANCEL
7 -	SPRING, UPPER BEARING
8 -	WASHER, THRUST
9 -	SCREW, PAN HD TAPPING
10 -	RETAINER, BEARING
11 -	BEARING ASM

Key No.	Part Name
12 -	BOLT, SHEAR (M6X1.0) WITH WASHER
14 -	HOUSING ASM, BRG & STRG
15 -	SWITCH, TURN SIGNAL
16 -	HOUSING ASM, LOCK CYL A/TRNS
17 -	SWITCH ASM, IGNITION
18 -	SCREW, IGN SWITCH
21 -	CABLE, PARK LOCK
31 -	JACKET ASM, STEERING COLUMN
32 -	BUSHING ASM, STRG COL JACKET
33 -	SHAFT ASM, STEERING COLUMN

2. Place shifter lever in Park position, then the ignition key in OFF-LOCK position and remove key.
3. Disconnect wire connector from interlock solenoid assembly.
4. Remove interlock solenoid mounting screws, then the interlock solenoid assembly.
5. Reverse procedure to install. **Torque** mounting screws to 21 inch lbs.

LOCK CYLINDER HOUSING

1. Remove steering wheel as described in the "Electrical" section of the appropriate vehicle section in the front of this manual.
2. Remove steering column from vehicle as described under "Steering Column, Replace."
3. Place key in RUN position and shift lever in PARK.
4. Drill off heads of two shear bolts using a ¼ inch drill bit.
5. Remove lock cylinder housing assembly, then the threaded ends of shear bolts from lock cylinder housing assembly.
6. Reverse procedure to install. Install lock cylinder housing with two shear bolts and tighten bolts until heads break off, approximately 97 inch lbs.

PARK LOCK CABLE
Removal

1. Remove steering wheel as described in the "Electrical" section of the appropriate vehicle section in the front of this manual.
2. Place key in RUN position, then disconnect park lock cable from lock cylinder housing assembly.
3. **On models with column shift,** disconnect park lock cable from shift gate assembly.

Installation

1. Place key in RUN position and shift lever in PARK position.
2. Snap connector body of cable assembly to lock cylinder, ensuring locking tab is fully engaged into lock cylinder housing.
3. **On models with column shift,** place key in OFF-LOCK position and pull key half way out of lock cylinder housing.
4. Route cable end fitting through park lock latch, then depress adjuster button and snap cable adjuster assembly to shift gate assembly.
5. Snap cable into cable retainer, then depress adjuster button and pull cable sheathing towards lock cylinder to remove lash from system.
6. Release sheathing, then release button.

SHIFT LEVER GATE & CLEVIS ASSEMBLY
Column Shift

1. Remove steering wheel as described in the "Electrical" section of the appropriate vehicle section in the front of this manual.

2. Remove shift lever, then the shift cable from shift cable ball stud.
3. Remove shoulder tapping screw, button head screw, shift pivot bushing and stud and clevis assembly.
4. Remove clevis spacer, shift lever spring, spring retainer, two flat head screws and shift lever gate assembly.
5. Reverse procedure to install, noting the following:
   a. **Torque** flat head screws to 14 ft. lbs, button head screw to 15 ft. lbs and shoulder tapping screw to 119 inch lbs.
   b. Lubricate clevis spacer.

STEERING COLUMN JACKET BUSHING ASSEMBLY, ORIENTATION PLATE CAM, TURN SIGNAL CANCEL CAM ASSEMBLY, UPPER BEARING SPRING, BEARING ASSEMBLY, STEERING COLUMN SHAFT ASSEMBLY, STEERING COLUMN HOUSING ASSEMBLY & STEERING COLUMN JACKET ASSEMBLY

Disassembly

1. Remove steering wheel as described in the "Electrical" section of the appropriate vehicle section in the front of this manual.
2. Remove turn signal switch mounting screws and turn signal switch, letting switch hang freely.
3. Remove wash/wipe switch mounting screws and wash/wipe switch, letting switch hang freely.
4. Remove retaining ring using lock plate adapter J 23653-91 and lock plate compressor J 23653-C or their equivalents to compress orientation plate cam and upper bearing spring. Discard retaining ring.
5. Remove orientation plate cam, turn signal cancel cam assembly, upper bearing spring, thrust washer, bearing retainer and bearing assembly. Discard bearing retainer retaining ring.
6. Remove steering column from vehicle as described under "Steering Column, Replace."
7. Inspect steering column for damage.
8. Remove steering column jacket bushing assembly, then the steering column shaft assembly from lower end of steering column jacket assembly.
9. Remove retaining ring from shaft assembly and discard, then the four pan head tapping screws.
10. Disconnect park lock cable from lock cylinder housing assembly.
11. **On models with column shift,** disconnect park lock cable from shift gate assembly.
12. **On all models,** remove bearing and steering housing assembly from steering column jacket assembly.

Assembly

Ensure all fasteners are securely seated before applying torque. Failure to do so may result in component damage or malfunctioning of steering column.

1. Assemble bearing and steering housing assembly to steering column jacket assembly using four pan head tapping screws. **Torque** screws to 47 inch lbs.
2. Install new retaining ring to lower groove of steering shaft assembly, ensuring ring is firmly seated in groove.
3. Install steering column shaft assembly into lower end of steering column jacket assembly until bottomed.
4. Place key in OFF-LOCK position, remove key, rotate shaft until lock bolt engages and locks shaft in position, then insert key.
5. Install steering column jacket bushing assembly and snap into position.
6. Install bearing assembly, then lubricate.
7. Install bearing retainer, thrust washer, upper bearing spring and turn signal cancel cam assembly. Lubricate turn signal cancel cam assembly with synthetic grease.
8. Install orientation plate cam, then a new retaining ring using lock plate adapter and lock plate compressor to compress orientation plate cam and upper bearing spring. Ensure retaining ring is firmly seated in groove.
9. Install turn signal switch, wash/wipe switch and park lock cable as previously described.
10. Install steering wheel as described in the "Electrical" section of the appropriate vehicle section in the front of this manual.
11. Install steering column as described under "Steering Column, Replace."

TILT COLUMN

Refer to **Figs. 48 through 50** when servicing these steering columns.

STEERING COLUMN COVERS

Refer to "Standard Columns" for procedure.

TURN SIGNAL SWITCH

Refer to "Standard Columns" for procedure.

WASH/WIPE SWITCH

Refer to "Standard Columns" for procedure.

IGNITION SWITCH

Refer to "Standard Columns" for procedure.

INTERLOCK SOLENOID ASSEMBLY
Column Shift

Refer to "Standard Columns" for procedure.

LOCK CYLINDER HOUSING

Refer to "Standard Columns" for procedure.

PARK LOCK CABLE

Refer to "Standard Columns" for procedure.

Fig. 49 Exploded view of tilt steering column. 1992-93 Achieva & Grand Am w/floor shift

Key No.	Part Name
1 - SWITCH, WASH/WIPE
2 - SCREW, SWITCH
3 - NUT, HEXAGON JAM (M14X1.5)
4 - RING, RETAINING
5 - CAM, ORIENTATION PLATE
6 - CAM ASM, TURN SIGNAL CANCEL
7 - SPRING, UPPER BEARING
8 - SEAT, INNER RACE
9 - RACE, INNER
10 - RETAINER, SPRING
11 - SPRING, WHEEL TILT
12 - BOLT, SHEAR (M6X1.0)
13 - PIN, PIVOT
14 - HOUSING ASM, BRG & STRG
15 - SWITCH, TURN SIGNAL

Key No.	Part Name
16 - HOUSING ASM, LOCK CYL A/TRNS
17 - SWITCH ASM, IGNITION
18 - SCREW, IGN SWITCH
21 - CABLE, PARK LOCK
31 - SUPPORT, WIRE
32 - SCREW, WIRE SUPPORT
33 - SHAFT ASM, STEERING
34 - SHAFT ASM, RACE & UPPER
35 - SPHERE, CENTERING
36 - SPRING, JOINT PRELOAD
37 - SHAFT ASM, LOWER STEERING
38 - SCREW, PAN HD TAPPING
39 - BUMPER, TILT
40 - SUPPORT, STRG COLUMN HOUSING
41 - JACKET ASM, STEERING COLUMN
42 - BUSHING ASM, STRG COL JACKET

Fig. 48 Exploded view of tilt steering column. Cavalier w/floor shift

Key No.	Part Name
1 - SWITCH, WASH/WIPE
2 - SCREW, SWITCH
3 - COVER, STRG COL, UPPER
4 - NUT, HEXAGON
5 - RING, RETAINING
6 - CAM, ORIENTATION PLATE
7 - CAM ASM, TURN SIGNAL CANCELLING
8 - SPRING, UPPER BEARING
9 - SEAT, INNER RACE
10 - RACE, INNER
11 - BOLT, SHEAR
13 - HOUSING ASM, STEERING COLUMN
14 - PIN, PIVOT
15 - LOCK CYL ASM, IGN SWITCH &
16 - SWITCH ASM, IGNITION
17 - SCREW, IGN SWITCH
18 - SCREW, WIRE SUPPORT
19 - SUPPORT, WIRE

Key No.	Part Name
19 - SUPPORT, WIRE
20 - LEVER, TILT
21 - SPRING, WHEEL TILT
22 - RETAINER, SPRING
23 - SWITCH, TURN SIGNAL
24 - SCREW, PAN HEAD 6-LOBED
25 - NUT, SPRING (U-TYPE)
26 - COVER, STRG COL, LOWER
27 - SCREW, PAN HEAD 6-LOBED
28 - SHAFT ASM, LOWER STEERING
29 - SPHERE, CENTERING
30 - SPRING, JOINT PRELOAD
31 - SHAFT ASM, RACE & UPPER
32 - SHAFT ASM, STEERING
33 - SCREW, HEX HD TAPPING
34 - BUMPER, TILT
35 - SUPPORT, STRG COLUMN HOUSING
36 - JACKET ASM, STEERING COLUMN
37 - BUSHING ASM, STRG COL JACKET

SHIFT LEVER GATE & CLEVIS ASSEMBLY

Column Shift

Refer to "Standard Columns" for procedure.

STEERING COLUMN JACKET BUSHING ASSEMBLY, ORIENTATION PLATE CAM, TURN SIGNAL CANCEL CAM ASSEMBLY, UPPER BEARING SPRING, BEARING ASSEMBLY, STEERING COLUMN SHAFT ASSEMBLY, STEERING COLUMN HOUSING ASSEMBLY & STEERING COLUMN JACKET ASSEMBLY

Disassembly

1. Remove steering wheel as described in the "Electrical" section of the appropriate vehicle section in the front of this manual.
2. Remove turn signal switch mounting screws and turn signal switch, letting switch hang freely.
3. Remove wash/wipe switch mounting screws and wash/wipe switch, letting switch hang freely.
4. Remove retaining ring using lock plate adapter J 23653-91 and lock plate compressor J 23653-C or their equivalents to compress orientation plate cam and upper bearing spring. Discard retaining ring.
5. Remove orientation plate cam, turn signal cancel cam assembly, upper bearing spring, inner race seat, and inner race.
6. Pull tilt lever bracket on column housing assembly and tilt column all the way up.
7. Remove steering column from vehicle as described under "Steering Column, Replace."
8. Inspect steering column for damage.
9. Remove steering column jacket bushing from lower end of jacket assembly, then insert a Phillips head screwdriver into square opening in spring retainer, push down and turn counterclockwise to release retainer and wheel tilt spring.
10. Remove spring retainer and tilt spring, then the two pivot pins using pivot pin remover J 21854-01 or equivalent.
11. Place lock cylinder in RUN position, then pull tilt lever to release column housing and remove column housing from housing support.
12. Remove wire support screw and wire support, then the steering shaft assembly from housing support.
13. Remove tilt bumpers from housing support with pliers, then the pan head screws and housing support from jacket assembly.
14. If necessary, service steering shaft assembly as follows:
    a. **Before separating upper and lower shafts, note relationship of upper shaft with alignment mark in threaded end at 12 o'clock position and lower shaft pinch bolt groove at 9 o'clock**

Key No.	Part Name
1	SWITCH, WASH/WIPE
2	SCREW, SWITCH
3	NUT, HEXAGON JAM (M14X1.5)
4	RING, RETAINING
5	CAM, ORIENTATION PLATE
6	CAM ASM; TURN SIGNAL CANCEL
7	SPRING, UPPER BEARING
8	SEAT, INNER RACE
9	RACE, INNER
10	RETAINER, SPRING
11	SPRING, WHEEL TILT
12	BOLT, SHEAR (M6X1.0)
13	PIN, PIVOT
14	HOUSING ASM, BRG & STRG
15	SWITCH, TURN SIGNAL
16	HOUSING ASM, LOCK CYL A/TRNS
17	SWITCH ASM, IGNITION
18	SCREW, IGN SWITCH
19	SOLENOID ASM, INTERLOCK
20	SCREW, SOLENOID
21	CABLE, PARK LOCK
22	SPACER, CLEVIS
23	CLEVIS ASM, STUD &
24	SCREW, SHOULDER TAPPING
25	RETAINER, SPRING
26	SPRING, SHIFT LEVER
27	SCREW, BUTTON HEAD
28	BUSHING, SHIFT PIVOT
29	SCREW, FLAT HEAD
30	GATE ASM, SHIFT LEVER
31	SUPPORT, WIRE
32	SCREW, WIRE SUPPORT
33	SHAFT ASM, STEERING
34	SHAFT ASM, RACE & UPPER
35	SPHERE, CENTERING
36	SPRING, JOINT PRELOAD
37	SHAFT ASM, LOWER STEERING
38	SCREW, PAN HD TAPPING
39	BUMPER, TILT
40	SUPPORT, STRG COLUMN HOUSING
41	JACKET ASM, STEERING COLUMN
42	BUSHING ASM, STRG COL JACKET

Fig. 50   Exploded view of tilt steering column. 1992-93 Skylark w/column shift

position. Refer to this alignment for proper reassembly.
    b. Position upper shaft 90° to lower shaft and separate, **Fig. 51**.
    c. Rotate centering sphere 90° and remove from upper shaft.
    d. Separate sphere halves and joint preload spring.

Assembly

Ensure all fasteners are securely seated before applying torque. Failure to do so may result in component damage or malfunctioning of steering column.

1. If necessary, assemble steering shaft as follows:

    a. Lubricate centering sphere halves and joint preload spring with lithium grease, then assemble spring between sphere halves with ends of spring in notches.
    b. Lubricate sphere end of upper shaft with lithium grease, then assemble sphere into upper shaft and rotate sphere 90°.
    c. Lubricate sphere end of lower shaft with lithium grease.
    d. Place alignment notch on threaded end of upper shaft at 12 o'clock, **Fig. 52**. Pinch bolt groove near end of lower shaft must be at 9 o'clock position.
    e. Position upper shaft 90° to lower

34-SHAFT ASM, RACE & UPPER
35-SPHERE, CENTERING
36-SPRING, JOINT PRELOAD
37-SHAFT ASM, LOWER STEERING

Fig. 51 Steering shaft & centering sphere alignment. 1991 Cutlass Calais, Grand Am, Skylark & Sunbird w/tilt column

shaft, then engage and straighten, **Fig. 51.**
2. Assemble housing support to jacket assembly with support screws. **Torque** screws to 12 ft. lbs.
3. Install tilt bumpers to housing support and snap into place.
4. Install steering shaft assembly into support housing.
5. Lubricate both bearings in column housing with lithium grease, then assemble column housing onto shaft assembly and column support.
6. Lubricate pivot pins with lithium grease, then install pivot pins until bottomed in housing. **Stake pivot pins to housing in three equally spaced locations. If there is no surface suitable for restaking, housing must be replaced.**
7. Pull tilt lever bracket on column housing assembly and tilt column all the way up.
8. Lubricate tilt spring with lithium grease, then install tilt spring with spring retainer. Ensure spring engages locating tab on support housing. Insert Phillips head screwdriver into square opening in spring retainer, push down and turn clockwise to lock in place.
9. Install wire support with wire support screw. **Torque** screw to 53 inch lbs.
10. Place key in OFF-LOCK position, remove key, rotate shaft until lock bolt engages and locks shaft in position.
11. Install inner race and inner race seat.
12. Install upper bearing spring and turn signal cancel cam assembly.
13. Install orientation plate cam, then a new retaining ring using lock plate adapter and lock plate compressor to compress orientation plate cam and upper bearing spring. Ensure retaining ring is firmly seated in groove.

14. Install turn signal switch, wash/wipe switch and park lock cable as previously described.
15. Install steering wheel as described in the "Electrical" section of the appropriate vehicle section in the front of this manual.

1992–93 Sunbird
STANDARD COLUMN

Refer to **Fig. 53** when servicing these steering columns.

SHAFT LOCK, TURN SIGNAL CANCEL CAM ASSEMBLY, UPPER BEARING SPRING, THRUST WASHER, BUZZER SWITCH ASSEMBLY, STEERING COLUMN LOCK CYLINDER SET
Disassembly

1. Remove steering wheel as described in the "Electrical" section of the appropriate vehicle section in the front of this manual.
2. Disconnect battery ground cable.
3. Remove shaft lock cover, then the shaft lock retaining ring using plate compressor J 23653-C or equivalent to depress shaft lock. Discard ring.
4. Remove shaft lock, turn signal cancelling cam assembly, upper bearing spring and thrust washer.
5. Move turn signal to the "right turn" position.
6. Remove multi-function lever and hazard knob assembly.
7. Remove screw and signal switch arm, then the turn signal switch screws.
8. Remove turn signal switch assembly and allow switch to hang freely.
9. Remove key from lock cylinder set, then the buzzer switch assembly.
10. Reinstall key in lock cylinder and turn to LOCK position.
11. Remove retaining screw, then the lock cylinder set.

Assembly

Ensure all fasteners are securely seated before applying torque. Failure to do so may result in component damage or malfunctioning of steering column.

34-SHAFT ASM, RACE & UPPER
37-SHAFT ASM, LOWER STEERING

Fig. 52 Upper shaft to lower shaft alignment. 1991 Cutlass Calais, Grand Am, Skylark & Sunbird w/tilt column

1. Install lock cylinder set and retaining screw. **Torque** screw to 40 inch lbs.
2. Remove key from lock cylinder set, then install buzzer switch assembly.
3. Re-install key in lock cylinder set, then turn key to LOCK position.
4. Install turn signal switch assembly and screws. **Torque** screws to 30 inch lbs.
5. Install signal switch arm and screw. **Torque** screw to 20 inch lbs.
6. Install hazard knob assembly and multi-function lever.
7. Install thrust washer, upper bearing spring and turn signal cancelling cam assembly. Lubricate cancelling cam with synthetic grease.
8. Install shaft lock and shaft lock retaining ring using plate compressor J 23653-C to depress shaft lock. Ring must be fully seated in groove.
9. Install shaft lock cover, then connect battery ground cable.
10. Install steering wheel as described in the "Electrical" section of the appropriate vehicle section in the front of this manual.

STEERING SHAFT ASSEMBLY, TURN SIGNAL SWITCH ASSEMBLY, STEERING COLUMN HOUSING ASSEMBLY, SWITCH ACTUATOR PIVOT ASSEMBLY, SPRING & BOLT ASSEMBLY, BEARING ASSEMBLY, SWITCH ACTUATOR SECTOR & IGNITION SWITCH ACTUATOR ASSEMBLY
Disassembly

1. Remove steering wheel as described in the "Electrical" section of the appropriate vehicle section in the front of this manual.
2. Disconnect battery ground cable.
3. Remove steering column from vehicle as described under "Steering Column, Replace."
4. Inspect steering column for damage.
5. Perform all disassembly steps from "Shaft Lock, Turn Signal Cancelling Cam Assembly, Upper Bearing Spring, Thrust Washer, Buzzer Switch Assembly & Steering Column Lock Cylinder Set" as previously described.

Service Kits

201-HSG ASM SERV SET, STRG COL
  -INCLUDES: 16,17,23,24,25
202-GREASE SERV KIT, (SYNTHETIC)
203-RACK SERV ASM, SW AC ROD &
  -INCLUDES: 20,21
204-ROD SERVICE KIT, DIMMER SWITCH
  -INCLUDES 47
205-SECTOR SERV KIT, IGN SW ACTR
  -INCLUDES 17

1-NUT, HEXAGON LOCKING (M14x1.5)
2-COVER, SHAFT LOCK
3-RING, RETAINING
4-LOCK, STEERING SHAFT
5-CAM ASM, TURN SIG CANCELLING
6-SPRING, UPPER BEARING
7-SCREW, BIND HD CROSS RECESS
8-SCREW, RD WASH HD (M4.2x1.41)
9-ARM, ACTUATOR SWITCH
10-SWITCH ASM, TURN SIGNAL
11-SCREW, HEX WASHER HD TAP
12-WASHER, THRUST
13-SWITCH ASM, BUZZER
15-SCREW, LOCK RETAINING
16-HOUSING ASM, STRG COL
17-SECTOR, SWITCH ACTUATOR
18-LOCK CYLINDER SET, STRG COL
19-SPRING, RACK PRELOAD
20-RACK, SWITCH ACTUATOR
21-ROD, SWITCH ACTUATOR
22-WASHER, SPRING THRUST
23-RETAINER, UPPER BEARING
24-BUSHING, BEARING RETAINING
25-BEARING ASM
26-BOLT ASM, SPRING &
27-WASHER, WAVE
28-LEVER, KEY RELEASE
29-PIN, SWITCH ACTUATOR PIVOT
30-PIVOT ASM, SWITCH ACTUATOR
31-SPRING, KEY RELEASE
33-PROTECTOR, WIRING
34-RING, RETAINING
35-SHAFT ASM, STEERING
37-BOWL, FLOOR SHIFT LEVER
38-SCREW, BIND HD C/REC
39-SHROUD, SHIFT BOWL
40-JACKET ASM, STRG COL
41-STUD, DIMR & IGN SW MOUNTING
42-SWITCH ASM, DIMMER
43-SWITCH ASM, IGNITION
44-NUT, HEX (#10-24)
45-SCREW, WASH HD (#10-24 x .25)
47-ROD, DIMMER SWITCH ACTUATOR
49-BOLT, FLANGED HEX HD
50-BRACKET ASM, STRG COL SUPT
51-BUSHING, STRG COL JACKET

Fig. 53 Exploded view of standard steering column (Part 2 of 2). 1992-93 Sunbird

Fig. 53 Exploded view of standard steering column (Part 1 of 2). 1992-93 Sunbird

6. Remove steering shaft assembly, then the retaining ring from shaft.
7. Inspect column shaft assembly for damage.
8. Remove four support bolts, then the steering column support bracket assembly.
9. Remove wiring protector, turn signal switch assembly, washer head screw and hex nut.
10. Remove dimmer switch, dimmer switch rod and switch mounting stud.
11. Remove ignition switch, two cross recess screws and ignition switch inhibitor housing assembly.
12. Remove cover screws and lock housing cover assembly with floor shift lever bowl and shift bowl shroud. Pull housing cover from jacket and remove upper bearing retainer.
13. Remove three cross recess screws, floor shift lever bowl with shift bowl shroud, then the shroud from bowl.
14. If necessary, disassemble steering column housing as follows:
    a. Remove switch actuator rack with spring and bolt assembly, then the spring and bolt assembly from switch actuator rack.
    b. Remove switch actuator rod from rack, then the spring thrust washer from spring and bolt assembly.
    c. Remove switch actuator sector, rack preload spring, switch actuator pivot pin and switch actuator pivot assembly.
    d. Remove bearing retaining bushing using a punch, then the bearing assembly using a punch.

Assembly

Ensure all fasteners are securely seated before applying torque. Failure to do so may result in component damage or malfunctioning of steering column.

Use bearing retainer bushing to aid in seating bearing assembly into housing assembly. Tab on bushing must be fully seated into slot in housing assembly.

1. If necessary, assemble steering column housing as follows:
    a. Install bearing assembly, bearing retaining bushing, switch actuator pivot assembly and switch actuator pivot pin. **Torque** pin to 27 inch lbs.
    b. Install rack preload spring and switch actuator sector.
    c. Assemble spring thrust washer to bolt assembly, switch actuator rod to switch actuator rack, then the spring and bolt assembly to switch actuator rack.
    d. Assemble spring and bolt assembly with switch actuator rack to housing assembly. **First tooth of rack must interact with first and second tooth of sector. With rack fully inserted, block tooth of sector will rest in block tooth of rack.**
2. Assemble retaining ring to shaft assembly, then the shaft assembly to jacket assembly. Lubricate with lithium grease.

3. Assemble shift bowl shroud to floor shift lever bowl, then the bowl with shroud to steering column housing assembly.
4. Install three cross recess screws, then **torque** to 17 inch lbs.
5. Install turn signal switch connector through column housing assembly, then the upper bearing retainer.
6. Assemble lock housing cover assembly with bowl and shroud to jacket assembly.
7. Install cover screws and tighten in a clockwise order finger tight, then **torque** screws in same order to 47 inch lbs.
8. Adjust ignition switch assembly by moving switch slider to extreme left position, then one detent to right, OFF-LOCK position. **New ignition switch will be pinned in OFF-LOCK position, remove plastic pin after switch is installed on column.**
9. Install ignition switch and mounting stud to jacket, then **torque** stud to 35 inch lbs.
10. Install dimmer switch rod, assemble dimmer switch assembly to rod, then install washer head screw and hex nut finger tight.
11. Adjust dimmer switch by placing a 3/32 inch drill bit in hole on switch to limit travel, position switch on column and push against dimmer switch rod to remove all lash, then remove drill bit. **Torque** screw and nut to 35 inch lbs.
12. Install wiring protector, steering column support bracket assembly, then the four mounting bolts. **Torque** bolts to 22 ft. lbs.
13. Perform all assembly steps from "Shaft Lock, Turn Signal Cancelling Cam Assembly, Upper Bearing Spring, Thrust Washer, Buzzer Switch Assembly & Steering Column Lock Cylinder Set" as previously described.

TILT COLUMN

Refer to **Fig. 54** when servicing these steering columns.

SHAFT LOCK, TURN SIGNAL CANCEL CAM ASSEMBLY, UPPER BEARING SPRING, UPPER BEARING INNER RACE SEAT, INNER RACE, BUZZER SWITCH ASSEMBLY, STEERING COLUMN LOCK CYLINDER SET

Disassembly

1. Remove steering wheel as described in the "Electrical" section of the appropriate vehicle section in the front of this manual.
2. Disconnect battery ground cable.
3. Remove shaft lock cover, then the shaft lock retaining ring using plate compressor J 23653-C or equivalent to depress shaft lock. Discard ring.
4. Remove shaft lock, turn signal cancelling cam assembly, upper bearing spring, upper bearing inner race seat and inner race.
5. Move turn signal to the right turn position.

6. Remove multi-function lever and hazard knob assembly.
7. Remove screw and signal switch arm, then the turn signal switch screws.
8. Remove turn signal switch assembly and allow switch to hang freely.
9. Remove key from lock cylinder set, then the buzzer switch assembly.
10. Reinstall key in lock cylinder and turn to LOCK position.
11. Remove lock retaining screw, then the lock cylinder.

Assembly

Ensure all fasteners are securely seated before applying torque. Failure to do so may result in component damage or malfunctioning of steering column.

1. Install lock cylinder and lock retaining screw. **Torque** screw to 22 inch lbs.
2. Remove key from lock cylinder set, then install buzzer switch assembly.
3. Re-install key in lock cylinder set, then turn key to LOCK position.
4. Install turn signal switch assembly and screws. **Torque** screws to 30 inch lbs.
5. Install signal switch arm and screw. **Torque** screw to 20 inch lbs.
6. Install hazard knob assembly and multi-function lever.
7. Install inner race, upper bearing inner race seat, upper bearing spring and turn signal cancelling cam assembly. Lubricate cancelling cam with synthetic grease.
8. Install shaft lock and shaft lock retaining ring using plate compressor J 23653-C to depress shaft lock. Ring must be fully seated in groove.
9. Install shaft lock cover, then connect battery ground cable.
10. Install steering wheel as described in the "Electrical" section of the appropriate vehicle section in the front of this manual.

LOCK HOUSING COVER ASSEMBLY, COLUMN HOUSING COVER END CAP, PIVOT & PULSE SWITCH ASSEMBLY, DIMMER SWITCH ROD ACTUATOR & TILT SPRING ASSEMBLY

Disassembly

1. Remove steering wheel as described in the "Electrical" section of the appropriate vehicle section in the front of this manual.
2. Disconnect battery ground cable.
3. Perform all disassembly steps from "Shaft Lock, Turn Signal Cancelling Cam Assembly, Upper Bearing Spring, Upper Bearing Inner Race Seat, Inner Race, Buzzer Switch Assembly & Steering Column Lock Cylinder Set" as previously described.
4. Remove tilt lever, cover screws and lock housing cover assembly. Let cover hang freely.
5. Remove column housing cover end cap with dimmer switch rod actuator, then the actuator from end cap.

1-NUT, HEX LOCKING (M14x1.5)
2-COVER, SHAFT LOCK
5-RING, RETAINING
6-LOCK, SHAFT
7-CAM ASM, TURN SIG CANCEL
8-SPRING, UPPER BEARING
9-SCREW, BNDG HD CR RECESS
10-SCREW, RD WASH HD (M4.2x1.41)
11-ARM, SIGNAL SWITCH
12-SWITCH ASM, TURN SIGNAL
13-SEAT, UPPER BRG INNER RACE
14-RACE, INNER
15-SCREW, PAN HD SOC TAP
16-SWITCH ASM, BUZZER
18-SCREW, LOCK RETAINING
19-COVER ASM, LOCK HOUSING
20-LOCK CYLINDER SET, STRG COL
21-ACTUATOR, DIMMER SW ROD
22-PIN, SWITCH ACTUATOR PIVOT
23-SWITCH ASM, PIVOT & (PULSE)
25-CAP, COL HSG COVER END
26-PROTECTOR, WIRING
27-PROTECTOR, WIRING (CRUISE)
30-HOUSING ASM, STRG COLUMN
31-BEARING ASM
32-BOLT, LOCK
33-SPRING, LOCK BOLT
34-SHOE, STEERING WHEEL LOCK
35-SHOE, STEERING WHEEL LOCK
37-SHAFT, DRIVE
38-PIN, DOWEL
39-PIN, PIVOT
40-SPRING, SHOE
41-SPRING, RELEASE LEVER
42-PIN, RELEASE LEVER
43-LEVER, SHOE RELEASE
44-RACK, SWITCH ACTUATOR
45-SPRING, RACK PRELOAD
46-HOUSING, STRG COLUMN
47-SECTOR, SWITCH ACTUATOR
48-SCREW, HEX WASHER HEAD
50-GUIDE, SPRING
51-SPRING, WHEEL TILT
52-RETAINER, SPRING
55-SHAFT ASM, STEERING
56-SHAFT ASM, RACE & UPPER
57-SPHERE, CENTERING

58-SPRING, JOINT PRELOAD
59-SHAFT ASM, LOWER STEERING
61-SCREW, SUPPORT
62-SUPPORT ASM, STRG COL HSG
63-PLATE, LOCK
71-SHROUD, STRG COL HOUSING
72-JACKET ASM, STRG COL
76-ACTUATOR ASM, IGN SWITCH
77-ROD, DIMMER SWITCH
78-SCREW, WASH HD (#10-24x.25)
79-NUT, HEXAGON (#10-24)
80-SWITCH ASM, IGNITION
81-STUD, DIMR & IGN SW MTG
82-SWITCH ASM, DIMMER
83-HOUSING ASM, IGN SW INHIBITOR
84-SCREW, PAN HD C/REC (4-24 x .25)
85-BOLT, FLDG HEX HD (M8 x 1.25)
86-BRACKET ASM, STRG COL SUPT
87-BUSHING, STRG COL JACKET

Service Kits

201-RACK SERV KIT, COL SECTOR &
  -INCLUDES: 14,31,33,44,47,48
202-SPRING SERV KIT, TILT COLUMN
  -INCLUDES: 13,14,39,50,51,52
203-SPHERE SERV KIT, TILT COLUMN
  -INCLUDES: 57,58
204-GREASE SERV KIT, (SYNTHETIC)
205-COVER SERV ASM, LOCK HOUSING
  -INCLUDES: 19

Fig. 54   Exploded view of tilt steering column (Part 2 of 2). 1992-93 Sunbird

Fig. 54   Exploded view of tilt steering column (Part 1 of 2). 1992-93 Sunbird

6. Remove switch actuator pivot pin, then the pivot and pulse switch assembly.
7. Remove spring retainer using a cross recess head screwdriver to push retainer down and turn clockwise to release.
8. Remove spring and spring guide.

Assembly

Ensure all fasteners are securely seated before applying torque. Failure to do so may result in component damage or malfunctioning of steering column.

1. Install spring guide and spring. Lubricate with lithium grease.
2. Install spring retainer using a cross recess head screwdriver to push retainer down and turn clockwise to lock in place.
3. Install pivot and pulse switch assembly to lock housing cover assembly, then the switch actuator pivot pin to switch and cover.
4. Install dimmer switch rod actuator to column housing cover end cap. Lubricate with lithium grease.
5. Install end cap with actuator to lock housing cover assembly. Bottom edge of dimmer switch rod actuator should rest on bend in dimmer switch rod.
6. Install lock housing cover assembly and mounting screws. Tighten screw in 12 o'clock position first, screw in 8 o' clock position second, and screw in 3 o'clock position third. **Torque** screws in same order to 80 inch lbs.
7. Install tilt lever.
8. Perform all assembly steps from "Shaft Lock, Turn Signal Cancelling Cam Assembly, Upper Bearing Spring, Upper Bearing Inner Race Seat, Inner Race, Buzzer Switch Assembly & Steering Column Lock Cylinder Set" as previously described.

TURN SIGNAL SWITCH ASSEMBLY, STEERING COLUMN HOUSING ASSEMBLY, STEERING WHEEL LOCK SHOE, SWITCH ACTUATOR SECTOR, SWITCH ACTUATOR RACK, BEARING ASSEMBLY, LOCK BOLT, STEERING SHAFT ASSEMBLY & STEERING COLUMN HOUSING SUPPORT ASSEMBLY

Disassembly

1. Remove steering wheel as described in the "Electrical" section of the appropriate vehicle section in the front of this manual.
2. Disconnect battery ground cable.
3. Remove steering column from vehicle as described under "Steering Column, Replace."
4. Inspect steering column for damage.
5. Perform all disassembly steps from "Lock Housing Cover Assembly, Column Housing Cover End Cap, Pivot & Pulse Switch Assembly, Dimmer Switch Rod Actuator & Tilt Spring Assembly" as previously described.

6. Remove turn signal switch assembly with lock housing cover assembly from steering column.
7. Remove four bolts and support bracket from steering column, then the wiring protectors and gently pull wire harness through column.
8. Remove pivot pins using pivot pin remover J 21854-01 or equivalent, then re-install tilt lever.
9. Remove steering column housing assembly, pull back on tilt lever and pull steering column housing assembly down and away from column.
10. If necessary, disassemble steering column housing as follows:
    a. Remove bearing assembly, hex head screw, lock bolt spring, lock bolt, switch actuator rack and rack preload spring.
    b. Remove driveshaft, switch actuator sector, then the release lever pin using lock shoe and release lever pin remover/installer J 22635 or equivalent.
    c. Remove shoe release lever, release lever spring, then the dowel pin using lock shoe and release lever pin remover/installer.
    d. Remove lock shoes and shoe springs.
11. If necessary, assemble steering column housing as follows:
    a. Install shoe springs and lock shoes, then the dowel pin using lock shoe and release lever pin remover/installer.
    b. Install release lever spring, shoe release lever, then the release lever pin using lock shoe and release lever pin remover/installer.
    c. Install switch actuator sector, driveshaft and rack preload spring, then assemble switch actuator rack to actuator sector.
    d. Assemble bearing assembly lubricated with lithium grease to column housing using steering column housing bearing installer J 38639 and driver handle J 8092 or their equivalents.
    e. Install lock bolt, lock bolt spring and hex head screw. **Torque** screw to 35 inch lbs.
12. Remove steering column jacket bushing, then the steering column shaft assembly.
13. Inspect steering column shaft assembly for damage, then mark upper shaft assembly and lower steering shaft assembly to ensure proper assembly.
14. If necessary, disassemble steering column shaft assembly as follows:
    a. Disassemble upper shaft assembly from lower steering shaft assembly. Tilt 90° to each other and disengage.
    b. Disassemble centering sphere from upper shaft assembly. Rotate sphere 90D and slip out.
    c. Remove joint preload spring from centering sphere.
15. If necessary, assemble steering column shaft assembly as follows:
    a. Install joint preload spring to centering sphere, then lubricate cen-

tering sphere with lithium grease, slip into upper shaft assembly and rotate sphere 90°.
    b. Install upper shaft assembly to lower steering shaft assembly. Align marks and tilt assemblies 90° to each other.
16. Remove support screws, then the column housing support assembly with dimmer switch rod from steering column jacket assembly. Remove rod from support.
17. Remove lock plate from steering column jacket assembly, then the steering column housing shroud.
18. Remove hex nut and screw, then the dimmer switch assembly from rod.
19. Remove mounting stud and ignition switch assembly with switch actuator assembly.
20. Remove switch actuator assembly from switch assembly, then the two pan head screws from ignition switch and ignition switch inhibitor housing assembly.
21. Remove ignition switch inhibitor from ignition switch.

Assembly

Ensure all fasteners are securely seated before applying torque. Failure to do so may result in component damage or malfunctioning of steering column.

1. Install shroud to jacket, lock plate to steering column jacket assembly, then the dimmer switch rod to loop in column housing support assembly.
2. Install support assembly and mounting screws. **Torque** mounting screws to 77 inch lbs.
3. Install actuator assembly to groove in housing support assembly, then the steering shaft assembly to jacket assembly. Lubricate with lithium grease.
4. Install tilt lever, then the column housing assembly to column.
5. Position column housing and align switch actuator rack with pin on end of ignition switch actuator rack.
6. Pull back on tilt lever, pushing column housing onto column housing support assembly.
7. Release tilt lever to lock shoes onto dowel pins, then remove tilt lever.
8. Install pivot pins, lubricate with lithium grease, then press pin until firmly seated, two places.
9. Install steering column jacket bushing. Lubricate outer surface with lithium grease. Bushing locator lug must seat in jacket notch.
10. Adjust ignition switch assembly by moving switch slider to extreme left position, then one detent to right, OFF-LOCK position. **New ignition switch, switch will be pinned in OFF-LOCK position. Remove plastic pin after switch is assembled to column.**
11. Install ignition switch and mounting stud, then **torque** stud to 35 inch lbs.
12. Install ignition switch inhibitor to ignition switch, then the two pan head screws. **Torque** screws to 30 inch lbs.

13. Install dimmer switch assembly to rod, then the screw and nut and tighten finger tight.
14. Adjust dimmer switch by placing a 3/32 inch drill bit in hole on switch to limit travel, position switch on column and push against dimmer switch rod to remove all lash, then remove drill bit. **Torque** screw and nut to 35 inch lbs.
15. Install turn signal switch assembly wire harness through lock housing cover assembly and steering column. Let switch hang freely.
16. Install wiring protectors, then the bracket with four bolts. **Torque** bolts to 22 ft. lbs.
17. Perform all assembly steps from "Lock Housing Cover Assembly, Column Housing Cover End CAp, Pivot & Pulse Switch Assembly, Dimmer Switch Rod Actuator & Tilt Spring Assembly" as previously described.
18. Install steering column into vehicle as described under "Steering Column, Replace."
19. Connect battery ground cable, then install steering wheel as described in the "Electrical" section of the appropriate vehicle section in the front of this manual.

Beretta & Corsica

STANDARD COLUMN

Disarm airbag as described under "Airbag System Disarming," then remove column as described under "Steering Column, Replace." The steering wheel must be straight and the column in the Lock position. **Care must be taken when handling column with a live inflator module. Never point bag deploy surface toward you, and never stand column on steering wheel. Accidental deployment in these positions may cause injury. Always face bag deploy surface toward open space to allow for unrestricted expansion.**

INFLATOR MODULE, COIL ASSEMBLY, SHAFT LOCK, TURN SIGNAL CANCELLING CAM, UPPER BEARING SPRING, THRUST WASHER, TURN SIGNAL SWITCH, BUZZER SWITCH, LOCK CYLINDER SET & CENTERING COIL ASSEMBLY

Refer to **Fig. 55** for exploded view of steering column.

Disassembly

1. Remove inflator module from steering wheel as follows:
   a. Remove Torx screws from back of steering wheel.
   b. Remove connector position assurance (CPA) and connector from rear of inflator module.
   c. Remove inflator module.
2. Remove horn connector to slip ring, then horn contact.
3. Remove steering wheel locknut.
4. Remove steering wheel using wheel puller J 1859-03 or equivalent. **When attaching puller to steering wheel, use care to prevent threading the side screws into the coil assembly.**
5. Remove coil assembly retaining ring.
6. Remove coil assembly off shaft end, allowing coil to hang freely. **The coil assembly will become uncentered if steering column is separated from gear and is allowed to rotate, or centering spring is pushed down letting hub rotate while coil is removed from column.**
7. Remove wave washer, then shaft lock spacer.
8. Using tool J-23653-C or equivalent, depress shaft lock, then remove shaft lock retaining ring.
9. Remove shaft lock, then the turn signal cancelling cam assembly.
10. Remove upper bearing spring, then thrust washer.
11. Place turn signal in Right Turn position.
12. Remove multi-function lever and hazard knob assembly.
13. Remove signal switch assembly, then turn signal switch assembly. Position turn signal switch out of way. If removal of switch is necessary, disconnect electrical connector at base of column and remove wiring protector, then gently pull wire harness through gear shift lever bowl, column housing and lock housing cover.
14. Remove coil assembly.
15. Remove key from cylinder lock and remove buzzer switch and clip, then reinstall key in cylinder lock and place key in Lock position.
16. Remove lock retaining screw and lock cylinder set.

Assembly

Ensure all fasteners are securely seated before applying required torque.

1. Install lock cylinder set, **torque** lock retaining screw to 40 inch lbs.
2. Place key in Run position, then install buzzer switch and clip.
3. Route turn signal switch wiring harness through lock housing cover, column housing and gear shift lever bowl.
4. Route coil assembly wire through lock housing cover, column housing and gear shift lever bowl and allow coil to hang freely.
5. Install turn signal switch, **torquing** attaching screws to 30 inch lbs.
6. Install switch arm, **torque** retaining screw to 20 inch lbs.
7. Install hazard knob, multi-function lever.
8. Install thrust washer, then the upper bearing spring.
9. Install turn signal cancelling cam assembly, then the shaft lock.
10. Using tool J-23653-C or equivalent to depress shaft lock, install shaft lock retaining ring. Ring must seat in groove on shaft.
11. Set steering shaft so that block teeth on upper steering shaft are at the 12 o'clock and 6 o'clock positions. The alignment mark at the end of shaft should be at 12 o'clock position. Set ignition switch to Lock position to ensure no damage occurs to the coil assembly.
12. Ensure coil assembly hub is centered, **Fig. 56.** The coil assembly will become uncentered if the column is separated from the steering gear and is allowed to rotate, or the coil is removed from the column without first locking in position with locking screw.
13. Install wave washer, then shaft lock spacer.
14. Install coil assembly, using horn tower on cancel cam on inner ring and projections on outer ring for alignment, then the coil assembly retaining ring.
15. Install steering wheel, then inflator module to steering wheel.

COLUMN HOUSING, SWITCH ACTUATOR PIVOT ASSEMBLY, LOCK BOLT, BEARING ASSEMBLY, SWITCH ACTUATOR, DIMMER & IGNITION SWITCH

Disassembly

1. Perform "Disassembly" steps for "Inflator Module, Coil Assembly, Shaft Lock, Turn Signal Cancelling Cam, Upper Bearing Spring, Thrust Washer, Turn Signal Switch, Buzzer Switch, Lock Cylinder Set & Centering Coil Assembly."
2. Remove dimmer switch attaching screw and hex nut, dimmer switch, then dimmer switch rod.
3. Remove ignition switch attaching screw, then ignition switch.
4. Remove steering column housing assembly, then floorshift bowl.
5. Remove upper bearing retainer, then floorshift bowl from housing cover.
6. Remove ignition switch actuator assembly with lock bolt and spring washer.
7. Remove switch actuator pivot pin, then pivot pin assembly.
8. Remove bearing retainer bushing, then bearing assembly.
9. Remove switch actuator sector, then rack preload spring.

Assembly

1. Install rack preload spring, then switch actuator sector.
2. Install bearing assembly, then bearing retainer bushing.
3. Install switch actuator pivot assembly, then pivot pin. **Torque** pivot pin to 29 inch lbs.
4. Install actuator rod to actuator rack.
5. Install ignition switch actuator assembly, lock bolt, then spring thrust washer.
6. Install upper retainer, then floorshift bowl. **Torque** floorshift bowl attaching screws to 16 inch lbs.
7. Install ignition switch. Switch must be in the "Off-Lock" position.
8. Adjust ignition switch as shown in **Fig. 51.**

27	RETAINER, UPPER BEARING
28	ROD, SWITCH ACTUATOR
29	BEARING ASM
31	PIN, SWITCH ACTUATOR PIVOT
32	PIVOT ASM, SWITCH ACTUATOR
36	PROTECTOR, WIRING
37	SPACER, SHAFT LOCK
38	SHROUD, CONNECTOR
39	RING, RETAINING
40	SHAFT ASM, STEERING COLUMN
43	BOWL, FLOORSHIFT
44	SCREW, BINDING HD CROSS RECESS
45	JACKET ASM, STEERING COLUMN
46	SWITCH ASM, IGNITION
47	STUD, DIMR & IGN SW MOUNTING
48	NUT, HEX (#10-24 x .25)
49	SCREW, WASHER HD (#10-24 x .25)
50	SWITCH ASM, DIMMER
51	ROD, DIMMER SWITCH
55	BUSHING ASM, STRG COL JACKET

Service Kits

201	COIL SERV KIT, INFL RESTRAINT
	-INCLUDES: 3,4,38
202	GREASE SERV KIT, (SYNTHETIC)

1	NUT, HEXAGON LOCKING (M14x1.5)
2	RING, RETAINING
3	COIL ASM, INFL RESTRAINT
4	WASHER, WAVE
5	RING, RETAINING
6	LOCK, SHAFT
7	CAM ASM, TURN SIG CANCELLING
8	SPRING, UPPER BEARING
9	SCREW, BINDING HD CROSS RECESS
10	SCREW, RD WASH HD (M4.2x1.41)
11	ARM, SIGNAL SWITCH
12	SWITCH ASM, TURN SIGNAL
13	SCREW, HEX WASHER HD TAPPING
14	WASHER, THRUST
15	SWITCH ASM, BUZZER
16	CLIP, BUZZER SWITCH RETAINING
17	SCREW, LOCK RETAINING
18	HOUSING ASM, STEERING COLUMN
19	SECTOR, SWITCH ACTUATOR
20	LOCK CYLINDER SET, STRG COLUMN
22	SPRING, RACK PRELOAD
23	RACK, SWITCH ACTUATOR
24	WASHER, SPRING THRUST
25	BOLT, LOCK
26	BUSHING, BEARING RETAINING

Fig. 55 Exploded view of standard steering column. Beretta & Corsica

Perform the following steps to center coil assembly:
A. Remove coil assembly.
B. Hold coil assembly with clear bottom up to see coil ribbon.
C. NOTE: There are two different styles of coils. One rotates clockwise and the other rotates counter-clockwise.
D. While holding coil assembly, depress spring lock to rotate hub in direction of arrow until it stops.
E. The coil ribbon should be wound up snug against center hub.
F. Rotate coil hub in opposite direction approximately two and a half (2-1/2) turns. Release spring lock between locking tabs in front of arrow.

Fig. 56 Centering coil assembly. Beretta & Corsica w/standard column

9. Install dimmer switch and adjust as follows:
   a. Place a 3/32 drill bit in hole on switch, **Fig. 58.**
   b. Place switch on column and push against switch rod to remove all lash, remove drill bit and **Torque** attaching nut and bolt to 35 inch lbs.
10. Perform "Assembly" steps for "Inflator Module, Coil Assembly, Shaft Lock, Turn Signal Cancelling Cam, Upper Bearing Spring, Thrust Washer, Turn Signal Switch, Buzzer Switch, Lock Cylinder Set & Centering Coil Assembly."

COLUMN JACKET BEARING ASSEMBLY, STEERING COLUMN SHAFT ASSEMBLY

Disassembly

1. Perform "Disassembly" steps for "Inflator Module, Coil Assembly, Shaft Lock, Turn Signal Cancelling Cam, Upper Bearing Spring, Thrust Washer, Turn Signal Switch, Buzzer Switch, Lock Cylinder Set & Centering Coil Assembly."
2. Perform "Disassembly" steps for "Column Housing, Switch Actuator Pivot Assembly, Lock Bolt, Bearing Assembly, Switch Actuator, Dimmer & Ignition Switch"
3. Remove steering column jacket bushing assembly, then column shaft assembly, **Fig. 59.**
4. Remove retaining ring from shaft.

MOVE SWITCH SLIDER TO EXTREME RIGHT POSITION AND THEN MOVE SLIDER ONE DETENT TO THE LEFT "OFF-LOCK"

SWITCH ASM. IGNITION

Fig. 57 Adjusting ignition switch. Beretta & Corsica w/standard column

Assembly

1. Install retaining ring onto shaft.
2. Install shaft, then bushing assembly. Tab on bushing must fit into slot on end of steering column jacket.
3. Perform "Disassembly" steps for "Column Housing, Switch Actuator Pivot Assembly, Lock Bolt, Bearing Assembly, Switch Actuator, Dimmer & Ignition Switch."
4. Perform "Disassembly" steps for "Inflator Module, Coil Assembly, Shaft Lock, Turn Signal Cancelling Cam, Upper Bearing Spring, Thrust Washer, Turn Signal Switch, Buzzer Switch, Lock Cylinder Set & Centering Coil Assembly."

TILT COLUMN

Disarm airbag as described under "Airbag System Disarming," then remove column as described under "Steering Column Replace." The steering wheel must be straight and the column in the Lock position. **Care must be taken when handling column with a live inflator module. Never point bag deploy surface toward you, and never stand column on steering wheel. Accidental deployment in these positions may cause injury. Always face bag deploy surface toward open space to allow for unrestricted expansion.**

INFLATOR MODULE, COIL ASSEMBLY, SHAFT LOCK, TURN SIGNAL CANCELLING CAM, UPPER BEARING SPRING, UPPER BEARING SEAT, INNER RACE TURN SIGNAL SWITCH, BUZZER SWITCH & LOCK CYLINDER SET

Refer to **Fig. 60** for exploded view of steering column.

Disassembly

1. Remove inflator module from steering wheel as follows:
   a. Remove Torx screws from back of steering wheel.
   b. Remove connector position assurance (CPA) and connector from rear of inflator module.
   c. Remove inflator module.
2. Remove horn connector to slip ring, then horn contact.
3. Remove steering wheel locknut.
4. Remove steering wheel using wheel puller J 1859-03 or equivalent. **When**

SWITCH ASM. DIMMER   3/32" DRILL BIT

Fig. 58 Adjusting dimmer switch. Beretta & Corsica w/standard column

39 RING, RETAINING
40 SHAFT ASM. STEERING COLUMN
45 JACKET ASM. STEERING COLUMN
55 BUSHING ASM. STRG COL JACKET

Fig. 59 Removing column jacket bushing & shaft assembly. Beretta & Corsica w/standard column

attaching puller to steering wheel, use care to prevent threading the side screws into the coil assembly.
5. Remove coil assembly retaining ring.
6. Remove coil assembly off shaft end, allowing coil to hang freely.
7. Using tool J-23653-C or equivalent, depress shaft lock, then remove shaft lock retaining ring.
8. Remove shaft lock, then the turn signal cancelling cam.
9. Remove upper bearing spring, then the upper bearing seat.
10. Remove inner race, then place turn signal in Right Turn position.
11. Remove signal switch arm attaching screw and the arm, then the turn signal switch attaching screws.
12. Remove hazard knob, then position turn signal switch out of way. If removal of switch is necessary, remove retainer spring and wiring protector, then gently pull wire harness through gear shift lever bowl, column housing and lock housing cover.
13. Remove coil assembly.
14. Remove key from cylinder lock and remove buzzer switch and clip, then reinstall key in cylinder lock and place key in Lock position.
15. Remove lock retaining screw and lock cylinder set.

Assembly

Ensure all fasteners are securely seated before applying required torque.

1. Install lock cylinder set, **torque** lock retaining screw to 22 inch lbs.
2. Place key in Run position, then install buzzer switch and clip.

43	LEVER, SHOE RELEASE
44	RACK, SWITCH ACTUATOR
45	SPRING, RACK PRELOAD
46	HOUSING, STRG COLUMN
48	WASHER, SPRING THRUST
50	GUIDE, SPRING
51	SPRING, WHEEL TILT
52	RETAINER, SPRING
55	SHAFT ASM, STEERING COLUMN
56	SHAFT ASM, RACE & UPPER
57	SPHERE, CENTERING
58	SPRING, JOINT PRELOAD
59	SHAFT ASM, LOWER STEERING
61	SCREW, SUPPORT
62	SUPPORT ASM, STRG COL HSG
63	SHROUD, STRG COL HOUSING
72	JACKET ASM, STRG COL
80	BEARING ASM, ADAPTER &
81	SWITCH ASM, IGNITION
82	SCREW, WASH HD (#10-24 x .25)
83	ACTUATOR ASM, IGNITION SWITCH
84	ROD, DIMMER SWITCH
85	NUT, HEXAGON (#10-24 x .25)
86	STUD, DIMR & IGN SW MOUNTING
87	SWITCH ASM, DIMMER

Service Kits

201	SPRING SERV KIT, TILT COLUMN
	-INCLUDES: 13,14,39,50,51,52
202	COIL SERV KIT, INFL RESTRAINT
	-INCLUDES: 3,4,28
203	SPHERE SERV KIT, TILT COLUMN
	-INCLUDES: 57,58
204	GREASE SERV KIT, (SYNTHETIC)

1	NUT, HEXAGON LOCKING (M14x1.5)
2	RING, RETAINING
3	COIL ASM, INFL RESTRAINT
4	WASHER, WAVE
5	RING, RETAINING
6	LOCK, SHAFT
7	CAM ASM, TURN SIG CANCELLING
8	SPRING, UPPER BEARING
9	SCREW, BINDING HD CROSS RECESS
10	SCREW, RD WASH HD (M4.2x1.41)
11	ARM, SIGNAL SWITCH
12	SWITCH ASM, TURN SIGNAL
13	SEAT, UPPER BRG INNER RACE
14	RACE, INNER
15	SCREW, PAN HD 6-LOBED SOC TAP
16	SWITCH ASM, BUZZER
18	SCREW, LOCK RETAINING
19	COVER ASM, LOCK HOUSING
20	LOCK CYLINDER SET, STRG COL
21	SCREW, FLT HD TAPPING
24	CAP, STRG COL HSG COVER END
25	ACTUATOR, DIMMER SWITCH ROD
26	PROTECTOR, WIRING
28	SHROUD, CONNECTOR
30	HOUSING ASM, STRG COLUMN
31	BEARING ASM
34	SHOE, STEERING WHEEL LOCK
35	SHOE, STEERING WHEEL LOCK
36	SHIELD, WIRE ABRASION
38	PIN, DOWEL
39	PIN, PIVOT
40	SPRING, SHOE
41	SPRING, RELEASE LEVER
42	PIN, RELEASE LEVER

Fig. 60 Exploded view of tilt steering column. Beretta & Corsica

32 BOLT, LOCK
38 PIN, DOWEL
44 RACK, SWITCH ACTUATOR
46 HOUSING, STRG COLUMN

31 BEARING ASM
34 SHOE, STRG WHEEL LOCK
35 SHOE, STRG WHEEL LOCK

42 PIN, RELEASE LEVER
43 LEVER, SHOE RELEASE

Fig. 61 Disassembling steering column housing. Beretta & Corsica w/tilt column

39 PIN, PIVOT

Fig. 62 Removing pivot pin. Beretta & Corsica w/tilt column

31 BEARING ASM
46 HOUSING, STRG COLUMN

Fig. 63 Installing bearing assembly. Beretta & Corsica w/tilt column

---

3. Route turn signal switch wiring harness through lock housing cover, column housing and gear shift lever bowl.
4. Route coil assembly wire through lock housing cover, column housing and gear shift lever bowl and allow coil to hang freely.
5. Install turn signal switch, **torquing** attaching screws to 30 inch lbs.
6. Install switch actuator pivot assembly, **torque** retaining screw to 20 inch lbs.
7. Install hazard knob, multi-function lever, then the inner race.
8. Install upper bearing inner race seat, then the upper bearing spring.
9. Install turn signal cancelling cam, then the shaft lock.
10. Using tool J-23653-C or equivalent to depress shaft lock, install shaft lock retaining ring, aligning to block tooth on shaft.
11. Ensure coil assembly hub is centered, **Fig. 56.** The coil assembly will become uncentered if the column is separated from the steering gear and is allowed to rotate, or the coil is removed from the column without first locking in position with locking screw.
12. Install wave washer.
13. Install coil assembly, using horn tower on cancel cam on inner ring and projections on outer ring for alignment, then the coil assembly retaining ring.
14. Install steering wheel, then inflator module to steering wheel.

LOCK HOUSING COVER, COVER END CAP, DIMMER SWITCH ROD ACTUATOR & TILT SPRING ASSEMBLY
Disassembly

1. Perform "Disassembly" steps for "Inflator Module, Coil Assembly, Shaft

Lock, Turn Signal Cancelling Cam, Upper Bearing Spring, Upper Bearing Seat, Inner Race Turn Signal Switch, Buzzer Switch & Lock Cylinder Set."
2. Remove lock housing cover attaching screws and the cover, then the tilt lever.
3. Remove cover housing end cap, then dimmer switch rod actuator.
4. Using a cross recess head screwdriver, remove spring retainer. Push retainer down and turn counterclockwise to release.
5. Remove spring and spring guide.

Assembly

Ensure all fasteners are securely seated before applying required torque.
1. Coat spring guide and spring with lithium grease and install them, then install spring retainer. Push retainer down and turn clockwise to lock into place.
2. Install dimmer switch rod actuator to dimmer switch rod.
3. Install cover housing end cap.
4. Install lock housing cover. Tighten screw in 12 o'clock position first, screw in 8 o'clock position second and screw in 3 o'clock position third, then **torque** screws to 80 inch lbs. in same order.
5. Perform "Assembly" steps for "Inflator Module, Coil Assembly, Shaft Lock, Turn Signal Cancelling Cam, Upper Bearing Spring, Upper Bearing Seat, Inner Race Turn Signal Switch, Buzzer Switch & Lock Cylinder Set."

COLUMN HOUSING, LOCK SHOES, SWITCH ACTUATOR RACK BEARINGS ASSEMBLY & LOCK BOLT ASSEMBLY
Disassembly

1. Perform "Disassembly" steps for "Inflator Module, Coil Assembly, Shaft Lock, Turn Signal Cancelling Cam, Upper Bearing Spring, Upper Bearing Seat, Inner Race Turn Signal Switch, Buzzer Switch & Lock Cylinder Set."
2. Perform "Disassembly" steps for "Lock Housing Cover, Cover End Cap, Dimmer Switch Rod Actuator & Tilt Spring Assembly."
3. Remove pivot pin using tool J 21854-01 or equivalent, then reinstall tilt lever.
4. Remove steering column housing by pulling back on tilt lever and pull

steering column housing down and away from steering column.
5. Disassemble steering column housing as follows:
   a. Remove bearing assembly, switch actuator rack, lock bolt and spring thrust washer, **Fig. 61.**
   b. Remove rack preload spring from housing.
   c. Remove release lever pin using tool J 22635, then shoe release lever.
   d. Remove dowel pin using tool J 22635 or equivalent, **Fig. 62.**
   e. Remove lock shoes and shoe springs.
   f. Reverse procedure to reassemble the steering column housing. When installing bearing assembly use tools J8092 and J 38629 or equivalent, **Fig. 63.**

Assembly

Ensure all fasteners are securely seated before applying required torque.
1. Install steering column housing to steering column as follows:
   a. Line up switch actuator rack with pin on end of ignition switch actuator assembly.
   b. Pull back on tilt lever, then push steering column housing onto steering column support assembly.
   c. Release tilt lever to lock shoes onto dowel pins.
   d. Remove tilt lever.
2. Lubricate pivot pins using suitable lithium grease, press pins in until firmly seated.
3. Perform "Assembly" steps for "Lock Housing Cover, Cover End Cap, Dimmer Switch Rod Actuator & Tilt Spring Assembly."
4. Perform "Assembly" steps for "Inflator Module, Coil Assembly, Shaft Lock, Turn Signal Cancelling Cam, Upper Bearing Spring, Upper Bearing Seat, Inner Race Turn Signal Switch, Buzzer Switch & Lock Cylinder Set."

[72] JACKET ASM. STRG COL
[81] SWITCH ASM. IGNITION
[82] SCREW, WASH HD (#10-24X.25)
[83] ACTUATOR ASM. IGNITION SWITCH
[85] NUT,HEX (#10-24X.25)
[86] STUD. DIMR & IGN SW MOUNTING
[87] SWITCH ASM. DIMMER

Fig. 64 Removing dimmer & ignition switch. Beretta & Corsica w/tilt column

SHAFT ASSEMBLY, COLUMN HOUSING SUPPORT, IGNITION SWITCH, DIMMER SWITCH & JACKET BUSHING ASSEMBLY

Disassembly

1. Perform "Disassembly" steps for "Inflator Module, Coil Assembly, Shaft Lock, Turn Signal Cancelling Cam, Upper Bearing Spring, Upper Bearing Seat, Inner Race Turn Signal Switch, Buzzer Switch & Lock Cylinder Set."
2. Perform "Disassembly" steps for "Lock Housing Cover, Cover End Cap, Dimmer Switch Rod Actuator & Tilt Spring Assembly."
3. Perform "Disassembly" steps for "Column Housing, Lock Shoes, Switch Actuator Rack Bearings Assembly & Lock Bolt Assembly."
4. Remove steering column shaft assembly. **Mark upper and lower shaft assemblies to ensure proper assembly.**
5. Remove steering column support screw, steering column support assembly, then dimmer switch rod from jacket assembly.
6. Remove column housing shroud from jacket.
7. Remove ignition switch and dimmer switch as shown in **Fig. 64.**.

Assembly

Ensure all fasteners are securely seated before applying required torque.
1. Install shroud to jacket, then dimmer switch rod to steering column support assembly.
2. Install support assembly, **torque** attaching screws to 47 inch lbs.
3. Install steering column shaft assembly. Refer to **Fig. 65** for proper shaft position.
4. Install steering column jacket bushing. Align tab on bushing with slot on end of jacket.
5. Install actuator assembly.
6. Perform "Disassembly" steps for "Column Housing, Lock Shoes, Switch Actuator Rack Bearings Assembly & Lock Bolt Assembly."

7. Perform "Disassembly" steps for "Lock Housing Cover, Cover End Cap, Dimmer Switch Rod Actuator & Tilt Spring Assembly."
8. Perform "Disassembly" steps for "Inflator Module, Coil Assembly, Shaft Lock, Turn Signal Cancelling Cam, Upper Bearing Spring, Upper Bearing Seat, Inner Race Turn Signal Switch, Buzzer Switch & Lock Cylinder Set."
9. Install ignition switch to jacket. Install with switch in Off-Lock position, and shift bowl must not be in Park position **Fig. 57.**
10. Install dimmer switch and adjust as follows:
    a. Place a 3/32 drill bit in hole on switch, **Fig. 58.**
    b. Place switch on column and push against switch rod to remove all lash, remove drill bit and **Torque** attaching nut and bolt to 35 inch lbs.

Cutlass Supreme, Grand Prix, Lumina & Regal

STANDARD COLUMN

Refer to **Fig. 66.** when servicing this column.

Floor shift models equipped with automatic transmission use an ignition switch inhibitor and park lock cable. On these models, the park lock cable must be disconnected from ignition switch inhibitor before steering column is removed from vehicle. When removal of steering column is necessary, proceed as follows:
1. Lower steering column to floor of vehicle.
2. Remove shield or other upper column housing.
3. Turn column lock cylinder to the On position.
4. Disconnect park lock cable from ignition switch inhibitor with small screwdriver or punch, **Fig. 67.**

TURN SIGNAL CANCEL CAM ASSEMBLY, PIVOT & PULSE SWITCH ASSEMBLY & TURN SIGNAL SWITCH ASSEMBLY

Disassembly

1. Remove nut retainer, jam nut and steering wheel.
2. Remove turn signal cancel cam assembly, hazard knob screw and hazard warning knob.
3. Position turn signal switch so that signal switch screws and housing cover screw can be removed through openings in switch.
4. Remove housing cover screw and column housing cover.
5. Disconnect wiring protector from opening in instrument panel bracket on jacket and bowl assembly and separate from wires.
6. Disconnect pivot and pulse switch connector from ignition and dimmer switch.
7. Remove pivot switch screw and pivot and pulse switch assembly.

[56] SHAFT ASM. RACE & UPPER
[57] SPHERE. CENTERING
[59] SHAFT ASM. LOWER STEERING

Fig. 65 Proper upper to lower shaft position. Beretta & Corsica w/tilt column

8. Remove turn signal switch screws and disconnect turn signal switch connector from ignition and dimmer switch assembly connector.
9. Remove seventeen-way lock from turn signal connector and disconnect wires on alarm or buzzer assembly from turn signal connector with special tool No. J 35689-A or equivalent, **Fig. 68.** Wrap wire ends with tape to protect during removal and installation.
10. Remove turn signal switch assembly from column.

Assembly

1. Install turn signal switch assembly and **torque** screws to 35 inch lbs.
2. Connect wires from alarm or buzzer assembly to turn signal switch connector.
3. Install seventeen-way secondary lock to turn signal connector and snap in place.
4. Connect turn signal switch connector to ignition and dimmer switch connector and snap in place.
5. Install pivot and pulse switch assembly and **torque** screw to 18 inch lbs.
6. Connect pivot switch connector to ignition and dimmer switch connector and snap in place.
7. Install wiring protector as follows:
    a. Wrap protector around all wires passing through instrument panel bracket opening.
    b. Close protector so that interlocking grooves engage and slide protector into instrument panel bracket opening on jacket and bowl assembly and snap in place.
8. Install column housing cover and **torque** screw to 35 inch lbs.
9. Install hazard warning knob and **torque** screw to 9 inch lbs.
10. Lubricate bottom side of cancel cam with lithium grease and install turn signal cancel cam assembly.
11. Install steering wheel and jam nut, **torque** jam nut to 30 inch lbs. and secure with nut retainer.

5-SPRING, UPPER BEARING
6-WASHER, THRUST
7-SCREW, PAN HD 6-LOBED SOC TAP
8-COVER, COLUMN HOUSING
9-KNOB, HAZARD WARNING
10-SCREW, OV HD C/REC (M3.5X1.27)
11-SWITCH ASM, TURN SIGNAL
12-SCREW, PAN HD 6-LOBED SOC TAP
13-HOUSING ASM, STRG COLUMN
14-HOUSING, STEERING COLUMN
15-BEARING ASM
16-SPACER, STRG COLUMN HOUSING
17-SHAFT ASM, STEERING
18-SCR, OVL HD 6-LOBED SOC TAP
19-SWITCH ASM, PIVOT & PULSE
20-PROTECTOR, WIRING
21-SWITCH ASM, BUZZER
22-SCREW, LOCK RETAINING
23-BOWL ASM, JACKET &
24-LOCK CYL SET, STRG COLUMN
25-SCREW, HEX WASHER HD TAPPING
26-SHIELD, BOWL
27-ADJUSTER ASM, PRNDL
28-BEARING ASM, ADAPTER &
29-SCREW, HEX WASHER HD TAPPING
30-SEAT, LOWER BEARING
31-SPRING, LOWER BEARING
32-RETAINER, LOWER SPRING
33-CAP, DIMMER SWITCH ROD
34-STUD DIMR & IGN SW MOUNTING
35-NUT, HEXAGON (#10-24)
36-ROD, DIMMER SW ACTUATOR
37-SWITCH ASM, COLUMN LOCK & IGN

1-NUT, HEXAGON JAM (M14X1.5)
2-CAM ASM, SPACER & CANCELLING

3-RING, RETAINING
4-WASHER, THRUST

Fig. 66 Exploded view of standard steering column. Cutlass Supreme, Grand Prix, Lumina & Regal

STEERING SHAFT ASSEMBLY, STEERING COLUMN HOUSING, BEARING ASSEMBLIES, ALARM ASSEMBLY & STEERING COLUMN LOCK CYLINDER.

Disassembly

1. Remove turn signal cancel cam assembly, pivot & pulse switch assembly & turn signal switch assembly as previously described.
2. Remove two lower spring retainers and discard.
3. Remove lower bearing spring and lower bearing seat.
4. Remove adapter screws, adapter and lower bearing assembly.
5. Turn lock cylinder to the Run position.
6. Place opening in retaining ring over flat on steering shaft, then remove retaining ring with a screwdriver and discard.

7. Remove thrust washer, upper bearing spring and washer.
8. Remove steering shaft from lower end of jacket and bowl assembly.
9. Remove housing screws and column housing.
10. Remove housing spacer and bearing with drift and discard.
11. Turn lock cylinder to the Off-Lock position and remove key.
12. Remove alarm assembly by lifting alarm tab with a screwdriver and gently pulling wires to remove.
13. Remove lock retaining screw and lock cylinder.
14. Remove rod cap from dimmer switch rod and jacket and bowl assembly.

Assembly

1. Install rod cap into jacket and bowl assembly.
2. Install lock cylinder and **torque** retaining retaining screw to 27 inch lbs.

3. Install alarm assembly by pushing down into retaining bore until bottomed with plastic tab covering lock retaining screw.
4. Lubricate bearing with lithium grease and press into housing with a 1½ inch socket until bottomed.
5. Install housing spacer and column housing and **torque** screw to 88 inch lbs.
6. Turn lock cylinder to the Run position and insert steering shaft into the lower end of jacket and bowl assembly until shaft rests against bearing. The shaft will extend 2½ inches beyond the highest surface of column housing when installed properly.
7. Install thrust washer, upper bearing spring and thrust washer.
8. Wrap a two inch wide piece of shim stock .005 inch, around the shaft and slip a new retaining ring up to the thrust washer. Use two long handled

Fig. 67 Disconnecting park lock cable. Cutlass Supreme, Grand Prix, Lumina & Regal w/floor shift & automatic transmission

Fig. 68 Disconnecting switch wires. Cutlass Supreme, Grand Prix, Lumina & Regal w/standard column

Fig. 69 Installing ignition switch & actuator. Cutlass Supreme, Grand Prix, Lumina & Regal w/standard column

Fig. 70 Adjusting dimmer switch. Cutlass Supreme, Grand Prix, Lumina & Regal w/standard column

screwdrivers and push on retaining ring until it seats in the retainer ring groove in shaft. Discard shim stock.
9. Install adapter and lower bearing assembly and **torque** adapter screws to 27 inch lbs.
10. Install lower bearing seat and lower bearing spring.
11. Install two new lower spring retainers and compress spring until retainers are positioned 1.14 inch from lower end of steering shaft.
12. Perform assembly steps for turn signal cancel cam assembly, pivot & pulse switch assembly & turn signal switch assembly as previously described.

IGNITION & DIMMER SWITCH ASSEMBLY
Disassembly
1. Place shift lever in the Park position and lock cylinder in the Off position.
2. Remove steering column from vehicle.
3. Disconnect turn signal switch and pivot and pulse switch connectors from ignition and dimmer switch assembly connector.
4. Remove bowl shield screw and nut and remove bowl shield.
5. Remove dimmer and ignition switch assembly as follows:
   a. Remove dimmer switch nut, upper mounting stud, then dimmer switch.
   b. Remove lower mounting stud and ignition switch from ignition switch actuator rod.
6. Remove dimmer switch actuator rod from rod cap.

Assembly
1. Place the ignition switch slider in the far left position and move back one detent to the right, Off-Lock position. **Fig. 69.**
2. Insert a 3/32 inch drill bit into the adjustment hole on ignition switch to hold switch slider in proper position during installation.
3. Install ignition switch to switch rod.
4. Install ignition switch to jacket and bowl assembly with lower mounting stud and **torque** stud to 35 inch lbs.
5. Remove drill bit from ignition switch and install dimmer switch actuator

rod, tab first, through hole in instrument panel bracket and hole in dimmer switch rod cap.
6. Tab on rod must engage wide slot in rod cap and snap in place.
7. Install dimmer switch onto actuator rod and dimmer switch assembly on lower mounting stud with dimmer switch nut and upper mounting stud.
8. Adjust dimmer switch by inserting a 3/32 inch drill bit through hole in switch and push switch against actuator rod to remove all lash. **Fig. 70.**
9. **Torque** dimmer switch nut and upper mounting stud to 35 inch lbs.
10. Install shield screw and bowl shield nut and **torque** shield screw to 53 inch lbs. and bowl shield nut to 35 inch lbs.
11. Connect turn signal switch and pivot and pulse switch connectors to ignition and dimmer switch connector and snap in place.

TILT COLUMN
Refer to **Fig. 71.** when servicing this column.

Floor shift models equipped with automatic transmission use an ignition switch inhibitor and park lock cable. On these models, the park lock cable must be disconnected from ignition switch inhibitor before steering column is removed from vehicle. When removal of steering column is necessary, proceed as follows:
1. Lower steering column to floor of vehicle.
2. Remove shield or other upper column housing.
3. Turn column lock cylinder to the On position.

4. Disconnect park lock cable from ignition switch inhibitor with small screwdriver or punch, **Fig. 67.**

TURN SIGNAL CANCEL CAM ASSEMBLY, PIVOT & PULSE SWITCH ASSEMBLY & TURN SIGNAL SWITCH ASSEMBLY
Disassembly
1. Remove nut retainer, jam nut and steering wheel.
2. Remove turn signal cancel cam assembly, hazard knob screw and hazard warning knob.
3. Position turn signal switch so that signal switch screws and housing cover screw can be removed through openings in switch.
4. Remove housing cover screw and column housing cover.
5. Disconnect wiring protector from opening in instrument panel bracket on jacket and bowl assembly and separate from wires.
6. Disconnect pivot and pulse switch connector from ignition and dimmer switch.
7. Remove pivot switch screw and pivot and pulse switch assembly.
8. Remove turn signal switch screws and disconnect turn signal switch connector from ignition and dimmer switch assembly connector.
9. Remove seventeen-way lock from turn signal connector and disconnect wires on alarm or buzzer assembly from turn signal connector with special tool No. J 35689-A or equivalent, **Fig. 68.** Wrap wire ends with tape to protect during removal and installation.
10. Remove turn signal switch assembly from column.

Assembly
1. Install turn signal switch assembly and **torque** screws to 35 inch lbs.
2. Connect wires from alarm or buzzer assembly to turn signal switch connector.
3. Install seventeen-way secondary lock to turn signal connector and snap in place.
4. Connect turn signal switch connector to ignition and dimmer switch connector and snap in place.

1 - NUT, HEXAGON JAM (M14X1.5)
2 - CAM ASM, SPACER & CANCELLING
3 - SCREW, PAN HD 6 - LOBED SOC TAP
4 - COVER, COLUMN HOUSING
5 - KNOB, HAZARD WARNING
6 - SCREW, OV HD C/REC (M3.5X1.27)
7 - SWITCH ASM, TURN SIGNAL
8 - CAP, HSG SHOE PIN RETAINER
9 - HOUSING ASM, SHAFT &
10 - PIN, PIVOT
11 - RETAINER, SPRING
12 - SPRING, WHEEL TILT
13 - GUIDE, TILT SPRING
14 - SCR, OVL HD 6 - LOBED SOC TAP
15 - SWITCH ASM, PIVOT & PULSE
16 - PROTECTOR, WIRING
17 - BUZZER SWITCH ASM
18 - SCREW, LOCK RETAINING
19 - BOWL ASM, JACKET &
20 - LOCK CYL SET, STRG COLUMN
21 - SCREW, HEX WASHER HD TAPPING
22 - SHIELD, BOWL
23 - ADJUSTER ASM, PRNDL
24 - BEARING ASM, ADAPTER &
25 - SCREW, HEX WASHER HD TAPPING
26 - SEAT, LOWER BEARING
27 - SPRING, LOWER BEARING
28 - RETAINER, LOWER SPRING
29 - SCR, OVL HD 6 - LOBED SOC TAP
30 - BRACKET ASM, TILT LEVER &
31 - BUMPER, COLUMN TILT
32 - CAP, DIMMER SWITCH ROD
33 - STUD, DIMR & IGN SW MOUNTING
34 - NUT, HEXAGON (#10 - 24)
35 - ROD, DIMMER SW ACTUATOR
36 - SWITCH ASM, IGNITION

Fig. 71 Exploded view of tilt steering column. Cutlass Supreme, Grand Prix, Lumina & Regal

5. Install pivot and pulse switch assembly and **torque** screw to 18 inch lbs.
6. Connect pivot switch connector to ignition and dimmer switch connector and snap in place.
7. Install wiring protector as follows:
   a. Wrap protector around all wires passing through instrument panel bracket opening.
   b. Close protector so that interlocking grooves engage and slide protector into instrument panel bracket opening on jacket and bowl assembly and snap in place.
8. Install column housing cover and **torque** screw to 35 inch lbs.
9. Install hazard warning knob and **torque** screw to 9 inch lbs.
10. Lubricate bottom side of cancel cam with lithium grease and install turn

signal cancel cam assembly.
11. Install steering wheel and jam nut, **torque** jam nut to 30 inch lbs. and secure with nut retainer.

TILT LEVER & BRACKET ASSEMBLY, WHEEL TILT SPRING, LOWER BEARING ASSEMBLY, STEERING SHAFT & HOUSING ASSEMBLY, ALARM ASSEMBLY, STEERING COLUMN LOCK CYLINDER, COLUMN TILT BUMPERS & JACKET & BOWL ASSEMBLY
Disassembly

1. Remove turn signal cancel cam assembly, pivot & pulse switch assembly & turn signal switch assembly as previously described.

2. Pull tilt lever and tilt column all the way up.
3. Insert Phillips tip screwdriver into square opening in spring retainer, push down and turn left to release retainer and wheel tilt spring.
4. Remove spring retainer, tilt spring and tilt spring guide.
5. Remove two lower spring retainers and discard.
6. Remove lower bearing spring and lower bearing seat.
7. Remove adapter screws, adapter and lower bearing assembly.
8. Remove two pivot pins from shaft and housing assembly with special tool No. J 21854-01 or equivalent.
9. Turn lock cylinder to the Run position and pull tilt lever to release shaft and housing assembly.

10. Remove shaft and housing assembly from jacket and bowl assembly.
11. Turn lock cylinder to the Off-Lock position and remove key.
12. Remove alarm assembly by lifting alarm tab with a screwdriver and gently pulling wires to remove.
13. Remove lock retaining screw and lock cylinder.
14. Remove column tilt bumpers with vise grips. If bumper is broken off use a 7/32 inch drill bit to remove remaining piece of bumper.
15. Remove tilt bracket screws and tilt lever and bracket assembly.
16. Remove rod cap from dimmer switch rod and jacket and bowl assembly.

Assembly

1. Install rod cap into jacket and bowl assembly.
2. Install tilt lever and bracket assembly into jacket and bowl assembly and **torque** tilt bracket screws to 35 inch lbs.
3. Install three tilt bumpers into jacket and bowl assembly until bottomed.
4. Install column lock cylinder and **torque** screw to 27 inch lbs.
5. Install alarm assembly by pushing down into retaining bore until bottomed with plastic tab covering lock retaining screw.
6. Insert key and turn lock cylinder to the Run position.
7. Install shaft and housing assembly.
8. Lubricate pivot pins with lithium grease and install into pivot holes in shaft and housing assembly until bottomed.
9. Pull tilt lever and tilt column all the way up.
10. Lubricate tilt spring guide with lithium grease and install tilt spring guide into tilt spring.
11. Install guide and tilt spring with spring retainer as follows:
    a. Ensure that recess in spring guide engages round locating tab in jacket and bowl assembly.
    b. Insert Phillips tip screwdriver into square opening in spring retainer, push down and turn right to lock in place.
12. Install adapter and lower bearing assembly and **torque** adapter screws to 27 inch lbs.
13. Install lower bearing seat and lower bearing spring.
14. Install two new lower spring retainers and compress spring until retainers are positioned 1.14 inch from lower end of steering shaft.
15. Perform assembly steps for turn signal cancel cam assembly, pivot & pulse switch assembly & turn signal switch assembly as previously described.

Ignition & Dimmer Switch Assembly

Refer to "Standard Columns" for procedure.

Bonneville, Caprice, Custom Cruiser, LeSabre, Park Avenue, 88 & 98 Less Supplemental Inflatable Restraint (SIR)

STANDARD COLUMN

SHAFT LOCK, TURN SIGNAL CANCELLING CAM, UPPER BEARING SPRING, TURN SWITCH ACTUATOR, BUZZER SWITCH & LOCK CYLINDER SET

Disassembly

Wheels of vehicle must be in straight ahead position. Failure to do so may cause improper alignment of some components during installation, resulting in column malfunction.
1. Place key in "lock" position.
2. Remove screws from back of steering wheel and horn pad, disconnecting horn lead from cam tower.
3. Remove retainer and hex nut, **Fig. 72**, then remove the steering wheel.
4. Depress shaft lock, then remove shaft lock retaining ring.
5. Remove shaft lock and shaft lock cover, then the turn signal cancelling cam.
6. Remove upper bearing spring, then the thrust washer.
7. Place turn signal in right turn position.
8. Remove switch actuator arm attaching screw and the arm, then the turn signal switch attaching screws, positioning switch out of way. If it is necessary to remove switch, remove wiring protector and hazard knob, then gently pull wire harness through gearshift lever bowl shroud and steering column housing.
9. Remove key from lock cylinder set and remove buzzer switch and clip, then reinsert key in lock cylinder set and turn to "lock" position.
10. Remove lock cylinder retaining screw and the lock cylinder set.

Assembly

1. Install lock cylinder set, torquing retaining screw to 22 inch lbs.
2. Place key in "run" position and install buzzer switch and clip.
3. Route turn signal switch wiring harness through steering column housing, gearshift bowl shroud and gearshift lever bowl and secure switch, torquing retaining screws to 22 inch lbs.
4. Install switch actuator arm, torquing attaching screw to 18 inch lbs.
5. Install thrust washer, then the upper bearing spring.
6. Install turn signal cancelling cam, then the shaft lock.
7. Depress shaft lock, then install shaft lock retaining ring.

8. Install steering wheel, then the hex nut and retainer.
9. Install horn pad and wiring protector.

STEERING COLUMN HOUSING, COVER END CAP, PIVOT & SWITCH ASSEMBLY, SWITCH ACTUATOR ROD/RACK, UPPER BEARING, DIMMER SWITCH & IGNITION SWITCH

Disassembly

1. Perform "Disassembly" steps for "Shaft Lock, Turn Signal Cancelling Cam, Upper Bearing Spring, Turn Switch Actuator, Buzzer Switch & Lock Cylinder Set."
2. Remove steering column housing and dimmer switch attaching screws and the dimmer switch hex nut, then the dimmer switch and mounting stud.
3. **On models equipped with cruise control,** unplug connector from base plate and remove multi-function lever.
4. **On all models,** remove ignition switch, then the dimmer switch rod.
5. Remove steering column housing, then the shift lever gate attaching screws and the shift lever gate.
6. Remove switch actuator rod and rack assembly, lock bolt assembly and spring thrust washer.
7. Remove switch actuator sector, then the upper bearing retainer.
8. Remove bearing retaining bushing and horn circuit contact, then the bearing assembly.
9. Remove housing cover attaching screw and cover, then the switch actuator pivot pin and pivot and switch assembly.

Assembly

1. Install pivot and switch assembly to steering column housing, then install switch actuator pivot pin.
2. Install housing cover and screw, then the bearing assembly.
3. Install bearing retaining bushing and horn circuit contact, then the switch actuator sector.
4. Install switch actuator rod and rack assembly and lock bolt assembly, then the shift lever gate and attaching screws.
5. **On models equipped with cruise control,** plug multi-function lever connector and cruise control wire on wash/wipe switch together and mount on base plate, then install multi-function lever.
6. **On all models,** install upper bearing retainer, then the steering column housing with attaching screws. Tighten screw in 12 o'clock position first, screw in 8 o'clock position second and screw in 4 o'clock position third, torquing to 80 inch lbs.
7. Install ignition switch and mounting stud, then adjust ignition switch, **Fig. 69.**
8. Install dimmer switch rod, then the dimmer switch and hex nut.
9. Adjust dimmer switch, **Fig. 73.**
10. Install dimmer switch attaching screw.

1	RETAINER	48	SPRING, SHIFT TUBE RETURN
2	NUT, HEXAGON	49	ADAPTER, LOWER BEARING
3	COVER, SHAFT LOCK	50	BEARING ASSY, ADAPTER &
4	RING, RETAINING	51	RETAINER, BEARING
5	LOCK, STEERING SHAFT	52	SCREW, HEX WASHER HEAD TAPPING
6	CAM ASSY, TURN SIGNAL CANCELLING	53	BEARING ASSY
7	SPRING, UPPER BEARING	54	RETAINER, BEARING ADAPTER
8	SCREW, BINDING HEAD CROSS RECESS	55	CLIP, LOWER BEARING ADAPTER
9	SCREW, ROUND WASHER HEAD		
10	ARM ASSY, SWITCH ACTUATOR		
11	SWITCH ASSY, TURN SIGNAL		
12	SCREW, HEX WASHER HEAD TAPPING		
13	WASHER, THRUST	60	RING, RETAINING
14	SWITCH ASSY, BUZZER	61	SHAFT ASSY, STEERING
15	CLIP, BUZZER SWITCH RETAINING	62	BUSHING ASSY, STEERING SHAFT
16	SCREW, LOCK RETAINING	63	SCREW, FLAT HEAD
17	HOUSING, STEERING COLUMN	64	WASHER, WAVE
18	SECTOR ASSY, SWITCH ACTUATOR	65	SEAL, DASH
19	LOCK CYLINDER SET, STEERING COLUMN	66	CUP, THRUST
20	BEARING ASSY		
21	BUSHING, BEARING RETAINING		
22	CONTACT, HORN CIRCUIT		SERVICE KITS
23	RETAINER, UPPER BEARING		
24	SWITCH ASSY, PIVOT &	201	HOUSING ASSY SERVICE KIT, STEERING COLUMN
25	BOLT ASSY, SPRING &	202	SHAFT REPAIR KIT, INJECTION STEERING
26	SPRING, RACK PRELOAD	203	SECTOR SERVICE KIT, IGNITION SWITCH ACTUATOR
27	RACK ASSY, SWITCH ACTUATOR ROD &		
28	COVER, HOUSING		
29	SCREW, BINDING HEAD CROSS RECESS		
30	SCREW, FLAT HEAD CROSS RECESS		
31	GATE, SHIFT LEVER		
32	WASHER, SPRING THRUST		
33	PIN, SWITCH ACTUATOR PIVOT		
34	SPRING, UPPER SHIFT LEVER		
35	BOWL, GEARSHIFT LEVER		
36	SHROUD, GEARSHIFT BOWL		
37	BEARING, BOWL LOWER		
38	JACKET ASSY, STEERING COLUMN		
39	PROTECTOR, WIRING		
40	ROD, DIMMER SWITCH ACTUATOR		
41	SWITCH ASSY, DIMMER		
42	SCREW, WASHER HEAD		
43	STUD, DIMMER & IGNITION SWITCH MOUNTING		
44	SWITCH ASSY, IGNITION		
45	NUT, HEXAGON		
46	TUBE ASSY, SHIFT		
47	WASHER, SPRING THRUST		

Fig. 72   Exploded view of standard steering column. Bonneville, Caprice, Custom Cruiser, LeSabre, Park Avenue, 88 & 98 less airbag (SIR)

11. Perform "Assembly" steps for "Shaft Lock, Turn Signal Cancelling Cam, Upper Bearing Spring, Turn Switch Actuator, Buzzer Switch & Lock Cylinder Set."

SHAFT & LOWER BEARING ASSEMBLY, GEARSHIFT LEVER BOWL SWITCH TUBE ASSEMBLY & LOWER BOWL BEARING

Disassembly

1. Remove screws from back of steering wheel and horn pad, disconnecting horn lead from cam tower.
2. Remove retainer and hex nut, then remove the steering wheel.
3. Remove steering column from vehicle.
4. Perform "Disassembly" steps 4 through 10 for "Shaft Lock, Turn Signal Cancelling Cam, Upper Bearing Spring, Turn Switch Actuator, Buzzer Switch & Lock Cylinder Set."
5. Perform "Disassembly" steps for "Steering Column Housing, Cover

64 SWITCH, DIMMER

Fig. 73   Adjusting dimmer switch. Bonneville, Caprice, Custom Cruiser, LeSabre, Park Avenue, 88 & 98 w/standard steering column

End Cap, Pivot & Switch Assembly, Switch Actuator Rod Rack, Upper Bearing, Dimmer Switch & Ignition Switch."
6. Remove lower bearing adapter clip, then the bearing adapter retainer.
7. Remove bearing assembly, then the lower bearing adapter.
8. Remove shift tube return spring and spring thrust washer, then the gear shift lever bowl and shroud.
9. Remove shift tube assembly, then the wave washer.
10. Remove lower bowl bearing.

Assembly

1. Install lower bowl bearing to jacket assembly.
2. Install wave washer, then the shift tube assembly.
3. Install gearshift lever bowl and shroud, then the shift tube return spring and spring thrust washer.
4. Install lower bearing adapter, then the bearing assembly.
5. Install bearing adapter retainer, then the lower bearing adapter clip.
6. Perform "Assembly" steps for "Steering Column Housing, Cover End Cap, Pivot & Switch Assembly, Switch Actuator Rod Rack, Upper Bearing, Dimmer Switch & Ignition Switch."
7. Install steering column in vehicle.
8. Perform "Assembly" steps for "Shaft Lock, Turn Signal Cancelling Cam, Upper Bearing Spring, Turn Switch Actuator, Buzzer Switch & Lock Cylinder Set."

TILT COLUMN

SHAFT LOCK, TURN SIGNAL CANCELLING CAM, UPPER BEARING SPRING, UPPER BEARING SEAT, INNER RACE, TURN SIGNAL SWITCH, BUZZER SWITCH & LOCK CYLINDER SET

Disassembly

Wheels of vehicle must be in straight ahead position. Failure to do so may cause improper alignment of some components during installation, resulting in column malfunction. Refer to **Fig. 74** for parts identification.

1. Place key in "lock" position.
2. Disconnect battery ground cable.
3. Remove screws from back of steering wheel and horn pad, disconnecting horn lead from cam tower.
4. Remove retainer and jam nut, then, using tool J-1859-03 or equivalent, the steering wheel.
5. Using tool J-23653-A or equivalent, depress shaft lock, then remove shaft lock retaining ring.
6. Remove shaft lock and shaft lock cover, then the turn signal cancelling cam.
7. Remove upper bearing spring, then the upper bearing seat.
8. Remove inner race.
9. Place turn signal in "right turn" position, then remove signal switch arm attaching screw and the arm.
10. Remove turn signal switch attaching screws and position switch out of way. If it is necessary to remove switch, remove wiring harness protector and hazard knob, then gently pull wire harness through gear shift lever bowl, column housing and lock housing cover.
11. Remove key from cylinder lock, and remove buzzer switch and clip, then reinsert key in cylinder lock and turn to "lock" position.
12. Remove lock retaining screw and lock cylinder set.

Assembly

1. Install lock cylinder set, torquing retaining screw to 26 inch lbs.
2. Place key in "run" position, then install buzzer switch and clip.
3. Route turn signal switch wiring harness through lock housing cover, column housing and gear shift lever bowl, then secure switch, torquing retaining screws to 26 inch lbs.
4. Install signal switch arm, torquing retaining screw to 18 inch lbs.
5. Install hazard knob, then the inner race.
6. Install upper bearing seat, then the upper bearing spring.
7. Install turn signal cancelling cam, then the shaft lock.
8. Depress shaft lock, then install shaft lock retaining ring.
9. Install steering wheel, then the jam nut and retainer.
10. Install horn pad, then the wiring harness protector.
11. Connect battery ground cable.

LOCK HOUSING COVER, COVER END CAP, PIVOT & SWITCH ASSEMBLY, DIMMER SWITCH ROD ACTUATOR & TILT SPRING ASSEMBLY

Disassembly

1. Perform "Disassembly" steps for "Shaft Lock, Turn Signal Cancelling Cam, Upper Bearing Spring, Upper Bearing Seat, Inner Race, Turn Signal Switch, Buzzer Switch & Lock Cylinder Set."
2. Remove lock housing cover attaching screws and cover, then the tilt lever.
3. Remove cover housing end cap and the dimmer switch rod actuator.
4. **On vehicles equipped with cruise control,** unplug cruise control connector and remove multi-function lever.
5. **On all models,** gently pull pivot switch wiring harness through column housing and gear shift lever bowl.
6. Remove pivot pin, then the pivot and switch assembly.
7. Remove spring retainer, then the spring and spring guide.

Assembly

1. Coat spring guide and spring with lithium grease and install, then install spring retainer.
2. Install pivot and switch assembly, then the pivot pin.
3. Route pivot and switch assembly wiring harness through gear shift lever bowl and column housing.
4. Install dimmer switch rod actuator, then the gear shift lever bowl, ensuring bottom edge of dimmer switch rod actuator rests on bend in dimmer switch rod.
5. Install cover housing end cap.
6. **On vehicles equipped with cruise control,** plug in cruise control connector and install multi-function lever.
7. **On all models,** Install lock housing cover. Tighten screw in 12 o'clock position first, screw in 8 o'clock position second and screw in 4 o'clock position third, then **torque** in same order to 89 inch lbs.
8. Perform "Assembly" steps for "Shaft Lock, Turn Signal Cancelling Cam, Upper Bearing Spring, Upper Bearing Seat, Inner Race, Turn Signal Switch, Buzzer Switch & Lock Cylinder Set."

COLUMN HOUSING, LOCK SHOES, ACTUATOR SECTOR ASSEMBLY, SWITCH ACTUATOR RACK, BEARINGS & LOCK BOLT ASSEMBLY

Disassembly

1. Perform "Disassembly" steps for "Shaft Lock, Turn Signal Cancelling Cam, Upper Bearing Spring, Upper Bearing Seat, Inner Race, Turn Signal Switch, Buzzer Switch & Lock Cylinder Set."
2. Perform "Disassembly" steps for "Lock Housing Cover, Cover End Cap, Pivot & Switch Assembly, Dimmer

Switch Rod Actuator & Tilt Spring Assembly."
3. Using pivot pin remover tool No. J-21854-01 or equivalent, remove pivot pins, **Fig. 75.**
4. Reinstall tilt lever.
5. Remove column housing assembly by pulling back on tilt lever and pulling housing down and away from column.
6. Remove driveshaft, then the switch actuator sector.
7. Remove switch actuator rack and rack preload spring, then the release lever pin and release lever.
8. Remove release lever spring, then the dowel pin.
9. Remove lock shoes and lock shoe springs, then the bearings.
10. Remove hex head bolt, then the lock bolt spring and lock bolt.

Assembly

1. Install bearings to column housing, then install driveshaft.
2. Install actuator sector, then the lock shoes.
3. Install dowel pin, then the lock shoe springs.
4. Install release lever spring, then the release lever.
5. Install release lever pin, then the rack preload spring.
6. Install switch actuator rack to actuator sector.
7. Install lock bolt and lock bolt spring, then the hex head bolt.
8. Install column housing assembly to column as follows:
   a. Position column housing assembly and align switch actuator rack with pin on end of actuator rod.
   b. Pull back on tilt lever, pushing column housing assembly onto column housing support assembly.
   c. Release tilt lever to lock shoes.
9. Remove tilt lever.
10. Lubricate pivot pins with lithium grease and install them.
11. Perform "Assembly" steps for "Lock Housing Cover, Cover End Cap, Pivot & Switch Assembly, Dimmer Switch Rod Actuator & Tilt Spring Assembly."
12. Perform "Assembly" steps for "Shaft Lock, Turn Signal Cancelling Cam, Upper Bearing Spring, Upper Bearing Seat, Inner Race, Turn Signal Switch, Buzzer Switch & Lock Cylinder Set."

SHAFT ASSEMBLY, COLUMN HOUSING SUPPORT, SHIFT TUBE ASSEMBLY, IGNITION SWITCH, DIMMER SWITCH & LOWER BEARING ASSEMBLY

Disassembly

1. Perform "Disassembly" steps for "Shaft Lock, Turn Signal Cancelling Cam, Upper Bearing Spring, Upper Bearing Seat, Inner Race, Turn Signal Switch, Buzzer Switch & Lock Cylinder Set."
2. Perform "Disassembly" steps for "Lock Housing Cover, Cover End Cap, Pivot & Switch Assembly, Dimmer Switch Rod Actuator & Tilt Spring Assembly."

82	STRAP, WIRE HARNESS
83	RETAINER, BEARING & SEAL
84	WASHER ASM, RETAINER
86	TUBE ASM, SHIFT
87	BEARING ASM, ADAPTER &
88	SCREW, HEX WASHER HD TAP
90	SEAT, LOWER BEARING
91	SPRING, LOWER BEARING
92	RETAINER, LOWER SPRING
93	CONNECTOR, AXIAL POS ASSUR
94	SUPPORT, STRG COL LOWER
95	BOLT, HEX FLNG HD (M6x1x14)
96	INTERLOCK ASM, SOLENOID &
97	SHIELD, INTERLOCK LEVER
98	LEVER ASM, INTLCK & BMPR
99	BUMPER, INTERLOCK LEVER
100	BUSHING, SOLENOID PIN
101	RING, RETAINING (METRIC 3CMI)
102	BOLT, HEX FLNG HD (M6x1x14)
103	SOLENOID ASM, INTERLOCK
104	SCREW, PAN HD 6-LOBED SOC TAP
105	SWITCH ASM, DIMMER

41	SPRING, RELEASE LEVER
42	PIN, RELEASE LEVER
43	LEVER, SHOE RELEASE
44	RACK, SWITCH ACTUATOR
45	SPRING, RACK PRELOAD
46	HOUSING, STRG COLUMN
47	SECTOR, SWITCH ACTUATOR
48	SCREW, HEX WASHER HEAD
50	GUIDE, SPRING
51	SPRING, WHEEL TILT
52	RETAINER, SPRING
55	SHAFT ASM, STEERING
56	SHAFT ASM, RACE & UPPER
57	SPHERE, CENTERING
58	SPRING, JOINT PRELOAD
59	SHAFT ASM, LOWER STEERING
61	SCREW, SUPPORT
62	SUPPORT ASM, STRG COL HSG
63	SUPPORT, STRG COL HSG
64	SCREW, OVL HD CROSS RECESS
65	GATE, SHIFT LEVER
66	RING, SHIFT TUBE RETAINING
67	WASHER, THRUST
68	PLATE, LOCK
69	WASHER, WAVE
70	SPRING, SHIFT LEVER
71	BOWL ASM, GEARSHIFT LEVER
72	JACKET ASM, STRG COL
76	ACTUATOR ASM, IGN SWITCH
77	ROD, DIMMER SWITCH
78	SCREW, WASH HD (#10-24x.25)
79	NUT, HEXAGON (#10-24)
80	SWITCH ASM, IGNITION & DIMR
81	STUD, DIMR & IGN SW MTG

1	NUT, HEX LOCKING (M14x1.5)
2	COVER, SHAFT LOCK
5	RING, RETAINING
6	LOCK SHAFT
7	CAM ASM, TURN SIG CANCEL
8	SPRING, UPPER BEARING
9	SCREW, BNDG HD CR RECESS
10	SCREW, RD WASH HD (M4.2x1.41)
11	ARM ASM, SIGNAL SWITCH
12	SWITCH ASM, TURN SIGNAL
13	SEAT, UPPER BRG INNER RACE
14	RACE, INNER
15	SCREW, PAN HD SOC TAP
16	SWITCH ASM, BUZZER
18	SCREW, LOCK RETAINING
19	COVER ASM, LOCK HOUSING
20	LOCK CYLINDER SET, STRG COL
21	ACTUATOR, DIMMER SW ROD
22	PIN, SWITCH ACTUATOR PIVOT
23	SWITCH ASM, PIVOT & (PULSE)
24	BASE PLATE, COL HSG CVR END
25	CAP, COL HSG COVER END
26	PROTECTOR, WIRING
30	HOUSING ASM, STRG COLUMN
31	BEARING ASM
32	BOLT, LOCK
33	SPRING, LOCK BOLT
34	SHOE, STEERING WHEEL LOCK
35	SHOE, STEERING WHEEL LOCK
36	SHIELD, WIRE PROTECTOR
37	SHAFT, DRIVE
38	PIN, DOWEL
39	PIN, PIVOT
40	SPRING, SHOE

Fig. 74 Exploded view of tilt steering column. 1991 Bonneville, LeSabre, Park Avenue, 88 & 98 less airbag (SIR)

23. PIN, PIVOT

Fig. 75 Removing pivot pins. Bonneville, Caprice, Custom Cruiser, Park Avenue, LeSabre, 88 & 98 w/tilt column less airbag (SIR)

68. SWITCH, DIMMER

Fig. 76 Adjusting dimmer switch. Bonneville, Caprice, Custom Cruiser, Park Avenue, LeSabre, 88 & 98 w/tilt column less airbag (SIR)

3. Perform "Disassembly" steps for "Column Housing, Lock Shoes, Actuator Sector Assembly, Switch Actuator Rack, Bearings & Lock Bolt Assembly."
4. Remove steering column from vehicle.
5. Remove bearing retainer, then the attaching screws and the lower bearing.
6. Remove shaft assembly then disconnect lower shaft.
7. Remove sphere from upper shaft, then the retainer clip from the sphere.
8. Remove housing support assembly attaching screws, then the housing support assembly and dimmer switch rod.
9. Remove hex nut and hex head bolt, then the dimmer switch and mounting stud.
10. Remove gear shift bowl.

Assembly

1. Install gear shift lever bowl to jacket, then the dimmer switch rod to housing support.
2. Install housing support assembly, torquing attaching screws to 80 inch lbs.
3. Install actuator rod assembly to track in housing support.
4. Install ignition switch and mounting stud, then adjust switch, **Fig. 69.**
5. Install retaining clip and sphere to upper shaft.
6. Install lower shaft to upper shaft with block tooth on shaft lower end of upper shaft at 12 o'clock position and notch at end of lower shaft at 4 o'clock position.
7. Lubricate shaft assembly with lithium grease and install to column.
8. Install column housing assembly to

1 SPRING SHOE	25 SHAFT LOCK RETAINER	49 COLUMN SUPPORT
2 PIVOT PIN	26 CARRIER SNAP RING RETAINER	50 LOWER STEERING SHAFT
3 DOWEL PIN	27 RETRACTED SHAFT BUMPER	51 CENTERING SPHERE
4 DRIVE SHAFT	28 SHAFT NUT	52 JOINT PRELOAD SPRING
5 STEERING WHEEL LOCK SHOE	29 SPACERS	53 RACE & STEERING YOKE
6 LOCK BOLT SPRING	30 WIRE PROTECTOR	54 LOCKING WEDGE
7 LOCK BOLT	31 COLUMN HOUSING END CAP	55 UPPER STEERING SHAFT
8 BEARING	32 SPRING RETAINER	56 TELESCOPE LOCKING ROD
9 SWITCH ACTUATOR PIVOT PIN	33 WHEEL TILT SPRING	57 SCREWS
10 DIMMER SWITCH ROD ACTUATOR	34 SPRING GUIDE	58 IGNITION SWITCH ASSEMBLY
11 SWITCH ACTUATOR PIVOT	35 SWITCH ACTUATOR SECTOR	59 BEARING
12 PIN PRELOAD	36 PIVOT PIN	60 LOWER BEARING ADAPTER
13 TILT LEVER OPENING SHIELD	37 STEERING COLUMN HOUSING	61 BEARING ADAPTER RETAINER
14 LOCK CYLINDER	38 RACK PRELOAD SPRING	62 SNAP RING
15 LOCK CYLINDER COVER	39 SWITCH ACTUATOR RACK	63 WASHER
16 BUZZER RETAINER CLIP	40 IGNITION SWITCH ACTUATOR	64 LOCK PLATE
17 BUZZER SWITCH	41 SHOE RELEASE LEVER	65 WAVE WASHER
18 INNER RACE	42 BEARING	66 SHIFT TUBE
19 INNER RACE SEAT	43 GEARSHIFT BOWL SHROUD	67 COWL SEAL
20 TURN SIGNAL SWITCH	44 GEARSHIFT LEVER BOWL	68 STEERING COLUMN JACKET
21 SIGNAL SWITCH ARM ASSEMBLY	45 LIFT LEVER SPRING	69 DIMMER SWITCH
22 UPPER BEARING SPRING	46 SHIFT TUBE RETAINING RING	70 DIMMER SWITCH ROD
23 CARRIER ASSEMBLY	47 SHIFT LEVER GATE	
24 STEERING SHAFT LOCK	48 DOWEL PIN	

Fig. 77 Exploded view of tilt/telescopic steering column. 1991-92 Brougham

column.
9. Position column assembly and align switch actuator rack with pin on end of actuator rod.
10. Pull back on tilt lever, pushing column housing assembly onto column housing support assembly.
11. Release tilt lever to lock shoes, then remove tilt lever.
12. Lubricate inner surface of lower bearing with lithium grease, then install bearing and retaining screws.
13. Install bearing retainer.
14. Install dimmer switch, hex nut and hex head bolt, then adjust dimmer switch, **Fig. 76.**
15. Install steering column to instrument panel.
16. Install tilt lever.
17. Perform "Assembly" steps for "Column Housing, Lock Shoes, Actuator Sector Assembly, Switch Actuator Rack, Bearings & Lock Bolt Assembly."
18. Perform "Assembly" steps for "Lock Housing Cover, Cover End Cap, Pivot & Switch Assembly, Dimmer Switch Rod Actuator & Tilt Spring Assembly."
19. Perform "Assembly" steps for "Shaft Lock, Turn Signal Cancelling Cam, Upper Bearing Spring, Upper Bearing Seat, Inner Race, Turn Signal Switch, Buzzer Switch & Lock Cylinder Set."

Brougham
TILT/TELESCOPIC COLUMN
Refer to **Fig. 77.** when servicing this column.

Disassembly
1. Disconnect battery ground cable, then remove column from vehicle.
2. Turn ignition switch to the Run position.
3. Remove horn pad, switch and horn connector.
4. Remove three small bolts and unscrew telescoping adjuster from shaft.

5. Remove telescoping lever from column, nut from steering column shaft and steering wheel.
6. Remove key warning buzzer and retaining clip.
7. Remove lock cylinder retaining screw inside lock housing column cover and lock cylinder from column.
8. Remove hazard switch, tilt column lever and turn signal/cruise control lever.
9. Remove lock housing column cover, lower column cover and fuse panel cover.
10. Disconnect harness connector, then remove wiring protector and multi-function turn signal switch from column.
11. Install tilt lever and place column in the full up position.
12. Remove upper bearing seat, inner race and bearing.
13. Remove tilt spring retainer, spring and guide.
14. Use a punch to remove driveshaft and sector.
15. Remove pivot pins using special tool No. J 21854-01 or equivalent, Fig. 75.
16. Tilt housing by pulling upward on tilt lever and pulling housing upward until it stops. Move housing to the right to disengage rack from actuator.
17. Remove race and upper shaft assembly from lower shaft at centering sphere.
18. Remove gearshift lever, gate and column support.
19. Remove lock plate, retaining ring and washers.
20. Remove shift tube from shift bowl using special tool No. J 23072 or equivalent.
21. Remove lower bearing and retainer.

Assembly

1. Install lower bearing and retainer.
2. Install gear shift tube to bowl using special tool No. J 23073-01 or equivalent.
3. Install lock plate, retaining ring and washers.
4. Install column support, gearshift lever and gate.
5. Install race and upper shaft assembly to lower shaft at centering sphere.
6. Install tilt housing and new pivot pins.
7. Install driveshaft and sector.
8. Install tilt spring, retainer and guide.
9. Install upper bearing, seat and inner race.
10. Install multi-function switch to column, wiring protector and connect harness connector.
11. Install fuse panel, lower column and lock housing column covers.
12. Install hazard switch, turn signal/cruise control and tilt column levers to column.
13. Install lock cylinder and retaining screw to column.
14. Install key warning buzzer and retaining clip.
15. Install steering wheel to column shaft and **torque** nut to 35 ft. lbs.
16. Install telescope locking lever on shaft and telescope adjuster.

17. Position locking lever and bolts along the marks made by the bolts when tightened, **torque** bolts to 35 inch lbs.
18. Check operation of telescoping lever for proper release and tightening within the lever's range of motion. Ensure that the wheel is free to telescope when the lever is all the way to the left and securely locked when lever is all the way to the right. If necessary adjust using the slotted locking lever bolt holes.
19. Install horn contact wire and horn pad assembly, then connect battery ground cable.

Century, Cutlass Ciera, Cutlass Cruiser & 6000

STANDARD COLUMN

Refer to **Fig. 78.** when servicing this column.

SHAFT LOCK, TURN SIGNAL CANCELLING CAM, UPPER BEARING SPRING, UPPER BEARING SEAT, INNER RACE, TURN SIGNAL SWITCH, ALARM ASSEMBLY & LOCK CYLINDER SET

Disassembly

1. Disconnect battery ground cable.
2. Gently pull up on horn pad to remove.
3. Disconnect horn lead by gently pushing down on lead and turning to the left, spring will then come out of cancelling cam tower.
4. Remove retainer, nut and steering wheel.
5. Remove shaft lock retaining ring using special tool No. J 23653-C or equivalent to depress shaft lock.
6. Remove shaft lock, turn signal cancelling cam, upper bearing spring and thrust washer.
7. Move turn signal to the "right turn" position.
8. Remove multi-function lever, screw and switch actuator arm.
9. Remove screws, hazard knob assembly and turn signal switch.
10. Remove wiring protector and gently pull harness through gearshift lever bowl, gearshift lever bowl shroud and lock cover assembly housing.
11. Remove key from lock cylinder and alarm assembly and clip.
12. Reinstall key and turn to the Lock position, remove lock retaining screw, then lock cylinder set.

Assembly

1. Install lock cylinder set and retaining screw and **torque** to 30 inch lbs.
2. Install key and turn to the Run position.
3. Install alarm assembly and clip.
4. Install turn signal switch harness through lock housing cover assembly, gearshift lever bowl and gearshift bowl shroud and connect.
5. Install turn signal switch and screws and **torque** to 35 inch lbs.
6. Install wiring protector, switch actua-

tor arm and screw and **torque** to 20 inch lbs.
7. Install hazard knob assembly, multi-function lever, thrust washer, upper bearing spring and turn signal cancelling cam.
8. Install shaft lock and shaft lock retaining ring using special tool No. J 23653-C to depress shaft lock.
9. Install steering wheel and nut and **torque** to 30 ft. lbs.
10. Install horn lead and pad, then connect battery ground cable.

LOCK HOUSING COVER ASSEMBLY, COVER END CAP, PIVOT & PULSE SWITCH ASSEMBLY, IGNITION SWITCH ACTUATOR, UPPER BEARING, SWITCH ACTUATOR SECTOR, DIMMER SWITCH & IGNITION SWITCH

Disassembly

1. Remove shaft lock, turn signal cancelling cam, upper bearing spring, upper bearing seat, inner race, turn signal switch, alarm assembly & lock cylinder set as previously described.
2. **On models equipped with cruise control,** remove housing cover end cap, disconnect multi-function lever connector and gently pull through shroud, bowl and cover and remove multi-function lever.
3. **On all models,** remove washer head screw, hex nut, dimmer switch and mounting stud.
4. Remove ignition switch, dimmer switch rod, cover screws and lock cover housing assembly.
5. Remove upper bearing retainer and gently pull pivot switch harness through gear shift bowl shroud and gear shift lever bowl.
6. Remove binding head cross recess screw, housing cover end cap and switch actuator pivot pin.
7. Remove pivot and pulse switch assembly, flat head cross recess screws and shift lever gate.
8. Remove ignition switch actuator assembly, spring and lock bolt assembly, spring thrust washer and rack preload spring.
9. Remove bearing retaining bushing and horn circuit contact.
10. Remove bearing assembly and switch actuator sector.

Assembly

1. Install switch actuator sector and bearing assembly.
2. Install bearing retaining bushing, horn circuit contact and rack preload spring.
3. Install ignition switch actuator assembly, spring and lock bolt assembly and spring thrust washer.
4. Install shift lever gate and **torque** screws to 44 inch lbs.
5. Install pivot and pulse switch assembly and switch actuator pivot pin.
6. **On models equipped with cruise control,** gently pull connector through cover assembly, bowl, and

Fig. 78 Exploded view of standard steering column. Century, Cutlass Ciera, Cutlass Cruiser & 6000

1	NUT, HEXAGON LOCKING (M14 × 1.5)
3	RING, RETAINING
4	LOCK, SHAFT
5	CAM ASM, TURN SIG CANCELLING
6	SPRING, UPPER BEARING
7	SCREW, BINDING HD CROSS RECESS
8	SCREW, RD WASH HD (M4.2 × 1.41)
9	ARM, SIGNAL SWITCH
10	SWITCH ASM, TURN SIGNAL
11	SCREW, HEX WASHER HD TAPPING
12	WASHER, THRUST
13	SWITCH ASM, BUZZER
14	CLIP, BUZZER SWITCH RETAINING
15	SCREW, LOCK RETAINING
16	COVER ASM, LOCK HOUSING
17	SECTOR, SWITCH ACTUATOR
18	LOCK CYLINDER SET, STRG COLUMN
19	GATE, SHIFT LEVER
20	SPRING, RACK PRELOAD
21	ACTUATOR ASM, IGNITION SWITCH
22	WASHER, SPRING THRUST
23	RETAINER, UPPER BEARING
24	BUSHING, BEARING RETAINING
25	BEARING ASM
26	BOLT ASM, SPRING &
27	CONTACT, HORN CIRCUIT
28	SCREW, FLAT HEAD CROSS RECESS
29	PIN, SWITCH ACTUATOR PIVOT
30	SWITCH ASM, PIVOT & (PULSE)
31	CAP, COL HSG COVER END
32	SCREW, BINDING HEAD CROSS RECESS
33	PROTECTOR, WIRING
34	RING, RETAINING
35	SHAFT ASM, STEERING COLUMN
36	SPRING, UPPER SHIFT LEVER
37	BOWL, GEARSHIFT LEVER
38	SHROUD, GEARSHIFT BOWL
39	BEARING, BOWL LOWER
40	JACKET ASM, STRG COL
41	STUD, DIMR & IGN SW MOUNTING
42	SWITCH ASM, DIMMER
43	SWITCH ASM, IGNITION
44	NUT, HEXAGON (#10-24 × .25)
45	SCREW, WASH HD (#10-24 × .25)
47	ROD, DIMMER SWITCH
48	TUBE ASM, SHIFT
49	SPRING, LOWER BEARING
50	BEARING ASM, ADAPTER &
51	SCREW, HEX WASHER HD TAPPING
52	RETAINER, BEARING & SEAL
53	SEAT, LOWER BEARING
54	SPRING, SHIFT TUBE RETURN
55	RETAINER, LOWER SPRING

shroud and connect, then install multi-function lever.

7. **On all models,** install housing cover end cap and screw and **torque** screw to 18 inch lbs.

8. Gently pull pivot switch harness through bowl and shroud and con-

nect.

9. Install upper bearing retainer, lock housing cover assembly and screws and **torque** screws to 97 inch lbs.

10. Install ignition switch and mounting stud and **torque** to 36 inch lbs.

11. Install dimmer switch rod, dimmer

switch and hex nut and **torque** to 36 inch lbs.

12. Perform assembly steps for shaft lock, turn signal cancelling cam, upper bearing spring, upper bearing seat, inner race, turn signal switch, alarm assembly & lock cylinder set as previously described.

SHAFT ASSEMBLY, ADAPTER & BEARING ASSEMBLY, GEARSHIFT LEVER BOWL, SHIFT TUBE ASSEMBLY & BOWL LOWER BEARING

Disassembly

1. Disconnect battery ground cable.
2. Gently pull up on horn pad to remove and disconnect horn lead by pushing down and turning left to remove from cancelling cam tower.
3. Remove retainer, nut and steering wheel.
4. Remove column from vehicle.
5. Remove bearing and seal retainer, lower spring retainer, lower bearing spring and lower bearing seat.
6. Remove hex head screws, adapter and bearing assembly and shift tube return spring.
7. Remove column shaft assembly and check for accident damage.
8. Remove retaining ring, gearshift lever bowl and shroud.
9. Remove upper shift lever spring from bowl, shift tube assembly and bowl lower bearing.

Assembly

1. Install lower bowl bearing to jacket assembly and upper shift lever spring to bowl.
2. Install shift tube assembly, gearshift lever bowl and shroud.
3. Install shift tube return spring, adapter and bearing assembly, lubricating inner surface with lithium grease.
4. Install screws and **torque** to 27 inch lbs.
5. Install lower bearing seat, lower bearing spring, bearing and seal retainer.
6. Install steering wheel and **torque** nut to 30 ft. lbs.
7. Install retainer, horn lead and pad and connect battery ground cable.

TILT COLUMN

Refer to **Fig. 79.** when servicing this column.

Shaft Lock, Turn Signal Cancelling Cam, Upper Bearing Spring, Upper Bearing Seat, Inner Race, Turn Signal Switch, Alarm Assembly & Lock Cylinder Set

Refer to "Standard Column" for disassembly procedure.

LOCK HOUSING COVER, COVER END CAP, PIVOT & PULSE SWITCH ASSEMBLY, DIMMER SWITCH ROD ACTUATOR & TILT SPRING ASSEMBLY

Disassembly

1. Remove shaft lock, turn signal cancelling cam, upper bearing spring, upper bearing seat, inner race, turn signal switch, alarm assembly & lock cylinder set as previously described.
2. **On models equipped with cruise control**, remove housing cover end cap, unplug connector and gently pull through bowl assembly, then remove multi-function lever.
3. **On all models**, remove cover screws and lock housing cover assembly.
4. Remove tilt lever, cover end cap and dimmer switch rod actuator.
5. Gently pull pivot switch harness through bowl assembly and column housing.
6. Remove pivot pin, pivot and pulse switch assembly, spring retainer, spring and spring guide.

Assembly

1. Install spring guide and spring coated with lithium grease.
2. Install spring retainer, pivot and pulse switch assembly and pivot pin.
3. Feed pivot and pulse switch assembly harness through column housing and bowl assembly and connect.
4. Install dimmer switch rod actuator to cover end cap.
5. Install cover end cap to lock housing cover assembly. Bottom edge of dimmer switch rod actuator should rest on bend in dimmer switch rod.
6. Install lock housing cover assembly.
7. **On models equipped with cruise control**, gently pull connector through column housing and bowl assembly and connect, then install multi-function lever.
8. **On all models**, install lock housing cover assembly screws and **torque** to 80 inch lbs. Screw in the 12 o'clock position first, 8 o'clock position second and the 4 o'clock position last.
9. Perform assembly steps for shaft lock, turn signal cancelling cam, upper bearing spring, upper bearing seat, inner race, turn signal switch, alarm assembly & lock cylinder set as previously described.

COLUMN HOUSING, LOCK SHOES, ACTUATOR SECTOR ASSEMBLY, SWITCH ACTUATOR RACK, BEARINGS & LOCK BOLT ASSEMBLY

Disassembly

1. Remove shaft lock, turn signal cancelling cam, upper bearing spring, upper bearing seat, inner race, turn signal switch, alarm assembly & lock cylinder set, lock housing cover, cover end cap, pivot & pulse switch assembly, dimmer switch rod actuator & tilt spring assembly as previously de-

1	NUT, HEXAGON LOCKING (M14 × 1.5)
3	RING, RETAINING
4	LOCK, SHAFT
5	CAM ASM, TURN SIG CANCELLING
6	SPRING, UPPER BEARING
7	SCREW, BINDING HD CROSS RECESS
8	SCREW, RD WASH HD (M4.2 × 1.41)
9	ARM, SIGNAL SWITCH
10	SWITCH ASM, TURN SIGNAL
11	SEAT, UPPER BEARING INNER RACE
12	RACE, INNER
13	SCREW, PAN HD 6-LOBED SOC TAP
14	SWITCH ASM, BUZZER
15	CLIP, BUZZER SWITCH RETAINING
16	SCREW, LOCK RETAINING
17	COVER ASM, LOCK HOUSING
18	LOCK CYLINDER SET, STRG COLUMN
19	ACTUATOR, DIMMER SWITCH ROD
20	PIN, SWITCH ACTUATOR PIVOT
21	SWITCH ASM, PIVOT & (PULSE)
22	CAP, COL HSG COVER END
23	PROTECTOR, WIRING
24	HOUSING ASM, STRG COLUMN
25	BEARING ASM
26	BOLT, LOCK
27	SPRING, LOCK BOLT
28	SHOE, STEERING WHEEL LOCK
29	SHOE, STEERING WHEEL LOCK
31	SHAFT, DRIVE
32	PIN, DOWEL
33	PIN, PIVOT
34	SPRING, SHOE
35	SPRING, RELEASE LEVER
36	PIN, RELEASE LEVER
37	LEVER, SHOE RELEASE
38	RACK, SWITCH ACTUATOR
39	SPRING, RACK PRELOAD
40	HOUSING, STRG COLUMN
41	SECTOR, SWITCH ACTUATOR
42	SCREW, HEX WASHER HEAD
43	GUIDE, SPRING
44	SPRING, WHEEL TILT
45	RETAINER, SPRING
46	SHAFT ASM, STEERING COLUMN
47	SHAFT ASM, RACE & UPPER
48	SPHERE, CENTERING
49	SPRING, JOINT PRELOAD
50	SHAFT ASM, LOWER STEERING
51	SCREW, SUPPORT
52	SUPPORT ASM, STRG COL HSG
53	SUPPORT, STRG COL HSG
54	SCREW, OVAL HD CROSS RECESS
55	GATE, SHIFT LEVER
56	RING, SHIFT TUBE RETAINING
57	WASHER, THRUST
58	PLATE, LOCK
59	WASHER, WAVE
60	SPRING, SHIFT LEVER
61	BOWL ASM, GEARSHIFT LEVER
62	JACKET ASM, STRG COL
63	ACTUATOR ASM, IGNITION SWITCH
64	SWITCH ASM, IGNITION
65	STUD, DIMR & IGN SW MOUNTING
66	SWITCH ASM, DIMMER
67	NUT, HEXAGON (#10-24 × .25)
68	SCREW, WASH HD (#10-24 × .25)
69	ROD, DIMMER SWITCH
70	TUBE ASM, SHIFT
71	BEARING ASM, ADAPTER &
72	SCREW, HEX WASHER HD TAPPING
73	RETAINER, BEARING & SEAL
74	SEAT, LOWER BEARING
75	SPRING, LOWER BEARING
76	RETAINER, LOWER SPRING

Fig. 79 Exploded view of tilt steering column. Century, Cutlass Ciera, Cutlass Cruiser & 6000

scribed.

2. Remove pivot pins using special tool No. J 21854-01 or equivalent, **Fig. 75.**
3. Reinstall tilt lever and remove column housing by pulling back on tilt lever and pulling housing down and away from column.
4. Remove driveshaft, switch actuator sector, switch actuator rack and rack preload spring.
5. Remove release lever pin, shoe release lever and release lever spring.
6. Remove dowel pin, lock shoes, shoe springs and bearing assembly.
7. Remove hex head screw, lock bolt spring and lock bolt.

Assembly

1. Install bearing assembly to column housing.
2. Install driveshaft, switch actuator sector and lock shoes.
3. Install dowel pin, shoe springs and release lever spring.
4. Install shoe release lever, release lever pin and rack preload spring.
5. Install switch actuator rack to switch actuator sector.
6. Install lock bolt, lock bolt spring and hex head screw. **Torque** screw to 37 inch lbs.
7. Install column housing to column. Position column housing and align switch actuator rack with pin on end of actuator assembly. pull back on tilt lever, pushing column housing onto column housing support assembly. Release tilt lever to lock shoes onto dowel pins.
8. Remove tilt lever and install pivot pins lubricated with lithium grease.
9. Perform assembly steps for shaft lock, turn signal cancelling cam, upper bearing spring, upper bearing seat, inner race, turn signal switch, alarm assembly & lock cylinder set, lock housing cover, cover end cap, pivot & pulse switch assembly, dimmer switch rod actuator & tilt spring assembly as previously described.

SHAFT ASSEMBLY, COLUMN HOUSING SUPPORT, SHIFT TUBE ASSEMBLY, IGNITION SWITCH, DIMMER SWITCH & LOWER BEARING ASSEMBLY

Disassembly

1. Remove shaft lock, turn signal cancelling cam, upper bearing spring, upper bearing seat, inner race, turn signal switch, alarm assembly & lock cylinder set, lock housing cover, cover end cap, pivot & pulse switch assembly, dimmer switch rod actuator & tilt spring assembly, column housing, lock shoes, actuator sector assembly, switch actuator rack, bearings & lock bolt assembly as previously described.
2. Remove column from vehicle.
3. Remove bearing and seal retainer, lower spring retainer, lower bearing spring and lower bearing seat.
4. Remove hex head screws, adapter and bearing assembly.
5. Remove column shaft assembly and

inspect for accident damage.

6. Mark upper and lower shaft assemblies to ensure proper assembly.
7. Remove upper shaft assembly, lower shaft assembly. Tilt 90° to each other and disengage.
8. Remove centering sphere from upper shaft assembly. Rotate sphere 90° and slip out.
9. Remove joint preload spring from centering sphere.
10. Remove screws, column housing support assembly and dimmer switch rod from steering column jacket assembly.
11. Remove rod from column housing support assembly and screws and shift lever gate from support assembly.
12. Remove hex nut, screw, dimmer switch assembly and mounting stud.
13. Remove ignition switch assembly and switch actuator assembly.
14. Remove switch actuator assembly from switch assembly.
15. Remove shift tube retaining ring, thrust washer and shift lever spring.
16. Remove shift tube using special tool No. J 23072 or equivalent.
17. Remove lock plate, wave washer and gearshift lever bowl.

Assembly

1. Install shift lever spring to gear shift lever bowl and gear shift lever bowl to shift tube jacket.
2. Install wave washer lubricated with lithium grease and lock plate.
3. Install shift tube using special tool No. J 23073 or equivalent.
4. Install thrust washer and shift tube retaining ring.
5. Install gate and screws to support assembly and **torque** screws to 27 inch lbs.
6. Install dimmer switch rod to support assembly.
7. Install column support assembly and **torque** screws to 80 inch lbs.
8. Install actuator assembly to track in housing support assembly.
9. Install joint preload spring to centering sphere.
10. Lubricate centering sphere with lithium grease and slip into upper shaft assembly and rotate 90°.
11. Ensure marks made on upper and lower shaft assemblies line up after assembly.
12. Install upper shaft assembly to lower shaft assembly, line up marks and tilt assemblies 90° to each other.
13. Install column shaft assembly lubricated with lithium grease to jacket assembly.
14. Perform assembly steps for shaft lock, turn signal cancelling cam, upper bearing spring, upper bearing seat, inner race, turn signal switch, alarm assembly & lock cylinder set, lock housing cover, cover end cap, pivot & pulse switch assembly, dimmer switch rod actuator & tilt spring assembly, column housing, lock shoes, actuator sector assembly, switch actuator rack, bearings & lock bolt assembly as pre-

viously described.

15. Install adapter and bearing assembly and lubricate inner surface with lithium grease.
16. Install screws and **torque** to 27 inch lbs.
17. Install lower bearing seat, lower bearing spring, lower spring retainer, bearing and seal retainer.
18. Install ignition switch assembly and mounting stud and **torque** to 36 inch lbs.
19. Install dimmer switch assembly, screw and nut and **torque** to 36 inch lbs.
20. Install column into vehicle.

Bonneville, Camaro, Corvette, DeVille, Firebird, Fleetwood, LeSabre, Park Avenue, Reatta, Riviera, Toronado, Trofeo, 88, 98, & 1991-92 Eldorado & Seville w/Supplemental Inflatable Restraint (SIR)

Disarm airbag system as described under "Airbag System Disarming," then remove column as described under "Steering Column, Replace." The steering wheel must be straight and the column in the Lock position. **Care must be taken when handling column with a live inflator module. Never point bag deploy surface toward you, and never stand column on steering wheel. Accidental deployment in these positions may cause injury. Always face bag deploy surface toward open space to allow for unrestricted expansion.**

COIL ASSEMBLY, SHAFT LOCK, TURN SIGNAL CANCELLING CAM, UPPER BEARING SPRING, UPPER BEARING SEAT, INNER RACE TURN SIGNAL SWITCH, BUZZER SWITCH & LOCK CYLINDER SET

Refer to **Figs. 80 through 89** when servicing this column.

Disassembly

Steering wheel replacement for the Riviera, Reatta, Trofeo and Toronado with airbag or redundant steering wheel controls has been revised by service bulletin No. 90-110-9.

Continued on page 27-60

50-GUIDE, SPRING
51-SPRING, WHEEL TILT
52-RETAINER, SPRING
55-SHAFT ASM, STEERING COLUMN
56-SHAFT ASM, RACE & UPPER
57-SPHERE, CENTERING
58-SPRING, JOINT PRELOAD
59-SHAFT ASM, LOWER STEERING
61-SCREW, SUPPORT
62-SUPPORT ASM, STRG COL HSG
63-SUPPORT, STRG COL HSG
64-SCREW, OVAL HD CROSS RECESS
65-GATE, SHIFT LEVER
66-RING, SHIFT TUBE RETAINING
67-WASHER, THRUST
68-PLATE, LOCK
69-WASHER, WAVE
70-SPRING, SHIFT LEVER
71-BOWL ASM, GEARSHIFT LEVER
72-JACKET ASM, STRG COL
76-ACTUATOR ASM, IGNITION SWITCH
77-ROD, DIMMER SWITCH
78-SCREW, WASH HD (#10-24 X .25)
79-NUT, HEXAGON (#10-24 X .25)
80-SWITCH ASM, DIMR & IGNITION
81-STUD, DIMR & IGN SW MOUNTING
86-TUBE ASM, SHIFT
87-BEARING ASM, ADAPTER &
88-SCREW, HEX WASHER HD TAPPING
89-RETAINER, BEARING & SEAL
90-SEAT, LOWER BEARING
91-SPRING, LOWER BEARING
92-RETAINER, LOWER SPRING

Service Kits

201-RACK SERV KIT, COLUMN SECTOR &
  -INCLUDES: 14,31,33,44,47,48
202-SPRING SERV KIT, TILT COLUMN
  -INCLUDES: 13,14,39,50,51,52
203-COIL SERV KIT, INFL RESTRAINT
  -INCLUDES: 3,4,27
204-SPHERE SERV KIT, TILT COLUMN
  -INCLUDES: 57,58

1-NUT, HEXAGON LOCKING (M14X1.5)
2-RING, RETAINING
3-COIL ASM, INFL RESTRAINT
4-WASHER, WAVE
5-RING, RETAINING
6-LOCK, SHAFT
7-CAM ASM, TURN SIG CANCELLING
8-SPRING, UPPER BEARING
9-SCREW, BINDING HD CROSS RECESS
10-SCREW, RD WASH HD (M4.2X1.41)
11-ARM, SIGNAL SWITCH
12-SWITCH ASM, TURN SIGNAL
13-SEAT, UPPER BEARING INNER RACE
14-RACE, INNER
15-SCREW, PAN HD 6-LOBED SOC TAP
16-SWITCH ASM, BUZZER
17-CLIP, BUZZER SWITCH RETAINING
18-SCREW, LOCK RETAINING
19-COVER ASM, LOCK HOUSING
20-LOCK CYLINDER SET, STRG COLUMN
21-ACTUATOR, DIMMER SWITCH ROD
22-PIN, SWITCH ACTUATOR PIVOT
23-SWITCH ASM, PIVOT & (PULSE)
24-BASE PLATE, COL HSG COVER END
25-CAP, COL HSG COVER END
26-PROTECTOR, WIRING
27-SHROUD, CONNECTOR
30-HOUSING ASM, STRG COLUMN
31-BEARING ASM
32-BOLT, LOCK
33-SPRING, LOCK BOLT
34-SHOE, STEERING WHEEL LOCK
35-SHOE, STEERING WHEEL LOCK
36-SHIELD, WIRE ABRASION
37-SHAFT, DRIVE
38-PIN, DOWEL
39-PIN, PIVOT
40-SPRING, SHOE
41-SPRING, RELEASE LEVER
42-PIN, RELEASE LEVER
43-LEVER, SHOE RELEASE
44-RACK, SWITCH ACTUATOR
45-SPRING, RACK PRELOAD
46-HOUSING, STRG COLUMN
47-SECTOR, SWITCH ACTUATOR
48-SCREW, HEX WASHER HEAD

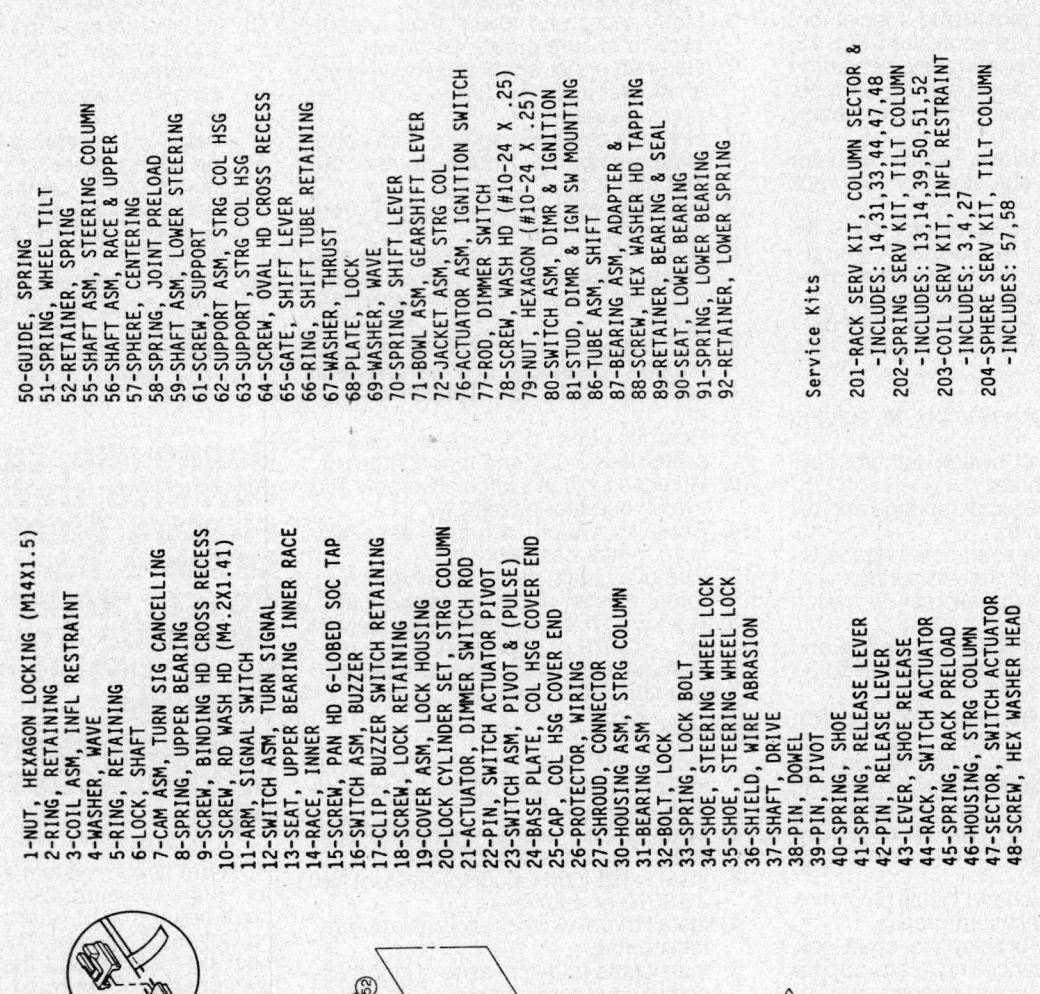

Fig. 80 Exploded view of steering column. 1991 DeVille & Fleetwood w/airbag (SIR)

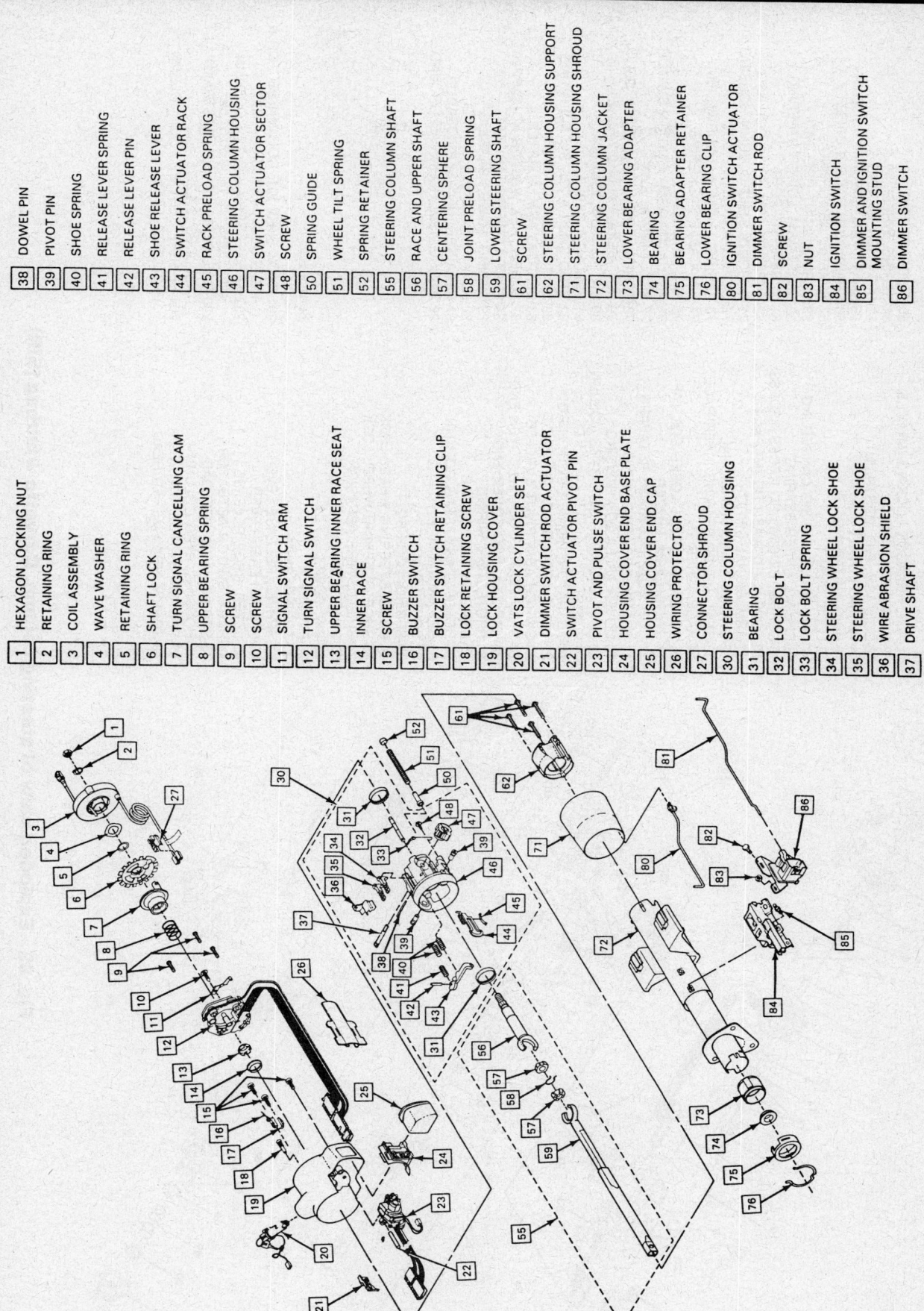

38	DOWEL PIN
39	PIVOT PIN
40	SHOE SPRING
41	RELEASE LEVER SPRING
42	RELEASE LEVER PIN
43	SHOE RELEASE LEVER
44	SWITCH ACTUATOR RACK
45	RACK PRELOAD SPRING
46	STEERING COLUMN HOUSING
47	SWITCH ACTUATOR SECTOR
48	SCREW
50	SPRING GUIDE
51	WHEEL TILT SPRING
52	SPRING RETAINER
55	STEERING COLUMN SHAFT
56	RACE AND UPPER SHAFT
57	CENTERING SPHERE
58	JOINT PRELOAD SPRING
59	LOWER STEERING SHAFT
61	SCREW
62	STEERING COLUMN HOUSING SUPPORT
71	STEERING COLUMN HOUSING SHROUD
72	STEERING COLUMN JACKET
73	LOWER BEARING ADAPTER
74	BEARING
75	BEARING ADAPTER RETAINER
76	LOWER BEARING CLIP
80	IGNITION SWITCH ACTUATOR
81	DIMMER SWITCH ROD
82	SCREW
83	NUT
84	IGNITION SWITCH
85	DIMMER AND IGNITION SWITCH MOUNTING STUD
86	DIMMER SWITCH

1	HEXAGON LOCKING NUT
2	RETAINING RING
3	COIL ASSEMBLY
4	WAVE WASHER
5	RETAINING RING
6	SHAFT LOCK
7	TURN SIGNAL CANCELLING CAM
8	UPPER BEARING SPRING
9	SCREW
10	SCREW
11	SIGNAL SWITCH ARM
12	TURN SIGNAL SWITCH
13	UPPER BEARING INNER RACE SEAT
14	INNER RACE
15	SCREW
16	BUZZER SWITCH
17	BUZZER SWITCH RETAINING CLIP
18	LOCK RETAINING SCREW
19	LOCK HOUSING COVER
20	VATS LOCK CYLINDER SET
21	DIMMER SWITCH ROD ACTUATOR
22	SWITCH ACTUATOR PIVOT PIN
23	PIVOT AND PULSE SWITCH
24	HOUSING COVER END BASE PLATE
25	HOUSING COVER END CAP
26	WIRING PROTECTOR
27	CONNECTOR SHROUD
30	STEERING COLUMN HOUSING
31	BEARING
32	LOCK BOLT
33	LOCK BOLT SPRING
34	STEERING WHEEL LOCK SHOE
35	STEERING WHEEL LOCK SHOE
36	WIRE ABRASION SHIELD
37	DRIVE SHAFT

Fig. 81 Exploded view of steering column. Camaro & Firebird w/airbag (SIR)

1-NUT, HEXAGON LOCKING (M14X1.5)
2-RING, RETAINING
3-COIL ASM, INFL RESTRAINT
4-WASHER, WAVE
5-RING, RETAINING
6-LOCK, SHAFT
7-CAM ASM, TURN SIG CANCELLING
8-SPRING, UPPER BEARING
9-SCREW, BINDING HD CROSS RECESS
10-SCREW, RD WASH HD (M4.2X1.41)
11-ARM, SIGNAL SWITCH
12-SWITCH ASM, TURN SIGNAL
13-SEAT, UPPER BEARING INNER RACE
14-RACE, INNER
15-SCREW, PAN HD 6-LOBED SOC TAP
16-SWITCH ASM, BUZZER
17-CLIP, BUZZER SWITCH RETAINING
18-SCREW, LOCK RETAINING
19-COVER ASM, LOCK HOUSING
20-LOCK CYLINDER SET, STRG COLUMN VATS
21-ACTUATOR, DIMMER SWITCH ROD
22-PIN, SWITCH ACTUATOR PIVOT
23-SWITCH ASM, PIVOT & (PULSE)
24-BASE PLATE, COL HSG COVER END
25-CAP, COL HSG COVER END
26-PROTECTOR, WIRING
27-SHROUD, CONNECTOR
30-HOUSING ASM, STRG COLUMN
31-BEARING ASM
32-BOLT, LOCK
33-SPRING, LOCK BOLT
34-SHOE, STEERING WHEEL LOCK
35-SHOE, STEERING WHEEL LOCK
36-SHIELD, WIRE ABRASION
37-SHAFT, DRIVE
38-PIN, DOWEL
39-PIN, PIVOT
40-SPRING, SHOE
41-SPRING, RELEASE LEVER
42-PIN, RELEASE LEVER
43-LEVER, SHOE RELEASE
44-RACK, SWITCH ACTUATOR
45-SPRING, RACK PRELOAD
46-HOUSING, STRG COLUMN
47-SECTOR, SWITCH ACTUATOR
48-SCREW, HEX WASHER HEAD

50-GUIDE, SPRING
51-SPRING, WHEEL TILT
52-RETAINER, SPRING
55-SHAFT ASM, STEERING COLUMN
56-SHAFT ASM, RACE & UPPER
57-SPHERE, CENTERING
58-SPRING, JOINT PRELOAD
59-SHAFT ASM, LOWER STEERING
61-SCREW, SUPPORT
62-SUPPORT ASM, STRG COL HSG
71-SHROUD, STRG COLUMN HOUSING
72-JACKET ASM, STRG COL
73-SPRING, CABLE BACKDRIVE
74-PIN, CABLE BACKDRIVE PIN
75-PIN, INHIBITOR
76-ACTUATOR ASM, IGNITION SWITCH
77-ROD, DIMMER SWITCH
78-SCREW, WASH HD (#10-24 X .25)
79-NUT, HEXAGON (#10-24 X .25)
80-SWITCH ASM, IGNITION
81-BRACKET, CABLE
82-STUD, DIMR & IGN SW MOUNTING
83-SWITCH ASM, DIMMER
86-BEARING ASM, ADAPTER &
87-SCREW, HEX WASHER HD TAPPING
88-SEAT, LOWER BEARING
89-SPRING, LOWER BEARING
90-RETAINER, LOWER SPRING
91-RETAINER (NON-SERVICEABLE)
92-WIRING ASM, HORN PAD GROUND

Service Kits

201-RACK SERV KIT, COLUMN SECTOR &
 -INCLUDES: 14,31,33,44,47,48
202-SPRING SERV KIT, TILT COLUMN
 -INCLUDES: 13,14,39,50,51,52
203-COIL SERV KIT, INFL RESTRAINT
 -INCLUDES: 3,4,27
204-SPHERE SERV KIT, TILT COLUMN
 -INCLUDES: 57,58

Fig. 82 Exploded view of steering column. Corvette w/airbag (SIR)

1-NUT, HEXAGON LOCKING (M14X1.5)
2-RING, RETAINING
3-COIL ASM, INFL RESTRAINT
4-WASHER, WAVE
5-RING, RETAINING
6-LOCK, SHAFT
7-CAM ASM, TURN SIG CANCELLING
8-SPRING, UPPER BEARING
9-SCREW, BINDING HD CROSS RECESS
12-SWITCH ASM, TURN SIGNAL
13-SEAT, UPPER BEARING INNER RACE
14-RACE, INNER
15-SCREW, PAN HD 6-LOBED SOC TAP
16-SWITCH ASM, BUZZER
18-SCREW, LOCK RETAINING
19-COVER ASM, LOCK HOUSING
20-LOCK CYLINDER SET, STRG COLUMN
PASS KEY
26-PROTECTOR, WIRING
28-SHROUD, CONNECTOR
30-HOUSING ASM, STRG COLUMN
31-BEARING ASM
32-BOLT, LOCK
34-SHOE, STEERING WHEEL LOCK
35-SHOE, STEERING WHEEL LOCK
36-SHIELD, WIRE ABRASION
38-PIN, DOWEL
39-PIN, PIVOT
40-SPRING, SHOE
41-SPRING, RELEASE LEVER
42-PIN, RELEASE LEVER
43-LEVER, SHOE RELEASE
44-RACK, SWITCH ACTUATOR
45-SPRING, RACK PRELOAD
46-HOUSING, STRG COLUMN
48-WASHER, SPRING THRUST

50-GUIDE, SPRING
51-SPRING, WHEEL TILT
52-RETAINER, SPRING
55-SHAFT ASM, STEERING COLUMN
56-SHAFT ASM, RACE & UPPER
57-SPHERE, CENTERING
58-SPRING, JOINT PRELOAD
59-SHAFT ASM, LOWER STEERING
61-SCREW, SUPPORT
62-SUPPORT ASM, STRG COL HSG
71-SHROUD, STRG COLUMN HOUSING
72-JACKET ASM, STRG COL
79-CLIP, CONVOLUTED CONDUIT
80-CONDUIT, CONVOLUTED
81-SWITCH ASM, IGNITION
82-SCREW, WASH HD (#10-24 X .25)
83-ACTUATOR ASM, IGNITION SWITCH
91-BEARING ASM, ADAPTER &
93-SCREW, HEX WASHER HD TAPPING
94-RETAINER, BEARING & SEAL
95-SEAT, LOWER BEARING
96-SPRING, LOWER BEARING
97-RETAINER, LOWER SPRING

Service Kits

201-RACK SERV KIT, COLUMN SECTOR &
-INCLUDES: 14,31,44
202-SPRING SERV KIT, TILT COLUMN
-INCLUDES: 13,14,39,50,51,52
203-COIL SERV KIT, INFL RESTRAINT
-INCLUDES: 3,4,28
204-SPHERE SERV KIT, TILT COLUMN
-INCLUDES: 57,58

Fig. 83   Exploded view of steering column. 1991-92 Eldorado & Seville w/airbag (SIR)

1-NUT, HEXAGON LOCKING (M14X1.5)
2-RING, RETAINING
3-COIL ASM, INFL RESTRAINT
4-WASHER, WAVE
5-RING, RETAINING
6-LOCK, SHAFT
7-CAM ASM, TURN SIG CANCELLING
8-SPRING, UPPER BEARING
9-SCREW, BINDING HD CROSS RECESS
10-SCREW, RD WASH HD (M4.2X1.41)
11-ARM, SIGNAL SWITCH
12-SWITCH ASM, TURN SIGNAL
13-SEAT, UPPER BEARING INNER RACE
14-RACE, INNER
15-SCREW, PAN HD 6-LOBED SOC TAP
16-SWITCH ASM, BUZZER
17-CLIP, BUZZER SWITCH RETAINING
18-SCREW, LOCK RETAINING
19-COVER ASM, LOCK HOUSING
20-LOCK CYLINDER SET, STRG COLUMN PASS KEY
21-ACTUATOR, DIMMER SWITCH ROD
22-PIN, SWITCH ACTUATOR PIVOT
23-SWITCH ASM, PIVOT & (PULSE)
24-BASE PLATE, COL HSG COVER END
25-CAP, COL HSG COVER END
26-PROTECTOR, WIRING
27-SCREW, FLT HD TAPPING
28-SHROUD, CONNECTOR
30-HOUSING ASM, STRG COLUMN
31-BEARING ASM
32-BOLT, LOCK
33-SPRING, LOCK BOLT
34-SHOE, STEERING WHEEL LOCK
35-SHOE, STEERING WHEEL LOCK
36-SHIELD, WIRE ABRASION
37-SHAFT, DRIVE
38-PIN, DOWEL
39-PIN, PIVOT
40-SPRING, SHOE
41-SPRING, RELEASE LEVER
42-PIN, RELEASE LEVER
43-LEVER, SHOE RELEASE
44-RACK, SWITCH ACTUATOR
45-SPRING, RACK PRELOAD

46-HOUSING, STRG COLUMN
47-SECTOR, SWITCH ACTUATOR
48-SCREW, HEX WASHER HEAD
50-GUIDE, SPRING
51-SPRING, WHEEL TILT
52-RETAINER, SPRING
55-SHAFT ASM, STEERING COLUMN
56-SHAFT ASM, RACE & UPPER
57-SPHERE, CENTERING
58-SPRING, JOINT PRELOAD
59-SHAFT ASM, LOWER STEERING
61-SCREW, SUPPORT
62-SUPPORT ASM, STRG COL HSG
71-SHROUD, STRG COLUMN HOUSING
72-JACKET ASM, STRG COL
79-CLIP, CONVOLUTED CONDUIT
80-CONDUIT, CONVOLUTED
81-SWITCH ASM, IGNITION
82-SCREW, WASH HD (#10-24 X .25)
83-ACTUATOR ASM, IGNITION SWITCH
84-ROD, DIMMER SWITCH
85-NUT, HEXAGON (#10-24 X .25)
86-STUD, DIMR & IGN SW MOUNTING
87-SWITCH ASM, DIMMER
91-BEARING ASM, ADAPTER &
93-SCREW, HEX WASHER HD TAPPING
94-RETAINER, BEARING & SEAL
95-SEAT, LOWER BEARING
96-SPRING, LOWER BEARING
97-RETAINER, LOWER SPRING

Service Kits

201-RACK SERV KIT, COLUMN SECTOR &
  -INCLUDES: 14,31,33,44,47,48
202-SPRING SERV KIT, TILT COLUMN
  -INCLUDES: 13,14,39,50,51,52
203-COIL SERV KIT, INFL RESTRAINT
  -INCLUDES: 3,4,28
204-SPHERE SERV KIT, TILT COLUMN
  -INCLUDES: 57,58

Fig. 84 Exploded view of steering column. Reatta & Riviera w/airbag (SIR)

Fig. 85   Exploded view of steering column. 1991 Park Avenue, 88 & 98 w/airbag (SIR)

1. NUT, HEXAGON LOCKING (M14 X 1.5)
2. RING, RETAINING
3. COL ASM, INFL RESTRAINT
4. RING, RETAINING
5. LOCK, SHAFT
6. CAM ASM, TURN SIG CANCELLING
7. SPRING, UPPER BEARING
8. SCREW, BINDING HD CROSS RECESS
9. SCREW, RD WASH HD (M4.2 X 1.41)
10. ARM, SIGNAL SWITCH
11. SWITCH ASM, TURN SIGNAL
12. GATE, SHIFT LEVER
13. SEAT, UPPER BEARING INNER RACE
14. RACE INNER
15. SCREW, PAN HD B-LOBED SOC TAP
16. SWITCH ASM, BUZZER
17. CLIP, BUZZER SWITCH RETAINING
18. SCREW, LOCK RETAINING
19. LOCK CYLINDER SET, STRG COLUMN
20. COVER, LOCK HOUSING
21. ACTUATOR, DIMMER SWITCH ROD
22. PIN, SWITCH ACTUATOR PIVOT
23. SWITCH ASM, PIVOT & PULSE
24. BASE PLATE, COL HSG COVER END
25. CAP, COL HSG COVER END
26. PROTECTOR, WIRING
27. CONNECTOR ASM, BODY
28. TERMINAL, POS ASSURANCE
29. HOUSING ASM, STRG COLUMN
30. BEARING ASM
31. BOLT, LOCK
32. SPRING, LOCK BOLT
33. SHOE, STEERING WHEEL LOCK
34. SHOE, STEERING WHEEL LOCK
35. SHAFT, DRIVE
36. PIN, DOWEL
37. PIN, PIVOT
38. SPRING, SHOE
39. PIN, RELEASE LEVER
40. SPRING, RELEASE LEVER
41. LEVER, SHOE RELEASE
42. SHAFT ASM, RACE & UPPER
43. SPRING, CENTERING
44. SPRING, JOINT PRELOAD
45. SHAFT ASM, LOWER STEERING
46. SHAFT ASM, STEERING
47. ACTUATOR ASM, IGNITION SWITCH
48. SPRING, RACK PRELOAD
49. RACK, SWITCH ACTUATOR
50. HOUSING, STRG COLUMN
51. SECTOR, SWITCH ACTUATOR
52. SCREW, HEX, WASHER HEAD
53. GUIDE, SPRING
54. SPRING WHEEL TILT
55. RETAINER, SPRING
56. SUPPORT, STRG COL HSG
57. PIN, DOWEL (SECONDARY)
58. PIN, DOWEL
59. SCREW, OVAL HEAD CROSS RECESS
60. GATE, SHIFT LEVER
61. RING, SHIFT TUBE RETAINING
62. WASHER, THRUST
63. PLATE, LOCK
64. WASHER, WAVE
65. SPRING, SHIFT LEVER
66. BOWL, ASM, GEAR SHIFT LEVER
67. JACKET ASM, STRG COL
68. SPRING, RETAINER
69. STUD, DIMM & IGN SW MOUNTING
70. SWITCH ASM IGN & BEAM CHANGE
71. NUT, HEXAGON (#10-24 X .25)
72. SCREW, WASH. HD #10-24 X .25)
73. ROD, DIMMER SWITCH
74. SUPPORT ASM, STRG COL HSG
75. SCREW, SUPPORT
76. TUBE ASM, SHAFT
77. BEARING ASM, ADAPTER
78. SCREW, HEX WASHER HD TAPPING
79. RETAINER, BEARING & SEAL
80. SEAT, LOWER BEARING
81. SPRING, LOWER BEARING
82. RETAINER, LOWER SPRING

SERVICE KITS
201. SWITCH ASM SERVICE KIT, PIVOT & INCLUDES: 21, # 22
202. RACK SERV KIT, COLUMN SELECTOR & INCLUDES: 13, 29, 31, 48, 50, & 51
203. SPRING SERV KIT, TILT COLUMN INCLUDES: 12, 13, 52, 53, & 54
204. COIL SERV KIT, INFL RESTRAINT INCLUDES: 2, 3, 26, & 27
205. COVER & SCR SERV KIT, LOCK HSG. INCLUDES: 17, 4, 19
206. SPHERE SERV KIT, TILT COLUMN INCLUDES: 42, 4 43

1-NUT, HEXAGON LOCKING (M14X1.5)
2-RING, RETAINING
3-COIL ASM, INFL RESTRAINT
4-WASHER, WAVE
5-RING, RETAINING
6-LOCK, SHAFT
7-CAM ASM, TURN SIG CANCELLING
8-SPRING, UPPER BEARING
9-SCREW, BINDING HD CROSS RECESS
10-SCREW, RD WASH HD (M4.2X1.41)
11-ARM, SIGNAL SWITCH
12-SWITCH ASM, TURN SIGNAL
13-SEAT, UPPER BEARING INNER RACE
14-RACE, INNER
15-SCREW, PAN HD 6-LOBED SOC TAP
16-SWITCH ASM, BUZZER
17-CLIP, BUZZER SWITCH RETAINING
18-SCREW, LOCK RETAINING
19-COVER ASM, LOCK HOUSING
20-LOCK CYLINDER SET, STRG COLUMN
    PASS KEY
21-ACTUATOR, DIMMER SWITCH ROD
22-PIN, SWITCH ACTUATOR PIVOT
23-SWITCH ASM, PIVOT & (PULSE)
24-BASE PLATE, COL HSG COVER END
25-CAP, COL HSG COVER END
26-PROTECTOR, WIRING
27-SCREW, FLT HD TAPPING
28-SHROUD, CONNECTOR
30-HOUSING ASM, STRG COLUMN
31-BEARING ASM
32-BOLT, LOCK
33-SPRING, LOCK BOLT
34-SHOE, STEERING WHEEL LOCK
35-SHOE, STEERING WHEEL LOCK
36-SHIELD, WIRE ABRASION
37-SHAFT, DRIVE
38-PIN, DOWEL
39-PIN, PIVOT
40-SPRING, SHOE
41-SPRING, RELEASE LEVER
42-PIN, RELEASE LEVER
43-LEVER, SHOE RELEASE
44-RACK, SWITCH ACTUATOR
45-SPRING, RACK PRELOAD
46-HOUSING, STRG COLUMN
47-SECTOR, SWITCH ACTUATOR
48-SCREW, HEX WASHER HEAD
50-GUIDE, SPRING
51-SPRING, WHEEL TILT
52-RETAINER, SPRING

55-SHAFT ASM, STEERING COLUMN
56-SHAFT ASM, RACE & UPPER
57-SPHERE, CENTERING
59-SPRING, JOINT PRELOAD
59-SHAFT ASM, LOWER STEERING
61-SCREW, SUPPORT
62-SUPPORT ASM, STRG COL HSG
63-SUPPORT, STRG COL HSG
64-SCREW, OVAL HD CROSS RECESS
65-GATE, SHIFT LEVER
66-RING, SHIFT TUBE RETAINING
67-WASHER, THRUST
68-PLATE, LOCK
69-WASHER, WAVE
70-SPRING, SHIFT LEVER
71-BOWL, GEARSHIFT LEVER
72-JACKET ASM, STRG COL
79-CLIP, CONVOLUTED CONDUIT
80-CONDUIT, CONVOLUTED
81-SWITCH ASM, IGNITION
82-SCREW, WASH HD (#10-24 X .25)
83-ACTUATOR ASM, IGNITION SWITCH
84-ROD, DIMMER SWITCH
85-NUT, HEXAGON (#10-24 X .25)
86-STUD, DIMR & IGN SW MOUNTING
87-SWITCH ASM, DIMMER
88-SHROUD, GEARSHIFT BOWL
90-TUBE ASM, SHIFT
91-BEARING ASM, ADAPTER &
92-CUP, LOWER BEARING
93-SCREW, HEX WASHER HD TAPPING
94-RETAINER, BEARING & SEAL
95-SEAT, LOWER BEARING
96-SPRING, LOWER BEARING
97-RETAINER, LOWER SPRING

Service Kits

201-RACK SERV KIT, COLUMN SECTOR &
    -INCLUDES: 14,31,33,44,47,48
202-SPRING SERV KIT, TILT COLUMN
    -INCLUDES: 13,14,39,50,51,52
203-COIL SERV KIT, INFL RESTRAINT
    -INCLUDES: 3,4,28
204-SPHERE SERV KIT, TILT COLUMN
    -INCLUDES: 57,58

Fig. 86 Exploded view of steering column. 1991 Toronado/Trofeo w/airbag (SIR)

61—SCREW, SUPPORT
62—SUPPORT ASM, STRG COL HSG
63—SUPPORT, STRG COL HSG
64—SCREW, OVL HD CROSS RECESS
65—GATE, SHIFT LEVER
66—RING, SHIFT TUBE RETAINING
67—WASHER, THRUST
68—PLATE, LOCK
69—WASHER, WAVE
70—SPRING, SHIFT LEVER
71—BOWL ASM, GEARSHIFT LEVER
72—JACKET ASM, STRG COL
76—ACTUATOR ASM, IGN SWITCH
77—ROD, DIMMER SWITCH
78—SCREW, WASH HD (#10—24x.25)
79—NUT, HEXAGON (#10—24)
80—SWITCH ASM, IGNITION & DIMR
81—STUD, DIMR & IGN SW MTG
82—STRAP, WIRE HARNESS
83—RETAINER, BEARING & SEAL
84—WASHER ASM, RETAINER
86—TUBE ASM, SHIFT
87—BEARING ASM, ADAPTER &
88—SCREW, HEX WASHER HD TAP
90—SEAT, LOWER BEARING
91—SPRING, LOWER BEARING
92—RETAINER, LOWER SPRING
93—CONNECTOR, AXIAL POS ASSUR
94—SUPPORT, STRG COL LOWER
95—BOLT, HEX FLNG HD (M6x1x14)
96—INTERLOCK ASM, SOLENOID &
97—SHIELD, INTERLOCK LEVER
98—LEVER ASM, INTLCK & BMPR
99—BUMPER, INTERLOCK LEVER
100—BUSHING, SOLENOID PIN
101—RING, RETAINING (METRIC 3CMI)
102—BOLT, HEX FLNG HD (M6x1x14)
103—SOLENOID ASM, INTERLOCK
104—SCREW, PAN HD 6—LOBED SOC
     TAP
105—SWITCH ASM, DIMMER

Service Kits

RACK SERV KIT, COL SECTOR &
  —INCLUDES: 14,31,33,44,47,48
SPRING SERV KIT, TILT COLUMN
  —INCLUDES: 13,14,39,50,51,52
COIL SERV KIT, INFL RESTRAINT
  —INCLUDES: 3,4,28
SPHERE SERV KIT, TILT COLUMN
  —INCLUDES: 57,58
GREASE SERV KIT, (SYNTHETIC)

**Fig. 87 Exploded view of tilt steering column
(Part 2 of 2). 1992-93 Bonneville, DeVille,
Fleetwood (FWD), LeSabre, Park Avenue, 88 &
98 w/airbag (SIR) & column shift**

1—NUT, HEX LOCKING (M14x1.5)
2—RING, RETAINING
3—COIL ASM, INFL RESTRAINT
4—WASHER, WAVE
5—RING, RETAINING
6—LOCK, SHAFT
7—CAM ASM, TURN SIG CANCEL
8—SPRING, UPPER BEARING
9—SCREW, BNDG HD CR RECESS
10—SCREW, RD WASH HD (M4.2x1.41)
11—ARM ASM, SIGNAL SWITCH
12—SWITCH ASM, TURN SIGNAL
13—SEAT, UPPER BRG INNER RACE
14—RACE, INNER
15—SCREW, PAN HD SOC TAP
16—SWITCH ASM, BUZZER
18—SCREW, LOCK RETAINING
19—COVER ASM, LOCK HOUSING
20—LOCK CYLINDER SET, STRG COL
     (PASS KEY)
21—ACTUATOR, DIMMER SW ROD
22—PIN, SWITCH ACTUATOR PIVOT
23—SWITCH ASM, PIVOT & (PULSE)
24—BASE PLATE, COL HSG CVR END
25—CAP, COL HSG COVER END
26—PROTECTOR, WIRING
27—SCREW, FLT HD TAPPING
28—SHROUD, CONNECTOR
30—HOUSING ASM, STRG COLUMN
31—BEARING ASM
32—BOLT, LOCK
33—SPRING, LOCK BOLT
34—SHOE, STRG WHEEL LOCK
35—SHOE, STRG WHEEL LOCK
36—SHIELD, WIRE PROTECTOR
37—SHAFT, DRIVE
38—PIN, DOWEL
39—PIN, PIVOT
40—SPRING, SHOE
41—SPRING, RELEASE LEVER
42—PIN, RELEASE LEVER
43—LEVER, SHOE RELEASE
44—RACK, SWITCH ACTUATOR
45—SPRING, RACK PRELOAD
46—HOUSING, STRG COLUMN
47—SECTOR, SWITCH ACTUATOR
48—SCREW, HEX WASHER HEAD
50—GUIDE, SPRING
51—SPRING, WHEEL TILT
52—RETAINER, SPRING
55—SHAFT ASM, STEERING
56—SHAFT ASM, RACE & UPPER
57—SPHERE, CENTERING
58—SPRING, JOINT PRELOAD
59—SHAFT ASM, LOWER STEERING

**Fig. 87 Exploded view of tilt steering column
(Part 1 of 2). 1992-93 Bonneville, DeVille,
Fleetwood (FWD), LeSabre, Park Avenue, 88 &
98 w/airbag (SIR) & column shift**

61-SCREW, SUPPORT
62-SUPPORT ASM, STRG COL HSG
63-PLATE, LOCK
71-SHROUD, STRG COLUMN HSG
72-JACKET ASM, STRG COL
79-CLIP, CONVOLUTED CONDUIT
80-CONDUIT, CONVOLUTED
81-SWITCH ASM, COL LOCK & IGN
82-SCREW, WASH HD (#10-24X.25)
83-ACTUATOR ASM, IGNITION SWITCH
84-ROD, DIMMER SWITCH
85-NUT, HEXAGON (#10-24)
86-STUD, DIMR & IGNITION SW MTG
87-SWITCH ASM, DIMMER
89-STRAP, WIRE HARNESS
91-BEARING ASM, ADAPTER &
93-SCREW, HEX WASHER HD TAP
94-SEAT, LOWER BEARING
95-SPRING, LOWER BEARING
96-RETAINER, LOWER SPRING
97-RETAINER, BEARING & SEAL
98-SEAL, STEERING SHAFT
99-BUSHING, SEAL RETAINING
106-SCREW, RD WASH HD (M4.2X1.41)
107-MODULE ASM, E & C INTERFACE

Service Kits

201-RACK SERV KIT, COL SECTOR &
-INCLUDES: 14,31,33,44,47,48
202-SPRING SERV KIT, TILT COLUMN
-INCLUDES: 13,14,39,50,51,52
203-COIL SERV KIT, INFL RESTRAINT
-INCLUDES: 3,4,28
204-SPHERE SERV KIT, TILT COLUMN
-INCLUDES: 57,58
205-GREASE SERV KIT, (SYNTHETIC)

Fig. 88 Exploded view of steering column (Part 2 of 2). 1992 Toronado & Trofeo w/airbag (SIR)

1-NUT, HEX LOCKING (M14x1.5)
2-RING, RETAINING
3-COIL ASM, INFL RESTRAINT
4-WASHER, WAVE
5-RING, RETAINING
6-LOCK, SHAFT
7-CAM ASM, TURN SIG CANCEL
8-SPRING, UPPER BEARING
9-SCREW, BNDG HD CR RECESS
10-SCREW, RD WASH HD (M4.2x1.41)
11-ARM ASM, SIGNAL SWITCH
12-SWITCH ASM, TURN SIGNAL
13-SEAT, UPPER BRG INNER RACE
14-RACE, INNER
15-SCREW, PAN HD SOC TAP
16-SWITCH ASM, BUZZER
18-SCREW, LOCK RETAINING
19-COVER ASM, LOCK HOUSING
20-LOCK CYLINDER SET, STRG COL
    PASS KEY
21-ACTUATOR, DIMMER SW ROD
22-PIN, SWITCH ACTUATOR PIVOT
23-SWITCH ASM, PIVOT & (PULSE)
24-BASE PLATE, COL HSG CVR END
25-CAP, COL HSG COVER END
26-PROTECTOR, WIRING
27-SCREW, FLT HD TAPPING
28-SHROUD, CONNECTOR
30-HOUSING ASM, STRG COLUMN
31-BEARING ASM
32-BOLT, LOCK
33-SPRING, LOCK BOLT
34-SHOE, STEERING WHEEL LOCK
35-SHOE, STEERING WHEEL LOCK
36-SHIELD, WIRE PROTECTOR
37-SHAFT, DRIVE
38-PIN, DOWEL
39-PIN, PIVOT
40-SPRING, SHOE
41-SPRING, RELEASE LEVER
42-PIN, RELEASE LEVER
43-LEVER, SHOE RELEASE
44-RACK, SWITCH ACTUATOR
45-SPRING, RACK PRELOAD
46-HOUSING, STRG COLUMN
47-SECTOR, SWITCH ACTUATOR
48-SCREW, HEX WASHER HEAD
50-GUIDE, SPRING
51-SPRING, WHEEL TILT
52-RETAINER, SPRING
55-SHAFT ASM, STEERING
56-SHAFT ASM, RACE & UPPER
57-SPHERE, CENTERING
58-SPRING, JOINT PRELOAD
59-SHAFT ASM, LOWER STEERING

Fig. 88 Exploded view of steering column (Part 1 of 2). 1992 Toronado & Trofeo w/airbag (SIR)

51-SPRING, WHEEL TILT
52-RETAINER, SPRING
55-SHAFT ASM, STEERING
56-SHAFT ASM, RACE & UPPER
57-SPHERE, CENTERING
58-SPRING, JOINT PRELOAD
59-SHAFT ASM, LOWER STEERING
61-SCREW, SUPPORT
62-SUPPORT ASM, STRG COL HSG
68-PLATE, LOCK
71-SHROUD, STRG COL HSG
72-JACKET ASM, STRG COL
76-ACTUATOR ASM, IGN SWITCH
77-ROD, DIMMER SWITCH
78-SCREW, WASH HD (#10-24x.25)
79-NUT, HEXAGON (#10-24)
80-SWITCH ASM, IGN & DIMMER
81-STUD, DIMR & IGN SW MTG
82-SWITCH ASM, DIMMER
83-STRAP, WIRE HARNESS
87-BEARING ASM, ADAPTER &
88-SCREW, HEX WASHER HD TAP
90-SEAT, LOWER BEARING
91-SPRING, LOWER BEARING
92-RETAINER, LOWER SPRING
93-RETAINER, BEARING & SEAL
94-WASHER ASM, RETAINER
95-BRACKET, E & C MODULE
96-MODULE ASM, E & C INTERFACE

Service Kits

201-RACK SERV KIT, COL SECTOR &
-INCLUDES: 14,31,33,44,47,48
202-SPRING SERV KIT, TILT COLUMN
-INCLUDES: 13,14,39,50,51,52
203-COIL SERV KIT, INFL RESTRAINT
-INCLUDES: 3,4,28
204-SPHERE SERV KIT, TILT COLUMN
-INCLUDES: 57,58
205-GREASE SERV KIT, (SYNTHETIC)

1-NUT, HEX LOCKING (M14x1.5)
2-RING, RETAINING
3-COIL ASM, INFL RESTRAINT
4-WASHER, WAVE
5-RING, RETAINING
6-LOCK, SHAFT
7-CAM ASM, TURN SIG CANCEL
8-SPRING, UPPER BEARING
9-SCREW, BNDG HD CR RECESS
10-SCREW, RD WASH HD (M4.2x1.41)
11-ARM ASM, SIGNAL SWITCH
12-SWITCH ASM, TURN SIGNAL
13-SEAT, UPPER BRG INNER RACE
14-RACE, INNER
15-SCREW, PAN HD SOC TAP
16-SWITCH ASM, BUZZER
18-SCREW, LOCK RETAINING
19-COVER ASM, LOCK HOUSING
20-LOCK CYLINDER SET, STRG COL (PASS KEY)
21-ACTUATOR, DIMMER SW ROD
22-PIN, SWITCH ACTUATOR PIVOT
23-SWITCH ASM, PIVOT & (PULSE)
24-BASE PLATE, COL HSG CVR END
25-CAP, COL HSG COVER END
26-PROTECTOR, WIRING
27-SCREW, FLT HD TAPPING
28-SHROUD, CONNECTOR
30-HOUSING ASM, STRG COLUMN
31-BEARING ASM
32-BOLT, LOCK
33-SPRING, LOCK BOLT
34-SHOE, STRG WHEEL LOCK
35-SHOE, STRG WHEEL LOCK
36-SHIELD, WIRE PROTECTOR
37-SHAFT, DRIVE
38-PIN, DOWEL
39-PIN, PIVOT
40-SPRING, SHOE
41-SPRING, RELEASE LEVER
42-PIN, RELEASE LEVER
43-LEVER, SHOE RELEASE
44-RACK, SWITCH ACTUATOR
45-SPRING, RACK PRELOAD
46-HOUSING, STRG COLUMN
47-SECTOR, SWITCH ACTUATOR
48-SCREW, HEX WASHER HEAD
50-GUIDE, SPRING

Fig. 89 Exploded view of tilt steering column (Part 2 of 2). 1992-93 Bonneville, 88 & 98 w/airbag (SIR) & floor shift

Fig. 89 Exploded view of tilt steering column (Part 1 of 2). 1992-93 Bonneville, 88 & 98 w/airbag (SIR) & floor shift

2. RING, RETAINING
3. COIL ASM, INFL RESTRAINT
F. LOCK SCREW

Fig. 90   Locking coil assembly. Bonneville, Camaro, Corvette, DeVille, Eldorado, Firebird, Fleetwood (FWD), LeSabre, Park Avenue, Reatta, Riviera, Seville, Toronado/Trofeo, 88 & 98 w/airbag (SIR)

26. CONNECTOR ASM, BODY
27. TERMINAL, POS ASSURANCE

Fig. 93   Assembling connector body. Bonneville, Camaro, Corvette, DeVille, Eldorado, Firebird, Fleetwood (FWD), LeSabre, Park Avenue, Reatta, Riviera, Seville, Toronado/Trofeo, 88 & 98 w/airbag (SIR)

Wheel of vehicle must be in straight ahead position and key must be in LOCK position.

1. Remove screws from back of steering wheel.
2. Remove restraint module from steering wheel.
3. Remove coil assembly plug from restraint module, then the horn contact from column.
4. Remove hexagon locking nut, then, using tool J-1859-03 or equivalent, the steering wheel. **On Riviera, Reatta, Trofeo and Toronado models, insert steering wheel puller bolts only four to six threads deep to prevent the bolts from going through the hub and damaging the coil assembly.**
5. Remove steering wheel shroud.
6. Remove lock screw from boss HOME position on coil assembly to CENTER LOCK position on coil assembly, **Fig. 90.**
7. Remove coil assembly retaining ring.
8. Remove coil assembly off shaft end, allowing coil to hang freely.
9. Using tool J-23653-A or equivalent, depress shaft lock, then remove shaft lock retaining ring.
10. Remove shaft lock, then the turn signal cancelling cam.
11. Remove upper bearing spring, then

26. CONNECTOR ASM, BODY
27. TERMINAL, POS ASSURANCE

Fig. 91   Disassembling connector body.

the upper bearing seat.

12. Remove inner race, then place turn signal in Right Turn position.
13. Remove signal switch arm attaching screw and the arm, then the turn signal switch attaching screws.
14. Remove hazard knob, then position turn signal switch out of way. If removal of switch is necessary, remove retainer spring and wiring protector, then gently pull wire harness through gear shift lever bowl, column housing and lock housing cover.
15. Remove coil assembly, if necessary, as follows:
    a. Disconnect POS assurance terminal, and, using tool J-35689-A or equivalent, disconnect wires from body connector assembly, **Fig. 91.**
    b. Tape wire ends, then gently pull wire through gear shift lever bowl, column housing, and lock housing cover.
16. Remove key from cylinder lock and remove buzzer switch and clip, then reinstall key in cylinder lock and place key in Lock position.
17. Remove lock retaining screw and lock cylinder set.

Assembly

Ensure all fasteners are securely seated before applying required torque.

1. Install lock cylinder set, **torquing** lock retaining screw to 26 inch lbs.
2. Place key in Run position, then install buzzer switch and clip.
3. Route turn signal switch wiring harness through lock housing cover, column housing and gear shift lever bowl.
4. Route coil assembly wire through lock housing cover, column housing and gear shift lever bowl and allow coil to hang freely.
5. Install turn signal switch, **torquing** attaching screws to 26 inch lbs.
6. Install wiring protector and retaining spring.
7. Install signal switch arm, **torquing** retaining screw to 18 inch lbs.
8. Install hazard knob, then the inner race.
9. Install upper bearing seat, then the upper bearing spring.
10. Install turn signal cancelling cam, then the shaft lock.
11. Using tool J-23653-A or equivalent to depress shaft lock, install shaft lock

Perform the following steps to center coil assembly:
A. Remove coil assembly (3) from column
B. Lock screw to boss "Home" position, allowing hub to rotate
C. Hold coil assembly housing in one hand with steering wheel connector up
D. Rotate coil hub counterclockwise until it stops. Turn coil over to inspect coil position through the clear bottom. The coil ribbon should be wound up snug against center hub.
E. Rotate coil hub clockwise approximately two and a half (2½) turns until "Center Lock" hole is even with the notch in coil housing
F. Hold hub in position while installing lock screw to "Center Lock" hole

Fig. 92   Centering coil assembly.

retaining ring, aligning to block tooth on shaft.
12. Ensure coil assembly hub is centered, **Fig. 92. The coil assembly will become uncentered if the column is separated from the steering gear and is allowed to rotate, or the coil is removed from the column without first locking in position with locking screw.**
13. Install coil assembly, using horn tower on cancel cam on inner ring and projections on outer ring for alignment, then the coil assembly retaining ring. **Move lock screw from CENTER LOCK position to HOME position on coil assembly.**
14. Install steering wheel and steering wheel shroud, then the hexagon locking nut.
15. Install coil assembly plug to air bag module and the horn contact into column.
16. Install steering wheel module to steering wheel.
17. Using tool J-35689-A or equivalent, connect wires to connector body assembly and install POS assurance terminal, **Fig. 93.**
18. Install screws to back of steering column, then connect battery ground cable.

LOCK HOUSING COVER, COVER END CAP, PIVOT & SWITCH ASSEMBLY, DIMMER SWITCH ROD ACTUATOR & TILT SPRING ASSEMBLY

Disassembly

1. Perform "Disassembly" steps for "Coil

Assembly, Shaft Lock, Turn Signal Cancelling Cam, Upper Bearing Spring, Upper Bearing Seat, Inner Race Turn Signal Switch, Buzzer Switch & Lock Cylinder Set."

2. Remove lock housing cover attaching screws and the cover, then the tilt lever.
3. Remove cover housing end cap, base plate, and dimmer switch rod actuator, then gently pull pivot switch wiring harness through column housing and gear shift lever bowl.
4. **On vehicles equipped with cruise control,** unplug connector from base plate and remove multi-function lever.
5. **On all models,** remove pivot pin, then the pivot and switch assembly.
6. Remove spring retainer, then the spring and spring guide.

Assembly

Ensure all fasteners are securely seated before applying required torque.
1. Coat spring guide and spring with lithium grease and install them, then install spring retainer.
2. Install pivot and pulse switch assembly, then the pivot pin.
3. Route lock housing cover wire harness through gear shift lever bowl and column housing.
4. Install dimmer switch rod actuator to base plate, then the base plate to gear shift lever bowl, ensuring bottom edge of dimmer switch rod actuator rests on bend in dimmer switch rod.
5. Install cover housing end cap.
6. **On vehicles equipped with cruise control,** plug multi-function lever connector and cruise control wires on wipe/wash switch together and mount on base plate and install multi-function lever.
7. **On all models,** install lock housing cover. Tighten screw in 12 o'clock position first, screw in 8 o'clock position second and screw in 4 o'clock position third, then **torque** screws to 89 inch lbs. in same order.
8. Perform "Assembly" steps for "Coil Assembly, Shaft Lock, Turn Signal Cancelling Cam, Upper Bearing Spring, Upper Bearing Seat, Inner Race Turn Signal Switch, Buzzer Switch & Lock Cylinder Set."

COLUMN HOUSING, LOCK SHOES, ACTUATOR SECTOR ASSEMBLY, SWITCH ACTUATOR RACK, BEARINGS & LOCK BOLT ASSEMBLY
Disassembly
1. Perform "Disassembly" steps for "Coil

Assembly, Shaft Lock, Turn Signal Cancelling Cam, Upper Bearing Spring, Upper Bearing Seat, Inner Race Turn Signal Switch, Buzzer Switch & Lock Cylinder Set."

2. Remove lock housing cover attaching screws and the cover, then the tilt lever.
3. Remove cover housing end cap, base plate and dimmer switch rod actuator, then gently pull pivot switch wire harness through column housing and gear shift lever bowl.
4. **On vehicles equipped with cruise control,** unplug connector from base plate and remove multi-function lever.
5. **On all models,** remove spring retainer, then the spring and spring guide.
6. Using tool J-21854-01 or equivalent, remove pivot pins, **Fig. 75,** then reinstall tilt lever.
7. Remove column housing assembly by pulling back on tilt lever and pulling housing down and away from column.
8. Remove driveshaft, then the switch actuator sector.
9. Remove switch actuator rack and rack preload spring, then the release lever pin.
10. Remove release lever, then the release lever spring.
11. Remove dowel pin, then the lock shoes.
12. Remove lock shoe springs, then the bearings.
13. Remove hex head bolt, then the lock bolt spring and lock bolt.

Assembly

Ensure all fasteners are securely seated before applying required torque.
1. Install bearings to column housing.
2. Install driveshaft, then the actuator sector.
3. Install lock shoes, then the dowel pin.
4. Install lock shoe springs, then the release lever spring.
5. Install release lever, then the release lever pin.
6. Install rack preload spring, then the switch actuator rack to actuator sector.
7. Install lock bolt, then the lock bolt spring.
8. Install hex head bolt.
9. Install column housing assembly to column as follows:
   a. Position column housing assembly and align switch actuator rack with pin on end of actuator rod.
   b. Pull back on tilt lever, pushing column housing assembly onto column housing support assembly, then release tilt lever to lock shoes.
10. Remove tilt lever.
11. Lubricate pivot pins with lithium grease and install them.
12. Perform "Assembly" steps for "Lock Housing Cover, Cover End Cap, Pivot

& Switch Assembly, Dimmer Switch Rod Actuator & Tilt Spring Assembly" and "Coil Assembly, Shaft Lock, Turn Signal Cancelling Cam, Upper Bearing Spring, Upper Bearing Seat, Inner Race Turn Signal Switch, Buzzer Switch & Lock Cylinder Set."

SHAFT ASSEMBLY, COLUMN HOUSING SUPPORT, SHIFT TUBE ASSEMBLY, IGNITION SWITCH, DIMMER SWITCH & LOWER BEARING ASSEMBLY
Disassembly

1. Perform "Disassembly" steps for "Coil Assembly, Shaft Lock, Turn Signal Cancelling Cam, Upper Bearing Spring, Upper Bearing Seat, Inner Race Turn Signal Switch, Buzzer Switch & Lock Cylinder Set."
2. Remove lock housing cover attaching screws and the cover, then the tilt lever.
3. Remove cover housing end cap, base plate and dimmer switch rod actuator, then gently pull pivot switch wire harness through column housing and gear shift lever bowl.
4. **On vehicles equipped with cruise control,** unplug connector from base plate and remove multi-function lever.
5. **On all models,** remove spring retainer, then the spring and spring guide.
6. Using tool J-21854-01 or equivalent, remove pivot pins, **Fig. 75,** then reinstall tilt lever.
7. Remove column housing assembly by pulling back on tilt lever and pulling housing down and away from column.
8. Remove steering column from vehicle. **Once steering column is removed from vehicle, the column is extremely susceptible to damage. Dropping column assembly on its end could collapse steering shaft or loosen plastic injections that maintain column rigidity. Leaning on column assembly may cause jacket to bend or deform. Any of the above damage may impair column's collapsible design. If it is necessary to remove steering wheel, use only the specified steering wheel puller. Under no conditions should end of shaft be hammered on because hammering could loosen plastic injections that maintain column rigidity.**
9. Remove bearing retainer, then the spring retainer.
10. Remove lower bearing spring, then the lower bearing seat.
11. Remove screws and lower bearing, then the shaft assembly. Check for accident damage.
12. Remove lower shaft.
13. Remove sphere from shaft assembly, then the retainer clip from sphere.
14. Remove housing support assembly retaining screws, then the housing

82. SWITCH, DIMMER

Fig. 94 Adjusting dimmer switch. Bonneville, Camaro, Corvette, DeVille, Eldorado, Firebird, Fleetwood (FWD), LeSabre, Park Avenue, Reatta, Riviera, Seville, Toronado/Trofeo, 88 & 98 w/airbag (SIR)

support assembly and dimmer switch rod.

15. Remove hex nut and hex head bolt, then the dimmer switch and mounting stud.
16. Remove ignition switch and actuator rod assembly, then the shift tube retaining ring.
17. Remove thrust washer, then the gear shift lever spring.
18. Using tool J-23072 or equivalent, remove shift tube.
19. Remove lock plate and wave washer, then the gear shift lever bowl.

Assembly

Ensure all fasteners are securely seated before applying required torque.

1. Install gear shift lever spring to gear shift lever bowl, then the gear shift lever bowl to the shift tube jacket.
2. Lubricate wave washer with lithium grease and install it.
3. Install lock plate, then, using tool J-23073-1-2-3 or equivalent, the shift tube.
4. Install thrust washer, then the shift tube retaining ring.
5. Install dimmer switch rod to housing support.
6. Install housing support assembly, **torquing** attaching bolts to 79 inch lbs.
7. Install actuator rod assembly to track in housing support.
8. Install retaining clip and sphere to shaft assembly.
9. Install lower shaft to shaft assembly with block tooth on shaft end of shaft assembly at 12 o'clock position and notch at lower end of shaft at 4 o'clock position.
10. Lubricate shaft assembly with lithium grease and install to column.
11. Perform "Assembly" steps for "Column Housing, Lock Shoes, Actuator Sector Assembly, Switch Actuator Rack, Bearings & Lock Bolt Assembly," "Lock Housing Cover, Cover End Cap, Pivot & Switch Assembly, Dimmer Switch Rod Actuator & Tilt Spring Assembly" and "Coil Assembly, Shaft Lock, Turn Signal Cancelling Cam, Upper Bearing Spring, Upper Bearing Seat, Inner Race Turn Signal Switch, Buzzer Switch & Lock Cylinder Set."
12. Lubricate inner surface of lower bear-

ing with lithium grease, then install lower bearing and screws.
13. Install lower bearing seat, then the lower bearing spring.
14. Install spring retainer, then the bearing retainer.
15. Install dimmer switch, hex nut and hex head bolt, then adjust dimmer switch, **Fig. 94.**
16. Install ignition switch and mounting stud, then adjust ignition switch, **Fig. 95.**
17. Install column to vehicle instrument panel.

1993 Eldorado & Seville

Disarm airbag system as described under "Airbag System Disarming," then remove column from vehicle as described under "Steering Column, Replace."

The steering wheel must be straight and the column in the LOCK position. **Care must be taken when handling column with a live inflator module. Never point bag deploy surface toward you, and never stand column on steering wheel. Accidental deployment in these positions may cause injury. Always face bag deploy surface toward open space to allow for unrestricted expansion.**

Refer to **Figs. 96 and 97** for steering column service procedures.

UPPER COLUMN

The upper column consists of the following components: airbag coil assembly, shaft lock, turn signal cancelling cam assembly, upper bearing spring, upper bearing inner race seat, inner race, turn signal switch assembly, buzzer switch assembly and the steering column pass key lock cylinder set.

Disassembly

1. Disable airbag system as described under "Airbag System Disarming."
2. Remove inflator module and steering wheel as described under "Steering Wheel, Replace," in the appropriate "Electrical" section.
3. Remove coil assembly retaining ring, then the coil assembly.
4. Remove wave washer, then using removal tool No. J 23653-C or equivalent to push down shaft lock, remove shaft lock retaining ring.
5. Remove shaft lock, then the turn signal cancelling cam assembly.
6. Remove upper bearing spring and upper bearing inner race seat.
7. Remove inner race, then move turn signal to "Right Turn" position (up).
8. Remove multi-function lever and hazard knob assembly.
9. Remove signal switch arm, then the turn signal switch screws.
10. Remove turn signal switch assembly as follows:
    a. Disconnect turn signal switch connector from the bulkhead connector.
    b. Remove wiring protector.
    c. Gently pull wire harness through column.
11. **Coil assembly will become un-**

MOVE SWITCH SLIDER TO EXTREME RIGHT POSITION AND THEN MOVE SLIDER ONE DETENT TO THE LEFT (OFF LOCK)

3/32" DRILL BIT IN HOLE TO LOCK SWITCH

36. SWITCH ASM, IGN & BEAM CHANGE

Fig. 95 Adjusting ignition switch. Bonneville, Camaro, Corvette, DeVille, Eldorado, Firebird, Fleetwood (FWD), LeSabre, Park Avenue, Reatta, Riviera, Seville, Toronado/Trofeo, 88 & 98

centered if the steering column is separated from the steering gear and is allowed to rotate; or if the centering spring is pushed down, letting the hub rotate while the coil is removed from the steering column.

12. Remove inflatable restraint coil assembly with wire harness from the coil assembly as follows:
    a. Remove the coil terminal from the vehicle harness.
    b. Remove yellow connector shroud from the black terminal connector.
    c. Remove wiring protector.
    d. Attach a length of mechanics wire to the coil terminal connector to aid in assembly.
    e. Gently pull wire through column.
13. Remove key from pass key lock cylinder set, **Fig. 98.**
14. Remove buzzer switch assembly, then reinsert key in pass key in lock cylinder. Ensure key is in LOCK position.
15. Remove lock retaining screw, then remove pass key lock cylinder and harness as follows:
    a. Disconnect pivot switch connector from bulkhead connector and remove 13-way secondary lock.
    b. Disconnect two terminals of pass key wire harness from cavities 12 and 13 of switch connector.
    c. Remove wiring protector, then attach a piece of mechanics wire to terminal to aid in reassembly.
    d. Remove retaining clip from housing cover and gently pull wire harness through column.

Assembly

Route wire from pass key lock cylinder as shown in **Fig. 99,** and snap retaining clip into hole in housing. **Failure to do so may result in component damage or malfunction of pass key lock cylinder.**

1. Install pass key lock cylinder as follows:
    a. Install wire terminal through column and snap retaining clip into hole in housing.
    b. Connect two terminals of pass key wire harness to cavities 12 and 13 of pivot switch connector.
    c. Attach 13-way secondary lock to switch connector.
    d. Connect switch connector to bulk-

61-SCREW, SUPPORT
62-SUPPORT ASM, STRG COL HSG
63-SUPPORT, STRG COL HSG
64-SCREW, OVL HD CROSS RECESS
65-GATE, SHIFT LEVER
66-RING, SHIFT TUBE RETAINING
67-WASHER, THRUST
68-PLATE, LOCK
69-WASHER, WAVE
70-SPRING, SHIFT LEVER
71-BOWL ASM, GEARSHIFT LEVER
72-SHROUD, GEARSHIFT BOWL
73-TUBE ASM, SHIFT
74-SCREW, WASH HD (#10-24X.25)
75-SOLENOID ASM, INTERLOCK
76-SCREW, HEX WASH HD (#10-24X.25)
77-BRACKET, SOLENOID
78-JACKET ASM, STRG COL
79-SPRING, BALL JOINT
80-ACTUATOR ASM, IGNITION SWITCH
81-SCREW, PAN HD SOC
82-RETAINER, CAM
83-CAM ASM, CABLE SHIFT
84-SWITCH ASM, IGNITION
85-NUT, HEXAGON
86-ADJUSTER ASM, PRNDL
87-STUD, DIMR & IGNITION SW MTG
88-ROD, DIMMER SWITCH
89-SWITCH ASM, DIMMER
90-BRACKET ASM, STUD &
91-BEARING ASM, ADAPTER &
92-SCREW, HEX WASHER HD TAP
93-SEAT, LOWER BEARING
94-SPRING, LOWER BEARING
95-RETAINER, LOWER SPRING
96-RETAINER, BEARING
97-SEAL, STEERING SHAFT
98-BUSHING, SEAL RETAINING
99-CONNECTOR, POS ASSURANCE TER
Service Kits

201-RACK SERV KIT, COL SECTOR &
   -INCLUDES: 15,31,33,44,47,48
202-SPRING SERV KIT, TILT COLUMN
   -INCLUDES: 14,15,39,50,51,52
203-COIL SERV KIT, INFL RESTRINT
   -INCLUDES: 3,4,5
204-SPHERE SERV KIT, TILT COLUMN
   -INCLUDES: 57,58
205-GREASE SERV KIT, (SYNTHETIC)

1-NUT, HEX LOCKING (M14x1.5)
2-RING, RETAINING
3-COIL ASM, INFL RESTRAINT
4-WASHER, WAVE
5-SHROUD, CONNECTOR
6-RING, RETAINING
7-LOCK, SHAFT
8-CAM ASM, TURN SIG CANCEL
9-SPRING, UPPER BEARING
10-SCREW, BNDG HD CR RECESS
11-SCREW, RD WASH HD (M4.2x1.41)
12-ARM ASM, SIGNAL SWITCH
13-SWITCH ASM, TURN SIGNAL
14-SEAT, UPPER BRG INNER RACE
15-RACE, INNER
16-SCREW, PAN HD SOC TAP
17-SWITCH ASM, BUZZER
18-SCREW, LOCK RETAINING
19-COVER ASM, LOCK HOUSING
20-LOCK CYLINDER SET, STRG COL
   PASS KEY
21-ACTUATOR, DIMMER SW ROD
22-PIN, SWITCH ACTUATOR PIVOT
23-SWITCH ASM, PIVOT & (PULSE)
24-BASE PLATE, COL HSG CVR END
25-CAP, COL HSG COVER END
26-PROTECTOR, WIRING
27-SCREW, FLT HD TAPPING
30-HOUSING ASM, STRG COLUMN
31-BEARING ASM
32-BOLT, LOCK
33-SPRING, LOCK BOLT
34-SHOE, STEERING WHEEL LOCK
35-SHOE, STEERING WHEEL LOCK
36-SHIELD, WIRE PROTECTOR
37-SHAFT, DRIVE
38-PIN, DOWEL
39-PIN, PIVOT
40-SPRING, SHOE
41-SPRING, RELEASE LEVER
42-PIN, RELEASE LEVER
43-LEVER, SHOE RELEASE
44-RACK, SWITCH ACTUATOR
45-SPRING, RACK PRELOAD
46-HOUSING, STRG COLUMN
47-SECTOR, SWITCH ACTUATOR
48-SCREW, HEX WASHER HEAD
50-GUIDE, SPRING
51-SPRING, WHEEL T,LT
52-RETAINER, SPRING
55-SHAFT ASM, STEERING
56-SHAFT ASM, RACE & UPPER
57-SPHERE, CENTERING
58-SPRING, JOINT PRELOAD
59-SHAFT ASM, LOWER STEERING

Fig. 96   Exploded view of column shift tilt steering column (Part 2 of 2). 1993 Eldorado & Seville

Fig. 96   Exploded view of column shift tilt steering column (Part 1 of 2). 1993 Eldorado & Seville

61-SCREW, SUPPORT
62-SUPPORT ASM, STRG COL HSG
71-SHROUD, STRG COL HSG
72-JACKET ASM, STRG COL
79-CLIP, CONVOLUTED CONDUIT
80-CONDUIT, CONVOLUTED
81-SWITCH ASM, IGNITION
82-SCREW, WASH HD (#10-24X.25)
83-ACTUATOR ASM, IGNITION SWITCH
84-ROD, DIMMER SWITCH
85-NUT, HEXAGON (#10-24)
86-STUD, DIMR & IGNITION SW MTG
87-SWITCH ASM, DIMMER
91-BEARING ASM, ADAPTER &
93-SCREW, HEX WASHER HD TAP
94-SEAT, LOWER BEARING
95-SPRING, LOWER BEARING
96-RETAINER, LOWER SPRING
97-RETAINER, BEARING
98-SEAL, STEERING SHAFT
99-BUSHING, SEAL RETAINING

Service Kits

201-RACK SERV KIT, COL SECTOR &
   -INCLUDES: 14,31,33,44,47,48
202-SPRING SERV KIT, TILT COLUMN
   -INCLUDES: 13,14,39,50,51,52
203-COIL SERV KIT, INFL RESTRINT
   -INCLUDES: 3,4,28
204-SPHERE SERV KIT, TILT COLUMN
   -INCLUDES: 57,58
205-GREASE SERV KIT, (SYNTHETIC)

1-NUT, HEX LOCKING (M14x1.5)
2-RING, RETAINING
3-COIL ASM, INFL RESTRAINT
4-WASHER, WAVE
5-RING, RETAINING
6-LOCK, SHAFT
7-CAM ASM, TURN SIG CANCEL
8-SPRING, UPPER BEARING
9-SCREW, BNDG HD CR RECESS
10-SCREW, RD WASH HD (M4.2x1.41)
11-ARM ASM, SIGNAL SWITCH
12-SWITCH ASM, TURN SIGNAL
13-SEAT, UPPER BRG INNER RACE
14-RACE, INNER
15-SCREW, PAN HD SOC TAP
16-SWITCH ASM, BUZZER
18-SCREW, LOCK RETAINING
19-COVER ASM, LOCK HOUSING
20-LOCK CYLINDER SET, STRG COL
   PASS KEY
21-ACTUATOR, DIMMER SW ROD
22-PIN, SWITCH ACTUATOR PIVOT
23-SWITCH ASM, PIVOT & (PULSE)
24-BASE PLATE, COL HSG CVR END
25-CAP, COL HSG COVER END
26-PROTECTOR, WIRING
27-SCREW, FLT HD TAPPING
28-SHROUD, CONNECTOR
30-HOUSING ASM, STRG COLUMN
31-BEARING ASM
32-BOLT, LOCK
33-SPRING, LOCK BOLT
34-SHOE, STEERING WHEEL LOCK
35-SHOE, STEERING WHEEL LOCK
36-SHIELD, WIRE PROTECTOR
37-SHAFT, DRIVE
38-PIN, DOWEL
39-PIN, PIVOT
40-SPRING, SHOE
41-SPRING, RELEASE LEVER
42-PIN, RELEASE LEVER
43-LEVER, SHOE RELEASE
44-RACK, SWITCH ACTUATOR
45-SPRING, RACK PRELOAD
46-HOUSING, STRG COLUMN
47-SECTOR, SWITCH ACTUATOR
48-SCREW, HEX WASHER HEAD
50-GUIDE, SPRING
51-SPRING, WHEEL TILT
52-RETAINER, SPRING
55-SHAFT ASM, STEERING
56-SHAFT ASM, RACE & UPPER
57-SPHERE, CENTERING
58-SPRING, JOINT PRELOAD
59-SHAFT ASM, LOWER STEERING

Fig. 97 Exploded view of console shift tilt steering column (Part 2 of 2). 1993 Eldorado & Seville

Fig. 97 Exploded view of console shift tilt steering column (Part 1 of 2). 1993 Eldorado & Seville

Fig. 98 Pass key wire connection locations. 1993 Eldorado & Seville

18 SCREW, LOCK RETAINING
20 LOCK CYLINDER SET, STRG COL (PASS KEY)

Fig. 99 Pass key wire installation. 1993 Eldorado, Fleetwood (RWD) & Seville

2 RING, RETAINING
3 COIL ASM, INFL RESTRAINT
8 CAM ASM, TURN SIG CANCEL

Fig. 101 Coil assembly installation. 1993 Eldorado, Fleetwood (RWD) & Seville

Fig. 100 Coil assembly centering procedure. 1993 Eldorado, Fleetwood (RWD) & Seville

---

head connector.
2. Install lock retaining screw. **Torque** to 22 inch lbs.
3. Install key from pass key lock cylinder set. Install buzzer switch assembly.
4. Reinstall key in pass key lock cylinder set. Ensure key is in LOCK position.
5. Install turn signal switch assembly wire harness through steering column. Let switch hang freely and connect switch electrical connector to bulkhead connector.
6. Install coil assembly wire harness through column. Let coil hang freely, then connect yellow connector shroud to black terminal connector and connect to the vehicle harness.
7. Install turn signal switch assembly and screw. **Torque** screw to 30 inch lbs.
8. Install signal switch arm and screws. **Torque** screws to 20 inch lbs.
9. Install hazard knob assembly and multi-function lever.
10. Install inner race, upper bearing inner race seat and the upper bearing spring.
11. Install turn signal cancelling cam assembly. Lubricate with synthetic grease.
12. Install shaft lock.
13. Install new shaft lock retaining ring using installation tool No. J 23653-C or equivalent, to push down shaft lock. **Ring must be firmly seated in groove on shaft.**
14. Set steering shaft so block tooth on upper steering shaft is at the 12 o'clock position and the wheels are facing straight ahead. Set ignition switch to LOCK position to ensure no damage occurs to the coil assembly.
15. Install wave washer.
16. **SIR coil assembly wires must be kept tight with no slack while installing SIR coil assembly. Failure to do so may cause wires to be kinked near the shaft lock area and cut when the steering wheel is turned.**
17. Ensure coil assembly is centered as follows:
    a. Remove coil assembly.
    b. Hold coil assembly with clear bottom up to see coil ribbon.
    c. There are two different styles of coils. One rotates clockwise and the other rotates counterclockwise.
    d. While holding coil assembly, depress spring lock to rotate hub in direction of arrow shown in **Fig.**

100, until is stops.
    e. The coil ribbon should be wound up tight against the center hub.
    f. Rotate coil hub in opposite direction approximately 2 1/2 turns. Release spring lock between locking tabs in front of arrow, **Fig. 100.**
18. Install coil assembly as follows:
    a. Pull wire tight while positioning SIR coil to the steering shaft.
    b. Align opening in coil with horn tower and "locating bump' between two tabs on housing cover, **Fig. 101.**
    c. Seat coil assembly into steering column.
19. Install coil assembly retaining ring. **Ring must be firmly seated in groove on shaft.**
20. Gently pull lower coil assembly, turn signal, pass key, and pivot wires to remove any wire kinks that may be inside steering column assembly. Failure to do so may cause damage to wire harness.
21. Install wiring protector.
22. Install steering wheel and enable airbag system.

HOUSING COVER

The housing cover consists of the following components: lock housing cover assembly, column housing cover end cap, pivot & pulse switch assembly, dimmer switch rod actuator and the tilt spring assembly.

Disassembly

1. Remove upper column as described under "Upper Column" disassembly procedures.
2. Remove housing end cap.
3. Remove cruise control and multi-function lever connectors from base plate and disconnect.
4. Remove multi-function lever.

5. Remove cover screws, then remove the tilt lever.
6. Remove lock housing cover assembly.
7. Remove base plate and dimmer switch rod actuator.
8. Remove switch actuator pivot pin, then the pivot and pulse switch assembly as follows:
    a. Allow switch to hang freely if removal is not required.
    b. Disconnect pivot and switch connector from bulkhead connector.
    c. Gently pull wire harness through column.
9. Remove spring retainer, spring and spring guide.

Assembly

1. Install spring guide and spring. Lubricate with lithium grease.
2. Using a cross recess screwdriver, push spring retainer down and turn clockwise to lock in place.
3. Install pivot and switch assembly to lock housing cover assembly.
4. Connect switch actuator pivot pin to switch and cover.
5. Pull pivot and switch assembly wire harness through steering column. Connect switch connector to bulkhead connector.
6. Install dimmer switch rod actuator to base plate. Lubricate with lithium grease.
7. Install base plate to lock housing cover assembly. Bottom edge of dimmer switch rod actuator must rest on bend in dimmer switch rod.
8. Install lock housing cover assembly.
9. Install screws. Tighten screw in 12 o'clock position first, 8 o'clock position second, and the screw in the 3 o'clock position last. **Torque** screws in same order to 80 inch lbs.
10. Connect multi-function lever and cruise control connectors together and mount on base plate.
11. Install housing cover end cap.
12. Assembly remainder of steering column as described under "Upper Column" assembly procedure.

MID COLUMN

The mid column consists of the following components: steering column housing assembly, steering wheel lock shoe, switch actuator sector, switch actuator rack, bearing assembly, lock bolt, steering column housing support assembly, steering shaft assembly and the shift tube assembly.

Disassembly

1. Disarm airbag system as described under "Airbag System Disarming."
2. Disconnect battery ground cable, then remove steering column from vehicle as described under "Steering Column, Replace."
3. Perform all disassembly steps described under "Housing Cover."
4. Remove pivot pins using pivot pin removal tool No. J 21854-01 or equivalent. Reinstall tilt lever.
5. Remove steering column housing assembly. Pull back on tilt lever and pull steering column housing assembly down and away from column.
6. Remove the following components to disassemble the steering column housing assembly:
   a. Bearing assembly.
   b. Wire abrasion shield.
   c. Hex head screw.
   d. Lock bolt spring.
   e. Lock bolt.
   f. Switch actuator rack and rack preload spring.
   g. Driveshaft.
   h. Switch actuator sector.
   i. Release lever pin using lock shoe and release lever pin tool No. J 22635 or equivalent.
   j. Shoe release lever.
   k. Release lever spring.
   l. Dowel pin using lock show and release lever pin tool No. J 22635 or equivalent.
   m. Lock shoes and shoe springs.
7. Remove lower spring retainer.
8. Remove bearing and seal retainer.
9. Remove lower spring retainer.
10. Remove lower bearing spring and lower bearing seat.
11. Remove hex head bolts, then the adapter and bearing assembly.
12. Remove steering column shaft assembly.
13. Mark upper shaft assembly and lower steering shaft assembly to ensure proper assembly. Failure to assemble properly will cause steering wheel to be turned 180°.
14. Disassemble steering column shaft assembly as follows:
    a. Separate upper shaft assembly from lower steering shaft assembly. Tilt 90° to each other and disengage.
    b. Separate centering sphere from upper shaft assembly by rotating sphere 90° and sliding out.
    c. Remove joint preload spring from centering sphere.
15. Remove support screws, then remove column housing support assembly with dimmer switch rod from the steering column jacket.

16. Remove oval head recess screws and shift lever gate from support.
17. Remove shift tube retaining ring, then the two thrust washers and the lock plate.
18. Remove wave washer and two thrust washers, then the gearshift lever bowl assembly with the gearshift bowl shroud and shift tube assembly.
19. Remove shroud from bowl.
20. Remove shift lever spring, then the shift tube from the bowl. Use a press is necessary.
21. Remove hex nut and pan head screw securing PRNDL adjuster assembly.
22. Remove PRNDL adjuster bracket and the dimmer switch assembly.
23. Remove dimmer and ignition switch mounting stud.
24. Remove ignition switch assembly from ignition switch actuator assembly.
25. Remove cam retainer.
26. Remove pan head screw and dimmer and ignition switch mounting stud.
27. Remove cable assembly with ignition switch actuator assembly as follows:
    a. Remove cable clip from upper location of steering column jacket assembly.
    b. Remove cable mounting clip from solenoid bracket.
    c. Remove ball joint socket from solenoid.
    d. Remove ball joint spring.
28. Remove hex washer head screw securing interlock solenoid assembly and solenoid bracket to steering column jacket assembly.
29. Remove hex washer head screws securing solenoid bracket to steering column jacket assembly.

Assembly

1. Install solenoid bracket. **Torque** screws to 35 inch lbs.
2. Install interlock solenoid assembly, then finger tighten hex washer head screw.
3. Connect terminal connector to interlock solenoid assembly.
4. Install cable assembly with ignition switch actuator assembly, as follows:
   a. Install cable clip to upper location of jacket assembly.
   b. Allow lower cable to hang free.
5. Install stud and bracket assembly. **Torque** screw and stud to 35 inch lbs.
6. Install cable shift cam assembly and cam retainer. **Torque** retainer to 35 inch lbs.
7. Assemble gate and screws to support. **Torque** screws to 33 inch lbs.
8. Install dimmer switch rod to column housing support assembly.
9. Install support assembly and screws. **Torque** screws to 88 inch lbs.
10. Install shift tube lever spring to gearshift lever bowl assembly.
11. Attach bowl to shift tube assembly using shift tube installation tool No. J 23073-1 or equivalent.
12. Install gearshift bowl shroud to bowl.
13. Install shift tube with bowl to steering column jacket assembly.
14. Install two thrust washers and wave washer. Lubricate wave washer with

lithium grease.
15. Install lock plate and two thrust washers.
16. Install shift tube retaining ring, then connect steering shaft assembly to jacket assembly.
17. Install tilt lever, then the column housing assembly to the column, as follows:
    a. Position column housing assembly and align switch actuator rack with pin on end of ignition switch actuator assembly.
    b. Pull back on tilt lever, pushing column housing assembly onto column housing support assembly.
    c. Release tilt lever to lock shoes and onto dowel pins.
    d. Remove tilt lever.
18. Install pivot pins. Lubricate with lithium grease, then press pin until firmly seated.
19. Install adapter and bearing assembly. Lubricate with lithium grease.
20. Install hex head screws. **Torque** to 30 inch lbs.
21. Install lower bearing seat and lower bearing spring. Press new lower spring retainer onto shaft to compress spring.
22. Measure distance from face of adapter and bearing assembly to lower spring retainer. Spring height must be 1.0 inch.
23. Install bearing and seal retainer, then the steering shaft seal.
24. Install seal retaining bushing and a new spring retainer.
25. Assemble remaining steering column components as described in the "Assembly" procedures.

1993 Fleetwood (RWD)

Disarm airbag system as described under "Airbag System Disarming," then remove column from vehicle as described under "Steering Column, Replace."

The steering wheel must be straight and the column in the LOCK position. **Care must be taken when handling column with a live inflator module. Never point bag deploy surface toward you, and never stand column on steering wheel. Accidental deployment in these positions may cause injury. Always face bag deploy surface toward open space to allow for unrestricted expansion.**

Refer to **Fig. 11** for steering column service procedures.

UPPER COLUMN

The upper column consists of the following components: inflatable restraint coil assembly, shaft lock, turn signal cancelling cam assembly, upper bearing spring, upper bearing inner race seat, inner race, turn signal switch assembly, buzzer switch assembly and the steering column pass key lock cylinder set.

Disassembly

1. Remove coil assembly retaining ring.
2. Remove inflatable restraint coil assembly, if required, as follows:
   a. Remove wave washer, then the

shaft lock retaining ring using lock plate compressor tool No. J 23635-C or equivalent, to push down on shaft.

  b. Remove shaft lock, then the turn signal cancelling cam assembly.
  c. Remove upper bearing spring and the upper bearing race seat.
  d. Remove inner race, then place turn signal lever to "RIGHT TURN" position (up).
  e. Remove multi-function lever and hazard knob assembly.
  f. Remove screws and the signal switch arm.
  g. Remove turn signal switch mounting screws, then remove the turn signal switch assembly by removing the wiring protector and gently pulling wire harness through the column.
  h. Remove wiring protector, then attach a piece of mechanics wire to terminal connector harness to ease reassembly.
  i. Gently pull wire through column and remove inflatable restraint coil assembly.
3. Remove key from pass key lock cylinder set.
4. Remove buzzer switch assembly, then reinsert key in pass key lock cylinder and move to LOCK position.
5. Remove lock retaining screw, then remove pass key lock cylinder and harness as follows:
  a. Disconnect cylinder harness connector from vehicle wire harness.
  b. Remove wiring protector.
  c. Attach a piece of mechanics wire to terminals to ease in reassembly.
  d. Gently pull wire harness through column.

Assembly

1. Install pass key lock cylinder as follows:
  a. Route wire from pass key lock cylinder as shown in **Fig. 99**, and snap retaining clip into hole in housing. **Failure to do so may result in component damage or malfunction of pass key lock cylinder.**
  b. Pull wire terminals through column and snap retaining clip into hole in housing.
  c. Connect cylinder harness connector to vehicle wire harness.
2. Install lock retaining screw. **Torque** to 22 inch lbs.
3. Remove key from pass key lock cylinder set, install buzzer switch assembly, then reinsert key in pass key lock cylinder set. Ensure key is in LOCK position.
4. Insert signal switch assembly wire harness through steering column. Allow switch to hang freely, then connect switch connector to vehicle wire harness.
5. Pull coil assembly wire harness through column, **Fig. 102**. Allow coil to hang freely.

INFL RESTRAINT COIL ASM AND TURN SIGNAL SWITCH WIRE HARNESSES THROUGH HERE. 5 O'CLOCK POSITION.

Fig. 102   Coil assembly wire installation. 1993 Fleetwood (RWD)

6. Install turn signal switch assembly and mounting screws. **Torque** mounting screws to 30 inch lbs.
7. Install signal switch arm and screws. **Torque** screws to 20 inch lbs.
8. Install hazard knob assembly and multi-function lever.
9. Install inner race, upper bearing inner race seat and upper bearing spring.
10. Install turn signal cancelling cam assembly. Lubricate with synthetic grease.
11. Install shaft lock, then the new shaft lock retaining ring using lock plate compressor tool No. J 23653-C or equivalent, to push down shaft lock. **Retaining ring must be firmly seated in groove on shaft.**
12. Set steering shaft so block tooth on upper steering shaft is at the 12 o'clock position and the wheels are straight ahead, then set ignition switch to LOCK position, to ensure no damage to coil assembly.
13. Install wave washer.
14. Coil assembly will become uncentered if the steering column is separated from the steering gear and is allowed to rotate, or if the centering spring is pushed down, allowing hub to rotate while coil is removed from column. If this occurs, center coil assembly by referring to **Fig. 100**, and performing the following:
  a. Ensure wheels are pointing straight ahead.
  b. Remove coil assembly.
  c. Hold coil assembly with clear bottom up to see coil ribbon.
  d. There are two different styles of coils, one rotates clockwise, the other rotates counterclockwise.
  e. While holding coil assembly, depress spring lock to rotate hub in direction of arrow, **Fig. 100**, until it stops.
  f. Coil ribbon should be wound up tightly against center hub.
  g. Rotate coil hub in opposite direction approximately 2 1/2 turns. Release spring lock between locking tabs in front of arrow.
15. If a new coil assembly is installed, assemble pre-centered coil assembly to steering column. Remove centering tab and dispose.
16. **SIR coil assembly wire must be kept tight with no slack while installing the coil assembly. failure to do so may cause wire to be kinked**

near shaft lock area and cut when the steering wheel is turned.
17. Ensure coil assembly is centered. If not, perform procedure described in step 14.
18. Install coil assembly as follows:
  a. Pull wire tight while positioning airbag coil to steering shaft.
  b. Align opening in coil with horn tower and "locating bump" between two tabs on housing cover, **Fig. 101.**
  c. Seat coil assembly into steering column.
19. Install coil assembly retaining ring. Ring must be firmly seated in groove on shaft.
20. Gently pull lower coil assembly, turn signal and pass key wires to remove any wire kinks that may be inside steering column assembly. Failure to do so may cause damage to wire harness.
21. Install wiring protector.
22. Enable airbag system as described under "Airbag System Arming."

HOUSING COVER

Refer to the 1993 Eldorado & Seville "Housing Cover" assembly and disassembly procedures for housing cover service.

MID COLUMN

Refer to the 1993 Eldorado & Seville "Mid Column" assembly and disassembly procedures for mid column service.

ATTACHMENT PLATE, SENSOR ASSEMBLY & STEERING SHAFT BUSHING ASSEMBLY

Disassembly

1. Remove steering column from vehicle as described under "Steering Column, Replace."
2. Remove lower bearing adapter clip, then the sensor assembly.
3. Remove bearing adapter retainer, then the steering shaft bushing assembly.

Assembly

1. Assemble steering shaft bushing assembly to jacket assembly. Lubricate inner surface of bushing with lithium grease.
2. Install bearing adapter retainer, then the sensor assembly.
3. Install lower bearing adapter clip.

Caprice, Custom Cruiser & Roadmaster w/Supplemental Inflatable Restraint (SIR)

STANDARD COLUMN

INFLATOR MODULE, STEERING WHEEL COIL ASSEMBLY, SHAFT LOCK, CANCELLING CAM, UPPER BEARING SPRING, UPPER BEARING SEAT, INNER RACE, TURN SIGNAL SWITCH, BUZZER SWITCH & LOCK CYLINDER SET

Disassembly

Refer to **Fig. 103** for exploded view of steering column.

With steering column, inflator module and steering wheel already removed as previously outlined in "Steering Column Replace," proceed as follows:

1. Place key in "lock" position.
2. Remove coil assembly retaining ring, slide coil assembly off end of shaft, then remove wave washer.
3. Remove shaft lock retaining ring using tool J 23653-C or equivalent to depress shaft lock. **Use a ½ inch wrench to hold the shaft of tool J 23653 or equivalent when releasing the nut. Failure to do so may cause tool to fly off the steering column causing personal injury.**
4. Remove shaft lock, then the turn signal cancelling cam.
5. Remove upper bearing spring, then the thrust washer.
6. Place turn signal in "right turn" position, then remove signal switch arm attaching screw and the arm.
7. Remove turn signal switch attaching screws and position switch out of way. If it is necessary to remove switch, remove wiring harness protector and hazard knob, then gently pull wire harness through gear shift lever bowl, column housing and lock housing cover.
8. If necessary remove coil assembly as follows:
   a. Remove connector from terminal connector.
   b. Remove wire protector, then attach a wire to the coil assembly connector at the base of the steering column.
   c. Pull wire through lock housing cover and gearshift bowl shroud.
9. Remove key from cylinder lock, and remove buzzer switch and clip, then reinsert key in cylinder lock and turn to "lock" position.
10. Remove lock retaining screw and lock cylinder set.

Assembly

1. Install lock cylinder set, torquing retaining screw to 22 inch lbs.
2. Place key in "run" position, then install buzzer switch and clip.
3. Route turn signal switch wiring harness through lock housing cover, column housing and gear shift lever bowl.
4. Place coil assembly wire through lock housing cover and gearshift bowl shroud.
5. Connect shroud connector to terminal connector.
6. Install turn signal and hazard warning switch.
7. Install signal switch arm, torquing retaining screw to 10 inch lbs.
8. Install hazard knob.
9. Install thrust washer, then the upper bearing spring.
10. Install turn signal cancelling cam, then the shaft lock.
11. Depress shaft lock, then install shaft lock retaining ring.
12. Install steering wheel and inflator module as outlined in "Steering Column Replace."

LOCK HOUSING COVER, COVER END CAP, PIVOT & PULSE SWITCH ASSEMBLY, IGNITION SWITCH ACTUATOR ASSEMBLY, LOCK BOLT, UPPER BEARING, SWITCH ACTUATOR SECTOR, DIMMER SWITCH & IGNITION SWITCH

Disassembly

1. Perform "Disassembly" steps for "Inflator Module, Steering Wheel Coil Assembly, Shaft Lock, Cancelling Cam, Upper Bearing Spring, Upper Bearing Seat, Inner Race, Turn Signal Switch, Buzzer Switch & Lock Cylinder Set."
2. **On models equipped with cruise control,** unplug multi-function lever and cruise control connectors, then remove multi-function lever.
3. **On all models,** remove lock housing cover attaching screws, then cover.
4. Remove lock bolt and spring thrust washer from ignition switch actuator.
5. Remove housing cover screws, then cover.
6. Remove switch actuator pivot pin, and pulse switch using pivot pin removal tool J 21854-01.
7. Remove shift lever gate attaching screws, then lever gate.
8. Remove retaining bushing, horn contact, then bearing assembly.
9. Remove switch actuator, then rack preload spring.
10. Remove dimmer switch attaching screws, then dimmer switch.
11. Remove ignition switch attaching screws, then ignition switch and actuator.

Assembly

1. Install rack preload spring, switch actuator, then bearing assembly.
2. Install bearing retaining bushing, then horn contact.
3. Install shift lever gate, **torque** attaching screws to 18 inch lbs.
4. Install pivot and pulse switch.
5. Install switch actuator pivot pin, **torque** to 27 inch lbs.
6. Install housing cover, **torque** attaching screws to 17 inch lbs.
7. Install switch actuator, lock bolt, then spring thrust washer.
8. Install upper bearing retainer, then lock cover housing. **Torque** cover housing attaching screws to 47 inch lbs.
9. Install ignition switch, **torque** attaching screw to 35 inch lbs. Ignition switch must be in Off-Unlock position and gearshift lever bowl must not be in park position.
10. Install dimmer switch actuator rod, then dimmer switch. **Torque** attaching screws to 28 inch lbs.
11. Perform "Assembly" steps for "Inflator Module, Steering Wheel Coil Assembly, Shaft Lock, Cancelling Cam, Upper Bearing Spring, Upper Bearing Seat, Inner Race, Turn Signal Switch, Buzzer Switch & Lock Cylinder Set."

SHAFT ASSEMBLY, ADAPTER & BEARING ASSEMBLY, GEARSHIFT LEVER BOWL, SHIFT TUBE ASSEMBLY & LOWER BOWL BEARING

1. Perform "Disassembly" steps for "Inflator Module, Steering Wheel Coil Assembly, Shaft Lock, Cancelling Cam, Upper Bearing Spring, Upper Bearing Seat, Inner Race, Turn Signal Switch, Buzzer Switch & Lock Cylinder Set."
2. Perform "Disassembly" steps for "Lock Housing Cover, Cover End Cap, Pivot & Pulse Switch Assembly, Ignition Switch Actuator Assembly, Lock Bolt, Upper Bearing, Switch Actuator Sector, Dimmer Switch & Ignition Switch
3. Remove steering column from vehicle as outlined in "Steering Column Replace."
4. Remove lower bearing adapter clip, bearing adapter retainer, then adapter and bearing assembly.
5. Remove lower bearing spring, spring thrust washer, then steering column shaft.
6. Remove retaining spring from column shaft.
7. Remove gearshift lever bowl from the gearshift bowl shroud.
8. Remove gearshift bowl shroud from the gearshift lever bowl.
9. Remove upper shift lever spring from gearshift lever bowl.
10. Remove shift tube, then bowl lower bearing from steering column jacket.
11. Reverse procedure to install.

TILT COLUMN

INFLATOR MODULE, STEERING WHEEL COIL ASSEMBLY, SHAFT LOCK, CANCELLING CAM, UPPER BEARING SPRING, UPPER BEARING SEAT, INNER RACE, TURN SIGNAL SWITCH, BUZZER SWITCH & LOCK CYLINDER SET

Disassembly

Refer to **Fig. 104** exploded view of steering column.

With steering column, inflator module

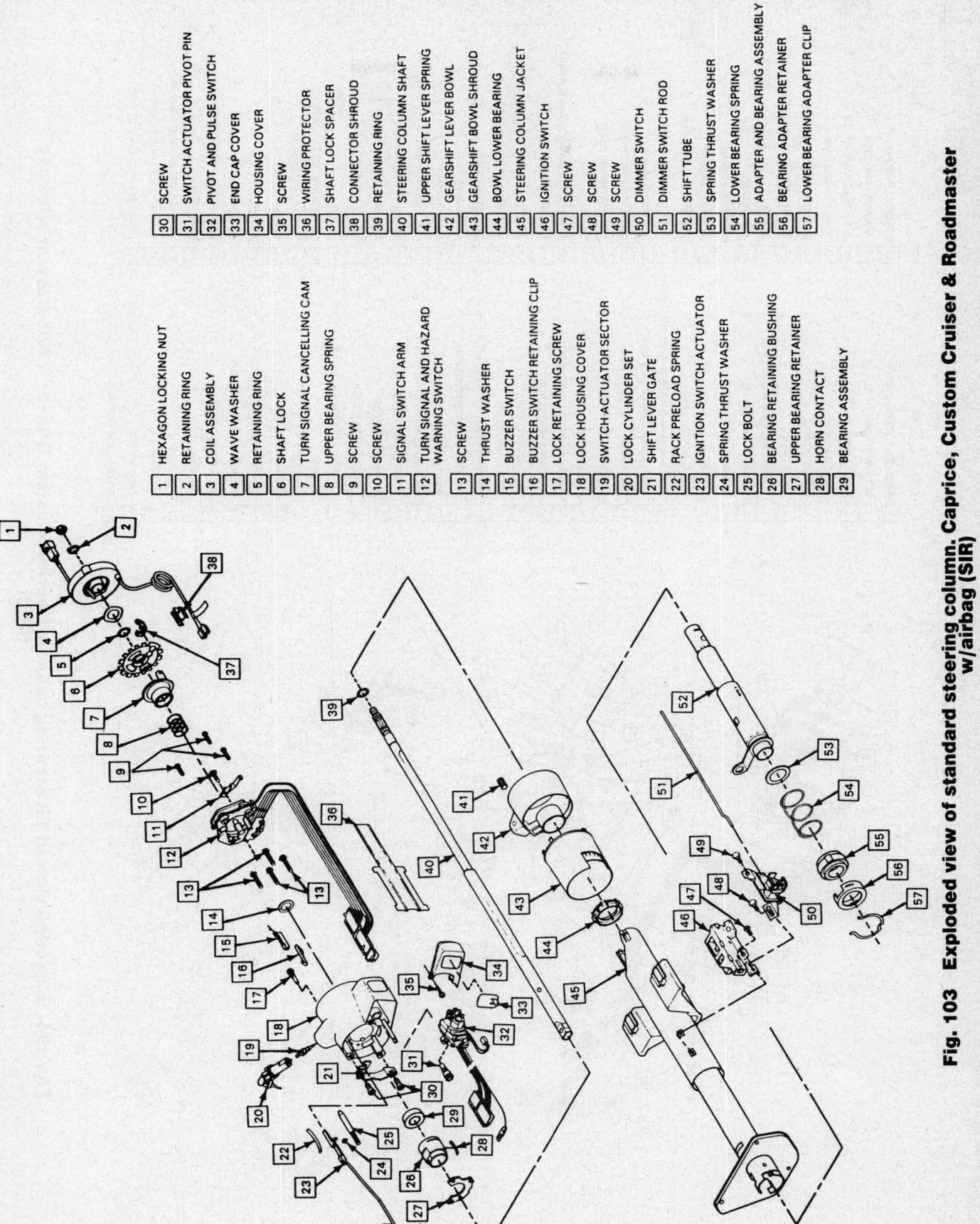

1	HEXAGON LOCKING NUT
2	RETAINING RING
3	COIL ASSEMBLY
4	WAVE WASHER
5	RETAINING RING
6	SHAFT LOCK
7	TURN SIGNAL CANCELLING CAM
8	UPPER BEARING SPRING
9	SCREW
10	SCREW
11	SIGNAL SWITCH ARM
12	TURN SIGNAL AND HAZARD WARNING SWITCH
13	SCREW
14	THRUST WASHER
15	BUZZER SWITCH
16	BUZZER SWITCH RETAINING CLIP
17	LOCK RETAINING SCREW
18	LOCK HOUSING COVER
19	SWITCH ACTUATOR SECTOR
20	LOCK CYLINDER SET
21	SHIFT LEVER GATE
22	RACK PRELOAD SPRING
23	IGNITION SWITCH ACTUATOR
24	SPRING THRUST WASHER
25	LOCK BOLT
26	BEARING RETAINING BUSHING
27	UPPER BEARING RETAINER
28	HORN CONTACT
29	BEARING ASSEMBLY

30	SCREW
31	SWITCH ACTUATOR PIVOT PIN
32	PIVOT AND PULSE SWITCH
33	END CAP COVER
34	HOUSING COVER
35	SCREW
36	WIRING PROTECTOR
37	SHAFT LOCK SPACER
38	CONNECTOR SHROUD
39	RETAINING RING
40	STEERING COLUMN SHAFT
41	UPPER SHIFT LEVER SPRING
42	GEARSHIFT LEVER BOWL
43	GEARSHIFT BOWL SHROUD
44	BOWL LOWER BEARING
45	STEERING COLUMN JACKET
46	IGNITION SWITCH
47	SCREW
48	SCREW
49	SCREW
50	DIMMER SWITCH
51	DIMMER SWITCH ROD
52	SHIFT TUBE
53	SPRING THRUST WASHER
54	LOWER BEARING SPRING
55	ADAPTER AND BEARING ASSEMBLY
56	BEARING ADAPTER RETAINER
57	LOWER BEARING ADAPTER CLIP

Fig. 103 Exploded view of standard steering column. Caprice, Custom Cruiser & Roadmaster w/airbag (SIR)

42	RELEASE LEVER PIN
43	SHOE RELEASE LEVER
44	SWITCH ACTUATOR RACK
45	RACK PRELOAD SPRING
46	STEERING COLUMN HOUSING
47	SWITCH ACTUATOR SECTOR
48	SCREW
50	SPRING GUIDE
51	WHEEL TILT SPRING
52	SPRING RETAINER
55	STEERING COLUMN SHAFT
56	RACE AND UPPER SHAFT
57	CENTERING SPHERE
58	JOINT PRELOAD SPRING
59	LOWER STEERING SHAFT
61	SCREW
63	STEERING COLUMN HOUSING SUPPORT
64	SCREW
65	SHIFT LEVER GATE
66	SHIFT TUBE RETAINING RING
67	THRUST WASHER
68	LOCK PLATE
69	WAVE WASHER
70	SHIFT LEVER SPRING
71	GEARSHIFT LEVER BOWL
72	STEERING COLUMN JACKET
81	IGNITION SWITCH
82	SCREW
83	IGNITION SWITCH ACTUATOR
84	DIMMER SWITCH ROD
85	SCREW
86	SCREW
87	DIMMER SWITCH
88	GEARSHIFT BOWL SHROUD
90	SHIFT TUBE
91	ADAPTER AND BEARING ASSEMBLY
92	BEARING ADAPTER RETAINER
93	LOWER BEARING ADAPTER CLIP

1	HEXAGON LOCKING UNIT
2	RETAINING RING
3	COIL ASSEMBLY
4	WAVE WASHER
5	RETAINING RING
6	SHAFT LOCK
7	TURN SIGNAL CANCELLING CAM
8	UPPER BEARING SPRING
9	SCREW
10	SCREW
11	SIGNAL SWITCH ARM
12	TURN SIGNAL AND HAZARD WARNING SWITCH
13	UPPER BEARING INNER RACE SEAT
14	INNER RACE
15	SCREW
16	BUZZER SWITCH
17	BUZZER SWITCH RETAINING CLIP
18	LOCK RETAINING SCREW
19	LOCK HOUSING COVER
20	LOCK CYLINDER SET
21	DIMMER SWITCH ROD ACTUATOR
22	SWITCH ACTUATOR PIVOT PIN
23	PIVOT AND PULSE SWITCH
24	HOUSING COVER END BASE PLATE
25	HOUSING COVER END CAP
26	WIRING PROTECTOR
28	CONNECTOR SHROUD
30	STEERING COLUMN HOUSING ASSEMBLY
31	BEARING
32	LOCK BOLT
33	LOCK BOLT SPRING
34	STEERING WHEEL LOCK SHOE
35	STEERING WHEEL LOCK SHOE
36	WIRE ABRASION SHIELD
37	DRIVE SHAFT
38	DOWEL PIN
39	PIVOT PIN
40	SHOE SPRING
41	RELEASE LEVER SPRING

Fig. 104 Exploded view of tilt steering column, Caprice, Custom Cruiser & Roadmaster w/airbag (SIR)

and steering wheel already removed as previously outlined in "Steering Column Replace," proceed as follows:

1. Place key in "lock" position.
2. Remove coil assembly retaining ring, slide coil assembly off end of shaft, then remove wave washer.
3. Remove shaft lock retaining ring using tool J 23653-C or equivalent to depress shaft lock. **Use a ½ inch wrench to hold the shaft of tool J 23653 or equivalent when releasing the nut. Failure to do so may cause tool to fly off the steering column causing personal injury.**
4. Remove shaft lock and shaft lock cover, then the turn signal cancelling cam.
5. Remove upper bearing spring, then the upper bearing seat.
6. Remove inner race.
7. Place turn signal in "right turn" position, then remove signal switch arm attaching screw and the arm.
8. Remove turn signal switch attaching screws and position switch out of way. If it is necessary to remove switch, remove wiring harness protector and hazard knob, then gently pull wire harness through gear shift lever bowl, column housing and lock housing cover.
9. If necessary remove coil assembly as follows:
   a. Remove connector from terminal connector.
   b. Remove wire protector, then attach a wire to the coil assembly connector at the base of the steering column.
   c. Pull wire through lock housing cover and gearshift bowl shroud.
10. Remove key from cylinder lock, and remove buzzer switch and clip, then reinsert key in cylinder lock and turn to "lock" position.
11. Remove lock retaining screw and lock cylinder set.

Assembly

1. Install lock cylinder set, torquing retaining screw to 22 inch lbs.
2. Place key in "run" position, then install buzzer switch and clip.
3. Route turn signal switch wiring harness through lock housing cover, column housing and gear shift lever bowl.
4. Place coil assembly wire through lock housing cover and gearshift bowl shroud.
5. Connect shroud connector to terminal connector.
6. Install turn signal and hazard warning switch.
7. Install signal switch arm, torquing retaining screw to 20 inch lbs.
8. Install hazard knob, then the inner race.
9. Install upper bearing seat, then the upper bearing spring.
10. Install turn signal cancelling cam, then the shaft lock.
11. Depress shaft lock, then install shaft lock retaining ring.

12. Install steering wheel and inflator module as outlined in "Steering Column Replace."

LOCK HOUSING COVER, COVER END CAP, PIVOT & SWITCH ASSEMBLY, DIMMER SWITCH ROD ACTUATOR & TILT SPRING ASSEMBLY

Disassembly

1. Perform "Disassembly" steps for "Inflator Module, Steering Wheel Coil Assembly, Shaft Lock, Turn Signal Cancelling Cam, Upper Bearing Spring, Upper Bearing Seat, Inner Race, Turn Signal Switch, Buzzer Switch & Lock Cylinder Set."
2. Remove lock housing cover attaching screws and cover, then the tilt lever.
3. Remove cover housing end cap and the dimmer switch rod actuator.
4. **On vehicles equipped with cruise control,** unplug cruise control connector and remove multi-function lever.
5. **On all models,** gently pull pivot switch wiring harness through column housing and gear shift lever bowl.
6. Remove pivot pin, then the pivot and switch assembly.
7. Remove pivot and pulse switch.
8. Remove spring retainer, then the spring and spring guide.

Assembly

1. Coat spring guide and spring with lithium grease and install, then install spring retainer.
2. Install pivot and switch assembly, then the pivot pin.
3. Attach actuator pivot pin to pivot and pulse switch, and lock housing cover.
4. Route pivot and pulse switch assembly wiring harness through gear shift lever bowl and column housing.
5. Install dimmer switch rod actuator, then the gear shift lever bowl, ensuring bottom edge of dimmer switch rod actuator rests on bend in dimmer switch rod.
6. Install cover housing end cap.
7. **On vehicles equipped with cruise control,** plug in cruise control connector and install multi-function lever.
8. **On all models,** Install lock housing cover. Tighten screw in 12 o'clock position first, screw in 8 o'clock position second and screw in 3 o'clock position third, then **torque** in same order to 80 inch lbs.
9. Perform "Assembly" steps for "Inflator Module, Steering Wheel Coil Assembly, Shaft Lock, Turn Signal Cancelling Cam, Upper Bearing Spring, Upper Bearing Seat, Inner Race, Turn Signal Switch, Buzzer Switch & Lock Cylinder Set."

COLUMN HOUSING, LOCK SHOES, ACTUATOR SECTOR ASSEMBLY, SWITCH ACTUATOR RACK, BEARINGS & LOCK BOLT ASSEMBLY

Disassembly

1. Perform "Disassembly" steps for "In-

flator Module, Steering Wheel Coil Assembly, Shaft Lock, Turn Signal Cancelling Cam, Upper Bearing Spring, Upper Bearing Seat, Inner Race, Turn Signal Switch, Buzzer Switch & Lock Cylinder Set."
2. Perform "Disassembly" steps for "Lock Housing Cover, Cover End Cap, Pivot & Switch Assembly, Dimmer Switch Rod Actuator & Tilt Spring Assembly."
3. Using pivot pin remover tool No. J-21854-01 or equivalent, remove pivot pins, **Fig. 75.**
4. Reinstall tilt lever.
5. Remove column housing assembly by pulling back on tilt lever and pulling housing down and away from column.
6. Remove driveshaft, then the switch actuator sector.
7. Remove switch actuator rack and rack preload spring, then the release lever pin and release lever.
8. Remove release lever spring, then the dowel pin.
9. Remove lock shoes and lock shoe springs, then the bearings.
10. Remove hex head bolt, then the lock bolt spring and lock bolt.

Assembly

1. Install bearings to column housing, then install driveshaft.
2. Install actuator sector, then the lock shoes.
3. Install dowel pin, then the lock shoe springs.
4. Install release lever spring, then the release lever.
5. Install release lever pin, then the rack preload spring.
6. Install switch actuator rack to actuator sector.
7. Install lock bolt and lock bolt spring, then the hex head bolt.
8. Install column housing assembly to column as follows:
   a. Position column housing assembly and align switch actuator rack with pin on end of actuator rod.
   b. Pull back on tilt lever, pushing column housing assembly onto column housing support assembly.
   c. Release tilt lever to lock shoes.
9. Remove tilt lever.
10. Lubricate pivot pins with lithium grease and install them.
11. Perform "Assembly" steps for "Lock Housing Cover, Cover End Cap, Pivot & Switch Assembly, Dimmer Switch Rod Actuator & Tilt Spring Assembly."
12. Perform "Assembly" steps for "Inflator Module, Steering Wheel Coil Assembly, Shaft Lock, Turn Signal Cancelling Cam, Upper Bearing Spring, Upper Bearing Seat, Inner Race, Turn Signal Switch, Buzzer Switch & Lock Cylinder Set."

SHAFT ASSEMBLY, COLUMN HOUSING SUPPORT, SHIFT TUBE ASSEMBLY, IGNITION SWITCH, DIMMER SWITCH & LOWER BEARING ASSEMBLY

Disassembly

1. Perform "Disassembly" steps for "Inflator Module, Steering Wheel Coil Assembly, Shaft Lock, Turn Signal Cancelling Cam, Upper Bearing Spring, Upper Bearing Seat, Inner Race, Turn Signal Switch, Buzzer Switch & Lock Cylinder Set."
2. Perform "Disassembly" steps for "Lock Housing Cover, Cover End Cap, Pivot & Switch Assembly, Dimmer Switch Rod Actuator & Tilt Spring Assembly."
3. Perform "Disassembly" steps for "Column Housing, Lock Shoes, Actuator Sector Assembly, Switch Actuator Rack, Bearings & Lock Bolt Assembly."
4. Remove steering column from vehicle as outlined in "Steering Column Replace."
5. Remove bearing retainer, then the attaching screws and the lower bearing.
6. Remove shaft assembly then disconnect lower shaft.
7. Remove centering sphere from upper shaft, then the retainer clip from the sphere.
8. Remove housing support assembly attaching screws, then the housing support assembly and dimmer switch rod.
9. Remove hex nut and hex head bolt, then the dimmer switch and mounting stud.
10. Remove ignition switch and ignition switch actuator.
11. Remove shift tube retaining ring, thrust washer, lock plate, wave washer, then shift tube using special tool J 23072 or equivalent.
12. Remove gear shift bowl.

Assembly

1. Install gear shift lever bowl to jacket, then the dimmer switch rod to housing support.
2. Install shift tube using special tool J 23073-01 or equivalent, wave washer, lock plate, thrust washer, then shift tube retaining ring.
3. Install dimmer switch rod to steering column housing support.
4. Install housing support assembly, torquing attaching screws to 30 inch lbs.
5. Install actuator rod assembly to track in housing support.
6. Install ignition switch and mounting stud, then adjust switch.
7. Install retaining clip and sphere to upper shaft.
8. Install lower shaft to upper shaft with block tooth on shaft lower end of upper shaft at 12 o'clock position and notch at end of lower shaft at 4 o'clock position.
9. Lubricate shaft assembly with lithium grease and install to column.
10. Install column housing assembly to column.

Fig. 105 Checking slide block. 1991 Storm

11. Position column assembly and align switch actuator rack with pin on end of actuator rod.
12. Pull back on tilt lever, pushing column housing assembly onto column housing support assembly.
13. Release tilt lever to lock shoes, then remove tilt lever.
14. Lubricate inner surface of lower bearing with lithium grease, then install bearing and retaining screws.
15. Install bearing retainer.
16. Install dimmer switch, hex nut and hex head bolt, then adjust dimmer switch.
17. Perform "Assembly" steps for "Column Housing, Lock Shoes, Actuator Sector Assembly, Switch Actuator Rack, Bearings & Lock Bolt Assembly."
18. Perform "Assembly" steps for "Lock Housing Cover, Cover End Cap, Pivot & Switch Assembly, Dimmer Switch Rod Actuator & Tilt Spring Assembly."
19. Perform "Assembly" steps for "Inflator Module, Steering Wheel Coil Assembly, Shaft Lock, Turn Signal Cancelling Cam, Upper Bearing Spring, Upper Bearing Seat, Inner Race, Turn Signal Switch, Buzzer Switch & Lock Cylinder Set."

Storm

Disarm airbag before servicing steering column. Refer to "Airbag System Disarming" for procedures.
The wheel must be straight and the column in the Lock position. **Care must be taken when handling column with a live inflator module. Never point bag deploy surface toward you, and never stand column on steering wheel. Accidental deployment in these positions may cause injury. Always face bag deploy surface toward open space to allow for unrestricted expansion.**

DISASSEMBLY

1. Remove the inflator module as follows:
   a. With the ignition switch in the Off position disconnect battery ground cable.
   b. Remove the SIR module screws and the SIR module.
2. Remove steering wheel retaining nut and steering wheel.
3. Remove horn switch screws and horn switch, rear steering wheel cover screws and rear cover.
4. Remove lower switch panel, dash lighter panel and hood release panel.
5. Remove lap air deflector and left lower dash trim panel.
6. Remove upper steering column mounting bolts and drop column down.
7. Remove two piece steering column cover, then disconnect coil assembly wiring harness from turn signal switch.
8. Remove four screws and coil assembly from turn signal switch.
9. Remove turn signal switch, then snap ring and spacer collar from steering shaft.
10. Remove ignition switch, then steering shaft from steering column.
11. Remove back drive cable and guide.
12. Inspect steering column for damage as follows:
    a. Check upper column tube bearing for abnormal noise or rotation difficulty, replace as necessary.
    b. Check slide block on steering column bracket assembly. Block be within .28 inch from the slots insert edge. **Fig. 105.** If measurement is not within specifications, replace column.

ASSEMBLY

1. Install guide onto column, then ignition switch.
2. Install steering shaft into column, then install collar and snap ring onto column.
3. Install turn signal switch onto column, then four screws and coil assembly onto turn signal switch.
4. Connect coil assembly wiring harness into turn signal switch.
5. Install two piece steering column cover, then install steering column and steering column mounting bolts and **torque** to 18 ft.lbs..
6. Install left lower dash trim panel and lap air deflector.
7. Install hood release panel, dash lighter panel and lower switch panel.
8. Install rear steering wheel cover, then connect horn contact switches into wheel.
9. Install steering wheel and retaining nut, **torque** nut to 25 ft. lbs.
10. Install SIR module and SIR module screws, **torque** screws to 44 inch lbs.
11. With the ignition switch in the Off position, connect the battery ground cable.
12. **When all service procedures have been completed, rearm airbag as outlined in "Airbag System Arming."**

1	STEERING SHAFT LOWER JOINT	7	STEERING WHEEL BUMPER
2	STEERING COLUMN ASSEMBLY	8	STEERING SHAFT NUT
3	STEERING COLUMN UPPER COVER	9	STEERING WHEEL PAD
4	TURN SIGNAL/DIMMER SWITCH	10	STEERING COLUMN LOWER COVER
5	GROUND WIRE	11	STEERING COLUMN UNDER COVER
6	STEERING WHEEL	12	STEERING LOCK ASSEMBLY

Fig. 106   Exploded view of steering column. Metro less airbag (SIR)

Metro Less Supplemental Inflatable Restraint (SIR)

Refer to **Figs. 18 through 21 and 106 through 108** when servicing this steering column.

Metro w/Supplemental Inflatable Restraint (SIR)

Disarm airbag before servicing steering column. Refer to "Airbag System Disarming" for procedures.

SIR COIL & TURN SIGNAL/DIMMER SWITCH

Remove steering wheel as outlined in "Steering Column Replace" in this section.
Refer to **Fig. 23** for exploded view of steering column.
1. Remove six screws retaining upper and lower steering column covers, then remove column covers.
2. Remove two electrical connectors from fuse box, one from the SIR harness, and one from the main wiring harness, **Fig. 109.**
3. Remove SIR coil and turn signal/dimmer switch attaching screws, then switch assembly.
4. Reverse procedure to install noting the following:
   a. Ensure that SIR coil is centered. If not position wheels of vehicle in the straightforward position.
   b. Check position of SIR coil, **Fig. 110.**
   c. If "Neutral" mark is at the alignment mark the coil is centered and no adjustment is necessary.
   d. If "R1" mark is close to the alignment mark coil is one rotation off to the right from its center state and needs to be adjusted on turn counterclockwise. The "R2" mark indicates that the coil is two rotations off.
   e. If "L1" mark is close to the alignment mark coil is one rotation off to the left from its center state and needs to be adjusted on turn clockwise. The "L2" mark indicates that the coil is two rotations off.
   f. To adjust remove SIR coil, hold coil lead at its base and turn in the direction specified in steps d and e. Then replace SIR coil.
   g. **When all service procedures have been completed, rearm airbag as described under "Airbag System Arming."**

STEERING COLUMN LOCK ASSEMBLY

Disarm airbag before servicing steering column. Refer to "Airbag System Disarming" for disarming procedures.
Remove steering wheel as outlined in "Steering Column Replace" in this section.
1. Remove ignition switch attaching screw, then switch.
2. Remove ignition key warning switch attaching screws, then switch.
3. Loosen and remove two steering column lock retaining bolts using a center punch, **Fig. 111. When using center punch do not damage aluminum parts of lock assembly.**
4. Turn ignition key to "ON" or "ACC" position, then remove lock assembly from steering column.
5. Reverse procedure to install.
6. **When all service procedures have been completed, rearm airbag as outlined in "Airbag System Arming."**

LeMans

STANDARD COLUMN

Refer to **Fig. 112** when servicing this column.

TURN SIGNAL SWITCH HOUSING ASSEMBLY, STEERING SHAFT ASSEMBLY, STEERING COLUMN HOUSING & IGNITION SWITCH HOUSING ASSEMBLY

Disassembly

1. Disconnect battery ground cable and remove steering wheel horn cap and horn leads.
2. Remove nut, retainer and steering wheel, then unclip contact ring from wheel if necessary.
3. Remove steering column as previously described in Steering Column, Replace section.
4. Remove alignment bushing from lower end of shaft assembly, then upper steering shaft spring.
5. Remove thrust washer, washer head tap screws and turn signal switch housing assembly.
6. Turn lock cylinder to the Run position and remove steering shaft from lower end of jacket assembly.
7. Remove shear bolts, shear bolt washers and ignition switch housing as follows:
   a. Drill off head of shear bolts down to shear bolt washers with a 1/4 inch drill bit.
   b. Separate washers and switch housing from column housing.
   c. Remove threaded end of shear bolts from ignition switch housing using vise grips.
8. Remove lock cylinder from ignition switch housing, ignition switch retaining screw and ignition switch assembly.
9. Remove shear bolts and column housing as follows:
   a. Drill off head of shear bolts with a 5/16 inch drill bit.
   b. Separate column housing from jacket assembly.
   c. Remove threaded end of shear bolts from Jacket assembly using vise grips.

Assembly

1. Install column housing to jacket assembly using "new" shear bolts and

REMOVAL

1) Set front wheels in the straightforward state and remove steering shaft joint cover.
2) Remove steering shaft joint bolts.

| 1 | STEERING SHAFT JOINT UPPER SIDE BOLT |
| 2 | STEERING SHAFT JOINT LOWER SIDE BOLT |

INSTALLATION

1) Align flat part of lower joint shaft with bolt hole of upper joint as shown. Then insert lower joint shaft into upper joint.

| 1 | LOWER JOINT ASSEMBLY |
| 2 | UPPER JOINT ASSEMBLY |

2) Be sure that front wheels and steering wheel are in straightforward state and insert lower joint into steering pinion shaft.
3) If steering column nuts were loosened in removal, torque lower bracket nuts to below specification first:

N·m	lb. ft.
14	10

And then torque upper bracket nuts to specification:

N·m	lb. ft.
14	10

4) Torque steering shaft joint bolts to specification:

N·m	lb. ft.
25	18

5) Install steering shaft joint cover.

6. REMOVE AND INSTALL HORN RELAY

REMOVAL

1) Disconnect negative battery cable.
2) Disconnect horn relay electrical connector.
3) Remove horn relay from mounting bracket, located near the front of the main fusebox.

INSTALLATION

1) Horn relay to mounting bracket.
2) Connect horn relay electrical connector.
3) Connect negative battery cable.
4) Verify proper horn relay operation.

Fig. 108 Steering shaft lower joint & horn relay removal & installation. Metro less airbag (SIR)

REMOVAL

1) Remove steering column. Refer to STEERING COLUMN REMOVAL.

| 1 | STEERING COLUMN |
| 2 | IGNITION SWITCH ASSEMBLY |

2) Using center punch as shown, loosen and remove steering lock mounting bolts. Use care not to damage aluminum part of steering lock body with center punch.

| 1 | CENTER PUNCH (WITH SHARP POINT) |
| 2 | IGNITION SWITCH MOUNTING BOLTS |

3) Turn ignition key to "ACC" or "ON" position and remove ignition switch assembly from steering column.

INSTALLATION

1) Position oblong hole of steering shaft in the center of hole in column.

| 1 | STEERING SHAFT |
| 2 | STEERING COLUMN |

2) Turn ignition key to "ACC" or "ON" position and install ignition switch assembly onto column.
3) Now turn ignition key to "LOCK" position and pull it out.
4) Align hub on ignition switch assembly with oblong hole of steering shaft and rotate shaft to ensure that steering shaft is locked.
5) Tighten two new bolts until head of each bolt is broken off.
6) Turn ignition key to "ACC" or "ON" position and check to be sure that steering shaft rotates smoothly. Also check for lock operation.
7) Install steering column. Refer to STEERING COLUMN INSTALLATION.

Fig. 107 Steering lock removal & installation. Metro less airbag (SIR)

1 SIR HARNESS
2 MAIN WIRE HARNESS (HORN)
3 SIR COIL AND TURN SIGNAL/DIMMER SWITCH HARNESS
4 FUSE BLOCK

Fig. 109   Electrical connector locations. Metro w/airbag (SIR)

torque until bolt head separates from body, approximately 11 ft. lbs.
2. Install ignition switch to ignition switch housing ensuring retaining pin engages ear on ignition switch. Ensure that the tab on the lock cylinder shaft and the slotted opening on the ignition switch are in alignment, the lock cylinder and ignition switch must be in the Run position prior to installation.
3. Install lock cylinder into ignition switch housing.
4. Install ignition switch housing to column housing using "new" shear bolts and washers and **torque** until bolt head separates from body, approximately 15 ft. lbs.
5. Turn lock cylinder to the Run position and install steering shaft assembly into lower end of jacket assembly until bottomed.
6. Turn lock cylinder to the Off-Lock position and remove key.
7. Rotate steering shaft until lock bolt engages and locks steering shaft in position.
8. Install signal switch housing to steering column housing with washer head tap screws and **torque** to 30 inch lbs.
9. Install alignment bushing over lower end of steering shaft and into lower end of jacket assembly.
10. Install steering column in car, refer to Steering Column, Replace section.
11. Install thrust washer and upper steering shaft spring on steering shaft.
12. Install contact ring if necessary, steering wheel, retainer and nut and **torque** nut to 13 ft. lbs.
13. Install horn leads and cap, then connect battery ground cable.

TILT COLUMN

Refer to **Fig. 113** when servicing this column.

TURN SIGNAL SWITCH HOUSING ASSEMBLY, STEERING SHAFT ASSEMBLY, STEERING COLUMN HOUSING & IGNITION SWITCH HOUSING ASSEMBLY

Disassembly

1. Disconnect battery ground cable and

1 SIR COIL
2 NEUTRAL MARK
3 ALIGNMENT MARK

Fig. 110   Checking position of SIR coil. Metro w/airbag (SIR)

remove steering wheel horn cap and horn leads.
2. Remove nut, retainer and steering wheel, then unclip contact ring from wheel if necessary.
3. Remove steering column as previously described in Steering Column, Replace section.
4. Remove alignment bushing from lower end of shaft assembly, then cancelling cam spring from upper end of shaft assembly.
5. Remove washer head tap screws and signal switch housing assembly.
6. Compress spring retainer and upper bearing spring with special tools No. J 36667 and J 23653-A or equivalent.
7. Remove retaining ring, spring retainer, upper bearing spring, inner race seat and inner race.
8. Pull tilt lever and tilt column all the way up.
9. Insert a Phillips tip screwdriver into square opening in spring retainer, push down and turn left to release retainer and tilt spring.
10. Remove spring retainer and tilt spring.
11. Remove two pivot pins using special tool No. J 21854-01 or equivalent.
12. Turn lock cylinder to the Run position and pull tilt lever to release column housing from housing support.
13. Remove shear bolts, shear bolt washers and ignition switch housing from column housing as follows:
   a. Drill off head of shear bolts down to shear bolt washers with a 1/4 inch drill bit.
   b. Separate washers and switch housing from column housing.
   c. Remove threaded end of shear bolts from ignition switch housing using vise grips.

1 CENTER PUNCH
2 STEERING COLUMN LOCK BOLTS

Fig. 111   Removing steering column lock bolts. Metro w/airbag (SIR)

14. Remove lock cylinder from ignition switch housing, ignition switch retaining screw and ignition switch assembly.
15. Remove steering shaft assembly from housing support.
16. Remove tilt bumpers using pliers.
17. Remove support screws and support housing from jacket assembly.
18. When necessary, the steering shaft assembly may be serviced as follows:
   a. Prior to separation of upper shaft and lower shaft, note relationship of upper shaft with lock bolt slot at 12 o'clock position and lower shaft pinch bolt groove at 7 o'clock position. Refer to this orientation for proper reassembly.
   b. Position upper shaft 90° to lower shaft and separate.
   c. Rotate centering sphere 90° and remove from upper shaft.
   d. Separate sphere halves and joint preload spring.

Assembly

1. Install housing support to jacket assembly with support screws and **torque** to 12 ft.lbs.
2. Install tilt bumpers to housing support and snap into place, then install steering shaft assembly into support housing.
3. Lubricate bearings in column housing with lithium grease and install column housing onto shaft assembly and housing support.
4. Lubricate pivot pins with lithium grease and install until bottomed in housing.
5. **Pivot pins must be staked to housing after installation. Stake each pin at three equally spaced locations.**
6. Pull tilt lever and tilt column all the way up.
7. Lubricate tilt spring with lithium grease and install tilt spring with spring retainer as follows:
   a. Make sure that spring engages locating tab on support housing.
   b. Insert a Phillips tip screwdriver into square opening in spring retainer, push down and turn right to lock in place.

1- NUT, HEXAGON
2- SPRING, UPPER STRG SHAFT
3- WASHER, THRUST
4- SCREW, WASHER HD TAP
5- HOUSING ASM, SIGNAL SWITCH
6- BOLT, SHEAR
7- BOLT, SHEAR
8- WASHER, SHEAR BOLT
9- HOUSING, STEERING COLUMN
10- JACKET ASM, STEERING COLUMN
11- BUSHING, ALIGNMENT
12- HOUSING ASM, IGN SWITCH
13- SCREW, IGN SWITCH RETAINING
14- SWITCH ASM, IGNITION
15- SHAFT ASM, STEERING COLUMN

Fig. 112   Exploded view of standard steering column. LeMans

8. Install ignition switch to ignition switch housing ensuring retaining pin engages ear on ignition switch. **Ensure that the tab on the lock cylinder shaft and the slotted opening on the ignition switch are in alignment, the lock cylinder and ignition switch must be in the Run position prior to installation.**
9. Install ignition switch retaining screw and hand tighten, approximately 2.7 inch lbs. of **torque**.
10. Install lock cylinder into ignition switch housing.
11. Install ignition switch housing to column housing using "new" shear bolts and washers and **torque** until bolt head separates from body, approximately 15 ft. lbs.
12. Turn lock cylinder to the Off-Lock position and remove key.
13. Rotate steering shaft assembly until lock bolt engages and locks steering shaft into position.
14. Install inner race, inner race seat, upper bearing spring and spring retainer.
15. Compress retainer and spring with special tools No. J 26667 and J 23653-A or equivalent.
16. Install retaining ring in groove on upper shaft.
17. Install signal switch housing to steering column housing with washer head tap screws and **torque** to 30 inch lbs.
18. Install alignment bushing over lower end of steering shaft and into lower end of jacket assembly.
19. Install steering column as previously described in Steering Column, Replace section.
20. Install cancelling cam spring on steering shaft.
21. Install contact ring if necessary, steering wheel, retainer and nut and

1- NUT, HEXAGON
2- SPRING, CANCELLING CAM
3- RING, RETAINING
4- RETAINER, SPRING
5- SPRING, UPPER BEARING
6- SCREW, HEX WASHER HD TAP
7- HOUSING ASM, SIGNAL SWITCH
8- SEAT, INNER RACE
9- RACE, INNER
10- BOLT, SHEAR
11- WASHER, SHEAR BOLT
12- HOUSING ASM, STEERING COLUMN
13- PIN, PIVOT
14- HOUSING ASM, IGN SWITCH
15- SWITCH ASM, IGNITION
16- SCREW, IGN SWITCH RETAINING
17- SPRING, WHEEL TILT
18- RETAINER, SPRING
19- SHAFT ASM, STEERING
20- SHAFT ASM, RACE & UPPER
21- SPHERE, CENTERING
22- SPRING, JOINT PRELOAD
23- SHAFT ASM, LOWER STEERING
24- BUMPER, TILT
25- SCREW, SUPPORT
26- SUPPORT, STRG COLUMN HOUSING
27- JACKET ASM, STEERING COLUMN

Fig. 113   Exploded view of tilt steering column. LeMans

1	COLUMN HOLE COVER	7	WHEEL PAD
2	INTERMEDIATE SHAFT	8	STEERING WHEEL
3	IGNITION HARNESS CONNECTOR	9	STEERING COLUMN TUBE
4	LOCK CYLINDER ASSEMBLY	10	LOWER COLUMN COVER
5	UPPER COLUMN COVER	11	LOWER INSTRUMENT FINISH PANEL
6	MULTI-FUNCTION SWITCH		

Fig. 114 Exploded view of steering column. 1991-92 Prizm

torque nut to 13 ft. lbs.

22. Install horn leads and cap, then connect battery ground cable.

STEERING SHAFT ASSEMBLY
Disassembly

1. When necessary, the steering shaft assembly may be serviced as follows:
   a. Prior to separation of upper shaft and lower shaft, note relationship of upper shaft with lock bolt slot at 12 o'clock position and lower shaft pinch bolt groove at 7 o'clock position. Refer to this orientation for proper reassembly.
   b. Position upper shaft 90° to lower shaft and separate.
   c. Rotate centering sphere 90° and remove from upper shaft.
   d. Separate sphere halves and joint preload spring.

Assembly

1. Lubricate centering sphere halves and joint preload spring with lithium grease and install spring between sphere halves with ends of spring in notches.
2. Lubricate sphere end of upper and lower shaft with lithium grease and install sphere into upper shaft and rotate sphere 90°
3. To ensure proper operation, align upper shaft and lower shaft by placing lock bolt slot on upper shaft at 12 o'clock position and pinch bolt groove near end of lower shaft at 7 o'clock position.
4. Position upper shaft 90° to lower shaft and install upper shaft to lower shaft and straighten.

1991–92 Prizm
STANDARD COLUMN

Refer to **Fig. 114** when servicing this column.

Disassembly

1. Disconnect battery ground cable.
2. Remove steering wheel pad, horn switch connector, shaft nut and steering wheel.
3. Remove steering column as previously described in Steering Column, Replace section.
4. Secure column assembly into a vise, making sure not to damage column.
5. Remove lock cylinder housing as follows:
   a. Using a centering punch, mark the center of the tapered-head bolts securing the lock cylinder housing
   b. Using a .12-.16 inch drill bit, drill into the bolts then remove with a suitable bolt extractor.
6. Remove main shaft as follows:
   a. Using snap ring pliers, remove upper snap ring.
   b. Remove shaft from column tube, then snap ring from shaft.
7. Remove upper column tube bearing and check for abnormal noise or rotation difficulty. If bearing is faulty, replace.
8. Remove lock cylinder assembly and check for proper operation. If cylinder is faulty, replace.
9. Remove column tube bushing using a screwdriver, inspect for damage and replace if necessary.

Assembly

1. Install column tube bushing, then upper column tube bearing.
2. Install main shaft into column tube as follows:
   a. Using snap ring pliers, install snap ring in the inside groove of the main shaft.
   b. Insert main shaft into tube.
   c. Using snap ring pliers, connect shaft snap ring to column.
3. Install lock cylinder assembly.
4. Install lock cylinder housing onto column with "new" tapered-head bolts and **torque** bolts until the bolt heads break off.
5. Install column assembly as described in Steering Column, Replace section.
6. Install steering wheel and nut, **torque** bolt to 25 ft. lbs.
7. Install horn switch connector and horn pad, then connect battery ground cable.

TILT COLUMN

Refer to **Figs. 114 and 115** when servicing this column.

Disassembly

1. Disconnect battery ground cable.
2. Remove steering wheel pad, horn switch connector, shaft nut and steering wheel.
3. Remove steering column as previously described in Steering Column, Replace section.
4. Secure column assembly into a vise, making sure not to damage column.
5. Remove lock cylinder housing as follows:

Fig. 115   Exploded view of tilt steering shaft. 1991-92 Prizm

a. Using a centering punch, mark the center of the tapered-head bolts securing the lock cylinder housing
b. Using a .12-.16 inch drill bit, drill into the bolts then remove with a suitable bolt extractor.
6. Remove two tension springs, then two bolts, two bushings and two compression springs.
7. Remove tilt levers retainers, then tilt pawls, two nuts and bolts and separate two pawls from collars.
8. Remove two pawl stoppers, then remove tilt lever, tilt sub-lever and lever lock bolt.
9. Remove lower column tube.
10. Remove column pivot bolts using special tools No. J 38256 or equivalent pivot bolt remover and a J 2619-01 or equivalent slide hammer, **Fig. 116.**
11. Separate upper and lower columns.
12. Remove mainshaft as follows;
    a. Using special tool No. J 38364 or equivalent spring compressor, compress main shaft spring.
    b. Remove shaft snap ring with snap ring pliers.
    c. Separate main shaft from column.
    d. Remove thrust collar and bearing.

Fig. 116   Removing pivot bolts. 1991-92 Prizm

e. Remove snap ring from shaft using snap ring pliers.
13. Remove wiring harness clamp, then steering support
14. Remove snap ring from lower column tube using snap ring pliers, then remove main shaft collar.
15. Inspect lock cylinder assembly to ensure that lock mechanism operates properly. Replace if necessary.
16. Remove column tube bushing with a screwdriver and inspect for damage or unusual wear. Replace if necessary.

Assembly

Prior to assembly of steering column, apply GM 1050109 or equivalent grease to all parts indicated in **Fig. 117**.
1. Install column tube bushing, then steering support to lower column.
2. **Torque** steering support to lower column bolts to 14 ft. lbs.
3. Install main shaft to column tube as follows:
    a. Using snap ring pliers, install snap ring.
    b. Install main shaft, bearing, collar and spring.
    c. Using special tool No. J 38364 or equivalent spring compressor, compress main shaft spring and install a "new" snap ring with snap ring pliers.
4. Install wire harness clamp to column.
5. Install main shaft with upper and lower columns.
6. **Select the proper pivot bolts to match the upper column. If the column is marked with a number 1 on the side, select a grooveless bolt; if the upper column is marked with a number 2, select a grooved bolt. When one bolt has been selected,**

Fig. 117   Tilt steering column grease points. 1991-92 Prizm

choose its opposite for the other side as both sides are different.

7. Install pivot bolts, driving in with a hammer.
8. Install tilt lever lock bolt, tilt lever and sub lever.
9. Select collars for tilt pawl, **Fig. 118**
10. Insert collars into tilt pawls and install temporarily.
11. Engage tilt lever side pawls at the center of the ratchet and **torque** pawl nut to 70 inch lbs.
12. Install two tilt levers and **torque** tilt lever retainer forward nuts to 70 inch lbs. and retainer rearward nuts to 89 inch lbs.
13. Install two compression springs with bushings in each end and **torque** spring bolts to 70 inch lbs.
14. Install two tension springs.
15. Install lock cylinder housing onto column with "new" tapered-head bolts and **torque** bolts until the bolt heads break off.
16. Install column assembly as described in Steering Column, Replace section.
17. Install steering wheel and nut, **torque** bolt to 25 ft. lbs.
18. Install horn switch connector and horn pad, then connect battery ground cable.

1993 Prizm

The steering column cannot be disassembled for repairs. Service of a faulty column is by replacement only.

TILT LEVER SIDE	TILT SUB LEVER SIDE	OUTER DIAMETER
1	5	11.504–11.514 mm (0.4529–0.4533")
2	6	11.499–11.509 mm (0.4527–0.4531")
3	7	11.494–11.504 mm (0.4525–0.4529")
4	8	11.488–11.498 mm (0.4523–0.4527")

Fig. 118   Selecting correct collars. 1991-92 Prizm

DISASSEMBLY

Refer to **Fig. 119,** for exploded view of steering column.
1. Disconnect combination switch electrical connector.
2. Loosen four screws and remove combination switch from steering column.
3. Remove ignition switch housing as follows:
   a. Using a suitable center punch, mark center of the tapered-head bolts securing the ignition switch housing.
   b. Using a .12-.16 inch (3-4 mm) drill bit, drill into tapered-head bolts.
   c. Remove two tapered-head bolts using a suitable bolt extractor, then remove the ignition switch housing.
4. Remove main shaft, noting the following:
   a. Using suitable snap ring pliers, remove upper snap ring.
   b. Remove shaft from steering column tube.
   c. Remove snap ring from shaft.

ASSEMBLY

1. Connect main shaft into column tube as follows:
   a. Using snap ring pliers, install snap ring to the inside groove of the main shaft.
   b. Insert main shaft into the tube.
   c. Using snap ring pliers, connect shaft snap ring to column.
2. Install ignition switch housing assembly to steering column, securing with two new tapered-head bolts. Tighten tapered-head bolts until heads snap off.
3. Install combination switch to steering column, securing with four screws.
4. Connect combination switch electrical connector.

306 KNEE BOLSTER
308 UPPER STEERING COLUMN COVER
309 COMBINATION SWITCH
310 SIDE TRIM COVERS
311 INFLATOR MODULE
312 LOWER STEERING COLUMN COVER
315 STEERING COLUMN ASSEMBLY
316 IGNITION SWITCH

Fig. 119 Exploded view of steering column. 1993 Prizm

PASSIVE RESTRAINT SYSTEMS

TABLE OF CONTENTS

Supplemental Inflatable Restraint (SIR) System

INDEX

Continued

PRECAUTIONS

AIRBAG SYSTEM DISARMING

1991 Park Avenue

When carrying a live inflator module, ensure bag and trim cover are pointed away from you. Never carry inflator module by the wires or connector on underside of module.

The diagnostic energy reserve module (DERM) can maintain voltage to cause a system deployment for up to ten minutes after the ignition switch is turned off and the battery is disconnected. Servicing the SIR system during this period may result in accidental deployment and personal injury.
1. Turn ignition switch to OFF position, then disconnect and tape battery

ground cable terminal.
2. Remove Connector Position Assurance (CPA), then disconnect yellow two-way SIR electrical connector at base of steering column.
3. Remove screws and/or nuts from back of steering wheel, then the inflator module from steering wheel.
4. Remove Connector Position Assurance (CPA), then disconnect coil assembly connector and horn lead.
5. Place inflator module on a bench or other surface with bag and trim cover facing up.

1991 88 & 98

The diagnostic energy reserve module (DERM) can maintain voltage to cause a system deployment for up to ten minutes after the ignition switch is turned off and the battery is disconnected. Servicing the SIR system during this period may result in accidental deployment and personal injury.

1. Turn ignition switch to OFF position, then remove I/P fuse 7 from fuse block.
2. Disconnect yellow two-way SIR electrical connector at base of steering column.

Beretta, Bonneville w/Single Airbag, Camaro, Century, Corsica, Corvette, Cutlass Ciera/Cruiser, DeVille, Eldorado, Firebird, Fleetwood (FWD), Fleetwood (RWD), LeSabre, Reatta, Riviera, Seville & Toronado/Trofeo & 1992–93 Park Avenue, 88 & 98

The diagnostic energy reserve module (DERM) can maintain voltage to cause a system deployment for up to ten minutes after the ignition switch is turned off and the battery is disconnected. Servicing the SIR system during this period may result in accidental deployment and personal injury.

1. Ensure front wheels are pointed straight ahead.
2. Turn ignition switch to LOCK position and remove SIR or AIRBAG fuse.
3. Remove left sound insulator. **Remove courtesy lamp from sound insulator, if necessary.**
4. Remove Connector Position Assurance (CPA), then disconnect yellow two-way SIR electrical connector at base of steering column.

Caprice, Custom Cruiser & Roadmaster

The diagnostic energy reserve module (DERM) can maintain voltage to cause a system deployment for up to ten minutes after the ignition switch is turned off and the battery is disconnected. Servicing the SIR system during this period may result in accidental deployment and personal injury.

1. Ensure front wheels are pointed straight ahead.
2. Turn ignition switch to LOCK position and remove SIR fuse from fuse block.
3. Remove Connector Position Assurance (CPA), then disconnect yellow two-way SIR electrical connector at base of steering column.

Bonneville w/Dual Airbags

The diagnostic energy reserve module (DERM) can maintain voltage to cause a system deployment for up to ten minutes after the ignition switch is turned off and the battery is disconnected. Servicing the SIR system during this period may result in accidental deployment and personal injury.

1. Ensure front wheels are pointed straight ahead.

2. Turn ignition switch to OFF position and remove SIR fuse from fuse panel.
3. Remove left and right sound insulators.
4. Remove Connector Position Assurance (CPA), then disconnect yellow two-way SIR electrical connector at base of steering column.
5. Remove Connector Position Assurance (CPA), then disconnect yellow two-way passenger inflator module connector at base of right side instrument panel, clipped to knee bolster.

Metro

The diagnostic energy reserve module (DERM) can maintain voltage to cause a system deployment for up to ten minutes after the ignition switch is turned off and the battery is disconnected. Servicing the SIR system during this period may result in accidental deployment and personal injury.

1. **On 1992-93 models,** place steering wheel so that wheels are pointing straight ahead, then turn ignition switch to LOCK position.
2. **On 1991 models,** turn ignition switch to OFF position.
3. **On all models,** remove SIR IG fuse from SIR fuse block.
4. Remove rear plastic access cover from inflator module housing.
5. Remove Connector Position Assurance (CPA), then disconnect yellow two-way SIR electrical connector inside inflator module housing.

1991 Storm

The diagnostic energy reserve module (DERM) can maintain voltage to cause a system deployment for up to ten minutes after the ignition switch is turned off and the battery is disconnected. Servicing the SIR system during this period may result in accidental deployment and personal injury.

1. Turn ignition switch to OFF position, then disconnect battery ground cable.
2. Remove fuses C-22 and C-23 from fuse box, then disconnect orange three-way connector at the base of the steering column.

1992–93 Storm

The diagnostic energy reserve module (DERM) can maintain voltage to cause a system deployment for up to ten minutes after the ignition switch is turned off and the battery is disconnected. Servicing the SIR system during this period may result in accidental deployment and personal injury.

1. Place steering wheel so that wheels are pointing straight ahead, then turn ignition switch to LOCK position.
2. Remove fuses C-22 and C-23 from fuse block.
3. Remove switch bezel from instrument panel, then disconnect electrical connector from switches.
4. Remove cigar lighter bezel from instrument panel, then disconnect cigar lighter electrical connectors.
5. Remove two screws and hood latch release handle from knee bolster,

then the three screws, three bolts and two nuts retaining the knee bolster.
6. Disconnect lap cooler air duct from knee bolster, then remove knee bolster from vehicle.
7. Remove Connector Position Assurance (CPA), then disconnect orange three-way connector at the base of the steering column.

Prizm

1. Ensure front wheels are pointed straight ahead, then turn ignition switch to LOCK position.
2. Remove IGN and CIG & RADIO fuse from junction block No. 1.
3. Remove Connector Position Assurance (CPA) and disconnect lower steering column (yellow two-cavity) connector at base of steering column.

AIRBAG SYSTEM ARMING

1991 Park Avenue

1. Turn ignition switch to OFF position, connect horn lead and coil assembly connector, then install Connector Position Assurance (CPA).
2. Install inflator module and secure to steering wheel using new screws and/or nuts.
3. **Torque** screws and/or nuts to 25 inch lbs.
4. Connect yellow two-way SIR electrical connector at base of steering column, then install Connector Position Assurance (CPA).
5. Install left sound insulator, then the SIR fuse into fuse block.
6. Turn ignition switch to RUN position and ensure "Inflatable Restraint" indicator flashes 7 to 9 times, then turns off.

1991 88 & 98

1. Connect yellow two-way SIR electrical connector at base of steering column.
2. Install I/P fuse 7 into fuse block, turn ignition switch to RUN position and ensure "Inflatable Restraint" indicator flashes 7 to 9 times, then turns off.

Beretta, Bonneville w/Single Airbag, Camaro, Century, Corsica, Corvette, Cutlass Ciera/Cruiser, DeVille, Eldorado, Firebird, Fleetwood (FWD), Fleetwood (RWD), LeSabre, Reatta, Riviera, Seville, Toronado, Trofeo & 1992–93 Park Avenue, 88 & 98

1. Connect yellow two-way SIR electrical connector, then install Connector Position Assurance (CPA).
2. Install left sound insulator. **Install courtesy lamp to sound insulator, if applicable.**
3. Install SIR fuse to fuse block, turn ignition switch to RUN position and ensure "Inflatable Restraint" lamp flashes 7 to 9 times, then turns off.

Caprice, Custom Cruiser & Roadmaster

1. Connect yellow two-way SIR electrical connector at base of column, then install Connector Position Assurance (CPA).
2. Install SIR fuse into fuse block, turn ignition switch to RUN position and ensure "Inflatable Restraint" lamp flashes 7 to 9 times and then turns off.

Bonneville w/Dual Airbags

1. Connect yellow two-way passenger inflator module connector at base of right side instrument panel, clipped to knee bolster, then install Connector Position Assurance (CPA).
2. Connect yellow two-way SIR electrical connector at base of steering column, then install Connector Position Assurance (CPA).
3. Install left and right sound insulators, then the SIR fuse into fuse panel.
4. Turn ignition switch to RUN position and ensure "Inflatable Restraint" lamp flashes 7 to 9 times, then turns off.

Metro

1. Turn ignition switch to LOCK position.
2. Connect yellow two-way SIR electrical connector inside inflator module housing, then install Connector Position Assurance (CPA).
3. Install SIR IG fuse into SIR fuse block, then the rear plastic access cover onto inflator module housing.
4. Turn ignition switch to RUN position and ensure "Inflatable Restraint" lamp flashes 7 to 9 times and then turns off.

1991 Storm

1. Turn ignition switch to OFF position, then connect orange three-way connector at the base of the steering column.
2. Install fuses C-22 and C-23 into fuse box, then connect battery ground cable.

1992-93 Storm

1. Turn ignition switch to OFF position, then connect orange three-way connector at the base of the steering column.
2. Connect lap cooler air duct to knee bolster, then install knee bolster.
3. **Torque** knee bolster bolts and nuts to 89 inch lbs.
4. Install hood latch release handle to knee bolster.
5. Connect cigar lighter electrical connector, then snap cigar lighter bezel into place on instrument panel.
6. Connect switch bezel electrical connectors, then snap switch bezel into place on instrument panel.

Prizm

1. Turn ignition switch to LOCK position.
2. Connect lower steering column yellow two-cavity connector.
3. Install IGN and CIG & RADIO fuses.
4. Turn ignition switch to ACC or ON positions and verify that the airbag indicator illuminates steady for approximately six seconds and then turns off.

DESCRIPTION

The Supplemental Inflatable Restraint (SIR) system supplements the normal restraint of the seat belt by deploying an airbag during an accident. The airbag deploys when the vehicle is involved in a front end collision of sufficient force. To further absorb the energy of an accident, there is a knee bolster (tie bar) located below the instrument panel in the driver area. The steering column is collapsible to also absorb force.

the main portions of the SIR system are the deployment loop and the diagnostic energy reserve module (DERM). The main function of the deployment loop is to supply current through the inflator module in the steering wheel which will cause deployment of the airbag in the event of an accident severe enough to warrant airbag deployment.

The deployment loop consists of the arming sensor, coil assembly, inflator module and discriminating sensors. The arming sensor switches power to the inflator module on the high side of the deployment loop. Either of the discrimination sensors can supply ground to the inflator module on the low side of the deployment loop. The inflator module is only supplied sufficient current to deploy when the arming sensor and at least one of the two discriminating sensors close simultaneously.

The diagnostic energy reserve module (DERM) supplies the deployment loop with a 36 volt loop reserve (36VLR) to assure sufficient energy to deploy the airbag if the ignition voltage is cut during an accident.

COMPONENT DESCRIPTION

DIAGNOSTIC ENERGY RESERVE MODULE (DERM)

The DERM is designed to perform the following functions in the SIR system:

1. **Energy reserve:** The DERM maintaining a 36 volt loop reserve (36VLR) energy supply to provide deployment energy for a few seconds if the vehicle voltage is low or if lost in a vehicle accident.
2. **Malfunction detection:** The DERM performs diagnostic monitoring of SIR system electrical components.
3. **Malfunction recording:** The DERM provides SIR system fault code information through a SCAN/TECH tool or the SIR warning lamp.
4. **Driver Notification:** The DERM warns the driver of SIR system faults by controlling the SIR warning lamp.
5. **Accident recording:** The DERM records the SIR system status during a vehicle accident.

The DERM is connected to the SIR harness by a 24-way connector. This harness connector utilizes a shorting bar across certain terminals in the contact area. This shorting bar connects the SIR warning lamp output to ground when the DERM connector is disconnected. This will cause the lamp to illuminate steady whenever the ignition switch is at the Run, Bulb Test, or Start positions with the DERM disconnected.

SIR CONTROL MODULE (PASSENGER COMPARTMENT SENSOR)

1991 88

The SIR control module contains the passenger compartment sensor and the inflatable restraint system diagnostics. The SIR control module diagnostic system monitors the accuracy of the inflatable restraint sensing components and wiring harness and controls the warning lamp.

The SIR control module monitors vehicle deceleration and combines this information with signals from the forward sensor to determine whether deployment is necessary. An electrical pulse is sent to the steering wheel module when a forward sensor closure, or a signal from the passenger compartment sensor, and an arming sensor closure occur simultaneously.

DUAL POLE ARMING SENSOR

The dual pole arming sensor is a dual pole switch located in the driver/passenger deployment loops power feed side (high side). The dual pole arming sensor is calibrated to close at low level velocity changes (lower than the discriminating sensors). This assures that both inflator modules are connected directly to the DERM's 36VLR or ignition 1 voltage when either discriminating sensor closes.

DISCRIMINATING SENSOR

The discriminating sensors are wired in parallel on the deployment loops ground side (low side). These sensors are calibrated to close with velocity changes severe enough to warrant deployment.

FORWARD SENSOR

The forward sensor is mechanically actuated and responds to a drop in vehicle speed. This sensor has a normally open switch, and distinguishes between deployment and non-deployment situations by means of a preset calibration which allows the sensor to close only with sufficient impact force. If an accident occurs, the contacts of the forward sensor close, completing an electrical circuit. If the contacts of the forward sensor close simultaneously with the contacts of the arming sensor, deployment occurs.

ARMING SENSOR

This sensor is a normally open mechanical switch that closes during deceleration encountered in an accident. The arming sensor is wired in series with the steering wheel module and provides backup to the other sensors. A parallel resistor in the arming sensor permits a small amount of current to flow through the initiator circuit for diagnostic purposes.

POWER SUPPLY

The power supply provides an increased voltage to the inflatable restraint system to guarantee deployment for low voltage conditions, perform limited internal diagnostics and monitor the reliability of the inflatable restraint harness at the 8 terminal connector.

ENERGY RESERVE MODULE

This module provides sufficient electrical energy to guarantee restraint deployment even if vehicle's battery is damaged or disconnected during deployment.

STEERING COLUMN & COIL ASSEMBLY

This system uses a collapsible steering column that incorporates a coil assembly which provides a continuous electrical connection between the SIR control module and the steering wheel module for the full range of steering wheel rotation.

RESISTOR MODULE

The resistor module is inserted in the SIR harness between the inflator module and the DERM. The resistor module allows the DERM to monitor the deployment loop for faults and also allows the DERM to detect when a deployment has occurred.

INFLATOR MODULES

The steering wheel module is composed of an inflator assembly, electrical initiator and inflatable bag which is installed in the steering wheel hub area and covered by a vinyl trim cover.

The passenger inflator module (if equipped) is composed of an inflator assembly, electrical initiator and inflatable bag which is installed in the instrument panel above the instrument panel compartment.

When an accident of sufficient force is sensed by the sensors, the inflatable bag is deployed by a gas producing generator. The trim cover then opens at seams which rupture as the system is deployed.

WARNING LAMP

The warning lamp is red and displays the words Inflatable Restraint. Refer to "Diagnosis and Testing" for further information on lamp operation.

KNEE BOLSTER

The knee bolster is an energy absorbing pad which controls the forward movement of the driver during an accident by restricting leg movement.

SIR WIRING HARNESS

This wiring harness interconnects the system components. The initiator circuit has special yellow shorting bar connectors which help prevent accidental deployment or tampering when the connector is disconnected.

The SIR wiring harness components are part of the body wire harness assembly. Sections of the harness which include more than one SIR wire are wrapped with yellow tape.

FUSE PANEL

Vehicles equipped with an airbag have a specially designed fuse panel which is located in the lower instrument panel trim pad and is hinged to swing out for easy access.

SAFETY & SERVICE PRECAUTIONS & WARNINGS

Safe handling of live and deployed steering wheel modules requires adhering to following procedures:

1. Always wear safety glasses when servicing an inflatable restraint system vehicle and when handling a steering wheel module.
2. Before servicing SIR system, wait 10 minutes after disconnecting battery voltage before servicing SIR system. This prevents accidental deployment and possible injury.
3. Extreme care must be taken when handling a sensor. This also pertains to the SIR control module which contains the passenger compartment sensor.
4. Never strike or jar a sensor in such a way that may cause deployment.
5. All sensors, the SIR system control module and the SIR control center mounting plate bolts must be carefully torqued to ensure proper operation.
6. The following components cannot be repaired, as these components are serviced only by replacement:
   a. Forward sensor
   b. Arming sensor
   c. Power supply
   d. Diagnostic energy reserve module (DERM)
   e. SIR control module
   f. Coil assembly
   g. Steering wheel module

HANDLING LIVE (UNDEPLOYED) MODULES

Special care is necessary when handling and storing a live (undeployed) inflator module. The rapid gas generation produced during deployment of the airbag could cause the inflator module or an object in front of the inflator module to be thrown through the air.

When carrying a live steering wheel module, be sure the bag and trim cover are pointed away from you. Never carry the inflator module by the wires or connector on the underside of the module. In case of accidental deployment, the bag will then deploy with minimal chance of injury.

When placing the steering wheel module on a bench or other surface, always face the bag and trim cover up, away from the surface. Never rest a steering column assembly on the steering wheel with the inflator face down and the column vertical. This is necessary so that a free space is provided to allow the airbag to expand in the unlikely event of accidental deployment.

HANDLING DEPLOYED MODULES

After the inflator module has been deployed, the surface of the airbag may contain a powdery residue. This powder consists primarily of corn starch (used to lubricate the airbag as it inflates) and by-products of the chemical reaction. Sodium hydroxide dust (similar to lye dust) is produced as a by-product of the deployment reaction. The sodium hydroxide then quickly reacts with atmospheric moisture and is converted to sodium carbonate and sodium bicarbonate (baking soda). Therefore, it is unlikely that sodium hydroxide will be present after deployment. Always wear safety glasses and gloves when handling a deployed module, and wash hands with mild soap and water afterward.

VEHICLE SCRAPPING

Some vehicle with SIR systems that have live (undeployed) inflator modules may have to be scrapped because they have completed their useful life or have been severely damaged in a non-deployment type accident. The following procedure should be followed when scrapping a vehicle with an undeployed module:

1. Place ignition switch in Off position.
2. Ensure steering wheel module is secured to steering wheel and that their is nobody in vehicle, and remove all loose objects from front seat.
3. Disconnect lower steering column connector and remove shorting clip from connector.
4. Cut lower steering column connector away from vehicle harness leaving at least 6 inches of wire at the connector.
5. Splice two 18 gauge wires, at least 20 feet long, into steering wheel module circuit wiring at base of steering column.
6. Stretch wires away from vehicle to their full length.
7. Apply 12 volts across wires to deploy module. **Do not touch steering wheel module area for 20 minutes, due to heat generated by deployment.**

AIRBAG DISPOSAL

When a deployed module has been removed from a vehicle, it may be disposed of with any other scrap material. Handle with gloves and safety glasses and wash hands after handling. **The steering wheel module must be deactivated prior to disposal. The module contains explosive material. Failure to deactivate before disposing may result in personal injury.**

WIRING DIAGRAMS & CONNECTOR IDENTIFICATION

Refer To **Figs. 1 through 23** for airbag system wiring diagrams.

Refer To **Figs. 24 through 37** for connector identification.

Continued on page 28-55

Fig. 1   SIR wiring circuit (Part 1 of 2). 1991 Beretta & Corsica

Fig. 1   SIR wiring circuit (Part 2 of 2). 1991 Beretta & Corsica

Fig. 2 SIR wiring circuit (Part 1 of 2). 1992-93 Beretta & Corsica

Fig. 2   SIR wiring circuit (Part 2 of 2). 1992-93 Beretta & Corsica

Fig. 3 SIR wiring circuit (Part 1 of 2). 1991-92 Camaro & Firebird

Fig. 3   SIR wiring circuit (Part 2 of 2). 1991-92 Camaro & Firebird

Fig. 4 SIR wiring circuit (Part 1 of 2). Caprice, Custom Cruiser & Roadmaster

Fig. 4   SIR wiring circuit (Part 2 of 2). Caprice, Custom Cruiser & Roadmaster

CAUTION: To avoid deployment when troubleshooting the SIR system do not use electrical test equipment, such as test lights, battery powered or A/C powered voltmeter, ohmmeter, etc., or any type of electrical equipment.

Fig. 5   SIR wiring circuit (Part 1 of 2). Corvette

Fig. 5   SIR wiring circuit (Part 2 of 2). Corvette

> **CAUTION:**   To avoid deployment when troubleshooting the SIR system do not use electrical test equipment, such as test lights, battery powered or A/C powered voltmeter, ohmmeter, etc., or any type of electrical equipment other than specified in this manual. Instructions in this manual must be followed carefully otherwise personal injury may result.

IMPORTANT:
WHEN DERM CONNECTOR IS DISCONNECTED, A SHORTING BAR IS CLOSED SHORTING TERMINAL "A1" TO TERMINAL "B1" ILLUMINATING THE INDICATOR.

Fig. 6   SIR wiring circuit (Part 1 of 2). DeVille & Fleetwood

Fig. 6 SIR wiring circuit (Part 2 of 2). DeVille & Fleetwood

Fig. 7   SIR wiring circuit (Part 1 of 2). 1991 Eldorado & Seville

Fig. 7   SIR wiring circuit (Part 2 of 2). 1991 Eldorado & Seville

Fig. 8   SIR wiring circuit (Part 1 of 2). 1992 Eldorado & Seville

Fig. 8 SIR wiring circuit (Part 2 of 2). 1992 Eldorado & Seville

Fig. 9   SIR wiring circuit (Part 1 of 2). 1991 Metro

Fig. 9   SIR wiring circuit (Part 2 of 2). 1991 Metro

Fig. 10   SIR wiring circuit (Part 1 of 2). 1992-93 Metro

CAUTION: To avoid deployment when troubleshooting the SIR system do not use electrical test equipment, such as test lights, battery powered or AC powered voltmeter, ohmmeter, etc., or any type of electrical equipment other than specified in this manual. Instructions in this manual must be followed carefully otherwise personal injury may result.

Fig. 10   SIR wiring circuit (Part 2 of 2). 1992-93 Metro

Fig. 11   SIR wiring circuit (Part 1 of 2). Reatta, Riviera, Toronado & Trofeo

Fig. 11   SIR wiring circuit (Part 2 of 2). Reatta, Riviera, Toronado & Trofeo

Fig. 12   SIR wiring circuit (Part 1 of 2). Storm

Fig. 12   SIR wiring circuit (Part 2 of 2). Storm

Fig. 13   SIR wiring circuit (Part 1 of 2). 1991 88

Fig. 13   SIR wiring circuit (Part 2 of 2). 1991 88

Fig. 14   SIR wiring circuit (Part 1 of 2). 1991 98

Fig. 14 SIR wiring circuit (Part 2 of 2). 1991 98

Fig. 15 SIR wiring circuit (Part 1 of 2). 1992-93 88 & 98

Fig. 15   SIR wiring circuit (Part 2 of 2). 1992-93 88 & 98

Fig. 16   SIR wiring circuit (Part 1 of 2). 1992-93 Bonneville w/single airbag

Fig. 16   SIR wiring circuit (Part 2 of 2). 1992-93 Bonneville w/single airbag

Fig. 17   SIR wiring circuit (Part 1 of 2). 1992-93 Bonneville w/dual airbags

Fig. 17   SIR wiring circuit (Part 2 of 2). 1992-93 Bonneville w/dual airbags

Fig. 18   SIR wiring circuit (Part 1 of 2). 1993 Century & Cutlass Ciera/Cruiser

Fig. 18 SIR wiring circuit (Part 2 of 2). 1993 Century & Cutlass Ciera/Cruiser

Fig. 19   SIR wiring circuit (Part 1 of 2). 1993 Camaro & Firebird

Fig. 19   SIR wiring circuit (Part 2 of 2). 1993 Camaro & Firebird

Fig. 20   SIR wiring circuit (Part 1 of 2). 1993 Eldorado & Seville

Fig. 20   SIR wiring circuit (Part 2 of 2). 1993 Eldorado & Seville

Fig. 21   SIR wiring circuit (Part 1 of 2). 1993 Fleetwood (RWD)

Fig. 21   SIR wiring circuit (Part 2 of 2). 1993 Fleetwood (RWD)

Fig. 22   SIR wiring circuit (Part 1 of 2). Prizm

Fig. 22   SIR wiring circuit (Part 2 of 2). Prizm

Fig. 23 SIR wiring circuit. LeSabre & Park Avenue

Fig. 24   SIR electrical connectors. Beretta, Corsica & 1991 Camaro & Firebird

Fig. 25   SIR electrical connectors. 1992 Camaro & Firebird

YELLOW

**MICRO-PACK
DERM**

YELLOW

**METRI-PACK 280
STEERING COLUMN CONNECTOR**

YELLOW

**METRI-PACK 280
BODY HARNESS CONNECTOR TO FORWARD
DISCRIMINATING SENSOR CONNECTOR**

YELLOW

**METRI-PACK 280
ARMING SENSOR**

YELLOW

**MICRO-PACK
RESISTOR MODULE**

**Fig. 26   SIR electrical connectors. 1991
Caprice, Custom Cruiser & Roadmaster**

**Fig. 27   SIR electrical connectors. 1992-93
Caprice, Custom Cruiser & Roadmaster**

Fig. 28   SIR electrical connectors. Corvette

Fig. 29 SIR electrical connectors. DeVille, Fleetwood, Reatta, Riviera, Toronado, Trofeo, 98, 1991 Eldorado, Seville, 1992-93 Bonneville w/single airbag & 88

Fig. 30 SIR electrical connectors. 1992 Eldorado & Seville

Fig. 31 SIR electrical connectors. 1992-93 Metro

Fig. 32 SIR electrical connectors. 1992-93 Storm

ALL SIR CONNECTORS ARE ORANGE EXCEPT DERM CONNECTOR. DERM CONNECTOR IS YELLOW.

Fig. 33 SIR electrical connectors. 1992-93 Bonneville w/dual airbags

Fig. 35 SIR electrical connectors. 1993 Camaro & Firebird

Fig. 34 SIR electrical connectors. 1993 Century & Cutlass Ciera/Cruiser

WIRE HARNESS & CONNECTOR REPAIR PROCEDURES

Special wiring repair procedures have been developed for use on the Supplemental Inflatable Restraint systems due to the sensitive nature of the circuitry.

The use of Terminal Repair Kit tool No. J-38125 or equivalent, contains special sealed splices for use in repairing SIR system wiring. A special crimping tool, heat torch and instruction manual for these splices are also included.

The critical features of the sealed splices are a special heat shrink sleeve with sealing adhesive to produce an environmentally sealed splice and a cross hatched core crimp to provide necessary contact integrity for the sensitive low energy circuits.

SIR CONNECTOR BODY & TERMINAL REPAIR

If any connector or terminal in the SIR wire harness, except pigtail, is damaged, the component should be repaired using one of the connector repair assembly packs. These kits include an instruction sheet and sealed splices which will be necessary to splice the new wires, connector and terminals to the harness.

If individual terminals are damaged on the DERM or resistor module, repair using the DERM/resistor terminal repair assem-bly pack. If individual terminals are damaged on any other SIR connection, the entire connection should be replaced using the appropriate repair assembly pack.

SIR PIGTAIL REPAIR

If the wiring pigtail is damaged, the entire component should be replaced.

SIR WIRE REPAIR

If any wire except the pigtail is damaged, the wire should be repaired by splicing in a new section of wire of the same gauge size. The sealed splices and crimping tool from J-38125 must be used for these splices.

COMPONENT LOCATION DIAGRAMS

1991 88

Refer to **Fig. 38** for component locations.

1991 98

Refer to **Fig. 39** for component locations.

1992-93 BONNEVILLE W/SINGLE AIRBAG, 88 & 98

Refer to **Fig. 40** for component locations.

1992-93 BONNEVILLE W/SINGLE AIRBAG, 88 & 98

Refer to **Fig. 40** for component locations.

1991 REATTA, RIVIERA, TORONADO & TROFEO

Refer to **Fig. 42** for component locations.

1992-93 RIVIERA, TORONADO & TROFEO

Refer to **Fig. 43** for component locations.

METRO

Refer to **Fig. 44** for component locations.

STORM

Refer to **Fig. 45** for component locations.

CAPRICE, CUSTOM CRUISER & ROADMASTER

Refer to **Fig. 46** for component locations.

1991 ELDORADO & SEVILLE

Refer to **Fig. 47** for component locations.

DEVILLE & FLEETWOOD

Refer to **Fig. 48** for component locations.

1992 ELDORADO & SEVILLE

Refer to **Fig. 49** for component locations.

CORVETTE

Refer to **Fig. 50** for component locations.

BERETTA & CORSICA

Refer to **Fig. 51** for component locations.

1991-92 CAMARO & FIREBIRD

Refer to **Fig. 52** for component locations.

1993 CAMARO & FIREBIRD

Refer to **Fig. 53** for component locations.

CENTURY & CUTLASS CIERA/CRUISER

Refer to **Fig. 54** for component locations.

Fig. 36   SIR electrical connectors. 1993 Fleetwood (RWD)

Fig. 37   SIR electrical connectors. Prizm

1993 ELDORADO & SEVILLE

Refer to **Fig. 55** for component locations.

1993 FLEETWOOD (RWD)

Refer to **Fig. 56** for component locations.

PRIZM

Refer to **Fig. 57** for component locations.

PARK AVENUE & 1992-93 LESABRE

The SIR coil assembly is located in the steering column underneath the steering wheel.
The inflator module is located in the steering column underneath the horn pad.
The dual sensor is located behind the center of the instrument panel.
The SIR resistor module is located behind the right hand kick panel.
The DERM is located behind the right hand kick panel.

The forward discriminating sensor is located in front of the radiator, attached to the upper tie bar.
The dual sensor is located behind the right hand side of the instrument panel, beneath the windshield.

DIAGNOSIS & TESTING

To avoid deployment when testing the SIR system, do not use electrical test equipment such as battery powered or A/C powered voltmeter or ohmmeter, or any type of electrical equipment other than those specified in this section. Do not use a non-powered probe type tester. Instructions in this section must be followed carefully, otherwise personal injury may result.

INTERMITTENTS

Most intermittents are caused by faulty connections or wiring, if an intermittent condition is suspected, check the following:

1. Poor mating of connector halves and/or terminals not fully seated in connector body.
2. Dirt or corrosion on terminals.
3. Improperly formed or damaged terminals.
4. Poor terminal to wire connection such as poor crimps, solder joints or crimping over wire insulation.
5. Wire insulation rubbed through causing short as wire touches other components.
6. Wire broken inside of insulation, this condition may show continuity.

DIAGNOSTIC TROUBLE CODE INTERPRETATION
Current Codes

Current codes are faults that are presently being detected or have not been successfully cleared because the malfunction still exists. If the battery has been disconnect, all current codes will be erased. **Do not disconnect battery if an SIR system malfunction exists and trouble codes have not been retrieved.**

History Codes

History codes are all faults detected since the DERM memory was last cleared. If a history code is present, the related malfunction may not necessarily exist. History codes may only be erased using a SCAN/TECH tool.

ACCESSING DIAGNOSTIC TROUBLE CODES

SCAN/TECH 1 TOOL DIAGNOSTICS

A SCAN/TECH 1 tool can be used to read current codes and history codes. The tool must be updated to communicate with the SIR system through a replaceable cartridge or a manufacturer's update before it can be used for SIR diagnosis. To use the SCAN/TECH 1 tool, connect it to the ALDL connector and turn the ignition switch ON. Follow the tool manufacturer's instructions for communication with the SIR system.

FLASH CODE DIAGNOSTICS

Except Eldorado, Reatta, Riviera, Seville, Toronado & Trofeo

Flash codes diagnostics can only be used to read current codes and to determine if history codes exist. To read current codes, ground terminal K of the ALDL connector with the ignition switch On.

The DERM displays the trouble codes by flashing the SIR warning lamp. Each code that is displayed will consist of a number of flashes which represents the first digit, followed by a 1/2 second pause, followed by a number of flashes which represent the second number. An example of trouble code 41 would be four flashes, followed by a 1/2 second pause, followed by one flash.

Each code is flashed once until all codes are displayed. The code sequence will repeat until terminal K of the ALDL connector is no longer grounded.

Two special codes exist when reading the flash codes. Code 12 will always be displayed when the flash codes are enabled. Code 12 is not an indication of a fault, but an indication that flash code mode has been started. Code 13 will be displayed only if no history codes are in memory. To read history codes, a SCAN/TECH tool must be used.

Eldorado & Seville

Trouble codes can be read by using the digital instrument panel cluster to display any stored codes. Enter diagnostics by pressing "OFF" and "WARM" simultaneously, then press "LOW" four times to enter the SIR system. Press "HI" to display any SIR codes. Refer to **Figs. 58 and 59.**

Reatta, Riviera, Toronado & Trofeo

Trouble codes can be read by using the digital instrument panel cluster to display any stored codes. Enter diagnostics by pressing "OFF" and "WARM" simultaneously, then press "LOW" four times to enter the SIR system. Press "HI" to display any SIR codes. Refer to **Fig. 60.**

CLEARING DIAGNOSTIC TROUBLE CODES

All current codes except code 51 will clear automatically when the malfunction causing the code is corrected and all conditions to clear have been satisfied. Current code 51 requires a SCAN/TECH tool to clear.

History codes can only be cleared by using a SCAN/TECH tool. All history codes except code 51 can be cleared.

INSPECTION REQUIRED AFTER AN ACCIDENT

All SIR components, including harness and brackets must be inspected after an accident. Any wire harness damage must be repaired only with the crimp and seal splice sleeves contained within kit J-38125. Any SIR components that are damaged or bent must be replaced with new parts even if deployment did not occur. **Never use SIR parts from another vehicle. This does not include remanufactured parts purchased from an authorized General Motors dealer. Never attempt to service SIR parts on your own. Service is by replacement only. Verify replacement inflator module part number as some inflator modules look identical but contain different internal components.**

Vehicles involved in accidents resulting in frame damage, major body or sheet metal damage, or where the steering column has been impacted, may also have a damaged or misaligned steering column. To check steering column for accident damage, refer to **Figs. 61 through 75.**

COMPONENT REPLACEMENT

ARMING SENSOR

Beretta & Corsica

1. Disarm airbag system as described under "Airbag System Disarming."
2. Remove glove compartment assembly.
3. Remove CPA and disconnect sensor electrical connector.
4. Remove sensor mounting bolts, then remove sensor.
5. Reverse procedure to install, noting the following:
   a. **Torque** mounting bolts to 80 inch lbs.
   b. Following installation, rearm airbag system as described under "Airbag System Arming."
   c. Turn ignition switch to the ON position and verify the "Inflatable Restraint" indicator flashes 7 to 9 times then turns off. If indicator does not respond, refer to "Diagnosis and Testing."

1991-92 Camaro & Firebird

1. Disarm airbag system as described under "Airbag System Disarming."
2. Remove knee bolster, as described

under "Component Replacement."
3. Remove upper console.
4. Remove arming sensor retaining bolts, then disconnect arming sensor electrical connector and remove arming sensor, **Fig. 76.**
5. Reverse procedure to install, noting the following:
   a. Install arming sensor with arrow pointing toward front of vehicle. **Torque** retaining bolts to 25 inch lbs.
   b. Following installation, rearm airbag system as described under "Airbag System Arming."
   c. Turn ignition switch to the ON position and verify the "Inflatable Restraint" indicator flashes 7 to 9 times then turns off. If indicator does not respond, refer to "Diagnosis and Testing."

Caprice, Custom Cruiser & Roadmaster

1. Disarm airbag system as described under "Airbag System Disarming."
2. Remove twilight sentinel module from bracket, if equipped.
3. Reposition dash mat for access, then disconnect CPA and arming sensor connector from body harness connector near top of instrument panel.
4. Remove mounting screws, then the arming sensor. **Fig. 77.**
5. Reverse procedure to install, noting the following:
   a. Following installation, rearm airbag system as described under "Airbag System Arming."
   b. Turn ignition switch to the ON position and verify the "Inflatable Restraint" indicator flashes 7 to 9 times then turns off. If indicator does not respond, refer to "Diagnosis and Testing."

Century & Cutlass Ciera/Cruiser

1. Disarm airbag system as described under "Airbag System Disarming."
2. Remove instrument panel compartment and right outlets.
3. Remove electrical connector from retainer, then release connector position assurance (CPA) from connector and disconnect the connector.
4. Loosen sensor mounting bolts and remove sensor.
5. Reverse procedure to install, noting the following:
   a. Tighten to specifications.
   b. Ensure arming sensor is correctly mounted to mounting bracket.
   c. Rearm airbag system as described under "Airbag System Arming."

Corvette

1. Disarm airbag system as described under "Airbag System Disarming."
2. Remove radio control.
3. Disconnect arming sensor connector from clip on RH knee bolster inner bracket.
4. Remove SIR wiring harness to arming sensor CPA and disconnect arming

sensor electrical connector.

5. Remove arming sensor retaining fasteners. **Fig. 78.**
6. Remove arming sensor.
7. Reverse procedure to install, noting the following:
   a. Install sensor with arrow pointing toward front of vehicle.
   b. **Torque** mounting bolts to 11 ft. lbs.
   c. **Torque** mounting nuts to 107 inch lbs.
   d. Rearm airbag system as described under "Airbag System Arming."
   e. Turn ignition switch to the ON position and verify the "Inflatable Restraint" indicator flashes 7 to 9 times then turns off.

DeVille, Eldorado, Fleetwood, LeSabre, Park Avenue, Riviera, Reatta, Toronado, Trofeo, 1991 Seville & 98

On these models, the arming sensor and passenger compartment sensor are removed as an assembly. Refer to "Dual Sensor, Replacement" for removal procedures.

Metro & Storm

1. Disarm airbag system as described under "Airbag System Disarming."
2. Disconnect battery ground cable.
3. Remove instrument panel assembly.
4. **On Storm models,** disconnect defroster duct from cowl.
5. **On all models,** remove CPA and disconnect electrical connector.
6. Loosen sensor mounting bolts and remove sensor.
7. Reverse procedure to install, noting the following:
   a. Install sensor with arrow pointing toward front of vehicle.
   b. **On Metro models, torque** mounting bolts to 53 inch lbs.
   c. **On Storm models, torque** mounting bolts to 89 inch lbs.
   d. **On all models,** rearm airbag system as described under "Airbag System Arming."
   e. Turn ignition switch to the ON position and verify the "Inflatable Restraint" indicator flashes 7 to 9 times then turns off.

1991 88

1. Disarm airbag system as described under "Airbag System Disarming."
2. Remove front seat (passenger seat only if independent).
3. Bend up carpet retention tabs, then roll back carpet to expose passenger compartment sensing system cover.
4. Remove screws securing cover, then the cover.
5. Disconnect arming sensor connectors and remove retaining pins.
6. Remove arming sensor attaching nuts and the sensor.
7. Reverse procedure to install, noting the following:

a. Install arming sensor with arrow pointing toward front of vehicle. **Torque** attaching nuts to 88 inch lbs.
b. Ensure sensing system cover to bracket attaching screws are fully driven, seated and not stripped.
c. Install front seat, then rearm airbag system as described under "Airbag System Arming."
d. Use tester J-36884 to verify proper voltage at SIR test connector, **Fig. 79.**

1992 Seville

1. Disarm airbag system as described under "Airbag System Disarming."
2. Remove glove compartment.
3. Disconnect connector position assurance and electrical connector from sensor.
4. Remove two sensor bolts and sensor.
5. Reverse procedure to install. Tighten to specifications.
6. Rearm airbag system as described under "Airbag System Arming."

DUAL SENSOR
DeVille & Fleetwood (FWD)

1. Disarm airbag system as described under "Airbag System Disarming."
2. Remove DERM as described under "Diagnostic Energy Reserve Module, Replace."
3. Remove nut retaining sensor connector.
4. Remove CPA and disconnect sensor electrical connector.
5. Remove nut retaining resistor module and two nuts retaining body computer module.
6. Remove DERM and body control module bracket.
7. Remove sensor mounting bolts and screws.
8. Remove sensor by rotating rear of sensor to disengage from mounting clip and pulling rearward.
9. Reverse procedure to install, noting the following:
   a. Install sensor with arrow pointing toward front of vehicle.
   b. Ensure front flange of sensor is engaged into spring clip on bracket.
   c. **Torque** mounting bolts to 84 inch lbs.
   d. **Torque** body computer module and resistor mounting nuts to 84 inch lbs.
   e. Following installation, rearm airbag system as described under "Airbag System Arming."
   f. Turn ignition switch to the ON position and verify the "Inflatable Restraint" indicator flashes 7 to 9 times then turns off.

Riviera, Reatta, Toronado, Trofeo, 1991 Seville & 1991-92 Eldorado

1. Disarm airbag system as described under "Airbag System Disarming."

2. Remove body computer module and glove compartment assembly.
3. Remove right side-glass defroster hose and position sound insulation away from cowl.
4. Disconnect sensor electrical connector and remove two retaining bolts.
5. Reverse procedure to install, noting the following:
   a. Install sensor with arrow pointing toward the front of vehicle.
   b. **Torque** sensor securing bolts to 98 inch lbs.
   c. Following installation, rearm airbag system as described under "Airbag System Arming."
   d. Turn ignition switch to the ON position and verify the "Inflatable Restraint" indicator flashes 7 to 9 times then turns off.

LeSabre, Park Avenue & 1991 98

1. Disarm airbag system as described under "Airbag System Disarming."
2. Remove instrument panel assembly.
3. Remove air distributor assembly, located behind I/P.
4. Remove push-type fastener retaining sensor electrical connector to theft deterrent/pass key control module bracket.
5. Remove CPA and dual sensor electrical connector.
6. Remove mounting bolts attaching sensor to front of dash.
7. Remove sensor by rotating rear of sensor to disengage from mounting clip and pulling rearward.
8. Reverse procedure to install, noting the following:
   a. Ensure front flange of sensor is engaged into spring clip on bracket.
   b. **Torque** mounting bolts to 84 inch lbs.
   c. Following installation, rearm airbag system as described under "Airbag System Arming."
   d. Turn ignition switch to the ON position and verify the "Inflatable Restraint" indicator flashes 7 to 9 times then turns off.

1992-93 88, 98 & Bonneville w/Single Airbag

1. Disarm airbag system as described under "Airbag System Disarming."
2. Remove instrument panel assembly.
3. Remove air distributor assembly.
4. Remove push type fastener retaining sensor pigtail to theft deterrent control module bracket.
5. Disconnect connector position assurance and sensor electrical connector.
6. Remove sensor mounting bolts.
7. Remove sensor by rotating rear of sensor to disengage from mounting clip and pulling rearward.
8. Reverse procedure to install. Tighten to specifications.
9. Rearm airbag system as described under "Airbag System Arming."

1992-93 Bonneville w/Dual Airbags

1. Disarm airbag system as described under "Airbag System Disarming."
2. Remove instrument panel assembly.
3. Disconnect connector position assurance and sensor electrical connector.
4. Remove steering column support bracket brace to pillar panel bolts.
5. Remove steering column support bracket brace to steering column support bracket bolts.
6. Remove steering column support bracket brace.
7. Remove attaching bolts and sensor.
8. Reverse procedure to install. Tighten to specifications.
9. Rearm airbag system as described under "Airbag System Arming."

DUAL POLE ARMING SENSOR

Use extreme caution when handling an airbag system sensor. Striking an airbag sensor could cause system deployment, resulting in personal injury and/or improper airbag system operation. All sensors and mounting bracket bolts must be properly tightened to ensure proper operation.

1993 Camaro & Firebird

1. Disarm airbag system as described under "Airbag System Disarming."
2. Remove center console.
3. Disconnect connector position assurance (CPA) connector and electrical connector from dual pole arming sensor.
4. Remove sensor fasteners, then remove dual pole arming sensor from vehicle.
5. Reverse procedure to install, noting the following:
   a. Tighten to specifications.
   b. Rearm airbag system as described under "Airbag System Arming."

1993 Eldorado & Seville

1. Disarm airbag as described under "Airbag System Disarming."
2. Remove glove compartment.
3. Remove four screws and the glove box unit from instrument panel, then remove passenger inflator module as described under "Passenger Inflator Module."
4. Remove two screws and one nut retaining radio chassis to bracket.
5. Disconnect electrical connectors and coax cable from radio chassis, then remove radio chassis from bracket.
6. Remove two screws retaining bracket assembly and set aside.
7. Disconnect connector position assurance (CPA) and electrical connector from sensor.
8. Loosen two bolts and remove dual pole arming sensor.
9. Reverse procedure to install, noting the following:
   a. Tighten mounting bolts to specifications.
   b. Rearm airbag system as described under "Airbag System Arming."

1993 Fleetwood (RWD)

1. Disarm airbag system as described under "Airbag System Disarming."
2. Remove accelerator pedal assembly.
3. Disconnect connector position assurance (CPA) and electrical connector.
4. Loosen fasteners from dual pole arming sensor.
5. Remove dual pole arming sensor.
6. Reverse procedure to install, noting the following:
   a. Tighten to specifications.
   b. Rearm airbag system as described under "Airbag System Arming."

PASSENGER COMPARTMENT SENSOR

Century & Cutlass Ciera/Cruiser

1. Disarm airbag system as described under "Airbag System Disarming."
2. Remove right sound insulator.
3. Remove sensor electrical connector from retainer, then release connector position assurance (CPA) from connector and disconnect connector.
4. Pull back carpet on tunnel for access to sensor.
5. Loosen sensor mounting bolts and remove sensor.
6. Reverse procedure to install, noting the following:
   a. Tighten to specifications.
   b. Rearm airbag system as described under "Airbag System Arming."

Beretta & Corsica

1. Disarm airbag system as described under "Airbag System Disarming."
2. Remove console, left front seat and track guides.
3. Remove left side shroud panel and left front center pillar lower trim and carpet restrainer.
4. Remove CPA and disconnect sensor electrical connector.
5. Lift carpet to gain access to electrical harness routing conduits. **Fig. 80.**
6. Remove sensor mounting bolts, then snap open conduits and remove sensor wiring.
7. Remove passenger compartment sensor.
8. Reverse procedure to install, noting the following:
   a. Install sensor with arrow pointing toward front of vehicle.
   b. **Torque** mounting bolts to 80 inch lbs.
   c. Following installation, rearm airbag system as described under "Airbag System Arming."
   d. Turn ignition switch to the ON position and verify the "Inflatable Restraint" indicator flashes 7 to 9 times then turns off.

DeVille, Eldorado, Fleetwood, LeSabre, Park Avenue, Reatta, Riviera, Seville, Toronado, Trofeo & 1991 98

The passenger compartment sensor

and arming sensor are removed as an assembly. Refer to "Dual Sensor" or "Dual Pole Arming Sensor" for removal procedure.

1991-92 Camaro & Firebird

1. Disarm airbag system as described under "Airbag System Disarming."
2. Remove knee bolster, refer to "Knee Bolster, Replace."
3. Remove console.
4. Remove heater air distribution duct.
5. Remove CPA and disconnect passenger compartment discriminating sensor electrical connector.
6. Remove sensor retaining bolts, then the sensor.
7. Reverse procedure to install, noting the following:
   a. Install sensor with arrow pointing toward front of vehicle. **Torque** bolts to 25 inch lbs.
   b. Following installation, rearm airbag system as described under "Airbag System Arming."
   c. Turn ignition switch to the ON position and verify the "Inflatable Restraint" indicator flashes 7 to 9 times then turns off.

1993 Camaro & Firebird

1. Disarm airbag system as described under "Airbag System Disarming."
2. Disconnect connector position assurance (CPA) and electrical connectors from sensor.
3. Loosen fasteners and remove passenger compartment sensor from vehicle.
4. Reverse procedure to install, noting the following:
   a. Tighten to specifications.
   b. Rearm airbag system as described under "Airbag System Arming."

Metro

1. Disarm airbag system as described under "Airbag System Disarming."
2. Disconnect battery ground cable.
3. Remove CPA and disconnect sensor electrical connector, below instrument panel, on right side of steering column.
4. Remove two mounting bolts, then remove sensor.
5. Reverse procedure to install, noting the following:
   a. Install sensor with arrow pointing toward front of vehicle.
   b. **Torque** mounting bolts to 53 inch lbs.
   c. Following installation, rearm airbag system as described under "Airbag System Arming."
   d. Turn ignition switch to the ON position and verify the "Inflatable Restraint" indicator flashes 7 to 9 times then turns off.

Storm

1. Disarm airbag system as described under "Airbag System Disarming."

2. Remove front console bracket.
3. Disconnect electrical connector clip and sensor connector.
4. Remove two mounting bolts securing sensor.
5. Remove sensor.
6. Reverse procedure to install, noting the following:
   a. Install sensor with arrow pointing towards front of vehicle.
   b. **Torque** mounting bolts to 89 inch lbs.
   c. Following installation, rearm airbag system as described under "Airbag System Arming."
   d. Turn ignition switch to the ON position and verify the "Inflatable Restraint" indicator flashes 7 to 9 times then turns off.

FORWARD DISCRIMINATING SENSOR

1992-93 88, 98 & BONNEVILLE

1. Disarm airbag system as described under "Airbag System Disarming."
2. Disconnect connector position assurance and sensor pigtail electrical connection.
3. Remove sensor pigtail wiring from clips.
4. Remove bolts and upper radiator tie bar to grill reveal molding.
5. Remove sensor bolts and sensor.
6. Reverse procedure to install. Tighten to specifications.
7. Rearm airbag system as described under "Airbag System Arming."

1993 CENTURY & CUTLASS CIERA/CRUISER

1. Disarm airbag system as described under "Airbag System Disarming."
2. Remove grille from front of vehicle.
3. Remove sensor electrical connector from retainer.
4. Release connector position assurance (CPA) from connector and disconnect connector.
5. Remove sensor mounting bolts, then remove the sensor.
6. Reverse procedure to install, noting the following:
   a. Ensure sensor arrow points toward front of vehicle.
   b. Tighten to specifications.
   c. Rearm airbag system as described under "Airbag System Arming."

1993 FLEETWOOD (RWD)

Left Sensor

1. Disarm airbag system as described under "Airbag System Disarming."
2. Disconnect Connector Position Assurance (CPA) and sensor electrical connector.
3. Remove sensor mounting fasteners, then remove sensor from vehicle.
4. Reverse procedure to install, noting the following:
   a. Ensure arrow on top of sensor is

pointing toward front of vehicle.
   b. Tighten to specifications.
   c. Rearm airbag system as described under "Airbag System Arming."

Right Sensor

1. Disarm airbag system as described under "Airbag System Disarming."
2. Remove battery, then disconnect Connector Position Assurance (CPA) and sensor electrical connector.
3. Remove sensor mounting fasteners, then remove sensor from vehicle.
4. Reverse procedure to install, noting the following:
   a. Ensure arrow on top of sensor is pointed toward front of vehicle.
   b. Tighten to specifications.
   c. Rearm airbag system as described under "Airbag System Arming."

1993 CAMARO & FIREBIRD

1. Disarm airbag system as described under "Airbag System Disarming."
2. Loosen sensor fasteners and lower sensor for access.
3. Disconnect connector position assurance (CPA) and electrical connectors.
4. Remove sensor from vehicle.
5. Reverse procedure to install, noting the following:
   a. Tighten to specifications.
   b. Rearm airbag system as described under "Airbag System Arming."

FORWARD SENSORS

BERETTA & CORSICA

1. Disarm airbag system as described under "Airbag System Disarming."
2. Remove right outer radiator upper air baffle.
3. Remove CPA and disconnect sensor electrical connector.
4. Remove wiring clips from upper radiator tie bar, then remove bolts securing bracket to upper radiator tie bar.
5. Remove nuts securing sensor to bracket.
6. Reverse procedure to install, noting the following:
   a. Install sensor with arrow pointing toward front of vehicle.
   b. **Torque** sensor mounting nuts and bolts to 80 inch lbs.
   c. Following installation, rearm airbag system as described under "Airbag System Arming."
   d. Turn ignition switch to the ON position and verify the "Inflatable Restraint" indicator flashes 7 to 9 times then turns off.

1991-92 CAMARO & FIREBIRD

1. Disarm airbag system as described under "Airbag System Disarming."
2. Remove air cleaner, then raise and support vehicle.
3. Remove radiator air upper baffle.
4. Remove CPA and disconnect Forward Discriminating Sensor electrical connector behind radiator support.
5. Remove forward discrimination sen-

sor retaining bolts, then the sensor, **Fig. 81.**
6. Reverse procedure to install, noting the following:
   a. Install forward discriminating sensor with arrow pointing toward front of vehicle. **Torque** bolts to 25 inch lbs.
   b. Following installation, rearm airbag system as described under "Airbag System Arming."
   c. Turn ignition switch to the ON position and verify the "Inflatable Restraint" indicator flashes 7 to 9 times then turns Off.

CAPRICE, CUSTOM CRUISER & ROADMASTER

Left & Right Sensors

1. Disarm airbag system as described under "Airbag System Disarming."
2. Remove battery if necessary for access to right sensor.
3. Remove radiator support baffle.
4. Disconnect CPA and electrical connector from radiator support.
5. Remove mounting screws from sensor, then remove sensor.
6. Reverse procedure to install, noting the following:
   a. Install sensor with arrow pointing toward front of vehicle.
   b. **Torque** mounting screws to 25 inch lbs.
   c. Following installation, rearm airbag system as described under "Airbag System Arming."
   d. Turn ignition switch to the ON position and verify the "Inflatable Restraint" indicator flashes 7 to 9 times then turns off.

CORVETTE

Left Sensor

1. Disarm airbag system as described under "Airbag System Disarming."
2. Remove battery, ECM and ECM support.
3. Remove sensor mounting bolts then disconnect sensor electrical connector and remove sensor from vehicle.
4. Reverse procedure to install, noting the following:
   a. Install sensor with arrow pointing toward front of vehicle.
   b. **Torque** mounting bolts to 11 ft. lbs.
   c. Following installation, rearm airbag system as described under "Airbag System Arming."
   d. Turn ignition switch to the ON position and verify the "Inflatable Restraint" indicator flashes 7 to 9 times then turns off.

Right Sensor

1. Disarm airbag system as described under "Airbag System Disarming."
2. Remove six front RH rocker panel retaining screws.

3. Remove right side front fender gill panel retaining bolts, then the fender.
4. Peel back rear portion of wheelwell to hood seal.
5. Remove right side lower wheelwell retaining bolts, then the wheelwell.
6. Remove two front windshield washer reservoir retaining bolts, then loosen remaining washer reservoir bolt.
7. Rotate reservoir to access sensor.
8. Remove sensor retaining bolts, then disconnect sensor electrical connector.
9. Reverse procedure to install, noting the following:
   a. Install sensor with arrow pointing toward front of vehicle.
   b. **Torque** mounting bolts to 11 ft. lbs.
   c. **Torque** reservoir mounting bolts to 54 inch lbs.
   d. **Torque** wheelwell to frame bolts to 80 inch lbs.
   e. Following installation, rearm airbag system as described under "Airbag System Arming."
   f. Turn ignition switch to the ON position and verify proper operation of "INFL REST" lamp.

DEVILLE, FLEETWOOD (FWD), LESABRE, PARK AVENUE & 98

1. Disarm airbag system as described under "Airbag System Disarming."
2. Disconnect forward sensor electrical connector, then remove harness retaining clips, **Fig. 82.**
3. Remove two sensor mounting bolts, then remove sensor.
4. Reverse procedure to install, noting the following:
   a. **Torque** sensor mounting bolts to 62 inch lbs.
   b. Following installation, rearm airbag system as described under "Airbag System Arming."
   c. Turn ignition switch to the ON position and verify the "Inflatable Restraint" indicator flashes 7 to 9 times then turns off.

REATTA, RIVIERA, TORONADO, TROFEO, 1991 ELDORADO & SEVILLE

1. Disarm airbag system as described under "Airbag System Disarming."
2. Disconnect battery ground cable.
3. Disconnect and remove wire harness conduit cover.
4. Disconnect CPA and sensor electrical connector.
5. Remove harness retaining clips and pull harness through radiator support brace.
6. Raise and support vehicle, then remove two tamper resistant bolts with insert bit tool No. J-38597 or equivalent.
7. Remove sensor from vehicle.
8. Reverse procedure to install, noting the following:
   a. Install sensor with arrow towards front of vehicle.
   b. **Torque** tamper resistant bolts to

98 inch lbs.
   c. Following installation, rearm airbag system as described under "Airbag System Arming."
   d. Turn ignition switch to the ON position and verify the "Inflatable Restraint" indicator flashes 7 to 9 times then turns off.

1992-93 ELDORADO & SEVILLE

Left Sensor

1. Disarm airbag system as described under "Airbag System Disarming."
2. Disconnect connector position assurance and sensor electrical connector.
3. Remove two sensor bolts and sensor.
4. Reverse procedure to install. Tighten to specifications.
5. Rearm airbag system as described under "Airbag System Arming."

Right Sensor

1. Disarm airbag system as described under "Airbag System Disarming."
2. Remove cruise control servo unit.
3. Remove two bolts retaining A/C accumulator bracket.
4. Remove screws retaining coolant reservoir to A/C accumulator bracket and wheelwell.
5. Move insulation on shock tower aside. Sensor connector should be visible.
6. Disconnect connector position assurance and sensor electrical connector.
7. Remove two sensor bolts and sensor.
8. Reverse procedure to install. Tighten to specifications.
9. Rearm airbag system as described under "Airbag System Arming."

METRO

1. Disarm airbag system as described under "Airbag System Disarming."
2. Disconnect battery ground cable.
3. Disconnect sensor connector from lamp support panel.
4. Remove CPA and sensor electrical connector.
5. Disconnect two sensor lead wire clamps and remove two sensor mounting bolts.
6. Remove sensor.
7. Reverse procedure to install, noting the following:
   a. Install sensor with arrow pointing toward front of vehicle.
   b. **Torque** mounting bolts to 98 inch lbs.
   c. Following installation, rearm airbag system as described under "Airbag System Arming."
   d. Turn ignition switch to the ON position and verify the "Inflatable Restraint" indicator flashes 7 to 9 times then turns off.

STORM

1. Disarm airbag system as described under "Airbag System Disarming."
2. Disconnect battery ground cable.
3. Raise and support vehicle, then dis-

connect sensor electrical connector. **Fig. 83.**
4. Remove three mounting bolts and sensor from radiator support brace.
5. Reverse procedure to install, noting the following:
   a. Install sensor with arrow pointing toward front of vehicle.
   b. **Torque** sensor mounting bolts to 97 inch lbs.
   c. Following installation, rearm airbag system as described under "Airbag System Arming."
   d. Turn ignition switch to the ON position and verify the "Inflatable Restraint" indicator flashes 7 to 9 times then turns off.

1991 88

1. Disarm airbag system as described under "Airbag System Disarming."
2. Remove grille attaching screws, then the grille.
3. Remove CPA and sensor connector from left fender in engine compartment.
4. Remove fasteners securing forward sensor to bracket.
5. Remove sensor.
6. Reverse procedure to install, noting the following:
   a. **Torque** fasteners to 62 inch lbs.
   b. Following installation, rearm airbag system as described under "Airbag System Arming."

PRIZM

1. Disarm airbag system as described under "Airbag System Disarming."
2. Raise and support vehicle, then remove retaining clips and wheelhousing from front wheelwell.
3. Disconnect forward sensor electrical connector.
4. Loosen two mounting bolts and remove forward sensor from vehicle. Discard mounting bolts following removal.
5. Reverse procedure to install, noting the following;
   a. Ensure forward sensor is installed with arrow on sensor pointing toward front of vehicle.
   b. Tighten to specifications.
   c. **Always secure with new mounting bolts.**
   d. Rearm airbag system as described under "Airbag System Arming."

CENTER SENSOR ASSEMBLY

Prizm

Do not open the center sensor assembly case for any reason. Touching the connector pins or soldered components may cause electrostatic discharge (ESD) damage. Repair of a faulty center sensor assembly is by replacement only.
1. Disarm airbag system as described under "Airbag System Disarming."
2. Disconnect battery ground cable, then

remove console from vehicle.
3. Remove three bolts and console mounting bracket from floor, then remove rear seat cushion.
4. Loosen rear floor carpet to gain access to center sensor assembly bolts.
5. Disconnect center sensor assembly connectors.
6. Remove three bolts and the center sensor assembly from vehicle.
7. Reverse procedure to install, noting the following:
   a. Tighten to specifications.
   b. Rearm airbag system as described under "Airbag System Arming."

POWER SUPPLY MODULE

1991 88
Removal

1. Disarm airbag system as described under "Airbag System Disarming."
2. Remove front seat (passenger seat only if independent).
3. Bend up carpet retention tabs, then roll back carpet to expose passenger compartment sensing system cover.
4. Remove screws securing cover, then the cover.
5. Remove two screws on side of power supply, then the connector retainer bracket.
6. Disconnect power supply connector from harness assembly.
7. Remove screw attaching power supply to bracket, then the power supply.

Installation

1. Install power supply, securing to mounting bracket with one screw.
2. Connect power supply connector to harness assembly.
3. Install power supply connector retainer bracket, securing with two screws.
4. Install sensing system cover to bracket, ensuring attaching screws are fully driven, seated and not stripped.
5. Install carpet in position and bend down carpet retention tabs.
6. Install front seat, then rearm airbag system as described under "Airbag System Arming."
7. Use tester J-36884 to verify proper voltage at SIR test connector, **Fig. 79.**

KNEE BOLSTER

Beretta, Corsica, 1991-92 Camaro & Firebird

1. Disarm airbag system as described under "Airbag System Disarming."
2. Remove knee bolster retaining screws, **Fig. 84.**
3. Reverse procedure to install, noting the following:
   a. Following installation, rearm airbag system as described under "Airbag System Arming."
   b. Turn ignition switch to the ON position and verify the "Inflatable Restraint" indicator flashes 7 to 9 times then turns off.

Caprice, Custom Cruiser & Roadmaster

1. Remove lower steering column trim panel.
2. Remove four bolster mounting screws.
3. Remove knee bolster.
4. Reverse procedure to install. **Torque** mounting screws to 53 inch lbs.

Corvette

1. Disarm airbag system as described under "Airbag System Disarming."
2. Remove lower trim panel.
3. Remove console side trim panel LH upper two screws. Rotate access panel down to remove two knee bolster retaining bolts.
4. Remove knee bolster inner and outer bracket retaining screws.
5. Disconnect lap air outlet duct from lower duct assembly.
6. Remove knee bolster.
7. Reverse procedure to install, noting the following:
   a. **Torque** bolster inner mounting bolts to 116 inch lbs.
   b. **Torque** bolster outer mounting bolts to 17 ft. lbs.
   c. Following installation, rearm airbag system as described under "Airbag System Arming."
   d. Turn ignition switch to the ON position and verify the proper operation of "INFL REST" lamp.

DeVille & Fleetwood

1. Disarm airbag system as described under "Airbag System Disarming."
2. Remove I/P lower trim panel.
3. Remove two twilight sentinel bracket retaining screws.
4. Remove two fuse block bracket retaining screws.
5. **On 1991 models,** remove two nuts from studs on instrument panel.
6. **On all models,** remove two knee bolster tie bar retaining screws, **Fig. 85.**
7. Remove left side instrument panel retaining bolt.
8. Reverse procedure to install, noting the following:
   a. Following installation, rearm airbag system as described under "Airbag System Arming."
   b. Turn ignition switch to the ON position and verify the "Inflatable Restraint" indicator flashes 7 to 9 times then turns off.

Eldorado & Seville

1. Remove center trim plate.
2. Remove five screws securing knee bolster.
3. Remove knee bolster.
4. Reverse procedure to install.

Metro

1. Remove lower steering column trim panel and steering column reinforcement plate.

2. Remove two lower instrument panel retaining screws.
3. Remove five mounting screws and knee bolster from instrument panel support member.
4. Reverse procedure to install.

Reatta & Riviera

1. Disarm airbag system as described under "Airbag System Disarming."
2. Remove instrument panel trim plate.
3. Remove front and rear console assemblies.
4. Remove six knee retaining bolster screws, then the knee bolster, **Fig. 86.**
5. Reverse procedure to install, noting the following:
   a. Following installation, rearm airbag system as described under "Airbag System Arming."
   b. Turn ignition switch to the ON position and verify the "Inflatable Restraint" indicator flashes 7 to 9 times then turns off.

Storm

1. Disarm airbag system as described under "Airbag System Disarming."
2. Remove left lower switch and dash lighter panel assemblies.
3. Remove hood release latch and cable.
4. Remove knee bolster.
5. Reverse procedure to install, noting the following:
   a. **Torque** knee bolster mounting nuts and bolts 89 inch lbs.
   b. Following installation, rearm airbag system as described under "Airbag System Arming."
   c. Turn ignition switch to the ON position and verify the "Inflatable Restraint" indicator flashes 7 to 9 times then turns off.

Toronado & Trofeo

1. Remove left side sound insulator.
2. Remove two bolster retaining screws, then remove the knee bolster.
3. Reverse procedure to install.

1991 88

1. Disarm airbag system as described under "Airbag System Disarming."
2. Remove trim pad between instrument panel and lower trim panel.
3. Remove screws along top of instrument panel lower trim panel.
4. Remove screws from left end of lower trim panel.
5. Remove screws from bottom of lower trim panel.
6. Disconnect electrical connectors as necessary to remove panel.
7. Reverse procedure to install, noting the following:
   a. Following installation, rearm airbag system as described under "Airbag System Arming."
   b. Ensure proper operation of airbag lamp.

Prizm

1. Remove retaining clips and left front sill plate.
2. Loosen two screws and remove hood latch release handle from knee bolster.
3. Remove two bolt covers from front of knee bolster.
4. Remove four bolts and the knee bolster from instrument panel, disconnecting lap cooler air outlet from lap cooler air duct.
5. Reverse procedure to install, noting the following:
   a. Tighten to specifications.
   b. Rearm airbag system as described under "Airbag System Arming."

DRIVER'S INFLATOR MODULE

Always wear safety glasses and gloves. Wash hands with mild soap and water after handling a deployed module.

METRO & STORM

1. Disarm airbag system as described under "Airbag System Disarming."
2. Disconnect battery ground cable.
3. Remove four screws from rear of steering wheel.
4. Disconnect electrical connector and carefully remove inflator module from steering wheel.
5. Reverse procedure to install, noting the following:
   a. **On Metro models, torque** mounting screws to 89 inch lbs.
   b. **On Storm models, torque** mounting screws to 44 inch lbs.
   c. Following installation, rearm airbag system as described under "Airbag System Arming."
   d. Turn ignition switch to the ON position and verify the "Inflatable Restraint" indicator flashes 7 to 9 times then turns off.

PRIZM

1. Disarm airbag system as described under "Airbag System Disarming."
2. Place front wheels in straight ahead position, then remove two side trim covers from steering column.
3. Remove two Torx screws and release connector position assurance (CPA) from inflator module.
4. Disconnect upper steering column connector and remove inflator module from steering wheel.
5. Reverse procedure to install, noting the following:
   a. Tighten to specifications.
   b. Rearm airbag system as described under "Airbag System Arming"

1991 88
Removal

1. Disarm airbag system as described under "Airbag System Disarming."
2. Remove three of the four module to

steering column attaching screws from back side of steering wheel.
3. While supporting module with one hand, remove fourth screw and disconnect the module connector, then tape the connector.
4. Disconnect horn lead.

Installation

1. While holding module with one hand, connect module connector and horn lead.
2. Place module in position and secure with one screw.
3. Install three remaining screws, ensuring all attaching bolts are fully driven, seated and not stripped.
4. Remove tape and rearm airbag system as described under "Airbag System Arming."

EXCEPT METRO, PRIZM, STORM & 1991 88

1. Disarm airbag system as described under "Airbag System Disarming."
2. Disconnect battery ground cable and wait ten minutes before removing inflator module.
3. Remove four bolts at rear of steering wheel, securing inflator module.
4. Rotate horn lead 1/4 turn and disconnect.
5. Disconnect electrical connectors and remove inflator module.
6. Reverse procedure to install, noting the following:
   a. **Torque** mounting screws to 25 inch lbs.
   b. Following installation, rearm airbag system as described under "Airbag System Arming."
   c. Turn ignition switch to the ON position and verify the "Inflatable Restraint" indicator flashes 7 to 9 times then turns off.

PASSENGER INFLATOR MODULE

1992-93 Bonneville

1. Disarm airbag system as described under "Airbag System Disarming."
2. Remove instrument panel assembly.
3. Remove inflator module to instrument panel nuts and bolts.
4. Remove inflator module.
5. Reverse procedure to install, noting the following:
   a. Tighten to specifications.
   b. Rearm airbag system as described under "Airbag System Arming."

1993 Eldorado & Seville

1. Disarm airbag system as described under "Airbag System Disarming."
2. Remove instrument panel upper trim panel.
3. Remove screw located behind trap door in rear of glove compartment retaining inflator module to bracket.
4. Remove four screws retaining inflator module to top of instrument panel.
5. Remove inflator module and wiring harness.

6. Reverse procedure to install, noting the following:
   a. Tighten to specifications.
   b. Rearm airbag system as described under "Airbag System Arming."

1993 Fleetwood (RWD)

1. Disarm airbag system as described under "Airbag System Disarming."
2. Remove upper trim pad from instrument panel.
3. Disconnect connector position assurance (CPA) and electrical connector.
4. Loosen inflator module fasteners, then remove passenger inflator module from vehicle.
5. Reverse procedure to install, noting the following:
   a. Tighten to specifications.
   b. Rearm airbag system as described under "Airbag System Arming."

1993 Camaro & Firebird

1. Disarm airbag system as described under "Airbag System Disarming."
2. Remove I/P carrier assembly.
3. Disconnect connector position assurance (CPA) and electrical connectors from passenger inflator module.
4. Loosen fasteners and remove inflator module from vehicle.
5. Reverse procedure to install, noting the following:
   a. Tighten to specifications.
   b. Rearm airbag system as described under "Airbag System Arming."

DIAGNOSTIC ENERGY RESERVE MODULE (DERM)

Do not open the DERM case for any reason. Touching the connector pins or soldered components may cause electrostatic discharge damage. Repair of a faulty DERM is by replacement only.

Beretta, Corsica, DeVille & Fleetwood (FWD)

1. Disarm airbag system as described under "Airbag System Disarming."
2. Remove right sound insulator.
3. Remove glove box assembly.
4. Loosen retaining nuts and slide DERM from bracket.
5. Unlatch orange connector lock then disconnect DERM electrical connector and remove DERM, **Fig. 87.**
6. Reverse procedure to install, noting the following:
   a. **Torque** DERM retaining nuts to 35 inch lbs.
   b. Following installation, rearm airbag system as described under "Airbag System Arming."
   c. Turn ignition switch to the ON position and verify the "Inflatable Restraint" indicator flashes 7 to 9 times then turns off.

1991-92 Camaro & Firebird

1. Disarm airbag system as described under "Airbag System Disarming."
2. Remove instrument panel pad.

3. Remove side window defogger duct and retaining screws.
4. Remove DERM upper and lower retaining screws, **Fig. 88.**
5. Unlatch orange lock and disconnect DERM electrical connector.
6. Reverse procedure to install, noting the following:
   a. Rearm airbag system as described under "Airbag System Arming."
   b. Turn ignition switch to the ON position and verify the "Inflatable Restraint" indicator flashes 7 to 9 times then turns off.

1993 Camaro & Firebird

1. Disarm airbag system as described under "Airbag System Disarming."
2. Remove right side lower sound insulator pad, then remove the I/P compartment door assembly.
3. Disconnect Connector Position Assurance (CPA) connector and electrical connector from DERM.
4. Remove DERM from vehicle.
5. Reverse procedure to install. Rearm airbag system as described under "Airbag System Arming."

Caprice, Custom Cruiser & Roadmaster

1. Disarm airbag system as described under "Airbag System Disarming."
2. Remove resistor module as described under "Resistor Module, Replacement."
3. Disconnect electrical connector from DERM and remove three nuts from DERM bracket.
4. Remove DERM and bracket as an assembly.
5. Loosen three nuts and remove DERM from bracket.
6. Reverse procedure to install, noting the following:
   a. **Torque** mounting nuts to 17 inch lbs.
   b. Following installation, rearm airbag system as described under "Airbag System Arming."
   c. Turn ignition switch to the ON position and verify the "Inflatable Restraint" indicator flashes 7 to 9 times then turns off.

Century & Cutlass Ciera/Cruiser

1. Disarm airbag system as described under "Airbag System Disarming."
2. Remove right sound insulator.
3. Remove accelerator pedal and bracket assembly.
4. Release connector position assurance (CPA), then disconnect DERM electrical connector.
5. Loosen nuts and remove DERM from vehicle.
6. Reverse procedure to install, noting the following:
   a. Tighten to specifications.
   b. Rearm airbag system as described under "Airbag System Arming."

Corvette

1. Disarm airbag system as described under "Airbag System Disarming."
2. Remove knee bolster inner bracket and radio control.
3. Remove SIR wiring harness to DERM CPA and disconnect electrical connectors.
4. Remove DERM.
5. Reverse procedure to install, noting the following:
   a. **Torque** knee bolster inner bracket and DERM bracket LH fasteners to 116 inch lbs.
   b. Following installation, rearm airbag system as described under "Airbag System Arming."
   c. Turn ignition switch to the ON position and verify the "Inflatable Restraint" indicator flashes 7 to 9 times then turns off.

Eldorado, Riviera, Reatta, Seville, Toronado & Trofeo

1. Disarm airbag system as described under "Airbag System Disarming."
2. Disconnect DERM electrical connector, **Fig. 89.**
3. Loosen DERM retaining nuts, located to the right of steering column.
4. Remove DERM from vehicle.
5. Reverse procedure to install, noting the following:
   a. Following installation, rearm airbag system as described under "Airbag System Arming."
   b. Turn ignition switch to the ON position and verify the "Inflatable Restraint" indicator flashes 7 to 9 times then turns off.

1993 Fleetwood (RWD)

1. Disarm airbag system as described under "Airbag System Disarming."
2. Disconnect connector position assurance (CPA) and electrical connector from DERM.
3. Disconnect electrical connector from Retained Accessory Power (RAP) relay.
4. Loosen DERM fasteners, then remove DERM bracket.
5. Loosen fasteners from Transmission Converter Clutch (TCC) disable relay, then remove TCC disable relay for clearance.
6. Remove DERM from vehicle.
7. Reverse procedure to install, noting the following:
   a. Tighten to specifications.
   b. Rearm airbag system as described under "Airbag System Arming."

Metro

1. Disarm airbag system as described under "Airbag System Disarming."
2. Disconnect battery ground cable.
3. Remove orange connector lock and disconnect DERM electrical connector.

4. From below instrument panel, at right side steering column, remove DERM mounting bracket from steering column support member.
5. Disconnect and remove resistor module from DERM mounting bracket, then remove DERM from bracket.
6. Reverse procedure to install, noting the following:
   a. Following installation, rearm airbag system as described under "Airbag System Arming."
   b. Turn ignition switch to the ON position and verify the "Inflatable Restraint" indicator flashes 7 to 9 times then turns off.

LeSabre & Park Avenue

1. Disarm airbag system as described under "Airbag System Disarming."
2. Remove RH sound insulator.
3. Remove remote accessory control module (RAC) from bracket. **Do not disconnect.**
4. Remove mounting bolt from DERM bracket. Slide DERM from bracket.
5. Disconnect electrical connector from DERM, then remove nut attaching bracket to DERM.
6. Reverse procedure to install, noting the following:
   a. **Torque** RH sound insulator mounting bolts to 19 inch lbs.
   b. **Torque** bracket attaching nut to 35 inch lbs.
   c. Following installation, rearm airbag system as described under "Airbag System Arming."
   d. Turn ignition switch to the ON position and verify the "Inflatable Restraint" indicator flashes 7 to 9 times then turns off.

Storm

1. Disarm airbag system as described under "Airbag System Disarming."
2. Disconnect battery ground cable.
3. Remove front console bracket and disconnect DERM electrical connector.
4. Remove four screws and nuts securing DERM yellow bracket.
5. Disconnect and remove resistor module from DERM mounting bracket.
6. Remove four retaining clips at DERM.
7. Remove DERM.
8. Reverse procedure to install, noting the following:
   a. **Torque** DERM yellow bracket retaining screws to 44 inch lbs.
   b. **Torque** yellow bracket retaining nuts to 35 inch lbs.
   c. Following installation, rearm airbag system as described under "Airbag System Arming."
   d. Turn ignition switch to the ON position and verify the "Inflatable Restraint" indicator flashes 7 to 9 times then turns off.

1992-93 88, 98 & Bonneville

1. Disarm airbag system as described under "Airbag System Disarming."
2. Remove instrument panel insert.
3. Remove remote accessory control module from multi-use bracket and position aside.
4. Remove spacer from underneath DERM.
5. Remove DERM from multi-use bracket by separating hook and loop tape, then disconnect electrical connector.
6. Reverse procedure to install.
7. Rearm airbag system as described under "Airbag System Arming."

ENERGY RESERVE MODULE

1991 88
Removal

1. Disarm airbag system as described under "Airbag System Disarming."
2. Remove front seat (passenger seat only if independent).
3. Bend up carpet retention tabs, then roll back carpet to expose SIR control center cover.
4. Remove cover, then remove screws securing energy reserve module to bracket.
5. Disconnect energy reserve module connector from harness assembly. **Wiggle connector when removing from module, do not attempt to pry up lock tabs on connector.**
6. Remove energy reserve module.

Installation

1. Install energy reserve module, securing to bracket with screws.
2. Connect energy reserve module connector to harness assembly.
3. Install sensing system cover to bracket, ensuring attaching screws are fully driven, seated and not stripped.
4. Install carpet in position and bend down carpet retention tabs.
5. Install front seat, then rearm airbag system as described under "Airbag System Arming."
6. Use tester J-36884 to verify proper voltage at SIR test connector, **Fig. 79.**

SIR DIAGNOSTIC MODULE

1991 88
Removal

Handle SIR control module carefully to avoid damaging passenger compartment sensor.
1. Disarm airbag system as described under "Airbag System Disarming."
2. Remove front seat (passenger seat only, if equipped with independent seats).
3. Bend up carpet retention tabs, then roll back carpet to expose passenger compartment sensing system cover.
4. Loosen screws and remove cover.

5. Disconnect sensor connector from harness assembly and the arming sensor connector.
6. Remove diagnostic module.
7. Remove SIR control module attaching nuts and the module. **Use care when handling a sensor. Never jar or strike the module in a manner which may cause deployment. Never apply voltage to a sensor when it is not rigidly attached to vehicle.**

Installation

1. Install SIR control module with arrow pointing toward front of vehicle.
2. Install module attaching bolts. **Torque to 88 inch lbs.**
3. Connect sensing connector to harness assembly, and the arming sensor.
4. Install sensor connector retaining pins.
5. Install sensing system cover to bracket, ensuring attaching screws are fully driven, seated and not stripped.
6. Install carpet in position and bend down carpet retention tabs.
7. Install front seat, then rearm airbag system as described under "Airbag System Arming."
8. Use tester J-36884 to verify proper voltage at SIR test connector, **Fig. 79.**

RESISTOR MODULE

Beretta & Corsica

1. Disarm airbag system as described under "Airbag System Disarming."
2. Remove tape securing resistor module to wiring harness.
3. Remove CPA and disconnect resistor module electrical connector.
4. Remove resistor module, **Fig. 90.**
5. Reverse procedure to install, noting the following:
   a. Following installation, rearm airbag system as described under "Airbag System Arming."
   b. Turn ignition switch to the ON position and verify the "Inflatable Restraint" indicator flashes 7 to 9 times then turns off.

1991-92 Camaro & Firebird

1. Disarm airbag system as described under "Airbag System Disarming."
2. Remove knee bolster, refer to "Knee Bolster, Replace."
3. Unsnap resistor module from left side tie bar, **Fig. 91,** then remove CPA and disconnect module electrical connector.
4. Reverse procedure to install, noting the following:
   a. Following installation, rearm airbag system as described under "Airbag System Arming."
   b. Turn ignition switch to the ON position and verify the "Inflatable Restraint" indicator flashes 7 to 9 times then turns off.

Caprice, Custom Cruiser & Roadmaster

1. Disarm airbag system as described under "Airbag System Disarming."
2. Disconnect CPA and electrical connector at resistor module.
3. Remove resistor module by sliding to the left on the DERM bracket.
4. Reverse procedure to install, noting the following:
   a. Following installation, rearm airbag system as described under "Airbag System Arming."
   b. Turn ignition switch to the ON position and verify the "Inflatable Restraint" indicator flashes 7 to 9 times then turns off.

Century & Cutlass Ciera/Cruiser

The resistor module is part of the SIR wiring harness and is taped to the I/P wiring harness. The resistor module is located level with and to the right of the radio.
1. Disarm airbag system as described under "Airbag System Disarming."
2. Remove radio.
3. Carefully cut tape attaching resistor module to the I/P wiring harness.
4. Release connector position assurance (CPA) and disconnect resistor module.
5. Remove resistor module from vehicle.
6. Reverse procedure to install. Rearm airbag system as described under "Airbag System Arming."

Corvette

1. Disarm airbag system as described under "Airbag System Disarming."
2. Remove radio control.
3. Disconnect resistor module from instrument carrier assembly.
4. Remove SIR wiring harness CPA and disconnect electrical connector from resistor module.
5. Remove resistor module.
6. Reverse procedure to install, noting the following:
   a. Following installation, rearm airbag system as described under "Airbag System Arming."
   b. Turn ignition switch to the ON position and verify the "Inflatable Restraint" indicator flashes 7 to 9 times then turns off.

DeVille & Fleetwood (FWD)

1. Disarm airbag system as described under "Airbag System Disarming."
2. Remove right sound insulator.
3. Remove glove box module.
4. Remove CPA, then disconnect resistor module electrical connector and remove module, **Fig. 92.**

5. Reverse procedure to install, noting the following:
   a. **On 1991 models, torque** body computer module mounting nut to 30 ft. lbs.
   b. **On all models,** rearm airbag system as described under "Airbag System Arming."
   c. Turn ignition switch to the ON position and verify the "Inflatable Restraint" indicator flashes 7 to 9 times then turns off.

1991 Eldorado & Seville

1. Disarm airbag system as described under "Airbag system Disarming."
2. Remove two center trim plate retaining screws, then the plate.
3. Remove knee bolster, refer to "Knee Bolster Replace."
4. Remove instrument panel steering column reinforcement plate.
5. Remove hood release lever, then unsnap module from bracket behind left side of instrument panel.
6. Remove CPA, then disconnect module electrical connector.
7. Remove module form vehicle.
8. Reverse procedure to install, noting the following:
   a. Following installation, rearm airbag system as described under "Airbag System Arming."
   b. Turn ignition switch to the ON position and verify the "Inflatable Restraint" indicator flashes 7 to 9 times then turns off.

1992-93 Eldorado & Seville

1. Disarm airbag system as described under "Airbag System Disarming."
2. Remove steering column opening filler trim.
3. Remove steering column opening bracket.
4. Disconnect connector position assurance and electrical connector.
5. Remove resistor module.
6. Reverse procedure to install.
7. Rearm airbag system as described under "Airbag System Arming."

Metro & Storm

The resistor module is removed with the DERM as an assembly. Refer to "Diagnostic Energy Reserve Module (DERM), Replace" for replacement procedure.

LeSabre & Park Avenue

1. Disarm airbag system as described

under "Airbag System Disarming."
2. Remove instrument panel lower trim plate, then the air vent deflector.
3. Remove three bolts and three screws securing glove compartment assembly to instrument panel.
4. Slide resistor module off of bracket.
5. Disconnect electrical connector and remove resistor module.
6. Reverse procedure to install, noting the following:
   a. **Torque** glove compartment bolts and screws to 17 inch lbs.
   b. Following installation, rearm airbag system as described under "Airbag System Arming."
   c. Turn ignition switch to the ON position and verify the "Inflatable Restraint" indicator flashes 7 to 9 times then turns off.

Reatta, Riviera, Toronado & Trofeo

1. Disarm airbag system as described under "Airbag System Disarming."
2. Disconnect battery ground cable.
3. Disconnect module from bracket behind left side of instrument panel.
4. Disconnect CPA and module electrical connector.
5. Remove resistor module.
6. Reverse procedure to install, noting the following:
   a. Following installation, rearm airbag system as described under "Airbag System Arming."
   b. Turn ignition switch to the ON position and verify the "Inflatable Restraint" indicator flashes 7 to 9 times then turns off.

1991 98

1. Disarm airbag system as described under "Airbag System Disarming."
2. Remove RH sound insulator.
3. Remove resistor module from multi-use bracket.
4. Disconnect resistor module electrical connector, then remove resistor module.
5. Revere procedure to install, noting the following:
   a. Following installation, rearm airbag system as described under "Airbag System Arming."
   b. Turn ignition switch to the ON position and verify the "Inflatable Restraint" indicator flashes 7 to 9 times then turns off.

1992-93 88, 98 & Bonneville w/Single Airbag

1. Disarm airbag system as described under "Airbag System Disarming."
2. Remove instrument panel compartment insert.
3. Remove resistor module from multi-use bracket.
4. Disconnect CPA and electrical connector from resistor module.
5. Reverse procedure to install.
6. Rearm airbag system as described under "Airbag System Arming."

SIR COIL ASSEMBLY
Camaro & Firebird

Refer to "Inflator Module Replace."

Except Camaro & Firebird

Refer to "Steering Column Service" in the "Steering Columns" section.

STEERING WHEEL
Removal

1. Disarm airbag system as described under "Airbag System Disarming."
2. Remove inflator module as previously described.
3. Remove two screws securing steering pad, then remove pad if equipped.
4. Disconnect electrical connectors and leads.
5. Remove retainer and nut, then remove steering wheel, using suitable steering wheel puller tool.

Installation

1. Align mark on steering wheel with mark on shaft, then install nut. **Torque** to 25-30 ft. lbs.
2. Install retainer, then the steering wheel module.
3. Connect horn lead and install pad if equipped, securing with two attaching screws.
4. Following installation, rearm airbag system as described under "Airbag System Arming."
5. Turn ignition switch to the ON position and verify the "Inflatable Restraint" indicator flashes 7 to 9 times then turns off.

TIGHTENING SPECIFICATIONS

Component	Torque/Inch Lbs.
Beretta & Corsica	
Arming Sensor Bolts	80
Diagnostic Energy Reserve Module Nuts	35
Forward Discriminating Sensor Bracket Bolts	80
Forward Discriminating Sensor Nuts	80
Knee Bolster Panel Screws	13
Nuts Securing Studs To Diagnostic Energy Reserve Module	22
Passenger Compartment Discriminating Sensor Bolts	80
1991-92 Camaro & Firebird	
Arming Sensor Bolt	25
Diagnostic Energy Reserve Module Screw	19
Forward Discriminating Sensor Bolt	25
Knee Bolster Screw	49
Passenger Compartment Discriminating Sensor Bolt	25
1993 Camaro & Firebird	
Arming Sensor Fastener	40
Forward Discriminating Sensor	89
Passenger Compartment Sensor	89
Passenger Inflator Module	25
Caprice, Custom Cruiser & Roadmaster	
Arming Sensor Mounting Screw	25
Diagnostic Energy Reserve Module Bracket Mounting Bolt ③	53
Diagnostic Energy Reserve Module Bracket Mounting Nut ②	17
Diagnostic Energy Reserve Module To Bracket Nut	17
Forward Discriminating Sensor Mounting Screw	25
Knee Bolster Deflector Mounting Bolt	89
Knee Bolster Mounting Bolt	53
Steering Column Lower Trim Panel Screw	17
Century & Cutlass Ciera/Cruiser	
DERM To Bracket Nuts	53
Front Discriminating Sensor Mounting Bolts	44
Passenger Compartment Discriminating Sensor Bolts	44
Corvette	
Arming Sensor Bolts	11 ①
Arming Sensor Nuts	107
Forward Discriminating Sensor Bolts ③	11 ①
Forward Discriminating Sensor Bolts ②	19 ①
Front Bumper Skid Bar To Drive Train & Front Suspension Frame Assembly Nuts	22 ①
Front Bumper Skid Bar To Power Steering Cooler Bolts	89
Front Bumper Skid Bar To Skid Plate Bracket Nuts	20 ①
Knee Bolster Inner Console Area Bolts ③	116
Knee Bolster Inner Console Area Bolts ②	89
Knee Bolster Outer Console Area Bolts ①	17 ①
I/P Inner Knee Bolster Bracket To Console Bracket Bolts ③	116

Component	Torque/Inch Lbs.
Corvette-Continued	
I/P Inner Knee Bolster Bracket To Console Bracket Bolts ②	89
I/P Inner Knee Bolster Bracket To Diagnostic Energy Reserve Module Bracket Area Bolts ③	116
I/P Inner Knee Bolster Bracket To Diagnostic Energy Reserve Module Bracket Area Bolts ②	89
DeVille & Fleetwood (FWD)	
BCM Retaining Nuts ③	33
DERM Nuts ③	35
DERM/BCM Bracket Screw ③	13
Dual Sensor ③	11 ①
Dual Sensor Pigtail Wiring To BCM Stud Nut ③	35
Forward Discriminating Sensor Bolts	82
Forward Discriminating Sensor Bracket Brace To Lower Radiator Tie Bar Bolts	84
Forward Discriminating Sensor Bracket To Brace Bolt	84
Forward Discriminating Sensor Bracket To Upper Radiator Tie Bolts	84
I/P Lower Brace Bolt	84
I/P Lower Brace Nut	84
I/P Column Reinforcement Plate Bolts	17
I/P Steering Column Filler Screws ③	13
Left Support Bracket Bolts ③	84
Passenger Compartment Discriminating/Arming Sensor Bolts	84
Resistor Module To BCM Stud Nut ③	35
Steering Column Upper Support Bracket Brace Assembly Bolts/Screws	84
Steering Column Upper Support Bracket Brace Assembly To Steering Column Upper Support Bracket Bolts	62
Eldorado & Seville	
Dual Pole Arming Sensor Mounting Bolts	98
Dual Sensor Mounting Bolts	98
Forward Discriminating Sensor Bracket Mounting Nuts & Bolts	98
Forward Discriminating Sensor Mounting Bolts	98
Left & Right Hand Discriminating Sensor Bolts ③	45
Passenger Inflator Module	18
Fleetwood (RWD)	
DERM Fasteners	17
Dual Pole Arming Sensor	25
Forward Discriminating Sensor	25
Passenger Inflator Module	89
Metro	
Arming Sensor Mounting Bolts	53
DERM Mounting Bracket Bolts ③	44
DERM To DERM Mounting Bracket Nuts ③	35
Forward Discriminating Sensor Mounting Bolts	98
Negative Battery Cable To Negative Battery Terminal Retainer ③	11 ①
Passenger Compartment Discriminating Sensor Mounting Bolts	53

Continued

TIGHTENING SPECIFICATIONS—Continued

Component	Torque/ Inch Lbs.
Park Avenue	
Dual Sensor Bolts ②	11 ①
Dual Sensor Bolts ③	84
Forward Discriminating Sensor Bracket Mounting Nuts & Bolts	84
Forward Discriminating Sensor Mounting Bolts ②	12 ①
Forward Discriminating Sensor Mounting Bolts ③	62
Inflator Module Bolts ②	17
Inflator Module Bolts ③	25
Knee Deflector Nuts & Bolts	89
Prizm	
Center Sensor Assembly Bolts	115
Console Mounting Bracket Bolts	89
Forward Sensor Bolts	18 ①
Inflator Module	78
Knee Bolster Bolts	89
LeSabre	
Dual Sensor Bolts	11 ①
Forward Discriminating Sensor Mounting Bolts	12 ①
Inflator Module Bolts	25
Knee Deflector Nuts & Bolts	89
Reatta, Riviera, Toronado & Trofeo	
Dual Sensor Mounting Bolts	98
Forward Discriminating Sensor Bracket Mounting Nuts & Bolts	98
Forward Discriminating Sensor Mounting Bolts	98
Storm	
Arming Sensor Mounting Bolts	89
Diagnostic Energy Reserve Module Yellow Bracket Retaining Nuts	35
Diagnostic Energy Reserve Module Yellow Bracket Retaining Screws	44
Forward Discriminating Sensor Mounting Bolts	97
Knee Bolster Assembly Retaining Nut & Bolt	89
Negative Battery Cable To Negative Battery Terminal Retainer ③	11 ①
Passenger Compartment Discriminating Sensor Mounting Bolts	89
1991 88	
Arming sensor Nuts	88

Component	Torque/ Inch Lbs.
1991 88-Continued	
Energy Reserve Module Screws	31
Forward Sensor Bolts	62
Forward Sensor Bracket Bolts	88
Passenger Compartment Sensor/Diagnostic Module Nuts	88
SIR Control Center Cover Screws	31
SIR Control Center Bracket Non-Self Tapping Screws	88
SIR Control Center Mounting Bracket Self Tapping Screw	44
SIR System Control Module Bolts	88
1991 98	
Diagnostic Energy Reserve Module Bolts	71
Diagnostic Energy Reserve Module Bracket Nut	35
Forward Discriminating Sensor Bolts	62
Forward Discriminating Sensor Bracket Bolts	84
Forward Discriminating Sensor Bracket Brace Bolts	84
Passenger Compartment Discriminating Sensor/ Arming Sensor Bolts	84
1992-93 88, 98 & Bonneville w/Single Airbag	
Forward Discriminating Sensor Bolts	12 ①
Forward Discriminating Sensor Bracket Bolts	84
Passenger Compartment Discriminating Sensor/ Arming Sensor Bolts	11 ①
Upper Radiator Tie Bar To Grill Reveal Molding Bolts	84
1992-93 Bonneville w/Dual Airbags	
Dual Pole Arming Sensor Bolts	53
Forward Discriminating Sensor Bolts	12 ①
Forward Discriminating Sensor Bracket Bolts	84
Passenger Compartment Discriminating Sensor Bolts	11 ①
Passenger Inflator Module Bolts	17
Passenger Inflator Module Nuts	89
Steering Column Support Bracket Brace To Pillar Panel Bolts	89
Steering Column Support Bracket Brace To Steering Column Support Bracket Bolts	62

① —Ft. lbs.
② —1991 only.
③ —1992-93 only.

1 FORWARD SENSOR
2 SIR WIRING HARNESS
3 INDICATOR LAMP
4 INFLATOR MODULE
5 PASSENGER COMPARTMENT SENSOR/ DIAGNOSTIC MODULE (PCSDM)
6 POWER SUPPLY MODULE
7 ARMING SENSOR
8 ENERGY RESERVE MODULE
9 TEST CONNECTOR
10 STEERING COLUMN AND COIL ASSEMBLY
11 STEERING WHEEL
12 KNEE BOLSTER
13 FUSE PANEL

Fig. 38   SIR component locations. 1991 88

1 FORWARD DISCRIMINATING SENSOR
2 DIAGNOSTIC ENERGY RESERVE MODULE (DERM)
3 RESISTOR MODULE
4 DUAL SENSOR
5 COIL ASSEMBLY
6 INFLATOR MODULE

Fig. 40   SIR component locations. 1992-93 88, 98 & Bonneville w/single airbag

1 INFLATOR MODULE
2 COIL ASSEMBLY
3 FORWARD DISCRIMINATING SENSOR
4 DUAL SENSOR
5 RESISTOR MODULE
6 DIAGNOSTIC ENERGY RESERVE MODULE (DERM)
7 INSTRUMENT PANEL

Fig. 39   SIR component locations. 1991 98

1 FORWARD DISCRIMINATING SENSOR
2 DIAGNOSTIC ENERGY RESERVE MODULE (DERM)
3 PASSENGER INFLATOR MODULE
4 PASSENGER COMPARTMENT DISCRIMINATING SENSOR
5 DUAL POLE ARMING SENSOR
6 COIL ASSEMBLY
7 DRIVER INFLATOR MODULE

Fig. 41   SIR component locations. 1992-93 Bonneville w/dual airbags

Fig. 42 SIR component locations. 1991 Reatta, Riviera, Toronado & Trofeo

Fig. 43 SIR component locations. 1992-93 Riviera, Toronado & Trofeo

① FORWARD DISCRIMINATING SENSOR
② DUAL SENSOR
③ SIR INFLATOR MODULE
④ SIR COIL ASSEMBLY
⑤ INDICATOR LAMP
⑥ DIAGNOSTIC/ENERGY RESERVE MODULE (DERM)
⑦ SIR RESISTOR MODULE
⑧ KNEE BOLSTER

900	RADIATOR CORE SUPPORT
901	HOOD LATCH
902	FORWARD DISCRIMINATING SENSOR
903	SIR HARNESS
904	ARMING SENSOR
905	EVAPORATOR CASE (IF EQUIPPED WITH A/C)
906	HEATER CASE
907	PASSENGER COMPARTMENT DISCRIMINATING SENSOR
908	RESISTOR MODULE
909	DERM
910	DERM MOUNTING BRACKET
911	INFLATOR MODULE
912	STEERING WHEEL
913	SIR COIL ASSEMBLY AND COMBINATION SWITCH ASSEMBLY
914	STEERING COLUMN

Fig. 44 SIR component locations. Metro

900	ARMING SENSOR
902	COWL PANEL
903	DERM CONNECTOR
904	CONSOLE BRACKET
905	DERM
906	STEERING WHEEL
907	SIR COIL ASSEMBLY (BEHIND STEERING WHEEL)
908	INFLATOR MODULE
909	TRANSAXLE CONTROL CABLE
910	PASSENGER COMPARTMENT DISCRIMINATING SENSOR
911	PASSENGER COMPARTMENT DISCRIMINATING SENSOR CONNECTOR
912	FLOOR PANEL
913	WIRING HARNESS RETAINER
914	JUNCTION CONNECTOR
915	RESISTOR MODULE
916	FORWARD DISCRIMINATING SENSOR CONNECTOR
917	FORWARD DISCRIMINATING SENSOR
918	CONDENSER FAN

Fig. 45 SIR component locations. Storm

Fig. 46 SIR component locations. Caprice, Custom Cruiser & Roadmaster

A	RADIATOR SUPPORT STRUCTURE	8	DERM
1	FORWARD DISCRIMINATING SENSOR	9	RESISTOR MODULE
2	FORWARD DISCRIMINATING SENSOR	13	SIR WIRING HARNESS
3	ARMING SENSOR	14	DERM CONNECTOR
4	COIL ASSEMBLY	15	RESISTOR MODULE CONNECTOR
5	INFLATOR MODULE	16	FUSE BLOCK

Fig. 47 SIR component locations. 1991 Eldorado & Seville

Fig. 48 SIR component locations. DeVille & Fleetwood

1	INFLATOR MODULE	4	DUAL SENSOR	6	DIAGNOSTIC ENERGY RESERVE MODULE (DERM)
2	COIL ASSEMBLY	5	RESISTOR MODULE	7	INSTRUMENT PANEL
3	FORWARD DISCRIMINATING SENSOR				

1	LH MIDRAIL SENSOR
2	FORWARD DISCRIMINATING SENSOR
3	RH MIDRAIL SENSOR
4	ARMING SENSOR
5	SIR INFLATOR MODULE
6	SIR COIL ASSEMBLY
7	INDICATOR LAMP
8	DIAGNOSTIC/ENERGY RESERVE MODULE (DERM)
9	SIR RESISTOR MODULE
10	KNEE BOLSTER

Fig. 49 SIR component locations. 1992 Eldorado & Seville

1 RESISTOR MODULE
2 RH FORWARD DISCRIMINATING SENSOR
3 ARMING SENSOR
4 DIAGNOSTIC ENERGY RESERVE MODULE (DERM)
5 INFLATABLE RESTRAINT WIRING HARNESS
6 YELLOW 2-WAY CONNECTOR AT THE BASE OF STEERING COLUMN
7 LH FORWARD DISCRIMINATING SENSOR
8 RH FRONT SIDE MEMBER
9 CENTRAL CONTROL MODULE (CCM)
10 INFLATOR MODULE
11 SIR COIL ASSEMBLY
12 LH FRONT SIDE MEMBER

Fig. 50 SIR component locations. Corvette

1 INFLATOR MODULE
2 RESISTOR MODULE
3 COIL ASSEMBLY
4 FORWARD DISCRIMINATING SENSOR
5 DIAGNOSTIC ENERGY RESERVE MODULE (DERM)
6 ARMING SENSOR
7 PASSENGER COMPARTMENT DISCRIMINATING SENSOR

Fig. 51 SIR component locations. Corsica & Beretta

FWD DISCRIMINATING SENSOR
DERM
COIL WIRE
RESISTOR MODULE
PASS CMPT DISCR SENSOR
INFLATOR MODULE
ARMING SENSOR

Fig. 52 SIR component locations. 1991-92 Camaro & Firebird

1 PASSENGER COMPARTMENT DISCRIMINATING SENSOR
2 STEERING COLUMN SUPPORT BRACKET
3 FRONT END TIE BAR
4 FORWARD DISCRIMINATING SENSOR
5 HVAC DUCT
6 DERM
7 SIR WIRING HARNESS
8 PASSENGER INFLATOR MODULE
9 LP COMPARTMENT DOOR ASSEMBLY
10 DUAL POLE ARMING SENSOR
11 FLOOR TUNNEL
12 SIR COIL ASSEMBLY
13 DRIVER INFLATOR MODULE
14 DRIVER INFLATOR MODULE HARNESS CONNECTOR

Fig. 53 SIR component locations. 1993 Camaro & Firebird

SUPPLEMENTAL INFLATABLE RESTRAINT (SIR) SYSTEM

Fig. 55   SIR component locations. 1993 Eldorado & Seville

1 LH MIDRAIL SENSOR
2 FORWARD DISCRIMINATING SENSOR
3 PASSENGER INFLATOR MODULE
4 PASSENGER INFLATOR MODULE CONNECTOR
5 "TRAP" DOOR
6 DUAL POLE ARMING SENSOR
7 DRIVER INFLATOR MODULE
8 SIR COIL ASSEMBLY
9 DERM
10 KNEE BOLSTER
11 SIR INDICATOR LAMP

Fig. 54   SIR component locations. Century & Cutlass Ciera/Cruiser

1 DERM
2 DERM BRACKET
3 DAYTIME RUNNING LAMPS (DRL) MODULE
4 AIR DISTRIBUTION DUCT
5 DATA LINK CONNECTOR
6 CRUISE CONTROL MODULE
7 FRONT END SUPPORT
8 FORWARD DISCRIMINATING SENSOR

9 SIR WIRING HARNESS
10 FORWARD LAMP INTERCONNECT
11 SIR COIL ASSEMBLY
12 INFLATOR MODULE
13 I/P CENTER SUPPORT
14 ARMING SENSOR
15 PASSENGER COMPARTMENT DISCRIMINATING SENSOR
16 TUNNEL

Fig. 57 SIR component locations. Prizm

903 CENTER SENSOR ASSEMBLY CONNECTOR B
904 CENTER SENSOR ASSEMBLY CONNECTOR
905 CENTER SENSOR ASSEMBLY
906 STEERING WHEEL
907 SRS COIL ASSEMBLY (BEHIND STEERING WHEEL)
908 INFLATOR MODULE
909 CENTER SENSOR ASSEMBLY CONNECTOR C
910 DRIVER'S SEAT
911 FRONT STRUT ASSEMBLY
912 WHEELWELL
916 FORWARD SENSOR CONNECTOR
917 FORWARD SENSOR

Fig. 56 SIR component locations. 1993 Fleetwood (RWD)

1 PASSENGER INFLATOR MODULE
2 CONNECTOR POSITION ASSURANCE (CPA)
3 PASSENGER INFLATOR MODULE JUMPER
4 PASSENGER INFLATOR MODULE BRACKET
5 INSTRUMENT PANEL
6 LH FORWARD DISCRIMINATING SENSOR
7 RH FORWARD DISCRIMINATING SENSOR
8 SIR WIRING HARNESS
9 SIR COIL ASSEMBLY
10 DRIVER INFLATOR MODULE
11 DRIVER INFLATOR MODULE HARNESS CONNECTOR
12 HORN LEAD
13 EBTCM
14 DERM
15 RAP POWER RELAY
16 DUAL POLE ARMING SENSOR
17 STEERING COLUMN SUPPORT

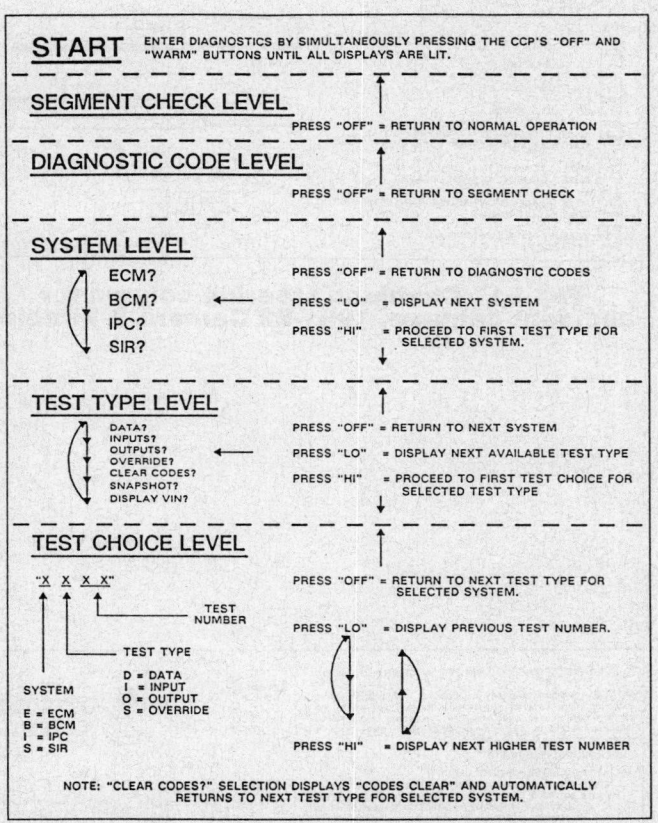

Fig. 58 On board diagnostics. 1991 Eldorado & Seville

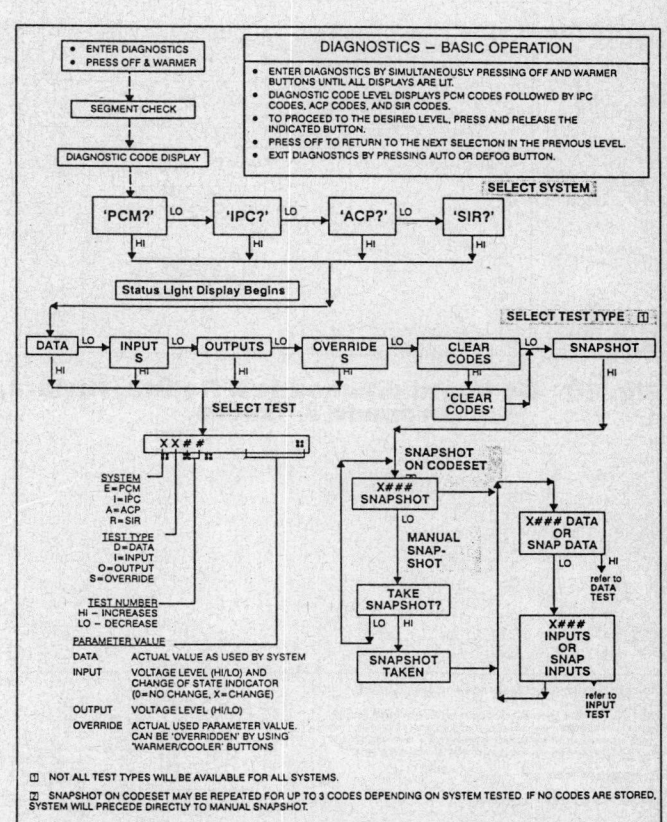

Fig. 59 On board diagnostics. 1992 Eldorado & Seville

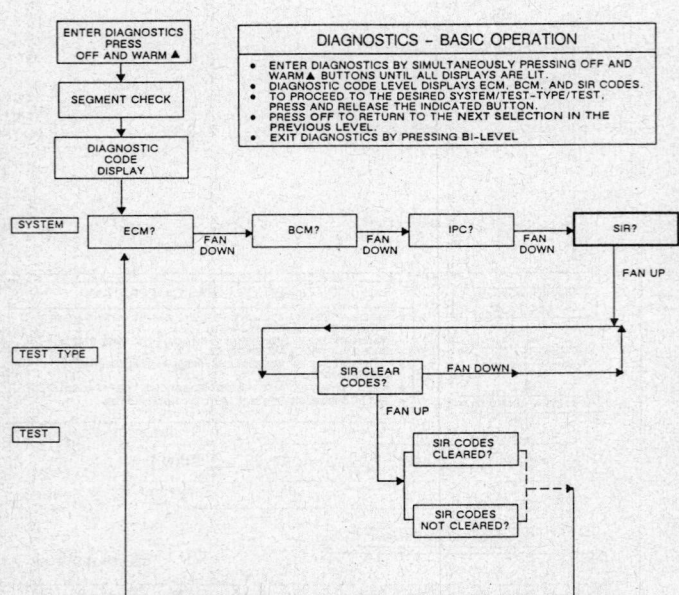

Fig. 60   On board diagnostics. Reatta, Riviera, Toronado & Trofeo

Fig. 61   Checking steering column for accident damage. 1991-92 Camaro & Firebird

Fig. 62   Checking steering column for accident damage. 1993 Camaro & Firebird

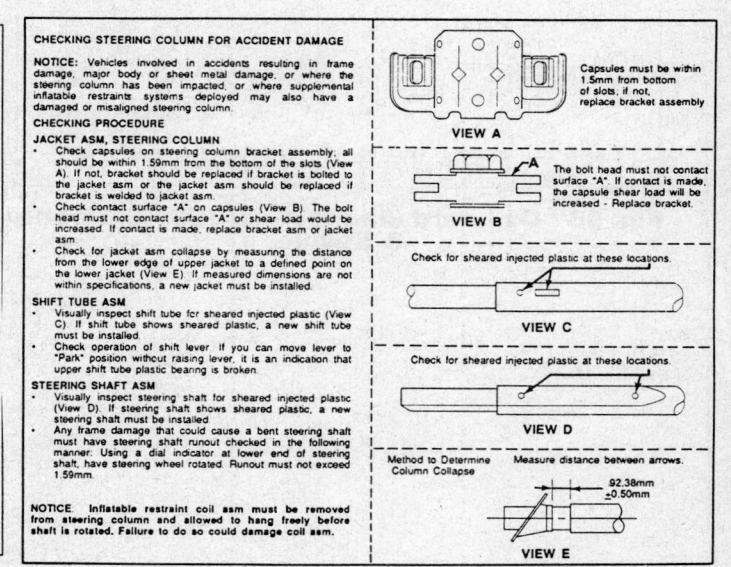

Fig. 63   Checking steering column for accident damage. 1991 Corsica & Beretta

Fig. 64   Checking steering column for accident damage. 1992-93 Corsica & Beretta

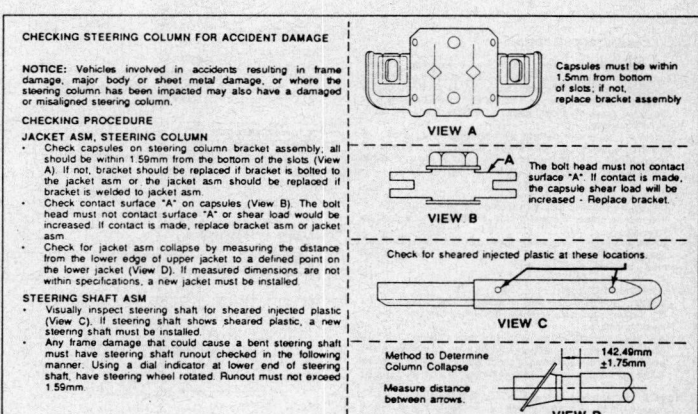

Fig. 65   Checking steering column for accident damage. 1991 Corvette

Fig. 66   Checking steering column for accident damage. 1992-93 Corvette

Fig. 67   Checking steering column for accident damage. Reatta & Riviera, 1991 Park Avenue, Toronado & Trofeo

CHECKING STEERING COLUMN FOR ACCIDENT DAMAGE

NOTICE: Vehicles involved in accidents resulting in frame damage, major body or sheet metal damage, or where the steering column has been impacted, or where supplemental inflatable restraints systems deployed may also have a damaged or misaligned steering column.

CHECKING PROCEDURE

JACKET ASM, STEERING COLUMN

- Check capsules on steering column bracket assembly; all must be securely seated in bracket slots and checked for any loose conditions when pushed or pulled by hand (View A). If not, bracket should be replaced if bracket is bolted to the jacket assembly or the jacket assembly should be replaced if bracket is welded to jacket assembly.
- Check for jacket asm collapse by measuring the distance from the lower edge of upper jacket to a defined point on the lower jacket (View D). If measured dimensions are not within specifications, a new jacket must be installed.

SHIFT TUBE ASM

- Visually inspect shift tube for sheared injected plastic (View B). If shift tube shows sheared plastic, a new shift tube must be installed.
- Check operation of shift lever. If you can move lever to "Park" position without raising lever, it is an indication that upper shift tube plastic bearing is broken.

STEERING SHAFT ASM

- Visually inspect steering shaft for sheared injected plastic (View C). If steering shaft shows sheared plastic, a new steering shaft must be installed.
- Any frame damage that could cause a bent steering shaft must have steering shaft runout checked in the following manner: Using a dial indicator at lower end of steering shaft, have steering wheel rotated. Runout must not exceed 1.59mm.

NOTICE: Inflatable restraint coil asm must be removed from steering column and allowed to hang freely before shaft is rotated. Failure to do so could damage coil asm.

VIEW A
(CAPSULES)
CHECK FOR ANY LOOSE CONDITION WHEN PUSHED OR PULLED BY HAND.

CHECK FOR SHEARED INJECTED PLASTIC AT THESE LOCATIONS.
VIEW B
(SHIFT TUBE)

CHECK FOR SHEARED INJECTED PLASTIC AT THESE LOCATIONS.
VIEW C
(STEERING SHAFT)

122.92 MM +/- .50 MM

VIEW D (METHOD TO DETERMINE COLUMN COLLAPSE) WITH LOWER BEARING REMOVED MEASURE DISTANCE BETWEEN ARROWS.

Fig. 68 Checking steering column for accident damage. 1992 Toronado & Trofeo

---

CHECKING STEERING COLUMN FOR ACCIDENT DAMAGE

NOTICE: Vehicles involved in accidents resulting in frame damage, major body or sheet metal damage, or where the steering column has been impacted, or where supplemental inflatable restraints systems deployed may also have a damaged or misaligned steering column.

CHECKING PROCEDURE

JACKET ASM, STEERING COLUMN

- Check capsules on steering column bracket assembly; all should be within 1.59mm from the bottom of the slots (View A). If not, bracket should be replaced if bracket is bolted to the jacket asm or the jacket asm should be replaced if bracket is welded to jacket asm.
- Check contact surface "A" on capsules (View B). The bolt head must not contact surface "A" or shear load would be increased. If contact is made, replace bracket asm or jacket asm.
- Check for jacket asm collapse by measuring the distance from the lower edge of upper jacket to a defined point on the lower jacket (View E). If measured dimensions are not within specifications, a new jacket must be installed.

SHIFT TUBE ASM

- Visually inspect shift tube for sheared injected plastic (View C). If shift tube shows sheared plastic, a new shift tube must be installed.
- Check operation of shift lever. If you can move lever to "Park" position without raising lever, it is an indication that upper shift tube plastic bearing is broken.

STEERING SHAFT ASM

- Visually inspect steering shaft for sheared injected plastic (View D). If steering shaft shows sheared plastic, a new steering shaft must be installed.
- Any frame damage that could cause a bent steering shaft must have steering shaft runout checked in the following manner: Using a dial indicator at lower end of steering shaft, have steering wheel rotated. Runout must not exceed 1.59mm.

NOTICE: Inflatable restraint coil asm must be removed from steering column and allowed to hang freely before shaft is rotated. Failure to do so could damage coil assembly.

1.59 MM

VIEW A
(CAPSULES)
CAPSULES MUST BE WITHIN 1.59 MM FROM BOTTOM OF SLOTS; IF NOT, REPLACE BRACKET OR JACKET.

VIEW B "A"
THE BOLT HEAD MUST NOT CONTACT SURFACE "A". IF CONTACT IS MADE, THE CAPSULE SHEAR LOAD WILL BE INCREASED. REPLACE BRACKET OR JACKET.

CHECK FOR SHEARED INJECTED PLASTIC AT THESE LOCATIONS.
VIEW C
(SHIFT TUBE)

CHECK FOR SHEARED INJECTED PLASTIC AT THESE LOCATIONS.
VIEW D
(STEERING SHAFT)

282.77 MM +/- .50 MM

VIEW E (METHOD TO DETERMINE COLUMN COLLAPSE) WITH LOWER BEARING REMOVED MEASURE DISTANCE BETWEEN ARROWS.

Fig. 69 Checking steering column for accident damage. Caprice, Custom Cruiser & Roadmaster

---

CHECKING STEERING COLUMN FOR ACCIDENT DAMAGE

NOTICE: Vehicles involved in accidents resulting in frame damage, major body or sheet metal damage, or where the steering column has been impacted may also have a damaged or misaligned steering column.

CHECKING PROCEDURE

JACKET ASM, STEERING COLUMN

- Check capsules on steering column bracket assembly; all should be within 1.59mm from the bottom of the slots (View A). If not, bracket should be replaced if bracket is bolted to the jacket asm or the jacket asm should be replaced if bracket is welded to jacket asm.
- Check contact surface "A" on capsules (View B). The bolt head must not contact surface "A" or shear load would be increased. If contact is made, replace bracket asm or jacket asm.
- Check for jacket asm collapse by measuring the distance from the lower edge of upper jacket to a defined point on the lower jacket (View E). If measured dimensions are not within specifications, a new jacket must be installed.

SHIFT TUBE ASM

- Visually inspect shift tube for sheared injected plastic (View C). If shift tube shows sheared plastic, a new shift tube must be installed.
- Check operation of shift lever. If you can move lever to "Park" position without raising lever, it is an indication that upper shift tube plastic bearing is broken.

STEERING SHAFT ASM

- Visually inspect steering shaft for sheared injected plastic (View D). If steering shaft shows sheared plastic, a new steering shaft must be installed.
- Any frame damage that could cause a bent steering shaft must have steering shaft runout checked in the following manner: Using a dial indicator at lower end of steering shaft, have steering wheel rotated. Runout must not exceed 1.59mm.

1.59 MM

VIEW A
(CAPSULES)
CAPSULES MUST BE WITHIN 1.59 MM FROM BOTTOM OF SLOTS; IF NOT, REPLACE BRACKET OR JACKET.

VIEW B "A"
THE BOLT HEAD MUST NOT CONTACT SURFACE "A". IF CONTACT IS MADE, THE CAPSULE SHEAR LOAD WILL BE INCREASED. REPLACE BRACKET OR JACKET.

CHECK FOR SHEARED INJECTED PLASTIC AT THESE LOCATIONS.
VIEW C
(SHIFT TUBE)

CHECK FOR SHEARED INJECTED PLASTIC AT THESE LOCATIONS.
VIEW D
(STEERING SHAFT)

114.85 MM +/- .50 MM

VIEW E (METHOD TO DETERMINE COLUMN COLLAPSE) WITH BEARING REMOVED MEASURE DISTANCE BETWEEN ARROWS.

Fig. 70 Checking steering column for accident damage. Century & Cutlass Ciera/Cruiser

---

CHECKING STEERING COLUMN FOR ACCIDENT DAMAGE

NOTICE: Vehicles involved in accidents resulting in frame damage, major body or sheet metal damage, or where the steering column has been impacted, or where supplemental inflatable restraints systems deployed may also have a damaged or misaligned steering column.

CHECKING PROCEDURE

JACKET ASM, STEERING COLUMN

- Check capsules on steering column bracket assembly; all should be within 1.5mm from the bottom of the slots (View A). If not, bracket should be replaced if bracket is bolted to the jacket asm or the jacket asm should be replaced if bracket is welded to jacket asm.
- Check contact surface "A" on capsules (View B). The bolt head must not contact surface "A". If contact is made, the capsule shear load would be increased. If contact is made, replace bracket asm or jacket asm.
- Check for jacket asm collapse by measuring the distance from the lower edge of upper jacket to a defined point on the lower jacket (View E). If measured dimensions are not within specifications, a new jacket must be installed.

SHIFT TUBE ASM

- Visually inspect shift tube for sheared injected plastic (View C). If shift tube shows sheared plastic, a new shift tube must be installed.
- Check operation of shift lever. If you can move lever to "Park" position without raising lever, it is an indication that upper shift tube plastic bearing is broken.

STEERING SHAFT ASM

- Visually inspect steering shaft for sheared injected plastic (View D). If steering shaft shows sheared plastic, a new steering shaft must be installed.
- Any frame damage that could cause a bent steering shaft must have steering shaft runout checked in the following manner: Using a dial indicator at lower end of steering shaft, have steering wheel rotated. Runout must not exceed 1.59mm.

NOTICE: Inflatable restraint coil asm must be removed from steering column and allowed to hang freely before shaft is rotated. Failure to do so could damage coil asm.

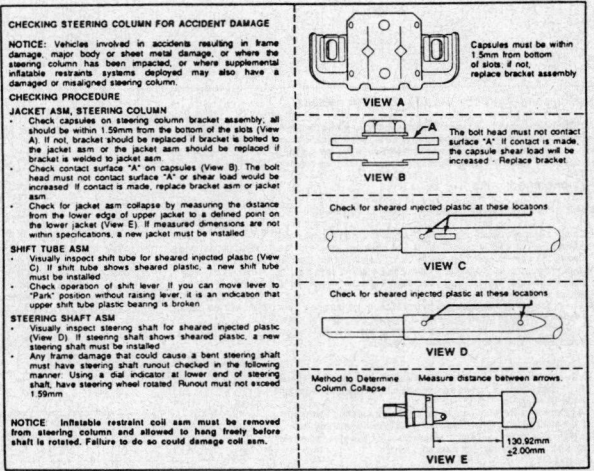

VIEW A
Capsules must be within 1.5mm from bottom of slots; if not, replace bracket assembly

VIEW B "A"
The bolt head must not contact surface "A". If contact is made, the capsule shear load will be increased - Replace bracket

Check for sheared injected plastic at these locations
VIEW C

Check for sheared injected plastic at these locations
VIEW D

Method to Determine Column Collapse   Measure distance between arrows.

VIEW E
130.92mm ±2.00mm

Fig. 71 Checking steering column for accident damage. 88, 98, 1991 DeVille & Fleetwood, 1992-93 Bonneville, LeSabre & Park Avenue

CHECKING STEERING COLUMN FOR ACCIDENT DAMAGE

NOTICE: Vehicles involved in accidents resulting in frame damage, major body or sheet metal damage, or where the steering column has been impacted, or where supplemental inflatable restraints deployed may also have a damaged or misaligned steering column.

CHECKING PROCEDURE

JACKET ASM, STEERING COLUMN
- Check capsules on steering column bracket assembly; all should be within 1.59mm from the bottom of the slots (View A). If not, bracket should be replaced if bracket is bolted to the jacket asm or the jacket asm should be replaced if bracket is welded to jacket asm.
- Check contact surface "A" on capsules (View B). The bolt head must not contact surface "A" or shear load would be increased. If contact is made, replace bracket asm or jacket asm.
- Check for jacket asm collapse by measuring the distance from the lower edge of upper jacket to a defined point on the lower jacket (View E). If measured dimensions are not within specifications, a new jacket must be installed.

SHIFT TUBE ASM
- Visually inspect shift tube for sheared injected plastic (View C). If shift tube shows sheared plastic, a new shift tube must be installed.
- Check operation of shift lever. If you can move lever to "Park" position without raising lever, it is an indication that upper shift tube plastic bearing is broken.

STEERING SHAFT ASM
- Visually inspect steering shaft for sheared injected plastic (View D). If steering shaft shows sheared plastic, a new steering shaft must be installed.
- Any frame damage that could cause a bent steering shaft must have steering shaft runout checked in the following manner: Using a dial indicator at lower end of steering shaft, have steering wheel rotated. Runout must not exceed 1.59mm.

NOTICE: Inflatable restraint coil asm must be removed from steering column and allowed to hang freely before shaft is rotated. Failure to do so could damage coil asm.

VIEW A

Capsules must be within 1.5mm from bottom of slots; if not, replace bracket assembly

VIEW B

The bolt head must not contact surface "A". If contact is made, the capsule shear load will be increased - Replace bracket.

Check for sheared injected plastic at these locations.

VIEW C

Check for sheared injected plastic at these locations.

VIEW D

Method to Determine Column Collapse — Measure distance between arrows.

132.60mm ±.50mm

VIEW E

Fig. 72 Checking steering column for accident damage. 1991 Eldorado & Seville

CHECKING STEERING COLUMN FOR ACCIDENT DAMAGE

NOTICE: Vehicles involved in accidents resulting in frame damage, major body or sheet metal damage, or where the steering column has been impacted, or where supplemental inflatable restraints systems deployed may also have a damaged or misaligned steering column.

CHECKING PROCEDURE

JACKET ASM, STEERING COLUMN
- Check capsules on steering column bracket assembly; all must be securely seated in bracket slots and checked for any loose conditions when pushed or pulled by hand (View A). If not, bracket should be replaced if bracket is bolted to the jacket assembly or the jacket assembly should be replaced if bracket is welded to jacket assembly.
- Check for jacket asm collapse by measuring the distance from the lower edge of upper jacket to a defined point on the lower jacket (View D). If measured dimensions are not within specifications, a new jacket must be installed.

SHIFT TUBE ASM
- Visually inspect shift tube for sheared injected plastic (View B). If shift tube shows sheared plastic, a new shift tube must be installed.
- Check operation of shift lever. If you can move lever to "Park" position without raising lever, it is an indication that upper shift tube plastic bearing is broken.

STEERING SHAFT ASM
- Visually inspect steering shaft for sheared injected plastic (View C). If steering shaft shows sheared plastic, a new steering shaft must be installed.
- Any frame damage that could cause a bent steering shaft must have steering shaft runout checked in the following manner: Using a dial indicator at lower end of steering shaft, have steering wheel rotated. Runout must not exceed 1.59mm.

NOTICE: Inflatable restraint coil asm must be removed from steering column and allowed to hang freely before shaft is rotated. Failure to do so could damage coil asm.

VIEW A (CAPSULES)
CHECK FOR ANY LOOSE CONDITION WHEN PUSHED OR PULLED BY HAND

CHECK FOR SHEARED INJECTED PLASTIC AT THESE LOCATIONS.
VIEW B (SHIFT TUBE)

CHECK FOR SHEARED INJECTED PLASTIC AT THESE LOCATIONS.
VIEW C (STEERING SHAFT)

127.13 MM +/- .50 MM

VIEW D (METHOD TO DETERMINE COLUMN COLLAPSE) MEASURE DISTANCE BETWEEN ARROWS.

Fig. 73 Checking steering column for accident damage. 1992-93 Eldorado & Seville

A   532.5 mm (20.96 INCHES)
1   STEERING COLUMN

Fig. 74 Checking steering column for accident damage. 1991 Metro

315

A

A   528 mm (20.79")
315 STEERING COLUMN

Fig. 75 Checking steering column for accident damage. 1992-93 Metro

FRT

8   ARMING SENSOR
22   FLOOR TUNNEL
23   CONNECTOR POSITION ASSURANCE
24   ELECTRICAL CONNECTOR
25   BOLT
26   CONSOLE MOUNTING BRACKET

Fig. 76 Arming sensor removal. 1991-92 Camaro & Firebird

A   STEERING COLUMN SUPPORT
4   ARMING SENSOR
11   SCREW

Fig. 77 Arming sensor removal. Caprice, Custom Cruiser & Roadmaster

Fig. 78   Arming sensor removal. Corvette

1	DERM
2	INSULATOR
3	FASTENERS • IF 2 BOLTS TIGHTEN TO 14 N·m (11 lb. ft.) • IF 2 NUTS TIGHTEN TO 12 N·m (107 lb. in.)
4	ARMING SENSOR
5	DERM BRACKET
6	INSULATORS
7	DERM RETAINER
8	DERM BOLTS

Fig. 79   Circuit test connector location. 1991 88

1	CONNECTOR POSITION ASSURANCE (CPA)
2	PASSENGER COMPARTMENT DISCRIMINATING SENSOR CONNECTOR
3	PASSENGER COMPARTMENT DISCRIMINATING SENSOR
4	PLASTIC WIRE ROUTING CONDUITS
5	BOLTS
6	NUT

Fig. 80   Passenger compartment sensor removal. Beretta & Corsica

1	FORWARD DISCRIMINATING SENSOR
2	BOLT
3	BOLT
4	FORWARD DISCRIMINATING SENSOR BRACKET
5	BRACE
6	CLIP

Fig. 82   Forward sensor removal. 1991 DeVille, Fleetwood, Park Avenue & 98

7	FORWARD DISCRIMINATING SENSOR
9	BOLT
10	RADIATOR SUPPORT
11	ELECTRICAL CONNECTOR
12	CONNECTOR POSITION ASSURANCE

Fig. 81   Forward sensor removal. 1991-92 Camaro & Firebird

1	ENGINE COOLING FAN
2	FORWARD SENSOR

Fig. 83   Forward sensor removal. Storm

8	BRACKET
9	TIE BAR
10	KNEE BOLSTER
11	SCREW COVER
12	SCREW
13	NUT

Fig. 84   Knee bolster replacement. 1991-92 Camaro & Firebird

1. NUT
2. KNEE BOLSTER (TIE BAR)
3. SCREW
4. BOLT
5. BOLT
6. BRACKET; FUSE BLOCK
7. SCREW; 1.9 N•M (17 LB-IN)
8. BRACKET; TWILIGHT SENTINEL

Fig. 85   Knee bolster replacement. DeVille & Fleetwood

1	INSTRUMENT PANEL
2	KNEE BOLSTER
3	SCREWS

Fig. 86   Knee bolster replacement. Riviera & Reatta

1. DASH
2. RESISTOR MODULE
3. NUT; 4 N•M (30 LB-FT)
4. BCM/DERM BRACKET
5. BOLT/SCREW
6. DIAGNOSTIC ENERGY RESERVE MODULE

Fig. 87   DERM replacement. Beretta, Corsica, DeVille & Fleetwood

4	DERM MODULE
13	INSTRUMENT PANEL
15	SCREW
16	INSTRUMENT PANEL TIE BAR

Fig. 88   DERM replacement. 1991-92 Camaro & Firebird

| 1 | MOUNTING BRACKET |
| 2 | DERM |

Fig. 89   DERM replacement. Eldorado, Riviera, Reatta, Seville, Toronado & Trofeo

1   RESISTOR MODULE

Fig. 90   Resistor module replacement. Beretta & Corsica

2	RESISTOR MODULE
13	INSTRUMENT PANEL
17	LEFT SIDE TIE BAR
18	CONNECTOR POSITION ASSURANCE

Fig. 91   Resistor module replacement. 1991-92 Camaro & Firebird

1. SIR DUAL SENSOR
2. SIR DUAL SENSOR CONNECTOR
3. BODY COMPUTER MODULE
4. SIR RESISTOR MODULE CONNECTOR
5. SIR RESISTOR MODULE
6. BODY COMPUTER MODULE CONNECTORS
7. AUTO DOOR LOCK MODULE
8. AIR CONDITIONING WIRING
9. ROOF AND HEADER WIRING
10. BODY HARNESS
11. RELAY PANEL ASSEMBLY
12. SCREW; 1.4 N•M (12 LB-IN)
13. ILLUMINATED ENTRY MODULE
14. ILLUMINATED ENTRY MODULE CONNECTOR
16. COURTESY LAMP
17. DOOR LOCK RELAY WIRING
18. DOOR LOCK RELAY
19. PROGRAMMER CONNECTOR
20. PROGRAMMER
21. DIAGNOSTIC ENERGY RESERVE MODULE CONNECTOR
22. DIAGNOSTIC ENERGY RESERVE MODULE

Fig. 92   Resistor module replacement. DeVille & Fleetwood

Automatic Safety Belt System

INDEX

DESCRIPTION

BROUGHAM

The automatic safety belt system allows the safety belts to remained fastened while occupants enter and exit the vehicle. The main components of the system include a passive restraint module, left hand and right hand door latch switches and left hand and right hand shoulder and lap belt retractor solenoids. The purpose of the system is to keep the safety belt retractor mechanisms from locking up while the front doors are being opened and closed.

Battery voltage is applied, at all times, to both door latch switches. Whenever a front door is opened, the front door latch switch closes, voltage is applied through the switch to the passive restraint module, and the module detects a door ajar input. When the input is detected, the passive restraint module applies battery voltage to the shoulder and lap belt retractor solenoids. The retractor solenoids are permanently grounded so they become energized as soon as voltage is applied from the passive restraint module. When the retractor solenoids are energized, the safety belt lock mechanisms are disabled. Therefore, when a front door is opened, the safety belt for that door will not be allowed to lock up and interfere with normal opening and closing of the door. The passive restraint module continues to apply battery voltage to the belt retractor solenoids for 1.5 to 5.5 seconds after both front doors have been closed. This time-out period prevents the safety belts from locking up in a door slamming or immediate door reopening situations.

In addition to receiving an input from the door latch switches, the passive restraint module also receives a vehicle speed signal from the vehicle speed sensor buffer. Whenever the passive restraint module determines a vehicle speed of over two miles per hour, the battery voltage signal applied to the belt retractor solenoids is cancelled. This feature ensures safety belt lockup whenever the vehicle is in motion, regardless of input from the door latch switches or the 1.5 to 5.5 second timer.

In order to provide constant operation, the passive restraint module receives battery voltage at all times and is permanently grounded.

LEMANS

The automatic safety belt system consists of a shoulder belt mounted to a carrier which moves along a guide rail between the A and B-pillars. When the front doors are opened, the shoulder belts move to the A-pillar. When the ignition switch is turned to "ON," the belts move to the B-pillar. This system also incorporates active lap belts which must be used with the motorized shoulder belts.

DIAGNOSIS & TESTING

BROUGHAM

Refer to wiring circuit, **Fig. 1**, and system diagnosis chart, **Fig. 2**, when diagnosing this system.

LEMANS

Refer to wiring circuit, **Fig. 3**, when performing the following diagnosis and testing procedures. Refer to the symptom table, **Fig. 4**, and related tests, **Figs. 5 through 14**, as directed.

COMPONENT REPLACEMENT

LEMANS

GUIDE RAIL

1. With belt locked at B-pillar, disconnect battery ground cable.
2. Remove shoulder belt from carrier.

3. **On hatchback models,** remove upper quarter trim panel.
4. **On all models,** remove guide rail trim panel.
5. Remove upper and lower bolts retaining lock mechanism.
6. Remove warning lamp switch from lock mechanism, then remove lock mechanism.
7. Loosen five retaining screws and remove guide rail.
8. Reverse procedure to install, noting the following:
   a. **Torque** mechanism to guide rail bolts to 26 ft. lbs.

DRIVE MOTOR ASSEMBLY

Hatchback

1. Disconnect battery ground cable.
2. Remove guide rail.
3. Remove bolts retaining drive motor and locking section.
4. Remove assembly by pulling down while turning the locking section 180°.
5. Reverse procedure to install, noting the following:
   a. **Torque** drive motor mounting bolts to 26 ft. lbs.
   b. **Torque** locking section mounting bolts to 15 ft. lbs.

Sedan

1. With belt locked at B-pillar, disconnect battery ground cable.
2. Remove front and rear sill plates.
3. Remove B-pillar upper and lower trim.
4. Remove two bolts, one screw and locking mechanism from guide rail.
5. Disconnect metal retaining clip and remove drive motor mounting nut.
6. Remove drive motor and disconnect electrical connector.
7. Reverse procedure to install, noting the following:
   a. **Torque** drive motor retaining nut to 26 ft. lbs.
   b. **Torque** locking mechanism screw and bolts to 15 ft. lbs.

Fig. 1 Automatic safety belt wiring circuit (Part 1 of 2). Brougham

Fig. 1   Automatic safety belt wiring circuit (Part 2 of 2). Brougham

TEST		RESULT	ACTION
A1.	Open LH front door. Backprobe PASSIVE RESTRAINT MODULE connector with a digital multimeter from cavity 3 to chassis ground. Measure voltage.	Less than 10.0 volts.	GO TO A11.
		More than 10.0 volts.	Leave multimeter connected and GO TO A2.
A2.	Close LH front door and wait 10 seconds. Measure voltage from PASSIVE RESTRAINT MODULE connector cavity 3 to chassis ground with all doors closed.	More than 10.0 volts.	GO TO A16.
		Less than 10.0 volts.	Leave multimeter connected and GO TO A3.
A3.	Open RH front door. Measure voltage from PASSIVE RESTRAINT MODULE connector cavity 3 to chassis ground.	Less than 10.0 volts.	GO TO A20.
		More than 10.0 volts.	Leave multimeter connected, close RH front door and GO TO A4.
A4.	Raise both rear wheels. Open LH front door. Start engine and place gear selector in "D." Increase rear wheel speed to 5 mph. Measure voltage from PASSIVE RESTRAINT MODULE connector cavity 3 to chassis ground.	More than 10.0 volts.	GO TO A22.
		Less than 10.0 volts.	Leave multimeter connected and GO TO A5.

Fig. 2   Automatic safety belt diagnostic chart (Part 1 of 5). Brougham

TEST	RESULT	ACTION
A5. Apply brake and reduce wheel speed to 0 mph. Place gear selector in "P." Measure voltage from PASSIVE RESTRAINT MODULE connector cavity 3 to chassis ground with LH front door still open.	More than 10.0 volts.	Replace PASSIVE RESTRAINT MODULE.
	Less than 10.0 volts.	Leave multimeter connected and GO TO A6.
A6. Turn ignition switch to "OFF." Close LH front door, wait 10 seconds and reopen LH front door. Measure voltage from PASSIVE RESTRAINT MODULE connector cavity 3 to chassis ground.	Less than 10.0 volts.	Replace PASSIVE RESTRAINT MODULE.
	More than 10.0 volts.	GO TO A7.
A7. Disconnect PASSIVE RESTRAINT MODULE connector. Disconnect LH FRONT SHOULDER BELT RETRACTOR SOLENOID. Connect a fused jumper from PASSIVE RESTRAINT MODULE connector cavity 1 to cavity 3. Listen for LH FRONT LAP BELT RETRACTOR SOLENOID operation while connecting jumper.	SOLENOID does not operate (Ltr Fuse or jumper fuse opens).	Repair short to ground in YEL (528) wire between PASSIVE RESTRAINT MODULE and SOLENOIDS.
	SOLENOID does not operate (fuses do not open).	Leave jumper connected and GO TO A24.
	SOLENOID operates.	Remove jumper and GO TO A8.
A8. Connect LH FRONT SHOULDER BELT RETRACTOR SOLENOID connector. Disconnect LH FRONT LAP BELT RETRACTOR SOLENOID connector. Reconnect fused jumper from PASSIVE RESTRAINT MODULE connector cavity 1 to cavity 3 and listen for LH FRONT SHOULDER BELT RETRACTOR SOLENOID operation.	SOLENOID does not operate.	Leave jumper connected and GO TO A26.
	SOLENOID operates.	Remove jumper and GO TO A9.
A9. Disconnect RH FRONT SHOULDER BELT RETRACTOR SOLENOID connector. Reconnect fused jumper from PASSIVE RESTRAINT MODULE connector cavity 1 to cavity 3. Listen for RH FRONT LAP BELT RETRACTOR SOLENOID operation while connecting jumper.	SOLENOID does not operate.	Leave jumper connected and GO TO A28.
	SOLENOID operates.	Remove jumper and GO TO A10.
A10. Connect RH FRONT SHOULDER BELT RETRACTOR SOLENOID connector. Disconnect RH FRONT LAP BELT RETRACTOR SOLENOID connector. Reconnect fused jumper from PASSIVE RESTRAINT MODULE connector cavity 1 to cavity 3 and listen for RH FRONT SHOULDER BELT RETRACTOR SOLENOID operation.	SOLENOID does not operate.	Leave jumper connected and GO TO A30.
	SOLENOID operates.	All systems diagnosed in this cell are functioning normally.

Fig. 2   Automatic safety belt diagnostic chart (Part 2 of 5). Brougham

TEST	RESULT	ACTION
A11. Disconnect PASSIVE RESTRAINT MODULE connector. Connect a digital multimeter from connector cavity 1 to chassis ground. Measure voltage.	Less than 10.0 volts.	Repair open in ORN (40) wire between FUSE BLOCK and PASSIVE RESTRAINT MODULE.
	More than 10.0 volts.	GO TO A12.
A12. Connect a digital multimeter from PASSIVE RESTRAINT MODULE connector cavity 5 to chassis ground. Measure resistance.	More than 0.3 ohms.	Repair BLK (151) ground wire.
	Less than 0.3 ohms.	GO TO A13.
A13. Connect a digital multimeter from PASSIVE RESTRAINT MODULE connector cavity 4 to chassis ground. Measure voltage with LH front door open.	More than 10.0 volts.	Check circuit (528) for a short to ground. If OK, replace PASSIVE RESTRAINT MODULE.
	Less than 10.0 volts.	GO TO A14.
A14. Backprobe LH FRONT DOOR LATCH SWITCH connector with a digital multimeter from cavity B to chassis ground. Measure voltage with LH front door open.	More than 10.0 volts.	Repair open in PNK (527) wire.
	Less than 10.0 volts.	GO TO A15.
A15. Backprobe LH FRONT DOOR LATCH SWITCH connector with a digital multimeter from cavity A to chassis ground. Measure voltage.	More than 10.0 volts.	Replace LH FRONT DOOR LATCH SWITCH.
	Less than 10.0 volts.	Repair open in ORN (340) or (40) wire between FUSE BLOCK and LH FRONT DOOR LATCH SWITCH.
A16. Disconnect PASSIVE RESTRAINT MODULE connector. Connect a digital multimeter from connector cavity 3 to chassis ground. Measure voltage.	More than 10.0 volts.	Repair short to voltage in YEL (528) wire.
	Less than 10.0 volts.	GO TO A17.
A17. Connect a digital multimeter from PASSIVE RESTRAINT MODULE connector cavity 4 to chassis ground. Measure voltage with both front doors closed.	Less than 10.0 volts.	Replace PASSIVE RESTRAINT MODULE.
	More than 10.0 volts.	Leave multimeter connected and GO TO A18.
A18. Disconnect LH FRONT DOOR LATCH SWITCH connector. Measure voltage from PASSIVE RESTRAINT MODULE connector cavity 4 to chassis ground.	Less than 10.0 volts.	Replace LH FRONT DOOR LATCH SWITCH.
	More than 10.0 volts.	GO TO A19.

Fig. 2   Automatic safety belt diagnostic chart (Part 3 of 5). Brougham

TEST	RESULT	ACTION
A19. Disconnect RH FRONT DOOR LATCH SWITCH connector. Measure voltage from PASSIVE RESTRAINT MODULE connector cavity 4 to chassis ground.	Less than 10.0 volts.	Replace RH FRONT DOOR LATCH SWITCH.
	More than 10.0 volts.	Repair short to voltage in PNK (527) wire.
A20. Backprobe RH FRONT DOOR LATCH SWITCH connector with a digital multimeter from cavity B to chassis ground. Measure voltage with RH front door open.	More than 10.0 volts.	Repair open in PNK (527) wire between RH FRONT DOOR LATCH SWITCH and C305.
	Less than 10.0 volts.	GO TO A21.
A21. Backprobe RH FRONT DOOR LATCH SWITCH connector with a digital multimeter from cavity A to chassis ground. Measure voltage.	More than 10.0 volts.	Replace RH FRONT DOOR LATCH SWITCH.
	Less than 10.0 volts.	Repair open in ORN (40) wire between S301 and RH FRONT DOOR LATCH SWITCH.
A22. Turn ignition switch to "OFF." Lower the vehicle so that only the RH rear wheel is capable of spinning. (Keep the LH rear wheel in contact with the floor while leaving some clearance between the floor and the RH rear wheel.) Backprobe PASSIVE RESTRAINT MODULE connector with a digital multimeter from cavity 2 to chassis ground. Turn ignition switch to "RUN" (do not start engine) and observe voltage reading while manually rotating RH rear wheel with gear selector in "DRIVE."	Voltage fluctuates from greater than 8 volts to less than 3 volts while RH rear wheel is rotated.	Replace PASSIVE RESTRAINT MODULE.
	Voltage does not fluctuate.	GO TO A23.
A23. Disconnect PASSIVE RESTRAINT MODULE connector and VEHICLE SPEED SENSOR BUFFER connector C1. Connect a digital multimeter from PASSIVE RESTRAINT MODULE connector cavity 2 to cavity C of VEHICLE SPEED SENSOR BUFFER connector C1. Measure resistance.	More than 0.3 ohms.	Repair LT BLU/BLK (824) wire between PASSIVE RESTRAINT MODULE and VEHICLE SPEED SENSOR BUFFER.
	Less than 0.3 ohms.	Repair terminal contact at cavity 2.
A24. Disconnect LH FRONT LAP BELT RETRACTOR SOLENOID connector. Connect a digital multimeter from connector cavity A to chassis ground. Measure voltage.	Less than 10.0 volts.	Repair open in YEL (528) wire between PASSIVE RESTRAINT MODULE and LH FRONT LAP BELT RETRACTOR SOLENOID.
	More than 10.0 volts.	Go to A25.

Fig. 2   Automatic safety belt diagnostic chart (Part 4 of 5). Brougham

TEST	RESULT	ACTION
A25. Connect a digital multimeter from LH FRONT LAP BELT RETRACTOR SOLENOID connector cavity B to chassis ground. Measure resistance.	More than 0.3 ohms.	Repair BLK (150) ground wire.
	Less than 0.3 ohms	Replace LH SAFETY BELT RETRACTOR ASSEMBLY.
A26. Disconnect LH FRONT SHOULDER BELT RETRACTOR SOLENOID connector. Connect a digital multimeter from connector cavity A to chassis ground. Measure voltage.	Less than 10.0 volts	Repair open in YEL (528) wire between S515 and LH FRONT SHOULDER BELT RETRACTOR SOLENOID
	More than 10.0 volts.	GO TO A27
A27. Connect a digital multimeter from LH FRONT SHOULDER BELT RETRACTOR SOLENOID connector cavity B to chassis ground. Measure resistance.	More than 0.3 ohms.	Repair BLK (150) ground wire.
	Less than 0.3 ohms.	Replace LH SAFETY BELT RETRACTOR ASSEMBLY.
A28. Disconnect RH FRONT LAP BELT RETRACTOR SOLENOID connector. Connect a digital multimeter from connector cavity A to chassis ground. Measure voltage.	Less than 10.0 volts.	Repair open in YEL (528) wire between S615 and RH FRONT LAP BELT RETRACTOR SOLENOID.
	More than 10.0 volts	GO TO A29
A29. Connect a digital multimeter from RH FRONT LAP BELT RETRACTOR SOLENOID connector cavity B to chassis ground. Measure resistance.	More than 0.3 ohms.	Repair BLK (150) ground wire.
	Less than 0.3 ohms.	Replace RH SAFETY BELT RETRACTOR ASSEMBLY.
A30. Disconnect RH FRONT SHOULDER BELT RETRACTOR SOLENOID connector. Connect a digital multimeter from connector cavity A to chassis ground. Measure voltage.	Less than 10.0 volts.	Repair open in YEL (528) wire between S615 and RH FRONT SHOULDER BELT RETRACTOR SOLENOID.
	More than 10.0 volts.	GO TO A31.
A31. Connect a digital multimeter from RH FRONT SHOULDER BELT RETRACTOR SOLENOID connector cavity B to chassis ground. Measure resistance.	More than 0.3 ohms.	Repair BLK (150) ground wire.
	Less than 0.3 ohms.	Replace RH SAFETY BELT RETRACTOR ASSEMBLY.

Fig. 2   Automatic safety belt diagnostic chart (Part 5 of 5). Brougham

Fig. 3   Automatic safety belt wiring circuit (Part 1 of 2). LeMans

Fig. 3   Automatic safety belt wiring circuit (Part 2 of 2). LeMans

SYMPTOM	DO TEST
Neither belt operates	A: Power and Ground Test
One belt remains in position at A-PILLAR	C: Shoulder Belt Motor and Switch Test
LAP BELTS Indicator remains on or does not come on	E: LAP BELTS Indicator Test F: Safety Belts Switch Test
Shoulder Belt Warning Indicator remains on after belt reaches B-PILLAR	B: Shoulder Belt Warning Indicator Test
Belt does not move freely while traveling on track	D: Belt Retractor Solenoid Test
Shoulder Belt Warning Indicator does not light	B: Shoulder Belt Warning Indicator Test

Fig. 4   Symptom table. LeMans

Measure: VOLTAGE
At: PASSIVE RESTRAINT CONTROL MODULE (Disconnected)
Condition:
- **Ignition Switch: RUN**

Measure Between	Correct Voltage	For Diagnosis
17 (RED/WHT) & Ground	Battery	See 1
17 (RED/WHT) & 22 (BLK)	Battery	See 2
20 (RED) & Ground	Battery	See 3

- If voltages are correct, replace Passive Restraint Control Module.
1. Check RED/WHT (3) wire for an open.
2. Check BLK (150) wire for an open.
3. Check RED (2) wire for an open.

Fig. 5   Test A, power & ground test. LeMans

Measure: VOLTAGE
At: PASSIVE RESTRAINT CONTROL MODULE CONNECTOR (Disconnected)
Condition:
- **Ignition in RUN or START**

Measure Between	Correct Voltage	For Diagnosis
10 (YEL) & Ground	Battery	See 1

- If voltage is correct, go to Test B; Table 2.
1. Check YEL (237) wire for an open. If wire is good, check bulb. Replace cluster if bulb is OK.

Fig. 6   Test B table 1, shoulder belt warning indicator test. LeMans

Measure: RESISTANCE
At: PASSIVE RESTRAINT CONTROL MODULE CONNECTOR (Disconnected)
Conditions:
- **Ignition: OFF**
- **Shoulder Belts at A-PILLAR**
- **Shoulder Belts Buckled**

Measure Between	Correct Measurement	For Diagnosis
19 (GRN/WHT) & Ground	More than 100 ohms	See 1
5 (GRN/WHT) & Ground	More than 100 ohms	See 1
3 (WHT/YEL) & Ground	Less than 10 ohms	See 2
6 (WHT/YEL) & Ground	Less than 10 ohms	See 2
• Shoulder Belts at B-PILLAR		
19 (GRN/WHT) & Ground	Less than 10 ohms	See 1
5 (GRN/WHT) & Ground	Less than 10 ohms	See 1
3 (WHT/YEL) & Ground	More than 100 ohms	See 2
6 (WHT/YEL) & Ground	More than 100 ohms	See 2
• LH and RH Doors Closed		
8 (WHT/BRN) & Ground	More than 100 ohms	See 3
9 (WHT/BRN) & Ground	More than 100 ohms	See 3
• LH and RH Doors open		
8 (WHT/BRN) & Ground	Less than 10 ohms	See 3
9 (WHT/BRN) & Ground	Less than 10 ohms	See 3

- If all measurements are correct, go to Table 3.
1. Replace respective Shoulder Belt Motor and A-PILLAR Switch.
2. Replace respective B-PILLAR Switch.
3. Check WHT/BRN (159) wire for an open or short to ground. If wire is OK, replace respective Door Jamb Switch.

Fig. 10   Test C table 2, shoulder belt motor and switch test. LeMans

Measure: VOLTAGE
At: CONNECTOR C310 (Disconnected)
Condition:
- **Ignition: RUN**

Measure Between	Correct Voltage	For Diagnosis
4 (GRN) & Ground	Battery	See 1
4 (GRN) & 3 (BLK)	Battery	See 2

- If all voltages are correct, go to Test B; Table 3.
1. Check GRN (964) wire for an open or short to ground. If wire is OK, replace Passive Restraint Control Module.
2. Check/repair BLK (150) wire for an open.

Fig. 7   Test B table 2, shoulder belt warning indicator test. LeMans

Measure: VOLTAGE
At: CONNECTOR C310 female half (LH)
**   CONNECTOR C311 female half (RH)**
**   (Disconnected)**
Condition:
- **Ignition in RUN**

Measure Between	Correct Voltage	For Diagnosis
8 (GRN/WHT) & Ground	Battery	See 1
8 (GRN/WHT) & 6 (BLK)	Battery	See 2
7 (WHT/YEL) & Ground	Battery	See 3
7 (WHT/YEL) & 3 (BLK)	Battery	See 2

- If all voltages are correct, go to Test B; Table 2.
1. Check GRN/WHT (964) or (944) for an open or short to ground. If wire is OK, replace Passive Restraint Control Module.
2. Repair open in BLK (150) wire.
3. Check WHT/YEL (942) or (945) wire for an open or short to ground. If wire is OK, replace Passive Restraint Control Module.

Fig. 9   Test C table 1, shoulder belt motor and switch test. LeMans

Connect: FUSED JUMPER
At: CONNECTOR C310 (Disconnected)
Condition:
- **Ignition: RUN**

Connect Between	Correct Result	For Diagnosis
4 (GRN) & 3 (BLK)	Shoulder Belt Indicator lights	See 1

- If result is correct, replace LH Shoulder Belt Switch.
1. Replace Passive Restraint Control Module.

Fig. 8   Test B table 3, shoulder belt warning indicator test. LeMans

Connect: FUSED JUMPER
At: C310 or C311 male half (Disconnected)
Condition:
    Terminal 1 Connected to positive battery
    with Fused Jumper

Connect Between	Correct Results	For Diagnosis
9 (BLU) & Ground	Motor Runs	See 1

- If the result is correct, replace Passive Restraint Control Module.
1. Replace respective Shoulder Belt Motor and A-PILLAR Switch.

Fig. 11   Test C table 3, shoulder belt motor and switch test. LeMans

Measure: VOLTAGE
At: PASSIVE RESTRAINT CONTROL
    MODULE CONNECTOR (Disconnected)
Condition:
- Ignition in RUN

Measure Between	Correct Voltage	For Diagnosis
13 (GRY) & Ground	Battery	See 1

- If voltage is correct, go to Test F.
1. Check bulb and GRY (947) wire for an open.

Fig. 13   Test E, lap belts indicator test. LeMans

Measure: VOLTAGE
At: SAFETY BELT SWITCH CONNECTOR
    (Disconnected)
Condition:
- Ignition in RUN

Measure Between	Correct Voltage	For Diagnosis
A (BLK) & Ground	Battery	See 1
A (BLK) & B (BLK)	Battery	See 2

- Reconnect: SAFETY BELT SWITCH
- Lap Belt: BUCKLED

| A (BLK) & B (BLK) | 12 volts | See 3 |

- Lap Belt: UNBUCKLED

| A (BLK) & B (BLK) | 0 Volts | See 3 |

- If all voltages are correct, replace Module.
1. Check BLK (238) wire for an open. If wires are good, replace Module.
2. Check BLK (151 and 150) wires for an open.
3. Replace SAFETY BELT Switch.

Fig. 14   Test F, safety belt switch test. LeMans

Measure: VOLTAGE
At: SUSPECT BELT RETRACTOR SOLENOID
    CONNECTOR (Disconnected)
Conditions:
- Ignition in RUN or START
- Doors: CLOSED
- Belt traveling between A-PILLAR and B-PILLAR

Measure Between	Correct Voltage	For Diagnosis
WHT/BLU & Ground	Battery	See 1
WHT/BLU & BLK	Battery	See 2

- If all voltage are correct, replace suspect solenoid.
1. Check WHT/BLU (941) wires for an open or a short to ground. If wires are good, replace module.
2. Check BLK (150) wires for an open.

Fig. 12   Test D, belt retractor solenoid test. LeMans

ACTIVE SUSPENSION SYSTEMS

TABLE OF CONTENTS

Application Chart

Model	Year	Type	Page No.	Model	Year	Type	Page No.
Bonneville	1991-93	Electronic Level Control	29-2	Park Avenue	1991-93	Electronic Level Control	29-2
Brougham	1991-92	Electronic Level Control	29-2		1993	Computer Command Ride Control	29-40
Caprice	1991-93	Electronic Level Control	29-2	Reatta	1991	Electronic Level Control	29-2
Corvette	1991-93	Selective Ride Control	29-31	Riviera	1991-93	Electronic Level Control	29-2
Custom Cruiser	1991-92	Electronic Level Control	29-2	Roadmaster	1991-93	Electronic Level Control	29-2
DeVille	1991-93	Computer Command Ride Control	29-40	Seville	1991-92	Computer Command Ride Control	29-40
	1991-93	Electronic Level Control	29-2		1991-93	Electronic Level Control	29-2
Eldorado	1991-93	Computer Command Ride Control	29-40		1993	Road Sensing Suspension	29-52
	1993	Electronic Level Control	29-2		1993	Speed Sensitive Suspension	29-48
	1993	Road Sensing Suspension	29-52	Toronado/Trofeo	1991-92	Electronic Level Control	29-2
	1993	Speed Sensitive Suspension	29-48	88	1991-93	Electronic Level Control	29-2
Fleetwood (FWD)	1991-92	Computer Command Ride Control	29-40		1993	Computer Command Ride Control	29-40
	1991-92	Electronic Level Control	29-2	98	1991-93	Electronic Level Control	29-2
Fleetwood (RWD)	1993	Electronic Level Control	29-2		1993	Computer Command Ride Control	29-40
LeSabre	1991-93	Electronic Level Control	29-2	6000	1991	Electronic Level Control	29-2
	1993	Computer Command Ride Control	29-40				

Electronic Level Controls (ELC)

INDEX

PRECAUTIONS

AIRBAG SYSTEM DISARMING

1991 Park Avenue

When carrying a live inflator module, ensure bag and trim cover are pointed away from you. Never carry inflator module by the wires or connector on underside of module.

The diagnostic energy reserve module (DERM) can maintain voltage to cause a system deployment for up to ten minutes after the ignition switch is turned off and the battery is disconnected. Servicing the SIR system during this period may result in accidental deployment and personal injury.

1. Turn ignition switch to OFF position, then disconnect and tape battery ground cable terminal.
2. Remove Connector Position Assurance (CPA), then disconnect yellow two-way SIR electrical connector at base of steering column.
3. Remove screws and/or nuts from back of steering wheel, then the inflator module from steering wheel.
4. Remove Connector Position Assurance (CPA), then disconnect coil assembly connector and horn lead.
5. Place inflator module on a bench or other surface with bag and trim cover facing Up.

1991 88 & 98

The diagnostic energy reserve module (DERM) can maintain voltage to cause a system deployment for up to ten minutes after the ignition switch is turned off and the battery is disconnected. Servicing the SIR system during this period may result in accidental deployment and personal injury.

1. Turn ignition switch to OFF position, then remove I/P fuse 7 from fuse block.
2. Disconnect yellow two-way SIR electrical connector at base of steering column.

Beretta, Bonneville w/Single Airbag, Camaro, Corsica, Corvette, DeVille, Eldorado, Firebird, Fleetwood (FWD), Fleetwood (RWD), LeSabre, Reatta, Riviera, Seville & Toronado/Trofeo & 1992–93 Park Avenue, 88 & 98

The diagnostic energy reserve module (DERM) can maintain voltage to cause a system deployment for up to ten minutes after the ignition switch is turned off and the battery is disconnected. Servicing the SIR system during this period may result in accidental deployment and personal injury.

1. Ensure front wheels are pointed straight ahead.
2. Turn ignition switch to LOCK position and remove SIR or AIRBAG fuse.
3. Remove left sound insulator. **Remove courtesy lamp from sound insulator, if necessary.**
4. Remove Connector Position Assurance (CPA), then disconnect yellow two-way SIR electrical connector at base of steering column.

Caprice, Custom Cruiser & Roadmaster

The diagnostic energy reserve module (DERM) can maintain voltage to cause a system deployment for up to ten minutes after the ignition switch is turned off and the battery is disconnected. Servicing the SIR system during this period may result in accidental deployment and personal injury.

1. Ensure front wheels are pointed straight ahead.
2. Turn ignition switch to LOCK position and remove SIR fuse from fuse block.
3. Remove Connector Position Assurance (CPA), then disconnect yellow two-way SIR electrical connector at base of steering column.

Bonneville w/Dual Airbags

The diagnostic energy reserve module (DERM) can maintain voltage to cause a system deployment for up to ten minutes after the ignition switch is turned off and the battery is disconnected. Servicing the SIR system during this period may result in accidental deployment and personal injury.

1. Ensure front wheels are pointed straight ahead.
2. Turn ignition switch to OFF position and remove SIR fuse from fuse panel.
3. Remove left and right sound insulators.
4. Remove Connector Position Assurance (CPA), then disconnect yellow two-way SIR electrical connector at base of steering column.
5. Remove Connector Position Assurance (CPA), then disconnect yellow two-way passenger inflator module connector at base of right side instrument panel, clipped to knee bolster.

Metro

The diagnostic energy reserve module (DERM) can maintain voltage to cause a system deployment for up to ten minutes after the ignition switch is turned off and the battery is disconnected. Servicing the SIR system during this period may result in accidental deployment and personal injury.

1. On 1992-93 models, place steering wheel so that wheels are pointing straight ahead, then turn ignition switch to LOCK position.
2. On 1991 models, turn ignition switch to OFF position.
3. On all models, remove SIR IG fuse from SIR fuse block.
4. Remove rear plastic access cover from inflator module housing.
5. Remove Connector Position Assurance (CPA), then disconnect yellow two-way SIR electrical connector inside inflator module housing.

1991 Storm

The diagnostic energy reserve module (DERM) can maintain voltage to cause a system deployment for up to ten minutes after the ignition switch is turned off and the battery is disconnected. Servicing the SIR system during this period may result in accidental deployment and personal injury.

1. Turn ignition switch to OFF position, then disconnect battery ground cable.
2. Remove fuses C-22 and C-23 from fuse box, then disconnect orange three-way connector at the base of the steering column.

1992–93 Storm

The diagnostic energy reserve module (DERM) can maintain voltage to cause a system deployment for up to ten minutes after the ignition switch is turned off and the battery is disconnected. Servicing the SIR system during this period may result in accidental deployment and personal injury.

1. Place steering wheel so that wheels are pointing straight ahead, then turn ignition switch to LOCK position.
2. Remove fuses C-22 and C-23 from fuse block.
3. Remove switch bezel from instrument panel, then disconnect electrical connector from switches.
4. Remove cigar lighter bezel from instrument panel, then disconnect cigar lighter electrical connectors.
5. Remove two screws and hood latch release handle from knee bolster, then the three screws, three bolts and two nuts retaining the knee bolster.
6. Disconnect lap cooler air duct from knee bolster, then remove knee bolster from vehicle.
7. Remove Connector Position Assurance (CPA), then disconnect orange three-way connector at the base of the steering column.

1993 Prizm

1. Ensure front wheels are pointed straight ahead, then turn ignition switch to LOCK position.
2. Remove IGN and CIG & RADIO fuse from junction block No. 1.
3. Remove Connector Position Assurance (CPA) and disconnect lower steering column (yellow two-cavity) connector at base of steering column.

AIRBAG SYSTEM ARMING

1991 Park Avenue

1. Turn ignition switch to OFF position, connect horn lead and coil assembly connector, then install Connector Position Assurance (CPA).
2. Install inflator module and secure to steering wheel using new screws and/or nuts.
3. **Torque** screws and/or nuts to 25 inch lbs.
4. Connect yellow two-way SIR electrical connector at base of steering column, then install Connector Position Assurance (CPA).
5. Install left sound insulator, then the SIR fuse into fuse block.
6. Turn ignition switch to RUN position and ensure that "Inflatable Restraint" indicator flashes 7 to 9 times, then turns off.

1991 88 & 98

1. Connect yellow two-way SIR electrical connector at base of steering column.
2. Install I/P fuse 7 into fuse block, turn ignition switch to RUN position and ensure that "Inflatable Restraint" indicator flashes 7 to 9 times, then turns off.

Beretta, Bonneville w/Single Airbag, Camaro, Corsica, Corvette, DeVille, Eldorado, Firebird, Fleetwood (FWD), Fleetwood (RWD), LeSabre, Reatta, Riviera, Seville, Toronado, Trofeo & 1992–93 Park Avenue, 88 & 98

1. Connect yellow two-way SIR electrical connector, then install Connector Position Assurance (CPA).
2. Install left sound insulator. **Install courtesy lamp to sound insulator, if applicable.**
3. Install SIR fuse to fuse block, turn ignition switch to RUN position and ensure that "Inflatable Restraint" lamp flashes 7 to 9 times, then turns off.

Caprice, Custom Cruiser & Roadmaster

1. Connect yellow two-way SIR electrical connector at base of column, then install Connector Position Assurance (CPA).
2. Install SIR fuse into fuse block, turn ignition switch to RUN position and ensure that "Inflatable Restraint" lamp flashes 7 to 9 times and then turns off.

Bonneville w/Dual Airbags

1. Connect yellow two-way passenger inflator module connector at base of right side instrument panel, clipped to knee bolster, then install Connector Position Assurance (CPA).
2. Connect yellow two-way SIR electrical connector at base of steering column, then install Connector Position Assurance (CPA).
3. Install left and right sound insulators, then the SIR fuse into fuse panel.
4. Turn ignition switch to RUN position and ensure that "Inflatable Restraint" lamp flashes 7 to 9 times, then turns off.

DESCRIPTION

The Electronic Level Control (ELC) system adjusts rear trim height in response to changes in vehicle loading. This system consists of an air compressor assembly, air dryer, exhaust solenoid, compressor relay, height sensor, air adjustable shocks and air tubing. The compressor is activated when the ignition is On and weight is added to the vehicle. The exhaust solenoid is connected directly to the positive side of the battery, allowing the system to exhaust when the ignition is Off and excess weight is removed.

SYSTEM COMPONENTS

Compressor

This assembly is a single-piston air pump powered by a 12 volt DC permanent magnet motor. The compressor head casting contains intake and exhaust valves plus a solenoid-operated exhaust valve which releases air from the system when energized. The compressor on Pontiac 6000 models is mounted under the body on the rear left side of the vehicle. On Bonneville, Brougham, Delta 88 & 98, Deville, Fleetwood and Park Avenue the compressor is located on the left side of the engine compartment. On Eldorado, Reatta, Riviera, Seville, Toronado and 1991-92 full size station wagons the compressor is located at the top of the rear suspension support.

Air Dryer

The air dryer, attached to the compressor outlet, performs two system functions. The dryer contains a dry chemical that absorbs moisture from the air before it is delivered to the shocks. Moisture is removed from the chemical and returned to the air when system is being exhausted. The air dryer also contains a valving arrangement that maintains a minimum air pressure of 7-14 psi in the shocks.

Exhaust Solenoid

The exhaust solenoid is located in the compressor head assembly and provides two functions. The solenoid exhausts air from the system when energized by the height sensor. It also acts as a blow-off valve to limit maximum pressure output of the compressor.

Compressor Relay

The compressor relay is controlled by the height sensor and completes the 12 volt circuit to the compressor.

Height Sensor

The height sensor controls two circuits, compressor relay coil ground circuit and exhaust solenoid coil ground circuit. To prevent energizing the compressor relay and exhaust solenoid circuits during normal ride motions, the sensor circuit provides a predetermined delay before the ground circuit is completed.

The sensor electronically limits compressor run time and exhaust solenoid energized time. This limit function is necessary to prevent continuous compressor operation in case of a system leak or continuous exhaust solenoid operation. This timer is reset whenever the ignition is turned Off and On, or height sensor exhaust or compressor signal changes.

The height sensor is mounted to the body frame in the rear of the vehicle. The sensor actuator arm is attached to the control arm by a short link.

Fig. 1   ELC wiring diagram. Bonneville

Air Adjustable Shocks

The shocks are constructed with a rubber-like sleeve attached to the dust tube and reservoir. This sleeve forms a flexible chamber which will extend the shock when air pressure is increased. In order to maintain proper operation and reliability, a minimum pressure of 7-14 psi must be maintained in the system at all times.

SYSTEM OPERATION

When a load is added to the vehicle, the body is moved down causing the height sensor arm to rotate upward. This movement activates the internal timing circuit which, after a predetermined delay of 8–15 seconds, grounds pin No. 3, thus completing the compressor relay circuit to ground. When the relay circuit is energized, the circuit to the compressor is complete, allowing the compressor to send pressurized air to the shocks.

As the shocks inflate, the vehicle body moves upward, causing the sensor arm to rotate downward. Once the body reaches its original height, the sensor opens the compressor relay circuit and shuts the compressor Off.

When excess load is removed from the rear of the vehicle, the body rises upward, which causes the sensor arm to rotate downward. This movement activates the internal timing circuit which, after a predetermined delay of 8-15 seconds, allows the sensor to complete the exhaust solenoid circuit to ground. With the solenoid energized, air exhausts from the shocks

back through the air dryer and exhaust solenoid valve.

As the vehicle body lowers, the height sensor arm is rotated upward until the vehicle reaches its original height. When this height is reached, the sensor opens the exhaust solenoid circuit which prevents air from escaping.

The height sensor position is checked when the ignition is turned On. If the height sensor indicates that it is not necessary to raise or lower the vehicle, the internal timer circuit is activated. After 40 seconds, the compressor will run for four seconds. This ensures the shocks are filled with the proper residual pressure (7-14 psi). If weight is added or removed from the vehicle during this 40 second delay, the air replenishment cycle will be overridden and the vehicle will raise or lower after normal delay.

DIAGNOSIS & TESTING

When diagnostic procedures require that vehicle be raised on a hoist, it is important that the rear axle assembly remains in the normal trim height position at all times. When a frame contact hoist is used, two additional jack stands should be used to support the rear axle or control arms in the normal trim height position.

ELECTRICAL DIAGNOSIS
Except Eldorado & Seville w/4.6L/V8-279 Engine

If ELC system is inoperative, check fuse

in the fuse block.

Refer to ELC wiring circuits, **Figs. 1 through 11** and diagnostic charts, **Figs. 12 through 30,** when performing electrical diagnosis on the ELC system.

Eldorado & Seville w/4.6L/V8-279 Engine

On these models the ELC system is controlled by the Road Sensing Suspension (RSS) control module. For diagnostic procedures on this system, refer to "Road Sensing Suspension."

RESIDUAL AIR CHECK

1. Remove air line from dryer fitting and attach air line from pressure gauge tool No. J 22124-A or equivalent to dryer fitting as shown in **Fig. 31.**
2. Disconnect electrical connection to pump and jumper 12 volt dark green wire terminal to run compressor. Pump should run until a pressure of 100 psi is reached.
3. Disconnect wiring from compressor exhaust solenoid and jumper 12 volt to one terminal and ground the other terminal to the exhaust system.
4. Air should be exhausted from the system until gauge indicates 7-14 psi.

COMPRESSOR/DRYER PERFORMANCE TEST

1. Disconnect wiring from compressor motor and exhaust solenoid terminals.
2. Disconnect existing pressure line from dryer and attach pressure gauge

Fig. 2 ELC wiring diagram. Brougham

tool No. J 22124-A or equivalent to dryer fitting.

3. Connect an ammeter to 12 volt source and to compressor.

4. Operate compressor and note the following:

   a. Current draw should not exceed 14 amps.

   b. When gauge reads at least 100 psi, turn compressor Off by disconnecting power supply and observe if pressure leaks down. Compressor should not leak below 90 psi. If compressor is permitted to run until it reaches maximum output pressure of 180 psi, the solenoid exhaust valve will act as a relief valve. The resulting leak down when compressor is shutoff will indicate a false leak.

   c. Refer to chart shown in **Fig. 32** if compressor fails to meet specification.

   d. If performance is satisfactory, install compressor and connect wiring and air lines.

ELC SYSTEM LEAK TEST

1. Tee pressure gauge tool No. J 22124-A into ELC system between dryer assembly and pressure regulator valve. Install so that shut-off valve is on the compressor side of gauge.

2. With shutoff valve open, apply service air pressure through service valve on gauge until gauge reads 100 psi.

3. If leak is indicated, close shutoff valve and continue to observe for pressure drop. Closing valve isolates the compressor from the rest of the system.

4. If gauge pressure continues to drop, leak is external to the compressor. Leak test all connections with soap and water or suitable leak test solution.

5. If gauge pressure does not continue to drop, leak is in the compressor. Refer to **Fig. 33** to check compressor for leaks.

6. If pressure builds up rapidly but vehicle does not raise, check for pinched air lines and stuck or binding shocks.

HEIGHT SENSOR OPERATIONAL CHECK

1. Turn ignition Off, then On. This will reset height sensor timer circuits.

2. Raise vehicle on hoist. Ensure rear wheels or axle housing are supported and that vehicle is at proper trim height.

3. Disconnect link from height sensor arm, then ensure sensor wiring and harness ground are connected properly.

4. Move sensor arm upward. There should be a delay of 8-15 seconds before compressor turns on and shocks start to inflate. As soon as shocks start to fill, stop compressor by

moving sensor arm down.

5. Move sensor arm down below position where compressor stopped. There should be a delay of 8-15 seconds before shocks start to deflate and vehicle lowers.

SYSTEM SERVICE

When repair or adjustment procedures require that vehicle be raised on a hoist, it is important that the rear axle assembly remains in the normal trim height position at all times. When a frame contact hoist is used, two additional jack stands should be used to support the rear axle or control arms in the normal trim height position.

HEIGHT SENSOR, ADJUST

The link should be properly attached to the sensor arm and track bar, when making this adjustment.

1. Loosen lock bolt that secures metal arm to height sensor plastic arm.

2. To raise vehicle trim height, move plastic arm upward and tighten lock bolt.

3. To lower vehicle trim height, follow step 1 and move plastic arm down.

4. If adjustment cannot be made, check for correct sensor.

Continued on page 29-22

Fig. 3 ELC wiring diagram. 1991–92 Caprice, Caprice Wagon, Custom Cruiser & Roadmaster

Fig. 4   ELC wiring diagram. DeVille & Fleetwood (FWD)

Fig. 5   ELC wiring diagram. Eldorado & Seville

Fig. 6 ELC wiring diagram. Reatta, Riviera, & Toronado/Trofeo

Fig. 7   ELC wiring diagram. 88 & 98

Fig. 8   ELC wiring diagram. 6000

Fig. 10 ELC wiring diagram. Fleetwood (RWD)

Fig. 9 ELC wiring diagram. 1993 Caprice & Roadmaster

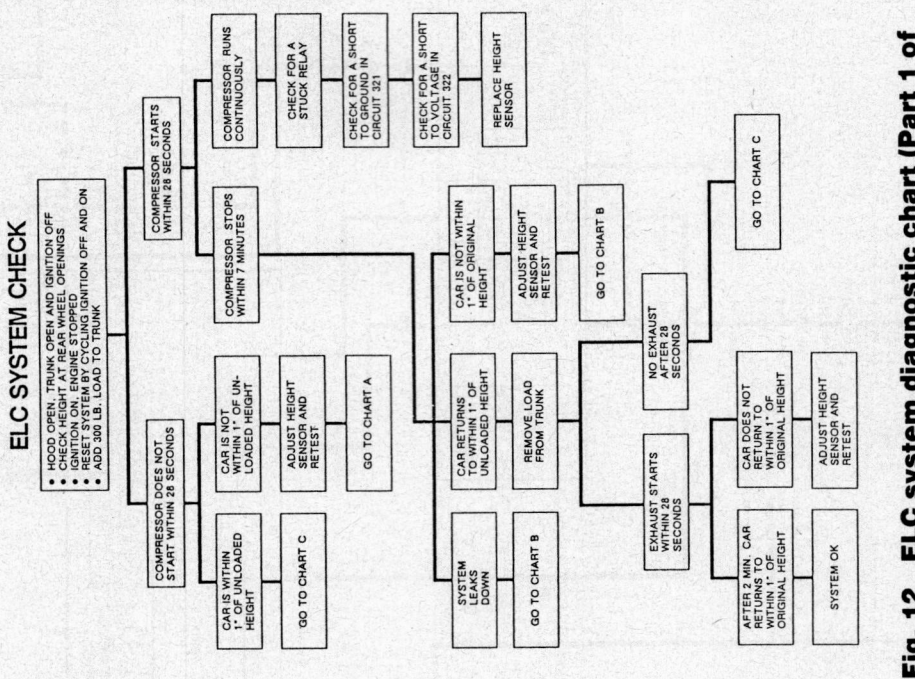

Fig. 12 ELC system diagnostic chart (Part 1 of 5). Brougham

Fig. 11 ELC wiring diagram. LeSabre & Park Avenue

CHART A – COMPRESSOR DOES NOT OPERATE

CHART D – RESET CIRCUIT OPERATIONAL CHECK

Fig. 12 ELC system diagnostic chart (Part 5 of 5). Brougham

Fig. 12 ELC system diagnostic chart (Part 2 of 5). Brougham

CHART B – IMPROPER OR CONTINUOUS EXHAUST

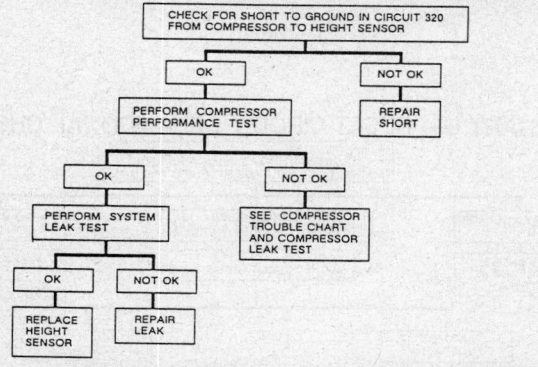

Fig. 12 ELC system diagnostic chart (Part 3 of 5). Brougham

CHART C – NO EXHAUST

ELC SYSTEM CHECK

Fig. 13 ELC system diagnostic chart (Part 1 of 5). Eldorado, Reatta, Riviera, Seville & Toronado/Trofeo

Fig. 12 ELC system diagnostic chart (Part 4 of 5). Brougham

CHART A – COMPRESSOR DOES NOT OPERATE

Fig. 13 ELC system diagnostic chart (Part 2 of 5). Eldorado, Reatta Riviera, Seville & Toronado/Trofeo

CHART B – IMPROPER OR CONTINUOUS EXHAUST

Fig. 13 ELC system diagnostic chart (Part 3 of 5). Eldorado, Reatta Riviera, Seville & Toronado/Trofeo

CHART C – NO EXHAUST

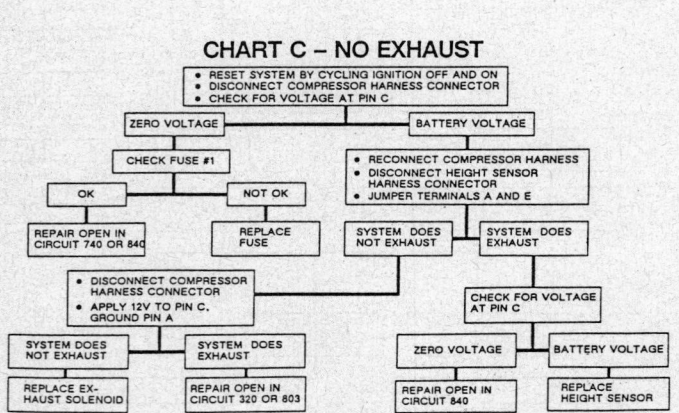

Fig. 13 ELC system diagnostic chart (Part 4 of 5). Eldorado, Reatta Riviera, Seville & Toronado/Trofeo

CHART D – RESET CIRCUIT OPERATIONAL CHECK

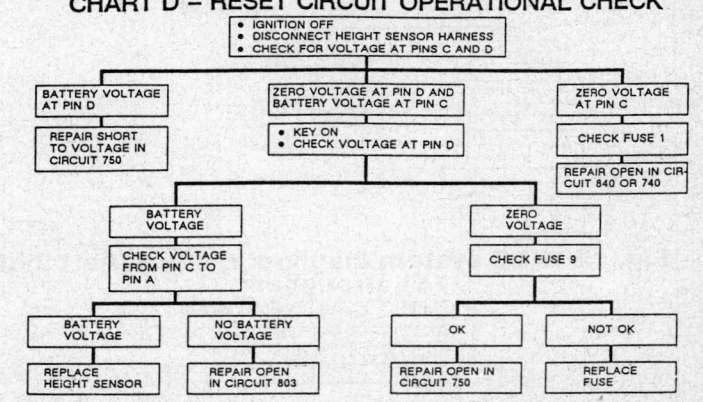

Fig. 13 ELC system diagnostic chart (Part 5 of 5). Eldorado, Reatta Riviera, Seville & Toronado/Trofeo

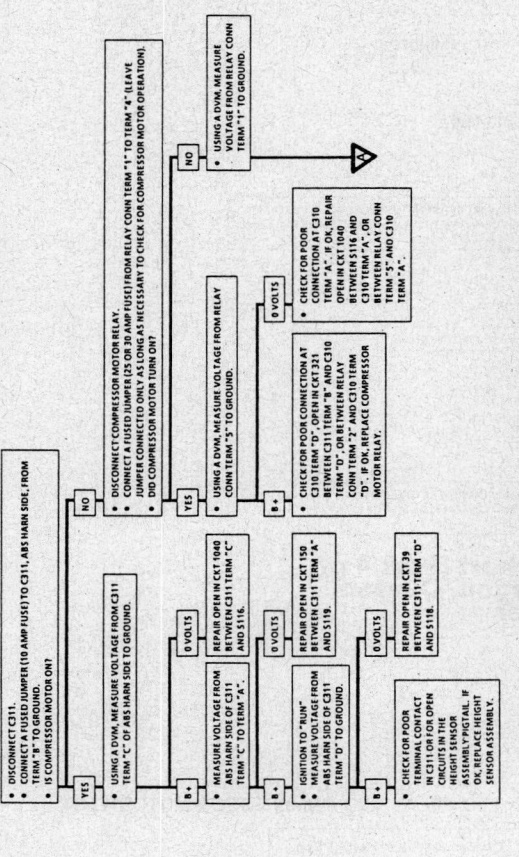

Fig. 15 ELC system diagnostic chart (Part 1 of 4). 1991–92 Caprice, Caprice Wagon, Custom Cruiser & Roadmaster

Fig. 15 ELC system diagnostic chart (Part 3 of 4). 1991–92 Caprice, Caprice Wagon, Custom Cruiser & Roadmaster

SYMPTOM	PROCEDURE
Compressor Motor does not turn "ON" to raise rear of vehicle.	Chart #1
ELC System does not vent to lower rear of vehicle (checks Exhaust Solenoid).	Chart #2
Compressor Motor runs continuously (longer than 7 minutes).	Chart #3
Compressor Motor runs for maximum run time (approximately 4.5 to 7 minutes) then stops.	Check for air leaks in the ELC System and for proper adjustment of the Height Sensor Assembly. If no air leaks are found and sensor is adjusted properly, check for a short to ground in CKT 320 between Height Sensor Assembly and Exhaust Solenoid. If OK, replace Height Sensor Assembly.
ELC system continuously relevels vehicle with no change in load.	Check for air leaks in the ELC System.

Fig. 14 ELC system symptom chart. 1991–92 Caprice, Caprice Wagon, Custom Cruiser & Roadmaster

Fig. 15 ELC system diagnostic chart (Part 2 of 4). 1991–92 Caprice, Caprice Wagon, Custom Cruiser & Roadmaster

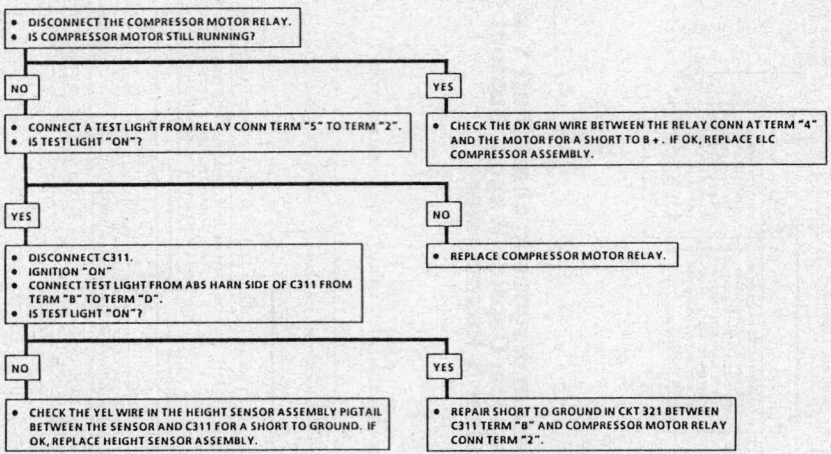

CHART #3
COMPRESSOR MOTOR RUNS CONTINUOUSLY (LONGER THAN 7 MINUTES)

Fig. 15   ELC system diagnostic chart (Part 4 of 4). 1991–92 Caprice, Caprice Wagon, Custom Cruiser & Roadmaster

SYMPTOM	FOR DIAGNOSIS
Compressor does not run	Do Test A
System does not exhaust	Do Test B
Compressor runs for more than 7 minutes; vehicle stays at maximum height	Disconnect the ELC Height Sensor connector • If the Compressor does not run, replace the ELC Height Sensor. • If the Compressor runs, check YEL (321) wire for a short to ground; check for sticking relay
Compressor runs for maximum time (7 minutes) then turns off; vehicle does not reach proper height	Do Test C
ELC Compressor Assembly cycles on and off frequently	Do Test C

Fig. 16   ELC system symptom chart. Bonneville, Deville, Fleetwood (FWD), 88 & 98

A: ELC RELAY AND COMPRESSOR MOTOR TEST

Fig. 17   ELC system diagnostic chart (Part 1 of 6). Bonneville, Deville, Fleetwood (FWD), 88 & 98

Fig. 17 ELC system diagnostic chart (Part 2 of 6). Bonneville, Deville, Fleetwood (FWD), 88 & 98

Fig. 17 ELC system diagnostic chart (Part 3 of 6). Bonneville, Deville, Fleetwood (FWD), 88 & 98

C: ELC HEIGHT SENSOR TEST (TABLE 1)

Measure: VOLTAGE

At: ELC HEIGHT SENSOR CONNECTOR (Disconnected)

Condition:
- Ignition Switch: RUN

Between	Voltage	Diagnosis
C (ORN) & Ground	Battery	See 1
C (ORN) & A (BLK)	Battery	See 2
D (BRN) & A (BLK)	Battery	See 3
B (YEL) & A (BLK)	Battery	See 4
E (WHT) & A (BLK)	Battery	See 5

- If all voltages are correct, reconnect the connector and go to Table 2.
1. Check/repair ORN (340) wire for an open (see schematic).
2. Check/repair BLK (154) wire for an open (see schematic).
3. Check/repair BRN (50) wire for an open (see schematic).
4. Check/repair YEL (321) wire for an open (see schematic).
5. Check/repair WHT (320) wire for an open or short to ground (see schematic).

Fig. 17 ELC system diagnostic chart (Part 4 of 6). Bonneville, Deville, Fleetwood (FWD), 88 & 98

Fig. 17 ELC system diagnostic chart (Part 5 of 6). Bonneville, Deville, Fleetwood (FWD), 88 & 98

Fig. 17 ELC system diagnostic chart (Part 6 of 6). Bonneville, Deville, Fleetwood (FWD), 88 & 98

SYMPTOM	PROCEDURE
Compressor Motor does not turn "ON" to raise rear of vehicle.	Chart #1
ELC System does not vent to lower rear of vehicle (checks Exhaust Solenoid).	Chart #2
Compressor Motor runs continuously (longer than 7 minutes).	Chart #3
Compressor Motor runs for maximum run time (approximately 4.5 to 7 minutes) then stops.	Check for air leaks in the ELC System and for proper adjustment of the Height Sensor Assembly. If OK, replace Height Sensor Assembly.
ELC System continuously re-levels vehicle with no change in load.	Check for air leaks in the ELC System.

Fig. 18 ELC system symptom chart. 1993 Caprice & Roadmaster

CHART #1
COMPRESSOR MOTOR DOES NOT TURN "ON" TO RAISE REAR OF VEHICLE

Fig. 19 ELC system diagnostic chart (Part 1 of 4). 1993 Caprice & Roadmaster

Fig. 19 ELC system diagnostic chart (Part 2 of 4). 1993 Caprice & Roadmaster

CHART #2
ELC SYSTEM DOES NOT VENT TO LOWER REAR OF VEHICLE (CHECKS EXHAUST SOLENOID)

Fig. 19 ELC system diagnostic chart (Part 3 of 4). 1993 Caprice & Roadmaster

CHART #3
COMPRESSOR MOTOR RUNS CONTINUOUSLY (LONGER THAN 7 MINUTES)

Fig. 19 ELC system diagnostic chart (Part 4 of 4). 1993 Caprice & Roadmaster

SYMPTOM	PROCEDURE
Compressor Motor does not turn "ON" to raise rear of vehicle.	Chart #1
ELC System does not vent to lower rear of vehicle (checks Exhaust Solenoid).	Chart #2
Compressor Motor runs continuously (longer than 7 minutes).	Chart #3
Compressor Motor runs for maximum run time (approximately 4.5 to 7 minutes) then stops.	Check for air leaks in the ELC System and for proper adjustment of the Height Sensor Assembly. If OK, replace Height Sensor Assembly.
ELC System continuously re-levels vehicle with no change in load.	Check for air leaks in the ELC System.
"LEVEL RIDE" Indicator inoperative, ELC System operates normally.	Check for an open in CKT 322 or CKT 1500. If OK, check bulb. If bulb is OK, remove cluster for service.

Fig. 20 ELC system symptom chart. Fleetwood RWD

CHART #1
COMPRESSOR MOTOR DOES NOT TURN "ON" TO RAISE REAR OF VEHICLE

Fig. 21 ELC system diagnostic chart (Part 1 of 4). Fleetwood RWD

Fig. 21 ELC system diagnostic chart (Part 2 of 4). Fleetwood RWD

CHART #2
ELC SYSTEM DOES NOT VENT TO LOWER REAR OF VEHICLE (CHECKS EXHAUST SOLENOID)

Fig. 21 ELC system diagnostic chart (Part 3 of 4). Fleetwood RWD

CHART #3
COMPRESSOR MOTOR RUNS CONTINUOUSLY (LONGER THAN 7 MINUTES)

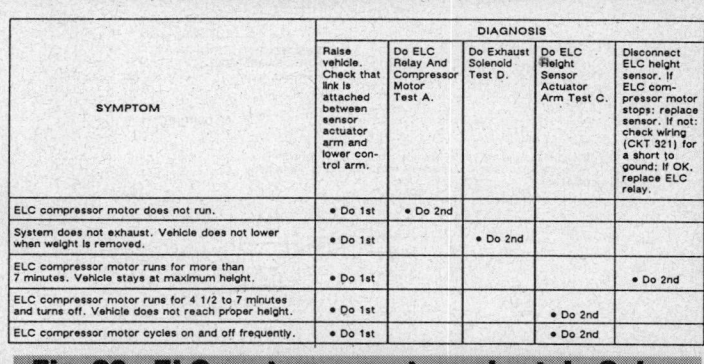

Fig. 21 ELC system diagnostic chart (Part 4 of 4). Fleetwood RWD

SYMPTOM	DIAGNOSIS				
	Raise vehicle. Check that link is attached between sensor actuator arm and lower control arm.	Do ELC Relay And Compressor Motor Test A.	Do Exhaust Solenoid Test D.	Do ELC Height Sensor Actuator Arm Test C.	Disconnect ELC height sensor. If ELC compressor motor stops: replace sensor. If not: check wiring (CKT 321) for a short to gound; If OK, replace ELC relay.
ELC compressor motor does not run.	• Do 1st	• Do 2nd			
System does not exhaust. Vehicle does not lower when weight is removed.	• Do 1st		• Do 2nd		
ELC compressor motor runs for more than 7 minutes. Vehicle stays at maximum height.	• Do 1st				• Do 2nd
ELC compressor motor runs for 4 1/2 to 7 minutes and turns off. Vehicle does not reach proper height.	• Do 1st			• Do 2nd	
ELC compressor motor cycles on and off frequently.	• Do 1st			• Do 2nd	

Fig. 22 ELC system symptom chart. LeSabre & Park Avenue

Fig. 23 ELC diagnostic chart (ELC relay & compressor motor test). LeSabre & Park Avenue

- ELC height sensor connector: disconnected
- Ignition switch: RUN

Battery voltage in each case. If not: check related wiring for an open or short to ground; check applicable in-line connectors (see schematic) for proper terminal contact; check appropriate fuses.

ELC HEIGHT
SENSOR CONNECTOR
(Harness side)

- If all measurements are correct: check ELC height sensor connector for proper terminal contact; if contact OK, go to ELC Height Sensor Actuator Arm Test C.

Fig. 24 ELC diagnostic chart (ELC height sensor voltage test). LeSabre & Park Avenue

- ELC height sensor connector: disconnected

[1] Jumper ELC height sensor connector as shown to pressurize system.

BLK
ELC HEIGHT
SENSOR CONNECTOR
(Harness side)

[2] If exhaust solenoid vents system: go to ELC Height Sensor Actuator Arm Test C; otherwise leave jumper in place and go to [3].

BLK
ELC HEIGHT
SENSOR CONNECTOR
(Harness side)

- ELC compressor assembly connector: disconnected

[3] If test lamp lights in both cases: check ELC compressor assembly (terminals A and C) and ELC height sensor (terminal E) pigtail connectors for proper terminal contact; check pigtail wiring for an open or short to ground; if wiring and contacts are OK, go to Air Dryer Test F. If test lamp does not light: check wiring (CKTS 320 and 340) for an open or short to ground.

BLK
ELC COMPRESSOR
ASSEMBLY CONNECTOR
(Harness side)

Fig. 26 ELC diagnostic chart (Exhaust solenoid test). LeSabre & Park Avenue

- ELC height sensor connector: connected
- Cycle ignition switch and then turn to RUN.
- Disconnect link from actuator arm and move actuator arm up as far as it goes,

Does ELC compressor motor run after 17-27 second delay?

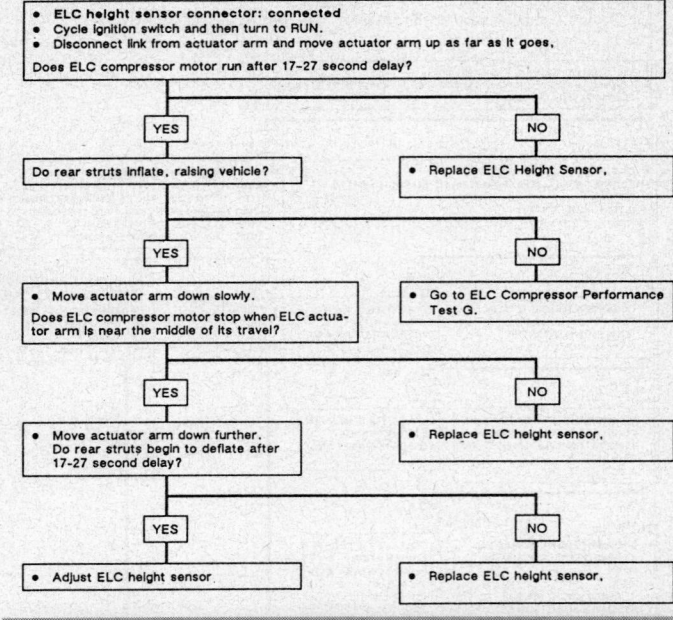

Fig. 25 ELC diagnostic chart (ELC height sensor actuator arm test). LeSabre & Park Avenue

- Remove ELC compressor assembly,
- Remove two motor case attaching screws.
- Pull case and magnet assembly off armature.

[1] Inspect inside motor case for any foreign material that could bind or lock up armature.

[2] Check that brush lead is not grounded.

[3] Check that brush lead ground connection is tight.

[4] Check that brush spring is properly positioned.

- If no defects can be found: replace motor/cylinder assembly,

Fig. 27 ELC diagnostic chart (ELC compressor inspection test). LeSabre & Park Avenue

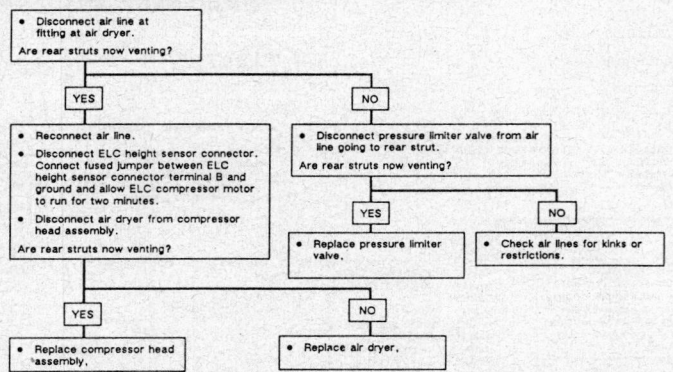

Fig. 28 ELC diagnostic chart (Air dryer test). LeSabre & Park Avenue

- Connect J 22124-A pressure gage to air dryer as shown.
- Close shut off valve (down).

[1] ELC COMPRESSOR ASSEMBLY

J 22124-A PRESSURE GAGE

SHUT OFF VALVE

- Disconnect ELC compressor assembly connector.
- Connect an ammeter capable of reading up to 20 AMPS to ELC compressor assembly connectors as shown.
- Disconnect link from ELC height sensor actuator arm and move actuator arm as far up as it goes.
- Observe ammeter and pressure gage while compressor runs.
- When pressure reaches 760 kPa (110 psi), move actuator arm down until ELC compressor motor stops.

Did compressor current draw exceed 14 amps?

[2]

BLK
ELC COMPRESSOR ASSEMBLY CONNECTOR (Harness half)

BLK
ELC COMPRESSOR ASSEMBLY CONNECTOR (Compressor half)

NO → YES

NO:
- Observe pressure gage for one minute.
Did pressure fall below 620 kPa (90 psi)?

YES:
- Replace motor/cylinder assembly.

NO → A (Continued)

YES:
- Do ELC Compressor Assembly Leak Test H.

Fig. 29 ELC diagnostic chart (ELC compressor performance test, part 1 of 2). LeSabre & Park Avenue

---

Continued ▽ A

- ELC height sensor connector: disconnected.
- Open shut off valve (up).
- Connect J 22124-A pressure gage in place of pressure limiter valve. Install so that the shut off valve is on compressor side of gage.
- Connect fused jumper between ELC height sensor connector (terminal B) and ground.
- Disconnect ELC height sensor fused jumper when pressure reaches 760 to 830 kPa (110 to 120 psi).
- Close shut off valve (down) and observe pressure gage for one minute.

Is pressure dropping?

ELC COMPRESSOR ASSEMBLY

J 22124-A PRESSURE GAGE

TO REAR STRUTS

YES:
- Leak test all connections with soap and water solution. Repair/replace as necessary.

NO:
- If pressure builds up rapidly and vehicle does not rise, check for pinched air lines or binding strut. If pressure builds at a normal rate, replace pressure limiter valve.

Fig. 29 ELC diagnostic chart (ELC compressor performance test, part 2 of 2). LeSabre & Park Avenue

[1] Connect J 22124-A pressure gage to dryer as shown. Close shut off valve (down).

[2] Run compressor to 690 kPa (100 psi) through gage valve.

[3] Using soap bubble solution, test locations called out below.

DRYER COVER
Replace dryer if leak is found.

DRYER O-RING CASTING BORE

J 22124-A PRESSURE GAGE

SHUT OFF VALVE

AROUND EDGE OF COVER GASKET
Check torque of head bolts before replacing gasket.

AROUND EDGE OF SOLENOID VALVE TERMINAL HOUSING
Replace compressor head assembly if leak is found.

HEAD CASTING AIR INTAKE AND EXHAUST ASSEMBLY
Replace compressor head assembly if leak is found.

- Repair/replace components where leak is found.

Fig. 30 ELC diagnostic chart (ELC compressor assembly leak test). LeSabre & Park Avenue

---

CURRENT DRAW TEST

AMMETER

[1]

PRESSURE OUTPUT TEST

[2]

[1] MOTOR GROUND LEAD
[2] SPECIAL TOOL J-22124-A

Fig. 31 Compressor performance test

MALFUNCTION	CORRECTION
1. Compressor runs but current draw exceeds 14 amps.	1. Replace compressor.
2. Compressor inoperative	2. Replace compressor.
3. Compressor output less than 758 kPa (110 psi)	3. Perform compressor/dryer leak test, if no leak is found, replace compressor.
4. Pressure leaks down to 0 kPa (0 psi)	4. Perform compressor/dryer leak test, and make corrections as required.
5. Pressure build up ok, but leaks down below 60 kPa (90 psi) before holding steady. (Does not go to 0 psi.)	5. Replace head assembly

Fig. 32 Compressor/Dryer trouble chart

1 ATTACH PRESSURE GAGE J 22124–A TO DRYER AND PRESSURIZE COMPRESSOR TO 690 kPa (100 PSI) THROUGH THE GAGE FILL–VALVE.

2 USING SOAP BUBBLE SOLUTION, CHECK ITEMS CALLED OUT BELOW:

A DRYER O-RING CASTING BORE

B AROUND EDGE OF COVER GASKET (IF LEAK IS FOUND, CHECK TORQUE OF COVER BOLTS BEFORE REPLACING GASKET)

C AROUND EDGE OF SOLENOID VALVE TERMINAL HOUSING (REPLACE HEAD ASSEMBLY IF LEAK IS FOUND)

D HEAD CASTING AIR INTAKE AND EXHAUST OPENING (REPLACE COMPRESSOR HEAD IF LEAK IS FOUND)

E COVER BOLTS (TIGHTEN BOLTS TO 4 N.m – 36 LB. IN.)

F DRYER COVER (REPLACE DRYER/EXHAUST/BLOCKER VALVE)

Fig. 33 Compressor leak test

[1] COMPRESSOR HEAD ASSEMBLY
[2] DRIER BRACKET
[3] AIR DRIER
[4] O'RING

Fig. 34 Air dryer assembly

[1] EXHAUST SOLENOID CONNECTOR
[2] HEAD ASSEMBLY
[3] CYLINDER AND MOTOR ASSEMBLY
[4] CYLINDER HEAD O'RING

Fig. 35 Compressor head assembly

Fig. 36 Air compressor, disassembled

SHIELD, COMPRESSOR & BRACKET, REPLACE

1. Disconnect battery ground cable.
2. Raise and support vehicle.
3. Remove compressor shield, if equipped, then deflate system.
4. Disconnect high pressure line at air dryer by revolving spring clip 90° while holding connector end and removing tube assembly.
5. Disconnect electrical connector from compressor pigtail harness.
6. Remove three compressor mounting screws, then the compressor.
7. Remove three compressor mounting bracket screws, then the bracket.
8. If replacing compressor assembly, remove dryer and dryer bracket.
9. Reverse procedure to install. After connecting battery ground cable, cy-cle ignition switch, then test system operation, looking for air leaks at dryer.

AIR DRYER, REPLACE

1. Remove compressor as described in "Shield, Compressor & Bracket, Replace."
2. Rotate dryer retainer spring 90° and pull dryer and O-ring out of compressor head assembly, **Fig. 34.**
3. Reverse procedure to install.

COMPRESSOR HEAD ASSEMBLY, REPLACE

1. Remove air dryer assembly as described in "Air Dryer, Replace."
2. Remove three compressor head mounting bolts and head assembly, **Fig. 35.**
3. Reverse procedure to install, using a new O-ring and **torquing** head mounting bolts to 36 inch lbs.

SOLENOID VALVE ASSEMBLY, REPLACE

If solenoid valve assembly requires replacement, it should be replaced with compressor head assembly. Refer to "Compressor Head Assembly, Replace."

HEIGHT SENSOR & BRACKET, REPLACE

1. Disconnect battery ground cable.
2. Raise and support vehicle.
3. Disconnect harness from sensor electrical connector by squeezing oval sides of the connector lock to release locking tabs.
4. Remove link from height sensor arm, then remove sensor mounting screws or nuts and the sensor.
5. Remove sensor mounting bracket to underbody attaching screws and remove bracket.
6. Reverse procedure to install, noting the following:
   a. When connecting harness to sensor electrical connector, push connector into sensor plug until sloped shoulder on rear edge of boss is visible in plug slot. Push oval connector lock onto plug until its two locking tabs snap over shoulder of sensor plug.
   b. Perform height sensor operational check and adjustment procedure as described in "Height Sensor Operational Check" and "Height Sensor, Adjustment."

AIR COMPRESSOR SERVICE
Disassembly

1. Remove the seven compressor cover screws, then the compressor cover and gasket, **Fig. 36.**
2. Remove head and solenoid assembly.
3. Remove two filters, exhaust valve, spring and air dryer O-ring from head assembly.
4. Remove solenoid from head by lifting slightly and sliding to the dryer outlet side.
5. Remove O-ring from solenoid assembly.

TORQUE BOLTS TO 4 N·m
(36 IN. LBS.) PER SEQUENCE

Fig. 37   Air compressor head tightening sequence

1. VISE WITH 3/16" SHIMS
2. STRUT
3. HOLD NUMBER 50 TORX
4. TURN 12 PT. BOX WRENCH
5. UPPER MOUNT

Fig. 38   Removing upper strut mount

1. OUTER CLAMP
2. STRUT

Fig. 39   Removing outer clamp

1. OUTER TUBE
2. "O" RING — LUBRICATE WITH SILICONE
3. "O" RING GROVE

Fig. 40   O-ring replacement

6. Remove head gasket from cylinder assembly.
7. Remove four mounting bracket screws, then the bracket and gasket. Note position of ground wire for installation.

Assembly

1. Install gasket and mounting bracket, then the ground wire and screws.
2. Install head gasket on cylinder assembly.
3. Install O-ring on solenoid assembly, then the solenoid in the head with valve opposite air dryer outlet.
4. Install two filters, exhaust valve and spring on head assembly.

5. Install gasket and cover on head assembly, then four short cover screws.
6. Install head and cover assembly to cylinder assembly using three long screws. **Torque** all seven screws in sequence, **Fig. 37,** to 36 inch lbs.
7. Install air dryer O-ring on compressor.

STRUT AIR BLADDER, REPLACE
Removal

1. Remove strut from vehicle.
2. Scribe alignment marks between upper mount and outer tube.
3. Clamp strut in a suitable vise using wooden blocks.

4. Remove upper mount from strut, **Fig. 38.**
5. Cut and remove outer clamp with a hacksaw, **Fig. 39.**
6. Cut air bladder from outer tube and slide the inner tube upward.
7. Remove O-ring from inside top of outer tube, **Fig. 40.**
8. Cut and remove inner clamp with a hacksaw, **Fig. 41.**
9. Remove air bladder from inner tube.

Installation

1. Lubricate new O-ring and O-ring groove with silicone lubricant. Install O-ring in groove, **Fig. 40.**
2. Apply silicone lubricant to inside top

1. INNER CLAMP
2. AIR BLADDER
3. STRUT

Fig. 41   Removing inner clamp

1. STRUT
2. J 34649 SEALING RING COMPRESSOR
3. AIR BLADDER
4. 6mm (1/4'')
5. 44mm (1 3/4'')
6. 102mm (4'')
7. INNER CLAMP
8. IMPACT WRENCH
9. SECOND FOLD DOWN

Fig. 43   Inner clamp & air bladder position

1. AIR BLADDER
2. LUBRICATE INSIDE OF AIR BLADDER 57mm (2 1/4'')
3. LUBRICATE OUTSIDE OF AIR BLADDER
4. FOLD BOTTOM OF AIR BLADDER BEFORE INSTALLATION

Fig. 42   Replacing air bladder

1. UPPER MOUNT
2. 90° ±2°
3. 58° ±2°
4. STRUT TO KNUCKLE MOUNT

Fig. 44   Air fitting position

of new air bladder and the entire outside of air bladder, **Fig. 42.**
3. Fold bottom of air bladder before installation on inner tube. Place air bladder over inner tube, continuing to fold bladder from the bottom up. Position top of air bladder as shown in **Fig. 43. Do not use tools to fold air bladder as damage may occur, causing air leakage.**
4. Place inner clamp in position as shown in **Fig. 43.** Tighten clamp with tool J-34649.
5. Fold bottom of air bladder upward and fold top of 4 inch section downward.
6. Apply silicone lubricant to polished diameter of inner shaft tube.
7. Place outer tube over air bladder and push downward against folded portion of bladder. **The outer tube must be completely seated over shaft.**
8. Install upper mount onto strut, aligning marks made during disassembly, and **torque** nut to 74 ft.lbs. **The upper mount and tube air fitting must be properly positioned with the bottom strut mount, Fig. 44.**
9. Apply silicone lubricant to outer tube.
10. Install air bladder over outer tube by folding upward over tube and push over tube.
11. Install and tighten hose clamp over grooved area of air bladder.
12. Support strut and partially inflate air bladder. Check for leaks with soap solution.
13. Install strut into vehicle.

VEHICLE TRIM HEIGHT CHECK
Trim heights are checked with tires at recommended pressure, fuel tank at capacity, front seat in rear position, no passengers and trunk empty, except for spare tire and jack.
Refer to **Figs. 45** through **55** for trim height measurements.

Continued on page 29-30

		SUSPENSION		ROCKER PANEL		WHEEL OPENING	
		Z	D	J	K	P	R
RIVIERA	mm	46	28	219	222	696	705
	in.	1.81	1.10	8.62	8.74	27.40	27.76
REATTA	mm	53	35	216	219	733	745
	in.	2.09	1.38	8.50	8.62	28.86	29.33

NOTE: "D" HEIGHT IS MEASURED ON THE REAR SIDE OF REAR SUSPENSION ASSEMBLY

REAR SUSPENSION

FRONT SUSPENSION

CENTERLINE OF REAR OUTER BUSHING BOLT
CENTERLINE OF REAR INNER BUSHING BOLT

CENTERLINE OF BUSHING BOLT
FRAME CRADLE
LOWEST POINT ON BALL JOINT HOUSING EXCLUDING GREASE FITTING

563 mm 22.17 in.
502 mm 19.75 in.
580 mm 22.84 in.
640 mm 25.20 in.
RIVIERA
REATTA
P,R
GROUND
J,K
GROUND

Fig. 46 Vehicle trim height measurements. Reatta & Riviera

ROCKER PANEL
GROUND
"J" or "K"
CENTERLINE OF AXLE
600 mm 23½ in.
600 mm 23½ in.
600 mm 23½ in.

CENTERLINE OF CONTROL ARM BOLT
LOWEST POINT ON GREASE FITTING (EXCEPT GREASE FITTING)
REAR
"D"

CENTERLINE OF CONTROL ARM BOLT
LOWEST POINT ON BALLJOINT HOUSING (EXCEPT GREASE FITTING)
FRONT
"Z"

TRIM HEIGHT CHECK PROCEDURE

1. VEHICLE MUST BE ON LEVEL GROUND.
2. TIRES MUST BE INFLATED TO PROPER PRESSURE.
3. FUEL TANK SHOULD BE FULL.
4. NO PASSENGERS OR ADDED WEIGHT SHOULD BE IN THE VEHICLE. THE TRUNK MUST BE EMPTY EXCEPT FOR THE SPARE TIRE AND JACK.
5. PLACE THE FRONT SEAT IN THE REAR POSITION.
6. IGNITION SWITCH ON TO ACTIVATE ELECTRONIC LEVEL CONTROL (ELC). (IF EQUIPPED)
7. "BOUNCE" THE CAR THREE TIMES AT THE FRONT AND REAR TO NORMALIZE THE SUSPENSION.
8. MEASURE FROM THE LOWEST POINT ON THE BALLJOINT HOUSING TO CONTROL ARM BOLT CENTERLINE AT "D" AND "Z" POSITIONS. (SEE ILLUSTRATIONS ABOVE)
9. MEASURE FROM KNOWN LEVEL FLOOR TO ROCKER PANEL AT "J" AND "K" POSITIONS. EXCEPT SSE MODELS.
10. MEASURE FROM KNOWN LEVEL FLOOR TO THE WHEEL OPENING AT "P" AND "R" POSITIONS.

MAXIMUM VARIATION SIDE TO SIDE & FRONT TO REAR IS 19MM (¾ IN)

LOAD CONDITIONS — COOLANT TO CAPACITY AND FULL TANK OF FUEL

"Z"	"D"	"P"	"R"	"J"	"K"
55-75 mm	70-90 mm	708-728 mm	710-730 mm	231-251 mm	231-251 mm
2 5/32-2 15/16 in.	2 3/4-3 9/16 in.	27 7/8-28 21/32 in.	27 15/16-28 3/4 in.	9 3/32-9 7/8 in.	9 3/32-9 7/8 in.

Fig. 45 Vehicle trim height measurements. Bonneville

Fig. 48 Vehicle trim height measurements. 1992 Toronado/Trofeo

	SUSPENSION				ROCKER PANEL				WHEEL OPENING	
	Z		D		J		K		P	R
TORONADO mm	57		34		231		231		706	718
in.	2.24		1.34		9.09		9.09		27.80	28.27

Fig. 47 Vehicle trim height measurements. 1991 Toronado/Trofeo

FRONT-"Z" DIMENSION

MINIMUM	TARGET	MAXIMUM
40 mm (1.58 in.)	46 mm (1.81 in.)	52 mm (2.05 in.)

REAR-"D" DIMENSION

MINIMUM	TARGET	MAXIMUM
17 mm (.67 in.)	24 mm (.95 in.)	31 mm (1.22 in.)

DIMENSIONS SHOWN ABOVE ARE FOR VEHICLE WITH CORRECT TIRE PRESSURE, FULL TANK OF FUEL, PROPERLY OPERATING ELC SYSTEM AND NO PASSENGERS OR ADDED WEIGHT IN CAR.

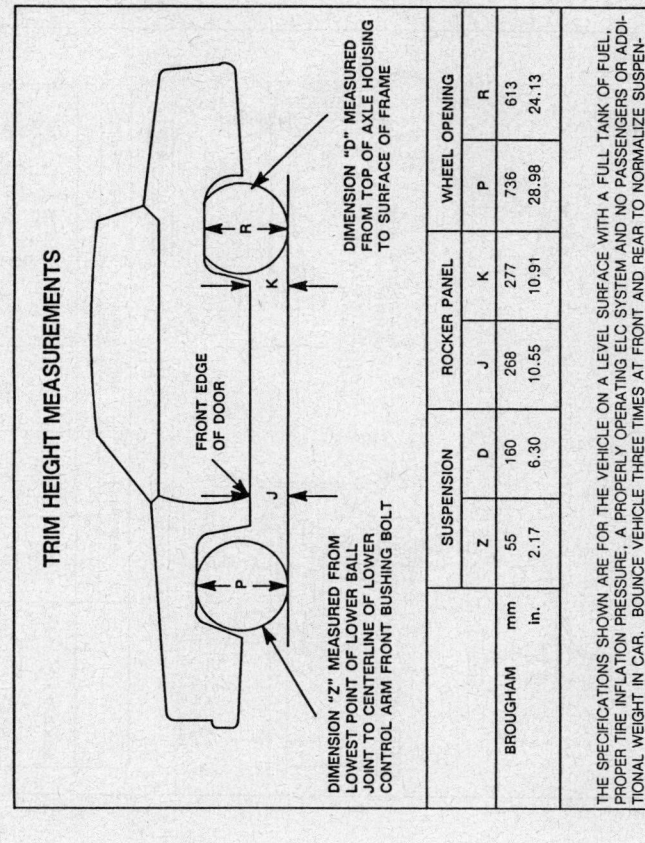

TRIM HEIGHT MEASUREMENTS

DIMENSION "D" MEASURED FROM TOP OF AXLE HOUSING TO SURFACE OF FRAME

FRONT EDGE OF DOOR

DIMENSION "Z" MEASURED FROM LOWEST POINT OF LOWER BALL JOINT TO CENTERLINE OF LOWER CONTROL ARM FRONT BUSHING BOLT

		SUSPENSION		ROCKER PANEL		WHEEL OPENING	
		Z	D	J	K	P	R
BROUGHAM	mm	55	160	268	277	736	613
	in.	2.17	6.30	10.55	10.91	28.98	24.13

THE SPECIFICATIONS SHOWN ARE FOR THE VEHICLE ON A LEVEL SURFACE WITH A FULL TANK OF FUEL, PROPER TIRE INFLATION PRESSURE, A PROPERLY OPERATING ELC SYSTEM AND NO PASSENGERS OR ADDITIONAL WEIGHT IN CAR. BOUNCE VEHICLE THREE TIMES AT FRONT AND REAR TO NORMALIZE SUSPENSION. MAXIMUM VARIATION SIDE TO SIDE IS 9 MM. ALL MEASUREMENTS ARE ±10 MM. (3/8 INCH).

Fig. 50   Vehicle trim height measurements. 1991–92 Cadillac Brougham

ROCKER PANEL

"J" OR "K"

GROUND

CENTERLINE OF CONTROL ARM BOLT

LOWEST POINT ON BALL JOINT HOUSING (EXCEPT GREASE FITTING)

REAR

"D"

600 MM 23 1/2 IN.

"K"

"J"

600 MM 23 1/2 IN.

CENTERLINE OF CONTROL ARM BOLT

LOWEST POINT ON BALL JOINT HOUSING (EXCEPT GREASE FITTING)

FRONT

"Z"

Eighty-Eight:
- D = 68-88 mm (2 11/16 - 3 7/16 in.)
- Z = 50-70 mm (1 15/16 - 2 3/4 in.)
- J = 229-249 mm (9 - 9 13/16 in.)
- K = 236-256 mm (9 9/32 - 10 1/16 in.)

LeSabre:
- D = 68-88 mm (2 11/16 - 3 7/16 in.)
- Z = 50-70 mm (1 15/16 - 2 3/4 in.)
- J = 229-249 mm (9 - 9 13/16 in.)
- K = 236-256 mm (9 9/32 - 10 1/16 in.)

Ninety-Eight:
- D = 68-88 mm (2 11/16 - 3 7/16 in.)
- Z = 50-70 mm (1 15/16 - 2 3/4 in.)
- J = 228-248 mm (9 - 9 13/16 in.)
- K = 230-250 mm (9 1/16 - 9 27/32 in.)

Park Avenue/Park Avenue Ultra:
- D = 68-88 mm (2 11/16 - 3 7/16 in.)
- Z = 50-70 mm (1 15/16 - 2 3/4 in.)
- J = 228-248 mm (9 - 9 13/16 in.)
- K = 230-250 mm (9 1/16 - 9 27/32 in.)

Fig. 49   Vehicle trim height measurements. LeSabre, Park Avenue, 88 & 98

Fig. 52 Vehicle trim height measurements. 1991 Eldorado & Seville

		SUSPENSION			ROCKER PANEL			WHEEL OPENING	
		Z	D		J	K		P	R
ELDORADO	mm	52	29		229	231		718	710
	in.	2.05	1.14		9.02	9.09		28.27	27.95
SEVILLE	mm	51	30		229	233		717	724
	in.	2.01	1.18		9.02	9.09		28.23	28.50

Fig. 51 Vehicle trim height measurements. 1993 Fleetwood RWD

MODEL	SUSPENSION	TIRE	J		K		P		R		D		Z	
			mm	INCH	mm	INCH	mm	INCH	mm	INCH	mm	INCH	mm	INCH
SEDAN	FE1	235-70	252	9.9	264	10.4	737	29.0	546	21.5	147	5.8	56	2.2
	FE2/F41	225-70	252	9.9	264	10.4	737	29.0	546	21.5	152	6.0	61	2.4

NOTE: Trim heights should be within ± 10 mm (0.4 inch).

TRIM HEIGHT CHECK PROCEDURE

1. VEHICLE MUST BE ON LEVEL GROUND.
2. TIRES MUST BE INFLATED TO PROPER PRESSURE.
3. FUEL TANK SHOULD BE FULL.
4. NO PASSENGERS OR ADDED WEIGHT SHOULD BE IN THE VEHICLE. THE TRUNK MUST BE EMPTY EXCEPT FOR THE SPARE TIRE AND JACK.
5. PLACE THE FRONT SEAT IN THE REAR POSITION.
6. IGNITION SWITCH ON TO ACTIVATE ELECTRONIC LEVEL CONTROL (ELC). (IF EQUIPPED)
7. "BOUNCE" THE CAR THREE TIMES AT THE FRONT AND REAR TO NORMALIZE THE SUSPENSION.
8. MEASURE FROM THE LOWEST POINT ON THE BALLJOINT HOUSING TO CONTROL ARM BOLT CENTERLINE AT "D" AND "Z" POSITIONS. (SEE ILLUSTRATIONS ABOVE)
9. MEASURE FROM KNOWN LEVEL FLOOR TO ROCKER PANEL AT "J" AND "K" POSITIONS. EXCEPT SSE MODELS.
10. MEASURE FROM KNOWN LEVEL FLOOR TO THE WHEEL OPENING AT "P" AND "R" POSITIONS.

MAXIMUM VARIATION SIDE TO SIDE & FRONT TO REAR IS 19MM (¾ IN)

LOAD CONDITIONS — COOLANT TO CAPACITY AND FULL TANK OF FUEL

"Z"	64-84 mm	2⁹⁄₆₄-3³⁄₈ in.
"D"	71-91 mm	2¹³⁄₆₄-3¹³⁄₃₂ in.
"P"	706-726 mm	27¹⁵⁄₆₄-28¹³⁄₆₄ in.
"R"	656-676 mm	25⁵⁄₆₄-26¹⁵⁄₆₄ in.
"J"	230-250 mm	9⁶⁄₆₄-9²⁵⁄₃₂ in.
"K"	230-250 mm	9⁶⁄₆₄-9²⁵⁄₃₂ in.

Fig. 54 Vehicle trim height measurements. DeVille & Fleetwood (FWD)

		SUSPENSION		ROCKER PANEL		WHEEL OPENING	
		Z	D	J	K	P	R
ELDORADO	mm	52	30	223	221	717	716
	in.	2.05	1.18	8.78	8.70	28.23	28.19
SEVILLE	mm	56	34	245	245	726	726
	in.	2.21	1.34	9.65	9.65	28.68	28.68
SEVILLE STS	mm	52	31	241	241	722	722
	in.	2.05	1.22	9.49	9.49	28.43	28.43

THE SPECIFICATIONS SHOWN ARE FOR THE VEHICLE ON A LEVEL SURFACE WITH A FULL TANK OF FUEL, PROPER TIRE INFLATION PRESSURE, NO PASSENGERS OR ADDITIONAL WEIGHT IN CAR, AND A PROPERLY OPERATING ELECTRONIC LEVEL CONTROL SYSTEM. BOUNCE VEHICLE THREE TIMES AT FRONT AND REAR TO NORMALIZE SUSPENSION. ALL MEASUREMENTS ARE ±10MM. MAXIMUM VARIATION SIDE TO SIDE IS 12 MM (0.5 INCH).

Fig. 53 Vehicle trim height measurements. 1992–93 Eldorado & Seville

TRIM HEIGHTS CHART

VEHICLE	SUSPENSION	TIRE	J		K		P		R	
			mm	INCH	mm	INCH	mm	INCH	mm	INCH
SEDAN	FE1	205-75	252.00	9.92	264.00	10.39	742.00	29.52	539.00	21.22
		225-70	252.00	9.92	264.00	10.39	742.00	29.52	539.00	21.22
	FE2	225-70	252.00	9.92	264.00	10.39	742.00	29.52	539.00	21.22
	Police	205-75	252.00	9.92	264.00	10.39	742.00	29.52	539.00	21.22
		225-75*	252.00	9.92	264.00	10.39	742.00	29.52	539.00	21.22
		235-70*	252.00	9.92	264.00	10.39	742.00	29.21	539.00	21.22
WAGON	ALL	225-75	252.00	9.92	264.00	10.39	742.00	29.21	550.00	21.65
		225-70	252.00	9.92	264.00	10.39	742.00	29.21	550.00	21.65

*Speed Rated Tires
NOTE: All dimensions shown are vertical to the ground. Trim heights should be within ± 10 mm (0.4 inch) to be considered correct.

Fig. 55   Vehicle trim height measurements. Caprice, Caprice Wagon, Custom Cruiser & Roadmaster

VEHICLE TRIM HEIGHT ADJUSTMENT

1. Loosen locknut securing metal arm to height sensor plastic arm, **Fig. 56.**
2. To increase trim height, move plastic actuator arm upward and tighten locknut.
3. To decrease trim height, move plastic actuator arm downward and tighten locknut.
4. If proper adjustment cannot be made, ensure correct height sensor is installed.

Fig. 56   Vehicle trim height adjustment

Selective Ride Control (SRC)

INDEX

SYMPTOM TABLE

SYMPTOM	PROCEDURE
Codes 13, 14, 21, 22	Chart #1
Codes 31, 32, 33, 34	Chart #2
Codes 41, 42, 43 (See Note 1 below)	Chart #3
Code 23 (See Note 2 below)	Chart #4
Cannot read codes	Chart #5

CODE DEFINITION

- Code 12 – Start of code sequence
- Code 13 – Left Rear time out
- Code 14 – Right Front time out
- Code 21 – Left Front time out
- Code 22 – Right Rear time out
- Code 23 – Loss of vehicle speed signal (See Note 2 below)
- Code 31 – Left Front out of position
- Code 32 – Right Front out of position
- Code 33 – Left Rear out of position
- Code 34 – Right Rear out of position
- Code 41 – Selective Ride Control Switch short to "B+"
- Code 42 – Selective Ride Control Switch open contacts (See Note 1 below)
- Code 43 – Selective Ride Control Switch open circuit

Note 1:

Code 42 will set if the Selective Ride Control Switch is not properly positioned in one of the three detent positions.

Note 2:

Code 23 will set if the Ignition Switch is cycled "ON/OFF" three times without driving vehicle. The "Service Ride Control" Indicator will turn "OFF" once the vehicle has been driven if the system is OK, but the code will remain as a history code and should be cleared to avoid future misdiagnosis.

Fig. 1   Symptom table. 1991

PRECAUTIONS

AIRBAG SYSTEM DISARMING

The diagnostic energy reserve module (DERM) can maintain voltage to cause a system deployment for up to ten minutes after the ignition switch is turned off and the battery is disconnected. Servicing the SIR system during this period may result in accidental deployment and personal injury.

1. Ensure front wheels are pointed straight ahead.
2. Turn ignition switch to LOCK position and remove SIR or AIRBAG fuse.
3. Remove left sound insulator. **Remove courtesy lamp from sound insulator, if necessary.**
4. Remove Connector Position Assurance (CPA), then disconnect yellow two-way SIR electrical connector at base of steering column.

AIRBAG SYSTEM ARMING

1. Connect yellow two-way SIR electrical connector, then install Connector Position Assurance (CPA).
2. Install left sound insulator. **Install courtesy lamp to sound insulator, if applicable.**
3. Install SIR fuse to fuse block, turn ignition switch to RUN position and ensure that "Inflatable Restraint" lamp flashes 7 to 9 times, then turns off.

DESCRIPTION

The Selective Ride Control (SRC) system is capable of setting the vehicle suspension to various damping positions by use of the SRC switch and/or automatically depending on vehicle speed input to SRC module. This system consists of front and rear adjustable shock absorbers, electrical actuators, a selective ride control switch and control module.

The selective ride control shock absorber operates in the same manner as the standard gas shock absorber. The shock absorbers are gas charged to reduce aeration (foaming) of shock fluid which results in unlimited damping control. They also reduce impact harshness and improve road isolation. An electrical actuator is positioned on top of each adjustable shock absorber. The control module is located in the left rear storage compartment behind the driver's seat and the control switch is located on the floor console.

SYSTEM COMPONENTS

Module

The SRC module provides electronic control logic and electrical output drive for the system, based on driver preference and vehicle speed input data. The SRC module receives its speed signal from the transmission VSS sensor assembly. Once a speed signal has been detected, the SRC module adjusts the damper valving to one of six specific settings according to vehicle speed and Select Ride Switch setting ("PERF" "SPORT" OR "TOUR.") The damping rate increases with vehicle speed and only within the selected setting. The SRC module has ability to store system trouble codes.

Electrical Actuators

This system utilizes external electrical actuators to adjust the valve position of each shock absorber as dictated by SRC module. The actuators consist of a bi-directional DC motor with an integral position feedback sensor. The SRC module can move the electrical actuators in either direction. The motor range of travel for valve adjustment while attached to shock absorber is from 0° to 90°. The SRC module determines position of the valve by counting ground pulses on position sensor input from the actuator position feedback sensors.

Shock Absorber

The shocks are pressurized gas type and provide damping by forcing oil through internal orifices to resist suspension movement. The variable damping feature is provided by changing orifice size. The orifice size is controlled by adjusting a shaft which extends through top of shock absorber. The shaft is turned by the electrical actuator, mounted on top of shock absorber.

Fig. 2 Selective ride wiring diagram (Part 1 of 2). 1991

Fig. 2 Selective ride wiring diagram (Part 2 of 2). 1991

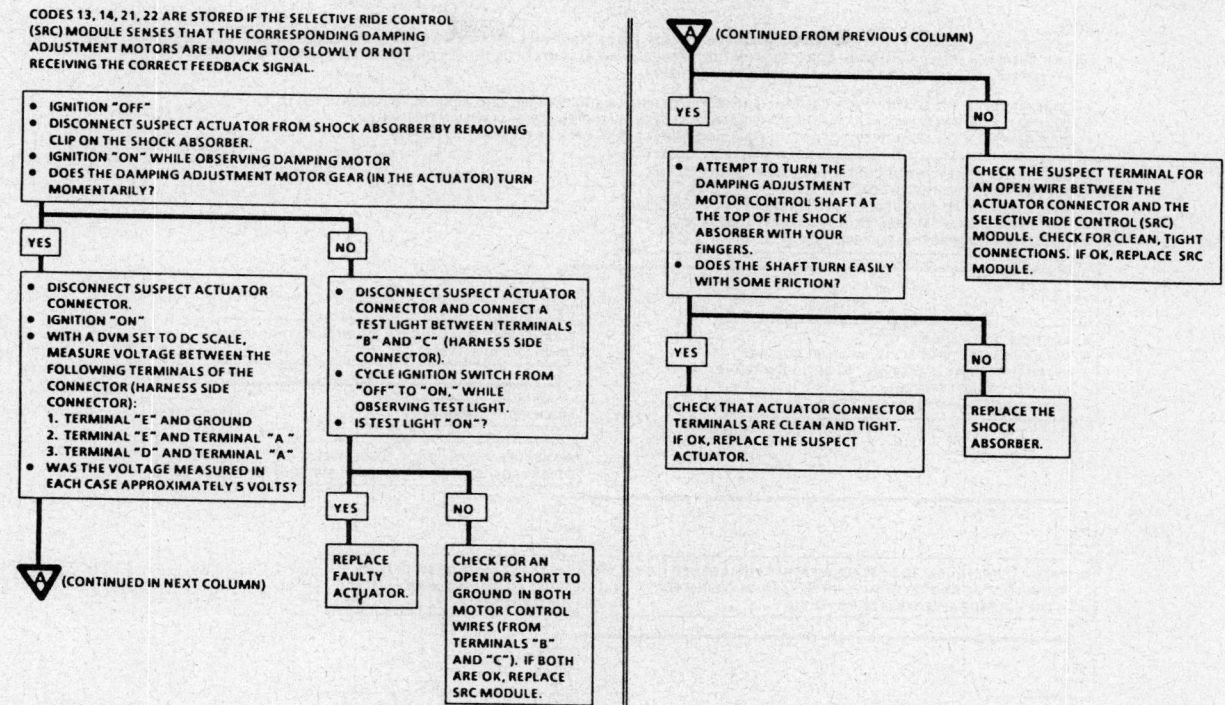

Fig. 3   Diagnosis chart 1. 1991

Fig. 4   Diagnosis chart 2. 1991

DIAGNOSIS & TESTING

Selective ride trouble codes may be read with the vehicle stopped using a Tech 1 with and 88-92 brake cartridge or by grounding terminal "C" of the Assembly Line Diagnostic Link (ALDL). Observe the "Service Ride Control" indicator with the ignition switch in "Run." The trouble codes are comprised of two digits. A digit is read by counting the number of flashes that occur within a half second of each other. The second digit will appear about one second after the first digit has gone.

Each code will repeat three times before the next code begins with a three second pause between codes. The entire trouble code sequence will reappear as long as terminal "C" is grounded. The trouble code display begins by showing code 12 three times, marking the beginning of the sequence.

If the diagnostic mode cannot be entered (no codes appear, not even 12), refer to **Fig. 1.**

When the diagnosis is complete and any necessary repairs have been made, the trouble codes must be cleared to prevent further misdiagnosis. To clear the system, select clear code function using Tech 1 with an 88-92 brake cartridge or ground pin "C" of the ALDL connector for two seconds and repeat the procedure twice for a total of three groundings.

On 1991 models, diagnose select ride control system by reading trouble codes stored in selective ride control module. Refer to **Fig. 1.** for symptom table chart, **Fig. 2,** for wiring diagram and **Figs. 3 through 7,** for trouble code diagnosis charts.

On 1992-93 models, diagnose selective ride control system by reading the trouble codes stored in the selective ride control module. Refer to **Fig. 8,** for system diagnosis chart, **Fig. 9,** for wiring diagram and **Figs. 10 through 15,** for trouble code diagnosis charts.

CHART #3
CODES 41, 42 OR 43 SET

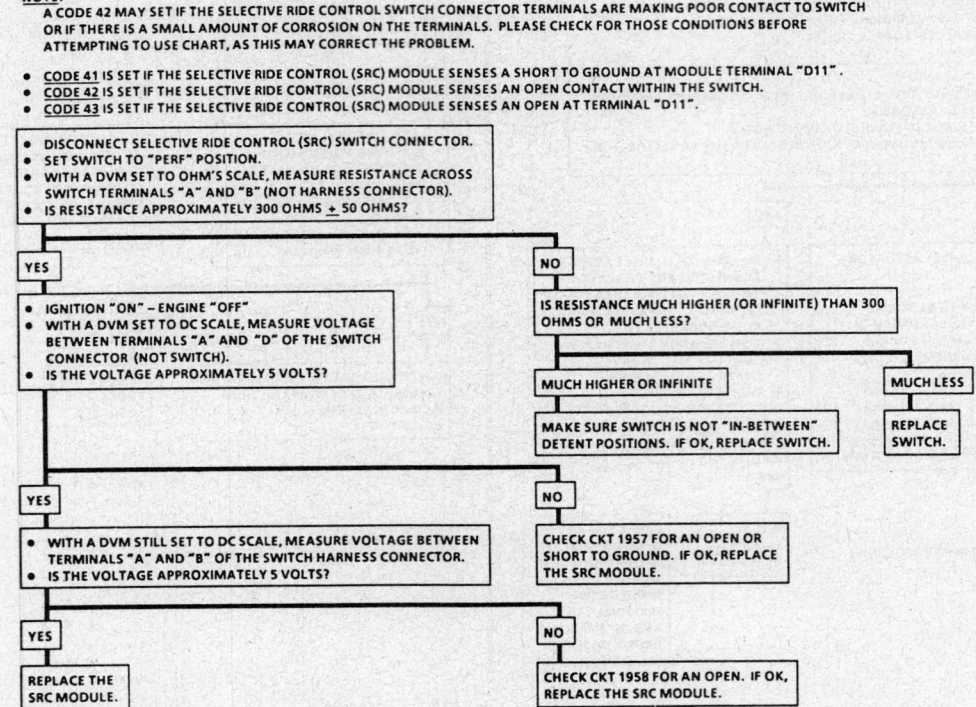

NOTE:
A CODE 42 MAY SET IF THE SELECTIVE RIDE CONTROL SWITCH CONNECTOR TERMINALS ARE MAKING POOR CONTACT TO SWITCH OR IF THERE IS A SMALL AMOUNT OF CORROSION ON THE TERMINALS. PLEASE CHECK FOR THOSE CONDITIONS BEFORE ATTEMPTING TO USE CHART, AS THIS MAY CORRECT THE PROBLEM.

- CODE 41 IS SET IF THE SELECTIVE RIDE CONTROL (SRC) MODULE SENSES A SHORT TO GROUND AT MODULE TERMINAL "D11".
- CODE 42 IS SET IF THE SELECTIVE RIDE CONTROL (SRC) MODULE SENSES AN OPEN CONTACT WITHIN THE SWITCH.
- CODE 43 IS SET IF THE SELECTIVE RIDE CONTROL (SRC) MODULE SENSES AN OPEN AT TERMINAL "D11".

Fig. 5   Diagnosis chart 3. 1991

CHART #4
CODE 23
LOSS OF VEHICLE SPEED

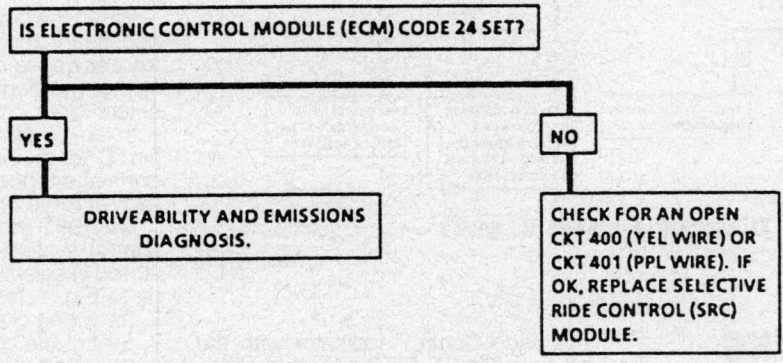

NOTE:
CODE 23 WILL SET IF THE IGNITION SWITCH IS CYCLED "ON" AND "OFF" THREE TIMES WITHOUT DRIVING THE VEHICLE. SYSTEM IS WORKING NORMALLY IF THE "SERVICE RIDE CONTROL" INDICATOR TURNS "OFF" AFTER DRIVING VEHICLE. CODE 23 WILL REMAIN AS A HISTORY CODE, AND SHOULD BE CLEARED TO PREVENT FUTURE MISDIAGNOSIS.

Fig. 6   Diagnosis chart 4. 1991

CHART #5
TROUBLE CODES CANNOT BE READ

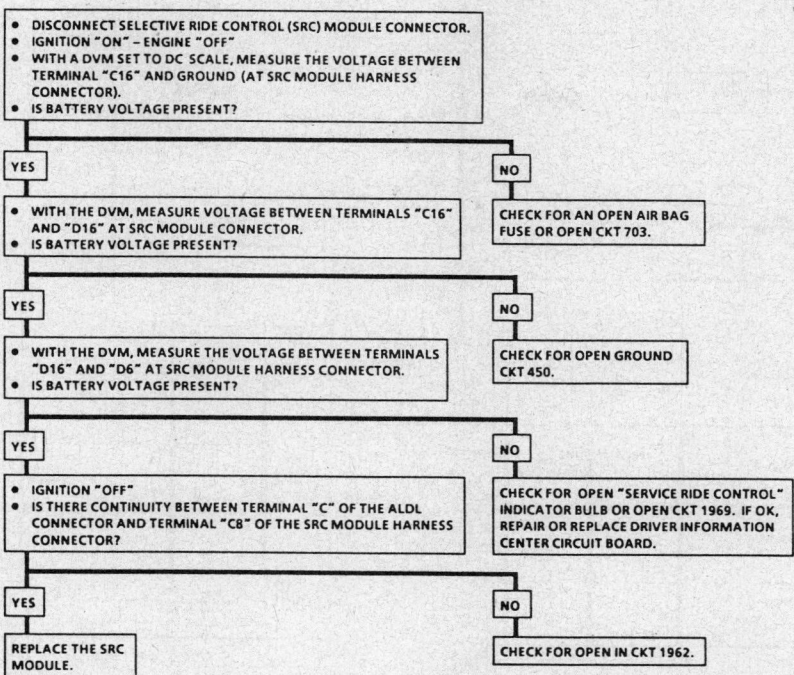

Fig. 7   Diagnosis chart 5. 1991

Fig. 8   System diagnosis chart. 1992–93

Fig. 9   Selective ride wiring diagram (Part 1 of 4). 1992

Fig. 9 Selective ride wiring diagram (Part 1 of 4). 1993

Fig. 9 Selective ride wiring diagram (Part 2 of 4). 1992–93

Fig. 9 Selective ride wiring diagram (Part 3 of 4). 1992–93

Fig. 9 Selective ride wiring diagram (Part 4 of 4). 1992–93

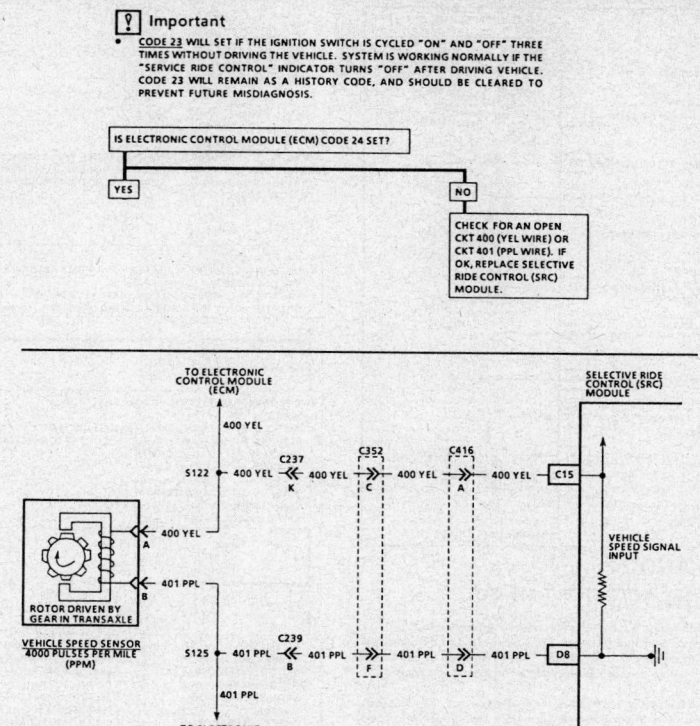

Important
- CODE 23 WILL SET IF THE IGNITION SWITCH IS CYCLED "ON" AND "OFF" THREE TIMES WITHOUT DRIVING THE VEHICLE. SYSTEM IS WORKING NORMALLY IF THE "SERVICE RIDE CONTROL" INDICATOR TURNS "OFF" AFTER DRIVING VEHICLE. CODE 23 WILL REMAIN AS A HISTORY CODE, AND SHOULD BE CLEARED TO PREVENT FUTURE MISDIAGNOSIS.

Fig. 10   Code 23, loss of vehicle speed signal. 1992–93

CODES 13 AND 22
LEFT REAR OR RIGHT REAR TIME-OUT

Circuit Description:

The Selective Ride Control (SRC) module supplies power and ground to the electrical actuators and can drive them in either direction, depending on the requested damper position. At each ignition cycle, the SRC module drives the actuators to a fail-safe position until a vehicle speed signal is received. This is referred to as system initialization. The electrical actuator has an integral Hall-effect sensor which reports the actuator's position to the SRC module by way of a position feedback circuit.

Codes 13 and 22 are stored in the SRC module's diagnostic memory if the module senses that the corresponding SRC modules electrical actuator is not moving or moving too slowly or not receiving the correct feedback signal.

Test Description: Number(s) below refer to circled number(s) on the diagnostic chart.

1. This test will determine if the actuator motor moves to the fail-safe position under system initialization.
2. If the actuator motor moved under system initialization the position feedback circuit is suspect. This test will determine if there is approximately 5 volts present on the position feedback circuits.
3. If the actuator motor did not move under system initialization, this test will determine if the actuator is receiving voltage from the SRC module. If no voltage is present, the circuit between the actuator and the SRC module or the SRC module is suspect. If voltage is present, the actuator is faulty.
4. This test will determine if there is physical damage to the shock absorber that is not allowing the adjustment shaft to turn or turn freely.

Fig. 11   Code 13 & 22, left rear or right rear time out. 1992–93

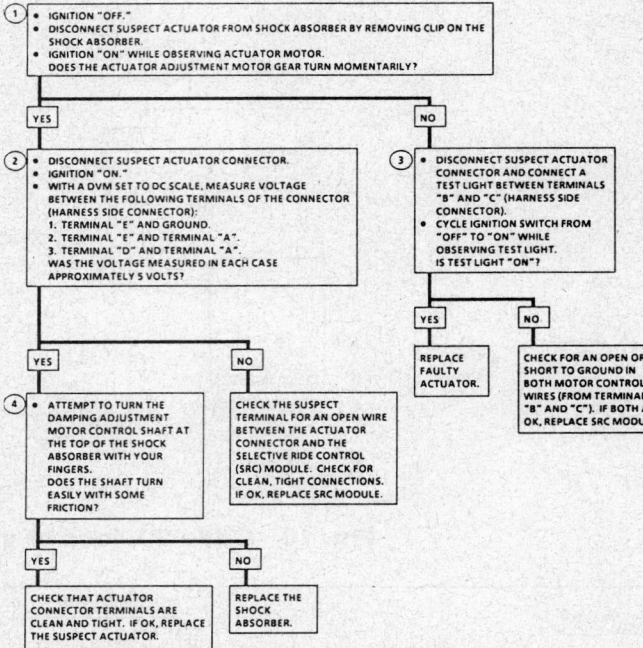

CODES 14 AND 21
RIGHT FRONT OR LEFT FRONT SRC ACTUATOR TIME-OUT

Circuit Description:

The Selective Ride Control (SRC) module supplies power and ground to the electrical actuators and can drive them in either direction, depending on the requested damper position. At each ignition cycle, the SRC module drives the actuators to a fail-safe position until a vehicle speed signal is received. This is referred to as system initialization. The electrical actuator has an integral Hall-effect sensor which reports the actuator's position to the SRC module by way of a position feedback circuit.

Codes 14 and 21 are stored in the SRC modules diagnostic memory if the module senses that the corresponding SRC module's electrical actuator is not moving or moving too slowly or not receiving the correct feedback signal.

Test Description: Number(s) below refer to circled number(s) on the diagnostic chart.

1. This test will determine if the actuator motor moves to the fail-safe position under system initialization.
2. If the actuator motor moved under system initialization, the position feedback circuit is suspect. This test will determine if there is approximately 5 volts present on the position feedback circuits.
3. If the actuator motor did not move under system initialization, this test will determine if the actuator is receiving voltage from the SRC module. If no voltage is present, the circuit between the actuator and the SRC module or the SRC module is suspect. If voltage is present, the actuator is faulty.
4. This test will determine if there is physical damage to the shock absorber that is not allowing the adjustment shaft to turn or turn freely.

Fig. 12   Code 14 & 21, right front or left front SRC actuator time out. 1992–93

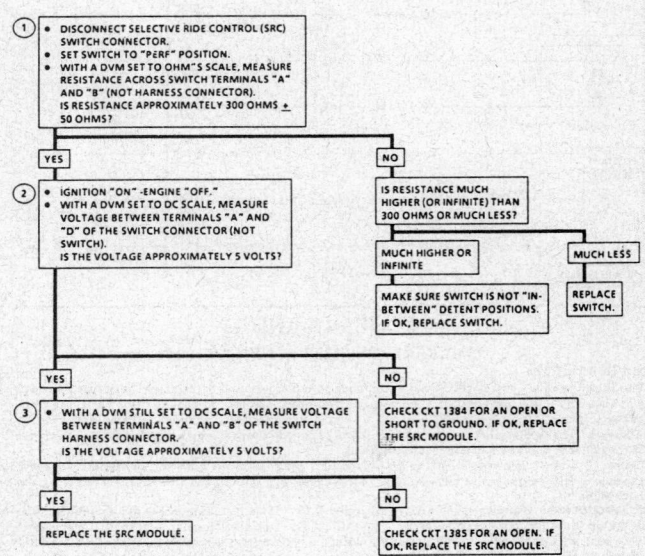

CODES 41, 42 AND 43
SELECTIVE RIDE CONTROL (SRC) SWITCH CIRCUIT FAULT

Circuit Description:

The selective ride control module inputs a 5 volt reference signal to the SRC switch which modifies that voltage to identify the selected position (tour, sport, perf.). A Code 41 will set if the SRC module senses a short to ground at module terminal "D11". A Code 42 will set if the SRC module senses an open contact in the SRC switch. A Code 43 will set if the SRC module senses an open at terminal "D11".

Test Description: Number(s) below refer to circled number(s) on the diagnostic chart.

Important
- A Code 42 may set if the selective ride control switch connector terminals are making poor contact to switch or if there is a small amount of corrosion on the terminals. Please check for those conditions before attempting to use the diagnosis chart. As this may correct the problem.

1. This test will determine if the switch is in the correct resistance range while in the "Perf" position. Always make sure the switch is all the way to the "Perf" position before performing this test.

2. This test will determine if the SRC switch is receiving the correct reference voltage from the SRC module.
3. This test will determine if the SRC module is faulty. If the switch is determined to be OK and is receiving the proper inputs from the SRC module but Codes 41, 42 or 43 are still present, the SRC module should be replaced.

Fig. 13   Code 41, 42 & 43, selective ride control switch circuit fault. 1992–93

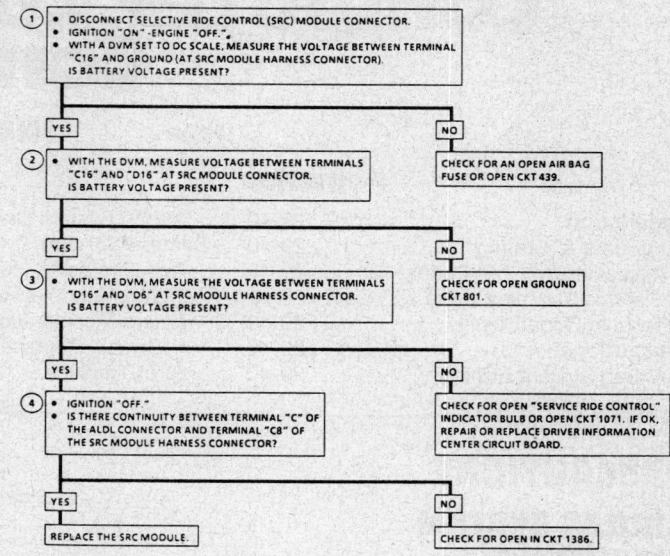

SELECTIVE RIDE CONTROL (SRC) FAULT CODES CANNOT BE READ

Circuit Description:

When the ignition switch is first turned "ON" (Run) system voltage is applied from the AIR BAG Fuse to the SRC module at the "Ignition 1" input terminal "C16". The SRC module responds by turning "ON" the "Service Ride Control" warning lamp for a few seconds while performing tests on the SRC system.

Grounding terminal "C" of the ALDL connector pulls the "Diagnostic Request" input terminal "C8" of the SRC module low and signals the module to enter the "Flash Code" diagnostic display mode.

Test Description: Number(s) below refer to circled number(s) on the diagnostic chart.
1. This test will determine if there is battery voltage at terminal "C16" (ignition input) of the Selective Ride Control (SRC) Module.
2. This test will determine if the SRC module has ground at terminal "D16".
3. This test will determine if battery voltage is present on CKT 1071 to turn the "Service Ride Control" lamp "ON."
4. This test will determine if there is an open in CKT 1386. If continuity is established on CKT 1386, then the SRC module has an internal fault and should be replaced.

Fig. 14   Selective ride control fault codes cannot be read. 1992–93

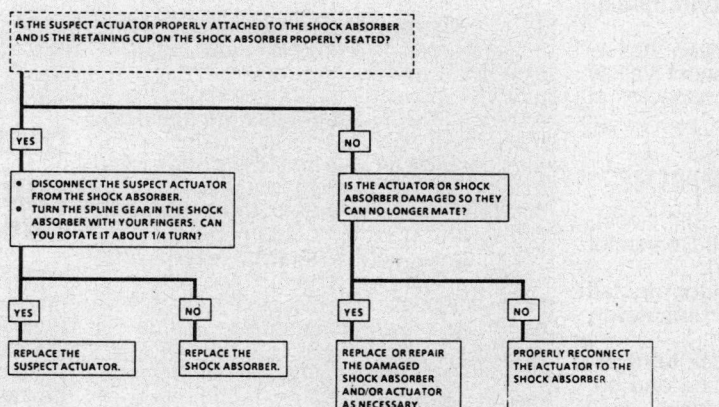

Fig. 15   Code 31, 32, 33 & 34, SRC actuator out of position. 1992–93

Computer Command Ride Control

INDEX

PRECAUTIONS

AIRBAG SYSTEM DISARMING

The diagnostic energy reserve module (DERM) can maintain voltage to cause a system deployment for up to ten minutes after the ignition switch is turned off and the battery is disconnected. Servicing the SIR system during this period may result in accidental deployment and personal injury.

1. Ensure front wheels are pointed straight ahead.
2. Turn ignition switch to LOCK position and remove SIR or AIRBAG fuse.
3. Remove left sound insulator. **Remove courtesy lamp from sound insulator, if necessary.**
4. Remove Connector Position Assurance (CPA), then disconnect yellow two-way SIR electrical connector at base of steering column.

AIRBAG SYSTEM ARMING

1. Connect yellow two-way SIR electrical connector, then install Connector Position Assurance (CPA).
2. Install left sound insulator. **Install courtesy lamp to sound insulator, if applicable.**
3. Install SIR fuse to fuse block, turn ignition switch to RUN position and ensure that "Inflatable Restraint" lamp flashes 7 to 9 times, then turns off.

DESCRIPTION

The Computer Command Ride Control (CCR) system **Fig. 1**, controls the vehicle's ride firmness by controlling an actuator in each of the four struts to increase ride firmness as speed increases. On three damping mode systems the three modes are comfort, normal and sport. On two damping mode systems the modes are firm and comfort. Damping mode selection is controlled by the CCR controller according to vehicle speed conditions, vehicle accelerometer input and any error conditions which may exist.

1	REAR STRUT
2	CCR CONTROL MODULE
3	ACCELEROMETER
4	DRIVER SELECT SWITCH
5	FRONT STRUT
6	POWER TRAIN CONTROL MODULE
7	WIRING HARNESS

Fig. 1 Computer Command Ride (CCR) system

On three-mode systems, the CCR controller located on a bracket under the driver's seat, controls and monitors the system. Using speed and accelerometer input signals the CCR determines the optimum mode strut valving. The controller monitors feedback signals from the struts to determine proper system operation. If the controller receives an incorrect feedback signal, a diagnostic trouble code is set in the controller and the fault indicator on the controller will light. The fault indicator will flash diagnostic trouble codes when the controller's diagnostic enable circuit is grounded.

On two-mode systems, the driver select switch determines the operating mode of the system. In the "Normal" switch position, the damping level depends on vehicle speed and accelerometer inputs. In the "Firm" switch position, the system will place the damping level in the firm mode regardless of vehicle speed and accelerometer inputs.

Each strut contains an electrical actuator that rotates a selector valve to a specific location commanded by the CCR controller. The selector valve contains different sized orifices which increase or decrease the strut's damping rate to control ride firmness.

The accelerometer/lateral acceleration switch is used for lift, dive or roll control. The switch will activate the sport mode on three damping mode systems or the firm mode on two damping mode systems when it detects any excessive lift, dive or roll. The system will then return to its speed dependent mode two seconds after the switch returns to its inactive state.

DIAGNOSIS & TESTING

TROUBLE CODE DISPLAY
TWO-MODE SYSTEMS

Any system error will cause both the driver select switch L.E.D.'s to be illuminated. The error display will exist as long as the the error code is active. If the fault corrects itself, the error display will no longer be illuminated, but the error code will be stored in the controller memory.

If the displays are not indicating an error condition, one or the other will be on to follow the driver select switch position, with the following exception. When the driver select switch is in the "Normal" position and the system is in the firm mode due to accelerometer input, the "Firm" L.E.D. will illuminate to show a shift to the firm mode. The "Normal" L.E.D. then will turn back on when the system returns to the comfort mode.

If a code is set, a one second self diagnostic test is performed at three minute intervals and whenever the driver select switch position is changed. Both L.E.D.'s will be on during this test and will go out if the fault code is corrected. If the fault still exists, the L.E.D.'s will remain on.

THREE-MODE SYSTEMS
LeSabre & Park Avenue

Any system error will cause the fault indicator to illuminate. The fault indicator remains lit as long as the diagnostic trouble code is active. If the fault corrects itself, the fault indicator will turn off, but the diagnostic trouble code will remain in the CCR controller's non-volatile memory.

If a diagnostic trouble code is set, a one second self-diagnostic test is performed at three minute intervals. The fault indicator comes on during this test and goes out if the fault is corrected. If the fault still exists, the indicator will remain on.

Eldorado & Seville

When the ignition switch is turned on the system performs a self-test that lasts for 7.5 seconds. The error lamp will remain on during the self-test. After the self-test, the control module will be in either the normal operating mode, error mode or reset mode. When the control module is in the "Normal Mode," the error lamp is on below 10 mph and goes off above 10 mph to indicate proper operation of the CCR system and to verify that the control module is receiving speed information. When the control module is in the "Error Mode," the error lamp is off below 10 mph and on above 10 mph. When the control module is in the "Reset Mode," the error lamp is turned off to indicate a CCR control module problem.

Any system error will cause a "SERVICE CCR SYSTEM" message to be displayed on the Driver Information Center (DIC). The message will be displayed as long as the error code is active. If the fault corrects itself, the "SERVICE CCR SYSTEM" message will turn off, but the error code will remain in the control module non-volatile memory.

If a code is set, a one second self-diagnostic test is performed at three minute intervals. The error lamp will remain on during this test and will go out if the fault is corrected. If the fault still exists, the lamp will be off below 10 mph and on above 10 mph.

DeVille, Fleetwood (FWD) & Sixty Special

Any system error will cause the "SERVICE CCR/SERVICE SSS" telltale lamp to illuminate. The error display will exist as long as the error code is active. If the fault corrects itself, the "SERVICE CCR/SERVICE SSS" telltale lamp will turn off, but the error code will be retained in the control module non-volatile memory.

If the code is set, a one second self-diagnostic test is performed at three minute intervals. The error lamp will be on during this test and will go out if the fault is corrected. If the fault still exists, the lamp will remain on.

ACCESSING TROUBLE CODES

The CCR diagnostic systems may be actuated by either of two methods.

Grounding the diagnostic enable circuit at pin ""C" of the ALDL connector or by using the control module wiring harness connector, **Figs. 2 through 5.** To read codes using the control module connector on models except LeSabre and Park Avenue, ground pin "D2" to pin "D16." To read codes using the control module connector on LeSabre and Park Avenue models, ground terminal "F2" of the connector.

Both driver select switch L.E.D.'s will blink in unison to transmit blink code diagnostics. Error codes can be read by counting the number of flashes of the L.E.D.'s. The error code display will start after pin D2 or F2 has been grounded for three seconds before beginning the blink code sequence. The sequence starts with a three second L.E.D. off period. Then code 12 is displayed three times to mark the beginning of the sequence. Next, each stored code is blinked out in ascending order. Each code is displayed three times before proceeding to the next code. If pins D2 and D16 remain connected or terminal F2 remains grounded, the entire error code sequence will repeat beginning with code 12 flashing three times. Refer to **Fig. 6** for an example of an error code format.

Refer to **Figs. 7, 8 and 9** for trouble code identification and description. Refer to **Figs. 10 through 13** for system wiring diagrams to help in the repair and diagnosis of the trouble codes.

CLEARING TROUBLE CODES

To clear error codes, connect one end of a jumper wire to pin "A" of the ALDL connector. Alternately plug into and remove the opposite end of the jumper from pin "C" three times. Hold each connection one second and pause one second between connections.

On models with driver switch L.E.D.'s, once the ALDL has been cleared, it will turn both the L.E.D.'s off for one second, and then turn them on for two seconds. If the L.E.D.'s do not go out, then the error codes have not been cleared successfully. Repeat clearing sequence.

SYSTEM SERVICE
CONTROL MODULE, REPLACE
Except Eldorado & Seville

1. Move driver seat forward.
2. **On LeSabre and Park Avenue models,** remove driver's seat.
3. **On models except LeSabre and Park Avenue,** cut carpet back under driver seat to expose the control module, **Figs. 14 and 15.**
4. **On all models,** disconnect control module electrical connector.
5. Remove control module retaining screws, then the control module.
6. Reverse procedure to install.

Eldorado & Seville

1. Open luggage compartment and remove front of trunk trim panel.

2. Disconnect control module electrical connector.
3. Remove control module to bracket retaining screws, then the control module.
4. Reverse procedure to install.

LATERAL ACCELERATION/ ACCELERATOR SWITCH, REPLACE
Except Eldorado & Seville

1. Move driver seat forward.
2. **On LeSabre and Park Avenue models,** remove driver's seat.
3. **On models except LeSabre and Park Avenue,** cut carpet back under driver seat to expose the switch, **Fig. 14.**
4. **On all models,** disconnect switch electrical connector.
5. Remove switch retaining screws, then the switch.
6. Reverse procedure to install.

Eldorado & Seville

1. Remove gear selector retaining clip and handle.
2. Remove two center console storage compartment assembly retaining screws, then the storage compartment from the center console.
3. Remove ashtray, then disconnect cigarette lighter electrical connector.
4. Remove ashtray housing assembly retaining screw, then the ashtray housing from the center console.
5. Remove five upper console retaining screws.
6. Remove upper console illumination bulbs and sockets, then the upper console assembly from lower console.
7. Remove lower console to bracket retaining screw and nuts.
8. Remove two console to instrument panel screws.
9. Remove support rod, then the lower console.
10. Cut carpet back approximately two inches to gain access to switch, **Fig. 16.**
11. Disconnect switch electrical connector.
12. Remove switch retaining screws, then the switch from frame rail.
13. Reverse procedure to install.

ACCELEROMETER, REPLACE

1. Move driver seat forward.
2. Cut carpet back under driver's seat to expose accelerometer, **Fig. 15.**
3. Disconnect accelerometer electrical connector.
4. Remove accelerometer retaining screws, then the accelerometer.
5. Reverse procedure to install.

STRUT, REPLACE

Refer to "Front Suspension & Steering" or "Rear Axle & Suspension" in appropriate chassis section.

DESCRIPTION	CKT.	CAV.		CAV.	CKT.	DESCRIPTION
GROUND	804	D16		C16	1176	IGNITION 3
		D15		C15	1020	MESSAGE OUTPUT
LR DRIVE	1010	D14		C14	1014	RR DRIVE
LF DRIVE	1002	D13		C13	1006	RF DRIVE
		D12		C12		
LF GROUND	1005	D11		C11		
RF GROUND	1009	D10		C10		
LR GROUND	1013	D9		C9		
RR GROUND	1017	D8		C8		
LATERAL ACCEL.	1308	D7		C7	817	SPEED SIGNAL
LF FEEDBACK	1004	D6		C6		
RF FEEDBACK	1008	D5		C5		
LR FEEDBACK	1012	D4		C4		
RR FEEDBACK	1016	D3		C3	1490	LIFT / DIVE SIGNAL
DIAGNOSTIC ENABLE	1050	D2		C2	1309	LATERAL ACCEL.
		D1		C1		

Fig. 2   Control module connector. Eldorado & Seville

Fig. 3   Control module connector. DeVille, Fleetwood (FWD) & Sixty Special

Fig. 4   Control module connector. 88 & 98

Code 12   Initialization (System Normal – No Error)
Code 23   Left Front Actuator Position Error
Code 24   Right Front Actuator Position Error
Code 25   Left Rear Actuator Position Error
Code 26   Right Rear Actuator Position Error
Code 31   Lift/Dive Signal Error
Code 32   Lateral Accelerator Switch Error
Code 34   Vehicle Speed Signal Error
Code 35   Speed Sensitive Steering Error

Fig. 7   Trouble code identification. DeVille, Fleetwood (FWD), LeSabre, Park Avenue & Sixty Special

Code 12   Initiation Code
Code 13   Left Front Actuator Over Current
Code 14   Right Front Actuator Over Current
Code 15   Left Rear Actuator Over Current
Code 16   Right Rear Actuator Over Current
Code 23   Left Front Actuator Position Error
Code 24   Right Front Actuator Position Error
Code 25   Left Rear Actuator Position Error
Code 26   Right Rear Actuator Position Error
Code 31   Lift / Dive Input Error
Code 32   Lateral Acceleration Switch Error

Fig. 8   Trouble code identification. Eldorado & Seville

Fig. 5   Control module connector. LeSabre & Park Avenue

Code 12   Initialization
Code 13   Left Front Actuator Over Current
Code 14   Right Front Actuator Over Current
Code 15   Left Rear Actuator Over Current
Code 16   Right Rear Actuator Over Current
Code 23   Left Front Actuator Position Error
Code 24   Right Front Actuator Position Error
Code 25   Left Rear Actuator Position Error
Code 26   Right Rear Actuator Position Error
Code 32   Mercury Switch Accelerometer Error
Code 33   Driver Select Switch Input Error
Code 34   Vehicle Speed Signal Error

Fig. 6   Example of error code format

Fig. 9   Trouble code identification. 88 & 98

Fig. 10   CCR wiring diagram (Part 1 of 2). DeVille, Fleetwood (FWD) & Sixty Special

Fig. 10   CCR wiring diagram (Part 2 of 2). DeVille, Fleetwood (FWD) & Sixty Special

Fig. 11   CCR wiring diagram (Part 1 of 2). 88 & 98

Fig. 11   CCR wiring diagram (Part 2 of 2). 88 & 98

Fig. 12 CCR wiring diagram (Part 2 of 3). Eldorado & Seville

Fig. 12 CCR wiring diagram (Part 1 of 3). Eldorado & Seville

Fig. 13 CCR wiring diagram (Part 1 of 3). LeSabre & Park Avenue

Fig. 12 CCR wiring diagram (Part 3 of 3). Eldorado & Seville

Fig. 13 CCR wiring diagram (Part 3 of 3). LeSabre & Park Avenue

Fig. 13 CCR wiring diagram (Part 2 of 3). LeSabre & Park Avenue

A   BAR, SEAT
1   CONTROL MODULE, CCR
3   SWITCH, LATERAL ACCELERATOR
7   SCREW (2)
8   CONNECTOR, ELECTRICAL
9   CONNECTOR, ELECTRICAL
10 SCREW (2)
11 BRACKET

Fig. 14   CCR control module & lateral accelerator switch mounting. DeVille, Fleetwood (FWD) & Sixty Special

Fig. 15   CCR control module & mercury switch accelerometer mounting. 88 & 98

Fig. 16   Lateral accelerator switch mounting. Eldorado & Seville

Speed Sensitive Suspension

INDEX

PRECAUTIONS

AIRBAG SYSTEM DISARMING

The diagnostic energy reserve module (DERM) can maintain voltage to cause a system deployment for up to ten minutes after the ignition switch is turned off and the battery is disconnected. Servicing the SIR system during this period may result in accidental deployment and personal injury.

1. Ensure front wheels are pointed straight ahead.
2. Turn ignition switch to LOCK position and remove SIR or AIRBAG fuse.
3. Remove left sound insulator. **Remove courtesy lamp from sound insulator, if necessary.**
4. Remove Connector Position Assurance (CPA), then disconnect yellow two-way SIR electrical connector at base of steering column.

AIRBAG SYSTEM ARMING

1. Connect yellow two-way SIR electrical connector, then install Connector Position Assurance (CPA).
2. Install left sound insulator. **Install courtesy lamp to sound insulator, if applicable.**

Fig. 1   Comparing damping mode to speed input

3. Install SIR fuse to fuse block, turn ignition switch to RUN position and ensure that "Inflatable Restraint" lamp flashes 7 to 9 times, then turns off.

DESCRIPTION

The Speed-Sensitive Suspension system control the firmness of the car's ride by automatically controlling an actuator in each of the four struts. The system has three damping modes; comfort, normal and firm. The control module determines damping mode selection according to vehicle speed conditions, lift/drive input, lateral acceleration switch input and any error conditions which may exist. When two demanded positions conflict, the system will go to the firmest damping position.

The control module located on the right electronics bay in the luggage compartment controls and monitors the speed-sensitive suspension system. The control module also controls the Speed-Sensitive Steering system. The control module receives speed, lift/dive and lateral acceleration input and determines the optimum mode strut valving for current operating conditions. The control module also receives feedback from the struts to determine proper system operation. If the control module receives an incorrect feedback signal for two successive ignition cycles, an error code will be set in memory and a "SERVICE RIDE CONTROL" message will be displayed on the driver information center.

Each strut contains an electrical actuator which rotates a selector valve to a specific location commanded by the control module. The selector valve contains different size orifices which will increase or decrease the damping rate of the strut to control ride firmness. The actuators are an integral part of the strut and cannot be serviced separately.

To determine which damping mode the system should be based on speed input, refer to **Fig. 1.**

DESCRIPTION	CKT.	CAV.					CAV.	CKT.	DESCRIPTION
GROUND	804	D16					C16	50	IGNITION 3
STEERING SOLENOID	1294	D15					C15	1020	MESSAGE OUTPUT
LR DRIVE	1010	D14					C14	1014	RR DRIVE
LF DRIVE	1002	D13					C13	1006	RF DRIVE
		D12					C12		
LF GROUND	1005	D11					C11		
RF GROUND	1009	D10					C10		
LR GROUND	1013	D9					C9		
RR GROUND	1017	D8					C8		
LATERAL ACCEL.	1308	D7					C7	817	SPEED SIGNAL
LF FEEDBACK	1004	D6					C6		
RF FEEDBACK	1008	D5					C5		
LR FEEDBACK	1012	D4					C4		
RR FEEDBACK	1016	D3					C3	1490	LIFT / DIVE SIGNAL
DIAGNOSTIC ENABLE	1045	D2					C2	1309	LATERAL ACCEL.
STEERING SOLENOID	1295	D1					C1		

Fig. 2   Control module connector

EXAMPLE:
- CODE 23 PRESENT
- DLC PIN 'C' GROUNDED BEFORE KEY–ON

1 SEC. PAUSE BETWEEN DIGITS

ON — —
ERROR LAMP STATUS
OFF — —

IGNITION OFF | 7.5 SEC. DELAY | CODE 12 FLASHED THREE TIMES | 3 SEC. PAUSE BETWEEN CODES | CODE 23 FLASHED THREE TIMES | CODES DISPLAYED IN ASCENDING ORDER

KEY–ON

Fig. 3   Example of trouble code sequence

Lift/drive input is received from the Powertrain Control Module (PCM). The system will go to the firm mode during wide open throttle to provide anti-lift. The system will go to the firm mode when there is a high deceleration rate to provide anti-drive.

The lateral acceleration switch (accelerometer) provides the control module with body roll information. The control module will command the struts to the firm mode when the switch senses lateral acceleration.

Each actuator provides a feedback voltage signifying the actuator position relative to a "Home" position. A single three volt pad signifies the home position which correlates to the first comfort damping position of the actuator, while subsequent zero to one volt pads signify the remaining damping positions. Each damping position is separated by a five volt pad.

DIAGNOSIS & TESTING
TROUBLE CODE DISPLAY

When the ignition switch is turned on the system performs a self-test which lasts 7.5 seconds. The error lamp will be on for this period. After the self-test, the control module may be in "Normal Operating Mode," "Error Mode" or "Reset Mode." When the control module is in the "Normal Operating Mode" the error lamp is on below 10 mph to indicate proper system operation and to verify that the control module is receiving speed information. When the control module is in "Error Mode" the error lamp is off below 10 mph and turns on above 10 mph. When the control module is in "Reset Mode" the error lamp is turned off to indicate a control module problem.

Any system error that is active for two successive ignition cycles will cause the "SERVICE RIDE CONTROL" message to be displayed on the driver information center (except for the accelerometer code 32 which is displayed immediately). The message will be displayed as long as the error code is active. If the fault code corrects itself, the "SERVICE RIDE CONTROL" message will turn off, but the error code will be stored in the control module's non-volatile memory.

If a code is set, a one second self-diagnosis test is performed at three minute intervals. The error lamp will be on during this test and will go out if the fault code is corrected. If the fault still exists, the lamp will be off below 10 mph and on above 10 mph.

ACCESSING TROUBLE CODES

The diagnostic system can be accessed by grounding the Diagnostic Enable circuit at pin "C" of the Diagnostic Link Connector (DLC) or by grounding pin "D2" to pin "D16" of the control module connector, **Fig. 2.** After pin "C" is grounded, the lamp will come on for 7.5 seconds before beginning the blink code diagnostic sequence.

This is followed by displaying code 12, three times to indicate the beginning of the sequence. Then each stored code is blinked out, in ascending order. Each code will be displayed three times before proceeding to the next code. When all codes have been read, the entire code sequence will repeat, beginning with code 12. The sequence will repeat until the Diagnostic Enable circuit is disconnected.

Codes are read by counting the number of flashes of the L.E.D. on the control module. A code 12 would be indicated by the lamp flashing once, followed by a one second pause, followed by two flashes with a half second pause between flashes. There is a three second pause between codes. Refer to **Fig. 3** for an example of a code sequence.

If the diagnostic mode is entered, and no codes are stored in memory, the control module will continually display code 12. System trouble codes are as follows:
Code 12: Initiation code.
Code 23: Left front actuator error.
Code 24: Right front actuator error.
Code 25: Left rear actuator error.
Code 26: Right rear actuator error.
Code 31: Lift/dive input error.
Code 32: Lateral acceleration switch error.
Code 35: Speed-sensitive steering error.

Refer to **Fig. 4,** for the system wiring diagram to help in the repair and diagnosis of the trouble codes.

CLEARING TROUBLE CODES

The error codes can be cleared by grounding the diagnostic enable circuit (pin "C" to pin "A" of the DLC or pin "D2" to pin "D16" of the control module connector) three times for approximately one second within 30 seconds. The control module will indicate that the codes are cleared by turning off the error lamp for one second. The codes cannot be cleared by disconnecting battery or control module connectors. When error codes are cleared, the ignition cycle counter is disabled until the control module completes a successful self-test. A code 31 (lift/dive error) requires a cycle of the ignition switch to retest.

SYSTEM SERVICE
CONTROL MODULE, REPLACE

1. Remove front of luggage compartment trim panel.
2. Disconnect control module electrical connector, **Fig. 5.**
3. Remove control module retaining screws, then the control module.
4. Reverse procedure to install.

LATERAL ACCELERATION SWITCH, REPLACE

1. Remove center console storage compartment by pulling up and out.
2. Remove shift handle retaining clip and shift handle.

Fig. 4 Speed-sensitive suspension system wiring diagram (Part 2 of 3)

Fig. 4 Speed-sensitive suspension system wiring diagram (Part 1 of 3)

1 CONTROL MODULE

Fig. 5 Control module mounting

1 LATERAL ACCELERATION SWITCH

Fig. 6 Lateral acceleration switch mounting

Fig. 4 Speed-sensitive suspension system wiring diagram (Part 3 of 3)

3. Remove console upper trim panel.
4. Disconnect cigarette lighter electrical connector.
5. Remove radio trim plate.
6. Remove two retaining nuts from bottom of radio control head.
7. Twist radio control head so that the right side is removed first in order to clear connectors on the left side.

8. Disconnect electrical connectors, then remove the radio.
9. Remove four console to instrument panel retaining screws.
10. Remove gear selector trim plate and PRNDL illumination lamp socket.
11. Remove two shifter plate upper mounting bolts, then the two shifter assembly to floor retaining nuts.

12. Working through the storage compartment opening, remove two console to floor retaining nuts.
13. Remove console blower air supply duct.
14. Slide console forward and disconnect electrical connectors.
15. Slide console rearward to clear shifter assembly, then remove center console.
16. Pull carpet rearward to gain access to lateral acceleration switch.
17. Disconnect lateral acceleration switch electrical connector, then remove switch from body rail, Fig. 6.
18. Reverse procedure to install.

STRUTS, REPLACE

Refer to "Front Suspension & Steering" and "Rear Axle & Suspension" sections of "Buick Reatta & Riviera, Cadillac Eldorado & Seville, Oldsmobile Toronado & Trofeo" for strut replacement procedures.

Road Sensing Suspension

INDEX

1 FRONT POSITION SENSOR
2 FRONT STRUT
3 FRONT ACCELEROMETER
4 SPEED SENSITIVE STEERING SOLENOID
5 RSS MODULE
6 REAR POSITION SENSOR
7 REAR SHOCK
8 ELC COMPRESSOR
9 REAR ACCELEROMETER
10 RESISTOR MODULE (NOT VISIBLE)

Fig. 1   Road Sensing Suspension (RSS) system

PRECAUTIONS
AIRBAG SYSTEM DISARMING

The diagnostic energy reserve module (DERM) can maintain voltage to cause a system deployment for up to ten minutes after the ignition switch is turned off and the battery is disconnected. Servicing the SIR system during this period may result in accidental deployment and personal injury.
1. Ensure front wheels are pointed straight ahead.
2. Turn ignition switch to LOCK position and remove SIR or AIRBAG fuse.
3. Remove left sound insulator. **Remove courtesy lamp from sound insulator, if necessary.**
4. Remove Connector Position Assurance (CPA), then disconnect yellow two-way SIR electrical connector at base of steering column.

AIRBAG SYSTEM ARMING

1. Connect yellow two-way SIR electrical connector, then install Connector Position Assurance (CPA).
2. Install left sound insulator. **Install courtesy lamp to sound insulator, if applicable.**

3. Install SIR fuse to fuse block, turn ignition switch to RUN position and ensure that "Inflatable Restraint" lamp flashes 7 to 9 times, then turns off.

DESCRIPTION

The Road Sensing Suspension/Real Time Damping (RSS/RTD) system **Fig. 1,** controls damping forces in the shock absorbers and struts in response to various road and driving conditions. The system is capable of making these changes within 10-15 milliseconds.

The RSS module receives the following inputs; vertical acceleration, wheel-to-body position, vehicle speed and lift/dive. The RSS module evaluates the input data and uses it to control the solenoid valves in each of the dampers independently to provide varied levels of suspension control.

The system also controls the Speed-Sensitive Steering (SSS) system and Electronic Level Control (ELC) system. The SSS system changes driver steering effort based on vehicle speed. The ELC system maintains proper vehicle trim height under various vehicle loading conditions.

SYSTEM COMPONENTS
RSS Module

The RSS module located on the right electronics bay in the luggage compartment controls the Road Sensing Suspension, Speed Sensitive Steering and Electronic Level Control Systems.

Position Sensors

Position sensors are mounted at each corner of the vehicle between a control arm and the body. The position sensors provide the system with relative wheel to body position and velocity. The rear position sensors input is also used by the Electronic Level Control (ELC) system for trim height information.

Accelerometer

An accelerometer is mounted on each corner of the vehicle. The accelerometer supplies the controller with the vertical acceleration of the body.

Speed Sensor

Vehicle speed input is received from the Powertrain Control Module (PCM) and is used to determine the amount of damper control and steering assist required.

Lift/Dive

Lift/dive input is received from the Powertrain Control Module (PCM). When the system receives a lift or dive signal it will adjust the suspension system to the firm position on all corners. The lift signal is calculated in the PCM based on throttle position, transmission gear and vehicle speed. The dive signal, calculated by the PCM, checks the rate of change in vehicle speed.

Damper

The damper contains a solenoid valve that is controlled by the RSS module. The solenoid provides two levels of damping, firm and soft. The soft mode is accomplished by switching the solenoid to the "ON" state, causing the damper oil to bypass the main damper valving. The firm mode is accomplished by switching the solenoid to the "OFF" state causing the damper oil to flow through the main damper valving. Each mode is much softer/firmer than a passive damper would be. The solenoid is an integral part of the damper and cannot be serviced separately.

RSS Resistor Module

The RSS resistor module is located in the luggage compartment in the right quarter panel, external to the RSS module and consists of four resistors inside a ceramic material. When a solenoid is switched to the "ON" state, full system voltage is applied for a short period of time to quickly activate the solenoid. It is undesirable to maintain this high current to the solenoid any longer than required, therefore a resistor is put into the circuit. This "Hold" mode provides enough current to hold the solenoid in the "ON" position.

Steering Solenoid

The steering solenoid valve is a device that is controlled to vary power assist levels. The solenoid is driven by the controller using pulse width modulation (varying the amount of time the solenoid is on) as a function of the vehicle speed. When the solenoid is in the "OFF" position, the vehicle will have full power steering assist.

Electronic Level Control (ELC) System

The ELC system automatically adjusts the rear trim height in response to vehicle loading. On vehicles with the 4.6L/V8-279 engine, the height sensing function is performed by the RSS rear position sensors. Rear trim height information is input from the rear position sensors to the RSS control module which controls the ELC compressor and exhaust solenoid information. Refer to "Electronic Level Controls" for system operation and on-vehicle service.

DIAGNOSIS & TESTING
TROUBLE CODE DISPLAY

The RSS control module continually monitors operating conditions for possible system malfunctions. By comparing system conditions against standard operating limits, certain circuit and component malfunctions can be detected. A four digit alpha-numeric trouble code is stored in the computer memory when a problem is detected by this self-diagnostic system.

ACCESSING TROUBLE CODES

To access trouble codes and perform system tests, refer to **Fig. 2.** When performing system diagnosis and repair, refer to **Fig. 3** for diagnostic information and **Figs. 4 and 5** for system wiring diagram and electrical connectors.

CLEARING TROUBLE CODES

To clear system trouble codes, refer to **Fig. 2.**

SYSTEM SERVICE
RSS MODULE, REPLACE

After replacing the RSS module it will be necessary to calibrate the new RSS module. A TECH 1 scan tool or suitable equivalent is required to calibrate the new RSS module.
1. Remove luggage compartment front trim panel.
2. Disconnect control module electrical connectors, **Fig. 6.**
3. Remove module from right electronics bay.
4. Reverse procedure to install, calibrate new module as follows:
   a. Ensure TECH 1 scan tool or suitable equivalent has latest version of chassis application program.
   b. Connect scan tool to Data Line Connector (DLC).
   c. Turn ignition key on, but do not start engine.
   d. Calibrate module per instructions on TECH 1 readout.
   e. After calibrating the RSS module, adjust vehicle trim height as described in "Trim Height, Adjustment."

TRIM HEIGHT, ADJUSTMENT

A TECH 1 scan tool or suitable equivalent is necessary to adjust vehicle trim height.
1. Place vehicle on a level surface, with doors closed and no passengers or extra weight in the car.
2. If any RTD rear position or rear damper codes are set, they must be repaired prior to adjusting trim height.
3. Check rear position sensor values in diagnostics (RTD parameters SD13 and SD14) to ensure they are in normal range as shown in **Fig. 3.** If parameters are not within normal range, check for bent position sensor brackets or disconnected sensors.
4. Check fuel level reading in IPC (data parameter ID40) and round up to nearest gallon.
5. Connect TECH 1 scan tool to DLC connector, then run ignition key to the "ON" position.
6. Adjust trim height per TECH 1 instructions, then remove TECH 1 from the vehicle.

RSS RESISTOR MODULE, REPLACE

The resistor module is receiving a high amount of current and can get very hot 480°F (250°C). Extreme care should be taken when replacing or working around the resistor module.
1. Remove luggage compartment trim panel.
2. Disconnect resistor module electrical connector, **Fig. 7.**
3. Remove resistor module from vehicle.
4. Reverse procedure to install.

FRONT RSS POSITION SENSOR, REPLACE

1. Raise and support vehicle.
2. Remove wheel and tire assembly.
3. Disconnect position sensor electrical connector, **Fig. 8.**
4. Disconnect wires from frame rail.
5. Unlatch sensor locking tabs and remove position sensor from upper and lower ball studs.
6. Reverse procedure to install.

REAR RSS POSITION SENSOR, REPLACE

1. Raise and support vehicle.
2. Remove wheel and tire assembly.
3. Disconnect sensor electrical connector, **Fig. 9.**
4. Disconnect wires from suspension support.
5. Unlatch sensor locking tabs and remove position sensor from upper and lower ball studs.
6. Reverse procedure to install.

FRONT RSS ACCELEROMETER, REPLACE

1. Disconnect accelerometer electrical connector, **Fig. 10.**
2. Depress accelerometer locking tab and remove from bracket.
3. Reverse procedure to install.

REAR RSS ACCELEROMETER, REPLACE

1. Raise and support vehicle.
2. Disconnect accelerometer electrical connector, **Fig. 11.**
3. Depress accelerometer locking tab and remove from bracket.
4. Reverse procedure to install.

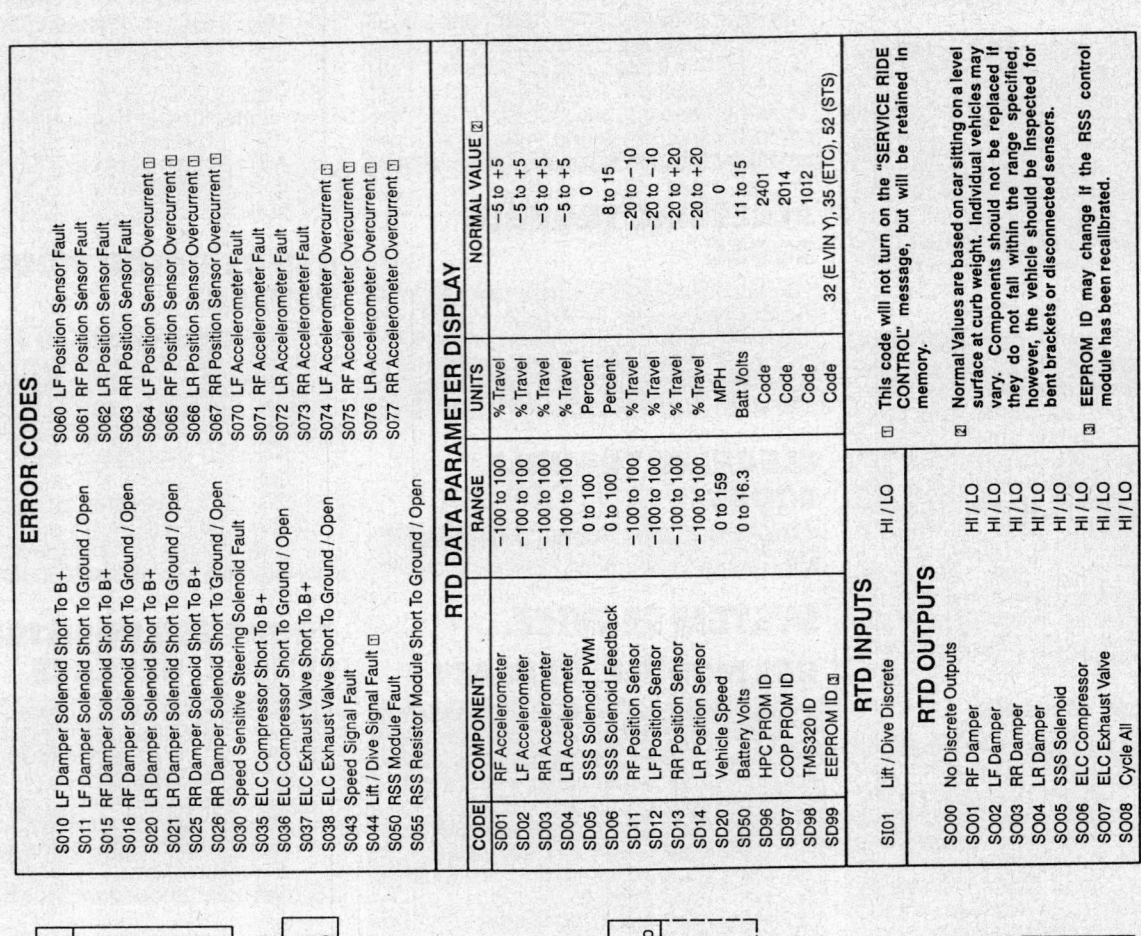

ERROR CODES

Code	Fault	Code	Fault
S010	LF Damper Solenoid Short To B+	S060	LF Position Sensor Fault
S011	LF Damper Solenoid Short To Ground / Open	S061	RF Position Sensor Fault
S015	RF Damper Solenoid Short To B+	S062	LR Position Sensor Fault
S016	RF Damper Solenoid Short To Ground / Open	S063	RR Position Sensor Fault
S020	LR Damper Solenoid Short To B+	S064	LF Position Sensor Overcurrent □
S021	LR Damper Solenoid Short To Ground / Open	S065	RF Position Sensor Overcurrent □
S025	RR Damper Solenoid Short To B+	S066	LR Position Sensor Overcurrent □
S026	RR Damper Solenoid Short To Ground / Open	S067	RR Position Sensor Overcurrent □
S030	Speed Sensitive Steering Solenoid Fault	S070	LF Accelerometer Fault
S035	ELC Compressor Short To B+	S071	RF Accelerometer Fault
S036	ELC Compressor Short To Ground / Open	S072	LR Accelerometer Fault
S037	ELC Exhaust Valve Short To B+	S073	RR Accelerometer Fault
S038	ELC Exhaust Valve Short To Ground / Open	S074	LF Accelerometer Overcurrent □
S043	Speed Signal Fault	S075	RF Accelerometer Overcurrent □
S044	Lift / Dive Signal Fault □	S076	LR Accelerometer Overcurrent □
S050	RSS Module Fault	S077	RR Accelerometer Overcurrent □
S055	RSS Resistor Module Short To Ground / Open		

RTD DATA PARAMETER DISPLAY

CODE	COMPONENT	RANGE	UNITS	NORMAL VALUE ☑
SD01	RF Accelerometer	−100 to 100	% Travel	−5 to +5
SD02	LF Accelerometer	−100 to 100	% Travel	−5 to +5
SD03	RR Accelerometer	−100 to 100	% Travel	−5 to +5
SD04	LR Accelerometer	−100 to 100	% Travel	−5 to +5
SD05	SSS Solenoid PWM	0 to 100	Percent	0
SD06	SSS Solenoid Feedback	0 to 100	Percent	8 to 15
SD11	RF Position Sensor	−100 to 100	% Travel	−20 to −10
SD12	LF Position Sensor	−100 to 100	% Travel	−20 to −10
SD13	RR Position Sensor	−100 to 100	% Travel	−20 to +20
SD14	LR Position Sensor	−100 to 100	% Travel	−20 to +20
SD20	Vehicle Speed	0 to 159	MPH	0
SD50	Battery Volts	0 to 16.3	Batt Volts	11 to 15
SD96	HPC PROM ID		Code	2401
SD97	COP PROM ID		Code	2014
SD98	TMS320 ID		Code	1012
SD99	EEPROM ID ☑		Code	32 (E VIN Y), 35 (ETC), 52 (STS)

RTD INPUTS

Code	Input	Value
SI01	Lift / Dive Discrete	HI / LO

RTD OUTPUTS

Code	Output	Value
SO00	No Discrete Outputs	
SO01	RF Damper	HI / LO
SO02	LF Damper	HI / LO
SO03	RR Damper	HI / LO
SO04	LR Damper	HI / LO
SO05	SSS Solenoid	HI / LO
SO06	ELC Compressor	HI / LO
SO07	ELC Exhaust Valve	HI / LO
SO08	Cycle All	HI / LO

□ This code will not turn on the "SERVICE RIDE CONTROL" message, but will be retained in memory.

☑ Normal Values are based on car sitting on a level surface at curb weight. Individual vehicles may vary. Components should not be replaced if they do not fall within the range specified, however, the vehicle should be inspected for bent brackets or disconnected sensors.

☑ EEPROM ID may change if the RSS control module has been recalibrated.

Fig. 3 Diagnostic information

Fig. 2 Operating vehicle self-diagnostic system

DIAGNOSTICS – BASIC OPERATION

- ENTER DIAGNOSTICS BY SIMULTANEOUSLY PRESSING OFF AND WARMER BUTTONS UNTIL ALL DISPLAYS ARE LIT.
- DIAGNOSTIC CODE LEVEL DISPLAYS PCM CODES FOLLOWED BY IPC CODES, ACP CODES, AND SIR CODES.
- TO PROCEED TO THE DESIRED LEVEL, PRESS AND RELEASE THE INDICATED BUTTON.
- PRESS OFF TO RETURN TO THE NEXT SELECTION IN THE PREVIOUS LEVEL.
- EXIT DIAGNOSTICS BY PRESSING AUTO OR DEFOG BUTTON.

KEY

To Select Another Test Press:
Hi – To Increment
Lo – To Decrement

• PROM ID Code Number Identifies An Individual Calibration And Is Periodically Updated;

Fig. 4 RSS system wiring diagram (Part 2 of 6)

Fig. 4 RSS system wiring diagram (Part 1 of 6)

Fig. 4 RSS system wiring diagram (Part 4 of 6)

Fig. 4 RSS system wiring diagram (Part 3 of 6)

Fig. 4 RSS system wiring diagram (Part 6 of 6)

Fig. 4 RSS system wiring diagram (Part 5 of 6)

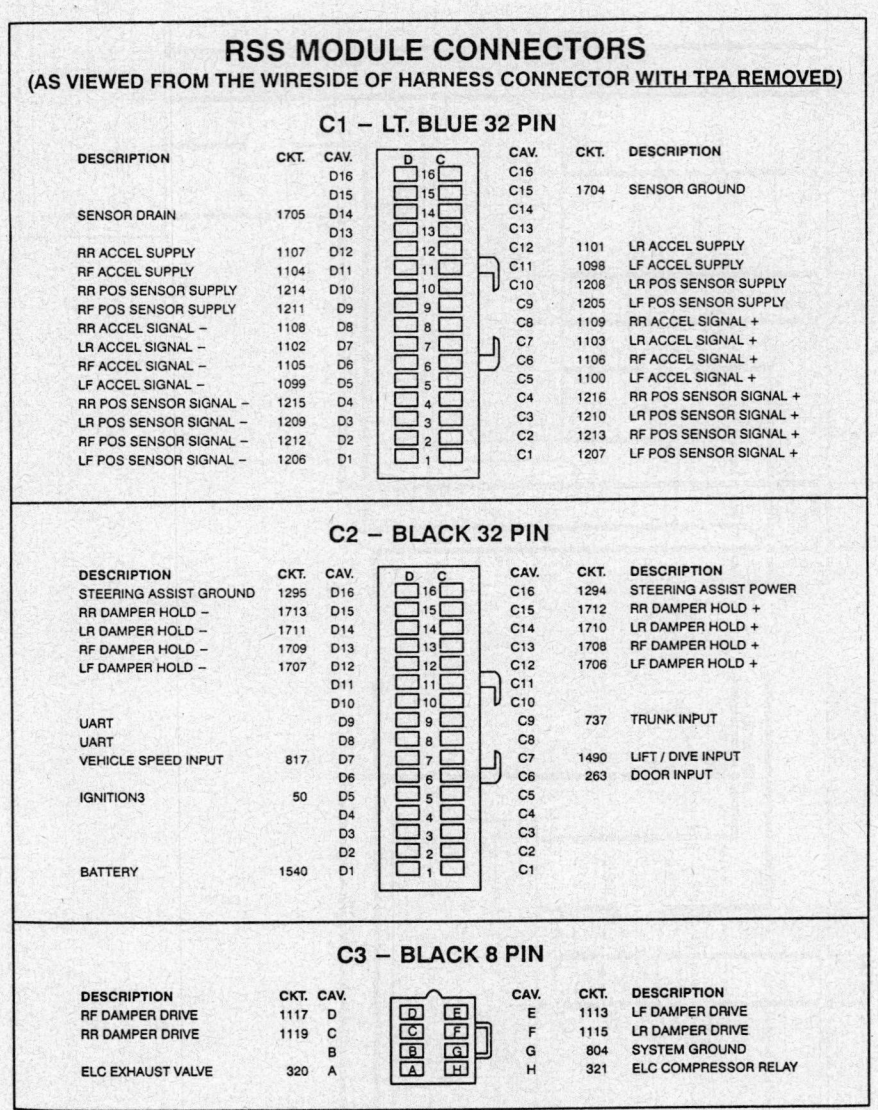

RSS MODULE CONNECTORS
(AS VIEWED FROM THE WIRESIDE OF HARNESS CONNECTOR <u>WITH TPA REMOVED</u>)

C1 – LT. BLUE 32 PIN

DESCRIPTION	CKT.	CAV.		CAV.	CKT.	DESCRIPTION
		D16		C16		
		D15		C15	1704	SENSOR GROUND
SENSOR DRAIN	1705	D14		C14		
		D13		C13		
RR ACCEL SUPPLY	1107	D12		C12	1101	LR ACCEL SUPPLY
RF ACCEL SUPPLY	1104	D11		C11	1098	LF ACCEL SUPPLY
RR POS SENSOR SUPPLY	1214	D10		C10	1208	LR POS SENSOR SUPPLY
RF POS SENSOR SUPPLY	1211	D9		C9	1205	LF POS SENSOR SUPPLY
RR ACCEL SIGNAL –	1108	D8		C8	1109	RR ACCEL SIGNAL +
LR ACCEL SIGNAL –	1102	D7		C7	1103	LR ACCEL SIGNAL +
RF ACCEL SIGNAL –	1105	D6		C6	1106	RF ACCEL SIGNAL +
LF ACCEL SIGNAL –	1099	D5		C5	1100	LF ACCEL SIGNAL +
RR POS SENSOR SIGNAL –	1215	D4		C4	1216	RR POS SENSOR SIGNAL +
LR POS SENSOR SIGNAL –	1209	D3		C3	1210	LR POS SENSOR SIGNAL +
RF POS SENSOR SIGNAL –	1212	D2		C2	1213	RF POS SENSOR SIGNAL +
LF POS SENSOR SIGNAL –	1206	D1		C1	1207	LF POS SENSOR SIGNAL +

C2 – BLACK 32 PIN

DESCRIPTION	CKT.	CAV.		CAV.	CKT.	DESCRIPTION
STEERING ASSIST GROUND	1295	D16		C16	1294	STEERING ASSIST POWER
RR DAMPER HOLD –	1713	D15		C15	1712	RR DAMPER HOLD +
LR DAMPER HOLD –	1711	D14		C14	1710	LR DAMPER HOLD +
RF DAMPER HOLD –	1709	D13		C13	1708	RF DAMPER HOLD +
LF DAMPER HOLD –	1707	D12		C12	1706	LF DAMPER HOLD +
		D11		C11		
		D10		C10		
UART		D9		C9	737	TRUNK INPUT
UART		D8		C8		
VEHICLE SPEED INPUT	817	D7		C7	1490	LIFT / DIVE INPUT
		D6		C6	263	DOOR INPUT
IGNITION3	50	D5		C5		
		D4		C4		
		D3		C3		
		D2		C2		
BATTERY	1540	D1		C1		

C3 – BLACK 8 PIN

DESCRIPTION	CKT.	CAV.		CAV.	CKT.	DESCRIPTION
RF DAMPER DRIVE	1117	D		E	1113	LF DAMPER DRIVE
RR DAMPER DRIVE	1119	C		F	1115	LR DAMPER DRIVE
		B		G	804	SYSTEM GROUND
ELC EXHAUST VALVE	320	A		H	321	ELC COMPRESSOR RELAY

Fig. 5   RSS system connectors

1 RSS MODULE
2 BLACK 8 PIN CONNECTOR (C3)
3 BLACK 32 PIN CONNECTOR (C2)
4 LT BLUE 32 PIN CONNECTOR (C1)
5 RIGHT ELECTRONICS BAY

FRONT OF CAR

Fig. 6   Replacing RSS control module

VIEW A

FRONT OF CAR

VIEW A

1 RSS RESISTOR MODULE
2 RIGHT TRUNK HINGE

Fig. 7   Replacing RSS resistor module

FRONT OF CAR

FRONT OF CAR

1 FRONT RSS POSITION SENSOR
2 UPPER BALL STUD
3 LOWER BALL STUD
4 LOWER CONTROL ARM
5 ROSEBUD ATTACHMENTS
6 POSITION SENSOR WIRING HARNESS
7 FRONT STRUT WIRING HARNESS

Fig. 8   Replacing front RSS position sensor

FRONT OF CAR

1. REAR RSS POSITION SENSOR
2. REAR SUSPENSION SUPPORT

Fig. 9   Replacing rear RSS position sensor

1. FRONT RSS ACCELEROMETER
2. FRONT STRUT TOWER

Fig. 10   Replacing front accelerometer

1. REAR RSS ACCELEROMETER
2. REAR SUSPENSION SUPPORT

Fig. 11   Replacing rear accelerometer

WIPER SYSTEM SERVICE

TABLE OF CONTENTS

Application Chart

Model	Year	System	Page No.
Achieva	1992-93	②	30-2
Beretta	1991-93	②	30-2
Bonneville	1991-93	②	30-2
Brougham	1991-92	①	30-23
Caprice	1991-93	②	30-2
Cavalier	1991-93	③	30-18
Century	1991-93	②	30-2
Corsica	1991-93	②	30-2
Corvette	1991-93	②	30-2
Custom Cruiser	1991-92	②	30-2
Cutlass Calais	1991	②	30-2
Cutlass Ciera	1991-93	②	30-2
Cutlass Cruiser	1991-93	②	30-2
Cutlass Supreme	1991-93	②	30-2
DeVille	1991-93	②	30-2
Eighty Eight	1991-93	②	30-2
Eldorado	1991-93	②	30-2
Fleetwood (FWD)	1991-92	②	30-2
Fleetwood (RWD)	1993	②	30-2
Grand Am	1991-93	②	30-2
Gran Prix	1991-93	②	30-2

Model	Year	System	Page No.
LeSabre	1991-93	②	30-2
Metro	1991-93	④	30-24
Lumina	1991-93	②	30-2
Ninety Eight	1991-93	②	30-2
Park Avenue	1991-93	②	30-2
Prizm	1991-93	④	30-24
Reatta	1991	②	30-2
Regal	1991-93	②	30-2
Riviera	1991-93	②	30-2
Roadmaster	1991-93	②	30-2
Seville	1991-93	②	30-2
Storm	1991-93	④	30-2
Sunbird	1991-93	③	30-18
Toronado	1991-92	②	30-2
Trofeo	1991-92	②	30-2
6000	1991	②	30-2

① —Multiplex pulse wiper system.
② —Permanent magnet depressed park system.
③ —Permanent magnet positive park system.
④ —One, two and three speed systems.

Permanent Magnet Depressed Park System

INDEX

DESCRIPTION

The Permanent Magnet Depressed Park (PMDP) windshield wiper and remote washer pump system consists of a depressed park wiper motor and a washer pump mounted on the washer fluid reservoir.

Based on the type of control switch used and whether an optional electronic printed circuit board is attached in the wiper cover, the system can serve as either a pulse type wiper system or a standard type system. Pulse timing and demand functions are controlled electronically on pulse systems. The pulse system also uses the vehicle speed signal to adjust the wiper delay time. The faster the vehicle is traveling, the shorter delay time between wipe cycles.

Electronic logic circuits on the pulse wiper system's printed circuit board establish all timing and washer commands. If the WASH switch is pressed, a wash is performed for as long as the switch is depressed. The wash action is followed by six seconds of dry wipes before shutoff. With the control switch in the LO or HI speed position, the respective brush circuit is completed to the 12 volt DC source and the wiper motor runs at that particular speed setting.

Moving the switch to the PULSE mode operates the wiper motor intermittently and the delay and be varied by moving the switch back and forth in the delay mode. An instantaneous wipe can be obtained by moving the switch to the MIST position.

Fig. 1 Wiper system circuit diagram. 1991–92 Except Camaro, Century, Corvette, Cutlass Ciera/Cutlass Cruiser, Firebird & 6000

DIAGNOSIS & TESTING

EXCEPT CORVETTE

1991–92

Refer to wiring circuit diagrams **Figs. 1 and 2**, wiper motor terminal checks **Figs. 3 and 4**, wiper switch tests **Fig. 5 through 8**, wiper/washer switch check charts **Figs. 9 and 10** and diagnosis charts **Figs. 11 through 22**, when performing system diagnosis and testing procedures.

1993

On models except Eldorado and Seville, refer to wiring circuits **Figs. 23 and 24**, connector terminal identification **Figs. 25 and 26** and diagnosis charts **Figs. 27 through 43**, when performing system diagnosis and testing procedures.

On Eldorado and Seville models, refer to wiring circuit diagram **Fig. 44**, wiper motor terminal check **Fig. 45** wiper switch tests **Figs. 46 and 47**, wiper/washer switch check chart **Fig. 48** and diagnosis charts **Figs. 49 through 58**, when performing system diagnosis and testing procedures.

CORVETTE

Refer to **Figs. 59 through 68** for system diagnosis charts.

Fig. 4 Wiper motor terminal check. 1991–92 Camaro, Century, Cutlass Ciera/Cutlass Cruiser, Firebird & 6000

Fig. 3 Wiper motor terminal check. 1991–92 Except Camaro, Century, Corvette, Cutlass Ciera/Cutlass Cruiser, Firebird & 6000

Fig. 2 Wiper system circuit diagram. 1991–92 Camaro, Century, Cutlass Ciera/Cutlass Cruiser, Firebird & 6000

Fig. 5 Wiper/washer switch test (standard). 1991–92 Except Camaro, Century, Corvette, Cutlass Ciera/Cutlass Cruiser, Firebird & 6000

Fig. 6 Wiper/washer switch test (standard). 1991–92 Camaro, Century, Cutlass Ciera/Cutlass Cruiser, Firebird & 6000

Fig. 7 Wiper/washer switch test (pulse). 1991–92 Except Camaro, Century, Corvette, Cutlass Ciera/Cutlass Cruiser, Firebird & 6000

Fig. 8 Wiper/washer switch test (pulse). 1991–92 Camaro, Century, Cutlass Ciera/Cutlass Cruiser, Firebird & 6000

SWITCH MODE	TERMINAL #	MIST	OFF	PULSE	LO	HI	WASH
PULSE	1	C TO 8	C TO 8	C TO 8	C TO 8	C TO 8	C TO 8
	2	B(+)	—	B(+)	B(+)	C TO 3	C TO 3
	3	B(+)	B(+)	—	B(+)	C TO 2	C TO 2
	4	—	—	—	—	—	—
	5	—	—	—	—	—	B(+)
	6	10-12V	10-12V	10-12V	10-12V	10-12V	B(+)
	7	GROUND	GROUND	GROUND	GROUND	GROUND	GROUND
	8	C TO 1	C TO 1	C TO 1	C TO 1	C TO 1	C TO 1
	9	—	—	—	—	B(+)	—
STANDARD	1	C TO 8	C TO 8	▨	C TO 8	C TO 8	C TO 8
	2	B(+)	—	▨	B(+)	C TO 3	C TO 3
	3	B(+)	B(+)	▨	B(+)	C TO 2	C TO 2
	4	—	—	▨	—	—	—
	5	—	—	▨	—	—	B(+)
	6	—	—	▨	—	—	—
	7	GROUND	GROUND	▨	GROUND	GROUND	GROUND
	8	C TO 1	C TO 1	▨	C TO 1	C TO 1	C TO 1
	9	—	—	▨	—	B(+)	—

C = CONTINUITY

Fig. 9 Wiper/washer switch check chart. 1991–92 Except Camaro, Century, Corvette, Cutlass Ciera/Cutlass Cruiser, Firebird & 6000

SWITCH MODE	TERMINAL #	MIST	OFF	PULSE	LO	HI †	WASH
PULSE	1	C	C	C	C	C	C
	2	B(+)	—	B(+)	B(+)	—	*B(+)
	3	B(+)	B(+)	—	B(+)	—	*B(+)
	4	—	—	—	—	—	—
	5	—	—	—	—	—	—
	6	10-12V	10-12V	10-12V	10-12V	10-12V	B(+)
	7	GROUND	GROUND	GROUND	GROUND	GROUND	GROUND
	8	C	C	C	C	C	C
	9	—	—	—	—	B(+)	—
STANDARD	1	C	C	▨	C	C	C
	2	—	—	▨	B(+)	—	*B(+)
	3	B(+)	B(+)	▨	—	—	*B(+)
	4	—	—	▨	—	—	—
	5	—	—	▨	—	—	—
	6	—	—	▨	—	—	B(+)
	7	—	GROUND	▨	GROUND	GROUND	GROUND
	8	C	C	▨	C	C	C
	9	—	—	▨	—	B(+)	—

C = CONTINUITY † TERMINALS #2 & #3 CONNECTED TOGETHER. *EXCEPT ON HI.

Fig. 10 Wiper/washer switch check chart. 1991–92 Camaro, Century, Cutlass Ciera/Cutlass Cruiser, Firebird & 6000

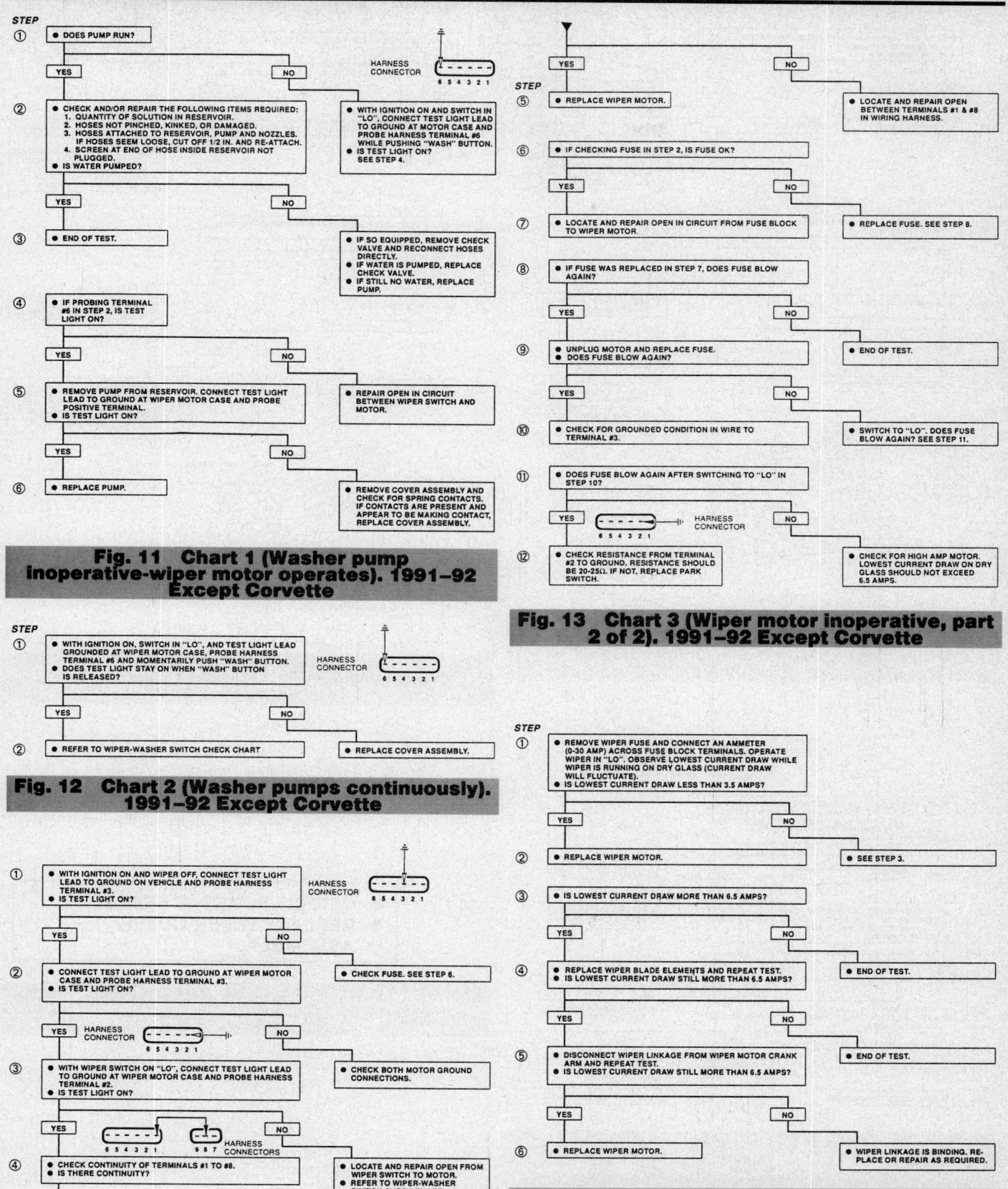

Fig. 11   Chart 1 (Washer pump inoperative-wiper motor operates). 1991–92 Except Corvette

Fig. 12   Chart 2 (Washer pumps continuously). 1991–92 Except Corvette

Fig. 13   Chart 3 (Wiper motor inoperative, part 1 of 2). 1991–92 Except Corvette

Fig. 13   Chart 3 (Wiper motor inoperative, part 2 of 2). 1991–92 Except Corvette

Fig. 14   Chart 4 (Intermittent wiper operation in "Delay," or "Lo" or "Hi" modes). 1991–92 Except Corvette

STEP

① • WITH IGNITION ON AND WIPER SWITCH OFF, PROBE HARNESS TERMINAL #2.
• IS TEST LIGHT ON?

YES / NO

HARNESS CONNECTOR
6 5 4 3 2 1

② • REFER TO WIPER-WASHER SWITCH CHECK CHART.

• REMOVE WIPER COVER ASSEMBLY. RECONNECT MOTOR WITHOUT COVER.
• WHEN MOTOR IS SWITCHED FROM "LO" TO "OFF" IS PARK SWITCH LATCH ARM IN POSITION TO CATCH DRIVE PAWL? (REFER TO ILLUSTRATION.) SEE STEP 3.

③ • IN STEP 2, IS PARK SWITCH LATCH IN POSITION TO CATCH DRIVE PAWL?

YES / NO

④ • IS DRIVE PAWL BENT?

YES / NO

• REPLACE PARK SWITCH OR COVER ASSEMBLY (PULSE ONLY).

⑤ • REPLACE WIPER MOTOR.

• CHECK SHAFT FOR ZERO END PLAY (SEE ILLUSTRATION). EXCESSIVE END PLAY WILL CAUSE DRIVE PAWL TO OVERRIDE LATCH.
• REPLACE WIPER MOTOR IF END PLAY EXISTS.

ROTATION   DRIVE PAWL

PRESS IN AND OUT HERE TO CHECK FOR ZERO SHAFT END PLAY

LATCH ARM   RELAY SLOT

Fig. 15   Chart 5 (Wiper will not park). 1991—92 except Camaro, Century, Corvette, Cutlass Ciera/Cutlass Cruiser, Firebird & 6000

STEP

① • WITH IGNITION ON AND WIPER SWITCH OFF, PROBE HARNESS TERMINAL #2.
• IS TEST LIGHT ON?

YES / NO

HARNESS CONNECTOR
6 5 4 3 2 1

② • REFER TO WIPER-WASHER SWITCH CHECK CHART, FIGURE 9.

• REMOVE WIPER COVER ASSEMBLY. RECONNECT MOTOR WITHOUT COVER.
• WHEN MOTOR IS SWITCHED FROM "LO" TO "OFF" IS PARK SWITCH LATCH ARM IN POSITION TO CATCH DRIVE PAWL? (REFER TO ILLUSTRATION.) SEE STEP 3.

③ • IN STEP 2, IS PARK SWITCH LATCH IN POSITION TO CATCH DRIVE PAWL?

YES / NO

④ • IS DRIVE PAWL BENT?

YES / NO

• REPLACE PARK SWITCH OR COVER ASSEMBLY (PULSE ONLY).

⑤ • REPLACE WIPER MOTOR.

• CHECK SHAFT FOR ZERO END PLAY (SEE ILLUSTRATION). EXCESSIVE END PLAY WILL CAUSE DRIVE PAWL TO OVERRIDE LATCH.
• REPLACE WIPER MOTOR IF END PLAY EXISTS.

ROTATION   DRIVE PAWL

PRESS IN AND OUT HERE TO CHECK FOR ZERO SHAFT END PLAY

LATCH ARM   RELAY SLOT

Fig. 16   Chart 5 (Wiper will not park). 1991—92 Camaro, Century, Cutlass Ciera/Cutlass Cruiser, Firebird & 6000

STEP

① • WITH VOLTMETER CONNECTED TO TERMINAL #6 AND GROUNDED AT MOTOR CASE, VARY "DELAY" MODE FROM MINIMUM DELAY TIME TO MAXIMUM DELAY TIME. VOLTAGE SHOULD VARY FROM A MAXIMUM TO MINIMUM.
• DOES VOLTAGE VARY?

YES / NO

HARNESS CONNECTOR
6 5 4 3 2 1

② • WITH IGNITION ON AND WIPER SWITCH ON MINIMUM DELAY, CONNECT TEST LIGHT LEAD TO GROUND AT WIPER MOTOR CASE AND PROBE HARNESS TERMINAL #2.
• IS TEST LIGHT ON?

YES / NO

• REFER TO WIPER-WASHER SWITCH CHECK CHART

③ • REMOVE COVER ASSEMBLY.
• ARE PARK SWITCH PULSE TERMINALS TOUCHING PADS ON ON CIRCUIT BOARD?

YES / NO

• REFER TO WIPER-WASHER SWITCH CHECK CHART

④ • REPLACE COVER ASSEMBLY.

• REPLACE SPRING CONTACTS.

Fig. 17   Chart 6 (No "Delay" or continuous "Delay"- motor operates in "Lo" and "Hi" modes). 1991—92 Except Corvette

---

① • CIRCUIT BOARD IS DEFECTIVE.
• REPLACE WIPER COVER ASSEMBLY.

Fig. 18   Chart 7 (Wiper stays in "Delay" during wash cycle started in "Delay"). 1991—92 Except Corvette

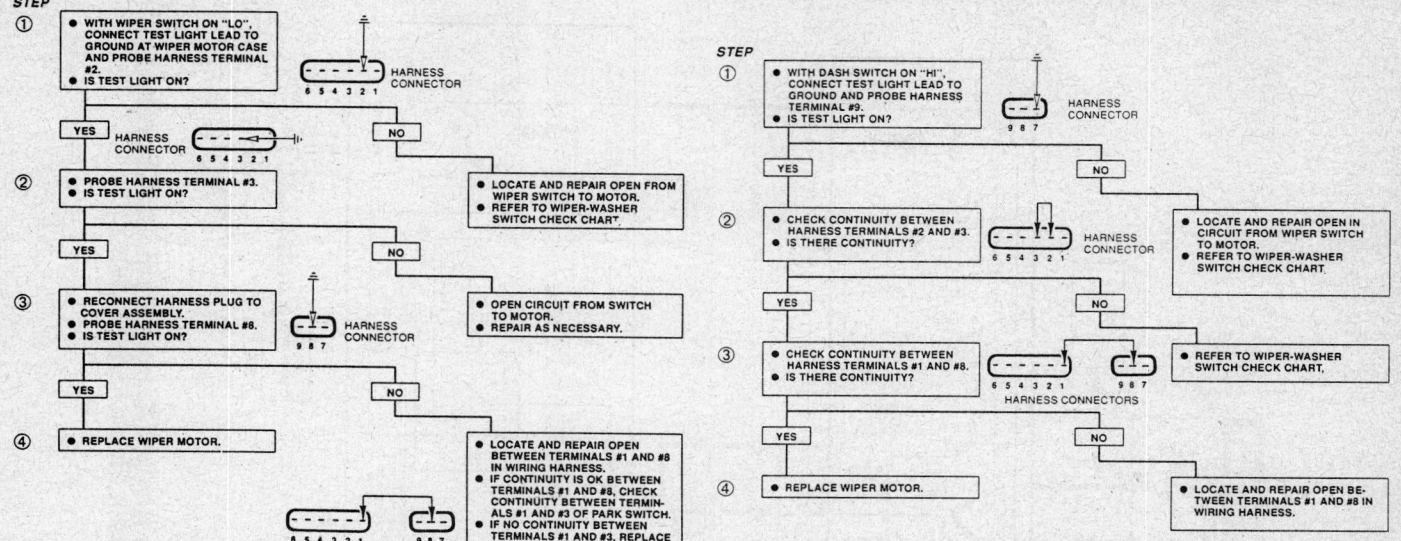

Fig. 19 Chart 8 (No "Lo" mode). 1991–92 Except Corvette

Fig. 20 Chart 9 (No "Hi" mode or blades cycle in & out of park with switch in "Hi"). 1991–92 except Camaro, Century, Corvette, Cutlass Ciera/Cutlass Cruiser, Firebird & 6000

Fig. 21 Chart 9 (No "Hi" mode or blades cycle in & out of park with switch in "Hi"). 1991–92 Camaro, Century, Cutlass Ciera/Cutlass Cruiser, Firebird & 6000

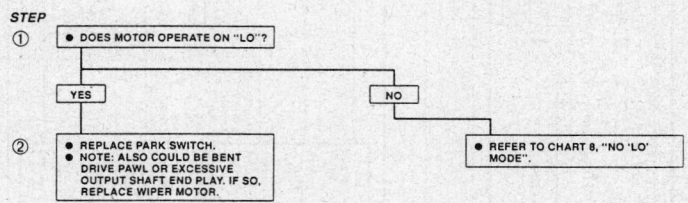

Fig. 22 Chart 10 (No "Hi" mode or blades cycle in & out of park with switch in "Hi"). 1991–92 Except Corvette

Fig. 24 Wiring circuit. 1993 Except Camaro, Corvette, Eldorado, Firebird & Seville

Fig. 23 Wiring circuit. 1993 Camaro & Firebird

A BLK
B YEL
C PPL
D DK GRN
E GRY

Fig. 25   Connector terminal identification. 1993 Camaro & Firebird

C1							C2		
F	E	D	C	B	A		A	B	C
PNK	DK BLU	RED	DK GRN	GRY	YEL		PPL	YEL	BLK

Fig. 26   Connector terminal identification. 1993 Except Camaro, Corvette, Eldorado, Firebird & Seville

- IGNITION SWITCH TO "RUN."
- BACKPROBE WITH A TEST LIGHT FROM WIPER/WASHER SWITCH CONN C215 TERM "D" TO GROUND.
  IS TEST LIGHT "ON"?

YES →
- WIPER SWITCH TO "HI".
- CONNECT TEST LIGHT FROM CONN C215 TERM "G" TO GROUND.
  IS TEST LIGHT "ON"?

NO → REPAIR OPEN OR POOR CONNECTION IN CKT 143 TO WIPER/WASHER SWITCH ASSEMBLY. IF FUSE 14 IS OPEN, CHECK FOR SHORT TO GROUND IN RELATED CKTS. RELATED CKTS WILL DEPEND ON WHETHER FUSE BLOWS BEFORE OR AFTER SYSTEM OPERATION.

YES →
- DISCONNECT WIPER MOTOR CONNECTOR.
- CONNECT TEST LIGHT FROM WIPER MOTOR CONN TERM "C" TO GROUND.
  IS TEST LIGHT "ON"?

NO → CHECK FOR POOR CONNECTION AT CONN C215 TERM "D" OR OPEN IN PIGTAIL (CKT 143) TO WIPER/WASHER SWITCH ASSEMBLY.
IF OK, REPLACE WIPER/WASHER SWITCH ASSEMBLY.

Fig. 27   Chart 1 (Wipers do not operate in any mode, part 1 of 2). 1993 Camaro & Firebird

YES →
- CONNECT TEST LIGHT FROM WIPER MOTOR CONN TERM "C" TO TERM "A".
  IS TEST LIGHT "ON"?

NO → REPAIR OPEN OR POOR CONNECTION IN CKT 92 BETWEEN CONN C215 AND WIPER MOTOR ASSEMBLY.
THEN, CONTINUE DIAGNOSIS IN OPPOSITE BOX OF CHART.

YES → CHECK FOR POOR CONNECTION TO WIPER MOTOR ASSEMBLY.
IF OK, RELACE WIPER MOTOR ASSEMBLY.

NO → REPAIR OPEN OR POOR CONNECTION IN GROUND CKT 150.

Fig. 27   Chart 1 (Wipers do not operate in any mode, part 2 of 2). 1993 Camaro & Firebird

- IGNITION SWITCH TO "RUN."
- WIPER SWITCH "OFF."
- DISCONNECT WIPER/WASHER SWITCH CONN C215.

WIPER MOTOR KEEPS RUNNING
- USING A DVM, MEASURE VOLTAGE FROM CONN C215 (VEHICLE SIDE) TERM "E" TO GROUND.

WIPER MOTOR PARKS
CHECK FOR SHORTED WIRES IN PIGTAIL TO WIPER/WASHER SWITCH ASSEMBLY.
IF OK, REPLACE WIPER/WASHER SWITCH ASSEMBLY.

MORE THAN 1 VOLT
- RECONNECT WIPER/WASHER SWITCH CONN C215.
- DISCONNECT WIPER MOTOR CONNECTOR.
- USING THE DVM, MEASURE VOLTAGE FROM WIPER MOTOR CONN TERM "D" TO GROUND.

LESS THAN 1 VOLT (APPROX. 0 VOLT)
- RECONNECT WIPER/WASHER SWITCH CONN C215.
- DISCONNECT WIPER MOTOR CONNECTOR.
- USING THE DVM, MEASURE VOLTAGE FROM WIPER MOTOR CONN TERM "C" TO GROUND.

MORE THAN 1 VOLT
REPAIR B+ CONNECTION TO CKT 113.

LESS THAN 1 VOLT
REPLACE WIPER MOTOR COVER ASSEMBLY.

0 VOLT
REPLACE WIPER MOTOR COVER ASSEMBLY.

B+
REPAIR SHORT TO B+ IN CKT 92.

Fig. 28   Chart 2 (Wipers run when switch is off). 1993 Camaro & Firebird

DO WIPERS OPERATE AT ALL WITH WIPER SWITCH IN "HI"?

YES →
- IGNITION SWITCH TO "RUN".
- WIPER SWITCH TO "HI".
- CONNECT A TEST LIGHT BETWEEN WIPER/WASHER SWITCH CONN C215 TERM "G" AND GROUND.
  IS TEST LIGHT "ON"?

NO → REPLACE WIPER/WASHER SWITCH ASSEMBLY.

YES →
- DISCONNECT WIPER MOTOR CONNECTOR.
- CONNECT TEST LIGHT BETWEEN HARNESS TERM "C" AND GROUND.
  IS TEST LIGHT "ON"?

NO → CHECK FOR POOR CONNECTION AT CONN C215 OR FOR OPEN IN PIGTAIL TO WIPER/WASHER SWITCH ASSEMBLY.
IF OK, REPLACE WIPER/WASHER SWITCH ASSEMBLY.

YES → CHECK FOR POOR CONNECTION TO WIPER MOTOR ASSEMBLY.
IF OK, REPLACE WIPER MOTOR ASSEMBLY.

NO → REPAIR OPEN IN CKT 92.

Fig. 29   Chart 3 (No high speed mode). 1993 Camaro & Firebird

- IGNITION SWITCH TO "RUN."
- WIPER SWITCH TO "LO."
- USING A DVM, MEASURE VOLTAGE FROM WIPER/WASHER SWITCH CONN C215 TERM "E" TO GROUND.

MORE THAN 1 VOLT
- DISCONNECT WIPER MOTOR CONNECTOR.
- USING THE DVM, MEASURE VOLTAGE FROM WIPER MOTOR CONN TERM "D" TO GROUND.

LESS THAN 1 VOLT (APPROX. 0 VOLT)
CHECK FOR POOR CONNECTION AT CONN C215 OR FOR OPEN IN PIGTAIL TO WIPER/WASHER SWITCH ASSEMBLY.
IF OK, REPLACE WIPER/WASHER SWITCH ASSEMBLY.

MORE THAN 1 VOLT
REPLACE WIPER MOTOR COVER ASSEMBLY.

LESS THAN 1 VOLT (APPROX. 0 VOLT)
REPAIR OPEN IN CKT 113.

Fig. 30   Chart 4 (Low speed, pulse delay & mist modes inoperative). 1993 Camaro & Firebird

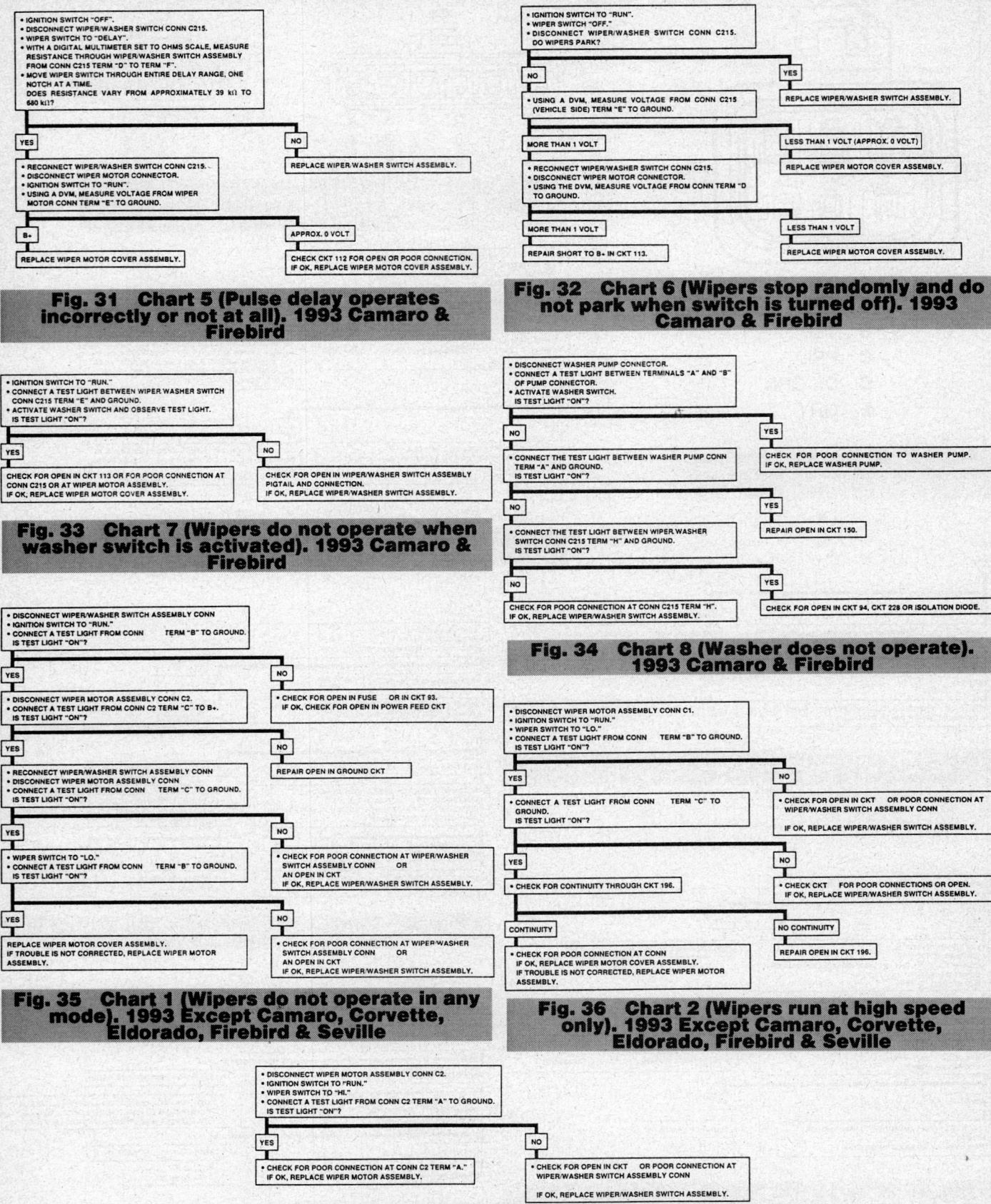

Fig. 31 Chart 5 (Pulse delay operates incorrectly or not at all). 1993 Camaro & Firebird

Fig. 32 Chart 6 (Wipers stop randomly and do not park when switch is turned off). 1993 Camaro & Firebird

Fig. 33 Chart 7 (Wipers do not operate when washer switch is activated). 1993 Camaro & Firebird

Fig. 34 Chart 8 (Washer does not operate). 1993 Camaro & Firebird

Fig. 35 Chart 1 (Wipers do not operate in any mode). 1993 Except Camaro, Corvette, Eldorado, Firebird & Seville

Fig. 36 Chart 2 (Wipers run at high speed only). 1993 Except Camaro, Corvette, Eldorado, Firebird & Seville

Fig. 37 Chart 3 (Wipers run at low speed only). 1993 Except Camaro, Corvette, Eldorado, Firebird & Seville

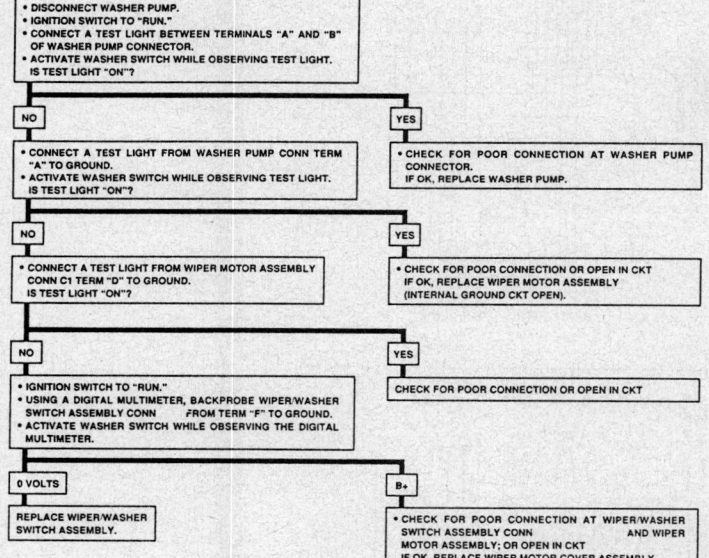

Fig. 38   Chart 4 (Wipers run intermittently in low or high speed settings). 1993 Except Camaro, Corvette, Eldorado, Firebird & Seville

Fig. 40   Chart 6 (Wipers cycle in and out of park position after wipers are shut off). 1993 Except Camaro, Corvette, Eldorado, Firebird & Seville

Fig. 42   Chart 8 (Washer will not operate). 1993 Except Camaro, Corvette, Eldorado, Firebird & Seville

Fig. 39   Chart 5 (Wipers will not turn off). 1993 Except Camaro, Corvette, Eldorado, Firebird & Seville

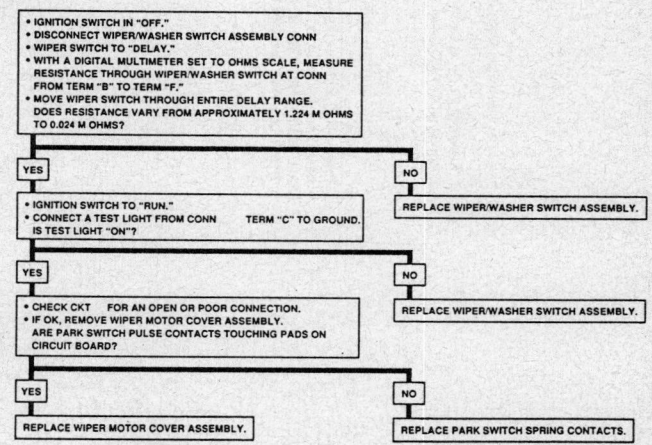

Fig. 41   Chart 7 (Pulse delay operates incorrectly or not at all). 1993 Except Camaro, Corvette, Eldorado, Firebird & Seville

Fig. 43   Chart 9 (Washer will not shut off). 1993 Except Camaro, Corvette, Eldorado, Firebird & Seville

NOTE: THE FOLLOWING PROCEDURES ASSUME THAT THE TECHNICIAN HAS CHECKED THE FOLLOWING:
1. CONTINUITY OF ALL HARNESS WIRES
2. WIPER MOTOR TO DASH MOUNTING SCREWS TIGHT
3. FUSES

WIPER MOTOR

CHECK FOR MOTOR OPERATION BEFORE REMOVING FROM VEHICLE. DISCONNECT ALL WIRING FROM WIPER AND PERFORM THE FOLLOWING CHECKS IN THIS ORDER:

TERMINAL A
TERMINAL B
TERMINAL C
TERMINAL D
TERMINAL E
TERMINAL F
TERMINAL G
TERMINAL H
TERMINAL I

IF WIPER MOTOR FUNCTIONS IN ALL MODES, GO TO WIPER-WASHER SWITCH CHECK CHART.

*IF A STANDARD TYPE MOTOR IS WIRED FOR THE PULSE CHECK, THE PARK RELAY WILL CLICK SHUT BUT THERE WILL BE NO OBSERVABLE MOTOR ACTION.

① LO SPEED   12V (+)

② HI SPEED   12V (+)

③ PARK   12V (+)

④ PULSE* (APPROX. 8 SEC. DELAY)   12V (+)   12V (+)   500 K

Fig. 45   Wiper motor terminal check. 1993 Eldorado & Seville

WIRING DIAGRAM
STANDARD & STANDARD/WASH-OUTWIPE WIPER ASSEMBLY

*MIST IS SPRING RETURN AND OPTIONAL

MIST OFF LO HI

WASH

IGNITION SWITCH

PUMP MOTOR ARM

A B C D E F G H —

WIRING DIAGRAM
PULSE & PULSE/WASH-OUTWIPE WIPER ASSEMBLY

INSTRUMENT PANEL SWITCH

MIST OFF PULSE LO HI

WASH

24 KΩ

1.2 MΩ

IGNITION SWITCH

PUMP MOTOR ARM

A B C D E F G H —

WIPER ASSEMBLY WIRING DIAGRAM

TRANSIENT SUPPRESSOR

PARK SWITCH
RUN (CLOSE BY RELAY)
PARK (OPEN BY MECH)

ELECTRONIC CIRCUIT BOARD

A B C D E F   G H —

WIPER MOTOR ARM

WIPER ASSEMBLY WIRING DIAGRAM

TRANSIENT SUPPRESSOR

PARK SWITCH
RUN (CLOSE BY RELAY)
PARK (OPEN BY MECH)

ELECTRONIC CIRCUIT BOARD

A B C D E F   G H —

WIPER MOTOR ARM

Fig. 44   Wiper system circuit diagram. 1993 Eldorado & Seville

Fig. 46   Wiper/washer switch test (standard). 1993 Eldorado & Seville

*MIST IS SPRING RETURN AND OPTIONAL

Fig. 47   Wiper/washer switch test (pulse). 1993 Eldorado & Seville

SWITCH MODE / TERMINAL		MIST	OFF	PULSE	LO	HI †	WASH
PULSE	A	C	C	C	C	C	C
	B	B(+)	—	B(+)	B(+)	—	*B(+)
	C	B(+)	B(+)	—	B(+)	—	*B(+)
	D	—	—	—	—	—	—
	E	—	—	—	—	—	—
	F	10-12V	10-12V	10-12V	10-12V	10-12V	B(+)
	G	GROUND	GROUND	GROUND	GROUND	GROUND	GROUND
	H	C	C	C	C	C	C
	I	—	—	—	—	B(+)	—
STANDARD	A		C		C	C	C
	B		—		B(+)	—	*B(+)
	C		B(+)		B(+)	—	*B(+)
	D		—		—	—	—
	E		—		—	—	—
	F		—		—	—	B(+)
	G		GROUND		GROUND	GROUND	GROUND
	H		C		C	C	C
	I		—		—	B(+)	—

C = CONTINUITY   † TERMINALS B & C CONNECTED TOGETHER   *EXCEPT ON HI.

Fig. 48   Wiper/washer switch check chart. 1993 Eldorado & Seville

STEP

① ● DOES PUMP RUN?

② ● CHECK AND/OR REPAIR THE FOLLOWING ITEMS REQUIRED:
   1. QUANTITY OF SOLUTION IN RESERVOIR.
   2. HOSES NOT PINCHED, KINKED, OR DAMAGED.
   3. HOSES ATTACHED TO RESERVOIR, PUMP AND NOZZLES. IF HOSES SEEM LOOSE, CUT OFF 1/2 IN. AND RE-ATTACH.
   4. SCREEN AT END OF HOSE INSIDE RESERVOIR NOT PLUGGED.
   ● IS WATER PUMPED?

③ ● END OF TEST.

④ ● IF PROBING TERMINAL F IN STEP 2, IS TEST LIGHT ON?

⑤ ● REMOVE PUMP FROM RESERVOIR. CONNECT TEST LIGHT LEAD TO GROUND AT WIPER MOTOR CASE AND PROBE POSITIVE TERMINAL.
   ● IS TEST LIGHT ON?

⑥ ● REPLACE PUMP.

HARNESS CONNECTOR   F E D C B A

● WITH IGNITION ON AND SWITCH IN "LO", CONNECT TEST LIGHT LEAD TO GROUND AT MOTOR CASE AND PROBE HARNESS TERMINAL #6 WHILE PUSHING "WASH" BUTTON.
● IS TEST LIGHT ON? SEE STEP 4.

● IF SO EQUIPPED, REMOVE CHECK VALVE AND RECONNECT HOSES DIRECTLY.
● IF WATER IS PUMPED, REPLACE CHECK VALVE.
● IF STILL NO WATER, REPLACE PUMP.

● REPAIR OPEN IN CIRCUIT BETWEEN WIPER SWITCH AND MOTOR.

● FOR PULSE SYSTEM, REMOVE COVER ASSEMBLY AND CHECK FOR SPRING CONTACTS. IF CONTACTS ARE PRESENT AND APPEAR TO BE MAKING CONTACT, REPLACE COVER ASSEMBLY.
● FOR NON-PULSE SYSTEM, REPLACE COVER ASSEMBLY.

Fig. 49   Chart 1 (Washer pump inoperative-wiper motor operates). 1993 Eldorado & Seville

STEP

① ● WITH IGNITION ON, SWITCH IN "LO", AND TEST LIGHT LEAD GROUNDED AT WIPER MOTOR CASE, PROBE HARNESS TERMINAL F AND MOMENTARILY PUSH "WASH" BUTTON.
   ● DOES TEST LIGHT STAY ON WHEN "WASH" BUTTON IS RELEASED?

HARNESS CONNECTOR   F E D C B A

② ● REFER TO WIPER-WASHER SWITCH CHECK CHART.

● REPLACE COVER ASSEMBLY.

Fig. 50   Chart 2 (Washer pumps continuously). 1993 Eldorado & Seville

① ● WITH IGNITION ON AND WIPER OFF, CONNECT TEST LIGHT LEAD TO GROUND ON VEHICLE AND PROBE HARNESS TERMINAL C.
   ● IS TEST LIGHT ON?

HARNESS CONNECTOR   F E D C B A

② ● CONNECT TEST LIGHT LEAD TO GROUND AT WIPER MOTOR CASE AND PROBE HARNESS TERMINAL C.
   ● IS TEST LIGHT ON?

● CHECK FUSE. SEE STEP 6.

③ HARNESS CONNECTOR   F E D C B A
   ● WITH WIPER SWITCH ON "LO", CONNECT TEST LIGHT LEAD TO GROUND AT WIPER MOTOR CASE AND PROBE HARNESS TERMINAL B.
   ● IS TEST LIGHT ON?

● CHECK BOTH MOTOR GROUND CONNECTIONS.

④ F E D C B A   I H G   HARNESS CONNECTORS
   ● CHECK CONTINUITY OF TERMINALS A TO H.
   ● IS THERE CONTINUITY?

● LOCATE AND REPAIR OPEN FROM WIPER SWITCH TO MOTOR.
● REFER TO WIPER-WASHER SWITCH CHECK CHART.

Fig. 51   Chart 3 (Wiper motor inoperative, part 1 of 2). 1993 Eldorado & Seville

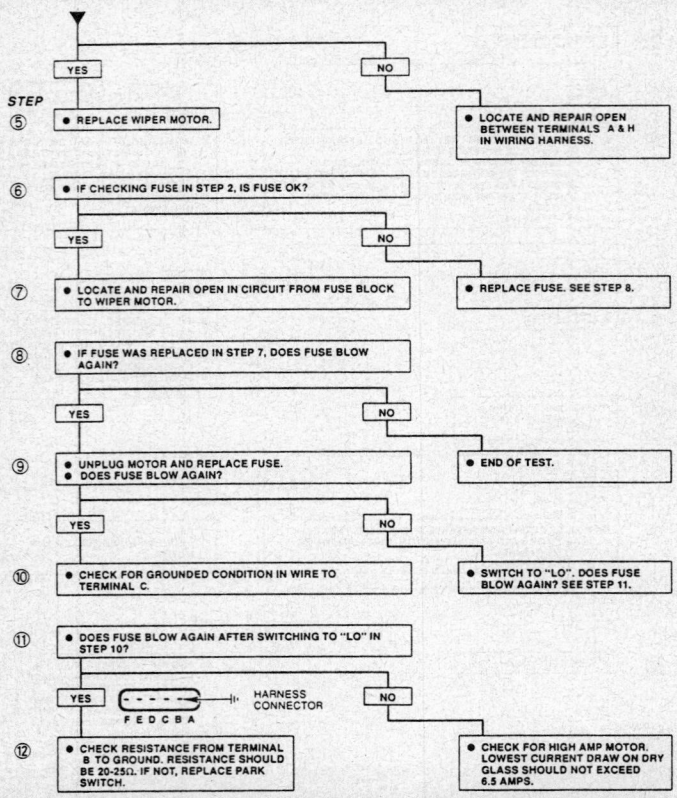

Fig. 51   Chart 3 (Wiper motor inoperative, part 2 of 2). 1993 Eldorado & Seville

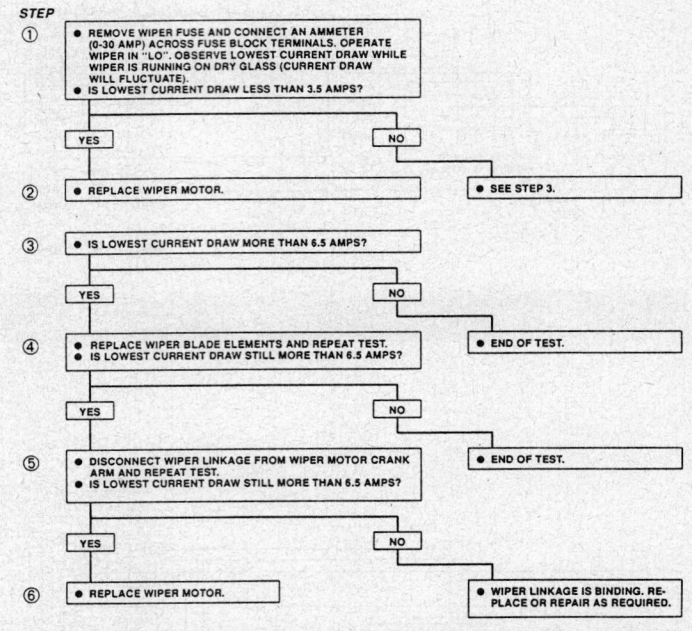

Fig. 52   Chart 4 (Intermittent wiper operation in "Delay," or "Lo" or "Hi" modes). 1993 Eldorado & Seville

Fig. 53   Chart 5 (Wiper will not park). 1991–92 except Camaro, Century, Corvette, Cutlass Ciera/Cutlass Cruiser, Firebird & 6000

Fig. 54   Chart 6 (No "Delay" or continuous "Delay"- motor operates in "Lo" and "Hi" modes). 1993 Eldorado & Seville

①
● CIRCUIT BOARD IS DEFECTIVE.
● REPLACE WIPER COVER ASSEMBLY.

Fig. 55   Chart 7 (Wiper stays in "Delay" during wash cycle started in "Delay"). 1993 Eldorado & Seville

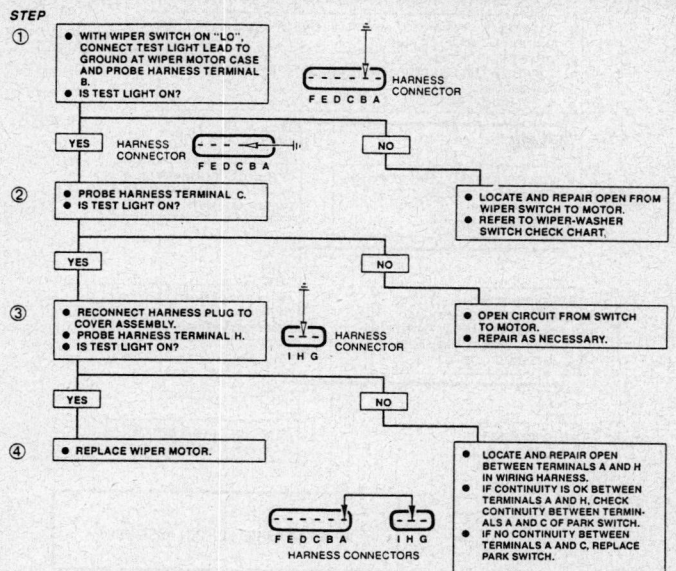

Fig. 56   Chart 8 (No "Lo" mode). 1993 Eldorado & Seville

Fig. 57   Chart 9 (No "Hi" mode or blades cycle in & out of park with switch in "Hi"). 1991–92 except Camaro, Century, Corvette, Cutlass Ciera/Cutlass Cruiser, Firebird & 6000

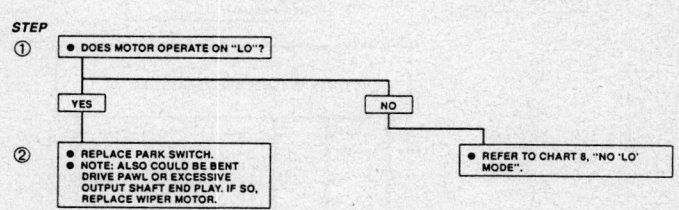

Fig. 58   Chart 10 (Blades cycle in & out of park with switch off). 1993 Eldorado & Seville

Fig. 59   Chart 1 (Wipers do not operate at any speed). 1991–92 Corvette

Fig. 60   Chart 1 (Wipers do not operate at any speed). 1993 Corvette

Fig. 61   Chart 2 (Wipers run at high speed only). 1991–92 Corvette

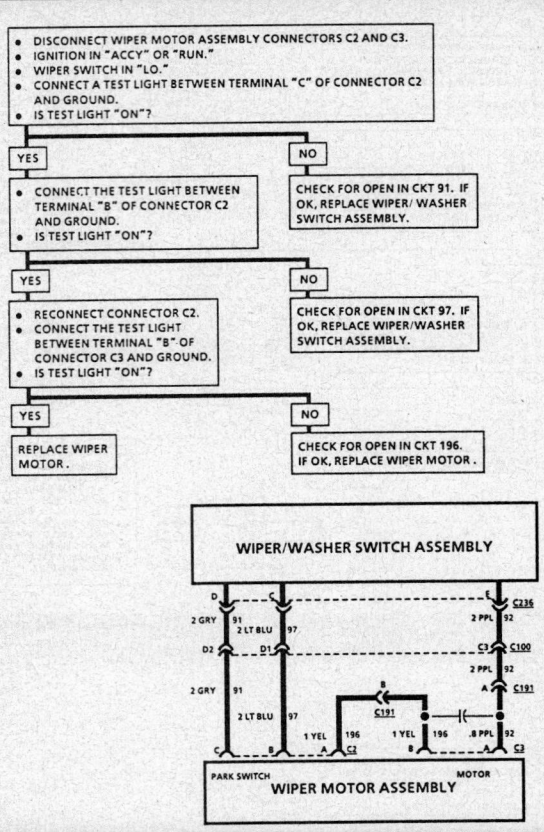

Fig. 62   Chart 2 (Wipers run at high speed only). 1993 Corvette

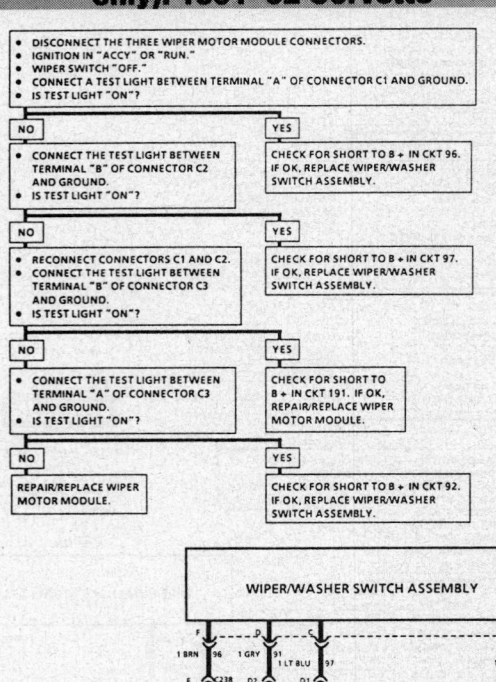

Fig. 63   Chart 3 (Wipers will not shut off). 1991–92 Corvette

Fig. 64   Chart 3 (Wipers will not shut off). 1993 Corvette

- DISCONNECT WIPER MOTOR MODULE CONNECTOR C3.
- IGNITION IN "ACCY" OR "RUN."
- WIPER SWITCH IN "HI."
- CONNECT A TEST LIGHT BETWEEN TERMINAL "A" OF CONNECTOR C3 AND GROUND.
- IS TEST LIGHT "ON"?

YES	NO
REPAIR/REPLACE WIPER MOTOR MODULE.	CHECK FOR OPEN IN CKT 92. IF OK, REPLACE WIPER/WASHER SWITCH ASSEMBLY.

- DISCONNECT WIPER MOTOR ASSEMBLY CONNECTOR C3.
- IGNITION IN "ACCY" OR "RUN."
- WIPER SWITCH IN "HI."
- CONNECT A TEST LIGHT BETWEEN TERMINAL "A" OF CONNECTOR C3 AND GROUND.
- IS TEST LIGHT "ON"?

YES	NO
REPLACE WIPER MOTOR .	CHECK FOR OPEN IN CKT 92. IF OK, REPLACE WIPER/WASHER SWITCH ASSEMBLY.

Fig. 65   Chart 4 (Wipers run at low speed only). 1991–92 Corvette

Fig. 66   Chart 4 (Wipers run at low speed only). 1993 Corvette

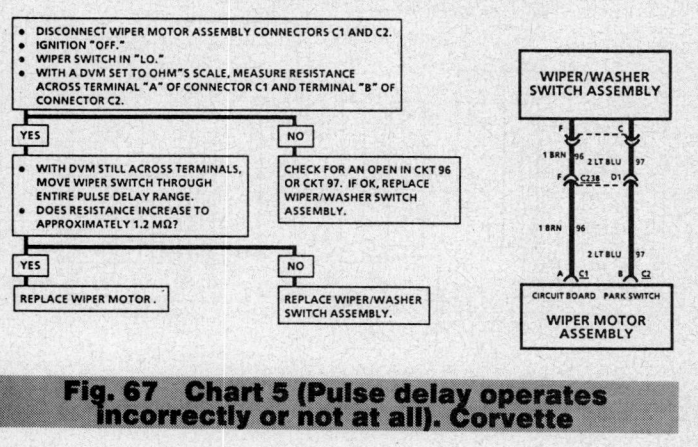

- DISCONNECT WIPER MOTOR ASSEMBLY CONNECTORS C1 AND C2.
- IGNITION "OFF."
- WIPER SWITCH IN "LO."
- WITH A DVM SET TO OHM"S SCALE, MEASURE RESISTANCE ACROSS TERMINAL "A" OF CONNECTOR C1 AND TERMINAL "B" OF CONNECTOR C2.

YES	NO
- WITH DVM STILL ACROSS TERMINALS, MOVE WIPER SWITCH THROUGH ENTIRE PULSE DELAY RANGE. - DOES RESISTANCE INCREASE TO APPROXIMATELY 1.2 MΩ?	CHECK FOR AN OPEN IN CKT 96 OR CKT 97. IF OK, REPLACE WIPER/WASHER SWITCH ASSEMBLY.

YES	NO
REPLACE WIPER MOTOR .	REPLACE WIPER/WASHER SWITCH ASSEMBLY.

Fig. 67   Chart 5 (Pulse delay operates incorrectly or not at all). Corvette

- DISCONNECT WASHER PUMP MOTOR CONNECTOR.
- IGNITION IN "ACCY" OR "RUN."
- CONNECT A TEST LIGHT BETWEEN TERMINALS "A" AND "B" OF WASHER PUMP MOTOR CONNECTOR.
- ACTIVATE WASHER SWITCH WHILE OBSERVING TEST LIGHT.
- TEST LIGHT SHOULD REMAIN "OFF." DOES IT?

YES	NO
- CONNECT THE TEST LIGHT BETWEEN TERMINAL "A" AND A GOOD GROUND. - ACTIVATE WASHER SWITCH. - TEST LIGHT SHOULD REMAIN "OFF." DOES IT?	REPLACE WASHER PUMP MOTOR.

YES	NO
- DISCONNECT WIPER MOTOR ASSEMBLY CONNECTORS C1 AND C2. - CONNECT THE TEST LIGHT BETWEEN TERMINAL "C" OF CONNECTOR C1 AND GROUND. - ACTIVATE WASHER SWITCH. - TEST LIGHT SHOULD REMAIN "OFF." DOES IT?	REPAIR OPEN IN GROUND CKT 150 (TERMINAL "B" OF PUMP CONNECTOR).

YES	NO
- CONNECT THE TEST LIGHT BETWEEN TERMINAL "A" OF CONNECTOR C1 AND GROUND. - ACTIVATE WASHER SWITCH. - IS TEST LIGHT "ON"?	REPAIR OPEN IN CKT 94.

YES	NO
- CONNECT THE TEST LIGHT BETWEEN TERMINAL "B" OF CONNECTOR C2 AND GROUND. - ACTIVATE WASHER SWITCH. - IS TEST LIGHT "ON"?	CHECK FOR OPEN IN CKT 96. IF OK, REPLACE WIPER/WASHER SWITCH ASSEMBLY.

YES	NO
REPLACE WIPER MOTOR.	CHECK FOR OPEN IN CKT 97. IF OK, REPLACE WIPER/WASHER SWITCH ASSEMBLY.

Fig. 68   Chart 6 (Washer will not operate). Corvette

Permanent Magnet Positive Park System

INDEX

Fig. 1   Wiper/washer wiring circuit (Standard). 1991–92

Fig. 2   Wiper/washer wiring circuit (Pulse). 1991–92

DESCRIPTION

This wiper/washer system consists of a permanent magnet positive park wiper motor, a washer pump mounted on the fluid reservoir and wiper/washer control switch.

This system can be used for a standard wiper/washer system or a pulse wiper/washer system. The standard type wiper/washer system is controlled directly by the wiper/washer control switch. The pulse type wiper/washer system has a printed circuit board enclosed in the wiper housing cover that controls system functions. The printed circuit board is controlled by the wiper/washer control switch.

DIAGNOSIS & TESTING
1991–92

To properly diagnose this system refer to wiring circuits **Figs. 1 and 2**, wiper motor on-vehicle check **Fig. 3**, wiper/washer switch tests **Figs. 4 and 5**, wiper/washer switch check chart **Fig. 6** and diagnosis charts **Figs. 7 through 17**.

1993

Refer to wiring circuits **Figs. 18 and 19**, and diagnosis charts **Figs. 20 through 25** when performing system diagnosis and testing procedures.

NOTE: THE FOLLOWING PROCEDURES ASSUME THAT THE TECHNICIAN HAS CHECKED THE FOLLOWING:
1. CONTINUITY OF ALL HARNESS WIRES
2. WIPER MOTOR MOUNTING BOLTS TIGHT
3. FUSES

CHECK WIPER MOTOR OPERATION BEFORE REMOVING FROM VEHICLE. DISCONNECT ALL WIRING FROM MOTOR AND PERFORM THE FOLLOWING CHECKS IN THIS ORDER:

IF WIPER MOTOR FUNCTIONS IN ALL MODES. GO TO WIPER-WASHER SWITCH CHECK CHART

Fig. 3   Wiper motor on-vehicle check. 1991–92

Fig. 4 Wiper/washer switch check (Standard). 1991–92

Fig. 5 Wiper/washer switch check (Pulse). 1991–92

SWITCH MODE / HARNESS TERMINAL	MIST	OFF	(PULSE) DELAY	LO	HI	WASH (while in OFF)
A	B(+)	B(+)	B(+)	B(+)	B(+)	B(+)
B	0V	0V	0V	0V	0V	0V
C	B(+)	0	B(+)	B(+)	B(+)	B(+)
D	0V	0V	0V	0V	B(+)	0V

Fig. 6 Wiper/washer switch check chart. 1991–92

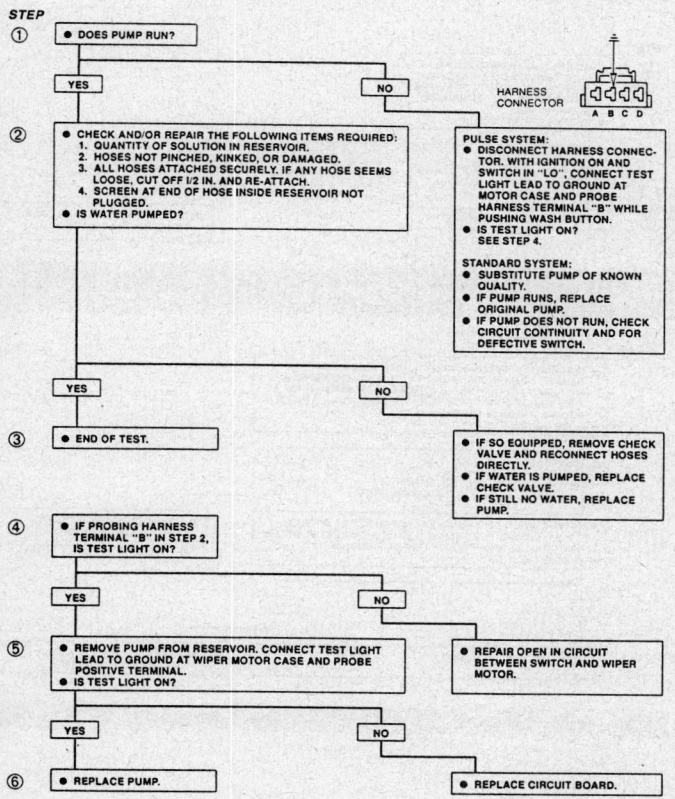

Fig. 7 Chart 1 (Washer pump inoperative). 1991–92

Fig. 8 Chart 2 (Washer pumps continuously). 1991–92

Fig. 9 Chart 3 (Wiper motor inoperative, part 1 of 2). 1991–92

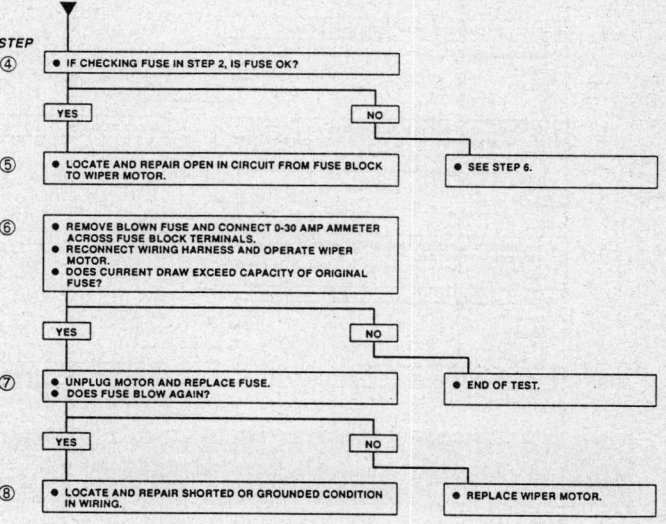

Fig. 9 Chart 3 (Wiper motor inoperative, part 2 of 2). 1991–92

STEP

① • DISCONNECT WIRING HARNESS. WITH IGNITION ON AND SWITCH IN "LO", CONNECT 12 VOLT SOURCE TO MOTOR TERMINAL #2.
• DOES WIPER RUN IN "LO"?

YES → NO → • REPLACE WIPER MOTOR.

② • CHECK FOR OPEN IN WIRE FROM MOTOR TERMINAL #2 TO WIPER SWITCH.
• IF WIRE IS OPEN, REPAIR.
• IF WIRE IS OK, REPLACE WIPER SWITCH.

Fig. 10   Chart 4 (No "LO" mode). 1991–92

STEP

① • DISCONNECT WIRING HARNESS. WITH IGNITION ON AND SWITCH IN "HI", CONNECT 12 VOLT SOURCE TO MOTOR TERMINAL #1.
• DOES WIPER RUN IN "HI"?

YES → NO → • REPLACE WIPER MOTOR.

② • CHECK FOR OPEN IN WIRE FROM MOTOR TERMINAL #1 TO WIPER SWITCH.
• IF WIRE IS OPEN, REPAIR.
• IF WIRE IS OK, REPLACE WIPER SWITCH.

Fig. 11   Chart 5 (No "HI" mode). 1991–92

STEP

① • DISCONNECT WIRING HARNESS. WITH IGNITION ON AND SWITCH "OFF" (PARK POSITION), CONNECT A JUMPER BETWEEN MOTOR TERMINALS #2 AND #3, AND A 12 VOLT SOURCE TO TERMINAL #4.
• DO BLADES PARK?

YES → NO → • REPLACE WIPER MOTOR.

② • WITH SWITCH STILL "OFF", CHECK FOR CURRENT FLOW BETWEEN HARNESS TERMINALS "B" AND "C".
• IS THERE CURRENT FLOW?

YES → NO → • CHECK FOR OPEN IN WIRE FROM HARNESS TERMINAL "C" TO SWITCH.
• IF WIRE IS OPEN, REPAIR.
• IF WIRE IS OK, REPLACE WIPER SWITCH.

③ • CHECK FOR OPEN IN WIRE FROM HARNESS TERMINAL "D" TO FUSE BLOCK AND REPAIR.

Fig. 12   Chart 6 (Wiper motor shuts off, but blades do not park). 1991–92

STEP

① • DISCONNECT WIRING HARNESS. WITH IGNITION ON AND SWITCH "OFF", CONNECT A JUMPER BETWEEN MOTOR TERMINALS #2 AND #3, AND A 12 VOLT SOURCE TO MOTOR TERMINAL #4.
• DOES MOTOR SHUT OFF?

YES → NO → • REPLACE WIPER MOTOR.

② • REPLACE WIPER SWITCH.

Fig. 13   Chart 7 (Wiper motor will not shut off). 1991–92

STEP

① • CHECK LINKAGE FOR CONNECTION TO WIPER MOTOR CRANK ARM.
• IS LINKAGE CONNECTED?

YES → NO → • CONNECT LINKAGE AND CHECK SYSTEM.

② • REPLACE WIPER MOTOR.

Fig. 15   Chart 9 (Wiper motor runs, but blades do not move). 1991–92

STEP

① • REMOVE WIPER FUSE AND CONNECT AN AMMETER (0-30 AMP) ACROSS FUSE BLOCK TERMINALS. OPERATE WIPER IN "HI". OBSERVE LOWEST CURRENT DRAW WHILE WIPER IS RUNNING ON DRY GLASS (CURRENT DRAW WILL FLUCTUATE).
• IS LOWEST CURRENT DRAW LESS THAN 5.0 AMPS?

YES → NO → • SEE STEP 3.

② • REPLACE WIPER MOTOR.

③ • IS LOWEST CURRENT DRAW MORE THAN 5.0 AMPS?

YES → NO → • END OF TEST.

④ • REPLACE WIPER BLADE ELEMENTS AND REPEAT TEST.
• IS LOWEST CURRENT DRAW STILL MORE THAN 5.0 AMPS?

YES → NO → • END OF TEST.

⑤ • DISCONNECT WIPER LINKAGE FROM WIPER MOTOR CRANK ARM AND REPEAT TEST.
• IS LOWEST CURRENT DRAW STILL MORE THAN 5.0 AMPS?

YES → NO → • WIPER LINKAGE IS BINDING. REPLACE OR REPAIR AS REQUIRED.

⑥ • REPLACE WIPER MOTOR.

Fig. 14   Chart 8 (Intermittent wiper operation in "LO" of "HI" modes, blades stop at random positions). 1991–92

STEP

① • DISCONNECT WIRING HARNESS. WITH IGNITION ON AND SWITCH "OFF" (PARK), CHECK FOR OPEN BETWEEN MOTOR TERMINAL #3 AND GROUND.
• IS OPEN CIRCUIT FOUND?

YES → NO → • CHECK ARM AND BLADE LOCATION AND/OR LINKAGE.

② • REPLACE WIPER MOTOR.

Fig. 16   Chart 10 (Blades park above park position). 1991–92

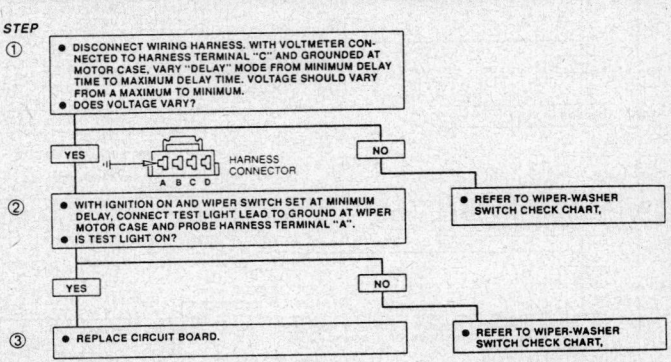

STEP

① • DISCONNECT WIRING HARNESS. WITH VOLTMETER CONNECTED TO HARNESS TERMINAL "C" AND GROUNDED AT MOTOR CASE, VARY "DELAY" MODE FROM MINIMUM DELAY TIME TO MAXIMUM TO MINIMUM. VOLTAGE SHOULD VARY FROM A MAXIMUM TO MINIMUM.
• DOES VOLTAGE VARY?

YES → NO → • REFER TO WIPER-WASHER SWITCH CHECK CHART.

② • WITH IGNITION ON AND WIPER SWITCH SET AT MINIMUM DELAY, CONNECT TEST LIGHT LEAD TO GROUND AT WIPER MOTOR CASE AND PROBE HARNESS TERMINAL "A".
• IS TEST LIGHT ON?

YES → NO → • REFER TO WIPER-WASHER SWITCH CHECK CHART.

③ • REPLACE CIRCUIT BOARD.

Fig. 17   Chart 11 (No "Delay" mode). 1991–92

Fig. 19 Wiper/washer system wiring circuit (Pulse). 1993

Fig. 18 Wiper/washer system wiring circuit (Standard). 1993

Fig. 20 Chart 1 (Wipers do not operate in any mode). 1993

Fig. 22 Chart 3 (Wipers run at low speed only). 1993

Fig. 23 Chart 4 (Wipers will not turn off). 1993

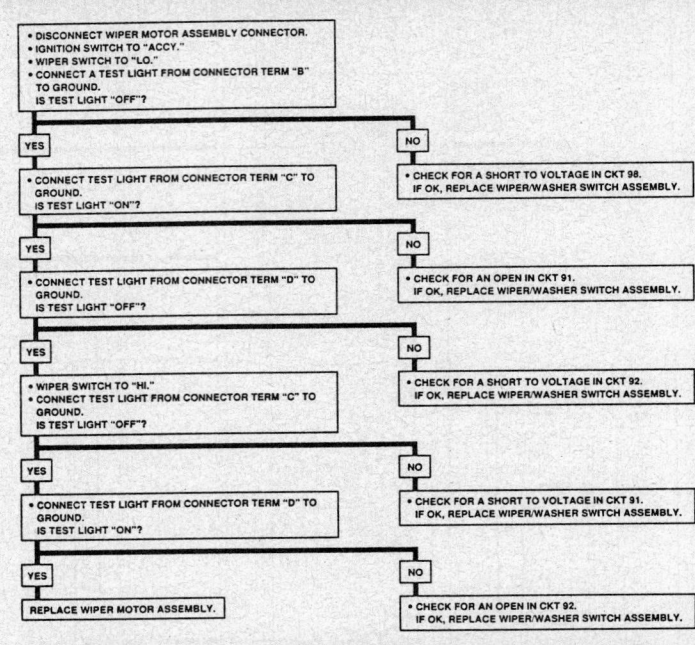

Fig. 21 Chart 2 (Wipers run at high speed only). 1993

Fig. 24 Chart 5 (Wipers run intermittently in low or high speed settings). 1993

Fig. 25 Chart 6 (Washer will not operate). 1993

Multiplex Pulse Wiper System

INDEX

Fig. 1   Wiper/washer system wiring circuit. 1991–92 Brougham

DESCRIPTION

The multiplex pulse wiper system provides a controlled wiping action. The system can be identified by a single electrical lead to the timing circuit.

The wiper switch in "DELAY" mode can be varied from minimum to a maximum position by moving the control knob. The delay can vary from 0 to 12 seconds depending on the position of the knob.

The multiplex pulse wiper motor less the washer pump is the same as the stack standard depressed park wiper motor except for the concealed electrical leads.

When the motor is at low speed the motor shunt field is connected directly to ground at the control switch and there is no external resistance.

When the motor is at medium speed the shunt field is connected to ground through two external resistors (one 20 lhm resistor located in the parking relay and one 13 ohm resistor located in the control switch). The resistors are connected in parallel which provides an equivalent resistance of approximately 8 ohms.

When the motor is at high speed the circuit is open at the control switch and completed to ground through the 20 ohm resistor in the parking relay.

When the motor is in the pulse or delay mode, the parking relay coil ground circuit is maintained at the control switch which keeps it energized. This maintains the 12 volt DC current to the pulse relay coil. The relay coil ground circuit is opened at the control switch and the timing circuit controls the ground circuit.

DIAGNOSIS & TESTING

Refer to wiring circuit **Fig. 1** and terminal identification in **Figs. 2 and 3** for continuity and ground checks.

1. WASHER PUMP RELAY TERMINALS
2. DARK GRAY COVER
3. TIMING CIRCUIT TERMINAL
4. BLACK WITH PINK STRIPE WIRE (12V DC TO MOTOR WINDINGS FROM PULSE RELAY)
5. BLACK WIRE (MOTOR SHUNT FIELD GROUND WIRE)
6. MOTOR GROMMET
7. RED WIRE (12V DC TO PULSE RELAY)
8. WIPER MOTOR TERMINALS (PARK RELAY)

Fig. 2   Multiplex pulse wiper motor & pump assembly (Cover in place). 1991–92 Brougham

1. WASHER PUMP RELAY
2. PARK RELAY
3. TIMING CIRCUIT ASSEMBLY
4. PULSE RELAY
5. SINGLE TIMING CIRCUIT TERMINAL

Fig. 3   Multiplex pulse wiper motor & pump assembly (Cover removed). 1991–92 Brougham

One, Two & Three Speed Systems (GEO)

INDEX

DESCRIPTION

METRO

Standard (Non-Pulse) Wiper Operation

When the wiper switch is on low, battery voltage is applied to the wiper motor through the blue wire. When the wiper switch is in high, battery voltage is applied directly to motor through the blue/red wire to the high speed brushes.

When the wiper switch is turned off, the run/park switch in the wiper motor is still in the Run position. Voltage is still applied to the wiper motor at the low speed brushes through the run/park switch, blue/white and blue wires.

Pulse Wiper Operation

When the wiper switch is in delay position, a shunt is applied to two of the inputs at the pulse wiper relay by the wiper switch to start the pulse operation. The pulse wiper relay momentarily supplies battery voltage to wiper switch to run wiper motor. The wiper blades make one sweep and reach park, the park/run switch opens. The wiper blades remain in park until the pulse wiper relay supplies battery voltage to start another sweep. The delay time between sweeps is determined by circuits in the pulse wiper relay.

PRIZM & STORM

Windshield wiper operation is controlled by a dash or steering column mounted switch. The wiper feed circuit is protected by a fuse which is located in the fuse block on most models, or in an inline fuse holder on some models with pulse wipers. A circuit breaker, integral with the motor brush holder, protects the motor against overload. Pulse wipers, available on most models, use a variable resistor, a pulse control module, and/or a modified wiper motor to provide a delay wipe mode.

DIAGNOSIS & TESTING

METRO

Refer to **Figs. 1 and 2,** for complete system diagnosis.

WIPER SWITCH TEST

Inspect wiper and washer switch for continuity, refer to **Fig. 3,** for switch connections.

WIPER MOTOR TEST

Low Speed Test

1. Using 12 volt battery, connect positive terminal to blue terminal on motor, and negative terminal to black lead wire **Fig. 4.**
2. Motor should rotate at 45 to 55 RPM.

High Speed Test

1. Using 12 volt battery, connect positive terminal to blue/red terminal on motor, and negative terminal to black lead wire **Fig. 4.**
2. Motor should rotate at 68 to 78 RPM.

Park Operation Test

1. Use 12 volt battery, connect positive terminal to yellow/blue terminal on motor, and negative terminal to black lead wire **Fig. 4.**
2. Using a jumper short the blue/white and blue terminals to each other.
3. Check whether motor shaft stops at a given position. **This position must conform to the start position.**
4. Repeat step 2 to confirm that shaft stops at the same position.

Checking Brush and Commutator

1. Check continuity between blue terminal and black lead wire.
2. If continuity is poor, check brush to commutator contact area.
3. If contact area is fouled, use suitable solvent to clean area. **When surface is coarse or burnt, use sandpaper to polish surface smooth.**
4. If necessary, replace brushes. **Replace brushes as a set.**

Intermittent Wiper Relay Test

1. Disconnect wiper/washer switch connector.
2. Using 12 volt battery, connect positive terminal to black terminal on connector, and negative terminal to yellow/blue terminal on connector **Fig. 5.**
3. Turn intermittent switch to OFF position, If an operating sound is heard from relay, it is operating properly. If no sound is heard, replace relay.

SYSTEM DIAGNOSIS

WIPER/WASHER — DIAGNOSTIC CHART A

	TEST	RESULT	ACTION
A1.	Turn ignition switch to "ON." Press Wash button.	FRONT WASHER PUMP operates, and wipers complete at least 1 sweep.	GO TO A2.
		FRONT WASHER PUMP does not operate.	GO TO A4.
		FRONT WASHER PUMP operates but wipers do not complete at least 1 full sweep.	GO TO A14.
		FRONT WASHER PUMP continues to operate after Wash Switch has been released.	GO TO A19.
		Wipers continue to operate continuously after Wash Switch has been released.	GO TO A20.
A2.	Press "LO" button.	Wipers operate at low speed.	GO TO A3.
		Wipers do not operate.	Replace FRONT WIPER/WASHER SWITCH.
		Wipers operate at high speed.	GO TO A8.
A3.	Press "HI" button.	Wipers operate at high speed.	All systems diagnosed are functioning normally.
		Wipers do not operate.	GO TO A10.
		Wipers operate at low speed.	GO TO A12.
A4.	Backprobe FRONT WIPER/WASHER SWITCH connector a test lamp from cavity 5 to chassis ground.	Test lamp does not light.	Repair open in YEL/BLU wire between JUNCTION BLOCK and FRONT WIPER/WASHER SWITCH.
		Test lamp lights.	GO TO A5.
A5.	Backprobe FRONT WIPER/WASHER SWITCH connector with a test lamp from cavity 7 to chassis ground. Press Wash button.	Test lamp does not light.	Replace FRONT WIPER/WASHER SWITCH.
		Test lamp lights.	GO TO A6.
A6.	Disconnect FRONT WASHER PUMP and FRONT WIPER/WASHER SWITCH connectors. Connect a digital multimeter from FRONT WASHER PUMP connector cavity 2 to FRONT WIPER/WASHER SWITCH connector cavity 7. Measure resistance.	More than 0.3 ohms.	Repair open in BLU/BLK wire between FRONT WIPER/WASHER SWITCH and FRONT WASHER PUMP.
		Less than 0.3 ohms.	GO TO A7.
A7.	Connect a digital multimeter from FRONT WASHER PUMP connector cavity 1 to chassis ground. Measure resistance.	More than 0.3 ohms.	Repair BLK ground wire between FRONT WASHER PUMP and G101 (XFi, Base, LSi – USA /Canada) or G200 (Convertible – USA).
		Less than 0.3 ohms.	Replace FRONT WASHER PUMP.
A8.	Backprobe FRONT WIPER MOTOR connector with a test lamp from cavity 1 to chassis ground.	Test lamp does not light.	Replace FRONT WIPER MOTOR.
		Test lamp lights.	GO TO A9.
A9.	Disconnect FRONT WIPER/WASHER SWITCH connector. Connect a test lamp from connector cavity 2 to chassis ground.	Test lamp lights.	Repair short to voltage in BLU/RED wire between FRONT WIPER/WASHER SWITCH and FRONT WIPER MOTOR.
		Test lamp does not light.	Replace FRONT WIPER/WASHER SWITCH.
A10.	Backprobe FRONT WIPER MOTOR connector with a test lamp from cavity 1 to chassis ground.	Test lamp lights.	Replace FRONT WIPER MOTOR.
		Test lamp does not light.	GO TO A11.
A11.	Backprobe FRONT WIPER/WASHER SWITCH with a test lamp from cavity 2 to chassis ground.	Test lamp lights.	Repair open in BLU/RED wire between FRONT WIPER/WASHER SWITCH and FRONT WIPER MOTOR.
		Test lamp does not light.	Replace FRONT WIPER/WASHER SWITCH.
A12.	Backprobe FRONT WIPER MOTOR connector with a test lamp from cavity 2 to chassis ground.	Test lamp does not light.	Replace FRONT WIPER MOTOR.
		Test lamp lights.	GO TO A13.
A13.	Disconnect FRONT WIPER/WASHER SWITCH connector. Connect a test lamp from connector cavity 6 to chassis ground.	Test lamp lights.	Repair short to voltage in BLU wire between FRONT WIPER/WASHER SWITCH and FRONT WIPER MOTOR.
		Test lamp does not light.	Replace FRONT WIPER/WASHER SWITCH.
A14.	Backprobe FRONT WIPER MOTOR connector with a test lamp from cavity 2 to chassis ground. Press Wash button.	Test lamp does not light.	Repair open in BLU wire between FRONT WIPER/WASHER SWITCH and FRONT WIPER MOTOR.
		Test lamp lights.	GO TO A15.
A15.	Backprobe FRONT WIPER MOTOR connector with a test lamp from cavity 4 to chassis ground. Press Wash button.	Test lamp does not light.	GO TO A16.
		Test lamp lights.	GO TO A17.
A16.	Backprobe JUNCTION BLOCK connector C8 with a test lamp from cavity 8 to chassis ground.	Test lamp lights.	Repair open in YEL/BLU wire between JUNCTION BLOCK and FRONT WIPER MOTOR.
		Test lamp does not light.	Replace JUNCTION BLOCK.
A17.	Manually move wipers up and out of PARK position. Backprobe FRONT WIPER MOTOR connector with a test lamp from cavity 3 to chassis ground.	Test lamp does not light.	Replace FRONT WIPER MOTOR.
		Test lamp lights.	GO TO A18.
A18.	Backprobe FRONT WIPER/WASHER SWITCH connector with a test lamp from cavity 4 to chassis ground.	Test lamp does not light.	Repair open in BLU/WHT wire between FRONT WIPER MOTOR and FRONT WIPER/WASHER SWITCH.
		Test lamp lights.	Replace FRONT WIPER/WASHER SWITCH.
A19.	Disconnect FRONT WIPER/WASHER SWITCH connector.	FRONT WASHER PUMP continues to operate.	Repair short to voltage in BLU/BLK wire between FRONT WIPER/WASHER SWITCH and FRONT WIPER MOTOR.
		FRONT WASHER PUMP stops operating.	Replace FRONT WIPER/WASHER SWITCH.
A20.	Disconnect FRONT WIPER/WASHER SWITCH connector.	Wipers continue to operate.	Repair short to voltage in BLU or BLU/WHT wire between FRONT WIPER/WASHER SWITCH and WIPER MOTOR.
		Wipers stop operating.	GO TO A21.
A21.	Make sure that wipers are in the fully down PARK position. Backprobe FRONT WIPER MOTOR connector with a test lamp from cavity 3 to chassis ground.	Test lamp lights.	Replace FRONT WIPER MOTOR.
		Test lamp does not light.	Replace FRONT WIPER/WASHER SWITCH.

Fig. 1 System diagnosis chart. Metro less pulse wiper

PRIZM

Refer to **Figs. 6 and 7,** for complete system diagnosis.

WIPER SWITCH TEST

Inspect wiper/washer switch for continuity, refer to **Fig. 8,** for switch connections.

WIPER MOTOR TEST
Low Speed Test

1. Using 12 volt battery, connect positive terminal to terminal 2 on motor, and negative terminal to wiper motor body **Fig. 9.**
2. Motor should rotate at 45 to 55 RPM.

High Speed Test

1. Using 12 volt battery, connect positive terminal to terminal 1 on motor, and negative terminal to wiper motor body **Fig. 10-44.**
2. Motor should rotate at 69 to 83 RPM.

Park Operation Test

1. Use 12 volt battery, connect positive terminal to terminal 2 on motor, and negative terminal to wiper motor body **Fig. 11.**
2. Operate wiper motor at low speed.
3. Check whether motor shaft stops at a given position. **Time this disconnection so that wipers stop in any position other than their rest position.**
4. Install jumper wire between terminals 2 and 3, **Fig. 12.**
5. Connect battery positive lead to terminal 4.
6. Check that wiper motor stops running at rest position. If wiper motor operation is not as specified, replace motor.

STORM

Refer to **Figs. 13 and 14,** for complete system diagnosis.

WIPER SWITCH TEST

Inspect wiper and washer switch for continuity, refer to **Figs. 15 and 36,** for switch connections.

WIPER MOTOR TEST
Low Speed Test

1. Using 12 volt battery, connect positive terminal to "LO" terminal on motor, and negative terminal to wiper motor body **Fig. 17.**
2. Motor should rotate at 45 to 55 RPM.

High Speed Test

1. Using 12 volt battery, connect positive terminal to "HI" terminal on motor, and negative terminal to wiper motor body **Fig. 17.**
2. Motor should rotate at 69 to 83 RPM.

Park Operation Test

1. Use 12 volt battery, connect positive terminal to "Park" terminal on motor, and negative terminal to wiper motor body **Fig. 17.**
2. Operate wiper motor at high speed.
3. Check whether motor shaft stops at a given position. **This position must conform to the start position.**
4. Repeat step 2 to confirm that shaft stops at the same position.

SYSTEM DIAGNOSIS

WIPER/WASHER: PULSE		DIAGNOSTIC CHART A	
	TEST	RESULT	ACTION
A1.	Turn ignition switch to "ON." Press Wash button.	FRONT WASHER PUMP operates, and wipers complete at least 1 sweep.	GO TO A2.
		FRONT WASHER PUMP does not operate.	GO TO A5.
		FRONT WASHER PUMP operates but wipers do not complete at least 1 full sweep.	GO TO A17.
		FRONT WASHER PUMP continues to operate after Wash Switch has been released.	GO TO A22.
		Wipers continue to operate continuously after Wash Switch has been released.	GO TO A23.
A2.	Press "LO" button.	Wipers operate at low speed.	GO TO A3.
		Wipers do not operate.	Replace FRONT WIPER/WASHER SWITCH.
		Wipers operate at high speed.	GO TO A9.
A3.	Press "HI" button.	Wipers operate at high speed.	GO TO A4.
		Wipers do not operate.	GO TO A11.
		Wipers operate at low speed.	GO TO A13.
A4.	Press "INT" button.	Wipers sweep once every 6 seconds.	All systems diagnosed are functioning normally.
		Wipers do not operate in the intermittent mode.	GO TO A15.
A5.	Backprobe FRONT WIPER/WASHER SWITCH connector with a test lamp from cavity 5 to chassis ground.	Test lamp does not light.	Repair open in YEL/BLU wire between JUNCTION BLOCK and FRONT WIPER/WASHER SWITCH.
		Test lamp lights.	GO TO A6.
A6.	Backprobe FRONT WIPER/WASHER SWITCH connector with a test lamp from cavity 7 to chassis ground. Press Wash button.	Test lamp does not light.	Replace FRONT WIPER/WASHER SWITCH.
		Test lamp lights.	GO TO A7.
A7.	Disconnect FRONT WASHER PUMP and FRONT WIPER/WASHER SWITCH connectors. Connect a digital multimeter from FRONT WASHER PUMP connector cavity 2 to FRONT WIPER/WASHER SWITCH connector cavity 7. Measure resistance.	More than 0.3 ohms.	Repair open in BLU/BLK wire between FRONT WIPER/WASHER SWITCH and FRONT WASHER PUMP.
		Less than 0.3 ohms.	GO TO A8.
A8.	Connect a digital multimeter from FRONT WASHER PUMP connector cavity 1 to chassis ground. Measure resistance.	More than 0.3 ohms.	Repair BLK ground wire between FRONT WASHER PUMP and G101 (XFi, Base, LSi – USA/Canada) or G200 (Convertible – USA).
		Less than 0.3 ohms.	Replace FRONT WASHER PUMP.
A9.	Backprobe FRONT WIPER MOTOR connector with a test lamp from cavity 1 to chassis ground.	Test lamp does not light.	Replace FRONT WIPER MOTOR.
		Test lamp lights.	GO TO A10.
A10.	Disconnect FRONT WIPER/WASHER SWITCH connector. Connect a test lamp from connector cavity 2 chassis ground.	Test lamp lights.	Repair short to voltage in BLU/RED wire between FRONT WIPER/WASHER SWITCH and FRONT WIPER MOTOR.
		Test lamp does not light.	Replace FRONT WIPER/WASHER SWITCH.
A11.	Backprobe FRONT WIPER MOTOR connector with a test lamp from cavity 1 to chassis ground.	Test lamp lights.	Replace FRONT WIPER MOTOR.
		Test lamp does not light.	GO TO A12.
A12.	Backprobe FRONT WIPER/WASHER SWITCH with a test lamp from cavity 2 to chassis ground.	Test lamp lights.	Repair open in BLU/RED wire between FRONT WIPER/WASHER SWITCH and FRONT WIPER MOTOR.
		Test lamp does not light.	Replace FRONT WIPER/WASHER SWITCH.
A13.	Backprobe FRONT WIPER MOTOR connector with a test lamp from cavity 2 to chassis ground.	Test lamp does not light.	Replace FRONT WIPER MOTOR.
		Test lamp lights.	GO TO A14.
A14.	Disconnect FRONT WIPER/WASHER SWITCH connector. Connect a test lamp from connector cavity 6 to chassis ground.	Test lamp lights.	Repair short to voltage in BLU wire between FRONT WIPER/WASHER SWITCH and FRONT WIPER MOTOR.
		Test lamp does not light.	Replace FRONT WIPER/WASHER SWITCH.
A15.	Disconnect FRONT WIPER/WASHER SWITCH connector. Connect a digital multimeter from connector cavity 1 to chassis ground. Measure resistance.	Less than 0.3 ohms.	Replace FRONT WIPER/WASHER SWITCH.
		More than 0.3 ohms.	GO TO A16.
A16.	Disconnect JUNCTION BLOCK connector C6. Connect a digital multimeter from JUNCTION BLOCK connector C6 to FRONT WIPER/WASHER connector cavity 1. Measure resistance.	More than 0.3 ohms.	Repair BLK ground wire between JUNCTION BLOCK and FRONT WIPER/WASHER SWITCH.
		Less than 0.3 ohms.	Replace JUNCTION BLOCK.
A17.	Backprobe FRONT WIPER MOTOR connector with a test lamp from cavity 2 to chassis ground. Press Wash button.	Test lamp does not light.	Repair open in BLU wire between FRONT WIPER/WASHER SWITCH and FRONT WIPER MOTOR.
		Test lamp lights.	GO TO A18.
A18.	Backprobe FRONT WIPER MOTOR connector with a test lamp from cavity 4 to chassis ground. Press Wash button.	Test lamp does not light.	GO TO A19.
		Test lamp lights.	GO TO A20.
A19.	Backprobe JUNCTION BLOCK connector C8 with a test lamp from cavity 8 to chassis ground.	Test lamp lights.	Repair open in YEL/BLU wire between JUNCTION BLOCK and FRONT WIPER MOTOR.
		Test lamp does not light.	Replace JUNCTION BLOCK.
A20.	Manually move wipers up and out of PARK position. Backprobe FRONT WIPER MOTOR connector with a test lamp from cavity 3 to chassis ground.	Test lamp does not light.	Replace FRONT WIPER MOTOR.
		Test lamp lights.	GO TO A21.
A21.	Backprobe FRONT WIPER/WASHER SWITCH connector with a test lamp from cavity 4 to chassis ground.	Test lamp does not light.	Repair open in BLU/WHT wire between FRONT WIPER MOTOR and FRONT WIPER/WASHER SWITCH.
		Test lamp lights.	Replace FRONT WIPER/WASHER SWITCH.
A22.	Disconnect FRONT WIPER/WASHER SWITCH connector.	FRONT WASHER PUMP continues to operate	Repair short to voltage in BLU/BLK wire between FRONT WIPER/WASHER SWITCH and FRONT WIPER MOTOR.
		FRONT WASHER PUMP stops operating.	Replace FRONT WIPER/WASHER SWITCH.
A23.	Disconnect FRONT WIPER/WASHER SWITCH connector.	Wipers continue to operate.	Repair short to voltage in BLU or BLU/WHT wire between FRONT WIPER/WASHER SWITCH and WIPER MOTOR.
		Wipers stop operating.	GO TO A24.
A24.	Make sure that wipers are in the fully down PARK position. Backprobe FRONT WIPER MOTOR connector with a test lamp from cavity 3 to chassis ground.	Test lamp lights.	Replace FRONT WIPER MOTOR.
		Test lamp does not light.	Replace FRONT WIPER/WASHER SWITCH.

Fig. 2   System diagnosis chart. Metro w/pulse wiper

BL/W : BLUE/WHITE
BL : BLUE
Y/BL : YELLOW/BLUE
BU/R : RED

BL/Y : BLUE/YELLOW
R/Y : RED/YELLOW
R/G : RED/GREEN
B : BLACK

Fig. 3 Wiper switch continuity chart. Metro

Fig. 4   Connections to operate two & three speed wiper motor independent of vehicle wiring

1. BATTERY
2. WIPER MOTOR
3. (+)-YELLOW/BLUE LEAD
4. (−)-BLACK LEAD
5. JUMPER

BL/R : BLUE/RED
BL/W : BLUE/WHITE
BL : BLUE
Y/BL : YELLOW/BLUE

Fig. 5   Intermittent wiper relay test connections. Metro

SYSTEM DIAGNOSIS

WIPER/WASHER	DIAGNOSTIC CHART A	
TEST	**RESULT**	**ACTION**
A1. Turn ignition switch to "ON." Press Wash Switch and release.	WINDSHIELD WASHER PUMP operates.	GO TO A2.
	WINDSHIELD WASHER PUMP does not operate.	GO TO A5.
A2. Turn WINDSHIELD WIPER SWITCH to the "MIST" position and release.	Wipers sweep once and return to PARK.	GO TO A3.
	Wipers do not sweep.	GO TO A12.
	Wipers sweep but do not return to PARK.	GO TO A16.
	Wipers sweep more than once.	GO TO A20.
A3. Turn WINDSHIELD WIPER SWITCH to the "LO" position.	Wipers sweep at low speed.	GO TO A4.
	Wipers do not sweep.	Replace WINDSHIELD WIPER SWITCH.
	Wipers operate in high speed.	GO TO A22.
A4. Turn WINDSHIELD WIPER SWITCH the to "HI" position.	Wipers operate at high speed.	All systems diagnosed are functioning normally.
	Wipers do not sweep.	GO TO A24.
	Wipers operate in low speed.	GO TO A26.
A5. Backprobe WINDSHIELD WASHER PUMP connector with a test lamp from cavity 2 to chassis ground.	Test lamp does not light.	GO TO A6.
	Test lamp lights.	GO TO A7.
A6. Backprobe JUNCTION BLOCK 1 connector C2 with a test lamp from cavity 4 to chassis ground.	Test lamp lights.	Repair open in BLU wire between JUNCTION BLOCK 1 and WINDSHIELD WASHER PUMP.
	Test lamp does not light.	Replace JUNCTION BLOCK 1.
A7. Disconnect WINDSHIELD WIPER SWITCH connector. Connect a test lamp from connector cavity 8 to chassis ground.	Test lamp does not light.	GO TO A8.
	Test lamp lights.	GO TO A11.
A8. Backprobe WINDSHIELD WASHER DIODE connector with a test lamp from cavity 2 to chassis ground.	Test lamp lights.	Repair open in BLU/RED wire between WINDSHIELD WASHER DIODE and WINDSHIELD WIPER SWITCH.
	Test lamp does not light.	GO TO A9.
A9. Backprobe WINDSHIELD WASHER DIODE connector with a test lamp from cavity 1 to chassis ground.	Test lamp lights.	Replace WINDSHIELD WASHER DIODE.
	Test lamp does not light.	GO TO A10.
A10. Backprobe WINDSHIELD WASHER PUMP connector with a test lamp from cavity 1 to chassis ground.	Test lamp lights.	Repair open in BLU/YEL wire between WINDSHIELD WASHER PUMP and WINDSHIELD WASHER DIODE.
	Test lamp does not light.	Replace WINDSHIELD WASHER PUMP.
A11. Connect a digital multimeter from WINDSHIELD WIPER SWITCH connector cavity 16 to chassis ground. Measure resistance.	More than 0.3 ohms.	Repair WHT/BLK ground wire between WINDSHIELD WIPER SWITCH and G200.
	Less than 0.3 ohms.	Replace WINDSHIELD WIPER SWITCH.

Fig. 6   System diagnosis chart (Part 1 of 2). Prizm less pulse wiper

GENERAL MOTORS—Wiper System Service

SYSTEM DIAGNOSIS

WIPER/WASHER		DIAGNOSTIC CHART A (CONT'D)	
TEST		**RESULT**	**ACTION**
A12.	Backprobe WINDSHIELD WIPER SWITCH connector with a test lamp from cavity 18 to chassis ground.	Test lamp does not light.	GO TO A13.
		Test lamp lights.	GO TO A14.
A13.	Backprobe JUNCTION BLOCK 1 connector C5 with a test lamp from cavity 7 to chassis ground.	Test lamp lights.	Replace JUNCTION BLOCK 3.
		Test lamp does not light.	Replace JUNCTION BLOCK 1.
A14.	Backprobe WINDSHIELD WIPER SWITCH connector with a test lamp from cavity 7 to chassis ground. Hold WINDSHIELD WIPER SWITCH in the "MIST" position.	Test lamp does not light.	Replace WINDSHIELD WIPER SWITCH.
		Test lamp lights.	GO TO A15.
A15.	Backprobe WINDSHIELD WIPER MOTOR connector with a test lamp from cavity 2 to chassis ground.	Test lamp does not light.	Repair open in BLU/BLK wire between WINDSHIELD WIPER SWITCH and WINDSHIELD WIPER MOTOR.
		Test lamp lights.	Replace WINDSHIELD WIPER MOTOR.
A16.	Backprobe WINDSHIELD WIPER MOTOR connector with a test lamp from cavity 4 to chassis ground.	Test lamp does not light.	GO TO A17.
		Test lamp lights.	GO TO A18.
A17.	Backprobe JUNCTION BLOCK 3 connector C2 with a test lamp from cavity 5 to chassis ground.	Test lamp lights.	Repair open in BLU wire between JUNCTION BLOCK 3 and WINDSHIELD WIPER MOTOR.
		Test lamp does not light.	Replace JUNCTION BLOCK 3.
A18.	Disconnect WINDSHIELD WIPER SWITCH connector. Connect a digital multimeter from terminal 4 to terminal 7 (WINDSHIELD WIPER SWITCH side). Measure resistance with WINDSHIELD WIPER SWITCH in "OFF."	More than 0.3 ohms.	Replace WINDSHIELD WIPER SWITCH.
		Less than 0.3 ohms.	GO TO A19.
A19.	Disconnect WINDSHIELD WIPER MOTOR connector. Connect a digital multimeter from WINDSHIELD WIPER SWITCH connector cavity 4 to WINDSHIELD WIPER MOTOR connector cavity 3. Measure resistance.	More than 0.3 ohms.	Repair open in BLU/WHT wire between WINDSHIELD WIPER SWITCH And WINDSHIELD WIPER MOTOR.
		Less than 0.3 ohms.	Replace WINDSHIELD WIPER MOTOR.
A20.	Disconnect WINDSHIELD WIPER MOTOR connector. Connect a test lamp from connector cavity 2 to chassis ground.	Test lamp does not light.	Replace WINDSHIELD WIPER MOTOR.
		Test lamp lights.	GO TO A21.
A21.	Disconnect WINDSHIELD WIPER SWITCH connector. Connect a test lamp from connector cavity 7 to chassis ground.	Test lamp lights.	Repair short to voltage in BLU/BLK wire between WINDSHIELD WIPER SWITCH and WINDSHIELD WIPER MOTOR.
		Test lamp does not light.	Replace WINDSHIELD WIPER SWITCH.
A22.	Disconnect WINDSHIELD WIPER MOTOR connector. Connect a test lamp from connector cavity 1 to chassis ground.	Test lamp does not light.	Replace WINDSHIELD WIPER MOTOR.
		Test lamp lights.	GO TO A23.
A23.	Disconnect WINDSHIELD WIPER SWITCH connector. Connect a test lamp from connector cavity 13 to chassis ground.	Test lamp lights.	Repair short to voltage in BLU/ORN wire between WINDSHIELD WIPER SWITCH and WINDSHIELD WIPER MOTOR.
		Test lamp does not light.	Replace WINDSHIELD WIPER SWITCH.
A24.	Backprobe WINDSHIELD WIPER SWITCH connector with a test lamp from cavity 13 to chassis ground.	Test lamp does not light.	Replace WINDSHIELD WIPER SWITCH.
		Test lamp lights.	GO TO A25.
A25.	Backprobe WINDSHIELD WIPER MOTOR connector with a test lamp from cavity 1 to chassis ground.	Test lamp does not light.	Repair open in BLU/ORN wire between WINDSHIELD WIPER and WINDSHIELD WIPER MOTOR.
		Test lamp lights.	Replace WINDSHIELD WIPER MOTOR.
A26.	Disconnect WINDSHIELD WIPER MOTOR connector. Connect a test lamp from connector cavity 2 to chassis ground.	Test lamp does not light.	Replace WINDSHIELD WIPER MOTOR.
		Test lamp lights.	GO TO A27.
A27.	Disconnect WINDSHIELD WIPER SWITCH connector. Connect a test lamp from connector cavity 7 to chassis ground.	Test lamp lights.	Repair short to voltage in BLU/BLK wire between WINDSHIELD WIPER SWITCH and WINDSHIELD WIPER MOTOR.
		Test lamp does not light.	Replace WINDSHIELD WIPER SWITCH.

Fig. 6   System diagnosis chart (Part 2 of 2). Prizm less pulse wiper

SYSTEM DIAGNOSIS

WIPER/WASHER: PULSE		DIAGNOSTIC CHART A	
	TEST	**RESULT**	**ACTION**
A1.	Turn ignition switch to "ON." Press Wash and release.	WINDSHIELD WASHER PUMP operates and wipers make 2-5 sweeps and return to PARK.	GO TO A2.
		WINDSHIELD WASHER PUMP does not operate.	GO TO A5.
		WINDSHIELD WASHER PUMP operates but wipers do not sweep.	GO TO A12.
		WINDSHIELD WASHER PUMP continues to operate.	GO TO A16.
		Wipers sweep but do not return to PARK.	GO TO A20.
		Wipers continue to operate.	GO TO A24.
A2.	Turn WINDSHIELD WIPER SWITCH to the "LO" position.	Wipers sweep at low speed.	GO TO A3.
		Wipers do not sweep.	Replace WINDSHIELD WIPER SWITCH.
		Wipers operate in high speed.	GO TO A26.
A3.	Turn WINDSHIELD WIPER SWITCH to the "III" position.	Wipers operate at high speed.	GO TO A4.
		Wipers do not sweep.	GO TO A28.
		Wipers operate in low speed.	GO TO A30.
A4.	Turn WINDSHIELD WIPER SWITCH to the "INT" position. Adjust delay time up and down.	Wipers operate in intermittent mode with delay times changing with adjustment.	All systems diagnosed are functioning normally.
		Wipers do not operate or do not operate in intermittent mode.	Replace WINDSHIELD WIPER SWITCH.
		Delay times do not change with adjustment.	Replace WINDSHIELD WIPER SWITCH.
A5.	Backprobe WINDSHIELD WASHER PUMP connector with a test lamp from cavity 2 to chassis ground.	Test lamp does not light.	GO TO A6.
		Test lamp lights.	GO TO A7.
A6.	Backprobe JUNCTION BLOCK 1 connector C2 with a test lamp from cavity 4 to chassis ground.	Test lamp lights.	Repair open in BLU wire between JUNCTION BLOCK 1 and WINDSHIELD WASHER PUMP.
		Test lamp does not light.	Replace JUNCTION BLOCK 1.
A7.	Backprobe WINDSHIELD WASHER PUMP connector with a test lamp from cavity 1 to chassis ground.	Test lamp does not light.	Replace WINDSHIELD WASHER PUMP.
		Test lamp lights.	GO TO A8.
A8.	Backprobe WINDSHIELD WASHER DIODE connector with a test lamp from cavity 1 to chassis ground.	Test lamp does not light.	Repair open in BLU/YEL wire between WINDSHIELD WASHER PUMP and WINDSHIELD WASHER DIODE.
		Test lamp lights.	GO TO A9.
A9.	Backprobe WINDSHIELD WASHER DIODE connector with a test lamp from cavity 2 to chassis ground.	Test lamp does not light.	Replace WINDSHIELD WASHER DIODE.
		Test lamp lights.	GO TO A10.
A10.	Backprobe WINDSHIELD WIPER SWITCH connector with a test lamp from cavity 8 to chassis ground.	Test lamp does not light.	Repair open in BLU/RED wire between WINDSHIELD WASHER DIODE and WINDSHIELD WIPER SWITCH.
		Test lamp lights.	GO TO A11.
A11.	Backprobe WINDSHIELD WIPER SWITCH connector with a digital multimeter from cavity 16 to chassis ground.	More than 0.3 ohms.	Repair WHT/BLK ground wire between WINDSHIELD WIPER SWITCH and G200.
		Less than 0.3 ohms.	Replace WINDSHIELD WIPER SWITCH.
A12.	Backprobe WINDSHIELD WIPER SWITCH connector with a test lamp from cavity 18 to chassis ground.	Test lamp does not light.	GO TO A13.
		Test lamp lights.	GO TO A14.
A13.	Backprobe JUNCTION BLOCK 1 connector C5 with a test lamp from cavity 7 to chassis ground.	Test lamp lights.	Replace JUNCTION BLOCK 3.
		Test lamp does not light.	Replace JUNCTION BLOCK 1.
A14.	Backprobe WINDSHIELD WIPER SWITCH connector with a test lamp from cavity 7 to chassis ground. Press Wash Switch.	Test lamp does not light.	Replace WINDSHIELD WIPER SWITCH.
		Test lamp lights.	GO TO A15.
A15.	Backprobe WINDSHIELD WIPER MOTOR connector with a test lamp from cavity 2 to chassis ground. Press Wash Switch.	Test lamp does not light.	Repair open in BLU/BLK wire between WINDSHIELD WIPER SWITCH and WINDSHIELD WIPER MOTOR.
		Test lamp lights.	Replace WINDSHIELD WIPER MOTOR.
A16.	Disconnect WINDSHIELD WIPER SWITCH connector.	WINDSHIELD WASHER PUMP stops.	Replace WINDSHIELD WIPER SWITCH.
		WINDSHIELD WASHER PUMP continues to operate.	GO TO A17.
A17.	Remove WINDSHIELD WASHER DIODE.	WINDSHIELD WASHER PUMP stops.	GO TO A18.
		WINDSHIELD WASHER PUMP continues to operate.	GO TO A19.

Fig. 7   System diagnosis chart (Part 1 of 2). Prizm w/pulse wiper

SYSTEM DIAGNOSIS

WIPER/WASHER: PULSE	DIAGNOSTIC CHART A (CONT'D)	
TEST	**RESULT**	**ACTION**
A18. Connect a digital multimeter from WINDSHIELD WIPER SWITCH connector cavity 8 to chassis ground. Measure resistance.	Less than infinite.	Repair short to ground in BLU/RED wire between WINDSHIELD WASHER DIODE and WINDSHIELD WIPER SWITCH.
	Infinite.	Replace WINDSHIELD WASHER DIODE.
A19. Disconnect WINDSHIELD WASHER PUMP connector. Connect a digital multimeter from connector cavity 1 to chassis ground. Measure resistance.	Less than infinite.	Repair short to ground in BLU/YEL wire between WINDSHIELD WASHER PUMP and WINDSHIELD WASHER DIODE.
	Infinite.	Replace WINDSHIELD WASHER PUMP.
A20. Backprobe WINDSHIELD WIPER MOTOR connector with a test lamp from cavity 4 to chassis ground.	Test lamp does not light.	GO TO A21.
	Test lamp lights.	GO TO A22.
A21. Backprobe JUNCTION BLOCK 3 connector C2 with a test lamp from cavity 5 to chassis ground.	Test lamp lights.	Repair open in BLU wire between JUNCTION BLOCK 3 and WINDSHIELD WIPER MOTOR.
	Test lamp does not light.	Replace JUNCTION BLOCK 3.
A22. Disconnect WINDSHIELD WIPER SWITCH connector. Connect a digital multimeter from connector terminal 4 to terminal 7 (WINDSHIELD WIPER SWITCH side). Measure resistance with WINDSHIELD WIPER SWITCH in "OFF."	More than 0.3 ohms.	Replace WINDSHIELD WIPER SWITCH.
	Less than 0.3 ohms.	GO TO A23.
A23. Disconnect WINDSHIELD WIPER MOTOR connector. Connect a digital multimeter from WINDSHIELD WIPER SWITCH connector cavity 4 to WINDSHIELD WIPER MOTOR connector cavity 3. Measure resistance.	More than 0.3 ohms.	Repair open in BLU/WHT wire between WINDSHIELD WIPER SWITCH and WINDSHIELD WIPER MOTOR.
	Less than 0.3 ohms.	Replace WINDSHIELD WIPER MOTOR.
A24. Disconnect WINDSHIELD WIPER MOTOR connector. Connect a test lamp from connector cavity 2 to chassis ground.	Test lamp does not light.	Replace WINDSHIELD WIPER MOTOR.
	Test lamp lights.	GO TO A25.
A25. Disconnect WINDSHIELD WIPER SWITCH connector. Connect a test lamp from connector cavity 7 to chassis ground.	Test lamp lights.	Repair short to voltage in BLU/BLK wire between WINDSHIELD WIPER SWITCH and WINDSHIELD WIPER MOTOR.
	Test lamp does not light.	Replace WINDSHIELD WIPER SWITCH.
A26. Disconnect WINDSHIELD WIPER MOTOR connector. Connect a test lamp from connector cavity 1 to chassis ground.	Test lamp does not light.	Replace WINDSHIELD WIPER MOTOR.
	Test lamp lights.	GO TO A27.
A27. Disconnect WINDSHIELD WIPER SWITCH connector. Connect a test lamp from connector cavity 13 to chassis ground.	Test lamp lights.	Repair short to voltage in BLU/ORN wire between WINDSHIELD WIPER SWITCH and WINDSHIELD WIPER MOTOR.
	Test lamp does not light.	Replace WINDSHIELD WIPER SWITCH.
A28. Backprobe WINDSHIELD WIPER MOTOR connector with a test lamp from cavity 1 to chassis ground.	Test lamp lights.	Replace WINDSHIELD WIPER MOTOR.
	Test lamp does not light.	GO TO A29.
A29. Backprobe WINDSHIELD WIPER SWITCH connector with a test lamp from cavity 13 to chassis ground.	Test lamp lights.	Repair open in BLU/ORN wire between WINDSHIELD WIPER SWITCH and WINDSHIELD WIPER MOTOR.
	Test lamp does not light.	Replace WINDSHIELD WIPER SWITCH.
A30. Disconnect WINDSHIELD WIPER MOTOR connector. Connect a test lamp from connector cavity 2 to chassis ground.	Test lamp does not light.	Replace WINDSHIELD WIPER MOTOR.
	Test lamp lights.	GO TO A31.
A31. Disconnect WINDSHIELD WIPER SWITCH connector. Connect a test lamp from connector cavity 7 to chassis ground.	Test lamp lights.	Repair short to voltage in BLU/BLK wire between WINDSHIELD WIPER SWITCH and WINDSHIELD WIPER MOTOR.
	Test lamp does not light.	Replace WINDSHIELD WIPER SWITCH.

Fig. 7   System diagnosis chart (Part 2 of 2). Prizm w/pulse wiper

Terminals		4	7	13	18	8	16
Switch position							
Wiper	MIST		○		○		
	OFF	○	○				
	INT	○	○				
	LO		○		○		
	HI			○	○		
Washer	OFF						
	ON					○	○

1	MULTI-FUNCTION SWITCH
2	ELECTRICAL CONNECTOR

Fig. 8   Windshield wiper switch. Prizm

1	TERMINAL 2
2	WIPER MOTOR
3	BATTERY

Fig. 9   Windshield wiper "Low" speed operation. Prizm

1	TERMINAL 1
2	WIPER MOTOR
3	BATTERY

Fig. 10   Windshield wiper "High" speed operation. Prizm

SYSTEM DIAGNOSIS

DIAGNOSTIC CHART A

WIPER/WASHER

TEST	RESULT	ACTION
A1. Turn ignition switch to "ON." Press WASH button.	WINDSHIELD WASHER PUMP operates.	GO TO A2.
	WINDSHIELD WASHER PUMP does not operate.	GO TO A5.
	WINDSHIELD WASHER PUMP continues to operate after WASH button has been released.	GO TO A10.
A2. Press "LO" button.	Wipers sweep at low speed.	GO TO A3.
	Wipers do not sweep.	GO TO A11.
A3. Press "HI" button.	Wipers sweep at high speed.	GO TO A16.
	Wipers do not sweep.	GO TO A4.
	Wipers sweep at low speed.	GO TO A18.
	Wipers do not sweep.	GO TO A20.
A4. Press "OFF" button.	Wipers complete 1 full sweep and stop.	All systems diagnosed are functioning normally.
	Wipers do not complete 1 full sweep.	GO TO A22.
	Wipers continue for more than 2 sweeps.	GO TO A25.
A5. Disconnect WINDSHIELD WASHER PUMP connector. Connect a digital multimeter from cavity 2 to chassis ground. Measure resistance.	More than 0.3 ohms.	Repair BLK ground wire between WINDSHIELD WASHER PUMP and G103.
	Less than 0.3 ohms.	GO TO A6.
A6. Connect a test lamp from WINDSHIELD WASHER PUMP connector cavity 1 to chassis ground. Press WASH button.	Test lamp lights.	Replace WINDSHIELD WASHER PUMP.
	Test lamp does not light.	GO TO A7.
A7. Backprobe WINDSHIELD WIPER/WASHER SWITCH connector with a test lamp from cavity 4 to chassis ground. Press WASH button.	Test lamp lights.	Repair open in BLU/YEL wire.
	Test lamp does not light.	GO TO A8.
A8. Backprobe WINDSHIELD WIPER/WASHER SWITCH connector with a test lamp from cavity 3 to chassis ground.	Test lamp lights.	Replace WINDSHIELD WIPER/WASHER SWITCH.
	Test lamp does not light.	GO TO A9.
A9. Backprobe JUNCTION BLOCK connector C4 with a test lamp from cavity 16 to chassis ground.	Test lamp does not light.	Replace JUNCTION BLOCK.
	Test lamp lights.	Repair open in BLU wire between JUNCTION BLOCK and WINDSHIELD WIPER/WASHER SWITCH.
A10. Disconnect WINDSHIELD WIPER/WASHER SWITCH connector.	WINDSHIELD WASHER PUMP stops.	Replace WINDSHIELD WIPER/WASHER SWITCH.
	WINDSHIELD WASHER PUMP continues to operate.	Repair short to voltage in BLU/YEL wire between WINDSHIELD WIPER/WASHER SWITCH and WINDSHIELD WASHER PUMP.
A11. Backprobe WINDSHIELD WIPER MOTOR connector with a fused jumper from cavity 2 to chassis ground.	WINDSHIELD WIPER MOTOR operates.	Remove jumper, GO TO A12.
	WINDSHIELD WIPER MOTOR does not operate.	Remove jumper, GO TO A14.
A12. Disconnect WINDSHIELD WIPER/WASHER SWITCH connector. Connect a digital multimeter from connector terminal 8 to chassis ground. Measure resistance.	More than 0.3 ohms.	GO TO A13.
	Less than 0.3 ohms.	Repair open in PNK/YEL wire between WINDSHIELD WIPER/WASHER SWITCH and WINDSHIELD WIPER MOTOR.
A13. Disconnect WINDSHIELD WIPER MOTOR connector. Connect a digital multimeter from WINDSHIELD WIPER MOTOR connector cavity 2 to WINDSHIELD WIPER/WASHER SWITCH connector terminal 7. Measure resistance.	Less than 0.3 ohms.	Replace WINDSHIELD WIPER/WASHER SWITCH.
	More than 0.3 ohms.	Repair open in PNK/YEL wire between WINDSHIELD WIPER/WASHER SWITCH and G201.
A14. Backprobe WINDSHIELD WIPER MOTOR connector with a test lamp from cavity 6 to chassis ground.	Test lamp lights.	Replace WINDSHIELD WIPER MOTOR.
	Test lamp does not light.	GO TO A15.
A15. Backprobe JUNCTION BLOCK connector C5 with a test lamp from cavity 9 to chassis ground.	Test lamp does not light.	Replace JUNCTION BLOCK.
	Test lamp lights.	Repair open in BLU wire between JUNCTION BLOCK and WINDSHIELD WIPER MOTOR.

Fig. 13 System diagnosis chart (Part 1 of 2). Storm less pulse wiper

Fig. 11 Windshield wiper terminal 2. Prizm

A — DISCONNECT TERMINAL 2
1 — TERMINAL 2
2 — WIPER MOTOR
3 — BATTERY

1 — TERMINAL 2
2 — JUMPER WIRE
3 — WIPER MOTOR
4 — TERMINAL 3
5 — BATTERY
6 — TERMINAL 4

Fig. 12 Windshield wiper "Park" operation. Prizm

SYSTEM DIAGNOSIS

WIPER/WASHER: PULSE — DIAGNOSTIC CHART A

TEST	RESULT	ACTION
A1. Turn ignition switch to "ON." Press WASH button for one to two seconds and release.	WINDSHIELD WASHER PUMP operates and wipers complete at least one sweep.	GO TO A2.
	WINDSHIELD WASHER PUMP does not operate.	GO TO A6.
	WINDSHIELD WASHER PUMP operates but wipers do not sweep.	GO TO A11.
	WINDSHIELD WASHER PUMP continues to operate after WASH button is released.	GO TO A19.
	Wipers continue for more than two sweeps after WASH button is released.	GO TO A21.
	Wipers do not complete at least one full sweep.	GO TO A28.
A2. Press and release OFF/MIST button.	Wipers complete one full sweep.	GO TO A3.
	Wipers do not operate.	GO TO A30.
A3. Press "INT" button.	Wipers complete one full sweep every four seconds.	GO TO A4.
	Wipers do not operate.	GO TO A31.
A4. Press "LO" button.	Wipers operate at low speed.	GO TO A5.
	Wipers do not operate.	Replace WINDSHIELD WIPER/WASHER SWITCH.
A5. Press "HI" button.	Wipers operate at high speed.	All systems diagnosed in this cell are functioning normally.
	Wipers do not operate.	GO TO A33.
A6. Disconnect WINDSHIELD WASHER PUMP connector. Connect a digital multimeter from cavity 2 to chassis ground. Measure resistance.	More than 0.3 ohms.	Repair BLK ground wire between WINDSHIELD WASHER PUMP and G103.
	Less than 0.3 ohms.	GO TO A7.
A7. Connect a test lamp from WINDSHIELD WASHER PUMP cavity 1 to chassis ground. Press and hold WASH button.	Test lamp lights.	Replace WINDSHIELD WASHER PUMP.
	Test lamp does not light.	GO TO A8.
A8. Backprobe WINDSHIELD WIPER/WASHER SWITCH with a test lamp from cavity 4 to chassis ground. Press and hold WASH button.	Test lamp lights.	Repair open in BLU/YEL wire between WINDSHIELD WIPER/WASHER SWITCH and WINDSHIELD WASHER PUMP.
	Test lamp does not light.	GO TO A9.
A9. Backprobe WINDSHIELD WIPER/WASHER SWITCH connector with a test lamp from cavity 3 to chassis ground.	Test lamp lights.	Replace WINDSHIELD WIPER/WASHER SWITCH.
	Test lamp does not light.	GO TO A10.
A10. Backprobe JUNCTION BLOCK connector C4 with a test lamp from cavity 16 to chassis ground.	Test lamp lights.	Replace JUNCTION BLOCK.
	Test lamp does not light.	Repair open in BLU wire between JUNCTION BLOCK and WINDSHIELD WIPER/WASHER SWITCH.
A11. Backprobe WINDSHIELD WIPER MOTOR connector with a test lamp from cavity 6 to chassis ground.	Test lamp does not light.	Repair open in BLU wire between JUNCTION BLOCK and WINDSHIELD WIPER MOTOR.
	Test lamp lights.	GO TO A12.
A12. Backprobe WINDSHIELD WIPER MOTOR connector with a fused jumper from cavity 2 to chassis ground.	WINDSHIELD WIPER MOTOR does not operate.	Replace WINDSHIELD WIPER MOTOR.
	WINDSHIELD WIPER MOTOR operates.	Remove jumper, GO TO A13.
A13. Disconnect INTERMITTENT WIPER RELAY connector. Connect a test lamp from cavity 11 to chassis ground.	Test lamp does not light.	Repair open in BLU wire between INTERMITTENT WIPER RELAY and S101.
	Test lamp lights.	GO TO A14.
A14. Connect a test lamp from cavity 8 to chassis ground. Press and hold WASH button.	Test lamp lights.	Repair open in BLU/YEL wire between INTERMITTENT WIPER RELAY and S100.
	Test lamp lights.	GO TO A15.

Fig. 14 System diagnosis chart (Part 1 of 2). Storm w/pulse wiper

SYSTEM DIAGNOSIS

WIPER/WASHER — DIAGNOSTIC CHART A (CONT'D)

TEST	RESULT	ACTION
A16. Disconnect WINDSHIELD WIPER MOTOR connector. Connect a digital multimeter from cavity 1 to chassis ground. Measure resistance.	Infinite.	Replace WINDSHIELD WIPER MOTOR.
	Less than infinite.	GO TO A17.
A17. Disconnect WINDSHIELD WIPER/WASHER SWITCH connector. Connect a digital multimeter from connector cavity 6 (switch side) to chassis ground. Measure resistance.	Less than infinite.	Replace WINDSHIELD WIPER/WASHER SWITCH.
	Infinite.	Repair short to ground in BLU/WHT wire between WINDSHIELD WIPER MOTOR and WINDSHIELD WIPER/WASHER SWITCH.
A18. Disconnect WINDSHIELD WIPER MOTOR connector. Connect a digital multimeter from cavity 1 chassis ground. Measure resistance.	Less than 0.3 ohms.	Replace WINDSHIELD WIPER MOTOR.
	More than 0.3 ohms.	GO TO A19.
A19. Backprobe WINDSHIELD WIPER/WASHER SWITCH connector with a digital multimeter from cavity 6 to chassis ground. Measure resistance.	More than 0.3 ohms.	Replace WINDSHIELD WIPER/WASHER SWITCH.
	Less than 0.3 ohms.	Repair open in BLU/WHT wire between WINDSHIELD WIPER/WASHER SWITCH and WINDSHIELD WIPER MOTOR.
A20. Disconnect WINDSHIELD WIPER MOTOR connector. Connect a digital multimeter from cavity 2 to chassis ground. Measure resistance.	Infinite.	Replace WINDSHIELD WIPER MOTOR.
	Less than infinite.	GO TO A21.
A21. Disconnect WINDSHIELD WIPER/WASHER SWITCH connector. Connect a digital multimeter from connector cavity 7 (switch side) to chassis ground. Measure resistance.	Less than infinite.	Replace WINDSHIELD WIPER/WASHER SWITCH.
	Infinite.	Repair short to ground in PNK/YEL wire between WINDSHIELD WIPER/WASHER SWITCH and WINDSHIELD WIPER MOTOR.
A22. Disconnect WINDSHIELD WIPER MOTOR connector. Connect a digital multimeter from cavity 4 to chassis ground. Measure resistance.	More than 0.3 ohms.	Repair BLK ground wire between WINDSHIELD WIPER MOTOR and G102.
	Less than 0.3 ohms.	GO TO A23.
A23. Connect a digital multimeter across WINDSHIELD WIPER MOTOR connector cavities 2 and 5. Measure resistance.	Less than 0.3 ohms.	Replace WINDSHIELD WIPER MOTOR.
	More than 0.3 ohms.	GO TO A24.
A24. Disconnect WINDSHIELD WIPER/WASHER SWITCH connector. Connect a digital multimeter from WINDSHIELD WIPER/WASHER SWITCH connector terminal 5 (wiring harness side) to WINDSHIELD WIPER MOTOR connector cavity 5. Measure resistance.	Less than 0.3 ohms.	Replace WINDSHIELD WIPER/WASHER SWITCH.
	More than 0.3 ohms.	Repair open in BLU/GRN wire between WINDSHIELD WIPER/WASHER SWITCH and WINDSHIELD WIPER MOTOR.
A25. Disconnect WINDSHIELD WIPER/WASHER SWITCH connector.	WINDSHIELD WIPER MOTOR continues to operate.	Repair short to ground in BLU/WHT or PNK/YEL wire between WINDSHIELD WIPER MOTOR and WINDSHIELD WIPER/WASHER SWITCH.
	WINDSHIELD WIPER MOTOR stops.	GO TO A26.
A26. Disconnect WINDSHIELD WIPER MOTOR connector. Connect a digital multimeter from cavity 5 to chassis ground. Measure resistance.	Infinite.	Replace WINDSHIELD WIPER/WASHER SWITCH.
	Less than infinite.	Repair short to ground in BLU/GRN wire between WINDSHIELD WIPER/WASHER SWITCH and WINDSHIELD WIPER MOTOR.

Fig. 13 System diagnosis chart (Part 2 of 2). Storm less pulse wiper

SYSTEM DIAGNOSIS

WIPER/WASHER: PULSE	DIAGNOSTIC CHART A (CONT'D)	
TEST	**RESULT**	**ACTION**
A15. Connect a digital multimeter from INTERMITTENT WIPER RELAY connector cavity 9 to chassis ground. Measure resistance.	More than 0.3 ohms.	Repair BLK ground wire between INTERMITTENT WIPER RELAY and G102.
	Less than 0.3 ohms.	GO TO A16.
A16. Connect a fused jumper from INTERMITTENT WIPER RELAY connector cavity 2 to chassis ground.	WINDSHIELD WIPER MOTOR operates.	Replace INTERMITTENT WIPER RELAY.
	WINDSHIELD WIPER MOTOR does not operate.	Remove jumper, GO TO A17.
A17. Backprobe WINDSHIELD WIPER/WASHER SWITCH connector with a fused jumper from cavity 5 to chassis ground.	WINDSHIELD WIPER MOTOR operates.	Repair open in BLU/GRN wire between WINDSHIELD WIPER/WASHER SWITCH and WINDSHIELD WASHER PUMP.
	WINDSHIELD WIPER MOTOR does not operate.	Remove jumper, GO TO A18.
A18. Backprobe WINDSHIELD WIPER/WASHER SWITCH connector with a fused jumper from cavity 7 to chassis ground.	WINDSHIELD WIPER MOTOR operates.	Replace WINDSHIELD WIPER/WASHER SWITCH.
	WINDSHIELD WIPER MOTOR does not operate.	Repair open in PNK/YEL wire between WINDSHIELD WIPER/WASHER SWITCH and WINDSHIELD WIPER MOTOR.
A19. Disconnect WINDSHIELD WIPER/WASHER SWITCH connector.	WINDSHIELD WASHER PUMP stops.	Replace WINDSHIELD WIPER/WASHER SWITCH.
	WINDSHIELD WASHER PUMP continues to operate.	GO TO A20.
A20. Disconnect INTERMITTENT WIPER RELAY connector.	WINDSHIELD WASHER PUMP stops.	Replace INTERMITTENT WIPER RELAY.
	WINDSHIELD WASHER PUMP continues to operate.	Repair short to voltage in BLU/YEL wire between WINDSHIELD WIPER/WASHER SWITCH, INTERMITTENT WIPER RELAY and WINDSHIELD WASHER PUMP.
A21. Disconnect INTERMITTENT WIPER RELAY connector.	WINDSHIELD WIPER MOTOR continues to operate.	GO TO A22.
	WINDSHIELD WIPER MOTOR stops.	GO TO A24.
A22. Disconnect WINDSHIELD WIPER/WASHER SWITCH connector.	WINDSHIELD WIPER MOTOR continues to operate.	Repair short to ground in BLU/WHT or PNK/YEL wire between WINDSHIELD WIPER/WASHER SWITCH and WINDSHIELD WIPER MOTOR.
	WINDSHIELD WIPER MOTOR stops.	GO TO A23.
A23. Connect a digital multimeter from INTERMITTENT WIPER RELAY connector cavity 2 to chassis ground. Measure resistance.	Infinite.	Replace WINDSHIELD WIPER/WASHER SWITCH.
	Less than infinite.	Repair short to ground in BLU/GRN wire between WINDSHIELD WIPER/WASHER SWITCH and INTERMITTENT WIPER RELAY.
A24. Connect a test lamp from INTERMITTENT WIPER RELAY connector cavity 4 to chassis ground. Press "LO" button.	Test lamp does not light.	GO TO A25.
	Test lamp lights only when wipers are in PARK position.	GO TO A26.
A25. Backprobe WINDSHIELD WIPER MOTOR connector with a test lamp from cavity 5 to chassis ground.	Test lamp does not light.	Replace WINDSHIELD WIPER MOTOR.
	Test lamp lights only when wipers are in PARK position.	Repair open in BLU/ORN wire between WINDSHIELD WIPER MOTOR and INTERMITTENT WIPER RELAY.
A26. Connect a digital multimeter from INTERMITTENT WIPER RELAY connector cavity 7 to chassis ground. Measure resistance.	Infinite.	Replace INTERMITTENT WIPER RELAY.
	Less than infinite.	GO TO A27.
A27. Disconnect WINDSHIELD WIPER/WASHER SWITCH connector. Connect a digital multimeter from cavity 9 (SWITCH side) to chassis ground. Measure resistance.	Less than infinite.	Replace WINDSHIELD WIPER/WASHER SWITCH.
	Infinite.	Repair short to ground in LT GRN/RED wire on WINDSHIELD WIPER/WASHER SWITCH.
A28. Disconnect INTERMITTENT WIPER RELAY connector.	Test lamp lights only when wipers are in PARK position.	Replace INTERMITTENT WIPER RELAY.
	Test lamp lit continuously.	GO TO A29.
A29. Connect a test lamp from cavity 4 to chassis ground. Press "LO" button. Disconnect WINDSHIELD WIPER MOTOR connector. Connect a test lamp from connector cavity 5 to chassis ground.	Test lamp does not light.	Replace WINDSHIELD WIPER MOTOR.
	Test lamp lights.	Repair short to voltage in BLU/ORN wire between WINDSHIELD WIPER MOTOR and INTERMITTENT WIPER RELAY.
A30. Disconnect WINDSHIELD WIPER/WASHER SWITCH connector. Connect a digital multimeter from connector terminal 8 to chassis ground. Measure resistance.	Less than 0.3 ohms.	Replace WINDSHIELD WIPER/WASHER SWITCH.
	More than 0.3 ohms.	Repair BLK ground wire between WINDSHIELD WIPER/WASHER SWITCH and G201.
A31. Turn ignition switch to "OFF." Disconnect INTERMITTENT WIPER RELAY connector. Connect a digital multimeter from cavity 7 to chassis ground. Measure resistance.	Less than 0.3 ohms.	Replace INTERMITTENT WIPER RELAY.
	More than 0.3 ohms.	GO TO A32.
A32. Backprobe WINDSHIELD WIPER/WASHER SWITCH connector with a digital multimeter from cavity 9 to chassis ground. Measure resistance.	More than 0.3 ohms.	Replace WINDSHIELD WIPER/WASHER SWITCH.
	Less than 0.3 ohms.	Repair open in LT GRN/RED wire between WINDSHIELD WIPER/WASHER SWITCH and INTERMITTENT WIPER RELAY.
A33. Backprobe WINDSHIELD WIPER MOTOR connector with a fused jumper from cavity 1 to chassis ground.	WINDSHIELD WIPER MOTOR does not operate.	Replace WINDSHIELD WIPER MOTOR.
	WINDSHIELD WIPER MOTOR operates.	Remove jumper, GO TO A34.
A34. Backprobe WINDSHIELD WIPER/WASHER SWITCH with a fused jumper from cavity 6 to chassis ground.	WINDSHIELD WIPER MOTOR operates.	Replace WINDSHIELD WIPER/WASHER SWITCH.
	WINDSHIELD WIPER MOTOR does not operate.	Repair open in BLU/WHT wire between WINDSHIELD WIPER/WASHER SWITCH and WINDSHIELD WIPER MOTOR.

Fig. 14   System diagnosis chart (Part 2 of 2). Storm w/pulse wiper

NO. SWITCH POSITION	3	4	6	7	8	9	1	2
🚗 (wiper)	o—o							
HI			o——————o					
LO				o———o				
INT					o———o		ILLUMINATION	
MIST				o———o				
OFF								

Fig. 15 Wiper switch continuity chart. Storm

NO. SWITCH POSITION	3	4	5	6	7	8	9	1	2
🚗 (wiper)	o—o								
HI				o———————o					
LO					o———o				
INT			o———o		o———o		ILLUMINATION	
MIST					o———o				
OFF			o———————o						

Fig. 16 Windshield wiper cable continuity chart. Storm

I-3

Fig. 17 Windshield wiper connections. Storm

B
NC
Low
High
Ground
Park

Rear Window Wiper Systems

INDEX

Fig. 1   Rear wiper motor assembly. Century, Cutlass Cruiser & 6000 wagons

Fig. 2   Rear wiper motor wiring schematic. Century, Cutlass Cruiser & 6000 wagons

Fig. 3   Rear window wiper switch test chart. Century, Cutlass Cruiser & 6000 wagons

REAR WINDOW WIPER SWITCH CHECK		
	SWITCH MODE	
TERMINAL	OFF	ON
A	B(+)	0V
B	0V	B(+)
C	GROUND	GROUND
D	0V	B(+)

Fig. 4   Rear wiper motor wiring schematic. Caprice, Custom Cruiser & Roadmaster wagons

DESCRIPTION

CENTURY, CUTLASS CRUISER & 6000 WAGONS

These vehicles use a one speed, 12 volt, DC permanent magnet motor, **Fig. 1.** The motor drives a gearbox which in turn drives a wiper pivot that provides an oscillating output to the arm and blade.

The system operates only with the ignition in Run position, but will park if the ignition is turned off.

There are three electrical terminals on the motor, **Fig. 2.** Terminals A, B and C are used when the motor is in Run mode. A and C are positive and B is ground.

When wiper switch is set to OFF, only motor terminals A and B are used, with A being positive and the circuit being completed through the closed park switch terminals. A cam on the gear then opens at Park position and the wiper shuts off.

The autopark module supplies power to the rear wiper motor to allow the wiper arm to park if the ignition switch is turned off while the wiper is operating.

CAPRICE, CUSTOM CRUISER & ROADMASTER WAGONS

These vehicles use a one speed permanent magnet motor. The motor drives a gearbox which in turn drives a wiper pivot that provides an oscillating output to the arm and blade.

METRO & PRIZM

These vehicles use a one speed type motor.

STORM

These vehicles use a one speed type motor and are equipped with a separate type washer pump and reservoir located behind rear end trim panel.

DIAGNOSIS & TESTING

CENTURY, CUTLASS CRUISER & 6000 WAGONS

Before removing wiper assembly from vehicle, perform the following:
1. Disconnect wiring harness and apply 12 volts to motor terminals A and C and connect ground to terminal B. The motor should run.
2. To test for proper parking, apply 12 volts to terminal A and connect ground to terminal B. The wiper should park and shutoff.

3. If results are correct in steps 1 and 2, the problem is in the wiring harness or switch. After checking all wires for continuity and ensuring fuses are satisfactory, check switch by turning ignition switch on and probing connector to dash switch. Results should be as shown, **Fig. 3,** with respect to vehicle ground.

CAPRICE, CUSTOM CRUISER & ROADMASTER WAGONS

1. To test for proper motor operation, disconnect wiring harness and apply 12 volts to terminals A and C of autopark module and ground terminal B, **Fig. 4.** Motor should run.
2. To test for proper park operation, apply 12 volts to terminal A and ground terminal B. The wiper should go into park position and shutoff.
3. If wiper motor does not run in steps one and two, refer to diagnostic chart in **Fig. 5 and 6.**

Fig. 5   Rear wiper system diagnosis chart (wiper inoperative). Caprice, Custom Cruiser & Roadmaster wagons

Fig. 6   Rear wiper system diagnosis chart (wiper will not park). Caprice, Custom Cruiser & Roadmaster wagons

TERMINAL	SWITCH MODE	
	OFF	ON
A	Battery Voltage	Battery Voltage
B	Ground	Ground
C	Zero Voltage	Battery Voltage

Fig. 7   Rear window wiper switch test chart. Caprice, Custom Cruiser & Roadmaster wagons

STORM

Refer to **Fig. 13**, for complete system diagnosis.

Motor Test

Using a digital multimeter, take measurements and compare the results to the specifications in **Fig. 14**. If the motor does not operate as specified, replace motor.

1. Connect battery positive lead to terminal 2, **Fig. 15**.
2. Connect battery negative lead to wiper motor body.
3. If wiper motor does not operate as specified in **Fig. 14**, replace motor.

Park Position Inspection

1. Connect battery positive lead to terminal 2, **Fig. 15**.
2. Connect battery negative lead to wiper motor body.
3. Remove battery positive lead from terminal 2. Time this disconnection so that the wiper stops in any position other than "Park" position.
4. If operation does not end in the "Park" position, replace wiper motor.

Switch Test

Using a voltmeter, perform tests in **Figs. 7**, with ignition switch ON. If the voltage is not as specified, replace switch.

METRO

Refer to **Fig. 8**, for complete system diagnosis.

PRIZM

Refer to **Fig. 9**, for complete system diagnosis.

Switch Test

Using a digital multimeter, perform continuity tests in **Fig. 10**. If the continuity is not as specified, replace switch.

Motor Test

1. Connect battery positive lead to terminal 2, **Fig. 11**.
2. Connect battery negative lead to wiper motor body.
3. If wiper motor does not operate, replace motor.

Park Position Inspection

1. Connect battery positive lead to terminal 1, install jumper between terminals 2 and 3, **Fig. 12**.
2. Connect battery negative lead to wiper motor body.
3. If operation does not end in the "Park" position, replace wiper motor.

SYSTEM DIAGNOSIS
REAR WIPER/WASHER
DIAGNOSTIC CHART A

TEST	RESULT	ACTION
A1. Press REAR WIPER SWITCH all the way to the WASH position.	Rear wiper sweeps and washer fluid is sprayed on rear window.	All systems diagnosed are functioning normally.
	Rear wiper sweeps but washer fluid is sprayed on front window.	GO TO A2.
	Rear wiper does not sweep.	GO TO A5.
	WASHER FLUID PUMP does not operate.	Check operation of front washer. If good, repair open in BLU/YEL wire between REAR WIPER SWITCH and S280.
A2. Backprobe WASHER CHANGE VALVE connector with a test lamp from cavity 2 to chassis ground.	Test lamp does not light.	Repair open in JUNCTION BLOCK 3 or in BLU wire between JUNCTION BLOCK 3 and WASHER CHANGE VALVE.
	Test lamp lights.	GO TO A3.
A3. Turn ignition switch to "OFF." Backprobe REAR WIPER SWITCH connector with a digital multimeter from cavity 1 to chassis ground. Measure resistance with switch pressed to WASH.	More than 0.3 ohms.	GO TO A4.
	Less than 0.3 ohms.	GO TO A5.
A4. Backprobe REAR WIPER SWITCH with a digital multimeter from cavity 8 to chassis ground. Measure resistance.	More than 0.3 ohms.	Repair open in WHT/BLK ground wire between REAR WIPER SWITCH and G201 (Base, LSi) or G200 (GSi).
	Less than 0.3 ohms.	Replace REAR WIPER SWITCH.
A5. Backprobe WASHER CHANGE VALVE connector with a digital multimeter from cavity 1 to chassis ground. Measure resistance with the REAR WIPER SWITCH pressed to WASH.	More than 0.3 ohms.	Repair open in PNK wire between WASHER CHANGE VALVE and REAR WIPER SWITCH.
	Less than 0.3 ohms.	Replace WASHER CHANGE VALVE.
A6. Backprobe REAR WIPER SWITCH connector with a test lamp from cavity 2 to chassis ground.	Test lamp does not light.	Repair open in BLU wire or JUNCTION BLOCK 3 between JUNCTION BLOCK 3 and REAR WIPER SWITCH.
	Test lamp lights.	GO TO A7.
A7. Backprobe REAR WIPER SWITCH connector with a test lamp from cavity 4 to chassis ground with switch pressed.	Test lamp does not light.	Replace REAR WIPER SWITCH.
	Test lamp lights.	GO TO A8.
A8. Backprobe REAR WIPER MOTOR connector with a test lamp from cavity 3 to chassis ground with REAR WIPER SWITCH pressed.	Test lamp does not light.	Repair open in PNK wire between REAR WIPER SWITCH and REAR WIPER MOTOR.
	Test lamp lights.	GO TO A9.
A9. Backprobe REAR WIPER MOTOR connector with a test lamp from cavity 1 to chassis ground.	Test lamp does not light.	Repair open in BLU wire between JUNCTION BLOCK 1 and REAR WIPER MOTOR.
	Test lamp lights.	GO TO A10.
A10. Disconnect REAR WIPER MOTOR connector and REAR WIPER SWITCH connector. Connect a digital multimeter from REAR WIPER MOTOR connector cavity 2 to REAR WIPER SWITCH connector cavity 3. Measure resistance.	Less than 0.3 ohms.	Replace REAR WIPER MOTOR.
	More than 0.3 ohms.	Repair open in PNK/BLK wire between REAR WIPER MOTOR and REAR WIPER SWITCH.

Fig. 9   System diagnosis chart. Prizm rear wiper

SYSTEM DIAGNOSIS
REAR WIPER/WASHER
DIAGNOSTIC CHART A

TEST	RESULT	ACTION
A1. Turn Rear Wiper Switch ON.	REAR WIPER MOTOR operates.	GO TO A2.
	REAR WIPER MOTOR does not operate.	GO TO A5.
A2. Turn Rear Wiper Switch OFF.	REAR WIPER MOTOR stops with wiper in PARK position.	GO TO A3.
	REAR WIPER MOTOR does not stop.	GO TO A9.
	Rear wiper does not return to PARK position.	GO TO A11.
A3. Press and hold Rear Washer Switch.	REAR WASHER PUMP and REAR WIPER MOTOR both operate.	GO TO A4.
	REAR WASHER PUMP does not operate.	Release switch and GO TO A14.
A4. Release Rear Washer Switch.	REAR WIPER MOTOR does not operate.	Replace REAR WIPER/WASHER SWITCH.
	REAR WASHER PUMP and REAR WIPER MOTOR both stop with wiper in PARK position.	All systems diagnosed are functioning normally.
	REAR WASHER PUMP and REAR WIPER MOTOR does not stop.	GO TO A17.
	REAR WIPER MOTOR does not stop or rear wiper does not return to PARK position.	Replace REAR WIPER/WASHER SWITCH.
A5. Backprobe REAR WIPER/WASHER SWITCH connector with a test lamp from cavity 5 to chassis ground.	Test lamp does not light.	Repair open in YEL/BLU wire between JUNCTION BLOCK and REAR WIPER/WASHER SWITCH.
	Test lamp lights.	GO TO A6.
A6. Turn Rear Wiper Switch ON. Backprobe REAR WIPER/WASHER SWITCH connector with a test lamp from cavity 2 to chassis ground.	Test lamp does not light.	Replace REAR WIPER/WASHER SWITCH.
	Test lamp lights.	GO TO A7.
A7. Backprobe REAR WIPER MOTOR connector with a test lamp from cavity 4 to chassis ground.	Test lamp does not light.	Repair open in ORN wire between REAR WIPER/WASHER SWITCH and REAR WIPER MOTOR.
	Test lamp lights.	GO TO A8.
A8. Backprobe REAR WIPER MOTOR with a digital multimeter from ground terminal to G400. Measure resistance.	More than 0.3 ohms.	Repair BLK ground wire between REAR WIPER MOTOR and G400.
	Less than 0.3 ohms.	Replace REAR WIPER MOTOR.
A9. Disconnect REAR WIPER/WASHER SWITCH connector.	REAR WIPER MOTOR continues to operate.	Repair short to voltage in ORN wire between REAR WIPER/WASHER SWITCH and REAR WIPER MOTOR.
	REAR WIPER MOTOR stops.	GO TO A10.
A10. Connect a digital multimeter across REAR WIPER/WASHER SWITCH terminals 2 and 5. Measure resistance.	Less than infinite.	Replace REAR WIPER/WASHER SWITCH.
	Infinite.	Replace REAR WIPER MOTOR.
A11. Backprobe REAR WIPER MOTOR connector with a test lamp from cavity 2 to chassis ground.	Test lamp does not light.	Repair open in YEL/BLU wire between JUNCTION BLOCK and REAR WIPER MOTOR.
	Test lamp lights.	GO TO A12.
A12. Backprobe REAR WIPER MOTOR connector with a test lamp from cavity 1 to chassis ground.	Test lamp does not light.	Replace REAR WIPER MOTOR.
	Test lamp lights.	GO TO A13.
A13. Backprobe REAR WIPER/WASHER SWITCH connector with a test lamp from cavity 3 to chassis ground.	Test lamp lights.	Repair open in BLU/ORN wire between REAR WIPER MOTOR and REAR WIPER/WASHER SWITCH.
	Test lamp does not light.	Replace REAR WIPER/WASHER SWITCH.
A14. Disconnect REAR WIPER/WASHER SWITCH connector. Connect a digital multimeter from cavity 6 to cavity 1. Measure resistance while pressing Rear Washer Switch.	More than 0.3 ohms.	Replace REAR WIPER/WASHER SWITCH.
	Less than 0.3 ohms.	Release switch and GO TO A15.
A15. Reconnect REAR WIPER/WASHER SWITCH connector. Backprobe REAR WASHER PUMP connector with a test lamp from cavity 2 to chassis ground while pressing Rear Washer Switch.	Test lamp does not light.	Repair open in BLK/GRN wire between REAR WIPER/WASHER SWITCH and REAR WASHER PUMP.
	Test lamp lights.	GO TO A16.
A16. Disconnect REAR WASHER PUMP connector. Connect a digital multimeter from cavity 1 to chassis ground. Measure resistance.	More than 0.3 ohms.	Repair BLK ground wire between REAR WASHER PUMP and G101.
	Less than 0.3 ohms.	Replace REAR WASHER PUMP.
A17. Disconnect REAR WIPER/WASHER SWITCH connector.	REAR WASHER PUMP stops.	Replace REAR WASHER PUMP.
	REAR WASHER PUMP continues to operate.	Repair short to voltage in BLK/GRN wire between REAR WIPER/WASHER SWITCH and REAR WASHER PUMP.

Fig. 8   System diagnosis chart. Metro rear wiper

1 TERMINAL 2
2 ELECTRICAL CONNECTOR
3 REAR WIPER MOTOR

Fig. 11 Rear wiper motor connections. Prizm

1 ELECTRICAL CONNECTOR
2 REAR WIPER-WASHER SWITCH

Terminals Switch position	1	2	3	4	7	8	11	12
OFF							⊙	⊙
ON		⊙	⊙				⊙	⊙
Wash		⊙		⊙	⊙			⊙

Fig. 10 Rear wiper switch connections. Prizm

1 ELECTRICAL CONNECTOR
2 TERMINAL 1
3 TERMINAL 2
4 TERMINAL 3
5 REAR WIPER MOTOR

Fig. 12 Rear wiper "Park" connections. Prizm

REAR WIPER MOTOR	SPECIFICATIONS
RATED VOLTAGE	12V
OPERATING VOLTAGE	10-15V
STARTING VOLTAGE	8V
TESTING VOLTAGE	13.5V
CURRENT AT 10 KG-CM LOAD AT 15 KG-CM LOAD	2.0A OR LESS 2.5A OR LESS
STALL CURRENT	9A OR LESS
INSULATION RESISTANCE	1MΩ (MINIMUM)
SPEED (AT 10 KG-CM LOAD)	34-44 RPM

Fig. 14 Rear wiper motor specifications. Storm

Fig. 15 Rear wiper motor connections. Storm

SYSTEM DIAGNOSIS

DIAGNOSTIC CHART A

WIPER/WASHER	TEST	RESULT	ACTION
A1.	Turn ignition switch to "ON." Press REAR WIPER/WASHER SWITCH to MIST/WASH (bottom of switch) and release.	REAR WASHER PUMP operates and REAR WIPER/WASHER MOTOR sweeps once.	GO TO A2.
		REAR WASHER PUMP operates but REAR WIPER MOTOR does not sweep.	GO TO A5.
		REAR WIPER MOTOR sweeps once but REAR WASHER PUMP does not operate.	GO TO A8.
		REAR WIPER MOTOR and REAR WASHER PUMP do not operate.	GO TO A11.
		REAR WIPER PUMP and REAR WIPER MOTOR operate but REAR WIPER MOTOR does not complete one sweep.	GO TO A13.
A2.	Press REAR WIPER/WASHER SWITCH to WIPER (first detent on top of switch).	REAR WIPER MOTOR operates.	GO TO A3.
		REAR WIPER MOTOR does not operate.	Replace REAR WIPER/WASHER SWITCH.
A3.	Press REAR WIPER/WASHER SWITCH to WIPER/WASHER (fully press top of switch).	REAR WIPER MOTOR and REAR WASHER PUMP operate.	GO TO A4.
		REAR WIPER MOTOR operates but REAR WASHER PUMP does not operate.	Replace REAR WIPER/WASHER SWITCH.
		REAR WASHER PUMP operates but REAR WIPER MOTOR does not operate.	Replace REAR WIPER/WASHER SWITCH.
A4.	Press REAR WIPER/WASHER SWITCH to OFF.	REAR WIPER MOTOR and REAR WASHER PUMP stop.	All systems diagnosed are functioning normally.
		REAR WIPER MOTOR or REAR WASHER PUMP continue to operate.	GO TO A15.
A5.	Disconnect REAR WIPER MOTOR connector. Connect a digital multimeter from cavity 3 to chassis ground. Measure resistance.	More than 0.3 ohms.	Repair BLK ground wire between REAR WIPER MOTOR and G401.
		Less than 0.3 ohms.	GO TO A6.
A6.	Connect a test lamp from REAR WIPER MOTOR connector cavity 2 to chassis ground. Observe test lamp while pressing REAR WIPER/WASHER SWITCH to MIST/WASH.	Test lamp lights.	Replace REAR WIPER MOTOR.
		Test lamp does not light.	GO TO A7.
A7.	Backprobe REAR WIPER/WASHER SWITCH connector with a test lamp from cavity 4 to chassis ground. Observe test lamp while pressing REAR WIPER/WASHER SWITCH to MIST/WASH.	Test lamp does not light.	Replace REAR WIPER/WASHER SWITCH.
		Test lamp lights.	Repair open in LT GRN/YEL wire between REAR WIPER/WASHER SWITCH and REAR WIPER MOTOR.
A8.	Disconnect REAR WASHER PUMP connector. Connect a digital multimeter from connector cavity 2 to chassis ground. Measure resistance.	More than 0.3 ohms.	Repair BLK ground wire between REAR WASHER PUMP and G404.
		Less than 0.3 ohms.	GO TO A9.
A9.	Connect a test lamp from REAR WASHER PUMP connector cavity 1 to chassis ground. Observe test lamp while pressing REAR WIPER/WASHER SWITCH to the MIST/WASH position.	Test lamp lights.	Replace REAR WASHER PUMP.
		Test lamp does not light.	GO TO A10.
A10.	Backprobe REAR WIPER/WASHER SWITCH connector with a test lamp from cavity 1 to chassis ground. Observe test lamp while pressing REAR WIPER/WASHER SWITCH to the MIST/WASH position.	Test lamp does not light.	Replace REAR WIPER/WASHER SWITCH.
		Test lamp lights.	Repair open in LT GRN/WHT wire between REAR WIPER/WASHER SWITCH and REAR WASHER PUMP.
A11.	Backprobe REAR WIPER/WASHER SWITCH connector with a test lamp from cavity 5 to chassis ground.	Test lamp lights.	Replace JUNCTION BLOCK.
		Test lamp does not light.	GO TO A12.
A12.	Backprobe JUNCTION BLOCK connector C4 with a test lamp from cavity 4 to chassis ground.	Test lamp does not light.	Replace JUNCTION BLOCK.
		Test lamp lights.	Repair open in LT GRN/BLK wire between JUNCTION BLOCK and REAR WIPER/WASHER SWITCH.
A13.	Backprobe REAR WIPER MOTOR connector with a test lamp from cavity 1 to chassis ground.	Test lamp does not light.	Replace REAR WIPER MOTOR.
		Test lamp lights.	GO TO A14.
A14.	Backprobe JUNCTION BLOCK connector C7 with a test lamp from cavity 2 to chassis ground.	Test lamp does not light.	Replace JUNCTION BLOCK.
		Test lamp lights.	Repair open in LT GRN/BLK wire between JUNCTION BLOCK and REAR WIPER MOTOR.
A15.	Disconnect REAR WIPER/WASHER SWITCH connector.	REAR WIPER MOTOR or REAR WASHER PUMP continues to operate.	Replace REAR WIPER/WASHER SWITCH.
		REAR WASHER PUMP continues to operate.	Repair short to voltage in LT GRN/YEL wire between REAR WIPER/WASHER SWITCH and REAR WIPER MOTOR.
		REAR WASHER PUMP continues to operate.	Repair short to voltage in LT GRN/WHT wire between REAR WIPER/WASHER SWITCH and REAR WASHER PUMP.

Fig. 13 System diagnosis chart. Storm rear wiper

SPEED CONTROL SYSTEMS

NOTE: Wire Code Identification And Symbol Identification Located In The Front Of This Manual Can Be Used As An Aid When Using Wiring Circuits Found In This Section.

TABLE OF CONTENTS

Application Chart

Year	Model	Type
BUICK		
Century	1991–93	2
LeSabre	1991	2
	1992–93	3
Park Avenue	1991–93	3
Reatta	1991	3
Regal	1991–93	2
Riviera	1991–93	3
Roadmaster	1991–92	2
	1993	5
Skylark	1991–93	2
CADILLAC		
Brougham	1991–92	1
DeVille	1991–93	1
Eldorado	1991–93	1
Fleetwood	1991–93	1
Seville	1991–93	1
CHEVROLET		
Beretta	1991–93	2
Camaro	1991–92	2
	1993	5
Caprice	1991–92	2
	1993	5
Cavalier	1991–93	2
Corsica	1991–93	2
Corvette	1991–93	2

Year	Model	Type
CHEVROLET-Continued		
Lumina	1991–93	2
GEO		
Prizm	1991–93	4
OLDSMOBILE		
Achieva	1992–93	2
Custom Cruiser	1991–92	2
Cutlass Calais	1991	2
Cutlass Ciera	1991–93	2
Cutlass Cruiser	1991–93	2
Cutlass Supreme	1991–93	2
Toronado/Trofeo	1991–93	3
88	1991	2
	1992–93	3
98	1991–93	3
PONTIAC		
Bonneville	1991	2
	1992–93	3
Firebird	1991–92	2
	1993	5
Grand Am	1991–93	2
Grand Prix	1991–93	2
LeMans	1991–92	2
Sunbird	1991–93	2
6000	1991	2

NOTE: On Vehicles Equipped With Airbags, Disarm Airbag As Outlined Under "Airbag Disarming" Before Any Diagnosis, Testing, Troubleshooting Or Repairs Are Performed. After All Diagnosis, Testing, Troubleshooting Or Repairs Have Been Completed, Rearm Airbag As Outlined Under "Airbag System Arming."

NOTE: Wire Color Code And Symbol Identification Located In The Front Of This Manual Can Be Used As An Aid When Using Wiring Circuits Found In This Section.

INDEX

PRECAUTIONS

AIRBAG SYSTEM DISARMING

DeVille, Eldorado, Seville & 1991—92 FLeetwood (FWD)

The diagnostic energy reserve module (DERM) can maintain voltage to cause a system deployment for up to ten minutes after the ignition switch is turned off and the battery is disconnected. Servicing the SIR system during this period may result in accidental deployment and personal injury.

1. Ensure front wheels are pointed straight ahead.
2. Turn ignition switch to LOCK position and remove SIR or AIRBAG fuse.
3. Remove left sound insulator. **Remove courtesy lamp from sound insulator, if necessary.**
4. Remove Connector Position Assurance (CPA), then disconnect yellow two-way SIR electrical connector at base of steering column.

AIRBAG SYSTEM ARMING

DeVille, Eldorado, Seville & 1991—92 Fleetwood (FWD)

1. Connect yellow two-way SIR electrical connector, then install Connector Position Assurance (CPA).
2. Install left sound insulator. **Install courtesy lamp to sound insulator, if applicable.**
3. Install SIR fuse to fuse block, turn ignition switch to RUN position and ensure that "Inflatable Restraint" lamp flashes 7 to 9 times, then turns off.

DESCRIPTION

This Cruise Control System utilizes vacuum to activate the throttle servo. Throttle position is changed when the servo unit diaphragm receives varying levels of vacuum, controlled by a solenoid valve. The solenoid valve modulates the vacuum signal to the servo in response to commands from the electronic controller. The electronic controller monitors signals from the engagement and instrument panel switches, electric brake release switch, and the speed sensor. The speed sensor, signals vehicle speed to the controller. These signals are used by the controller to activate the solenoid valve, regulating the level of vacuum to the servo diaphragm. This system uses two brake release switches. An electric brake release, mounted on the brake pedal support, turns the system Off and vents the servo diaphragm to the atmosphere through the solenoid valve. A second brake release switch, a vacuum release valve also located on the brake pedal support, vents the servo unit to the atmosphere.

ELECTRONIC CONTROLLER

The ECM or PCM receives input signals from the cruise control engagement switches, instrument panel switch, brake release switch, drive switch and speed sensor.

On models equipped with DFI or PFI, the ECM or PCM also receives engine control signals. The ECM then processes these signals and transmits a command signal to the solenoid valve, regulating vacuum to the servo unit diaphragm.

CRUISE CONTROL MODULE

Brougham

The cruise control module (CCM) receives signals from the cruise engagement, instrument panel, and electric brake release switches, and servo position and speed sensors. The CCM then process this information and transmits signals to the vacuum and vent valves in the servo to control vehicle speed.

SPEED SENSOR

Except 1991—92 Brougham

On front wheel drive vehicles the speed sensor is mounted in the transaxle. A magnet rotates near a coil, producing voltage pulses in the coil. As speed increases, so do the number of voltage pulses per second.

The speed sensor buffer takes the sensor/voltage pulses from the sensor and uses them to close two solid state output switches. Each output terminal is switched to ground at a rate that is proportional to the speed of the car. The speedometer and the ECM are switched at 4000 pulses per mile. **The output switches in the speed sensor are solid state. Self-powered test lights or ohmmeters should not be used to test them. Do not measure the resistance at the outputs of the buffer.**

1991—92 Brougham

The vehicle speed sensor (VSS) is located at the rear of the transmission. The VSS is a permanent magnet generator consisting of a field coil and permanent magnet stator that produces AC voltage. When the vehicle is in motion an impulse is sent to the vehicle speed buffer. The information is then sent to the speedometer, engine control module, cruise control module, and passive restraint module at a rate of 4004 or 2002 pulses per minute.

VACUUM CONTROL VALVE

The vacuum control valve operates in response to a signal from the PCM, ECM or electronic controller and opens when the system is engaged. When the valve is opened, vacuum is available to the servo unit solenoid valve to regulate the servo unit. When the cruise control is disengaged, the vacuum control valve is closed.

SERVO UNIT SOLENOID VALVE

The solenoid valve modulates the vacuum signal to the servo unit in response to commands from the BCM, ECM or electronic controller in order for the throttle to be in proper position for desired cruise speed.

SERVO UNIT

The servo unit is essentially a vacuum activated variable diaphragm. It positions the throttle when the system is in operation through a bead chain actuator, combination chain and cable actuator or rod actuator depending on model of vehicle.

To operate the servo unit, a controlled vacuum provided by the servo unit solenoid valve is applied to the servo diaphragm, drawing the diaphragm inward, pulling the actuator to operate the throttle.

BRAKE RELEASE SWITCHES

The Cruise Control system utilizes an electrical brake release switch and a vacuum release valve.

The electric brake release switch cuts off the voltage supplied through the instrument panel switch to the electronic controller when the brake pedal is depressed. The vacuum release valve operates after the electric release switch disengages. It serves as a back-up release system and opens a port that vents the servo unit to atmospheric pressure, allowing the throttle to return to the idle position.

INSTRUMENT PANEL SWITCH

Except 1991—92 DeVille, Eldorado, Fleetwood (FWD) & Seville

This instrument panel mounted switch provides electrical power to the cruise control system. When switch is in Off position, the system cannot be engaged. When switch is in On-Auto position, the amber light next to the words Cruise Control is lit and system may be engaged with the switch located on the turn signal lever at any speed above 25 mph. When system is engaged, a green light is illuminated adjacent to the word Auto.

ENGAGEMENT SWITCH OPERATION, CRUISE MODE

The turn signal lever mounted engagement switch has several modes of operation. With the switch in the On-Auto position, the engagement switch operates as follows:

Switch In Fully Released Position

1. System not operational.
2. System has been engaged previously. The electronic controller is supplying control voltage to the servo unit solenoid valve. The servo unit solenoid valve regulates vacuum to the servo unit which maintains throttle position for desired speed.

Push Button Depressed & Held

After using accelerator pedal to obtain desired speed, the operator can then momentarily depress the push button switch. The electronic controller will provide a control voltage to the servo unit solenoid valve and apply the required vacuum to the servo unit to maintain set speed. When a decrease in speed is desired, the operator may depress and hold the push button with no accelerator pedal pressure. The electronic controller then signals the servo unit solenoid valve to vent the servo unit to atmosphere, closing the throttle. When push button is released, vehicle will cruise at new desired speed.

Slide Lever Actuation

This switch allows the operator to resume a previously set speed after braking or accelerating. Depressing and releasing the slide switch above 25 mph, will accelerate vehicle until previously set speed is reached. If operator desires to advance speed from set speed, actuating and holding slide switch will accelerate vehicle until slide switch is released. Vehicle will now maintain new set speed.

SET/COAST BUTTON SWITCH

This switch has two positions, Normal and Depressed.

Set Position

With vehicle speed above approximately 25 mph and instrument panel switch in On position, pressing and releasing set/coast button will cause the cruise speed to be set at speed vehicle was travelling at when button was released, ± 1 mph. The system will cruise until either the instrument panel switch is moved to Off position, the ignition switch is turned off and/or the set/coast button is pushed in fully and held. Depressing the brake pedal releases the cruise, but not the resume capability.

Coast (Trim) Position

Cruise speed can be changed with the set/coast switch fully depressed. Cruise speed can be increased by accelerating to desired cruise speed, then fully depressing and releasing switch. When switch is released, a new cruise speed is set. To decrease cruise speed, fully depress and hold switch, then decelerate to desired cruise speed and release switch.

Tap Down Position

The cruise speed can be decreased in 1 mph increments by tapping the set/coast switch. With cruise control engaged and operating, quickly depress and release or tap switch. Each tap of switch will decrease cruise speed 1 mph to a maximum 10 mph decrease in cruise speed. This feature can be used to lower the cruise speed below the 25 mph minimum setting to as low as 16 mph.

ROUTE CRUISE CONTROL CABLE ASM UNDER SPARK PLUG WIRES, T.V. CABLE, AND ACCELERATOR CABLE.

VIEW B

VIEW A

HOLES IN BLADE

VIEW A

SERVO BLADE SELECT CABLE HOLE BASED ON MINIMUM CABLE SLACK.

SERVO BLADE SELECT CABLE HOLE BASED ON MINIMUM CABLE SLACK.

VIEW B

CABLE ADJUSTMENT
1. WITH ENGINE OFF (ISC) IDLE SPEED MOTOR MUST BE RETRACTED UNTIL THE THROTTLE LEVER IS CLEAR OF THE ISC PLUNGER. REFER TO SECTION 6E FOR PROCEDURE.
2. ATTACH CABLE ASM. TO THROTTLE LEVER AND SELECT THE CABLE HOLE ON SERVO BLADE BASED ON MINIMUM CABLE SLACK. (SEE VIEW B).

1 CRUISE CONTROL SERVO
2 CRUISE CONTROL CABLE ASM
3 RETAINER
4 THROTTLE LEVER
5 COVER AIR CLEANER ASM
6 ACCELERATOR CABLE
7 HOUSING
8 THROTTLE VALVE CABLE

Fig. 1 T.V. cable adjustment. Eldorado, Seville, DeVille & 1991–92 Fleetwood (FWD)

RESUME/ACCEL SWITCH

This switch has two positions. When switch is **momentarily** moved toward the R/A position after braking, cruise control operation will be returned to last set speed.

If switch is held in R/A position for more than 1 second, the system reverts to the Accel mode. To accelerate vehicle, move switch to R/A position and hold until vehicle reaches desired increased speed. When switch is released, speed vehicle has accelerated to becomes new cruise speed. In order to use Accel mode, the cruise instrument panel switch must be in On position and vehicle speed must be above 25 mph.

Tap Up Position

This feature allows the cruise speed to be increased in 1 mph increments up to 10 mph by quickly pressing switch toward R/A position and quickly releasing switch.

LASH LEARN
4.6L Northstar Engine

The cruise control system utilizes a lash learn system to compensate for any minor misadjustments in the servo linkage due to tolerance stack-up or build error. The leash learn term is generally calculated when the PCM receives a cruise set command and the throttle is fully relaxed. The PCM calculates the servo position movement to offset the throttle position movement. The PCM uses this value to subsequent servo position commands.

To perform lash learn, perform the following procedure:
1. Drive vehicle to approximately 50 mph.
2. Take foot off accelerator for three seconds.
3. Engage cruise SET/COATS button.

TROUBLESHOOTING
PRELIMINARY CHECKS
1991–92 Brougham

1. Check cruise control fuse.
2. Check cruise control servo linkage adjustment, and vacuum hose routings.
3. Check vacuum hoses for leaks, kinks, or restrictions.

1991–92 DeVille & Fleetwood (FWD)

1. Disarm airbag system as described under "Airbag System Disarming."
2. Check cruise control servo linkage adjustment, and vacuum hose routings.
3. Check vacuum hoses for leaks, kinks, or restrictions.
4. Check for sticking, leaking, or plugged vacuum release valve.
5. Rearm airbag system as described under "Airbag System Arming."

Eldorado & Seville

1. Disarm airbag system as described under "Airbag System Disarming."
2. Check cruise fuse 8 for proper operation by observing the battery no charge indicator, with ignition switch in run and engine off
3. Check transaxle position switch by observing the PRNDL display.
4. Check vacuum hoses for leaks, kinks, and other restrictions.
5. Check cruise control servo linkage. If necessary to adjust, refer to **Fig. 1** for procedure.
6. Rearm airbag system as described under "Airbag System Arming."

ROAD TEST

Perform the following road test and note system operation. If a cause for the observed malfunction cannot be determined by following troubleshooting procedures, proceed to "System Diagnosis."

1991—92 DeVille & Fleetwood (FWD)

Refer to **Fig. 2,** when performing vehicle road test.

Brougham

Perform road test with cruise control switch on and vehicle speed above 25 mph.

1. Place engagement switch in Set/Coast position, then release it. Cruise engage indicator should light and vehicle should maintain speed.
2. Hold engage switch in Set/Coast position with foot off accelerator. Vehicle should coast at a slower speed.
3. Release Set/Coast switch. Cruise control should engage and hold a slower speed above 25 mph.
4. Place engage switch in Resume/Accel position and hold it there. Vehicle should accelerate.
5. Release engage switch. Vehicle should hold new faster speed.
6. Tap brake pedal. Vehicle should coast slower.
7. Place engage switch in Resume/Accel position momentarily. Vehicle should accelerate to former set speed.
8. While cruising, accelerate, then remove foot from accelerator pedal. Vehicle should coast back to set speed.
9. While cruising, tap engage switch to Resume/Accel position. Vehicle speed should increase with each tap 1 mph.
10. While cruising, tap engage switch to Set/Coast position. Vehicle speed should decrease 1 mph for each tap down to 25 mph.
11. Place cruise control switch in Off position. Cruise control should turn off.

Eldorado & Seville

Perform road test with cruise switch in On position and vehicle speed above 25 mph.

1. Momentarily depress set/coast switch in steering wheel pad and ensure vehicle maintains speed.
2. Hold set/coast switch in with foot off accelerator and ensure vehicle coasts down to a lower speed.
3. Release set/coast switch and ensure cruise control engages and holds slower speed if speed is greater than 25 mph.
4. Slide and hold resume/accelerate switch in and ensure vehicle accelerates.
5. Release resume/accelerate switch and ensure vehicle holds new, faster speed.
6. Tap brake pedal and ensure vehicle coasts.
7. Slide resume/accelerate switch and ensure vehicle accelerates to speed set before tapping of brake pedal.
8. Tap set/coast switch and ensure vehicle speed decreases 1 mph for each tap.
9. Tap resume/accelerate switch and

ACTION	NORMAL RESULT
Drive vehicle faster than 25 mph Press Cruise Switch to ON Momentarily depress Set/Coast Switch	Vehicle maintains speed CRUISE Indicator lights when the switch is released and the system is engaged
Hold Set/Coast switch in, foot off accelerator	Vehicle coasts to a slower speed
Release Set/Coast Switch	Cruise Control engages and holds the slower speed, if the new speed remains above 25 mph
Depress and hold Resume/Accel Switch in	Vehicle accelerates
Release Resume/Accel Switch	Vehicle holds new faster speed
Tap Brake Pedal	Vehicle coasts
Depress and release Resume/Accel Switch	Vehicle accelerates to speed set prior to Brake Pedal tap
Tap Set/Coast Switch	Vehicle speed decreases 1 mph for each tap (can be tapped down to 25 mph)
Tap Resume/Accel Switch	Vehicle speed increases 1 mph for each tap
Move Cruise Switch to OFF	Cruise Control releases to manual operation

Fig. 2   Road test system check. 1991—92 DeVille & Fleetwood (FWD)

ensure vehicle speed increases 1 mph for each tap.
10. Slide cruise switch in righthand switch assembly to Off position and ensure cruise control releases to manual operation.

SYSTEM DIAGNOSIS & TESTING

DeVille & 1991—92 Fleetwood (FWD)

SELF-DIAGNOSTIC SYSTEM

In the process of controlling the various subsystems, the ECM and PCM continually monitor operating conditions for possible malfunctions. By comparing system conditions against standard operating limits certain circuits and component malfunctions can be detected. A two digit numerical code is stored in the computer memory when a problem is detected by this self diagnostic system.

If the ECM diagnostics detect a fault, the cruise control system will be inhibited for the entire ignition cycle. The faults that may inhibit the cruise control system are as follows::

1. Fault with vehicle speed sensor or throttle position sensor circuit.
2. Cruise control requested above 90 mph.
3. A rapid rise in RPM's.
4. Difference between vehicle speed and set speed is too high.
5. Transaxle is shifted to neutral position.
6. ECM detects battery voltage either too high or too low.
7. Acceleration is too high.
8. Coolant temperature is too high.
9. **On 1991-92 models,** a cruise control servo position sensor is shorted or grounded.
10. The cruise is On, brake is not depressed an the PCM output is HI when it should be LOW, or vice-versa.
11. A throttle angle greater than 20° and the servo position sensor indicates a stroke greater than commanded.
12. Servo position sensor indicates that the servo is still engaged after cruise control has been disengaged.
13. Vehicle speed cycles from 30 mph or greater to 0 mph with no VCC brake switch input, and the PCM will record 10 of these consecutively.
14. Park neutral switch is closed when the vehicle is in 4th gear with speed between 23 and 35 mph for 10 seconds.

Codes other than described may be stored in the control module memory and displayed when the system is accessed to diagnose cruise control malfunctions. It may be necessary to identify and diagnose the failures caused by these additional codes in order to ensure proper system operation. For complete diagnosis of the system, refer to the "Fuel Injection Section" in the MOTOR's Auto Engine Tune Up & Electronic Manual.

Intermittent Problem Diagnosis

Trouble codes displayed during the first pass of ECM diagnostic codes, but not the second pass, are considered intermittent. Intermittent trouble codes are those that the ECM previously determined to be faulty but later tested good. If the code is intermittent, most charts will refer to a special note. **Do not bypass the charts when checking intermittent conditions.** Failure to check an intermittent condition may result in replacement of good components.

Many intermittent problems are caused by poor electrical connections. Diagnosis should start with visual and physical inspection of connectors which are related with the code.

Entering Self-Diagnostic Mode

1. Turn ignition switch on.
2. Simultaneously depress the Off and Warmer buttons on the climate control panel and hold buttons until all display panel segments are illuminated which indicates the beginning of

the diagnostic readout. The purpose of illuminating the two display panels is to ensure that all segments are working. **If any segments are are inoperative, the affected display panel must be replaced.**

3. After the display segment check is completed, any stored trouble code will be displayed on the data center. These two-digit codes will be displayed with a prefix of either E or F to designate which computer sensed the malfunction. If a trouble code is displayed, or if the self-diagnostics system cannot be accessed, a defect has been sensed in the vehicle's electronic control system. To diagnose these malfunctions, refer to the "Fuel Injection Section" in the MOTOR's Auto Engine Tune Up & Electronics manual.

4. After all codes are displayed or if no trouble codes are stored, the code .7.0 will appear on the display.

Code .7.0

Code .7.0 is a decision point. When this code is displayed, the diagnostic feature relevant to the current malfunction can be selected. The two diagnostic modes relevant to cruise control diagnosis, ECM switch tests and ECM output cycling, are detailed below.

Clearing Trouble Codes

The trouble codes stored in the system memory can be cleared to aid in diagnosing intermittent conditions. To clear codes, proceed as follows:

1. Enter diagnostic mode as outlined.
2. To clear engine control module (ECM) codes, simultaneously depress the Off and HI buttons on the climate control panel and hold the buttons until the code E.0.0 is displayed.
3. To clear body control module (BCM) codes, simultaneously depress the Off and LO buttons on the climate control panel and hold until the code F.0.0 is displayed.
4. After E.0.0 and F.0.0 are displayed, the code .7.0 will be displayed. With this code displayed, turn off ignition and leave ignition off for at least 10 seconds before re-entering the diagnostic mode.

Exiting Self-Diagnostic Mode

To exit the self-diagnostic mode, depress the AUTO button on the climate control panel or turn of ignition for at least 10 seconds.

ECM/PCM SWITCH TEST SERIES

To perform the switch test series, the engine must be running and the code .7.0 must be displayed on the data center panel. To begin the test sequence, depress and release the brake pedal, and the test will begin as soon as the display changes from code .7.0 to code E.7.1. If the code does not change, check brake switch feed to the ECM and check for defective ECM.

The ECM will display a code for each switch, in sequence, and if the switch does not operate properly, the ECM will store the code as a trouble code. In addition, the appropriate switch must be cycled within 10 seconds after its code is displayed or the ECM will store a trouble code associated with that switch. When performing the following tests, refer to wiring diagrams and connector points on **Figs. 3 through 8** and **Figs. 9 through 20** for diagnostic tests. Perform switch tests as follows:

1. With code E.7.1 displayed, depress and release brake pedal again to test cruise control brake switch circuit.
2. With code E.7.2 displayed, depress accelerator pedal from idle position to open throttle, then slowly release pedal. As throttle is moved the ECM tests throttle switch for proper operation.
3. **On 1991 models,** with code E.7.3 displayed, move transmission selector into reverse, then neutral to test operation of park/neutral switch.
4. **On 1992 models,** with code E.7.3 displayed, is not a valid test.
5. **On all models,** with code E.7.5 displayed, turn cruise control instrument panel switch from off to on, then back to off to test operation of switch. Refer to **Fig. 9** for further testing procedure. For intermittent codes proceed as follows:
   a. The amber cruise-on indicator can be used to monitor the cruise dash switch status. Turn dash switch on and wiggle wiring and connectors. If switch or circuit from the fuse to switch are open, the amber light will blink out.
   b. If cruise fuse blows intermittently, turn switch on, then wiggle wiring, connectors and cruise steering column switch. If circuit becomes grounded, fuse will blow.
6. With code E.7.6 displayed and with instrument panel cruise control switch on, depress and release set/coast button to test set/coast button operation. Refer to **Fig. 10** for further testing procedure. For intermittent codes proceed as follows:
   a. Turn cruise dash switch to on and backprobe ECM B4 with a voltmeter to ground. B4 should show 12 volts with set/coast depressed and 0 volts with switch released. While observing meter, cycle switch and wiggle wiring and connectors.
7. With code E.7.7 displayed and with instrument panel cruise control switch on, depress and release resume/acceleration switch to test operation of switch. Refer to **Fig. 11** for further testing procedure. For intermittent codes proceed as follows:
   a. Turn cruise dash switch to on and backprobe ECM B6 with a voltmeter to ground. B6 should show 12 volts with resume/acceleration switch depressed and 0 volts with switch released. While observing meter, cycle switch and wiggle wiring and connectors.
8. With code E.7.8 displayed, turn steer-

ing wheel to full lock in both directions, then return wheel to straight ahead position to test power steering pressure switch operation.

9. When the switch tests are completed, the ECM will go back and display codes for switches which did not test properly.
10. Check circuit between each switch that failed and the ECM, test switches individually, repair as needed, then clear trouble codes and retest system.
11. If malfunction persists, refer to "Fuel Injection Section" in the MOTOR Auto Engine Tune Up & Electronics manual.

ECM OUTPUT CYCLING

ECM output cycling can be tested after code E.9.5 is displayed on the data center. Code E.9.5 can be reached by depressing the HI button on the climate control panel when code .7.0 is displayed. The ECM output cycling mode, code E.9.6, will then cycle ECM outputs on and off. To enter output cycling mode, proceed as follows:

1. With engine running, turn instrument panel cruise control switch to ON position to allow cruise control outputs to cycle.
2. Turn ignition off, then within 2 seconds turn ignition back on.
3. Enter self-diagnostic mode and obtain code E.9.5 as outlined above.
4. Every 3 seconds devices will be cycled.
5. Depress HI button on climate control panel to advance device testing and depress LO button to return to E0.0 (cycle none).
6. **On all models,** if the system fails to operate as outlined, check wiring between effected component and ECM, test components individually, repair as needed, then clear trouble codes and repeat test. If malfunction persists, refer to "Fuel Injection Section" in the MOTOR's Auto Engine Tune Up & Electronics Manual.

Eldorado & Seville

SELF-DIAGNOSTIC SYSTEM

In the process of controlling the various subsystems, the ECM and BCM continually monitor operating conditions for possible malfunctions. By comparing system conditions against standard operating limits certain circuits and component malfunctions can be detected. A three digit numerical code is stored in the computer memory when a problem is detected by this self diagnostic system.

ENTERING SELF-DIAGNOSTIC MODE

To enter diagnostic service mode, turn ignition on, then depress Off and Warm buttons on the climate control panel (CCP). Hold buttons until all display panel segments illuminate, indicating the beginning of diagnostic readout. The two display panels must be illuminated, except for turn signal lights, to ensure all segments are

Continued on page 31-14

Fig. 3   Wiring diagram (Part 1 of 2). 1991 DeVille & Fleetwood (FWD)

Fig. 3   Wiring diagram (Part 2 of 2). 1991 DeVille & Fleetwood (FWD)

Fig. 4 Wiring diagram (Part 2 of 2). 1992 DeVille & Fleetwood (FWD)

Fig. 4 Wiring diagram (Part 1 of 2). 1992 DeVille & Fleetwood (FWD)

Fig. 5 Wiring diagram (Part 1 of 2). 1993 DeVille

Fig. 5 Wiring diagram (Part 2 of 2). 1993 DeVille

CIRCUIT DESCRIPTION	CIRCUIT NUMBER	PCM (2A/B) BLACK	CIRCUIT NUMBER	CIRCUIT DESCRIPTION
BATTERY	480	1	435	EGR SOLENOID
N/C		2	776	TRANS INPUT P
C/C POSITION HI	398	3		N/C
C/C POSITION LO	399	4		
N/C		5	469	SENSOR GROUND
N/C		6	439	IGNITION
N/C		7	427	THROTTLE SWITCH
COOLING FAN RELAY #2	1270	8	800	UART SERIAL DATA
SPEED SENSOR INPUT LO	400	9	800	UART SERIAL DATA
SPEED SENSOR INPUT HI	401	10	419	CHECK ENGINE SIGNAL
4000 PULSE SPEED OUTPUT #1	389	11	1269	COOLING FAN RELAY #1
4000 PULSE SPEED OUTPUT #2	917	12	450	PCM GROUND

SINGLE CAVITY METRI PAK CONNECTOR

Fig. 6   PCM connector (Part 1 of 3). 1991 DeVille & Fleetwood (FWD)

CIRCUIT DESCRIPTION	CIRCUIT NUMBER	PCM (1C/D) BLACK	CIRCUIT NUMBER	CIRCUIT DESCRIPTION
PCM GROUND	450	1		N/C
C/C ON–OFF	397	2	86	C/C ENABLE
C/C SET/COAST	84	3	87	C/C RESUME
N/C		4	420	VCC BRAKE
N/C		5	633	CAM HI
PCM GROUND	450	6		N/C
PCM GROUND	450	7	424	BYPASS
EST REFERENCE PULSE HI	430	8	423	EST
EST REFERENCE/CAM LO	453	9	495	POWER STEERING SW.
N/C		10	772	TRANS INPUT B
N/C		11	841	INJECTOR 1
HEATED W/S	637	12	878	INJECTOR 8
INJECTOR 2	842	13	846	INJECTOR 6
INJECTOR 7	877	14	474	5V REFERENCE
INJECTOR 5	845	15	844	INJECTOR 4
INJECTOR 3	843	16	480	BATTERY

SINGLE CAVITY METRI PAK CONNECTOR

Fig. 6   PCM connector (Part 2 of 3). 1991 DeVille & Fleetwood (FWD)

NOTE: THE TPA STRAIN RELIEVERS IN THIS CONNECTOR WILL BE MARKED AS C AND D

CIRCUIT DESCRIPTION	CIRCUIT NUMBER	PCM (3E/F) GREEN	CIRCUIT NUMBER	CIRCUIT DESCRIPTION
FUEL PUMP RELAY	465	1	425	ISC HI
C/C VENT	403	2	426	ISC LO
C/C SOURCE	402	3	491	SERIAL DATA IN
A/C CLUTCH RELAY	366	4	1222	SHIFT B
VCC MOD	108	5	526	SERAL DATA OUT
VCC SOLENOID	422	6	1490	COMPUTER RIDE
TRANS INPUT C	773	7	428	CANISTER PURGE
TRANS INPUT A	771	8		N/C
N/C		9		N/C
PASS KEY THEFT SYSTEM	229	10	1223	SHIFT A
N/C		11	476	SENSOR GND
N/C		12	451	FIXED SPARK
TPS SIGNAL	417	13	120	FUEL PUMP FEEDBACK
N/C		14	412	OXYGEN SENSOR
MAP SIGNAL	432	15	413	OXYGEN SENSOR
MAT SIGNAL	472	16	410	COOLANT TEMP

Fig. 6   PCM connector (Part 3 of 3). 1991 DeVille & Fleetwood (FWD)

CIRCUIT DESCRIPTION	CIRCUIT NUMBER	PCM (2A/B) BLACK	CIRCUIT NUMBER	CIRCUIT DESCRIPTION
BATTERY	480	1	435	EGR SOLENOID
N/C		2	776	TRANS PRNDL INPUT PARITY
C/C SERVO POSITION SENSOR	398	3		N/C
C/C SERVO POSITION SENSOR	399	4		N/C
N/C		5	476	MAP/MAT SENSOR GROUND
LEFT O2 SENSOR LO	413	6	1276	IGNITION
LEFT O2 SENSOR HI	1589	7	427	THROTTLE SWITCH
HIGH SPEED COOLING FAN RLY	1270	8	800	UART SERIAL DATA
SPEED SENSOR INPUT LO	401	9	800	UART SERIAL DATA
SPEED SENSOR INPUT HI	400	10	419	'SERVICE ENGINE SOON' LIGHT
4K SPEED OUTPUT TO IPC	818	11	1269	LOW SPEED COOLING FAN RLY
4K SPEED OUTPUT TO CCR	817	12	450	PCM GROUND

Fig. 7   PCM connector (Part 1 of 3). 1992 DeVille & Fleetwood (FWD)

CIRCUIT DESCRIPTION	CIRCUIT NUMBER	PCM (1C/D) BLACK	CIRCUIT NUMBER	CIRCUIT DESCRIPTION
PCM GROUND	450	1	1586	OVERSPEED ALARM (EXP)
C/C ON–OFF	397	2	86	C/C BRAKE SWITCH
C/C SET/COAST	84	3	87	C/C RESUME
N/C		4	420	VCC BRAKE SWITCH
N/C		5	633	CAM SENSOR INPUT
PCM GROUND	450	6		N/C
PCM GROUND	450	7	424	EST BYPASS
EST REFERENCE PULSE HI	430	8	423	EST OUTPUT
EST REFERENCE/CAM LO	453	9	816	POWER STEERING SW.
N/C		10	772	TRANS PRNDL INPUT B
N/C		11	841	INJECTOR 1
HEATED W.S. REQUEST	637	12	878	INJECTOR 8
INJECTOR 2	842	13	846	INJECTOR 6
INJECTOR 7	877	14	474	5V REFERENCE
INJECTOR 5	845	15	844	INJECTOR 4
INJECTOR 3	843	16	480	BATTERY

Fig. 7   PCM connector (Part 2 of 3). 1992 DeVille & Fleetwood (FWD)

CIRCUIT DESCRIPTION	CIRCUIT NUMBER	PCM (3E/F) GREEN	CIRCUIT NUMBER	CIRCUIT DESCRIPTION
FUEL PUMP RELAY	465	1	425	ISC HI
C/C VENT SOLENOID	403	2	426	ISC LO
C/C VAC SOLENOID	402	3		N/C
A/C CLUTCH RELAY	762	4	1223	SHIFT B SOLENOID
VCC MOD	446	5		N/C
VCC SOLENOID	422	6	1490	CCR LIFT/DIVE OUTPUT
TRANS PRNDL INPUT C	773	7	428	CANISTER PURGE SOLND
TRANS PRNDL INPUT A	771	8		N/C
N/C		9		N/C
PASS–KEY FUEL ENABLE	229	10	1222	SHIFT A SOLENOID
N/C		11	1076	CTS/TPS SENSOR GROUND
N/C		12	462	FIXED SPARK/SET TIMING
TPS SIGNAL	417	13	120	FUEL PUMP FEEDBACK
N/C		14	412	RIGHT O2 SENSOR HI
MAP SIGNAL	432	15	413	RIGHT O2 SENSOR LO
MAT SIGNAL	472	16	410	COOLANT TEMP SIGNAL

Fig. 7   PCM connector (Part 3 of 3). 1992 DeVille & Fleetwood (FWD)

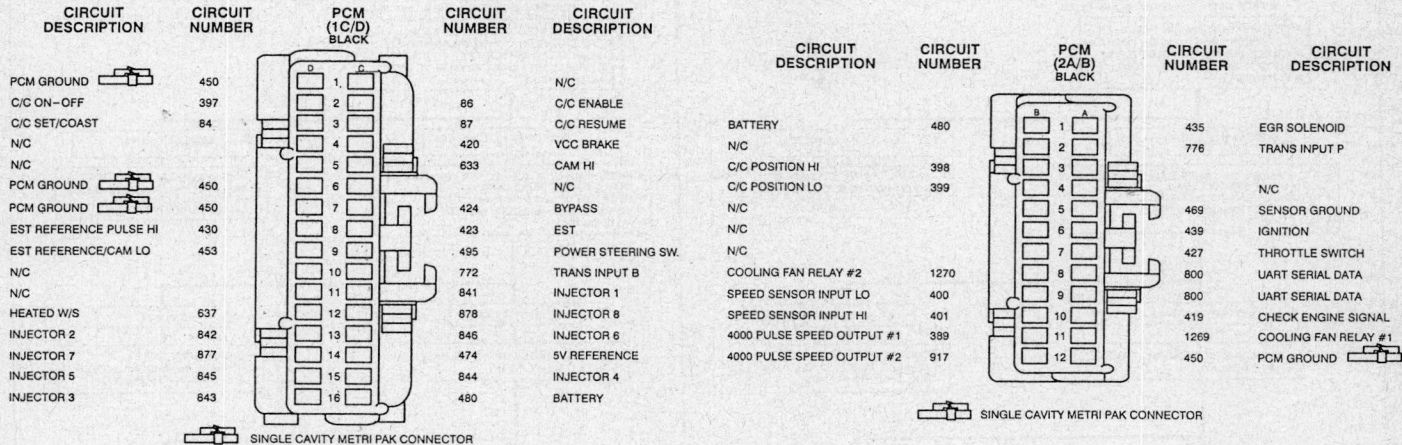

CIRCUIT DESCRIPTION	CIRCUIT NUMBER	PCM (1C/D) BLACK	CIRCUIT NUMBER	CIRCUIT DESCRIPTION
PCM GROUND	450	1		N/C
C/C ON–OFF	397	2	86	C/C ENABLE
C/C SET/COAST	84	3	87	C/C RESUME
N/C		4	420	VCC BRAKE
N/C		5	633	CAM HI
PCM GROUND	450	6		N/C
PCM GROUND	450	7	424	BYPASS
EST REFERENCE PULSE HI	430	8	423	EST
EST REFERENCE/CAM LO	453	9	495	POWER STEERING SW.
N/C		10	772	TRANS INPUT B
N/C		11	841	INJECTOR 1
HEATED W/S	637	12	878	INJECTOR 8
INJECTOR 2	842	13	846	INJECTOR 6
INJECTOR 7	877	14	474	5V REFERENCE
INJECTOR 5	845	15	844	INJECTOR 4
INJECTOR 3	843	16	480	BATTERY

SINGLE CAVITY METRI PAK CONNECTOR

Fig. 8   PCM connector (Part 1 of 3). 1993 DeVille

CIRCUIT DESCRIPTION	CIRCUIT NUMBER	PCM (2A/B) BLACK	CIRCUIT NUMBER	CIRCUIT DESCRIPTION
BATTERY	480	1	435	EGR SOLENOID
N/C		2	776	TRANS INPUT P
C/C POSITION HI	398	3		
C/C POSITION LO	399	4		N/C
N/C		5	469	SENSOR GROUND
N/C		6	439	IGNITION
N/C		7	427	THROTTLE SWITCH
COOLING FAN RELAY #2	1270	8	800	UART SERIAL DATA
SPEED SENSOR INPUT LO	400	9	800	UART SERIAL DATA
SPEED SENSOR INPUT HI	401	10	419	CHECK ENGINE SIGNAL
4000 PULSE SPEED OUTPUT #1	389	11	1269	COOLING FAN RELAY #1
4000 PULSE SPEED OUTPUT #2	917	12	450	PCM GROUND

SINGLE CAVITY METRI PAK CONNECTOR

Fig. 8   PCM connector (Part 2 of 3). 1993 DeVille

NOTE: THE TPA STRAIN RELIEVERS IN THIS CONNECTOR WILL BE MARKED AS C AND D

CIRCUIT DESCRIPTION	CIRCUIT NUMBER	PCM (3E/F) GREEN	CIRCUIT NUMBER	CIRCUIT DESCRIPTION
FUEL PUMP RELAY	465	1	425	ISC HI
C/C VENT	403	2	426	ISC LO
C/C SOURCE	402	3	491	SERIAL DATA IN
A/C CLUTCH RELAY	366	4	1222	SHIFT B
VCC MOD	108	5	526	SERAL DATA OUT
VCC SOLENOID	422	6	1490	COMPUTER RIDE
TRANS INPUT C	773	7	428	CANISTER PURGE
TRANS INPUT A	771	8		N/C
N/C		9		N/C
PASS KEY THEFT SYSTEM	229	10	1223	SHIFT A
N/C		11	476	SENSOR GND
N/C		12	451	FIXED SPARK
TPS SIGNAL	417	13	120	FUEL PUMP FEEDBACK
N/C		14	412	OXYGEN SENSOR
MAP SIGNAL	432	15	413	OXYGEN SENSOR
MAT SIGNAL	472	16	410	COOLANT TEMP

Fig. 8   PCM connector (Part 3 of 3). 1993 DeVille

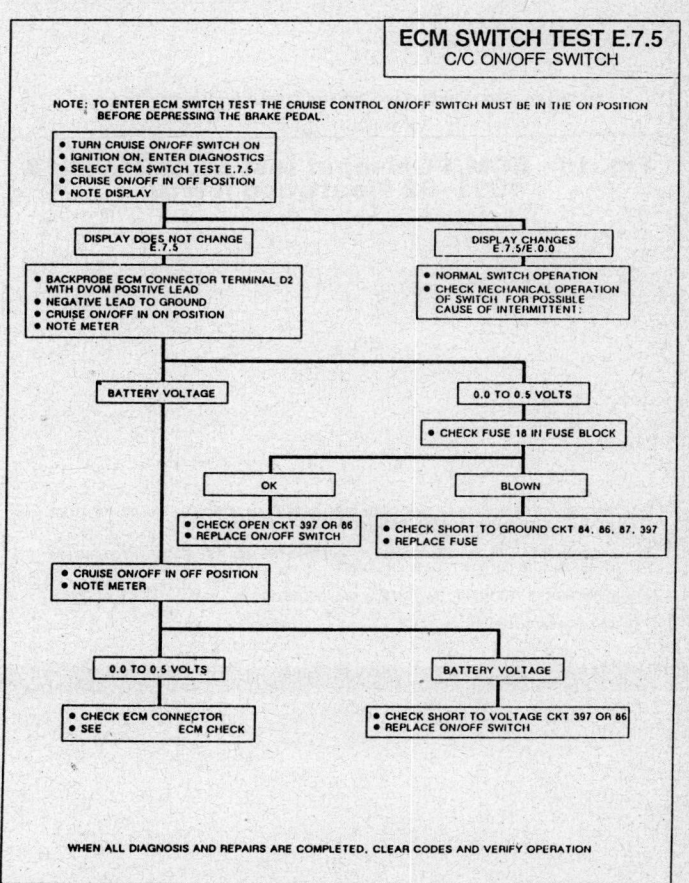

Fig. 9   ECM/PCM input test E7.5. DeVille & 1991–92 Fleetwood (FWD)

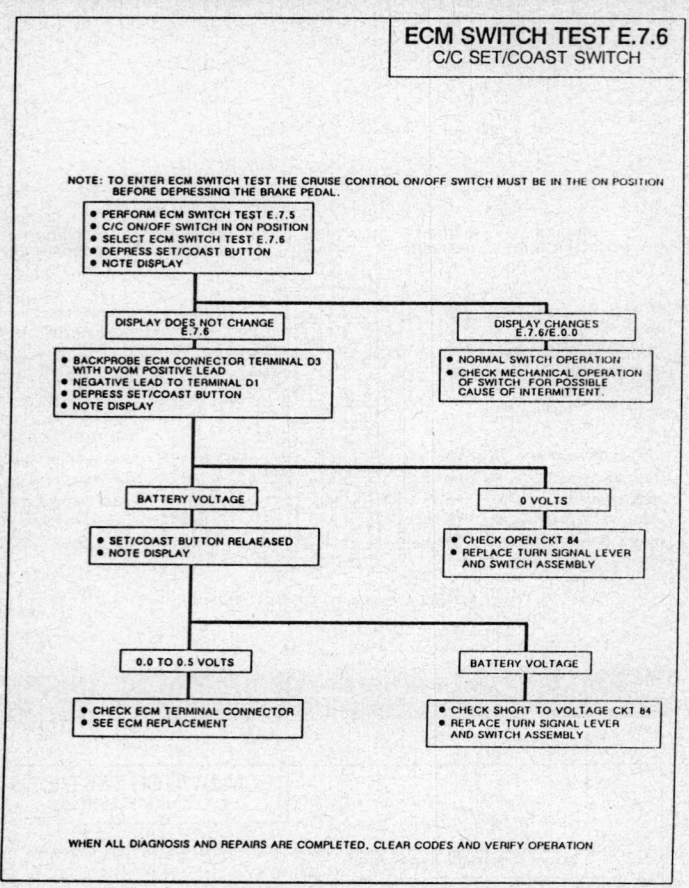

Fig. 10 ECM/PCM input test E7.6. DeVille & 1991–92 Fleetwood (FWD)

Fig. 11 ECM/PCM input test E7.7. DeVille & 1991–92 Fleetwood (FWD)

- THE PRIMARY PURPOSE OF THIS CODE IS TO DETECT AN ACTION OF THE DRIVER THAT COULD CAUSE AN UNSAFE CONDITION OR DAMAGE TO THE VEHICLE.
- THIS CODE CAN BE DRIVER INDUCED BY SHIFTING THE GEAR SELECTOR INTO NEUTRAL WHEN THE CRUISE CONTROL IS ENGAGED.
- A FAILURE OF THE PRNDL SWITCH MAY CAUSE THE CODE TO SET.
- CHECK FOR CODE E91.

Fig. 12   DTC test EO60. 1993 DeVille

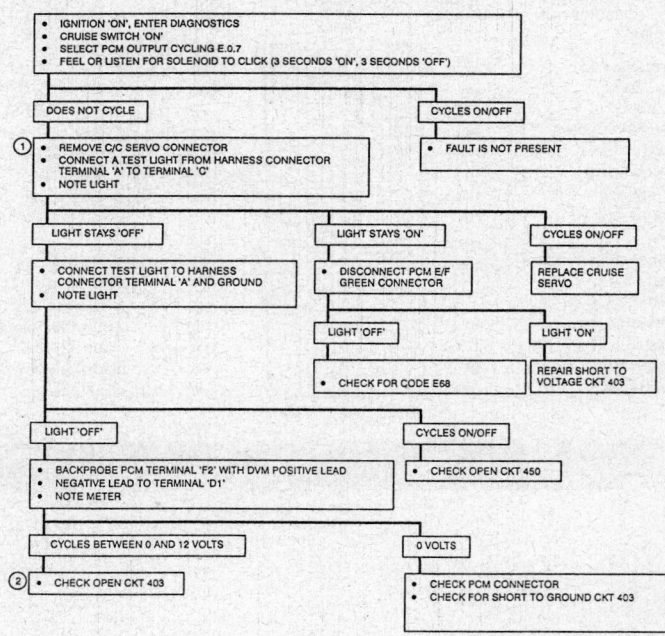

WHEN ALL DIAGNOSIS AND REPAIRS ARE COMPLETED, CLEAR CODES AND VERIFY OPERATION

Fig. 13   DTC test EO61. 1993 DeVille

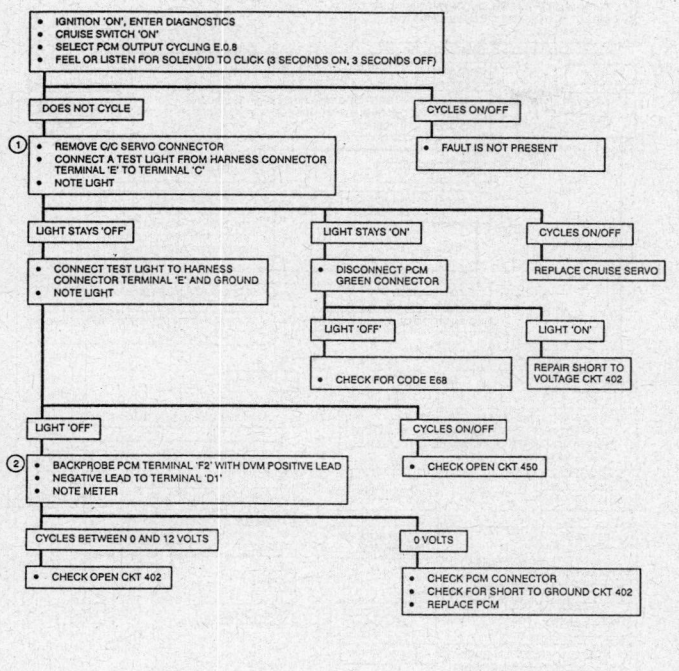

Fig. 14   DTC test EO62. 1993 DeVille

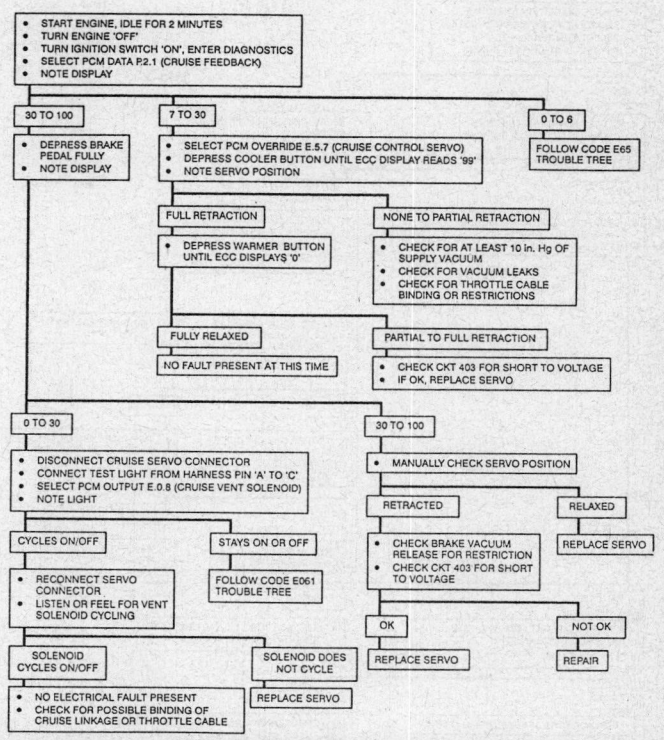

Fig. 15   DTC test EO63. 1993 DeVille

- Code E64 sets when the vehicle speed increases greater that 16 MPH in one second with the cruise engaged (4 mph in .25 second)
- If code E64 is set, cruise control will disengage and Code E64 is stored in memory.
- Most occurrences of Code E64 are caused by wheelspin due to icy or wet conditions
- If Code E64 is found and no other cruise control faults exists, clear codes and road test vehicle.

WHEN ALL DIAGNOSIS AND REPAIRS ARE COMPLETED, CLEAR CODES AND VERIFY OPERATION

Fig. 16   DTC test EO64. 1993 DeVille

THIS CODE WILL SET IF ENGINE RPM EXCEEDS 4800 RPM. THIS MAY OCCUR ON SLIPPERY PAVEMENT, EXTENDED WIDE OPEN THROTTLE ACCELERATION, OR FOR SOME MECHANICAL PROBLEMS (SUCH AS TRANSMISSION SLIPPAGE). UNDER THESE CONDITIONS, CODE E066 WILL SET AND SHOULD BE CONSIDERED NORMAL. THE DRIVER SHOULD BE CONSIDERED NORMAL. THE DRIVER SHOULD BE ADVISED WHY THE CRUISE DISENGAGED. CLEAR THE CODE AND ROAD TEST VEHICLE TO VERIFY NORMAL OPERATION.

WHEN ALL DIAGNOSIS AND REPAIRS ARE COMPLETED, CLEAR CODES AND VERIFY OPERATION

Fig. 18   DTC test EO66. 1993 DeVille

Fig. 17   DTC test EO65. 1993 DeVille

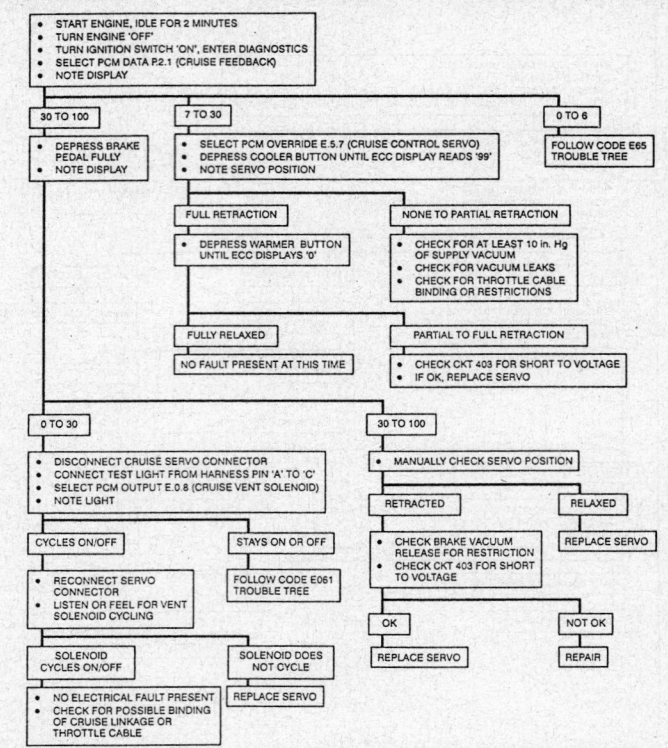

operating. **Do not attempt diagnosis unless all segments appear, as an improper diagnosis may result.** If any segments are inoperative, the display panel must be replaced.

ACCESSING CODES

After the diagnostic service mode is entered, any trouble codes stored in the computer memory will be displayed, **Fig. 21.** ECM codes will be displayed first, then BCM codes. Codes will also be accompanied by Current or History. History indicates the failure was not present the last time the code was tested. Current indicates the fault still exists. At any time during the display of trouble codes the Low button on the CCP is depressed, the display of codes will be bypassed. At any time during the display of trouble codes the Reset/Recall button on the DIC is depressed, the system will exit diagnostic service mode and go back to normal vehicle operation. Refer to **Figs. 22 through 46,** for trouble codes EO/PO60 through EO/PO69 and EO/PO99 and **Fig. 47 through 54** for ECM/PCM input test diagnostics.

DIAGNOSTIC TEST PROCEDURES

After trouble codes have been displayed, the diagnostic service mode can be used to further test the speed control system. To do so, refer to **Fig. 21,** and proceed as follows:

1. Following the display of trouble codes, the first available system level

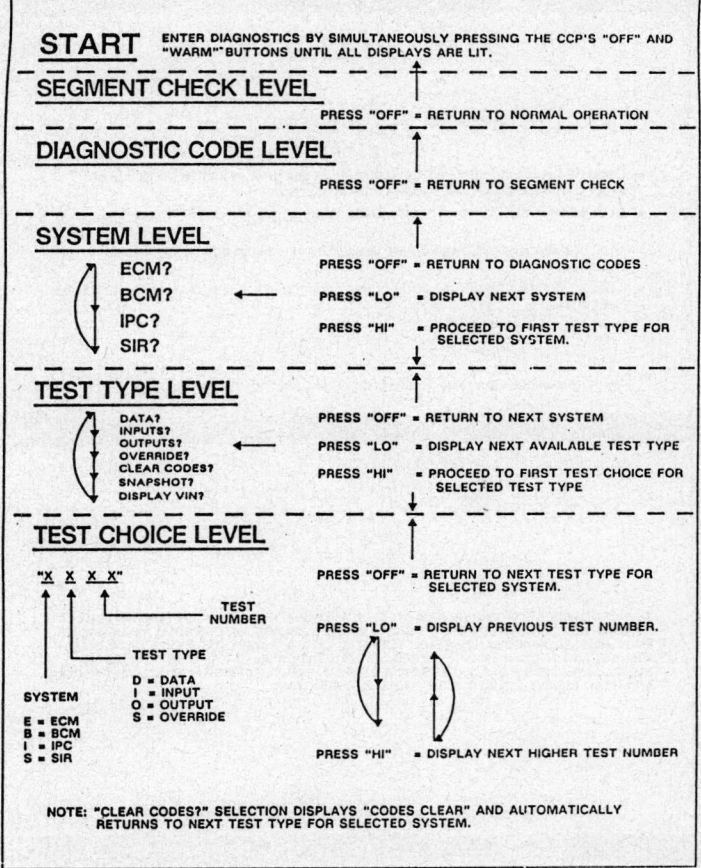

Fig. 21 Operating service mode. Eldorado & Seville

will be displayed, which is the ECM system.

2. **On all models,** depress Hi button on the CCP. This will display "Data," the first available test type.
3. Press Lo button on the CCP to display "Input," the test type level for speed control system testing.
4. Depress Hi button on the CCP. This will displayed the first test type. At this point, press Hi button until the correct test type appears as listed below under the applicable model year.
5. To display the previous test, press Lo button. To return to previous test type, press Off.

Cruise Control Inoperative

If cruise control is inoperative, enter ECM "Input" tests and perform the following, referring to wiring diagrams and connector points, **Figs. 55 through 61,** and ECM replacement check. If cruise system does function, but indicator does not light, proceed to step 13.

1. With ignition switch in Run position, select ECM input test E182.
2. If ECM does not display LO with cruise control switch off, or does not display Hi with cruise control switch on, refer to **Figs. 47 and 48.** For intermittent codes proceed as follows:
   a. The amber cruise on indicator can be used to monitor cruise dash switch status. Turn dash switch on and wiggle wiring and connectors. If switch or circuit from fuse to switch are open, amber light will blink out.
   b. If cruise 3A fuse blows intermittently, turn switch on, wiggle wiring, connectors, cruise steering column switch. If circuit becomes grounded, the fuse will blow.
3. If ECM displays LO with cruise switch on and displays HI with cruise switch on, select input test E170, on all models, turn ignition switch to Run position and cruise switch on.
4. If ECM does not display LO with brake pedal depressed, or does not display HI with brake pedal released, refer to **Figs. 49 and 50.**
5. If ECM displays LO with brake pedal and HI with brake pedal released, select ECM input test E184, on all models turn ignition switch to Run position and cruise control on.
6. If ECM does not display HI with Resume/Accelerate switch depressed, or does not display LO with resume/accelerate switch released, refer to **Figs. 51 and 52.** For intermittent codes proceed as follows:
   a. Turn cruise dash switch to on and backprobe ECM B6 with a voltmeter to ground, B6 should show 12 volts with Resume/Accelerate depressed and 0 volts with Resume/Accelerate released. Cycle switch while observing the meter, wiggle wiring and connectors.
7. If ECM displays HI with resume/accelerate switch depressed and displays LO with resume accelerate switch released, select ECM input

test E183, on all models, turn ignition switch to Run position and cruise switch on.
8. If ECM does not display HI with resume/accelerate switch depressed, or does not display LO with resume/accelerate switch released, refer to **Figs. 53 and 54.** For intermittent codes proceed as follows:
   a. Turn cruise dash switch to on and backprobe ECM B4 with a voltmeter to ground. B4 should show 12 volts with resume/accelerate depressed and 0 volts with resume/accelerate released. Cycle switch while observing meter, wiggle wiring and connectors.
9. If ECM displays HI when resume/accelerate switch is depressed and displays LO when resume/accelerate switch is released, run engine for 2 minutes, then turn engine off and select ECM override test ES04.
10. Vary override from 0 to 99, then to 0 again.
11. If cruise control servo does not pull fully in and then release, check vacuum source and hoses for leaks, kinks or restrictions and check servo linkage for mechanical binding, then replace cruise control servo as necessary.
12. If cruise control servo pulls fully in and then releases, replace ECM.
13. If cruise On indicator does not light, but cruise system does function, proceed as follows:
    a. Remove right switch assembly and connect test lamp between connector terminals B4 and BC1.
    b. If lamp does not illuminate, check flex circuit 804, repairing as necessary.

CLEARING CODES

The trouble codes stored in the system memory can be cleared to aid in diagnosing intermittent conditions. To clear codes, proceed as follows:

1. Enter diagnostic service mode as outlined.
2. Follow steps 1 and 2 under "Diagnostic Test Procedures."
3. Depress LO button on the CCP until clear codes is displayed.
4. Depress HI button on the CCP, this will start the erasing process. **Note the following.**
   a. Selection of the clear codes test type will result in the message clear codes being displayed along with the selected system name. This message will appear for 3 seconds to indicate that all stored trouble codes have been erased from that system's memory. After 3 seconds the display will automatically return to the next available test type for the selected system.

EXITING DIAGNOSTIC SERVICE MODE

To exit the diagnostic service mode, depress the Reset/Recall button on the DIC or turn the ignition switch off.

Brougham

TEST PROCEDURES
1991–92

Refer to **Figs. 62 and 63** for test procedures.

When performing diagnostic tests, refer to **Fig. 64** for wiring diagrams, and **Fig. 65** for connector pin identification.

ELECTRICAL TESTING

Before proceeding with electrical tests on, ensure all test equipment such as test lights and voltmeters are in good working order, inspect cruise control fuse and replace as necessary, inspect all vacuum hoses for leaks and check for adequate system vacuum.

ELECTRIC BRAKE RELEASE SWITCH
On Vehicle

1. Turn ignition to On position and the instrument panel switch to On-Auto position.
2. Connect test light to suitable ground.
3. Probe brown wire at brake switch connector. Lamp should illuminate.
4. With probe still attached to brown wire, check switch adjustment. Light should go out when brake pedal is depressed $1/8$-$1/2$ inch.
5. If lamp did not illuminate in step 3, probe wire in adjacent connector cavity.
6. If lamp illuminates, adjust or replace switch as necessary.
7. If lamp does not illuminate, repair wiring to switch.

Off Vehicle

Using self powered test lamp, lamp should be off with switch plunger extended, and should illuminate with switch plunger fully depressed.

INSTRUMENT PANEL & ENGAGEMENT SWITCHES

1. Turn ignition switch to On position.
2. Connect test light to ground.
3. Probe three terminals of turn signal lever cruise harness connector with instrument panel switch in both Off and On-Auto positions. With switch in Off position, there should be no power at any terminal. With switch in On-Auto position, test lamp should illuminate at B cavity. and amber indicator should light.
4. Probe cavity D and depress Set/Coast switch. Lamp should illuminate.
5. Probe cavity C and depress Resume/Accel switch. Lamp should illuminate.
6. If results are satisfactory in step 3, but lamp does not illuminate in step 4 or 5, replace turn signal lever engagement switch.

ACTION	NORMAL RESULT	FOR DIAGNOSIS
• PERFORM SELF-DIAGNOSTIC SYSTEM CHECK	AND RECORD AND DIAGNOSE ANY STORED CODES	
• INSPECT CRUISE CONTROL SERVO THROTTLE ACTUATING CABLE, CRUISE BRAKE SWITCH AND VCC BRAKE SWITCH FOR PROPER ADJUSTMENT (A MISADJUSTED CABLE WILL CAUSE SURGING AND BINDING).		
• INSPECT VACUUM LINES FOR KINKS, RESTRICTIONS, AND DETERIORATION		
• ENTER DIAGNOSTICS AND SELECT ECM INPUT E182		
CRUISE SWITCH OFF	E182 DISPLAYS LO	REFER TO INPUT TEST E182
CRUISE SWITCH ON	E182 DISPLAYS HI	
• LEAVE CRUISE SWITCH ON AND SELECT ECM INPUT E170		
DEPRESS BRAKE PEDAL	E170 DISPLAYS LO	REFER TO INPUT TEST E170
RELEASE BRAKE PEDAL	E170 DISPLAYS HI	
• SELECT ECM INPUT E171		
DEPRESS BRAKE PEDAL	E171 DISPLAYS LO	REFER TO INPUT TEST E171
RELEASE BRAKE PEDAL	E171 DISPLAYS HI	
• SELECT ECM INPUT E184		
SLIDE CRUISE SWITCH TO RESUME/ ACCEL POSITION	E184 DISPLAYS HI	REFER TO INPUT TEST E184
RELEASE CRUISE SWITCH	E184 DISPLAYS LO	
DEPRESS SET/COAST SWITCH	E184 DISPLAYS LO	CHECK CKTS 84 AND 87 FOR A WIRE TO WIRE SHORT. IF OK, REPLACE MULTI-FUNCTION LEVER
• SELECT ECM INPUT TEST E183 (LEAVE CRUISE SWITCH ON)		
DEPRESS SET/COAST SWITCH	E183 DISPLAYS HI	REFER TO INPUT TEST E183
RELEASE SET/COAST SWITCH	E183 DISPLAYS LO	
SLIDE CRUISE SWITCH TO RESUME/ ACCEL POSITION	E183 DISPLAYS LO	CHECK CKTS 84 AND 87 FOR A WIRE TO WIRE SHORT. IF OK, REPLACE MULTI-FUNCTION LEVER
• IF ALL RESULTS ARE NORMAL, GO TO TEST B: CRUISE CONTROL OUTPUT TEST		

Fig. 22   Diagnostic procedure, A: Isolation test. 1992 Eldorado & Seville

① CHECKS CRUISE CONTROL SERVO OPERATION, SERVO THROTTLE LINKAGE, AND VACUUM.

② CHECKS VACUUM LINES FOR RESTRICTIONS AND SERVO/THROTTLE LINKAGE FOR BINDING.

WHEN ALL DIAGNOSIS AND REPAIRS ARE COMPLETED VERIFY OPERATION

Fig. 23   Diagnostic procedure, B: Cruise control output test. 1992 Eldorado & Seville

AMBER ON LAMP INOPERATIVE OR MALFUNCTIONING

1. Turn ignition switch to On position.
2. Place instrument panel switch in On-Auto position.
3. If amber On switch does not illuminate, check for burned out lamp, open ground wire, open connector, inoperative switch, blown fuse or printed circuit.
4. Place instrument panel switch in Off position.
5. If amber On light illuminates, check for shorted leads or inoperative switch.

GREEN CRUISE LAMP INOPERATIVE OR MALFUNCTIONING

1. If road test indicates that system controls speed, but green indicator light is not illuminated, check for burned out lamp or open in pink wire of cavity B between switch connector and controller connector.
2. Turn ignition switch to On position and place instrument panel switch in On-Auto position, then ground cavity B in controller connector. If green lamp illuminates, replace controller.
3. If green indicator remains on when system is not controlling speed, check for short in harness between switch and controller connector and, if there is no short, replace controller.
4. Ensure amber light is illuminated to confirm power supply.

ENGAGE SWITCH & HARNESS

1. Disconnect turn lever engage switch from harness.
2. Using ohmmeter, test turn lever engage switch as follows:
   a. Place engage switch in released position. There should be no continuity between any two terminals.
   b. Depress engage switch slide. There should be continuity only between yellow and green wire terminals.
   c. Depress engage switch push button. There should be continuity only between green and red wire terminals.
3. If results are not correct in steps a, b or c, replace engagement switch and harness.
4. Connect one lead of ohmmeter to steering column mounting bracket and check each terminal. If any terminal indicates continuity, replace lever and harness.

Adjustments
CABLE OR ROD ADJUSTMENT

A cable is used in this system. The servo unit positions the throttle linkage through the use of a cable. To adjust this cable turn engine to the "Off" position. Retract idle speed control (ISC) motor plunger, **throttle lever must not touch ISC plunger.** Connect cruise control cable to servo hole blade, **Fig. 1,** that allows minimum slack.

BRAKE RELEASE SWITCH ADJUSTMENT

With brake pedal depressed, push cruise control/stoplight switch fully into retainer, then pull brake pedal fully back to rest position. Switch will back out of retainer and adjust automatically. **On vehicles equipped with anti-lock brakes,** release brake pedal and allow to come to rest. Brake release switch contacts should open at 1/8-1/2 inch pedal travel, measured at centerline of brake pedal pad. Actuation of stop lamp contact is 3/16 after cruise control contact opens.

VACUUM RELEASE VALVE ADJUSTMENT

With brake pedal depressed, push vacuum valve switch all the way into the retaining clip. Pull the brake pedal to the stop to automatically adjust the valve. **On vehicle equipped with anti-lock brakes,** release pedal and allow to come to rest. Vacuum dump valve assembly should open at 1-1 5/16 inch pedal travel, measured at centerline of brake pedal pad.

Continued on page 31-36

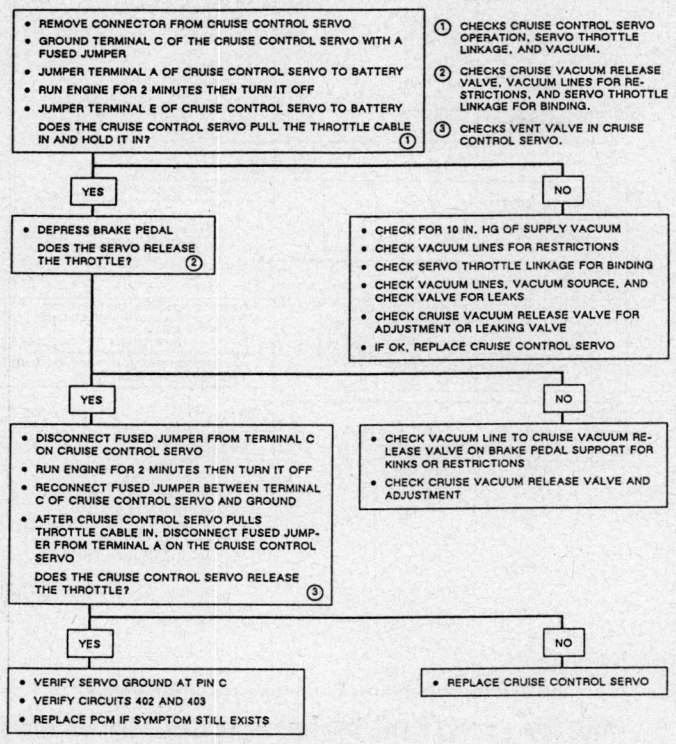

Fig. 24 Diagnostic procedure, C: Cruise control servo test. 1992 Eldorado & Seville

ACTION	NORMAL RESULT	FOR DIAGNOSIS
• PERFORM SELF-DIAGNOSTIC SYSTEM CHECK		AND RECORD AND DIAGNOSE ANY STORED CODES
• INSPECT CRUISE CONTROL SERVO THROTTLE ACTUATING CABLE, STOP/BTSI/CRUISE BRAKE SWITCH AND TCC BRAKE SWITCH FOR PROPER ADJUSTMENT (A MISADJUSTED CABLE WILL CAUSE SURGING AND BINDING).		
• INSPECT VACUUM LINES FOR KINKS, RESTRICTIONS, AND DETERIORATION		
• ENTER DIAGNOSTICS AND SELECT PCM INPUT PI82		
CRUISE SWITCH OFF	PI82 DISPLAYS LO	SEE ①
CRUISE SWITCH ON	PI82 DISPLAYS HI	SEE ②
• LEAVE CRUISE SWITCH ON AND SELECT PCM INPUT PI70		
DEPRESS BRAKE PEDAL	PI70 DISPLAYS LO	SEE ③
RELEASE BRAKE PEDAL	PI70 DISPLAYS HI	SEE ④
• SELECT PCM INPUT PI71		
DEPRESS BRAKE PEDAL	PI71 DISPLAYS LO	SEE ⑤
RELEASE BRAKE PEDAL	PI71 DISPLAYS HI	SEE ⑤
• SELECT PCM INPUT PI84		
SLIDE CRUISE SWITCH TO RESUME/ ACCEL POSITION	PI84 DISPLAYS HI	SEE ⑥
RELEASE CRUISE SWITCH	PI84 DISPLAYS LO	SEE ⑦
DEPRESS SET/COAST SWITCH	PI84 DISPLAYS LO	CHECK CKTS 84 AND 87 FOR A WIRE TO WIRE SHORT. IF OK, REPLACE MULTI-FUNCTION LEVER
• SELECT PCM INPUT TEST PI83 (LEAVE CRUISE SWITCH ON)		
DEPRESS SET/COAST SWITCH	PI83 DISPLAYS HI	SEE ⑧
RELEASE SET/COAST SWITCH	PI83 DISPLAYS LO	SEE ⑨
SLIDE CRUISE SWITCH TO RESUME/ ACCEL POSITION	PI83 DISPLAYS LO	CHECK CKTS 84 AND 87 FOR A WIRE TO WIRE SHORT. IF OK, REPLACE MULTI-FUNCTION LEVER

• IF ALL RESULTS ARE NORMAL, GO TO TEST B: CRUISE CONTROL OUTPUT TEST

① SHORT TO VOLTAGE IN CKTS 397 OR 85.
SHORTED CRUISE CONTROL SWITCH

② FUSE D5, CRUISE CONTROL SWITCH OR CKTS
250, 397 OPEN.
CKT 250, 397 OR 86 SHORTED TO GROUND

③ STOP/BTSI/ CRUISE BRAKE SWITCH MISADJUSTED
OR DEFECTIVE.
SHORT TO VOLTAGE IN CKT 86

④ STOP/BTSI/CRUISE BRAKE SWITCH OPEN OR MIS-
ADJUSTED.
OPEN-IN CKTS 397 OR 86

⑤ REFER TO CODE P090 DIAGNOSIS IN SECTION 6E

⑥ OPEN RESUME/ACCEL SWITCH OR CKT 87

⑦ SHORTED RESUME/ACCEL SWITCH.
SHORT TO VOLTAGE IN CKT 87

⑧ OPEN SET/COAST SWITCH OR CKT 84

⑨ SHORTED SET/COAST SWITCH.
SHORT TO VOLTAGE IN CKT 84

• IF ALL CHECKS AND TERMINAL CONTACT ARE OK, REPLACE PCM

Fig. 25 Diagnostic procedure, A: Isolation test. 1993 Eldorado & Seville

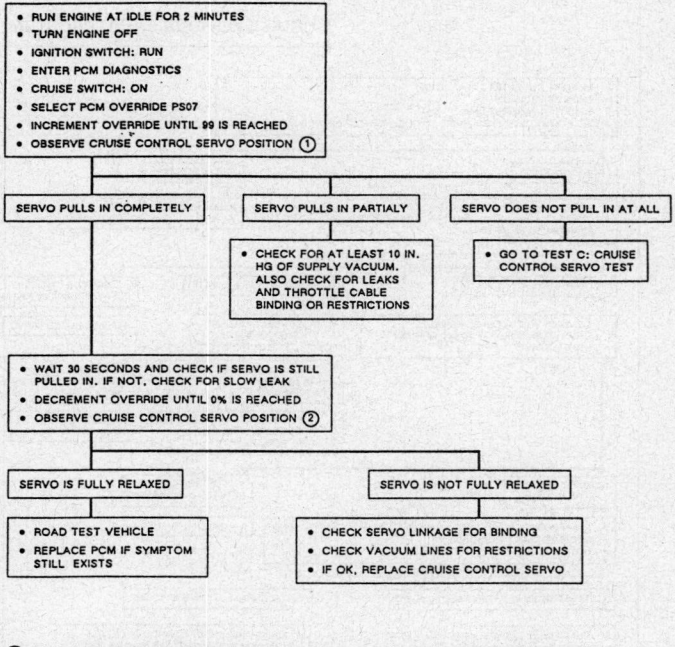

① CHECKS CRUISE CONTROL SERVO OPERATION, SERVO THROTTLE LINKAGE, AND VACUUM.
② CHECKS VACUUM LINES FOR RESTRICTIONS AND SERVO THROTTLE LINKAGE FOR BINDING.

WHEN ALL DIAGNOSIS AND REPAIRS ARE COMPLETED, PERFORM LASH LEARN PROCEDURE (NORTHSTAR ONLY) AND VERIFY OPERATION

Fig. 26 Diagnostic procedure, B: Cruise control output test. 1993 Eldorado & Seville

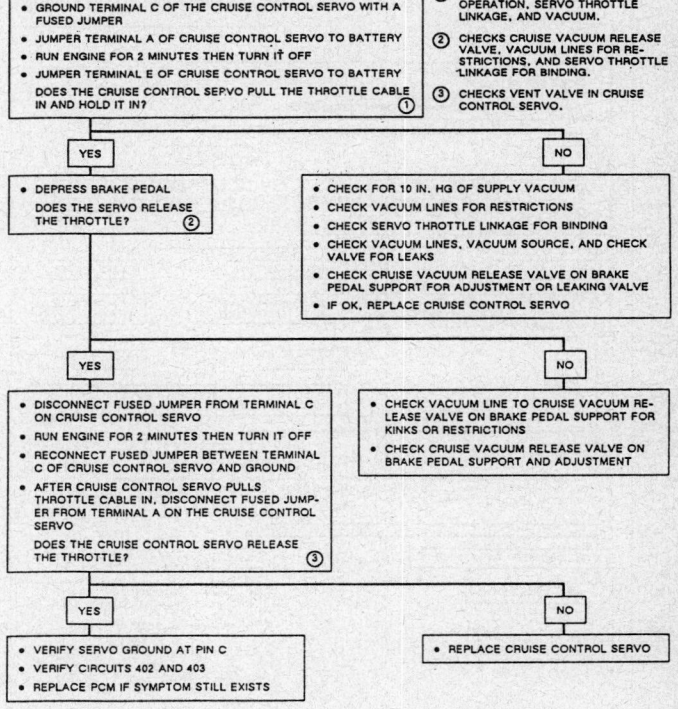

WHEN ALL DIAGNOSIS AND REPAIRS ARE COMPLETED, PERFORM LASH LEARN PROCEDURE (NORTHSTAR ONLY) AND VERIFY OPERATION

Fig. 27 Diagnostic procedure, C: Cruise control servo test. 1993 Eldorado & Seville

PCM CODE E060

CRUISE-NOT IN DRIVE

- THE PRIMARY PURPOSE OF THIS CODE IS TO DETECT AN ACTION OF THE DRIVE THAT COULD CAUSE AN UNSAFE CONDITION OR DAMAGE TO THE VEHICLE.
- THIS CODE CAN BE DRIVER INDUCED BY SHIFTING THE GEAR SELECTOR INTO NEUTRAL WHEN THE CRUISE CONTROL IS ENGAGED.
- A FAILURE OF THE PRNDL SWITCH MAY CAUSE THE CODE TO SET.
- CHECK FOR CODE E091.

Fig. 28   DTC test PO60. Eldorado & Seville w/4.9L engine

WHEN ALL DIAGNOSIS AND REPAIRS ARE COMPLETED, CLEAR CODES AND VERIFY OPERATION

Fig. 29   DTC test PO60. 1993 Eldorado & Seville w/4.6L Northstar engine

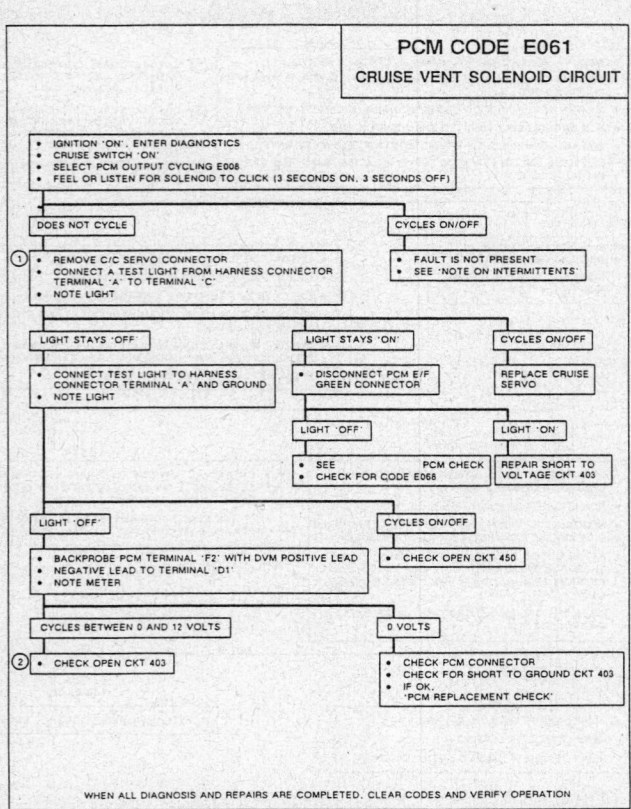

Fig. 30   DTC test PO61 (Part 1 of 3). 1991 Eldorado & Seville w/4.9L engine

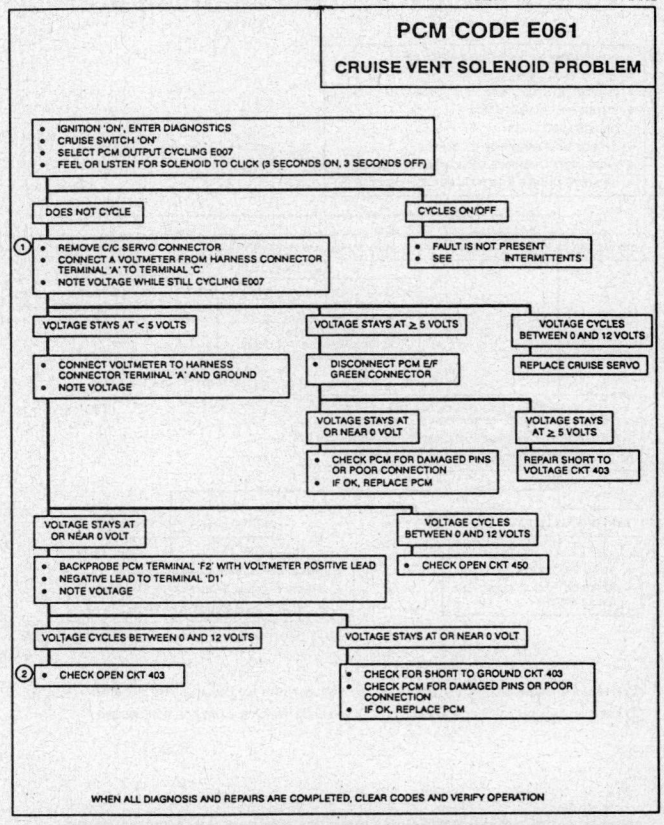

Fig. 30   DTC test PO61 (Part 2 of 3). 1992 Eldorado & Seville w/4.9L engine

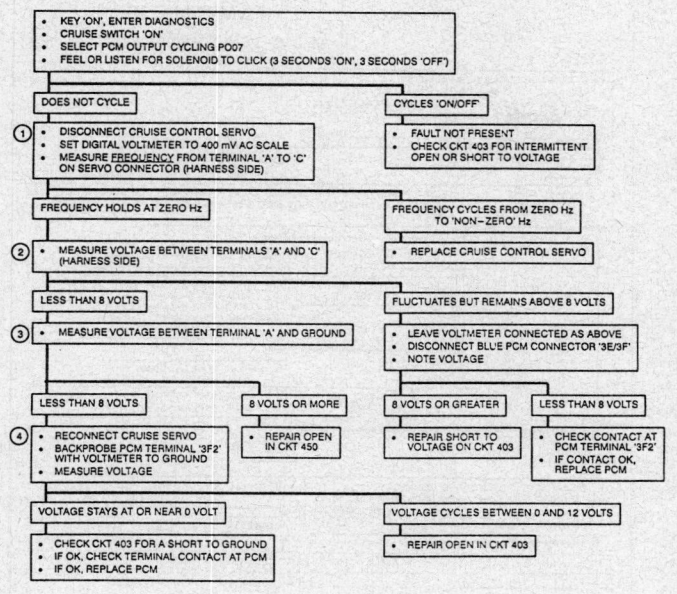

Fig. 30   DTC test PO61 (Part 3 of 3). 1993 Eldorado & Seville w/4.9L engine

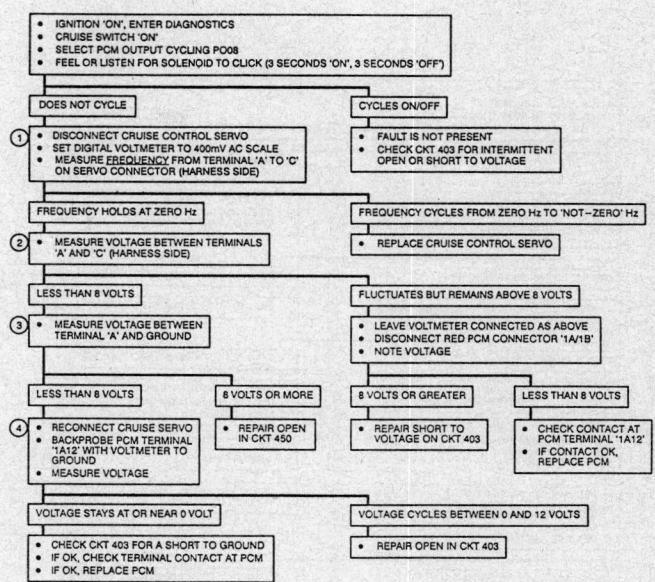

Fig. 31   DTC test PO61. 1993 Eldorado & Seville w/4.6L Northstar engine

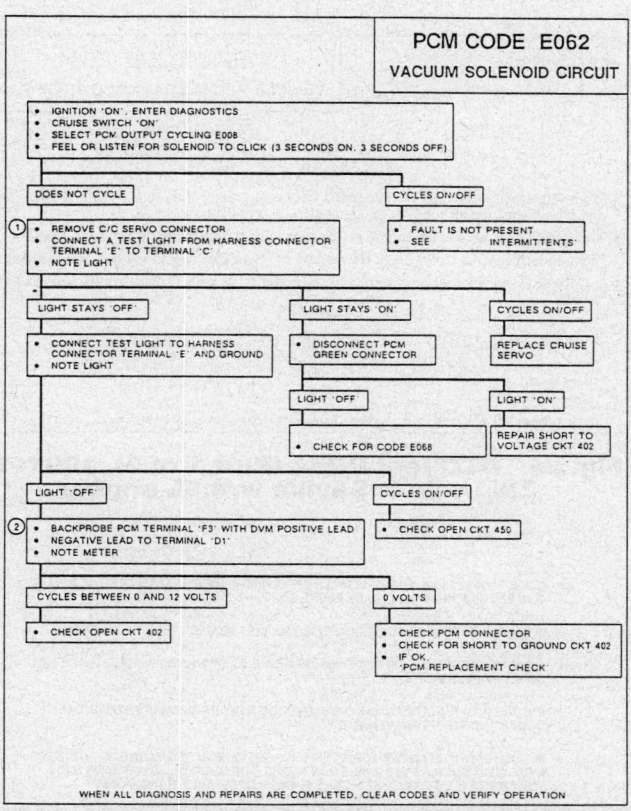

Fig. 32   DTC test PO62 (Part 1 of 2). 1991 Eldorado & Seville w/4.9L engine

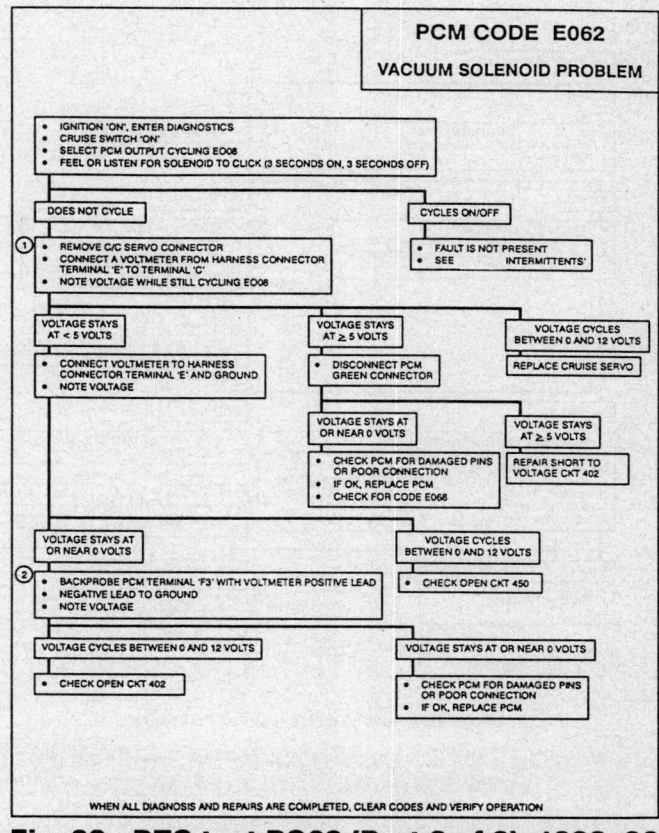

Fig. 32   DTC test PO62 (Part 2 of 2). 1992–93 Eldorado & Seville w/4.9L engine

Fig. 33   DTC test PO62. 1993 Eldorado & Seville w/4.6L Northstar engine

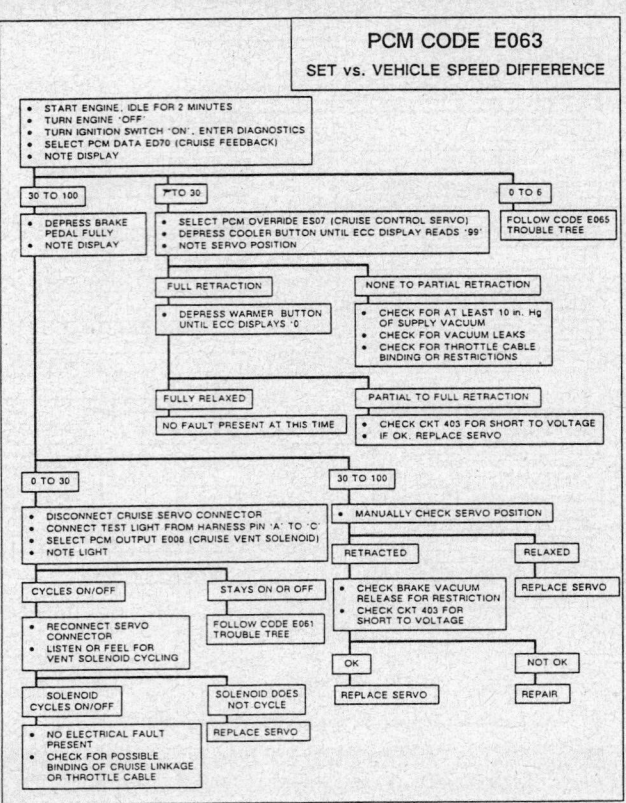

Fig. 34   DTC test PO63. Eldorado & Seville w/4.9L engine

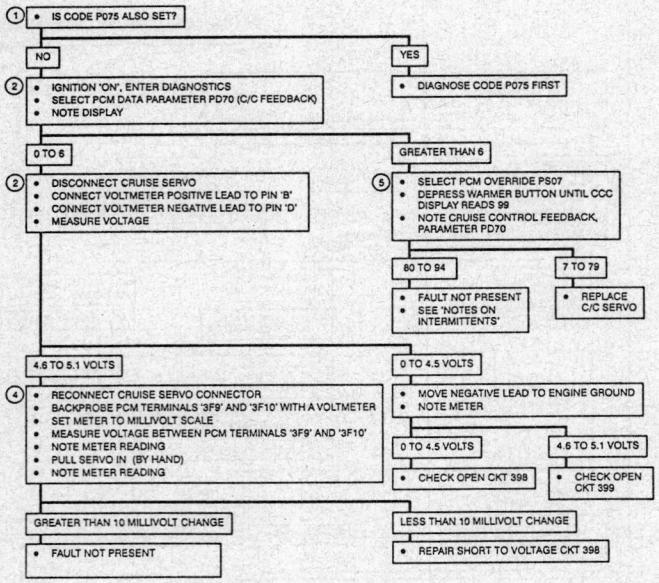

Fig. 35   DTC test PO63. 1993 Eldorado & Seville w/4.6L Northstar engine

Fig. 36   DTC test PO64 (Part 1 of 2). 1991–92 Eldorado & Seville w/4.9L engine

- CODE P064 SETS WHEN THE VEHICLE SPEED INCREASES GREATER THAT 16 MPH IN ONE SECOND WITH THE CRUISE ENGAGED.

- IF CODE P064 IS SET, CRUISE CONTROL WILL DISENGAGE.

- MOST OCCURRENCES OF CODE P064 ARE CAUSED BY WHEELSPIN DUE TO ICY, WET OR SLIPPERY CONDITIONS.

- IF CODE P064 IS FOUND AND NO OTHER CRUISE CONTROL FAULTS EXISTS, CLEAR CODES AND ROAD TEST VEHICLE.

- IF CODE P075 IS ALSO SET, LOOK FOR SOURCES OF ELECTROMAGNETIC INTERFERENCE (EMI), SUCH AS VSS WIRES RUN ALONG SIDE SPARK PLUG WIRES OR HIGH POWER TRANSMITTERS (LIKE MOBILE RADIOS) OPERATING IN THE VICINITY.

Fig. 36   DTC test PO64 (Part 2 of 2). 1993 Eldorado & Seville w/4.9L engine

- CODE P064 SETS WHEN THE VEHICLE SPEED INCREASES GREATER THAN 16 MPH IN ONE SECOND WITH THE CRUISE ENGAGED.

- IF CODE P064 IS SET, CRUISE CONTROL WILL DISENGAGE.

- MOST OCCURRENCES OF CODE P064 ARE CAUSED BY WHEELSPIN DUE TO ICY, WET OR SLIPPERY CONDITIONS.

- IF CODE P064 IS FOUND AND NO OTHER CRUISE CONTROL FAULTS EXISTS, CLEAR CODES AND ROAD TEST VEHICLE.

- IF CODE P075 IS ALSO SET, LOOK FOR SOURCES OF ELECTROMAGNETIC INTERFERENCE (EMI), SUCH AS VSS WIRES RUN ALONG SIDE SPARK PLUG WIRES OR HIGH POWER TRANSMITTERS (LIKE MOBILE RADIOS) OPERATING IN THE VICINITY.

Fig. 37 DTC test PO64. 1993 Eldorado & Seville w/4.6L Northstar engine

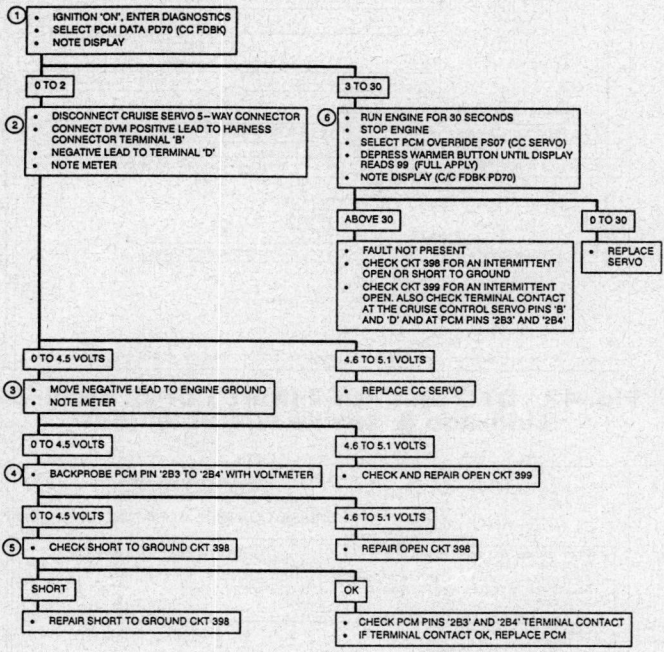

Fig. 38 DTC test PO65 (Part 2 of 2). 1993 Eldorado & Seville w/4.9L engine

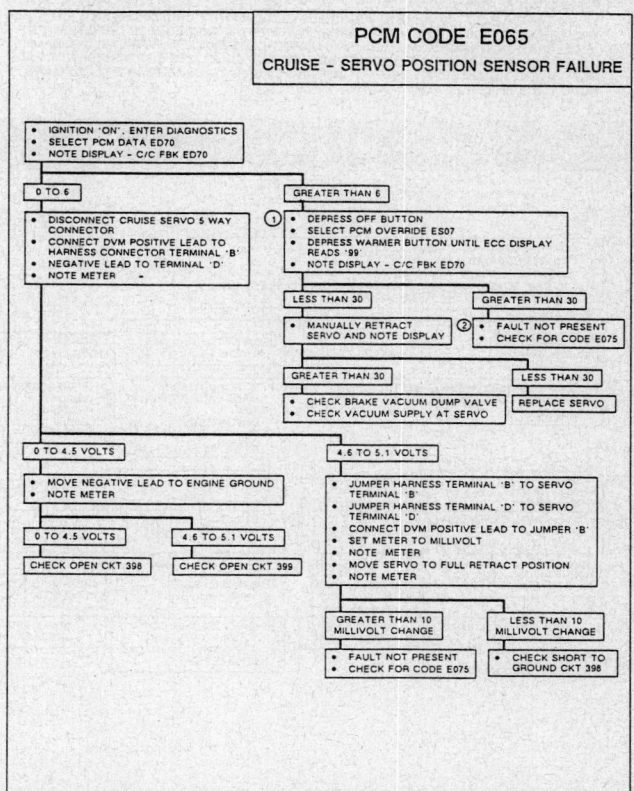

Fig. 38 DTC test PO65 (Part 1 of 2). 1991–92 Eldorado & Seville w/4.9L engine

PCM CODE E066

CRUISE-ENGINE RPM TOO HIGH

THIS CODE WILL SET IF ENGINE RPM EXCEEDS 4800 RPM. THIS MAY OCCUR ON SLIPPERY PAVEMENT, EXTENDED WIDE OPEN THROTTLE ACCELERATION, OR FOR SOME MECHANICAL PROBLEMS (SUCH AS TRANSMISSION SLIPPAGE). UNDER THESE CONDITIONS, CODE E066 WILL SET AND SHOULD BE CONSIDERED NORMAL. THE DRIVER SHOULD BE CONSIDERED NORMAL. THE DRIVER SHOULD BE ADVISED WHY THE CRUISE DISENGAGED. CLEAR THE CODE AND ROAD TEST VEHICLE TO VERIFY NORMAL OPERATION.

WHEN ALL DIAGNOSIS AND REPAIRS ARE COMPLETED, CLEAR CODES AND VERIFY OPERATION.

Fig. 40 DTC test PO66. Eldorado & Seville w/4.9L engine

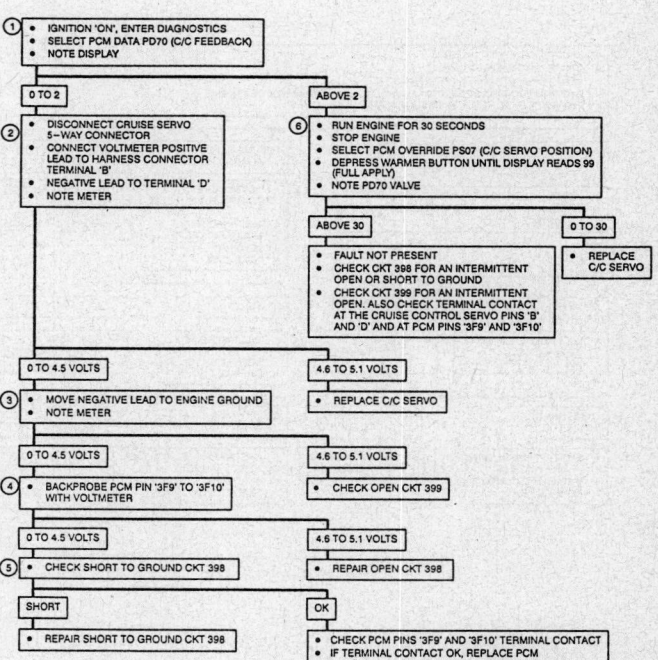

WHEN ALL DIAGNOSIS AND REPAIRS ARE COMPLETED, CLEAR CODES AND VERIFY OPERATION

Fig. 39 DTC test PO65. 1993 Eldorado & Seville w/4.6L Northstar engine

GENERAL MOTORS–Speed Control Systems

THIS CODE WILL SET IF ENGINE RPM EXCEEDS 5975 RPM WITH CRUISE CONTROL ENGAGED. THIS MAY OCCUR ON ICY, WET, OR SLIPPERY PAVEMENT, EXTENDED WIDE OPEN THROTTLE ACCELERATION, OR FOR SOME MECHANICAL PROBLEMS (SUCH AS TRANSAXLE SLIPPAGE). UNDER THESE CONDITIONS, CODE P066 WILL SET AND SHOULD BE CONSIDERED NORMAL. THE DRIVER SHOULD BE ADVISED WHY THE CRUISE DISENGAGED. CLEAR THE CODE AND ROAD TEST VEHICLE TO VERIFY NORMAL OPERATION.

Fig. 41   DTC test PO66. 1993 Eldorado & Seville w/4.6L Northstar engine

WHEN ALL DIAGNOSIS AND REPAIRS ARE COMPLETED, CLEAR CODES AND VERIFY OPERATION

Fig. 42   DTC test PO67 (Part 2 of 2). 1993 Eldorado & Seville w/4.9L engine

WHEN ALL DIAGNOSIS AND REPAIRS ARE COMPLETED, CLEAR CODES AND VERIFY OPERATION

Fig. 43   DTC test PO67. 1993 Eldorado & Seville w/4.6L Northstar engine

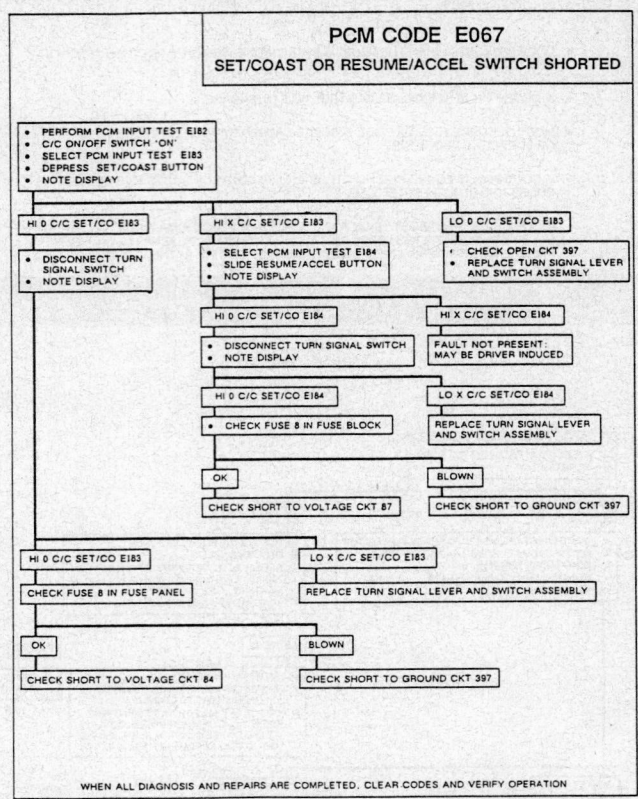

WHEN ALL DIAGNOSIS AND REPAIRS ARE COMPLETED, CLEAR CODES AND VERIFY OPERATION

Fig. 42   DTC test PO67 (Part 1 of 2). 1991–92 Eldorado & Seville w/4.9L engine

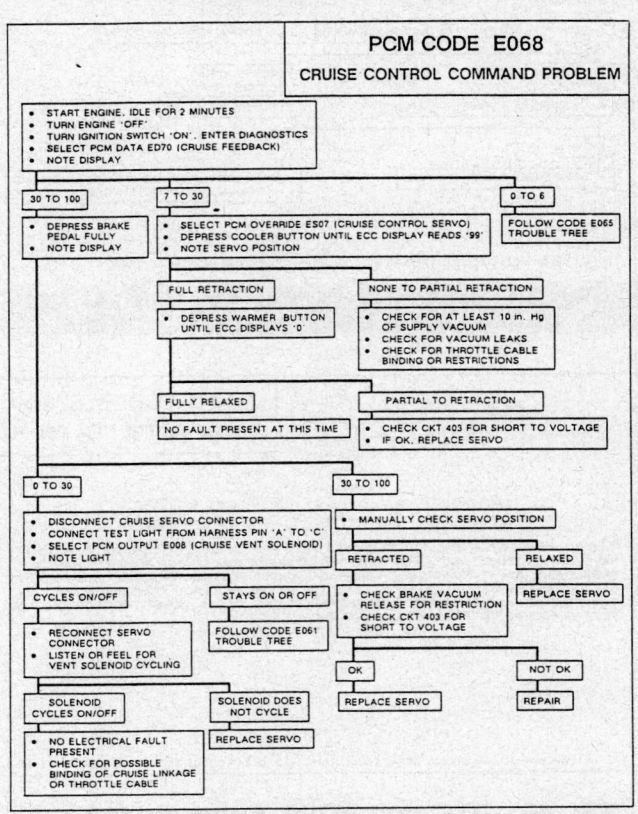

Fig. 44   DTC test PO68 (Part 1 of 2). 1991–92 Eldorado & Seville w/4.9L engine

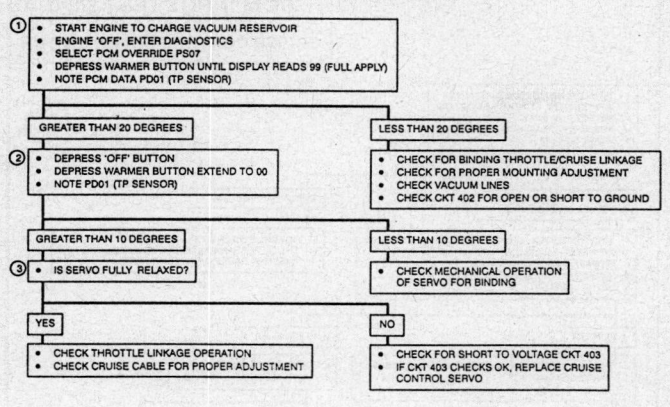

NOTE: IF SET, DIAGNOSE CODES P021, P022, P061, P062 AND P065 FIRST

Fig. 44   DTC test PO68 (Part 2 of 2). 1993 Eldorado & Seville w/4.9L engine

NOTE: IF SET, DIAGNOSE CODES P021, P022, P061, P062 AND P065 FIRST

NOTE: INSPECT SERVO, SERVO BRACKET, AND THROTTLE CABLE BRACKET FOR PROPER FIT AND ALIGNMENT. ALSO INSPECT CABLES FOR BINDING, PROPER CONNECTION AND ADJUSTMENT.

Fig. 45   DTC test PO68. 1993 Eldorado & Seville w/4.6L Northstar engine

- THIS DIAGNOSTIC TROUBLE CODE SETS WHEN TRACTION CONTROL AND CRUISE CONTROL ARE ACTIVE AT THE SAME TIME.
- IF DIAGNOSTIC TROUBLE CODE P069 SETS, CRUISE CONTROL WILL BE DISENGAGED
- CHECK FOR TRACTION CONTROL CODES.
- MOST CASES OF DIAGNOSTIC TROUBLE CODE P069 ARE CAUSED BY WHEEL SPIN UNDER ICY, WET, OR SLIPPERY CONDITIONS WHILE CRUISE ACTIVE.
- IF NO OTHER CRUISE CONTROL OR TRACTION CONTROL FAULTS EXIST, CLEAR CODES AND VERIFY CORRECT CRUISE AND TRACTION CONTROL OPERATION.

WHEN ALL DIAGNOSIS AND REPAIRS ARE COMPLETED, CLEAR CODES AND VERIFY OPERATION

Fig. 46   DTC test PO69. Eldorado & Seville w/4.6L Northstar engine

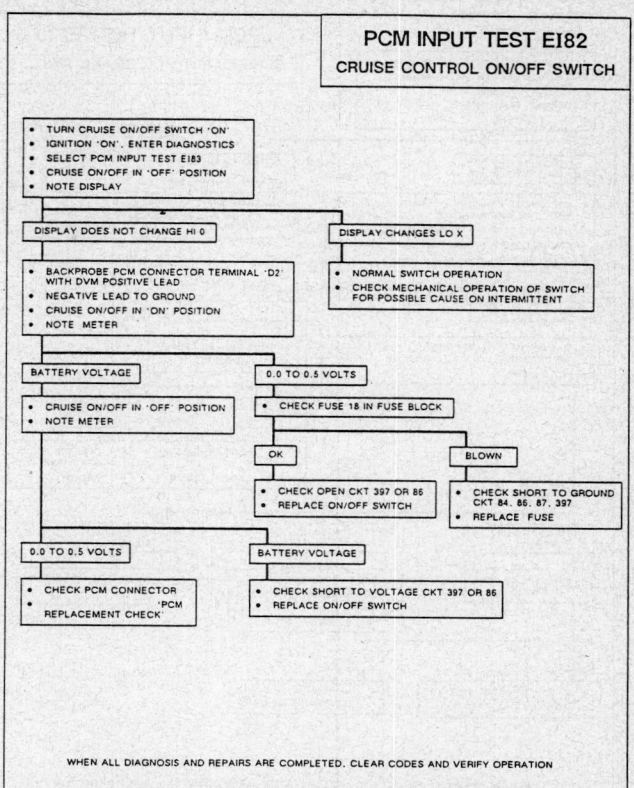

Fig. 47   PCM input test E182. 1991 Eldorado & Seville

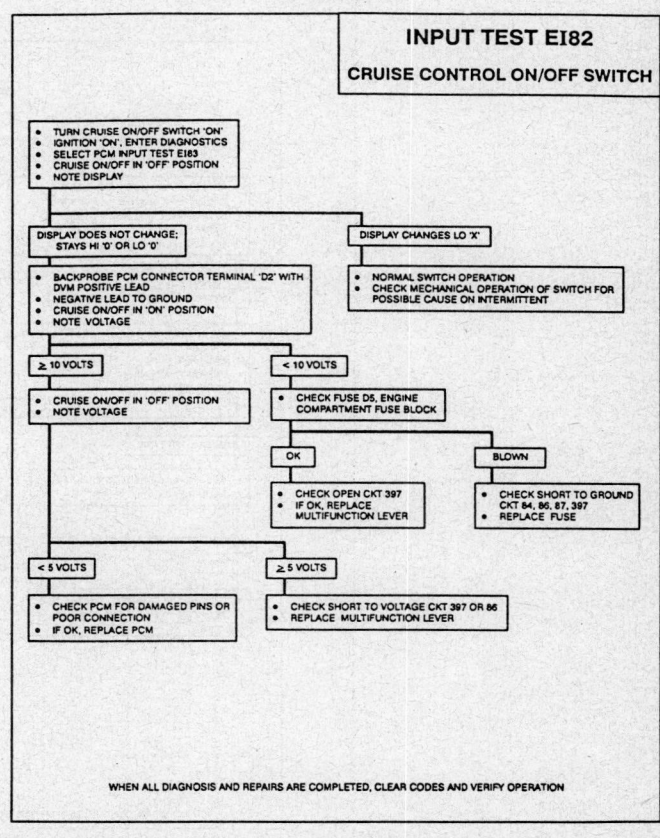

Fig. 48   PCM input test E182. 1992 Eldorado & Seville

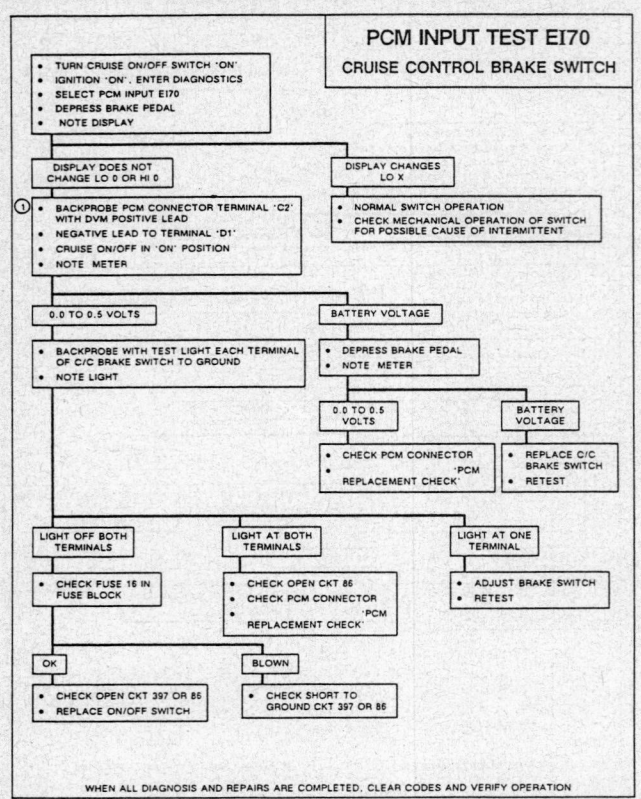

Fig. 49   PCM input test E170. 1991 Eldorado & Seville

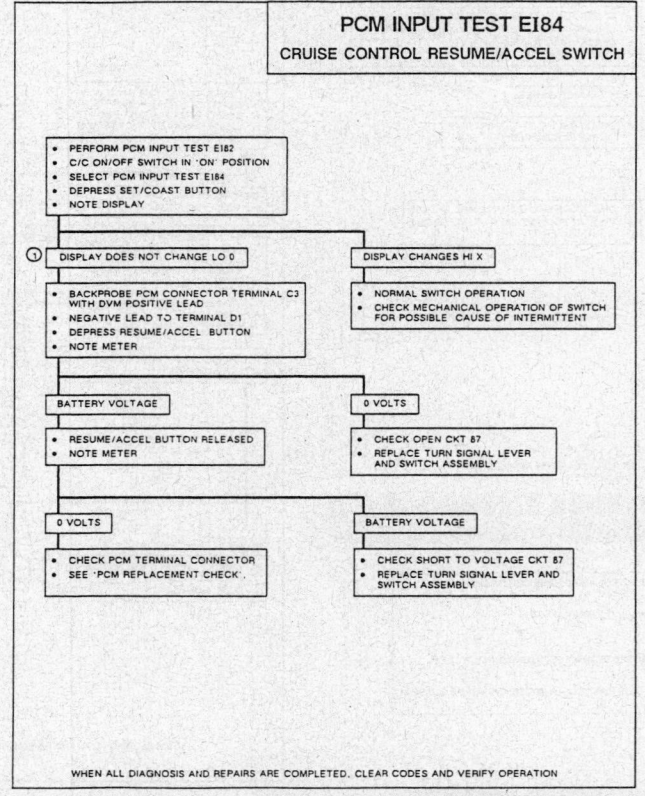

Fig. 50   PCM input test E170. 1992 Eldorado & Seville

Fig. 51   PCM input test E184. 1991 Eldorado & Seville

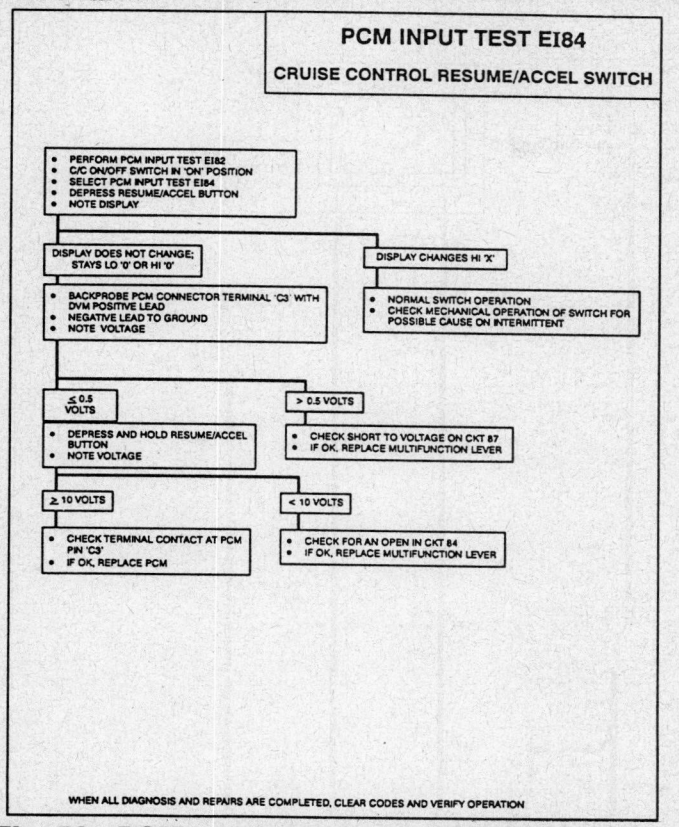

Fig. 52   PCM input test E184. 1992 Eldorado & Seville

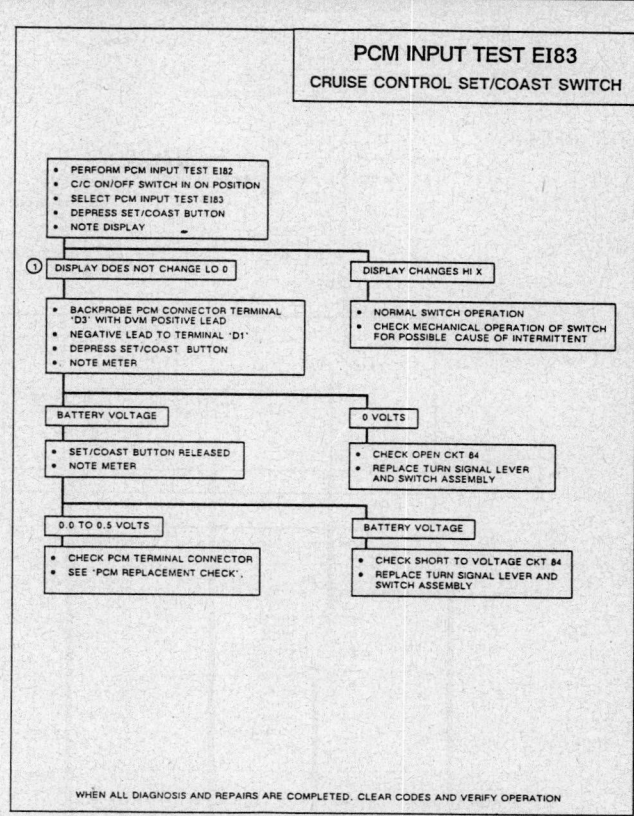

Fig. 53   PCM input test E183. 1991 Eldorado & Seville

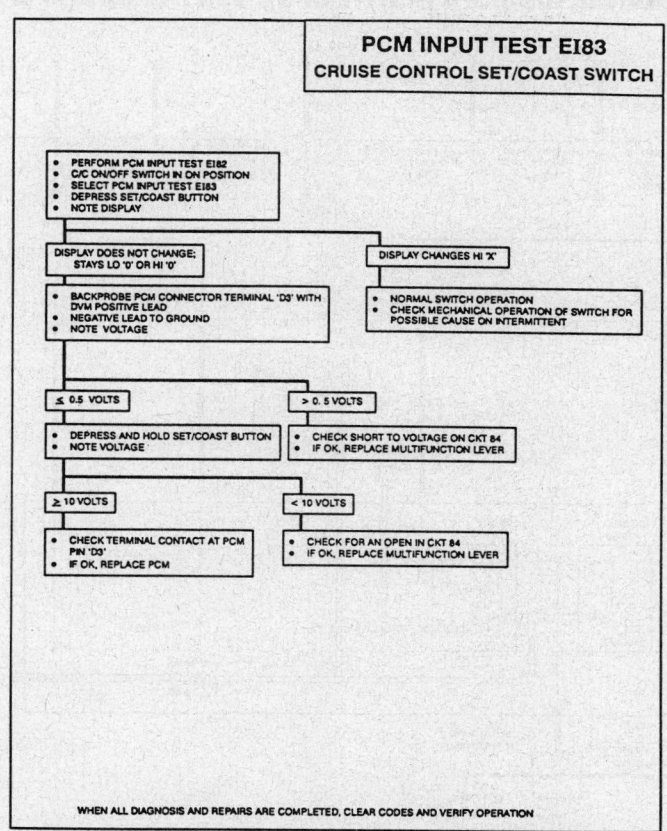

Fig. 54   PCM input test E183. 1992 Eldorado & Seville

Fig. 55   Wiring diagram (Part 1 of 2). 1991 Eldorado & Seville

Fig. 55   Wiring diagram (Part 2 of 2). 1991 Eldorado & Seville

Fig. 56 Wiring diagram (Part 2 of 2). 1992 Eldorado & Seville

Fig. 56 Wiring diagram (Part 1 of 2). 1992 Eldorado & Seville

Fig. 57 Wiring diagram (Part 2 of 2). 1993 Eldorado & Seville

Fig. 57 Wiring diagram (Part 1 of 2). 1993 Eldorado & Seville

Fig. 58 ECM connector (Part 1 of 3). 1991 Eldorado & Seville

CIRCUIT DESCRIPTION	CIRCUIT NUMBER	ECM (2A/B) BLACK	CIRCUIT NUMBER	CIRCUIT DESCRIPTION
BATTERY	480	1	435	EGR SOLENOID
N/C		2	434	PARK/NEUTRAL
C/C POSITION HI	398	3	815	POWER STEERING SW.
C/C POSITION LO	399	4		N/C
N/C		5	476A	SENSOR GROUND
LEFT O_2 SENSOR	413	6	339	IGNITION
LEFT O_2 SENSOR	912	7	427	THROTTLE SWITCH
COOLING FAN RELAY #2	536	8	800	UART SERIAL DATA OUT
SPEED SENSOR INPUT LO	401	9	800	UART SERIAL DATA IN
SPEED SENSOR INPUT HI	400	10	325	CHECK ENGINE SIGNAL
4000 PULSE SPEED OUTPUT #1	817	11	535	COOLING FAN RELAY #1
N/C	818	12	450	ECM GROUND

Fig. 59 PCM connector (Part 1 of 3). 1992 Eldorado & Seville

CIRCUIT DESCRIPTION	CIRCUIT NUMBER	PCM (2A/B) BLACK	CIRCUIT NUMBER	CIRCUIT DESCRIPTION
BATTERY	480	1	435	EGR SOLENOID
N/C		2	776	TRANS PRNDL INPUT PARITY
C/C SERVO POSITION SENSOR	398	3		N/C
C/C SERVO POSITION SENSOR	399	4		N/C
N/C		5	476	MAP/MAT SENSOR GROUND
LEFT O_2 SENSOR LO	413	6	1276	IGNITION
LEFT O_2 SENSOR HI	1589	7	427	THROTTLE SWITCH
HIGH SPEED COOLING FAN RLY	1270	8	800	UART SERIAL DATA
SPEED SENSOR INPUT LO	401	9	800	UART SERIAL DATA
SPEED SENSOR INPUT HI	400	10	419	'SERVICE ENGINE SOON' LIGHT
4K SPEED OUTPUT TO IPC	818	11	1269	LOW SPEED COOLING FAN RLY
4K SPEED OUTPUT TO CCR	817	12	450	PCM GROUND

Fig. 58 ECM connector (Part 2 of 3). 1991 Eldorado & Seville

CIRCUIT DESCRIPTION	CIRCUIT NUMBER	ECM (1C/D) BLACK	CIRCUIT NUMBER	CIRCUIT DESCRIPTION
ECM GROUND	450	1		N/C
C/C ON-OFF	397	2	86	C/C ENABLE
C/C SET/COAST	84	3	87	C/C RESUME
N/C		4	420	VCC BRAKE
N/C		5	633	CAM HI
ECM GROUND	450	6		N/C
ECM GROUND	450	7	424	BYPASS
EST REFERENCE PULSE HI	430	8	423	EST
EST REFERENCE/CAM LO	453	9	816	POWER STEERING SW
N/C		10	438	3RD GEAR SW.
N/C		11	841	INJECTOR 1
N/C		12	878	INJECTOR 8
INJECTOR 2	842	13	846	INJECTOR 6
INJECTOR 7	877	14	474	5V REFERENCE
INJECTOR 5	845	15	844	INJECTOR 4
INJECTOR 3	843	16	480	BATTERY

Fig. 59 PCM connector (Part 2 of 3). 1992 Eldorado & Seville

CIRCUIT DESCRIPTION	CIRCUIT NUMBER	PCM (1C/D) BLACK	CIRCUIT NUMBER	CIRCUIT DESCRIPTION
PCM GROUND	450	1	1586	OVERSPEED ALARM (EXP)
C/C ON-OFF	397	2	86	C/C BRAKE SWITCH
C/C SET/COAST	84	3	87	C/C RESUME
N/C		4	420	VCC BRAKE
N/C		5	633	CAM SENSOR INPUT
PCM GROUND	450	6		N/C
PCM GROUND	450	7	424	EST BYPASS
EST REFERENCE PULSE HI	430	8	423	EST OUTPUT
EST REFERENCE/CAM LO	453	9	816	POWER STEERING SW.
N/C		10	772	TRANS PRNDL INPUT B
N/C		11	841	INJECTOR 1
HEATED W.S. REQUEST	637	12	878	INJECTOR 8
INJECTOR 2	842	13	846	INJECTOR 6
INJECTOR 7	877	14	474	5V REFERENCE
INJECTOR 5	845	15	844	INJECTOR 4
INJECTOR 3	843	16	480	BATTERY

Fig. 58 ECM connector (Part 3 of 3). 1991 Eldorado & Seville

CIRCUIT DESCRIPTION	CIRCUIT NUMBER	ECM (3E/F) GREEN	CIRCUIT NUMBER	CIRCUIT DESCRIPTION
FUEL PUMP RELAY	465	1	425	ISC HI
C/C VENT	403	2	426	ISC LO
C/C SOURCE	402	3		N/C
A/C CLUTCH RELAY	762	4		N/C
N/C		5		N/C
VCC SOLENOID	422	6	436	AIR SWITCH VALVE
4TH GEAR SW.	446	7	428	CANISTER PURGE
N/C		8		N/C
N/C		9	429	AIR DIVERT VALVE
PASS KEY SYSTEM	229	10		N/C
N/C		11	976	SENSOR GND
N/C		12	462	FIXED SPARK
TPS SIGNAL	417	13	120	FUEL PUMP FEEDBACK
N/C		14	412	RIGHT O_2 SENSOR HI
MAP SIGNAL	432	15	413	RIGHT O_2 SENSOR LO
MAT SIGNAL	472	16	410	COOLANT TEMP

Fig. 59 PCM connector (Part 3 of 3). 1992 Eldorado & Seville

CIRCUIT DESCRIPTION	CIRCUIT NUMBER	PCM (3E/F) GREEN	CIRCUIT NUMBER	CIRCUIT DESCRIPTION
FUEL PUMP RELAY	465	1	425	ISC HI
C/C VENT SOLENOID	403	2	426	ISC LO
C/C VAC SOLENOID	402	3		N/C
A/C CLUTCH RELAY	762	4	1223	SHIFT B SOLENOID
VCC MOD	446	5		N/C
VCC SOLENOID	422	6	1490	CCR LIFT/DIVE OUTPUT
TRANS PRNDL INPUT C	773	7	428	CANISTER PURGE SOLND
TRANS PRNDL INPUT A	771	8		N/C
N/C		9		N/C
PASS-KEY FUEL ENABLE	229	10	1222	SHIFT A SOLENOID
N/C		11	1076	CTS/TPS SENSOR GROUND
N/C		12	462	FIXED SPARK/SET TIMING
TPS SIGNAL	417	13	120	FUEL PUMP FEEDBACK
N/C		14	412	RIGHT O_2 SENSOR HI
MAP SIGNAL	432	15	413	RIGHT O_2 SENSOR LO
MAT SIGNAL	472	16	410	COOLANT TEMP SIGNAL

BLACK
Micro-Pack 100

POWERTRAIN CONTROL MODULE (PCM)-2A/2B

CAVITY	WIRE COLOR	CIRCUIT NUMBER	DESCRIPTION
2A1	GRY	435	EGR Solenoid Control*
2A2	WHT	776	Transaxle Range Switch Input Parity
2A3	—	—	NOT USED
2A4	—	—	NOT USED
2A5	BLK/PNK	476	IAT & MAP Sensor Return
2A6	PNK/WHT	1276	Ignition 1
2A7	PNK	427	Throttle Switch Input
2A8	TAN	800	UART Data Line
2A9	TAN	800	UART Data Line
2A10	BRN/WHT	419	SERVICE ENGINE SOON Indicator Control
2A11	GRY/BLK	1269	Cooling Fan Low Speed Control
2A12	BLK/WHT	450	Ground
2B1	ORN	480	Battery
2B2	—	—	NOT USED
2B3	TAN	398	Cruise Servo Position Sensor Input HI
2B4	LT BLU/BLK	399	Cruise Servo Position Sensor Input LO
2B5	—	—	NOT USED
2B6	TAN	413	Front Oxygen Sensor LO*
2B7	PPL	1589	Front Oxygen Sensor HI*
2B8	DK GRN/WHT	1270	Cooling Fan High Speed Control
2B9	PPL	401	Vehicle Speed Sensor Input LO
2B10	YEL	400	Vehicle Speed Sensor Input HI
2B11	RED/WHT	818	Vehicle Speed Output (4,000 PPM)
2B12	DK GRN/WHT	817	Vehicle Speed Output (4,000 PPM)

* WIRING IS PRESENT WITH UNLEADED FUEL SYSTEMS NA5, NB2 OR NN5

Fig. 60 PCM connector (Part 2 of 2), 1993 Eldorado & Seville w/4.9L engine

BLACK
Micro-Pack 100

POWERTRAIN CONTROL MODULE (PCM)-1C/1D

CAVITY	WIRE COLOR	CIRCUIT NUMBER	DESCRIPTION
1C1	BRN/WHT	1586	Vehicle Speed Output (2,000 PPM) (with Leaded Fuel System NM8)
1C2	BRN	86	Cruise Brake Switch Input
1C3	GRY/BLK	87	Cruise Resume/Accel Input
1C4	PPL	420	TCC Brake Switch Input
1C5	BRN/WHT	633	Cam HI Input
1C6	—	—	NOT USED
1C7	TAN/BLK	424	Bypass Spark Output
1C8	WHT	423	Ignition Control
1C9	DK BLU/WHT	816	Power Steering Pressure Input
1C10	YEL	772	Transaxle Range Switch Input B
1C11	BLK	841	Injector 1 Control
1C12	DK BLU/WHT	878	Injector 8 Control
1C13	BLK/YEL	846	Injector 6 Control
1C14	GRY	474	5 Volt Reference
1C15	BLK/LT BLU	844	Injector 4 Control
1C16	ORN	480	Battery
1D1	BLK/WHT	450	Ground
1D2	GRY	397	Cruise Enable Input
1D3	DK BLU	84	Cruise Set/Coast Input
1D4	—	—	NOT USED
1D5	—	—	NOT USED
1D6	BLK/WHT	450	Ground
1D7	BLK/WHT	450	Ground
1D8	PPL/WHT	430	Dist Reference HI Input (Engine RPM)
1D9	BLK/RED	453	Cam Reference Lo Input
1D10	—	—	NOT USED
1D11	—	—	NOT USED
1D12	WHT	637	Fast Idle Request Input
1D13	BLK/LT GRN	842	Injector 2 Control
1D14	RED/BLK	877	Injector 7 Control
1D15	BLK/WHT	845	Injector 5 Control
1D16	BLK/PNK	843	Injector 3 Control

Fig. 60 PCM connector (Part 1 of 2), 1993 Eldorado & Seville w/4.9L engine

BLUE

Micro-Pack 100

POWERTRAIN CONTROL MODULE (PCM)-3E/3F

CAVITY	WIRE COLOR	CIRCUIT NUMBER	DESCRIPTION
3E1	BLK/RED	453	REF LO Input
3E2	PPL/WHT	430	4X REF HI Input
3E3	—	—	NOT USED
3E4	LT GRN	1222	Transaxle Shift A Solenoid Control
3E5	YEL/BLK	1223	Transaxle Shift B Solenoid Control
3E6	DK GRN	1433	Starter Inhibit Output
3E7	—	—	NOT USED
3E8	—	—	NOT USED
3E9	DK BLU	426	ISC Motor Control
3E10	LT BLU	425	ISC Motor Control
3E11	LT BLU	1715	Delivered Torque Output
3E12	DK GRN/YEL	428	Evaporative Emission Solenoid Control
3E13	TAN/BLK	422	Torque Converter Clutch Solenoid Control
3E14	—	—	NOT USED
3E15	DK GRN/YEL	762	A/C Compressor Clutch Relay Control
3E16	GRY	474	5 Volt Reference
3F1	LT BLU/BLK	647	24X REF HI Input
3F2	BRN/WHT	633	Cam HI Input
3F3	WHT	423	Ignition Control
3F4	TAN/BLK	424	Bypass Spark Output
3F5	BRN/WHT	419	SERVICE ENGINE SOON Indicator Control
3F6	—	—	NOT USED
3F7	DK GRN/WHT	1270	Cooling Fan High Speed Control
3F8	GRY/BLK	1269	Cooling Fan Low Speed Control
3F9	TAN	398	Servo Position Sensor Input (HI)
3F10	LT BLU/BLK	399	Servo Position Sensor Input (LO)
3F11	PPL	1490	Lift/Dive Signal Output
3F12	—	—	NOT USED
3F13	TAN	413	Front Heated Oxygen Sensor Input (HI)
3F14	PPL	412	Front Heated Oxygen Sensor Input (LO)
3F15	TAN	413	Rear Heated Oxygen Sensor Input (LO)
3F16	PPL	1589	Rear Heated Oxygen Sensor Input (HI)

Fig. 61 PCM connector (Part 2 of 2). 1993 Eldorado & Seville w/4.6L Northstar engine

WHITE

Micro-Pack 100

POWERTRAIN CONTROL MODULE (PCM)-2C/2D

CAVITY	WIRE COLOR	CIRCUIT NUMBER	DESCRIPTION
2C1	BLK/PNK	476	Sensor Return
2C2	BLK/WHT	450	Ground
2C3	BLK/WHT	450	Ground
2C4	ORN	480	Battery
2C5	PNK/BLK	750	Ignition 3
2C6	GRY	1714	Desired Torque Input
2C7	ORN	1725	Extended Travel Brake Switch Input
2C8	DK BLU	229	Cranking Fuel Enable
2C9	BRN	1456	EGR Valve Feedback
2C10	—	—	NOT USED
2C11	TAN	472	IAT Sensor Input
2C12	TAN	800	UART Data Line
2C13	TAN	800	UART Data Line
2C14	RED	225	Generator Control/Feedback
2C15	LT BLU/WHT	1229	Transaxle Pressure Control Solenoid Enable
2C16	RED/BLK	1228	Transaxle Pressure Solenoid Control
2D1	BLK/ORN	469	Sensor Return
2D2	BLK/WHT	450	Ground
2D3	BLK/WHT	450	Ground
2D4	ORN	480	Battery
2D5	PPL/WHT	1276	Ignition 1
2D6	PNK	114	Oil Level Switch Input
2D7	WHT	637	Fast Idle Request Input
2D8	PNK	427	Throttle Position Switch Input
2D9	ORN/BLK	434	Park/Neutral Input
2D10	YEL	1726	Brake Booster Vacuum Sensor Input
2D11	—	—	NOT USED
2D12	BRN	86	Cruise Brake Switch Input
2D13	PPL	420	TCC Brake Switch Input
2D14	GRY	397	Cruise Enable Input
2D15	DK BLU	84	Set/Coast Input
2D16	GRY/BLK	87	Resume/Accel Input

Fig. 61 PCM connector (Part 1 of 2). 1993 Eldorado & Seville w/4.6L Northstar engine

Connect: QUICK CHECKER (J34185, SPECMO QC-3 OR EQUIVALENT) or DIGITAL MULTIMETER
At: CRUISE CONTROL MODULE CONNECTOR (Disconnected)
Conditions:
- Ignore status of lights not mentioned in Quick Checker column steps.
- Ignition Switch: RUN
- When making any resistance measurements throughout this test, turn the Ignition Switch to OFF. Failure to do so could cause incorrect results and misdiagnosis.

Step	Condition	With Quick Checker, Correct Response	Without Quick Checker, Using Digital Multimeter			For Different Response:
			Meter Range	Connector Terminals	Correct Response	
1	Cruise Switch OFF	—	200 ohms	J & Ground	0 ohms	Check BLK ground wire for an open
	Cruise Switch OFF	All lights off	20 VDC	A & J, L & J, M & J, G & J	0 volts	See 3, 2
2	Cruise Switch ON	ON/OFF Light On	20 VDC	A & J	Battery voltage	See 1, 6, 2
		BRK Light On	20 VDC	G & J	Battery voltage	See 1, 4
		LAMP light On	20 VDC	B & J	Battery voltage	See 1, 2
		VENT Light On	200 ohms	C & J	30 to 55 ohms	See 1, 6, 5
		VAC Light On	200 ohms	K & J	30 to 55 ohms	See 1, 6, 5
		SPS Light On	200 ohms	F & H	15 to 20 ohms	See 1, 6, 5
		RA Light Off	20 VDC	M & J	0 volts	See 3, 7
		SC Light Off	20 VDC	L & J	0 volts	See 3, 7

Fig. 62 Diagnostic procedure, A: Isolation test (Part 1 of 3). 1991–92 Brougham

Step	Condition					
3	Cruise Switch ON, Set Switch pressed	SC Light On	20 VDC	L & J	Battery voltage	See 1, 8
		VAC & SHORT Lights OFF	—	—	—	Check CKT 402 for a short to ground. If OK see 5.
		R A Light Off	20 VDC	M & J	0 volts	See 9, 7
4	Cruise Switch in R A	R A Light On	20 VDC	M & J	Battery voltage	See 1, 8
		VENT & SHORT Lights OFF	—	—	—	Check CKT 403 for a short to ground. If OK see 5.
		SC Light Off	20 VDC	L & J	0 volts	See 10, 7
5	Cruise Switch ON, drive wheels turned by hand	VSS Light flashes On and Off	20 VDC	A & D	Pulses between approximately battery voltage and less than 2 volts	See 1, 6, 11.
6	Quick Checker not connected	—	200 ohms	F & J	Open in circuit (infinite resistance)	See 12
7	Quick Checker not connected	—	200 ohms	F & C	Open in circuit (infinite resistance)	See 13
8	Quick Checker not connected	—	200 ohms	F & K	Open in circuit (infinite resistance)	
9	Quick Checker not connected	—	200 ohms	H & C	Open in circuit (infinite resistance)	

Fig. 62 Diagnostic procedure, A: Isolation test (Part 2 of 3). 1991–92 Brougham

| 10 | Quick Checker not connected | — | 200 ohms | H & K | Open in circuit (infinite resistance) | See 13 |

- **If all measurements are correct, go to Test C: Servo Actuation Test.**

POSSIBLE CAUSES OF INCORRECT RESULTS

1. Open or high resistance circuit. Check circuit connected to terminals listed under Digital Meter.
2. Check Cruise Control Switch (see schematic).
3. Short to battery voltage. Check circuit connected to terminals listed under Digital Meter.
4. Check Brake Switch and related wiring.
5. Check Cruise Control Servo (see Cruise Control Servo Test "B").
6. Short to ground. Check circuit connected to terminals listed under Digital Meter.
7. Shorted Engage Switch.
8. Open Engage Switch.
9. Short to CKT 84.
10. Short to CKT 87.
11. Replace Vehicle Speed Sensor Buffer.
12. Disconnect Servo and repeat Step 6.
   - D If open circuit is now measured replace Cruise Control Servo.
   - D If continuity is still measured, repair short to ground in circuit 398.
13. Check Cruise Control Module and Servo for shorted connector terminals. Check harness wiring between Cruise Control Module and Servo for wire to wire shorts.

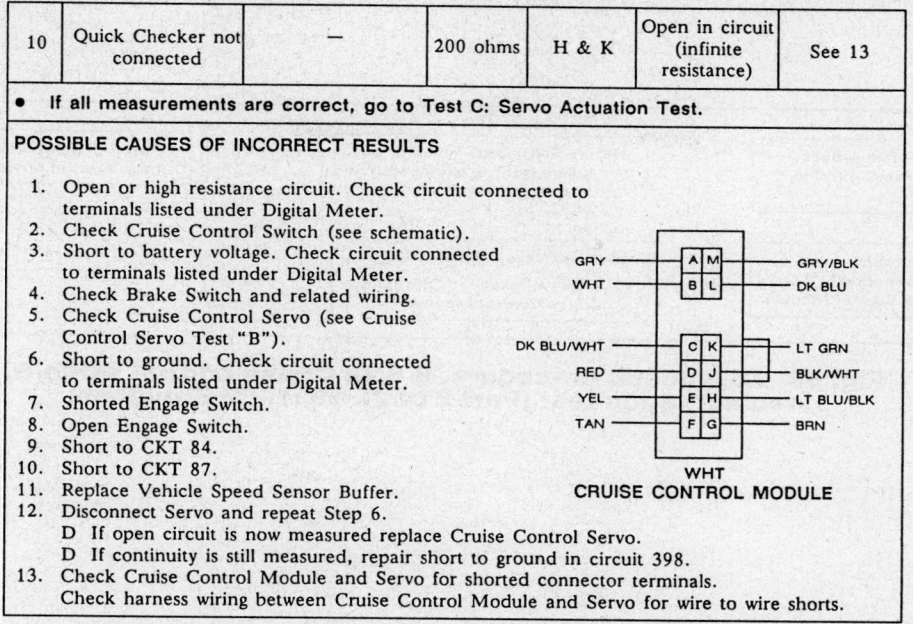

Fig. 62 Diagnostic procedure, A: Isolation test (Part 3 of 3). 1991–92 Brougham

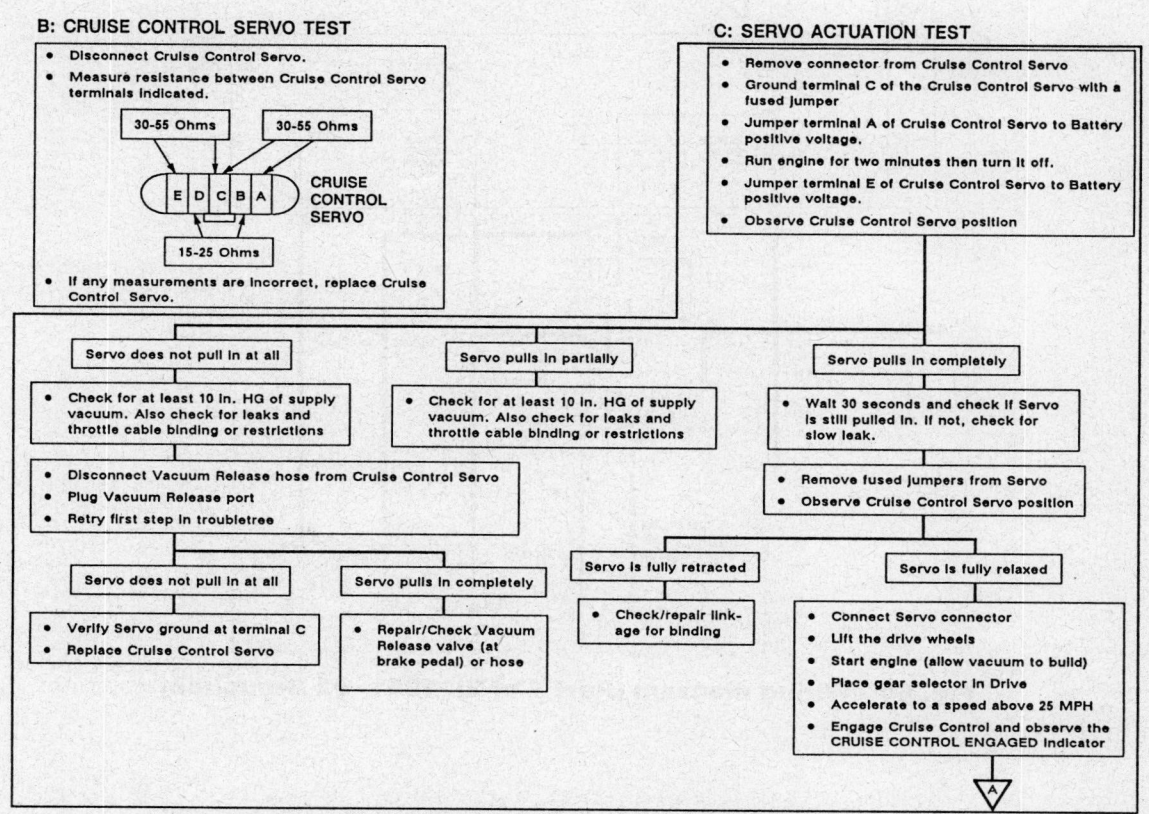

Fig. 63 Diagnostic procedure, B & C: Cruise control servo & servo actuation test (Part 1 of 2). 1991–92 Brougham

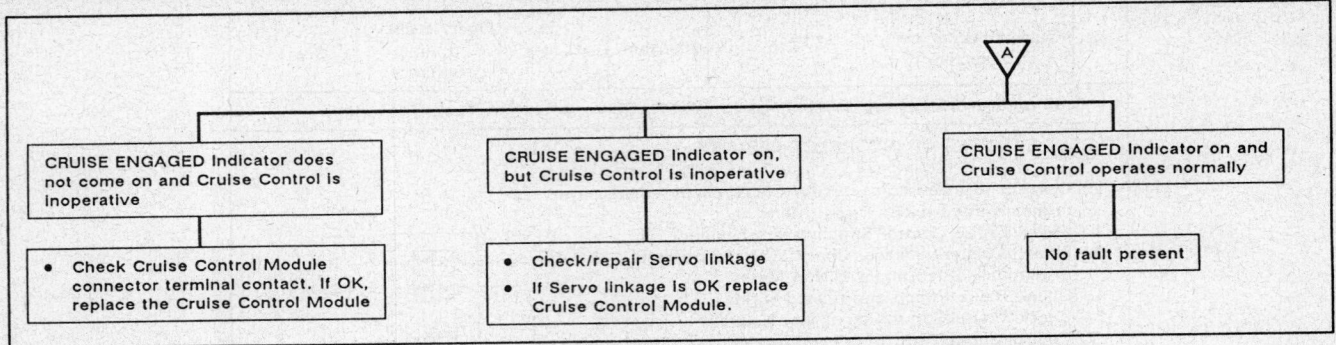

**Fig. 63   Diagnostic procedure, B & C: Cruise control servo &
servo actuation test (Part 2 of 2). 1991–92 Brougham**

Fig. 64   Wiring diagram (Part 1 of 2). 1991–92 Brougham

Fig. 64   Wiring diagram (Part 2 of 2). 1991–92 Brougham

WHITE

Printed Circuit (Edgeboard-ECM)
CRUISE CONTROL MODULE

CAVITY	WIRE COLOR SOCKET HALF	CIRCUIT NUMBER
A	GRA	397
B	YEL	400
C	DK BLU/WHT	403
D	DK GRN	389
E	—	—
F	TAN	398
G	BRN	86
H	LT BLU/BLK	399
J	BLK	151
K	LT GRN	402
L	DK BLU	84
M	GRA/BLK	87

Fig. 65   Control module connector pin locations. 1991–92 Brougham

Component Replacement

CRUISE CONTROL CABLE

1992 Fleetwood (FWD) & 1992–93 DeVille

Refer to **Fig. 66** when performing this procedure.
1. Remove air cleaner housing lid and throttle body intake ductwork.
2. Remove retainer at servo, then remove cable from rear bracket by releasing lock tangs.
3. Remove accelerator cable, clip and cruise control cable from air cleaner housing.
4. Remove accelerator cable and cruise control cable from front bracket by releasing locking tang.
5. Disconnect cruise control cable from throttle lever, then remove cable.
6. Reverse procedure to install, adjusting cable as outlined.

SERVO UNIT

Brougham

1. Disconnect electrical connector and vacuum hoses.
2. Disconnect throttle cable, throttle actuating chain or actuating rod from servo unit.
3. Remove screws securing servo unit and servo unit solenoid valve assembly to mounting bracket.
4. Reverse procedure to install. **Torque** servo unit mounting bracket screws 10-15 inch lbs.

1991 DeVille & Fleetwood (FWD)

Refer to **Fig. 67**, for replacement procedure.

1992 Fleetwood (FWD) & 1992–93 DeVille

1. Disconnect cruise control cable at retainer.
2. Disconnect vacuum hoses and electrical connector.
3. Remove mounting bracket and nut, then servo and bracket assembly.
4. Remove servo retaining screws, then servo.
5. Reverse procedure to install. **Torque** servo to bracket screws to 12 inch lbs. **Torque** mounting bracket nut and bolt to 13 ft. lbs. Adjust cruise control cable as outlined.6

Eldorado & Seville

1. Disconnect electrical connector from servo unit.
2. Remove vacuum hoses from servo unit.
3. Disconnect throttle cable or throttle actuator rod from servo unit.
4. Remove screws securing servo unit to mounting bracket.
5. Reverse procedure to install. **Torque** servo unit mounting bracket screws 11-15 inch lbs.

1	SCREW; 1.4 N·m (12 LB-FT)	10	BRACKET
2	BRACKET	11	ACCELERATOR CONTROL CABLE
3	SERVO ASSEMBLY	12	AIR CLEANER COVER ASSEMBLY
4	GENERATOR	13	CLIP
5	BOLT; 17 N·m (13 LB-FT)	14	AIR CLEANER HOUSING ASSEMBLY
6	NUT; 17 N·m (13 LB-FT)	15	THROTTLE VALVE CABLE ASSEMBLY
7	RETAINER	16	BRACKET
8	SERVO CABLE		
9	SERVO BLADE		

Fig. 66 Cruise control replacement. 1992 Fleetwood (FWD) & 1992–93 DeVille

ELECTRIC BRAKE RELEASE SWITCH & VACUUM DUMP VALVE

Electric Brake Release Switch

An inoperative switch must be replaced. Install new switch and adjust as described under "Brake Release Switch Adjustment" previously outlined.

Vacuum Dump Valve

An inoperative switch must be replaced. Install new switch and adjust as described under "Vacuum Release Valve" previously outlined.

ENGAGEMENT SWITCH

The engagement switch cannot be serviced. The complete turn signal lever must be replaced as an assembly.

1. Disconnect battery ground cable.
2. Remove steering column lower cover and remove tape securing wire to column.
3. Disconnect cruise control switch connector and attach a suitable piece of wire to switch connector.
4. Remove turn signal lever by pulling it out of the detent retaining clip inside the steering column. **On some models, it may be necessary to remove steering wheel.**
5. Pull harness up gently so guide wire can be used to install new unit.
6. Reverse procedure to install.

SPEED SENSOR & HARNESS

Access to the speed sensor and harness assembly is gained by partially removing the speedometer cluster and disconnecting the electrical connector at the

1. SCREW; 1.4 N•M (12 LB-IN)
2. BRACKET
3. SERVO ASSEMBLY
4. GENERATOR
5. BOLT; 17 N•M (13 LB-FT)
6. NUT; 17 N•M (13 LB-FT)
7. RETAINER
8. SERVO CABLE
9. SERVO BLADE
10. BRACKET
11. ACCELERATOR CONTROL CABLE
12. AIR CLEANER COVER ASSEMBLY
13. CLIP
14. AIR CLEANER HOUSING ASSEMBLY
15. THROTTLE VALVE CABLE ASSEMBLY
16. BRACKET

Fig. 67 Cruise control servo. DeVille & 1991–92 Fleetwood (FWD)

cluster and electronic controller ends of the harness. Refer to "Instrument Cluster, Replace" for partial removal of the speedometer cluster.

BUFFER AMPLIFIER
1991–92 Brougham

1. Disconnect battery ground cable.

2. Remove RH hush panel, then two screws from ECM bracket.
3. Disconnect electrical connector, then buffer amplifier.
4. Reverse procedure to install.

CONTROLLER
1991–92 Brougham

1. Remove radio.

2. Disconnect cruise module electrical connectors.
3. Remove control module attaching screws to right of steering column, then remove module.
4. Reverse procedure to install.

DeVille & 1991–92 Fleetwood (FWD)

1. Remove steering column lower cover.
2. Disconnect electrical connectors from controller.
3. Remove screws securing controller to steering column lower cover.
4. Reverse procedure to install.

Eldorado & Seville

1. Disconnect battery ground cable.
2. Remove lower instrument panel cover.
3. Unclip relay panel from twilight sentinel amplifier and cruise control controller mounting bracket, located to the left of the steering column.
4. Remove screws securing controller mounting bracket to instrument panel assembly.
5. Lower mounting bracket and disconnect electrical connectors from cruise control controller.
6. Remove screws securing controller to mounting bracket and remove controller.
7. Reverse procedure to install.

SERVO UNIT SOLENOID VALVE

1. Remove screw securing solenoid valve to servo unit.
2. Disconnect vacuum hose and electrical connector and pull solenoid valve away from the servo unit.
3. Reverse procedure to install.

VACUUM CONTROL SOLENOID VALVE

1. Disconnect one electrical connector and two vacuum hoses from valve.
2. Remove screw securing valve to servo unit mounting bracket on front of dash bracket.
3. Reverse procedure to install.

NOTE: On Vehicles Equipped With Airbags, Disarm Airbag As Outlined Under "Airbag System Disarming" Before Any Diagnosis, Testing, Troubleshooting Or Repairs Are Performed. After All Diagnosis, Testing, Troubleshooting Or Repairs Have Been Completed, Rearm Airbag As Outlined Under "Airbag System Arming."

NOTE: Wire Color Code Identification And Symbol Identification Located In The Front Of This Manual Can Be Used As An Aid When Using The Wiring Circuits Found In This Section.

INDEX

PRECAUTIONS

AIRBAG SYSTEM DISARMING

Beretta, Corsica, Corvette, LeSabre & 1991–92 Camaro & Firebird

The diagnostic energy reserve module (DERM) can maintain voltage to cause a system deployment for up to ten minutes after the ignition switch is turned off and the battery is disconnected. Servicing the SIR system during this period may result in accidental deployment and personal injury.

1. Ensure front wheels are pointed straight ahead.
2. Turn ignition switch to LOCK position and remove SIR or AIRBAG fuse.
3. Remove left sound insulator. **Remove courtesy lamp from sound insula-**tor, if necessary.
4. Remove Connector Position Assurance (CPA), then disconnect yellow two-way SIR electrical connector at base of steering column.

1991 88

The diagnostic energy reserve module (DERM) can maintain voltage to cause a system deployment for up to ten minutes after the ignition switch is turned off and the battery is discon-

nected. Servicing the SIR system during this period may result in accidental deployment and personal injury.
1. Turn ignition switch to OFF position, then remove I/P fuse 7 from fuse block.
2. Disconnect yellow two-way SIR electrical connector at base of steering column.

1991–92 Caprice, Custom Cruiser & Roadmaster

The diagnostic energy reserve module (DERM) can maintain voltage to cause a system deployment for up to ten minutes after the ignition switch is turned off and the battery is disconnected. Servicing the SIR system during this period may result in accidental deployment and personal injury.
1. Ensure front wheels are pointed straight ahead.
2. Turn ignition switch to LOCK position and remove SIR fuse from fuse block.
3. Remove Connector Position Assurance (CPA), then disconnect yellow two-way SIR electrical connector at base of steering column.

AIRBAG SYSTEM ARMING

Beretta, Corsica, Corvette, LeSabre & 1991–92 Camaro & Firebird

1. Connect yellow two-way SIR electrical connector, then install Connector Position Assurance (CPA).
2. Install left sound insulator. **Install courtesy lamp to sound insulator, if applicable.**
3. Install SIR fuse to fuse block, turn ignition switch to RUN position and ensure that "Inflatable Restraint" lamp flashes 7 to 9 times, then turns off.

1991 88

1. Connect yellow two-way SIR electrical connector at base of steering column.
2. Install I/P fuse 7 into fuse block, turn ignition switch to RUN position and ensure that "Inflatable Restraint" indicator flashes 7 to 9 times, then turns off.

1991–92 Caprice, Custom Cruiser & Roadmaster

The diagnostic energy reserve module (DERM) can maintain voltage to cause a system deployment for up to ten minutes after the ignition switch is turned off and the battery is disconnected. Servicing the SIR system during this period may result in accidental deployment and personal injury.
1. Ensure front wheels are pointed straight ahead.
2. Turn ignition switch to Lock position and remove SIR or AIR BAG fuse from fuse block.
3. Remove Connector Position Assurance (CPA), then disconnect yellow two-way SIR electrical connector at base of steering column.

DESCRIPTION

This system consists of a mode control assembly, electronic controller (module), Vehicle Speed Sensor (VSS) buffer amplifier, servo unit, and release switches and valves. The servo unit maintains vehicle speed (throttle position) by trapping vacuum in its diaphragm chamber at servo positions determined by the control module. The module monitors mode control switch position, signals from the VSS buffer amplifier, servo position and release switch operation, then operates vacuum valves within the servo unit to control servo operation and vehicle speed. The module also contains a speed limiting function which prevents system operation at speeds below approximately 25 mph.

The mode control assembly consists of a 3 position slide-type switch and a set/coast switch button. To operate the system, the slide switch must be in on position and vehicle speed must be above 25 mph. The system is engaged at the desired speed by fully depressing, then releasing the set/coast button. Cruise speed can be increased from the set position by accelerating vehicle to desired speed, then pressing and releasing button. In order to decrease speed, the set/coast button is held in the fully-depressed position (disengaging system), then released when the desired speed is reached. The system can be disengaged at any time by depressing the brake or clutch pedal, or by moving the slide switch to off position.

If the system is disengaged by depressing the brake or clutch pedal, the last set speed will be retained in the module memory until the slide switch or ignition switch is moved to off position. Momentarily moving the slide switch to the resume/accel. position will cause the vehicle to accelerate to the last set speed and maintain that speed. If the slide switch is held in the resume/accel. position, the vehicle will continue to accelerate until the switch is released. When the switch is released, the speed that the vehicle accelerated to becomes the new set speed.

The slide switch also allows a tap-up function to increase cruise set speed in 1 mph increments. With the cruise control engaged and operating, tapping-up is done by pressing the slide switch to the resume position, then quickly releasing it. This procedure can be repeated 10 times before the system must be reset to a new speed in the conventional manner.

SYSTEM COMPONENTS
SPEED SENSOR

On models with conventional instrument panels, a speedometer frame mounted optic head is used to pick up light reflected by a speedometer cable mounted blade. The reflected light is produced by a light emitting diode (L.E.D.). As the speedometer cable mounted blade enters the L.E.D. light beam, the light is reflected into the optic head. From there, the light enters a photocell in the optic head and produces a low power speed signal. This signal is sent to a buffer for amplification and conditioning, then to the controller.

On models with electronic speedometers or electronic instrumentation, a transmission mounted speed sensor is used. This sensor utilizes a permanent magnet (PM) to generate vehicle speed information to the controller. Some models use a buffer amplifier to modify the sensor output.

CRUISE CONTROL MODULE

The module will interpret the position of the servo, the position of the control switches and the output of the speed sensor. In response to these inputs, the module electrically signals the opening or closing of the vent and vacuum solenoid valves in the servo.

The module is mounted on the dash support bracket at the right side of the steering column, but is integral with the ECM on some models with certain engines.

VACUUM RELEASE VALVE

The vacuum release valve provides an additional vent to atmosphere for the servo unit when the brake pedal is held in the depressed position. The venting is spring actuated and occurs within the free travel of the brake pedal arm.

COMBINATION VACUUM RELEASE VALVE/CONVERTER CLUTCH SWITCH

This combination valve and switch is used on vehicles equipped with a lock-up torque converter. The vacuum release valve portion operates identically to the release valve previously described. At the same time, the converter clutch switch contacts open and the locking clutch mechanism in the transmission is disengaged.

COMBINATION CRUISE/STOP LIGHT SWITCH

A separately mounted vacuum release valve is used with this combination switch. When the brake pedal is depressed, the switch resets the cruise function to a non-cruise condition and illuminates the brake lights. Two sets of electrical contacts are used in the switch: one to operate the stop lights, and the other to operate the cruise release function.

CLUTCH SWITCH

The clutch switch is used on vehicles equipped with manual transmission. When the clutch pedal is depressed, the cruise function is disconnected and will remain so after the pedal is released.

SERVO UNIT

The servo unit, **Fig. 1**, operates the throttle in response to signals from the electronic controller.

During a steady speed cruise condition, both vacuum and vent valves are closed or sealed. The servo holds a constant vacuum on the diaphragm and places no flow requirements on the vacuum source.

During vehicle deceleration, the vacuum

INTERNAL VIEW

TO VACUUM SUPPLY

TO VACUUM BRAKE RELEASE VALVE

1. SERVO
2. VACUUM SOLENOID AND VALVE (NORMALLY CLOSED)
3. COIL
4. VARIABLE INDUCTANCE POSITION SENSOR
5. VENT SOLENOID AIR VALVE (NORMALLY OPEN)
6. STEEL CORE
7. SERVO BLADE

Fig. 1   Servo unit

Connect: QUICK CHECKER (J34185, SPECMO QC-3 OR EQUIVALENT) or DIGITAL MULTI-METER
At: CRUISE CONTROL MODULE CONNECTOR (Disconnected)
Condition:
- **Ignition Switch: RUN**

TEST	Condition	With Quick Checker, Correct Response	Without Quick Checker, Using Digital Multi-Meter			For Different Response, Do Test:
			Meter Range	Connector Terminals	Correct Response	
1	Cruise Switch OFF	—	200 ohms	J & Ground	0 ohms	B
		All Lights OFF	20 VDC	A & J	0 volts	A
			20 VDC	M & J	0 volts	A
2	Cruise Switch ON	ON/OFF Light On	20 VDC	A & J	Battery voltage	B
		BRK Light On	20 VDC	G & J	Battery voltage	C
		VENT Light On	200 ohms	C & J	30 to 55 ohms	D
		VAC Light On	200 ohms	K & J	30 to 55 ohms	E
		SPS Light On	200 ohms	F & H	15 to 25 ohms	F
		RA Light Off	20 VDC	M & J	0 volts	A
		SC Light Off	20 VDC	L & J	0 volts	A

Fig. 2   Cruise control system diagnosis chart (Part 1 of 2). 1991 Bonneville

TEST	Condition	With Quick Checker, Correct Response	Without Quick Checker, Using Digital Multi-Meter			For Different Response, Do Test:
			Meter Range	Connector Terminals	Correct Response	
3	Cruise Switch ON, Set Switch pressed	SC Light On	20 VDC	L & J	Battery voltage	G
		VAC & SHORT Lights Off	200 ohms	K & J	30 to 55 ohms	H
4	Cruise Switch in R/A	ON/OFF Light On	20 VDC	A & J	Battery voltage	B
		RA Light On	20 VDC	M & J	Battery voltage	I
		VENT & SHORT Lights Off	200 ohms	C & J	30 to 55 ohms	J
5	Cruise Switch ON, drive wheels turned by hand	VSS Light flashes On and Off	20 VDC	A & D	Pulses between approximately battery voltage and less than 7 volts	K, L
6	Run engine for one minute, then turn it off. With Ignition Switch in RUN and holding Cruise Switch in R/A, press Set Switch, wait for Cruise Control Servo to pull in and release Set Switch	Vacuum holds the servo all the way in	Connect fused jumper from C to M and from K to L before operating switches		Vacuum holds the servo all the way in	M
7	Quick Checker not connected	—	200 ohms	F & J	Over range	N

- If all the responses were correct, replace the Cruise Control Module. Check for proper operation.

Fig. 2   Cruise control system diagnosis chart (Part 2 of 2). 1991 Bonneville

Connect: QUICK CHECK (J-34185, SPECMO QC-3 OR EQUIVALENT) OR DIGITAL VOLTMETER
At: CRUISE CONTROL MODULE CONNECTOR (Disconnected)
Condition:
- **Ignition Switch: RUN**

Test	Condition	With Quick Checker, Correct Response	Without Quick Checker, Using a Digital Meter			For Different Response, Do Test:
			Meter Range	Connector Terminals	Correct Response	
1	Cruise Switch: OFF	—	200 ohms	J & Ground	0 ohms	B
		All Lights Off	20 VDC	A & J	0 volts	A
			20 VDC	M & J	0 volts	A
	(Digital Cluster Only)	LAMP Light On	20 VDC	B & J	Battery voltage	O
2	Cruise Switch: ON	ON/OFF Light On	20 VDC	A & J	Battery voltage	B
		BRK Light On	20 VDC	G & J	Battery voltage	C
		VENT Light On	200 ohms	C & J	30 to 55 ohms	D
		VAC Light On	200 ohms	K & J	30 to 55 ohms	E
		SPS Light On	200 ohms	F & H	15 to 25 ohms	F
		RA Light Off	20 VDC	M & J	0 volts	A
		SC Light Off	20 VDC	L & J	0 volts	A
3	Cruise Switch ON Set Switch pressed	SC Light On	20 VDC	L & J	Battery voltage	G
		VAC & SHORT Lights Off	200 ohms	K & J	30 to 55 Ohms	H
4	Cruise Switch in R/A	ON/OFF Light ON	20 VDC	A & J	Battery voltage	B
		RA Light On	20 VDC	M & J	Battery voltage	I
		VENT & SHORT Lights Off	200 ohms	C & J	30 to 55 ohms	J
5	Cruise Switch ON, drive wheels turned by hand	VSS Light flashes On and Off	20 VDC	A & D	Pulses between approximately battery voltage and less than 7 volts	K, L
6	Run engine for one minute, then turn it off. With Ignition Switch in RUN, and holding Cruise Switch in R/A, press Set Switch, wait for Servo to pull in and release Set Switch	Vacuum holds the servo all the way in	Connect fused jumpers from C to M and from K to L before operating switches		Vacuum holds the servo all the way in	M
7	Quick Checker not connected	—	200 ohms	F & J	Over range	N

- If all the responses were correct, replace the Cruise Control Module and check for proper operation.

Fig. 3   Cruise control system diagnostic chart. 1991-92 LeMans

solenoid is energized by the controller to open vacuum valve to vacuum source. Throttle angle is increased by increased vacuum level in the servo, and the vent remains closed.

During vehicle acceleration, the vent solenoid is de-energized by the controller to open the vent valve to atmosphere. This reduces vacuum in the servo and allows throttle return spring to decrease throttle angle while the vacuum valve remains closed.

SERVICE PRECAUTIONS

On vehicles equipped with ABS brake system, the hydraulic accumulator, when fully charged contains brake fluid at high pressure. Before disconnecting any lines, hoses or fittings, ensure accumulator is full depressurized. Failure to do so may result in personal injury.

To depressurize the hydraulic accumulator, turn the ignition to the Off position or disconnect negative battery cable, pump brake pedal a minimum of 40 times at approximately 50 lbs. of force. A noticeable change in pedal feel will occur when accumulator is fully discharged.

DIAGNOSIS & TESTING 1991 Models Except Corvette, Cutlass Supreme, Grand Prix, LeSabre, Lumina, Park Avenue, Regal, 88 & 98

TROUBLESHOOTING

1. Check vacuum hoses for leaks, kinks and restrictions, and the cruise control servo linkage for proper slack.

2. If system works except for tap-up and tap-down functions, replace cruise control module.

ROAD TEST

1. Drive vehicle at speed greater than 25 mph, place cruise switch in On position and depress set button at end of multi-function lever. Cruise indicator should illuminate and vehicle should maintain speed.
2. With foot off accelerator, hold set button in. Vehicle should coast at a slower speed.

Connect: QUICK CHECKER (J 34185, SPECMO QC-3 OR EQUIVALENT) or DIGITAL MULTIMETER
At: CRUISE CONTROL MODULE CONNECTOR (Disconnected) –
Conditions:
• Ignition Switch: RUN
• Test with quick Checker (J 34185 or equivalent) or Digital Multimeter

Check	Condition	With Quick Checker, Correct Response	Without Quick Checker, Using a Digital Meter			For Different Result, Do Test:
			Meter Range	Connector Terminals	Correct Result	
1	Cruise Switch OFF	—	200 ohms	J & Ground	0 ohms	B
			20 VDC	A & J	0 volts	
		All Lights Off	20 VDC	M & J	0 volts	A
2	Cruise Switch ON	ON/OFF Light On	20 VDC	A & J	Battery voltage	B
		BRK Light On	20 VDC	G & J	Battery voltage	C
		VENT Light On	200 ohms	C & J	30 to 55 ohms	D
		VAC Light On	200 ohms	K & J	30 to 55 ohms	E
		SPS Light On	200 ohms	F & H	15 to 25 ohms	F
		RA Light Off	20 VDC	M & J	0 volts	A
		SC Light Off	20 VDC	L & J	0 volts	A

**Fig. 4   Cruise control system diagnostic chart
(Part 1 of 2). 1991–92 Camaro & Firebird**

Check	Condition	With Quick Checker, Correct Response	Without Quick Checker, Using a Digital Meter			For Different Result, Do Test
			Meter Range	Connector Terminals	Correct Result	
3	Cruise Switch ON Set Switch pressed	SC Light On	20 VDC	L & J	Battery voltage	G
		VAC & SHORT Lights Off	200 ohms	K & J	30 to 55 ohms	H
4	Cruise Switch in R/A	ON/OFF Light ON	20 VDC	A & J	Battery voltage	B
		RA Light On	20 VDC	M & J	Battery voltage	I
		VENT & SHORT Lights Off	200 ohms	C & J	30 to 55 ohms	J
5	Cruise Switch ON, drive wheels turned by hand	VSS Light flashes On and Off	20 VDC	A & D	Pulses between approximately battery voltage and less than 7 volts	K, L
6	Run engine for one minute, then turn it off. With Ignition Switch in RUN and holding Cruise Switch in R/A, press Set Switch, wait for Servo to pull in, and release Set Switch.	Vacuum holds the servo all the way in	Connect fused jumpers from C to M and from K to L before operating switches		Vacuum holds the servo all the way in	M
7	Quick Checker not connected		200 ohms	F & J	Over range	N
8	Quick Checker not connected	—	200 ohms	F & C	Open circuit (infinite resistance)	
9	Quick Checker not connected	—	200 ohms	F & K	Open circuit (infinite resistance)	O
10	Quick Checker not connected	—	200 ohms	H & C	Open circuit (infinite resistance)	
11	Quick Checker not connected	—	200 ohms	H & K	Open circuit (infinite resistance)	

• If all results are correct, replace Cruise Control Module and check for normal operation.

**Fig. 4   Cruise control system diagnostic chart
(Part 2 of 2). 1991–92 Camaro & Firebird**

3. Release set button. If new speed is greater than 25 mph, cruise control should engage and hold slower speed.
4. Slide cruise switch to Resume/Accel position and hold it there. Vehicle should accelerate.
5. Release cruise switch back to On position. Vehicle should hold new, faster speed.
6. Tap brake pedal. Vehicle should coast slower and cruise indicator should go out.
7. Slide cruise control switch momentarily to Resume/Accel position. Cruise indicator should illuminate and vehicle should accelerate to former set speed.
8. While cruising, accelerate, then remove foot from accelerator pedal. Vehicle should coast back to set speed.
9. While cruising, tap cruise switch to Resume/Accel position. Vehicle speed should decrease 1 mph for each tap up to ten.
10. While cruising, tap set button. Vehicle speed should decrease 1 mph for each tap down to 25 mph.
11. Slide cruise control switch to Off position. Cruise control should turn off and cruise indicator should go out.

SYSTEM DIAGNOSIS, 1991 BERETTA, BONNEVILLE, CORSICA & 1991–92 CAMARO, FIREBIRD & LEMANS

Perform tests as shown, **Figs. 2 through 4.** If results are other than specified, perform designated test. **Do not press set switch and Resume/Accel position of cruise switch at same time while engine is running. If quick checker displays a short light, release switches immediately.**

When performing the following tests refer to wiring diagram and control module pin connectors **Figs. 5 through 8,** for basic outlines.

TEST A
Except Beretta & Corsica
1. Check for shorts to voltage in wires to terminals A, G, L and M of cruise control module.
2. If wires are satisfactory, replace multi-function lever.

Beretta & Corsica
1. Check for short to voltage in wires to terminals A (gray wire) G (dark green wire) L (dark blue wire) and M (gray black wire) of cruise control module.
2. If wires are satisfactory, check multi-function lever and cruise control switches for a short, replacing as necessary.

Fig. 5   Typical cruise control wiring diagram (Part 1 of 2). 1991 Bonneville & LeMans

Fig. 5   Typical cruise control wiring diagram (Part 2 of 2). 1991 Bonneville & LeMans

Fig. 6   Cruise control wiring diagram (Part 1 of 2). 1991–92 Camaro & Firebird

Fig. 6   Cruise control wiring diagram (Part 2 of 2). 1991–92 Camaro & Firebird

Fig. 7 Cruise control module connector pin location

TEST B

1991–92 LeMans

1. Check gages, cruise, and radio fuses, as equipped, or fuse No. 13.
2. Ensure terminal J of cruise control module is grounded.
3. Disconnect connector C223 check for battery voltage at terminal A (red wire) with ignition in Run position. If battery voltage is not available, check red wire and fuse box auxiliary connector.
4. Check continuity between terminals A (red wire) and B (gray wire) of connector C223 with cruise switch in On position. If there is no continuity, replace multi-function switch.
5. Check for open in gray wire (circuit 397) between terminal B of connector C223 and terminal A of cruise control module connector.

Cavalier, Ciera, Sunbird & 6000

1. Check radio fuse.
2. Ensure terminal J of cruise control module is grounded.
3. Disconnect connector C235 and check for battery voltage at terminal A (brown/white wire) with ignition in Run position. If battery voltage is not available on 6000, check yellow wire (circuit 43) or brown/white wire (circuit 141). If battery voltage is not available on Cavalier, Ciera or Sunbird, check brown/white wire (circuit 141).
4. Check continuity between terminals A (blue wire) and B (green wire) of connector C235 with cruise switch in On position. If there is no continuity, replace multi-function lever.
5. Check for open in gray wire (circuit 397) between terminal B of connector C235 and terminal A of cruise control module connector.

1991 Bonneville

1. Check gages and radio fuses, or No. 18 (Bonneville).
2. Ensure terminal J of cruise control module is grounded.
3. Disconnect connector C235 or C211 (1991-92 Camaro and Firebird) and check for battery voltage at terminal A (yellow wire on Calais) (pink/black wire all other models) with ignition in Run position. If battery voltage is not available, check pink/black wire (circuit 141, Caprice and LeSabre, and Custom Cruiser; circuit 43, Skylark

and Grand Am; circuit 239, Bonneville; circuit 39 Camaro and Firebird) and yellow wire (circuit 43, Calais, Grand Am, and Skylark).
4. Check continuity between terminals A (blue wire) and B (green wire, except Bonneville; red wire, Bonneville) of connector C235 with cruise switch in On position. If there is no continuity, replace multi-function lever.
5. Check for open in gray wire (circuit 397) between terminal B of connector C235 (except Camaro and Firebird) or C211 (1991-92 Camaro and Firebird) and terminal A of cruise control module connector.

Beretta & Corsica

1. Check fuse No. 14.
2. Ensure terminal L (black wire) of cruise control module is grounded.
3. Disconnect connector C235 and check for battery voltage at terminal A (brown/white wire) of harness half with ignition switch in Run position. If battery voltage is not available, check brown/white wire (circuit 141) for an open.
4. Check continuity between terminals A (blue wire) and C (green wire) of pin half of connector C235 with cruise switch in On position. If there is no continuity, check multi-function lever and cruise control switches for an open, replacing as necessary.
5. Check for an open in gray wire (circuit 397) between terminal C of connector C235 and terminal A of cruise control module connector.

TEST C

1. Check for open in brake or clutch switch.
2. **On 1991 Bonneville,** check for open in brown/white wire (circuit 86) to terminal G of cruise control module.
3. **On Beretta and Corsica,** check brown wire (circuit 86) for an open.
4. **On Camaro and Firebird,** check for an open in brown wire (circuit 86) gray/white wire or gray wire (circuit 397).
5. **On LeMans,** check for open in gray and gray/black wires between the cruise control module, brake switch and clutch switch.

TEST D

1. If measurement is less than 30 ohms, proceed to test J. Otherwise, remove connector from cruise control servo and measure resistance between terminals A and C of servo.
2. If resistance is greater than 55 ohms, replace cruise control servo.
3. If resistance is less than 55 ohms, check for open in dark blue or dark blue/white wire (circuit 403) between terminal C of cruise control module and terminal A of cruise control servo. Ensure terminal C of servo connector is grounded.

TEST E

1. If measurement was less than 30

Fig. 8 Cruise control module connector pin location

ohms, proceed to test H. Otherwise, remove connector from cruise control servo and measure resistance between terminals E and C of servo.
2. If resistance is greater than 55 ohms, replace cruise control servo.
3. If resistance is less than 55 ohms, check for open in light green wire (circuit 402) between terminal K of cruise control module and terminal E of cruise control servo. Ensure terminal C of servo connector is grounded.

TEST F

1. If measurement was less than 15 ohms, proceed to test N. Otherwise, remove connector from cruise control servo and measure resistance between terminals B and D of servo.
2. If resistance is greater than 25 ohms, replace cruise control servo.
3. If resistance is less than 25 ohms, check for open in light blue/black and light blue wires (circuit 399) between terminal H of cruise control module and terminal D of cruise control servo. Also, check for open in tan wire (circuit 398) between terminal F of module and terminal B of servo.

TEST G

Except Beretta, Corsica & 1991–92 Camaro & Firebird

1. Disconnect connector C235 (except LeMans) or C223 (LeMans) and check switch continuity between terminals B (green wire, gray wire on LeMans) and D (red wire, C (red wire) with set switch pressed.
2. If there is no continuity, replace multi-function lever.
3. If there is continuity, check for open in dark blue wire (circuit 84) between terminal D of connector C235 (except LeMans) or C223 (LeMans) and terminal L of cruise control module.

Beretta & Corsica

1. Disconnect connector C235 and check switch continuity between terminals C and D of pin half with set/coast switch depressed.
2. If there is no continuity, check multi-function lever and cruise control switches for an open, replacing as necessary.
3. If switches are not open, check for an open in dark blue wire (circuit 84) be-

tween terminal D of connector C235 and terminal J of cruise control module.

1991–92 Camaro & Firebird

1. Disconnect connector C211 and check switch continuity between terminals L and K of the pin half with the set switch pressed.
2. If there is no continuity, replace multi-function lever.
3. If the switch is not open, check for an open in dark blue wire (circuit 84) between terminal K of connector C211 and terminal L of cruise control module.

TEST H

1. Remove connector from servo and measure resistance between terminals C and E of servo.
2. If resistance is less than 30 ohms, replace cruise control servo.
3. **Except on Caprice,** if resistance is 30 ohms or greater, check for short to ground in light green wire (circuit 402) from terminal K of cruise control module to terminal E of cruise control servo.
4. **On Caprice,** if resistance is 30 ohms or greater, check for a short to ground in dark blue wire (circuit 403) from terminal C of cruise control module and terminal A of cruise control servo.

TEST I

Except Beretta, Corsica & 1991–92 Camaro & Firebird

1. Disconnect connector C235 (except LeMans) or C223 (LeMans) and check switch continuity between terminals A and C or D with cruise switch in Resume/Accel position.
2. If there is no continuity, replace multi-function lever.
3. If there is continuity, check for open in gray/black wire or gray/white wire (circuit 87, except Caprice and LeMans or dark green wire (circuit 83, Caprice and LeMans between terminal C (except 1991 Bonneville) or D (Calais and Ciera) of connector C235 (except LeMans) or C223 (LeMans) and terminal M of cruise control module.

Beretta & Corsica

1. Disconnect connector C235 and check switch continuity between terminals A and B of pin half with resume/accel switch pressed.
2. If there is no continuity, check multi-function lever and cruise control switches for an open.
3. If switches are not open, check for an open in gray/black wire (circuit 87) between terminal B of connector C235 and terminal terminal M of cruise control module.

1991–92 Camaro & Firebird

1. Disconnect C211 and check switch continuity between terminals M and J of the pin half with the cruise switch in resume/accel position.
2. If there is no continuity, replace multi-function lever.

3. If the switch does not open, check for open in gray/black wire (circuit 87), between terminal J of connector C211 and terminal M of cruise control module.

TEST J

1. Remove connector from cruise control servo and measure resistance between terminals A and C of servo.
2. If resistance is less than 30 ohms, replace cruise control servo.
3. If resistance is 30 ohms or greater, check for short to ground in dark blue/white wire or dark blue wire (circuit 403) from terminal C of cruise control module to terminal A of cruise control servo.

TEST K

If VSS light does not illuminate, or voltage between terminals A and D remains less than 7 volts or less than 4 volts check for open in red wire (circuit 381) brown or brown/red wire (circuit 437) gray/black wire (circuit 938) yellow wire (circuit 400) or green/white or dark green wire (circuit 389) from vehicle speed sensor buffer or ECM.

TEST L

If VSS light does not go off or battery voltage remains between terminals A and D, check for short to ground on red wire (circuit 381) brown or brown/red wire (circuit 437) gray/black wire (circuit 938) yellow wire (circuit 400) or green/white or dark green wire (circuit 389) from vehicle speed sensor buffer or ECM.

TEST M

1. Check for blocked or leaking vacuum source. If vacuum source is satisfactory, plug vacuum release port and repeat test 6, **Figs. 2 through 4.**
2. If vacuum now holds throttle open, repair or replace vacuum release valve or the hose to the valve.
3. If test still fails, replace cruise control servo.

TEST N

1. Disconnect cruise control servo connector and repeat test 7, **Figs. 2 through 4.**
2. If resistance is now over range, replace cruise control servo.
3. If resistance is still low, repair short in tan wire (circuit 398) from terminal F of cruise control module to terminal B of cruise control servo.

TEST O,

Except Beretta & Corsica

If all other tests in **Figs. 2 through 5** were satisfactory, replace cruise control servo.

Beretta & Corsica

1. Check resistance between grounds G100 and G101.
2. If resistance exceeds .1 ohm, clean and tighten both grounds and the negative battery cable. If ground circuit is suspect, add a ground strap between engine block and bulkhead.
3. If resistance is less than .1 ohm, replace cruise control module and check for normal operation.

1991–92 SYSTEM DIAGNOSIS, EXCEPT BONNEVILLE, CAMARO, CAPRICE, CUSTOM CRUISER, FIREBIRD, LEMANS, ROADMASTER & 1992–93 ACHIEVA, BERETTA, CORSICA, GRAND AM & SKYLARK

Perform test as shown, **Fig. 9.** If results are other than specified, perform designated test. **Do not press set switch and Resume/Accel position of cruise switch at same time while engine is running. If quick checker displays a short light, release switches immediately.**

When performing the following tests refer to wiring diagrams **Figs. 10 through 13,** and control module pin connectors **Figs. 7, 8 and 14.**

TEST E

1. Check for shorts to voltage in wires to terminals A, G, L and M of cruise control module.
2. If wires are satisfactory, check multi-function lever and cruise control switch for a short.
3. If switch is satisfactory, replace multi-function lever.

TEST F

Beretta & Corsica

1. Check fuse No. 14.
2. Ensure terminal J (black wire) of cruise control module is grounded.
3. Disconnect connector C235 and check for battery voltage at terminal A (brown/white wire) of harness half with ignition switch in Run position. If battery voltage is not available, check brown/white wire (circuit 141) for an open.
4. Check continuity between terminals A (brown wire) and C (gray wire) of pin half of connector C235 with cruise switch in On position. If there is no continuity, check multi-function lever and cruise control switches for an open, replacing as necessary.
5. Check for an open in gray wire (circuit 397) between terminal A of connector C235 and terminal A of cruise control module connector.

Cavalier

1. Check cruise fuse.
2. Ensure terminal J (black wire) of cruise control module is grounded.
3. Disconnect connector C235 and check for battery voltage at terminal A (brown/white wire) of harness half with ignition switch in Run position. If battery voltage is not available, check brown/white wire (circuit 141) for an open.
4. Check continuity between terminals A (black wire) and B (black wire) of pin half of connector C235 with cruise

Connect: QUICK CHECKER (J34185, SPECMO QC-3 OR EQUIVALENT) or DIGITAL MULTI-METER
At: CRUISE CONTROL MODULE CONNECTOR (Disconnected)
Conditions:
- Ignition Switch: RUN
- When making any resistance measurements throughout this test, turn the Ignition Switch to OFF. Failure to do so could cause incorrect results and misdiagnosis

Step	Action	With Quick Checker, Correct Response	Without Quick Checker, Using a Digital Multi-Meter			For Different Result, Do Test
			Meter Range	Connector Terminals	Correct Response	
1	Cruise Switch OFF	–	200 ohms	J & Ground	0 ohms	Check BLK wire for an open
		All the lights off	20 VDC	A & J	0 volts	E
			20 VDC	M & J	0 volts	
2	Cruise Switch ON	ON/OFF Light on	20 VDC	A & J	Battery voltage	F
		BRK Light on	20 VDC	G & J	Battery voltage	G
		VENT Light on	200 ohms	C & J	30 to 55 ohms	H
		VAC Light on	200 ohms	K & J	30 to 55 ohms	I
		SPS Light on	200 ohms	F & H	15 to 25 ohms	J
		RA Light off	20 VDC	M & J	0 volts	E
		SC Light off	20 VDC	L & J	0 volts	E
3	Cruise Switch ON, Set/Coast Switch pressed	SC Light on	20 VDC	L & J	Battery voltage	K
		VAC & SHORT Lights off	–	–	–	L
4	Resume/Accel/Switch pressed	ON/OFF Light on	–	–	–	F
		RA Light on	20 VDC	M & J	Battery voltage	M
		VENT & SHORT Lights off	–	–	–	N

Fig. 9   Cruise control system diagnosis chart (Part 1 of 2). 1991–92 Except Bonneville, Camaro, Caprice, Custom Cruiser, Firebird, LeMans, Roadmaster & 1992 Achieva, Beretta, Corsica, Grand Am & Skylark

Step	Action	With Quick Checker, Correct Response	Without Quick Checker, Using a Digital Multi-Meter			For Different Result, Do Test
			Meter Range	Connector Terminals	Correct Response	
5	Cruise Switch ON, drive wheels turned by hand	VSS Light flashes on and off	20 VDC	A & D	Pulses between approximately battery voltage and less than 7 volts	O, P
6	Quick Checker not connected	–	200 ohms	F & J	Open circuit (infinite resistance)	Q
7	Quick Checker not connected	–	200 ohms	F & C	Open circuit (infinite resistance)	R
8	Quick Checker not connected	–	200 ohms	F & K	Open circuit (infinite resistance)	R
9	Quick Checker not connected	–	200 ohms	H & C	Open circuit (infinite resistance)	R
10	Quick Checker not connected	–	200 ohms	H & K	Open circuit (infinite resistance)	R

- If all measurements are correct, go to Test S: Servo Actuation Test

Fig. 9   Cruise control system diagnosis chart (Part 2 of 2). 1991–92 Except Bonneville, Camaro, Caprice, Custom Cruiser, Firebird, LeMans, Roadmaster & 1992 Achieva, Beretta, Corsica, Grand Am & Skylark

switch in On position. If there is no continuity, check multi-function lever and cruise control switches for an open, replacing as necessary.
5. Check for an open in gray wire (circuit 397) between terminal D of connector C235 and terminal A of cruise control module connector.

Cutlass Calais, Grand Am, Skylark & Sunbird
1. Check radio fuse.

2. Ensure terminal J of cruise control module is grounded.
3. Disconnect connector C235 and check for battery voltage at terminal A (yellow wire) with ignition in Run position. If battery voltage is not available, check yellow wire (circuit 43).
4. Check continuity between terminals A (black wire) and B (black wire) of connector C235 with cruise switch in On position. If there is no continuity, re-

place multi-function lever.
5. Check for open in gray wire (circuit 397) between terminal B of connector C235 and terminal A of cruise control module connector.

Century, Cutlass Ciera, Cutlass Cruiser & 6000
1. Check radio fuse.
2. Ensure terminal J of cruise control module is grounded.

Fig. 10 Wiring diagram (Part 1 of 2). 1991 Beretta & Corsica

Fig. 10 Wiring diagram (Part 2 of 2). 1991 Beretta & Corsica

Fig. 11   Typical wiring diagram (Part 1 of 2). Century, Cutlass Ciera/Cutlass Cruiser & 1991 6000

Fig. 11   Typical wiring diagram (Part 2 of 2). Century, Cutlass Ciera/Cutlass Cruiser & 1991 6000

3. Disconnect row E of connector C206 and check for battery voltage at terminal E1 (brown/white wire) with ignition in Run position. If battery voltage is not available, check brown/white wire (circuit 141).
4. Check continuity between terminals E1 and E2 of connector C206 with cruise switch in On position. If there is no continuity, replace multi-function lever.
5. Check for open in gray wire (circuit 397) between terminal E2 of connector C206 and terminal A of cruise control module connector.

TEST G

1. Check for open in brake or clutch switch.
2. **On Beretta and Corsica models,** check brown wire (circuit 86), dark green wire (circuit 986), brown and brown/white (circuit 379), for an open.
3. **On Cutlass Calais, Grand Am and Skylark models,** check brown/white wire (circuit 86), or gray wire (circuit 986), for an open.
4. **On Cavalier and Sunbird models,** check brown (circuit 86), or brown/white wire (circuit 379), for an open.
5. **On Century, Cutlass Ciera, Cutlass Cruiser and 6000 models,** check for an open in brown wire (circuit 86) and gray wire (circuit 397) to the brake switch.

TEST H

1. If measurement is less than 30 ohms, proceed to test N. Otherwise, remove connector from cruise control servo and measure resistance between terminals A and C of servo.
2. If resistance is greater than 55 ohms, replace cruise control servo.
3. If resistance is less than 55 ohms, check for open in dark blue or dark blue/white wire (circuit 403) between terminal C of cruise control module and terminal A of cruise control servo. Ensure terminal C of servo connector is grounded.

TEST I

1. If measurement was less than 30 ohms, proceed to test L. Otherwise, remove connector from cruise control servo and measure resistance between terminals E and C of servo.
2. If resistance is greater than 55 ohms, replace cruise control servo.
3. If resistance is less than 55 ohms, check for open in light green wire (circuit 402) between terminal K of cruise control module and terminal E of cruise control servo. Ensure terminal C of servo connector is grounded.

TEST J

1. If measurement was less than 15 ohms, proceed to test Q. Otherwise, remove connector from cruise control servo and measure resistance between terminals B and D of servo.
2. If resistance is greater than 25 ohms, replace cruise control servo.

Fig. 12 Typical wiring diagram (Part 1 of 2). 1991 Cutlass Calais, Grand Am & Skylark

Fig. 12 Typical wiring diagram (Part 2 of 2). 1991 Cutlass Calais, Grand Am & Skylark

3. If resistance is less than 25 ohms, check for open in light blue/black or light blue wire (circuit 399) between terminal H of cruise control module and terminal D of cruise control servo. Also, check for open in tan wire (circuit 398) between terminal F of module and terminal B of servo.

TEST K

Beretta & Corsica

1. Disconnect connector C235 and check switch continuity between terminals A (Gray wire) and D (Black wire) of pin half with set/coast switch depressed.
2. If there is no continuity, check multi-function lever and cruise control switches for an open, replacing as necessary.
3. If switches are not open, check for an open in dark blue wire (circuit 84) between terminal D of connector C235 and terminal L of cruise control module.

Cavalier, Cutlass Calais, Grand Am, Skylark & Sunbird

1. Disconnect connector C235 and check switch continuity between terminals B (black wire) and D (black wire) with set switch pressed.
2. If there is no continuity, replace multi-function lever.
3. If there is continuity, check for open in dark blue wire (circuit 84) between terminal D and terminal L of cruise control module.

Century, Cutlass Ciera, Cutlass Cruiser & 6000

1. Disconnect row E of connector C206 and check switch continuity between terminals E2 and E3 with set switch pressed.
2. If there is no continuity, replace multi-function lever.
3. If there is continuity, check for open in dark blue wire (circuit 84) between terminal E2 of connector C206 and terminal L of cruise control module.

TEST L

1. Remove connector from servo and measure resistance between terminals C and E of servo.
2. If resistance is less than 30 ohms, replace cruise control servo.
3. If resistance is 30 ohms or greater, check for short to ground in light green wire (circuit 402) from terminal K of cruise control module to terminal E of cruise control servo.

TEST M

Beretta & Corsica

1. Disconnect connector C235 and check switch continuity between terminals C (brown wire) and B (red wire) of pin half with resume/accel switch pressed.
2. If there is no continuity, check multi-function lever and cruise control switches for an open.

Fig. 13 Typical wiring diagram (Part 1 of 2). Cavalier & Sunbird

Fig. 13 Typical wiring diagram (Part 2 of 2). Cavalier & Sunbird

3. If switches are not open, check for an open in gray/black wire (circuit 87) between terminal B of connector C235 and terminal terminal M of cruise control module.

Cavalier, Cutlass Calais, Grand Am, Skylark & Sunbird

1. Disconnect connector C235 and check switch continuity between terminals A and C with cruise switch in Resume/Accel position.
2. If there is no continuity, replace multi-function lever.
3. If there is continuity, check for open in gray/black wire (circuit 87) between terminal C and terminal M of cruise control module.

Century, Cutlass Ciera, Cutlass Cruiser & 6000

1. Disconnect row E of connector C206 and check switch continuity between terminals E1 and E4 with cruise switch in Resume/Accel position.
2. If there is no continuity, replace multi-function lever.
3. If there is continuity, check for open in gray/black wire (circuit 87) between terminal E4 of connector C206 and terminal M of cruise control module.

TEST N

1. Remove connector from cruise control servo and measure resistance between terminals A and C of servo.
2. If resistance is less than 30 ohms, replace cruise control servo.
3. If resistance is 30 ohms or greater, check for short to ground in dark blue/white wire or dark blue wire (circuit 403) from terminal C of cruise control module to terminal A of cruise control servo.

TEST O

Corsica & Beretta

If VSS light does not illuminate, or voltage between terminals A and D remains less than 7 volts check for open in red wire (circuit 381) and dark green/white (circuit 817) wires.

Cutlass Calais, Grand Am & Skylark

If VSS light does not illuminate, or voltage between terminals A and D remains less than 7 volts check for open in dark green wire (circuit 389) from the engine control module .

Cavalier & Sunbird

If VSS light does not illuminate, or voltage between terminals A and D remains less than 7 volts check for open in red wire (circuit 381) from the engine control module .

Century, Cutlass Ciera, Cutlass Cruiser & 6000

If VSS light does not illuminate, or voltage between terminals A and D remains less than 7 volts check for open in red wire (circuit 381).

Fig. 14 Cruise control module connector C206 pin location. Century, Cutlass Ciera/Cutlass Cruiser, Custom Cruiser & 1991 6000

TEST P

Corsica & Beretta

If VSS light does not go off or battery voltage remains between terminals A and D, check for short to ground on red wire (circuit 381) and dark green/white (circuit 817) wires.

Cutlass Calais, Grand Am & Skylark

If VSS light does not go off or battery voltage remains between terminals A and D, check for short to ground on dark green wire (circuit 389) from the engine control module.

Cavalier & Sunbird

If VSS light does not go off or battery voltage remains between terminals A and D, check for short to ground on red wire (circuit 381) from the engine control module.

Century, Cutlass Ciera, Cutlass Cruiser & 6000

If VSS light does not go off, or battery voltage remains between terminals A and D remains less than 7 volts check for short to ground in red wire (circuit 381).

TEST Q

1. Disconnect cruise control servo connector and repeat test 6, **Fig. 9.**
2. If resistance is now over range, replace cruise control servo.
3. If resistance is still low repair short in tan wire (circuit 398) from terminal F of cruise control module to terminal B of cruise control servo.

TEST R

1. Disconnect cruise control servo connector and repeat test 7, 8, 9 and 10 **Fig. 9.** Perform test on the cruise control servo (male side).
2. If circuit is now open check cruise control servo connector and cruise control module connector for corrosion. Repair wire if connector is OK.
3. If resistance is still low, check cruise control servo terminals for corrosion. Replace cruise control servo if connectors are OK.

TEST S

When performing servo actuation test S refer to **Fig. 15.**

1992–93 Achieva, Beretta, Corsica, Grand Am & Skylark

Perform tests in isolation chart, **Fig. 16.** If results are incorrect perform tests in diagnostic charts, **Fig. 17 through 30.** Do not press both the set switch and Resume/Accel position of cruise switch at same time with engine running. If quick checker displays a short light, release switches immediately.

When performing the following tests, refer to **Figs. 31 through 33,** for wiring diagram and control module pin locations, **Fig. 8.**

1991–92 Caprice, Custom Cruiser & Roadmaster

When diagnosing and testing system refer to **Figs. 34 through 40,** for diagnostic charts, and **Figs. 41 through 43** for wiring diagrams.

Corvette

TROUBLESHOOTING

1. Check for open cruise fuse.
2. Check for vacuum leaks in cruise control servo vacuum lines.
3. Check cruise control cable for looseness, binding, and connection at throttle body.
4. Ensure proper terminal mating at connectors, then check for corrosion or bent terminals.

SYSTEM DIAGNOSIS

When diagnosing and testing system refer to **Figs. 44 and 45,** for wiring diagrams.

Refer to **Figs. 46 through 49,** for symptom and system diagnosis.

Cutlass Supreme, Grand Prix, Lumina, Regal & 1991 LeSabre & 88

TROUBLESHOOTING

1991 LeSabre

For troubleshooting and system diagnostic procedures, refer to **Figs. 50 through 54.** NOTE: On **Fig. 50** E1 circuit is a pink/black wire.

Cutlass Supreme, Grand Prix, Regal & 1991 88

1. Check vacuum hoses for leaks, kinks and/or restrictions.
2. Check cruise control servo linkage for proper slack.
3. If system works except for tap-up and tap-down functions, replace cruise control module.

ROAD TEST

1. Drive vehicle at speed greater than 25 mph, place cruise switch in On position and depress set button at end of multi-function lever. Cruise indicator should illuminate and vehicle should maintain speed.
2. With foot off accelerator, hold set button in. Vehicle should coast at a slower speed.
3. Release set button. If new speed is greater than 25 mph, cruise control should engage and hold slower speed.
4. Slide cruise switch to Resume/Accel position and hold it there. Vehicle should accelerate.
5. Release cruise switch back to On position. Vehicle should hold new, faster speed.
6. Tap brake pedal. Vehicle should coast slower and cruise indicator should go out.
7. Slide cruise control switch momentarily to Resume/Accel position. Cruise indicator should illuminate and vehicle should accelerate to former set speed.
8. While cruising, accelerate, then remove foot from accelerator pedal. Vehicle should coast back to set speed.
9. While cruising, tap cruise switch to Resume/Accel position. Vehicle speed should decrease 1 mph for each tap up to ten.
10. While cruising, tap set button. Vehicle speed should decrease 1 mph for each tap down to 25 mph.
11. Slide cruise control switch to Off position. Cruise control should turn off and cruise indicator should go out.

SYSTEM DIAGNOSIS

Perform tests in diagnostic chart, **Figs. 2, and 55 through 57.** If results are incorrect perform designated test. **Do not press both the set switch and Resume/Accel position of cruise switch at same time with engine running. If quick checker displays a short light, release switches immediately.**

When performing the following tests, refer to **Figs. 7, 8, 14 and 58 through 61.** for wiring diagram and control module pin locations.

For system diagnosis on 1991 LeSabre, refer to "Troubleshooting" section.

TEST A

1991 88

1. Check for shorts to voltage in wires to terminals G (brown wire, except Cutlass Supreme and Grand Prix w/manual transaxle; brown/white wire, Cutlass Supreme and Grand Prix w/manual transaxle) A (gray wire) M (gray/black wire) and L (dark blue wire) of cruise control module.
2. If wires are satisfactory, replace multi-function lever.

Cutlass Supreme, Grand Prix, Lumina & Regal

1. Check for shorts to voltage in wires to

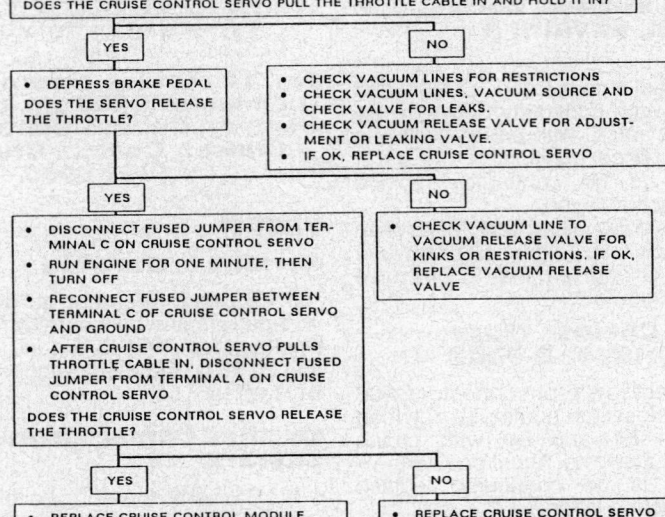

- ECM CONNECTORS CONNECTED
- REMOVE CONNECTOR FROM CRUISE CONTROL SERVO
- GROUND TERMINAL C OF THE CRUISE CONTROL SERVO WITH A FUSED JUMPER
- JUMPER TERMINAL A OF CRUISE CONTROL SERVO TO BATTERY
- RUN ENGINE FOR ONE MINUTE THEN TURN IT OFF
- JUMPER TERMINAL E OF CRUISE CONTROL SERVO TO BATTERY

DOES THE CRUISE CONTROL SERVO PULL THE THROTTLE CABLE IN AND HOLD IT IN?

Fig. 15 Servo actuation test S. Except 1993 Camaro, Caprice, Firebird LeMans & Roadmaster

CHART #1
ISOLATION TEST

Connect: QUICK CHECKER (J 34185, SPECMO QC-3 OR EQUIVALENT) or DIGITAL MULTI-METER
At: CRUISE CONTROL MODULE CONNECTOR (Disconnected)
Condition:
- Ignition Switch: "RUN"
- When making any resistance measurements throughout this test, turn the Ignition Switch to "OFF." Failure to do so could cause incorrect results and misdiagnosis.

Note: Ignore status of lights not mentioned in quick checker column steps.

STEP	Condition	With Quick Checker, Correct Response	Without Quick Checker, Using Digital Multi-meter			For Different Response, Do Chart #:
			Meter Range	Connector Terminals	Correct Response	
1	Cruise Switch "OFF"	—	200 ohms	J & Ground	0 ohms	Check CKT 450 for an open
		All lights off	20 VDC	A & J	0 volts	2
			20 VDC	M & J	0 volts	
2	Cruise Switch "ON"	ON/OFF Light On	20 VDC	A & J	Battery voltage	3
		BRK Light On	20 VDC	G & J	Battery voltage	4
		VENT Light On	200 ohms	C & J	30 to 55 ohms	5
		VAC Light On	200 ohms	K & J	30 to 55 ohms	6
		SPS Light On	200 ohms	F & H	15 to 25 ohms	7
		R/A Light Off	20 VDC	M & J	0 volts	2
		SC Light Off	20 VDC	L & J	0 volts	
3	Cruise Switch "ON," Set Switch pressed	SC Light On	20 VDC	L & J	Battery voltage	8
		VAC & SHORT Lights Off	—	—	—	9
4	Cruise Switch in "RES/ACC"	ON/OFF Light On	—	—	—	3
		R/A Light On	20 VDC	M & J	Battery voltage	10
		VENT & SHORT Lights Off	—	—	—	11
5	Cruise Switch "ON," drive wheels turned by hand	VSS Light flashes On and Off	20 VDC	A & D	Pulses between approximately battery voltage and less than 7 volts	12
6	Quick Checker not connected	—	200 ohms	F & J	Open in circuit (infinite resistance)	13
7	Quick Checker not connected	—	200 ohms	F & C	Open in circuit (infinite resistance)	
8	Quick Checker not connected	—	200 ohms	F & K	Open in circuit (infinite resistance)	14
9	Quick Checker not connected	—	200 ohms	H & C	Open in circuit (infinite resistance)	
10	Quick Checker not connected	—	200 ohms	H & K	Open in circuit (infinite resistance)	

D If all measurements are correct, go to Chart #15: Servo Actuation Test.

Fig. 16 Cruise control system isolation test Chart 1, 1992–93 Achieva, Beretta, Corsica, Grand Am & Skylark

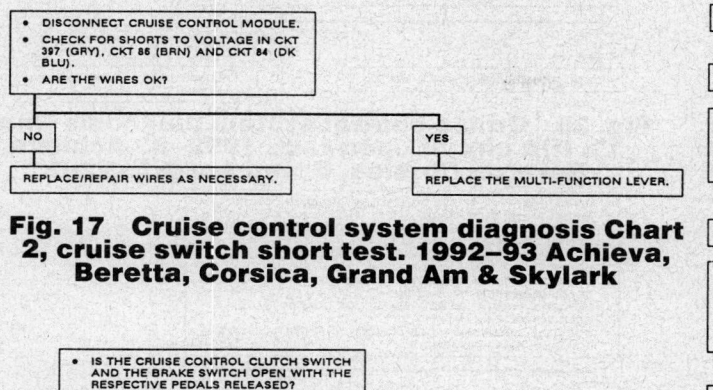

Fig. 17   Cruise control system diagnosis Chart 2, cruise switch short test. 1992–93 Achieva, Beretta, Corsica, Grand Am & Skylark

Fig. 19   Cruise control system diagnosis Chart 4, brake circuit open test. 1992–93 Achieva, Beretta, Corsica, Grand Am & Skylark

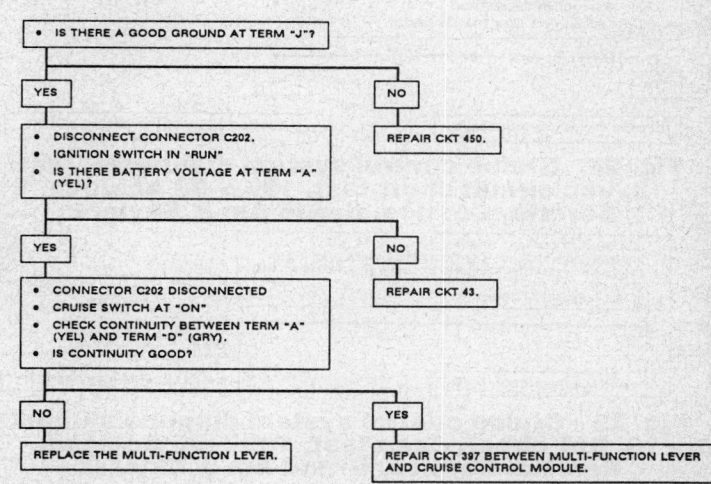

Fig. 18   Cruise control system diagnosis Chart 3, power circuit open test. 1992–93 Achieva, Beretta, Corsica, Grand Am & Skylark

Fig. 20   Cruise control system diagnosis Chart 5, vent circuit open test. 1992–93 Achieva, Beretta, Corsica, Grand Am & Skylark

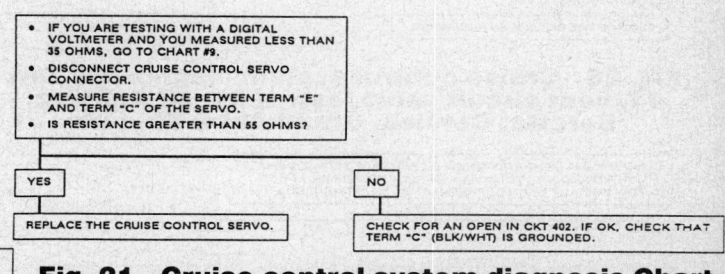

Fig. 21   Cruise control system diagnosis Chart 6, vac circuit open test. 1992–93 Achieva, Beretta, Corsica, Grand Am & Skylark

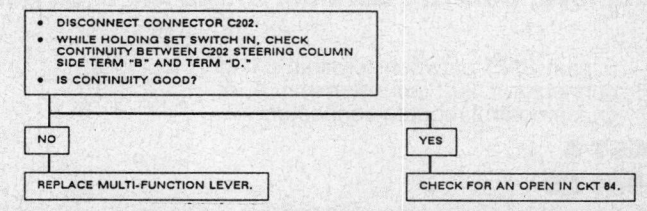

Fig. 22   Cruise control system diagnosis Chart 7, sps circuit open test. 1992–93 Achieva, Beretta, Corsica, Grand Am & Skylark

Fig. 23   Cruise control system diagnosis Chart 8, sc circuit open test. 1992–93 Achieva, Beretta, Corsica, Grand Am & Skylark

terminals A, G, M, and L terminals of cruise control module.
2. If wires are satisfactory, replace multi-function lever.

TEST B
1991 88
1. Check fuse No. 18.
2. Ensure terminal J of cruise control module is grounded.
3. Disconnect connector C202 and check for battery voltage at terminal E1 (pink/black wire) with ignition switch in Run position. If battery volt-

age is not available, check pink/black wire (circuit 239).
4. Check continuity between terminals E1 (pink wire) and E2 (gray wire) of connector C202 with cruise switch in On position. If there is no continuity, replace multi-function lever.
5. Check for an open in gray wire (circuit 397) between terminal E2 of connector C202 and terminal A of cruise control module connector.

Cutlass Supreme, Grand Prix, Lumina & Regal
1. Check instrument cluster fuse.

2. Ensure terminal J of cruise control module connector is grounded.
3. Disconnect connector C202 and check for battery voltage at terminal E12 (pink/black wire) of female half with ignition switch in Run position. If battery voltage is not available, check pink/black wire (circuit 750).
4. Check continuity between terminals E1 (gray wire) and E12 (pink/black wire) of male half of connector C202 with cruise switch in On position. If there is no continuity, replace multi-function lever.
5. Check for open in gray/white wire

Fig. 24 Cruise control system diagnosis Chart 9, vac circuit short test. 1992–93 Achieva, Beretta, Corsica, Grand Am & Skylark

Fig. 25 Cruise control system diagnosis Chart 10, R/A circuit open test. 1992–93 Achieva, Beretta, Corsica, Grand Am & Skylark

Fig. 26 Cruise control system diagnosis Chart 11, vent circuit short test. 1992–93 Achieva, Beretta, Corsica, Grand Am & Skylark

Fig. 27 Cruise control system diagnosis Chart 12, vss circuit open/short test. 1992–93 Achieva, Beretta, Corsica, Grand Am & Skylark

(circuit 397) between terminal E1 of connector C202 and terminal A of cruise control module connector.

TEST C

1991 88

1. Check for open in cruise/brake switch.
2. Check for open in brown wire (circuit 86) and gray wire (circuit 397).

TEST D

1. If measurement was less than 30 ohms, proceed to test J. Otherwise, re-move connector from cruise control servo and measure resistance be-tween terminals A and C of servo.
2. If resistance is greater than 55 ohms, replace cruise servo.
3. If resistance is less than 55 ohms, check for open in dark blue/white wire (circuit 403, LeSabre and Lumi-na) or dark blue wire (circuit 403, Grand Prix and Regal) or light/green wire (circuit 402 1991 88) between terminal C of cruise control module and terminal A of cruise control servo.

Ensure terminal C of cruise control servo connector is grounded.

TEST E

1. If measurement is less than 30 ohms, proceed to test H. Otherwise, remove connector from cruise control servo and measure resistance between ter-minals E and C of cruise control servo.
2. If resistance is greater than 55 ohms, replace cruise control servo.
3. If resistance is less than 55 ohms, check for open in light green wire (circuit 402) between terminal K of cruise control module and terminal E of cruise control servo. Ensure termi-nal C of cruise control servo connec-tor is grounded.

Fig. 28 Cruise control system diagnosis Chart 13, R/A circuit open test. 1992–93 Achieva, Beretta, Corsica, Grand Am & Skylark

Fig. 29 Cruise control system diagnosis Chart 14, servo test. 1992–93 Achieva, Beretta, Corsica, Grand Am & Skylark

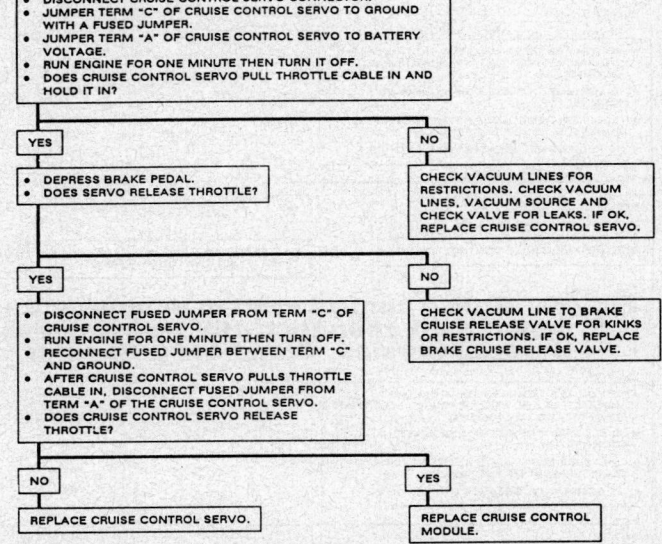

Fig. 30 Cruise control system diagnosis Chart 15, servo actuation test. 1992–93 Achieva, Beretta, Corsica, Grand Am & Skylark

TEST F

1. If measurement is less than 15 ohms, proceed to test N ot test M on 1991 88. Otherwise, remove connector from cruise control servo and mea-sure resistance between terminals B and D of cruise control servo.
2. If resistance is greater than 25 ohms, replace cruise control servo.
3. If resistance is less than 25 ohms, check for open in light blue/black wire (circuit 399) between terminal H of cruise control module and terminal D of cruise control servo. Also, check for open in tan wire (circuit 398) between terminal F of cruise control module and terminal B of cruise control servo.

Fig. 31   Wiring diagram (Part 2 of 2). 1992-93 Achieva & Grand Am

Fig. 31   Wiring diagram (Part 1 of 2). 1992-93 Achieva, Beretta, Corsica & Grand Am

Fig. 32 Wiring diagram (Part 2 of 2). 1992–93 Beretta & Corsica

Fig. 32 Wiring diagram (Part 1 of 2). 1992–93 Beretta & Corsica

Fig. 33 Wiring diagram (Part 2 of 2). 1992-93 Skylark

Fig. 33 Wiring diagram (Part 1 of 2). 1992-93 Skylark

**Fig. 34   Cruise control system diagnosis Chart 1, cruise control will not engage (Part 1 of 3).
1991 Caprice, Custom Cruiser & Roadmaster**

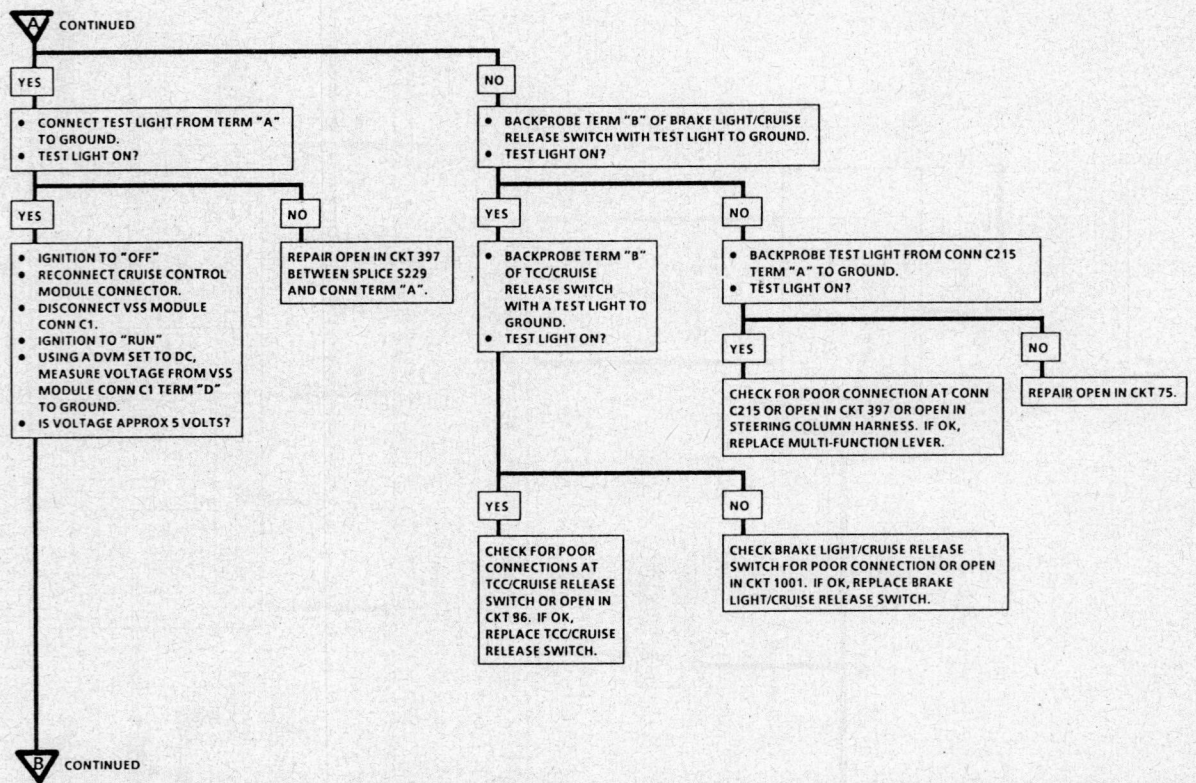

**Fig. 34   Cruise control system diagnosis Chart 1, cruise control will not engage (Part 2 of 3).
1991 Caprice, Custom Cruiser & Roadmaster**

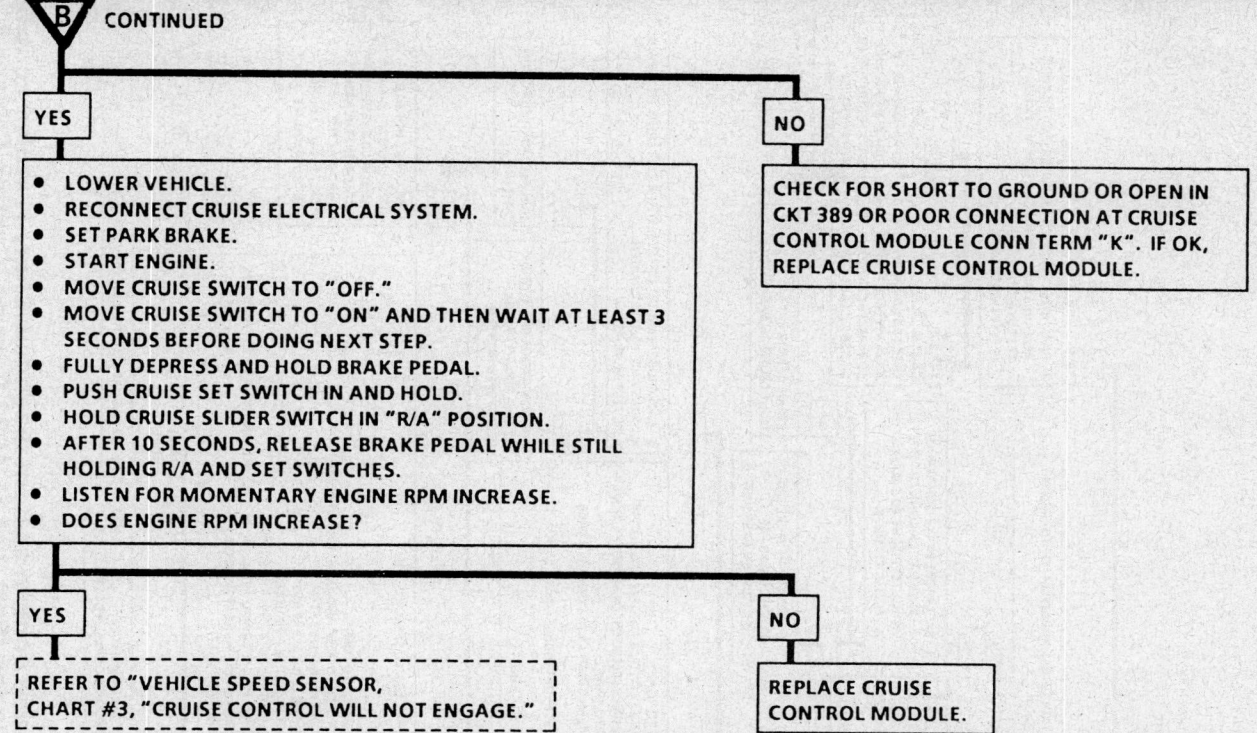

Fig. 34 Cruise control system diagnosis Chart 1, cruise control will not engage (Part 3 of 3). 1991 Caprice, Custom Cruiser & Roadmaster

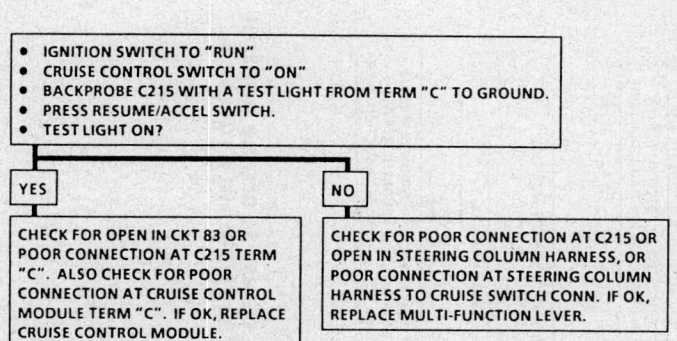

Fig. 35 Cruise control system diagnosis Chart 2, cruise control will not resume, accelerate, tap-up or tap-down. 1991 Caprice, Custom Cruiser & Roadmaster

Fig. 36 Cruise control system diagnosis Chart 3, cruise control will not engage (Vehicle speed sensor). 1991 Caprice, Custom Cruiser & Roadmaster

TEST G
1991 88

1. Disconnect connector C202 and check switch continuity between terminals E2 (gray wire) and E3 (dark blue wire) with set switch depressed.
2. If there is no continuity, replace multi-function lever.
3. If there is continuity, check for open in dark blue wire (circuit 84) between terminal E3 of connector C202 and terminal L of cruise control module.

Cutlass Supreme, Grand Prix, Lumina & Regal

1. Disconnect connector C202 and check switch continuity between terminals E1 (gray wire) and E2 (dark blue wire) of male (female on Regal) half with set switch depressed.
2. If there is no continuity, replace multi-function lever.
3. If there is continuity, check for open in dark blue wire (circuit 84) between terminal E2 of connector C202 and terminal L of cruise control module.

TEST H

1. Remove connector from cruise control servo and measure resistance between terminals C and E of cruise control servo connector.
2. If resistance is less than 30 ohms, replace cruise control servo.
3. If resistance is 30 ohms or greater, check for short to ground in light green wire (circuit 402) between terminal K of cruise control module and terminal E of cruise control servo.

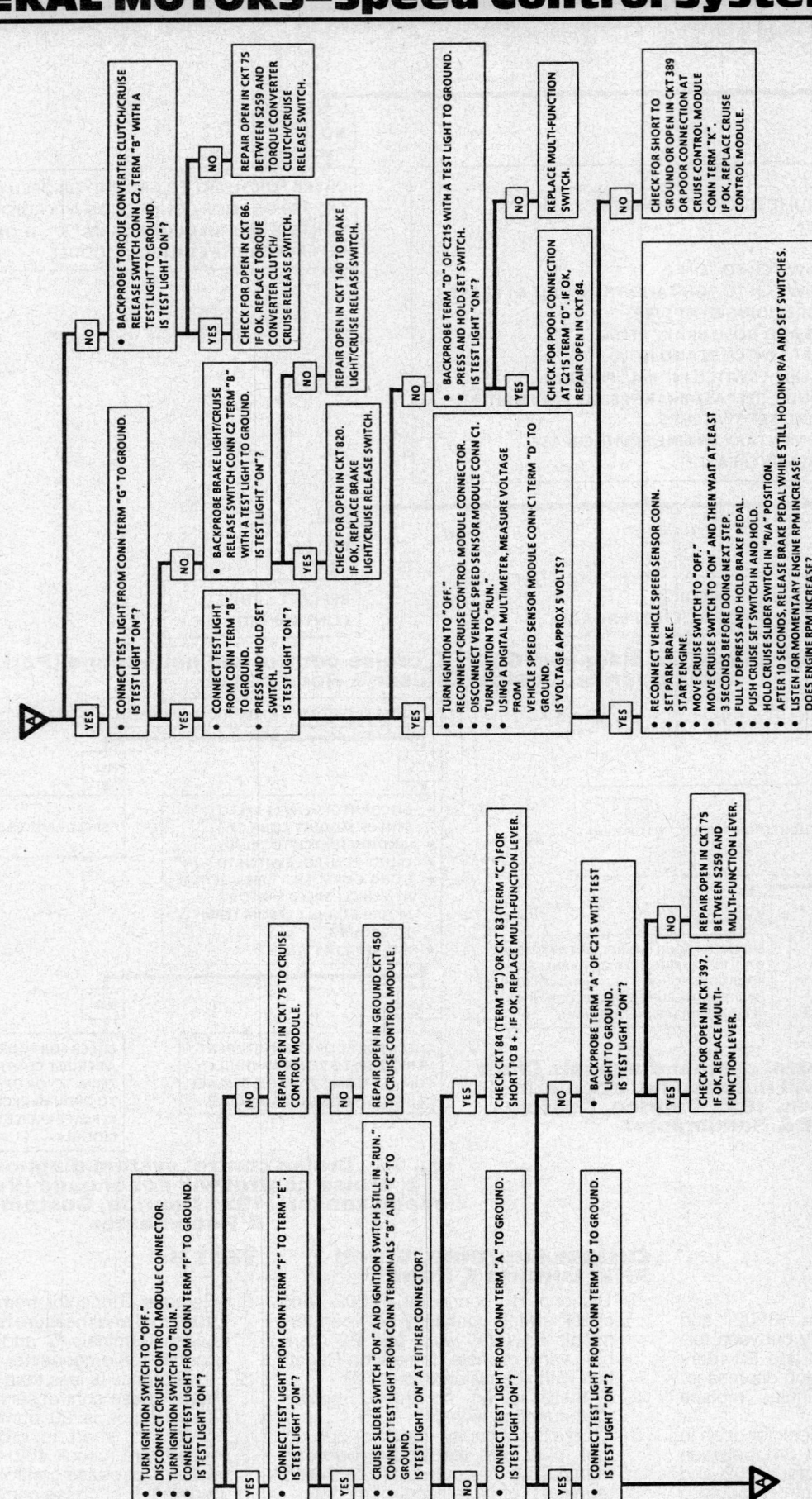

Fig. 37 Cruise control system diagnosis Chart 1, cruise control will not engage (Part 2 of 2). 1992 Caprice, Custom Cruiser & Roadmaster

Fig. 37 Cruise control system diagnosis Chart 1, cruise control will not engage (Part 1 of 2). 1992 Caprice, Custom Cruiser & Roadmaster

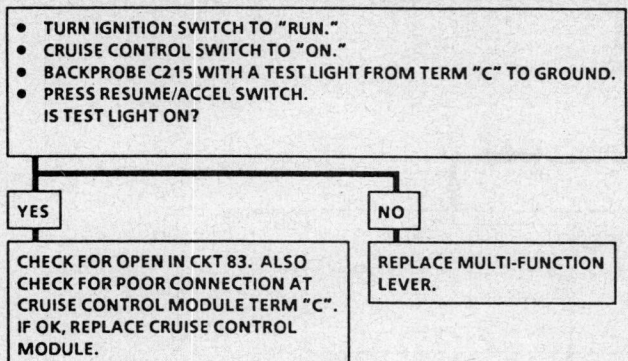

Fig. 38 Cruise control system diagnosis Chart 2, cruise control will not resume, accelerate, tap-up or tap-down. 1992 Caprice, Custom Cruiser & Roadmaster

Fig. 40 Cruise control system diagnosis Chart 4, cruise indicator on at all times. 1991–92 Roadmaster

Fig. 39 Cruise control system diagnosis Chart 3, cruise indicator inoperative. 1991-92 Roadmaster

TEST I
1991 88
1. Disconnect connector C202 and check switch continuity between terminals E1 (pink/black wire, 1991 88) and E4 (black wire) with cruise switch in Resume/Accel position.
2. If there is no continuity, replace multi-function lever.
3. If there is continuity, check for open in gray/black wire (circuit 87) between terminal E4 of connector C202 and terminal M of cruise control module.

Cutlass Supreme, Grand Prix, Lumina & Regal
1. Disconnect connector C202 and check cruise switch continuity between terminals E12 and E13 of male half of connector C202 with cruise switch in Resume/Accel position.
2. If there is no continuity, replace multi-function lever.
3. If there is continuity, check for open in gray/black wire (circuit 87) between terminal E13 of connector C202 and terminal M of cruise control module.

TEST J
Except 1991 88
1. Remove connector from cruise control servo and measure resistance between terminals A and C of cruise control servo.

2. If resistance is less than 30 ohms, replace cruise control servo.
3. **On 1991 models,** if resistance is greater than 30 ohms, check for a short to ground in the wire from terminal C of the cruise control module to terminal A of the cruise control servo.

1991 88
For servo actuation test J, refer to **Fig. 62.**

TEST K
1991 88
1. Remove connector from cruise control servo, measure resistance between terminals A and C of servo.
2. If resistance is less than 30 ohms, replace cruise control servo.
3. If resistance is greater than 30 ohms, check for short to ground in dark blue/white wire (circuit 403) from terminal C of cruise control module and terminal A of cruise control servo.

TEST L
1991 88
If VSS light does not illuminate, or voltage between terminals A and D remains less than 1 volts check for open in red wire (circuit 381) of vehicle speed sensor buffer.

TEST M
Cutlass Supreme, Grand Prix, Lumina & Regal
1. Disconnect the cruise control servo connector and repeat test 6 of the isolation test **Fig. 55.**
2. If resistance is now open, replace cruise control test.
3. If resistance is still low, repair short in wire from terminal H of the cruise control module to terminal D of the cruise control servo.

1991 88
If VSS light does not go off or battery voltage remains between terminals A and D, check for short to ground in red wire (circuit 381) of vehicle speed sensor buffer.

TEST N
Except Cutlass Supreme, Grand Prix, Lumina & Regal
1. Disconnect cruise control servo connector and repeat test 7, **Figs. 2 and 57.**
2. If resistance is now over range, replace cruise control servo.
3. If resistance is still low, check for short in tan wire (circuit 398) from terminal F of cruise control module to terminal B of cruise control servo.

Cutlass Supreme, Grand Prix, Lumina & Regal
1. Disconnect cruise control servo connector and repeat test 7, 8, 9 and 10 **Fig. 55.**
2. If resistance is now open, check the cruise control servo connector and cruise control module connector for corrosion between terminals. If OK, repair shorted wire.
3. If resistance is still low, check servo terminals for corrosion.

TEST O
1991 88
1. Disconnect cruise control servo and repeat test 7, 8, 9 and 10.
2. If measurement shows a open circuit, check cruise control servo and module connectors for corrosion between terminals. If OK, check for shorted wire.
3. If resistance is still low, check servo terminals for corrosion. If OK replace cruise control servo.

Continued on page 31-76

Fig. 41   Typical wiring diagram (Part 1 of 2). 1991 Caprice, Custom Cruiser & Roadmaster

Fig. 41   Typical wiring diagram (Part 2 of 2). 1991 Caprice, Custom Cruiser & Roadmaster

TYPE 2

Fig. 43 Wiring diagram. 1992 Roadmaster

Fig. 42 Wiring diagram. 1992 Caprice & Custom Cruiser

Fig. 44 Cruise control wiring diagram, (Part 1 of 2). 1991 Corvette

Fig. 44 Cruise control wiring diagram, (Part 2 of 2). 1991 Corvette

Fig. 45 Cruise control wiring diagram, (Part 2 of 2). 1992–93 Corvette

Fig. 45 Cruise control wiring diagram, (Part 1 of 2). 1992–93 Corvette

SYMPTOM	PROCEDURE
Cruise will not engage.	Chart #1
Cruise will not maintain set speed or cruise surges.	Chart #2
Does not resume, accelerate or tap up	Chart #3

Fig. 46   Cruise control symptom chart. Corvette

Fig. 47   Cruise control system diagnosis; Chart 1 (Part 1 of 3). Corvette

Fig. 47   Cruise control system diagnosis; Chart 1 (Part 2 of 3). Corvette

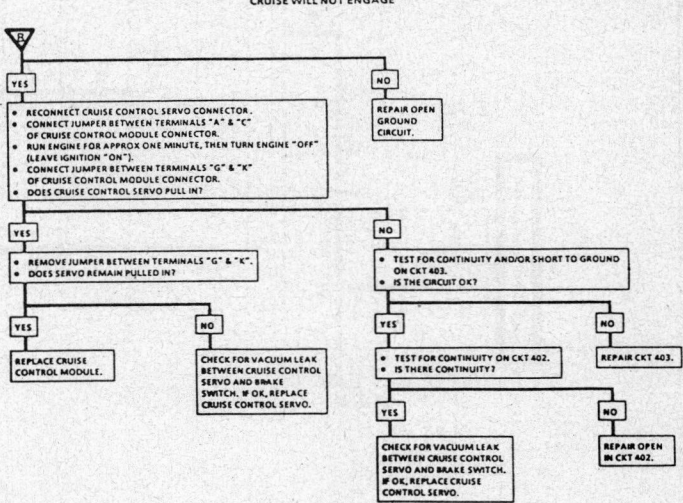

Fig. 47   Cruise control system diagnosis; Chart 1 (Part 3 of 3). Corvette

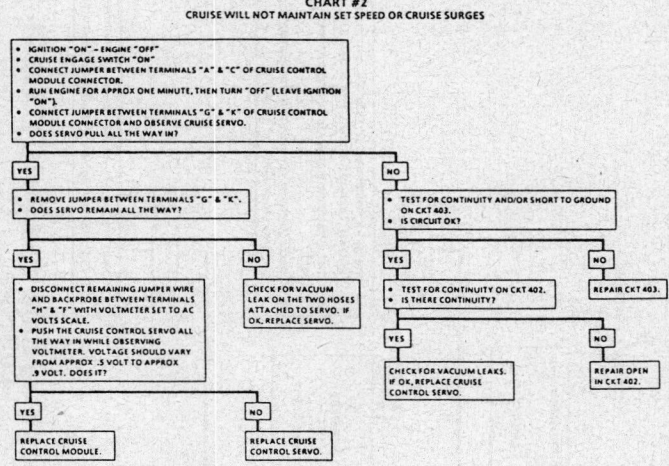

Fig. 48 Cruise control system diagnosis; Chart 2. Corvette

Fig. 49 Cruise control system diagnosis; Chart 3. Corvette

SYMPTOM	DIAGNOSIS				
	If a quick checker is available, do Cruise Control Module Test A. If a quick checker is not available, do Cruise Control Module Test B.	Replace Cruise Control Module.	Check for binding servo linkage or throttle linkage. Check vacuum lines for leaks or blockage.	Check YEL (494) wire to ECM for an open or short to ground.	Do Cruise Control Vacuum Test C.
All or some cruise control functions do not operate.	• Do 2nd	• Do 3rd	• Do 1st		
No tap up or tap down operation, otherwise system OK.		•			
Vehicle surges with cruise control engaged.	• Do 2nd	• Do 5th	• Do 1st	• Do 3rd	• Do 4th

Fig. 50 Troubleshooting procedure. 1991 LeSabre

- **Cruise Switch: ON**
- Raise car and slowly turn drive wheels by hand.

11 Pulses between battery voltage and less than 1 volt. If not, see Vehicle Speed Sensor.

WHT

CRUISE CONTROL MODULE CONNECTOR

Fig. 51   Cruise control system diagnosis; Test B (Part 3 of 3). 1991 LeSabre

CRUISE CONTROL SERVO

To battery

To battery

- Apply approximately 15" Hg of vacuum with hand pump to vacuum port.
- Does vacuum pull in and hold in Cruise Control Servo vacuum actuator?

YES →
- Check for restricted or kinked vacuum supply hose to Vacuum Tank or Cruise Control Servo.
- Check vacuum supply hose and connections for leaks.
- Check Vacuum Check Valve for correct operation (i.e. not stuck open or closed).

NO →
- Plug vacuum release port.
- Apply approximately 15" Hg of vacuum with hand pump to vacuum port.
- Does vacuum pull in and hold Cruise Control Servo vacuum actuator?

YES →
- Check for leak in vacuum hose and connections.
- If OK, adjust/replace Vacuum Release Valve.

NO →
- Replace Cruise Control Servo.

Fig. 52   Cruise control system diagnosis, (Test C). 1991 LeSabre

6 Battery voltage with Cruise Control Switch at ON or R/A, 0 volts with Cruise Control Switch at OFF. If not, check wiring to C206. If OK, do Cruise Switch Test E.

2 Battery voltage with Cruise Control Switch at ON or R/A, 0 volts with Cruise Control Switch at OFF. If not, check wiring to C206. If wiring is OK, do Cruise Switch Test E.

4 Battery voltage with cruise control Set Switch depressed, 0 volts released. If not, check wiring to C206. If wiring is OK, do Cruise Switch Test E.

3 Battery voltage. If not, check wire and Instrument Cluster printed circuit. If OK, replace Instrument Cluster,

1 Ground. If not, check wire.

5 Battery voltage with Cruise Switch at ON and brake pedal released. 0 volts with brake pedal depressed. If not, check related wiring. If related wiring is OK, adjust/replace Cruise/Brake Switch.

7 Battery voltage. If not check wire. If wire is OK, replace ECM.

WHT

CRUISE CONTROL MODULE CONNECTOR

Fig. 51   Cruise control system diagnosis; Test B (Part 1 of 3). 1991 LeSabre

8 30-55 ohms.

9 15-25 ohms.

10 30-55 ohms.

WHT

CRUISE CONTROL MODULE CONNECTOR

- If any measurement is not correct, check related wiring to Cruise Control Servo. If wiring is OK, replace Cruise Control Servo.

Fig. 51   Cruise control system diagnosis; Test B (Part 2 of 3). 1991 LeSabre

- Cruise Control Servo connector: disconnected
- If any measurement is incorrect, replace Cruise Control Servo.

Fig. 53   Cruise control system diagnosis, (Test D). 1991 LeSabre

- Remove connector C206 from mounting bracket. Separate connector and measure resistance at steering column half.
- X indicates continuity. O indicates open.
- If any measurement is incorrect, check steering column wiring and Multi-Function Lever connector. If OK, replace Multi-Function Lever.

WIRE COLORS SWITCH POSITION	BLK	DK BLU	GRY	PNK
Cruise Switch: OFF	O	O	O	O
Cruise Switch: ON	O	O	X	X
Cruise Switch: ON SET button: depressed (hold)	O	X	X	X
Cruise Switch: R/A (hold)	X	O	X	X

Fig. 54   Cruise control system diagnosis, (Test E). 1991 LeSabre

Connect: QUICK CHECKER (J-34185, SPECMO QC-3 OR EQUIVALENT) or VOLT-OHMETER
At: CRUISE CONTROL MODULE CONNECTOR (Disconnected)
Conditions:
- Ignition Switch: RUN
- When making resistance measurements throughout this text, turn Ignition Switch to off. Failure to do so could cause incorrect results and misdiagnosis.
- Test with quick checker (J-34185 or equivalent) or digital meter

| Test | Condition | With quick checker, Correct Response | Without quick checker, Using a Digital Meter | | | For Different Response, do Test: |
			Meter Range	Connector Terminals	Connector Response	
1	Cruise Switch OFF	–	200 ohms	J & Ground	0 ohms	B
		All lights Off	20 VDC	A & J	0 volts	A
			20 VDC	M & J	0 volts	
2	Cruise Switch ON	ON/OFF Light on	20 VDC	A & J	Battery voltage	B
		BRK Light on	20 VDC	G & J	Battery voltage	C
		VENT Light on	200 ohms	C & J	30 to 55 ohms	D
		VAC Light on	200 ohms	K & J	30 to 55 ohms	E
		SPS Light on	200 ohms	F & H	15 to 25 ohms	F
		RA Light off	20 VDC	M & J	0 volts	A
		SC Light off	20 VDC	L & J	0 volts	A

Fig. 55   Cruise control system isolation test (Part 1 of 2). Cutlass Supreme, Grand Prix, Lumina & Regal

| Test | Condition | With quick checker Correct Response | Without quick checker Using a Digital Meter | | | For Different Response, do Test: |
			Meter Range	Connector Terminals	Connector Response	
3	Cruise Switch ON, Set Switch pressed	SC Light on	20 VDC	L & J	Battery voltage	G
		VAC & SHORT Lights off	not applicable	not applicable	not applicable	H
4	Cruise Switch in R/A	ON/OFF Light on	not applicable	not applicable	not applicable	B
		RA Light on	20 VDC	M & J	Battery voltage	I
		VENT & SHORT Lights off	not applicable	not applicable	not applicable	J
5	Cruise Switch ON, drive wheels turned by hand	VSS Light flashes on and off	20 VDC	A & D	Pulses between approximately battery voltage and less than 7 volts	K, L
6	Quick checker not connected	–	200 ohms	H & J	Open Circuit (infinite resistance)	M
7	Quick checker not connected	–	200 ohms	F & C	Open Circuit (infinite resistance)	N
8	Quick checker not connected	–	200 ohms	F & K	Open Circuit (infinite resistance)	N
9	Quick checker not connected	–	200 ohms	H & C	Open Circuit (infinite resistance)	N
10	Quick checker not connected	–	200 ohms	H & K	Open Circuit (infinite resistance)	N

- If all responses were correct, go to Test O: Servo Actuation Test

Fig. 55   Cruise control system isolation test (Part 2 of 2). Cutlass Supreme, Grand Prix, Lumina & Regal

- Remove connector from Cruise Control Servo
- Ground terminal C of the Cruise Control Servo with a fused jumper
- Jumper terminal A of Cruise Control Servo to Battery
- Run engine for one minute then turn it off
- Jumper terminal E of Cruise Control Servo to Battery

Does the Cruise Control Servo pull the throttle cable in and hold it in?

YES

- Depress brake pedal

Does the Servo release the throttle?

NO

- Check vacuum lines for restrictions
- Check vacuum lines, vacuum source, check valve for leaks
- Check Brake Cruise Release Valve for adjustment or leaking valve
- Replace Cruise Control Servo

YES

- Disconnect fused jumper from terminal C on Cruise Control Servo
- Run engine for one minute, then turn off
- Reconnect fused jumper between terminal C of Cruise Control Servo and ground
- After Cruise Control Servo pulls throttle cable in, disconnect Fused Jumper from terminal A on the Cruise Control Servo

Does the Cruise Control Servo release the throttle?

NO

- Check vacuum line to Cruise Control Check Valve for kinks or restrictions. If OK, replace Cruise Control Check Valve

YES

- Replace Cruise Control Module

NO

- Replace Cruise Control Servo

Fig. 56   Cruise control system test "O," servo actuation test. Cutlass Supreme, Grand Prix, Lumina & Regal

Connect: QUICK CHECKER (J 34185, SPECMO QC-3, or EQUIVALENT) or VOLT-OHMMETER
At: CRUISE CONTROL MODULE CONNECTOR (Disconnected)
Conditions:
- Ignition Switch: RUN
- When making any resistance measurements throughout this test, turn the Ignition Switch to OFF. Failure to do so could cause incorrect results and misdiagnosis.

Check	Action	With Quick Checker, Correct Response	Without Quick Checker, Using a Digital Meter			For Different Result, Do Test
			Meter Range	Connector Terminals	Correct Response	
1	Cruise Switch OFF	—	200 ohms	J & Ground	0 ohms	B
		All lights off	20 VDC	A & J, L & J M & J, G & J	0 volts	A
2	Cruise Switch ON	ON/OFF light on	20 VDC	A & J	Battery voltage	B
		BRK light on	20 VDC	G & J	Battery voltage	C
		VENT light on	200 ohms	C & J	30 to 55 ohms	D
		VAC light on	200 ohms	K & J	30 to 55 ohms	E
		SPS light on	200 ohms	F & H	15 to 25 ohms	F
		RA light off	20 VDC	M & J	0 volts	A
		SC light off	20 VDC	L & J	0 volts	A
3	Cruise Switch ON, Set Switch pressed and held	SC light on	20 VDC	L & J	Battery voltage	G
		VAC & SHORT lights off	N/A	N/A	N/A	H
4	Cruise Switch in R/A	ON/OFF light on	N/A	N/A	N/A	B
		RA light on	20 VDC	M & J	Battery voltage	I
		VENT & SHORT lights off	N/A	N/A	N/A	K
5	Cruise Switch ON, drive wheels turned by hand	VSS light flashes on and off	20 VDC	A & D	Pulses between approximately battery voltage and less than 7 volts	L, M
6	Quick checker not connected	—	200 ohms	H & J	Open Circuit (infinite resistance)	N
7	Quick checker not connected	—	200 ohms	F & C	Open Circuit (infinite resistance)	O
8	Quick checker not connected	—	200 ohms	F & K	Open Circuit (infinite resistance)	O
9	Quick checker not connected	—	200 ohms	H & C	Open Circuit (infinite resistance)	O
10	Quick checker not connected	—	200 ohms	H & K	Open Circuit (infinite resistance)	O

- If all results are correct, go to Test J: Servo Actuation Test.

Fig. 57   Cruise control system isolation test. 1991 88

Fig. 58 Cruise control wiring diagram. 1991 LeSabre

Fig. 59   Cruise control wiring diagram (Part 1 of 2). Cutlass Supreme, Grand Prix & Lumina

Fig. 59   Cruise control wiring diagram (Part 2 of 2). Cutlass Supreme, Grand Prix & Lumina

Fig. 60 Cruise control wiring diagram (Part 1 of 2). Regal

Fig. 60 Cruise control wiring diagram (Part 2 of 2). Regal

Fig. 61   Cruise control wiring diagram, (Part 1 of 2). 1991 88

Fig. 61   Cruise control wiring diagram, (Part 2 of 2). 1991 88

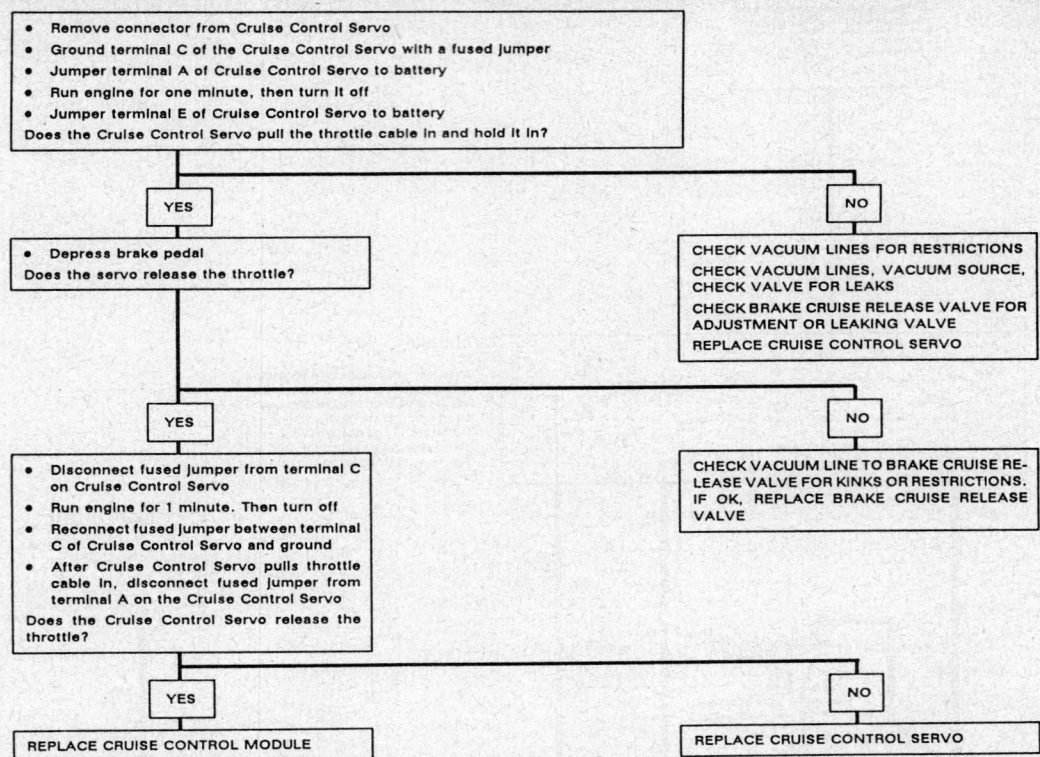

Fig. 62   Servo actuation test J. 1991 88

COMPONENT DIAGNOSIS & TESTING
ELECTRIC BRAKE RELEASE SWITCH

1. Turn ignition switch to On position.
2. Connect test light to ground.
3. Probe brown wire at brake switch connector. Lamp should illuminate.
4. Check switch adjustment, with probe still at brown wire, depressing brake pedal 1/8-1/2 inch. Light should go out.
5. If lamp did not illuminate in step 3, probe wire in adjacent connector cavity. If lamp illuminates, adjust or replace switch as necessary. If light does not illuminate, check wiring to switch.

COMPONENT REPLACEMENT
SERVO UNIT

1. Disconnect servo assembly electrical connector.
2. Disconnect vacuum hoses.
3. Disconnect actuating chain, cable or rod from servo assembly.
4. Remove servo assembly and servo unit solenoid valve assembly to mounting bracket attaching screws, then remove servo assembly.
5. Reverse procedure to install. **Torque** servo assembly to bracket attaching screws to 14-18 inch lbs.

ENGAGEMENT SWITCH

Refer to appropriate electrical section for multi-function switch replacement procedures.

ADJUSTMENTS
SPEED CONTROLS, ADJUST
CABLE, ADJUST

1. Ensure cable assembly in cable and servo bracket.
2. Pull servo assembly cable and toward servo without moving throttle body lever.
3. If one of the holes in the servo tab aligns with cable pin, connect pin to tab with retainer.
4. If tab hole does not align with pin, move cable from servo assembly until next closest tab hole lines up, then connect pin to tab with retainer. **Do not stretch cable to make adjustment, as the engine will not be able to return to idle.**

SERVO ROD, ADJUST

1. Ensure engine high idle speed is properly adjusted, turn off engine, the set carburetor choke to hot idle position.
2. Remove servo rod retainer, then adjust rod and install retainer in hole which provides some clearance between retainer and servo bushing. Clearance must not exceed width of one hole.

ELECTRIC & VACUUM RELEASE SWITCHES, ADJUST

1. With brake pedal fully depressed, insert switch into retainer until valve seats fully.
2. **On vehicles equipped with anti-lock brakes,** release brake pedal and allow to come to rest.
3. **On models less ABS brakes,** pull brake pedal rearward against pedal stop until clicking sounds are no longer heard.
4. Release brake pedal, then repeat step 2 and ensure clicking is not present.

ELECTRIC BRAKE RELEASE SWITCH & VACUUM RELEASE VALVE ADJUSTMENT

The switch assembly and valve assembly cannot be adjusted until brake booster pushrod is assembled to brake pedal assembly. Adjustment is as follows:

1. Depress brake pedal and switch assembly and valve assembly into their proper retaining clips until fully seated.
2. **On vehicles equipped with anti-lock brakes,** release brake pedal and allow to come to rest.
3. **On models less anti-lock brakes,** slowly pull pedal back to its fully retracted position. The switch assembly and valve assembly will move within their retainers to their adjusted position.
4. The following brake pedal travel distances may be used to check for a properly adjusted cruise control and stop lamp switch assembly and vacuum release valve assembly.
a. Cruise control switch contacts must open at 1/8-1/2 inch pedal

travel, measured at centerline of brake pedal pad. **Nominal actuation of stop lamp contacts is** $3/16$ **inch after cruise control contacts open.**

b. Vacuum release valve assembly

must open at $1^{1}/16$–$1^{5}/16$ inches pedal travel, measured at centerline of brake pedal pad.

CLUTCH ELECTRIC RELEASE SWITCH ADJUSTMENT

1. Ensure clutch release switch is fully

seated in retainer.

2. Pull clutch pedal pad upward. **Do not exert an upward force on the clutch pedal of more than 20 lbs, or damage to clutch master cylinder retaining ring may result.**

Type 3

NOTE: On Vehicles Equipped With Airbags, Disarm Airbag As Outlined Under "Airbag System Disarming" Before Any Diagnosis, Testing, Troubleshooting Or Repairs Are Performed. After All Diagnosis, Testing, Troubleshooting Or Repairs Have Been Completed, Rearm Airbag As Outlined Under "Airbag System Arming."

NOTE: Wire Color Code Identification And Symbol Identification Located In The Front Of This Manual Can Be Used As An Aid When Using The Wiring Circuits Found In This Section.

INDEX

PRECAUTIONS
AIRBAG SYSTEM DISARMING

1991 PARK AVENUE

When carrying a live inflator module, ensure bag and trim cover are pointed away from you. Never carry inflator module by the wires or connector on underside of module.

The diagnostic energy reserve module (DERM) can maintain voltage to cause a system deployment for up to ten minutes after the ignition switch is turned off and the battery is disconnected. Servicing the SIR system during this period may result in accidental deployment and personal injury.

1. Turn ignition switch to OFF position, then disconnect and tape battery ground cable terminal.
2. Remove Connector Position Assurance (CPA), then disconnect yellow two-way SIR electrical connector at base of steering column.
3. Remove screws and/or nuts from back of steering wheel, then the inflator module from steering wheel.
4. Remove Connector Position Assurance (CPA), then disconnect coil assembly connector and horn lead.
5. Place inflator module on a bench or other surface with bag and trim cover facing Up.

RIVIERA, TORONADO/TROFEO, 1991 REATTA & 1992-93 BONNEVILLE, LESABRE, PARK AVENUE, 88 & 98

The diagnostic energy reserve module (DERM) can maintain voltage to cause a system deployment for up to ten minutes after the ignition switch is turned off and the battery is disconnected. Servicing the SIR system during this period may result in accidental deployment and personal injury.

1. Ensure front wheels are pointed straight ahead.
2. Turn ignition switch to LOCK position and remove SIR or AIRBAG fuse.
3. **On models except Bonneville w/dual airbags, remove left sound insulator. Remove courtesy lamp from sound insulator, if necessary.**
4. On Bonneville w/dual airbags, remove left and right sound insulators.
5. Remove Connector Position Assurance (CPA), then disconnect yellow two-way SIR electrical connector at base of steering column.

1991 98

The diagnostic energy reserve module (DERM) can maintain voltage to cause a system deployment for up to ten minutes after the ignition switch is turned off and the battery is disconnected. Servicing the SIR system during this period may result in accidental deployment and personal injury.

1. Turn ignition switch to OFF position, then remove I/P fuse 7 from fuse block.
2. Disconnect yellow two-way SIR electrical connector at base of steering column.

AIRBAG SYSTEM ARMING

1991 PARK AVENUE

1. Turn ignition switch to OFF position, connect horn lead and coil assembly connector, then install Connector Position Assurance (CPA).
2. Install inflator module and secure to steering wheel using new screws and/or nuts.
3. **Torque** screws and/or nuts to 25 inch lbs.
4. Connect yellow two-way SIR electrical connector at base of steering column, then install Connector Position Assurance (CPA).
5. Install left sound insulator, then the SIR fuse into fuse block.
6. Turn ignition switch to RUN position and ensure that "Inflatable Restraint" indicator flashes 7 to 9 times, then turns off.

RIVIERA, TORONADO/TROFEO, 1991 REATTA & 1992–93 BONNEVILLE, LESABRE, PARK AVENUE, 88 & 98

1. Connect yellow two-way SIR electrical connector, then install Connector Position Assurance (CPA).
2. **On models except Bonneville w/dual airbags,** install left sound insulator. **Install courtesy lamp to sound insulator, if applicable.**
3. **On Bonneville w/dual airbags,** install left and right sound insulators, then the SIR fuse into fuse panel.
4. Install SIR fuse to fuse block, turn ignition switch to RUN position and ensure that "Inflatable Restraint" lamp flashes 7 to 9 times, then turns off.

1991 98

1. Connect yellow two-way SIR electrical connector at base of steering column.
2. Install I/P fuse 7 into fuse block, turn ignition switch to RUN position and ensure that "Inflatable Restraint" indicator flashes 7 to 9 times, then turns off.

DESCRIPTION

This system is basically the same as Type 2, excepting the fact that on this type the function of the cruise control module is performed by the PCM. The main parts of the cruise control system are the mode control switches, PCM, servo unit, vehicle speed sensor, vacuum supply, electrical and vacuum release switches, and electrical harness. The cruise system uses vacuum to operate a throttle servo. The PCM monitors vehicle speed and servo position to operate the servo vacuum and vent valves to maintain desired speed.

ROAD TEST

1. Drive vehicle at speed greater than 25 mph, place cruise switch in On position and depress set button at end of multi-function lever. Cruise indicator should illuminate and vehicle should maintain speed.
2. With foot off accelerator, hold set button in. Vehicle should coast at a slower speed.
3. Release set button. If new speed is greater than 25 mph, cruise control should engage and hold slower speed.
4. Slide cruise switch to Resume/Accel position and hold it there. Vehicle should accelerate.
5. Release cruise switch back to On position. Vehicle should hold new, faster speed.
6. Tap brake pedal. Vehicle should coast slower and cruise indicator should go out.
7. Slide cruise control switch momentarily to Resume/Accel position. Cruise indicator should illuminate and vehicle should accelerate to former set speed.
8. While cruising, accelerate, then remove foot from accelerator pedal. Vehicle should coast back to set speed.
9. While cruising, tap cruise switch to Resume/Accel position. Vehicle speed should decrease 1 mph for each tap up to ten.
10. While cruising, tap set button. Vehicle speed should decrease 1 mph for each tap down to 25 mph.
11. Slide cruise control switch to Off position. Cruise control should turn off and cruise indicator should go out.

SERVICE PRECAUTIONS

On vehicles equipped with ABS brake system, the hydraulic accumulator, when fully charged contains brake fluid at high pressure. Before disconnecting any lines, hoses or fittings, ensure accumulator is full depressurized. Failure to do so may result in personal injury.

To depressurize the hydraulic accumulator, turn the ignition to the Off position or disconnect negative battery cable, pump brake pedal a minimum of 40 times at approximately 50 lbs. of force. A noticeable change in pedal feel will occur when accumulator is fully discharged.

SYSTEM DIAGNOSIS & TESTING

The operation of the cruise control system is integral with the Body Control Module (BCM) or Power Control Module (PCM). The BCM or PCM monitors the cruise control system and other systems by comparing the actual operating conditions to standard values stored in memory. When certain system malfunctions are detected, a three digit trouble code is stored in the BCM memory. These trouble codes can be displayed to aid in system diagnosis. In this manner, the speed control system can be diagnosed by accessing fault codes, if they exist, that pertain to the speed control system.

Codes other than those described below may be stored in the BCM memory and displayed when the system is accessed to diagnose cruise control malfunctions. It may be necessary to diagnose these codes and identify the non-speed control related failure in order to ensure proper speed control system operation. For further diagnosis of other systems related to the BCM, refer to MOTOR's "Auto Engine Tune Up & Electronic Manual."

ENTERING DIAGNOSTIC SERVICE MODE

PARK AVENUE, RIVIERA, 98, 1991–92 TORONADO/TROFEO, 1992–93 BONNEVILLE, LESABRE, 88 & 1991 REATTA

Connect TECH 1 Diagnostic Scan tool or equivalent to DLC (ALDL) connector, **Figs. 1 and 2,** which is located under the instrument panel and is sometimes covered by a plastic cover.

ACCESSING DIAGNOSTIC CODES

Terminal B of the connector is the diagnostic terminal and is grounded by connecting it to terminal A (internal ECM/PCM/VCM/ ground). Once terminals A and B have been connected, the ignition switch must be moved to the On position with the engine not running. The Service Engine Soon light should flash Diagnostic Trouble Code (DTC) 12 three times consecutively. The flash sequence should be as follows: flash, pause, flash-flash, long pause, flash, pause, flash-flash, long pause, flash, pause, flash-flash. DTC 12 indicates that the system is operating properly. If DTC 12 is not indicated, a problem is present within the diagnostic system itself.

Following the output of DTC 12, the Service Engine Soon light will indicate a diagnostic trouble code three times, if present, or it will continue to output DTC 12.If more than one code is present, the codes will be output in lowest number to highest with each code being output three times.

TERMINAL IDENTIFICATION

A	GROUND	E	SERIAL DATA
B	DIAGNOSTIC TERMINAL	F	TCC (IF USED)
C	A.I.R. (IF USED)	G	FUEL PUMP (IF USED)
D	SERVICE ENGINE SOON LIGHT (IF USED)	M	SERIAL DATA (IF USED)

Fig. 1   DLC (ALDL) connector. 1991–92

TERMINAL IDENTIFICATION

A	GROUND	F	TCC (IF USED)
B	DIAGNOSTIC TERMINAL	M	SERIAL DATA
E	SERIAL DATA (IF USED)		

Fig. 2   DLC connector. 1993

DIAGNOSTIC TEST PROCEDURES

When diagnosing and testing system, refer to **Figs. 3 through 11,** for wiring diagrams, and **Figs. 12 through 25** for cruise control system check, and trouble code diagnostic charts.

CLEARING CODES

To clear code the ECM must power feed must be disconnected for at least 30 seconds. Depending how vehicle is equipped, the power feed can be disconnected at the ECM fuse in the fuse box, the inline fuse holder at the battery, or the positive battery terminal pigtail connector.

COMPONENT DIAGNOSIS & TESTING

ELECTRIC BRAKE RELEASE SWITCH

1. Turn ignition switch to On position.
2. Connect test light to ground.
3. Probe brown wire at brake switch connector. Lamp should illuminate.
4. Check switch adjustment, with probe still at brown wire, depressing brake pedal $1/8-1/2$ inch. Light should go out.
5. If light did not illuminate in step 3, probe wire in adjacent connector cavity. If lamp illuminates, adjust or replace switch as necessary. If light does not illuminate, check wiring to switch.

VACUUM RELEASE VALVES

An inoperative valve must be replaced. Ensure vacuum hose to switch is firmly connected and that it is not cracked or deteriorated. Vacuum source and hoses should be checked for improper routing, leaks, kinks or restrictions.

ADJUSTMENTS

CRUISE CONTROL CABLE

Adjust cruise control cable to minimum slack as follows:
1. Ensure throttle lever is in idle position with engine off.
2. Pull servo assembly end of cable toward servo blade.
3. If hole in servo blade is aligned with cable pin, install pin in that hole and install retainer.

4. If hole does not align with pin, install pin in next hole away from servo assembly. **Do not stretch cable.**

ELECTRIC BRAKE RELEASE SWITCH & VACUUM RELEASE/VCC SWITCH

The switch assembly and valve assembly cannot be adjusted until brake booster pushrod is assembled to brake pedal assembly. Adjustment is as follows:
1. Depress brake pedal and install switch assembly and valve assembly into their proper retaining clips until fully seated.
2. **On vehicles equipped with anti-lock brakes,** release brake pedal and allow to come to rest.
3. **On vehicles less ABS brakes,** slowly pull pedal back to its fully retracted position. The switch assembly and valve assembly will move within their retainers to their adjusted position.
4. **On all models,** the following brake pedal travel distances may be used to check for a properly adjusted cruise control and stop lamp switch assembly and vacuum release valve assembly.
   a. Cruise control switch contacts must open at .88-1.2 inch pedal travel, measured at centerline of brake pedal pad. **Nominal actuation of stop lamp contacts is .4 inch after cruise control contacts open.**
   b. Vacuum release valve assembly must open at $1 1/16-1 5/16$ inches pedal travel, measured at centerline of brake pedal pad.

COMPONENT REPLACEMENT

SERVO UNIT

RIVIERA

1. Disconnect electrical connector and vacuum hoses.
2. Disconnect throttle actuating chain, cable or rod from servo unit.
3. Remove 3 screws retaining servo unit and servo unit solenoid valve assembly to mounting bracket and remove servo.

4. Reverse procedure to install. **Torque servo unit to mounting bracket attaching screws to 10-15 inch lbs.**

EXCEPT RIVIERA

1. Remove throttle body intake ductwork, then disconnect retainer at servo blade.
2. Disconnect cruise control cable at from servo bracket by release locking tangs.
3. Disconnect vacuum hoses and electrical connector.
4. Remove servo bracket nuts, servo and bracket assembly.
5. Remove bolts retaining servo to bracket, then servo.
6. Reverse procedure to install noting the following:
   a. Tighten servo to bracket bolts to 14 ft. lbs.
   b. Tighten servo bracket nuts to 20 ft. lbs.
   c. **Retainer must be installed with tang secured over cable stud head.**

ENGAGEMENT SWITCH

The cruise control engagement switch is part of the multi-function lever, which must be replaced as an assembly. Refer to individual car chapter.

CRUISE/SHIFT INTERLOCK/BRAKE SWITCH

1. Remove sound insulator, then electrical connectors.
2. Disconnect vacuum hose, then remove switch by carefully pulling switch rearward.
3. Disassemble brake switches, **Fig. 26.**
4. Reverse procedure to install.

CRUISE CONTROL CABLE

1. Disconnect cruise control cable from throttle lever by removing retainer.
2. Remove retainer at servo blade.
3. Disconnect cable from servo bracket by releasing lock tangs, **Fig. 27.**
4. Remove cable.
5. Reverse procedure to install noting the following:
   a. **Conduit fittings at both ends must have locking tangs expanded and locked in attaching holes.**

Fig. 3 Wiring diagram (Part 1 of 2). Riviera & 1991 Reatta

Fig. 3 Wiring diagram (Part 2 of 2). Riviera & 1991 Reatta

Fig. 4   Wiring diagram (Part 1 of 2). 1991–92 Toronado/Trofeo

Fig. 4   Wiring diagram (Part 2 of 2). 1991–92 Toronado/Trofeo

Fig. 5   Wiring diagram (Part 1 of 2). 1991 98

Fig. 5   Wiring diagram (Part 2 of 2). 1991 98

Fig. 6   Wiring diagram (Part 1 of 2). 1992 88

Fig. 6   Wiring diagram (Part 2 of 2). 1992 88

Fig. 7 Wiring diagram (Part 1 of 2). 1992–93 98 & 1993 88

Fig. 7 Wiring diagram (Part 2 of 2). 1992–93 98 & 1993 88

Fig. 8 Wiring diagram. 1991–92 Park Avenue & 1992 LeSabre

Fig. 9 Wiring diagram. 1993 LeSabre & Park Avenue

Fig. 10 Wiring diagram. 1992 Bonneville

Fig. 11 Wiring diagram. 1993 Bonneville

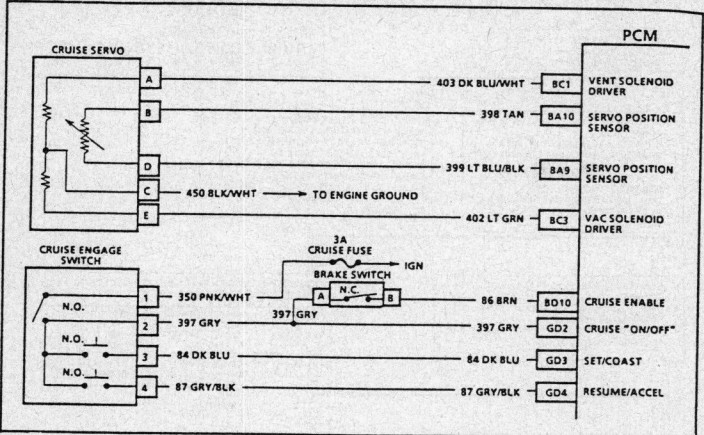

Fig. 12   Cruise control system check & trouble code wiring diagram. 1991–92

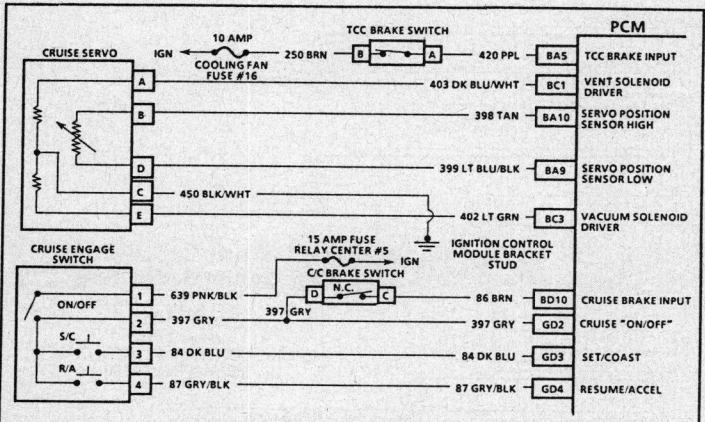

Fig. 13   Cruise control system check & trouble code wiring diagram. 1993 except Riviera

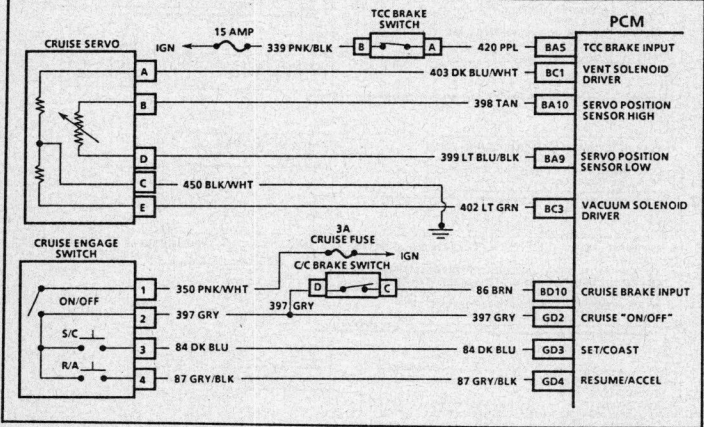

Fig. 14   Cruise control system check & trouble code wiring diagram. 1993 Riviera

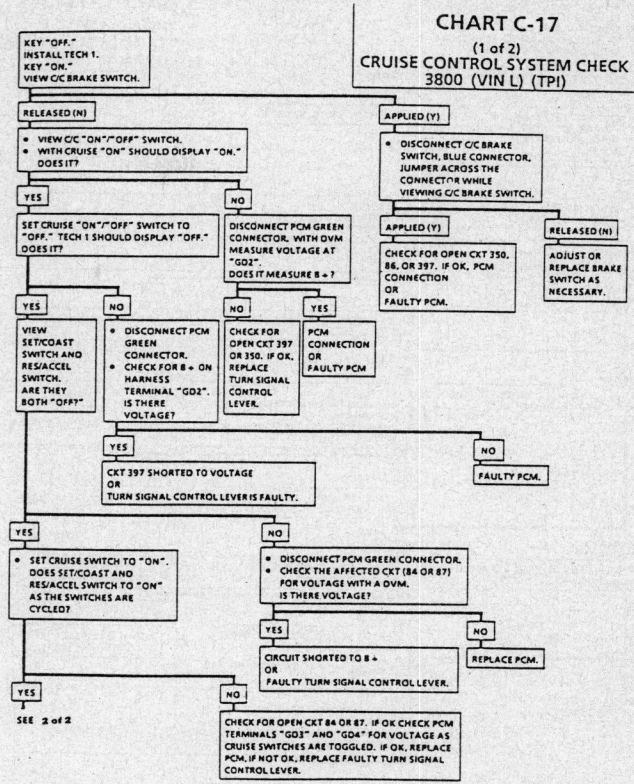

Fig. 15   Chart C-17, cruise control system check (Part 1 of 2). 1991–92

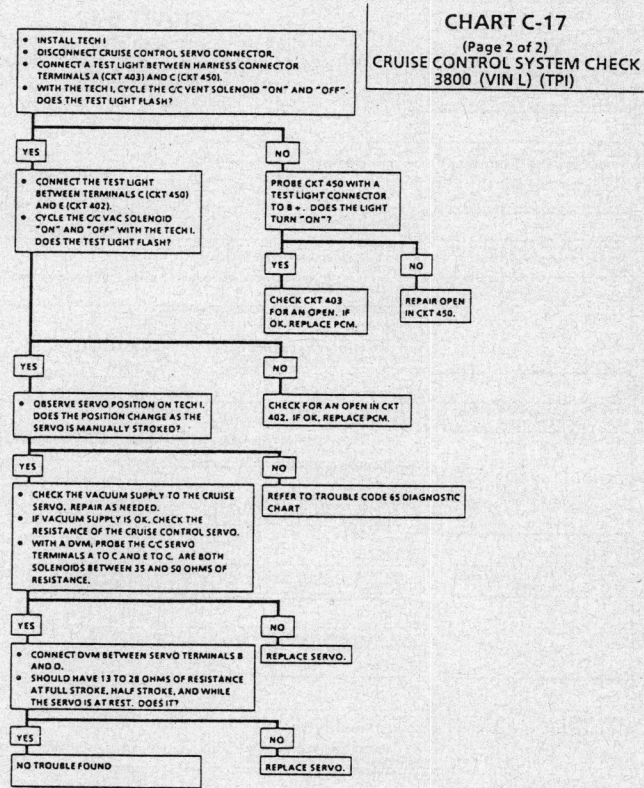

Fig. 15   Chart C-17, cruise control system check (Part 2 of 2). 1991–92

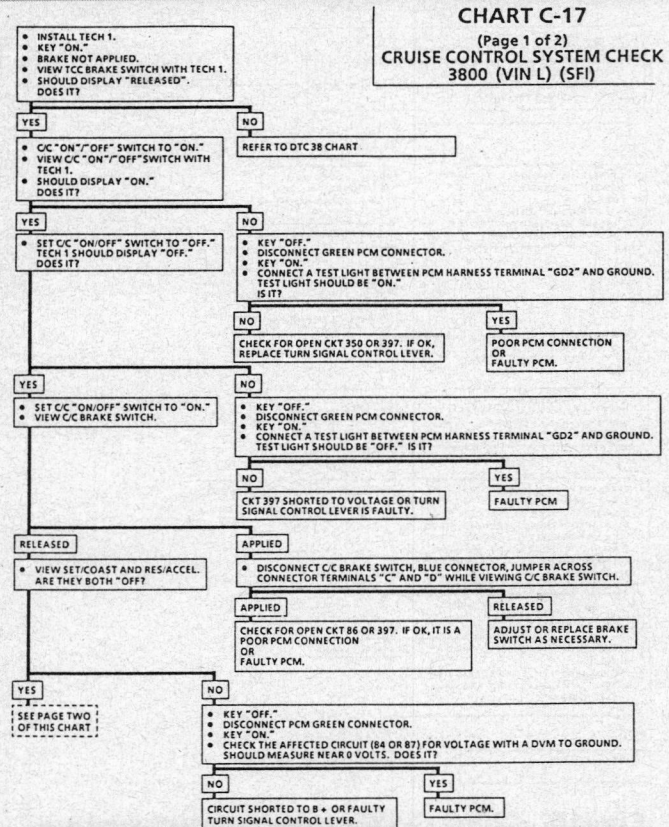

Fig. 16   Chart C-17, cruise control system check (Part 1 of 2). 1993 except Riviera

Fig. 16   Chart C-17, cruise control system check (Part 2 of 2). 1993 except Riviera

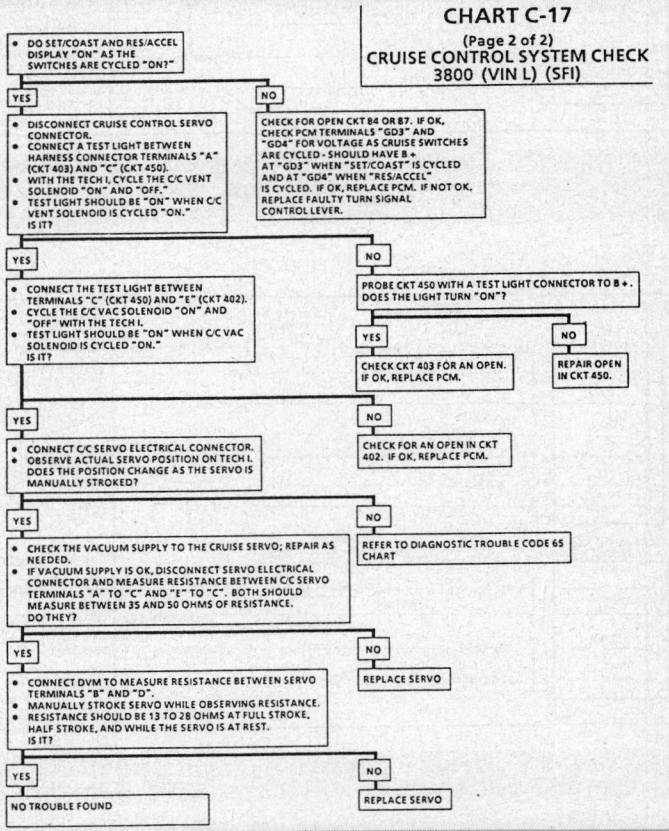

Fig. 17   Chart C-17, cruise control system check (Part 1 of 2). 1993 Riviera

Fig. 17   Chart C-17, cruise control system check (Part 2 of 2). 1993 Riviera

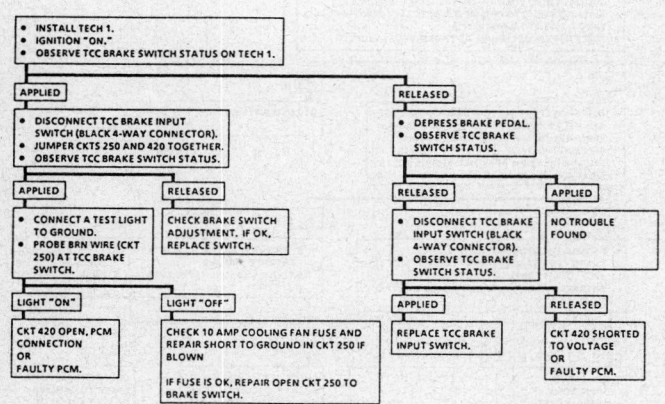

DTC 38
TCC BRAKE INPUT CIRCUIT
3800 (VIN 1) (SFI)

- INSTALL TECH 1.
- IGNITION "ON."
- OBSERVE TCC BRAKE SWITCH STATUS ON TECH 1.

APPLIED
- DISCONNECT TCC BRAKE INPUT SWITCH (BLACK 4-WAY CONNECTOR).
- JUMPER CKTS 250 AND 420 TOGETHER.
- OBSERVE TCC BRAKE SWITCH STATUS.

APPLIED
- CONNECT A TEST LIGHT TO GROUND.
- PROBE BRN WIRE (CKT 250) AT TCC BRAKE SWITCH.

RELEASED
CHECK BRAKE SWITCH ADJUSTMENT. IF OK, REPLACE SWITCH.

LIGHT "ON"
CKT 420 OPEN, PCM CONNECTION OR FAULTY PCM.

LIGHT "OFF"
CHECK 10 AMP COOLING FAN FUSE AND REPAIR SHORT TO GROUND IN CKT 250 IF BLOWN

IF FUSE IS OK, REPAIR OPEN CKT 250 TO BRAKE SWITCH.

RELEASED
- DEPRESS BRAKE PEDAL.
- OBSERVE TCC BRAKE SWITCH STATUS.

RELEASED
- DISCONNECT TCC BRAKE INPUT SWITCH (BLACK 4-WAY CONNECTOR).
- OBSERVE TCC BRAKE SWITCH STATUS.

APPLIED
NO TROUBLE FOUND

APPLIED
REPLACE TCC BRAKE INPUT SWITCH.

RELEASED
CKT 420 SHORTED TO VOLTAGE OR FAULTY PCM.

Fig. 18   Trouble code 38. 1993 except Riviera

DTC 38
BRAKE INPUT CIRCUIT
3800 (VIN L) (SFI)

- INSTALL TECH 1.
- IGNITION "ON."
- "SCAN" TCC BRAKE SWITCH. TECH 1 DISPLAYS:

"APPLIED"
- DISCONNECT BRAKE INPUT SWITCH.
- JUMPER CKTS 339 AND 420 TOGETHER.
- TECH 1 DISPLAYS:

"APPLIED"
- CONNECT A TEST LIGHT TO GROUND.
- PROBE PNK/BLK WIRE CKT 339 AT BRAKE SWITCH.

"RELEASED"
CHECK BRAKE INPUT SWITCH ADJUSTMENT. IF OK, REPLACE SWITCH.

LIGHT "ON"
CKT 420 OPEN, PCM CONNECTION OR FAULTY PCM.

LIGHT "OFF"
CHECK 15 AMP FUSE FOR CKT 339 AND REPAIR SHORT TO GROUND IF BLOWN. IF OK, REPAIR OPEN CKT 339 TO BRAKE SWITCH.

"RELEASED"
- DEPRESS BRAKE PEDAL.
- TECH 1 DISPLAYS:

"RELEASED"
- DISCONNECT BRAKE INPUT SWITCH.
- TECH 1 DISPLAYS:

"APPLIED"
NO TROUBLE FOUND.

"APPLIED"
REPLACE BRAKE INPUT SWITCH.

"RELEASED"
CKT 420 SHORTED TO VOLTAGE OR FAULTY PCM.

Fig. 19   Trouble code 38. 1993 Riviera

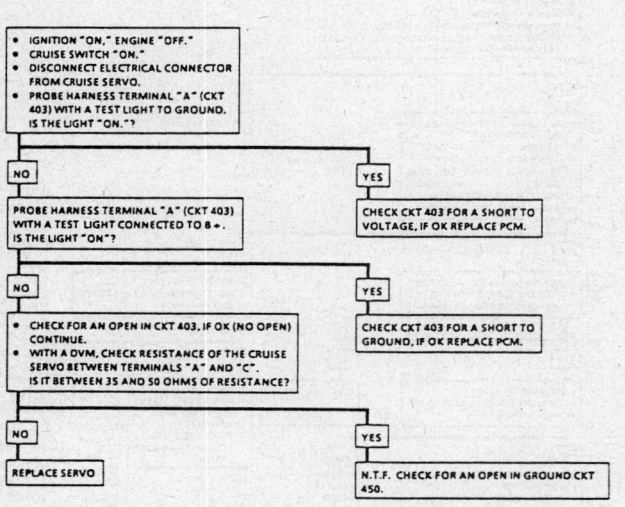

CODE 61
CRUISE VENT SOLENOID CIRCUIT
3800 (VIN L) (TPI)

- IGNITION "ON," ENGINE "OFF."
- CRUISE SWITCH "ON."
- DISCONNECT ELECTRICAL CONNECTOR FROM CRUISE SERVO.
- PROBE HARNESS TERMINAL "A" (CKT 403) WITH A TEST LIGHT TO GROUND. IS THE LIGHT "ON."?

NO
PROBE HARNESS TERMINAL "A" (CKT 403) WITH A TEST LIGHT CONNECTED TO B+. IS THE LIGHT "ON"?

YES
CHECK CKT 403 FOR A SHORT TO VOLTAGE, IF OK REPLACE PCM.

NO
- CHECK FOR AN OPEN IN CKT 403, IF OK (NO OPEN) CONTINUE.
- WITH A DVM, CHECK RESISTANCE OF THE CRUISE SERVO BETWEEN TERMINALS "A" AND "C". IS IT BETWEEN 35 AND 50 OHMS OF RESISTANCE?

YES
CHECK CKT 403 FOR A SHORT TO GROUND, IF OK REPLACE PCM.

NO
REPLACE SERVO

YES
N.T.F. CHECK FOR AN OPEN IN GROUND CKT 450.

Fig. 20   Trouble code 61. 1991–92

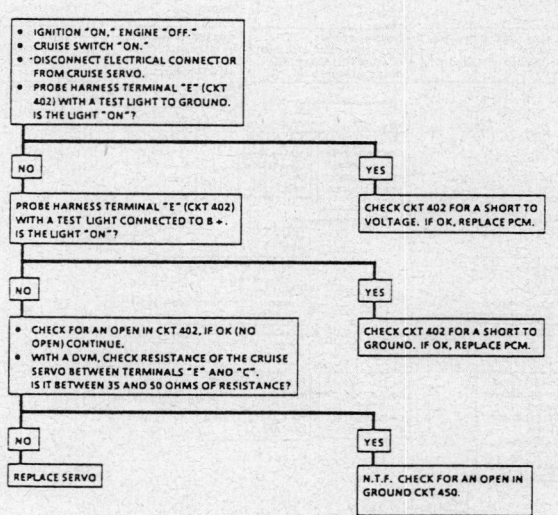

CODE 62
CRUISE VAC SOLENOID CIRCUIT
3800 (VIN L) (TPI)

- IGNITION "ON," ENGINE "OFF."
- CRUISE SWITCH "ON."
- DISCONNECT ELECTRICAL CONNECTOR FROM CRUISE SERVO.
- PROBE HARNESS TERMINAL "E" (CKT 402) WITH A TEST LIGHT TO GROUND. IS THE LIGHT "ON"?

NO
PROBE HARNESS TERMINAL "E" (CKT 402) WITH A TEST LIGHT CONNECTED TO B+. IS THE LIGHT "ON"?

YES
CHECK CKT 402 FOR A SHORT TO VOLTAGE. IF OK, REPLACE PCM.

NO
- CHECK FOR AN OPEN IN CKT 402, IF OK (NO OPEN) CONTINUE.
- WITH A DVM, CHECK RESISTANCE OF THE CRUISE SERVO BETWEEN TERMINALS "E" AND "C". IS IT BETWEEN 35 AND 50 OHMS OF RESISTANCE?

YES
CHECK CKT 402 FOR A SHORT TO GROUND. IF OK, REPLACE PCM.

NO
REPLACE SERVO

YES
N.T.F. CHECK FOR AN OPEN IN GROUND CKT 450.

Fig. 21   Trouble code 62. 1991–92

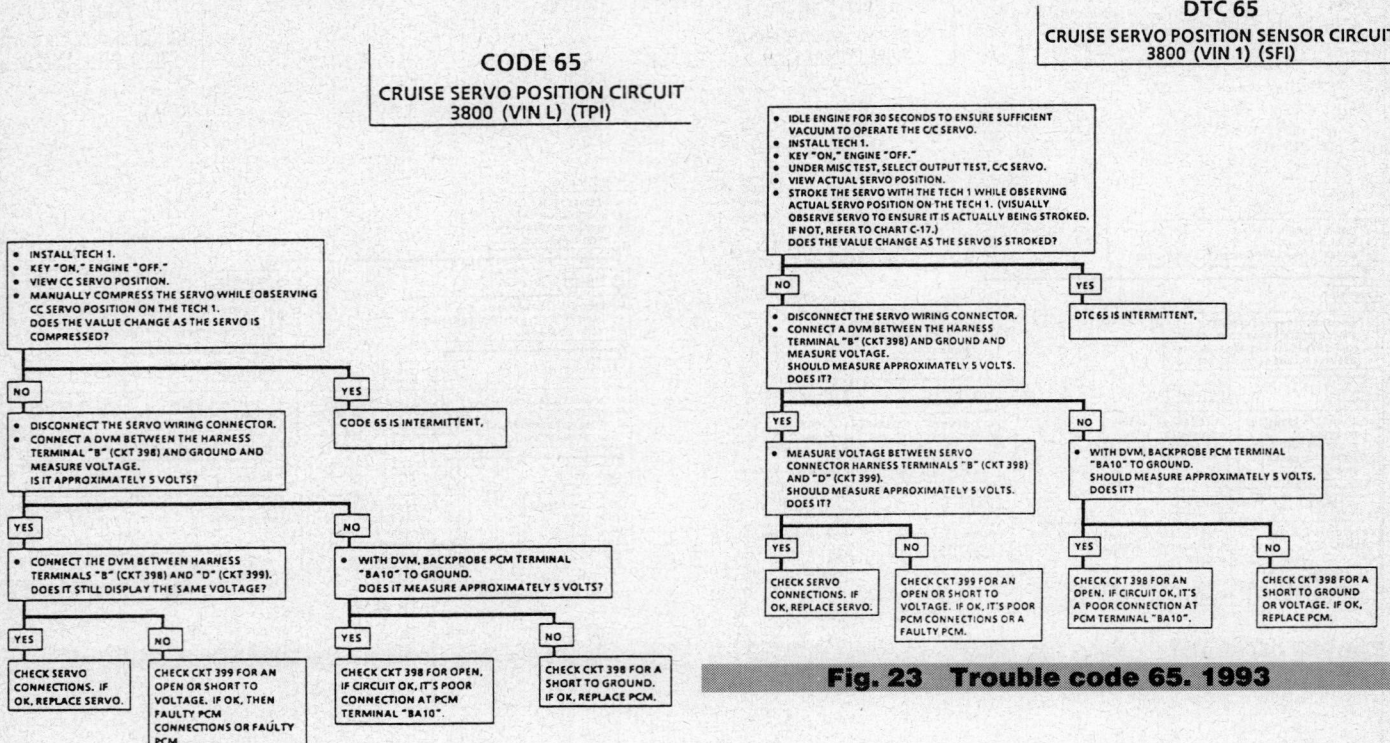

Fig. 22   Trouble code 65. 1991–92

Fig. 23   Trouble code 65. 1993

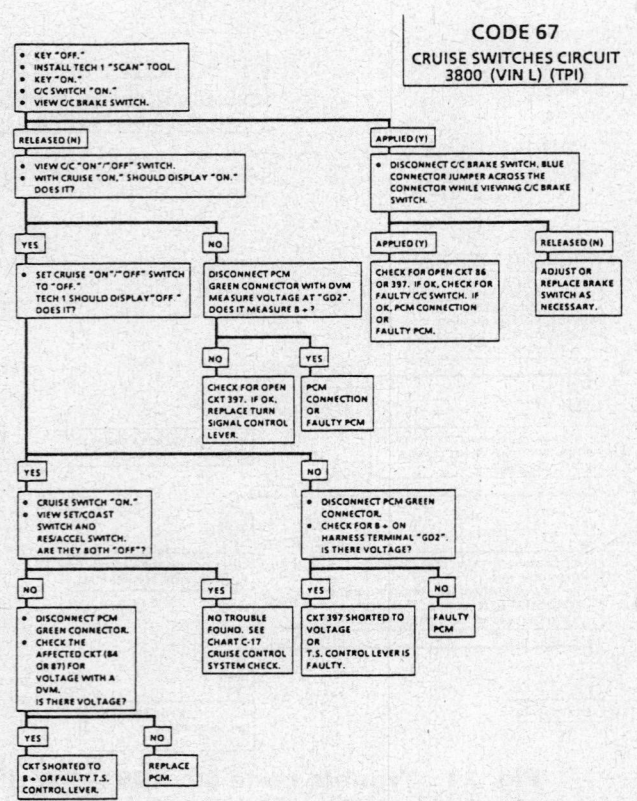

Fig. 24   Trouble code 67. 1991–92

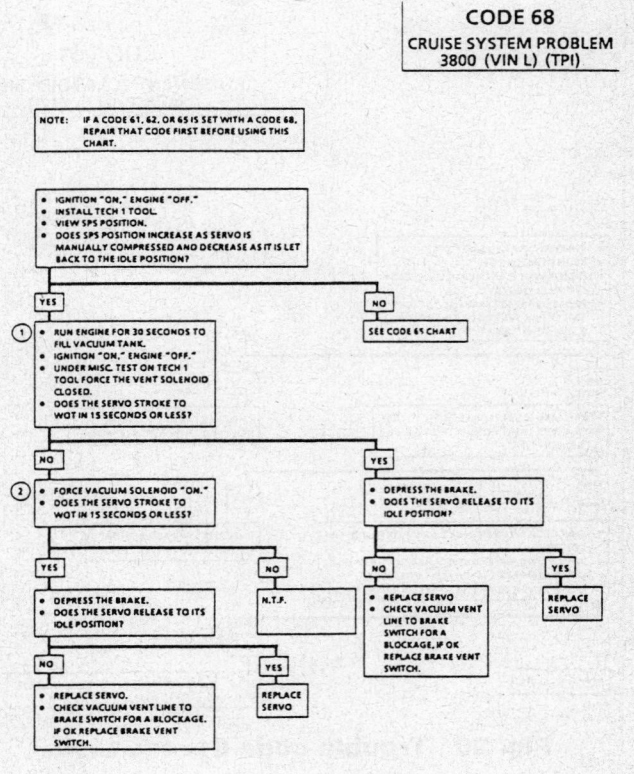

Fig. 25   Trouble code 68. 1991–92

1. STEERING COLUMN SUPPORT
2. MODULAR BRAKE PEDAL MOUNTING BRACKET
3. VACUUM RELEASE VALVE HOSE
4. TCC/ANTILOCK BRAKE SWITCH CONNECTOR
5. STOPLAMP SWITCH CONNECTOR
6. CRUISE/SHIFT INTERLOCK/BRAKE SWITCH CONNECTOR
7. CRUISE/SHIFT INTERLOCK/BRAKE SWITCH
8. TCC/ANTILOCK BRAKE SWITCH
9. RETAINER

Fig. 26   Cruise/shift interlock/brake switch disassembly. 1993 except Riviera

1. THROTTLE BODY
2. RETAINER; MUST BE INSTALLED WITH TANG SECURED OVER CABLE STUD HEAD
3. CRUISE CONTROL CABLE
4. ACCELERATOR CABLE
5. CONDUIT FITTING; MUST HAVE LOCKING TANGS EXPANDED AND LOCKED IN ATTACHING HOLES (VIEW B)
6. FUEL PIPES
7. SERVO BRACKET
8. SERVO BLADE; SELECT HOLE FOR MINIMUM CABLE SLACK
9. CRUISE CONTROL SERVO
10. LOCKING TANGS; EXPAND AND LOCK ON BRACKET AS SHOWN
11. BRACKET (ACCELERATOR OR SERVO)
12. SCREW/BOLT; 1.6 N·M (15 LB-IN)
13. NUT; 27 N·M (20 LB-FT)
14. TRANS. CABLE BRACKET STUDS

Fig. 27   Cruise control cable removal

Type 4

NOTE: Wire Color Code And Symbol Identification Located In The Front Of This Manual Can Be Used As An Aid When Using Wiring Circuits Found In This Section.

INDEX

PRECAUTIONS

AIRBAG SYSTEM DISARMING

1. Ensure front wheels are pointed straight ahead, then turn ignition switch to LOCK position.
2. Remove IGN and CIG & RADIO fuse from junction block No. 1.

3. Remove Connector Position Assurance (CPA) and disconnect lower steering column (yellow two-cavity) connector at base of steering column.

AIRBAG SYSTEM ARMING

1. Turn ignition switch to LOCK position.
2. Connect lower steering column yellow two-cavity connector.
3. Install IGN and CIG & RADIO fuses.

4. Turn ignition switch to ACC or ON positions and verify that the airbag indicator illuminates steady for approximately six seconds and then turns off.

DESCRIPTION

1991–92

This system automatically adjusts the

opening of the engine throttle valve so that a selected vehicle speed can be maintained during favorable driving conditions. When system is engaged, the vehicle maintains a constant speed regardless of terrain.

1993

The cruise control system maintains a selected speed under normal driving conditions. Steep grades up or down may cause variations in the selected speeds. This cruise control system has the ability to cruise, coast, resume speed, accelerate and -tap-up- or -tap-down-.

The main system components of the cruise control system are the cruise control module (CCM), the actuator, cruise control switch and vehicle speed sensor (VSS).

The CCM and actuator are the two main components that allow the system to control and maintain desired vehicle speed. The CCM monitors vehicle speed and provides cruise control actuator with the necessary command to maintain and change vehicle speed in response to inputs from the cruise control switch. Cruise control operation is disengaged when the CCM receives a cancel signal from the parking brake switch, stoplamp switch, brake fluid level switch, cruise control switch, park/neutral (PNP) switch (automatic transaxles) or clutch pedal position (CPP) interrupt switch (manual transaxles).

SYSTEM COMPONENTS
CRUISE CONTROL MODULE (CCM)
1993

The cruise control module is mounted on the center console under the radio. The main function of the CCM is to monitor and act upon input signals from the cruise control switch and VSS. There are four different kinds of input signals received by the CCM: ON/OFF, speed control, throttle position and cancel. The ON/OFF signal is provided by the cruise control switch and activates and deactivates the cruise control system. The speed control input signal to the CCM is provided by the cruise control switch and VSS. Speed control input signals from the cruise control switch are the RES/ACC (resume/accelerate) signal and the SET/COAST signal; these signals are also used to initiate the -tap-up- and -tap-down- functions. The CCM uses these signals in addition to the signal from the VSS to determine and maintain or alter vehicle speed in accordance with the driver's commands. The throttle position signals to the CCM are provided by the actuator and the idle switch inside the throttle position (TP) sensor. These signals allow the CCM to constantly monitor throttle position during cruise control operation. The cancel signal are provided by the cruise control switch CANCEL signal, the parking brake switch, stoplamp switch, brake fluid level switch, park/neutral (PNP) switch (automatic transaxles) or clutch pedal position (CPP) interrupt switch (manual transaxles).

CRUISE CONTROL ACTUATOR
1993

The actuator is mounted to the right inner fender. The actuator consists of a DC servo motor, a worm gear, a throttle angle sensor (potentiometer) and a magnetic clutch.

VEHICLE SPEED SENSOR
1993

The VSS is an electronic relay that is mounted on the transaxle. As the transaxle's output shaft turns, the VSS provides the speedometer with vehicle speed input (voltage pulses).

CLUTCH PEDAL POSITION (CPP) INTERRUPT SWITCH (MANUAL TRANSAXLES)
1993

The clutch pedal position (CPP) interrupt switch is mounted directly above the clutch pedal. Whenever the clutch pedal is depressed, the CPP interrupt switch closes and provides a ground to the CCM. The CCM disengages cruise control operation when this ground signal is sensed.

PARK/NEUTRAL POSITION (PNP) SWITCH (AUTOMATIC TRANSAXLES)
1993

The park/neutral position (PNP) switch is mounted to the transaxle. Whenever the manual selector lever is placed in Park or Neutral, the PNP closes and provides a ground to the CCM. The CCM disengages cruise control operation when this ground signal is sensed.

BRAKE FLUID LEVEL SWITCH
1993

The brake fluid level switch is mounted inside the brake fluid reservoir. Whenever the brake fluid level drops below a specified level, the brake fluid level switch closes and provides a ground to the CCM. The CCM disengages cruise control operation when this ground signal is sensed.

PARKING BRAKE SWITCH
1993

The parking brake switch is located in the center console directly under the parking brake. Whenever the parking brake is engaged, the switch closes and provides a ground to the CCM. The CCM disengages cruise control operation when this ground signal is sensed.

STOPLAMP SWITCH
1993

The stoplamp switch is located under the instrument panel directly above the brake pedal. Whenever the brake pedal is depressed, one set of stoplamp switches close and provide a ground to the CCM. The CCM disengages cruise control operation when this ground signal is sensed. When the brake pedal is depressed, another set of stoplamp switch contacts open,

and the voltage circuit from the CCM to the magnetic clutch inside the actuator is interrupted. With voltage removed from the magnetic clutch, the actuator's DC servo motor is disengaged from the worm gear and the throttle is permitted to return to the idle position. This feature is provided to ensure cancellation of the cruise control system operation during vehicle braking.

THROTTLE POSITION SENSOR
1993

The throttle position (TP) sensor is located on the throttle body. Whenever the throttle is in the idle position, the idle switch contacts within the TP sensor close and provide a ground to the CCM.

POWERTRAIN CONTROL MODULE (PCM)
1993

On vehicles equipped with four-speed automatic transaxles, the CCM receives a shift solenoid number 2 signal. This signal informs the CCM that the transaxle is in second or third gear and is out of the OVERDRIVE mode.

CRUISE ON-OFF SWITCH
1993

The On-Off switch is a temporary contact type button located on the end of the cruise control switch. The purpose of the switch is turn the cruise control system on and off.

RES/ACC SWITCH
1993

The RES/ACC (resume/accelerate) switch returns cruise control operation to the last speed setting after a cancel signal is received by the CCM. If acceleration during cruise speed is desired, move cruise control switch upward into RES/ACC position and hold it there until desired speed is attained.

The RES/ACC switch can also be used to -tap-up- vehicle speed. Tapping-up is accomplished by quickly moving cruise control switch up into RES/ACC position and releasing it. Tapping-up will increase vehicle speed in 1 mph increments.

SET/COAST SWITCH
1993

The SET/COAST witch is activated when the cruise control switch is moved downward. The vehicle will cruise at the speed when the switch was activated. By moving the switch downward and holding it there, the cruise control system will disengage and the throttle will return to idle position. The SET/COAST switch can lso be used to -tap-down- vehicle speed. -Tapping-down- is performed by quickly moving and releasing the SET/COAST switch. This will decrease vehicle speed in 1 mph increments.

Symptom	Read	Result	Circuits
• Cruise control switch indicator blinks five times or • Cruise control system does not set or • Cruise control system does not operate.	Type B Codes	11	• Actuator • Cruise Control Module
		21	• Speed Sensor • Cruise Control Module
		23	• Check speedometer cable operation • Actuator • Speed Sensor • Vacuum Pump and Hose • Vacuum Switch • Cruise Control Module
		31	• Engage Switch • Cruise Control Module
		33	• Engage Switch • Cruise Control Module
	Type A Code 5	No Code	• Speed Sensor • Cruise Control Module
		OK	• Cruise Control Switch • Engage Switch • Stoplamp Switch • Clutch or Neutral Start Switch • Parking Brake Switch • Check speedometer cable operation • Actuator • Cruise Control Module • Vacuum Hose and Brake Fluid
Setting speed deviated on high or low speed.	Type A Code 3	OK	• Check speedometer cable operation • Speed Sensor • Vacuum Pump • Vacuum Switch • Actuator • Cruise Control Module
		No Code	• Speed Sensor
Vehicle speed fluctuates when control switch is turned to "SET/COAST."			• Speed Sensor • Check speedometer cable operation • Actuator • Cruise Control Module
Setting speed does not cancel when the brake pedal is depressed.	Type A Code 4	OK	• Actuator • Stoplamp Switch • Cruise Control Module
		No Code	• Stoplamp Switch • Cruise Control Module
Setting speed does not cancel when the parking brake is applied.	Type A Code 4	OK	• Actuator • Cruise Control Module
		No Code	• Parking Brake Switch • Cruise Control Module

Fig. 1 Cruise control system troubleshooting chart (Part 1 of 2). 1991–92

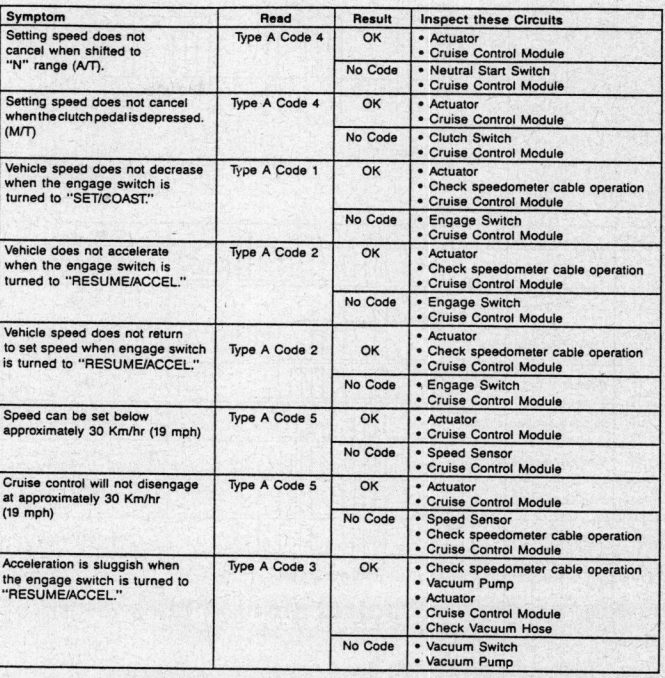

Symptom	Read	Result	Inspect these Circuits
Setting speed does not cancel when shifted to "N" range (A/T).	Type A Code 4	OK	• Actuator • Cruise Control Module
		No Code	• Neutral Start Switch • Cruise Control Module
Setting speed does not cancel when the clutch pedal is depressed. (M/T)	Type A Code 4	OK	• Actuator • Cruise Control Module
		No Code	• Clutch Switch • Cruise Control Module
Vehicle speed does not decrease when the engage switch is turned to "SET/COAST."	Type A Code 1	OK	• Actuator • Check speedometer cable operation • Cruise Control Module
		No Code	• Engage Switch • Cruise Control Module
Vehicle does not accelerate when the engage switch is turned to "RESUME/ACCEL."	Type A Code 2	OK	• Actuator • Check speedometer cable operation • Cruise Control Module
		No Code	• Engage Switch • Cruise Control Module
Vehicle speed does not return to set speed when engage switch is turned to "RESUME/ACCEL."	Type A Code 2	OK	• Actuator • Check speedometer cable operation • Cruise Control Module
		No Code	• Engage Switch • Cruise Control Module
Speed can be set below approximately 30 Km/hr (19 mph)	Type A Code 5	OK	• Actuator • Cruise Control Module
		No Code	• Speed Sensor • Cruise Control Module
Cruise control will not disengage at approximately 30 Km/hr (19 mph)	Type A Code 5	OK	• Actuator • Cruise Control Module
		No Code	• Speed Sensor • Check speedometer cable operation • Cruise Control Module
Acceleration is sluggish when the engage switch is turned to "RESUME/ACCEL."	Type A Code 3	OK	• Check speedometer cable operation • Vacuum Pump • Actuator • Cruise Control Module • Check Vacuum Hose
		No Code	• Vacuum Switch • Vacuum Pump

Fig. 1 Cruise control system troubleshooting chart (Part 2 of 2). 1991–92

NO.	CONDITIONS	INDICATOR CODE	DIAGNOSIS
1	"SET/COAST" on		"SET/COAST" circuit is normal.
2	"RESUME/ACCEL" on		"RESUME/ACCEL" circuit is normal.
3	Vacuum switch on		Vacuum switch circuit is normal.
4	Each cancel switch on (Stoplamp switch, Parking brake switch, Clutch switch, Neutral start switch)		Each cancel switch circuit is normal.
5	Drive 40 km/h (25 mph) or over		Speed sensor circuit is normal.
6	Drive 30 km/h (19 mph) or below		Speed sensor circuit is normal.

Fig. 2 Type A code chart. 1991–92

	INDICATION CODE	DIAGNOSIS
	ON OFF	Normal.
11	ON OFF	Actuator circuit is abnormal.
21	ON OFF	Speed sensor signal circuit is abnormal.
23	ON OFF	*Vehicle speed has decreased 16 km/h (10 mph) or more from the set speed.
31	ON OFF	"RESUME/ACCEL" circuit is abnormal.
33	ON OFF	"RESUME/ACCEL" and "SET/COAST" circuit is abnormal.

*If the set speed is maintained when the control switch is set again at "SET/COAST," there is no malfunction.

Fig. 3 Type B code chart. 1991–92

OPERATION

SETTING DESIRED SPEED
1991–92

Turn main switch to On position. The indicator lamp will illuminate. Depress accelerator pedal to obtain desired speed above 25 mph. Turn control switch downward toward Set (Coast), then release it. This will set the system at the speed the vehicle was moving at when the switch was released.

TEMPORARY ACCELERATION
1991–92

Accelerate by depressing accelerator pedal. When accelerator pedal is released, the vehicle will automatically slow to the preset speed.

RESETTING AT A HIGHER SPEED
1991–92

Turn control switch upward toward Resume (Accel). The vehicle speed will keep increasing until the control switch is released. Release control switch when desired speed is reached. **On vehicles with automatic transmission, overdrive is released during acceleration and is restored when the control switch is released.**

RESETTING AT LOWER SPEED
1991–92

Turn control switch downward toward Set (Coast). The vehicle speed will continue decreasing until control switch is released. Release control switch at desired speed.

CANCELLING THE PRESET SPEED
1991–92

Once the preset speed has been set, it may be cancelled by doing any of the following:
1. Depress brake pedal.
2. Depress clutch pedal (vehicles with manual transmission).
3. Place shift lever at Neutral position (vehicles with automatic transmission).
4. Slightly pull the parking brake lever.
5. Turn main switch to Off position.

RESUMING THE PRESET SPEED
1991–92

Automatic cruising is only temporarily cancelled by steps 1 through 4 under Cancelling The Preset Speed if vehicle has not decelerated to below 25 mph. The preset speed will be resumed when the control switch is turned upward toward Resume (Accel).

TROUBLESHOOTING

1991–92

1. Refer to charts, **Fig. 1.**
2. If instructed to read a type A code, refer to **Fig. 2** and proceed as follows:

EXAMPLE: Vehicle Speed Sensor (VSS) (DTC 21)

CODE	DIAGNOSTIC AREA	MODE		FAILURE
—	Normal*	ON OFF		—
11	Actuator DC Servo Motor			Short
12	Actuator Magnetic Clutch			Short
13	Actuator			Open
21	Vehicle Speed Sensor (VSS)			Open or Short
23	Vehicle Speed Sensor (VSS)			Vehicle Speed Input 16 km/h (10 mph) lower than Set Speed
32	Cruise Control Switch			Short
34	Cruise Control Switch			Incorrect Voltage

* FAILURE WITHIN ELECTRONIC CIRCUIT IF FLASHED ON-OFF 5 TIMES ONLY

Fig. 4   Cruise control module diagnostic trouble code chart. 1993

a. Turn ignition switch on.
b. Turn set/coast switch on.
c. Push main switch on.
d. Turn set/coast switch off.
e. Meet conditions listed in chart. **Checking of No. 4 code is done with front of vehicle raised and supported and with engine idling.**
f. Read diagnostic code on main switch indicator. If there is no indication code, refer to Diagnosis.
3. If instructed to read type B codes, refer to **Fig. 3** and proceed as follows:
a. If, while driving with cruise control on, the system is cancelled by a malfunction in either the actuator or the speed sensor, the main switch indicator will blink 5 times.
b. While driving at a speed of no more than 10 mph, press set/coast switch three times within two seconds. **In order to save diagnostic code(s) when a malfunction has occurred, always inspect with ignition and main switches on. Should the power be cut, the diagnostic code(s) will be erased from the computer memory. If there is no indication code, refer to Diagnosis.**

1993

Refer to **Figs. 4 and 5** for diagnostic trouble code interpretation and CCM connector identification.

SYSTEM DIAGNOSIS & TESTING

1991–92

Refer to **Figs. 6 through 15**, when diagnosing system, and **Figs. 16 and 17** for wiring diagram and terminal identification.

1993

Refer to **Figs. 18 through 35**, when diagnosing system, and **Fig. 36 through 38** for cruise control system, starter and stoplamp wiring diagrams.

COMPONENT DIAGNOSIS & TESTING

CRUISE CONTROL MODULE

1991–92

Refer to **Fig. 39** to test cruise control module.

CRUISE CONTROL SWITCH

1991–92

To test control switch, refer to **Fig. 40**.

CLUTCH SWITCH

1991–92

1. Disconnect clutch switch electrical connector.
2. Connect digital multimeter, J34029-A, or equivalent, to clutch switch terminals 1 and 2.
3. With clutch pedal depressed, ensure continuity.
4. With clutch pedal released, ensure no continuity.
5. If results are not as indicated, replace clutch switch.

SPEED SENSOR

1991–92

Refer to **Fig. 10**, to test speed sensor.

STOPLAMP SWITCH

1991–92

Refer to **Fig. 41** to test stoplamp switch.

PARKING BRAKE SWITCH

1991–92

1. Disconnect parking brake switch electrical connectors.
2. Ensure continuity between terminals with parking brake engaged.
3. No continuity should be indicated between terminals with parking brake returned.
4. If results are not as indicated, replace parking brake switch.

ACTUATOR

1991–92

1. Ensure control cable freeplay is less than .39 inch, **Fig. 42**, adjusting as necessary.
2. Using a digital multimeter, J43029-A, or equivalent, measure resistance values between terminals 2 and 3, then measure resistance between terminals 1 and 3.
3. If resistance is not approximately 30 ohms between terminals 2 and 3, and approximately 68 ohms between ter-

---

BACK VIEW OF CCM CONNECTOR

CAVITY	WIRE COLOR	CIRCUIT	VOLTAGE
1	RED/WHT	BATTERY POWER	12V
2	BLK (VIN 6 AND VIN 8 – M/T) BLK/WHT (VIN 8 – A/T)	CLUTCH PEDAL DEPRESSED SIGNAL (M/T) "P" OR "N" SIGNAL (A/T)	12V ①
3	RED/BLK	PARKING BRAKE AND BRAKE FLUID LEVEL SWITCH SIGNAL	12V ②
4	WHT/BLU	CRUISE "ON-OFF" SIGNAL	12V ③
5	GRN/RED	"CRUISE" INDICATOR CONTROL	12V ④
6	—	NOT USED	—
7	—	NOT USED	—
8	PPL	DIAGNOSTIC REQUEST SIGNAL	12V
9	RED	O/D CUT CONTROL (VIN 8 – A/T)	12V ⑤
10	GRN/BLK	MAGNETIC CLUTCH CONTROL	0V* ⑥
11	RED/BLK	DC SERVO MOTOR – CLOSE	0V* ⑦
12	RED/GRN	DC SERVO MOTOR – OPEN	0V* ⑧
13	WHT/BLK	GROUND	0V*
14	BLK/YEL	IGNITION POWER	12V
15	RED/GRN	MEMORY POWER	12V
16	GRN/WHT	BRAKE SIGNAL	0V* ⑨
17	—	NOT USED	—
18	GRN/BLK	RES/ACC, SET/COAST AND CANCEL SWITCH SIGNAL	12V ⑩
19	—	NOT USED	—
20	PPL/WHT	VEHICLE SPEED INPUT	⑪
21	—	NOT USED	—
22	BRN/WHT	SHIFT SOLENOID NUMBER 2 SIGNAL (VIN 8 – A/T)	0V* ⑫
23	BLU	IDLE SWITCH SIGNAL	0V* ⑬
24	BLU/ORN	REFERENCE VOLTAGE (THROTTLE ANGLE SENSOR)	5V
25	LT GRN	THROTTLE ANGLE INPUT	⑭
26	BLU/RED	THROTTLE ANGLE SENSOR GROUND	0V*

* LESS THAN 1.0 VOLTS
① 0V WITH PNP OR CPP INTERRUPT SWITCH CLOSED
② 0V WITH PARKING BRAKE OR BRAKE FLUID LEVEL SWITCH CLOSED
③ MOMENTARY 0V WITH BUTTON PRESSED
④ 0V WITH "CRUISE" INDICATOR LIT
⑤ 0V WITH "OVERDRIVE" AND CRUISE CONTROL ENGAGED AND ENGINE UNDER A HEAVY LOAD
⑥ 12V WITH CRUISE CONTROL ENGAGED
⑦ 12V WITH DC SERVO MOTOR CLOSE SIDE ENERGIZED
⑧ 12V WITH DC SERVO MOTOR OPEN SIDE ENERGIZED
⑨ 12V WITH BRAKE PEDAL DEPRESSED
⑩ 0.7–2.5V WITH CRUISE CONTROL SWITCH IN RES/ACC POSITION 2.4–4.6V WITH CRUISE CONTROL SWITCH IN SET/COAST POSITION 4.1–7.2V WITH CRUISE CONTROL SWITCH IN CANCEL POSITION
⑪ VARIES WITH VEHICLE SPEED 0–5V
⑫ 12V WITH TRANSAXLE IN 2ND OR 3RD GEAR
⑬ 12V WITH IDLE SWITCH OPEN
⑭ VOLTAGE VARIES WITH THROTTLE POSITION

Fig. 5   Cruise control connector identification chart. 1993

minals 1 and 3, replace actuator.
4. Disconnect actuator electrical connector.
5. Connect positive lead from battery to terminals 1 and 2 and the negative lead to terminal 3.
6. Using a hand held vacuum pump, J23738-A, or equivalent, slowly apply vacuum from 0 to 11.8 inches Hg, ensuring control cable can be pulled smoothly.
7. Disconnect terminal 1 and 2, then check control cable returns to original position, and vacuum returns to 0 inches Hg.
8. If results are not as indicated, replace actuator.

VACUUM PUMP

1991–92

1. Connect a hand held vacuum pump, J23738-A, or equivalent, to actuator side of vacuum pump.
2. Connect positive battery terminal to terminal 1 of vacuum pump.
3. Connect negative battery lead to terminal 2.
4. Ensure vacuum of 7.87 inches Hg or above.
5. If results are not as indicated, replace vacuum pump.

VACUUM SWITCH

1991–92

1. Ensure no continuity between vacuum switch terminal 1 and 2 with vacuum of 6.30 to 7.08 inches Hg applied.
2. Ensure no continuity between terminals with no vacuum applied.
3. If results are not as indicated, replace switch.

NEUTRAL SAFETY SWITCH

1991–92

1. Disconnect neutral safety switch electrical connector.
2. Connect a digital multimeter, J34029-A, or equivalent, to neutral safety switch terminals 1 and 2, then test continuity with switch in "P" and "N" position.
3. Ensure continuity between terminals 3 and 4 with switch in "R" position.
4. If results are not as indicated, replace neutral safety switch.

COMPONENT REPLACEMENT

CLUTCH PEDAL POSITION (CPP) INTERRUPT SWITCH (MANUAL TRANSAXLES)

1993

1. Disconnect battery ground cable.
2. Remove two cover plates from knee bolster.
3. Disconnect hood release cable from hood release lever and bracket.
4. Remove four bolts and knee bolster from instrument panel.

5. Disconnect electrical connector from ABS data link connector (DLC), if equipped.
6. Remove one screw and left side ventilation from left side duct outlet.
7. Disconnect CPP interrupt switch electrical connector from CPP interrupt switch, **Fig. 43**, then loosen CPP interrupt switch locknut.
8. Remove CPP interrupt switch locknut and switch by turning counterclockwise.
9. Reverse procedure to install noting the following:
   a. Tighten CPP interrupt switch locknut to 89 inch lbs.
   b. Tighten knee bolster bolts to 89 inch lbs.
   c. Tighten battery ground cable to 11 ft. lbs.

CRUISE CONTROL ACTUATOR

1991–92

1. Remove actuator electrical connector, then remove vacuum hose.
2. Remove actuator cover attaching screws, then remove cover.
3. Remove control cable as outlined previously.
4. Remove actuator attaching nuts.
5. Reverse procedure to install.

1993

1. Disconnect battery ground cable.
2. Remove actuator cover, then loosen cable locknuts.
3. Disconnect control cable from actuator lever and bracket.
4. Disconnect actuator electrical connector.
5. Remove three bolts from actuator, then actuator and brackets.
6. Reverse procedure to install noting the following:
   a. Tighten actuator bolts to 89 inch lbs.
   b. Inspect cable for excessive wear or loose fit, replace as necessary.
   c. Tighten cable locknuts to 44 ft. lbs.

CRUISE CONTROL CABLE

1991–92

1. Remove actuator cover attaching screws.
2. Disconnect control cable from actuator assembly.
3. Remove left lower dash trim panel.
4. Remove inner cable plate attaching nuts.
5. Remove outer cable plate attaching bolt.
6. Remove control cable from cable plate, then remove cable.
7. Reverse procedure to install.

1993

1. Remove actuator cover, then loosen cable locknuts.
2. Disconnect control cable from actuator lever and bracket.
3. Disconnect cable from three underhood guide clips, **Fig. 44**.

4. Remove cable from cruise control bellcrank above accelerator pedal, **Fig. 44**.
5. Unclip cable grommet at bulkhead.
6. Remove control cable.
7. Reverse procedure to install noting the following:
   a. Inspect cable for fraying, loose fit or excessive wear, replace as necessary.
   b. Tighten cable locknuts to 44 inch. lbs.

CRUISE CONTROL MODULE (CCM)

1993

1. Disconnect battery ground cable.
2. **On automatic transaxles,** move shifter to -L- (Low) position.
3. **On manual transaxles,** remove gear shift knob and boot from lever, then move shifter to 4th gear.
4. **On all models,** remove center console trim bezel, then disconnect electrical connectors from rear defogger switch, hazard switch and cigar lighter at rear of center console trim bezel.
5. Remove center console tray, then four screws and radio.
6. Disconnect electrical connectors and antenna lead from rear of radio.
7. Remove five screws and rear console from vehicle.
8. **On automatic transaxles,** remove shifter trim bezel from center console.
9. **On all models,** Remove two screws and center console from vehicle.
10. Disconnect CCM electrical connector, then remove two bolts and CCM from vehicle.
11. Reverse procedure to install noting the following:
    a. Tighten CCM bolts to 89 inch lbs.
    b. Tighten battery ground cable to 11 ft. lbs.

CRUISE CONTROL SWITCH

1993

1. Disable airbag system as outlined under -Airbag System Disarming.-
2. Remove inflator module from steering wheel as follows:
   a. Place front wheels in straight ahead position.
   b. Remove side trim covers from steering wheel.
   c. Remove two Torx head screws, release connector position assurance (CPA) and disconnect upper steering column connector, **Fig. 45**.
   d. Remove inflator module from steering wheel.
3. Disconnect cruise control switch electrical connector from airbag coil assembly, **Fig. 46**.
4. Open terminal position assurance (TPA) on top of cruise control switch electrical connector using a terminal remove from J 38125-A terminal repair kit or equivalent.
5. Disconnect black wire from cruise

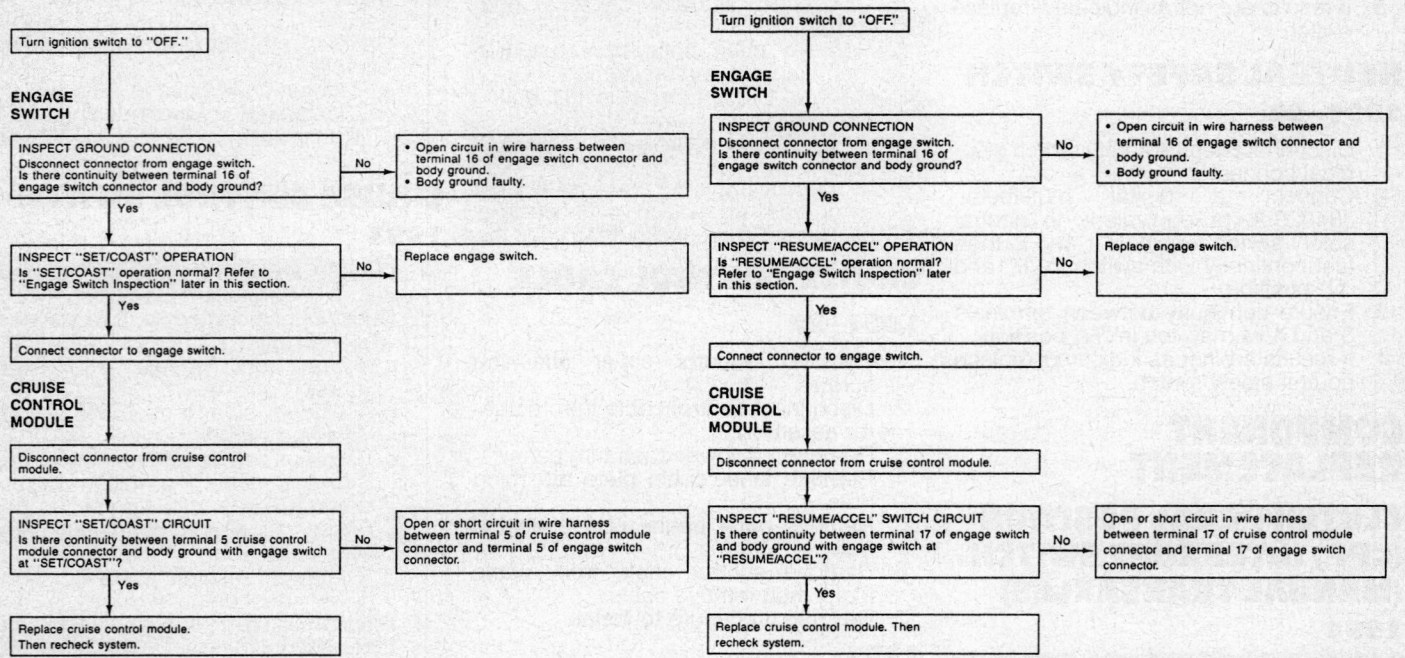

Fig. 6   Cruise control switch circuit diagnosis (Part 1 of 2). 1991—92

Fig. 6   Cruise control switch circuit diagnosis (Part 2 of 2). 1991—92

Fig. 7   Engage switch "Set/Coast" circuit diagnosis. 1991—92

Fig. 8   Engage switch "Resume/Accel" circuit diagnosis. 1991—92

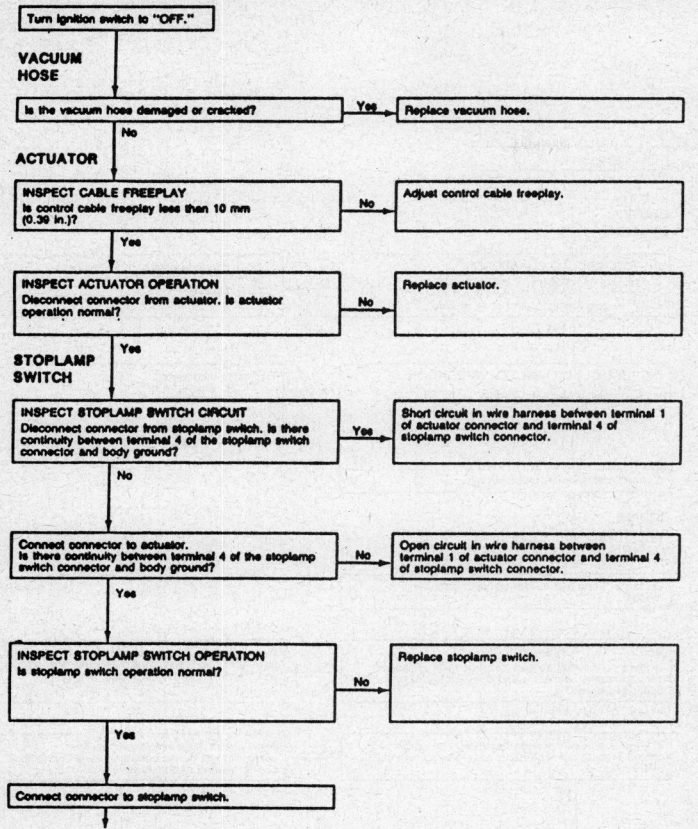

Fig. 9   Actuator circuit diagnosis (Part 1 of 2).
1991–92

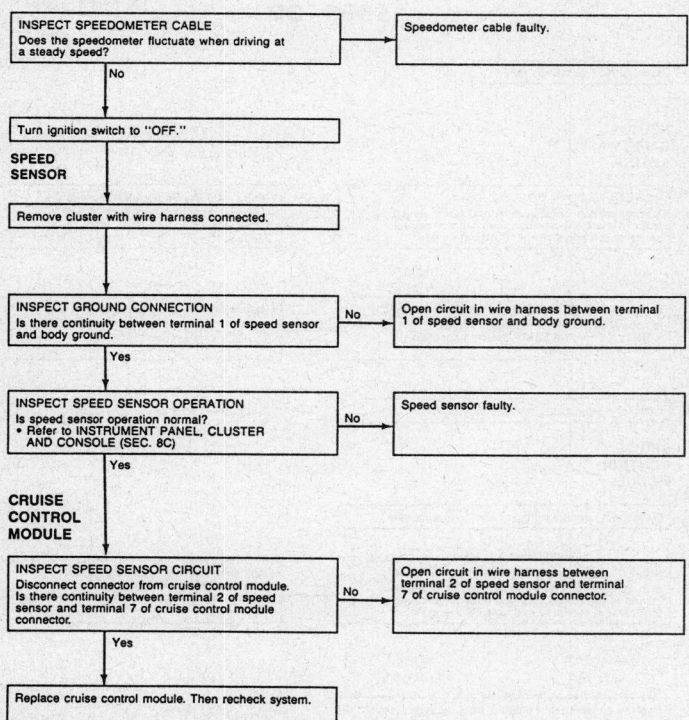

Fig. 10   Speed sensor circuit diagnosis.
1991–92

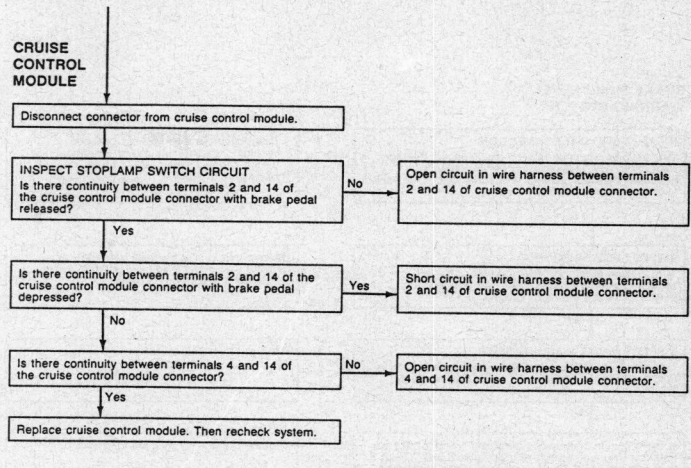

Fig. 9   Actuator circuit diagnosis (Part 2 of 2).
1991–92

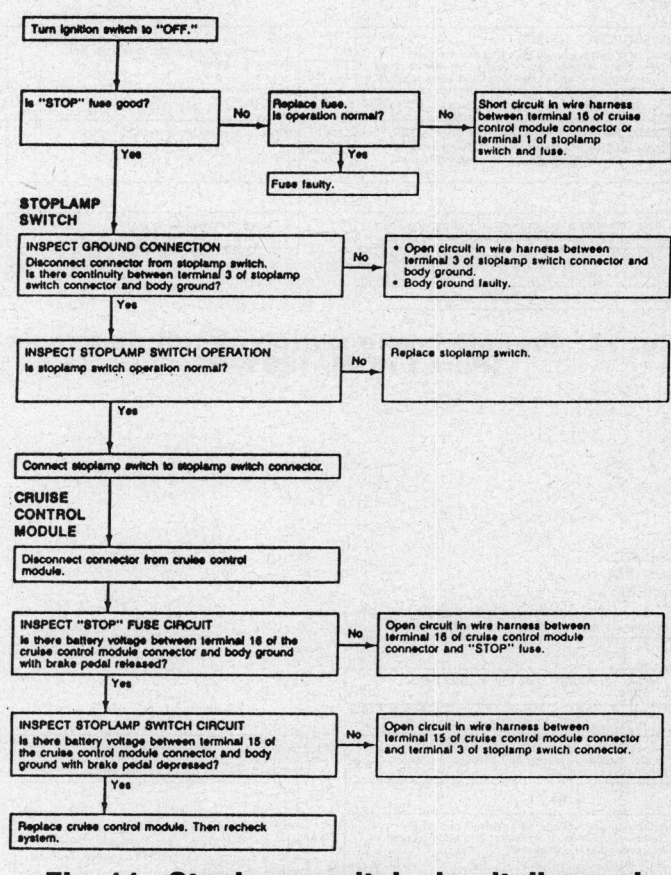

Fig. 11   Stoplamp switch circuit diagnosis.
1991–92

control switch electrical connector using a terminal remove from J 38125-A terminal repair kit or equivalent.
6. Remove three screws and cruise control switch from steering wheel.
7. Reverse procedure to install. Reactivate airbag as outlined under "Airbag System Arming."

Continued on page 31-117

Fig. 12　Parking brake switch circuit diagnosis (Part 1 of 2). 1991–92

Fig. 13　Clutch switch circuit diagnosis. 1991–92

Fig. 12　Parking brake switch circuit diagnosis (Part 2 of 2). 1991–92

Fig. 14　Neutral safety switch circuit diagnosis. 1991–92

Fig. 15 Vacuum circuit diagnosis (Part 1 of 2). 1991–92

Fig. 15 Vacuum circuit diagnosis (Part 2 of 2). 1991–92

Fig. 16 Cruise control system wiring diagram. 1991–92

Fig. 17 Cruise control system connector terminal identification. 1991–92

Fig. 18 Cruise control module on-board diagnostic (OBD) system check (Part 1 of 5). 1993

Fig. 18 Cruise control module on-board diagnostic (OBD) system check (Part 2 of 5). 1993

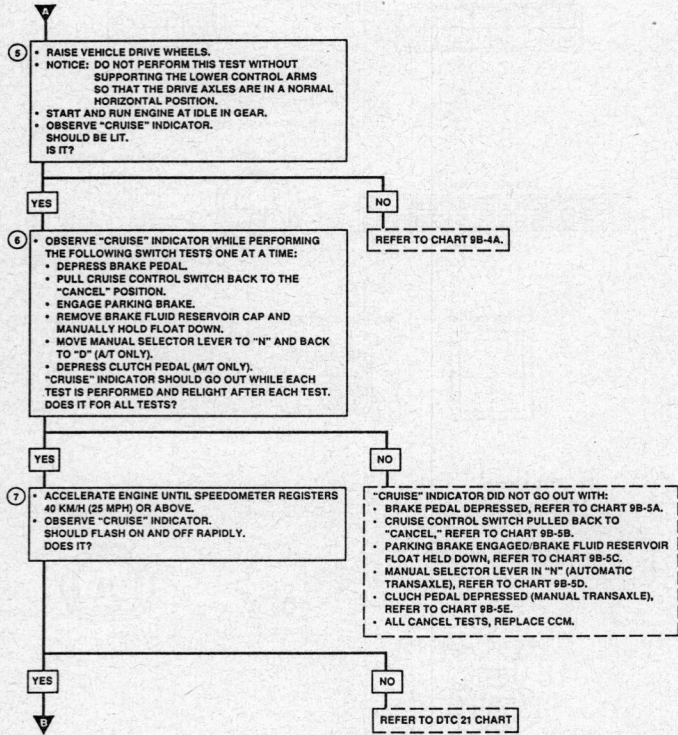

Fig. 18 Cruise control module on-board diagnostic (OBD) system check (Part 3 of 5). 1993

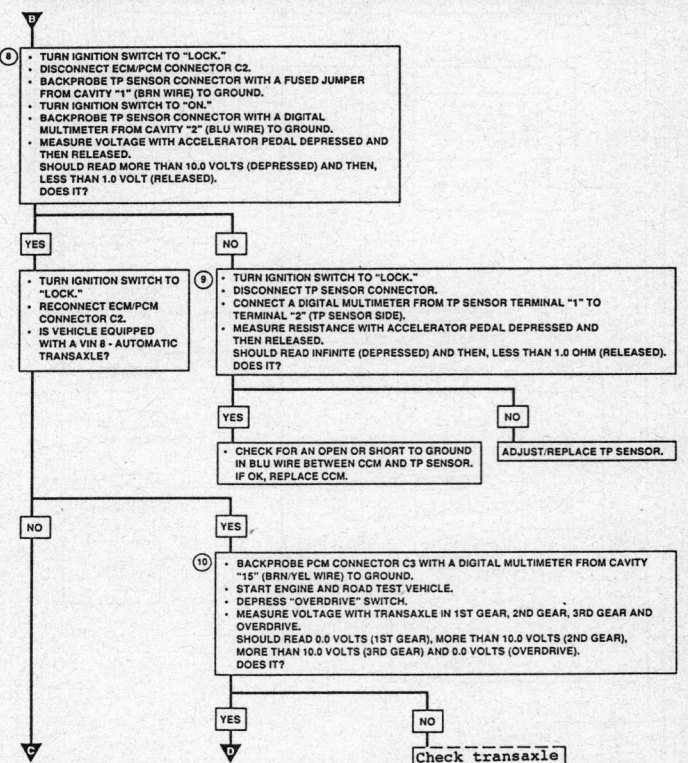

Fig. 18 Cruise control module on-board diagnostic (OBD) system check (Part 4 of 5). 1993

Fig. 18   Cruise control module on-board diagnostic (OBD) system check (Part 5 of 5). 1993

Fig. 19   Cruise control chart 9B-1, –CRUISE– indicator does not light (Part 1 of 4). 1993

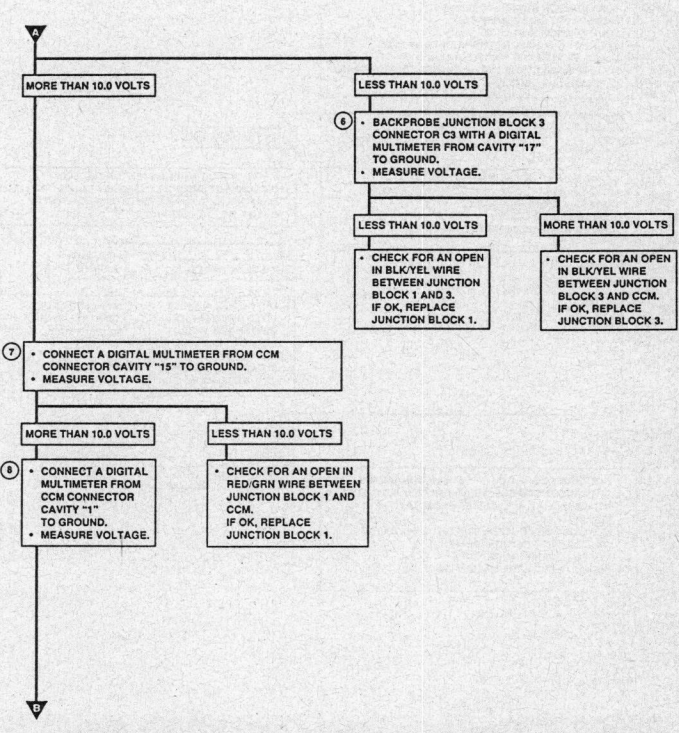

Fig. 19   Cruise control chart 9B-1, –CRUISE– indicator does not light (Part 2 of 4). 1993

Fig. 19   Cruise control chart 9B-1, –CRUISE– indicator does not light (Part 3 of 4). 1993

Fig. 19 Cruise control chart 9B-1, –CRUISE– indicator does not light (Part 4 of 4). 1993

Fig. 20 Cruise control chart 9B-2, –CRUISE– indicator does not flash SET/COAST test (Part 1 of 3). 1993

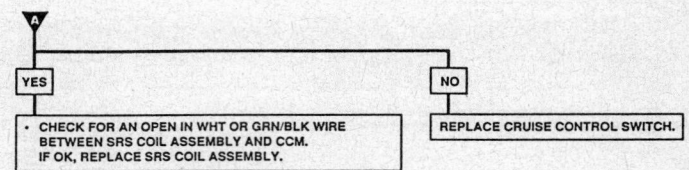

Fig. 20 Cruise control chart 9B-2, –CRUISE– indicator does not flash SET/COAST test (Part 3 of 3). 1993

Fig. 20 Cruise control chart 9B-2, –CRUISE– indicator does not flash SET/COAST test (Part 2 of 3). 1993

Fig. 21 Cruise control chart 9B-3, –CRUISE– indicator does not flash RES/ACC test (Part 1 of 2). 1993

IMPORTANT: BE SURE THAT CCM OBD SYSTEM CHECK HAS BEEN PERFORMED BEFORE CONTINUING DIAGNOSIS.

FROM CCM OBD SYSTEM CHECK.

①
- TURN IGNITION SWITCH TO "LOCK."
- DISCONNECT CCM CONNECTOR.
- CONNECT A DIGITAL MULTIMETER FROM CCM CONNECTOR CAVITY "18" TO GROUND.
- MOVE CRUISE CONTROL SWITCH UP TO "RES / ACC" POSITION AND HOLD.
- MEASURE RESISTANCE. SHOULD BE APPROXIMATELY 70 OHMS. IS IT?

NO → REPLACE CRUISE CONTROL SWITCH.

YES → REPLACE CCM.

Fig. 21 Cruise control chart 9B-3, –CRUISE– indicator does not flash RES/ACC test (Part 2 of 2). 1993

Fig. 22 Cruise control chart 9B-4A, –CRUISE– indicator does not light during CANCEL switch test (Part 1 of 2). 1993

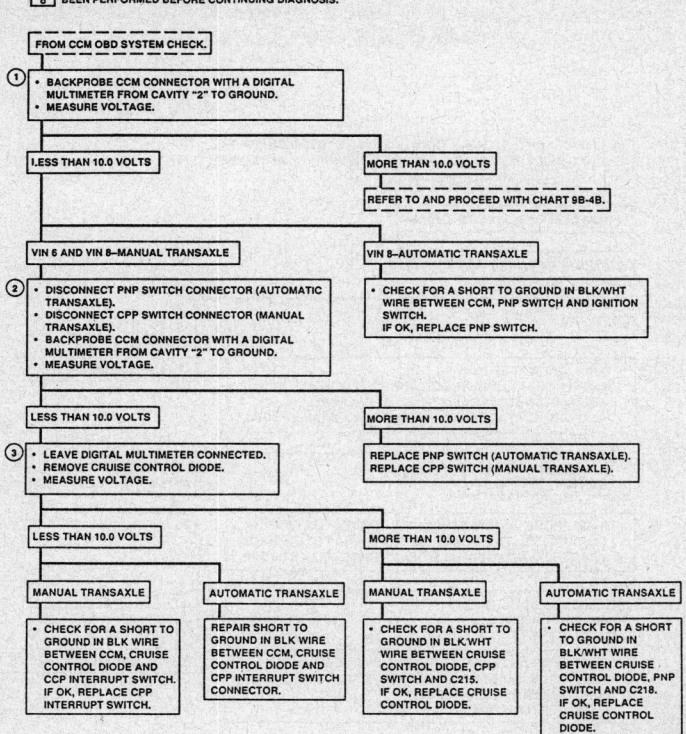

IMPORTANT: BE SURE THAT CCM OBD SYSTEM CHECK HAS BEEN PERFORMED BEFORE CONTINUING DIAGNOSIS.

FROM CCM OBD SYSTEM CHECK.

①
- BACKPROBE CCM CONNECTOR WITH A DIGITAL MULTIMETER FROM CAVITY "2" TO GROUND.
- MEASURE VOLTAGE.

LESS THAN 10.0 VOLTS

MORE THAN 10.0 VOLTS → REFER TO AND PROCEED WITH CHART 9-B-4B.

VIN 6 AND VIN 8–MANUAL TRANSAXLE

VIN 8–AUTOMATIC TRANSAXLE

②
- DISCONNECT PNP SWITCH CONNECTOR (AUTOMATIC TRANSAXLE).
- DISCONNECT CPP SWITCH CONNECTOR (MANUAL TRANSAXLE).
- BACKPROBE CCM CONNECTOR WITH A DIGITAL MULTIMETER FROM CAVITY "2" TO GROUND.
- MEASURE VOLTAGE.

- CHECK FOR A SHORT TO GROUND IN BLK/WHT WIRE BETWEEN CCM, PNP SWITCH AND IGNITION SWITCH. IF OK, REPLACE PNP SWITCH.

LESS THAN 10.0 VOLTS

MORE THAN 10.0 VOLTS → REPLACE PNP SWITCH (AUTOMATIC TRANSAXLE). REPLACE CPP SWITCH (MANUAL TRANSAXLE).

③
- LEAVE DIGITAL MULTIMETER CONNECTED.
- REMOVE CRUISE CONTROL DIODE.
- MEASURE VOLTAGE.

LESS THAN 10.0 VOLTS

MORE THAN 10.0 VOLTS

MANUAL TRANSAXLE	AUTOMATIC TRANSAXLE	MANUAL TRANSAXLE	AUTOMATIC TRANSAXLE
• CHECK FOR A SHORT TO GROUND IN BLK WIRE BETWEEN CCM, CRUISE CONTROL DIODE AND CCP INTERRUPT SWITCH. IF OK, REPLACE CPP INTERRUPT SWITCH.	• REPAIR SHORT TO GROUND IN BLK WIRE BETWEEN CRUISE CONTROL DIODE AND C215. IF OK, REPLACE CPP INTERRUPT SWITCH CONNECTOR.	• CHECK FOR A SHORT TO GROUND IN BLK/WHT WIRE BETWEEN CRUISE CONTROL DIODE, CPP SWITCH AND C215. IF OK, REPLACE CRUISE CONTROL DIODE.	• CHECK FOR A SHORT TO GROUND IN BLK/WHT WIRE BETWEEN CRUISE CONTROL DIODE, PNP SWITCH AND C218. IF OK, REPLACE CRUISE CONTROL DIODE.

Fig. 22 Cruise control chart 9B-4A, –CRUISE– indicator does not light during CANCEL switch test (Part 2 of 2). 1993

Fig. 23 Cruise control chart 9B-4B, –CRUISE– indicator does not light during CANCEL switch test (Part 1 of 3). 1993

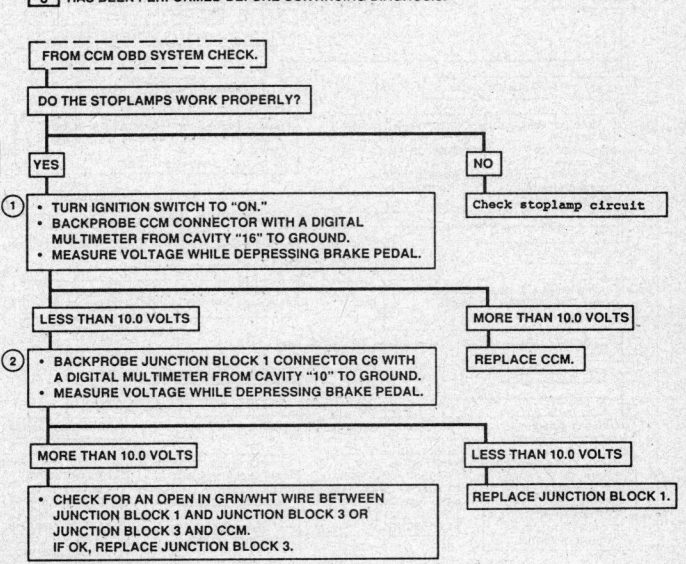

IMPORTANT: BE SURE THAT CCM OBD SYSTEM CHECK AND CHART 9B-4A HAVE BEEN PERFORMED BEFORE CONTINUING DIAGNOSIS.

FROM CHART 9B-4A.

① • PLACE TRANSAXLE IN PARK.
• TURN IGNITION SWITCH TO "LOCK."
• DISCONNECT CCM CONNECTOR.
• CONNECT A DIGITAL MULTIMETER FROM CCM CONNECTOR CAVITY "16" TO GROUND.
• TURN IGNITION SWITCH TO "ON."
• MEASURE VOLTAGE.

LESS THAN 1.0 VOLT   MORE THAN 1.0 VOLT

Check stoplamp circuit

② • CONNECT A DIGITAL MULTIMETER FROM CCM CONNECTOR CAVITY "3" TO GROUND.
• MEASURE RESISTANCE.

LESS THAN INFINITE   INFINITE

③ • CONNECT A DIGITAL MULTIMETER FROM CCM CONNECTOR CAVITY "18" TO GROUND.
• MEASURE RESISTANCE.

LESS THAN INFINITE   INFINITE

REPLACE CRUISE CONTROL SWITCH.   PROBLEM IS NOT IN CANCEL SWITCH CIRCUITRY.

Fig. 23   Cruise control chart 9B-4B, –CRUISE– indicator does not light during CANCEL switch test (Part 2 of 3). 1993

A

④ • LEAVE DIGITAL MULTIMETER CONNECTED.
• DISCONNECT PARKING BRAKE SWITCH CONNECTOR.
• MEASURE RESISTANCE FROM CCM CONNECTOR CAVITY "3" TO GROUND.

LESS THAN INFINITE   INFINITE

⑤ • LEAVE DIGITAL MULTIMETER CONNECTED.
• DISCONNECT BRAKE FLUID LEVEL SWITCH CONNECTOR.
• MEASURE RESISTANCE FROM CCM CONNECTOR CAVITY "3" TO GROUND.

REPLACE PARKING BRAKE SWITCH.

LESS THAN INFINITE   INFINITE

• CHECK FOR A SHORT TO GROUND IN RED/BLK WIRE BETWEEN PARKING BRAKE SWITCH AND JUNCTION BLOCK 3, CCM AND JUNCTION BLOCK 3 OR JUNCTION BLOCK 3 AND BRAKE FLUID LEVEL SWITCH.
IF OK, REPLACE JUNCTION BLOCK 3.

REPLACE BRAKE FLUID LEVEL SWITCH.

Fig. 23   Cruise control chart 9B-4B, –CRUISE– indicator does not light during CANCEL switch test (Part 3 of 3). 1993

HOT AT ALL TIMES

JUNCTION BLOCK 1
STOP FUSE 15 AMP
14 C5
RED/WHT
2 C203
RED/WHT
2
STOPLAMP SWITCH CLOSED WITH BRAKE PEDAL DEPRESSED
1
GRN/WHT
1 C203
GRN/WHT
18 C5   10 C6
JUNCTION BLOCK 1

GRN/WHT
2 C4
2 C3
JUNCTION BLOCK 3

GRN/WHT
16
BRAKE SIGNAL
CRUISE CONTROL MODULE (CCM)

Fig. 24   Cruise control chart 9B-5A, –CRUISE– indicator does not go out during CANCEL test (Stoplamp switch circuit, Part 1 of 2). 1993

IMPORTANT: BE SURE THAT CCM OBD SYSTEM CHECK HAS BEEN PERFORMED BEFORE CONTINUING DIAGNOSIS.

FROM CCM OBD SYSTEM CHECK.

DO THE STOPLAMPS WORK PROPERLY?

YES   NO

① • TURN IGNITION SWITCH TO "ON."
• BACKPROBE CCM CONNECTOR WITH A DIGITAL MULTIMETER FROM CAVITY "16" TO GROUND.
• MEASURE VOLTAGE WHILE DEPRESSING BRAKE PEDAL.

Check stoplamp circuit

LESS THAN 10.0 VOLTS   MORE THAN 10.0 VOLTS

② • BACKPROBE JUNCTION BLOCK 1 CONNECTOR C6 WITH A DIGITAL MULTIMETER FROM CAVITY "10" TO GROUND.
• MEASURE VOLTAGE WHILE DEPRESSING BRAKE PEDAL.

REPLACE CCM.

MORE THAN 10.0 VOLTS   LESS THAN 10.0 VOLTS

• CHECK FOR AN OPEN IN GRN/WHT WIRE BETWEEN JUNCTION BLOCK 1 AND JUNCTION BLOCK 3 OR JUNCTION BLOCK 3 AND CCM.
IF OK, REPLACE JUNCTION BLOCK 3.

REPLACE JUNCTION BLOCK 1.

Fig. 24   Cruise control chart 9B-5A, –CRUISE– indicator does not go out during CANCEL test (Stoplamp switch circuit, Part 2 of 2). 1993

Fig. 25 Cruise control chart 9B-5B, —CRUISE— indicator does not go out during CANCEL test (Cruise control CANCEL switch circuit, Part 1 of 2). 1993

IMPORTANT: BE SURE THAT CCM OBD SYSTEM CHECK HAS BEEN PERFORMED BEFORE CONTINUING DIAGNOSIS.

Fig. 25 Cruise control chart 9B-5B, —CRUISE— indicator does not go out during CANCEL test (Cruise control CANCEL switch circuit, Part 2 of 2). 1993

IMPORTANT: BE SURE THAT THE CCM OBD SYSTEM CHECK HAS BEEN PERFORMED BEFORE CONTINUING DIAGNOSIS.

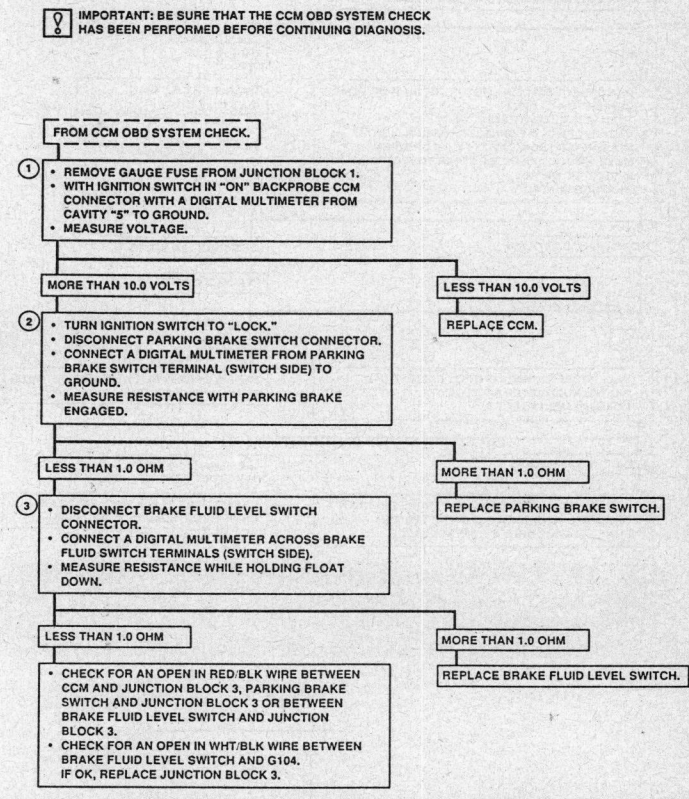

Fig. 26 Cruise control chart 9B-5C, —CRUISE— indicator does not go out during CANCEL test (Parking brake/brake fluid level switch circuit, Part 2 of 2). 1993

Fig. 26 Cruise control chart 9B-5C, —CRUISE— indicator does not go out during CANCEL test (Parking brake/brake fluid level switch circuit, Part 1 of 2). 1993

Fig. 27 Cruise control chart 9B-5D, —CRUISE— indicator does not go out during CANCEL test (PNP switch circuit-Automatic transaxle, Part 1 of 2). 1993

IMPORTANT: BE SURE THAT CCM OBD SYSTEM CHECK HAS BEEN PERFORMED BEFORE CONTINUING DIAGNOSIS.

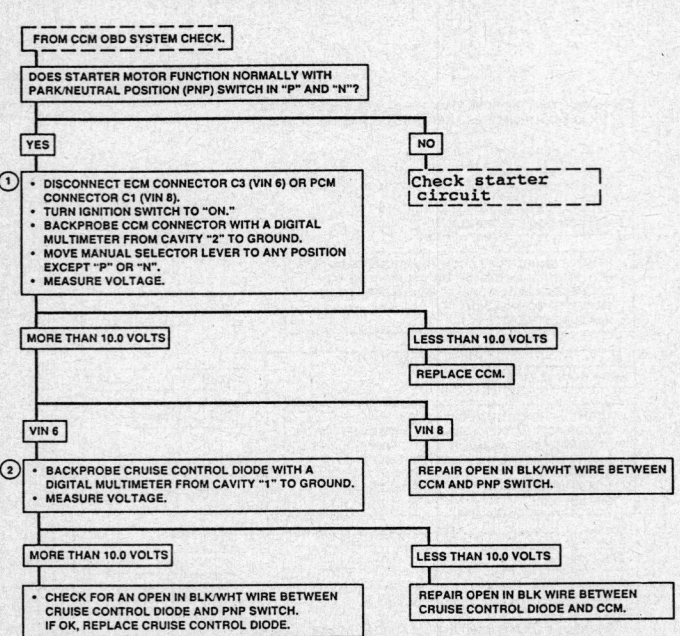

Fig. 27 Cruise control chart 9B-5D, —CRUISE— indicator does not go out during CANCEL test (PNP switch circuit-Automatic transaxle, Part 2 of 2). 1993

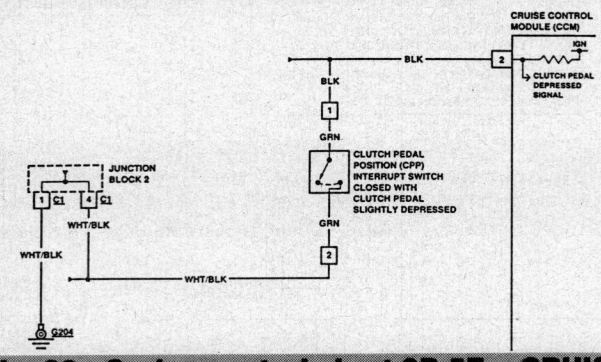

Fig. 28 Cruise control chart 9B-5E, —CRUISE— indicator does not go out during CANCEL test (CPP interrupt switch circuit-Manual transaxle, Part 1 of 2). 1993

IMPORTANT: BE SURE THAT CCM OBD SYSTEM CHECK HAS BEEN PERFORMED BEFORE CONTINUING DIAGNOSIS.

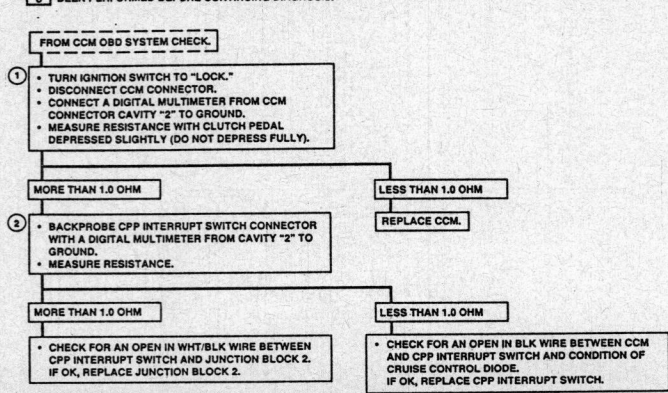

Fig. 28 Cruise control chart 9B-5E, —CRUISE— indicator does not go out during CANCEL test (CPP interrupt switch circuit-Manual transaxle, Part 2 of 2). 1993

Fig. 29 DTC 11, overvoltage on motor open circuit, Part 1 of 3). 1993

IMPORTANT: BE SURE THAT CCM OBD SYSTEM CHECK HAS BEEN PERFORMED BEFORE CONTINUING DIAGNOSIS.

Fig. 29 DTC 11, overvoltage on motor open circuit, Part 2 of 3). 1993

A

⑤
- LEAVE GROUND AND POWER CONNECTED TO TERMINALS "4" AND "5."
- CONNECT A FUSED JUMPER FROM CRUISE CONTROL ACTUATOR CONNECTOR TERMINAL "7" (ACTUATOR SIDE) TO GROUND.
- CONNECT A FUSED JUMPER FROM CRUISE CONTROL ACTUATOR CONNECTOR TERMINAL "6" (ACTUATOR SIDE) TO B+.
- OBSERVE CRUISE CONTROL ACTUATOR ARM. SHOULD MOVE SMOOTHLY TO THE OPEN POSITION WITH MOTOR STOPPING WHEN FULLY OPEN. DOES IT?

YES → ⑥
- REVERSE POWER AND GROUND CONNECTIONS ON TERMINALS "6" AND "7."
- OBSERVE CRUISE CONTROL ACTUATOR ARM. SHOULD MOVE SMOOTHLY TO THE CLOSE POSITION WITH MOTOR STOPPING WHEN FULLY CLOSED. DOES IT?

NO → REPLACE CRUISE CONTROL ACTUATOR.

YES → REPLACE CCM.

NO → REPLACE CRUISE CONTROL ACTUATOR.

Fig. 29   DTC 11, overvoltage on motor open circuit, Part 3 of 3). 1993

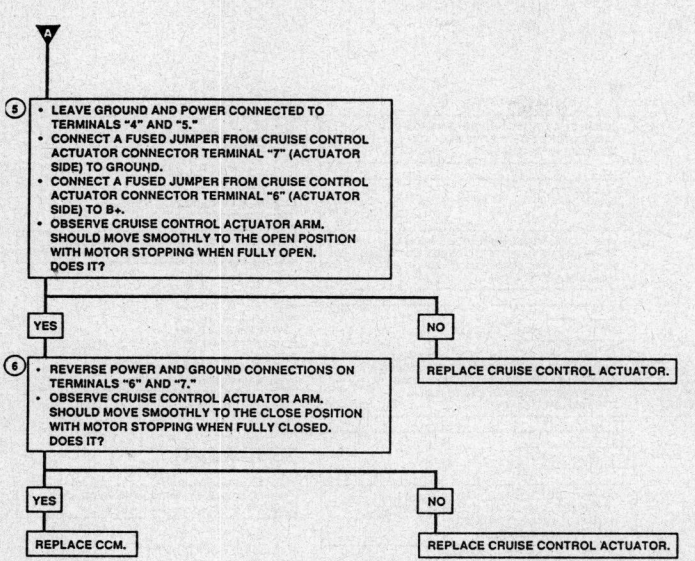

IMPORTANT: BE SURE THAT CCM OBD SYSTEM CHECK HAS BEEN PERFORMED BEFORE CONTINUING DIAGNOSIS.

FROM CCM OBD SYSTEM CHECK.

①
- TURN IGNITION SWITCH TO "LOCK."
- DISCONNECT CCM CONNECTOR.
- TURN IGNITION SWITCH TO "ON."
- CONNECT A DIGITAL MULTIMETER FROM CCM CONNECTOR CAVITY "10" TO GROUND.
- MEASURE VOLTAGE. SHOULD BE ZERO VOLTS. IS IT?

YES → ②
- LEAVE DIGITAL MULTIMETER CONNECTED.
- DISCONNECT CRUISE CONTROL ACTUATOR CONNECTOR.
- MEASURE RESISTANCE FROM CCM CONNECTOR CAVITY "10" TO GROUND.

NO → REPAIR SHORT TO VOLTAGE IN GRN/BLK OR RED/YEL WIRE BETWEEN CCM AND CRUISE CONTROL ACTUATOR.

INFINITE → ③
- CONNECT A DIGITAL MULTIMETER FROM CRUISE CONTROL ACTUATOR CONNECTOR CAVITY "5" TO CCM CONNECTOR CAVITY "10."
- MEASURE RESISTANCE.

LESS THAN INFINITE → REPAIR SHORT TO GROUND IN GRN/BLK OR RED/YEL WIRE BETWEEN STOPLAMP SWITCH AND CRUISE CONTROL ACTUATOR OR STOPLAMP SWITCH AND CCM.

LESS THAN 1.0 OHM → ④
- CONNECT A DIGITAL MULTIMETER FROM CRUISE CONTROL ACTUATOR CONNECTOR CAVITY "4" TO GROUND.
- MEASURE RESISTANCE.

MORE THAN 1.0 OHM → ⑤
- BACKPROBE STOPLAMP SWITCH CONNECTOR CAVITIES "3" AND "4" WITH A DIGITAL MULTIMETER.
- MEASURE RESISTANCE.

LESS THAN 1.0 OHM →

MORE THAN 1.0 OHM → REPAIR OPEN IN WHT/BLK WIRE BETWEEN CRUISE CONTROL ACTUATOR AND G104.

LESS THAN 1.0 OHM → REPAIR OPEN IN GRN/BLK OR RED/YEL WIRE BETWEEN CRUISE CONTROL ACTUATOR AND STOPLAMP SWITCH OR CCM AND STOPLAMP SWITCH.

MORE THAN 1.0 OHM → REPLACE STOPLAMP SWITCH.

A

Fig. 30   DTC 12, overvoltage on magnetic clutch circuit, Part 2 of 3). 1993

Fig. 30   DTC 12, overvoltage on magnetic clutch circuit, Part 1 of 3). 1993

A

- MOVE CRUISE CONTROL ACTUATOR ARM BACK AND FORTH. SHOULD MOVE FREELY. DOES IT?

YES →
- CONNECT A FUSED JUMPER FROM CRUISE CONTROL ACTUATOR CONNECTOR TERMINAL "4" (ACTUATOR SIDE) TO GROUND.
- CONNECT A FUSED JUMPER FROM CRUISE CONTROL ACTUATOR CONNECTOR TERMINAL "5" (ACTUATOR SIDE) TO B+.
- ATTEMPT TO MOVE CRUISE CONTROL ACTUATOR ARM. SHOULD NOT MOVE FREELY. DOES IT?

NO → REPLACE CRUISE CONTROL ACTUATOR.

YES → REPLACE CRUISE CONTROL ACTUATOR.

NO → REPLACE CCM.

Fig. 30   DTC 12, overvoltage on magnetic clutch circuit, Part 3 of 3). 1993

Fig. 31   DTC 13, open motor circuit or abnormal throttle angle sensor signal (Part 1 of 5). 1993

Fig. 31   DTC 13, open motor circuit or abnormal throttle angle sensor signal (Part 2 of 5). 1993

Fig. 31   DTC 13, open motor circuit or abnormal throttle angle sensor signal (Part 3 of 5). 1993

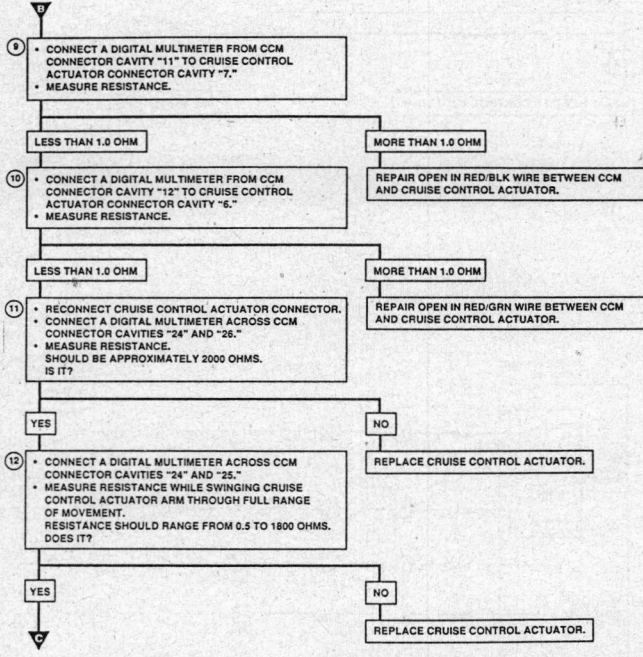

Fig. 31   DTC 13, open motor circuit or abnormal throttle angle sensor signal (Part 4 of 5). 1993

Fig. 31   DTC 13, open motor circuit or abnormal throttle angle sensor signal (Part 5 of 5). 1993

Fig. 32   DTC 21, vehicle speed sensor (Open/shorted circuit, Part 1 of 3). 1993

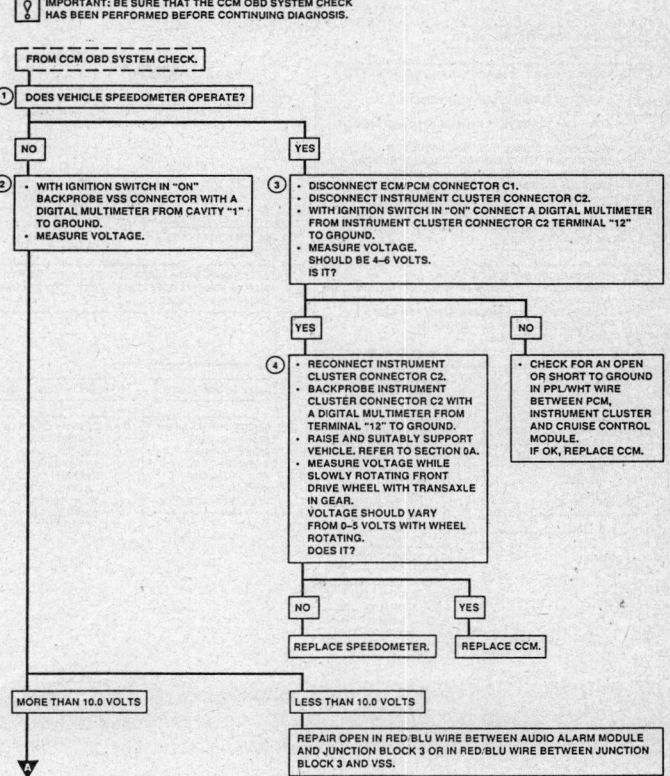

Fig. 32   DTC 21, vehicle speed sensor (Open/shorted circuit, Part 2 of 3). 1993

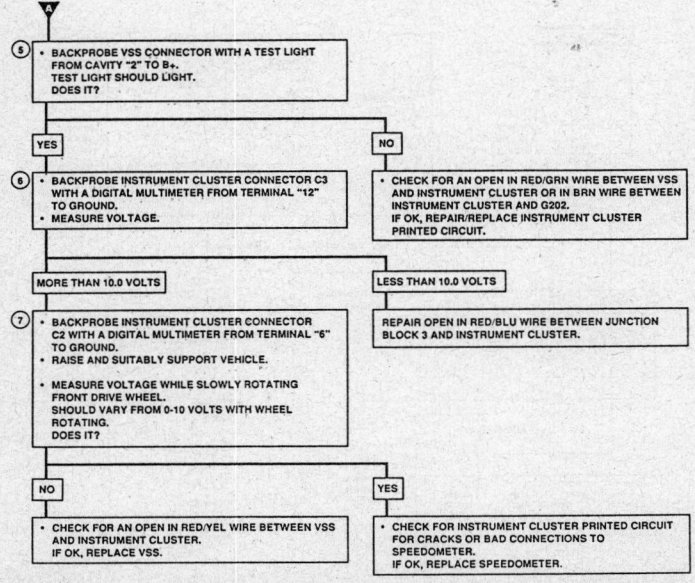

Fig. 32   DTC 21, vehicle speed sensor (Open/shorted circuit, Part 3 of 3). 1993

Fig. 33   DTC 23, vehicle speed drops more than 10 mph under set speed (Part 1 of 4). 1993

Fig. 33   DTC 23, vehicle speed drops more than 10 mph under set speed (Part 2 of 4). 1993

Fig. 33   DTC 23, vehicle speed drops more than 10 mph under set speed (Part 3 of 4). 1993

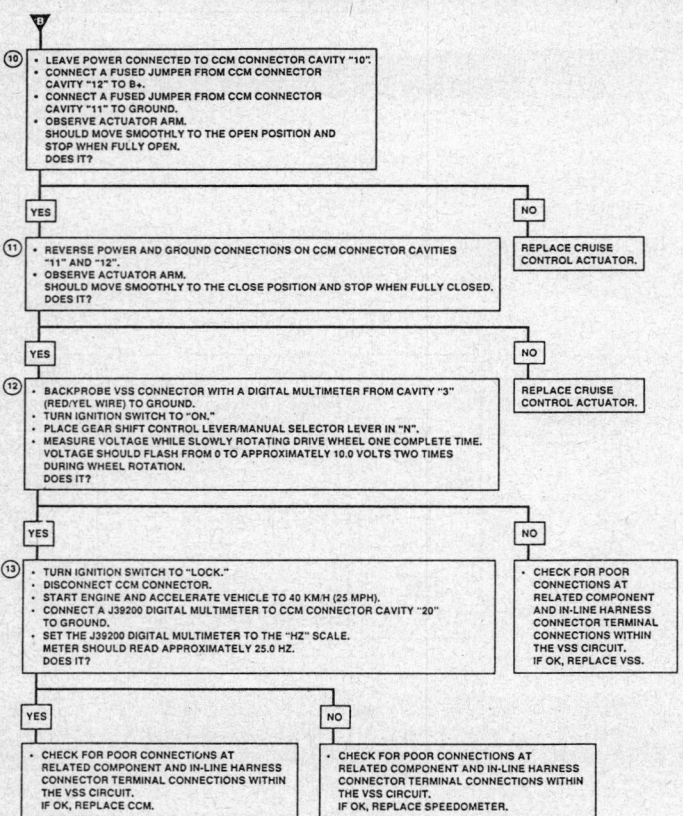

Fig. 33   DTC 23, vehicle speed drops more than 10 mph under set speed (Part 4 of 4). 1993

Fig. 34   DTC 32, cruise control switch shorted (Part 1 of 3). 1993

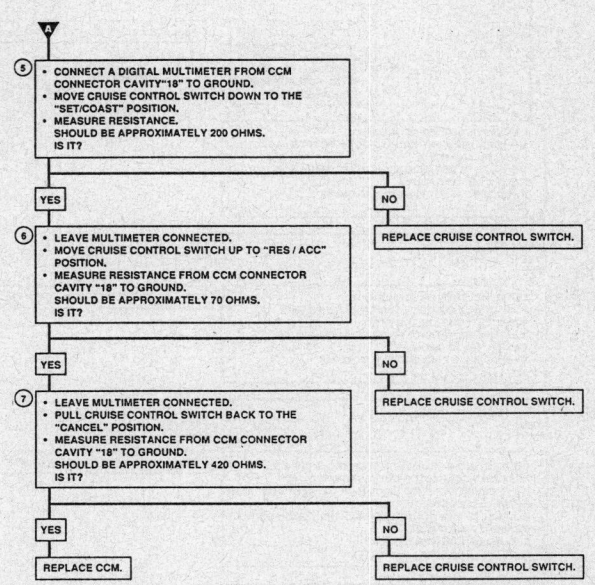

Fig. 34   DTC 32, cruise control switch shorted (Part 3 of 3). 1993

Fig. 34   DTC 32, cruise control switch shorted (Part 2 of 3). 1993

Fig. 35   DTC 34, abnormal signal from cruise control switch (Part 1 of 3). 1993

Fig. 35   DTC 34, abnormal signal from cruise control switch (Part 2 of 3). 1993

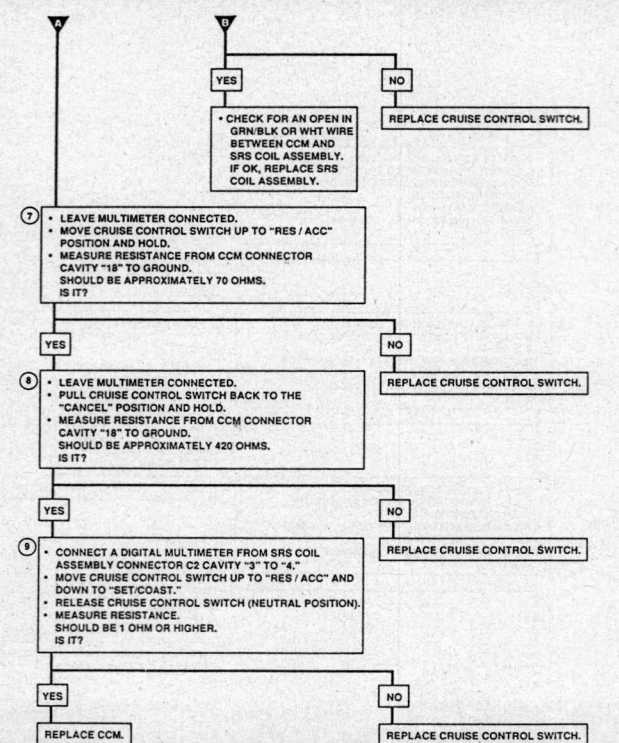

Fig. 35   DTC 34, abnormal signal from cruise control switch (Part 3 of 3). 1993

Fig. 36   Cruise control module wiring diagram (Part 1 of 5). 1993

Fig. 36   Cruise control module wiring diagram (Part 2 of 5). 1993

Fig. 36   Cruise control module wiring diagram (Part 3 of 5). 1993

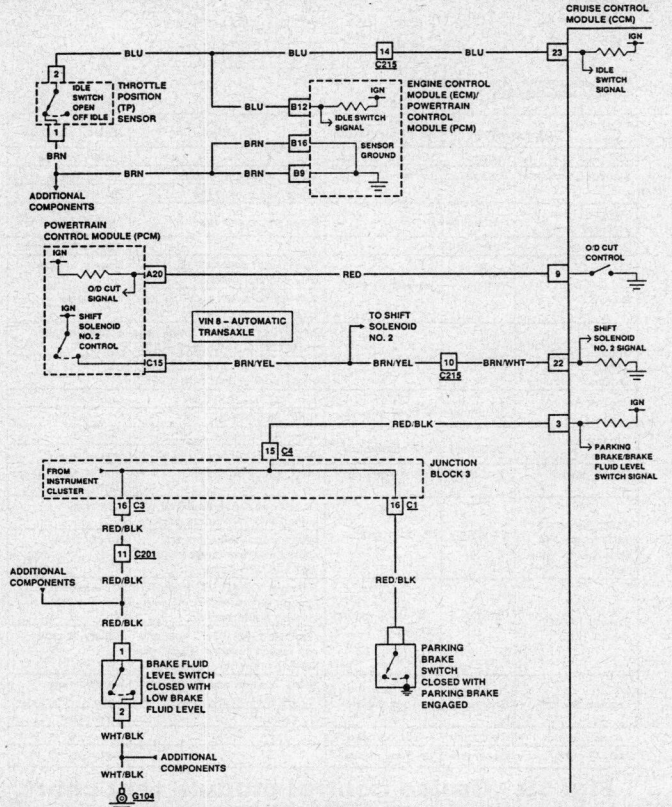

Fig. 36 Cruise control module wiring diagram (Part 4 of 5). 1993

Fig. 36 Cruise control module wiring diagram (Part 5 of 5). 1993

Fig. 37 Starter wiring diagram (Part 1 of 2). 1993

Fig. 37 Starter wiring diagram (Part 2 of 2). 1993

Fig. 38 Stoplamp wiring diagram. 1993

Connection or measure item	Check for	Tester connection	Condition	Specified value
"STOP" Fuse	Voltage	16—Body ground	—	Battery voltage
Stoplamp Switch	Voltage	15—16	Brake pedal depressed	No voltage
			Brake pedal released	Battery voltage
Stoplamp Switch (Release Valve)	Resistance	2—14	Brake pedal released	Approx. 68 ohms
Control Valve	Resistance	4—14	—	Approx. 30 ohms
Cruise Control Switch	Voltage	10—Body ground	Turn ignition switch to "RUN" and cruise control switch to "CRUISE"	Battery voltage
			Turn ignition switch to "RUN" and cruise control switch to "OFF"	No voltage
Cruise Control Switch (indicator circuit)	Voltage	3—Body ground	Turn ignition switch to "RUN" and cruise control switch to "CRUISE"	Battery voltage
			Turn ignition switch to "RUN" and cruise control switch to "OFF"	No voltage
Engage Switch "SET/COAST"	Continuity	5—Body ground	Turn "SET/COAST" on	Continuity
			Turn "SET/COAST" off	No continuity
Engage Switch "RESUME/ACCEL"	Continuity	17—Body ground	Turn "RESUME/ACCEL" on	Continuity
			Turn "RESUME/ACCEL" off	No continuity
Speed Sensor	Continuity	7—Body ground	Vehicle moving slowly	1 pulse each 40 cm (15.75 in.)
Clutch Switch (M/T) or Neutral Start Switch (A/T)	Continuity	11—Body ground	Clutch pedal depressed or shifted into "N" range	Continuity
			Clutch pedal released or shifted into any range except "N" and "P" range	No continuity
Parking Brake Switch	Voltage	12—Body ground	Remove "CHARGE" fuse. Turn ignition switch to "RUN" with parking brake applied.	No voltage
			Remove "CHARGE" fuse and turn ignition switch to "RUN" with parking brake lever released.	Battery voltage
Vacuum Switch	Continuity	9—Body ground	Apply vacuum approx.170 mmHg (6.69 in. Hg. 22.7 kPa)	No continuity
			No vacuum	Continuity
Vacuum Pump	Continuity	1—Body ground	—	Continuity
Body Ground	Continuity	13—Body ground	—	Continuity

Fig. 39 Cruise control module test chart. 1991—92

Fig. 40 Testing cruise control switch. 1991—92

Terminals — Switch Position	1	2	3	4
Switch free (Brake pedal depressed)	o—		—o	
Switch pin pushed in (Brake pedal released)		o—		—o

1 TERMINAL 1
2 TERMINAL 2
3 TERMINAL 3
4 TERMINAL 4
5 STOPLAMP SWITCH

Fig. 41 Testing stop light switch. 1991—92

1 ACTUATOR
2 CONTROL CABLE

Fig. 42 Checking control cable freeplay. 1991—92

904 CLUTCH PEDAL POSITION (CPP) INTERRUPT
    SWITCH
918 ELECTRICAL CONNECTOR
922 CPP INTERRUPT SWITCH LOCKNUT

**Fig. 43 Clutch pedal position
(CPP) interrupt switch
location. 1993**

311 INFLATOR MODULE
314 UPPER STEERING COLUMN CONNECTOR
323 CONNECTOR POSITION ASSURANCE (CPA)

**Fig. 45 Inflator module
removal. 1993**

ENGAGEMENT SWITCH

1991–92

The cruise control engagement switch
is part of the multi-function lever, which
must be replaced as an assembly. Refer to
individual car chapter.

PARK/NEUTRAL POSITION
(PNP) SWITCH
(AUTOMATIC
TRANSAXLES)

1993

1. Disconnect battery ground cable, then
   place shifter in Neutral position.
2. Raise and support vehicle.
3. Remove six splash shield bolts and
   splash shield.
4. Remove one nut, one lock washer
   and shift select cable from manual lever.
5. Disconnect PNP electrical connector.
6. Remove one nut, one lock washer
   and manual lever from manual shaft.

923 CRUISE CONTROL ACTUATOR COVER
924 CRUISE CONTROL ACTUATOR
925 CRUISE CONTROL ACTUATOR MOUNTING
    BRACKET
926 GUIDE CLIP
927 CRUISE CONTROL CABLE LOCKNUTS
928 CRUISE CONTROL CABLE
929 CRUISE CONTROL CABLE BELLCRANK

**Fig. 44 Cruise control actuator components.
1993**

918 ELECTRICAL CONNECTOR
919 CRUISE CONTROL SWITCH
920 CRUISE CONTROL SWITCH SCREWS

**Fig. 46 Cruise control switch
location. 1993**

A STOPLAMP SWITCH CLEARANCE
  0.5 – 2.4 mm (0.02 – 0.09")
501 BRAKE PEDAL
504 STOPLAMP SWITCH
505 STOPLAMP SWITCH
    LOCKNUT

**Fig. 48 Stoplamp switch
clearance. 1993**

Unstake lock plate behind manual
shaft nut.
7. Remove manual shaft nut and lock
   plate from PNP switch, then PNP

A NEUTRAL BASIC LINE
B PNP SWITCH SLEEVE GROOVE
711 PNP SWITCH BOLTS

**Fig. 47 Park/neutral position
(PNP) switch adjustment. 1993**

switch bolts and switch.
8. Reverse procedure to install noting
   the following:
   a. Tighten manual shaft nut to 61
      inch lbs.
   b. Adjust PNP switch by aligning neu-
      tral basic line scribed in PNP
      switch with groove in PNP switch
      sleeve, Fig. 47.
   c. Tighten PNP switch to 48 inch lbs.
   d. Tighten manual lever nut to 106
      inch lbs.
   e. Adjust shift select cable by rotating
      manual lever counterclockwise un-
      til it reaches Park position. Rotate
      manual lever clockwise two detent
      positions until manual lever is in
      Neutral position. Install shift select
      cable into manual lever and secure
      with cable nut. Pull cable taut mak-
      ing sure no deflection exists.
   f. Tighten shift select cable to 115
      inch lbs.
   g. Tighten left splash shield bolts to
      44 inch lbs.
   h. Tighten battery ground cable to 11
      ft. lbs.
9. Ensure proper operation of PNP
   switch by performing the following
   steps:

a. Apply parking brake and block wheels.
b. With shifter in Park, turn start engine and verify starter operation, then stop engine and turn engine Off with key in On position.
c. Move shifter to Neutral, turn start engine and verify starter operation.
d. Verify that starter does not operate in Drive, 2nd, Low or Reverse.

STOPLAMP SWITCH

1993

1. Disconnect battery ground cable, then slide hood latch release cable sideways to release from holder.
2. Disconnect hood release cable from hood latch release lever.
3. Remove two screws and hood latch release lever from knee bolster.
4. Remove two cover plates, two screws, four bolts and knee bolster from instrument panel.
5. Remove left side ventilation duct from left side duct outlet.
6. Disconnect stoplamp electrical connector from stoplamp switch, then

loosen stoplamp switch locknut, **Fig. 48.**
7. Remove stoplamp switch locknut, then stoplamp switch.
8. Reverse procedure to install noting the following:
   a. Adjust stoplamp switch. Turn switch until distance between end of switch plunger and end of threaded portion of switch is within .02-.09 inch.
   b. Tighten stoplamp switch locknut to 89 inch lbs.
   c. Tighten knee bolster bolts to 124 inch lbs.
   d. Tighten battery ground cable to 11 ft. lbs.

VACUUM PUMP

1991–92

1. Disconnect vacuum pump electrical connector.
2. Disconnect vacuum hoses.
3. Remove vacuum pump attaching bolts, then remove vacuum pump.
4. Reverse procedure to install.

VACUUM SWITCH

1991–92

1. Disconnect vacuum switch electrical connector.
2. Disconnect vacuum switch vacuum hose.
3. Unscrew vacuum switch, then remove vacuum switch.
4. Reverse procedure to install.

ADJUSTMENTS

SPEED CONTROLS, ADJUST

1991–92

This system utilizes the actuator cable for adjustment. Check that the cables are properly installed. Measure the cable stroke to where the throttle valve begins to open. If the cable stroke is not approximately .39 inches with a slight amount of freeplay, adjustment is required. Loosen cable tightening nut and carefully position cable forward until specification is met. **Do not stretch cable.**

Type 5

NOTE: On Vehicles Equipped With Airbags, Disarm Airbag As Outlined Under "Airbag System Disarming" Before Any Diagnosis, Testing, Troubleshooting Or Repairs Are Performed. After All Diagnosis, Testing, Troubleshooting Or Repairs Have Been Completed, Rearm Airbag As Outlined Under "Airbag System Arming."

NOTE: Wire Color Code And Symbol Identification Located In The Front Of This Manual Can Be Used As An Aid When Using Wiring Circuits Found In This Manual.

INDEX

PRECAUTIONS

AIRBAG SYSTEM DISARMING

1993 CAMARO & FIREBIRD

The diagnostic energy reserve module (DERM) can maintain voltage to cause a system deployment for up to ten minutes after the ignition switch is turned off and the battery is disconnected. Servicing the SIR system during this period may result in accidental

deployment and personal injury.
1. Ensure front wheels are pointed straight ahead.
2. Turn ignition switch to Lock position and remove SIR or AIRBAG fuse.
3. Remove left sound insulator. **Remove courtesy lamp from sound insulator, if necessary.**
4. Remove Connector Position Assurance (CPA), then disconnect yellow two-way SIR electrical connector at base of steering column.
5. Remove instrument panel door assembly, then Connector Position As-

surance (CPA) and yellow 24-way DERM harness connector.

1993 CAPRICE, FLEETWOOD (RWD) & ROADMASTER

The diagnostic energy reserve module (DERM) can maintain voltage to cause a system deployment for up to ten minutes after the ignition switch is turned off and the battery is disconnected. Servicing the SIR system during this period may result in accidental deployment and personal injury.
1. Ensure front wheels are pointed

straight ahead.
2. Turn ignition switch to Lock position and remove SIR fuse from fuse block.
3. Remove Connector Position Assurance (CPA), then disconnect yellow two-way SIR electrical connector at base of steering column.

AIRBAG SYSTEM ARMING
1993 CAMARO & FIREBIRD

1. Install instrument panel door assembly, then Connector Position Assurance (CPA) and yellow 24-way DERM harness connector.
2. Connect yellow two-way SIR electrical connector, then install Connector Position Assurance (CPA).
3. Install left sound insulator. **Install courtesy lamp to sound insulator, if applicable.**
4. Install SIR fuse to fuse block, turn ignition switch to Run position and ensure that "Inflatable Restraint" lamp flashes 7 to 9 times, then shuts off.

1993 CAPRICE, FLEETWOOD (RWD) & ROADMASTER

The diagnostic energy reserve module (DERM) can maintain voltage to cause a system deployment for up to ten minutes after the ignition switch is turned off and the battery is disconnected. Servicing the SIR system during this period may result in accidental deployment and personal injury.
1. Ensure front wheels are pointed straight ahead.
2. Turn ignition switch to Lock position and remove SIR or AIR BAG fuse from fuse block.
3. Remove Connector Position Assurance (CPA), then disconnect yellow two-way SIR electrical connector at base of steering column.

DESCRIPTION

The main parts of the cruise control system are the functional control switches, cruise control module assembly, vehicle speed sensor assembly and cruise control release switch, stop lamp and torque converter clutch (TCC) switch, and clutch on 5.7L engines (Camaro and Firebird) or clutch anticipate switch assemblies on 3.4L engines (Camaro and Firebird).

The cruise control system uses a cruise control module assembly to obtain the desired vehicle cruise speed. Two important components in the module assembly assist in this. The first is electronic controller and second is an electric stepper motor. The controller monitors vehicle speed and operates the electric stepper motor. The motor moves a ribbon and throttle linkage, in response to the controller, to maintain the desired cruise speed. The cruise control module assembly contains a low speed limit which will prevent the system from operation during speeds below 25 mph. The operation of the controller is controlled by functional switches located on the turn signal and headlamp switch and cruise control actuator and windshield wiper/washer lever assembly.

Cruise control release switch, stop lamp and clutch or clutch anticipate switch assemblies are provided to disengage the cruise system. The switch assemblies are mounted on the brake and accelerator and clutch pedal bracket. When the brake pedal or clutch pedal is depressed, the cruise control system is electrically disengaged and the throttle is returned to idle position.

SYSTEM COMPONENTS
SPEED SENSOR
1993 Camaro & Firebird

The vehicle speed sensor is mounted to the automatic transmission and produces and alternating current (ac) signal. The frequency of this signal is proportional to the speed in which the transmission output shaft rotates, which is proportional to the speed of the vehicle.

The ac signal produced by the sensor is supplied to the engine control module (ECM), cruise control module and instrument cluster. The signal is transmitted at a rate of 4000 pulses per mile. The ECM, cruise control module and speedometer internally convert the number of pulses per miles per second to determine vehicle speed.

SPEED SENSOR BUFFER
1993 Caprice, Fleetwood (RWD) & Roadmaster

The vehicle speed sensor (VSS) buffer receives a signal from the VSS (permanent magnet generator) indicating vehicle speed. The buffer processes the signal which is then sent to the engine control module (ECM), cruise control module and speedometer.

CRUISE CONTROL MODULE
1993 Camaro, Caprice, Firebird, Fleetwood (RWD) & Roadmaster

On Camaro and Firebird models, the module is mounted on the left engine compartment inner side rail. On Caprice, Fleetwood (RWD) and Roadmaster models, the module is mounted on the left wheelhouse panel near the master cylinder. The module has an electronic controller and an electric stepper motor to vary the throttle with each different cruise mode. The module is not serviceable.

DIAGNOSIS & TROUBLESHOOTING

Refer to **Figs. 1 through 34** for cruise control and vehicle speed sensor wiring diagrams, diagnosis and troubleshooting. After repairs, verify the operation of the cruise control system by performing the following procedure:
1. Set parking brake, then start engine.
2. Move cruise switch to Off, then move cruise switch to On and wait at least three seconds before proceeding.
3. Fully depress and hold brake pedal, then push cruise switch in and hold.
4. Hold cruise slider switch in R/A posi-

tion, then after ten seconds, release brake pedal while holding R/A and Set switches.
5. Engine RPM should increase momentarily then return to normal.

ADJUSTMENTS
CRUISE CONTROL CABLE
1993 CAMARO & FIREBIRD

With throttle closed, lock cable conduit by pressing down on lock tab. When cable is in unlocked position and throttle is closed, cable adjustment spring removes appropriate amount of slack. Lock button must be fully extended to allow proper adjustment spring operation prior to locking.

1993 CAPRICE, FLEETWOOD (RWD) w/V4U COACHBUILDER OPTION EQUIPMENT & ROADMASTER

1. Remove air cleaner and resonator.
2. Unlock cable conduit at support bracket.
3. With throttle closed, lock cable conduit by pressing down on lock tab.
4. When cable is in unlocked position and throttle is closed, cable adjustment spring removes appropriate amount of slack.
5. Lock button must be fully extended to allow proper adjustment spring operation prior to locking.
6. Install air cleaner and resonator.

ACCELERATOR CABLE LESS V4U COACHBUILDER OPTION EQUIPMENT
FLEETWOOD (RWD)

The accelerator control and cruise control assembly is serviced as an assembly. The cruise control cable is a non-adjustable but the accelerator cable requires adjustment after installation.
1. Press accelerator cable adjuster button and hold.
2. Position accelerator cable adjuster in non-adjusted position, **Fig. 35.** Pull cable casing away from adjuster so that casing will be at its longest position.
3. Release accelerator cable adjuster button.
4. Using moderate foot pressure (approximately 50 ft. lbs. of force), press accelerator pedal down to wide open throttle position; several clicks of the accelerator cable should be heard.

CRUISE CONTROL SWITCH ASSEMBLIES
1993 CAMARO & FIREBIRD

The release switch assembly must be adjusted at the same time the stop lamp and torque converter clutch (TCC) switch is adjusted. The clutch switch assembly or clutch anticipate switch assembly cannot be adjusted until clutch pedal assembly is installed. **Proper stop lamp switch ad-**

justment is essential. Improper adjustment will cause brake drag and excessive brake lining wear. Refer to **Fig. 36** when performing this procedure.

1. Depress brake pedal or clutch pedal and insert release switch assembly, stop lamp and TCC switch assembly and clutch switch or clutch anticipate switch assembly into pedal assembly with bracket until retainer on release switch, stop lamp and TCC switch assembly and clutch switch or clutch anticipate switch assembly is fully seated.
2. **Ensure proper amount of force is applied to brake pedal assembly during adjustment. Excessive force could damage vacuum booster, too little force could result in dragging brakes.**
3. Slowly pull brake or clutch pedal rearward with 50 pounds of force until click sounds can no longer be heard. Release switch assembly, stop lamp and TCC switch assembly and clutch switch or clutch anticipate switch will have moved retainers to their original positions.
4. Release switch and stop lamp and TCC switch contacts should be open at 1 inch or less of pedal travel and occur at same time or before beginning of braking. The brake pedal can travel up to 1 inch before cruise control disengages.

1993 CAPRICE, FLEETWOOD (RWD) & ROADMASTER

The release switch and stop lamp switch cannot be adjusted until after the brake booster pushrod is assembled to brake pedal assembly. Refer to **Fig. 37** when performing this procedure.

1. Depress brake pedal and insert release switch and stop lamp switch assembly into retainers until fully seated.
2. Slowly release brake pedal back to its original position. Release switch and stop lamp switch assemblies will move within retainers to their adjusted position.
3. The following brake pedal travel distances can be used to check for properly adjusted release switch and stop lamp switch assemblies:
   a. Release switch and stop lamp switch assemblies contacts must be open at $1/8$–$1/2$ inch brake pedal travel, measured at centerline of brake pedal pad.
   b. Nominal actuation of stop lamp switch contacts is about $3/16$ inch after cruise switch control contacts close.

TV CABLE LESS V4U COACHBUILDER OPTION EQUIPMENT
FLEETWOOD (RWD)

The TV cable setting synchronizes the TV cable assembly and the throttle body. If unset, shifting problems and premature transmission wear may result. This procedure sets the accelerator cable from the

throttle body and TV cable from adjuster to automatic transmission. The TV cable requires no periodic adjustment.

1. Stop engine, then remove cover, shield and inner cover, **Fig. 38.**
2. Put accelerator control cable from adjuster to throttle body in non-adjusted position by pressing button and slide out to fully stretched position, then releasing button.
3. Put TV cable from adjuster to automatic transmission in non-adjusted position by flipping toggle switch up.
4. Insert $1/8$ inch drill bit, grooved side up, through cams. If bit goes down further, it will hit gear and bind adjuster assembly.
5. Set torque wrench to 35 inch lbs. Insert torque wrench with $1/4$ inch drive extension through round hole in top of first pulley and into square hole in second pulley. Tighten relaxer cams to 35 inch lbs. Once relaxer cams are tightened, maintain torque with wrench until after toggle switch on TV cable is flipped down to lock setting.
6. Remove torque wrench with extension and drill bit, then install inner cover, shield and cover.
7. Install TECH 1 with mass storage cartridge to vehicle.
8. Fully depress accelerator pedal while monitoring throttle angle on TECH 1. Throttle angle must be 90 percent or above. If throttle angle is below 90 percent, repeat cable setting as outlined.

TV CABLE w/V4U COACHBUILDER OPTION EQUIPMENT
FLEETWOOD (RWD)

Setting of the cable must be done by rotating throttle body injector throttle lever at the throttle body. Do not use accelerator pedal to rotate throttle body injector throttle lever.

1. Stop engine, then remove air cleaner.
2. Depress and hold down readjust button at engine end of TV cable assembly.
3. Move slider **Fig. 39** rearward until it stops.
4. Release adjust button, then rotate throttle body injector throttle lever to its -full-travel position.-
5. Slider must move toward throttle body injector lever assembly when injector throttle lever is rotated to its -full-travel position.-
6. Install air cleaner, then ensure cable moves freely after engine has been warmed up.

COMPONENT REPLACEMENT
CRUISE CONTROL CABLE
1993 CAMARO, CAPRICE, FIREBIRD, FLEETWOOD (RWD) w/V4U COACHBUILDER OPTION EQUIPMENT & ROADMASTER

The cable is connected between the

cruise control module and throttle body lever.

1. **On 1993 Caprice, Fleetwood (RWD) and Roadmaster models,** remove air cleaner and resonator.
2. Remove cable and conduit from engine bracket, **Fig. 40.**
3. Remove cable end fitting from throttle body lever stud.
4. Remove cruise control retainer at module.
5. Remove cable from module as follows:
   a. Compress conduit tangs, **Fig. 41,** and pull out of module housing.
   b. Disconnect cable bead from cruise motor band end fitting on module, **Fig. 41.**
   c. Note routing and remove cable.
6. Reverse procedure to install noting the following:
   a. **Ribbon must not be twisted;** slide cable conduit fitting over ribbon and snap into module housing ensuring both tangs are engaged.
   b. Adjust cable as outlined.

ACCELERATOR & CRUISE CONTROL CABLE ADJUSTER
FLEETWOOD (RWD)

1. Remove cover and shield from adjuster, then squeeze tabs on side of cover to remove, **Fig. 42.**
2. Remove accelerator control and cruise control cable as outlined.
3. Remove accelerator control and automatic transmission TV as outlined.
4. Disconnect electrical connector, then loosen bolts/screws and reposition module.
5. Remove adjuster and bracket assembly from vehicle.
6. Remove bracket nuts, then bracket from adjuster.
7. Remove bracket from adjuster, then retainers and bolts/screws.
8. Reverse procedure to install noting the following:
   a. Tighten bracket bracket nuts to 71 inch lbs.
   b. Tighten module bolts/screws to 71 inch lbs.
   c. Adjust automatic transmission TV cable as outlined.
   d. Adjust accelerator cable (without V4U Coachbuilder Equipment Option) as outlined.

ACCELERATOR CONTROL & CRUISE CONTROL CABLE LESS V4U COACHBUILDER EQUIPMENT OPTION
FLEETWOOD (RWD)

1. Remove cover and shield from adjuster, then clip from cable and cover from adjuster, **Fig. 43.**
2. Using a small flat-bladed tool, release lock tab on cable assembly while sliding cable casing out of adjuster.
3. Remove beads of cable from slots in

Fig. 1 Cruise control wiring diagram (Part 2 of 2). 1993 Camaro & Firebird

Fig. 1 Cruise control wiring diagram (Part 1 of 2). 1993 Camaro & Firebird

Fig. 3 Cruise control wiring diagram. 1993 Fleetwood (RWD)

Fig. 2 Cruise control wiring diagram. 1993 Caprice

Fig. 5 Cruise control system check (Part 1 of 2)

ACTION	NORMAL RESULTS
[1] • Drive vehicle above 25 mph. • Cruise Switch to "ON." • Depress Set Switch once and release. • Remove foot from accelerator pedal.	Vehicle maintains set speed.
[2] • Depress and hold Set Switch until vehicle speed decreases by 4 to 5 mph. • Release Set Switch.	Vehicle decelerates and maintains a new lower set speed, if speed is above 25 mph.
[3] • Depress and hold R/A Switch until vehicle speed increases by 4 to 5 mph. • Release R/A Switch.	Vehicle accelerates and maintains a new higher set speed.
[4] • Depress brake pedal slightly.	Cruise Control disengages. Memory unchanged.
[5] • Depress R/A Switch once and release.	Vehicle accelerates to and maintains previous set speed.
[6] • Depress R/A Switch once and release (less than 3/4 of a second).	Vehicle speed increases by 1 mph and maintains new set speed.

Fig. 5 Cruise control system check (Part 2 of 2)

ACTION	NORMAL RESULTS
[7] • Depress Set Switch once and release (less than 3/8 of a second).	Vehicle speed decreases by 1 mph and maintains new set speed.
[8] • Depress Set and R/A Switches simultaneously.	Vehicle put in Non-Cruise mode with memory unchanged.
[9] • Depress R/A Switch once and release.	Vehicle accelerates to and maintains previous set speed.
[10] • Cruise Switch to "OFF."	Cruise Control disengages. Memory is lost.

Fig. 6 Cruise control symptom table. 1993 Camaro & Firebird

SYMPTOM		PROCEDURE
Cruise Control will not engage. Speedometer operates normally.		Chart #1
Cruise Control will not resume, accelerate, tap-up or tap-down.		Chart #2

Fig. 4 Cruise control wiring diagram. 1993 Roadmaster

SYMPTOM	PROCEDURE
Cruise Control will not engage.	Chart #1
Cruise Control will not resume, accelerate, tap-up or tap-down.	Chart #2

Fig. 7 Cruise control symptom table. 1993 Caprice & Roadmaster

SYMPTOM	PROCEDURE
Cruise Control will not engage.	Chart #1
Cruise Control will not resume, accelerate, tap-up or tap-down.	Chart #2
"CRUISE ENGAGED" Indicator inoperative.	Chart #3
"CRUISE ENGAGED" Indicator on at all times.	Chart #4

Fig. 8 Cruise control symptom table. 1993 Fleetwood (RWD)

CHART #1
CRUISE CONTROL WILL NOT ENGAGE
(ASSUMES SPEEDOMETER OPERATES NORMALLY)

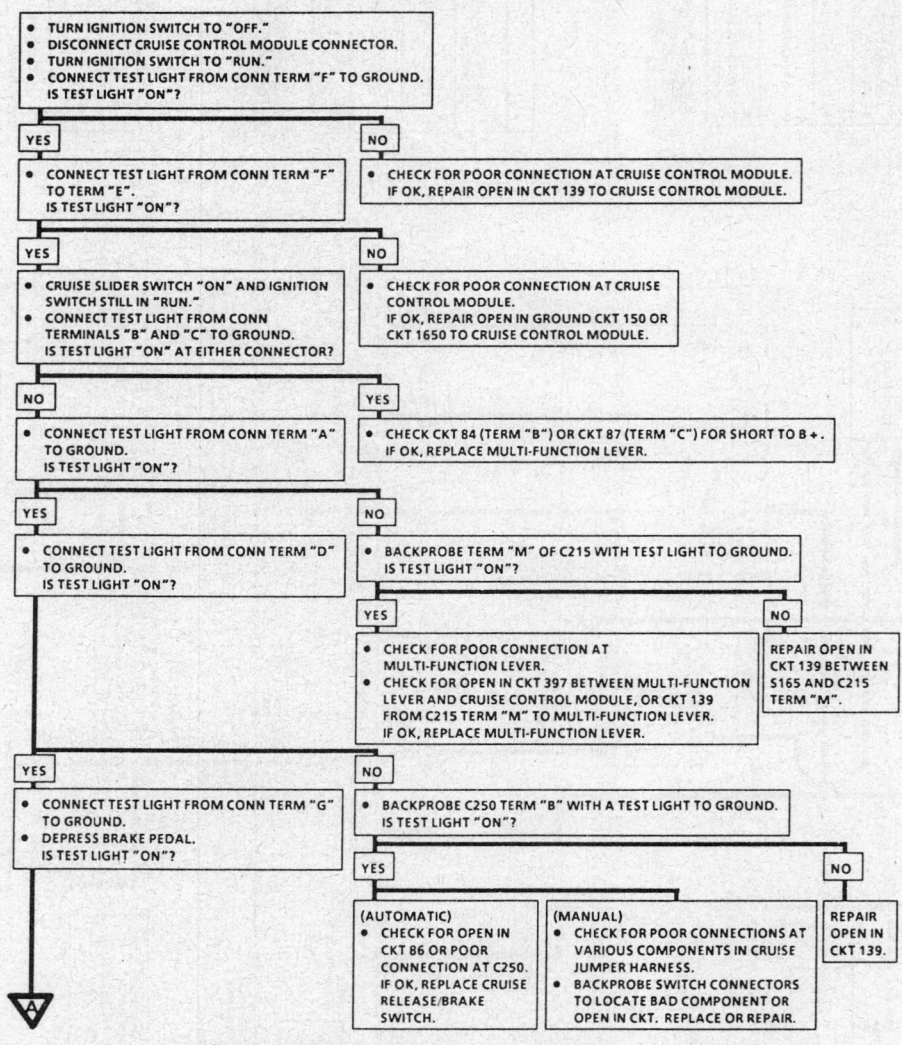

Fig. 9 Cruise control troubleshooting chart No. 1 (Part 1 of 2). 1993 Camaro & Firebird

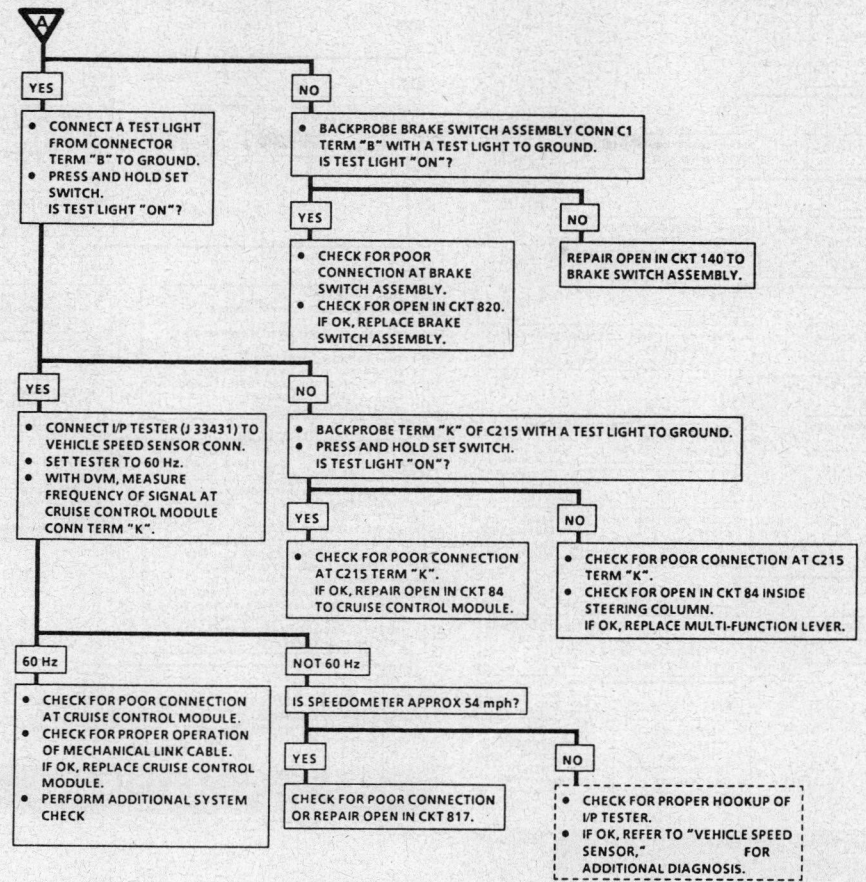

Fig. 9   Cruise control troubleshooting chart No. 1 (Part 2 of 2). 1993 Camaro & Firebird

CHART #2
CRUISE CONTROL WILL NOT RESUME, ACCELERATE, TAP-UP OR TAP-DOWN

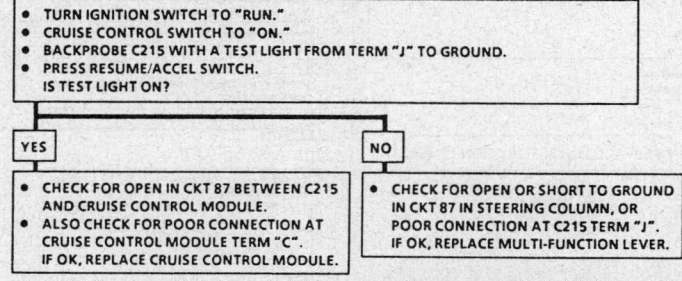

Fig. 10   Cruise control troubleshooting chart No. 2. 1993 Camaro & Firebird

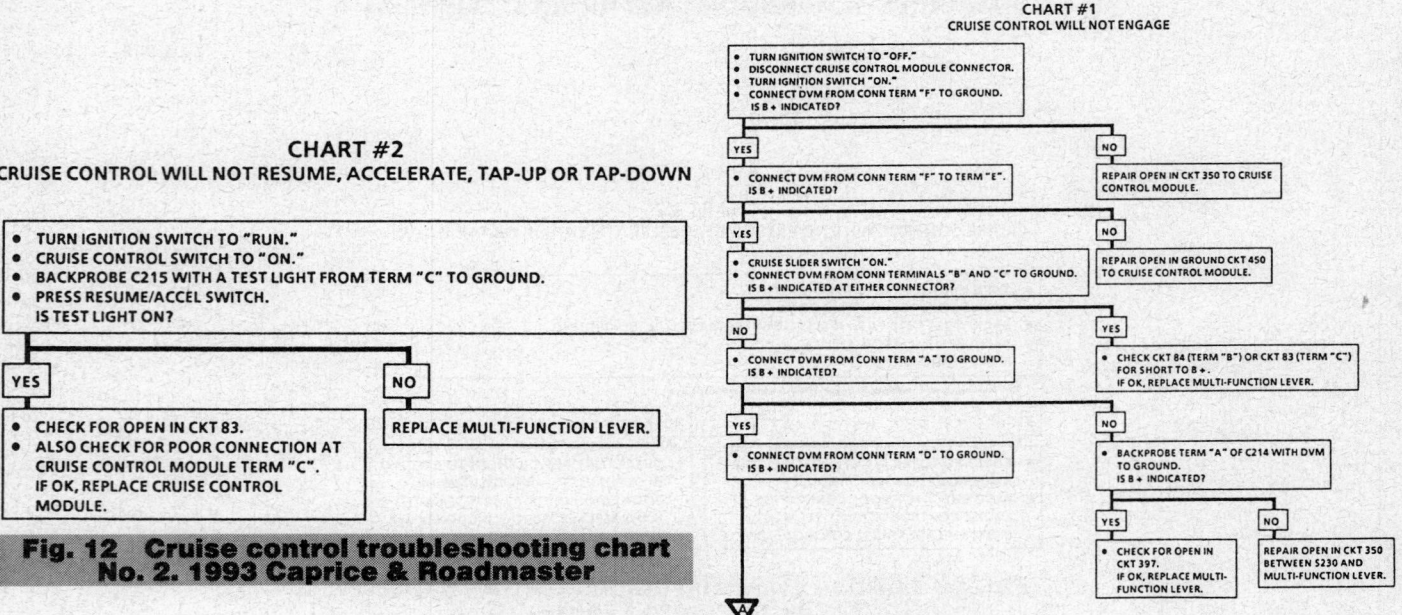

CHART #1
CRUISE CONTROL WILL NOT ENGAGE

- TURN IGNITION SWITCH TO "OFF."
- DISCONNECT CRUISE CONTROL MODULE CONNECTOR.
- TURN IGNITION SWITCH TO "RUN."
- CONNECT TEST LIGHT FROM CONN TERM "F" TO GROUND. IS TEST LIGHT "ON"?

YES → • CONNECT TEST LIGHT FROM CONN TERM "F" TO TERM "E". IS TEST LIGHT "ON"?

NO → REPAIR OPEN IN CKT 75 TO CRUISE CONTROL MODULE.

YES → • CRUISE SLIDER SWITCH "ON" AND IGNITION SWITCH STILL IN "RUN."
• CONNECT TEST LIGHT FROM CONN TERMINALS "B" AND "C" TO GROUND. IS TEST LIGHT "ON" AT EITHER CONNECTOR?

NO → REPAIR OPEN IN GROUND CKT 450 TO CRUISE CONTROL MODULE.

NO → • CONNECT TEST LIGHT FROM CONN TERM "A" TO GROUND. IS TEST LIGHT "ON"?

YES → • CHECK CKT 84 (TERM "B") OR CKT 83 (TERM "C") FOR SHORT TO B +. IF OK, REPLACE MULTI-FUNCTION LEVER.

YES → • CONNECT TEST LIGHT FROM CONN TERM "D" TO GROUND. IS TEST LIGHT "ON"?

NO → • BACKPROBE TERM "A" OF C215 WITH TEST LIGHT TO GROUND. IS TEST LIGHT "ON"?

YES → • CHECK FOR OPEN IN CKT 397. IF OK, REPLACE MULTI-FUNCTION LEVER.

NO → REPAIR OPEN IN CKT 75 BETWEEN S259 AND MULTI-FUNCTION LEVER.

YES → • CONNECT TEST LIGHT FROM CONN TERM "G" TO GROUND.
• DEPRESS BRAKE PEDAL. IS TEST LIGHT "ON"?

NO → • BACKPROBE TORQUE CONVERTER CLUTCH/CRUISE RELEASE SWITCH CONN C2, TERM "B" WITH A TEST LIGHT TO GROUND. IS TEST LIGHT "ON"?

YES → • CHECK FOR OPEN IN CKT 86. IF OK, REPLACE TORQUE CONVERTER CLUTCH/CRUISE RELEASE SWITCH.

NO → REPAIR OPEN IN CKT 75 BETWEEN S259 AND TORQUE CONVERTER CLUTCH/CRUISE RELEASE SWITCH.

Fig. 11   Cruise control troubleshooting chart No. 1 (Part 1 of 2). 1993 Caprice & Roadmaster

CHART #1 (continued)
CRUISE CONTROL WILL NOT ENGAGE

YES → • CONNECT A TEST LIGHT FROM CONNECTOR TERM "B" TO GROUND
• PRESS AND HOLD SET SWITCH. IS TEST LIGHT "ON"?

NO → • BACKPROBE BRAKE LIGHT/CRUISE RELEASE SWITCH CONN TERM "B" WITH A TEST LIGHT TO GROUND. IS TEST LIGHT "ON"?

YES → • CHECK FOR OPEN IN CKT 820. IF OK, REPLACE BRAKE LIGHT/CRUISE RELEASE SWITCH.

NO → REPAIR OPEN IN CKT 140 TO BRAKE LIGHT/CRUISE RELEASE SWITCH.

YES → • TURN IGNITION TO "OFF."
• RECONNECT CRUISE CONTROL MODULE CONNECTOR.
• DISCONNECT VEHICLE SPEED SENSOR MODULE CONN C1.
• TURN IGNITION TO "RUN."
• USING A DIGITAL MULTIMETER, MEASURE VOLTAGE FROM VEHICLE SPEED SENSOR MODULE CONN C1 TERM "D" TO GROUND. IS VOLTAGE APPROX 5 VOLTS?

NO → • BACKPROBE TERM "D" OF C215 WITH A TEST LIGHT TO GROUND.
• PRESS AND HOLD SET SWITCH. IS TEST LIGHT "ON"?

YES → • CHECK FOR POOR CONNECTION AT C215 TERM "D". IF OK, REPAIR OPEN IN CKT 84.

NO → REPLACE MULTI-FUNCTION LEVER IF THERE IS NO OPEN IN CKT 84 INSIDE STEERING COLUMN.

YES → • RECONNECT VEHICLE SPEED SENSOR CONN.
• SET PARK BRAKE.
• START ENGINE.
• MOVE CRUISE SWITCH TO "OFF."
• MOVE CRUISE SWITCH TO "ON" AND THEN WAIT AT LEAST 3 SECONDS BEFORE DOING NEXT STEP.
• FULLY DEPRESS AND HOLD BRAKE PEDAL.
• PUSH CRUISE SET SWITCH IN AND HOLD.
• HOLD CRUISE SLIDER SWITCH IN "R/A" POSITION.
• AFTER 10 SECONDS, RELEASE BRAKE PEDAL WHILE STILL HOLDING R/A AND SET SWITCHES.
• LISTEN FOR MOMENTARY ENGINE RPM INCREASE. DOES ENGINE RPM INCREASE?

NO → • CHECK FOR SHORT TO GROUND OR OPEN IN CKT 389 OR POOR CONNECTION AT CRUISE CONTROL MODULE CONN TERM "K". IF OK, REPLACE CRUISE CONTROL MODULE.

YES → REFER TO "VEHICLE SPEED SENSOR," CHART #3, "CRUISE CONTROL WILL NOT ENGAGE."

NO → REPLACE CRUISE CONTROL MODULE.

Fig. 11   Cruise control troubleshooting chart No. 1 (Part 2 of 2). 1993 Caprice & Roadmaster

CHART #2
CRUISE CONTROL WILL NOT RESUME, ACCELERATE, TAP-UP OR TAP-DOWN

- TURN IGNITION SWITCH TO "RUN."
- CRUISE CONTROL SWITCH TO "ON."
- BACKPROBE C215 WITH A TEST LIGHT FROM TERM "C" TO GROUND.
- PRESS RESUME/ACCEL SWITCH. IS TEST LIGHT ON?

YES → • CHECK FOR OPEN IN CKT 83.
• ALSO CHECK FOR POOR CONNECTION AT CRUISE CONTROL MODULE TERM "C". IF OK, REPLACE CRUISE CONTROL MODULE.

NO → REPLACE MULTI-FUNCTION LEVER.

Fig. 12   Cruise control troubleshooting chart No. 2. 1993 Caprice & Roadmaster

CHART #1
CRUISE CONTROL WILL NOT ENGAGE

- TURN IGNITION SWITCH TO "OFF."
- DISCONNECT CRUISE CONTROL MODULE CONNECTOR.
- TURN IGNITION SWITCH TO "ON."
- CONNECT DVM FROM CONN TERM "F" TO GROUND. IS B + INDICATED?

YES → • CONNECT DVM FROM CONN TERM "F" TO TERM "E". IS B + INDICATED?

NO → REPAIR OPEN IN CKT 350 TO CRUISE CONTROL MODULE.

YES → • CRUISE SLIDER SWITCH "ON."
• CONNECT DVM FROM CONN TERMINALS "B" AND "C" TO GROUND. IS B + INDICATED AT EITHER CONNECTOR?

NO → REPAIR OPEN IN GROUND CKT 450 TO CRUISE CONTROL MODULE.

NO → • CONNECT DVM FROM CONN TERM "A" TO GROUND. IS B + INDICATED?

YES → • CHECK CKT 84 (TERM "B") OR CKT 83 (TERM "C") FOR SHORT TO B +. IF OK, REPLACE MULTI-FUNCTION LEVER.

YES → • CONNECT DVM FROM CONN TERM "D" TO GROUND. IS B + INDICATED?

NO → • BACKPROBE TERM "A" OF C214 WITH DVM TO GROUND. IS B + INDICATED?

YES → • CHECK FOR OPEN IN CKT 397. IF OK, REPLACE MULTI-FUNCTION LEVER.

NO → REPAIR OPEN IN CKT 350 BETWEEN S230 AND MULTI-FUNCTION LEVER.

Fig. 13   Cruise control troubleshooting chart No. 1 (Part 1 of 2). 1993 Fleetwood (RWD)

CHART #1 (continued)
CRUISE CONTROL WILL NOT ENGAGE

YES / **NO**

- **YES** branch:
  - CONNECT DVM FROM CONN TERM "G" TO GROUND. IS B + INDICATED?

- **NO** branch:
  - BACKPROBE CRUISE CONTROL RELEASE SWITCH CONN C2, TERM "B" WITH A DVM TO GROUND. IS B + INDICATED?

NO (from left):
- CONNECT DVM FROM CONN TERM "B" TO GROUND.
- PRESS AND HOLD SET SWITCH. IS B + INDICATED?

YES:
- DISCONNECT STOP LIGHT SWITCH CONN C2.
- PROBE TERM "C" OF SWITCH CONN C2 WITH A DVM TO GROUND. IS B + INDICATED?

YES (under release switch NO/YES):
- CHECK FOR OPEN IN CKT 86. IF OK, REPLACE CRUISE CONTROL RELEASE SWITCH.

NO:
- BACKPROBE INSTRUMENT CLUSTER CONN C2 TERM "11" WITH A DVM TO GROUND. IS B + INDICATED?

YES (short):
- REPAIR SHORT TO BATTERY VOLTAGE IN CKT 820.

NO:
- CHECK ADJUSTMENT OF STOP LIGHT SWITCH. IF OK, REPLACE STOP LIGHT SWITCH.

YES:
- REPAIR OPEN IN CKT 1656 BETWEEN CRUISE CONTROL RELEASE SWITCH AND S211.

NO:
- REPAIR OPEN IN CKT 39 BETWEEN S201 AND INSTRUMENT CLUSTER CONN C2 TERM "11".

YES (left lower):
- TURN IGNITION TO "OFF."
- RECONNECT CRUISE CONTROL MODULE CONNECTOR.
- DISCONNECT VEHICLE SPEED SENSOR MODULE CONN C1.
- TURN IGNITION "ON."
- USING A DVM, MEASURE VOLTAGE FROM VEHICLE SPEED SENSOR MODULE CONN C1 TERM "C" TO GROUND. IS VOLTAGE APPROX 5–7 VOLTS?

- BACKPROBE TERM "D" OF C214 WITH A DVM TO GROUND.
- PRESS AND HOLD SET SWITCH. IS B + INDICATED?

YES:
- CHECK FOR POOR CONNECTION AT C214 TERM "D". IF OK, REPAIR OPEN IN CKT 84.

NO:
- REPLACE MULTI-FUNCTION SWITCH IF CKT 84 IS NOT OPEN INSIDE COLUMN.

YES (lower left big box):
- RECONNECT VEHICLE SPEED SENSOR CONN.
- SET PARK BRAKE.
- START ENGINE.
- MOVE CRUISE SWITCH TO "OFF."
- MOVE CRUISE SWITCH TO "ON" AND THEN WAIT AT LEAST 3 SECONDS BEFORE DOING NEXT STEP.
- FULLY DEPRESS AND HOLD BRAKE PEDAL.
- PUSH CRUISE SET SWITCH IN AND HOLD.
- HOLD CRUISE SLIDER SWITCH IN "R/A" POSITION.
- AFTER 10 SECONDS, RELEASE BRAKE PEDAL WHILE STILL HOLDING R/A AND SET SWITCHES.
- LISTEN FOR MOMENTARY ENGINE RPM INCREASE. DOES ENGINE RPM INCREASE?

- CHECK FOR SHORT TO GROUND IN ENTIRE CKT 818.
- CHECK FOR OPEN IN CKT 818 FROM CRUISE CONTROL MODULE TERM "K" TO VSS MODULE CONN C1 TERM "C". IF OK, REPLACE CRUISE CONTROL MODULE.

YES:
- CHECK FOR POOR CONNECTION AT VEHICLE SPEED SENSOR MODULE CONN C1 TERM "C". IF OK, REPLACE VEHICLE SPEED SENSOR MODULE.

NO:
- REPLACE CRUISE CONTROL MODULE.

Fig. 13   Cruise control troubleshooting chart No. 1 (Part 2 of 2). 1993 Fleetwood (RWD)

CHART #2
CRUISE CONTROL WILL NOT RESUME, ACCELERATE, TAP-UP OR TAP-DOWN

- TURN IGNITION SWITCH "ON."
- CRUISE CONTROL SWITCH TO "ON."
- BACKPROBE C214 WITH A DVM FROM TERM "C" TO GROUND.
- PRESS RESUME/ACCEL SWITCH. IS B + INDICATED?

YES:
- CHECK FOR OPEN IN CKT 83.
- ALSO CHECK FOR POOR CONNECTION AT CRUISE CONTROL MODULE TERM "C". IF OK, REPLACE CRUISE CONTROL MODULE.

NO:
- REPLACE MULTI-FUNCTION LEVER.

Fig. 14   Cruise control troubleshooting chart No. 2. 1993 Fleetwood (RWD)

CHART #3
"CRUISE ENGAGED" INDICATOR INOPERATIVE

- DISCONNECT CRUISE CONTROL MODULE CONNECTOR.
- TURN IGNITION SWITCH "ON."
- MEASURE VOLTAGE FROM CRUISE CONTROL MODULE CONN TERM "J" TO GROUND.

B +:
- CHECK FOR POOR CONNECTION AT CRUISE CONTROL MODULE CONN TERM "J". IF OK, REPLACE CRUISE CONTROL MODULE.

0 VOLT:
- CHECK FOR POOR CONNECTION AT C200 TERM "G8", INSTRUMENT CLUSTER CONN C2 TERM "13" OR "CRUISE" INDICATOR LAMP, OR OPEN IN CKT 85.

Fig. 15   Cruise control troubleshooting chart No. 3. 1993 Fleetwood (RWD)

CHART #4
"CRUISE ENGAGED" INDICATOR ON AT ALL TIMES

- TURN IGNITION SWITCH "ON."
- CRUISE CONTROL SWITCH "OFF."
- DISCONNECT CRUISE CONTROL MODULE. IS "CRUISE" INDICATOR ON?

YES:
- CHECK FOR SHORT TO GROUND ON CKT 85. IF OK, SERVICE INSTRUMENT CLUSTER.

NO:
- REPLACE CRUISE CONTROL MODULE.

Fig. 16   Cruise control troubleshooting chart No. 4. 1993 Fleetwood (RWD)

Fig. 17   Vehicle speed sensor wiring diagram. 1993 Camaro & Firebird

SYMPTOM	PROCEDURE	
Speedometer and Cruise Control inoperative; Code 24 not set.	Chart #1	
Speedometer inoperative. Code 24 not set. Cruise Control operates.	Check for open, short to ground or short to B + in CKT 817 between S242 and Instrument Cluster Connector. Also check for poor connection at terminal "B12". If OK, service Instrument Cluster.	

Fig. 18   Vehicle speed sensor symptom table. 1993 CAMARO & Firebird

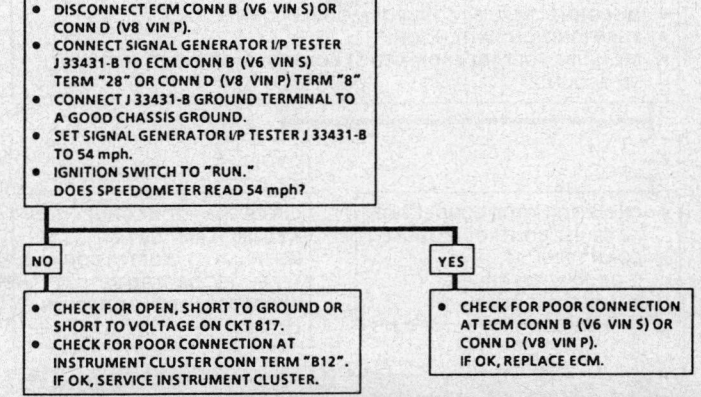

CHART #1
SPEEDOMETER AND CRUISE CONTROL INOPERATIVE; CODE 24 NOT SET

- DISCONNECT ECM CONN B (V6 VIN S) OR CONN D (V8 VIN P).
- CONNECT SIGNAL GENERATOR I/P TESTER J 33431-B TO ECM CONN B (V6 VIN S) TERM "28" OR CONN D (V8 VIN P) TERM "8"
- CONNECT J 33431-B GROUND TERMINAL TO A GOOD CHASSIS GROUND.
- SET SIGNAL GENERATOR I/P TESTER J 33431-B TO 54 mph.
- IGNITION SWITCH TO "RUN." DOES SPEEDOMETER READ 54 mph?

NO
- CHECK FOR OPEN, SHORT TO GROUND OR SHORT TO VOLTAGE ON CKT 817.
- CHECK FOR POOR CONNECTION AT INSTRUMENT CLUSTER CONN TERM "B12". IF OK, SERVICE INSTRUMENT CLUSTER.

YES
- CHECK FOR POOR CONNECTION AT ECM CONN B (V6 VIN S) OR CONN D (V8 VIN P). IF OK, REPLACE ECM.

Fig. 19   Vehicle speed sensor troubleshooting chart No. 1. 1993 Camaro & Firebird

Fig. 21 Vehicle speed sensor wiring diagram. 1993 Fleetwood (RWD)

Fig. 20 Vehicle speed sensor wiring diagram. 1993 Caprice

Fig. 23   Vehicle speed sensor wiring diagram. 1993 Roadmaster Wagon

Fig. 22   Vehicle speed sensor wiring diagram. 1993 Roadmaster Sedan

CHART #1

SPEEDOMETER INOPERATIVE AND ECM CODE 24 IS SET

- IGNITION SWITCH TO "RUN."
- USING A DIGITAL MULTIMETER, MEASURE THE VOLTAGE FROM VEHICLE SPEED SENSOR MODULE CONN C1 TERM "H" TO GROUND.

0 VOLT → REPAIR OPEN IN CKT 439 TO VEHICLE SPEED SENSOR MODULE.

B+ → USING A DIGITAL MULTIMETER, MEASURE THE VOLTAGE AT VEHICLE SPEED SENSOR MODULE CONN C1 FROM TERM "H" TO TERM "A".

0 VOLT → REPAIR OPEN IN CKT 450 TO VEHICLE SPEED SENSOR MODULE.

B+ →
- DISCONNECT VEHICLE SPEED SENSOR CONNECTOR.
- USING A J 33431-B SIGNAL GENERATOR AND INSTRUMENT PANEL TESTER WITH A J 33431-4 ADAPTER, BACKPROBE VEHICLE SPEED SENSOR CONN WITH THE J 33431-4 RED LEAD TO TERM "A" AND THE J 33431-4 BLACK LEAD TO CHASSIS GROUND.
- SET J 33431-B TO 54 MPH, 60 Hz.
- J 33431-B "ON."
- DOES SPEEDOMETER READ APPROX 85 k/hr (54 mph)?

YES →
- REMOVE THE J 33431-4 BLACK LEAD FROM CHASSIS GROUND.
- BACKPROBE THE VEHICLE SPEED SENSOR CONN TERM "B", WITH THE J 33431-4 BLACK LEAD, KEEPING THE RED LEAD CONNECTED TO TERM "A". DOES SPEEDOMETER READ APPROX 85 k/hr (54 mph)?

NO →
- CHECK FOR SHORT TO GROUND OR VOLTAGE IN CKT 401.
- CHECK FOR POOR CONNECTION AT VEHICLE SPEED SENSOR MODULE CONN C2 TERM "C" OR C204 TERM "A5", OR OPEN IN CKT 401. IF OK, REPLACE VEHICLE SPEED SENSOR MODULE.

YES →
- CHECK FOR POOR CONNECTIONS AT VEHICLE SPEED SENSOR. IF OK, REPLACE VEHICLE SPEED SENSOR.

NO →
- CHECK FOR SHORT TO VOLTAGE IN CKT 400.
- CHECK FOR POOR CONNECTION AT VEHICLE SPEED SENSOR MODULE CONN C2 TERM "A" OR C204 TERM "A3", OR OPEN IN CKT 400. IF OK, REPLACE VEHICLE SPEED SENSOR MODULE.

Fig. 26 Vehicle speed sensor troubleshooting chart No. 1. 1993 Caprice & Roadmaster

SYMPTOM	PROCEDURE
Speedometer inoperative and ECM Code 24 is set.	Chart #1
Speedometer operative and ECM Code 24 is set.	See DTC 24
Speedometer inoperative or inaccurate.	Chart #2
Cruise Control does not engage.	Chart #3

Fig. 24 Vehicle speed sensor symptom table. 1993 Caprice & Roadmaster

SYMPTOM	PROCEDURE
Speedometer inoperative and ECM Code 24 is set.	Chart #1
Speedometer operative and ECM Code 24 is set.	See DTC 24
Speedometer inoperative or inaccurate.	Chart #2

Fig. 25 Vehicle speed sensor symptom table. 1993 Fleetwood (RWD)

Fig. 27 Vehicle speed sensor troubleshooting chart No. 1, 1993 Fleetwood (RWD)

Fig. 28 Vehicle speed sensor troubleshooting chart No. 2, 1993 Caprice

Fig. 29 Vehicle speed sensor troubleshooting chart No. 2, 1993 Roadmaster

CHART #3

CRUISE CONTROL DOES NOT ENGAGE

IMPORTANT:

- PERFORM CHART #1, "CRUISE CONTROL WILL NOT ENGAGE," BEFORE PROCEEDING.

DOES SPEEDOMETER FUNCTION NORMALLY?

NO → REFER TO CHART #2, "SPEEDOMETER INOPERATIVE OR INACCURATE."

YES →
- DISCONNECT AUDIO ALARM MODULE CONN C22 (SEDAN).
- DISCONNECT POWER STEERING CONTROL MODULE CONNECTOR (SEDAN).
- DISCONNECT VEHICLE SPEED SENSOR MODULE CONN C1.
- IGNITION SWITCH TO "RUN."
- CRUISE CONTROL SWITCH TO "ON."
- USING A DIGITAL MULTIMETER, MEASURE VOLTAGE AT VEHICLE SPEED SENSOR MODULE CONN C1 FROM TERM "D" TO GROUND. IS IT APPROX 5 VOLTS?

NO →
- CHECK FOR POOR CONNECTION AT CRUISE CONTROL MODULE TERM "K" OR OPEN OR SHORT TO GROUND IN CKT 389.
- CHECK FOR SHORT TO GROUND THROUGH AUDIO ALARM MODULE OR POWER STEERING CONTROL MODULE (SEDAN). IF OK, REPLACE CRUISE CONTROL MODULE.

YES →
- CHECK FOR POOR CONNECTION AT VEHICLE SPEED SENSOR MODULE CONN C1 TERM "D". IF OK, REPLACE VEHICLE SPEED SENSOR MODULE.

Fig. 31 Vehicle speed sensor troubleshooting chart No. 3. 1993 Roadmaster

① ASSUMES SPEEDOMETER IS WORKING OK.
- RAISE DRIVE WHEELS.
- WITH ENGINE IDLING IN GEAR, SCAN TOOL SHOULD DISPLAY MPH ABOVE 0. DOES IT?

NO →
- ENGINE STILL IDLING IN GEAR.
- BACKPROBE CKT 437 AT 37-WAY CONNECTOR WITH VOLTMETER TO GROUND.
- IS VOLTAGE VARYING BETWEEN 1 AND 12 VOLTS?

YES → DTC 24 IS INTERMITTENT.

NO →
② - IGNITION "OFF."
- DISCONNECT VSS BUFFER MODULE.
- IGNITION "ON."
- BACKPROBE CKT 437 AT 37-WAY CONNECTOR WITH VOLTMETER TO GROUND.
- SHOULD DISPLAY 10 VOLTS OR MORE. DOES IT?

YES → FAULTY ECM

NO → CKT 437 OPEN BETWEEN 37-WAY CONNECTOR AND VSS BUFFER MODULE CONNECTOR OR FAULTY VSS BUFFER MODULE.

YES → CKT 437 SHORTED TO GROUND, OPEN BETWEEN ECM AND 37-WAY CONNECTOR, FAULTY CONNECTION OR FAULTY ECM.

Fig. 33 Vehicle speed sensor DTC 24. 1993 Caprice & Roadmaster

CHART #3

CRUISE CONTROL DOES NOT ENGAGE

IMPORTANT:

- PERFORM CHART #1, "CRUISE CONTROL WILL NOT ENGAGE," BEFORE PROCEEDING.

DOES SPEEDOMETER FUNCTION NORMALLY?

NO → REFER TO CHART #2, "SPEEDOMETER INOPERATIVE OR INACCURATE."

YES →
- DISCONNECT VEHICLE SPEED SENSOR MODULE CONN C1.
- IGNITION SWITCH TO "RUN."
- CRUISE CONTROL SWITCH TO "ON."
- USING A DIGITAL MULTIMETER, MEASURE VOLTAGE AT VEHICLE SPEED SENSOR MODULE CONN C1 FROM TERM "D" TO GROUND. IS IT APPROX 5 VOLTS?

NO →
- CHECK FOR POOR CONNECTION AT CRUISE CONTROL MODULE TERM "K" OR OPEN OR SHORT TO GROUND IN CKT 389. IF OK, REPLACE CRUISE CONTROL MODULE.

YES →
- CHECK FOR POOR CONNECTION AT VEHICLE SPEED SENSOR MODULE CONN C1 TERM "D". IF OK, REPLACE VEHICLE SPEED SENSOR MODULE.

Fig. 30 Vehicle speed sensor troubleshooting chart No. 3. 1993 Caprice

CHART #2

SPEEDOMETER INOPERATIVE OR INACCURATE

ECM CODE 24 SET?

YES → REFER TO CHART #1, "SPEEDOMETER INOPERATIVE AND ECM CODE 24 IS SET."

NO →
- DISCONNECT VEHICLE SPEED SENSOR MODULE CONN C1
- USING A J 33431-B SIGNAL GENERATOR AND INSTRUMENT PANEL TESTER WITH A J 33431-4 ADAPTER, CONNECT THE RED LEAD TO THE VEHICLE SPEED SENSOR MODULE CONN C1 TERM "C" AND THE BLACK LEAD TO CHASSIS GROUND.
- SET J 33431-B TO 54 mph, 60 Hz.
- IGNITION SWITCH TO "RUN."
- J 33431-B "ON."
- DOES SPEEDOMETER READ APPROX 85 k/hr (54 mph)?

YES →
- CHECK FOR POOR CONNECTION AT VEHICLE SPEED SENSOR MODULE CONN C1 TERM "C". IF OK, REPLACE VEHICLE SPEED SENSOR MODULE.

NO →
- CHECK FOR SHORT TO VOLTAGE OR SHORT TO GROUND IN CKT 818.
- CHECK FOR OPEN IN CKT 818 OR POOR CONNECTION AT C200 TERM "E2" OR INSTRUMENT CLUSTER CONN TERM "B11". IF OK, SERVICE INSTRUMENT CLUSTER.

Fig. 32 Vehicle speed sensor troubleshooting chart No. 2. 1993 Fleetwood (RWD)

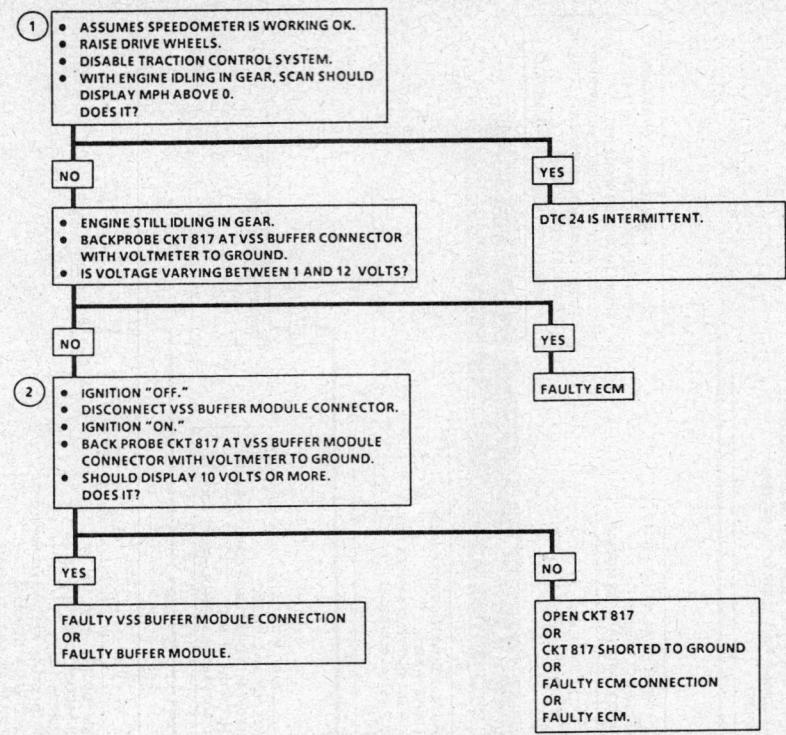

Fig. 34 Vehicle speed sensor DTC 24. 1993 Fleetwood (RWD)

A CABLE, CRUISE CONTROL
B CABLE, ACCELERATOR
C ADJUSTER, ACCELERATOR CABLE
1 MODULE ASSEMBLY, CRUISE CONTROL
21 CABLE ASSEMBLY, ACCELERATOR CONTROL AND CRUISE CONTROL
22 ADJUSTER ASSEMBLY, ACCELERATOR CONTROL AND CRUISE CONTROL CABLE

Fig. 35 Accelerator control and cruise control cable assembly. 1993 Fleetwood (RWD) less V4U Coachbuilder Equipment Option

A MANUAL TRANSMISSION
B AUTOMATIC TRANSMISSION
C CONNECTOR, ELECTRICAL
D CONNECTOR, ELECTRICAL
E CONNECTOR, ELECTRICAL
F CONNECTOR, ELECTRICAL
G CONNECTOR, ELECTRICAL
H WITH 3.4L L32 ENGINE
J WITH 5.7L LT1 ENGINE
4 SWITCH ASSEMBLY, CRUISE CONTROL CLUTCH ANTICIPATE
5 SWITCH ASSEMBLY, CRUISE CONTROL CLUTCH
6 SWITCH ASSEMBLY, CRUISE CONTROL RELEASE
7 SWITCH ASSEMBLY, STOPLAMP AND TORQUE CONVERTER CLUTCH
19 SWITCH ASSEMBLY, CLUTCH START
20 PEDAL ASSEMBLY, BRAKE AND ACCELERATOR AND CLUTCH (WITH BRACKET)
21 PEDAL ASSEMBLY, BRAKE AND ACCELERATOR (WITH BRACKET)

Fig. 36 Exploded view of cruise control switch assembly. 1993 Camaro & Firebird

adjuster, then cable from cruise control module as follows:
  a. Compress conduit tangs and pull out of module.
  b. Disconnect cable bead from cruise motor ribbon end fitting on module, **Fig. 44.**
4. Remove cable from accelerator pedal and body, then cable from vehicle.
5. Reverse procedure to install noting the following:
  a. **Ribbon must not be twisted.** Slide end fitting over ribbon and install in module until tangs snap in place.
  b. Adjust accelerator cable as out-

lined (without V4U Coachbuilder Equipment Option).

CRUISE CONTROL MODULE
1993 CAMARO & FIREBIRD

1. Remove accelerator control cable splash shield screws and bolts, then splash shield.
2. Remove left hand front bumper fascia lower deflector, **Fig. 45** as follows:
  a. Remove retainer, then bolts and

screws from front lower deflector and wheelhouse panel liner.
  b. Remove bolts and screws from front lower deflector and radiator air lower deflector.
  c. Remove retainers from front lower deflector and radiator lower baffle.
  d. Remove front lower deflector by sliding outward from radiator lower deflector and wheelhouse panel liner.
3. Remove cruise control cover to ac-

2 BRACKET ASSEMBLY, BRAKE PEDAL
3 PEDAL ASSEMBLY, BRAKE
4 RETAINER, STOPLAMP SWITCH
5 SWITCH ASSEMBLY, STOPLAMP
6 SWITCH ASSEMBLY, CRUISE CONTROL RELEASE
7 RETAINER, CRUISE CONTROL RELEASE SWITCH

Fig. 37 Cruise control release switch & stop lamp switch assemblies. 1993 Caprice & Roadmaster

A SLIDER AGAINST FITTING (ZERO OR RESET POSITION)
B TO TRANSMISSION
C TO THROTTLE BODY
825 CABLE ASSEMBLY, AUTOMATIC TRANSMISSION TV
900 TAB, AUTOMATIC TRANSMISSION TV CABLE RESET
901 SLIDER, AUTOMATIC TRANSMISSION TV CABLE

Fig. 39 Automatic transmission TV cable readjustment. 1993 Fleetwood (RWD) w/V4U Coachbuilder Equipment Option

A 1/8" DRILL BIT (FOR ADJUSTMENT ONLY)
B ADJUSTMENT HOLE
C 1/4" DRIVE TORQUE WRENCH ACCESS HOLE (ADJUSTMENT ONLY)
D COVER, CABLE ADJUSTER INNER
825 CABLE ASSEMBLY, AUTOMATIC TRANSMISSION TV
828 ADJUSTER ASSEMBLY, ACCELERATOR CONTROL AND CRUISE CONTROL SERVO CABLE
831 COVER, ACCELERATOR CONTROL AND CRUISE CONTROL SERVO CABLE ADJUSTER
832 CABLE ASSEMBLY, CRUISE CONTROL SERVO
834 CABLE ASSEMBLY, ACCELERATOR PEDAL
838 CABLE ASSEMBLY, ACCELERATOR CONTROL SERVO
839 SHIELD, ACCELERATOR CONTROL CABLE SPLASH (PLASTIC OUTER SHIELD)

Fig. 38 Accelerator control & cruise control servo cable adjuster. 1993 Fleetwood (RWD) less V4U Coachbuilder Equipment Option

A RIBBON
B RIBBON MUST NOT BE TWISTED
C MARKINGS IN YELLOW FOR LT1 ENGINE, PINK FOR L32 ENGINE
D BEAD
11 MODULE ASSEMBLY, CRUISE CONTROL
14 CABLE ASSEMBLY, CRUISE CONTROL

Fig. 40 Cruise control cable retainer removal

A CONDUIT
B TANG
C HOUSING
D END FITTING
11 MODULE ASSEMBLY, CRUISE CONTROL
14 CABLE ASSEMBLY, CRUISE CONTROL
18 RETAINER, CRUISE CONTROL

Fig. 41 Cruise control cable removal

cess connectors, then disconnect electrical connector from cruise control module.
4. Disconnect cruise control cable from module, then remove bolts and screws.
5. Remove module with bracket, **Fig. 45**, then module from bracket.
6. Reverse procedure to install noting the following:
   a. Tighten cruise control module to bracket screws and bolts to 53 ft. lbs.
   b. Tighten cruise control module to left engine compartment inner side rail screws and bolts to 89 ft. lbs.
   c. Tighten radiator air lower deflector and front lower deflector screws and bolts to 49 ft. lbs.
   d. Tighten accelerator cable splash shield screws and bolts to 17 ft. lbs.

1993 CAPRICE & ROADMASTER

1. Disconnect battery ground cable.
2. Disconnect electrical connector from module, **Fig. 46**.
3. Disconnect cruise control cable from module, then remove bolts and screws.

4. Remove module and plugs.
5. Remove plugs from module if a new module is being installed.
6. Reverse procedure to install noting the following:
   a. Align holes in accelerator and cruise control adjuster bracket to holes in wheelhouse panel and position module on wheelhouse panel.
   b. Tighten module bolts and screws to 71 ft. lbs.
   c. Adjust cable, if necessary, as outlined.

CRUISE CONTROL SWITCH ASSEMBLIES

1993 CAMARO & FIREBIRD

1. Remove left hand instrument panel sound insulator, then disconnect electrical connectors.
2. Remove release switch assembly, stop lamp and TCC switch assembly and clutch switch or clutch anticipate switch, if equipped from pedal with bracket, **Fig. 36**.
3. Reverse procedure to install. Adjust as outlined.

ENGAGEMENT SWITCH

The engagement switch is not serviceable. The complete turn signal, headlamp dimmer switch, cruise control actuator and windshield wiper/washer must be replaced as an assembly.
1. Disconnect battery ground cable.
2. Remove steering column access cov-

A RIBBON
B BEAD
1 MODULE ASSEMBLY, CRUISE CONTROL
21 CABLE ASSEMBLY, ACCELERATOR CONTROL
    AND CRUISE CONTROL

Fig. 43 Cable bead to cruise control module assembly. 1993 Fleetwood (RWD)

A COVER
B CABLE, CRUISE CONTROL
C CABLE, AUTOMATIC TRANSMISSION TV
D CABLE, ACCELERATOR
E CABLE, ACCELERATOR TO THROTTLE BODY INJECTOR
1 MODULE ASSEMBLY, CRUISE CONTROL
15 BRACKET ASSEMBLY, ACCELERATOR CONTROL AND CRUISE CONTROL CABLE
16 NUT, ACCELERATOR CONTROL AND CRUISE CONTROL CABLE BRACKET, 8.0 N·m (71 LB. IN.)
19 BOLT/SCREW, CRUISE CONTROL MODULE, 8.0 N·m (71 LB. IN.)
20 RETAINER, CRUISE CONTROL MODULE
21 CABLE ASSEMBLY, ACCELERATOR CONTROL AND CRUISE CONTROL
22 ADJUSTER ASSEMBLY, ACCELERATOR CONTROL AND CRUISE CONTROL CABLE
23 CABLE ASSEMBLY, ACCELERATOR CONTROL AND AUTOMATIC TRANSMISSION TV
25 SHIELD ASSEMBLY, ACCELERATOR CONTROL AND CRUISE CONTROL CABLE ADJUSTER
26 COVER, ACCELERATOR CONTROL AND CRUISE CONTROL CABLE ADJUSTER

Fig. 42 Accelerator control & cruise control cable adjuster removal. 1993 Fleetwood (RWD) less V4U Coachbuilder Equipment Option

19 RETAINER, FRONT BUMPER FASCIA LOWER DEFLECTOR
20 DEFLECTOR, FRONT BUMPER FASCIA LOWER
21 BOLT/SCREW, RADIATOR AIR LOWER DEFLECTOR
22 BOLT/SCREW, FRONT BUMPER FASCIA LOWER DEFLECTOR
35 BOLT/SCREW, FRONT BUMPER FASCIA LOWER DEFLECTOR
36 RETAINER, FRONT BUMPER FASCIA LOWER DEFLECTOR
37 BAFFLE, RADIATOR AIR LOWER
38 LINER, FRONT WHEELHOUSE PANEL
39 DEFLECTOR, RADIATOR AIR LOWER

Fig. 44 Front bumper fascia lower deflector removal. 1993 Camaro & Firebird

A CONNECTOR, ELECTRICAL
10 BOLT/SCREW, CRUISE CONTROL, 6 N·m (53 LB. IN.)
11 MODULE ASSEMBLY, CRUISE CONTROL
12 BRACKET ASSEMBLY, CRUISE CONTROL MODULE
13 COVER, CRUISE CONTROL
14 CABLE ASSEMBLY, CRUISE CONTROL
15 HARNESS ASSEMBLY, FORWARD LAMP WIRING
16 BOLT/SCREW, CRUISE CONTROL MODULE BRACKET, 10 N·m (89 LB. IN.)
17 RAIL ASSEMBLY, ENGINE COMPARTMENT INNER SIDE

Fig. 45 Cruise control module removal. 1993 Camaro & Firebird

A CONNECTOR, ELECTRICAL
1 MODULE ASSEMBLY, CRUISE CONTROL
19 BOLT/SCREW, CRUISE CONTROL MODULE, 8 N·m (71 LB. IN.)
20 PLUG, FRONT WHEELHOUSE PANEL HOLE

Fig. 46 Cruise control module removal. 1993 Caprice & Roadmaster

er, then disconnect electrical connector; ensure windshield wiper switch is in Off position.
3. Remove lever assembly by pulling straight out.
4. Reverse procedure to install.

RELEASE SWITCH & STOP LAMP SWITCH

1993 CAPRICE & ROADMASTER

1. Disconnect electrical connectors, then remove release switch and stop lamp switch assemblies from retainers, **Fig. 37**.
2. Remove retainers from bracket.
3. Reverse procedure to install. Adjust as outlined.

TROUBLESHOOTING SUPPLEMENT

INDEX

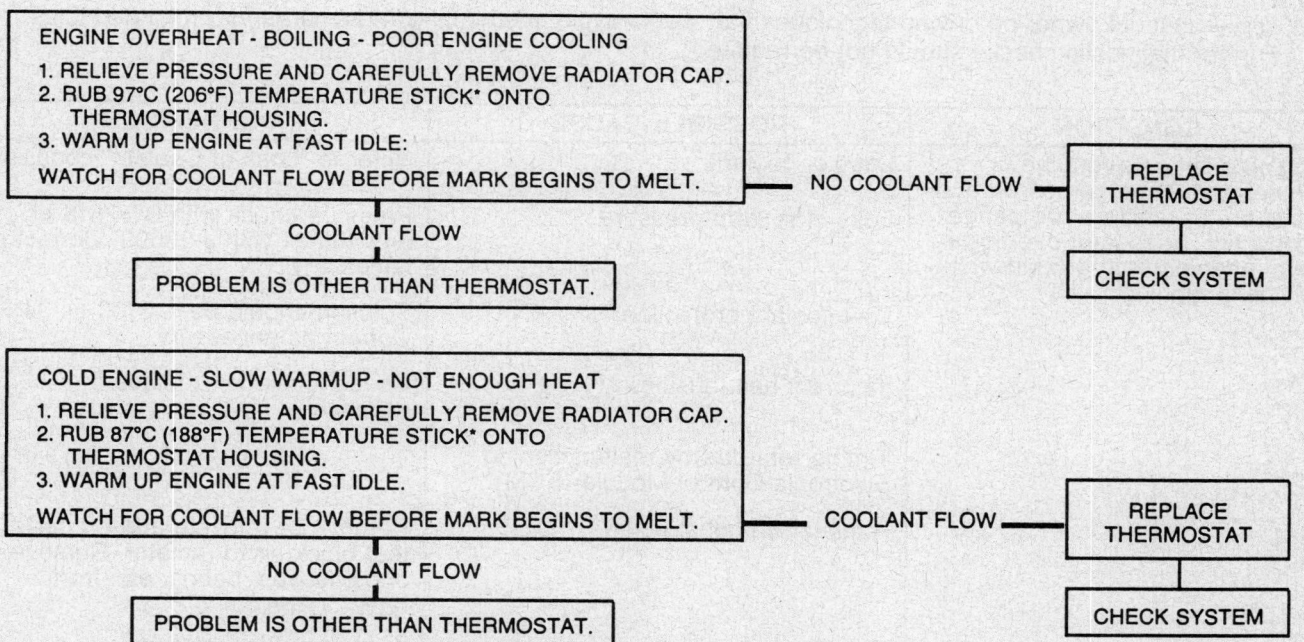

ENGINE OVERHEAT - BOILING - POOR ENGINE COOLING

1. RELIEVE PRESSURE AND CAREFULLY REMOVE RADIATOR CAP.
2. RUB 97°C (206°F) TEMPERATURE STICK* ONTO THERMOSTAT HOUSING.
3. WARM UP ENGINE AT FAST IDLE:

WATCH FOR COOLANT FLOW BEFORE MARK BEGINS TO MELT. — NO COOLANT FLOW — REPLACE THERMOSTAT / CHECK SYSTEM

COOLANT FLOW

PROBLEM IS OTHER THAN THERMOSTAT.

COLD ENGINE - SLOW WARMUP - NOT ENOUGH HEAT

1. RELIEVE PRESSURE AND CAREFULLY REMOVE RADIATOR CAP.
2. RUB 87°C (188°F) TEMPERATURE STICK* ONTO THERMOSTAT HOUSING.
3. WARM UP ENGINE AT FAST IDLE.

WATCH FOR COOLANT FLOW BEFORE MARK BEGINS TO MELT. — COOLANT FLOW — REPLACE THERMOSTAT / CHECK SYSTEM

NO COOLANT FLOW

PROBLEM IS OTHER THAN THERMOSTAT.

* NOTE: THE TEMPERATURE STICK IS A PENCIL LIKE DEVICE WHICH HAS A WAX MATERIAL CONTAINING CERTAIN CHEMICALS WHICH MELT AT A GIVEN TEMPERATURE. TEMPERATURE STICKS CAN BE USED TO DETERMINE A THERMOSTAT'S OPERATING TEMPERATURE BY RUBBING 87°C (188°F) AND 97°C (206°F) STICKS ON THE THERMOSTAT HOUSING. THE MARKS MADE BY THE STICKS SHOULD MELT WHEN COOLANT TEMPERATURES OF 87°C (188°F) AND 97°C (206°F) ARE REACHED, RESPECTIVELY. THESE TEMPERATURES ARE THE NORMAL OPERATING RANGE OF THE THERMOSTAT.

Fig. 1   Thermostat

COOLING SYSTEM DIAGNOSIS

1. Does overheating occur while pulling a trailer?

   Yes — how heavy trailer? If trailer weight is greater than 454 kg (1,000 lbs.) and vehicle is equipped with normal duty cooling system, a heavy duty cooling package is required (per trailer hauling specs.). Further diagnostic checks should not be required.

2. Is vehicle equipped with add-on or after market air conditioning system?

   Yes — was heavy duty radiator installed with the system? If not, install heavy duty radiator for the vehicle model involved. Further diagnostic checks should not be required.

3. Is overheating occurring after prolonged idle in gear, A/C system operating?

   Yes — instruct owner on driving techniques that would avoid overheating, such as:
   a. Idle in Neutral as much as possible — increase engine RPM to get coolant flow through radiator.
   b. Turn A/C system off during extended idles if overheating is indicated by hot lamp or temperature gage. Further diagnostic checks should not be required.

4. Is overheating occurring after prolonged driving in slow city traffic, traffic jams, etc?

   Yes — instruct owner on driving techniques that would avoid overheating — same as for prolonged idles. Further diagnostic checks should not be required.

CONDITION	POSSIBLE CAUSE	CORRECTION
Engine overheats (engine temperature lamp comes on and stays on, or temperature gauge shows hot, or coolant overflows from reservoir onto ground while engine is running.	Loss of coolant.	Refer to "Loss of Coolant" condition.
	Loss of system pressure.	Pressure check with BT-7518 or J-24460-01 with J-23699. Correct as necessary.
	Low coolant protection.	Solution should be −37°C (−34°F). Correct as necessary.
	Incorrect belt tension.	Check tensioner, replace if necessary.
	Timing retarded by malfunctioning Electronic Control Module (ECM).	
	Radiator fins obstructed.	Remove or relocate add-on parts that block air to radiator. Remove bugs, leaves, debris, etc. from radiator fins.
	Cooling system passages blocked by rust or scale.	Drain and flush the system. Repair as necessary.
	Reservoir hose pinched or kinked.	Reroute or replace hose as necessary.
	Cooling fan inoperative.	

Fig. 2   Cooling system (Part 1 of 3)

COOLING SYSTEM DIAGNOSIS (CONTINUED)		
CONDITION	**POSSIBLE CAUSE**	**CORRECTION**
Engine overheats (engine temperature lamp comes on and stays on, or temperature gauge shows hot, or coolant overflows from reservoir onto ground while engine is running. (cont'd.)	Loose, damaged and/or missing deflector.	Repair or replace as necessary.
	Thermostat stuck in closed position.	Replace thermostat.
	Faulty coolant pump.	Replace coolant pump.
	Incorrect radiator.	Install correct radiator.
Loss of coolant.	Leaking radiator.	Repair or replace as necessary.
	Faulty cooling system pressure cap.	Replace cap.
	Leaking coolant reservoir or hose.	Replace reservoir or hose as necessary.
	Loose or damaged hoses or connections.	Repair or replace hoses or clamps as necessary.
	Coolant pump seal leaking.	Replace coolant pump.
	Coolant pump gasket leaking.	Replace gasket.
	Improper cylinder head bolt torque.	Tighten bolts to specifications, replace cylinder head gasket(s) if required.
	Leaking intake manifold or cylinder head or gaskets, cylinder head or block core plug, heater core.	Repair or replace as necessary.
Engine fails to reach normal operating temperature. (Cool air from heater.)	Thermostat stuck open. Incorrect thermostat.	Replace thermostat. Install correct thermostat.
	Coolant below add mark.	Add coolant as necessary. Use correct solution.
Hot lamp on or high temperature gage reading, no loss of coolant.	Faulty engine temperature switch or circuit.	

Fig. 2   Cooling system (Part 2 of 3)

A. Problems not requiring disassembly of cooling system —

  1. Large obstructions blocking radiator or condenser

    a. Auxiliary oil coolers — relocate
    b. Ice, mud or snow — remove

  2. Engine oil overfill — check engine oil dipstick

  3. Incorrect radiator for application — install correct radiator

  4. Missing or damaged lower air baffle — repair or replace as necessary

B. Problems requiring disassembly of cooling system —

  1. Incorrect or damaged fan — repair or replace as necessary

  2. Faulty emission system components (could cause overheating at idle) — replace faulty component

    a. PCV valve
    b. TVS or TCS

  3. Pressure check cooling system with pressure cap installed

  4. Faulty coolant pump — replace coolant pump

  5. Plugged radiator tubes

  6. Internal system leaks

    a. Head gasket
    b. Cracked block
    c. Timing chain/belt cover
    d. Intake manifold gasket

  7. Plugged coolant passages in cylinder head(s) — remove head(s) and check visually

Fig. 2   Cooling system (Part 3 of 3)

SYMPTOM	POSSIBLE CAUSES/CORRECTIONS
BODY/CHASSIS — GENERAL	
Abnormal noise	• Control arm bushings or tie rod ends worn: Inspect and replace as needed.
	• Spring improperly positioned: Reposition spring.
	• Stabilizer shaft loose: Inspect mounting bolts and links; torque to specifications.
	• Strut or strut mounting worn: Inspect and service as needed.
	• Suspension bolts loose: Torque to specifications.
	• Suspension components damaged: Inspect and repair/replace components as needed.
	• Wheel nuts loose: Inspect wheel for out of round lug holes; torque nuts to specifications.
	• Wheel covers: Repair/replace.
	• Steering gear loose. Torque mounting bolts to specifications.
Body leans or sways in corners	• Springs broken or sagging: Inspect and service as needed.
	• Stabilizer shaft loose: Inspect mounting bolts and links: torque to specifications.
	• Strut worn: Inspect and service as needed.
	• Vehicle overloaded: Reduce load.
	• Tire pressure(s) incorrect: Inflate to specifications.
"Dog" tracking	• Frame to underbody alignment incorrect: Inspect and service as needed.
	• Rear control arm damaged or bushings worn: Repair/replace components, as needed.
	• Rear toe incorrect: Check and perform alignment.
	• Faulty or bent rear suspension component: Repair/replace components as needed.
Low or uneven trim height	• Springs incorrect, broken, sagging or weak: Inspect and service as needed.
	• Vehicle overloaded: Reduce load.
	• Tire pressure(s) incorrect: Inflate to specifications.
Suspension bottoms	• Springs incorrect, broken, sagging or weak: Inspect and service as needed.
	• Strut worn: Inspect and service as needed.
	• Vehicle overloaded: Reduce load.

Fig. 3   Front suspension, steering & wheel alignment (Part 1 of 5)

SYMPTOM	POSSIBLE CAUSES/CORRECTIONS
RIDE	
Too harsh	• Incorrect springs: Determine correct component(s) and install.
	• Incorrect strut: Determine correct component(s) and install.
	• Tire pressure(s) incorrect: Inflate to specifications.
Too soft	• Springs sagging or incorrect: Inspect and service as needed.
	• Strut worn: Inspect and service as needed.
	• Tire pressure(s) incorrect: Inflate to specifications.
SHIMMY, SHAKE OR VIBRATION	• Brake rotor imbalance: Refinish and/or replace as needed.
	• Brake rotor(s) warped (vibration occurs during braking): Refinish and/or replace as needed.
	• Ball joints worn: Inspect and replace as needed.
	• Excessive loaded radial runout of tire and wheel: Balance wheel/tire, correct tire non-uniformity, and recheck for vibration. If still present and runout exceeds specifications, replace wheel.
	• Tie rod ends worn: Replace as needed.
	• Tire pressure(s) incorrect: Inflate to specifications.
	• Tire(s)/wheel(s) out of balance: Balance as needed.
	• Tire(s)/wheel(s) out of round: Service and/or replace as needed.
	• Excessive wheel or wheel stud runout: Service and/or replace as needed.
	• Wheel trim imbalance: Adjust trim and balance as needed.
	• Wheel bearings worn: Replace hub and bearing.
STEERING	
Erratic when braking	• Caster uneven or incorrect: Inspect components for wear and perform alignment.
	• Control arm loose: Inspect control arm, bushings, ball joint and mounting hardware; replace and/or torque to specifications.
	• Rotors warped: Refinish and/or replace as needed.
	• Springs broken or sagging: Inspect and service as needed.
	• Wheel bearings worn: Replace hub and bearing.

Fig. 3   Front suspension, steering & wheel alignment (Part 2 of 5)

SYMPTOM	POSSIBLE CAUSES/CORRECTIONS
STEERING (Continued)	
Erratic when braking (Continued)	• Wheel caliper leaking: Inspect and service as needed.
Hard steering	• Bind or catch in steering gear: Check for correct rack bearing preload and for steering gear damage; adjust and/or replace, as needed.
	• Low fluid; excessive internal leakage of steering components: Add fluid, as needed.
	• Steering gear loose: Torque mounting bolts to specifications.
	• Intermediate shaft bolt torque too high: Torque to specifications.
Poor returnability	• Ball joints binding: Inspect and replace as needed.
	• Front wheel alignment: Check and perform alignment.
	• Steering gear valve sticking: Flush and bleed system; if symptom persists, service partial steering gear.
	• Steering gear loose: Torque mounting bolts to specifications.
	• Intermediate shaft bolt torque too high: Torque to specifications.
	• Lower coupling binding on steering gear: Inspect and repair/replace components as needed.
	• Rack preload misadjusted (too tight): Torque to specifications.
	• Steering column binding: Check column alignment, mounting, and bearings; adjust, repair and/or replace, as needed.
	• Tire pressures incorrect: Inflate to specifications.
Steering wheel kick-back	• Air in power steering system: Inspect and bleed system.
	• Joints from column to steering gear loose or worn: Check for correct torque; replace components as needed.
	• Steering gear loose: Torque mounting bolts to specifications.
	• Tie rod ends loose: Inspect and replace as needed.

Fig. 3 Front suspension, steering & wheel alignment (Part 3 of 5)

SYMPTOM	POSSIBLE CAUSES/CORRECTIONS
STEERING (Continued)	
Steering wheel kick-back (Continued)	• Wheel bearings worn: Replace hub and bearings.
	• See "Too Much Play In Steering."
Steering wheel surges or jerks	• Hydraulic system: Diagnose and service as needed.
	• Low fluid level: Add fluid, as needed.
	• Pump drive belt loose: Adjust or replace as needed. See specific engine section.
	• Steering gear valve sluggish: Flush and bleed system; if symptom persists, service partial steering gear.
Too much play in steering	• Joints from column to steering gear loose or worn: Check for correct torque; replace components as needed.
	• Steering gear loose: Torque mounting bolts to specifications.
	• Wheel bearings worn: Replace hub and bearing.
Wander or poor steering stability	• Front or rear wheel alignment: Check and perform alignment.
	• Rack preload misadjusted (too loose): Torque to specifications.
	• Springs broken or sagging: Inspect and service as needed.
	• Stabilizer shaft loose: Inspect mounting bolts and links; torque to specifications.
	• Strut worn: Inspect and service as needed.
	• Tires uneven/misaligned: Service and/or replace as needed. Check and perform alignment.
TIRES/WHEELS	
Abnormal/excessive wear	• Front or rear wheel alignment; excessive toe: Inspect components for wear and perform alignment.
	• Hard driving.
	• Tire pressure low: Inflate to specifications.
	• Springs broken or sagging: Inspect and service as needed.

Fig. 3 Front suspension, steering & wheel alignment (Part 4 of 5)

SYMPTOM	POSSIBLE CAUSES/CORRECTIONS
TIRES/WHEELS (Continued)	
Abnormal/excessive wear (Continued)	• Strut(s) worn: Inspect and service as needed.
	• Tires not rotated properly: Inspect tire(s); service and/or replace as needed.
	• Tire(s) out of balance: Balance as needed.
	• Vehicle overloaded: Reduce load.
Scuffed	• Excessive speed on turns.
	• Control arm bent or twisted: Inspect and replace as needed.
	• Toe incorrect: Check and perform alignment.
Cupped	• Ball joint worn: Replace ball joint.
	• Front or rear wheel alignment: Check and perform alignment.
	• Strut worn: Inspect and service as needed.
	• Tire/wheel runout excessive: Service and/or replace as needed.
	• Wheel bearing worn: Replace hub and bearing.
	• Steering gear loose: Torque mounting bolts to specifications.
Wheel tramp	• Improper strut action: Service and/or replace as needed.
	• Tire/wheel out of balance: Balance as needed.
	• Blister or bump on tire.
VEHICLE LEADS/PULLS	• Front brakes dragging:
	• Front wheel alignment: Check and perform alignment.
	• Radial tire lateral force: Inspect tire(s); service and/or replace as needed.
	• Steering gear valve off center (unbalanced). Inspect and adjust.
	• Springs broken or sagging: Inspect and service as needed.
	• Tire pressure incorrect: Inflate to specifications.
	• Tires mismatched/uneven: Service and/or replace as needed.

Fig. 3 Front suspension, steering & wheel alignment (Part 5 of 5)

ENGINE REBUILDING SPECIFICATIONS

CYLINDER HEAD, VALVE GUIDES & VALVE SEATS

*All Measurements Given In Inches, Unless Otherwise Specified.

Engine Liter/CID/VIN	Year	Cylinder Head Warpage Limit	Cylinder Head Overall Thickness	Valve Guides Standard Inside Diameter	Stem To Guide Clearance Intake	Stem To Guide Clearance Exhaust	Seat Angle	Valve Seats Seat Width Intake	Valve Seats Seat Width Exhaust	Runout
1.0L/3-61/5,6	1991	.002	—	.2165-.2170	.0008-.0021	.0014-.0024	45°	.0512-.0590	.0512-.0590	—
1.0L/3-61/6	1992-93	.002	—	.2165-.2174	.0008-.0021	.0018-.0028	45°	.0512-.0590	.0512-.0590	—
1.6L/4-97/6 ①	1991	—	—	.2770-.2780	.0008-.0020	.0016-.0028	46°	.0500-.0701	.0500-.0701	.002
	1992-93	—	3.77	.2780 ⑨	.0008-.0020	.0016-.0028	46°	.0500-.0701	.0500-.0701	.002
1.6L/4-97/6 ②	1991-92	.002	—	—	.0031	.0039	45°	.0390-.0551	.0390-.0551	—
1.6L/4-97/5 ③	1991-92	.002	—	.2366-.2374	.0010-.0024	.0012-.0026	45°	.0390-.0551	.0390-.0551	—
1.6L/4-97/5,6 ④ ⑤	1991	—	—	—	.0009	.0012	—	.0870	.0790	—
1.6L/4-97/6 ④	1992-93	.0158	—	—	.0009	.0012	—	.0870	.0790	—
1.8L/4-108/8 ⑭	1993	.002	—	.2366-.2374	.0010-.0024	.0012-.0026	45°	.039-.055	.039-.055	—
1.8L/4-110/8 ⑤	1992-93	.008	—	—	.0009	.0012	—	.0870	.0790	—
2.0L/4-121/K,M,H	1991-93	⑥	—	.2766-.2772	.0006-.0017	.0012-.0024	45°	.0500-.0701	.0500-.0701	.002
2.2L/4-133/G,4	1991-93	⑥	—	—	.0011-.0026	.0014-.0030	46°	.0490-.0590	.0630-.0750	.002
2.3L/4-138/A,D,3	1991-93	.008	—	.2762-.2772	.0010-.0027	.0015-.0032	45°	.0370-.0748	.0370-.0748	—
2.5L/4-151/R	1991-92	.007	—	—	.0011-.0027	.0013-.0040	46°	.0350-.0750	.0580-.1050	.002
3.1L/V6-192/T,V	1991-93	⑥	—	—	.0010-.0027	.0010-.0027	46°	.0610-.0730	.0670-.0790	.001
3.3L/V6-204/N	1991-93	.002	—	—	.0015-.0035	.0015-.0035	45°	.0600-.0800	.0900-.1100	.002
3.4L/V6-204/X	1991-93	.004	—	—	.0011-.0026	.0014-.0031	46°	.0490-.0590	.0630-.0750	⑩
3.8L/V6-231/C,L,1	1991-93	—	—	—	.0015-.0035	.0015-.0032	45°	.0600-.0800	.0900-.1100	.002
4.3L/V6-262/Z	1991-93	—	—	—	.0011-.0027	.0011-.0027	46°	⑪	.0620-.0930	.002
4.5L/V8-273/5	1991	—	—	.343	.0010-.0030	.0020-.0040	45°	.0620	.0930	.004
4.6L/V8-279/Y	1993	.002	—	.235	.001-.003	.002-.004	46°	.003	.0035	.002
4.9L/V8-300/B	1991-92	—	—	.343	.0010-.0030	.0020-.0040	45°	.0620	.0930	.004
5.0L/V8-305/E,F	1991-93	—	—	—	.0011-.0027	.0011-.0027	46°	⑪	⑫	.002
5.0L/V8-307/Y	1991	.006	—	—	.0010-.0027	.0015-.0032	⑦	.0370-.0750	.0500-.1000	⑧
5.7L/V8-350/7,8	1991-93	—	—	—	.0011-.0027	.0011-.0027	46°	⑪	⑫	.002
5.7L/V8-350/P	1992-93	—	—	—	.0011-.0027	.0011-.0027	46°	.030-.050	.060-.080	.002
5.7L/V8-350/J	1991-93	—	—	—	⑬	.0014-.0030	44°	.0569-.0734	.0569-.0734	.004

①—LeMans.
②—Prizm w/4A-FE 16 valve engine.
③—Prizm w/GSI 4A-GE 16 valve engine.
④—Storm w/12 valve engine.
⑤—Storm w/16 valve engine.
⑥—Maximum surface refinish, .010 inch.
⑦—Intake, 45°; exhaust, 31°.
⑧—Intake, .002 inch; exhaust, .004 inch.
⑨—Minimum.
⑩—1991, .004 inch; 1992-93, .002 inch.
⑪—1991, .0310-.0620 inch; 1992-93, .0350-.0600 inch.
⑫—1991, .0620-.0930 inch; 1992-93, .0600-.0940 inch.
⑬—1991, .0012-.0026 inch; 1992-93, .0012-.0394 inch.
⑭—Prizm w/16-valve engine.

VALVES & VALVE SPRINGS

All Measurements Given In Inches, Unless Otherwise Specified.

| Engine Liter/CID/VIN | Year | Valves | | | | | | | Valve Springs | | | | |
| | | Stem Diameter | | Clearance | | | | | | | | | |
		Intake	Exhaust	Intake	Exhaust	Face Angle	Margin ①	Free Length	Installed Height	Seated Press. Pounds @ Inches	Comp. Press. Pounds @ Inches	Out Of Square Limit
1.0L/3-61/5,6	1991	.2148-.2157	.2146-.2151	—	—	45°	②	1.6035	1.28	41-47.2 @ 1.28	—	.079
1.0L/3-61/6	1992-93	.2148-.2157	.2142-.2144	—	—	45°	②	1.6035	1.28	41-47.2 @ 1.28	—	.079
1.6L/4-97/6 ④	1991	.2755-.2760	.2747-.2758	—	—	46°	—	—	1.24	62 @ 1.24	140 @ .85	—
	1992-93	.276 ①	.275 ①	—	—	46°	—	—	1.24	62 @ 1.24	140 @ .85	—
1.6L/4-97/6 ⑤	1991-93	.2350-.2356	.2348-.2354	.006-.010 ③	.008-.012 ③	45.5°	.020	1.724	—	—	—	.098
1.6L/4-97/5 ⑥	1991-92	.2350-.2356	.2348-.2354	.006-.010 ③	.008-.012 ③	45.5°	.0315	1.6177	—	—	—	.098
1.6L/4-97/6 ⑦	1991-93	.2335	.2335	.006 ③	.010 ③	—	.0315	⑧	—	—	—	—
1.6L/4-97/5 ⑨	1991	.2335	.2335	.004-.008 ③	.008-.012 ③	—	.0315	—	—	—	—	—
1.8L/4-110/8 ⑨	1992-93	.232	.232	—	—	—	.0315	—	—	—	—	—
1.8L/4-108/8 ⑯	1993	.2350-.2356	.2348-.2354	.0010-.0024	.0012-.0026	45	.031-.047	1.5185	—	37.3 @ 1.248	—	.079
2.0L/4-121/K,M,H	1991-93	.2755-.2760	.2747-.2753	—	—	46°	.031	—	1.476	⑩	165-179 @ 1.043	—
2.2L/4-133/G	1991	—	—	—	—	45°	.031	2.06	1.61	100-110 @ 1.61	208-222 @ 1.22	—
2.2L/4-133/4	1992-93	—	—	—	—	45°	.031	1.89	1.64	79-85 @ 1.64	225-233 @ 1.25	—
2.3L/4-138/A,D,3	1991-93	.2745-.2752	.2740-.2747	—	—	⑪	—	—	1.437	71-79 @ 1.4370	⑫	—
2.5L/4-151/R	1991-92	—	—	—	—	45°	—	㉑	1.68	75 @ 1.68	173 @ 1.24	—
3.1L/V6-192/T,V	1991-93	—	—	—	—	45°	—	1.91	1.5748	90 @ 1.701	215 @ 1.291	—
3.3L/V6-204/N	1991-93	—	—	—	—	45°	.025	1.981	1.69-1.75	76-84 @ 1.750	200-220 @ 1.315	—
3.4L/V6-204/X	1991-93	—	—	—	—	45°	—	1.66	1.40	75 @ 1.40	180 @ 1.03	—
3.8L/V6-231/C,L,1	1991-93	—	—	—	—	45°	.025	1.981	1.69-1.75	76-84 @ 1.75	200-220 @ 1.315	—
4.3L/V6-262/Z	1991-93	—	—	—	—	45°	—	2.03	1.69-1.71	76-84 @ 1.70	194-206 @ 1.25	—
4.5L/V8-273/5	1991	.3413-.3420	.3401-.3408	—	—	45°	⑭	2.125	1.73	68-76 @ 1.73	214-232 @ 1.35	—
4.6L/V8-279/Y,8	1993	.2331-.2339	.2331-.2339	.001-.003	.001-.003	45°	—	1.575	1.19	53 @ 1.19	109 @ .823	—
4.9L/V8-300/B	1991-93	.3413-.3420	.3401-.3408	—	—	45°	⑭	㉒	1.73	68-76 @ 1.73	214-232 @ 1.35	—
5.0L/V8-305/E,F	1991-93	—	—	—	—	45°	.031	2.03 ⑬	⑮	76-84 @ 1.7	194-206 @ 1.25	—
5.7L/V8-350/7,8	1991-93	—	—	—	—	45°	—	2.03 ⑬	⑮	76-84 @ 1.7	194-206 @ 1.25	—
5.7L/V8-350/P	1992-93	—	—	—	—	45°	—	2.01	1.78	81-89 @ 1.78	252-272 @ 1.31	—
5.7L/V8-350/J	1991-93	—	—	—	—	45°	—	⑰	⑱	⑲	⑳	—

① —Minimum.
② —Intake, .039 inch; exhaust, .047 inch.
③ —Cold.
④ —LeMans.
⑤ —Prizm w/4A-FE 16 valve engine.
⑥ —Prizm w/GSI 4A-GE 16 valve engine.
⑦ —Storm w/12 valve engine.
⑧ —Intake, 1.73 inch; exhaust, 1.67 inch.
⑨ —Storm w/16 valve engine.
⑩ —VIN K, 63-71 lbs. @ 1.476 inch; VIN M, 74-82 lbs. @ 1.476 inch.
⑪ —Intake, 44°; exhaust, 44.5°.
⑫ —1991, 188-202 lbs. @ 1.0433 inch; 1992, 193-207 @ 1.0433 inch.
⑬ —Damper spring, 1.86 inch.
⑭ —Intake, .005 inch; exhaust, .030 inch.
⑮ —1991, Intake, 1.7187 inch; exhaust, 1.5937 inch; 1992-93, 1.7 inch.
⑯ —Prizm w/16 valve engine.
⑰ —Inner spring, 1.54 inch; outer spring, 1.71 inch.
⑱ —Inner spring, 1.18 inch; outer spring, 1.34 inch.
⑲ —Inner spring, 34.2-37.8 lbs. @ 1.18

Continued

VALVES & VALVE SPRINGS-Continued

inch; outer spring, 64.1-76.4 lbs. @ 1.34 inch.
⑳ —Inner spring, 75.5-81.8 lbs. @ .79

inch; outer spring, 146.8-166.4 lbs. @ .95 inch.

㉑ —1991, 2.20 inch; 1992–93, 2.01 inch.
㉒ —1991, 2.125 inch; 1992–93, 1.95 inch.

CYLINDER BLOCK

*All Measurements Given In Inches, Unless Otherwise Specified.

Engine Liter/CID/VIN	Year	Cylinder Bore Diameter (Std.)	Cylinder Bore Taper Max.	Cylinder Bore Out of Round Max.
1.0L/3-61/5,6	1991-93	①	.0039	.0039
1.6L/4-97/6 ②	1991-93	3.110	.0005	.0005
1.6L/4-97/5,6 ③ ④	1991-93	—	.0005	.005
1.6L/4-97/5,6 ⑤ ⑥	1991	3.1496-3.1512	.005	.005
1.6L/4-97/6 ⑤	1992-93	3.1496-3.1512	.005	.005
1.8L/4-108/8 ⑪	1993	3.1890-3.2177	.005	.005
1.8L/4-110/8 ⑥	1992-93	3.1496-3.1508	.005	.005
2.0L/4-121/K,M,H	1991	3.3852-3.3868	.0005	.0005
2.2L/4-133/G,4	1991-93	3.5036-3.5043	.0005	.0005
2.3L/4-138/A,D,3	1991-93	3.6217-3.6223	.0003	.0004
2.5L/4-151/R	1991-92	4.0000	.005	.001
3.1L/V6-192/T,V	1991-93	3.5045-3.5052	.0005	.0005
3.3L/V6-204/N	1991-93	3.700	.0005	.0004
3.4L/V6-204/X	1991-93	3.6213-3.6224	—	.0003
3.8L/V6-231/C,L,1	1991-93	3.800	.0005	.0004
4.3L/V6-262/Z	1991	3.9995-4.0025	⑦	.001
	1992-93	⑨	⑦	.001
4.5L/V8-273/5	1991	⑧	.0005	.0008
4.6L/V8-279/Y,9	1993	3.6807-3.6815	.0004	.0008
4.9L/V8-300/B	1992-93	⑧	⑩	.0008
5.0L/V8-305/E,F	1991-93	3.7350-3.7385	⑦	.001
5.7L/V8-350/7,8,P	1991-93	⑨	⑦	.001
5.7L/V8-350/J	1991-93	3.8971-3.8981	—	—

① —Cylinder bore diameter Nos. are stamped on the top of the block in sequence. No. 1, 2.9138-2.9142 inch & No. 2, 2.9134-2.9138 inch.
② —LeMans.
③ —Prizm w/4A-FE 16 valve engine, VIN 6.
④ —Prizm w/GSI 4A-GE 16 valve engine, VIN 5.

⑤ —Storm w/12 valve engine.
⑥ —Storm w/16 valve engine.
⑦ —Thrust side, .0005 inch; relief side, .0010 inch.
⑧ —Nominal cylinder bore diameter, 3.622 inches. Liner protrusion, flush to .0032 inch above block deck. Maximum variation between liners, .0039 inch. Piston & liner are

matched set & must be replaced as an assembly if liner protrusion, taper, out of round or piston to liner clearance are not within specifications.
⑨ —1991, 3.9995-4.0025 inch; 1992–93, 4.0007-4.0017 inch.
⑩ —1991, .0005 inch; 1992–93, .0248 inch.
⑪ —Prizm w/16-valve engine.

PISTONS, PINS & RINGS

*All Measurements Given In Inches, Unless Otherwise Specified.

Engine Liter/CID/VIN	Year	Piston Diameter (Std.)	Piston Clearance	Piston Pin Diameter①	Piston Pin To Piston Clearance	Piston Ring End Gap② Comp.	Piston Ring End Gap② Oil	Piston Ring Side Clearance Comp.	Piston Ring Side Clearance Oil
1.0L/3-60/5,6	1991-93	2.9122-2.9129	.0008-.0015	—	—	.0079	.0079	③	—
1.6L/4-97/6 ⑥	1991	3.110	.0008	.7200	.0003-.0004	.0118	—	⑦	—
	1992-93	3.110	.0008	.7200	.0003-.0004	.01-.02	—	⑦	—
1.6L/4-97/6 ⑧	1991-93	⑨	.0024-.0031	—	—	④	.0039	⑤	—
1.6L/4-97/5 ⑩	1991-92	⑪	.0039-.0047	.7876-.7880	.0002-.0003	⑫	.0059	.0012-.0028	.0039-.0236
1.6L/4-97/5,6 ⑬ ⑭	1991	⑮	.0024-.0031	.7094-.7095	—	⑯	.0039	⑰	.0039-.0236
1.6L/4-97/6 ⑬	1992-93	㉛	.0011-.0019	.7094-.7095	—	⑯	.0039	㉜	.0039-.0236
1.8L/4-108/8 ㉕	1993	㊴	.0008-.0015	—	—	㊵	.0039-.0177	—	.0033-.0041
1.8L/4-110/8 ⑭	1992-93	⑮	.0019-.0027	.7871-.7872	—	㉝	.0039	㉞	—
2.0L/4-121/K,M,H	1991-93	⑱	⑲	.8264-.8267	.0004-.0005	⑳	—	㉑	—
2.2L/4-133/G,4	1991-93	—	.0007-.0017	.8000-.8002	.0004-.0009	.010	.010	.0019	.0019
2.3L/4-138/A,D,3	1991-93	3.6203-3.6210	.0007-.0020	.8660-.8661	㉒	㉓	.0157	㉔	—
2.5L/4-151/R	1991-92	—	.0014-.0022	.9270-.9280	.0003-.0005	.0118	.0196	㉖	.0149-.0551
3.1L/V6-192/T,V	1991-93	3.5029-3.5037	.0009-.0022	.9052-.9054	.0004-.0008	㉗	.010	.0020-.0035	.008
3.3L/V6-204/N	1991-93	—	.0004-.0022	.9053-.9055	.0004-.0008	.010	㉟	.0013-.0031	.0011-.0081
3.4L/V6-204/X	1991-93	3.6208-3.6215	.0009-.0023	.9052-.9054	.00046-.00093	㉚	.010	.0016-.0035	.008-.0019
3.8L/V6-231/C,L,1	1991-93	—	.0004-.0022	.9053-.9055	.0004-.0008	.010	.015	.0013-.0031	.0011-.0081
4.3L/V6-262/Z	1991	—	.0007-.0017	.9270-.9273	.0002-.0003	.010	.015	.0012-.0032	.002-.007
	1992-93	—	.0007-.0017	.9270-.9273	.0004-.0008	.010-.017	.015	.0014-.0032	.0014-.0032
4.5L/V8-273/5	1991	—	.0010-.0018	.8656-.8661	.0002-.0004	.015	.010	.016-.0037	㉘
4.6L/V8-279/Y,9	1993	—	.0004-.0020	.865-.866	—	.010-016	.010-.030	.002-.004	㉘
4.9L/V8-300/B	1991-93	—	.0004-.0020	.8659-.8661	.0003-.0007	.012	.0004	.016-.0037	㉘
5.0L/V8-305/E,F	1991-93	—	㊱	.9270-.9273	.0002-.0003	㊲	.015	.0012-.0032	.002-.007
5.7L/V8-350/7,8	1991-93	—	㊳	.9270-.9273	.0002-.0003	㊲	.015	.0012-.0032	.002-.007
5.7L/V8-350/P	1992-93	—	.0007-.0021	.9270-.9271	.0005-.0008	㊲	.010	.0012-.0032	.002-.007
5.7L/V8-350/J	1991-93	—	—	.9841-.9843	.0002-.0007	㉙	.012	.002-.003	.001-.002

①—Pistons & pins are matched set & should be replaced as an assembly.
②—Minimum.
③—Top ring, .0012-.0027 inch; 2nd ring, .0008-.0023 inch.
④—Top ring, .0098 inch; 2nd ring, .0059 inch.
⑤—Top ring, .0016-.0031 inch; 2nd ring, .0012-.0028 inch.
⑥—LeMans.
⑦—Top ring, .0024-.0036 inch; 2nd ring, .0019-.0032 inch.
⑧—Prizm w/4A-FE 16 valve engine.
⑨—There are three standard sizes of pistons marked with a No. on top. No. 1, 3.1862-3.1866 inch; No. 2, 3.1866-3.1870 inch; No. 3, 3.1870-3.1874 inch.
⑩—Prizm w/GSI 4A-GE 16 valve engine.
⑪—There are three standard sizes of pistons marked w/a No. on top. No. 1, 3.1846-3.1850 inch; No. 2, 3.1850-3.1854 inch; No. 3, 3.1854-3.1858 inch.
⑫—Top ring, .0098 inch; 2nd ring, .0079 inch.
⑬—Storm w/12 valve engine.
⑭—Storm w/16 valve engine.
⑮—There are three standard sizes of pistons marked with a No. on top.

No. 1, 3.1473-3.1477 inch; No. 2, 3.1477-3.1481 inch; No. 3, 3.1481-3.1485 inch.
⑯—Top ring, .0011 inch; 2nd ring, .0018 inch.
⑰—Top ring, .0018-.0031 inch; 2nd ring, .0008-.0024 inch.
⑱—VIN K & H, 3.3844-3.3860 inch; VIN M, 3.3837-3.3852 inch.
⑲—VIN K & H, .0004-.0012 inch; VIN M, .0012-.0020 inch.
⑳—Top ring, .0098 inch; 2nd ring, .0118 inch.
㉑—Top ring, .0024-.0036 inch; 2nd ring, .0019-.0032 inch.
㉒—VIN A, .0003-.0006 inch. 1991 VIN D, .00008-.00040 inch. 1992-93 VIN D & 3, .00007-.00043 inch.
㉓—1991 top ring, .0138 inch; 2nd ring, .0157 inch.
㉔—1991 VIN A: top ring, .0027-.0047 inch; 2nd ring, .0157-.0031 inch. 1991 VIN D: top ring, .0019-.0039 inch; 2nd ring, .0157-.0031 inch.
㉕—Prizm w/16-valve engine.
㉖—Top ring, .0020-.0031 inch; 2nd ring, .0011-.0031 inch.
㉗—Top ring, .010 inch; 2nd ring, .020 inch.
㉘—Zero clearance; side sealing ring.

㉙—Top ring, .016 inch; 2nd ring, .031 inch.
㉚—Top ring, .012 inch; 2nd ring, .019 inch.
㉛—There are three standard sizes of pistons marked with a letter on top. A, 3.1480-3.1484 inch; B, 3.1484-3.1488-8 inch; C, 3.1488-3.1492 inch.
㉜—Top ring, .00117-.00315 inch; 2nd ring, .00078-.00236 inch.
㉝—Top ring, .00110-.0157 inch; 2nd ring, .0177-.0236 inch.
㉞—Top ring, .00177-.00315 inch; 2nd ring, .00078-.00236 inch.
㉟—1991, .010 inch; 1992-93, .015 inch.
㊱—1991, .0007-.0017 inch; 1992-93, .0007-.0021 inch.
㊲—1991, .010 inch; 1992-93, Top ring, .010 inch; 2nd ring, .018 inch.
㊳—1991, .0007-.0021 inch; 1992-93, .0005-.0022 inch.
㊴—There are three standard sizes of pistons marked with a No. on top. No. 1, 3.1852-3.1856 inch; No. 2, 3.1856-3.1860 inch; No. 3, 3.1860-3.1864 inch.
㊵—Top ring, .0098-.0138 inch; lower ring, .0138-.0234 inch.

CAMSHAFT & LIFTERS

*All Measurements Given In Inches, Unless Otherwise Specified.

Engine Liter/CID/ VIN	Year	Camshaft Journal Diameter	Maximum Journal Run-out	Camshaft Bearing Clearance	Camshaft Endplay	Rocker Arm Oil Clearance	Lifter Bore Diameter	Lifter Diameter	Lifter To Bore Clearance
1.0L/3-60/5,6	1991-93	①	.0039	.0008-.0024	—	—	1.2205-1.2214	1.2188-1.2194	.0010-.0025
1.6L/4-97/6 ②	1991-93	③	—	.0018-.0035	.0035-.0083	—	—	—	—
1.6L/4-97/6 ④	1991—93	⑤	.0016	.0014-.0028	.0043	—	—	—	.0006-.0018
1.6L/4-97/5 ⑥	1991-92	1.0610-1.0616	.0016	.0014-.0028	.0031-.0075	—	—	1.1014-1.1018	.0006-.0008
1.6L/4-97/6 ⑦	1991-93	1.0157	.0040	.0059	.008	.0002-.0008	—	—	—
1.6L/4-97/5 ⑧	1991	1.0157	.0040	.0059	.008	—	—	1.218	—
1.8L/4-108/8 ⑪	1993	.9035-.9041	.0016	—	—	—	—	—	—
1.8L/4-110/8 ⑧	1992-93	1.0157	.0039	.0059	.008	—	—	1.219	—
2.0L/4-121/K,M,H	1991-93	⑨	—	.0011-.0035	.0016-.0063	—	—	—	—
2.2L/4-133/G,4	1991-93	1.867-1.869	—	.0010-.0039	—	—	—	—	—
2.3L/4-138/A,D,3	1991-93	⑩	—	.0019-.0043	.0010-.0088	—	—	—	.0005-.0023
2.5L/4-151/R	1991-92	1.869	—	.0007-.0027	.0015-.0050	—	.8435-.8444	.8412-.8427	.0006-.0023
3.1L/V6-192/T,V	1991-93	1.8678-1.8815	—	.0001-.0004	—	—	—	—	—
3.3L/V6-204/N	1991-93	1.785-1.786	—	⑫	—	—	—	—	—
3.4L/V6-204/X	1991	2.165-2.166	—	.0015-.0035	—	—	—	—	—
	1992-93	2.1643-2.1647	—	.0019-.0040	—	—	—	—	—
3.8L/V6-231/C,L,1	1991-93	1.785-1.786	—	.0005-.0035	—	—	—	—	—
4.3L/V6-262/Z	1991-93	1.8682-1.8692	—	—	⑬	—	—	—	—
4.5L/V8-273/5	1991	—	.002	.0018-.0037	—	—	—	—	.0007-.0027
4.6L/V8-279/Y,9	1993	1.061-1.062	—	.002-.003	—	—	1.2992	1..297-1.298	.001-.003
4.9L/V8-300/B	1991-93	—	.0009	.0018-.0037	—	—	—	—	.0007-.0027
5.0L/V8-305/E,F	1991-93	1.8682-1.8692	—	—	.004-.012	—	—	—	—
5.7L/V8-350/7,8,P	1991-93	1.8682-1.8692	—	—	.004-.012	—	—	—	—
5.7L/V8-350/J	1991-93	1.140-1.141	—	—	.0055-.0138	—	—	—	—

① —Journal No. 1, 1.0220-1.0228; journal No. 2 & 3, 1.1795-1.1803.
② —LeMans.
③ —Journal No. 1, 1.5520-1.5530 inch; journal No. 2, 1.5624-1.5630 inch; journal No. 3, 1.5722-1.5730 inch; journal No. 4, 1.5820-1.5828 inch; journal No. 5, 1.5919-1.5927 inch.
④ —Prizm w/4A-FE 16 valve engine.
⑤ —Journal No. 1, .9822 inch; journal No. 2, 3, 4 & 5, .9035 inch.
⑥ —Prizm w/GSI 4A-GE 16 valve engine.
⑦ —Storm w/12 valve engine.
⑧ —Storm w/16 valve engine.
⑨ —Journal No. 1, 1.6706-1.6712; No. 2, 1.6812-1.6818; No. 3, 1.6911-1.6917; No. 4, 1.7009-1.7015; No. 5, 1.7100-1.7106.
⑩ —1991 VIN A & 1991 VIN D: journal No. 1, 1.5720-1.5728 inch; journal No. 2, 3, 4 & 5, 1.3751 1.3759 inch.
⑪ —Prizm w/16-valve engine.
⑫ —1991, .0005-.0035 inch; 1992-93, journals 1 & 4, .0016-.0044 inch & journals 2 & 3, .0019-.0047 inch.
⑬ —1991, .004-.012 inch; 1992-93, .001-.009 inch.

OIL PUMP

*All Measurements Given In Inches, Unless Otherwise Specified.

Engine Liter/CID/ VIN	Year	Gear Backlash	Gear To Body Clearance	Gear Endplay ①	Gear Pocket Depth	Gear Pocket Diameter	Pump Gear Thickness	Pump Gear Diameter	Relief Valve To Body Clearance
1.0L/3-60/5,6	1991-93	—	.0122	.0059	—	—	—	—	—
1.6L/4-97/6 ②	1991-93	.004-.008	.0043-.0074	.001-.004	.3948-.3968	③	—	④	—
1.6L/4-97/6 ⑤	1991-93	.0138	.0039	.0079	—	—	—	—	—
1.6L/4-97/5 ⑥	1991	.0012	.004	.0078	—	—	—	—	—
	1992	.0138	.0039	.0079	—	—	—	—	—
1.6L/4-97/5,6 ⑦ ⑧	1991	.0012	.004	.0078	—	—	—	—	—
1.6L/4-97/6 ⑦	1992-93	.0012	.004	.0078	—	—	—	—	—
1.8L/4-108/8 ⑧	1993	—	.0031-.0079	.0010-.0039	—	—	—	—	—
1.8L/4-110/8 ⑧	1992-93	.0012	.004	.008	—	—	—	—	—
2.0L/4-121/K,M,H	1991-93	.004-.008	.0043-.0074	.001-.004	.395-.397	③	—	④	—
2.2L/4-133/G,4	1991-93	.004-.008	.0015-.0040	.002-.006	1.195-1.198	1.503-1.506	1.199-1.200	1.498-1.500	.0015-.0035
2.3L/4-138/A,D,3	1991-93	.0091-.0201	—	.0059	.6736-.6756	2.1273-2.1292	.6727-.6731	2.124-2.126	—
2.5L/4-151/R	1991-92	—	—	—	.514-.516	—	.511-.512	—	—
3.1L/V6-192/T ⑨	1991-93	.0037-.0077	.003-.004	.0016-.0067	1.195-1.198	1.503-1.506	1.199-1.200	1.498-1.500	.0015-.0035

OIL PUMP-Continued

Engine Liter/CID/VIN	Year	Gear Backlash	Gear To Body Clearance	Gear Endplay①	Gear Pocket Depth	Gear Pocket Diameter	Pump Gear Thickness	Pump Gear Diameter	Relief Valve To Body Clearance
3.1L/V6-192/T⑩	1991-93	.0037-.0077	.003-.004	.002-.006	1.202-1.205	1.504-1.506	1.199-1.200	1.498-1.500	.0015-.0035
3.3L/V6-204/N	1991-93	—	.008-.015	.001-.0035	.4610-.4625	3.508-3.512	—	—	.0015-.0030
3.4L/V6-204/X	1991-93	⑪	⑪	⑪	⑪	⑪	⑪	⑪	⑪
3.8L/V6-231/C,L,1	1991-93	.006	.008-.015	.0010-.0035	.4610-.4625	3.508-3.512	—	—	.0015-.0030
4.3L/V6-262/Z	1991-93	⑪	⑪	⑪	⑪	⑪	⑪	⑪	⑪
4.5L/V8-273/5	1991	.0010-.0013	.0018-.0031	—	—	—	—	—	—
4.9L/V8-300/B	1991-93	⑪	⑪	⑪	⑪	⑪	⑪	⑪	⑪
5.0L/V8-305/E,F	1991-93	⑪	⑪	⑪	⑪	⑪	⑪	⑪	⑪
5.7L/V8-350/7,8,P	1991-93	⑪	⑪	⑪	⑪	⑪	⑪	⑪	⑪
5.7L/V8-350/J	1991-93	⑪	⑪	⑪	⑪	⑪	⑪	⑪	⑪

①—Measured between pump cover & end of gears using straightedge & feeler gauge.
②—LeMans.
③—Inner gear, 1.614-1.615 inch; outer gear, 3.231-3.234 inch.
④—Inner gear, 1.612-1.613 inch; outer gear, 3.2248-3.2269 inch.
⑤—Prizm w/4A-FE 16 valve engine.
⑥—Prizm w/GSI 4A-GE 16 valve engine.
⑦—Storm w/12 valve engine.
⑧—Storm w/16 valve engine.
⑨—Aluminum body pump.
⑩—Cast iron body pump.
⑪—Pump components are not serviced separately. If any component is damaged or worn, pump should be replaced.

CRANKSHAFT, BEARINGS & CONNECTING RODS

*All Measurements Given In Inches, Unless Otherwise Specified.

Engine Liter/CID/VIN	Year	Crankshaft Standard Journal Diameter Main Bearing	Crankshaft Standard Journal Diameter Crank Pin	Out of Round All①	Taper All①	Bearing Clearance Main Bearings	Bearing Clearance Connecting Rod Bearings	Thrust Bearing Clearance	Connecting Rods Pin Bore Diameter	Connecting Rods Side Clearance
1.0L/3-61/5,6	1991-93	②	1.6529-1.6535	.0004	.0004	.0008-.0015	.0012-.0019	.0044-.0122	—	.0039-.0078
1.6L/4-97/6③	1991	2.1653	1.6918-1.6920	.0002	.0002	.0006-.0020	.0007-.0025	.0047-.0138	—	.0028-.0095
	1992-93	2.17	1.6918-1.6920	.0002	.0002	.0006-.0020	.00177-.00354	.0047-.0138	—	.0028-.0095
1.6L/4-97/6④	1991-93	1.8891-1.8898	1.5742-1.5748	.008	.008	.0006-.0013	.0008-.0020	.0118	—	.0059-.0098
1.6L/4-97/5⑤	1991-92	1.8891-1.8898	1.6529-1.6535	.0004	.0004	.0006-.0013	.0008-.0020	.0008-.0087	—	.0059-.0098
1.6L/4-97/6⑥	1991-93	2.0440-2.0448	1.5722-1.5728	.0020	.0020	.0008-.0020	.0008-.0018	.0024-.0095	—	.0079-.0138
1.6L/4-97/5⑦	1991	2.0440-2.0448	1.5722-1.5728	.0020	.0020	.0008-.0020	.0010-.0023	.0024-.0095	—	.0079-.0138
1.8L/4-108/8⑪	1993	⑰	—	.0008	.0008	.0006-.0039	.0008-.0031	.0008-.0118	—	.0008-.0031
1.8L/4-110/8⑦	1992-93	2.0440-2.0448	1.8083-1.8089	.0002	.0002	.00079-.00199	—	.0024-.0095	—	—
2.0L/4-121/K,M,H	1991-93	2.2828-2.2833	1.9279-1.9287	.0002	.0002	.0006-.0016	.0007-.0025	.0028-.0118	—	.0028-.0095
2.2L/4-133/G,4	1991-93	2.4945-2.4954	1.9983-1.9994	.0002	.0002	.0006-.0019	.0010-.0031	.002-.007	—	.0039-.0149
2.3L/4-138/A,D,3	1991-93	2.0470-2.0480	1.8887-1.8897	.0005	.0005	.0005-.0023	.0005-.0020	.0034-.0095	—	.0059-.0177
2.5L/4-151/R	1991-92	2.300	2.00	.0005	.0005	.0005-.0022	.0005-.0027	⑫	—	.0059-.0236
3.1L/V6-192/T,V	1991-93	2.6473-2.6483	1.9983-1.9994	.0002	.0002	.0012-.0030	.0011-.0034	.0012-.0030	—	.014-.027
3.3L/V6-204/N	1991-93	2.4988-2.4998	2.2487-2.2499	.0003	.0003	⑬	⑭	.003-.011	—	.003-.015
3.4L/V6-204/X	1991-93	2.6473-2.6479	1.9987-1.9994	.0002	.0002	.0013-.0030	.0011-.0032	.0013-.0030	—	.014-.025
3.8L/V6-231/C,L,1	1991-93	2.4988-2.4998	2.2487-2.2499	.0003	.0003	⑬	⑭	.003-.011	—	.003-.015
4.3L/V6-262/Z	1991-93	⑧ ⑮	2.2487-2.2498	.0002	.0002	⑨	.0013-.0035	.001-.007	—	.006-.014
4.5L/V8-273/5	1991	2.6354-2.6364	1.927	.0003	—	⑩	—	.0010-.007	—	.008-.020
4.6L/V8-279/Y,9	1993	2.52	—	.0005	.0005	.0005-.003	.001-.003	—	—	.008-.020
4.9L/V8-300/B	1991-93	2.6354-2.6364	1.927-1.928	.0003	—	⑩		.0010-.007	—	.008-.020
5.0L/V8-305/E,F	1991-93	⑧	2.0893-2.0998	.0002	.0002	⑨	.0013-.0035	.001-.007	—	.006-.014
5.7L/V8-350/7,8,P	1991-93	⑧	2.0893-2.0998	.0002	.0002	⑨	.0013-.0035	.001-.007	—	.006-.014
5.7L/V8-350/J	1991-93	2.755-2.756	2.0993-2.1000	.0003	.0002	.0007-.0023	.0007-.0027	⑯	—	.008-.028

①—Maximum.
②—The counter weights of No. 1 cylinder have four stamped numbers, they indicate the journal diameters at bearing caps respectively. No. 1, 1.7714-1.7716 inch; No. 2, 1.7712-1.7714 inch & No. 3, 1.7710-1.7712 inch.
③—LeMans.
④—Prizm w/4A-FE engine.
⑤—Prizm w/4A-GE 16 valve engine.
⑥—Storm w/12 valve engine.
⑦—Storm w/16 valve engine.
⑧—1991 models: journal No. 1, 2.4488-2.4493 inch; journal No. 2, 3 & 4, 2.4481-2.4490 inches; journal No. 5, 2.4481-2.4488 inches.
⑨—Journal No. 1, .0008-.0020 inch; journal No. 2, 3 & 4, .0011-.0020 inch; journal No. 5, .0017-.0032 inch.
⑩—Journal No. 1, .0008-.0031 inch; journal No. 2, 3, 4 & 5, .0016-.0039 inch.
⑪—Prizm w/16-valve engine.
⑫—1991, .0005-.0220 inch; 1992-93, .0005-.016 inch.
⑬—1991, .0003-.0018 inch; 1992-93, .0008-.0022 inch.
⑭—1991, .0003-.0026 inch; 1992-93, .0008-.0022 inch.
⑮—1992-93 models: journal No. 1, .0008-.0020 inch; journal No. 2, 3, 4, .0011-.0023 inch; journal No. 5, .0017-.0032 inch.
⑯—1991, .0006-.0010 inch; 1992-93, .010-.040 inch.
⑰—Stamping No. 1, 2.0482-2.0485; stamping No. 2, 2.0485-2.0487; stamping No. 3, 2.0487-2.0489.

SATURN

INDEX OF SERVICE OPERATIONS

Continued

SATURN

INDEX OF SERVICE OPERATIONS-Continued

SPECIFICATIONS

GENERAL ENGINE SPECIFICATIONS

Year	Engine, Liter/CID	Fuel Injection System	Bore & Stoke	Compression Ratio	Net H.P. @ RPM	Maximum Torque, Ft. Lbs. @ RPM	Normal Oil Pressure ①
1991	1.9L/4-116②	TBI④	3.23 X 3.55	9.3	85@5000	107@2400	36
	1.9L/4-116③	MPFI⑤	3.23 X 3.55	9.5	124@6000	119@4800	36
1992	1.9L/4-116②	TBI④	3.23 X 3.55	9.3	85@5000	107@2400	36
	1.9L/4-116③	MPFI⑤	3.23 X 3.55	9.5	124@5600	119@4800	36
1993	1.9L/4-116②	TBI④	3.23 X 3.55	9.3	85@5000	107@2400	36
	1.9L/4-116③	MPFI⑤	3.23 X 3.55	9.5	124@5600	119@4800	36
1994	1.9L/4-116②	TBI④	3.23 X 3.55	9.3	85@5000	107@2400	36
	1.9L/4-116③	MPFI⑤	3.23 X 3.55	9.5	124@5600	119@4800	36

①—At 2000 RPM.
②—SOHC-Single overhead cam.
③—DOHC-Dual overhead cam.
④—Throttle body injection.
⑤—Multi-point fuel injection.

TUNE UP SPECIFICATIONS

Spark Plug Gap	Ignition Timing, BTDC				Curb Idle Speed		Fast Idle Speed		Fuel Pump Pressure
	Firing Order	Man. Trans.	Auto Trans.	Mark Fig.	Man. Trans.	Auto Trans.	Man. Trans.	Auto Trans.	
.040	1-3-4-2	—	—	—	①	②	③	③	58–94

①—On SOHC, 700–800 RPM, on DOHC, 800–900 RPM in Neutral.
②—On SOHC, 600–700 RPM, on DOHC, 700–800 RPM in Drive.
③—Controlled by idle air control (IAC) valve.

WHEEL ALIGNMENT SPECIFICATIONS

FRONT WHEEL

Model	Caster Angle, Degrees		Camber Angle, Degrees				Toe, Degrees
			Limits		Desired		
	Limits	Desired	Left	Right	Left	Right	
All	+1.2 to +2.7	+1.7	−1.2 to +.65	−1 to +1	0	0	0 to +.4

WHEEL ALIGNMENT SPECIFICATIONS—Continued
REAR WHEEL

Model	Camber Angle, Degrees		Toe, Degrees
	Limits	Desired	
All	−1.55 to 0.0	−.6	0 to +.40

COOLING SYSTEM & CAPACITY DATA

Engine, Liter/CID	Cooling Capacity, Qts.		Radiator Cap Relief Pressure, Lbs.	Thermo. Opening Temp.	Fuel Tank, Gals.	Engine Oil, Qts.	Transaxle Oil	
	Less A/C	With A/C					Man. Trans., Qts.	Auto Trans., Qts.
1.9L/4-116	7	7	13–20	190	13.2	4①	2.6	3.75②

①—Change w/filter.
②—Fluid change w/pressure filter.

LUBRICANT DATA

Model	Lubricant Type			
	Transaxle		Power Steering	Brake System
	Manual	Automatic		
All	Dexron IIE	Dexron IIE	①	②

①—Must meet GM specification 9985010.
②—Delco Supreme II or DOT 3.

ELECTRICAL
INDEX

PRECAUTIONS
AIRBAG SYSTEM DISARMING

1. Place ignition in OFF position, then remove Supplemental Inflatable Restraint (SIR) fuse.
2. Remove connector position assurance (CPA) device from yellow two way SIR connector at base of steering column.

AIRBAG SYSTEM REARMING

1. Place ignition in Off position, then connect yellow two way SIR connector at base of steering column, then install CPA device to connector.
2. Install SIR fuse.
3. Turn ignition switch to Run position, then ensure AIRBAG lamp flashes 7 to 9 times, then remains Off.

FUSE PANEL & FLASHER LOCATION

The underhood junction block is located at the lefthand front of the engine compartment at the fender apron. The instrument panel junction block is located behind the center instrument panel in front of the console.

STARTER REPLACE

1. **On models with airbag**, disarm air-

Fig. 1 Neutral start switch removal

bag system as described under 'Precautions."
2. **On all models,** disconnect battery ground cable.
3. Remove air inlet tube and fresh air hose, on DOHC models, lift resonator upward to disengage from engine support bracket.
4. Remove upper starter attaching bolt through access hole near intake manifold support bracket.
5. Raise and support vehicle.
6. **On 1991-93 models,** remove starter shield pin using pliers, then lift shield upward to release from solenoid.
7. **On 1994 models,** remove starter shield by pulling outward to release bottom of shield, then lift shield upward to right to remove.
8. **On all models,** disconnect starter electrical connectors and position aside.
9. Remove lower starter attaching bolt.
10. **On 1991—93 models,** remove rear starter support bracket attaching bolt.
11. **On 1991-93 models,** rotate starter until bracket clears axle shaft support bracket, pull rearward toward lefthand side of vehicle to remove.
12. **On 1994 models,** pull starter rearward, toward lefthand side of vehicle to remove.
13. **On all models,** reverse procedure to install. Torque starter attaching bolts to 26 ft. lbs., starter bracket bolts to 22 ft. lbs. on 1991-93 models or 27 ft. lbs. on 1994 models, starter solenoid terminal to 44 inch lbs. and starter positive terminal to 89 inch lbs. on 1991-93 models or 71 inch lbs. on 1994 models.
14. **On models with airbag,** rearm airbag system as described under "Precautions."

IGNITION LOCK
REPLACE

1. **On models with airbag,** disarm airbag system as described under "Precautions."
2. **On all models,** disconnect battery ground cable.
3. Remove ignition lock bezel.
4. Remove upper steering column filler panel.
5. Insert ignition key to switch, then rotate to ACC position.
6. Depress square locking button at top of ignition lock assembly, then remove lock cylinder.

7. Reverse procedure to install, noting the following:
   a. **On models with airbag,** rearm airbag system as described under "Precautions."

CLUTCH START SWITCH
REPLACE

1. **On models with airbag,** disarm airbag system as described under "Precautions."
2. **On all models,** disconnect battery ground cable.
3. Disconnect clutch switch electrical connector.
4. Remove clutch switch attaching bolt, then remove switch.
5. Reverse procedure to install Torque clutch switch attaching bolt to 89 inch lbs.
6. **On models with airbag,** rearm airbag system as described under "Precautions."

NEUTRAL START SWITCH
REPLACE

1. **On DOHC models,** remove air filter box, then lift resonator upward to disengage from support bracket.
2. **On all models,** remove air induction tube.
3. Disconnect gear selector switch electrical connector.
4. Disconnect control lever shift cable.
5. Remove control lever shaft attaching nut, then remove manual lever, noting lever position, **Fig. 1.**
6. Remove two selector switch to transaxle case attaching bolts, then remove switch.
7. Reverse procedure to install, noting the following:
   a. **Torque** manual lever to control shaft attaching nut to 8 ft. lbs.
   b. Adjust switch, place transaxle in D4 position, then using a suitable ohmmeter, check for continuity across terminals, **Fig. 2,** if continuity is not indicated, rotate switch until continuity is present.
   c. **Torque** switch to case bolts to 142 inch lbs.
   d. **Torque** air induction tube to 15 inch lbs.

BACK-UP LAMP SWITCH
REPLACE

1. **On models equipped with ABS,** remove air induction tube.
2. **On all models,** disconnect back-up light electrical connectors.
3. Unscrew switch, then remove.
4. Reverse procedure to install. **Torque** switch to 23 ft. lbs.

Fig. 2 Neutral start switch adjustment

STEERING WHEEL
REPLACE

1. **On models with airbag,** disarm airbag system as described under "Precautions."
2. **On all models,** install a protective cover over the driver's seat.
3. Disconnect battery ground cable.
4. Pull edge of horn pad to unclip.
5. Disconnect horn pad electrical connectors, then remove pad.
6. Remove steering column shaft clip, then remove wheel attaching nut.
7. Using steering wheel puller tool No. J-1859-03 or equivalent, remove steering wheel.
8. Reverse procedure to install noting the following:
   a. **Torque** steering wheel attaching nut to 30 ft. lbs.
   b. **On models with airbag,** rearm airbag system as described under "Precautions."

INSTRUMENT CLUSTER
REPLACE

1. **On models with airbag,** disarm airbag system as described under "Precautions."
2. **On all models,** disconnect battery ground cable.
3. Remove instrument panel left and right end cap attaching screw, then pull rearward to unclip.
4. **On 1991 models,** remove lighter trim bezel.
5. **On all models,** remove left and right lower trim panel extensions by disconnecting from Velcro fasteners, then pull rearward at upper clips to remove.
6. **On 1993-94 models,** disconnect traction control/fog lamp electrical connector.
7. **On all models,** remove center air outlet trim panel by pulling outward, starting at bottom of panel and working upward.
8. Remove trim panel extension strip by

Fig. 3 Connector position assurance removal

Fig. 4 Instrument cluster removal

Fig. 5 Windshield cowl trim panel removal

pulling rearward to unclip.
9. Remove cluster trim panel attaching screws, then pull rearward to unclip.
10. Remove connect position assurance devices, **Fig. 3**, and disconnect electrical connectors from instrument panel lighting rheostat and rear window defogger switches.
11. Remove instrument cluster trim panel.
12. Remove instrument cluster attaching screws, **Fig. 4**, then pull rearward to gain access.
13. Disconnect cluster electrical connectors by depressing retainer legs, then remove instrument cluster.
14. Reverse procedure to install noting the following:
   a. **On models with airbag,** rearm airbag system as described under "Precautions."

RADIO
REPLACE

1. **On models with airbag,** disarm airbag system as described under "Precautions."
2. **On all models,** disconnect battery ground cable.
3. Remove instrument panel center air outlet trim panel, by pulling rearward to unclip, start at bottom and work upward.
4. **On 1993-94 models,** disconnect traction control/fog lamp electrical connector.
5. **On all models,** remove radio attaching screws, then slide radio rearward.
6. Disconnect radio electrical connectors and antenna.
7. Reverse procedure to install noting the following:
   a. **On models with airbag,** rearm airbag system as described under "Precautions."

WIPER MOTOR
REPLACE

1. Disconnect battery ground cable.
2. Remove wiper arm finish cap and attaching screw.
3. Lift wiper blade assembly from windshield, then remove wiper arm from pivot.
4. Remove cowl trim panel, **Fig. 5.**
5. Using a 13 mm wrench, move wiper motor crank arm to 12 o'clock position to access rear wiper module fasteners.

6. Remove wiper module attaching screws, then lift module to disconnect motor and module electrical connectors.
7. Remove wiper module, then move wiper motor crank arm to 9 o'clock or park position.
8. Remove crank arm nut, then disconnect crank arm from motor shaft.
9. Remove wiper motor attaching nut and bolts, then remove motor from transmission.
10. Reverse procedure to install. **Torque** wiper motor crank arm on wiper motor shaft to 21 ft. lbs., wiper module to 89 inch lbs. and wiper arms to 19 ft. lbs.

WIPER MOTOR TRANSMISSION
REPLACE

Refer to "Wiper Motor, Replace" for wiper motor transmission replacement procedure.

BLOWER MOTOR
REPLACE

1. **On models with airbag,** disarm airbag system as described under "Precautions."
2. **On all models,** disconnect battery ground cable.
3. Remove right instrument panel lower sound insulator, if equipped.
4. Disconnect blower motor electrical connector.
5. Remove blower motor attaching screws, then remove motor.
6. Reverse procedure to install noting the following:
   a. **On models with airbag,** rearm airbag system as described under "Precautions."

HEATER CORE
REPLACE

1. **On models with airbag,** disarm airbag system as described under "Precautions."
2. **On all models,** disconnect battery ground cable, then drain coolant.
3. Raise and support vehicle.
4. Move heater hose clamps upward.
5. Lower vehicle.
6. **On DOHC models,** remove air cleaner housing cover and air induction at intake manifold.

7. **On SOHC models,** remove air cleaner housing.
8. **On all models,** remove heater hoses at core, then blow coolant from heater core with an air hose.
9. Disconnect left and right center instrument panel trim panel Velcro tabs, then pull outward to unclip.
10. Remove lower heater duct attaching screws, then drop straight down and slide out sideways, **Fig. 6.** Use caution to not damage the rear floor heater duct seal.
11. Release temperature cable hold-down clip from lower heater core cover by lifting upward on plastic tab while down on top of cable, **Fig. 7.**
12. Depress temperature valve pin, then pull temperature cable straight out.
13. Remove heater core cover attaching screws, then remove.
14. Remove lower heater core cover.
15. Remove heater core pipe clamp attaching screw.
16. Remove lower heater core retainer attaching screws.
17. Remove heater core.
18. Reverse procedure to install noting the following:
   a. **On models with airbag,** rearm airbag system as described under "Precautions."

EVAPORATOR CORE
REPLACE

1. **On models with airbag,** disarm airbag system as described under "Precautions."
2. **On all models,** disconnect battery cable.
3. Discharge A/C system, then drain cooling system.
4. **On DOHC models,** remove air cleaner cover and air induction hose at intake manifold.
5. **On SOHC models,** remove air cleaner housing.
6. **On all models,** remove suction hose and liquid line from thermal expansion valve.
7. Place protective cover over A/C hoses, lines and expansion module to prevent A/C contamination.

Fig. 6 Lower heater duct removal

Fig. 7 Temperature cable release

Fig. 8 Upper instrument panel removal

Fig. 9 Instrument panel removal

Fig. 10 Windshield defroster nozzle removal

Fig. 11 Front dash seal removal

8. Remove thermal expansion valve from evaporator.
9. Raise and support vehicle.
10. Move heater core inlet and outlet clamps up.
11. Lower vehicle.
12. Remove heater core hoses, then using an air hose, blow excess coolant from heater core.
13. Remove left and right instrument panel end caps.
14. Remove left and right center instrument panel extensions by disconnecting lower Velcro fasteners, then pulling rearward to unclip.
15. Remove center air outlet trim panel by pulling outward, start at bottom then work upward.
16. **On 1993-94 models,** disconnect traction control/fog lamp electrical connector.
17. **On all models,** unclip trim panel extension strip.
18. Remove upper trim panel screw cap. then remove upper trim panel, **Fig. 8.**
19. Lift upper trim panel to disengage clips at rear edge.
20. Pull panel rearward out of clips at bottom of windshield, then remove upper trim panel.
21. Open glove compartment.
22. Remove cluster trim panel four attaching screws, then pull upward to unclip.
23. Remove lockpins, then disconnect electrical connectors from instrument panel lighting rheostat and rear window defogger switches and Connec-

tor Position Assurance (CPA) devices, **Fig. 3.**
24. Remove instrument cluster, then remove glove box attaching screws, then remove glove compartment.
25. Remove ALDL attaching screws, then ALDL connector.
26. Remove steering column filler panel attaching screws. Do not scratch console with mounting tabs.
27. Remove hood release lever.
28. Remove instrument cluster attaching screws, then pull rearward.
29. Disconnect cluster electrical connectors, then remove cluster.
30. Remove radio and HVAC control panels.
31. Disconnect lighter connector, then remove lighter bulb holder by rotating counterclockwise and pull straight rearward.
32. Apply parking brake, then lift and remove parking brake filler panel at rear edge.
33. **On models equipped with manual transaxle,** remove gear shift knob by pulling straight upward.
34. **On all models,** remove ashtray, then unclip ashtray bulb holder.
35. Remove window/mirror switch by lifting at back edge and pulling rearward.
36. Remove lockpins and disconnect window/mirror electrical connectors.
37. Remove console rear storage compartment liner.

38. Remove console side screws, then remove console rear compartment attaching screws.
39. Lift rear of console, push seat belt bezels from console.
40. Remove instrument fuse block attaching screws, then remove dash reinforcement ground wire.
41. Remove instrument panel junction block electrical connector and attaching screw.
42. **On models equipped with automatic transaxle,** disconnect two way instrument panel to body electrical connector and CPA devices.
43. **On all models,** remove antenna hold-down clips and electrical connectors.
44. Loosen floor shifter assembly.
45. Remove attaching nuts and bolts, then lift lower reinforcement bracket from stud, then slide bracket rearward.
46. Remove instrument panel retainer and reinforcement bracket attaching screws and nuts, **Fig. 9.**
47. Remove steering column attaching screws, then lower steering column to seat, then cover steering column.
48. Remove instrument panel assembly.
49. Lift rear heater duct from mounting bolt, then remove. Do not remove rear foam seal.
50. Remove center air outlet duct attaching screws, then remove.

Fig. 12   Mode valve removal

Fig. 13   Upper air inlet case removal

Fig. 14   Evaporator removal

51. Remove windshield defroster nozzle from mode valve assembly, **Fig. 10.**
52. Rotate front of defroster nozzle up and away from windshield, then remove.
53. Remove CPA devices and disconnect blower motor resistor connector.
54. Remove HVAC module hold-down clips and disconnect electrical connector.
55. Disconnect blower motor and recirc motor electrical connectors.
56. Remove HVAC module attaching screws and nuts, then remove module.

57. Remove and discard drain, heater core pipes, evaporator block and evaporator pipe O-ring front of dash seals, **Fig. 11.**
58. Remove mode valve assembly attaching screws, **Fig. 12,** then lift mode valve assembly upward to remove.
59. Remove upper air inlet case attaching screws, then lift upward to remove, **Fig. 13.**
60. Remove evaporator pipe clamp at-

taching screws, then lift evaporator upward to remove, **Fig. 14.**
61. Reverse procedure to install, noting the following:
   a. **Torque** steering column attaching screws to 33 ft. lbs.
   b. **Torque** thermal expansion valve to evaporator to 89 ft. lbs.
   c. **Torque** thermal expansion valve liquid and suction lines to 19 ft. lbs.
   d. **On models with airbag,** rearm airbag system as described under "Precautions."

1.9L/4-116 ENGINE

INDEX

Fig. 1   Motion restrictor removal. 1991 w/DOHC

PRECAUTIONS

AIRBAG SYSTEM DISARMING

1. Place ignition in OFF position, then remove Supplemental Inflatable Restraint (SIR) fuse.
2. Remove connector position assurance (CPA) device from yellow two way SIR connector at base of steering column.

AIRBAG SYSTEM REARMING

1. Place ignition in Off position, then connect yellow two way SIR connector at base of steering column, then install CPA device to connector.
2. Install SIR fuse.

3. Turn ignition switch to Run position, then ensure AIRBAG lamp flashes 7 to 9 times, then remains Off.

ENGINE MOUNTS
REPLACE

1991

1. **On models equipped with DOHC engine and manual transaxle**, remove crosscar duct, then remove engine motion restrictor, **Fig. 1.**
2. **On all models,** raise and support vehicle.
3. Remove right wheel assembly and inner fender splash shield.
4. Remove engine mount to cradle attaching nut, **Fig. 2.**
5. Place a jack stand and block of wood below the oil pan, then remove weight from engine mount.
6. Remove engine mount to engine attaching bolts, then raise powertrain to remove mount.
7. Reverse procedure to install.

1992–94

1. **On models with airbag,** disarm airbag system as described under "Precautions."
2. **On all models,** remove two engine mount to midrail bracket attaching nuts, **Fig. 3.**
3. Position a floor jack under oil pan. Using a block of wood between pan and floor jack, raise engine enough to unload mount.
4. Remove three engine to front cover attaching nuts **Fig. 4,** then remove engine mount.
5. Reverse procedure to install noting the following:
   a. Tighten mount to midrail bracket and engine mount to front cover attaching nuts to specifications.

Fig. 2   Lower engine mount removal. 1991

   b. **On models with airbag,** rearm airbag system as described under "Precautions."

ENGINE
REPLACE

1. **On models with airbag,** disarm airbag system as described under "Precautions."
2. **On all models,** disconnect battery ground cable, remove coolant bottle cap, then drain coolant.
3. **On DOHC models,** lift resonator upward to disengage from engine service support bracket.
4. **On all models,** remove air cleaner assembly.
5. Disconnect the following electrical connectors:
   a. Two coolant temperature sensors.
   b. Oxygen sensor and clip, at front transaxle mount bracket.

Fig. 3 Engine mount to midrail bracket removal. 1992–94

Fig. 4 Engine mount to front cover removal. 1992–94

Fig. 5 Fuel line removal

Fig. 6 Transaxle shifter cable removal

Fig. 7 Support between torque strut & cradle. 1992–94

   c. Idles air control valve.
   d. Two ignition coil connectors.
   e. Manifold absolute pressure sensor.
   f. EGR solenoid.
   g. Brake booster hose at booster or intake manifold.
   h. Two grounds located rear of cylinder head at transaxle.
   i. Injector connectors.
6. Disconnect transaxle connectors as follows:
   a. Three neutral safety/selector switch.
   b. Valve body actuator.
   c. Turbine speed sensor.
   d. Temperature sensor.
   e. Back-up light switch.
7. Disconnect accelerator cables.
8. Bleed fuel pressure using tool No. SST 9127E or equivalent into a suitable container, then disconnect fuel lines using tool No. SA9157E or equivalent, **Fig. 5. Place a cloth around fitting before disconnecting.**
9. Using wire, tie fuel lines to brake master cylinder, to prevent fuel leakage.
10. Disconnect upper radiator hose and de-aeration hose at engine.
11. Disconnect A/C compressor and position aside.
12. Pinch tabs to disconnect and plug cooler lines at transaxle, then wrap transaxle cooler line fittings with a cloth.

13. **On models equipped with automatic transaxle,** disconnect shifter cable, **Fig. 6.**
14. **On models equipped with manual transaxle,** proceed as follows:
   a. Remove hydraulic damper to clutch housing stud nuts, then slide damper and bracket from studs.
   b. Rotate clutch actuator 1/4 turn counterclockwise while pushing toward housing to disengage connector and remove.
   c. Position clutch hydraulic system aside.
15. **On al models,** secure radiator, condenser and fan module to front crossbar using wire.
16. Raise and support vehicle.
17. Remove front wheel assemblies, then front and side shields from cradle.
18. Remove brake caliper bracket attaching bolts, then position caliper aside.
19. Disconnect lower radiator and heater inlet and return hoses at engine.
20. Disconnect steering shaft and power steering pressure switch electrical connector, if equipped.
21. Remove front exhaust pipe, catalytic converter, then powertrain stiffener bracket. **On 1991 models,** remove powertrain stiffening bracket bolts and bracket. **Do not remove torque restrictor bracket to transaxle.**
22. **On all models,** remove automatic transaxle flywheel cover and torque converter to flexplate attaching bolts.
23. Remove alternator and starter shields.
24. Disconnect the following electrical connectors:
   a. Starter feed.
   b. Alternator feed.
   c. Oil pressure sensor.
   d. Knock sensor.
   e. Crankshaft position sensor.
   f. EVO solenoid, if equipped.
   g. Vehicle speed sensor.
   h. Canister purge solenoid.
   i. PCM/EC and oxygen sensor.
   j. ABS wheel sensor ground connectors, if equipped.
25. Unclip brake lines from rear of cradle, then remove electrical harness from engine, then low vehicle, to lay electrical harness on underhood junction

block and battery cover.
26. **On 1992-94 models with a torque axis mount system,** place a one inch by one inch by 2 inch long block of wood between torque strut and cradle, **Fig. 7.**
27. **On 1991 models,** remove three right-hand upper engine torque axis mount to front cover nuts, then two mount to midrail bracket nuts allowing engine to rest on block of wood.
28. **On all models,** position suitable powertrain support dolly and two four inch by four inch by 36 inch wood pieces to support cradle.
29. Remove cradle to body attaching bolts, then lower cradle, ensuring two large rear cradle spacers are attached.
30. Install suitable engine lifting equipment.
31. Remove spark plug wire ends at ignition module.
32. Remove power steering pump with bracket, then using wire, attach in upright position to steering gear or cradle.
33. Remove transaxle housing attaching bolts.
34. Remove front engine mount, then disconnect motion restrictor, if required.
35. Place 1/2 inch by one inch by three inch block of wood below axle shaft.
36. Remove starter bracket.
37. **On DOHC models,** remove intake manifold bracket.

Fig. 8 Engine strut bracket & torque strut removal. 1992–94

Fig. 9 Fuel pressure bleed

Upper Side

8 4 1 5

7 3 2 6 9

Lower Side

Fig. 10 Intake manifold tightening sequence. SOHC

38. **On all models,** remove three axle shaft bracket bolts, then allow bracket to rotate rearward. It may be necessary to lift engine slightly to allow clearance between starter bracket and driveshaft bracket.
39. **On 1992-94 models with axis mount system,** place a four by four by six inch long block of wood under transaxle housing.
40. **On 1991 models,** remove front engine mount assembly, then disconnect motion restrictor cable used with DOHC engines with manual transaxles.
41. **On 1992-94 models,** the engine strut bracket and torque strut are removed as an assembly. The engine may have to lifted just enough for the engine strut removal, **Fig. 8.**
42. **On all models,** remove four transaxle housing attaching bolts.
43. Carefully lift engine, then install to engine stand.
44. Remove the following:
    a. Starter and alternator.
    b. Water pump.
    c. Oil Pressure sending unit.
    d. Knock sensor.
    e. Crankshaft position sensor.
    f. Clutch assembly (flexplate) and flywheel.
    g. Using tool No. SST SA9123 E or equivalent, cut oil pan seal from front cover oil seal rear seal carrier, then remove oil pan and filter.
    h. Oil pick up tube.
    i. **On DOHC models,** remove baffle plate.
45. Reverse procedure to install. **On models with airbag,** rearm airbag system as described under "Precautions."

INTAKE MANIFOLD REPLACE

SOHC

1. Disconnect battery ground cable, then drain engine coolant.
2. Remove air cleaner assembly, then disconnect fresh air hose at cam cover.
3. Remove PCV hose.
4. Connect tool No. SA9127E or equivalent to fuel pressure, **Fig. 9,** when fuel line is disconnected wrap with a cloth before disconnecting.
5. Install fuel bleed hose to suitable container, then open valve to bleed system, once pressure is bled, remove tool.
6. Remove fuel line bracket bolt, then using tool No. SA9157E or equivalent, disconnect fuel supply and return lines.
7. Disconnect throttle cable from throttle body, then remove bracket attaching nuts.
8. Disconnect the following electrical connectors:
    a. Fuel injectors.
    b. Idle air control (IAC).
    c. Throttle position sensor (TPS).
    d. EGR valve.
    e. Manifold absolute pressure sensor.
9. Remove wires with tubes, the position harness onto fuel relay.
10. Disconnect and label TBI tube module assembly vacuum hoses.
11. Disconnect heater hose, then remove cylinder head coolant outlet de-aeration line fitting and clamps, then position aside.
12. Remove intake manifold support bracket to block attaching bolt, then remove accessory drive belt.
13. Remove power steering pump attaching bolts, then position aside.
14. Remove intake manifold attaching nuts, then remove manifold and gasket.
15. Reverse procedure to install. Tighten intake manifold attaching nuts to specifications in sequence as shown in, **Fig. 10.**

DOHC

1. Disconnect battery ground cable, then drain engine coolant.
2. Remove air inlet tube/resonator assembly, then disconnect fresh air hose at cam cover, lift resonator up-ward to disengage from engine.
3. Remove PCV hose.
4. Connect tool No. SA9127E or equivalent to fuel pressure, **Fig. 9,** when fuel line is disconnected wrap with a cloth before disconnecting.
5. Install fuel bleed hose to suitable container, then open valve to bleed system, once pressure is bled, remove tool.
6. Remove fuel line bracket bolt, then using tool No. SA9157E or equivalent, disconnect fuel supply and return lines.
7. Disconnect throttle cable from throttle body, then remove bracket attaching nuts.
8. Disconnect the following electrical connectors:
    a. Fuel injectors.
    b. Idle air control (IAC).
    c. Throttle position sensor (TPS).
    d. Manifold absolute pressure sensor.
9. Disconnect heater and de-aeration hoses at intake manifold outlet.
10. Disconnect EGR solenoid vacuum hose.
11. Position electrical harness over brake master cylinder.
12. Remove intake manifold support bracket to block attaching bolt, then remove accessory drive belt.
13. Remove power steering pump attaching bolts, then position aside.
14. Remove upper intake manifold attaching nuts.
15. Raise and support vehicle, then remove lower power steering unit bracket.
16. Remove intake manifold bracket attaching bolt.
17. Disconnect canister purge relay and brake booster vacuum hose.
18. Remove lower intake manifold attaching stud, then lower vehicle, remove manifold.
19. Reverse procedure to install. Tighten intake manifold attaching nuts to specifications in sequence as shown in, **Fig. 11.**

Upper Side

5	2	3
7	4	1	6

Lower Side

Fig. 11   Intake manifold tightening sequence. DOHC

EXHAUST MANIFOLD REPLACE

1. Disconnect battery ground cable.
2. Raise and support vehicle.
3. **On 1991-92 models,** remove exhaust pipe to manifold attaching nuts, then lower pipe and discard gasket.
4. **On all models,** lower vehicle.
5. Remove A/C compressor and rear compressor bracket.
6. **On 1993-94 models,** remove two front exhaust pipe to engine stiffening bracket attaching bolts.
7. **On all models,** disconnect oxygen sensor electrical connector, then remove sensor.
8. Remove exhaust manifold attaching nuts, then remove manifold and discard gasket.
9. Reverse procedure to install. Tighten exhaust manifold attaching nuts to specification in sequence, **Fig. 12.**

CYLINDER HEAD REPLACE

SOHC

1. Disconnect battery ground cable, then remove coolant bottle cap.
2. Drain coolant from engine and radiator.
3. Remove air cleaner and air inlet duct, then disconnect PCV and fresh air hose.
4. Disconnect accelerator cable from TBI throttle lever and bracket from intake manifold.
5. Disconnect the following electrical connectors:
   a. Coolant temperature and PCM connectors.
   b. Injectors.
   c. Idle air control valve.
   d. Manifold air pressure sensor.
   e. Throttle position switch.
   f. Spark plug wires.
   g. Oxygen sensor.
   h. A/C Compressor.

SOHC				DOHC	
Upper Side				Upper Side	
8	4	1	5	2	3
7	3	2	6	4	1	5
Lower Side				Lower Side	

Fig. 12   Exhaust manifold tightening sequence

Fig. 14   Crankshaft damper removal

6. Position electrical harness on underhood junction block.
7. Disconnect and label the following vacuum hoses:
   a. Canister purge valve.
   b. EGR valve.
   c. MAP sensor.
   d. Brake booster at intake manifold or brake booster.
   e. TBI assembly.
8. Disconnect upper radiator hose at cylinder head, heater hose at intake manifold and de-aeration hose at TBI assembly.
9. Using tool No. SA9127E or equivalent, bleed fuel pressure into suitable container.
10. Remove fuel line clamp to intake manifold bas attaching bolt.
11. Disconnect fuel supply and return lines at TBI assembly, then remove lower intake manifold support bracket stud.
12. **On 1992-94 models with a torque axis mount system,** unclip lower splash shield and place a one by one by 2 inch long block of wood between torque strut and cradle.
13. Remove three righthand upper engine torque axis mount to front cover attaching nuts, allowing engine to rest on block of wood.

Fig. 13   Valve cover removal. SOHC

14. **On all models,** remove accessory drive belt.
15. Disconnect de-aeration line at cylinder head water outlet and support bracket then remove rocker cover, **Fig. 13.**
16. Remove three A/C compressor front bracket to cylinder head attaching bolts, then rear bracket attaching bolts, then position compressor aside.
17. Remove power steering pump bracket attaching bolts, then position pump aside.
18. Raise and support vehicle, then drain engine oil.
19. Remove lefthand wheel assembly and splash shield.
20. Remove drive belt tensioner.
21. Using a universal three jaw puller, **Fig. 14,** while holding damper, remove front crankshaft damper assembly. **Do not pry against cover.**
22. Using tool No. SA9104 E or equivalent with flat side toward crankshaft sprocket, to hold front crankshaft timing sprocket.
23. Remove four front oil pan attaching bolts and 14 front cover attaching bolts.
24. Using tool No. SA9123E or equivalent, cut RTV seal from front cover.
25. Using front cover pry tangs, remove cover, then remove and discard two oil gallery transfer seals.
26. **Positioning crankshaft 90° off top dead center (TDC) ensures pistons will not contact valves during assembly.**
27. Rotate crankshaft clockwise, viewed from crankshaft accessory belt end, ensuring timing mark on crankshaft sprocket and keyway align with main bearing cap split line.
28. Remove timing chain, tensioner, guides, camshaft sprocket and chained, using a 7/8 inch wrench to hold camshaft when removing sprocket, **Fig. 15.**
29. Remove TBI assembly, discard gasket, then cover intake manifold opening.
30. Using a six point socket, uniformly loosen and remove ten head bolts in sequence shown, **Fig. 16.**
31. Lift cylinder head from cylinder block dowels.
32. Reverse procedure to install, noting

Fig. 15 Timing chain removal. SOHC

Fig. 16 Cylinder head bolt loosening sequence

Intake Side

8 4 1 5 9

7 3 2 6 10

Exhaust Side

Fig. 17 Cylinder head bolt tightening sequence

Fig. 20 Crankshaft sprocket & block timing mark

Fig. 18 Crankshaft at 90° past TDC

Fig. 19 Camshaft at No. 1 TDC. SOHC

Fig. 21 Timing chain installation. SOHC

the following:

a. Install cylinder head bolts in sequence shown, **Fig. 17,**
b. Ensure crankshaft is 90° past TDC, **Fig. 18,** as required, position camshaft to No. 1 TDC by loosely installing sprocket and rotating clockwise until timing pin may be installed, **Fig. 19.**
c. Rotate crankshaft counterclockwise until No. 1 cylinder is TDC, crankshaft sprocket timing mark will align with cylinder block timing mark, **Fig. 20.**
d. One silver link plate aligns to camshaft sprocket pip marks and another paired link plates align with crankshaft sprocket tooth that is

located at the 6 o'clock position. Crankshaft sprocket pip mark must be aligned with block timing mark.
e. Place timing chain over camshaft sprocket and under crankshaft sprocket, camshaft sprocket FRT letters must face forward, **Fig. 21.**
f. **Keep excess chain slack to chain tensioner side of cylinder block when installing timing chain.**
g. Install camshaft sprocket timing pin, using a 3/16 inch drill, **Fig. 19.**
h. Install camshaft washer and bolt, tighten to specifications, while holding cam.
i. Install chain guides.

DOHC

1. Disconnect battery ground cable, then remove coolant bottle cap.
2. Drain coolant from radiator and engine.
3. Remove air cleaner cover and air inlet duct, lift resonator upward to disengage button from engine support bracket.
4. Disconnect cam cover air hose at cam cover.
5. Disconnect accelerator cable from throttle body and intake manifold bracket.
6. Remove the following electrical connectors:
   a. Coolant temperature gauge and PCM connectors.
   b. Injector connectors.

c. Idle air control valve.
d. Throttle position switch.
e. Manifold air pressure sensor.
f. Remove oxygen sensor.
g. Remove spark plug wires.
h. A/C compressor.
7. Lay electrical harness onto underhood junction block and battery cover.
8. Disconnect and label the following vacuum hoses:
   a. Canister purge valve.
   b. PCV valve at cam cover.
   c. EGR valve.
   d. Fuel regulator.
   e. Throttle body connector.
9. Disconnect the following hose clamps using tool No. SA911E or equivalent:
   a. Upper radiator head at cylinder

Fig. 22 Crankshaft sprocket & keyway alignment. DOHC

Fig. 23 Crankshaft alignment. DOHC

Intake Side

12	6	8	9
	3	1	2	4
11	5	7	10

Exhaust Side

Fig. 24 Cam cover tightening sequence. DOHC

head outlet.
b. De-aeration hose at intake manifold.
c. Heater hose at intake manifold or front of dash.
d. Vacuum brake booster hose.
10. Using tool No. SA9127E or equivalent, bleed fuel pressure into suitable container.
11. Remove fuel line clamp to intake manifold bas attaching bolt.
12. Using tool No. SA9157E or equivalent, disconnect fuel supply and return line to fuel rail.
13. Disconnect fuel line at regulator.
14. Remove upper intake manifold support bracket attaching bolt.
15. **On 1992-94 models, with a torque axis mount system,** unclip lower splash shield and place a one by one by 2 inch long block of wood between torque strut and cradle.
16. Remove three righthand upper engine torque axis mount to front cover attaching nuts, allowing engine to rest on block of wood.
17. **On all models,** remove accessory drive belt and tensioner. Do not remove water pump pulley.
18. **On 1992-94 models,** accessory drive belt idler pulley must be removed to allow front cover to be removed.
19. **On all models,** remove camshaft cover assembly.
20. Remove power steering pump bracket attaching bolts, then position pump aside.
21. Remove A/C compressor front and rear bracket attaching bolts, then position compressor aside.
22. Raise and support vehicle, then drain engine oil.
23. Remove left wheel assembly and splash shield.
24. Remove intake manifold bracket to intake manifold attaching bolts.
25. Remove front damper assembly, hold damper with a strap wrench or 3/4 inch square by 12 inch long piece of wood wedged between damper spoke and rear, lower side of front cover.
26. Using a universal three jaw puller, **Fig. 14,** while holding damper, remove front crankshaft damper assembly. **Do not pry against cover.**

27. Disconnect exhaust pipe from exhaust manifold.
28. Install tool No. SA9104E or equivalent with flat side toward sprocket to hold sprocket.
29. Remove four front oil pan bolts, the using tool No. SA9123E or equivalent, cut seal from front cover.
30. Remove front cover attaching bolts, then use a screwdriver to pry front cover from cylinder block.
31. **Position crankshaft 90° off top dead center ensures pistons will not contact valves upon assembly.**
32. Rotate crankshaft clockwise, viewed from crankshaft accessory belt end, ensuring timing mark on sprocket and keyway align with main bearing cap split line, **Fig. 22.**
33. Remove timing chain tensioner, guides, camshaft sprockets and chain, then using a 7/8 inch wrench to hold camshaft while removing sprocket bolts. **Do place fingers or tools between camshaft sprocket and chain during removal or assembly.**
34. Loosen and remove cylinder head bolts in sequence, **Fig. 16.**
35. Lift cylinder head from dowels on engine block, then remove head.
36. Reverse to install, noting the following:
a. Install cylinder head bolts in sequence shown, **Fig. 17,**
b. Ensure crankshaft is 90° past TDC, **Fig. 18,** install camshaft timing gears attaching bolts and washer, the letters FRT on sprocket must face forward away from cylinder head, then hold camshafts while tightening bolts to specifications. **Do not torque camshaft attaching bolts against 3/16 inch timing pins as cylinder head damage may result.**
c. Turn camshaft up to No. 1 TDC by rotating camshaft and sprocket until timing pins can be installed.
d. Rotate crankshaft counterclockwise until No. 1 cylinder is TDC, crankshaft sprocket timing mark will align with cylinder block timing mark, **Fig. 20.**
e. Two separated silver link plates align to camshaft sprocket pip marks and another two paired link

plates align crankshaft sprocket tooth that is located at the 6 o'clock position. Crankshaft sprocket pip mark must be aligned with block timing mark.
f. Place timing chain over camshaft sprockets and under crankshaft sprocket.
g. **Keep excess chain slack to chain tensioner side (movable guide) of cylinder block when installing timing chain or camshaft sprockets will not be correctly timed.**
h. Position silver colored link plates over pip mark on cam sprocket, then position crankshaft sprocket tooth that is pointed downward at 6 o'clock position between two silver colored links. Crankshaft sprocket pip mark should be aligned with block timing mark.
i. Align timing pin holes, crankshaft sprocket pip mark with block mark, colored links with camshaft and crankshaft, **Fig. 23.**
j. Install cam covers, tighten to sequence, **Fig. 24,** to specifications.

CAMSHAFT LIFT SPECIFICATIONS

Engine	Intake	Exhaust
SOHC	.2531–.2556	.2531–.2556
DOHC	.3528–.3559	.3409–.3441

VALVE ADJUSTMENT

This engine is equipped with hydraulic lifters so no adjustment is available.

VALVE GUIDES

Valve guides are an integral part of the cylinder head and are pressed in. If valve stem clearance becomes excessive, the valve guides must be reamed to the oversize and the oversize valves installed. Valves are available in .010 inch oversize.

Fig. 25   Pressurizing cylinder

Fig. 26   Front cover tightening sequence. SOHC

Fig. 27   Front cover tightening sequence. DOHC

Fig. 28   Timing chain length inspection

Fig. 29   Timing chain guide track wear

Fig. 30   Timing chain tensioner check

VALVE SPRING & SEALS REPLACE

1. Disconnect battery ground cable.
2. **On SOHC models,** remove spark plugs, rocker cover and rocker arm assemblies.
3. **On DOHC models,** remove spark plugs, cam cover and camshaft.
4. **On all models,** install angle supports tool No. SA9127E or equivalent, then on SOHC engines, use four M8 X 25 mm bolts, and DOHC engines use four M6 X 25 mm bolts to mount supports to end rocker arm shaft threaded holes with support flange toward center of cylinder head, then **torque** to 124 inch lbs. on SOHC models, or 89 inch lbs. on DOHC models.
5. While sliding rods through support, install compressor lever arm assembly.
6. Install spark plug adapter tool SA9127E or equivalent, to each cylinder.
7. With piston at TDC, pressurize cylinder to 100 psi, **Fig. 25.**
8. Tap compressor lever with plastic mallet while applying slight amount of pressure to breaker bar.
9. Position lever over valve spring, then use a ¹⁄₂ inch breaker bar to compress spring.
10. Remove valve spring cap retainers, then release spring tension.
11. Remove cap and spring.
12. Using tool No. SA9102E or equivalent, remove valve stem seal.
13. Reverse procedure to install.

FRONT COVER REPLACE

1. Disconnect battery ground cable.
2. **On 1992-94 models with a torque axis mount system,** unclip lower splash shield and place a one by one by 2 inch long block of wood between torque strut and cradle.
3. Remove three righthand upper engine torque axis mount to front cover attaching nuts, allowing engine to rest on block of wood.
4. **On all models,** remove accessory drive belt, idler pulley, tensioner, crankshaft damper and power steering pump.
5. Remove front cover attaching bolts.
6. Using a screwdriver, pry front cover at upper and lower corners to remove.
7. Reverse procedure to install. Tighten attaching bolts to specifications, in sequence, **Figs. 26 and 27.**

TIMING CHAIN REPLACE

SOHC

Refer to "Cylinder Head, Replace" for timing chain replacement procedure.
1. Inspect timing chain as follows:
   a. Inspect chain for wear and damaged links.
   b. Using ruler, measure chain inner diameter, standard I.D. is

16.50-16.61 inch and service limit is 16.77 inch, **Fig. 28.**
   c. Inspect chain guides for wear and cracks, measure chain track wear, standard is 0.0 inch, service limit is .0984 inch, **Fig. 29.**
   d. Inspect timing sprocket teeth on crankshaft, camshaft and key for wear. Inspect camshaft thrust plate and sprocket thrust surface for cracks and wear.
   e. Inspect tensioner operation, release plunger lock, ensuring piston moves freely.
   f. Ensure oil feed hole is open, submerge tensioner in oil or solvent, depress plunger and check flow from tensioner body, check cylinder block port for blockage.
   g. With timing chain and guides installed, measure plunger travel, **Fig. 30,** standard is .0696-.438 inch, service limit is .8626 inch.

DOHC

Refer to "Cylinder Head, Replace" for timing chain replacement procedure.
1. Inspect timing chain as follows:
   a. Inspect chain for wear and damaged links.
   b. Using a ruler, measure chain inner diameter, standard I.D. is 22.83-22.95 inch and service limit is 23.15 inch, **Fig. 28.**
   c. Inspect chain guides for wear and cracks, measure chain track wear,

Fig. 31   No. 1 cylinder at TDC. DOHC

Fig. 32   Camshaft front support fixture. DOHC

Fig. 33   Camshaft support fixture installation. DOHC

standard is 0.0 inch, service limit is .0984 inch, **Fig. 29.**

   d. Inspect timing sprocket teeth on crankshaft, camshaft and key for wear. Inspect camshaft thrust plate and sprocket thrust surface for cracks and wear.

   e. Inspect tensioner operation, release plunger lock, ensuring piston moves freely.

   f. Ensure oil feed hole is open, submerge tensioner in oil or solvent, depress plunger and check flow from tensioner body, check cylinder block port for blockage.

   g. With timing chain and guides installed, measure plunger travel, **Fig. 30,** standard is .045-.388 inch, service limit is .8626 inch.

CAMSHAFT
REPLACE
SOHC

1. Remove cylinder head as outlined under "Cylinder Head, Replace."
2. Remove spark plugs.
3. Remove intake and exhaust manifold attaching nuts, then remove.
4. Remove rocker arm assembly attaching bolts, then remove remove two rocker arm shafts and rocker arm guide plates and lifters.
5. Remove battery cover and battery, then using suitable punch and hammer, remove rear camshaft plug.
6. Measure camshaft thrust clearance while moving camshaft back and forth, using a dial indicator. Standard thrust is .028-.0079 inches and service limit is .0098 inch. If clearance is not as indicated, replace camshaft and/or thrust plate.
7. Remove camshaft from either end of cylinder head.
8. Reverse procedure to install, noting the following:
   a. If camshaft is removed through rear of cylinder head, install new plug.
   b. If camshaft is removed through front, install new Torx screws.

Fig. 34   Camshaft removal. DOHC

DOHC

1. Disconnect battery ground cable.
2. Remove spark plug wires, accessory drive belt, EGR valve solenoid attaching screw, PCV fresh air hose and cam cover assembly.
3. Position No. 1 cylinder to TDC, **Fig. 31,** align damper mark with front cover arrow mark.
4. Hold camshaft using a 7/8 inch open end wrench, then remove camshaft timing sprocket attaching bolts and washer.
5. **On 1992-94 models,** install front support fixture, align two holes in each camshaft sprocket, sprocket adapter and front support fixture, install but do not tighten four attaching nut, **Fig. 32.**
6. **On all models** install suitable camshaft sprocket adapter to each camshaft, but do not tighten pilot bolts, **Fig. 33.**
7. Remove upper timing chain guide and front camshaft bearing caps.
8. **On 1991 models,** install front support fixture, align two holes in each camshaft sprocket, sprocket adapter and front support fixture, install but do not tighten four attaching nut, **Fig. 32.**
9. **On all models,** using a 7/8 inch wrench, hold camshaft, then **torque** sprocket pilot bolts to 18 ft. lbs.
10. Move camshaft sprocket off end of each camshaft onto sprocket adapter, **Fig. 34.**
11. Install four 3/8 inch nuts and bolts with blocks through camshaft sprocket, sprocket adapter and front support fixture, install steel blocks against rearward side of camshaft sprocket. **Torque** nuts and bolts to 18 ft. lbs.

12. Install two 6 mm front support fixture hex bolts to front cover, **torque** bolts to 7 ft. lbs.
13. While holding camshaft with a 7/8 inch wrench, remove camshaft sprocket pilot bolt.
14. Move cam rearward enough to ensure camshaft end is no longer inside sprocket pilot.
15. Loosen and remove camshaft bearing cap attaching bolts in several passes. **If lifters are removed, keep in order for installation, store lifters with camshaft contact facing downward.**
16. Reverse procedure to install.

PISTON & ROD ASSEMBLY

Assemble the piston and connecting rod by aligning the mark on top of the piston with the front of the engine. Assemble connecting rod to the piston with the bearing tang slots directed toward the exhaust manifold, **Fig. 35.**

PISTON, PINS & RINGS

Pistons are available in .005 inch (.125 mm) and .0157 inch (.400 mm) oversizes.

To check piston fit in bore, using a micrometer, measure piston diameter at right angle to piston pin hole center line, .20 inch (5 mm) from bottom of piston. Piston diameter plus piston clearance minus .002 inch allowance for finish honing will give piston size to be bored to.

CRANKSHAFT REAR OIL SEAL
REPLACE

1. Disconnect battery ground cable.
2. Remove transaxle, flywheel, cover and two lower oil pan bolts.
3. Using a suitable rolling head pry bar or pinch bar, separate rear seal carrier from cylinder block.
4. Remove oil seal with a screwdriver.
5. Reverse procedure to install. Using tool No. SA 9121E or equivalent, install seal.

OIL PAN
REPLACE

1. Disable airbag system as outlined under "Precautions."

Fig. 35   Piston assembly

Fig. 36   Oil pump body clearance

Fig. 37   Oil pump tip clearance

Fig. 38   Oil pump end to end clearance

2. Drain engine oil, then remove front exhaust pipe.
3. **On 1991 models,** remove engine stiffening bracket and flywheel cover.
4. **On all models,** remove right side tire, splash shield and vibration damper.
5. Loosen, but do not remove, four front engine mount attaching bolts about ½ inch.
6. Remove oil pan attaching bolts, on models equipped with manual transaxle, a suitable 8mm flexible socket may be used to access rear oil pan bolts next o flywheel.
7. Pry front engine mount away from cylinder block to allow oil pan removal.
8. Using RTV removal tool No. SAE9123E or equivalent, drive sharp edge between pan and block.
9. Drive tool around pan to shear seal, then using a suitable rubber mallet, tap pan sideways to remove.
10. Reverse procedure to install, apply .160 inch bead RTV to inside edge of oil panel groove.

OIL PUMP
REPLACE

1. Disconnect battery ground cable.
2. Raise and support vehicle.
3. Drain engine oil.
4. Remove righthand front wheel assembly and splash shield.
5. Using a universal three jaw puller, **Fig. 14,** while holding damper, remove front crankshaft damper assembly. **Do not pry against cover.**
6. **On 1992-94 models,** the accessory drive belt idler pulley must be re-

moved to allow front cover to be removed and replaced in vehicle.
7. **On all models,** remove engine accessory drive belt.
8. Remove power steering pump and position aside.
9. Remove belt tensioner.
10. **On SOHC models,** remove rocker cover.
11. **On DOHC models,** remove cam cover.
12. **On 1992-94 models,** remove three righthand upper engine torque axis mount to front cover attaching nuts, allowing engine to rest on block of wood.
13. **On all models,** using tool No. SA9104 E or equivalent with flat side toward crankshaft sprocket, to hold front crankshaft timing sprocket.
14. Remove four front oil pan attaching bolts and 14 front cover attaching bolts.
15. Using tool No. SA9123E or equivalent, cut RTV seal from front cover.
16. Using front cover pry tangs, remove cover, then remove and discard two oil gallery transfer seals.
17. Reverse procedure to install.

OIL PUMP SERVICE
DISASSEMBLE

1. Remove cover plate attaching bolts, then remove drive and riven rotor.
2. Remove and discard relief valve using tool No. SA9103E or equivalent.

INSPECTION

1. Inspect body clearance as follows:
   a. Using a feeler gauge, measure clearance between driven rotor and pump body, **Fig. 36.**
   b. Standard clearance should be .006-.011 inch and maximum clearance is .0042 inch.
   c. If clearance is greater than maximum, replace oil pump rotor set.
2. Inspect tip clearance using a feeler gauge between both rotor tips, **Fig. 37,** clearance should be .006 inch.
3. Inspect end to end clearance as follows:
   a. Using a feeler gauge, measure clearance between side of gear rotor assembly and cover plate, **Fig. 38.**
   b. Standard clearance should be .0016-.0049 inch and maximum clearance is .005 inch.

ASSEMBLE

1. Using a screwdriver or punch, remove front cover oil seal.
2. Install new oil seal using tool No. SA9140E or equivalent and a press or hammer.
3. Coat relief valve with engine oil, then using tool No. SA9103E or equivalent and a hammer, install relief valve.
4. Pack oil pump assembly with petroleum jelly.
5. Install drive and driven rotors to pump body with chamfer toward front oil seal.
6. Install pump body cover and tighten bolts to specifications.

BELT TENSION DATA

Belt	New Lbs.	Used Lbs.
Accessory	50—65	45

SERPENTINE DRIVE BELTS

BELT ROUTING

Refer to **Fig. 39,** for serpentine belt routing.

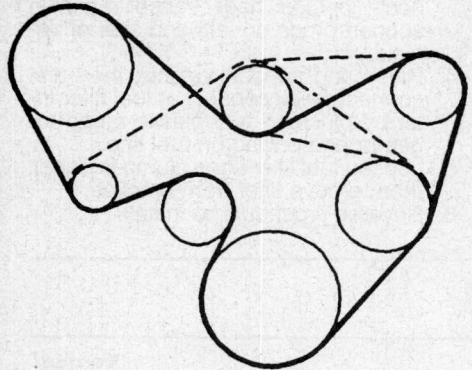

Fig. 39   Serpentine belt routing

Fig. 40   Belt tensioner removal

Fig. 41   Belt tensioner arm

BELT TENSIONER, REPLACE

Tensioner internal components are nor serviceable, do not disassemble tensioner.
1. Disconnect battery ground cable.
2. On 1992-94 models with a torque axis mount system, unclip lower splash shield and place a one by one by 2 inch long block of wood between torque strut and cradle.
3. Remove three righthand upper engine torque axis mount to front cover attaching nuts, allowing engine to rest on block of wood.
4. **On all models,** remove belt as outlined under "Belt, Replace."
5. Remove power steering pump with bracket.
6. Remove tensioner upper and lower attaching bolts, **Fig. 40.**
7. Install a pry bar between steel engine mount and steel frame rail, then move engine slightly toward drivers fender, as required, then remove tensioner.
8. Reverse procedure to install.

BELT, REPLACE

Removal

1. Disconnect battery ground cable.
2. Using suitable 14 mm or ⁹/₁₆ inch wrench, depress tensioner arm, **Fig. 41.**
3. Remove belt from A/C compressor and idler pulley, then remove belt.

Installation

1. Route belt over all pulleys, except front cover idler or A/C compressor.
2. Using 14 mm or ⁹/₁₆ inch wrench, depress tensioner arm, **Fig. 41.**
3. Install belt to idler pulley and A/C compressor.
4. Tighten idler pulley to specifications.

COOLING SYSTEM BLEED

These engines do not require a special bleed procedure. After filling cooling system, run engine and allow to reach normal operating temperature with pressure cap off. Air will then automatically bleed through cap opening.

THERMOSTAT REPLACE

REMOVAL

Do not remove pressure cap while engine is running or when engine is still warm.
1. Remove engine drain plug at right front of engine, to drain coolant from radiator, then open draincock at lower part of radiator. Ensure coolant level is below thermostat housing.
2. Disconnect lower radiator hose at thermostat housing using Snap On Tool HCP10 or equivalent, then remove two water inlet housing retaining bolts.
3. Remove water inlet and thermostat as an assembly, then remove and discard O-ring.
4. Remove thermostat element with service tool provided with replacement part. The new part will not function correctly if oil comes in contact with part. If oil is found in coolant, flush entire system before replacing thermostat.
5. Ensure no damage or seat deterioration is found within water inlet housing. Use care not to damage machined aluminum surfaces.

INSTALLATION

1. Install new thermostat with service tool provided, ensuring tangs are properly seated in the legs and the piston is correctly positioned in water inlet housing.
2. Install new O-ring on the water inlet housing, then the water inlet housing, thermostat into cylinder block.
3. Install retaining bolts and tighten to specifications.
4. Close radiator and engine drain plugs and tighten to specification.
5. Install lower radiator hose. Ensure vehicle is on level surface.
6. Fill coolant system using only recommended mixture of 50/50 mixture of water and non phosphate ethylene glycol-base coolant.
7. Start engine and run for several minutes, then fill cooling system surge tank to full cold line.
8. Install pressure cap and check for leaks.

WATER PUMP REPLACE

1. Disconnect battery ground cable, then drain coolant.
2. Raise and support vehicle.
3. Remove right wheel assembly, then inner wheelwell splash shield.
4. Remove A/C compressor attaching bolts, then position aside.
5. Place one inch wood block between crankshaft and water pump pulley, then remove water pump bolts and allow pulley to hang on pump hub.
6. Remove water pump attaching bolts, then remove water pump and discard gasket.
7. Reverse procedure to install. Tighten water pump bolts to specification in criss cross pattern.

FUEL PUMP REPLACE

1. Remove fuel tank as follows:
   a. Remove fuel filler cap.
   b. Disconnect battery ground cable.
   c. When fuel line is disconnected or removed wrap fuel fitting in cloth before disconnecting.
   d. Remove fuel delivery line Schraeder valve cap, in engine compartment.
   e. Using tool No. SA9127E or equivalent, on Schraeder valve, released fuel system pressure.
   f. Raise and support rear of vehicle 28 inches higher than front.
   g. Place container below fuel tank fill neck hose, then loosen connecting tube and vent hose clamps.
   h. Wrap a cloth around filler neck connecting tube, then remove tube from tank.
   i. Using a socket extension, push filler neck check ball into fuel tank.
   j. Install siphon hose in fuel tank through fuel filler, then siphon fuel from tank into a container.
   k. Remove fill neck bracket, then disconnect fuel supply and return lines.
   l. Remove fuel tank support straps,

then disconnect electrical connector.

m. Remove fuel tank assembly.

2. Using tool No. SA9156E or equivalent, remove fuel pump module cam lock ring.
3. Lift assembly at 45° angle to remove.
4. Remove and discard large fuel pump module to tank O-ring.
5. Reverse procedure to install.

FUEL FILTER REPLACE

1. Disconnect battery ground cable.
2. Disconnect fresh air inlet hose from rocker cam cover, then remove air inlet tube.
3. Place a shop towel around fuel line, using tool No. SA9157E or equivalent, disconnect large fuel line quick connect, located near intake manifold support brace on lefthand side of vehicle.
4. Raise and support vehicle, then disconnect quick connect at fuel filter inlet by pinching two plastic tangs together and pulling on fuel line.
5. Loosen fuel filter band clamp fastener, then remove filter from bracket.
6. Reverse procedure to install.

TIGHTENING SPECIFICATIONS

Component	Torque/Ft. Lbs.	Component	Torque/Ft. Lbs.
A/C Compressor Front Bracket To Block	35	EGR Solenoid Bracket ③	89 ①
A/C Compressor Front/Rear Bracket To Head	22	EGR Solenoid Bracket ②	19
A/C Compressor To Front Bracket	35	EGR Valve Nut To Head	21
A/C Compressor To Rear Bracket	22	EGR Valve Stud To Head	62 ①
Accelerator Bracket To Front Dash	106 ①	Engine Block Heater To Block	18
Accelerator Cable Bracket To Intake Manifold	19	Engine Lift Bracket To Block ⑥	36
Accelerator Control Cable Stud ②	62 ①	Engine Lift Bracket To Block ⑥	22
Air Cleaner Duct Clamp	15 ①	Engine Mount To Front Cover	7
Air Cleaner/Resonator Bolts	89 ①	Engine Support Bracket	28
Air Cleaner/Resonator Clamps	18 ①	ESC Knock Sensor	133 ①
Alternator Positive Terminal	89 ①	Exhaust Manifold Studs To Front Pipe	115 ①
Alternator To Block	27	Exhaust Manifold Studs To Head	106 ①
Axle Shaft Intermediate Bracket To Block	41	Exhaust Manifold To Head ②	16
Battery Cable	151 ①	Exhaust Manifold To Head ③	23
Battery Cable To Alternator	7	Exhaust Pipe To Converter	33
Belt Idler Pulley To Front Cover	33	Flexplate To Converter	41
Belt Tensioner Pulley	22	Flexplate To Crankshaft	44
Belt Tensioner To Block	22	Flywheel/Flexplate Cover	89 ①
Block Oil Gallery Plug	22	Flywheel To Crankshaft	59
Camshaft Bearing Cap To Head ③	124 ①	Front Cover To Block (Center)	89 ①
Camshaft Cover To Head ③	89 ①	Front Cover To Block (Perimeter)	22
Camshaft Sprocket To Camshaft	75	Front Engine Mount To Block	52
Camshaft Thrust Bearing To Head ②	18	Fuel Canister Bracket To Frame Rail	22
Canister Band Clamp	31 ①	Fuel Line Support Bracket	22
Canister Purge Solenoid To Block	22	Fuel Line Support Clip	106 ①
Catalytic Converter To Isolator	19	Fuel Rail To Intake Manifold	22
Clutch Pressure Plate To Flywheel	19	Fuel Return Pipe Nut To Pressure Regulator ③	133 ①
Connecting Rod Cap To Rod	33	Fuel Supply Pipe ③	18
Coolant/Cylinder Block Heater	19	Fuel Tank Fill Hose	27 ①
Coolant Drain Plug	26	Fuel Tank Fill Pipe	18 ①
Coolant Temperature Sensor	71 ①	Fuel Tank Fill Pipe Bracket	53 ①
Cradle To Body	151	Fuel Tank Straps	25
Crankshaft Bearing Cap To Block	37	Fuel/Vapor Line To Body	27 ①
Crankshaft Damper To Crankshaft	159	Heater Outlet To Intake Manifold	19
Crankshaft Position Sensor	80 ①	Heater Return Nipple	37
Crankshaft Rear Oil Seal Carrier To Block	97 ①	Idle Air Control Sensor	28
Cylinder Head Bolts ②	④	Idle Air Control Valve	18 ①
Cylinder Head Bolts ③	⑦	Ignition Module To Transaxle Case	71 ①
Cylinder Head Core Hole Plug	53 ①	Induction Air Sensor	44 ①
Cylinder Head Water Jacket ③	55	Intake Manifold Bracket To Block (LH)	22
De-Aeration Line Clamp ②	80 ①	Intake Manifold Bracket To Block (RH) ③	41
De-Aeration Line Fitting To Head	97 ①	Intake Manifold Bracket To Manifold ②	21
De-Aeration Line Nut To Head ②	151 ①	Intake Manifold Bracket To Manifold ③	22
De-Aeration Line To Cam Cover	53 ①		

Continued

TIGHTENING SPECIFICATIONS—Continued

Component	Torque/ Ft. Lbs.
Intake Manifold Stud To Fuel Line Clamp ②	62 ①
Intake Manifold Stud To Head	106 ①
Intake Manifold Stud To Head (P/S Bracket) ②	188 ①
Intake Manifold Stud To Head (P/S Bracket) ③	22
Intake Manifold To Head	22
MAP Sensor ②	53 ①
MAP Sensor ③	27
Motion Restrictor Bracket	40
Motion Restrictor To Side Of Block	22
Mount To Midrail Bracket	⑧
Oil Baffle Plate To Block	41
Oil Drain Plug	26
Oil Filter	⑤
Oil Pan To Block	80 ①
Oil Pickup Tube ③	133 ①
Oil Pipe Bracket To Block ③	133 ①
Oil Pipe Bracket To Block ②	41
Oil Pressure Sensor	26
Oil Pump Cover	97 ①
Oxygen Sensor	19
Power Steering Hoses	20
Power Steering Pump Bracket	22
Power Steering Pump To Bracket	28
Power Steering Return Hose Clamp	18 ①
Radiator Upper Bracket	89 ①
Rear Engine Mount To Block	35
Rocker Arm Cover To Head ②	22
Rocker Arm Shaft To Head	19
Spark Plug	20
Starter Bracket To Starter	89 ①
Starter Motor	27
Starter Motor Bracket To Axle Shaft	22
Starter Positive Terminal	89 ①
Starter Solenoid Terminal	35 ①

Component	Torque/ Ft. Lbs.
Steering Joint To Gear	35
Stiffening Bracket	40
Strut To Knuckle	148
TBI Assembly Fuel Line	19
TBI Assembly To Air Intake Manifold	24
TBI Injector	18 ①
Thermostat Housing To Block	22
Throttle Body To Air Intake Manifold ③	23
Throttle Position Sensor	18 ①
Timing Chain Guides	19
Timing Chain Tensioner	168 ①
Transaxle Case To Block (Lower)	96
Transaxle Case To Block (Upper)	66
Transaxle Lower Mount To Cradle	41
Transaxle Lower Mount To Transaxle	23
Transaxle Rear Mount	36
Vapor Canister To Body	22
Vehicle Speed Sensor	19 ①
Water Pump	22
Water Pump Pulley	18

① —Inch lbs.
② —SOHC.
③ —DOHC.
④ —Tighten in sequence to 22 ft. lbs., then to 33 ft. lbs., then install Tool No. SA9140E or equivalent, calibrate to zero, then in sequence turn each bolt another 90°.
⑤ —Tighten to gasket, then turn and additional ¾ to 1 turn.
⑥ —Less A/C.
⑦ —Tighten in sequence to 22 ft. lbs., then to 37 ft. lbs., then install Tool No. SA9140E or equivalent, calibrate to zero, then in sequence turn each bolt another 90°.
⑧ —1991–93 models, 52 ft. lbs., 1994 models, 37 ft. lbs.

CLUTCH & MANUAL TRANSAXLE

INDEX

Fig. 1   Clutch pedal height

Fig. 2   Measuring pressure plate

Fig. 3   Measuring flywheel

PRECAUTIONS

AIRBAG SYSTEM DISARMING

1. Place ignition in OFF position, then remove Supplemental Inflatable Restraint (SIR) fuse.
2. Remove connector position assurance (CPA) device from yellow two way SIR connector at base of steering column.

AIRBAG SYSTEM REARMING

1. Place ignition in Off position, then connect yellow two way SIR connector at base of steering column, then install CPA device to connector.
2. Install SIR fuse.
3. Turn ignition switch to Run position, then ensure AIRBAG lamp flashes 7 to 9 times, then remains Off.

ADJUSTMENTS

CLUTCH PEDAL HEIGHT

The hydraulic clutch system provides automatic clutch adjustment, therefore, there is no adjustment provision. The clutch pedal height can be measured, **Fig. 1**, 5.3-6.2 inch should be indicated. If not, check carpet or floor mat under pedal, a faulty bushing or damaged pedal may be indicated.

CLUTCH
REPLACE

REMOVAL & INSPECTION

1. **On models with airbag,** disarm airbag system as described under "Precautions."
2. **On all models,** remove transaxle as outlined under "Transaxle, Replace."
3. Remove unsnap release fork and bearing from ball stud to remove.
4. Slide release bearing from release fork, then check release bearing for excessive play or minimal drag, replace as required. **Do not wash bearing in solvent.**
5. Using a feeler gauge, measure between pressure plate and flywheel, .205-.287 inch should be indicated, if not, replace clutch disc.
6. Remove pressure plate to flywheel attaching bolts in progressive crisscross pattern.
7. Remove pressure plate and clutch disc.
8. Inspect pressure plate for excessive wear, chatter marks, cracks or overheating, replace as required. **Random black spotting on friction surface is normal.**
9. Using a straightedge and feeler gauge, measure pressure plate warpage, **Fig. 2**, maximum warpage is .006 inch.
10. Inspect clutch disc for oil, burnt spots, loose damper springs, hub and rivets, replace as required.
11. Inspect flywheel ring gear for wear or damage, replace as required.
12. Measure flywheel thickness, **Fig. 3**, minimum thickness is 1.102 inch, replace is required.
13. Using a dial indicator, measure flywheel runout, push crankshaft forward to take up thrust bearing clearance, maximum runout is .006 inch, replace as required.
14. Remove flywheel to crankshaft attaching bolts, then remove flywheel.

INSTALLATION

1. Install flywheel to crankshaft attaching bolts, then tighten in order, **Fig. 4**, to specifications.
2. Install clutch disc and pressure plate, with pressure plate yellow dot aligned with flywheel mark, then start pressure plate to flywheel bolts.
3. Install clutch disc alignment tool No. SA9145T or equivalent, until bottoms out in crankshaft.
4. Tighten bolts in crisscross pattern to specifications.
5. Remove clutch alignment tool, then install fork clip.
6. Lube fork pivot using high temperature grease part No. 21005995 or equivalent, then install release bearing to fork. **Do not lube release bearing or quill.**
7. Install release fork and bearing to ball stud.
8. Lube input shaft splines, then install transaxle assembly.
9. **On models with airbag,** rearm airbag system as described under "Precautions."

Fig. 4   Flywheel tightening sequence

SLAVE CYLINDER
REPLACE

1. Disable airbag system as outlined under "Precautions," then block clutch pedal.
2. **On DOHC models,** lift resonator upward, to disengage from engine bracket.
3. **On all models,** remove air induction tube.
4. Rotate actuator 1/4 turn counterclockwise while pushing toward housing to disengage, then remove actuator from clutch housing. **Removal of hydraulic damper prior to actuator removal will result in a broken hydraulic line.**
5. Remove hydraulic damper to clutch housing attaching nuts, then slide damper and bracket assembly from studs.
6. Remove clutch pedal pin to slave cylinder pushrod attaching clip, then disconnect pushrod from pedal.
7. Turn slave cylinder about 1/8 turn clockwise, then remove.
8. Reverse procedure to install.

CLUTCH BLEED
PROCEDURE

The hydraulic system is serviced as a unit, it has been filled with fluid and bled of air. If the system requires any fluid, check the hydraulic components for leakage. Remove the slave cylinder from the clutch housing and check for leakage at the piston, a slightly wet surface is normal, if excessive, replace system.

Use only DOT 3 brake fluid. **Do not use mineral oil or a paraffin bas oil in the hydraulic system as damage to rubber**

parts will occur. Clean the cap and sides of reservoir before removing cap, then remove diaphragm. Carefully replace diaphragm and cover after filling.

TRANSAXLE
REPLACE

1. **On models with airbag,** disarm airbag system as described under "Precautions."
2. **On all models,** disconnect battery ground cable.
3. **On models equipped with SOHC engine,** remove two air inlet duct attaching screws, disconnect air temperature sensor electrical connector, then remove air inlet duct.
4. **On models equipped with DOHC engine,** remove two cross car duct attaching screws, disconnect air temperature sensor electrical connector, then remove cross car duct.
5. **On models equipped with DOHC engine,** loosen flex tube to air box clamp, remove three air body attaching screws, then remove air box.
6. **On 1992-94 models,** remove transaxle strut to cradle bracket attaching bolt, the loosen transaxle strut to transaxle bracket attaching bolt and position strut aside.
7. **On all models,** disconnect the following electrical connectors:
   a. Back-up light switch.
   b. Vehicle speed sensor.
   c. Remove and discard vent tube clip.
   d. Two upper clutch housing ground terminals.
   e. Oxygen sensor from clutch housing.
8. **On 1991 models with DOHC engine,** remove right front cradle to engine cable bracket attaching nut.
9. **On all models,** remove upper clutch housing the engine bolts, then install four inch guide bolts in upper rear clutch housing bolt hole.
10. Remove DIS coil attaching screws, then remove.
11. **On 1991 models,** loosen two front transaxle mount bolts.
12. **On all models,** remove shift cables from shift arms and clutch housing, **Fig. 5.**
13. Turn clutch slave cylinder 1/4 counterclockwise while pushing into clutch housing, then remove cylinder.
14. Secure radiator to upper support with mechanics wire.
15. Install engine lifting equipment.
16. Raise and support vehicle, then drain transaxle fluid.
17. Remove front wheels, then right, left and front splash shields.
18. **On 1991 models,** remove engine mount to cradle attaching nuts.
19. **On 1992-94 models,** remove engine strut cradle bracket to cradle fasteners.
20. **On all models,** remove transaxle to cradle mount.

Fig. 5   Shift cable removal

21. Remove front exhaust pipe.
22. Remove steering gear to cradle attaching bolts and support steering gear with suitable wire.
23. Remove brake line bracket push pin at rear of cradle.
24. **On 1991 models,** remove two transaxle front mount to cradle attaching bolts.
25. **On 1991 models,** loosen, but do not remove, transaxle rear mount pivot bolt, remove four rear mount to bracket attaching bolts, then position rear mount aside.
26. **On all models,** remove engine to transaxle stiffening bracket.
27. Remove clutch housing dust cover.
28. Remove and discard lower ball joint cotter pins, then loosen nut to top of bolt thread.
29. Using tool No. SA9132S or equivalent, separate ball joint from lower control arm. **On models with ABS, outer CV joint has a speed sensor ring, failure to use the proper tool will result in loss of ABS or system damage.**
30. Using suitable large screwdriver or pry bar, separate left side axle from transaxle, pull axle slightly rearward and install axle seal protector tool No. SA91112T or equivalent.
31. Position a suitable powertrain support dolly and two four inch by four inch by 36 inch wood pieces to support cradle.
32. Remove cradle to body attaching bolts, then lower cradle, ensuring two large rear cradle spacers are attached.
33. Support transaxle with a jack stand.
34. Using a screwdriver or pry bar, separate left axle from transaxle. **Do not allow tool to contact or damage axle seal.**
35. Separate transaxle from engine enough to clear intermediate shaft, then lower transaxle to remove.
36. Reverse procedure to install. **On models with airbag,** rearm airbag system as described under "Precautions."

TIGHTENING SPECIFICATIONS

Component	Torque/ Ft. Lbs.
Air Box	89①
Clutch Fork Stabilizer	18
Clutch Housing Dust Cover	89①
Clutch Housing To Engine Stud	74
Clutch Hydraulic Damper Nuts	18
Converter Housing Ground Terminal	18
Cradle Bracket To Cradle	52②
Down Pipe To Convertor	33
Down Pipe To Exhaust Manifold	23
Down Pipe To Stiffening Bracket	23
Engine Mount To Cradle	66
Flex Tube	18①
Flywheel	59
Front Transaxle Mount To Cradle	35④
Ignition Module	61①
Lower Ball Joint	55
Lower Converter Housing	96
Lower Transaxle Mount	③

Component	Torque/ Ft. Lbs.
Pressure Plate	18
Rear Pitch Restrictor	40④
Rear Transaxle Mount	⑥
Steering Gear To Cradle	40
Strut Cradle Bracket To Cradle	52②
Tie Rod End	33
Transaxle Bracket To Transaxle	40②
Transaxle Drain Plug	40⑤
Transaxle Stiffening Bracket	35
Transaxle Strut To Cradle	52②
Transaxle Strut To Transaxle Bracket	52②
Wheel Lug Nuts	100

①—Inch lbs.
②—1992–94 models.
③—1991 models, 35 ft. lbs., 1992–94 models
④—1991 models.
⑤—1993–94 models do not require drain plug seal replacement.
⑥—1991 models, 40 ft. lb., 1992–94 models, 52 ft. lbs.

REAR AXLE & SUSPENSION

INDEX

HUB & BEARING
REPLACE
DRUM BRAKES

1. Raise and support vehicle, then remove wheel assembly.
2. Remove brake drum, then four hub to knuckle attaching bolts, then remove.
3. Reverse procedure to install.

DISC BRAKES

1. Raise and support vehicle, then remove wheel assembly.
2. **On models equipped with ABS,** disconnect wheel speed sensor electrical connector.
3. **On all models,** remove caliper to knuckle attaching bolts, then hang caliper with wire.
4. Remove brake rotor, then four hub to knuckle attaching bolts, remove hub.
5. Reverse procedure to install.

KNUCKLE
REPLACE
DISC BRAKES

1. Raise and support vehicle, then re-

move wheel assembly.
2. Disconnect ABS wheel speed sensor electrical connector.
3. Remove caliper to knuckle attaching bolts. Suspend caliper with mechanics wire, then remove rotor.
4. Remove hub to knuckle attaching bolts, then remove hub and backing plate.
5. Loosen but do not remove lateral link to knuckle attaching bolts.
6. Loosen but do not remove strut to knuckle attaching bolts.
7. Remove trailing arm to knuckle attaching nut, then arm to body bolts.
8. Remove lateral link to knuckle attaching nuts, then remove knuckle to strut bolts, remove knuckle.
9. Reverse procedure to install.

DRUM BRAKES

1. Raise and support vehicle.
2. Remove wheel assembly and brake drum.
3. Remove hub to knuckle attaching bolts, then remove hub.
4. Using wire, position brake assembly aside.

5. Loosen but do not remove lateral link and strut to knuckle attaching bolts.
6. Remove trailing arm to knuckle attaching nut, then arm to body bolts, then slide arm from knuckle.
7. Remove link and strut to knuckle attaching bolts, then remove link.
8. Reverse procedure to install.

STRUT
REPLACE

1. **On Coupe models,** remove rear seat bottom cushion, then right and left interior rocker panel molding.
2. **On Coupe models,** remove left and right interior rear sail panel.
3. **On Sedan models,** remove left or right interior C-pillar molding.
4. **On all models,** fold down rear seats, then remove rear set bolsters.
5. **On Coupe models,** remove cargo area package shelf attaching screws and carpet.
6. **On all models,** remove speaker grilles and seat belt bezel, then separate belts from shelf.

Fig. 1   Exploded view of rear suspension

Fig. 2   Brake line removal

7. Raise and support vehicle, then remove wheel assembly.
8. Loosen but do not remove steering knuckle to strut attaching nuts.
9. Using a floor jack, support knuckle, then remove upper strut attaching nuts.
10. **On models equipped with ABS,** disconnect ABS electrical harness from strut.
11. **On all models,** remove strut to knuckle nuts, then remove strut.
12. Reverse procedure to install.

TRAILING ARM
REPLACE

1. Raise and support vehicle.
2. Remove wheel assemblies.
3. Remove trailing arm to knuckle attaching nut, **Fig. 1.**
4. Remove trailing arm to body attaching bolts, then slide arm from knuckle.
5. Reverse procedure to install.

LATERAL LINK
REPLACE

1. To remove front lateral link, remove fuel tank as follows:
   a. Remove fuel filler cap.
   b. Disconnect battery ground cable.
   c. When fuel line is disconnected or removed, wrap fuel fitting in cloth before disconnecting.
   d. Remove fuel delivery line Schraeder valve cap, in engine compartment.
   e. Using tool No. SA9127E or equivalent, on Schraeder valve, released fuel system pressure.
   f. Raise and support rear of vehicle 28 inches higher than front.
   g. Place a container below fuel tank fill neck hose, then loosen connecting tube and vent hose clamps.
   h. Wrap cloth around filler neck connecting tube, then remove tube from tank.
   i. Using a socket extension, push filler neck check ball into fuel tank.
   j. Install siphon hose in fuel tank through fuel filler, then siphon fuel from tank into container.
   k. Remove fill neck bracket, then disconnect fuel supply and return lines.
   l. Remove fuel tank support straps, then disconnect electrical connector.
   m. Remove fuel tank assembly.
2. Raise and support vehicle, then remove wheel assembly.
3. Remove lateral link to knuckle attaching bolt, then lateral link to crossmember bolts, **Fig. 1.**
4. Remove lateral link.
5. Reverse procedure to install.

STABILIZER BAR
REPLACE

1. Raise and support vehicle, then remove wheel assembly.
2. Position drain container at left rear brake line, then disconnect and plug left brake line.
3. Remove right and left stabilizer bar link to knuckle attaching nuts, then bar to crossmember nuts.
4. Loosen but do not remove lateral link to knuckle attaching bolts, the remove trailing arm to knuckle and arm to body attaching nuts.
5. Slide trailing arm from knuckle, then remove lateral link bolt, swing link downward.
6. Disconnect brake lines from crossmember, **Fig. 2.**
7. Remove stabilizer bar.
8. Reverse procedure to install.

TIGHTENING SPECIFICATIONS

Component	Torque/ Ft. Lbs.	Component	Torque/ Ft. Lbs.
ABS Electrical Harness	53①	**Fuel Tank Straps**	30
Brake Line	14	**Fuel Vent & Fill Line Clamps**	25①
Crossmember To Body	89	**Hub To Knuckle**	63
Front Lateral Link To Crossmember (Bolt)	126	**Lateral Link To Knuckle**	122
Front Lateral Link To Crossmember (Nut)	89	**Rear Caliper To Knuckle**	63
Fuel Fill Neck Bracket	53①	**Rear Lateral Link To Crossmember**	89

Continued

TIGHTENING SPECIFICATIONS—Continued

Component	Torque/ Ft. Lbs.
Stabilizer Bar Link To Bracket	30
Stabilizer Bar To Crossmember	41
Stabilizer Bar To Link	30
Strut Shaft Nut	37
Strut To Knuckle	148
Trailing Arm To Body	89
Trailing Arm To Knuckle	74
Upper Strut Nuts	21
Wheel Lug Nut	100

① —Inch lbs.

FRONT SUSPENSION & STEERING

INDEX

Fig. 1 Brake rotor removal

Fig. 2 Exploded view of front suspension

PRECAUTIONS
AIRBAG SYSTEM DISARMING

1. Place ignition in OFF position, then remove Supplemental Inflatable Restraint (SIR) fuse.
2. Remove connector position assurance (CPA) device from yellow two way SIR connector at base of steering column.

AIRBAG SYSTEM REARMING

1. Place ignition in Off position, then connect yellow two way SIR connector at base of steering column, then install CPA device to connector.
2. Install SIR fuse.
3. Turn ignition switch to Run position, then ensure AIRBAG lamp flashes 7 to 9 times, then remains Off.

HUB & BEARING & STEERING KNUCKLE REPLACE

1. Depress brake pedal, then loosen axle to hub nut.
2. Raise and support vehicle, then remove wheel assembly.
3. Remove caliper to knuckle attaching bolts. Suspend caliper with mechanics wire.

Fig. 3   Wheel bearing/hub removal

Fig. 4   Hub vise installation

Fig. 6   Bearing removal

Fig. 5   Inner bearing race removal

4. Loosen but do not remove knuckle to strut attaching bolts.
5. If rotor is difficult to remove, use two M8 X 1.25 self tapping bolts, to remove, **Fig. 1.**
6. Remove axle nut and washer, then remove and discard lower control arm ball stud cotter pin.
7. Loosen castle nut until level with top of ball stud.
8. Remove and discard tie rod cotter pin.
9. Remove tie rod and castle nut.
10. Using tool No. SA9132A or equivalent, separate lower control arm from knuckle. **Do not use wedge type tool to separate or ABS speed sensor ring or seal damage may occur.**
11. Remove lower ball joint castle nut, **Fig. 2.**
12. Using tool No. SA91100C or equivalent, separate tie rod end from steering knuckle.
13. **On models equipped with ABS brakes,** disconnect wheel speed sensor electrical connector.
14. **On all models,** support or suspend drive axle assembly.
15. Remove strut to knuckle attaching bolts, then remove knuckle and hub assembly. If difficult to separate axle from hub, tap end of drive axle shaft using a block of wood and hammer. **Do not hammer end of axle.**
16. Reverse procedure to install.

HUB & BEARING SERVICE

1. Remove splash shields, then ABS wheel speed sensor, is equipped.
2. Install wheel bearing/hub removal tool No. SA9159S or equivalent, **Fig. 3,** then place assembly in a soft jawed vise, **Fig. 4.**
3. Hold hub drive with a wrench. Tighten driver screw to remove hub.
4. Install inner race puller, **Fig. 5,** then remove inner bearing race.
5. Remove steering knuckle from vise, then remove bridge retainer and bridge.
6. Remove bridge snap ring using snap ring pliers.
7. Using knuckle support tube and small driver, **Fig. 6,** press out bearing.
8. Reverse to assemble.

BALL JOINT
REPLACE
LOWER

The ball joint and the lower control arm are a unit and serviced as an assembly, refer to "Control Arm, Replace" for replacement procedure.

STRUT
REPLACE
REMOVAL

1. Raise and support vehicle, then remove wheel assembly.
2. **On models equipped with ABS,** disconnect wheel speed sensor electrical connector bracket.
3. **On all models,** loosen but do not remove steering knuckle to strut housing attaching bolts.
4. Place a floor jack below lower control arm and support.
5. Remove upper strut attaching nuts.
6. Slowly raise vehicle, then lower strut assembly.
7. Remove knuckle to housing attaching bolts, **Fig. 2,** then place cloth over CV joint seal.
8. Remove strut assembly.

DISASSEMBLE

1. Using spring compressor tool No. SA9155C or equivalent and holding fixture, compress spring to unload upper strut mount.
2. While holding strut shaft, remove strut

shaft nut.
3. Release spring compressor, then tilt strut assembly outward.
4. Remove upper strut assembly, check for damage. replace as required.
5. Remove strut spring and dust shield, inspect for damage, replace as required.
6. Remove strut.

ASSEMBLE

1. Place strut in compressor tool, then attach with strut to knuckle bolt, through lower mounting hole.
2. Extend strut shaft to travel limit.
3. Install dust shield, spring, spring isolator and mount, ensuring spring is properly seated in seat and isolator.
4. Compress spring, then install strut shaft attaching nut and tighten to specifications.

INSTALLATION

1. Install upper strut attaching nuts, tighten to specification.
2. Install strut to steering knuckle attaching bolts, tighten to specification.
3. **On models equipped with ABS brakes,** install sensor electrical connector bracket, tighten to specifications.
4. **On all models,** install wheel and tighten nuts to specifications.
5. Lower vehicle.

COIL SPRING
REPLACE

Refer to "Strut, Replace" for coil spring removal procedure.

CONTROL ARM
REPLACE
LOWER

1. Raise and support vehicle, then re-

move wheel assembly.

2. Remove and discard lower control arm ball stud cotter pin.
3. Loosen lower control ball stud castle nut until level with top of ball stud.
4. Using tool No. SA9132S or equivalent, separate lower control arm from knuckle. **Do not use wedge type tool or ABS speed sensor ring or seal may be damaged.**
5. Remove lower control arm ball stud castle nut.
6. Remove inner front fender splash shield.
7. Remove lower control arm to cradle attaching nut and bolt, **Fig. 2.**
8. Remove lower control arm to tension strut attaching nut, then remove arm.
9. Reverse procedure to install.

Fig. 7   Belt spring tension release

TENSION STRUT
REPLACE

1. Raise and support vehicle, then remove wheel assembly.
2. Remove and discard lower control arm ball stud cotter pin.
3. Loosen but do not remove left lower control arm ball stud castle nut.
4. **For lefthand side of vehicle,** proceed as follows:
   a. Using tool No. SA9132S or equivalent, separate lower control arm from steering knuckle. **Do not use wedge type tool or ABS speed sensor ring or seal damage may occur.**
   b. Remove lower control arm ball joint castle nut.
   c. Remove left front inner fender splash shield.
   d. Remove lower control arm to cradle attaching nut and bolt.
5. **For righthand side of vehicle,** proceed as follows:
   a. Turn wheel left to gain access, then remove tension strut to lower control arm attaching nut and washer.
6. **For both sides,** remove tension strut to cradle bracket attaching bolts.
7. Remove tension strut and left control

arm assembly.

8. Remove control arm to tension strut attaching nut and washer, then separate.
9. Reverse procedure to install.

MANUAL STEERING GEAR
REPLACE

1. Disconnect battery ground cable.
2. Raise and support vehicle.
3. Remove front wheel assemblies.
4. Remove and discard tie rod end cotter pins.
5. Using tool No. SA91100C or equivalent, remove tie rod end from steering knuckle. **Do not separate joint with wedge type tool or damage may result.**
6. Remove left inner fender splash shield.
7. Loosen intermediate shaft cover from steering gear, then raise slightly, remove pinch bolt.
8. Remove steering gear cradle attaching bolts, then remove through left fenderwell.
9. Reverse procedure to install.

POWER STEERING GEAR
REPLACE

1. Disconnect battery ground cable.
2. Raise and support vehicle.
3. Remove and discard tie rod end cotter pins.
4. Remove tie rod end to knuckle castle nuts.
5. Using tool No. SA91100C or equivalent, remove tie rod end from steering knuckle. **Do not separate joint using wedge-type tool or damage may result.**
6. Remove left inner fender splash shield.
7. Loosen intermediate shaft cover from steering gear, then raise slightly, remove pinch bolt.
8. Disconnect power steering pressure switch, then place drain container below pressure and return hoses.
9. Disconnect pressure and return hoses and allow system to drain.
10. Remove steering gear attaching bolts, then remove through left fenderwell.
11. Reverse procedure to install.

POWER STEERING PUMP
REPLACE

1. Disconnect battery ground cable.
2. Remove power steering pump reservoir fill cap.
3. Raise and support vehicle.
4. Place a drain pan below steering gear hoses.
5. Remove steering gear hoses and allow system to drain. **Do not rotate steering wheel.**
6. Using a box end wrench, relieve spring tension from accessory drive belt, then remove belt, **Fig. 7.**
7. **On models equipped with DOHC,** remove pump to intake manifold bracket, then pump to engine block bracket.
8. **On all models,** remove pump to engine block attaching bolts, then raise pump to disconnect EVO electrical connector.
9. Remove pump and hose assembly, then remove hoses.
10. Reverse procedure to install.

TIGHTENING SPECIFICATIONS

Component	Torque/ Ft. Lbs.	Component	Torque/ Ft. Lbs.
ABS Electrical Connector Bracket	6	Pump To Engine Block Bolts	28
Axle To Hub Nut	148	Pump To Engine Block Bracket ①	22
Ball Joint Stud Castle Nut	55	Pump To Intake Manifold Bracket ①	22
Brake Dust Shield	18	Steering Gear Cradle Bolts	40
Caliper Bracket To Knuckle	81	Strut Shaft Nut	37
Control Arm To Cradle (Bolt)	92	Strut To Steering Knuckle	148
Control Arm To Cradle (Nut)	74	Tension Strut Bracket To Cradle	103
Control Arm To Tension Strut	106	Tie Rod End To Steering Knuckle	33
Intermediate Shaft To Steering Gear Pinch Bolt	35	Upper Strut Mount	21
Power Steering Pump Bracket	28	Wheel Lug Nuts	100
Power Steering Pressure & Return Line Fittings	20	① —DOHC.	

WHEEL ALIGNMENT

INDEX

Fig. 1   Front & rear camber adjustment

Fig. 2   Rear toe adjustment

Fig. 3   Measuring vehicle trim height

PRELIMINARY INSPECTION

1. Road test vehicle.
2. Inspect tires for proper inflation, wear pattern or out of round condition.
3. Inspect suspension and steering components for wear and damage.
4. Inspect strut bushings for wear or damage.
5. Inspect vehicle ride height.

FRONT WHEEL ALIGNMENT

Rear wheel alignment must be set to specifications before front alignment adjustment.

CASTER

1. Lock steering wheel in straight ahead position.
2. Remove upper strut mount attaching nuts.
3. Slide strut forward or rearward, to adjust, 1.57 inch will change caster by about 1/2°. **Body attachment holes may need to be filed or ground into oval slots, to allow enough front to rear strut movement to adjust caster to specifications, do not exceed .354 inch in slot width.**
4. Install upper strut mount attaching nuts, then **torque** to 74 ft. lbs.
5. Recheck caster angle.

CAMBER

1. Lock steering wheel in straight ahead position.
2. Loosen two strut to knuckle fasteners, then pull or push to adjust.
3. If more then three degrees or camber is desired, check for bent suspension components.
4. If suspension is ok, proceed as follows:
   a. Raise and support vehicle.
   b. Remove wheel assembly.
   c. Remove strut to knuckle attaching bolts, then separate knuckle from strut bracket.
   d. Using a file or grinder, remove material from strut bracket lower hole, **Fig. 1.**
   e. To increase negative camber, remove from outside hole, to increase positive camber, remove from inside hole.
   f. **Torque** strut to knuckle attaching bolts to 148 ft. lbs.
   g. Install wheel assembly, **torque** wheel lug nuts to 100 ft. lbs., then recheck camber setting, lower vehicle.

TOE IN

1. Lock steering wheel in straight ahead position.
2. Loosen left and right outer tie rod jam nuts.
3. Turn inner tie rod, by flats, to change toe.
4. After adjustment, **torque** outer tie rod end jam nuts 74 ft. lbs.
5. **Ensure seals do not become twisted.**
6. Recheck toe angle.

REAR WHEEL ALIGNMENT

CASTER

Rear wheel caster is not adjustable.

CAMBER

1. Loosen two strut to knuckle fasteners, then pull or push to adjust.
2. If more then 1.5° of camber is desired, check for bent suspension components.
3. If suspension is ok, proceed as follows:
   a. Raise and support vehicle.
   b. Remove wheel assembly.
   c. Remove strut to knuckle attaching bolts, then separate knuckle from strut bracket.
   d. Using a file or grinder, remove material from strut bracket lower hole, **Fig. 1.**
   e. To increase negative camber, remove from outside hole, to increase positive camber, remove from inside hole.
   f. **Torque** strut to knuckle attaching bolts to 148 ft. lbs.
   g. Install wheel assembly, **torque** wheel lug nuts to 100 ft. lbs., then recheck camber setting, lower vehicle.

TOE IN

1. Loosen rearmost lateral link to crossmember attaching bolts.
2. Using tool No. SA9158C or equivalent, move lateral link to adjust, **Fig. 2.**
3. **Torque** lateral link to 89 ft. lbs.
4. Recheck toe, then repeat for other wheel.

VEHICLE RIDE HEIGHT

1. Place vehicle on level surface.
2. If fuel tank is not full, the following weight must be added to the trunk, to simulate a full tank:

a. ¹/₈ tank, add 70 lbs.
b. ¹/₄ tank, add 60 lbs.
c. ³/₈ tank, add 50 lbs.
d. ¹/₂ tank, add 40 lbs.
e. ⁵/₈ tank, add 30 lbs.
f. ³/₄ tank, add 20 lbs.
g. ⁷/₈ tank, add 10 lbs.

3. Bounce front and rear suspension to allow suspension to settle.
4. With front tire pressure of 30 psi and rear of 26 psi, measure vehicle ride height, **Fig. 3.**
5. Measure from front (A) or rear (B) of rocker flange, to locate vehicle height measuring points J (front rocker height) and K (rear rocker height).
6. **On Sedan models,** A is 4.6 inch and B is 4.1 inch.
7. **On Coupe models,** A is 5.9 inch and B is 5.4 inch.
8. **On all models,** measure vehicle height from level surface, to bottom horizontal surface of rocker panel. **Do not measure from rocker/jacking flange**
9. **On Coupe models,** J should be 7.8-9.1 inch and K should be 7.9-9.4 inch.
10. **On Sedan models,** J should be 7.8-9.0 inch and K should be 8.0-9.3 inch.
11. **On Coupe SC 1 models with aluminum wheels,** J should be 8.2-9.1 inch and K should be 8.3—9.5 inch.
12. **On Wagon models,** J should be 7.8-9.1 inch and K should be 8.1—9.5 inch.
13. **On all models,** when measuring alignment angles, vehicle trim height must be accurate, if not, add or remove weight until height is correct.

AIR CONDITIONING

TABLE OF CONTENTS

Troubleshooting

INDEX

PRELIMINARY CHECKS

Most A/C system malfunctions can be detected by a thorough inspection of the system and components.
1. Check the air intake duct, lower air deflector, condenser to radiator seal and the rear hood seal for missing or damaged parts.
2. Check outer surfaces of radiator and condenser cores to ensure air flow is not blocked by dirt, leaves or other matter.
3. Check for kinks in hoses and lines and refrigerant leaks using an electronic leak detector.
4. Check for a worn or loose compressor belt or malfunctioning belt tensioner.
5. Check blower motor operation at all speeds.
6. With blower on High, check for equal distribution of air out of all outlets.
7. Check operation of control mode lever and the distribution of air from the designated outlets.
8. Press "Recirc" button with blower on high. A noticeable increase in air flow and sound should occur. Indicator should illuminate.
9. Start engine and run until normal operating temperature is reached.
10. Check operation of temperature control lever and air outlet temperature from hot to cold.
11. Press "A/C" button. Indicator should illuminate.
12. Check compressor for clutch engagement, slippage or noise.
13. Check electric cooling fan operation with A/C on.
14. Turn A/C off. Compressor clutch should disengage.

LEAK TESTS

Whenever a refrigerant leak is suspected in the system or a service operation performed which results in disturbing lines or connections, it is recommended to test for leaks.

LIQUID LEAK DETECTORS

There are a number of locations on the air conditioning system where a liquid leak detector solution may be used to pinpoint refrigerant leaks. Apply soap solution to the area in question. Any indication of bubbles will indicate a system leak.

ELECTRONIC LEAK DETECTORS

For restricted access areas, an electronic leak detector J-23400 or equivalent should be used.

The H-10 leak detector No. J-26934 or equivalent, is a 110 volt AC powered tester, while the refrigerant leak detector No. J-29547 or equivalent, is a portable, battery operated model. Both models provide visual and/or audible signals to indicate leak detection.

The successful use of electronic leak detectors depends upon carefully following the manufacturer's instructions regarding calibration, operation and maintenance.

Battery condition is especially important to the accuracy of the portable battery powered model and is monitored by a low battery indicator.

System Testing

INDEX

If the ambient air temperature is . . .	The pressure gauge should read–(P.S.I.)	The pressure gauge should read–(P.S.I.)	The right center air should read–(°F)
DEGREES °F	SUCTION	DISCHARGE	OUTLET °F
70	25~30	140~190	40~45
80	25~32	200~250	45~50
90	25~34	260~310	50~55
100	27~35	320~370	55~60

Fig. 1   Service stall test specifications

If the ambient air temperature is . . .	The pressure gauge should read–(P.S.I.)	The pressure gauge should read–(P.S.I.)	The right center air should read–(°F)
DEGREES °F	SUCTION	DISCHARGE	OUTLET °F
70	30~36	100~120	41~51
80	28~34	130~160	42~52
90	25~31	170~200	44~54
100	24~30	220~260	47~57

Fig. 2   45 MPH test specifications

GENERAL PRECAUTIONS

The freon refrigerant used is also known as R-12. It is colorless and odorless both as a gas and a liquid. Since it boils (vaporizes) at −21.7°F, it will usually be in a vapor state when being handled. If a portion of the liquid coolant should come in contact with the hands or face, note that its temperature momentarily will be at least −22°F.

Protective goggles should be worn when opening any refrigerant lines. If liquid coolant does touch the eyes, bathe eyes quickly in cold water, then apply a bland disinfectant oil. See an eye doctor.

When checking a system for leaks with a torch type leak detector, do not breathe the vapors coming from the flame. Do not discharge refrigerant near a live flame. A poisonous phosgene gas is produced when R-12 is burned.

Never allow the temperature of refrigerant drums to exceed 125°F. The excessive increase in temperature will cause a corresponding increase in pressure which may cause the safety plug to release or the drum to burst.

when connecting and disconnecting service gauges on an A/C system, ensure gauge hand valves are fully closed and compressor service valves, if equipped, are in the back-seated (fully counterclockwise) position. Do not disconnect hoses from service port adapters, if used, while gauges are connected to the A/C system.

To disconnect hoses, always remove adapter from service port. Do not disconnect hoses from gauge manifold while connected to the A/C system, as refrigerant will be rapidly discharged.

After disconnecting gauge lines, check the valve areas to be sure service valves are correctly seated and Schraeder valves, if used, are not leaking.

PERFORMANCE TEST

SERVICE STALL TEST

Record the manifold gauge pressures and outlet temperature with the following preset vehicle conditions:
1. Install thermometer in right center outlet.
2. Open doors and windows to stabilize interior temperature with outside ambient air temperature.
3. Press "Recirc" button.
4. Set temperature lever to full cold.
5. Select 3rd blower speed.
6. Press "A/C" button.
7. With engine warm, run at 2000 RPM.
8. Continue running until system pressures and outlet temperature stabilize (three to five minutes).
9. Record pressure and temperature.
10. Compare readings to normal system performance chart, **Fig. 1.**

45 MPH TEST

Recorded manifold gauge pressures and outlet temperature with the vehicle conditions listed under "Service Stall Test," except for the following conditions:
1. "Recirc" off (outside air).
2. Vehicle running at 45 MPH with engine fully warm.
3. Compare readings to normal system performance chart, **Fig. 2.**

System Service
INDEX

Fig. 1 Low pressure gauge hose connection

Fig. 2 High pressure gauge hose connection

Fig. 3 High & low side schraeder valve locations

MANIFOLD GAUGE INSTALLATION

Always wear goggles and wrap a clean cloth around fittings, valves and connections when performing work that involves opening the refrigerant system.

Ensure gauges read zero before installing manifold gauge set.

1. Close both hand valves of manifold gauge set.
2. Connect low pressure (blue) gauge hose to suction service port, located on the suction pipe, **Fig. 1**.
3. Hand tighten gauge hose nut, then connect adapter to high pressure gauge hose, **Fig. 2**.
4. Connect high pressure (red) gauge hose to discharge service port, located on the discharge pipe.
5. Hand tighten adapter hose nut to discharge service port.

OIL CHARGE

ADDING OIL

Adding oil to the A/C system should take place after recovery and before evacuation procedure.

1. Remove refrigeration discharge hose at the compressor pipe connection.
2. Pour the correct quantity of new Saturn compressor oil, or equivalent, into the discharge hose pipe.
3. Always lubricate new O-rings with clean compressor oil prior to assembly.
4. Properly connect hose to compressor with new O-ring. Add new oil to components before installation.

OIL CHARGE REQUIREMENTS

The A/C system requires 200 cc of Saturn Compressor Oil or equivalent.

New oil quantities must be added to the system during component replacement, as follows:

1. **Compressor:** Remove, drain and measure oil. Drain replacement compressor. Add same amount of new compressor oil as was drained from removed compressor.
2. **Evaporator:** Add three ounces of new compressor oil.
3. **Condenser:** Add one ounce of new compressor oil.
4. **Receiver-Dehydrator:** Add one ounce of new compressor oil.

SYSTEM EVACUATION

1. Connect manifold gauge set and vacuum pump to high and low side schraeder valves, **Fig. 3**.
2. Turn vacuum pump on and slowly open high and low side valves to pump. Allow system to evacuate for 20-30 minutes. Note vacuum gauge reading.
3. Close high and low side valves. Shut-off vacuum pump.
4. Watch low side gauge for vacuum loss (1-3 minutes).
5. If loss is less than 1 inch Hg., from level recorded in step 2, proceed to "System Charging."
6. If vacuum loss is greater than 1 inch Hg., from level recorded in step 2, charge with with 1/2 lb. of R-12 refrigerant.

7. Leak test, repair leaks and re-test. Disconnect high side adapter from service port and check for vacuum loss before leak testing.

SYSTEM CHARGING

Never remove a gauge line from its adapter when line is connected to the A/C system. Always remove the line adapter from the service fitting to disconnect a line. Do not remove charging hose at the gauge set while attached to the service low-side fitting. This will result in a complete discharge of the system due to the depressed schraeder valve in service low-side fitting and may cause personal injury due to escaping R-12.

1. Open R-12 source valve and allow 1 lb. of liquid R-12 to flow into system through low-side service fitting, **Fig. 4**.
2. As soon as 1 lb. has been added to system, start engine, set A/C control to upper outlets, temperature lever to max cold, blower speed on high and push A/C compressor button to the On position (button should illuminate).
3. Slowly draw in remainder of refrigerant charge.
4. Turn off R-12 source valve and run engine for 30 seconds to clear lines and gauges.
5. With engine running, remove the charging low-side hose adapter from the suction pipe service fitting. Remove quickly to avoid excess refrigerant escaping from the system.
6. Ensure an O-ring seal is inside of caps before installation, because cap is primary seal for A/C service fittings.

Failure to tighten cap will result in re-frigerant leakage.
7. Install protective caps on service fittings and hand tighten.
8. Turn engine off, then check system for leaks with electronic leak detector.

DRUM METHOD

Place R-12 drum on scale and note total weight before charging. Watch scale during charging to determine amount of R-12 used.
1. Connect manifold gauge set as follows:
   a. Connect low pressure gauge hose to low pressure service fitting on suction pipe at rear of compressor, **Fig. 4.** Do not connect high pressure line to A/C system.
   b. Connect center hose to R-12 source.
2. Open valve on drum to start flow of refrigerant.

Fig. 4 System charging valve connections

CHARGING STATION METHOD

Follow charging station manufacturer's instructions with the following exceptions:

1. Do not connect high pressure line to air conditioning system.
2. Keep high pressure valve on the charging station closed at all times.
3. Perform the entire evacuation and charge procedure through the low-side pressure service fitting on the suction pipe, **Fig. 4.**
4. Following these procedures will prevent accidental high-side vehicle system pressure being subjected to the charging station in the event an error is made in valve sequence during compressor operation to pull in the R-12 charge.

SERVICE VALVE LOCATION

Refer to **Figs. 1 through 4** for service valve locations.

A/C Data Table

Model	Year	Refrigerant Capacity, Lbs.	Refrigeration Oil		Compressor Clutch Air Gap, Inch
			Total System Capacity, Qts.	Compressor Oil Level	
All	1991-92	2.25	.212①	②	.012-.024

① —200 cc.
② —Oil level may not be checked. If replacement is necessary, measure amount removed from old compressor, then add same amount to new compressor.

COOLING FANS

NOTE: Wire Code And Symbol Identification Located In The Front Of This Manual Can Be Used As An Aid When Using Wiring Circuits Found In This Section.

INDEX

SYSTEM DESCRIPTION

On vehicles with A/C, the cooling fan has five unequally spaced blades to provide air flow through the radiator and condenser. the fan is driven by an electric motor which is attached to the radiator support. The fan motor is activated by a coolant temperature switch.

On models less A/C, the cooling fan has four unequally spaced blades that have curled tips to provide minimum noise. A fan shroud is used to prevent recirculation of air around the fan.

DIAGNOSIS & TESTING

Refer to **Fig. 1** for electric cooling fan wiring circuit.

COOLING FAN INOPERATIVE

Refer to **Fig. 2** for electric cooling fan inoperative diagnosis.

COOLING FAN OPERATES CONSTANTLY

Refer to **Fig. 3** for electric cooling fan operates constantly diagnosis.

COMPONENT REPLACEMENT

COOLING FAN ASSEMBLY

1. Disconnect battery ground cable.

Fig. 1   Cooling fan wiring circuit

2. **On DOHC models,** remove intake air ducts and temperature sensor connector.
3. **On all models,** remove wiring harness from cooling fan motor.
4. Loosen and remove top hold-down bolts from cooling fan assembly.
5. **On models with automatic transaxles and A/C,** it may be necessary to loosen the top transaxle oil cooler line for clearance.

6. **On all models,** lift cooling fan off of lower mounting brackets. Move assembly to left and rotate counterclockwise while lifting upward past upper radiator hose.
7. Remove cooling fan assembly from vehicle.
8. Reverse procedure to install.

COOLING FAN MOTOR

1. Remove cooling fan assembly as described under "Cooling Fan Assembly, Replace."
2. While holding fan, remove fan to motor nut (lefthand thread). Pull fan off of motor shaft.
3. Remove screws securing fan motor to shroud.
4. Remove motor from fan shroud.
5. Reverse procedure to install. **Torque** motor nut to 27-44 inch lbs.

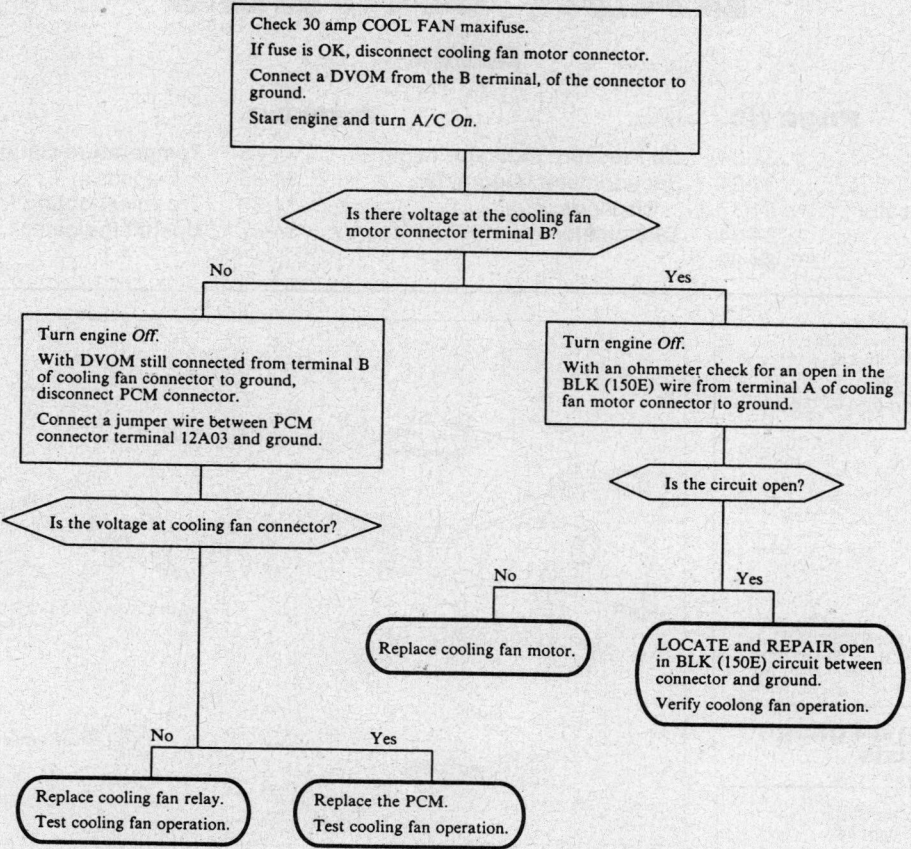

Fig. 2   Cooling fan inoperative diagnosis

Check 30 amp COOL FAN maxifuse.

If fuse is OK, disconnect cooling fan motor connector.

Connect a DVOM from the B terminal, of the connector to ground.

Start engine and turn A/C *On*.

Is there voltage at the cooling fan motor connector terminal B?

No

Turn engine *Off*.

With DVOM still connected from terminal B of cooling fan connector to ground, disconnect PCM connector.

Connect a jumper wire between PCM connector terminal 12A03 and ground.

Is the voltage at cooling fan connector?

No

Replace cooling fan relay.
Test cooling fan operation.

Yes

Replace the PCM.
Test cooling fan operation.

Yes

Turn engine *Off*.

With an ohmmeter check for an open in the BLK (150E) wire from terminal A of cooling fan motor connector to ground.

Is the circuit open?

No

Replace cooling fan motor.

Yes

LOCATE and REPAIR open in BLK (150E) circuit between connector and ground.

Verify coolong fan operation.

Fig. 3   Cooling fan operates constantly diagnosis

Disconnect negative battery cable.

Remove cooling fan relay.

Connect negative battery cable.

Does cooling fan still operate?

No

Replace engine cooling fan relay.

If the fan operates with a new relay, check for a short to ground in the DK GRN/WHT (335) wire to the PCM.

If a short is found, repair.

If no short, replace PCM.

Yes

Repair short to power in BLK/PNK (702) wire from underhood junction block to cooling fan motor.

DASH GAUGES

INDEX

IMPORTANT: To diagnose the cluster correctly, all diagnostic steps must be completed and followed in order.

IMPORTANT: Allow a short time for the gage to stabilize.

DIAGNOSTIC STEP	INPUT RESISTANCE	FUEL GAGE READING
1.	31Ω	At FULL or slightly above
2.	44.5Ω	At FULL or slightly below
3.	92Ω	At MID or slightly above
4.	106Ω	At MID or slightly below
5.	204Ω	At EMPTY or slightly above
6.	301Ω	At EMPTY or slightly below

Fig. 1   Fuel level gauge diagnosis

IMPORTANT: To diagnose the cluster correctly, all diagnostic steps must be completed and followed in order.

IMPORTANT: Allow a short time for the gage to stabilize.

DIAGNOSTIC STEP	INPUT RESISTANCE	READING
1.	5000Ω	At COLD mark or slightly below
2.	560Ω	At COLD mark or slightly above
3.	183Ω	At MID mark or slightly below
4.	151Ω	At MID mark or slightly above
5.	65Ω	At HOT mark or slightly below
6.	54Ω	At HOT mark or slightly above

Fig. 3   Temperature gauge diagnosis

Fig. 2   Temperature gauge sensor connector locations

IMPORTANT: To diagnose the cluster correctly, all diagnostic steps must be completed and followed in order.

IMPORTANT: Allow a short time for the gage to stabilize.

DIAGNOSTIC STEP	INPUT RESISTANCE	READING
1.	5Ω	At LOW mark or slightly below
2.	15Ω	At LOW mark or slightly above
3.	68Ω	At MID mark or slightly below
4.	89Ω	At MID mark or slightly above
5.	145Ω	At 3/4 mark or slightly below
6.	222Ω	At 3/4 mark or slightly above

Fig. 4   Oil pressure gauge diagnosis

FUEL LEVEL GAUGE

The fuel gauge receives a variable resistance signal from the fuel sender, located in the fuel tank. This signal is a function of the amount of fuel remaining in the tank. This variable resistance regulates the current through the coil windings of the fuel gauge, which in turn deflects the gauge pointer.

DIAGNOSIS

1. Disconnect in-line fuel connector, located in the rear compartment on the driver side behind the carpet.

2. Using cluster tester tool No. SA9205Z or equivalent, and a digital multimeter (set to OHMS scale), connect the leads to terminals B and C of the connector going to the front of the vehicle.
3. Turn ignition switch to Run position (do not start engine).
4. Set resistances as shown in **Fig. 1.**
5. If fuel gauge reading is not accurate, replace cluster.

TEMPERATURE GAUGE

The temperature gauge receives a variable resistance signal from the coolant temperature gauge sender. This variable resistance regulates the current through the coil windings of the temperature gauge, which in turn deflects the gauge pointer.

DIAGNOSIS

1. Disconnect coolant temperature sensor connector, located on the upper front left side of engine, **Fig. 2.**
2. Using cluster tester tool No. SA9205Z or equivalent, and a digital multimeter (set to OHMS scale), connect one lead to coolant temperature sensor connector and the other lead to en-

gine ground.
3. Turn ignition to Run position (do not start engine).
4. Set input resistances as shown in **Fig. 3.**
5. If temperature gauge is not accurate, replace cluster.

OIL PRESSURE GAUGE

The oil pressure gauge receives a variable resistance signal from the oil pres-

X — Most Probable Cause(s)
● — Possible Causes

COMPLAINT–CONDITION	IGN4 Fuse	IGN1 Fuse	IP Batt Fuse	HB TT Fuse	INJ Fuse	Circuit 153T	Circuit 153K	Circuit 30A/30/30B	Circuit 803B/803/803A	Circuit 135/135A	Circuit 31/31A	Circuit 11E	Circuit 990A/990	Circuit 419/419A or 419AA	Circuit 33B	Circuit 33B/33C/153P	Circuit 33B/33E	Circuit 33B/33/155E	Circuit 35/35A or 35AA	Circuit 231/231A	Circuit 231/231A	Circuit 231/231B	Circuit 25/25A	Circuit 237A/237	Circuit 237A/237/981/155RR	Circuit 237A/237/238/155LL	Circuit 996/996A	Circuit 456/456A	Circuit 1290	Circuit 153S	Circuit 68/68A
Only the Highbeam Telltale Operable	X																														
High Beam Telltale Inoperable		X	X									●																			
Only Highbeam Telltale and Low Coolant Level Telltale Operable		X																													
Low Coolant level Telltale Inoperable						X																								X	
Fuel Level Gage always on E								X	X																						
Fuel Level Gage always on F								X																							
Engine Temp Gage always on C									X																						
Engine Temp Gage always on H									X																						
Oil Pressure Gage always on L										X																					
Oil Pressure Gage always on H										X																					

Fig. 5   Dash gauge & cluster troubleshooting (Part 1 of 4)

X — Most Probable Cause(s)
● — Possible Causes

COMPLAINT–CONDITION	Circuit 1932	Circuit 1936/2A	Circuit 940	Circuit 39C	Circuit 39E	Circuit 817B/817A/817E or 817EE	Circuit 3B	Circuit 121A/121	Circuit 8J	Circuit 139F/68/68A	Circuit 663	Circuit 664	Ignition Switch	I/P cluster	DIS Module	Fuel Level Gage Sensor	Coolant Temp Gage Sensor	Oil Pressure Switch/Sensor	Coolant Level Switch	Passive Restraint control Module	PCM	Low Brake Fluid Switch	ABS Control Module	Parking Brake Switch	Headlamp Switch	Oil Pressure Switch	Generator	Passive Restraint Latch Switch	Driver's Lap Belt Switch	Highbeam Telltale Bulb	Circuit 153Y / 153Z / 153G	Circuit 3A
Only the Highbeam Telltale Operable	X													●																		
High Beam Telltale Inoperable		X	X																						●					X	●	
Highbeam Telltale and Low Coolant Level Telltale Operable				X	X									●																		X
Low Coolant level Telltale Inoperable						X			X					●					●													
Speedometer, Odometer Inoperable				X	X									X							●											
Tachometer Inoperable								X						●	●																	
Fuel Level Gage always on E														●		●																
Fuel Level Gage always on F														●		●																
Engine Temp Gage always on C														●			●															
Engine Temp Gage always on H														●			●															
Oil Pressure Gage always on L														●				●														
Oil Pressure Gage always on H														●				●														
Fuel Level, Engine Temp, Oil Pressure Gages always on E.C.L. respectively												X																				

Fig. 5   Dash gauge & cluster troubleshooting (Part 2 of 4)

sure sender/switch. This variable resistance regulates the current through the coil windings of the oil pressure gauge, which in turn deflects the gauge pointer.

DIAGNOSIS

1. Disconnect oil pressure sender/switch connector, located on right side of engine.
2. Using cluster tester tool No. SA9205Z or equivalent, and a digital multimeter (set to OHMS scale), connect one lead to oil pressure sender/switch connector and one lead to engine ground.
3. Turn ignition switch to Run position (do not start engine).
4. Set input resistances as shown in **Fig. 4.**
5. If oil pressure gauge reading is not correct, replace cluster.

OIL PRESSURE INDICATOR LAMP

The oil pressure indicator lamp is switched to round by the oil pressure switch. When the lamp is switched to ground, ignition voltage flows through the lamp, allowing it to illuminate. This indicates that oil pressure has dropped below a specified limit.

X — Most Probable Cause(s)
● — Possible Causes

Fig. 5 Dash gauge & cluster troubleshooting (Part 3 of 4)

COMPLAINT–CONDITION	IGN4 Fuse	IGN1 Fuse	IP Batt Fuse	HB TT Fuse	INJ Fuse	Circuit 153T	Circuit 153K	Circuit 30A/30/30B	Circuit 803B/803/803A	Circuit 135/135A	Circuit 31/31A	Circuit 11E	Circuit 1625A/1625	Circuit 419/419A or 419AA	Circuit 33B	Circuit 33B/33C/153P	Circuit 33B/33E	Circuit 33B/33/155E	Circuit 35/35A or 35AA	Circuit 231/231A	Circuit 231/231A	Circuit 231/231B	Circuit 25/25A	Circuit 237A/237	Circuit 237A/237/981/155RR	Circuit 237A/237/238/155LL	Circuit 996/996A	Circuit 456/456A	Circuit 1290	Circuit 153S
Lapbelt Telltale Inoperable													X																	
Service Engine Soon Telltale Inoperable														X																
Brake Telltale Never On															X															
Brake Telltale Always On																X	X	X												
Engine Temp Telltale Inoperable																				X										
Highbeam Telltale Always On												X																		
Oil Pressure Telltale Inoperable																								X	X					
Charge Telltale Inoperable																										X				
Left Turn Signal Indicator does not Flash																														
Right Turn Signal Indicator does not Flash																														
Seatbelt Telltale Never On																											X			
Seatbelt Telltale Always On																												X	X	
Shift to D2 Telltale Telltale Inoperable																													X	
Upshift Telltale Inoperable																														X

X — Most Probable Cause(s)
● — Possible Causes

Fig. 5 Dash gauge & cluster troubleshooting (Part 4 of 4)

COMPLAINT–CONDITION	Circuit 1932/3A	Circuit 1936	Circuit 940	Circuit 39C	Circuit 39E	Circuit 817B/817A/817E or 817EE	Circuit 3B	Circuit 121A/121	Circuit 8J	Circuit 139F/68/68A	Circuit 663	Circuit 664	Battery Cable 2C/2B	Ignition Switch	I/P Cluster	Dis Module	Fuel Level Gage Sensor	Coolant Temp Gage Sensor	Oil Pressure Switch/Sensor	Coolant Level Switch	Passive restraint Control Module	PCM	Low Brake Fluid Switch	ABS Control Module	Parking Brake Switch	Headlamp Switch	Oil Pressure Switch	Generator	Passive Restraint Latch Switch	Driver's Lap Belt Switch	I/P Cluster Telltale Bulb
Lapbelt Telltale Inoperable															●						●									●	X
Service Engine Soon Telltale Inoperable															●							●									X
Brake Telltale Never On															●								●	●	●	●					
Brake Telltale Always On															●									●							X
Engine Temp Telltale Inoperable															●																X
Highbeam Telltale Always On															●											●					X
Oil Pressure Telltale Inoperable															●												●				X
Charge Telltale Inoperable															●													●			X
Left Turn Signal Indicator does not Flash											X				●																X
Right Turn Signal Indicator does not Flash												X			●																X
Seatbelt Telltale Never On															●														●		
Seatbelt Telltale Always On															●														●		
Shift to D2 Telltale Inoperable															●								●								X
Upshift Telltale Inoperable															●																X

SPEEDOMETER/ODOMETER

The speedometer receives vehicle speed information from the powertrain control module (PCM). The vehicle speed signal is passed through an RC filter to the input of the speedometer/odometer drive integrated circuit (IC), located in the instrument cluster. The high-to-low edge of the square wave input triggers the IC to produce a well defined pulse of current to the moving coil inside the speedometer gauge. The IC also counts the input transitions and uses this information to drive the stepper motor for both odometers. The vehicle completes one mile for every 4983 pulses received from the PCM.

DIAGNOSIS

If the speedometer or odometer is inoperative, a voltmeter can be used to see if there is an active signal present. Since the duty cycle of the signal is always 50 percent, the voltage will be averaged.

If a correct signal is received, half ignition voltage will be present. If the signal is stuck high, full ignition voltage will be present. If signal is shorted to ground, zero volts will be present.

TACHOMETER

The tachometer receives engine RPM information from the distributorless ignition system (DIS) module. The engine RPM signal is buffered by an RC filter/limiting diode and sent to the tachometer drive integrated circuit (IC), both located within the instrument cluster. The IC receives a low-to-high square wave signal, and produces a well defined pulse of current to the moving coil inside the tachometer. The engine completes one revolution for every two pulses received from the DIS module.

LOW COOLANT LEVEL INDICATOR

The low coolant indicator lamp is connected to ground by an 820 ohm, 1/2 watt resistor, located in the instrument cluster. When the coolant level is adequate, it is pulled up to IGNITION 1 by the coolant level switch. If the coolant level is below a specified level, this switch opens and the input level drops to GROUND. This signal activates a counter integrated circuit (IC) which, after a 8-12 second delay, drives an NPN transistor and turns on the indicator lamp. This indicates that the coolant level is low.

During engine start-up, the LOW COOLANT indicator lamp is illuminated, for 2-3 seconds, by the integrated circuit built into the instrument cluster for a bulb check.

UPSHIFT INDICATOR LAMP

The upshift indicator lamp is pulled to ground by the powertrain control module (PCM). When the lamp is pulled to ground, ignition voltage flows through the lamp, allowing it to illuminate. This indicates when to shift to the next highest gear for maximum fuel mileage.

TROUBLESHOOTING

Refer to **Fig. 5,** for dash gauges and cluster troubleshooting.

STARTER MOTORS

INDEX

X — Most Probable Cause(s)
● — Possible Causes

COMPLAINT–CONDITION \ CAUSE	IGN3 Fuse	Circuit 151A	Circuit 1930A	Circuit 5/6/6B (Manual Trans only)	Circuit 5A/6A/6X (Auto Trans only)	Circuit 2B	Ignition Switch	Clutch Starter Switch	Neutral Starter Switch	Starter Motor/Solenoid	Battery	Engine Mechanical	Flywheel–Pinion gap	Extreme Cold	Mating Surfaces	Theft Deterrent
Starter Dead, No Click From Solenoid	X		X	X	X		●	●	●	X	X					●
Starter Dead, Solenoid Does Click						X				X	X	●		●		
Starter Cranks Slowly	X									●	X	●		●	●	
Starter Does Not Engage										X			●			

Fig. 1   Troubleshooting (Part 1 of 3)

DESCRIPTION

Automatic transmission models use a 1.876 hp (1.4 kW) planetary gear reduction starter. While manual transmission models use a 1.072 hp (0.8 kW) planetary gear reduction starter.

These planetary gear reduction starters consist of an armature, a frame with permanent magnet poles, a planetary drive mechanism, a solenoid, and a housing. The starters use a planetary gear drive between the armature and motor pinion. The gear drive allows the use of permanent magnets eliminating heat that normally would be produced by coil fields, and also simplifies motor construction since there are no internal field coils and connections.

TROUBLESHOOTING

Refer to **Fig. 1,** for starter motor troubleshooting.

DIAGNOSIS & TESTING

ON-VEHICLE STARTER TEST

Ensure battery is in satisfactory condition before performing test. If battery power is insufficient, the start motor will not function properly.

Electronic System Tester tool No. SA9154Z or equivalent, is required for the following starter system test.

1. Connect red and black tester cables to battery. Place gray inductive current pick-up around positive battery cable.
2. Ensure arrow on gray inductive current pick-up is pointing toward starter motor solenoid.
3. Disable ignition system by disconnecting electrical connection at ignition module.
4. Press "Starter Test" button on system tester.
5. Position tester so the display can be seen from driver's seat. When display reads "Crank Engine," turn ignition to Start position.
6. Tester will continue to display "Crank Engine" for 15 seconds.
7. The System Tester will display the following information:
   a. Cranking Amps: This displays the average amperage drawn by the starter motor during cranking. Refer to **Fig. 2,** for normal operation amperage specifications.
   b. Cranking Voltage: This displays the average battery voltage during cranking. If the voltage is below 9.5 volts, ensure battery is in satisfactory condition and properly charged. Correct cranking voltage and a slow stator indicates loose or corroded cables.
   c. Good Starter/Bad Starter: If display reads "Bad Starter," replace starter motor only after determining there is no engine mechanical malfunctions or flywheel binding problems.

Fig. 1 Troubleshooting (Part 3 of 3)

COMPLAINT	POSSIBLE CAUSE	CORRECTION
No click, no crank during starting.	If voltage at the starter switch terminal is less than 9 volts, then the control circuit is the probable cause.	Check starter ground: a. paint on mounting surface b. battery negative ground. c. other loose connections
	If voltage at the starter switch terminal is greater than 9 volts, then the motor is the probable root cause.	Replace the starter motor.
Click, no crank during startup.	If voltage at the starter switch terminal is greater than 6 volts, possible causes could be damaged internal starter ground, excess solenoid temperature, excess voltage drop between the brushes and commutator, or defect at internal solenoid connection.	Replace the starter motor.
	If voltage at the starter switch terminal is greater than 6 volts a possible cause could be the radial and axial fit between the pinion and flywheel.	Replace starter or flywheel, whichever is found to be damaged.
	Check distance between the flywheel and pinion, check flywheel runout.	NOTE: Saturn starter motors are not to be shimmed.
Starter motor continues to run with pinion extended after starting.	Starter motor internal short (at contact assembly or solenoid coil) or external short between battery and switch terminal.	Check external ring terminals and wires for possible touching between battery and switch terminal lead. If no external short exists, replace starter motor.
Starter motor continues to run with pinion retracted after startup.	Internal starter motor damage; either electrical (welded contact, short between motor and battery terminal) or mechanical (contact rod).	Replace starter motor.
Whine on disengagement after starting.	Internal starter motor mechanical problem (spline to drive interference, shift mechanism hang-up, plunger hang-up) or pinion to ring rear interference.	Replace starter motor. Check flywheel to pinion distance and runout.
Noisy during starting.	Internal starter motor problem: gear noise or pole rub with armature.	Replace starter motor.

Fig. 1 Troubleshooting (Part 2 of 3)

Complaint/Condition	Possible Causes	Correction
High pitched whine during cranking (before the engine fires over), but engine cranks and starts.	The distance between the flywheel and starter pinion is too great. Check the flywheel for damage such as a bent flywheel or excessive or unusual wear patterns.	Start the engine and carefully touch the outside diameter of the flywheel with chalk or crayon to show high point of tooth runout when the engine is turned off.
		Turn the engine off and rotate the engine by hand so that the marked teeth are in the area of inspection. If the runout is present, the flywheel may have to be replaced. If no runout exists, check the starter drive gear and starter housing for any unusual conditions that would cause it not to mesh properly. If a problem exists, replace the starter motor. IMPORTANT: starter motors are not shimmed.
High pitched whine after engine fires over as key is being released (starter hang-in, or solenoid weak).	The distance between the flywheel and starter pinion is too small.	Check flywheel runout if it is acceptable, replace the starter motor. IMPORTANT: The starter motor is not shimmed for service.
A loud whoop after the engine fires over; but while the starter is still engaged. May sound like a siren if engine is revved while the starter is engaged.	The most probable cause is a damaged or over-running clutch.	Replace the starter motor.
A rumble or growl, or in several cases a knock as the starter motor is coasting down to a stop after starting the engine.	The most probable cause is a bent or unbalanced starter armature.	Replace the starter motor.
High pitched whine during starting.	Check the flywheel for damage such as a bent flywheel or unusual wear patterns.	Start the engine and, using chalk, mark the high point of the tooth runout when the engine is turned off. If the runout is present, the flywheel may have to be replaced. If no runout exists, the starter gear or housing may be preventing the gears from meshing properly. If a condition exists, replace the starter motor.
High pitched whine after the engine fires over.	Check flywheel runout.	If flywheel runout is acceptable, replace the starter motor.
Loud whoop after the engine fires over.	Starter motor.	Replace the starter motor.
Rumble or knock as starter motor coasts down after starting.	Starter motor.	Replace the starter motor.

CLUTCH START SWITCH

1. Check resistance through switch.
2. Circuit should be open with clutch is engaged.
3. Less than two ohms should exist when clutch is fully depressed.

Room Temperature: 5°–27°C (40°–80°F)	80–120 amps
Hot Engine: Coolant above 50°C (120°F)	70 – 110 amps
Cold Engine: 5°C (40°F)	90 – 130 amps

Fig. 2 Cranking amperage specifications

NEUTRAL START SWITCH

1. Check resistance through switch from Pin A to Pin B.
2. Circuit should be open when transaxle shifter is in R, 3 or 2.
3. Resistance should be less than 2 ohms when transaxle shifter is in P or N.

ALTERNATORS

NOTE: Wire Code And Symbol Identification Located In The Front Of This Manual Can Be Used As An Aid When Using Wiring Circuits Found In This Section.

INDEX

X — Most Probable Cause(s)
• — Possible Causes

COMPLAINT–CONDITION	IGN4 Fuse	IGN3 Fuse	IGN1 Fuse	Circuit 15A (Battery Ground)	Circuit 2C/2B	Circuit 1932	Circuit 1930A	Curcuit 3A	Circuit 300/250A/250	Circuit 39C	Circuit 25/25A	I/P Cluster	Generator	Ignition Switch	Excessive Electrical Load	Constant Running at Low RPM	Loose Belt	Broken Belt	Loose Mounting Bolts	Parasitic Load
Charge Warning Telltale Lamp Does Not Light	X		X		X			X			X	X	•	•	•					
Charge Warning Telltale Lamp stays on with Engine on													X	•	•		•	•	•	
Battery is Undercharged				X	X								•		•		•	•		X
Battery is Overcharged													X							
Lights Dim at Idle															X	•	•	X		
Lights Dim at Over 1000 RPM																	X	•	•	
Mechanical Noise													•				X		•	
Radio Noise/Hum or Whistle													•							
Output Exceeds 16V													X							

Fig. 1 Alternator system troubleshooting chart

DESCRIPTION

The alternator is constructed of a rotor mounted on bearings in two end frames, a stator assembly, six silicon diodes, an internally mounted voltage regulator and an integral mounted shield. the alternator develops AC voltages which are converted to DC current by a rectifier circuit.

The Powertrain Control Module (PCM) monitors battery voltage and will increase idle speed if battery voltage drops below a calibrated amount.

TROUBLESHOOTING

Refer to **Fig. 1** for alternator system troubleshooting procedures and **Fig. 2**, for alternator system wiring circuit.

DIAGNOSIS & TESTING

PRECAUTIONS

Before connecting any test equipment to alternator, ensure engine and ignition are off and drive belt is at correct tension.

CHARGING SYSTEM FUNCTION TEST

1. Turn ignition key to Off position. Charge indicator lamp should be off.
2. Turn ignition key to On position. Charge indicator lamp should be on.
3. Crank engine. Charge indicator lamp should turn off and stay off once the engine is running.

ALTERNATOR TEST

Electronic System Tester tool No. SA9154Z or equivalent, is required for the following starter system test.

1. Clean battery terminals and attach Electronic System Tester clamps to appropriate terminals.
2. Clamp current probe to wire leading to battery ground terminal. Arrow on probe should point toward battery.
3. Press "Charging System Test." The display should show the correct number of cylinders.
4. Run engine at 2000 RPM until display flashes "Maintain 2000 RPM."
5. Hold at 2000 RPM until counter counts down from ten seconds.
6. When ten seconds are over, run engine at idle until display reads "Maintain Idle." Hold this momentarily until the display reads "Test Complete."
7. Press "Continue" to see results. The Electronic System Tester will display voltage and current output of the alternator as follows:
   a. Voltage output should be above 13 volts.
   b. Current output should be a minimum of 60 amps.
8. If alternator does not meet the above specifications:
   a. Verify battery is charged correctly.
   b. Ensure vehicle does not have any excessive electrical loads.
   c. Replace alternator.
   d. Repeat test to verify repairs.

Fig. 2   Charging system wiring circuit (Part 1 of 2)

Fig. 2   Charging system wiring circuit (Part 2 of 2)

DISC BRAKES

INDEX

Fig. 1   Center console removal

PARKING BRAKE ADJUST

1. Disconnect battery ground cable.
2. Remove center console assembly as follows:
   a. **On models with automatic transaxles,** tape release button in on the shift lever.
   b. **On models with manual transaxles,** remove shifter knob.
   c. **On all models,** remove liner in rear storage tray and remove two screws under liner.
   d. Remove two screws on front side of console, then apply parking brake and remove trim plate below park brake lever by lifting at rear edge and working plate up evenly.
   e. Remove both ash trays, then disconnect front ash tray light from console.
   f. **On models with power windows and mirrors,** remove window/mirror switch by pushing switch forward and lifting rear edge. Disconnect electrical connectors.
   g. **On all models,** remove side trim panels from center console.
   h. Lift rear of console, **Fig. 1.** Release and push out both seat belt bezels from below console.
   i. Lift console out while feeding seat belts through console.
3. Raise and support vehicle.
4. Pull parking brake lever to third click from released position.

5. Tighten adjuster nut, **Fig. 2,** until slight brake drag is felt at rear wheel.
6. Apply and release parking brake several times.
7. Pull lever up to second click. There should be no brake drag at rear wheels.
8. Pull brake lever to third click. There should be slight drag at rear wheels. Adjust if necessary.
9. Pull lever to fourth click. Rear wheels should not turn by hand.
10. Reverse procedure to install center console assembly.

BRAKE SYSTEM BLEED

Use only DOT 3 brake fluid from a clean sealed container. **Do not use DOT 5 silicone fluid.** Do not allow fluid to come in contact with painted surfaces.

MANUAL PROCEDURE

1. Fill master cylinder reservoir, ensure reservoir is at least half full during bleed procedure.
2. If master cylinder is suspected to have air in its bore, proceed as follows:
   a. Loosen front master cylinder brake line.
   b. Using a container, allow brake fluid to flow from front master cylinder port.
   c. Install and tighten brake line to master cylinder.
   d. Slowly depress brake pedal one time and hold.
   e. Loosen front master cylinder brake line to purge air, then tighten brake line, then release pedal.
   f. Repeat until all air is bleed from cylinder.
3. If caliper or wheel cylinder is suspected, proceed as follows:
   a. Install a wrench over bleeder valve, then install a piece of transparent hose over bleeder nipple, submerge other end in transparent container of clean new brake fluid.
   b. Loosen bleeder screw.
   c. Apply brake pedal slowly and hold.
   d. Tighten bleeder screw.
   e. Release brake pedal.
   f. Repeat procedure until all air is removed from brake lines.

Fig. 2   Parking brake adjustment

4. If more than one brake line is to be bled, bleed in sequence:
   a. Right rear.
   b. Left front.
   c. Left rear.
   d. Right front.
5. Check brake pedal for sponginess, if indicated, repeat procedure.
6. When bleeding is complete, check and fill reservoir.

PRESSURE PROCEDURE

1. Clean brake fluid reservoir cap, then remove cap.
2. Fill master cylinder.
3. Install bleeder adapter tool No. SA9150BR or equivalent, to brake fluid reservoir.
4. Connect a suitable pressure bleeder to adapter.
5. Charge pressure bleeder to 20-25 psi.
6. Perform steps 2 through 6 under "Manual Procedure" for to complete bleeding process.

FRONT DISC BRAKE
BRAKE PADS, REPLACE

1. Raise and support vehicle.
2. Remove front wheel assemblies.
3. Remove caliper lockpin.
4. Pivot caliper upward around guide pin.
5. Remove brake pads.
6. Remove two pad clips from caliper support.
7. Reverse procedure to install.

Fig. 3   Rear caliper piston removal

CALIPER, REPLACE

1. Raise and support vehicle.
2. Remove wheel assemblies.
3. Disconnect caliper brake fluid lines and plug opening.
4. Remove caliper lockpin, guide pin and pin boots.
5. Remove caliper from caliper support, ensuring not to damage pin boots.
6. Remove brake pads.
7. Remove two pad clips from caliper support.
8. Reverse procedure to install.

CALIPER SERVICE

Disassemble

1. Inspect lockpin and guide pin boots for damage. replace as required.
2. Inspect piston boot and lockpin for damage, replace as required.
3. Using a small screwdriver, remove piston boot ring and boot.
4. Pad caliper interior with a suitable cushion, then apply non-lubricated compressed air to caliper inlet hole to remove piston.
5. Remove piston seal, then bleeder valve and cap.
6. Clean all parts in clean denatured alcohol, then dry with non-lubricated compressed air, then blow out all caliper body and bleeder valve passages.
7. Inspect piston for damage, replace as required.
8. Inspect caliper bore for damage, slight corrosion may be removed using suitable crocus cloth, is excessive damage, replace caliper. **Do not hone caliper bore.**
9. Inspect seal groove for damage, replace as required.

Assemble

1. Install bleeder valve.
2. Lubricate piston seal using clean brake fluid, then install, ensuring seal is not twisted.
3. Install lubricated piston boot to piston.
4. Install lubricated piston to body, push

---

piston to bottom of bore.
5. Install boot ring, ensure piston boot outer edge is smoothly seated in counterbore, work boot ring into groove near open end of caliper bore. **Do not pinch piston ring between boot ring and body.**
6. Lift piston boot inner edge to release trapped air, then install caliper and bleed brake system.

REAR DISC BRAKE

BRAKE PADS, REPLACE

1. Raise and support vehicle.
2. Remove wheel assemblies.
3. Remove caliper lockpin and guide pin.
4. Remove caliper from support and suspend with mechanics wire.
5. Remove brake pads from caliper support.
6. Remove two pad clips from caliper support.
7. Reverse procedure to install.

CALIPER, REPLACE

1. Raise and support vehicle.
2. Remove wheel assemblies.
3. Disconnect caliper brake fluid lines and plug opening.
4. Slip parking brake cable end from brake lever, then using cable release tool No. SA9151BR or equivalent, remove cable outer housing.
5. Remove caliper lockpin and guide pin.
6. Remove caliper from caliper support, ensuring not to damage pin boots.
7. Remove lockpin and guide pins from caliper support.
8. Reverse procedure to install.

CALIPER SERVICE

Disassemble

1. Inspect lockpin and guide pin boots for damage. replace as required.
2. Inspect piston boot and lockpin for damage, replace as required.
3. Using a small screwdriver, remove piston boot ring and boot.
4. Pad caliper interior with suitable cushion, then apply non-lubricated compressed air to caliper inlet hole to remove piston **Fig. 3.**
5. Remove piston seal, then bleeder valve and cap.
6. Clean all parts in clean denatured alcohol, then dry with non-lubricated compressed air, then blow out all caliper body and bleeder valve passages.
7. Inspect piston for damage, replace as required.
8. Inspect caliper bore for damage, slight corrosion may be removed using suitable crocus cloth, is excessive dam-

---

Fig. 4   Rear caliper piston installation

age, replace caliper. **Do not hone caliper bore.**
9. Inspect seal groove for damage, replace as required.

Assemble

1. Install bleeder valve and cap.
2. Lubricate piston seal using clean brake fluid, then install, ensuring seal is not twisted.
3. Install lubricated piston boot to piston.
4. Install lubricated piston to body, push piston by hand, then install tool No. SA91110NE or equivalent to piston slots, rotate piston clockwise to install, **Fig. 4.**
5. Install boot ring, ensure piston boot outer edge is smoothly seated in counterbore, work boot ring into groove near open end of caliper bore. **Do not pinch piston ring between boot ring and body.**
6. Lift piston boot inner edge to release trapped air, then install caliper and bleed brake system.

PARKING CABLE
REPLACE

1. Remove console as described under "Parking Brake, Adjust."
2. Remove adjuster nut, equalizer and cable from threaded rod.
3. Using tool No. SA9151BR or equivalent, remove parking brake cables from console bracket.
4. Raise and support vehicle.
5. Remove park brake grommet and cable assembly from floor pan.
6. Remove trailing arm/park brake cable to to body attaching fasteners.
7. Remove cable attaching nut at floor pan.
8. Disconnect cable from caliper lever, then using tool No. SA9151BR or equivalent, remove cable from brake, then remove from vehicle.
9. Reverse procedure to install.

DISC BRAKE ROTOR SPECIFICATIONS

Year	New Thickness	Minimum Refinish Thickness ①	Discard Thickness	Thickness Variation (Parallelism)	Lateral Runout (T.I.R.)
SATURN					
1991-94 ②	.710	.633	6.25	—	—
1991-94 ③	.430	.370	.350	—	—

① —All brake rotors have a discard dimension cast into them. This is a wear dimension, not a refinish dimension. Any rotor that does not meet specifications should be discarded.
②—Front.
③—Rear.

TIGHTENING SPECIFICATIONS

Component	Torque/ Ft. Lbs.
Brake Lever To Floor Bolt	35
Brake Lever To Floor Nut	23
Brake Line To Master Cylinder	18
Brake Pedal Pivot	16
Brake Pipe To Body	20
Master Cylinder To Brake Booster	20
Backing Plate To Knuckle ③	63
Bleed Valve ②	97 ①
Bleed Valve ③	66 ①
Brake Dust Shield ②	18
Brake Hose To Caliper ②	32
Brake Hose To Caliper ③	32
Brake Line To Brake Hose (RL) ③	14

Component	Torque/ Ft. Lbs.
Brake Line To Wheel Cylinder ②	32
Brake Pipe To Brake Hose ②	18
Brake Pipe To Brake Hose ③	168 ①
Caliper Lock & Guide Pins	27
Caliper Mount Bracket ②	81
Caliper To Caliper Support ②	27
Caliper To Knuckle ③	63
Wheel Lug Nuts	103
Wheel Speed Sensor To Knuckle ②	89 ①

① —Inch lbs.
② —Front.
③ —Rear.

DRUM BRAKES

INDEX

REMOVAL

1. Release parking brake.
2. Raise and support vehicle.
3. Remove rear wheels.
4. Remove brake drum. **Do not pry against brake backing plate.**
5. Remove lower return spring, **Fig. 1.**
6. Remove adjuster spring.
7. Remove leading brake shoe hold-down, spring and pin.
8. Remove adjuster assembly and lever. If difficult, pull leading shoe toward front of vehicle, then remove or turn star wheel on adjuster to shorten length.
9. Twist shoe from upper return spring engagement to remove.
10. Remove parking brake shoe upper return spring.
11. Remove park brake shoe hold-down cup, spring and pin.

12. Push park brake lever into cable spring to remove park brake cable from lever.
13. Remove park brake lever retainer and wave washer and separate from park brake shoe.
14. Reverse procedure to install.

INSPECTION

1. Inspect adjuster assembly, ensuring screw threads turn smoothly into nut over full threaded length.
2. Inspect wheel cylinder for damage, leakage or seizure, replace as required.

INSTALLATION

1. Lubricate adjuster assembly, adjuster lever surface, backing plate at shoe contact pads and park brake lever pin

Fig. 1   Rear brake assembly

2. Install park brake lever assembly.
3. Install park brake cable, through cable spring onto brake lever.
4. Install park brake shoe, hold-down pin, spring and cup.
5. Install long, straight end of upper return spring to park brake shoe.

6. Install other end of return spring to back of leading shoe.
7. While pulling leading shoe toward front of vehicle, install adjuster assembly.
8. Install adjuster lever.
9. Install leading brake shoe by installing hold-down pin, spring and cup.

10. Install adjuster spring.
11. Install lower return spring.
12. Using brake drum clearance tool No. SA91109NE or equivalent, drum inner diameter, then measure brake shoe assembly outer diameter, adjust brake adjuster to obtain .050 inch measurement less than drum inner diameter.

DRUM BRAKE SPECIFICATIONS

Model	Brake Drum I.D., Inch	Minimum Refinish Diameter, Inch	Discard Diameter, Inch
All	.787	.790	7.93

TIGHTENING SPECIFICATIONS

Component	Torque/Ft. Lbs.	Component	Torque/Ft. Lbs.
Backing Plate To Knuckle	63	Brake Pipe To Brake Hose	168 ①
Bleed Valve	66 ①	Wheel Cylinder To Backing Plate	89 ①
Brake Line To Brake Hose (RL)	14	Wheel Lug Nuts	103

①—Inch lbs.

AUTOMATIC TRANSAXLE

INDEX

PRECAUTIONS

AIRBAG SYSTEM DISARMING

1. Place ignition in OFF position, then remove Supplemental Inflatable Restraint (SIR) fuse.
2. Remove connector position assurance (CPA) device from yellow two way SIR connector at base of steering column.

AIRBAG SYSTEM REARMING

1. Place ignition in Off position, then connect yellow two way SIR connector at base of steering column, then install CPA device to connector.
2. Install SIR fuse.
3. Turn ignition switch to Run position, then ensure AIRBAG lamp flashes 7 to 9 times, then remains Off.

IDENTIFICATION

The transaxle identification plate is located on the torque converter housing, **Fig. 1.**

DESCRIPTION

This automatic four speed transaxle is a fully automatic unit consisting of four multiple disc clutches, a four element torque converter with a lock up clutch, 1st gear sprag clutch and a servo actuated dog clutch.

The transaxle uses and electronic control system. The unit uses five electrohydraulic actuators in conjunction with a powertrain control module (PCM) and its sensors to control shift timing, shift feel and on-board diagnostics.

MAINTENANCE

FLUID LEVEL CHECK

1. Start engine and allow to reach normal operating temperature.
2. Position vehicle on level surface.
3. Apply parking brake.
4. Move selector through all gears.
5. Move gear selector to P (park) position.
6. Allow engine to idle for three minutes with accessories off.
7. Check fluid level, color and condition.

FLUID CHANGE

1. Fluid may be drained when operating temperature of 190-200°F is reached.
2. Turn engine off, then raise and support vehicle.
3. Remove transaxle drain plug, then allow fluid five minutes to drain.

Fig. 1   Transaxle identification

4. Install new drain plug washer and drain plug, the **torque** plug to 40 ft. lbs.
5. Fill transaxle with to correct fluid level.

TROUBLESHOOTING

Refer to **Fig. 2**, for transaxle troubleshooting.

IN-VEHICLE REPAIRS

SELECTOR SWITCH, REPLACE

Removal

1. Remove air induction tube.
2. **On models equipped with DOHC engine,** remove air filter box, then lift resonator upward to disengage from service support bracket.
3. **On all models,** disconnect gear selector switch electrical connector.
4. Remove control lever shaft attaching nut, then remove manual lever, noting position.
5. Remove two selector switch to transaxle case attaching bolts, then remove.

Installation

1. Install switch to transaxle, then install switch to case attaching bolt and finger tighten.
2. Install manual lever to control shaft attaching nut, then tighten to specifications.
3. Adjust switch as follows:
   a. Place transaxle in D4 position, then using a suitable ohmmeter check for continuity across selector switch terminals, if continuity is not indicated, rotate switch until continuity is present.
   b. Tighten switch to case attaching bolts to specifications, then recheck for continuity.
4. Install cable to control lever, then ad-

just cable as outlined under "Shift Cable, Replace."
5. Connect switch electrical connector.
6. Install air induction tube and tighten attaching bolts to specifications.

SHIFT CABLE, REPLACE
Removal

1. Remove console assembly as follows:
   a. Tape release button on shifter lever handle.
   b. Remove rear storage tray liner, then remove two screws below liner.
   c. Remove two front console attaching screws.
   d. Apply parking brake, then remove trim panel below park brake lever.
   e. Remove ashtrays, then disconnect front ashtray electrical connector.
   f. **On models equipped with power window/mirrors,** lift window/lock/mirror switch rear edge, slide switch rearward, then disconnect electrical connectors.
   g. **On all models,** remove side trim panels.
   h. Lift rear of console, then from below console, release and push out seat belt bezels.
   i. Lift console while feeding seat belts through console.
2. Position shifter in second gear, then disconnect cable end from shifter.
3. Depress two cable tabs on cable housing, then remove cable from shifter assembly.
4. Remove air induction tube.
5. Disconnect cable from shifter lever.
6. Depress two cable retaining tabs, then remove cable from converter housing.
7. Raise and support vehicle.
8. Remove cable grommet from front of dash, then remove two attaching nuts and feed grommet plate through dash hole.

Installation

1. Feed cable and plate through front of dash, then install plat and tighten attaching nuts to specifications.
2. Connect cable to shift lever assembly.
3. Install cable housing to shifter assembly.
4. Install console assembly.
5. Install cable to converter housing.
6. Ensure transaxle and shifter are in park position.
7. Release cable adjustment lock tab, using a screwdriver, to pry lock tab up, then lift with hand.
8. Connect cable to shift lever, then install retainer.
9. Move cable housing back and forth in adjuster, noting endplay:
   a. Center cable housing in middle of endplay.
   b. Press in lock tab.
   c. Verify correct operation.
10. Install air induction tube.

PARK LOCK CABLE, REPLACE
Removal

1. Remove console assembly as outlined under "Shift Cable, Replace."
2. Remove three ignition switch bezel attaching screws, then remove bezel.
3. Place ignition switch on, depress cable retaining tab, then remove cable from ignition module.
4. Unsnap park lock cable end terminal from shifter plastic lock out lever.
5. Depress cable housing end fitting tabs, then remove cable from shifter assembly.
6. Remove cable, noting cable routing.

Installation

1. Ensure cable is routed through accelerator pedal bracket retainer.
2. Install cable, route cable same as cable was removed.
3. Turn ignition on, install cassette end of cable to ignition module, then turn ignition off.
4. Install park lock cable fitting end to shifter assembly, ensuring completely seated.
5. Using a screwdriver, lift cable end fitting lock tab to allow housing to move freely in end fitting.
6. Attach park lock cable end terminal to plastic lock out lever on shifter.
7. Adjust park lock cable as follows:
   a. With ignition off, shifter in park, depress cable end fitting lock and remove adjustment clip from new cable end terminal.
   b. If connecting a cable that does not have an adjustment clip, adjust clip to provide .005 inch gap between cable and end and cable to park lock connector.
8. Verify park lock operation as follows:
   a. With ignition off and shifter in park, attempt to shift lever out of park, lever should not shift out of park.
   b. Turn ignition to on position, then attempt to shift lever out of park, lever should shift out of park.

X — Most Probable Cause(s)
● — Possible Causes

COMPLAINT–CONDITION	MAT	CTS	Dis. Primary	Dis. Secondary	Fuel Delivery System	EGR System	TPS	MAP Sensor	Eng. Vac.	Engine Mech. System	PCM/TC Calibration	Trans. 1st Gear Hyd./Mech.	Trans. Line Act. System	Trans. 2nd Act. System	Trans. 3rd Act. System	Trans. 4th Act. System	Trans. TCC Act. System	Trans. Hydra/Mech.	Trans. Perf/Norm Sw.	Shift to 2 Lt. Circuit	PRNDL Sel. Circuit	Brake Switch Circuit	Trans. Master Enable Circuit	Clutch Clearance	Gear Clearance Incorrect	1st Clutch Defective	2nd Clutch Defective	3rd Clutch Defective	4th Clutch Defective	Park Pawl Mech.	Reverse Fork Mech.	TCC Defective	Input Shaft Nut
Trans Hard Up–Shift:	X	●	●		●	X	●	X			●		X					●	●					X				●		'			
1st–2nd													X	●													●	●					
2nd–3rd													X	●	●													●	●				
3rd–4th													X		●	●																	
Trans Vibration:			●	●													X	X															
While Cruising			●	●													●	X															
Idling			●	●					●									X															
Accelerating			●	●													●	X															
Cold Ambient			●	●													●	X															
Normal Operating Temperature			●	●													●	X															
Cold Engine	X	●															●	●															
Decelerating					●												●	●															
Accessory Load			●														●	X															
Under Load			●														●	X															
Always			●														●	X															
Trans Shudder:			●	●	●					●					●	●	●	●															
Acceleration				X										●	●	●	●																
Normal Operating Temperature				●													●	●															
Deceleration																	●	●															
Braking																									●								
Under Load		●	X	●	●									●	●	●	●	●															
2nd Gear			X												●		X	●															
3rd Gear			X		●											●	X	●															
4th Gear			X			X										●	X	●															
Reverse			●														●	X															

Fig. 2 Troubleshooting chart (Part 1 of 2)

c. With lever out of park, turn ignition to off position, key should be able to be removed from ignition.

d. Attempt to shift lever to park, this should not be allowed.

e. Turn ignition off, then attempt to remove ignition key, removal should occur.

f. If steps a through e are not as indicated, re-adjust cable.

9. Install lower ignition switch bezel attaching screws.

10. Install console assembly.

VALVE BODY, REPLACE
Removal

1. Disconnect battery terminals. **Disconnect ground terminal first.**
2. Remove battery shield, then battery.
3. Remove battery tray.
4. Loosen transaxle connector bolt, then disconnect electrical connector.
5. **On models equipped with ABS,** remove master cylinder to booster attaching nuts, then lift cylinder slightly to remove valve body cover, then position cylinder back on booster studs.
6. **On all models,** remove valve body cover attaching bolts.
7. Remove eleven valve body to case bolts as shown in **Fig. 3.**

Installation

1. Install manual valve to manual link with manual valve flat facing upwards.
2. Lower valve body, then install manual link to manual valve.
3. Valve body to case attaching bolts must be placed in the valve body prior to installation, **Fig. 4.**
4. Clean and lubricate attaching bolts with Dexron II or equivalent.
5. Tighten valve body bolts in sequence, **Fig. 5,** to specifications.
6. Tighten valve body to case attaching bolts in sequence, **Fig. 6,** to specifications.
7. Using suitable carburetor cleaner, clean valve body cover gasket surface, then install valve body cover attaching bolts, in sequence, **Fig. 7,** and tighten to specifications.
8. **On models equipped with ABS,** install master cylinder to booster at-taching nuts, then tighten to specifications.
9. **On all models,** connector transaxle electrical connector, then tighten connector attaching bolt to specifications.
10. Install battery tray, then tighten attaching bolts to specifications.
11. Install battery and battery shield attaching bolts, then tighten to specifications.
12. Connect battery terminals. **Connect positive terminal first to prevent arcing.**

TRANSAXLE
REPLACE

1. **On models with airbag,** disarm airbag system as described under "Precautions."
2. **On all models,** disconnect battery ground cable, then remove air induction tube.
3. **On DOHC models,** lift resonator upward to disengage from engine service support bracket.

X — Most Probable Cause(s)
● — Possible Causes

COMPLAINT–CONDITION	MAT	CTS	Dis. Primary	Dis. Secondary	Fuel Delivery System	EGR System	TPS	MAP Sensor	Eng. Vac.	Engine Mech. System	PCM/TCM Calibration	Trans. 1st Gear Hyd./Mech.	Trans. Line Act. System	Trans. 2nd Act. System	Trans. 3rd Act. System	Trans. 4th Act. System	Trans. TCC Act. System	Trans. Hydra./Mech.	Trans. Perf/Norm Sw.	Shift to 2 Lt. Circuit	PRNDL Sel. Circuit	Brake Switch Circuit	Trans. Master Enable Circuit	Clutch Clearance	Gear Clearance Incorrect	1st Clutch Defective	2nd Clutch Defective	3rd Clutch Defective	4th Clutch Defective	Park Pawl Mech.	Reverse Fork Mech.	TCC Defective	Input Shaft Nut
Trans Hard Downshift			●				●						X						●		●						●	●	●				
Accelerating													X							X							●	●	●				
Decelerating													X					X		X													
Shift to Two (2) Light													X					X															
Trans Slipping:													X	●	●	●	●									●	●	●	●			●	
Accelerating													X	●	●	●	●									●	●	●	●				
Normal Operating Temperature												●	X	●	●	●	●																
Cold Engine													X	●	●	●	●									●	●	●	●				
From Launch												●	X																				
1st Gear													X													X							
2nd Gear														X													X						●
3rd Gear															X													●					
4th Gear																X													●				
Reverse														X			X										X						
TCC																	X															X	
Trans Gear Missing:													X	●	●	●	●				●		●			●	●	●	●			X	
Reverse														●													X				X		
Drives in Neutral																								X	●	●	●	●	●				
Trans No Park																														X			
Trans Stuck In Park																														X			
Trans Hunting/Gears, TCC:		●			X	X	X	●	●				X	X	X	X		●		●	X												
While Cruising		●			X	X	X	●											●														
Cold Engine	X				●	●	●							●	●	●	●				●												
Under Load					X	X	X						●	●	●	●	●																

Fig. 2   Troubleshooting chart (Part 2 of 2)

Fig. 3   Valve body to case bolt removal

DO NOT REMOVE

f. Unclip oxygen sensor wire retainer from converter housing.
5. Remove top two converter housing to engine bolts, then insert suitable M12 x 1.75 x 100mm (4 inch) guide bolt with bolt head cut off, to top rear converter housing bolt hole.
6. Remove and discard DIS module to housing attaching bolts, then remove wire module coil to coolant outlet.
7. Loosen two front transaxle mount to transaxle bolts.
8. Secure radiator to upper radiator support with mechanics wire.
9. Install suitable engine support equipment, as follows:
   a. Install support bar feet on outer edge od shock tower.
   b. Connect bar hooks to engine support brackets.
   c. Position stabilizer foot on engine block to right of engine oil dipstick.
   d. Adjust hooks, then stabilize to remove looseness.
10. Raise and support vehicle, then drain transaxle fluid.
11. Remove front wheel assemblies.
12. Remove right, left and front splash shields.

DOWEL BOLT
DOWEL BOLT

Fig. 4   Valve body to case bolt location

13. Remove and discard outer cotter pin from lower ball joints, loosen attaching nut, then back off until top of nut is even with top of threads.
14. Using ball joint tool No. SA9132S or equivalent, separate ball joint from steering knuckle. **On models with ABS, outer CV joint has speed sensor ring, incorrect tool usage may**

4. **On all models,** disconnect the following electrical connectors:
   a. Actuator connector.
   b. Vehicle and turbine speed sensor.
   c. Transaxle temperature sensor.
   d. Selector switch connector.
   e. Two ground terminals from top two converter housing bolts.

Fig. 5 Valve body bolt tightening sequence

Fig. 6 Valve body to case bolt tightening sequence

Fig. 7 Valve body cover bolt tightening sequence

25. Depress transaxle connector plastic tabs, then pull cooler lines from transaxle, then install 3/8 inch rubber hose between cooler lines to prevent leakage and dirt from entering lines.

26. Using suitable powertrain support dolly and two 4 inch x 4 inch x 36 inch pieces of wood support cradle on dolly.

27. Remove four cradle to body attaching bolts, then lower cradle from vehicle, ensuring two large spacing washers between cradle and body are attached to prevent loss.

28. Lower vehicle, lower transaxle side of engine support bar hook enough to allow valve body cover to clear frame rail, then raise vehicle. **It may be requires to lower rear of transaxle to clear body by adjusting engine support equipment.**

29. Support transaxle with a suitable jack.

30. Using a large screwdriver or pry bar, separate lefthand side axle from transaxle. **Do not allow pry tool to contact axle seal or seal damage may occur.**

result in ring damage or loss of ABS.

15. Remove down pipe to manifold attaching nuts, then down pipe to powertrain stiffening bracket bolts, then down pipe to catalytic converter attaching bolts, then remove down pipe and discard front exhaust pipe to manifold and converter gaskets.

16. Remove engine to transaxle mount bracket attaching bolts, then remove bracket.

17. Remove rear transaxle mount bracket to transaxle bolts, then loosen mount attaching bolt to allow bracket to hang.

18. Remove right side steering rack to cradle bolt, then back out bolt on left side as far as possible.

19. Disconnect brake line from rear cradle bracket.

20. Remove dust cover to converter housing attaching bolts, then remove cover.

21. Remove torque converter to flywheel attaching bolts.

22. Remove front transaxle mount to cradle attaching nuts.

23. Remove lower engine mount to cradle attaching nuts.

24. Remove lower transaxle mount to cradle attaching nuts.

31. Remove lower converter housing to engine attaching bolts, then install a suitable guide bolt to lower front converter housing.
32. Separate transaxle from engine, then lower enough to reach transaxle shifter cable.
33. Disconnect shifter cable, then remove shifter cable from converter housing.
34. Lower transaxle, then using cooler cleaner tool No. SA-165T or equivalent clean oil cooler and lines.
35. Reverse procedure to install, noting the following:

a. **On models with airbag,** rearm airbag system as described under "Precautions."
b. **On all models,** tighten bolts and nuts to specifications.

TIGHTENING SPECIFICATIONS

Component	Torque/ Ft. Lbs.
Actuator Cover	97①
Actuator Valve Body Bolts	97①
Air Induction Tube To Air Box Clamp	15①
Air Induction Tube To Battery Tray	62①
Bracket To Intermediate Shaft	40
Brake Master Cylinder To Booster	20
Converter Housing To Case	18
Converter Housing To Engine Studs	74
Converter Housing To Lower Engine	96
Cradle To Body	151
Distributorless Ignition System (DIS) Module	62①
Dust Cover To Converter Housing	89①
Engine Mount To Cradle Stud	67
Engine Mount	35
Exhaust Down Pipe To Catalytic Converter	33
Exhaust Down Pipe To Stiffening Bracket	23
Flywheel To Crankshaft	59
Ground Terminal To Converter Housing	18
Input Shaft Clamp	110
Input Shaft Nut	110
Intake Bracket	22
Intermediate Shaft Support	47
Lower Ball Joint Nut	55②
Oil Cooler Line Fitting	22
Oil Cooler Line To Radiator	20
Output Shaft Nut	110
Park Pawl Assembly	22
Park Sense Switch To Console	53①
Rear Cover To Case	15

Component	Torque/ Ft. Lbs.
Rear Idle Shaft Cap	15
Rear Pitch Restrictor To Transaxle	40
Servo Cover Seal To Cover	15
Shifter To Floor	19
Starter Bracket To Intermediate Shaft	22
Stator Shaft Bolts	22
Steering Rack To Cradle	40
Tie Rod End To Knuckle	33②
Torque Converter To Flexplate	52
Transaxle Connector Bolt	27①
Transaxle Drain Plug	41
Transaxle Driver Side Mount To Cradle	40
Transaxle Front Cradle Nuts To Studs	35
Transaxle Mount To Transaxle	35
Transaxle Oil Indicator Tube	106①
Transaxle Passenger Side Mount To Cradle	40
Transaxle Pump Bolt	80①
Transaxle Shifter Cable To Plate	62①
Transaxle Temperature Sensor	70①
Turbine Speed Sensor	124①
Valve Body Cover Bolt	89①
Valve Body To Case	97①
Vehicle Speed Sensor	124①
Wheel Lug Nuts	103

①—Inch lbs.
②—Tighten, then align nut slot to cotter pin hole.

FRONT WHEEL DRIVE AXLE

INDEX

DESCRIPTION

The drive axle assembly, **Fig. 1,** consists of a tri-pot joint and an outer constant velocity (CV) joint, connected to an axle shaft. The outer CV joint has the ability to swivel, while the tri-pot joint has the ability to both swivel and move in and out. The right side of the vehicle incorporates an intermediate shaft, allowing the left and right axle shafts to be of equal length.

The drive axle should be inspected periodically for damage and wear.

TROUBLESHOOTING

CLICKING NOISE IN TURNS

Worn or damaged outboard joint(s).

CLUNK WHEN ACCELERATING FROM COAST TO DRIVE

Worn or damaged inboard tri-pot joint(s).

SHUDDER OR VIBRATION DURING ACCELERATION

1. Excessive C.V. joint angle.
2. Incorrect toe in or out.
3. Incorrect trim height.
4. Worn or damaged inboard or outboard C.V. joint(s).

VIBRATION AT HIGHWAY SPEEDS

1. Out of balance front tires or wheels.
2. Out of round front tires.
3. Worn C.V. joint(s).
4. Binding or tight C.V. joint(s).

DRIVE SHAFT REPLACE

REMOVAL

1. Depress brake pedal and loosen drive axle nut.
2. Raise and support vehicle, then remove front wheel and tire assembly and front inner splash shield. **If left drive axle or intermediate shaft is being removed, drain fluid from transaxle.**

Fig. 1   Disassembled view of drive shaft

3. Remove drive axle nut and washer, **Fig. 2.**
4. Remove and discard lower control arm to steering knuckle cotter pin.
5. Loosen lower control arm to steering knuckle castle nut to the point where top of castle nut is even with top of ball stud. **Do not remove castle nut at this time.**
6. Separate lower control arm from steering knuckle, using removal tool No. SA9132S or equivalent, **Fig. 3.** Do

Fig. 2 Drive shaft nut & washer removal

Fig. 3 Separating lower ball joint

Fig. 4 Separating outer tie rod end

Fig. 5 Separating lower ball joint from steering knuckle

Fig. 6 Separating axle from hub

Fig. 7 Supporting drive axle assembly

not use a wedge type tool to separate joint.
7. Remove and discard outer tie rod cotter pin, then remove tie rod end castle nut.
8. Separate tie rod end from steering knuckle, using removal tool No. SA91100C or equivalent, **Fig. 4. Do not use a wedge type tool to separate joint.**
9. Remove lower control arm to steering knuckle castle nut.
10. Position a long pry bar at the proper cradle and tension strut locations, then pull down on pry bar, separating lower control arm ball stud from steering knuckle, **Fig. 5.** Pull steering knuckle away from ball stud.
11. While pulling knuckle/strut assembly away from vehicle, pull outer end of drive axle out of wheel hub. If difficulty is encountered separating axle from hub, tap on end of drive axle shaft using a block of wood and a hammer, **Fig. 6.**
12. Support or suspend drive axle assembly with mechanics wire, **Fig. 7.**
13. **When removing right side drive axle,** remove drive axle from intermediate shaft by tapping axle at correct location with a hammer, using a block of wood between hammer and drive axle, **Fig. 8.** Separate drive axle from intermediate shaft and remove from vehicle.
14. **When removing left side drive axle,**

remove drive axle by inserting a large screwdriver at correct location and prying axle out of transaxle, **Fig. 9. When inserting screwdriver between transaxle and drive axle, do not contact transaxle oil seal.** Remove drive axle from vehicle.

INSTALLATION
1. **When installing left side drive axle,** install transaxle seal protector tool No. SA91112T or equivalent, into transaxle, **Fig. 10.**
2. After drive axle splines have safely passed transaxle oil seal, remove seal protector and fully seat drive axle into transaxle.
3. **When installing right side drive axle,** insert inner end of drive axle onto outer end of intermediate driveshaft and push firmly to engage axle retaining ring.
4. **When installing both drive axles,** insert outer end or drive axle into wheel hub. Do not install drive axle to hub washer or nut at this time.
5. Install lower control arm ball stud into steering knuckle. Install ball stud castle nut but do not tighten at this time.
6. Install tie rod end to steering knuckle with castle nut and new cotter pin. **Torque** castle nut to 33 ft. lbs.
7. **Torque** ball joint stud castle nut to 55 ft. lbs. and install new cotter pin.
8. Install new axle to hub washer and nut. **Torque** axle nut to 145 ft. lbs.

9. Install front inner fender splash shield.
10. **Remove rust or corrosion from wheel mounting surfaces and brake rotors and drums. Failure to do so can cause wheel lug nuts to loosen in service.**
11. Position wheel onto hub and install wheel nuts. **Torque** nuts in criss cross pattern to 103 ft. lbs.
12. Lower vehicle from hoist and fill transaxle to correct level with proper lubricant, if necessary.
13. Connect battery ground cable.

INTERMEDIATE DRIVE SHAFT
REPLACE
REMOVAL
1. Disconnect battery ground cable.
2. Remove right side drive axle as described under "Drive Axle, Replace."
3. **On DOHC engine models,** remove intermediate shaft support bracket to intake manifold bracket fasteners.
4. **On all models,** remove starter motor bracket to intermediate shaft bracket fastener.
5. Remove intermediate shaft support bracket to engine block fasteners.
6. Remove intermediate drive assembly from vehicle.

Fig. 8   Right drive axle from intermediate shaft removal

Fig. 9   Left drive axle from transaxle removal

Fig. 10   Transaxle seal protector installed in transaxle

Fig. 11   Deflector ring from axle removal

Fig. 12   Outer CV joint retaining clamps removal

Fig. 13   Disconnecting race retaining ring

INSTALLATION

1. Install transaxle seal protector tool No. SA91112T or equivalent, **Fig. 10.**
2. Install intermediate driveshaft into transaxle. **Do not contact oil seal with shaft splines. The splines can damage oil seal.**
3. After intermediate driveshaft splines have safely passed transaxle oil seal, remove seal protector and fully seat intermediate driveshaft into transaxle.
4. Install intermediate driveshaft to engine block. **Torque** bolts to 40 ft. lbs.
5. **On DOHC engine models,** install intermediate shaft support bracket to intake manifold bracket. **Torque** bolts to 33 ft. lbs.
6. **On all models,** install starter motor bracket to intermediate shaft bracket. **Torque** bolts to 22 ft. lbs.

DRIVE SHAFT SERVICE
DISASSEMBLY

1. Clamp axle shaft in a vise.
2. If drive axle has a damaged deflector ring, remove ring from CV outer race using a brass drift and hammer and discard, **Fig. 11.**
3. Remove outer CV joint and seal as follows:
   a. Cut seal retaining clamps on CV

Fig. 14   CV joint ball removal

joint seal with side cutters or a flat screw driver. Disengage outer band from inner band at retainer peg and discard clamp, **Fig. 12.**
   b. Separate joint seal from CV joint race at large diameter and slide seal along axle shaft away from joint.
   c. Wipe excess grease from face of CV inner race.
   d. Spread ears on race retaining ring with snap ring pliers No. SA9198C or equivalent, and remove CV joint assembly from axle shaft, **Fig. 13.**
   e. Remove axle seal from shaft.
4. Disassemble CV joint as follows:

a. Using a brass drift, gently tap on cage until tilted enough to remove first ball, **Fig. 14.** Remove remaining balls in similar manner.
b. With all balls removed, pivot cage and inner race 90° to center line of outer race with cage windows aligned with lands of outer race, then lift out cage and inner race.
c. Rotate inner race up and out of cage.
d. Thoroughly clean all CV joint parts and allow to dry.
5. Remove tri-pot joint and seal as follows:
   a. Cut eared seal retaining clamp on tri-pot seal using side cutters and discard.
   b. Remove and discard earless clamp, using a small bladed screwdriver.
   c. Separate seal from tri-pot housing at large diameter and slide seal along axle shaft away from joint.
   d. Wipe excess grease from face of tri-pot spider and inside of tri-pot housing, then remove tri-pot housing from spider and shaft, **Fig. 15.**
   e. Spread spacer ring with snap ring pliers SA9198C or equivalent and slide spacer ring and tri-pot spider back on axle, **Fig. 16.**
   f. Remove spider retaining ring from groove on axle shaft and slide spi-

Fig. 15 Separating tri-pot housing from spider & shaft

Fig. 16 Spider assembly retaining ring from shaft removal

Fig. 17 Crimping small CV joint retaining clamp

Fig. 18 Crimping large CV joint retaining clamp

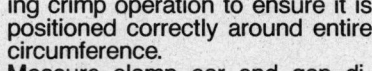

Fig. 19 Deflecting ring installation

Fig. 20 Crimping small tri-pot seal retaining ring

der assembly off shaft. **Handle tri-pot spider assembly with care. Tri-pot balls and needle rollers mat separate from spider trunions.**

  g. Remove seal from axle shaft, then thoroughly degrease housing and allow to dry.

ASSEMBLY

1. Assembly CV joint as follows:
  a. Inspect parts for unusual wear, cracks and other damage. Replace joint assembly if needed.
  b. Place a light coat of grease on all inner and outer race grooves, then insert and rotate inner race into cage.
  c. Install cage and inner race into outer race with windows of cage aligned with lines of outer race.
  d. Install balls using a brass drift to gently rotate and position cage and inner race.
  e. Pack assembled joint with grease provided with service kit.
2. Install outer CV joint and seal as follows:
  a. Install small retaining clamp on neck of new seal. Do not crimp.
  b. Slide seal onto axle shaft and locate neck of seal in proper position in seal groove on axle shaft.
  c. Crimp seal retaining clamp with tool No. SA9203C or equivalent, **Fig. 17.** Check clamp location dur-

ing crimp operation to ensure it is positioned correctly around entire circumference.
  d. Measure clamp ear end gap dimension and recrimp if necessary.
  e. Place approximately half of grease provided in kit, inside seal and pack CV with remaining grease.
  f. Position large seal retaining clamp around seal. **Ensure retaining ring side of inner race faces axle shaft prior to installation.**
  g. Push CV joint onto axle shaft until retaining ring is seated in groove on axle shaft.
  h. Slide large diameter of seal over outside of CV joint race and locate lip of seal in housing groove.
  i. Crimp seal retaining clamp with tool No. SA9203C or equivalent, **Fig. 18.** Check clamp location during crimp operation to ensure it is positioned correctly around entire circumference.
  j. Measure clamp ear end gap dimension and recrimp if necessary.
  k. Position deflecting ring at CV joint outer race, if removed.
  l. Using tool No. SA9160C or equivalent and a M20 x 1.0 nut, tighten nut until deflector bottoms against shoulder of CV outer race, **Fig. 19.**
3. Install tri-pot joint and seal as follows:
  a. Inspect tri-pot joint components for unusual wear, cracks and other damage and replace if needed.

  b. Clean shaft. If rust is present in seal mounting area, remove rust with wire brush.
  c. Install small seal retaining clamp on neck of seal. Do not crimp.
  d. Slide seal onto shaft and locate neck of seal in proper position in seal groove on axle shaft.
  e. Crimp seal retaining clamp with tool No. SA9203C or equivalent, **Fig. 20.** Check clamp location during crimp operation to ensure it is positioned correctly around entire circumference.
  f. Measure clamp ear end gap dimension and recrimp if necessary, then install spacer ring on axle shaft and beyond second groove.
  g. Slide tri-pot spider assembly past spider retaining ring groove. **Ensure counterbored surface of tri-pot spider faces end of shaft after installation.**
  h. Install spider retaining ring in groove of axle shaft with snap ring pliers No. SA9198C or equivalent, then slide tri-pot spider towards end of shaft and reseat spacer ring in groove on axle.
  i. Place approximately half of the grease provided in kit in side seal and use the remainder to pack tri-pot housing.
  j. Install new convolute retainer over seal. **Joint must be assembled with convolute retainer in posi-**

SATURN

Fig. 21 Tri-pot assembly at proper vehicle dimension

tion . Seal damage will result if joint is not assembled to correct dimension.

k. Position seal retaining clamp around large diameter of seal, then slide tri-pot housing over tri-pot spider assembly on shaft.

l. Slide large diameter of seal over outside of tri-pot housing and locate lip of seal in housing groove.

m. Position tri-pot assembly at proper vehicle dimension, **Fig. 21**.

n. Place large seal retaining clamp around seal and close with tool No. SA9161C or equivalent, **Fig. 22**.

Fig. 22 Tri-pot large retaining clamp installation

HYDRAULIC BRAKE SYSTEM
INDEX

DESCRIPTION

These vehicles use a diagonally split hydraulic system, **Fig. 1**. This system combines the left front and right rear brake on one hydraulic circuit, while the right front and left rear are on the other.

Installed in master cylinder are integral brake proportioning valves, which limit the fluid pressure to the rear brakes after a predetermined rear brake pressure has been reached. These valves are used to minimize the occurance of rear wheel lock-up when the brakes are applied and the vehicle is lightly loaded in the rear.

A brake fluid level sensor, located in the brake fluid reservoir, will activate the brake warning lamp if the brake fluid becomes low. After the brake fluid level is corrected and a moderately high brake pedal force is applied, the brake warning lamp should go off.

TROUBLESHOOTING

When troubleshooting the hydraulic brake system, perform the following checks and inspections. If a malfunction still exists within the system, refer to the brake system diagnosis chart, **Fig. 2**, and the troubleshooting chart, **Fig. 3**.

ROAD TESTING

When testing brakes, ensure the road is level and dry. Test brakes at both light and heavy pedal pressure. Do not lock up brakes or slide tires during a brake test.

Fig. 1 Diagonally split brake system

Check the tires on the vehicle before performing a brake test. Tires should be equally inflated, identical in size and of equal tread pattern. Excessive camber and caster will cause the brakes to pull. An overloaded vehicle will also brake erratically.

FLUID LEAKS

Start engine and depress the brake pedal. If the pedal gradually falls under cons-

tant pressure, the hydraulic system may be leaking. Raise and support vehicle and check all tubing lines and backing plates for signs of leakage. It may be necessary to lift or remove the carpeting or floor mats to check for booster or master cylinder leakage.

BRAKE SYSTEM BLEEDING

Brake fluid is corrosive to painted sur-

X — Most Probable Cause(s)
● — Possible Causes

Fig. 2 Brake diagnosis chart

COMPLAINT–CONDITION	Low Brake Fluid Level	Leaking Brake Line or Connection	Leaking Wheel Cylinder or Piston Seal	Leaking Master Cylinder	Air in Brake System	Contaminated or Improper Brake Fluid	Leaking Vacuum System	Restricted Air Passage in Vacuum Booster	Damaged Vacuum Booster	Worn Out Brake Lining	Glazed Brake Lining	Uneven Brake Lining Wear	Incorrect Lining Material	Contaminated Brake Lining	Linings Damaged by Abusive Use	Excessive Brake Lining Dust	Heat Spotted/Scored Drums/Rotors	Out-of-Round Brake Drums	Improper Rotor Thickness Variation	Excessive Lateral Runout	Faulty Automatic Adjusters	Incorrect Wheel Cylinder Sizes	Weak or Incorrect Brake Shoe Springs	Brake Asm. Bolts Missing or Loose	Insufficient Brake Shoe Guide Lubricant	Restricted Fluid Passage	Sticking Wheel Cylinder Piston	Incorrect Stoplamp Switch Adjustment	Brake Pedal Linkage Interference/Binding	Improperly Adjusted Park Brake
Excessive Brake Pedal Travel	●	●	●	●	X							●								●	●				●					
Brake Pedal Travel Gradually Increases		X	X	X																							●	●		
Excessive Brake Pedal Effort	●						X	●	●	●	X			●								●					●	●		
Excessive Braking Action			●						●	●	●	●		X	X	X	●					●	●							
Brakes Slow to Respond							●	●	X	●																	●	●		●
Brakes Slow to Release							●		●	●																●	●	●	X	
Brakes Drag							●		●		●										●		X	●	●	●	●		X	●
Uneven Braking Action (Side-to-Side)		●	●						●	●	●	●	X	●	X	●				●	●						●	●		
Uneven Braking Action (Front-to-Rear)		●			●				●	●	●	●	X	●	X	●											●	●		
Scraping Noise from Brakes												●	●	●	●	●							X	●	X					
Brakes Squeak During Application										●	●	●	●	●	●	●	●				●				●		X			
Brakes Squeak During Stop										●	●	●	●	●	X	●	●								X	●				
Brakes Pulsate (Roughness)																	X	X	X	●										
Brakes Groan at End of Stop										●									●							●				
Brake Warning Lamp Glows	X	●	●	●																										

faces. Care must be taken not to allow brake fluid to come in contact with painted surfaces on vehicle.

MANUAL PROCEDURE

1. Fill master cylinder reservoir with Dot 3 type brake fluid. Keep reservoir at least half full during bleeding procedure.
2. If master cylinder is suspected to have air trapped inside, it must be bled before bleeding brake lines. Bleed master cylinder as follows:
   a. Depress brake pedal slowly one time and hold.
   b. Loosen front brake line at master cylinder and allow brake fluid to flow from front master cylinder port, then tighten front brake line to master cylinder.
   c. Repeat sequence until all air is removed from master cylinder bore.
3. Loosen, then slightly retighten bleeder valves at all four wheels. Repair any broken, stripped or frozen valves at this time.
4. Proceed to appropriate wheel first and follow set sequence according to "Bleed Sequence."
5. Place transparent tube over bleeder valve, then allow tube to hang down into transparent container. Ensure end of tube is submerged in clean brake fluid.
6. Instruct an assistant to slowly depress brake pedal one time and hold.
7. Crack open bleeder valve, purging air from cylinder. Retighten bleeder screw and slowly release pedal.
8. Repeat steps 6 and 7 until all air is bled from system.
9. Check fluid level after bleeding each wheel and fill as necessary.

PRESSURE PROCEDURE

Pressure bleeding equipment must be the diaphragm type. It must have a rubber diaphragm between the air supply and the brake fluid to prevent air, moisture and other contaminants from entering brake system.

1. Clean brake fluid reservoir cap and area around cap, then remove cap.
2. Fill master cylinder reservoir with Dot 3 type brake fluid.
3. Install bleeder adapter tool No. SA9150BR or equivalent to brake fluid reservoir, **Fig. 4.**
4. Connect pressure bleeder to adapter and set pressure to 20-25 psi.
5. Loosen front brake line at master cylinder and allow brake fluid to flow from front master cylinder port until all air is bled, then tighten front brake line to master cylinder.
6. Open each bleeder valve until all air is bled, then tighten bleeder screw.
7. Remove pressure bleeder and ensure fluid level is full.

BLEED SEQUENCE

All models: RR-LF-LR-RF.

HYDRAULIC SYSTEM FLUSH

If brake fluid is old, rusty or contaminated, or whenever new parts are installed in hydraulic system, the system must be flushed. Bleed brakes, allowing at least one quart of clean brake fluid to pass through system. Any rubber parts in hydraulic system which were exposed to contaminated fluid must be replaced.

MASTER CYLINDER REPLACE

1. Disconnect battery ground cable.
2. Remove brake fluid level sensor electrical connector from master cylinder reservoir.
3. Remove brake line fitting nuts from master cylinder. **Plug open lines and fittings to prevent brake fluid loss and contamination.**
4. Remove two master cylinder to brake booster attaching nuts and master cylinder.
5. Reverse procedure to install.

FLUID RESERVOIR REPLACE

1. Remove master cylinder from vehicle as described under "Master Cylinder, Replace."
2. Wipe reservoir cap clean, remove cap and inspect reservoir cap and diaphragm for cuts, nicks or deformation. Replace damaged parts as necessary.
3. Drain brake fluid from reservoir.
4. **On models equipped with anti-lock brakes,** remove modulator and motor pack from master cylinder.
5. **On all models,** remove brake fluid level sensor.

Fig. 3 Brake pedal feel diagnosis chart (Part 2 of 6)

Complaint/Condition	Possible Cause(s)	Correction(s)
Excessive Pedal Effort	Leaking or damaged vacuum booster (i.e. cut diaphragm, restricted vacuum hose, damaged vacuum check valve, cracked power piston, restricted air passages)	Replace booster.
	Worn out brake linings (glazed)	Replace linings.
	Damage to braking surface of rotor or drum.	Replace rotor or drum.
	Crimped brake line or collapsed brake hose.	Replace line or hose.
	Engine out of specifications.	Check engine to specification.
Pedal Goes to the Floor	Low fluid level, large amount of air in system.	Bleed brake system.
	Broken brake line or brake hose.	Replace line or hose.
	Cut, torn or nicked master cylinder secondary seals.	Repair or replace master cylinder.
	Brake pedal not connected to push rod.	Check connection and repair.
	Wheel cylinder or caliper piston falls out.	Check assembly and repair.

Fig. 3 Brake pedal feel diagnosis chart (Part 1 of 6)

Complaint/Condition	Possible Cause(s)	Correction(s)
Pedal Feel		
Excessive Pedal Travel	Air in brake system.	Bleed brake system.
	Front or rear brakes not adjusting to lining wear.	Check adjuster mechanism and replace or repair as needed.
	Leaking wheel cylinder or caliper piston seal.	Replace wheel cylinder or overhaul caliper
	Leaking at brake line or hose connections.	Tighten connection. Replace line or hose.
	Internal master cylinder seal leak.	Overhaul or replace master cylinder.
	Uneven lining wear or damaged lining.	Replace lining.
	Rotor or drum out of specifications (i.e. rotor too thin, parallelism, out of round, bell shaped etc.).	Replace rotor, or drum.
	Improper vacuum booster to master cylinder length.	Replace booster and pushrod.
Pedal Creeps Down	Internal master cylinder seal leak or defective master cylinder bore.	Repair or replace master cylinder.
	Leaking wheel cylinder or caliper piston seal.	Replace wheel cylinder or overhaul caliper
	Leaking at brake line or hose connections.	Tighten connection. Replace lines or hose.
	Damaged vacuum booster check valve or grommet.	Replace check valve and grommet.
Pedal Pulses	Rotor or drum out of specifications (i.e. lateral runout, parallelism, out of round, bell shaped etc.).	Replace or turn rotor or drum.
	Worn out linings or linings wearing unevenly.	Replace linings.
	Wheel bearings worn.	Replace wheel bearing.
	Damaged suspension, knuckle or axle.	Replace defective parts.

Fig. 3 Brake pedal feel diagnosis chart (Part 4 of 6)

Complaint/Condition	Possible Cause(s)	Correction(s)
Performance		
Brake Pull Left/Right	Caliper pistons sticking.	Overhaul caliper and replace piston.
	Loose wheel bearings or suspension attachments.	Replace wheel bearings or tighten suspension attachments.
	Worn suspension components.	Replace suspension components.
	Loose steering or steering gear.	Repair or replace steering components.
	Uneven wear on tires, tires not properly inflated or incorrect tires for vehicle.	Check tire and replace if necessary.
	Uneven worn linings.	Replace linings.
	Front suspension out of line.	Align suspension.
	Restricted brake line or hose.	Replace line or hose.
Brakes Grab	Contaminated brake linings.	Replace linings.
	Damage to braking surface of rotors or drums.	Replace rotors or drums.
	Rotor or drum out of specifications (i.e. lateral runout, parallelism, out of round, bell shaped, etc.).	Replace or turn rotor or drum.
	Damaged vacuum booster.	Replace booster.
Brakes Drag	Caliper pistons stuck.	Overhaul caliper and replace piston.
	Corroded caliper bolts. Caliper will not retract.	Replace bolts and bolt boots.
	Compensating port or bypass hole in master cylinder clogged.	Clean master cylinder and rebuild.
	Worn or damaged drum brake return springs.	Replace drum brake springs.
	Contaminated or improper brake fluid, rubber seals are swollen.	Flush brake system and replace all rubber parts including hoses.
	Parking brake not releasing.	Check cable and cable attachments.
	Self-adjusters over adjusting for lining wear.	Overhaul or replace adjusters.
	Improper vacuum booster push rod length.	Gage booster push rod and replace if needed.
Brake Action Uneven (Front – Rear)	Uneven wear on tires, tires improperly inflated or incorrect tires installed.	Check tires and replace if needed.
	Proportioning valve not functioning properly.	Replace master cylinder.
	Linings wearing unevenly front to rear.	Replace linings.
	Fluid leak in system.	Check system for leaks and repair or replace components.
	Hot spots or worn surface on drum or rotor.	Replace drum or rotor.

Fig. 3 Brake pedal feel diagnosis chart (Part 3 of 6)

Complaint/Condition	Possible Cause(s)	Correction(s)
Noise		
Squeal/Scrape While Not Braking	Worn linings, sensor scraping on rotor (normal).	Replace linings.
	Loose drum brake component (spring, lever, adjuster, etc.).	Check drum brake and repair.
	Loose front suspension attachments.	Tighten attachments or replace.
	Caliper interference with rotor.	Check clearance and repair.
	Bent or cracked suspension parts.	Replace components.
	Drum or rotor contacting backing plate or dust shield.	Check clearance and repair.
Squeal/Scrape While Braking	Linings worn out, shoe contacting drum or rotor.	Replace linings.
	Lack of lubrication on backing plate or on adjuster screw.	Lubricate backing plate or adjuster screw.
	Lack of lubrication on caliper sliding surfaces.	Lubricate.
	Lack of lubrication on brake pedal attachments.	Lubricate.
	Damage to insulator between disc brake shoe and caliper piston.	Replace insulator and pads as needed.
	Hot spots or worn surface on drum or rotor.	Replace rotor or drum.
	Weak hold down springs or worn drum brake components.	Replace drum brake springs.
Chatters/Rattles	Hot spots or worn surface on drum or rotor.	Replace drum or rotor.
	Rotor or drum out of specifications (i.e. lateral runout, parallelism, out of round, bell shaped, etc.).	Replace or turn rotor or drum.
	Lining contaminated with foreign substances.	Replace linings.
	Linings wearing unevenly.	Replace linings.
	Bent or loose brake shoes.	Replace show and linings.
	Weak or broken retractor springs.	Replace drum brake springs.
	Loose brake cable, brake line, or ABS wiring.	Check cable or line connection and tighten or replace as needed.
Groans (at/near stop)	Linings worn out.	Replace linings.
	Incorrect or damaged lining material.	Replace linings.
	Hot spots or worn surface on drum or rotor.	Replace drum or rotor.
	Cracked or bent knuckle or suspension parts.	Replace suspension component.
	Loose suspension.	Tighten suspension or replace.

Complaint/Condition	Possible Cause(s)	Correction(s)
Brakes Slow to Release	Caliper piston sticking.	Overhaul caliper and replace piston.
	Corroded caliper bolts. Caliper will not retract.	Replace bolts and bolt boots.
	Contaminated or improper brake fluid, rubber seals are swollen.	Flush brake system and replace all rubber parts including hoses.
	Worn caliper piston seals.	Overhaul calipers.
	Worn or damaged drum brake return springs.	Replace drum brake springs.
	Worn or damaged master cylinder seals.	Overhaul master cylinder.
	Damage to mechanical action of brake pedal.	Check pedal and repair or replace.
Slow Response/Excessive Stopping Distance	Rotor not turned to proper surface finish.	Check rotor surface finish and turn rotor or replace.
	Linings not adjusting properly, damaged self–adjusters or worn piston seal.	Overhaul drum brake or caliper.
	Caliper pistons sticking.	Overhaul caliper and replace piston.
	Worn or glazed linings.	Replace linings.
	Proportioning valve not functioning properly.	Replace master cylinder.
Odor	Linings over heated.	
	Lining contaminated with foreign substances.	Replace lining.
Poor Fuel Economy	Linings over heated.	
	Egg shaped drum or bent rotor/knuckle.	Replace drum, rotor or knuckle.

Fig. 3   Brake pedal feel diagnosis chart (Part 5 of 6)

Complaint/Condition	Possible Cause(s)	Correction(s)
Telltale		
Red (Brake) Telltale On	Park brake on.	Release park brake.
	Low brake fluid level in master cylinder (check for leaks).	Fill reservoir. Check for leaks.
	Improperly adjusted park brake switch.	Check park brake switch connection and adjustment.
	Damaged park brake switch or switch circuit.	Replace switch or repair circuit.
	Antilock brake system (ABS) problem	Refer to ABS
Amber (ABS) Telltale On (Solid/Flashing)	Refer to ABS	
Parking Brake		
Does Not Hold	Park brake not adjusted properly.	Adjust park brake.
	Brakes not adjusting properly.	Check brake adjusters and repair or replace as needed.
	Linings worn out.	Replace linings.
	Linings contaminated with foreign material.	Replace linings.
	Cable disconnected from lever.	Connect cable.
	Lever bent or loose.	Replace lever.
	Cable slipping.	Replace cable.
Does Not Release	Park brake cables binding.	Check cable and cable attachments.
	Release lever broken or binding.	Replace park brake lever.
Parking Brake Lever Hard to Apply	Lack of lubrication on apply mechanism.	Lubricate apply mechanism.
	Park brake cables binding.	Check cables and cable attachments.

Fig. 3   Brake pedal feel diagnosis chart (Part 6 of 6)

Fig. 4   Brake pressure bleeder adapter installation

Fig. 5   Master cylinder reservoir spring pin removal

Fig. 6   Removing reservoir & O-rings from cylinder body

Fig. 7   Master cylinder retainer clip removal

Fig. 8   Removing master cylinder pistons w/air pressure

6. Place master cylinder in vice. **Do not clamp on master cylinder body.**
7. Drive out spring pins using a 1/8 inch punch, **Fig. 5.**
8. Pull reservoir out of cylinder body, then remove O-rings from grooves in reservoir bayonets, **Fig. 6.**
9. Clean reservoir with clean denatured alcohol and inspect reservoir for cracks or deformation. Replace reservoir if damaged.
10. Reverse procedure to install using new O-rings.

MASTER CYLINDER OVERHAUL

DISASSEMBLY

1. Remove master cylinder from vehicle

as described under "Master Cylinder, Replace."
2. Wipe reservoir cap clean, remove cap and inspect reservoir cap and diaphragm for cuts, nicks or deformation. Replace damaged parts as necessary.
3. Drain brake fluid from reservoir.
4. **On models equipped with anti-lock brakes,** remove modulator and motor pack from master cylinder.
5. **On all models,** remove brake fluid level sensor.
6. Remove reservoir as described under "Fluid Reservoir, Replace."
7. While depressing master cylinder piston, remove retainer clip, **Fig. 7.**
8. Apply low pressure non-lubricated compressed air into upper brake fluid output port, **Fig. 8.** This will facilitate removal of primary and secondary piston assemblies as well as spring and spring retainer.
9. Clean all parts with clean denatured alcohol. Dry with unlubricated, low pressure compressed air. Blow out all passages in cylinder body.
10. Inspect pistons and seals for nicks, cuts, cracks, wear or corrosion. Replace all worn or damaged parts.
11. Inspect master cylinder bore for scoring or corrosion. If cylinder bore is damaged, replace master cylinder. Do not hone master cylinder bore.

ASSEMBLY

1. Lubricate secondary seal and master cylinder bore with clean brake fluid.
2. Install spring and secondary piston assembly into master cylinder bore, **Fig. 9.**

Fig. 9   Master cylinder piston & seal installation

3. Lubricate primary seal and master cylinder bore with clean brake fluid.
4. Install primary piston assembly into master cylinder bore.
5. While depressing master cylinder piston, install retainer clip.
6. Install reservoir as described under "Fluid Reservoir, Replace."
7. Install brake fluid level sensor.
8. **On models equipped with anti-lock brakes,** install modulator and motor pack from master cylinder.
9. **On all models,** install master cylinder into vehicle as described under "Master Cylinder, Replace."

WHEEL CYLINDER OVERHAUL

Wheel cylinders on these models are non-serviceable and must be replaced as an assembly.

POWER BRAKE UNITS

INDEX

DESCRIPTION

The vacuum brake booster is a single diaphragm vacuum suspended unit. Engine vacuum is provided to the booster through a hose and a vacuum check valve. When the brakes are not applied, internal valves within the booster provide vacuum to both sides of the diaphragm. When the brakes are applied, air at atmospheric pressure is applied to one side of the diaphragm. Since a higher pressure now exists on one side of the diaphragm than the other, a force is created, assisting the brake application.

Fig. 1   Brake booster mounting

BRAKE BOOSTER REPLACE

1. Disconnect battery ground cable and remove air cleaner.
2. **On models with anti-lock brakes,** remove battery, battery box and tray.
3. **On all models,** remove two master cylinder to brake booster nuts and move master cylinder away from

booster without bending brake lines.
4. Disconnect vacuum hose from vacuum check valve.
5. Remove booster pushrod retainer and washer, then remove pushrod from brake pedal pin, **Fig. 1.**

6. Remove four nuts attaching brake booster, then remove booster from vehicle.
7. Reverse procedure to install. **Torque** booster to body nuts and master cylinder to booster nuts to 20 ft. lbs.

BRAKE BOOSTER OVERHAUL
Vacuum brake boosters on these vehicles are non-serviceable and must be replaced as an assembly.

ANTI-LOCK BRAKES

INDEX

Fig. 1   Anti-lock brake system

DESCRIPTION
The Anti-Lock Brake System (ABS) **Fig. 1,** minimizes wheel lockup during heavy braking on most road surfaces. The system performs this function by monitoring wheel speed and controlling the brake fluid pressure during braking. This allows the driver to retain directional stability and better steering capability.

DIAGNOSIS & TESTING
This system contains a sophisticated onboard diagnostic system that can by accessed with a bidirectional "SCAN" tool. **To properly diagnose the ABS system, a SATURN bidirectional scan tool or equivalent is necessary.** The scan tool can be used to identify system faults as specifically as possible including whether

or not the fault is intermittent. The scan tool can also be used to monitor the input and output signals of the Anti-Lock Brake Control Module (ABCM), manually control system components and perform automated functional tests. Using the scan tool allows for accurate fault confirmation and repair verification. Refer to **Fig. 2** for ABS scan tool information.

GENERAL INFORMATION		KEY ON	EXPLANATION
T-Codes	xxx	No	Indicates if trouble codes are present
LF Wheel SPD MPH	xx	0 MPH	Speed of left front wheel
RF Wheel SPD MPH	xx	0 MPH	Speed of right front wheel
LR Wheel SPD MPH	xx	0 MPH	Speed of left rear wheel
RR Wheel SPD MPH	xx	0 MPH	Speed of right rear wheel
Vehicle REF MPH	xx	0 MPH	Filtered average of all 4 wheel speeds
LF Solenoid	xxx	Off	Solenoid status (on during ABS stop)
RF Solenoid	xxx	Off	Solenoid status (on during ABS stop)
LF Command AMP	xx.x	0.0	Desired motor current during ABS stop
LF Sensed AMP	xx.x	0.0	Actual motor current during ABS stop
RF Command AMP	xx.x	0.0	Desired motor current during ABS stop
RF Sensed AMP	xx.x	0.0	Actual motor current during ABS stop
R Command AMP	xx.x	0.0	Desired motor current during ABS stop
R Sensed AMP	xx.x	0.0	Actual motor current during ABS stop
BAT Enable V	xx.x	12.6	Ignition voltage to ABS control module
LF Brake	xxxxxxx	Release	Motor direction during ABS stop
RF Brake	xxxxxxx	Release	Motor direction during ABS stop
Brake Switch	xxx	Off	Current status of brake switch
Drake Switch Cycled	xxx	No	Has brake switch been on this IGN cycle?
Brake Switch Open	xxx	No	Indicate an open brake switch circuit
ABS TT xxx		On	Status of ABS telltale
ABS TT Flash	xxx	Off	Indicated telltale is flashing
Enable Relay	xxx	On	Indicated status of ABS Enable Relay
ABS Stop	xxx	No	Indicated if vehicle is in an ABS stop
Brake TT	xxx	Off	Indicates status of ABS telltale
Brake TT Open	xxx	No	Indicates an open brake telltale circuit
25 MPH Reached	xxx	No	Has 25 MPH been reached this IGN cycle?

Fig. 2   ABS scan tool information

VISUAL/PHYSICAL UNDERHOOD INSPECTION

Before beginning any system diagnosis, it is important that a careful visual and physical inspection be performed. Inspect all vacuum hoses for correct routing, pinches, cuts or disconnects. Inspect all wires in the engine compartment and to wheel speed sensors for proper routing and connections.

ANTI-LOCK TELLTALE LAMP & RED BRAKE WARNING LAMP

The Anti-Lock Telltale lamp, located in the instrument cluster, has several functions. If the lamp comes on solid, a malfunction has occurred and the ABS system has been disabled and should be serviced as soon as possible. If the telltale lamp is flashing, a malfunction has occurred, but the ABS system is still operational. The vehicle should still be serviced as soon as possible. Because the telltale lamp is also used to perform a bulb and system check, it will come on with the key on and the engine not running. When the engine is started, the lamp will turn off after approximately three seconds. If the telltale lamp remains on or begins to flash, the self-diagnostic system has detected a malfunction.

The red brake telltale lamp will light if any of the following conditions are met: low brake fluid in the master cylinder, parking brake switch is closed, activated by the ABCM.

READING TROUBLE CODES

When performing ABS system diagnosis refer to wiring circuits, **Fig. 3 or 4**, system electrical connectors **Fig. 5** and ABCM pin identification **Fig. 6**.

To access trouble codes, connect the SATURN scan tool or suitable equivalent to the ALDL connector located under the instrument panel. The scan tool can now communicate directly to the ABCM. Any code(s) stored in the ABCM memory can now be displayed. When an ABS fault is detected, the ABS telltale lamp is lit and code(s) are placed in the General Information Table (Current Codes). When the ignition is switched off, the current codes are moved to the Malf History Table (Past Codes) and cleared from the General Information Table (Current Codes).

Refer to the "Diagnostic Chart Index" for code description and chart location.

CLEARING TROUBLE CODES

Current codes are cleared every time the ignition is turned off. To clear Malf History (Past Codes) select "Clear Codes" function on the scan tool. Past codes will clear themselves after 100 ignition cycles with no fault occurring. **Disconnecting power to the ABCM has no effect on stored codes.**

INTERMITTENTS

Most intermittent malfunctions are caused by loose or damaged electrical wiring and connectors. The scan tool can be used in several ways to aid in intermittent diagnosis. Connect scan tool to the ALDL connector with the engine not running, then manipulate wiring harnesses or components under the hood while observing the scan tool. Leaving scan tool connected to the ALDL connector, drive vehicle under conditions similar to those present when the ABS fault first occurred. If the problem seems to be related to certain parameters that can be checked with the scan tool, they should be checked at

this time. If there does not seem to be any correlation between the problem and any specific circuit, the scan tool can be checked on each position, watching for a period of time to see if there is any change in the readings that would indicate an intermittent malfunction.

The ABCM has the ability to take a snapshot of data with the last code stored. This can be done using the Malf History function of the scan tool and can be very useful when trying to diagnose an intermittent code.

SYSTEM SERVICE

ANTI-LOCK BRAKE CONTROL MODULE (ABCM), REPLACE

The ABCM is located under the instrument panel, to the left of the steering column. The ABCM and Powertrain Control Module (PCM) are located in the same carrier. The ABCM is outboard of the PCM, closest to the lefthand side kick panel.
1. Disconnect battery ground cable.
2. Remove connector position assurance locking pin from 2-way ABCM connector, then disconnect connector, **Fig. 74**.
3. Disconnect 32-way ABCM connector, then turn ABCM retaining screw 1/4 turn.
4. Remove module by pulling downward. **Avoid snagging wiring.**
5. Reverse procedure to install. **The ABCM contains a Electronically Erasable Programmable Read Only Memory (EE PROM) that must be reprogrammed when a service replacement module is installed or a Code 82 will result.**

Continued on page 34-88

Fig. 3   Anti-lock brake system wiring circuit. 1991-92 models (Part 1 of 2)

Fig. 3   Anti-lock brake system wiring circuit. 1991-92 models (Part 2 of 2)

Fig. 4   Anti-lock brake system wiring circuit. 1993–94 models (Part 1 of 3)

Fig. 4   Anti-lock brake system wiring circuit. 1993–94 models (Part 2 of 3)

Fig. 4 Anti-lock brake system wiring circuit. 1993–94 models (Part 3 of 3)

Fig. 5 Anti-lock brake system electrical connectors

Fig. 6   ABCM pin identification

DIAGNOSTIC CHART INDEX

Trouble Code	Description	Year	Page No.	Fig. No.
	No Scan Data	1991-94	34-67	7
Code 11	**Telltale Circuit Open Or Grounded**	1991-92	34-67	8
Code 12	**Telltale Or Traction LED Fault**	1993-94	34-67	9
Code 13	**Telltale Circuit Shorted To B+**	1991-92	34-69	10
Code 14	**Switched Battery Circuit Open**	1991-93	34-69	11
Code 14	**Switched Battery Circuit Open**	1994	34-69	12
Code 15	**Switched Battery Circuit Shorted B+**	1991-93	34-70	13
Code 15	**Switched Battery Circuit Shorted B+**	1994	34-70	14
Code 16	**Enable Relay Coil Circuit Open**	1991-93	34-70	15
Code 16	**Enable Relay Coil Circuit Open**	1994	34-71	16
Code 17	**Enable Relay Coil Circuit Grounded**	1991-93	34-71	17
Code 17	**Enable Relay Coil Circuit Grounded**	1994	34-71	18
Code 18	**Enable Relay Coil Circuit Shorted To B+**	1991-93	34-72	19
Code 18	**Enable Relay Coil Circuit Shorted To B+**	1994	34-72	20
Code 21	**LF Wheel Speed=0 MPH**	1991-94	34-72	21
Code 22	**RF Wheel Speed=0 MPH**	1991—94	34-73	22
Code 23	**LR Wheel Speed=0 MPH**	1991-94	34-73	23
Code 24	**RR Wheel Speed=0 MPH**	1991-94	34-74	24
Code 25	**LF Wheel Speed Acceleration Fault**	1991-94	34-74	25
Code 26	**RF Wheel Speed Acceleration Fault**	1991-94	34-75	26
Code 27	**LR Wheel Speed Acceleration Fault**	1991-94	34-75	27
Code 28	**RR Wheel Speed Acceleration Fault**	1991-94	34-76	28
Code 31	**Any Two Wheel Speeds=0**	1991-94	34-76	29
Code 36	**System Voltage Low**	1991-94	34-77	30

Continued

DIAGNOSTIC CHART INDEX—Continued

Trouble Code	Description	Year	Page No.	Fig. No.
Code 37	ABS System Voltage High	1991–94	34-77	31
Code 38	Left Front ESB Does Not Hold Motor	1991–94	34-77	32
Code 41	Right Front ESB Does Not Hold Motor	1991–94	34-78	33
Code 42	Rear ESB Does Not Hold Motor	1991–94	34-78	34
Code 44	LF Motor Frozen	1991–94	34-78	35
Code 45	RF Motor Frozen	1991–94	34-78	36
Code 46	Rear Motor Frozen	1991–94	34-78	37
Code 47	LF Motor Circuit Current Low	1991–94	34-79	38
Code 48	RF Motor Circuit Current Low	1991–94	34-79	39
Code 51	Rear Motor Circuit Current Low	1991–94	34-79	40
Code 52	LF In Release Too Long	1991–94	34-79	41
Code 53	RF In Release Too Long	1991–94	34-80	42
Code 54	Rear In Release Too Long	1991–94	34-80	43
Code 55	Motor Circuit Fault Detected	1991–94	34-80	44
Code 56	LF Motor Circuit Open	1991–94	34-80	45
Code 57	LF Motor Circuit Grounded	1991–94	34-81	46
Code 58	LF Motor Circuit Shorted To B+	1991-92	34-81	47
Code 58	LF Motor Circuit Shorted To B+	1993-94	34-81	48
Code 61	RF Motor Circuit Open	1991-92	34-81	49
Code 61	RF Motor Circuit Open	1993-94	34-82	50
Code 62	RF Motor Circuit Grounded	1991–94	34-82	51
Code 63	RF Motor Circuit Shorted To B+	1991–94	34-82	52
Code 64	Rear Motor Circuit Open	1991-92	34-82	53
Code 64	Rear Motor Circuit Open	1993-94	34-83	54
Code 65	Rear Motor Circuit Grounded	1991–94	34-83	55
Code 66	Rear Motor Circuit Shorted To B+	1991–94	34-83	56
Code 76	Solenoid Circuit 1288 Open Or Shorted To B+	1991-93	34-83	57
Code 76	Solenoid Circuit 1288 Open Or Shorted To B+	1994	34-84	58
Code 77	Solenoid Circuit 1288 Grounded	1991–94	34-84	59
Code 78	Solenoid Circuit 1289 Open Or Shorted To B+	1991–94	34-84	60
Code 81	Solenoid Circuit 1289 Grounded	1991–94	34-84	61
Code 82	ABS Calibration Fault	1991-92	34-85	62
Code 82	ABS Calibration Fault	1993-94	34-85	63
Code 86	ABS Turned On Red Brake Telltale	1991–94	34-85	64
Code 87	Red Brake Telltale Circuit Open	1991–94	34-85	65
Code 88	Red Brake Telltale Circuit Shorted To B+	1991-92	34-86	66
Code 88	Red Brake Telltale Circuit Shorted To B+	1993-94	34-86	67
Code 91	Brake Switch Circuit Open During Normal Stop	1991–94	34-86	68
Code 92	Brake Switch Circuit Open During ABS Stop	1991–94	34-86	69
Code 93	Brake Switch Circuit Open On Initialization	1991–94	34-87	70
Code 94	Brake Switch Circuit Always Closed	1991–94	34-87	71
Code 95	Stop Lamp Circuit Open NO TAG	1991–94	34-87	72
Code 96	Stop Lamp Circuit Open Or Grounds Open	1991–94	34-87	73

Fig. 7   No scan data

Fig. 8   Code 11, telltale circuit open or grounded. 1991-92 models

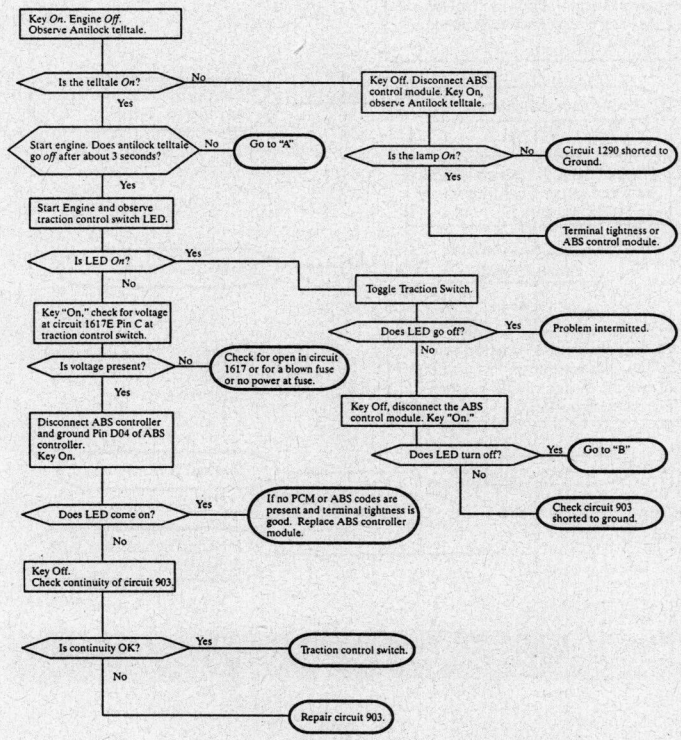

Fig. 9   Code 12, telltale or traction LED fault. 1993-94 models (Part 1 of 2)

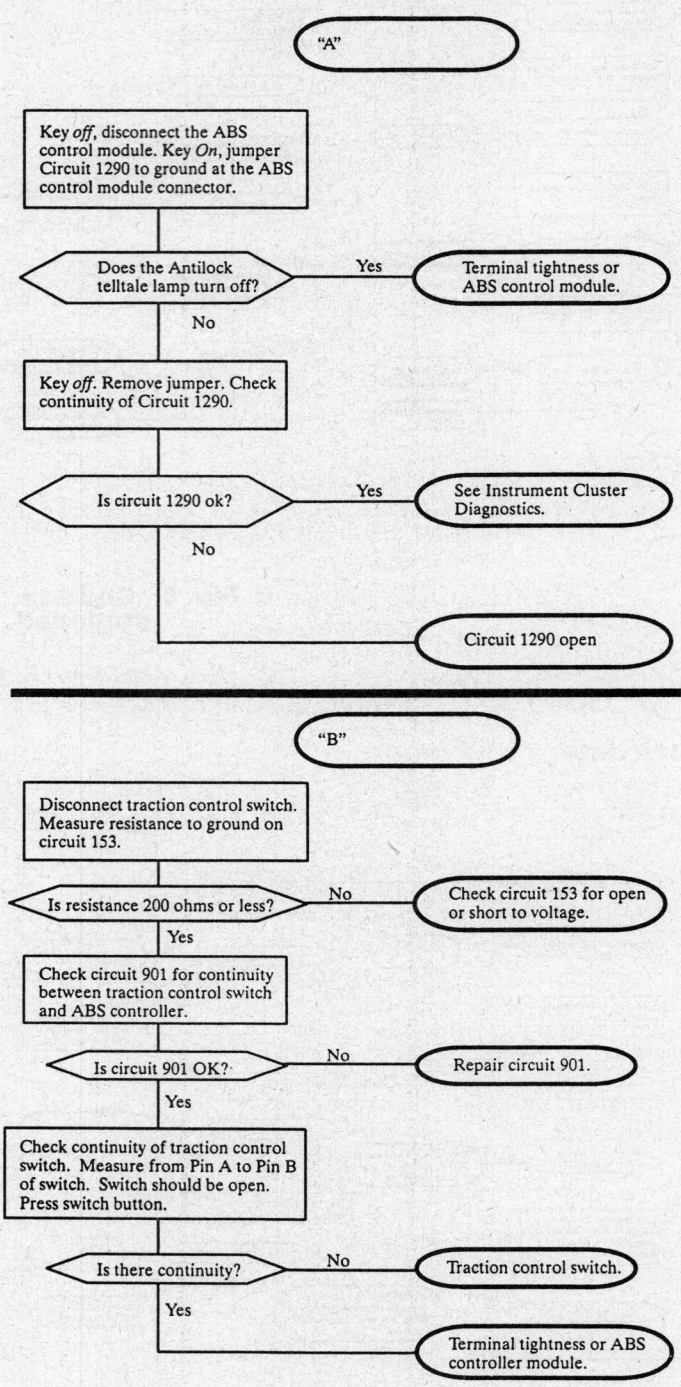

Fig. 9   Code 12, telltale or traction LED fault. 1993-94 models (Part 2 of 2)

Fig. 10   Code 13, telltale circuit shorted to B+. 1991-92 models

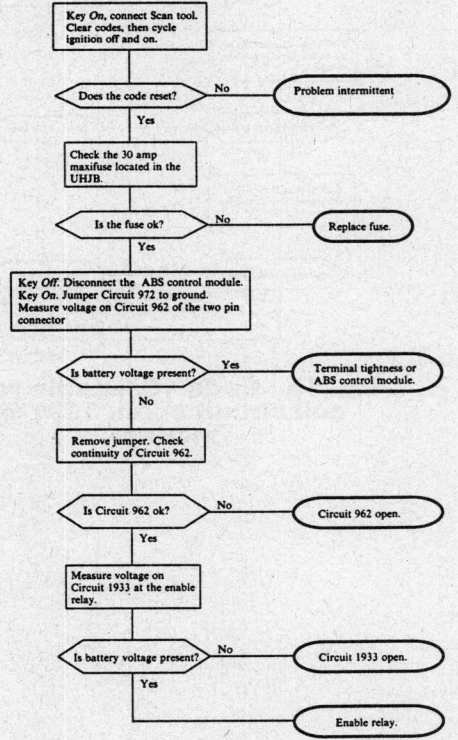

Fig. 11   Code 14, switched battery circuit open. 1991-93 models

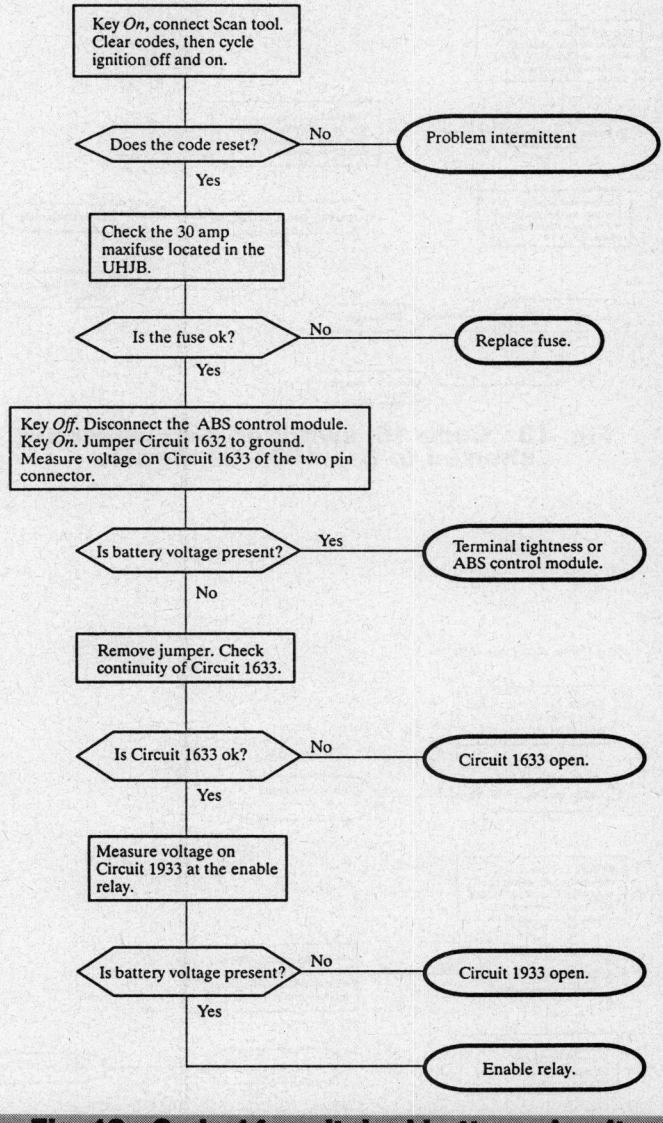

Fig. 12   Code 14, switched battery circuit open. 1994 models

If code 17 is set, do code 17 chart first.

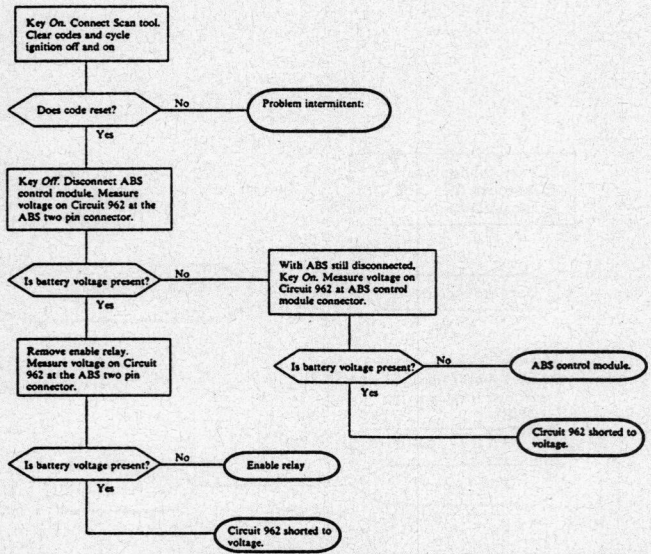

Fig. 13   Code 15, switched battery circuit shorted to B+. 1991-93 models

If Flag 17 is set, do Flag 17 chart first.

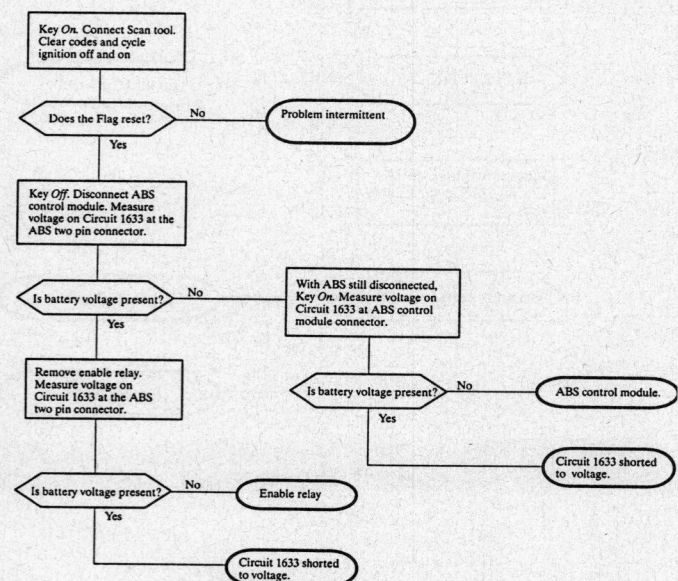

Fig. 14   Code 15, switched battery circuit shorted to B+. 1994 models

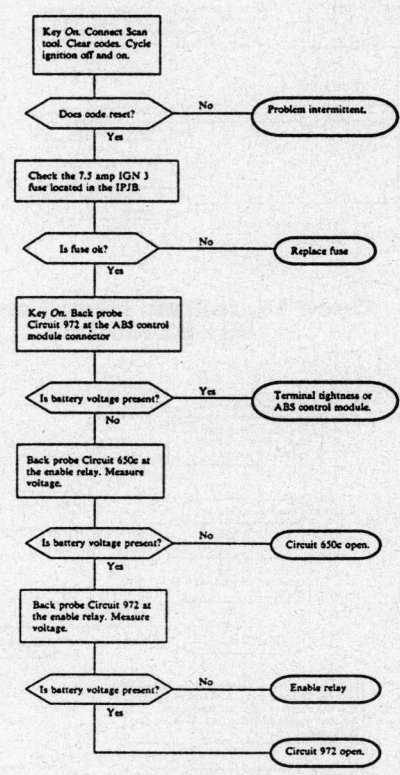

Fig. 15   Code 16, enable relay coil circuit open. 1991-93 models

Fig. 16   Code 16, enable relay coil circuit open. 1994 models

Fig. 17   Code 17, enable relay coil circuit grounded. 1991-93 models

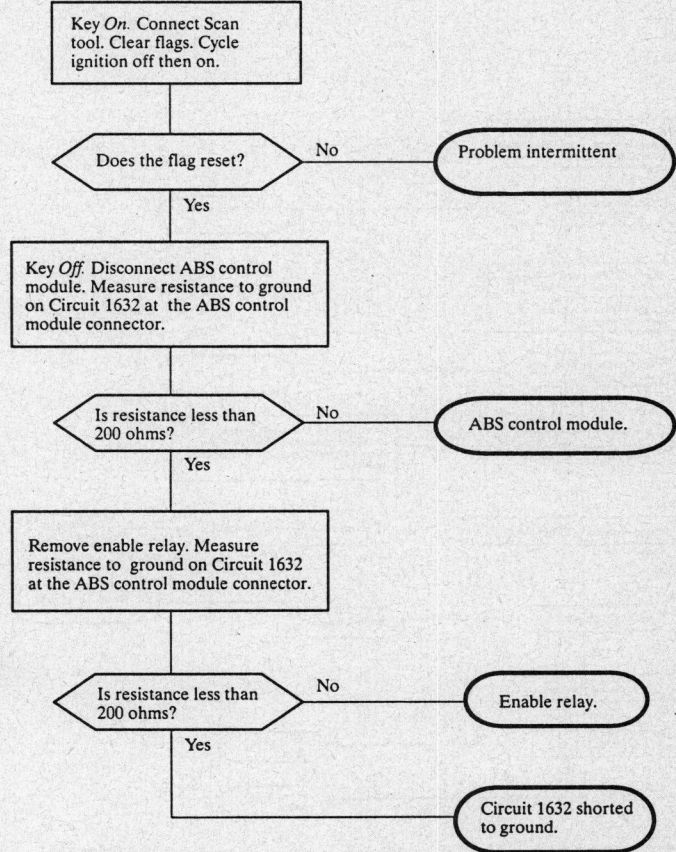

Fig. 18   Code 17, enable relay coil circuit grounded. 1994 models

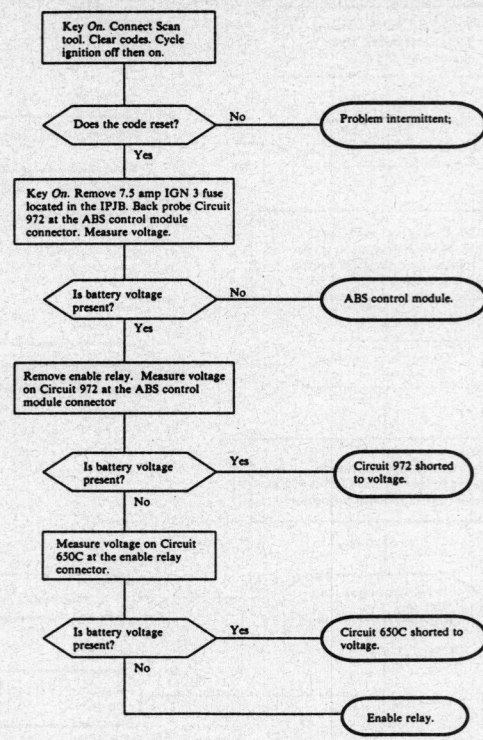

Fig. 19   Code 18, enable relay coil circuit shorted to B+. 1991-93 models

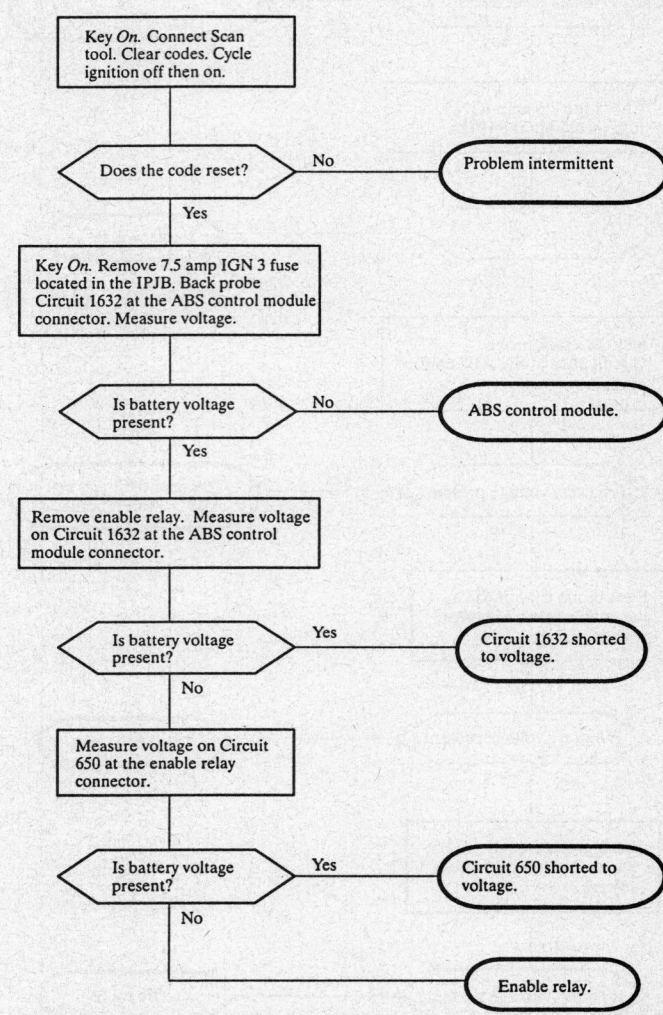

Fig. 20   Code 18, enable relay coil circuit shorted to B+. 1994 models

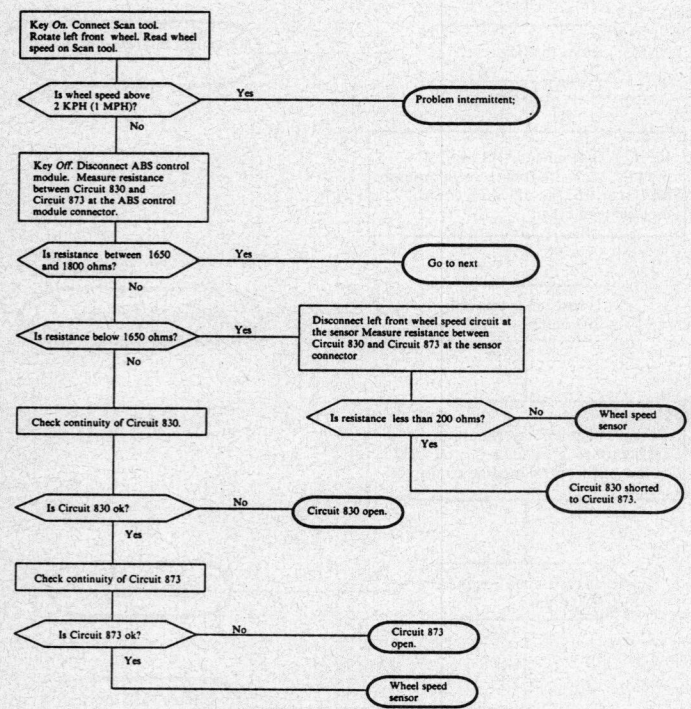

Fig. 21   Code 21, LF wheel speed=0 MPH (Part 1 of 2)

Fig. 21   Code 21, LF wheel speed=0 MPH (Part 2 of 2)

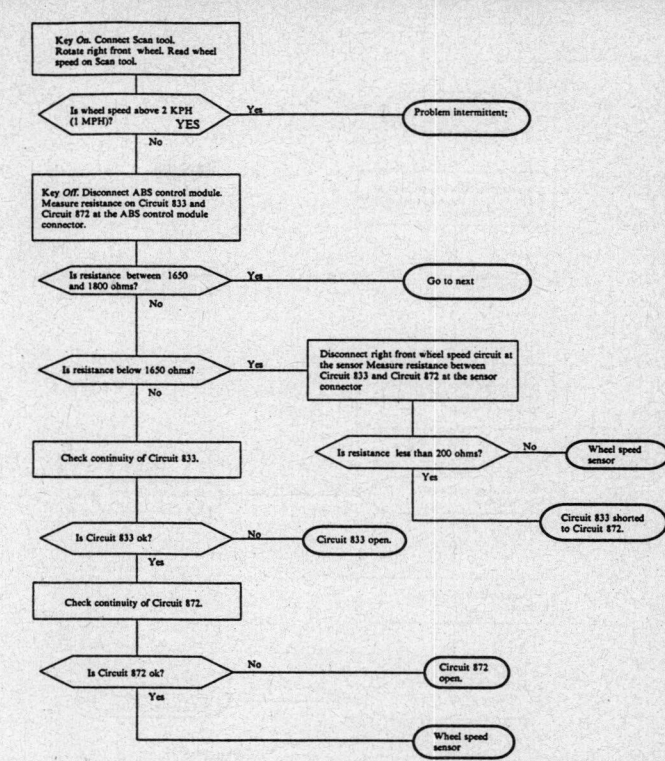

Fig. 22   Code 22, RF wheel speed=0 MPH (Part 1 of 2)

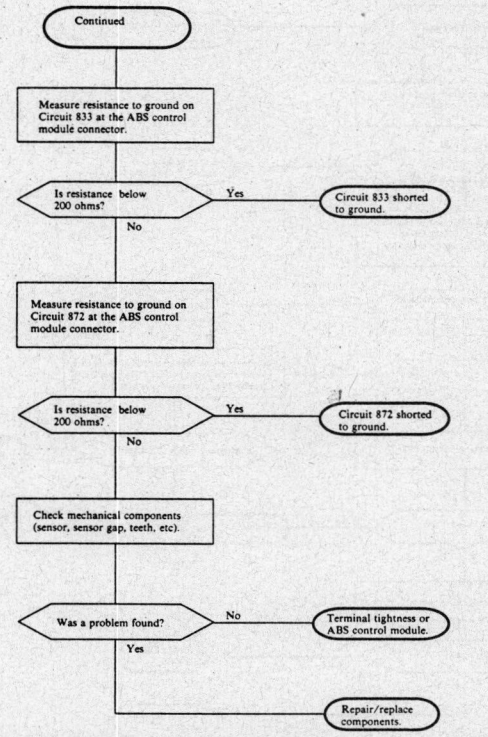

Fig. 22   Code 22, RF wheel speed=0 MPH (Part 2 of 2)

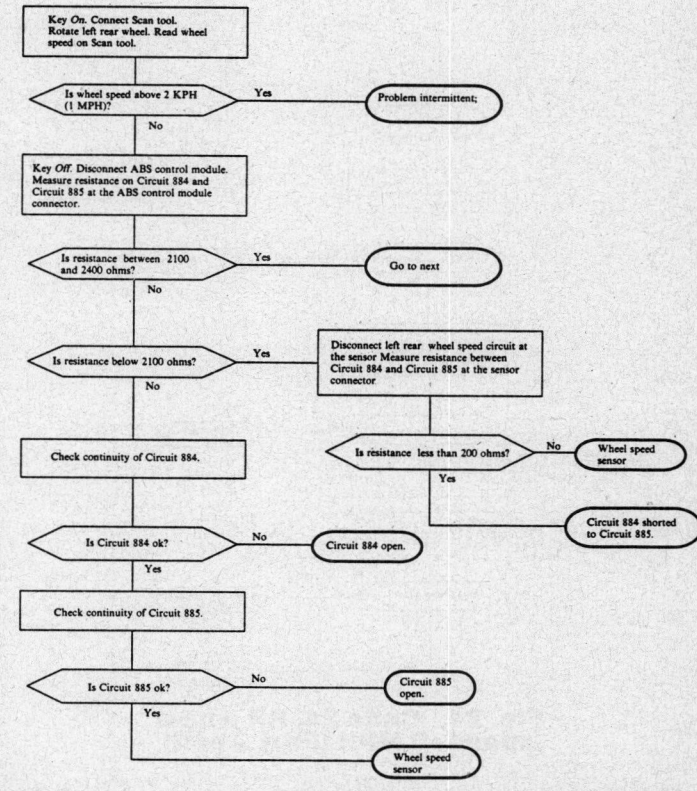

Fig. 23   Code 23, LR wheel speed=0 MPH (Part 1 of 2)

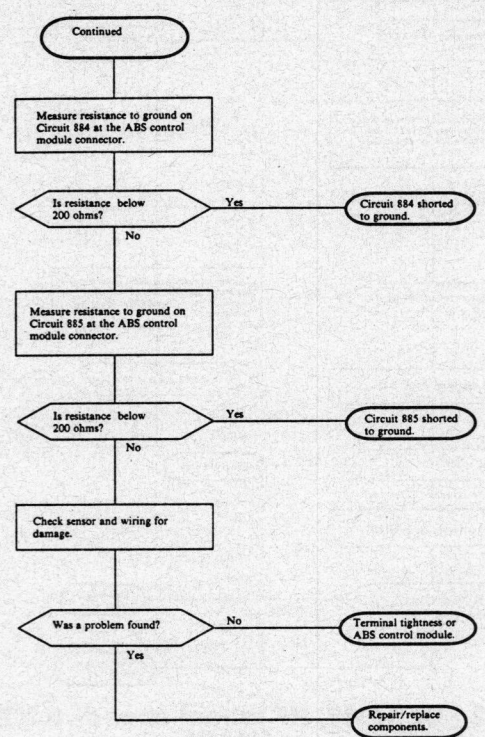

Fig. 23   Code 23, LR wheel speed=0 MPH (Part 2 of 2)

Fig. 24   Code 24, RR wheel speed=0 MPH (Part 2 of 2)

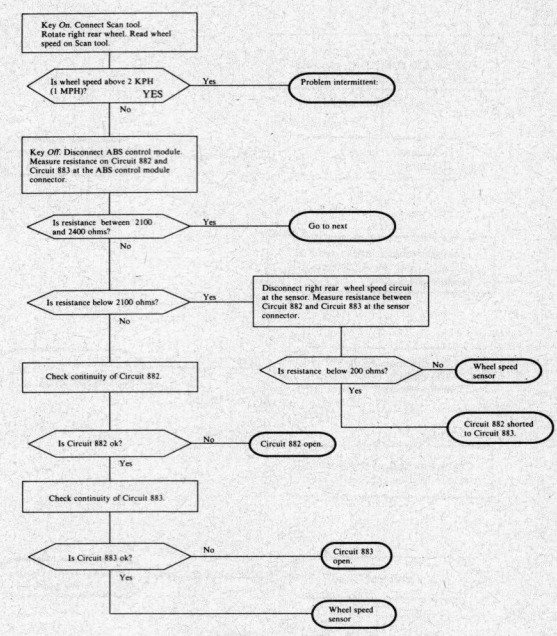

Fig. 24   Code 24, RR wheel speed=0 MPH (Part 1 of 2)

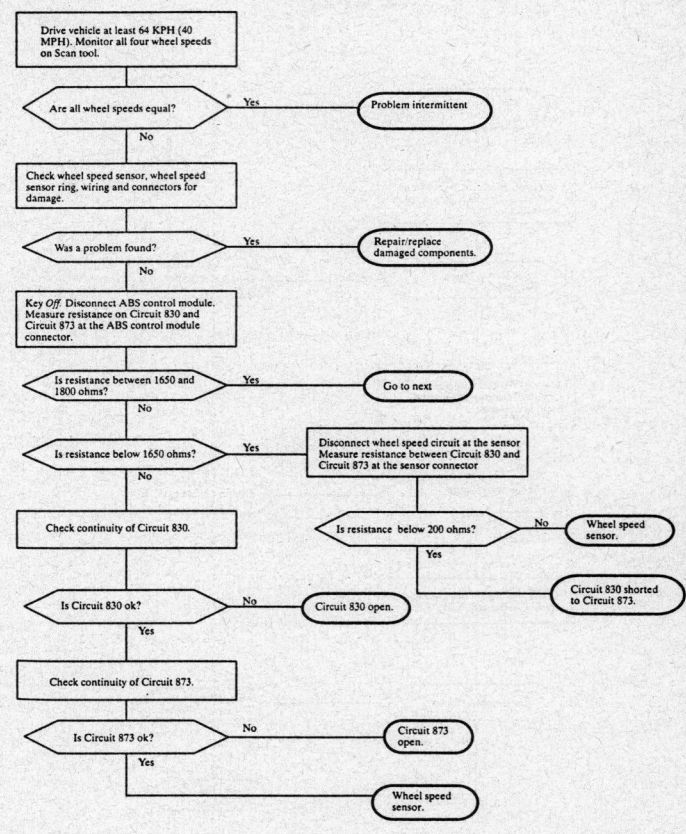

Fig. 25   Code 25, LF wheel speed acceleration fault (Part 1 of 2)

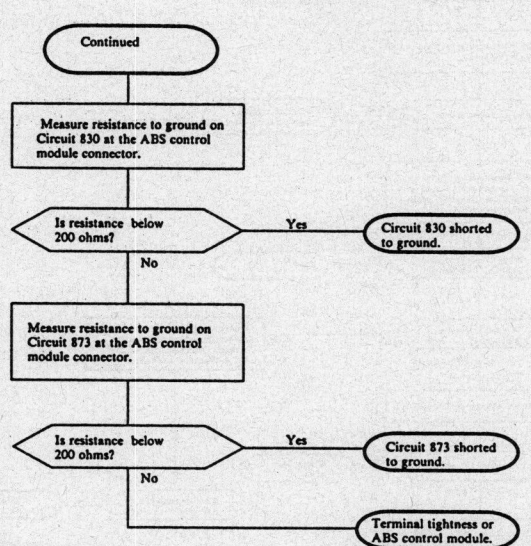

Fig. 25   Code 25, LF wheel speed acceleration fault (Part 2 of 2)

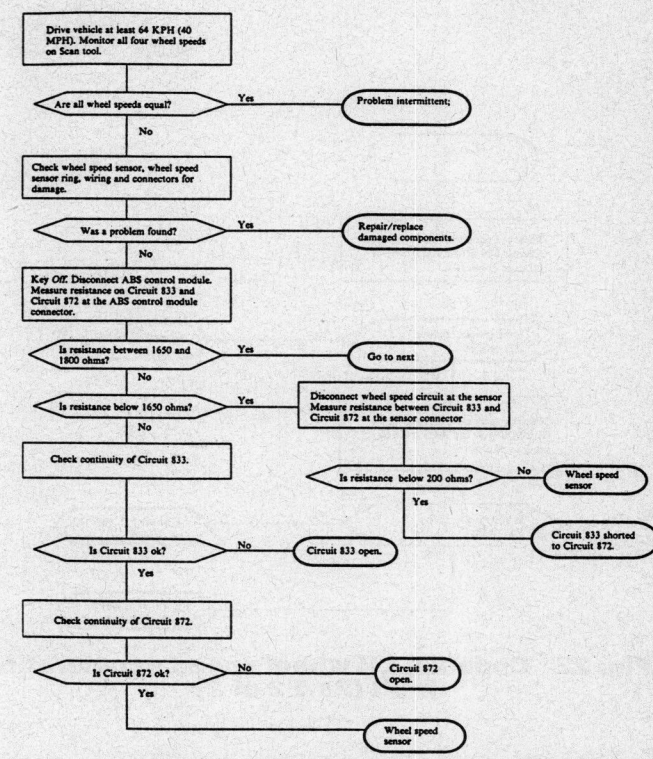

Fig. 26   Code 26, RF wheel speed acceleration fault (Part 1 of 2)

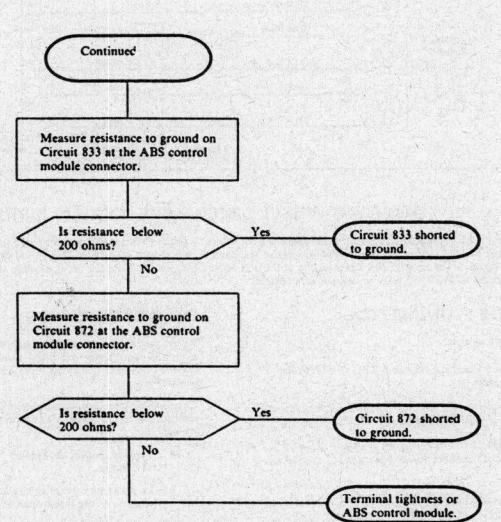

Fig. 26   Code 26, RF wheel speed acceleration fault (Part 2 of 2)

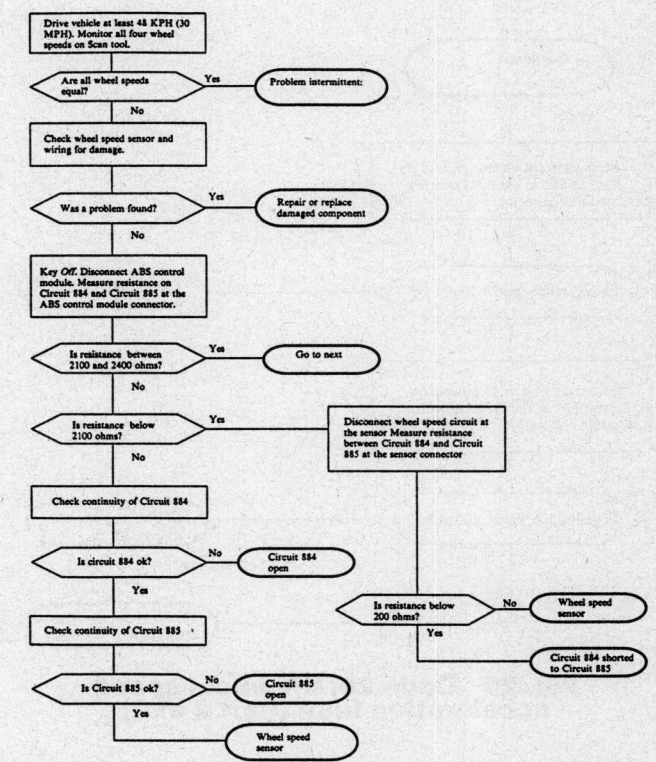

Fig. 27   Code 27, LR wheel speed acceleration fault (Part 1 of 2)

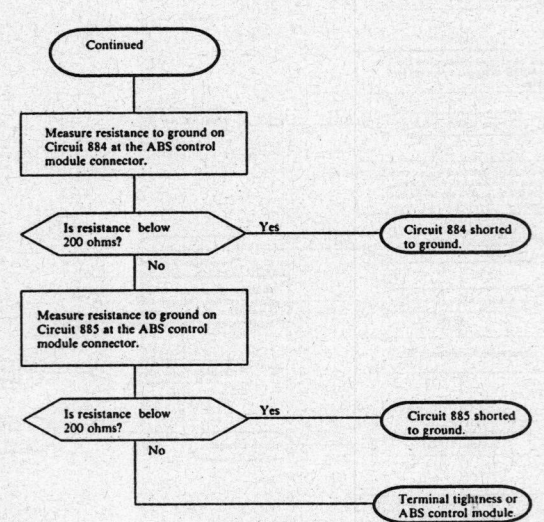

Fig. 27   Code 27, LR wheel speed acceleration fault (Part 2 of 2)

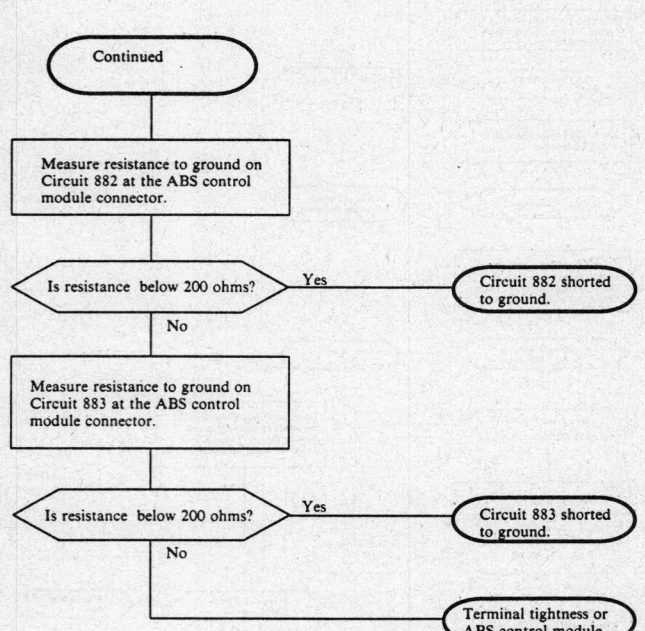

Fig. 28   Code 28, RR wheel speed acceleration fault (Part 2 of 2)

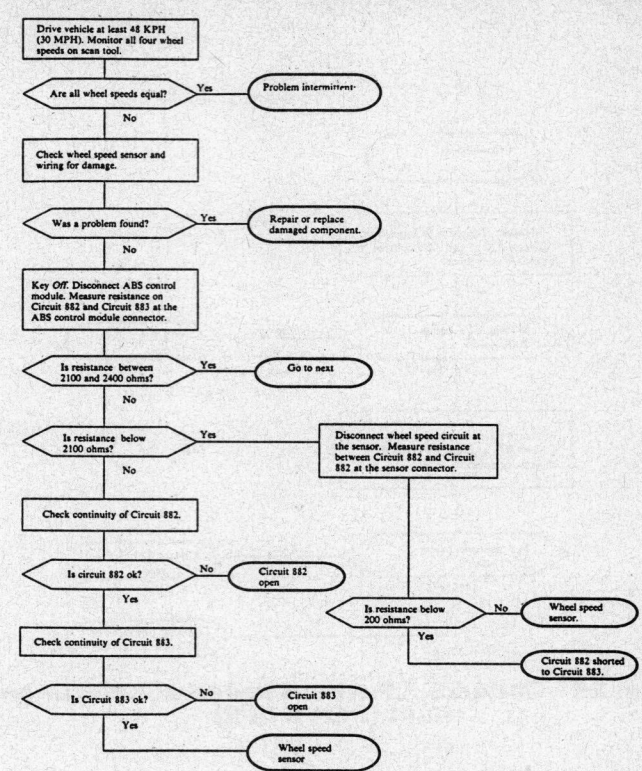

Fig. 28   Code 28, RR wheel speed acceleration fault (Part 1 of 2)

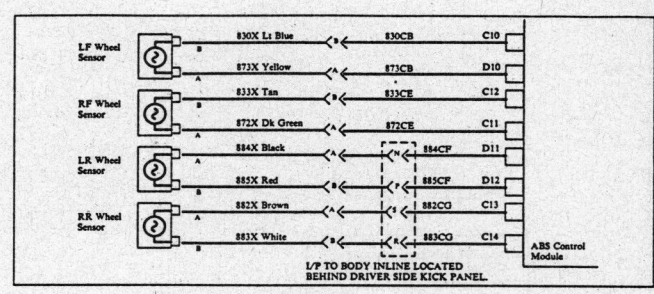

ANY TWO WHEEL SPEEDS ARE 0 KPH (0 MPH)

The four wheel speed sensors monitor the speed of each wheel by placing a magnetic coupling next to a toothed ring mounted on the axle of each front wheel and in the hub and bearing of each rear wheel. The signal changes with the wheel speed. If the wheel speed signal is seen at 0 MPH on any two wheels while the car is moving, the control module will disable all ABS and turn on the Antilock telltale.

CODE PARAMETERS

Code 31 sets if:

Any two wheel speeds Are 0 KPH (0 MPH) for 60 seconds.

This code can set anytime vehicle is moving faster then 16 KPH (10 MPH) and not in ABS braking.

The vehicle should be driven at speeds above 16 KPH (10 MPH) to check for reappearance of this failure.

DIAGNOSIS

Diagnose Code 31 by connecting the Scan tool and either driving the vehicle or rotating each wheel by hand to determine which wheel speeds equal 0 KPH (0 MPH). When the faulty wheel sensors are identified, proceed with the corresponding Wheel Speed = 0 trouble tree (Codes 21, 22, 23, or 24). Closely inspect the connectors in the circuitry, since this is the most likely cause of a Code 31.

If both rear wheel speeds = 0 KPH (0 MPH), check the inline connector located behind the driver side kick panel for a bad connection or the body extension harness to the rear axle harness connector for a bad connection.

DIAGNOSTIC AIDS

Before proceeding make a thorough visual inspection of the wheel speed sensor circuitry. Closely inspect the inline connector(s) since this is the most likely area for opens or shorts.

Connect the Scan tool, spin the wheel by hand, and monitor the wheel speed. Make a comparison with other wheels.

- Visually inspect the sensors for a loose fastener or damage.
- Using an ohmmeter to check resistance, shake wires to locate intermittents.

Check the tightness of the female terminal grip with a spare male terminal.

When attempting to diagnose an intermittent problem, use the Scan tool* to review supplemental diagnostic information. The supplemental data can be used to duplicate a problem.

* Select Malf History from Scan tool ABS menu.

Intermittents or opens suspected to be at the connectors can be detected by using a Diagnostic Service Probe. Voltage can be read on wires without disconnecting any connectors.

**Fig. 29   Code 31, any two wheel speeds = 0.
1991-92, 1994 models**

Fig. 30 Code 36, ABS system voltage low (Part 1 of 2)

Fig. 30 Code 36, ABS system voltage low (Part 2 of 2)

Fig. 31 Code 37, ABS system voltage high

Fig. 32 Code 38, left front ESB does not hold motor

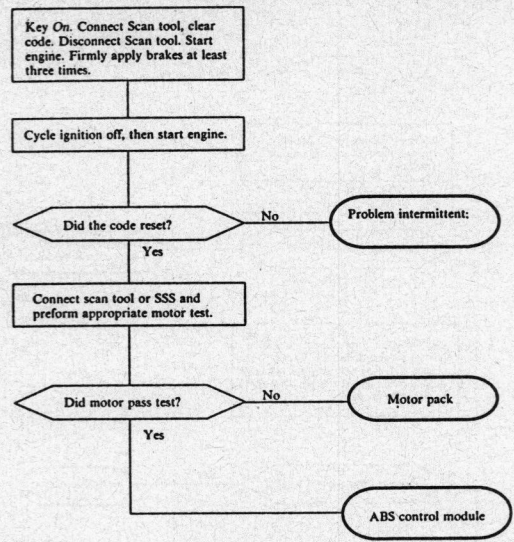

Fig. 33   Code 41, right front ESB does not hold motor

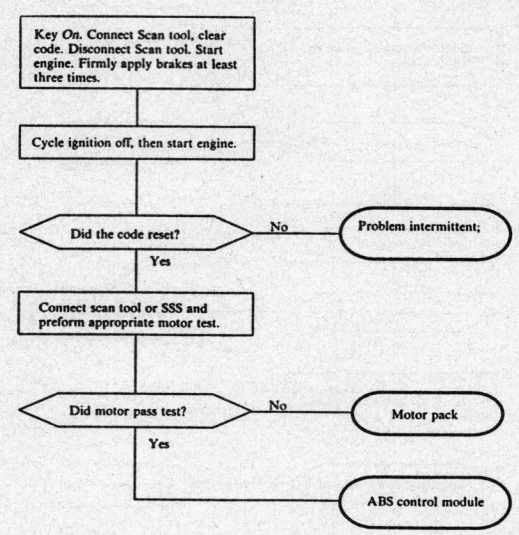

Fig. 34   Code 42, rear ESB does not hold motor

Fig. 35   Code 44, LF motor frozen

Fig. 37   Code 46, rear motor frozen

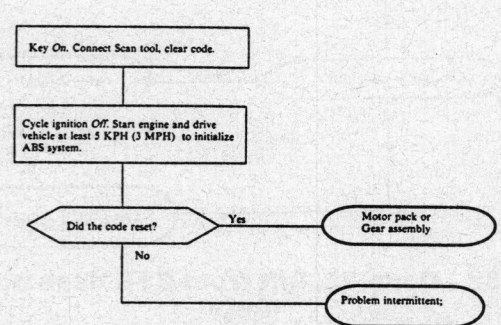

Fig. 36   Code 45, RF motor frozen

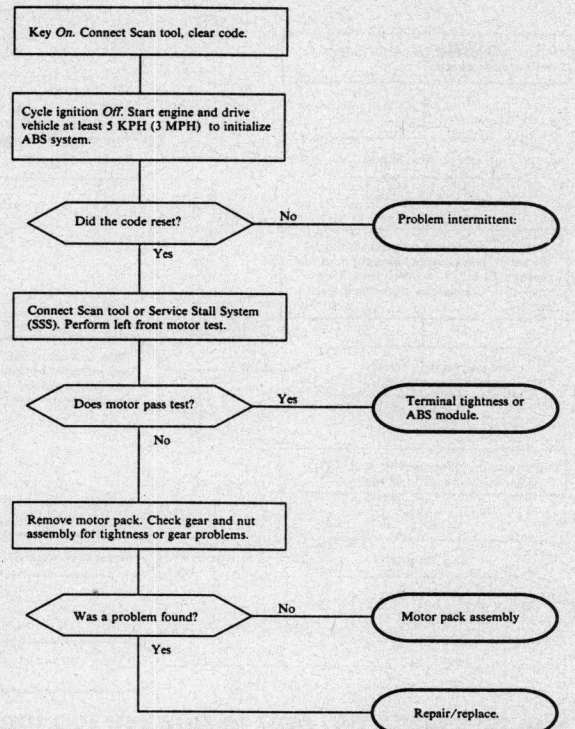

Fig. 38   Code 47, LF motor circuit current low

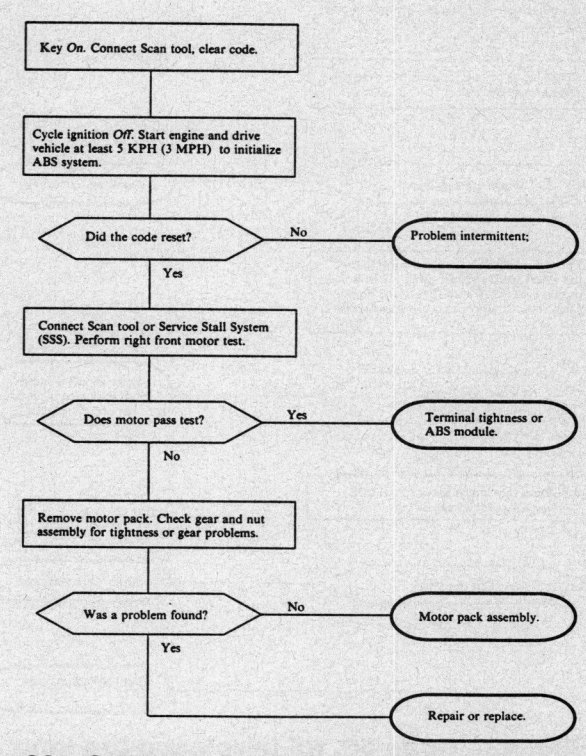

Fig. 39   Code 48, RF motor circuit current low

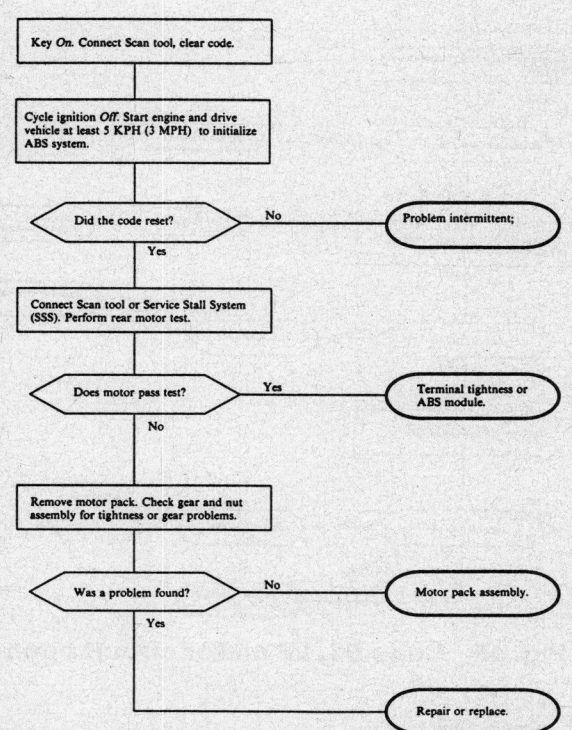

Fig. 40   Code 51, rear motor circuit current low

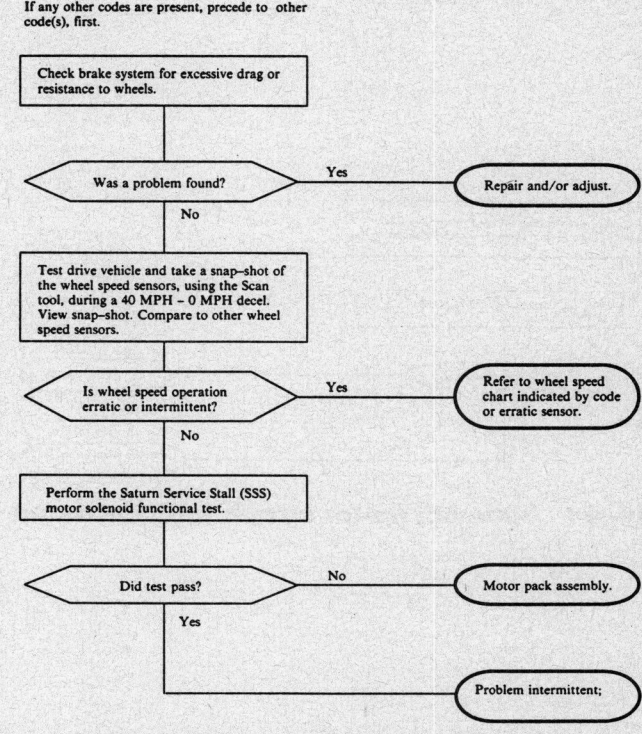

Fig. 41   Code 52, LF in release too long

If any other codes are present, precede to other code(s) first.

Check brake system for excessive drag or resistance to wheels.

Was a problem found? —Yes→ Repair and/or adjust.

No

Test drive vehicle and take a snap–shot of the wheel speed sensors, using the Scan tool, during a 40 MPH – 0 MPH decel. View snap–shot. Compare to other wheel speed sensors.

Is wheel speed operation erratic or intermittent? —Yes→ Refer to wheel speed chart indicated by code or erratic sensor.

No

Perform the Saturn Service Stall (SSS) motor solenoid functional test.

Did test pass? —No→ Motor pack assembly.

Yes

Problem intermittent;

Fig. 42   Code 53, RF in release too long

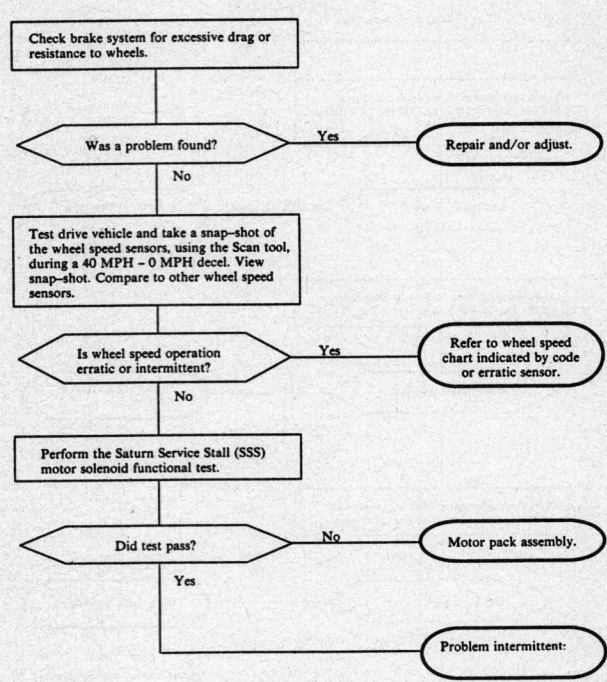

If any other codes are present, precede to code(s).

Check brake system for excessive drag or resistance to wheels.

Was a problem found? —Yes→ Repair and/or adjust.

No

Test drive vehicle and take a snap–shot of the wheel speed sensors, using the Scan tool, during a 40 MPH – 0 MPH decel. View snap–shot. Compare to other wheel speed sensors.

Is wheel speed operation erratic or intermittent? —Yes→ Refer to wheel speed chart indicated by code or erratic sensor.

No

Perform the Saturn Service Stall (SSS) motor solenoid functional test.

Did test pass? —No→ Motor pack assembly.

Yes

Problem intermittent:

Fig. 43   Code 54, rear in release too long

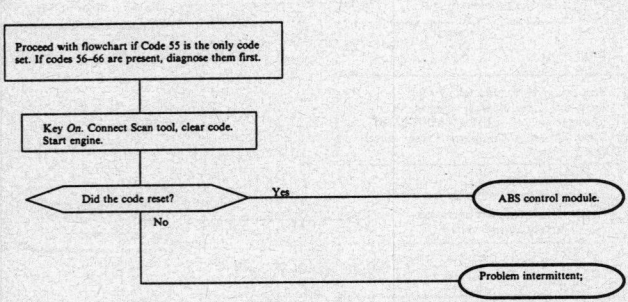

Proceed with flowchart if Code 55 is the only code set. If codes 56–66 are present, diagnose them first.

Key On. Connect Scan tool, clear code. Start engine.

Did the code reset? —Yes→ ABS control module.

No

Problem intermittent;

Fig. 44   Code 55, motor circuit fault detected

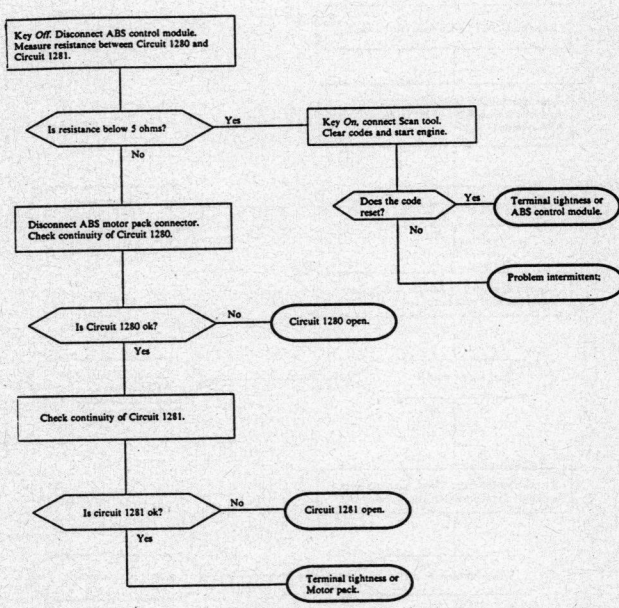

Key Off. Disconnect ABS control module. Measure resistance between Circuit 1280 and Circuit 1281.

Is resistance below 5 ohms? —Yes→ Key On, connect Scan tool. Clear codes and start engine.

No

Does the code reset? —Yes→ Terminal tightness or ABS control module.

No

Problem intermittent;

Disconnect ABS motor pack connector. Check continuity of Circuit 1280.

Is Circuit 1280 ok? —No→ Circuit 1280 open.

Yes

Check continuity of Circuit 1281.

Is circuit 1281 ok? —No→ Circuit 1281 open.

Yes

Terminal tightness or Motor pack.

Fig. 45   Code 56, LF motor circuit open

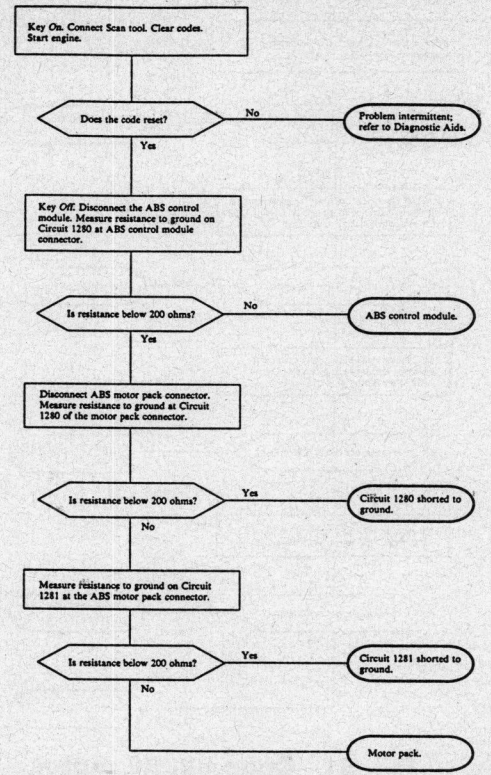

Fig. 46   Code 57, LF motor circuit grounded

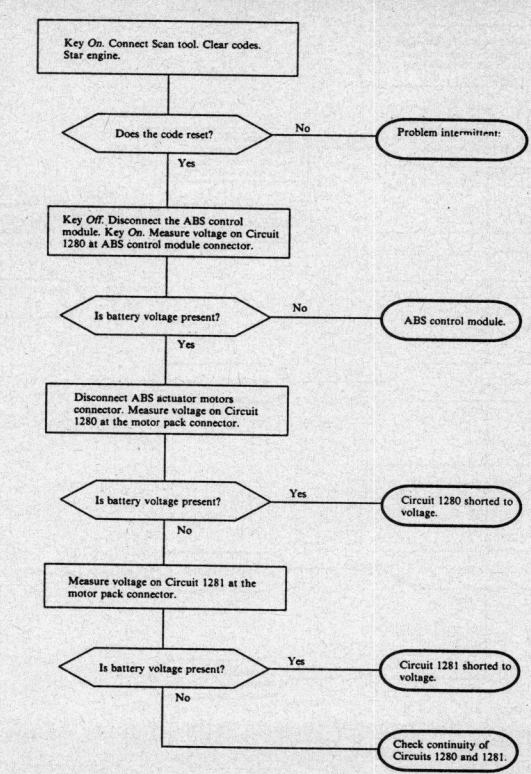

Fig. 47   Code 58, LF motor circuit shorted to B+. 1991-92 models

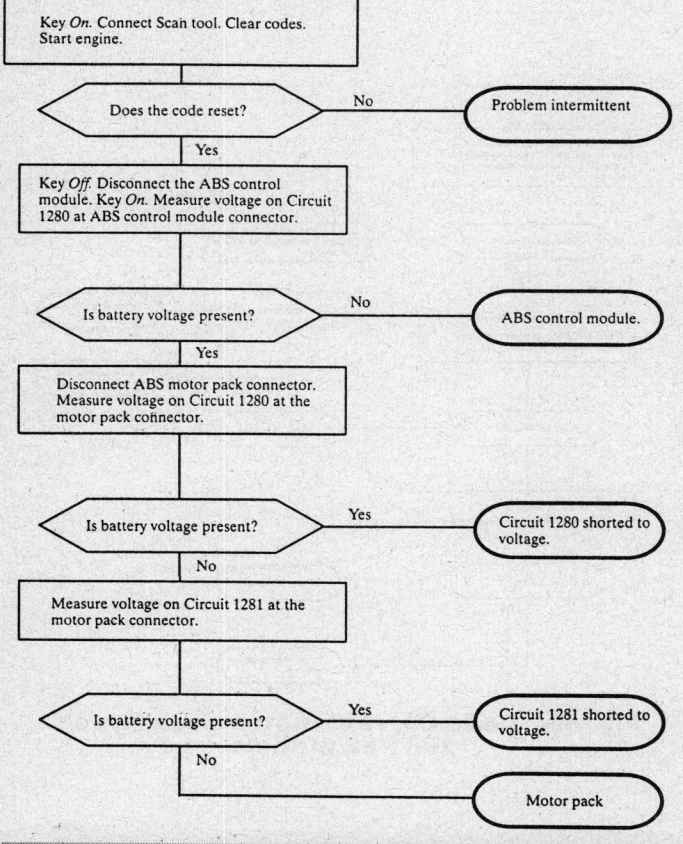

Fig. 48   Code 58, LF motor circuit shorted to B+. 1993-94 models

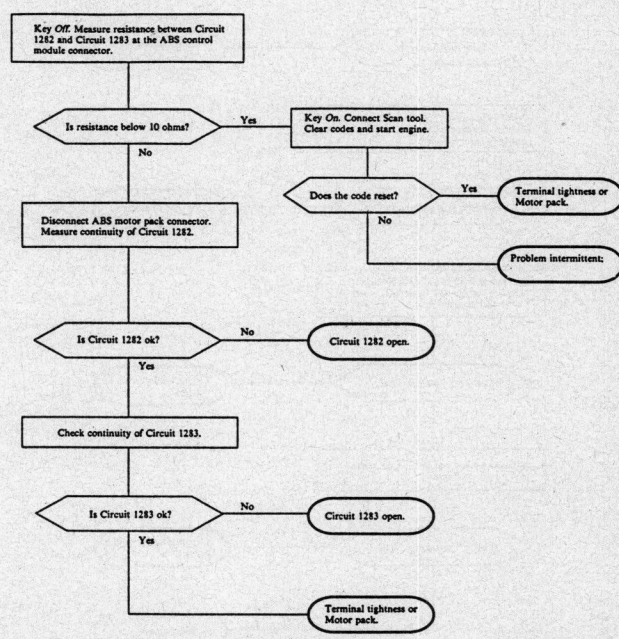

Fig. 49   Code 61, RF motor circuit open. 1991-92 models

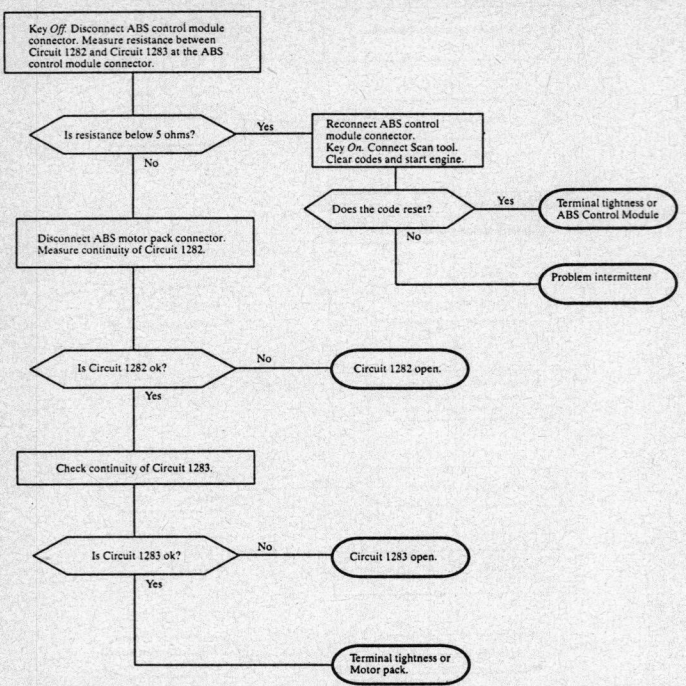

**Fig. 50   Code 61, RF motor circuit open.
1993-94 models**

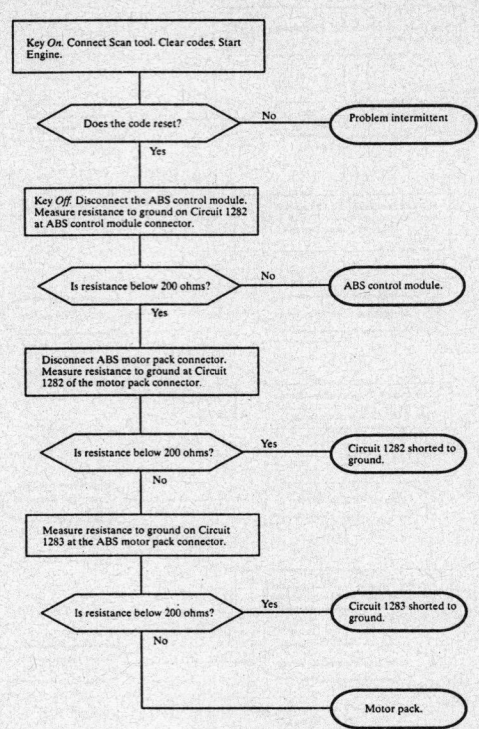

**Fig. 51   Code 62, RF motor
circuit grounded**

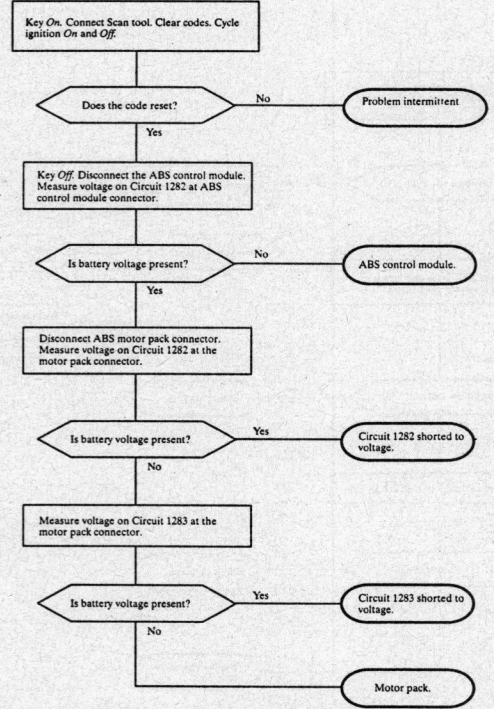

**Fig. 52   Code 63, RF motor
circuit shorted to B+**

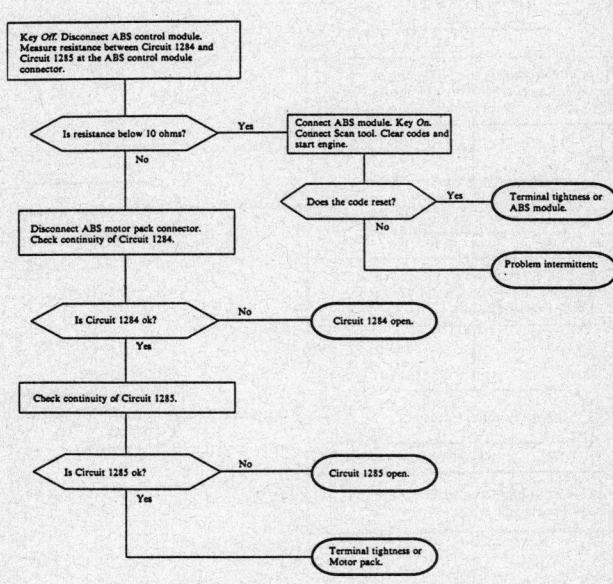

**Fig. 53   Code 64, rear motor circuit open.
1991-92 models**

Fig. 54   Code 64, rear motor circuit open. 1993-94 models

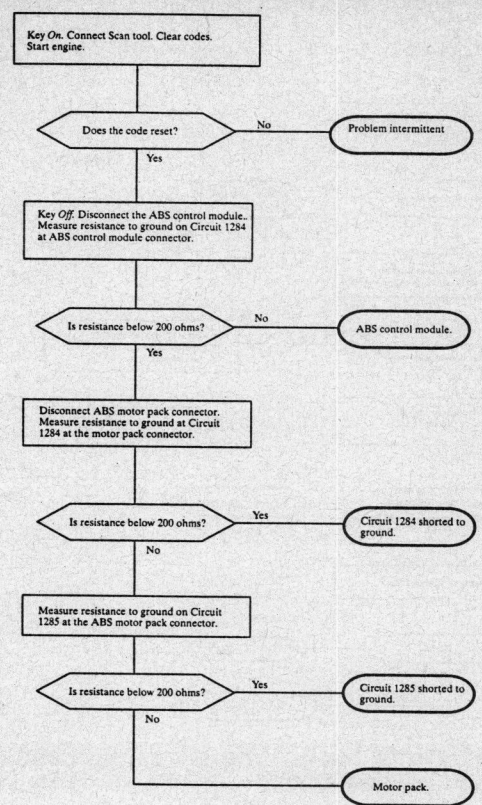

Fig. 55   Code 65, rear motor circuit grounded

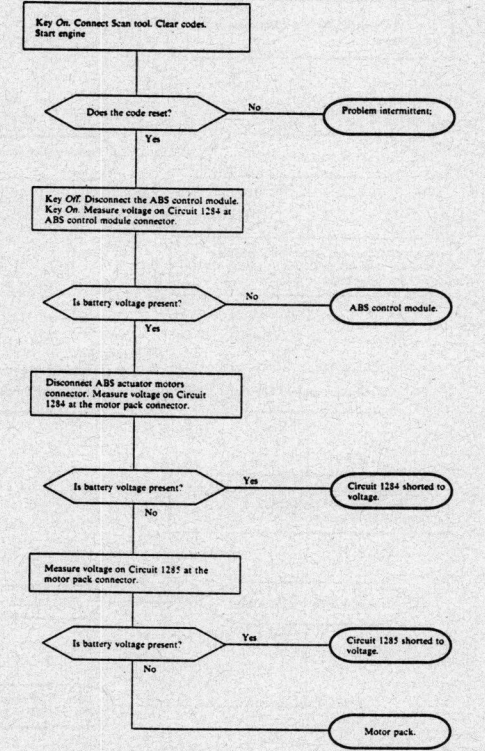

Fig. 56   Code 66, rear motor circuit shorted to B+

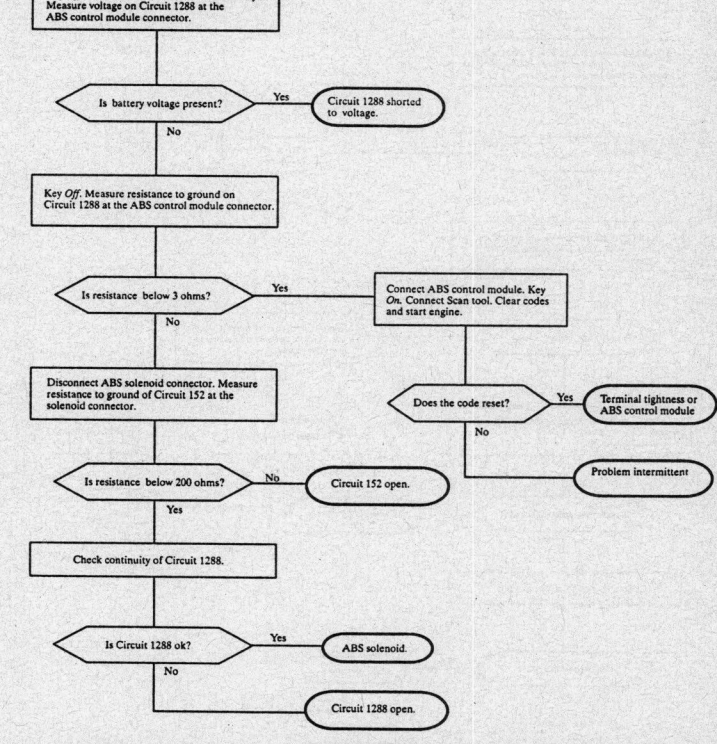

Fig. 57   Code 76, solenoid circuit 1288 open or shorted to B+. 1991-93 models

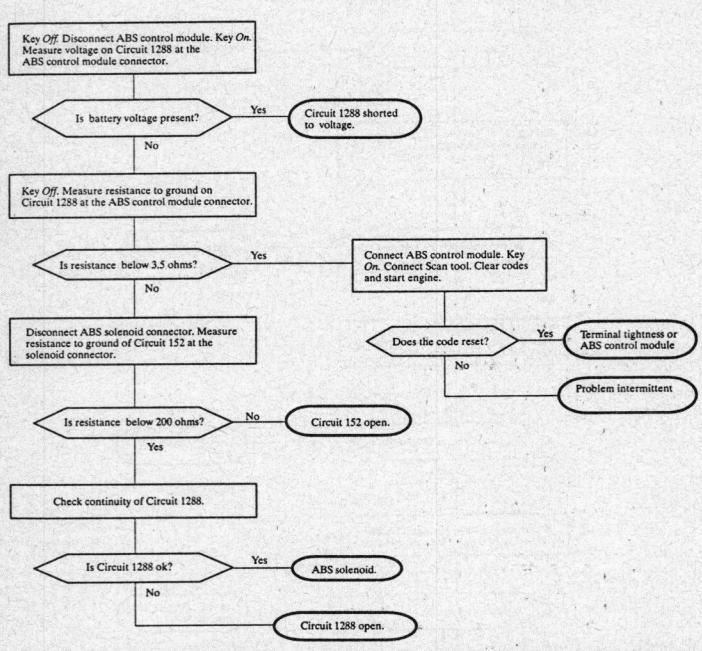

Fig. 58   Code 76, solenoid circuit 1288 open or shorted to B+. 1994 models

Fig. 59   Code 77, solenoid circuit 1288 grounded

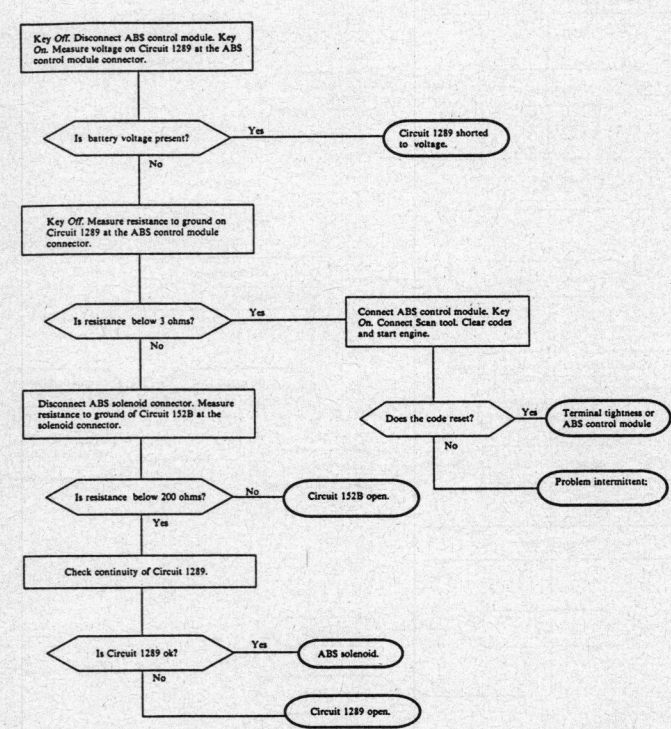

Fig. 60   Code 78, solenoid circuit 1289 open or shorted to B+

Fig. 61   Code 81, solenoid circuit 1289 grounded

Fig. 62   Code 82, ABS calibration fault. 1991-92 models

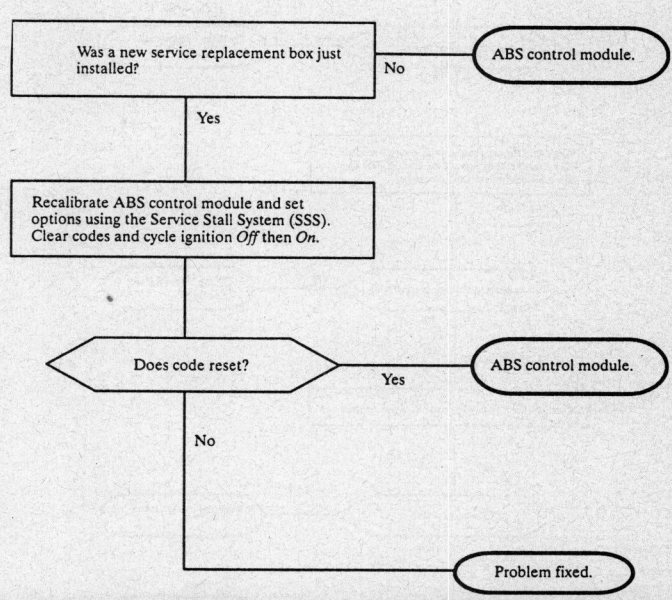

Fig. 63   Code 82, ABS calibration fault. 1993-94 models

RED BRAKE TELLTALE COMMANDED ON BY ABS CONTROL MODULE

The Brake warning telltale can be turned on by the ABS control module in the event that base brake performance is degraded by an ABS fault (such as an open rear motor circuit when the piston is not home).

CODE PARAMETERS

ABS Code 86 will set if:

The ABS control module commands the Brake telltale to turn on.

DIAGNOSTIC AIDS

This code is set to provide notification that the ABS control module turned on the brake telltale.

Diagnose the accompanying ABS codes first. If the brake telltale remains on after the ABS fault is corrected, diagnose the problem associated with the brake telltale (park brake switch, low brake fluid, etc.).

Code 86 should only set in conjunction with another ABS code. If Code 86 sets alone, the ABS control module should be replaced.

Fig. 64   Code 86, ABS turned on red brake telltale

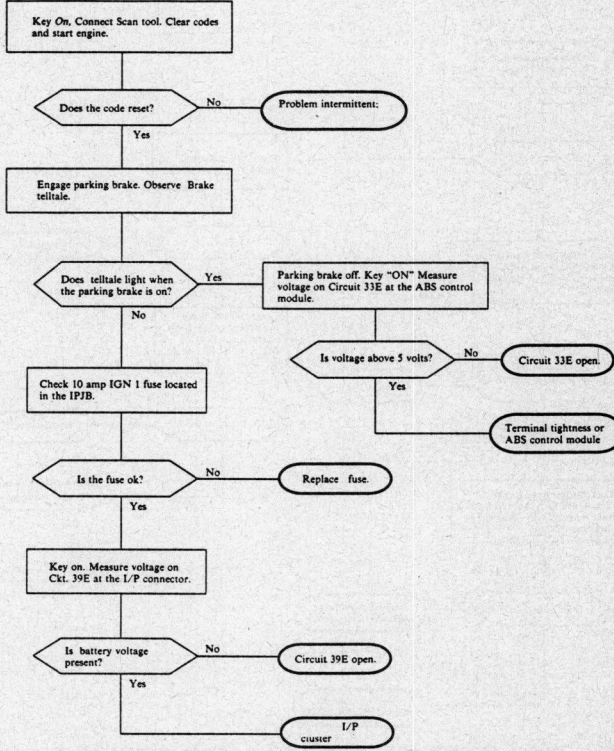

Fig. 65   Code 87, red brake telltale circuit open

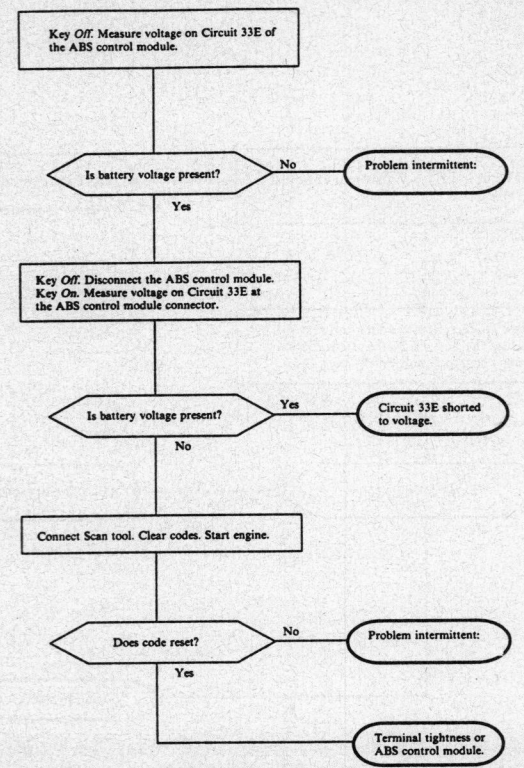

Fig. 66   Code 88, red brake telltale circuit shorted to B+. 1991-92 models

Fig. 67   Code 88, red brake telltale circuit shorted to B+. 1993-94 models

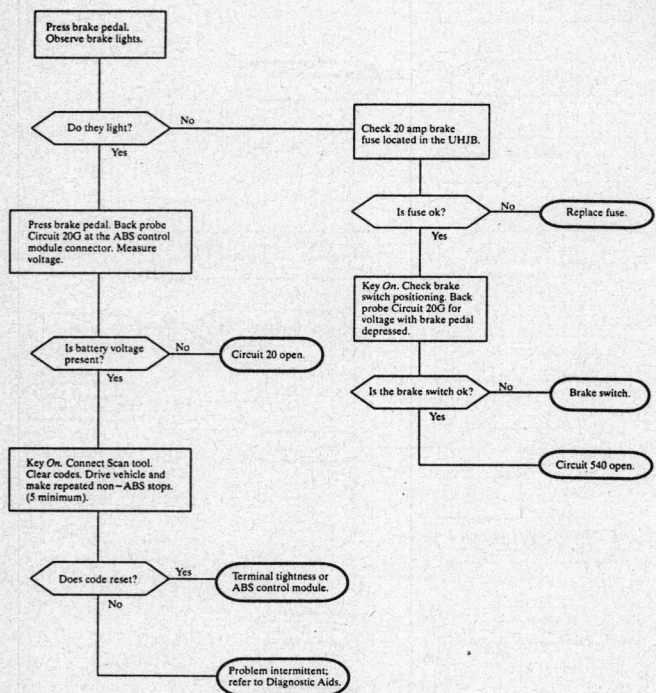

Fig. 68   Code 91, brake switch circuit open during normal stop

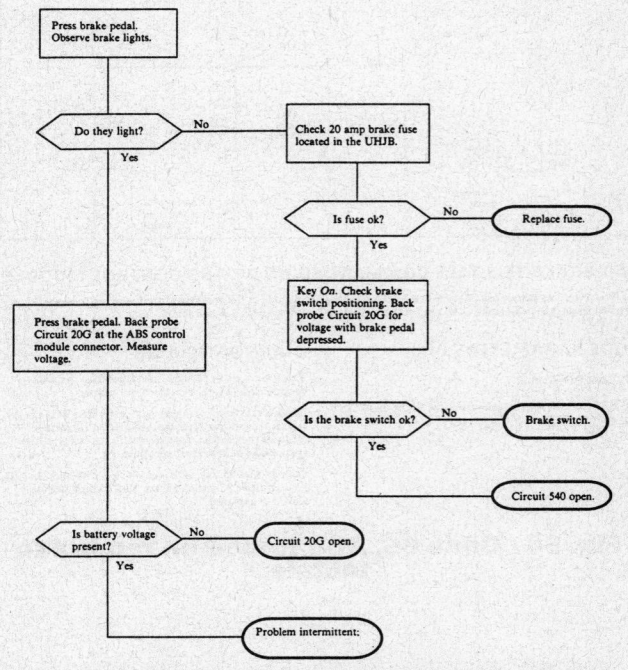

Fig. 69   Code 92, brake switch circuit open during ABS stop

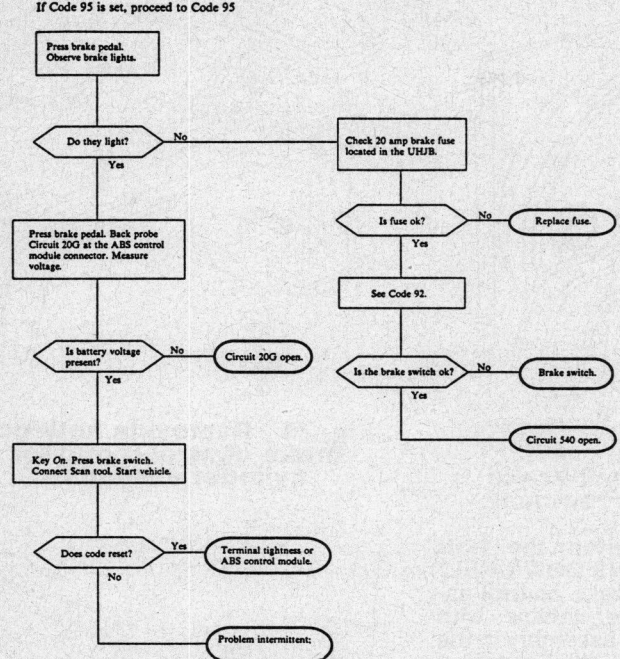

Fig. 70   Code 93, brake switch circuit open on initialization

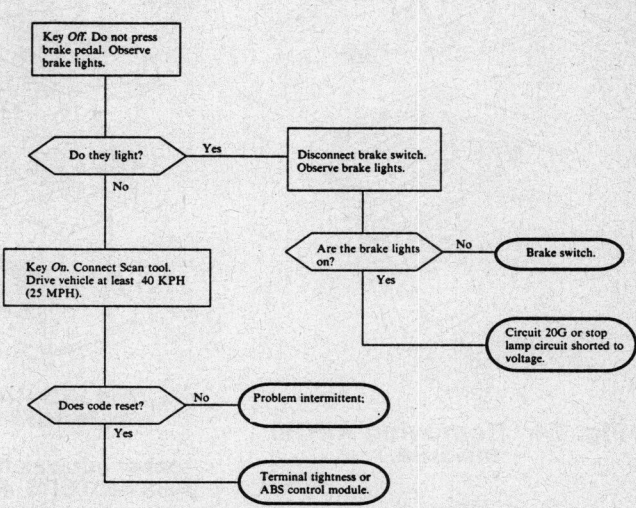

Fig. 71   Code 94, brake switch circuit always closed

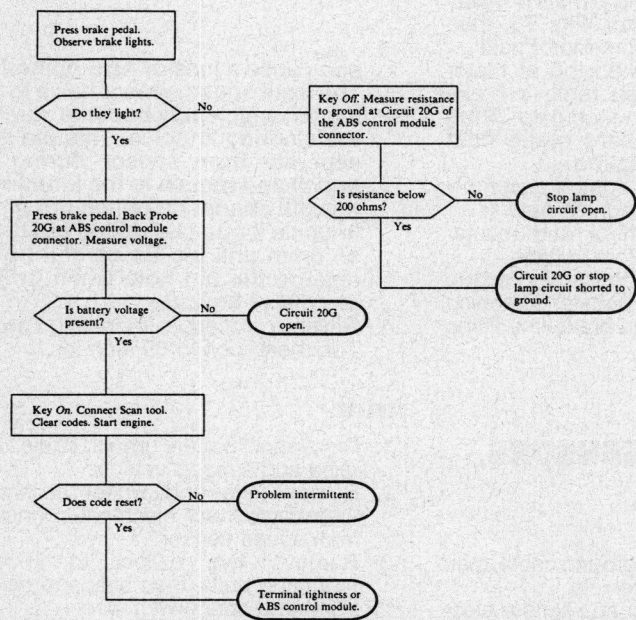

Fig. 72   Code 95, stop lamp circuit open NO TAG

Fig. 73   Code 96, stop lamp circuit open or grounds open

Fig. 74   Removing ABCM module

Fig. 77   Front speed sensor replacement

Fig. 75   Anti-lock brake solenoid valve removal

Fig. 76   Removing anti-lock brake control & master cylinder assembly

Fig. 78   Rear hub & bearing assembly replacement

ANTI-LOCK BRAKE SOLENOID VALVE, REPLACE

1. Disconnect battery ground cable.
2. Clean dirt from solenoid valve and area around solenoid.
2. Disconnect electrical connector from solenoid valve, **Fig. 75.**
3. Remove two solenoid to modulator Torx head retaining screws, then the solenoid from the modulator.
4. Reverse procedure to install, and **torque** Torx retaining screws to 45 inch lbs. **There are two different designs of solenoids used on this ABS system. The solenoids are not interchangeable. Each is identified by an eight digit number on the top of the solenoid. Ensure correct solenoid is installed.**

ANTI-LOCK BRAKE CONTROL & MASTER CYLINDER ASSEMBLY, REPLACE

The control assembly drive gears are under spring tension and will turn during disassembly if not unloaded. To remove tension, use the SATURN scan tool or equivalent to perform the "RUN ABS MOTORS, PISTONS DOWN-REL" before removing the brake control assembly. Do not drive vehicle with anti-lock brake control assembly in the tension released position. Excessive brake pedal travel and reduced brake effectiveness could occur. Always perform "RUN ABS MOTORS, PISTONS UP-HOME" before driving vehicle.

1. Disconnect battery cables, then remove battery from vehicle.
2. Disconnect two electrical connectors from solenoid valves, then the brake fluid level sensor connector at the master cylinder.
3. Remove CPA locking pin from 6-way motor pack connector, **Fig. 76,** then detach connector from motor pack.
4. Place a shop cloth on top of motor pack assembly, then remove brake line fitting nuts from modulator. **Plug open lines to prevent brake fluid loss and contamination.**
5. Remove two brake control assembly to brake booster attaching nuts.
6. Remove brake control and master cylinder assembly from vehicle.
7. Reverse procedure to install. **Torque** assembly to brake booster attaching nuts to 20 ft. lbs. and brake line fitting nuts to 18 ft. lbs.

WHEEL SPEED SENSORS, REPLACE
Front

1. Disconnect battery ground cable, then raise and support vehicle.
2. Disconnect wheel speed sensor electrical connector, **Fig. 77.**
3. Remove wheel speed sensor to steering knuckle Torx head bolt, then the wheel speed sensor. **When removing speed sensor, be careful not to damage speed sensor ring. Even a minor scratch on the sensor ring**

can cause a loss of ABS operation. The front speed sensor has a locating pin which may become stuck in the steering knuckle. This pin may separate from sensor during removal and remain in the knuckle. If this pin cannot be pulled out of the knuckle it must be drilled out using an 8mm drill bit. Be careful not to enlarge the pin hole when drilling pin out of knuckle.

4. Reverse procedure to install. **Torque** Torx head bolt to 89 inch lbs.

Rear

1. Disconnect battery ground cable, then raise and support vehicle.
2. Remove tire and wheel assembly, then disconnect electrical connector from speed sensor.
3. Remove two caliper to knuckle mounting bolts, then suspend caliper from strut spring with wire.
4. Remove rotor from hub, then the four hub to knuckle attaching bolts, **Fig. 78.**
5. Remove hub and bearing assembly.
6. Reverse procedure to install, **torque** hub to knuckle bolts and caliper to knuckle bolts to 63 ft. lbs.

ABS SYSTEM BLEEDING

Before bleeding the rear brakes, the rear displacement cylinder pistons must be returned to the topmost position. Using a SATURN scan tool or suitable equivalent, perform "RUN ABS MOTORS, PISTON UP-HOME." This will run the pistons to the top of their travel.

Use only Dot 3 brake fluid from a clean and sealed container. Do not use Dot 5 brake fluid.

PRESSURE BLEEDING

1. Remove master cylinder cover and ensure reservoir is properly filled.
2. Connect bleeder adapter tool No. SA9150BR or equivalent to master cylinder reservoir.
3. Connect bleeder adapter to pressure bleeding equipment.
4. Connect a clear plastic bleeder hose to modulator assembly rearward bleeder valve and submerge other end of hose into clean container partially filled with brake fluid.
5. Adjust pressure bleeding equipment to 5-10 psi, then wait approximately 30 seconds to ensure that there is no leakage.
6. Adjust pressure bleed equipment to 30-35 psi.
7. To bleed ABS hydraulic modulator and master cylinder, proceed as follows:
   a. Slowly open rearward bleeder valve and allow fluid to flow until no air is seen in fluid, then **torque** valve to 65 inch lbs.
   b. Attach bleeder hose to modulator assembly forward bleeder hose.
   c. Slowly open forward bleeder valve and allow fluid to flow until no air is seen in fluid, then **torque** valve to 65 inch lbs.
8. To bleed wheel brakes, proceed as follows:
   a. Raise and support vehicle.
   b. Attach bleeder hose to bleeder valve of right rear wheel and submerge other end of hose into clean container partially filled with brake fluid.
   c. Loosen bleeder valve and allow fluid to flow until air bubbles are no longer present, then close valve.
   d. Repeat steps b and c, first for left rear wheel, then the right front caliper, then the left front caliper.
9. Road test vehicle, to verify brake performance.

MANUAL BLEEDING

1. Ensure that brake fluid reservoir is properly filled.
2. Attach bleeder hose to modulator assembly rearward bleed valve and submerge other end of hose in clean container partially filled with brake fluid.
3. Pump brake pedal several times, then slowly open bleeder valve 1/2 to 3/4 turns.

4. Depress brake pedal and hold until fluid begins to flow.
5. Close valve and repeat steps 3 and 4 on forward valve. Once fluid is seen to flow from both the forward and rearward valves, modulator valve and master cylinder are filled sufficiently with fluid. However, these components may not be purged of air. At this point, bleed the wheel brakes.
6. Raise and support vehicle.
7. Attach bleeder hose to bleeder valve of right rear wheel and submerge other end of hose in clean container partially filled with brake fluid.
8. Open bleeder valve and slowly depress brake pedal, then close valve and slowly release brake pedal. Wait five seconds to proceed.
9. Repeat step 8 until brake pedal feels firm and no air bubbles are observed in bleeder hose.
10. Repeat steps 7, 8 and 9, first for left rear wheel, then the right front caliper, then the left front caliper.
11. Lower vehicle and attach bleeder hose to rearward bleeder valve.
12. Depress brake pedal using moderate pressure, then slowly open bleeder valve 1/2 to 3/4 turns and allow fluid to flow.
13. Close valve and release brake pedal, then wait five seconds to proceed.
14. Repeat steps 12 and 13 until all air is purged from system.
15. Road test vehicle to verify brake performance.

MANUAL STEERING GEAR

INDEX

DESCRIPTION

The manual steering system is a rack and pinion design. The major components of the steering system are the steering wheel, steering column and shaft, intermediate shaft, manual steering gear, tie rods and steering knuckles.

When the steering wheel is turned, the steering shaft turns the intermediate shaft which turns the pinion of the steering gear. The gear teeth on the pinion mesh with the mating teeth on the straight rack inside the steering gear. Rotation of the pinion converts to a straight-line motion of the rack across the vehicle that moves the tie rods either left or right. This motion causes the steering knuckle to pivot either clockwise or counterclockwise, steering the front wheels.

TROUBLESHOOTING

Refer to **Fig. 1** for manual steering system troubleshooting.

BEARING PRELOAD ADJUST

The following adjustment should be made with the front wheels raised and the steering wheel centered.

1. Loosen adjuster plug locknut on steering gear housing.
2. Turn adjuster plug clockwise until it bottoms in steering gear housing, **Fig. 2.**
3. **Torque** adjuster plug to 106 inch lbs.
4. Back-off adjuster plug 50-70° (approximately one flat of nut).
5. **Torque** locknut, while holding adjuster plug, to 52 ft. lbs.
6. Check steering wheel returnability following adjustment.

Complaint/Condition	Possible Cause(s)	Correction(s)
Hard Steering	Front tire(s) improperly inflated.	Inflate tire(s) correctly.
	Improperly adjusted, improperly lubricated or damaged steering gear.	Adjust, lubricate (check for damaged seals) or replace steering gear.
	Worn or binding lower control arm ball stud(s).	Replace lower control arm(s).
	Worn or binding inner or outer tie rod end(s).	Replace inner or outer tie rod end(s).
	Worn or binding upper strut mount(s).	Replace mount(s).
	Worn or binding intermediate shaft joint(s).	Replace intermediate shaft.
	Binding within steering column or intermediate shaft boot.	Correct condition.
Poor return of steering wheel to center	Front tire(s) improperly inflated.	Inflate tire(s) correctly.
	Improperly adjusted, improperly lubricated or damaged steering gear.	Adjust, lubricate (check for damaged seals) or replace steering gear.
	Worn or binding lower control arm ball stud(s).	Replace lower control arm(s).
	Worn or binding inner or outer tie rod end(s).	Replace inner or outer tie rod end(s).
	Worn or binding upper strut mount(s).	Replace mount(s).
	Worn or binding intermediate shaft joint(s).	Replace intermediate shaft.
	Binding within steering column or intermediate shaft boot.	Correct condition.
	Incorrect front wheel caster.	Adjust front wheel caster.
Excessive free play in steering	Wheel bearing(s) worn.	Replace wheel bearing(s).
	Steering gear mounting bolt(s) loose.	Tighten bolt(s).
	Steering gear out of adjustment or worn.	Adjust or replace steering gear.
	Inner or outer steering tie rod(s) worn.	Replace tie rod(s).
	Lower control arm ball stud(s) worn.	Replace lower control arm(s).
	Tension strut bushings worn.	Replace bushings.
Rattle clunking noise in steering	Inner or outer tie rod end(s) worn.	Replace tie rod end(s).
	Steering gear out of adjustment or worn.	Adjust or replace steering gear.
	Intermediate shaft joint(s) worn.	Replace intermediate shaft.
	Steering gear mounting bolt(s) loose.	Tighten bolt(s).
	Worn wheel bearing(s).	Replace wheel bearing(s).

Fig. 1   Steering system troubleshooting

BACK OFF 50° TO 70° (APPROX. ONE FLAT)

Fig. 2   Bearing preload adjustment

POWER STEERING
INDEX

DESCRIPTION
STEERING SYSTEM

The power steering system is a rack and pinion design, featuring an Electronic Variable Orifice (EVO) design pump.

Unlike conventional power steering systems, the EVO feature adjusts the amount of steering assist according to the speed of the vehicle, which is monitored by a vehicle speed sensor (VSS). This information is read electronically by the Powertrain Control Module (PCM), which commands the EVO actuator to control the power steering pump output flow.

At low speeds, where high levels of assist are desired, the EVO actuator is open further, providing more flow to the steering gear and greater assist. At higher speeds, the actuator is closed further, providing less pump flow and less steering assist and improved road feeling. All of the additional flow of the pump that is not needed by the gear is allowed to return to the reservoir through a bypass.

POWER STEERING PRESSURE SWITCH

The power steering pressure switch is an input to the powertrain control module (PCM). If the pressure exceeds 450-650 psi, the switch opens, signalling to the PCM to increase engine idle RPM and turn the A/C compressor off to compensate for the additional load of the power steering pump.

EVO ACTUATOR

The EVO actuator is a 10 ohm linear solenoid. The PCM controls the current to the high and low side of the actuator so current control is retained in the presence of any output fault condition.

The control of the actuator is accomplished by pulse width modulating (PWM) voltage to the actuator ad monitoring the actual current flow. The PCM varies the PWM signal in order to make the actual current equal to the desired current.

SYSTEM BLEEDING

1. With engine off, front wheels raised and turned completely left, check reservoir fluid level. Add fluid if necessary.
2. Bleed system by turning wheels from side to side several times, without contacting stops.
3. Start engine and check fluid level. Add fluid if necessary.
4. Return steering wheel to straight ahead position, lower front wheels and allow engine to idle for two to three minutes.
5. Road test vehicle to ensure steering functions normally and is free from noise.

TROUBLESHOOTING

Refer to **Fig. 1** for power steering system troubleshooting.

Complaint/Condition	Possible Cause(s)	Correction(s)
Hard Steering	Front tire(s) improperly inflated.	Inflate tire(s) correctly.
	Improperly adjusted, improperly lubricated or damaged steering gear.	Adjust, lubricate (check for damaged seals) or replace steering gear.
	Worn or binding lower control arm ball stud(s).	Replace lower control arm(s).
	Worn or binding inner or outer tie rod(s).	Replace inner or outer tie rod end(s).
	Worn or binding upper strut mount(s).	Replace mount(s).
	Worn or binding intermediate shaft joint(s).	Replace intermediate shaft.
	Accessory drive belt loose.	Check accessory drive belt tension.
	Power steering fluid level low.	Add power steering fluid.
	Insufficient power steering pump pressure.	Repair or replace power steering pump.
	Faulty EVO actuator.	Replace EVO actuator.
	Restricted or leaking power steering hoses.	Replace hoses or tighten hose connections.
	High internal leakage in steering gear.	Replace steering gear.
	Excessive front wheel caster.	Adjust front wheel caster.
	Binding within steering column or intermediate shaft boot.	Correct condition.
Poor return of steering wheel to center	Front tire(s) improperly inflated.	Inflate tire(s) correctly.
	Improperly adjusted, improperly lubricated or binding steering gear.	Adjust, lubricate (check for damaged seals) or replace steering gear.
	Incorrect front wheel caster.	Adjust front wheel caster.
	Worn or binding inner or outer tie rod end(s).	Replace inner or outer tie rod end(s).
	Worn or binding upper strut mount(s).	Replace mount(s).
	Worn or binding intermediate shaft joint(s).	Replace intermediate shaft.
	Binding within steering column or intermediate shaft boot.	Correct condition.
Excessive free play in steering	Wheel bearing(s) worn.	Replace wheel bearing(s).
	Steering gear mounting bolt(s) loose.	Tighten bolt(s).
	Steering gear out of adjustment or worn.	Adjust or replace steering gear.
	Inner or outer steering tie rod(s).	Replace tie rod(s).
	Lower control arm ball stud(s) worn.	Replace lower control arm(s).
	Tension strut bushings worn.	Replace bushings.

Fig. 1   Power steering system troubleshooting (Part 1 of 3)

Complaint/Condition	Possible Cause(s)	Correction(s)
Rattling noise in power steering pump	Vane(s) sticking in rotor slot(s).	Clean rotor/vanes or replace component(s).
	Worn pump shaft bearing.	Replace bearing, pump or housing.
Swishing noise in power steering pump	Damaged flow control valve.	Replace flow control valve.
Whining noise in power steering pump	Pump shaft being scored.	Correct condition.

Fig. 1   Power steering system troubleshooting (Part 3 of 3)

Complaint/Condition	Possible Cause(s)	Correction(s)
Rattle clunking noise in steering	Inner or outer tie rod end(s) worn.	Replace inner or outer tie rod end(s).
	Steering gear out of adjustment or worn.	Adjust or replace steering gear.
	Intermediate shaft joint(s) worn.	Replace intermediate shaft.
	Steering gear mounting bolt(s) loose.	Tighten bolt(s).
	Worn wheel bearing(s).	Replace wheel bearing(s).
Momentary increase in steering effort when steering wheel is turned quickly	High internal leakage in steering gear.	Replace steering gear.
	Low power steering fluid level.	Correct power steering fluid level.
	Insufficient pump pressure.	Repair or replace power steering pump.
	Damaged EVO actuator.	Replace actuator.
	Damaged handwheel sensor (Coupe only).	Replace handwheel sensor.
	EVO electrical circuit malfunction.	Correct condition.
Steering wheel surges or jerks when turning at low speeds	Insufficient power steering pump pressure.	Repair or replace power steering pump.
	High internal leakage in steering gear.	Replace steering gear.
	Loose accessory drive belt.	Check accessory drive belt tension.
Insufficient system pressure – caused by pump	Flow control valve stuck or inoperative.	Free or replace flow control valve.
	EVO system malfunction.	EVO system
	Pressure plate not flat against pump ring.	Correct condition.
	Worn pump ring.	Replace pump ring.
	Scored pressure, thrust plate or rotor.	Replace components.
	Vane(s) sticking in rotor slot(s).	Clean rotor/vanes or replace component(s).
	Cracked or broken thrust, or pressure plate.	Replace components.
Insufficient system pressure – caused by steering gear	Scored steering gear housing bore.	Replace steering gear.
	Leaking steering gear piston seals or inner rack seal.	Replace steering gear.
Growling noise in power steering pump	Excessive back pressure in hoses or steering gear caused by restriction.	Eliminate restriction.
	Scored pressure plate, thrust plate or rotor.	Replace component(s)
	Worn pump ring.	Replace pump ring.
	Air in power steering fluid.	Add power steering and bleed system.
	Pump mounting loose.	Tighten pump mounting.
	Restricted fluid lines.	Eliminate restriction.

Fig. 1   Power steering system troubleshooting (Part 2 of 3)

14. If flow rate is greater then 1 gallon per minute, steering gear is leaking internally and must be replaced.

EVO SUBSYSTEM TEST

1. Disconnect high pressure line at power steering pump and install Power Steering System Tester tool No. SA9134C or equivalent.
2. Connect a Powertrain Diagnostic Tool (PDT) to ALDL diagnostic port. Follow tool manufacturer's instructions.
3. Open gate valve on steering system tester.
4. Run engine until normal operating temperature is reached. Replace any power steering fluid lost during tester installation, then bleed system if necessary.
5. Select "EVO Subsystem Test" using the PDT tool, in the special test menu.
6. Using the PDT, command the EVO actuator to provide "full assist." Record power steering fluid flow rate, as indicated on the power steering system tester. If flow rate is not between 2.35-2.85 gallons per minute, replace EVO actuator.
7. Using the PDT, command the EVO actuator to provide "no assist." Record fluid flow rate, as indicated on steering tester. If flow rate is not between 0.4-0.9 gallons per minute, replace EVO actuator.

DIAGNOSIS & TESTING

HYDRAULIC SYSTEM TEST

1. Disconnect high pressure line at steering gear and install power steering system tester tool No. SA9134C or equivalent.
2. Open gate valve on power steering system tester.
3. Run engine until it has reached normal operating temperature. Replace any power steering fluid lost during tester installation, then bleed system if necessary.
4. With engine idling, record pressure and flow rate. If the pressure reading is greater than 150 psi, stop engine and check power steering lines for restrictions. **Do not turn steering wheel while performing this test.**
5. Slowly close gate valve until 700 psi is indicated on the power steering tester. Record pressure and flow rate.
6. Flow rate should not drop more than 1 gallon per minute from flow rate recorded in step 4.
7. If flow rate drops more than 1 gallon per minute, replace ring, rotor and the vanes in the pump. Also inspect pressure plate and thrust plates for wear.
8. Completely close and open gate valve three times. **Do not close gate valve for more than five seconds at a time.** Record fluid pressure each time the valve is closed.
9. If all three readings are not within 50 psi, replace flow control valve.
10. With gate valve open, increase engine speed to 1600 RPM and record fluid pressure and flow rate. **Do not turn steering wheel.**
11. Flow rate should not vary more than 1 gallon per minute from the flow rate recorded in step 4.
12. Ensure flow control valve moves freely in pump housing. Inspect valve for burrs.
13. Turn steering wheel completely to left, then completely to right. Record fluid pressure and flow rate at each stop.

Fig. 2   Steering gear bearing preload adjustment

Fig. 3   EVO actuator replacement

Fig. 4   EVO actuator O-ring locations

Fig. 5   Pump retaining ring removal

Fig. 6   Pump internal component removal

Fig. 7   Pump housing O-ring seal, dowel pins and driveshaft seal removal

STEERING GEAR BEARING PRELOAD
ADJUST

The following adjustment should be made with the front wheel raised and the steering wheel centered.
1. Loosen adjuster plug locknut on steering gear housing.
2. Turn adjuster plug clockwise until it bottoms in steering gear housing, **Fig. 2.**
3. **Torque** adjuster plug to 106 inch lbs.
4. Back-off adjuster plug 50-70° (approximately one flat of nut).
5. **Torque** locknut, while holding adjuster plug, to 52 ft. lbs.
6. Check steering wheel returnability following adjustment.

PRESSURE SWITCH
REPLACE

1. Disconnect battery ground cable, then raise and support vehicle.
2. Disconnect electrical connection at power steering pressure switch.
3. Remove switch.
4. Reverse procedure to install, noting the following:
   a. Inspect O-ring and replace if necessary.
   b. **Torque** switch to 97 inch lbs.

Fig. 8   Removing rotor, vanes, ring and thrust plate from driveshaft

ELECTRONIC VARIABLE ORIFICE (EVO) ACTUATOR
REPLACE

1. Disconnect battery ground cable.
2. Remove pump from vehicle, then disconnect EVO electrical connector locating clip.
3. Remove EVO actuator assembly using socket removal tool No. SA91116C or equivalent, **Fig. 3.** Do not pivot socket tool during removal.

4. Remove discharge fitting from actuator.
5. Remove three O-ring seals from actuator. Note size and location of O-ring seals.
6. Reverse procedure to install, noting the following:
   a. Refer to **Fig. 4** for three O-ring seals locations.
   b. **Torque** EVO actuator to 46 ft. lbs.
   c. Install pump and bleed power steering system.

STEERING PUMP OVERHAUL

DISASSEMBLY

1. Remove power steering pump from vehicle.
2. Remove reservoir retaining clips from reservoir assembly.
3. Remove reservoir from housing.
4. Remove O-ring seal from pump housing, then remove pulley using puller tool No. SA9162C or equivalent.
5. Remove three power steering pump to bracket fasteners and remove bracket from pump.
6. Remove EVO actuator assembly using removal tool No. SA9116C or equivalent.
7. Remove flow control valve and spring.

Fig. 9   Driveshaft/rotor/thrust plate assembly

Fig. 10   Pump ring dowel pins & pump ring assembly

Fig. 11   Pressure plate assembly

8. Remove retaining ring, **Fig. 5,** as follows:
   a. Use a C-clamp (one side on end cover, the other on pump driveshaft) to depress end cover, easing removal of retaining ring.
   b. Insert a piece of wood between C-clamp and pump driveshaft.
   c. Place a punch into pump housing access hole and remove retaining ring.
9. Gently push on driveshaft to assist in removing end cover.
10. Remove internal pump components in two groups, **Fig. 6,** as follows:
    a. Remove end cover, O-ring, pressure plate spring and pressure plate.
    b. Remove driveshaft with pump rotor, pump vanes, pump ring, thrust plate and shaft retaining ring.
11. Remove O-ring seal (A), two dowel pins (B) and driveshaft seal (C) from pump housing, **Fig. 7.**
12. Remove pressure plate, pressure plate spring and O-ring from end cover.
13. Remove shaft retaining ring from driveshaft.
14. Remove pump rotor, pump vanes, pump ring and thrust plate from driveshaft, **Fig. 8.**
15. Separate pump rotor, pump vanes and pump ring.
16. Clean all parts with new power steering fluid.
17. Inspect pump ring, pump vanes, thrust plate and driveshaft for scoring, pitting or chatter marks.
18. Replace any damaged components. Do not attempt to remove damage with abrasive cleaners.
19. A wavy pattern on pump ring face will be present with low mileage and should not be mistaken for pre-mature wear or damage.

ASSEMBLY

1. Lubricate driveshaft with new power steering fluid.
2. Install new driveshaft seal into pump housing using a suitably sized socket as a driver.
3. Install thrust plate and pump rotor onto driveshaft.
4. Install driveshaft/rotor/thrust plate assembly into housing, **Fig. 9.**
5. Install pump ring dowel pins into pump housing through thrust plate. Install pump ring (with holes correctly positioned onto dowel pins) into housing, **Fig. 10.**
6. Pump ring face has a indentation on one side near the dowel hole. The ring must be installed with the indentation facing up. **If ring is installed upside down, the pump will not function.**
7. Install vanes into pump rotor. Vanes may be installed in either direction.
8. Lubricate new pump housing O-ring with power steering fluid and install into groove in housing.
9. Align pressure plate dowel holes with dowel pins and install plate into housing.
10. Position pressure plate spring against pressure plate. Lubricate new end cover O-ring with power steering fluid and install onto end cover, **Fig. 11.**
11. Lubricate outer edit of end cover with power steering fluid, then press end cover into pump housing.
12. Install retaining ring into groove in pump housing, with ring opening near access hole in housing. Ensure ring is fully seated in housing groove.
13. Install three O-ring seals onto EVO actuator, if removed during disassembly procedure. **Install three seals (A, B and C) in correct position as shown in Fig. 4.**
14. Correctly position EVO actuator and discharge fitting to pump assembly, **Fig. 3.**
15. **Torque** EVO actuator with installation tool NO. SA9116C or equivalent, to 46 ft. lbs., **Fig. 3.**
16. Install power steering pump bracket onto power steering pump with three fasteners. **Torque** to 28 ft. lbs.
17. Install pump pulley using installation tool No. SA9162C or equivalent.
18. Lubricate new reservoir O-ring with power steering fluid and install onto reservoir.
19. Install reservoir into pump housing. Push reservoir straight into housing, then install retaining clips.
20. Install pump into vehicle and bleed power steering system.

DASH PANEL SERVICE

INDEX

Fig. 1   Upper trim panel removal

Fig. 2   Cluster trim panel removal

Fig. 3   Instrument cluster removal

Fig. 4   Steering column filler panel removal

PRECAUTIONS

AIRBAG SYSTEM DISARMING

1. Place ignition in OFF position, then remove Supplemental Inflatable Restraint (SIR) fuse.
2. Remove connector position assurance (CPA) device from yellow two way SIR connector at base of steering column.

AIRBAG SYSTEM REARMING

1. Place ignition in Off position, then connect yellow two way SIR connector at base of steering column, then install CPA device to connector.
2. Install SIR fuse.
3. Turn ignition switch to Run position, then ensure AIRBAG lamp flashes 7 to 9 times, then remains Off.

DASH PANEL REPLACE

1. Disable airbag system as described under "Precautions."
2. Disconnect battery ground cable, then remove left and right end cap assembly by removing end cap attachment screw and pulling out board to disconnect retainer clips.
3. **On 1991 models,** remove cigar lighter trim bezel.
4. **On all models,** remove left and right lower trim panel extensions by disconnecting lower velcro fasteners and pulling out at upper clip locations.
5. Carefully remove center air outlet/trim panel by pulling outward at clip locations. Start at bottom and work up. Do not use instruments that may damage trim panel.
6. **On 1993-94 models,** disconnect traction control/fog lamp electrical connector.
7. **On all models,** remove trim panel extension strip by pulling outward at clip locations.
8. Remove upper trim panel screw caps by carefully prying with a small screwdriver, then remove upper trim panel screws.
9. Lift upper trim panel to disengage clips at rear edge, **Fig. 1.**
10. Remove upper trim panel by pulling rearward out of clips at bottom of windshield.
11. Remove screws and pull cluster trim panel rearward to disengage retainers, **Fig. 2.**
12. Remove connector position assurance (CPA) devices and disconnect electrical connectors from instrument panel lighting rheostat and rear win-

Fig. 5   Instrument panel junction block

dow defrost switches. Remove cluster trim panel.
13. Remove screws and pull instrument panel cluster out enough to disconnect electrical connectors.
14. Disconnect electrical connector by depressing retainer legs. **Fig. 3.** Remove instrument cluster.
15. Remove wiring harness clips from dash reinforcement.
16. Loosen screws and remove assembly line diagnostic link connector.
17. Loosen screws and remove steering column filler panel, **Fig. 4.**
18. Remove hood release lever screw.
19. Remove radio and HVAC dash control assembly.
20. Disconnect cigarette lighter electrical connector.
21. Remove cigarette lighter bulb holder by rotating counterclockwise and pulling straight out.
22. Apply parking brake, then remove parking brake filler panel by carefully lifting at rear edge.

Fig. 6   Two-way instrument panel connector

Fig. 7   Floor shifter bracket removal

Fig. 8   Instrument panel & reinforcement bracket screw locations

23. **On models with manual transaxles,** remove gear selector knob by pulling straight up.
24. **On models with automatic transaxles,** move gear selector to No. 2 position.
25. **On models with power windows,** remove ashtray and disconnect ashtray bulb holder.
26. Remove window/mirror switch by sliding switch forward, then lifting rear edge.
27. **On models with standard windows,** remove connector position assurance (CPA) devices and disconnect window/mirror electrical connectors, then remove console.

28. **On all models,** loosen screws and remove instrument panel junction block from dash reinforcement, **Fig. 5.**
29. Remove ground wire from dash reinforcement, then loosen screw and remove rear electrical connector from instrument panel fuse block.
30. Remove CPA device and disconnect two-way instrument panel to body harness connector, **Fig. 6.**
31. Remove wire harness and antenna hold-down clips from instrument panel reinforcement.
32. Loosen floor shifter assembly. Remove two nuts, lift lower reinforcement bracket off of studs and slide bracket rearward, **Fig. 7.**
33. Loosen mounting nuts and lower

cruise control module, if equipped.
34. Remove screws and nuts from instrument panel retainer and reinforcement bracket, **Fig. 8.**
35. Remove bolts and lower steering column assembly onto front seat.
36. Carefully remove instrument panel/retainer assembly.
37. Reverse procedure to install, noting the following:
    a. Feed fuse block and wire harness through lower reinforcement and into position.
    b. **Torque** steering column retaining bolts to 26 ft. lbs.
    c. Rearm airbag system as described under "Precautions."

STEERING COLUMNS

INDEX

PRECAUTIONS

AIRBAG SYSTEM DISARMING

1. Place ignition in OFF position, then remove Supplemental Inflatable Restraint (SIR) fuse.
2. Remove connector position assurance (CPA) device from yellow two way SIR connector at base of steering column.

AIRBAG SYSTEM REARMING

1. Place ignition in Off position, then connect yellow two way SIR connector at base of steering column, then install CPA device to connector.
2. Install SIR fuse.
3. Turn ignition switch to Run position, then ensure AIRBAG lamp flashes 7 to 9 times, then remains Off.

STEERING COLUMN REPLACE

REMOVAL

1. Disconnect battery ground cable.
2. Remove steering wheel as follows:
    a. Pull on edge of horn pad to release from steering wheel.
    b. Disconnect electrical wires and remove horn pad.
    c. Remove clip on end of steering column shaft, then remove steering wheel retaining nut.
    d. Attach steering wheel puller tool and remove wheel from column.
3. Remove two screws and upper steering column cover.
4. Remove ignition lock bezel. Remove two screws and the lower steering column cover.
5. Remove left and right lower trim panel extensions by disconnecting lower velcro fasteners and pulling panels

out of two upper fasteners, **Fig. 1.**
6. Remove center trim plate by pulling on bottom to disengage lower fasteners, then pull top of trim plate to disengage upper fasteners, **Fig. 2.**
7. Remove trim panel extension strip by pulling out at fastener locations.
8. Remove both upper trim panel screw caps, **Fig. 3,** then remove two screws and lift panel to disengage six clips at rear edge.
9. Slide panel out of three clips at windshield and remove upper panel. Remove trim panel extension strip by pulling out at fastener locations, **Fig. 3.**
10. Remove four screws and lift cluster trim panel to disengage rear retainers, **Fig. 4.** Disconnect harness from rear window defroster and thermostat switches, then remove trim panel.
11. Remove six screws to remove steering column opening filler assembly, **Fig. 5.**
12. Remove connector position assur-

Fig. 1 Lower trim panel removal

Fig. 2 Center trim plate removal

Fig. 3 Upper trim panel removal

Fig. 4 Cluster trim panel removal

Fig. 5 Steering column opening filler removal

Fig. 6 Handwheel sensor replacement

ance (CPA) device and disconnect wires from lower control switch.

13. Disconnect lever control switch connector, then disconnect ignition switch from ignition module.
14. Remove two upper steering column bolts. Carefully lower steering column onto front seat.
15. Remove upper bolt from intermediate shaft and disconnect shaft from column.
16. **On Coupe models,** disconnect handwheel sensor electrical sensor.
17. **On all models,** remove two bolts to disconnect steering column at hinge point.
18. Remove steering column from vehicle.
19. **On Coupe models,** remove handwheel sensor from lower steering column support bracket by releasing both sensor locking tabs and remove sensor from column.
20. **On all models,** position steering column in a vise at the upper bracket. Using a center punch, mark center of shear bolts on ignition module assembly.
21. Drill a small hole (¹⁄₈ inch) in shear bolts at the center mark. Remove shear bolts with a screw extractor. Remove ignition module assembly and clamp from column.

INSTALLATION

1. Using new shear bolts, install ignition module onto steering column. Tighten shear bolts until heads break off.
2. **On Coupe models,** install handwheel sensor onto steering column. Position electrical connector to top of column and attach to lower support bracket by snapping sensor locking tabs into bracket.
3. **On all models,** install steering column at hinge point.
4. Connect intermediate shaft. **Torque** bolt to 33 ft. lbs.
5. **On Coupe models,** connect handwheel sensor electrical sensor.
6. **On all models,** raise steering column up to instrument panel and install two bolts. **Torque** to 26 ft. lbs.
7. Install lever control switch by fitting into bottom locating holes on ignition module. Tighten lower screw first to ensure correct location.
8. Install ignition switch to ignition module.
9. Install steering column opening filler.
10. Install cluster trim panel.
11. Install instrument panel top cover. Use six new clips.
12. Install trim panel extension strip, center trim plate and lower trim panel extensions.

13. Install steering column covers.
14. Install steering wheel. **Torque** retaining nut to 30 ft. lbs.
15. Connect battery ground cable.

HANDWHEEL SENSOR REPLACE

COUPE

1. Rotate steering wheel until clamp bolt at lower steering column intermediate shaft joint is accessible.
2. Remove clamp bolt at lower steering column intermediate shaft joint, **Fig. 6**
3. Slide intermediate shaft off lower steering column.
4. Remove handwheel sensor from lower steering column support bracket by releasing both sensor locking tabs.
5. Rotate handwheel sensor 180° until electrical connector is easily accessible, then disconnect electrical connector from sensor.
6. Remove handwheel sensor.
7. Reverse procedure to install, noting the following:
   a. Ensure electrical connector is facing up.
   b. **Torque** intermediate shaft pinch bolt to 35 ft. lbs.

PASSIVE RESTRAINTS

TABLE OF CONTENTS

Supplemental Inflatable Restraint (SIR)

INDEX

AIRBAG SYSTEM DISARMING

1. Point wheels straight ahead by turning steering wheel.
2. Turn ignition to Off position, then disconnect and tape battery ground terminal.
3. Remove airbag fuse.
4. Remove connector position assurance (CPA) device from yellow two-way SIR connector at base of steering column, then disconnect connector.

AIRBAG SYSTEM REARMING

1. Turn ignition switch to Off position.
2. Connect yellow two-way SIR connector at base of steering column and install Connector Position Assurance (CPA) device to connector.
3. Install airbag fuse.
4. Turn ignition switch to RUN position. Ensure "airbag" telltale lamp flashes seven times, then remains off.

PRECAUTIONS

Safe handling of live and deployed air-bag modules requires following the following procedures:

1. Perform SIR diagnostic system check under "Reading and Diagnosing Codes" as the first and last task during diagnosis and service.
2. Before attempting service on or around SIR components or wiring, disarm the SIR system as described under "Airbag System Disarming."
3. The Diagnostic Energy Reserve Module (DERM) maintains voltage after the ignition switch is turned to OFF and the battery is disconnected. Wait 10 minutes for this backup power to discharge before performing any service on the SIR system.
4. Inspect SIR system components after an accident that may or may not involve airbag deployment.
5. Use special electrical connector adapters when performing diagnostic tests.
6. Replace wiring terminals with special repair kits.
7. Never strike or jar a sensor in a way that could cause deployment.
8. If a sensor or DERM is dropped from a height greater than 2 feet or shows any signs of damage, replace the component.
9. Use caution in ensuring proper location of the sensors to the vehicle structure. The keying of the sensors to the structure through differently sized mounting holes and the wiring harness must not be modified for any reason.
10. All sensor and mounting bracket bolts must be carefully torqued to assure proper operation.
11. Never power up the SIR system when any sensor is not rigidly attached to the vehicle.
12. Avoid touching the DERM terminals to prevent damage due to electrostatic discharge.

HANDLING LIVE (UNDEPLOYED) AIRBAG MODULES

Special care is necessary when handling and storing a live (undeployed) inflator module. The rapid gas generation produced during deployment of the airbag could cause the inflator module or an object in front of the inflator module to be thrown through the air.

When carrying a live inflator module, be sure the airbag and trim cover are pointed away from you. Never carry the inflator module by the wires or by the connector on the underside of the module. In case of accidental deployment, the airbag will deploy with minimal chance of injury.

When placing the steering wheel module on a bench or other surface, always face the airbag and trim cover away from the surface. Never rest a steering wheel with the inflator face down and the column vertical. A free space must be provided to allow for airbag expansion in case of accidental deployment.

HANDLING DEPLOYED MODULES

After the airbag has been deployed, the surface of the airbag may contain a powdery residue. This powder consists primarily of corn starch (used to lubricate the airbag as it inflates) and by-products of the chemical reaction. Sodium hydroxide dust (similar to lye dust) is produced as a by-product of the deployment reaction. The sodium hydroxide then quickly reacts with atmospheric moisture and is converted to sodium carbonate and sodium bicarbonate (baking soda). Therefore, it is unlikely that sodium hydroxide will be present after deployment. Always wear safety glasses and gloves when handling a deployed module, and wash hands with mild soap and water afterward.

VEHICLE SCRAPPING

Some SIR equipped vehicles that have live (undeployed) inflator modules may have to be scrapped because they have completed their useful life or have been severely damaged in a non-deployment type accident. The following procedure should be followed when scrapping a vehicle with an undeployed module.

1. Place ignition switch in Off position.
2. Ensure inflator module is secured to steering wheel.
3. Remove all loose objects from front seat and module cover.
4. Disconnect yellow two-way connector at base of steering column.
5. Cut yellow two-way connector away from vehicle harness leaving at least 6 inches of wire at the connector.
6. Splice two 18 gauge wires, 15 feet long, into steering wheel module circuit wiring at base of steering column.
7. Ensure vehicle interior is free of all people and loose or flammable objects.
8. Stretch wires away from vehicle to their full length.
9. Apply 12 volts across wires to deploy module. Do not touch metal areas of inflator module for 10 minutes due to heat generated by deployment.

AIRBAG DISPOSAL

When a deployed module has been removed from a vehicle, it may be disposed of with any other scrap material. Handle with gloves and safety glasses and wash hands after handling. The inflator module must be deactivated prior to disposal. Failure to deactivate before disposing may result in personal injury since the module contains explosive material.

1. BOLT/SCREW–ARMING SENSOR
2. SENSOR ASM–INFL RST PASS COMPT (ARMING SENSOR)
3. RESISTOR MODULE I/P HARNESS
4. DERM BRKT
5. NUT–DERM BRKT
6. MODULE ASM–INFL RST (DERM)
7. BOLT/SCREW–INFL RST F/END SH MET SEN
8. SENSOR ASM–INFL RST F/END SH MET (DISCRIMINATING SENSORS)
9. BOLT/SCREW–INFL MODULE
10. SIR STEERING WHEEL
11. SIR COIL ASM CONNECTOR
12. INFLATOR MODULE

Fig. 1   SIR component location & wiring view

DESCRIPTION

The supplemental inflatable restraint (SIR) system, **Fig. 1** supplements the driver seat belt to provide additional protection in a frontal crash. The system deploys an airbag from the center of the steering wheel during a frontal crash of sufficient force.

SIR SYSTEM COMPONENTS

DIAGNOSTIC ENERGY RESERVE MODULE

The diagnostic energy reserve module (DERM) provides reserve energy to the deployment loop. It also performs diagnostic monitoring of all SIR system electrical components. The DERM warns the driver of system faults via the "airbag" telltale.

Do not open the DERM case for any reason. Touching connector pins or soldered components may cause electrostatic discharge damage. Do not at-

tempt to repair of a faulty DERM. It is serviced only by replacement.

"AIRBAG" TELLTALE

The "airbag" telltale notifies the driver of SIR system faults. The lamp is operational whenever the ignition switch is in the Run or Start position.

The telltale also verifies lamp and DERM operation by flashing seven times when the ignition switch is first turned On.

ARMING SENSOR

The arming sensor is located on the power feed side of the deployment loop. When it senses severe changes in vehicle velocity, it provides current to the inflator module in preparation for deployment.

The sensor is located in the instrument panel near the glove box.

DISCRIMINATING SENSORS

Discriminating sensors are located on

Fig. 2   SIR coil assembly

1. SIR COIL ASSEMBLY
2. INFLATOR MODULE CONNECTOR
3. STEERING COLUMN CONNECTOR

the ground side of the deployment loop. When they sense severe changes in vehicle velocity, they provide ground to the inflator module in preparation for deployment.

The sensors are located on the radiator support outboard of the radiator.

SIR COIL ASSEMBLY

The SIR coil assembly, **Fig. 2** consists of six current-carrying circuits in the deployment loop. The coil allows rotation of the steering wheel while maintaining contact between the deployment loop and the inflator module.

INFLATOR MODULE

The inflator module is located in the steering wheel hub beneath the trim cover. The inflator module consists of an inflatable bag, an inflator (canister of gas generating material) and an initiating device.

RESISTOR MODULE

The resistor module consists of resistors in the SIR harness between the DERM and the steering column. It is mounted on the DERM bracket. The resistor module allows the DERM to monitor the deployment loop for faults while limiting current flow to a non-deployment level.

STEERING COLUMN

The steering column is energy absorbing and is designed to compress in a frontal crash to decrease the chance of injury to the driver.

KNEE BOLSTER & SEAT

The knee bolster and seat are used to absorb energy and control the driver's forward movement during a frontal crash by limiting leg movement.

DEPLOYMENT LOOP

The deployment loop is a circuit that supplies current to the inflator module, located in the steering wheel hub, to deploy the airbag.

OPERATION

When the vehicle is in a frontal crash of sufficient force to close the arming sensor and at least one of the discriminating sensors simultaneously, current flows through the deployment loop, **Fig. 3**. The arming sensor supplies the current, while the discriminating sensor(s) provide the ground. Current passing through the initiator ignites the inflator (a canister of gas generating material) inside the inflator module. The gas produced from this reaction rapidly inflates the airbag. The DERM records the system status during a vehicle accident.

WIRING DIAGRAM & CONNECTOR IDENTIFICATION

Refer to **Figs. 4 and 5** for wiring diagram and connector identification.

WIRING HARNESS & CONNECTOR REPAIR

Special wiring repair procedures have been developed for use on the SIR systems due to the sensitive nature of the circuitry.

The use of connector repair kit tool No. SA9138Z or equivalent, contains special sealed splices for use in repairing SIR system wiring. A special crimping tool, heat torch and instruction manual for these splices are also included.

The critical features of the sealed splices are a special heat shrink sleeve with sealing adhesive to produce an environmentally sealed splice and a cross hatched core crimp to provide necessary contact integrity for the sensitive low energy circuits.

DIAGNOSIS & TESTING

To avoid deployment when troubleshooting the SIR system, do not use electrical test equipment such as a battery powered or AC powered voltmeter, ohmmeter, etc., or any type of electrical equipment other than specified. Do not use a non-powered probe type tester. Instructions in this section must be followed carefully, otherwise personal injury may result.

DIAGNOSTIC TROUBLE CODE TYPES

Current Codes

Current codes are faults that are presently being detected or have not been successfully cleared because the malfunction

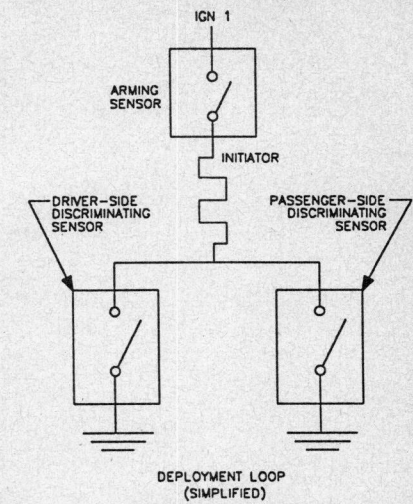

Fig. 3   Deployment loop

still exists. If the battery has been disconnected, all current codes will be erased. **Do not disconnect battery if an SIR system malfunction exists and trouble codes have not been retrieved.**

History Codes

History codes are all faults detected since the DERM memory was last cleared. If a history code is present, the related malfunction may not necessarily exist. History codes may only be erased using a SCAN/TECH tool.

ACCESSING DIAGNOSTIC TROUBLE CODES

To access trouble codes, refer to diagnostic system check, **Fig. 6**

READING TROUBLE CODES

To read and diagnose trouble codes, refer to **Figs. 7 through 28.**

AFTER ACCIDENT INSPECTION

In all types of accidents, regardless of airbag deployment, visually inspect the following components and their mounting points and replace as required:
1. Inflator module
2. Steering wheel
3. SIR coil assembly
4. Steering column
5. Knee bolster and instrument panel mounting attachments
6. Driver seat and belts
7. Discriminating sensors
8. Arming sensors
9. DERM
10. Resistor module

Sensors in the damaged area should be replaced, even if the sensors do not appear to be damaged. Do not attempt to determine whether a sensor is OK, always replace the sensor if it is located in a damaged area.

Fig. 4   SIR system wiring diagram

Also inspect the SIR coil assembly wiring and steering wheel for signs of scorching, melting, or other damage due to excessive heat. If the coil assembly wiring or steering wheel is damaged, replace them. Check the steering column and wheel dimensions to determine if they are damaged.

Do not attempt to repair the forward discriminating sensors, the arming sensor, the DERM, the resistor module, the SIR coil assembly, the inflator module, the steering wheel or the steering column. Service of these items is replacement only. Verify the replacement part numbers.

Never use SIR parts from another vehicle.

Proper operation of the sensors and the SIR system requires that any repairs to the vehicle structure return it to its original production configuration.

SYSTEM SERVICE

INFLATOR MODULE, REPLACE

1. Disarm SIR system as outlined under "Airbag System Disarming."
2. Remove four inflator module screws, then lift module out of steering wheel. Discard screws.
3. Remove connector positive assurance (CPA), then disconnect connector and remove inflator module.
4. Reverse procedure to install, noting the following:
    a. **Torque** new inflator module screws to 89 in. lbs. **Never reuse old screws.**
    b. Rearm SIR system as outlined under "Airbag System Rearming."

STEERING WHEEL, REPLACE

1. Disarm SIR system as outlined under "Airbag System Disarming."
2. Remove inflator module as described under "Inflator Module, Replace."
3. Disconnect cruise control switch, if equipped, then the horn switch connector.
4. Remove steering wheel attaching nut, then discard nut.
5. Install steering wheel puller onto steering wheel and remove steering wheel, feeding wiring through wheel.
6. Insert yellow tab into SIR coil assembly to prevent SIR coil from rotating. If tab is not available, tape coil.
7. Reverse procedure to install, noting the following:

Continued on page 34-110

Fig. 5   SIR connectors

DIAGNOSTIC CHART INDEX

Diagnostic chart	Description	Year	Page No.	Fig. No.
—	SIR Diagnostic System Check	1993–94	34-102	6
Chart A	"Airbag" Telltale Lamp Stays On Steady	1993–94	34-102	7
Chart B	"Airbag" Telltale Lamp Does Not Come On	1993–94	34-102	8
Chart C	"Airbag" Telltale Lamp Does Not Stay On Steady During Crank	1993–94	34-103	9
Chart D	DERM Cannot Communicate With PDT	1993–94	34-103	10
Chart E	History Code Diagnosis	1993–94	34-103	11
Code 21	Steering Column Circuit Resistance Too High	1993–94	34-104	12
Code 22	Steering Column Circuit Resistance Too Low	1993–94	34-104	13
Code 21 & 22	Steering Column Circuit Resistance Undetermined	1993–94	34-105	14
Code 23	Steering Column Circuit Voltage Too High	1993–94	34-105	15
Code 24	Steering Column Circuit Voltage Too Low	1993–94	34-106	16
Code 25	Short To Battery In Steering Column Circuit	1993–94	34-107	17
Code 26	Open In Steering Column Circuit	1993–94	34-107	18
Code 31	Open 36 VLR To Deployment Loop	1993–94	34-107	19
Code 32	Grounded 36 VLR To Deployment Loop	1993–94	34-108	20
Code 33	Steering Diode Shorted In Arming Sensor	1993–94	34-108	21
Code 34	Open In Ignition 1 Feed To Deployment Loop	1993–94	34-108	22
Code 35	Discriminating Sensor Open	1993–94	34-108	23
Code 41/42	Deployment Loop Energy Reserve Voltage Fault	1993–94	34-109	24
Code 51	Accident Detected	1993–94	34-109	25
Code 52	EEPROM Accident Data Area Full	1993–94	34-109	26
Code 61	Force Low Or "Airbag" Telltale Lamp Circuit Failure	1993–94	34-109	27
Code 61	Internal DERM Fault	1993–94	34-109	28

Important: Record all codes — cycle and history.

Fig. 6 SIR diagnostic system check

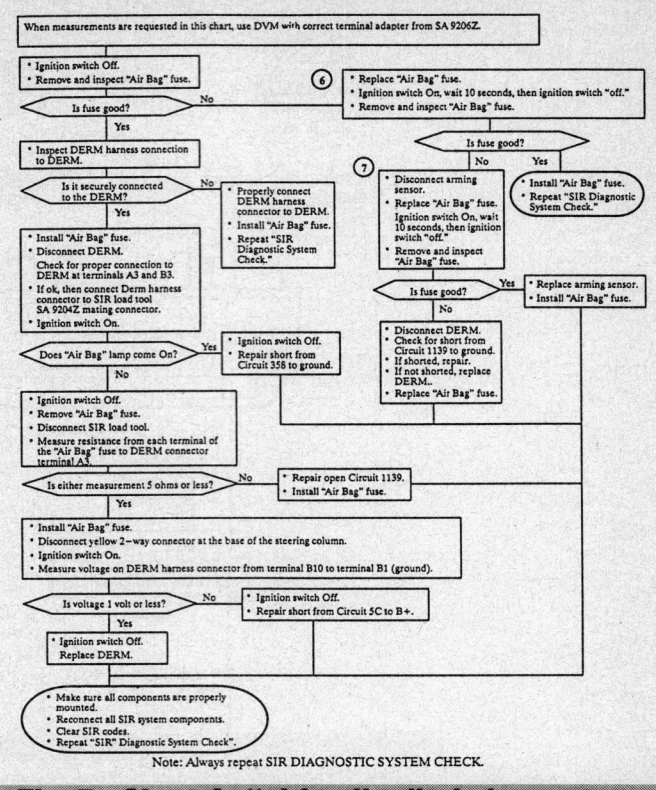

Fig. 7 Chart A, "airbag" telltale lamp stays On steady

Fig. 8 Chart B, "airbag" telltale lamp does not come On (Part 1 of 2)

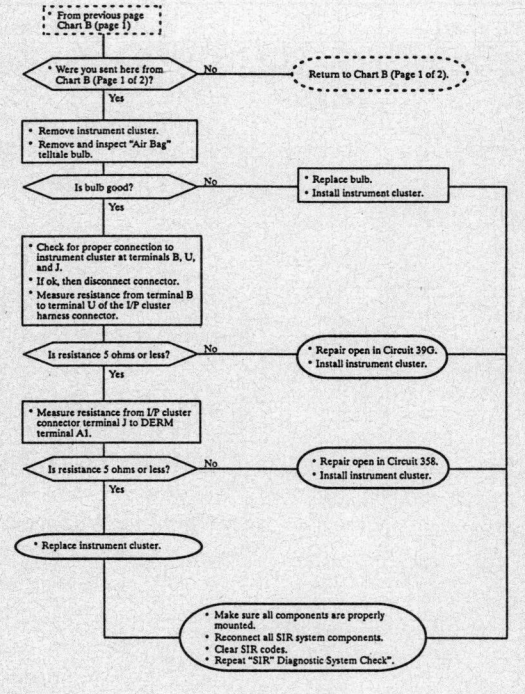

Fig. 8 Chart B, "airbag" telltale lamp does not come On (Part 2 of 2)

Fig. 9   Chart C, "airbag" telltale lamp does not stay on steady during crank

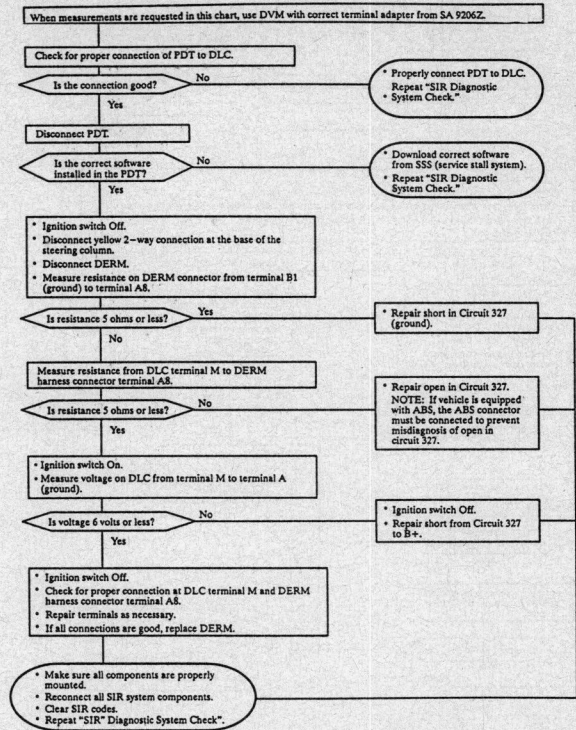

Fig. 10   Chart D, DERM cannot communicate with PDT

When measurements are requested in this chart, use SA 91114 NE DVM with the correct terminal adapter from SA 9206Z. When a check for proper connection is requested, refer to "Intermittents/History Codes/Poor Connection" in Section 1.

• If Code 51 is set	• Go to Code 51 Chart
• If Code 52 is set	• Go to Code 52 Chart
• If Code 71 is set	• Go to Code 71 Chart
• If Code 33 is set	• Go to Code 33 Chart
• Is History Code 21, 22, 24, or 26 set?	• Check for intermittent shorts or grounds within the steering column. With the ignition "ON", engine at idle, slowly turn the steering wheel from full lock left to full lock right a number of times. Observe the "Air Bag" telltale. If the light comes "ON" a code is now current. With the wheel in this position, return to the "SIR Diagnostic System Check."
• Is History Code 41 or 42 set?	• Inspect 36VLR CKT 236 between DERM and arming sensor for intermittent shorts to ground or voltage. Repair as needed following wiring repair procedures and using tool SA 9138Z. • Clear SIR Codes and repeat "SIR Diagnostic System Check."
• Is History Code 61 set?	• This code will set if IGN 1 Fuse or the "Air Bag" telltale lamp is open or removed. If a wiring fault existed in CKT 39 and has been repaired, clear codes and repeat "SIR Diagnostic System Check." • If no known fault existed in CKT 39, inspect CKT 688 between resistor module and DERM, and CKT 358 between "Air Bag" telltale and DERM. Check both circuits for poor connection, open, shorts to ground, or voltage. Repair as needed following wiring repair procedures and using tool SA 9138Z.
• Is History Code 35 set?	• Inspect CKT 349 between driver and passenger side discriminating sensors, CKT 1003E and CKT 1003C. An intermittent open in any of these CKTs will cause this code. Assure proper connections at these sensors. Repair circuits as needed following wiring repair procedures and using tool SA 9138Z. • Clear SIR Codes and repeat "SIR Diagnostic System Check."
• Is History Code 23 set?	• Inspect 36VLR CKT 236 for shorts to CKTs 347, 348, or 349. Assure proper connections at the arming and discriminating sensors. Inspect for connector damage. Repair or replace as needed following wiring repair procedures and using tool SA 9138Z. • Clear SIR Codes and repeat "SIR Diagnostic System Check."
• Are History Codes 33 and 42 set with any of the following? A) No other codes B) Code 41 C) Code 61	• Problem is likely to be an intermittent short to system voltage in 36VLR circuit. • Inspect wiring between DERM and arming sensor, if wiring is cut, pinched or shorted, repair as needed following wiring repair procedures and using tool SA 9138Z. • Clear SIR Codes and repeat "SIR Diagnostic System Check."
• Are History Codes 32 and 42 set with any of the following? A) No other codes B) Code 41 C) Code 61	• Problem is likely to be an intermittent short to ground in 36VLR circuit. • Inspect wiring between DERM and arming sensor, if wiring is cut, pinched or shorted, repair as needed following wiring repair procedures and using tool SA 9138Z. • Clear SIR Codes and repeat "SIR Diagnostic System Check."
• Are History codes 24 and 31 set with any of the following: A) No other codes B) Code 61	• Problem is likely to be an intermittent open in 36VLR circuit. • Inspect wiring between DERM and arming sensor, if wiring is cut, pinched or shorted, repair as needed following wiring repair procedures and using tool SA 9138Z. • Clear SIR Codes and repeat "SIR Diagnostic System Check."

Fig. 11   Chart E, history code diagnosis (Part 1 of 2)

• Are both History Codes 21 and 22 set?	• Inspect CKT 714 for intermittent open and CKT 688 for intermittent short between DERM and resistor module. Repair as needed following wiring repair procedures and using tool SA 9138Z. Assure proper connection at DERM and resistor module, assure CPAs (connector position assurance locks) are installed. • Clear SIR Codes and repeat "SIR Diagnostic System Check."
• Are History Codes 24, 26 and 34 set?	• Inspect CKT 752 for opens or shorts to ground. Repair as needed following wiring repair procedures and using tool SA 9138Z. • Clear SIR Codes and repeat "SIR Diagnostic System Check."
• Are History Codes 24 and 34 set?	• Inspect for shorts to ground or voltage on CKTs 347, 348, 349, 688, 714, 752 or 753 repair as needed following wiring repair procedures and using tool SA 9138Z. • Clear SIR Codes and repeat "SIR Diagnostic System Check."
• Are History Codes 23 and 34 set?	• Inspect for shorts from CKT 236 to CKTs 347, 348 or 349. • Clear SIR Codes and repeat "SIR Diagnostic System Check."
• Is History Code 31 set?	• Inspect 36VLR CKT 236 between DERM and arming sensor for intermittent open. Assure good connection at DERM and arming sensor. Assure CPAs are installed (connector position assurance locks). Repair as needed following wiring repair procedures and using tool SA 9138Z. • Clear SIR Codes and repeat "SIR Diagnostic System Check."
• Is History Code 34 set?	• Inspect CKT 1139 between "Air Bag" fuse and arming sensor for intermittent open. Assure good connection at arming sensor. Assure CPAs are installed (connector position assurance locks). Repair as needed following wiring repair procedures and using tool SA 9138Z. • Clear SIR Codes and repeat "SIR Diagnostic System Check."

• For aid in diagnosing other history codes, refer to the specific chart for that code.
• Always repeat "SIR Diagnostic System Check."

Fig. 11   Chart E, history code diagnosis (Part 2 of 2)

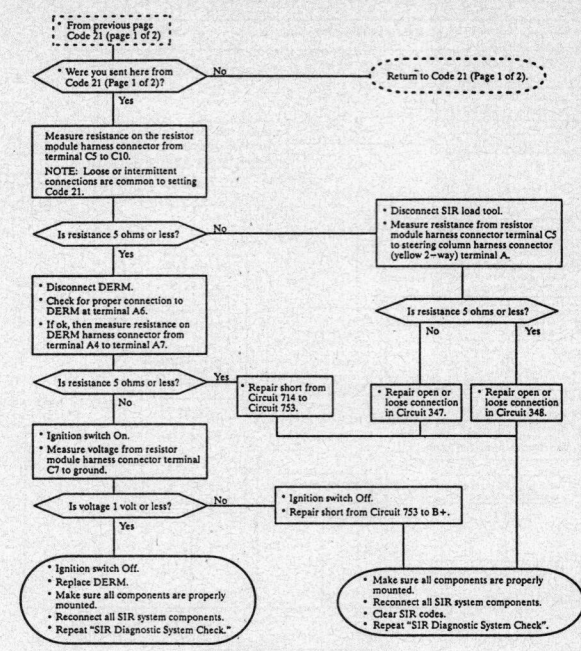

Fig. 12   Code 21, steering column circuit resistance too high (Part 1 of 2)

Fig. 12   Code 21, steering column circuit resistance too high (Part 2 of 2)

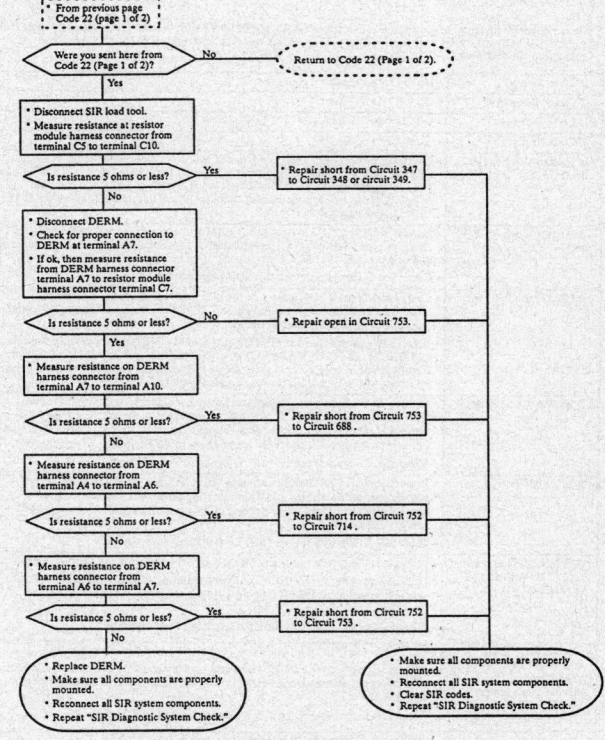

Fig. 13   Code 22, steering column circuit resistance too low (Part 1 of 2)

Fig. 13   Code 22, steering column circuit resistance too low (Part 2 of 2)

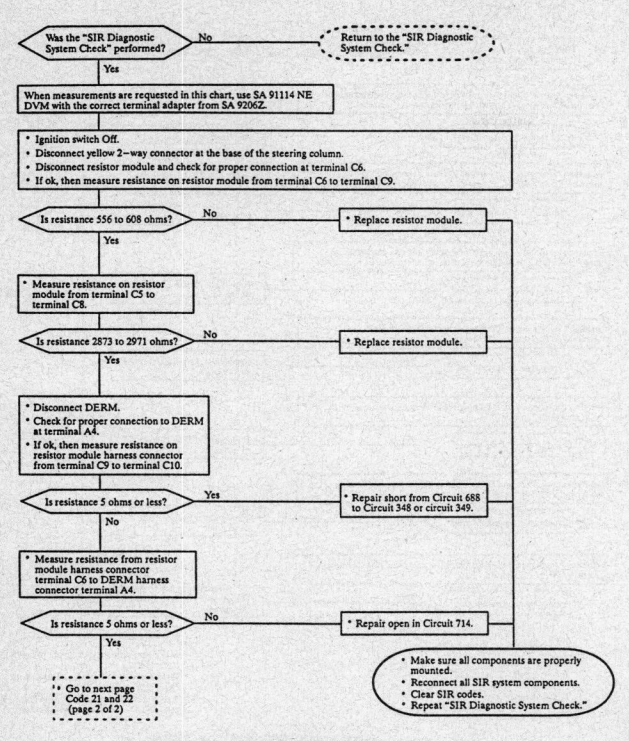

Note: Always repeat SIR DIAGNOSTIC SYSTEM CHECK.

Fig. 14   Code 21 & 22, steering column circuit resistance undetermined (Part 1 of 2)

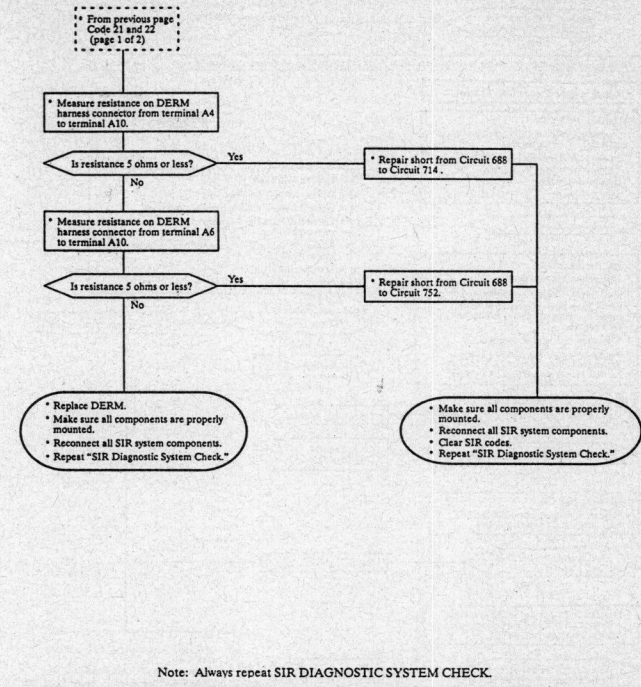

Note: Always repeat SIR DIAGNOSTIC SYSTEM CHECK.

Fig. 14   Code 21 & 22, steering column circuit resistance undetermined (Part 2 of 2)

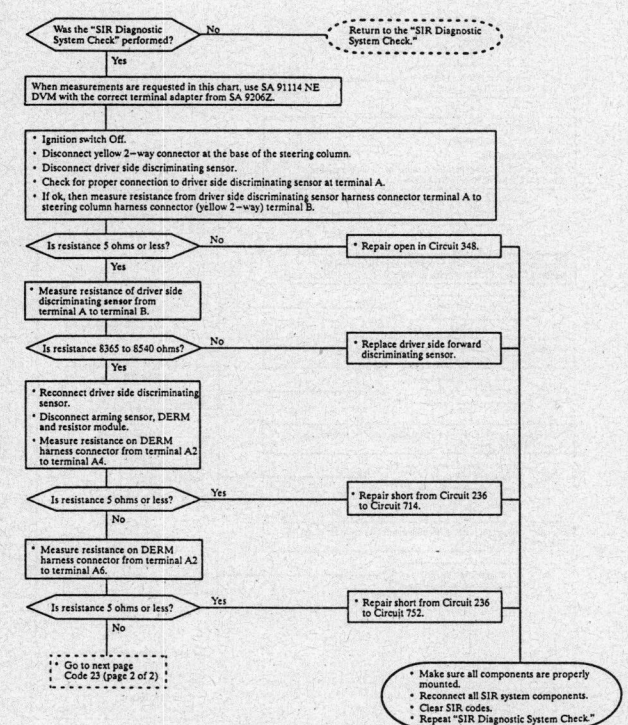

Note: Always repeat SIR DIAGNOSTIC SYSTEM CHECK.

Fig. 15   Code 23, steering column circuit voltage too high (Part 1 of 2)

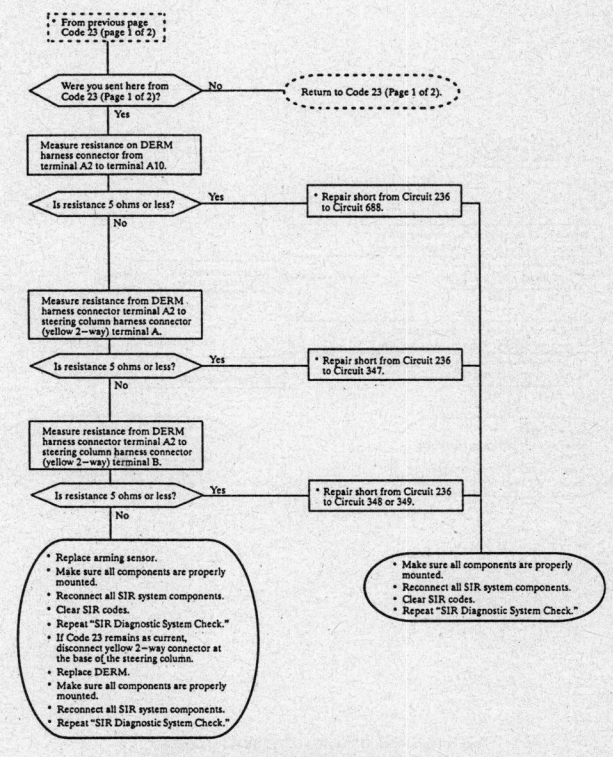

Note: Always repeat SIR DIAGNOSTIC SYSTEM CHECK.

Fig. 15   Code 23, steering column circuit voltage too high (Part 2 of 2)

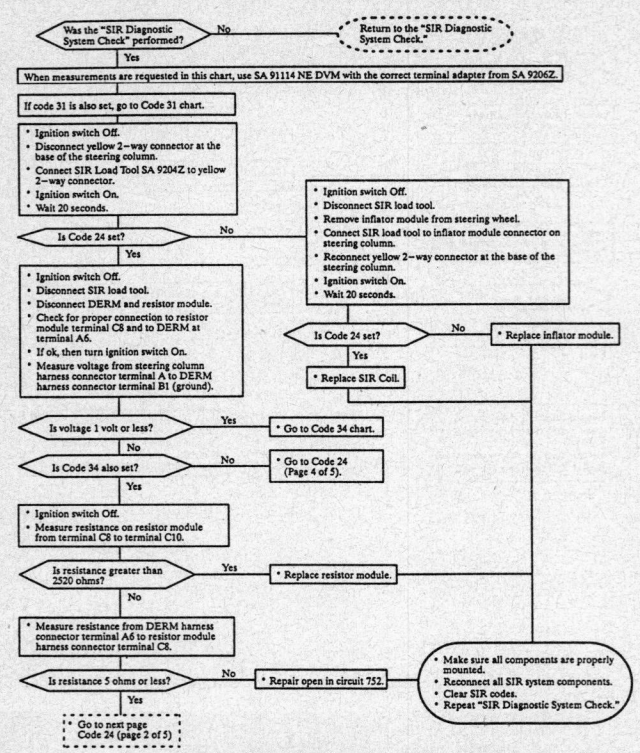

Fig. 16   Code 24, steering column circuit voltage too low (Part 1 of 5)

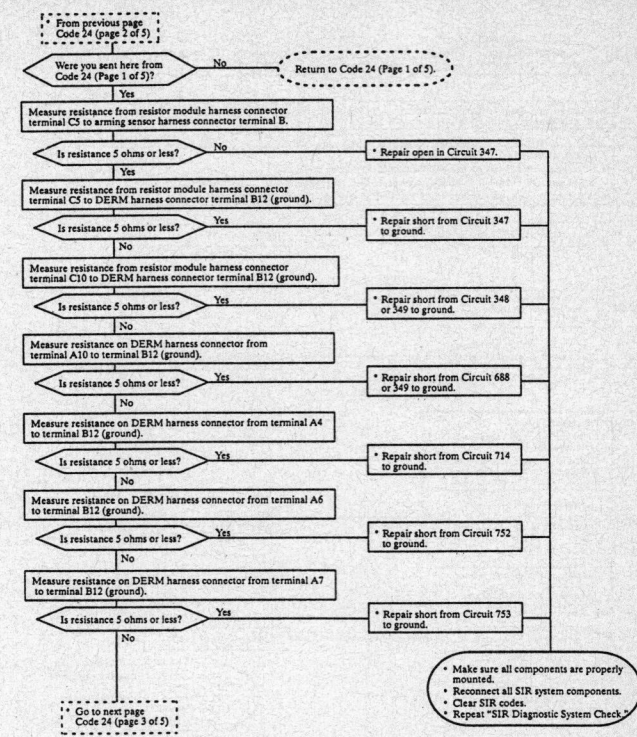

Fig. 16   Code 24, steering column circuit voltage too low (Part 2 of 5)

Fig. 16   Code 24, steering column circuit voltage too low (Part 3 of 5)

Fig. 16   Code 24, steering column circuit voltage too low (Part 4 of 5)

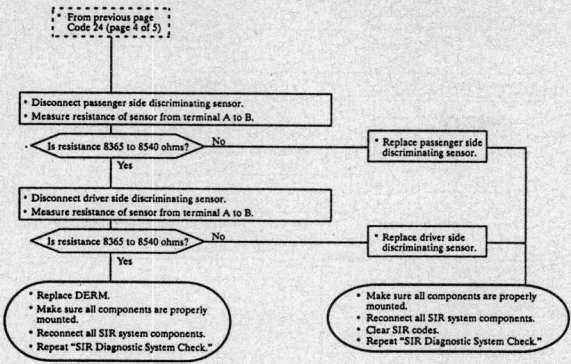

Fig. 16 Code 24, steering column circuit voltage too low (Part 5 of 5)

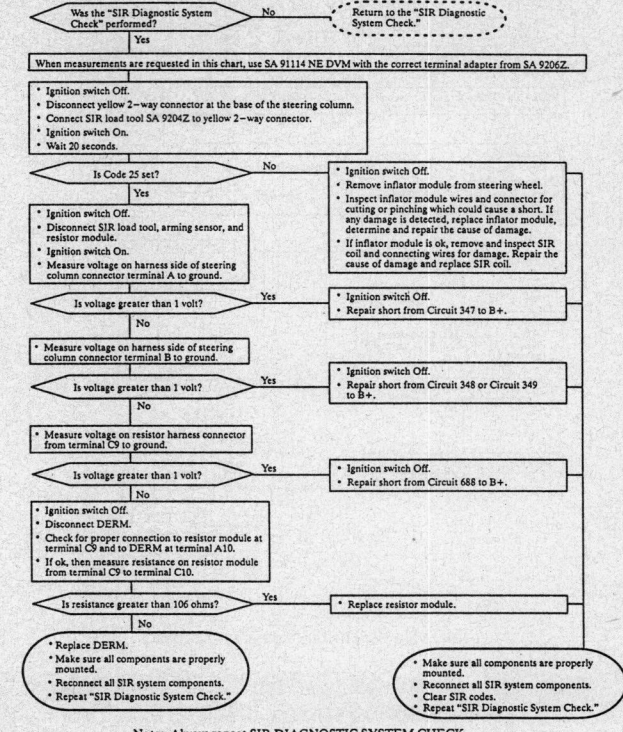

Fig. 17 Code 25, short to battery in steering column circuit

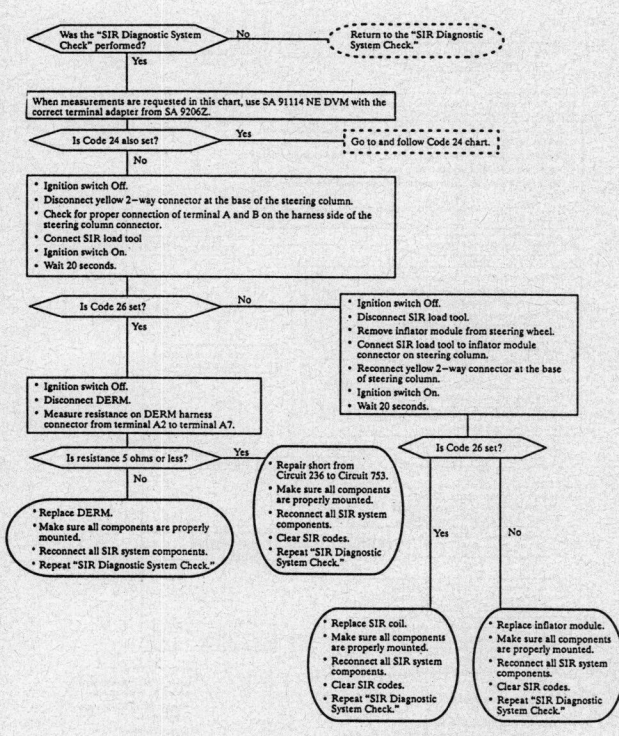

Fig. 18 Code 26, open in steering column circuit

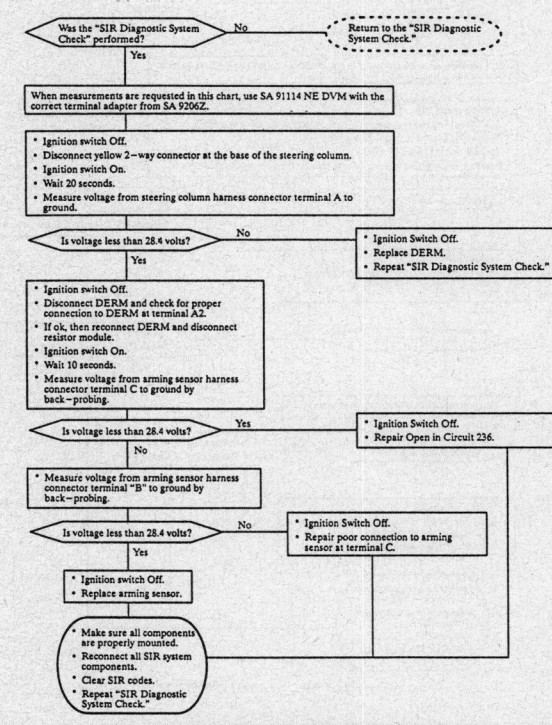

Fig. 19 Code 31, open 36 VLR to deployment loop

Fig. 20   Code 32, grounded 36 VLR to deployment loop

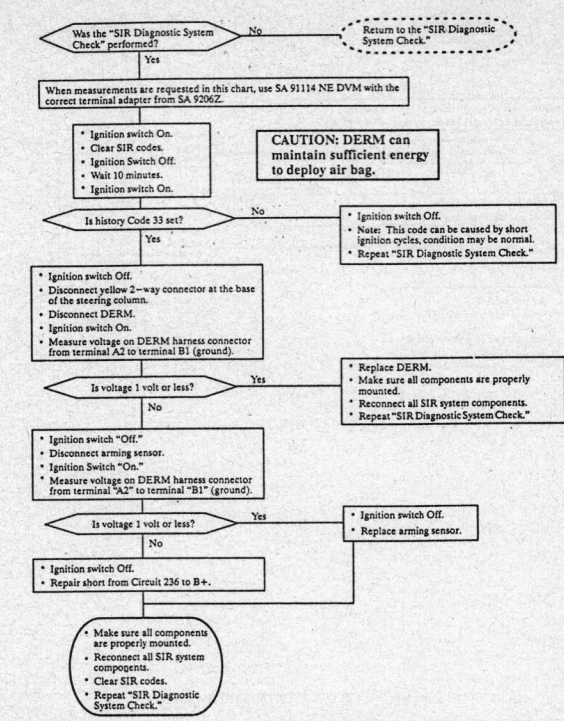

Fig. 21   Code 33, steering diode shorted in arming sensor

Fig. 22   Code 34, open in ignition 1 feed to deployment loop

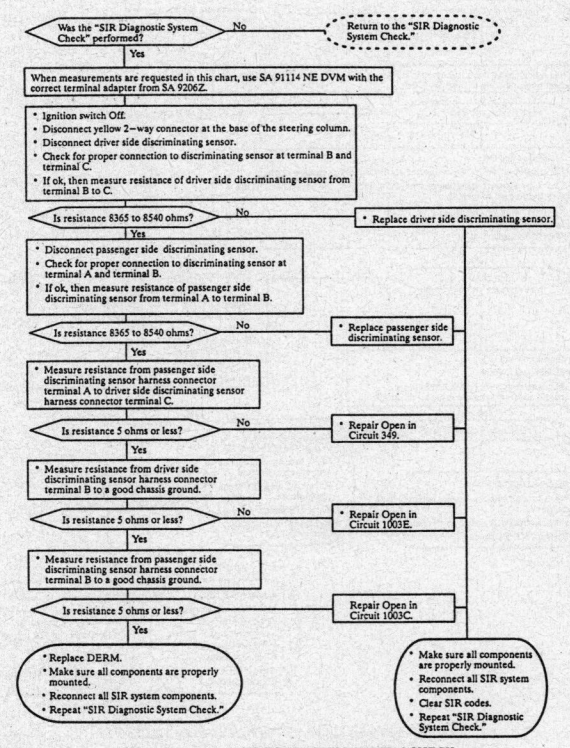

Fig. 23   Code 35, discriminating sensor open

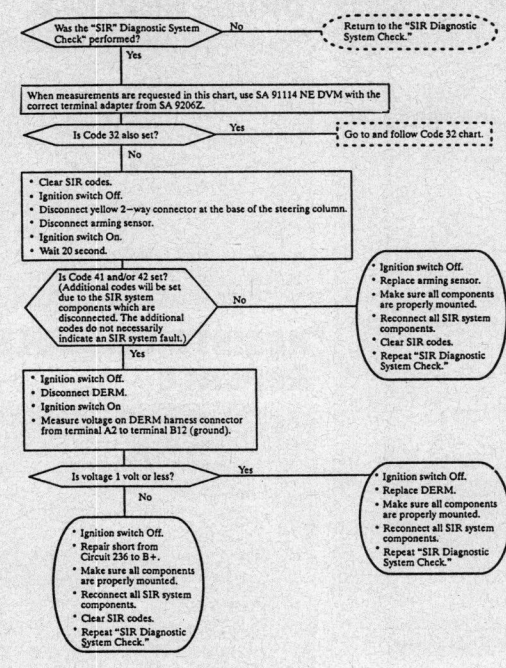

Note: Always repeat SIR DIAGNOSTIC SYSTEM CHECK.

Fig. 24   Code 41/42, deployment loop energy reserve voltage fault

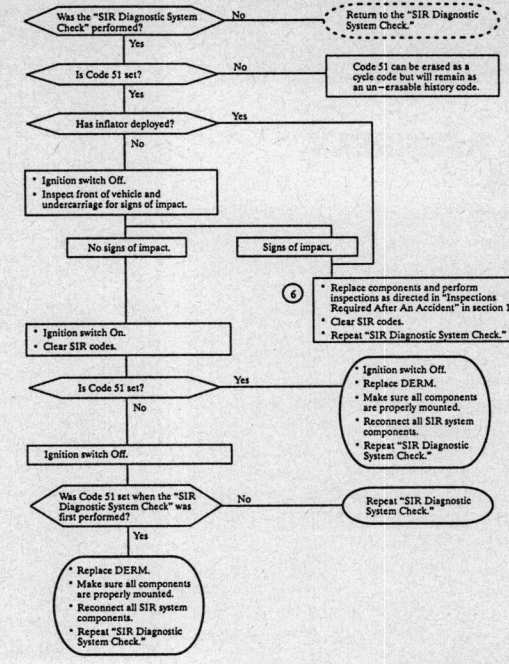

Note: Always repeat SIR DIAGNOSTIC SYSTEM CHECK.

Fig. 25   Code 51, accident detected

Note: Always repeat SIR DIAGNOSTIC SYSTEM CHECK.

Fig. 26   Code 52, EEPROM accident data area full

Note: Always repeat SIR DIAGNOSTIC SYSTEM CHECK.

Fig. 28   Code 71, internal DERM fault

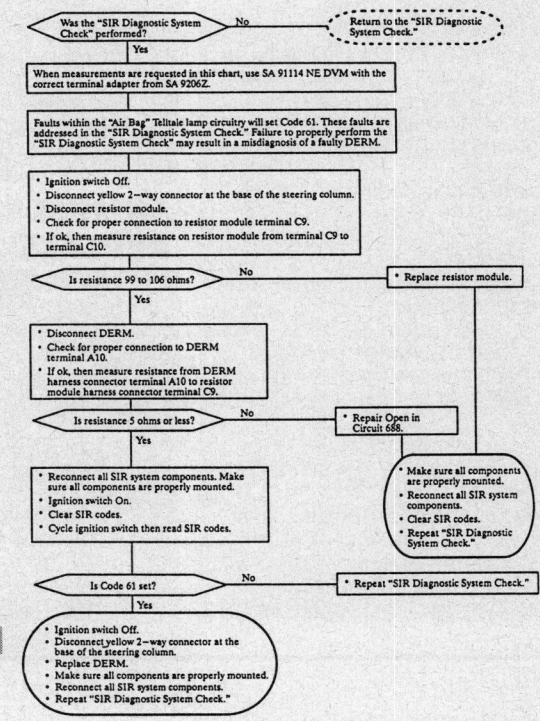

Note: Always repeat SIR DIAGNOSTIC SYSTEM CHECK.

Fig. 27   Code 61, force low or "airbag" telltale lamp circuit failure

SATURN

a. **Torque** new steering wheel attaching nut to 30 ft. lbs.
b. Rearm SIR system as outlined under "Airbag System Rearming."

SIR COIL ASSEMBLY, REPLACE

1. Disarm SIR system as outlined under "Airbag System Disarming."
2. Remove steering wheel as described under "Steering Wheel, Replace."
3. Remove upper and lower steering column shrouds.
4. Align front wheels to straight ahead position and remove SIR coil assembly from lever control switch. **If coil is removed without wheels facing straight ahead and steering wheel has not been moved, original coil can be reinstalled if the coil hub also has not been rotated.**
5. Route pigtail of SIR coil down steering column and install SIR coil to lever control switch.
6. Route wiring through steering wheel.
7. Reverse steps 1 through 3 to install, noting the following:
   a. Rearm SIR system as outlined under "Airbag System Rearming."

STEERING COLUMN, REPLACE

1. Disarm SIR system as outlined under "Airbag System Disarming."
2. Remove steering wheel as described under "Steering Wheel, Replace."
3. Remove upper steering column shroud screws and shroud.
4. Remove ignition lock bezel, then the lower steering column cover screws and cover.
5. Remove lefthand and righthand lower trim panel extensions.
6. Remove center plate and trim panel extension strip.
7. Remove upper dash trim panel screw caps, screws and panel.
8. Remove four cluster trim panel screws, then disengage retainers.
9. Disconnect harness from rear window defog and instrument panel dimmer switches.
10. Remove cluster trim panel.
11. Remove six knee bolster screws and knee bolster.
12. Remove connector position assurance (CPA) device and disconnect connectors from lever control switch.
13. Remove lever control switch.
14. Remove two ignition switch screws

and disconnect switch from ignition module.
15. Remove steering column bolts and lower column onto front seat.
16. Remove upper bolt from intermediate shaft and disconnect shaft from column.
17. Remove steering column from vehicle.
18. Position steering column in vise at upper bracket, then use center punch to mark center of shear bolts on ignition module assembly.
19. Drill small hole at center mark of shear bolts, then remove bolts with shear extractor.
20. Remove ignition module assembly and clamp from steering column.
21. Reverse procedure to install, noting the following:
   a. Install new shear bolts on ignition module assembly, tightening until heads break off.
   b. **Torque** intermediate shaft bolt to 33 ft. lbs.
   c. **Torque** steering column upper bolts to 26 ft. lbs.
   d. Rearm SIR system as outlined under "Airbag System Rearming."

DISCRIMINATING SENSORS, REPLACE

1. Disarm SIR system as outlined under "Disarming SIR System."
2. Remove bolts and sensor from upper radiator support.
3. Remove connector position assurance (CPA) device and disconnect connector. Note position and routing of wiring for installation reference.
4. Reverse procedure to install, noting the following:
   a. **Torque** sensor bolts to 89 in. lbs.
   b. Rearm SIR system as outlined under "Airbag System Rearming."

ARMING SENSOR, REPLACE

1. Disarm SIR system as outlined under "Airbag System Disarming."
2. Remove upper dash trim panel screw caps, screws and panel.
3. Remove arming sensor bolts, then the arming sensor from cross-car beam.
4. Remove connector position assurance (CPA) device and disconnect connector.
5. Reverse procedure to install, noting the following:
   a. **Torque** arming sensor bolts to 71 in. lbs.
   b. Rearm SIR system as outlined under "Airbag System Rearming."

DERM, REPLACE

1. Disarm SIR system as outlined under "Airbag System Disarming."
2. Remove upper trim panel screw caps, screws and panel.
3. Pulling DERM straight up, remove from bracket.
4. Pull lock tab up and push connector lock down to disconnect connector.
5. Reverse procedure to install, noting the following:
   a. Rearm SIR system as outlined under "Airbag System Rearming."

RESISTOR MODULE, REPLACE

1. Disarm SIR system as outlined under "Airbag System Disarming."
2. Remove DERM as described under "DERM, Removal."
3. Remove DERM bracket nuts, then pull bracket off studs.
4. Remove connector position assurance (CPA) device and disconnect connector.
5. Squeezing back of clips, remove resistor module.
6. Reverse procedure to install, noting the following:
   a. Tighten DERM bracket nuts to 71 in. lbs.
   b. Rearm SIR system as outlined under "Airbag System Rearming."

KNEE BOLSTER, REPLACE

If knee bolster shows any visible damage, it should be replaced, not repaired.
1. Disarm SIR system as outlined under "Airbag System Disarming."
2. Remove lefthand and righthand lower trim panel extensions.
3. Remove center air outlet/trim panel.
4. Remove upper trim panel screw caps, screws and panel.
5. Open glove box.
6. Tilt steering wheel down.
7. Remove four cluster trim panel screws, then disengage panel from retainers.
8. Remove connector position assurance (CPA) devices and disconnect electrical connectors from instrument panel lighting rheostat and rear window defogger switches.
9. Remove cluster trim panel.
10. Remove screws and data link connector (DLC).
11. Remove knee bolster screws and knee bolster.
12. Reverse procedure to install. Rearm SIR system as outlined under "Airbag System Rearming."

Automatic Seat Belts

NOTE: Wire Code And Symbol Identification Located In The Front Of This Manual Can Be Used As An Aid When Using Wiring Circuits Found In This Section.

INDEX

DESCRIPTION

The passive restraint control module (PRCM), located in the console, controls the power for the passive restraint belt system and the lap and shoulder belt reminder system. The system allows independent operation of both front shoulder belts.

OPERATION

The PRCM controls shoulder belt operation according to conditions detected by the PRCM through inputs received from various switches. The PRCM receives these signals and operates the shoulder belts according to its internal program.

Under normal operation, the shoulder belt will move to the B-pillar when the ignition switch is ON and the door is closed, or the vehicle speed is greater than 13 mph.

The shoulder belt moves to the A-pillar when the door opens and vehicle speed is less than 13 mph.

On the driver's side, the shoulder belt will move to the A-pillar if the ignition is OFF and the key is removed from the ignition.

TROUBLESHOOTING

Refer to the wiring circuit, **Fig. 1,** along with the system troubleshooting chart, **Fig. 2,** when troubleshooting the automatic seat belt system.

SYSTEM SERVICE

RETRACTOR, REPLACE

1. **On models with manual transaxle,** remove transaxle shift knob.
2. **On models with automatic transaxle,** tape release button in depressed position on shift lever handle.
3. **On all models,** remove liner in rear storage tray and remove two screws below the liner.

4. Remove two screws on front sides of console.
5. Apply parking brake and remove trim plate below park brake lever by lifting at rear edge and working the plate up evenly.
6. Remove both ashtrays, then disconnect front ashtray lamp from console.
7. **On models with power windows,** remove window/mirror switch by sliding switch forward then lifting rear edge. Disconnect switch electrical connectors.
8. **On all models,** remove center console side trim panels, then lift rear of console. From below console, release and push out both seat belt bezels, **Fig. 3.**
9. Remove center fastener, then the retractor anchor bolts.
10. Remove retractors. Disconnect electrical connector on driver's side.
11. Reverse procedure to install, noting the following:
    a. Apply Loctite 242 threadlocker or equivalent, to all restraint bolts/nuts prior to installation.
    b. **Torque** retractor anchor bolts to 35 ft. lbs.
    c. To ease installation, fully recline both front seats and set front of console over shifter.

TRACK ASSEMBLY, REPLACE

1. Remove instrument panel end cap, **Fig. 4.**
2. Remove instrument panel top cover by removing screw caps and screws. Lift panel at rear edge to disengage clips and slide panel out of clips at windshield, **Fig. 5.** Use caution when removing top cover to keep from scratching garnish moldings.
3. Remove screw in top of front lower garnish molding.
4. **On Coupe models,** remove coat hook.

5. **On all models,** starting at front of molding, pull firmly on molding at clip locations to remove. Partially remove front garnish/sill molding at center pillar garnish molding, **Fig. 6.**
6. Partially remove rear garnish/sill molding and remove center pillar lower molding fasteners. Release center pillar lower molding from center pillar, **Fig. 7.**
7. Slide lap belt through center pillar lower molding and remove molding, **Fig. 7.**
8. Disconnect wiring harness leading to shoulder belt track assembly.
9. Remove shoulder belt track assembly, **Fig. 8.**
10. Reverse procedure to install, noting the following:
    a. Apply Loctite No. 242 threadlocker or equivalent, to all restraint bolts/nuts before installation.
    b. **Torque** two bottom guide tube clip bolts to 27 inch lbs.
    c. **Torque** all other guide track bolts to 53 inch lbs.
    d. **Torque** shoulder belt upper anchor Torx head bolt to 30 ft. lbs.

PASSIVE RESTRAINT CONTROL MODULE (PRCM), REPLACE

1. Remove access panel above PRCM in center console.
2. Remove four screws securing center console.
3. Raise parking brake handle as far as possible.
4. Raise center console from rear until access to PRCM is possible from rear of console.
5. Gently press plastic tab at rear of PRCM and lift up at same time.
6. Disconnect electrical connectors and remove from rear.
7. Reverse procedure to install.

Fig. 1 Automatic seat belt wiring circuit (Part 1 of 2)

Fig. 1   Automatic seat belt wiring circuit (Part 2 of 2)

CAUSE — COMPLAINT–CONDITION	IP Batt Fuse	IGN4 Fuse	IGN1 fuse	Prest Fuse (Passive Restraint)	GND. CKT. 155C/155Y	GND. CKT. 159A, 159B, 155P	GND. CKT. 158A, 158B, 155L	GND. CKT. 238, 155L	GND. CKT. 1622, 155RR	GND. CKT. 1620, 1621, 155R	GND. CKT. 1623, 1624, 155J	CKT. 3A, 39A	CKT. 640, 1936	CKT. 817, 817A, 817E	CKT. 1618, 1619	CKT. 1637, 1629	CKT. 39C, 1625A, 237A	CKT. 80A/80B	Passive Restraint Control Module	Battery	Chime Module	Intermittent Connection	Friction/Binding Extreme Cold
Mouse Stuck:																							
Both at B Pillar	•		X	X									X						•	•			
Both at A Pillar	•	•	X	X	X							X	X						•	•			
One at B the Other at A	•		X	X									X						•	•			
One at B the Other Okay									X	X					X	X							
One at A the Other Okay									X	X					X	X							
One or Both in Middle	•	•	X	X															•	•			X
Slow Mouse																					X		X
Jerky Mouse																						X	X
No Lap Telltale					X														•				
No Shoulder Telltale						X													•				
Chime Inappropriate					X	X															X		
No Driver Side Release with Key Out																			•				
Shoulder TT Always On									X	X	X												X

X — Most Probable Cause(s)
● — Possible Causes

Fig. 2   Automatic seat belt system troubleshooting

Fig. 3   Seat belt bezel removal

Fig. 4   Instrument panel end cap removal

Fig. 5   Instrument panel top cover removal

Fig. 6   Front garnish/sill molding removal

Fig. 7   Center pillar lower molding removal

Fig. 8   Track assembly replacement

WIPER SYSTEMS

NOTE: Wire Code And Symbol Identification Located In The Front Of This Manual Can Be Used As An Aid When Using Wiring Circuits Found In This Section.

INDEX

Fig. 1 Wiper system troubleshooting chart

(X — Most Probable Cause(s); • — Possible Causes)

COMPLAINT-CONDITION	WIPER/WASHER SYSTEM	IGN4 Fuse	Wiper Fuse	Circuit 153R	Circuit 153F	Circuit 150J	Circuit 92	Circuit 96	Circuit 1932/493	Circuit 94A/94	Ignition Switch	Column Switch	Battery	Wiper Motor/Module	Washer Pump	Washer Fluid Hose	Friction	Over Torque of Mounting Bolts
Wipers do not work at all	X	X	X	X					X		•	•	•	•			•	
Works on HI speed only										X		•		•				
HI speed does not work				X		X					X		•					
Works on INTERMITTENT only											X		•					
INTERMITTENT does not work											•		•					
Slow wipers		•						•				X					X	
Jerky wipers				X				X				•					X	
Wipers stop, then restart after several minutes												•					X	
Wipers on with switch on OFF					X	X			•									
Wipers work when engine being cranked																		
Excessive motor noise												X					•	X
No washer fluid on windshield															X			
Washer pump does not work				X			X					•						
Washer fluid pressure low												•			X	X		

DESCRIPTION

The windshield wiper and washer system consists of a stalk mounted switch, a windshield wiper motor/control module, a two-speed wiper motor and a washer pump motor.

The windshield wipers and washers operate with the ignition in the Run or Acc positions.

TROUBLESHOOTING

Refer to **Fig. 1,** for troubleshooting the wiper/washer system.

DIAGNOSIS & TESTING

WIPER MODULE

1. Check the circuits, connectors and terminals that are attached to the wiper terminal, **Fig. 2.**
2. Test wiper module in vehicle. It must be connected to the windshield wiper switch to work properly.
3. Wiper module and motor are serviced as an assembly. Repair is by replacement only.
4. Check terminals and connections for damage and corrosion.

WIPER SWITCH

Test resistance between pin A and C. Refer to **Fig. 3** for correct resistance specifications.

SYSTEM PERFORMANCE TEST

1. Turn ignition switch to ACC position and turn wiper switch to "Intermittent 1" position.
   a. Wipers should immediately activate.
   b. On "Intermittent 1," the time interval between cycles (one cycle being one back-and-forth motion of the blades) should be two seconds.
   c. On "Intermittent 2," the interval should be seven seconds.
   d. On "Intermittent 3,"the interval should be 12 seconds.
2. Start engine and put wiper switch on "Low" speed position. Wipers should immediately activate and speed should be 42-53 cycles per minute.
3. Put wiper switch on "High" speed position. Wipers should activate within one second and have a speed of 61-73 cycles per minute on a wet windshield.
4. Push down on wiper switch to the "Mist" position. Wipers should cycle once as long as the switch is being held.
5. Pull wiper switch to "Wash" position. Washer pump and wipers should both activate within one second. Wipers should cycle twice and washer pump should remain on as long as the switch lever is being pulled into the position. The wipers will complete two cycles before parking after the wash is complete.
6. With wipers on "Low" speed, crank engine. Wipers should stop moving and start again once the ignition is back in the RUN position.

Fig. 2 Wiper system wiring circuit

Measure Resistance from Pin C to Pin A.	
Switch Position	Resistance in OHMS *
OFF	OPEN
LOW	300 ohms (.300 k ohms)
HIGH	300 ohms (.300 k ohms)
MIST	300 ohms (.300 k ohms)
INT. 1	2090 ohms (2.09 k ohms)
INT. 2	990 ohms (.990 k ohms)
INT. 3	560 ohms (.560 k ohms)
WASH	130 ohms (.13 k ohms)

* Resistance measurements should be ± 10 %

Check for continuity from Pin A to Pin B of the
Column Switch. There should be less than ONE (1)
OHM when the switch is in HIGH; and OPEN
when switch is in any other position.

**Fig. 3 Wiper switch
resistance specifications**

SPEED CONTROL SYSTEM

NOTE: Wire Code And Symbol Identification Located In The Front Of This Manual Can Be Used As An Aid When Using Wiring Circuits Found In This Section.

INDEX

DESCRIPTION & OPERATION

The system consists of a cruise control module, located in the passenger compartment on the driver's side above the accelerator pedal between the steering column and HVAC control head, control switches, cruise brake switch and on models equipped with manual transmission, a cruise clutch switch.

The completely electronic system does not require vacuum or a vacuum servo motor to control throttle movement. A cable from the cruise control module pulls the accelerator linkage at the accelerator pedal.

The on/off switch enables and disables the speed control system. In the on position the cruise control will activate and in the off position the cruise control will immediately be disabled.

When the cruise in enabled, depressing the set/coast switch will engage the cruise. When cruise is engaged the cruise control module will maintain the desired speed within one mph. When the set/coast switch is held down the vehicle speed will coast down until the switch is released.

If the vehicle has been in the cruise control engage mode, and cruise has been disabled by pressing the brake or clutch switch, then vehicle can return to the previous cruise set by momentarily depressing the resume/accel switch one time.

The vehicle speed in miles per hour is used for tap up and tap down cruise speed adjustments. Once tap up or tap down button is depressed, vehicle speed will increase or decrease by one mph for each time the switch is depressed.

The cruise control system has five circuits linking it to various input signals and a ground circuit. The IGN3 circuit sends ignition on signal to the module when the switch is in the on position. The cruise control switch supplies battery power to the power-up module, through the enable circuit. The vehicle speed information comes from the powertrain control module (PCM) at 4987 pulses per minutes, on all models except Coupe, or 4995 pulses per minute on Coupe models. The cruise con-

trol module receives input from the set/coast/resume/accel switch, located on the steering wheel. The cruise control module determines the command by the amount of voltage received. Brake and clutch switch inputs are received when the pedal is depressed to disengage the system.

DIAGNOSIS & TESTING

SYSTEM PERFORMANCE TEST

Perform the following procedure to confirm speed control system is operating correctly.

1. Test drive vehicle at 25 mph or more, ensuring speed controls operate with switch in On position.
2. Depress set/coast switch for a minimum of 1 second to engage speed controls.
3. Release accelerator pedal, ensuring car maintains speed.
4. Depress brake or clutch to disengage system, ensuring vehicle decelerates.
5. Depress resume/accelerate switch for at least 1 second, vehicle should resume original speed.
6. Depress resume/accelerate switch for 1.5–4.5 seconds, vehicle speed should increase by one mph.
7. Repeat step 6.
8. Turn speed control on/off switch to off position, vehicle should decelerate.

ELECTRICAL TEST

Refer to **Fig. 1**, for electrical wiring circuit.
1. Remove CPA from cruise control module electrical connector.
2. Disconnect module electrical connector, then install cruise/cluster tester connector.
3. Install module electrical connector to tester.
4. Plug cruise/cluster tester power cord to lighter.
5. Select road or shop tester mode.
6. Perform the following diagnostic tests:
   a. For inoperative cruise control system, refer to **Fig. 2**.

b. For intermittent cruise operation, refer to **Fig. 3**.
c. For vehicle road test, refer to **Fig. 4**.

COMPONENT TESTING

BRAKE & CLUTCH SWITCH

With switch depressed, switch contacts should be closed, continuity exists. With switch depressed, switch contacts should be open, no continuity should exist.

SYSTEM SERVICE

CRUISE CONTROL MODULE, REPLACE

1. Disconnect battery ground cable.
2. Remove connector position assurance (CPA), then disconnect cruise control electrical connector.
3. Disconnect speed control cable from accelerator pedal.
4. Remove module attaching nuts, then remove.
5. Reverse procedure to install. **Torque** module attaching nuts to 44 inch lbs.

SPEED CONTROL SWITCH, REPLACE

1. Disconnect battery ground cable.
2. Carefully pry switch button from horn pad.
3. Disconnect switch electrical connector, then remove switch.
4. Reverse procedure to install.

BRAKE SWITCH, REPLACE

1. Disconnect battery ground cable.
2. Disconnect clutch switch electrical connector.
3. Remove switch attaching bolt, then remove switch.
4. Reverse procedure to install. **Torque** switch bolt to 89 inch lbs.

CLUTCH SWITCH, REPLACE

1. Disconnect battery ground cable.
2. Disconnect clutch switch electrical connector.
3. Remove switch attaching bolt, then

Fig. 1 Speed control wiring circuit

remove switch.
4. Reverse procedure to install. **Torque switch bolt to 89 inch lbs.**

STEERING COLUMN SLIP RING, REPLACE

1. Disconnect battery ground cable.
2. Remove steering wheel horn pad, then disconnect electrical connector.
3. Remove steering wheel attaching nut.
4. Remove steering wheel with a standard steering wheel puller tool.
5. Remove upper and lower steering column covers.
6. Remove three electrical harness attaching screws, then disconnect electrical connectors.
7. Remove steering column slip ring.
8. Reverse procedure to install.

ADJUSTMENTS
CONTROL CABLE
With Scan Tool

1. Install scan tool according to manufacturers instructions.
2. Check throttle position sensor voltage, tighten or loosen cable. If cable is too tight then loosen by turning cable until scan tool reads 0 or quits moving, then loosen two more turns. If cable is too loose, then tighten cable until TPS has a reading, then loosen two adjuster two turns.
3. If slug at end of cruise control to throttle cable comes off and cable comes out of cruise control module, replace speed control module. The cable and adjuster assembly may be replaced separately only if slug has not been separated from cable at module end of assembly.
4. Adjust cable by pulling forward and

turning ring on adjuster until TPS voltage reads 0 volts, then loosen two more turns.

Less Scan Tool

1. Remove air intake tube at throttle body.
2. Check throttle blade position.
3. Adjust cable by pulling forward and turning ring on adjuster until throttle blade if fully closed, then loosen two more turns.
4. install air intake tube.
5. Cable and adjuster assembly are not repairable, replace as an assembly. Do not remove cable and adjuster from cruise control module.

BRAKE & CLUTCH SWITCH, ADJUST

Loosen switch attaching bolts, then slide forward or rearward. Switch plunger should be fully depressed with brake pedal released.

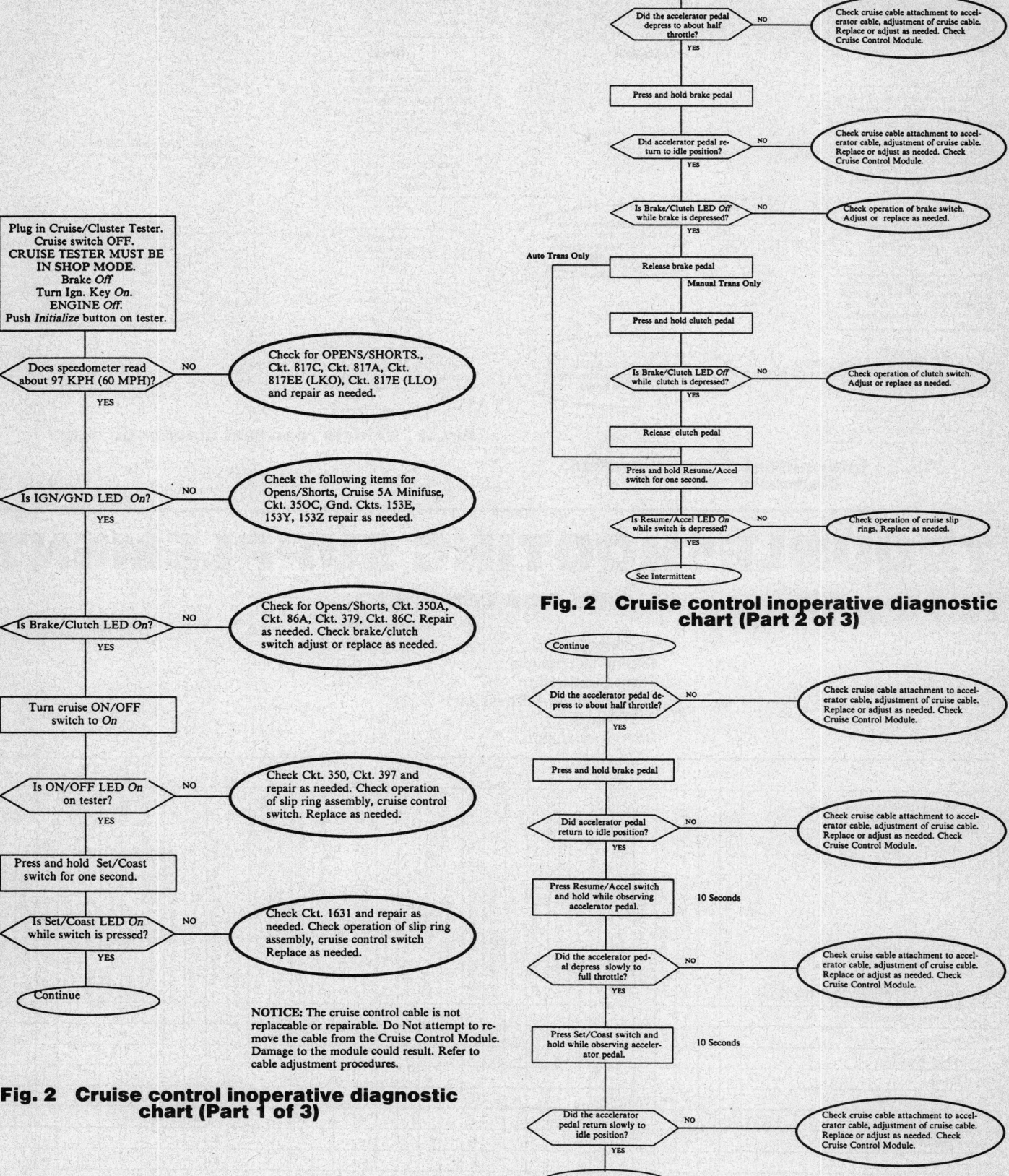

Plug in Cruise/Cluster Tester.
Cruise switch OFF.
CRUISE TESTER MUST BE
IN SHOP MODE.
Brake *Off*
Turn Ign. Key *On.*
ENGINE *Off.*
Push *Initialize* **button on tester.**

Does speedometer read about 97 KPH (60 MPH)? — NO → Check for OPENS/SHORTS., Ckt. 817C, Ckt. 817A, Ckt. 817EE (LKO), Ckt. 817E (LLO) and repair as needed.

Is IGN/GND LED *On?* — NO → Check the following items for Opens/Shorts, Cruise 5A Minifuse, Ckt. 35OC, Gnd. Ckts. 153E, 153Y, 153Z repair as needed.

Is Brake/Clutch LED *On?* — NO → Check for Opens/Shorts, Ckt. 350A, Ckt. 86A, Ckt. 379, Ckt. 86C. Repair as needed. Check brake/clutch switch adjust or replace as needed.

Turn cruise ON/OFF switch to *On*

Is ON/OFF LED *On* on tester? — NO → Check Ckt. 350, Ckt. 397 and repair as needed. Check operation of slip ring assembly, cruise control switch. Replace as needed.

Press and hold Set/Coast switch for one second.

Is Set/Coast LED *On* while switch is pressed? — NO → Check Ckt. 1631 and repair as needed. Check operation of slip ring assembly, cruise control switch Replace as needed.

Continue

NOTICE: The cruise control cable is not replaceable or repairable. Do Not attempt to remove the cable from the Cruise Control Module. Damage to the module could result. Refer to cable adjustment procedures.

Fig. 2   Cruise control inoperative diagnostic chart (Part 1 of 3)

Continue

Did the accelerator pedal depress to about half throttle? — NO → Check cruise cable attachment to accelerator cable, adjustment of cruise cable. Replace or adjust as needed. Check Cruise Control Module.

Press and hold brake pedal

Did accelerator pedal return to idle position? — NO → Check cruise cable attachment to accelerator cable, adjustment of cruise cable. Replace or adjust as needed. Check Cruise Control Module.

Is Brake/Clutch LED *Off* while brake is depressed? — NO → Check operation of brake switch. Adjust or replace as needed.

Auto Trans Only

Release brake pedal

Manual Trans Only

Press and hold clutch pedal

Is Brake/Clutch LED *Off* while clutch is depressed? — NO → Check operation of clutch switch. Adjust or replace as needed.

Release clutch pedal

Press and hold Resume/Accel switch for one second.

Is Resume/Accel LED *On* while switch is depressed? — NO → Check operation of cruise slip rings. Replace as needed.

See Intermittent

Fig. 2   Cruise control inoperative diagnostic chart (Part 2 of 3)

Continue

Did the accelerator pedal depress to about half throttle? — NO → Check cruise cable attachment to accelerator cable, adjustment of cruise cable. Replace or adjust as needed. Check Cruise Control Module.

Press and hold brake pedal

Did accelerator pedal return to idle position? — NO → Check cruise cable attachment to accelerator cable, adjustment of cruise cable. Replace or adjust as needed. Check Cruise Control Module.

Press Resume/Accel switch and hold while observing accelerator pedal.   10 Seconds

Did the accelerator pedal depress slowly to full throttle? — NO → Check cruise cable attachment to accelerator cable, adjustment of cruise cable. Replace or adjust as needed. Check Cruise Control Module.

Press Set/Coast switch and hold while observing accelerator pedal.   10 Seconds

Did the accelerator pedal return slowly to idle position? — NO → Check cruise cable attachment to accelerator cable, adjustment of cruise cable. Replace or adjust as needed. Check Cruise Control Module.

See Intermittent

Fig. 2   Cruise control inoperative diagnostic chart (Part 3 of 3)

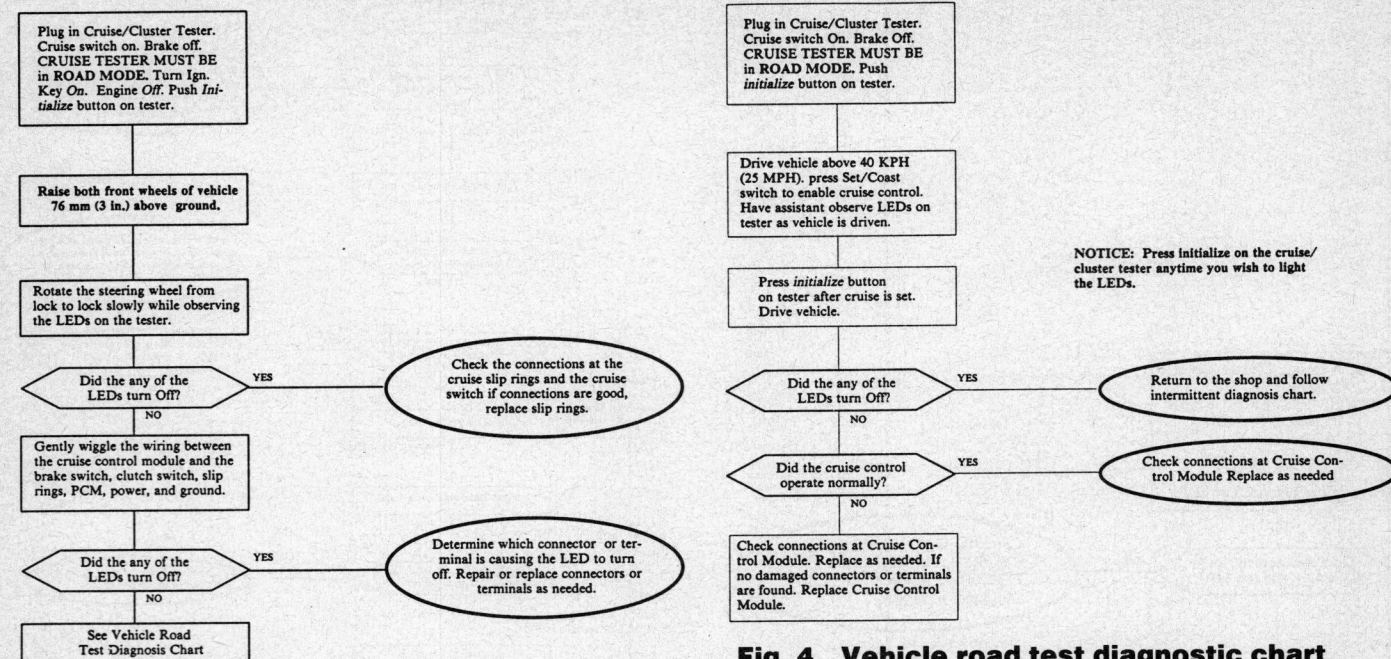

Fig. 3   Intermittent cruise operation diagnostic chart

Fig. 4   Vehicle road test diagnostic chart

TROUBLESHOOTING SUPPLEMENT

TABLE OF CONTENTS

X — Most Probable Cause(s)
● — Possible Causes

CAUSE

COMPLAINT–CONDITION	Engine Mechanical Operation	Head Gasket Blow-By or Seal Leakage	Faulty Damper, Flywheel, or Torque Converter Balance	Valve Leakage	Broken or Scored Pistons/Rings	Worn Pistons/Rings	Incorrect Main or Rod Bearing Clearance	Damaged Crankshaft or Main/Rod Bearings	Damaged/Worn Camshaft	Faulty Lifter or Guide Plate	Faulty Rocker Arm (Base)	Worn/Misaligned Timing Gear, Chain, or Key	Low Cylinder Compression	Worn or Scored Cylinder Bore	Throttle Linkage	Timing Retarded (Crankshaft/Ignition)	Timing Advanced (Crankshaft/Ignition)	Powertrain Mounts	Fuel Line or Clamps	Long Idle Periods	Cracked Cylinder Head or Wall	Engine Overloaded/Excessive Speed	Improper Starting Procedures	Debris or Fluid in Cylinder(s)	Faulty PCV Valve	Valve, Seals, and Guides	Starter, Cables, or Battery	Incorrect/Faulty Oil Filter	Powertrain Mounts/Adjustment	Trans. Second Gear Start	Lifter/Belt Tensioner Noisy
High Crankcase Pressure		●			X	X							●																		
Ticking Noise										X	●																	X			X
Mechanical Knocks				●	●	●	X			●	●							●	●					●					●		
Fuel Knocks																●	●	●													●
Excessive Engine Vibration		●	●					●								●	●	X											●		
Seized Engine Component					●	●	●	●					●											●							
Low Cylinder Compression		●		●	X	●																		●							
High Cylinder Leakage		●		X	X	●							●																		

Fig. 1   Engine mechanical (Part 1 of 2)

X — Most Probable Cause(s)
● — Possible Causes

COMPLAINT–CONDITION	Engine Mechanical Operation	Head Gasket Blow-By or Seal Leakage	Faulty Damper, Flywheel, or	Torque Converter Balance/Faulty	Valve Leakage/Valve Springs	Broken or Scored Pistons/Rings	Worn Pistons/Rings	Incorrect Main or Rod Bearing Clearance	Damaged Crankshaft or Main/	Rod Bearings	Damaged/Worn Camshaft	Faulty Lifter or Guide Plate	Faulty Rocker Arm (SOHC)	Worn/Misaligned Timing Gear, Chain, or Key	Low Cylinder Compression	Worn or Scored Cylinder Bore	Throttle Linkage	Timing Retarded (Crankshaft/Ignition)	Timing Advanced (Crankshaft/Ignition)	Engine Mount/Bolts	Fuel Line or Clamps	Long Idle Periods	Cracked Cylinder Head or Wall	Engine Overloaded/Excessive Speed	Improper Starting Procedures	Debris or Fluid in Cylinder(s)	Faulty PCV Valve	Valve, Seals, and Guides	Starter, Cables, or Battery	Incorrect/Faulty Oil Filter	Powertrain Mounts/Adjustment	Trans. Second Gear Start	Lifter/Belt Tensioner Noisy
Low/Loss of Power		●			●	●	●				●	●	●	●	X	●	●	●	●					●							●	●	X
Hard to Start					●	●	●				●				●	●		●	●						X				●				
Will Not Start — Hot					●	●	●								●	●													X				
Will Not Start — Cold					●	●	●								●	●									X				●				
Engine Starts and Stalls																																	
Engine Misfires/Backfires						●					●			X																			
Rough/Erratic Idle																											●						
Poor Acceleration															●																		
Excessive Acceleration Smoke																		●	●														
Excessive White Smoke		X																					●										
Black Smoke Under Load											●	●	●	●	●	●																	
Blue Smoke						X	●					●	●		●	●							●					●					
Excessive Lube Consumption		●				●	●	●								●											●	●		●	●		
Excessive Fuel Consumption		●			●	●	●				●	●	●					●	●		●			●	●								●
Excessive Coolant Consumption		X																					●										
Lube Oil Leaks		●				●	●																					●					
Lube Oil Contaminated		●																															
Coolant Contaminated		●																															
High Coolant Temperature		●																															
Low Coolant Temperature																																	
High Oil Sump Temperature																																	
No Heat From Heater		●																															
Crankcase Sludge						●	●															●											
Low Oil Pressure								●	●		●																						
High Oil Pressure																																	

Fig. 1 Engine mechanical (Part 2 of 2)

X — Most Probable Cause(s)
● — Possible Causes

Fig. 2 — Cooling system

COMPLAINT–CONDITION	Cooling System	Quality/Grade of Coolant	Low Coolant Level	Faulty or Incorrect Pressure Cap	Inaccurate Temperature Gauge or Sensor	Obstructed Radiator/Heater Flow	Faulty Operation of Fan Motor/Relay	Faulty Thermostat	Faulty Water Pump/Seal	Restricted Coolant Flow or Leak (Intake Manifold/Cylinder Head)	Faulty Fan Shroud	Faulty Air Inlet Duct	Plugged or Misrouted De-Aeration Line	High Coolant Temperature	Low Coolant Temperature	Radiator/Heater Core Damage	Obstructed Heater or Fill Hose	Faulty Accessory Drive Belt	Low Coolant Light On	Hose Clamps	Cylinder Block or Head	Intake Manifold
Low/Loss of Power																						
Hard to Start																						
Will Not Start — Hot																						
Will Not Start — Cold																						
Engine Starts and Stalls																						
Engine Misfires/Backfires																						
Rough/Erratic Idle																						
Poor Acceleration																						
Excessive Acceleration Smoke																						
Excessive White Smoke																					●	
Black Smoke Under Load																						
Blue Smoke																						
Excessive Lube Consumption																						
Excessive Fuel Consumption																						
Excessive Coolant Consumption/Leak									●	●						●				●	X	●
Lube Oil Leaks																						
Lube Oil Contaminated																						
Coolant Contaminated																						
High Coolant Temperature	●	X	X	X	●	X	●	●	●	●		●	X	●					●	●		
Low Coolant Temperature																						
High Oil Sump Temperature		●	●	●				●	●	●		●	●	●				●	●	●		
No Heat From Heater		●															●	●	●			
Crankcase Sludge																						
Low Oil Pressure																						
High Oil Pressure																						

Fig. 2 Cooling system

X — Most Probable Cause(s)
● — Possible Causes

FUEL, EXHAUST AND EMISSION SYSTEMS

COMPLAINT–CONDITION	Fuel Quality/No Fuel	Throttle Shaft	Throttle Blade/Bore Dirty (Min. Air)	Throttle Return Spring	Throttle Stop Lever	Throttle Cable	Faulty Injector	Injector Leak at Tip	Rich Injector	Lean Injector	Fuel Leak (Lines, Regulator, Tank)	IAC System	IAC Whistle	Injector Noise	Fuel Line/Fuel Pump Noise	Faulty Fuel Pump/Relay	Clogged/Pinched Fuel Line/Filter	Fuel Canister Purge System	Faulty Pressure Regulator	Low Fuel Pressure	High Fuel Pressure	EGR Valve Stuck Open	Oxygen Sensor	PCV Valve	PCM/EC (EEPROM)	Manifold Absolute Pressure Sensor	Throttle Position Sensor	EGR Valve/Passageway Closed	Crank Position Sensor	Coolant Temperature Sensor	Knock Sensor	Vacuum Leaks	Improper Starting Procedure
Hard Start/No Start	●						●	X	●	●		●				X	●	●		X		●				●	●		X	●			●
Stalling/Stumbling	●		X	●	●		●		●	●						●	●		●	●		X	●	●		●	●	X	●	X		●	
Rough/Erratic Idle	●	●	●	●	●			X	●	●		X				●	●		●	●			●	●		●		X	●	●		●	
High Idle		●		●	●	●			●	●		X							●							●				●		X	
Low Power	X					●	●									●	●		●		●					●		●	●	●		●	
Poor Fuel Economy	●						●	●	●	●	●								●		●									●	●	●	
Backfires								●	●							●			●										●	●	●	
Noises Miscellaneous													●	●	●	●																	
Sulfur Odor							●	●	●											●			●			●							
Fuel Odor											●							X						●									
Excessive Smoke							●		●	●														●									
Run On/Dieseling									●																								
Surges/Hesitates		●					●		●	●						X	●		●					●				X	●			●	
Engine Hydraulic Lock							●												●														
Sticky Throttle		●	X	●		X																					●						
Spark Knock		X																				X						X				●	

Fig. 3 Fuel, exhaust & emission systems (Part 1 of 2)

X — Most Probable Cause(s)
● — Possible Causes

FUEL, EXHAUST AND EMISSION SYSTEMS

COMPLAINT–CONDION	Speedometer Calibration	Wheel Alignment	Tire Pressure	Overloading	Ignition System	Brake System	Air Temperature Sensor	Altitude (Thin Air)	Engine Mechanical	Induction Clog/Air Filter	Converter Plugged/Damaged	Exhaust Pipe Collapsed/Bent	Muffler Plugged/Damaged	A/C On	Excessive Speed	Cruise Control Cable Adj.	Powertrain Mounts/Adjustment	Restricted Air Intake	Plugged Air Filter	Emission Control Sensors	Spark Plugs/Wires	PCV Valve	Vacuum Lines	Fuel System	Exhaust System Leaks
Hard Start/No Start					X				●	●	●	●	●	●		●		●	●	●				X	
Stalling/Stumbling					X				●	●										X				X	
Rough/Erratic Idle (Vibration)					●				●								X								
High Idle																		X		X		X	X		
Low Power				X	●	●			●	●	X	X	X	X	X					X				●	
Poor Fuel Economy	●	●	●	X	●	●	●	●	●	●				●	X					X				X	
Backfires					X						●	●	●							●					
Noises Miscellaneous											●	●	●											●	X
Sulfur Odor											●														
Fuel Odor																								X	
Excessive Smoke									●											●				●	
Run On/Dieseling																									
Surges/Hesitates					X						●					●				X				●	
Engine Hydraulic Lock									●															●	
Sticky Throttle																									
Spark Knock or Knock									●											X					
Failed Emission Test:					●													●	●	●	●	●	●	●	X
High HC					X				X											●	X	X	X	●	
High CO																		●	X	●	X			X	●

Fig. 3 Fuel, exhaust & emission systems (Part 2 of 2)

Complaint/Condition	Possible Cause(s)	Correction(s)
Vehicle pulls	Mismatched, unevenly worn or improperly inflated tire(s).	Replace or inflate tire(s) correctly.
	Improper front or rear wheel alignment.	Correct wheel alignment.
	Worn or bent suspension component(s).	Replace component(s).
	Worn wheel bearings.	Replace wheel bearings.
	Steering gear out of adjustment or worn.	Replace or adjust steering gear.
	Sagging spring(s).	Replace damaged spring(s).
	Worn strut(s).	Replace worn strut(s).
Abnormal or excessive tire wear	Worn suspension component(s).	Replace component(s).
	Hard driving.	Advice customer.
	Tire(s) improperly inflated.	Inflate tire(s) correctly.
	Worn strut(s).	Replace worn strut(s).
Excessive body roll/pitching	Tension strut bent or broken.	Replace tension strut.
	Rear stabilizer bar or stabilizer bar links bent or broken.	Replace stabilizer bar/stabilizer links.
	Broken or sagging spring(s).	Replace damaged spring(s).
	Tire(s) improperly inflated.	Inflate tire(s) correctly.
	Strut(s) worn.	Replace worn strut(s).
Suspension bottoming	Weak spring(s).	Replace weak spring(s).
Front wheel shimmy	Tire(s) worn, out of round or improperly inflated.	Replace or inflate tire(s).
	Wheel(s) out of balance.	Balance wheel(s).
	Worn strut(s).	Replace worn strut(s).
	Wheel alignment incorrect.	Correct front wheel alignment
	Wheel bearing(s) worn.	Replace worn bearing(s).
	Ball stud(s) worn.	Replace worn ball stud(s).
	Lower control arm bushing(s) worn or damaged.	Replace lower control arm(s).
	Tension strut bushing(s) worn or damaged.	Replace worn or damaged bu1g(s).

Fig. 4   Front suspension

Complaint/Condition	Possible Cause(s)	Correction(s)
Vehicle pulls	Mismatched, unevenly worn or improperly inflated tire(s).	Replace or inflate tire(s) corly.
	Improper front or rear wheel alignment.	Correct wheel alignment.
	Worn or bent front or rear suspension component(s).	Replace component(s).
	Worn wheel bearing(s).	Replace wheel bearing(s).
	Steering gear out of adjustment or worn.	Replace or adjust steering .
	Damaged or sagging spring(s).	Replace spring(s).
Abnormal or excessive tire wear	Improper front or rear wheel alignment.	Correct wheel alignment.
	Worn strut(s).	Replace strut(s).
	Worn or bent front or rear suspension component(s).	Replace component(s).
	Hard driving.	Advise customer.
	Tire(s) improperly inflated.	Inflate tire(s) correctly.
Excessive body roll/pitching	Worn strut(s).	Replace worn strut(s).
	Tension strut bent or broken.	Replace tension strut.
	Rear stabilizer bar or stabilizer bar links bent or broken.	Replace stabilizer bar/dizer bar links.
	Broken or sagging springs(s).	Replace damaged sprir
	Tire(s) improperly inflated.	Inflate tire(s) correctly

Fig. 5   Rear suspension

ENGINE REBUILDING SPECIFICATIONS

NOTE: All Specifications Given In Inches Unless Otherwise Noted.

INDEX

CYLNDER HEAD, VALVE GUIDES & VALVE SEATS

* All Specifications Given In Inches, Unless Otherwise Specified.

Engine, Liter/CID	Cylinder Head Warpage Limit	Cynder Head Overall Tickness	Valve Guides Standard I.D.	Stem To Guide Clearance Intake	Stem To Guide Clearance Exhaust	Seat Angle	Valve Seats Seat Width Intake	Valve Seats Seat Width Exhaust	Runout
1.9L/4-116 SOHC	①	4.14–4.454	.2751–.2761	.0010–.0025	.0015–.0032	44.5–45.5°	.0394–.0512	.0512–.0630	—
1.9L/4-116 DOHC	①	4.449–4.428	.275–.276	.0010–.0025	.0015–.0032	44.5–45.5°	.031–.048	.041–.058	—

SOHC—single overhead cam.
DOHC—dual overhead cam.

①—Longitudinal deck, .004 inch; transverse deck, .002 inch.

VALVES & VALVE SPRINGS

* All Specifications Given In Inches, Unless Otherwise Specified.

Engine, Liter/CID	Valves Stem Diameter Intake	Valves Stem Diameter Exhaust	Clearance① Intake	Clearance① Exhaust	Face Angle	Margin Min.	Valves Springs Free Length	Seated Press., Lbs. @ Inches	Comp. Press., Lbs. @ Inches	Out Of Square Limit
1.9L/4-116 SOHC	.2736–.2741	.2736–.2741	.001–.0025	.0015–.002	44.75–45.25°	②	1.8898–1.9134	76–87 @ 1.61	202–211@1.28	.100
1.9L/4-116 DOHC	.2736–.2741	.2729–.2736	.001–.0025	.0015–.0032	45–45.5°	.0295	1.61	66–77@1.34	163–180 @ .984	.100

SOHC—Single overhead cam.
DOHC—Dual overhead cam.

①—Between valve guide bushing & valve.

②—Intake width, .035 inch; exhaust width, .039 inch.

CYLINDER BLOCK

* All Specifications Given In Inches, Unless Otherwise Specified.

Model	Cylinder Bore Dia. (Std.)	Cylinder Bore Taper, Max.	Cylinder Bore Out Of Round, Max.
1.9L/4-116	①	.0020	.0020

①—Cylinder bes 1, 2 & 3; 3.2280–3.2287 inches. Cylder bore No. 4; 3.2283–3.22 inches.

SATURN

PISTONS, PINS & RINGS

* All Specifications Given In Inches, Unless Otherwise Specified.

Model	Piston Diameter (Std.) ①	Piston Clearance ④	Piston Pin Diameter ② ③	Piston Pin To Piston Clearance	Piston Ring End Gap, Min. Comp.	Piston Ring End Gap, Min. Oil	Piston Ring Side Clearance Comp. ⑤	Piston Ring Side Clearance Oil
1.9L/4-116	3.2270–3.2277		.7676–.7677	.0001–.0004	.0098	.0098		—

①—Measured at .20 inch from bottom of piston.
②—Pistons & pins are matched set and should be replaced as an assembly.
③—Minimum.
④—Bore 1, 2 & 3, .0002–.0017 inch; bore 4, .006–.0021 inch.
⑤—Top ring, .0016–.0035 inch; 2nd ring, .0012.0031 inch.

CAMSHAFT & LIFTERS

* All Specifications Given In Inches, Unless Otherwise Specified.

Engine, Liter/CID	Camshaft Journal Diameter	Maximum Journal Runout	Camshaft Bearing Clearance	Camshaft Endplay	Rocker Arm Oil Clearance	Lifter Bore Diameter	Lifter Diameter	Lifter To Bore Clearance
1.9L/4-116 SOHC	1.7480–1.7490	.0028	.0020–.0040	.0028–.0079	—	—	.8420–.8427	.007–.0024
1.9L/4-116 DOHC	1.1398–1.1406	.004	.0012–.0030	.0020–.008	—	—	1.2976–1.2982	.0010–.0026

SOHC—Single overhead cam.
DOHC—Dual overhead cam.

OIL PUMP

* All Specifications Given In Inches, Unless Otherwise Specified.

Engine, Liter/CID	Body To Side Clearance	Gear To Body Clearance	Tip Clearance	Gear Pocket Depth	Gear Pocket Diameter	Pump Gear Thickness	Pump Gear Diameter	Relief Valve To Body Clearance
1.9L/4-116	.0042	.005	.006	—	—	—	—	—

CRANKSHAFT, BEARING & CONNECTING RODS

* All Specifications Given In Inches, Unless Otherwise Specified.

Engine, Liter/CID	Crankshaft Standard Journal Diameter Main Bearing	Crankshaft Standard Journal Diameter Crank Pin	Out Of Round, All ①	Taper, All ①	Bearing Clearance Main Bearings	Bearing Clearance Connecting Rod Bearings	Thrust Bearing Clearance	Connecting Rod Pin Bore Diameter	Connecting Rod Side Clearance
1.9L/4-116	2.2438–2.2444	1.8500–1.8508	.0004	.0004	.0002–.002	.0002–.0009	—	.7679–.7685	.0065–.0222

①—Maximum.

DECIMAL & MILLIMETER EQUIVALENTS

INCH	INCH	MM		INCH	INCH	MM		INCH	INCH	MM
1/64	.015625	.397		23/64	.359375	9.128		11/16	.6875	17.462
1/32	.03125	.794		3/8	.375	9.525		45/64	.703125	17.859
3/64	.046875	1.191		25/64	.390625	9.922		23/32	.71875	18.265
1/16	.0625	1.587		13/32	.40625	10.319		47/64	.734375	18.653
5/64	.078125	1.984		27/64	.421875	10.716		3/4	.75	19.050
3/32	.09375	2.381		7/16	.4375	11.113		49/64	.765625	19.447
7/64	.109375	2.778		29/64	.453125	11.509		25/32	.78125	19.884
1/8	.125	3.175		15/32	.46875	11.906		51/64	.796875	20.240
9/64	.140625	3.572		31/64	.484375	12.303		13/16	.8125	20.637
5/32	.15625	3.969		1/2	.5	12.700		53/64	.828125	21.034
11/64	.171875	4.366		33/64	.515625	13.097		27/32	.84375	21.431
3/16	.1875	4.762		17/32	.53125	13.494		55/64	.859375	21.828
13/64	.203125	5.159		35/64	.546875	13.890		7/8	.875	22.225
7/32	.21875	5.556		9/16	.5625	14.287		57/64	.890625	22.622
15/64	.234375	5.953		37/64	.578125	14.684		29.32	.90625	23.019
1/4	.25	6.350		19/32	.59375	15.081		59/64	.921875	23.415
17/64	.265625	6.747		39/64	.609375	15.478		15/16	.9375	23.812
9/32	.28125	7.144		5/8	.625	15.875		61/64	.953125	24.209
19/64	.296875	7.541		41/64	.640625	16.272		31/32	.96875	24.606
5/16	.3125	7.937		21/32	.65625	16.669		63/64	.984375	25.003
21/64	.328125	8.334		43/64	.671875	17.065		1		25.400
11/32	.34375	8.731								

Special Service Tools

Throughout this manual references are made to and illustrations may depict the use of special tools required to perform certain jobs. These special tools can generally be ordered through the dealers of the make vehicle being serviced. It is also suggested that you check with local automotive supply firms as they also supply tools manufactured by other firms that will assist in the performance of these jobs. The vehicle manufacturers special tools are supplied by:

Chrysler Corporation . . . . Miller Special Tools
SPX Corporation
12842 Farmington Rd.
Livonia, Michigan 48150

Ford Motor Company . . . . Owatonna Tool Company
Owatonna, Minnesota 55060

General Motors . . . . Kent-Moore
SPX Corporation
29784 Little Mack
Roseville, Michigan 48066

Manual Information Locator

Operation/Subject/Topic	Auto Repair Manual	Auto Engine Tune Up & Electronics Manual
Airbags	X	—
Air Conditioning	X	—
AIR Systems	—	X
All-Wheel Drive Systems	X	—
Alternator Specifications	X	—
Alternator Systems	X	—
Anti-Lock Brake Systems	X	—
Automatic Transaxle In-Vehicle Service	X	—
Automatic Transmission In-Vehicle Service	X	—
Axle Shaft Service	X	—
Back-Up Light Switch, Replace	X	—
Balance Shaft Service	X	—
Ball Joint Service	X	—
Belt Tension Data	X	—
Blower Motor, Replace	X	—
Brake Booster Service	X	—
Brake Service	X	—
Camber Adjustment	X	—
Camshaft Service	X	—
Capacity Data	X	—
Carburetor Adjustments	—	X
Carburetor Overhaul	—	X
Caster Adjustment	X	—
Catalytic Converters	—	X
Clutch Service	X	—
Clutch Start Switch, Replace	X	—
Coil Spring, Replace	X	—
Compression Check	—	X
Compression Pressures	—	X
Computer System Diagnostics	—	X
Computer System Identification	—	X
Computer Terminal Connector Identification	—	X
Computerized Engine Control Systems	—	X
Control Arm Service	X	—
Cooling System Bleed	X	—
Cooling System Data	X	—
Crankshaft Pulley, Replace	X	—
Crankshaft Rear Oil Seal Service	X	—
Cruise Control Systems	X	—
Cylinder Block Specifications	X	—
Cylinder Head Service	X	—
Cylinder Head Specifications	X	—
Cylinder Head, Replace	X	—
Cylinder Liner, Replace	X	—
Dash Panel Service	X	—
Differential Service	X	—
Dimmer Switch, Replace	X	—
Disc Brake Service	X	—
Distributor Service	—	X
Distributor, Replace	X	X
Distributorless Ignition Systems	—	X
Drive Axle Service	X	—
Drive Belt Tension Data	X	—
Drum Brake Service	X	—
EGR System	—	X
Electric Engine Cooling Fans	X	—
Electric Fuel Pumps	X	X
Electrical Symbol Identification	X	X
Electronic Fuel Injection	—	X
Electronic Ignition	—	X
Electronic Instrumentation	—	X
Electronic Level Controls	X	—
Emission Control Application Charts	—	X
Emission Controls	—	X
Emission Vacuum Hose Routing	—	X
Engine Compartment Reference Diagrams	—	X
Engine Cooling Fans	X	—
Engine Electronic Control Module, Replace	—	X
Engine Electronic Control Unit, Replace	—	X
Engine Front Cover Service	X	—
Engine Mounts, Replace	X	—
Engine Oil Seal Service	X	—
Engine Rebuilding Specifications	X	—
Engine Repairs	X	—
Engine Sensor Location	—	X
Engine Sensor Replacement	—	X
Engine Sensor Specification Charts	—	X
Engine Specifications	X	—
Engine System Identification Charts	—	X
Engine Tightening Specifications	X	—
Engine, Replace	X	—
Evaporator Core, Replace	X	—
Exhaust Gas Recirculation (EGR) Systems	—	X
Exhaust Manifold, Replace	X	—
Fast Idle Speed Adjustment	—	X
Feedback Carburetors	—	X
Flasher Location	X	—
Front Drive Axle Service	X	—
Front Wheel Alignment	X	—
Fuel Control System Identification	—	X
Fuel Filter, Replace	X	—
Fuel Injection Systems	—	X
Fuel Injector Cleaning Procedures	—	X
Fuel Injector, Replace	—	X
Fuel Pump Pressure Specifications	X	X
Fuel Pump Pressure Test	—	X
Fuel Pump Replacement	X	X
Fuse Panel Location	X	—
General Engine Specifications	X	—
Headlight Switch, Replace	X	—
Heated Air Cleaners	—	X